SCOTT

2004
STANDARD POSTAGE STAMP CATALOGUE

ONE HUNDRED AND SIXTIETH EDITION IN SIX VOLUMES

VOLUME 3
COUNTRIES OF THE WORLD
G-I

EDITOR	James E. Kloetzel
ASSOCIATE EDITOR	William A. Jones
ASSISTANT EDITOR /NEW ISSUES & VALUING	Martin J. Frankevicz
VALUING ANALYST	Leonard J. Gellman
DESIGN MANAGER	Teresa M. Wenrick
IMAGE COORDINATOR	Nancy S. Martin
ELECTRONIC MEDIA MANAGER	Mark Kaufman
MARKETING/SALES DIRECTOR	William Fay
ADVERTISING	Renee Davis
CIRCULATION / PRODUCT PROMOTION MANAGER	Tim Wagner
EDITORIAL DIRECTOR/AMOS PRESS INC.	Michael Laurence

Released June 2003

Includes New Stamp Listings through the May, 2003 *Scott Stamp Monthly* Catalogue Update

Scott Publishing Co.

911 Vandemark Road, Sidney, OH 45365-0828

A division of AMOS PRESS, INC., publishers of *Linn's Stamp News, Coin World* and *Cars & Parts* magazine.

Table of Contents

See Volume 1 for United States, United Nations and Countries of the World A-B.
See Volumes 2, 4 through 6 for Countries of the World C-F, J-Z

Volume 2: C-F
Volume 4: J-O
Volume 5: P-Sl
Volume 6: So-Z

Scott Publishing Mission Statement

The Scott Publishing Team exists to serve the recreational, educational and commercial hobby needs of stamp collectors and dealers.

We strive to set the industry standard for philatelic information and products by developing and providing goods that help collectors identify, value, organize and present their collections.

Quality customer service is, and will continue to be, our highest priority. We aspire toward achieving total customer satisfaction.

ISBN 0-89487-313-X

Library of Congress Card No. 2-3301

You'll meet all kinds of interesting people inside the pages of Scott Stamp Monthly!

ENTERTAINING

INFORMATIVE

PROVOCATIVE

Every month you'll find:

- Entertaining and informative articles written by the hobby's leading authors and columnists.
- The very latest information on the world's new stamps in the Catalogue Update. Each month you get Scott numbers and photos for nearly 1,000 stamps.
- A magazine that serves an important function in the hobby, providing the latest information on new stamp issues, including illustrations and other details not available in other philatelic publications.
- Automatic enrollment into the Amos Advantage Program that can save you up 30% off stamp supplies, accessories, supplements, books and catalogues!

NEW!
Scott Stamp Monthly now available online!
Go to:
www.scottonline.com
to subscribe to our online edition!

Order online at:

www.amosadvantage.com

Call toll-free:

1-800-448-3611

write:

P.O. Box 828, Sidney, OH 45365-0828

(Offer valid only for U.S. subscribers. Canadian and International subscribers add $15.00 for postage.)

Scott Publishing Co.

SCOTT 911 VANDEMARK ROAD, SIDNEY, OHIO 45365 937-498-0802

Dear Scott Catalogue User:

Almost 14,000 value changes occur in this year's Volume 3 of the *2004 Scott Standard Postage Stamp Catalogue*. Volume 3 contains countries of the world G-I. The stamps of the British and Italian areas lead the way with almost 3,000 value changes each. Also showing significant changes are Iran, India, Ireland, Grenada/Grenada Grenadines and the German States. All told, much of the activity for Volume 3 is in the stamps of the British Commonwealth. Also, continuing the trend seen in Volume 1 and 2 and fueled by active buying in Europe, stamps with the Europa theme continue their strong upward movement in Volume 3.

What about value changes for 2004?

To begin, it is noteworthy that most of the value changes made this year in Volume 3 are upward, and many are unusually strong.

Leading the way in the 2004 catalog are the stamps of Great Britain and the Channel Islands with almost 3,000 value changes. Starting with the penny black, Scott 1, the strong positive trend continues for the first 250 stamps through 1946. The penny black rises to $3,250 unused and $190 used in the 2004 catalog, from $3,000 unused and $180 used last year. In more modern issues, strong positive movement is also seen among the Machin Heads.

Another area receiving a great deal of attention this year is the stamps of the Italian area where more than 2,700 stamps see their values changed. The changes cover almost all facets of that collecting area, starting with Italian States and continuing through Italy proper, Italian Offices Abroad and the Aegean Islands. For the stamps of the classic era of Italian States, changes are strongly upward. The first stamp of Modena, Scott 1, picturing the coat of arms in black on green paper, rises to $1,450 unused and $100 used in the 2004 catalog, from $1,050 unused and $87.50 used last year.

Values for Italian airmail stamps prior to WWII also provide a strong showing with used values leading the way. A new note has been added in the airmail section indicating that values for used airmail stamps are for postally used examples with legible cancellations. Also noted is that forged cancels on Nos. C1-C105 abound, and expertization is strongly recommended. The airmail set issued with the 1937 Summer Exhibition for Child Welfare, Scott C89-C94, soars to $100 in mint, never-hinged condition, $42 unused and $291.25 used in the 2004 catalog, from $75 in mint, never-hinged condition, $34.75 unused and $81.50 used last year. Stamps of Italian Offices Abroad are also broadly higher, most in the ten-percent range, and stamps of the Aegean Islands show similar upward movement.

The value changes for India are split almost evenly between India proper, the Convention States, and the Feudatory States. For India proper, most changes are in the 1950-75 time frame and show very strong upward movement. The set of 20 definitives issued from 1975-88 climbs to $49 in mint, never-hinged condition and $12.75 used in the 2004 catalog, from $33.70 mint, never hinged and $8.50 used in 2003. These changes are mild compared to some of the value increases seen in the Convention States of Faridkot and Gwalior. There, some of the minor error varieties have risen by almost a factor of ten. In the Feudatory States of Cochin, Dhar, Duttia and Faridkot, strong increases also occur.

This year, a major review of Iranian stamps takes place covering the period from the classics to the stamps of the late 1970s. More than 1,500 values have been changed with the trend being strongly upward. A good example of the increases that occur is the 16-stamp definitive issue of 1898 picturing lions on the low values and Shah Muzaffar-ed-Din on the higher values. The set almost doubles in value to $120 unused and $64.45 used in the 2004 catalog, from $66 unused and $32.70 used last year.

Almost 850 value changes appear for the popular collecting area of Ireland. Stamps with the Europa theme and stamps issued during the 1990s show a strong upward trend. One startling increase, clearly showing the strength of Europa issues, is the 1960 issue, Scott 175-176. This 2-stamp set soars to $75 in mint, never-hinged condition and $29 used in the 2004 catalog, from $29.50 mint, never hinged and $24 used in 2003.

The stamps of the German States have regained some of the ground they lost last year. Almost all early material shows increases of around ten to twenty percent. Typical of this is the first stamp of Hamburg, the one-half schilling black with numeral value on the Coat of Arms, Scott 1. The stamp rises to $70 unused and $450 used this year, from $62.50 unused and $375 used in the 2003 catalog.

Where are the editorial enhancements?

The major editorial changes to Volume 3 are the continuing image-scanning project; the reorganization of modern German and Italian definitive sets; the addition of a number of minor stamp varieties in the British area; and the addition of stamps and sets for Guadeloupe, Indo-China, Inini and Iran, among others.

The Scott image-scanning project has benefited over the past year by the assistance of many collectors and dealers. Many more stamp images appear in 2004 versus 2003, but we still have more progress to make before we can call this task completed. We thank all of those who have helped along the way, be it with the loan of a single stamp or dozens of stamps.

For Germany, the definitive set of 1992-2000 featuring famous women, Scott 1723-1735, has been closed and renumbered. The same is true for the definitive set of 1994-2001 featuring historic sites, Scott 1838-1861. Similar renumbering also occurs for two modern Italian definitive sets of the 1990s, Scott 1863-1868 and 2229-2247.

In Great Britain and the Channel Islands, a number of new minor varieties have been added. Interested collectors can review the Catalog Number Additions, Deletions & Changes list on page 1121 to determine specific additions.

In Honduras, the Scott editors have restored the 2-real black surcharge on the 2-real Coat-of-Arms black stamp on green paper of the Comayagua Issue, Scott 8. Experts now agree that this is a genuine issue.

In Iran, the previous 5-centime minor shade variety of the 1885 definitive set, Scott 62a, has been identified as a lithographed emergency predecessor of the 1885-86 typographed series. This issue has been elevated to major number status and assigned a new number, Scott 59A. Three shade varieties and an imperforate have also been added as minor varieties of this new major stamp. Additionally, Scott 215 has been deleted because experts now feel that it only exists as a forgery. Finally, a new set, Scott 516-523, has been added for the 1909 definitives overprinted "Stagecoach Stations" in French and Farsi.

Continuing with additions made this year to the French areas in Volume 2, new stamps have been added for Guadeloupe, Indo-China and Inini that reflect stamps issued in WWII by the French Vichy government. For Guadeloupe, the issues consist of regular postage No. 163A, semi-postals Nos. B11A-B11B, airmail semi-postals Nos. CB1-CB3 and postage-due stamps Nos. J37A-J37C. The new Indo-China Scott numbers are 226A-226D, B21A-B21B, C18A-C18O and CB2-CB5. The new Inini listings appear as Nos. 46-49, B9-B10 and CB1-CB3.

Values for never-hinged stamps have been added for unused sets and singles throughout Volume 3, and footnotes throughout the catalog have been added or modified.

Happy collecting,

James E Kloetzel

James E. Kloetzel/Catalogue Editor

Acknowledgments

Our appreciation and gratitude go to the following individuals who have assisted us in preparing information included in the 2004 Scott Catalogues. Some helpers prefer anonymity. These individuals have generously shared their stamp knowledge with others through the medium of the Scott Catalogue.

Those who follow provided information that is in addition to the hundreds of dealer price lists and advertisements and scores of auction catalogues and realizations that were used in producing the catalogue values. It is from those noted here that we have been able to obtain information on items not normally seen in published lists and advertisements. Support from these people goes beyond data leading to catalogue values, for they also are key to editorial changes.

A special acknowledgment to Liane and Sergio Sismondo of The Classic Collector for their extraordinary assistance and knowledge sharing that has aided in the preparation of this year's Standard and Classic Specialized Catalogues.

Dr. Karl Agre
Donald R. Alexander (China Stamp Society)
A. R. Allison (Orange Free State Study Circle)
B. J. Ammel (The Nile Post)
Robert Ausubel (Great Britain Collectors Club)
Dr. H.U. Bantz
John Barone (Stamptracks)
Jack Hagop Barsoumian (International Stamp Co.)
Tim Bartshe (Philatelic Society for Greater Southern Africa)
William Batty-Smith (Sarawak Specialists' Society)
Jules K. Beck (Latin American Philatelic Society)
Roger S. Brody
Keith & Margie Brown
Mike Bush (Joseph V. Bush, Inc.)
Lawrence A. Bustillo (Suburban Stamp Inc.)
A. Bryan Camarda (University Stamp Co.)
Richard A. Champagne
Henry Chlanda
Bob Coale
Robert Comeau
Laurie Conrad
Frank D. Correl
Andrew Cronin (Canadian Society of Russian Philately)
William T. Crowe (The Philatelic Foundation)
Tony L. Crumbley (Carolina Coin & Stamp, Inc.)
Norman S. Davis
Tony Davis
Tom Derbyshire (University Stamp Co.)
John DeStefanis
Kenneth E. Diehl
Bob Dumaine (Sam Houston Duck Co.)
William S. Dunn
Esi Ebrani
Paul G. Eckman
Peter R. Feltus
Leon Finik (Loral Stamps)
Henry Fisher
Geoffrey Flack
Joseph E. Foley (Eire Philatelic Association)
Jeffrey M. Forster
Bob Genisol (Sultan Stamp Center)
Daniel E. Grau
Fred F. Gregory
Michael H. Grollnek
Harry Hagendorf
Calvet M. Hahn
Joe Hahn (Paraguay Collectors Club)
Ted Hallock
Erich E. Hamm (Philactica)
Alan Hanks
John B. Head
Bruce Hecht (Bruce L. Hecht Co.)
Robert R. Hegland
Lee H. Hill, Jr.
John-Paul Himka
Robert W. Hisey
Harold Hite
Armen Hovsepian (ArmenStamp)
Jack R. Hughes (Fellowship of Samoa Specialists)
Philip J. Hughes (Croatian Philatelic Society)
Wilson Hulme
Kalman V. Illyefalvi (Society for Hungarian Philately)
Eric Jackson
Michael Jaffe (Michael Jaffe Stamps, Inc.)
Peter C. Jeannopoulos
Richard A. Johnson
Allan Katz (Ventura Stamp Company)
Stanford M. Katz
Lewis Kaufman
Dr. James W. Kerr
Charles F. Kezbers
Juri Kirsimagi (Estonian Philatelic Society)
Janet Klug
William V. Kriebel
John R. Lewis (The William Henry Stamp Co.)
Ulf Lindahl (Ethiopian Philatelic Society)
William A. Litle
Gary B. Little (Luxembourg Collectors Club)
Pedro Llach (Filatelia Llach S.L.)
B. Lucas (Iran Philatelic Study Circle)
George Luzitano
Dennis Lynch
Nick Markov (Italia Stamp Co.)
Marilyn R. Mattke
William K. McDaniel
Mark S. Miller
Allen Mintz (United Postal Stationery Society)
Chuck Q. Moo
William E. Mooz
David Mordant (Postmark and Postal History Society of Southern Africa)
Gary M. Morris (Pacific Midwest Co.)
Bruce M. Moyer (Moyer Stamps & Collectibles)
Richard H. Muller (Richard's Stamps)
James Natale
Victor Ostolaza
Dr. Everett L. Parker (St. Helena, Ascension & Tristan da Cunha Philatelic Society)
John E. Pearson (Pittwater Philatelic Service)
John Pedneault
Donald J. Peterson (International Philippine Philatelic Society)
Stanley M. Piller (Stanley M. Piller & Associates)
Todor Drumev Popov
Peter W. W. Powell
Bob Prager (Gary Posner, Inc.)
Stephen Radin (Albany Stamp Co.)
Ghassan D. Riachi
Ron Rice
Omar Rodriguez
Michael Rogers (Michael Rogers, Inc.)
Jon W. Rose
Michael Ruggiero
Frans H.A. Rummens (American Society for Netherlands Philately)
Christopher Rupp (Rupp Brothers Rare Stamps)
Mehrdad Sadri (Persiphila)
Richard H. Salz
Jacques C. Schiff, Jr. (Jacques C. Schiff, Jr., Inc.)
Bernard Seckler (Fine Arts Philatelists)
F. Burton Sellers
Charles F. Shreve (Shreves Philatelic Galleries, Inc.)
Jeff Siddiqui (Pakistan Philatelic Study Circle)
Sergio & Liane Sismondo (The Classic Collector)
Jack Solens (Armstrong Philatelics)
Christopher Smith
Ekrem Spahich (Croatian Philatelic Society)
Frits Staal
Richard Stambaugh
Frank J. Stanley, III
Richard Stark
Philip & Henry Stevens (postalstationery.com)
Mark Stucker
James F. Taff
Peter Thy (Philatelic Society for Greater Southern Africa)
Glenn Tjia (Quality Philatelics)
Scott R. Trepel (Siegel Auction Galleries, Inc.)
A.J. Ultee
Xavier Verbeck (American Belgian Philatelic Society)
Philip T. Wall
Daniel C. Warren
Richard A. Washburn
Giana Wayman (Asociacion Filatélica de Costa Rica)
William R. Weiss, Jr. (Weiss Philatelics)
Ed Wener (Indigo)
Ken Whitby
Don White (Dunedin Stamp Centre)
Kirk Wolford (Kirk's Stamp Company)
Robert F. Yacano (K-Line Philippines)
Ralph Yorio
John P. Zuckerman (Siegel Auction Galleries, Inc.)
Alfonso G. Zulueta, Jr.

Addresses, Telephone Numbers, Web Sites, E-Mail Addresses of General & Specialized Philatelic Societies

Collectors can contact the following groups for information about the philately of the areas within the scope of these societies, or inquire about membership in these groups. Aside from the general societies, we limit this list to groups that specialize in particular fields of philately, particular areas covered by the Scott Standard Postage Stamp Catalogue, and topical groups. Many more specialized philatelic societies exist than those listed below. These addresses were compiled in January 2002, and are, to the best of our knowledge, correct and current. Groups should inform the editors of address changes whenever they occur. The editors also want to hear from other such specialized groups not listed.

Unless otherwise noted all website addresses begin with http://

American Philatelic Society
PO Box 8000
State College PA 16803
Ph: (814) 237-3803
www.stamps.org
E-mail: relamb@stamps.org

American Stamp Dealers' Association
Joseph Savarese
3 School St.
Glen Cove NY 11542
Ph: (516) 759-7000
www.asdaonline.com
E-mail: asda@erols.com

International Society of Worldwide Stamp Collectors
Anthony Zollo
PO Box 150407
Lufkin TX 75915-0407
www.iswsc.org
E-mail: stamptmf@frontiernet.net

Junior Philatelists of America
Jennifer Arnold
PO Box 2625
Albany OR 97321
www.jpastamps.org
E-mail: exec.sec@jpastamps.org

Royal Philatelic Society
41 Devonshire Place
London, United Kingdom W1G 6JY

Royal Philatelic Society of Canada
PO Box 929, Station Q
Toronto, ON, Canada M4T 2P1
Ph: (888) 285-4143
www.rpsc.org
E-mail: info@rpsc.org

Groups focusing on fields or aspects found in worldwide philately (some may cover U.S. area only)

American Air Mail Society
Stephen Reinhard
PO Box 110
Mineola NY 11501
ourworld.compuserve.com/homepages/aams/
E-mail: sr1501@aol.com

American First Day Cover Society
Douglas Kelsey
PO Box 65960
Tucson AZ 85728-5960
Ph: (520) 321-0880
www.afdcs.org
E-mail: afdcs@aol.com

American Revenue Association
Eric Jackson
PO Box 728
Leesport PA 19533-0728
Ph: (610) 926-6200
www.revenuer.org
E-mail: eric@revenuer.com

American Topical Association
Ray E. Cartier
PO Box 57
Arlington TX 76004-0057
Ph: (817) 274-1181
home.prcn.org/~pauld/ata/
E-mail: americantopical@msn.com

Errors, Freaks and Oddities Collectors Club
Jim McDevitt
PO Box 1126
Kingsland GA 31548
Ph: (912) 729-1573
E-mail: cwouscg@aol.com

Fakes and Forgeries Study Group
Anthony Torres
107 Hoover Rd.
Rochester NY 14617-3611
E-mail: ajtorres@rochester.rr.com

First Issues Collectors Club
Kurt Streepy
608 Whitethorn Way
Bloomington IN 47403
Ph: (812) 339-6229
E-mail: kstreepy@msn.com

International Philatelic Society of Joint Stamp Issues Collectors
Richard Zimmermann
124, Avenue Guy de Coubertin
Saint Remy Les Chevreuse, France F-78470
perso.clubinternet.fr/rzimmerm/index.htm
E-mail: rzimmerm@club-internet.fr

National Duck Stamp Collectors Society
Anthony J. Monico
PO Box 43
Harleysville PA 19438-0043
www.hwcn.org/link/ndscs
E-mail: ndscs@hwcn.org

No Value Identified Club
Albert Sauvanet
Le Clos Royal B, Boulevard des Pas Enchantes
St. Sebastien-sur Loire, France 44230
E-mail: alain.vailly@irin.univ_nantes.fr

The Perfins Club
Bob Szymanski
10 Clarridge Circle
Milford MA 01757
E-mail: perfinman@attbi.com

Post Mark Collectors Club
David Proulx
7629 Homestead Drive
Baldwinsville NY 13027
E-mail: stampdance@baldcom.net

Postal History Society
Kalman V. Illyefalvi
8207 Daren Court
Pikesville MD 21208-2211
Ph: (410) 653-0665

Precancel Stamp Society
176 Bent Pine Hill
North Wales PA 19454
Ph: (215) 368-6082
E-mail: abentpine1@aol.com

United Postal Stationery Society
Cora Collins
PO Box 1792
Norfolk VA 23501-1792
Ph: (757) 420-3487
www.upss.org
E-mail: poststat@juno.com

Groups focusing on U.S. area philately as covered in the Standard Catalogue

Canal Zone Study Group
Richard H. Salz
60 27th Ave.
San Francisco CA 94121

Carriers and Locals Society
John D. Bowman
PO Box 382436
Birmingham AL 35238-2436
Ph: (205) 967-6200
www.pennypost.org
E-mail: jdbowman@atlantabroadband.com

Confederate Stamp Alliance
Richard L. Calhoun
PO Box 581
Mt. Prospect IL 60056-0581

Hawaiian Philatelic Society
Kay H. Hoke
PO Box 10115
Honolulu HI 96816-0115
Ph: (808) 521-5721
E-mail: bannan@pixi.com

Plate Number Coil Collectors Club
Gene C. Trinks
3603 Bellows Court
Troy MI 48083
www.pnc3.org
E-mail: gctrinks@sprynet.com

United Nations Philatelists
Blanton Clement, Jr.
292 Springdale Terrace
Yardley PA 19067-3421
www.unpi.com
E-mail: bclemjr@aol.com

United States Stamp Society
Executive Secretary
PO Box 6634
Katy TX 77491-6631
www.usstamps.org

U.S. Cancellation Club
Roger Rhoads
3 Ruthana Way
Hockessin DE 19707
www.geocities.com/athens/2088/usccome.htm
E-mail: rrrhoads@aol.com

U.S. Philatelic Classics Society
Mark D. Rogers
PO Box 80708
Austin TX 78708-0708
www.uspcs.org
E-mail: mrogers23@austin.rr.com

Groups focusing on philately of foreign countries or regions

Aden & Somaliland Study Group
Gary Brown
PO Box 106
Briar Hill, Victoria, Australia 3088
E-mail: garyjohn951@optushome.com.au

Albania Study Circle
Paul Eckman
PO Box 39880
Los Angeles CA 90039
members.netscapeonline.co.uk/johnsphipps/index.html
E-mail: peckman797@earthlink.net

American Society of Polar Philatelists (Antarctic areas)
Alan Warren
PO Box 39
Exton PA 19341-0039
south-pole.com/aspp.htm
E-mail: alanwar@att.net

Andorran Philatelic Study Circle
D. Hope
17 Hawthorn Dr.
Stalybridge, Cheshire, United Kingdom SK15 1UE
www.chy-an-piran.demon.co.uk/
E-mail: apsc@chy-an-piran.demon.co.uk

Australian States Study Circle
Ben Palmer
GPO 1751
Sydney, N.S.W., Australia 1043

Austria Philatelic Society
Ralph Schneider
PO Box 23049
Belleville IL 62223
Ph: (618) 277-6152
www.apsus.esmartweb.com
E-mail: rsstamps@aol.com

American Belgian Philatelic Society
Kenneth L. Costilow
621 Virginius Dr.
Virginia Beach VA 23452-4417
Ph: (757) 463-6081
groups.hamptonroads.com/ABPS
E-mail: kcos32@home.com

Bechuanalands and Botswana Society
Neville Midwood
69 Porlock Lane
Furzton, Milton Keynes, United Kingdom MK4 1JY
www.netcomuk.co.uk/~midsoft/bbsoc.html
E-mail: runnerpo@netcomuk.co.uk

Bermuda Collectors Society
Thomas J. McMahon
PO Box 1949
Stuart FL 34995

Brazil Philatelic Association
Kurt Ottenheimer
462 West Walnut St.
Long Beach NY 11561
Ph: (516) 431-3412
E-mail: oak462@juno.com

British Caribbean Philatelic Study Group
Dr. Reuben A. Ramkissoon
3011 White Oak Lane
Oak Brook IL 60523-2513

British North America Philatelic Society (Canada & Provinces)
H. P. Jacobi
5295 Moncton St.
Richmond, B.C., Canada V7E 3B2
www.bnaps.org
E-mail: beaver@telus.net

British West Indies Study Circle
W. Clary Holt
PO Drawer 59
Burlington NC 27216
Ph: (336) 227-7461

Burma Philatelic Study Circle
A. Meech
7208 91st Ave.
Edmonton, AB, Canada T6B 0R8
E-mail: ameech@telusplanet.net

Ceylon Study Group
R. W. P. Frost
42 Lonsdale Road, Cannington
Bridgewater, Somerset, United Kingdom TA5 2JS

China Stamp Society
Paul H. Gault
PO Box 20711
Columbus OH 43220
www.chinastampsociety.org
E-mail: secretary@chinastampsociety.org

Colombia/Panama Philatelic Study Group
PO Box 2245
El Cajon CA 92021
E-mail: jimacross@juno.com

Society for Costa Rica Collectors
Dr. Hector R. Mena
PO Box 14831
Baton Rouge LA 70808
www.socorico.org
E-mail: hrmena@aol.com

Croatian Philatelic Society (Croatia & other Balkan areas)
Ekrem Spahich
502 Romero, PO Box 696
Fritch TX 79036-0696
Ph: (806) 857-0129
www.croatianmall.com/cps/
E-mail: ou812@arn.net

Cuban Philatelic Society of America
Ernesto Cuesta
PO Box 34434
Bethesda MD 20827
www.philat.com/cpsa

Cyprus Study Circle
Jim Wigmore
19 Riversmeet, Appledore
Bideford, N. Devon, United Kingdom EX39 1RE
www.geocities.com/cyprusstudycircle
E-mail: istug@aol.com

Society for Czechoslovak Philately
Robert T. Cossaboom
PO Box 25332
Scott AFB IL 62225-0332
www.czechoslovakphilately.com
E-mail: klfck1@aol.com

Danish West Indies Study Unit of the Scandinavian Collectors Club
John L. Dubois
Thermalogic Corp.
22 Kane Industrial Drive
Hudson MA 01749
Ph: (800) 343-4492
dwi.thlogic.com
E-mail: jld@thlogic.com

East Africa Study Circle
Ken Hewitt
16 Ashleigh Road
Solihull, United Kingdom B91 1AE
E-mail: 106602.2410@compuserve.com

Egypt Study Circle
Mike Murphy
109 Chadwick Road
London, United Kingdom SE15 4PY
E-mail: egyptstudycircle@hotmail.com

Estonian Philatelic Society
Juri Kirsimagi
29 Clifford Ave.
Pelham NY 10803

Ethiopian Philatelic Society
Ulf Lindahl
640 S. Pine Creek Rd.
Fairfield CT 06430
Ph: (203) 255-8005
members.home.net/fbheiser/ethiopia5.htm
E-mail: ulindahl@optonline.net

Falkland Islands Philatelic Study Group
Carl J. Faulkner
Williams Inn, On-the-Green
Williamstown MA 01267-2620
Ph: (413) 458-9371

Faroe Islands Study Circle
Norman Hudson
28 Enfield Road
Ellesmere Port, Cheshire, United Kingdom CH65 8BY
www.pherber.com/fisc/fisc.html
E-mail: jntropics@hotmail.com

Former French Colonies Specialist Society
BP 628
75367 Paris Cedex 08, France
www.ifrance.com/colfra
E-mail: clubcolfra@aol.com

France & Colonies Philatelic Society
Walter Parshall
103 Spruce St.
Bloomfield NJ 07003-3514

Germany Philatelic Society
PO Box 779
Arnold MD 21012-4779
www.gps.nu
E-mail: germanyphilatelic@starpower.net

German Democratic Republic Study Group of the German Philatelic Society
Ken Lawrence
PO Box 8040
State College PA 16803-8040
Ph: (814) 237-3803
E-mail: apsken@aol.com

Gibraltar Study Circle
D. Brook
80 Farm Road
Weston Super Mare, Avon, United Kingdom BS22 8BD
www.abel.co.uk/~stirrups/GSC.HTM
E-mail: drstirrups@dundee.ac.uk

Great Britain Collectors Club
Parker A. Bailey, Jr.
PO Box 773
Merrimack NH 03054-0773
www.gbstamps.com/gbcc
E-mail: pbaileyjr@worldnet.att.net

Hellenic Philatelic Society of America (Greece and related areas)
Dr. Nicholas Asimakopulos
541 Cedar Hill Ave.
Wyckoff NJ 07481
Ph: (201) 447-6262

International Society of Guatemala Collectors
Mrs. Mae Vignola
105 22nd Ave.
San Francisco CA 94121

Haiti Philatelic Society
Ubaldo Del Toro
5709 Marble Archway
Alexandria VA 22315
E-mail: u007ubi@aol.com

Honduras Collectors Club
Jeff Brasor
PO Box 143383
Irving TX 75014

Hong Kong Stamp Society
Dr. An-Min Chung
3300 Darby Rd. Cottage 503
Haverford PA 19041-1064

Society for Hungarian Philately
Robert Morgan
2201 Roscomare Rd.
Los Angeles CA 90077-2222
www.hungarianphilately.org
E-mail: h.alanhoover@lycosemail.com

India Study Circle
John Warren
PO Box 7326
Washington DC 20044
Ph: (202) 564-6876
E-mail: warren.john@epa.gov

Indian Ocean Study Circle
K. B. Fitton
50 Firlands
Weybridge, Surrey, United Kingdom KT13 0HR
www.stampdomain.com/iosc
E-mail: keithfitton@intonet.co.uk

Society of Indo-China Philatelists
Norman S. Davis
PO Box 290406
Brooklyn NY 11229

Iran Philatelic Study Circle
Darrell R. Hill
1410 Broadway
Bethlehem PA 18015-4025
www.iranphilatelic.org
E-mail: d.r.hill@att.net

Eire Philatelic Association (Ireland)
Myron G. Hill III
PO Box 1210
College Park MD 20741-1210
eirephilatelicassoc.org
E-mail: mhill@radix.net

Society of Israel Philatelists
Paul S. Aufrichtig
300 East 42nd St.
New York NY 10017

Italy and Colonies Study Circle
Andrew D'Anneo
1085 Dunweal Lane
Calistoga CA 94515
E-mail: audanneo@napanet.net

International Society for Japanese Philately
Kenneth Kamholz
PO Box 1283
Haddonfield NJ 08033
www.isjp.org
E-mail: isjp@home.com

Korea Stamp Society
John E. Talmage
PO Box 6889
Oak Ridge TN 37831
www.pennfamily.org/KSS-USA
E-mail: jtalmage@usit.net

Latin American Philatelic Society
Piet Steen
197 Pembina Ave.
Hinton, AB, Canada T7V 2B2

Latvian Philatelic Society
Aris Birze
569 Rougemount Dr.
Pickering, ON, Canada L1W 2C1

Liberian Philatelic Society
William Thomas Lockard
PO Box 106
Wellston OH 45692
Ph: (740) 384-2020
E-mail: tlockard@zoomnet.net

Liechtenstudy USA (Liechtenstein)
Ralph Schneider
PO Box 23049
Belleville IL 62223
Ph: (618) 277-6152
www.rschneiderstamps.com/Liechtenstudy.htm
E-mail: rsstamps@aol.com

Lithuania Philatelic Society
John Variakojis
3715 W. 68th St.
Chicago IL 60629
Ph: (773) 585-8649
www.filatelija.lt/lps/
E-mail: variakojis@earthlink.net

Luxembourg Collectors Club
Gary B. Little
3304 Plateau Dr.
Belmont CA 94002-1312
www.luxcentral.com/stamps/LCC
E-mail: lcc@luxcentral.com

Malaya Study Group
Joe Robertson
12 Lisa Court
Downsland Road
Basingstoke, Hampshire, United Kingdom RG21 8TU
home.freeuk.net/johnmorgan/msg.htm

Malta Study Circle
Alec Webster
50 Worcester Road
Sutton, Surrey, United Kingdom SM2 6QB
E-mail: alecwebster50@hotmail.com

Mexico-Elmhurst Philatelic Society International
David Pietsch
PO Box 50997
Irvine CA 92619-0997
E-mail: mepsi@msn.com

Society for Moroccan and Tunisian Philately
206, bld. Pereire
75017 Paris, France
members.aol.com/Jhaik5814
E-mail: jhaik5814@aol.com

Nepal & Tibet Philatelic Study Group
Roger D. Skinner
1020 Covington Road
Los Altos CA 94024-5003
Ph: (650) 968-4163
fuchs-online.com/ntpsc/

American Society of Netherlands Philately
Jan Enthoven
221 Coachlite Ct. S.
Onalaska WI 54650
Ph: (608) 781-8612
www.cs.cornell.edu/Info/People/aswin /NL/neth
E-mail: jenthoven@centurytel.net

New Zealand Society of Great Britain
Keith C. Collins
13 Briton Crescent
Sanderstead, Surrey, United Kingdom CR2 0JN
www.cs.stir.ac.uk/~rgc/nzsgb
E-mail: rgc@cs.stir.ac.uk

Nicaragua Study Group
Erick Rodriguez
11817 S.W. 11th St.
Miami FL 33184-2501
clubs.yahoo.com/clubs/nicaraguastudygroup
E-mail: nsgsec@yahoo.com

Society of Australasian Specialists/ Oceania
Henry Bateman
PO Box 4862
Monroe LA 71211-4862
Ph: (800) 571-0293
members.aol.com/stampsho/saso.html
E-mail: hbateman@jam.rr.com

Orange Free State Study Circle
J. R. Stroud
28 Oxford St.
Burnham-on-sea, Somerset, United Kingdom TA8 1LQ
www.ofssc.org
E-mail: jrstroud@classicfm.net

Pacific Islands Study Group
John Ray
24 Woodvale Avenue
London, United Kingdom SE25 4AE
www.pisc.org.uk
E-mail: john.ray@bigfoot.com

Pakistan Philatelic Study Circle
Jeff Siddiqui
PO Box 7002
Lynnwood WA 98046
E-mail: jeffsiddiqui@msn.com

Centro de Filatelistas Independientes de Panama
Vladimir Berrio-Lemm
Apartado 0835-348
Panama, 10, Panama
E-mail: filatelia@cwpanama.net

Papuan Philatelic Society
Steven Zirinsky
PO Box 49, Ansonia Station
New York NY 10023
E-mail: szirinsky@compuserve.com

International Philippine Philatelic Society
Robert F. Yacano
PO Box 100
Toast NC 27049
Ph: (336) 783-0768
E-mail: yacano@advi.net

Pitcairn Islands Study Group
Nelson A. L. Weller
2940 Wesleyan Lane
Winston-Salem NC 27106
Ph: (336) 724-6384
E-mail: nalweller@aol.com

Plebiscite-Memel-Saar Study Group of the German Philatelic Society
Clay Wallace
100 Lark Court
Alamo CA 94507
E-mail: wallacec@earthlink.net

Polonus Philatelic Society (Poland)
Arkadius Walinski
7414 Lincoln Ave. - D
Skokie IL 60076-3898
Ph: (847) 674-4286

International Society for Portuguese Philately
Clyde Homen
1491 Bonnie View Rd.
Hollister CA 95023-5117
www.portugalstamps.com
E-mail: cjh@hollinet.com

Rhodesian Study Circle
William R. Wallace
PO Box 16381
San Francisco CA 94116
www.rhodesianstudycircle.org.uk
E-mail: bwall8rscr@earthlink.net

Canadian Society of Russian Philately
Andrew Cronin
PO Box 5722, Station A
Toronto, ON, Canada M5W 1P2
Ph: (905) 764-8968
www3.sympatico.ca/postrider/postrider
E-mail: postrider@sympatico.ca

Rossica Society of Russian Philately
Gerald D. Seiflow
27 N. Wacker Drive #167
Chicago IL 60606-3203
www.rossica.org
E-mail: ged.seiflow@rossica.org

Ryukyu Philatelic Specialist Society
Carmine J. DiVincenzo
PO Box 381
Clayton CA 94517-0381

St. Helena, Ascension & Tristan Da Cunha Philatelic Society
Dr. Everett L. Parker
HC 76, Box 32
Greenville ME 04441-9727
Ph: (207) 695-3163
ourworld.compuserve.com/homepages/ ST_HELENA_ASCEN_TDC
E-mail: eparker@prexar.com

St. Pierre & Miquelon Philatelic Society
David Salovey
320 Knights Corner
Stony Point NY 10980
E-mail: jamestaylor@wavehome.com

Associated Collectors of El Salvador
Jeff Brasor
PO Box 143383
Irving TX 75014

Fellowship of Samoa Specialists
Jack R. Hughes
PO Box 1260
Boston MA 02117-1260
members.aol.com/tongaJan/foss.html

Sarawak Specialists' Society
Stu Leven
4031 Samson Way
San Jose CA 95124-3733
Ph: (408) 978-0193
www.britborneostamps.org.uk
E-mail: stulev@ix.netcom.com

Scandinavian Collectors Club
Donald B. Brent
PO Box 13196
El Cajon CA 92020
www.scc-online.org
E-mail: dbrent47@sprynet.com

Slovakia Stamp Society
Jack Benchik
PO Box 555
Notre Dame IN 46556

Philatelic Society for Greater Southern Africa
William C. Brooks VI
PO Box 4158
Cucamonga CA 91729-4158
Ph: (909) 484-2806
www.homestead.com/psgsa/index.html
E-mail: bbrooks@hss.co.sbcounty.gov

Spanish Philatelic Society
Robert H. Penn
1108 Walnut Drive
Danielsville PA 18038
Ph: (610) 767-6793

Sudan Study Group
Charles Hass
PO Box 3435
Nashua NH 03061-3435
Ph: (603) 888-4160
E-mail: hassstamps@aol.com

American Helvetia Philatelic Society (Switzerland, Liechtenstein)
Richard T. Hall
PO Box 15053
Asheville NC 28813-0053
www.swiss-stamps.org
E-mail: secretary@swiss-stamps.org

Tannu Tuva Collectors Society
Ken Simon
513 Sixth Ave. So.
Lake Worth FL 33460-4507
Ph: (561) 588-5954
www.seflin.org/tuva
E-mail: p003115b@pb.seflin.org

Society for Thai Philately
H. R. Blakeney
PO Box 25644
Oklahoma City OK 73125
E-mail: HRBlakeney@aol.com

Transvaal Study Circle
J. Woolgar
132 Dale Street
Chatham, Kent ME4 6QH, United Kingdom
www.transvaalsc.org

Ottoman and Near East Philatelic Society (Turkey and related areas)
Bob Stuchell
193 Valley Stream Lane
Wayne PA 19087
E-mail: president@oneps.org

Ukrainian Philatelic & Numismatic Society
George Slusarczuk
PO Box 303
Southfields NY 10975-0303
www.upns.org
E-mail: Yurko@warwick.net

Vatican Philatelic Society
Sal Quinonez
2 Aldersgate, Apt. 119
Riverhead NY 11901
Ph: (516) 727-6426

British Virgin Islands Philatelic Society
Roger Downing
PO Box 11156
St. Thomas VI 00801-1156
Ph: (284) 494-2762
www.islandsun.com/FEATURES/bviphil9198.html
E-mail: issun@candwbvi.net

West Africa Study Circle
Dr. Peter Newroth
33-520 Marsett Place
Victoria, BC, Canada V8Z 7J1
ourworld.compuserve.com/homepages/ FrankWalton

Western Australia Study Group
Brian Pope
PO Box 423
Claremont, Western Australia, Australia 6910

Yugoslavia Study Group of the Croatian Philatelic Society
Michael Lenard
1514 North 3rd Ave.
Wausau WI 54401
Ph: (715) 675-2833
E-mail: mjlenard@aol.com

Topical Groups

Americana Unit
Dennis Dengel
17 Peckham Rd.
Poughkeepsie NY 12603-2018
www.americanaunit.org
E-mail: info@americanaunit.org

Astronomy Study Unit
George Young
PO Box 632
Tewksbury MA 01876-0632
Ph: (978) 851-8283
www.fandm.edu/departments/astronomy/miscell/astunit.html
E-mail: george-young@msn.com

Bicycle Stamp Club
Norman Batho
358 Iverson Place
East Windsor NJ 08520
Ph: (609) 448-9547
members.tripod.com/~bicyclestamps
E-mail: normbatho@worldnet.att.net

Biology Unit
Alan Hanks
34 Seaton Dr.
Aurora, ON, Canada L4G 2K1
Ph: (905) 727-6993

Bird Stamp Society
G. P. Horsman
9 Cowley Drive, Worthy Down
Winchester, Hants., United Kingdom
SO21 2OW

Canadiana Study Unit
John Peebles
PO Box 3262, Station "A"
London, ON, Canada N6A 4K3
E-mail: john.peebles@odyssey.on.ca

Captain Cook Study Unit
Brian P. Sandford
173 Minuteman Dr.
Concord MA 01742-1923
www.captaincookstudyunit.com/
E-mail: USagent@captaincookstudyu-nit. com/

Casey Jones Railroad Unit
Oliver C. Atchison
PO Box 31631
San Francisco CA 94131-0631
Ph: (415) 648-8057
www.uqp.de/cjr/index.htm
E-mail: cjrrunit@aol.com

Cats on Stamps Study Unit
Mary Ann Brown
3006 Wade Rd.
Durham NC 27705

Chemistry & Physics on Stamps Study Unit
Dr. Roland Hirsch
20458 Water Point Lane
Germantown MD 20874
www.cpossu.org
E-mail: rfhirsch@cpossu.org

Chess on Stamps Study Unit
Anne Kasonic
7625 County Road #153
Interlaken NY 14847
www.iglobal.net/home/reott/stamps1.htm#cossu
E-mail: akasonic@epix.net

Christmas Philatelic Club
Linda Lawrence
312 Northwood Drive
Lexington KY 40505
Ph: (606) 293-0151
www.hwcn.org/link/cpc
E-mail: stamplinda@aol.com

Christopher Columbus Philatelic Society
Donald R. Ager
PO Box 71
Hillsboro NH 03244-0071
Ph: (603) 464-5379
E-mail: meganddon@conknet.com

Collectors of Religion on Stamps
Verna Shackleton
425 North Linwood Avenue #110
Appleton WI 54914
Ph: (920) 734-2417
www.powernetonline.com/~corosec/coros1.htm
E-mail: corosec@powernetonline.com

Dogs on Stamps Study Unit
Morris Raskin
202A Newport Rd.
Monroe Township NJ 08831
Ph: (609) 655-7411
www.dossu.org
E-mail: mraskin@nerc.com

Earth's Physical Features Study Group
Fred Klein
515 Magdalena Ave.
Los Altos CA 94024
www.philately.com/society_news/earths _physical.htm

Ebony Society of Philatelic Events and Reflections (African-American topicals)
Sanford L. Byrd
PO Box 8888
Corpus Christi, TX 78468-8888
www.slsabyrd.com/esper.htm
E-mail: esper@str.rr.com

Embroidery, Stitchery, Textile Unit
Helen N. Cushman
1001 Genter St., Apt. 9H
La Jolla CA 92037
Ph: (619) 459-1194

Europa Study Unit
Hank Klos
PO Box 611
Bensenville IL 60106
E-mail: eunity@aol.com or klosh@clearnet.org

Fine & Performing Arts
Ruth Richards
10393 Derby Dr.
Laurel MD 20723
E-mail: bersec@aol.com

Fire Service in Philately
Brian R. Engler, Sr.
726 1/2 W. Tilghman St.
Allentown PA 18102-2324
Ph: (610) 433-2782
E-mail: brenglersr@enter.net

Gay & Lesbian History on Stamps Club
Joe Petronie
PO Box 190842
Dallas TX 75219-0842
www.glhsc.org
E-mail: glhsc@aol.com

Gems, Minerals & Jewelry Study Group
George Young
PO Box 632
Tewksbury MA 01876-0632
Ph: (978) 851-8283
www.rockhounds.com/rockshop/gmjsuapp.txt
E-mail: george-young@msn.com

Graphics Philately Association
Mark Winnegrad
PO Box 380
Bronx NY 10462-0380

Journalists, Authors & Poets on Stamps
Sol Baltimore
28742 Blackstone Dr.
Lathrup Village MI 48076

Lighthouse Stamp Society
Dalene Thomas
8612 West Warren Lane
Lakewood CO 80227-2352
Ph: (303) 986-6620
www.lighthousestampsociety.org
E-mail: dalene1@wideopenwest.com

Lions International Stamp Club
John Bargus
304-2777 Barry Rd. RR 2
Mill Bay, BC, Canada V0R 2P0
Ph: (250) 743-5782

Mahatma Gandhi On Stamps Study Circle
Pramod Shivagunde
Pratik Clinic, Akluj
Solapur, Maharashtra, India 413101
E-mail: drnanda@bom6.vsnl.net.in

Mask Study Unit
Carolyn Weber
1220 Johnson Drive, Villa 104
Ventura CA 93003-0540
www.home.prcn.org/~pauld/ata/units/masks.htm
E-mail: kencar@venturalink.net

Masonic Study Unit
Stanley R. Longenecker
930 Wood St.
Mount Joy PA 17552-1926
E-mail: natsco@usa.net

Mathematical Study Unit
Estelle Buccino
5615 Glenwood Rd.
Bethesda MD 20817-6727
Ph: (301) 718-8898
www.math.ttu.edu/msu/
E-mail: m.strauss@ttu.edu

Medical Subjects Unit
Dr. Frederick C. Skvara
PO Box 6228
Bridgewater NJ 08807
E-mail: fcskvara@bellatlantic.net

Mesoamerican Archeology Study Unit
Chris Moser
PO Box 1442
Riverside CA 92502
www.masu.homestead.com/info.html
E-mail:cmoser@ci.riverside.ca.us

Napoleonic Age Philatelists
Ken Berry
7513 Clayton Dr.
Oklahoma City OK 73132-5636
Ph: (405) 721-0044
E-mail: krb2@earthlink.net

Old World Archeological Study Unit
Eileen Meier
PO Box 369
Palmyra VA 22963

Parachute Study Group
Bill Wickert
3348 Clubhouse Road
Virginia Beach VA 23452-5339
Ph: (757) 486-3614
E-mail: bw47psg@worldnet.att.net

Petroleum Philatelic Society International
Linda W. Corwin
5427 Pine Springs Court
Conroe TX 77304
Ph: (936) 441-0216
E-mail: corwin@pdq.net

Philatelic Computing Study Group
Robert de Violini
PO Box 5025
Oxnard CA 93031-5025
www.pcsg.org
E-mail: dviolini@west.net

Philatelic Lepidopterists' Association
Alan Hanks
34 Seaton Dr.
Aurora, ON, Canada L4G 2K1
Ph: (905) 727-6933

Philatelic Music Circle
Cathleen Osborne
PO Box 1781
Sequim WA 98382
Ph: (360) 683-6373
www.stampshows.com/pmc.html

Rainbow Study Unit
Shirley Sutton
PO Box 37
Lone Pine, AB, Canada T0G 1M0
Ph: (780) 584-2268
E-mail: george-young@msn.com

Rotary on Stamps Unit
Donald Fiery
PO Box 333
Hanover PA 17331
Ph: (717) 632-8921

Scouts on Stamps Society International
Carl Schauer
PO Box 526
Belen NM 87002
Ph: (505) 864-0098
www.sossi.org
E-mail: rfrank@sossi.org

Ships on Stamps Unit
Robert Stuckert
2750 Highway 21 East
Paint Lick KY 40461
Ph: (859) 925-4901
www.shipsonstamps.org

Space Unit
Carmine Torrisi
PO Box 780241
Maspeth NY 11378
Ph: (718) 386-7882
stargate.1usa.com/stamps/
E-mail: ctorrisi1@juno.com

Sports Philatelists International
Margaret Jones
5310 Lindenwood Ave.
St. Louis MO 63109-1758
www.geocities.com/colosseum/track/6279

Stamps on Stamps Collectors Club
William Critzer
1360 Trinity Drive
Menlo Park CA 94025
Ph: (650) 234-1136
www.stampsonstamps.org
E-mail: wllmcritz@aol.com

Windmill Study Unit
Walter J. Hollien
PO Box 346
Long Valley NJ 07853-0346

Wine on Stamps Study Unit
James D. Crum
816 Kingsbury Ct.
Arroyo Grande CA 93420-4517
Ph: (805) 489-3559
E-mail: jdakcrum@aol.com

Women on Stamps Study Unit
Hugh Gottfried
2232 26th St.
Santa Monica CA 90405-1902
Ph: (310) 452-1442
E-mail: hgottfri@lausd.k12.ca.us

Zeppelin Collectors Club
Cheryl Ganz
PO Box A3843
Chicago IL 60690-3843

Expertizing Services

The following organizations will, for a fee, provide expert opinions about stamps submitted to them. Collectors should contact these organizations to find out about their fees and requirements before submitting philatelic material to them. The listing of these groups here is not intended as an endorsement by Scott Publishing Co.

General Expertizing Services

American Philatelic Expertizing Service (a service of the American Philatelic Society)
PO Box 8000
State College PA 16803
Ph: (814) 237-3803
Fax: (814) 237-6128
www.stamps.org
E-mail: ambristo@stamps.org
Areas of Expertise: Worldwide

B. P. A. Expertising, Ltd.
PO Box 137
Leatherhead, Surrey, United Kingdom KT22 0RG
E-mail: sec.bpa@tcom.co.uk
Areas of Expertise: British Commonwealth, Great Britain, Classics of Europe, South America and the Far East

Philatelic Foundation
501 Fifth Ave., Rm. 1901
New York NY 10017
Areas of Expertise: U.S. & Worldwide

Professional Stamp Experts
PO Box 6170
Newport Beach CA 92658
Ph: (877) STAMP-88
Fax: (949) 833-7955
www.collectors.com/pse
E-mail: pseinfo@collectors.com
Areas of Expertise: Stamps and covers of U.S., U.S. Possessions, British Commonwealth

Royal Philatelic Society Expert Committee
41 Devonshire Place
London, United Kingdom W1N 1PE
www.rpsl.org.uk/experts.html
E-mail: experts@rpsl.org.uk
Areas of Expertise: All

Expertizing Services Covering Specific Fields Or Countries

Canadian Society of Russian Philately Expertizing Service
PO Box 5722, Station A
Toronto, ON, Canada M5W 1P2
Fax: (416)932-0853
Areas of Expertise: Russian areas

China Stamp Society Expertizing Service
1050 West Blue Ridge Blvd
Kansas City MO 64145
Ph: (816) 942-6300
E-mail: hjmesq@aol.com
Areas of Expertise: China

Confederate Stamp Alliance Authentication Service
c/o Patricia A. Kaufmann
10194 N. Old State Road
Lincoln DE 19960-9797
Ph: (302) 422-2656
Fax: (302) 424-1990
www.webuystamps.com/csaauth.htm
E-mail: trish@ce.net
Areas of Expertise: Confederate stamps and postal history

Croatian Philatelic Society Expertizing Service
PO Box 696
Fritch TX 79036-0696
Ph: (806) 857-0129
E-mail: ou812@arn.net
Areas of Expertise: Croatia and other Balkan areas

Errors, Freaks and Oddities Collectors
Club Expertizing Service
138 East Lakemont Dr.
Kingsland GA 31548
Ph: (912) 729-1573
Areas of Expertise: U.S. errors, freaks and oddities

Estonian Philatelic Society Expertizing Service
39 Clafford Lane
Melville NY 11747
Ph: (516) 421-2078
E-mail: esto4@aol.com
Areas of Expertise: Estonia

Hawaiian Philatelic Society Expertizing Service
PO Box 10115
Honolulu HI 96816-0115
Areas of Expertise: Hawaii

Hong Kong Stamp Society Expertizing Service
PO Box 206
Glenside PA 19038
Fax: (215) 576-6850
Areas of Expertise: Hong Kong

International Association of Philatelics Experts
United States Associate members:

Paul Buchsbayew
119 W. 57th St.
New York NY 10019
Ph: (212) 977-7734
Fax: (212) 977-8653
Areas of Expertise: Russia, Soviet Union

William T. Crowe
(see Philatelic Foundation)

John Lievsay
(see American Philatelic Expertizing Service and Philatelic Foundation)
Areas of Expertise: France

Robert W. Lyman
P.O. Box 348
Irvington on Hudson NY 10533
Ph and Fax: (914) 591-6937
Areas of Expertise: British North America, New Zealand

Robert Odenweller
P.O. Box 401
Bernardsville, NJ 07924-0401
Ph and Fax: (908) 766-5460
Areas of Expertise: New Zealand, Samoa to 1900

Alex Rendon
P.O. Box 323
Massapequa NY 11762
Ph and Fax: (516) 795-0464
Areas of Expertise: Bolivia, Colombia, Colombian States

Sergio Sismondo
10035 Carousel Center Dr.
Syracuse NY 13290-0001
Ph: (315) 422-2331
Fax: (315) 422-2956
Areas of Expertise: Cape of Good Hope, Canada, British North America

International Society for Japanese Philately Expertizing Committee
32 King James Court
Staten Island NY 10308-2910
Ph: (718) 227-5229
Areas of Expertise: Japan and related areas, except WWII Japanese Occupation issues

International Society for Portuguese Philately Expertizing Service
PO Box 43146
Philadelphia PA 19129-3146
Ph: (215) 843-2106
Fax: (215) 843-2106
E-mail: s.s.washburne@worldnet.att.net
Areas of Expertise: Portugal and colonies

Mexico-Elmhurst Philatelic Society International Expert Committee
PO Box 1133
West Covina CA 91793
Areas of Expertise: Mexico

Philatelic Society for Greater Southern Africa Expert Panel
13955 W. 30th Ave.
Golden CO 80401
Areas of expertise: Entire South and South West Africa area, Bechuanalands, Basutoland, Swaziland

Ryukyu Philatelic Specialist Society Expertizing Service
1710 Buena Vista Ave.
Spring Valley CA 91977-4458
Ph: (619) 697-3205
Areas of Expertise: Ryukyu Islands

Ukrainian Philatelic & Numismatic Society Expertizing Service
30552 Dell Lane
Warren MI 48092-1862
Ph: (810) 751-5754
Areas of Expertise: Ukraine, Western Ukraine

V. G. Greene Philatelic Research Foundation
Box 100, First Canadian Place
Toronto, ON, Canada M5X 1B2
Ph: (416) 863-4593
Fax: (416) 863-4592
Areas of Expertise: British North America

Information on Catalogue Values, Grade and Condition

Catalogue Value

The Scott Catalogue value is a retail value; that is, an amount you could expect to pay for a stamp in the grade of Very Fine with no faults. Any exceptions to the grade valued will be noted in the text. The general introduction on the following pages and the individual section introductions further explain the type of material that is valued. The value listed for any given stamp is a reference that reflects recent actual dealer selling prices for that item.

Dealer retail price lists, public auction results, published prices in advertising and individual solicitation of retail prices from dealers, collectors and specialty organizations have been used in establishing the values found in this catalogue. Scott Publishing Co. values stamps, but Scott is not a company engaged in the business of buying and selling stamps as a dealer.

Use this catalogue as a guide for buying and selling. The actual price you pay for a stamp may be higher or lower than the catalogue value because of many different factors, including the amount of personal service a dealer offers, or increased or decreased interest in the country or topic represented by a stamp or set. An item may occasionally be offered at a lower price as a "loss leader," or as part of a special sale. You also may obtain an item inexpensively at public auction because of little interest at that time or as part of a large lot.

Stamps that are of a lesser grade than Very Fine, or those with condition problems, generally trade at lower prices than those given in this catalogue. Stamps of exceptional quality in both grade and condition often command higher prices than those listed.

Values for pre-1900 unused issues are for stamps with approximately half or more of their original gum. Stamps with most or all of their original gum may be expected to sell for more, and stamps with less than half of their original gum may be expected to sell for somewhat less than the values listed. On rarer stamps, it may be expected that the original gum will be somewhat more disturbed than it will be on more common issues. Post-1900 unused issues are assumed to have full original gum. From breakpoints in most countries' listings, stamps are valued as never hinged, due to the wide availability of stamps in that condition. These notations are prominently placed in the listings and in the country information preceding the listings. Some countries also feature listings with dual values for hinged and never-hinged stamps.

Grade

A stamp's grade and condition are crucial to its value. The accompanying illustrations show examples of Very Fine stamps from different time periods, along with examples of stamps in Fine to Very Fine and Extremely Fine grades as points of reference.

FINE stamps (illustrations not shown) have designs that are noticeably off center on two sides. Imperforate stamps may have small margins, and earlier issues may show the design touching one edge of the stamp design. For perforated stamps, perfs may barely clear the design on one side, and very early issues normally will have the perforations slightly cutting into the design. Used stamps may have heavier than usual cancellations.

FINE-VERY FINE stamps may be somewhat off center on one side, or slightly off center on two sides. Imperforate stamps will have two margins of at least normal size, and the design will not touch any edge. For perforated stamps, the perfs are well clear of the design, but are still noticeably off center. *However, early issues of a country may be printed in such a way that the design naturally is very close to the edges. In these cases, the perforations may cut into the design very slightly.* Used stamps will not have a cancellation that detracts from the design.

VERY FINE stamps may be slightly off center on one side, but the design will be well clear of the edge. The stamp will present a nice, balanced appearance. Imperforate stamps will have three normal-sized margins. *However, early issues of many countries may be printed in such a way that the perforations may touch the design on one or more sides. Where this is the case, a boxed note will be found defining the centering and margins of the stamps being valued.* Used stamps will have light or otherwise neat cancellations. This is the grade used to establish Scott Catalogue values.

EXTREMELY FINE stamps are close to being perfectly centered. Imperforate stamps will have even margins that are larger than normal. Even the earliest perforated issues will have perforations clear of the design on all sides.

Scott Publishing Co. recognizes that there is no formally enforced grading scheme for postage stamps, and that the final price you pay or obtain for a stamp will be determined by individual agreement at the time of transaction.

Condition

Grade addresses only centering and (for used stamps) cancellation. *Condition* refers to factors other than grade that affect a stamp's desirability.

Factors that can increase the value of a stamp include exceptionally wide margins, particularly fresh color, the presence of selvage, and plate or die varieties. Unusual cancels on used stamps (particularly those of the 19th century) can greatly enhance their value as well.

Factors other than faults that decrease the value of a stamp include loss of original gum, regumming, a hinge remnant or foreign object adhering to the gum, natural inclusions, straight edges, and markings or notations applied by collectors or dealers.

Faults include missing pieces, tears, pin or other holes, surface scuffs, thin spots, creases, toning, short or pulled perforations, clipped perforations, oxidation or other forms of color changelings, soiling, stains, and such man-made changes as reperforations or the chemical removal or lightening of a cancellation.

Grading Illustrations

On the following two pages are illustrations of various stamps from countries appearing in this volume. These stamps are arranged by country, and they represent early or important issues that are often found in widely different grades in the marketplace. The editors believe the illustrations will prove useful in showing the margin size and centering that will be seen on the various issues.

In addition to the matters of margin size and centering, collectors are reminded that the very fine stamps valued in the Scott catalogues also will possess fresh color and intact perforations, and they will be free from defects.

Most examples shown are computer-manipulated images made from single digitized master illustrations.

Stamp Illustrations Used in the Catalogue

It is important to note that the stamp images used for identification purposes in this catlaogue may not be indicative of the grade of stamp being valued. Refer to the written discussion of grades on this page and to the grading illustrations on the following two pages for grading information.

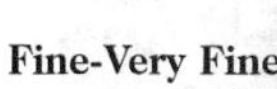

SCOTT CATALOGUES VALUE STAMPS IN THIS GRADE

Very Fine

Extremely Fine

Fine-Very Fine

SCOTT CATALOGUES VALUE STAMPS IN THIS GRADE

Very Fine

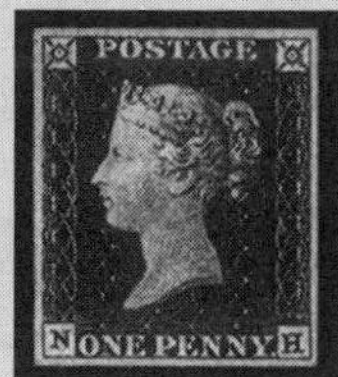

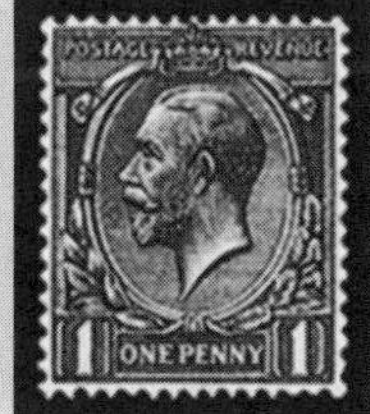

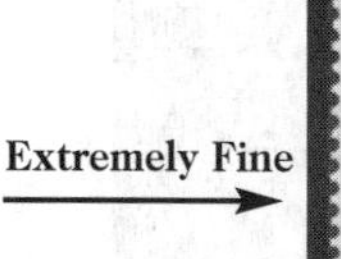

Fine-Very Fine

SCOTT CATALOGUES VALUE STAMPS IN THIS GRADE

Very Fine

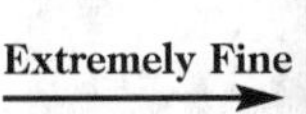

Fine-Very Fine

SCOTT CATALOGUES VALUE STAMPS IN THIS GRADE

Very Fine

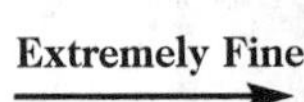

For purposes of helping to determine the gum condition and value of an unused stamp, Scott Publishing Co. presents the following chart which details different gum conditions and indicates how the conditions correlate with the Scott values for unused stamps. Used together, the Illustrated Grading Chart on the previous pages and this Illustrated Gum Chart should allow catalogue users to better understand the grade and gum condition of stamps valued in the Scott catalogues.

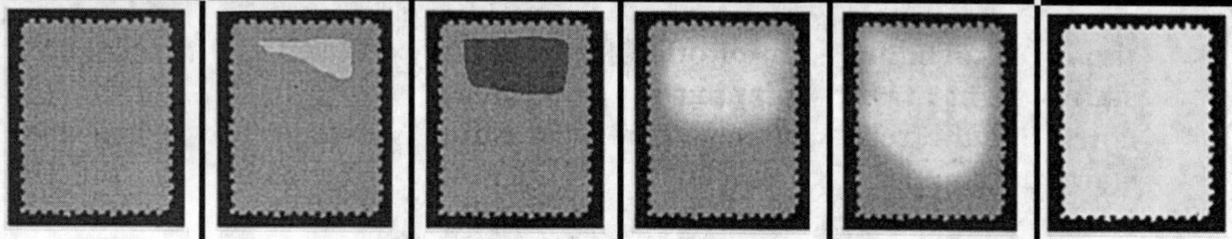

Gum Categories:	MINT N.H.	ORIGINAL GUM (O.G.)				NO GUM
	Mint Never Hinged *Free from any disturbance*	**Lightly Hinged** *Faint impression of a removed hinge over a small area*	**Hinge Mark or Remnant** *Prominent hinged spot with part or all of the hinge remaining*	**Large part o.g.** *Approximately half or more of the gum intact*	**Small part o.g.** *Approximately less than half of the gum intact*	**No gum** *Only if issued with gum*
Commonly Used Symbol:	★★	★	★	★	★	(★)
Pre-1900 Issues (Pre-1890 for U.S.)	*Very fine pre-1900 stamps in these categories trade at a premium over Scott value*			Scott Value for "Unused"		Scott "No Gum" listings for selected unused classic stamps
From 1900 to break-points for listings of never-hinged stamps	Scott "Never Hinged" listings for selected unused stamps	Scott Value for "Unused" (Actual value will be affected by the degree of hinging of the full o.g.)				
From breakpoints noted for many countries	Scott Value for "Unused"					

Never Hinged (NH; ★★): A never-hinged stamp will have full original gum that will have no hinge mark or disturbance. The presence of an expertizer's mark does not disqualify a stamp from this designation.

Original Gum (OG; ★): Pre-1900 stamps should have approximately half or more of their original gum. On rarer stamps, it may be expected that the original gum will be somewhat more disturbed that it will be on more common issues. Post-1900 stamps should have full original gum. Original gum will show some disturbance caused by a previous hinge(s) which may be present or entirely removed. The actual value of a post-1900 stamp will be affected by the degree of hinging of the full original gum.

Disturbed Original Gum: Gum showing noticeable effects of humidity, climate or hinging over more than half of the gum. The significance of gum disturbance in valuing a stamp in any of the Original Gum categories depends on the degree of disturbance, the rarity and normal gum condition of the issue and other variables affecting quality.

Regummed (RG; (★)): A regummed stamp is a stamp without gum that has had some type of gum privately applied at a time after it was issued. This normally is done to deceive collectors and/or dealers into thinking that the stamp has original gum and therefore has a higher value. A regummed stamp is considered the same as a stamp with none of its original gum for purposes of grading.

Catalogue Listing Policy

It is the intent of Scott Publishing Co. to list all postage stamps of the world in the *Scott Standard Postage Stamp Catalogue.* The only strict criteria for listing is that stamps be decreed legal for postage by the issuing country and that the issuing country actually have an operating postal system. Whether the primary intent of issuing a given stamp or set was for sale to postal patrons or to stamp collectors is not part of our listing criteria. Scott's role is to provide basic comprehensive postage stamp information. It is up to each stamp collector to choose which items to include in a collection.

It is Scott's objective to seek reasons why a stamp should be listed, rather than why it should not. Nevertheless, there are certain types of items that will not be listed. These include the following:

1. Unissued items that are not officially distributed or released by the issuing postal authority. Even if such a stamp is "accidentally" distributed to the philatelic or even postal market, it remains unissued. If such items are officially issued at a later date by the country, they will be listed. Unissued items consist of those that have been printed and then held from sale for reasons such as change in government, errors found on stamps or something deemed objectionable about a stamp subject or design.
2. Stamps "issued" by non-existent postal entities or fantasy countries, such as Nagaland, Occusi-Ambeno, Staffa, Sedang, Torres Straits and others.
3. Semi-official or unofficial items not required for postage. Examples include items issued by private agencies for their own express services. When such items are required for delivery, or are valid as prepayment of postage, they are listed.
4. Local stamps issued for local use only. Postage stamps issued by governments specifically for "domestic" use, such as Haiti Scott 219-228, or the United States non-denominated stamps, are not considered to be locals, since they are valid for postage throughout the country of origin.
5. Items not valid for postal use. For example, a few countries have issued souvenir sheets that are not valid for postage. This area also includes a number of worldwide charity labels (some denominated) that do not pay postage.
6. Intentional varieties, such as imperforate stamps that look like their perforated counterparts and are issued in very small quantities. These are often controlled issues intended for speculation.
7. Items distributed by the issuing government only to a limited group, such as a stamp club, philatelic exhibition or a single stamp dealer, and later brought to market at inflated prices. These items normally will be included in a footnote.

The fact that a stamp has been used successfully as postage, even on international mail, is not in itself sufficient proof that it was legitimately issued. Numerous examples of so-called stamps from non-existent countries are known to have been used to post letters that have successfully passed through the international mail system.

There are certain items that are subject to interpretation. When a stamp falls outside our specifications, it may be listed along with a cautionary footnote.

A number of factors are considered in our approach to analyzing how a stamp is listed. The following list of factors is presented to share with you, the catalogue user, the complexity of the listing process.

Additional printings — "Additional printings" of a previously issued stamp may range from an item that is totally different to cases where it is impossible to differentiate from the original. At least a minor number (a small-letter suffix) is assigned if there is a distinct change in stamp shade, noticeably redrawn design, or a significantly different perforation measurement. A major number (numeral or numeral and capital-letter combination) is assigned if the editors feel the "additional printing" is sufficiently different from the original that it constitutes a different issue.

Commemoratives — Where practical, commemoratives with the same theme are placed in a set. For example, the U.S. Civil War Centennial set of 1961-65 and the Constitution Bicentennial series of 1989-90 appear as sets. Countries such as Japan and Korea issue such material on a regular basis, with an announced, or at least predictable, number of stamps known in advance. Occasionally, however, stamp sets that were released over a period of years have been separated. Appropriately placed footnotes will guide you to each set's continuation.

Definitive sets — Blocks of numbers generally have been reserved for definitive sets, based on previous experience with any given country. If a few more stamps were issued in a set than originally expected, they often have been inserted into the original set with a capital-letter suffix, such as U.S. Scott 1059A. If it appears that many more stamps than the originally allotted block will be released before the set is completed, a new block of numbers will be reserved, with the original one being closed off. In some cases, such as the British Machin Head series or the U.S. Transportation and Great Americans series, several blocks of numbers exist. Appropriately placed footnotes will guide you to each set's continuation.

New country — Membership in the Universal Postal Union is not a consideration for listing status or order of placement within the catalogue. The index will tell you in what volume or page number the listings begin.

"No release date" items — The amount of information available for any given stamp issue varies greatly from country to country and even from time to time. Extremely comprehensive information about new stamps is available from some countries well before the stamps are released. By contrast some countries do not provide information about stamps or release dates. Most countries, however, fall between these extremes. A country may provide denominations or subjects of stamps from upcoming issues that are not issued as planned. Sometimes, philatelic agencies, those private firms hired to represent countries, add these later-issued items to sets well after the formal release date. This time period can range from weeks to years. If these items were officially released by the country, they will be added to the appropriate spot in the set. In many cases, the specific release date of a stamp or set of stamps may never be known.

Overprints — The color of an overprint is always noted if it is other than black. Where more than one color of ink has been used on overprints of a single set, the color used is noted. Early overprint and surcharge illustrations were altered to prevent their use by forgers.

Se-tenants — Connected stamps of differing features (se-tenants) will be listed in the format most commonly collected. This includes pairs, blocks or larger multiples. Se-tenant units are not always symmetrical. An example is Australia Scott 508, which is a block of seven stamps. If the stamps are primarily collected as a unit, the major number may be assigned to the multiple, with minors going to each component stamp. In cases where continuous-design or other unit se-tenants will receive significant postal use, each stamp is given a major Scott number listing. This includes issues from the United States, Canada, Germany and Great Britain, for example.

Understanding the Listings

On the opposite page is an enlarged "typical" listing from this catalogue. Below are detailed explanations of each of the highlighted parts of the listing.

A Scott number — Scott catalogue numbers are used to identify specific items when buying, selling or trading stamps. Each listed postage stamp from every country has a unique Scott catalogue number. Therefore, Germany Scott 99, for example, can only refer to a single stamp. Although the Scott catalogue usually lists stamps in chronological order by date of issue, there are exceptions. When a country has issued a set of stamps over a period of time, those stamps within the set are kept together without regard to date of issue. This follows the normal collecting approach of keeping stamps in their natural sets.

When a country issues a set of stamps over a period of time, a group of consecutive catalogue numbers is reserved for the stamps in that set, as issued. If that group of numbers proves to be too few, capital-letter suffixes, such as "A" or "B," may be added to existing numbers to create enough catalogue numbers to cover all items in the set. A capital-letter suffix indicates a major Scott catalogue number listing. Scott uses a suffix letter only once. Therefore, a catalogue number listing with a capital-letter suffix will not also be found with the same letter (lower case) used as a minor-letter listing. If there is a Scott 16A in a set, for example, there will not also be a Scott 16a. However, a minor-letter "a" listing may be added to a major number containing an "A" suffix (Scott 16Aa, for example).

Suffix letters are cumulative. A minor "b" variety of Scott 16A would be Scott 16Ab, not Scott 16b.

There are times when a reserved block of Scott catalogue numbers is too large for a set, leaving some numbers unused. Such gaps in the numbering sequence also occur when the catalogue editors move an item's listing elsewhere or have removed it entirely from the catalogue. Scott does not attempt to account for every possible number, but rather attempts to assure that each stamp is assigned its own number.

Scott numbers designating regular postage normally are only numerals. Scott numbers for other types of stamps, such as air post, semi-postal, postal tax, postage due, occupation and others have a prefix consisting of one or more capital letters or a combination of numerals and capital letters.

B Illustration number — Illustration or design-type numbers are used to identify each catalogue illustration. For most sets, the lowest face-value stamp is shown. It then serves as an example of the basic design approach for other stamps not illustrated. Where more than one stamp use the same illustration number, but have differences in design, the design paragraph or the description line clearly indicates the design on each stamp not illustrated. Where there are both vertical and horizontal designs in a set, a single illustration may be used, with the exceptions noted in the design paragraph or description line.

When an illustration is followed by a lower-case letter in parentheses, such as "A2(b)," the trailing letter indicates which overprint or surcharge illustration applies.

Illustrations normally are 70 percent of the original size of the stamp. An effort has been made to note all illustrations not illustrated at that percentage. Virtually all souvenir sheet illustrations are reduced even more. Overprints and surcharges are shown at 100 percent of their original size if shown alone, but are 70 percent of original size if shown on stamps. In some cases, the illustration will be placed above the set, between listings or omitted completely. Overprint and surcharge illustrations are not placed in this catalogue for purposes of expertizing stamps.

C Paper color — The color of a stamp's paper is noted in italic type when the paper used is not white.

D Listing styles — There are two principal types of catalogue listings: major and minor.

Major listings are in a larger type style than minor listings. The catalogue number is a numeral that can be found with or without a capital-letter suffix, and with or without a prefix.

Minor listings are in a smaller type style and have a small-letter suffix or (if the listing immediately follows that of the major number) may show only the letter. These listings identify a variety of the major item. Examples include perforation, color, watermark or printing method differences, multiples (some souvenir sheets, booklet panes and se-tenant combinations), and singles of multiples.

Examples of major number listings include 16, 28A, B97, C13A, 10N5, and 10N6A. Examples of minor numbers are 16a and C13Ab.

E Basic information about a stamp or set — Introducing each stamp issue is a small section (usually a line listing) of basic information about a stamp or set. This section normally includes the date of issue, method of printing, perforation, watermark and, sometimes, some additional information of note. *Printing method, perforation and watermark apply to the following sets until a change is noted.* Stamps created by overprinting or surcharging previous issues are assumed to have the same perforation, watermark and printing method as the original. Dates of issue are as precise as Scott is able to confirm and often reflect the dates on first-day covers, rather than the actual date of release.

F Denomination — This normally refers to the face value of the stamp; that is, the cost of the unused stamp at the post office at the time of issue. When a denomination is shown in parentheses, it does not appear on the stamp. This includes the non-denominated stamps of the United States, Brazil and Great Britain, for example.

G Color or other description — This area provides information to solidify identification of a stamp. In many recent cases, a description of the stamp design appears in this space, rather than a listing of colors.

H Year of issue — In stamp sets that have been released in a period that spans more than a year, the number shown in parentheses is the year that stamp first appeared. Stamps without a date appeared during the first year of the issue. Dates are not always given for minor varieties.

I Value unused and Value used — The Scott catalogue values are based on stamps that are in a grade of Very Fine unless stated otherwise. Unused values refer to items that have not seen postal, revenue or any other duty for which they were intended. Pre-1900 unused stamps that were issued with gum must have at least most of their original gum. Later issues are assumed to have full original gum. From breakpoints specified in most countries' listings, stamps are valued as never hinged. Stamps issued without gum are noted. Modern issues with PVA or other synthetic adhesives may appear ungummed. Self-adhesive stamps are valued as appearing undisturbed on their original backing paper. For a more detailed explanation of these values, please see the "Catalogue Value," "Condition" and "Understanding Valuing Notations" sections elsewhere in this introduction.

In some cases, where used stamps are more valuable than unused stamps, the value is for an example with a contemporaneous cancel, rather than a modern cancel or a smudge or other unclear marking. For those stamps that were released for postal and fiscal purposes, the used value represents a postally used stamp. Stamps with revenue cancels generally sell for less. Scott values for used self-adhesive stamps are for examples either on piece or off piece.

J Changes in basic set information — Bold type is used to show any changes in the basic data given for a set of stamps. This includes perforation differences from one stamp to the next or a different paper, printing method or watermark.

K Total value of a set — The total value of sets of three or more stamps issued after 1900 are shown. The set line also notes the range of Scott numbers and total number of stamps included in the grouping. The actual value of a set consisting predominantly of stamps having the minimum value of twenty cents may be less than the total value shown. Similary, the actual value or catalogue value of se-tenant pairs or of blocks consisting of stamps having the minimum value of twenty cents may be less than the catalogue values of the component parts.

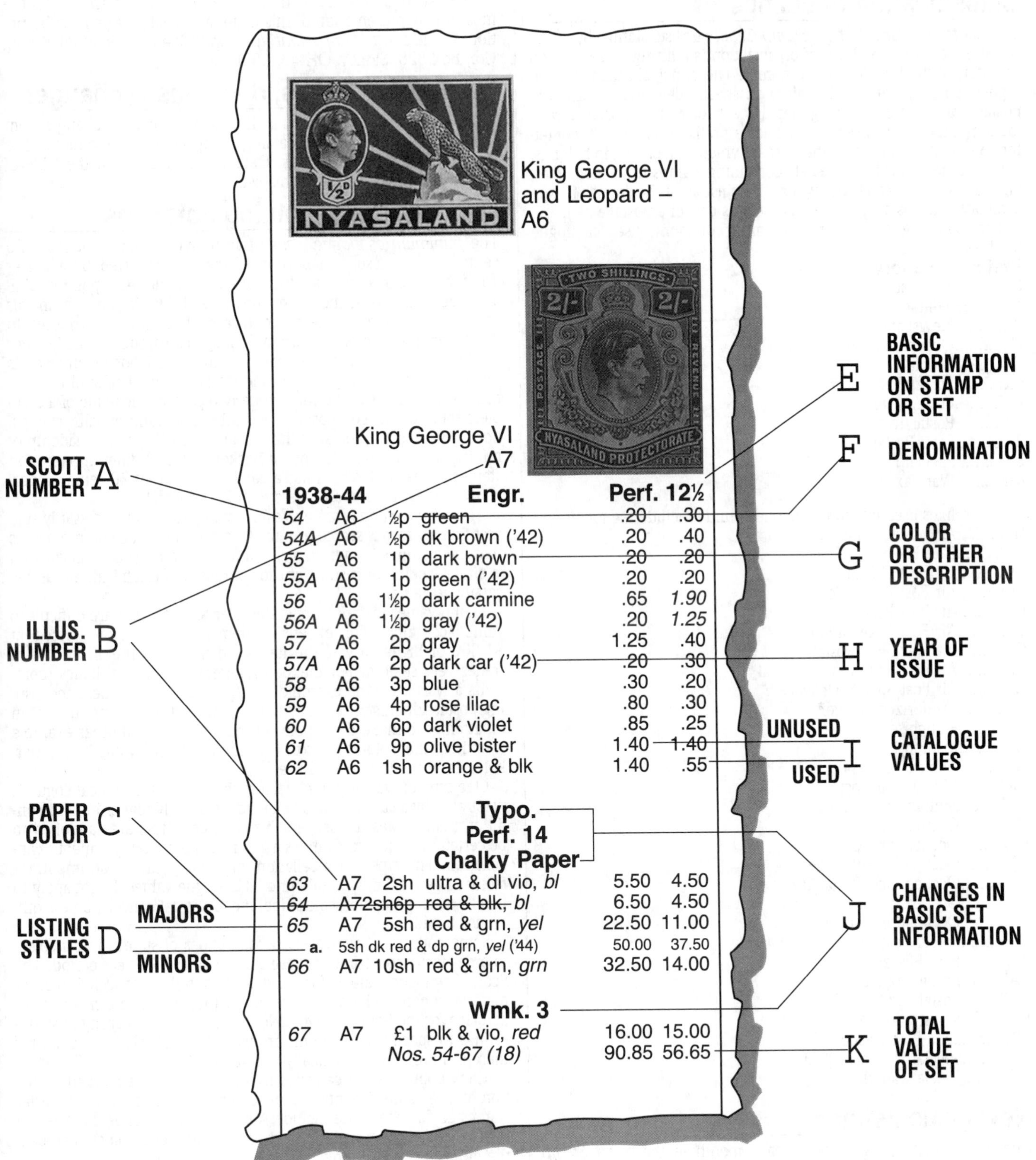
NYASALAND
King George VI and Leopard – A6
TWO SHILLINGS
2/- 2/-
POSTAGE REVENUE
NYASALAND PROTECTORATE
King George VI A7
1938-44 Engr. Perf. 12½
54 A6 ½p green .20 .30
54A A6 ½p dk brown ('42) .20 .40
55 A6 1p dark brown .20 .20
55A A6 1p green ('42) .20 .20
56 A6 1½p dark carmine .65 1.90
56A A6 1½p gray ('42) .20 1.25
57 A6 2p gray 1.25 .40
57A A6 2p dark car ('42) .20 .30
58 A6 3p blue .30 .20
59 A6 4p rose lilac .80 .30
60 A6 6p dark violet .85 .25
61 A6 9p olive bister 1.40 1.40
62 A6 1sh orange & blk 1.40 .55
Typo.
Perf. 14
Chalky Paper
63 A7 2sh ultra & dl vio, bl 5.50 4.50
64 A7 2sh6p red & blk, bl 6.50 4.50
65 A7 5sh red & grn, yel 22.50 11.00
a. 5sh dk red & dp grn, yel ('44) 50.00 37.50
66 A7 10sh red & grn, grn 32.50 14.00
Wmk. 3
67 A7 £1 blk & vio, red 16.00 15.00
Nos. 54-67 (18) 90.85 56.65
SCOTT NUMBER A
ILLUS. NUMBER B
PAPER COLOR C
LISTING STYLES D
MAJORS
MINORS
E BASIC INFORMATION ON STAMP OR SET
F DENOMINATION
G COLOR OR OTHER DESCRIPTION
H YEAR OF ISSUE
UNUSED
USED
I CATALOGUE VALUES
J CHANGES IN BASIC SET INFORMATION
K TOTAL VALUE OF SET

Special Notices

Classification of stamps

The *Scott Standard Postage Stamp Catalogue* lists stamps by country of issue. The next level of organization is a listing by section on the basis of the function of the stamps. The principal sections cover regular postage, semi-postal, air post, special delivery, registration, postage due and other categories. Except for regular postage, catalogue numbers for all sections include a prefix letter (or number-letter combination) denoting the class to which a given stamp belongs. When some countries issue sets containing stamps from more than one category, the catalogue will at times list all of the stamps in one category (such as air post stamps listed as part of a postage set).

The following is a listing of the most commonly used catalogue prefixes.

Prefix ...Category
C ....Air Post
M...........Military
P............Newspaper
N ....Occupation - Regular Issues
O ....Official
Q ....Parcel Post
J.............Postage Due
RA ....Postal Tax
B............Semi-Postal
E............Special Delivery
MR ....War Tax

Other prefixes used by more than one country include the following:
H ....Acknowledgment of Receipt
I.............Late Fee
CO.........Air Post Official
CQ.........Air Post Parcel Post
RAC ....Air Post Postal Tax
CF..........Air Post Registration
CB ....Air Post Semi-Postal
CBO.......Air Post Semi-Postal Official
CE ....Air Post Special Delivery
EY..........Authorized Delivery
S ....Franchise
G ....Insured Letter
GY ....Marine Insurance
MC ....Military Air Post
MQ........Military Parcel Post
NC.........Occupation - Air Post
NO.........Occupation - Official
NJ ....Occupation - Postage Due
NRA.......Occupation - Postal Tax
NB ....Occupation - Semi-Postal
NE ....Occupation - Special Delivery
QY ....Parcel Post Authorized Delivery
AR ....Postal-fiscal
RAJ ....Postal Tax Due
RAB ....Postal Tax Semi-Postal
F............Registration
EB..........Semi-Postal Special Delivery
EO ....Special Delivery Official
QE ....Special Handling

New issue listings

Updates to this catalogue appear each month in the *Scott Stamp Monthly* magazine. Included in this update are additions to the listings of countries found in the *Scott Standard Postage Stamp Catalogue* and the *Specialized Catalogue of United States Stamps*, as well as corrections and updates to current editions of this catalogue.

From time to time there will be changes in the final listings of stamps from the *Scott Stamp Monthly* to the next edition of the catalogue. This occurs as more information about certain stamps or sets becomes available.

The catalogue update section of the *Scott Stamp Monthly* is the most timely presentation of this material available. Annual subscriptions to the *Scott Stamp Monthly* are available from Scott Publishing Co., Box 828, Sidney, OH 45365-0828.

Number additions, deletions & changes

A listing of catalogue number additions, deletions and changes from the previous edition of the catalogue appears in each volume. See Catalogue Number Additions, Deletions & Changes in the table of contents for the location of this list.

Understanding valuing notations

The *minimum catalogue value* of an individual stamp or set is 20 cents. This represents a portion of the cost incurred by a dealer when he prepares an individual stamp for resale. As a point of philatelic-economic fact, the lower the value shown for an item in this catalogue, the greater the percentage of that value is attributed to dealer mark up and profit margin. In many cases, such as the 20-cent minimum value, that price does not cover the labor or other costs involved with stocking it as an individual stamp. The sum of minimum values in a set does not properly represent the value of a complete set primarily composed of a number of minimum-value stamps, nor does the sum represent the actual value of a packet made up of minimum-value stamps. Thus a packet of 1,000 different common stamps — each of which has a catalogue value of 20-cents — normally sells for considerably less than 200 dollars!

The *absence of a retail value* for a stamp does not necessarily suggest that a stamp is scarce or rare. A dash in the value column means that the stamp is known in a stated form or variety, but information is either lacking or insufficient for purposes of establishing a usable catalogue value.

Stamp values in *italics* generally refer to items that are difficult to value accurately. For expensive items, such as those priced at $1,000 or higher, a value in italics indicates that the affected item trades very seldom. For inexpensive items, a value in italics represents a warning. One example is a "blocked" issue where the issuing postal administration may have controlled one stamp in a set in an attempt to make the whole set more valuable. Another example is an item that sold at an extreme multiple of face value in the marketplace at the time of its issue.

One type of warning to collectors that appears in the catalogue is illustrated by a stamp that is valued considerably higher in used condition than it is as unused. In this case, collectors are cautioned to be certain the used version has a genuine and contemporaneous cancellation. The type of cancellation on a stamp can be an important factor in determining its sale price. Catalogue values do not apply to fiscal, telegraph or non-contemporaneous postal cancels, unless otherwise noted.

Some countries have released back issues of stamps in canceled-to-order form, sometimes covering as much as a 10-year period. The Scott Catalogue values for used stamps reflect canceled-to-order material when such stamps are found to predominate in the marketplace for the issue involved. Notes frequently appear in the stamp listings to specify which items are valued as canceled-to-order, or if there is a premium for postally used examples.

Many countries sell canceled-to-order stamps at a marked reduction of face value. Countries that sell or have sold canceled-to-order stamps at *full* face value include Australia, Netherlands, France and Switzerland. It may be almost impossible to identify such stamps if the gum has been removed, because official government canceling devices are used. Postally used copies of these items on cover, however, are usually worth more than the canceled-to-order stamps with original gum.

Abbreviations

Scott Publishing Co. uses a consistent set of abbreviations throughout this catalogue to conserve space, while still providing necessary information.

COLOR ABBREVIATIONS

amb.....amber
anil......aniline
ap........apple
aqua.....aquamarine
az........azure
bis........bister
bl.........blue
bld.......blood
blk.......black
bril.......brilliant
brn.......brown
brnsh...brownish
brnz.....bronze
brt.......bright
brnt.....burnt
car.......carmine
cer.......cerise
chlky....chalky
cham...chamois
chnt.....chestnut
choc.....chocolate
chr.......chrome
cit........citron
cl.........claret
cob......cobalt
cop......copper
crim.....crimson
cr.........cream
dk........dark
dl.........dull
dp........deep
db........drab
emer....emerald
gldn.....golden
grysh....grayish
grn.......green
grnsh...greenish
hel.......heliotrope
hn........henna
ind.......indigo
int........intense
lav.......lavender
lem......lemon
lil.........lilac
lt..........light
mag.....magenta
man.....manila
mar......maroon
mv.......mauve
multi....multicolored
mlky....milky
myr......myrtle
ol.........olive
olvn.....olivine
org.......orange
pck......peacock
pnksh...pinkish
Prus.....Prussian
pur.......purple
redsh...reddish
res.......reseda
ros.......rosine
ryl........royal
sal........salmon
saph.....sapphire
scar......scarlet
sep.......sepia
sien......sienna
sil........silver
sl.........slate
stl........steel
turq.....turquoise
ultra.....ultramarine
Ven......Venetian
ver.......vermilion
vio.......violet
yel.......yellow
yelsh....yellowish

When no color is given for an overprint or surcharge, black is the color used. Abbreviations for colors used for overprints and surcharges include: "(B)" or "(Blk)," black; "(Bl)," blue; "(R)," red; and "(G)," green.

Additional abbreviations in this catalogue are shown below:

Adm. ....Administration
AFL................American Federation of Labor
Anniv..............Anniversary
APS ....American Philatelic Society
Assoc. ....Association
ASSR. ....Autonomous Soviet Socialist Republic
b.....................Born
BEP ....Bureau of Engraving and Printing
Bicent. ....Bicentennial
Bklt.................Booklet
Brit. ....British
btwn................Between
Bur..................Bureau
c. or ca. ....Circa
Cat. ....Catalogue
Cent. ....Centennial, century, centenary
CIO ....Congress of Industrial Organizations
Conf. ....Conference
Cong................Congress
Cpl. ....Corporal
CTO ....Canceled to order
d......................Died
Dbl. ....Double
EKU.................Earliest known use
Engr.................Engraved
Exhib...............Exhibition
Expo................Exposition
Fed. ....Federation
GB...................Great Britain
Gen. ....General
GPO ....General post office
Horiz. ....Horizontal
Imperf..............Imperforate
Impt. ....Imprint
Intl. ....International
Invtd................Inverted
L......................Left
Lieut., lt...........Lieutenant
Litho................Lithographed
LL....................Lower left
LR ....Lower right
mm..................Millimeter
Ms...................Manuscript
Natl. ....National
No...................Number
NY...................New York
NYC ....New York City
Ovpt. ....Overprint
Ovptd. ....Overprinted
P......................Plate number
Perf..................Perforated, perforation
Phil...................Philatelic
Photo................Photogravure
PO....................Post office
Pr.....................Pair
P.R...................Puerto Rico
Prec..................Precancel, precanceled
Pres..................President
PTT ....Post, Telephone and Telegraph
Rio...................Rio de Janeiro
Sgt...................Sergeant
Soc. ....Society
Souv. ....Souvenir
SSR..................Soviet Socialist Republic, see ASSR
St.....................Saint, street
Surch................Surcharge
Typo. ....Typographed
UL....................Upper left
Unwmkd. ....Unwatermarked
UPU ....Universal Postal Union
UR....................Upper Right
US....................United States
USPOD.............United States Post Office Department
USSR ....Union of Soviet Socialist Republics
Vert. ....Vertical
VP ....Vice president
Wmk. ....Watermark
Wmkd. ....Watermarked
WWI ....World War I
WWII ....World War II

Examination

Scott Publishing Co. will not comment upon the genuineness, grade or condition of stamps, because of the time and responsibility involved. Rather, there are several expertizing groups that undertake this work for both collectors and dealers. Neither will Scott Publishing Co. appraise or identify philatelic material. The company cannot take responsibility for unsolicited stamps or covers sent by individuals.

How to order from your dealer

When ordering stamps from a dealer, it is not necessary to write the full description of a stamp as listed in this catalogue. All you need is the name of the country, the Scott catalogue number and whether the desired item is unused or used. For example, "Japan Scott 422 unused" is sufficient to identify the unused stamp of Japan listed as "422 A206 5y brown."

Basic Stamp Information

A stamp collector's knowledge of the combined elements that make a given stamp issue unique determines his or her ability to identify stamps. These elements include paper, watermark, method of separation, printing, design and gum. On the following pages each of these important areas is briefly described.

Paper

Paper is an organic material composed of a compacted weave of cellulose fibers and generally formed into sheets. Paper used to print stamps may be manufactured in sheets, or it may have been part of a large roll (called a web) before being cut to size. The fibers most often used to create paper on which stamps are printed include bark, wood, straw and certain grasses. In many cases, linen or cotton rags have been added for greater strength and durability. Grinding, bleaching, cooking and rinsing these raw fibers reduces them to a slushy pulp, referred to by paper makers as "stuff." Sizing and, sometimes, coloring matter is added to the pulp to make different types of finished paper.

After the stuff is prepared, it is poured onto sieve-like frames that allow the water to run off, while retaining the matted pulp. As fibers fall onto the screen and are held by gravity, they form a natural weave that will later hold the paper together. If the screen has metal bits that are formed into letters or images attached, it leaves slightly thinned areas on the paper. These are called watermarks.

When the stuff is almost dry, it is passed under pressure through smooth or engraved rollers - dandy rolls - or placed between cloth in a press to be flattened and dried.

Stamp paper falls broadly into two types: wove and laid. The nature of the surface of the frame onto which the pulp is first deposited causes the differences in appearance between the two. If the surface is smooth and even, the paper will be of fairly uniform texture throughout. This is known as *wove paper*. Early papermaking machines poured the pulp onto a continuously circulating web of felt, but modern machines feed the pulp onto a cloth-like screen made of closely interwoven fine wires. This paper, when held to a light, will show little dots or points very close together. The proper name for this is "wire wove," but the type is still considered wove. Any U.S. or British stamp printed after 1880 will serve as an example of wire wove paper.

Closely spaced parallel wires, with cross wires at wider intervals, make up the frames used for what is known as *laid paper*. A greater thickness of the pulp will settle between the wires. The paper, when held to a light, will show alternate light and dark lines. The spacing and the thickness of the lines may vary, but on any one sheet of paper they are all alike. See Russia Scott 31-38 for examples of laid paper.

Batonne, from the French word meaning "a staff," is a term used if the lines in the paper are spaced quite far apart, like the printed ruling on a writing tablet. Batonne paper may be either wove or laid. If laid, fine laid lines can be seen between the batons.

Quadrille is the term used when the lines in the paper form little squares. *Oblong quadrille* is the term used when rectangles, rather than squares, are formed. See Mexico-Guadalajara Scott 35-37 for examples of oblong quadrille paper.

Paper also is classified as thick or thin, hard or soft, and by color if dye is added during manufacture. Such colors may include yellowish, greenish, bluish and reddish.

Brief explanations of other types of paper used for printing stamps, as well as examples, follow.

Pelure — Pelure paper is a very thin, hard and often brittle paper that is sometimes bluish or grayish in appearance. See Serbia Scott 169-170.

Native — This is a term applied to handmade papers used to produce some of the early stamps of the Indian states. Stamps printed on native paper may be expected to display various natural inclusions that are normal and do not negatively affect value. Japanese paper, originally made of mulberry fibers and rice flour, is part of this group. See Japan Scott 1-18.

Manila — This type of paper is often used to make stamped envelopes and wrappers. It is a coarse-textured stock, usually smooth on one side and rough on the other. A variety of colors of manila paper exist, but the most common range is yellowish-brown.

Silk — Introduced by the British in 1847 as a safeguard against counterfeiting, silk paper contains bits of colored silk thread scattered throughout. The density of these fibers varies greatly and can include as few as one fiber per stamp or hundreds. U.S. revenue Scott R152 is a good example of an easy-to-identify silk paper stamp.

Silk-thread paper has uninterrupted threads of colored silk arranged so that one or more threads run through the stamp or postal stationery. See Great Britain Scott 5-6 and Switzerland Scott 14-19.

Granite — Filled with minute cloth or colored paper fibers of various colors and lengths, granite paper should not be confused with either type of silk paper. Austria Scott 172-175 and a number of Swiss stamps are examples of granite paper.

Chalky — A chalk-like substance coats the surface of chalky paper to discourage the cleaning and reuse of canceled stamps, as well as to provide a smoother, more acceptable printing surface. Because the designs of stamps printed on chalky paper are imprinted on what is often a water-soluble coating, any attempt to remove a cancellation will destroy the stamp. *Do not soak these stamps in any fluid.* To remove a stamp printed on chalky paper from an envelope, wet the paper from underneath the stamp until the gum dissolves enough to release the stamp from the paper. See St. Kitts-Nevis Scott 89-90 for examples of stamps printed on this type of chalky paper.

India — Another name for this paper, originally introduced from China about 1750, is "China Paper." It is a thin, opaque paper often used for plate and die proofs by many countries.

Double — In philately, the term double paper has two distinct meanings. The first is a two-ply paper, usually a combination of a thick and a thin sheet, joined during manufacture. This type was used experimentally as a means to discourage the reuse of stamps.

The design is printed on the thin paper. Any attempt to remove a cancellation would destroy the design. U.S. Scott 158 and other Banknote-era stamps exist on this form of double paper.

The second type of double paper occurs on a rotary press, when the end of one paper roll, or web, is affixed to the next roll to save time feeding the paper through the press. Stamp designs are printed over the joined paper and, if overlooked by inspectors, may get into post office stocks.

Goldbeater's Skin — This type of paper was used for the 1866 issue of Prussia, and was a tough, translucent paper. The design was printed in reverse on the back of the stamp, and the gum applied over the printing. It is impossible to remove stamps printed on this type of paper from the paper to which they are affixed without destroying the design.

Ribbed — Ribbed paper has an uneven, corrugated surface made by passing the paper through ridged rollers. This type exists on some copies of U.S. Scott 156-165.

Various other substances, or substrates, have been used for stamp manufacture, including wood, aluminum, copper, silver and gold foil, plastic, and silk and cotton fabrics.

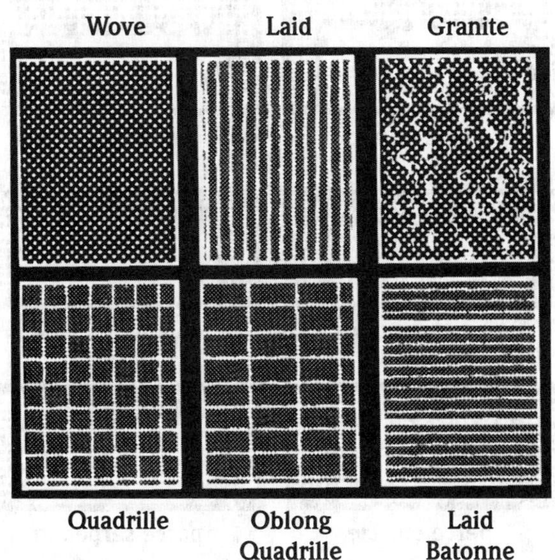

Watermarks

Watermarks are an integral part of some papers. They are formed in the process of paper manufacture. Watermarks consist of small designs, formed of wire or cut from metal and soldered to the surface of the mold or, sometimes, on the dandy roll. The designs may be in the form of crowns, stars, anchors, letters or other characters or symbols. These pieces of metal - known in the paper-making industry as "bits" - impress a design into the paper. The design sometimes may be seen by holding the stamp to the light. Some are more easily seen with a watermark detector. This important tool is a small black tray into which a stamp is placed face down and dampened with a fast-evaporating watermark detection fluid that brings up the watermark image in the form of dark lines against a lighter background. These dark lines are the thinner areas of the paper known as the watermark. Some watermarks are extremely difficult to locate, due to either a faint impression, watermark location or the color of the stamp. There also are electric watermark detectors that come with plastic filter disks of various colors. The disks neutralize the color of the stamp, permitting the watermark to be seen more easily.

Multiple watermarks of Crown Agents and Burma

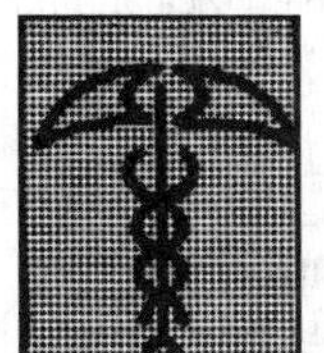
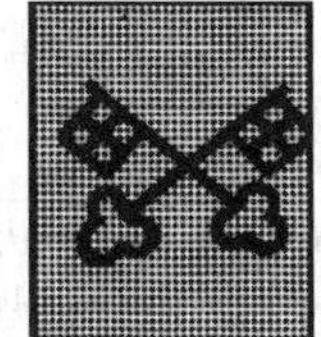

Watermarks of Uruguay, Vatican City and Jamaica

WARNING: Some inks used in the photogravure process dissolve in watermark fluids (Please see the section on Soluble Printing Inks). Also, see "chalky paper."

Watermarks may be found normal, reversed, inverted, reversed and inverted, sideways or diagonal, as seen from the back of the stamp. The relationship of watermark to stamp design depends on the position of the printing plates or how paper is fed through the press. On machine-made paper, watermarks normally are read from right to left. The design is repeated closely throughout the sheet in a "multiple-watermark design." In a "sheet watermark," the design appears only once on the sheet, but extends over many stamps. Individual stamps may carry only a small fraction or none of the watermark.

"Marginal watermarks" occur in the margins of sheets or panes of stamps. They occur on the outside border of paper (ostensibly outside the area where stamps are to be printed). A large row of letters may spell the name of the country or the manufacturer of the paper, or a border of lines may appear. Careless press feeding may cause parts of these letters and/or lines to show on stamps of the outer row of a pane.

Soluble Printing Inks

WARNING: Most stamp colors are permanent; that is, they are not seriously affected by short-term exposure to light or water. Many colors, especially of modern inks, fade from excessive exposure to light. There are stamps printed with inks that dissolve easily in water or in fluids used to detect watermarks. Use of these inks was intentional to prevent the removal of cancellations. Water affects all aniline inks, those on so-called safety paper and some photogravure printings - all such inks are known as *fugitive colors. Removal from paper of such stamps requires care and alternatives to traditional soaking.*

Separation

"Separation" is the general term used to describe methods used to separate stamps. The three standard forms currently in use are perforating, rouletting and die-cutting. These methods are done during the stamp production process, after printing. Sometimes these methods are done on-press or sometimes as a separate step. The earliest issues, such as the 1840 Penny Black of Great Britain (Scott 1), did not have any means provided for separation. It was expected the stamps would be cut apart with scissors or folded and torn. These are examples of imperforate stamps. Many stamps were first issued in imperforate formats and were later issued with perforations. Therefore, care must be observed in buying single imperforate stamps to be certain they were issued imperforate and are not perforated copies that have been altered by having the perforations trimmed away. Stamps issued imperforate usually are valued as singles. However, imperforate varieties of normally perforated stamps should be collected in pairs or larger pieces as indisputable evidence of their imperforate character.

PERFORATION

The chief style of separation of stamps, and the one that is in almost universal use today, is perforating. By this process, paper between the stamps is cut away in a line of holes, usually round, leaving little bridges of paper between the stamps to hold them together. Some types of perforation, such as hyphen-hole perfs, can be confused with roulettes, but a close visual inspection reveals that paper has been removed. The little perforation bridges, which project from the stamp when it is torn from the pane, are called the teeth of the perforation.

As the size of the perforation is sometimes the only way to differentiate between two otherwise identical stamps, it is necessary to be able to accurately measure and describe them. This is done with a perforation gauge, usually a ruler-like device that has dots or graduated lines to show how many perforations may be counted in the space of two centimeters. Two centimeters is the space universally adopted in which to measure perforations.

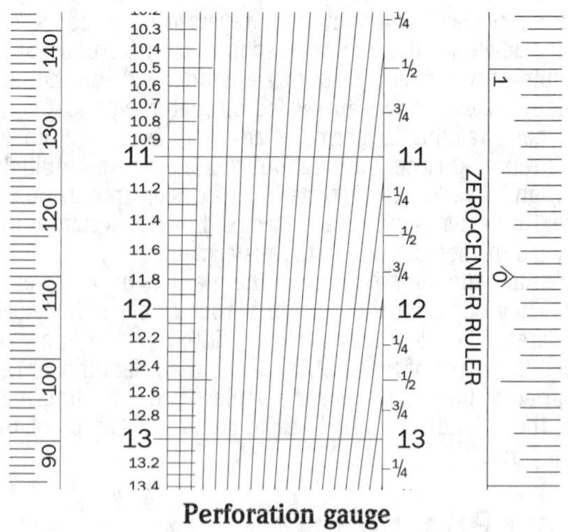

Perforation gauge

To measure a stamp, run it along the gauge until the dots on it fit exactly into the perforations of the stamp. If you are using a graduated-line perforation gauge, simply slide the stamp along the surface until the lines on the gauge perfectly project from the center of the bridges or holes. The number to the side of the line of dots or lines that fit the stamp's perforation is the measurement. For example, an "11" means that 11 perforations fit between two centimeters. The description of the stamp therefore is "perf. 11." If the gauge of the perforations on the top and bottom of a stamp differs from that on the sides, the result is what is known as *compound perforations.* In measuring compound perforations, the gauge at top and bottom is always given first, then the sides. Thus, a stamp that measures 11 at top and bottom and 10 1/2 at the sides is "perf. 11 x 10 1/2." See U.S. Scott 632-642 for examples of compound perforations.

Stamps also are known with perforations different on three or all four sides. Descriptions of such items are clockwise, beginning with the top of the stamp.

A perforation with small holes and teeth close together is a "fine perforation." One with large holes and teeth far apart is a "coarse perforation." Holes that are jagged, rather than clean-cut, are "rough perforations." *Blind perforations* are the slight impressions left by the perforating pins if they fail to puncture the paper. Multiples of stamps showing blind perforations may command a slight premium over normally perforated stamps.

The term *syncopated perfs* describes intentional irregularities in the perforations. The earliest form was used by the Netherlands from 1925-33, where holes were omitted to create distinctive patterns. Beginning in 1992, Great Britain has used an oval perforation to help prevent counterfeiting. Several other countries have started using the oval perfs or other syncopated perf patterns.

A new type of perforation, still primarily used for postal stationery, is known as microperfs. Microperfs are tiny perforations (in some cases hundreds of holes per two centimeters) that allows items to be intentionally separated very easily, while not accidentally breaking apart as easily as standard perforations. These are not currently measured or differentiated by size, as are standard perforations.

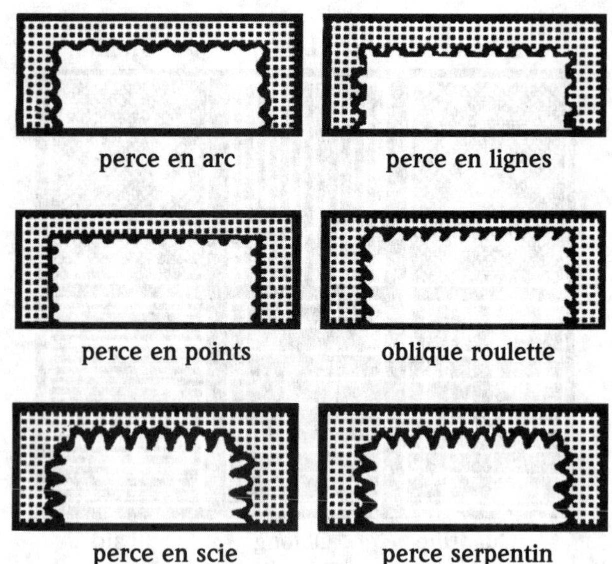

ROULETTING

In rouletting, the stamp paper is cut partly or wholly through, with no paper removed. In perforating, some paper is removed. Rouletting derives its name from the French roulette, a spur-like wheel. As the wheel is rolled over the paper, each point makes a small cut. The number of cuts made in a two-centimeter space determines the gauge of the roulette, just as the number of perforations in two centimeters determines the gauge of the perforation.

The shape and arrangement of the teeth on the wheels varies. Various roulette types generally carry French names:

Perce en lignes - rouletted in lines. The paper receives short, straight cuts in lines. This is the most common type of rouletting. See Mexico Scott 500.

Perce en points - pin-rouletted. This differs from a small perforation because no paper is removed, although round, equidistant holes are pricked through the paper. See Mexico Scott 242-256.

Perce en arc and *perce en scie* - pierced in an arc or saw-toothed designs, forming half circles or small triangles. See Hanover (German States) Scott 25-29.

Perce en serpentin - serpentine roulettes. The cuts form a serpentine or wavy line. See Brunswick (German States) Scott 13-18.

Once again, no paper is removed by these processes, leaving the stamps easily separated, but closely attached.

DIE-CUTTING

The third major form of stamp separation is die-cutting. This is a method where a die in the pattern of separation is created that later cuts the stamp paper in a stroke motion. Although some standard stamps bear die-cut perforations, this process is primarily used for self-adhesive postage stamps. Die-cutting can appear in straight lines, such as U.S. Scott 2522, shapes, such as U.S. Scott 1551, or imitating the appearance of perforations, such as New Zealand Scott 935A and 935B.

Printing Processes

ENGRAVING (Intaglio, Line-engraving, Etching)

Master die — The initial operation in the process of line engraving is making the master die. The die is a small, flat block of softened steel upon which the stamp design is recess engraved in reverse.

Master die

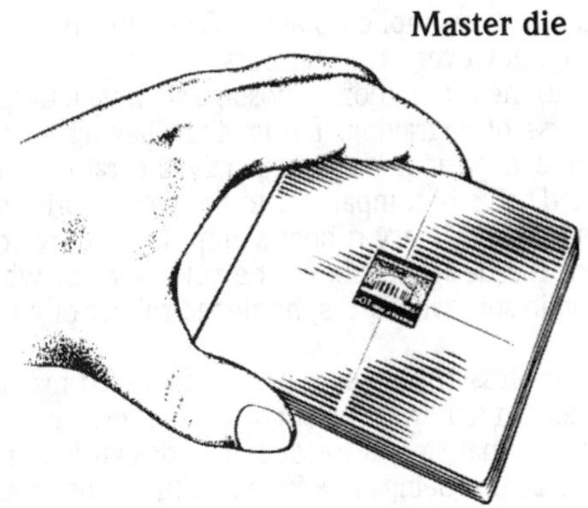

Photographic reduction of the original art is made to the appropriate size. It then serves as a tracing guide for the initial outline of the design. The engraver lightly traces the design on the steel with his graver, then slowly works the design until it is completed. At various points during the engraving process, the engraver hand-inks the die and makes an impression to check his progress. These are known as progressive die proofs. After completion of the engraving, the die is hardened to withstand the stress and pressures of later transfer operations.

Transfer roll

Transfer roll — Next is production of the transfer roll that, as the name implies, is the medium used to transfer the subject from the master die to the printing plate. A blank roll of soft steel, mounted on a mandrel, is placed under the bearers of the transfer press to allow it to roll freely on its axis. The hardened die is placed on the bed of the press and the face of the transfer roll is applied to the die, under pressure. The bed or the roll is then rocked back and forth under increasing pressure, until the soft steel of the roll is forced into every engraved line of the die. The resulting impression on the roll is known as a "relief" or a "relief transfer." The engraved image is now positive in appearance and stands out from the steel. After the required number of reliefs are "rocked in," the soft steel transfer roll is hardened.

Different flaws may occur during the relief process. A defective relief may occur during the rocking in process because of a minute piece of foreign material lodging on the die, or some other cause. Imperfections in the steel of the transfer roll may result in a breaking away of parts of the design. This is known as a relief break, which will show up on finished stamps as small, unprinted areas. If a damaged relief remains in use, it will transfer a repeating defect to the plate. Deliberate alterations of reliefs sometimes occur. "Altered reliefs" designate these changed conditions.

Plate — The final step in pre-printing production is the making of the printing plate. A flat piece of soft steel replaces the die on the bed of the transfer press. One of the reliefs on the transfer roll is positioned over this soft steel. Position, or layout, dots determine the correct position on the plate. The dots have been lightly marked on the plate in advance. After the correct position of the relief is determined, the design is rocked in by following the same method used in making the transfer roll. The difference is that this time the image is being transferred from the transfer roll, rather than to it. Once the design is entered on the plate, it appears in reverse and is recessed. There are as many transfers entered on the plate as there are subjects printed on the sheet of stamps. It is during this process that double and shifted transfers occur, as well as re-entries. These are the result of improperly entered images that have not been properly burnished out prior to rocking in a new image.

Modern siderography processes, such as those used by the U.S. Bureau of Engraving and Printing, involve an automated form of rocking designs in on preformed cylindrical printing sleeves. The same process also allows for easier removal and re-entry of worn images right on the sleeve.

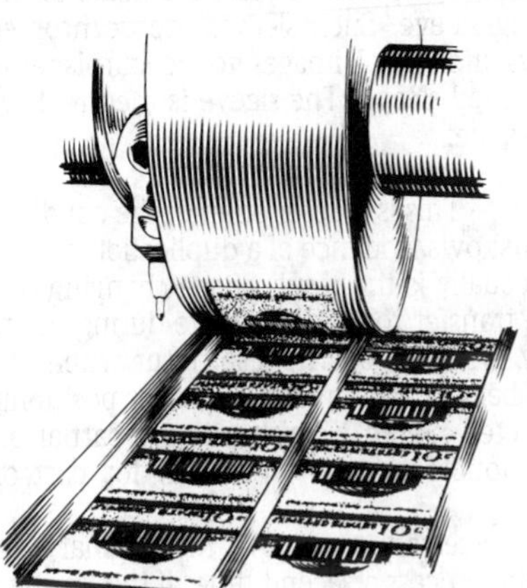

Transferring the design to the plate

Following the entering of the required transfers on the plate, the position dots, layout dots and lines, scratches and other markings generally are burnished out. Added at this time by the siderographer are any required *guide lines, plate numbers* or other *marginal markings.* The plate is then hand-inked and a proof impression is taken. This is known as a plate proof. If the impression is approved, the plate is machined for fitting onto the press, is hardened and sent to the plate vault ready for use.

On press, the plate is inked and the surface is automatically wiped clean, leaving ink only in the recessed lines. Paper is then forced under pressure into the engraved recessed lines, thereby receiving the ink. Thus, the ink lines on engraved stamps are slightly raised, and slight depressions (debossing) occur on the back of the stamp. Prior to the advent of modern high-speed presses and more advanced ink formulations, paper had to be dampened before receiving the ink. This sometimes led to uneven shrinkage by the time the stamps were perforated, resulting in improperly perforated stamps, or misperfs. Newer presses use drier paper, thus both *wet* and *dry printings* exist on some stamps.

Rotary Press — Until 1914, only flat plates were used to print engraved stamps. Rotary press printing was introduced in 1914, and slowly spread. Some countries still use flat-plate printing.

After approval of the plate proof, older *rotary press plates* require additional machining. They are curved to fit the press cylinder. "Gripper slots" are cut into the back of each plate to receive the "grippers," which hold the plate securely on the press. The plate is then hardened. Stamps printed from these bent rotary press plates are longer or wider than the same stamps printed from flat-plate presses. The stretching of the plate during the curving process is what causes this distortion.

Re-entry — To execute a re-entry on a flat plate, the transfer roll is re-applied to the plate, often at some time after its first use on the press. Worn-out designs can be resharpened by carefully burnishing out the original image and re-entering it from the transfer roll. If the original impression has not been sufficiently removed and the transfer roll is not precisely in line with the remaining impression, the resulting double transfer will make the re-entry obvious. If the registration is true, a re-entry may be difficult or impossible to distinguish. Sometimes a stamp printed from a successful re-entry is identified by having a much sharper and clearer impression than its neighbors. With the advent of rotary presses, post-press re-entries were not possible. After a plate was curved for the rotary press, it was impossible to make a re-entry. This is because the plate had already been bent once (with the design distorted).

However, with the introduction of the previously mentioned modern-style siderography machines, entries are made to the preformed cylindrical printing sleeve. Such sleeves are dechromed and softened. This allows individual images to be burnished out and re-entered on the curved sleeve. The sleeve is then rechromed, resulting in longer press life.

Double Transfer — This is a description of the condition of a transfer on a plate that shows evidence of a duplication of all, or a portion of the design. It usually is the result of the changing of the registration between the transfer roll and the plate during the rocking in of the original entry. Double transfers also occur when only a portion of the design has been rocked in and improper positioning is noted. If the worker elected not to burnish out the partial or completed design, a strong double transfer will occur for part or all of the design.

It sometimes is necessary to remove the original transfer from a plate and repeat the process a second time. If the finished re-worked image shows traces of the original impression, attributable to incomplete burnishing, the result is a partial double transfer.

With the modern automatic machines mentioned previously, double transfers are all but impossible to create. Those partially doubled images on stamps printed from such sleeves are more than likely re-entries, rather than true double transfers.

Re-engraved — Alterations to a stamp design are sometimes necessary after some stamps have been printed. In some cases, either the original die or the actual printing plate may have its "temper" drawn (softened), and the design will be re-cut. The resulting impressions from such a re-engraved die or plate may differ slightly from the original issue, and are known as "re-engraved." If the alteration was made to the master die, all future printings will be consistently different from the original. If alterations were made to the printing plate, each altered stamp on the plate will be slightly different from each other, allowing specialists to reconstruct a complete printing plate.

Dropped Transfers — If an impression from the transfer roll has not been properly placed, a dropped transfer may occur. The final stamp image will appear obviously out of line with its neighbors.

Short Transfer — Sometimes a transfer roll is not rocked its entire length when entering a transfer onto a plate. As a result, the finished transfer on the plate fails to show the complete design, and the finished stamp will have an incomplete design printed. This is known as a "short transfer." U.S. Scott No. 8 is a good example of a short transfer.

TYPOGRAPHY (Letterpress, Surface Printing, Flexography, Dry Offset, High Etch)

Although the word "Typography" is obsolete as a term describing a printing method, it was the accepted term throughout the first century of postage stamps. Therefore, appropriate Scott listings in this catalogue refer to typographed stamps. The current term for this form of printing, however, is "letterpress."

As it relates to the production of postage stamps, letterpress printing is the reverse of engraving. Rather than having recessed areas trap the ink and deposit it on paper, only the raised areas of the design are inked. This is comparable to the type of printing seen by inking and using an ordinary rubber stamp. Letterpress includes all printing where the design is above the surface area, whether it is wood, metal or, in some instances, hardened rubber or polymer plastic.

For most letterpress-printed stamps, the engraved master is made in much the same manner as for engraved stamps. In this instance, however, an additional step is needed. The design is transferred to another surface before being transferred to the transfer roll. In this way, the transfer roll has a recessed stamp design, rather than one done in relief. This makes the printing areas on the final plate raised, or relief areas.

For less-detailed stamps of the 19th century, the area on the die not used as a printing surface was cut away, leaving the surface area raised. The original die was then reproduced by stereotyping or electrotyping. The resulting electrotypes were assembled in the required number and format of the desired sheet of stamps. The plate used in printing the stamps was an electroplate of these assembled electrotypes.

Once the final letterpress plates are created, ink is applied to the raised surface and the pressure of the press transfers the ink impression to the paper. In contrast to engraving, the fine lines of letterpress are impressed on the surface of the stamp, leaving a debossed surface. When viewed from the back (as on a typewritten page), the corresponding line work on the stamp will be raised slightly (embossed) above the surface.

PHOTOGRAVURE (Gravure, Rotogravure, Heliogravure)

In this process, the basic principles of photography are applied to a chemically sensitized metal plate, rather than photographic paper. The design is transferred photographically to the plate through a halftone, or dot-matrix screen, breaking the reproduction into tiny dots. The plate is treated chemically and the dots form depressions, called cells, of varying depths and diameters, depending on the degrees of shade in the design. Then, like engraving, ink is applied to the plate and the surface is wiped clean. This leaves ink in the tiny cells that is lifted out and deposited on the paper when it is pressed against the plate.

Gravure is most often used for multicolored stamps, generally using the three primary colors (red, yellow and blue) and black. By varying the dot matrix pattern and density of these colors, virtually any color can be reproduced. A typical full-color gravure stamp will be created from four printing cylinders (one for each color). The original multicolored image will have been photographically separated into its component colors.

Modern gravure printing may use computer-generated dot-matrix screens, and modern plates may be of various types including metal-coated plastic. The catalogue designation of Photogravure (or "Photo") covers any of these older and more modern gravure methods of printing.

For examples of the first photogravure stamps printed (1914), see Bavaria Scott 94-114.

LITHOGRAPHY (Offset Lithography, Stone Lithography, Dilitho, Planography, Collotype)

The principle that oil and water do not mix is the basis for lithography. The stamp design is drawn by hand or transferred from engraving to the surface of a lithographic stone or metal plate in a greasy (oily) substance. This oily substance holds the ink, which will later be transferred to the paper. The stone (or plate) is wet with an acid fluid, causing it to repel the printing ink in all areas not covered by the greasy substance.

Transfer paper is used to transfer the design from the original stone or plate. A series of duplicate transfers are grouped and, in turn, transferred to the final printing plate.

Photolithography — The application of photographic processes to lithography. This process allows greater flexibility of design, related to use of halftone screens combined with line work. Unlike photogravure or engraving, this process can allow large, solid areas to be printed.

Offset — A refinement of the lithographic process. A rubber-covered blanket cylinder takes the impression from the inked lithographic plate. From the "blanket" the impression is *offset* or transferred to the paper. Greater flexibility and speed are the principal reasons offset printing has largely displaced lithography. The term "lithography" covers both processes, and results are almost identical.

EMBOSSED (Relief) Printing

Embossing, not considered one of the four main printing types, is a method in which the design first is sunk into the metal of the die. Printing is done against a yielding platen, such as leather or linoleum. The platen is forced into the depression of the die, thus forming the design on the paper in relief. This process is often used for metallic inks.

Embossing may be done without color (see Sardinia Scott 4-6); with color printed around the embossed area (see Great Britain Scott 5 and most U.S. envelopes); and with color in exact registration with the embossed subject (see Canada Scott 656-657).

HOLOGRAMS

For objects to appear as holograms on stamps, a model exactly the same size as it is to appear on the hologram must be created. Rather than using photographic film to capture the image, holography records an image on a photoresist material. In processing, chemicals eat away at certain exposed areas, leaving a pattern of constructive and destructive interference. When the phororesist is developed, the result is a pattern of uneven ridges that acts as a mold. This mold is then coated with metal, and the resulting form is used to press copies in much the same way phonograph records are produced.

A typical reflective hologram used for stamps consists of a reproduction of the uneven patterns on a plastic film that is applied to a reflective background, usually a silver or gold foil. Light is reflected off the background through the film, making the pattern present on the film visible. Because of the uneven pattern of the film, the viewer will perceive the objects in their proper three-dimensional relationships with appropriate brightness.

The first hologram on a stamp was produced by Austria in 1988 (Scott 1441).

FOIL APPLICATION

A modern tecnique of applying color to stamps involves the application of metallic foil to the stamp paper. A pattern of foil is applied to the stamp paper by use of a stamping die. The foil usually is flat, but it may be textured. Canada Scott 1735 has three different foil applications in pearl, bronze and gold. The gold foil was textured using a chemical-etch copper embossing die. The printing of this stamp also involved two-color offset lithography plus embossing.

COMBINATION PRINTINGS

Sometimes two or even three printing methods are combined in producing stamps. In these cases, such as Austria Scott 933 or Canada 1735 (described in the preceding paragraph), the multiple-printing technique can be determined by studing the individual characteristics of each printing type. A few stamps, such as Singapore Scott 684-684A, combine as many as three of the four major printing types (lithography, engraving and typography). When this is done it often indicates the incorporation of security devices against counterfeiting.

INK COLORS

Inks or colored papers used in stamp printing often are of mineral origin, although there are numerous examples of organic-based pigments. As a general rule, organic-based pigments are far more subject to varieties and change than those of mineral-based origin.

The appearance of any given color on a stamp may be affected by many aspects, including printing variations, light, color of paper, aging and chemical alterations.

Numerous printing variations may be observed. Heavier pressure or inking will cause a more intense color, while slight interruptions in the ink feed or lighter impressions will cause a lighter appearance. Stamps printed in the same color by water-based and solvent-based inks can differ significantly in appearance. This affects several stamps in the U.S. Prominent Americans series. Hand-mixed ink formulas (primarily from the 19th century) produced under different conditions (humidity and temperature) account for notable color variations in early printings of the same stamp (see U.S. Scott 248-250, 279B, for example). Different sources of pigment can also result in significant differences in color.

Light exposure and aging are closely related in the way they affect stamp color. Both eventually break down the ink and fade colors, so that a carefully kept stamp may differ significantly in color from an identical copy that has been exposed to light. If stamps are exposed to light either intentionally or accidentally, their colors can be faded or completely changed in some cases.

Papers of different quality and consistency used for the same stamp printing may affect color appearance. Most pelure papers, for example, show a richer color when compared with wove or laid papers. See Russia Scott 181a, for an example of this effect.

The very nature of the printing processes can cause a variety of differences in shades or hues of the same stamp. Some of these shades are scarcer than others, and are of particular interest to the advanced collector.

Luminescence

All forms of tagged stamps fall under the general category of luminescence. Within this broad category is fluorescence, dealing with forms of tagging visible under longwave ultraviolet light, and phosphorescence, which deals with tagging visible only under shortwave light. Phosphorescence leaves an afterglow and fluorescence does not. These treated stamps show up in a range of different colors when exposed to UV light. The differing wavelengths of the light activates the tagging material, making it glow in various colors that usually serve different mail processing purposes.

Intentional tagging is a post-World War II phenomenon, brought about by the increased literacy rate and rapidly growing mail volume. It was one of several answers to the problem of the need for more automated mail processes. Early tagged stamps served the purpose of triggering machines to separate different types of mail. A natural outgrowth was to also use the signal to trigger machines that faced all envelopes the same way and canceled them.

Tagged stamps come in many different forms. Some tagged stamps have luminescent shapes or images imprinted on them as a form of security device. Others have blocks (United States), stripes, frames (South Africa and Canada), overall coatings (United States), bars (Great Britain and Canada) and many other types. Some types of tagging are even mixed in with the pigmented printing ink (Australia Scott 366, Netherlands Scott 478 and U.S. Scott 1359 and 2443).

The means of applying taggant to stamps differs as much as the intended purposes for the stamps. The most common form of tagging is a coating applied to the surface of the printed stamp. Since the taggant ink is frequently invisible except under UV light, it does not interfere with the appearance of the stamp. Another common application is the use of phosphored papers. In this case the paper itself either has a coating of taggant applied before the stamp is printed, has taggant applied during the papermaking process (incorporating it into the fibers), or has the taggant mixed into the coating of the paper. The latter method, among others, is currently in use in the United States.

Many countries now use tagging in various forms to either expedite mail handling or to serve as a printing security device against counterfeiting. Following the introduction of tagged stamps for public use in 1959 by Great Britain, other countries have steadily joined the parade. Among those are Germany (1961); Canada and Denmark (1962); United States, Australia, France and Switzerland (1963); Belgium and Japan (1966); Sweden and Norway (1967); Italy (1968); and Russia (1969). Since then, many other countries have begun using forms of tagging, including Brazil, China, Czechoslovakia, Hong Kong, Guatemala, Indonesia, Israel, Lithuania, Luxembourg, Netherlands, Penrhyn Islands, Portugal, St. Vincent, Singapore, South Africa, Spain and Sweden to name a few.

In some cases, including United States, Canada, Great Britain and Switzerland, stamps were released both with and without tagging. Many of these were released during each country's experimental period. Tagged and untagged versions are listed for the aforementioned countries and are noted in some other countries' listings. For at least a few stamps, the experimentally tagged version is worth far more than its untagged counterpart, such as the 1963 experimental tagged version of France Scott 1024.

In some cases, luminescent varieties of stamps were inadvertently created. Several Russian stamps, for example, sport highly fluorescent ink that was not intended as a form of tagging. Older stamps, such as early U.S. postage dues, can be positively identified by the use of UV light, since the organic ink used has become slightly fluorescent over time. Other stamps, such as Austria Scott 70a-82a (varnish bars) and Obock Scott 46-64 (printed quadrille lines), have become fluorescent over time.

Various fluorescent substances have been added to paper to make it appear brighter. These optical brightners, as they are known, greatly affect the appearance of the stamp under UV light. The brightest of these is known as Hi-Brite paper. These paper varieties are beyond the scope of the Scott Catalogue.

Shortwave UV light also is used extensively in expertizing, since each form of paper has its own fluorescent characteristics that are impossible to perfectly match. It is therefore a simple matter to detect filled thins, added perforation teeth and other alterations that involve the addition of paper. UV light also is used to examine stamps that have had cancels chemically removed and for other purposes as well.

Gum

The Illustrated Gum Chart in the first part of this introduction shows and defines various types of gum condition. Because gum condition has an important impact on the value of unused stamps, we recommend studying this chart and the accompanying text carefully.

The gum on the back of a stamp may be shiny, dull, smooth, rough, dark, white, colored or tinted. Most stamp gumming adhesives use gum arabic or dextrine as a base. Certain polymers such as polyvinyl alcohol (PVA) have been used extensively since World War II.

The *Scott Standard Postage Stamp Catalogue* does not list items by types of gum. The *Scott Specialized Catalogue of United States Stamps* does differentiate among some types of gum for certain issues.

Reprints of stamps may have gum differing from the original issues. In addition, some countries have used different gum formulas for different seasons. These adhesives have different properties that may become more apparent over time.

Many stamps have been issued without gum, and the catalogue will note this fact. See, for example, United States Scott 40-47. Sometimes, gum may have been removed to preserve the stamp. Germany Scott B68, for example, has a highly acidic gum that eventually destroys the stamps. This item is valued in the catalogue with gum removed.

Reprints and Reissues

These are impressions of stamps (usually obsolete) made from the original plates or stones. If they are valid for postage and reproduce obsolete issues (such as U.S. Scott 102-111), the stamps are *reissues.* If they are from current issues, they are designated as *second, third,* etc., *printing.* If designated for a particular purpose, they are called *special printings.*

When special printings are not valid for postage, but are made from original dies and plates by authorized persons, they are *official reprints. Private reprints* are made from the original plates and dies by private hands. An example of a private reprint is that of the 1871-1932 reprints made from the original die of the 1845 New Haven, Conn., postmaster's provisional. *Official reproductions* or imitations are made from new dies and plates by government authorization. Scott will list those reissues that are valid for postage if they differ significantly from the original printing.

The U.S. government made special printings of its first postage stamps in 1875. Produced were official imitations of the first two stamps (listed as Scott 3-4), reprints of the demonetized pre-1861 issues (Scott 40-47) and reissues of the 1861 stamps, the 1869 stamps and the then-current 1875 denominations. Even though the official imitations and the reprints were not valid for postage, Scott lists all of these U.S. special printings.

Most reprints or reissues differ slightly from the original stamp in some characteristic, such as gum, paper, perforation, color or watermark. Sometimes the details are followed so meticulously that only a student of that specific stamp is able to distinguish the reprint or reissue from the original.

Remainders and Canceled to Order

Some countries sell their stock of old stamps when a new issue replaces them. To avoid postal use, the *remainders* usually are canceled with a punch hole, a heavy line or bar, or a more-or-less regular-looking cancellation. The most famous merchant of remainders was Nicholas F. Seebeck. In the 1880s and 1890s, he arranged printing contracts between the Hamilton Bank Note Co., of which he was a director, and several Central and South American countries. The contracts provided that the plates and all remainders of the yearly issues became the property of Hamilton. Seebeck saw to it that ample stock remained. The "Seebecks," both remainders and reprints, were standard packet fillers for decades.

Some countries also issue stamps *canceled-to-order (CTO),* either in sheets with original gum or stuck onto pieces of paper or envelopes and canceled. Such CTO items generally are worth less than postally used stamps. In cases where the CTO material is far more prevalent in the marketplace than postally used examples, the catalogue value relates to the CTO examples, with postally used examples noted as premium items. Most CTOs can be detected by the presence of gum. However, as the CTO practice goes back at least to 1885, the gum inevitably has been soaked off some stamps so they could pass as postally used. The normally applied postmarks usually differ slightly from standard postmarks, and specialists are able to tell the difference. When applied individually to envelopes by philatelically minded persons, CTO material is known as *favor canceled* and generally sells at large discounts.

Cinderellas and Facsimiles

Cinderella is a catch-all term used by stamp collectors to describe phantoms, fantasies, bogus items, municipal issues, exhibition seals, local revenues, transportation stamps, labels, poster stamps and many other types of items. Some cinderella collectors include in their collections local postage issues, telegraph stamps, essays and proofs, forgeries and counterfeits.

A *fantasy* is an adhesive created for a nonexistent stamp-issuing authority. Fantasy items range from imaginary countries (Occusi-Ambeno, Kingdom of Sedang, Principality of Trinidad or Torres Straits), to non-existent locals (Winans City Post), or nonexistent transportation lines (McRobish & Co.'s Acapulco-San Francisco Line).

On the other hand, if the entity exists and could have issued stamps (but did not) or was known to have issued other stamps, the items are considered *bogus* stamps. These would include the Mormon postage stamps of Utah, S. Allan Taylor's Guatemala and Paraguay inventions, the propaganda issues for the South Moluccas and the adhesives of the Page & Keyes local post of Boston.

Phantoms is another term for both fantasy and bogus issues.

Facsimiles are copies or imitations made to represent original stamps, but which do not pretend to be originals. A catalogue illustration is such a facsimile. Illustrations from the Moens catalogue of the last century were occasionally colored and passed off as stamps. Since the beginning of stamp collecting, facsimiles have been made for collectors as space fillers or for reference. They often carry the word "facsimile," "falsch" (German), "sanko" or "mozo" (Japanese), or "faux" (French) overprinted on the face or stamped on the back. Unfortunately, over the years a number of these items have had fake cancels applied over the facsimile notation and have been passed off as genuine.

Forgeries and Counterfeits

Forgeries and counterfeits have been with philately virtually from the beginning of stamp production. Over time, the terminology for the two has been used interchangeably. Although both forgeries and counterfeits are reproductions of stamps, the purposes behind their creation differ considerably.

Among specialists there is an increasing movement to more specifically define such items. Although there is no universally accepted terminology, we feel the following definitions most closely mirror the items and their purposes as they are currently defined.

Forgeries (also often referred to as *Counterfeits*) are reproductions of genuine stamps that have been created to defraud collectors. Such spurious items first appeared on the market around 1860, and most old-time collections contain one or more. Many are crude and easily spotted, but some can deceive experts.

An important supplier of these early philatelic forgeries was the Hamburg printer Gebruder Spiro. Many others with reputations in this craft included S. Allan Taylor, George Hussey, James Chute, George Forune, Benjamin & Sarpy, Julius Goldner, E. Oneglia and L.H. Mercier. Among the noted 20th-century forgers were Francois Fournier, Jean Sperati and the prolific Raoul DeThuin.

Forgeries may be complete replications, or they may be genuine stamps altered to resemble a scarcer (and more valuable) type. Most forgeries, particularly those of rare stamps, are worth only a small fraction of the value of a genuine example, but a few types, created by some of the most notable forgers, such as Sperati, can be worth as much or more than the genuine. Fraudulently produced copies are known of most classic rarities and many medium-priced stamps.

In addition to rare stamps, large numbers of common 19th- and early 20th-century stamps were forged to supply stamps to the early packet trade. Many can still be easily found. Few new philatelic forgeries have appeared in recent decades. Successful imitation of well-engraved work is virtually impossible. It has proven far easier to produce a fake by altering a genuine stamp than to duplicate a stamp completely.

Counterfeit (also often referred to as *Postal Counterfeit* or *Postal Forgery*) is the term generally applied to reproductions of stamps that have been created to defraud the government of revenue. Such items usually are created at the time a stamp is current and, in some cases, are hard to detect. Because most counterfeits are seized when the perpetrator is captured, postal counterfeits, particularly used on cover, are usually worth much more than a genuine example to specialists. The first postal counterfeit was of Spain's 4-cuarto carmine of 1854 (the real one is Scott 25). Apparently, the counterfeiters were not satisfied with their first version, which is now very scarce, and they soon created an engraved counterfeit, which is common. Postal counterfeits quickly followed in Austria, Naples, Sardinia and the Roman States. They have since been created in many other countries as well, including the United States.

An infamous counterfeit to defraud the government is the 1-shilling Great Britain "Stock Exchange" forgery of 1872, used on telegraph forms at the exchange that year. The stamp escaped detection until a stamp dealer noticed it in 1898.

Fakes

Fakes are genuine stamps altered in some way to make them more desirable. One student of this part of stamp collecting has estimated that by the 1950s more than 30,000 varieties of fakes were known. That number has grown greatly since then. The widespread existence of fakes makes it important for stamp collectors to study their philatelic holdings and use relevant literature. Likewise, collectors should buy from reputable dealers who guarantee their stamps and make full and prompt refunds should a purchased item be declared faked or altered by some mutually agreed-upon authority. Because fakes always have some genuine characteristics, it is not always possible to obtain unanimous agreement among experts regarding specific items. These students may change their opinions as philatelic knowledge increases. More than 80 percent of all fakes on the philatelic market today are regummed, reperforated (or perforated for the first time), or bear forged overprints, surcharges or cancellations.

Stamps can be chemically treated to alter or eliminate colors. For example, a pale rose stamp can be re-colored to resemble a blue shade of high market value. In other cases, treated stamps can be made to resemble missing color varieties. Designs may be changed by painting, or a stroke or a dot added or bleached out to turn an ordinary variety into a seemingly scarcer stamp. Part of a stamp can be bleached and reprinted in a different version, achieving an inverted center or frame. Margins can be added or repairs done so deceptively that the stamps move from the "repaired" into the "fake" category.

Fakers have not left the backs of the stamps untouched either. They may create false watermarks, add fake grills or press out genuine grills. A thin India paper proof may be glued onto a thicker backing to create the appearance an issued stamp, or a proof printed on cardboard may be shaved down and perforated to resemble a stamp. Silk threads are impressed into paper and stamps have been split so that a rare paper variety is added to an otherwise inexpensive stamp. The most common treatment to the back of a stamp, however, is regumming.

Some in the business of faking stamps have openly advertised foolproof application of "original gum" to stamps that lack it, although most publications now ban such ads from their pages. It is believed that very few early stamps have survived without being hinged. The large number of never-hinged examples of such earlier material offered for sale thus suggests the widespread extent of regumming activity. Regumming also may be used to hide repairs or thin spots. Dipping the stamp into watermark fluid, or examining it under longwave ultraviolet light often will reveal these flaws.

Fakers also tamper with separations. Ingenious ways to add margins are known. Perforated wide-margin stamps may be falsely represented as imperforate when trimmed. Reperforating is commonly done to create scarce coil or perforation varieties, and to eliminate the naturally occurring straight-edge stamps found in sheet margin positions of many earlier issues. Custom has made straight-edged stamps less desirable. Fakers have obliged by perforating straight-edged stamps so that many are now uncommon, if not rare.

Another fertile field for the faker is that of overprints, surcharges and cancellations. The forging of rare surcharges or overprints began in the 1880s or 1890s. These forgeries are sometimes difficult to detect, but experts have identified almost all. Occasionally, overprints or cancellations are removed to create non-overprinted stamps or seemingly unused items. This is most commonly done by removing a manuscript cancel to make a stamp resemble an unused example. "SPECIMEN" overprints may be removed by scraping and repainting to create non-overprinted varieties. Fakers use inexpensive revenues or pen-canceled stamps to generate unused stamps for further faking by adding other markings. The quartz lamp or UV lamp and a high-powered magnifying glass help to easily detect removed cancellations.

The bigger problem, however, is the addition of overprints, surcharges or cancellations - many with such precision that they are very difficult to ascertain. Plating of the stamps or the overprint can be an important method of detection.

Fake postmarks may range from many spurious fancy cancellations to a host of markings applied to transatlantic covers, to adding normally appearing postmarks to definitives of some countries with stamps that are valued far higher used than unused. With the increased popularity of cover collecting, and the widespread interest in postal history, a fertile new field for fakers has come about. Some have tried to create entire covers. Others specialize in adding stamps, tied by fake cancellations, to genuine stampless covers, or replacing less expensive or damaged stamps with more valuable ones. Detailed study of postal rates in effect at the time a cover in question was mailed, including the analysis of each handstamp used during the period, ink analysis and similar techniques, usually will unmask the fraud.

Restoration and Repairs

Scott Publishing Co. bases its catalogue values on stamps that are free of defects and otherwise meet the standards set forth earlier in this introduction. Most stamp collectors desire to have the finest copy of an item possible. Even within given grading categories there are variances. This leads to a controversial practice that is not defined in any universal manner: stamp *restoration.*

There are broad differences of opinion about what is permissible when it comes to restoration. Carefully applying a soft eraser to a stamp or cover to remove light soiling is one form of restoration, as is washing a stamp in mild soap and water to clean it. These are fairly accepted forms of restoration. More severe forms of restoration include pressing out creases or removing stains caused by tape. To what degree each of these is acceptable is dependent upon the individual situation. Further along the spectrum is the freshening of a stamp's color by removing oxide build-up or the effects of wax paper left next to stamps shipped to the tropics.

At some point in this spectrum the concept of *repair* replaces that of restoration. Repairs include filling thin spots, mending tears by reweaving or adding a missing perforation tooth. Regumming stamps may have been acceptable as a restoration or repair technique many decades ago, but today it is considered a form of fakery.

Restored stamps may or may not sell at a discount, and it is possible that the value of individual restored items may be enhanced over that of their pre-restoration state. Specific situations dictate the resultant value of such an item. Repaired stamps sell at substantial discounts from the value of sound stamps.

Terminology

Booklets — Many countries have issued stamps in small booklets for the convenience of users. This idea continues to become increasingly popular in many countries. Booklets have been issued in many sizes and forms, often with advertising on the covers, the panes of stamps or on the interleaving.

The panes used in booklets may be printed from special plates or made from regular sheets. All panes from booklets issued by the United States and many from those of other countries contain stamps that are straight edged on the sides, but perforated between. Others are distinguished by orientation of watermark or other identifying features. Any stamp-like unit in the pane, either printed or blank, that is not a postage stamp, is considered to be a *label* in the catalogue listings.

Scott lists and values booklet panes. Complete booklets also are listed and valued. Individual booklet panes are listed only when they are not fashioned from existing sheet stamps and, therefore, are identifiable from their sheet stamp counterparts.

Panes usually do not have a used value assigned to them because there is little market activity for used booklet panes, even though many exist used and there is some demand for them.

Cancellations — The marks or obliterations put on stamps by postal authorities to show that they have performed service and to prevent their reuse are known as cancellations. If the marking is made with a pen, it is considered a "pen cancel." When the location of the post office appears in the marking, it is a "town cancellation." A "postmark" is technically any postal marking, but in practice the term generally is applied to a town cancellation with a date. When calling attention to a cause or celebration, the marking is known as a "slogan cancellation." Many other types and styles of cancellations exist, such as duplex, numerals, targets, fancy and others. See also "precancels," below.

Coil Stamps — These are stamps that are issued in rolls for use in dispensers, affixing and vending machines. Those coils of the United States, Canada, Sweden and some other countries are perforated horizontally or vertically only, with the outer edges imperforate. Coil stamps of some countries, such as Great Britain and Germany, are perforated on all four sides and may in some cases be distinguished from their sheet stamp counterparts by watermarks, counting numbers on the reverse or other means.

Covers — Entire envelopes, with or without adhesive postage stamps, that have passed through the mail and bear postal or other markings of philatelic interest are known as covers. Before the introduction of envelopes in about 1840, people folded letters and wrote the address on the outside. Some people covered their letters with an extra sheet of paper on the outside for the address, producing the term "cover." Used airletter sheets, stamped envelopes and other items of postal stationery also are considered covers.

Errors — Stamps that have some major, consistent, unintentional deviation from the normal are considered errors. Errors include, but are not limited to, missing or wrong colors, wrong paper, wrong watermarks, inverted centers or frames on multicolor printing, inverted or missing surcharges or overprints, double impressions, missing perforations and others. Factually wrong or misspelled information, if it appears on all examples of a stamp, are not considered errors in the true sense of the word. They are errors of design. Inconsistent or randomly appearing items, such as misperfs or color shifts, are classified as freaks.

Color-Omitted Errors — This term refers to stamps where a missing color is caused by the complete failure of the printing plate to deliver ink to the stamp paper or any other paper. Generally, this is caused by the printing plate not being engaged on the press or the ink station running dry of ink during printing.

Color-Missing Errors — This term refers to stamps where a color or colors were printed somewhere but do not appear on the finished stamp. There are four different classes of color-missing errors, and the catalog indicates with a two-letter code appended to each such listing what caused the color to be missing:

FO = A *foldover* of the stamp sheet during printing may block ink from appearing on a stamp. Instead, the color will appear on the back of the foldover (where it might fall on the back of the selvage or perhaps on the back of another stamp).

EP = A piece of *extraneous paper* falling across the plate or stamp paper will receive the printed ink. When the extraneous paper is removed, an unprinted portion of stamp paper remains and shows partially or totally missing colors.

CM = A misregistration of the printing plates during printing will result in a *color misregistration*, and such a misregistration may result in a color not appearing on the finished stamp.

PS = A *perforation shift* after printing may remove a color from the finished stamp. Normally, this will occur on a row of stamps at the edge of the stamp pane.

Overprints and Surcharges — Overprinting involves applying wording or design elements over an already existing stamp. Overprints can be used to alter the place of use (such as "Canal Zone" on U.S. stamps), to adapt them for a special purpose ("Porto" on Denmark's 1913-20 regular issues for use as postage due stamps, Scott J1-J7) or to commemorate a special occasion (United States Scott 647-648).

A *surcharge* is a form of overprint that changes or restates the face value of a stamp or piece of postal stationery.

Surcharges and overprints may be handstamped, typeset or, occasionally, lithographed or engraved. A few hand-written overprints and surcharges are known.

Precancels — Stamps that are canceled before they are placed in the mail are known as precancels. Precanceling usually is done to expedite the handling of large mailings and generally allow the affected mail pieces to skip certain phases of mail handling.

In the United States, precancellations generally identified the point of origin; that is, the city and state. This information appeared across the face of the stamp, usually centered between parallel lines. More recently, bureau precancels retained the parallel lines, but the city and state designations were dropped. Recent coils have a service inscription that is present on the original printing plate. These show the mail service paid for by the stamp. Since these stamps are not intended to receive further cancellations when used as intended, they are considered precancels. Such items often do not have parallel lines as part of the precancellation.

In France, the abbreviation *Affranchts* in a semicircle together with the word *Postes* is the general form of precancel in use. Belgian precancellations usually appear in a box in which the name of the city appears. Netherlands precancels have the name of the city enclosed between concentric circles, sometimes called a "lifesaver." Precancellations of other countries usually follow these patterns, but may be any arrangement of bars, boxes and city names.

Precancels are listed in the Scott catalogues only if the precancel changes the denomination (Belgium Scott 477-478); if the precanceled stamp is different from the non-precanceled version (such as untagged U.S. precancels); or if the stamp exists only precanceled (France Scott 1096-1099, U.S. Scott 2265).

Proofs and Essays — Proofs are impressions taken from an approved die, plate or stone in which the design and color are the same as the stamp issued to the public. Trial color proofs are impressions taken from approved dies, plates or stones in colors that vary from the final version. An essay is the impression of a design that differs in some way from the issued stamp. "Progressive die proofs" generally are considered to be essays.

Provisionals — These are stamps that are issued on short notice and intended for temporary use pending the arrival of regular issues. They usually are issued to meet such contingencies as changes in government or currency, shortage of necessary postage values or military occupation.

During the 1840s, postmasters in certain American cities issued stamps that were valid only at specific post offices. In 1861, postmasters of the Confederate States also issued stamps with limited validity. Both of these examples are known as "postmaster's provisionals."

Se-tenant — This term refers to an unsevered pair, strip or block of stamps that differ in design, denomination or overprint.

Unless the se-tenant item has a continuous design (see U.S. Scott 1451a, 1694a) the stamps do not have to be in the same order as shown in the catalogue (see U.S. Scott 2158a).

Specimens — The Universal Postal Union required member nations to send samples of all stamps they released into service to the International Bureau in Switzerland. Member nations of the UPU received these specimens as samples of what stamps were valid for postage. Many are overprinted, handstamped or initial-perforated "Specimen," "Canceled" or "Muestra." Some are marked with bars across the denominations (China-Taiwan), punched holes (Czechoslovakia) or back inscriptions (Mongolia).

Stamps distributed to government officials or for publicity purposes, and stamps submitted by private security printers for official approval, also may receive such defacements.

The previously described defacement markings prevent postal use, and all such items generally are known as "specimens."

Tete Beche — This term describes a pair of stamps in which one is upside down in relation to the other. Some of these are the result of intentional sheet arrangements, such as Morocco Scott B10-B11. Others occurred when one or more electrotypes accidentally were placed upside down on the plate, such as Colombia Scott 57a. Separation of the tete-beche stamps, of course, destroys the tete beche variety.

Currency Conversion

Country	Dollar	Pound	S Franc	Yen	HK Dollar	Euro	Cdn Dollar	Aus Dollar
Australia	1.6793	2.6436	1.2258	0.0141	0.2146	1.8014	1.1123	-----
Canada	1.5049	2.3767	0.1020	0.0127	0.1929	1.6196	-----	0.8990
European Union	0.9292	1.4675	0.6804	0.0078	0.1191	-----	0.6174	0.5551
Hong Kong	7.8003	12.319	5.7120	0.0657	-----	8.3946	5.1833	4.6600
Japan	118.75	187.54	86.958	-----	15.224	127.80	78.909	70.942
Switzerland	1.3656	2.1567	-----	0.0115	0.1751	1.4697	0.9074	0.8158
United Kingdom	0.6332	-----	0.4637	0.0053	0.0812	0.6814	0.4208	0.3783
United States	-----	1.5793	0.7323	0.0084	0.1282	1.0762	0.6645	0.5974

Country	Currency	U.S. $ Equiv.
Gabon	Community of French Africa (CFA) franc	.0016
Gambia	dalasy	.0416
Georgia	lari	.4601
Germany	euro	1.0762
Ghana	cedi	.0001
Gibraltar	pound	1.5793
Great Britain	pound	1.5793
Alderney	pound	1.5793
Guernsey	pound	1.5793
Jersey	pound	1.5793
Isle of Man	pound	1.5793
Greece	euro	1.0762
Greenland	Danish krone	.1448
Grenada	East Caribbean dollar	.3745
Grenada Grenadines	East Caribbean dollar	.3745
Guatemala	quetzal	.1273
Guinea	franc	.0005
Guinea-Bissau	CFA franc	.0016
Guyana	dollar	.0056
Haiti	gourde	.0221
Honduras	lempira	.0587
Hong Kong	dollar	.1282
Hungary	forint	.0044
Iceland	krona	.0127
India	rupee	.0210
Indonesia	rupiah	.0001
Ireland	euro	1.0762
Israel	shekel	.2051
Italy	euro	1.0762
Ivory Coast	CFA franc	.0016

*Source: **Wall Street Journal** Feb. 24, 2003. Figures reflect values as of Feb. 21, 2003.*

COMMON DESIGN TYPES

Pictured in this section are issues where one illustration has been used for a number of countries in the Catalogue. Not included in this section are overprinted stamps or those issues which are illustrated in each country.

EUROPA

Europa, 1956

The design symbolizing the cooperation among the six countries comprising the Coal and Steel Community is illustrated in each country.

Belgium 496-497
France 805-806
Germany 748-749
Italy 715-716
Luxembourg 318-320
Netherlands 368-369

Europa, 1958

"E" and Dove — CD1

European Postal Union at the service of European integration.

1958, Sept. 13

Belgium 527-528
France 889-890
Germany 790-791
Italy 750-751
Luxembourg 341-343
Netherlands 375-376
Saar 317-318

Europa, 1959

6-Link Enless Chain — CD2

1959, Sept. 19

Belgium 536-537
France 929-930
Germany 805-806
Italy 791-792
Luxembourg 354-355
Netherlands 379-380

Europa, 1960

19-Spoke Wheel CD3

First anniversary of the establishment of C.E.P.T. (Conference Europeenne des Administrations des Postes et des Telecommunications.) The spokes symbolize the 19 founding members of the Conference.

1960, Sept.

Belgium 553-554
Denmark 379
Finland 376-377
France 970-971
Germany 818-820
Great Britain 377-378
Greece 688
Iceland 327-328
Ireland 175-176
Italy 809-810
Luxembourg 374-375
Netherlands 385-386
Norway 387
Portugal 866-867
Spain 941-942
Sweden 562-563
Switzerland 400-401
Turkey 1493-1494

Europa, 1961

19 Doves Flying as One — CD4

The 19 doves represent the 19 members of the Conference of European Postal and Telecommunications Administrations C.E.P.T.

1961-62

Belgium 572-573
Cyprus 201-203
France 1005-1006
Germany 844-845
Great Britain 383-384
Greece 718-719
Iceland 340-341
Italy 845-846
Luxembourg 382-383
Netherlands 387-388
Spain 1010-1011
Switzerland 410-411
Turkey 1518-1520

Europa, 1962

Young Tree with 19 Leaves CD5

The 19 leaves represent the 19 original members of C.E.P.T.

1962-63

Belgium 582-583
Cyprus 219-221
France 1045-1046
Germany 852-853
Greece 739-740
Iceland 348-349
Ireland 184-185
Italy 860-861
Luxembourg 386-387
Netherlands 394-395
Norway 414-415
Switzerland 416-417
Turkey 1553-1555

Europa, 1963

Stylized Links, Symbolizing Unity — CD6

1963, Sept.

Belgium 598-599
Cyprus 229-231
Finland 419
France 1074-1075
Germany 867-868
Greece 768-769
Iceland 357-358
Ireland 188-189
Italy 880-881
Luxembourg 403-404
Netherlands 416-417
Norway 441-442
Switzerland 429
Turkey 1602-1603

Europa, 1964

Symbolic Daisy — CD7

5th anniversary of the establishment of C.E.P.T. The 22 petals of the flower symbolize the 22 members of the Conference.

1964, Sept.

Austria 738
Belgium 614-615
Cyprus 244-246
France 1109-1110
Germany 897-898
Greece 801-802
Iceland 367-368
Ireland 196-197
Italy 894-895
Luxembourg 411-412
Monaco 590-591
Netherlands 428-429
Norway 458
Portugal 931-933
Spain 1262-1263
Switzerland 438-439
Turkey 1628-1629

Europa, 1965

Leaves and "Fruit" CD8

1965

Belgium 636-637
Cyprus 262-264
Finland 437
France 1131-1132
Germany 934-935
Greece 833-834
Iceland 375-376
Ireland 204-205
Italy 915-916
Luxembourg 432-433
Monaco 616-617
Netherlands 438-439
Norway 475-476
Portugal 958-960
Switzerland 469
Turkey 1665-1666

Europa, 1966

Symbolic Sailboat — CD9

1966, Sept.

Andorra, French 172
Belgium 675-676
Cyprus 275-277
France 1163-1164
Germany 963-964
Greece 862-863
Iceland 384-385
Ireland 216-217
Italy 942-943
Liechtenstein 415
Luxembourg 440-441
Monaco 639-640
Netherlands 441-442
Norway 496-497
Portugal 980-982
Switzerland 477-478
Turkey 1718-1719

Europa, 1967

Cogwheels CD10

1967

Andorra, French 174-175
Belgium 688-689
Cyprus 297-299
France 1178-1179
Germany 969-970
Greece 891-892
Iceland 389-390
Ireland 232-233
Italy 951-952
Liechtenstein 420
Luxembourg 449-450
Monaco 669-670
Netherlands 444-447
Norway 504-505
Portugal 994-996
Spain 1465-1466
Switzerland 482
Turkey B120-B121

Europa, 1968

Golden Key with C.E.P.T. Emblem CD11

1968

Andorra, French 182-183
Belgium 705-706
Cyprus 314-316
France 1209-1210
Germany 983-984
Greece 916-917
Iceland 395-396
Ireland 242-243
Italy 979-980
Liechtenstein 442
Luxembourg 466-467
Monaco 689-691
Netherlands 452-453
Portugal 1019-1021
San Marino 687
Spain 1526
Turkey 1775-1776

Europa, 1969

"EUROPA" and "CEPT" CD12

Tenth anniversary of C.E.P.T.

1969

Andorra, French 188-189
Austria 837
Belgium 718-719
Cyprus 326-328
Denmark 458
Finland 483
France 1245-1246
Germany 996-997
Great Britain 585
Greece 947-948
Iceland 406-407
Ireland 270-271
Italy 1000-1001
Liechtenstein 453
Luxembourg 474-475
Monaco 722-724
Netherlands 475-476
Norway 533-534
Portugal 1038-1040
San Marino 701-702
Spain 1567
Sweden 814-816

Switzerland 500-501
Turkey 1799-1800
Vatican 470-472
Yugoslavia 1003-1004

Europa, 1970

Interwoven Threads
CD13

1970

Andorra, French 196-197
Belgium 741-742
Cyprus 340-342
France 1271-1272
Germany 1018-1019
Greece 985, 987
Iceland 420-421
Ireland 279-281
Italy 1013-1014
Liechtenstein 470
Luxembourg 489-490
Monaco 768-770
Netherlands 483-484
Portugal 1060-1062
San Marino 729-730
Spain 1607
Switzerland 515-516
Turkey 1848-1849
Yugoslavia 1024-1025

Europa, 1971

"Fraternity, Cooperation, Common Effort"
CD14

1971

Andorra, French 205-206
Belgium 803-804
Cyprus 365-367
Finland 504
France 1304
Germany 1064-1065
Greece 1029-1030
Iceland 429-430
Ireland 305-306
Italy 1038-1039
Liechtenstein 485
Luxembourg 500-501
Malta 425-427
Monaco 797-799
Netherlands 488-489
Portugal 1094-1096
San Marino 749-750
Spain 1675-1676
Switzerland 531-532
Turkey 1876-1877
Yugoslavia 1052-1053

Europa, 1972

Sparkles, Symbolic of Communications
CD15

1972

Andorra, French 210-211
Andorra, Spanish 62
Belgium 825-826
Cyprus 380-382
Finland 512-513
France 1341
Germany 1089-1090
Greece 1049-1050
Iceland 439-440
Ireland 316-317
Italy 1065-1066
Liechtenstein 504
Luxembourg 512-513
Malta 450-453
Monaco 831-832
Netherlands 494-495
Portugal 1141-1143
San Marino 771-772
Spain 1718
Switzerland 544-545
Turkey 1907-1908
Yugoslavia 1100-1101

Europa, 1973

Post Horn and Arrows
CD16

1973

Andorra, French 319-320
Andorra, Spanish 76
Belgium 839-840
Cyprus 396-398
Finland 526
France 1367
Germany 1114-1115
Greece 1090-1092
Iceland 447-448
Ireland 329-330
Italy 1108-1109
Liechtenstein 528-529
Luxembourg 523-524
Malta 469-471
Monaco 866-867
Netherlands 504-505
Norway 604-605
Portugal 1170-1172
San Marino 802-803
Spain 1753
Switzerland 580-581
Turkey 1935-1936
Yugoslavia 1138-1139

Europa, 2000

CD17

2000

Albania 2621-2622
Andorra, French 522
Andorra, Spanish 262
Armenia 610-611
Austria 1814
Azerbaijan 698-699
Belarus 350
Belgium 1818
Bosnia & Herzegovina (Moslem) 358
Bosnia & Herzegovina (Serb) 111-112
Croatia 428-429
Cyprus 959
Czech Republic 3120
Denmark 1189
Estonia 394
Faroe Islands 376
Finland 1129
Aland Islands 166
France 2771
Georgia 228-229
Germany 2086-2087
Gibraltar 837-840
Great Britain (Guernsey) 805-809
Great Britain (Jersey) 935-936
Great Britain (Isle of Man) 883
Greece 1959
Greenland 363
Hungary 3699-3700
Iceland 910
Ireland 1230-1231
Italy 2349
Latvia 504
Liechtenstein 1178
Lithuania 668
Luxembourg 1035
Macedonia 187
Malta 1011-1012
Moldova 355
Monaco 2161-2162
Poland 3519
Portugal 2358
Portugal (Azores) 455
Portugal (Madeira) 208
Romania 4370
Russia 6589
San Marino 1480
Slovakia 355
Slovenia 424
Spain 3036
Sweden 2394
Switzerland 1074
Turkey 2762
Turkish Rep. of Northern Cyprus 500
Ukraine 379
Vatican City 115

The Gibraltar stamps are similar to the stamp illustrated, but none have the design shown above. All other sets listed above include at least one stamp with the design shown, but some include stamps with entirely different designs. Bulgaria Nos. 4131-4132 are Europa stamps with completely different designs.

PORTUGAL & COLONIES
Vasco da Gama

Fleet Departing
CD20

Fleet Arriving at Calicut — CD21

Embarking at Rastello
CD22

Muse of History
CD23

San Gabriel, da Gama and Camoens
CD24

Archangel Gabriel, the Patron Saint
CD25

Flagship San Gabriel — CD26

Vasco da Gama — CD27

Fourth centenary of Vasco da Gama's discovery of the route to India.

1898

Azores 93-100
Macao 67-74
Madeira 37-44
Portugal 147-154
Port. Africa 1-8
Port. Congo 75-98
Port. India 189-196
St. Thomas & Prince Islands 170-193
Timor 45-52

Pombal
POSTAL TAX
POSTAL TAX DUES

Marquis de Pombal — CD28

Planning Reconstruction of Lisbon, 1755 — CD29

Pombal Monument, Lisbon — CD30

Sebastiao Jose de Carvalho e Mello, Marquis de Pombal (1699-1782), statesman, rebuilt Lisbon after earthquake of 1755. Tax was for the erection of Pombal monument. Obligatory on all mail on certain days throughout the year. Postal Tax Dues are inscribed "Multa."

1925

Angola RA1-RA3, RAJ1-RAJ3
Azores RA9-RA11, RAJ2-RAJ4
Cape Verde RA1-RA3, RAJ1-RAJ3
Macao RA1-RA3, RAJ1-RAJ3
Madeira RA1-RA3, RAJ1-RAJ3
Mozambique RA1-RA3, RAJ1-RAJ3
Nyassa RA1-RA3, RAJ1-RAJ3
Portugal RA11-RA13, RAJ2-RAJ4
Port. Guinea RA1-RA3, RAJ1-RAJ3
Port. India RA1-RA3, RAJ1-RAJ3
St. Thomas & Prince Islands RA1-RA3, RAJ1-RAJ3
Timor RA1-RA3, RAJ1-RAJ3

Vasco da Gama
CD34

Mousinho de Albuquerque
CD35

Dam
CD36

Prince Henry the Navigator
CD37

Affonso de Albuquerque
CD38

Plane over Globe
CD39

1938-39

Angola 274-291, C1-C9
Cape Verde 234-251, C1-C9
Macao 289-305, C7-C15
Mozambique 270-287, C1-C9
Port. Guinea 233-250. C1-C9
Port. India 439-453, C1-C8
St. Thomas & Prince Islands ... 302-319, 323-340, C1-C18
Timor 223-239, C1-C9

Lady of Fatima

Our Lady of the Rosary, Fatima, Portugal — CD40

1948-49

Angola	315-318
Cape Verde	266
Macao	336
Mozambique	325-328
Port. Guinea	271
Port. India	480
St. Thomas & Prince Islands	351
Timor	254

A souvenir sheet of 9 stamps was issued in 1951 to mark the extension of the 1950 Holy Year. The sheet contains: Angola No. 316, Cape Verde No. 266, Macao No. 336, Mozambique No. 325, Portuguese Guinea No. 271, Portuguese India Nos. 480, 485, St. Thomas & Prince Islands No. 351, Timor No. 254. The sheet also contains a portrait of Pope Pius XII and is inscribed "Encerramento do Ano Santo, Fatima 1951." It was sold for 11 escudos.

Holy Year

Church Bells and Dove CD41

Angel Holding Candelabra CD42

Holy Year, 1950.

1950-51

Angola	331-332
Cape Verde	268-269
Macao	339-340
Mozambique	330-331
Port. Guinea	273-274
Port. India	490-491, 496-503
St. Thomas & Prince Islands	353-354
Timor	258-259

A souvenir sheet of 8 stamps was issued in 1951 to mark the extension of the Holy Year. The sheet contains: Angola No. 331, Cape Verde No. 269, Macao No. 340, Mozambique No. 331, Portuguese Guinea No. 275, Portuguese India No. 490, St. Thomas & Prince Islands No. 354, Timor No. 258, some with colors changed. The sheet contains doves and is inscribed 'Encerramento do Ano Santo, Fatima 1951.' It was sold for 17 escudos.

Holy Year Conclusion

Our Lady of Fatima — CD43

Conclusion of Holy Year. Sheets contain alternate vertical rows of stamps and labels bearing quotation from Pope Pius XII, different for each colony.

1951

Angola	357
Cape Verde	270
Macao	352
Mozambique	356
Port. Guinea	275
Port. India	506
St. Thomas & Prince Islands	355
Timor	270

Medical Congress

CD44

First National Congress of Tropical Medicine, Lisbon, 1952. Each stamp has a different design.

1952

Angola	358
Cape Verde	287
Macao	364
Mozambique	359
Port. Guinea	276
Port. India	516
St. Thomas & Prince Islands	356
Timor	271

Postage Due Stamps

CD45

1952

Angola	J37-J42
Cape Verde	J31-J36
Macao	J53-J58
Mozambique	J51-J56
Port. Guinea	J40-J45
Port. India	J47-J52
St. Thomas & Prince Islands	J52-J57
Timor	J31-J36

Sao Paulo

Father Manuel de Nobrege and View of Sao Paulo — CD46

Founding of Sao Paulo, Brazil, 400th anniv.

1954

Angola	385
Cape Verde	297
Macao	382
Mozambique	395
Port. Guinea	291
Port. India	530
St. Thomas & Prince Islands	369
Timor	279

Tropical Medicine Congress

CD47

Sixth International Congress for Tropical Medicine and Malaria, Lisbon, Sept. 1958. Each stamp shows a different plant.

1958

Angola	409
Cape Verde	303
Macao	392
Mozambique	404
Port. Guinea	295
Port. India	569
St. Thomas & Prince Islands	371
Timor	289

Sports

CD48

Each stamp shows a different sport.

1962

Angola	433-438
Cape Verde	320-325
Macao	394-399
Mozambique	424-429
Port. Guinea	299-304
St. Thomas & Prince Islands	374-379
Timor	313-318

Anti-Malaria

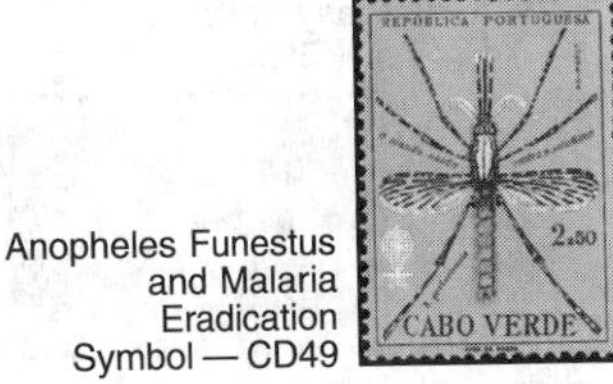

Anopheles Funestus and Malaria Eradication Symbol — CD49

World Health Organization drive to eradicate malaria.

1962

Angola	439
Cape Verde	326
Macao	400
Mozambique	430
Port. Guinea	305
St. Thomas & Prince Islands	380
Timor	319

Airline Anniversary

Map of Africa, Super Constellation and Jet Liner — CD50

Tenth anniversary of Transportes Aereos Portugueses (TAP).

1963

Angola	490
Cape Verde	327
Mozambique	434
Port. Guinea	318
St. Thomas & Prince Islands	381

National Overseas Bank

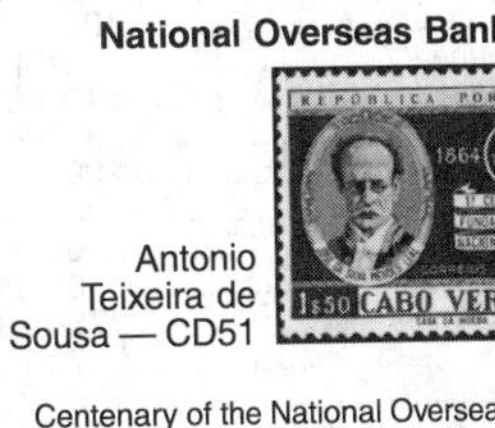

Antonio Teixeira de Sousa — CD51

Centenary of the National Overseas Bank of Portugal.

1964, May 16

Angola	509
Cape Verde	328
Port. Guinea	319
St. Thomas & Prince Islands	382
Timor	320

ITU

ITU Emblem and the Archangel Gabriel — CD52

International Communications Union, Cent.

1965, May 17

Angola	511
Cape Verde	329
Macao	402
Mozambique	464
Port. Guinea	320
St. Thomas & Prince Islands	383
Timor	321

National Revolution

CD53

40th anniv. of the National Revolution. Different buildings on each stamp.

1966, May 28

Angola	525
Cape Verde	338
Macao	403
Mozambique	465
Port. Guinea	329
St. Thomas & Prince Islands	392
Timor	322

Navy Club

CD54

Centenary of Portugal's Navy Club. Each stamp has a different design.

1967, Jan. 31

Angola	527-528
Cape Verde	339-340
Macao	412-413
Mozambique	478-479
Port. Guinea	330-331
St. Thomas & Prince Islands	393-394
Timor	323-324

Admiral Coutinho

CD55

Centenary of the birth of Admiral Carlos Viegas Gago Coutinho (1869-1959), explorer and aviation pioneer. Each stamp has a different design.

1969, Feb. 17

Angola	547
Cape Verde	355
Macao	417
Mozambique	484
Port. Guinea	335
St. Thomas & Prince Islands	397
Timor	335

Administration Reform

Luiz Augusto Rebello da Silva — CD56

Centenary of the administration reforms of the overseas territories.

1969, Sept. 25

Angola	549
Cape Verde	357
Macao	419
Mozambique	491
Port. Guinea	337
St. Thomas & Prince Islands	399
Timor	338

Marshal Carmona

CD57

Birth centenary of Marshal Antonio Oscar Carmona de Fragoso (1869-1951), President of Portugal. Each stamp has a different design.

1970, Nov. 15

Angola	563
Cape Verde	359
Macao	422
Mozambique	493
Port. Guinea	340
St. Thomas & Prince Islands	403
Timor	341

Olympic Games

CD59

20th Olympic Games, Munich, Aug. 26-Sept. 11. Each stamp shows a different sport.

1972, June 20

Angola	569
Cape Verde	361
Macao	426
Mozambique	504
Port. Guinea	342
St. Thomas & Prince Islands	408
Timor	343

Lisbon-Rio de Janeiro Flight

CD60

50th anniversary of the Lisbon to Rio de Janeiro flight by Arturo de Sacadura and Coutinho, March 30-June 5, 1922. Each stamp shows a different stage of the flight.

1972, Sept. 20

Angola	570
Cape Verde	362
Macao	427
Mozambique	505
Port. Guinea	343
St. Thomas & Prince Islands	409
Timor	344

WMO Centenary

WMO Emblem — CD61

Centenary of international meterological cooperation.

1973, Dec. 15

Angola	571
Cape Verde	363
Macao	429
Mozambique	509
Port. Guinea	344
St. Thomas & Prince Islands	410
Timor	345

FRENCH COMMUNITY

Upper Volta can be found under Burkina Faso in Vol. 1

Madagascar can be found under Malagasy in Vol. 3

Colonial Exposition

People of French Empire CD70

Women's Heads CD71

France Showing Way to Civilization CD72

"Colonial Commerce" CD73

International Colonial Exposition, Paris.

1931

Cameroun	213-216
Chad	60-63
Dahomey	97-100
Fr. Guiana	152-155
Fr. Guinea	116-119
Fr. India	100-103
Fr. Polynesia	76-79
Fr. Sudan	102-105
Gabon	120-123
Guadeloupe	138-141
Indo-China	140-142
Ivory Coast	92-95
Madagascar	169-172
Martinique	129-132
Mauritania	65-68
Middle Congo	61-64
New Caledonia	176-179
Niger	73-76
Reunion	122-125
St. Pierre & Miquelon	132-135
Senegal	138-141
Somali Coast	135-138
Togo	254-257
Ubangi-Shari	82-85
Upper Volta	66-69
Wallis & Futuna Isls.	85-88

Paris International Exposition Colonial Arts Exposition

"Colonial Resources" CD74 CD77

Overseas Commerce CD75

Exposition Building and Women CD76

"France and the Empire" CD78

Cultural Treasures of the Colonies CD79

Souvenir sheets contain one imperf. stamp.

1937

Cameroun	217-222A
Dahomey	101-107
Fr. Equatorial Africa	27-32, 73
Fr. Guiana	162-168
Fr. Guinea	120-126
Fr. India	104-110
Fr. Polynesia	117-123
Fr. Sudan	106-112
Guadeloupe	148-154
Indo-China	193-199
Inini	41
Ivory Coast	152-158
Kwangchowan	132
Madagascar	191-197
Martinique	179-185
Mauritania	69-75
New Caledonia	208-214
Niger	72-83
Reunion	167-173
St. Pierre & Miquelon	165-171
Senegal	172-178
Somali Coast	139-145
Togo	258-264
Wallis & Futuna Isls.	89

Curie

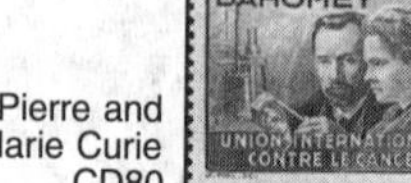

Pierre and Marie Curie CD80

40th anniversary of the discovery of radium. The surtax was for the benefit of the Intl. Union for the Control of Cancer.

1938

Cameroun	B1
Cuba	B1-B2
Dahomey	B2
France	B76
Fr. Equatorial Africa	B1
Fr. Guiana	B3
Fr. Guinea	B2
Fr. India	B6
Fr. Polynesia	B5
Fr. Sudan	B1
Guadeloupe	B3
Indo-China	B14
Ivory Coast	B2
Madagascar	B2
Martinique	B2
Mauritania	B3
New Caledonia	B4
Niger	B1
Reunion	B4
St. Pierre & Miquelon	B3
Senegal	B3
Somali Coast	B2
Togo	B1

Caillie

Rene Caille and Map of Northwestern Africa — CD81

Death centenary of Rene Caillie (1799-1838), French explorer. All three denominations exist with colony name omitted.

1939

Dahomey	108-110
Fr. Guinea	161-163
Fr. Sudan	113-115
Ivory Coast	160-162
Mauritania	109-111
Niger	84-86
Senegal	188-190
Togo	265-267

New York World's Fair

Natives and New York Skyline CD82

1939

Cameroun	223-224
Dahomey	111-112
Fr. Equatorial Africa	78-79
Fr. Guiana	169-170
Fr. Guinea	164-165
Fr. India	111-112
Fr. Polynesia	124-125
Fr. Sudan	116-117
Guadeloupe	155-156
Indo-China	203-204
Inini	42-43
Ivory Coast	163-164
Kwangchowan	121-122
Madagascar	209-210
Martinique	186-187
Mauritania	112-113
New Caledonia	215-216
Niger	87-88
Reunion	174-175
St. Pierre & Miquelon	205-206
Senegal	191-192
Somali Coast	179-180
Togo	268-269
Wallis & Futuna Isls.	90-91

French Revolution

Storming of the Bastille CD83

French Revolution, 150th anniv. The surtax was for the defense of the colonies.

1939

Cameroun	B2-B6
Dahomey	B3-B7
Fr. Equatorial Africa	B4-B8, CB1
Fr. Guiana	B4-B8, CB1
Fr. Guinea	B3-B7
Fr. India	B7-B11
Fr. Polynesia	B6-B10, CB1
Fr. Sudan	B2-B6
Guadeloupe	B4-B8
Indo-China	B15-B19, CB1
Inini	B1-B5
Ivory Coast	B3-B7

Kwangchowan B1-B5
Madagascar.................... B3-B7, CB1
Martinique.................................B3-B7
Mauritania.................................B4-B8
New Caledonia................ B5-B9, CB1
Niger..B2-B6
Reunion B5-B9, CB1
St. Pierre & Miquelon.................B4-B8
Senegal B4-B8, CB1
Somali Coast..............................B3-B7
Togo...B2-B6
Wallis & Futuna Isls. B1-B5

Plane over Coastal Area CD85

All five denominations exist with colony name omitted.

1940

Dahomey C1-C5
Fr. Guinea C1-C5
Fr. Sudan................................. C1-C5
Ivory Coast C1-C5
Mauritania................................ C1-C5
Niger.. C1-C5
Senegal C12-C16
Togo... C1-C5

Defense of the Empire

Colonial Infantryman — CD86

1941

Cameroun B13B
Dahomey B13
Fr. Equatorial Africa B8B
Fr. Guiana B10
Fr. Guinea B13
Fr. India B13
Fr. Polynesia............................... B12
Fr. Sudan.................................... B12
Guadeloupe B10
Indo-China B19B
Inini B7
Ivory Coast B13
Kwangchowan B7
Madagascar.................................. B9
Martinique..................................... B9
Mauritania................................... B14
New Caledonia............................ B11
Niger.. B12
Reunion B11
St. Pierre & Miquelon B8B
Senegal B14
Somali Coast.................................. B9
Togo... B10B
Wallis & Futuna Isls. B7

Colonial Education Fund

CD86a

1942

Cameroun CB3
Dahomey CB4
Fr. Equatorial Africa CB5
Fr. Guiana CB4
Fr. Guinea CB4
Fr. India CB3
Fr. Polynesia............................. CB4
Fr. Sudan.................................. CB4
Kwangchowan CB4

Cross of Lorraine & Four-motor Plane CD87

1941-5

Cameroun C1-C7
Fr. Equatorial Africa C17-C23
Fr. Guiana C9-C10
Fr. India C1-C6
Fr. Polynesia............................. C3-C9
Fr. West Africa C1-C3
Guadeloupe C1-C2
Madagascar........................... C37-C43
Martinique................................. C1-C2
New Caledonia C7-C13
Reunion C18-C24
St. Pierre & Miquelon C1-C7
Somali Coast C1-C7

Transport Plane CD88

Caravan and Plane CD89

1942

Dahomey C6-C13
Fr. Guinea C6-C13
Fr. Sudan............................... C6-C13
Ivory Coast C6-C13
Mauritania.............................. C6-C13
Niger....................................... C6-C13
Senegal C17-C25
Togo.. C6-C13

Red Cross

Marianne CD90

The surtax was for the French Red Cross and national relief.

1944

Cameroun B28
Fr. Equatorial Africa B38
Fr. Guiana B12
Fr. India B14
Fr. Polynesia................................. B13
Fr. West Africa B1
Guadeloupe B12
Madagascar................................... B15
Martinique..................................... B11
New Caledonia.............................. B13
Reunion B15
St. Pierre & Miquelon B13
Somali Coast................................. B13
Wallis & Futuna Isls. B9

Eboue

CD91

Felix Eboue, first French colonial administrator to proclaim resistance to Germany after French surrender in World War II.

1945

Cameroun 296-297
Fr. Equatorial Africa 156-157
Fr. Guiana 171-172
Fr. India 210-211
Fr. Polynesia........................... 150-151
Fr. West Africa 15-16
Guadeloupe 187-188
Madagascar............................. 259-260
Martinique............................... 196-197
New Caledonia......................... 274-275
Reunion 238-239
St. Pierre & Miquelon 322-323
Somali Coast........................... 238-239

Victory

Victory — CD92

European victory of the Allied Nations in World War II.

1946, May 8

Cameroun C8
Fr. Equatorial Africa C24
Fr. Guiana C11
Fr. India C7
Fr. Polynesia................................. C10
Fr. West Africa C4
Guadeloupe C3
Indo-China C19
Madagascar................................... C44
Martinique....................................... C3
New Caledonia.............................. C14
Reunion C25
St. Pierre & Miquelon C8
Somali Coast.................................... C8
Wallis & Futuna Isls. C1

Chad to Rhine

Leclerc's Departure from Chad — CD93

Battle at Cufra Oasis — CD94

Tanks in Action, Mareth — CD95

Normandy Invasion — CD96

Entering Paris — CD97

Liberation of Strasbourg — CD98

"Chad to the Rhine" march, 1942-44, by Gen. Jacques Leclerc's column, later French 2nd Armored Division.

1946, June 6

Cameroun C9-C14
Fr. Equatorial Africa C25-C30
Fr. Guiana C12-C17
Fr. India C8-C13
Fr. Polynesia........................... C11-C16
Fr. West Africa C5-C10
Guadeloupe C4-C9
Indo-China C20-C25
Madagascar............................. C45-C50
Martinique.................................... C4-C9
New Caledonia........................ C15-C20
Reunion C26-C31
St. Pierre & Miquelon C9-C14
Somali Coast............................. C9-C14
Wallis & Futuna Isls. C2-C7

UPU

French Colonials, Globe and Plane — CD99

Universal Postal Union, 75th anniv.

1949, July 4

Cameroun C29
Fr. Equatorial Africa C34
Fr. India C17
Fr. Polynesia.................................. C20
Fr. West Africa C15
Indo-China C26
Madagascar.................................... C55
New Caledonia............................... C24
St. Pierre & Miquelon C18
Somali Coast................................... C18
Togo.. C18
Wallis & Futuna Isls. C10

Tropical Medicine

Doctor Treating Infant CD100

The surtax was for charitable work.

1950

Cameroun B29
Fr. Equatorial Africa B39
Fr. India B15
Fr. Polynesia................................... B14
Fr. West Africa B3
Madagascar...................................... B17
New Caledonia................................ B14
St. Pierre & Miquelon B14
Somali Coast.................................... B14
Togo... B11

Military Medal

Medal, Early Marine and Colonial Soldier — CD101

Centenary of the creation of the French Military Medal.

1952

Cameroun ... 332
Comoro Isls. ... 39
Fr. Equatorial Africa ... 186
Fr. India ... 233
Fr. Polynesia ... 179
Fr. West Africa ... 57
Madagascar ... 286
New Caledonia ... 295
St. Pierre & Miquelon ... 345
Somali Coast ... 267
Togo ... 327
Wallis & Futuna Isls. ... 149

Liberation

Allied Landing, Victory Sign and Cross of Lorraine — CD102

Liberation of France, 10th anniv.

1954, June 6

Cameroun ... C32
Comoro Isls. ... C4
Fr. Equatorial Africa ... C38
Fr. India ... C18
Fr. Polynesia ... C22
Fr. West Africa ... C17
Madagascar ... C57
New Caledonia ... C25
St. Pierre & Miquelon ... C19
Somali Coast ... C19
Togo ... C19
Wallis & Futuna Isls. ... C11

FIDES

Plowmen CD103

Efforts of FIDES, the Economic and Social Development Fund for Overseas Possessions (Fonds d' Investissement pour le Developpement Economique et Social). Each stamp has a different design.

1956

Cameroun ... 326-329
Comoro Isls. ... 43
Fr. Polynesia ... 181
Fr. West Africa ... 65-72
Madagascar ... 292-295
New Caledonia ... 303
Somali Coast ... 268
Togo ... 331

Flower

CD104

Each stamp shows a different flower.

1958-9

Cameroun ... 333
Comoro Isls. ... 45
Fr. Equatorial Africa ... 200-201
Fr. Polynesia ... 192
Fr. So. & Antarctic Terr. ... 11
Fr. West Africa ... 79-83
Madagascar ... 301-302
New Caledonia ... 304-305
St. Pierre & Miquelon ... 357
Somali Coast ... 270
Togo ... 348-349
Wallis & Futuna Isls. ... 152

Human Rights

Sun, Dove and U.N. Emblem CD105

10th anniversary of the signing of the Universal Declaration of Human Rights.

1958

Comoro Isls. ... 44
Fr. Equatorial Africa ... 202
Fr. Polynesia ... 191
Fr. West Africa ... 85
Madagascar ... 300
New Caledonia ... 306
St. Pierre & Miquelon ... 356
Somali Coast ... 274
Wallis & Futuna Isls. ... 153

C.C.T.A.

CD106

Commission for Technical Cooperation in Africa south of the Sahara, 10th anniv.

1960

Cameroun ... 335
Cent. Africa ... 3
Chad ... 66
Congo, P.R. ... 90
Dahomey ... 138
Gabon ... 150
Ivory Coast ... 180
Madagascar ... 317
Mali ... 9
Mauritania ... 117
Niger ... 104
Upper Volta ... 89

Air Afrique, 1961

Modern and Ancient Africa, Map and Planes — CD107

Founding of Air Afrique (African Airlines).

1961-62

Cameroun ... C37
Cent. Africa ... C5
Chad ... C7
Congo, P.R. ... C5
Dahomey ... C17
Gabon ... C5
Ivory Coast ... C18
Mauritania ... C17
Niger ... C22
Senegal ... C31
Upper Volta ... C4

Anti-Malaria

CD108

World Health Organization drive to eradicate malaria.

1962, Apr. 7

Cameroun ... B36
Cent. Africa ... B1
Chad ... B1
Comoro Isls. ... B1
Congo, P.R. ... B3
Dahomey ... B15
Gabon ... B4
Ivory Coast ... B15
Madagascar ... B19
Mali ... B1
Mauritania ... B16
Niger ... B14
Senegal ... B16
Somali Coast ... B15
Upper Volta ... B1

Abidjan Games

CD109

Abidjan Games, Ivory Coast, Dec. 24-31, 1961. Each stamp shows a different sport.

1962

Chad ... 83-84
Cent. Africa ... 19-20
Congo, P.R. ... 103-104
Gabon ... 163-164, C6
Niger ... 109-111
Upper Volta ... 103-105

African and Malagasy Union

Flag of Union CD110

First anniversary of the Union.

1962, Sept. 8

Cameroun ... 373
Cent. Africa ... 21
Chad ... 85
Congo, P.R. ... 105
Dahomey ... 155
Gabon ... 165
Ivory Coast ... 198
Madagascar ... 332
Mauritania ... 170
Niger ... 112
Senegal ... 211
Upper Volta ... 106

Telstar

Telstar and Globe Showing Andover and Pleumeur-Bodou — CD111

First television connection of the United States and Europe through the Telstar satellite, July 11-12, 1962.

1962-63

Andorra, French ... 154
Comoro Isls. ... C7
Fr. Polynesia ... C29
Fr. So. & Antarctic Terr. ... C5
New Caledonia ... C33
Somali Coast ... C31
St. Pierre & Miquelon ... C26
Wallis & Futuna Isls. ... C17

Freedom From Hunger

World Map and Wheat Emblem CD112

U.N. Food and Agriculture Organization's "Freedom from Hunger" campaign.

1963, Mar. 21

Cameroun ... B37-B38
Cent. Africa ... B2
Chad ... B2
Congo, P.R. ... B4
Dahomey ... B16
Gabon ... B5
Ivory Coast ... B16
Madagascar ... B21
Mauritania ... B17
Niger ... B15
Senegal ... B17
Upper Volta ... B2

Red Cross Centenary

CD113

Centenary of the International Red Cross.

1963, Sept. 2

Comoro Isls. ... 55
Fr. Polynesia ... 205
New Caledonia ... 328
St. Pierre & Miquelon ... 367
Somali Coast ... 297
Wallis & Futuna Isls. ... 165

African Postal Union, 1963

UAMPT Emblem, Radio Masts, Plane and Mail CD114

Establishment of the African and Malagasy Posts and Telecommunications Union.

1963, Sept. 8

Cameroun ... C47
Cent. Africa ... C10
Chad ... C9
Congo, P.R. ... C13
Dahomey ... C19
Gabon ... C13
Ivory Coast ... C25
Madagascar ... C75
Mauritania ... C22
Niger ... C27
Rwanda ... 36
Senegal ... C32
Upper Volta ... C9

Air Afrique, 1963

Symbols of Flight — CD115

First anniversary of Air Afrique and inauguration of DC-8 service.

1963, Nov. 19

Cameroun C48
Chad C10
Congo, P.R. C14
Gabon C18
Ivory Coast C26
Mauritania C26
Niger C35
Senegal C33

Europafrica

Europe and Africa Linked — CD116

Signing of an economic agreement between the European Economic Community and the African and Malagasy Union, Yaounde, Cameroun, July 20, 1963.

1963-64

Cameroun 402
Chad C11
Cent. Africa C12
Congo, P.R. C16
Gabon C19
Ivory Coast 217
Niger C43
Upper Volta C11

Human Rights

Scales of Justice and Globe CD117

15th anniversary of the Universal Declaration of Human Rights.

1963, Dec. 10

Comoro Isls. 58
Fr. Polynesia 206
New Caledonia 329
St. Pierre & Miquelon 368
Somali Coast 300
Wallis & Futuna Isls. 166

PHILATEC

Stamp Album, Champs Elysees Palace and Horses of Marly CD118

Intl. Philatelic and Postal Techniques Exhibition, Paris, June 5-21, 1964.

1963-64

Comoro Isls. 60
France 1078
Fr. Polynesia 207
New Caledonia 341
St. Pierre & Miquelon 369
Somali Coast 301
Wallis & Futuna Isls. 167

Cooperation

CD119

Cooperation between France and the French-speaking countries of Africa and Madagascar.

1964

Cameroun 409-410
Cent. Africa 39
Chad 103
Congo, P.R. 121
Dahomey 193
France 1111
Gabon 175
Ivory Coast 221
Madagascar 360
Mauritania 181
Niger 143
Senegal 236
Togo 495

ITU

Telegraph, Syncom Satellite and ITU Emblem CD120

Intl. Telecommunication Union, Cent.

1965, May 17

Comoro Isls. C14
Fr. Polynesia C33
Fr. So. & Antarctic Terr. C8
New Caledonia C40
New Hebrides 124-125
St. Pierre & Miquelon C29
Somali Coast C36
Wallis & Futuna Isls. C20

French Satellite A-1

Diamant Rocket and Launching Installation — CD121

Launching of France's first satellite, Nov. 26, 1965.

1965-66

Comoro Isls. C15-C16
France 1137-1138
Fr. Polynesia C40-C41
Fr. So. & Antarctic Terr. C9-C10
New Caledonia C44-C45
St. Pierre & Miquelon C30-C31
Somali Coast C39-C40
Wallis & Futuna Isls. C22-C23

French Satellite D-1

D-1 Satellite in Orbit — CD122

Launching of the D-1 satellite at Hammaguir, Algeria, Feb. 17, 1966.

1966

Comoro Isls. C17
France 1148
Fr. Polynesia C42
Fr. So. & Antarctic Terr. C11
New Caledonia C46
St. Pierre & Miquelon C32
Somali Coast C49
Wallis & Futuna Isls. C24

Air Afrique, 1966

Planes and Air Afrique Emblem — CD123

Introduction of DC-8F planes by Air Afrique.

1966

Cameroun C79
Cent. Africa C35
Chad C26
Congo, P.R. C42
Dahomey C42
Gabon C47
Ivory Coast C32
Mauritania C57
Niger C63
Senegal C47
Togo C54
Upper Volta C31

African Postal Union, 1967

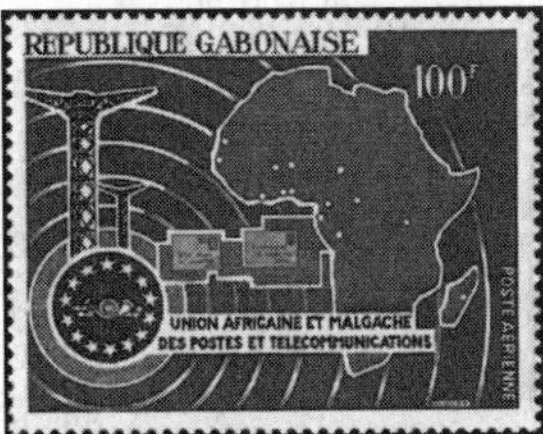

Telecommunications Symbols and Map of Africa — CD124

Fifth anniversary of the establishment of the African and Malagasy Union of Posts and Telecommunications, UAMPT.

1967

Cameroun C90
Cent. Africa C46
Chad C37
Congo, P.R. C57
Dahomey C61
Gabon C58
Ivory Coast C34
Madagascar C85
Mauritania C65
Niger C75
Rwanda C1-C3
Senegal C60
Togo C81
Upper Volta C50

Monetary Union

Gold Token of the Ashantis, 17-18th Centuries — CD125

West African Monetary Union, 5th anniv.

1967, Nov. 4

Dahomey 244
Ivory Coast 259
Mauritania 238
Niger 204
Senegal 294
Togo 623
Upper Volta 181

WHO Anniversary

Sun, Flowers and WHO Emblem CD126

World Health Organization, 20th anniv.

1968, May 4

Afars & Issas 317
Comoro Isls. 73
Fr. Polynesia 241-242
Fr. So. & Antarctic Terr. 31
New Caledonia 367
St. Pierre & Miquelon 377
Wallis & Futuna Isls. 169

Human Rights Year

Human Rights Flame — CD127

1968, Aug. 10

Afars & Issas 322-323
Comoro Isls. 76
Fr. Polynesia 243-244
Fr. So. & Antarctic Terr. 32
New Caledonia 369
St. Pierre & Miquelon 382
Wallis & Futuna Isls. 170

2nd PHILEXAFRIQUE

CD128

Opening of PHILEXAFRIQUE, Abidjan, Feb. 14. Each stamp shows a local scene and stamp.

1969, Feb. 14

Cameroun C118
Cent. Africa C65
Chad C48
Congo, P.R. C77
Dahomey C94
Gabon C82
Ivory Coast C38-C40
Madagascar C92
Mali C65

Mauritania.......................................C80
Niger..C104
Senegal...C68
Togo..C104
Upper Volta......................................C62

Concorde

Concorde in Flight CD129

First flight of the prototype Concorde supersonic plane at Toulouse, Mar. 1, 1969.

1969

Afars & Issas.................................C56
Comoro Isls.....................................C29
France..C42
Fr. Polynesia....................................C50
Fr. So. & Antarctic Terr. C18
New Caledonia.................................C63
St. Pierre & Miquelon.....................C40
Wallis & Futuna Isls. C30

Development Bank

Bank Emblem — CD130

African Development Bank, fifth anniv.

1969

Cameroun...499
Chad..217
Congo, P.R..................................181-182
Ivory Coast.......................................281
Mali...127-128
Mauritania...267
Niger..220
Senegal..317-318
Upper Volta.......................................201

ILO

ILO Headquarters, Geneva, and Emblem — CD131

Intl. Labor Organization, 50th anniv.

1969-70

Afars & Issas....................................337
Comoro Isls...83
Fr. Polynesia.................................251-252
Fr. So. & Antarctic Terr. 35
New Caledonia....................................379
St. Pierre & Miquelon..........................396
Wallis & Futuna Isls. 172

ASECNA

Map of Africa, Plane and Airport CD132

10th anniversary of the Agency for the Security of Aerial Navigation in Africa and Madagascar (ASECNA, Agence pour la Securite de la Navigation Aerienne en Afrique et a Madagascar).

1969-70

Cameroun...500
Cent. Africa.......................................119
Chad..222
Congo, P.R...197
Dahomey..269
Gabon...260
Ivory Coast...287
Mali...130
Niger...221
Senegal...321
Upper Volta...204

U.P.U. Headquarters

CD133

New Universal Postal Union headquarters, Bern, Switzerland.

1970

Afars & Issas.......................................342
Algeria...443
Cameroun......................................503-504
Cent. Africa..125
Chad...225
Comoro Isls..84
Congo, P.R...216
Fr. Polynesia..................................261-262
Fr. So. & Antarctic Terr. 36
Gabon...258
Ivory Coast...295
Madagascar..444
Mali..134-135
Mauritania..283
New Caledonia......................................382
Niger...231-232
St. Pierre & Miquelon.....................397-398
Senegal...328-329
Tunisia..535
Wallis & Futuna Isls. 173

De Gaulle

CD134

First anniversary of the death of Charles de Gaulle, (1890-1970), President of France.

1971-72

Afars & Issas..................................356-357
Comoro Isls.....................................104-105
France..1322-1325
Fr. Polynesia...................................270-271
Fr. So. & Antarctic Terr. 52-53
New Caledonia................................393-394
Reunion...377, 380
St. Pierre & Miquelon......................417-418
Wallis & Futuna Isls. 177-178

African Postal Union, 1971

UAMPT Building, Brazzaville, Congo — CD135

10th anniversary of the establishment of the African and Malagasy Posts and Telecommunications Union, UAMPT. Each stamp has a different native design.

1971, Nov. 13

Cameroun..C177
Cent. Africa.......................................C89
Chad..C94
Congo, P.R.......................................C136
Dahomey...C146
Gabon..C120
Ivory Coast...C47
Mauritania...C113
Niger..C164
Rwanda..C8
Senegal...C105
Togo..C166
Upper Volta..C97

West African Monetary Union

African Couple, City, Village and Commemorative Coin — CD136

West African Monetary Union, 10th anniv.

1972, Nov. 2

Dahomey...300
Ivory Coast..331
Mauritania...299
Niger...258
Senegal..374
Togo..825
Upper Volta..280

African Postal Union, 1973

Telecommunications Symbols and Map of Africa — CD137

11th anniversary of the African and Malagasy Posts and Telecommunications Union (UAMPT).

1973, Sept. 12

Cameroun..574
Cent. Africa...194
Chad..294
Congo, P.R...289
Dahomey..311
Gabon..320
Ivory Coast..361
Madagascar..500
Mauritania..304
Niger..287
Rwanda..540
Senegal..393
Togo...849
Upper Volta..297

Philexafrique II — Essen

CD138

CD139

Designs: Indigenous fauna, local and German stamps. Types CD138-CD139 printed horizontally and vertically se-tenant in sheets of 10 (2x5). Label between horizontal pairs alternately commemoratives Philexafrique II, Libreville, Gabon, June 1978, and 2nd International Stamp Fair, Essen, Germany, Nov. 1-5.

1978-1979

Benin...C285-C286
Central Africa.............................C200-C201
Chad..C238-C239
Congo Republic..........................C245-C246
Djibouti......................................C121-C122
Gabon..C215-C216
Ivory Coast.....................................C64-C65
Mali..C356-C357
Mauritania..................................C185-C186
Niger..C291-C292
Rwanda...C12-C13
Senegal.......................................C146-C147

BRITISH COMMONWEALTH OF NATIONS

The listings follow established trade practices when these issues are offered as units by dealers. The Peace issue, for example, includes only one stamp from the Indian state of Hyderabad. The U.P.U. issue includes the Egypt set. Pairs are included for those varieties issues with bilingual designs se-tenant.

Silver Jubilee

Windsor Castle and King George V CD301

Reign of King George V, 25th anniv.

1935

Antigua..77-80
Ascension...33-36
Bahamas...92-95
Barbados...186-189
Basutoland..11-14
Bechuanaland Protectorate..............117-120
Bermuda...100-103
British Guiana..................................223-226
British Honduras..............................108-111
Cayman Islands...................................81-84
Ceylon...260-263
Cyprus..136-139
Dominica...90-93
Falkland Islands...................................77-80
Fiji..110-113
Gambia...125-128
Gibraltar...100-103
Gilbert & Ellice Islands.........................33-36
Gold Coast..108-111
Grenada..124-127
Hong Kong.......................................147-150
Jamaica...109-112
Kenya, Uganda, Tanganyika................42-45
Leeward Islands...................................96-99
Malta..184-187
Mauritius..204-207
Montserrat..85-88
Newfoundland..................................226-229
Nigeria...34-37
Northern Rhodesia...............................18-21
Nyasaland Protectorate........................47-50
St. Helena..111-114
St. Kitts-Nevis......................................72-75
St. Lucia...91-94
St. Vincent.......................................134-137
Seychelles..118-121
Sierra Leone.....................................166-169
Solomon Islands...................................60-63
Somaliland Protectorate.......................77-80
Straits Settlements............................213-216
Swaziland...20-23
Trinidad & Tobago...............................43-46
Turks & Caicos Islands........................71-74
Virgin Islands.......................................69-72

The following have different designs but are included in the omnibus set:

Great Britain.....................................226-229
Offices in Morocco...... 67-70, 226-229, 422-425, 508-510
Australia..152-154
Canada..211-216
Cook Islands......................................98-100
India..142-148
Nauru...31-34
New Guinea..46-47
New Zealand....................................199-201
Niue...67-69

Papua 114-117
Samoa 163-165
South Africa 68-71
Southern Rhodesia 33-36
South-West Africa 121-124

249 stamps

Coronation

Queen Elizabeth and King George VI CD302

1937

Aden 13-15
Antigua 81-83
Ascension 37-39
Bahamas 97-99
Barbados 190-192
Basutoland 15-17
Bechuanaland Protectorate 121-123
Bermuda 115-117
British Guiana 227-229
British Honduras 112-114
Cayman Islands 97-99
Ceylon 275-277
Cyprus 140-142
Dominica 94-96
Falkland Islands 81-83
Fiji 114-116
Gambia 129-131
Gibraltar 104-106
Gilbert & Ellice Islands 37-39
Gold Coast 112-114
Grenada 128-130
Hong Kong 151-153
Jamaica 113-115
Kenya, Uganda, Tanganyika 60-62
Leeward Islands 100-102
Malta 188-190
Mauritius 208-210
Montserrat 89-91
Newfoundland 230-232
Nigeria 50-52
Northern Rhodesia 22-24
Nyasaland Protectorate 51-53
St. Helena 115-117
St. Kitts-Nevis 76-78
St. Lucia 107-109
St. Vincent 138-140
Seychelles 122-124
Sierra Leone 170-172
Solomon Islands 64-66
Somaliland Protectorate 81-83
Straits Settlements 235-237
Swaziland 24-26
Trinidad & Tobago 47-49
Turks & Caicos Islands 75-77
Virgin Islands 73-75

The following have different designs but are included in the omnibus set:

Great Britain 234
Offices in Morocco 82, 439, 514
Canada 237
Cook Islands 109-111
Nauru 35-38
Newfoundland 233-243
New Guinea 48-51
New Zealand 223-225
Niue 70-72
Papua 118-121
South Africa 74-78
Southern Rhodesia 38-41
South-West Africa 125-132

202 stamps

Peace

King George VI and Parliament Buildings, London CD303

Return to peace at the close of World War II.

1945-46

Aden 28-29
Antigua 96-97
Ascension 50-51
Bahamas 130-131
Barbados 207-208
Bermuda 131-132
British Guiana 242-243
British Honduras 127-128
Cayman Islands 112-113
Ceylon 293-294
Cyprus 156-157
Dominica 112-113
Falkland Islands 97-98
Falkland Islands Dep. 1L9-1L10
Fiji 137-138
Gambia 144-145
Gibraltar 119-120
Gilbert & Ellice Islands 52-53
Gold Coast 128-129
Grenada 143-144
Jamaica 136-137
Kenya, Uganda, Tanganyika 90-91
Leeward Islands 116-117
Malta 206-207
Mauritius 223-224
Montserrat 104-105
Nigeria 71-72
Northern Rhodesia 46-47
Nyasaland Protectorate 82-83
Pitcairn Island 9-10
St. Helena 128-129
St. Kitts-Nevis 91-92
St. Lucia 127-128
St. Vincent 152-153
Seychelles 149-150
Sierra Leone 186-187
Solomon Islands 80-81
Somaliland Protectorate 108-109
Trinidad & Tobago 62-63
Turks & Caicos Islands 90-91
Virgin Islands 88-89

The following have different designs but are included in the omnibus set:

Great Britain 264-265
Offices in Morocco 523-524
Aden
Kathiri State of Seiyun 12-13
Qu'aiti State of Shihr and Mukalla 12-13
Australia 200-202
Basutoland 29-31
Bechuanaland Protectorate 137-139
Burma 66-69
Cook Islands 127-130
Hong Kong 174-175
India 195-198
Hyderabad 51
New Zealand 247-257
Niue 90-93
Pakistan-Bahawalpur O16
Samoa 191-194
South Africa 100-102
Southern Rhodesia 67-70
South-West Africa 153-155
Swaziland 38-40
Zanzibar 222-223

164 stamps

Silver Wedding

King George VI and Queen Elizabeth

CD304 CD305

1948-49

Aden 30-31
Kathiri State of Seiyun 14-15
Qu'aiti State of Shihr and Mukalla 14-15
Antigua 98-99
Ascension 52-53
Bahamas 148-149
Barbados 210-211
Basutoland 39-40
Bechuanaland Protectorate 147-148
Bermuda 133-134
British Guiana 244-245
British Honduras 129-130
Cayman Islands 116-117
Cyprus 158-159
Dominica 114-115
Falkland Islands 99-100
Falkland Islands Dep. 1L11-1L12
Fiji 139-140
Gambia 146-147
Gibraltar 121-122
Gilbert & Ellice Islands 54-55
Gold Coast 142-143
Grenada 145-146
Hong Kong 178-179
Jamaica 138-139
Kenya, Uganda, Tanganyika 92-93
Leeward Islands 118-119
Malaya
Johore 128-129
Kedah 55-56
Kelantan 44-45
Malacca 1-2
Negri Sembilan 36-37
Pahang 44-45
Penang 1-2
Perak 99-100
Perlis 1-2
Selangor 74-75
Trengganu 47-48
Malta 223-224
Mauritius 229-230
Montserrat 106-107
Nigeria 73-74
North Borneo 238-239
Northern Rhodesia 48-49
Nyasaland Protectorate 85-86
Pitcairn Island 11-12
St. Helena 130-131
St. Kitts-Nevis 93-94
St. Lucia 129-130
St. Vincent 154-155
Sarawak 174-175
Seychelles 151-152
Sierra Leone 188-189
Singapore 21-22
Solomon Islands 82-83
Somaliland Protectorate 110-111
Swaziland 48-49
Trinidad & Tobago 64-65
Turks & Caicos Islands 92-93
Virgin Islands 90-91
Zanzibar 224-225

The following have different designs but are included in the omnibus set:

Great Britain 267-268
Offices in Morocco 93-94, 525-526
Bahrain 62-63
Kuwait 82-83
Oman 25-26
South Africa 106
South-West Africa 159

138 stamps

U.P.U.

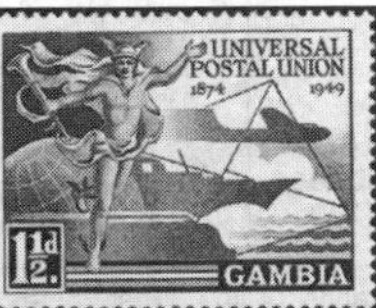

Mercury and Symbols of Communications — CD306

Plane, Ship and Hemispheres — CD307

Mercury Scattering Letters over Globe CD308

U.P.U. Monument, Bern CD309

Universal Postal Union, 75th anniversary.

1949

Aden 32-35
Kathiri State of Seiyun 16-19
Qu'aiti State of Shihr and Mukalla 16-19
Antigua 100-103
Ascension 57-60
Bahamas 150-153
Barbados 212-215
Basutoland 41-44
Bechuanaland Protectorate 149-152
Bermuda 138-141
British Guiana 246-249
British Honduras 137-140
Brunei 79-82
Cayman Islands 118-121
Cyprus 160-163
Dominica 116-119
Falkland Islands 103-106
Falkland Islands Dep. 1L14-1L17
Fiji 141-144
Gambia 148-151
Gibraltar 123-126
Gilbert & Ellice Islands 56-59
Gold Coast 144-147
Grenada 147-150
Hong Kong 180-183
Jamaica 142-145
Kenya, Uganda, Tanganyika 94-97
Leeward Islands 126-129
Malaya
Johore 151-154
Kedah 57-60
Kelantan 46-49
Malacca 18-21
Negri Sembilan 59-62
Pahang 46-49
Penang 23-26
Perak 101-104
Perlis 3-6
Selangor 76-79
Trengganu 49-52
Malta 225-228
Mauritius 231-234
Montserrat 108-111
New Hebrides, British 62-65
New Hebrides, French 79-82
Nigeria 75-78
North Borneo 240-243
Northern Rhodesia 50-53
Nyasaland Protectorate 87-90
Pitcairn Islands 13-16
St. Helena 132-135
St. Kitts-Nevis 95-98
St. Lucia 131-134
St. Vincent 170-173
Sarawak 176-179
Seychelles 153-156
Sierra Leone 190-193
Singapore 23-26
Solomon Islands 84-87
Somaliland Protectorate 112-115
Southern Rhodesia 71-72
Swaziland 50-53
Tonga 87-90
Trinidad & Tobago 66-69
Turks & Caicos Islands 101-104
Virgin Islands 92-95
Zanzibar 226-229

The following have different designs but are included in the omnibus set:

Great Britain 276-279
Offices in Morocco 546-549
Australia 223
Bahrain 68-71
Burma 116-121
Ceylon 304-306
Egypt 281-283
India 223-226
Kuwait 89-92
Oman 31-34
Pakistan-Bahawalpur 26-29, O25-O28
South Africa 109-111
South-West Africa 160-162

319 stamps

University

Arms of University College CD310

Alice, Princess of Athlone CD311

1948 opening of University College of the West Indies at Jamaica.

1951

Antigua ... 104-105
Barbados ... 228-229
British Guiana ... 250-251
British Honduras ... 141-142
Dominica ... 120-121
Grenada ... 164-165
Jamaica ... 146-147
Leeward Islands ... 130-131
Montserrat ... 112-113
St. Kitts-Nevis ... 105-106
St. Lucia ... 149-150
St. Vincent ... 174-175
Trinidad & Tobago ... 70-71
Virgin Islands ... 96-97

28 stamps

Coronation

Queen Elizabeth II — CD312

1953

Aden ... 47
  Kathiri State of Seiyun ... 28
  Qu'aiti State of Shihr and Mukalla ... 28
Antigua ... 106
Ascension ... 61
Bahamas ... 157
Barbados ... 234
Basutoland ... 45
Bechuanaland Protectorate ... 153
Bermuda ... 142
British Guiana ... 252
British Honduras ... 143
Cayman Islands ... 150
Cyprus ... 167
Dominica ... 141
Falkland Islands ... 121
Falkland Islands Dependencies ... 1L18
Fiji ... 145
Gambia ... 152
Gibraltar ... 131
Gilbert & Ellice Islands ... 60
Gold Coast ... 160
Grenada ... 170
Hong Kong ... 184
Jamaica ... 153
Kenya, Uganda, Tanganyika ... 101
Leeward Islands ... 132
Malaya
  Johore ... 155
  Kedah ... 82
  Kelantan ... 71
  Malacca ... 27
  Negri Sembilan ... 63
  Pahang ... 71
  Penang ... 27
  Perak ... 126
  Perlis ... 28
  Selangor ... 101
  Trengganu ... 74
Malta ... 241
Mauritius ... 250
Montserrat ... 127
New Hebrides, British ... 77
Nigeria ... 79
North Borneo ... 260
Northern Rhodesia ... 60
Nyasaland Protectorate ... 96
Pitcairn ... 19
St. Helena ... 139
St. Kitts-Nevis ... 119
St. Lucia ... 156
St. Vincent ... 185
Sarawak ... 196
Seychelles ... 172
Sierra Leone ... 194
Singapore ... 27
Solomon Islands ... 88
Somaliland Protectorate ... 127
Swaziland ... 54
Trinidad & Tobago ... 84
Tristan da Cunha ... 13
Turks & Caicos Islands ... 118
Virgin Islands ... 114

The following have different designs but are included in the omnibus set:

Great Britain ... 313-316
  Offices in Morocco ... 579-582
Australia ... 259-261
Bahrain ... 92-95
Canada ... 330
Ceylon ... 317
Cook Islands ... 145-146
Kuwait ... 113-116
New Zealand ... 280-284
Niue ... 104-105
Oman ... 52-55
Samoa ... 214-215
South Africa ... 192
Southern Rhodesia ... 80
South-West Africa ... 244-248
Tokelau Islands ... 4

106 stamps

Royal Visit 1953

Separate designs for each country for the visit of Queen Elizabeth II and the Duke of Edinburgh.

1953

Aden ... 62
Australia ... 267-269
Bermuda ... 163
Ceylon ... 318
Fiji ... 146
Gibraltar ... 146
Jamaica ... 154
Kenya, Uganda, Tanganyika ... 102
Malta ... 242
New Zealand ... 286-287

13 stamps

West Indies Federation

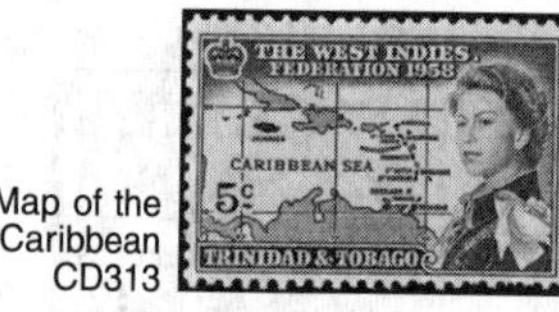

Map of the Caribbean CD313

Federation of the West Indies, April 22, 1958.

1958

Antigua ... 122-124
Barbados ... 248-250
Dominica ... 161-163
Grenada ... 184-186
Jamaica ... 175-177
Montserrat ... 143-145
St. Kitts-Nevis ... 136-138
St. Lucia ... 170-172
St. Vincent ... 198-200
Trinidad & Tobago ... 86-88

30 stamps

Freedom from Hunger

Protein Food CD314

U.N. Food and Agricultural Organization's "Freedom from Hunger" campaign.

1963

Aden ... 65
Antigua ... 133
Ascension ... 89
Bahamas ... 180
Basutoland ... 83
Bechuanaland Protectorate ... 194
Bermuda ... 192
British Guiana ... 271
British Honduras ... 179
Brunei ... 100
Cayman Islands ... 168
Dominica ... 181
Falkland Islands ... 146
Fiji ... 198
Gambia ... 172
Gibraltar ... 161
Gilbert & Ellice Islands ... 76
Grenada ... 190
Hong Kong ... 218
Malta ... 291
Mauritius ... 270
Montserrat ... 150
New Hebrides, British ... 93
North Borneo ... 296
Pitcairn ... 35
St. Helena ... 173
St. Lucia ... 179
St. Vincent ... 201
Sarawak ... 212
Seychelles ... 213
Solomon Islands ... 109
Swaziland ... 108
Tonga ... 127
Tristan da Cunha ... 68
Turks & Caicos Islands ... 138
Virgin Islands ... 140
Zanzibar ... 280

37 stamps

Red Cross Centenary

Red Cross and Elizabeth II CD315

1963

Antigua ... 134-135
Ascension ... 90-91
Bahamas ... 183-184
Basutoland ... 84-85
Bechuanaland Protectorate ... 195-196
Bermuda ... 193-194
British Guiana ... 272-273
British Honduras ... 180-181
Cayman Islands ... 169-170
Dominica ... 182-183
Falkland Islands ... 147-148
Fiji ... 203-204
Gambia ... 173-174
Gibraltar ... 162-163
Gilbert & Ellice Islands ... 77-78
Grenada ... 191-192
Hong Kong ... 219-220
Jamaica ... 203-204
Malta ... 292-293
Mauritius ... 271-272
Montserrat ... 151-152
New Hebrides, British ... 94-95
Pitcairn Islands ... 36-37
St. Helena ... 174-175
St. Kitts-Nevis ... 143-144
St. Lucia ... 180-181
St. Vincent ... 202-203
Seychelles ... 214-215
Solomon Islands ... 110-111
South Arabia ... 1-2
Swaziland ... 109-110
Tonga ... 134-135
Tristan da Cunha ... 69-70
Turks & Caicos Islands ... 139-140
Virgin Islands ... 141-142

70 stamps

Shakespeare

Shakespeare Memorial Theatre, Stratford-on-Avon — CD316

400th anniversary of the birth of William Shakespeare.

1964

Antigua ... 151
Bahamas ... 201
Bechuanaland Protectorate ... 197
Cayman Islands ... 171
Dominica ... 184
Falkland Islands ... 149
Gambia ... 192
Gibraltar ... 164
Montserrat ... 153
St. Lucia ... 196
Turks & Caicos Islands ... 141
Virgin Islands ... 143

12 stamps

ITU

ITU Emblem CD317

Intl. Telecommunication Union, cent.

1965

Antigua ... 153-154
Ascension ... 92-93
Bahamas ... 219-220
Barbados ... 265-266
Basutoland ... 101-102
Bechuanaland Protectorate ... 202-203
Bermuda ... 196-197
British Guiana ... 293-294
British Honduras ... 187-188
Brunei ... 116-117
Cayman Islands ... 172-173
Dominica ... 185-186
Falkland Islands ... 154-155
Fiji ... 211-212
Gibraltar ... 167-168
Gilbert & Ellice Islands ... 87-88
Grenada ... 205-206
Hong Kong ... 221-222
Mauritius ... 291-292
Montserrat ... 157-158
New Hebrides, British ... 108-109
Pitcairn Islands ... 52-53
St. Helena ... 180-181
St. Kitts-Nevis ... 163-164
St. Lucia ... 197-198
St. Vincent ... 224-225
Seychelles ... 218-219
Solomon Islands ... 126-127
Swaziland ... 115-116
Tristan da Cunha ... 85-86
Turks & Caicos Islands ... 142-143
Virgin Islands ... 159-160

64 stamps

Intl. Cooperation Year

ICY Emblem CD318

1965

Antigua ... 155-156
Ascension ... 94-95
Bahamas ... 222-223
Basutoland ... 103-104
Bechuanaland Protectorate ... 204-205
Bermuda ... 199-200
British Guiana ... 295-296
British Honduras ... 189-190
Brunei ... 118-119
Cayman Islands ... 174-175
Dominica ... 187-188
Falkland Islands ... 156-157
Fiji ... 213-214
Gibraltar ... 169-170
Gilbert & Ellice Islands ... 104-105
Grenada ... 207-208
Hong Kong ... 223-224
Mauritius ... 293-294
Montserrat ... 176-177
New Hebrides, British ... 110-111
New Hebrides, French ... 126-127
Pitcairn Islands ... 54-55

St. Helena 182-183
St. Kitts-Nevis 165-166
St. Lucia 199-200
Seychelles 220-221
Solomon Islands 143-144
South Arabia 17-18
Swaziland 117-118
Tristan da Cunha 87-88
Turks & Caicos Islands 144-145
Virgin Islands 161-162

64 stamps

Churchill Memorial

Winston Churchill and St. Paul's, London, During Air Attack
CD319

1966

Antigua 157-160
Ascension 96-99
Bahamas 224-227
Barbados 281-284
Basutoland 105-108
Bechuanaland Protectorate 206-209
Bermuda 201-204
British Antarctic Territory 16-19
British Honduras 191-194
Brunei 120-123
Cayman Islands 176-179
Dominica 189-192
Falkland Islands 158-161
Fiji 215-218
Gibraltar 171-174
Gilbert & Ellice Islands 106-109
Grenada 209-212
Hong Kong 225-228
Mauritius 295-298
Montserrat 178-181
New Hebrides, British 112-115
New Hebrides, French 128-131
Pitcairn Islands 56-59
St. Helena 184-187
St. Kitts-Nevis 167-170
St. Lucia 201-204
St. Vincent 241-244
Seychelles 222-225
Solomon Islands 145-148
South Arabia 19-22
Swaziland 119-122
Tristan da Cunha 89-92
Turks & Caicos Islands 146-149
Virgin Islands 163-166

136 stamps

Royal Visit, 1966

Queen Elizabeth II and Prince Philip
CD320

Caribbean visit, Feb. 4 - Mar. 6, 1966.

1966

Antigua 161-162
Bahamas 228-229
Barbados 285-286
British Guiana 299-300
Cayman Islands 180-181
Dominica 193-194
Grenada 213-214
Montserrat 182-183
St. Kitts-Nevis 171-172
St. Lucia 205-206
St. Vincent 245-246
Turks & Caicos Islands 150-151
Virgin Islands 167-168

26 stamps

World Cup Soccer

Soccer Player and Jules Rimet Cup
CD321

World Cup Soccer Championship, Wembley, England, July 11-30.

1966

Antigua 163-164
Ascension 100-101
Bahamas 245-246
Bermuda 205-206
Brunei 124-125
Cayman Islands 182-183
Dominica 195-196
Fiji 219-220
Gibraltar 175-176
Gilbert & Ellice Islands 125-126
Grenada 230-231
New Hebrides, British 116-117
New Hebrides, French 132-133
Pitcairn Islands 60-61
St. Helena 188-189
St. Kitts-Nevis 173-174
St. Lucia 207-208
Seychelles 226-227
Solomon Islands 167-168
South Arabia 23-24
Tristan da Cunha 93-94

42 stamps

WHO Headquarters

World Health Organization Headquarters, Geneva — CD322

1966

Antigua 165-166
Ascension 102-103
Bahamas 247-248
Brunei 126-127
Cayman Islands 184-185
Dominica 197-198
Fiji 224-225
Gibraltar 180-181
Gilbert & Ellice Islands 127-128
Grenada 232-233
Hong Kong 229-230
Montserrat 184-185
New Hebrides, British 118-119
New Hebrides, French 134-135
Pitcairn Islands 62-63
St. Helena 190-191
St. Kitts-Nevis 177-178
St. Lucia 209-210
St. Vincent 247-248
Seychelles 228-229
Solomon Islands 169-170
South Arabia 25-26
Tristan da Cunha 99-100

46 stamps

UNESCO Anniversary

"Education" — CD323

"Science" (Wheat ears & flask enclosing globe). "Culture" (lyre & columns). 20th anniversary of the UNESCO.

1966-67

Antigua 183-185
Ascension 108-110
Bahamas 249-251
Barbados 287-289
Bermuda 207-209
Brunei 128-130
Cayman Islands 186-188
Dominica 199-201
Gibraltar 183-185
Gilbert & Ellice Islands 129-131
Grenada 234-236
Hong Kong 231-233
Mauritius 299-301
Montserrat 186-188
New Hebrides, British 120-122
New Hebrides, French 136-138
Pitcairn Islands 64-66
St. Helena 192-194
St. Kitts-Nevis 179-181
St. Lucia 211-213
St. Vincent 249-251
Seychelles 230-232
Solomon Islands 171-173
South Arabia 27-29
Swaziland 123-125
Tristan da Cunha 101-103
Turks & Caicos Islands 155-157
Virgin Islands 176-178

84 stamps

Silver Wedding, 1972

Queen Elizabeth II and Prince Philip — CD324

Designs: borders differ for each country.

1972

Anguilla 161-162
Antigua 295-296
Ascension 164-165
Bahamas 344-345
Bermuda 296-297
British Antarctic Territory 43-44
British Honduras 306-307
British Indian Ocean Territory 48-49
Brunei 186-187
Cayman Islands 304-305
Dominica 352-353
Falkland Islands 223-224
Fiji 328-329
Gibraltar 292-293
Gilbert & Ellice Islands 206-207
Grenada 466-467
Hong Kong 271-272
Montserrat 286-287
New Hebrides, British 169-170
Pitcairn Islands 127-128
St. Helena 271-272
St. Kitts-Nevis 257-258
St. Lucia 328-329
St.Vincent 344-345
Seychelles 309-310
Solomon Islands 248-249
South Georgia 35-36
Tristan da Cunha 178-179
Turks & Caicos Islands 257-258
Virgin Islands 241-242

60 stamps

Princess Anne's Wedding

Princess Anne and Mark Phillips — CD325

Wedding of Princess Anne and Mark Phillips, Nov. 14, 1973.

1973

Anguilla 179-180
Ascension 177-178
Belize 325-326
Bermuda 302-303
British Antarctic Territory 60-61
Cayman Islands 320-321
Falkland Islands 225-226
Gibraltar 305-306
Gilbert & Ellice Islands 216-217
Hong Kong 289-290
Montserrat 300-301
Pitcairn Island 135-136
St. Helena 277-278
St. Kitts-Nevis 274-275
St. Lucia 349-350
St. Vincent 358-359
St. Vincent Grenadines 1-2
Seychelles 311-312
Solomon Islands 259-260
South Georgia 37-38
Tristan da Cunha 189-190
Turks & Caicos Islands 286-287
Virgin Islands 260-261

44 stamps

Elizabeth II Coronation Anniv.

CD326

CD327

CD328

Designs: Royal and local beasts in heraldic form and simulated stonework. Portrait of Elizabeth II by Peter Grugeon. 25th anniversary of coronation of Queen Elizabeth II.

1978

Ascension 229
Barbados 474
Belize 397
British Antarctic Territory 71
Cayman Islands 404
Christmas Island 87
Falkland Islands 275
Fiji 384
Gambia 380
Gilbert Islands 312
Mauritius 464
New Hebrides, British 258
St. Helena 317
St. Kitts-Nevis 354
Samoa 472
Solomon Islands 368
South Georgia 51
Swaziland 302
Tristan da Cunha 238
Virgin Islands 337

20 sheets

Queen Mother Elizabeth's 80th Birthday

CD330

Designs: Photographs of Queen Mother Elizabeth. Falkland Islands issued in sheets of 50; others in sheets of 9.

1980

Ascension 261
Bermuda 401
Cayman Islands 443
Falkland Islands 305
Gambia 412
Gibraltar 393
Hong Kong 364
Pitcairn Islands 193
St. Helena 341
Samoa 532
Solomon Islands 426
Tristan da Cunha 277

12 stamps

Royal Wedding, 1981

Prince Charles and Lady Diana — CD331

Wedding of Charles, Prince of Wales, and Lady Diana Spencer, St. Paul's Cathedral, London, July 29, 1981.

1981

Antigua 623-625
Ascension 294-296
Barbados 547-549
Barbuda 497-499
Bermuda 412-414
Brunei 268-270
Cayman Islands 471-473
Dominica 701-703
Falkland Islands 324-326
Falkland Islands Dep. 1L59-1L61
Fiji 442-444
Gambia 426-428
Ghana 759-761
Grenada 1051-1053
Grenada Grenadines 440-443
Hong Kong 373-375
Jamaica 500-503
Lesotho 335-337
Maldive Islands 906-908
Mauritius 520-522
Norfolk Island 280-282
Pitcairn Islands 206-208
St. Helena 353-355
St. Lucia 543-545
Samoa 558-560
Sierra Leone 509-517
Solomon Islands 450-452
Swaziland 382-384
Tristan da Cunha 294-296
Turks & Caicos Islands 486-488
Caicos Island 8-10
Uganda 314-316
Vanuatu 308-310
Virgin Islands 406-408

Princess Diana

CD332

CD333

Designs: Photographs and portrait of Princess Diana, wedding or honeymoon photographs, royal residences, arms of issuing country. Portrait photograph by Clive Friend. Souvenir sheet margins show family tree, various people related to the princess. 21st birthday of Princess Diana of Wales, July 1.

1982

Antigua 663-666
Ascension 313-316
Bahamas 510-513
Barbados 585-588
Barbuda 544-546
British Antarctic Territory 92-95
Cayman Islands 486-489
Dominica 773-776
Falkland Islands 348-351
Falkland Islands Dep. 1L72-1L75
Fiji 470-473
Gambia 447-450
Grenada 1101A-1105
Grenada Grenadines 485-491
Lesotho 372-375
Maldive Islands 952-955
Mauritius 548-551
Pitcairn Islands 213-216
St. Helena 372-375
St. Lucia 591-594
Sierra Leone 531-534
Solomon Islands 471-474
Swaziland 406-409
Tristan da Cunha 310-313
Turks and Caicos Islands 530A-534
Virgin Islands 430-433

250th anniv. of first edition of Lloyd's List (shipping news publication) & of Lloyd's marine insurance.

CD335

Designs: First page of early edition of the list; historical ships, modern transportation or harbor scenes.

1984

Ascension 351-354
Bahamas 555-558
Barbados 627-630
Cayes of Belize 10-13
Cayman Islands 522-525
Falkland Islands 404-407
Fiji 509-512
Gambia 519-522
Mauritius 587-590
Nauru 280-283
St. Helena 412-415
Samoa 624-627
Seychelles 538-541
Solomon Islands 521-524
Vanuatu 368-371
Virgin Islands 466-469

Queen Mother 85th Birthday

CD336

Designs: Photographs tracing the life of the Queen Mother, Elizabeth. The high value in each set pictures the same photograph taken of the Queen Mother holding the infant Prince Henry.

1985

Ascension 372-376
Bahamas 580-584
Barbados 660-664
Bermuda 469-473
Falkland Islands 420-424
Falkland Islands Dep. 1L92-1L96
Fiji 531-535
Hong Kong 447-450
Jamaica 599-603
Mauritius 604-608
Norfolk Island 364-368
Pitcairn Islands 253-257
St. Helena 428-432
Samoa 649-653
Seychelles 567-571
Solomon Islands 543-547
Swaziland 476-480
Tristan da Cunha 372-376
Vanuatu 392-396
Zil Elwannyen Sesel 101-105

Queen Elizabeth II, 60th Birthday

CD337

1986, April 21

Ascension 389-393
Bahamas 592-596
Barbados 675-679
Bermuda 499-503
Cayman Islands 555-559
Falkland Islands 441-445
Fiji 544-548
Hong Kong 465-469
Jamaica 620-624
Kiribati 470-474
Mauritius 629-633
Papua New Guinea 640-644
Pitcairn Islands 270-274
St. Helena 451-455
Samoa 670-674
Seychelles 592-596
Solomon Islands 562-566
South Georgia 101-105
Swaziland 490-494
Tristan da Cunha 388-392
Vanuatu 414-418
Zambia 343-347
Zil Elwannyen Sesel 114-118

Royal Wedding

Marriage of Prince Andrew and Sarah Ferguson CD338

1986, July 23

Ascension 399-400
Bahamas 602-603
Barbados 687-688
Cayman Islands 560-561
Jamaica 629-630
Pitcairn Islands 275-276
St. Helena 460-461
St. Kitts 181-182
Seychelles 602-603
Solomon Islands 567-568
Tristan da Cunha 397-398
Zambia 348-349
Zil Elwannyen Sesel 119-120

Queen Elizabeth II, 60th Birthday

Queen Elizabeth II & Prince Philip, 1947 Wedding Portrait — CD339

Designs: Photographs tracing the life of Queen Elizabeth II.

1986

Anguilla 674-677
Antigua 925-928
Barbuda 783-786
Dominica 950-953
Gambia 611-614
Grenada 1371-1374
Grenada Grenadines 749-752
Lesotho 531-534
Maldive Islands 1172-1175
Sierra Leone 760-763
Uganda 495-498

Royal Wedding, 1986

CD340

Designs: Photographs of Prince Andrew and Sarah Ferguson during courtship, engagement and marriage.

1986

Antigua 939-942
Barbuda 809-812
Dominica 970-973
Gambia 635-638
Grenada 1385-1388
Grenada Grenadines 758-761
Lesotho 545-548
Maldive Islands 1181-1184
Sierra Leone 769-772
Uganda 510-513

Lloyds of London, 300th Anniv.

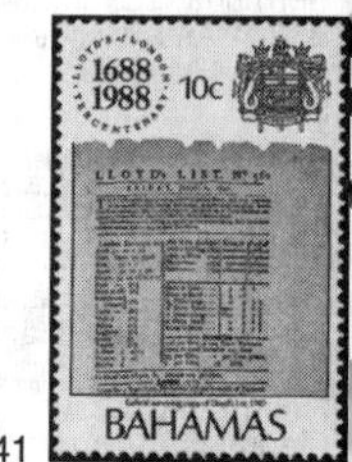

CD341

Designs: 17th century aspects of Lloyds, representations of each country's individual connections with Lloyds and publicized disasters insured by the organization.

1986

Ascension 454-457
Bahamas 655-658
Barbados 731-734
Bermuda 541-544
Falkland Islands 481-484
Liberia 1101-1104
Malawi 534-537
Nevis 571-574
St. Helena 501-504
St. Lucia 923-926
Seychelles 649-652
Solomon Islands 627-630
South Georgia 131-134
Trinidad & Tobago 484-487
Tristan da Cunha 439-442
Vanuatu 485-488
Zil Elwannyen Sesel 146-149

Moon Landing, 20th Anniv.

CD342

Designs: Equipment, crew photographs, spacecraft, official emblems and report profiles created for the Apollo Missions. Two stamps in each set are square in format rather than like the stamp shown; see individual country listings for more information.

1989

Ascension Is. 468-472
Bahamas 674-678
Belize 916-920
Kiribati 517-521
Liberia 1125-1129
Nevis 586-590
St. Kitts 248-252

Samoa 760-764
Seychelles 676-680
Solomon Islands 643-647
Vanuatu 507-511
Zil Elwannyen Sesel 154-158

Queen Mother, 90th Birthday

CD343

CD344

Designs: Portraits of Queen Elizabeth, the Queen Mother. See individual country listings for more information.

1990

Ascension Is. 491-492
Bahamas 698-699
Barbados 782-783
British Antarctic Territory 170-171
British Indian Ocean Territory 106-107
Cayman Islands 622-623
Falkland Islands 524-525
Kenya 527-528
Kiribati 555-556
Liberia 1145-1146
Pitcairn Islands 336-337
St. Helena 532-533
St. Lucia 969-970
Seychelles 710-711
Solomon Islands 671-672
South Georgia 143-144
Swaziland 565-566
Tristan da Cunha 480-481
Zil Elwannyen Sesel 171-172

Queen Elizabeth II, 65th Birthday, and Prince Philip, 70th Birthday

CD345

CD346

Designs: Portraits of Queen Elizabeth II and Prince Philip differ for each country. Printed in sheets of 10 + 5 labels (3 different) between. Stamps alternate, producing 5 different triptychs.

1991

Ascension Is. 505-506
Bahamas 730-731
Belize 969-970
Bermuda 617-618
Kiribati 571-572
Mauritius 733-734
Pitcairn Islands 348-349
St. Helena 554-555
St. Kitts 318-319
Samoa 790-791
Seychelles 723-724
Solomon Islands 688-689
South Georgia 149-150
Swaziland 586-587
Vanuatu 540-541
Zil Elwannyen Sesel 177-178

Royal Family Birthday, Anniversary

CD347

Queen Elizabeth II, 65th birthday, Charles and Diana, 10th wedding anniversary: Various photographs of Queen Elizabeth II, Prince Philip, Prince Charles, Princess Diana and their sons William and Henry.

1991

Antigua 1446-1455
Barbuda 1229-1238
Dominica 1328-1337
Gambia 1080-1089
Grenada 2006-2015
Grenada Grenadines 1331-1340
Guyana 2440-2451
Lesotho 871-875
Maldive Islands 1533-1542
Nevis 666-675
St. Vincent 1485-1494
St. Vincent Grenadines 769-778
Sierra Leone 1387-1396
Turks & Caicos Islands 913-922
Uganda 918-927

Queen Elizabeth II's Accession to the Throne, 40th Anniv.

CD348

CD349

Various photographs of Queen Elizabeth II with local Scenes.

1992 - CD348

Antigua 1513-1518
Barbuda 1306-1309
Dominica 1414-1419
Gambia 1172-1177
Grenada 2047-2052
Grenada Grenadines 1368-1373
Lesotho 881-885
Maldive Islands 1637-1642
Nevis 702-707
St. Vincent 1582-1587
St. Vincent Grenadines 829-834
Sierra Leone 1482-1487
Turks and Caicos Islands 978-987
Uganda 990-995
Virgin Islands 742-746

1992 - CD349

Ascension Islands 531-535
Bahamas 744-748
Bermuda 623-627
British Indian Ocean Territory 119-123
Cayman Islands 648-652
Falkland Islands 549-553
Gibraltar 605-609
Hong Kong 619-623
Kenya 563-567
Kiribati 582-586
Pitcairn Islands 362-366
St. Helena 570-574
St. Kitts 332-336
Samoa 805-809
Seychelles 734-738
Solomon Islands 708-712
South Georgia 157-161
Tristan da Cunha 508-512
Vanuatu 555-559
Zambia 561-565
Zil Elwannyen Sesel 183-187

Royal Air Force, 75th Anniversary

CD350

1993

Ascension 557-561
Bahamas 771-775
Barbados 842-846
Belize 1003-1008
Bermuda 648-651
British Indian Ocean Territory 136-140
Falkland Is. 573-577
Fiji 687-691
Montserrat 830-834
St. Kitts 351-355

Royal Air Force, 80th Anniv.

Design CD350 Re-inscribed

1998

Ascension 697-701
Bahamas 907-911
British Indian Ocean Terr 198-202
Cayman Islands 754-758
Fiji 814-818
Gibraltar 755-759
Samoa 957-961
Turks & Caicos Islands 1258-1265
Tuvalu 763-767
Virgin Islands 879-883

End of World War II, 50th Anniv.

CD351

CD352

1995

Ascension 613-617
Bahamas 824-828
Barbados 891-895
Belize 1047-1050
British Indian Ocean Territory 163-167
Cayman Islands 704-708
Falkland Islands 634-638
Fiji 720-724
Kiribati 662-668
Liberia 1175-1179
Mauritius 803-805
St. Helena 646-654
St. Kitts 389-393
St. Lucia 1018-1022
Samoa 890-894
Solomon Islands 799-803
South Georgia & S. Sandwich Is. 198-200
Tristan da Cunha 562-566

UN, 50th Anniv.

CD353

1995

Bahamas 839-842
Barbados 901-904
Belize 1055-1058
Jamaica 847-851
Liberia 1187-1190
Mauritius 813-816
Pitcairn Islands 436-439
St. Kitts 398-401
St. Lucia 1023-1026
Samoa 900-903
Tristan da Cunha 568-571
Virgin Islands 807-810

Queen Elizabeth, 70th Birthday

CD354

1996

Ascension 632-635
British Antarctic Territory 240-243
British Indian Ocean Territory 176-180
Falkland Islands 653-657
Pitcairn Islands 446-449
St. Helena 672-676
Samoa 912-916
Tokelau 223-227
Tristan da Cunha 576-579
Virgin Islands 824-828

Diana, Princess of Wales (1961-97)

CD355

1998

Ascension 696
Bahamas 901A-902
Barbados 950
Belize 1091
Bermuda 753
Botswana 659-663
British Antarctic Territory 258
British Indian Ocean Terr. 197
Cayman Islands 752A-753
Falkland Islands 694
Fiji 819-820
Gibraltar 754
Kiribati 719A-720
Namibia 909
Niue 706
Norfolk Island 644-645
Papua New Guinea 937
Pitcairn Islands 487
St. Helena 711
St. Kitts 437A-438
Samoa 955A-956
Seycelles 802
Solomon Islands 866-867
South Georgia & S. Sandwich Islands 220
Tokelau 253
Tonga 980

Niuafo'ou..201
Tristan da Cunha.............................618
Tuvalu 762
Vanuatu 719
Virgin Islands....................................878

Wedding of Prince Edward and Sophie Rhys-Jones

CD356

1999

Ascension.................................729-730
Cayman Islands........................775-776
Falkland Islands 729-730
Pitcairn Islands.........................505-506
St. Helena 733-734
Samoa..971-972
Tristan da Cunha......................636-637
Virgin Islands............................908-909

1st Manned Moon Landing, 30th Anniv.

CD357

1999

Ascension.................................731-735
Bahamas 942-946
Barbados...................................967-971
Bermuda...778
Cayman Islands.........................777-781
Fiji..853-857
Jamaica 889-893
Kirbati 746-750
Nauru...465-469
St. Kitts......................................460-464
Samoa.......................................973-977
Solomon Islands.......................875-879
Tuvalu 800-804
Virgin Islands............................910-914

Queen Mother's Century

CD358

1999

Ascension..................................736-740
Bahamas 951-955
Cayman Islands.........................782-786
Falkland Islands 734-738
Fiji..858-862
Norfolk Island 688-692
St. Helena 740-744
Samoa.......................................978-982
Solomon Islands........................880-884
South Georgia & South
Sandwich Islands 231-235
Tristan da Cunha......................638-642
Tuvalu 805-809

Prince William, 18th Birthday

CD359

2000

Ascension.................................755-759
Cayman Islands........................797-801
Falkland Islands 762-766
Fiji...889-893
South Georgia 257-261
and South Sandwich Islands
Tristan da Cunha......................664-668
Virgin Islands............................925-929

Reign of Queen Elizabeth II, 50th Anniv.

CD360

2002

Ascension.................................790-794
Bahamas 1033-1037
Barbados...............................1019-1023
Belize.....................................1152-1156
Bermuda..................................822-826
British Antarctic Territory..........307-311
British Indian Ocean Territory 239-243
Cayman Islands........................844-848
Falkland Islands 804-808
Gibraltar....................................896-900
Jamaica 952-956
Nauru..491-495
Norfolk Island 758-762
Papua New Guinea..............1019-1023
Pitcairn Islands..................................552
St. Helena 788-792
St. Lucia 1146-1150
Solomon Islands........................931-935
South Georgia & So. Sandwich Is........ 274-278
Swaziland 706-710
Tokelau 302-306
Tonga..1059
Niuafo'ou.......................................239
Tristan da Cunha......................706-710
Virgin Islands............................967-971

Queen Mother Elizabeth (1900-2002)

CD361

2002

Ascension.................................799-801
Bahamas 1044-1046
Bermuda...................................834-836
British Antarctic Territory..........312-314
British Indian Ocean Territory 245-247
Cayman Islands........................857-861
Falkland Islands 812-816
Nauru..499-501
Pitcairn Islands.........................561-565
St. Helena 808-812
St. Lucia 1155-1159
Seychelles..830
Solomon Islands........................945-947
South Georgia & So. Sandwich Isls..... 281-285
Tokelau 312-314
Tristan da Cunha......................715-717
Virgin Islands............................979-983

Dies of British Colonial Stamps

DIE A

DIE B

DIE A:
1. The lines in the groundwork vary in thickness and are not uniformly straight.
2. The seventh and eighth lines from the top, in the groundwork, converge where they meet the head.
3. There is a small dash in the upper part of the second jewel in the band of the crown.
4. The vertical color line in front of the throat stops at the sixth line of shading on the neck.

DIE B:
1. The lines in the groundwork are all thin and straight.
2. All the lines of the background are parallel.
3. There is no dash in the upper part of the second jewel in the band of the crown.
4. The vertical color line in front of the throat stops at the eighth line of shading on the neck.

DIE I

DIE II

DIE I:
1. The base of the crown is well below the level of the inner white line around the vignette.
2. The labels inscribed "POSTAGE" and "REVENUE" are cut square at the top.
3. There is a white "bud" on the outer side of the main stem of the curved ornaments in each lower corner.
4. The second (thick) line below the country name has the ends next to the crown cut diagonally.

DIE Ia.
1 as die II.
2 and 3 as die I.

DIE Ib.
1 and 3 as die II.
2 as die I.

DIE II:
1. The base of the crown is aligned with the underside of the white line around the vignette.
2. The labels curve inward at the top inner corners.
3. The "bud" has been removed from the outer curve of the ornaments in each corner.
4. The second line below the country name has the ends next to the crown cut vertically.

British Colonial and Crown Agents Watermarks

Wmk. 1
Crown and C C

Wmk. 2
Crown and C A

Wmk. 3
Multiple Crown and C A

Wmk. 4
Multiple Crown and Script C A

Wmk. 4a

Wmk. 314
St. Edward's Crown and C A Multiple

Wmk. 373

Wmk. 384

Watermarks 1 to 4, 314, 373, and 384, common to many British territories, are illustrated here to avoid duplication.

The letters "CC" of Wmk. 1 identify the paper as having been made for the use of the Crown Colonies, while the letters "CA" of the others stand for "Crown Agents." Both Wmks. 1 and 2 were used on stamps printed by De La Rue & Co.

Wmk. 3 was adopted in 1904; Wmk. 4 in 1921; Wmk. 314 in 1957; Wmk. 373 in 1974; and Wmk. 384 in 1985.

In Wmk. 4a, a non-matching crown of the general St. Edwards type (bulging on both sides at top) was substituted for one of the Wmk. 4 crowns which fell off the dandy roll. The non-matching crown occurs in 1950-52 printings in a horizontal row of crowns on certain regular stamps of Johore and Seychelles, and on various postage due stamps of Barbados, Basutoland, British Guiana, Gold Coast, Grenada, Northern Rhodesia, St. Lucia, Swaziland and Trinidad and Tobago. A variation of Wmk. 4a, with the non-matching crown in a horizontal row of crown-CA-crown, occurs on regular stamps of Bahamas, St. Kitts-Nevis and Singapore.

Wmk. 314 was intentionally used sideways, starting in 1966. When a stamp was issued with Wmk. 314 both upright and sideways, the sideways varieties usually are listed also – with minor numbers. In many of the later issues, Wmk. 314 is slightly visible.

Wmk. 373 is usually only faintly visible.

British Commonwealth of Nations

Dominions, Colonies, Territories, Offices and Independent Members

Comprising stamps of the British Commonwealth and associated nations.

A strict observance of technicalities would bar some or all of the stamps listed under Burma, Ireland, Kuwait, Nepal, New Republic, Orange Free State, Samoa, South Africa, South-West Africa, Stellaland, Sudan, Swaziland, the two Transvaal Republics and others but these are included for the convenience of collectors.

1. Great Britain

Great Britain: Including England, Scotland, Wales and Northern Ireland.

2. The Dominions, Present and Past

AUSTRALIA

The Commonwealth of Australia was proclaimed on January 1, 1901. It consists of six former colonies as follows:

New South Wales
Queensland
South Australia
Victoria
Tasmania
Western Australia

Territories belonging to, or administered by Australia: Australian Antarctic Territory, Christmas Island, Cocos (Keeling) Islands, Nauru, New Guinea, Norfolk Island, Papua New Guinea.

CANADA

The Dominion of Canada was created by the British North America Act in 1867. The following provinces were former separate colonies and issued postage stamps:

British Columbia and Vancouver Island
New Brunswick
Newfoundland
Nova Scotia
Prince Edward Island

FIJI

The colony of Fiji became an independent nation with dominion status on Oct. 10, 1970.

GHANA

This state came into existence Mar. 6, 1957, with dominion status. It consists of the former colony of the Gold Coast and the Trusteeship Territory of Togoland. Ghana became a republic July 1, 1960.

INDIA

The Republic of India was inaugurated on January 26, 1950. It succeeded the Dominion of India which was proclaimed August 15, 1947, when the former Empire of India was divided into Pakistan and the Union of India. The Republic is composed of about 40 predominantly Hindu states of three classes: governor's provinces, chief commissioner's provinces and princely states. India also has various territories, such as the Andaman and Nicobar Islands.

The old Empire of India was a federation of British India and the native states. The more important princely states were autonomous. Of the more than 700 Indian states, these 43 are familiar names to philatelists because of their postage stamps.

CONVENTION STATES

Chamba
Faridkot
Gwalior
Jhind
Nabha
Patiala

NATIVE FEUDATORY STATES

Alwar
Bahawalpur
Bamra
Barwani
Bhopal
Bhor
Bijawar
Bundi
Bussahir
Charkhari
Cochin
Dhar
Duttia
Faridkot (1879-85)
Hyderabad
Idar
Indore
Jaipur
Jammu
Jammu and Kashmir
Jasdan
Jhalawar
Jhind (1875-76)
Kashmir
Kishangarh
Las Bela
Morvi
Nandgaon
Nowanuggur
Orchha
Poonch
Rajpeepla
Sirmur
Soruth
Travancore
Wadhwan

NEW ZEALAND

Became a dominion on September 26, 1907. The following islands and territories are, or have been, administered by New Zealand:

Aitutaki
Cook Islands (Rarotonga)
Niue
Penrhyn
Ross Dependency
Samoa (Western Samoa)
Tokelau Islands

PAKISTAN

The Republic of Pakistan was proclaimed March 23, 1956. It succeeded the Dominion which was proclaimed August 15, 1947. It is made up of all or part of several Moslem provinces and various districts of the former Empire of India, including Bahawalpur and Las Bela. Pakistan withdrew from the Commonwealth in 1972.

SOUTH AFRICA

Under the terms of the South African Act (1909) the self-governing colonies of Cape of Good Hope, Natal, Orange River Colony and Transvaal united on May 31, 1910, to form the Union of South Africa. It became an independent republic May 3, 1961.

Under the terms of the Treaty of Versailles, South-West Africa, formerly German South-West Africa, was mandated to the Union of South Africa.

SRI LANKA (CEYLON)

The Dominion of Ceylon was proclaimed February 4, 1948. The island had been a Crown Colony from 1802 until then. On May 22, 1972, Ceylon became the Republic of Sri Lanka.

3. Colonies, Past and Present; ControlledTerritory and Independent Members of the Commonwealth

Aden
Aitutaki
Antigua
Ascension
Bahamas
Bahrain
Bangladesh
Barbados
Barbuda
Basutoland
Batum
Bechuanaland
Bechuanaland Prot.
Belize
Bermuda
Botswana
British Antarctic Territory
British Central Africa
British Columbia and Vancouver Island
British East Africa
British Guiana

British Honduras
British Indian Ocean Territory
British New Guinea
British Solomon Islands
British Somaliland
Brunei
Burma
Bushire
Cameroons
Cape of Good Hope
Cayman Islands
Christmas Island
Cocos (Keeling) Islands
Cook Islands
Crete,
  British Administration
Cyprus
Dominica
East Africa & Uganda
  Protectorates
Egypt
Falkland Islands
Fiji
Gambia
German East Africa
Gibraltar
Gilbert Islands
Gilbert & Ellice Islands
Gold Coast
Grenada
Griqualand West
Guernsey
Guyana
Heligoland
Hong Kong
Indian Native States
  (see India)
Ionian Islands
Jamaica
Jersey
Kenya
Kenya, Uganda & Tanzania
Kuwait
Labuan
Lagos
Leeward Islands
Lesotho
Madagascar
Malawi
Malaya
  Federated Malay States
  Johore
  Kedah
  Kelantan
  Malacca
  Negri Sembilan
  Pahang
  Penang
  Perak
  Perlis
  Selangor
  Singapore
  Sungei Ujong
  Trengganu
Malaysia
Maldive Islands
Malta
Man, Isle of
Mauritius
Mesopotamia
Montserrat
Muscat
Namibia
Natal
Nauru
Nevis
New Britain
New Brunswick
Newfoundland
New Guinea
New Hebrides
New Republic
New South Wales
Niger Coast Protectorate
Nigeria
Niue
Norfolk Island
North Borneo
Northern Nigeria
Northern Rhodesia
North West Pacific Islands
Nova Scotia
Nyasaland Protectorate
Oman
Orange River Colony
Palestine
Papua New Guinea
Penrhyn Island
Pitcairn Islands
Prince Edward Island
Queensland
Rhodesia
Rhodesia & Nyasaland
Ross Dependency
Sabah
St. Christopher
St. Helena
St. Kitts
St. Kitts-Nevis-Anguilla
St. Lucia
St. Vincent
Samoa
Sarawak
Seychelles
Sierra Leone
Solomon Islands
Somaliland Protectorate
South Arabia
South Australia
South Georgia
Southern Nigeria
Southern Rhodesia
South-West Africa
Stellaland
Straits Settlements
Sudan
Swaziland
Tanganyika
Tanzania
Tasmania
Tobago
Togo
Tokelau Islands
Tonga
Transvaal
Trinidad
Trinidad and Tobago
Tristan da Cunha
Trucial States
Turks and Caicos
Turks Islands
Tuvalu
Uganda
United Arab Emirates
Victoria
Virgin Islands
Western Australia
Zambia
Zanzibar
Zululand

POST OFFICES IN FOREIGN COUNTRIES

Africa
  East Africa Forces
  Middle East Forces
Bangkok
China
Morocco
Turkish Empire

Colonies, Former Colonies, Offices, Territories Controlled by Parent States

Belgium

Belgian Congo
Ruanda-Urundi

Denmark

Danish West Indies
Faroe Islands
Greenland
Iceland

Finland

Aland Islands

France

COLONIES PAST AND PRESENT, CONTROLLED TERRITORIES

Afars & Issas, Territory of
Alaouites
Alexandretta
Algeria
Alsace & Lorraine
Anjouan
Annam & Tonkin
Benin
Cambodia (Khmer)
Cameroun
Castellorizo
Chad
Cilicia
Cochin China
Comoro Islands
Dahomey
Diego Suarez
Djibouti (Somali Coast)
Fezzan
French Congo
French Equatorial Africa
French Guiana
French Guinea
French India
French Morocco
French Polynesia (Oceania)
French Southern & Antarctic Territories
French Sudan
French West Africa
Gabon
Germany
Ghadames
Grand Comoro
Guadeloupe
Indo-China
Inini
Ivory Coast
Laos
Latakia
Lebanon
Madagascar
Martinique
Mauritania
Mayotte
Memel
Middle Congo
Moheli
New Caledonia
New Hebrides
Niger Territory
Nossi-Be
Obock
Reunion
Rouad, Ile
Ste.-Marie de Madagascar
St. Pierre & Miquelon
Senegal
Senegambia & Niger
Somali Coast
Syria
Tahiti
Togo
Tunisia
Ubangi-Shari
Upper Senegal & Niger
Upper Volta
Viet Nam
Wallis & Futuna Islands

POST OFFICES IN FOREIGN COUNTRIES

China
Crete
Egypt
Turkish Empire
Zanzibar

Germany

EARLY STATES

Baden
Bavaria
Bergedorf
Bremen
Brunswick
Hamburg
Hanover
Lubeck
Mecklenburg-Schwerin
Mecklenburg-Strelitz
Oldenburg
Prussia
Saxony
Schleswig-Holstein
Wurttemberg

FORMER COLONIES

Cameroun (Kamerun)
Caroline Islands
German East Africa
German New Guinea
German South-West Africa
Kiauchau
Mariana Islands
Marshall Islands
Samoa
Togo

Italy

EARLY STATES

Modena
Parma
Romagna
Roman States
Sardinia
Tuscany
Two Sicilies
  Naples
  Neapolitan Provinces
  Sicily

FORMER COLONIES, CONTROLLED TERRITORIES, OCCUPATION AREAS

Aegean Islands
  Calimno (Calino)
  Caso
  Cos (Coo)
  Karki (Carchi)
  Leros (Lero)
  Lipso
  Nisiros (Nisiro)
  Patmos (Patmo)
  Piscopi
  Rodi (Rhodes)
  Scarpanto
  Simi
  Stampalia
Castellorizo
Corfu
Cyrenaica
Eritrea
Ethiopia (Abyssinia)
Fiume
Ionian Islands
  Cephalonia
  Ithaca
  Paxos
Italian East Africa
Libya
Oltre Giuba
Saseno
Somalia (Italian Somaliland)
Tripolitania

POST OFFICES IN FOREIGN COUNTRIES

"ESTERO"*
Austria
China
  Peking
  Tientsin
Crete
Tripoli
Turkish Empire
  Constantinople
  Durazzo
  Janina
Jerusalem
Salonika
Scutari
Smyrna
Valona

*Stamps overprinted "ESTERO" were used in various parts of the world.

Netherlands

Aruba
Netherlands Antilles (Curacao)
Netherlands Indies
Netherlands New Guinea
Surinam (Dutch Guiana)

Portugal

COLONIES PAST AND PRESENT, CONTROLLED TERRITORIES

Angola
Angra
Azores
Cape Verde
Funchal
Horta
Inhambane
Kionga
Lourenco Marques
Macao
Madeira
Mozambique
Mozambique Co.
Nyassa
Ponta Delgada
Portuguese Africa
Portuguese Congo
Portuguese Guinea
Portuguese India
Quelimane
St. Thomas & Prince Islands
Tete
Timor
Zambezia

Russia

ALLIED TERRITORIES AND REPUBLICS, OCCUPATION AREAS

Armenia
Aunus (Olonets)
Azerbaijan
Batum
Estonia
Far Eastern Republic
Georgia
Karelia
Latvia
Lithuania
North Ingermanland
Ostland
Russian Turkestan
Siberia
South Russia
Tannu Tuva
Transcaucasian Fed. Republics
Ukraine
Wenden (Livonia)
Western Ukraine

Spain

COLONIES PAST AND PRESENT, CONTROLLED TERRITORIES

Aguera, La
Cape Juby
Cuba
Elobey, Annobon & Corisco
Fernando Po
Ifni
Mariana Islands
Philippines
Puerto Rico
Rio de Oro
Rio Muni
Spanish Guinea
Spanish Morocco
Spanish Sahara
Spanish West Africa

POST OFFICES IN FOREIGN COUNTRIES

Morocco
Tangier
Tetuan

GABON

ga-'bōⁿ

LOCATION — West coast of Africa, at the equator
GOVT. — Republic
AREA — 102,089 sq. mi.
POP. — 1,225,853 (1999 est.)
CAPITAL — Libreville

Gabon originally was under the control of French West Africa. In 1886, it was united with French Congo. In 1904, Gabon was granted a certain degree of colonial autonomy which prevailed until 1934, when it merged with French Equatorial Africa. Gabon Republic was proclaimed November 28, 1958.

100 Centimes = 1 Franc

Catalogue values for unused stamps in this country are for Never Hinged items, beginning with Scott 148 in the regular postage section, Scott B4 in the semi-postal section, Scott C1 in the airpost section, Scott CB1 in the airpost semi-postal section, Scott J34 in the postage due section, and Scott O1 in the officials section.

Watermark

Wmk. 385

Stamps of French Colonies of 1881-86 Handstamp Surcharged in Black:

a

b

1886 Unwmk. *Perf. 14x13½*

No.	Type	Description	Unused	Used
1	A9	5c on 20c red, *grn* (a)	325.00	300.00
2	A9	10c on 20c red, *grn* (b)	325.00	300.00
3	A9	25c on 20c red, *grn* (b)	45.00	30.00
e.		56 dots around "GAB"	*4,250.*	1,000.
4	A9	50c on 15c bl (b)	900.00	*950.00*
5	A9	75c on 15c bl (b)	1,150.	*1,250.*

Nos. 1-3 exist with double surcharge of numeral; No. 3 with "GAB" double or inverted, or with "25" double.

On Nos. 3 and 5 the surcharge slants down; on No. 4 it slants up. The number of dots varies.

Counterfeits of Nos. 1-15 exist.

Handstamp Surcharged in Black—c **15**

1888-89

No.	Type	Description	Unused	Used
6	A9	15c on 10c blk, *lav*	*3,750.*	800.
7	A9	15c on 1fr brnz grn, *straw*	*1,500.*	750.
8	A9	25c on 5c grn, *grnsh*	925.	160.
9	A9	25c on 10c blk, *lav*	*3,750.*	1,200.
10	A9	25c on 75c car, *rose*	*2,100.*	900.

Official reprints exist.

Postage Due Stamps of French Colonies Handstamp Surcharged in Black—d

1889 *Imperf.*

No.	Type	Description	Unused	Used
11	D1	15c on 5c black	175.	160.
12	D1	15c on 30c black	*3,250.*	*2,250.*
13	D1	25c on 20c black	70.00	50.00

Nos. 11 and 13 exist with "GABON," "TIMBRE" or "25" double; "TIMBRE" or "15" omitted, etc.

A8

1889 Typeset

No.	Type	Description	Unused	Used
14	A8	15c blk, *rose*	1,100.	700.
15	A8	25c blk, *green*	700.	550.

Ten varieties of each. Nos. 14-15 exist with "GAB" inverted or omitted, and with small "f" in "Francaise."

Navigation and Commerce — A9

1904-07 Typo. *Perf. 14x13½*
Name of Colony in Blue or Carmine

No.	Type	Description	Unused	Used
16	A9	1c blk, *lil bl*	.50	.50
a.		"GABON" double	175.00	
17	A9	2c brn, *buff*	.50	.50
18	A9	4c claret, *lav*	1.00	1.00
19	A9	5c yellow green	1.50	1.50
20	A9	10c rose	4.00	4.00
21	A9	15c gray	4.00	4.00
22	A9	20c red, *grn*	6.50	6.50
23	A9	25c blue	3.75	3.75
24	A9	30c yel brn	8.50	8.50
25	A9	35c blk, *yel* ('06)	14.00	14.00
26	A9	40c red, *straw*	11.00	11.00
27	A9	45c blk, *gray grn* ('07)	19.00	19.00
28	A9	50c brn, *az*	8.50	8.50
29	A9	75c dp vio, *org*	14.00	14.00
30	A9	1fr brnz grn, *straw*	25.00	25.00
31	A9	2fr vio, *rose*	52.50	52.50
32	A9	5fr lil, *lav*	95.00	95.00
		Nos. 16-32 (17)	269.25	269.25

Perf. 13½x14 stamps are counterfeits.
For surcharges see Nos. 72-84.

Fang Warrior — A10

Fang Woman — A12

Libreville A11

Inscribed: "Congo Français"

1910 *Perf. 13½x14*

No.	Type	Description	Unused	Used
33	A10	1c choc & org	1.25	1.25
34	A10	2c black & choc	1.25	1.25
35	A10	4c vio & dp bl	1.50	1.50
36	A10	5c ol gray & grn	2.50	2.50
37	A10	10c red & car	3.50	3.50
38	A10	20c choc & dk vio	3.50	3.50
39	A11	25c dp bl & choc	3.00	3.00
40	A11	30c gray blk & red	20.00	20.00
41	A11	35c dk vio & grn	10.00	10.00
42	A11	40c choc & ultra	16.00	16.00
43	A11	45c carmine & vio	24.00	24.00
44	A11	50c bl grn & gray	37.50	37.50
45	A11	75c org & choc	62.50	62.50
46	A12	1fr dk brn & bis	62.50	62.50
47	A12	2fr carmine & brn	190.00	190.00
48	A12	5fr blue & choc	190.00	190.00
		Nos. 33-48 (16)	629.00	629.00

Inscribed: "Afrique Equatoriale"

1910-22

No.	Type	Description	Unused	Used
49	A10	1c choc & org	.20	.20
50	A10	2c black & choc	.20	.20
a.		2c gray black & deep olive	.30	.20
51	A10	4c vio & dp bl	.25	.25
52	A10	5c ol gray & grn	.35	.25
53	A10	5c gray blk & ocher ('22)	.55	.55
54	A10	10c red & car	.60	.55
55	A10	10c yel grn & bl grn ('22)	.55	.55
56	A10	15c brn vio & rose ('18)	.45	.35
57	A10	20c ol brn & dk vio	9.50	6.50
58	A11	25c dp bl & choc	.55	.45
59	A11	25c Prus bl & blk ('22)	.70	.70
60	A11	30c gray blk & red	.80	.60
61	A11	30c rose & red ('22)	.90	.85
62	A11	35c dk vio & grn	.45	*.55*
63	A11	40c choc & ultra	.80	.60
64	A11	45c carmine & vio	.70	.60
65	A11	45c blk & red ('22)	1.00	1.00
66	A11	50c bl grn & gray	.90	.70
67	A11	50c dk bl & bl ('22)	.70	.70
68	A11	75c org & choc	3.25	3.00
69	A12	1fr dk brn & bis	1.60	1.60
70	A12	2fr car & brn	2.75	2.40
71	A12	5fr blue & choc	4.75	4.25
		Nos. 49-71 (23)	32.50	27.40

For overprints & surcharges see #85-119, B1-B3.

Stamps of 1904-07 Surcharged in Black or Carmine

1912

No.	Type	Description	Unused	Used
72	A9	5c on 2c brn, *buff*	.60	.60
73	A9	5c on 4c cl, *lav* (C)	.60	.60
74	A9	5c on 15c gray (C)	.35	.35
75	A9	5c on 20c red, *grn*	.35	.35
76	A9	5c on 25c bl (C)	.35	.35
77	A9	5c on 30c pale brn (C)	.35	.35
78	A9	10c on 40c red, *straw*	.35	.35
79	A9	10c on 45c blk, *gray grn* (C)	.60	.60
80	A9	10c on 50c brn, *az* (C)	.60	.60
81	A9	10c on 75c dp vio, *org*	.60	.60
82	A9	10c on 1fr brnz grn, *straw*	.60	.60
83	A9	10c on 2fr vio, *rose*	.65	.65
a.		Inverted surcharge	200.00	200.00
84	A9	10c on 5fr lil, *lav*	2.25	2.25
		Nos. 72-84 (13)	8.25	8.25

Two spacings between the surcharged numerals are found on Nos. 72 to 84.

Stamps of 1910-22 Overprinted in Black, Blue or Carmine

On A10, A12

On A11

1924-31

No.	Type	Description	Unused	Used
85	A10	1c brown & org	.20	.20
86	A10	2c blk & choc (Bl)	.30	.30
87	A10	4c violet & ind	.20	.20
88	A10	5c gray blk & ocher	.30	.30
89	A10	10c yel grn & bl grn	.60	.60
a.		Double overprint (Bk & Bl)	100.00	100.00
90	A10	10c dk bl & brn ('26) (C)	.20	.20
91	A10	15c brn vio & rose (Bl)	.60	.60
92	A10	15c rose & brn vio ('31) (Bl)	.75	.75
93	A10	20c ol brn & dk vio (C)	.60	.60
a.		Inverted overprint	125.00	125.00
94	A11	25c Prus bl & blk (C)	.45	.45
95	A11	30c rose & red (Bl)	.45	.45
96	A11	30c blk & org ('26)	.45	.45
97	A11	30c dk grn & bl grn ('28)	.60	.60
98	A11	35c dk vio & grn (Bl)	.40	.40
99	A11	40c choc & ultra (C)	.30	.30
100	A11	45c blk & red (Bl)	.80	.80
101	A11	50c dk bl & bl (C)	.45	.45
102	A11	50c car & grn ('26)	.45	.45
103	A11	65c dp bl & red org ('28)	2.40	2.40
104	A11	75c org & brn (Bl)	1.10	1.10
105	A11	90c brn red & rose ('30)	1.75	1.50
106	A12	1fr dk brn & bis	.95	.95
107	A12	1.10fr dl grn & rose red ('28)	3.50	3.25
108	A12	1.50fr pale bl & dk bl ('30)	.75	.75
109	A12	2fr rose & brn	1.00	1.00
110	A12	3fr red vio ('30)	4.50	4.00
111	A12	5fr dp bl & choc	3.25	3.25
		Nos. 85-111 (27)	27.30	26.30

Types of 1924-31 Issues Surcharged with New Values in Black or Carmine

1925-28

No.	Type	Description	Unused	Used
112	A12	65c on 1fr ol grn & brn	.65	.65
113	A12	85c on 1fr ol grn & brn	.75	.75
114	A11	90c on 75c brn red & cer ('27)	.95	.95
115	A12	1.25fr on 1fr dk bl & ultra (C)	.45	.45
116	A12	1.50fr on 1fr lt bl & dk bl ('27)	.95	.95
117	A12	3fr on 5fr mag & ol brn	4.50	4.50
118	A12	10fr on 5fr org brn & grn ('27)	8.25	8.25
119	A12	20fr on 5fr red vio & org red ('27)	7.50	7.50
		Nos. 112-119 (8)	24.00	24.00

Bars cover the old denominations on #114-119.

Common Design Types pictured following the introduction.

Colonial Exposition Issue
Common Design Types

1931 *Perf. 12½*
Name of Country in Black

No.	Type	Description	Unused	Used
120	CD70	40c dp green	1.75	1.75
121	CD71	50c violet	1.75	1.75
122	CD72	90c red orange	1.75	1.75
123	CD73	1.50fr dull blue	2.50	2.50
		Nos. 120-123 (4)	7.75	7.75

Timber Raft on Ogowe River A16

Count Savorgnan de Brazza — A17

Village of Setta Kemma A18

1932-33 Photo. *Perf. 13x13½*

No.	Type	Description	Unused	Used
124	A16	1c brown violet	.20	.20
125	A16	2c blk, *rose*	.20	.20
126	A16	4c green	.20	.20
127	A16	5c grnsh blue	.20	.20
128	A16	10c red, *yel*	.20	.20
129	A16	15c red, *grn*	.50	.30

130 A16	20c	deep red	.50	.30
131 A16	25c	brown red	.25	.20
132 A17	30c	yellow grn	.75	.55
133 A17	40c	brown vio	.90	.50
134 A17	45c	blk, *dl grn*	.90	.80
135 A17	50c	red brown	.60	.40
136 A17	65c	Prus blue	3.25	3.00
137 A17	75c	blk, *red org*	1.60	1.40
138 A17	90c	rose red	1.75	1.25
139 A17	1fr	yel grn, *bl*	17.50	12.50
140 A18	1.25fr	dp vio ('33)	1.10	.80
141 A18	1.50fr	dull blue	1.75	.90
142 A18	1.75fr	dp green ('33)	1.40	.60
143 A18	2fr	brn red	17.50	12.50
144 A18	3fr	yel grn, *bl*	3.00	2.50
145 A18	5fr	red brown	3.75	3.00
146 A18	10fr	blk, *red org*	17.00	14.00
147 A18	20fr	dk violet	27.50	22.50
		Nos. 124-147 (24)	102.50	79.00

See French Equatorial Africa No. 192 for stamp inscribed "Gabon" and "Afrique Equatoriale Francaise."

Catalogue values for all unused stamps in this section, from this point to the end of the section, are for Never Hinged items.

Republic

Prime Minister Leon Mba — A19

Flag & Map of Gabon & UN Emblem — A20

Unwmk.

1959, Nov. 28 Engr. *Perf. 13*

148 A19 15fr shown .20 .20
149 A19 25fr Mba, profile .20 .20

Proclamation of the Republic, 1st anniv.

Imperforates
Most Gabon stamps from 1959 onward exist imperforate in issued and trial colors, and also in small presentation sheets in issued colors.

C.C.T.A. Issue
Common Design Type

1960, May 21 Engr. *Perf. 13*

150 CD106 50fr vio brn & Prus bl .55 .55

1961, Feb. 9

151 A20 15fr multi .20 .20
152 A20 25fr multi .20 .20
153 A20 85fr multi .80 .60
Nos. 151-153 (3) 1.20 1.00

Gabon's admission to United Nations.

Combretum A21

1fr, 5fr, Tulip tree, vert. 2fr, 3fr, Yellow cassia.

1961, July 4 Unwmk. *Perf. 13*

154 A21 50c rose red & grn .20 .20
155 A21 1fr sl grn, red & bis .20 .20
156 A21 2fr dk grn & yel .20 .20
157 A21 3fr ol grn & yel .20 .20
158 A21 5fr multi .20 .20
159 A21 10fr grn & rose red .20 .20
Nos. 154-159 (6) 1.20 1.20

President Leon Mba — A22

1962 Engr.

160 A22 15fr indigo, car & grn .20 .20
161 A22 20fr brn blk, car & grn .20 .20
162 A22 25fr brn, car & grn .20 .20
Nos. 160-162 (3) .60 .60

Abidjan Games Issue
Common Design Type

1962, July 21 Photo. *Perf. 12½x12*

163 CD109 20fr Foot race, start .20 .20
164 CD109 50fr Soccer .55 .40
Nos. 163-164,C6 (3) 2.35 1.60

African-Malgache Union Issue
Common Design Type

1962, Sept. 8 *Perf. 12½x12*

165 CD110 30fr emer, bluish grn, red & gold .65 .50

Captain Ntchorere and Flags of France and Gabon A23

1962, Nov. 23 *Perf. 12*

166 A23 80fr multi .80 .60

Capt. Ntchorere, who died for France, 6/7/40.

Waves Around Globe A23a

Design: 100fr, Orbit patterns around globe.

1963, Sept. 19 Photo. *Perf. 12½*

167 A23a 25fr ultra, grn & org .25 .20
168 A23a 100fr grn, ultra & red brn 1.10 1.10

Issued to publicize space communications.

UNESCO Emblem, Scales and Tree A23b

1963, Dec. 10 Engr. *Perf. 13*

169 A23b 25fr grn, dk gray & red brn .25 .20

15th anniv. of the Universal Declaration of Human Rights.

Barograph and WMO Emblem A23c

1964, Mar. 23 Unwmk. *Perf. 13*

170 A23c 25fr ol bis, sl grn & ultra .30 .25

UN's 4th World Meteorological Day, Mar. 23.

Arms of Gabon — A24

1964, June 15 Photo. *Perf. 13x12½*

171 A24 25fr ocher & multi .30 .20

Tarpon A25

Designs: 60fr, Gorilla, vert. 80fr, Buffalo.

1964, July 15 Engr. *Perf. 13*

172 A25 30fr brn red, bl & blk .50 .20
173 A25 60fr brn, grn & brn red 1.00 .35
174 A25 80fr dk bl, grn & red brn 1.25 .60
Nos. 172-174 (3) 2.75 1.15

Cooperation Issue
Common Design Type

1964, Nov. 7

175 CD119 25fr gray, dk brn & lt bl .30 .20

Dissotis Rotundifolia — A26

5fr, Gloriosa superba. 15fr, Eulophia horsfallii.

1964, Nov. 16 Photo. *Perf. 12x12½*
Flowers in Natural Colors

176 A26 3fr deep grn .20 .20
177 A26 5fr green .25 .20
178 A26 15fr dark brn .45 .25
Nos. 176-178 (3) .90 .65

Sun and IQSY Emblem A27

1965, Feb. 25 *Perf. 12½x12*

179 A27 85fr multi .85 .50

International Quiet Sun Year, 1964-65.

Morse Telegraph A28

1965, May 17 Engr. *Perf. 13*

180 A28 30fr multi .35 .25

Cent. of the ITU.

Manganese Crusher, Moanda A29

Design: 60fr, Uranium mining, Mounana.

1965, June 15 Unwmk. *Perf. 13*

181 A29 15fr brt bl, pur & red .25 .20
182 A29 60fr brn, brt bl & red .75 .40

Issued to publicize Gabon's mineral wealth.

Field Ball — A30

Okoukoue Dance — A31

1965, July 15 Engr. *Perf. 13*

183 A30 25fr brt grn, blk & red .30 .20

1st African Games, Brazzaville, 7/18-25. See #C35.

1965, Sept. 15 *Perf. 13*

Design: 60fr, Mukudji dance.

184 A31 25fr brn, grn & yel .25 .20
185 A31 60fr blk, dk red & brn .70 .40

Abraham Lincoln A32

1965, Sept. 28 Photo. *Perf. 12½x13*

186 A32 50fr vio bl, blk, gold & buff .50 .35

Centenary of death of Abraham Lincoln.

Old & New Post Offices and Mail Transport A33

1965, Dec. 18 Engr. *Perf. 13*

187 A33 30fr bl, brt grn & choc .30 .20

Issued for Stamp Day, 1965.

Balumbu Mask — A34

Intl. Negro Arts Festival, Dakar, Senegal, Apr. 1-24:
10fr, Fang ancestral figure, Byeri. 25fr, Fang mask. 30fr, Okuyi mask, Myene. 85fr, Bakota leather mask.

1966, Apr. 18 Photo. *Perf. 12x12½*

188 A34 5fr red, brn, blk & buff .20 .20
189 A34 10fr brt grnsh bl, dk brn & yel .25 .20
190 A34 25fr multicolored .45 .20
191 A34 30fr mar, yel & blk .55 .20
192 A34 85fr multicolored 1.25 .50
Nos. 188-192 (5) 2.70 1.30

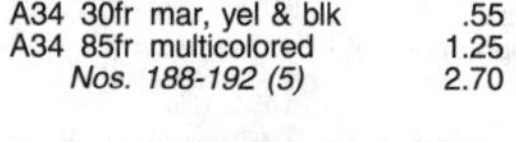

WHO Headquarters, Geneva — A35

1966, May 3 Photo. *Perf. 12½x13*

193 A35 50fr org yel, ultra & blk .50 .30

Inauguration of the WHO Headquarters, Geneva.

Mother Learning to Write — A36

Soccer Player — A37

1966, June 22 Photo. *Perf. 12x12½*

194 A36 30fr multi .35 .20

UNESCO literacy campaign.

1966, July 15 Engr. *Perf. 13*

Design: 90fr, Player facing left.

195 A37 25fr brn, grn & ultra .25 .20
196 A37 90fr ultra & dk pur 1.00 .60
Nos. 195-196,C45 (3) 2.75 1.45

8th World Cup Soccer Championship, Wembley, England, July 11-30.

Timber Industry — A38

Economic development: 85fr, Offshore oil rigs.

1966, Aug. 17 *Perf. 13*

197 A38 20fr red brn, lil & dk grn .25 .20
198 A38 85fr dk brn, brt bl & brt grn 1.10 .40

Woman with Children at Bank Window A39

1966, Sept. 23 Engr. *Perf. 13*

199 A39 25fr brt bl, vio brn & sl grn .25 .20

Issued to publicize Savings Banks.

Scouts Around Campfire A40

50fr, Boy Scout pledging ceremony, vert.

1966, Oct. 17 Engr. *Perf. 13*

200 A40 30fr sl bl, car & dk brn .30 .20
201 A40 50fr Prus bl, brn red & dk brn .55 .30

Issued to honor Gabon's Boy Scouts.

Sikorsky S-43 Hydroplane and Map of West Africa A41

1966, Dec. 17 Photo. *Perf. 12½x12*

202 A41 30fr multi .40 .25

Stamp Day and for the 30th anniv. of the 1st air-mail service from Libreville to Port Gentil.

Hippopotami — A42

Animals: 2fr, African crocodiles. 3fr, Water chevrotain. 5fr, Chimpanzees. 10fr, Elephants. 20fr, Leopards.

1967, Jan. 5 Photo. *Perf. 13x14*

203 A42 1fr multi .20 .20
204 A42 2fr multi .20 .20
205 A42 3fr multi .20 .20
206 A42 5fr multi .20 .20
207 A42 10fr multi .50 .25
208 A42 20fr multi 1.00 .30
Nos. 203-208 (6) 2.30 1.35

Lions International Emblem — A43

50fr, Lions emblem, map of Gabon and globe.

1967, Jan. 14 *Perf. 12½x13*

209 A43 30fr multicolored .30 .20
210 A43 40fr blue & multi .50 .25
a. Strip of 2, #209-210 + label 1.00 1.00

50th anniv. of Lions Intl.

Carnival Masks — A44

1967, Feb. 4 Photo. *Perf. 12x12½*

211 A44 30fr brn, yel bis & bl .35 .20

Libreville Carnival, Feb. 4-7.

"Transportation" and Tourist Year Emblem — A45

1967, Feb. 15 *Perf. 12½x13*

212 A45 30fr multi .35 .20

International Tourist Year, 1967.

Olympic Diving Tower, Mexico City — A46

Symbolic of Atomic Energy Agency — A47

1968 Olympic Games: 30fr, Sun, snow crystals and Olympic rings. 50fr, Ice skating rink and view of Grenoble.

1967, Mar. 18 Engr. *Perf. 13*

213 A46 25fr dk vio, grnsh bl & ultra .25 .20
214 A46 30fr grn, red lil & mar .30 .20
215 A46 50fr ultra, grn & brn .55 .35
Nos. 213-215 (3) 1.10 .75

1967, Apr. 15 Engr. *Perf. 13*

216 A47 30fr red brn, dk grn & ultra .35 .20

International Atomic Energy Agency.

Pope Paul VI, Papal Arms and Libreville Cathedral A48

1967, June 1 Engr. *Perf. 13*

217 A48 30fr ultra, grn & blk .35 .20

"Populorum progressio" encyclical by Pope Paul VI concerning underdeveloped countries.

Flags, Tree, Logger, Map of Gabon and Mask — A49

1967, June 24 Engr. *Perf. 13*

218 A49 30fr multi .30 .20

EXPO '67, International Exhibition, Montreal, Apr. 28-Oct. 27, 1967.

Europafrica Issue, 1967

Map of Europe and Africa and Products A50

1967, July 18 Photo. *Perf. 12½x12*

219 A50 50fr multi .50 .20

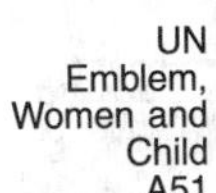

UN Emblem, Women and Child A51

1967, Aug. 10 Engr. *Perf. 13*

220 A51 75fr brt blue, dk brn & emer .75 .30

United Nations Commission for Women.

19th Century Mail Ships — A52

Design: No. 222, Modern mail ships.

1967, Nov. 17 Photo. *Perf. 12½*

221 A52 30fr multi .45 .25
222 A52 30fr multi .45 .25
a. Pair, #221-222 1.10 1.10

Stamp Day. No. 222a has continuous design.

Draconea Fragrans — A53

Trees: 10fr, Pycnanthus angolensis. 20fr, Disthemonanthus benthamianus.

1967, Dec. 5 Engr. *Perf. 13*
Size: 22x36mm

223 A53 5fr bl, emer & brn .35 .20
224 A53 10fr grn, dk grn & bl .45 .25
225 A53 20fr rose red, grn & ol .60 .35
Nos. 223-225,C61-C62 (5) 4.05 2.05

For booklet pane see No. C62a.

WHO Regional Office A54

1968, Apr. 8 Engr. *Perf. 13*

226 A54 20fr multi .25 .20

20th anniv. of the WHO.

Dam, Power Station and UNESCO Emblem A55

1968, June 18 Engr. *Perf. 13*

227 A55 15fr lake, org & Prus bl .25 .20

Hydrological Decade (UNESCO), 1965-74.

Pres. Albert Bernard Bongo — A56

30fr, Pres. Bongo & arms of Gabon in background.

1968, June 24 Photo. *Perf. 12x12½*

228 A56 25fr grn, buff & blk .20 .20
229 A56 30fr rose lil, lt bl & blk .25 .20

Tanker, Refinery, and Map of Area Served — A56a

1968, July 30 Photo. *Perf. 12½*

230 A56a 30fr multi .30 .20

Port Gentil (Gabon) Refinery opening, 6/12/68.

Open Book, Child and UNESCO Emblem A57

1968, Sept. 10 Engr. *Perf. 13*

231 A57 25fr vio bl, dl red & brn .25 .20

Issued for International Literacy Day.

A58

A60

A59

1968, Oct. 15 Engr. *Perf. 13*

232 A58 20fr Coffee .25 .20
233 A58 40fr Cacao .45 .20

1968, Nov. 23 Engr. *Perf. 13*

234 A59 30fr "La Junon" .60 .25

Issued for Stamp Day.

1968, Dec. 10

Lawyer, globe and human rights flame.

235 A60 20fr blk, bl grn & car .25 .20

International Human Rights Year.

Okanda Gap — A61

Designs: 15fr, Barracuda. 25fr, Kinguele Waterfall, vert. 30fr, Sitatunga trophies, vert.

1969, Mar. 28 Engr. *Perf. 13*

236 A61 10fr brn, bl & sl grn .20 .20
237 A61 15fr brn red, emer & ind .70 .20
238 A61 25fr bl, pur & ol .30 .20
239 A61 30fr multi .55 .25
Nos. 236-239 (4) 1.75 .85

Year of African Tourism, 1969.

Mvet (Musical Instrument) A62

Musical Instruments: 30fr, Ngombi harp. 50fr, Ebele and Mbe drums. 100fr, Medzang xylophone.

1969, June 6 Engr. *Perf. 13*

240 A62 25fr plum, ol & dp car .20 .20
241 A62 30fr red brn, ol & dk brn .25 .20
242 A62 50fr plum, ol & dp car .45 .25
243 A62 100fr red brn, ol & dk brn 1.00 .45
a. Min. sheet of 4, #240-243 2.50 2.50
Nos. 240-243 (4) 1.90 1.10

Aframomum Polyanthum (Zingiberaceae) A63

Tree of Life A64

African Plants: 2fr, Chlamydocola chlamydantha (Sterculiaceae). 5fr, Costus dinklagei (Zingiberaceae). 10fr, Cola rostrata (Sterculiaceae). 20fr, Dischistocalyx grandifolius (Acanthaceae).

1969, July 15 Photo. *Perf. 12x12½*

244 A63 1fr multi .20 .20
245 A63 2fr lt ol & multi .20 .20
246 A63 5fr multi .20 .20
247 A63 10fr slate & multi .30 .20
248 A63 20fr yel & multi .50 .25
Nos. 244-248 (5) 1.40 1.05

1969, Aug. 17 Photo.

249 A64 25fr multi .25 .20

National renovation.

Drilling for Oil on Land — A65

Workers and ILO Emblem — A66

Design: 50fr, Offshore drilling station.

1969, Sept. 13 *Perf. 12x12½*

250 A65 25fr multi .20 .20
251 A65 50fr multi .25 .20
a. Strip of 2, #250-251 + label .70 .70

20th anniv. of the ELF-SPAFE oil operations in Gabon.

1969, Oct. 29 Engr. *Perf. 13*

252 A66 30fr bl, sl grn & dp car .25 .20

50th anniv. of the ILO.

Arms of Port Gentil — A67

Coats of Arms: 20fr, Lambarene. 30fr, Libreville.

1969, Nov. 19 Photo. *Perf. 12*

253 A67 20fr red, gold, sil & blk .20 .20
254 A67 25fr bl, blk & gold .20 .20
255 A67 30fr bl & multi .20 .25
Nos. 253-255 (3) .60 .65

See Nos. 267-269, 291-293, 321-326, 340-348, 409-417, 492-501.

Canoe Mail Transport A68

1969, Dec. 18 Engr. *Perf. 13*

256 A68 30fr brt grn, grnsh bl & red brn .35 .20

Issued for Stamp Day 1969.

Satellite, Globe, TV Screen and ITU Emblem A69

1970, May 17 Engr. *Perf. 13*

257 A69 25fr dk bl, dk red brn & blk .25 .20

International Telecommunications Day.

UPU Headquarters Issue
Common Design Type

1970, May 20 Engr. *Perf. 13*

258 CD133 30fr brt grn, brt rose lil & brn .45 .25

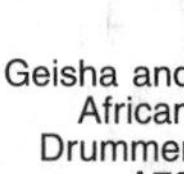

Geisha and African Drummer A70

1970, May 27 Photo. *Perf. 12½x12*

259 A70 30fr ultra & multi .25 .20

EXPO '70 Intl. Exhibition, Osaka, Japan, 3/15-9/13.

ASECNA Issue
Common Design Type

1970, Aug. 26 Engr. *Perf. 13*

260 CD132 100fr brt grn & bl grn .90 .55

UN Emblem, Globe, Dove and Charts A71

1970, Oct. 24 Photo. *Perf. 12½x12*

261 A71 30fr Prus bl & multi .30 .20

25th anniversary of the United Nations.

Bushbucks A72

Designs: 15fr, Pels scaly-tailed flying squirrel. 25fr, Gray-cheeked monkey, vert. 40fr, African golden cat. 60fr, Sevaline genet.

1970, Dec. 14 Photo. *Perf. 12½x13*

262 A72 5fr yel grn & multi .20 .20
263 A72 15fr red org & blk .35 .25
264 A72 25fr vio & multi .85 .35
265 A72 40fr red & multi 1.40 .60
266 A72 60fr bl & multi 2.10 1.00
Nos. 262-266 (5) 4.90 2.40

Coats of Arms Type of 1969

20fr, Mouila. 25fr, Bitam. 30fr, Oyem.

1971, Feb. 16 Photo. *Perf. 12*

267 A67 20fr ver, blk, sil & gold .20 .20
268 A67 25fr emer, gold & blk .25 .20
269 A67 30fr emer, gold, blk & red .30 .20
Nos. 267-269 (3) .75 .60

Men of Four Races and Emblem — A73

1971, Mar. 21 Engr. *Perf. 13*

270 A73 40fr multi .35 .20

Intl. year against racial discrimination.

Map of Africa and Telecommunications System — A74

1971, Apr. 30 Photo. *Perf. 13*

271 A74 30fr org & multi .25 .20

Pan-African telecommunications system.

Charaxes Smaragdalis — A75

Butterflies: 10fr, Euxanthe crossleyi. 15fr, Epiphora rectifascia. 25fr, Imbrasia bouvieri.

1971, May 26 Photo. *Perf. 13*

272 A75 5fr yel & multi .50 .20
273 A75 10fr bl & multi 1.10 .40
274 A75 15fr grn & multi 2.00 .60
275 A75 25fr ol & multi 2.40 .80
Nos. 272-275 (4) 6.00 2.00

Hertzian Center, Nkol Ogoum A76

1971, June 17 Engr. *Perf. 13*

276 A76 40fr grn, blk & dk car .30 .20

3rd World Telecommunications Day.

Mother Nursing Child A77

1971, Aug. 17 Engr. *Perf. 13*

277 A77 30fr lil rose, sep & ocher .30 .20

Gabonese social security system, 15th anniv.

UN Headquarters and Emblem — A78

1971, Sept. 30 Photo. *Perf. 13*

278 A78 30fr red & multi .25 .20

10th anniv. of Gabon's admission to the UN.

Large Egret — A79

Birds: 40fr, African gray parrot. 50fr, Woodland Kingfisher. 75fr, Cameroon bareheaded rock-fowl. 100fr, Gold Coast touraco.

1971, Oct. 12 Litho. *Perf. 13*

279 A79 30fr multi .45 .20
280 A79 40fr multi .70 .35
281 A79 50fr multi .85 .40
282 A79 75fr multi 1.25 .60
283 A79 100fr multi 1.75 .90
Nos. 279-283 (5) 5.00 2.45

Asystasia Volgeliana A80

Designs: Flowers of Acanthus Family after paintings by Noel Hallé.

1972, Apr. 4 Photo. *Perf. 13*

284 A80 5fr pale cit & multi .20 .20
285 A80 10fr multi .25 .20
286 A80 20fr multi .40 .25
287 A80 30fr lil rose & multi .50 .30
288 A80 40fr dk grn & multi 1.00 .40
289 A80 65fr red & multi 1.50 .60
Nos. 284-289 (6) 3.85 1.95

Louis Pasteur — A81

1972, May 15 Engr. *Perf. 13*

290 A81 80fr dp org, pur & grn .35 .20

Sesquicentennial of the birth of Louis Pasteur (1822-1895), scientist and bacteriologist.

Arms Type of 1969

30fr, Franceville. 40fr, Makokou. 60fr, Tchibanga.

1972, June 2 Photo. *Perf. 12*

291 A67 30fr sil & multi .20 .20
292 A67 40fr grn & multi .30 .20
293 A67 60fr blk, grn & sil .50 .25
Nos. 291-293 (3) 1.00 .65

Globe and Telecommunications Symbols — A81a

1972, July 25 *Perf. 13x12½*

294 A81a 40fr blk, yel & org .30 .20

4th World Telecommunications Day.

Nat King Cole — A82

Black American Jazz Musicians: 60fr, Sidney Bechet. 100fr, Louis Armstrong.

1972, Sept. 1 Photo. *Perf. 13x13½*

295 A82 40fr bl & multi .75 .20
296 A82 60fr org & multi 1.25 .40
297 A82 100fr multi 2.00 .60
Nos. 295-297 (3) 4.00 1.20

Blanding's Rear-fanged Snake — A83

Designs: 2fr, Beauty snake. 3fr, Eggeating snake. 15fr, Striped ground snake. 25fr, Jameson's mamba. 50fr, Gabon viper.

1972, Oct. 2 Litho. *Perf. 13*

298 A83 1fr lem & multi .20 .20
299 A83 2fr red brn & multi .20 .20
300 A83 3fr brn org & multi .20 .20
301 A83 15fr multi .20 .20
302 A83 25fr grn & multi .25 .20
303 A83 50fr multi .50 .25
Nos. 298-303 (6) 1.55 1.25

See Nos. 330-332, 354-357.

Dr. Armauer G. Hansen, Lambarene Leprosarium — A84

1973, Jan. 28 Engr. *Perf. 13*

304 A84 30fr Prus grn, sl grn & brn .25 .20

Centenary of the discovery of the Hansen bacillus, the cause of leprosy.

Charaxes Candiope — A85

Designs: Various butterflies.

1973, Feb. 23 Litho. *Perf. 13*

305 A85 10fr *shown* .35 .20
306 A85 15fr *Eunica pechueli* .55 .20
307 A85 20fr *Cyrestis camillus* .90 .25
308 A85 30fr *Charaxes castor* 1.10 .30
309 A85 40fr *Charaxes ameliae* 1.25 .55
310 A85 50fr *Pseudacrea boisduvali* 1.50 .65
Nos. 305-310 (6) 5.65 2.15

Balloon of Santos-Dumont, 1901 — A86

History of Aviation: 1fr, Montgolfier's balloon, 1783, vert. 3fr, Octave Chanute's biplane, 1896. 4fr, Clement Ader's Plane III, 1897. 5fr, Louis Bleriot crossing the Channel, 1909. 10fr, Fabre's hydroplane, 1910.

1973, May 3 Engr. *Perf. 13*

311 A86 1fr grn, sl grn & dk red .20 .20
312 A86 2fr sl grn & brt bl .20 .20
313 A86 3fr bl, sl & org .20 .20
314 A86 4fr lil & dk pur .50 .20
315 A86 5fr slate grn & org .80 .25
316 A86 10fr rose lil & Prus bl 1.40 .35
Nos. 311-316 (6) 3.30 1.40

1977 Coil Stamp

316A A86 10fr aqua .20 .20

No. 316A has red control numbers on back of every 10th stamp.

INTERPOL Emblem — A87

1973, June 26 Engr. *Perf. 13*

317 A87 40fr magenta & ultra .25 .20

50th anniversary of the International Criminal Police Organization (INTERPOL).

Earth Station "2 Decembre" A88

1973, July 2 Engr. *Perf. 13*

318 A88 40fr slate grn, bl & brn .25 .20

Party Headquarters, Libreville — A89

1973, Aug. 17 Photo.

319 A89 30fr multi .20 .20

African Postal Union Issue

Common Design Type

1973, Sept. 12 Engr. *Perf. 13*

320 CD137 100fr red lil, pur & bl .60 .40

Arms Type of 1969

5fr, Gamba. 10fr, Ogowe-Lolo. 15fr, Fougamou. 30fr, Kango. 40fr, Booue. 60fr, Koula-Moutou.

1973-74 Photo. *Perf. 12*

321 A67 5fr bl & multi ('74) .20 .20
322 A67 10fr blk, red & gold ('74) .20 .20
323 A67 15fr grn & multi ('74) .20 .20
324 A67 30fr red & multi .25 .20
325 A67 40fr red & multi .25 .20
326 A67 60fr emer & multi .40 .20
Nos. 321-326 (6) 1.50 1.20

Issued #321-323, 2/13; #324-326, 10/4.

St. Teresa of Lisieux — A90

40fr, St. Teresa and Jesus carrying cross.

1973, Dec. 4 Photo. *Perf. 13*

327 A90 30fr blk & multi .25 .20
328 A90 40fr blk & multi .30 .25

St. Teresa of the Infant Jesus (Thérèse Martin, 1873-97), Carmelite nun.

Human Rights Flame — A91

1973, Dec. 10 Engr.

329 A91 20fr grn, red & ultra .20 .20

25th anniversary of the Universal Declaration of Human Rights.

Wildlife Type of 1972

Monkeys: 40fr, Mangabey. 60fr, Cercopithecus cephus. 80fr, Mona monkey.

1974, Mar. 20 Litho. *Perf. 14*

330 A83 40fr gray grn & multi .20 .20
331 A83 60fr lt bl & multi .35 .20
332 A83 80fr lil rose & multi .45 .25
Nos. 330-332 (3) 1.00 .65

Ogowe River at Lambarene A93

50fr, Cape Estérias. 75fr, Poubara rope bridge.

1974, July 30 Photo. *Perf. 13x13½*

333 A93 30fr multi .20 .20
334 A93 50fr multi .25 .20
335 A93 75fr multi .40 .25
Nos. 333-335 (3) .85 .65

Manioc A94

Design: 50fr, Palms and dates.

1974, Nov. 13 Photo. *Perf. 13x12½*

336 A94 40fr org red & multi .25 .20
337 A94 50fr bister & multi .25 .20

UDEAC Issue

Presidents and Flags of Cameroun, CAR, Congo, Gabon and Meeting Center — A95

1974, Dec. 8 Photo. *Perf. 13*

338 A95 40fr multi .25 .20

See No. C156.

Hôtel du Dialogue — A96

1975, Jan. 20 Photo. *Perf. 13*

339 A96 50fr multi .25 .20

Opening of Hôtel du Dialogue.

Arms Type of 1969

5fr, Ogowe-Ivindo. 10fr, Moabi. #342, Moanda. #343, Nyanga. 25fr, Mandji. #345, Mekambo. #346, Omboué. 60fr, Minvoul. 90fr, Mayumba.

1975-77 Photo. *Perf. 12*

340 A67 5fr red & multi .20 .20
341 A67 10fr gold & multi .20 .20
342 A67 15fr red, sil & blk .20 .20
343 A67 15fr bl & multi .20 .20
344 A67 25fr grn & multi .20 .20
345 A67 50fr blk, gold & red .25 .20
346 A67 50fr multi .25 .20
347 A67 60fr multi .35 .20
348 A67 90fr multi .45 .25
Nos. 340-348 (9) 2.30 1.85

Issued: #340-342, Jan. 21, 1975; #343-345, Aug. 17, 1976; #346-348, July 12, 1977.

Map of Africa with Lion's Head, and Lions Emblem — A97

1975, May 2 Typo. *Perf. 13*

349 A97 50fr grn & multi .25 .20

Lions Club 17th congress, District 403, Libreville.

Hertzian Wave Transmitter Network, Map of Gabon A98

1975, July 8 Engr. *Perf. 13*

350 A98 40fr multi		.25	.20

City and Rural Women, Car, Train and Building — A99

1975, July 22 Engr. *Perf. 13*

351 A99 50fr car, bl & brn		.35	.20

International Women's Year 1975.

Scoutmaster Ange Mba, Emblems and Rope — A100

Design: 50fr, Hand holding rope, Scout, camp, Boy Scout and Nordjamb 75 emblems.

1975, July 29

352 A100 40fr multi	.25	.20
353 A100 50fr grn, red & dk brn	.35	.20

Nordjamb 75, 14th Boy Scout Jamboree, Lillehammer, Norway, July 29-Aug. 7.

Wildlife Type of 1972

Fish: 30fr, Lutjanus goreensis. 40fr, Galeoides decadactylus. 50fr, Sardinella aurita. 120fr, Scarus hoefleri.

1975, Sept. 22 Litho. *Perf. 14*

354 A83 30fr multi	.20	.20
355 A83 40fr multi	.25	.20
356 A83 50fr multi	.25	.20
357 A83 120fr multi	.65	.45
Nos. 354-357 (4)	1.35	1.05

Agro-Industrial Complex — A102

1975, Dec. 15 Litho. *Perf. 12½*

358 A102 60fr multi	.35	.25

Inauguration of Agro-Industrial Complex, Franceville.

Tchibanga Bridge — A103

Bridges of Gabon: 10fr, Mouila. 40fr, Kango. 50fr, Lambaréné, vert.

1976, Jan. 30 Engr. *Perf. 13*

359 A103 5fr multi	.20	.20
360 A103 10fr multi	.20	.20
361 A103 40fr multi	.20	.20
362 A103 50fr multi	.25	.20
Nos. 359-362 (4)	.85	.80

Telephones 1876 and 1976, Satellite, A. G. Bell — A104

1976, Mar. 10 Engr. *Perf. 13*

363 A104 60fr dk bl, grn & sl grn	.35	.25

Centenary of first telephone call by Alexander Graham Bell, Mar. 10, 1876.

Msgr. Jean Remy Bessieux — A105

1976, Apr. 30 Engr. *Perf. 13*

364 A105 50fr grn, bl & sepia	.25	.20

Death centenary of Msgr. Bessieux.

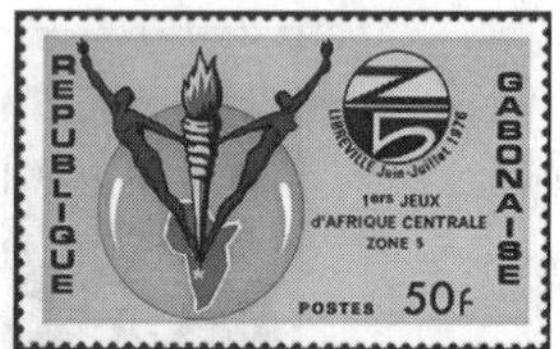

Athletes, Torch, Map of Africa, Games Emblem — A106

1976, June 25 Photo. *Perf. 13x12½*

365 A106 50fr multi	.25	.20
366 A106 60fr org & multi	.35	.25

First Central African Games (Zone 5), Libreville, June-July.

Motobécane, France — A107

Motorcycles: 5fr, Bultaco, Spain. 10fr, Suzuki, Japan. 20fr, Kawasaki, Japan. 100fr, Harley-Davidson, US.

1976, July 20 Litho. *Perf. 12½*

367 A107 3fr multi	.20	.20
368 A107 5fr org & multi	.20	.20
369 A107 10fr bl & multi	.20	.20
370 A107 20fr multi	.20	.20
371 A107 100fr car & multi	.55	.40
Nos. 367-371 (5)	1.35	1.20

Rice A108

1976, Oct. 15 Litho. *Perf. 13x13½*

372 A108 50fr shown	.25	.20
373 A108 60fr Pepper plants	.35	.25

1977, Apr. 22 Litho. *Perf. 13x13½*

50fr, Banana plantation. 60fr, Peanut market.

374 A108 50fr multi	.25	.20
375 A108 60fr multi	.35	.25

Telecommunications Emblem and Telephone — A109

1977, May 17 *Perf. 13*

376 A109 60fr multi	.35	.25

World Telecommunications Day.

View of Oyem A110

50fr, Cape Lopez. 70fr, Lebamba Cave.

1977, June 9 Litho. *Perf. 12½*

377 A110 50fr multi	.25	.20
378 A110 60fr multi	.35	.25
379 A110 70fr multi	.40	.25
Nos. 377-379 (3)	1.00	.70

Conference Hall — A111

1977, June 23 Photo. *Perf. 13x12½*

380 A111 100fr multi	.55	.40

Meeting of the OAU, Libreville.

Arms of Gabon — A112

1977 Engr. *Perf. 13*

Size: 23x36mm

381 A112 50fr blue	.25	.20

Size: 17x23mm

382 A112 60fr orange	.35	.20
a. Booklet pane of 5	1.90	
383 A112 80fr red	.40	.35
Nos. 381-383 (3)	1.00	.75

#381 issued in coils, #382 in booklets only. Issued: #381-382, June 23; #383, Sept.

Modern Buildings, Libreville — A113

1977, Aug. 17 Litho. *Perf. 12*

387 A113 50fr multi	.25	.20

National Festival 1977.

Paris to Vienna, 1902 — A114

Renault Automobiles: 10fr, Coupé 1 2 CV, 1921. 30fr, Torpédo Scaphandrier, 1925. 40fr, Reinastella 40 CV, 1929. 100fr, Nerva Grand Sport, 1937. 150fr, Voiturette 1 CV, 1899. 200fr, Alpine Renault V6, 1977.

1977, Aug 30 Engr. *Perf. 13*

388 A114 5fr multi	.20	.20
389 A114 10fr multi	.20	.20
390 A114 30fr multi	.20	.20
391 A114 40fr multi	.20	.20
392 A114 100fr multi	.40	.30
Nos. 388-392 (5)	1.20	1.10

Miniature Sheet

393 Sheet of 2 + label	2.00	2.00
a. A114 150fr multi	.75	.75
b. A114 200fr multi	1.00	1.00

Louis Renault, French automobile pioneer, birth centenary. Nos. 383a-393b are perf. on 3 sides, without perforation between stamps and center label showing dark brown portrait of Renault.

See Nos. 395-400.

Globe A115

1978, Feb. 21 Engr. *Perf. 13x12½*

394 A115 80fr multi	.40	.35

World Leprosy Day.

Automobile Type of 1977

Citroen Cars: 10fr, Cabriolet, 1922. 50fr, Taxi, 1927. 60fr, Berline, 1932. 80fr, Berline, 1934. 150fr, Torpedo, 1919. 200fr, Berline, 1948. 250fr, Pallas, 1975.

1978, May 9 Engr. *Perf. 13*

395 A114 10fr multi	.20	.20
396 A114 50fr multi	.35	.25
397 A114 60fr multi	.40	.25
398 A114 80fr multi	.55	.35
399 A114 200fr multi	1.40	.65
Nos. 395-399 (5)	2.90	1.70

Miniature Sheet

400 Sheet of 2	2.25	2.25
a. A114 150fr multi	.75	.75
b. A114 250fr multi	1.25	1.25

Andre Citroen (1878-1935), automobile designer and manufacturer.

Ndjole on Ogowe River — A116

Views: 40fr, Lambarene lake district. 50fr, Owendo Harbor.

1978, May 17 Litho. *Perf. 12½*

401 A116 30fr multi	.20	.20
402 A116 40fr multi	.25	.20
403 A116 50fr multi	.35	.20
Nos. 401-403 (3)	.80	.60

Sternotomis Mirabilis — A117

Anti- Apartheid Emblem — A118

Various Coleopteras.

1978, June 21 Photo. *Perf. 12½x13*

404 A117 20fr multi	.20	.20
405 A117 60fr multi	.40	.25
406 A117 75fr multi	.50	.30
407 A117 80fr multi	.55	.35
Nos. 404-407 (4)	1.65	1.10

1978, July 25 Engr. *Perf. 13*

408 A118 80fr multi .55 .35

Arms Type of 1969

1978-80 Photo. *Perf. 12*

409 A67 5fr Oyem	.20	.20
410 A67 5fr Ogowe-Maritime ('79)	.20	.20
411 A67 10fr Lastoursville ('79)	.20	.20
412 A67 10fr Haut-Ogooue ('80)	.20	.20
413 A67 15fr M'Bigou ('79)	.20	.20
414 A67 20fr Estuaire ('80)	.20	.20
415 A67 30fr Bitam ('80)	.20	.20
416 A67 40fr Okondja	.25	.20
417 A67 60fr Mimongo	.35	.25
Nos. 409-417 (9)	2.00	1.85

A119

1978, Oct. 24 Engr. *Perf. 13*

419 A119 80fr multi .55 .35

UNESCO campaign to save the Acropolis.

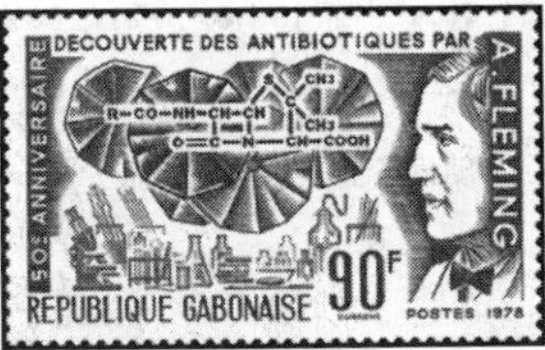

Penicillin Formula, — A120

1978, Nov. 21 Engr. *Perf. 13*

420 A120 90fr multi .60 .40

Alexander Fleming's discovery of antibiotics, 50th anniversary.

The Visitation — A121

80fr, Massacre of the Innocents. Woodcarvings from St. Michael's Church, Libreville.

1978, Dec. 15 Photo.

421 A121 60fr gold & multi	.40	.25
422 A121 80fr gold & multi	.55	.35

Christmas 1978. See Nos. 437-438.

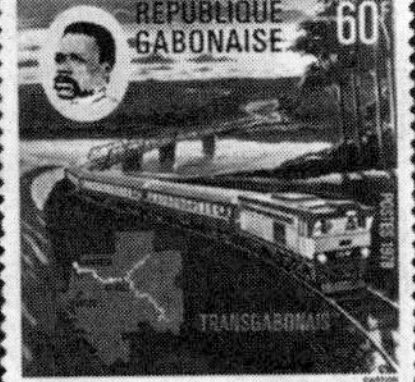

Train and Map A122

1978, Dec. 27 Litho. *Perf. 12½*

423 A122 60fr multi .40 .25

Inauguration of Trans-Gabon Railroad, Libreville to Njolé.

A123

Pre-Olympic Year (Kremlin Towers, Olympic Emblem, Ancestral Figure and): 80fr, Long jump, vert. 100fr, Yachts.

1979, May 15 Engr. *Perf. 13*

424 A123 60fr multi	.40	.25
425 A123 80fr multi	.55	.35
426 A123 100fr multi	.65	.40
a. Miniature sheet of 3, #424-426	1.60	1.60
Nos. 424-426 (3)	1.60	1.00

Rowland Hill, Messenger and Gabon No. O9 — A124

Allamanda Schottii A125

Designs: 80fr, Bakota mask and tulip tree flowers, vert. 150fr, Pigeon, UPU emblem, truck and canoe. No. 430b, Gloriosa superba. No. 430c, Phaeomeria magnifica, vert. No. 430d, Berlinia bracteosa, vert.

1979, June 8 Photo. *Perf. 13*

427 A124 50fr multi	.35	.20
428 A124 80fr multi	.55	.35

Engr.

429 A124 150fr multi	1.00	.60
Nos. 427-429 (3)	1.90	1.15

Souvenir Sheet

Photo. *Perf. 14*

430 Sheet of 4	3.00	3.00
a. A125 100fr multicolored	.65	
b. A125 100fr multicolored	.65	
c. A125 100fr multicolored	.65	
d. A125 100fr multicolored	.65	

Philexafrique II, Libreville, June 8-17. Nos. 427-429 each printed in sheets of 10 with 5 labels showing exhibition emblem. No. 427 also commemorates Sir Rowland Hill (1795-1879), originator of penny postage. No. 430 has label with exhibition emblem.

IYC Emblem, Globe, Child with Bird — A126

1979, June 15 Engr. *Perf. 13*

431 A126 100fr multi .65 .40

International Year of the Child.

"TELECOM 79" — A127

1979, Sept. 18 Litho. *Perf. 13x12½*

432 A127 80fr multi .55 .25

3rd World Telecommunications Exhibition, Geneva, Sept. 20-26.

Sugar Cane Harvest — A128

1979, Oct. 9 Photo. *Perf. 12½x13*

433 A128 25fr shown	.20	.20
434 A128 30fr Yams	.20	.20

Judo Throw — A129

1979, Oct. 23 Engr. *Perf. 13*

435 A129 40fr multi .25 .20

World Judo Championships, Paris, Dec.

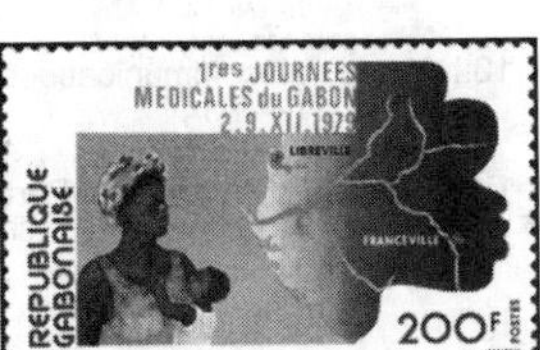

Mother and Child, Map of Congo River Basin — A130

1979, Dec. 2 Litho. *Perf. 12*

436 A130 200fr multi 1.40 .65

Medical Week, Dec. 2-9.

Christmas Type of 1978

Wood Carvings, St. Michael's Church, Libreville: 60fr, Flight into Egypt. 80fr, The Circumcision.

1979, Dec. 12 Photo. *Perf. 13*

437 A121 60fr multi	.40	.20
438 A121 80fr multi	.55	.25

Pres. Omar Bongo — A131

1979-80 Litho. *Perf. 12½*

439 A131 60fr multi	.40	.20
440 A131 80fr multi	.55	.25

Bongo's 44th birthday (#439); re-election and inauguration (#440).

Issued: 60fr, 12/30/79; 80fr, 2/27/80.

OPEC, 20th Anniv. — A132

1980, Mar. 27 Litho. *Perf. 13½x13*

441 A132 50fr multi .35 .20

Donguila Church — A133

1980 Apr. 3 Litho. *Perf. 12½*

442 A133 60fr shown	.40	.20
443 A133 80fr Bizengobibere Church	.55	.25

Easter 1980.

De Brazza (1852-1905), Map of Gabon with Franceville A134

1980, June 30 Litho. *Perf. 12½*

444 A134 165fr multi 1.10 .55

Franceville Foundation centenary, founded by Savorgnan De Brazza.

20th Anniversary of Independence — A135

1980, Aug. 17 Photo. *Perf. 13*

445 A135 60fr Leon Mba and Omar Bongo .40 .20

World Tourism Conference, Manila, Sept. 27 — A136

1980, Sept. 10 **Engr.**
446 A136 80fr multi .55 .25

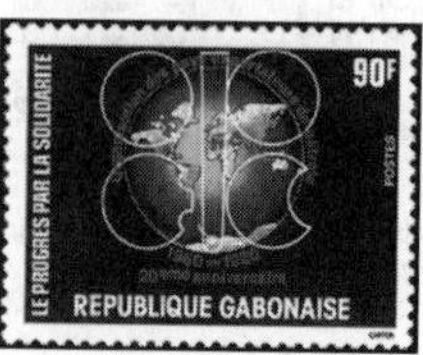

20th Anniversary of OPEC A137

1980, Sept. 15 **Litho.** ***Perf. 12½***
447 A137 90fr shown .60 .30
448 A137 120fr Men Holding OPEC emblem, vert. .80 .40

Pseudochelidon Eurystomina A138

1980, Oct. 15 **Photo.** ***Perf. 14x14½***
449 A138 50fr *shown* .35 .20
450 A138 60fr *Merops nubicus* .40 .20
451 A138 80fr *Pitta angolensis* .55 .25
452 A138 150fr *Scotopelia peli* 1.00 .50
Nos. 449-452 (4) 2.30 1.15

Statue of Bull, Bizangobibere Church — A139

1980, Dec. 10 **Photo.** ***Perf. 14x14½***
453 A139 60fr shown .40 .20
454 A139 80fr Male statue .55 .25

Christmas 1980.

Heinrich von Stephan — A140

1981, Jan. 7 **Engr.** ***Perf. 13***
455 A140 90fr brn & dk brn .60 .30

Von Stephan (1831-97), UPU founder.

13th Anniversary of National Renovation Movement — A141

1981, Mar. 12 **Litho.** ***Perf. 13x12½***
456 A141 60fr multi .40 .20

Lion Statue, Bizangobibere A142

1981, Apr. 12 **Photo.** ***Perf. 14x14½***
457 A142 75fr multi .50 .25
458 A142 100fr multi .65 .35

Easter 1981.

Port Gentil Lions Club Banner — A143

1981, May 1 **Litho.** ***Perf. 12½***
459 A143 60fr shown .40 .20
460 A143 75fr District 403 .50 .25
461 A143 80fr Libreville Cocotiers .55 .25
462 A143 100fr Libreville Hibiscus .65 .35
463 A143 165fr Ekwata 1.10 .55
464 A143 200fr Haut-Ogooue 1.40 .65
Nos. 459-464 (6) 4.60 2.25

Lions International, 23rd Congress of District 403, Libreville, May 1-3.

13th World Telecommunications Day — A144

1981, May 17 **Photo.** ***Perf. 13***
465 A144 125fr multi .80 .40

Unity, Work and Justice A145

R.P. Klaine (Missionary), 70th Death Anniv. A146

1981-96? **Photo.** ***Perf. 13***
466 A145 5fr beige & blk .20 .20
467 A145 10fr pale lil & blk .20 .20
468 A145 15fr brt yel grn & blk .20 .20
469 A145 20fr pink & blk .20 .20
470 A145 25fr vio & blk .20 .20
471 A145 40fr red org & blk .25 .20
472 A145 50fr bluish grn & blk .35 .20
473 A145 75fr bis brn & blk .50 .25
473A A145 90fr lt bl & blk ('83) .25 .20
474 A145 100fr yel & blk .65 .35
474A A145 125fr grn & blk ('83) .35 .20
474B A145 150fr brt pink & blk ('86) .40 .20
474C A145 175fr grnish bl & blk ('96)
Nos. 466-474B (12) 3.75 2.60

See Nos. 862-871.

1981, July 2 **Litho.**

90fr, Archbishop Walker, 110th birth anniv.

475 A146 70fr multi .45 .25
476 A146 90fr multi .60 .30

Map of Gabon and Scout Sign — A147

Intl. Year of the Disabled — A148

1981, July 16 ***Perf. 12½***
477 A147 75fr multi .50 .25

4th Pan-African Scouting Congress, Abidjan, Aug.

No. 477 Overprinted: DAKAR / 28e CONFERENCE / MONDIALE DU / SCOUTISME

1981, July 23
478 A147 75fr multi .50 .25

28th World Scouting Conf., Dakar, Aug.

1981, Aug. 6 **Engr.** ***Perf. 13***
479 A148 100fr multi .65 .35

Hypolimnas Salmacis A149

1981, Sept. 10 **Litho.** ***Perf. 14½x14***
480 A149 75fr shown .50 .25
481 A149 100fr Euphaedra themis .65 .35
482 A149 150fr Amauris niavius 1.00 .50
483 A149 250fr Cymothoe lucasi 1.60 .80
Nos. 480-483 (4) 3.75 1.90

Paul as Harlequin, by Pablo Picasso (1881-1973) A150

1981, Sept. 25 ***Perf. 14½x13½***
484 A150 500fr multi 3.50 1.60

World Food Day — A151

1981, Oct. 16 **Engr.** ***Perf. 13***
485 A151 350fr multi 2.25 1.25

Traditional Hairstyle — A152

Designs: Various hairstyles.

1981, Nov. 12 **Litho.** ***Perf. 14½x15***
486 A152 75fr multi .50 .20
487 A152 100fr multi .65 .35
488 A152 125fr multi .80 .40
489 A152 200fr multi 1.40 .65
a. Souvenir sheet of 4, #486-489 3.50 1.60
Nos. 486-489 (4) 3.35 1.60

See Nos. 609A-609B, 676.

Christmas 1981 A153

Designs: Children's drawings.

1981, Dec. 10 ***Perf. 14½x14***
490 A153 75fr Girls dancing .50 .25
491 A153 100fr Dinner .65 .35

Arms Type of 1969

Perf. 12, 13 (#495-497)

1982-92 **Photo.**
492 A67 75fr Moyen-Ogooue .50 .25
493 A67 90fr Cocobeach .25 .20
494 A67 100fr Woleu-N'tem .65 .35
495 A67 100fr Lambarene .40 .20
496 A67 100fr Port Gentil District .90 .45
497 A67 100fr Medouneu .90 .45
498 A67 125fr Mouila .35 .20
499 A67 135fr N'Djole .40 .20
500 A67 150fr N'Gounie 1.00 .50
501 A67 160fr Leconi .55 .30
Nos. 492-501 (10) 5.90 3.10

Issued: #492, 494, 500, 1/13/82; #493, 498, 499, 8/7/84; #496, 4/17/91; #497, 8/12/82.

A154

1982, Feb. 16 Litho. *Perf. 13*
502 A154 100fr multi .65 .35

Visit of Pope John Paul II, Feb. 17-19.

A155

1982, Mar. 31 Engr. *Perf. 13*
503 A155 75fr black .50 .25

Alfred de Musset (1810-1857), writer.

Merchant Navy Ships A156

1982, Apr. 7 Litho. *Perf. 14½x14*
504 A156 75fr Timber carrier .50 .25
505 A156 100fr Freighter .65 .35
506 A156 200fr Oil tanker 1.40 .65
Nos. 504-506 (3) 2.55 1.25

See Nos. 588, 599.

TB Bacillus Centenary — A157

1982, Apr. 24 Litho. *Perf. 13*
507 A157 100fr multi .65 .35

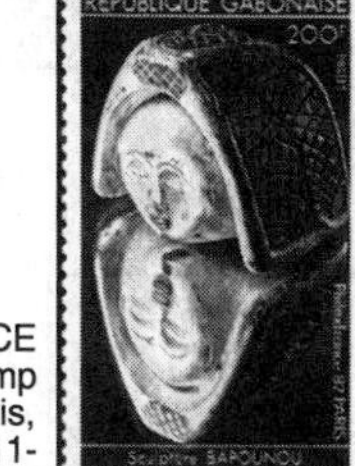

PHILEXFRANCE '82 Stamp Exhibition, Paris, June 11-21 — A158

1982, Apr. 28 *Perf. 12½*
508 A158 100fr Rope bridge .65 .35
509 A158 200fr Sculptured head 1.40 .65
a. Pair, #508-509 + label 2.10 1.50

14th World Telecommunications Day — A159

1982, May 17 *Perf. 13*
510 A159 75fr multi .50 .25

1982 World Cup — A160

Designs: Various soccer players.

1982, May 19 *Perf. 14x14½*
511 A160 100fr multi .65 .35
512 A160 125fr multi .80 .40
513 A160 200fr multi 1.40 .65
a. Souvenir sheet of 3, #511-513, perf. 14½ 2.75 1.50
Nos. 511-513 (3) 2.85 1.40

For overprints see Nos. 516-518.

2nd UN Conf. on Peaceful Uses of Outer Space, Vienna, Aug. 9-21 — A161

1982, July 7 Engr. *Perf. 13*
514 A161 250fr Satellites 1.60 .80

White Carnations A162

Designs: Various carnations.

1982, June 9 Photo. *Perf. 14½x14*
515 Strip of 3 2.25 1.10
a. A162 75fr multi .50 .25
b. A162 100fr multi .65 .35
c. A162 175fr multi 1.10 .50

Nos. 511-513a Overprinted in Red with Semi-Finalists or Finalists

1982, Aug. 19 Litho. *Perf. 14x14½*
516 A160 100fr multi .65 .35
517 A160 125fr multi .80 .40
518 A160 200fr multi 1.40 .65
a. Souvenir sheet of 3 3.00 1.50
Nos. 516-518 (3) 2.85 1.40

Italy's victory in 1982 World Cup.

Phyllonotus Duplex A163

1982, Sept. 22 *Perf. 14½x14*
519 A163 75fr shown .50 .25
520 A163 100fr Chama crenulata .65 .35
521 A163 125fr Cardium hians .85 .40
Nos. 519-521 (3) 2.00 1.00

Okouyi Mask — A164

1982, Oct. 13 Litho. *Perf. 14x14½*
522 A164 75fr shown .50 .25
523 A164 100fr Ondoumbo reliquary .65 .35
524 A164 150fr Tsogho statuette 1.00 .50
525 A164 250fr Fang bellows 1.60 .80
Nos. 522-525 (4) 3.75 1.90

Christmas 1982 — A165

1983, Dec. 15 Litho. *Perf. 14x14½*
526 A165 100fr St. Francis Xavier Church .65 .35

Trans-Gabon Railroad Inauguration — A166

1983, Jan. 18 *Perf. 12½*
527 A166 75fr multi .50 .25

5th African Highway Conference, Libreville, Feb. 6-11 — A167

1983, Feb. 2 *Perf. 13*
528 A167 100fr multi .65 .35

15th Anniv. of Natl. Renewal — A168

Provincial Symbols: a. Bakota mask, Ogowe Ivindo. b. Butterfly, Ogowe Lolo. c. Buffalo, Nyanga. d. Isogho hairdo, Ngounie. e. Tarpon, Ogowe Maritime. f. Manganese, Haut Ogowe. g. Crocodiles, Moyen Ogowe. h. Coffee plant. i. Epitorium trochiformis.

1983, Mar. 12 Litho. *Perf. 13x13½*
529 Strip of 9 + label 6.50 3.50
a. A168 75fr multi .50 .25
b. A168 90fr multi .55 .30
c. A168 90fr multi .60 .30
d. A168 100fr multi .65 .35
e. A168 125fr multi .80 .40
f. A168 125fr multi .80 .40
g. A168 125fr multi .80 .40
h. A168 135fr multi .90 .45
i. A168 135fr multi .90 .45

25th Anniv. of Intl. Maritime Org. — A169

1983, Mar. 17 *Perf. 13*
530 A169 125fr multi .80 .40

Pelican A170

1983, Apr. 20 Litho. *Perf. 15x14½*
531 A170 90fr Water musk deer .60 .30
532 A170 125fr shown .80 .40
533 A170 225fr Elephant 1.50 .75
534 A170 400fr Iguana 2.50 1.25
a. Souv. sheet of 4, #531-534 5.75 2.75
Nos. 531-534 (4) 5.40 2.70

25th Anniv. of UN Economic Commission for Africa A171

1983, Apr. 29 Litho. *Perf. 12½*
535 A171 125fr multi .80 .40

15th World Telecommunications Day — A172

1983, May 17 Litho. *Perf. 13*
536 A172 90fr multi .60 .30
537 A172 90fr multi .60 .30
a. Pair, #536-537 1.25 .65

Denomination of No. 536 in lower right, No. 537, upper left.

Nkoltang Earth Satellite Station — A173

1983, July 2
538 A173 125fr multi .80 .40

10th anniv. of station; WCY.

Ivindo River Rapids — A174

1983, Sept. 7 Engr. *Perf. 13*

539 A174 90fr shown .60 .30
540 A174 125fr Ogooue River .80 .40
541 A174 185fr Wonga Wongue Preserve 1.25 .60
542 A174 350fr Coastal view 2.25 1.25
Nos. 539-542 (4) 4.90 2.55

Hand Drum, Mahongwe A175

Harmful Insects — A176

1983, Oct. 12 Litho. *Perf. 14x14½*

543 A175 90fr shown .30 .20
544 A175 125fr Okoukoue dancer .40 .20
545 A175 135fr Four-stringed fiddle .40 .25
546 A175 260fr Ndoumou dancer .80 .35
Nos. 543-546 (4) 1.90 1.00

1983, Nov. 9

547 A176 90fr Glossinidae .30 .20
548 A176 125fr Belonogaster junceus .40 .20
549 A176 300fr Aedes aegypti 1.00 .45
550 A176 350fr Mylabris 1.25 .60
Nos. 547-550 (4) 2.95 1.45

Christmas 1983 — A177

Wood Carvings, St. Michael's Church, Libreville.

Perf. 14½x13½

1983, Dec. 14 Litho.

551 A177 90fr Adultress .30 .20
552 A177 125fr Good Samaritan .40 .20

Boeing 737, No. 202 — A178

1984, Jan. 12 *Perf. 13x12½*

553 A178 125fr shown .40 .20
554 A178 225fr Lufthansa jet, Germany No. C2 .70 .40
a. Pair, #553-554 + label 1.10 .60

19th World UPU Congress, Hamburg, June 19-26.

3rd Anniv. of Africa 1 Radio Transmitter — A179

1984, Feb. 7 Litho. *Perf. 12½*

555 A179 125fr multi .40 .20

Local Flowers — A180

Various flowers.

1984, Apr. 18 Litho. *Perf. 14x15*

556 A180 90fr multi .30 .20
557 A180 125fr multi .40 .20
558 A180 135fr multi .40 .25
559 A180 350fr multi 1.25 .60
Nos. 556-559 (4) 2.35 1.25

Fruit Trees A181

1984, Mar. 1 Litho. *Perf. 14½x14*

560 A181 90fr Coconut .30 .20
561 A181 100fr Papaya .30 .20
562 A181 125fr Mango .40 .20
563 A181 250fr Banana .80 .40
Nos. 560-563 (4) 1.80 1.00

World Telecommunications Day — A182

1984, May 17 *Perf. 13x13½*

564 A182 125fr multi .40 .20

Black Jazz Musicians A183

1984, July 5 *Perf. 12½*

565 A183 90fr Lionel Hampton .30 .20
566 A183 125fr Charlie Parker .40 .20
567 A183 260fr Erroll Garner .80 .40
Nos. 565-567 (3) 1.50 .80

View of Medouneu — A184

1984, Sept. 1 Litho. *Perf. 13*

568 A184 90fr shown .30 .20
569 A184 125fr Canoes, Ogooue River .40 .20
570 A184 165fr Railroad .55 .25
Nos. 568-570 (3) 1.25 .65

15th World UPU Day — A185

1984, Oct. 9 Litho. *Perf. 13½*

571 A185 125fr UPU emblem, globe, mail .40 .20

40th Anniv., International Civil Aviation Organization — A186

1984, Dec. 1 Litho. *Perf. 13½*

572 A186 125fr Icarus .35 .20

Masks — A186a

1984, Oct. 30 Litho. *Perf. 14x15*

572A A186a 90fr Kouele
572D A186a 250fr Kota du Sud

The editors would like to examine the 125fr and 150fr stamps of this set.

Christmas — A187

1984, Dec. 14 Litho. *Perf. 12½*

573 A187 90fr St. Michael's Church Libreville .25 .20
574 A187 125fr St. Michael's, diff. .35 .20
a. Pair, #573-574 .60 .35

World Leprosy Day — A188

1985, Jan. 27 Litho. *Perf. 12½*

575 A188 125fr Hospital, Libreville .35 .20

International Youth Year — A189

1985, Feb. 6 Litho. *Perf. 13x12½*

576 A189 125fr Silhouttes, wreath .35 .20

Birds A190

1984 Litho. *Perf. 15x14*

577 A190 90fr Crowned crane .25 .20
578 A190 125fr Hummingbird .35 .20
579 A190 150fr Toucan .40 .20
Nos. 577-579 (3) 1.00 .60

Silhouettes, Emblem — A191

1985, Mar. 20 *Perf. 12½*

580 A191 125fr brt ultra, red & bl .35 .20

Cultural and Technical Cooperation Agency, 15th anniv.

Wildlife A192

1985, Apr. 17 *Perf. 15x14*

581 A192 90fr Aulacode .25 .20
582 A192 100fr Porcupine .25 .20
583 A192 125fr Giant pangolin .35 .20
584 A192 350fr Antelope .90 .40
a. Souvenir sheet of 4, #581-584 1.90 .90
Nos. 581-584 (4) 1.75 1.00

Georges Damas Aleka, Composer A193

1985, Apr. 30 *Perf. 13*

585 A193 90fr Portrait, La Concorde score .25 .20

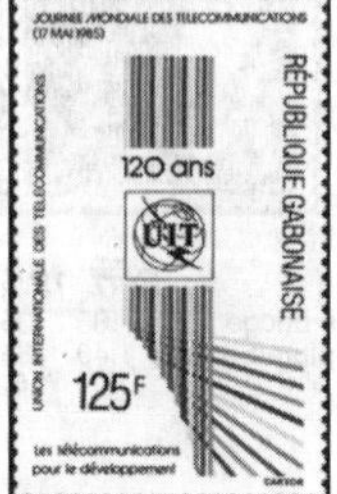

A194

A195

1985, May 17 *Perf. 13½*
586 A194 125fr multi .35 .20

World Telecommunications Day. ITU, 120th anniv.

1985, June 9
587 A195 90fr Emblem .25 .20

J.O.C., 30th anniv.

Merchant Navy Ships Type of 1982

1985, July 1 *Perf. 15x14*
588 A156 185fr Freighter Mpassa .55 .25

Posts and Telecommunications Administration, 20th Anniv. — A196

1985, July 25 *Perf. 13*
589 A196 90fr Headquarters .25 .20

President Bongo — A197

1985, Aug. 17 *Perf. 14*
590 A197 250fr multi .70 .40
591 A197 500fr multi 1.50 .80
a. Pair, #590-591 + 3 labels 2.25 1.50

Imperf

Size: 120x90mm

592 A197 1000fr View of Libreville 3.00 1.50
Nos. 590-592 (3) 5.20 2.70

Natl. Independence, 25th anniv.
No. 592 has non-denominated vignettes of Nos. 590-591.

Org. of Petroleum Exporting Countries, 25th Anniv. — A198

1985, Sept. 25 *Perf. 13½*
593 A198 350fr multi 1.00 .50

Intl. Center of the Bantu Civilizations — A199

1985, Nov. 16 **Litho.** *Perf. 15x14*
594 A199 185fr multi .60 .30

St. Andrew's Church, Libreville — A199a

Design: 125fr, Church interior, horiz.

Perf. 14x15, 15x14

1985, Dec. **Litho.**
594A A199a 90fr multicolored
594B A199a 125fr multicolored

Christmas.

UNESCO, 25th Anniv. — A200

1986, Jan. 5 **Litho.** *Perf. 12½*
595 A200 100fr multi .50 .25

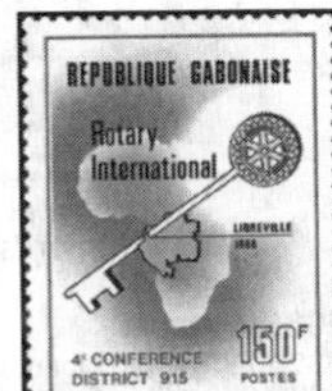
A201

1986, May 1 **Litho.** *Perf. 13½*
596 A201 150fr multi .80 .40

Rotary Intl. District 915, 4th conf.

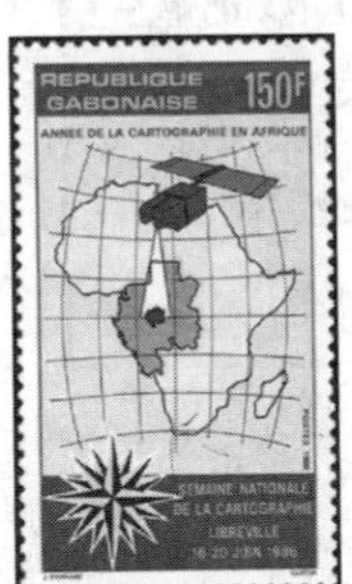
A202

1986, June 16 **Litho.** *Perf. 12½*
597 A202 150fr multi .80 .40

Natl. Week of Cartography, Libreville, June 16-20.

Coffee Flowers, Berries, Beans — A203

1986, Aug. 27 **Litho.** *Perf. 12½*
598 A203 125fr multi .75 .35

Organization of African and Madagascar Coffee Producers, 25th anniv.

Merchant Navy Ships Type of 1982

1986, June 24 **Litho.** *Perf. 15x14*
599 A156 250fr Merchantman L'Abanga 1.40 .70

Natl. Postage Stamp, Cent. — A205

1986, July 10 *Perf. 13½x14½*
600 A205 500fr Boats, No. 4 3.00 1.50

Flowering Plants — A206

1986, July 23 *Perf. 14½x15*
601 A206 100fr Allamanda nerifolia .60 .30
602 A206 150fr Musa cultivar .90 .45
603 A206 160fr Dissotis decumbens .95 .50
604 A206 350fr Campylospermum laeve 2.25 1.10
Nos. 601-604 (4) 4.70 2.35

Butterflies A207

1986, Sept. 18 **Litho.** *Perf. 15x14*
605 A207 150fr Machaon .80 .40
606 A207 290fr Urania 1.60 .80

St. Pierre Church, Libreville A208

1986, Dec. 23 **Litho.** *Perf. 15x14½*
607 A208 500fr multi 2.75 1.40

Christmas.

Trans-Gabon Railway from Owendo to Franceville, Inauguration — A209

1986, Dec. 30 *Perf. 13*
608 A209 90fr multi .50 .25

Souvenir Sheet

609 A209 250fr multi 1.40 .70

Traditional Hairstyles Type of 1981

1986 **Litho.** *Perf. 14x15*
609A A152 100fr black, gray & yellow
609B A152 150fr tan, black & red brown 1.00 .50

Fish A210

1987, Jan. 15 *Perf. 15x14½*
610 A210 90fr Adioryx bastatus .50 .25
611 A210 125fr Scarus boefleri .65 .30
612 A210 225fr Cephalacanthus volitans 1.25 .60
613 A210 350fr Dasyatis marmorata 2.00 .95
a. Souv. sheet of 4, Nos. 610-613 5.75 2.90
Nos. 610-613 (4) 4.40 2.10

No. 613a issued Oct. 1987.

Raoul Follereau (1903-1977) A211

1987, Jan. 23 *Perf. 12½*
614 A211 125fr multi .70 .35

World Leprosy Day.

Pres. Bongo Accepting the 1986 Dag Hammarskjold Peace Prize — A212

1987, Mar. 31 **Litho.** *Perf. 13*
615 A212 125fr multi .70 .35

World Telecommunications Day — A213

1987, May 17 **Litho.** *Perf. 13½*
616 A213 90fr multi .50 .25

Lions Club of Gabon, 30th Anniv. — A214

1987, July 18 **Litho.** *Perf. 12x12½*
617 A214 90fr multi .50 .25

Pierre de Coubertin, Father of the Modern Olympics A215

1987, Aug. 29
618 A215 200fr multi 1.10 .55

Lions Club Intl., 70th Anniv. — A216

1987, Oct. 1
619 A216 165fr multi .90 .45

World Post Day — A217

1987, Oct. 9 Litho. *Perf. 13½*
620 A217 125fr multi .85 .40

Seashells A218

1987, Oct. *Perf. 15x14*
621 A218 90fr Natica fanel .60 .30
622 A218 125fr Natica fulminea cruentata .85 .40
a. Souv. sheet of 2, Nos. 621-622 1.50 .75

Intl. Year of Shelter for the Homeless — A219

1987, Oct. 5 *Perf. 12½*
623 A219 90fr multi .65 .30

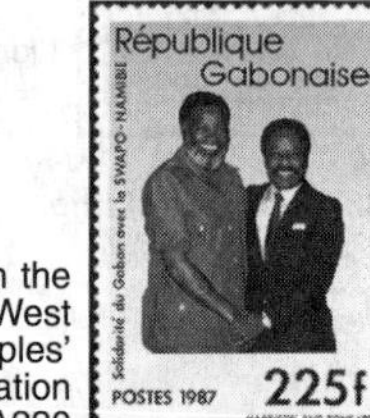

Solidarity with the South West African Peoples' Organization (SWAPO) — A220

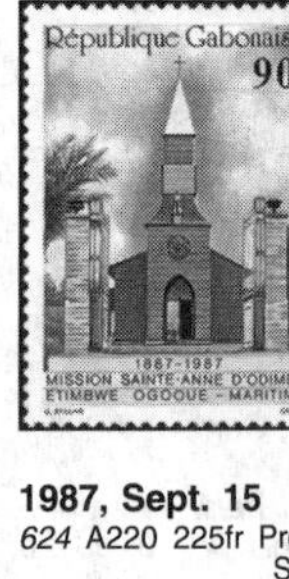

St. Anna of Odimba Mission — A221

1987, Sept. 15 Litho. *Perf. 14½x15*
624 A220 225fr Pres. Bongo, SWAPO leader 1.60 .80

1987, Nov. 2 *Perf. 13½*
625 A221 90fr multi .65 .30

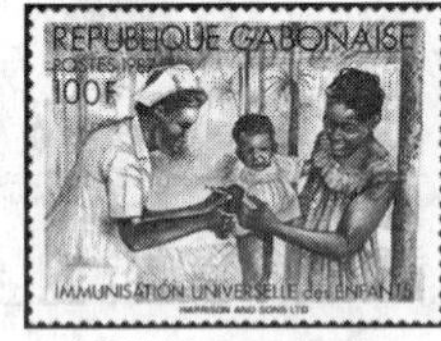

Universal Child Immunization — A222

1987, Nov. 16 *Perf. 15x14½*
626 A222 100fr multi .70 .35

20th Anniv. of the Presidency of Omar Bongo A223

1987, Dec. 2 *Perf. 14½x13½*
627 A223 1000fr multi 7.25 3.50

Christmas A224

1987, Dec. 15 *Perf. 15x14½*
628 A224 90fr St. Therese Church, Oyem .65 .30

1988 Winter Olympics, Calgary — A225

1987, Dec. 30 *Perf. 13½x14½*
629 A225 125fr multi .90 .45

Medicinal Plants — A226

1988, Jan. 26 Litho. *Perf. 14x15*
630 A226 90fr Cassia occidentalis .65 .30
631 A226 125fr Tabernanthe iboga .90 .45
632 A226 225fr Cassia alata 1.60 .80
633 A226 350fr Anthocleista schweinfurthii 2.50 1.25
a. Miniature sheet of 4, #630-633 5.75 2.75
Nos. 630-633 (4) 5.65 2.80

World Wildlife Fund — A227

African forest elephant, *Loxodonta africana cyclotis.*

1988, Feb. 29 Litho. *Perf. 13½*
634 A227 25fr multi 1.60 .25
635 A227 40fr multi, diff. 2.40 .40
636 A227 50fr multi, diff. 4.00 .45
637 A227 100fr multi, diff. 6.50 .90
Nos. 634-637 (4) 14.50 2.00

Traditional Musical Instruments — A228

1988, Feb. 17 *Perf. 14*
638 A228 90fr Obamba hochet .85 .40
639 A228 100fr Fang sanza, vert. .95 .50
640 A228 125fr Mitsogho harp, vert. 1.25 .60
641 A228 165fr Fang xylophone 1.50 .80
a. Souv. sheet of 4, Nos. 638-641 4.50 2.25
Nos. 638-641 (4) 4.55 2.30

World Cup Rugby — A229

Perf. 13½x14½
1987, June 10 Litho.
642 A229 350fr multi 2.50 1.25

Delta Post Office Inauguration — A230

1988, Mar. 9
643 A230 90fr multi .60 .30

World Telecommunications Day — A231

1988, May 17 *Perf. 13½*
644 A231 125fr multi .85 .40

Storming of the Bastille, July 14, 1789 — A232

1988, May 30 Litho. *Perf. 13*
645 A232 125fr multi .85 .40

PHILEXFRANCE '89.

Intl. Fund for Agricultural Development (IFAD), 10th Anniv. — A233

1988, June 20 *Perf. 13½*
646 A233 350fr multi 2.40 1.25

Intl. Red Cross and Red Crescent Organizations, 125th Annivs. — A234

1988, July 15 Litho. *Perf. 12½*
647 A234 125fr multi .80 .40

1988 Summer Olympics, Seoul A235

1988, Sept. 17 Litho. *Perf. 15x14*
648 A235 90fr Tennis .60 .30
649 A235 100fr Swimming .70 .35
650 A235 350fr Running 2.40 1.10
651 A235 500fr Hurdles 3.25 1.60
a. Souv. sheet of 4, #648-651 7.00 3.50
Nos. 648-651 (4) 6.95 3.35

World Post Day A236

1988, Oct. 9 *Perf. 13½*
652 A236 125fr blk, brt yel & brt blue .85 .40

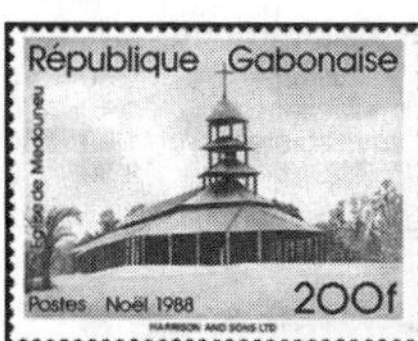

Christmas
A237

1988, Dec. 20 Litho. *Perf. 15x14*

653 A237 200fr Medouneu Church 1.25 .65

Natica Fanel
A237a

1988 Litho. *Perf. 15x14*

653A A237a 90fr shown
653B A237a 125fr Natica sp.
c. Souv. sheet of 2, #653A-653B

A238

A239

1989, Feb. 21 *Perf. 13½*

654 A238 175fr multi 1.10 .60

Chaine des Rotisseurs in Gabon, 10th anniv.

1989, Mar. 6 Litho. *Perf. 13½*

655 A239 125fr multi .75 .40

Rabi Kounga oil field. See No. 707.

Traditional Games — A240

Perf. 13½x14½

1989, Mar. 20 Litho.

656 A240 90fr multicolored .60 .30

Birds — A241

1989, Apr. 17 Litho. *Perf. 14x15*

657 A241 100fr White-tufted bittern .60 .30
658 A241 175fr Gabon gray parakeet 1.10 .50
659 A241 200fr Pygmy hornbill 1.25 .60
660 A241 500fr Pope's martin 3.00 1.50
a. Souv. sheet of 4, Nos. 657-660 5.75 3.00
Nos. 657-660 (4) 5.95 2.90

See Nos. 750-753.

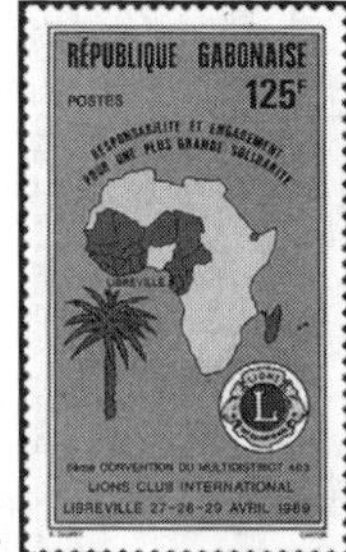

A242

1989, Apr. 27 *Perf. 13*

661 A242 125fr multi .75 .40

8th Convention of Lions Intl. District 403, Libreville, Apr. 27-29.

World Telecommunications Day — A243

1989, May 17 *Perf. 13½*

662 A243 300fr multi 1.75 .90

PHILEXFRANCE '89 — A244

Symbols of the French revolution, 1789.

Wmk. 385

1989, July 7 Litho. *Perf. 13*

663 A244 175fr multi 1.10 .60

French Revolution, Bicent. — A245

1989, July 14

664 A245 500fr multi 3.25 1.60

Fruit — A246

Perf. 14½x15

1989, May 30 Litho. Unwmk.

665 A246 90fr Coconuts .65 .30
666 A246 125fr Cabosse .85 .40
667 A246 175fr Pineapple 1.25 .60
668 A246 250fr Breadfruit 1.75 .90
a. Souv. sheet of 4, #665-668 4.50 2.25
Nos. 665-668 (4) 4.50 2.20

AIMF, 10th Anniv. — A247

1989, July 27 Litho. *Perf. 13*

669 A247 100fr multi .65 .30

African Development Bank, 25th Anniv. — A248

1989, Aug. 2 Litho. *Perf. 13*

670 A248 100fr multi .60 .30

Apples and Oranges, by Cezanne (1839-1906) — A249

Perf. 13½x14½

1989, June 22 Litho.

671 A249 500fr multicolored 3.25 1.60

1990 World Cup Soccer Championships, Italy — A250

Various athletes.

Perf. 15x14½

1989, Aug. 23 Litho. Unwmk.

672 A250 100fr shown .65 .35
673 A250 175fr multi, diff. 1.25 .60
674 A250 300fr multi, diff. 2.10 1.10
675 A250 500fr multi, diff. 3.50 1.75
a. Souv. sheet of 4, #672-675 7.50 3.75
Nos. 672-675 (4) 7.50 3.80

Traditional Hair Style Type of 1981

1989, Sept. 16 *Perf. 14½x15*

676 A152 175fr gray, black & vio 1.25 .60

Post Day — A252

1989, Sept. 10 Litho. *Perf. 12*

Granite Paper

677 A252 175fr multicolored 1.40 .70

Postal Service, 125th Anniv. (in 1987) — A255

Perf. 13½x14½

1989 Litho. Unwmk.

681 A255 90fr multicolored .65 .30

Dated 1988.

St. Louis Church, Port Gentil
A256

1989, Dec. 15 Litho. *Perf. 15x14*

682 A256 100fr multicolored .80 .40

Christmas. See Nos. 725-726, 757.

L'Ogooue', N'Gomo
A256a

1989 Litho. *Perf. 15x14*

682A A256a 100fr multicolored

Libreville Coat of Arms — A257

Wmk. 385

1990, Mar. 12 Litho. *Perf. 13½*

683 A257 100fr multicolored .80 .40

World Health Day — A258

1990, Apr. 7 Litho. *Perf. 13*

684 A258 400fr multicolored 3.25 1.60

Souvenir Sheet

Prehistoric Tools
A259

1990, Feb. 14 Litho. *Perf. 15x14*

685 Sheet of 4 7.00 3.50
a. A259 100fr Hand axe .70 .40
b. A259 175fr Knife blade 1.25 .65
c. A259 300fr Arrowhead 2.10 1.10
d. A259 400fr Double bladed hand axe 2.75 1.50

See Nos. 727-730.

Souvenir Sheet

Fauna — A260

Illustration reduced.

1990, Apr. 13 *Perf. 14*
686 A260 Sheet of 4 8.50 4.25
a. 100fr Cercopitheque .90 .45
b. 175fr Potamocherus Porcus 1.55 .75
c. 200fr Antelope 1.75 .85
d. 500fr Mandrill 4.50 2.25

First Postage Stamps, 150th Anniv. — A261

1991, Jan. 9 Litho. *Perf. 13½x14½*
687 A261 500fr multicolored 4.50 2.25

Independence, 30th Anniv. — A263

1990, Aug. 17 Litho. *Perf. 13*
693 A263 100fr multicolored .90 .45

Mushrooms — A263a

Various mushrooms.

1990 Litho. *Perf. 15x14*
693A A263a 100fr multicolored
693B A263a 175fr multicolored
693C A263a 300fr multicolored
693D A263a 500fr multicolored

Organization of Petroleum Exporting Countries (OPEC), 30th anniv. — A264

1990, Sept. 19 Litho. *Perf. 13*
694 A264 200fr multicolored 1.75 .90

1990 World Cup Soccer Championships, Italy — A264a

1990, June 8 Litho. *Perf. 15x14*
694A A264a 100fr Goalie making save
694B A264a 175fr multicolored
694D A264a 500fr Player celebrating

A 300fr stamp exists with the set.

A265

1990, Oct. 9 *Perf. 13½*
695 A265 175fr blue, yel & blk 1.60 .80

World Post Day.

Traditional Bwiti Dancer A265a

1990 Litho. *Perf. 15x14*
695A A265a 100fr Ndjembe dancers
695B A265a 175fr shown

Flowers A266

1991, Jan. 9 Litho. *Perf. 15x14*
696 A266 100fr Frangipanier .90 .45
697 A266 175fr Boule de feu 1.50 .75
698 A266 200fr Flamboyant 1.75 .85
699 A266 300fr Rose de porcelaine 2.75 1.25
a. Souvenir sheet of 4, #696-699 7.00 3.50
Nos. 696-699 (4) 6.90 3.30

Petroglyphs — A267

1991, Feb. 26 Litho. *Perf. 15x14*
700 A267 100fr Lizard figure .90 .45
701 A267 175fr Triangular figure 1.50 .75
702 A267 300fr Incused lines 2.75 1.25
703 A267 500fr Concentric circles, circles in lines 4.50 2.25
a. Souvenir sheet of 4, #700-703 9.50 4.75
Nos. 700-703 (4) 9.65 4.70

Rubber Trees — A268

1991, Mar. 20 Litho. *Perf. 14x15*
705 A268 100fr multicolored .90 .45

World Telecommunications Day — A269

1991, May 17 Litho. *Perf. 13½*
706 A269 175fr multicolored 1.40 .70

Rabi Kounga Oil Field Type of 1989

1991 Litho. *Perf. 13½*
707 A239 175fr multicolored

Ngounie Women Washing Clothes A271

1991, July 17 Litho. *Perf. 13½*
708 A271 100fr multicolored .90 .45

A272

A273

Designs: Craftsmen.

1991, June 19 *Perf. 14x15*
709 A272 100fr Basket maker .90 .45
710 A272 175fr Wood carver 1.50 .75
711 A272 200fr Weaver 1.75 .90
712 A272 500fr Thatch maker 4.50 2.25
Nos. 709-712 (4) 8.65 4.35

1991, Aug. 18 Litho. *Perf. 14x15*

Gabonese Medals: 100fr, Equatorial Knight's Star. 175fr, Equatorial Officer's Star. 200fr, Equatorial Commander's Star.

Gray Background
713 A273 100fr multicolored .80 .40
714 A273 175fr multicolored 1.40 .70
715 A273 200fr multicolored 1.60 .80
Nos. 713-715 (3) 3.80 1.90

See Nos. 735-737.

Fishing in Gabon A274

1991, Sept. 18 *Perf. 15x14*
716 A274 100fr Bow-net fishing .80 .40
717 A274 175fr Trammel fishing 1.40 .70
718 A274 200fr Net fishing 1.60 .80
719 A274 300fr Seine fishing 2.40 1.25
a. Souvenir sheet of 4, #716-719 6.25 3.00
Nos. 716-719 (4) 6.20 3.15

World Post Day — A275

Termite Mounds — A276

1991, Oct. 9 *Perf. 13½*
720 A275 175fr blue & multi 1.40 .70

See Nos. 749, 786.

1991, Nov. 6 *Perf. 14x15*
721 A276 100fr Phallic .80 .40
722 A276 175fr Cathedral 1.40 .70
723 A276 200fr Mushroom 1.60 .80
724 A276 300fr Arboreal 2.40 1.25
Nos. 721-724 (4) 6.20 3.15

Church Type of 1989

1991, Dec. 18 Litho. *Perf. 15x14*
725 A256 100fr Church of Makokou .80 .40
726 A256 100fr Church of Dibwangui .80 .40

Christmas. No. 725 inscribed 1990.

Prehistoric Tools Type of 1990

Pottery: 100fr, Neolithic pot. 175fr, Bottle, 8th cent. 200fr, Vase, 8th cent. 300fr, Vase, 8th cent, diff.

1992, Jan. 9 Litho. *Perf. 14x15*
727 A259 100fr multi, vert. .80 .40
728 A259 175fr multi, vert. 1.40 .70
729 A259 200fr multi, vert. 1.60 .80
730 A259 300fr multi, vert. 2.40 1.25
a. Sheet of 4, #727-730 6.25 3.00
Nos. 727-730 (4) 6.20 3.15

Occupations A277

1992, Feb. 5
731 A277 100fr Basket maker .80 .40
732 A277 175fr Blacksmith 1.40 .70
733 A277 200fr Boat builder 1.60 .80

734 A277 300fr Hairdresser 2.40 1.25
  a. Souvenir sheet of 4, #731-734 6.25 3.00
  Nos. 731-734 (4) 6.20 3.15

No. 734a issued Feb. 9.

Gabonese Medals Type of 1991

Designs: 100fr, Equatorial Grand Officer's Star. 175fr, Grand Cross of Dignity and Equatorial Star. 200fr, Order of Merit.

1992, Mar. 18 Litho. *Perf. 14x15*
Aquamarine Background

735 A273 100fr multicolored .75 .40
736 A273 175fr multicolored 1.50 .70
737 A273 200fr multicolored 1.75 .80
  Nos. 735-737 (3) 4.00 1.90

A278

A279

1992, Apr. 19 *Perf. 13*
738 A278 500fr multicolored 4.25 2.10

Konrad Adenauer (1876-1967), German Statesman.

1992, May 17 *Perf. 13½*
739 A279 175fr multicolored 1.50 .75

World Telecommunications Day.

Butterflies A280

1992, June 10 Litho. *Perf. 15x14*
740 A280 100fr Graphium policenes .90 .45
741 A280 175fr Acraea egina 1.60 .80

A281

A282

1992, July 25 *Perf. 14x15*
742 A281 100fr Cycling .90 .45
743 A281 175fr Boxing 1.60 .80
744 A281 200fr Pole vault 1.75 .90
  Nos. 742-744 (3) 4.25 2.15

1992 Summer Olympics, Barcelona.

1992, Sept. 16 Litho. *Perf. 14x15*

Tribal masks.

745 A282 100fr Fang .90 .45
746 A282 175fr Mpongwe 1.60 .80
747 A282 200fr Kwele 1.75 .90
748 A282 300fr Pounou 2.75 1.40
  a. Souvenir sheet of 4, #745-748 7.00 3.50
  Nos. 745-748 (4) 7.00 3.55

World Post Day Type of 1991 Inscribed 1992

1992, Oct. 9 Litho. *Perf. 13½*
749 A275 175fr bl grn & multi 1.50 .75

Bird Type of 1989

1992, Nov. 4 Litho. *Perf. 14x15*
750 A241 100fr African owl .85 .40
751 A241 175fr Coliou strie 1.50 .75
752 A241 200fr Vulture 1.60 .85
753 A241 300fr Giant kingfisher 2.50 1.25
  a. Souvenir sheet of 4, #750-753 6.50 3.25
  Nos. 750-753 (4) 6.45 3.25

Cattle A283

Various scenes of cattle in pasture.

1992, Dec. 10 *Perf. 15x14*
754 A283 100fr multicolored .80 .40
755 A283 175fr multicolored 1.40 .70
756 A283 200fr multicolored 1.60 .80
  Nos. 754-756 (3) 3.80 1.90

Church Type of 1989

1992, Dec. 16
757 A256 100fr Tchibanga Church .80 .40

Christmas.

Intl. Conference on Nutrition, Rome — A284

1992, Dec. 20 *Perf. 13½*
758 A284 100fr multicolored .80 .40

Shells A285

1993, Jan. 6 Litho. *Perf. 15x14*
759 A285 100fr Pugilina .80 .40
760 A285 175fr Conus pulcher 1.40 .70
761 A285 200fr Fusinus 1.60 .80
762 A285 300fr Cymatium 2.40 1.25
  a. Souvenir sheet, #759-762 13.00 6.50
  Nos. 759-762 (4) 6.20 3.15

World Leprosy Day A286

1993, Jan. 28 *Perf. 13½*
763 A286 175fr multicolored 1.40 .70

Fernan-Vaz Mission A287

1993, Feb. 3 *Perf. 15x14*
764 A287 175fr multicolored 1.40 .70

Chappe's Semaphore Telegraph, Bicent. — A288

Designs: 100fr, Claude Chappe (1763-1805), engineer and inventor. 175fr, Chappe's signaling device and code. 200fr, Emile Baudot (1845-1903), devising telegraph code, early telegraph equipment. 300fr, Modern satellite, electronic chip and fiber optics.

1993, Mar. 10 Litho. *Perf. 13½*
765 A288 100fr multicolored .85 .40
766 A288 175fr multicolored 1.40 .70
767 A288 200fr multicolored 1.60 .85
768 A288 300fr multicolored 2.50 1.25
  a. Souvenir sheet of 4, #765-768 6.50 3.25
  Nos. 765-768 (4) 6.35 3.20

Albert Schweitzer's Arrival in Lambarene, 80th Anniv. — A289

1993, Apr. 6 Litho. *Perf. 13*
769 A289 500fr multicolored 4.75 2.25
  a. Booklet pane of 1 4.75

Booklet Stamps
Size: 26x37mm
Perf. 13½

770 A289 250fr Feeding chickens 2.25 1.10
  a. Booklet pane of 4 9.00
771 A289 250fr Holding babies 2.25 1.10
  a. Booklet pane of 4 9.00
  Nos. 769-771 (3) 9.25 4.45

Booklet containing one of each pane sold for 3000fr.

Nicolaus Copernicus, Heliocentric Solar System A290

1993, May 5 Litho. *Perf. 15x14*
772 A290 175fr multicolored 1.40 .70

Polska '93.

A291

A292

1993, May 17 *Perf. 13½*
773 A291 175fr multicolored 1.40 .70

World Telecommunications Day.

1993, June 9 Litho. *Perf. 14*

Traditional Wine Making: 100fr, Still. 175fr, Extracting juice from palm roots. 200fr, Man in palm tree.

774 A292 100fr multicolored .85 .40
775 A292 175fr multicolored 1.40 .70
776 A292 200fr multicolored 1.60 .80
  a. Souvenir sheet of 3, #774-776 4.00 2.00
  Nos. 774-776 (3) 3.85 1.90

Crustaceans — A293

1993, July 21 Litho. *Perf. 15x14*
777 A293 100fr Spiny lobster .75 .40
778 A293 175fr Violin crab 1.25 .65
779 A293 200fr Crayfish 1.50 .75
780 A293 300fr Spider crab 2.25 1.10
  Nos. 777-780 (4) 5.75 2.90

Paris '94 — A294

1993, Aug. 10 Litho. *Perf. 13*
781 A294 100fr multicolored .85 .40

Animal Traps A295

1993, Sept. 15 Litho. *Perf. 15x14*
782 A295 100fr Squirrel .40 .20
783 A295 175fr Small game .70 .35
784 A295 200fr Large game .80 .40
785 A295 300fr Palm rat 1.25 .60
  a. Souvenir sheet of 4, #782-785 3.25 1.75
  Nos. 782-785 (4) 3.15 1.55

World Post Day Type of 1991 Inscribed 1993

1993, Oct. 9 *Perf. 13½*
786 A275 175fr yellow & multi .70 .35

Making Bamboo Toys — A296

1993, Oct. 20 *Perf. 11½*
787 A296 100fr multicolored .40 .20

Tourism A297

1993, Nov. 16

788 A297 100fr Leconi Canyon .40 .20
789 A297 175fr La Lope Valley .70 .35

Christmas A298

1993, Dec. 20 ***Perf. 15x14***

790 A298 100fr Catholic Mission, Mandji .40 .20

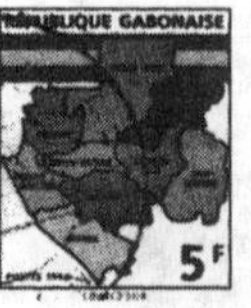

Provincial Map — A299

1994 **Litho.** ***Perf. 14½***

791 A299 5fr yellow & multi
792 A299 10fr multicolored
793 A299 25fr multi
795 A299 75fr violet & multi
796 A299 100fr pink & multi
797 A299 175fr blue & multi

Issued: 5fr, 75fr, 100fr, 1/28/94.

Numbers have been reserved for 2 additional values in this set released between 1993 and 1994. The editors would like to examine the other stamps.

Vision of Gabon's Future — A300

1994, Oct. 5 **Litho.** ***Perf. 14½***

798 A300 500fr multicolored *3.00 1.50*

1994 World Cup Soccer Championships, US — A301

Designs: a, 100fr, Hands on soccer ball. b, 175fr, Two players, ball in air. c, 200fr, Legs of players. d, 300fr, Player, ball.

1994, Apr. 5 ***Perf. 15x14***

799 A301 Sheet of 4, #a.-d. *6.00 3.00*

Miniature Sheets of 12

Prehistoric Wildlife — A302

No. 800: a, Sordes. b, Diplodocus (d-e, g-h). c, Eudimorphodon (b). d, Dimetrodon (a). e, Anuroenathus. f, Deinonychus, pachycephalosaurus (e). g, Triceratops (j). h, Hadrosaur (i, k-l). i, Genus Meganeura. j, Longisquama. k, Oviraptor. l, Monoclonius.

No. 801: a, Pistosaurus (d-e, h). b, Pteranodon (c). c, Coelophysis. d, Xenacanthus (g). e, Ischyodus (f, h-i). f, Placochelys. g, Dunkleosteus (j). h, Cymbospondylus (i). i, Enchodus. j, Paracybeloides (k). k, Nautiliod (h). l, Palaeospondylus.

No. 802: a, Tyrannosaurus rex (d). b, Apatosaurus (a, d-e). c, Dimorphodon. d, Stegasaurus (a, e). e, Archaeopteryx. f, Protoceratops. g, Ichthyosaur. h, Phobosuchus, deltoptychius. i, Parasaurolophus (f). j, Scapanorhynchus (g). k, Spathobathis, plesiosaurus (j, l). l, Cladoselacho.

1995, Sept. 4 **Litho.** ***Perf. 14***

800 A302 125fr #a.-l. 6.50 3.25
801 A302 225fr #a.-l. 11.00 5.50
802 A302 260fr #a.-l. 12.50 6.25
Nos. 800-802 (3) 30.00 15.00

Singapore '95 (#800).

Miniature Sheets

Nobel Prize Fund Established, Cent. — A303

Recipients: No. 803a, Walter H. Brattain, physics, 1956. b, Carl F. Cori, medicine, 1947. c, Gerty T. Cori, medicine, 1947. d, Owen Chamberlain, physics, 1959. e, Christian Anfinsen, chemistry, 1972. f, George de Hevesy, chemistry, 1943. g, Kenichi Fukui, chemistry, 1981. h, Elie Wiesel, peace, 1986. i, Carl F. Braun, physics, 1909.

No. 804: a, Georg Wittig, chemistry, 1979. b, Charles Dawes, peace, 1925. c, Frederic Mistral, literature, 1904. d, Juan Jimenez, literature, 1956. e, Michael S. Brown, medicine, 1985. f, Guglielmo Marconi, physics, 1909. g, Werner Forssmann, medicine, 1956. h, Francis W. Aston, chemistry, 1922. i, Martin Ryle, physics, 1974.

No. 805: a, Leon Jouhaux, peace, 1951. b, Rudolf L. Mossbauer, physics, 1961. c, George Seferis, literature, 1963. d, James Chadwick, physics, 1935. e, Aung San Suu Kyi, peace, 1991. f, John H. Nothrop, chemistry, 1946. g, Eduard Buchner, chemistry, 1907. h, Hans A. Bethe, physics, 1967. i, Nils Dalen, physics, 1912.

No. 806, Hermann Hesse, literature, 1946. No. 807, Albert Schweitzer, peace, 1952. No. 808, Nelson Mandela, peace, 1993.

1995, Oct. 18 **Litho.** ***Perf. 14***

Sheets of 9

803 A303 125fr #a.-i. 4.50 2.25
804 A303 225fr #a.-i. 8.00 4.00
805 A303 260fr #a.-i. 9.50 4.75
Nos. 803-805 (3) 22.00 11.00

Souvenir Sheets

806-808 A303 1500fr each 6.00 3.00

Monseigneur Bessieux (1803-76), Evangelist A306

1995, Dec. 25 **Litho.** ***Perf. 13***

811 A306 500fr multicolored 2.75 1.40

Miniature Sheet of 8

A307

World War II, 50th Anniv. A308

Designs: a, German generals planning attack. b, Afrika Korps troops ride tanks into El Agheila. c, German artillary fires on British positions in Tobruk. d, British soldiers surrender. e, British soldiers break siege of Tobruk. f, Allies advancing though barbed wire, El Alamein. g, German tanks retreat to Tunis. h, German tank surrenders.

1996, Jan. 29 ***Perf. 14***

812 A307 125fr #a.-h. + label 5.50 2.75

1996, Jan. 26 **Litho.** ***Perf. 14***

Designs: No. 813a, Pres. Franklin D. Roosevelt. b, Pres. Harry S Truman. c, Gen. George Marshall.

1000fr, Flags of US, Great Britain, USSR.

813 A308 225fr Strip of 3, #a.-c. 3.75 1.90

Souvenir Sheet

814 A308 1000fr multicolored 5.50 2.75

No. 813 was issued in sheets of 9 stamps.

Dogs — A309

China '96: a, Dalmatian. b, Basset hound. c, Harrier. d, German Shepherd. e, Bernese bouvier. f, Pug. g, West highland white terrier. h, Akita.

1996, May 13 **Litho.** ***Perf. 14***

815 A309 125fr Sheet of 8, #a.-h. 4.00 2.00

St. Pius X Catholic Mission, 10th Anniv. A310

Mgr. Marcel Lefebvre, interior of mission.

1996, Mar. 4 ***Perf. 13½***

816 A310 100fr yellow & multi .40 .20
817 A310 125fr blue & multi .50 .25

Rotary, Intl. A311

Rotary emblem and: 125fr, UN flag. 225fr, Natl. flag of Gabon. 260fr, Rotary, Intl. flag. 1500fr, Olympic flag.

1996, July 3 **Litho.** ***Perf. 14***

818-820 A311 Set of 3 1.75 .90

Souvenir Sheet

821 A311 1500fr multicolored 6.00 3.00

Boy Scouts — A312

Designs: 125fr, Scout sign. 225fr, Constructing a lean-to. 260fr, Camping. 1500fr, Lord Baden-Powell.

1996, July 15

822-824 A312 Set of 3 2.40 1.25

Souvenir Sheet

825 A312 1500fr multicolored 5.00 2.50

Cercopithecus Solatus — A313

1996, Mar. 6 ***Perf. 13½x13***

826 A313 500fr multicolored 2.00 1.00

Fight Against AIDS — A314

Shells — A315

1996, Apr. 3 ***Perf. 13½x13***

827 A314 500fr multicolored 2.00 1.00

1996 ***Perf. 13½x13, 13x13½***

Designs: 100fr, Fusinus caparti. 260fr, Hexaplex rosarium. 500fr, Conus pulcher, horiz.

828-830 A315 Set of 3 3.50 1.75

1996 Summer Olympic Games, Atlanta A316

1996, May 8 ***Perf. 11½***

831 A316 225fr Boxing .75 .40
832 A316 500fr Relay race 1.75 .90

Campaign Against Use of Illegal Drugs A317

1996, Aug. 6 **Litho.** ***Perf. 11½***

833 A317 500fr multicolored 2.00 1.00

Contemporary Paintings, by H. Moundounga A318

1996, Sept. 10

834 A318 100fr Girl .40 .20
835 A318 125fr Three faces .50 .25
836 A318 225fr Eyes .90 .45
a. Souvenir Sheet, #834-836 1.75 .90
Nos. 834-836 (3) 1.80 .90

China '96 — A319

Temple in winter. Illustration reduced.

1996, May 13 Litho. *Perf. 14*

837 A319 500fr multicolored 2.00 1.00

No. 837 was not available until March 1997.

Environmental Protection — A320

Endangered species: 100fr, Galago alleni, vert. 125fr, Perodicticus potto. 225fr, Orycteropus afer. 260fr, Manis gigantea.

1996, June 5 *Perf. 13½*

838-841 A320 Set of 4 2.75 1.40

Children's Paintings A321

Designs: 100fr, Woman's arms encircling world, vert. 125fr, People forming circle around animals. 225fr, Slaughtering of elephants, vert.

1996, Dec. 25 Litho. *Perf. 11½*

842-844 A321 Set of 3 1.75 .90

Dated 1996.

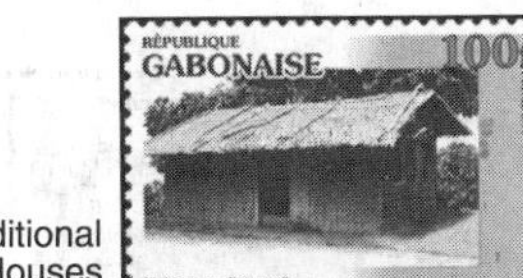

Traditional Houses A322

100fr, Mud & stick cabin. 125fr, Pygmy hut. 225fr, Bark-sided cabins. 260fr, Wood-sided cabins.

1996, Nov. 6

845-848 A322 Set of 4 2.75 1.40
a. Souvenir sheet, #845-848 2.75 1.40

A323

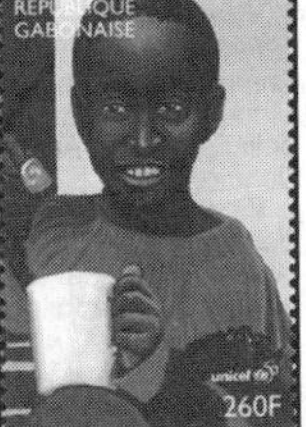

A324

1996, Oct. 10

849 A323 500fr multicolored 2.00 1.00

Investiture of Pres. Nelson Mandela, 3rd anniv.

1997, Apr. 9 Litho. *Perf. 14*

UNICEF, 50th Anniv.: No. 850: a, Boy holding cup. b, Girl holding cup. c, Boy eating. 1500fr, Boy holding plate.

850 A324 260fr Sheet of 3, #a.-c. 3.25 1.60

Souvenir Sheet

851 A324 1500fr multicolored 6.00 3.00

UNESCO, 50th Anniv. A325

No. 852: a, Kyoto, Japan. b, Puma, Los Katios Natl. Park, Colombia. c, Abu Simbel Monument, Egypt. d, Old Rauma, Finland. e, Rotunda, City of Vicenza, Italy. f, Homes, China. g, Port of Salvador, Brazil. h, Delos Ruins, Greece.

No. 853: a, Fasil Ghebbi Monument, Gondar Region, Ethiopia. b, Victoria Falls, Zambia. c, Zambezi Plains, Chewore Safari Areas, Zimbabwe. d, Nature Reserve, Niger. e, Banc D'Arguin Natl. Park, Mauritania. f, Gorée Island, Senegal. g, Djémila Ruins, Algeria. h, Mosque, Medina of Fez, Morocco.

1000fr, Terracotta warriors, Mausoleum of first Qin Emperor, China.

1997, Apr. 16

Sheets of 8 + Label

852-853 A325 225fr #a.-h., each 7.50 3.75

Souvenir Sheet

854 A325 1000fr multicolored 4.00 2.00

A326

City Arms.

1997, Mar. 12 Litho. *Perf. 11½x12*

855 A326 100fr N'Dendé .40 .20
856 A326 125fr Libreville .50 .25
857 A326 225fr Mitzic .90 .45
Nos. 855-857 (3) 1.80 .90

A327

1997, July 1 *Perf. 14*

Return of Hong Kong to China: 125fr, Skyline. 225fr, Skyline, diff. 260fr, Skyline at night, horiz. 500fr, Skyline at night, Deng Xiaoping (1904-97), horiz.

858-861 A327 Set of 4 4.50 2.25

Nos. 858-859 were each issued in sheets of 4. Nos. 860-861 are 59x28mm and were issued in sheets of 3.

Unity, Work and Justice Type of 1981

1994-95 Litho. *Perf. 12*

862 A145 5fr green blue & black
863 A145 10fr orange & black
864 A145 25fr grey lilac & black
865 A145 50fr salmon & black
867 A145 100fr pink & black
868 A145 125fr yellow green & black
869 A145 175fr yellow & black
870 A145 225fr green & black

Perf. 12x11½

1994-95 Litho *Perf. 12*

871 A145 260fr lt blue & black

Issued: 50fr, 125fr, 9/30/95; others, 9/20/94.

A number has been reserved for an additional value in this set. The editors would like to examine it.

Paintings — A328

1995, Oct. 10 Litho. *Perf. 14*

872 A328 100fr Woman
873 A328 125fr Stylized women
873A A328 225fr Masked Face

Raponda Walker, 25th Death Anniv. — A329

Masks — A330

1995, June 7 *Perf. 13½*

874 A329 500fr multicolored

1995

875 A330 100fr Bateke
876 A330 125fr Bavili
877 A330 225fr Fang
878 A330 260fr Bandjabi

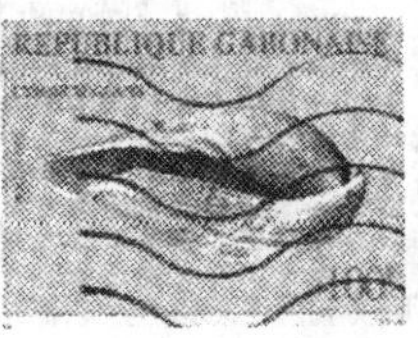

Shells A331

1995

879 A331 100fr Cymbium glans
880 A331 125fr Muricidae murey
880A A331 225fr Siliquaria — —
881 A331 260fr Strombus latus

The editors suspect that additional stamps may have been issued in this set and would like to examine any examples.

Saint-Exupery French Cultural Center — A332

1996 *Perf. 13x13½*

883 A332 100fr black & multi
884 A332 125fr blue & multi
885 A332 225fr red & multi

Inter-Continental Hotel, 50th Anniv. — A333

1996 *Perf. 13½*

886 A333 125fr creme & blue

Early Post Offices A333a

1996, July 20 Litho. *Perf. 12x11½*

886A A333a 100fr Port Gentil, 1917
886B A333a 125fr Cap-Lopez, 1888
886C A333a 225fr Libreville, 1862

Flowers, Butterflies, Moths, Insects — A334

Designs, vert: 125fr, Rubra tigridia pauonia, pieridae. 225fr, Acraeidae, strelitzia reginae. 260fr, Zautedeschia aethiopica, zonabris oculata. 500fr, Bee orchid, iron prominent moth caterpillar.

No. 891: a, Liliaceae. b, Macrophylla, phoebis philea. c, Theaceae amugashita. d, Lilium american cultivars, vanessa atalanta. e, Hybrids, hippodamia convergens. f, Sibine stimulea, iridaceae.

No. 892: a, Kalmialati. b, G. gandavensis, calopteryx maculata. c, Narcissus pseudonarcissus. d, Ipheton uniflorum, Tlemaris thysbe. e, Rudbackia hirta. f, Tritida grandiflora, danaus plexippus.

No. 893, Papilion zellicaon, geranium pelargonium, vert. No. 894, Anax jumus, gladstoniana, vert.

1997, Aug. 11 Litho. *Perf. 14*

887-890 A334 Set of 4 4.50 2.25

Sheets of 6

891-892 A334 260fr #a.-f., each 6.25 6.25

Souvenir Sheets

893-894 A334 1500fr each 6.00 6.00

Protection of Indigenous Animals — A335

100fr, Dendrohyrax arboreus. 125fr, Galago elegantulus. 225fr, Stephanoaetus coronatus.

1997, June 5 *Perf. 13½x13*

895-897 A335 Set of 3 1.50 .75
897a Souvenir sheet of 3, #895-897 1.75 .90

Gabonese Art — A336

Designs: 100fr, Droits de Creatures, vert. 125fr, Ambassadeur, vert. 225fr, Hallucinations.

1997, May 8 ***Perf. 13½x13, 13x13½***

898-900 A336 Set of 3 1.50 .75
900a Souvenir sheet of 1, #900 .80 .40

Air Gabon, 20th Anniv. A337

1997, June 1 ***Perf. 13x13½***

901 A337 125fr multicolored .45 .25
902 A337 225fr multicolored .80 .40

A338

A339

1997 **Litho.** ***Perf. 13½x13***

903 A338 225fr multicolored .75 .40

First ACP Summit, Libreville.

1997, Oct. 8 ***Perf. 13½x13***

904 A339 225fr multicolored .75 .40

Lions Club in Gabon, 40th anniv.

AIPLF, 30th Anniv. A340

1997, Oct. 30 ***Perf. 12x11½***

905 A340 260fr multicolored .90 .45

A341

1997, Nov. 11 ***Perf. 14x14½***

906 A341 500fr multicolored 1.75 .85

Paul Gondjout, 1st pres. of the natl. assembly.

A342

1997, Nov. 17 ***Perf. 11½x12***

907 A342 500fr multicolored 1.75 .85

Heinrich von Stephan (1831-97).

A343

Diana, Princess of Wales (1961-97) - #908: a, 500fr. b, 300fr. c, 260fr. d, 225fr. e, f, 125fr. No. 909, Diana in white dress.

1998, Feb. 10 **Litho.** ***Perf. 13½***

908 A343 Sheet of 6, #a.-f. 5.25 2.50

Souvenir Sheet

909 A343 3000fr multicolored 10.00 5.00

A344

1998, June 4 **Litho.** ***Perf. 13½x13***

District Arms: 100fr, Akieni. 125fr, Pana. 225fr, Lebamba.

910-912 A344 Set of 3 1.50 .75

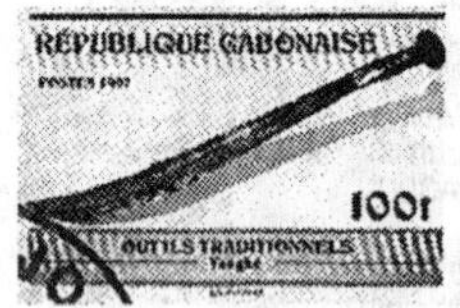

Traditional Tools A345

100fr, Yanghe. 125fr, Ikanga. 225fr, Ivedili.

1997, Nov. 5 **Litho.** ***Perf. 14***

913-915 A345 Set of 3

New Horizons Foundation A346

1998 **Litho.** ***Perf. 13x13½***

916 A346 225fr multicolored .75 .40

Protected Animals — A347

Designs: 100fr, Hippopotamus amphibius. 125fr, Sylvicapra grimmia. 225fr, Pelecanus rufescens.

1998 ***Perf. 13½x13***

917 A347 100fr multicolored .35 .20
918 A347 125fr multicolored .45 .20
919 A347 225fr multicolored .75 .40
a. Souvenir sheet, #917-919 1.60 .80

A348

A349

Various soccer plays, country flags in background: 100fr, 125fr, 225fr, 260fr.

1998, July 10 **Litho.** ***Perf. 13½x13***

920-923 A348 Set of 4 2.50 1.25
923a Sheet of 4, #920-923 2.50 1.25

1998 World Cup Soccer Championships, France.

1998

924 A349 260fr multicolored .90 .45

ACCT, 26th Anniv.

Elimination of Land Mines — A350

1998 **Litho.** ***Perf. 11½x12***

925 A350 260fr multicolored .95 .50

Gandhi — A351

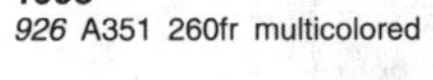

1998

926 A351 260fr multicolored .95 .50

Mother Teresa (1910-97) — A352

1998

927 A352 500fr multicolored 1.75 .90

Deng Xiaoping (1904-97) — A353

1998

928 A353 500fr multicolored 1.75 .90

Intl. Year of the Ocean A354

1999 **Litho.** ***Perf. 11½***

929 A354 125fr multicolored .45 .25

Dated 1998.

Wooden Tools — A355

1999

930 A355 100fr Mortier .35 .20
931 A355 125fr Pilon .45 .25

Dated 1998.

Universal Declaration of Human Rights A356

1999

932 A356 225fr multicolored .80 .40

Dated 1998.

Space Exploration — A357

#933, Gemini 7. #934, Skylab. #935, Atlas Moon Explorer. #936, Space Shuttle.

#937: a, Venera 4. b, TDRS. c, Sputnik II. d, Zond II. e, Untethered walk. f, Intelsat 6. g, Luna 16. h, Sputnik III. i, Vostok V. j, Lunar explorer. k, 2nd lunar landing. l, Conrad and Surveyor.

#938: a, Sputnik. b, Mariner 2. c, Apollo 11 Lunar Module. d, Gemini 7. e, Mir. f, Atlas Moon Explorer. g, Space Shuttle Orbit. h, Hubbell. i, Soyuz. j, Apollo 11 re-entry. k, Skylab. l, Venture Star.

#939: a, Lunar landing II. b, Gemini 7. c, Venture Star. d, Hubbell.

#940, Shuttle launch. #941, Untethered walk. #942, Apollo II. #943, Lunar landing module.

1999, Apr. 30 **Litho.** ***Perf. 14***

933-936 A357 Set of 4 3.25 1.60

Sheets of 12

937 A357 100fr #a.-l. 4.25 2.25
938 A357 125fr #a.-l. 5.25 2.75

Sheet of 4

939 A357 225fr #a.-d. 3.00 1.50

Souvenir Sheets

940-943 A357 1500fr each 5.00 2.50

Moon landing, 30th anniv.

Traditional Weapons - A358

Designs: 100fr, Sagaie. 125fr, Arbalète. 225fr, Couteau et jet.

1999 *Perf. 13*
944-946 A358 Set of 3 1.50 .75

Folklore — A358a

Designs: 125fr, Mitsogho reliquary.

1999 **Litho.** ***Perf. 13¼***
946A A358a 125fr multi

The editors suspect that additional stamps may have been issued in this set and would like to examine any examples.

Democracy A359

1999 **Litho.** ***Perf. 11¾***
947 A359 100fr multicolored .30 .20

UPU, 125th Anniv. A360

100fr, People, map. 225fr, Emblem, letters, vert. 260fr, Great Wall of China, vert.

1999
948 A360 100fr multicolored .30 .20
949 A360 225fr multicolored .70 .35
950 A360 260fr multicolored .80 .40
Nos. 948-950 (3) 1.80 .95

Manufacture of Aspirin, Cent. — A361

1999
951 A361 225fr multicolored .70 .35

PhilexFrance '99 — A362

1999, July 2 **Litho.** ***Perf. 13***
952 A362 225fr multi *.70 .70*

No. 952 has a holographic image. Soaking in water may affect hologram.

Central African Economic and Monetary Community Days — A364

Map of Africa and: 125fr, Circle of member's flags. 225fr, Rows of member's flags.

1999 **Litho.** ***Perf. 14½***
954-955 A364 Set of 2 1.00 1.00

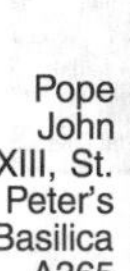

Pope John XXIII, St. Peter's Basilica A365

1999 **Litho.** ***Perf. 11¾***
956 A365 100fr multi .35 .35

Announcement of 2nd Vatican Council, 40th anniv., Christmas.

Unity, Work and Justice Type of 1981

1999 **Litho.** ***Perf. 11¾***
Granite Paper
959 A145 40fr lil & blk .20 .20

Shells A365a

Designs: 100fr, Harpa doris. 125fr, Thais haemastoma. 225fr, Cassis tessellata.

1999 **Litho.** ***Perf. 13x13½***
964-966 A365a Set of 3 1.60 1.60

Fish A365b

Designs: 100fr, Epinephelus marginatus, mugil cephalus. 125fr, Brycinus macrolepidotus. 225fr, Oreochromis schwebischi. 260fr, Pomadasys peroteti, caranx hippos, ethmalosa fimbriata.

1999
967-970 A365b Set of 4 2.40 2.40

Expo 2000, Hanover A366

2000 **Litho.** ***Perf. 11¾x11½***
971 A366 225fr multi .65 .65

Protected Animals A367

Designs: 125fr, Haliaetus vocifer. 225fr, Panthera pardus. 260fr, Panthera leo.

2000
972-974 A367 Set of 3 1.75 1.75

Events of the 20th Century A368

Designs: 100fr, Universal Declaration of Human Rights, vert. 125fr, World War II. 225fr, First man on the moon.

2000 ***Perf. 11½x11¾, 11¾x11½***
975-977 A368 Set of 3 1.25 1.25

Scientific Achievements of the 20th Century — A369

Designs: 100fr, Microprocessor, 1971. 125fr, Nuclear reactor, 1942. 225fr, Structure of DNA, 1953.

2000 ***Perf. 11¾x11½***
978-980 A369 Set of 3 1.25 1.25

Tourism A370

100fr, Pygmy village. 125fr, Lake region. 225fr, Poubara Waterfall. 260fr, Mt. Brazza.

2000 ***Perf. 13x13½***
981-984 A370 Set of 4 2.00 2.00

Y2K Bug — A371

2000 ***Perf. 11½x11¾***
985 A371 225fr multi .65 .65

Dr. Albert Schweitzer (1875-1965) A372

2000 ***Perf. 13¼x13***
986 A372 260fr multi .80 .80

A373

Trains — A374

Designs: No. 987, 100fr, Japanese Hikari trains. 125fr, Hungarian Bo-Bo electric locomotive. No. 989, 500fr, Pakistani electric locomotive. No. 990, 500fr, Belgian locomotive.

No. 991: a, 100fr, Korean Bo-Bo locomotive. b, 100fr, Moroccan electric locomotive. c, 100fr, Spanish electric locomotive. d, 500fr, Yugoslavian Type J2-441. e, 500fr, Chinese electric locomotive. f, 500fr, Norwegian Type E115.

No. 992: a, 100fr, Portuguese Diesel-electric locomotive. b, 100fr, Japanese mag-lev train. c, 100fr, Long Island Railroad diesel car. d, 500fr, German Type 103. e, 500fr, Romanian Co-Co locomotive. f, 500fr, English HST.

No. 993, 1500fr, English train "The Advanced." No. 994, 1500fr, French TGV 001. No. 995, 1500fr, Austrian Transalpine train. No. 996, 1500fr, Stourbridge Lion. No. 997, 1500fr, Puffing Billy, vert. No. 998, 1500fr, Union Pacific 4-8-8-4 Big Boy, vert. No. 999, French TGV, vert.

Illustration A374 reduced.

Perf. 13¼x13¾, 13¾x13¼

2000, Dec. 10 **Litho.**
987-990 A373 Set of 4 3.50 3.50

Sheets of 6, #a-f
991-992 A373 Set of 2 10.00 10.00

Souvenir Sheets
993-995 A373 Set of 3 12.50 12.50
996-999 A374 Set of 4 17.00 17.00

A375

Prehistoric Animals — A376

Designs: No. 1000, 100fr, Archaeopteryx. No. 1001, 100fr, Velociraptor, vert. No. 1002, 125fr, Torosaurus. No. 1003, 125fr, Corythosaurus, vert. No. 1004, 225fr, Pachycephalosaurus, vert. No. 1005, 500fr, Parasaurolophus.

No. 1006, 100fr, Pterodactylus. No. 1007, 125fr, Allosaurus. No. 1008, 125fr, Struthiomimus, vert. No. 1009, 225fr, Psittacosaurus, vert. No. 1010, 260fr, Parasauraolophus, vert. No. 1011, 500fr, Acanthostega.

No. 1012: a, 125fr, Camarasaurus. b, 125fr, Rhamphorhynchus. c, 125fr, Saltasaurus. d, 225fr, Camptosaurus. e, 225fr, Megalosaurus. f, 225fr, Allosaurus. g, 260fr, Anchisaurus. h, 260fr, Dilophosaurus. i, 260fr, Massospondylus.

No. 1013: a, 100fr, Stegosaurus. b, 100fr, Pteranodon. c, 100fr, Carnotaurus. d, 125fr, Iguanodon. e, 125fr, Pentaceratops. f, 125fr, Styracosaurus. g, 500fr, Deinonychus. h, 500fr, Stegoceras. i, 500fr, Struthiomimus.

No. 1014: a, 125fr, Volcano. b, 125fr, Pterodactylus. c, 125fr, Dimorphodon. d, 125fr, Alamosaurus. e, 225fr, Psittacosaurus. f, 225fr, Deinonychus. g, 225fr, Dromiceiomimus. h, 225fr, Yangchuanosaurus. i, 260fr, Protorosaurus. j, 260fr, Triceratops. k, 260fr, Daspletosaurus. l, 260fr, Pentaceratops.

No. 1015: a, 125fr, Brachiosaurus. b, 125fr, Scaphognathus. c, Mountain and sun. d, 125fr, Pteranodon. e, 225fr, Tyrannosaurus. f, 225fr, Ichthyosaurus. g, 225fr, Macroplata. h, 225fr, Dilophosaurus. i, 500fr, Stegosaurus. j, 500fr, Thecodontosaurus. k, 500fr, Saltosaurus. l, 500fr, Pachyrhinosaurus.

No. 1016, 225fr: a, Tyrannosaurus. b, Criorhynchus. c, Pterodactylus. d, Albertosaurus. e, Dromiceiomimus. f, Opisthocoelicaudia. g, Brachiosaurus. h, Pachycephalosaurus. i, Parasaurolophus. j, Edmontosaurus. k, Pentaceratops. l, Corythosaurus.

No. 1017, 260fr: a, Peteinosaurus. b, Volcanoes. c, Acanthostega. d, Ceresiosaurus. e, Pliosaur. f, Stethacanthus. g, Ichthyosaur. h, Pholidogaster. i, Gerrothorax. j, Diplocaulus. k, Mixosaurus. l, Echinoceras raricostatum.

No. 1018, 1500fr, Tyrannosaurus Rex. No. 1019, 1500fr, Arrhinoceratops. No. 1020, 1500fr, Argentinosaurus, vert. No. 1021, 1500fr, Cetiosaurus, vert. No. 1022, 1500fr, Archaeopteryx. No. 1023, Saltasaurus, vert.

2000, Dec. 20

1000-1005 A375 Set of 6 3.25 3.25
1006-1011 A376 Set of 6 3.75 3.75

Sheets of 9, #a-i

1012-1013 A375 Set of 2 11.00 11.00

Sheets of 12, #a-l

1014-1015 A375 Set of 2 16.00 16.00
1016-1017 A376 Set of 2 16.00 16.00

Souvenir Sheets

1018-1021 A375 Set of 4 17.00 17.00
1022-1023 A376 Set of 2 8.25 8.25

No. 1021 contains one 42x56mm stamp.

Train Type of 2000 and

A377

Designs: 100fr, German Type 201. No. 1025, 225fr, German Type 112. No. 1026, 225fr, ICT. No. 1027, 260fr, ICE.

No. 1028, 260fr, French Electric BB9004. No. 1029, 260fr, French Type 232U 4-8-2. No. 1030, 500fr, French Type 241C 4-8-2 "Mountain." No. 1031, 500fr, German TEE.

No. 1032: a, 125fr, German Type 41. b, 125fr, Type 39. c, 125fr, German Type 10. d, 500fr, German Type 99. e, 500fr, German Type 58. f, 500fr, German Type 44.

No. 1033: a, 225fr, German Type 229. b, 225fr, Type 152. c, 225fr, German Type 101. d, 500fr, German Type 250. e, 500fr, German Type 232. f, 500fr, Type 216.

No. 1034: a, 125fr, Prussian Type P8 4-6-0. b, 125fr, Bavarian Type S3/6 4-6-2. c, 125fr, German Type 01 4-6-2. d, 500fr, German Electric "Crocodile." e, 500fr, Swiss Electric Type Be 4/6. f, 500fr, Swiss Electric Type Ae 6/6.

No. 1035: a, 125fr, Stirling 8ft Single 4-2-2 "No. 1," UK. b, 125fr, Greeley Pacific Type A3 4-6-2 "Flying Scotsman," UK. c, 125fr, Stanier Coronation Type 4-6-2 "Coronation Scot," UK. d, 500fr, Baldwin 4-4-0 "The General," US. e, Class J1 Hudson 4-8-4, US. f, "Super Chief" Diesel-electric, US.

No. 1036, 1500fr, Type 91. No. 1037, 1500fr, Type 57. No. 1038, Greeley Pacific Type A4 4-6-2 "Silver Link," UK. No. 1039, J Type 4-8-4, US.

Perf. 13¼x13½, 13½x13¼

2000? Litho.

1024-1027 A374 Set of 4 2.25 2.25
1028-1031 A377 Set of 4 4.25 4.25

Sheets of 6, #a-f

1032-1033 A374 Set of 2 11.00 11.00
1034-1035 A377 Set of 2 10.50 10.50

Souvenir Sheets

1036-1037 A374 Set of 2 8.25 8.25
1038-1039 A377 Set of 2 8.25 8.25

Nos. 1038-1039 each contain one 56x42mm stamp.

Scientific Achievements of the 20th Century Type of 2000

Designs: 100fr, Isolation of insulin, 1921. 125fr, Invention of television, 1921. 225fr, Invention of the calculator, 1951.

2001, July 27 Litho. *Perf. 11¾x11½*

1040-1042 A369 Set of 3 1.25 1.25

SEMI-POSTAL STAMPS

No. 37 Surcharged in Red

1916 Unwmk. *Perf. 13½x14*

B1 A10 10c + 5c red & car 10.00 10.00
a. Double surcharge 100.00 *110.00*

Same Surcharge on No. 54 in Red

B2 A10 10c + 5c red & car 16.00 16.00
a. Double surcharge 100.00 *110.00*

No. 54 Surcharged in Red

1917

B3 A10 10c + 5c red & car .70 .70

Catalogue values for unused stamps in this section, from this point to the end of the section, are for Never Hinged items.

Republic Anti-Malaria Issue

Common Design Type

1962, Apr. 7 Engr. *Perf. 12½x12*

B4 CD108 25fr + 5fr yel grn .75 .75

WHO drive to eradicate malaria.

Freedom from Hunger Issue

Common Design Type

1963, Mar. 21 Unwmk. *Perf. 13*

B5 CD112 25fr + 5fr dk red, grn & brn .60 .60

Red Cross — SP1

1997, May 8 Litho. *Perf. 13½x13*

B6 SP1 150fr +75fr multi .75 .60

AIR POST STAMPS

Catalogue values for unused stamps in this section are for Never Hinged items.

Dr. Albert Schweitzer — AP1

Unwmk.

1960, July 23 Engr. *Perf. 13*

C1 AP1 200fr grn, dl red brn & ultra 3.00 2.00

For surcharge see No. C11.

Workmen Felling Tree — AP2

1960, Oct. 8

C2 AP2 100fr red brn, grn & blk 2.75 1.00

5th World Forestry Cong., Seattle, WA, Aug. 29-Sept. 10.

Olympic Games Issue

French Equatorial Africa No. C37 Surcharged in Red Like Chad No. C1

AP2a

1960, Dec. 15

C3 AP2a 250fr on 500fr grnsh blk, blk & slate 5.25 5.25

17th Olympic Games, Rome, 8/25-9/11.

Lyre-tailed Honey Guide — AP3

1961, May 30 *Perf. 13*

C4 AP3 50fr sl grn, red brn & ultra 1.00 .60

See Nos. C14-C17.

Air Afrique Issue

Common Design Type

1962, Feb. 17 Engr. *Perf. 13*

C5 CD107 500fr sl grn, blk & bis 7.50 4.00

Long Jump — AP3a

1962, July 21 Photo. *Perf. 12x12½*

C6 AP3a 100fr dk & lt bl, brn & blk 1.60 1.00

Issued to publicize the Abidjan Games.

Breguet 14, 1928 — AP4

Development of air transport: 20fr, Dragon biplane transport. 60fr, Caravelle jet. 85fr, Rocket-propelled aircraft.

1962, Sept. 4 Engr. *Perf. 13*

C7 AP4 10fr dl red brn & sl .35 .20
C8 AP4 20fr dk bl, sl & ocher .55 .25
C9 AP4 60fr dk sl grn, blk & brn 1.25 .55
C10 AP4 85fr dk bl, blk & org 2.10 1.25
a. Souv. sheet of 4, #C7-C10 5.00 5.00
Nos. C7-C10 (4) 4.25 2.25

Gabon's 1st phil. exhib., Libreville, Sept. 2-9.

No. C1 Surcharged in Red: "100F/JUBILE GABONAIS/1913-1963"

1963, Apr. 18

C11 AP1 100fr on 200fr 2.00 1.00

50th anniv. of Dr. Albert Schweitzer's arrival in Gabon.

Post Office, Libreville — AP5

1963, Apr. 28 Photo. *Perf. 13x12*

C12 AP5 100fr multi 1.10 .65

African Postal Union Issue

Common Design Type

1963, Sept. 8 Unwmk. *Perf. 12½*

C13 CD114 85fr brt car, ocher & red 1.10 .60

Bird Type of 1961

Birds: 100fr, Johanna's sunbird. 200fr, Blue-headed bee-eater, vert. 250fr, Crowned hawk-eagle, vert. 500fr, Narina trogon, vert.

1963-64 Engr. *Perf. 13*

C14 AP3 100fr dk grn, vio bl & car 2.50 .95
C15 AP3 200fr ol, vio bl & red 4.25 2.10
C16 AP3 250fr grn, blk & dk brn ('64) 8.25 3.00
C17 AP3 500fr multi 9.00 4.00
Nos. C14-C17 (4) 24.00 10.05

1963 Air Afrique Issue

Common Design Type

1963, Nov. 19 Photo. *Perf. 13x12*

C18 CD115 50fr lt vio, gray, blk & grn .75 .40

Europafrica Issue

Common Design Type

1963, Nov. 30 *Perf. 12x13*

C19 CD116 50fr vio, yel & dk brn .90 .50

Chiefs of State Issue

REPUBLIQUE GABONAISE
POSTE AERIENNE
100F
President TOMBALBAYE
President DACKO
President MBA
President MASSAMBA-DEBAT
5me ANNIVERSAIRE DE LA CONFERENCE DES CHEFS D'ETAT D'AFRIQUE EQUATORIALE

Map and Presidents of Chad, Congo, Gabon and CAR — AP5a

1964, June 23 *Perf. 12½*

C20 AP5a 100fr multi 1.25 .70

See note after Central African Republic No. C19.

Europafrica Issue, 1964

Globe and Emblems of Industry and Agriculture — AP6

1964, July 20 *Perf. 12x13*
C21 AP6 50fr red, olive & blue .85 .50

See note after Cameroun No. 402.

Start of Race — AP7

Athletes (Greek): 50fr, Massage at gymnasium, vert. 100fr, Anointing with oil before game, vert. 200fr, Four athletes.

1964, July 30 **Engr.** *Perf. 13*
C22 AP7 25fr sl grn, dk brn & org .40 .25
C23 AP7 50fr dk brn, sl grn & org brn .85 .35
C24 AP7 100fr vio bl, ol grn & dk brn 1.75 .65
C25 AP7 200fr dk brn, mag & org red 2.75 1.40
a. Min. sheet of 4, #C22-C25 7.50 7.50
Nos. C22-C25 (4) 5.75 2.65

18th Olympic Games, Tokyo, Oct. 10-25.

Communications Symbols — AP7a

1964, Nov. 2 **Litho.** *Perf. 12½x13*
C26 AP7a 25fr lt grn, dk brn & lt red brn .45 .20

See note after Chad No. C19.

John F. Kennedy (1917-63) — AP8

1964, Nov. 23 **Photo.** *Perf. 12½*
C27 AP8 100fr grn, org & blk 1.25 1.00
a. Souv. sheet of 4 5.00 5.00

Telephone Operator, Nurse and Police Woman — AP9

1964, Dec. 5 **Engr.** *Perf. 13*
C28 AP9 50fr car, bl & chocolate .75 .35

Social evolution of Gabonese women.

World Map and ICY Emblem — AP10

1965, Mar. 25 **Unwmk.** *Perf. 13*
C29 AP10 50fr org, Prus bl & grnsh bl .65 .40

International Cooperation Year.

Merchant Ship, 17th Century — AP11

25fr, Galleon, 16th cent., vert. 85fr, Frigate, 18th cent., vert. 100fr, Brig, 19th cent.

1965, Apr. 22 **Photo.** *Perf. 13*
C30 AP11 25fr lilac & multi .50 .40
C31 AP11 50fr yellow & multi 1.10 .60
C32 AP11 85fr multi 1.90 .90
C33 AP11 100fr multi 2.50 1.10
Nos. C30-C33 (4) 6.00 3.00

Red Cross Nurse Carrying Sick Child — AP12

1965, June 25 **Engr.** *Perf. 13*
C34 AP12 100fr brn, slate grn & red 1.10 .50

Issued for the Gabonese Red Cross.

Women's Basketball AP13

1965, July 15 **Unwmk.**
C35 AP13 100fr sep, red org & brt lil 1.25 .65

African Games, Brazzaville, July 18-25.

Maps of Europe and Africa — AP14

1965, July 26 **Photo.** *Perf. 13x12*
C36 AP14 50fr multi 1.00 .40

See note after Cameroun No. 421.

Pres. Leon Mba AP15

1965, Aug. 17 *Perf. 12½*
C37 AP15 25fr multi .45 .35

Fifth anniversary of independence.

Sir Winston Churchill and Microphones — AP16

1965, Sept. 28 **Photo.** *Perf. 12½*
C38 AP16 100fr gold, blk & bl 1.25 .70

Sir Winston Spencer Churchill (1874-1965), statesman and World War II leader.

Dr. Albert Schweitzer — AP17

Embossed on Gold Foil
Die-cut Perf. 14½, Approx.

1965, Dec. 4
C39 AP17 1000fr gold 32.50 32.50

Dr. Albert Schweitzer (1875-1965), medical missionary, theologian and musician.

Pope John XXIII and St. Peter's — AP18

1965, Dec. 10 **Photo.** *Perf. 13x12½*
C40 AP18 85fr multi .85 .60

Issued in memory of Pope John XXIII.

Anti-Malaria Treatment AP19

1966, Apr. 8 **Photo.** *Perf. 12½*
C41 AP19 50fr shown .75 .50
a. Min. sheet of 4 4.00 4.00
C42 AP19 100fr First aid 1.25 .75
a. Min. sheet of 4 8.00 8.00

Issued for the Red Cross.

Diamant Rocket, A-1 Satellite and Map of Africa — AP20

90fr, FR-1 satellite, Diamant rocket and earth.

1966, May 18 **Engr.** *Perf. 13*
C43 AP20 30fr dk pur, brt bl & red brn .40 .20
C44 AP20 90fr brt lil, red & pur 1.10 .50

French achievements in space.

Soccer and World Map — AP21

1966, July 15 **Engr.** *Perf. 13*
C45 AP21 100fr slate & brn red 1.50 .65

8th World Soccer Cup Championship, Wembley, England, July 11-30.

Symbols of Industry and Transportation AP22

1966, July 26 **Photo.** *Perf. 12x13*
C46 AP22 50fr multi .60 .25

3rd anniv. of the economic agreement between the European Economic Community and the African and Malgache Union.

Air Afrique Issue, 1966
Common Design Type

1966, Aug. 31 **Photo.** *Perf. 13*
C47 CD123 30fr org, blk & gray .35 .20

Student and UNESCO Emblem — AP23

1966, Nov. 4 Engr. *Perf. 13*
C48 AP23 100fr dl bl, ocher & blk 1.00 .55

20th anniv. of UNESCO.

Libreville Airport — AP24

1966, Nov. 21 Engr. *Perf. 13*
C49 AP24 200fr dp bl & red brn 2.25 .80

Inauguration of Libreville Airport.

Farman 190 — AP25

Planes: 300fr, De Havilland Heron. 500fr, Potez 56.

1967, Apr. 1 Engr. *Perf. 13*
C50 AP25 200fr ultra, lil & bl grn 2.00 .55
C51 AP25 300fr brn, lil & brt bl 3.25 .75
C52 AP25 500fr brn car, dk grn & indigo 5.75 2.50
Nos. C50-C52 (3) 11.00 3.80

For surcharge see No. C128.

Planes, Runways and ICAO Emblem — AP26

1967, May 19 Engr. *Perf. 13*
C53 AP26 100fr plum, brt bl & yel grn 1.10 .55

International Civil Aviation Organization.

Blood Donor and Bottles — AP27

100fr, Human heart and transfusion apparatus.

1967, June 26 Photo. *Perf. 12½*
C54 AP27 50fr ocher, red & sl .75 .30
a. Souvenir sheet of 4 3.00 3.00

C55 AP27 100fr yel grn, red & gray 1.50 .60
a. Souvenir sheet of 4 5.00 5.00

Issued for the Red Cross. Nos. C54a, C55a each contain 2 vertical tête bêche pairs.

Jamboree Emblem and Symbols of Orientation AP28

1967, Aug. 1 Engr. *Perf. 13*

Design: 100fr, Jamboree emblem, maps and Scouts of Africa and America.

C56 AP28 50fr multi .50 .30
C57 AP28 100fr brt grn, dp car & bl 1.10 .70

12th Boy Scout World Jamboree, Farragut State Park, Idaho, Aug. 1-9.

African Postal Union Issue, 1967

Common Design Type

1967, Sept. 9 Engr. *Perf. 13*
C58 CD124 100fr dl bl, ol & red brn .90 .50

Mission Church — AP29

1967, Oct. 18 Engr. *Perf. 13*
C59 AP29 100fr brt bl, dk grn & blk 1.10 .60

125th anniv. of the arrival of American Protestant missionaries in Baraka-Libreville.

UN Emblem, Sword, Book and People — AP30

1967, Nov. 7 Photo. *Perf. 13*
C60 AP30 60fr dk red, vio bl & bis .65 .35

UN Commission on Human Rights.

Tree Type of Regular Issue

Designs: 50fr, Baillonella toxisperma. 100fr, Aucoumea klaineana.

1967, Dec. 5 Engr. *Perf. 13*
Size: 26½x47½mm
C61 A53 50fr grn, brt bl & brn .90 .50
C62 A53 100fr multi 1.75 .75
a. Bklt. pane of 5, #223-225, C61-C62 with gutter btwn. 4.50 4.50

Konrad Adenauer AP31

1968, Feb. 20 Photo. *Perf. 12½*
C63 AP31 100fr blk, dl org & red 1.25 .45
a. Souvenir sheet of 4 5.00 5.00

Issued in memory of Konrad Adenauer (1876-1967), chancellor of West Germany (1949-63). No. C63a includes 1967 CEPT (Europa) emblem.

Madonna of the Rosary by Murillo AP32

90fr, Christ in Bonds, by Luis de Morales. 100fr, St. John on Patmos, by Juan Mates.

1968, July 9 Photo. *Perf. 12½x12*
C64 AP32 60fr multi .65 .30
C65 AP32 90fr multi 1.00 .40
C66 AP32 100fr multi, horiz. 1.10 .60
Nos. C64-C66 (3) 2.75 1.30

See #C77, C102-C104, C132-C133, C146-C148.

Europafrica Issue

Stylized Knot — AP32a

1968, July 23 Photo. *Perf. 13*
C67 AP32a 50fr yel brn, emer & lt ultra .60 .30

See note after Congo Republic No. C69.

Support for Red Cross — AP33

50fr, Distribution of Red Cross gifts.

1968, Aug. 13
C68 AP33 50fr multi .50 .25
C69 AP33 100fr multi 1.10 .50
a. Bklt. pane of 2, #C68, C69 with gutter btwn. 1.75 1.75

Issued for the Red Cross.

High Jump — AP34

1968, Sept. 3 Engr.
C70 AP34 25fr shown .30 .20
C71 AP34 30fr Bicycling, vert. .40 .20
C72 AP34 100fr Judo, vert. 1.00 .40
C73 AP34 200fr Boxing 1.75 .75
a. Bklt. pane of 4, #C70-C71, C72-C73 with gutter btwn. 4.75 4.75
Nos. C70-C73 (4) 3.45 1.55

Issued to publicize the 19th Summer Olympic Games, Mexico City, Oct. 12-27.

Pres. Mba, Flag and Arms of Gabon AP35

Embossed on Gold Foil

1968, Nov. 28 *Perf. 14½*
C74 AP35 1000fr gold, grn, yel & dk bl 11.00 11.00

Death of Pres. Léon Mba (1902-67), 1st anniv.

Pres. Bongo, Maps of Gabon and Owendo Harbor — AP36

1968, Dec. 16 Photo. *Perf. 12½*
C75 AP36 25fr shown .30 .20
C76 AP36 30fr Owendo Harbor .40 .20
a. Strip of 2, #C75-C76 + label .75 .60

Laying of the foundation stone for Owendo Harbor, June 24, 1968.

PHILEXAFRIQUE Issue

Painting Type of 1968

Design: 100fr, The Convent of St. Mary of the Angels, by Francois Marius Granet.

1969, Jan. 8 Photo. *Perf. 12½x12*
C77 AP32 100fr multi 1.75 1.75

Issued to publicize PHILEXAFRIQUE Philatelic Exhibition in Abidjan, Feb. 14-23. Printed with alternating brown label.

Mahatma Gandhi — AP37

Portraits: 30fr, John F. Kennedy. 50fr, Robert F. Kennedy. 100fr, Martin Luther King, Jr.

1969, Jan. 15 *Perf. 12½*
C78 AP37 25fr pink & blk .35 .20
C79 AP37 30fr lt yel grn & blk .35 .20
C80 AP37 50fr lt bl & blk .55 .20
C81 AP37 100fr brt rose lil & blk 1.00 .40
a. Souv. sheet of 4, #C78-C81 2.50 2.50
Nos. C78-C81 (4) 2.25 1.00

Issued to honor exponents of non-violence.

2nd PHILEXAFRIQUE Issue

Common Design Type

1969, Feb. 14 Engr. *Perf. 13*
C82 CD128 50fr grn, ind & red brn .90 .75

Battle of Rivoli, by Henri Philippoteaux — AP39

100fr, The Oath of the Army, by Jacques Louis David. 250fr, Napoleon with the Children on the Terrace in St. Cloud, by Louis Ducis.

1969, Apr. 23 Photo. *Perf. 12½x12*

C83 AP39 50fr brn & multi 1.10 .60
C84 AP39 100fr grn & multi 1.25 1.00
C85 AP39 250fr lil & multi 5.00 2.75
Nos. C83-C85 (3) 7.35 4.35

Birth bicentenary of Napoleon I.

Red Cross Plane, Nurse and Biafran Children — AP40

20fr, Dispensary, ambulance & supplies. 25fr, Physician & nurse in children's ward. 30fr, Dispensary & playing children.

1969, June 20 Photo. *Perf. 14x13½*

C86 AP40 15fr lt ultra, dk brn & red .25 .20
C87 AP40 20fr emer, blk, brn & red .35 .20
C88 AP40 25fr grnsh bl, dk brn & red .35 .20
C89 AP40 30fr org yel, dk brn & red .40 .20
Nos. C86-C89 (4) 1.35 .80

Red Cross help for Biafra.

A souvenir sheet contains four stamps similar to Nos. C86-C89, but lithographed and rouletted 13x13½. Gray margin with red inscription and Red Cross. Size: 118x75mm. Sold in cardboard folder. Value $1.20.

Astronauts and Lunar Landing Module, Apollo 11 — AP41

Embossed on Gold Foil

1969, July 25 *Die-cut Perf. 10½x10*

C90 AP41 1000fr gold 10.00 10.00

See note after Algeria No. 427.

African and European Heads and Symbols — AP42

Icarus and Sun — AP43

Europafrica Issue, 1970

1970, June 5 Photo. *Perf. 12x13*

C91 AP42 50fr multi .55 .30

1970, June 10 Engr. *Perf. 13*

Designs: 100fr, Leonardo da Vinci's flying man, 1519. 200fr, Jules Verne's space shell approaching moon, 1865.

C92 AP43 25fr ultra, red & org .40 .20
C93 AP43 100fr ocher, plum & sl grn .80 .45
C94 AP43 200fr gray, ultra & dk car 2.00 .90
a. Min. sheet of 3, #C92-C94 3.75 3.75
Nos. C92-C94 (3) 3.20 1.55

UAMPT Emblem AP44

Embossed on Gold Foil

1970, June 18 *Die-cut Perf. 12½*

C95 AP44 200fr gold, yel grn & bl 1.90 1.10

Meeting of the Afro-Malagasy Union of Posts & Telecommuncations (UAMPT), Libreville, 6/17-23.

Throwing Knives AP45

Gabonese Weapons: 30fr, Assegai and crossbow, vert. 50fr, War knives, vert. 90fr, Dagger and sheath.

1970, July 10 Engr. *Perf. 13*

C96 AP45 25fr multi .30 .20
C97 AP45 30fr multi .40 .20
C98 AP45 50fr multi .55 .25
C99 AP45 90fr multi 1.10 .45
a. Min. sheet of 4, #C96-C99 2.25 2.25
Nos. C96-C99 (4) 2.35 1.10

Japanese Masks, Mt. Fuji and Torii at Miyajima — AP46

Embossed on Gold Foil

1970, July 31 *Die-cut Perf. 10*

C100 AP46 1000fr multi 10.00 10.00

Issued to publicize EXPO '70 International Exhibition, Osaka, Japan, Mar. 15-Sept. 13.

Pres. Albert Bernard Bongo — AP47

Lithographed; Gold Embossed

1970, Aug. 17 *Perf. 12½*

C101 AP47 200fr multi 2.25 1.10

10th anniversary of independence.

Painting Type of 1968

Paintings: 50fr, Portrait of a Young Man, School of Raphael. 100fr, Portrait of Jeanne d'Aragon, by Raphael. 200fr, Madonna with Blue Diadem, by Raphael.

1970, Oct. 16 Photo. *Perf. 12½x12*

C102 AP32 50fr multi .55 .30
C102A AP32 100fr blue & multi 1.10 .40
C102B AP32 200fr brown & multi 2.10 1.00
Nos. C102-C102B (3) 3.75 1.70

Raphael (1483-1520).

Miniature Sheets

Sikorsky S-32 — AP47a

Hugo Junkers — AP47b

1970, Dec. 5 Litho. *Perf. 12*

C103 Sheet of 8
a. AP47a 15fr shown
b. AP47a 25fr Fokker "Southern Cross"
c. AP47a 40fr Dornier DO-18
d. AP47a 60fr Dornier DO-X
e. AP47a 80fr Breguet "Bizerte"
f. AP47a 125fr Douglas "Cloudster"
g. AP47a 150fr De Havilland DH-2
h. AP47a 200fr Vickers "Vimi"

C104 Sheet of 4 10.00 10.00
a. AP47b 200fr shown
b. AP47b 300fr Claude Dornier
c. AP47b 400fr Anthony Fokker
d. AP47b 500fr Igor Sikorsky

Imperf

C105 Sheet of 8
a. AP47a 10fr Dornier "Spatz"
b. AP47a 20fr Douglas DC-3
c. AP47a 30fr Dornier DO-7 "Wal"
d. AP47a 50fr Sikorsky S-38
e. AP47a 75fr De Havilland "Moth"
f. AP47a 100fr Supermarine "Spitfire"
g. AP47a 125fr Breguet XIX
h. AP47a 150fr Fokker "Universal"

Size: 80x90mm

C106 AP47b 1000fr Claude Dornier

Claude Dornier (1884-1969), aviation pioneer. No. C104 exists imperf.

Presidents Bongo and Pompidou — AP48

1971, Feb. 11 Photo. *Perf. 13*

C107 AP48 50fr multi 1.00 .60

Visit of Georges Pompidou, Pres. of France.

Apollo 14 — AP48a

1971, Feb. 19 *Perf. 14*

Yellow Inscriptions

C108 15fr Lift off
C108A 25fr Achieving orbit
C108B 40fr Lunar module descent
C108C 55fr Lunar landing
C108D 75fr Lunar liftoff
C108E 120fr Earth re-entry

Souvenir Sheet

C108F Sheet of 2
g. AP48a 100fr Modules attached
h. AP48a 100fr like #C108E

Nos. C108-C108F exist imperf. with white inscriptions.

Flowers and Plane — AP49

25fr, Carnations. 40fr, Roses. 55fr, Daffodils. 75fr, Orchids. 120fr, Tulips.

1971, May 7 Litho. *Perf. 13½x14*

C109 AP49 15fr yellow & multi .25 .20
C109A AP49 25fr multi .30 .20
C109B AP49 40fr pink & multi .55 .25
C109C AP49 55fr blue & multi .70 .30
C110 AP49 75fr multi 1.25 .40
C111 AP49 120fr green & multi 1.50 .50
a. Souv. sheet of 2, #C110-C111 3.00 3.00
Nos. C109-C111 (6) 4.55 1.85

"Flowers by air."

Napoleon's Death Mask AP50

Designs: 200fr, Longwood, St. Helena, by Jacques Marchand, horiz. 500fr, Sarcophagus in Les Invalides, Paris.

1971, May 12 Photo. *Perf. 13*

C112 AP50 100fr gold & multi 1.40 .55
C113 AP50 200fr gold & multi 2.10 .95
C114 AP50 500fr gold & multi 5.50 2.50
Nos. C112-C114 (3) 9.00 4.00

Napoleon Bonaparte (1769-1821).

Souvenir Sheet

Charles de Gaulle — AP51

Designs: 40fr, President de Gaulle. 80fr, General de Gaulle. 100fr, Quotation.

1971, June 18 Photo. *Perf. 12½*

C115 AP51 Sheet of 5 4.00 4.00
a. 40fr dark red & multi .40 .40
b. 80fr dark green & multi .40 .40
c. 100fr green, brown & yel 1.00 1.00

In memory of Gen. Charles de Gaulle (1890-1970), Pres. of France.
For surcharge see No. C126.

Red Crosses AP52

1971, June 29

C116 AP52 50fr multicolored .60 .30

For the Red Cross of Gabon.
For surcharge see No. C143.

Uranium — AP53

1971, July 20 Photo. *Perf. 13x12½*

C117 AP53 85fr shown 1.60 .80
C118 AP53 90fr Manganese 1.90 1.00

Landing Module over Moon — AP54

Embossed on Gold Foil

1971, July 30 *Die-cut Perf. 10*

C119 AP54 1500fr multi 14.00 14.00

Apollo 11 and 15 US moon missions.

African Postal Union Issue, 1971

Common Design Type

Design: 100fr, Bakota copper mask and UAMPT building, Brazzaville, Congo.

1971, Nov. 13 Photo. *Perf. 13x13½*

C120 CD135 100fr bl & multi .90 .45

Ski Jump and Miyajima Torii AP55

130fr, Speed skating and Japanese temple.

1972, Jan. 31 Engr. *Perf. 13*

C121 AP55 40fr hn brn, sl grn & vio bl .50 .25
C122 AP55 130fr hn brn, sl grn & vio bl 1.25 .50
a. Strip of 2, #C121-C122 + label 2.25 1.75

11th Winter Olympic Games, Sapporo, Japan, Feb. 3-13.

The Basin and Grand Canal, by Vanvitelli — AP56

Paintings: 70fr, Rialto Bridge, by Canaletto (erroneously inscribed Caffi), vert. 140fr, Santa Maria della Salute, by Vanvitelli, vert.

1972, Feb. 7 Photo. *Perf. 13*

C123 AP56 60fr gold & multi .75 .35
C124 AP56 70fr gold & multi 1.00 .50
C125 AP56 140fr gold & multi 1.75 .75
Nos. C123-C125 (3) 3.50 1.60

UNESCO campaign to save Venice.

No. C115 Surcharged in Brown and Gold

Souvenir Sheet

1972, Feb. 11 *Perf. 12½*

C126 AP51 Sheet of 5 7.00 7.00
a. 60fr on 40fr multi 1.00 1.00
b. 120fr on 80fr multi 2.00 2.00
c. 180fr on 100fr multi 3.00 3.00

Publicity for the erection of a memorial for Charles de Gaulle. Nos. C126a-C126b have surcharge and Cross of Lorraine in gold, 2 bars obliterating old denomination in brown; No. C126c has surcharge, cross and bars in brown. Two Lorraine Crosses and inscription (MEMORIAL DU GENERAL DE GAULLE) in brown added in margin.

Hotel Inter-Continental, Libreville — AP57

1972, Feb. 26 Engr. *Perf. 13*

C127 AP57 40fr bl, sl grn & org brn .45 .25

No. C51 Surcharged

1972, Mar. 3

C128 AP25 50fr on 300fr multi .50 .30

Official visit of the Grand Master of the Knights of Malta, March 3.

Discobolus, by Alcamenes AP58

Designs: 100fr, Doryphoros, by Polycletus. 140fr, Borghese gladiator, by Agasias.

1972, May 10 Engr. *Perf. 13*

C129 AP58 30fr rose cl & gray .35 .35
C130 AP58 100fr rose cl & gray .95 .45
C131 AP58 140fr rose cl & gray 1.25 .60
a. Min. of sheet of 3, #C129-C131 2.75 2.75
Nos. C129-C131 (3) 2.55 1.40

20th Olympic Games, Munich, 8/26-9/10.
For surcharges see Nos. C134-C136.

Painting Type of 1968

Paintings: 30fr, Adoration of the Magi, by Peter Brueghel, the Elder, horiz. 40fr, Madonna and Child, by Marco Basaiti.

1972, Oct. 30 Photo. *Perf. 13*

C132 AP32 30fr gold & multi .25 .20
C133 AP32 40fr gold & multi .35 .20

Christmas 1972.

Nos. C129-C131 Surcharged with New Value, Two Bars and Names of Athletes.

1972, Dec. 5 Engr. *Perf. 13*

C134 AP58 40fr on 30fr .35 .20
C135 AP58 120fr on 100fr 1.00 .50
C136 AP58 170fr on 140fr 1.50 .80
Nos. C134-C136 (3) 2.85 1.50

Gold medal winners in 20th Olympic Games: Daniel Morelon, France, Bicycling (C134); Kipchoge Keino, Kenya, steeplechase (C135); Mark Spitz, US, swimming (C136).

Globe with Space Orbits, Simulated Stamps — AP59

1973, Feb. 20 Photo. *Perf. 13*

C137 AP59 100fr multi .80 .40
a. Souv. sheet of 4, perf. 12x12½ 3.75 3.75

PHILEXGABON 1973, Phil. Exhib., Libreville, Feb. 19-26. No. C137a exists imperf.

DC10-30 "Libreville" over Libreville Airport — AP60

1973, Mar. 19 Typo. *Perf. 13*

C138 AP60 40fr blue & multi .35 .20

Kinguélé Hydroelectric Station — AP61

Design: 40fr, Kinguélé Dam.

1973, June 19 Engr. *Perf. 13*

C139 AP61 30fr slate grn & dk ol .20 .20
C140 AP61 40fr slate grn, dk ol & bl .25 .20
a. Strip of 2, #C139-C140 + label .50 .50

Hydroelectric installations at Kinguélé.

M'Bigou Stone Sculpture, Woman's Head — AP62

Design: 200fr, Sculpture, man's head.

1973, July 5

C141 AP62 100fr blk, bl & grn .80 .55
C142 AP62 200fr grn, sep & sl grn 1.60 1.00

No. C116 Surcharged with New Value, 2 Bars, and Overprinted in Ultramarine: "SECHERESSE SOLIDARITE AFRICAINE"

1973, Aug. 16 Photo. *Perf. 12½*

C143 AP52 100fr on 50fr multi .80 .50

African solidarity in drought emergency.

Astronauts and Lunar Rover on Moon — AP63

1973, Sept. 6 Engr. *Perf. 13*

C144 AP63 500fr multi 2.75 1.75

Apollo 17 US moon mission, 12/7-19/73.

Presidents Houphouet Boigny (Ivory Coast) and De Gaulle — AP64

1974, Apr. 30 Engr. *Perf. 13*

C145 AP64 40fr rose lilac & indigo .20 .20

30th anniv. of the Conf. of Brazzaville.

Painting Type of 1968

Impressionist Paintings: 40fr, Pleasure Boats, by Claude Monet, horiz. 50fr, Ballet Dancer, by Edgar Degas. 130fr, Young Girl with Flowers, by Auguste Renoir.

1974, June 11 Photo. *Perf. 13*

C146 AP32 40fr gold & multi .20 .20
C147 AP32 50fr gold & multi .25 .20
C148 AP32 130fr gold & multi .70 .40
Nos. C146-C148 (3) 1.15 .80

Astronaut on Moon, Eagle and Emblems
AP65

1974, July 20 Engr. *Perf. 13*
C149 AP65 200fr multi 1.10 .70

First men on the moon, 5th anniversary.

UPU Emblem, Letters, Pigeon
AP66

UPU cent.: 300fr, UPU emblem, letters, pigeons, diff.

1974, Oct. 9 Engr. *Perf. 13*
C150 AP66 150fr lt bl & Prus bl .75 .45
C151 AP66 300fr org & claret 1.50 .80

Space Docking, US and USSR Crafts
AP67

1974, Oct. 23 Engr. *Perf. 13*
C152 AP67 1000fr grn, red & sl 5.50 3.50

Russo-American space cooperation.
For overprint see No. C169.

Soccer and Games Emblem — AP68

Designs: Soccer actions.

1974, Oct. 25
C153 AP68 40fr grn, red & brn .20 .20
C154 AP68 65fr red, brn & grn .30 .20
C155 AP68 100fr grn, red & brn .50 .30
a. Souv. sheet of 3, #C153-C155 + 3 labels 1.10 1.10
Nos. C153-C155 (3) 1.00 .70

World Cup Soccer Championship, Munich, June 13-July 7.

UDEAC Issue

Presidents and Flags of Cameroun, CAR, Gabon and Congo — AP68a

1974, Dec. 8 Photo. *Perf. 13*
C156 AP68a 100fr gold & multi .60 .40

Annunciation, Tapestry, 15th Century — AP69

Christmas: 40fr, Visitation from 15th century tapestry, Notre Dame de Beaune, vert.

1974, Dec. 11
C157 AP69 40fr gold & multi .25 .20
C158 AP69 50fr gold & multi .35 .20

Dr. Schweitzer and Lambarene Hospital — AP70

1975, Jan. 14 Engr. *Perf. 13*
C159 AP70 500fr multi 2.50 1.75

Dr. Albert Schweitzer (1875-1965), medical missionary, birth centenary.

Crucifixion, by Bellini — AP71

Paintings: 150fr, Resurrection, Burgundian School, c. 1500.

1975, Apr. 8 Photo. *Perf. 13½*
Size: 26x45mm
C160 AP71 140fr gold & multi .90 .50
Size: 36x48mm
Perf. 13
C161 AP71 150fr gold & multi 1.00 .50

Easter 1975.

Marc Seguin Locomotive, 1829 — AP72

Locomotives: 25fr, The Iron Duke, 1847. 40fr, Thomas Rogers, 1895. 50fr, The Soviet 272, 1934.

1975, Apr. 8 Engr. *Perf. 13*
C162 AP72 20fr multi .20 .20
C163 AP72 25fr multi .20 .20
C164 AP72 40fr multi .20 .20
C165 AP72 50fr lil & multi .25 .20
Nos. C162-C165 (4) .85 .80

Swimming Pool, Montreal Olympic Games' Emblem — AP73

Designs: 150fr, Boxing ring and emblem. 300fr, Stadium, aerial view, and emblem.

1975, Sept. 30 Litho. *Perf. 13x12½*
C166 AP73 100fr multi .40 .25
C167 AP73 150fr multi .60 .40
C168 AP73 300fr multi 1.25 .85
a. Min. sheet of 3, #C166-C168 2.25 2.25
Nos. C166-C168 (3) 2.25 1.50

Pre-Olympic Year 1975.

No. C152 Surcharged in Violet Blue: "JONCTION / 17 Juillet 1975"

1975, Oct. 20 Engr. *Perf. 13*
C169 AP67 1000fr multi 5.50 3.75

Apollo-Soyuz link-up in space, July 17, 1975.

Annunciation, by Maurice Denis — AP74

Painting: 50fr, Virgin and Child with Two Saints, by Fra Filippo Lippi.

1975, Dec. 9 Photo. *Perf. 13*
C170 AP74 40fr gold & multi .25 .20
C171 AP74 50fr gold & multi .35 .20

Christmas 1975.

Concorde and Globe — AP75

1975, Dec. 29 Engr. *Perf. 13*
C172 AP75 500fr bl, vio bl & red 2.50 1.90

For overprint see No. C198.

No. C172 Surcharged

1976, Jan. 21
C173 AP75 1000fr on 500fr 5.50 3.75

Nos. C172-C173 for the 1st commercial flight of supersonic jet Concorde from Paris to Rio, Jan. 21.

Slalom and Olympic Games Emblem — AP76

Design: 250fr, Speed skating and Winter Olympic Games emblem.

1976, Apr. 22 Engr. *Perf. 13*
C174 AP76 100fr blk, bl & red .40 .30
C175 AP76 250fr blk, bl & red 1.00 .70
a. Souvenir sheet 1.50 1.50

12th Winter Olympic Games, Innsbruck, Austria, Feb. 4-15. No. C175a contains 100fr and 250fr stamps in continuous design with additional inscription and skier between, but without perforations between the design elements.

Size of perforated area: 125x27mm; size of sheet: 169x90mm.

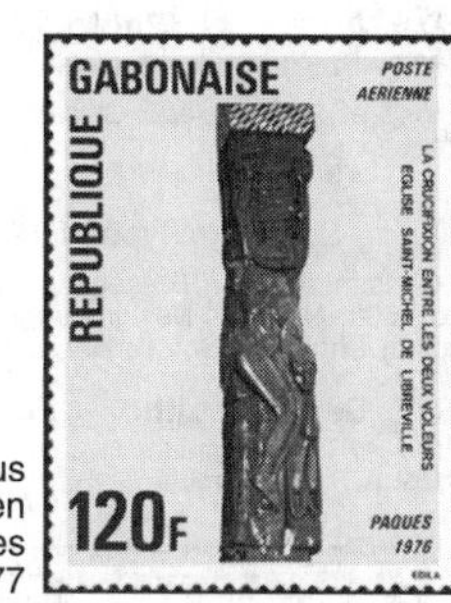

Jesus Between the Thieves
AP77

Design: 130fr, St. Thomas putting finger into wounds of Jesus. Both designs after wood carvings in Church of St. Michael, Libreville.

1976, Apr. 28 Litho. *Perf. 12½x13*
C176 AP77 120fr multi .65 .40
C177 AP77 130fr multi .70 .50

Easter 1976. See #C188-C189, C220-C221.

Boston Tea Party — AP78

Designs: 150fr, Battle of New York. 200fr, Demolition of statue of George III.

1976, May 3 Engr. *Perf. 13*
C178 AP78 100fr multi .55 .40
C179 AP78 150fr multi .80 .55
C180 AP78 200fr multi 1.10 .65
a. Triptych, #C178-C180 + 2 labels 2.75 2.25

American Bicentennial.

Nos. C178-C180 Overprinted: "4 JUILLET 1976"

1976, July 4 Engr. *Perf. 13*
C181 AP78 100fr multi .55 .40
C182 AP78 150fr multi .80 .55
C183 AP78 200fr multi 1.10 .65
a. Triptych, #C181-C183 + 2 labels 2.75 2.25

Independence Day.

Running — AP79

200fr, Soccer. 260fr, High jump.

1976, July 27 Litho. *Perf. 12½*
C184 AP79 100fr multi .40 .30
C185 AP79 200fr multi .80 .50
C186 AP79 260fr multi 1.00 .70
a. Souv. sheet of 3, #C184-C186, perf. 13 2.25 2.25
Nos. C184-C186 (3) 2.20 1.50

21st Olympic Games, Montreal, Canada, July 17-Aug. 1.

Presidents Giscard d'Estaing and Bongo — AP80

1976, Aug. 5 Photo. *Perf. 13*
C187 AP80 60fr blue & multi .35 .20

Visit of Pres. Valèrie Giscard d'Estaing of France.

Sculpture Type of 1976

Christmas: 50fr, Presentation at the Temple. 60fr, Nativity. Designs after wood Carvings in Church of St. Michael, Libreville.

1976, Dec. 6 Litho. *Perf. 12½x13*
C188 AP77 50fr multi .25 .20
C189 AP77 60fr multi .35 .25

Oklo Fossil Reactor — AP81

1976, Dec. 15 Litho. *Perf. 13*
C190 AP81 60fr red & multi .35 .25

The Last Supper, by Juste de Gand — AP82

100fr, The Deposition, by Nicolas Poussin.

1977, Mar. 25 Litho. *Perf. 12½*
C191 AP82 50fr gold & multi .25 .20
C192 AP82 100fr gold & multi .55 .40

Easter 1977.

Air Gabon Plane and Insigne — AP83

1977, June 3 Litho. *Perf. 12½*
C193 AP83 60fr multi .35 .25

Air Gabon's first intercontinental route.

Beethoven, Piano and Score — AP84

1977, June 15 Engr. *Perf. 13*
C194 AP84 260fr slate 1.40 .90

Ludwig van Beethoven (1770-1827).

Lindbergh and Spirit of St. Louis — AP85

1977, Sept. 13 Engr. *Perf. 13*
C195 AP85 500fr multi 2.50 1.60

Charles A. Lindbergh's solo transatlantic flight from NY to Paris, 50th anniv.

Soccer — AP86

1977, Oct. 18 Photo. *Perf. 13x12½*
C196 AP86 250fr multi 1.40 .90

Elimination games, World Soccer Cup, Buenos Aires, 1978.

Viking on Mars AP87

1977, Nov. 17 Engr. *Perf. 13*
C197 AP87 1000fr multi 5.50 2.75

Viking, US space probe.

No. C172 Overprinted: "PARIS NEW-YORK / PREMIER VOL / 22.11.77"

1977, Nov. 22 Engr. *Perf. 13*
C198 AP75 500fr multi 2.75 2.00

Concorde, 1st commercial flight, Paris to NYC.

Lion Hunt, by Rubens — AP88

Rubens Paintings: 80fr, Hippopotamus Hunt. 200fr, Head of Black Man, vert.

1977, Nov. 24 Litho. *Perf. 13*
C199 AP88 60fr gold & multi .35 .25
C200 AP88 80fr gold & multi .45 .35
C201 AP88 200fr gold & multi 1.10 .80
a. Souv. sheet of 3, #C199-C201 1.90 1.90
Nos. C199-C201 (3) 1.90 1.40

Peter Paul Rubens (1577-1640).

Adoration of the Kings, by Rubens — AP89

Design: 80fr, Flight into Egypt, by Rubens.

1977, Dec. 15 Litho. *Perf. 12½*
C202 AP89 60fr gold & multi .35 .25
C203 AP89 80fr gold & multi .45 .35

Christmas 1977; Peter Paul Rubens.

Paul Gauguin, Self-Portrait AP90

150fr, Flowers in vase and Maori statuette.

1978, Feb. 8 Litho. *Perf. 12½x12*
C204 AP90 150fr multi .80 .40
C205 AP90 300fr multi 1.60 .80

Paul Gauguin (1848-1903), French painter.

Pres. Bongo, Map of Gabon, Plane and Train AP91

Lithographed; Gold Embossed

1978, Mar. 12 *Perf. 12½*
C206 AP91 500fr multi 2.50 1.40

10th anniversary of national renewal.

Soccer and Argentina '78 Emblem — AP92

Argentina '78 Emblem and: 120fr, Three soccer players. 200fr, Jules Rimet Cup, vert.

1978, July 18 Engr. *Perf. 13*
C207 AP92 100fr red, grn & brn .40 .20
C208 AP92 120fr grn, red & brn .50 .30
C209 AP92 200fr brn & red .80 .40
a. Min. sheet of 3, #C207-C209 1.75 1.75
Nos. C207-C209 (3) 1.70 .90

11th World Cup Soccer Championship, Argentina, June 1-25.

Nos. C207-C209a Overprinted in Ultramarine or Black:
a. ARGENTINE / HOLLANDE / 3-1
b. BRESIL / ITALIE / 2-1
c. CHAMPION / DU MONDE 1978 / ARGENTINE

1978, July 21 Engr. *Perf. 13*
C210 AP92(a) 100fr multi .55 .25
C211 AP92(b) 120fr multi .65 .35
C212 AP92(c) 200fr multi 1.10 .55
a. Min. sheet of 3 (Bk) 2.50 2.50
Nos. C210-C212 (3) 2.30 1.15

Argentina's World Cup victory.

Albrecht Dürer (age 13), Self-portrait AP93

Design: 250fr, Lucas de Leyde, by Dürer.

1978, Sept. 15 Engr. *Perf. 13*
C213 AP93 100fr red brn & slate .55 .25
C214 AP93 250fr blk & red brn 1.40 .65

Dürer (1474-1528), German painter.

Philexafrique II-Essen Issue

Common Design Types

Designs: No. C215, Gorilla and Gabon No. 280. No. C216, Stork and Saxony No. 1.

1978, Nov. 1 Litho. *Perf. 13x12½*
C215 CD138 100fr multi .55 .25
C216 CD139 100fr multi .55 .25
a. Pair, #C215-C216 + label 1.10 .50

#C216a exists with two different labels: one for PHILEXAFRIQUE II and one for ESSEN '78.

Wright Brothers and Flyer AP94

1978, Dec. 19 Engr. *Perf. 13*
C217 AP94 380fr multi 2.00 1.00

75th anniversary of 1st powered flight.

Pope John Paul II AP95

Design: 200fr, Popes Paul VI and John Paul I, St. Peter's Basilica and Square, horiz.

1979, Jan. 24 Litho. *Perf. 12½*
C218 AP95 100fr multi .55 .25
C219 AP95 200fr multi 1.10 .55

Sculpture Type of 1976

Easter: 100fr, Disciples recognizing Jesus in the breaking of the bread. 150fr, Jesus appearing to Mary Magdalene. Designs after wood carvings in Church of St. Michael, Libreville.

1979, Apr. 10 Litho. *Perf. 12½x13*
C220 AP77 100fr multi .65 .35
C221 AP77 150fr multi 1.00 .50

Capt. Cook and Ships AP96

1979, July 10 Engr. *Perf. 13*

C222 AP96 500fr multi	3.50	1.60

Capt. James Cook (1728-1779), explorer, death bicentenary.

Flags and Map of England and France, Bleriot, Bleriot XI — AP97

Aviation Retrospect: 1000fr, Astronauts walking on moon (gold embossed inset).

Perf. 12½x12, 12

1979, Aug. 8 Litho.

C223 AP97 250fr multi	1.60	.80
C224 AP97 1000fr multi	6.50	3.50

1st flight over English Channel, 70th anniv.; Apollo 11 moon landing, 10th anniv.

Rotary Emblem, Map of Africa, Head — AP98

1979, Sept. 25 Photo. *Perf. 13*

C225 AP98 80fr multi	.55	.25

Rotary International, 75th anniversary.

Eugene Jamot, Tsetse Fly — AP99

1979, Nov. 23 Engr. *Perf. 13*

C226 AP99 300fr multi	2.00	1.00

Eugene Jamot (1879-1937), discoverer of sleeping sickness cure.

Bobsledding, Lake Placid '80 Emblem AP100

1980, Feb. 25 Litho. *Perf. 12½*

C227 AP100 100fr shown	.60	.35
C228 AP100 200fr Ski jump	1.40	.65
a. Souv. sheet of 2, #C227-C228	2.00	1.00

13th Winter Olympic Games, Lake Placid, NY, Feb. 12-24.

Jean Ingres AP101

1980, May 14 Engr. *Perf. 13*

C229 AP101 100fr shown	.65	.35
C230 AP101 200fr Jacques Offenbach	1.40	.65
C231 AP101 360fr Gustave Flaubert	2.25	1.25
Nos. C229-C231 (3)	4.30	2.25

12th World Telecommunications Day — AP102

1980, May 17 Litho. *Perf. 12½*

C232 AP102 80fr multi	.55	.25

Costes, Bellonte and Plane — AP103

Design: 1000fr, Mermoz, sea plane.

1980, July 16 Engr. *Perf. 13*

C233 AP103 165fr multi	1.10	.55
C234 AP103 1000fr multi	6.50	3.50

1st North Atlantic crossing, 50th anniv.; 1st South Atlantic air mail service, 50th anniv.

Running, Moscow '80 Emblem AP104

1980, July 25 Litho.

C235 AP104 50fr shown	.35	.20
C236 AP104 100fr Pole vault	.65	.35
C237 AP104 250fr Boxing	1.50	.80
a. Souv. sheet of 3, #C235-C237	2.50	1.40
Nos. C235-C237 (3)	2.50	1.35

22nd Summer Olympic Games, Moscow, July 19-Aug. 3.

Nos. C235-C237a Overprinted in Red, Brown, Ultramarine or Black

50fr: YIFTER (Eth.) / NYAMBUI (Tanz.) / MAANINKA (Finl.) / 5000 Metres
100fr: KOZIAKIEWICZ (Pol.) / (record du monde) / VOLKOV (Urss) et / SLUSARSKI (Pol.)
250fr: WELTERS / ALDAMA (Cuba) / MUGABI (Oug.) / KRUBER (Rda) / et SZCZERDA (Pol.)

1980, Sept. 25 Litho. *Perf. 13*

C238 AP104 50fr (R, vert. & horiz.)	.35	.20
C239 AP104 100fr (Br)	.65	.35
C240 AP104 250fr (U)	1.50	.80
a. Souv. sheet of 3 (Blk)	2.50	1.40
Nos. C238-C240 (3)	2.50	1.35

Pres. Charles de Gaulle AP105

1980, Nov. 9 Photo. *Perf. 13*

C241 AP105 100fr shown	.60	.35
C242 AP105 200fr Pres. & Mrs. de Gaulle	1.40	.65
a. Souv. sheet of 2, #C241-C242	2.00	1.00

Pres. Charles de Gaulle (1890-1970).

AP106

1981, Feb. 19 Litho. *Perf. 13*

C243 AP106 60fr Soccer Players	.40	.20
C244 AP106 190fr Soccer player	1.40	.65

ESPANA '82 World Cup Soccer Championship.

AP107

1981, Mar. 26 Litho. *Perf. 13*

Spacecraft and Astronauts: 250fr, Yuri Gagarin. 500fr, Alan B. Shepard.

C245 AP107 150fr multi	1.00	.50
C246 AP107 250fr multi	1.60	.80
C247 AP107 500fr multi	3.50	1.60
a. Souv. sheet of 3, #C245-C247, perf. 12½	6.25	3.25
Nos. C245-C247 (3)	6.10	2.90

200th anniv. of discovery of Uranus by William Herschel (1738-1822).

Map of Africa and Emblems AP108

1981, June 1 Litho. *Perf. 12½*

C248 AP108 100fr multi	.65	.35

Electric Power Distribution Union, 7th Congress, Libreville, June 1-5.

D-51 Steam Locomotive, Japan, and SNCF Turbotrain TGV-001, France — AP109

200th Birth Anniv. of George Stephenson: 100fr, B&O Mallet 7100, US, Prussian T3 steam locomotive. 350fr, Stephenson and his Rocket, BB Alsthom electric locomotive, Central Africa.

1981, June 4 Engr. *Perf. 13*

C249 AP109 75fr multi	.50	.25
C250 AP109 100fr multi	.65	.35
C251 AP109 350fr multi	2.25	1.10
a. Souvenir sheet of 3	3.50	1.90
Nos. C249-C251 (3)	3.40	1.70

#C251a contains #C249-C251 in changed colors.

No. C251a Overprinted in 1 line across 3 stamps: 26 fevrier 1981-Record du monde de vitesse 380 km a l'heure
Souvenir Sheet

1981, June 13 Engr. *Perf. 13*

C252 AP109 Sheet of 3	3.50	1.90

New world railroad speed record, set Feb. 26.

Intl. Letter Writing Week, Oct. 9-16 — AP110

1981, Oct. 9 Photo. *Perf. 13*

C253 AP110 200fr multi	1.40	.65

Souvenir Sheet

22nd Anniv. of Independence — AP110a

Illustration reduced.

1982 Typo. *Perf. 13x12½*
Self-Adhesive

C253A AP110a 2000fr multicolored

Printed on wood.

Still Life with a Mandolin, by George Braque (1882-1963) — AP111

Design: 350fr, Boy Blowing Bubbles, by Edouard Manet (1832-1883), vert.

Perf. 13x12½, 12½x13

1982, Oct. 5 Litho.

C254 AP111 300fr multi	2.00	1.00
C255 AP111 350fr multi	2.25	1.25

Pre-olympic Year — AP112

Manned Flight Bicentenary AP113

1983, Feb. 16 Litho. *Perf. 13*

C256 AP112 90fr Gymnast	.45	.25
C257 AP112 350fr Wind surfing	1.75	.90

1983, June 1 Engr. *Perf. 13*

Balloons.

C258 AP113 100fr Transatlantic flight, 5th anniv.	.65	.35
C259 AP113 125fr Montgolfiere, 1783	.80	.40
C260 AP113 350fr Rozier's balloon, 1783	2.25	1.25
Nos. C258-C260 (3)	3.70	2.00

Lady with Unicorn, by Raphael (1483-1520) AP114

1983, June 19 *Perf. 12½x13*

C261 AP114 1000fr multi	6.50	3.50

1984 Winter Olympics — AP115

1984, Feb. 8 Litho. *Perf. 12½*

C262 AP115 125fr Hockey	.40	.20
C263 AP115 350fr Figure skaters	1.10	.55

See No. C268.

Paris-Libreville-Paris Air Race, Mar. 15-28 — AP116

1984, Mar. 15 Litho. *Perf. 13x12½*

C264 AP116 500fr Planes, emblem	1.60	.80

The Racetrack, by Edgar Degas — AP117

1984, Mar. 21 *Perf. 13*

C265 AP117 500fr multi	1.60	.80

1984 Summer Olympics AP118

Hamburg '84 Philatelic Exhibition — AP119

Illustration AP119 reduced.

1984, May 31 Litho. *Perf. 12½*

C266 AP118 90fr Basketball	.30	.20
C267 AP118 125fr Running	.40	.20

Souvenir Sheet

Nos. C262-C263, C266-C267 with Added Inscriptions

1984, Oct. 3 Litho. *Perf. 13*

C268 Sheet of 4	2.00	1.00
a. AP118 90fr MEDAILLE D'OR: U.S.A.	.25	.20
b. AP118 125fr MEDAILLE D'OR: KORIR	.35	.20
c. AP115 125fr Hockey sur glace: U.R.S.S.	.35	.20
d. AP115 350fr Danse couple: J. Torvill-C. Dean	1.00	.50

Souvenir Sheet

1984 Typo. *Perf. 13x12½*
Self-Adhesive

C268A AP119 1000fr multi

Printed on wood.

Dr. Albert Schweitzer (1875-1965) AP119a

1985, Sept. 5 Litho. *Perf. 12½*

C269 AP119a 350fr multi	1.00	.50

Flags of Gabon, UN AP120

1985, Sept. 20

C270 AP120 225fr multi	.65	.35

Admission of Gabon to UN, 25th anniv.

Central Post Office, Libreville, UPU and Gabon Postal Emblems — AP121

1985, Oct. 9

C271 AP121 300fr multi	1.00	.50

World Post Day.

UN, 40th Anniv. — AP122

1985, Oct. 24 Litho. *Perf. 12½*

C272 AP122 350fr multi	1.25	.55

PHILEXAFRICA '85, Lome, Togo — AP123

1985, Oct. 30 *Perf. 13*

C273 AP123 100fr Scout campsite	.35	.20
C274 AP123 150fr Telecommunications, transportation	.55	.25
a. Pair, #C273-C274 + label	.90	.50

Gabon's Gift to the UN — AP124

Design: Mother and Child, carved wood statue, and UN emblem.

1986, Mar. 15 Litho. *Perf. 13½*

C275 AP124 350fr multi	1.75	.85

Lastour Arriving in Gabon — AP125

1986, Mar. 25 Litho. *Perf. 12½*

C276 AP125 100fr multi	.55	.30

Lastoursville, cent.

World Telecommunications Day — AP126

1986, May 17 *Perf. 13½*

C277 AP126 300fr multi	1.60	.80

1986 World Cup Soccer Championships, Mexico — AP127

1986, May 31 *Perf. 12½*

C278 AP127 100fr Goal .55 .30
C279 AP127 150fr Dribbling, religious carving .80 .40
C280 AP127 250fr Players, map, soccer cup 1.40 .70
C281 AP127 350fr Stadium, flags 1.90 .95
a. Souv. sheet of 4, #C278-C281 4.75 2.40
Nos. C278-C281 (4) 4.65 2.35

For overprints see Nos. C283-C286.

World Post Day — AP128

1986, Oct. 9 **Litho.** *Perf. 12½*

C282 AP128 500fr multi 2.75 1.40

Nos. C278-C281 Ovptd. "ARGENTINA 3 -R.F.A 2" in One or Two Lines in Red

1986, Oct. 23 **Litho.** *Perf. 12½*

C283 AP127 100fr multi .55 .30
C284 AP127 150fr multi .80 .40
C285 AP127 250fr multi 1.40 .70
C286 AP127 350fr multi 1.90 .95
Nos. C283-C286 (4) 4.65 2.35

The Renewal, 19th Anniv. AP129

1987, Mar. 12 **Litho.** *Perf. 13*

C287 AP129 500fr multi 2.75 1.40

Konrad Adenauer (1876-1967), West German Chancellor AP130

1987, Apr. 15 *Perf. 12x12½*

C288 AP130 300fr mar, chlky bl & blk 1.60 .85

Schweitzer and Medical Settlement — AP131

1988, Apr. 17 **Litho.** *Perf. 12½x12*

C289 AP131 500fr multi 3.50 1.75

Dr. Albert Schweitzer (1875-1965), missionary physician and founder of the hospital and medical settlement, Lambarene, Gabon.

Port Gentil Refinery, 20th Anniv. — AP132

1988, Sept. 1 **Litho.** *Perf. 13½*

C290 AP132 350fr multi 2.40 1.25

De Gaulle's Call for French Resistance, 50th Anniv. — AP133

1990, June 18 **Litho.** *Perf. 13*

C291 AP133 500fr multicolored 3.50 1.75

Port of Marseilles by J. B. Jongkind (1819-1891) — AP134

1991, Feb. 9 **Litho.** *Perf. 13*

C292 AP134 500fr multicolored 4.50 2.25

Discovery of America, 500th Anniv. — AP135

1992, Oct. 12 **Litho.** *Perf. 13*

C293 AP135 500fr multicolored 4.25 2.10

Antoine de Saint-Exupery (1900-44) — AP136

1994 **Litho.** *Perf. 13*

C294 AP136 500fr multicolored *3.00 1.50*

Opening of the Channel Tunnel — AP137

1994

C295 AP137 500fr multicolored *3.00 1.50*

AIR POST SEMI-POSTAL STAMPS

Catalogue values for unused stamps in this section are for Never Hinged items.

Ramses II Paying Homage to Four Gods, Wadi-es-Sabua — SPAP1

Unwmk.

1964, Mar. 9 **Engr.** *Perf. 13*

CB1 SPAP1 10fr + 5fr dk bl & bis brn .70 .70
CB2 SPAP1 25fr + 5fr dk car rose & vio bl .90 .90
CB3 SPAP1 50fr + 5fr sl grn & claret 1.40 1.40
Nos. CB1-CB3 (3) 3.00 3.00

UNESCO world campaign to save historic monuments in Nubia.

POSTAGE DUE STAMPS

Postage Due Stamps of France Overprinted

1928 **Unwmk.** *Perf. 14x13½*

J1 D2 5c light blue .20 .20
J2 D2 10c gray brown .20 .20
J3 D2 20c olive green .70 .70
J4 D2 25c bright rose .75 .75
J5 D2 30c light red 1.10 1.10
J6 D2 45c blue green 1.10 1.10
J7 D2 50c brown violet 1.60 1.60
J8 D2 60c yellow brown 1.60 1.60
J9 D2 1fr red brown 1.60 1.60
J10 D2 2fr orange red 2.40 2.40
J11 D2 3fr bright violet 2.75 2.75
Nos. J1-J11 (11) 14.00 14.00

Chief Makoko, de Brazza's Aide — D3

Count Savorgnan de Brazza — D4

1930 **Typo.** *Perf. 13½x14*

J12 D3 5c dk bl & olive .75 .75
J13 D3 10c dk red & brn .80 .80
J14 D3 20c green & brn 1.10 1.10
J15 D3 25c lt bl & brn 1.10 1.10
J16 D3 30c bis brn & Prus bl 1.60 1.60
J17 D3 45c Prus bl & ol 2.40 2.40
J18 D3 50c red vio & brn 2.75 2.75
J19 D3 60c gray lil & bl blk 4.75 4.75
J20 D4 1fr bis brn & bl blk 6.50 6.50
J21 D4 2fr violet & brn 8.50 8.50
J22 D4 3fr dp red & brn 9.75 9.75
Nos. J12-J22 (11) 40.00 40.00

Fang Woman — D5

1932 **Photo.** *Perf. 13x13½*

J23 D5 5c dk bl, *bl* .85 .85
J24 D5 10c red brown 1.00 1.00
J25 D5 20c chocolate 1.50 1.50
J26 D5 25c yel grn, *bl* 1.40 1.40
J27 D5 30c car rose 1.50 1.50
J28 D5 45c red org, *yel* 5.00 5.00
J29 D5 50c dk violet 1.75 1.75
J30 D5 60c dull blue 2.50 2.50
J31 D5 1fr blk, *red org* 6.00 6.00
J32 D5 2fr dark green 7.00 7.00
J33 D5 3fr rose lake 6.50 6.50
Nos. J23-J33 (11) 35.00 35.00

Catalogue values for unused stamps in this section, from this point to the end of the section, are for Never Hinged items.

Republic

Pineapple — D6

Unwmk.

1962, Dec. 10 **Engr.** *Perf. 11*

J34 D6 50c shown .20 .20
J35 D6 50c Mangoes .20 .20
a. Pair, #J34-J35 .25
J36 D6 1fr Avocados .20 .20
J37 D6 1fr Tangerines .20 .20
a. Pair, #J36-J37 .25
J38 D6 2fr Coconuts .20 .20
J39 D6 2fr Grapefruit .20 .20
a. Pair, #J38-J39 .25
J40 D6 5fr Oranges .30 .30
J41 D6 5fr Papaya .30 .30
a. Pair, #J40-J41 .60
J42 D6 10fr Breadfruit .65 .65
J43 D6 10fr Guavas .65 .65
a. Pair, #J42-J43 1.30
J44 D6 25fr Lemons .75 .75
J45 D6 25fr Bananas .75 .75
a. Pair, #J44-J45 1.50
Nos. J34-J45 (12) 4.60 4.60

Pairs se-tenant at the base.

Charaxes Candiope — D7

Butterflies: 10fr, Charaxes ameliae. 25fr, Cyrestis camillus. 50fr, Charaxes castor. 100fr, Pseudacrea boisduvali.

1978, July 4 **Litho.** *Perf. 13*

J46 D7 5fr multi .20 .20
J47 D7 10fr multi .20 .20
J48 D7 25fr multi .25 .25
J49 D7 50fr multi .70 .45
J50 D7 100fr multi 1.40 .80
Nos. J46-J50 (5) 2.75 1.90

OFFICIAL STAMPS

Catalogue values for unused stamps in this section are for Never Hinged items.

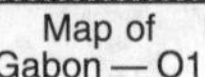

Map of Gabon — O1

Flag of Gabon — O2

Designs: 25fr, 30fr, Flag of Gabon. 50fr, 85fr, 100fr, 200fr, Coat of Arms.

1968 Unwmk. Photo. *Perf. 14*

O1 O1 1fr olive & multi .20 .20
O2 O1 2fr multi .20 .20
O3 O1 5fr lilac & multi .20 .20
O4 O1 10fr emer & multi .20 .20
O5 O1 25fr brn & multi .30 .20
O6 O1 30fr org & multi .30 .20
O7 O1 50fr multi .50 .20
O8 O1 85fr multi .90 .30
O9 O1 100fr yel & multi 1.25 .40
O10 O1 200fr gray & multi 2.25 1.00
Nos. O1-O10 (10) 6.30 3.10

1971-84 Typo. *Perf. 13x14*

O11 O2 5fr multi ('81) .20 .20
O12 O2 10fr multi .20 .20
O13 O2 20fr multi ('81) .20 .20
O14 O2 25fr multi ('84) .20 .20
O15 O2 30fr multi ('78) .25 .20
O16 O2 40fr multi ('72) .45 .25
O17 O2 50fr multi ('76) .55 .20
O18 O2 60fr multi ('77) .60 .25
O19 O2 75fr multi ('81) .30 .20
O20 O2 80fr multi ('77) .90 .40
O21 O2 100fr multi ('78) .65 .25
O22 O2 500fr multi ('78) 3.50 1.25
Nos. O11-O22 (12) 8.00 3.80

GAMBIA

'gam-bē-ə

LOCATION — Extending inland from the mouth of the Gambia River on the west coast of Africa
GOVT. — Republic in British Commonwealth
AREA — 4,068 sq. mi.
POP. — 1,087,000 (1995 est.)
CAPITAL — Banjul

The British Crown Colony and Protectorate of Gambia became independent in 1965 and a republic in 1970.

12 Pence = 1 Shilling
100 Bututs = 1 Dalasy (1971)

Catalogue values for unused stamps in this country are for Never Hinged items, beginning with Scott 144.

Queen Victoria
A1 A2

Typographed and Embossed

1869, Jan. Unwmk. *Imperf.*

1 A1 4p pale brown 400. 200.
a. 4p brown 450. 160.
2 A1 6p deep blue 400. 150.
a. 6p blue *475.* *140.*
b. 6p pale blue *2,250.* *1,250.*

1874, Aug. Wmk. 1

3 A1 4p pale brown 325. 175.
a. 4p brown 325. 175.
4 A1 6p blue 275. 175.
a. 6p deep blue 275. 200.
b. Panel sloping down from left to right 475. 275.

The name panel sloping down variety is from a top right corner position. A top left corner position exists with a less noticeable sloping of the panel down from right to left; it is worth less.

1880, June *Perf. 14*

5 A1 ½p orange 5.50 *10.50*
6 A1 1p maroon 3.50 *5.00*
7 A1 2p rose 17.00 9.00
8 A1 3p ultra 40.00 21.00
9 A1 4p brown 125.00 12.00
10 A1 6p blue 65.00 37.50
a. Panel sloping down from left to right 225.00 110.00
11 A1 1sh green 160.00 100.00
Nos. 5-11 (7) 416.00 195.00

The watermark on Nos. 5-11 exists both upright and sideways.
See footnote following No. 4.

1886-87 Wmk. 2 Sideways

12 A1 ½p green ('87) 2.25 *2.00*
13 A1 1p rose car ('87) 4.00 *5.25*
a. 1p maroon *15,000.*
14 2p deep orange 1.50 *7.00*
b. 2p orange 8.50 5.50
15 A1 2½p ultramarine 1.25 1.00
16 A1 3p slate 4.00 *13.00*
17 A1 4p brown 3.50 1.75
18 A1 6p slate green 9.75 *40.00*
a. 6p pale olive green 55.00 50.00
b. 6p bronze green 24.00 *45.00*
c. As "a," panel sloping down from left to right 150.00 125.00
d. As "b," panel sloping down from left to right 55.00 *80.00*
19 A1 1sh violet 3.75 *15.00*
a. 1sh purple 3.50 *15.00*
Nos. 12-19 (8) 30.00 *85.00*

See footnote following No. 4.

1898, Jan. Typo. Wmk. 2

20 A2 ½p gray green 1.75 1.75
21 A2 1p carmine rose 1.25 .75
22 A2 2p brn org & pur 4.00 *3.50*
23 A2 2½p ultramarine 1.50 *1.50*
24 A2 3p red vio & ultra 12.50 *12.00*
25 A2 4p brown & ultra 4.50 *20.00*
26 A2 6p ol grn & car rose 9.00 *17.50*
27 A2 1sh vio & green 20.00 *42.50*
Nos. 20-27 (8) 54.50 *99.50*

King Edward VII — A3

1902-05 *Perf. 14*

28 A3 ½p green 1.75 *2.00*
29 A3 1p car rose 1.25 .75
30 A3 2p org & pur 3.00 1.50
31 A3 2½p ultramarine 21.00 14.50
32 A3 3p red vio & ultra 11.00 2.75
33 A3 4p brn & ultra 2.75 *19.00*
34 A3 6p ol grn & rose 3.00 *10.00*
35 A3 1sh bluish vio & green 42.50 *67.50*
36 A3 1sh6p grn & red, *yel* 5.00 *14.50*
37 A3 2sh black & org 37.50 *47.50*
38 A3 2sh6p pur & brn, *yel* 13.00 *47.50*
39 A3 3sh red & grn, *yel* 20.00 *47.50*
Nos. 28-39 (12) 161.75 *275.00*

Numerals of 5p, 7½p, 10p, 1sh6p, 2sh6p and 3sh of type A3 are in color on plain tablet.
Issued: 1p, 3/13; ½p, 3p, 4/19; 2p, 2½p, 4p, 6p, 1sh, 2sh, 6/14; 1sh6p, 2sh6p, 3sh, 4/6/05.
For surcharges, see Nos. 65-66.

1904-09 Wmk. 3

41 A3 ½p green 2.00 .30
42 A3 1p car rose 3.00 .20
a. 1p carmine ('09) 3.00 .20
43 A3 2p org & pur ('06) 8.50 3.50
44 A3 2p gray ('09) 1.50 5.00
45 A3 2½p ultramarine 3.00 3.00
46 A3 3p red vio & ultra 3.75 2.00
47 A3 3p vio, *yel* ('09) 2.75 .75
48 A3 4p brn & ultra ('06) 13.00 *25.00*
49 A3 4p blk & red, *yel* ('09) .75 .65
50 A3 5p gray & black 9.00 *10.00*
51 A3 5p org & vio ('09) 1.50 1.25
52 A3 6p ol grn & rose ('06) 12.00 *25.00*
53 A3 6p dull vio ('09) 1.75 1.75
54 A3 7½p blue grn & red 6.00 *20.00*
55 A3 7½p brn & ultra ('09) 1.90 1.75
56 A3 10p ol bis & red 15.00 *20.00*
57 A3 10p ol grn & car rose ('09) 2.50 5.00
58 A3 1sh violet & grn 16.00 *35.00*
59 A3 1sh blk, *grn* ('09) 3.00 *10.00*
60 A3 1sh 6p vio & grn ('09) 8.00 *25.00*
61 A3 2sh black & org 55.00 *62.50*
62 A3 2sh vio & bl, *bl* ('09) 12.00 *15.00*
63 A3 2sh 6p blk & red, *bl* ('09) 20.00 19.00
64 A3 3sh yel & grn ('09) 25.00 *35.00*
Nos. 41-64 (24) 226.90 *326.65*

Nos. 38-39 Surcharged in Black:

a

b

Type a (I) - The word "PENNY" is 5mm from the horizontal bars.
Type a (II) - "PENNY" is 4mm from the bars.

1906, Apr. Wmk. 2

65 A3 ½p on 2sh6p, type I 47.50 *57.50*
a. Type II 47.50 *57.50*
66 A3 1p on 3sh 55.00 35.00
a. Double surcharge *1,800.* *4,500.*

King George V — A4

1912-22 Wmk. 3

70 A4 ½p green .65 *.90*
71 A4 1p carmine 1.25 .25
a. 1p scarlet 2.25 .80
72 A4 1½p ol brn & grn .25 .25
73 A4 2p gray .40 *2.25*
74 A4 2½p ultramarine 3.50 2.25
75 A4 3p violet, *yel* .25 .25
76 A4 4p blk & red, *yel* .65 *7.50*
77 A4 5p orange & vio .60 *1.25*
78 A4 6p dl vio & red violet .60 *1.50*
79 A4 7½p brn & ultra .90 *5.00*
80 A4 10p ol grn & car rose 1.75 *15.00*
81 A4 1sh blk, *green* 1.25 .90
a. 1sh black, *emerald* .75 *15.00*
82 A4 1sh6p vio & green 7.00 *9.00*
83 A4 2sh vio & bl, *bl* 2.25 *5.50*
84 A4 2sh6p blk & red, *bl* 2.50 *11.50*
85 A4 3sh yel & green 7.00 *17.50*
86 A4 5sh grn & red, *yel* ('22) *55.00* *80.00*
Nos. 70-86 (17) *85.80* *160.80*

Numerals of 1½p, 5p, 7½p, 10p, 1sh6p, 2sh, 2sh6p, 3sh, 4sh and 5sh of type A3 are in color on colorless tablet. No. 86 is on chalky paper.

1921-22 Wmk. 4

87 A4 ½p green .25 *11.50*
88 A4 1p carmine .90 *3.50*
89 A4 1½p ol grn & bl grn 1.25 *10.00*
90 A4 2p gray .90 *1.75*
91 A4 2½p ultramarine .50 *4.75*
92 A4 5p org & violet 1.60 *13.00*
93 A4 6p dl vio & red vio 1.60 *13.00*
94 A4 7½p brn & ultra 1.75 *22.50*
95 A4 10p yel grn & car rose 6.25 *12.50*
96 A4 4sh blk & red ('22) *45.00* *82.50*
Nos. 87-96 (10) *60.00* *175.00*

No. 96 is on chalky paper.

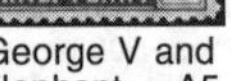

George V and Elephant — A5

George V — A6

1922-27 Engr. Wmk. 4

Head and Shield in Black

102 A5 ½p green .45 .45
103 A5 1p brown .60 .20
104 A5 1½p carmine .70 .20
105 A5 2p gray .85 1.60
106 A5 2½p orange .80 *8.75*
107 A5 3p ultramarine .75 .20
108 A5 4p car, *org* ('27) 3.50 *14.50*
109 A5 5p yellow green 1.75 *8.00*
110 A5 6p claret 1.10 .25
111 A5 7½p vio, *yel* ('27) 6.00 *35.00*
112 A5 10p blue 4.00 *14.50*
113 A6 1sh vio, *org* ('24) 2.00 .85
114 A6 1sh6p blue 8.50 *9.75*
115 A6 2sh vio, *blue* 3.25 *3.50*
116 A6 2sh6p dark green 3.25 *7.75*
117 A6 3sh aniline vio 10.00 *32.50*
a. 3sh black purple 175.00 *350.00*
118 A6 4sh brown 3.50 *13.00*
119 A6 5sh dk grn, *yel* ('26) 10.00 *29.00*
120 A6 10sh yellow green 60.00 *80.00*
Nos. 102-120 (19) 121.00 *260.00*

1922, Sept. 1 Wmk. 3

Head & Shield in Black

121 A5 4p carmine, *yel* 2.25 *2.00*
122 A5 7½p violet, *yel* 2.75 *5.00*
123 A6 1sh violet, *orange* 6.00 *16.00*
124 A6 5sh dk green, *yel* 29.00 *77.50*
Nos. 121-124 (4) 40.00 *100.50*

Common Design Types pictured following the introduction.

Silver Jubilee Issue

Common Design Type

1935, May 6 Wmk. 4 *Perf. 11x12*

125 CD301 1½p carmine & bl .45 .35
126 CD301 3p ultra & brn .55 *.90*
127 CD301 6p ol grn & lt bl 1.00 *1.75*
128 CD301 1sh brn vio & ind 3.00 *4.00*
Nos. 125-128 (4) 5.00 *7.00*
Set, never hinged 9.50

Coronation Issue

Common Design Type

1937, May 12 *Perf. 11x11½*

129 CD302 1p brown .20 .20
130 CD302 1½p dark carmine .20 .20
131 CD302 3p deep ultra .35 .25
Nos. 129-131 (3) .75 .65
Set, never hinged 1.25

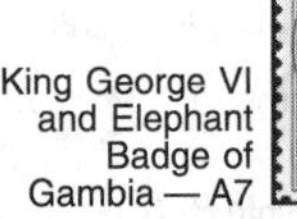

King George VI and Elephant Badge of Gambia — A7

1938-46 *Perf. 12*

132 A7 ½p bl grn & blk .20 *.45*
133 A7 1p brn & red vio .20 *.40*
134 A7 1½p rose red & brn lake .25 1.75
134A A7 1½p gray black & ultra ('44) .20 1.25
135 A7 2p gray black & ultra 1.50 2.50
135A A7 2p rose red & brn lake ('43) .50 1.75
136 A7 3p blue & brt bl .30 .20
136A A7 5p dk vio brn & olive ('41) .35 .35
137 A7 6p plum & ol grn 1.00 .30
138 A7 1sh vio & sl blk 1.25 .20
138A A7 1sh3p bl & choc ('46) 1.25 2.00
139 A7 2sh bl & dp rose 3.00 2.50
140 A7 2sh6p sl grn & sep 7.50 1.60
141 A7 4sh dk vio & red orange 12.50 2.00
142 A7 5sh org red & dk blue 12.50 3.25
143 A7 10sh blk & yel org 12.50 5.50
Nos. 132-143 (16) 55.00 26.00
Set, never hinged 80.00

Issued: 5p, 3/13; #135A, 10/1; #134A, 1/2; 1sh3p, 11/28; others, 4/1.

Catalogue values for unused stamps in this section, from this point to the end of the section, are for Never Hinged items.

Peace Issue

Common Design Type

1946, Aug. 6 Engr. *Perf. 13½*

144 CD303 1½p black .20 .20
145 CD303 3p deep blue .20 .20

Silver Wedding Issue

Common Design Types

1948, Dec. 24 Photo. *Perf. 14x14½*

146 CD304 1½p black .25 .20

Perf. 11½x11

Engr.; Name Typo.

147 CD305 £1 purple 11.50 *13.00*

UPU Issue
Common Design Types
Engr.; Name Typo. on 3p, 6p
Perf. 13½, 11x11½

1949, Oct. 10 **Wmk. 4**

No.	Type	Description	Unused	Used
148	CD306	1½p slate	.30	.55
149	CD307	3p indigo	1.40	1.00
150	CD308	6p red lilac	.40	.40
151	CD309	1sh violet	.40	.30
		Nos. 148-151 (4)	2.50	2.25

Coronation Issue
Common Design Type

1953, June 2 Engr. ***Perf. 13½x13***

No.	Type	Description	Unused	Used
152	CD312	1½p dk blue & black	.40	.40

Palm Wine Tapping — A8

Palm Leaf and Elizabeth II, by Annigoni — A9

Designs: 1p, 1sh3p, Cutter. 1½p, 5sh, Wolof woman. 2½p, 2sh, Barra canoe. 3p, 10sh, "Lady Wright." 4p, 4sh, James Island. 1sh, 2sh6p, Woman farming. £1, Elephant badge of Gambia.

1953, Nov. 2 ***Perf. 13½***

No.	Type	Description	Unused	Used
153	A8	½p dk green & car	.25	.20
154	A8	1p dk brn & ultra	.35	.35
155	A8	1½p gray & dk brn	.20	.45
156	A8	2½p car & black	.35	.60
157	A8	3p pur & indigo	.30	.20
158	A8	4p dp blue & blk	.50	1.50
159	A8	6p dp plum & brn	.30	.20
160	A8	1sh green & yel brn	.50	.45
161	A8	1sh3p blue & vio bl	8.25	.45
162	A8	2sh car & indigo	5.75	3.00
163	A8	2sh6p brn & bl grn	3.25	1.40
164	A8	4sh brn org & dp bl	9.00	2.75
165	A8	5sh ultra & red brn	2.00	1.40
166	A8	10sh dk yel green & ultra	16.00	6.25
167	A8	£1 black & bl grn	12.50	8.00
		Nos. 153-167 (15)	59.50	27.20

Wmk. 314

1961, Dec. 2 Engr. ***Perf. 11½***

Design: 3p, 6p, Map of West Africa.

No.	Type	Description	Unused	Used
168	A9	2p lilac & green	.20	.20
169	A9	3p brown & Prus grn	.60	.20
170	A9	6p car rose & dk blue	.60	.60
171	A9	1sh3p green & violet	.60	2.00
		Nos. 168-171 (4)	2.00	3.00

Visit of Elizabeth II to Gambia, Dec., 1961.

Freedom from Hunger Issue
Common Design Type

1963, June 4 Photo. ***Perf. 14x14½***

No.	Type	Description	Unused	Used
172	CD314	1sh3p car rose	.55	.20

Red Cross Centenary Issue
Common Design Type

1963, Sept. 2 Litho. ***Perf. 13***

No.	Type	Description	Unused	Used
173	CD315	2p black & red	.20	.20
174	CD315	1sh3p ultra & red	.65	.50

Beautiful Long-tailed Sunbird — A10

Birds: 1p, Yellow-mantled whydah. 1½p, Cattle egret. 2p, Yellow-bellied parrot. 3p, Ring-necked parakeet. 4p, Amethyst starling. 6p, Village weaver. 1sh, Rufous-crowned roller. 1sh3p, Red-eyed turtle dove. 2sh6p, Double-spurred francolin. 5sh, Palm-nut vulture. 10sh, Orange-cheeked waxbill. £1, Emerald cuckoo.

Perf. 12½x13

1963, Nov. 4 Photo. Wmk. 314
Multicolored Design & Inscription

No.	Type	Description	Unused	Used
175	A10	½p rose buff	.25	.55
176	A10	1p gray green	.25	.25
177	A10	1½p pale violet	1.40	.65
178	A10	2p buff	1.40	.65
179	A10	3p light gray	1.40	.65
180	A10	4p lt yel green	1.40	.70
181	A10	6p light blue	1.40	.20
182	A10	1sh pale grysh grn	1.00	.20
183	A10	1sh3p light blue	10.00	1.25
184	A10	2sh6p pale green	7.50	2.40
185	A10	5sh blue	7.50	2.75
186	A10	10sh tan	10.50	6.75
187	A10	£1 pale rose	22.50	13.00
		Nos. 175-187 (13)	66.50	30.00

For overprints see Nos. 188-191, 193-205.

Nos. 176, 179, 182 and 183 Overprinted: "SELF GOVERNMENT/1963"

1963, Nov. 7

No.	Type	Description	Unused	Used
188	A10	1p multicolored	.20	.20
189	A10	3p multicolored	.20	.20
190	A10	1sh multicolored	.25	.25
191	A10	1sh3p multicolored	.35	.35
		Nos. 188-191 (4)	1.00	1.00

Shakespeare Issue
Common Design Type

1964, Apr. 23 Photo. ***Perf. 14x14½***

No.	Type	Description	Unused	Used
192	CD316	6p ultramarine	.25	.20

Nos. 175-187 Overprinted: "INDEPENDENCE / 1965"

Perf. 12½x13

1965, Feb. 18 Photo. Wmk. 314
Multicolored Design & Inscription

No.	Type	Description	Unused	Used
193	A10	½p rose buff	.30	.55
194	A10	1p gray green	.30	.20
195	A10	1½ pale violet	.55	.55
196	A10	2p buff	.70	.25
197	A10	3p light gray	.70	.20
198	A10	4p lt yel green	.70	.75
199	A10	6p light blue	.70	.20
200	A10	1sh pale grysh grn	.70	.20
201	A10	1sh3p light blue	.70	.20
202	A10	2sh6p pale green	.70	.50
203	A10	5sh blue	.70	.65
204	A10	10sh tan	1.50	1.25
205	A10	£1 pale rose	5.75	6.25
		Nos. 193-205 (13)	14.00	11.75

In the overprint, "1965" is flush at left side under "Independence" on the ½p, 1½p, 6p, 1sh3p and 2sh6p; it is centered on the others.

Flag of Gambia over Gambia River — A11

Design: 2p, 1sh6p, Coat of arms.

1965, Feb. 18 Unwmk. ***Perf. 14***

No.	Type	Description	Unused	Used
206	A11	½p slate & multi	.20	.20
207	A11	2p lt brown & multi	.20	.20
208	A11	7½p dk brown & multi	.35	.30
209	A11	1sh6p lt green & multi	.50	.25
		Nos. 206-209 (4)	1.25	.95

Gambia's Independence.

ITU Emblem, Old and New Communication Equipment — A12

1965, May 17 Photo. ***Perf. 14½x14***

No.	Type	Description	Unused	Used
210	A12	1p dull blue & silver	.25	.20
211	A12	1sh6p violet & gold	.75	.30

Cent. of the ITU.

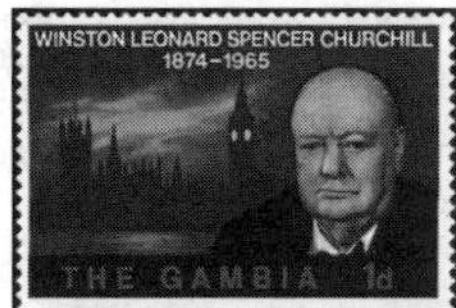

Winston Churchill and Parliament — A13

1966, Jan. 24 ***Perf. 14x14½***

No.	Type	Description	Unused	Used
212	A13	1p multicolored	.20	.20
213	A13	6p multicolored	.30	.20
214	A13	1sh6p multicolored	.50	.60
		Nos. 212-214 (3)	1.00	1.00

Sir Winston Leonard Spencer Churchill, statesman and WWII leader.

Red-cheeked Cordon Bleu and Emblem — A14

Birds: 1p, White-faced tree duck. 1½p, Red-throated bee eater. 2p, Pied kingfisher. 3p, Yellow-crowned bishop. 4p, Fish eagle. 6p, Bruce's green pigeon. 1sh, Blue-bellied roller. 1sh6p, African pigmy kingfisher. 2sh6p, Spur-winged goose. 5sh, Little woodpecker. 10sh, Violet plantain eater. £1, Pintailed whydah, vert.

Perf. 12½x13

1966, Feb. 18 Photo. Unwmk.
Size: 29x25mm
Multicolored Design & Inscription

No.	Type	Description	Unused	Used
215	A14	½p gray	.75	.30
216	A14	1p bluish green	.25	.30
217	A14	1½p yel green	.25	.30
218	A14	2p rose lilac	4.00	.35
219	A14	3p lilac	.25	.20
220	A14	4p blue	.40	.25
221	A14	6p gray	.30	.20
222	A14	1sh light green	.30	.20
223	A14	1sh6p bright blue	.75	.25
224	A14	2sh6p tan	.75	.50
225	A14	5sh gray green	.75	.75
226	A14	10sh ocher	.75	2.25

Perf. 14x14½
Size: 25x39mm

No.	Type	Description	Unused	Used
227	A14	£1 pink	1.00	5.00
		Nos. 215-227 (13)	10.50	10.85

Coat of Arms, Old and New Views of Bathurst — A15

Photo.; Silver Impressed (Arms)
1966, June 24 ***Perf. 14½x14***

No.	Type	Description	Unused	Used
228	A15	1p orange & dk brn	.20	.20
229	A15	2p lt ultra & dk brn	.20	.20
230	A15	6p emer & dk brown	.20	.20
231	A15	1sh6p brt pink & dk brn	.25	.25
		Nos. 228-231 (4)	.85	.85

150th anniv. of the founding of Bathurst.

Adonis and Atlantic Hotels and ITY Emblem — A16

Photo.; Silver Impressed (Emblem)
1967, Dec. 20 ***Perf. 14½x14***

No.	Type	Description	Unused	Used
232	A16	2p lt yel green & brn	.20	.20
233	A16	1sh orange & brown	.20	.20
234	A16	1sh6p lilac rose & brn	.20	.20
		Nos. 232-234 (3)	.60	.60

International Tourist Year.

Handcuffs and Human Rights Flame A17

Intl. Human Rights Year: 1sh, Fort Bullen. 5sh, Methodist Church.

1968, July 15 Photo. ***Perf. 14x13***

No.	Type	Description	Unused	Used
235	A17	1p gold & multi	.20	.20
236	A17	1sh gold & multi	.20	.20
237	A17	5sh gold & multi	.40	.50
		Nos. 235-237 (3)	.80	.90

Gambia #1, Victoria and Elizabeth II — A18

Designs: 6p, Gambia #2, Victoria & Elizabeth II. 2sh6p, Gambia #1-2, Elizabeth II.

Photo. and Embossed
Perf. 14x13½

1969, Jan. 20 Wmk. 314

No.	Type	Description	Unused	Used
238	A18	4p dull yel & dk brn	.20	.20
239	A18	6p dp yel grn & bl	.20	.20
240	A18	2sh6p dk bl gray, brn & bl	.60	.75
		Nos. 238-240 (3)	1.00	1.15

Centenary of Gambian postage stamps.

Dornier Wal, Route Gambia to Brazil and Lufthansa Emblem — A19

2p, Plane & ship Westfalen, route Gambia to Brazil & Lufthansa emblem. 1sh6p, Zeppelin, route Gambia to Brazil & Lufthansa emblem.

Perf. 13½x14

1969, Dec. 15 Litho. Unwmk.

No.	Type	Description	Unused	Used
241	A19	2p pink, org red & blk	.55	.20
242	A19	1sh buff, dl yel & blk	.55	.20
243	A19	1sh6p lt bl, ultra & blk	.65	1.10
		Nos. 241-243 (3)	1.75	1.50

35th anniversary of pioneer air services.

Runner, Flag and Arms of Gambia A20

1970, July 16 ***Perf. 14½x14***
Flag in Red, Blue & Green

No.	Type	Description	Unused	Used
244	A20	1p pink & brown	.20	.20
245	A20	1sh ultra & brown	.20	.20
246	A20	5sh green & brown	.40	.40
		Nos. 244-246 (3)	.80	.80

9th Commonwealth Games, Edinburgh, Scotland, July 16-25.

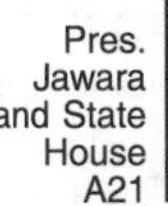

Pres. Jawara and State House A21

Republic Day, Apr. 24, 1970: 1sh, Pres. Sir Dauda Kairaba Jawara, vert. 1sh6p, Pres. Jawara and Gambia flag, vert.

1970, Nov. 2 Litho. *Perf. 14*
247 A21 2p gray & multi .20 .20
248 A21 1sh multicolored .20 .20
249 A21 1sh6p pink & multi .35 .35
Nos. 247-249 (3) .75 .75

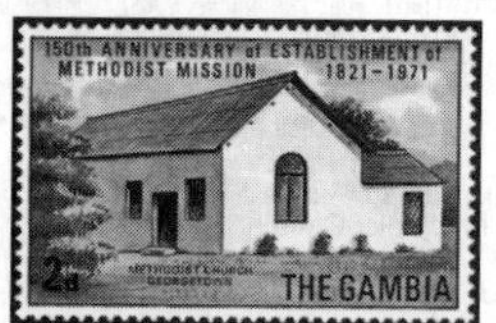

Methodist Church, Georgetown — A22

Designs: 1sh, Map of Africa and cross, vert. 1sh6p, John Wesley.

1971, Apr. 16 Unwmk. *Perf. 14*
250 A22 2p multicolored .20 .20
251 A22 1sh vio blue & multi .20 .20
252 A22 1sh6p green & multi .35 .35
Nos. 250-252 (3) .75 .75

Establishment of Methodist Mission, 150th anniv.

Yellowfin Tuna A23

Fish from Gambian Waters: 4b, Peters' mormyrid. 6b, Tropical two-wing flying fish. 8b, African sleeper goby. 10b, Yellowtail snapper. 13b, Rock hind. 25b, West African eel cat. 38b, Tiger shark. 50b, Electric catfish. 63b, Swamp eel. 1.25d, Smalltooth sawfish. 2.50d, Barracuda. 5d, Brown bullhead.

1971, July 1 Litho. *Perf. 14*
Fish in Natural Colors
253 A23 2b blue .20 .20
254 A23 4b lemon .20 .20
255 A23 6b lt blue green .20 .20
256 A23 8b orange brown .20 .20
257 A23 10b lt Prus blue .20 .20
258 A23 13b orange yel .20 .20
259 A23 25b green .30 .30
260 A23 38b brick red .35 .35
261 A23 50b Prus blue .60 .50
262 A23 63b bister .70 *1.00*
263 A23 1.25d yel green 1.25 *2.00*
264 A23 2.50d deep rose 2.50 *3.50*
265 A23 5d ultramarine 5.00 *6.00*
Nos. 253-265 (13) 11.90 *14.85*

Mungo Park, Scottish Landscape, Map of Gambia Basin — A24

Map of Gambia River Basin and: 25b, Park traveling in dugout canoe. 37b, Park's death under attack at Busa Rapids.

Perf. 13½x14
1971, Sept. 10 Litho. Unwmk.
270 A24 4b ultra & multi .20 .20
271 A24 25b yel green & multi .65 .30
272 A24 37b brick red & multi 1.00 *1.75*
Nos. 270-272 (3) 1.85 2.25

Mungo Park (1771-1806), Scottish explorer of the Gambia and Niger Rivers.

Radio Gambia and Pres. Jawara A25

Designs: 25b, Map showing area reached by Radio Gambia. 37b, Like 4b.

1972, July 1 *Perf. 14*
273 A25 4b black & dull yel .20 .20
274 A25 25b black, blue & red .20 *.25*
275 A25 37b black & yel green .40 *.75*
Nos. 273-275 (3) .80 1.20

Radio Gambia, 10th anniv., May 1.

High Jump A26

1972, Aug. 31 *Perf. 13½*
276 A26 4b emerald & multi .20 .20
277 A26 25b lt ultra & multi .20 .20
278 A26 37b red & multi .35 .35
Nos. 276-278 (3) .75 .75

20th Olympic Games, Munich, 8/26-9/11.

Mandingo Woman — A27

Designs: 25b, Musician playing Mandingo 21-stringed lute (kora). 37b, Map of Mali empire and area of Mandingo language.

1972, Oct. 18 Litho. *Perf. 14x14½*
279 A27 2b rose red & multi .20 .20
280 A27 25b lt ultra & multi .30 .30
281 A27 37b emerald & multi .50 .50
Nos. 279-281 (3) 1.00 1.00

International Conference on Mandingo Studies, London, June 30-July 3.

Ship Model with Lanterns A28

Christmas: 2b, Lighted ship (lantern) carried by boys.

1972, Dec. 1 Litho. *Perf. 13x13½*
282 A28 2b violet & multi .20 .20
283 A28 1.25d blue & multi .80 .80

Peanuts, FAO Emblem — A29

1973, Mar. 31 Litho. *Perf. 14½x14*
284 A29 2b red & multi .20 .20
285 A29 25b lt blue & multi .25 .25
286 A29 37b emerald & multi .40 .40
Nos. 284-286 (3) .85 .85

Freedom from Hunger, 2nd UN development campaign.

Planting and Drying Rice — A30

Oil Palms — A31

Cassava A32

1973, Apr. 30 *Perf. 14½x14*
287 A30 2b shown .20 .20
288 A30 25b Sorghum (Guinea corn) .20 .20
289 A30 37b Rice crop .30 .30

1973, July 16
290 A31 2b shown .20 .20
291 A31 25b Limes .25 .25
292 A31 37b Oil palm fruits .45 .45

1973, Oct. 15
293 A32 2b shown .20 .20
294 A32 50b Cotton .45 .45
Nos. 287-294 (8) 2.25 2.25

Gambian agriculture.

OAU Emblem — A33

1973, Nov. 1 Unwmk. *Perf. 13½x13*
295 A33 4b green, yel & black .20 .20
296 A33 25b dp mag, yel & black .25 .25
297 A33 37b blue, yel & black .25 .25
Nos. 295-297 (3) .70 .70

10th anniv. of the OAU.

Red Cross — A34

Perf. 14½x14
1973, Nov. 30 Wmk. 314
298 A34 4b red & black .20 .20
299 A34 25b ultra, red & black .25 .25
300 A34 37b emer, red & black .30 .30
Nos. 298-300 (3) .75 .75

25th anniv. of Gambia Red Cross Soc.

Flag of Gambia and Arms of Banjul — A35

Perf. 13½x13
1973, Dec. 17 Litho. Unwmk.
301 A35 4b yel green & multi .20 .20
302 A35 25b ver & multi .25 .25
303 A35 37b lt ultra & multi .25 .25
Nos. 301-303 (3) .70 .70

Change of name of Bathurst to Banjul and of St. Mary's Island to Banjul Island.

UPU Emblem — A36

1974, Aug. 24 Litho. *Perf. 13½x13*
304 A36 4b lilac & multi .20 .20
305 A36 37b blue & multi .35 .35

Centenary of Universal Postal Union.

Churchill at Harrow — A37

Churchill in Uniform of 4th Hussars — A38

Designs: 50b, Churchill as Prime Minister.

1974, Nov. 30 Litho. *Perf. 13½*
306 A37 4b multicolored .20 .20
307 A38 37b multicolored .30 .25
308 A38 50b multicolored .50 *.65*
Nos. 306-308 (3) 1.00 *1.10*

Sir Winston Churchill (1874-1965).

WPY Emblem, Races of Man A39

Symbolic Designs and WPY Emblem: 37b, Races multiplying and dividing like atom. 50b, World population.

1974, Dec. 16 Litho. *Perf. 14*
309 A39 4b multicolored .20 .20
310 A39 37b multicolored .20 .20
311 A39 50b multicolored .25 .25
Nos. 309-311 (3) .65 .65

World Population Year.

Dr. Schweitzer and Hospital, Lambarene — A40

50b, Dr. Schweitzer examining patient. 1.25d, Dr. Schweitzer in boat on Ogowe River.

1975, Jan. 14 Litho. *Perf. 14*
312 A40 10b multicolored .20 .20
313 A40 50b multicolored .40 .25
314 A40 1.25d multicolored .90 .75
Nos. 312-314 (3) 1.50 1.20

Dr. Albert Schweitzer (1875-1965), medical missionary, birth centenary.

Peace Dove A41

10b, Gambia flag. 50b, Gambia coat of arms. 1.25d, Map of Gambia & Gambia River.

1975, Feb. 18 *Perf. 13*

315	A41	4b	multicolored	.20	.20
316	A41	10b	multicolored	.20	.20
317	A41	50b	multicolored	.20	.20
318	A41	1.25d	multicolored	.40	.40
			Nos. 315-318 (4)	1.00	1.00

10th anniversary of independence.

Public Services Graph, A.D.B. Emblem A42

David, by Michelangelo A43

African Development Bank Emblem and: 50b, Plant symbolizing growth of Africa, fed by Development Bank. 1.25d, A.D.B. emblem surrounded by symbols of water, education, roads and hospitals.

1975, Mar. 31 Litho. *Perf. 14*

319	A42	10b	multicolored	.20	.20
320	A42	50b	multicolored	.30	.25
321	A42	1.25d	multicolored	.50	*.55*
			Nos. 319-321 (3)	1.00	1.00

African Development Bank, 10th anniv.

1975, Nov. 14 *Perf. 14½*

Bas-reliefs by Michelangelo: 50b, Madonna of the Steps. 1.25d, Battle of the Centaurs, horiz.

322	A43	10b	dull blue & multi	.20	.20
323	A43	50b	sepia & multi	.40	.40
324	A43	1.25d	green & multi	1.00	1.00
			Nos. 322-324 (3)	1.60	1.60

Michelangelo Buonarroti (1475-1564), Italian painter, sculptor and architect.

Gambia High School A44

Designs: 50b, Pupil in laboratory and school emblem. 1.50d, School emblem.

1975, Nov. 17

325	A44	10b	multicolored	.20	.20
326	A44	50b	multicolored	.20	.20
327	A44	1.50d	multicolored	.60	.60
			Nos. 325-327 (3)	1.00	1.00

Gambia High School, centenary.

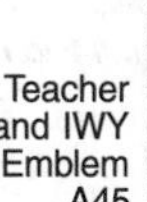

Teacher and IWY Emblem A45

IWY: 10b, Women planting rice. 50b, Nurse holding baby. 1.50d, Woman traffic officer.

1975, Dec. 15 Litho. *Perf. 14½*

328	A45	4b	yellow & multi	.20	.20
329	A45	10b	multicolored	.20	.20
330	A45	50b	multicolored	.40	.20
331	A45	1.50d	blue & multi	.70	.30
			Nos. 328-331 (4)	1.50	.90

Woman Golfer A46

Designs: 50b, Golfer addressing ball. 1.50d, Golfer finishing iron shot.

1976, Feb. 18 Litho. *Perf. 14½*

332	A46	10b	multicolored	.75	.20
333	A46	50b	multicolored	1.75	.25
334	A46	1.50d	multicolored	2.50	1.00
			Nos. 332-334 (3)	5.00	1.45

11th anniversary of independence.

American Militiaman — A47

American Bicent.: 50b, Continental Army soldier. 1.25d, Declaration of Independence.

1976, May 15 Litho. *Perf. 14x13½*

335	A47	25b	multicolored	.25	.20
336	A47	50b	multicolored	.55	.40
337	A47	1.25d	multicolored	1.00	1.00
	a.		Souvenir sheet of 3, #335-337	2.75	*4.50*
			Nos. 335-337 (3)	1.80	1.60

Mother and Child, Christmas Decoration — A48

1976, Oct. 28 Litho. *Perf. 14*

338	A48	10b	lt ultra & multi	.20	.20
339	A48	50b	rose & multi	.20	.20
340	A48	1.25d	yel grn & multi	.60	.50
			Nos. 338-340 (3)	1.00	.90

Christmas.

Serval Cat and Wildlife Fund Emblem — A49

Designs: 25b, Harnessed antelope. 50b, Sitatunga. 1.25d, Leopard.

1976, Nov. 29 *Perf. 13½x14*

341	A49	10b	multicolored	*8.00*	.40
342	A49	25b	multicolored	*10.50*	.40
343	A49	50b	multicolored	*18.00*	.75
344	A49	1.25d	multicolored	*32.50*	*5.00*
	a.		Souvenir sheet of 4, #341-344	*80.00*	*10.00*
			Nos. 341-344 (4)	*69.00*	*6.55*

Abuko Nature Reserve.

Queen's Visit, 1961 — A50

Designs: 50b, The spurs and jeweled sword. 1.25d, The oblation of the sword.

1977, Feb. 7 Litho. *Perf. 13½x14*

345	A50	25b	multicolored	.20	.20
346	A50	50b	multicolored	.20	.20
347	A50	1.25d	multicolored	.60	*.60*
			Nos. 345-347 (3)	1.00	*1.00*

25th anniv. of the reign of Elizabeth II.

Festival Emblem and Weaver A51

1977, Jan. 12 Litho. *Perf. 14*

348	A51	25b	multicolored	.20	.20
349	A51	50b	multicolored	.30	.30
350	A51	1.25d	multicolored	.75	.75
	a.		Souvenir sheet of 3, #348-350	2.00	*3.00*
			Nos. 348-350 (3)	1.25	1.25

2nd World Black and African Festival, Lagos, Nigeria, Jan. 15-Feb. 12.

Stone Circles, near Kuntaur A52

Tourism: 50b, Ruins of Fort on James Island. 1.25d, Mungo Park Monument.

1977, Feb. 18 Litho. *Perf. 14½*

351	A52	25b	multicolored	.20	.20
352	A52	50b	multicolored	.30	.30
353	A52	1.25d	multicolored	.75	.75
			Nos. 351-353 (3)	1.25	1.25

Clerodendrum Splendens — A53

Flowers and Shrubs: 4b, White water lily. 6b, Fireball lily. 8b, Mussaenda elegans. 10b, Broad-leaved ground orchid. 13b, Fiber plant. 25b, False kapok. 38b, Baobab. 50b, Coral tree. 63b, Gloriosa lily. 1.25d, Bell-flowered mimosa. 2.50d, Kindin dolo. 5d, African tulip tree. 6b, 8b, 10b, 13b, 25b, 38b, 1.25d, 2.50d, vertical.

1977, July 1 Litho. *Perf. 14½*

354	A53	2b	multicolored	.20	.20
355	A53	4b	multicolored	.20	*.25*
356	A53	6b	multicolored	.20	*.25*
357	A53	8b	multicolored	.20	.20
358	A53	10b	multicolored	2.00	.25
359	A53	13b	yellow & multi	.20	*.30*
	a.		Pale olive background	*3.00*	*3.00*
360	A53	25b	multicolored	.20	.20
361	A53	38b	multicolored	.25	*.45*
362	A53	50b	multicolored	.35	.35
363	A53	63b	multicolored	.40	*.50*
364	A53	1.25d	multicolored	.60	*1.25*
365	A53	2.50d	multicolored	.65	*1.25*
366	A53	5d	multicolored	1.00	*2.00*
			Nos. 354-366 (13)	6.45	*7.45*

For surcharges see Nos. 390A-390C.

Crowned Crane, Nile Crocodile, Bush Buck — A54

Madonna, Flight into Egypt, by Rubens — A55

Designs: 25b, Banjul Declaration, excerpt, flag colors. 50b, Banjul Declaration. 1.25d, Climbing lily, butterfly and moth.

1977, Oct. 15 Litho. *Perf. 14*

367	A54	10b	lt blue & black	.20	.20
368	A54	25b	multicolored	.30	.20
369	A54	50b	multicolored	.55	.25
370	A54	1.25d	red & black	1.75	.75
			Nos. 367-370 (4)	2.80	1.40

Banjul Declaration, for the conservation of flora and fauna, Feb. 18, 1977.

1977, Dec. 15 Litho. *Perf. 14x13½*

Rubens Paintings: 25b, Education of Mary by St. Ann. 50b, Child's head. 1d, Madonna surrounded by saints.

371	A55	10b	multicolored	.20	.20
372	A55	25b	multicolored	.25	.25
373	A55	50b	multicolored	.55	.35
374	A55	1d	multicolored	1.00	1.00
			Nos. 371-374 (4)	2.00	1.80

Peter Paul Rubens (1577-1640). Nos. 371-374 printed in sheets of 5 stamps and decorative label.

Dome of the Rock, Jerusalem — A56

1978, Jan. 3 Litho. *Perf. 14½*

375	A56	8b	olive green & multi	*.60*	*.30*
376	A56	25b	red & multi	*2.50*	*1.25*

Palestinian fighters and their families.

Walking on Greased Pole — A57

Verreaux's Eagle Owl — A58

Designs: 50b, Pillow fight on greased pole. 1.25d, Rowers in long boat.

1978, Feb. 18 *Perf. 14*

377	A57	10b	multicolored	.20	.20
378	A57	50b	multicolored	.30	.20
379	A57	1.25d	multicolored	.50	.50
			Nos. 377-379 (3)	1.00	.90

Independence Regatta celebrating 13th anniversary of independence.

Elizabeth II Coronation Anniversary Issue

Souvenir Sheet

Common Design Types

1978, Apr. 15 Litho. *Perf. 15*

380		Sheet of 6	1.50	1.50
	a.	CD326 1d White grayhound of Richmond	.30	.30
	b.	CD327 1d Elizabeth II	.30	.30
	c.	CD328 1d Lion	.30	.30

No. 380 contains 2 se-tenant strips of Nos. 380a-380c, separated by horizontal gutter with commemorative and descriptive inscriptions.

1978, Oct. 28 Litho. Perf. 14x13½

Birds of Prey and Wildlife Fund Emblem: 25b, Lizard buzzard. 50b, West African harrier hawk. 1.25d, Long-crested hawk eagle.

381 A58 20b multicolored 16.00 .75
382 A58 25b multicolored 16.00 .75
383 A58 50b multicolored 22.50 2.50
384 A58 1.25d multicolored 30.00 10.00
Nos. 381-384 (4) 84.50 14.00

Abuko Nature Reserve.

MV Lady Wright A59

New river vessels: 25b, River vessel Lady Chilel Jawara. 1d, Cross section of Lady Chilel Jawara.

1978, Dec. 1 Litho. Perf. 14½

385 A59 8b multicolored .20 .20
386 A59 25b multicolored .40 .30
387 A59 1d multicolored 1.40 1.25
Nos. 385-387 (3) 2.00 1.75

Motorized Police A60

1979, Feb. 18 Litho. Perf. 14

388 A60 10b shown .75 .20
389 A60 50b Fire engine 1.25 .30
390 A60 1.25d Ambulance 2.00 1.00
Nos. 388-390 (3) 4.00 1.50

14th anniversary of independence.

Nos. 359, 363-364 Surcharged

1979 Litho. Perf. 14½

390A A53 25b on 13b multi .25 .35
390B A53 25b on 63b multi .20 .20
390C A53 25b on 1.25d multi .20 .20
Nos. 390A-390C (3) .65 .75

Issued: #390A, 3/5; others, 3/26.

Ramsgate Sands, by William P. Frith — A61

Designs: 10b, 25b, IYC emblem and details from painting shown on 1d. 25b, vert.

1979, May 25 Litho. Perf. 14

Size: 38x21mm, 21x38mm

391 A61 10b multicolored .20 .20
392 A61 25b multicolored .20 .20

Size: 56x21mm

393 A61 1d multicolored .85 .85
Nos. 391-393 (3) 1.25 1.25

International Year of the Child.

Gambia No. 15, Maltese Cross Postmark A62

Gambian Stamps and Maltese Cross Postmark: 25b, #1. 50b, #208. 1.25d, #125.

1979, Aug. 16 Litho. Perf. 14½

394 A62 10b multicolored .20 .20
395 A62 25b multicolored .20 .20
396 A62 50b multicolored .20 .30
397 A62 1.25d multicolored .50 .70
a. Souvenir sheet of 1 1.25 1.40
Nos. 394-397 (4) 1.10 1.40

Sir Rowland Hill (1795-1879), originator of penny postage.

Abuko Earth Station, Construction — A63

Telecommunications: 50b, Newly opened station. 1d, Intelsat satellites orbiting earth.

1979, Sept. 20 Litho. Perf. 14

398 A63 25b multicolored .20 .20
399 A63 50b multicolored .30 .30
400 A63 1d multicolored .50 .50
Nos. 398-400 (3) 1.00 1.00

Apollo 11 Lift-off — A64

1979, Oct. 17 Litho. Perf. 14

401 A64 25b shown .20 .20
402 A64 38b Orbiting moon .25 .25
403 A64 50b Splashdown .55 .55
a. Souvenir booklet 4.00
b. Pane, 2 each 25b, 38b, 50b 1.90
c. Pane of 1 (2d Lunar module) 1.75
Nos. 401-403 (3) 1.00 1.00

Apollo 11 moon landing, 10th anniversary. No. 403a contains Nos. 403b-403c printed on peelable, self-adhesive paper backing with Apollo 11 emblems on back. Stamps and panes are die-cut and have 1 to 3 sides rouletted 9½.

Large Spotted Acraea, Wildlife Fund Emblem — A65

Wildlife Fund Emblem and Butterflies: 50b, Yellow pansy. 1d, Veined swallowtail. 1.25d, Foxy charaxes.

1980, Jan. 3 Litho. Perf. 13½x14

404 A65 25b multicolored 10.50 .40
405 A65 50b multicolored 13.50 .75
406 A65 1d multicolored 21.00 2.00
407 A65 1.25d multicolored 21.00 2.25
a. Souvenir sheet of 4, #404-407 75.00 9.00
Nos. 404-407 (4) 66.00 5.40

Abuko Nature Reserve.

Steam Launch "Vampire" — A66

1980, May 6 Litho. Perf. 14½

408 A66 10b shown .20 .20
409 A66 25b "Lady Denham" .30 .20

Perf. 13½x14½

Size: 49x21mm

410 A66 50b "Mansa Kila Ba" .35 .25
411 A66 1.25d "Prince of Wales" .55 .60
Nos. 408-411 (4) 1.40 1.25

London 80 Intl. Stamp Exhib., May 6-14.
For surcharge see No. 497A.

Queen Mother Elizabeth Birthday Issue

Common Design Type

1980, Aug. 4 Litho. Perf. 14

412 CD330 67b multicolored .40 .50

Phoenician Trading Vessel — A67

1980, Oct. 2 Litho. Perf. 14½

413 A67 8b shown .20 .20
414 A67 67b Egyptian seagoing ship .50 .30
415 A67 75b Portuguese caravel .60 .40
416 A67 1d Spanish galleon .80 .60
Nos. 413-416 (4) 2.10 1.50

Virgin and Child, by Francesco de Mura — A68

Christmas: 67b, Praying Virgin with Crown of Stars, by Correggio. 75b, Rest on the Flight, after Correggio.

1980, Dec. 18 Litho. Perf. 14

417 A68 8b multicolored .20 .20
418 A68 67b multicolored .25 .25
419 A68 75b multicolored .40 .40
Nos. 417-419 (3) .85 .85

New Atlantic Hotel, Conference Emblem — A69

1981, Feb. 18 Litho. Perf. 14

420 A69 25b shown .20 .20
421 A69 75b Ancient stone circle .40 .40
422 A69 85b Conference emblem .55 .55
Nos. 420-422 (3) 1.15 1.15

World Tourism Conference, Manila, Sept. 27 and 16th anniversary of independence.

13th World Telecomunications Day — A70

1981, May 17 Litho. Perf. 14

423 A70 50b No. 399 .50 .35
424 A70 50b No. 313 .50 .35
425 A70 85b ITU, WHO emblems .85 .60
Nos. 423-425 (3) 1.85 1.30

Royal Wedding Issue

Common Design Type

1981, July 22 Litho. Perf. 13½x13

426 CD331 75b Bouquet .25 .25
427 CD331 1d Charles .35 .35
428 CD331 1.25d Couple .40 .40
Nos. 426-428 (3) 1.00 1.00

For surcharges see Nos. 439, 497C.

Planting Rice Seedlings A71

1981, Sept. 4 Litho. Perf. 14

429 A71 10b shown .20 .20
430 A71 50b Spraying .30 .35
431 A71 85b Winnowing and drying .50 .55
Nos. 429-431 (3) 1.00 1.10

West African Rice Development Assoc., 10th anniv.

Abuko Nature Reserve A72

Designs: Wildlife Fund emblem and reptiles.

1981, Nov. 17 Litho. Perf. 14

432 A72 40b Bosc's monitor 12.50 .50
433 A72 60b Dwarf crocodile 13.50 1.00
434 A72 80b Royal python 17.00 2.00
435 A72 85b Chameleon 17.00 2.00
Nos. 432-435 (4) 60.00 5.50

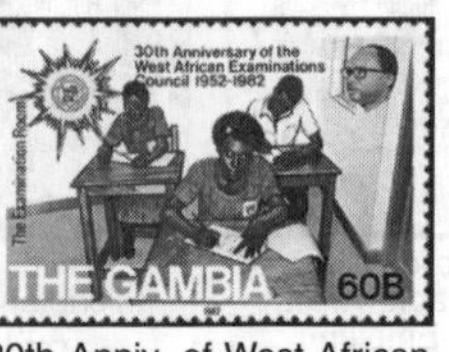

30th Anniv. of West African Examinations Council — A73

1982, Mar. 16 Litho. Perf. 14

436 A73 60b Test room .60 .40
437 A73 85b 1st high school .75 .55
438 A73 1.10d Council office 1.00 .75
Nos. 436-438 (3) 2.35 1.70

No. 426 Surcharged

1982, Apr. 19 Litho. Perf. 13½x13

439 CD331 60b on 75b multi 1.75 2.25

Scouting Year A74

1982, May Perf. 14

440 A74 85b Tree planting 1.50 1.00
441 A74 1.25d Woodworking 1.75 1.75
442 A74 1.27d Baden-Powell 2.00 2.50
Nos. 440-442 (3) 5.25 5.25

1982 World Cup A75

1982, June 13 Litho. Perf. 14

443 A75 10b Team .20 .20
444 A75 1.10d Players 1.00 .75
445 A75 1.25d Stadium 1.00 .80
446 A75 1.55d Cup 1.10 1.00
a. Souvenir sheet of 4, #443-446 5.50 5.50
Nos. 443-446 (4) 3.30 2.75

For surcharge see No. 497B.

Princess Diana Issue

Common Design Type

1982, July 1 Perf. 14½x14

447 CD333 10b Arms .20 .20
448 CD333 85b Diana .65 .65
449 CD333 1.10d Wedding .85 .85
450 CD333 2.50d Portrait 1.75 1.75
Nos. 447-450 (4) 3.45 3.45

For surcharge see No. 479D.

Economic Community of West African States Development A76

Designs: 10b, Yundum Experimental Farm. 60b, Banjul/Kaolack Microwave Tower. 90b, Soap Factory, Denton Bridge Banjul. 1.25d, Control Tower, Yundum.

1982, Nov. 5 Litho. *Perf. 14x14½*

451 A76 10b multicolored .30 .20
452 A76 60b multicolored 2.10 *2.40*
453 A76 90b multicolored 2.10 *3.25*
454 A76 1.25d multicolored 3.00 *3.75*
Nos. 451-454 (4) 7.50 9.60

Kassina Cassinoides — A77

1982, Dec. Litho. *Perf. 14*

455 A77 10b shown 1.25 .20
456 A77 20b Hylarana galamensis 2.25 .30
457 A77 85b Euphlyctis occipitalis 3.50 2.00
458 A77 2d Kassina senegalensis 5.00 *9.00*
Nos. 455-458 (4) 12.00 11.50

A78

1983, Mar. 14 Wmk. 373 *Perf. 12*

459 A78 10b Globe showing Gambia .20 .20
460 A78 60b Batik cloth .25 *.35*
461 A78 1.10d Bagging peanuts .45 *.60*
462 A78 2.10d Flag .70 *1.10*
Nos. 459-462 (4) 1.60 2.25

Commonwealth Day.

Sisters of St. Joseph of Cluny Centenary — A79

1983, Apr. 8 Litho. *Perf. 14*

463 A79 10b Founder Anne Marie Javouhey, vert. .20 .20
464 A79 85b Javouhey with children, house .50 .50

River Boats A80

1983, July 11 Litho. *Perf. 14*

465 A80 1b Canoes .20 .20
466 A80 2b Upstream ferry .20 .20
467 A80 3b Dredging vessel .20 .20
468 A80 4b Harbor launch .20 .20
469 A80 5b Freighter .20 .20
470 A80 10b 60-foot launch .20 .20
471 A80 20b Multi-purpose vessel .20 .20
472 A80 30b Large sailing canoe .20 .20
473 A80 40b Passenger-cargo ferry .20 .20
474 A80 50b Cargo liner, diff. .25 .25
475 A80 75b Fishing boats .45 .45
476 A80 1d Peanut river train .55 .50
477 A80 1.25d Groundnutter .70 *.75*
478 A80 2.50d Banjul-Barra ferry 1.50 *2.00*
479 A80 5d Binlang Bolong 3.25 *4.25*
480 A80 10d Passenger-cargo ferry, diff. 6.00 *7.50*
Nos. 465-480 (16) 14.50 *17.50*

For overprints see Nos. 523-524.

World Communications Year — A81

1983, Oct. 10

481 A81 10b Local ferry .20 .20
482 A81 85b GPO telex, Banjul .60 .60
483 A81 90b Radio Gambia .65 .65
484 A81 1.10d Loading mail, Yundum Airport .80 .80
Nos. 481-484 (4) 2.25 2.25

Osprey, Breeding Range A82

Designs: Birds, Maps of Europe and Africa.

1983, Sept. 12 Litho. *Perf. 14*

485 A82 10b multicolored 1.75 .50
486 A82 60b multicolored 3.00 2.75
487 A82 85b multicolored 3.50 3.25
488 A82 1.10d multicolored 3.75 *5.50*
Nos. 485-488 (4) 12.00 12.00

Raphael, 500th Birth Anniv. A83

Details from St. Paul Preaching at Athens.

1983, Nov. 1 Litho. *Perf. 14*

489 A83 60b multicolored .55 .55
490 A83 85b multicolored .70 .70
491 A83 1d multicolored .75 .75
Nos. 489-491 (3) 2.00 2.00

Souvenir Sheet

492 A83 2d multi, vert. 1.75 1.50

Manned Flight, 200th Anniv. A84

Flown covers and: 60b, Montgolfier Balloon. 85b, British Caledonian Aircraft. 96b, Junkers Airplane. 1.25d, Lunar module. 4d, Zeppelin.

1983, Dec. 12 Litho. *Perf. 14*

493 A84 60b multicolored .35 .35
494 A84 85b multicolored .45 .45
a. Bklt. pane, 2 each #493, 494 1.90
495 A84 90b multicolored .45 .45
496 A84 1.25d multicolored .50 .50
a. Bklt. pane, 2 each #495, 496 2.75
Nos. 493-496 (4) 1.75 1.75

Souvenir Sheet

497 A84 4d multicolored 9.00 9.00

No. 497 issued in booklet containing Nos. 497, 494a, 496a.

Nos. 411, 445, 428 and 449 Surcharged with Black Bars and New Value

Perfs. as before

1983, Dec. 14 Litho.

497A A66 1.50d on 1.25d, #411
497B A75 1.50d on 1.25d, #445
497C CD331 2d on 1.25d, #428
497D CD333 2d on 1.10d, #449

The status of Nos. 497A-497D is questioned.

Easter A85

Various Disney characters painting Easter eggs.

1984, Apr. 15 Litho. *Perf. 11*

498 A85 1b multicolored .20 .20
499 A85 2b multicolored .20 .20
500 A85 3b multicolored .20 .20
501 A85 4b multicolored .20 .20
502 A85 5b multicolored .20 .20
503 A85 10b multicolored .20 .20
504 A85 60b multicolored .40 .40
505 A85 90b multicolored .65 .65
506 A85 5d multicolored 2.75 2.75
Nos. 498-506 (9) 5.00 5.00

Souvenir Sheet

Perf. 14

507 A85 5d multicolored 5.00 5.00

1984 Summer Olympics A86

1984, Mar. 30 Litho. *Perf. 14*

508 A86 60b Shot put, vert. .30 .30
509 A86 85b High jump .45 .45
510 A86 90b Wrestling, vert. .45 .45
511 A86 1d Gymnastics, vert. .50 .50
512 A86 1.25d Swimming .60 .60
513 A86 2d Diving 1.00 1.00
Nos. 508-513 (6) 3.30 3.30

Souvenir Sheet

514 A86 5d Yachting, vert. 3.00 3.00

For overprints see Nos. 570-576.

Nile Crododile A87

1984, May 23

515 A87 4b Young hatching *2.50* *.50*
516 A87 6b Adult carrying young *2.50* *.50*
517 A87 90b Adult *18.00* *4.00*
518 A87 1.50d Adult, diff. *22.50* *5.00*
a. Souvenir sheet of 4, #514-518 *6.00* *6.00*
Nos. 515-518 (4) *45.50* *10.00*

Lloyd's List Issue

Common Design Type

1984, June 1 Litho. *Perf. 14*

519 CD335 60b Banjul Port .70 .60
520 CD335 85b Bulk cargo carrier .90 .90
521 CD335 90b Sinking of the Dagomba .90 *1.10*
522 CD335 1.25d 19th-cent. frigate 1.50 *1.90*
Nos. 519-522 (4) 4.00 4.50

Nos. 478-479 Overprinted: "19th UPU / CONGRESS HAMBURG"

1984, June 19 Litho. *Perf. 14*

523 A80 2.50d multicolored 1.40 *1.75*
524 A80 5d multicolored 2.75 *3.50*

1984 Summer Olympics A88

1984, July 28 Litho. *Perf. 14*

525 A88 60b Running .35 .35
526 A88 85b Long jump .50 .50
527 A88 90b Running, diff. .50 .50
528 A88 1.25d Long jump, diff. .65 .65
Nos. 525-528 (4) 2.00 2.00

Gambia-South America Transatlantic Flight, 50th Anniv. — A89

1984, Nov. 1 Litho. *Perf. 14*

529 A89 60b Graf Zeppelin D-LZ127 1.25 1.10
530 A89 85b Dornier Wal on S.S. Westfalen 1.75 *1.90*
531 A89 90b Dornier DO-18 D-ABYM 1.90 *2.75*
532 A89 1.25d Dornier Wal D-2069 1.90 *3.00*
Nos. 529-532 (4) 6.80 8.75

Butterflies and Marine Life A90

1984, Nov. 27

533 A90 10b Antanartia hippomene .35 .25
534 A90 55b Penaeus duorarum .40 .35
535 A90 75b Caretta caretta .65 .50
536 A90 85b Pseudacraea eurytus .95 *1.00*
537 A90 90b Charaxes lactitinctus .95 *1.00*
538 A90 1.50d Physalia .95 *1.00*
539 A90 2.35d Uca pugilator 1.75 *1.90*
540 A90 3d Graphium pylades 2.50 *4.25*
Nos. 533-540 (8) 8.50 *10.25*

Souvenir Sheets

541 A90 5d Eurema hapale 10.00 10.00
542 A90 5d Cowrie snail 4.00 *4.00*

UN Child Survival Campaign A91

1985, Feb. 27

543 A91 10b Oral rehydration therapy .20 .20
544 A91 85b Growth monitoring .45 .45
545 A91 1.10d Breast-feeding .55 .55
546 A91 1.50d Universal immunization .65 .65
Nos. 543-546 (4) 1.85 1.85

UN Decade for Women A92

Design: 1d, 1.25d, Woman working in office.

1985, Mar. 11

547 A92 60b multicolored .30 .30
548 A92 85b multicolored .45 .45
549 A92 1d multicolored .60 .60
550 A92 1.25d multicolored .65 .65
Nos. 547-550 (4) 2.00 2.00

Audubon Birth Bicent. — A93

Queen Mother, 85th Birthday — A94

Illustrations of North American bird species by John J. Audubon (1785-1851).

1985, July 15

551 A93 60b Cathartes aura 1.40 .90
552 A93 85b Anhinga anhinga 1.60 1.60
553 A93 1.50d Butoroides striatus 2.00 3.50
554 A93 5d Aix sponsa 3.25 6.00
Nos. 551-554 (4) 8.25 12.00

Souvenir Sheet

555 A93 10d Gavia immer 5.50 5.50

1985, July 24

556 A94 85b Inspecting troops .35 .35
557 A94 3d Portrait 1.10 1.10
558 A94 5d Portrait, diff. 2.00 2.00
Nos. 556-558 (3) 3.45 3.45

Souvenir Sheet

559 A94 10d On parade with Prince Charles 4.00 4.00

Life on the Mississippi, by Mark Twain (1835-1910) — A95

Walt Disney characters. The 60b, 85b, 2.35d, 5d and No. 569 show scenes from "Faithful John" by the brothers Grimm.

1985, Oct. 30

560 A95 60b Portrait .55 .55
561 A95 85b Treasure .70 .70
562 A95 1.50d Helm of Calamity Jane 1.50 1.50
563 A95 2d Antebellum Mansion, Missouri Shore 1.75 1.75
564 A95 2.35d Music 1.75 1.75
565 A95 2.50d Measuring Channel Depth, Natchez 2.00 2.00
566 A95 3d Card Game aboard the Gold Dust 2.25 2.25
567 A95 5d Statue 2.75 2.75
Nos. 560-567 (8) 13.25 13.25

Souvenir Sheet

568 A95 10d Landing, St. Louis 7.00 6.50
569 A95 10d Goofy 8.50 8.50

Nos. 508-514 Ovptd. "GOLD MEDALIST" or "GOLD MEDAL," Name of Winner and Country

60b, Claudia Losch, West Germany, women's shot put. 85b, Ulrike Meyfarth, West Germany, women's high jump. 90b, Pasquale Passarelli, West Germany, 126-pound Greco-Roman wrestling. 1d, Li Ning, China, men's gymnastic floor exercises. 1.25d, Michael Gross, West Germany, men's 100-meter butterfly and 200-meter freestyle swimming. 2d, Sylvie Bernier, Canada, women's springboard diving. 5d, US, Star Class yachting.

1985, Nov. 11 ***Perf. 14***

570 A86 60b multicolored .40 .30
571 A86 85b multicolored .50 .40
572 A86 90b multicolored .50 .45
573 A86 1d multicolored .50 .50
574 A86 1.25d multicolored .75 .65
575 A86 2d multicolored 1.00 1.00
Nos. 570-575 (6) 3.65 3.30

Souvenir Sheet

576 A86 5d multicolored 2.50 2.50

UN 40th Anniv. A97

Views of Banjul.

1985, Nov. 15

577 A97 85b Independence Stadium .45 .45
578 A97 2d Central Bank 1.10 1.10
579 A97 4d Port 2.25 2.25
580 A97 6d Oyster Creek Bridge 3.50 3.50
Nos. 577-580 (4) 7.30 7.30

Natl. independence, 20th anniv.

UN FAO, 40th Anniv. A98

1985, Nov. 15

581 A98 60b Corn .30 .30
582 A98 1.10d Paddy .60 .60
583 A98 3d Cow, calf 1.75 1.75
584 A98 5d Fruit 2.75 2.75
Nos. 581-584 (4) 5.40 5.40

Diocese of Gambia and Guinea, 50th Anniv. A99

Designs: 60b, Fishermen, Fotoba, Guinea. 85b, St. Mary's Primary School, Banjul. 1.10d, St. Mary's Cathedral, Banjul. 1.50d, Mobile Dispensary at Christy, Kunda, 1935-45.

1985, Dec. 24

585 A99 60b multicolored .30 .30
586 A99 85b multicolored .45 .45
587 A99 1.10d multicolored .50 *.60*
588 A99 1.50d multicolored .75 *.90*
Nos. 585-588 (4) 2.00 *2.25*

Girl Guides, 75th Anniv. — A100

Christmas — A101

1985, Dec. 27

589 A100 60b Application, horiz. .30 .30
590 A100 85b 2nd Bathurst, horiz. .45 .45
591 A100 1.50d Lady Baden-Powell .90 .90
592 A100 5d Rosamond Fowlis, leader 2.75 2.75
Nos. 589-592 (4) 4.40 4.40

Souvenir Sheet

593 A100 10d Guides 5.50 5.50

1985, Dec. 27 ***Perf. 15***

Painting details: 60b, Virgin and Child, by Dirck Bouts (c. 1400-1475). 85b, The Annunciation, by Robert Campin (c. 1378-1444). 1.50d, Adoration of the Shepherds, by Gerard David (c. 1460-1523). 5d, The Nativity, by Gerard David. 10d, Adoration of the Magi, by Hieronymus Bosch (1450-1516).

594 A101 60b multicolored .30 .30
595 A101 85b multicolored .45 .45
596 A101 1.50d multicolored .90 .90
597 A101 5d multicolored 1.75 1.75
Nos. 594-597 (4) 3.40 3.40

Souvenir Sheet

598 A101 10d multicolored 4.75 4.75

Intl. Youth Year A102

1985, Dec. 31 ***Perf. 14***

599 A102 60b Mother's helper .30 .30
600 A102 85b Wrestling .45 .45
601 A102 1.10d Griot storyteller .60 .60
602 A102 1.50d Crocodile pool .90 .90
Nos. 599-602 (4) 2.25 2.25

Souvenir Sheet

603 A102 5d Cow herder 2.75 2.75

A103

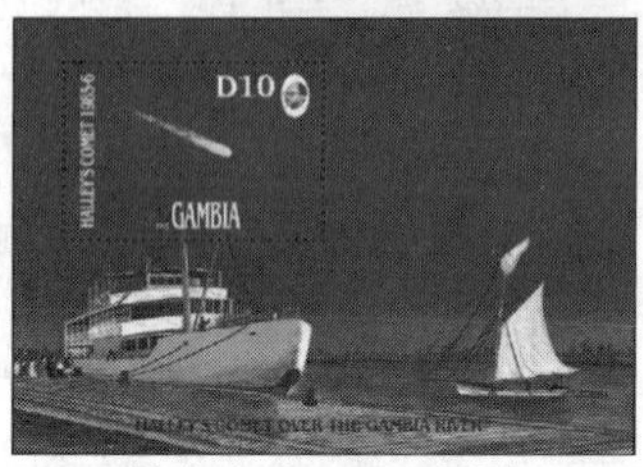

Halley's Comet — A104

Designs: 10b, Maria Mitchell (1818-1889), American astronomer, Kitt Peak Natl. Observatory, Papago Indian Reservation, Arizona. 20b, Apollo 11, Neil Armstrong steps on moon, 1969. 75b, Skylab 4, Kohoutek Comet, 1973. 1d, NASA Infrared Astronomical Satellite, 1983. 2d, Comet sighting, 1577, Turkish art. No. 609, NASA Intl. Cometary Explorer satellite. No. 610, Comet.

1986, Mar.

604 A103 10b multicolored .30 .20
605 A103 20b multicolored .50 .20
606 A103 75b multicolored .75 .50
607 A103 1d multicolored 1.00 .75
608 A103 2d multicolored 1.40 1.25
609 A103 10d multicolored 4.00 *4.50*
Nos. 604-609 (6) 7.95 *7.40*

Souvenir Sheet

610 A104 10d multicolored 5.00 *5.75*

For overprints see Nos. 650-656.

Queen Elizabeth II, 60th Birthday
Common Design Type

Designs: 1d, Royal family at Royal Tournament, 1936. 2.50d, Christening, 1983. No. 613, State visit to West Germany, 1978. No. 614, At Balmoral, 1935.

1986, Apr. 21

611 CD339 1d lt yel bis & blk .40 .40
612 CD339 2.50d pale green & multi .75 .75
613 CD339 10d dl lil & multi 2.50 *3.00*
Nos. 611-613 (3) 3.65 *4.15*

Souvenir Sheet

614 CD339 10d tan & black 3.50 3.50

1986 World Cup Soccer Championships, Mexico — A105

1986, May 2

615 A105 75b Block .45 .45
616 A105 1d Kneeing the ball .65 .65
617 A105 2.50d Kick 2.00 2.00
618 A105 10d Heading the ball 5.00 *5.50*
Nos. 615-618 (4) 8.10 *8.60*

Souvenir Sheet

619 A105 10d Goalie catching ball 6.50 5.50

For overprints see Nos. 639-643.

AMERIPEX '86 — A106

Exhibition emblem, automobiles and flags: 25b, 1986 Mercedes 500, Germany. 75b, 1935 Cord 810, US. 1d, 1957 Borgward Isabella Coupe, Germany. 1.25d, 1985-6 Lamborghini Countach, Italy. 2d, 1955 Ford Thunderbird, US. 2.25d, 1956 Citroen DS19, France. 5d, 1936 Bugatti Atlante, France. 10d, 1936 Horch 853, Germany. No. 628, 1913 Benz 8/20, Germany. No. 629, 1924 Steiger 10/50, Germany.

1986, May 22 ***Perf. 15***

620 A106 25b multi .20 .20
621 A106 75b multi .50 .40
622 A106 1d multi .75 .60
623 A106 1.25d multi .80 .70
624 A106 2d multi 1.00 *1.10*
625 A106 2.25d multi 1.00 *1.25*
626 A106 5d multi 2.00 *2.75*
627 A106 10d multi 4.00 *4.50*
Nos. 620-627 (8) 10.25 *11.50*

Souvenir Sheets

628 A106 12d multi 4.50 6.00
629 A106 12d multi 4.50 6.00

Karl Benz automobile cent.

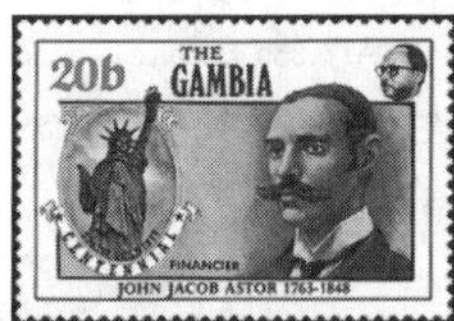

Statue of Liberty, Cent. A107

Statue and famous emigrants: 20b, John Jacob Astor (1763-1848), financier. 1d, Jacob Riis (1849-1914), journalist. 1.25d, Igor Sikorsky (1889-1972), aeronautics engineer. 5d, Charles Boyer (1899-1978), actor. 10d, Statue, vert.

1986, June 10 ***Perf. 14***

630 A107 20b multicolored .20 .20
631 A107 1d multicolored .60 .60
632 A107 1.25d multicolored .70 .70
633 A107 5d multicolored 2.75 2.75
Nos. 630-633 (4) 4.25 4.25

Souvenir Sheet

634 A107 10d multicolored 5.50 5.50

Royal Wedding Issue, 1986
Common Design Type

1d, Engagement of Prince Andrew and Sarah Ferguson. 2.50d, Andrew. 4d, Andrew in flight uniform, other helicopter pilot. 7d, Couple, diff.

1986, July 23

635 CD340 1d multi .55 .55
636 CD340 2.50d multi 1.25 1.25
637 CD340 4d multi 2.00 2.00
Nos. 635-637 (3) 3.80 3.80

Souvenir Sheet

638 CD340 7d multi 3.75 3.75

Nos. 615-619 Overprinted "WINNERS / Argentina 3 / W. Germany 2" in Gold

1986, Sept. 16 Litho. ***Perf. 14***

639 A105 75b multicolored .35 .35
640 A105 1d multicolored .55 .55
641 A105 2.50d multicolored 1.40 1.40
642 A105 10d multicolored 5.00 5.00
Nos. 639-642 (4) 7.30 7.30

Souvenir Sheet

643 A105 10d multicolored 5.00 5.00

Christmas, STOCKHOLMIA '86 — A108

Disney characters mailing letters in various countries.

1986, Nov. 4 ***Perf. 11***

No.	Type	Denom.	Description	Unused	Used
644	A108	1d	Great Britain	.75	.50
645	A108	1.25d	United States	.80	.70
646	A108	2d	France	1.25	1.25
647	A108	2.35d	Australia	1.40	1.40
648	A108	5d	Germany	2.00	2.00
			Nos. 644-648 (5)	6.20	5.85

Souvenir Sheet

No.	Type	Denom.	Description	Unused	Used
649	A108	10d	Sweden	5.00	5.00

Nos. 604-610 Ovptd. with Halley's Comet Logo in Silver

1986, Oct. 21 Litho. ***Perf. 14***

No.	Type	Denom.	Description	Unused	Used
650	A103	10b	multicolored	.25	.20
651	A103	20b	multicolored	.50	.20
652	A103	75b	multicolored	.75	.50
653	A103	1d	multicolored	.90	.60
654	A103	2d	multicolored	1.25	*1.50*
655	A103	10d	multicolored	3.50	*4.50*
			Nos. 650-655 (6)	7.15	*7.50*

Souvenir Sheet

No.	Type	Denom.	Description	Unused	Used
656	A104	10d	multicolored	3.50	3.50

Marc Chagall (1887-1985), Artist A109

Paintings, ceramicware, sculpture: 75b, Snowing. 85b, The Boat, 1957. 1d, Maternity, 1913. 1.25d, The Flute Player. 2.35d, Lovers and the Beast, 1957. 4d,Fishes at Saint Jean. 5d, Entering the Ring, 1968. 10d, Three Acrobats, 1956. No. 665, The Sabbath. No. 666, The Cattle Driver.

1987, Feb. 6 **Litho.**

No.	Type	Denom.	Description	Unused	Used
657	A109	75b	multi	.30	.25
658	A109	85b	multi	.35	.30
659	A109	1d	multi	.45	.40
660	A109	1.25d	multi	.55	.50
661	A109	2.35d	multi	.90	.80
662	A109	4d	multi	1.40	1.25
663	A109	5d	multi	1.75	1.50
664	A109	10d	multi	2.75	2.50

Sizes: 110x95mm, 110x68mm

Imperf

No.	Type	Denom.	Description	Unused	Used
665	A109	12d	multi	4.00	4.00
666	A109	12d	multi	4.00	4.00
			Nos. 657-666 (10)	16.45	15.50

Musical Instruments — A110

Various instruments from the Mandingo Empire.

1987, Jan. 21 Litho. ***Perf. 15***

No.	Type	Denom.	Description	Unused	Used
667	A110	75b	Bugarab, tabala	.20	.20
668	A110	1d	Balaphong, fiddle	.30	.30
669	A110	1.25d	Bolongbato, konting	.35	.35
670	A110	10d	Koras	1.75	*2.50*
			Nos. 667-670 (4)	2.60	3.35

Souvenir Sheet

No.	Type	Denom.	Description	Unused	Used
671	A110	12d	Sabarrs	2.50	*3.00*

Nos. 669-670 vert.
For overprints see Nos. 750, 856-860.

America's Cup A111

1987, Apr. 3 ***Perf. 14***

No.	Type	Denom.	Description	Unused	Used
672	A111	20b	America, 1851	.20	.20
673	A111	1d	Courageous, 1974	.30	.30
674	A111	2.50d	Volunteer, 1887	.70	.70
675	A111	10d	Intrepid, 1967	3.00	3.00
			Nos. 672-675 (4)	4.20	4.20

Souvenir Sheet

No.	Type	Denom.	Description	Unused	Used
676	A111	12d	Australia II, 1983	3.75	3.75

For overprint see No. 751.

Statue of Liberty, Cent. A112

Photographs of restoration and unveiling in 1986.

1987, Apr. 9 **Litho.**

No.	Type	Denom.	Description	Unused	Used
677	A112	1b	Shoulder, torch	.20	.20
678	A112	2b	Operation Sail flotilla	.20	.20
679	A112	3b	Tall ship, ships	.20	.20
680	A112	5b	Luxury liner, aircraft carrier	.20	.20
681	A112	50b	Statue's coiffure	.35	.35
682	A112	75b	Coiffure, diff.	.50	.50
683	A112	1d	Workmen scaling statue	.65	.65
684	A112	1.25d	Back of statue	.75	.75
685	A112	10d	Front of Statue	3.75	3.50
686	A112	12d	Side of statue	4.00	3.50
			Nos. 677-686 (10)	10.80	10.05

Nos. 677, 681-686 vert.

Flowers from Abuko Nature Reserve — A113

75b, Lantana camara. 1d, Clerodendrum thomsoniae. 1.50d, Haemanthus multiflorus. 1.70d, Gloriosa simplex. 1.75d, Combretum microphyllum. 2.25d, Eulophia guineensis. 5d, Erythrina senegalensis. 15d, Dichrostachys glomerata.

#691, Costus spectabilis. #691A, Strophanthus preussii.

1987, May 25

No.	Type	Denom.	Description	Unused	Used
687	A113	75b	multi	.20	.20
687A	A113	1d	multi	.25	.25
688	A113	1.50d	multi	.40	.40
688A	A113	1.70d	multi	.45	.45
689	A113	1.75d	multi	.45	.45
689A	A113	2.25d	multi	.60	.60
689B	A113	5d	multi	1.40	1.40
690	A113	15d	multi	3.25	*3.75*
			Nos. 687-690 (8)	7.00	*7.50*

Souvenir Sheets

No.	Type	Denom.	Description	Unused	Used
691	A113	15d	shown	3.25	*3.75*
691A	A113	15d	multi	3.25	*3.75*

#691-691A are continuous designs.
For overprint see No. 752.

CAPEX '87 A115

Various buses.

1987, June 15

No.	Type	Denom.	Description	Unused	Used
692	A115	20b	multi, vert.	.35	.20
693	A115	75b	multi	.50	.25
694	A115	1d	multi	1.25	.75
695	A115	10d	multi, vert.	2.50	2.00
			Nos. 692-695 (4)	4.60	3.20

Souvenir Sheet

No.	Type	Denom.	Description	Unused	Used
696	A115	12d	multi	3.75	3.75

For overprint see No. 749.

1988 Summer Olympics, Seoul A116

1987, July 3

No.	Type	Denom.	Description	Unused	Used
697	A116	50b	Women's basketball	.20	.20
698	A116	1d	Volleyball	.50	.30
699	A116	3d	Field hockey	1.00	.90
700	A116	10d	Handball	3.00	3.00
			Nos. 697-700 (4)	4.70	4.40

Souvenir Sheet

No.	Type	Denom.	Description	Unused	Used
701	A116	15d	Soccer	4.00	4.00

Nos. 697-698 vert.

A117

The Twelve Days of Christmas, Medieval Counting Song — A118

Designs: 20b, Partridge in a pear tree. 40b, 2 turtle doves. 60b, 3 French hens. 75b, 4 calling birds. 1d, 5 golden rings. 1.25d, 6 geese a-laying. 1.50d, 7 swans a-swimming. 2d, 8 maids a-milking. 3d, 9 ladies dancing. 5d, 10 lords a-leaping. 10d, 11 pipers piping. 12d, 12 drummers drumming.

Miniature Sheet

1987, Nov. 2 Litho. ***Perf. 14***

No.	Type	Denom.	Description	Unused	Used
702			Sheet of 12	10.00	10.00
a.	A117	20b	multicolored	.20	.20
b.	A117	40b	multicolored	.20	.20
c.	A117	60b	multicolored	.20	.20
d.	A117	75b	multicolored	.20	.20
e.	A117	1d	multicolored	.30	.30
f.	A117	1.25d	multicolored	.35	.35
g.	A117	1.50d	multicolored	.45	.45
h.	A117	2d	multicolored	.55	.55
i.	A117	3d	multicolored	.90	.90
j.	A117	5d	multicolored	1.40	1.40
k.	A117	10d	multicolored	2.75	2.75
l.	A117	12d	multicolored	3.25	3.25

Souvenir Sheet

No.	Type	Denom.	Description	Unused	Used
703	A118	15d	multi	4.00	*4.50*

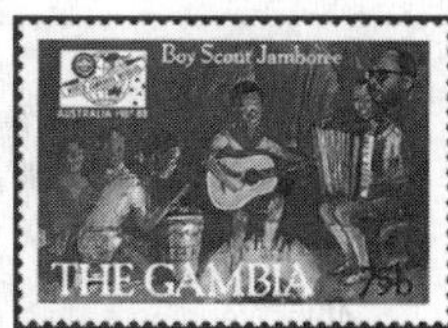

16th Boy Scout Jamboree, Australia, 1987-88 A119

1987, Nov. 9

No.	Type	Denom.	Description	Unused	Used
704	A119	75b	Singing around campfire	.20	.20
705	A119	1d	Nature study, African katydid	.40	.30
706	A119	1.25d	Bird watching, red-tailed tropicbird	.50	.40
707	A119	12d	Boarding bus	3.50	3.50
			Nos. 704-707 (4)	4.60	4.40

Souvenir Sheet

No.	Type	Denom.	Description	Unused	Used
708	A119	15d	Nature study	4.50	4.50

Mickey Mouse, 60th Anniv. — A120

Disney animated characters and historic locomotives: 60b, Richard Trevithick's locomotive, 1804. 75b, Empire State Express 999, 1893. 1d, George Stephenson's Rocket, 1829. 1.25d, Santa Fe Mountain 2-10-2, 1920. 2d, Class GG-1 Pennsylvania, 1933. 5d, Stourbridge Lion, 1829. 10d, Best Friend of Charleston, 1830. 12d, M10001 Union Pacific, 1934. No. 717, Tres Grande Vitesse-SNCF, 1981, France. No. 718, The General, Western & Atlantic, 1855.

1987, Dec. 9 Litho. ***Perf. 14x13½***

No.	Type	Denom.	Description	Unused	Used
709	A120	60b	multicolored	.20	.20
710	A120	75b	multicolored	.25	.25
711	A120	1d	multicolored	.30	.30
712	A120	1.25d	multicolored	.40	.40
713	A120	2d	multicolored	.60	.60
714	A120	5d	multicolored	1.50	1.50
715	A120	10d	multicolored	3.00	3.00
716	A120	12d	multicolored	3.50	3.50
			Nos. 709-716 (8)	9.75	9.75

Souvenir Sheets

No.	Type	Denom.	Description	Unused	Used
717	A120	15d	multicolored	4.25	4.25
718	A120	15d	multicolored	4.25	4.25

Fauna and Flora A121

1988, Feb. 9 Litho. ***Perf. 15***

No.	Type	Denom.	Description	Unused	Used
719	A121	50b	Duiker, acacia	.20	.20
720	A121	75b	Red-billed hornbill, casuarina	.20	.20
721	A121	90b	West African dwarf crocodile, rice	.25	.25
722	A121	1d	Leopard, papyrus	.25	.25
723	A121	1.25d	Crested cranes, millet	.35	.35
724	A121	2d	Waterbuck, baobab tree	.55	.55
725	A121	3d	Oribi, Senegal palm	.80	.80
726	A121	5d	Hippopotamus, papaya	1.40	1.40
			Nos. 719-726 (8)	4.00	4.00

Souvenir Sheets

No.	Type	Denom.	Description	Unused	Used
727	A121	12d	Great white pelican	2.50	2.50
728	A121	12d	Red-throated bee-eater	2.50	2.50

Nos. 720, 722, 724, 726 and 728 vert.

40th Wedding Anniv. of Queen Elizabeth II and Prince Philip — A122

1988, Mar. 15 *Perf. 14*

729 A122 75b Wedding portrait, 1947 .20 .20
730 A122 1d Couple at leisure .25 .25
731 A122 3d Wedding portrait, diff. .75 .75
732 A122 10d Couple, c. 1987 2.50 2.50
Nos. 729-732 (4) 3.70 3.70

Souvenir Sheet

733 A122 15d Wedding party 3.50 3.50

1988 Summer Olympics, Seoul A123

1988, May 3 Litho. *Perf. 14*

734 A123 1d Archery, vert. .20 .20
735 A123 1.25d Boxing, vert. .20 .20
736 A123 5d Gymnastics, vert. 1.00 *1.25*
737 A123 10d 100-Meter sprint 2.25 *2.50*
Nos. 734-737 (4) 3.65 *4.15*

Souvenir Sheet

738 A123 15d Award ceremony, Olympic stadium 4.00 4.00

Anniversaries & Events — A124

Designs: 50b, Red Cross flag. 75b, Friendship 7, piloted by John Glenn, 1963. 1d, British Airways Concorde jet. 1.25d, Spirit of St. Louis, piloted by Charles Lindbergh, 1927. 2d, X-15, piloted by Major William Knight, 1967. 3d, Bell X-1, piloted by Capt. Charles Yeager, 1947. 10d, Spanish galleon, British warship, 1588. 12d, The Titanic. No. 747, Kangaroo and joey. No. 748, Cathedral, modern church, vert.

1988, May 15

739 A124 50b multicolored .50 .50
740 A124 75b multicolored .50 .50
741 A124 1d multicolored .75 .75
742 A124 1.25d multicolored .75 .75
743 A124 2d multicolored 1.00 1.00
744 A124 3d multicolored 1.25 1.25
745 A124 10d multicolored 3.25 3.25
746 A124 12d multicolored 3.75 3.75
Nos. 739-746 (8) 11.75 11.75

Souvenir Sheets

747 A124 15d multicolored 3.50 3.50
748 A124 15d multicolored 3.50 3.50

Intl. Red Cross, 125th anniv. (50b); first American in space, 25th anniv. in 1987 (75b); 1st London-New York scheduled Concorde flight, 10th anniv. in 1987 (1d); first solo trans-atlantic flight, 60th anniv. in 1987 (1.25d); fastest speed flown, 6.72 Mach, 20th anniv. in 1987 (2d); 1st supersonic flight, 40th anniv. in 1987 (3d); defeat of the Spanish Armada, 400th anniv. (10d); maiden voyage of the Titanic, 75th anniv. in 1987 (12d); founding of Australia, bicentennial (No. 747); and founding of Berlin, 750th anniv. in 1987 (No. 748).

Nos. 694, 670, 675 and 690 Ovptd. for Philatelic Exhibitions

a

b

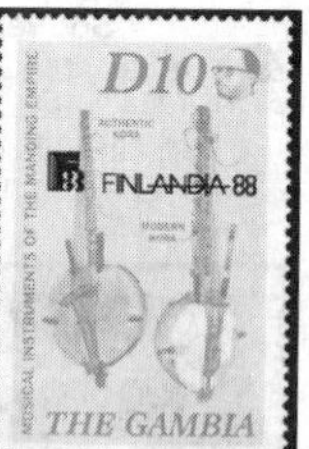

c

d

1988, Apr. 19 Litho. *Perf. 14, 15*

749 A115(a) 1d multi .30 .30
750 A110(b) 10d multi 2.25 2.25
751 A111(c) 10d multi 2.25 2.25
752 A113(d) 15d multi 3.00 3.00
Nos. 749-752 (4) 7.80 7.80

Paintings by Titian A125

Designs: 25b, Emperor Charles V, 1549. 50b, St. Margaret and the Dragon, 1565. 60b, Ranuccio Farnese, 1542. 75b, Tarquin and Lucretia, 1570. 1d, The Knight of Malta, c. 1550. 5d, Spain Succouring Faith, 1571. 10d, Doge Francesco Venier, 1555. 12d, Doge Grimani Before the Faith, c. 1555-1576. No. 761, Jealous Husband, 1511. No. 762, Venus Blindfolding Cupid, 1560.

1988, July 7 Litho. *Perf. 13½x14*

753 A125 25b multicolored .20 .20
754 A125 50b multicolored .30 .30
755 A125 60b multicolored .35 .35
756 A125 75b multicolored .50 .50
757 A125 1d multicolored .60 .60
758 A125 5d multicolored 2.00 2.00
759 A125 10d multicolored 3.25 3.25
760 A125 12d multicolored 3.75 3.75
Nos. 753-760 (8) 10.95 10.95

Souvenir Sheets

761 A125 15d multicolored 3.50 3.50
762 A125 15d multicolored 3.50 3.50

Tribute to John F. Kennedy A126

1988, Sept. 1 Litho. *Perf. 14*

763 A126 75b Sailing .20 .20
764 A126 1d Peace Corps enactment .30 .30
765 A126 1.25d Public address, vert. .40 .40
766 A126 12d Grave, Arlington Natl. Cemetery 2.75 2.75
Nos. 763-766 (4) 3.65 3.65

Souvenir Sheet

767 A126 15d Kennedy, vert. 3.50 3.50

Entertainers — A127

20b, Emmett Lee Kelly (1898-1979), clown. 1d, Gambia Natl. Ensemble. 1.25d, Jackie Gleason (1916-87), comedian, & The Honeymooners cast. 1.50d, Stan Laurel (1890-1965) & Oliver Hardy (1892-1957), film comedy team. 2.50d, Yul Brynner (c. 1920-85), actor. 3d, Cary Grant (1904-86), actor. 10d, Danny Kaye (1918-87), comedian, actor. 20d, Charlie Chaplin (1889-1977), comedian, actor. #776, Harpo (1893-1964), Chico (1891-1961), Zeppo (1901-79) & Groucho (1890-1977) Marx, comedy team. #777, Fred Astaire (1899-1987) & Rita Hayworth (1918-87), dancers & film stars. #768-775 vert.

1988, Nov. 9 Litho.

768 A127 20b multi .20 .20
769 A127 1d multi .30 .30
770 A127 1.25d multi .40 .40
771 A127 1.50d multi .45 .45
772 A127 2.50d multi .75 .75
773 A127 3d multi .90 .90
774 A127 10d multi 3.00 3.00
775 A127 20d multi 5.50 5.50
Nos. 768-775 (8) 11.50 11.50

Souvenir Sheets

776 A127 15d multi 4.50 4.50
777 A127 15d multi 4.50 4.50

Kelly's name is spelled incorrectly; Brynner's and Grant's dates are incorrect.

Zeppelin LZ7 Deutschland, 1910 — A128

Transportation innovations: 50b, Stephenson's Locomotion, 1825. 75b, General Motors Sun Racer, 1987. 1d, Sprague's Premiere, 1888. 1.25d, Gold Rush bicycle, 1986. 2.50d, 1st Liquid-fuel rocket, invented by Robert Goddard, 1925. 10d, Orukter Amphibolos, 1805. 12d, Sovereign of the Seas, 1988. No. 786, USS Nautilus, 1954, vert. No. 787, Fulton's Nautilus, early 19th cent.

1988, Nov. 21 Litho. *Perf. 14*

778 A128 25b multi .35 .25
779 A128 50b multi .60 .40
780 A128 75b multi .70 .55
781 A128 1d multi .85 .70
782 A128 1.25d multi .85 .75
783 A128 2.50d multi 1.25 1.00
784 A128 10d multi 3.00 3.00
785 A128 12d multi 3.50 3.50
Nos. 778-785 (8) 11.10 10.15

Souvenir Sheets

786 A128 15d multi 3.50 3.50
787 A128 15d multi 3.50 3.50

Discovery of America, 500th Anniv. (in 1992) A129

Designs: 50b, Caravel, Henry the Navigator (1394-1460), Prince of Portugal, and coat of arms, vert. 75b, Jesse Ramsden's sextant, map of Africa, arms, vert. 1d, Hour glass, 15th cent., and map, vert. 1.25d, Henry and Vasco da Gama, vert. 2.50d, Da Gama and 15th cent. caravel, vert. 5d, Mungo Park (1771-1806), Scottish explorer, arms and map of Gambia River. 10d, Map of west African coast, 1563. 12d, Portuguese caravel, arms. No. 796, Caravel off the Gambian coast, 15th cent., vert. No. 797, European ship off Gambian coast, 15th cent., vert.

1988, Dec. 1 Litho. *Perf. 14*

788 A129 50b multi .50 .50
789 A129 75b multi .60 .60
790 A129 1d multi .70 .70
791 A129 1.25d multi .85 .85
792 A129 2.50d multi 1.25 1.25
793 A129 5d shown 2.00 2.00
794 A129 10d multi 3.25 3.25
795 A129 12d multi 3.50 3.50
Nos. 788-795 (8) 12.65 12.65

Souvenir Sheets

796 A129 15d multi 3.75 3.75
797 A129 15d multi 3.75 3.75

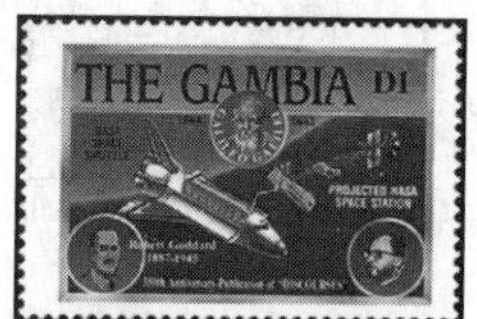

Space Achievements — A130

Galileo and: 50b, Futuristic aerospace plane and Ernst Mach (1838-1916), Austrian physicist, vert. 75b, OAO III astronomical satellite and Niels Bohr (1885-1962), Danish physicist and Nobel lauerate in 1922, vert. 1d, NASA space shuttle, future space station and Robert Goddard (1882-1945), American rocket scientist. 1.25d, Flyby of probe past Jupiter, 1979, and Edward Barnard (1857-1923), American astronomer who discovered Jupiter's 5th satellite in 1892. 2d, Hubble Space Telescope and George Hale (1868-1938), American astronomer, vert. 3d, Precision measurement of the distance between the Earth and the Moon by laser and Albert A. Michelson (1852-1931), Nobel laureate in 1907 for research on the speed of light. 10d, HEAO-2 Einstein orbital satellite and Albert Einstein, vert. 20d, Voyager, 1st circumnavigation of the world without refueling, 1987, and the Wright Brothers. No. 806, Moon Ganymede passing the Great Red Spot on Jupiter. No. 807, Apollo and Neil Armstrong, 1st man on the Moon, July 20, 1969, vert.

1988, Dec. 12 *Perf. 14*

798 A130 50b multi .20 .20
799 A130 75b multi .20 .20
800 A130 1d multi .30 .30
801 A130 1.25d multi .40 .40
802 A130 2d multi .60 .60
803 A130 3d multi .90 .90
804 A130 10d multi 2.50 2.50
805 A130 20d multi 4.50 4.50
Nos. 798-805 (8) 9.60 9.60

Souvenir Sheets

806 A130 15d multi 4.50 4.50
807 A130 15d multi 4.50 4.50

350th anniv. of the publication of Discourses, by Galileo.

Army Day A131

1989, Feb. 10 Litho. *Perf. 14*

808 A131 75b Troops on parade .20 .20
809 A131 1d Regimental flags .30 .30
810 A131 1.25d Drummer, vert. .40 .40
811 A131 10d Atlantic Shooting Cup winner, vert. 2.50 2.50
812 A131 15d Assault course, vert. 4.00 4.00
813 A131 20d 105-mm gun 4.50 4.50
Nos. 808-813 (6) 11.90 11.90

Miniature Sheet

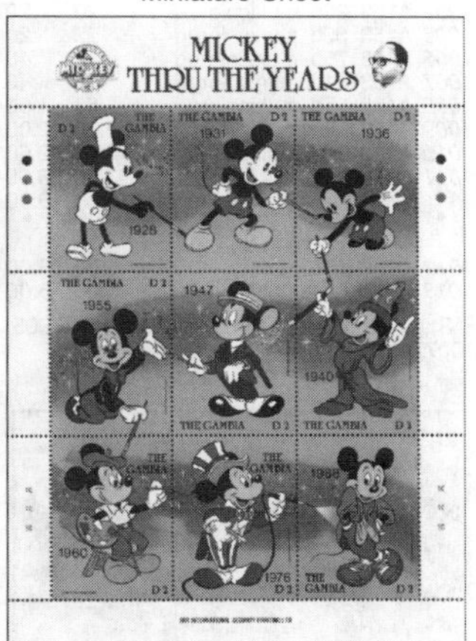

Mickey Mouse, 60th Anniv. (in 1988) — A132

Mickey Mouse through the years: a, 1928. b, 1931. c, 1936. d, 1955. e, 1947. f, 1940. g, 1960. h, 1976. i, 1988. 15d, Birthday party.

1989, Apr. 6 Litho. *Perf. 13x13½*

814	A132	Sheet of 9	5.50	5.50
a.-i.		2d any single	.60	.60

Size: 139x110mm

Imperf

815	A132	15d multi	4.50	4.50

Easter A133

Paintings by Rubens: 50b, Le Coup de Lance, 1620. 75b, The Flagellation of Christ, 1617. 1d, The Lamentation for Christ, c. 1617. 1.25d, Descent from the Cross, c. 1611. 2d, The Holy Trinity, c. 1617. 5d, The Doubting Thomas. 10d, Lamentation over Christ, 1614. 12d, Lamentation over Christ with the Virgin and St. John, c. 1613. No. 824, The Last Supper, c. 1631. No. 825, The Raising of the Cross, c. 1610.

1989, Apr. 14 *Perf. 13½x14*

816	A133	50b multi	.20	.20
817	A133	75b multi	.25	.25
818	A133	1d multi	.30	.30
819	A133	1.25d multi	.40	.40
820	A133	2d multi	.65	.65
821	A133	5d multi	1.50	1.50
822	A133	10d multi	2.50	2.50
823	A133	12d multi	3.00	3.00
		Nos. 816-823 (8)	8.80	8.80

Souvenir Sheets

824	A133	15d multi	3.50	3.50
825	A133	15d multi	3.50	3.50

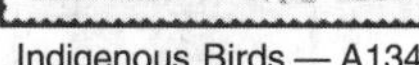

Indigenous Birds — A134

1989, Apr. 24 *Perf. 14*

826	A134	20b African emerald cuckoo	.40	.25
827	A134	60b Gray-headed bush shrike	.50	.40
828	A134	75b Crowned crane	.60	.45
829	A134	1d Secretary bird	.60	.45
830	A134	2d Red-billed hornbill	.65	.65
831	A134	5d Superb sunbird	1.60	1.60
832	A134	10d Little owl	3.25	3.25
833	A134	12d Bateleur eagle	3.75	3.75
		Nos. 826-833 (8)	11.35	10.80

Souvenir Sheets

834	A134	15d Red-billed fire finch	4.50	4.50
835	A134	15d Ostriches	4.50	4.50

Indigenous Butterflies — A135

1989, May 15

836	A135	50b Papilio antimachus	.20	.20
837	A135	75b Euphaedra neophron	.25	.25
838	A135	1d Aterica rabena	.30	.30
839	A135	1.25d Salamis parhassus	.40	.40
840	A135	5d Precis rhadama	1.60	1.60
841	A135	10d Papilio demodocus	2.75	2.75
842	A135	12d Charaxes etesippe	3.25	3.25
843	A135	15d Danaus formosa	4.00	4.00
		Nos. 836-843 (8)	12.75	12.75

Souvenir Sheets

844	A135	15d Euphaedra ceres	4.75	4.75
845	A135	15d Cymothoe pluto	4.75	4.75

Trains of Africa A136

Designs: 50b, Nigerian coal train, 1959. 75b, 14A Class 2-6-6-2 Garratt. 1d, British (Pacific) in Sudan. 1.25d, American 0-8-0, 1925. 5d, Scottish 4-8-2, 1955. 7d, Scottish 4-8-2, 1926. 10d, British 4-6-0. 12d, American-made 2-6-0 in Ghana. No. 854, British 2-8-2 Class 25 facing forward, vert. No. 855, Class 25 facing left, vert.

1989, June 15 Litho. *Perf. 14*

846	A136	50b multi	.20	.20
847	A136	75b multi	.25	.25
848	A136	1d multi	.35	.35
849	A136	1.25d multi	.50	.50
850	A136	5d multi	1.60	1.60
851	A136	7d multi	2.00	2.00
852	A136	10d multi	3.00	3.00
853	A136	12d multi	3.50	3.50
		Nos. 846-853 (8)	11.40	11.40

Souvenir Sheets

854	A136	15d multi	4.00	4.00
855	A136	15d multi	4.00	4.00

Nos. 667-671 Ovptd. "PHILEXFRANCE / '89"

1989, June 23 Litho. *Perf. 15*

856	A110	75b multi	.25	.25
857	A110	1d multi	.30	.30
858	A110	1.25d multi	.45	.45
859	A110	10d multi	2.00	2.00
		Nos. 856-859 (4)	3.00	3.00

Souvenir Sheet

860	A110	12d multi	3.00	3.00

Paintings by Japanese Artists A137

Paintings by Hiroshige unless noted otherwise: 50b, Sparrow and Bamboo. 75b, Peonies and a Canary, by Hokusai. 1d, Crane and Marsh Grasses. 1.25d, Crossbill and Thistle, by Hokusai. 2d, Cuckoo and Azalea, by Hokusai. 5d, Parrot on a Pine Branch. 10d, Mandarin Ducks in a Stream. 12d, Bullfinch and Drooping Cherry, by Hokusai. No. 869, Tit and Peony, horiz. No. 870, Peony and Butterfly, by Shigenobu, horiz.

1989, July 7 *Perf. 13½x14, 14x13½*

861	A137	50b multi	.20	.20
862	A137	75b multi	.25	.25
863	A137	1d multi	.30	.30
864	A137	1.25d multi	.40	.40
865	A137	2d multi	.60	.60
866	A137	5d multi	1.50	1.50
867	A137	10d multi	3.25	3.25
868	A137	12d multi	3.50	3.50
		Nos. 861-868 (8)	10.00	10.00

Souvenir Sheets

869	A137	15d multi	4.00	4.00
870	A137	15d multi	4.00	4.00

1990 World Cup Soccer Championships, Italy — A138

Various athletes and Italian landmarks: 75b, Rialto Bridge, Venice. 1.25d, The Baptistery, Pisa. 7d, Casino San Remo. 12d, The Colosseum, Rome. No. 875, St. Mark's Cathedral, Venice, vert. No. 876, Piazza Colonna, Rome.

1989, Aug 25 *Perf. 14*

871	A138	75b multi	.35	.35
872	A138	1.25b multi	.50	.50
873	A138	7d multi	2.25	2.25
874	A138	12d multi	3.50	3.50
		Nos. 871-874 (4)	6.60	6.60

Souvenir Sheets

875	A138	15d multi	4.00	4.00
876	A138	15d multi	4.00	4.00

Medicinal Plants — A139

1989, Sept. 18 Litho. *Perf. 14*

877	A139	20b *Vitex doniana*	.20	.20
878	A139	50b *Ricinus communis*	.20	.20
879	A139	75b *Palisota hirsuta*	.20	.20
880	A139	1d *Smilax kraussiana*	.30	.30
881	A139	1.25d *Aspilia africana*	.35	.35
882	A139	5d *Newbouldia laevis*	1.40	1.40
883	A139	8d *Monodora tenuifolia*	2.25	2.25
884	A139	10d *Gossypium arboreum*	2.75	2.75
		Nos. 877-884 (8)	7.65	7.65

Souvenir Sheets

885	A139	15d *Kigelia africana*	4.00	4.00
886	A139	15d *Spathodea campanulata*	4.00	4.00

Fish A140

1989, Oct. 19 Litho. *Perf.*

887	A140	20b Lookdown	.20	.20
888	A140	75b Boarfish	.45	.45
889	A140	1d Gray triggerfish	.50	.50
890	A140	1.25d Skipjack tuna	.60	.60
891	A140	2d Bermuda chub	.80	.80
892	A140	4d Atlantic manta	1.60	1.60
893	A140	5d Striped mullet	2.00	2.00
894	A140	10d Ladyfish	3.00	3.00
		Nos. 887-894 (8)	9.15	9.15

Souvenir Sheet

895	A140	15d Porcupinefish	4.50	4.50
896	A140	15d Shortfin makos	4.50	4.50

Souvenir Sheet

The White House, Washington, DC — A141

1989, Nov. 17 Litho. *Perf. 14*

897	A141	10d multicolored	2.75	2.75

World Stamp Expo '89.

World Stamp Expo '89, Washington, DC — A142

Disney characters riding carousel horses: 20b, Daniel Muller Indian pony. 50b, Herschell-Spillman steed. 75b, Gustav Dentzel stander. 1d, Muller armored stander. 1.25d, Jumper from the Smithsonian Collection. 2d, Illion "American Beauty." 8d, Zalar jumper. 10d, Parker buckling. No. 906, Philadelphia Tobaggan Co. Carousel, Elitch Gardens, Denver, CO. No. 907, PTC Roman chariot.

1989, Nov. 29 Litho. *Perf. 14x13½*

898	A142	20b multicolored	.40	.20
899	A142	50b multicolored	.60	.30
900	A142	75b multicolored	.70	.40
901	A142	1d multicolored	.75	.50
902	A142	1.25d multicolored	.80	.75
903	A142	2d multicolored	1.00	1.00
904	A142	8d multicolored	3.00	3.00
905	A142	10d multicolored	3.25	3.25
		Nos. 898-905 (8)	10.50	9.40

Souvenir Sheets

906	A142	12d multicolored	4.00	4.00
907	A142	12d multicolored	4.00	4.00

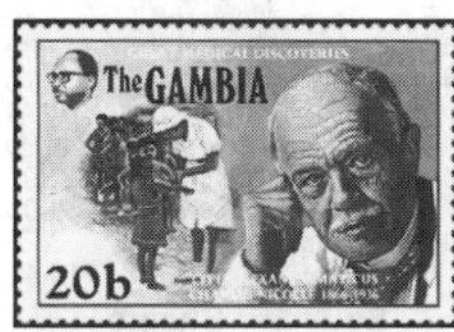

Nobel Prize Winners for Physiology and Great Medical Pioneers — A143

20b, Charles Nicolle (1866-1936), France, 1928 Prize, discovered transmission of typhus by body lice. 50b, Paul Ehrlich (1854-1915), Germany, 1908 Prize, immunology research. 75b, Selman Waksman (1888-1973), Russian-American, 1952 Prize, discovered antibiotic streptomycin, used to treat tuberculosis. 1d, Edward Jenner (1749-1823), Great Britain, discovered smallpox vaccine. 1.25d, Robert Koch (1843-1910), 1905 Prize, isolated the tubercle bacillus. 5d, Sir Alexander Fleming (1881-1955), Scotland, 1945 Prize, developed penicillin. 8d, Max Theiler (1899-1972), US, 1951 Prize, developed yellow fever vaccine. 10d, Louis Pasteur (1822-95), France, proved the germ theory of infection.
#916, C-9 Nightingale Aeromedical Airlift. #917, Hughes Vicking helicopter used in airlift.

1989, Dec. 12 *Perf. 14*

908	A143	20b multicolored	.30	.25
909	A143	50b multicolored	.50	.40
910	A143	75b multicolored	.65	.50
911	A143	1d multicolored	.70	.60
912	A143	1.25d multicolored	.80	.70
913	A143	5d multicolored	1.60	1.60
914	A143	8d multicolored	2.50	2.50
915	A143	10d multicolored	3.25	3.25
		Nos. 908-915 (8)	10.30	9.80

Souvenir Sheets

916	A143	15d multicolored	4.25	4.25
917	A143	15d multicolored	4.25	4.25

Orchids — A144

1989, Dec. 18 *Perf. 14*

918 A144 20b *Bulbophyllum lepidum* .25 .25
919 A144 75b *Tridactyle tridactylites* .45 .45
920 A144 1d *Vanilla imperialis* .60 .60
921 A144 1.25d *Oeceoclades maculata* .70 .70
922 A144 2d *Polystachya affinis* 1.00 1.00
923 A144 4d *Ancistrochilus rothschildianus* 1.75 1.75
924 A144 5d *Angraecum distichum* 2.00 2.00
925 A144 10d *Liparis guineensis* 3.25 3.25
Nos. 918-925 (8) 10.00 10.00

Souvenir Sheets

926 A144 15d *Eulophia guineensis* 4.25 4.25
927 A144 15d *Plectrelminthus caudatus* 4.25 4.25

Christmas — A145

Disney characters and classic automobiles: 20b, 1922 Pierce Arrow. 50b, 1919 Spyker. 75b, 1929 Packard. 1d, 1920 Daimler. 1.25d, 1924 Hispano Suiza. 2d, Opel Laubfrosch, 1924-27. 10d, 1927 Vauxhall 30/98. 12d, 1923 Peerless. No. 936, 1930 Bentley Supercharged, Santa Claus. No. 937, 1928 Stutz Blackhawk Speedster, picnic.

1989, Dec. 19 **Litho.** *Perf. 14*

928 A145 20b multicolored .40 .20
929 A145 50b multicolored .60 .35
930 A145 75b multicolored .70 .45
931 A145 1d multicolored .75 .50
932 A145 1.25d multicolored .80 .70
933 A145 2d multicolored .90 .90
934 A145 10d multicolored 3.00 3.00
935 A145 12d multicolored 3.25 3.25
Nos. 928-935 (8) 10.40 9.35

Souvenir Sheets

936 A145 15d multicolored 4.75 4.75
937 A145 15d multicolored 4.75 4.75

Wimbledon Tennis Champions A146

1st Moon Landing, 20th Anniv. (in 1989) A147

1990, Jan. 2 **Litho.** *Perf. 15x14½*

938 A146 20b John Newcombe .20 .20
939 A146 20b G.W. Hillyard .20 .20
a. Pair, #938-939 .25 .25
940 A146 50b Roy Emerson .20 .20
941 A146 50b Dorothy Chambers .20 .20
a. Pair, #940-941 .25 .25
942 A146 75b Donald Budge .20 .20
943 A146 75b Suzanne Lenglen .20 .20
a. Pair, #942-943 .40 .40
944 A146 1d Laurence Doherty .25 .25
945 A146 1d Helen Wills Moody .25 .25
a. Pair, #944-945 .50 .50
946 A146 1.25d Bjorn Borg .30 .30
947 A146 1.25d Maureen Connolly .30 .30
a. Pair, #946-947 .60 .60
948 A146 4d Jean Borotra .85 .85
949 A146 4d Maria Bueno .85 .85
a. Pair, #948-949 1.75 1.75
950 A146 5d Anthony Wilding 1.10 1.10
951 A146 5d Louise Brough 1.10 1.10
a. Pair, #950-951 2.25 2.25
952 A146 7d Fred Perry 1.50 1.50
953 A146 7d Margaret Court 1.50 1.50
a. Pair, #952-953 3.00 3.00
954 A146 10d Bill Tilden 2.00 2.00
955 A146 10d Billie Jean King 2.00 2.00
a. Pair, #954-955 4.00 4.00
956 A146 12d Rod Laver 2.25 2.25
957 A146 12d Martina Navratilova 2.25 2.25
a. Pair, #956-957 4.50 4.50
Nos. 938-957 (20) 17.70 17.70

Souvenir Sheets

958 A146 15d Rod Laver, diff. 4.50 4.50
959 A146 15d Martina Navratilova, diff. 4.50 4.50

1990, Feb. 16 *Perf. 14*

Designs: 20b, *Eagle* lunar module descending, horiz. 50b, Apollo 11 liftoff. 75b, Astronaut descending ladder, horiz. 1d, Astronaut, US flag over Sea of Tranquillity, horiz. 1.25d, Mission emblem. 1.75d, Crew, horiz. 8d, Lunar module, Sea of Tranquillity, horiz. 12d, Recovery of command module *Columbia* after splashdown. No. 968, Neil Armstrong returning to *Eagle.* No. 969, View of Earth.

960 A147 20b multicolored .25 .25
961 A147 50b multicolored .35 .25
962 A147 75b multicolored .50 .35
963 A147 1d multicolored .55 .40
964 A147 1.25d multicolored .65 .50
965 A147 1.75d multicolored .80 .75
966 A147 8d multicolored 2.25 2.25
967 A147 12d multicolored 2.75 2.75
Nos. 960-967 (8) 8.10 7.50

Souvenir Sheets

968 A147 15d multicolored 3.75 3.75
969 A147 15d multicolored 3.75 3.75

Miniature Sheet

Birds of Africa A148

Designs: a, White-faced owl. b, Village weaver. c, Red-throated bee eater. d, Brown harrier eagle. e, Red bishop. f, Scarlet-chested sunbird. g, Red-billed hornbill. h, Mosque swallow. i, White-faced tree duck. j, African fish eagle. k, Great white pelican. l, Carmine bee eater. m, Hadada ibis. n, Crocodile plover. o, Yellow-bellied sunbird. p, African skimmer. q, Woodland kingfisher. r, Jacana. s, Pygmy goose. t, Hamerkop.

1990, Apr. 12 **Litho.** *Perf. 14*

970 Sheet of 20 8.00 8.00
a.-t. A148 1.25d any single .40 .40

RAF World War II Fighter Planes A149

Designs: 10b, Bristol Blenheim Mk-1. 20b, Battle. 50b, Blenheim 4. 60b, Wellington 1C. 75b, Whitley 5. 1d, Hampden Mk-1. 1.25d, Spitfire 1A and Hurricane 1. 2d, Avro Manchester. 3d, Stirling. 5d, Handley Page Halifax B-2. 10d, Lancaster B-3. 12d, Mosquito B-4. No. 983, Lancaster B-3 over Hamburg. No. 984, Spitfire 1, Battle of Britain.

1990, Apr. 18 *Perf. 14*

971 A149 10b multicolored .25 .20
972 A149 20b multicolored .35 .20
973 A149 50b multicolored .45 .30
974 A149 60b multicolored .50 .30
975 A149 75b multicolored .50 .35
976 A149 1d multicolored .60 .35
977 A149 1.25d multicolored .70 .40
978 A149 2d multicolored .75 .40
979 A149 3d multicolored 1.00 .90
980 A149 5d multicolored 1.25 1.25
981 A149 10d multicolored 2.50 2.50
982 A149 12d multicolored 3.00 3.00
Nos. 971-982 (12) 11.85 10.15

Souvenir Sheets

983 A149 15d multicolored 4.50 4.50
984 A149 15d multicolored 4.50 4.50

Independence, 25th Anniv. — A150

Designs: 3d, Sir Dawda Jawara, President. 12d, Jet and map showing airport. 18d, National arms.

1990, June 5 **Litho.** *Perf. 14*

985 A150 1d multicolored .20 .20
986 A150 3d multicolored .60 .60
987 A150 12d multicolored 3.00 3.00
Nos. 985-987 (3) 3.80 3.80

Souvenir Sheet

988 A150 18d multicolored 3.75 3.75

Baobab Tree A151

1990, June 14 **Litho.** *Perf. 14*

989 A151 5b shown .20 .20
990 A151 10b Woodcarving .20 .20
991 A151 20b Pres. Jawara .20 .20
992 A151 50b Map .20 .20
993 A151 75b Batik fabric .20 .20
994 A151 1d Bakau Beach Resort .25 .25
995 A151 1.25d Tendaba Camp .30 .30
996 A151 2d Shrimp industry .45 .45
997 A151 5d Peanut oil mill .75 .75
998 A151 10d Pottery, kora 1.50 1.50
999 A151 15d Ansellia Africana orchid 3.75 3.75
1000 A151 30d Ancient stone rings, Euryphene gambiae 6.25 6.25
Nos. 989-1000 (12) 14.25 14.25

Nos. 990, 999 vert.

Penny Black, 150th Anniv. A152

1990, June 18

1001 A152 1.25d brt bl & blk .50 .35
1002 A152 12d dark red & blk 3.50 3.50

Souvenir Sheet

1003 A152 15d sil, bis & blk 4.25 4.25

Mickey Visits England — A153

Walt Disney characters at: 20b, 10 Downing Street. 50b, Trafalgar Square. 75b, Cliffs of Dover. 1d, Tower of London. 5d, Hampton Court Palace. 8d, Magdalen Tower, Oxford University. 10d, Old London Bridge. 12d, Rosetta Stone, British Museum. No. 1012, Picadilly Circus. No. 1013, Houses of Parliament and Big Ben on the River Thames.

1990, June 19 *Perf. 14x13½*

1004 A153 20b multicolored .20 .20
1005 A153 50b multicolored .20 .20
1006 A153 75b multicolored .40 .40
1007 A153 1d multicolored .40 .40
1008 A153 5d multicolored 1.60 1.60
1009 A153 8d multicolored 2.00 2.00
1010 A153 10d multicolored 2.50 2.50
1011 A153 12d multicolored 3.00 3.00
Nos. 1004-1011 (8) 10.30 10.30

Souvenir Sheets

1012 A153 18d multicolored 5.00 5.00
1013 A153 18d multicolored 5.00 5.00

Stamp World London '90. Nos. 1004-1005, 1007, 1009 vert.

A154

1990, July 19 *Perf. 14*

1014 6d Girl facing left 1.60 1.60
1015 6d Young girl, diff. 1.60 1.60
1016 6d Seated in chair 1.60 1.60
a. A154 Strip of 3, #1014-1016 4.80 4.80

Souvenir Sheet

1017 A154 18d like No. 1014 4.00 4.00

A156

A157

Players from participating countries.

1990, Sept. 24 **Litho.** *Perf. 14*

1018 A156 1d Italy .30 .30
1019 A156 1.25d Argentina .40 .40
1020 A156 3d Costa Rica .90 .90
1021 A156 5d UAE 1.40 1.40
Nos. 1018-1021 (4) 3.00 3.00

Souvenir Sheets

1022 A156 18d Holland 4.50 4.50
1023 A156 18d Romania 4.50 4.50

World Cup Soccer Championships, Italy.

1990, Nov. 1 **Litho.** *Perf. 14*

1024 A157 20b Men's discus .20 .20
1025 A157 50b Men's 100-meter race .20 .20
1026 A157 75b Women's 400-meter race .20 .20
1027 A157 1d Men's 200-meter race .30 .30
1028 A157 1.25d Rhythmic gymnastics .35 .35
1029 A157 3d Soccer .85 .85
1030 A157 10d Men's marathon 3.00 3.00
1031 A157 12d Tornado class sailing 3.50 3.50
Nos. 1024-1031 (8) 8.60 8.60

Souvenir Sheets

1032 A157 15d Parade of flags 4.25 4.25
1033 A157 15d Stadium, card section 4.25 4.25

1992 Summer Olympics, Barcelona.

Christmas A158

Entire paintings or different details from: 20b, 7d, The Annunciation with St. Emidius by

Crivelli. 50b, The Annunciation by Campin. 75b, The Solly Madonna by Raphael. 1.25d, The Tempi Madonna by Raphael. 2d, Madonna of the Linen Window by Raphael. 10d, The Orleans Madonna by Raphael. 15d, Madonna and Child by Crivelli. No. 1042, The Niccolini-Cowper Madonna by Raphael.

1990, Dec. 24 Litho. *Perf. 13½x14*

1034	A158	20b	multicolored	.20	.20
1035	A158	50b	multicolored	.20	.20
1036	A158	75b	multicolored	.20	.20
1037	A158	1.25d	multicolored	.35	.35
1038	A158	2d	multicolored	.55	.55
1039	A158	7d	multicolored	1.75	1.75
1040	A158	10d	multicolored	2.25	2.25
1041	A158	15d	multicolored	3.00	3.00
			Nos. 1034-1041 (8)	8.50	8.50

Souvenir Sheet

1042	A158	15d	multicolored	4.25	4.25

Peter Paul Rubens (1577-1640), Painter — A159

Entire paintings or different details from: 20b, 75b, 10d, No. 1054, The Lion Hunt. 1d, 1.25d, 3d, 15d, The Tiger Hunt. 5d, No. 1055, The Boar Hunt. No. 1056, The Crocodile and Hippopotamus Hunt. No. 1057, Saint George Slays the Dragon, vert.

1990, Dec. 24 Litho. *Perf. 14x13½*

1046	A159	20b	multicolored	.20	.20
1047	A159	75b	multicolored	.20	.20
1048	A159	1d	multicolored	.30	.30
1049	A159	1.25d	multicolored	.40	.40
1050	A159	3d	multicolored	.90	.90
1051	A159	5d	multicolored	1.50	1.50
1052	A159	10d	multicolored	2.50	2.50
1053	A159	15d	multicolored	3.50	3.50
			Nos. 1046-1053 (8)	9.50	9.50

Souvenir Sheets

1054	A159	15d	multicolored	3.50	3.50
1055	A159	15d	multicolored	3.50	3.50
1056	A159	15d	multicolored	3.50	3.50
1057	A159	15d	multicolored	3.50	3.50

World Summit for Children A160

1991, Jan. 7 Litho. *Perf. 14*

1058	A160	1d	multicolored	.50	.50

Intl. Literacy Year — A161

Walt Disney characters in "The Sword in the Stone": No. 1059a, Wart and Sir Kay. b, Merlin reading book. c, Wart learning geography. d, Wart writing on blackboard. e, Wart as bird, Madam Mim. f, Merlin and Madam Mim. g, Mim as dragon. h, Wart pulling sword from stone. i, Wart as King of England. No. 1060, Merlin, Wart in forest, vert. No. 1061, Knight trying to remove sword from stone, vert.

1991, Feb. 14 Litho. *Perf. 14x13½*

1059	A161	3d	Min. sheet of 9, #1059a-1059i	8.00	8.00

Souvenir Sheets

1060	A161	20d	multicolored	6.50	6.50
1061	A161	20d	multicolored	6.50	6.50

Miniature Sheets

Wildlife A162

No. 1062: a, Bebearia senegalensis. b, Graphium ridleyanus. c, Precis antilope. d, Charaxes ameliae. e, Addax. f, Sassaby. g, Civet. h, Green monkey. i, Spurwing goose. j, Red-billed hornbill. k, Osprey. l, Glossy ibis. m, Egyptian plover. n, Golden-tailed woodpecker. o, Green woodhoopoe. p, Gaboon viper.

No. 1063: a, Red-billed firefinch. b, Leaflove. c, Piacpiac. d, Emerald cuckoo. e, Red colobus monkey. f, African elephant. g, Duiker. h, Giant eland. i, Oribi. j, West African dwarf crocodile. k, Crowned crane. l, Jackal. m, Yellow-throated longclaw. n, Abyssinian ground hornbill. o, Papilio hesperus. p, Papilio antimachus.

No. 1064: a, Martial eagle. b, Red-cheeked cordon-bleu. c, Red bishop. d, Great white pelican. e, Patas monkey. f, Vervet monkey. g, Roan antelope. h, Western hartebeest. i, Waterbuck. j, Warthog. k, Spotted hyena. l, Olive baboon. m, Palla decius. n, Acraea pharsalus. o, Neptidopsis ophione. p, Acraea caecilia.

No. 1065, African spoonbill, vert. No. 1066, Lion, vert. No. 1067, Buffalo weaver, vert.

1991, May 31 Litho. *Perf. 14*

Sheets of 16

1062	A162	1d	#a.-p.	4.50	4.50
1063	A162	1.50d	#a.-p.	6.50	6.50
1064	A162	5d	#a.-p.	20.00	20.00
			Nos. 1062-1064 (3)	31.00	31.00

Souvenir Sheets

1065	A162	18d	multicolored	5.00	5.00
1066	A162	18d	multicolored	5.00	5.00
1067	A162	18d	multicolored	5.00	5.00

Butterflies — A163

Designs: 20b, Papilio dardanus. 50b, Bematistes poggei. 1d, Vanessa cardiu. 1.50d, Amphicallia tigris. 3d, Hypolimnes dexithea. 8d, Acraea egina. 10d, Salmis temora. 15d, Precis octavia. No. 1076, Danaus chrysippus. No. 1077, Charaxes jasius. No. 1078, Papilio demodocus. No. 1079, Papilio nireus.

1991, June 1 Litho. *Perf. 14*

1068	A163	20b	multicolored	.20	.20
1069	A163	50b	multicolored	.20	.20
1070	A163	1d	multicolored	.30	.30
1071	A163	1.50d	multicolored	.50	.50
1072	A163	3d	multicolored	.90	.90
1073	A163	8d	multicolored	2.40	2.40
1074	A163	10d	multicolored	3.00	3.00
1075	A163	15d	multicolored	4.50	4.50
			Nos. 1068-1075 (8)	12.00	12.00

Souvenir Sheets

1076	A163	18d	multicolored	5.50	5.50
1077	A163	18d	multicolored	5.50	5.50
1078	A163	18d	multicolored	4.75	4.75
1079	A163	18d	multicolored	4.75	4.75

While Nos. 1078-1079 have same release date as Nos. 1068-1077, the dollar value of Nos. 1078-1079 were lower when they were released.

Royal Family Birthday, Anniversary

Common Design Type

1991, Aug. 12 Litho. *Perf. 14*

1080	CD347	20b	multi	.20	.20
1081	CD347	50b	multi	.20	.20
1082	CD347	75b	multi	.20	.20
1083	CD347	1d	multi	.30	.30
1084	CD347	1.25d	multi	.40	.40
1085	CD347	1.50d	multi	.45	.45
1086	CD347	12d	multi	3.50	3.50
1087	CD347	15d	multi	4.50	4.50
			Nos. 1080-1087 (8)	9.75	9.75

Souvenir Sheets

1088	CD347	18d	Elizabeth, Philip	4.50	4.50
1089	CD347	18d	Diana, sons, Charles	4.50	4.50

20b, 75b, 1.50d, 15d, No. 1089, Charles and Diana, 10th wedding anniversary. Others, Queen Elizabeth II, 65th birthday.

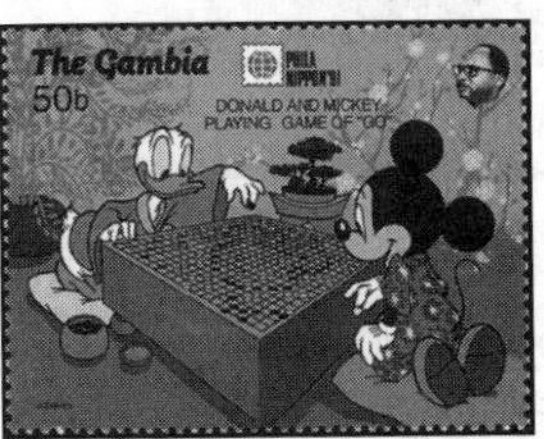

Phila Nippon '91 — A164

Walt Disney characters playing Japanese games and sports: 50b, Donald Duck and Mickey Mouse playing Go. 75b, Morty, Ferdie and Pete sumo wrestling. 1d, Minnie Mouse, Clarabelle, Daisy Duck playing battledore and shuttlecock. 1.25d, Goofy, Mickey at Okinawa bullfight, vert. 5d, Mickey as a Hawk Hunter Tagari, vert. 7d, Mickey, Minnie, and Donald play Jan-Ken-Pon, vert. 10d, Goofy as archer. 15d, Morty, Ferdie fly Japanese kites, vert. No. 1098, Goofy batting in Japanese baseball game, vert. No. 1099, Mickey, Scrooge McDuck playing Japanese football, vert. No. 1100, Mickey fly fishing, vert. No. 1101, Mickey climbing Mt. Fuji, vert.

Perf. 14x13½, 13½x14

1991, Aug. 22 Litho.

1090	A164	50b	multicolored	.20	.20
1091	A164	75b	multicolored	.20	.20
1092	A164	1d	multicolored	.30	.30
1093	A164	1.25d	multicolored	.40	.40
1094	A164	5d	multicolored	1.50	1.50
1095	A164	7d	multicolored	2.10	2.10
1096	A164	10d	multicolored	3.00	3.00
1097	A164	15d	multicolored	4.50	4.50
			Nos. 1090-1097 (8)	12.20	12.20

Souvenir Sheets

1098	A164	20d	multicolored	6.00	6.00
1099	A164	20d	multicolored	6.00	6.00
1100	A164	20d	multicolored	6.00	6.00
1101	A164	20d	multicolored	6.00	6.00

Intl. Literacy Year — A165

Walt Disney characters in scenes from Rudyard Kipling's "Just So Stories": 50b, How the Whale Got His Throat. 75b, How the Camel Got His Hump. 1d, How the Leopard Got His Spots. 1.25d, The Elephant's Child. 1.50d, Singsong of Old Man Kangaroo. 7d, The Crab that Played with the Sea. 10d, The Cat that Walked by Himself. 15d, The Butterfly that Stamped. No. 1110, How the Alphabet was Made, vert. No. 1111, The Beginning of the Armadillos. No. 1112, How the First Letter was Written, vert. No. 1113, How the Rhinoceros Got His Skin.

1991, Aug. 28 Litho. *Perf. 14x13½*

1102	A165	50b	multicolored	.20	.20
1103	A165	75b	multicolored	.20	.20
1104	A165	1d	multicolored	.30	.30
1105	A165	1.25d	multicolored	.40	.40
1106	A165	1.50d	multicolored	.45	.45
1107	A165	7d	multicolored	2.10	2.10
1108	A165	10d	multicolored	3.00	3.00
1109	A165	15d	multicolored	4.50	4.50
			Nos. 1102-1109 (8)	11.15	11.15

Souvenir Sheets

Perf. 13½x14, 14x13½

1110	A165	20d	multicolored	6.00	6.00
1111	A165	20d	multicolored	6.00	6.00
1112	A165	20d	multicolored	4.50	4.50
1113	A165	20d	multicolored	4.50	4.50

While Nos. 1112-1113 have the same issue date as Nos. 1102-1111, the dollar value of Nos. 1112-1113 was lower when they were released.

Train Cabooses — A166

No. 1114: a, Steel cupola, Canadian Pacific. b, Four-wheel, Cumberland and Pennsylvania. c, Mexican slim gauge. d, All steel cupola, Northern Pacific. e, Four-wheel, Morristown & Erie. f, Streamlined cupola, Burlington Northern. g, Caboose coach, McCloud River. h, Wide vision, Santa Fe. i, Wide vision, Frisco.

No. 1115: a, Narrow gauge, Oahu Railway. b, Standard brake-van, British Railways. c, Wide view steel, Union Pacific. d, Four-wheel, Belt Railway of Chicago. e, Four-wheel, McCloud River. f, Logging, Angelina County Lumber Co. g, Narrow gauge, Coahuila & Zacatecas. h, Three-foot gauge, United Railways of Yucatan. i, Steel cupola, Rio Grande.

No. 1116: a, Four-wheel, Colorado & Southern. b, Transfer, Santa Fe. c, Wooden cupola, Canadian National. d, Transfer steel, Union Pacific. e, Caboose coach, Virginia & Truckee. f, Standard brake-van, British. g, Narrow gauge, Intl. Railways of Central America. h, Steel cupola, Northern Pacific. i, Wood, Burlington Northern.

No. 1117, Pennsylvania electric, vert. No. 1118, Unidentified caboose, trainman with flag, vert. No. 1119, Unidentified green wooden caboose behind yellow freight car.

1991, Sept. 12 Litho. *Perf. 14x13½*

Sheets of 9

1114	A166	1d	#a.-i.	3.00	3.00
1115	A166	2d	#a.-i.	4.00	4.00
1116	A166	1.50d	#a.-i.	3.00	3.00
			Nos. 1114-1116 (3)	10.00	10.00

Souvenir Sheets

Perf. 12x13, 13x12

1117	A166	20d	multicolored	6.00	6.00
1118	A166	20d	multicolored	4.50	4.50
1119	A166	20d	multicolored	4.50	4.50

While Nos. 1115-1116 and 1118-1119 have the same issue date as Nos. 1114 and 1117, the dollar value of Nos. 1115-1116 and 1118-1119 was lower when they were released.

Fish — A167

1991, Oct. 28 Litho. *Perf. 14x14½*

1120	A167	20b	Tiger shark	.20	.20
1121	A167	25b	Common jewel fish	.20	.20
1122	A167	50b	Five spot fish	.20	.20
1123	A167	75b	Smalltooth sawfish	.20	.20
1124	A167	1d	Five spot tilapia	.30	.30
1125	A167	1.25d	Dwarf jewel fish	.30	.30
1126	A167	1.50d	Five spot jewel fish	.45	.45
1127	A167	3d	Bumphead	.90	.90
1128	A167	10d	Egyptian mouth-brooder	3.00	3.00
1129	A167	15d	Burton's mouth-brooder	3.25	3.25
			Nos. 1120-1129 (10)	9.00	9.00

Souvenir Sheets

1130	A167	18d	Great barracuda	4.00	4.00
1131	A167	18d	Yellowtail snapper	4.00	4.00

While Nos. 1120-1122, 1125, 1129-1131 have the same issue date as Nos. 1123-1124, 1126-1128 the dollar value of Nos. 1120-1122, 1125, 1129-1130 was lower when they were released.

Hummel Figurines — A168

20b, #1141a, Girl and boy waving handkerchiefs. 75b, #1140a, Boy and girl under umbrella. 1d, #1140b, Two girls wearing scarfs. 1.50d, #1140c, Girl and boy in window with flower box. 2.50d, #1141b, Two girls with basket. 5d, #1141c, Boy wearing long pants, boy wearing shorts. 10d, #1141d, Two girls on fence. 15d, #1140d, Boy with stick, girl with bag.

1991, Nov. 4 Litho. *Perf. 14*

1132	A168	20b	multicolored	.20	.20
1133	A168	75b	multicolored	.20	.20
1134	A168	1d	multicolored	.30	.30
1135	A168	1.50d	multicolored	.55	.55
1136	A168	2.50d	multicolored	.75	.75
1137	A168	5d	multicolored	1.50	1.50
1138	A168	10d	multicolored	3.00	3.00
1139	A168	15d	multicolored	4.50	4.50
			Nos. 1132-1139 (8)	11.00	11.00

Souvenir Sheets of 4

1140	A168	4d	#a.-d.	4.75	4.75
1141	A168	5d	#a.-d.	6.00	6.00

Paintings by Vincent Van Gogh A169

Designs: 20b, The Old Cemetery Tower at Nuenen in the Snow, horiz. 25b, Head of a Peasant Woman with White Cap. 50b, The Green Parrot. 75b, Vase with Carnations. 1d, Vase with Red Gladioli. 1.25b, Beach at Scheveningen in Calm Weather, horiz. 1.50d, Boy Cutting Grass with a Sickle, horiz. 2d, Coleus Plant in a Flowerpot. 3d, Self-portrait, spring-summer 1887. 4d, Self-portrait. 5d, Self-portrait, diff. 6d, Self-portrait, spring 1887. 8d, Still Life with a Bottle, Two Glasses, Cheese and Bread. 10d, Still Life with Cabbage, Clogs and Potatoes, horiz. 12d, Montmartre: The Street Lamps. 15d, Head of a Peasant Woman with Brownish Cap. No. 1158, Arles: View From the Wheat Fields. No. 1159, Autumn Landscape. No. 1160, Montmartre: Quarry, The Mills, horiz. No. 1161, The Potato Eaters, horiz.

Perf. 13½x14, 14x13½

1991, Dec. 5 Litho.

1142	A169	20b	multicolored	.20	.20
1143	A169	25b	multicolored	.20	.20
1144	A169	50b	multicolored	.20	.20
1145	A169	75b	multicolored	.20	.20
1146	A169	1d	multicolored	.20	.20
1147	A169	1.25d	multicolored	.35	.35
1148	A169	1.50d	multicolored	.35	.35
1149	A169	2d	multicolored	.55	.55
1150	A169	3d	multicolored	.70	.70
1151	A169	4d	multicolored	1.25	1.25
1152	A169	5d	multicolored	1.50	1.50
1153	A169	6d	multicolored	1.40	1.40
1154	A169	8d	multicolored	2.40	2.40
1155	A169	10d	multicolored	2.25	2.25
1156	A169	12d	multicolored	2.75	2.75
1157	A169	15d	multicolored	4.50	4.50

Size: 127x102mm

Imperf

1158	A169	20d	multicolored	6.00	6.00
1159	A169	20d	multicolored	6.00	6.00
1160	A169	20d	multicolored	4.50	4.50
1161	A169	20d	multicolored	4.50	4.50
			Nos. 1142-1161 (20)	40.00	40.00

While Nos. 1142-1143, 1146, 1148, 1150, 1153, 1155-1156, 1160-1161 have the same issue date as Nos. 1144-1145, 1147, 1149, 1151-1152, 1154, 1157-1159, the dollar value of Nos. 1142-1143, 1146, 1148, 1150, 1153, 1155-1156, 1160-1161 was lower when they were released.

Christmas A170

Paintings by Fra Angelico: 20b, The Madonna of Humility. 50b, Madonna and Child with Angels. 75b, The Virgin and Child with Angels. 1d, Annunciation. 1.25d, Presentation in the Temple. 5d, Annunciation, diff. 10d, Madonna della Stella. 15d, Naming of St. John the Baptist. No. 1170, Annunciation and Adoration of the Magi. No. 1171, Coronation of the Virgin.

1991, Dec. 23 *Perf. 12*

1162	A170	20b	multicolored	.20	.20
1163	A170	50b	multicolored	.20	.20
1164	A170	75b	multicolored	.20	.20
1165	A170	1d	multicolored	.30	.30
1166	A170	1.25d	multicolored	.40	.40
1167	A170	5d	multicolored	1.50	1.50
1168	A170	10d	multicolored	2.00	2.00
1169	A170	15d	multicolored	3.50	3.50
			Nos. 1162-1169 (8)	8.30	8.30

Souvenir Sheets

Perf. 14½

1170	A170	20d	multicolored	4.00	4.00
1171	A170	20d	multicolored	4.00	4.00

Queen Elizabeth II's Accession to the Throne, 40th Anniv.

Common Design Type

1992, Feb. 6 Litho. *Perf. 14*

1172	CD348	20b	multicolored	.20	.20
1173	CD348	50b	multicolored	.20	.20
1174	CD348	1d	multicolored	.20	.20
1175	CD348	15d	multicolored	3.25	3.25
			Nos. 1172-1175 (4)	3.85	3.85

Souvenir Sheets

1176	CD348	20d	Queen at left, yacht	4.50	4.50
1177	CD348	20d	Queen at right, boat	4.50	4.50

Famous Blues Musicians — A171

1992, Feb. 12 *Perf. 14*

1178	A171	20b	Son House	.20	.20
1179	A171	25b	W. C. Handy	.20	.20
1180	A171	50b	Muddy Waters	.20	.20
1181	A171	75b	Lightnin Hopkins	.20	.20
1182	A171	1d	Ma Rainey	.20	.20
1183	A171	1.25d	Mance Lipscomb	.30	.30
1184	A171	1.50d	Mahalia Jackson	.35	.35
1185	A171	2d	Ella Fitzgerald	.45	.45
1186	A171	3d	Howlin Wolf	.70	.70
1187	A171	5d	Bessie Smith	1.10	1.10
1188	A171	7d	Leadbelly	1.50	1.50
1189	A171	10d	Joe Willie Wilkins	2.25	2.25
			Nos. 1178-1189 (12)	7.65	7.65

Souvenir Sheets

1190	A171	20d	Gambian string drummer	4.50	4.50
1191	A171	20d	Elvis Presley	4.50	4.50
1192	A171	20d	Billie Holiday	4.50	4.50

While all stamps have the same issue date the dollar value of some was lower when they actually were released.

A172

Papal Visit, 1992 — A172a

Designs: 1d, Pope John Paul II. 1.25d, Pope, Pres. Dwada Jawara. 20d, Flags, Papal arms. 25d, Pope at Mass.
Illustration A172a reduced.

1992, Feb. 23 Litho. *Perf. 14*

1193	A172	1d	multicolored	.20	.20
1194	A172	1.25d	multicolored	.30	.30
1195	A172	20d	multicolored	4.50	4.50
			Nos. 1193-1195 (3)	5.00	5.00

Souvenir Sheet

1196	A172	25d	multicolored	5.50	5.50

Embossed

Perf. 12

Without Gum

Size: 65x43mm

1196A	A172a	50d	gold	*25.00*	

No. 1196A was not available until late 1993, exists imperf on large card.

1992 Summer Olympics, Barcelona A173

20b, Map & Nadia Comaneci, gymnastics, Romania, 1976. 50b, D. Moorcraft, 5000 meters, Great Britain, 1984. 75b, M. Nemeth, javelin, Hungary, 1976. 1d, J. Pedraza, 20k walking, Mexico, 1968. 1.25d, Map, Spanish Arms & flag, Yachting soling class, Brazil, 1984. 1.50d, Spanish building, Field hockey, East Germany, 1984. 12d, Map & Michael Jordan, basketball, US, 1984. 15d, V. Borzov, 100 meters, USSR, 1972. #1201, Flamenco dancer, vert. #1206, Map & Bull.

1992, Mar. 6 Litho. *Perf. 14*

1197	A173	20b	multicolored	.20	.20
1198	A173	50b	multicolored	.20	.20
1199	A173	75b	multicolored	.20	.20
1200	A173	1d	multicolored	.30	.30
1201	A173	1.25d	multicolored	.30	.30
1202	A173	1.50d	multicolored	.35	.35
1203	A173	12d	multicolored	2.75	2.75
1204	A173	15d	multicolored	4.50	4.50
			Nos. 1197-1204 (8)	8.80	8.80

Souvenir Sheet

1205	A173	20d	multicolored	6.00	6.00
1206	A173	20d	multicolored	4.50	4.50

While Nos. 1197, 1201-1203, 1206 have the same issue date as Nos. 1198-1200, 1204-1205, the value of Nos. 1197, 1201-1203, 1206 was lower when they were released.

Easter A174

Paintings: 20b, Christ Presented to the People, by Rembrandt. 50b, Christ Carrying the Cross, by Mathias Grunewald. 75b, The Crucifixion, by Mathias Grunewald. 1d, The Crucifixion, by Rubens. 1.25d, The Road to Calvary (detail), by Tintoretto. 1.50d, The Road to Calvary (entire), by Tintoretto. 15d, The Crucifixion, by Masaccio. 20d, Descent from the Cross (detail), by Rembrandt. No. 1215, Crowning with Thorns (detail), by Titian. No. 1216, Crowning with Thorns, by Anthony Van Dyck.

1992, Apr. 16 Litho. *Perf. 13½*

1207	A174	20b	multicolored	.20	.20
1208	A174	50b	multicolored	.20	.20
1209	A174	75b	multicolored	.20	.20
1210	A174	1d	multicolored	.25	.25
1211	A174	1.25d	multicolored	.30	.30
1212	A174	1.50d	multicolored	.35	.35
1213	A174	15d	multicolored	3.50	3.50
1214	A174	20d	multicolored	4.50	4.50
			Nos. 1207-1214 (8)	9.50	9.50

Souvenir Sheets

1215	A174	25d	multicolored	5.25	5.25
1216	A174	25d	multicolored	5.25	5.25

World Columbian Stamp Expo, Chicago A175

Walt Disney characters in Chicago: 50b, Mickey at Navy pier. 1d, Mickey floats by Wrigley Building. 1.25d, Donald graduates from University of Chicago. 12d, Goofy at Chicago's Adler Planetarium. No. 1221, Goofy above Chicago at the Hancock Center, horiz.

1992, Apr. 8 Litho. *Perf. 13½x14*

1217	A175	50b	multicolored	.20	.20
1218	A175	1d	multicolored	.20	.20
1219	A175	1.25d	multicolored	.30	.30
1220	A175	12d	multicolored	2.75	2.75
			Nos. 1217-1220 (4)	3.45	3.45

Souvenir Sheet

Perf. 14x13½

1221	A175	18d	multicolored	4.00	4.00

No. 1220 has name spelled "Alder."

Granada '92 — A176

Mickey Mouse as Columbus: 20b, With map. 75b, Ideas rejected. 1.50d, Explores America. 15d, Returns to Spain. No. 1231, Embarks for America.

1992, Apr. 8 *Perf. 13½x14*

1227	A176	20b	multicolored	.20	.20
1228	A176	75b	multicolored	.20	.20
1229	A176	1.50d	multicolored	.35	.35
1230	A176	15d	multicolored	3.50	3.50
			Nos. 1227-1230 (4)	4.25	4.25

Souvenir Sheet

1231	A176	18d	multicolored	4.00	4.00

Flowers — A177

1992, July 21 Litho. *Perf. 14*

1237	A177	20b	Hibiscus	.20	.20
1238	A177	50b	Calabash nutmeg	.20	.20
1239	A177	75b	Silk cotton tree	.20	.20
1240	A177	1d	Oncoba	.25	.25
1241	A177	1.25d	Paintbrush plant	.30	.30
1242	A177	1.50d	Tree gardenia	.40	.40
1243	A177	2d	Glory bower	.45	.45
1244	A177	5d	Ashanti blood	1.25	1.25

1245 A177 10d African peach 2.50 2.50
1246 A177 12d Butterfly bush 3.00 3.00
1247 A177 15d Crepe ginger 3.75 3.75
1248 A177 18d Spider tresses 4.00 4.00
Nos. 1237-1248 (12) 16.50 16.50

Souvenir Sheets

1249 A177 20d Water lily 4.50 4.50
1250 A177 20d Bougainvillea 5.00 5.00
1251 A177 20d Baobab tree 5.00 5.00
1252 A177 20d Climbing pea 5.00 5.00

While Nos. 1240, 1242, 1244, 1247, 1250 have the same release date as Nos. 1237, 1241, 1243, 1248-1249, their values in relation to the dollar were higher when they were released.

Riverboats — A178

Riverboat and waterway: 20b, Joven Antonia, Gambia River. 50b, Dresden, Elbe River. 75b, Medway Queen, Medway River. 1d, Lady Wright, Gambia River. 1.25d, Devin, Vltava River. 1.50d, Lady Chilel, Gambia River. 5d, Robert Fulton, Hudson River. 10d, Coonawarra, Murray River. 12d, Nakusp, Columbia River. 15d, Lucy Ashton, Firth of Clyde. No. 1263, Rudesheim, Rhine River. No. 1264, City of Cairo, Mississippi River.

1992, Aug. 3 Litho. *Perf. 14*

1253 A178 20b multicolored .20 .20
1254 A178 50b multicolored .20 .20
1255 A178 75b multicolored .20 .20
1256 A178 1d multicolored .20 .20
1257 A178 1.25d multicolored .25 .25
1258 A178 1.50d multicolored .35 .35
1259 A178 5d multicolored 1.10 1.10
1260 A178 10d multicolored 2.25 2.25
1261 A178 12d multicolored 2.75 2.75
1262 A178 15d multicolored 3.50 3.50
Nos. 1253-1262 (10) 11.00 11.00

Souvenir Sheets

1263 A178 20d multicolored 4.50 4.50
1264 A178 20d multicolored 4.50 4.50

Miniature Sheet

World War II in the Pacific — A179

Designs: a, USS Pennsylvania. b, Japanese attack begins. c, USS Ward sinking Japanese submarine. d, Ford Naval Air Station under attack. e, News bulletin announcing attack. f, Front page of Honolulu Star-Bulletin. g, Japanese invade Guam. h, US recovers Wake Island. i, Doolittle raids Japan from USS Hornet. j, Battle of Midway.

1992 Litho. *Perf. 14½x15*

1265 A179 2d Sheet of 10, #a.-j. 4.50 4.50

1992 Summer Olympics, Barcelona A180

Designs: 20b, Women's double sculls. 50b, Kayak, vert. 75b, Women's precision rapid-fire shooting. 1d, Judo, vert. 1.25d, Javelin, vert. 1.50d, Gymnastics, vault, vert. 3d, Windsurfing, vert. 5d, High jump. No. 1274, Women's 200-meter backstroke. No. 1275, Table tennis.

1992, Aug. 10 Litho. *Perf. 14*

1266 A180 20b multicolored .20 .20
1267 A180 50b multicolored .20 .20
1268 A180 75b multicolored .20 .20
1269 A180 1d multicolored .25 .25
1270 A180 1.25d multicolored .30 .30
1271 A180 1.50d multicolored .35 .35
1272 A180 3d multicolored .75 .75
1273 A180 5d multicolored 1.25 1.25
Nos. 1266-1273 (8) 3.50 3.50

Souvenir Sheets

1274 A180 18d multicolored 4.50 4.50
1275 A180 18d multicolored 4.50 4.50

1992 Winter Olympics, Albertville — A181

Designs: 2d, Downhill skiing, vert. 10d, Four-man bobsled, vert. 12d, Ski jumping, vert. 15d, Slalom skiing.
No. 1280, Men's 500-meter speedskating. No. 1281, Pairs figure skating, vert.

1992, Aug. 10 Litho. *Perf. 14*

1276-1279 A181 Set of 4 10.00 10.00

Souvenir Sheets

1280-1281 A181 18d each 4.50 4.50

Dinosaurs — A182

20b, Dryosaurus. 25b, Saurolophus. 50b, #1291, Allosaurus. 75b, Fabrosaurus. 1d, Deinonychus. 1.25d, #1292A, Cetiosaurus. 1.50d, Camptosaurus. 2d, #1292, Ornithosuchus. 3d, Spinosaurus. 5d, Ornithomimus. 10d, Kentrosaurus. 12d, Schlermochus.

1992, Sept. 21 Litho. *Perf. 14*

1283 A182 20b multi .20 .20
1284 A182 25b multi .20 .20
1284A A182 50b multi .20 .20
1284B A182 75b multi .20 .20
1284C A182 1d multi .25 .25
1285 A182 1.25d multi .30 .30
1286 A182 1.50d multi .35 .35
1286A A182 2d multi .50 .50
1287 A182 3d multi .75 .75
1288 A182 5d multi 1.25 1.25
1289 A182 10d multi 2.50 2.50
1290 A182 12d multi 3.00 3.00
Nos. 1283-1290 (12) 9.70 9.70

Souvenir Sheets

1291 A182 25d multi 6.00 6.00
1292 A182 25d multi 6.00 6.00
1292A A182 25d multi 6.00 6.00

Genoa '92.

Walt Disney's Goofy, 60th Anniv. — A183

Scenes from Disney cartoon films: 50b, Orphan's Benefit, 1934, 1941. 75b, Moose Hunters, 1937. 1d, Mickey's Amateurs, 1937. 1.25d, Lonesome Ghosts, 1937. 5d, Boat Builders, 1938. 7d, The Whalers, 1938. 10d, Goofy and Wilbur, 1939. 15d, Saludos Amigos, 1941. No. 1301, The Band Concert, 1935, vert. No. 1302, Goofy today, vert.

1992 Litho. *Perf. 14x13½*

1293 A183 50b multicolored .20 .20
1294 A183 75b multicolored .20 .20
1295 A183 1d multicolored .20 .20
1296 A183 1.25d multicolored .30 .30
1297 A183 5d multicolored 1.10 1.10
1298 A183 7d multicolored 1.75 1.75
1299 A183 10d multicolored 2.50 2.50
1300 A183 15d multicolored 3.50 3.50
Nos. 1293-1300 (8) 9.75 9.75

Souvenir Sheets

Perf. 13½x14

1301 A183 20d multicolored 4.50 4.50
1302 A183 20d multicolored 5.00 5.00

Discovery of America, 500th Anniv. A184

5d, Santa Maria. 12d, Pinta, Santa Maria, and Nina. 18d, Tree branch, green-winged macaw.

1992, Oct. Litho. *Perf. 14*

1303 A184 5d multi 1.10 1.10
1304 A184 12d multi 2.75 2.75

Souvenir Sheet

1305 A184 18d multi, vert. 4.00 4.00

Golf — A186

Pres. Jarwara playing golf and: 20b, Map, flag of Australia. 1d, Trophy, Gambian flag. 1.50d, Gambian flag. 2d, Map, flag of Japan. 3d, Map, flag of US. 5d, Trophy, 1985, Gambian flag (small portrait only). #1312, Map, flag of Scotland. 12d, Map, flag of Italy. #1312B, Pres. Jawara about to tee off. #1312C, Gambian flag (small portrait).

1992 Litho. *Perf. 14*

1306 A186 20b multi .20 .20
1307 A186 1d multi .25 .25
1308 A186 1.50d multi .35 .35
1309 A186 2d multi .50 .50
1310 A186 3d multi .75 .75
1311 A186 5d multi 1.25 1.25
1312 A186 10d multi 2.50 2.50
1312A A186 12d multi 3.00 3.00
Nos. 1306-1312A (8) 8.80 8.80

Souvenir Sheets

1312B A186 10d multi 2.50 2.50
1312C A186 18d multi, horiz. 4.00 4.00

No. 1306, Royal Melbourne Golf Course, Australia. No. 1309, Shinonoseki Golf Course, Japan. No. 1310, US Open, Pebble Beach. No. 1312, St. Andrew's Golf Course, Scotland. No. 1312A, Italian Open, Monticello, Milan.
Issued: 20b, 2d, 5d, #1312, 1312B, Dec. 8; others, Oct.

Souvenir Sheet

Ellis Island, New York City — A187

1992, Oct. 28 Litho. *Perf. 14*

1313 A187 18d multicolored 4.50 4.50

Postage Stamp Mega Event '92, New York City.

Christmas A188

Details or entire paintings: 50b, The Holy Family, by Raphael. 75b, Madonna and Child with St. Elizabeth and the Infant St. John (Small Holy Family), by Raphael. 1d, The Holy Family as the Little Holy Family, by Raphael. 1.25d, Escape to Egypt, by Broederlam. 1.50d, Flight Into Egypt, by Isenbrant. No. 1319, The Flight into Egypt, by Cosimo Tura. No. 1320, Flight into Egypt, by Master of Hoogstraelen. No. 1321, The Holy Family, by El Greco. 4d, The Holy Family, by Bernard Van Orley. 5d, Holy Family with Infant Jesus Sleeping, by Charles Le Brun. 10d, Rest on the Flight to Egypt, by Gentileschi. 12d, Rest on the Flight to Egypt, by Orazio Gentileschi. No. 1326, The Holy Family, by Giorgione. No. 1327, Rest on the Flight to Egypt, by Simone Cantarino. No. 1328, The Flight to Egypt, by Vittore Carpaccio.

1992, Nov. 3 Litho. *Perf. 13½x14*

1314 A188 50b multicolored .20 .20
1315 A188 75b multicolored .20 .20
1316 A188 1d multicolored .25 .25
1317 A188 1.25d multicolored .30 .30
1318 A188 1.50d multicolored .40 .40
1319 A188 2d multicolored .45 .45
1320 A188 2d multicolored .50 .50
1321 A188 2d multicolored .50 .50
1322 A188 4d multicolored 1.00 1.00
1323 A188 5d multicolored 1.25 1.25
1324 A188 10d multicolored 2.00 2.00
1325 A188 12d multicolored 2.25 2.25
Nos. 1314-1325 (12) 9.30 9.30

Souvenir Sheets

1326 A188 25d multicolored 4.50 4.50
1327 A188 25d multicolored 4.50 4.50
1328 A188 25d multicolored 4.50 4.50

A189

A190

A191

A192

A193

A194

Anniversaries and Events — A195

Designs: No. 1329, Ariane 4 rocket. No. 1330, Berlin airlift, Konrad Adenauer. No. 1331, LZ127 Graf Zeppelin. 6d, Jentink's duiker. 7d, World map. 9d, Wolfgang Amadeus Mozart. No. 1335, America's Cup yacht Enterprise, 1930. No. 1336, Imperial parrot. No. 1337, Lions Intl. emblem. No. 1338, American Space shuttle. 15d, Prisoners of war returning home, Adenauer. 18d, First rigid airship, LZ1. No. 1341, European Space Agency's Hermes space shuttle. No. 1342, Scene from "The Marriage of Figaro." No. 1343, Face of Adenauer. No. 1344, Count Ferdinand von Zeppelin. No. 1345, Earth as seen from space.

1992-93 Litho. *Perf. 14*

1329 A189 2d multicolored .50 .50
1330 A191 2d multicolored .50 .50
1331 A191 2d multicolored .50 .50
1332 A192 6d multicolored 1.50 1.50
1333 A193 7d multicolored 1.75 1.75
1334 A190 9d multicolored 2.25 2.25
1335 A194 10d multicolored 2.50 2.50
1336 A192 10d multicolored 2.50 2.50
1337 A195 10d multicolored 2.50 2.50
1338 A189 12d multicolored 3.00 3.00
1339 A191 15d multicolored 3.75 3.75
1340 A191 18d multicolored 4.50 4.50
Nos. 1329-1340 (12) 25.75 25.75

Souvenir Sheets

1341 A189 18d multicolored 4.00 4.00
1342 A190 18d multicolored 4.00 4.00
1343 A191 18d multicolored 4.00 4.00
1344 A191 18d multicolored 4.00 4.00
1345 A192 18d multicolored 4.00 4.00

Intl. Space Year (#1329, 1338, 1341). Wolfgang Amadeus Mozart, bicent. of death (#1334, 1342). Konrad Adenauer, 25th anniv. of death (#1330, 1339, 1343). Count Zeppelin, 75th anniv. of death (#1331, 1340, 1344). Earth Summit, Rio de Janeiro (#1332, 1336, 1345). Intl. Conf. on Nutrition, Rome (#1333). America's Cup yacht race (#1335). Lions Intl., 75th anniv. (#1337).

Issued: #1333, 1335, 1339, 1343, 1/93; others, 12/92.

Peace Corps, 25th Anniv. A196

1993, Feb.

1346 A196 2d multicolored .50 .50

Elvis Presley, 15th Anniv. of Death (in 1992) — A197

a, Portrait. b, With guitar. c, Holding microphone.

1993

1347 A197 3d Strip of 3, #a.-c. 2.25 2.25

Miniature Sheets

Baseball Films — A198

Movie and stars: No. 1348a, Casey at the Bat, Wallace Beery, 1927, Elliott Gould, 1986. b, Babe Comes Home, Anna Q. Nilsson, Babe Ruth, 1927. c, Elmer the Great, Joe E. Brown, 1933. d, The Naughty Nineties, Bud Abbott and Lou Costello, 1945. e, Take Me Out to the Ball Game, Frank Sinatra, Gene Kelly, Esther Williams, 1949. f, Damn Yankees, Tab Hunter, Gwen Verdon, 1958. g, The Pride of St. Louis, Dan Dailey, 1952. h, Brewster's Millions, John Candy, Richard Pryor, 1985.

No. 1349a, The Jackie Robinson Story, Jackie Robinson, Ruby Dee, 1950. b, Bang the Drum Slowly, Robert DeNiro, 1973. c, The Bingo Long Traveling All-Stars & Motor Kings, James Earl Jones, Billy Dee Williams, 1976. d, Bull Durham, Kevin Costner, Susan Sarandon, 1988. e, Eight Men Out, eight actors, 1988. f, Field of Dreams, Ray Liotta, 1989. g, Major League, Charlie Sheet, 1989. h, Mr. Baseball, Tom Selleck, 1992.

#1350, The Babe, John Goodman, 1992. #1351, The Natural, Robert Redford. #1351A, The Winning Team, Ronald Reagan. #1351B, A League of Their Own, Tom Hanks, Madonna.

1993, Mar. 25 Litho. *Perf. 13*

Sheets of 8

1348 A198 3d #a.-h. 6.00 6.00
1349 A198 3d #a.-h. 6.00 6.00

Souvenir Sheet

1350 A198 20d multi 5.00 5.00
1351 A198 20d multi, vert. 5.00 5.00
1351A A198 20d multi 5.00 5.00
1351B A198 20d multi, vert. 5.00 5.00

Miniature Sheets

Louvre Museum, Bicent. — A199

Details from paintings, by Jacques-Louis David (1748-1825): Nos. 1352a-b, Oath of the Horatii (diff. details). c, The Love of Paris & Helen. d, Rape of the Sabine Women. e, Leonidas of Thermopylae. f-h, Napoleon Crowning Josephine (left, center, right).

Details from paintings, by Antoine (c. 1588-1648) and Louis (1593-1648) Le Nain: No. 1353a, Inside Home of Peasants. b-c, The Tobacco Smokers (diff. details). d, The Cart. e, Peasants' Meal. f-g, Interior Portraits (diff. details). h, The Forge.

Details or entire paintings, by Leonardo Da Vinci: No. 1354a, St. John the Baptist. b, Virgin of the Rocks. c, Bacchus. d, Woman from the Court of Milan. e, The Virgin of the Rocks (detail). f, Mona Lisa. g, Mona Lisa (detail of hands). h, Two Horsemen, Study of the Horse.

No. 1355, Allegory of Victory, by Mathieu Le Nain (1607-1677). No. 1356, The Artist and Her Daughter, by Elisabeth Vigee-Lebrun (1755-1842).

1993, Jan. 7 Litho. *Perf. 12*

Sheets of 8

1352 A199 3d #a.-h. 6.00 6.00
1353 A199 3d #a.-h. 6.00 6.00
1354 A199 3d #a.-h. 6.00 6.00

Souvenir Sheets

Perf. 14½

1355 A199 20d multicolored 5.00 5.00
1356 A199 20d multicolored 5.00 5.00

#1355-1356 each contain 1 55x88mm stamp.

Miniature Sheet

Animals of West Africa — A200

Designs: No. 1358a, Giraffe. b, Baboon. c, Caracal. d, Large-spotted genet. e, Bushbuck. f, Red-fronted gazelle. g, Red-flanked duiker. h, Cape buffalo. i, African civet. j, Side-striped jackal. k, Ratel. l, Striped polecat.

No. 1359a, Vervet. b, Blackish-green guenon. c, Long-tailed pangolin. d, Leopard. e, Elephant. f, Hunting dog. g, Spotted hyena. h, Lion. i, Hippopotamus. j, Nile crocodile. k, Aardvark. l, Warthog.

1993, Apr. 5 Litho. *Perf. 14*

Sheets of 12

1358 A200 2d #a.-l. 9.00 9.00
1359 A200 5d #a.-l. 9.00 9.00

Souvenir Sheet

1360 A200 20d like #1359b 5.00 5.00

No. 1360 printed in continuous design with black frameline around stamp. A number has been reserved for an additional value in this set.

Long-Tailed Pangolin — A201

Pangolin in various positions on tree limb.

1993, Apr. 5

1362 A201 1.25d multicolored .45 .45
1363 A201 1.50d multicolored .60 .60
1364 A201 2d multicolored .70 .70
1365 A201 5d multicolored 1.75 1.75
Nos. 1362-1365 (4) 3.50 3.50

Souvenir Sheet

1366 A201 20d like #1363 7.50 7.50

World Wildlife Federation.

Birds

A202 A203

Designs: 1.25d, Osprey. 1.50d, Egyptian vulture, horiz. 2d, Martial eagle. 3d, Ruppell's griffon vulture, horiz. 5d, Auger buzzard. 8d, Greater kestrel. 10d, Secretary bird. 15d, Bateleur eagle, horiz.

No. 1375a, Rose-ringed parakeet. b, Variable sunbird. c, Red-billed hornbill. d, Red-billed fire-finch. e, Common go-away bird. f, Crimson-breasted shrike. g, Gray-headed bush-shrike. h, Nicator. i, Egyptian plover. j, Congo peacock. k, Greater painted snipe. l, Crowned crane.

#1376, Verreaux's eagle. #1377, Tawny owl.

1993, Apr. 15 Litho. *Perf. 14*

1367 A202 1.25d multicolored .30 .30
1368 A202 1.50d multicolored .40 .40
1369 A202 2d multicolored .50 .50
1370 A202 3d multicolored .75 .75
1371 A202 5d multicolored 1.25 1.25
1372 A202 8d multicolored 2.00 2.00
1373 A202 10d multicolored 2.50 2.50
1374 A202 15d multicolored 3.75 3.75
Nos. 1367-1374 (8) 11.45 11.45

Miniature Sheet of 12

1375 A203 2d #a.-l. 6.00 6.00

Souvenir Sheets

1376 A202 20d multicolored 5.00 5.00
1377 A202 20d multicolored 5.00 5.00

#1376-1377 each contain 1 56x42mm stamp.

Aviation Anniversaries — A204

Designs: No. 1379, Guyot balloon, 1785, vert. No. 1380, Dr. Hugo Eckener, zeppelin LZ3 in flight. No. 1381, Sopwith Snipe. No. 1382, Eckener, LZ3 moored to ground. 8d, Eckener, Graf Zeppelin. 10d, Balloon, Comte D'Artois, 1785, vert. 15d, Royal Aircraft Factory S.E.5. No. 1386, Avro 504K. No. 1387, Eckener, LZ3 in flight, diff. No. 1388, Blanchard's flying ship, 1785, vert.

1993, May Litho. *Perf. 14*

1379 A204 2d multicolored .50 .50
1380 A204 2d multicolored .50 .50
1381 A204 5d multicolored 1.25 1.25
1382 A204 5d multicolored 1.25 1.25
1383 A204 8d multicolored 2.00 2.00
1384 A204 10d multicolored 2.50 2.50
1385 A204 15d multicolored 3.75 3.75
Nos. 1379-1385 (7) 11.75 11.75

Souvenir Sheets

1386 A204 20d multicolored 5.00 5.00
1387 A204 20d multicolored 5.00 5.00
1388 A204 20d multicolored 5.00 5.00

Dr. Hugo Eckener, 125th birth anniv. (#1380, 1382, 1383, 1387). Royal Air Force, 75th anniv. (#1381, 1385, 1386).

Nos. 1379, 1384, 1388 are airmail.

Miniature Sheet

Coronation of Queen Elizabeth II, 40th Anniv. A205

Designs: a, 2d, Official coronation photograph. b, 5d, Orb and Scepter. c, 8d, Winston Churchill. d, 10d, Queen during Trooping of the Color.

20d, Portrait, by Joe King, 1972.

1993, June 2 *Perf. 13½x14*

1389 A205 Sheet, 2 ea #a.-d. 10.00 10.00

Souvenir Sheet

Perf. 14

1390 A205 20d multicolored 5.50 5.50

No. 1390 contains one 28x42mm stamp.

Miniature Sheet

A206

Benz Automobiles: a, 1894 Benz Velo. b, 1894 Benz. c, 1885 Benz. d, 1905 Benz Mannheim. e, 1892 Benz. f, 1900 Benz, blue. g, 1911 Benz. h, 1893 Benz Velo. i, 1900 Benz, black. j, 1900 Benz, red. k, 1911 Benz, front view. l, 1885 Benz, rear view.

No. 1393, 20d, 1900 Benz, diff.

Ford automobiles: No. 1392a, Henry Ford, age 30, 1910 Model T. b, 1896, green seat. c, Henry Ford with Barney Oldfield and 1902 racing car, 999. d, 1896, Henry Ford with bicycle. e, 1903 Model A. f, 1908 Model T, top down. g, 1908 Model T, top up. h, 1906 Model K. i, 1931 Model A. j, 1906 Model A. k, 1906 Model N. l, 1905 Model F.

No. 1394, 1896, red seat.

1993, June 7 ***Perf. 14***

Sheets of 12

1391 A206 2d #a.-l. 6.00 6.00
1392 A206 2d #a.-l. 6.00 6.00

Souvenir Sheet

1393 A206 20d multicolored 5.00 5.00
1394 A206 20d multicolored 5.00 5.00

1st Benz 4-wheel automobile, cent. (#1391, 1393).

1st engine by Henry Ford, cent. (#1392, 1394).

Miniature Sheets

Entertainers — A207

Designs: No. 1395a, Buddy Holly. b, Otis Redding. c, Bill Haley. d, Dinah Washington. e, Musical instruments. f, Ritchie Valens. g, Clyde McPhatter. h, Elvis Presley.

#1396a-1396i, Various pictures of Madonna.

#1397a-1397i, Various pictures of Elvis Presley.

#1398a-1398i, Various pictures of Marilyn Monroe.

1993, July 26 Litho. ***Perf. 14***

Sheets of 8 & 9

1395 A207 3d #a.-h. 6.00 6.00
1396 A207 3d #a,-i. 6.75 6.75
1397 A207 3d #a,-i. 6.75 6.75
1398 A207 3d #a.-i. 6.75 6.75
Nos. 1395-1398 (4) 26.25 26.25

Cats and Dogs A208

Cats: No. 1399a, Siamese. b, Colorpoint longhair. c, Burmese. d, Birman. e, Snowshoe. f, Tonkinese. g, Foreign shorthair. h, Balinese. i, Oriental shorthair. j, Foreign shorthair, diff. k, Colorpoint longhair, diff. l, Colorpoint longhair, diff.

No. 1401, Colorpoint shorthair, vert. No. 1402, Burmese, vert.

Dogs: No. 1400a, Shih tzu. b, Skye terrier. c, Berner laufhund. d, Boxer. e, Welsh corgi (Queen Elizabeth II). f, Dumfrieshire. g, Lurcher. h, Welsh corgi (Princess Anne). i, Pekinese. j, Papillon. k, Otterhound. l, Pug.

No. 1403, Long-haired dachshund. No. 1404, Cairn terrier.

1993, Sept. 13 Litho. ***Perf. 14***

Sheets of 12

1399 A208 2d #a.-l. 6.00 6.00
1400 A208 2d #a.-i. 6.00 6.00

Souvenir Sheets

1401 A208 20d multicolored 5.00 5.00
1402 A208 20d multicolored 5.00 5.00
1403 A208 20d multicolored 5.00 5.00
1404 A208 20d multicolored 5.00 5.00

Taipei '93 — A209

#1405, Fawang Si Pagoda, Song Shan Mt., Henan. #1406, Wanshoubao Pagoda, Shashi. #1407, Red Pavilion, Shibaozhai. #1408, Songyue Si Pagoda, Song Shan Mt., Henan. #1409, Bond Center, Hong Kong. #1410, Tianning Si Pagoda, Beijing. #1411, Xuanzhuang Pagoda, Xian, Shenxi. #1412, Forbidden City, Beijing.

Tang Dynasty funerary objects - #1413: a, Camel. b, Horse and female rider. c, Camel, diff. d, Yellow-glazed horse. e, Camel, diff. f, Horse with saddle.

Pottery - #1414: a, Vase. b, Small wine cup. c, Fahua type Mei-ping vase. d, Urn vase, export ware. e, Tureen. f, Lidded Potiche.

#1415, Standing Buddhas,Hallway of Upper Huayan Si Temple, Datong, horiz. #1416, Seated Buddha, Main Hall, Shanhua Si Temple, Datong.

1993, Sept. 27 Litho. ***Perf. 14***

1405 A209 20b multicolored .20 .20
1406 A209 20b multicolored .20 .20
1407 A209 2d multicolored .50 .50
1408 A209 2d multicolored .50 .50
1409 A209 5d multicolored 1.25 1.25
1410 A209 5d multicolored 1.25 1.25
1411 A209 15d multicolored 3.75 3.75
1412 A209 15d multicolored 3.75 3.75
Nos. 1405-1412 (8) 11.40 11.40

Miniature Sheets of 6

1413 A209 5d #a.-f. 7.50 7.50
1414 A209 5d #a.-f. 7.50 7.50

Souvenir Sheets

1415 A209 18d multicolored 4.50 4.50
1416 A209 18d multicolored 4.50 4.50

With Bangkok '93 Emblem

#1417, Sanctuary of Prasat Phanom Wan. #1418, Lai Kham Vihan, Chiang Mai. #1419, Spirit Shrine, Bangkok. #1420, Walking Buddha, Wat Phra Si Ratana Mahathat. #1421, Buddha, Sukhothai's Wat Mahathat. #1422, Gopura of Prasat Phanom Rung. #1423, Prang of Prasat Hin Phimai. #1424, Slender Chedis, Wat Yai Chai, Mongkon.

Thai painting - #1425: a, Early Fruit Stand. b, Scene in Chinese Style, Wat Bovornivet. c, Buddha Descends from Tauatimsa. d, Sang Thong Tales, Lai Kham Vihan. e, The Damned in Hell, Wah Suthat. f, King Sanjaya Travels on Elephant, Wat Suwannaram.

Thai Buddha sculpture - #1426: a, U Thong C, 14th-15th cent. b, Adorned Seated, 17th cent. c, Phra Chai, 19th cent. d, Bronze, 14th cent. e, U Thong A, bronze. f, Crowned, 14th-15th cent.

#1427, Ceramics, horiz. #1428, Character in Khon, dance drama.

1993

1417 A209 20b multicolored .20 .20
1418 A209 20b multicolored .20 .20
1419 A209 2d multicolored .50 .50
1420 A209 2d multicolored .50 .50
1421 A209 5d multicolored 1.25 1.25
1422 A209 5d multicolored 1.25 1.25
1423 A209 15d multicolored 3.75 3.75
1424 A209 15d multicolored 3.75 3.75
Nos. 1417-1424 (8) 11.40 11.40

Miniature Sheets of 6

1425 A209 5d #a.-f. 7.50 7.50
1426 A209 5d #a.-f. 7.50 7.50

Souvenir Sheets

1427 A209 18d multicolored 4.50 4.50
1428 A209 18d multicolored 4.50 4.50

With Indopex '93 Emblem

Designs: No. 1429, Pura Taman Ayun (garden temple), Mengwi, Bali. No. 1430, Natl. monument with statue of Prince Diponegoro, Jakarta. No. 1431, Candi Jawi, East Java. No. 1432, Guardian at Singosari Palace, East Java. No. 1433, Monument of Irian Jaya, (liberation), Jakarta. No. 1434, Central Temple, Prambanan complex, Lara Djonggrang. No. 1435, "Date of the Year Temple," Panataran complex, East Java. No. 1436, Brahma & Siva Temples, Loro Jonggrang, Java.

Masks: No. 1437a, Telek Luh. b, Jero Gde. c, Barong Macan. d, Monkey. e, Mata Gde. f, Jauk Kras.

Paintings: No. 1438a, Tree Mask, Soedibio, 1978. b, Dry Lizard, Hendra Gunawan, 1977. c, The Corn Eater, Sudjana Kerton, 1988. d, Night Watchman, Djoko Pekik, 1988. e, Hunger, Kerton, 1984. f, Arje Player, Soedjojono, 1971.

No. 1439, Stone carving, Brahma & Gods, Borobudur, Java, horiz. No. 1440, Effigies of the Dead, Torajaland, horiz.

1993, Sept. 27 Litho. ***Perf. 14***

1429 A209 20b multicolored .20 .20
1430 A209 20b multicolored .20 .20
1431 A209 2d multicolored .50 .50
1432 A209 2d multicolored .50 .50
1433 A209 5d multicolored 1.25 1.25
1434 A209 5d multicolored 1.25 1.25
1435 A209 15d multicolored 3.75 3.75
1436 A209 15d multicolored 3.75 3.75
Nos. 1429-1436 (8) 11.40 11.40

Miniature Sheets of 6

1437 A209 5d #a.-f. 7.50 7.50
1438 A209 5d #a.-f. 7.50 7.50

Souvenir Sheets

1439 A209 18d multicolored 4.50 4.50
1440 A209 18d multicolored 4.50 4.50

Miniature Sheet

Casey at the Bat — A210

Nos. 1441-1443: Characters and scenes from Disney's animated film Casey at the Bat.

1993, Oct. 25 Litho. ***Perf. 14x13½***

1441 A210 2d Sheet of 9, #a.-i. 4.50 4.50

Souvenir Sheets

1442 A210 20d multicolored 5.00 5.00

Perf. 13½x14

1443 A210 20d multi, vert. 5.00 5.00

Picasso — A211

Paintings: 2d, Woman with a Comb, 1906. 5d, The Mirror, 1932. 7d, Woman on a Pillow, 1969. 18d, The Three Dancers, 1925.

1993, Oct. 7 Litho. ***Perf. 14***

1444-1446 A211 Set of 4 3.50 3.50

Souvenir Sheet

1447 A211 18d multicolored 4.50 4.50

Copernicus A212

1993, Oct. 7 ***Perf. 14***

5d, Early astronomical instrument. 10d, Telescope.

1448-1449 A212 Set of 2 3.75 3.75

Souvenir Sheet

Perf. 12x13

1450 A212 18d Copernicus 4.50 4.50

Polska '93 A213

Paintings: 2d, Pont-Nuef, Paris, by Rudzka-Cybisowa, 1932. No. 1452, 10d, Honegger's Liturgical Symphony, by Bogusz, 1973. No. 1453, 10d, Niedzica castle. 18d, When You Enter Here, Whisper My Name Soundlessly, by Waniek, 1973.

1993, Oct. 7 ***Perf. 14***

1451-1453 A213 Set of 3 5.50 5.50

Souvenir Sheet

1454 A213 18d multicolored 4.50 4.50

1994 World Cup Soccer Championships, US — A214

Players, country: 1.25d, Hannich, Hungary; Stopyra, France. 1.50d, Labd, Morocco; Lineker, England. 2d, Segota, Canada; Morozov, Russia. 3d, Roger Milla, Cameroun. 5d, Rodax, Australia; Weiss, Czech Republic. 10d, Claesen, Belgium; Bossis & Amoros, France. 12d, Candida, Brazil; Ramirez, Costa Rica. 15d, Silva, Brazil; Platini, France. No. 1463, Muller, Brazil; McDonald, Ireland, horiz. No. 1463A, Buchwald and Matthaeus, Germany; Maradona, Argentina, horiz.

1993, Nov. 22 ***Perf. 13½x14***

1455 A214 1.25d multi .30 .30
1456 A214 1.50d multi .40 .40
1457 A214 2d multi .50 .50
1458 A214 3d multi .75 .75
1459 A214 5d multi 1.25 1.25
1460 A214 10d multi 2.50 2.50
1461 A214 12d multi 3.00 3.00
1462 A214 15d multi 3.75 3.75
Nos. 1455-1462 (8) 12.45 12.45

Souvenir Sheets

Perf. 13

1463 A214 25d multi 6.25 6.25
1463A A214 25d multi 6.25 6.25

Christmas A215

Designs: 25b, 2d (No. 1467), 15d, Details or entire painting, Adoration of the Magi, by Rubens.

Details or entire woodcut by Durer: 1d, Holy Family with Joachim & Anna. 1.50d, The Annunciation, Life of the Virgin. 2d (No. 1468), The Virgin Mary Worshipped by Albrecht Bonstetten. 7d, Virgin on a Throne, Crowned by an Angel. 10d, The Holy Family with Two Angels in a Portico (detail).

Souvenir Sheets: No. 1472, 20d, Adoration of the Magi, by Rubens. No. 1473, 20d, The Holy Family with Two Angels in a Portico, (entire), by Durer, horiz.

1993, Dec. 1 ***Perf. 13½x14, 14x13½***

1464-1473 A215 Set of 10 20.00 20.00

Fine Art — A216

Paintings by Rembrandt: 50b, A Man in a Cap. No. 1476, Man with a Gold Helmet. 7d, A Franciscan Monk. 15d, The Apostle Paul. 20d, Dr. Tulp Demonstrating the Anatomy of the Arm, horiz.

Paintings by Matisse: 1.50d, Portrait of Pierre Matisse. No. 1477, Portrait of Auguste Pellerin (II). 5d, Andre Derain. 12d, The Young Sailor (II). No. 1483, Pianist and Checker Players, horiz.

1993, Dec. 15 ***Perf. 13½x14***

1474 A216	50b	multicolored	.20	.20
1475 A216	1.50d	multicolored	.40	.40
1476 A216	2d	multicolored	.50	.50
1477 A216	2d	multicolored	.50	.50
1478 A216	5d	multicolored	1.25	1.25
1479 A216	7d	multicolored	1.75	1.75
1480 A216	12d	multicolored	3.00	3.00
1481 A216	15d	multicolored	3.75	3.75
	Nos. 1474-1481 (8)		11.35	11.35

Souvenir Sheets

Perf. 14x13½

1482 A216	20d	multicolored	5.00	5.00
1483 A216	20d	multicolored	5.00	5.00

Winter Sports A217

Disney characters portraying sports: 50b, Ski ballet. 75b, Pairs figure skating. 1d, Speed skating. 1.25d, Biathlon. 4d, 4-Man bobsled. 5d, Luge. 7d, Figure skating. 10d, Downhill skiing. 15d, Ice hockey.

No. 1493, Cross country skiing. No. 1494, Mogul skiing.

1993, Dec. 20 ***Perf. 13½x14***

1484-1492 A217 Set of 9 11.00 11.00

Souvenir Sheets

1493-1494 A217 20d each 4.50 4.50

A218

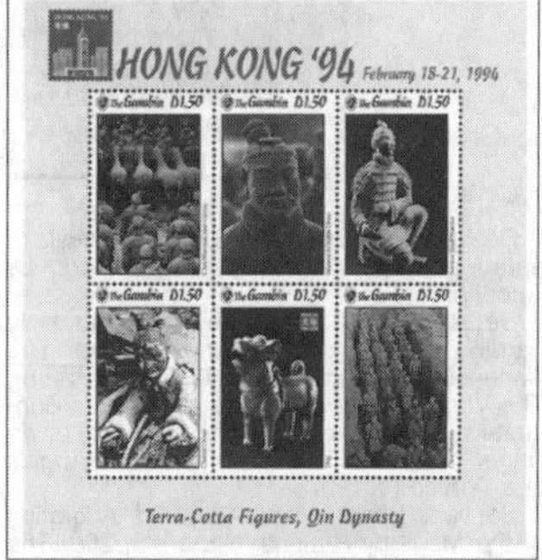
Hong Kong '94 — A219

Stamps, painting, Spring Garden-1846, by M. Bruce: No. 1495, Hong Kong #357, left detail. No. 1496, Right detail, #1000.

Museum of Qin Figures, Shaanxi Province, Tomb of First Emperor: No. 1497a, Qin warriors, horses. b, Warrior in battle dress. c, Armor clad warrior. d, Chariot driver. e, Dog. f, Qin warriors.

No. 1498, Show emblem, Hong Kong #253, vert.

1994, Feb. 18 Litho. ***Perf. 14***

1495 A218	1.50d	multicolored	.50	.40
1496 A218	1.50d	multicolored	.50	.40
a.	Pair, #1495-1496		1.00	.75

Miniature Sheet of 6

1497 A219 1.50d #a.-f. 3.00 3.00

Souvenir Sheet

1498 A218 20d multicolored 5.00 5.00

Nos. 1495-1496 issued in sheets of 5 pairs. No. 1496a is a continuous design.

New Year 1994 (Year of the Dog) (#1497e, #1498).

New Year 1994 (Year of the Dog) A220

Disney characters: 25b, Pluto the Racer. 50b, Fifi. 75b, Pluto, Jr. 1.25d, Goofy and Bowser. 1.50d, Butch. 2d, Toliver. 3d, Ronnie. 5d, Primo. 8d, Pluto's kid brother. 10d, Army mascot. 12d, Pluto and Dinah's pups. 18d, Bent Tail, Junior.

#1511, Pluto, Dinah. #1512, Eega Beeva, Dog Pflip, Goofy, horiz. #1513, Dinah's pups, Pluto.

1994, Apr. 11 Litho. ***Perf. 13½x14***

1499-1510 A220 Set of 12 12.50 12.50

Souvenir Sheets

1511 A220 20d multicolored 4.50 4.50

Perf. 14x13½, 13½x14

1512 A220 20d multicolored 4.50 4.50
1513 A220 20d multicolored 4.50 4.50

Orchids A221

Designs: 1d, Oeceoclades maculata. 1.25d, Angraecum distichum. 2d, Plectrelminthus caudatus. 5d, Tridactyle tridactylites. 8d, Bulbophyllum lepidum. 10d, Angraecum eburneum. 12d, Eulophia guineensis. 15d, Angraecum eichleranum.

No. 1522, Ancistrochilus rothschildianus. No. 1523, Vanilla imperialis.

1994, May 1 ***Perf. 14***

1514 A221	1d	multicolored	.25	.25
1515 A221	1.25d	multicolored	.30	.30
1516 A221	2d	multicolored	.50	.50
1517 A221	5d	multicolored	1.25	1.25
1518 A221	8d	multicolored	2.00	2.00
1519 A221	10d	multicolored	2.50	2.50
1520 A221	12d	multicolored	3.00	3.00
1521 A221	15d	multicolored	3.75	3.75
	Nos. 1514-1521 (8)		13.55	13.55

Souvenir Sheets

1522 A221	25d	multicolored	6.25	6.25
1523 A221	25d	multicolored	6.25	6.25

Easter A222

Disney characters celebrate Easter: 25b, 4d, 8d, 12d, Ludwig von Drake. 50b, Minnie, Daisy. 3d, Mickey. 5d, Donald. 10d, Goofy.

#1532, Von Drake. #1533, Mickey, Minnie.

1994, Apr. 11 Litho. ***Perf. 13½x14***

1524-1531 A222 Set of 8 11.50 11.50

Souvenir Sheets

1532-1533 A222 20d each 5.00 5.00

Miniature Sheets of 6 or 8

Sierra Club, Cent. A223

Various views of: No. 1534a-1534b, Prince William Sound. c-d, The Serengeti. e-f, Ross Island.

No. 1535: a-c, Briksdal Fjord, vert. d-f, Yosemite, vert.

No. 1536: a-b, Tibetan Plateau, vert. c-d, Yellowstone, vert. e, Ross Island, vert. f, The Serengeti, vert. g, Mount Erebus, vert. h, Ansel Adams Wilderness, vert.

No. 1537: a-b, Ansel Adams Wilderness. c-d, Mount Erebus. e, Prince William Sound. f, Yellowstone. g, Tibetan Plateau. h, Sierra Club emblem.

1994, Apr. 25 ***Perf. 14***

1534-1535 A223 5d #a.-f, each 7.50 7.50
1536-1537 A223 5d #a.-h, ea 10.00 10.00

Miniature Sheets of 12

Paintings of Cats A224

No. 1538: a, The Arena, by Harold Weston. b, Cat Killing a Bird, by Picasso. c, Cat and Butterfly, by Hokusai. d, Winter: Cat on a Cushion, by Steinlen. e, Rattown Tigers, by Prang. f, Cat on the Floor, by Steinlen. g, Cat and Kittens. h, Cats Looking Over a Fence, by Prang. i, Little White Kittens into Mischief, by Ives. j, Cat Bathing, by Hiroshige. k, Playtime, by Tuck. l, Summer: Cat on a Balustrade, by Steinlen.

No. 1539, vert.: a, Girl with a Kitten, by Perronneau. b, Still Life with Cat and Fish, by Chardin. c, Tinkle a Cat. d, Naughty Puss! e, Cats, by Steinlen. f, Girl in Red with Cat and Dog, by Phillips. g, Cat, Butterfly and Begonia, by Haronobu. h, Cat and Kitten, by Higgins. i, Woman with a Cat, by Renoir. j, Minnie from Outskirts of Village, by Thrall. k, The Fisher, by Tuck. l, Artist and His Family, by Vaenius.

No. 1540, The Morning Rising, by Lepicie. No. 1541, The Graham Children, by Hogarth, vert.

1994, July 11 Litho. ***Perf. 14***

1538-1539 A224 5d #a.-l, ea 15.00 15.00

Souvenir Sheets

1540-1541 A224 20d each 5.00 5.00

Monkeys — A225

Designs: 1d, Patas. 1.50d, Collared mangabey. 2d, Black and white colobus. 5d, Mona. 8d, Kirk's colobus. 10d, Vervet. 12d, Red colobus. 15d, Guinea baboon.

Heads of: No. 1550, Collared mangabey. No. 1551, Guinea baboon.

1994, Aug. 1 Litho. ***Perf. 14***

1542-1549 A225 Set of 8 12.00 12.00

Souvenir Sheets

1550-1551 A225 25d each 5.50 5.50

D-Day, 50th Anniv. A226

Designs: 50b, Free Dutch sloop Soema joins attack. 75b, HMS Belfast fires on beach defenses. 1d, USS Texas hits Point Du Hoc. 2d, Free French cruiser George Leygues.

20d, HMS Ramillies.

1994, Aug. 16

1552-1555 A226 Set of 4 1.00 1.00

Souvenir Sheet

1556 A226 20d multicolored 4.50 4.50

Miniature Sheet of 9

First Manned Moon Landing, 25th Anniv. A227

Designs: a, Yuri Gagarin. b, Valentina Tereshkova. c, Ham (chimpanzee). d, Alexei Leonov. e, Neil Armstrong. f, Svetlana Y. Savitskaya. g. Marc Garneau. h, Vladimir Komarov. i, Ulf Merbold.

30d, Neil Armstrong, Edwin "Buzz" Aldrin, Michael Collins at press conference.

1994, Aug. 16

1557 A227 2d #a.-i. 4.00 4.00

Souvenir Sheet

1558 A227 30d multicolored 6.00 6.00

A228

PHILAKOREA '94 — A229

Designs: 50b, Kungnakchon Hall, Naejangsa. 2d, Kettle of Popchusa. 3d, Pomun Tourist Resort.

Paper screen panels, episode from Sanguozhi, 18th cent. Choson Dynasty: a, Warriors on horseback. b, Soldiers atop fort. c, Shooting with bows and arrows. d, Bowing before horse & rider. e, Fight on horseback. f, h, Charging on horses. g, Trudging through valley. i, j, Living peacefully.

20d, Traditional tombstone guardian, Taenung, vert.

1994, Aug. 16 ***Perf. 14, 13½ (#1562)***

1559-1561 A228 Set of 3 1.10 1.10

Miniature Sheet of 10

1562 A229 1d #a.-j. 2.00 2.00

Souvenir Sheet

1563 A228 20d multicolored 4.00 4.00

A230

Intl. Olympic Committee, Cent. — A231

Designs: 1.50d, Daley Thompson, Great Britain, decathalon, 1980, 1984. 5d, Heide Marie Rosendohl, Germany, long jump, 1972. 20d, Team Sweden, ice hockey, 1994.

1994, Aug. 16 ***Perf. 14***

1564 A230 1.50d multicolored .30 .30
1565 A230 5d multicolored 1.00 1.00

Souvenir Sheet

1566 A231 20d multicolored 4.00 4.00

Butterflies A232

Designs: 1d, Mylothris rhodope. 1.25d, Iolaphilus menas. 2d, Neptis nemetes. 5d, Antanartia delius. 8d, Acraea caecilia. 10d, Papilio nireus. 12d, Pipilio menestheus. 15d, Iolaphilus julus.
#1575, Colotis evippe. #1576, Bematistes epaea.

1994, Aug. 18 ***Perf. 14***

1567-1574 A232 Set of 8 11.00 11.00

Souvenir Sheets

1575-1576 A232 25d each 5.00 5.00

1994 World Cup Soccer Championships, US — A233

Designs: 50b, Bobby Charlton, England. 75b, Ferenc Puskas, Hungary. 1d, Paolo Rossi, Italy. 2d, Biri Biri, Gambian playing for Spain. 3d, Diego Maradona, Argentina. 8d, Johan Cruyff, Netherlands. 10d, Franz Beckenbauer, Germany. 15d, Thomas Dooley, US.
No. 1585, Pele, Brazil. No. 1586, Gordon Banks, England.

1994, Sept. 1

1577-1584 A233 Set of 8 8.00 8.00

Souvenir Sheets

1585-1586 A233 25d each 5.00 5.00

Miniature Sheets of 9

Mushrooms A234

Designs: No. 1587a, Agaricus campestris. b, Lepista nuda. c, Podaxis pistillaris. d, Oudemansiella radicata. e, Schizophyllum commune. f, Chlorophyllum molybdites. g, Hypholoma fasciculare. h, Mycena pura. i, Ganoderma lucidum.
No. 1588a, Suillus luteus. b, Bolbitius vitellinus. c, Clitocybe nebularis. d, Omphalotus olearius. e, Auricularia auricula. f, Macrolepiota rhacodes. g, Volvariella volvacea. h, Psilocybe coprophila. i, Suillus granulatus.
No. 1589, Cyathus striatus. No. 1590, Leucoagaricus naucina.

1994, Sept. 30

1587-1588 A234 5d #a.-i, each 9.00 9.00

Souvenir Sheets

1589-1590 A234 20d each 4.00 4.00

Christmas A235

French paintings: 50b, Expectant Madonna with St. Joseph, by unknown artist. 75b, Rest of the Holy Family, by Louis Le Nain. 1d, Rest on the Flight into Egypt, by Antoine Watteau. No. 1594, 2d, Noon, by Claude Lorrain. No. 1595, 2d, Rest on the Flight into Egypt, by Francois Boucher. No. 1596, 2d, Rest on the Flight into Egypt, by Jean-Honore Fragonard. 10d, The Holy Family, by Nicolas Poussin. 12d, Mystical Marriage of St. Catherine, by Pierre-Francois Mignard.
No. 1599, The Nativity by Torchlight, by Louis Le Nain. No. 1600, Adoration of the Shepherds, by Mathieu Le Nain.

1994, Dec. 5 Litho. ***Perf. 13½x14***

1591-1598 A235 Set of 8 6.75 6.75

Souvenir Sheets

1599-1600 A235 25d each 5.75 5.75

Miniature Sheet of 9

Marilyn Monroe (1926-62), Actress — A236

No. 1601a-1601i, Various portraits.
No. 1602, Wearing red dress. No. 1603, Wearing long, dangling earrings.

1995, Jan. 8 Litho. ***Perf. 14***

1601 A236 4d #a.-i. 7.25 7.25

Souvenir Sheets

1602-1603 A236 25d each 5.00 5.00

Miniature Sheet of 9

Elvis Presley (1935-77), Entertainer A237

Portraits: a, As child. b, Singing, later years. c, With mother. d, With wife, Priscilla. e, With gold medallion. f, Wearing army uniform. g, Singing, younger years. h, Wearing hat. i, With daughter, Lisa Marie.

1995, Jan. 8

1604 A237 4d #a.-i. 7.25 7.25

Miniature Sheets of 12

Dinosaurs A238

No. 1605: a, Pteranodon. b, Archaeopteryx. c, Rhamphorhynchus. d, Ornithomimus. e, Stegosaurus. f, Heterodontosaurus. g, Lystrosaurus. h, Euoplocephalus. i, Coelophysis. j, Staurilosaurus. k, Giantoperis. l, Diarthrognathus.
No. 1606: a, Archaeopteryx, diff. b, Vangehuanosaurus. c, Ceolophysis, diff. d, Plateosaurus. e, Baryonyx. f, Ornitholestes. g, Dryosaurus. h, Estemmenosuchus. i, Macroplata. j, Shonisaurus. k, Muraeonosaurus. l, Archelon.
No. 1607, Bactrosaurus. No. 1608, Tyrannosaurus, vert. No. 1609, Triceratops, vert. No. 1610, Spinosaurus.

1995 Litho. ***Perf. 14***

1605 A238 2d #a.-l. 5.25 5.25
1606 A238 3d #a.-l. 8.00 8.00

Souvenir Sheets

1607 A238 20d multi 4.50 4.50
1608 A238 22d multi 4.75 4.75
1609-1610 A238 25d each 5.50 5.50

Miniature Sheet of 4

New Year 1995 (Year of the Boar) — A239

Stylized boars. Chinese inscriptions in: a, Green. b, Blue violet. c, White. d, Black.
10d, Three boars.

1995, May 4 ***Perf. 14½***

1611 A239 3d #a.-d. 2.75 2.75

Souvenir Sheet

1612 A239 10d multicolored 2.25 2.25

Water Birds A240

Designs: 2d, Great white egret. 8d, Hammerkop. 10d, Shoveler. 12d, Crowned crane.
#1617: a, Pintail. b, Fulvous tree duck (a). c, Garganey. d, White-faced tree duck. e, White-backed duck. f, Egyptian goose. g, Pigmy goose. h, Little bittern (k). i, Redshank. j, Ringed plover. k, Black-winged stilt. l, Squacco heron (k).
#1618, Ferruginous duck. #1619, Moorhen.

1995, May 8 ***Perf. 14***

1613-1616 A240 Set of 4 7.00 7.00

Miniature Sheet of 12

1617 A240 3d #a.-l. 8.00 8.00

Souvenir Sheets

1618-1619 A240 25d each 5.50 5.50

ECOWAS — A241

2d, Free movement of people in Gambia. 5d, Captain Yaya AJJ Jammeh, Chairman of Arm Force Provisional Ruling Council, Head of State.

1995, May 30 Litho. ***Perf. 14***

1620 A241 2d multicolored .45 .45
1621 A241 5d multicolored 1.10 1.10

Marine Life A242

No. 1622, vert: a, Multicolored parrot fish. b, Sparisoma viride. c, Queen parrot fish. d, Bicolor parrot fish.
No. 1623: a, Leatherback turtle. b, Tiger shark. c, Surgeon fish. d, Emperor angelfish. e, Blue parro fish. f, Triggerfish. g, Sea horse. h, Lionfish. i, Moray eel. j, Red fin butterflyfish. k, Octopus. l, Ray.
No. 1624, Holacanthus ciliaris. No. 1625, Angelichthys isabelita.

1995, June 20

1622 A242 8d Strip of 4, #a.-d. 7.00 7.00

Miniature Sheet of 12

1623 A242 3d #a.-l. 8.00 8.00

Souvenir Sheets

1624-1625 A242 25d each 5.50 5.50

UN, 50th Anniv. — A243

#1626: a, 3d, Girls. b, 5d, Woman helping girl at blackboard. c, 8d, Girl writing on blackboard.
25d, Nurse holding baby on scales.

1995, July 6

1626 A243 Strip of 3, #a.-c. 3.50 3.50

Souvenir Sheet

1627 A243 25d multicolored 5.50 5.50

Miniature Sheet of 8

World War II Motion Pictures A244

Movie stars: No. 1628a, Peter Lawford. b, Gene Tierney, Dana Andrews. c, Groucho, Gummo Marx. d, James Stewart. e, Chico, Harpo Marx. f, Tyrone Power. g, Cary Grant, Ingrid Bergman. h, Veronica Lake.
Motion pictures: No. 1629, A Lady Fights Back. No. 1630, Desert Victory.

1995, July 6

1628 A244 3d #a.-h. + label 5.25 5.25

Souvenir Sheets

1629-1630 A244 25d each 5.50 5.50

Miniature Sheet of 6

VJ Day, 50th Anniv. A245

No. 1631: a, Fairey Firefly. b, Fairey Barracuda II. c, Vickers Supermarine Seafire II. d, HMS Repulse. e, HMS Illustrious. f, HMS Exeter.
25d, Bomber being shot down by 3-stack cruiser.

1995, Aug. 1

1631 A245 5d #a.-f. + label 6.75 6.75

Souvenir Sheet

1632 A245 25d multicolored 5.50 5.50

A246

A247

Carrying sacks of grain: No. 1633a, 3d, Woman in pink. b, 5d, Two people. c, 8d, Man.
25d, Fisherman with net.

1995, Aug. 1 Litho. *Perf. 14*
1633 A246 Strip of 3, #a.-c. 3.50 3.50

Souvenir Sheet

1634 A246 25d multicolored 5.50 5.50

FAO, 50th Anniv. No. 1633 is a continuous design.

1995, Aug. 1

Nobel Prize Winners: 2d, Kenichi Fukui, chemistry, 1981. 3d, Gustav Stresemann, peace, 1929. 5d, Thomas Mann, literature, 1929. 8d, Albert Schweitzer, peace, 1952. 12d, Leo Esaki, physics, 1973. 15d, Lech Walsea, peace, 1983.

No. 1635: a, Marie Curie, chemistry, 1911. b, Adolf Butenandt, chemistry, 1939. c, Tonegawa Susumu, medicine, 1987. d, Nelly Sachs, literature, 1966. e, Kawabata Yasunari, literature, 1968. f, Yukawa Hideki, physics, 1949. g, Paul Ehrlich, medicine, 1908. h, Sato Eisaku, peace, 1974. i, Carl von Ossietzky, peace, 1935.

25d, Willy Brandt, peace, 1971.

1634A-1634F A247 Set of 6 10.00 10.00

Miniature Sheet of 9

1635 A247 5d #a.-i. 10.00 10.00

Souvenir Sheet

1636 A247 25d multicolored 5.50 5.50

Rotary Intl., 50th Anniv. A248

Designs: 15d, Paul Haris, Rotary emblem. 20d, Natl. flag, Rotary emblem.

1995, Aug. 1
1637 A248 15d multicolored 3.25 3.25

Souvenir Sheet

1638 A248 20d multicolored 4.50 4.50

Miniature Sheets of 3

1995 Boy Scout Jamboree, Holland — A249

How to tie the lariat: No. 1639: a, First step. b, Second step. c, Completed.

How to tie bowline: No. 1640: a, 12d, First step. b, 10d, Second step. c, 5d, Completed.

No. 1641, Bowline used to lift injured scout. No. 1642, Hitch used in lifesaving lift.

1995, Aug. 1
1639 A249 2d #a.-c. 1.40 1.40
1640 A249 #a.-c. 6.00 6.00

Souvenir Sheets

1641-1642 A249 25d each 5.50 5.50

Queen Mother, 95th Birthday A250

No. 1643: a, Drawing. b, Bright blue hat, dress. c, Formal portrait. d, Green hat, dress. 25d, Pale blue & white dress, blue hat.

1995, Aug. 1 *Perf. 13½14*
1643 A250 5d Strip or block of 4, #a.-d. 4.50 4.50

Souvenir Sheet

1644 A250 25d multicolored 5.50 5.50

No. 1643 was issued in sheets of 8 stamps.

Nos. 1643-1644 exist with black frame and overprint in sheet margin "In Memoriam 1900-2002" in one or two lines.

1996 Summer Olympics, Atlanta A251

Designs: 1d, Bruce Jenner, US, decathlon. 1.25d, Greg Louganis, US, diving. 1.50d, Michael Gross, Germany 50-meter butterfly. 2d, Vasily Alexeev, USSR, weight lifting. 3d, Patrick Ewing, US, Juan Antonio Corbalan, Spain, basketball. 5d, Men's volleyball, US v. Brazil. 10d, John Svenden, West Germany, Armando Fernandez, US, water polo. 15d, Pertti Karppinen, Finland, single sculls.

No. 1653, vert: a, Stefano Cerioni, Italy, fencing. b, Alberto Covo, Italy, 10,000-meter run. c, Mary Lou Retton, US, women's gymnastics. d, Vladimir Artemov, USSR, men's gymnastics. e, Florence Griffith-Joyner, US, 400-meter relay. f, Brazil, soccer. g, Nelson Valis, US, 1000-meter sprint cycling. h, Cheryl Miller, US, women's basketball.

No. 1654, Karen Stives, US, equestrian. No. 1655, Edwin Moses, US, 400-meter hurdles, vert.

1995, Aug. 17
1645-1652 A251 Set of 8 8.50 8.50

Miniature Sheet of 8

1653 A251 3d #a.-h. 5.25 5.25

Souvenir Sheets

1654-1655 A251 25d each 5.50 5.50

Volleyball, cent. (#1650).

Rotary, Intl., 90th Anniv., 1995 Boy Scout Jamboree, Holland — A252

Designs: 2d, Gambia Rotary contributing to education. No. 1657, 5d, Wood Badge course, Yundum, 1980. No. 1658, 5d, M.J.E. Sambou, organizing scout commissioner, vert.

1995, Sept. 5
1656-1658 A252 Set of 3 2.75 2.75

Flowers — A253

Designs: 2d, Zantedeschia rehmannii. 5d, Euadenia eminens. 10d, Passiflora vitifolia. 15d, Dietes grandiflora.

No. 1663: a, Canarina abyssinica. b, Nerine bowdenii. c, Zantedeschia aethiopica. d, Aframomum sceptrum. e, Schotia brachypetala. f, Catharanthus roseus. g, Protea grandiceps. h, Plumbago capensis. i, Uncarina grandidieri.

No. 1664: a, Kigelia africana. b, Hibiscus schizopetalus. c, Dombeya mastersii. d, Agapanthus orientalis. e, Strelitzia reginae. f, Spathodea campanulata. g, Rhodolaena bakeriana. h, Gazania rigens. i, Ixianthes retzioides.

No. 1665, Eulophia quartiniana. No. 1666, Gloriosa simplex.

1995, Oct. 2 Litho. *Perf. 14*
1659-1662 A253 Set of 4 7.00 7.00

Miniature Sheets of 9

1663-1664 A253 3d #a.-i., each 6.00 6.00

Souvenir Sheets

1665-1666 A253 25d each 5.50 5.50

SOS Children's Villages A254

#1667, 2d, Children playing near houses. #1668, 2d, Aid worker with child, vert. 5d, Children.

1995, Oct. 9 Litho. *Perf. 14*
1667-1669 A254 Set of 3 2.00 2.00

Miniature Sheets of 9

Entertainers A255

Rock & roll stars: #1670: a, Roy Orbison. b, Mick Jagger. c, Bruce Springsteen. d, Jimi Hendrix. e, Bill Haley. f, Gene Vincent. g, Buddy Holly. h, Jerry Lee Lewis. i, Chuck Berry.

#1671a-1671i, Various pictures of James Dean.

#1672, James Dean. #1673, Elvis Presley.

1995, Dec. 1 Litho. *Perf. 13½x14*
1670 A255 3d #a.-i. 6.00 6.00
1671 A255 3d #a.-i. 6.00 6.00

Souvenir Sheets

1672-1673 A255 25d each 5.50 5.50

Motion pictures, cent. (#1671-1672).

Christmas A256

Details or entire paintings: 75b, Madonna of the, Valley. 1d, Madonna, by Giotto. 2d, The Flight into Egypt, by Luca Giordano. 5d, The Epiphany, by Bondone. 8d, Virgin & Child, by Burgkmair. 12d, Madonna, by Bellini.

No. 1680, Mother and Child, by Rubens. No. 1681, The Christ, by Carpaccio.

1995, Dec. 18
1674-1679 A256 Set of 6 6.25 6.25

Souvenir Sheets

1680-1681 A256 25d each 5.50 5.50

Banjul Intl. Airport A257

1995, Dec. 21 Litho. *Perf. 14*
1682-1685 A257 1d, 2d, 3d, 5d, set of 4 2.50 2.50

UPU, 121st Anniv. — A258

1995, Dec. 21
1686-1689 A258 1d, 2d, 3d, 7d, set of 4 2.75 2.75

Marine Life A259

Designs: 2d, Commerson's dolphin. 5d, Narwhal. 8d, True's beaked whale. 10d, Rough-toothed dolphin.

Dolphins: No. 1694a, Northern rightwhale. b, Spotted. c, Common. d, Pacific white-sided. e, Atlantic humpbacked. f, Atlantic white-sided. g, White-beaked. h, Striped. i, Risso's.

Whales: No. 1695a, Bryde's. b, Sperm. c, Humpback. d, Sei. e, Blue. f, Gray. g, Fin. h, Killer. i, Right.

#1696, Beluga, clymene dolphin. #1697, Bowhead whale, dall's porpoise, blue shark.

1995, Dec. 22
1690-1693 A259 Set of 4 5.50 5.50

Miniature Sheets of 9

1694-1695 A259 3d #a.-i., each 6.00 6.00

Souvenir Sheets

1696-1697 A259 25d each 5.50 5.50

Cowboys and American Indians — A260

Disney characters portraying Amerian Indians or in western scenes: 15b, Pete, Seminole. 20b, Donald, Chinook. 25b, Huey, Dewey, Louie, Blackfoot. 30b, Sharp shooter Minnie. 40b, Bull-riding Donald. 50b, Cattle-branding Mickey. 2d, Donald, Tlingit. 3d, Bronco-busting Mickey. 12d, Trick-roping Grandma Duck. No. 1707, 15d, Goofy the ranch hand. No. 1708, 15d, Mickey, Pomo. 20d, Minnie, Goofy, Navaho.

No. 1710, Minnie, Massachusetts Tribe. No. 1711, Pluto singing, vert. No. 1712, Donald with rope around neck, vert. No. 1712, Minnie, Shoshoni, vert.

1995, Dec. 22 *Perf. 14x13½*
1698-1709 A260 Set of 12 15.00 15.00

Souvenir Sheets

1710-1713 A260 25d each 5.50 5.50

New Year 1996 (Year of the Rat) — A261

Various stylized rats: Nos. 1714a, 63b. b, 75b. c, 1.50d. d, 4d.

No. 1715a, like #1714a. b, like #1714d. c, like #1714c. d, like #1714b.

No. 1716, Two rats.

1996, Jan. 2 *Perf. 14½*
1714 A261 Strip of 4, #a.-d. 1.50 1.50

Miniature Sheet

1715 A261 3d Sheet of 4, #a.-d. 2.75 2.75

Souvenir Sheet

1716 A261 10d multicolored 2.25 2.25

#1714 issued in sheets of 16 stamps.

Miniature Sheets of 8 + Label

Paintings from Metropolitan Museum of Art — A262

Details or entire paintings: No. 1717: a, Don Tiburcio Pérez y Cuervo, by Goya. b, Jean Antoine Moltedo, by J.A.D. Ingres. c, The Letter, by Corot. d, General Etienne Maurice Gerard, by J.L. David. e, Portrait of the Artist, by Van Gogh. f, Joseph Henri Altés, by Degas. g, Princess de Broglie, by Ingres. h, Lady at the Table, by Cassatt.

No. 1718: a, Broken Eggs, by Greuze. b, Johann Joachim Winckelmann, by Mengs. c, Col. George K.H. Coussmaker, by Reynolds. d, Self Portrait with Pupils, by Labille-Guiard. e, Courtesan Holding a Fan, by Utamaro. f, The Woodgatherers, by Gainsborough. g, Mr. Grace D. Elliott, by Gainsborough. h, The Drummond Children, by Raeburn.

No. 1719: a, Sunflowers, by Monet. b, Still Life with Pansies, by Fantin-Latour. c, Parisians Enjoying the Park, by Monet. d, La Mére Larchevêque, by Pissarro. e, Rue de L'Epicerie, Rouen, by Pissarro. f, The Abduction of Rebecca, by Delacroix. g, Daughter, Abraham-Ben-Chimol, by Delacroix. h, Christ on Lake of Gennesaret, by Delacroix.

No. 1720: a, Henry Frederick, Prince of Wales, by Peake. b, Saints Peter, Martha, Mary & Leonard, by Correggio. c, Marriage Feast at Cana, by Juan de Flandes. d, Portrait of one of Wedigh Family, by Holbein. e, Guillaume Budé, by Clouet. f, Portrait of a Cardinal, by El Greco. g, St. Jerome as a Cardinal, by El Greco. h, Portrait of a Man, by Titian.

No. 1721, The Harvesters, by Bruegel. No. 1722, The Creation of the World and the Expulsion from Paradise, by Giovanni de Paolo. No. 1723, Henry IV at the Battle of Ivry, by Rubens. No. 1724, The Israelites Gathering Manna in the Desert, by Rubens.

1996, Jan. 29 Litho. *Perf. 13½x14*

1717-1720 A262 4d #a.-h., each 7.00 7.00

Souvenir Sheets

Perf. 14

1721-1724 A262 25d each 5.50 5.50

Nos. 1721-1724 each contain one 85x57mm stamp.

No. 1723 is actually in the Uffizi Gallery in Florence; No. 1724 in the Los Angeles County Museum of Art.

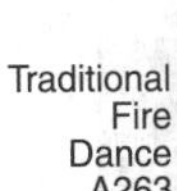

Traditional Fire Dance A263

Designs: 1d, Blowing fire from mouth, vert. 2d, as 1d, diff. 3d, Holding sticks of fire at leg, vert. 7d, Holding out two sticks of fire.

1996, Jan. 29 Litho. *Perf. 14*

1725-1728 A263 Set of 4 3.00 3.00

Disney Charaters Performing Good Deeds — A264

Designs: 1d, Community blood drive. 4d, Adopt-a-pet. 5d, Christmas giving for the needy. 10d, Teaching outdoor skills. 15d, Teaching reading. 20d, Volunteer fire fighters.

No. 1735, Highway volunteers. No. 1736, Counting whales.

1996, Apr. 12 Litho. *Perf. 13½x14*

1729-1734 A264 Set of 6 12.00 12.00

Souvenir Sheets

1735-1736 A264 25d each 5.50 5.50

Bruce Lee (1940-73), Martial Arts Expert — A265

#1737: Various portraits. 25d, In fighting stance.

1996, Apr. 1 Litho. *Perf. 14*

1737 A265 3d Sheet of 9, #a.-i. 6.00 6.00

Souvenir Sheet

1738 A265 25d multicolored 5.50 5.50

China '96, 9th Asian Intl. Philatelic Exhibition (#1737).

African Wildlife A266

15d, African civet.

#1740: a, Roan antelope. b, Lesser bush baby. c, Leopard. d, Guinea forest red colobus. e, Kob. f, Common eland.

#1741: a, African buffalo. b, Topi. c, Vervet. d, Hippopotamus. e, Waterbuck. f, Senegal chameleon. g, Western green mamba. h, Slender snouted crocodile (i). i, Adanson's mud turtle.

No. 1742, Lion. No. 1743, Chimpanzee.

1996, Apr. 15 Litho. *Perf. 14*

1739 A266 15d multicolored 3.25 3.25
1740 A266 3d Block of 6, #a.-f. 4.00 4.00
1741 A266 4d Sheet of 9, #a.-i. 8.00 8.00

Souvenir Sheets

1742-1743 A266 25d each 5.50 5.50

#1740 issued in sheets of 12 stamps.

Queen Elizabeth II, 70th Birthday A267

#1744: a, Portrait wearing blue dress. b, Wearing white dress, crown. c, Younger picture, crown.

25d, Buckingham Palace, horiz.

1996, May 9 Litho. *Perf. 13½x14*

1744 A267 8d Strip of 3, #a.-c. 5.25 5.25

Souvenir Sheet

Perf. 14x13½

1745 A267 25d multicolored 5.50 5.50

No. 1744 was issued in sheets of 9 stamps with each strip in a different order.

Sheets of 6

Classic Cars and Fire Engines A268

Classic cars: #1746: a, 1912 Fiat Tipo 510, Italy. b, 1936 Toyota Model 4B Phaeton, Japan. c, 1924 NAG C4B, Germany. d, 1903 Cadillac, US. e, 1925 Bentley, Great Britain. f, 1909 Renault Model AX, France.

Fire engines: #1747: a, 1850 Pumper Hose Cart, US. b, 1891 Steam Fire Engine, US. c, 1864 Lausitzer, Germany. d, 1902 Chemical Engine, Great Britain. e, 1904 Motor Fire Engine, Great Britain. f, 1860 Colonia No. 5, Germany.

No. 1748, 1917 Mitsubishi Model A, Japan. No. 1749, 1865 Amoskeag steamer, US.

1996, May 27 *Perf. 14*

1746-1747 A268 4d #a.-f., each 5.25 5.25

Souvenir Sheets

1748-1749 A268 25d each 5.50 5.50

Euro '96, 1996 European Soccer Championships, England — A269

Team pictures: #1750, Bulgaria. #1751, Croatia. #1752, Czech Republic. #1753, Denmark. #1754, England. #1755, France. #1756, Germany. #1757, Holland. #1758, Italy. #1759, Portugal. #1760, Romania. #1761, Russia. #1762, Scotland. #1763, Spain. #1764, Switzerland. #1765, Turkey.

#1766, Hristo Stoitchkov, Bulgaria, vert. #1767, Davor Suker, Croatia, vert. #1768, Pavel Hapal, Czech Republic. #1769, 1992 Denmark team, European championship winners. #1770, Bryan Robson, England, vert. #1771, 1984 Championship cup won by French team, vert. #1772, Jüegen Klinsmann, Germany. #1773, Ruud Gullit, Holland, vert. #1774, Roberto Baggio, Italy, vert. #1775, Eusebio, Portugal, vert. #1776, Gheorge Hagi, Romania, vert. #1777, Oleg Salenko, Russia, vert. #1778, Gary McAllister, Scotland, vert. #1779, Juan Goikoetxea, Spain, vert. #1780, Christophe Ohrel, Switzerland, vert. #1781, Hami Mandirali, Turkey, vert.

1996, June 8 Litho. *Perf. 14*

1750-1765 A269 2d Set of 16 7.00 7.00

Souvenir Sheets

1766-1781 A269 25d each 5.50 5.50

Nos. 1750-1765 each exist in miniature sheets of 8 + 1 label.

See Nos. 1808-1819.

1996 Summer Olympic Games, Atlanta — A270

1912 Olympics, Stockholm: 1d, Ray Ewry, standing high jump. 2d, Fanny Durack, freestyle swimming. 5d, Stadium, scenes in Stocholm. 10d, Jim Thorpe, decathlon, pentathlon.

Winners in past Olympics: 1786: a, Japanese volleyball team, 1964. b, Li Neng, floor exercises, 1984. c, Sergei Bubka, pole vault, 1988. d, Nadia Comaneci, all around gymnastics, 1976. e, Edwin Moses, 400-meter hurdles, 1984. f, Vitaly Shcherbo, all around gymnastics, 1992. g, Evelyn Ashford, 100-meters, 1984. h, Muhammad Ali, light heavyweight boxing, 1960. i, Carl Lewis, C. Smith, 400-meters relay, 1984.

1992 Olympians: #1787a, Fu Mingxia, platform diving. b, Heike Henkel, high jump. c, Spanish soccer team. d, Jackie Joyner-Kersee, heptathlon. e, Tatiana Gutsu, all around gymnastics. f, Michael Johnson, 400-meters. g, Lin Li, 200-meter individual medley. h, Gail Devers, 100-meters. i, Mike Powell, long jump.

No. 1788, Michael Gross, swimming, 1984, 1988, horiz. No. 1789, Ulrike Meyfarth, high jump, 1972, 1984.

1996, July 18 Litho. *Perf. 14*

1782-1785 A270 Set of 4 4.00 4.00

Sheets of 9

1786-1787 A270 3d #a.-i., each 6.00 6.00

Souvenir Sheets

1788-1789 A270 25d each 5.50 5.50

Jerusalem, 3000th Anniv. — A271

1.50d, Roman costume, Pillar of Absalem. 2d, Turkish costume, Gate of Mercy. 3d, Greek costume, Church of the Holy Sepulcher. 10d, Western Wall of the Temple Mount, Hasidic costume.

25d, Emblem, King David Tower, vert.

1996, July 25

1790-1793 A271 Set of 4 3.50 3.50

Souvenir Sheet

1794 A271 25d multicolored 5.50 5.50

Radio, Cent. A272

1d, Glenn Miller. 4d, Louis Armstrong. 5d, Nat King Cole. 10d, Andrews Sisters.

25d, Harry S Truman.

1996, July 25 *Perf. 13½x14*

1795-1798 A272 Set of 4 4.50 4.50

Souvenir Sheet

1799 A272 25d multicolored 5.50 5.50

UNICEF, 50th Anniv. — A273

Designs: 63b, Boy holding shoes. 3d, Girl receiving vaccination. 8d, Boy with soup ladle. 10d, Girl with blanket.

25d, Boy receiving vaccination, horiz.

1996, July 25 *Perf. 14*

1800-1803 A273 Set of 4 4.25 4.25

Souvenir Sheet

1804 A273 25d multicolored 5.50 5.50

A274

A275

#1805: a, John F. Kennedy. b, Jacqueline Kennedy Onassis. c, Willy Brandt. d, Marilyn Monroe. e, Mao Tse Tung. f, Sung Ching Ling. g, Charles de Gaulle. h, Marlene Dietrich.

Nos. 1806-1807: Various portraits of Jacqueline Kennedy Onassis (1929-94).

1996, Aug. 22

1805 A274 5d Sheet of 8, #a.-h. 8.75 8.75
1806 A275 5d Sheet of 9, #a.-i. 9.00 9.00

Souvenir Sheet

1807 A274 25d multicolored 5.50 5.50

#1751-1752, 1754, 1756, 1758, 1761, and #1767-1768, 1770, 1772, 1774, 1777 With Added Inscriptions

1996, Aug. 26

1808-1813 A269 2d Set of 6 2.75 2.75

Souvenir Sheets

1814-1819 A269 25d each 5.50 5.50

Nos. 1808-1813 were issued in sheets of 8 + 1 label. Inscriptions on Nos. 1808-1813 and in sheet margins of Nos. 1814-1819 show date of game, teams competing, and final score. Margin of the miniature sheets show additional information about individual games, and name of Germany as winner.

Team or team player shown as follows: Croatia (#1808, 1814), Czech Republic (#1809, 1815), England (#1810, 1816), Germany (#1811, 1817), Italy (#1812, 1818), Russia (#1813, 1819).

Richard Petty, NASCAR Driving Champion A276

Designs: No. 1820a, 1969 Ford. b, Richard Petty. c, 1978 Dodge Magnum. d, 1987 Pontiac. e, 1989 Pontiac. f, 1975 Dodge Daytona. 25d, 1972 Plymouth.

1996, Aug. 27

1820 A276 5d Sheet of 6, #a.-f. 6.50 6.50

Souvenir Sheet

1821 A276 25d multicolored 5.50 5.50

No. 1821 contains one 85x28mm stamp.

Elvis Presley's 1st "Hit" Year, 40th Anniv. A277

Designs: Various portraits.

1996, Sept. 8 Litho. *Perf. 13½x14*

1822 A277 5d Sheet of 6, #a.-f. 6.50 6.50

Supermarine S6B's Schneider Trophy Victory, 65th Anniv. — A278

Spitfire aircraft: #1823: a, PR XIX, Royal Swedish Air Force. b, MK VB, US Army Air. c, MK VC, French Air Force. d, MK VB, Soviet Air Force. e, MK IXE, Netherlands East Indies Air Force. f, MK IXE, Israeli Defense Force. g, MK VIII, Royal Australian Air Force. h, MK VB, Turkish Air Force. i, PR XI, Royal Danish Air Force.

#1823: k, K5054, first prototype aircraft. l, K9787, first production aircraft. m, MK 1A, "Battle of Britain." n, LF MK IXE, D-Day invasion markings. o, MK XII, first "Griffon" engined model. p, MK XIVC, SEAC markings. q, PR XIX, Royal Swedish Air Force. r, PR MK XIX. s, FMK 22/24 final variant.

#1824, The Supermarine S.6B S1595. #1824A, Supermarine S.6B S1595 seaplane.

1996, Sept. 13 Litho. *Perf. 14*

Sheets of 9

1823 A278 4d #a.-i. 8.00 8.00
1823J A278 4d #k.-s. 8.00 8.00

Souvenir Sheets

1824 A278 25d multicolored 5.50 5.50
1824A A278 25d multicolored 5.50 5.50

A279

A280

1996, Sept. 8 Litho. *Perf. 14*

1825 A279 5d multicolored 1.10 1.10

Bob Dylan (b. 1941), singer, songwriter. Issued in sheets of 16.

1996, Oct. 22 Litho. *Perf. 14*

Birds: 50b, Egyptian plover. 63b, Painted snipe. 75b, Golden-breasted bunting. 1d, Bateleur. 1.50d, Didric cuckoo. 2d, European turtle dove. 3d, Village weaver. 4d, European roller. 5d, Cut-throat. 10d, Hoopoe. 15d, White-faced scops-owl. 20d, Narina trogan. 25d, Pied kingfisher. 30d, Common kestrel.

1826	A280	50b	multicolored	.20	.20
1827	A280	63b	multicolored	.20	.20
1828	A280	75b	multicolored	.20	.20
1829	A280	1d	multicolored	.25	.25
1830	A280	1.50d	multicolored	.30	.30
1831	A280	2d	multicolored	.45	.45
1832	A280	3d	multicolored	.60	.60
1833	A280	4d	multicolored	.90	.90
1834	A280	5d	multicolored	1.10	1.10
1835	A280	10d	multicolored	2.25	2.25
1836	A280	15d	multicolored	3.25	3.25
1837	A280	20d	multicolored	4.50	4.50
1838	A280	25d	multicolored	5.50	5.50
1839	A280	30d	multicolored	6.50	6.50
	Nos. 1826-1839 (14)			26.20	26.20

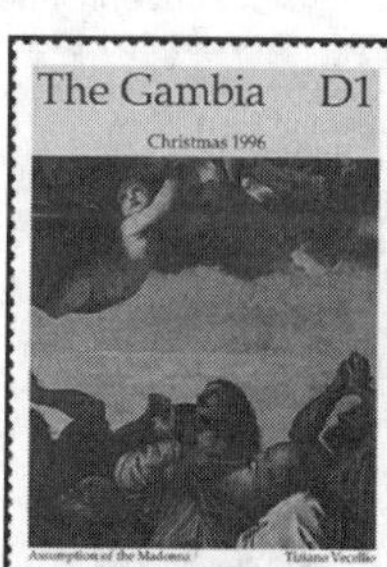

Christmas A281

Details of painting, Assumption of the Madonna, by Titian: 1d, Watching assumption, cherub, clouds. 1.50d, Cherubs. 2d, Cherub. 3d, Cherub holding up cloud, outstretched arms below. 10d, People watching assumption. 15d, Cherubs pointing.

No. 1846, Adoration of the Child, by Filippo Lippi, horiz. No. 1847, Virgin and Child with Infant St. John, by Raphael.

1996, Nov. 18 *Perf. 13½x14*

1840-1845 A281 Set of 6 7.25 7.25

Souvenir Sheets

1846-1847 A281 25d each 5.50 5.50

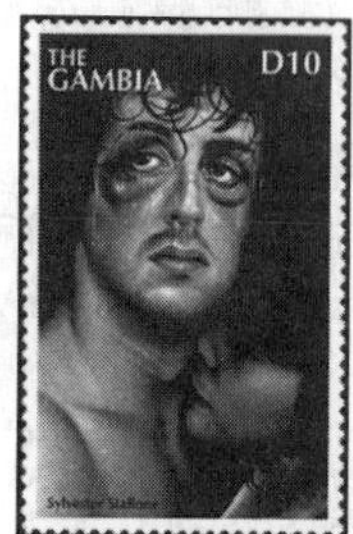

Sylvester Stallone in Movie, "Rocky" — A282

1996, Nov. 21 Litho. *Perf. 14*

1848 A282 10d Sheet of 3 6.50 6.50

Development Projects — A283

Designs: 63b, 2d, Arch 22, vert. 1d, Tractor, rice development project. 1.50d, Worker in rice paddy, vert. 3d, Banjul Intl. Airport Terminal Building. 5d, Chamoi Bridge.

No. 1855, Workers in rice paddy. No. 1856, Statue in front of Arch 22, vert.

1996 Litho. *Perf. 14*

1849-1854 A283 Set of 6 3.00 3.00

Souvenir Sheets

1855 A283 20d multicolored 4.50 4.50
1856 A283 25d multicolored 5.50 5.50

New Year 1997 (Year of the Ox) — A284

Various stylized oxen, background color: #1857-1858 (#1858 all 3d): a, 63b, orange. b, 75b, purple. c, 1.50d, blue green. d, 4d, yellow orange.

10d, Ox with baby lying on its back.

1997, Jan. 16 *Perf. 15*

1857 A284 Strip of 4, #a.-d. 1.50 1.50
1858 A284 3d Sheet of 4, #a.-d. 2.50 2.50

Souvenir Sheet

Perf. 14

1859 A284 10d multicolored 2.25 2.25

No. 1859 contains one 43x29mm stamp.

Mickey's Journey to the West — A285

Nos. 1860a-1860f, 1861a-1861f, Scenes from Disney's "Monkey King."

No. 1862, Donald, Mickey, vert. No. 1863, Wu-Kong Sun (The Monkey King), monkeys, Mickey. No. 1864, Mickey, Intelligent Tortoise, Master San Tang. No. 1865, Mickey, Minnie obtaining Buddhist scriptures.

1997, Jan. 28 *Perf. 14x13½*

1860 A285 2d Sheet of 6, #a.-f. 2.40 2.40
  g. No. 1860 overprinted 2.50 2.50
1861 A285 3d Sheet of 6, #a.-f. 3.50 3.50
  g. No. 1861 overprinted 3.75 3.75

Souvenir Sheets

1862 A285 5d multi 1.00 1.00
  a. No. 1862 overprinted 1.00 1.00
1863-1864 A285 10d each 2.00 2.00
  a. Nos. 1863-1864 overprinted, each 2.00 2.00
1865 A285 15d multi 3.00 3.00
  a. No. 1865 overprinted 3.00 3.00

Nos. 1860g, 1861g are overprinted in red in sheet margin: "70TH ANNIVERSARY OF MICKEY & MINNIE," and in black with "Happy Birthday," Mickey Mouse, and "1998" in emblem. Nos. 1862a, 1863a, 1864a, 1865a are overprinted in black in sheet margin with just "Happy Birthday" emblem.

Souvenir Sheet

Deng Xiaoping — A286

#1867, like #1866. Illustration reduced.

1996, May 13 Litho. *Perf. 13*

1866 A286 5d multicolored 1.10 1.10

Litho. & Embossed

Die Cut 9

Size: 95x56mm

1867 A286 300d gold

China '96. Nos. 1866-1867 were not available until March 1997.

Jackie Chan, Action Film Actor — A287

A287a

Various portraits.

#1869A, like #1868g. Illustration reduced.

1997, Feb. 12 *Perf. 14*

1868 A287 4d Sheet of 8, #a.-h. 6.50 6.50

Souvenir Sheet

1869 A287 25d multi, horiz. 5.00 5.00

Litho. & Embossed

Perf. 9

Without Gum

1869A A287a 300d gold & multi

Endangered Species — A288

No. 1870: a, Clouded leopard. b, Audouin's gull. c, Leatherback turtle. d, White-eared pheasant. e, Kakapo. f, Right whale. g, Black-footed ferret. h, Dwarf lemur. i, Peacock pheasant. j, Brown hyena. k, Cougar. l, Gharial. m, Monk seal. n, Mountain gorilla. o, Blyth's tragopan. p, Malayan tapir. q, Black rhinoceros. r, Polar bear. s, Red colobus. t, Tiger.

No. 1871: a, Arabian oryx. b, Baiji. c, Ruffed lemur. d, California condor. e, Blue-headed quail-dove. f, Numbat. g, Congo peacock. h, White uakari. i, Eskimo curlew. j, Gouldian finch. k, Coelacanth. l, Toucan barbet. m, Snow leopard. n, Queen Alexandra's birdwing. o, Dalmatian pelican. p, Chaco tortoise. q, Medong catfish. r, Helmeted hornbill. s, White-eyed river martin. t, Fluminense swallowtail.

No. 1872, Giant panda. No. 1873, Humpback whale. No. 1874, Japanese crane.

1997, Feb. 24

Sheets of 20

1870-1871 A288 1.50d #a.-t., ea 8.00 8.00

Souvenir Sheets

1872-1874 A288 25d each 5.00 5.00

Hong Kong '97 (Nos. 1870-1871).

Jungle Book — A289

a, Monkey facing right. b, Bear. c, Elephant. d, Monkey facing left. e, Panther, butterfly. f, Buffalo. g, Mandrill. h, Tiger. i, Wolf. j, Cobra. k, Mongoose. l, Child's face, flower.

1997

1875 A289 3d Sheet of 12, #a.-l. 7.25 7.25

Mushrooms — A290

1d, Polyporus squamosus. 3d, Armillaria tabescens. 5d, Collybia velutipes. 10d, Sarcoscypha coccinea.

No. 1880, vert: a, Amanita caesarea. b, Lepiota procera. c, Hygophorus psittacinus. d, Russula xerampelina. e, Laccaria amethystina. f, Coprinus micaceus. g, Boletus edulis. h, Morchella esculenta. i, Otidea auricula.

25d, Volvariella bombycina.

1997, Mar. 10 Litho. *Perf. 14*

1876-1879 A290 Set of 4 3.75 3.75
1880 A290 4d Sheet of 9, #a.-i. 5.50 5.50

Souvenir Sheet

1881 A290 25d multicolored 5.00 5.00

UNESCO, 50th Anniv. — A291

World Heritage sites: 1d, Horyu-Ji, Japan. 2d, Great Wall, China. 3d, City of Ayutthaya, Thailand. 4d, Ascension Convent, Santa Maria, Philippines. 10d, Dragons, Komodo Natl. Park, Indonesia. 15d, Timbuktu, Mali.

Various sites in Japan, vert: No. 1888: a, g, h. Kyoto. b, Himeji-Jo. c, d, Horyu-Ji. e, f, Yakushma.

Various sites in China, vert: No. 1889: a, b, c, Mogao Caves. d, e, Great Wall. f, g, h, Imperial Palace.

Various sites, vert: No. 1890: a, Mt. Nimba Strict Nature Reserve, Guinea. b, Banc D'Argun Natl. Park, Mauritania. c, Marrakesh, Morocco. d, Ichkeul Natl. Park, Tunisia. e, Mali. f, Salonga Natl. Park, Zaire. g, Timgad, Algeria. h, Benin.

Various sites in Germany: No. 1891: a, b, c, Bamberg. d, e, Maulbronn.

Various sites in Greece: No. 1892: a, d, e, Ruins in Delphi. b, c, City of Rhodes.

Various sites in Japan: No. 1893: a, b, Shirakami-Sanchi. c, d, e, Himeji-Jo.

No. 1894, Cloisters, Santa Maria de Alcobaca, Portugal, No. 1895, Kyoto, Japan. No. 1896, Ruins of Kilwa Kisiwani, Tanzania. No. 1897, Plitvice Lakes Natl. Park, Croatia.

1997, Mar. 24

1882-1887 A291 Set of 6 7.75 7.75

Sheets of 8 + Label

1888-1890 A291 4d #a.-h., each 7.00 7.00

Sheets of 5 + Label

1891-1893 A291 5d #a.-e., each 5.50 5.50

Souvenir Sheets

1894-1897 A291 25d each 5.50 5.50

Birds — A292

40d, Temminck's courser. 50d, European bee-eater. 100d, Green-winged teal.

1997, Mar. 25 Litho. *Perf. 14*

1898 A292 40d multicolored 8.00 8.00
1899 A292 50d multicolored 10.00 10.00
1900 A292 100d multicolored 20.00 20.00
Nos. 1898-1900 (3) 38.00 38.00

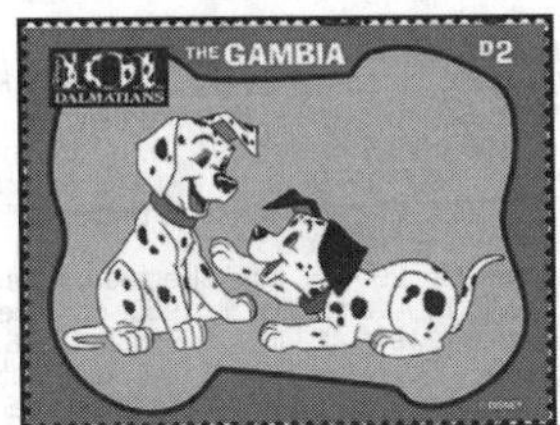

Disney's 101 Dalmatians — A293

Designs, vert: #1901: a, Dipstick. b, Fidget. c, Jewel. d, Lucky. e, Two-Tone. f, Wizzer.

#1902a-1902i, Various "Playful Puppies."

#1903a-1903i, Various "Mischievous puppies."

#1904, Hiding under sheep. #1905, Cruella. #1906, Looking at picture. #1907, Distributing mail, vert. #1908, Into paint. #1909, Playing video game.

1997, May 1 *Perf. 13½x14, 14x13½*

1901 A293 50b Sheet of 6, #a.-f. .60 .60
1902 A293 2d Sheet of 9, #a.-i. 3.50 3.50
1903 A293 3d Sheet of 9, #a.-i. 5.50 5.50

Souvenir Sheets

1904-1909 A293 25d each 5.00 5.00

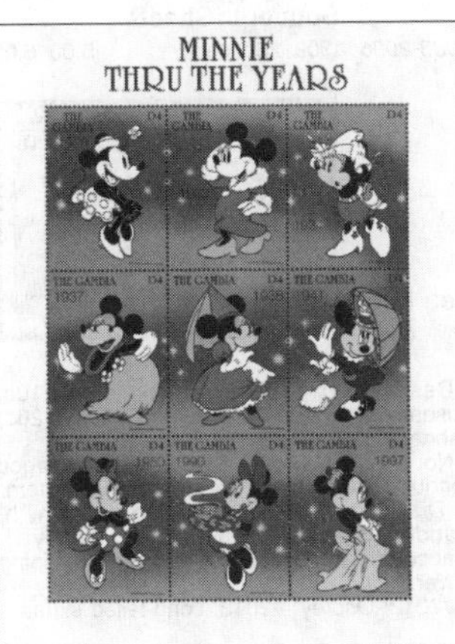

Minnie Thru the Years — A294

Minnie in various scenes dated: a, 1928. b, 1933. c, 1934. d, 1937. e, 1938. f, 1941. g, 1950. h, 1990. i, 1997.

25d, 1987.

1997, May 1 *Perf. 13½x14*

1910 A294 4d Sheet of 9, #a.-i. 7.25 7.25

Souvenir Sheet

1911 A294 25d multicolored 5.00 5.00

Juventus (World Club Soccer Champions), Cent. — A295

Designs: a, Juventus, 1897. b, Player from early years, emblems. c, Giampiero Boniperti. d, Roberto Bettega. e, European/ South American Cup, 1996. f, Drawing in celebration of cent.

1997, May 9 Litho. *Perf. 14x13½*

1912 A295 5d Sheet of 6, #a.-f. 6.00 6.00

Queen Elizabeth II, Prince Philip, 50th Wedding Anniv. A296

No. 1913: a, Queen. b, Royal Arms. c, Queen, Prince Philip. d, Queen holding flowers, Prince saluting. e, Royal Yacht Britannia. f, Prince Philip.

20d, Queen in red hat.

1997, May 20 *Perf. 14*

1913 A296 4d Sheet of 6, #a.-f. 4.75 4.75

Souvenir Sheet

1914 A296 20d multicolored 4.00 4.00

Paul P. Harris (1868-1947), Founder of Rotary Intl. — A297

Rotary emblem, portrait of Harris and: 10d, Tree of friendship planted by Sydney W. Pascall, Rotary Pres. 1931-32.

25d, Emblem, preserve planet earth.

1997, May 20 Litho. *Perf. 14*

1915 A297 10d multicolored 2.00 2.00

Souvenir Sheet

1916 A297 25d multicolored 5.00 5.00

Heinrich von Stephan (1831-97), Founder of UPU A298

Portrait of Von Stephan and: No. 1917: a, Otto von Bismarck. b, UPU emblem. c, Two-horse team and wagon, Boston, 1900.

25d, Hamburg-Lübeck postilion, 1828.

1997, May 20

1917 A298 5d Sheet of 3, #a.-c. 3.00 3.00

Souvenir Sheet

1918 A298 25d multicolored 5.00 5.00

PACIFIC 97.

Chernobyl Disaster, 10th Anniv. A299

Designs: No. 1919, Chabad's Children of Chernobyl. No. 1920, UNESCO.

1997, May 20 Litho. *Perf. 13½x14*

1919 A299 15d multicolored 3.00 3.00
1920 A299 15d multicolored 3.00 3.00

Grimm's Fairy Tales A300

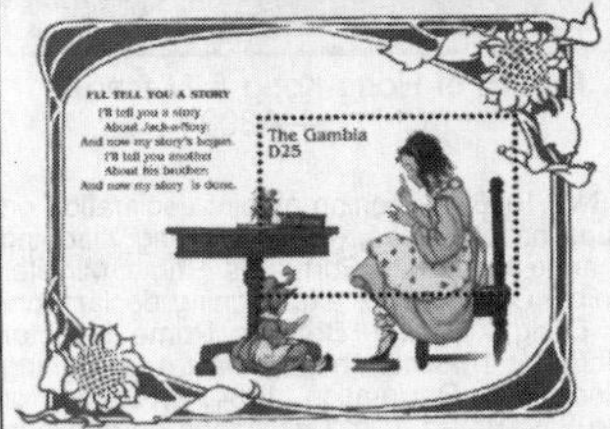

Mother Goose — A301

Scenes from "Little Red Riding Hood:" No. 1921: a, Grandmother's house. b, Little Red Riding Hood. c, Wolf.

No. 1922, Little Red Riding Hood, wolf, horiz. No. 1923, Girl seated on chair from "I'll Tell You a Story."

1997, May 20 *Perf. 13½x14*

1921 A300 10d Sheet of 3, #a.-c. 6.00 6.00

Souvenir Sheets

Perf. 14x13½

1922 A300 10d multicolored 2.00 2.00

Perf. 14

1923 A301 25d multicolored 5.00 5.00

Paintings, by Hiroshige (1797-1858) A302

No. 1924: a, Morning Glory and Cricket. b, Dragonfly and Begonia. c, Two Ducks Swimming among Reeds. d, A Black-Naped Oriole Perched on a Stem of Rose Mallow. e, A Pheasant on a Snow-covered Pine. f, A Cuckoo Flying through the Rain.

No. 1925: a, An Egret among Rushes. b, Peacock and Peonies. c, Three Wild Geese Flying across the Moon. d, A Cock in the Snow. e, A Pheasant and Bracken. f, Peonies.

No. 1926: a, Sparrow and Bamboo. b, Mandarin Ducks on an Icy Pond with Brown Leaves Falling. c, Blossoming Plum Tree. d, Java Sparrow and Magnolia. e, Chinese Bellflowers and Miscanthus. f, A Small Black Bird Clinging to a Tendril of Ivy.

No. 1927: a, Sparrows and Camellia in Snow. b, Parrot on a Branch of Pine. c, A Long-tailed Blue Bird on a Branch of Flowering Plum. d, Sparrow and Bamboo. e, Bird in a Tree. f, A Wild Duck Swimming beneath Snow-laden Reeds.

No. 1928: a, Kingfisher above a Yellow-flowered Water Plant. b, Wagtail and Roses. c, A Mandarin Duck on a Snowy Bank. d, A Japanese White-eye on a Persimmon Branch. e, Sparrows and Camellia in Snow. f, Kingfisher and Moon above a Yellow-flowered Water Plant.

No. 1929: a, Sparrow and Bamboo. b, Birds Flying over Waves. c, Blossoming Plum Tree with Full Moon. d, Kingfisher and Iris. e, A Blue-and-white Flycatcher on a Hibiscus Flower. f, Mandarin Ducks in Snowfall.

Unidentified paintings of: No. 1930, Falcon on perch. No. 1931, Two birds seated on branch. No. 1932, Kingfisher above Iris. No. 1933, Like #1925c. No. 1934, Bird on grapevine. No. 1935, Small bird in flowering tree.

1997, May 20 ***Perf. 14***

Sheets of 6

1924-1926 A302 4d #a.-f., each 4.75 4.75
1927-1929 A302 5d #a.-f., each 6.00 6.00

Souvenir Sheets

1930-1935 A302 25d each 5.00 5.00

Return of Hong Kong & Macao to China — A303

No. 1936: a, Signing of joint declaration on question of Macao, 1987. b, Deng Xiaoping sharing toast with Portugal's Prime Minister Anibal Cavaco Silva after signing declaration. c, Deng Xiaoping, Britain's Prime Minister Margaret Thatcher sharing toast after signing Sino-British Declaration, 1984. d, Signing of the Sino-British Joint Declaration on question of Hong Kong, 1984.

No. 1937: a, Sir Henry Pottinger, 1st governor of Hong Kong, 1841-44, Hong Kong Island ceded to Britain, 1843. b, Sir Hercules Robinson, governor 1859-65, Kowloon ceded to Britain, 1860. c, Sir Henry Blake, governor 1898-1903, New Territories leased to Britain, 1899.

No. 1938: a, Ships in harbor, Sir Henry Pottinger. b, Suspension bridge, Chris Patten, governor of Hong Kong, 1992-1997. c, Skyline at night, C.H. Tung, first Chinese chief executive, 1997.

No. 1939: a, Signing of Treaty of Nanking, 1842. b, Signing of Japanese surrender document, 1945. c, Signing of Sino-British Joint Declaration on question of Hong Kong, 1984, diff.

Illustration reduced.

1997, July 1

1936 A303 3d Sheet of 4, #a.-d. 2.40 2.40
1937 A303 4d Sheet of 3, #a.-c. 2.40 2.40
1938 A303 5d Sheet of 3, #a.-c. 3.00 3.00
1939 A303 6d Sheet of 3, #a.-c. 3.50 3.50

Wonders of the World — A304

Designs: 63b, Great Mosque at Samarra, Iraq, vert. 75b, Moai stone faces, Easter Island. 1d, Golden Gate Bridge, San Francisco. 1.50d, Statue of Liberty, New York, vert. 2d, Parthenon, Greece. 3d, Pyramid of the Sun, Teotihuacán, Mexico.

No. 1946: a, Rock of Gibraltar. b, St. Peter's Basilica, Vatican City. c, Santa Sophia, Istanbul. d, Gateway Arch, St. Louis. e, Great Wall of China. f, Carcassonne, France.

No. 1947: a, Stonehenge, England. b, Hughes HK-1 Hercules "Spruce Goose" airplane. c, Hoverspeed catamaran, Great Britain. d, Jet powered "Thrust 2." e, Djoser Step Pyramid, Egypt. f, Mallard steam locomotive.

No. 1948, Grand Canyon of the Colorado River, Arizona. No. 1949, Mt. Everest, Nepal. No. 1950, Washington Monument, Washington, DC.

1997, July 15

Size #1940, 1943: 24x38mm

1940-1945 A304 Set of 6 1.75 1.75

Sheets of 6

1946-1947 A304 5d #a.-f., each 6.00 6.00

Souvenir Sheets

1948-1950 A304 25d each 5.00 5.00

1993 Winter Olympics, Nagano A305

Designs: 5d, Downhill skiing. 10d, Luge. 15d, Speed skating. 20d, Ice hockey.

No. 1955: a, Luge, diff. b, Ice hockey (goalie). c, 4-man bobsled. d, Ski jumping. e, Curling. f, Women's figure skating. g, Speed skating, diff. h, Biathlon. i, Downhill skiing, diff.

No. 1956, vert: a, 2-man bobsled. b, Freestyle skiing. c, Speed skating, diff. d, Downhill skiing, diff. e, Women's figure skating, diff. f, Slalom skiing. g, Pairs figure skating. h, Cross-country skiing. i, Ski jumping, diff.

No. 1957, Female figure skater, vert. No. 1958, 2-man bobsled, diff.

1997, July 21 **Litho.** ***Perf. 14***

1951-1954 A305 Set of 4 10.00 10.00

Sheets of 9

1955-1956 A305 5d #a.-i., ea 9.00 9.00

Souvenir Sheets

1957-1958 A305 25d each 5.00 5.00

Cats A306

Designs: 63b, Scottish fold. 1.50d, American curl. 2d, British bi-color. 3d, Devon rex. 6d, Silver tabby 20d, Abyssinian.

No. 1965: a, Burmilla. b, Blue Burmese. c, Korat. d, British tabby. e, Foreign white. f, Somali.

No. 1966, Cornish rex. No. 1967, Siamese.

1997, Aug. 12

1959-1964 A306 Set of 6 6.75 6.75
1965 A306 5d Sheet of 6, #a.-f. 6.00 6.00

Souvenir Sheets

1966-1967 A306 25d each 5.00 5.00

Dinosaurs A307

50b, Coelophysis, ornitholestes. 63b, Spinosaurus. 75b, Kentrosaurus. 1d, Ceratosaurus. 1.50d, Stygimoloch. 2d, Troodon. 3d, Velociraptor. 4d, Triceratops. 5d, Protoceratops. 10d, Ornithomimus. 15d, Stegosaurus. 20d, Ankylosaurus saichania.

#1980: a, Anurognathus. b, Pteranodon. c, Pterosaurus. d, Saltasaurus. e, Agathaumus. f, Stegosaurus. g, Albertosaurus libratus. h, 4 Lesothosaurus. i, 7 Lesothosaurus.

#1981: a, Tarbosaurus bataar. b, Brachiosaurus. c, Styracosasaurus. d, Baryonyx. e, Coelophysis. f, Carnotaurus. g, Compsognathus longipes. h, Compsognathus-elegant jaw. i, Stenonychosaurus.

#1982, Deinonychus. #1983, Seismosaurus.

1997, June 23 **Litho.** ***Perf. 14***

1968-1979 A307 Set of 12 13.00 13.00

Sheets of 6

1980-1981 A307 4d #a.-i., ea 2.40 2.40

Souvenir Sheets

1982-1983 A307 25d each 5.00 5.00

No. 1982 contains one 50x38mm stamp. No. 1983 contains one 89x28mm stamp.

Dogs A308

Designs: 75b, Dalmatian. 1d, Rottweiler. 3d, Newfoundland. 4d, Great Dane. 10d, Old English sheepdog. 15d, Queensland heeler.

No. 1990: a, Akita. b, Welsh corgi. c, German shepherd. d, St. Bernard. e, Bullmastiff. f, Malamute.

#1991, Doberman pinscher. #1992, Boxer.

1997, Aug. 12

1984-1989 A308 Set of 6 6.75 6.75
1990 A308 5d Sheet of 6, #a.-f. 6.00 6.00

Souvenir Sheets

1991-1992 A308 25d each 5.00 5.00

1998 World Cup Soccer Championships, France — A309

Winning teams: 1d, Uruguay, 1950. 1.50d, W. Germany, 1954. 2d, Brazil, 1970. 3d, Brazil, 1962. 5d, Italy, 1938. 10d, Uruguay, 1930.

No. 1999: a, Brazil, 1994. b, Argentina, 1986. c, Brazil, 1970. d, Italy, 1934. e, Uruguay, 1958. f, England, 1966. g, Brazil, 1962. h, W. Germany, 1990.

Players: No. 2000: a, Mario Kempes, Argentina, 1978. b, Ademir, Brazil, 1950. c. Muller, W. Germany, 1970. d, Lineker, England, 1986. e, Eusebio, Portugal, 1966. f, Schillaci, Italy, 1990. g, Lata, Poland, 1974. h, Rossi, Italy, 1982.

No. 2001, vert: a, Kinkladze, Georgia. b, Shearer, England. c, Dani, Portugal. d, Weah, Liberia. e, Ravanelli, Italy. f, Raducioiu, Romania. g, Peter Schmeichel, Denmark. h, Bergkamp, Holland.

No. 2002, vert: a, Moore, England, 1966. b, Fritzwalter, W. Germany, 1954. c, Beckenbauer, W. Germany, 1974. d, Zoff, Italy, 1982. e, Maradona, Argentina, 1986. f, Passarella, Argentina, 1978. g, Matthäus, W. Germany, 1990. h, Dunga, Brazil, 1994.

No. 2003, Pele, Brazil. No. 2004, Eusebio, Portugal. No. 2005, Juninho, Brazil. No. 2006, Philippe Albert, Belgium.

1997, Sept. 4 ***Perf. 14x13½, 13½x14***

1993-1998 A309 Set of 6 4.50 4.50

Sheets of 8 + Label

1999-2002 A309 4d #a.-h., each 6.50 6.50

Souvenir Sheets

2003-2006 A309 25d each 5.00 5.00

Sea Birds A310

Designs: 5d, Red-legged cormorant. 10d, Roseate tern. 15d, Blue-footed booby. 20d, Sanderling.

No. 2011: a, Brown pelican. b, Galapagos penguin. c, Red billed tropic bird. d, Little tern. e, Dunlin. f, Kittiwake. g, Atlantic puffin. h, Wandering albatross. i, Masked booby. j, Glaucous winged gull. k, Artic tern. l, Piping plover.

#2012, Osprey. #2013, Long-tailed skua.

1997, Aug. 4 **Litho.** ***Perf. 14***

2007-2010 A310 Set of 4 10.00 10.00
2011 A310 3d Sheet of 12, #a.-l. 7.25 7.25

Souvenir Sheets

2012-2013 A310 23d each 4.50 4.50

A311

Diana, Princess of Wales (1961-97) — A312

Various portraits.

1997, Nov. 26 **Litho.** ***Perf. 14***

2014 A311 10d Sheet of 4, #a.-d. 8.00 8.00

Souvenir Sheet

2015 A312 25d multicolored 5.00 5.00

Christmas A313

Entire paintings or details: 1d, Angel, by Rembrandt. 1.50d, Initiation into the Rites of Dionysus, in Villa dei Misteri, Pompeii. 2d, Pair of Erotes with Purple Cloaks. 3d, The Ecstasy of Saint Teresa, by Gianlorenzo Bernini (carving). 5d, Annunciation, by Mathias Grunewald. 10d, Angel Playing the Organ, by Stefan Lochner.

No. 2022, The Rest on the Flight into Egypt, by Caravaggio. No. 2023, Education of Cupid, by Titian.

1997, Dec. 8

2016-2021 A313 Set of 6 4.50 4.50

Souvenir Sheets

2022-2023 A313 25d each 5.00 5.00

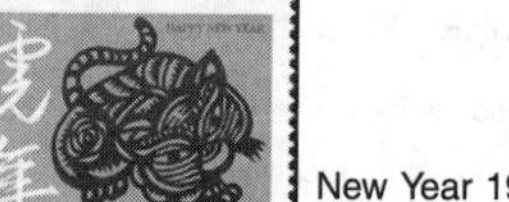

New Year 1998 (Year of the Tiger) — A314

Various stylized tigers: No. 2024: a, yellow brown background. b, purple background. c, brown background. d, orange background.

10d, Tiger, landscape.

1998, Jan. 5 **Litho.** ***Perf. 14½***

2024 A314 3d Sheet of 4, #a.-d. 2.40 2.40

Souvenir Sheet

Perf. 14

2025 A314 10d multicolored 2.00 2.00

No. 2025 contains one 38x24mm stamp.

Trains A315

No. 2026: a, Electric Train, Scotland. b, Beaconsfield, China. c, TGV, France. d, People Mover, England. e, ICE train, Germany. f, Montmartre Funicular, France.

No. 2027: a, SD70 Burlington Northern, US. b, Mallard, England. c, Baldwin 4-8-0, Peru. d, Sweden Rail. e, Rack Train, Amberawa-Java. f, Beyer-Peacock, Pakistan.

No. 2028, Monorail, England. No. 2029, Southern Pacific, US.

1998, May 19 Litho. *Perf. 14*

Sheets of 6

2026-2027 A315 5d #a.-f., each 6.00 6.00

Souvenir Sheets

2028-2029 A315 25d each 5.00 5.00

Flowers A316

Designs, vert: 75b, Daffodil. 1.50d, Transvaal daisy. 3d, Torchlily. 4d, Ancistrochilus rothschildianus. 10d, Polystachya vulcanica. 15d, Gladiolus.

No. 2036: a, Adenium multiflorum. b, Huernia namaquensis. c, Gloriosa superba. d, Strelitzia reginae. e, Passiflora mollissima. f, Bauhinia variegata.

No. 2037, Aerangis rhodosticta, vert. No. 2038, Ansella gigantea, vert.

1998, June 2 Litho. *Perf. 14*

2030-2035 A316 Set of 6 6.75 6.75
2036 A316 5d Sheet of 6, #a.-f. 6.00 6.00

Souvenir Sheets

2037-2038 A316 25d each 5.00 5.00

Historical Aircraft A317

No. 2039: a, Short Type 38, 1913. b, Fokker F.VII B 3m, 1925. c, Junkers F-13, 1919. d, Pitcairn "Mailwing," 1927. e, Douglas, 1920. f, Curtiss "Condor," 1934.

No. 2040: a, Wright Brothers, 1903. b, Curtiss, 1910. c, Farman, 1907. d, Bristol, 1911. e, Antoinette, 1908. f, Sopwith "Bat Boat," 1912.

No. 2041, Albatross, 1913. No. 2042, Boeing 247, 1932.

1998, June 10

Sheets of 6

2039-2040 A317 5d #a.-f., each 6.00 6.00

Souvenir Sheets

2041-2042 A317 25d each 5.00 5.00

Nos. 2041-2042 each contain one 85x28mm stamp.

Disney's "Mulan" A318

Characters from the animated movie - No. 2043: a, Mulan. b, Mushu. c, Little Brother. d, Cri-Kee. e, Grandmother Fa. f, Fa Li. g, Fa Zhou. h, Mulan and Khan.

No. 2044: a, Mulan riding Khan. b, Shang. c, Chi Fu. d, Chien-Po. e, Yao. f, Ling. g, Shan-Yu. h, Mulan, Shang & Mushu.

No. 2045, Mulan. No. 2046, Mulan riding Khan, diff. No. 2047, Mulan jumping in air. No. 2048, Mulan looking at Shang (in margin).

1998, July 1 Litho. *Perf. 13½x14*

2043 A318 4d Sheet of 8, #a.-h. 6.50 6.50
2044 A318 5d Sheet of 8, #a.-h. 8.00 8.00

Souvenir Sheets

2045-2048 A318 25d each 5.00 5.00

Ferrari Automobiles — A318a

No. 2048A: c, 365 GTB/4. d, Daytona. e, 1966 275 GTB.
25d, 365 GTB/4, diff.
Illustration reduced.

1998, Oct. 29 Litho. *Perf. 14*

2048A A318a 10d Sheet of 3, #c-e 5.50 5.50

Souvenir Sheet

Perf. 13¾x14¼

2048B A318a 25d multi 4.50 4.50

No. 2048A contains three 39x25mm stamps.

A319

A320

Famous People of the 20th Cent. - Jazz musicians - No. 2049: a, Sidney Bechet (1897-1959). b, Bechet playing clarinet. c, "Duke" Ellington conducting band. d, Ellington (1899-1974). e, Louis Armstrong (1900-71). f, Armstrong playing trumpet. g, Charlie "Bird" Parker playing saxophone. h, Parker (1920-55).

Composers - No. 2050: a, Cole Porter (1893-1964). b, "Born to Dance," by Porter. c, "Porgy and Bess," by George Gershwin. d, Gershwin (1898-1937). e, Richard Rodgers (1902-79) & Oscar Hammerstein II (1895-1960). f, "The King and I," by Rodgers & Hammerstein. g, "West Side Story," by Leonard Bernstein. h, Bernstein (1918-90).

No. 2051, Ella Fitzgerald (1917-96). No. 2052, Irving Berlin (1888-1989), "Oh How I Hate to Get Up in the Morning."

1998, Oct. 12 Litho. *Perf. 14*

Sheets of 8

2049-2050 A319 4d #a.-h., each 6.50 6.50

Souvenir Sheets

2051-2052 A319 25d each 5.00 5.00

Nos. 2049b-2049c, 2049f-2049g, 2050b-2050c, 2050f-2050g are 53x38mm.

1998, Oct. 25

Sinking of the Titanic - No. 2053: a, Capt. Edward J. Smith. b, Molly Brown. c, News of the disaster breaks. d, Benjamin Guggenheim. e, Isidor Strauss. f, Ida Strauss.

No. 2054, Picture of ship on postcard. No. 2055, Ship sinking. No. 2056, Remains of ship lying on bottom of ocean years later.

2053 A320 5d Sheet of 6, #a.-f. 6.00 6.00

Souvenir Sheets

2054-2056 A320 25d each 5.00 5.00

Diana, Princess of Wales (1961-97) A321

1998, Oct. 29 *Perf. 14½x14*

2057 A321 10d multicolored 2.00 2.00

Issued in sheets of 6.

Pablo Picasso (1881-1973) — A322

Paintings: 3d, Death of Casagemas, 1901. 5d, Seated Woman, 1920, vert. 10d, Mother and Child, 1907, vert.

25d, Child Playing with a Toy Truck, 1953, vert.

1998, Oct. 29 *Perf. 14½*

2058-2060 A322 Set of 3 3.50 3.50

Souvenir Sheet

2061 A322 25d multicolored 5.00 5.00

A323

A324

Mahatma Gandhi (1869-1948) - No. 2062: a, Age 62, 1932. b, Age 60, 1930, with Sarojini Naidu. c, Age 61, 1931, spinning yarn. d, Age 47, 1916.

25d, Age 61, 1931.

1998, Oct. 29 *Perf. 14*

2062 A323 10d Sheet of 4, #a.-d. 4.00 4.00

Souvenir Sheet

2063 A323 25d multicolored 5.00 5.00

Nos. 2062b-2062c are 53x39mm.

1998

Ships: 2d, Chinese Junk. 3d, HMS Victory. 10d, County Class Destroyer. 15d, Viking Longboat.

#2068, horiz: a, HMS Dreadnought. b, Truxton Class Cruiser. c, Queen Mary. d, Canberra. e, Queen Elizabeth. f, Queen Elizabeth 2.

#2069: a, Santa Maria. b, Mary Rose. c, Mayflower. d, Ark Royal. e, HMS Beagle. f, HMS Bounty.

#2070, Cuty Sark. #2071, Sovereign of the Seas.

2064-2067 A324 Set of 4 6.00 6.00

Sheets of 6

2068-2069 A324 5d #a.-f., each 6.00 6.00

Souvenir Sheets

2070-2071 A324 25d each 5.00 5.00

No. 2070 contains one 42x56mm stamp; No. 2071, one 56x42mm stamp.

1998 World Scouting Jamboree, Chile — A325

No. 2072: a, Scout handclasp. b, Small boat sailing. c, Scout salute.

No. 2073, Lord Robert Baden-Powell.

1998, Oct. 29 Litho. *Perf. 14*

2072 A325 10d Sheet of 3, #a.-c. 6.00 6.00

Souvenir Sheet

2073 A325 25d multicolored 5.00 5.00

Royal Air Force, 80th Anniv. A326

No. 2074: a, Sepecat Jaguar GR1. b, BAe Harrier GR7. c, Panavia Tornado GR1 firing Sidewinder AIM 9-L missle. d, Panavia Tornado GR1 on afterburner.

No. 2075: a, Sepecat Jaguar GR1A in low visibility gray finish. b, Panavia Tornado GR1A. c, Sepecat Jaguar GR1A in Bosnia theater camouflage finish. d, BAe Hawk 200.

No. 2076: a, Panavia Tornado GR1 flying left. b, BAe Hawk TIA. c, Sepecat Jaguar GR1A. d, Panavia Tornado GR1 flying right.

20d, Eurofighters. No. 2078, Biplane, hawk's head. No. 2079, Lightning, Eurofighter. No. 2080, Biplane, hawk in flight. No. 2081, Lancaster, Eurofighter. No. 2082, Biplane, hawk perched.

1998, Oct. 29

Sheets of 4

2074-2075 A326 5d #a.-d., each 4.00 4.00
2076 A326 7d #a.-d. 5.50 5.50

Souvenir Sheets

2077 A326 20d mult 4.00 4.00
2078-2082 A326 25d multi, each 5.00 5.00

Paintings by Eugène Delacroix (1798-1863) — A327

No. 2083: a, Mule Drivers from Tetuan. b, Encampment of Arab Mule Drivers. c, An Orange Seller. d, The Banks of the River. e, View of Tangier from the Seashore. f, Arab Horses Fighting in a Stable. g, Horses at the Trough. h, The Combat of the Giaour and Hassan.

No. 2084, vert: a, Moroccan from Tangier Standing. b, A Man of Tangier. c, Young Arab Standing with a Rifle. d, Moroccan Chieftan. e, Jewish Bride of Tangiers. f, Seated Jewess from Morocco. g, A seated Arab. h, Young Arab Seated by a Wall.

No. 2085: a, Turk Seated on a Sofa Smoking. b, View of Tangier from North African and Spanish Album. c, The Spanish Coast at Salobrena from North African and Spanish Album. d, The Aissaouas. e, Sea View from the Heights of Dieppe. f, An Arab Fantasy. g, Arab Comic Fantasy. h, An Arab Camp at Night.

Details: No. 2086, Self-portrait, vert. No. 2087, Two Women of Algiers in Their Apartment. No. 2088, Massacre of Chios.

1998, Oct. 29

Sheets of 8

2083-2085 A327 4d #a.-h., each 6.50 6.50

Souvenir Sheets

2086-2088 A327 25d each 5.00 5.00

Christmas — A328

1d, Beagle in sock. 2d, Giraffe, wreath. 3d, Rainbow bee eater, ribbon, ornament. 4d, Adult deer. 5d, Fawn. 10d, Irish red and white setter in package.

No. 2095, Brown classic tabby kitten. No. 2096, Basset hound, rough collie.

1998, Nov. 23

2089-2094 A328 Set of 6 5.00 5.00

Souvenir Sheets

2095-2096 A328 25d each 5.00 5.00

New Year 1999 (Year of the Rabbit) — A329

Stylized rabbits, background color: a, Olive brown. b, Green blue. c, Red brown. d, Pale orange.

1999, Jan. 4 Litho. *Perf. 14½*

2097 A329 3d Sheet of 4, #a.-d. 2.40 2.40

Souvenir Sheet

2098 A329 10d multicolored 2.00 2.00

No. 2098 contains one 39x24mm stamp.

Disney's Jungle Book A330

Characters - #2099: a, Mowgli, King Louie (bear). b, Mowgli, snake, c, Flunky Monkey. d, Monkey singing. e, Girl. f, Mowgli, Flunky Monkey. g, Mowgli, buzzards. h, Shere Khan (tiger).

No. 2100, Baby elephant, horiz. No. 2101, King Louie, horiz.

1999, Mar. 11 Litho. *Perf. 13½x14*

2099 A330 5d Sheet of 8, #a.-h. 7.25 7.25

Souvenir Sheets

2100-2101 A330 25d each 4.50 4.50

Australia '99, World Stamp Expo A331

African butterflies - #2102: a, Golden piper. b, Citrus swallowtail. c, Azure hairstreak. d, Two-tailed pasha. e, Blue pansy. f, African leaf butterfly.

No. 2103: a, Plain tiger. b, Blue swallowtail. c, Papilio mnesheus. d, Common opal. e, Forest green. f, Boisduval's false acraea.

No. 2104, Pirate butterfly, vert. No. 2105, Two-tailed pasha, vert.

1999, Apr. 12 Litho. *Perf. 14*

Sheets of 6

2102-2103 A331 6d #a.-f., each 6.50 6.50

Souvenir Sheets

2104-2105 A331 25d each 4.50 4.50

Wedding of Prince and Sophie Rhys-Jones A332

Various portraits of couple showing Sophie with - #2106: a, Blue collar. b, Long hair. c, Red collar.

25d, Couple, horiz.

1999, June 19 Litho. *Perf. 13½*

2106 A332 10d Sheet of 3, #a.-c. 5.50 5.50

Souvenir Sheet

2107 A332 25d multicolored 4.50 4.50

IBRA '99, World Philatelic Exhibition, Nuremberg — A333

Exhibition emblem, Adler 2-3-2 steam engine and: 4d, Samoa #104d. 5d, Samoa #55.

Emblem, sailing ship Friedrech August and: 10d, Samoa #64, #65. 15d, Samoa #67.

25d, Cover with Samoa #67 (part), 68.

Illustration reduced.

1999, July 6 *Perf. 14x14¼*

2108-2111 A333 Set of 4 6.25 6.25

Souvenir Sheet

2112 A333 25d multicolored 4.50 2.25

No. 2112 contains one 60x40mm stamp.

Apollo 11 Moon Landing, 30th Anniv. — A334

No. 2113: a, Bell X-14A VTOL aircraft. b, Lunar landing practice rig. c, Early prototype lander. d, Zero gravity training. e, Jet pack training. f, Lunar lander pilot training.

No. 2114, Apollo 11 Eagle, horiz. No. 2115, Apollo 11 splash down, horiz.

1999, July 6 *Perf. 14*

2113 A334 6d Sheet of 6, #a.-f. 6.50 6.50

Souvenir Sheets

2114-2115 A334 25d each 4.50 4.50

Souvenir Sheets

PhilexFrance '99, World Philatelic Exhibition — A335

Early railroads: #2116, Road-railer carriage. #2117, 2-2-2 Passenger locomotive, 1846.

Illustration reduced.

1999, July 6 *Perf. 13¾*

2116-2117 A335 25d each 4.50 2.25

Roots Homecoming Festival — A336

1d, Cannon, Freedom Post, Juffureh. 2d, Fort Bullen, Barra. 3d, James Fort Island.

1999, June 21 Litho. *Perf. 14*

2118-2120 A336 Set of 3 1.10 1.10

UN Rights of the Child, 10th Anniv. — A337

Pictures of children: a, With head down on table. b, Drinking from cup. c, Drawing on paper.

25d, Child smiling under umbrella.

1999, July 6

2121 A337 10d Sheet of 3, #a.-c. 5.50 5.50

Souvenir Sheet

2122 A337 25d multicolored 4.50 4.50

Johann Wolfgang von Goethe (1749-1832), Poet — A338

Designs: a, Faust quaffs the spirit's nectar. b, Portraits of Goethe and Friedrich von Schiller (1759-1805). c, Faust contemplates mortality.

25d, Portrait of Goethe, vert.

1999, July 6

2123 A338 15d Sheet of 3, #a.-c. 8.00 8.00

Souvenir Sheet

2124 A338 25d multicolored 4.50 4.50

Paintings by Hokusai (1760-1849) A339

Details or entire paintings - #2125: a, Bunshosei. b, Overthrower of Castles, Overthrower of Nations. c, Bee on Wild Rose. d, Sei Shonagon. e, Kuan-Yu. f, The Fifth Month.

#2126: a, Exotic Beauty. b, Wind (2 people). c, Dancing Monkey. d, Lady and Maiden on an Outing. e, Wind (3 people). f, Courtesan with Fan.

No. 2127, People on the Balcony of Sazaido. No. 2128, Caocao before the Battle of Chibi.

1999, July 6 *Perf. 13¾*

Sheets of 6

2125-2126 A339 5d #a.-f., each 5.50 5.50

Souvenir Sheets

2127-2128 A339 25d each 4.50 4.50

Sea Birds A340

2d, American oystercatcher. 3d, Blue-footed booby. 10d, Western gull. 15d, Brown pelican.

No. 2133: a, Atlantic puffin. b, Red-tailed tropicbird. c, Reddish egret. d, Laughing gull. e, Great white egret. f, Northern gannet. g, Forster's tern. h, Great cormorant. i, Razor bill.

No. 2134: a, Adélie penguin. b, Black skimmer. c, Erect-crested penguin. d, Heerman's gull. e, Glaucous-winged gull. f, Layson albatross. g, White pelican. h, Tufted puffin. i, Black guillemot.

No. 2135: a, Razor bill. b, Shelduck. c, Sandwich tern. d, Arctic skua. e, Gannet. f, Common gull.

No. 2136, Pelicans. No. 2137, California gull. No. 2138, Gentoo penguin.

1999, Aug. 1 *Perf. 14*

2129-2132 A340 Set of 4 5.50 5.50

Sheets of 9

2133-2134 A340 4d #a.-i., each 6.50 6.50

2135 A340 5d Sheet of 6, #a.-f. 5.50 5.50

Souvenir Sheets

2136-2138 A340 25d each 4.50 4.50

Nos. 2135-2138 have continuous designs.

Prehistoric Amimals — A341

No. 2139: a, Diatryma. b, Pteranodon. c, Stegodon. d, Icaronycteris. e, Archaeopteryx. f, Chasmatosaurus. g, Tytthostonyx. h, Hyaenodon. i, Uintatherium. j, Hesperocyon. k, Ambelodon. l, Indricotherium.

No. 2140: a, Carnotaurus. b, Quetzalcoatlus. c, Peteinosaurus. d, Prenocephale. e, Hesperornis. f, Coelophysis. g, Camptosaurus. h, Panderichthys. i, Garudimimus. j, Cacops. k, Ichthyostega. l, Scutellosaurus.

No. 2141, Lepisosteus. No. 2142, Sabertooth cat. No. 2143, Deinonychus. No. 2144, Microceratops.

1999, Aug. 1

Sheets of 12

2139-2140 A341 3d #a.-l., each 6.50 6.50

Souvenir Sheets

2141-2144 A341 25d each 4.50 4.50

Queen Mother, 100th Birthday (in 2000) — A342

No. 2145: a, Duchess of York, Princess Elizabeth, 1928. b, Lady Elizabeth Bowles-Lyon, 1923. c, Queen Elizabeth, 1946. d, Queen Mother, Prince Harry.

25d, Queen Mother celebrating 89th birthday, 1989.

1999, Aug. 4

2145 A342 10d Sheet of 4, #a.-d. + label 7.25 7.25

Souvenir Sheet

Perf. 13¾

2146 A342 25d multicolored 4.50 4.50

No. 2146 contains one 38x51mm stamp. Margins of sheets are embossed.

Orchids — A343

Designs: 2d, Sophrocattleya. 3d, Cattleya. 4d, Brassolaeliocattleya. 5d, Brassoepidendrum. 10d, Sophrolaeliocattleya. 15d, Iwanagaara.

No. 2153: a, Brassolaeliocattleya (yellow). b, Cattleytonia. c, Laeliocattleya (yellow). d, Miltonia. e, Cattleya forbesii. f, Odontoglossum cervantesii.

No. 2154: a, Lycaste macrobulbon. b, Laeliocattleya (red). c, Brassocattleya (pink). d, Cattleya, diff. e, Brassocattleya (speckled). f, Brassolaeliocattleya (yellow & red).

No. 2155, Unnamed. No. 2156, Brassolaeliocattleya (white & red).

1999, Aug. 1 Litho. *Perf. 14*

2147-2152 A343 Set of 6 6.50 6.50

Sheets of 6

2153-2154 A343 6d #a.-f., each 6.00 6.00
2155-2156 A343 25d each 4.25 4.25

Marine Fauna A344

Designs: 1d, Sea gull. 1.50d, Portuguese man-of-war. 5d, Walrus. 10d, Manatee.

No. 2161: a, Anglefish. b, Leafy sea dragon. c, Hawksbill turtle. d, Mandarin fish. e, Candy cane sea star. f, Plate coral. g. Butterflyfish. h, Coral polyp. i, Hermit crab. j, Strawberry shrimp. k, Giant blue clam. l, Sea cucumber.

No. 2162: a, Whale shark. b, Gray reef shark. c, New ZEngland octopus. d, Puffer fish. e, Lionfish. f, Squid. g, Chambered nautilus. h, Clown fish. i, Moray eel. j, Spiny lobster. k, Sotted ray. l, Clown anemone.

25d, Common dolphin.

1999, Aug. 1

2157-2160 A344 Set of 4 3.00 3.00

Sheets of 12

2161-2162 A344 3d #a.-l., each 6.00 6.00
2163 A343 25d multicolored 4.25 4.25

Galapagos Islands Marine Fauna — A345

#2164: a, Swallow-tailed gull. b, Frigate bird. c, Red-footed booby. d, Galapagos hawk. e, Great blue heron. f, Masked booby. g, Bottlenose dolphins. h, Black grunts. i, Surgeonfish. j, Stingray. k, Pilot whales. l, Pacific green sea turtle. m, Shark. n, Sea lion. o, Marine iguana. p, Pacific manta ray. q, Moorish idol. r, Galapagos penguin. s, Silver grunts. t, Sea urchin. u, Wrasse. v, Almaco amberjack. w, Blue-chin parrotfish. x, Yellow sea urchin. y, Lobster. z, Grouper. aa, Scorpionfish. ab, Squirrelfish. ac, Octopus. ad, King angelfish. ae, Horned shark. af, Galapagos hogfish. ag, Puffer fish. ah, Moray eel. ai, Orange tube corals. aj, Whitestripe chromis. ak, Longnose hawkfish. al, Sea cucumber, am, Spotted hawkfish. an, Zebra moray eel.

25d, Emperor penguins.

1999, Aug. 1

Sheet of 40

2164 A345 1.50d #a.-an. 10.00 10.00

Souvenir Sheet

2165 A345 25d multicolored 4.25 4.25

Souvenir Sheet

1999 Return of Macao to People's Republic of China — A346

No. 2166: a, Temple of A-ma. b, Border gate. c, Ruins of St. Paul's Cathedral.

Illustration reduced.

1999, Aug. 20 Litho. *Perf. 14*

2166 A346 7d Sheet of 3, #a-c 3.75 3.75

Space Exploration A347

Designs: 1d, Telstar I, horiz. 1.50d, Skylab. 2d, Mars 3 orbiter and lander. 3d, COBE. 10d, Astronaut Bruce McCandless. 15d, Apollo 13.

#2173: a, German V-2 rocket. b, Delta Straight 8. c, Ariane 4. d, Mercury on Atlas rocket. e, Saturn 1B. f, Cassini.

#2174, horiz.: a, Mariner 4. b, Viking Mars orbiter and lander. c, Giotto. d, Luna 9. e, Galileo.

#2175, horiz.: a, Soviet Vostok 1. b, Apollo command and service modules. c, Mecury capsule. d, Apollo 16 lunar module. e, Gemini 8. f, Soviet Soyuz.

#2176, Apollo-Soyuz, horiz. #2177, Mars Pathfinder, horiz.

1999

2167-2172 A347 Set of 6 5.50 5.50

Sheets of 6

2173-2175 A347 6d #a.-f., each 6.00 6.00
2176-2177 A347 25d each 4.25 4.25

#2176-2177 contain one 57x43mm stamp.

John F. Kennedy, Jr. (1960-99) A348

Designs: a, In 1961. b, In 1970s. c, In 1997.

1999, Dec. 7

2178 A348 15d Sheet of 3, #a.-c. 7.75 7.75

Flowers — A349

Various flower photographs making up a photomosaic of Princess Diana.

1999, Dec. 31 Litho. *Perf. 13¾*

2179 A349 3d Sheet of 8, #a.-h. 4.25 4.25

See No. 2290.

Millennium A350

Highlights of 1450-1500 - #2180: a, Da Vinci designs 1st flying machine. b, Gutenberg prints the Bible. c, 1st book in color printed. d, Ivan III becomes Grand Prince of Moscow. e, Ottomans capture Constantinople. f, Ming emperors rebuild Great Wall of China. g, Lorenzo de Medici begins rule in Florence. h, Henry VII becomes first Tudor king of England. i, Vasco da Gama sails to India. j, Aragon and Castile unite. k, Birth of Desiderius Erasmus. l, Cabot explores No. America. m, Henry VI wages War of the Roses. n, Bartholomeu Dias discovers Cape of Good Hope. o, Matthias Corvinus (Hunyadi) becomes king of Hungary. p, Columbus sails to America (60x40mm). q, Girolamo Savonarola burned at stake.

Highlights of 1900-1910 - #2181: a, Max Planck develops quantum theory. b, Graf Ferdinand von Zeppelin constructs first airship. c, Marconi sends 1st transatlantic message. d, Queen Victoria dies. e, 1st Nobel Prize. f, Boer War ends. g, Wright Brothers' 1st flight. h, 1st teddy bears made in Germany. i, Work begins on Panama Canal. j, Einstein develops theory of relativity. k, 1905 revolution in Russia. l, San Francisco earthquake. m, Color photography developed by Louis Lumière. n, Picasso paints "Les Demoiselles d'Avignon." o, Peary reaches North Pole. p, Model T appears (60x40mm). q, 1st kibbutz founded in Holy Land.

2000, Feb. 1 *Perf. 12¾x12½*

Sheets of 17

2180-2181 A350 3d a.-q., ea 8.75 8.75

Inscriptions are misspelled on several stamps on No. 2181.

New Year 2000 (Year of the Dragon) A351

Various dragons and Chinese characters with background colors: a, Blue green. b, Brownish gray. c, Red orange (purple dragon). d, Orange.

15d, Dull orange.

2000, Feb. 5 *Perf. 14x14½*

2182 A351 5d Sheet of 4, #a.-d. 3.50 3.50

Souvenir Sheet

Perf. 14

2183 A351 15d multi 2.60 2.60

#2183 contains one 42x28mm stamp.

African Wildlife A352

Designs: 50b, Indri. 75b, Nubian ibex. 1d, Grevy's zebra, vert. 2d, Bongo, vert. 3d, White rhinoceros. 4d, Lesser galago. 5d, Okapi, vert. 10d, Mhorr gazelle, vert.

No. 2192: a, Giant sable antelope. b, Greater kudu. c, Somali wild ass. d, Dorcas gazelle. e, Addax. f, Pelzeln's gazelle.

No. 2193: a, Cheetah. b, Chimpanzee. c, Angwantibo. d, Black rhinoceros. e, Bontebok. f, Giant eland.

No. 2194: a, Mountain gorilla. b, Black-faced impala. c, Crowned lemur. d, Long-tailed ground roller. e, Brown hyena. f, Mountain zebra.

No. 2195: a, Sacred ibis. b, Mauritius kestrel. c, Barbary leopard. d, Radiated tortoise. e, Pygmy hippopotamus. f, Bald ibis.

No. 2196, Aye-aye. No. 2197, Black lechwe, vert. No. 2198, Nile crocodile. No. 2199, African elephant.

2000, Feb. 18 *Perf. 14*

2184-2191 A352 00d Set of 8 4.50 4.50

Sheets of 6, #a.-f.

2192 A352 5d multi 5.25 5.25
2193 A352 6d multi 6.25 6.25
2194-2195 A352 7d each 7.25 7.25

Souvenir Sheets

2196-2199 A352 25d each 4.25 4.25

AmeriStamp Expo, Portland, Ore. (#2194).

The Three Stooges — A353

No. 2200: a, Curly pulling Moe's hair. b, Curly caught in wringer. c, Curly, Moe with drill. d, Moe pulling Larry's hair. e, Moe. f, Moe sticking finger in Curly's nose. g, Stooges pointing. h, Skull biting Curly's nose. i, Shemp.

No. 2201, Larry with crown. No. 2202, Curly on telephone, vert.

2000, Jan. 14 Litho. *Perf. 13¼*

2200 A353 5d Sheet of 9, #a.-i. 7.50 7.50

Souvenir Sheets

2201-2202 A353 25d each 4.25 4.25

I Love Lucy — A354

No. 2203: a, Lucy on sofa. b, Lucy, Ricky. c, Fred, Lucy, and Ethel. d, Lucy standing. e, Lucy, Ricky embracing. f, Lucy looking in mirror. g, Lucy with fists clenched. h, Lucy, Ricky on sofa. i, Lucy and Ethel.

No. 2204, Lucy, Ricky embracing, vert. No. 2205, Lucy looking in mirror, vert.

2000, Jan. 14 Litho. *Perf. 13¼*

2203 A354 5d Sheet of 9, #a.-i. 7.50 7.50

Souvenir Sheets

2204-2205 A354 25d each 4.25 4.25

Betty Boop A355

No. 2206: a, In green and yellow outfit. b, In red dress. c, In red shirt and blue jeans. d, In green and brown outfit. e, Seated in chair. f, In orange shirt and blue jeans. g, In fur coat. h, In pink dress. i, With dumbbell and water bottle.

No. 2207, In yellow flowered dress. No. 2208, In bathtub.

2000, Jan. 14 Litho. *Perf. 13¼*

2206 A355 5d Sheet of 9, #a.-i. 7.50 7.50

Souvenir Sheets

2207-2208 A355 25d each 4.25 4.25

Paintings of Anthony Van Dyck — A356

No. 2209: a, Samson and Delilah, c. 1619-20. b, Samson and Delilah sketch, 1618-20. c, Samson and Delilah, c. 1628-30.

No. 2210: a, The Adoration of the Shepherds. b, The Rest on the Flight to Egypt - The Virgin of the Partridges. c, Suffer the Little Children to Come Unto Me. d, Christ and the Moneychangers. e, Feast at the House of Simon the Pharisee. f, The Lamentation Over the Dead Christ.

No. 2211, vert.: a, Anton Giulo Brignole-Sale. b, Paolina Adorno Brignole-Sale. c, Battina Balbi Durazzo. d, Portrait of a Man of the Cattaneo Family. e, Portrait of a Woman. f, Elena Grimaldi Cattaneo.

No. 2212, vert.: a, A Genoese Senator. b, A Seated Gentlewoman. c, The Senator's Wife. d, A Genoese Lady - The Marchesa Balbi. e, Polyxena Spinola, Marchesa de Legones. f, Agostino Pallavicini.

No. 2213, vert.: a, Prince Rupert of the Palatinate. b, William II of Nassau and Orange. c, Prince Charles Louis of the Palatinate. d, Prince Rupert, Count Palatine. e, The Princess Mary. f, Prince Charles Louis, Count Palatine.

No. 2214, vert.: a, Sir George Villiers and Lady Katherine Manners as Adonis and Venus. b, Lady Mary Villiers with Lord Arran. c, Rachel de Ruvigny, Countess Southampton as Fortune. d, Venus at Forge of Vulcan. e, Daedalus and Icarus. f, The Clipping of Cupid's Wing.

No. 2215, A Man with His Son. No. 2216, Prince Charles Louis, Elector Palatine and His Brother, Prince Rupert of the Palatinate, vert. No. 2217, Venetia, Lady Digby, as Prudence, vert. No. 2218, Drunken Silenus, vert. No. 2219, Portrait of a Genoese Lady, vert. No. 2220, Charles II as Prince of Wales, vert. No. 2221, William II, Prince of Orange, and His Bride, Mary, Princess Royal of England, vert. No. 2222, The Three Eldest Children of Charles I, vert.

2000, May 1 ***Perf. 13¾***

2209 A356 5d Sheet of 3, #a.-c. 2.50 2.50

Sheets of 6, #a.-f.

2210-2214 A356 5d each 5.00 5.00

Souvenir Sheets

2215-2222 A356 25d each 4.25 4.25

Papal Visits — A357

1991-92 Visits - No. 2223: a, Portugal. b, Poland. c, Hungary. d, Brazil. e, Senegal. f, Gambia. g, Guinea. h, Angola. i, Sao Tomé. j, Dominican Republic.

1993 Visits - No. 2224: a, Benin. b, Uganda. c, Sudan. d, Albania. e, Spain. f, Jamaica. g, Mexico. h, United States. i, Lithuania. j, Latvia.

1993-95 Visits - No. 2225: a, Estonia. b, Croatia. c, Philippines. d, Papua New Guinea. e, Australia. f, Sri Lanka. g, Czech Republic. h, Belgium. i, Slovakia. j, Cameroon.

1995-96 Visits - No. 2226: a, South Africa. b, Kenya. c, United States. d, United Nations. e, Guatemala. f, Nicaragua. g, El Salvador. h, Venezuela. i, Tunisia. j, Slovenia.

1996-98 Visits - No. 2227: a, Germany. b, Hungary. c, France, 1996. d, Bosnia. e, Czech Republic. f, Lebanon. g, Poland. h, France, 1997. i, Brazil. j, Cuba.

1998-99 Visits - No. 2228: a, Nigeria. b, Austria. c, Croatia. d, Mexico. e, United States. f, Romania. g, Poland. h, Slovenia. i, India. j, Georgia.

No. 2229, Pope rekindles Eternal Flame. No. 2230, Pope blesses Holy Land. No. 2231, Pope places prayer on Western Wall. No. 2232, Pope assisted by Israeli president and prime minister. No. 2233, Pope prays at Western Wall. No. 2234, Pope receives Bible from chief rabbis. No. 2235, Pope touches bowl of soil. No. 2236, Pope at Yad Vashem, horiz.

Illustration reduced.

2000, May 15 **Litho.** ***Perf. 13¾***

Sheets of 10, #a.-j, + 2 labels

2223-2228 A357 6d each 9.50 9.50

Souvenir Sheets

Perf. 14½x14¾, 14¾x14½ (#2236)

2229-2236 A357 25d each 4.00 4.00

Stamps from Nos. 2223-2228 are 28x47mm.

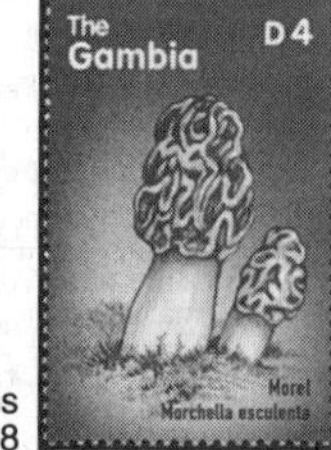

Mushrooms A358

Designs: 4d, Morel. 5d, Chanterelle. 15d, Knight cap. 20d, Spindle.

No. 2241: a, Yellow parasol. b, Mottle-gill. c, Poplar field cap. d, Caesar's. e, Flame shield-cap. f, Lilac bonnet.

No. 2242: a, Common puffball. b, Earth star. c, Silky volvar. d, Stump puffball. e, Spindle-stemmed bolete. f, Fox-orange cort.

No. 2243, Red-stemmed tough shank. No. 2244, St. George's.

2000, May 15 ***Perf. 14***

2237-2240 A358 Set of 4 7.00 7.00

Sheets of 6, #a.-f.

2241-2242 A358 7d each 6.75 6.75

Souvenir Sheets

2243-2244 A358 25d each 4.00 4.00

First Zeppelin Flight, Cent. — A359

No. 2245: a, LZ-10. b. LZ-127. c, LZ-129. 25d, LZ-130.

Illustration reduced.

2000, May 1 **Litho.** ***Perf. 14***

2245 A359 15d Sheet of 3, #a-c 7.00 7.00

Souvenir Sheet

2246 A359 25d multi 4.00 4.00

No. 2246 contains one 50x38mm stamp.

Prince William, 18th Birthday — A360

No. 2247: a, As child. b, In sweater. c, In suit, with flowers. d, In suit.

25d, With Prince Harry.

Illustration reduced.

2000, May 1 ***Perf. 14***

2247 A360 7d Sheet of 4, #a-d 4.50 4.50

Souvenir Sheet

Perf. 13¾

2248 A360 25d multi 4.00 4.00

No. 2248 contains one 38x50mm stamp.

Berlin Film Festival, 50th Anniv. — A361

No. 2249: a, Pane. Amore e Fantasia. b, Richard III. c, Smultronstället (Wild Strawberries). d, The Defiant Ones. e, The Living Desert. f, A Bout de Souffle.

25d, Twelve Angry Men.

Illustration reduced.

2000, May 1 ***Perf. 14***

2249 A361 7d Sheet of 6, #a-f 6.50 6.50

Souvenir Sheet

2250 A361 25d multi 4.00 4.00

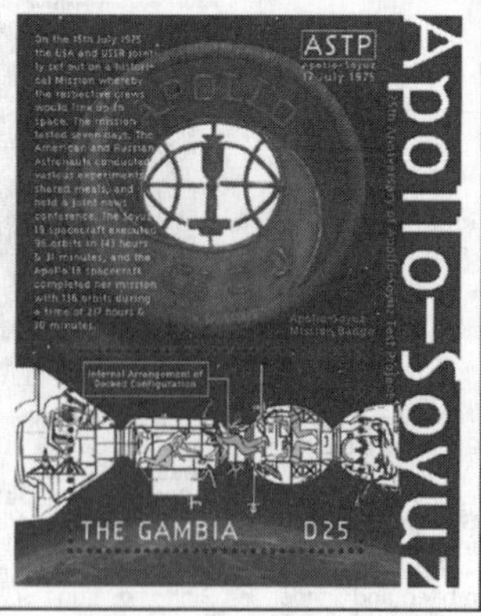

Apollo-Soyuz Mission, 25th Anniv. — A362

No. 2251: a, Donald K. Slayton. b, Thomas P. Stafford. c, Vance D. Brand.

25d, Diagram of docked spacecraft.

Illustration reduced.

2000, May 1

2251 A362 15d Sheet of 3, #a-c 7.00 7.00

Souvenir Sheet

2252 A362 25d multi 4.00 4.00

Souvenir Sheet

2000 Summer Olympics, Sydney — A363

No. 2253: a, Paavo Nurmi. b, Basketball. c, Panathenian Stadium, Athens and Greek flag. d, Ancient Greek chariot racing.

Illustration reduced.

2000, May 1

2253 A363 6d Sheet of 4, #a-d 3.75 3.75

Public Railways, 175th Anniv. — A364

No. 2254: a, Locomotion No. 1, George Stephenson. b, Chesapeake.

Illustration reduced.

2000, May 1

2254 A364 15d Sheet of 2, #a-b 4.75 4.75

Johann Sebastian Bach (1685-1750) — A365

Illustration reduced.

2000, May 1

2255 A365 25d multi 4.00 4.00

Popes — A366

No. 2256: a, Pope Felix IV, 526-30. b, Gelasius I, 492-96. c, Gregory I, 590-604. d, Gregory IX, 1227-41. e, Gregory XII, 1406-15. f, Honorius III, 1216-27.

No. 2257: a, Gregory XIII, 1572-85. b, Urban II, 1088-99. c, Sixtus I, 115-125. d, Pius IX, 1846-78. e, Pius IV, 1559-65. f, Paschal I, 817-24.

No. 2258: a, Alexander VII, 1655-67. b, Benedict XI, 1303-04. c, Calixtus III, 1455-58. d, Celestine V, 1294. e, Clement IX, 1667-69. f, Fabian, 236-50.

No. 2259, Peter, 33-64. No. 2260, Damasus I, 366-384. No. 2261, John I, 523-526.

Illustration reduced.

2000, July 26 **Litho.** ***Perf. 13¾***

Sheets of 6, #a-f

2256-2258 A366 7d each 6.25 6.25

Souvenir Sheets

2259-2261 A366 25d each 3.75 3.75

Butterflies A367

1.50d, Amphicalia tigris. 2d, Myrina silenus. 3d, Chrysiridia madagascarensis. 5d, Papilionidae. 10d, Dasiothia medea.

2000, Aug. 7 ***Perf. 14¾x14***

2262-2266 A367 Set of 5 3.25 3.25

Souvenir Sheet

Albert Einstein (1879-1955) — A368

2000, May 1 Litho. *Perf. 14¼*

2267 A368 25d multi 3.50 3.50

Space — A369

No. 2268: a, Uhuru. b, Rosat. c, I.U.E. d, Astro E. e, Exosat. f, Chandra.

No. 2269, vert.: a, Helios. b, Solar Max. c, SOHO. d, O.S.O. e, Special rocket launch. f, I.M.P.

No. 2270, XMM. No. 2271, 25d, Cassini Huygens.

Illustration reduced.

2000, May 1 *Perf. 14*

Sheets of 6, #a-f

2268-2269 A369 7d Set of 2 11.50 11.50

Souvenir Sheets

2270-2271 A369 25d Set of 2 6.75 6.75

The Stamp Show 2000, London; World Stamp Expo 2000, Anaheim.

Monarchs — A370

No. 2272: a, Charles I of Great Britain, 1625-49. b, Clovis III, king of the Franks (691-95).

No. 2273, 7d: a, Charles II of France, 885-887. b, Catherine de Medici of France, 1547-59. c, Boris Godunov of Russia, 1598-1605. d, Basil III of Russia, 1505-33. e, Anne of Great Britain, 1702-14. f, Charles IX of France, 1560-74.

No. 2274: a, James IV of Scotland, 1488-1513. b, James V of Scotland, 1513-42. c, James VI of Scotland, 1567-1625. d, Mary of Scotland, 1542-67. e, Mary of Great Britain, 1689-94. f, Elizabeth II, of Great Britain, 1952-present.

#2275, James Francis Edward Stuart. #2276, James IV of Scotland. #2277, Bahadur Shah of India, 1837-57.

Illustration reduced.

2000, July 26 *Perf. 13¾*

2272 A370 7d Sheet of 2, #a-b 1.90 1.90

Sheets of 6, #a-f

2273-2274 A370 7d Set of 2 11.50 11.50

Souvenir Sheets

2275-2277 A370 25d Set of 3 10.00 10.00

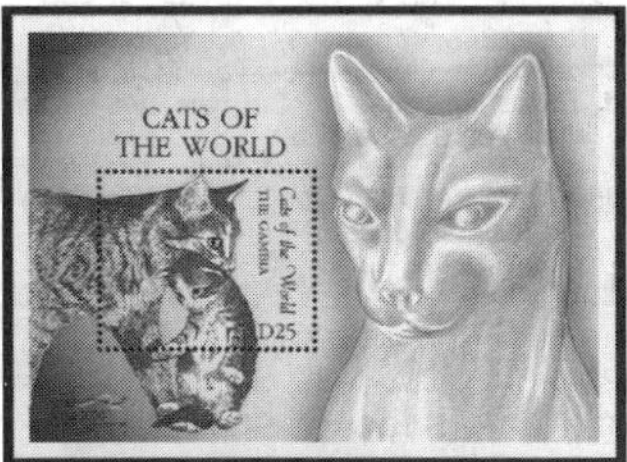

Puppies — A371

Designs: 1d, West Highland terrier. 1.50d, Bernese mountain dog. 3d, Yorkshire terrier. 4d, West Highland terrrier, diff. 10d, Chow chow. 15d, Poodle.

No. 2284: a, Border collie (brown and white). b, Border collie (black, brown and white). c, Yorkshire terrier. d, German shepherd. e, Beagle. f, Spaniel.

2000, Aug. 7 *Perf. 14¼*

2278-2283 A371 Set of 6 4.75 4.75

2284 A371 7d Sheet of 6, #a-f 5.75 5.75

Souvenir Sheet

2285 A371 25d Boxer 3.50 3.50

The Stamp Show 2000, London (Nos. 2284-2285).

Cats — A372

No. 2286, 4d: a, Egyptian mau. b, Singapura. c, American shorthair. d, Cornish rex. e, Birman. f, Scottish fold. g, Turkish angora. h, Turkish van.

No. 2287, 5d: a, Ragdoll. b, Bombay. c, Korat. d, Somali. e, British shorthair. f, American curl. g, Maine coon cat. h, Like No. 2286h.

No. 2288, Cat and kitten. No. 2289, Cat.

Illustration reduced.

2000, Aug. 7

Sheets of 8, #a-h

2286-2287 A372 Set of 2 9.75 9.75

Souvenir Sheets

2288-2289 A372 25d Set of 2 6.75 6.75

The Stamp Show 2000, London.

Flower Photomosaic Type of 1999 and

Queen Mother, 100th Birthday — A373

Designs: No. 2090, Various flower photographs making up a photomosaic of the Queen Mother. No. 2290I: Various photos of religious scenes making up a photomosaic of Pope John Paul II.

Illustration reduced.

2000, Aug. 7 Litho. *Perf. 13¾*

2290 A349 5d Sheet of 8, #a-h 5.50 5.50

2290I A349 6d Sheet of 8, #j-q 6.75 6.75

Litho. & Embossed

Without Gum

Die Cut 9x8¾

2291 A373 85d multi

Issued: Nos. 2290, 2291 8/7. No. 2290I, 8/8.

European Soccer Championships — A374

No. 2292, horiz. - Czech Republic: a, Nedved. b, Team photo. c, Maier. d, Antonin Panenka. e, Selessin Stadium, Liege. f, Patrik Berger.

No. 2293, horiz. - England: a, Alan Shearer. b, Team photo. c, David Seaman. d, Sol Campbell. e, Philips Stadium, Eindhoven. f, Southgate.

No. 2294, horiz. - Norway: a, Leonardsen. b, Team photo. c, Mykland. d, Solbakken. e, Rekdal.

No. 2295, horiz. - Slovenia: a, Aleksander Knavs. b, Team photo. c, Zlatko Zahovic. d, Ales Ceh. e, Stade Communal, Charleroi. f, Miran Pavlin.

No. 2296, horiz. - Sweden: a, Ljungberg. b, Team photo. c, Andersson. d, Nilsson. e, Schwarz.

No. 2297, horiz. - Turkey: a, Yalcin. b, Team photo. c, Buruk. d, Erdem. e, King Baudouin Stadium. f, Korkut.

No. 2298, Czech Republic coach, Jozef Chovanec. No. 2299, England coach Kevin Keegan. No. 2300, Norway coach Nils-Johan Semb. No. 2301, Slovenia coach Srecko Katanec. No. 2302 Sweden coaches, Söderberg and Lagerbäck. No. 2303, Turkey coach Mustafa Denizli.

Illustration reduced.

2000, Aug. 7 Litho. *Perf. 13¾*

Sheets of 6

2292	A374 7d #a-f	5.75	5.75
2293	A374 7d #a-f	5.75	5.75
2294	A374 7d #a-e, 2292e	5.75	5.75
2295	A374 7d #a-f	5.75	5.75
2296	A374 7d #a-e, 2293e	5.75	5.75
2297	A374 7d #a-f	5.75	5.75
	Nos. 2292-2297 (6)	34.50	34.50

Souvenir Sheets

2298-2303 A374 25d Set of 6 21.00 21.00

Paintings of Birds — A375

Designs: 1.50d, A White Pheasant and Other Fowl in a Classical Landscape, by Abraham Bisschop. 3d, Salmon-crested Cockatoo, by Bartolomeo Bimbi. 4d, A Great Bustard Cock and Other Birds, by Ludger Tom Ring. 15d, A Great Black-backed Gull and Other Birds, by Jokob Bogdani.

No. 2308: a, Peacocks, Hens and Mouse, by Tobias Stranover. b, Lady in a Red Jacket Feeding a Parrot, by Frans van Mieris. c, Birds by a Pool, by Melchior de Hondecoeter. d, Ganymede and the Eagle, by Peter Paul Rubens. e, Leda and the Swan, by Cesare de Sesto. f, Ducks and Ducklings at the Foot of a Tree in a Mediterranean Landscape, by Adriaen van Oolen. g, Portrait of the Falconer Robert Cheseman Carrying a Hooded Falcon, by Hans Holbein. h, A Golden Pheasant on a Stone Plinth, with Other Birds, by Jacobus Vonck.

No. 2309, horiz.: a, Still Life of Birds, by Caravaggio (hanging dead birds, basket). b, Turkeys with Young and Rock Doves, by Johan Wenzel Peter. c, The Threatened Swan, by Jan Asselyn. d, Still Life of Fruit and Birds in a Landscape, by Jakab Bogdany. e, Mobbing the Owl, by Tobias Stranover (owl at right, other birds). f, A Concert of Birds, by Hondecoeter (owl, cockatoo at center). g, Owls and Young Ones, by William Tomkins. h, Birds by a Stream, by Jean Baptiste Oudry.

No. 2310, 25d, The King Eagle Pursued to the Sun, by Philip Reinagle. No. 2311, 25d, Still Life of Birds, by Georg Flegl, horiz.

2000, Oct. 2 *Perf. 13½*

2304-2307 A375 Set of 4 3.25 3.25

Sheets of 8, #a-h

2308-2309 A375 5d Set of 2 11.00 11.00

Souvenir Sheets

2310-2311 A375 25d Set of 2 6.75 6.75

Descriptions of paintings are in margins on Nos. 2308-2311.

Paintings from the Prado — A376

No. 2312: a, The Madonna of the Fish, by Raphael. b, The Holy Family with a Lamb, by Raphael. c, The Madonna of the Stair, by Andrea del Sarto. d, Moneychanger from The Moneychanger and his Wife, by Marinus van Reymerswaele. e, Madonna and Child by Jan Gossaert. f, Wife from The Moneychanger and his Wife.

No. 2313: a, Bearded man from St. Benedict's Supper, by Juan Andres Ricci. b, Our Lady of the Immaculate Conception, by Francisco de Zurbarán. c, Monk with candle from St. Benedict's Supper. d, The Penitient Magdalen, by José de Ribera. e, Christ as Man of Sorrows, by Antonion de Pereda. f, St. Jerome, by Pereda.

No. 2314: a, Children with a Shell, by Bartolomé Esteban Murillo. b, Our Lady of the Immaculate Conception, by Murillo. c, The Good Shepherd, by Murillo. d, Woman with red headdress from The Parasol, by Francisco de Goya. e, A Rural Gift, by Ramon Bayeu. f, Woman with blue headdress from The Parasol.

No. 2315: a, Queen Isabella Farnese, by Jean Ranc. b, Young Woman Seen from the Back, by Jean-Baptiste Greuze. c, Charles III as a Child, by Ranc. d, James Bourdieu, by Sir Joshua Reynolds. e, Dr. Isaac Henrique Sequeira, by Thomas Gainsbourough. f, Portrait of a Clergyman, by Reynolds.

No. 2316: a, Portrait of a Young Woman, by Zacarias González Velázquez. b, The Painter Francisco de Goya, by Vicente Lopez Portaña. c, Portrait of a Girl, by Rafael Tejeo Diaz. d, Mary, from The Nativity, by Federico Barocci. e, Madonna and Child with St. John, by Correggio. f, Jesus, from The Nativity.

No. 2317: a, St. Andrew, by Francisco Rizi. b, Christ Crucified, by Diego Velázquez. c, St. Onuphrius, by Francisco Collantes. d, Charles II, by Juan Carreño de Miranda. e, St. Sebastian, by Carreño de Miranda. f, Peter Ivanovich Potemkin, by Carreño de Miranda.

No. 2318, The Defense of Cádiz Against the English, by Zurbarán. No. 2319, The Surrender of Juliers, by Jusepe Leonardo. No. 2320, The Holy Family with a Bird, by Murillo. No. 2321, Danäe, by Titian, horiz. No. 2322, Venus and Adonis, by Paolo Veronese, horiz. No. 2323, Jacob's Dream, by Ribera.

Illustration reduced.

2000, Oct. 6 *Perf. 12x12¼, 12¼x12*

Sheets of 6, #a-f

2312-2317 A376 6d Set of 6 30.00 30.00

Souvenir Sheets

2318-2323 A376 25d Set of 6 20.00 20.00

Espana 2000, Intl. Philatelic Exhibition.

Battle of Britain, 60th Anniv. — A377

No. 2324, horiz.: a, Hurricane downing German BF109. b, Spitfire over River Thames. c, Flight Lt. Denys E. Gilliam attacking German Dornier 217 planes. d, Hurricanes heading to intercept Luftwaffe bombers. e, Hurricanes returning to Croydon. f, G.A. Langley in combat with BF109. g, Bristol Blenheim IV over

English Channel. h, Spitfires taking off from Hornchurch.

No. 2325, horiz.: a, Plane from 29th Blenheim Squadron heading to Norwegian coast. b, Luftwaffe pilot Helmut Wick downs RAF pilot John Cock. c, Spitfire downs Dornier 217 off Dover. d, Bristol Beaufighter IIF on patrol. e, Bolton-Paul Defiants intercept Luftwaffe bombers. f, Spitfire in dogfite with German Stuka JU-87 divebomber. g, Spitfire and Hurricane fly over London and River Thames. h, Gloster Gladiator.

No. 2326, Group Captain Frank Carey. No. 2327, German Commander Adolf Joseph Ferdinand Galland.

Illustration reduced.

2000, Oct. 16 *Perf. 14*

Sheets of 8, #a-h

2324-2325 A377 5d Set of 2 11.00 11.00

Souvenir Sheets

2326-2327 A377 25d Set of 2 6.75 6.75

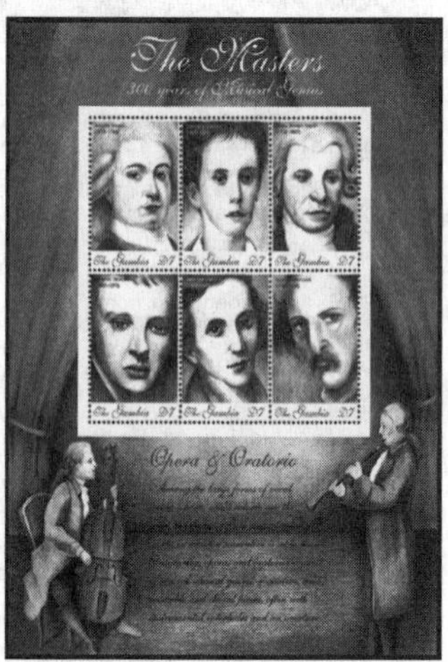

Composers — A378

No. 2328, 7d: a, Antonio Vivaldi. b, Giacomo Puccini. c, Franz Joseph Haydn. d, Leopold Stokowski. e, Felix Mendelssohn. f, Gaetano Donizetti.

No. 2329, 7d: a, Witold Lutoslawski. b, William Sterndale Bennett. c, Wolfgang Amadeus Mozart. d, Ludwig van Beethoven. e, Sergei Rachmaninoff. f, Peter Ilich Tchaikovsky.

No. 2330, 25d, Manuel de Falla. No. 2331, 25d, Fréderic Chopin.

Illustration reduced.

2000, Oct. 2 Litho. *Perf. 13¾x13¼*

Sheets of 6, #a-f

2328-2329 A378 Set of 2 11.50 11.50

Souvenir Sheets

2330-2331 A378 Set of 2 6.75 6.75

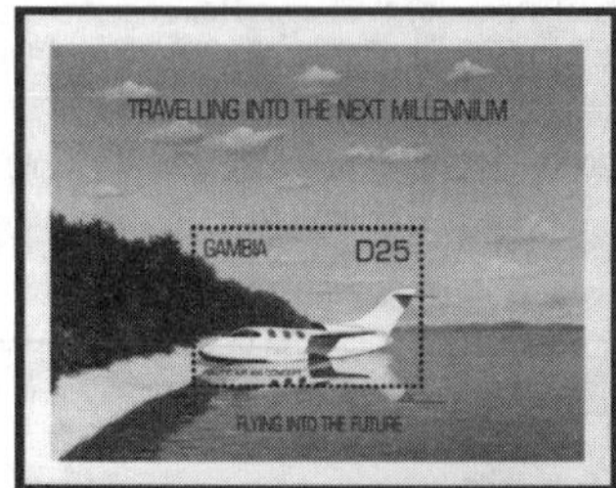

Transportation of the Future — A379

No. 2332 - Automobiles, 7d: b, Mazda RX-Evolv. c, Isuzu Kai. d, Ford 021C. e, Pontiac GTO. f, Chevrolet CERV III. g, Toyota Will VI.

No. 2333, Aircraft, 7d: a, Blended wing body, BWB-1. b, Boeing 767-400 ERX. c, Lockheed concept. d, Boeing X. e, American National Aerospace plane X-30 concept. f, Hotol taking off from Russian AN-225.

No. 2334, Trains, 8d: a, Maglev train MLU-002. b, Magnetic rail car. c, Monorail above ground concept. d, Seattle Monorail. e, Monorail above cabin concept. f, Monorail concept.

No. 2335 - Watercraft, 8d: h, Pendolare concept boat. i, Planesail boat. j, Airfoil concept. k, Ferry Sea Coaster concept. l, Shinaitoku Matu new sail technology. m, Supersport luxury yacht concept.

No. 2335G, 25d, Nautic Air 400 concept. No. 2335H, 25d, Maglev train. No. 2334I, 25d, Honda Sprocket concept. No. 2335J, 25d, Triton, US Coast Guard concept.

Illustration reduced.

2000, Oct. 2 *Perf. 14*

Sheets of 6, #a-f

2332 A379 7d Sheet of 6, #b-g 5.75 5.75
2333-2334 A379 Set of 2 12.00 12.00
2335 A379 8d Sheet of 6, #h-m 6.75 6.75

Souvenir Sheets

2335G-2335H A379 Set of 2 6.75 6.75
2335I A379 25d multi 3.50 3.50
2335J A379 25d multi 3.50 3.50

Nos. 2335 and 2335A contain one 56x41mm stamp.

Massacre of Israeli Olympic Athletes, 1972 — A380

No. 2336, horiz.: a, Moshe Weinberg. b, Eliezer Halffin. c, Mark Slavin. d, Ze'ev Friedman. e, Joseph Romano. f, Kahat Shor. g, David Berger. h, Joseph Gottfreund. i, Andrei Schpitzer. j, Amitsur Shapira. k, Yaakov Springer. l, Olympic poster.

Illustration reduced.

2000, Nov. 9

2336 A380 4d Sheet of 12, #a-l 6.50 6.50

Souvenir Sheet

2337 A380 25d Torchbearer 3.50 3.50

Ships A381

Designs: 5d, Spanish Armada. 10d, Brazilian river gunboat Colombo. 15d, Russian Navy mine carrier Jenissel. 20d, Japanese battleship Yamato.

No. 2342, 7d: a, British first-rate battleship, 18th cent. b, Spanish galleon, 16th cent. c, Russian four-masted barque, 20th cent. d, Henri Grace à Dieu with flag on stern, 16th cent. e, Frontispiece of John Dee's Arte of Navigation, 16th cent. f, British ironclad, 19th cent.

No. 2343, 7d: a, Chinese junk, 18th cent. b, Two-masted cog, 15th cent. c, Henri Grace à Dieu, no flag on stern, 16th cent. d, St. Brendan and monks at sea, 6th cent. e, Figurehead. f, British carrack, 16th cent.

No. 2344, 25d, Challenger, 19th cent. No. 2345, 25d, Golden Hind, 16th cent.

2000, Oct. 2 Litho. *Perf. 14*

2338-2341 A381 Set of 4 6.50 6.50

Sheets of 6, #a-f

2342-2343 A381 Set of 2 11.00 11.00

Souvenir Sheets

2344-2345 A381 Set of 2 6.50 6.50

Birds — A382

No. 2346, 7d, vert.: a, Pied flycatcher. b, Blackcap. c, Stonechat. d, Nightingale. e, Black-headed tchagra. f, Yellow wagtail.

No. 2347, 7d, vert.: a, Gray parrot. b, Great spotted cuckoo. c, Bar-tailed trogon. d, African hobby. e, Green turaco. f, Trumpeter hornbill.

No. 2348, 7d, vert.: a, Yellow-rumped tinkerbird. b, Greater honeyguide. c, Hoopoe. d, European roller. e, Carmine bee-eater. f, White-throated bee-eater.

#2349, 25d, European bee-eater. #2350, 25d, Bateleur. #2351, 25d, Secretary bird.

Illustration reduced.

2000, Oct. 2 *Perf. 13¾x13¼*

Sheets of 6, #a-f

2346-2348 A382 Set of 3 16.00 16.00

Souvenir Sheets

2349-2351 A382 Set of 3 9.75 9.75

Ferrari Automobiles — A383

4d, 3335P. 5d, 5125. 10d, 312P. 25d, 330P4.

2000, Nov. 15 *Perf. 14*

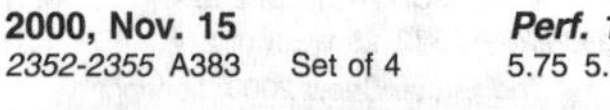

2352-2355 A383 Set of 4 5.75 5.75

12th Classic Automobile Marathon — A384

No. 2356: a, Morgan. b, Rover. c, Marmon. d, Rolls Royce Silver Cloud. e, Rolls Royce Phantom. f, Mercedes 680S. g, Mercedes 74. h, Invicta.

No. 2357: a, Allard. b, Ford coupe. c, Citroen Pilot. d, Packard (white). e, Austin A90. f, Bentley. g, Packard (red). h, Aston Martin.

No. 2358, Cadillac. No. 2359, Morris Minor.

2000, Nov. 15

Sheets of 8, #a-h

2356-2357 A384 5d Set of 2 10.50 10.50

Souvenir Sheets

2358-2359 A384 25d Set of 2 6.50 6.50

Queen Mother, 100th Birthday — A385

2000, Aug. 7 Litho. *Perf. 14*

2360 A385 7d multi .90 .90

Printed in sheets of 6.

The Horse in Art A386

Designs: 4d, At Full Stretch, by John Skeaping. 5d, The Burton, by Lionel Edwards. 10d, A Game of Polo, by Li Lin. 15d, St. George and the Dragon, by Raphael, vert.

No. 2365, 7d: a, Horses Emerging From the Sea, by Eugène Delacroix. b, The Ninth Duke of Marlborough on a Grey Horse, by Sir Alfred Munnings. c, Ovid in Exile Amongst the Scythians, by Delacroix. d, Early Morning Gallop, by Skeaping. e, Mare and Foal, by Munnings. f, Detail from Three-a-side Polo at Simla, by Edwards.

No. 2366, 7d, vert.: a, A Lady Hawking, by E. J. H. Vernet. b, Captain Robert Orme, by Sir Joshua Reynolds. c, Napoleon Crossing the Alps, by Jacques-Louis David. d, Nobby Gray, by Munnings. e, Amateur Jockeys Near a Carriage, by Edgar Degas. f, Detail from Three-a-side Polo at Simla, diff.

No. 2367, 25d, The Reckoning, by George Morland. No. 2368, 25d, One of the Family, by Frederic G. Cotman.

2000, Oct. 2

2361-2364 A386 Set of 4 4.50 4.50

Sheets of 6, #a-f

2365-2366 A386 Set of 2 11.00 11.00

Souvenir Sheets

2367-2368 A386 Set of 2 6.50 6.50

New Year 2001 (Year of the Snake) — A387

No. 2369: a, Vermilion background. b, Purple background. c, Dark blue background. d, Light green background.

Illustration reduced.

2001, Jan. 2

2369 A387 4d Sheet of 4, #a-d 2.10 2.10

Souvenir Sheet

2370 A387 15d Snake 2.00 2.00

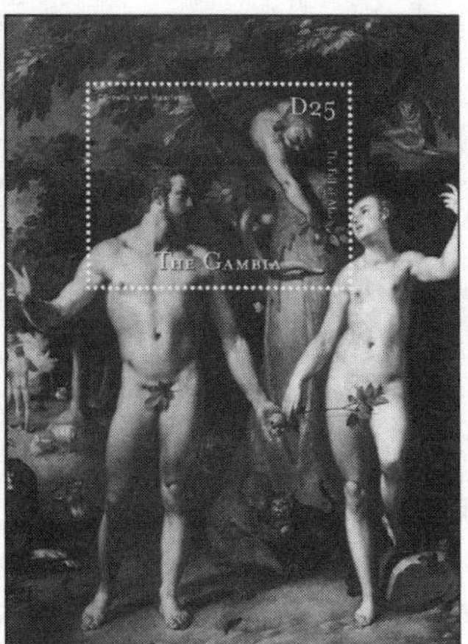

Rijksmuseum, Amsterdam, Bicent. (in 2000) — A388

No. 2371, 7d, vert.: a, Vessels in a Strong wind, by Jan Porcellis. b, Seascape in the Morning, by Simon de Vlieger. c, Travelers at a Country Inn, by Isaack van Ostade. d, Orpheus with Animals in a Landscape, by Aelbert Cuyp. e, Italian With a Mountain Plateau, by Cornelis van Poelenburch. f, Boatmen and hill from Boatman Moored on a Lake Shore, by Adam Pynacker.

No. 2372, 7d, vert.: a, Cow, boatmen and sailboat from Boatmen Moored on a Lake Shore. b, The Ford in the River, by Jan Baptist Weenix. c, Two Horses Near a Gate in a Meadow, by Paulus Potter. d, Cows and Sheep at a Stream, by Karel Dujardin. e, Violin player from The Duet, by Cornelis Saftleven. f, Lute player from The Duet.

No. 2373, 7d, vert.: a, Teapot from Still Life With Turkey Pie, by Pieter Claesz. b, Bouquet of Flowers in a Vase, by Ambrosius Bosschaert. c, Vase from Still Life With Flowers, Fruit and Shells, by Balthasar van der Ast. d, Flowers and fruit from Still Life With Flowers, Fruit and Shells. e, Tulips in a Vase, by Hans Boulenger. f, Laid Table With Cheese and Fruit, by Floris van Dijck.

No. 2374, 7d, vert.: a, Turkey, from Still Life With Turkey Pie. b, Still Life With Gilt Goblet, by Willem Claesz Heda. c, Still Life With Lobster and Nautilus Cup, by Jan Davidsz de Heem. d, Bacchanal, by Moses van Uyttenbroeck. e, The Anatomy Lesson of Dr. Nicolaes Tulp, by Rembrandt. f, Johannes Lutma, by Jacob Backer.

No. 2375, 7d, vert.: a, The Meagre Company, by Frans Hals and Pieter Codde. b, The Twins Clara and Aelbert de Bray, by Salomon de Bray. c, Self-portrait, by Ferdinand Bol. d, Ambulatory of the New Church in Delft, with the Tomb of Willem the Silent, by Gerard Houckgeest. e, View of the Tomb of Willem in the New Church in Delft, by Emanuel de Witte. f, Mountainous Landscape, by Hercules Segers.

No. 2376, 7d, vert.: a, Lute player from Gallant Company by Codde. b, Men and archway from Gallant Company. c, Man on bended knee from The Marriage of Willem van Loon and Margaretha Bas, by Jan Miense Molenaer. d, Crowd from The Marriage of Willen van Loon and Margaretha Bas. e, Woman in black robe from The Marriage of Willem van Loon and Margaretha Bas. f, Johanna Le Maire, by Nicolaes Eliasz Pickenoy.

No. 2377, 25d, The Fall of Man, by Cornelis van Haarlem. No. 2378, 25d, The Art Gallery of Jan Gildemeester Jansz, by Jan Ekels II. No. 2379, 25d, View of the Nieuwe Kerk and the Rear of the Town Hall in Amsterdam, by Isaak Outwater. No. 2380, 25d, The Spendthrift, by Cornelis Troost. No. 2381, 25d, Morning Ride on the Beach, by Anton Mauve. No. 2382, 25d, Meadow Landscape With Cattle, by Willen Roelofs.

Illustration reduced.

2001, Jan. 15 ***Perf. 13¾***

Sheets of 6, #a-f

2371-2376 A388 Set of 6 32.50 32.50

Souvenir Sheets

2377-2382 A388 Set of 6 20.00 20.00

The Wizard of Oz, Cent. (in 2000) — A389

No. 2383, 7d: a, Witch of the North. b, Poppies. c, Dorothy's house. d, Witch of the East. e, Dorothy. f, The Wizard.

No. 2384, 7d: a, Witch's wolf. b, Witch's forest. c, Witch's monkeys. d, Dorothy in poppies. e, Queen Mouse. f, Witch and evil bees.

No. 2385, 7d: a, Cowardly Lion. b, Land of Oz. c, Tin Man. d, Scarecrow. e, Toto. f, Munchkins.

No. 2386, 27d, Green Maiden. No. 2387, 27d, Gate keeper. No. 2388, 27d, Dorothy at crossroads, horiz.

Illustration reduced.

2001, Jan. 30

Sheets of 6, #a-f

2383-2385 A389 Set of 3 16.00 16.00

Souvenir Sheets

2386-2388 A389 Set of 3 10.50 10.50

History of the Theater — A390

No. 2389, 6d: a, Terra cotta statue. b, Tragic masks of King Priam. c, Euripides. d, Terra cotta statues of actors portraying drunks. e, Scene from Chinese play. f, Indian actors. g, Scene from Noh play, Japan. h, Scene from Clytemnestra.

No. 2390, 6d: a, William Shakespeare. b, Johann Wolfgang von Goethe. c, Moliere. d, Henrik Ibsen. e, George Bernard Shaw. f, Anton Chekhov. g, Sholom Aleichem. h, Tennessee Williams.

No. 2391, 25d, Sarah Bernhardt, vert. No. 2392, 25d, John Barrymore, vert.

Illustration reduced.

2001, Jan. 30 ***Perf. 14***

Sheets of 8, #a-h

2389-2390 A390 Set of 2 12.50 12.50

Souvenir Sheet

2391-2392 A390 Set of 2 6.50 6.50

Pokémon — A391

No. 2393: a, Beedrill. b, Arbok. c, Machop. d, Vileplume. e, Clefairy. f, Poliwhirl.

Illustration reduced.

2001, Feb. 1 ***Perf. 13¾***

2393 A391 7d Sheet of 6, #a-f 5.50 5.50

Souvenir Sheet

2394 A391 25d Articuno 3.25 3.25

Orchids — A392

Designs: 1.50d, Encyclia alata. 2d, Dendrobium lasiantherum. 3d, Cymbidiella pardalina. No. 2398, 4d, Cymbidium lowianum. 5d, Cypripedium irapeanum. 15d, Doritas pulcherrima.

No. 2401: a, Epidendrum pseudepidendrum. b, Eriopsis biloba. c, Masdevallia coccinea. d, Odontoglossum lindleyanum. e, Oerstedella wallisii. f, Paphiopedilum acmodontum. g, Laelia rubescens. h, Huntleya wallisii. i, Lycaste longiscapa. j, Maxillaria variabilis. k, Mexicoa ghiesbrechtiana. l, Miltoniopsis phalaenopsis.

No. 2402: a, Sobralia candida. b, Phragmipedium basseae. c, Phaius tankervilleae. d, Vanda rothchildiana. e, Telipogon pulchera. f, Rossioglossum insleayi.

No. 2403, 25d, Chaubardia heteroclita. No. 2404, 25d, Cychnoches loddigesii. No. 2405, 25d, Cattleya dowiana.

2001, Feb. 1 **Litho.** ***Perf. 14***

2395-2400 A392 Set of 6 5.50 5.50
2401 A392 4d Sheet of 12, #a-l 8.50 8.50
2402 A392 7d Sheet of 6, #a-f 7.50 7.50

Souvenir Sheets

2403-2405 A392 Set of 3 13.50 13.50

Hong Kong 2001 Stamp Exhibition (Nos. 2401-2405).

Medicinal Plants — A393

Designs: 3d, Pokeweed. 5d, Bay laurel. 10d, Coltsfoot. 15d, Marshmallow.

No. 2410, 8d, vert.: a, Restharrow. b, White willow. c, Sweet serge. d, Passion flower. e, Rosemary. f, Pepper.

No. 2411, 8d, vert.: a, Succory. b, Dandelion. c, Garlic. d, Hemp agrimony. e, Star thistle. f, Cypress.

No. 2412, 25d, Arbutus, vert. No. 2413, 25d, Olive, vert.

2001, Mar. 1

2406-2409 A393 Set of 4 5.75 5.75

Sheets of 6, #a-f

2410-2411 A393 Set of 2 17.00 17.00

Souvenir Sheets

2412-2413 A393 Set of 2 8.75 8.75

Japanese Art — A394

Designs: 1d, Mount Fuji and Tea Fields, by Matsuoka Eikyu. 2d, One heron from Herons and Flowers, by Okamo Shuki. No. 2416, 3d, Two herons from Herons and Flowers. No. 2417, 3d, The Realm of Gods in Yingzhou, by Tomioka Tessai. No. 2418, 4d, Peach Blossom Spring in Wuling, by Tessai. No. 2419, 4d, Egret, by Takeuchi Seiho. No. 2420, 5d, Spring Colors of the Lake and Mountains, by Shoda Gyokan. No. 2421, 5d, Sparrows, by Seiho. No. 2422, 10d, Red Lotus and White Goose, by Goun Saku. No. 2423, 10d, Portrait of Ushiwakamaru, by Kano Osanobu. 15d, Woman Selling Flowers, by Ito Shoha. 20d, The Sound of the Ocean, by Matsumoto Ichiyo.

No. 2426 - Birds and Flowers of the Twelve Months, by Sakai Hoitsu, 5d: a, Red and white flowers, bird on branch. b, Yellow flowers, bird flying. c, White flowers, bird on branch. d, Blue flowers. e, Sun, white and blue flowers. f, Red and white flowers.

No. 2427 - Birds and Flowers of the Twelve Months, by Hoitsu, 5d: a, Insect in sky, red pink and white flowers. b, Blue irises. c, Red, white light blue flowers. d, Fruit on tree. e, Bird standing in water. f, Snow-covered tree.

No. 2428 - Birds and Flowers, by Soga Chokuan, 7d: a, White flowers. b, Rooster at R. c, Roosters at L, red flower at R. d, Rooster at R, white flowers. e, Birds in sky. f, Roosters at L and R, white and red flowers. g, Roosters at L and R. Rooster at L, tree and red flowers.

No. 2429 - The Four Accomplishments, by Kaiho Yusho, 7d: a, Table. b, Two people near tree. c, Rock and hill. d, Two people. e, Rock and tree. f, One person. g, Three people. h, Three people, table.

No. 2430 - Book of Lacquer Paintings, by Shibata Zeshin: a, Flower. b, Birds. c, Butterfly on flower. d, Lobster.

No. 2431, 30d, Untitled painting (Yanagibashi at Ryogoku), by Utagawa Kuniyoshi, horiz. No. 2431, 30d, Poppies, by Tsuchida Bakusen, horiz. No. 2432, 30d, Puppies and Morning Glories, by Yamaguchi Soken, horiz. No. 2434, 30d, Deep Pool, by Nishimura Goun, horiz. No. 2435, 30d, Spring Farming Near a Riverside Village, by Mori Getsujo, horiz.

2001, Apr. 17

2414-2425 A394 Set of 12 14.50 14.50

Sheets of 6, #a-f

2426-2427 A394 Set of 2 10.50 10.50

Sheets of 8, #a-h

2428-2429 A394 Set of 2 20.00 20.00
2430 A394 10d Sheet of 4, #a-d 7.00 7.00

Imperf.

Size: 118x88mm

2431-2435 A394 Set of 5 26.00 26.00

Nos. 2428-2430 contain 28x42mm stamps. Phila Nippon '01, Japan.

Butterflies Type of 2000

Designs: 7d, Salamis temora. 8d, Cyrestus camillus. 20d, Papilio demodocus. 25d, Danaus chrysippus.

2001 ***Perf. 14¾x14***

2436-2439 A367 Set of 4 10.50 10.50

I Love Lucy Type of 2000

No. 2440: a, Lucy singing. b, Lucy with tambourine. c, Lucy with Ricky and Ethel. d, Lucy. e, Ethel and Ricky at piano. f, Ethel and Ricky on bench. g, Lucy at typewriter. h, Ethel singing. i, Lucy on bench.

No. 2441, 25d, Like #2440a, vert. No. 2442, 25d, Like #2440d, vert.

2001 ***Perf. 13¾***

2440 A354 5d Sheet of 9, #a-i 8.00 8.00

Souvenir Sheets

2441-2442 A354 Set of 2 8.75 8.75

Horses — A395

No. 2443, 7d, Head of: a, Akhal-Teke. b, Palomino. c, Kladruber. d, Paint Horse. e, Pinto. f, Kabardin.

No. 2444, 7d, horiz: a, Akhal-Teke. b, Kladruber. c, Palomino. d, Pinto. e, Paint Horse. f, Kabardin.

2001 **Litho.** ***Perf. 14***

Sheets of 6, #a-f

2443-2444 A395 Set of 2 10.50 10.50

Souvenir Sheet

2445 A395 25d Palomino 3.25 3.25

Three Stooges Type of 2000

No. 2446: a, Shemp as angel. b, Larry, Moe, Shemp, wearing feathered hats. c, Moe, Shemp and Larry wearing hospital uniforms. d, Larry with hammer, Shemp with gun, Moe. e, Moe, Larry, Shemp with woman. f, Moe and Shemp wearing tams. g, Moe, Larry, wagon wheel. h, Shemp, Moe, Larry in bus driver uniforms. i, Shemp hitting Larry and Moe.

No. 2447, 25d, Curly with telephone, skull, vert. No. 2448, 25d, Shemp on Moe's back, vert.

2001 ***Perf. 13¾***

2446 A353 5d Sheet of 9, #a-i 5.75 5.75

Souvenir Sheets

2447-2448 A353 Set of 2 6.25 6.25

I Love Lucy Type of 2000

No. 2449 : a, Lucy crawling on building ledge. b, Lucy standing against wall, arms outstretched. c, Lucy in apartment. d, Lucy reclining on ledge. e, Lucy with hand on forehead. f, Lucy reclining against wall. g, Ricky, bound and gagged Lucy. h, Lucy on sofa. i, Lucy, robber.

No. 2450, 25d, Lucy, robber, vert. No. 2451, 25d, Bound and gagged Lucy, seated Ethel, vert.

2001

2449 A354 5d Sheet of 9, #a-i 5.75 5.75

Souvenir Sheets

2450-2451 A354 Set of 2 6.25 6.25

Butterfly Type of 2000

2001 ***Perf. 14¾x14***

2452 A367 50d Coeliades forestan 6.25 6.25

2452A A367 75d Ornithoptera alexandrae 9.25 9.25

2452B A367 100dMorpho cypris 12.50 12.50

Queen Victoria (1819-1901) — A396

No. 2453, horiz.: a, Reading speech from throne. b, Benjamin Disraeli. c, Riding in procession from Parliament.

2001, Apr. 26 ***Perf. 14***

2453 A396 15d Sheet of 3, #a-c 5.75 5.75

Souvenir Sheet

2454 A396 25d Portrait 3.25 3.25

Queen Elizabeth II, 75th Birthday — A397

No. 2456: a, In uniform. b, In pink hat. c, Wearing crown, facing R. d, Wearing crown, facing L.

2001, Apr. 26 ***Perf. 14***

2455 A397 15d Sheet of 4, #a-d 7.50 7.50

Souvenir Sheet

2456 A397 25d In wedding dress 3.25 3.25

Flowers — A398

Designs: 1d, Disa unifloria. 4d, Monodora myristica. 6d, Clappertonia ficifolia. 20d, Calanthe rosea.

No. 2461, 7d: a, Vanilla planifolia. b, Strelitzia reginae. c, Gladiolus cardinalis. d, Arctotis venusta. e, Protea obtusifolia. f, Geissorhiza rochensis.

No. 2462, 7d: a, Canarina abyssinica. b, Amorphophallus abyssinicus. c, Calanthe rosea, diff. d, Gloriosa simplex. e, Clappertonia ficifolia, diff. f, Ansellia gigantea.

No. 2463, 25d, Arctoris venusta, diff. No. 2464, 25d, Geissorhiza rochensis, horiz.

2001, Mar. 1 **Litho.** ***Perf. 14***

2457-2460 A398 Set of 4 4.25 4.25

Sheets of 6, #a-f

2461-2462 A398 Set of 2 11.50 11.50

Souvenir Sheets

2463-2464 A398 Set of 2 6.75 6.75

Photomosaic of Queen Elizabeth II — A399

2001, Apr. 26

2465 A399 8d multi 1.00 1.00

Printed in sheets of 8, with and without marginal inscription "In Celebration of the 50th Anniversary of H. M. Queen Elizabeth II's Accession to the Throne.'

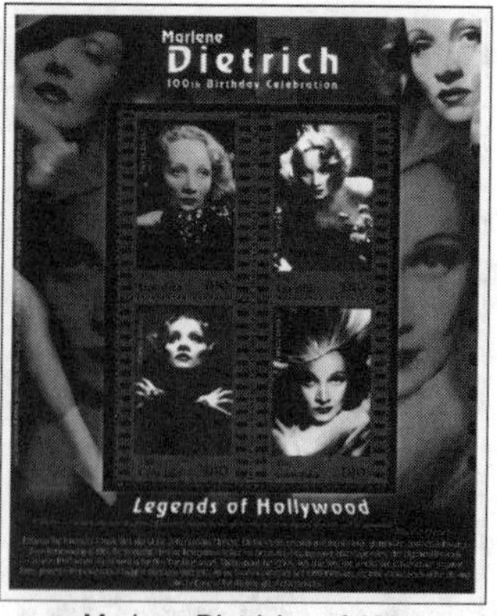

Marlene Dietrich — A400

No. 2466: a, With head on forearm. b, With bare shoulder. c, With arms crossed. d, Wearing hat.

2001, Apr. 26 ***Perf. 13¾***

2466 A400 10d Sheet of 4, #a-d 5.25 5.25

Mao Zedong (1893-1976) — A401

No. 2467: a, In 1935. b, In 1949. c, In 1951. 25d, In 1928.

2001, Apr. 26 ***Perf. 14***

2467 A401 15d Sheet of 3, #a-c 5.75 5.75

Souvenir Sheet

2468 A401 25d multi 3.25 3.25

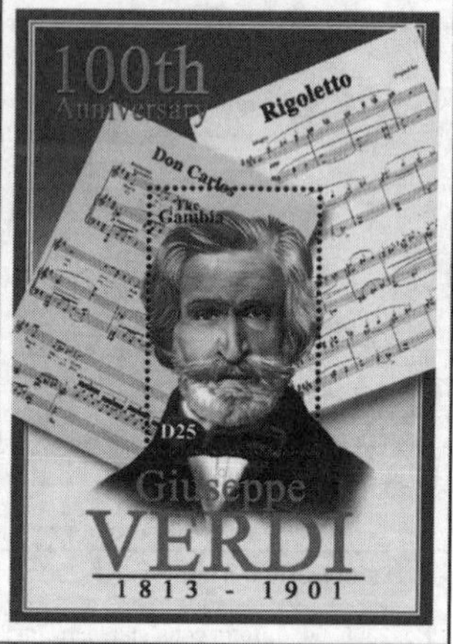

Giuseppe Verdi (1813-1901), Opera Composer — A402

No. 2469: a, Verdi with gray hair. b, Score and perfromers from La Traviata. c, Score and performer from Aida. d, Verdi with brown hair.

25d, Verdi and scores of Don Carlos and Rigoletto.

2001, Apr. 26

2469 A402 10d Sheet of 4, #a-d 5.25 5.25

Souvenir Sheet

2470 A402 25d multi 3.25 3.25

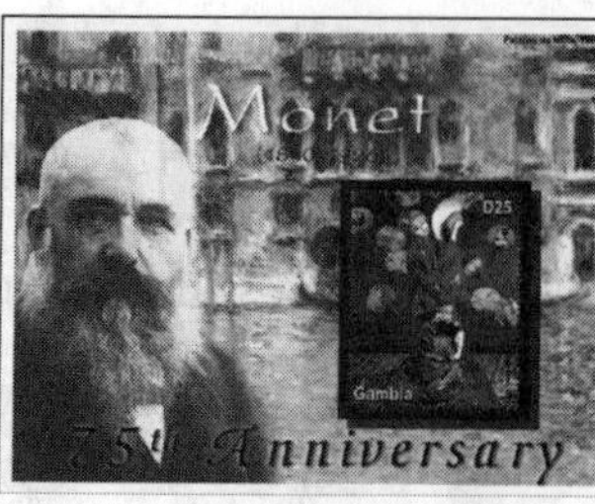

Monet Paintings — A403

No. 2471, horiz.: a, Madame Monet on the Sofa. b, The Picnic. c, The Luncheon. d, Jean Monet on His Mechanical Horse.

25d, La Japonaise.

2001, Apr. 26 ***Perf. 13¾***

2471 A403 10d Sheet of 4, #a-d 5.25 5.25

Souvenir Sheet

2472 A403 25d multi 3.25 3.25

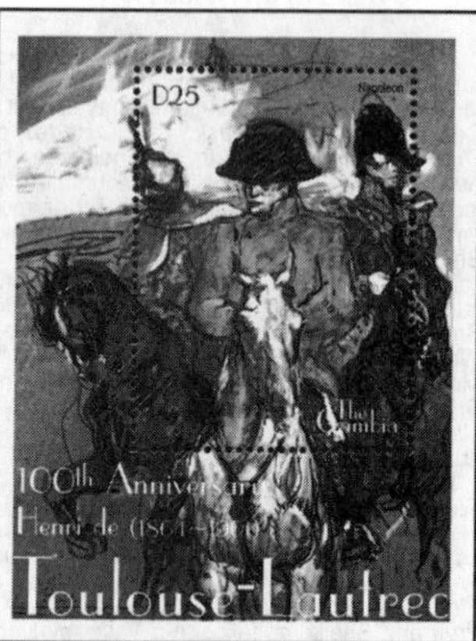

Toulouse-Lautrec Paintings — A404

No. 2473: a, At Le Rat Mort. b, The Milliner. c, Messaline.

25d, Napoleon.

2001, Apr. 26

2473 A404 7d Sheet of 3, #a-c 2.75 2.75

Souvenir Sheet

2474 A404 25d multi 3.25 3.25

Orchids — A405

Designs: 3d, Orchis morio. 4d, Fulophia speciosa. 5d, Angraecum leonis. 15d, Oeceoclades maculata.

No. 2479, 8d: a, Ceratostylis retisquama. b, Rangaeris rhipsalisocia. c, Phaius hybrid. d, Disa hybrid. e, Disa uniflora. f, Angraecum leonis.

No. 2480, 8d, horiz.: a, Satyrium erectum. b, Aeranthes grandiose. c, Aerangis somasticta. d, Polystachya bella. e, Eulophia guineensis. f, Disa blackii.

No. 2481, 25d, Aerangis curnowiana. No. 2482, 25d, Disa kirstenbosch pride.

2001, June 15 ***Perf. 14***

2475-2478 A405 Set of 4 3.50 3.50

Sheets of 6, #a-f

2479-2480 A405 Set of 2 12.00 12.00

Souvenir Sheets

2481-2482 A405 Set of 2 6.25 6.25

Belgica 2001 Intl. Stamp Exhibition, Brussels (#2479-2480).

SOS Children's Village A406

2001, July 2

2483 A406 10d multi 1.25 1.25

Flora & Fauna A407

Designs: 2d, Hoopoe. 3d, Great spotted cuckoo. 4d, Plain tiger butterfly. 5d, Zebra duiker. 10d, Sooty managbey. 20d, Greater kudu.

No. 2490, 8d: a, Hippopotamus. b, Elephant. c, Parusta simplex. d, Gray heron. e, Charaxes imperialis. f, Gloriosa simplex.

No. 2491, 8d: a, Alpine swift. b, Blotched genet. c, Thomas' galago. d, Carmine bee-eater. e, Tree pangolin. f, Campbell's monkey.

No. 2492, 8d: a, Gray parrot. b, Rachel's weaver. c, European bee-eater. d, River kingfisher. e, Red river hog. f, Bushbuck.

No. 2493, 8d: a, Blue diadem butterfly. b, Fire-footed rope squirrel. c, Clappertonia ficifolia. d, Costus spectabilis. e, African migrant butterfly. f, Giant African snail.

No. 2494, 25d, Long-tailed pangolin, vert. No. 2495, 25d, Eurasian kestrel, vert.

2001, July 16

2484-2489 A407 Set of 6 5.50 5.50

Sheets of 6, #a-f

2490-2493 A407 Set of 4 24.00 24.00

Souvenir Sheets

2494-2495 A407 Set of 2 6.25 6.25

A408

Ducks and Geese — A409

Designs: 2d, Blue-winged teal. No. 2497, 3d, Red-crested pochard. No. 2498, 4d, Falcated teal. No. 2499, 5d, Mandarin duck. No. 2500, 10d, King eider. 15d, Hooded merganser.

No. 2502, 3d, Wood duck. No. 2503, 4d, Mallard. No. 2504, 5d, Barrow's goldeneye. No. 2505, 10d, Bufflehead.

No. 2506, 7d, horiz.: a, Barrow's goldeneye. b, Harlequin duck. c, Pintail. d, Black-bellied whistling duck. e, Cinnamon teal. f, Surf scoter.

No. 2507, 7d, horiz.: a, Black scoter. b, Black duck. c, Green-winged teal. d, Bufflehead. e, Red-breasted merganser. f, Fulvous whistling duck.

No. 2508, 8d: a, European wigeon. b, Mallard. c, Garganey. d, Pintail, diff. e, Shoveler. f, Green-winged teal.

No. 2509, 8d: a, Black duck. b, Bufflehead. c, Cinnamon teal, diff. d, Goldeneye. e, Ruddy shelduck. f, Ferruginous duck.

No. 2510, 8d: a, Masked duck. b, Old squaw. c, Ring-necked duck. d, Harlequin duck, diff. e, Redhead. f, Canvasback.

No. 2511, 25d, American wigeon. No. 2512, 25d, Wood duck. No. 2513, 25d, Baikal teal.

No. 2514, 25d, Green-winged teal, horiz. No. 2515, 25d, Canada geese, horiz.

2001, July 16

2496-2501 A408 Set of 6 4.75 4.75
2502-2505 A409 Set of 4 2.75 2.75

Sheets of 6, #a-f

2506-2507 A409 Set of 2 10.00 10.00
2508-2510 A408 Set of 3 17.50 17.50

Souvenir Sheets

2511-2513 A408 Set of 3 9.00 9.00
2514-2515 A409 Set of 2 6.00 6.00

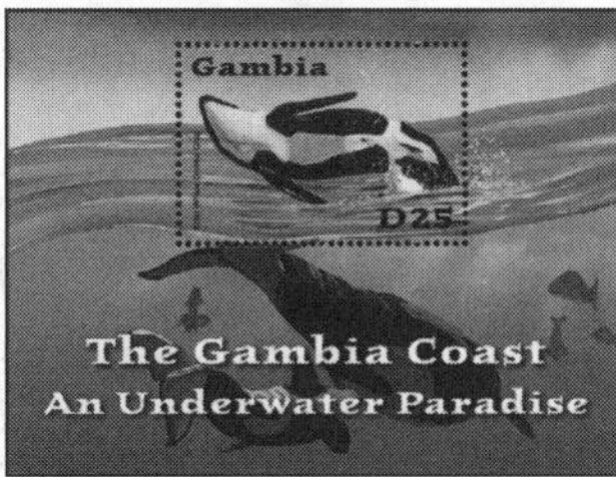

Cetaceans — A410

No. 2516, 7d: a, Killer whale (denomination at UR). b, Sperm whale (denomination at UR). c, Strap-toothed whale. d, Humpback whale. e, Southern right whale. f, Beluga.

No. 2517, 7d: a, Killer whale (denomination at LR). b, Sperm whale (denomination at LR). c, Narwhal. d, Gray whale. e, Blue whale. f, Northern right whale.

No. 2518, 25d, Killer whale. No. 2519, 25d, Humpback whale.

2001, July 16 ***Sheets of 6, #a-f***

2516-2517 A410 Set of 2 10.00 10.00

Souvenir Sheets

2518-2519 A410 Set of 2 6.00 6.00

A411

Trains A412

Designs: 2d, Rheingold Express. No. 2521, 10d, Amtrak train. No. 2522, 15d, The Blue Train. 20d, Cisalpino.

4d, Eurostar. No. 2525, 7d, Mallard. No. 2526, 10d, Rocket. No. 2527, TGV.

No. 2528, 7d: a, Eurostar, diff. b, Flying Hamburger. c, Coast Starlight. d, Tres Grande Vitesse. e, Golden Arrow. f, Shinkanzen "Max."

No. 2529, 7d: a, Siliguri to Darjeeling, India train. b, California Zephyr. c, Flying Scotsman. d, Trans-Siberian Express. e, Indian-Pacific. f, Thunersee.

No. 2530, 8d: a, Le Shuttle. b, Nord Express. c, 2-6-0, Switzerland. d, Duchess. e, Balkan Express. f, Class 44 2-10-0, Germany.

No. 2531, 8d: a, 7029 Clun Castle. b, Puffing Billy. c, ICE Electric. d, 4-4-2 S, Belgium. e, 2-8-2, Germany. f, PLM Coupe-Vents.

No. 2532, 25d, Cape Town to Victoria Falls train. No. 2533, 25d, The Southerner.

No. 2534, 25d, Stanier Class 5 4-6-0. No. 2535, 25d, Flying Scotsman, diff.

2001, July 31 ***Perf. 14***

2520-2523 A411 Set of 4 5.75 5.75
2524-2527 A412 Set of 4 4.50 4.50

Sheets of 6, #a-f

2528-2529 A411 Set of 2 10.00 10.00
2530-2531 A412 Set of 2 12.00 12.00

Souvenir Sheets

2532-2533 A411 Set of 2 6.00 6.00
2534-2535 A412 Set of 2 6.00 6.00

British Royal Navy — A413

Designs: 3d, St. Andrew, 1600s. 4d, Fleet maneuvers, 1914. 10d, HMS Illustrious, 1899. 15d, Battle of North Foreland, 1666.

No. 2540, 7d, horiz.: a, Mary Rose, 1512. b, Attack off Quebec, 1759. c, Armada campaign, 1588. d, Battle of Scheveningen, 1653. e, Blanche captures La Pique, 1795. f, Embarkation at Dover, 1520.

No. 2541, 7d, horiz. - Battles: a, Quiberon Bay, 1759. b, Barfleur, 1692. c, Nile, 1798. d, Trafalgar, 1805. e, Jutland, 1916. f, Camperdown, 1797.

No. 2542, 7d, horiz.: a, Battle of Navarino, 1827. b, Sinking of Eurydice, 1878. c, HMS Pantaloon captures Borboleta, 1845. d, Dardanelles, 1915. e, HMS Pickle captures Bolodora, 1829. f, HMS Invincible and Inflexible, Battle of the Falklands, 1914.

No. 2543, 25d, Ark Royal, 1582, horiz. No. 2544, 25d, Sovereign of the Seas, 1637, horiz.

2001, Sept. 6 **Litho.**

2536-2539 A413 Set of 4 3.75 3.75

Sheets of 6, #a-f

2540-2542 A413 Set of 3 15.00 15.00

Souvenir Sheets

2543-2544 A413 Set of 2 6.00 6.00

2002 World Cup Soccer Championships, Japan and Korea — A414

Jules Rimet Trophy and: 2d, Netherlands flag and player. 3d, Argentina flag and player. 4d, Ibaraki Kashima Stadium, Japan, horiz. 5d, George Best and Northern Ireland flag. 10d, Dino Zoff and Italian flag. 15d, Poster for 1938 tournament, France.

25d, Pat Bonner making save for Ireland.

2001, Sept. 6

2545-2550 A414 Set of 6 4.75 4.75

Souvenir Sheet

2551 A414 25d multi 3.00 3.00

No. 2551 contains one 56x42mm stamp.

European Royalty — A415

No. 2552: a, King Harald V, Queen Sonja, Norway. b, Queen Margrethe II, Denmark. c, King Carl XVI Gustaf and Queen Silvia, Sweden. d, King Juan Carlos, Queen Sofia, Spain. e, Queen Beatrix, Netherlands. f, King Albert II, Queen Paola, Belgium.

No. 2553, 25d, Crown Prince Haakon, Princess Mette-Marit, Norway. No. 2554, 25d, King Juan Carlos, Spain, vert.

Perf. 14¼x14½, 14½x14¼

2001, Nov. 15

2552 A415 7d Sheet of 6, #a-f 5.00 5.00

Souvenir Sheets

2553-2554 A415 Set of 2 5.75 5.75

Queen Mother Type of 1999

No. 2555: a, Duchess of York, Princess Elizabeth, 1928. b, Lady Elizabeth Bowes-Lyon, 1923. c, Queen Elizabeth, 1946. d, Queen Mother, Prince Harry.

40d, Queen Mother celebrating 89th birthday, 1989.

2001, Dec. 13 ***Perf. 14***

2555 A342 15d Sheet of 4, #a-d + label 7.00 7.00

Souvenir Sheet

Perf. 13¾

2556 A342 40d multi 4.50 4.50

No. 2556 contains one 38x50mm stamp.

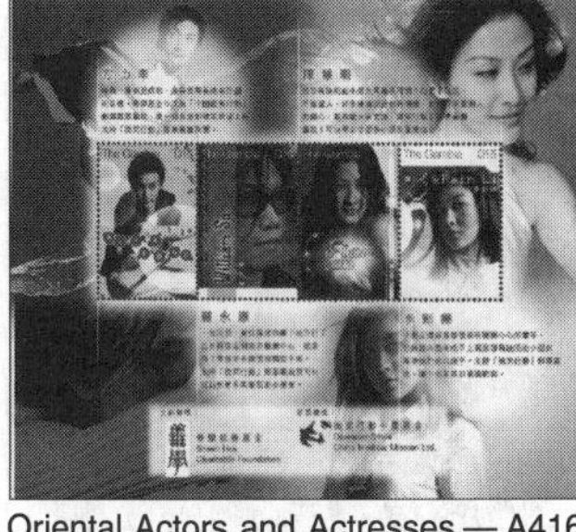

Oriental Actors and Actresses — A416

No. 2557, 15d: a, Alex Fong. b, William So. c, Flora Chan. d, Rain Li.

No. 2558, 15d - Kelly Chen: a, Close-up. b, As child, with cherry. c, On swing. d, As child, with hand above eyes.

No. 2559, 15d - Jacky Cheung: a, At L, laughing, looking to R. b, Looking forward, mouth open. c, At R, laughing, looking L. d, Looking forward, mouth closed.

No. 2560, 15d - Andy Hui, and Chinese characters at: a, L (pink suit). b, R (yellow suit). c, L (yellow suit). d, R (pink suit).

No. 2561, 15d - Miriam Yeung, with roses and petals at: a, LR. b, LL. c, UR. d, UL.

2001, Nov. 5 Litho. ***Perf. 13¾x13¼***

Sheets of 4, #a-d

2557-2561 A416 Set of 5 35.00 35.00

New Year 2002 (Year of the Horse) — A417

No. 2562 - Denomination at: a, UR. b, UL. c, LR. d, LL.

20d, African zebra.

2001, Dec. 26 ***Perf. 13***

2562 A417 6d Miniature sheet of 4, #a-d 2.75 2.75

Souvenir Sheet

Perf. 12½x13

2563 A417 20d multi 2.25 2.25

No. 2563 contains one 68x31mm triangular stamp.

Jacqueline Kennedy Onassis (1929-94) — A418

No. 2564: a, As baby. b, At age 6. c, Engagement to J.F.K. d, In wedding gown, 1955. e, In 1960. f, In 1980.
30d, At wedding to Aristotle Onassis.

2002, Jan. 24 ***Perf. 14***
2564 A418 7d Sheet of 6, #a-f 5.00 5.00

Souvenir Sheet

2565 A418 30d multi 3.50 3.50

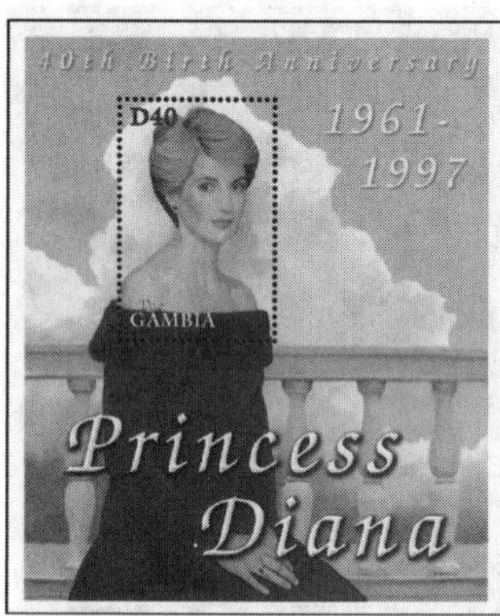

Princess Diana (1961-97) — A419

No. 2566 - Diana and: a, Coral rose. b, White rose. c, Yellow rose. d, Purple rose.
40d, Portrait.

2002, Jan. 24
2566 A419 15d Sheet of 4, #a-d 7.00 7.00

Souvenir Sheet

2567 A419 40d multi 4.75 4.75

Moths
A420

Designs: 2d, Tiger moth. 3d, Hawk moth. No. 2570, 10d, Pericopid moth. 15d, Spurge hawk.
No. 2572, 10d (50x38mm): a, Sloane's urania. b, Saturniid moth. c, Black witch moth. d, Burnet moth on plant. e, Day-flying moth. f, Lime hawk moth.
No. 2573, 10d (50x38mm): a, Emperor moth. b, Millar's tiger. c, Hawk moth, diff. d, Phrygionis privignara. e, Burnet moth, waterfall. f, Urania leilus.
No. 2574, 40d, Emerald moth. No. 2575, 40d, Red under-wing moth, vert.

Perf. 14, 13¾ (#2572-2573)

2002, Jan. 24
2568-2571 A420 Set of 4 3.50 3.50

Sheets of 6, #a-f

2572-2573 A420 Set of 2 14.00 14.00

Souvenir Sheets

2574-2575 A420 Set of 2 9.25 9.25

United We Stand — A421

2002, Feb. 6 ***Perf. 13¾x13¼***
2576 A421 20d multi 2.25 2.25

Issued in sheets of 4.

Reign of Queen Elizabeth II, 50th Anniv. — A422

No. 2577: a, With beige hat. b, With red hat. c, With blue hat. d, Near vehicle.
40d, Wearing uniform.

2002, Feb. 6 ***Perf. 14½***
2577 A422 15d Sheet of 4, #a-d 6.75 6.75

Souvenir Sheet

2578 A422 40d multi 4.50 4.50

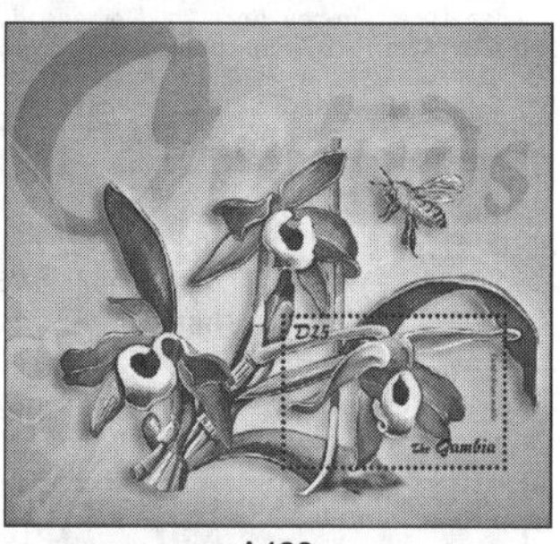

A423

Orchids — A424

No. 2579, vert.: a, Machu piechu. b, Masdevallia copper angel. c, Masdevallia hirtzi. d, Tuakau canoy.
No. 2580: a, Eriopsis sceptrum. b, Sarcanthopsis muellem. c, Bougainville white. d, Telipogon klotzchianus.
No. 2581, 7d: a, Richard Mueller. b, Colmanara wildcat. c, Cycnoches chlorochilon. d, Vanda coerylea. e, Disa blackii. f, Unnamed.
No. 2582, 7d: a, Seagulls beaulu queen. b, Hazel Boyd. c, Costa Rica. d, Dendrobium infudibulum. e, Disa hybrid. f, Chysis.
No. 2583, 6d, horiz.: a, Spathoglottis portus-finschii. b, Dendrobium macrophyllum. c, Grammaneis ellisii. d, Stanhopea wardii. e, Dendrobium nindi. f, Dendrobium williamsianum.
No. 2584, 7d: a, Seutieama steeli. b, Dendrobium inaequale. c, Dendrobium lasiathera. d, Calypso bulbosa. e, Vanda hindsii. f, Dendrobium violaceoflavens.
No. 2585, 8d, horiz.: a, Phaleonopsis rosenstomii. b, Cypripedium guttatum. c, Cypripedium reginae. d, Dendrobium engae. e, Diplocaulobium hydrophilum. f, Dendrobium cuthbertsonii.
No. 2586, 25d, Dendrobium nobile. No. 2587, 25d, Ancidium alliance, vert.
No. 2588, 25d, Menadenium labiosum. No. 2589, 25d, Dendrobium spectabile. No. 2590, 25d, Dendrobium canaliculatum, horiz.

2001, June 15 Litho. ***Perf. 14***
2579 A423 7d Sheet of 4, #a-d 2.50 2.50
2580 A424 10d Sheet of 4, #a-d 3.60 3.60

Sheets of 6, #a-f

2581-2582 A423 Set of 2 7.75 7.75
2583-2585 A424 Set of 3 11.50 11.50

Souvenir Sheets

2586-2587 A423 Set of 2 4.50 4.50
2588-2590 A424 Set of 3 6.75 6.75

Nos. 2579-2590 were not available until 2002. Belgica 2001 Intl. Stamp Exhibition (#2579).

Wildlife
A425

Designs: 2d, Martial eagle. 4d, Lion. 5d, Aardvark. 10d, Lion cub, vert.
No. 2595, 7d: a, Lion cub. b, Water buffalo. c, Topi. d, Hyena. e, Secretary bird. f, Genet.
No. 2596, 7d: a, Reedbuck. b, Hippopotamus. c, Waterbuck and malachite kingfisher. d, Hoopoe. e, White pelican. f, Waterbuck.
No. 2597, 25d, Hippopotamus. No. 2598, 25d, Crocodile.

2001, July 16
2591-2594 A425 Set of 4 1.90 1.90

Sheets of 6, #a-f

2595-2596 A425 Set of 2 7.75 7.75

Souvenir Sheets

2597-2598 A425 Set of 2 4.50 4.50

Nos. 2591-2598 were not available until 2002.

Pres. Theodore Roosevelt (1858-1919) — A426

No. 2599: a, Wearing hat and uniform. b, Close-up. c, With hand on chair. d, Wearing hat and neckerchief.
40d, Close-up, diff.

2002, Jan. 24
2599 A426 15d Sheet of 4, #a-d 7.00 7.00

Souvenir Sheet

2600 A426 40d multi 4.75 4.75

Betty Boop — A427

No. 2602, 40d, With gray ribbon in hair, horiz. No. 2603, 40d, With ice cream sundae.

2002, Feb. 13 ***Perf. 13¾***
2601 A427 7d shown .80 .80

Souvenir Sheets

2602-2603 A427 Set of 2 9.00 9.00

No. 2601 was issued in sheets of 9.

Shirley Temple in "Little Miss Broadway" — A428

No. 2604, horiz.: a, With man and old woman. b, Close-up. c, Waving. d, Holding man's tie. e, At hotel desk with men. f, Woman watching Temple point to tooth.
No. 2605: a, Dancing with young man. b, Dancing with old man with hat. c, Sitting with boy. d, Holding hands with old man.
30d, Wearing tiara and dancing with young man.

2002, Feb. 13
2604 A428 8d Sheet of 6, #a-f 5.50 5.50
2605 A428 10d Sheet of 4, #a-d 4.50 4.50

Souvenir Sheet

2606 A428 30d multi 3.50 3.50

2002 Winter Olympics, Salt Lake City — A429

Designs: No. 2607, 20d, Curling. No. 2608, 20d, Ski jumping.

2002, Mar. 18 ***Perf. 14***
2607-2608 A429 Set of 2 4.50 4.50
a. Souvenir sheet, #2607-2608 4.50 4.50

Chiune Sugihara, Japanese Diplomat Who Saved Jews in World War II — A430

2002, Apr. 29 ***Perf. 13½x13¼***
2609 A430 10d multi 1.10 1.10

Printed in sheets of 4.

Intl. Year of Mountains — A431

No. 2610: a, Winkler Tower, Italy. b, Mt. Huanstan Chico, Peru. c, Hodaka Mountains, Japan. d, Mustagh Ata, Kashmir.
40d, Mt. Myoko, Japan.

2002, July 1 ***Perf. 13¼x13½***
2610 A431 15d Sheet of 4, #a-d 6.50 6.50

Souvenir Sheet

2611 A431 40d multi 4.25 4.25

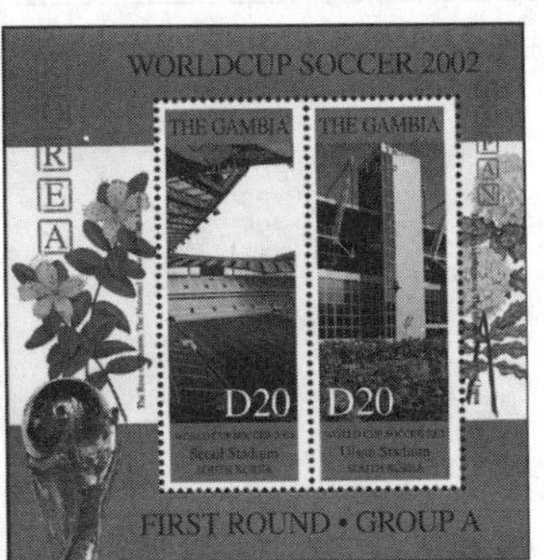
2002 World Cup Soccer Championships, Japan and Korea — A432

Players, dates and locations of matches - No. 2612, 9d: a, France v. Senegal. b, Uruguay v. Denmark. c, France v. Uruguay. d, Denmark v. Senegal. e, Denmark v. France. f, Senegal v. Uruguay.

No. 2613, 9d: a, Paraguay v. South Africa. b, Spain v. Slovenia. c, Spain v. Paraguay. d, South Africa v. Slovenia. e, South Africa v. Spain. f, Slovenia v. Paraguay.

No. 2614, 9d: a, Brazil v. Turkey. b, China v. Costa Rica. c, Brazil v. China. d, Costa Rica v. Turkey. e, Costa Rica v. Brazil. f, Turkey v. China.

No. 2615, 9d: a, South Korea v. Poland. b, US v. Portugal. c, South Korea v. US. d, Portugal v. Poland. e, Portugal v. South Korea. f, Poland v. US.

No. 2616, 9d: a, Germany v. Saudi Arabia. b, Ireland v. Cameroun. c, Germany v. Ireland. d, Cameroun v. Saudi Arabia. e, Cameroun v. Germany. f, Saudi Arabia v. Ireland.

No. 2617, 9d: a, England v. Sweden. b, Argentina v. Nigeria. c, Sweden v. Nigeria. d, Argentina v. England. e, Sweden v. Argentina. f, Nigeria v. England.

No. 2618, 9d: a, Croatia v. Mexico. b, Italy v. Ecuador. c, Italy v. Croatia. d, Mexico v. Ecuador. e, Mexico v. Italy. f, Ecuador v. Croatia.

No. 2619, 9d: a, Japan v. Belgium. b, Russia v. Tunisia. c, Japan v. Russia. d, Tunisia v. Belgium. e, Tunisia v. Japan. f, Belgium v. Russia.

Stadia and dates of matches between - No. 2620, 20d: a, France v. Senegal. b, Uruguay v. Denmark.

No. 2621, 20d: a, France v. Uruguay. b, Denmark v. Senegal.

No. 2622, 20d: a, Denmark v. France. b, Senegal v. Uruguay.

No. 2623, 20d: a, Paraguay v. South Africa. b, Spain v. Slovenia.

No. 2624, 20d: a, Spain v. Paraguay. b, South Africa v. Slovenia.

No. 2625, 20d, a, South Africa v. Spain. b, Slovenia v. Paraguay.

No. 2626, 20d: a, Brazil v. Turkey. b, China v. Costa Rica.

No. 2627, 20d: a, Brazil v. China. b, Costa Rica v. Turkey.

No. 2628, 20d: a, Costa Rica v. Brazil. b, Turkey v. China.

No. 2629, 20d: a, South Korea v. Poland. b, US v. Portugal.

No. 2630, 20d: a, South Korea v. US. b, Portugal v. Poland.

No. 2631, 20d: a, Portugal v. South Korea. b, Poland v. US.

No. 2632, 20d: a, Germany v. Saudi Arabia. b, Ireland v. Cameroun.

No. 2633, 20d: a, Germany v. Ireland. b, Cameroun v. Saudi Arabia.

No. 2634, 20d: a, Cameroun v. Germany. b, Saudi Arabia v. Ireland.

No. 2635, 20d: a, England v. Sweden. b, Argentina v. Nigeria.

No. 2636, 20d: a, Sweden v. Nigeria. b, Argentina v. England.

No. 2637, 20d: a, Sweden v. Argentina. b, Nigeria v. England.

No. 2638, 20d: a, Croatia v. Mexico. b, Italy v. Ecuador.

No. 2639, 20d: a, Italy v. Croatia. b, Mexico v. Ecuador.

No. 2640, 20d: a, Mexico v. Italy. b, Ecuador v. Croatia.

No. 2641, 20d: a, Japan v. Belgium. b, Russia v. Tunisia.

No. 2642, 20d: a, Japan v. Russia. b, Tunisia v. Belgium.

No. 2643, 20d: a, Tunisia v. Japan. b, Belgium v. Russia.

2002, July 1 *Perf. 13¼*

Sheets of 6, #a-f

2612-2619 A432 Set of 8 47.50 47.50

Souvenir Sheets

2620-2643 A432 Set of 24 100.00 100.00

See Nos. 2654-2656 for sheets with match results.

Popeye — A433

No. 2644, 10d: a, Popeye on cross-country skis. b, Popeye ski jumping. c, Popeye slaloming. d, Popeye snowboarding.

No. 2645, 10d: a, Swee'Pea on sled. b, Olive Oyl on skis. c, Brutus. d, Wimpy on ice skates.

No. 2646, 25d, Popeye and Olive in bobsled. No. 2647, 25d, Brutus playing hockey. No. 2648, 25d, Olive on ice skates. No. 2649, 25d, Popeye speed skating, horiz.

2002, June 17 **Litho.** *Perf. 14*

Sheets of 6, #a-f

2644-2645 A433 Set of 2 8.50 8.50

Souvenir Sheets

2646-2649 A433 Set of 4 11.00 11.00

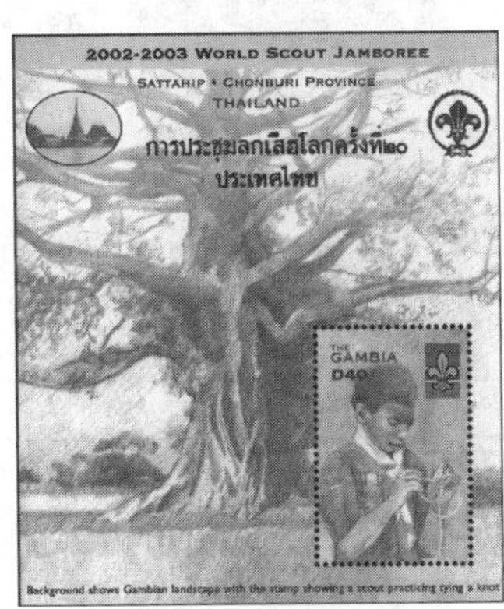
20th World Scout Jamboree, Thailand — A434

No. 2650: a, Scout with bugle. b, Scout making fire. c, Scout fishing.

40d, Scout tying knot.

2002, July 1 *Perf. 13½x13¼*

2650 A434 15d Sheet of 3, #a-c 4.75 4.75

Souvenir Sheet

2651 A434 40d multi 4.25 4.25

Intl. Year of Ecotourism — A435

No. 2652: a, Bird-of-Paradise flower. b, Goliath heron. c, Baobab tree. d, Roan antelope. e, Red tip butterfly. f, Egyptian cobra.

No. 2653, Yellow-billed stork.

2002, July 1

2652 A435 9d Sheet of 6, #a-d 5.75 5.75

Souvenir Sheet

2653 A435 9d multi .95 .95

Nos. 2616, 2617 and 2619 Redrawn With Match Scores

No. 2654, 9d: a, Germany 8, Saudi Arabia 0. b, Ireland 1, Cameroun 1. c, Germany 1, Ireland 1. d, Cameroun 1, Saudi Arabia 0. e, Cameroun 0, Germany 2. f, Saudi Arabia 0, Ireland 3

No. 2655, 9d: a, England 1, Sweden 1. b, Argentina 1, Nigeria 0. c, Sweden 2, Nigeria 1. d, Argentina 0, England 1. e, Sweden 1, Argentina 1. f, Nigeria 0, England 0.

No. 2656, 9d: a, Japan 2, Belgium 2. b, Russia 2, Tunisia 0. c, Japan 1, Russia 0. d, Tunisia 1, Belgium 1. e, Japan 2, Tunisia 0. f, Belgium 3, Russia 2.

2002, July 15 *Perf. 13¼*

Sheets of 6, #a-f

2654-2656 A432 Set of 3 17.00 17.00

Elvis Presley (1935-77) A436

2002, Aug. 19 *Perf. 13½x13¾*

2657 A436 5d multi .50 .50

Things from the Netherlands — A437

Netherlands Lighthouses — A438

Netherlands Postage Stamps, 150th Anniv. — A439

Women's Traditional Costumes of the Netherlands — A440

No. 2658: a, Farm. b, Porcelain. c, Building. d, Ice skaters. e, Cheese, flowers and wooden shoes. f, Prince Willem-Alexander and his bride.

No. 2659: a, Den Helder. b, Terschelling. c, Maasvlakte. d, Ijmuiden. e, Westkapelle. f, Breskens.

No. 2660: a, Netherlands #1. b, Netherlands #B72. c, Netherlands #279. d, Netherlands #586. e, Netherlands #620. f, Netherlands #1108a.

No. 2661: a, Woman from Friesland (plaid headdress). b, Back of woman from Utrecht. c, Woman and child from Noord-Holland.

2002, Aug. 30 *Perf. 13½x13¼*

2658 A437 10d Sheet of 6, #a-f 6.00 6.00

2659 A438 10d Sheet of 6, #a-f 6.00 6.00

Perf. 13¼x13½

2660 A439 10d Sheet of 6, #a-f 6.00 6.00

Perf. 13¼

2661 A440 20d Sheet of 3, #a-c 6.00 6.00

Amphilex 2002 Intl. Stamp Exhibition, Amsterdam.

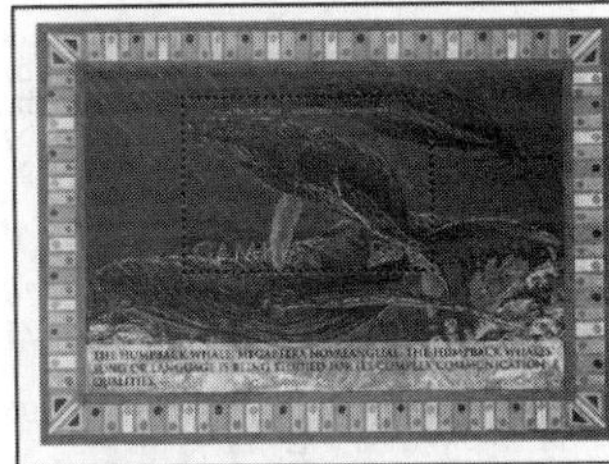
Marine Mammals and Flowers — A441

No. 2662, 10d: a, Blue whale. b, Pan-tropical spotted dolphin. c, Killer whale. d, Minke whale. e, Sperm whale. f, Pilot whale.

No. 2663, 10d: a, Juba-jamba. b, Devil's tongue. c, Rattle box. d, Vernonia purpurea. e, Seaside purslane. f, Fireball lily.

No. 2664, 50d, Humpback whale. No. 2665, 50d, Cape weed, swamp arum, vert.

2002, Sept. 23 *Perf. 14*

Sheets of 6, #a-f

2662-2663 A441 Set of 2 10.50 10.50

Souvenir Sheets

2664-2665 A441 Set of 2 9.00 9.00

A442

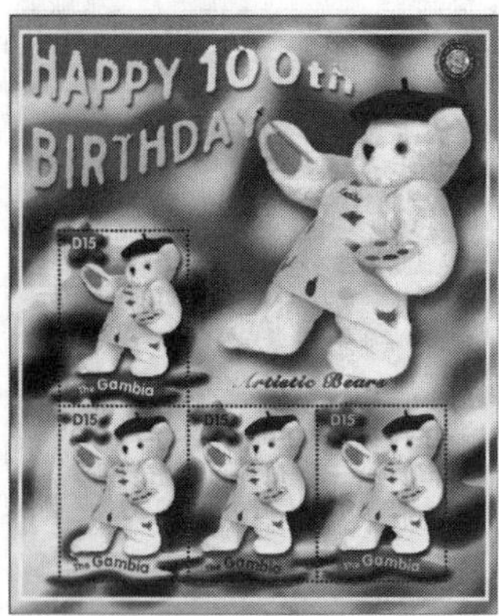

Teddy Bears, Cent. — A443

No. 2666: a, Bear with green feathered cap. b, Bear with beer stein. c, Bear with flower bouquet. d, Bear with mountain hat.

No. 2667 - Color of denomination and country name: a, White. b, Red violet. c, Blue violet. d, Green.

2002, Oct. 21 ***Perf. 14***

2666 A442 15d Sheet of 4, #a-d 5.50 5.50

Perf. 14¼

2667 A443 15d Sheet of 4, #a-d 5.50 5.50

Christmas — A444

Designs: 3d, Madonna of Loreto, by Perugino. 5d, Madonna della Consolazione, by Perugino. 7d, Adoration of the Shepherds, by Perugino. 15d, Transfiguration of Christ, by Giovanni Bellini. 35d, Adoration of the Magi, by Perugino.

45d, Christ Blessing, by Bellini.

2002, Nov. 4 ***Perf. 14***

2668-2672 A444 Set of 5 5.75 5.75

Souvenir Sheet

2673 A444 45d multi 4.00 4.00

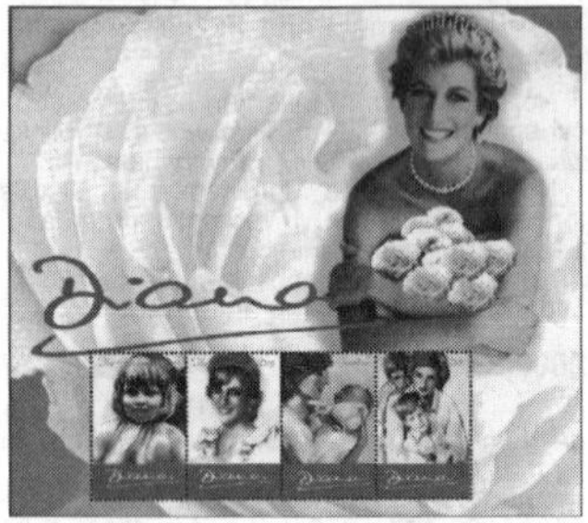

Princess Diana (1961-97) — A445

No. 2674, 15d - With red panel at bottom: a, As child. b, Wearing tiara. c, Holding baby. d, With children.

No. 2675, 15d: a, Wearing red hat. b, Wearing red and white hat. c, Wearing white gown. d, Wearing black gown and choker.

2002, Nov. 18

Sheets of 4, #a-d

2674-2675 A445 Set of 2 10.50 10.50

Souvenir Sheet

Gold-banded Forester Butterfly — A446

2002 **Litho.** ***Perf. 14***

2676 A446 60d multi 5.25 5.25

Birds — A447

No. 2677: a, Black-crowned crane. b, Barn owl. c, African pygmy kingfisher. d, Audouin's gull. e, Royal tern. f, Blue-bellied roller.

2002

2677 A447 7d Sheet of 6, #a-f 3.75 3.75

Pres. John F. Kennedy (1917-63) — A448

No. 2678, 15d: a, With daughter Caroline. b, At typewriter. c, At wedding to Jacqueline. d, With Jacqueline.

No. 2679, 15d, vert: a, In naval uniform. b, As child. c, Wearing shirt with open collar. d, At microphone.

2002, Nov. 8

Sheets of 4, #a-d

2678-2679 A448 Set of 2 10.50 10.50

A449

Trains
A450

Designs: 2d, Paris, Lyon & Mediterranean Railway. 3d, Zugspitz rack train, Germany. No. 2682, 10d, Austrian State Railway Class 210. 15d, State Railway of Saxony.

4d, 1922 Great Britain Class A1 4-6-2. 5d, 1957 Tee four car train. No. 2686, 7d, 1928 German Rheingold Mitropa car. 8d, 1900 German Gerda 4-4-0.

No. 2688, 7d: a, French Natl. Railway Series 68. b, French Natl. Railway Mistral. c, Prussian State Railway. d, Austrian Southern Railway. e, Paris-Orleans Railway. f, German Federal Railway E10.

No. 2689, 7d: a, Royal Prussian Union Railway. b, Austrian Federal Railway. c, German Rugen steam locomotive. d, Rh B Ge 2/4 electric locomotive. e, Panoramic Express, Switzerland. f, Brunig steam engine, Swiss Natl. Railway.

No. 2690, 10d: a, 1813 Puffing Billy, Great Britain. b, Adler, Germany, 1836. c, 1906 German 4-6-0. d, Class 132 Co-Co, Germany.

No. 2691, 10d: a, 1832 Brother Jonathan 4-2-0, US. b, Medoc Class 2-4-0, Germany and Switzerland, 1857. c, 1908 German Class S 3/6 4-6-2. d, 1959 German Class VT 11.5.

No. 2692, 10d: a, 1843 Beuth 2-2-2, Germany. b, 1852 Crampton 4-2-0, France. c, 1932 Sut 877 Flying Hamburger, Germany. d, 1970 Class 103.1 Co-Co, Germany.

No. 2693, 25d, German Federal Railway V200. No. 2694, 25d, German Federal Railway Trans-Europe Express.

No. 2695, 25d, 1953 VT10.5, Germany. No. 2696, 25d,1973 Class ET 403 four-car electric, Germany.

2002

2680-2683	A449	Set of 4	2.60	2.60
2684-2687	A450	Set of 4	2.10	2.10

Sheets of 6, #a-f

2688-2689	A449	Set of 2	7.25	7.25

Sheets of 4, #a-d

2690-2692	A450	Set of 3	10.50	10.50

Souvenir Sheets

2693-2694	A449	Set of 2	4.50	4.50
2695-2696	A450	Set of 2	4.50	4.50

New Year 2003 (Year of the Ram) — A451

No. 2697: a, Tan background, brown ram. b, Purple background. c, Brown background, orange ram. d, Orange background, purple and red ram.

2003, Jan. 27 ***Perf. 13¾***

2697 A451 10d Sheet of 4, #a-d 3.25 3.25

GEORGIA

ˈjor-jə

LOCATION — South of Russia, bordering on the Black Sea and occupying the entire western part of Trans-Caucasia
GOVT. — Republic
AREA — 26,900 sq. mi.
POP. — 5,066,499 (1999 est.)
CAPITAL — Tbilisi (Tiflis)

Georgia was formerly a province of the Russian Empire and later a part of the Transcaucasian Federation of Soviet Republics. Stamps of Georgia were replaced in 1923 by those of Transcaucasian Federated Republics.

On Mar. 1, 1994, Georgia joined the Commonwealth of Independent States.

100 Kopecks = 1 Ruble
100 Kopecks = 1 Coupon (1993)
100 Tetri = 1 Lari (Sept. 25, 1995)

Catalogue values for unused stamps in this country are for Never Hinged items, beginning with Scott 75 in the regular postage section, and Scott B10 in the semi-postal section.

Tiflis

A 6k local stamp, imperforate and embossed without color on white paper, was issued in November, 1857, at Tiflis by authority of the viceroy. The square design shows a coat of arms.

National Republic

St. George
A1 A2

Perf. 11½, Imperf.

1919 Litho. Unwmk.

No.	Type	Description	Unused	Used
12	A1	10k blue	.20	.20
13	A1	40k red orange	.20	.20
a.		Tête bêche pair	10.00	10.00
14	A1	50k emerald	.20	.20
15	A1	60k red	.20	.20
16	A1	70k claret	.20	*.25*
17	A2	1r orange brown	.20	*.25*
		Nos. 12-17 (6)	1.20	1.30

Queen Thamar — A3

1920 ***Perf. 11½, Imperf.***

No.	Type	Description	Unused	Used
18	A3	2r red brown	.30	.30
19	A3	3r gray blue	.20	*.30*
20	A3	5r orange	.30	*.60*
		Nos. 18-20 (3)	.80	*1.20*

Nos. 12-20 with parts of design inverted, sideways or omitted are fraudulent varieties.

Overprints meaning "Day of the National Guard, 12, 12, 1920" (5 lines) and "Recognition of Independence, 27, 1, 1921" (4 lines) were applied, probably in Italy, to remainders taken by government officials who fled when Russian forces occupied Georgia.

"Constantinople" and new values were unofficially surcharged on stamps of 1919-20 by a consul in Turkey.

Soviet Socialist Republic

Soldier with Flag — A5

Peasant Sowing Grain — A6

Industry and Agriculture — A7

1922 Unwmk. ***Perf. 11½***

No.	Type	Description	Unused	Used
26	A5	500r rose	3.50	3.25
27	A6	1000r bister brown	3.50	3.25
28	A7	2000r slate	6.50	6.00
29	A7	3000r brown	6.50	6.00
30	A7	5000r green	6.50	6.00
		Nos. 26-30 (5)	26.50	24.50

Forgeries exist of Nos. 26-30.

Nos. 26 to 30 exist imperforate but were not so issued. Value for set, $65.

Nos. 26-30 Handstamped with New Values in Violet

1923

No.	Type	Description	Unused	Used
36	A6	10,000r on 1000r	5.00	5.00
a.		Black surcharge	10.00	*15.00*
b.		20,000r on 1000r	200.00	
37	A7	15,000r on 2000r, blk surch.	4.75	*6.50*
a.		Violet surcharge	15.00	15.00
38	A5	20,000r on 500r	4.50	*6.50*
a.		Black surcharge	10.00	4.00
39	A7	40,000r on 5000r	4.00	4.00
a.		Black surcharge	7.00	*8.00*
40	A7	80,000r on 3000r	4.50	*6.50*
a.		Black surcharge	6.50	*10.00*
		Nos. 36-40 (5)	22.75	*28.50*

There were two types of the handstamped surcharges, with the numerals 5½mm and 6½mm high. The impressions are often too indistinct to measure or even to distinguish the numerals.

Double and inverted surcharges exist, as is usual with handstamps.

Printed Surcharge in Black

No.	Type	Description	Unused	Used
43	A6	10,000r on 1000r	5.75	*6.50*
44	A7	15,000r on 2000r	3.75	*4.00*
45	A5	20,000r on 500r	1.60	*2.00*
46	A7	40,000r on 5000r	3.00	*3.75*
47	A7	80,000r on 3000r	3.50	*4.00*
		Nos. 43-47 (5)	17.60	20.25

Nos. 43, 45, 46 and 47 exist imperforate but were not so issued. Value $25 each.

Russian Stamps of 1909-18 Handstamp Surcharged

Type I surcharge measures 20x5½mm.
Type II surcharge measures 22x7¼mm.

1923 ***Perf. 14½x15***

No.	Type	Description	Unused	Used
48	A14	10,000r on 7k lt bl	150.00	150.00
49	A11	15,000r on 15k red brn & bl (I)	10.00	10.00
a.		Type II	10.00	10.00

Type I Surcharge Handstamped on Armenia No. 141

No.	Type	Description	Unused	Used
50	A11	15,000r on 5r on 15k red brn & bl	150.00	*200.00*
a.		Type II		
		Nos. 48-50 (3)	310.00	*360.00*

Russian Stamps and Types of 1909-18 Surcharged in Dark Blue or Black

1923 ***Perf. 11½, 14½x15***

No.	Type	Description	Unused	Used
51	A14	75,000r on 1k org	3.00	*4.25*
a.		Imperf.	50.00	*75.00*
52	A14	200,000r on 5k cl	3.50	*4.75*
53	A8	300,000r on 20k bl & car (Bk)	3.50	*4.75*
a.		Dark blue surcharge	50.00	*75.00*
54	A14	350,000r on 3k red	5.50	*7.25*
a.		Imperf.	6.00	*7.25*

Imperf

No.	Type	Description	Unused	Used
55	A14	700,000r on 2k grn	6.50	*8.00*
a.		Perf. 14½x15	27.50	*32.50*
		Nos. 51-55 (5)	22.00	*29.00*

Catalogue values for unused stamps in this section, from this point to the end of the section, are for Never Hinged items.

Republic

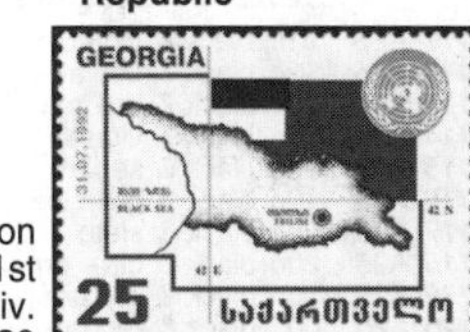

Admission to UN, 1st Anniv. A20

Map, flag, UN emblem.

1993, July 31 Litho. ***Perf. 13***

No.	Type	Description	Unused	Used
73	A20	25r green & multi	*.50*	.50
74	A20	50r brown & multi	*.85*	.85
75	A20	100r violet & multi	*1.75*	1.75
a.		Souvenir sheet of 3, #73-75 + label	*3.25*	3.25
		Nos. 73-75 (3)	*3.10*	3.10

Natl. Arms, Flag — A21

Fresco, 18th Cent. — A22

Apostle Simon, 11th Cent. — A23

Three Women, by Lado Gudiashvili A24

1993, Oct. 11 Photo. ***Perf. 12x11½***

No.	Type	Description	Unused	Used
76	A21	50k multicolored	*.25*	.25

Litho.

Perf. 12x12½

No.	Type	Description	Unused	Used
77	A22	50k multicolored	*.25*	.25
78	A23	1c multicolored	*.75*	.75
79	A24	1c multicolored	*.75*	.75
		Nos. 76-79 (4)	*2.00*	2.00

Nos. 76, 78-79 dated 1992.
For surcharges see Nos. 80-83, 93-95.

Surcharged in Claret, Black, or Blue

1994, May 31 Photo. ***Perf. 12x11½***

No.	Type	Description	Unused	Used
80	A21	5000c on 50k #76 (C)	*.20*	*.20*

Litho.

Perf. 12x12½

No.	Type	Description	Unused	Used
81	A22	5000c on 50k #77 (Blk)	*.20*	*.20*
82	A23	10,000c on 1c #78 (Bl)	*.25*	*.25*
83	A24	10,000c on 1c #79 (C)	*.25*	*.25*
		Nos. 80-83 (4)	*.90*	*.90*

Size and location of surcharge varies.

Places of Worship — A25

30c, Mtskheta Church. 40c, Gelati Church. 50c, Nikortsminda Church. 60c, Ikorta Church. 70c, Samtavisi Church. 80c, Bolnisi Zion Synagogue. 90c, Gremi Citadel Church.

1993, Oct. 11 Litho. ***Perf. 13½***

No.	Type	Description	Unused	Used
84	A25	30c blue	*.25*	.25
85	A25	40c red brown	*.30*	.30
86	A25	50c olive brown	*.40*	.40
87	A25	60c rose carmine	*.50*	.50
88	A25	70c rose lake	*.60*	.60
89	A25	80c green	*.65*	.65
90	A25	90c slate	*.75*	.75
		Nos. 84-90 (7)	*3.45*	3.45

See Nos. 111-120.

Niko Nikoladze (1843-1928) — A26

1994, May 31 Litho. ***Perf. 13½***

No.	Type	Description	Unused	Used
91	A26	150c black & gold	*.45*	.45

UPU, 120th Anniv. A27

1994, May 30

No.	Type	Description	Unused	Used
92	A27	200c multicolored	*.55*	.55

Nos. 77-79 Surcharged in Green or Red

1994 **Litho.** ***Perf. 12x12½***

93 A22 200c on 50k #77 *.35* .35
94 A23 300c on 1c #78 (R) *.45* .45
95 A24 500c on 1c #79 *.70* .70
Nos. 93-95 (3) *1.50* 1.50

A27a

A28

1994, Oct. 9 **Litho.** ***Perf. 14***

95A A27a 100c shown *.75* .75
95B A27a 200c Monument *1.50* 1.50

All Georgian Congress.

1995, Mar. 28 **Litho.** ***Perf. 14½***

Georgia Natl. Olympic Committee: 10c, Intl. year of sport & Olympic ideal. 15c, Olympic congress, cent. 20c, Intl. Olympic Committee, cent. 25c, Olympic truce.

96-99 A28 Set of 4 *2.50* 2.50

Dated 1994.

Paintings by Niko Piromanashvili (1862-1918) — A29

#100, Three Princes Carousing on the Grass. #101, Still life. #102, Georgian Woman with a Tambourine, vert. #103, Bear on a Moonlit Night, vert. #104, Woman with a Tankard of Beer, vert. #105, Deer, vert. #106, Fisherman, vert. #107, Giraffe, vert. #108, Boy on a Donkey, vert. #109, Brooder with Chicks.
#110, Family Picnicking.

1995, Mar. 29 **Litho.** ***Perf. 14***

100-109 A29 20c Set of 10 *4.75* 4.75

Souvenir Sheet

110 A29 100c multicolored *2.00* 2.00

Churches Type of 1993

10c

20c

400c

1c, #120, Metechi, 1278-1289. 2c, #117, Alaverdi, 11th cent. 3c, #116, Dranda, 8th cent. #114, Sveti-Zchoveli, 1010-1019. #115, Kumurdo, 964. #118, Anauri, 17th cent. #119, Bitschvinta, 10th cent.

1995 **Litho.** ***Perf. 14***

Size: 25½x39mm

111 A25 1c black & violet *1.00* 1.00
112 A25 2c black & sepia *1.00* 1.00
113 A25 3c black & red brn *1.00* 1.00
114 A25 10c black & violet *1.00* 1.00
115 A25 10c black & sepia *1.00* 1.00
116 A25 10c black & grn blue *1.00* 1.00
117 A25 20c black & slate *1.00* 1.00
118 A25 20c black & olive grn *1.00* 1.00
119 A25 400c black & org brn *1.00* 1.00
120 A25 400c black & red brn *1.00* 1.00
Nos. 111-120 (10) *10.00* 10.00

Paolo Iashvili (1894-1937) — A30

1995, Apr. 1

125 A30 300c multicolored *.75* .75

Prehistoric Animals — A31

#126, Brontosaurus. #127, Saurolophus. #128, Scolosaurus. #129, Triceratops. #130, Parasaurolophus. #131, Ceratosaurus. #132, Deinonichus. #133, Tyrannosaurus. #134, Stegosaurus.
#135: a, Pterodactylus (d). b, Rhamphophynghus (c, e). c, Pteranodon. d, Spinosaurus. e, Tyrannosaurus (f, h, i). f, Velociraptor. g, Monoklonius. h, Ornithomimus. i, Mastodon.
100c, Deinonychus.

1995 **Litho.** ***Perf. 14***

126-134 A31 15c Set of 9 *4.00* 4.00

Miniature Sheet of 9

135 A31 15c #a.-i. *5.00*

Souvenir Sheet

136 A31 100c multicolored *3.75* 3.75

Issued: #126-134, 5/12.

UNESCO World Heritage Sites A32

100c, Bagrati Cathedral. 500c, Jvari of Mtskhetha.

1995, Aug. 30 **Litho.** ***Perf. 14***

137 A32 100c multi *.50* .50

Souvenir Sheet

138 A32 500c multi, vert. *2.75* 2.75

Miniature Sheet

Wildlife Painting A33

Design: #a.-p., Various animals and birds.

1995, Aug. 4

139 A33 15c Sheet of 16, #a.-p. *5.00* *5.00*

Miniature Sheets of 16

Birds A34

Designs: Nos. 140a-140p, Various songbirds. Nos. 141a-141p, Various raptors.
No. 142, Songbird. No. 143, Owl.

1996, Feb. 26 **Litho.** ***Perf. 14***

140-141 A34 15t #a.-p., each *5.00*

Souvenir Sheets

142-143 A34 100t each *3.00*

Miniature Sheet

Fauna and Flora A35

a, Stork's head. b, Stork's body (a, f), berries. c, Snake (d, g, h). d, Moth. e, Lizard. f, Songbirds. g, Insect, flowers. h, Bee on flower. i, Butterfly, flower. j, Frog, lily (f). k, Snail. l, Turtle (p). m. Lobster. n, Sea plant, eel (o). o, Fish. p, Salamander.

1996, Mar. 14 **Litho.** ***Perf. 14***

144 A35 10t Sheet of 16, #a.-p. 5.50 5.50

Dinosaurs — A36

Illustration reduced.

1996, Apr. 24 **Litho.** ***Perf. 14***

145 A36 10t Sheet of 9, #a.-i. *3.50*

Intl. Olympic Committee, Cent. — A37

Georgian Olympians, landmarks from earlier Summer Olympic Games: 1t, Helsinki, 1952. 2t, Melbourne, 1956. 3t, Rome, 1960. 4t, Tokyo, 1964. 5t, Mexico City, 1968. 6t, Munich, 1972. 7t, Montreal, 1976. 8t, Moscow, 1980. 9t, Seoul, 1988. 10t, Barcelona, 1992.
Early Greek: 50t, Wrestlers. 70t, Runner.

1996, Aug. 16 **Litho.** ***Perf. 14***

146-155 A37 Set of 10 4.50 4.50

Souvenir Sheets

156 A37 50t multicolored 4.00 4.00
157 A37 70t multicolored 5.00 5.00

Olymphilex '96 (#157).

Paintings — A38

Designs: 10t, Citizens of Paris, by Lado Gudiashvili. 20t, Abstract, by Wassily Kandinsky. 30t, Still Life, by David Kakabadze. 50t, Three Painters, by Shalva Kikodze.
80t, Portrait of Niko Pirosmani, by Pablo Picasso.

1996, Aug. 2 **Litho.** ***Perf. 14***

158 A38 10t multicolored .25 .25
159 A38 20t multicolored .50 .50
160 A38 30t multicolored .75 .75
161 A38 50t multicolored 1.00 1.00

Size: 72x90mm

Imperf

162 A38 80t multicolored 1.75 1.75
Nos. 158-162 (5) 4.25 4.25

A39

1996, Dec. 25 **Litho.** ***Perf. 13x14***

163 A39 30t Anton I (1720-88) *.80* *.80*

Ivan Javakhishvili (1876-1940), Writer — A40

1997, Mar. 6 ***Perf. 14***

164 A40 50t multicolored *1.10* *1.10*

UN, 50th Anniv. A41

1997, Mar. 5 **Litho.** ***Perf. 14***

165 A41 30t purple & blue *.75* *.75*
166 A41 125t red & blue *2.75* *2.75*

Dogs — A42

Designs: 10t, Rottweiler. 30t, Gordon setter. 50t, St. Bernard. 60t, English bulldog. 70t, Caucasian sheep dog.
125t, Caucasian sheep dog, diff.

1997, June 2 **Litho.** ***Perf. 14***

167 A42 10t multicolored *.25* *.25*
168 A42 30t multicolored *.60* *.60*
169 A42 50t multicolored *1.10* *1.10*
170 A42 60t multicolored *1.25* *1.25*

171 A42	70t multicolored	1.50	1.50
a.	Sheet of 6, #167-172	6.50	
	Nos. 167-171 (5)	4.70	4.70

Souvenir Sheet

172 A42	125t multicolored	3.00	3.00

No. 171a contains stamp from No. 172 without the continuous design. Issued: 2/27/98.

Animated Film Characters — A43

Designs: a, 20t, Two mice talking. b, 30t, Man in bed. c, 40t, Balloons, bear, girl on cloud. d, 50t, Animals dancing, tree. e, 60t, Duck dressed as woman, tree.

1997, July 15 Litho. Perf. 14

173 A43	Strip of 5, #a.-e.	5.00	5.00

Georgian Women's Team, Winners of 1996 World Chess Olympiad — A44

No. 174: a, Maia Chiburdanidze, Nona Gaprindashvili, Nana Ioseliani, Nino Gurieli, 1992 winners. b, Chiburdanidze, Ioseliani, Ketevan Arakhamia, Gurieli, 1994 winners. c, Chiburdanidze, Ioseliani, Arakhamia, Gurieli, 1996 winners.

No. 175: a, 20t, Vice-Champion Nana Alexandria, 1975, 1981. b, 40t, Chiburdanidze, 1978, 1981 (Vice-Champion), 1984, 1986, 1991. c, 20t, Ioseliani, 1988, 1993. d, 50t, Gaprindashvili, 1962, 1965, 1969, 1972, 1975 (Vice-Champion).

1997, July 21 Litho. Imperf.

174 A44	30t Sheet of 3, #a.-d.+ label	2.25	2.25
175 A44	Sheet of 4, #a.-d.	3.50	3.50

Nos. 174-175 have simulated perforations.

A45

1998 Winter Olympic Games, Nagano A46

Stylized skier - #176: a, 20t. b, 30t. c, 40t. d, 50t.

Early hand-made winter apparel, equipment - No. 177: a, 20t, Snow shoe, hat, gloves. b, 30t, Scarf, snow shoe. c, 40t, Sled, gloves. d, 50t, Scarf, snow shoe.

No. 178, Stylized skier, diff. No. 179, Man's feet with snow shoes.

1998, Feb. 8 Litho. Perf. 14

176 A45	Sheet of 4, #a.-d.	4.00
177 A46	Sheet of 4, #a.-d.	4.00

Souvenir Sheets

178 A45	70t multicolored	2.00
179 A46	70t multicolored	2.00

Moscow '97 — A47

Tiflis local postage stamp of 1857.

1997, Oct. 17 Litho. Perf. 13x14

180 A47	80t multicolored	1.75

Souvenir Sheet

181 A47	1 l multicolored	2.25

Prince Vakhushti Bargrationi (1696-1758) — A48

40t, Map of Georgia, 1745, portrait. 80t, Portrait.

1997, Oct. 9

182 A48	40t multi	.90
183 A48	80t multi, vert.	1.75

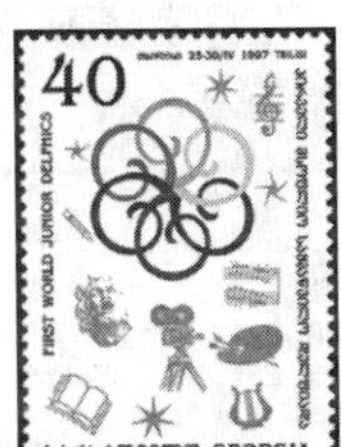

World Delphic Congress — A49

40t, Symbols of education, art & music, 1st World Junior Delphics. 80t, Building on mountaintop, 2nd World Delphic Cong.

1997, Nov. 24 Litho. Perf. 14

184 A49	40t multicolored	1.00
185 A49	80t multicolored	2.00

Voyage of Jason and the Argonauts A50

Plate and Vase Paintings: a, 30t, Greek galley from Rhodes, terracotta plate, 700-650BC. b, 40t, Preparation for Battle, vase painting, 460BC. c, 50t, Boreades, Phineus & Harpy, vase painting, 6th cent. d, 60t, Punishment of King Amicus, vase painting, 420-400BC. e, 70t, Argonauts in Colchis, vase painting, 4th cent. BC. f, 80t, The Dragon Vomiting Jason, vase painting, 490-485BC.

1998, June 23 Litho. Perf. 13x13½

186 A50	Sheet of 6, #a.-f.	7.50

Independence, 80th Anniv. — A51

1998, Dec. 25 Litho. Perf. 14

187 A51	80t multicolored	1.75	1.75

Horses A52

Various breeds.

1998, Dec. 22

188 A52	10t multicolored	.25	.25
189 A52	40t multicolored	.90	.90
190 A52	70t multicolored	1.40	1.40
191 A52	80t multicolored	1.60	1.60
	Nos. 188-191 (4)	4.15	4.15

Souvenir Sheet

Imperf

192 A52	100t multicolored	2.00	2.00

No. 192 has simulated perfs.

Locomotives — A53

Various locomotives built at Tbilisi Locomotives Works.

1998, Dec. 24

193 A53	10t multicolored	.25	.25
194 A53	30t multicolored	.70	.70
195 A53	40t multicolored	.85	.85
196 A53	50t multicolored	1.10	1.10
197 A53	80t multicolored	1.90	1.90
	Nos. 193-197 (5)	4.80	4.80

Souvenir Sheet

198 A53	100t multicolored	2.25	2.25

Europa A54

1998, Dec. 31 Litho. Perf. 13x12¾

199 A54	(80t) Berikaoba	1.50	1.50
200 A54	(100t) Chiakokonoba	1.90	1.90

Wildlife A55

10t, Vormela peregusna guld. 40t, Hyaena hyaena. 80t, Ursus arctos syriacus. 100t, Capra aegagrus erxleber.

1999, Feb. Litho. Perf. 14x13½

201 A55	10t multicolored	.25	.25
202 A55	40t multicolored	.95	.95
203 A55	80t multicolored	1.90	1.90
	Nos. 201-203 (3)	3.10	3.10

Souvenir Sheet

Imperf

204 A55	100t multicolored	2.40	2.40

Dated 1998. No. 204 has simulated perfs.

Ancient and Modern Bridges of Tbilisi A56

Bridges: a, 10t, Michael. b, 40t, Saarbruken. c, 50t, N. Baratashvili. d, 60t, Mukhrani. e, 70t, Avlabari. f, 80t, Metekhi.

1999, Feb. Perf. 13½x14

205 A56	Sheet of 6, #a.-f.	7.00	7.00

Mustela Lutreola, Worldwide Fund for Wildlife A57

1999, Apr. 27 Litho. Perf. 13x12¾

206 A57	(10t) Standing in water	.20	.20
207 A57	(20t) Feeding	.50	.20
208 A57	(30t) Two standing	.80	.30
209 A57	(60t) In burrow	1.75	.75
a.	Block of 4, #206-209	3.25	3.25

Nos. 206-209 were issued in sheets of 10 of each denomination and as se-tenant blocks of 4 in sheets of 20. The stamps from the se-tenant sheets have thicker lettering in the country and Latin names. Singles from the se-tenant sheets of 20 and from the individual sheetlets of 10 are of equal value.

Europa — A58

(80t), Batsara-Babaneury Reserve. (100t), Lagodekhy Reserve.

1999, Apr. 28 Litho. Perf. 12¾x13

210 A58	(80t) multi	1.75	1.75
211 A58	(100t) multi	2.10	2.10

Council of Europe, 50th Anniv. — A59

1999, Nov. Litho. Perf. 12¾

212 A59	50t shown	1.75	1.75
213 A59	80t Latin letters	2.75	2.75

Georgian Olympic Committee, 10th Anniv. A60

1999, Nov. Perf. 13¾

214 A60	20t multi	.70	.70
215 A60	50t multi	1.75	1.75

Butterflies A61

Designs: 10t, Iphiclides podalirius. 20t, Parnassius apollo. 50t, Colias aurorina herrich-schaffer. 80t, Tomares romanovi.

1999, Nov.

216	A61	10t multi	*.35*	*.35*
217	A61	20t multi	*.70*	*.70*
218	A61	50t multi	*1.75*	*1.75*
219	A61	80t multi	*2.75*	*2.75*
		Nos. 216-219 (4)	*5.55*	*5.55*

UPU, 125th Anniv. — A62

1999, Nov. ***Perf. 13¼x13½***

220	A62	20t shown	*.70*	*.70*
221	A62	80t Letter writer	*2.75*	*2.75*

Trucks A63

1999, Dec. ***Perf. 13¾***

Color of Truck

222	A63	20t green	*.70*	*.70*
223	A63	40t red & yellow	*1.25*	*1.25*
224	A63	50t blue & white	*1.60*	*1.60*
225	A63	80t red & white	*2.60*	*2.60*
		Nos. 222-225 (4)	*6.15*	*6.15*

Souvenir Sheet

226	A63	100t red	*3.25*	*3.25*

Souvenir Sheet

Svaneti, World Heritage Site — A64

1999, Dec. ***Perf. 12¾***

227	A64	100t multi	*3.50*	*3.50*

Europa, 2000

Common Design Type

Denominations: 80t, 100t.

2000, Mar. 31 Litho. ***Perf. 12¾x13***

228-229	CD17	Set of 2	*5.50*	*5.50*

Scenes from "The Knight in a Tiger's Skin," by Shota Rustaveli A65

Denominations: 10t, 20t, 30t, 50t, 60t.

2000, May 8 ***Perf. 14¼x13¾***

230-234	A65	Set of 5	*3.00*	*3.00*

Souvenir Sheet

235	A65	80t multi + label	*1.40*	*1.40*

Christianity, 2000th Anniv. — A66

Icons: 20t, St. Nino the Preacher. 50t, The Savior. 80t, The Virgin Hodigitria.

2000, May 10 ***Perf. 13¾***

236-238	A66	Set of 3	*4.25*	*4.25*

Souvenir Sheet

Georgian State System, 3000th Anniv. — A67

Illustration reduced.

2000, May 11 ***Perf. 13***

239	A67	100t multi	*3.50*	*3.50*

Fish — A68

Various fish: 10t, 20t, 30t, 50t, 80t.

2000, May 12 ***Perf. 13¾x13¼***

240-244	A68	Set of 5	*4.75*	*4.75*

David Saradjishvili (1848-1911), Brandy Maker A69

2000, Sept. 20 Litho. ***Perf. 14¼x14***

245	A69	80t multi	*1.60*	*1.60*

2000 Summer Olympics, Sydney — A70

No. 246: a, 20t, Runner at left. b, 50t, Runner at center. c, 80t, Runner at right.

Illustration reduced.

2000 Sept. 20 ***Perf. 13¾***

246	A70	Strip of 3, #a-c	*4.25*	*4.25*

Millennium — A71

No. 247: a, 20t, "1999." b, 50t, "2000." c, 80t, "2001."

Illustration reduced.

2000, Sept. 20

247	A71	Strip of 3, #a-c	*4.00*	*4.00*

Joint Georgia-Russia Space Reflector Project — A72

Designs: 20t, Astronauts at work. 80t, Reflector.

2000, Dec. 11 Litho. ***Perf. 13¾***

248-249	A72	Set of 2	*3.00*	*3.00*

Human Rights in Europe, 50th Anniv. A73

Denomination colors: 50t, Orange brown. 80t, Blue.

2000, Dec. 12 ***Perf. 14¼x14***

250-251	A73	Set of 2	*3.00*	*3.00*

Mushrooms A74

Designs: 10t, Cantharellus cibarius. 20t, Agaricus campestris. 30t, Armillariella mella. 50t, Russula adusta. 80t, Cortinarus violaceus.

2000, Dec. 14 ***Perf. 13¼x13½***

252-256	A74	Set of 5	*5.00*	*5.00*

UN High Commissioner for Refugees, 50th Anniv. — A75

2000, Dec. 14 ***Perf. 13½x14***

257	A75	50t multi	*1.25*	*1.25*

Houses of Worship Type of 1993

Unidentified buildings. Colors: 10t, Brown. 50t, Blue.

2000, Dec. 18 ***Perf. 13¼x13***

Size: 24x32mm

258-259	A25	Set of 2	*1.90*	*1.90*

Writers — A76

Designs: 30t, Alexander Kazbegi (1848-93). 40t, Jakob Gogebashvili (1840-1912). 50t, Vadja Pshavela (1861-1915). 70t, Akaki Tsereteli (1840-1915). 80t, Ilia Chavchavadze (1837-1907).

2000, Dec. 19 ***Perf. 13¼x13¾***

260-264	A76	Set of 5	*5.75*	*5.75*

Alexander Kartveli (1896-1977), Aircraft Designer — A77

Designs: 10t, P-47D Thunderbolt. 20t, F-84. 80t, F-105D Thunderchief.

2000, Dec. 20 ***Perf. 13¾x14***

265-267	A77	Set of 3	*3.25*	*3.25*

Souvenir Sheet

Perf. 13

268	A77	100t Portrait, vert.	*3.00*	*3.00*

Fire Fighting Service, 175th Anniv. — A78

2000, Dec. 24 ***Perf. 13¾x14***

269	A78	50t multi	*1.10*	*1.10*

Europa — A79

Designs: 40t, Ritsa Lake. 80t, Borjomi Park.

2001, Sept. 10 Litho. ***Perf. 12½x13***

270-271	A79	Set of 2	*3.00*	*3.00*
a.		Booklet pane, 2 each #270-271, perf. 12½x13 on 3 sides	*6.00*	
		Booklet, #271a	*6.00*	

Great Silk Route A80

2001, Sept. 20 ***Perf. 13x12½***

272	A80	20t shown	*.50*	*.50*

Souvenir Sheet

273	A80	80t Like 20t, no emblem	*2.00*	*2.00*

Kutaisi Synagogue — A81

2001, Sept. 13 Litho. ***Perf. 13x14***
274 A81 140t multi *4.75 4.75*

First Europe-Asia Chess Match — A82

2001, Sept. 18 Litho. ***Perf. 13¾***
275 A82 1 l multi *3.00 3.00*

Poets — A83

No. 276: a, Taras Shevchenko (1814-61), Ukrainian poet. b, Akaki Tsereteli (1840-1915), Georgian poet.

2001, Dec. 19 ***Perf. 13***
276 A83 50t Horiz. pair, #a-b *1.90 1.90*

See Ukraine No. 445.

Georgian National Ballet — A84

Designs: 30t, Dancers Iliko Sukhishvili (1907-85) and Nino Ramishvili (1910-2000), sketch for dance "Mtiuluri." 50t, Dancers, sketch for dance "Samaya." 80t, Sukhishvili, Ramishvili, and sketch for dance "Jeirani."

2002, Feb. 11 ***Perf. 13½x13¼***
277-279 A84 Set of 3 *4.75 4.75*

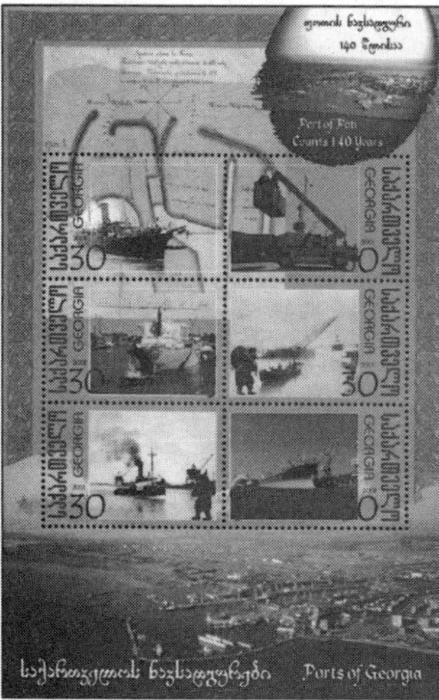

Port of Poti, 140th Anniv. — A85

No. 280: a, Map, ship (black and white photograph). b, Mobile container crane, containers. c, Ship and tugboat, cargo hauler. d, Cargo hauler, small boat, container crane lifting container (black and white photograph). e, Ship, cargo hauler (black and white photograph). f, Cargo hauler, large ship.

2002, Feb. 11 ***Perf. 13¼x13½***
280 A85 30t Sheet of 6, #a-f *5.25 5.25*

A86

Ashot Kurapalatl Opiza — A87

2002, Feb. 11 ***Perf. 13¼x13½***
281 A86 100t blue *2.00 2.00*

Perf. 13¼
282 A87 5 l brown *10.00 10.00*

Europa — A88

Designs: 40t, Georgian Circus. 80t, Tbilisi Circus.

2002, Mar. 22 ***Perf. 13½x13¼***
283-284 A88 Set of 2 *5.00 5.00*
a. Booklet pane, 2 each #283-284, perf. 13½x13¼ on 3 sides *10.00*
Booklet, #284a *10.00*

SEMI-POSTAL STAMPS

SP1

SP2

SP3

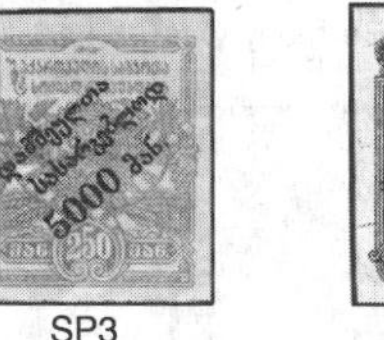

SP4

Surcharge in Red or Black

1922 Unwmk. ***Perf. 11½***
B1 SP1 1000r on 50r vio (R) .50 *2.00*
B2 SP2 3000r on 100r brn red .50 *2.00*
B3 SP3 5000r on 250r gray grn .50 *2.00*
B4 SP4 10,000r on 25r blue (R) .50 *2.00*
Nos. B1-B4 (4) 2.00 *8.00*

Nos. B1-B4 exist imperf but were not so issued. Values slightly more than perforated examples.

Georgian Natl. Olympic Committee SP10

1994, May 27 Litho. ***Perf. 13½***
B10 SP10 100c +50c multi .50 .50

UNICEF, 50th Anniv. SP11

Children's paintings: 20t+5t, People on ladder above rainbow, vert. 30t+10t, Animal character.

Perf. 13x14, 14x13
1996, Dec. 20 Litho.
B11 SP11 20t +5t multi *.75 .75*
B12 SP11 30t +10t multi *1.00 1.00*

In Remembrance of Sept. 11, 2001 Terrorist Attacks — SP12

2001, Dec. 31 Litho. ***Perf. 13x13¼***
B13 SP12 30t +10t multi *1.25 1.25*

Souvenir Sheet

B14 SP12 120t +10t multi *4.00 4.00*

GERMAN EAST AFRICA

'jər-mən 'ēst 'a-fri-kə

LOCATION — In East Africa, bordering on the Indian Ocean
GOVT. — German Colony
AREA — 384,180 sq. mi.
POP. — 7,680,132 (1913)
CAPITAL — Dar-es Salaam

Following World War I, the greater part of this German Colonial possession was mandated to Great Britain. The British ceded to the Belgians the provinces of Ruanda and Urundi (Belgian East Africa). The Kionga triangle was awarded to the Portuguese and became part of the Mozambique Colony. The remaining area became the British Mandated Territory of Tanganyika.

64 Pesa = 1 Rupee
100 Heller = 1 Rupee (1905)
100 Centimes = 1 Franc (1916)
12 Pence = 1 Shilling (1916)
100 Cents = 1 Rupee (1917)
12 Pence = 1 Shilling 100 Cents = 1 Rupee (1917)

Stamps of Germany Surcharged in Black

Nos. 1-5

Nos. 6-10

1893 Unwmk. ***Perf. 13½x14½***

Surcharge 15¼mm long

1 A9 2pes on 3pf brown 32.50 45.00
2 A9 3pes on 5pf green 37.50 45.00
3 A10 5pes on 10pf car 25.00 22.50

Surcharge 16¼mm long

4 A10 10pes on 20pf ultra 17.50 12.00

Surcharge 16¾mm long

5 A10 25pes on 50pf red brn 32.50 26.00
Nos. 1-5 (5) 145.00 150.50

The surcharge also comes 16¾mm on #1; 14¼ or 16¼mm on #2-3; 17½mm on #5. See the *Scott Classic Catalogue* for listings of these spacings.

1896
6 A9 2pes on 3pf dk brn 1.60 *30.00*
a. 2pes on 3pf light brown 22.50 *35.00*
b. 2pes on 3pf grayish brown 9.25 8.50
c. 2pes on 3pf reddish brown 32.50 *80.00*
7 A9 3pes on 5pf green 2.00 *3.50*
8 A10 5pes on 10pf car 2.10 *3.50*
9 A10 10pes on 20pf ultra 4.25 *4.25*
10 A10 25pes on 50pf red brn 18.00 *22.50*
Nos. 6-10 (5) 27.95 *63.75*

A5

Kaiser's Yacht "Hohenzollern" — A6

1900 Typo. ***Perf. 14***
11 A5 2p brown 2.25 1.25
12 A5 3p green 2.25 1.60
13 A5 5p carmine 2.75 2.00
14 A5 10p ultra 4.25 4.00
15 A5 15p org & blk, *sal* 4.25 5.25
16 A5 20p lake & blk 6.00 12.00
17 A5 25p pur & blk, *sal* 6.00 12.00
18 A5 40p lake & blk, *rose* 7.25 *18.00*

Engr.

Perf. 14½x14
19 A6 1r claret 16.00 *45.00*
20 A6 2r yellow green 8.00 *72.50*
21 A6 3r car & slate 60.00 *160.00*
Nos. 11-21 (11) 119.00 *333.60*

Value in Heller

1905 Typo. ***Perf. 14***
22 A5 2½h brown 1.75 1.40
23 A5 4h dk olive green 5.25 4.00
a. 4h green 8.00 8.50
b. 4h dark yellowish green 5.25 10.00
24 A5 7½h carmine 6.50 1.10
25 A5 15h ultra 12.50 4.25
26 A5 20h org & blk, *yel* 8.00 12.00
27 A5 30h lake & blk 8.00 5.00
28 A5 45h pur & blk 16.00 26.00
29 A5 60h lake & blk, *rose* 16.00 *72.50*
Nos. 22-29 (8) 74.00 *126.25*

1905-16 Wmk. Lozenges (125)
31 A5 2½h brown ('06) .80 .65
32 A5 4h green ('06) .80 .45
b. Booklet pane of 4 + 2 labels 35.00
c. Booklet pane of 5 + label *150.00*
33 A5 7½h car ('06) .90 .45
b. Booklet pane of 4 + 2 labels 35.00
c. Booklet pane of 5 + label *190.00*
34 A5 15h ultra ('06) 1.90 1.00
35 A5 20h org & blk, *yel* ('11) 2.00 *11.00*
36 A5 30h lake & blk ('09) 2.10 *6.00*
37 A5 45h pur & blk ('06) 4.25 *40.00*
38 A5 60h lake & blk, *rose* 25.00 *140.00*

Engr.

Perf. 14½x14
39 A6 1r red ('16) 6.50 *17,500.*
40 A6 2r yellow green 32.50
41 A6 3r car & slate ('08) 21.00 *175.00*
Nos. 31-41 (11) 97.75

No. 40 was never placed in use.

Forged cancellations are found on #35-39, 41.

OCCUPATION STAMPS

Issued Under Belgian Occupation

Stamps of Belgian Congo, 1915, Handstamped "RUANDA" in Black or Blue

1916 **Unwmk.** ***Perf. 13½ to 15***

No.	Type	Description	Unused	Used
N1	A29	5c green & blk	21.00	
N2	A30	10c carmine & blk	21.00	
N3	A21	15c blue grn & blk	42.50	
N4	A31	25c blue & blk	21.00	
N5	A23	40c brown red & blk	21.00	
N6	A24	50c brown lake & blk	30.00	
N7	A25	1fr olive bis & blk	150.00	
N8	A27	5fr ocher & blk	*2,150.*	
		Nos. N1-N7 (7)	306.50	

Stamps of Belgian Congo, 1915, Handstamped "URUNDI" in Black or Blue

No.	Type	Description	Unused	Used
N9	A29	5c green & blk	21.00	
N10	A30	10c carmine & blk	21.00	
N11	A21	15c bl grn & blk	42.50	
N12	A31	25c blue & blk	21.00	
N13	A23	40c brn red & blk	21.00	
N14	A24	50c brn lake & blk	30.00	
N15	A25	1fr ol bis & blk	150.00	
N16	A27	5fr ocher & blk	*2,150.*	
		Nos. N9-N15 (7)	306.50	

Stamps of Belgian Congo overprinted "Karema," "Kigoma" and "Tabora" were not officially authorized.

Nos. N1-N16 exist with forged overprint.

Stamps of Belgian Congo, 1915, Overprinted in Dark Blue

1916 ***Perf. 12½ to 15***

No.	Type	Description	Unused	Used
N17	A29	5c green & blk	.65	.25
b.		Inverted overprint	150.00	—
N18	A30	10c carmine & blk	.90	.35
N19	A21	15c bl grn & blk	.65	.25
N20	A31	25c blue & blk	5.25	1.40
N21	A23	40c brn red & blk	11.00	4.25
N22	A24	50c brn lake & blk	13.00	4.50
N23	A25	1fr olive bis & blk	2.25	.55
N24	A27	5fr ocher & blk	2.25	1.60
		Nos. N17-N24 (8)	35.95	13.15

Nos. N17-N18, N20-N22 Surcharged in Black or Red

1922

No.	Type	Description	Unused	Used
N25	A24	5c on 50c brn lake & blk	.35	.35
N26	A29	10c on 5c grn & blk (R)	.35	.30
N27	A23	25c on 40c brn red & blk (R)	2.25	1.25
N28	A30	30c on 10c car & blk	.35	.25
N29	A31	50c on 25c bl & blk (R)	.35	.25
		Nos. N25-N29 (5)	3.65	2.40

No. N25 has the surcharge at each side.

Issued Under British Occupation

Stamps of Nyasaland Protectorate, 1913-15 Overprinted

1916 **Wmk. 3** ***Perf. 14***

No.	Type	Description	Unused	Used
N101	A3	½p green	1.40	*7.25*
a.		Double overprint (R & Bk)		
N102	A3	1p carmine	1.50	*3.25*
N103	A3	3p violet, *yel*	7.00	*16.00*
a.		Double overprint		*8,500.*
N104	A3	4p scar & blk, *yel*	27.50	*37.50*
N105	A3	1sh black, *green*	27.50	*40.00*
		Nos. N101-N105 (5)	64.90	*104.00*

"N.F." stands for "Nyasaland Force."

Stamps of East Africa and Uganda, 1912-14, Overprinted in Black or Red

1917

No.	Type	Description	Unused	Used
N106	A3	1c black (R)	.20	*.75*
N107	A3	3c blue green	.20	.20
N108	A3	6c carmine	.20	.20
N109	A3	10c brown orange	.40	.40
a.		Inverted overprint		
N110	A3	12c gray	.40	*2.00*
N111	A3	15c ultramarine	.65	*1.75*
N112	A3	25c scar & blk, *yel*	.75	*3.25*
N113	A3	50c violet & blk	.75	*3.25*
N114	A3	75c blk, *bl grn,* olive back (R)	1.00	*4.25*
a.		75c black, *emerald* (R)	3.00	*42.50*

Overprinted

No.	Type	Description	Unused	Used
N115	A4	1r blk, *green*(R)	2.40	*6.75*
a.		1r black, *emerald* (R)	4.25	*42.50*
N116	A4	2r blk & red, *bl*	7.25	*37.50*
N117	A4	3r gray grn & vio	12.50	*67.50*
N118	A4	4r grn & red, *yel*	16.00	*80.00*
N119	A4	5r dl vio & ultra	35.00	*80.00*
N120	A4	10r grn & red, *grn*	62.50	*275.00*
a.		10r grn & red, *emerald*	67.50	*275.00*
N121	A3	20r vio & blk, *red*	175.00	*350.00*
N122	A3	50r gray grn & red	500.00	*725.00*
		Nos. N106-N120 (15)	140.20	*562.80*

See Tanganyika for "G.E.A." overprints on stamps inscribed "East Africa and Uganda Protectorates" with watermark 4.

SEMI-POSTAL STAMPS

Issued under Belgian Occupation

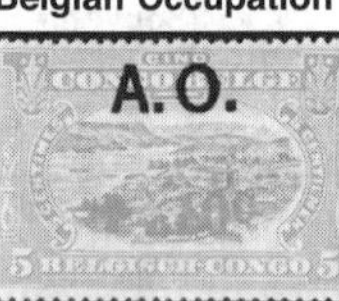

Semi-Postal Stamps of Belgian Congo, 1918, Overprinted

1918 **Unwmk.** ***Perf. 14, 15***

No.	Type	Description	Unused	Used
NB1	A29	5c + 10c grn & bl	.45	.45
NB2	A30	10c + 15c car & bl	.45	.45
NB3	A21	15c + 20c bl grn & bl	.45	.45
NB4	A31	25c + 25c dp & pale bl	.45	.45
NB5	A23	40c + 40c brn red & bl	.65	.65
NB6	A24	50c + 50c brn lake & bl	.85	.85
NB7	A25	1fr + 1fr ol bis & bl	2.40	2.40
NB8	A27	5fr + 5fr ocher & bl	7.25	7.25
NB9	A28	10fr + 10fr grn & bl	60.00	60.00
		Nos. NB1-NB9 (9)	72.95	72.95

The letters "A.O." are the initials of "Afrique Orientale" (East Africa).

GERMAN NEW GUINEA

j@r-m @n n# gi-n$

LOCATION — A group of islands in the west Pacific Ocean, including a part of New Guinea and adjacent islands of the Bismarck Archipelago.

GOVT. — German Protectorate

AREA — 93,000 sq. mi.

POP. — 601,427 (1913)

CAPITAL — Herbertshohe (later Kokopo)

The islands were occupied by Australian troops during World War I and renamed "New Britain." By covenant of the League of Nations they were made a mandated territory of Australia in 1920. The old name of "New Guinea" has since been restored. Postage stamps were issued under all regimes. For other listings see New Britain (1914-15), North West Pacific Islands (1915-22) and New Guinea in Vol. 4.

100 Pfennig = 1 Mark

Stamps of Germany Overprinted in Black

1897-99 **Unwmk.** ***Perf. 13½x14½***

No.	Type	Description	Unused	Used
1	A9	3pf brown	6.50	*8.00*
a.		3pf reddish brown ('99)	32.50	*65.00*
b.		3pf yellow brown ('99)	25.00	*45.00*
2	A9	5pf green	3.25	*4.25*
3	A10	10pf carmine	5.25	*7.25*
4	A10	20pf ultra	7.25	*11.00*
5	A10	25pf orange ('98)	22.50	*42.50*
a.		Inverted overprint	*2,750.*	
6	A10	50pf red brown	22.50	*35.00*
		Nos. 1-6 (6)	67.25	*108.00*

A3

Kaiser's Yacht "Hohenzollern" — A4

1901 **Typo.** ***Perf. 14***

No.	Type	Description	Unused	Used
7	A3	3pf brown	.85	1.00
8	A3	5pf green	6.00	1.00
9	A3	10pf carmine	20.00	1.90
10	A3	20pf ultra	1.25	*2.25*
11	A3	25pf org & blk, *yel*	1.25	*12.00*
12	A3	30pf org & blk, *sal*	1.25	*16.00*
13	A3	40pf lake & blk	1.25	*18.00*
14	A3	50pf pur & blk, *sal*	1.60	*16.00*
15	A3	80pf lake & blk, *rose*	3.00	*22.50*

Engr.

Perf. 14½x14

No.	Type	Description	Unused	Used
16	A4	1m carmine	3.25	*42.50*
17	A4	2m blue	5.00	*62.50*
18	A4	3m black vio	6.00	*125.00*
19	A4	5m slate & car	110.00	*375.00*
		Nos. 7-19 (13)	160.70	*695.65*

Fake cancellations exist on Nos. 10-19.

The stamps of German New Guinea overprinted "G.R.I." and new values in British currency were all used in New Britain and are listed under that country as Nos. 1-29C, O1-2.

A5

A6

Wmk. Lozenges (125)

1914-19 **Typo.** ***Perf. 14***

No.	Type	Description	Unused	Used
20	A3	3pf brown ('19)	.60	
21	A5	5pf green	1.40	
22	A5	10pf carmine	1.40	

Engr.

Perf. 14½x14

No.	Type	Description	Unused	Used
23	A6	5m slate & carmine	15.00	
		Nos. 20-23 (4)	18.40	

Nos. 20-23 were never placed in use.

Nos. 21-23 have "NEUGUINEA" as one word without a hyphen.

GERMAN SOUTH WEST AFRICA

'jər-mən 'sauth 'west 'a-fri-kə

LOCATION — In southwest Africa, bordering on the South Atlantic
GOVT. — German Colony
AREA — 322,450 sq. mi. (1913)
POP. — 94,372 (1913)
CAPITAL — Windhoek

The Colony was occupied by South African troops during World War I and in 1920 was mandated to the Union of South Africa by the League of Nations. See South West Africa in Vol. 6.

100 Pfennig = 1 Mark

Stamps of Germany Overprinted

1897 Unwmk. *Perf. 13½x14½*

1 A9 3pf dark brown 6.00 *10.00*
a. 3pf yellow brown 35.00 —
2 A9 5pf green 4.00 3.00
3 A10 10pf carmine 16.00 14.00
4 A10 20pf ultra 3.75 4.50
5 A10 25pf orange 240.00 15,000.
6 A10 50pf red brown 250.00

Nos. 5 and 6 were prepared for issue but were not sent to the Colony.

Overprinted "Deutsch-Südwestafrika"

1899

7 A9 3pf dark brown 3.50 *16.00*
a. 3pf reddish brown 12.50 *65.00*
b. 3pf yellow brown 5.50 *10.00*
8 A9 5pf green 2.50 1.75
9 A10 10pf carmine 2.60 2.10
10 A10 20pf ultra 10.00 11.00
11 A10 25pf orange 275.00 *325.00*
12 A10 50pf red brown 10.00 8.50

Kaiser's Yacht "Hohenzollern"
A3 A4

1900 Typo. *Perf. 14*

13 A3 3pf brown 5.00 1.10
14 A3 5pf green 20.00 .60
15 A3 10pf carmine 16.00 .65
16 A3 20pf ultra 30.00 1.10
17 A3 25pf org & blk, *yel* 1.75 *4.00*
18 A3 30pf org & blk, *sal* 15.00 2.25
19 A3 40pf lake & blk 1.75 *2.50*
20 A3 50pf pur & blk, *sal* 2.10 1.75
21 A3 80pf lake & blk, *rose* 2.10 *6.75*

Engr.

Perf. 14½x14

22 A4 1m carmine 25.00 *25.00*
23 A4 2m blue 22.50 *30.00*
24 A4 3m black vio 27.50 *35.00*
25 A4 5m slate & car 125.00 125.00
Nos. 13-25 (13) 293.70 *235.70*

Wmk. Lozenges (125)

1906-19 Typo. *Perf. 14*

26 A3 3pf brown ('09) .75 *6.00*
27 A3 5pf green .75 *1.10*
b. Bklt. pane of 6 (2 #27, 4 #28) 35.00
c. Booklet pane of 5 + label 150.00
28 A3 10pf carmine .90 *1.40*
b. Booklet pane of 5 + label 190.00
29 A3 20pf ultra ('11) .90 *3.00*
30 A3 30pf org & blk, *buff* ('11) 5.00 *200.00*

Engr.

Perf. 14½x14

31 A4 1m carmine ('12) 6.75 *32.50*
32 A4 2m blue ('11) 8.50 *22.50*
33 A4 3m blk vio ('19) 8.00
a. 3m gray violet 17.50
34 A4 5m slate & car 17.50 *250.00*
a. 5m slate & rose red 37.50
Nos. 26-34 (9) 49.05

Nos. 33, 33a, 34a were never placed in use.
Forged cancellations are found on #30-32, 34.

GERMAN STATES

'jər-mən 'stāts

Watermarks

Wmk. 92- 17mm wide

Wmk. 93- 14mm wide

Wmk. 94- Horiz. Wavy Lines Wide Apart

Wmk. 95v- Vert. Wavy Lines Close Together

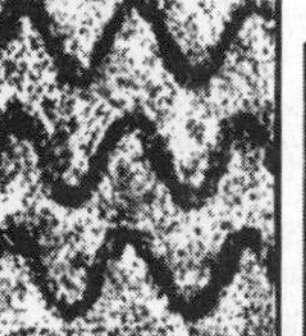

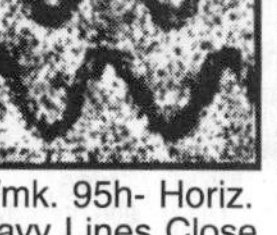

Wmk. 95h- Horiz. Wavy Lines Close Together

Wmk. 102- Post Horn

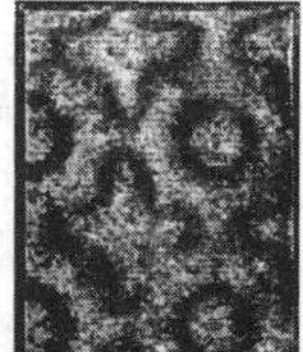

Wmk. 116- Crosses and Circles

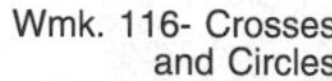

Wmk. 128- Wavy Lines

Wmk. 130- Wreath of Oak Leaves

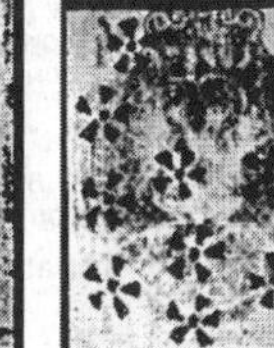

Wmk. 148- Small Flowers

Wmk. 162- Laurel Wreath

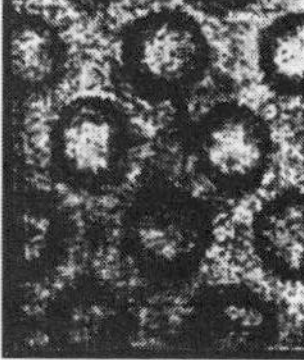

Wmk. 192- Circles

BADEN

LOCATION — In southwestern Germany
GOVT. — Grand Duchy
AREA — 5,817 sq. mi.
POP. — 1,432,000 (1864)
CAPITAL — Karlsruhe (principal city)

Baden was a member of the German Confederation. In 1870 it became part of the German Empire.

60 Kreuzer = 1 Gulden

Values for unused stamps are for examples with original gum as defined in the catalogue introduction except for Nos. 1-9 which are valued without gum. Very fine examples of Nos. 1-9 will have one or two margins touching the framelines due to the very narrow spacing of the stamps on the plates. Stamps with margins clear of the framelines on all four sides are scarce and sell for considerably more.

A1

1851-52 Unwmk. Typo. *Imperf.*

1 A1 1kr blk, *dk buff* 200.00 190.00
2 A1 3kr blk, *yellow* 100.00 10.50
3 A1 6kr blk, *yel grn* 325.00 35.00
4 A1 9kr blk, *lil rose* 65.00 17.00
Nos. 1-4 (4) 690.00 252.50

Thin Paper (First Printing, 1851)

1a A1 1kr black, *buff* 1,450. 575.00
2a A1 3kr black, *orange* 500.00 27.50
3a A1 6kr blk, *blue green* 1,650. 65.00
4a A1 9kr black, *deep rose* 2,000. 125.00
4b A1 9kr blk, *bl grn* (error) — —

1853-58

6 A1 1kr black 110.00 19.00
a. Tête bêche gutter pair *21,500.*
7 A1 3kr black, *green* 110.00 4.75
8 A1 3kr black, *bl* ('58) 500.00 24.00
a. Printed on both sides
9 A1 6kr black, *yellow* 190.00 16.00
Nos. 6-9 (4) 910.00 63.75

Reissues (1865) of Nos. 1, 2, 3, 6, 7 and 8 exist on thick paper and No. 9 on thin paper; the color of the last is brighter than that of the original.

Coat of Arms
A2 A3

1860-62 *Perf. 13½*

10 A2 1kr black 57.50 17.50
12 A2 3kr ultra ('61) 65.00 13.00
a. 3kr Prussian blue 225.00 40.00
13 A2 6kr red org ('61) 75.00 47.50
a. 6kr yellow orange ('62) 150.00 57.50
14 A2 9kr rose ('61) 190.00 125.00
Nos. 10-14 (4) 387.50 203.00

Copies of Nos. 10-14 and 18 with all perforations intact sell for considerably more.

1862 *Perf. 10*

15 A2 1kr black 45.00 57.50
a. 1kr silver gray 5,250.
16 A2 6kr prussian blue 87.50 50.00
17 A2 9kr brown 65.00 55.00
a. 9kr dark brown 275.00 225.00

Perf. 13½

18 A3 3kr rose 1,650. 275.00

1862-65 *Perf. 10*

19 A3 1kr black ('64) 35.00 9.50
a. 1kr silver gray 1,650.
20 A3 3kr rose 35.00 1.25
a. Imperf. 29,000. 14,500.
22 A3 6kr ultra ('65) 5.75 17.50
a. 6kr Prussian blue ('64) 450.00 52.50
23 A3 9kr brown ('64) 10.50 20.00
a. 9kr bister 300.00 70.00
b. Printed on both sides 4,350.
24 A3 18kr green 300.00 450.00
25 A3 30kr deep orange 22.50 1,050.
a. 30kr yellow orange 110.00 1,750.

Forged cancellations are known on #25, 28a.

A4

1868

26 A4 1kr green 3.00 3.50
27 A4 3kr rose 1.75 1.25
28 A4 7kr dull blue 15.00 26.00
a. 7kr sky blue 32.50 75.00
Nos. 26-28 (3) 19.75 30.75

The postage stamps of Baden were superseded by those of the German Empire on Jan. 1, 1872, but Official stamps were used during the year 1905.

Stamps of the Baden sector of the French Occupation Zone of Germany, issued in 1947-49, are listed under Germany, Occupation Issues.

RURAL POSTAGE DUE STAMPS

RU1

1862 **Unwmk.** *Perf. 10*

Thin Paper

LJ1 RU1 1kr blk, *yellow* 3.00 225.00
a. Thick paper 110.00 450.00
LJ2 RU1 3kr blk, *yellow* 1.75 87.50
a. Thick paper 87.50 300.00
LJ3 RU1 12kr blk, *yellow* 26.00 10,000.
a. Half used as 6kr on cover 15,000.
b. Quarter used as 3kr on cover —
Nos. LJ1-LJ3 (3) 30.75

On #LJ3, "LAND-POST" is a straight line. Paper of #LJ1a, LJ2a is darker yellow. Forged cancellations abound on #LJ1-LJ3.

OFFICIAL STAMPS
See Germany Nos. OL16-OL21.

BAVARIA

LOCATION — In southern Germany
GOVT. — Kingdom
AREA — 30,562 sq. mi. (1920)
POP. — 7,150,146 (1919)
CAPITAL — Munich

Bavaria was a member of the German Confederation and became part of the German Empire in 1870. After World War I, it declared itself a republic. It lost its postal autonomy on Mar. 31, 1920.

60 Kreuzer = 1 Gulden
100 Pfennig = 1 Mark (1874)

Values for unused stamps are for examples with original gum as defined in the catalogue introduction. Unused examples of the 1849-78 issues without gum sell for about 50-60% of the figures quoted.

A1

Broken Circle — A1a

1849 **Unwmk.** **Typo.** *Imperf.*

1 A1 1kr black 575.00 1,450.
a. 1kr deep black 1,750. 2,350.
b. Tête bêche pair 52,500.

With Silk Thread

2 A1a 3kr blue 35.00 2.00
a. 3kr greenish blue 35.00 2.00
b. 3kr deep blue 35.00 2.00
3 A1a 6kr brown 5,000. 160.00

No. 1 exists with silk thread but only as an essay.

Complete circle — A2

Coat of Arms — A3

1850-58 **With Silk Thread**

4 A2 1kr pink 140.00 14.50
5 A2 6kr brown 32.50 4.50
a. Half used as 3kr on cover 13,750.
6 A2 9kr yellow green 45.00 10.50
a. 9kr blue green ('53) 5,000. 125.00
7 A2 12kr red ('58) 92.50 100.00
8 A2 18kr yellow ('54) 95.00 160.00
Nos. 4-8 (5) 405.00 289.50

1862

9 A2 1kr yellow 47.50 14.00
10 A1a 3kr rose 110.00 1.75
a. 3kr carmine 35.00 3.75
11 A2 6kr blue 50.00 7.00
a. 6kr ultra 1,750. 6,000.
b. Half used as 3kr on cover 7,000.
12 A2 9kr bister 82.50 10.50
13 A2 12kr yellow grn 65.00 47.50
a. Half used as 6kr on cover 14,500.
14 A2 18kr ver red 700.00 110.00
a. 18kr pale red 110.00 350.00
Nos. 9-14 (6) 1,055. 190.75

No. 11a was not put in use.

1867-68 **Embossed**

15 A3 1kr yellow grn 47.50 7.00
a. 1kr dark blue green 225.00 30.00
16 A3 3kr rose 47.50 1.10
a. Printed on both sides 3,500.
17 A3 6kr ultra 32.50 13.00
a. Half used as 3kr on cover 29,000.
18 A3 6kr bister ('68) 57.50 35.00
a. Half used as 3kr on cover 14,500.
19 A3 7kr ultra ('68) 300.00 9.25
20 A3 9kr bister 32.50 24.00
21 A3 12kr lilac 260.00 70.00
22 A3 18kr red 100.00 125.00
Nos. 15-22 (8) 877.50 284.35

The paper of the 1867-68 issues often shows ribbed or laid lines.

1870-72 **Wmk. 92** *Perf. 11½*

Without Silk Thread

23 A3 1kr green 8.75 1.00
24 A3 3kr rose 17.50 .55
25 A3 6kr bister 24.00 22.50
26 A3 7kr ultra 2.25 2.50
a. 7kr Prussian blue 14.50 8.75
27 A3 9kr pale brn ('72) 3.25 2.75
28 A3 10kr yellow 3.50 10.00
29 A3 12kr lilac 875.00 3,250.
30 A3 18kr dull brick red 7.00 10.00
b. 18kr dark brick red 87.50 50.00

The paper of the 1870-75 issues frequently appears to be laid with the lines either close or wide apart.
See Nos. 33-37.
Reprints exist.

Wmk. 93

23a A3 1kr 75.00 7.00
24a A3 3kr 70.00 1.75
25a A3 6kr 125.00 52.50
26b A3 7kr 92.50 26.00
27a A3 9kr 200.00 350.00
28a A3 10kr 175.00 260.00
29a A3 12kr 260.00 800.00
30a A3 18kr dull brick red 300.00 125.00
c. 18kr dark brick red 200.00 175.00

A4

A5

1874-75 **Wmk. 92** *Imperf.*

31 A4 1m violet 450.00 57.50

Perf. 11½

32 A4 1m violet ('75) 150.00 35.00

See Nos. 46-47, 54-57, 73-76.

1875 **Wmk. 94**

33 A3 1kr green .50 17.00
34 A3 3kr rose .50 3.00
35 A3 7kr ultra 2.50 200.00
36 A3 10kr yellow 22.50 190.00
37 A3 18kr red 17.50 45.00
Nos. 33-37 (5) 43.50 455.00

False cancellations exist on #29, 29a, 33-37.

1876-78 **Embossed** *Perf. 11½*

38 A5 3pf lt green 22.50 1.10
39 A5 5pf dk green 57.50 8.00
40 A5 5pf lilac ('78) 110.00 14.50
41 A5 10pf rose 110.00 .45
42 A5 20pf ultra 125.00 2.25
43 A5 25pf yellow brn 110.00 4.00
44 A5 50pf scarlet 37.50 3.75
45 A5 50pf brown ('78) 575.00 20.00
46 A4 1m violet 1,400. 65.00
47 A4 2m orange 15.00 5.75

The paper of the 1876-78 issue often shows ribbed lines.
See Nos. 48-53, 58-72. For overprints and surcharge see Nos. 237, O1-O5.

1881-1906 **Wmk. 95v** *Perf. 11½*

48 A5 3pf green 9.25 .35
a. Imperf. 300.00 1,450.
49 A5 5pf lilac 13.00 1.00
50 A5 10pf carmine 8.75 .30
a. Imperf. 300.00 1,450.
51 A5 20pf ultra 10.50 .50
52 A5 25pf yellow brn 87.50 2.75
53 A5 50pf deep brown 110.00 2.50
54 A4 1m rose lilac ('00) 1.75 1.10
a. 1m red lilac, toned paper 50.00 2.40
55 A4 2m orange ('01) 2.50 3.50
a. Toned paper ('90) 57.50 8.00
56 A4 3m olive gray ('00) 14.50 17.50
a. White paper ('06) 110.00 400.00
57 A4 5m yellow grn ('00) 14.50 17.50
a. White paper ('06) 110.00 300.00
Nos. 48-57 (10) 272.25 47.00

Nos. 56-57 are on toned paper. A 2m lilac was not regularly issued.

1888-1900 **Wmk. 95h** *Perf. 14½*

58 A5 2pf gray ('00) 1.25 .35
59 A5 3pf green 7.50 1.60
60 A5 3pf brown ('00) .20 .30
61 A5 5pf lilac 17.00 2.75
62 A5 5pf dk green ('00) .20 .30
63 A5 10pf carmine .25 .30
64 A5 20pf ultra .25 .30
65 A5 25pf yellow brn 22.50 4.75
66 A5 25pf orange ('00) .25 .45
67 A5 30pf olive grn ('00) .30 .55
68 A5 40pf yellow ('00) .30 .75
69 A5 50pf dp brown 45.00 2.50
70 A5 50pf maroon ('00) .25 1.10
71 A5 80pf lilac ('00) 1.75 3.00
Nos. 58-71 (14) 97.00 19.00

Nos. 59, 61, 65, 69 and 70 are on toned paper; Nos. 67-68 on white.

Toned Paper

58a A5 2pf ('99) 8.75 2.75
60a A5 3pf ('90) 7.50 .30
62a A5 5pf ('90) 7.50 .30
63a A5 10pf 4.75 .30
b. 10pf imperf 57.50 140.00
64a A5 20pf 7.00 1.00
66a A5 25pf ('90) 11.50 1.25
70a A5 50pf ('90) 35.00 1.60
71a A5 80pf ('99) 22.50 6.50

1911 **Wmk. 95v**

72 A5 5pf dark green .50 7.50

1911 **Wmk. 95h** *Perf. 11½*

73 A4 1m rose lilac 3.00 22.50
74 A4 2m orange 13.00 30.00
75 A4 3m olive gray 13.00 45.00
76 A4 5m pale yel grn 13.00 45.00
Nos. 73-76 (4) 42.00 142.50

See note after No. 91 concerning used values.

A6

A7

Prince Regent Luitpold
A8

Perf. 14x14½

1911 **Wmk. 95h** **Litho.**

77 A6 3pf brn, *gray brn* .20 .20
a. "911" for "1911" 225.00 225.00
78 A6 5pf dk grn, *grn* .20 .20
a. Tête bêche pair 3.50 8.50
b. Booklet pane of 4 + 2 labels 77.50 125.00
c. Bklt. pane of 5 + label 175.00 300.00
d. Bklt. pane of 6 27.50
79 A6 10pf scar, *buff* .20 .20
a. Tête bêche pair 4.50 50.00
b. "911" for "1911" 12.00 12.00
d. Booklet pane of 5 + label 52.50 24.00
80 A6 20pf dp bl, *bl* 1.50 .60
81 A6 25pf vio brn, *buff* 2.50 1.00

Perf. 11½

Wmk. 95v

82 A7 30pf org buff, *buff* 1.25 .70
83 A7 40pf ol grn, *buff* 2.40 .70
84 A7 50pf cl, *gray brn* 2.00 1.10
84A A7 60pf dk grn, *buff* 2.00 1.10
85 A7 80pf vio, *gray brn* 7.00 3.75
86 A8 1m brn, *gray brn* 2.00 1.00
87 A8 2m dk grn, *grn* 2.00 5.00
88 A8 3m lake, *buff* 10.00 29.00
89 A8 5m dk bl, *buff* 8.75 20.00
90 A8 10m org, *yel* 17.50 32.50
91 A8 20m blk brn, *yel* 14.50 16.00
Nos. 77-91 (16) 74.00 113.05

90th birthday of Prince Regent Luitpold.
All values exist in 2 types except #84A.
Nos. 77-84, 85-91 exist imperf.

Used values: Nos. 73-76 and 77-91 often were canceled en masse for accounting purposes. These cancels are perfectly clear, and used values are for stamps canceled thus. Postally used examples are worth about twice as much.

Prince Regent Luitpold — A9

1911, June 10 **Unwmk.**

92 A9 5pf grn, yel & blk .35 .70
b. Horiz. pair, imperf. btwn. 110.00 175.00
93 A9 10pf rose, yel & blk .55 1.10
b. Pair, imperf. between 110.00 175.00

Silver Jubilee of Prince Regent Luitpold.

A10

A11

King Ludwig III
A12 A13

Perf. 14x14½

1914-20 Wmk. 95h Photo.

94 A10 2pf gray ('18) .20 *1.00*
95 A10 3pf brown .20 *1.00*
96 A10 5pf yellow grn .90 *1.10*
a. 5pf dark green .90 1.10
b. Tête bêche pair 2.40 7.75
c. Booklet pane of 5 + 1 label 10.50 40.00
97 A10 7½pf dp green ('16) .20 *1.10*
a. Tête bêche pair 1.50 *4.75*
b. Booklet pane of 6 10.00
98 A10 10pf vermilion 1.10 *1.10*
a. Tête bêche pair 2.40 7.75
b. Booklet pane of 5 + 1 label 10.50 40.00
99 A10 10pf car rose ('16) .20 *1.00*
100 A10 15pf ver ('16) .20 *1.00*
a. Tête bêche pair 1.50 4.75
b. Booklet pane of 5 + 1 label 4.25 15.00
101 A10 15pf car ('20) 1.25 *22.50*
102 A10 20pf blue .20 *1.00*
103 A10 25pf gray .20 *1.00*
104 A10 30pf orange .70 *1.00*
105 A10 40pf olive grn .20 *1.10*
106 A10 50pf red brn .20 *1.10*
107 A10 60pf blue grn .70 *1.10*
108 A10 80pf violet .20 *1.10*

Perf. 11½

Wmk. 95v

109 A11 1m brown .20 *1.10*
110 A11 2m violet .20 *1.90*
111 A11 3m scarlet .25 *4.00*

Wmk. 95h

112 A12 5m deep blue .30 *8.00*
113 A12 10m yellow grn 1.10 *40.00*
114 A12 20m brown 2.00 *57.50*
Nos. 94-114 (21) 10.70 149.70

See #117-135. For ovpts. and surcharges see #115, 136-175, 193-236, B1-B3.

Used Values

of Nos. 94-275, B1-B3 are for postally used stamps. Canceled-to-order stamps, which abound, sell for same prices as unused.

No. 94 Surcharged

1916 Wmk. 95h ***Perf. 14x14½***

115 A13 2½pf on 2pf gray .20 .75
a. Double surcharge

Ludwig III Types of 1914-20

1916-20 ***Imperf.***

117 A10 2pf gray .20 *7.75*
118 A10 3pf brown .20 *9.50*
119 A10 5pf pale yel grn .20 *7.75*
120 A10 7½pf dp green .20 *7.75*
a. Tête bêche pair 2.50 4.75
121 A10 10pf car rose .20 *7.75*
122 A10 15pf vermilion .20 *7.75*
a. Tête bêche pair 2.50 4.75
123 A10 20pf blue .20 *9.50*
124 A10 25pf gray .20 *9.50*
125 A10 30pf orange .20 *9.50*
126 A10 40pf olive grn .20 *9.50*
127 A10 50pf red brown .20 *9.50*
128 A10 60pf dark green .20 *10.50*
129 A10 80pf violet .20 *10.50*
130 A11 1m brown .25 *10.50*
131 A11 2m violet .25 *13.00*
132 A11 3m scarlet .35 *17.00*
133 A12 5m deep blue .60 *24.00*
134 A12 10m yellow green 1.00 *45.00*
135 A12 20m brown 1.40 *72.50*
Nos. 117-135 (19) 6.45 298.75

Stamps and Type of 1914-20 Overprinted:

a

b

Wmk. 95h or 95v

1919 ***Perf. 14x14½***

Overprint "a"

136 A10 3pf brown .20 *.80*
137 A10 5pf yellow grn .20 *.80*
138 A10 7½pf deep green .20 *.80*
139 A10 10pf car rose .20 *.80*
140 A10 15pf vermilion .20 *.80*
141 A10 20pf blue .20 *.80*
142 A10 25pf gray .20 *.80*
143 A10 30pf orange .20 *.80*
144 A10 35pf orange .20 *1.50*
a. Without overprint 77.50
145 A10 40pf olive grn .20 *.90*
146 A10 50pf red brown .20 *.90*
147 A10 60pf dark green .20 *.90*
148 A10 75pf red brown .20 *.75*
a. Without overprint 18.00 *175.00*
149 A10 80pf violet .20 *1.00*

Perf. 11½

Overprint "a"

150 A11 1m brown .20 *.90*
151 A11 2m violet .20 *1.00*
152 A11 3m scarlet .30 *2.75*

Overprint "b"

153 A12 5m deep blue .70 *7.75*
154 A12 10m yellow green .75 *30.00*
155 A12 20m dk brown 1.25 *30.00*
Nos. 136-155 (20) 6.20 84.75

Inverted overprints exist on Nos. 137-143, 145-147, 149. Value, each $15.

Double overprints exist on Nos. 137, 139, 143, 145, 150. Values, $30-$75.

Imperf

Overprint "a"

156 A10 3pf brown .20 *10.50*
157 A10 5pf pale yel grn .20 *10.50*
158 A10 7½pf dp green .20 *10.50*
159 A10 10pf car rose .20 *10.50*
160 A10 15pf vermilion .20 *10.50*
161 A10 20pf blue .20 *10.50*
162 A10 25pf gray .20 *10.50*
163 A10 30pf orange .20 *10.50*
164 A10 35pf orange .20 *13.00*
a. Without overprint 10.50
165 A10 40pf olive grn .20 *10.50*
166 A10 50pf red brown .20 *10.50*
167 A10 60pf dk green .20 *10.50*
168 A10 75pf red brown .20 *13.00*
a. Without overprint 150.00
169 A10 80pf violet .20 *13.00*
170 A11 1m brown .20 *16.00*
171 A11 2m violet .30 *18.00*
172 A11 3m scarlet .45 *26.00*

Overprint "b"

173 A12 5m deep blue .60 *32.50*
174 A12 10m yellow grn .75 *47.50*
175 A12 20m brown 1.50 *47.50*
Nos. 156-175 (20) 6.60 342.00

Stamps of Germany 1906-19 Overprinted

1919 Wmk. 125 ***Perf. 14, 14½***

176 A22 2½pf gray .20 *.70*
177 A16 3pf brown .20 *.70*
178 A16 5pf green .20 *.70*
179 A22 7½pf orange .20 *.75*
180 A16 10pf carmine .20 *1.00*
181 A22 15pf dk violet .20 *.80*
a. Double overprint 300.00 *925.00*
182 A16 20pf ultra .20 *.70*
183 A16 25pf org & blk, *yel* .20 *1.00*
184 A22 35pf red brown .20 *1.10*
185 A16 40pf lake & blk .20 *1.10*
186 A16 75pf green & blk .25 *1.50*
187 A16 80pf lake & blk, *rose* .25 *2.00*
188 A17 1m car rose .60 *3.00*
189 A21 2m dull blue .90 *6.25*
190 A19 3m gray violet .90 *8.25*
191 A20 5m slate & car .90 *8.25*
a. Inverted overprint *2,850.*
Nos. 176-191 (16) 5.80 *37.80*

Bavarian Stamps of 1914-16 Overprinted:

c

d

Wmk. 95h or 95v

1919-20 ***Perf. 14x14½***

Overprint "c"

193 A10 3pf brown .20 *1.00*
194 A10 5pf yellow grn .20 *.75*
195 A10 7½pf dp green .20 *10.50*
196 A10 10pf car rose .20 *.75*
197 A10 15pf vermilion .20 *.75*
198 A10 20pf blue .20 *.75*
199 A10 25pf gray .20 *1.00*
200 A10 30pf orange .20 *1.00*
201 A10 40pf olive grn .20 *9.25*
202 A10 50pf red brown .20 *1.25*
203 A10 60pf dk green .20 *9.25*
204 A10 75pf olive bister .25 *9.25*
205 A10 80pf violet .20 *2.40*

Perf. 11½

Overprint "c"

206 A11 1m brown .20 *1.75*
207 A11 2m violet .20 *3.25*
208 A11 3m scarlet .25 *4.75*

Overprint "d"

209 A12 5m deep blue .50 *11.50*
210 A12 10m yellow grn 1.00 *24.00*
211 A12 20m dk brown 1.50 *40.00*
Nos. 193-211 (19) 6.30 133.15

Imperf

Overprint "c"

212 A10 3pf brown .20 *7.75*
213 A10 5pf pale yel grn .20 *7.75*
214 A10 7½pf deep green .20 *17.00*
215 A10 10pf car rose .20 *7.75*
216 A10 15pf vermilion .20 *7.75*
217 A10 20pf blue .20 *7.75*
a. Double overprint 40.00
218 A10 25pf gray .20 *7.75*
219 A10 30pf orange .20 *9.25*
220 A10 40pf olive grn .20 *9.25*
221 A10 50pf red brn .20 *9.25*
222 A10 60pf dk green .20 *9.25*
223 A10 75pf olive bis .20 *24.00*
a. Without overprint 4.00
224 A10 80pf violet .20 *9.25*
225 A11 1m brown .20 *14.50*
226 A11 2m violet .20 *14.50*
227 A11 3m scarlet .35 *18.00*

Overprint "d"

228 A12 5m deep blue .50 *26.00*
229 A12 10m yellow grn 1.00 *45.00*
230 A12 20m brown 1.40 *72.50*
Nos. 212-230 (19) 6.25 324.25

Ludwig Type of 1914, Printed in Various Colors and Surcharged

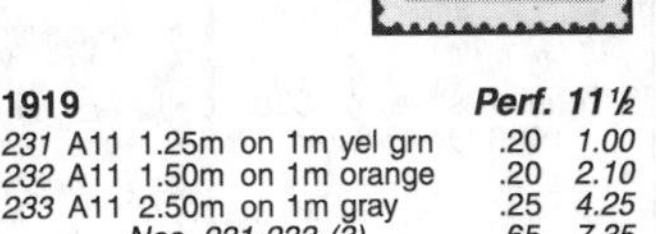

1919 ***Perf. 11½***

231 A11 1.25m on 1m yel grn .20 *1.00*
232 A11 1.50m on 1m orange .20 *2.10*
233 A11 2.50m on 1m gray .25 *4.25*
Nos. 231-233 (3) .65 *7.35*

1920 ***Imperf.***

234 A11 1.25m on 1m yel grn .20 *24.00*
a. Without surcharge 250.00
235 A11 1.50m on 1m org .20 *24.00*
a. Without surcharge 5.25
236 A11 2.50m on 1m gray .25 *24.00*
a. Without surcharge 5.25
Nos. 234-236 (3) .65 *72.00*

No. 60 Surcharged in Dark Blue

1920 ***Perf. 14½***

237 A5 20pf on 3pf brown .20 *1.00*
a. Inverted surcharge 5.25 *21.00*
b. Double surcharge 62.50 *150.00*

Plowman
A14

"Electricity" Harnessing Light to a Water Wheel
A15

Sower — A16

Madonna and Child — A17

von Kaulbach's "Genius" — A18

TWENTY PFENNIG
Type I - Foot of "2" turns downward.
Type II - Foot of "2" turns upward.

Perf. 14x14½

1920 Wmk. 95h Typo.

238 A14 5pf yellow grn .20 *.80*
239 A14 10pf orange .20 *.80*
240 A14 15pf carmine .20 *.80*
241 A15 20pf violet (I) .20 *.80*
a. 20pf violet (II) 6.25 *925.00*
242 A15 30pf dp blue .20 *.90*
243 A15 40pf brown .20 *.90*
244 A16 50pf vermilion .20 *1.00*
245 A16 60pf blue green .20 *1.50*
246 A16 75pf lilac rose .20 *1.50*

Perf. 12x11½

Wmk. 95v

247 A17 1m car & gray .25 *1.50*
248 A17 1¼m ultra & ol bis .20 *1.50*
249 A17 1½m dk grn & gray .20 *2.10*
250 A17 2½m blk & gray .20 *10.50*

Perf. 11½x12

Wmk. 95h

251 A18 3m pale blue .35 *9.25*
252 A18 5m orange .35 *9.25*
253 A18 10m deep green .60 *17.50*
254 A18 20m black .95 *24.00*
Nos. 238-254 (17) 4.90

Imperf. Pairs

238a A14 5pf yellow grn 42.50 300.00
239a A14 10pf orange 100.00
241b A15 20pf violet (I) 42.50
243a A15 40pf brown 92.50
244a A16 50pf vermilion 26.00
245a A16 60pf blue green 30.00
246a A16 75pf lilac rose 30.00
247a A17 1m car & gray 5.25 21.00
248a A17 1¼m ultra & ol bis 5.25 21.00
249a A17 1½m dk grn & gray 5.25 21.00
250a A17 2½m blk & gray 9.25 52.50
251a A18 3m pale blue 9.25 52.50
252a A18 5m orange 9.25 52.50
253a A18 10m deep green 9.25 52.50
254a A18 20m black 9.25 52.50

Perf. 12x11½

1920 Litho. Wmk. 95v

255 A17 2½m black & gray .35 *26.00*

On No. 255 the background dots are small, hazy and irregularly spaced. On No. 250 they are large, clear, round, white and regularly spaced in rows. The backs of the typo. stamps usually show a raised impression of parts of the design.

Stamps and Types of Preceding Issue Overprinted

1920

256 A14 5pf yellow green .20 *.90*
a. Inverted overprint 21.00
b. Imperf., pair 30.00 300.00
257 A14 10pf orange .20 *.90*
a. Imperf., pair 30.00 300.00
258 A14 15pf carmine .20 *.90*
259 A15 20pf violet .20 *.90*
a. Inverted overprint 21.00 525.00
b. Double overprint 10.50
c. Imperf., pair 40.00
260 A15 30pf deep blue .20 *.90*
a. Inverted overprint 21.00
b. Imperf., pair 40.00 300.00
261 A15 40pf brown .20 *.90*
a. Inverted overprint 21.00 350.00
b. Imperf., pair 40.00

262 A16 50pf vermilion .20 *1.50*
263 A16 60pf blue green .20 *.80*
264 A16 75pf lilac rose .25 *3.00*
265 A16 80pf dark blue .25 *1.75*
a. Without overprint *77.50*
b. Imperf., pair 40.00

Overprinted in Black or Red

266 A17 1m car & gray .25 *1.40*
a. Imperf., pair 40.00 300.00
b. Inverted overprint 37.50
267 A17 1¼m ultra & ol bis .25 *1.40*
a. Imperf., pair 40.00
268 A17 1½m dk grn & gray .30 *2.10*
a. Imperf., pair 40.00
269 A17 2m vio & ol bis .50 *2.50*
a. Without overprint 26.00
b. Imperf., pair 40.00
270 A17 2½m (#250) (R) .20 *1.75*
c. Imperf., pair 40.00
270A A17 2½m (#255) (R) .35 *62.50*
b. Imperf., pair 40.00

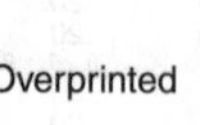

Overprinted

271 A18 3m pale blue 1.75 *5.75*
272 A18 4m dull red 2.10 *6.75*
a. Without overprint 37.50
273 A18 5m orange 1.75 *6.25*
274 A18 10m dp green 2.10 *7.75*
275 A18 20m black 4.00 *8.25*
Nos. 256-275 (21) 15.65 118.85

Nos. 256-275 were available for postage through all Germany, but were used almost exclusively in Bavaria.

SEMI-POSTAL STAMPS

Regular Issue of 1914-20 Surcharged in Black

1919 Wmk. 95h *Perf. 14x14½*
B1 A10 10pf + 5pf car rose .25 *1.25*
a. Inverted surcharge 21.00 *52.50*
b. Surcharge on back 40.00
c. Imperf., pair 250.00
B2 A10 15pf + 5pf ver .25 *1.25*
a. Inverted surcharge 21.00 *52.50*
b. Imperf., pair 150.00
B3 A10 20pf + 5pf blue .25 *1.50*
a. Inverted surcharge 21.00 *52.50*
b. Imperf., pair 300.00
Nos. B1-B3 (3) .75 *4.00*

Surtax was for wounded war veterans.

POSTAGE DUE STAMPS

D1

D2

With Silk Thread

1862 Typeset Unwmk. *Imperf.*
J1 D1 3kr black 95.00 250.00
a. "Empfange" 300.00 *775.00*

Without Silk Thread

1870 Typo. Wmk. 93 *Perf. 11½*
J2 D1 1kr black 8.00 *575.00*
a. Wmk. 92 35.00 *1,300.*
J3 D1 3kr black 8.00 *350.00*
a. Wmk. 92 35.00 700.00

Type of 1876 Regular Issue Overprinted in Red "Vom Empfänger zahlbar"

1876 Wmk. 94
J4 D2 3pf gray 11.00 *29.00*
J5 D2 5pf gray 8.00 *13.00*
J6 D2 10pf gray 2.50 1.00
Nos. J4-J6 (3) 21.50 *43.00*

1883 Wmk. 95v
J7 D2 3pf gray 65.00 *75.00*
J8 D2 5pf gray 42.50 47.50
J9 D2 10pf gray 1.75 .45
a. "Empfanper" 110.00 110.00
b. "zahlhar" 57.50 57.50
c. Imperf. 70.00
Nos. J7-J9 (3) 109.25 *122.95*

1895-1903 Wmk. 95h *Perf. 14½*
J10 D2 2pf gray .50 *1.10*
J11 D2 3pf gray ('03) .45 *2.00*
J12 D2 5pf gray ('03) .80 *1.40*
J13 D2 10pf gray ('03) .50 *.70*
Nos. J10-J13 (4) 2.25 *5.20*

1888

Rose-toned Paper

J10a D2 2pf gray 1.50 *3.50*
J11a D2 3pf gray 2.00 *1.75*
b. Inverted overprint *1,750.*
J12a D2 5pf gray 2.00 2.00
J13a D2 10pf gray 2.00 .85
b. As "a," double overprint *1,750.*
Nos. J10a-J13a (4) 7.50 8.10

No. J13b was used at Pirmasens.

Surcharged in Red in Each Corner

1895
J14 D2 2pf on 3pf gray *35,000.*

At least six copies exist, all used in Aichach.

OFFICIAL STAMPS

Nos. 77-81, 84, 95-96, 98-99, 102 perforated with a large E were issued for official use in 1912-16.

Regular Issue of 1888-1900 Overprinted

1908 Wmk. 95h *Perf. 14½*
O1 A5 3pf dk brown (R) .60 *2.50*
O2 A5 5pf dk green (R) .20 .20
O3 A5 10pf carmine (G) .20 .20
O4 A5 20pf ultra (R) .25 .40
O5 A5 50pf maroon 2.75 *4.75*
Nos. O1-O5 (5) 4.00 *8.05*

Nos. O1-O5 were issued for the use of railway officials. "E" stands for "Eisenbahn."

Coat of Arms — O1

1916-17 Typo. *Perf. 11½*
O6 O1 3pf bister brn .20 *.40*
O7 O1 5pf yellow grn .20 *.40*
O8 O1 7½pf grn, *grn* .20 *.30*
O9 O1 7½pf grn ('17) .20 *.25*
O10 O1 10pf deep rose .20 *.25*
O11 O1 15pf red, *buff* .25 *.30*
O12 O1 15pf red ('17) .20 *.40*
O13 O1 20pf dp bl, *bl* 1.00 *1.50*
O14 O1 20pf dp blue ('17) .20 *.25*
O15 O1 25pf gray .20 *.30*
O16 O1 30pf orange .20 *.30*
O17 O1 60pf dark green .20 *.30*
O18 O1 1m dl vio, *gray* .45 *1.50*
O19 O1 1m maroon ('17) 1.50 *350.00*
Nos. O6-O19 (14) 5.20 356.45

Used Values of Nos. O6-O69 are for postally used stamps. Canceled-to-order stamps, which abound, sell for same prices as unused.

Official Stamps and Type of 1916-17 Overprinted

1918
O20 O1 3pf bister brn .20 *7.75*
O21 O1 5pf yellow green .20 *.80*
O22 O1 7½pf gray green .20 *7.75*
O23 O1 10pf deep rose .20 *.80*
O24 O1 15pf red .20 *.80*
O25 O1 20pf blue .20 *.80*
O26 O1 25pf gray .20 *.80*
O27 O1 30pf orange .20 *.80*
O28 O1 35pf orange .20 *.80*
O29 O1 50pf olive gray .20 *1.00*
O30 O1 60pf dark green .20 *7.75*
O31 O1 75pf red brown .25 *2.10*
O32 O1 1m dl vio, *gray* .60 *7.75*
O33 O1 1m maroon 2.40 *250.00*
Nos. O20-O33 (14) 5.45 289.70

O2

O3

O4

1920 Typo. *Perf. 14x14½*
O34 O2 5pf yellow grn .20 *4.00*
O35 O2 10pf orange .20 *4.00*
O36 O2 15pf carmine .20 *4.00*
O37 O2 20pf violet .20 *4.00*
O38 O2 30pf dark blue .20 *5.25*
O39 O2 40pf bister .20 *5.25*

Perf. 14½x14

Wmk. 95v

O40 O3 50pf vermilion .20 *16.00*
O41 O3 60pf blue green .20 *6.75*
O42 O3 70pf dk violet .20 *18.00*
a. Imperf., pair 21.00
O43 O3 75pf deep rose .20 *22.50*
O44 O3 80pf dull blue .20 *22.50*
O45 O3 90pf olive green .20 *32.50*
O46 O4 1m dark brown .20 *29.00*
a. Imperf., pair 57.50
O47 O4 1¼m green .20 *40.00*
O48 O4 1½m vermilion .20 *42.50*
a. Imperf. pair 19.00
O49 O4 2½m deep blue .20 *47.50*
a. Imperf. pair 57.50
O50 O4 3m dark red .20 *57.50*
a. Imperf. pair 16.00
O51 O4 5m black 1.25 *72.50*
a. Imperf., pair 57.50
Nos. O34-O51 (18) 4.65 433.75

Stamps of Preceding Issue Overprinted

1920, Apr. 1
O52 O2 5pf yellow green .20 *2.10*
a. Imperf., pair 21.00
O53 O2 10pf orange .20 *1.25*
O54 O2 15pf carmine .20 *1.25*
O55 O2 20pf violet .20 *1.00*
O56 O2 30pf dark blue .20 *.90*
O57 O2 40pf bister .20 *.90*
O58 O3 50pf vermilion .20 *.90*
a. Imperf., pair 21.00
O59 O3 60pf blue green .20 *.90*
O60 O3 70pf dark violet 1.25 *1.75*
O61 O3 75pf deep rose .25 *.90*
O62 O3 80pf dull blue .20 *.90*
O63 O3 90pf olive green 1.00 *2.10*

Similar Ovpt., Words 8mm apart

O64 O4 1m dark brown .20 *.90*
a. Imperf., pair 21.00
O65 O4 1¼m green .20 *.90*
O66 O4 1½m vermilion .20 *.90*
O67 O4 2½m deep blue .20 *.90*
a. Imperf., pair 30.00
O68 O4 3m dark red .20 *.90*
O69 O4 5m black 6.25 *20.00*
Nos. O52-O69 (18) 11.55 39.35

Nos. O52-O69 could be used in all parts of Germany, but were almost exclusively used in Bavaria.

BERGEDORF

LOCATION — A town in northern Germany.

POP. — 2,989 (1861)

Originally Bergedorf belonged jointly to the Free City of Hamburg and the Free City of Lübeck. In 1867 it was purchased by Hamburg.

16 Schillings = 1 Mark

Values for unused stamps are for examples with original gum as defined in the catalogue introduction. Copies without gum sell for about 40% of the figures quoted. Values for used stamps are for examples canceled with parallel bars. Copies bearing dated town postmarks sell for more.

Combined Arms of Lübeck and Hamburg

A1 A2 A3

A4

A5

1861-67 Unwmk. Litho. *Imperf.*
1 A1 ½s blk, *pale bl* 35.00 *525.00*
a. ½s black, *blue* ('67) 100.00 *3,750.*
2 A3 1s blk, *white* 35.00 *250.00*
a. Tête bêche pair, vertical 200.00
b. Tête bêche pair, horiz. 260.00
3 A4 1½s blk, *yellow* 14.50 *1,000.*
a. Tête bêche pair *125.00*
4 A2 3s blue, *pink* 18.00 *1,250.*
5 A5 4s blk, *brown* 18.00 *1,600.*
Nos. 1-5 (5) 120.50 4,625.

Counterfeit cancellations are plentiful.

No. 3 exists in a tête bêche gutter pair. Value, unused $325.

The ½s on violet and 3s on rose, listed previously, as well as a 1s and 1½s on thick paper and 4s on light rose brown, come from proof sheets and were never placed in use. A 1½ "SCHILLINGE" (instead of SCHILLING) also exists only as a proof.

REPRINTS

½ SCHILLING

There is a dot in the upper part of the right branch of "N" of "EIN." The upper part of the shield is blank or almost blank. The horizontal bar of "H" in "HALBER" is generally defective.

1 SCHILLING

The "1" in the corners is generally with foot. The central horizontal bar of the "E" of "EIN" is separated from the vertical branch by a black line. The "A" of "POSTMARKE" has the horizontal bar incomplete or missing. The horizontal bar of the "H" of "SCHILLING" is separated from the vertical branches by a dark line at each side, sometimes the bar is missing.

1½ SCHILLINGE

There is a small triangle under the right side of the tower, exactly over the "R" of "POSTMARKE."

3 SCHILLINGE

The head of the eagle is not shaded. The horizontal bar of the second "E" of "BERGEDORF" is separated from the vertical branch by a thin line. There is generally a colored dot in the lower half of the "S" of "POSTMARKE."

4 SCHILLINGE

The upper part of the shield is blank or has two or three small dashes. In most of the reprints there is a diagonal dash across the wavy lines of the groundwork at the right of "I" and "E" of "VIER."

Reprints, value $1 each.

These stamps were superseded by those of the North German Confederation in 1868.

BREMEN

LOCATION — In northwestern Germany
AREA — 99 sq. mi.
POP. — 122,402 (1871)

Bremen was a Free City and member of the German Confederation. In 1870 it became part of the German Empire.

22 Grote = 10 Silbergroschen

Values for unused stamps are for examples with original gum as defined in the catalogue introduction. Copies without gum sell for about 50-60% the figures quoted.

Coat of Arms — A1

THREE GROTE
I II III

Type I - The central part of the scroll below the word Bremen is crossed by one vertical line.
Type II - The center of the scroll is crossed by two vertical lines.
Type III - The center of the scroll is crossed by three vertical lines.

1855 Unwmk. Litho. *Imperf.*
Horizontally Laid Paper
1 A1 3gr black, *blue* 150.00 210.00
Vertically Laid Paper
1A A1 3gr black, *blue* 210.00 450.00

No. 1 can be found with parts of a papermaker's watermark, consisting of lilies. Value: unused $900; used $1,250.
See Nos. 9-10.

A2 A3

FIVE GROTE

Type I - The shading at the left of the ribbon containing "funf Grote" runs downward from the shield.
Type II - The shading at the left of the ribbon containing "funf Grote" runs upward.

1856-60 Wove Paper
2 A2 5gr blk, *rose* 110.00 225.00
a. Printed on both sides
b. "Marken" (not issued) 9.00
3 A2 7gr blk, *yel* ('60) 175.00 *525.00*
4 A3 5sgr green ('59) 110.00 260.00
a. Chalky paper 40.00 *375.00*
b. 5sgr yellow green 95.00 175.00

See Nos. 6, 8, 12-13, 15.

A4 A5

1861-63 *Serpentine Roulette*
5 A4 2gr orange ('63) 240.00 *1,150.*
a. 2gr red orange 350.00 *2,250.*
b. Chalky paper 300.00 *2,400.*
6 A2 5gr blk, *rose* ('62) 110.00 150.00
a. Horiz. pair, imperf between —
7 A5 10gr black 350.00 *700.00*
8 A3 5sgr yellow green ('63) 350.00 175.00
a. Chalky paper 425.00 350.00
b. 5sgr green 225.00 150.00

See Nos. 11, 14.

1863
Horizontally (H) or Vertically (V) Laid Paper
9 A1 3gr blk, *blue* (V) 275.00 450.00
a. 3gr black, *blue* (H) 875.00 *2,250.*

1866-67 *Perf. 13*
10 A1 3gr black, *blue* 57.50 225.00
Wove Paper
11 A4 2gr orange 55.00 *175.00*
a. 2gr red orange 140.00 *400.00*
b. Horiz. pair, imperf. btwn. 2,250.
12 A2 5gr blk, *rose* 95.00 *200.00*
a. Horiz. pair, imperf. btwn. 700.00 —
13 A2 7gr blk, *yel* ('67) 110.00 *3,250.*
14 A5 10gr black ('67) 150.00 *800.00*
15 A3 5sgr green 110.00 *2,900.*
a. 5sgr yellow green 150.00 150.00
b. As "a," chalky paper 225.00 225.00

The stamps of Bremen were superseded by those of the North German Confederation on Jan. 1, 1868.

BRUNSWICK

LOCATION — In northern Germany
GOVT. — Duchy
AREA — 1,417 sq. mi.
POP. — 349,367 (1880)
CAPITAL — Brunswick

Brunswick was a member of the German Confederation and, in 1870 became part of the German Empire.

12 Pfennigs = 1 Gutegroschen
30 Silbergroschen (Groschen) = 24 Gutegroschen = 1 Thaler

Values for unused stamps are for examples with original gum as defined in the catalogue introduction except for Nos. 1-3 which are valued without gum. Nos. 1-3 with original gum sell for much higher prices, and Nos. 4-26 without gum sell for about 50-60% of the figures quoted.

The "Leaping Saxon Horse" — A1

The ½gr has white denomination and "Gr" in right oval.

1852 Unwmk. Typo. *Imperf.*
1 A1 1sgr rose 1,450. 225.00
2 A1 2sgr blue 1,050. 190.00
a. Half used as 1sgr on cover —
3 A1 3sgr vermilion 1,050. 175.00

See Nos. 4-11, 13-22.

1853-63 Wmk. 102
4 A1 ¼ggr blk, *brn*('56) 575.00 190.00
5 A1 ⅓sgr black ('56) 110.00 250.00
6 A1 ½gr blk, *grn*('63) 17.50 *175.00*
7 A1 1sgr blk, *orange* 300.00 42.50
a. 1sgr black, *orange buff* 300.00 50.00
8 A1 1sgr blk, *yel* ('61) 300.00 35.00
a. Diagonal half used as ½sgr on cover *14,500.*
9 A1 2sgr blk, *blue* 225.00 42.50
a. Diagonal half used as 1sgr on cover *7,000.*
b. Vertical half used as 1sgr on cover *14,500.*
10 A1 3sgr blk, *rose* 350.00 57.50
11 A1 3sgr rose ('62) 450.00 160.00

A3 A4

1857
12 A3 Four ¼ggr blk, *brn*('57) 30.00 70.00
a. Four ¼ggr blk, *yel brown* — 150.00

The bister on white paper was not issued. Value $5.25.

1864 *Serpentine Roulette 16*
13 A1 ⅓sgr black 350.00 *1,650.*
14 A1 ½gr blk, *green* 150.00 *2,350.*
15 A1 1sgr blk, *yellow* *2,300.* *1,150.*
16 A1 1sgr yellow 300.00 100.00
17 A1 2sgr blk, *blue* 300.00 250.00
a. Half used as 1sgr on cover *9,000.*
18 A1 3sgr rose 575.00 375.00
Rouletted 12
20 A1 1sgr blk, *yellow* *8,750.*
21 A1 1sgr yellow 475.00 250.00
22 A1 3sgr rose — *2,000.*

#13, 16, 18, 21-22 are on white paper.
Faked roulettes of Nos. 13-22 exist.

Serpentine Roulette
1865 Embossed Unwmk.
23 A4 ⅓gr black 20.00 *250.00*
24 A4 1gr carmine 1.75 *35.00*
25 A4 2gr ultra 6.50 *90.00*
a. 2gr gray blue 6.50 *90.00*
c. Half used as 1sgr on cover *14,000.*
26 A4 3gr brown 5.25 *100.00*
Nos. 23-26 (4) 33.50 475.00

Faked cancellations of Nos. 5-26 exist.

Imperf., Pair
23a A4 ⅓gr 70.00
24a A4 1gr 22.50
25b A4 2gr 60.00
26a A4 3gr 70.00

Stamps of Brunswick were superseded by those of the North German Confederation on Jan. 1, 1868.

HAMBURG

LOCATION — Northern Germany
GOVT. — Free City
AREA — 160 sq. mi.
POP. — 453,869 (1880)
CAPITAL — Hamburg

Hamburg was a member of the German Confederation and became part of the German Empire in 1870.

16 Schillings = 1 Mark

Values for unused stamps are for examples with original gum as defined in the catalogue introduction. Copies without gum sell for about 50-60% of the figures quoted.

Value Numeral on Arms — A1

1859 Typo. Wmk. 128 *Imperf.*
1 A1 ½s black 70.00 *450.00*
2 A1 1s brown 70.00 *57.50*
3 A1 2s red 70.00 *80.00*
4 A1 3s blue 70.00 *95.00*
5 A1 4s yellow green 52.50 *1,050.*
a. 4s green 87.50 *950.00*
b. Double impression —
6 A1 7s orange 65.00 30.00
7 A1 9s yellow 150.00 *1,450.*

See Nos. 13-21.

A2 A3

1864 Litho.
9 A2 1¼s gray 65.00 57.50
a. 1¼s lilac 110.00 70.00
b. 1¼s red lilac 110.00 57.50
c. 1¼s blue 350.00 *700.00*
d. 1¼s greenish gray 87.50 *77.50*
12 A3 2½s green 110.00 *110.00*

See Nos. 22-23.

The 1¼s and 2½s have been reprinted on watermarked and unwatermarked paper.

1864-65 Typo. *Perf. 13½*
13 A1 ½s black 4.25 7.75
a. Horiz. pair, imperf between 52.50
14 A1 1s brown 8.75 11.50
a. Half used as ½s on cover *14,000.*
b. Horiz. pair, imperf between 350.00 *575.00*
15 A1 2s red 10.50 16.00
17 A1 3s ultra 27.50 27.50
a. Imperf., pair 110.00
b. Horiz. pair, imperf vert.
c. 3s blue 32.50 25.00
18 A1 4s green 7.00 14.50
19 A1 7s orange 110.00 87.50
20 A1 7s violet ('65) 7.50 12.50
a. Imperf., pair 210.00
21 A1 9s yellow 18.00 *1,500.*
a. Vert. pair, imperf. btwn. 300.00
Litho.
22 A2 1¼s lilac 57.50 8.75
a. 1¼s red lilac 57.50 8.75
b. 1¼s violet 57.50 7.00
23 A3 2½s yellow grn 87.50 21.00
a. 2½s blue green 87.50 22.50

The 1¼s has been reprinted on watermarked and unwatermarked paper; the 2½s on unwatermarked paper.

A4 A5

Rouletted 10
1866 Unwmk. Embossed
24 A4 1¼s violet 30.00 27.50
a. 1¼s red violet 57.50 52.50
25 A5 1½s rose 5.75 *95.00*

Reprints:
1¼s: The rosettes between the words of the inscription have a well-defined open circle in the center of the originals, while in the reprints this circle is filled up.
In the upper part of the top of the "g" of "Schilling", there is a thin vertical line which is missing in the reprints.
The two lower lines of the triangle in the upper left corner are of different thicknesses in the originals while in the reprints they are of equal thickness.
The labels at the right and left containing the inscriptions are 2¾mm in width in the originals while they are 2½mm in reprints.
1½s: The originals are printed on thinner paper than the reprints. This is easily seen by turning the stamps over, when on the originals the color and impression will clearly show through, which is not the case in the reprints.
The vertical stroke of the upper part of the "g" in Schilling is very short on the originals, scarcely crossing the top line, while in the reprints it almost touches the center of the "g."
The lower part of the "g" of Schilling in the originals, barely touches the inner line of the frame, in some stamps it does not touch it at all, while in the reprints the whole stroke runs into the inner line of the frame.

A6

1867 Typo. Wmk. 128 *Perf. 13½*
26 A6 2½s dull green 8.75 *57.50*
a. 2½s dark green 45.00 *70.00*
b. Imperf., pair 190.00
c. Horiz. pair, imperf between 70.00

Forged cancellations exist on almost all stamps of Hamburg, especially on Nos. 4, 7, 21 and 25.
Nos. 1-23 and 26 exist without watermark, but they come from the same sheets as the watermarked stamps.
The stamps of Hamburg were superseded by those of the North German Confederation on Jan. 1, 1868.

HANOVER

LOCATION — Northern Germany
GOVT. — Kingdom
AREA — 14,893 sq. mi.
POP. — 3,191,000
CAPITAL — Hanover

Hanover was a member of the German Confederation and became in 1866 a province of Prussia.

10 Pfennigs = 1 Groschen
24 Gute Groschen = 1 Thaler
30 Silbergroschen = 1 Thaler (1858)

Values for unused stamps are for examples with original gum as defined in the catalogue introduction. Copies without gum sell for about 50-60% of the figures quoted.

Coat of Arms
A1 A2

Wmk. Square Frame

1850 Rose Gum Typo. *Imperf.*
1 A1 1g g blk, *gray bl* 2,100. 35.00

See Nos. 2, 11.

The reprints have white gum and no watermark.

1851-55 Wmk. 130
2 A1 1g g blk, *gray grn* 70.00 5.00
a. 1g g black, *yellow green* 450.00 24.00
3 A2 1/30th blk, *salmon* 87.50 37.50
a. 1/30th black, *crimson* ('55) 87.50 37.50
b. Bisect on cover —
5 A2 1/15th blk, *gray bl* 140.00 57.50
a. Bisect on cover —
6 A2 1/10th blk, *yellow* 175.00 45.00
a. 1/10th black, *orange* 175.00 45.00
Nos. 2-6 (4) 472.50 145.00

Bisects Nos. 3b, 5a, 12a and 13a were used for ½g.

See Nos. 8, 12-13.

The 1/10th has been reprinted on unwatermarked paper, with white gum.

Crown and Numeral — A3

1853 Wmk. 130
7 A3 3pf rose 350.00 240.00

See Nos. 9, 16-17, 25.

The reprints of No. 7 have white gum.

Fine Network in Second Color

1855 Unwmk.
8 A2 1/10th black & org 175.00 110.00
a. 1/10th black & yellow 300.00 175.00

No. 8 with olive yellow network and other values with fine network are essays.

Large Network in Second Color

1856-57
9 A3 3pf rose & blk 225.00 210.00
a. 3pf rose & gray 300.00 275.00
11 A1 1g black & grn g 57.50 6.50
12 A2 1/30th black & rose 110.00 25.00
a. Bisect on cover 12,000.
13 A2 1/15th black & blue 87.50 55.00
a. Bisect on cover 5,750.
14 A2 1/10th blk & org ('57) 575.00 42.50

The reprints have white gum, and the network does not cover all the outer margin.

Without Network

1859-63
16 A3 3pf pink 57.50 65.00
a. 3pf carmine rose 97.50 110.00
17 A3 3pf grn (Drei Zehntel) ('63) 300.00 725.00

Copies of No. 25 with rouletting trimmed off sometimes pretend to be No. 17. Minimum size of No. 17 acknowledged as genuine: 21½x24½mm.

The reprints of No. 16 have pink gum instead of red; the extremities of the banderol point downward instead of outward.

Crown and Post Horn — A7

King George V — A8

1859-61 *Imperf.*
18 A7 ½g black ('60) 50.00 160.00
a. Rose gum 225.00 275.00
19 A8 1g rose 2.25 2.00
a. 1g vio rose 25.00 20.00
b. 1g carmine 14.00 17.50
c. Half used as ½g on cover 10,000.
20 A8 2g ultra 14.00 25.00
a. Half used as 1g on cover 7,500.
22 A8 3g yellow 125.00 45.00
a. 3g orange yellow 110.00 70.00
23 A8 3g brown ('61) 20.00 40.00
a. One third used as 1g on cover —
24 A8 10g green ('61) 210.00 675.00

Reprints of ½g are on thick toned paper with yellowish gum. Originals are on white paper with rose or white gum. Reprints exist tête bêche.

Reprints of 3g yellow and 3g brown have white or pinkish gum. Originals have rose or orange gum.

1864 White Gum *Perce en Arc 16*
25 A3 3pf grn (Drei Zehntel) 24.00 45.00
26 A7 ½g black 200.00 200.00
27 A8 1g rose 5.75 2.40
28 A8 2g ultra 87.50 45.00
a. Half used as 1g on cover —
29 A8 3g brown 50.00 55.00
Nos. 25-29 (5) 367.25 347.40

Reprints of 3g are percé en arc 13½.

Rose Gum
25a A3 3pf green 57.50 57.50
26a A7 ½g black 350.00 300.00
27a A8 1g rose 30.00 18.00
29a A8 3g brown 875.00 900.00

The stamps of Prussia superseded those of Hanover on Oct. 1, 1866.

LUBECK

LOCATION — Situated on an arm of the Baltic Sea between the former German States of Holstein and Mecklenburg.
GOVT. — Free City and State
AREA — 115 sq. mi.
POP. — 136,413
CAPITAL — Lubeck

Lubeck was a member of the German Confederation and became part of the German Empire in 1870.

16 Schillings = 1 Mark

Values for Nos. 1-7 unused are for copies without gum. Copies with gum sell for about twice the figures quoted. Values for Nos. 8-14 unused are for examples with original gum as defined in the catalogue introduction. Nos. 8-14 without gum sell for about 50-60% of the figures quoted.

Coat of Arms — A1

1859 Litho. Wmk. 148 *Imperf.*
1 A1 ½g gray lilac 300.00 *1,300.*
2 A1 1s orange 300.00 *1,300.*
3 A1 2s brown 13.00 *140.00*
a. Value in words reads "ZWEI EIN HALB" 250.00 *5,250.*
4 A1 2½s rose 29.00 *525.00*
5 A1 4s green 13.00 *425.00*

1862 Unwmk.
6 A1 ½s lilac 9.25 *1,150.*
7 A1 1s yellow orange 17.00 *1,150.*

The reprints of the 1859-62 issues are unwatermarked and printed in bright colors.

A2

A3

1863 *Rouletted 11½*

Eagle embossed
8 A2 ½s green 26.00 *40.00*
9 A2 1s orange 82.50 *92.50*
a. Rouletted 10 125.00 *300.00*
10 A2 2s rose 16.00 *37.50*
11 A2 2½s ultra 35.00 *250.00*
12 A2 4s bister 26.00 *67.50*
Nos. 8-12 (5) 185.50 *487.50*

The reprints are imperforate and without embossing.

1864 Litho. *Imperf.*
13 A3 1¼s dark brown 26.00 *26.00*
a. 1¼s reddish brown 17.00 *47.50*

A4

1865 *Rouletted 11½*

Eagle embossed
14 A4 1½s red lilac 17.00 *52.50*

The reprints are imperforate and without embossing.

Counterfeit cancellations are found on #1-14.

The stamps of Lübeck were superseded by those of the North German Confederation on Jan. 1, 1868.

MECKLENBURG-SCHWERIN

LOCATION — In northern Germany, bordering on the Baltic Sea.
GOVT. — Grand Duchy
AREA — 5,065 sq. mi. (approx.)
POP. — 674,000 (approx.)
CAPITAL — Schwerin

Mecklenburg-Schwerin was a member of the German Confederation and became part of the German Empire in 1870.

48 Schillings = 1 Thaler

Values for unused stamps are for examples with original gum as defined in the catalogue introduction. Copies without gum sell for about 70% of the figures quoted.

Coat of Arms
A1 A2

1856 Unwmk. Typo. *Imperf.*
1 A1 Four ¼s red 92.50 77.50
a. ¼s red 9.25 7.75
2 A2 3s orange yellow 52.50 32.50
3 A2 5s blue 150.00 *175.00*
Nos. 1-3 (3) 295.00 *285.00*

See Nos. 4, 6-8.

A3

1864-67 *Rouletted 11½*
4 A1 Four ¼s red *2,000.* *1,300.*
a. ¼s red 125.00 175.00
5 A3 Four ¼s red 40.00 35.00
a. ¼s red 5.25 5.25
6 A2 2s gray lil ('67) 92.50 *1,150.*
a. 2s red violet ('66) 150.00 150.00

7 A2 3s org yel, wide margin ('67) 26.00 *200.00*
a. Narrow margin ('65) 110.00 77.50
8 A2 5s bister brn 92.50 *150.00*
a. Thick paper 150.00 *225.00*

The overall size of #7, including margin, is 24½x24½mm. That of #7a is 23½x23mm.

Counterfeit cancellations exist on those stamps valued higher used than unused.

These stamps were superseded by those of the North German Confederation on Jan. 1, 1868.

MECKLENBURG-STRELITZ

LOCATION — In northern Germany, divided by Mecklenburg-Schwerin
GOVT. — Grand Duchy
AREA — 1,131 sq. mi.
POP. — 106,347
CAPITAL — Neustrelitz

Mecklenburg-Strelitz was a member of the German Confederation and became part of the German Empire in 1870.

30 Silbergroschen = 48 Schillings = 1 Thaler

Values for unused stamps are for examples with original gum as defined in the catalogue introduction. Copies without gum sell for about 50% of the figures quoted.

Coat of Arms
A1 A2

Rouletted 11½

1864 Unwmk. Embossed
1 A1 ¼sg orange 110. *1,850.*
a. ¼sg yellow orange 250. *3,500.*
2 A1 ⅓sg green 42.50 *925.*
a. ⅓sg dark green 92.50 *1,850.*
3 A1 1sch violet 200. *2,450.*
4 A2 1sg rose 100. 125.
5 A2 2sg ultra 24. *525.*
6 A2 3sg bister 21. *1,050.*

Counterfeit cancellations abound.

These stamps were superseded by those of the North German Confederation in 1868.

OLDENBURG

LOCATION — In northwestern Germany, bordering on the North Sea.
GOVT. — Grand Duchy
AREA — 2,482 sq. mi.
POP. — 483,042 (1910)
CAPITAL — Oldenburg

Oldenburg was a member of the German Confederation and became part of the German Empire in 1870.

30 Silbergroschen = 1 Thaler
30 Groschen = 1 Thaler

Values for unused stamps are for examples with original gum as defined in the catalogue introduction. Copies without gum sell for about 50% of the figures quoted.

A1 A2

1852-55 Unwmk. Litho. *Imperf.*
1 A1 1/30th blk, *blue* 240.00 16.00
2 A1 1/15th blk, *rose* 525.00 52.50
3 A1 1/10th blk, *yellow* 525.00 52.50
4 A2 ⅓sgr blk, *grn*('55) 800.00 800.00

There are three types of Nos. 1 and 2.

A3

A4

1859

5 A3 ⅓g blk, *green* 1,750. *2,100.*
6 A3 1g blk, *blue* 475.00 29.00
7 A3 2g blk, *rose* 625.00 400.00
8 A3 3g blk, *yellow* 625.00 400.00
a. "OLBENBURG" 975.00 825.00

See Nos. 10, 13-15.

1861

9 A4 ¼g orange 200.00 *2,600.*
10 A3 ⅓g green 300.00 *575.00*
a. ⅓g bluish green 300.00 *575.00*
b. ⅓g moss green 1,150. *1,850.*
c. "OLDEIBURG" *475.00 775.00*
d. "Dritto" *475.00 775.00*
e. "Drittd" *475.00 775.00*
f. Printed on both sides *4,000.*
12 A4 ½g redsh brn 275.00 325.00
a. ½g dark brown 275.00 325.00
13 A3 1g blue 140.00 100.00
a. 1g gray blue 300.00 160.00
b. Printed on both sides *3,000.*
14 A3 2g red 275.00 275.00
15 A3 3g yellow 275.00 250.00
a. "OLDEIBURG" *475.00 475.00*
b. Printed on both sides *4,000.*

Forged cancellations are found on Nos. 9, 10, 12 and their minor varieties.

Coat of Arms — A5

1862 Embossed *Rouletted 11½*

16 A5 ⅓g green 125.00 125.00
17 A5 ½g orange 125.00 62.50
a. ½g orange red 150.00 92.50
18 A5 1g rose 72.50 9.25
19 A5 2g ultra 125.00 30.00
20 A5 3g bister 140.00 32.50

1867 *Rouletted 10*

21 A5 ⅓g green 14.50 *350.00*
22 A5 ½g orange 14.50 *240.00*
23 A5 1g rose 6.25 *30.00*
a. Half used as ½g on cover —
24 A5 2g ultra 6.25 *250.00*
25 A5 3g bister 16.00 *210.00*
Nos. 21-25 (5) 57.50 1,080.

Forged cancellations are found on #21-25.

The stamps of Oldenburg were replaced by those of the North German Confederation on Jan. 1, 1868.

PRUSSIA

LOCATION — The greater part of northern Germany.
GOVT. — Independent Kingdom
AREA — 134,650 sq. mi.
POP. — 40,165,219 (1910)
CAPITAL — Berlin

Prussia was a member of the German Confederation and became part of the German Empire in 1870.

12 Pfennigs = 1 Silbergroschen
60 Kreuzer = 1 Gulden (1867)

Values for unused stamps are for examples with original gum as defined in the catalogue introduction. Copies without gum sell for about 50% of the figures quoted.

King Frederick William IV
A1 A2

1850-56 Engr. Wmk. 162 *Imperf.*
Background of Crossed Lines

1 A1 4pf yel grn ('56) 72.50 47.50
a. 4pf dark green 100.00 77.50
2 A1 6pf (½sg) red org 52.50 30.00
3 A2 1sg black, *rose* 52.50 5.25
a. 1sg black, *bright red* *14,500.* 275.00
4 A2 2sg black, *blue* 72.50 10.50
a. Half used as 1sg on cover —
5 A2 3sg black, *yellow* 67.50 7.75
a. 3sg black, *orange buff* 210.00 21.00
Nos. 1-5 (5) 317.50 101.00

See Nos. 10-13.

Reprints exist on watermarked and unwatermarked paper.

A3

A4

Solid Background

1857 Typo. Unwmk.

6 A3 1sg rose 210.00 24.00
a. 1sg carmine rose 225.00 30.00
7 A3 2sg blue 825.00 52.50
a. 2sg dark blue 1,150. 77.50
b. Half used as 1sg on cover —
8 A3 3sg orange 100.00 26.00
a. 3sg yellow 1,050. 62.50
b. 3sg deep orange 525.00 77.50
Nos. 6-8 (3) 1,135. 102.50

The reprints of Nos. 6-8 inclusive have a period instead of a colon after "SILBERGR."

Background of Crossed Lines

1858-60 Typo.

9 A4 4pf green 47.50 21.00

Engr.

10 A1 6pf (½sg) org ('59) 125.00 100.00
a. 6pf (½sg) brick red 175.00 125.00

Typo.

11 A2 1sg rose 21.00 1.50
12 A2 2sg blue 72.50 10.50
a. 2sg dark blue 100.00 26.00
b. Half used as 1sg on cover —
13 A2 3sg orange 62.50 9.25
a. 3sg yellow 92.50 10.50
Nos. 9-13 (5) 328.50 142.25

Coat of Arms
A6 A7

1861-65 Embossed *Rouletted 11½*

14 A6 3pf red lilac ('67) 17.00 24.00
a. 3pf red violet ('65) 210.00 175.00
15 A6 4pf yellow green 6.25 5.25
a. 4pf green 26.00 26.00
16 A6 6pf orange 6.25 9.25
a. 6pf vermilion 77.50 40.00
17 A7 1sg rose 2.10 .50
18 A7 2sg ultra 6.25 1.00
a. 2sg blue 250.00 21.00
20 A7 3sg bister 5.75 1.25
a. 3sg gray brown ('65) 250.00 21.00
Nos. 14-20 (6) 43.60 41.25

A8

A9

Typographed in Reverse on Paper Resembling Goldbeater's Skin

1866 *Rouletted 10*

21 A8 10sg rose 47.50 *47.50*
22 A9 30sg blue 57.50 *92.50*

Perfect copies of #21-22 are extremely rare.

A10

1867 Embossed *Rouletted 16*

23 A10 1kr green 16.00 *26.00*
24 A10 2kr orange 26.00 *57.50*
25 A10 3kr rose 13.00 *16.00*
26 A10 6kr ultra 13.00 *26.00*
27 A10 9kr bister brown 17.00 *29.00*
Nos. 23-27 (5) 85.00 *154.50*

Imperforate stamps of the above sets are proofs.

The stamps of Prussia were superseded by those of the North German Confederation on Jan. 1, 1868.

OFFICIAL STAMPS
See Germany Nos. OL1-OL15.

SAXONY

LOCATION — In central Germany
GOVT. — Kingdom
AREA — 5,787 sq. mi.
POP. — 2,500,000 (approx.)
CAPITAL — Dresden

Saxony was a member of the German Confederation and became a part of the German Empire in 1870.

10 Pfennigs = 1 Neu-Groschen
30 Neu-Groschen = 1 Thaler

Values for unused stamps are for examples with original gum as defined in the catalogue introduction. Copies without gum sell for about 50-60% of the figures quoted.

A1

1850 Unwmk. Typo. *Imperf.*

1 A1 3pf brick red *4,250. 4,000.*
a. 3pf cherry red *7,000. 10,000.*
b. 3pf brown red *7,000. 7,000.*

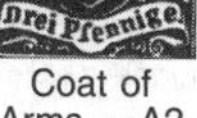
Coat of Arms — A2

Frederick Augustus II — A3

1851

2 A2 3pf green 77.50 62.50
a. 3pf yellow green 775.00 250.00

Nos. 2 and 2a are valued with the margin just touching the design in one or two places. Copies with margins all around sell considerably higher.

1851-52 Engr.

3 A3 ½ng black, *gray* 40.00 6.25
a. ½ng pale blue (error) *14,500.*
5 A3 1ng black, *rose* 62.50 5.25
6 A3 2ng black, *pale bl* 150.00 30.00
7 A3 2ng blk, *dk bl*('52) 475.00 29.00
8 A3 3ng black, *yellow* 100.00 13.00
Nos. 3-8 (5) 827.50 83.50

King John I — A4

1855-60

9 A4 ½ng black, *gray* 6.25 1.50
a. "1½" at left or right — —
10 A4 1ng black, *rose* 6.25 1.50
11 A4 2ng black, *dark blue* 13.00 6.25
a. 2ng black, *blue* 47.50 20.00
12 A4 3ng black, *yellow* 13.00 4.00
13 A4 5ng ver ('56) 52.50 37.50
a. 5ng orange brown ('60) 150.00 *175.00*
b. 5ng deep brown ('57) *475.00* 125.00
14 A4 10ng blue ('56) 150.00 150.00

The ½ng is found in 3 types, the 1ng in 2.

In 1861 the 5ng and 10ng were printed on hard, brittle, translucent paper.

A5

A6

Typo.; Arms Embossed

1863 *Perf. 13*

15 A5 3pf blue green 1.00 *17.00*
a. 3pf yellow green 26.00 *40.00*
16 A5 ½ng orange .60 1.00
a. ½ng red orange 13.00 3.00
17 A6 1ng rose .75 1.50
a. Vert. pair, imperf. between *150.00*
b. Horiz. pair, imperf. between *250.00*
18 A6 2ng blue 1.25 3.25
a. 2ng dark blue 7.75 18.00
19 A6 3ng red brown 1.50 6.25
a. 3ng bister brown 13.00 4.75
20 A6 5ng dull violet 21.00 *29.00*
a. 5ng gray violet 6.25 *210.00*
b. 5ng gray blue 10.50 *26.00*
c. 5ng slate 16.00 *125.00*

The stamps of Saxony were superseded on Jan. 1, 1868, by those of the North German Confederation.

SCHLESWIG-HOLSTEIN

LOCATION — In northern Germany.
GOVT. — Duchies
AREA — 7,338 sq. mi.
POP. — 1,519,000 (approx.)
CAPITAL — Schleswig

Schleswig-Holstein was an autonomous territory from 1848 to 1851 when it came under Danish rule. In 1864, it was occupied by Prussia and Austria, and in 1866 it became a province of Prussia.

16 Schillings = 1 Mark

Values for unused stamps are for examples with original gum as defined in the catalogue introduction. Copies without gum sell for about 50% of the figures quoted.

Coat of Arms — A1

Typographed; Arms Embossed
1850 Unwmk. *Imperf.*
With Silk Threads

1 A1 1s dl bl & grnsh bl 210.00 *4,000.*
a. 1s Prussian blue 475.00
2 A1 2s rose & pink 375.00 *5,250.*
a. 2s deep pink & rose 475.00
b. Double embossing *2,250.*

Forged cancellations are found on Nos. 1-2, 5-7, 9, 16 and 19.

A2

A3

1865 Typo. *Rouletted 11½*

3 A2 ⅓s rose 21.00 *29.00*
4 A2 1⅓s green 11.50 *14.50*
5 A3 1⅓s red lilac 29.00 *77.50*
6 A2 2s ultra 29.00 *140.00*
7 A3 4s bister 40.00 *775.00*
Nos. 3-7 (5) 130.50

Schleswig

A4

A5

1864 Typo. *Rouletted 11½*
8 A4 1⅓s green 29.00 13.00
9 A4 4s carmine 62.50 300.00

1865 *Rouletted 10, 11½*
10 A4 ½s green 21.00 35.00
11 A4 1⅓s red lilac 35.00 16.00
a. 1⅓s gray lilac ('67) 175.00 52.50
b. Half of #11a used as ⅔s on cover 23,000.
12 A5 1⅓s rose 19.00 40.00
13 A4 2s ultra 19.00 30.00
14 A4 4s bister 21.00 52.50
Nos. 10-14 (5) 115.00 173.50

Holstein

A6

A7

Type I - Small lettering in frame. Wavy lines in spandrels close together.

Type II - Small lettering in frame. Wavy lines wider apart.

Type III - Larger lettering in frame and no periods after "H R Z G." Wavy lines as II.

1864 Litho. *Imperf.*
15 A6 1¼s bl & gray, I 32.50 35.00
a. Half used as ⅝s on cover 7,000.
16 A6 1¼s bl & gray, II 525.00 2,250.
a. Half used as ⅝s on cover 17,500.
17 A6 1¼s bl & gray, III 30.00 40.00
a. Half used as ⅝s on cover 5,750.

1864 Typo. *Rouletted 8*
18 A7 1¼s blue & rose 26.00 13.00
a. Half used as ⅝s on cover 1,450.

A8

1865 *Rouletted 8*
19 A8 ½s green 40.00 62.50
20 A8 1⅓s red lilac 30.00 16.00
21 A8 2s blue 32.50 30.00
Nos. 19-21 (3) 102.50 108.50

A9

A10

1865-66 *Rouletted 7 and 8*
22 A9 1¼s red lilac ('66) 47.50 17.00
a. Half used as ⅝s on cover 17,500.
23 A10 1⅓s carmine 40.00 29.00
24 A9 2s blue ('66) 92.50 92.50
25 A10 4s bister 37.50 52.50
Nos. 22-25 (4) 217.50 191.00

These stamps were superseded by those of North German Confederation on Jan. 1, 1868.

THURN AND TAXIS

A princely house which, prior to the formation of the German Empire, enjoyed the privilege of a postal monopoly. These stamps were superseded on July 1, 1867, by those of Prussia, followed by those of the North German Postal District on Jan. 1, 1868, and later by stamps of the German Empire on Jan. 1, 1872.

Values for unused stamps are for examples with original gum as defined in the catalogue introduction. Copies without gum sell for about 50% of the figures quoted.

NORTHERN DISTRICT

30 Silbergroschen or Groschen = 1 Thaler

A1

A2

1852-58 Unwmk. Typo. *Imperf.*
1 A1 ¼sgr blk, *red brn*('54) 100.00 26.00
2 A1 ⅓sgr blk, *buff*('58) 47.50 100.00
3 A1 ½sgr blk, *green* 250.00 16.00
4 A1 1sgr blk, *dk bl* 525.00 62.50
5 A1 1sgr blk, *lt bl*('53) 300.00 9.25
6 A1 2sgr blk, *rose* 325.00 16.00
a Half used as 1sgr on cover 4,500.
7 A1 3sgr blk, *brownish yellow* 400.00 24.00
a. 3sgr blk, *pale orange yellow* 325.00 65.00

Reprints of Nos. 1-12, 15-20, 23-24, were made in 1910. They have "ND" in script on the back. Value, $6 each.

1859-60
8 A1 ¼sgr red ('60) 26.00 30.00
9 A1 ⅓gr green 100.00 47.50
10 A1 1sgr blue 100.00 21.00
11 A1 2sgr rose ('60) 57.50 40.00
12 A1 3sgr red brn ('60) 57.50 52.50
13 A2 5sgr lilac .75 150.00
14 A2 10sgr orange 1.00 375.00

Excellent forged cancellations exist on Nos. 13 and 14. For reprints, see note after No. 7.

1862-63
15 A1 ¼sgr black ('63) 13.00 30.00
16 A1 ⅓sgr green ('63) 18.00 100.00
17 A1 ½sgr orange yellow 40.00 24.00
18 A1 1sgr rose ('63) 26.00 16.00
19 A1 2sgr blue ('63) 21.00 47.50
20 A1 3sgr bister ('63) 10.50 24.00
Nos. 15-20 (6) 128.50 241.50

For reprints, see note after No. 7.

1865 *Rouletted*
21 A1 ¼sgr black 5.25 325.00
22 A1 ⅓sgr green 7.75 175.00
23 A1 ½sgr yellow 17.00 26.00
24 A1 1sgr rose 17.00 16.00
25 A1 2sgr blue 1.00 52.50
26 A1 3sgr bister 1.75 21.00
Nos. 21-26 (6) 49.75 615.50

For reprints, see note after No. 7.

1866 *Rouletted in Colored Lines*
27 A1 ¼sgr black .90 1,050.
28 A1 ⅓sgr green .90 475.00
29 A1 ½sgr yellow .90 100.00
30 A1 1sgr rose .90 47.50
a. Horizontal pair without rouletting between 77.50
b. Half used as ½sgr on cover —
31 A1 2sgr blue .90 475.00
32 A1 3sgr bister .90 125.00
Nos. 27-32 (6) 5.40 2,272.

Forged cancellations on Nos. 2, 13-14, 15-16, 21-22, 25-32 are plentiful.

SOUTHERN DISTRICT

60 Kreuzer = 1 Gulden

A1

A2

1852-53 Unwmk. *Imperf.*
42 A1 1kr blk, *lt grn* 92.50 7.75
43 A1 3kr blk, *dk bl* 350.00 24.00
44 A1 3kr blk, *bl* ('53) 300.00 7.75
45 A1 6kr blk, *rose* 475.00 5.25
46 A1 9kr blk, *brownish yellow* 325.00 7.75
a. 9kr blk, *pale orange yellow* 275.00 18.00

Reprints of Nos. 42-50, 53-56 were made in 1910. Each has "ND" in script on the back. Value, each $6.

1859
47 A1 1kr green 9.25 6.25
48 A1 3kr blue 225.00 11.50
49 A1 6kr rose 225.00 32.50
50 A1 9kr yellow 225.00 47.50
51 A2 15kr lilac 1.00 77.50
52 A2 30kr orange 1.00 210.00

Forged cancellations exist on Nos. 51 and 52. For reprints, see note after No. 46.

1862
53 A1 3kr rose 5.25 16.00
54 A1 6kr blue 5.25 16.00
55 A1 9kr bister 5.25 16.00
Nos. 53-55 (3) 15.75 48.00

For reprints, see note after No. 46.

1865 *Rouletted*
56 A1 1kr green 8.25 10.50
57 A1 3kr rose 13.00 5.25
58 A1 6kr blue 1.00 16.00
59 A1 9kr bister 1.50 18.00
Nos. 56-59 (4) 23.75 49.75

For reprint of No. 56, see note after No. 46.

1867 *Rouletted in Colored Lines*
60 A1 1kr green .90 18.00
61 A1 3kr rose .90 16.00
62 A1 6kr blue .90 26.00
63 A1 9kr bister .90 26.00
Nos. 60-63 (4) 3.60 86.00

Forged cancellations exist on Nos. 51-52, 58-63.

The Thurn & Taxis Stamps, Northern and Southern Districts, were replaced on July 1, 1867, by those of Prussia.

WURTTEMBERG

LOCATION — In southern Germany
GOVT. — Kingdom
AREA — 7,530 sq. mi.
POP. — 2,580,000 (approx.)
CAPITAL — Stuttgart

Württemberg was a member of the German Confederation and became a part of the German Empire in 1870. It gave up its postal autonomy on March 31, 1902, but official stamps were issued until 1923.

16 Kreuzer = 1 Gulden
100 Pfennigs = 1 Mark (1875)

Values for unused stamps are for examples with original gum as defined in the catalogue introduction. Unused copies without gum of Nos. 1-46 sell for about 60-70% of the figures quoted. Unused copies without gum of Nos. 47-54 sell for about 50% of the figures quoted.

A1

A1a

1851-52 Unwmk. Typo. *Imperf.*
1 A1 1kr blk, *buff* 575.00 62.50
a. 1kr black, *straw* 2,600. 300.00
2 A1 3kr blk, *yellow* 175.00 4.00
a. 3kr black, *orange* 2,300. 210.00
4 A1 6kr blk, *yel grn* 1,050. 24.00
a. 6kr black, *blue green* 2,000. 35.00
5 A1 9kr blk, *rose* 3,500. 24.00
6 A1a 18kr blk, *dl vio* ('52) 1,050. 400.00

On the "reprints" the letters of "Württemberg" are smaller, especially the first "e"; the right branch of the "r's" of Württemberg runs upward in the reprints and downward in the originals.

Coat of Arms — A2

With Orange Silk Threads
Typographed and Embossed

1857
7 A2 1kr yellow brown 375.00 47.50
a. 1kr dark brown 750.00 175.00
9 A2 3kr yellow orange 210.00 4.75
10 A2 6kr green 375.00 35.00
11 A2 9kr carmine rose 625.00 35.00
12 A2 18kr blue 1,850. 875.00

Very fine examples of Nos. 7-12 with have one or two margins touching, but not cutting, the frameline.

See Nos. 13-46, 53.

The reprints have red or yellow silk threads and are printed 2mm apart, while the originals are ¾mm apart.

1859 Without Silk Threads
13 A2 1kr brown 400.00 52.50
a. 1kr dark brown 1,450. 525.00
15 A2 3kr yellow org 175.00 4.75
16 A2 6kr green 7,000. 77.50
17 A2 9kr car rose 925.00 40.00
18 A2 18kr dark blue 2,200. 1,300.

The colors of the reprints are brighter; they are also printed 2mm apart instead of 1¼mm.

1860 *Perf. 13½*
19 A2 1kr brown 800.00 92.50
20 A2 3kr yellow org 210.00 5.25
21 A2 6kr green 2,200. 77.50
22 A2 9kr carmine 875.00 82.50

1861 Thin Paper
23 A2 1kr brown 400.00 92.50
a. 1kr black brown 475.00 110.00
25 A2 3kr yellow org 47.50 21.00
26 A2 6kr green 175.00 40.00
27 A2 9kr rose 525.00 100.00
a. 9kr claret 575.00 150.00
29 A2 18kr dark blue 1,150. 925.00

Copies of Nos. 23-29 with all perforations intact sell for considerably more.

1862 *Perf. 10*
30 A2 1kr black brown 210.00 175.00
31 A2 3kr yellow orange 300.00 21.00
32 A2 6kr green 225.00 77.50
33 A2 9kr claret 2,300. 475.00

1863
34 A2 1kr yellow grn 29.00 7.75
a. 1kr green 250.00 62.50
36 A2 3kr rose 210.00 2.50
a. 3kr dark claret 1,150. 175.00
37 A2 6kr blue 100.00 35.00
39 A2 9kr yellow brn 525.00 110.00
a. 9kr red brown 160.00 32.50
b. 9kr black brown 775.00 110.00
40 A2 18kr orange 775.00 250.00

1865-68 *Rouletted 10*
41 A2 1kr yellow grn 26.00 5.25
a. 1kr dark green 400.00 175.00
42 A2 3kr rose 26.00 1.50
a. 3kr claret 1,450. 1,700.
43 A2 6kr blue 160.00 32.50
44 A2 7kr slate bl ('68) 700.00 92.50
45 A2 9kr bister brn ('66) 1,150. 52.50
a. 9kr red brown 875.00 77.50
46 A2 18kr orange ('67) 1,300. 750.00

A3

1869-73 Typo. & Embossed
47 A3 1kr yellow grn 18.00 1.25
48 A3 2kr orange 110.00 82.50
49 A3 3kr rose 9.25 .75
50 A3 7kr blue 40.00 10.50
51 A3 9kr lt brn ('73) 52.50 29.00
52 A3 14kr orange 52.50 29.00
a. 14kr lemon yellow 1,050. 1,050.
Nos. 47-52 (6) 282.25 153.00

See No. 54.

1873 *Imperf.*
53 A2 70kr red violet 1,300. 2,900.
a. 70kr violet 2,200. 4,000.

Nos. 53 and 53a have single or double lines of fine black dots printed in the gutters between the stamps.

1874 *Perf. 11½x11*
54 A3 1kr yellow green 72.50 29.00

A4

A5

1875-1900 Typo.

55 A4 2pf sl gray ('94) 1.25 .60
56 A4 3pf green 13.00 1.00
57 A4 3pf brn ('90) .50 .40
a. Imperf. pair 100.00
58 A4 5pf violet 5.25 .50
59 A4 5pf grn ('90) 1.00 .40
a. 5pf blue green 200.00 18.00
b. Imperf., pair 100.00
60 A4 10pf carmine .75 .50
a. 10pf rose 52.50 .60
b. Imperf., pair 52.50
61 A4 20pf ultra .75 .50
a. 20pf dull blue .75 .50
b. Imperf., pair 100.00
62 A4 25pf red brn 77.50 6.25
63 A4 25pf orange ('90) 1.75 .75
a. Imperf., pair 100.00
64 A5 30pf org & blk ('00) 2.10 2.50
65 A5 40pf dp rose & blk ('00) 2.50 3.50
66 A4 50pf gray 525.00 26.00
67 A4 50pf gray grn 40.00 3.00
68 A4 50pf pur brn ('90) 1.75 .60
a. 50pf red brown 250.00 32.50
b. Imperf., pair 100.00
69 A4 2m yellow 575.00 160.00
70 A4 2m ver, *buff* ('79) 1,450. 82.50
71 A5 2m org & blk ('83) 5.75 6.25
Telegraph cancel 2.10
a. 2m yellow & black 275.00 35.00
b. Imperf., pair 100.00
Telegraph cancel 16.00
72 A5 5m bl & blk ('81) 29.00 *110.00*
Telegraph cancel 47.50
a. Double impression of figure of value 125.00

No. 70 has "Unverkauflich" (not for sale) printed on its back to remind postal clerks that it, like No. 69, was for their use and not to be sold to the public.

The regular postage stamps of Württemberg were superseded by those of the German Empire in 1902. Official stamps were in use until 1923.

WURTTEMBERG OFFICIAL STAMPS

For the Communal Authorities

O1

Perf. 11½x11

1875-1900 Typo. Unwmk.

O1 O1 2pf slate gray ('00) 1.00 .60
O2 O1 3pf brown ('96) 1.00 .50
O3 O1 5pf violet 26.00 1.00
a. Imperf., pair *2,900.*
O4 O1 5pf blue grn ('90) 1.00 .60
a. Imperf., pair 35.00
O5 O1 10pf rose 5.25 1.00
a. Imperf., pair 62.50
O6 O1 25pf orange ('00) 16.00 3.00
Nos. O1-O6 (6) 50.25 6.70

See Nos. O12-O32. For overprints and surcharges see Nos. O7-O11, O40-O52, O59-O93.

Used Values
When italicized, used values for Nos. O7-O183 are for favor-canceled copies. Postally used copies command a premium.

Stamps of Previous Issues Overprinted in Black

1906, Jan. 30

O7 O1 2pf slate gray 29.00 52.50
O8 O1 3pf dk brown 10.50 7.75
O9 O1 5pf green 3.00 2.10
O10 O1 10pf deep rose 3.00 2.40
O11 O1 25pf orange 32.50 52.50
Nos. O7-O11 (5) 78.00 117.25

Centenary of Kingdom of Württemberg.

Nos. O7-O11 also exist imperf but it is doubtful if they were ever issued in that condition.

Value Nos. O7-O11 canceled-to-order, $26.00.

1906-21 Wmk. 116

O12 O1 2pf slate gray 2.50 *.20*
O13 O1 2½pf gray blk ('16) .40 *.20*
O14 O1 3pf dk brown .50 *.20*
O15 O1 5pf green .50 *.20*
O16 O1 7½pf orange ('16) .40 *.20*
O17 O1 10pf dp rose .50 *.20*
O18 O1 10pf orange ('21) .20 *.20*
O19 O1 15pf yellow brn ('16) 1.00 *.20*
O20 O1 15pf dk violet ('17) .50 *.20*
O21 O1 20pf dp ultra ('11) 1.00 *.20*
O22 O1 20pf dp green ('21) .20 *.20*
O23 O1 25pf orange .50 *.20*
O24 O1 25pf brn & blk ('17) .70 *.20*
O25 O1 35pf brown ('19) 1.00 *.60*
O26 O1 40pf rose red ('21) .20 *.20*
O27 O1 50pf rose lake ('11) 9.25 *.20*
O28 O1 50pf vio brn ('21) .20 *.20*
O29 O1 60pf olive grn ('21) .25 *.20*
O30 O1 1.25m emerald ('21) .20 *.20*
O31 O1 2m gray ('21) .20 *.20*
O32 O1 3m brown ('21) .25 *.20*
Nos. O12-O32 (21) 20.45 *4.60*

No. O24 contains solid black numerals.

Nos. O12-O32 exist imperf. Value, each pair, $6-$16.

O3

Perf. 14½x14

1916, Oct. 6 Typo. Unwmk.

O33 O3 2½pf slate 1.00 *.90*
O34 O3 7½pf orange 1.00 *.90*
O35 O3 10pf car rose 1.00 *.90*
O36 O3 15pf yellow brn 1.00 *.90*
O37 O3 20pf blue 1.00 *.90*
O38 O3 25pf gray blk 2.50 *.90*
O39 O3 50pf red brown 5.25 *.90*
Nos. O33-O39 (7) 12.75 *6.30*

25th year of the reign of King Wilhelm II.

Stamps of 1900-06 Surcharged

Perf. 11½x11

1916, Sept. 10 Wmk. 116

O40 O1 25pf on 25pf orange 2.10 *.50*
a. Without wmk. 21.00

No. O13 Surcharged in Blue

1919 Wmk. 116

O42 O1 2pf on 2½pf gray blk .50 *.30*

Official Stamps of 1906-19 Overprinted

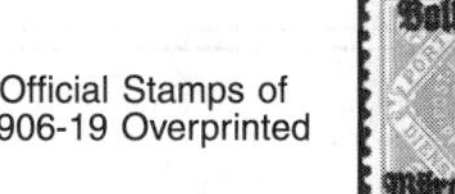

1919

O43 O1 2½pf gray blk .25 *.40*
O44 O1 3pf dk brown 7.75 *.40*
O45 O1 5pf green .25 *.40*
O46 O1 7½pf orange .50 *.40*
O47 O1 10pf rose .25 *.40*
O48 O1 15pf purple .25 *.40*
O49 O1 20pf ultra .25 *.40*
O50 O1 25pf brown & blk .25 *.40*
O51 O1 35pf brown 3.00 *.40*
O52 O1 50pf red brown 3.50 *.40*
Nos. O43-O52 (10) 16.25 *4.00*

Stag — O4

Wmk. 192

1920, Mar. 19 Litho. *Perf. 14½*

O53 O4 10pf maroon .75 *1.00*
O54 O4 15pf brown .75 *1.00*
O55 O4 20pf indigo .75 *1.00*
O56 O4 30pf deep green .75 *1.00*
O57 O4 50pf yellow .75 *1.00*
O58 O4 75pf bister 1.50 *1.00*
Nos. O53-O58 (6) 5.25 *6.00*

Official Stamps of 1906-19 Overprinted

Perf. 11½x11

1920, Apr. 1 Wmk. 116

O59 O1 5pf green 2.50 6.75
O60 O1 10pf deep rose 1.50 3.00
O61 O1 15pf dp violet 1.50 3.25
O62 O1 20pf ultra 2.50 5.75
a. Wmk. 192 3.00 5.75
O63 O1 50pf red brown 3.00 11.50
Nos. O59-O63 (5) 11.00 30.25

Nos. O59 to O63 were available for official postage throughout all Germany but were used almost exclusively in Württemberg.

Stamps of 1917-21 Surcharged in Black, Red or Blue

1923

O64 O1 5m on 10pf orange .20 *.20*
O65 O1 10m on 15pf dp violet .20 *.20*
O66 O1 12m on 40pf rose red .20 *.20*
O67 O1 20m on 10pf orange .20 *.20*
O68 O1 25m on 20pf green .20 *.20*
O69 O1 40m on 20pf green .20 *.20*
O70 O1 50m on 60pf olive grn .20 *.20*

Surcharged

O71 O1 60m on 1.25m emerald .20 *.20*
O72 O1 100m on 40pf rose red .20 *.20*
O73 O1 200m on 2m gray (R) .20 *.20*
O74 O1 300m on 50pf red brn (Bl) .20 *.20*
O75 O1 400m on 3m brn (Bl) .20 *.20*
O76 O1 1000m on 60pf ol grn .20 *.25*
O77 O1 2000m on 1.25m emerald .20 *.25*
Nos. O64-O77 (14) 2.80 *2.90*

Abbreviations:
Th = (Tausend) Thousand
Mil = (Million) Million
Mlrd = (Milliarde) Billion

Surcharged

1923

O78 O1 5th m on 10pf orange .20 *.25*
O79 O1 20th m on 40pf rose red .20 *.25*
O80 O1 50th m on 15pf violet .20 *.25*
O81 O1 75th m on 2m gray .95 *.25*
O82 O1 100th m on 20pf green .20 *.25*
O83 O1 250th m on 3m brown .20 *.25*

Surcharged

O84 O1 1mil m on 60pf ol grn .75 *.25*
O85 O1 2mil m on 50pf red brn .20 *.25*
O86 O1 5mil m on 1.25m emer .20 *.25*

Surcharged

O87 O1 4 mlrd m on 50pf red brn 1.75 *.25*
O88 O1 10 mlrd m on 3m brn 1.75 *.25*
Nos. O78-O88 (11) 6.60 *2.75*

No. O23 Surcharged with New Values in Rentenpfennig as

1923, Dec.

O89 O1 3pf on 25pf orange .25 *.25*
O90 O1 5pf on 25pf orange .25 *.25*
O91 O1 10pf on 25pf orange .25 *.25*
O92 O1 20pf on 25pf orange .25 *.25*
O93 O1 50pf on 25pf orange .50 *.25*
Nos. O89-O93 (5) 1.50 *1.25*

For the State Authorities

O6

Perf. 11½x11

1881-1902 Typo. Unwmk.

O94 O6 2pf sl gray ('96) 1.00 .75
O95 O6 3pf green 16.00 2.50
O96 O6 3pf dk brown ('90) 1.00 .50
O97 O6 5pf violet 4.00 .90
O98 O6 5pf green ('90) 1.50 .50
O99 O6 10pf rose 2.50 .75
O100 O6 20pf ultra .60 .75
O101 O6 25pf brown 24.00 4.75
O102 O6 25pf orange ('90) 4.00 .60
O103 O6 30pf org & blk ('02) 1.00 1.25
O104 O6 40pf dp rose & blk ('02) 1.00 1.50
O105 O6 50pf gray grn 5.25 5.75
O106 O6 50pf maroon ('91) 1.00 2.10
a. 50pf red brown ('90) 150.00 *1,100.*
O107 O6 1m yellow 47.50 125.00
O108 O6 1m violet ('90) 4.75 10.50
Nos. O94-O108 (15) 115.10 *158.10*

See #O119-O135. For overprints & surcharges see #O109-O118, O146-O164, O176-O183.

Overprinted in Black

1906

O109 O6 2pf slate gray 21.00 *4.00*
O110 O6 3pf dk brown 4.00 *4.00*
O111 O6 5pf green 3.00 *4.00*
O112 O6 10pf dp rose 3.00 *4.00*
O113 O6 20pf ultra 3.00 *4.00*
O114 O6 25pf orange 6.25 *4.00*
O115 O6 30pf org & blk 6.25 *4.00*
O116 O6 40pf dp rose & blk 24.00 *4.00*
O117 O6 50pf red brown 24.00 *4.00*
O118 O6 1m purple 47.50 *4.00*
Nos. O109-O118 (10) 142.00 40.00

Cent. of the kingdom of Wüttemberg.

Nos. O109 to O118 are also found imperforate, but it is doubtful if they were ever issued in that condition.

1906-19 Wmk. 116

No.	Design	Description	Unused	Used
O119	O6	2pf slate gray	.30	*.20*
O120	O6	2½pf gray blk ('16)	.35	*.20*
O121	O6	3pf dk brown	.30	*.20*
O122	O6	5pf green	.30	*.20*
O123	O6	7½pf orange ('16)	.35	*.20*
O124	O6	10pf deep rose	.30	*.20*
O125	O6	15pf yel brn ('16)	.35	*.20*
O126	O6	15pf purple ('17)	.50	*.25*
O127	O6	20pf ultra	.40	*.20*
O128	O6	25pf orange	.30	*.20*
O129	O6	25pf brn & blk ('17)	.25	*.20*
O130	O6	30pf org & blk	.30	*.20*
O131	O6	35pf brown ('19)	1.00	*2.10*
O132	O6	40pf dp rose & blk	.30	*.20*
O133	O6	50pf red brown	.30	*.20*
O134	O6	1m purple	1.50	*.20*
O135	O6	1m sl & blk ('17)	1.50	*.50*
		Nos. O119-O135 (17)	8.60	*5.65*

King Wilhelm II — O8

1916 Unwmk. Typo. *Perf. 14*

No.	Design	Description	Unused	Used
O136	O8	2½pf slate	.50	*.45*
O137	O8	7½pf orange	.50	*.45*
O138	O8	10pf carmine	.50	*.45*
O139	O8	15pf yellow brn	.50	*.45*
O140	O8	20pf blue	.50	*.45*
O141	O8	25pf gray blk	1.00	*.45*
O142	O8	30pf green	1.00	*.45*
O143	O8	40pf claret	1.50	*.45*
O144	O8	50pf red brn	2.10	*.45*
O145	O8	1m violet	2.10	*.45*
		Nos. O136-O145 (10)	10.20	*4.50*

25th year of the reign of King Wilhelm II.

Stamps of 1890-1906 Surcharged

1916-19 Wmk. 116 *Perf. 11½x11*

No.	Design	Description	Unused	Used
O146	O6	25pf on 25pf orange	1.75	*.50*
a.		Without watermark	24.00	7,000.
O147	O6	50pf on 50pf red brn	1.00	*.60*
a.		Inverted surcharge	24.00	

Beware of fake cancels on No. O146a.

No. O120 Surcharged in Blue

1919 Wmk. 116

No.	Design	Description	Unused	Used
O149	O6	2pf on 2½pf gray blk	1.00	*1.00*

Official Stamps of 1890-1919 Overprinted

1919

No.	Design	Description	Unused	Used
O150	O6	2½pf gray blk	.35	*.25*
O151	O6	3pf dk brown	5.25	*.50*
a.		Without watermark	35.00	
O152	O6	5pf green	.25	*.25*
O153	O6	7½pf orange	.25	*.25*
O154	O6	10pf rose	.25	*.25*
O155	O6	15pf purple	.25	*.25*
O156	O6	20pf ultra	.25	*.25*
O157	O6	25pf brn & blk	.25	*.25*
a.		Inverted overprint	62.50	*125.00*
O158	O6	30pf org & blk	.50	*.25*
a.		Inverted overprint	175.00	*275.00*
O159	O6	35pf brown	.35	*.25*
O160	O6	40pf rose & blk	.35	*.25*
O161	O6	50pf claret	.50	*.40*
O162	O6	1m slate & blk	.60	*.50*
		Nos. O150-O162 (13)	9.40	*3.90*

Nos. O151, O151a Surcharged in Carmine

1920 Wmk. 116

No.	Design	Description	Unused	Used
O164	O6	75pf on 3pf dk brn	.75	*.75*
a.		Without watermark	52.50	*13.00*

View of Stuttgart O9

10pf, 50pf, 2.50m, 3m, View of Stuttgart. 15pf, 75pf, View of Ulm. 20pf, 1m, View of Tubingen. 30pf, 1.25m, View of Ellwangen.

Wmk. 192

1920, Mar. 25 Typo. *Perf. 14½*

No.	Design	Description	Unused	Used
O166	O9	10pf maroon	.40	*.75*
O167	O9	15pf brown	.40	*.75*
O168	O9	20pf indigo	.40	*.75*
O169	O9	30pf blue grn	.40	*.75*
O170	O9	50pf yellow	.40	*.75*
O171	O9	75pf bister	.40	*.75*
O172	O9	1m orange red	.40	*.75*
O173	O9	1.25m dp violet	.40	*.75*
O174	O9	2.50m dark ultra	1.00	*.75*
O175	O9	3m yellow grn	1.50	*.75*
		Nos. O166-O175 (10)	5.70	*7.50*

Official Stamps of 1906-19 Overprinted

1920 Wmk. 116 *Perf. 11½x11*

No.	Design	Description	Unused	Used
O176	O6	5pf green	1.50	*2.50*
O177	O6	10pf deep rose	1.00	*2.10*
O178	O6	15pf purple	1.00	*2.10*
O179	O6	20pf ultra	1.00	*.90*
a.		Wmk. 192	77.50	*210.00*
O180	O6	30pf orange & blk	1.00	*2.50*
O181	O6	40pf dp rose & blk	1.00	*2.10*
O182	O6	50pf red brown	1.00	*2.50*
O183	O6	1m slate & blk	1.50	*5.25*
		Nos. O177-O183 (7)	7.50	17.45

The note after No. O63 will also apply to Nos. O176-O183.

NORTH GERMAN CONFEDERATION

Northern District
30 Groschen = 1 Thaler
Southern District
60 Kreuzer = 1 Gulden
Hamburg
16 Schillings = 1 Mark

Values for unused stamps are for examples with original gum as defined in the catalogue introduction. Copies without gum sell for about 50% of the figures quoted.

A1

A2

Rouletted 8½ to 10, 11 to 12½ and Compound

1868 Typo. Unwmk.

No.	Design	Description	Unused	Used
1	A1	¼gr red lilac	10.50	7.75
2	A1	⅓gr green	21.00	2.10
3	A1	½gr orange	21.00	1.50
4	A1	1gr rose	10.50	.50
b.		Half used as ½gr on cover		—
5	A1	2gr ultra	52.50	1.00
6	A1	5gr bister	52.50	5.25
7	A2	1kr green	24.00	5.25
8	A2	2kr orange	35.00	29.00
9	A2	3kr rose	24.00	1.00
10	A2	7kr ultra	100.00	6.75
11	A2	18kr bister	24.00	40.00
		Nos. 1-11 (11)	375.00	100.10

See Nos. 13-23.

Imperf

No.	Design	Description	Unused	Used
1a	A1	¼gr red lilac	110.00	—
2a	A1	⅓gr green	62.50	—
3a	A1	½gr orange	92.50	—
4a	A1	1gr rose	52.50	—
5a	A1	2gr ultra	175.00	—
6a	A1	5gr bister	175.00	—
7a	A2	1kr green	47.50	*77.50*
8a	A2	2kr orange	125.00	62.50
9a	A2	3kr rose	52.50	67.50
10a	A2	7kr ultra	240.00	*450.00*
11a	A2	18kr bister	240.00	*450.00*

A3

1868

No.	Design	Description	Unused	Used
12	A3	(½s) lilac brown	67.50	35.00

See No. 24.

1869 *Perf. 13½x14*

No.	Design	Description	Unused	Used
13	A1	¼gr lilac	9.25	8.75
a.		¼gr red violet	16.00	12.50
14	A1	⅓gr green	3.00	1.00
15	A1	½gr orange	3.00	1.00
16	A1	1gr rose	2.50	.50
17	A1	2gr ultra	4.75	.75
18	A1	5gr bister	5.25	5.25
19	A2	1kr green	7.75	5.25
20	A2	2kr orange	24.00	*62.50*
21	A2	3kr rose	4.75	1.00
22	A2	7kr ultra	7.25	5.75
23	A2	18kr bister	92.50	*1,150.*
		Nos. 13-23 (11)	164.00	

Counterfeit cancels exist on No. 23.

1869

No.	Design	Description	Unused	Used
24	A3	(½s) dull violet brown	3.00	5.25

A4

A5

Perf. 14x13½

No.	Design	Description	Unused	Used
25	A4	10gr gray	210.00	250.00
		Pen cancellation		40.00
26	A5	30gr blue	150.00	*700.00*
		Pen cancellation		*77.50*

Counterfeit cancels exist on No. 26.

See Germany designs A2, A3 and A8 for similar stamps.

OFFICIAL STAMPS

O1

1870 Unwmk. Typo. *Perf. 14½x14*

No.	Design	Description	Unused	Used
O1	O1	¼gr black & buff	16.00	*29.00*
O2	O1	⅓gr black & buff	6.25	*13.00*
O3	O1	½gr black & buff	1.75	*2.10*
O4	O1	1gr black & buff	1.75	.50
O5	O1	2gr black & buff	4.75	2.50
O6	O1	1kr black & gray	21.00	*160.00*
O7	O1	2kr black & gray	52.50	*950.00*
O8	O1	3kr black & gray	16.00	*30.00*
O9	O1	7kr black & gray	29.00	*175.00*
		Nos. O1-O9 (9)	149.00	1,362.

Counterfeit cancels exist on Nos. O6-O9.

The stamps of the North German Confederation were replaced by those of the German Empire on Jan. 1, 1872.

GERMANY

'jər-mə-nē

LOCATION — In northern Europe bordering on the Baltic and North Seas
AREA — 182,104 sq. mi. (until 1945)
POP. — 67,032,242 (1946)
CAPITAL — Berlin

In 1949 the Russian occupied areas became a separate country, the German Democratic Republic. The country was reunified Oct. 3, 1990.

30 Silbergroschen or Groschen = 1 Thaler
60 Kreuzer = 1 Gulden
100 Pfennigs = 1 Mark (1875)
100 Pfennigs = 1 Deutsche Mark (1948)
100 Cents = 1 Euro (2002)

Catalogue values for unused stamps in this country are for Never Hinged items, beginning with Scott 722 in the regular postage section, Scott B338 in the semi-postal section, Scott C61 in the airpost section, Scott 9N103 in the Berlin regular postage section and Scott 9NB12 in the Berlin semi-postal section.

Watermarks

Wmk. 48- Diagonal Zigzag Lines

Wmk. 116- Crosses and Circles

Wmk. 125- Lozenges

Wmk. 126- Network

Wmk. 127- Quatrefoils

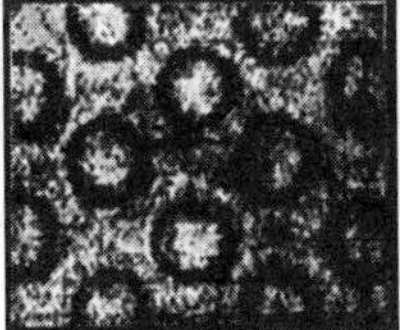
Wmk. 192- Circles

Wmk. 223- Eagle

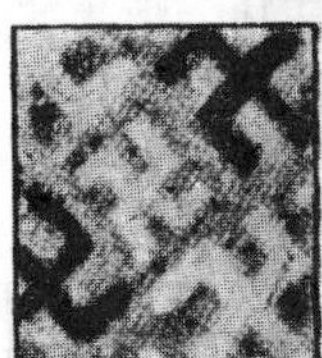
Wmk. 237- Swastikas

Wmk. 241- Cross

Wmk. 284- "DEUTSCHE POST" Multiple

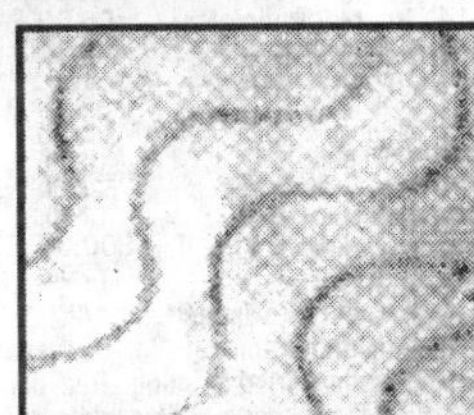
Wmk. 285- Marbleized Pattern

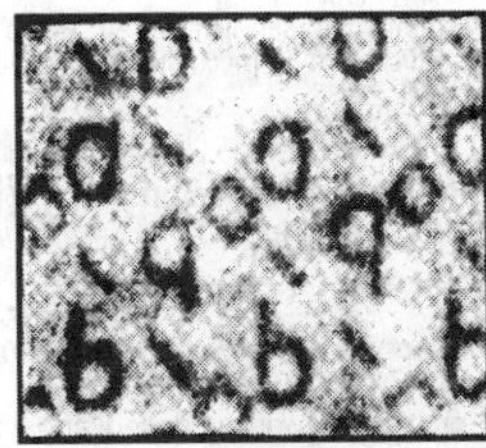
Wmk. 286- D P Multiple

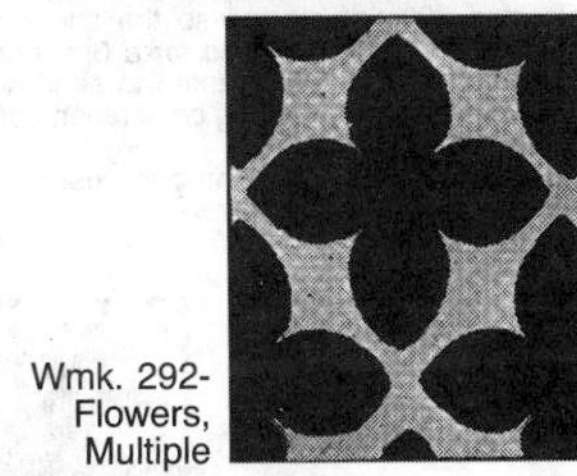
Wmk. 292- Flowers, Multiple

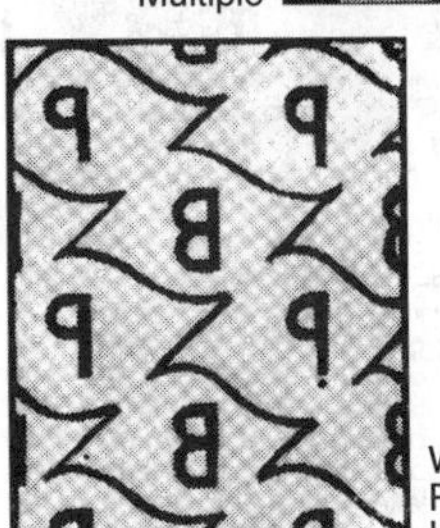
Wmk. 295- B P and Zigzag Lines

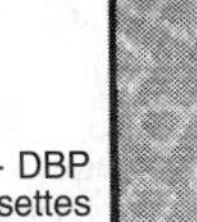
Wmk. 304- DBP and Rosettes Multiple

Empire

Values for unused stamps are for examples with original gum as defined in the catalogue introduction. Any exceptions are specifically mentioned.

Imperial Eagle — A1

Typographed, Center Embossed
1872 Unwmk. *Perf. 13½x14½*
Eagle with small shield

1	A1	¼gr violet	190.00	80.00
2	A1	⅓gr green	400.00	26.00
a.		Imperf.		—
3	A1	½gr red orange	850.00	35.00
a.		½gr orange yellow	975.00	35.00
4	A1	1gr rose	225.00	4.50
a.		Imperf.		
b.		Half used as ½gr on cover		*32,500.*
5	A1	2gr ultra	1,150.	11.50
a.		Imperf.		*7,000.*
6	A1	5gr bister	525.00	70.00
a.		Imperf.		*7,000.*
7	A1	1kr green	500.00	45.00
8	A1	2kr orange	32.50	*140.00*
a.		2kr red orange	450.00	225.00
9	A1	3kr rose	1,300.	10.00
10	A1	7kr ultra	1,750.	80.00
11	A1	18kr bister	425.00	300.00

Values for imperforates are for copies postmarked at Leipzig (⅓gr), Coblenz (1gr), Hoengen (2gr) and Leutersdorf (5gr).

A2

A3

1872 Typo. *Perf. 14½x13½*

12	A2	10gr gray	45.00	*1,050.*
		Pen cancellation		60.00
13	A3	30gr blue	92.50	*1,850.*
		Pen cancellation		400.00

For similar designs see A8, North German Confederation A4, A5.

A4

A5

Center Embossed
1872 *Perf. 13½x14½*
Eagle with large shield

14	A4	¼gr violet	57.50	75.00
15	A4	⅓gr yellow green	26.00	11.50
a.		⅓gr blue green	100.00	87.50
16	A4	½gr orange	32.50	3.50
a.		Imperf.		
17	A4	1gr rose	37.50	1.75
a.		Imperf.		*14,000.*
b.		Half used as ½gr on cover		*32,500.*
18	A4	2gr ultra	17.50	3.75
19	A4	2½gr orange brn	1,650.	50.00
a.		2½gr lilac brown	*3,750.*	300.00
20	A4	5gr bister	26.00	26.00
a.		Imperf.		*5,250.*
21	A4	1kr yellow green	29.00	22.50
a.		1kr blue green	325.00	350.00
22	A4	2kr orange	425.00	*1,750.*
23	A4	3kr rose	20.00	3.25
24	A4	7kr ultra	26.00	*60.00*
25	A4	9kr red brown	250.00	210.00
a.		9kr lilac brown	1,250.	400.00
26	A4	18kr bister	29.00	*1,600.*

Values for Nos. 17a and 20a are for copies postmarked at Potsdam (1gr), Damgarten or Anklam (5gr).

#14-26 with embossing inverted are fraudulent.

1874
Brown Surcharge

27	A5	2½gr on 2½gr brn	32.50	35.00
28	A5	9kr on 9kr brown	60.00	*250.00*

A6

A7

"Pfennige"
1875-77 Typo.

29	A6	3pf blue green	50.00	4.50
30	A6	5pf violet	85.00	2.40

Center Embossed

31	A7	10pf rose	35.00	.75
32	A7	20pf ultra	400.00	1.00
33	A7	25pf red brown	425.00	14.50
34	A7	50pf gray	1,100.	9.75
35	A7	50pf ol gray ('77)	1,300.	11.00

See Nos. 37-42. For surcharges see Offices in Turkey Nos. 1-6.

A8

1875-90 Typo. *Perf. 14½x13½*

36	A8	2m brownish pur ('90)	60.00	2.50
a.		2m purple	350.00	110.00
b.		2m dull vio pur ('89)	1,250.	55.00

No. 36a used is valued as a stamp with cds cancel dated between Jan. 1875 and Nov. 17, 1884.

Wmk125

Types of 1875-77, "Pfennig" without final "e"

1880-83 ***Perf. 13½x14½***

37	A6	3pf yel green	2.75	.70
a.		Imperf.		
38	A6	5pf violet	1.25	.70

Center Embossed

39	A7	10pf red	7.25	.70
a.		Imperf.	*300.00*	
40	A7	20pf brt ultra	5.25	.70
41	A7	25pf dull rose brn	13.00	2.50
a.		25pf red brown, thick paper ('83)	160.00	3.25
42	A7	50pf dp grayish ol grn	6.50	.70
a.		50pf olive green	175.00	1.00
		Nos. 37-42 (6)	36.00	6.00

Values for Nos. 37-42 are for stamps on thin paper. Those on thick paper sell for considerably more.

A9

A10

1889-1900 ***Perf. 13½x14½***

45	A9	2pf gray ('00)	.45	.60
a.		"REIGHSPOST"	50.00	*125.00*
		Never hinged	160.00	
46	A9	3pf brown	1.40	.70
a.		3pf yellow brown	8.00	.65
b.		Imperf.	150.00	—
		Never hinged	350.00	
c.		3pf reddish brown	45.00	7.25
47	A9	5pf blue green	1.10	.65
48	A10	10pf carmine	1.40	.65
a.		Imperf.	200.00	
		Never hinged	600.00	
49	A10	20pf ultra	6.50	.65
a.		20pf Prus blue	350.00	97.50
50	A10	25pf orange ('90)	26.00	1.25
a.		Imperf.	175.00	
		Never hinged	575.00	
51	A10	50pf chocolate	22.50	.70
a.		50pf copper brown	275.00	8.50
b.		Imperf.	300.00	
		Never hinged	375.00	
		Nos. 45-51 (7)	59.35	5.20
		Set, never hinged	300.00	

For surcharges and overprints see Offices in China Nos. 1-6, 16, Offices in Morocco 1-6, Offices in Turkey 8-12.

Germania — A11

1900, Jan. 1 ***Perf. 14***

52	A11	2pf gray	.65	.45
a.		Imperf.	325.00	
		Never hinged	1,450.	
53	A11	3pf brown	.65	.75
a.		Imperf.	325.00	
		Never hinged	1,450.	
54	A11	5pf green	.90	.45
55	A11	10pf carmine	1.60	.55
a.		Imperf.	40.00	
		Never hinged	92.50	
56	A11	20pf ultra	6.50	.45
57	A11	25pf orange & blk, *yel*	11.00	4.00
58	A11	30pf orange & blk, *sal*	16.00	.65
59	A11	40pf lake & black	20.00	1.00
60	A11	50pf pur & blk, *sal*	20.00	.85
61	A11	80pf lake & blk, *rose*	32.50	2.00
		Nos. 52-61 (10)	109.80	11.15
		Set, never hinged	700.00	

Early printings of Nos. 57-61 had "REICHSPOST" in taller and thicker letters than on the ordinary stamps.

For surcharges see Nos. 65B, Offices in China 17-32, Offices in Morocco 7-15, 32A, Offices in Turkey 13-20, 25-27.

"REICHSPOST" Larger

57a	A11	25pf	*1,150.*	*3,200.*
58a	A11	30pf	*1,150.*	*3,200.*
59a	A11	40pf	*1,150.*	*3,200.*
60a	A11	50pf	*1,150.*	*3,200.*
61a	A11	80pf	*1,150.*	*3,200.*

General Post Office in Berlin — A12

"Union of North and South Germany" A13

Unveiling Kaiser Wilhelm I Memorial, Berlin — A14

Wilhelm II Speaking at Empire's 25th Anniversary Celebration A15

Two types of 5m:
I - "5" is thick; "M" has slight serifs.
II - "5" thinner; "M" has distinct serifs.

Engr. ***Perf. 14½x14***

62	A12	1m carmine rose	82.50	1.60
		Never hinged	350.00	
a.		Imperf.	*2,300.*	
63	A13	2m gray blue	65.00	5.25
		Never hinged	400.00	
64	A14	3m black violet	85.00	40.00
		Never hinged	525.00	
65	A15	5m slate & car, I	1,100.	*1,650.*
		Never hinged	3,500.	
d.		Red and white retouched	300.00	*325.00*
		Never hinged	1,200.	
e.		White only retouched	525.00	*525.00*
		Never hinged	1,450.	
65A	A15	5m slate & car, II	300.00	300.00
		Never hinged	1,200.	

Nos. 62-65 exist perf. 11 1/2.

The vignette and frame of No. 65 usually did not align perfectly during printing. Red paint was use to retouch the vignette and/or white paint was used to retouch the inner frame.

No. 62a is without gum.

For surcharges see Offices in China Nos. 33-36A, Offices in Morocco 16-19A, Offices in Turkey 2-24B, 28-30.

Half of No. 54 Handstamp Surcharged in Violet

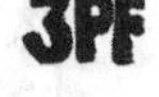

1901 ***Perf. 14***

65B	A11	3pf on half of 5pf	*7,600.*	*5,850.*
		Never hinged	*20,000.*	

This provisional was produced aboard the German cruiser Vineta. The purser, with the ship commander's approval, surcharged and bisected 300 5pf stamps so the ship's post office could meet the need for a 3pf (printed matter rate). The crew wanted to send home U.S. newspapers reporting celebrations of the Kaiser's birthday.

Forgeries exist and improper usages as well.

A16

1902 **Typo.**

65C	A16	2pf gray	1.25	.45
66	A16	3pf brown	.65	.75
a.		"DFUTSCHES"	8.50	*35.00*
		Never hinged	26.00	
67	A16	5pf green	2.00	.75
68	A16	10pf carmine	6.50	.55
69	A16	20pf ultra	26.00	.75
70	A16	25pf org & blk, *yel*	40.00	1.60
71	A16	30pf org & blk, *sal*	45.00	.45
72	A16	40pf lake & blk	60.00	.85
73	A16	50pf pur & blk, *buff*	60.00	.90
74	A16	80pf lake & blk, *rose*	125.00	2.25
		Nos. 65C-74 (10)	366.40	9.30
		Set, never hinged	1,450.	

Nos. 65C-74 exist imperf. Value, set $2,000.

See Nos. 80-91, 118-119, 121-132, 169, 174, 210. For surcharges see Nos. 133-136, B1, Offices in China 37-42, 47-52, Offices in Morocco 20-28, 33-41, 45-53, Offices in Turkey 31-38, 43-50, 55-59.

A17

A18

A19

A20

Perf. 14, 14¼-14½

Engr.

75	A17	1m carmine rose	210.00	2.25
a.		Imperf.	800.00	—
76	A18	2m gray blue	72.50	85.00
77	A19	3m black violet	65.00	16.00
a.		Imperf.	800.00	—
78	A20	5m slate & car	190.00	16.00
a.		Imperf.	800.00	—

See Nos. 92, 94-95, 102, 111-113. For surcharges see Nos. 115-116, Offices in China 43, 45-46, 53, 55-56, Offices in Morocco 29, 31-32, 42, 44, 54, 56-57, Offices in Turkey 39, 41-42, 51, 53-54.

A21

79	A21	2m gray blue	100.00	4.25
a.		Imperf.	700.00	—
		Never hinged	2,000.	
		Nos. 75-79 (5)	637.50	123.50
		Set, never hinged	2,850.	

See Nos. 93, 114. For surcharges see Nos. 117, Offices in China 44, 54, Offices in Morocco 30, 43, 55, Offices in Turkey 40, 52.

1905-19 Typo. Wmk. 125 ***Perf. 14***

80	A16	2pf gray	1.10	*2.00*
81	A16	3pf brown	.50	*1.10*
82	A16	5pf green (shades)	.50	1.10
b.		Bklt. pane of 5 + label ('11)	200.00	400.00
		Never hinged	400.00	
c.		Bklt. pane of 4 + 2 labels ('10)	325.00	650.00
		Never hinged	650.00	
d.		Bklt. pane of 2 + 4 labels ('12)	200.00	400.00
		Never hinged	400.00	
e.		Bklt. pane, #82 + 5 #83 ('17)	57.50	150.00
		Never hinged	150.00	
f.		Bklt. pane, 2 #82 + 4 #83 ('20)	15.00	37.50
		Never hinged	37.50	
g.		Bklt. pane, 4 #82 + 2 #83 ('19)	15.00	37.50
		Never hinged	37.50	
83	A16	10pf red	.50	*1.10*
b.		Bklt. pane of 5 + label ('10)	275.00	550.00
		Never hinged	550.00	
c.		Bklt. pane of 4 + 2 labels ('12)	250.00	500.00
		Never hinged	500.00	
d.		10pf carmine red	1.25	1.10
84	A16	20pf blue vio ('18)	.50	*1.10*
a.		20pf light blue	9.75	3.00
		Never hinged	40.00	
b.		20pf ultramarine	6.50	1.10
		Never hinged	35.00	
c.		Imperf.	525.00	*2,300.*
		Never hinged	1,450.	
d.		Half used as 10pf on cover		575.00
85	A16	25pf org & blk, *yel*	.50	*1.10*

86	A16 30pf org & blk, *buff*	.50	*1.10*
a.	30pf org & blk, *cr*	20.00	*57.50*
	Never hinged	57.50	
87	A16 40pf lake & black	.75	*1.10*
88	A16 50pf pur & blk, *buff*	.50	*1.10*
89	A16 60pf magenta	1.00	1.10
a.	60pf red violet	10.00	7.50
	Never hinged	37.50	
90	A16 75pf green & blk ('19)	.20	*1.10*
91	A16 80pf lake & blk, *rose*	.90	*1.50*

Perf. 14½ (25x17 holes)

Engr.

92	A17 1m carmine rose	1.75	1.10
93	A21 2m brt blue	4.00	3.50
a.	2m gray blue	32.50	22.50
	Never hinged	110.00	
94	A19 3m violet gray	1.75	*3.50*
b.	3m black-brown violet	10.00	22.50
	Never hinged	22.50	
95	A20 5m slate & car	1.60	*2.75*
a.	Center inverted	*40,000.*	*60,000.*
	Nos. 80-95 (16)	16.55	*25.35*
	Set, never hinged	42.50	

Pre-war printings of Nos. 80-91 have brighter colors and white instead of yellow gum. They sell for considerably more than the wartime printings which are valued here. No. 80 exists only from a pre-war printing.

Nos. 92a-95b also exist in both pre-war and wartime printings. Prices are for pre-war printings. Wartime printings sell for considerably more.

Nos. 92-95 exist only from a wartime printing. The 1m-5m also exist perf 14¼-14¾ (26x17 holes) in both pre-war and wartime printings. Both of these printings are much more expensive than Nos. 92-95. See the Scott Classic Specialized Catalogue for detailed listings.

Labels in No. 82c contain an "X." The version with advertising is worth 3 times as much. No. 82f has three 10pf stamps in the top row. The version with 3 on the bottom row is worth 4 times as much.

No. 84d was used at Field Post Office No. 107 in 1915, and at Field Post Office No. 766 during 1917.

Surcharged and overprinted stamps of designs A16-A22 are listed under Allenstein, Belgium, Danzig, France, Latvia, Lithuania, Marienwerder, Memel, Poland, Romania, Saar and Upper Silesia.

A22

1916-19 **Typo.**

96	A22 2pf lt gray ('18)	.20	*3.00*
97	A22 2½pf lt gray	.20	.85
98	A22 7½pf red orange	.20	1.10
b.	Bklt. pane, 4 #98 + 2 #100	82.50	200.00
	Never hinged	200.00	
c.	Bklt. pane, 2 #98 + 4 #99	70.00	175.00
	Never hinged	175.00	
d.	Bklt. pane, 2 #98 + 4 #100	82.50	200.00
	Never hinged	200.00	
e.	Bklt. pane, 2 #82 + 4 #98	24.00	57.50
	Never hinged	57.50	
f.	7½pf yellow orange	3.00	1.10
99	A22 15pf yellow brown	2.25	1.10
100	A22 15pf dk violet ('17)	.20	*1.10*
b.	Bklt. pane, 4 #82 + 2 #100	82.50	200.00
	Never hinged	200.00	
c.	Bklt. pane, 2 #83 + 4 #100	57.50	150.00
	Never hinged	150.00	
101	A22 35pf red brown ('19)	.20	*1.10*
	Nos. 96-101 (6)	3.25	*8.25*
	Set, never hinged	10.00	

See No. 120. For surcharge see No. B2.

Nos. 98e and 100c have the 2 stamps first in the bottom row.

Type of 1902

1920 Engr. Wmk. 192 ***Perf. 14½***

102	A19 3m black violet	1,450.	*2,900.*
	Never hinged	3,500.	

Republic

National Assembly Issue

A23

A24

Rebuilding Germany — A25

Designs: A23, Live Stump of Tree Symbolizing that Germany will Survive her Difficulties. A24, New Shoots from Oak Stump Symbolical of New Government.

Perf. 13x13½

1919-20 Unwmk. Typo.

105	A23 10pf carmine rose	.20	1.10
106	A24 15pf choc & blue	.20	1.10
107	A25 25pf green & red	.20	1.10
108	A25 30pf red vio & red ('20)	.20	1.10
	Nos. 105-108 (4)	.80	4.40
	Set, never hinged	2.00	

"1019" instead of "1919" is the result of broken type.

Types of 1902

Perf. 15x14½

1920 Wmk. 125 Offset

111	A17 1m red	1.50	1.25
112	A17 1.25m green	1.25	1.25
113	A17 1.50m yellow brown	.20	*1.25*
114	A21 2.50m lilac rose	.20	*1.00*
a.	2.50m magenta	1.25	1.50
b.	2.50m brown lilac	.35	1.25
	Nos. 111-114 (4)	3.15	*4.75*
	Set, never hinged	12.50	

Nos. 111, 112 and 113 differ from the illustration in many minor respects. The numerals of Nos. 75 and 92 are outlined, with shaded background. Those of No. 111 are plain, with solid background and flags have been added to the top of the building, at right and left.

Types of 1902 Surcharged

1920 Engr. ***Perf. 14½***

115	A17 1.25m on 1m green	.35	*4.75*
116	A17 1.50m on 1m org brn	.25	*5.25*
117	A21 2.50m on 2m lilac rose	7.25	*175.00*
	Nos. 115-117 (3)	7.85	
	Set, never hinged	20.00	

Germania Types of 1902-16

1920 Typo. ***Perf. 14, 14½***

118	A16 5pf brown	.20	*.95*
119	A16 10pf orange	.20	*.95*
a.	Tête bêche pair	.65	*4.50*
	Never hinged	1.60	
d.	Bklt. pane, 4 #119 + 2 #123	1.90	10.00
	Never hinged	4.75	
120	A22 15pf violet brn	.20	*1.00*
a.	Imperf.	32.50	
	Never hinged	85.00	
c.	Bklt. pane, 4 #84 + 2 #120	4.75	11.50
	Never hinged	11.50	
121	A16 20pf green	.20	*.95*
a.	Imperf.		210.00
123	A16 30pf dull blue	.20	*.90*
a.	Tête bêche pair	.65	*5.25*
	Never hinged	1.60	
d.	Bklt. pane, 2 #123 + 4 #124	1.90	10.00
	Never hinged	4.75	
124	A16 40pf carmine rose	.20	*.95*
a.	Tête bêche pair	.65	*4.50*
	Never hinged	1.60	
b.	Imperf.	125.00	625.00
	Never hinged	325.00	
d.	Bklt. pane, 2 #124 + 4 #126	3.50	32.50
	Never hinged	8.75	
125	A16 50pf red lilac	.40	*1.40*
126	A16 60pf olive green	.20	*.90*
a.	Tête bêche pair	.55	*7.50*
	Never hinged	1.40	
c.	Imperf.	125.00	
	Never hinged	325.00	
127	A16 75pf red violet	.20	*.90*
128	A16 80pf blue violet	.20	*.95*
a.	Imperf.	125.00	
	Never hinged	325.00	
129	A16 1m violet & grn	.20	*.90*
a.	Imperf.	70.00	
130	A16 1¼m ver & mag	.20	*.90*
131	A16 2m carmine & bl	.45	*.90*
132	A16 4m black & rose	.20	*1.10*
	Nos. 118-132 (14)	3.25	*13.65*
	Set, never hinged	8.25	

Stamps of 1920 Surcharged:

No. 133

No. 135

Nos. 134, 136

1921, Aug.

133	A16 1.60m on 5pf	.20	1.10
134	A16 3m on 1¼m	.20	1.10
135	A16 5m on 75pf (G)	.20	1.10
136	A16 10m on 75pf	.25	1.10
	Nos. 133-136 (4)	.85	4.40
	Set, never hinged	2.25	

In 1920 the current stamps of Bavaria were overprinted "Deutsches Reich". These stamps were available for postage throughout Germany, but because they were used almost exclusively in Bavaria, they are listed among the issues of that state.

A26

Iron Workers A27

Miners A28

Farmers A29

Post Horn A30

Numeral of Value — A31

Plowing A32

Wmk. Lozenges (125)

1921 Typo. *Perf. 14*

137 A26 5pf claret .20 1.60
138 A26 10pf olive green .20 1.00
a. Tête bêche pair .65 *18.00*
Never hinged 1.60
b. Bklt. pane, 5 #138 + 1 #141 3.50 47.50
Never hinged 8.75
139 A26 15pf grnsh blue .20 1.00
140 A26 25pf dark brown .20 1.00
141 A26 30pf blue green .20 1.00
a. Tête bêche pair .60 *14.50*
Never hinged 1.50
b. Bklt. pane, 2 #124 + 4 #141 3.75 32.50
Never hinged 9.25
142 A26 40pf red orange .20 1.00
143 A26 50pf violet .25 1.10
144 A27 60pf red violet .20 1.00
145 A27 80pf carmine rose .20 *4.50*
146 A28 100pf yellow grn .25 *1.50*
147 A28 120pf ultra .20 1.00
148 A29 150pf orange .20 *1.50*
149 A29 160pf slate grn .20 *6.50*
150 A30 2m dp vio & rose .30 *3.00*
151 A30 3m red & yel .30 *13.00*
152 A30 4m dp grn & yel grn .20 *3.00*

Engr.

153 A31 5m orange .25 *1.10*
154 A31 10m carmine rose .35 *2.00*
155 A32 20m indigo & grn .80 *2.25*
a. Green background inverted 150.00 *700.00*
Never hinged 525.00
Nos. 137-155 (19) 4.90 *48.05*
Set, never hinged 13.00

See Nos. 156-209, 211, 222-223, 225, 227. For surcharges and overprints see Nos. 241-245, 247-248, 261-262, 273-276, B6-B7, O24.

1922 Litho. *Perf. 14½x14*

156 A31 100m brown vio, *buff* .20 1.00
157 A31 200m rose, *buff* .20 1.00
158 A31 300m green, *buff* .20 1.00
159 A31 400m bis brn, *buff* .35 *1.75*
160 A31 500m orange, *buff* .20 1.00
Nos. 156-160 (5) 1.15 *5.75*
Set, never hinged 2.75

Postally Used vs. CTO

Values quoted for canceled copies of the 1921-1923 issues are for postally used stamps. These bring higher prices than the plentiful canceled-to-order specimens made by applying genuine handstamps to remainders. C.T.O. examples sell for about the same price as unused stamps. Certification of postal usage by competent authorities is necessary.

Perf. 14, 14½

1921-22 Typo. Wmk. 126

161 A26 5pf claret .60 *150.00*
162 A26 10pf olive grn 3.50 *125.00*
163 A26 15pf grnsh blue .50 *160.00*
164 A26 25pf dark brown .20 *2.75*
165 A26 30pf blue green .75 *260.00*
166 A26 40pf red orange .20 *3.50*
167 A26 50pf violet ('21) .20 1.10
168 A27 60pf red violet .20 *17.00*
169 A16 75pf red violet .25 *1.75*
170 A26 75pf deep ultra .20 *2.75*
171 A27 80pf car rose .35 *47.50*
172 A28 100pf olive green .20 1.10
a. Imperf. 26.00 575.00
Never hinged 65.00
173 A28 120pf ultra .60 *87.50*
174 A16 1¼m ver & mag .20 *1.00*
175 A29 150pf orange .20 1.00
a. Imperf. 5.25
Never hinged 14.00
176 A29 160pf slate green .60 *125.00*
177 A30 2m violet & rose .20 1.00
178 A30 3m red & yel ('21) .20 1.00
a. Imperf. 10.50 275.00
Never hinged 32.50
179 A30 4m dp grn & yel grn .20 1.00
180 A30 5m org & yel .20 1.25
a. Imperf. 125.00
181 A30 10m car & pale rose .20 1.00
a. Pale rose (background) omitted 29.00 750.00
182 A30 20m violet & org .20 1.00
183 A30 30m brown & yel .20 1.00
184 A30 50m dk green & vio .20 1.00
Nos. 161-184 (24) 10.35
Set, never hinged 27.50

1922-23

SIX MARKS:
Type I - Numerals upright.
Type II - Numerals leaning toward the right and slightly thinner.

EIGHT MARKS:
Type I - Numerals 2½mm wide with thick strokes.
Type II - Numerals 2mm wide with thinner strokes.

185 A30 2m blue violet .20 1.00
a. Imperf. 125.00
186 A30 3m red .20 .85
187 A30 4m dark green .20 1.00
a. Imperf. 7.50
188 A30 5m orange .20 1.00
a. Imperf. 100.00
189 A30 6m dark blue (II) .20 1.00
a. 6m dark blue (I) .20 .25
b. Imperf. 100.00
190 A30 8m olive green (I) .20 1.10
a. 8m olive green (II) .35 *35.00*
191 A30 20m dk violet ('23) .20 1.00
192 A30 30m pur brn ('23) .20 *6.50*
193 A30 40m lt green .20 1.40

Engr.

194 A31 5m orange .25 1.00
a. Imperf. 125.00
195 A31 10m carmine rose .50 1.75
196 A32 20m indigo & grn .20 3.00
a. Imperf. 150.00
b. Green background inverted 26.00 *350.00*
Nos. 185-196 (12) 2.75 20.60
Set, never hinged 8.00

1922-23 Litho. *Perf. 14½x14*

198 A31 50m indigo .20 1.10
199 A31 100m brn vio, *buff* ('23) .20 .75
200 A31 200m rose, *buff* ('23) .20 1.10
201 A31 300m grn, *buff* ('23) .20 .75
202 A31 400m bis brn, *buff* ('23) .20 .75
203 A31 500m org, *buff* ('23) .20 .75
204 A31 1000m gray ('23) .20 .75
205 A31 2000m blue ('23) .30 1.10
206 A31 3000m brown ('23) .20 2.40
207 A31 4000m violet ('23) .20 1.10
a. Imperf. 20.00 110.00
Never hinged 42.50
208 A31 5000m gray grn ('23) .25 1.10
a. Imperf. 32.50 160.00
Never hinged 85.00
209 A31 100,000m ver ('23) .20 .75
a. Imperf. 32.50
Never hinged 85.00
Nos. 198-209 (12) 2.55 12.40
Set, never hinged 4.75

1920-22 Wmk. 127 Typo.

210 A16 1¼m ver & mag 400.00 650.00
Never hinged 1,050.
211 A30 50m grn & vio ('22) 1.00 *700.00*
Never hinged 3.00

Wmk. 127 was intended for use only in printing revenue stamps.

Arms of Munich — A33

Wmk. Network (126)

1922, Apr. 22 Typo. *Perf. 13x13½*

212 A33 1¼m claret .20 1.10
213 A33 2m dark violet .20 1.10
214 A33 3m vermilion .20 1.10
215 A33 4m deep blue .20 1.10

Wmk. Lozenges (125)

216 A33 10m brown, *buff* .50 2.25
217 A33 20m lilac rose, *pink* 3.00 8.00
Nos. 212-217 (6) 4.30 14.65
Set, never hinged 13.00

Munich Industrial Fair.

Type of 1921 and

Miners — A34

A35

1922-23 Wmk. 126 *Perf. 14*

221 A34 5m orange .20 *12.00*
222 A29 10m dull blue ('22) .20 1.00
223 A29 12m vermilion ('22) .20 1.00
224 A34 20m red lilac .20 1.00
225 A29 25m olive brown .20 1.00
226 A34 30m olive green .20 *1.75*
227 A29 40m green .20 1.00
228 A34 50m grnsh blue .30 *100.00*
229 A35 100m violet .20 1.10
230 A35 200m carmine rose .20 1.10
231 A35 300m green .20 1.00
232 A35 400m dark brown .20 *5.00*
233 A35 500m red orange .20 *5.25*
234 A35 1000m slate .20 1.00
Nos. 221-234 (14) 2.90
Set, never hinged 4.50

The 50m was issued only in vertical coils.
Nos. 222-223 exist imperf.
For surcharges and overprints see Nos. 246, 249-260, 263-271, 277, 310, B5, O22-O23, O25-O28.

Wartburg Castle — A36

Cathedral of Cologne — A37

1923 Engr.

237 A36 5000m deep blue .20 *2.10*
a. Imperf. 2.25 *575.00*
Never hinged 575.00
238 A37 10,000m brn ol .25 *3.25*
Set, never hinged 1.25

Abbreviations:
Th = (Tausend) Thousand
Mil = (Million) Million
Mlrd = (Milliarde) Billion

A38

1923 Typo.

238A A38 5th m grnsh blue .20 *14.50*
b. Imperf. 80.00
Never hinged 200.00
239 A38 50th m bister .20 1.10
a. Imperf. 10.00 *1,450.*
Never hinged 24.00
240 A38 75th m dark violet .20 *9.25*
Set, never hinged .65

For surcharges see Nos. 272, 278.

Stamps and Types of 1922-23 Surcharged in Black, Blue, Green or Brown with Bars over Original Value

Wmk. Lozenges (125)

1923 *Perf. 14*

241 A26 8th m on 30pf .20 1.25
a. "8" inverted 16.00 *250.00*
Never hinged 50.00

Wmk. Network (126)

242 A26 5th m on 40pf .20 *1.25*
242A A26 8th m on 30pf 13.00 *3,500.*
243 A29 15th m on 40m .20 1.10
244 A29 20th m on 12m .20 1.25
a. Inverted surcharge
245 A29 20th m on 25m .20 *2.00*
246 A35 20th m on 200m .20 1.50
a. Inverted surcharge 52.50 575.00
Never hinged 125.00
247 A29 25th m on 25m .20 *13.00*
248 A29 30th m on 10m dp bl .20 1.00
a. Inverted surcharge 60.00
Never hinged 140.00
249 A35 30th m on 200m pale bl (Bl) .20 1.00
a. Without surcharge 100.00
Never hinged 200.00
250 A35 75th m on 300m yel grn .20 *13.00*
a. Imperf. 40.00
Never hinged 82.50
251 A35 75th m on 400m yel grn .20 1.25
252 A35 75th m on 1000m yel grn .20 1.50
a. Without surcharge 100.00
Never hinged 200.00
253 A35 100th m on 100m .20 *1.40*
a. Double surcharge 110.00
Never hinged 275.00
b. Inverted surcharge 13.00
Never hinged 32.50
254 A35 100th m on 400m bluish grn (G) .20 1.00
a. Imperf. 45.00 475.00
Never hinged 100.00
b. Without surcharge 100.00
Never hinged 200.00
255 A35 125th m on 1000m sal .20 1.40
256 A35 250th m on 200m .20 *4.75*
a. Inverted surcharge 26.00
Never hinged 70.00
b. Double surcharge 40.00
Never hinged 100.00
257 A35 250th m on 300m dp grn .20 *14.50*
a. Inverted surcharge 26.00
Never hinged 70.00
258 A35 250th m on 400m .20 *14.50*
a. Inverted surcharge 20.00
Never hinged 57.50
259 A35 250th m on 500m pink .20 1.00
a. Imperf. 45.00
Never hinged 92.50
260 A35 250th m on 500m red org .20 *14.50*
a. Double surcharge 24.00
Never hinged 52.50
b. Inverted surcharge 22.50
Never hinged 65.00
261 A26 800th m on 5pf lt grn (G) .20 *3.50*
a. Imperf. 26.00 125.00
Never hinged 77.50
262 A26 800th m on 10pf lt grn (G) .20 *4.00*
a. Imperf. 26.00
Never hinged 77.50
263 A35 800th m on 200m .20 *57.50*
a. Double surcharge 65.00
Never hinged 160.00
b. Inverted surcharge 32.50
Never hinged 85.00
264 A35 800th m on 300m lt grn (G) .20 *4.00*
a. Black surcharge 37.50
265 A35 800th m on 400m dk brn .20 *13.00*
a. Inverted surcharge 32.50
Never hinged 85.00
b. Double surcharge 40.00
Never hinged 110.00
266 A35 800th m on 400m lt grn (G) .20 *3.50*
267 A35 800th m on 500m lt grn (G) .20 *1,150.*
a. 800th m on 500m red org (Bk) 32.50
268 A35 800th m on 1000m lt grn (G) .20 1.10
269 A35 2mil m on 200m rose red .20 1.10
b. 2mil m on 200m car rose (#230) *1,150.*
Never hinged 2,600.
270 A35 2mil m on 300m dp grn .20 *1.50*
a. Inverted surcharge 32.50
Never hinged 85.00
b. Double surcharge 40.00
Never hinged 110.00
271 A35 2mil m on 500m dl rose .20 *6.00*
272 A38 2mil m on 5th m dl rose .20 1.10
b. Imperf. 37.50 110.00

Nos. 264a, 267a were not put in use.

Serrate Roulette 13½

273 A26 400th m on 15pf bis (Br) .20 *4.00*
a. Imperf. 40.00 175.00
Never hinged 87.50
274 A26 400th m on 25pf bis (Br) .20 *4.00*
a. Imperf. 75.00 *175.00*
Never hinged 125.00
275 A26 400th m on 30pf bis (Br) .20 *4.00*
a. Imperf. 29.00
Never hinged 75.00
276 A26 400th m on 40pf bis (Br) .20 *4.00*
a. Imperf. 29.00
Never hinged 75.00

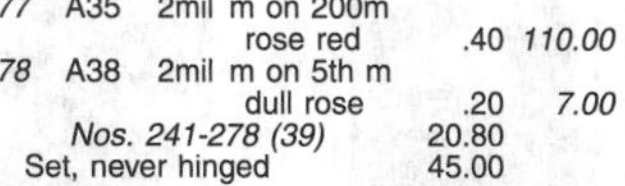

277 A35 2mil m on 200m rose red .40 110.00
278 A38 2mil m on 5th m dull rose .20 7.00
Nos. 241-278 (39) 20.80
Set, never hinged 45.00

Nos. 273-276 and 278 exist without surcharge. Value, $225-275 each.

A39

A39a

The stamps of types A39 and A39a usually have the value darker than the rest of the design.

1923 Wmk. 126 Perf. 14

280 A39 500th m brown .20 2.25
281 A39 1mil m grnsh bl .20 1.10
a. Imperf. 40.00 225.00
Never hinged 92.50
282 A39 2mil m dull vio .20 18.00
284 A39 4mil m yel grn .20 1.25
a. Value double 52.50
Never hinged 125.00
b. Imperf. 32.50
Never hinged 80.00
285 A39 5mil m rose .20 1.00
286 A39 10mil m red .20 .85
a. Value double 45.00 425.00
Never hinged 110.00
287 A39 20mil m ultra .20 1.25
288 A39 30mil m red brn .20 8.50
289 A39 50mil m dull ol grn .20 1.25
a. Imperf. 40.00 225.00
Never hinged 92.50
b. Value inverted 35.00
290 A39 100mil m gray .20 .85
291 A39 200mil m bis brn .20 .85
a. Imperf. 17.50
Never hinged 47.50
293 A39 500mil m ol grn .20 .85
294 A39a 1mlrd m choc .25 1.10
295 A39a 2mlrd m pale brn & grn .20 1.25
296 A39a 5mlrd m yellow & brn .20 1.10
297 A39a 10mlrd m ap grn & grn .20 1.10
a. Imperf. 26.00 200.00
Never hinged 65.00
298 A39a 20mlrd m bluish grn & brn .20 1.50
299 A39a 50mlrd m bl & dp bl .20 30.00
Nos. 280-299 (18) 3.65
Set, never hinged 6.25

The variety "value omitted" exists on Nos. 280-281, 284-287, 290-291, 293-294, 296, 298-299 and 307. Values $26 to $65 hinged, $65 to $160 never hinged.

See Nos. 301-309. For surcharges and overprints see Nos. 311-321, O40-O46.

Serrate Roulette 13½

301 A39 10mil m red .40 40.00
302 A39 20mil m ultra .40 250.00
303 A39 50mil m dull grn .40 5.50
304 A39 200mil m bis brn .40 10.50
305 A39a 1mlrd m choc .40 6.50
306 A39a 2mlrd m pale brn & grn .40 3.25
307 A39a 5mlrd m yel & brn .60 2.00
308 A39a 20mlrd m bluish grn & brn .60 9.75
309 A39a 50mlrd m bl & dp bl 1.50 525.00
Nos. 301-309 (9) 5.10
Set, never hinged 14.50

Stamps and Types of 1923 Surcharged with New Values

1923 Perf. 14

310 A35 1mlrd m on 100m vio .20 25.00
a. Inverted surcharge 87.50
Never hinged 225.00
b. Deep reddish purple 50.00 2,750.
Never hinged 125.00
311 A39 5mlrd m on 2mil m .20 110.00
a. Inverted surcharge 16.00
Never hinged 45.00
b. Double surcharge 40.00
Never hinged 100.00
312 A39 5mlrd m on 4mil m .20 21.00
a. Inverted surcharge 22.50 700.00
Never hinged 65.00
b. Double surcharge 32.50
Never hinged 85.00
313 A39 5mlrd m on 10mil m .20 2.25
a. Inverted surcharge 13.00 700.00
Never hinged 42.50
b. Double surcharge 32.50
Never hinged 85.00
314 A39 10mlrd m on 20mil m .20 2.50
a. Double surcharge 40.00
Never hinged 110.00
b. Inverted surcharge 22.50
Never hinged 65.00
315 A39 10mlrd m on 50mil m .20 2.10
a. Inverted surcharge 16.00 650.00
Never hinged 45.00
b. Double surcharge 40.00
Never hinged 110.00
316 A39 10mlrd m on 100mil m .20 6.50
a. Inverted surcharge 22.50 1,000.
Never hinged 65.00
b. Double surcharge 40.00
Never hinged 110.00
Nos. 310-316 (7) 1.40
Set, never hinged 4.00

No. 310b was issued in Bavaria only and is known as the Hitler provisional. Excellent forgeries exist.

Serrate Roulette 13½

319 A39 5mlrd m on 10mil m 1.50 160.00
a. Inverted surcharge 20.00
Never hinged 60.00
b. Double surcharge 20.00
Never hinged 52.50
320 A39 10mlrd m on 20mil m 4.50 85.00
321 A39 10mlrd m on 50mil m 1.50 35.00
a. Inverted surcharge 20.00
Never hinged 60.00
Nos. 319-321 (3) 7.50
Set, never hinged 17.50

A40

German Eagle — A41

1923 Perf. 14

323 A40 3pf brown .30 .20
324 A40 5pf dark green .30 .20
325 A40 10pf carmine .30 .20
326 A40 20pf deep ultra .85 .30
327 A40 50pf orange 2.25 .75
328 A40 100pf brn vio 7.25 .85
Nos. 323-328 (6) 11.25 2.50
Set, never hinged 65.00

For overprints see Nos. O47-O52.

Imperf.

323a A40 3pf 110.00 200.00
324a A40 5pf 60.00 —
325a A40 10pf 100.00 150.00
326a A40 20pf 110.00 200.00
327a A40 50pf 125.00 275.00
328a A40 100pf 125.00 —
Nos. 323a-328a (6) 630.00
Set, never hinged 1,300.

Value Omitted

323b A40 3pf 150.00 225.00
324b A40 5pf 150.00 225.00
325b A40 10pf 150.00
326b A40 20pf 150.00
327b A40 50pf 150.00
328b A40 100pf 150.00
Nos. 323b-328b (6) 900.00
Set, never hinged 1,750.

1924 Wmk. 126

330 A41 3pf lt brown .25 .20
331 A41 5pf lt green .25 .20
332 A41 10pf vermilion .30 .20
333 A41 20pf dull blue 1.60 .20
334 A41 30pf rose lilac 1.60 .35
335 A41 40pf olive green 11.00 .55
336 A41 50pf orange 12.00 .90
Nos. 330-336 (7) 27.00
Set, never hinged 225.00

The values above 5pf have "Pf" in the upper right corner.

For overprints see Nos. O53-O61.

Imperf.

330a A41 3pf 125.00 300.00
331a A41 5pf 160.00 300.00
332a A41 10pf 200.00
333a A41 20pf 150.00
334a A41 30pf 150.00
335a A41 40pf 175.00
Nos. 330a-335a (6) 960.00 600.00
Set, never hinged 1,950.

Rheinstein Castle — A43

View of Cologne A44

Marienburg Castle — A45

1924 Engr. Wmk. 126

337 A43 1m green 9.25 2.00
338 A44 2m blue 16.00 1.75
339 A45 3m claret 18.00 4.50
Nos. 337-339 (3) 43.25 8.25
Set, never hinged 125.00

See No. 387.

Dr. Heinrich von Stephan
A46 A47

1924-28 Typo.

340 A46 10pf dark green .45 .20
341 A46 20pf dark blue 1.10 .45
342 A47 60pf red brown 3.25 .45
a. Chalky paper ('28) 18.00 3.50
343 A47 80pf slate 8.50 1.10
Nos. 340-343 (4) 13.30 2.20
Set, never hinged 65.00

Universal Postal Union, 50th anniversary.
No. 340 exists imperf. Value $300.

Traffic Wheel — A48

German Eagle Watching Rhine Valley — A49

1925, May 30 Perf. 13½x13

345 A48 5pf deep green 2.75 4.50
346 A48 10pf vermilion 3.25 8.50
Set, never hinged 32.50

German Traffic Exhibition, Munich, May 30-Oct. 11, 1925.

1925 Perf. 14

347 A49 5pf green .35 .25
348 A49 10pf vermilion .70 .25
349 A49 20pf deep blue 4.00 .90
Nos. 347-349 (3) 5.05 1.40
Set, never hinged 26.00

1000 years' union of the Rhineland with Germany.

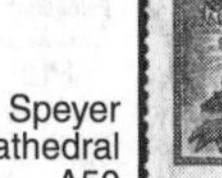

Speyer Cathedral A50

1925, Sept. 11 Engr.

350 A50 5m dull green 30.00 13.00
Never hinged 110.00

Johann Wolfgang von Goethe — A51

Designs: 3pf, 25pf, Goethe. 5pf, Friedrich von Schiller. 8pf, 20pf, Ludwig van Beethoven. 10pf, Frederick the Great. 15pf, Immanuel Kant. 30pf, Gotthold Ephraim Lessing. 40pf, Gottfried Wilhelm Leibnitz. 50pf, Johann Sebastian Bach. 80pf, Albrecht Durer.

1926-27 Typo. Perf. 14

351 A51 3pf olive brown .45 .20
352 A51 3pf bister ('27) .90 .20
353 A51 5pf dark green .90 .20
b. 5pf light green ('27) .90 .20
Never hinged 6.50
354 A51 8pf blue grn ('27) .90 .20
355 A51 10pf carmine .90 .20
356 A51 15pf vermilion 2.00 .20
a. Booklet pane of 8 + 2 labels 225.00
Never hinged 550.00
357 A51 20pf myrtle grn 9.25 .90
358 A51 25pf blue 3.00 .70
359 A51 30pf olive grn 5.50 .40
360 A51 40pf dp violet 9.75 .45
361 A51 50pf brown 12.50 5.00
362 A51 80pf chocolate 26.00 3.75
Nos. 351-362 (12) 72.05 12.40
Set, never hinged 725.00

Nos. 351-354, 356 and 357 exist imperf. Value each $175.

Nos. 354, 356 and 358 Overprinted

1927, Oct. 10

363 A51 8pf blue green 14.50 50.00
364 A51 15pf vermilion 14.50 50.00
365 A51 25pf blue 14.50 50.00
Nos. 363-365 (3) 43.50 150.00
Set, never hinged 150.00

"I.A.A." stands for "Internationales Arbeitsamt," (Intl. Labor Bureau), an agency of the League of Nations. Issued in connection with a meeting of the I.A.A. in Berlin, Oct. 10-15, 1927, they were on sale to the public.

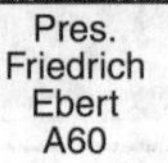

Pres. Friedrich Ebert
A60

Pres. Paul von Hindenburg
A61

1928-32 Typo. *Perf. 14*

366	A60	3pf bister	.20	.25
367	A61	4pf lt blue ('31)	.60	.25
a.		Tête bêche pair	4.00	8.00
		Never hinged	8.00	
b.		Bklt. pane of 9 + label	20.00	50.00
		Never hinged	50.00	
368	A61	5pf lt green	.35	.25
a.		Tête bêche pair	3.25	6.50
		Never hinged	6.50	
b.		Imperf.	110.00	
		Never hinged	225.00	
c.		Bklt. pane of 6 + 4 labels	16.00	40.00
		Never hinged	40.00	
d.		Bklt. pane, 4 #368 + 6 #369	20.00	50.00
		Never hinged	50.00	
369	A60	6pf lt olive grn ('32)	.65	.20
a.		Bklt. pane, 2 #369 + 8 #373	35.00	85.00
		Never hinged	85.00	
370	A60	8pf dark green	.20	.25
a.		Tête bêche pair	3.25	6.50
		Never hinged	6.50	
371	A60	10pf vermilion	1.60	1.40
372	A60	10pf red violet ('30)	.80	.35
373	A61	12pf orange ('32)	1.00	.20
a.		Tête bêche pair	8.00	16.00
		Never hinged	16.00	
374	A61	15pf car rose	.55	.25
a.		Tête bêche pair	4.00	8.00
		Never hinged	8.00	
b.		Bklt. pane 6 + 4 labels	18.00	45.00
		Never hinged	45.00	
375	A60	20pf Prus green	5.50	3.00
a.		Imperf.	275.00	
		Never hinged	550.00	
376	A60	20pf gray ('30)	5.25	.35
377	A61	25pf blue	6.50	.45
378	A60	30pf olive green	4.25	.35
379	A61	40pf violet	11.00	.45
380	A60	45pf orange	8.00	2.00
381	A61	50pf brown	8.00	1.25
382	A60	60pf orange brn	10.00	1.75
383	A61	80pf chocolate	18.00	4.00
384	A61	80pf yel bis ('30)	8.00	1.50
		Nos. 366-384 (19)	90.45	18.50
		Set, never hinged	825.00	

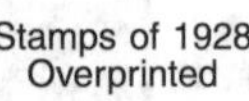

Stamps of 1928 Overprinted

1930, June 30

385	A60	8pf dark green	.90	.45
386	A61	15pf carmine rose	.90	.45
		Set, never hinged	10.50	

Issued in commemoration of the final evacuation of the Rhineland by the Allied forces.

View of Cologne
A63

1930 Engr. Wmk. 126

Inscribed: "Reichsmark"

387	A63	2m dark blue	26.00	10.50
		Never hinged	92.50	

A type of design A43 in green exists with "Reichsmark" instead of "Mark." It was not issued, though some examples are known in private hands.

Pres. von Hindenburg
A64

Frederick the Great
A65

1932, Oct. 1 Typo. Wmk. 126

391	A64	4pf blue	.45	.30
392	A64	5pf brt green	.65	.30
393	A64	12pf dp orange	4.00	.30
394	A64	15pf dk red	3.25	*8.50*
395	A64	25pf ultra	1.00	.50
396	A64	40pf violet	16.00	1.25
397	A64	50pf brown	5.25	*9.75*
		Nos. 391-397 (7)	30.60	20.90
		Set, never hinged	110.00	

85th birthday of von Hindenburg.

See Nos. 401-431, 436-441. For surcharges and overprints see France #N27-58, Luxembourg #N1-16 and Poland #N17-29.

1933, Apr. 12 Photo.

398	A65	6pf dk green	.55	.70
a.		Tête bêche pair	4.50	12.00
		Never hinged	9.25	
399	A65	12pf carmine	.55	.70
a.		Tête bêche pair	4.50	12.00
		Never hinged	9.25	
b.		Bklt. pane of 5 + label	14.50	35.00
		Never hinged	35.00	
400	A65	25pf ultra	32.50	18.00
		Nos. 398-400 (3)	33.60	19.40
		Set, never hinged	210.00	

Celebration of Potsdam Day.

Hindenburg Type of 1932

1933 Typo.

401	A64	3pf olive bister	10.50	.40
402	A64	4pf dull blue	3.25	.40
403	A64	6pf dk green	1.60	.35
404	A64	8pf dp orange	5.25	.40
a.		Bklt. pane, 3 #404 + 5 #406	57.50	140.00
		Never hinged	140.00	
b.		Open "D"	13.00	3.25
		Never hinged	30.00	
405	A64	10pf chocolate	3.25	.45
406	A64	12pf dp carmine	2.00	.35
a.		Bklt. pane, 4 #392 + 4 #406	32.50	80.00
		Never hinged	80.00	
407	A64	15pf maroon	4.50	*20.00*
408	A64	20pf brt blue	6.00	1.75
409	A64	30pf olive grn	6.00	1.10
410	A64	40pf red violet	24.00	2.50
411	A64	50pf dk grn & blk	13.00	2.00
412	A64	60pf claret & blk	24.00	.75
413	A64	80pf dk blue & blk	8.00	.90
414	A64	100pf orange & blk	21.00	10.00
		Nos. 401-414 (14)	132.35	*41.35*
		Set, never hinged	800.00	

Hindenburg Type of 1932

1933-36 Wmk. 237 *Perf. 14*

415	A64	1pf black	.20	.20
a.		Bklt. pane, 4 #415, 3 #417, label	3.50	8.50
		Never hinged	8.50	
b.		Bklt. pane, 3 #415, 3 #416 + 2 #418	4.75	12.00
		Never hinged	12.00	
c.		Bklt. pane, 2 #415, 5 #420, label	7.00	17.50
		Never hinged	17.50	
d.		Bklt. pane, 4 #415 + 4 #422	2.75	6.50
		Never hinged	6.50	
416	A64	3pf olive bis ('34)	.20	.20
a.		Bklt. pane, 4 #416 + 4 #418	2.40	5.75
		Never hinged	5.75	
b.		Bklt. pane, 4 #416 + 4 #419	2.40	5.75
		Never hinged	5.75	
c.		Bklt. pane, 6 #416, 1 #422, label	2.00	5.00
		Never hinged	5.00	
417	A64	4pf dull blue ('34)	.20	.20
a.		Bklt. pane, 3 #417, 4 #422, label	5.75	14.50
		Never hinged	14.50	
418	A64	5pf brt green ('34)	.20	.20
a.		Bklt. pane, 2 #418, 5 #419, label	3.00	7.50
		Never hinged	7.50	
b.		Bklt. pane, 2 #418, 3 #419 + 3 #420	3.50	8.75
		Never hinged	8.75	
c.		Bklt. pane, 4 #418 + 4 #420	3.00	7.50
		Never hinged	7.50	
419	A64	6pf dk green ('34)	.20	.20
a.		Bklt. pane of 7 + label	7.00	17.50
		Never hinged	17.50	
c.		Bklt. pane, 1 #419, 6 #422, label	15.00	37.50
		Never hinged	37.50	
420	A64	8pf dp orange ('34)	.20	.20
a.		Bklt. pane, 3 #420, 4 #422, label	3.00	7.50
		Never hinged	7.50	
b.		Open "D"	3.50	3.50
		Never hinged	10.00	
421	A64	10pf choc ('34)	.20	.20
422	A64	12pf dp car ('34)	.20	.20
a.		Bklt. pane of 7 + label	7.00	17.50
		Never hinged	17.50	
423	A64	15pf maroon ('34)	.25	.20
424	A64	20pf brt blue ('34)	.35	.20
425	A64	25pf ultra ('34)	.35	.20
426	A64	30pf olive grn ('34)	.60	.20
427	A64	40pf red violet ('34)	.60	.25
428	A64	50pf dk grn & blk ('34)	2.25	.30
429	A64	60pf claret & blk ('34)	.60	.30
430	A64	80pf dk bl & blk ('36)	1.75	.95
431	A64	100pf org & blk ('34)	2.25	.55
		Nos. 415-431 (17)	10.60	4.75
		Set, never hinged	55.00	

Karl Peters — A66

Swastika, Sun and Nuremberg Castle — A70

Designs: 3pf, Franz Adolf E. Lüderitz. 6pf, Dr. Gustav Nachtigal. 25pf, Hermann von Wissmann.

1934, June 30 *Perf. 13x13½*

432	A66	3pf brown & choc	2.00	*4.25*
433	A66	6pf dk grn & choc	1.00	.75
434	A66	12pf dk car & choc	1.60	.75
435	A66	25pf brt blue & choc	8.00	15.00
		Nos. 432-435 (4)	12.60	20.75
		Set, never hinged	125.00	

Issued in remembrance of the lost colonies of Germany.

Hindenburg Memorial Issue

Type of 1932

With Black Border

1934, Sept. 4 *Perf. 14*

436	A64	3pf olive bister	.65	.30
437	A64	5pf brt green	.65	.45
438	A64	6pf dk green	1.25	.25
439	A64	8pf vermilion	2.00	.25
440	A64	12pf deep carmine	2.00	.25
441	A64	25pf ultra	6.00	5.75
		Nos. 436-441 (6)	12.55	7.25
		Set, never hinged	92.50	

1934, Sept. 1 Photo.

442	A70	6pf dark green	2.50	.25
443	A70	12pf dark carmine	3.00	.25
		Set, never hinged	55.00	

Nazi Congress at Nuremberg.
Imperfs exist. Value, each $400.

Allegory "Saar Belongs to Germany"
A71

German Eagle
A72

1934, Aug. 26 Typo. Wmk. 237

444	A71	6pf dark green	2.50	.25
445	A72	12pf dark carmine	3.00	.25
		Set, never hinged	55.00	

Issued to mark the Saar Plebiscite.

Friedrich von Schiller
A73

Germania Welcoming Home the Saar
A74

1934, Nov. 5

446	A73	6pf green	2.25	.25
447	A73	12pf carmine	4.00	.25
		Set, never hinged	65.00	

175th anniv. of the birth of von Schiller.

1935, Jan. 16 Photo.

448	A74	3pf brown	.30	.90
449	A74	6pf dark green	.30	.40
450	A74	12pf lake	1.60	.40
451	A74	25pf dark blue	6.50	5.75
		Nos. 448-451 (4)	8.70	7.45
		Set, never hinged	72.50	

Return of the Saar to Germany.

German Soldier
A75

Wreath and Swastika
A76

1935, Mar. 15

452	A75	6pf dark green	.60	1.10
453	A75	12pf copper red	.60	1.10
		Set, never hinged	11.50	

Issued to commemorate War Heroes' Day.

1935, Apr. 26 Unwmk.

454	A76	6pf dark green	.60	.90
455	A76	12pf crimson	.75	.90
		Set, never hinged	16.00	

Young Workers' Professional Competitions.

Heinrich Schütz — A77

"The Eagle" — A80

Wmk. Swastikas (237)

1935, June 21 Engr. *Perf. 14*

456	A77	6pf shown	.40	.25
457	A77	12pf Bach	.60	.25
458	A77	25pf Handel	1.00	.75
		Nos. 456-458 (3)	2.00	1.25
		Set, never hinged	20.00	

Schutz-Bach-Handel celebration.

1935, July 10 *Perf. 14*

Designs: 12pf, Modern express train. 25pf, "The Hamburg Flyer." 40pf, Streamlined locomotive.

459	A80	6pf dark green	.80	.40
460	A80	12pf copper red	.80	.40
461	A80	25pf ultra	4.50	1.40
462	A80	40pf red violet	7.50	1.40
		Nos. 459-462 (4)	13.60	3.60
		Set, never hinged	85.00	

Centenary of railroad in Germany.
Exist imperf. Value, $225 each.

Bugler of Hitler Youth Movement
A84

Eagle and Swastika over Nuremberg
A85

1935, July 25 Photo.

463	A84	6pf deep green	1.00	1.75
464	A84	15pf brown lake	1.25	2.00
		Set, never hinged	14.50	

Hitler Youth Meeting.

1935, Aug. 30 Engr.

465	A85	6pf gray green	.65	.25
466	A85	12pf dark carmine	1.50	.25
		Set, never hinged	11.50	

1935 Nazi Congress at Nuremberg.

Nazi Flag Bearer and Feldherrnhalle at Munich — A86

Airplane — A87

1935, Nov. 5 Photo. *Perf. 13½*

467 A86 3pf brown .25 .40
468 A86 12pf dark carmine .35 .40
Set, never hinged 9.50

12th anniv. of the 1st Hitler "Putsch" at Munich, Nov. 9, 1923.

1936, Jan. 6

469 A87 40pf sapphire 4.25 2.00
Never hinged 35.00

10th anniv. of the Lufthansa air service.

Gottlieb Daimler — A88

Carl Benz — A89

1936, Feb. 15 *Perf. 14*

470 A88 6pf dark green .35 .40
471 A89 12pf copper red .40 .55
Set, never hinged 9.75

The 50th anniv. of the automobile; Intl. Automobile and Motorcycle Show, Berlin.

Otto von Guericke A90

Symbolical of Municipalities A91

1936, May 4

472 A90 6pf dark green .25 .30
Never hinged .90

250th anniv. of the death of the German inventor, Otto von Guericke, May 11, 1686.

1936, June 3

473 A91 3pf dark brown .20 .25
474 A91 5pf deep green .20 .25
475 A91 12pf lake .25 .45
476 A91 25pf dark ultra .45 .90
Nos. 473-476 (4) 1.10 1.85
Set, never hinged 13.00

6th Intl. Cong. of Municipalities, June 7-13.

Allegory of Recreation Congress A92

Salute to Swastika A93

1936, June 30

477 A92 6pf dark green .30 .40
478 A92 15pf deep claret .50 .80
Set, never hinged 11.00

World Congress for Vacation and Recreation held at Hamburg.

1936, Sept. 3 *Perf. 14*

479 A93 6pf deep green .30 .30
480 A93 12pf copper red .40 .40
Set, never hinged 10.00

The 1936 Nazi Congress.

Shield Bearer — A94

German and Austrian Carrying Nazi Flag — A95

1937, Mar. 3 Engr. Unwmk.

481 A94 3pf brown .20 .25
482 A94 6pf green .20 .25
483 A94 12pf carmine .45 .40
Nos. 481-483 (3) .85 .90
Set, never hinged 9.25

The Reich's Air Protection League.

Wmk. Swastikas (237)

1938, Apr. 8 Photo. *Perf. 14x13½*

Size: 23x28mm

484 A95 6pf dark green .20 .30
Never hinged .70

Unwmk. *Perf. 12½*

Size: 21½x26mm

485 A95 6pf deep green .20 .45
Never hinged .80

Union of Austria and Germany.

Cathedral Island A96

Hermann Goering Stadium A97

Town Hall, Breslau — A98

Centennial Hall, Breslau — A99

1938, June 21 Engr. *Perf. 14*

486 A96 3pf dark brown .20 .25
487 A97 6pf deep green .20 .25
488 A98 12pf copper red .25 .25
489 A99 15pf violet brown .55 .60
Nos. 486-489 (4) 1.20 1.35
Set, never hinged 10.50

16th German Gymnastic and Sports Festival held at Breslau, July 23-31, 1938.

Nazi Emblem — A100

1939, Apr. 4 Photo. Wmk. 237

490 A100 6pf dark green 1.00 2.40
491 A100 12pf deep carmine 1.25 2.40
Set, never hinged 16.00

Young Workers' Professional Competitions.

St. Mary's Church — A101

The Krantor, Danzig — A102

1939, Sept. 18

492 A101 6pf dark green .20 .35
493 A102 12pf orange red .25 .50
Set, never hinged 2.75

Unification of Danzig with the Reich.

Johannes Gutenberg and Library at Leipzig — A103

6pf, "High House," Leipzig. 12pf, Old Town Hall, Leipzig. 25pf, View of Leipzig Fair.

Inscribed "Leipziger Messe"

Perf. 10½

1940, Mar. 3 Photo. Unwmk.

494 A103 3pf dark brown .20 .30
495 A103 6pf dk gray green .20 .30
496 A103 12pf henna brown .20 .30
497 A103 25pf ultra .40 .85
Nos. 494-497 (4) 1.00 1.75
Set, never hinged 5.50

Leipzig Fair.

House of Nations, Leipzig — A107

6pf, Concert Hall, Leipzig. 12pf, Leipzig Fair Office. 25pf, Railroad Terminal, Leipzig.

Inscribed: "Reichsmesse Leipzig, 1941"

1941, Mar. 1 *Perf. 14x13½*

498 A107 3pf brown .20 .60
499 A107 6pf green .20 .60
500 A107 12pf dark red .25 .75
501 A107 25pf bright blue .55 1.10
Nos. 498-501 (4) 1.20 3.05
Set, never hinged 7.25

Leipzig Fair.

Fashion Allegory — A111

Vienna Fair Hall — A112

"Burgtheater" A113

Monument to Prince Eugene A114

1941, Mar. 8 *Perf. 13½x14*

502 A111 3pf dark red brown .20 .40
503 A112 6pf brt blue grn .20 .40
504 A113 12pf scarlet .20 .45
505 A114 25pf bright blue .50 1.10
Nos. 502-505 (4) 1.10 2.35
Set, never hinged 7.00

Vienna Fair.

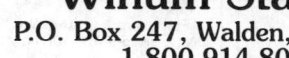

A115

Adolf Hitler — A116

1941-44 Typo. Perf. 14
Size: 18½x22½mm
506 A115 1pf gray black .20 .20
a. Bklt. pane, 4 #506 + 4 #509 .80 2.00
Never hinged 2.00
507 A115 3pf lt brown .20 .20
a. Bklt. pane, 6 #507 + 2 #510 .80 2.00
Never hinged 2.00
508 A115 4pf slate .20 .20
a. Bklt. pane, 4 #508, 2 #511 + 2 labels .80 2.00
Never hinged 2.00
509 A115 5pf dp yellow grn .20 .20
510 A115 6pf purple .20 .20
a. Bklt. pane of 7 + label 4.25 10.50
Never hinged 10.50
511 A115 8pf red .20 .20
511A A115 10pf dk brown ('42) .20 .20
511B A115 12pf carmine ('42) .20 .20

Engr.
512 A115 10pf dark brown .30 .20
513 A115 12pf brt carmine .30 .20
a. Bklt. pane of 6 + 2 labels 2.40 5.75
Never hinged 5.75
514 A115 15pf brown lake .20 .20
515 A115 16pf peacock green .20 .70
516 A115 20pf blue .20 .20
517 A115 24pf orange brown .20 .80

Size: 21½x26mm
518 A115 25pf brt ultra .20 .20
519 A115 30pf olive green .20 .20
520 A115 40pf brt red vio .20 .20
521 A115 50pf myrtle green .20 .20
522 A115 60pf dk red brown .20 .20
523 A115 80pf indigo .20 .25
524 A116 1m dk slate grn ('44) .25 2.75
a. Perf. 12½ ('42) .80 3.50
525 A116 2m violet ('44) .60 2.75
a. Perf. 12½ ('42) 1.00 32.50

Perf. 12½
526 A116 3m cop red ('42) .80 5.75
a. Perf. 14 ('44) 1.25 4.50
527 A116 5m dark blue ('42) 1.50 16.00
a. Perf. 14 ('44) 2.25 7.50
Nos. 506-527 (24) 7.35 32.40
Set, #506-527, never hinged 14.50
Set, #524a-527a, never hinged 16.00

Nos. 507, 510, 511, 511A, 511B, 520, 524-526 exist imperf.
For surcharge see No. MQ3. For overprints see Russia Nos. N9-N48.

Storm Trooper Emblem A117

Adolf Hitler A118

1942, Aug. 8 Photo. Perf. 14
528 A117 6pf purple .20 .60
Never hinged .60

War Effort Day of the Storm Troopers.

1944 Engr.
529 A118 42pf bright green .20 .80
Never hinged .20

Exists imperf. Value $140.

A119

1946 Typo. Wmk. 284 Perf. 14
Size: 18x22mm
530 A119 1pf black .20 .80
531 A119 2pf black .20 .20
532 A119 3pf yellow brn .20 1.25
533 A119 4pf slate .20 1.25
534 A119 5pf yellow grn .20 .40
535 A119 6pf purple .20 .20
536 A119 8pf dp ver .20 .20
537 A119 10pf chocolate .20 .20
538 A119 12pf bright red .20 .20
539 A119 12pf slate gray .20 .20
a. Bklt. pane, 5 #539 + 3 #542 6.50 52.50
Never hinged 14.50
540 A119 15pf violet brn .20 2.10
541 A119 15pf lt yel grn .20 .20
542 A119 16pf slate green .20 .20
543 A119 20pf lt blue .20 .20
544 A119 24pf orange brn .20 .20
545 A119 25pf brt ultra .20 2.50
546 A119 25pf orange yel .20 .55
547 A119 30pf olive .20 .20
548 A119 40pf red violet .20 .20
549 A119 42pf emerald .50 18.00
550 A119 45pf brt red .20 .25
551 A119 50pf dk ol grn .20 .20
552 A119 60pf brown red .20 .20
553 A119 75pf deep ultra .20 .20
554 A119 80pf dark blue .20 .20
555 A119 84pf emerald .20 .20

Size: 24½x29½mm
556 A119 1m olive green .20 .20
Nos. 530-556 (27) 30.70
Set, never hinged 4.25

Imperf. copies of Nos. 543, 544 and 548 are usually from the souvenir sheet No. B295. Most other denominations exist imperf.
For overprints see Nos. 585A-599, 9N64, 10N17-10N21.

Planting Olive A120

Sower A121

Laborer A122

Reaping Wheat A123

Germany Reaching for Peace — A124

Heinrich von Stephan — A125

1947-48 Perf. 14
557 A120 2pf brown blk .20 .25
558 A120 6pf purple .20 .20
559 A121 8pf red .20 .20
560 A121 10pf yel grn ('48) .20 .25
561 A122 12pf gray .20 .20
562 A120 15pf choc ('48) .20 1.10
563 A123 16pf dk bl grn .20 .25
564 A121 20pf blue .20 .25
565 A123 24pf brown org .20 .25
566 A120 25pf orange yel .20 .25
567 A122 30pf red ('48) .20 .50
568 A121 40pf red vio .20 .25
569 A123 50pf ultra ('48) .20 .50
571 A122 60pf red brn ('48) .20 .40
a. 60pf brown red .20 .25
572 A122 80pf dark blue .20 .35
573 A123 84pf emerald .20 .35

Engr.
574 A124 1m olive .20 .25
575 A124 2m dk brown vio .20 .25
576 A124 3m copper red .20 8.00
577 A124 5m dk blue ('48) .55 32.50
Nos. 557-577 (20) 46.55
Set, never hinged 4.00

Used examples of Nos. 576-577 with expertized postal cancellations sell for much more.
For overprints see Nos. 600-633, 9N1-9N34, 9N65-9N67, 10N1-10N16.

1947, May 15 Litho.
578 A125 24pf orange brown .20 .25
579 A125 75pf dark blue .20 .60
Set, never hinged .30

50th anniv. of the death of Heinrich von Stephan, 1st postmaster general of the German Empire.

Leipzig Fair Issues
Type of Semi-Postal Stamp of 1947

12pf, Maximilian I granting charter, 1497. 75pf, Estimating and collecting taxes, 1365.

Perf. 13½x13
1947, Sept. 2 Litho. Wmk. 284
580 SP252 12pf carmine .20 .60
581 SP252 75pf dk vio blue .20 1.10
Set, never hinged .25

Type of Semi-Postal Stamp of 1947, Dated 1948

50pf, Merchants at customs barrier, 1388. 84pf, Arranging stocks of merchandise, 1433.

1948, Mar. 2 Engr.
582 SP252 50pf deep blue .20 .40
583 SP252 84pf green .20 .65
Set, never hinged .25

Exist imperf. Value, each, $400.

Hanover Fair Issue

Weighing Goods for Export — A126

1948, May 22 Typo. Perf. 14
584 A126 24pf deep carmine .20 .55
585 A126 50pf ultra .20 .80
c. Pair, #584-585 1.75 12.50
Pair, never hinged 4.50
Set, never hinged .30

For Use in the United States and British Zones
Stamps of Germany 1946-47 Overprinted in Black

a

b

Overprint Type "a" on 1946 Numeral Issue

1948 Wmk. 284 Perf. 14
585A A119 2pf black 2.00 21.00
585B A119 8pf dp ver 4.50 40.00
586 A119 10pf chocolate .25 3.25
586A A119 12pf bright red 3.25 30.00
586B A119 12pf slate gray 60.00 375.00
586C A119 15pf violet brn 3.25 30.00
587 A119 15pf lt yel grn 1.10 10.50
587A A119 16pf slate green 19.00 125.00
587B A119 24pf orange brn 32.50 150.00
587C A119 25pf brt ultra 6.50 40.00
588 A119 25pf orange yel .55 6.50
589 A119 30pf olive .55 6.50
589A A119 40pf red violet 24.00 150.00
590 A119 45pf brt red .80 6.50
591 A119 50pf dk olive grn .80 6.50
592 A119 75pf dp ultra 2.00 18.00
593 A119 84pf emerald 2.00 18.00
Nos. 585A-593 (17) 163.05
Set, never hinged 325.00

Same, Overprinted Type "b"
593A A119 2pf black 9.25 50.00
593B A119 8pf dp ver 16.00 77.50
593C A119 10pf chocolate 14.50 77.50
593D A119 12pf bright red 4.50 40.00
593E A119 12pf slate gray 125.00 725.00
593F A119 15pf violet brown 4.50 30.00
594 A119 15pf lt yel grn .30 5.25
594A A119 16pf slate grn 16.00 110.00
594B A119 24pf org brn 18.00 140.00
594C A119 25pf brt ultra 5.25 37.50
594D A119 25pf orange yel 16.00 110.00
595 A119 30pf olive .55 4.25
595A A119 40pf red violet 24.00 160.00
596 A119 45pf bright red 1.10 7.50
597 A119 50pf dk ol grn 1.10 7.50
598 A119 75pf dp ultra 1.25 9.00
599 A119 84pf emerald 1.25 7.50
Nos. 593A-599 (17) 258.55
Set, never hinged 500.00

Nine other denominations of type A119 (1, 3, 4, 5, 6, 20, 42, 60 and 80pf) were also overprinted with types "a" and "b." These overprints were not authorized, but the stamps were sold at post offices and tolerated for postal use. Forgeries exist.
The overprints on Nos. 585A-599 have been extensively counterfeited.

Overprint Type "a" on Stamps and Types of 1947 Pictorial Issue
600 A120 2pf brown black .20 .20
601 A120 6pf purple .20 .20
602 A121 8pf dp vermilion .20 .20
603 A121 10pf yellow green .20 .20
604 A122 12pf slate gray .20 .20
605 A120 15pf chocolate 2.75 8.50
606 A123 16pf dk blue green .55 1.60
607 A121 20pf blue .20 .65
608 A123 24pf brown orange .20 .20
609 A120 25pf orange yellow .20 .40
610 A122 30pf red 1.00 3.25
611 A121 40pf red violet .25 .65
612 A123 50pf ultra .30 .65
614 A122 60pf red brown .30 .65
a. 60pf brown red 17.00 125.00
Never hinged 32.50
615 A122 80pf dark blue .55 1.60
616 A123 84pf emerald 1.25 4.25
Nos. 600-616 (16) 8.55 23.40
Set, never hinged 13.00

Same, Overprinted Type "b"
617 A120 2pf brown black .30 .95
618 A120 6pf purple .30 .95
619 A121 8pf red .30 .95
620 A121 10pf yellow green .20 .20
621 A122 12pf gray .30 1.00
622 A120 15pf chocolate .20 .40
623 A123 16pf dk blue green .20 .20
624 A121 20pf blue .20 .20
625 A123 24pf brown orange .25 1.00
626 A120 25pf orange yel 3.00 9.50
627 A122 30pf red .20 .40
628 A121 40pf red violet .20 .35
629 A123 50pf ultra .20 .35
631 A122 60pf red brown .20 .40
a. 60pf brown red .90 2.50
Never hinged 1.60
632 A122 80pf dark blue .20 .45
633 A123 84pf emerald .30 .95
Nos. 617-633 (16) 6.55 18.25
Set, never hinged 11.00

Most of Nos. 585A-633 exist with inverted and double overprints.

Frankfurt Town Hall A127

Our Lady's Church, Munich A128

Cologne Cathedral A129

Brandenburg Gate, Berlin A130

Holsten Gate, Lübeck — A131

Two types of mark values:
Type I - Four horiz. lines in stairs.
Type II - Seven horizontal lines.

Perf. 11½x11, 11
1948-51 Litho. Wmk. 286
634 A127 2pf black .20 .20
a. Perf. 14 1.00 3.50
635 A128 4pf orange brown .20 .20
a. Perf. 14 .50 .20
636 A129 5pf blue .20 .20
a. Perf. 14 .65 .20
637 A128 6pf orange brown .20 .25
638 A128 6pf orange .20 .20
a. Perf. 14 5.25 3.25
639 A127 8pf orange yel .20 .25
640 A128 8pf dk slate blue .20 .20

641 A129 10pf green .20 .20
a. Perf. 14 .65 .20
642 A128 15pf orange .75 3.25
643 A127 15pf violet .45 .20
a. Perf. 14 4.00 .20
644 A127 16pf bluish green .25 .40
645 A127 20pf blue .40 1.60
646 A130 20pf carmine .25 .20
a. Perf. 14 1.60 .20
647 A130 24pf carmine .20 .20
648 A129 25pf vermilion .40 .20
a. Perf. 14 6.50 *20.00*
649 A130 30pf blue .50 .20
a. Perf. 14 9.75 .20
650 A128 30pf scarlet 1.00 *3.25*
651 A129 40pf rose lilac .65 .25
a. Perf. 14 6.50 .25
652 A130 50pf ultra .55 *1.10*
653 A128 50pf bluish green .65 .20
a. Perf. 14 60.00 .20
654 A129 60pf violet brn 26.00 .20
a. Perf. 14 1.00 .20
655 A130 80pf red violet 1.10 .20
a. Perf. 14 40.00 .20
656 A128 84pf rose violet .65 3.00
657 A129 90pf rose lilac 1.10 .20
a. Perf. 14 60.00 .25

Perf. 11, 11x11½

658 A131 1m yellow grn (I) 13.00 .45
a. Perf. 14 (II) ('51) 52.50 .20
b. Perf. 11 (II) 16.00 .20
659 A131 2m violet (I) 12.00 .45
a. Type II 20.00 .20
660 A131 3m car rose (I) 13.00 2.00
a. Type II 65.00 .65
661 A131 5m blue (I) 20.00 17.50
a. Type II 80.00 2.50
Nos. 634-661 (28) 94.50 36.75
Set, never hinged 190.00
Set, 634a-658a, never hinged 450.00
Set, 658b-661a, never hinged 325.00

Imperforates of many values exist.

Specialists collect Nos. 634-661 with watermark in four positions: upright, D's facing left; upright, D's facing right; sideways, D's facing up; sideways, D's facing down.

Two types of perforation: line and comb. Nos. 634-657 are found both perf. 11 and 11½x11.

Herman Hildebrant Wedigh — A132

Wmk. 116

1949, Apr. 22 Engr. *Perf. 14*

662 A132 10pf green 1.00 *1.75*
663 A132 20pf carmine rose 1.00 *1.75*
664 A132 30pf blue 1.25 2.50
a. Sheet of 3, #662-664 26.00 *160.00*
Sheet, never hinged 72.50
Nos. 662-664 (3) 3.25 6.00
Set, never hinged 7.25

Hanover Export Fair, 1949.
No. 664a sold for 1 mark.

Federal Republic

AREA—95,520 sq. mi.
POP.—62,040,000 (1974 est.)
CAPITAL—Bonn

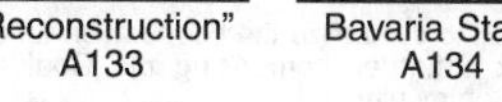

"Reconstruction" A133

Bavaria Stamp A134

1949, Sept. 7 Litho. Wmk. 286

665 A133 10pf blue green 13.50 *16.00*
666 A133 20pf rose carmine 16.00 *20.00*
Set, never hinged 80.00

Opening of the first Federal Assembly. Exist imperf. Value, each $425.

Wmk. 285

1949, Sept. 30 Litho. *Perf. 14*

Design: 30pf, Bavaria 6kr.

667 A134 20pf red & dull blue 17.50 *30.00*
668 A134 30pf dull blue & choc 29.00 *52.50*
Set, never hinged 70.00

Cent. of German postage stamps. See No. B309.

Heinrich von Stephan, General Post Office and Guild House, Bern A135

1949, Oct. 9 Wmk. 286

669 A135 30pf ultra 19.00 *32.50*
Never hinged 52.50

75th anniv. of the UPU.

Numeral and Post Horn — A136

1951-52 Typo. Wmk. 295

670 A136 2pf yellow grn .30 .75
671 A136 4pf yellow brn .30 .20
a. Booklet pane, 3 #671 + 3 #673 + 4 #677 92.50 300.00
Never hinged 300.00
672 A136 5pf dp rose vio 1.60 .20
673 A136 6pf orange 4.00 2.50
674 A136 8pf gray 4.50 6.50
675 A136 10pf dk green .65 .20
a. Booklet pane, 4 #675 + 5 #677 + label 92.50 190.00
Never hinged 300.00
676 A136 15pf purple 9.00 .75
677 A136 20pf carmine .65 .20
678 A136 25pf dk rose lake 20.00 4.00

Engr.

Size: 20x24½mm

679 A136 30pf blue 11.00 .25
680 A136 40pf rose lilac ('52) 30.00 .25
681 A136 50pf blue gray ('52) 40.00 .25
682 A136 60pf brown ('52) 30.00 .25
683 A136 70pf dp yel ('52) 110.00 10.50
684 A136 80pf carmine ('52) 125.00 1.50
685 A136 90pf yel grn ('52) 125.00 1.75
Nos. 670-685 (16) 512.00 30.05
Set, never hinged 1,650.

Imperfs. exist of #671, 673, 675, 681 & 684.

W. K. Roentgen A137

Mona Lisa A138

1951, Dec. 10

686 A137 30pf blue 26.00 14.50
Never hinged 62.50

50th anniv. of the awarding of the Nobel prize in physics to Wilhelm K. Roentgen.

Wmk. 285

1952, Apr. 15 Litho. *Perf. 13½*

687 A138 5pf multicolored .35 *.80*
Never hinged .90

500th anniv. of the birth of Leonardo da Vinci.

N. A. Otto — A139

Martin Luther — A140

Wmk. 295

1952, July 25 Engr. *Perf. 14*

688 A139 30pf deep blue 13.00 13.00
Never hinged 25.00

75th anniv. of the four-cycle gas engine.

1952, July 25

689 A140 10pf green 3.50 4.00
Never hinged 12.00

Issued to publicize the Lutheran World Federation Assembly, Hanover, 1952.

Freighter Off Heligoland A141

Carl Schurz A142

1952, Sept. 6

690 A141 20pf red 5.50 5.00
Never hinged 13.00

Return of Heligoland, Mar. 1, 1952.

Wmk. 285

1952, Sept. 17 Litho. *Perf. 13½*

691 A142 20pf blue, blk & brn org 5.50 6.50
Never hinged 16.00

Centenary of Carl Schurz's arrival in America.

Thurn and Taxis Postilion A143

Philipp Reis — A144

1952, Oct. 25

692 A143 10pf multicolored 2.50 1.75
Never hinged 6.50

1st Thurn and Taxis stamp, cent.

1952, Oct. 27 Photo. *Perf. 14*

693 A144 30pf blue 16.00 13.00
Never hinged 40.00

75 years of telephone service in Germany.

"Prevent Traffic Accidents" — A145

1953, Mar. 30 Litho. Wmk. 285

694 A145 20pf blk, red & bl grn 5.50 3.50
Never hinged 14.50

Justus von Liebig — A146

Red Cross and Compass — A147

1953, May 12 Engr. Wmk. 295

695 A146 30pf dark blue 12.50 20.00
Never hinged 40.00

150th anniv. of the birth of Justus von Liebig, chemist.

Perf. 14x13½

1953, May 8 Litho. Wmk. 285

696 A147 10pf dp ol grn & red 4.00 5.50
Never hinged 18.00

125th anniv. of the birth of Henri Dunant, founder of the Red Cross.

War Prisoner and Barbed Wire — A148

Train and Hand Signal — A149

Typographed and Embossed

1953, May 9 Unwmk. *Perf. 14*

697 A148 10pf gray & black 1.60 .25
Never hinged 5.50

Issued in memory of the prisoners of war.

Wmk. 295

1953, June 20 Engr. *Perf. 14*

Designs: 10pf, Pigeon and planes. 20pf, Automobiles and traffic signal. 30pf, Ship, barges and buoy.

698 A149 4pf brown 2.00 3.25
699 A149 10pf deep green 4.00 5.00
700 A149 20pf red 5.25 8.50
701 A149 30pf deep ultra 16.00 20.00
Nos. 698-701 (4) 27.25 36.75
Set, never hinged 65.00

Exhibition of Transport and Communications, Munich, 1953.

Pres. Theodor Heuss — A150

1954-60 Typo. *Perf. 14*

Size: 18½x22mm

702 A150 2pf citron .20 .20
a. Booklet pane, 5 #702, 4 #704 + label ('55) 20.00 65.00
Never hinged 35.00
b. Booklet pane, 3 #702, 6 #704 + label ('56) 2.75 8.50
Never hinged 6.00
c. Booklet pane, 3 #702, 1 #707, 5 #708 + label ('56) 6.50 20.00
Never hinged 14.50
703 A150 4pf orange brn .20 .20
704 A150 5pf rose lilac .20 .20
a. Booklet pane, 2 #704, 7 #708 + label ('55) 20.00 65.00
Never hinged 35.00
705 A150 6pf lt brown .20 *.45*
706 A150 7pf bluish green .20 .20
707 A150 8pf gray .20 *.35*
708 A150 10pf green .20 .20
a. Booklet pane, 4 #708, 5 #710 + label ('55) 20.00 65.00
Never hinged 35.00
709 A150 15pf ultra .20 .25
710 A150 20pf dk car rose .20 .20
711 A150 25pf red brown .25 .35

Engr.

Size: 19½x24mm

712 A150 30pf blue 4.00 3.25
713 A150 40pf red violet 1.60 .20
714 A150 50pf gray 60.00 .35
715 A150 60pf red brown 13.00 .35
716 A150 70pf olive 4.00 1.25
717 A150 80pf deep rose .65 3.50
718 A150 90pf deep green 4.00 1.60

Size: 24½x29½mm

719 A150 1m olive green .45 .20
720 A150 2m lt vio blue .65 .90
721 A150 3m deep plum 1.60 1.60
Nos. 702-721 (20) 92.00 15.80
Set, never hinged 225.00

Coils and sheets of 100 were issued of the 5, 7, 10, 15, 20, 25, 40 and 70pf. Every fifth coil stamp has a control number on the back.

Printings of Nos. 704, 706, 708-711 and 708b were made on fluorescent paper beginning in 1960.

Nos. 702, 709, 714 exist imperf. Value about $375 each.

See Nos. 737b, 755-761.

Catalogue values for unused stamps in this section, from this point to the end of the section, are for Never Hinged items.

Paul Ehrlich and Emil von Behring — A151

15th Century Printer — A152

Wmk. 285

1954, Mar. 13 Litho. *Perf. 13½*
722 A151 10pf dark green 9.75 3.00

Centenary of the births of Paul Ehrlich and Emil von Behring, medical researchers.
Exists imperf. Value $1,000.

1954, May 5 Typo. Wmk. 295
723 A152 4pf chocolate .90 .35

500th anniversary of the publication of Gutenberg's 42-line Bible. Design from woodcut by Jost Amman.

Bishop's Miter and Sword — A153
Carl F. Gauss — A154

Engraved; Center Embossed

1954, June 5 Unwmk. *Perf. 13½x14*
724 A153 20pf gray & red 7.25 3.50

Martyrdom of Saint Boniface, 1200th anniv.

Wmk. 295

1955, Feb. 23 Engr. *Perf. 14*
725 A154 10pf deep green 4.25 .35

Cent. of the death of Carl Friedrich Gauss, mathematician.

A155

A156

Wmk. 304

1955, May 7 Litho. *Perf. 13½*
726 A155 10pf green 4.25 1.25

Cent. of the birth of Oskar von Miller, electrical engineer.

Engraved and Embossed

1955, May 9 Unwmk. *Perf. 13½x14*
727 A156 40pf blue 14.50 4.75

Friedrich von Schiller, poet, 150th death anniv.

1906 Automobile A157

Wmk. 304

1955, June 1 Typo. *Perf. 13½*
728 A157 20pf red & black 9.25 4.25

German postal motor-bus service, 50th anniv.

Arms of Baden-Württemberg A158

Globe and Atomic Symbol A159

Perf. 13x13½

1955, June 15 Litho. Wmk. 295
729 A158 7pf lemon, blk & brn red 3.00 3.25
730 A158 10pf lemon, blk & grn 5.50 2.00
a. Value omitted *390.00 360.00*

Baden-Wurttemberg Exhibition, Stuttgart, 1955.

1955, June 24 Photo. *Perf. 13½x14*
731 A159 20pf rose brown 9.25 .75

Issued to encourage scientific research.

Orb and Symbols of Battle — A160

Photogravure and Embossed
Perf. 14x13½

1955, Aug. 10 Unwmk.
732 A160 20pf red lilac 7.75 3.25

Issued in honor of Augsburg and the millenium of the Battle on the Lechfeld.

Family in Flight — A161

Railroad Signal, Tracks — A162

1955, Aug. 2 Engr. Wmk. 304
733 A161 20pf brown lake 3.25 .40

Ten years of German expatriation. See No. 930.

Perf. 13½x14

1955, Oct. 5 Litho. Wmk. 304
734 A162 20pf red & black 9.25 1.75

European Timetable conf. at Wiesbaden, Oct. 5-15, 1955.

A163

A164

Stifter monument and sylized Trees.

1955, Oct. 22 Engr.
735 A163 10pf dark green 3.25 1.75

150th anniv. of the birth of Adalbert Stifter, poet.

Lithographed and Embossed
Perf. 14x13½

1955, Oct. 24 Unwmk.
736 A164 10pf UN emblem 3.25 3.50

United Nations Day, Oct. 24, 1955.

Numeral A165

Numeral and Signature A166

1955-58 Wmk. 304 Typo. *Perf. 14*
737 A165 1pf gray .20 .20

Wmk. 295

737A A165 1pf gray ('58) 7.00 *12.50*
b. Bklt. pane of 10 (#707, 2 each #737A, #704, #708, 3 #710) 20.00 45.00

No. 737A was issued only in the booklet pane, No. 737b. No. 737 was issued on fluorescent paper in 1963.

1956, Jan. 7 Engr. Wmk. 304
738 A166 20pf dark red 6.00 2.25

125th anniv. of the birth of Heinrich von Stephan, co-founder of the UPU.

Clavichord A167

1956, Jan. 27 Litho.
739 A167 10pf dull lilac .65 .25

200th anniv. of the birth of Wolfgang Amadeus Mozart, composer.

Heinrich Heine, Poet, Death Cent. — A168

Perf. 13x13½

1956, Feb. 17 Wmk. 295
740 A168 10pf ol grn & blk 2.50 2.60

Old Buildings, Lüneburg A169

Wmk. 304

1956, May 2 Engr. *Perf. 14*
741 A169 20pf dull red 6.50 6.50

Millenary of Lüneburg.

Olympic Rings A170

Robert Schumann A171

1956, June 9 *Perf. 13½x14*
742 A170 10pf slate green .65 .40

Issued to publicize the Olympic year, 1956.

1956, July 28 Litho. Unwmk.
743 A171 10pf citron, blk & red .60 .25

Schumann, composer, death cent.

Synod Emblem — A172

Thomas Mann — A173

Perf. 13½x13

1956, Aug. 8 Wmk. 304
744 A172 10pf green 3.00 3.00
745 A172 20pf brown carmine 3.50 4.25

Meeting of German Protestants (Evangelical Synod), Frankfurt-on-Main, Aug. 8-12.

1956, Aug. 11 Engr. *Perf. 13½x14*
746 A173 20pf pale rose vio 2.50 1.90

1st anniv. of the death of Thomas Mann, novelist.

Maria Laach Abbey — A174

"Rebuilding Europe" — A175

1956, Aug. 24 Photo. *Perf. 13x13½*
747 A174 20pf brn lake & gray 2.00 1.40

800th anniv. of the dedication of the Maria Laach Abbey.

Europa Issue, 1956

1956, Sept. 15 Engr. *Perf. 14*
748 A175 10pf green 1.00 .20
749 A175 40pf blue 6.25 .90

Issued to symbolize the cooperation among the six countries comprising the Coal and Steel Community.

Plan of Cologne Cathedral and Hand — A176

1956, Aug. 29 Litho. *Perf. 13x13½*
750 A176 10pf gray grn & red brn 2.25 2.00

77th meeting of German Catholics, Cologne, Aug. 29.

Map of the World and Policeman's Hand — A177

1956, Sept. 1 ***Perf. 13½x13***
751 A177 20pf red org, grn & blk 2.50 2.00

Issued on the occasion of the International Police Show, Essen, Sept. 1-23.

Pigeon Holding Letter — A178

1956, Oct. 27 **Engr.** ***Perf. 14***
752 A178 10pf green 1.25 .50

Issued to publicize the Day of the Stamp.

Cemetery Crosses — A179

1956, Nov. 17 ***Perf. 14x13½***
753 A179 10pf slate 1.25 .45

Issued to commemorate the people of Germany who died during WWII and to promote the Society for the Care of Military Cemeteries.

Saar Coat of Arms — A180

1957, Jan. 2 **Litho.** ***Perf. 13x13½***
754 A180 10pf bluish grn & brn .40 .35

Return of the Saar to Germany. See Saar #262.

Heuss Type of 1954

1956-57 **Wmk. 304** **Engr.** ***Perf. 14***
Size: 18½x22mm

755 A150 30pf slate green .35 .50
756 A150 40pf lt ultra 1.60 .20
757 A150 50pf olive .65 .20
758 A150 60pf lt brown 2.50 .35
759 A150 70pf violet 9.25 .35
760 A150 80pf red orange 4.50 1.60
761 A150 90pf bluish green 14.50 .70
Nos. 755-761 (7) 33.35 3.90

Nos. 755-756 were printed on both ordinary and fluorescent paper; Nos. 757-761 only on ordinary paper. Issue dates: 40pf, 1956. Others, 1957.

The 40pf and 70pf were also issued in coils. Every fifth coil stamp has control number on back.

Heinrich Hertz — A181

1957, Feb. 22 **Litho.** ***Perf. 14***
762 A181 10pf lt green & blk 1.10 .40

Heinrich Hertz, physicist, birth cent.

Paul Gerhardt — A182

1957, May 18 **Engr.**
763 A182 20pf carmine lake .45 .35

350th anniv. of the birth of Paul Gerhardt, Lutheran clergyman and hymn writer.

Tulip and Post Horn — A183

1957, June 8
764 A183 20pf red orange .45 .35

Flora & Philately Exhib., Cologne, June 8-10.

Arms of Aschaffenburg, 1332 — A184

Perf. 13x13½
1957, June 15 **Wmk. 304**
765 A184 20pf dp salmon & blk .45 .35

1000th anniv. of the founding of the Abbey and town of Aschaffenburg.

Scholars (Sapiens Manuscript) A185

1957, June 24 ***Perf. 13½x13***
766 A185 10pf blk, bl grn & red org .35 .25

Founding of Freiburg University, 500th anniv.

Modern Passenger Freighter — A186

1957, June 25 ***Perf. 13½x14***
767 A186 15pf brt blue, blk & red .90 .75

Merchant Marine Day, June 25.

Liebig Laboratory A187

1957, July 3 **Engr.** ***Perf. 14x13½***
768 A187 10pf dark green .35 .35

350th anniv. of the Justus Liebig School at Ludwig University, Giessen.

Albert Ballin — A188

Perf. 13½x14
1957, Aug. 15 **Litho.** **Wmk. 304**
769 A188 20pf dk car rose & blk 1.10 .35

Cent. of the birth of Albert Ballin, founder of the Hamburg-America Steamship Line.

Television Screen — A189

1957, Aug. 23 **Engr.** ***Perf. 14x13½***
770 A189 10pf blue vio & grn .35 .35

Issued to publicize the television industry.

Europa Issue, 1957

"United Europe" A190

Lithographed; Tree Embossed
1957-58 **Unwmk.** ***Perf. 14x13½***
771 A190 10pf yel grn & lt bl .35 .20
a. Imperf. *240.00 240.00*
772 A190 40pf dk bl & lt bl 3.50 .25

Wmk. 304
772A A190 10pf yel grn & lt bl 5.50 6.50
Nos. 771-772A (3) 9.35 6.95

A united Europe for peace and prosperity. Issued: #771-772, 9/16; #772A, 8/1958.

Water Lily — A191

European Robin — A192

Wmk. 304
1957, Oct. 4 **Litho.** ***Perf. 14***
773 A191 10pf yel grn & org yel .30 .30
774 A192 20pf multicolored .50 .30

Protection of wild animals and plants.

Carrier Pigeons — A193

Baron vom Stein — A194

1957, Oct. 5
775 A193 20pf dp car & blk .75 .35

Intl. Letter Writing Week, Oct. 6-12.

1957, Oct. 26 **Engr.** ***Perf. 13½x14***
776 A194 20pf red 1.25 .50

200th anniv. of the birth of Baron Heinrich Friedrich vom und zum Stein, Prussian statesman.

Leo Baeck — A195

Landschaft Building, Stuttgart — A196

1957, Nov. 2
777 A195 20pf dark red 1.25 .50

1st anniv. of the death of Rabbi Leo Baeck of Berlin.

Perf. 13x13½
1957, Nov. 16 **Litho.** **Wmk. 304**
778 A196 10pf dk grn & yel grn .70 .35

500th anniversary of the Wurttemberg Landtag (Assembly).

Coach — A197

"Max and Moritz" — A198

1957, Nov. 26 **Engr.** ***Perf. 14***
779 A197 10pf olive green .65 .30

Centenary of the death of Joseph V. Eichendorff, poet.

1958, Jan. 9 **Litho.** ***Perf. 13½x13***

Design: 20pf, Wilhelm Busch.

780 A198 10pf lt ol grn & blk .20 .20
781 A198 20pf red & black .60 .30

50th anniv. of the death of Wilhelm Busch, humorist.

"Prevent Forest Fires" — A199

1958, Mar. 5 ***Perf. 14***
782 A199 20pf brt red & blk .55 .35

Rudolf Diesel A200

1958, Mar. 18 Engr. *Perf. 14*
783 A200 10pf dk blue grn .30 .25

Centenary of the birth of Rudolf Diesel, inventor.

Giraffe and Lion — A201

View of Old Munich — A202

Perf. 13x13½
1958, May 7 Litho. Wmk. 304
784 A201 10pf brt yel grn & blk .45 .30

Zoo at Frankfort on the Main, cent.
Exists imperf. Value $225.

1958, May 22 Engr. *Perf. 14x13½*
785 A202 20pf dark red .45 .30

800th anniversary of Munich.

Market Cross, Trier — A203

Heraldic Eagle 5m Coin — A204

1958, June 3
786 A203 20pf dark red & black .45 .30

Millennium of the market of Trier (Treves).

1958, June 20 Litho. *Perf. 13x13½*
787 A204 20pf red & black .45 .30

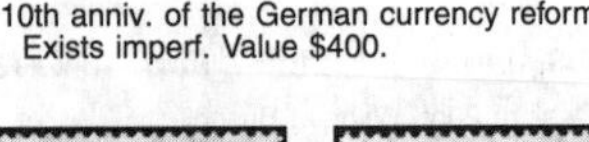

10th anniv. of the German currency reform.
Exists imperf. Value $400.

Turner Emblem and Oak Leaf A205

Schulze-Delitzsch A206

Perf. 13½x14
1958, July 21 Wmk. 304
788 A205 10pf gray, blk & dl grn .30 .35

150 years of German Turners and on the occasion of the 1958 Turner festival.

1958, Aug. 29 Engr. *Perf. 13½x14*
789 A206 10pf yellow green .40 .25

150th anniv. of the birth of Hermann Schulze-Delitzsch, founder of German trade organizations.

Common Design Types pictured following the introduction.

Europa Issue, 1958
Common Design Type

1958, Sept. 13 Litho.
Size: 24½x30mm

790 CD1 10pf yel grn & blue .25 .20
791 CD1 40pf lt blue & red 2.25 .30

Nicolaus Cusanus (Nikolaus Krebs) A207

Pres. Theodor Heuss A208

1958, Dec. 3 Litho. *Perf. 14x13½*
792 A207 20pf dk car rose & blk .40 .25

500th anniv. of the Cusanus Hospice at Kues, founded by Cardinal Nicolaus (1401-64).
Exists imperf. Value $250.

1959 Wmk. 304 *Perf. 14*
793 A208 7pf blue green .20 .20
794 A208 10pf green .35 .20
795 A208 20pf dk car rose .35 .20

Engr.

796 A208 40pf blue 10.50 .80
797 A208 70pf deep purple 3.25 .45
Nos. 793-797 (5) 14.65 1.85

Nos. 793-795 were issued in sheets of 100 and in coils. Every fifth coil stamp has a control number on the back.
An experimental booklet containing one pane of 10 of No. 794 was sold at Darmstadt in 1960. Value $650.

Jakob Fugger — A209

Adam Riese — A210

1959, Mar. 6 *Perf. 13x13½*
798 A209 20pf dk red & black .35 .30

500th anniversary of the birth of Jakob Fugger the Rich, businessman and banker.

1959, Mar. 28 *Perf. 13½x13*
799 A210 10pf ol grn & blk .35 .30

Adam Riese (c. 1492-1559), arithmetic teacher, 400th death anniversary.

Alexander von Humboldt — A211

Buildings, Buxtehude A212

1959, May 6 Engr. *Perf. 13½x14*
800 A211 40pf blue 1.40 1.10

Alexander von Humboldt (1769-1859), naturalist and geographer, death centenary.

1959, June 20 Litho. *Perf. 14*
801 A212 20pf lt blue, ver & blk .35 .30

Millennium of town of Buxtehude.

Holy Coat of Trier — A213

Lithographed; Coat Embossed
1959, July 18 Wmk. 304 *Perf. 14*
802 A213 20pf dull cl, buff & blk .35 .30

Showing of the seamless robe of Christ at the Cathedral of Trier, July 19-Sept. 20.

Synod Emblem — A214

1959, Aug. 12 Litho.
803 A214 10pf grn, brt vio & blk .25 .25

Meeting of German Protestants (Evangelical Synod), Munich, Aug. 12-16.

Souvenir Sheet

A215

Portraits: 10pf, George Friedrich Handel. 15pf, Louis Spohr. 20pf, Ludwig van Beethoven. 25pf, Joseph Haydn. 40pf, Felix Mendelssohn-Bartholdy.

Perf. 14x13½
1959, Sept. 8 Engr. Wmk. 304
804 A215 Sheet of 5 21.00 *42.50*
a. 10pf deep green 2.50 4.50
b. 15pf blue 2.50 4.50
c. 20pf dark carmine 2.50 3.00
d. 25pf brown 2.50 6.00
e. 40pf dark blue 2.50 4.50

Opening of Beethoven Hall in Bonn and to honor various anniversaries of German composers.

Europa Issue, 1959
Common Design Type

1959, Sept. 19 Litho. *Perf. 13½x14*
Size: 24x29½mm

805 CD2 10pf olive green .20 .20
806 CD2 40pf dark blue .90 .35

Uprooted Oak Emblem — A216

1960, Apr. 7 *Perf. 13½x13*
807 A216 10pf grn, blk & lil .20 .20
808 A216 40pf bl, blk & org 1.75 1.50

World Refugee Year, 7/1/59-6/30/60.

Philipp Melanchthon A217

Symbols of Christ's Sufferings A218

1960, Apr. 19 *Perf. 13½x14*
809 A217 20pf dk car rose & blk 1.10 1.00

400th anniversary of the death of Philipp Melanchthon, co-worker of Martin Luther in the German Reformation.

1960, May 17 *Perf. 14x13½*
810 A218 10pf Prus grn, gray & ocher .25 .25

1960 Passion Play, Oberammergau, Bavaria.

Dove, Chalice and Crucifix — A219

1960, July 30 Engr. *Perf. 14x13½*
811 A219 10pf dull green .50 .40
812 A219 20pf maroon .65 .60

37th Eucharistic World Congress, Munich.

Wrestlers and Olympic Rings — A220

Sport scenes from Greek urns: 10pf, Sprinters. 20pf, Discus and Javelin throwers. 40pf, Chariot race.

1960, Aug. 8 Wmk. 304
813 A220 7pf red brown .20 .20
814 A220 10pf olive green .35 .20
815 A220 20pf vermilion .35 .20
816 A220 40pf dark blue .90 .90
Nos. 813-816 (4) 1.80 1.50

17th Olympic Games, Rome, 8/25-9/11.

Hildesheim Cathedral, Miters, Cross and Crosier — A221

1960, Sept. 6 Engr. *Perf. 13½x14*
817 A221 20pf claret .65 .35

St. Bernward (960-1022) and St. Godehard (960-1038), bishops.

Europa Issue, 1960
Common Design Type

1960, Sept. 19 Wmk. 304
Size: 30x25mm

818 CD3 10pf ol grn & yel grn .20 .20
819 CD3 20pf brt red & lt red .50 .20
820 CD3 40pf bl & lt bl 1.00 .85
Nos. 818-820 (3) 1.70 1.25

George C. Marshall A222

Steam Locomotive A223

1960, Oct. 15 Litho. *Perf. 13x13½*

821 A222 40pf dp blue & blk 2.10 1.50

Issued to honor George C. Marshall, US general and statesman.

1960, Dec. 7 *Perf. 13½x14*

822 A223 10pf ol bis & blk .25 .25

125th anniversary of German railroads.

St. George — A224

Wmk. 304

1961, Apr. 23 Engr. *Perf. 14*

823 A224 10pf green .20 .20

Honoring Boy Scouts of the world on St. George's Day (patron saint of Boy Scouts).

Albrecht Dürer — A225

Portraits: 5pf, Albertus Magnus. 7pf, St. Elizabeth of Thuringia. 8pf, Johann Gutenberg. 15pf, Martin Luther. 20pf, Johann Sebastian Bach. 25pf, Balthasar Neumann. 30pf, Immanuel Kant. 40pf, Gotthold Ephraim Lessing. 50pf, Johann Wolfgang von Goethe. 60pf, Friedrich von Schiller. 70pf, Ludwig van Beethoven. 80pf, Heinrich von Kleist. 90pf, Prof. Franz Oppenheimer. 1m, Annette von Droste-Hülshoff. 2m, Gerhart Hauptmann.

1961-64 Typo. *Perf. 14*

Fluorescent or Ordinary Paper

824 A225 5pf olive .20 .20
b. Tête bêche pair ('63) .45 .80
825 A225 7pf dark bister .20 .20
826 A225 8pf lilac .20 .20
827 A225 10pf olive green .20 .20
b. Tête bêche pair .45 1.25
828 A225 15pf blue .20 .20
b. Tête bêche pair ('63) .80 1.90
829 A225 20pf dk red .20 .20
b. Tête bêche pair ('63) .55 1.60
830 A225 25pf orange brn .20 .20

Engr.

831 A225 30pf gray .20 .20
832 A225 40pf blue .20 .20
833 A225 50pf red brown .30 .20
834 A225 60pf dk car rose ('62) .30 .20
835 A225 70pf grnsh black .20 .20
a. 70pf deep green .45 .20
836 A225 80pf brown .35 .35
837 A225 90pf yel ol ('64) .30 .30
838 A225 1m violet blue .35 .20
839 A225 2m yel grn ('62) 2.50 .35
Nos. 824-839 (16) 6.10 3.60

Nos. 824-825, 827-830, 832, 834-835, 835a were issued in coils as well as in sheets. Every fifth coil stamp has a black control number on the back.

Nos. 824-839, including booklet panes and tête bêche pairs, were printed on fluorescent paper. Nos. 824-829 and 832 were also printed on ordinary paper.

Gottlieb Daimler's Car of 1886 and Signature A226

Design: 20pf, Carl Benz's 3-wheel car of 1886 and signature.

1961, July 3 Litho.

840 A226 10pf green & blk .20 .20
841 A226 20pf brick red & blk .30 .25

75 years of motorized traffic.

Messenger, Nuremberg, 18th Century — A227

Cathedral, Speyer — A228

Photogravure and Engraved

1961, Aug. 31 Wmk. 304 *Perf. 14*

842 A227 7pf brown red & blk .20 .20

Issued to publicize the exhibition "The Letter in Five Centuries," Nuremberg.

1961, Sept. 2 Engr.

843 A228 20pf vermilion .25 .30

900th anniversary of Speyer Cathedral.

Europa Issue, 1961

Common Design Type

1961, Sept. 18 Litho.

Size: 28½x18½mm

844 CD4 10pf olive green .20 .20
845 CD4 40pf violet blue .30 .30

No. 844 was printed on both ordinary and fluorescent paper.

Reis Telephone A229

Wmk. 304

1961, Oct. 26 Engr. *Perf. 14*

846 A229 10pf green .20 .20

Cent. of the demonstration of the 1st telephone by Philipp Reis.

Wilhelm Emanuel von Ketteler — A230

1961, Dec. 22 Litho.

847 A230 10pf olive grn & blk .20 .20

Sesquicentennial of the birth of von Ketteler, Bishop of Mainz and pioneer in social development.

Fluorescent Paper was introduced for all stamps, starting with No. 848. Of the stamps before No. 848, those issued on both ordinary and fluorescent paper include Nos. 704, 706, 708-711, 737, 755-756, 824-829, 832, 844. Those issued only on fluorescent paper (up to No. 848) include Nos. 708b, 830-831, 833-839 and 842.

Drusus Stone and Old View of Mainz — A231

Notes and Tuning Fork — A232

1962, May 10 Engr. Wmk. 304

848 A231 20pf deep claret .20 .20

The 2000th anniversary of Mainz.

1962, July 12 Litho. *Perf. 14*

849 A232 20pf red & black .20 .25

Issued to show appreciation of choral singing. The music is from the choral movement for three voices "In dulci jubilo" from "Musae Sioniae" by Michael Praetorius.

"Faith, Thanksgiving, Service" A233

1962, Aug. 22 Engr. Unwmk.

850 A233 20pf magenta .20 .25

79th meeting of German Catholics, Hanover, Aug. 22-29.

Open Bible, Chrismon and Chalice — A234

1962, Sept. 11 Litho. Wmk. 304

851 A234 20pf vermilion & blk .25 .25

Württemberg Bible Society, 150th anniv.

Europa Issue, 1962

Common Design Type

1962, Sept. 17 Engr.

Size: 28x23mm

852 CD5 10pf green .20 .20
853 CD5 40pf blue .35 .35

"Bread for the World" — A235

Lithographed and Embossed

1962, Nov. 23 *Perf. 14*

854 A235 20pf brown red & blk .20 .25

Issued in connection with the Advent Collection of the Protestant Church in Germany.

Mother and Child Receiving Gift Parcel — A236

1963, Feb. 9 Engr.

855 A236 20pf dark carmine .20 .25

Issued to express gratitude to the American organizations, CRALOG (Council of Relief Agencies Licensed to Operate in Germany) and CARE (Cooperative for American Remittances to Everywhere), for help during 1946-1962.

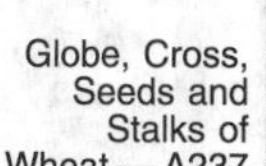

Globe, Cross, Seeds and Stalks of Wheat — A237

Checkered Lily — A238

Lithographed and Engraved

1963, Feb. 27 Wmk. 304 *Perf. 14*

856 A237 20pf gray, blk & red .20 .25

German Catholic "Misereor" (I have compassion) campaign against hunger and illness.

1963, Apr. 28 Litho. Unwmk.

Flowers: 15pf, Lady's slipper. 20pf, Columbine. 40pf, Beach thistle.

857 A238 10pf multicolored .20 .20
858 A238 15pf multicolored .20 .20
859 A238 20pf multicolored .20 .20
860 A238 40pf multicolored .30 .25
Nos. 857-860 (4) .90 .85

Flora and Philately Exhibition, Hamburg.

Heidelberg Catechism A239

1963, May 2 Litho. & Engr.

861 A239 20pf dp org, brn org & blk .25 .25

400th anniv. of the Heidelberg Catechism, containing the doctrine of the reformed church.

Cross of Golgotha, Darkened Sun and Moon — A240

1963, May 4 Litho. Wmk. 304

862 A240 10pf grn, dp car, blk & vio .20 .20

Consecration of the Regina Martyrum Church, Berlin-Plötzensee, in memory of the victims of Nazism.

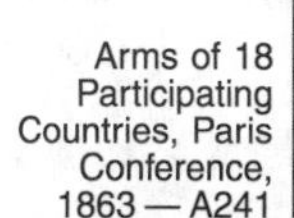

Arms of 18 Participating Countries, Paris Conference, 1863 — A241

Map Showing New Railroad Link, German and Danish Flags — A242

1963, May 7 Engr.

863 A241 40pf violet blue .35 .35

1st Intl. Postal Conf., Paris, 1863, cent.

1963, May 14 Litho. Unwmk.

864 A242 20pf multi .20 .20

Inauguration of the "Bird Flight Line" railroad link between Germany and Denmark.

Cross — A243

Lithographed and Embossed

1963, May 24 Unwmk. *Perf. 14*

865 A243 20pf magenta, red & yel .20 .20

Cent. of the founding of the Intl. Red Cross in connection with the German Red Cross cent. celebrations, Munster, May 24-26.

Synod Emblem and Crown of Barbed Wire — A244

Perf. 13½x13

1963, July 24 Litho. Wmk. 304

866 A244 20pf dp orange & blk .25 .25

Meeting of German Protestants (Evangelical Synod), Dortmund, July 24-28.

Europa Issue, 1963

Common Design Type

1963, Sept. 14 Engr. *Perf. 14*

Size: 28x23½mm

867 CD6 15pf green .20 .20
868 CD6 20pf red .20 .20

Old Town Hall, Hanover A245

State Capitals: #870, Hamburg harbor, 775th anniv. #871, North Ferry pier, Kiel. #872, National Theater, Munich. #873, Fountain & building, Wiesbaden. #874, Reichstag Building,Berlin. #875, Gutenberg Museum, Mainz. #876, Jan Wellem (Johann Wilhelm II, 1658-1716) statue, Dusseldorf. #877, City Hall, Bonn. #878, City Hall, Bremen. #879, View of Stuttgart. #879A, Ludwig's Church, Saarbrucken.

1964-65 Litho. Unwmk. *Perf. 14*

869	A245 20pf gray, blk & red	.20	.20
870	A245 20pf multicolored	.20	.20
871	A245 20pf multicolored	.20	.20
872	A245 20pf multicolored	.20	.20
873	A245 20pf multicolored	.20	.20
874	A245 20pf blue, blk, & grn	.20	.20
875	A245 20pf multicolored	.20	.20
876	A245 20pf multicolored	.20	.20
877	A245 20pf multi ('65)	.20	.20
878	A245 20pf multi ('65)	.20	.20
879	A245 20pf multi ('65)	.20	.20
879A	A245 20pf multi ('65)	.20	.20
	Nos. 869-879A (12)	2.40	2.40

View of Ottobeuren Abbey — A246

Lithographed and Engraved

1964, May 29 *Perf. 14*

880 A246 20pf pink, red & blk .20 .20

Ottobeuren Benedictine Abbey, 1200th anniv.

Pres. Heinrich Lübke — A247

Sophie Scholl — A248

1964, July 1 Litho. *Perf. 14*

881 A247 20pf carmine .20 .20
882 A247 40pf ultra .20 .20

Lübke's re-election. See Nos. 974-975.

1964, July 20 Litho. & Engr.

Designs: No. 884, Ludwig Beck. No. 885, Dietrich Bonhoeffer. No. 886, Alfred Delp. No. 887, Karl Friedrich Goerdeler. No. 888, Wilhelm Leuschner. No. 889, Count James von Moltke. No. 890, Count Claus Schenk von Stauffenberg.

883 A248 20pf blue gray & blk	.55	*1.00*
884 A248 20pf blue gray & blk	.55	*1.00*
885 A248 20pf blue gray & blk	.55	*1.00*
886 A248 20pf blue gray & blk	.55	*1.00*
887 A248 20pf blue gray & blk	.55	*1.00*
888 A248 20pf blue gray & blk	.55	*1.00*
889 A248 20pf blue gray & blk	.55	*1.00*
890 A248 20pf blue gray & blk	.55	*1.00*
Nos. 883-890 (8)	4.40	8.00

Issued to honor the German resistance to the Nazis, 1943-45. Printed in sheet of eight, containing one each of Nos. 883-890, se-tenant. Size: 148x105mm. The stamps were valid; the sheet was not, though widely used.

John Calvin — A249

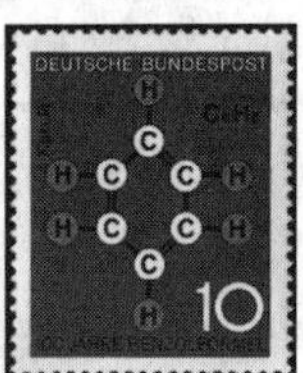

Benzene Ring, Kekulé's Formula — A250

1964, Aug. 3 Litho. *Perf. 14*

891 A249 20pf red & black .20 .20

Issued to honor the meeting of the International Union of the Reformed Churches in Germany, Frankfort on the Main, Aug. 3-13.

1964, Aug. 14 Unwmk. *Perf. 14*

Designs: 15pf, Cerenkov radiation, reactor in operation. 20pf, German gas engine.

892 A250 10pf dk brn, brt grn & blk	.20	.20
893 A250 15pf brt grn, ultra & blk	.20	.20
894 A250 20pf red, grn & blk	.20	.20
Nos. 892-894 (3)	.60	.60

Progress in science and technology: 10pf, centenary of benzene formula by August Friedrich Kekulé; 15pf, 25 years of nuclear fission, Hahn and Strassmann; 20pf, centenary of German internal combustion engine, Nikolaus August Otto and Eugen Langen.

Ferdinand Lasalle — A251

Radiating Sun — A252

1964, Aug. 31 Litho.

895 A251 20pf slate bl & blk .20 .20

Cent. of the death of Ferdinand Lasalle, a founder of the German Labor Movement.

1964, Sept. 2 Engr. Wmk. 304

896 A252 20pf gray & red .20 .20

80th meeting of German Catholics, Stuttgart, Sept. 2-6. The inscription from Romans 12:2: ". . . be ye transformed through the renewing of your mind."

Europa Issue, 1964

Common Design Type

1964, Sept. 14 Litho. Unwmk.

Size: 23x29mm

897 CD7 15pf yellow grn & lil .20 .20
898 CD7 20pf rose & lilac .20 .20

Judo — A253

1964, Oct. 10

899 A253 20pf multicolored .20 .20

18th Olympic Games, Tokyo, Oct. 10-25.

Prussian Eagle — A254

Lithographed and Embossed

1964, Oct. 30 Unwmk. *Perf. 14*

900 A254 20pf brown org & blk .20 .20

250 years of the Court of Accounts in Germany, founded as the Royal Prussian Upper Chamber of Accounts.

John F. Kennedy (1917-63) A255

Castle Gate, Ellwangen A256

1964, Nov. 21 Engr. Wmk. 304

901 A255 40pf dark blue .25 .25

1964-66 Typo. Unwmk.

Designs: (German buildings through 12 centuries): 10pf, Wall pavilion, Zwinger, Dresden. 15pf, Tegel Castle, Berlin. 20pf, Portico, Lorsch. 40pf, Trifels Fortress, Palatinate. 60pf, Treptow Gate, Neubrandenburg. 70pf, Osthofen Gate, Soest. 80pf, Elling Gate, Weissenburg.

903 A256 10pf brown ('65)	.20	.20
904 A256 15pf dk green ('65)	.20	.20
b. Tête bêche pair ('65)	.90	1.00
905 A256 20pf brown red ('65)	.20	.20
b. Tête bêche pair ('66)	1.00	1.00

Engr.

908 A256 40pf violet bl ('65)	.20	.20
909 A256 50pf olive bister	.35	.20
910 A256 60pf rose red	.75	.25
911 A256 70pf dark green ('65)	.90	.25
912 A256 80pf chocolate	.75	.20
Nos. 903-912 (8)	3.55	1.70

Nos. 903-905, 908, 910-912 were issued in sheets of 100 and in coils. Every fifth coil stamp has a black control number on the back.

Illustrations from the Works of Matthias Claudius A257

Otto von Bismarck by Franz von Lenbach — A258

1965, Jan. 21 Engr. *Perf. 14*

917 A257 20pf black & red .20 .20

150th anniv. of the death of Matthias Claudius, poet and editor of the "Wandsbecker Bothe." Exists imperf. Value $350.

1965, Apr. 1 Litho. *Perf. 14*

918 A258 20pf black & dull red .20 .20

Prince Otto von Bismarck (1815-1898), Prussian statesman and 1st chancellor of the German Empire.

Exists imperf. Value $250.

Jet Plane and Space Capsule — A259

Bouquet of Flowers — A260

Designs: 5pf, Traffic lights and signs. 10pf, Communications satellite and ground station. 15pf, Old and new post buses. 20pf, Semaphore telegraph and telecommunication tower. 40pf, Old and new railroad engines. 70pf, Sailing ship and ocean liner.

1965

919 A259 5pf gray & multi	.20	.20
920 A259 10pf multicolored	.20	.20
921 A259 15pf multicolored	.20	.20
922 A259 20pf maroon & multi	.20	.20
923 A259 40pf dk blue & multi	.20	.20
924 A259 60pf dull vio, yel & lt bl	.20	.20
925 A259 70pf multicolored	.25	.25
Nos. 919-925 (7)	1.45	1.45

Intl. Transport and Communications Exhib., Munich, June 25-Oct. 30. No. 924 also for the 10th anniv. of the reopening of air service by Lufthansa. Issued: 60pf, 4/1; others, 6/25.

No. 919 exists imperf.

1965, May 1 Litho.

926 A260 15pf multicolored .20 .20

75th anniv. of May Day celebration in Germany.

ITU Emblem — A261

Adolph Kolping — A262

1965, May 17 Unwmk. *Perf. 14*

927 A261 40pf dp blue & blk .25 .25

Cent. of the ITU.

1965, May 26 Typo.

928 A262 20pf black, gray & red .20 .20

Kolping (1813-65). founder of the Catholic Unions of Journeymen, the Kolpingwork.

Rescue Ship — A263

1965, May 29 Litho. & Engr.

929 A263 20pf red & black .20 .20

Cent. of the German Sea Rescue Service.

Type of 1955 dated "1945-1965"

Perf. 14x13½

1965, July 28 Engr. Wmk. 304

930 A161 20pf gray .20 .20

20 years of German expatriation.

Synod Emblem and Labyrinth — A264

Lithographed and Engraved

Perf. 13½x14

1965, July 28 Unwmk.

931 A264 20pf dp bl, grnsh bl & blk .20 .20

12th meeting of German Protestants (Evangelical Synod), Cologne, July 28-Aug. 1.

Waves and Stuttgart Television Tower — A265

1965, July 28 Litho. *Perf. 13½x13*

932 A265 20pf dp bl, blk & brt pink .20 .20

Issued to publicize the German Radio Exhibition, Stuttgart, Aug. 27-Sept. 5.

Stamps of Thurn and Taxis, 1852-59 A266

1965, Aug. 28 *Perf. 14*

933 A266 20pf multicolored .20 .20

125th anniv. of the introduction of postage stamps in Great Britain.

Europa Issue, 1965

Common Design Type

Perf. 14x13½

1965, Sept. 27 Engr. Wmk. 304

Size: 28x23mm

934 CD8 15pf green .20 .20
935 CD8 20pf dull red .20 .20

Nordertor, Flensburg A267

Brandenburg Gate A268

Designs: 5pf, Berlin Gate, Stettin. 10pf, Wall Pavilion, Zwinger, Dresden. 20pf, Portico, Lorsch. 40pf, Trifels Fortress, Palatinate. 50pf, Castle Gate, Ellwangen. 60pf, Treptow Gate, Neubrandenburg. 70pf, Osthofen Gate, Soest. 80pf, Elling Gate, Weissenburg. 90pf, Zschocke Ladies' Home, Königsberg. 1m, Melanchthon House, Wittenberg. 1.10m, Trinity Hospital, Hildesheim. 1.30m, Tegel Castle, Berlin. 2m, Löwenberg, Town Hall, interior view.

1966-69 Unwmk. Engr. *Perf. 14*

936 A267	5pf olive		.20	.20
937 A267	10pf dk brn ('67)		.20	.20
939 A267	20pf dk grn ('67)		.20	.20
940 A267	30pf yellow green		.20	.20
941 A267	30pf red ('67)		.20	.20
942 A267	40pf olive bis ('67)		.25	.25
943 A267	50pf blue ('67)		.35	.20
944 A267	60pf dp org ('67)		2.00	1.10
945 A267	70pf slate grn ('67)		.90	.20
946 A267	80pf red brown ('67)		1.60	.80
947 A267	90pf black		.65	.25
948 A267	1m dull blue		.65	.20
949 A267	1.10m red brown		.65	.25
950 A267	1.30m green ('69)		1.60	.60
951 A267	2m purple		1.60	.35
	Nos. 936-951 (15)		11.25	5.20

1966-68 Typo. *Perf. 14*

952 A268 10pf chocolate		.20	.20
a.	Bklt. pane, 4 #952, 2 #953, 4 #954 ('67)	3.25	3.25
b.	Tête bêche pair	.60	.30
c.	Bklt. pane, 2 #952, 4 #953	2.00	2.00
953 A268 20pf deep green		.25	.20
a.	Tête bêche pair ('68)	.65	.65
b.	Bklt. pane, 2 #953, 2 #954	1.25	1.25
954 A268 30pf red		.25	.20
a.	Tête bêche pair ('68)	.80	.80
955 A268 50pf dark blue		1.00	.25
956 A268 100pf dark blue ('67)		7.75	.40
Nos. 952-956 (5)		9.45	1.25

Nos. 952-956 were issued in sheets of 100 and in coils. Every fifth coil stamp has a black control number on the back.

Nathan Söderblom A269

Cardinal von Galen A270

1966, Jan. 15 Litho. *Perf. 13x13½*

959 A269 20pf dull lilac & blk .20 .20

Soderblom (1866-1931),Swedish Protestant theologian, who worked for the union of Christian churches and received 1930 Nobel Peace Prize.

1966, Mar. 22 Litho. *Perf. 14*

960 A270 20pf dp lil rose, sal pink & blk .20 .20

Clemens August Cardinal Count von Galen (1878-1946), anti-Nazi Bishop of Munster.

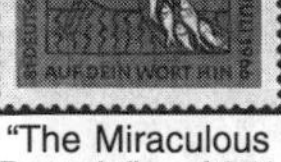

"The Miraculous Draught" — A271

G. W. Leibniz — A272

1966, July 13 Litho. *Perf. 14*

961 A271 30pf dp orange & blk .20 .20

81st meeting of German Catholics, Bamberg, July 13-17.

1966, Aug. 24 Unwmk. *Perf. 14*

962 A272 30pf rose car, pink & blk .20 .20

Gottfried Wilhelm Leibniz (1646-1716), philosopher and mathematician.

Europa Issue, 1966

Common Design Type

1966, Sept. 24 *Perf. 14*

Size: 23x28½mm

963 CD9 20pf multicolored .20 .20
964 CD9 30pf multicolored .20 .20

Diagram of Three-Phase Transmission A273

UNICEF Emblem A274

1966, Sept. 28 Litho.

965 A273 20pf shown .20 .20
966 A273 30pf Dynamo .20 .20

Progress in science and technology: 20pf, 75th anniv. of three-phase power transmission; 30pf, cent.y of discovery by Werner von Siemens of the dynamoelectric principle.

1966, Oct. 24 Litho. *Perf. 14*

967 A274 30pf red, blk & gray .20 .20

Awarding of the 1965 Nobel Peace Prize to UNICEF.

Werner von Siemens (1816-92), Electrical Engineer and Inventor — A275

1966, Dec. 13 Engr. *Perf. 14*

968 A275 30pf maroon .20 .20

Europa Issue, 1967

Common Design Type

1967, May 2 Photo. *Perf. 14*

Size: 23x28mm

969 CD10 20pf multi .20 .20
970 CD10 30pf multi .20 .20

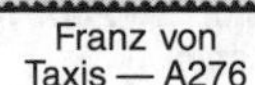

Franz von Taxis — A276

"Peace Is Among Us" — A277

Lithographed and Engraved

1967, June 3 *Perf. 14*

971 A276 30pf dp orange & blk .20 .20

450th anniv. of the death of Franz von Taxis, founder of the Taxis (Thurn and Taxis) postal system.

1967, June 21

972 A277 30pf brt pink & blk .20 .20

13th meeting of German Protestants (Evangelical Synod), Hanover, June 21-25.

Friedrich von Bodelschwingh A278

Perf. 13½x13

1967, July 1 Litho. Unwmk.

973 A278 30pf redsh brown & blk .20 .20

Cent. of Bethel Institution (for the incurable). Friedrich von Bodelschwingh (1877-1946), manager of Bethel (1910-46) & son of the founder.

Lübke Type of 1964

1967, Oct. 14 Litho. *Perf. 14*

974 A247 30pf carmine .20 .20
975 A247 50pf ultra .30 .25

Re-election of President Heinrich Lübke.

The Wartburg, Eisenach A279

1967, Oct. 31 Engr. *Perf. 14*

976 A279 30pf red .25 .25

450th anniversary of the Reformation.

Cross and Map of South America — A280

Koenig Printing Press — A281

1967, Nov. 17 Photo. *Perf. 14*

977 A280 30pf multicolored .20 .20

"Adveniat," aid movement of German Catholics for the Latin American church.

1968, Jan. 12 Litho. *Perf. 14*

Designs: 20pf, Zinc sulfide and lead sulfide crystals. 30pf, Schematic diagram of a microscope.

978 A281 10pf multicolored .20 .20
979 A281 20pf multicolored .20 .20
980 A281 30pf multicolored .20 .20
Nos. 978-980 (3) .60 .60

Progress in science and technology: 10pf, 150th anniv. of the Koenig printing press; 20pf, 1000th anniv. of mining in the Harz Mountains; 30pf, cent. of scientific microscope construction.

Symbols of Various Crafts A282

1968, Mar. 8 Litho. *Perf. 14*

981 A282 30pf multicolored .20 .20

Traditions and progress of the crafts. Exists imperf. Value $250.

Souvenir Sheet

Adenauer, Churchill, de Gasperi and Schuman — A283

Portraits: 10pf, Winston S. Churchill. 20pf, Alcide de Gasperi. 30pf, Robert Schuman. 50pf, Konrad Adenauer.

1968, Apr. 19 Litho. *Perf. 14*

Black Inscriptions

982 A283	Sheet of 4	2.00	2.00
a.	10pf dark red brown	.20	.20
b.	20pf green	.25	.25
c.	30pf dark red	.45	.45
d.	50pf bright blue	.65	.65

1st anniv. of the death of Konrad Adenauer (1876-1967), chancellor of West Germany (1949-63), and honoring leaders in building a united Europe.

Europa Issue, 1968

Common Design Type

1968, Apr. 29 Photo.

Size: 29x24½mm

983 CD11 20pf green, yel & brn .20 .20
984 CD11 30pf car, yel & brn .20 .20

Karl Marx (1818-83) A284

Lithographed and Engraved

1968, Apr. 29 ***Perf. 14***
985 A284 30pf red, black & gray .20 .20

Pierre de Coubertin — A285

1968, June 6 Unwmk. ***Perf. 14***
986 A285 30pf lilac & dk pur .20 .20
Nos. 986,B434-B437 (5) 1.55 1.55

19th Olympic Games, Mexico City, 10/12-27.

Opening Bars, "Die Meistersinger von Nurnberg," by Wagner — A286

Lithographed and Photogravure

1968, June 21
987 A286 30pf gray, blk & fawn .20 .20

Cent. of the 1st performance of Richard Wagner's "Die Meistersinger von Nurnberg."

Konrad Adenauer (1876-1967) A287

1968, July 19 Litho. ***Perf. 14***
988 A287 30pf dp orange & blk .25 .20

Cross and Dove in Center of Universe A288

1968, July 19 Litho. & Engr.
989 A288 20pf brt grn, bl blk & yel .20 .20

Issued to publicize the 82nd meeting of German Catholics, Essen, Sept. 4-8.

North German Confederation Nos. 4 and 10 — A289

1968, Sept. 5 Engr. ***Perf. 14***
990 A289 30pf cop red, gray vio & blk .20 .20

Cent. of the stamps of the North German Confederation.

Arrows Symbolizing Determination A290

Human Rights Flame A291

1968, Sept. 26 Photo. ***Perf. 14***
991 A290 30pf multi .20 .20

Centenary of the German trade unions.

1968, Dec. 10 Photo. ***Perf. 14***
992 A291 30pf multicolored .20 .20

International Human Rights Year.

Junkers 52 A292

Design: 30pf, Boeing 707.

1969, Feb. 6 Litho. ***Perf. 14***
993 A292 20pf green & multi .35 .20
994 A292 30pf red & multi .50 .20

50th anniv. of German airmail service.

Five-pointed Star — A293

1969, Apr. 28 Litho. ***Perf. 13½x13***
995 A293 30pf red & multi .35 .20

50th anniv. of the ILO.

Europa Issue, 1969
Common Design Type

1969, Apr. 28 Photo. ***Perf. 14***
Size: 29x23mm
996 CD12 20pf green, blue & yel .25 .20
997 CD12 30pf red brn, yel & blk .35 .20

Heraldic Eagles of Federal and Weimar Republics A294

1969, May 23 Photo. ***Perf. 14***
998 A294 30pf red, black & gold .80 .25

German Basic Law, 20th anniv., and the proclamation of the Weimar Constitution, 50th anniv.

Crosses — A295

1969, June 4 Litho. & Engr.
999 A295 30pf dk violet bl & cream .35 .20

German War Graves Commission, 50th anniv.

Seashore A296

1969, June 4 ***Perf. 14***
1000 A296 10pf shown .20 .20
1001 A296 20pf Foothills .50 .25
1002 A296 30pf Mountains .25 .20
1003 A296 50pf Riverbed .65 .40
Nos. 1000-1003 (4) 1.60 1.05

Issued to publicize Nature Protection.

"Hungry for Justice" — A297

1969, July 7 Litho. ***Perf. 14***
1004 A297 30pf multicolored .35 .20

14th meeting of German Protestants (Evangelical Synod), Stuttgart, July 16-20.

Electromagnetic Field — A298

1969, Aug. 11 Litho. ***Perf. 14***
1005 A298 30pf red & multi .35 .20

Issued to publicize the German Radio Exhibition, Stuttgart, Aug. 29-Sept. 7.

Maltese Cross — A299

1969, Aug. 11 ***Perf. 13x13½***
1006 A299 30pf red & black .40 .20

Maltese Relief Service, founded 1955, world-wide activities in social services, first aid and disaster assistance.

Souvenir Sheet

Marie Juchacz, Marie-Elisabeth Lüders and Helene Weber — A300

1969, Aug. 11 Engr. ***Perf. 14***
1007 A300 Sheet of 3 .65 .50
a. 10pf olive .20 .20
b. 20pf dark green .20 .20
c. 30pf lake .20 .20

50th anniv. of universal women's suffrage, Marie Juchacz (1879-1956), Marie-Elisabeth Lüders (1878-1966) and Helene Weber (1881-1962) were members of the German Reichstag.

Bavaria No. 16 — A301

Brine Pipe Line — A302

1969, Sept. 4 Litho. & Embossed
1008 A301 30pf gray & rose .30 .20

23rd meeting of the Federation of German Philatelists, Sept. 6, the 70th Philatelists' Day, Sept. 7, and the phil. exhib. "120 Years of Bavarian Stamps" in Garmish-Partenkirchen, Sept. 4-7.

1969, Sept. 4 Litho. ***Perf. 13½x13***
1009 A302 20pf multicolored .25 .20

350th anniversary of the Brine Pipe Line from Traunstein to Bad Reichenhall.

Rothenburg ob der Tauber — A303

Lithographed and Engraved

1969, Sept. 4 ***Perf. 14***
1010 A303 30pf dark red & blk .30 .20

See #1047-1049, 1067-1069A, 1106-1110.

Pope John XXIII (1881-1963) A304

Mahatma Gandhi (1869-1948) A305

1969, Oct. 2 Engr. ***Perf. 13½x14***
1011 A304 30pf dark red .30 .20

1969, Oct. 2 **Litho.**
1012 A305 20pf yellow grn & blk .25 .20

Ernst Moritz Arndt A306

Ludwig van Beethoven A307

1969, Nov. 13 Litho. & Engr.
1013 A306 30pf gray & maroon .30 .20

Arndt (1769-1860), historian, poet and member of German National Assembly.

1970, Mar. 20 ***Perf. 13½x14***

Portraits: 20pf, Georg Wilhelm Hegel (1770-1831), philosopher. 30pf, Friedrich Hölderlin (1770-1843), poet.

1014 A307 10pf pale vio & blk .60 .20
1015 A307 20pf olive & blk .30 .20
1016 A307 30pf rose & blk .30 .20
Nos. 1014-1016 (3) 1.20 .60

Saar No. 171 A308

1970, Apr. 29 Photo. *Perf. 14x13½*
1017 A308 30pf blk, red & gray grn .30 .20

Issued to publicize the SABRIA National Stamp Exhibition, Saarbrucken, Apr. 29-May 4. No. 1017 was issued Apr. 29 at the SABRIA post office in Saarbrucken, on May 4 throughout Germany.

Europa Issue, 1970
Common Design Type

1970, May 4 Engr. *Perf. 14x13½*
Size: 28x23mm
1018 CD13 20pf green .25 .20
1019 CD13 30pf red .30 .20

Münchhausen on His Severed Horse — A309

1970, May 11 Litho. *Perf. 13½x13*
1020 A309 20pf multicolored .25 .20

Soldier and storyteller Count Hieronymus C. F. von Münchhausen (1720-97).

Seagoing Vessel and Underpass A310

Nurse Assisting Elderly Woman — A311

1970, June 18 Litho. *Perf. 14*
1021 A310 20pf multicolored .25 .20

North Sea-Baltic Sea Canal, 75th anniv.

1970 Photo.

5pf, Welder (industrial protection). 10pf, Mountain climbers (rescuer bringing down casualty). 30pf, Fireman. 50pf, Stretcher bearer, casualty & ambulance. 70pf, Rescuer & drowning boy.

1022 A311 5pf dull blue & multi .20 .20
1023 A311 10pf brown & multi .20 .20
1024 A311 20pf green & multi .25 .20
1025 A311 30pf red & multi .55 .20
1026 A311 50pf blue & multi .55 .25
1027 A311 70pf green & multi .65 .55
Nos. 1022-1027 (6) 2.40 1.60

Honoring various voluntary services. Issued: 20pf, 30pf, 6/18; others, 9/21.

Pres. Gustav Heinemann A312

Cross Seen through Glass A313

1970-73 Engr. *Perf. 14*
1028 A312 5pf dark gray .20 .20
1029 A312 10pf brown .20 .20
1030 A312 20pf green .20 .20
1030A A312 25pf dp yellow grn .25 .20
1031 A312 30pf red brown .25 .20
1032 A312 40pf brown org .25 .20
1033 A312 50pf dark blue 1.25 .20
1034 A312 60pf blue .45 .20
1035 A312 70pf dark brown .60 .25
1036 A312 80pf slate grn .60 .25
1037 A312 90pf magenta 1.10 1.00
1038 A312 1m olive .80 .25
1038A A312 110pf olive gray .85 .35
1039 A312 120pf ocher 1.00 .45
1040 A312 130pf ocher 1.10 .50
1040A A312 140pf dk blue grn 1.25 .70
1041 A312 150pf purple 1.25 .35
1042 A312 160pf orange 1.40 .60
1042A A312 170pf orange 1.40 .30
1043 A312 190pf deep claret 1.90 .45
1044 A312 2m deep violet 1.50 .25
Nos. 1028-1044 (21) 17.80 7.30

Issued: 5pf, 1m, 7/23/70; 10, 20pf, 10/23/70; 30, 90pf, 2m, 1/7/71; 40, 50, 70, 80pf, 4/8/71; 60pf, 6/25/71; 25pf, 8/27/71; 120, 160pf, 3/8/72; 130pf, 6/20/72; 150pf, 7/5/72; 170pf, 9/11/72; 110, 140, 190pf, 1/16/73.

1970, Aug. 25 Litho.
1045 A313 20pf emerald & yellow .25 .20

Issued to publicize the world mission of Catholic missionaries who bring the Gospel to all peoples.

Cross A314

Comenius A315

1970, Sept. 4 *Perf. 13x13½*
1046 A314 20pf multicolored .20 .25

Issued to publicize the 83rd meeting of German Catholics, Trier, Sept. 9-13.

Town Type of 1969

Designs: No. 1047, View of Cochem and Moselle River. No. 1048, Cathedral and view of Freiburg im Breisgau. No. 1049, View of Oberammergau.

1970 Litho. *Perf. 14*
1047 A303 20pf apple grn & blk .30 .20
1048 A303 20pf green & dk brn .30 .20
1049 A303 30pf dp orange & blk .30 .20
Nos. 1047-1049 (3) .90 .60

Issued: #1047, 9/21; #1048, 11/4; #1049, 5/11.

1970, Nov. 12 *Perf. 13½x14*
1050 A315 30pf dark red & blk .30 .20

John Amos Comenius (1592-1670), theologian and educator.

Friedrich Engels — A316

Imperial Eagle, 1872 — A317

1970, Nov. 27 Litho. *Perf. 14*
1051 A316 50pf red & vio blue .80 .45

Engels (1820-95), socialist, collaborator with Marx.

1971, Jan. 18 Litho. *Perf. 13½x14*
1052 A317 30pf multicolored .80 .20

Centenary of the German Empire.

Friedrich Ebert (Germany No. 378) — A318

Molecule Diagram Textile Pattern — A319

1971, Jan. 18 *Perf. 13*
1053 A318 30pf red brn, ol & blk .80 .20

Ebert (1871-1925), 1st Pres. of the German Republic.

1971, Feb. 18 Litho. *Perf. 13½x13*
1054 A319 20pf brt grn, red & blk .20 .20

Synthetic textile fiber research, 125th anniversary.

School Crossing — A320

Signal to Pass — A321

Traffic Signs: 20pf, Proceed with caution. 30pf, Stop. 50pf, Pedestrian crossing.

1971, Feb. 18 *Perf. 14*
1055 A320 10pf black, ultra & red .20 .20
1056 A320 20pf black, red & grn .25 .20
1057 A320 30pf black, gray & red .30 .20
1058 A320 50pf black, ultra & red .60 .30
Nos. 1055-1058 (4) 1.35 .90

New traffic rules, effective Mar. 1, 1971.

1971, Apr. 16 Photo. *Perf. 14*

Traffic Signs: 10pf, Warning signal. 20pf, Drive at right. 30pf, "Observe pedestrian crossings."

1059 A321 5pf blue, blk & car .20 .20
1060 A321 10pf multicolored .20 .20
1061 A321 20pf brt grn, blk & car .30 .20
1062 A321 30pf carmine & multi .40 .20
Nos. 1059-1062 (4) 1.10 .80

New traffic rules, effective Mar. 1, 1971.

Luther Facing Charles V, Woodcut by Rabus — A322

Thomas à Kempis — A323

1971, Mar. 18 *Perf. 14*
1063 A322 30pf red & black .40 .20

450th anniversary of the Diet of Worms.

Europa Issue, 1971
Common Design Type

1971, May 3 Photo. *Perf. 14*
Size: 28½x23mm
1064 CD14 20pf green, gold & blk .20 .20
1065 CD14 30pf dp car, gold & blk .35 .20

1971, May 3 Engr.
1066 A323 30pf red & black .35 .20

500th anniversary of the death of Thomas à Kempis (1379-1471), Augustinian monk, author of "The Imitation of Christ."

Town Type of 1969

20pf, View of Goslar. #1068, View of Nuremberg. #1069, Heligoland. 40pf, Heidelberg.

1971-72 Litho. & Engr. *Perf. 14*
1067 A303 20pf brt green & blk .30 .20
1068 A303 30pf vermilion & blk .35 .20
1069 A303 30pf lt grn & blk ('72) .35 .20
1069A A303 40pf orange & blk ('72) .40 .20
Nos. 1067-1069A (4) 1.40 .80

Issued: 20pf, 9/15; #1068, 5/21; #1069, 1069A, 10/20.

Dürer's Signature A324

1971, May 21 Engr.
1070 A324 30pf copper red & blk .75 .20

500th anniversary of the birth of Albrecht Dürer (1471-1528), painter and engraver.

Congress Emblem — A325

Illustration from New Astronomy, by Kepler — A326

1971, May 28 Litho. *Perf. 13½x13*
1071 A325 30pf red, orange & blk .30 .20

Ecumenical Meeting at Pentecost of the German Evangelical and Catholic Churches, Augsburg, June 2-5.

1971, June 25 Photo. *Perf. 14*
1072 A326 30pf brt car, gold & blk .35 .20

Johannes Kepler (1571-1630), astronomer.

Dante Alighieri — A327

"Matches Cause Fires" — A328

1971, Sept. 3 Engr. *Perf. 14*
1073 A327 10pf black .20 .20

650th anniversary of the death of Dante Alighieri (1265-1321), poet.

1971-74 Typo. *Perf. 14*

Designs: 10pf, Broken ladder. 20pf, Hand and circular saw. 25pf, "Alcohol and automobile." 30pf, Safety helmets prevent injury. 40pf, Defective plug. 50pf, Nail sticking from board. 60pf, 70pf, Traffic safety (ball rolling before car). 1m, Hoisted cargo. 1.50m, Fenced-in open manhole.

1074 A328 5pf orange .20 .20
a. Bklt. pane, 2 each #1074, 1077-1079 ('74) 4.50 4.50
1075 A328 10pf dark brown .20 .20
a. Bklt. pane, 4 #1075, 2 #1078 2.50 2.50
b. Bklt. pane, 2 each #1075-1076, 1078-1079 ('75) 4.50 4.50
c. Bklt. pane, 2 each #1079, 1075, 1078, 1076 10.00 12.00
1076 A328 20pf purple .25 .20
1077 A328 25pf green .35 .20
1078 A328 30pf dark red .30 .20
1079 A328 40pf rose claret .30 .20
1080 A328 50pf Prus blue 1.60 .20
1081 A328 60pf violet blue 1.00 .35
1082 A328 70pf green & vio bl .80 .25
1083 A328 100pf olive 1.40 .20
1085 A328 150pf red brown 4.25 .65
Nos. 1074-1085 (11) 10.65 2.85

Accident prevention.

Issued in sheets of 100 and in coils. Every fifth coil stamp has a control number on the back.

Issued: 25pf, 60pf, 9/10; 5pf, 10/29; 10pf, 30pf, 3/8/72; 40pf, 6/20/72; 20pf, 100pf, 7/5/72; 150pf, 9/11/72; 50pf, 1/16/73; 70pf, 6/5/73.

Deaconesses A329

Senefelder's Lithography Press — A330

1972, Jan. 20 Litho. *Perf. 13x13½*
1087 A329 25pf green, blk & gray .30 .20

Wilhelm Löhe (1808-1872), founder of the Deaconesses Training Institute at Neuendettelsau.

1972, Apr. 14 Litho. *Perf. 13½x13*
1088 A330 25pf multicolored .30 .20

175th anniv. of the invention of the lithographic printing process by Alois Senefelder in 1796.

Europa Issue 1972
Common Design Type

1972, May 2 Photo. *Perf. 13½x14*
Size: 23x29mm
1089 CD15 25pf yel grn, dk bl & yel .25 .20
1090 CD15 30pf pale rose, dk & lt bl .40 .20

Lucas Cranach, by Dürer A331

Archer in Wheelchair A332

Lithographed and Engraved
1972, May 18 *Perf. 14*
1091 A331 25pf green, buff & blk .35 .20

Cranach (1472-1553), painter and engraver.

1972, July 18 Litho. *Perf. 14*
1092 A332 40pf yel, blk & red brn .75 .20

21st Stoke-Mandeville Games for the Paralyzed, Heidelberg, Aug. 1-10.

Kurt Schumacher A333

Post Horn and Decree — A334

1972, Aug. 18 Litho. & Engr.
1093 A333 40pf red & black .55 .20

Schumacher (1895-1952), 1st chairman of the German Social Democratic Party.

1972, Aug. 18 Photo.
1094 A334 40pf gold, car & blk .45 .20

Centenary of the German Postal Museum, Berlin. Design shows page from Heinrich von Stephan's decree establishing the museum.

Open Book — A335

Music by Heinrich Schütz — A336

1972, Sept. 11 Photo. *Perf. 13x13½*
1095 A335 40pf red & multi .40 .20

International Book Year 1972.

Lithographed and Engraved
1972, Sept. 29 *Perf. 14*
1096 A336 40pf multicolored .50 .20

300th anniversary of the death of Heinrich Schütz (1585-1672), composer.

Carnival Dancers A337

1972, Nov. 10 Litho. *Perf. 14*
1097 A337 40pf red & multi .70 .20

Cologne Carnival sesquicentennial.

Heinrich Heine (1797-1856), Poet — A338

1972, Dec. 13 Litho. *Perf. 14*
1098 A338 40pf rose, blk & red .70 .20

"Bread for the World" A339

1972, Dec. 13 Photo. *Perf. 14*
1099 A339 30pf green & red .35 .25

14th "Bread for the World-Developing Peace" campaign of the Protestant Church in Germany.

Würzburg Cathedral, 13th Century Seal—A340

1972, Dec. 13 Litho.
1100 A340 40pf dp car, lil rose & blk .35 .20

Synod 72, meeting of Catholic bishoprics, Würzburg.

Colors of France and Germany Interlaced — A340a

1973, Jan. 22 Litho. *Perf. 14*
Size: 51x28mm
1101 A340a 40pf multicolored .80 .20

10th anniversary of the Franco-German Cooperation Treaty.

Meteorological Map — A341

1973, Feb. 19 Litho. *Perf. 14*
1102 A341 30pf multicolored .30 .20

Cent. of intl. meteorological cooperation.

Radio Tower and "Interpol" A342

1973, Feb. 19 *Perf. 13½x13*
1103 A342 40pf blk & red .40 .20

50th anniversary of International Criminal Police Organization (INTERPOL).

Nicolaus Copernicus and Solar System — A343

1973, Feb. 19 *Perf. 14*
1104 A343 40pf blk & red .80 .20

Festival Poster — A344

Maximilian Kolbe — A345

1973, Mar. 15 Photo. *Perf. 14*
1105 A344 40pf multicolored .40 .20

German Turner Festival, Stuttgart, 6/12-17.

Town Type of 1969

Designs: 30pf, Saarbrücken. No. 1107, Ship in Hamburg Harbor. No. 1108, Rüdesheim. No. 1109, Aachen. No. 1110, Ships, Bremen Harbor.

1973 Lithographed and Engraved
1106 A303 30pf yel grn & blk .35 .20
1107 A303 40pf red & blk .70 .20
1108 A303 40pf org & blk .50 .20
1109 A303 40pf brn red & blk .50 .20
1110 A303 40pf red & blk .50 .20
Nos. 1106-1110 (5) 2.55 1.00

Issued: #1107-1108, 3/15; others 10/19.

Europa Issue 1973
Common Design Type

1973, Apr. 30 Photo. *Perf. 13½x14*
Size: 38½x21mm
1114 CD16 30pf grn, lt grn & yel .35 .20
1115 CD16 40pf dp mag, lil & yel .40 .20

1973, May 25 Litho. *Perf. 14*
1116 A345 40pf red, blk & brn .35 .20

Maximilian Kolbe (1894-1941), Polish priest who died in Auschwitz and was beatified in 1971.

"R" for Roswitha — A346

"Not by Bread Alone" — A347

1973, May 25
1117 A346 40pf red, blk & yel .35 .20

Millenary of the death of Roswitha of Gandersheim, Germany's first poetess.

1973, May 25 Photo.
1118 A347 30pf multicolored .30 .20

15th meeting of German Protestants (Evangelical Synod), Dusseldorf, June 27-July 1.

Environment Emblem and "Waste" — A348

30pf, "Water." 40pf, "Noise." 70pf, "Air."

1973, June 5 **Litho.**

1119 A348 25pf multicolored .30 .20
1120 A348 30pf multicolored .35 .20
1121 A348 40pf org & multi .55 .20
1122 A348 70pf ultra & multi .95 .60
Nos. 1119-1122 (4) 2.15 1.20

International environment protection and Environment Day, June 5.

Reconstructed Model of Schickard's Calculator A349

1973, June 12

1123 A349 40pf org & multi .40 .35

350th anniv. of the calculator built by Prof. Wilhelm Shickard, University of Tubingen.

Otto Wels (1873-1939), Leader of German Social Democratic Party — A350

1973, Sept. 14 **Litho.** ***Perf. 14***

1124 A350 40pf magenta & lilac .40 .20

Lubeck Cathedral — A351

1973, Sept. 14 **Litho. & Engr.**

1125 A351 40pf blk & multi .70 .20

800th anniversary of Lubeck Cathedral.

Emblems from UN and German Flags A352

1973, Sept. 21 **Litho.**

1126 A352 40pf multicolored .95 .20

Germany's admission to the UN.

Radio and Speaker, 1923 — A353

1973, Oct. 19 **Photo.** ***Perf. 14***

1127 A353 30pf brt grn & multi .30 .20

50 years of German broadcasting.

Luise Otto-Peters A354

1974, Jan. 15 **Litho. & Engr.**

1128 A354 40pf shown .55 .35
1129 A354 40pf Helene Lange .55 .35
1130 A354 40pf Gertrud Bäumer .55 .35
1131 A354 40pf Rosa Luxemburg .55 .35
Nos. 1128-1131 (4) 2.20 1.40

Honoring German women writers and leaders in political and women's movements.

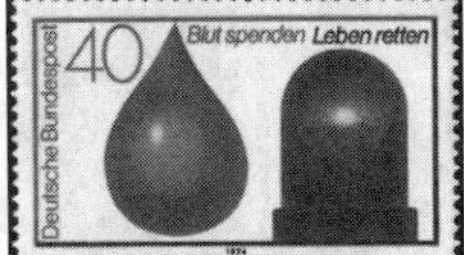

Drop of Blood and Police Car Light A355

1974, Feb. 15 **Photo.** ***Perf. 14***

1132 A355 40pf carmine & ultra .60 .20

Blood donor service in conjunction with accident emergency service.

Handicapped People — A356

1974, Feb. 15 **Litho.** ***Perf. 14***

1133 A356 40pf red & blk .60 .20

Rehabilitation of the handicapped.

Thomas Aquinas Teaching A357

1974, Feb. 15

1134 A357 40pf blk & red .40 .20

St. Thomas Aquinas (1225-1274), scholastic philosopher.

Girls under Trees, by August Macke — A358

Paintings: No. 1135, Deer in Red, by Franz Marc. 40pf, Portrait in Blue, by Alexej von Jawlensky, vert. 50pf, Pechstein (man) Asleep, by Erich Heckel, vert. 70pf, "Big Still-life," by Max Beckmann. 120pf, Old Farmer, by Ernst Ludwig Kirchner, vert.

1974 **Photo.**

1135 A358 30pf multicolored .35 .20
1136 A358 30pf multicolored .35 .20
1137 A358 40pf multicolored .45 .20
1138 A358 50pf multicolored .60 .20
1139 A358 70pf multicolored .80 .60
1140 A358 120pf multicolored 1.60 1.00
Nos. 1135-1140 (6) 4.15 2.40

German expressionist painters.
Issued: #1135, 1137, Feb. 15; #1136, 1138, Aug. 16; #1139-1140, Oct. 29.

Young Man, by Lehmbruck A359

Immanuel Kant A360

Europa: 40pf, Kneeling Woman, by Wilhelm Lehmbruck.

1974, Apr. 17 **Litho.** ***Perf. 14***

1141 A359 30pf multicolored .35 .20
1142 A359 40pf multicolored .40 .20

1974 **Litho. and Engr.** ***Perf. 14***

1143 A360 40pf Klopstock .40 .20

Engr.

1144 A360 90pf shown 1.50 .25

Friedrich Gottlieb Klopstock (1724-1803), poet, and Immanuel Kant (1724-1804), philosopher.
Issue dates: 40pf, May 15; 90pf, Apr. 17.

Souvenir Sheet

Federal Eagle and Flag — A361

1974, May 15 **Litho. & Embossed**

1145 A361 40pf gray & multi 1.00 .90

Federal Republic of Germany, 25th anniv.

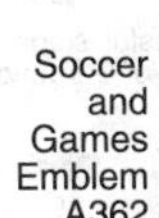

Soccer and Games Emblem A362

Design: 40pf, Three soccer players.

1974, May 15 **Litho.**

1146 A362 30pf grn & multi .60 .20
1147 A362 40pf org & multi 1.25 .20

World Cup Soccer Championship, Munich, June 13-July 7.

Crowned Cross Emblem of Diaconate A363

Landscape A364

1974, May 15

1148 A363 40pf multicolored .40 .20

125th anniversary of the Diaconal Association of the German Protestant Church.

1974, May 15

1149 A364 30pf multicolored .30 .20

To promote hiking and youth hostels.

Broken Bars of Prison Window A365

1974, July 16 **Litho.** ***Perf. 14x13½***

1150 A365 70pf violet bl & blk .75 .30

"Amnesty International," an organization for the protection of the rights of political, nonviolent, prisoners.

Hans Holbein, Self-portrait A366

Lithographed and Engraved

1974, July 16 ***Perf. 13½x14***

1151 A366 50pf multicolored .60 .20

Hans Holbein the Elder (c. 1470-1524), painter.

Man and Woman Looking at Moon, by Friedrich — A367

1974, Aug. 16 **Photo.** ***Perf. 14***

1152 A367 50pf multicolored .70 .20

Caspar David Friedrich (1774-1840), German Romantic painter.

Swiss and German 19th Century Mail Boxes — A368

1974, Oct. 29 **Litho.** ***Perf. 14***

1153 A368 50pf red & multi .80 .25

Centenary of Universal Postal Union.

Mothers and Foundation Emblem — A369

1975, Jan. 15 **Litho.** ***Perf. 13***

1154 A369 50pf multicolored .50 .20

Convalescent Mothers' Foundation, 25th anniversary.

Annette Kolb (1875-1967), Writer — A370

German women writers: 40pf, Ricarda Huch (1864-1947), writer. 50pf, Else Lasker-Schüler (1869-1945), poetess. 70pf, Gertrud von Le Fort (1876-1971), writer.

Lithographed and Engraved

1975, Jan. 15 ***Perf. 14***

1155 A370 30pf brown & multi .50 .20
1156 A370 40pf multicolored .40 .20
1157 A370 50pf claret & multi .40 .20
1158 A370 70pf blue & multi .80 .65
Nos. 1155-1158 (4) 2.10 1.25

Dr. Albert Schweitzer — A371

Design: 40pf, Hans Böckler.

1975 **Engr.**
1159 A371 40pf grn & blk .50 .20
1160 A371 70pf bl & blk 1.25 .30

Böckler (1875-1951), German Workers' Union leader, and of Dr. Albert Schweitzer (1875-1965), medical missionary. Issued: 40pf, Feb. 14; 70pf, Jan. 15.

Head, by Michelangelo A372

Plan of St. Peter's, Rome A373

1975, Feb. 14 **Photo.** ***Perf. 14***
1161 A372 70pf vio bl & blk 1.10 .85

Michelangelo Buonarroti (1475-1564), Italian sculptor, painter and architect.

1975, Feb. 14
1162 A373 50pf red & multi .50 .20

Holy Year 1975, the "Year of Reconciliation."

Ice Hockey A374

1975, Feb. 14 **Litho.** ***Perf. 14***
1163 A374 50pf bl & multi .70 .20

Ice Hockey World Championship, Munich and Düsseldorf, Apr. 3-19.

Concentric Group, by Oskar Schlemmer — A375

Europa: 50pf, Bauhaus Staircase, painting by Oskar Schlemmer (1888-1943) and CEPT emblem.

1975, Apr. 15 **Litho. & Engr.**
1164 A375 40pf gray & multi .40 .20
1165 A375 50pf gray & multi .55 .20

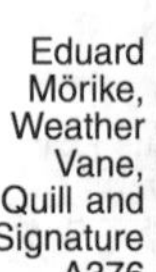

Eduard Mörike, Weather Vane, Quill and Signature A376

1975, May 15
1166 A376 40pf multicolored .35 .20

Eduard Mörike (1804-75), pastor and poet.

Joust, from Jousting Book of William IV A377

1975, May 15 **Photo.** ***Perf. 14***
1167 A377 50pf multicolored .70 .20

500th anniv. of the Wedding of Landshut, (last Duke of Landshut married the daughter of King of Poland, now a yearly local festival).

Cathedral of Mainz A378

1975, May 15 **Litho. & Engr.**
1168 A378 40pf multicolored .70 .20

Millennium of the Cathedral of Mainz.

View of Neuss, Woodcut A379

Satellite A380

1975, May 15
1169 A379 50pf multicolored .50 .20

500th anniv. of the unsuccessful siege of Neuss by Duke Charles the Bold of Burgundy.

1975-82 **Engr.** ***Perf. 14***

1170	A380	5pf	Shown	.20	.20
1171	A380	10pf	Electric train	.20	.20
1172	A380	20pf	Old Weser lighthouse	.20	.20
1173	A380	30pf	Rescue helicopter	.20	.20
1174	A380	40pf	Space shuttle	.25	.20
1175	A380	50pf	Radar station	.35	.20
1176	A380	60pf	X-ray machine	.45	.20
1177	A380	70pf	Shipbuilding	.50	.20
1178	A380	80pf	Tractor	.60	.20
1179	A380	100pf	Bituminous coal excavator	.65	.20
1180	A380	110pf	Color TV camera	.90	.25
1181	A380	120pf	Chemical plant	.85	.25
1182	A380	130pf	Brewery	1.10	.25
1183	A380	140pf	Heating plant, Licterfelde	.95	.35
1184	A380	150pf	Power shovel	1.75	.50
1185	A380	160pf	Blast furnace	1.40	.45
1186	A380	180pf	Payloader	1.60	.50
1187	A380	190pf	As #1184	1.60	.35
1188	A380	200pf	Oil drilling	1.40	.25
1189	A380	230pf	Frankfurt Airport	2.10	.50
1190	A380	250pf	Airport	2.40	.70
1191	A380	300pf	Electro. RR	2.40	.90
1192	A380	500pf	Effelsberg radio telescope	3.50	.65
			Nos. 1170-1192 (23)	25.55	7.90

Issued: 40, 50, 100pf, 5/15; 10, 30, 70pf, 8/14; 80, 120, 160pf, 10/15; 5, 140, 200pf, 11/14; 20, 500pf, 2/17/76; 60pf, 11/16/78; 230pf, 5/17/79; 150, 180pf, 7/12/79; 110, 130, 300pf, 6/16/82; 190, 250pf, 7/15/82.

Market and Town Hall, Alsfeld A381

#1197, Plönlein Corner, Siebers Tower and Kobolzeller Gate, Rothenburg. #1198, Town Hall (Steipe), Trier. #1199, View of Xanten.

1975, July 15 **Litho. & Engr.**
1196 A381 50pf multicolored .60 .45
1197 A381 50pf multicolored .60 .45
1198 A381 50pf multicolored .60 .45
1199 A381 50pf multicolored .60 .45
Nos. 1196-1199 (4) 2.40 1.80

European Architectural Heritage Year.

Three Stages of Drug Addiction A382

1975, Aug. 14 **Photo.** ***Perf. 14***
1200 A382 40pf multicolored .35 .20

Fight against drug abuse.

Matthias Erzberger A383

1975, Aug. 14 **Engr.**
1201 A383 50pf red & black .50 .20

Erzberger (1875-1921), statesman, signer of Compiègne Armistice (1918) at end of World War I.

Sign of Royal Prussian Post, 1776 — A384

1975, Aug. 14 **Litho.**
1202 A384 10pf blue & multi .30 .20

Stamp Day, 1975, and 76th German Philatelists' Day, Sept. 21.

Souvenir Sheet

Gustav Stresemann, Ludwig Quidde, Carl von Ossietzky — A385

1975, Nov. 14 **Engr.** ***Perf. 14***
1203 A385 Sheet of 3 1.60 1.40
a.-c. 50pf, single stamp .50 .45

German winners of Nobel Peace Prize. No. 1203 has litho. marginal inscription.

Olympic Rings, Symbolic Mountains A386

1976, Jan. 5 **Litho. & Engr.**
1204 A386 50pf red & multi .55 .20

12th Winter Olympic Games, Innsbruck, Austria, Feb. 4-15.

Konrad Adenauer — A387

1976, Jan. 5 **Engr.**
1205 A387 50pf dark slate green 1.10 .20

Konrad Adenauer (1876-1967), Chancellor (1949-63).

Books by Hans Sachs — A388

1976, Jan. 5 **Litho.**
1206 A388 40pf multicolored .50 .20

Hans Sachs (1494-1576), poet (meistersinger), 400th death anniversary.

Junkers F 13, 1926 — A389

1976, Jan. 5
1207 A389 50pf multicolored .75 .20

Lufthansa, 50th anniversary.

German Eagle — A390

1976, Feb. 17 **Photo.** ***Perf. 14***
1208 A390 50pf red, blk & gold .55 .20

Federal Constitutional Court, 25th anniv.

"EG" A391

1976, Apr. 6 **Photo.** ***Perf. 14***
1209 A391 40pf red & multi .55 .20

European Coal and Steel Community, 25th anniversary.

Wuppertal Suspension Train — A392

1976, Apr. 6 **Litho.**
1210 A392 50pf multicolored .65 .20

Wuppertal suspension railroad, 75th anniv.

Girl Selling Trinkets and Prints — A393

Europa: 50pf, Boy selling copperplate prints, and CEPT emblem. Ludwigsburg china figurines, c. 1765.

1976, May 13 **Photo.**

1211 A393 40pf olive & multi .35 .20
1212 A393 50pf scarlet & multi .60 .20

Dr. Carl Sonnenschein A394

1976, May 13 **Litho.**

1213 A394 50pf carmine & multi .55 .20

Sonnenschein (1876-1929), Roman Catholic clergyman and social reformer.

Weber Conducting "Freischutz" in Covent Garden — A395

1976, May 13

1214 A395 50pf red brown & blk .60 .20

Carl Maria von Weber (1786-1826), composer, 150th death anniversary.

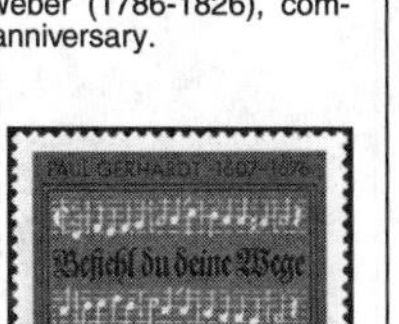

Hymn, by Paul Gerhardt A396

1976, May 13 **Engr. & Litho.**

1215 A396 40pf multicolored .35 .20

Gerhardt (1607-76), Lutheran hymn writer.

Carl Schurz, American Flag, Capitol A397

1976, May 13 **Litho.**

1216 A397 70pf multicolored .75 .25

American Bicentennial.

Modern Stage A398

1976, July 14 **Litho.** ***Perf. 14***

1217 A398 50pf multicolored .75 .20

Bayreuth Festival, centenary.

Bronze Ritual Chariot c. 1000 B.C. A399

Archaeological Treasures: 40pf, Celtic gold vessel, 5th-4th centuries B.C. 50pf, Celtic silver torque, 2nd-1st centuries B.C. 120pf, Roman cup with masks, 1st century A.D.

1976, July 14

1218 A399 30pf multicolored .30 .25
1219 A399 40pf multicolored .45 .25
1220 A399 50pf multicolored .55 .25
1221 A399 120pf multicolored 1.40 1.10
Nos. 1218-1221 (4) 2.70 1.85

Golden Plover A400 — "Simplicissimus Teutsch" A401

1976, Aug. 17

1222 A400 50pf multicolored .75 .20

Protection of birds.

1976, Aug. 17

1223 A401 40pf multicolored .75 .20

Johann Jacob Christoph von Grimmelshausen, 300th birth anniversary; author of the "Adventures of Simplicissimus Teutsch."

Imperial Post Emblem, Höchst am Main, 18th Cent. — A402 — Caroline Neuber as Medea — A403

1976, Oct. 14 **Litho.** ***Perf. 14***

1224 A402 10pf brown & multi .25 .20

Stamp Day.

1976, Nov. 16 **Photo.**

German Actresses: 40pf, Sophie Schröder (1781-1868) as Sappho. 50pf, Louise Dumont (1862-1932) as Hedda Gabler. 70pf, Hermine Körner (1878-1960) as Lady Macbeth.

1225 A403 30pf multicolored .35 .20
1226 A403 40pf multicolored .35 .20
1227 A403 50pf multicolored .55 .25
1228 A403 70pf multicolored .80 .70
Nos. 1225-1228 (4) 2.05 1.35

Palais de l'Europe, Strasbourg — A404

1977, Jan. 13 **Engr.** ***Perf. 14***

1229 A404 140pf green & blk 1.40 .45

Inauguration of the new Council of Europe Headquarters, Jan. 28.

Scenes from Till Eulenspiegel A405 — Pfaueninsel Castle A406

1977, Jan. 13 **Litho.**

1230 A405 50pf multicolored .45 .20

Till Eulenspiegel (d. 1350), roguish fool and hero, his adventures reported in book of same name.

1977-79 **Typo.** ***Perf. 14***

1231 A406 10pf Glucksburg .20 .20
a. Bklt. pane, 4 #1231, 2 each #1234, 1236 3.00 3.00
b. Bklt. pane, 4 #1231, 2 #1234, 2 #1310 2.25 2.25
c. Bklt. pane, 4 #1231, 2 #1310, 2 #1312 1.90 1.90
d. Bklt. pane, 2 each #1231, 1234, 1310-1311 6.25 6.25
1232 A406 20pf Shown .20 .20
1233 A406 25pf Gemen .30 .20
1234 A406 30pf Ludwigstein .25 .20
1235 A406 40pf Eltz .45 .20
1236 A406 50pf Neuschwanstein .50 .20
1237 A406 60pf Marksburg .65 .20
1238 A406 70pf Mespelbrunn .50 .20
1239 A406 90pf Vischerenburg 1.00 .30
1240 A406 190pf Pfaueninsel 1.60 .55
1240A A406 200pf Burresheim 2.00 .55
1241 A406 210pf Schwanenburg 2.25 .60
1242 A406 230pf Lichtenberg 2.25 .60
Nos. 1231-1242 (13) 12.15 4.20

See Nos. 1308-1315.

Issued in sheets of 100 and in coils. Every fifth coil stamp has control number on the back.

Issued: 60, 200pf, 1/13; 40, 190pf, 2/16; 10, 30pf, 4/14; 50, 70pf, 5/17; 230pf, 11/16/78; 25, 90pf, 1/11/79; 20, 210pf, 2/14/79.

Souvenir Sheet

German Art Nouveau — A407

Designs: 30pf, Floral ornament. 70pf, Athena, poster by Franz von Stuck. 90pf, Chair, c. 1902.

1977, Feb. 16 **Litho.** ***Perf. 14***

1243 A407 Sheet of 3 1.75 1.25
a. 30pf multicolored .25 .20
b. 70pf multicolored .50 .45
c. 90pf multicolored .80 .65

1st German Art Nouveau Exhib., 75th anniv.

Jean Monnet A408

1977, Feb. 16

1244 A408 50pf black & yellow .50 .20

Jean Monnet (1888-1979), French proponent of unification of Europe, became first Honorary Citizen of Europe in Apr. 1976.

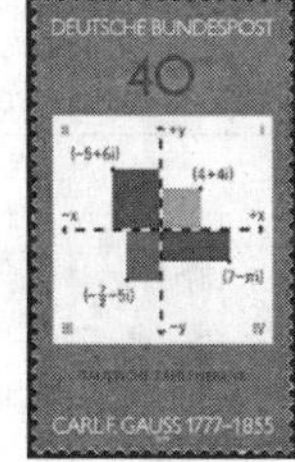

Flower Show Emblem A409 — Gauss Plane of Complex Numbers A410

1977, Apr. 14

1245 A409 50pf green & multi .55 .20

25th Federal Horticultural Show, Stuttgart, Apr. 29-Oct. 23.

1977, Apr. 14

1246 A410 40pf silver & multi .75 .20

Carl Friedrich Gauss (1777-1855), mathematician, 200th birth anniversary.

Barbarossa Head, Cappenberg Reliquary — A411

1977, Apr. 14

1247 A411 40pf multicolored .75 .20

Staufer Year 1977. "Time of the Hohenstaufen" Exhibition, Stuttgart, Mar. 25-June 5, in connection with the 25th anniversary of Baden-Wurttemberg.

Rhön Highway A412

Europa: 50pf, Rhine, Siebengebirge and train.

1977, May 7 **Litho. & Engr.**

1248 A412 40pf brt green & blk .45 .20
1249 A412 50pf brt red & blk .55 .20

Rubens, Self-portrait A413 — Ulm Cathedral A414

1977, May 17 **Engr.**

1250 A413 30pf brown black .55 .20

Peter Paul Rubens (1577-1640), Flemish painter, 400th birth anniversary.

1977, May 17 **Litho. & Engr.**

1251 A414 40pf blue & sepia .45 .20

600th anniversary of Ulm Cathedral.

Madonna, Oldest Rector's Seal A415 — Landgrave Philipp, Great Seal of University A416

1977, May 17 **Photo.**

1252 A415 50pf indigo & org red .65 .20
1253 A416 50pf indigo & org red .65 .20

Mainz University, 500th anniv. (No. 1252); Marburg University, 450th anniv. (No. 1253).

Morning, by Runge — A417

1977, July 13 **Litho.** ***Perf. 14***

1254 A417 60pf blue & multi .65 .25

Philipp Otto Runge (1777-1810), painter.

Bishop Ketteler's Coat of Arms — A418

1977, July 13

1255 A418 50pf multicolored .55 .20

Wilhelm Emmanuel von Ketteler (1811-1877), Bishop of Mainz, Reichstag member and social reformer, death centenary.

Fritz von Bodelschwingh A419

1977, July 13 Litho. & Engr.

1256 A419 50pf multicolored .55 .20

Pastor Fritz von Bodelschwingh (1877-1946), manager of Bethel Institute (for the incurable sick), birth centenary.

Jesus as Teacher, Great Seal of University — A420

1977, Aug. 16 Photo.

1257 A420 50pf multicolored .70 .20

Tübingen University, 500th anniversary.

Golden Hat, Schifferstadt, Bronze Age — A421

1977, Aug. 16 Litho.

Archaeological heritage: 120pf, Gilt helmet, from Prince's Tomb, Krefeld-Gellep. 200pf, Bronze Centaur's head, Schwarzenacker.

1258 A421 30pf multicolored .35 .20
1259 A421 120pf multicolored 1.25 .80
1260 A421 200pf multicolored 1.60 1.25
Nos. 1258-1260 (3) 3.20 2.25

Telephone Operator and Switchboard, 1881 — A422

1977, Oct. 13 Litho. *Perf. 14*

1261 A422 50pf multicolored .70 .20

German telephone centenary.

Arms of Hamburg, Post Emblem, c. 1861 — A423

Wilhelm Hauff — A424

1977, Oct. 13

1262 A423 10pf multicolored .25 .20

Stamp Day.

1977, Nov. 10 Photo. *Perf. 14*

1263 A424 40pf multicolored .35 .20

Wilhelm Hauff (1802-1827), writer and fabulist, 150th death anniversary.

Traveling Surgeon A425

Book Cover, by Alexander Schröder A426

1977, Nov. 10 Litho.

1264 A425 50pf multicolored .55 .20

Dr. Johann Andreas Eisenbarth (1663-1727), traveling surgeon and adventurer.

1978, Jan. 12 Litho. *Perf. 14*

1265 A426 50pf multicolored .50 .20

Rudolf Alexander Schröder (1878-1962), writer, designer, Lutheran minister.

"Refugees" — A427

1978, Jan. 12 Photo.

1266 A427 50pf multicolored .50 .20

Friedland Aid Society for displaced Germans, 20th anniversary.

Souvenir Sheet

Gerhart Hauptmann, Hermann Hesse, Thomas Mann — A428

1978, Feb. 16 Litho. *Perf. 14*

1267 A428 Sheet of 3 1.60 1.00
a. 30pf multicolored .30 .20
b. 50pf multicolored .45 .25
c. 70pf multicolored .65 .45

German winners of Nobel Literature Prize.

Martin Buber (1878-1965), Writer and Philosopher A429

1978, Feb. 16

1268 A429 50pf multicolored .50 .20

Museum Tower and Observatory — A430

1978, Apr. 13 Litho. *Perf. 14*

1269 A430 50pf multicolored .50 .20

German Museum for Natural Sciences and Technology, Munich, 75th anniversary.

Old City Halls A431

Europa: 40pf, Bamberg. 50pf, Regensburg. 70pf, Esslingen on Neckar.

Lithographed and Engraved

1978, May 22 *Perf. 14*

1270 A431 40pf multicolored .45 .20
1271 A431 50pf multicolored .80 .20
1272 A431 70pf multicolored .90 .45
Nos. 1270-1272 (3) 2.15 .85

Pied Piper of Hamelin A432

1978, May 22 Litho.

1273 A432 50pf multicolored .60 .20

The Pied Piper led 130 children of Hamelin away never to be seen again.

Janusz Korczak — A433

Fossil Bat — A434

1978, July 13 Litho. *Perf. 14*

1274 A433 90pf multicolored .90 .35

Dr. Janusz Korczak (1878-1942), physician, educator, proponent of children's rights.

1978, July 13

200pf, Eohippus (primitive horse), horiz.

1275 A434 80pf multicolored 1.25 .95
1276 A434 200pf multicolored 1.40 1.25

Archaeological heritage from Messel open-cast mine, c. 50 million years old.

Parliament, Bonn — A435

1978, Aug. 17 Litho. *Perf. 14*

1277 A435 70pf multicolored .95 .25

65th Interparliamentary Conf., Bonn, Sept. 3-14.

A436

Rose Window, Freiburg Cathedral.

1978, Aug. 17

1278 A436 40pf multicolored .35 .20

85th Congress of German Catholics, Freiburg, Sept. 13-17.

A437

1978, Aug. 17

Brentano as Butterfly, by Luise Duttenhofer.

1279 A437 30pf multicolored .35 .20

Clemens Brentano (1778-1842), poet.

A438

1978, Aug. 17

1280 A438 50pf multicolored .55 .20

European Human Rights Convention, 25th anniversary.

Baden Posthouse Sign, c. 1825 — A439

Saxony No. 1 with "World Philatelic Movement" Cancel — A440

1978, Oct. 12 Litho. *Perf. 14*

1281 A439 40pf multicolored .35 .20
1282 A440 50pf multicolored .35 .20
a. Pair, #1281-1282 .95 .75

Stamp Day and German Philatelists' Meeting, Frankfurt am Main, Oct. 12-15.

Easter at Walchensee, by Lovis Corinth — A441

Impressionist Paintings: 70pf, Horseman on Shore, by Max Liebermann, vert. 120pf, Lady with Cat, by Max Slevogt, vert.

1978, Nov. 16 Photo. *Perf. 14*

1283 A441 50pf multicolored .45 .30
1284 A441 70pf multicolored .70 .40
1285 A441 120pf multicolored 1.25 1.00
Nos. 1283-1285 (3) 2.40 1.70

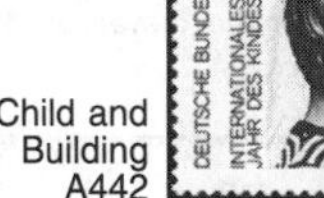

Child and Building A442

1979, Jan. 11 Photo.

1286 A442 60pf black & rose .65 .20

International Year of the Child and 20th anniv. of Declaration of Children's Rights.

Agnes Miegel — A443

Film — A444

1979, Feb. 14 Photo. *Perf. 14*

1287 A443 60pf multicolored .45 .20

Agnes Miegel (1879-1964), poet.

1979, Feb. 14 Litho.

1288 A444 50pf black & green .55 .20

25th German Short-Film Festival, Oberhausen, Apr. 23-28.

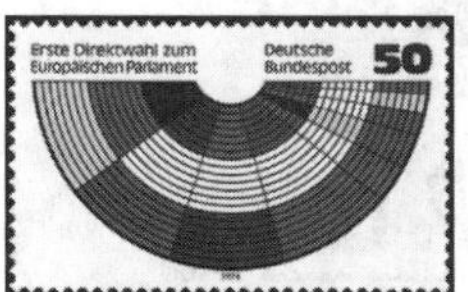

Parliament Benches in Flag Colors of Members — A445

1979, Feb. 14

1289 A445 50pf multicolored .60 .20

European Parliament, first direct elections, June 7-10, 1979.

Emblems of Road Rescue Services A446

1979, Feb. 14

1290 A446 50pf multicolored .55 .20

A447

Europa: 50pf, Telegraph office, 1863. 60pf, Post Office window, 1854.

1979, May 17 Litho. *Perf. 14*

1291 A447 50pf multicolored .45 .20
1292 A447 60pf multicolored .65 .20

A448

1979, May 17 Photo.

1293 A448 60pf red & black .60 .20

Anne Frank (1929-45), author, Nazi victim.

First Electric Train, 1879 Berlin Exhibition A449

1979, May 17 Litho.

1294 A449 60pf multicolored .70 .20

Intl. Transportation Exhib., Hamburg.

Hand Setting Radio Dial A450

1979, July 12 Litho. *Perf. 14*

1295 A450 60pf multicolored .60 .20

World Administrative Radio Conference, Geneva, Sept. 24-Dec. 1.

Moses Receiving Tablets of the Law, by Lucas Cranach — A451

1979, July 12 Litho. & Engr.

1296 A451 50pf black & blue grn .70 .20

450th anniv. of Martin Luther's Catechism.

Cross and Charlemagne's Emblem — A452

1979, July 12 Litho. & Embossed

1297 A452 50pf multicolored .55 .20

1979 pilgrimage to Aachen.

Hildegard von Bingen with Manuscript A453

1979, Aug. 9 Litho.

1298 A453 110pf multicolored .95 .30

Hildegard von Bingen, Benedictine nun, mystic and writer, 800th death anniversary.

Diagram of Einstein's Photoelectric Effect — A454

Designs: No. 1300, Otto Hahn's diagram of the splitting of the uranium nucleus. No. 1301, Max von Laue's atom arrangement in crystals.

1979, Aug. 9 Photo.

1299 A454 60pf multicolored .65 .25
1300 A454 60pf multicolored 1.10 .25
1301 A454 60pf multicolored .65 .25
Nos. 1299-1301 (3) 2.40 .75

Birth centenaries of German Nobel Prize winners: Albert Einstein, physics, 1921; Otto Hahn, chemistry, 1944; Max von Laue, physics, 1914.

Pilot on Board — A455

Lithographed and Engraved

1979, Oct. 11 *Perf. 14*

1302 A455 60pf multicolored .55 .20

Three centuries of pilots' regulations.

Birds in Garden, by Paul Klee — A456

1979, Nov. 14 Photo.

1303 A456 90pf multicolored .80 .30

Paul Klee (1879-1940), Swiss artist.

Mephistopheles and Faust — A457

1979, Nov. 14 Litho.

1304 A457 60pf multicolored .80 .20

Doctor Johannes Faust.

Energy Conservation A458

1979, Nov. 14 *Perf. 13x13½*

1305 A458 40pf multicolored .45 .20

Castle Type A406 of 1977-79

1979-82 Typo. *Perf. 14*

1308 35pf Lichtenstein .35 .20
1309 40pf Wolfsburg .40 .20
1310 50pf Inzlingen .45 .20
1311 60pf Rheydt .60 .20
1312 80pf Wilhelmsthal .75 .20
1313 120pf Charlottenburg 1.10 .35
1314 280pf Ahrensburg 2.75 .25
1315 300pf Herrenhausen 2.75 .25
Nos. 1308-1315 (8) 9.15 1.85

Issued: 60pf, 11/14; 40pf, 50pf, 2/14/80; 35pf, 80pf, 300pf, 6/16/82; 120pf, 280pf, 7/15/82.

Iphigenia, by Anselm Feuerbach — A459

1980, Jan. 10 Litho.

1321 A459 50pf multicolored .70 .20

Anselm Feuerbach (1829-1880), historical and portrait painter.

Flags of NATO and Members A460

1980, Jan. 10

1322 A460 100pf multicolored 1.10 .55

Germany's membership in NATO, 25th anniv.

Osnabruck, 1,200th Anniversary — A461

1980, Jan. 10 Litho. & Engr.

1323 A461 60pf multicolored .60 .20

Götz von Berlichingen, Painting on Glass — A462

1980, Jan. 10 Litho.

1324 A462 60pf multicolored .65 .20

Götz von Berlichingen (1480-1562), knight.

Duden Dictionary, Old and New Editions — A463

1980, Jan. 14

1325 A463 60pf multicolored .60 .20

Konrad Duden's German Language Dictionary, centenary of publication.

German Association for Public and Private Social Welfare Centenary — A464

1980, Apr. 10

1326 A464 60pf multicolored .60 .20

A465

Emperor Frederick I (Barbarossa) and Sons, Welf Chronicles, 12th century.

1980, Apr. 10
1327 A465 60pf multicolored .70 .20

Imperial Diet of Geinhausen, 800th anniv.

A466

1980, May 8 **Litho.** ***Perf. 14***

Europa: 50pf, Albertus Magnus (1193-1280), saint and doctor of the Church. 60pf, Gottfried Wilhelm Leibniz (1646-1716), philosopher.

1328 A466 50pf multicolored .60 .20
1329 A466 60pf multicolored .80 .20

Confession of Augsburg, Engraving, 1630 — A467

1980, May 8
1330 A467 50pf multicolored .50 .20

Reading of Confession of Augsburg to Charles V (first official creed of Lutheran Church), 400th anniversary.

Nature Preserves A468

1980, May 8 **Photo.**
1331 A468 40pf multicolored .70 .20

Oscillogram Pulses and Ear — A469

Lithographed and Embossed

1980, July 10 ***Perf. 14***
1332 A469 90pf multicolored .90 .25

16th Intl. Cong. for the Training and Education of the Hard of Hearing, Hamburg, 8/4-8.

Book of Daily Bible Readings, Title Page, 1731 A470

1980, July 10 **Litho.**
1333 A470 50pf multicolored .55 .20

Moravian Brethren's Book of Daily Bible Readings, 250th edition.

St. Benedict of Nursia, 1500th Birth Anniv. — A471

1980, July 10 ***Perf. 13x13½***
1334 A471 50pf multicolored .55 .20

Helping Hand — A472

1980, Aug. 14 **Litho. & Engr.**
1335 A472 60pf multicolored .65 .20

Dr. Friedrich Joseph Haass (1780-1853), physician and philanthropist.

Marie von Ebner-Eschenbach (1830-1916), Writer — A473

1980, Aug. 14 **Photo.**
1336 A473 60pf multicolored .65 .20

Ship's Rigging A474

1980, Aug. 14 **Litho.**
1337 A474 60pf multicolored 1.00 .20

Gorch Fock (pen name of Johan Kinau) (1880-1916), poet and dramatist.

Hoeing, Pressing Grapes, Wine Cellar, 14th Century Woodcuts A475

1980, Oct. 9 **Litho.** ***Perf. 14***
1338 A475 50pf multicolored .55 .20

Wine production in Central Europe, 2000th anniversary.

Setting Final Stone in South Tower, Cologne Cathedral — A476

1980, Oct. 9
1339 A476 60pf multicolored 1.10 .20

Completion of Cologne Cathedral, cent.

Landscape with Fir Trees, by Altdorfer — A477

Lithographed and Engraved

1980, Nov. 13 ***Perf. 14***
1340 A477 40pf multicolored .45 .20

Albrecht Altdorfer (1480-1538), painter and engraver.

Elly Heuss-Knapp A478

1981, Jan. 15 **Photo.**
1341 A478 60pf multicolored .65 .20

Elly Heuss-Knapp (1881-1951), founded Elly Heuss-Knapp Foundation (Rest and Recuperation for Mothers).

International Year of the Disabled — A479

1981, Jan. 15 **Litho.**
1342 A479 60pf multicolored .65 .20

European Urban Renaissance — A480

1981, Jan. 15 **Litho. & Engr.**
1343 A480 60pf multicolored .65 .20

Georg Philipp Telemann, Title Page of "Singet dem Herrn" Cantata — A481

1981, Feb. 12 **Photo.**
1344 A481 60pf multicolored .65 .20

Georg Telemann (1681-1767), composer.

Foreign Guest Worker Integration — A482

1981, Feb. 12 **Litho.**
1345 A482 50pf multicolored .55 .20

Preservation of the Environment A483

1981, Feb. 12
1346 A483 60pf multicolored .75 .20

European Patent Office Centenary A484

1981, Feb. 12
1347 A484 60pf multicolored .65 .20

A485

1981, Feb. 12 ***Perf. 13x13½***
1348 A485 40pf Chest scintigram .40 .20

Early examination for the prevention of cancer.

A486

1981, May 7 **Litho.** ***Perf. 14***

50pf, South German couple dancing in regional costumes. 60pf, Northern couple.

1349 A486 50pf multicolored .45 .20
1350 A486 60pf multicolored .65 .20

Europa.

19th German Protestant Convention, Hamburg, June 17-21 — A487

1981, May 7 **Photo.**
1351 A487 50pf multicolored .60 .20

A488

1981, May 7 **Litho.**
1352 A488 60pf Altar figures .60 .20

Tilman Riemenschneider (1460-1531), sculptor, 450th death anniversary.

A489

1981, July 16 **Litho.** ***Perf. 14***
1353 A489 110pf multicolored 1.25 .45

Georg von Neumayer polar research station.

Energy Conservation Research — A490

1981, July 16
1354 A490 50pf Solar generator .60 .20

Wildlife Protection A491

1981, July 16
1355 A491 60pf Baby coot .75 .20

Cooperation in Third World Development — A492

1981, July 16
1356 A492 90pf multicolored .90 .35

Wilhelm Raabe (1831-1910), Poet — A493

1981, Aug. 13 **Litho. & Engr.**
1357 A493 50pf dk green & green .60 .20

Statement of Constitutional Freedom (Fundamental Concept of Democracy) — A494

1981, Aug. 13 **Litho.** ***Perf. 14***
1358 A494 40pf shown .55 .20
1359 A494 50pf Separation of powers .55 .20
1360 A494 60pf Sovereignty of the people .80 .20
Nos. 1358-1360 (3) 1.90 .60

A495

People by Mailcoach, lithograph, 1855.

1981, Oct. 8 **Litho.**
1361 A495 60pf multicolored .85 .20

Stamp Day, Oct. 25.

A496

1981, Nov. 12 **Litho.** ***Perf. 14***
1362 A496 100pf multicolored 1.10 .25

Antarctic Treaty, 20th anniv.

St. Elizabeth of Thuringia, 750th Anniv. of Death — A497

1981, Nov. 12
1363 A497 50pf multicolored .70 .20

Karl von Clausewitz, by W. Wach — A498

1981, Nov. 12 **Photo.**
1364 A498 60pf multicolored .85 .20

Prussian general and writer, (1780-1831).

Social Insurance Centenary — A499

1981, Nov. 12
1365 A499 60pf multicolored .65 .20

Pear-shaped Pot with Lid, 1715 — A500

1982, Jan. 13 **Litho.**
1366 A500 60pf multicolored .65 .20

Johann Friedrich Bottger (1682-1719), originator of Dresden china, 300th birth anniv.

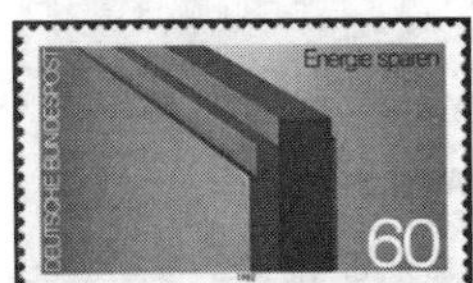

Energy Conservation — A501

1982, Jan. 13
1367 A501 60pf multicolored .65 .20

A502

Illustration from The Town Band of Bremen (folktale).

1982, Jan. 13
1368 A502 40pf red & black .45 .20

A503

1982, Feb. 18 **Photo.**
1369 A503 60pf multicolored 1.60 .20

Johann Wolfgang von Goethe (1749-1832), by Georg Melchior Kraus, 1776.

Robert Koch (1843-1910), Discoverer of Tubercle Bacillus, (1882) — A504

1982, Feb. 18
1370 A504 50pf multicolored 1.90 .20

Die Fromme Helene, by Wilhelm Busch (1832-1908) A505

1982, Apr. 15 **Litho.** ***Perf. 13½x14***
1371 A505 50pf multicolored .80 .20

Europa 1982 A506

1982, May 5 **Litho.** ***Perf. 14***
1372 A506 50pf Hambach Meeting sesquicentennial .70 .20
1373 A506 60pf Treaties of Rome, 1957-1982 .90 .20

Kiel Regatta Week Centenary — A507

1982, May 5
1374 A507 60pf multicolored .80 .20

Young Men's Christian Assoc. (YMCA) Centenary — A508

1982, May 5
1375 A508 50pf multicolored .60 .20

"Don't Drink and Drive" A509

1982, July 15 **Photo.**
1376 A509 80pf red & black .80 .20

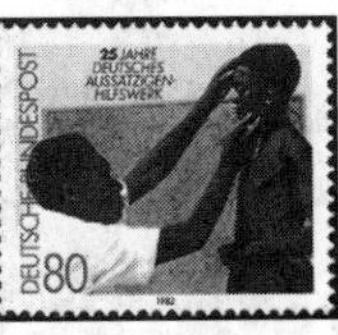

25th Anniv. of German Lepers' Org. — A510

1982, July 15 **Photo.**
1377 A510 80pf multicolored .80 .20

Prevent Water Pollution A511

1982, July 15
1378 A511 120pf multicolored 1.75 .25

Urea Model and Synthesis Formula A512

1982, Aug. 12 **Photo.**
1379 A512 50pf multicolored .60 .20

Friedrich Wohler (1800-1882), chemist, discoverer of organic chemistry.

St. Francis Preaching to the Birds, by Giotto — A513

1982, Aug. 12 **Litho.**
1380 A513 60pf multicolored .65 .20

800th birth anniv. of St. Francis of Assisi and 87th German Catholics Cong., Dusseldorf, 9/1-5.

James Franck, Max Born — A514

1982, Aug. 12 **Litho. & Engr.**
1381 A514 80pf multicolored .75 .20

James Franck (1882-1964) and Max Born (1882-1970), Nobel Prize physicists, developed quantum theory.

Stamp Day, Oct. 24 A515

1982, Oct. 14 **Photo.** ***Perf. 14***
1382 A515 80pf Poster 1.10 .20

400th Anniv. of the Gregorian Calendar — A516

Design: Calendar illumination, by Johannes Rasch, 1586.

1982, Oct. 14 **Litho.**
1383 A516 60pf multicolored .65 .20

A517

Presidents: a, Theodor Heuss, 1949-59. b, Heinrich Lubke, 1959-69. c, Gustav Heinemann, 1969-74. d, Walter Scheel, 1974-79. e, Karl Carstens, 1979-84.

1982, Nov. 10
1384 Sheet of 5 4.00 3.50
a.-e. A517 80pf, single stamp .65 .65

A518

1983, Jan. 13 **Litho.** ***Perf. 14***
1385 A518 80pf gray & black 1.25 .25

Edith Stein (d. 1942), philospher and Carmelite Nun.

Persecution and Resistance, 1933-1945 — A519

1983, Jan. 13
1386 A519 80pf multicolored 1.10 .25

Light Space Modulator, 1930 — A520

Walter Gropius (1883-1969), Founder of Bauhaus Architecture: 60pf, Sanctuary, zinc lithograph, 1942. 80pf, Bauhaus Archives, Berlin, 1979.

1983, Feb. 8
1387 A520 50pf multicolored .65 .20
1388 A520 60pf multicolored .85 .20
1389 A520 80pf multicolored 1.00 .25
Nos. 1387-1389 (3) 2.50 .65

Federahannes, Swabian-Alemannic Carnival — A521

1983, Feb. 8
1390 A521 60pf multicolored .70 .20

4th Intl. Horticultural Show, Munich, Apr. 28-Oct. 9 — A522

1983, Apr. 12 **Litho.** ***Perf. 14***
1391 A522 60pf multicolored .70 .20

Europa 1983
A523

Discoveries: 60pf, Printing press by Johannes Guttenburg. 80pf, Electromagnetic waves by Heinrich Hertz.

1983, May 5 **Litho.** ***Perf. 14***
1392 A523 60pf Movable type 1.25 .20
1393 A523 80pf Resonant circuit, electric flux lines .85 .25

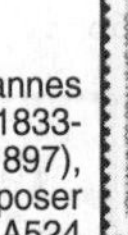

Johannes Brahms (1833-1897), Composer
A524

1983, May 5 **Photo.**
1394 A524 80pf multicolored 1.25 .25

Franz Kafka (1883-1924), Writer — A525

1983, May 5
1395 A525 80pf Signature, Tyn Church, Prague 1.10 .25

Beer Pureness Law, 450th Anniv.
A526

1983, May 5 **Litho.**
1396 A526 80pf Brewers, engraving, 1677 1.25 .25

300th Anniv. of Immigration to US — A527

1983, May 5 **Litho. & Engr.**
1397 A527 80pf Concord 1.25 .25

See US No. 2040.

Children and Road Safety
A528

1983, July 14 **Litho.** ***Perf. 14***
1398 A528 80pf multicolored 1.00 .25

50th Intl. Auto Show, Frankfurt, Sept. 15-25
A529

1983, July 14
1399 A529 60pf multicolored .65 .20

Otto Warburg — A530

1983, Aug. 11 **Photo.** ***Perf. 14***
1400 A530 50pf multicolored .55 .20

Warburg (1883-1970), pioneer of modern biochemistry, 1931 Nobel prize winner in medicine.

Christoph Martin Wieland (1733-1813), Poet — A531

1983, Aug. 11 **Litho.**
1401 A531 80pf multicolored .90 .25

10th Anniv. of UN Membership — A532

1983, Aug. 11 **Photo.**
1402 A532 80pf multicolored 1.10 .25

Rauhe Haus Orphanage Sesquicentennial — A533

1983, Aug. 11 **Litho.**
1403 A533 80pf multicolored .90 .25

Survey and Measuring Maps — A534

1983, Aug. 11
1404 A534 120pf multicolored 1.25 .30

Intl. Union of Geodesy and Geophysics Gen. Assembly, Hamburg, Aug. 15-26.

Stamp Day — A535

1983, Oct. 13 **Litho.** ***Perf. 13½***
1405 A535 80pf Postrider 1.10 .25

Martin Luther (1483-1546)
A536

1983, Oct. 13 ***Perf. 14***
1406 A536 80pf Engraving by G. Konig 1.60 .25

Customs Union Sesquicentennial — A537

1983, Nov. 10
1407 A537 60pf multicolored 1.40 .20

Territorial Authorities (Federation, Land, Communities) — A538

1983, Nov. 10 **Litho.**
1408 A538 80pf multicolored 1.10 .25

Trier, 2000th Anniv.
A539

1984, Jan. 12 **Litho. & Engr.**
1409 A539 80pf Black Gate, 175 A.D. 1.25 .25

Philipp Reis (1834-1874) Physicist and Inventor — A540

1984, Jan. 12 **Litho.**
1410 A540 80pf multicolored 1.25 .25

Gregor Mendel (1822-1884), Basic Laws of Heredity — A541

1984, Jan. 12 **Litho.**
1411 A541 50pf multicolored .80 .20

500th Anniv. of Michelstadt Town Hall — A542

1984, Feb. 16 **Litho.**
1412 A542 60pf multicolored .80 .20

350th Anniv. of Oberammergau Passion Play — A543

1984, Feb. 16 **Photo.**
1413 A543 60pf multicolored .80 .20

Second Election of Parliament, June 17 — A544

1984, Apr. 12 **Litho.** ***Perf. 13½***
1414 A544 80pf multicolored 1.10 .25

Europa (1959-1984) A545

1984, May 8 **Photo.** ***Perf. 14***
1415 A545 60pf multicolored .85 .20
1416 A545 80pf multicolored 1.00 .20

A546

1984, May 8 **Engr.**
1417 A546 60pf multicolored .65 .20

Nursery Rhyme Illustration, by Ludwig Richter (1803-84).

A547

1984, May 8
1418 A547 80pf Statue, 1693 .90 .25

St. Norbert von Xanten (1080-1134).

Barmer Theological Declaration, 50th Anniv. — A548

1984, May 8 **Litho.**
1419 A548 80pf Cross, text .90 .25

Souvenir Sheet

1984 UPU Congress A549

1984, June 19 **Litho.** ***Perf. 14***
1420 Sheet of 3 2.75 2.25
a. A549 60pf Letter sorting, 19th cent. .50 .45
b. A549 80pf Scanner .65 .60
c. A549 120pf H. von Stephan, founder 1.10 1.00

City of Neuss Bimillenium A550

1984, June 19 **Litho. & Engr.**
1421 A550 80pf Tomb of Oclatius .90 .25

Friedrich Wilhelm Bessel (1784-1846), Astronomer A551

1984, June 19
1422 A551 80pf Bessel function diagram .90 .25

88th German Catholic Convention, Munich, July 4-8 — A552

1984, June 19 **Photo.**
1423 A552 60pf Pope Pius XII .65 .20

Town Hall, Duderstadt — A553

1984, Aug. 21 **Litho.** ***Perf. 14***
1424 A553 60pf multicolored .65 .20

Medieval Document, Computer — A554

1984, Aug. 21
1425 A554 70pf multicolored .90 .25

10th Intl. Archives Congress, Bonn.

German Electron Synchrotron (DESY) Research Center, Hamburg — A555

1984, Aug. 21 **Photo.**
1426 A555 80pf multicolored 1.10 .25

Schleswig-Holstein Canal Bicentenary — A556

1984, Aug. 21 **Litho.**
1427 A556 80pf Knoop lock 1.10 .25

Stamp Day A557

1984, Oct. 18 **Litho.** ***Perf. 14***
1428 A557 80pf Imperial Taxis Posthouse, Augsburg 1.25 .25

Anti-smoking Campaign — A558

1984, Nov. 8 **Litho.**
1429 A558 60pf Match, text .80 .20

Equal Rights for Men and Women — A559

1984, Nov. 8
1430 A559 80pf Male & female symbols 1.00 .25

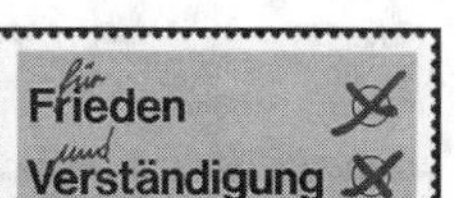

Peace and Understanding — A560

1984, Nov. 8
1431 A560 80pf Text 1.00 .25

Augsburg, 2000th Anniv. — A561

1985, Jan. 10 **Litho.**
1432 A561 80pf Roman Emperor Augustus, Augsburg buildings 1.00 .25

Philipp Jakob Spener, Religious Leader (1635-1705) A562

1985, Jan. 10 **Litho.**
1433 A562 80pf multicolored .90 .25

Deutches Wortebuch — A563

1985, Jan. 10 **Litho.**
1434 A563 80pf Bros. Grimm, text 1.10 .25

Romano Guardini, Theologist (1885-1968) A564

1985, Jan. 10 **Litho.**
1435 A564 80pf multicolored .90 .25

Market and Coinage Rights in Verden, 1000th Anniv. A565

1985, Feb. 21 **Litho.**
1436 A565 60pf multicolored 1.10 .20

German-Danish Border Areas and Flags — A566

1985, Feb. 21
1437 A566 80pf multicolored 1.10 .25

Bonn-Copenhagen declarations on mutual minorities, 30th anniv.

Johann Peter Hebel (1760-1826), Poet — A567

1985, Apr. 16 **Litho.**
1438 A567 80pf multicolored .90 .25

Egon Erwin Kisch (1885-1948), Journalist A568

1985, Apr. 16 **Litho.**
1439 A568 60pf Kisch using telephone .80 .20

Europa 1985 — A569

European Music Year: 60pf, Georg Friedrich Handel. 80pf, Johann Sebastian Bach.

1985, May 7 **Photo.**
1440 A569 60pf Portrait of Handel 1.25 .20
1441 A569 80pf Portrait of Bach 1.25 .30

Dominikus Zimmermann (1685-1766), Architect — A570

1985, May 7 **Photo.**
1442 A570 70pf Stucco column .80 .25

St. George's Cathedral, 750th Anniv. — A571

1985, May 7 **Litho.** ***Perf. 14***
1443 A571 60pf Cathedral, Limburg .80 .25

Father Josef Kentenich (1885-1968) — A572

1985, May 7 **Litho.**
1444 A572 80pf Portrait .90 .25

Forest Conservation A573

1985, July 16 **Litho.** ***Perf. 14***
1445 A573 80pf Clock, forest 1.10 .25

Intl. Youth Year A574

1985, July 16 ***Perf. 14***
1446 A574 60pf Scouts, scouting and IYY emblems .65 .25

30th World Scouting Conf., Munich, 7/15-19.

Frankfurt Stock Exchange, 400th Anniv. — A575

Design: Bourse, est. 1879, and Frankfurt Eagle, the exchange emblem.

1985, Aug. 13 ***Perf. 14x14½***
1447 A575 80pf multicolored 1.00 .25

The Sunday Walk, by Carl Spitzweg (1808-85) A576

1985, Aug. 13
1448 A576 60pf multicolored 1.10 .25

Fritz Reuter (1810-1874), Dialect Author — A577

1985, Oct. 15 **Litho.** ***Perf. 14***
1449 A577 80pf Portrait, manuscript 1.10 .25

Departure of the 1st Train from Nuremberg to Furth, 1835 — A578

1985, Nov. 12 **Litho.** ***Perf. 14x14½***
1450 A578 80pf Adler locomotive 1.10 .25

Founder Johannes Scharrer (1785-1844), German Railways 150th anniv.

Reintegration of German World War II Refugees, 40th Anniv. — A579

1985, Nov. 12 ***Perf. 14***
1451 A579 80pf multicolored 1.10 .25

Natl. Armed Forces, 30th Anniv. A580

1985, Nov. 12 ***Perf. 14x14½***
1452 A580 80pf Iron Cross, natl. colors 1.75 .25

Benz Tricycle, Saloon Car, 1912, and Modern Automobile — A581

1986, Jan. 16 **Litho.** ***Perf. 14***
1453 A581 80pf multicolored 1.10 .25

Automobile cent.

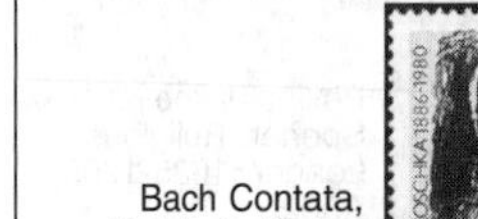

Bad Hersfeld, 1250th Anniv. A582

1986, Feb. 13 **Litho.** ***Perf. 14***
1454 A582 60pf multicolored .80 .25

Bach Contata, Detail, by Oskar Kokoschka (1886-1980) A583

1986, Feb. 13
1455 A583 80pf Self portrait .90 .25

Halley's Comet A584

1986, Feb. 13
1456 A584 80pf multicolored 1.10 .25

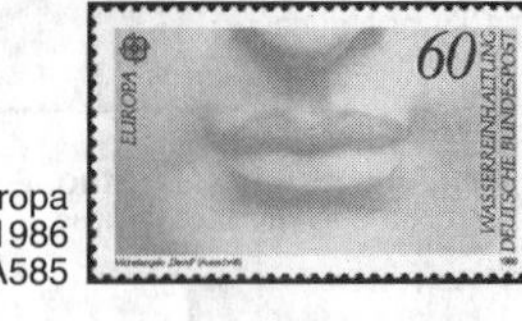

Europa 1986 A585

Details from Michelangelo's David: 60pf, Mouth (pure water). 80pf, Nose, (pure air).

1986, May 5 **Photo.** ***Perf. 14***
1457 A585 60pf multicolored .80 .20
1458 A585 80pf multicolored .90 .20

St. Johannis Monastery, Walsrode — A586

1986, May 5 **Litho. & Engr.**
1459 A586 60pf multicolored .80 .25

Monastery millennium and town of Walsrode, 603rd anniv.

King Ludwig II of Bavaria (1845-1886), Neuschwanstein Castle — A587

1986, May 5 **Litho.**
1460 A587 60pf multicolored 1.25 .25

Karl Barth (1886-1968), Protestant Theologian A588

1986, May 5 **Engr.**
1461 A588 80pf blk, dk red & red lil 1.00 .25

Religion, Science, Friendship and Fatherland — A589

1986, May 5 **Litho.**
1462 A589 80pf multicolored 1.00 .25

Union of German Catholic Students, 100th assembly, Frankfurt, June 12-15.

Carl Maria von Weber (1786-1826), Mass in E-flat Major — A590

1986, June 20 **Litho.** ***Perf. 14***
1463 A590 80pf multicolored 1.25 .25

Franz Liszt and Signature A591

1986, June 20
1464 A591 80pf dk blue & dk org 1.10 .25

Intl. Peace Year A592

1986, June 20
1465 A592 80pf multicolored 1.10 .25

Souvenir Sheet

Reichstag, Berlin — A593

Historic buildings: b, Koening Museum, Bonn. c, Parliament, Bonn.

1986, June 20
1466 Sheet of 3 3.25 2.50
a.-c. A593 80pf, any single .80 .70

European Satellite Technology — A594

Design: TV-SAT/TDF-1 over Europe.

1986, June 20
1467 A594 80pf multicolored 1.40 .25

Augsburg Cathedral Stained Glass Window A595

1986, Aug. 14 ***Perf. 14***
1468 A595 80pf multicolored 1.40 .25

Monuments protection.

King Frederick the Great (1712-1786) A596

1986, Aug. 14
1469 A596 80pf multicolored 1.75 .25

German Skat Congress, Cent. — A597

1986, Aug. 14
1470 A597 80pf Tournament card 1.10 .25

Organization for Economic Cooperation and Development, 25th Anniv. — A598

1986, Aug. 14

1471 A598 80pf multicolored 1.10 .25

Heidelberg University, 600th Anniv. — A599

1986, Oct. 16 **Litho.**

1472 A599 80pf multicolored 1.25 .25

Stagecoach, Stamps from 1975-1984 — A600

1986, Oct. 16

1473 A600 80pf multicolored 1.25 .25

Stamp Day, 50th Anniv.

A601 A602

1986, Nov. 13 **Litho.** ***Perf. 14***

1474 A601 70pf multicolored .80 .25

Mary Wigman (1886-1973), dancer.

1986-91 **Engr.** ***Perf. 14***

Famous Women: 5pf, Emma Ihrer (1857-1911), politician, labor leader. 10pf, Paula Modersohn-Becker (1876-1907), painter. 20pf, Cilly Aussem (1909-63), tennis champion. 30pf, Kathe Kollwitz (1867-1945), painter, graphic artist. 40pf, Maria Sibylla Merian (1647-1717), naturalist, painter. 50pf, Christine Teusch (1888-1968), minister of education and cultural affairs. 60pf, Dorothea Erxleben (1715-62), physician. 70pf, Elisabet Boehm (1859-1943), social organizer. 80pf, Clara Schumann (1819-96), pianist, composer. 100pf, Therese Giehse (1898-1975), actress. 120pf, Elisabeth Selbert (1896-1986), politician. 130pf, Lise Meitner (1878-1968), physicist. 140pf, Cecile Vogt (1875-1962), neurologist. 150pf, Sophie Scholl (1921-43), member of anti-Nazi resistance. 170pf, Hannah Arendt (1906-75), American political scientist. 180pf, Lotte Lehmann (1888-1976), soprano. 200pf, Bertha von Suttner (1843-1914), 1905 Nobel Peace Prize winner. 240pf, Mathilde Franziska Anneke, (1817-84), American author. 250pf, Queen Louise of Prussia (1776-1810). 300pf, Fanny Hensel (1805-47), composer-conductor. 350pf, Hedwig Dransfeld (1871-1925), women's rights activist. 500pf, Alice Salomon (1872-1948), feminist and social activist.

1475	A602	5pf multi	.20	.20
1476	A602	10pf multi	.20	.20
1477	A602	20pf multi	.20	.20
1478	A602	30pf multi	.30	.20
1479	A602	40pf multi	.40	.20
1480	A602	50pf multi	.45	.20
1481	A602	60pf multi	.60	.20
1482	A602	70pf multi	.85	.45
1483	A602	80pf multi	.70	.20
1484	A602	100pf multi	.70	.25
1485	A602	120pf multi	1.00	.40
1486	A602	130pf multi	1.60	.40
1487	A602	140pf multi	2.00	.80
1488	A602	150pf multi	2.40	.90
1489	A602	170pf multi	1.40	.25
1490	A602	180pf multi	1.50	.60
1491	A602	200pf multi	.95	.45
1492	A602	240pf multi	1.90	.80
1493	A602	250pf multi	2.50	.95
1493A	A602	300pf multi	1.50	.60
1494	A602	350pf multi	2.75	1.40
1494A	A602	500pf multi	3.50	1.50
	Nos. 1475-1494A (22)		27.60	11.35

Issued: 50pf, 80pf, 11/18; 40pf, 60pf, 9/17/87; 120pf, 11/7/87; 10pf, 4/14/88; 20pf, 130pf, 5/5/88; 100pf, 170pf, 240pf, 350pf, 11/10/88; 500pf, 1/12/89; 5pf, 2/9/89; 180pf, 250pf, 7/13/89; 140pf, 300pf, 8/10/89; 30pf, 70pf, 1/8/91; 150pf, 200pf, 2/14/91.

See #1723/1735, Berlin #9N516-9N532.

Advent Collection for Church Projects in Latin America, 25th Anniv. A603

1986, Nov. 13 **Litho.** ***Perf. 14***

1495 A603 80pf multicolored .80 .25

Berlin, 750th Anniv. — A604

1987, Jan. 15 **Litho.**

1496 A604 80pf multicolored 1.25 .40

Archbishop's Residence at Wurzburg, 1719-44 A605

1987, Jan. 15 **Photo.**

1497 A605 80pf multicolored 1.00 .25

Balthasar Neumann (1687-1753), Baroque architect.

Ludwig Erhard (1897-1977), Economist, Chancellor 1963-66 A606

1987, Jan. 15

1498 A606 80pf multicolored 1.25 .25

1987 Census — A607

1987, Jan. 15 **Litho.**

1499 A607 80pf Federal Eagle 1.10 .25

Clemenswerth Hunting Castle, 250th Anniv. — A608

1987, Feb. 12 **Litho.**

1500 A608 60pf multicolored .90 .20

Joseph von Fraunhofer (1787-1826), Optician, Physicist — A609

1987, Feb. 12 **Litho. & Engr.**

1501 A609 80pf Light spectrum diagram .90 .25

Karl May (1842-1912), Novelist — A610

1987, Feb. 12 **Photo.**

1502 A610 80pf Apache Chief Winnetou 1.00 .25

Papal Arms, Madonna and Child, Buildings in Kevelaer — A611

1987, Apr. 9 **Litho.**

1503 A611 80pf multicolored 1.10 .25

State visit of Pope John Paul II, Apr. 30-May 4; 17th Marian and 10th Mariological World Congress, Kevelaer, Sept. 11-20.

German Choral Soc., 125th Anniv. A612

1987, Apr. 9

1504 A612 80pf multicolored 1.00 .25

Europa 1987 A613

Modern architecture: 60pf, German Pavilion, designed by Ludwig Mies van der Rohe, 1928 World's Fair, Barcelona. 80pf, Kohlbrand Bridge, 1974, Hamburg, designed by Thyssen Engineering.

1987, May 5 **Litho.**

1505 A613 60pf multicolored .70 .25
1506 A613 80pf multicolored 1.10 .25

Organ Pipes, Signature A614

1987, May 5

1507 A614 80pf multicolored .80 .25

Dietrich Buxtehude (c. 1637-1707), composer.

Wilhelm Kaisen (1887-1979), Bremen City Senate President — A615

1987, May 5

1508 A615 80pf multicolored 1.00 .25

Johann Albrecht Bengel (1687-1752), Lutheran Theologian — A616

1987, May 5 **Photo.** ***Perf. 14***

1509 A616 80pf multicolored .90 .25

Kurt Schwitters (1887-1948), Artist — A617

1987, May 5 **Litho.**

1510 A617 80pf multicolored .90 .25

Rotary Intl. Convention, Munich, June 7-10 — A618

1987, May 5 **Photo.**

1511 A618 70pf multicolored 1.00 .25

Dulmen's Wild Horses, Merfelder Bruch Nature Reserve A619

1987, May 5

1512 A619 60pf multicolored 1.10 .25

European Environmental Conservation Year.

Bishopric of Bremen, 1200th Anniv. A620

Design: Charlemagne, Bremen Cathedral, city arms, Bishop Willehad.

1987, July 16 **Litho.** ***Perf. 14***

1513 A620 80pf multicolored .80 .25

7th European Rifleman's Festival, Lippstadt, Sept. 12-13 — A621

1987, Aug. 20 **Litho.** ***Perf. 14***

1514 A621 80pf multicolored .80 .25

Stamp Day — A622

1987, Oct. 15 **Litho.**
1515 A622 80pf Postmen, 1897 .80 .50

Historic Sites and Objects — A623

Designs: 5pf, Brunswick Lion. 10pf, Frankfurt Airport. 20pf, No. 1526, Queen Nefertiti of Egypt, bust, Egyptian Museum, Berlin. 30pf, Corner tower, Celle Castle, 14th cent. 33pf, 120pf, Schleswig Cathedral. 38pf, 280pf, Statue of Roland, Bremen. 40pf, Chile House, Hamburg. 41pf, 170pf, Russian church, Wiesbaden. 45pf, Rastatt Castle. 50pf, Filigree tracery on spires, Freiburg Cathedral. 60pf, Bavaria Munich, bronze statue above the Theresienwiese, Hall of Fame. No. 1527, Heligoland. 80pf, Entrance to Zollern II coal mine, Dortmund. 90pf, 140pf, Bronze flagon from Reinheim. 100pf, Altotting Chapel, Bavaria. 200pf, Magdeburg Cathedral. 300pf, Hambach Castle. 350pf, Externsteine Bridge near Horn-Bad Meinberg. 400pf, Opera House, Dresden. 450pf, New Gate, Neubrandenburg. 500pf, State Theatre, Cottbus. 700pf, German Theater, Berlin.

1987-96 **Typo.** ***Perf. 14***

1515A	A623	5pf	multi	.20	.20
1516	A623	10pf	multi	.20	.20
1517	A623	20pf	multi	.20	.20
1518	A623	30pf	multi	.30	.20
1519	A623	33pf	tmulti	.30	.20
1520	A623	38pf	multi	.45	.25
1521	A623	40pf	multi	.25	.25
1522	A623	41pf	multi	.35	.20
1523	A623	45pf	multi	.25	.30
1524	A623	50pf	multi	.30	.20
1525	A623	60pf	multi	.35	.20
1526	A623	70pf	multi	.60	.20
1527	A623	70pf	multi	.35	.20
1528	A623	80pf	multi	.40	.20
a.	Bklt. pane, 4 10pf, 2 50pf, 2 80pf ('89)			2.25	2.25
b.	Bklt. pane, 2 each 20pf, 80pf			1.50	1.50
1529	A623	90pf	multi	1.00	.45
1530	A623	100pf	multi	.75	.20
a.	Bklt. pane, 2 each 10, 60, 80, 100pf			4.25	4.25
b.	Bklt. pane, 2 each 20, 50, 80, 100pf			4.25	4.25
c.	Booklet pane, 10 #1530			8.00	8.00
	Complete booklet, #1530c			8.00	
d.	Booklet pane, 4 #1516, 2 each #1524, 1528, 1530			4.25	4.25
	Complete booklet, #1530d			4.25	
1531	A623	120pf	multi	1.10	.50
1532	A623	140pf	multi	1.25	.35
1533	A623	170pf	multi	1.40	.30
1534	A623	200pf	lmulti	1.40	.40
1535	A623	280pf	multi	3.00	1.10
1536	A623	300pf	multi	2.25	.20
1537	A623	350pf	multi	2.75	.20
1538	A623	400pf	multi	3.00	.30
1539	A623	450pf	multi	3.50	.40
1540	A623	500pf	multi	3.75	.50
1540A	A623	700pf	multi	5.25	1.25
	Nos. 1515A-1540A (27)			34.90	9.15

Issued: 30, 50, 60, 80pf, 11/6/87; 10, 300pf, 1/14/88; 120pf, #1526, 7/14/88; 40, 90, 280pf, 8/11/88; 20, 33, 38, 140pf, 1/12/89; 100, 350pf, 2/9/89; 5pf, 2/15/90; 45p, #1527, 6/21/90; 170pf, 6/4/91; 400pf, 10/10/91; 450pf, 8/13/92; 200pf, 4/15/93; 500pf, 6/17/93; 41pf, 8/12/93; 700pf, 9/16/93; #1530b, 11/9/94; #1530d, 8/14/96.

See #1655-1663, 1838-60, Berlin #9N543-9N557.

Christoph Willibald Gluck (1714-1787), Composer, and Score from the Opera Armide — A624

1987, Nov. 6 ***Perf. 14***
1541 A624 60pf car lake & dk gray .70 .20

Gerhart Hauptmann (1862-1946), Playwright — A625

1987, Nov. 6 **Litho.**
1542 A625 80pf black & brick red 1.00 .25

German Agro Action Organization, 125th Anniv. — A626

1987, Nov. 6 **Photo.**
1543 A626 80pf Rice field 1.00 .25

Mainz Carnival, 150th Anniv. — A627

1988, Jan. 14 **Litho.** ***Perf. 14***
1544 A627 60pf Jester .70 .25

Jacob Kaiser (1888-1961), Labor Leader — A628

1988, Jan. 14 **Litho. & Engr.**
1545 A628 80pf black .85 .25

Franco-German Cooperation Treaty, 25th Anniv. — A629

1988, Jan. 14
1546 A629 80pf Adenauer, De Gaulle 1.10 .45

See France No. 2086.

Beatification of Edith Stein and Rupert Mayer by Pope John Paul II in 1987 — A630

1988, Jan. 14 **Photo.**
1547 A630 80pf brown, blk & ver .80 .25

A631

Woodcut (detail) by Ludwig Richter.

1988, Feb. 18 **Litho.**
1548 A631 60pf multicolored .70 .25

Woodcut inspired by poem Solitude of the Green Woods, by Baron Joseph von Eichendorff (1788-1857).

A632

1988, Feb. 18 **Photo.**
1549 A632 80pf dk red & brn blk 1.00 .25

Arthur Schopenhauer (1788-1860), philosopher.

Friedrich Wilhelm Raiffeisen (1818-1888), Economist — A633

1988, Feb. 18 **Litho.**
1550 A633 80pf black & brt yel grn 1.25 .25

The German Raiffeisen Assoc., an agricultural cooperative credit soc., was founded by Raiffeisen.

Ulrich Reichsritter von Hutten (1488-1523), Humanist — A634

Design: Detail from an engraving published with Hutten's *Conquestiones.*

1988, Apr. 14 **Litho. & Engr.**
1551 A634 80pf multicolored .85 .45

Europa 1988 A635

Transport and communication: 60pf, Airbus A320. 80pf, Integrated Services Digital Network (ISDN) system.

1988, May 5 **Litho.**
1552 A635 60pf multicolored .85 .30
1553 A635 80pf multicolored .60 .30

City of Dusseldorf, 700th Anniv. — A636

1988, May 5
1554 A636 60pf multicolored .70 .25

Cologne University, 600th Anniv. — A637

1988, May 5
1555 A637 80pf multicolored .85 .25

Jean Monnet (1888-1979), French Statesman A638

1988, May 5
1556 A638 80pf multicolored .85 .25

Theodor Storm (1817-1888), Poet, Novelist — A639

1988, May 5
1557 A639 80pf multicolored .85 .25

German Volunteer Service, 25th Anniv. — A640

1988, May 5
1558 A640 80pf multicolored .85 .25

Town of Meersburg, Millennium — A641

1988, July 14 **Litho.** ***Perf. 14***
1559 A641 60pf multicolored .60 .25

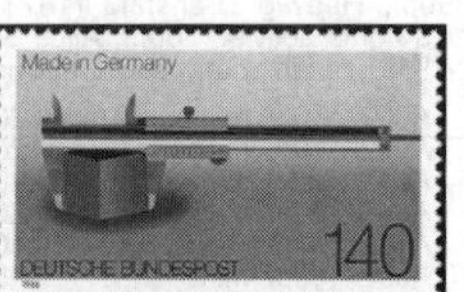

Leopold Gmelin (1788-1853), Chemist A642

1988, July 14 **Litho. & Engr.**
1560 A642 80pf multicolored .75 .25

Vernier Scale as a Symbol of Precision and Quality — A643

1988, July 14 **Litho.**
1561 A643 140pf multicolored 1.50 .60

Made in Germany.

August Bebel (1840-1913), Founder of the Social Democratic Party — A644

1988, Aug. 11 **Photo.**
1562 A644 80pf multicolored 1.00 .25

Intl. Red Cross, 125th Anniv. — A645

1988, Oct. 13 **Litho. & Engr.**
1563 A645 80pf scarlet & black 1.00 .25

Stamp Day — A646

1988, Oct. 13 **Litho.**
1564 A646 20pf Carrier pigeon .40 .20

1st Nazi Pogrom, Nov. 9, 1938 A647

Star, "Remembering is the secret of redemption," & burning synagogue in Baden-Baden.

1988, Oct. 13 **Photo.**
1565 A647 80pf dull pale pur & blk .75 .25

Postage Stamps for Bethel, Cent. A648

1988, Nov. 10 **Litho.**
1566 A648 60pf multicolored .85 .25

The Postage Stamps for Bethel program was founded by Pastor Friedrich V. Bodelschwingh to employ disabled residents of Bethel.

Samaritan Association of Workers (ASB) Rescue Service, Cent. — A649

1988, Nov. 10
1567 A649 80pf multicolored .85 .25

Bonn Bimillennium — A650

1989, Jan. 12 **Litho.**
1568 A650 80pf multicolored 1.25 .45

Bonn as capital of the federal republic, 40th anniv.

Bluxao I, 1955, by Willi Baumeister (1889-1955) — A651

1989, Jan. 12
1569 A651 60pf multicolored .75 .25

Misereor and Brot fur die Welt, 30th Annivs. A652

1989, Jan. 12 **Photo.**
1570 A652 80pf Barren and verdant soil .85 .25

Church organizations helping Third World nations to become self-sufficient in food production.

Cats in the Attic, Woodcut by Gerhard Marcks (1889-1981) — A653

1989, Feb. 9 **Litho.** ***Perf. 14***
1571 A653 60pf multicolored .75 .25

European Parliament 3rd Elections, June 18 — A654

Flags of member nations.

1989, Apr. 20 **Litho.**
1572 A654 100pf multicolored 1.50 .55

Europa 1989 A655

1989, May 5
1573 A655 60pf Kites .65 .25
1574 A655 100pf Puppets 1.10 .30

Hamburg Harbor, 800th Anniv. A656

1989, May 5
1575 A656 60pf multicolored .75 .25

Cosmas Damian Asam (1686-1739), Painter, Architect A657

1989, May 5 **Litho. & Engr.**
1576 A657 60pf Fresco .60 .25

Federal Republic of Germany, 40th Anniv. — A658

1989, May 5 **Photo.**
1577 A658 100pf Natl. crest, flag, presidents' signatures 1.10 .45

Council of Europe, 40th Anniv. — A659

1989, May 5 ***Perf. 14***
1578 A659 100pf Parliamentary Assembly, stars 1.00 .45

Franz Xaver Gabelsberger (1789-1849), Inventor of a German Shorthand — A660

1989, May 5 **Litho.**
1579 A660 100pf multicolored 1.10 .45

Sts. Kilian, Colman and Totnan (d. 689), Martyred Missionaries, and Clover — A661

1989, June 15 **Litho.**
1580 A661 100pf multicolored 1.00 .45

See Ireland No. 748.

Friedrich Silcher (1789-1860), Composer, and *Lorelai* Score — A662

1989, June 15
1581 A662 80pf multicolored .75 .25

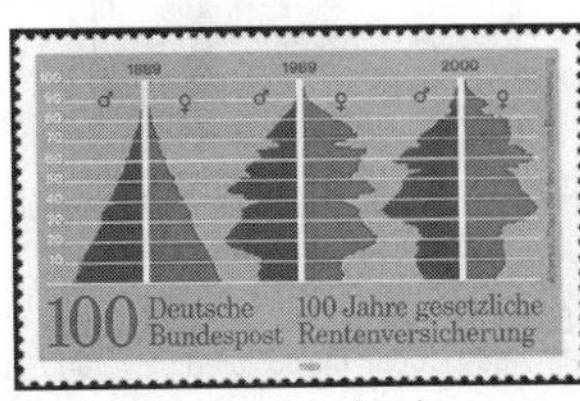

Social Security Pension Insurance, Cent. — A663

1989, June 15
1582 A663 100pf dull ultra, bl & ver 1.00 .45

Friedrich List (1789-1846), Economist — A664

1989, July 13 **Engr.** ***Perf. 14***
1583 A664 170pf black & dark red 1.75 .65

Summer Evening, 1905, by Heinrich Vogler — A665

Summer Evening, 1905, by Heinrich Vogler — A665

1989, July 13 **Litho.**
1584 A665 60pf multicolored .60 .25

Worpswede Artists' Village, cent.

A666

1989, July 13 **Photo.**
1585 A666 100pf slate grn, blk & gray .80 .45

Reverend Paul Schneider (d. 1939), martyr of Buchenwald concentration camp.

A667

1989, Aug. 10 **Litho.**
1586 A667 60pf multicolored .75 .25

Frankfurt Cathedral, 750th anniv.

Child Welfare A668

1989, Aug. 10 ***Perf. 14***
1587 A668 100pf multicolored .80 .45

Trade Union of the Mining and Power Industries, Cent. — A669

1989, Aug. 10 ***Perf. 14***
1588 A669 100pf multicolored .80 .45

Reinhold Maier (1889-1971), Politician A670

1989, Oct. 12 **Litho.**
1589 A670 100pf multicolored 1.00 .45

Restoration of St. James Church Organ, Constructed by Arp Schnitger, 1689 — A671

1989, Nov. 16
1590 A671 60pf multicolored .75 .25

Speyer, 2000th Anniv. A672

1990, Jan. 12 **Litho.** ***Perf. 14x14½***
1591 A672 60pf multicolored .75 .25

A673

Design: *The Young Post Rider,* an Engraving by Albrecht Durer.

Litho. & Engr.

1990, Jan. 12 ***Perf. 14***
1592 A673 100pf buff, vio brn & gray 1.40 .45

Postal communications in Europe, 500th anniv. See Austria No. 1486, Belgium No. 1332 and DDR No. 2791.

A674

1990, Jan. 12 **Litho.**
1593 A674 100pf multicolored .85 .45

Riesling Vineyards, 500th anniv.

Addition of Lubeck to the UNESCO World Heritage List, 1987 A675

1990, Jan. 12 **Litho. & Engr.**
1594 A675 100pf multicolored .85 .45

Seal of Col. Spittler, 1400, and Teutonic Order Heraldic Emblem A676

1990, Feb. 15 **Litho.**
1595 A676 100pf multicolored 1.10 .45

Teutonic Order, 800th anniv.

Seal of Frederick II and Galleria Reception Hall at the Frankfurt Fair A677

1990, Feb. 15
1596 A677 100pf multicolored 1.10 .45

Granting of fair privileges to Frankfurt by Frederick II, 750th anniv.

Youth Science and Technology Competition, 25th Anniv. — A678

1990, Feb. 15
1597 A678 100pf multicolored 1.00 .45

Nature and Environmental Protection — A679

1990, Feb. 15
1598 A679 100pf North Sea 1.40 .45

Labor Day, Cent. A680

1990, Apr. 19 **Photo.** ***Perf. 14***
1599 A680 100pf dark red & blk .85 .45

German Assoc. of Housewives, 75th Anniv. — A681

1990, Apr. 19 **Litho.**
1600 A681 100pf multicolored .85 .45

Europa A682

Post offices in Frankfurt am Main: 60pf, Thurn and Taxis Palace. 100pf, Modern Giro office.

1990, May 3 **Litho.**
1601 A682 60pf multicolored .90 .35
1602 A682 100pf multicolored 1.25 .40

German Students' Fraternity, 175th Anniv. — A683

1990, May 3 **Litho. & Engr.**
1603 A683 100pf multicolored 1.10 .45

Intl. Telecommunication Union, 125th Anniv. — A684

1990, May 3 **Litho.**
1604 A684 100pf multicolored .85 .45

German Life Boat Institution, 125th Anniv. — A685

1990, May 3
1605 A685 60pf multicolored .85 .45

Wilhelm Leuschner (1890-1944), Politician A686

1990, May 3 **Litho. & Engr.**
1606 A686 100pf lt gray violet 1.10 .45

Rummelsberg Diaconal Institution, Cent. — A687

1990, May 3 **Litho.**
1607 A687 100pf multicolored .85 .45

Charter of German Expellees, 40th Anniv. — A688

1990, June 21 **Photo.**
1608 A688 100pf multicolored 1.00 .45

Intl. Chamber of Commerce, 30th Universal Congress — A689

1990, June 21 **Litho.**
1609 A689 80pf multicolored .85 .55

Matthias Claudius (1740-1815), Writer — A691

1990, Aug. 9 **Litho.**
1611 A691 100pf multicolored 1.00 .30

Reunified Germany

AREA—137,179 sq. mi.
POP.—82,087,361 (1999 est.)
CAPITAL—Berlin

German Reunification — A692

1990, Oct. 3 **Litho.** ***Perf. 14***
1612 A692 50pf black, red & yel .70 .30
1613 A692 100pf black, red & yel 1.25 .45

First Postage Stamps, 150th Anniv. — A693

1990, Oct. 11 **Litho.**
1614 A693 100pf multicolored 1.00 .30

Heinrich Schliemann (1822-1890), Archaeologist — A694

1990, Oct. 11
1615 A694 60pf multicolored .85 .25

See Greece No. 1705.

Kathe Dorsch (1912-1957), Actress — A695

1990, Nov. 6 **Photo.**
1616 A695 100pf red & violet 1.00 .45

Opening of Berlin Wall, 1st Anniv. — A696

1990, Nov. 6 **Photo.** ***Perf. 14***
1617 A696 50pf shown .60 .30
1618 A696 100pf Brandenburg Gate 1.10 .50

Souvenir Sheet

1619 Sheet of 2 2.00 1.75
a. A696 50pf like No. 1617 .70 .60
b. A696 100pf like No. 1618 1.00 .90

Rainbow continuous on stamps from #1619.

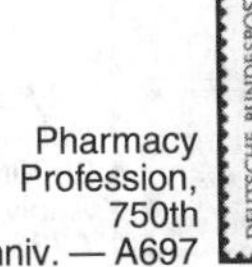

Pharmacy Profession, 750th Anniv. — A697

1991, Jan. 8 **Litho.**
1620 A697 100pf multicolored 1.10 .45

Hanover, 750th Anniv. — A698

1991, Jan. 8
1621 A698 60pf multicolored .85 .30

Brandenburg Gate, Bicentennial — A699

1991, Jan. 8 **Litho. & Engr.**
1622 A699 100pf gray, dk bl & red 1.40 .30

A700

1991, Jan. 8 **Photo.**
1623 A700 60pf multicolored .75 .30

Erich Buchholz (1891-1972), painter and architect.

A701

1991, Jan. 8 **Litho.**
1624 A701 100pf multicolored 1.00 .30

Walter Eucken (1891-1950), economist.

25th Intl. Tourism Exchange, Berlin — A702

1991, Jan. 8
1625 A702 100pf multicolored 1.00 .30

Souvenir Sheet

World Bobsled Championships, Altenberg — A703

1991, Jan. 8 ***Perf. 12½x13***
1626 A703 100pf multicolored 1.40 1.25

Friedrich Spee von Langenfeld (1591-1635), Poet — A704

1991, Feb. 14 **Litho.** ***Perf. 14***
1627 A704 100pf multicolored 1.00 .30

A705

1991, Feb. 14
1628 A705 100pf multicolored 1.00 .30

Ludwig Windthorst (1812-1891), politician.

A706

1991, Mar. 12
1629 A706 60pf multicolored .70 .30

Jan von Werth (1591-1652), general.

Flowers A707

1991, Mar. 12 ***Perf. 13***
1630 A707 30pf Schweizer mannschild .30 .20
1631 A707 50pf Wulfens primel (primula) .45 .25
1632 A707 80pf Sommerenzian (gentian) .75 .35
1633 A707 100pf Preiselbeere (cranberry) 1.00 .50
1634 A707 350pf Alpenedelweiss 3.00 1.75
Nos. 1630-1634 (5) 5.50 3.05

Battle of Legnica, 750th Anniv. A708

Litho. & Engr.

1991, Apr. 9 ***Perf. 14***
1635 A708 100pf multicolored 1.00 .60

See Poland No. 3019.

Choral Singing Academy of Berlin, Bicent. A709

1991, Apr. 9
1636 A709 100pf multicolored 1.00 .45

Lette Foundation, 125th Anniv. — A710

1991, Apr. 9 **Photo.**
1637 A710 100pf multicolored 1.00 .30

Historic Aircraft A711

1991, Apr. 9
1638 A711 30pf Junkers F13, 1930 .30 .20
1639 A711 50pf Grade Eindecker, 1909 .45 .20
1640 A711 100pf Fokker FIII, 1922 1.25 .30
1641 A711 165pf Graf Zeppelin LZ 127, 1928 1.75 1.50
Nos. 1638-1641 (4) 3.75 2.20

Europa A712

Satellites: 60pf, ERS-1. 100pf, Copernicus.

1991, May 2 **Litho.** ***Perf. 14***
1642 A712 60pf multicolored .85 .30
1643 A712 100pf multicolored 1.40 .30

Town Charters, 700th Anniv. — A713

Design: Arms of Bernkastel, Mayen, Montabaur, Saarburg, Welschbillig, and Wittlich.

1991, May 2
1644 A713 60pf multicolored .70 .30

Max Reger (1873-1916), Composer — A714

1991, May 2
1645 A714 100pf multicolored 1.10 .30

Inter-City Express Railway A715

1991, May 2
1646 A715 60pf multicolored .70 .30

18th World Gas Congress, Berlin — A716

Designs: 60pf, Wilhelm August Lampadius (1772-1842), chemist. 100pf, Gas street lamp.

1991, June 4 **Litho.** ***Perf. 13x12½***
1647 A716 60pf lt blue & black .60 .25
1648 A716 100pf lt blue & black .90 .35
a. Pair, #1647-1648 + label 1.75 1.60

Sea Birds — A717

Designs: 60pf, Kampflaufer, Philomachus pugnax. 80pf, Zwergseeschwalbe, Sterna albifrons. 100pf, Ringelgans, Branta bernicla. 140pf, Seeadler, Haliaeetus albicilla.

1991, June 4 **Litho.** ***Perf. 14***
1649 A717 60pf multicolored .60 .30
1650 A717 80pf multicolored .90 .50
1651 A717 100of multicolored .90 .50
1652 A717 140pf multicolored 1.50 1.25
Nos. 1649-1652 (4) 3.90 2.55

Paul Wallot (1841-1912), Architect — A718

Litho. & Engr.

1991, June 4 ***Perf. 14***
1653 A718 100pf multicolored 1.10 .30

Historic Sites Type of 1987

Designs: No. 1655, Frankfurt Airport. No. 1656, Wernigerode Town Hall. 60pf, Rastatt Castle. 80pf, Bavaria Munich, bronze statue above the Theresienwiese, Hall of Fame. No. 1663, Heligoland. No. 1664, Schwerin Castle. 110pf, Regensburg Stone Bridge.

1991-2001 Litho. ***Die Cut, Imperf.***
Self-Adhesive

1655 A623	10pf multi		.25	.20
1656 A623	10pf multi		.20	.20
1659 A623	60pf multi		.55	.50
1661 A623	80pf multi		.65	.60
1663 A623	100pf multi		1.00	.90
a.	Bklt. pane, 2 each #1655, 1659, 1661, 1663		5.00	
1664 A623	100pf multi		.90	.45
1666 A623	110pf multi		1.00	.50
a.	Booklet, 2 each #1656, 1664, 8 #1666		10.50	
	Nos. 1655-1666 (7)		4.55	3.35

Issued: #1655, 1659, 1661, 1663, June 4. Nos. 1656, 1664, 110pf, 5/25/01.

Nos. 1655, 1659, 1661, 1663 issued on peelable paper backing serving as booklet cover.

This is an expanding set. Numbers will change if necessary.

Dragonflies A719

50pf, #1671, Libellula depressa. #1672, 70pf, Sympetrum sanguineum. #1673, 80pf, Cordulegaster boltonii. #1674, 100pf, Aeshna viridis.

1991, July 9 Photo. ***Perf. 14***

1670 A719	50pf multicolored	.50	.25
1671 A719	60pf multicolored	.90	.50
1672 A719	60pf multicolored	.90	.50
1673 A719	60pf multicolored	.90	.50
1674 A719	60pf multicolored	.90	.50
a.	Block of 4, #1671-1674	3.75	2.75
1675 A719	70pf multicolored	.75	.50
1676 A719	80pf multicolored	.80	.50
1677 A719	100pf multicolored	.85	.55
	Nos. 1670-1677 (8)	6.50	3.80

Traffic Safety A720

1991, July 9 **Litho.**
1678 A720 100pf multicolored 1.10 .45

Geneva Convention on Refugees, 40th Anniv. — A721

1991, July 9
1679 A721 100pf blk, gray & pink 1.00 .30

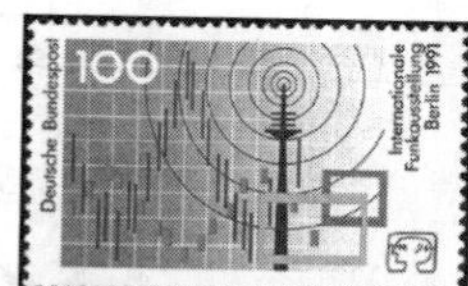

Intl. Radio Exhibition, Berlin — A722

1991, July 9
1680 A722 100pf multicolored 1.00 .30

Reinold von Thadden-Trieglaff (1891-1976), Founder of German Protestant Convention — A723

1991, Aug. 8 Litho. ***Perf. 14***
1681 A723 100pf multicolored 1.00 .30

August Heinrich Hoffman von Fallersleben (1798-1874), Poet and Philologist — A724

1991, Aug. 8
1682 A724 100pf multicolored 1.10 .30

German national anthem, 150th anniv.

3-Phase Energy Transmission, Cent. — A725

1991, Aug. 8
1683 A725 170pf multicolored 1.75 .75

Rhine-Ruhr Harbor, Duisburg, 275th Anniv. — A726

1991, Sept. 12 Litho. ***Perf. 14***
1684 A726 100pf multicolored 1.00 .30

Souvenir Sheet

Theodor Korner (1791-1813), Poet — A727

1991, Sept. 12 ***Perf. 13x12½***
1685 A727 Sheet of 2 2.25 .95
a. 60pf Sword and pen .60 .60
b. 100pf Portrait .90 .90

Hans Albers (1891-1960), Actor — A728

1991, Sept. 12 Photo. ***Perf. 14***
1686 A728 100pf multicolored 1.40 .30

Postman, Spreewald Region A729

1991, Oct. 10 Litho. ***Perf. 14***
1687 A729 100pf multicolored 1.00 .30

Stamp Day.

Bird Monument by Max Ernst — A730

1991, Oct. 10
1688 A730 100pf multicolored 1.00 .30

Sorbian Legends A731

1991, Nov. 5 ***Perf. 13***
1689 A731 60pf Fiddler, water sprite .60 .30
1690 A731 100pf Midday woman, woman from Nochten 1.10 .30

Souvenir Sheet

Wolfgang Amadeus Mozart, Death Bicent. — A732

1991, Nov. 5 Litho. ***Perf. 14***
1691 A732 100pf multicolored 1.75 1.60

Otto Dix (1891-1969), Painter — A733

Designs: 60pf, Portrait of the Dancer Anita Berber. 100pf, Self-portrait.

1991, Nov. 5 Photo. ***Perf. 14***
1692 A733 60pf multicolored .60 .30
1693 A733 100pf multicolored 1.25 .30

Julius Leber (1891-1945), Politician A734

1991, Nov. 5 **Litho.**
1694 A734 100pf black & red 1.00 .30

Nelly Sachs (1891-1970), Writer — A735

1991, Nov. 5
1695 A735 100pf violet 1.00 .30

City of Koblenz, 2000th Anniv. A736

1992, Jan. 9 ***Perf. 13x12½***
1696 A736 60pf multicolored 1.00 .30

Terre Des Hommes Child Welfare Organization, 25th Anniv. — A737

1992, Jan. 9 Litho. ***Perf. 14***
1697 A737 100pf multicolored 1.25 .45

Martin Niemoller (1892-1984), Theologian A738

1992, Jan. 9
1698 A738 100pf multicolored .90 .30

BADEN-WÜRTTEMBERG DEUTSCHE BUNDESPOST 100

Coats of Arms of States of the Federal Republic of Germany A739

1992-94 ***Perf. 13½***

1699	100pf Baden-Wurttemberg	.95	.50
1700	100pf Bavaria	.95	.50
1701	100pf Berlin	.95	.50
1702	100pf Brandenburg	.95	.50
1703	100pf Bremen	.95	.50
1704	100pf Hamburg	.95	.50
1705	100pf Hesse	.95	.50
1706	100pf Mecklenburg-Western Pomerania	.95	.50
1707	100pf Lower Saxony	.95	.50
1708	100pf North Rhine - Westphalia	.95	.50
1709	100pf Rhineland-Palatinate	.95	.50
1710	100pf Saar	.95	.50
1711	100pf Saxony	.95	.50
1712	100pf Saxony-Anhalt	.95	.50

1713 100pf Schleswig-Holstein .95 .50
1714 100pf Thuringia .95 .50
Nos. 1699-1714 (16) 15.20 8.00

See #B818.

Issued: #1699, 1/9/92; #1700, 3/12/92; #1701, 6/11/92; #1702, 7/16/92; #1703, 8/13/92; #1704, 9/10/92; #1705, 3/11/93; #1706, 6/17/93; #1707, 7/15/93; #1708, 8/12/93; #1709, 9/16/93; #1710, 1/13/94; #1711, 3/10/94; #1712, 6/16/94; #1713, 7/14/94; #1714, 9/8/94.

Famous Women Type of 1986

80pf, Rahel Varnhagen von Ense (1771-1833), pioneer in women's movement. No. 1724, Elisabeth Schwarzhaupt (1901-86), politician. No. 1725, Louise Henriette of Orange (1627-67), mother of Frederick, King of Prussia. No. 1726, Grethe Weiser (1903-70), actress. No. 1727, Marlene Dietrich (1901-92), actress. No. 1728, Käte Strobel (1907-96), government minister. No. 1729, Marie-Elisabeth Lüders (1878-1966), politician. No. 1730, Marieluise Fleisser (1901-74), writer. No. 1731, Maria Probst (1902-67), politician. No. 1732, Nelly Sachs (1891-1970), writer. 400pf, Charlotte von Stein (1742-1827), confidant of Goethe. 440pf, Gret Palucca (1902-93), dancer. 450pf, Hedwig Courths-Mahler (1867-1950), novelist.

1992-2000 Engr. *Perf. 14*

1723 A602 80pf blue & brown .45 .30
1724 A602 100pf green & org brown 1.00 .30
1725 A602 100pf violet & bister .65 .30
1726 A602 100pf ol bis & bl grn .80 .70
1727 A602 110pf vio & dk brn .60 .30
1728 A602 110pf ol & red brn .80 .70
1729 A602 220pf grn bl & vio bl 1.25 .70
1730 A602 220pf grn & brn 1.60 1.25
1731 A602 300pf deep blue & brown 2.25 1.50
1732 A602 300pf brn & vio 2.10 1.50
1733 A602 400pf lake & blk 3.50 1.25
1734 A602 440pf dp vio & dk car 3.25 2.50
1735 A602 450pf brt blue & blue 3.75 1.75
Nos. 1723-1735 (13) 22.00 13.05

Issued: 400pf, 1/9/92; 450pf, 6/11/92; 80pf, #1725, 10/13/94; #1727, 8/14/97; #1729, 8/28/97; #1724, #1730, 10/16/97; 440pf, 10/8/98; #1726, 1727, 11/9/00; Nos. 1730, 1732, 1/11/01.

Arthur Honegger (1892-1955), Composer A740

1992, Feb. 6 Photo. *Perf. 14*
1736 A740 100pf sepia & black 1.00 .45

Ferdinand von Zeppelin (1838-1917), Airship Builder — A741

1992, Feb. 6 Litho.
1737 A741 165pf multicolored 1.75 .75

City of Kiel, 750th Anniv. A742

1992, Mar. 12
1738 A742 60pf multicolored .75 .30

Konrad Adenauer A743

1992, Mar. 12 Photo.
1739 A743 100pf black & dull org 1.25 .30

Ernst Jakob Renz (1815-1892), Circus Director — A744

1992, Mar. 12 Litho.
1740 A744 100pf multicolored 1.00 .30

Berlin Sugar Institute, 125th Anniv. A745

1992, Mar. 12 *Perf. 13x12½*
1741 A745 100pf multicolored 1.00 .45

Johann Adam Schall von Bell (1592-1666), Astronomer and Missionary — A746

1992, Apr. 9 Litho. *Perf. 13x12½*
1742 A746 140pf multicolored 1.50 .60

Erfurt, Capital of Thuringia, 1250th Anniv. — A747

1992, May 7 Litho. *Perf. 14*
1743 A747 60pf multicolored .75 .30

Discovery of America, 500th Anniv. — A748

Europa: 60pf, Woodcut illustrating letters from Columbus, 1493. 100pf, Rene de Laudonniere and Chief Athore by Jacques le Moyne de Morgues, 1564.

1992, May 7 *Perf. 13½*
1744 A748 60pf multicolored .65 .30
1745 A748 100pf multicolored 1.10 .30

A749

1992, May 7 *Perf. 13*
1746 A749 100pf multicolored 1.10 .40

Order of Merit, 150th anniv.

A750

1992, May 7 Litho. *Perf. 14*
1747 A750 100pf multicolored 1.10 .45

St. Ludgerus, 1250th birth anniv.

Adam Riese (1492-1559), Mathematician — A751

1992, May 7
1748 A751 100pf multicolored 1.10 .40

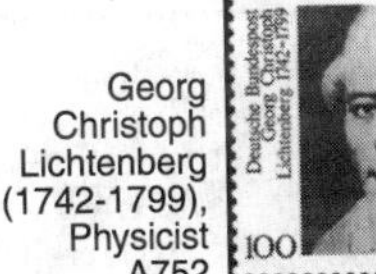

Georg Christoph Lichtenberg (1742-1799), Physicist A752

1992, June 11 Litho. *Perf. 14*
1749 A752 100pf multicolored 1.10 .45

20th Century Paintings — A753

Designs: 60pf, Landscape with a Horse, by Franz Marc (1880-1916). 100pf, Fashion Shop, by August Macke (1887-1914). 170pf, Murnau with a Rainbow, by Vassily Kandinsky (1866-1944).

1992, June 11 Litho. *Perf. 14*
1750 A753 60pf multicolored .60 .30
1751 A753 100pf multicolored .90 .45
1752 A753 170pf multicolored 1.50 .75
Nos. 1750-1752 (3) 3.00 1.50

See Nos. 1878-1880.

Leipzig Botanical Garden A754

1992, July 16 Litho. *Perf. 13x12½*
1753 A754 60pf multicolored .75 .30

Family Living — A755

1992, July 16 *Perf. 13½*
1754 A755 100pf multicolored 1.10 .30

17th World Congress on Home Economics, Hanover — A756

1992, July 16 Photo. *Perf. 14*
1755 A756 100pf multicolored 1.10 .45

Egid Quirin Asam (1692-1750), Architect and Sculptor — A757

1992, Aug. 13 Litho. *Perf. 14*
1756 A757 60pf multicolored .75 .30

German State Opera, Berlin, 250th Anniv. A758

1992, Aug. 13
1757 A758 80pf multicolored .85 .30

Federation of German Amateur Theaters, Cent. — A759

1992, Aug. 13
1758 A759 100pf multicolored 1.10 .30

Construction of First Globe by Martin Behaim, 500th Anniv. — A760

1992, Sept. 10 *Perf. 13½*
1759 A760 60pf multicolored .85 .30

Opening of Main-Danube Canal — A761

1992, Sept. 10 *Perf. 14*
1760 A761 100pf multicolored 1.10 .30

Werner Bergengruen (1892-1964), Writer — A762

1992, Sept. 10
1761 A762 100pf blk, bl & gray 1.10 .30

Jewelry & Watch Industries in Pforzheim, 225th Anniv. — A763

1992, Sept. 10
1762 A763 100pf multicolored 1.10 .30

Balloon Post — A764

1992, Oct. 15 Litho. *Perf. 14*
1763 A764 100pf multicolored 1.10 .30

Stamp Day.

Hugo Distler (1908-1942), Composer A765

1992, Oct. 15
1764 A765 100pf violet & black 1.10 .30

Association of German Plant and Machine Builders, Cent. — A766

1992, Oct. 15 Litho. & Engr.
1765 A766 170pf multicolored 1.50 .75

Single European Market A767

1992, Nov. 5 Litho. *Perf. 14*
1766 A767 100pf multicolored 1.10 .30

Jochen Klepper (1903-1942), Writer — A768

Litho. & Engr.
1992, Nov. 5 *Perf. 14*
1767 A768 100pf multicolored 1.10 .30

A769

1992, Nov. 5 Photo.
1768 A769 100pf sepia & black 1.10 .30

Werner von Siemens (1816-1892), electrical engineer.

A770

1992, Nov. 5 Litho.
1769 A770 100pf multicolored 1.10 .30

Gebhard Leberecht von Blucher (1742-1819), Commander of Prussian Army.

City of Munster, 1200th Anniv. — A771

1993, Jan. 14 Litho. *Perf. 14*
1770 A771 60pf multicolored .85 .30

Sir Isaac Newton, Scientist A772

1993, Jan. 14 Litho. & Engr.
1771 A772 100pf multicolored .85 .30

North German Naval Observatory, Hamburg, 125th Anniv. — A773

1993, Jan. 14 Litho. *Perf. 13x12½*
1772 A773 100pf multicolored .85 .30

Health and Safety in Workplace — A774

1993, Jan. 14 Photo. *Perf. 14*
1773 A774 100pf blk, yel & bl .85 .30

Association of German Electrical Engineers, Cent. — A775

1993, Jan. 14
1774 A775 170pf multicolored 1.50 .75

Leipzig Gewandhaus Orchestra, 250th Anniv. — A776

1993, Feb. 11 Litho. *Perf. 13x12½*
1775 A776 100pf black & gold .90 .30

St. John of Nepomuk, 600th Death Anniv. — A777

1993, Mar. 11
1776 A777 100pf multicolored .90 .30

New Postal Codes A778

1993, Mar. 11 *Perf. 14*
1777 A778 100pf multicolored 1.25 .30

20th Century German Paintings — A779

Designs: No. 1778, Cafe, by George Grosz (1893-1959). No. 1779, Sea and Sun, by Otto Pankok (1893-1966). No. 1780, Audience, by A. Paul Weber (1893-1980).

1993, Mar. 11
1778 A779 100pf multicolored 1.00 .60
1779 A779 100pf multicolored 1.00 .60
1780 A779 100pf multicolored 1.00 .60
Nos. 1778-1780 (3) 3.00 1.80

See Nos. 1863-1865, 1922-1924.

Benedictine Abbeys of Maria Laach and Bursfelde, 900th Anniv. — A780

Litho. & Engr.
1993, Apr. 15 *Perf. 14*
1781 A780 80pf multicolored .90 .30

5th Intl. Horticultural Show, Stuttgart — A781

1993, Apr. 15 Litho. *Perf. 13x12½*
1782 A781 100pf multicolored .90 .30

Contemporary Art — A782

Europa: 80pf, Storage Place, by Joseph Beuys (1921-1986). 100pf, Homage to the Square, by Joseph Albers (1888-1976).

1993, May 5 Litho. *Perf. 13½x14*
1783 A782 80pf multicolored .95 .50
1784 A782 100pf multicolored .95 .50

Dahlwitz Hoppegarten (Hippodrome), Berlin, 125th Anniv. — A783

1993, May 5 Litho. *Perf. 14*
1785 A783 80pf multicolored .80 .45

Lake Constance Steamer Hohentwiel — A784

1993, May 5 Photo.
1786 A784 100pf multicolored .90 .30

See Austria No. 1618, Switzerland No. 931.

Schulpforta School for Boys, 450th Anniv. — A785

1993, May 5 Litho.
1787 A785 100pf multicolored .90 .30

Coburger Convent, 125th Anniv. A786

1993, May 5 Litho. & Engr.
1788 A786 100pf black, green & red .90 .30

City of Potsdam, 1000th Anniv. A787

1993, June 17 Litho. *Perf. 13x12½*
1789 A787 80pf multicolored .95 .30

German UNICEF Committee, 40th Anniv. — A788

1993, June 17 **Litho.**
1790 A788 100pf multicolored .90 .30

Friedrich Holderlin (1770-1843), Writer — A789

1993, June 17 **Photo.** ***Perf. 14***
1791 A789 100pf multicolored .90 .30

Hans Fallada (1893-1947), Novelist — A790

1993, July 15
1792 A790 100pf multicolored .90 .30

Scenic Regions in Germany — A791

1993-96 **Litho.** ***Perf. 14***
Denominations 100pf

1793 A791	Rugen Island	.90	.45
1794 A791	Harz Mountains	.90	.45
1795 A791	Rhon Mountains	.90	.45
1796 A791	Bavarian Alps	.85	.45
1797 A791	Ore Mountains	.85	.45
1798 A791	Main River Valley	.85	.45
1799 A791	Mecklenburg lake district	.85	.45
1800 A791	Franconian Switzerland	.90	.55
1801 A791	Upper Lusatia	.90	.55
1802 A791	Sauerland	.90	.55
1803 A791	Havel River, Berlin	.90	.55
1804 A791	Holstein Switzerland	.90	.55
1805 A791	Saale	.90	.55
1806 A791	Spreewald	.90	.55
1807 A791	Eifel	.90	.55
	Nos. 1793-1807 (15)	13.30	7.55

Issued: #1793-1795, 7/15/93; #1796-1799, 7/14/94; #1800-1803, 7/6/95; #1804-1807, 4/11/96.

See #1938, 1974-1976, 2072-2073.

Mathias Klotz (1653-1743), Violin Maker — A792

1993, Aug. 12 **Litho.** ***Perf. 13x12½***
1808 A792 80pf multicolored .80 .30

Heinrich George (1893-1946), Actor — A793

1993, Aug. 12 ***Perf. 14***
1809 A793 100pf multicolored .90 .30

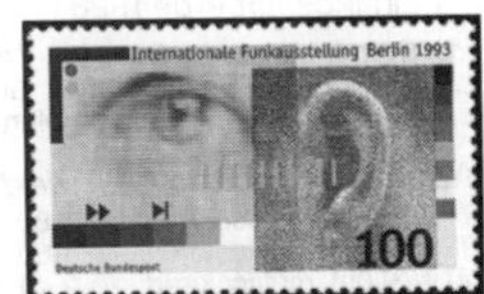

Intl. Radio Exhibition, Berlin — A794

1993, Aug. 12
1810 A794 100pf multicolored .90 .30

Hans Leip (1893-1983), Poet and Painter A795

1993, Sept. 16 **Litho.** ***Perf. 13***
1811 A795 100pf red, black & blue 1.10 .30

Birger Forell (1893-1958), Swedish Priest — A796

1993, Sept. 16 ***Perf. 14***
1812 A796 100pf multicolored 1.10 .30

Souvenir Sheet

For the Children — A797

1993, Sept. 16
1813 A797 100pf multicolored 1.10 1.10

Peter I. Tchaikovsky (1840-93), Composer — A798

1993, Oct. 14
1814 A798 80pf multicolored .90 .30

Max Reinhardt (1873-1943), Theatrical Director — A799

1993, Oct. 14
1815 A799 100pf buff, black & red 1.10 .30

St. Hedwig of Silesia, 750th Death Anniv. — A800

1993, Oct. 14
1816 A800 100pf multicolored 1.10 .30

See Poland No. 3176.

Paracelsus (1493-1541), Physician, Teacher — A801

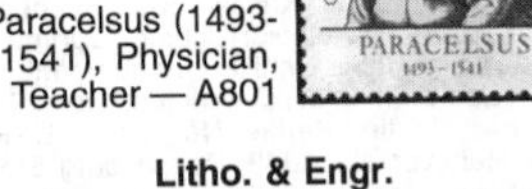

Litho. & Engr.
1993, Nov. 10 ***Perf. 14***
1817 A801 100pf multicolored 1.10 .30

Claudio Monteverdi (1567-1643), Composer — A802

1993, Nov. 10 **Litho.** ***Perf. 13x12½***
1818 A802 100pf multicolored 1.10 .30

Willy Brandt (1913-92), Statesman A803

1993, Nov. 10 ***Perf. 14***
1819 A803 100pf multicolored 1.25 .45

Staade, 1000th Anniv. A804

Litho. & Engr.
1994, Jan. 13. ***Perf. 14***
1820 A804 80pf multicolored .80 .35

Intl. Year of the Family A805

1994, Jan. 13 **Litho.**
1821 A805 100pf multicolored .95 .45

Heinrich Hertz (1857-94), Physicist — A806

1994, Jan. 13 ***Perf. 13x12½***
1822 A806 200pf multicolored 1.75 .80

Frankfurt Am Main, 1200th Anniv. A807

1994, Feb. 10
1823 A807 80pf multicolored .80 .35

Fulda, 1250th Anniv. A808

1994, Mar. 10 ***Perf. 14***
1824 A808 80pf multicolored .80 .35

German Women's Associations, German Women's Council, Cent. — A809

1994, Mar. 10 ***Perf. 13x12½***
1825 A809 100pf black, red & yellow .95 .45

Fourth European Parliamentary Elections — A810

1994, Mar. 10 ***Perf. 14***
1826 A810 100pf multicolored 1.10 .45

Foreigners in Germany: Living Together — A811

1994, Mar. 10
1827 A811 100pf multicolored .95 .45

Church of Our Lady, Munich, 500th Anniv. A812

1994, Apr. 14 **Litho.** ***Perf. 14***
1828 A812 100pf multicolored 1.10 .45

Europa A813

Designs: 80pf, Ohm's Law, by Georg Simon Ohm. 100pf, Quantum theory, by Max Planck.

1994, May 5 **Photo.**

1829 A813 80pf multicolored .80 .35
1830 A813 100pf multicolored .70 .45

Souvenir Sheet

Carl Hagenbeck (1844-1913), Circus Director, Animal Trainer, and Berlin Zoo, 150th Anniv. — A814

Designs: a, Hagenbeck, circus animals, zoo entrance. b, Zoo entrance, animals.

1994, May 5 **Litho.**

1831 A814 Sheet of 2 2.75 2.50
a. 100pf multicolored .80 .75
b. 200pf multicolored 1.75 1.60

Hans Pfitzner (1869-1949), Composer, Conductor — A815

1994, May 5

1832 A815 100pf multicolored .95 .45

Spandau Fortress, 400th Anniv. A816

1994, June 16 **Litho.** ***Perf. 14***

1833 A816 80pf multicolored .80 .35

Herzogsagmuhle, Social Welfare Organization, Cent. — A817

1994, June 16 ***Perf. 13***

1834 A817 100pf blue, yel & blk .95 .45

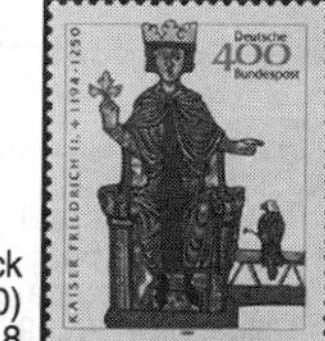

Emperor Frederick II (1194-1250) A818

1994, June 16 ***Perf. 13½x14***

1835 A818 400pf multicolored 3.25 2.25

Souvenir Sheet

Attempt to Assassinate Hitler, 50th Anniv. — A819

1994, July 20 **Litho.** ***Perf. 14***

1836 A819 100pf multicolored 1.10 1.10

Historic Sites Type of 1987

10pf, Wernigerode Town Hall. No. 20pf, Böttcherstrasse, Bremen. 1840, Berus Monument, Uberherrn. No. 1841, 47pf, Wilhelmshöhe Hillside Park, Kassel. 50pf, Kirchheim Castle. 80pf, St. Reinoldi Church, Dortmund. No. 1844, Goethe-Schiller Monument, No. 1845, Schwerin Castle, Weimar. No. 1846, Bellevue Castle, Berlin. No. 1847, EXPO 2000, Hanover. No. 1848, Regensburg Stone Bridge. No. 1849, Brühl's Terrace, Dresden. 300pf, Grimma Town Hall. No. 1850, St. Nikolai Cathedral, Greifswald. 400pf, Wartburg Castle, Eisenach. No. 1853, Town hall, Bremen. No. 1854, Cologne Cathedral. No. 1855, Holsten Gate, Lübeck. No. 1856, Heidelberg Castle. 550pf, Town Hall, Suhl-Heinrichs. 640pf, Speyer Cathedral. 720pf, Hildesheim Town Hall. 690pf, St. Michael's Church, Hamburg.

1994-2001 **Typo.** ***Perf. 14***

1838 A623 10pf multi .20 .20
1839 A623 20pf dk bl & brn org .20 .20
1840 A623 47pf green & gray .40 .20
1841 A623 47pf dk grn & gray .45 .25
1842 A623 50pf vio brn & beige .45 .20
1843 A623 80pf dull grn & sepia .75 .35
1844 A623 100pf blue & black .80 .30
a. Booklet pane of 10 8.00
Complete booklet, #1848a 8.00
1845 A623 100pf multi .80 .30
1846 A623 110pf dark gray & buff .90 .20
a. Booklet pane of 10 8.75
Complete booklet, #1849a 8.75
1847 A623 110pf org & bl .90 .35
a. Booklet pane of 10 8.75
Complete booklet, #1850a 8.75
1848 A623 110pf multi .90 .20
a. Booklet pane of 10 8.75
Booklet, #1850Bc 8.75
1849 A623 220pf grn & blk 1.75 .55
1850 A623 220pf multi 1.75 .35
1851 A623 300pf brn & ind 2.40 .35
1852 A623 400pf vio brn & beige 3.75 1.75
1853 A623 440pf multicolored 3.50 1.00
1854 A623 440pf blk & gray 4.00 2.00
1855 A623 510pf red brn & ind 4.00 1.25
1856 A623 510pf brn & bis brn 4.75 2.25
1857 A623 550pf multicolored 4.50 1.25
1858 A623 640pf rose brn & gray bl 5.00 1.40
1859 A623 690pf blk & grn 5.50 1.60
1860 A623 720pf dk gray & lil 6.25 3.25
Nos. 1838-1860 (23) 53.90 19.75

Issued: 550pf, 8/11/94; 640pf, 8/10/95; 690pf, 6/13/96; 47pf, 7/17/97; #1846, 220pf, #1853, 8/14/97: #1844, #1855, 8/28/97; #1847, 9/10/98; 10pf, #1848, 300pf, 9/28/00; #1845, 1/11/01. No. 1841, 80pf, 4/5/01. 720pf, 7/2/01. No. 1854, 8/9/01. 50pf, #1852, 9/5/01. 20pf, #1856, 11/8/01.

Johann Gottfried Herder (1744-1803), Theologian A820

1994, Aug. 11 **Photo.** ***Perf. 14***

1862 A820 80pf multicolored .80 .35

Paintings Type of 1993

Designs: 100pf, Maika, by Christian Schad. 200pf, Landscape, by Erich Heckel. 300pf, Couple Lying on Grass, by Gabriele Munter.

1994, Aug. 11 **Litho.** ***Perf. 14***

1863 A779 100pf multicolored .80 .50
1864 A779 200pf multicolored 1.60 1.10
1865 A779 300pf multicolored 2.40 1.60
Nos. 1863-1865 (3) 4.80 3.20

Ethnological Museum, Leipzig, 125th Anniv. — A821

1994, Sept. 8 **Litho.** ***Perf. 13x12½***

1866 A821 80pf multicolored .80 .35

Hermann von Helmholtz (1821-94), Scientist — A822

Litho. & Engr.

1994, Sept. 8 ***Perf. 13½x14***

1867 A822 100pf multicolored .95 .35

Willi Richter (1894-1972), Politician, Labor Leader — A823

1994, Sept. 8 **Litho.**

1868 A823 100pf multicolored .95 .50

Souvenir Sheet

For the Children — A824

1994, Sept. 8 ***Perf. 14***

1869 A824 100pf multicolored 1.10 1.00

Hans Sachs (1494-1576), Singer & Poet — A825

1994, Oct. 13 **Engr.** ***Perf. 13½x14***

1870 A825 100pf olive & maroon .95 .50

St. Wolfgang (924-94), Bishop of Regensburg A826

1994, Oct. 13 **Litho.** ***Perf. 14***

1871 A826 100pf multicolored .95 .50

Mail Delivery, Spreewald Region, c. 1900 — A827

1994, Oct. 13

1872 A827 100pf multicolored .95 .50

Stamp Day.

Quedlinburg, 1000th Anniv. — A828

Litho. & Engr.

1994, Nov. 9 ***Perf. 14***

1873 A828 80pf multicolored .80 .35

Opening of the Berlin Wall, 5th Anniv. A829

1994, Nov. 9 **Litho.** ***Perf. 13x12½***

1874 A829 100pf black, org & yel .95 .50

Natl. Assoc. for Preservation of German Graves Abroad, 75th Anniv. — A830

1994, Nov. 9 ***Perf. 14***

1875 A830 100pf black & red .95 .50

Theodore Fontane (1819-98), Poet — A831

1994, Nov. 9 ***Perf. 13½x14***

1876 A831 100pf multicolored .95 .50

Baron Friedrich von Steuben (1730-94) A832

1994, Nov. 9 ***Perf. 14***

1877 A832 100pf multicolored .95 .50

Paintings Type of 1992

Designs: 100pf, The Water Tower in Bremen, by Franz Radziwill. 200pf, Still Life with a Cat, by Georg Schrimpf. 300pf, An Estate in Dangast, by Karl Schmidt-Rottluff.

1995, Jan. 12 Litho. *Perf. 14*

1878 A753 100pf multicolored 1.00 .50
1879 A753 200pf multicolored 2.00 .90
1880 A753 300pf multicolored 3.00 1.40
Nos. 1878-1880 (3) 6.00 2.80

Province of Gera, 1000th Anniv. — A833

1995, Jan. 12 *Perf. 13½x13*

1881 A833 80pf multicolored .75 .40

Diet of Worms, 500th Anniv. A834

1995, Jan. 12 *Perf. 13x12½*

1882 A834 100pf multicolored .90 .55

Frederick William of Brandenburg, the Great Elector (1620-88) A835

1995, Feb. 9 Litho. *Perf. 14*

1883 A835 300pf multicolored 3.00 1.90

Conf. of General Convention on Climate, Berlin — A836

1995, Mar. 9 Litho. *Perf. 14*

1884 A836 100pf multicolored .90 .55

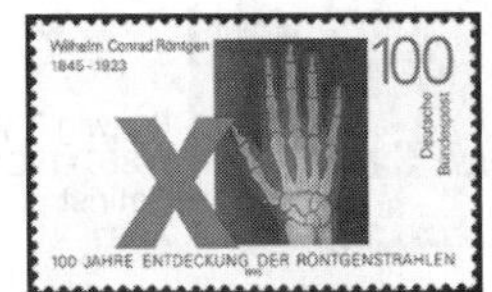

W.K. Roentgen (1845-1923) — A837

1995, Mar. 9

1885 A837 100pf multicolored .90 .55

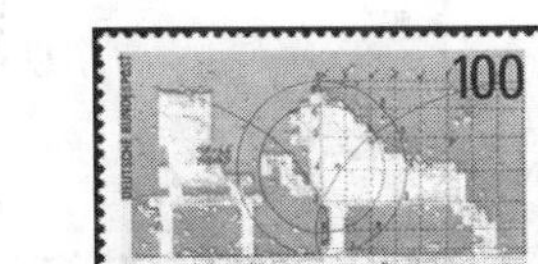

Carolo-Wilhelmina Technical University, Braunschweig, 250th Anniv. — A838

1995, Mar. 9

1886 A838 100pf multicolored .90 .55

Former State of Mecklenburg, 1000th Anniv. — A839

1995, Mar. 9

1887 A839 100pf multicolored .90 .55

City of Regensburg, 750th Anniv. — A840

1995, Apr. 6 Litho. *Perf. 14*

1888 A840 80pf multicolored .75 .35

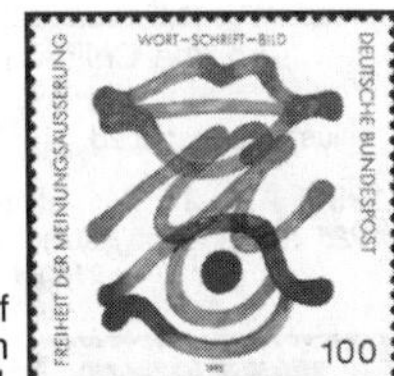

Freedom of Expression A841

1995, Apr. 6 Photo.

1889 A841 100pf multicolored .90 .55

Dietrich Bonhoeffer (1906-45), Protestant Theologian — A842

1995, Apr. 6

1890 A842 100pf multicolored .90 .55

Johann Conrad Schlaun (1695-1773), Architect A843

1995, Apr. 6 Litho. *Perf. 13*

1891 A843 200pf multicolored 1.90 1.10

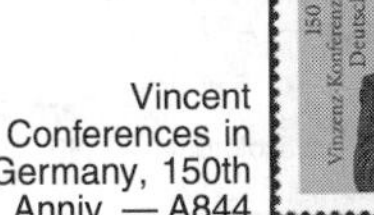

Vincent Conferences in Germany, 150th Anniv. — A844

1995, May 5 Litho. *Perf. 14*

1892 A844 100pf multicolored .90 .55

Schiller Society, Cent. — A845

1995, May 5 Photo.

1893 A845 100pf multicolored .90 .55

End of World War II, 50th Anniv. — A846

Designs: No. 1894, End of the war. 200pf, Moving towards United Europe.

No. 1896, Liberation of concentration camps. No. 1897: a, Destruction of buildings. b, Refugees.

1995, May 5 Litho. *Perf. 14*

1894 A846 100pf red & black 1.00 .85
1895 A846 200pf bl, gray, yel & blk 2.00 1.10

Souvenir Sheets

1896 A846 100pf multicolored 1.10 1.10
1897 Sheet of 2 2.25 2.25
a.-b. A846 100pf any single 1.10 1.10

Europa (#1894-1895).

Kiel Canal, Cent. — A847

1995, June 8 Litho. *Perf. 14*

1898 A847 80pf multicolored .75 .40

UN, 50th Anniv. — A848

1995, June 8

1899 A848 100pf gold, lil & gray .90 .55

Radio, Cent. A849

1995, June 8

1900 A849 100pf Marconi, wireless apparatus .90 .55

See Ireland Nos. 973-974, San Marino Nos. 1336-1337, Vatican City Nos. 978-979.

Carl Orff (1895-1982), Composer — A850

1995, July 6 Litho. *Perf. 13x13½*

1901 A850 100pf multicolored .90 .55

Henry the Lion, Duke of Bavaria (1129-95) A851

1995, July 6 *Perf. 14*

1902 A851 400pf multicolored 4.00 2.50

Kaiser Wilhelm Memorial Church, Berlin, Cent. — A852

1995, Aug. 10 Photo. *Perf. 14*

1903 A852 100pf multicolored .90 .55

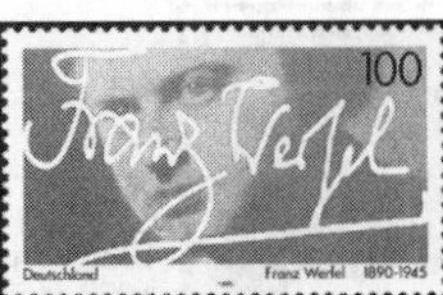

Franz Werfel (1890-1945), Author — A853

1995, Aug. 10 Litho.

1904 A853 100pf multicolored .90 .55

Franz Josef Strauss (1915-88), Politician A854

1995, Sept. 6 Photo. *Perf. 14x13½*

1905 A854 100pf multicolored .90 .55

Souvenir Sheet

German Film, Cent. — A855

Illustration reduced.

1995, Sept. 6 *Perf. 14*

1906 A855 Sheet of 3 3.75 3.50
a. 80pf Metropolis .75 .70
b. 100pf Little Superman .90 .80
c. 200pf The Sky Over Berlin 2.10 1.90

Kurt Schumacher (1895-1952), Politician A856

1995, Oct. 12 Litho. *Perf. 13*

1907 A856 100pf multicolored .90 .55

Souvenir Sheet

For the Children — A857

Illustration reduced.

1995, Oct. 12 *Perf. 14*

1908 A857 100pf multicolored 1.10 1.10

Leopold von Ranke (1795-1886), Historian A858

1995, Nov. 9 Litho. *Perf. 14*
1909 A858 80pf multicolored .75 .40

Paul Hindemith (1895-1963), Composer A859

1995, Nov. 9
1910 A859 100pf multicolored .90 .55

Nobel Prize Fund Established, Cent. — A860

1995, Nov. 9 Litho. & Engr.
1911 A860 100pf Nobel, last will .90 .55

See Sweden Nos. 2155-2158.

CARE, 50th Anniv. A861

1995, Nov. 9 Litho. *Perf. 13x12½*
1912 A861 100pf multicolored .90 .55

Victims of a Divided Germany, 1945-89 A862

1995, Nov. 9 *Perf. 14*
1913 A862 100pf Berlin Wall .90 .55

Borussia Dortmund, Soccer Champions — A863

1995, Dec. 6 Photo. *Perf. 14*
1914 A863 100pf multicolored .90 .60

Children's Missionary Work in Germany, Cent. — A864

1996, Jan. 11 Litho. *Perf. 14*
1915 A864 100pf multicolored .90 .55

Friedrich von Bodelschwingh (1877-1946), Protestant Theologian A865

1996, Jan. 11 *Perf. 13½*
1916 A865 100pf black & red .90 .55

Martin Luther (1483-1546), Theologian A866

1996, Feb. 8 Litho. *Perf. 14*
1917 A866 100pf multicolored .90 .55

Philipp Franz von Siebold (1796-1866), Physician and Diplomat — A867

1996, Feb. 17 *Perf. 13x12½*
1918 A867 100pf multicolored .90 .55

Cathedral Square, Halberstadt, 1000th Anniv. — A868

1996, Mar. 7 Litho. *Perf. 13*
1919 A868 80pf multicolored .75 .40

August Cardinal Graf von Galen (1878-1946) A869

1996, Mar. 7 *Perf. 13½*
1920 A869 100pf bl, gray & bis .90 .55

Giovanni Battista Tiepolo (1696-1770), Painter — A870

1996, Mar. 7 *Perf. 13*
1921 A870 200pf multicolored 1.90 1.00

20th Century German Paintings Type of 1993

Designs: 100pf, Sitting Female Nude, by Max Pechstein (1881-1955). 200pf, Abstract For Wilhelm Runge, by Georg Muche (1895-1987). 300pf, Still Life with Guitar, Book and Vase, by Helmut Kolle (1899-1931).

1996, Mar. 7 *Perf. 14*
1922 A779 100pf multicolored 1.00 .90
1923 A779 200pf multicolored 2.00 1.50
1924 A779 300pf multicolored 2.50 2.25
Nos. 1922-1924 (3) 5.50 4.65

Souvenir Sheet

For the Children — A871

Illustration reduced.

1996, Apr. 11 Litho. *Perf. 14*
1925 A871 100pf Racing messenger 1.10 1.00

Famous Women — A872

Europa: 80pf, Self-portrait, by Paula Modersohn-Becker (1876-1907). 100pf, Self-portrait, by Käthe Kollwitz (1867-1945).

1996, May 3
1926 A872 80pf multicolored .75 .35
1927 A872 100pf red & black .90 .55

Freising's Right to Hold Markets, 1000th Anniv. A873

1996, May 3
1928 A873 100pf multicolored .90 .55

Wolfgang Borchert (1921-47), Writer — A874

1996, May 3 *Perf. 13*
1929 A874 100pf multicolored .90 .55

Ruhr Festival, Recklinghausen, 50th Anniv. — A875

1996, May 3
1930 A875 100pf multicolored .90 .55

German Theater Assoc., 150th Anniv. — A876

1996, May 3 Photo. *Perf. 14*
1931 A876 200pf multicolored 1.90 1.00

Academy of Arts in Berlin, 300th Anniv. A877

1996, June 13 Litho. *Perf. 13*
1932 A877 100pf multicolored .90 .55

Gottfried Wilhelm Leibniz (1646-1716), Mathematician, Philosopher — A878

1996, June 13 *Perf. 14*
1933 A878 100pf multicolored .90 .55

City of Heidelberg, 800th Anniv. — A879

1996, July 18 Litho. *Perf. 14*
1934 A879 100pf multicolored .90 .55
Complete booklet, 10 #1934 10.00

UNICEF, 50th Anniv. A880

1996, July 18
1935 A880 100pf multicolored .90 .55

Ludwig Thoma (1867-1921), Satirist A881

1996, July 18 *Perf. 13x13½*
1936 A881 100pf multicolored .90 .55

Souvenir Sheet

German Natl. Parks A882

1996, July 18 *Perf. 14*
1937 Sheet of 3 6.50 6.00
a. A882 100pf Coastal 1.00 .90
b. A882 200pf Mudflat 1.75 1.60
c. A882 300pf Sea-inlet 2.75 2.50

Scenic Regions Type of 1993

"Gendarmenmarkt," central district of Berlin.

1996, Aug. 14 Litho. *Perf. 14*
1938 A791 100pf multicolored .90 .55

Assoc. of German Philatelists, 50th Anniv. — A883

1996, Aug. 14 Photo. *Perf. 14*
1939 A883 100pf multicolored .90 .55

Paul Lincke (1866-1946), Musician, Composer A884

1996, Aug. 14 Litho. *Perf. 13*
1940 A884 100pf multicolored .90 .55

UNESCO World Cultural Heritage A885

Design: Closed blast furnace, Völklingen.

1996, Aug. 14 *Perf. 13½*
1941 A885 100pf multicolored .90 .55

German Civil Code, Cent. — A886

1996, Aug. 14
1942 A886 300pf multicolored 2.75 1.50

Borussia Dortmund, Champion Soccer Club — A887

1996, Aug. 27
1943 A887 100pf multicolored .90 .55

Life Without Drugs A888

1996, Sept. 12 Photo. *Perf. 14*
1944 A888 100pf multicolored .90 .55

UNESCO World Cultural Heritage A889

Design: Old Town, Bamberg

1996, Sept. 12 Litho. *Perf. 14*
1945 A889 100pf multicolored .90 .55

Homeopathic Medicine, Bicent. — A890

Samuel Hahnemann (1755-1843), physician.

1996, Sept. 12 Litho. *Perf. 14*
1946 A890 400pf multicolored 3.75 3.50

Anton Bruckner (1824-96), Composer A891

1996, Oct. 9 Litho. *Perf. 13*
1947 A891 100pf multicolored .90 .55

Donaueschingen Music Festival, 75th Anniv. — A892

1996, Oct. 18 Litho. *Perf. 13½*
1948 A892 100pf multicolored .90 .55

Baron Ferdinand von Mueller (1825-96), Scientist — A893

Litho. & Engr.

1996, Oct. 18 *Perf. 14*
1949 A893 100pf multicolored .90 .55

See Australia No. 1566.

Carl Zuckmayer (1896-1977), Playwright A894

1996, Nov. 14 Litho. *Perf. 13*
1950 A894 100pf red, gray & blue .90 .55

Carlo Schmid (1896-1979), Politician, Scholar & Writer — A895

1996, Dec. 3 Photo. *Perf. 14*
1951 A895 100pf multicolored .90 .55

Franz Schubert (1797-1828), Composer A896

1997, Jan. 16 Litho. *Perf. 14*
1952 A896 100pf multicolored .90 .55

Sepp Herberger (1897-1977), Soccer Coach — A897

1997, Jan. 16
1953 A897 100pf multicolored .90 .55

Traffic Safety for Children A898

1997, Jan. 16
1954 A898 100pf multicolored .90 .55

See No. 1979.

Philipp Melanchthon (1497-1560), Protestant Reformer A899

1997, Feb. 4 Litho. *Perf. 14*
1955 A899 100pf multicolored .90 .55

Cologne Carnival, 175th Anniv. — A900

1997, Feb. 4
1956 A900 100pf multicolored .90 .55

Chancellor Ludwig Erhard (1897-1977) A901

1997, Feb. 4 Photo.
1957 A901 100pf multicolored .90 .55

Leipzig Fair, 500th Anniv. A902

1997, Mar. 6 *Perf. 13x12½*
1958 A902 100pf red, sil & blue .90 .55

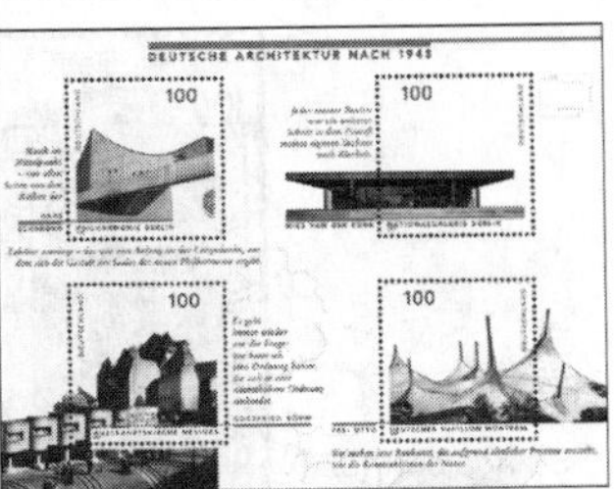

German Architecture after 1945 — A903

Building, architect: a, Berlin Philharmonic, by Hans Scharoun. b, New National Gallery, Berlin, by Ludwig Mies van der Rohe. c, St. Mary, Queen of Peace Church, Neviges, by Gottfried Böhm. d, German Pavilion, 1967 World's Fair, Montreal, by Frei Otto.

1997, Mar. 6 Litho. *Perf. 14*
1959 A903 Sheet of 4 4.50 4.50
a.-d. 100pf any single 1.00 1.00

City of Straubing, 1100th Anniv. — A904

1997, Mar. 10 *Perf. 13x12½*
1960 A904 100pf multicolored .90 .55

Heinrich von Stephan (1831-97) — A905

1997, Apr. 8 Litho. *Perf. 14*
1961 A905 100pf multicolored .90 .55

Augustusburg and Falkenlust Castles, UNESCO World Heritage Sites — A906

1997, Apr. 8
1962 A906 100pf multicolored .90 .55

Idar-Oberstein Gem & Jewelry Industry, 500th Anniv. — A907

1997, Apr. 8 *Perf. 13½*
1963 A907 300pf multicolored 2.75 1.00

St. Adalbert (956-997) — A908

1997, Apr. 23 Engr. *Perf. 14*
1964 A908 100pf deep violet .90 .55

See Poland #3337, Czech Republic #3012, Hungary #3569, Vatican City #1040.

Stories and Legends A909

Europa: 80pf, Fisherman and his Wife. 100pf, Rübezahl of Riesengebirge (Giant Mountains).

1997, May 5 Litho. *Perf. 14*
1965 A909 80pf multicolored .75 .40
1966 A909 100pf multicolored .90 .60

Sister Cities Movement, 50th Anniv. — A910

1997, May 5
1967 A910 100pf multicolored .90 .55

Souvenir Sheet

Society for Protection of German Forests, 50th Anniv. — A911

1997, May 5
1968 A911 Sheet of 2 3.25 3.25
a. 100pf multicolored 1.00 1.00
b. 200pf multicolored 2.00 2.00

Fr. Sebastian Kneipp (1821-97), Hydrotherapist A912

1997, June 9 *Perf. 13*
1969 A912 100pf multicolored .90 .55

Marshall Plan, 50th Anniv. A913

1997, June 9 *Perf. 13*
1970 A913 100pf multicolored .90 .55

"Documenta" Intl. Exhibition of Modern Art, Kassel — A914

Designs: a, Composition, by Fritz Winter, 1956. b, Mouth No. 15, by Tom Wesselmann, 1968. c, Quathlamba, by Frank Stella, 1964. d, Video sculpture, Beuys/Bois, by Nam June Paik.

1997, June 20 Litho. *Perf. 14*
1971 A914 100pf Sheet of 4, #a.-d. 4.25 4.25

Müngsten Bridge, Cent. — A915

1997, June 20 Litho. *Perf. 13½*
1972 A915 100pf multicolored .90 .55

Souvenir Sheet

For the Children — A916

Illustration reduced.

1997, July 17 Photo. *Perf. 13½*
1973 A916 100pf multicolored 1.10 1.10

Scenic Regions Type of 1993

#1974, Bavarian Forest. #1975, Lüneburg Heath. #1976, North German Moorland.

1997, Aug. 28 Litho. *Perf. 14*
1974 A791 110pf multicolored 1.00 .60
1975 A791 110pf multicolored 1.00 .60
1976 A791 110pf multicolored 1.00 .60
Nos. 1974-1976 (3) 3.00 1.80

Centenary of Rudolf Diesel's Engine A917

1997, Aug. 28 *Perf. 13*
1977 A917 300pf blue & gray 2.75 1.00

Cultivation of Potatoes in Germany, 350th Anniv. — A918

1997, Sept. 17 Litho. *Perf. 13*
1978 A918 300pf multicolored 2.75 1.00

Traffic Safety for Children Type

1997, Oct. 9 Litho. *Perf. 14*
1979 A898 10pf like #1954 .20 .20

Felix Mendelssohn-Bartholdy (1809-47), Composer — A919

1997, Oct. 9 *Perf. 13x13½*
1980 A919 110pf multicolored 1.00 .60

FC Bayern Munchen, 1997 German Soccer Champions — A920

1997, Oct. 16 Photo. *Perf. 14*
1981 A920 110pf multicolored 1.00 .60

Third Saar-Lorraine-Luxembourg Summit — A921

1997, Oct. 16 Litho.
1982 A921 110pf multicolored 1.00 .60

See Luxembourg #972, France #2613.

Charitable Assoc. of the German Catholic Church, Cent. — A922

1997, Nov. 6 Photo. *Perf. 14*
1983 A922 110pf multicolored 1.00 .60

Heinrich Heine (1797-1856), Poet — A923

1997, Nov. 6 Litho. *Perf. 13*
1984 A923 110pf multicolored *1.00 .60*

No. 1984 was sold in sheets of 10. It was withdrawn from sale 11/18/97, because runes associated with Nazi Germany were printed on the decorative selvage of the sheet. It was again placed on sale in sheets with runes removed.

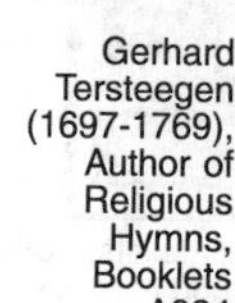

Gerhard Tersteegen (1697-1769), Author of Religious Hymns, Booklets A924

1997, Nov. 6 *Perf. 14*
1985 A924 110pf multicolored 1.00 .60

Thomas Dehler (1897-1967), Politician — A925

1997, Nov. 6
1986 A925 110pf multicolored 1.00 .60

Cistercian Monastery Maulbronn, UNESCO World Heritage Site — A926

1998, Jan. 22 Litho. *Perf. 14*
1987 A926 100pf multicolored .90 .50

Glienicke Bridge, Berlin — A927

1998, Jan. 22
1988 A927 110pf multicolored 1.00 .60

City of Nördlingen, 1100th Anniv. — A928

1998, Jan. 22
1989 A928 110pf multicolored 1.00 .60
a. Booklet pane of 10 9.50
Complete booklet, #1989a + 20 self-adhesive labels 9.50

Bertolt Brecht (1898-1956), Playwright A929

1998, Feb. 5
1990 A929 110pf multicolored 1.00 .60

Max Planck Society for Advancement of Science, 50th Anniv. — A930

1998, Feb. 5
1991 A930 110pf multicolored 1.00 .60

Town of Bad Frankenhausen, 1000th Anniv. — A931

1998, Mar. 12 Litho. *Perf. 13*
1992 A931 110pf multicolored 1.00 .60

Peace of Westphalia, End of Thirty Years' War, 350th Anniv. — A932

1998, Mar. 12 *Perf. 14*
1993 A932 110pf black & red 1.00 .60

German State Parliament Buildings — A933

Designs: No. 1994, Baden-Württemberg. No. 1995, Bavaria. No. 1996, Chamber of Deputies, Berlin. No. 1997, Brandenburg.

1998, Mar. 12
1994 A933 110pf multicolored 1.00 .60
1995 A933 110pf multicolored 1.00 .60
1996 A933 110pf multicolored 1.00 .60
1997 A933 110pf multicolored 1.00 .60
Nos. 1994-1997 (4) 4.00 2.40

See Nos 2027, 2029-2031, 2074-2076.

Hildegard von Bingen (1098-1179), Christian Mystic — A934

1998, Apr. 16
1998 A934 100pf multicolored .90 .55

Cistercian Abbey of St. Marienstern, Panschwitz-Kuckau, 750th Anniv. — A935

1998, Apr. 16 *Perf. 13x12½*
1999 A935 110pf multicolored 1.00 .60

Souvenir Sheet

For the Children — A936

Illustration reduced.

1998, Apr. 16 *Perf. 14*
2000 A936 110pf multicolored 1.00 1.00

Bayreuth Opera, 250th Anniv. — A937

Illustration reduced.

1998, Apr. 16 *Perf. 13½*
2001 A937 300pf multicolored 3.00 1.00

Ernst Jünger (1895-1998), Writer — A938

1998, Apr. 22 *Perf. 14*
2002 A938 110pf multicolored 1.00 .60

German Rural Women's Assoc. A939

1998, May 7 Litho. *Perf. 13*
2003 A939 110pf multicolored 1.00 .60

Europa and German Reunification Day — A940

1998, May 7 *Perf. 14½x14*
2004 A940 110pf multicolored 1.00 .60

Souvenir Sheet

German Constitution — A941

Designs: a, Parliamentary Council, Bonn, 1948, convening to draw up constitution. b, Natl. Assembly, St. Paul's Church, Frankfurt, 1848, electing pan-German constitutional Parliament.

1998, May 7 *Perf. 14*
2005 A941 Sheet of 2 3.25 3.25
a. 110pf multicolored 1.00 1.00
b. 220pf multicolored 2.00 2.00

Congress of German Catholics, 150th Anniv. — A942

1998, June 10 Litho. *Perf. 13x13½*
2006 A942 110pf multicolored 1.00 .60

Deutsche Mark, 50th Anniv. — A943

1998, June 19 *Perf. 13*
2007 A943 110pf multicolored 1.00 .60

German Cultivation of Hops — A944

1998, July 16 Litho. *Perf. 13*
2008 A944 110pf multicolored 1.00 .60

Founding of the European Central Bank, Frankfurt am Main — A945

1998, July 16 Photo. *Perf. 14*
2009 A945 110pf multicolored 1.00 .60

Souvenir Sheet

Saxon Switzerland Natl. Park — A945a

Illustration reduced.

1998, July 16 Litho. *Perf. 14*
2009A A945a Sheet of 2 3.25 3.25
b. 110pf multicolored 1.00 1.00
c. 220pf multicolored 2.00 2.00

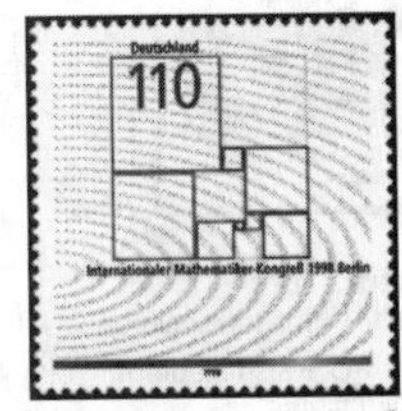

1998 Intl. Congress of Mathematicians, Berlin — A946

1998, Aug. 20 Photo. *Perf. 14x13½*
2010 A946 110pf multicolored 1.00 .60

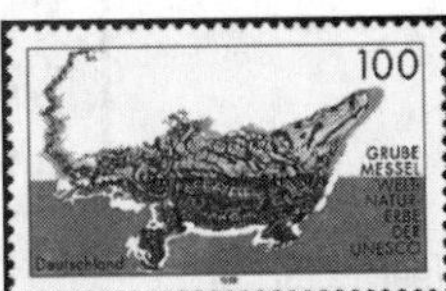

Grube Messel Fossil Beds A947

Würzburg Palace, Germany — A948

UNESCO World Heritage Sites: No. 2013, Puning Temple, Chengde, People's Republic of China.

1998, Aug. 20 Litho. *Perf. 13x12½*
2011 A947 100pf multicolored .90 .55

Perf. 13½x14
2012 A948 110pf multicolored 1.00 .60
2013 A948 110pf multicolored 1.00 .60

See China People's Republic #2887-2888.

Souvenir Sheet

20th Cent. German Design — A949

Designs: a, Glassware, by Peter Behrens, 1910. b, Teapot, by Marianne Brandt, 1924. c, Desk lamp, by Wilhelm Wagenfeld, 1924. d, "Wassily" chair, by Marcel Breuer, 1926.

1998, Aug. 20 *Perf. 14*
2014 Sheet of 4 4.50 4.50
a.-d. A949 110pf any single 1.10 1.10

See No. 2051.

Manfred Hausmann (1898-1986), Author — A950

1998, Sept. 10 Litho. *Perf. 14*
2015 A950 110pf multicolored 1.00 .60

A951

1998, Sept. 10
2016 A951 110pf multicolored 1.00 .60

Team 1 FC Kaiserslautern, 1998 German soccer champions.

Prevent Child Abuse — A952

1998, Sept. 10
2017 A952 110pf black & red 1.00 .60

Francke Charitable Institutions, Halle, 300th Anniv. — A953

1998, Sept. 10 ***Perf. 13***
2018 A953 110pf Building 1.00 .60

Mail Boat, "Hiorten" A954

1998, Oct. 8 Litho. ***Perf. 14***
2019 A954 110pf multicolored 1.00 .60

Stamp Day.

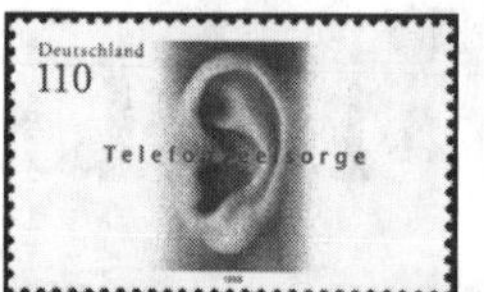

Telephone Help Lines for People in Distress — A955

1998, Oct. 8 ***Perf. 13x12½***
2020 A955 110pf multicolored 1.00 .60

Günther Ramin (1898-1956), Organist, Choir Leader — A956

1998, Oct. 8 Photo. ***Perf. 14x14½***
2021 A956 300pf multicolored 3.00 1.00

Saxony State Orchestra, Dresden, 450th Anniv. — A957

1998, Nov. 12 Litho. ***Perf. 14***
2022 A957 300pf multicolored 3.00 1.00

Universal Delcaration of Human Rights, 50th Anniv. — A958

1998, Nov. 12 ***Perf. 13x12½***
2023 A958 110pf multicolored 1.00 .60

See No. B848.

Weimar, 1999 European City of Culture, 1100th Anniv. — A959

1999, Jan. 14 Litho. ***Perf. 14***
2024 A959 100pf multicolored .90 .60
a. Booklet pane of 10 9.50
Complete booklet, #2024a + 20 labels 9.50

The self-adhesive labels are part of the booklet cover.

International Year of the Elderly A960

1999, Jan. 14 ***Perf. 13***
2025 A960 110pf multicolored 1.00 .60

Katharina von Bora (1499-1552), Wife of Martin Luther, from Painting by Lucas Cranach A961

1999, Jan. 14 ***Perf. 14***
2026 A961 110pf multicolored 1.00 .60

State Parliaments Type of 1998

The Hessian Parliament.

1999, Jan. 14
2027 A933 110pf multicolored 1.00 .60

Erich Kästner (1899-1974), Writer — A963

1999, Feb. 18 Litho. ***Perf. 13***
2028 A963 300pf multicolored 3.00 1.00

State Parliaments Type of 1998

Buildings: No. 2029, Hamburg. No. 2030, Mecklenburg-Western Pomerania. No. 2031, Bremen City Parliament.

1999 Litho. ***Perf. 14***
2029 A933 110pf multicolored 1.00 .60
2030 A933 110pf multicolored 1.00 .60
2031 A933 110pf multicolored 1.00 .60
Nos. 2029-2031 (3) 3.00 1.80

Issued: #2029-2030, 3/11; #2031, 4/27.

NATO, 50th Anniv. A963a

1999, Mar. 11 **Photo.**
2032 A963a 110pf multicolored 1.00 .60

Fraunhofer Society, 50th Anniv. — A964

1999, Mar. 11 Litho. ***Perf. 13***
2033 A964 110pf multicolored 1.00 .60

Expo 2000, Hanover A965

1999, Apr. 27
2034 A965 110pf multicolored 1.00 .60

See No. 2083.

German Automobile Club, Cent. — A966

1999, Apr. 27 **Photo.**
2035 A966 110pf multicolored 1.00 .60

German Cancer Relief Organization, 25th Anniv. — A967

1999, Apr. 27 Litho. ***Perf. 13***
2036 A967 110pf multicolored 1.00 .60

Knights of St. John of Jerusalem and Knights of Malta, 900th Anniv. — A968

1999, May 4
2037 A968 110pf multicolored 1.00 .60

Berlin Airlift, 1948-49 A969

1999, May 4 Photo. ***Perf. 14***
2038 A969 110pf multicolored 1.00 .60

Council of Europe, 50th Anniv. — A970

1999, May 4 Litho. ***Perf. 13***
2039 A970 110pf multicolored 1.00 .60

Souvenir Sheet

Berchtesgaden Natl. Park — A971

1999, May 4 ***Perf. 14***
2040 A971 110pf multicolored 1.00 .60

Europa.

Souvenir Sheet

Basic Law, 50th Anniv. — A972

Illustration reduced.

1999, May 21 Litho. ***Perf. 14***
2041 A972 110pf multicolored 1.00 .60

Souvenir Sheet

Federal Republic of Germany, 50th Anniv. — A973

Scenes from 1949, 1999: a, Leaders gathering, session of Parliament. b, Child carrying wood, child picking flower. c, Building "The Wall," people walking where "The Wall" has been removed. d, Soldiers, government assembly.

1999, May 21
2042 Sheet of 4 4.25 4.25
a.-d. A973 110pf any single 1.00 .60

SOS Children's Village, 50th Anniv. — A974

1999, June 10 Litho. ***Perf. 13¾x14***
2043 A974 110pf multicolored 1.00 .60

Paderborn Bishopric, 1200th Anniv. — A975

1999, June 10 ***Perf. 14***
2044 A975 110pf multicolored 1.00 .60

Johann Strauss, the Younger (1825-99) A976

1999, June 10 Photo. ***Perf. 13¾***
2045 A976 300pf multicolored 3.00 1.00

Dominikus-Ringeisen Institution, Ursberg, 115th Anniv. — A977

1999, July 15 **Litho.**
2046 A977 110pf multicolored 1.00 .60

Pres. Gustav Heinemann (1899-1976) A978

1999, July 15
2047 A978 110pf multicolored 1.00 .60

Cultural Foundation of the Federal States — A979

Sculpture: 110pf, Old Woman Smiling, by Ernst Barlach (1870-1938). 220pf, Bust of a Thinker, by Wilhelm Lehmbruck (1881-1919).

1999, July 15 Photo. ***Perf. 14***
2048 A979 110pf multicolored 1.00 .60
2049 A979 220pf multicolored 2.00 1.25

First Peace Conference in The Hague, Cent. — A980

1999, July 15 Litho. ***Perf. 13¼x13***
2050 A980 300pf multicolored 3.00 1.50

20th Cent. German Design Type of 1998

Souvenir Sheet

Designs: a, HF1 Television set, by Herbert Hirche, 1958. b, Knife, fork, spoon and teaspoon, by Peter Raacke, 1959. c, Pearl bottle, by Günter Kupetz, 1969. d, "Transrapid," Maglev train, by Alexander Neumeister, 1982.

1999, Aug. 12 Litho. ***Perf. 14***
Souvenir Sheet
2051 Sheet of 4 4.25 4.25
a.-d. A949 110pf any single 1.00 .60

Johann Wolfgang von Goethe (1749-1832), Poet — A981

1999, Aug. 12 ***Perf. 13¾***
2052 A981 110pf multicolored 1.00 .60

Souvenir Sheet

For the Children — A982

Illustration reduced.

1999, Aug. 12 ***Perf. 13¼***
2053 A982 110pf multicolored 1.00 .60

Bayern München, 1999 German Soccer Champions — A983

1999, Sept. 16 Litho. ***Perf. 14***
2054 A983 110pf multicolored 1.00 .60

Federal Association of German Book Traders Peace Prize, 50th Anniv. — A984

1999, Sept. 16 Photo. ***Perf. 13¾***
2055 A984 110pf multicolored 1.00 .60

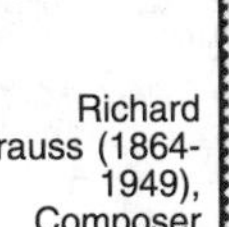

Richard Strauss (1864-1949), Composer A985

1999, Sept. 16 Litho. ***Perf. 13¼***
2056 A985 300pf multicolored 3.00 1.00

Göltzsch Valley Bridge A986

1999, Oct. 14 Litho. ***Perf. 14***
2057 A986 110pf multicolored 1.00 .60

German Federation of Trade Unions, 50th Anniv. — A987

1999, Oct. 14
2058 A987 110pf red & black 1.00 .60

Endangered Species A988

1999, Nov. 4 Litho. ***Perf. 13¾***
2059 A988 100pf Large horse-shoe bat .90 .55

EXPO 2000, Hanover A989

2000, Jan. 13 Litho. ***Perf. 14x14¼***
2060 A989 100pf multi .90 .55

See No. 2094.

Holy Year 2000 — A990

2000, Jan. 13 ***Perf. 13¾***
2061 A990 110pf multi 1.00 .60

Completion of Aachen Cathedral, 1200th Anniv. — A991

2000, Jan. 13
2062 A991 110pf Charlemagne 1.00 .60

German Soccer Assoc., Cent. — A992

2000, Jan. 13 **Photo.**
2063 A992 110pf multi 1.00 .60

Value is for copy with surrounding selvage.

Herbert Wehner (1906-90), Politician A993

2000, Jan. 13
2064 A993 110pf multi 1.00 .60

Albert Schweitzer (1875-1965), Humanitarian A994

2000, Jan. 13 Litho. ***Perf. 14x13¾***
2065 A994 110pf multi 1.00 .60

Prevention of Violence Against Women — A995

2000, Jan. 13 ***Perf. 14***
2066 A995 110pf multi 1.00 .60

Berlin Intl. Film Festival, 50th Anniv. A996

2000, Feb. 17 Litho. ***Perf. 14***
2067 A996 100pf multi .90 .55

Johannes Gutenberg (c. 1400-1468) A997

2000, Feb. 17 ***Perf. 13¾***
2068 A997 110pf red & black 1.00 .60

Friedrich Ebert (1871-1925), President of German Reich — A998

2000, Feb. 17 **Photo.**
2069 A998 110pf multi 1.00 .60

Düsseldorf Carnival, 175th Anniv. — A999

2000, Feb. 17 Litho. *Perf. 13x13½*

2070 A999 110pf multi 1.00 .60

Kurt Weill (1900-50), Composer — A1000

2000, Feb. 17 *Perf. 14*

2071 A1000 300pf multi 3.00 1.00

Scenic Regions Type of 1993

Design: #2072, Passau. #2073, Saar River bend, Mettlach.

2000 Litho. *Perf. 13¾x14*

2072 A791 110pf multi 1.00 .60
2073 A791 110pf multi 1.00 .60

Issued: No. 2072, 3/16.

State Parliament Building Type

#2074, Lower Saxony. #2075, North Rhine-Westphalia. #2076, Rhineland-Palatinate. #2077, Saarland.

2000 Litho. *Perf. 13¾x14*

2074 A933 110pf multi 1.00 .60
2075 A933 110pf multi 1.00 .60
2076 A933 110pf multi 1.00 .60

Perf. 14

2077 A933 110pf multi 1.00 .60
Nos. 2074-2077 (4) 4.00 2.40

Issued: #2074, 3/16; #2075, 4/13; #2076, 8/14; #2077, 11/9.

Pinwheel A1001

2000, Mar. 16 Litho. *Perf. 13¾*

2078 A1001 110pf multi 1.00 .60

Souvenir Sheet

Hainich National Park — A1002

Illustration reduced.

2000, Mar. 16 *Perf. 13¼*

2079 A1002 110pf multi 1.00 .60

Blue Wonder Bridge, Dresden A1003

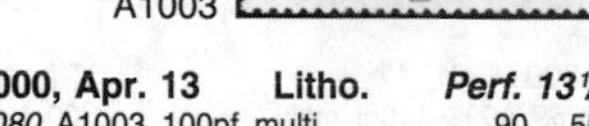

2000, Apr. 13 Litho. *Perf. 13¼*

2080 A1003 100pf multi .90 .55

Cultural Foundation Type of 1999

Designs: 110pf, The Expulsion from Paradise, sculpture by Leonhard Kern. 220pf, Silver table fountain, 1652-53, by Melchior Gelb.

2000, Apr. 13 *Perf. 14x14¼*

2081 A979 110pf multi 1.00 .60
2082 A979 220pf multi 2.00 1.50

Expo 2000 Type of 1999

2000, Apr. 13 *Die Cut Perf. 11*

Booklet Stamp
Self-Adhesive

2083 A965 110pf multi 1.00 .60
a. Booklet pane of 10 10.00

No. 2083a is a complete booklet.

Griefswald, 750th Anniv. — A1004

Litho. & Engr.

2000, Apr. 13 *Perf. 14x14¼*

2084 A1004 110pf multi 1.00 .60

Nikolaus Ludwig von Zinzendorf (1700-60), Religious Leader A1005

2000, May 12 Photo. *Perf. 13¾*

2085 A1005 110pf multi 1.00 .60

Europa, 2000

Common Design Type

2000, May 12 Litho. *Perf. 13¾*

2086 CD17 110pf multi 1.00 .60

Booklet Stamp
Self-Adhesive
Die Cut Perf. 10¾

2087 CD17 110pf multi 1.00 .60
a. Complete booklet of 10 10.00

Einkommende Zeitungen, First Daily Newspaper, 350th Anniv. — A1006

2000, June 8 Litho. *Perf. 13¾x14*

2088 A1006 110pf multi 1.00 .60

Chambers of Handicrafts in Germany, Cent. — A1007

2000, June 8 *Perf. 14*

2089 A1007 300pf gray & org 3.00 1.00

Zugspitze Weather Station, Cent. — A1008

2000, July 13 Litho. *Perf. 13¾x14*

2090 A1008 100pf multi .90 .55

Federal Disaster Relief Organization, 50th Anniv. — A1009

2000, July 13 *Perf. 14*

2091 A1009 110pf multi 1.00 .60

Johann Sebastian Bach (1685-1750) A1010

2000, July 13 *Perf. 13¼*

2092 A1010 110pf multi 1.00 .60

First Zeppelin Flight, Cent. — A1011

2000, July 13

2093 A1011 110pf multi 1.00 .60

Expo 2000 Type of 2000

110pf, Expo emblem, Earth, fingerprint.

2000, Aug. 14 Litho. *Perf. 14x14¼*

2094 A989 110pf multi 1.00 .60

Friedrich Nietzsche (1844-1900), Philosopher A1012

2000, Aug. 14 *Perf. 13¼*

2095 A1012 110pf multi 1.00 .60

Ernst Wiechert (1887-1950), Writer A1013

2000, Aug. 14 *Perf. 13¾*

2096 A1013 110pf multi 1.00 .60

"For You" — A1014

2000, Sept. 14 Litho. *Perf. 13x13¼*

2097 A1014 100pf multi .90 .55

Souvenir Sheet

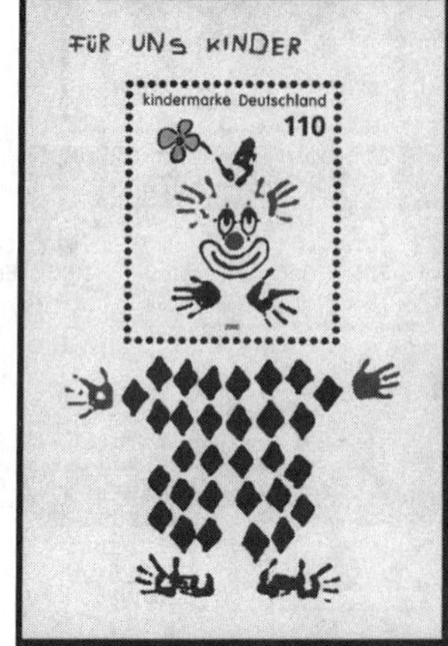

For the Children — A1015

2000, Sept. 14 *Perf. 13¾x14*

2098 A1015 110pf multi 1.00 .60

Adolph Kolping (1813-65) A1016

2000, Sept. 14 *Perf. 13¼*

2099 A1016 110pf multi 1.00 .60

Kolping Society, 150th anniv.

Federal Court of Justice, 50th Anniv. A1017

Litho. & Engr.

2000, Sept. 14 *Perf. 14x14¼*

2100 A1017 110pf multi 1.00 .60

Bernhard Nocht Institute for Tropical Medicine, Cent. — A1018

2000, Sept. 14 Litho. *Perf. 13¾x14*

2101 A1018 300pf multi 2.75 1.40

Reunification of Germany, 10th Anniv. A1019

2000, Sept. 28 ***Perf. 13¼***
2102 A1019 110pf multi 1.00 .60

Stamp Day — A1020

2000, Oct. 12 Litho. ***Perf. 13x13¼***
2103 A1020 110pf multi 1.00 .60

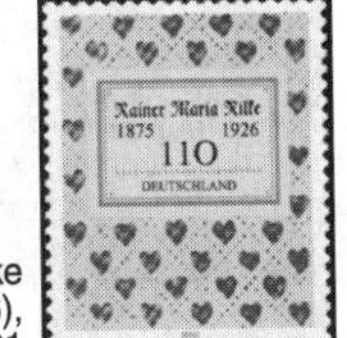

Rainer Maria Rilke (1875-1926), Poet — A1021

2000, Nov. 9 Litho. ***Perf. 13¼x13½***
2104 A1021 110pf multi 1.00 .60

Arnold Bode (1900-77), Artist — A1022

2000, Nov. 9 ***Perf. 13¼***
2105 A1022 110pf red & black 1.00 .60

Leonhart Fuchs (1501-66), Botanist A1023

2001, Jan. 11 Litho. ***Perf. 13¾***
2106 A1023 100pf multi .90 .55

Kingdom of Prussia, 300th Anniv. A1024

2001, Jan. 11 ***Perf. 14***
2107 A1024 110pf multi 1.00 .60

Association of Disabled War Veterans, 50th Anniv. — A1025

2001, Jan. 11 Photo. ***Perf. 14***
2108 A1025 110pf multi 1.00 .60

Youth Helpline Federation — A1026

2001, Jan. 11 Litho. ***Perf. 13¾x14***
2109 A1026 110pf multi 1.00 .60

Albert Lortzing (1801-51), Opera Composer A1027

2001, Jan. 11 ***Perf. 13¾***
2110 A1027 110pf multi 1.00 .60

Martin Bucer (1491-1551), Theologian A1028

2001, Feb. 8 Litho. ***Perf. 13¾***
2111 A1028 110pf multi 1.00 .60

Johann Heinrich Voss (1751-1826), Translator of Greek Classics A1029

2001, Feb. 8 ***Perf. 13¼***
2112 A1029 300pf multi 2.75 1.40

State Parliament Type of 1998

Design: No. 2113, Saxony. No. 2114, Saxony-Anhalt. No. 2115, Schleswig-Holstein. No. 2116, Thuringia.

2001 Litho. ***Perf. 13¾x14***
2113 A933 110pf multi 1.00 .50
2114 A933 110pf multi 1.00 .50
2115 A933 110pf multi .95 .50
2116 A933 110pf multi 1.00 .50
Nos. 2113-2116 (4) 3.95 2.00

Issued: No. 2113, 3/8/01. No. 2114, 5/10. No. 2115, 7/12. No. 2116, 9/5.

Erich Ollenhauer (1901-63), Politician — A1030

2001, Mar. 8 Litho. ***Perf. 14***
2117 A1030 110pf multi 1.00 .50

Karl Arnold (1901-58), Politician A1031

2001, Mar. 8 ***Perf. 13¼***
2118 A1031 110pf multi 1.00 .50

Federal Border Police, 50th Anniv. A1032

2001, Mar. 8 Litho. ***Perf. 13¾***
2119 A1032 110pf multi 1.00 .50

Rendsburg Railway Bridge — A1033

2001, Apr. 5 Litho. ***Perf. 14***
2120 A1033 100pf multi .95 .50

Folk Music — A1034

2001, Apr. 5 ***Perf. 13x13½***
2121 A1034 110pf multi 1.00 .50

"Post!" A1035

2001, Apr. 5 Photo. ***Perf. 14***
2122 A1035 110pf multi 1.00 .50

Goethe Institute, 50th Anniv. — A1036

2001, Apr. 5 Litho.
2123 A1036 300pf multi 2.75 1.40

Endangered Species — A1037

Designs: No. 2124, Mountain gorilla. No. 2125, Indian rhinoceros.

2001, May 10 Litho. ***Perf. 14***
2124 A1037 110pf multi 1.00 .50
2125 A1037 110pf multi 1.00 .50

See Nos. 2132-2133.

Europa A1038

2001, May 10 ***Perf. 13¾***
2126 A1038 110pf multi 1.00 .50

Werner Egk (1901-83), Composer — A1039

2001, May 10 ***Perf. 14***
2127 A1039 110pf multi 1.00 .50

St. Catherine's Monastery, 750th Anniv., Oceanographic Museum, 50th Anniv. — A1040

2001, June 13 Litho. ***Perf. 13x13¼***
2128 A1040 110pf multi 1.00 .50

Catholic Court Church, Dresden, 250th Anniv. A1041

2001, June 13 ***Perf. 13¼***
2129 A1041 110pf multi 1.00 .50

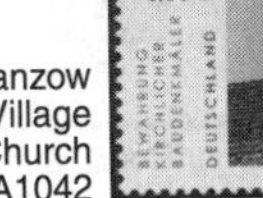

Canzow Village Church A1042

2001, July 12 Photo. ***Perf. 14x14¼***
2130 A1042 110pf multi .95 .50

Conservation of sacred monuments.

Souvenir Sheet

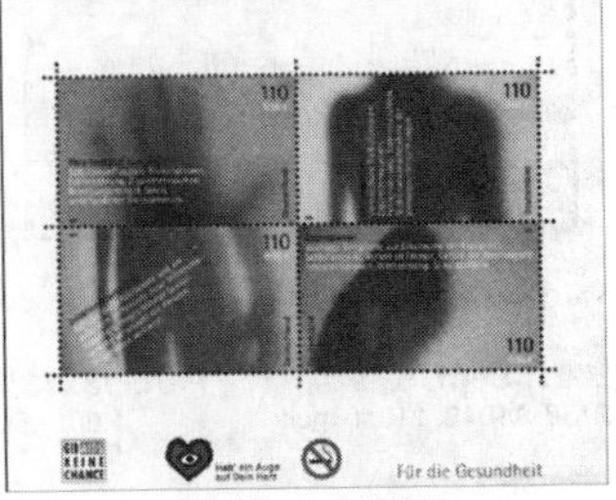

Health — A1043

No. 2131: a, Hand (circulatory diseases). b, Chest (cancer). c, Abdomen (infectious diseases). d, Head (depression).

2001, July 12 Litho. *Perf. 13x13½*
2131 A1043 Sheet of 4 4.00 2.00
a.-d. 110pf Any single 1.00 .50

Endangered Species Type of 2001
Die Cut Perf. 11¼x11
2001, July 12 Litho.
Booklet Stamps
Self-Adhesive

2132 A1037 110pf Like #2124 1.00 .50
2133 A1037 110pf Like #2125 1.00 .50
a. Booklet, 5 each #2132-2133 10.00

Furth Dragon Lancing Festival A1044

2001, Aug. 9 Litho. *Perf. 13¼*
2134 A1044 100pf multi .95 .45

Himmelsberg Lime Tree Natural Monument — A1045

2001 *Perf. 13¾x14*
2135 A1045 110pf multi 1.00 .50
Die Cut Perf. 9¾x10½
2135A A1045 110pf multi 1.00 .50
b. Booklet of 20 20.00

Issued: No. 2135, 8/9; No. 2135A, 9/13.

Lifelong Learning A1046

2001, Aug. 9 *Perf. 14*
2136 A1046 110pf multi 1.00 .50

Federal Constitutional Court, 50th Anniv. — A1047

2001, Sept. 5
2137 A1047 110pf multi 1.00 .50

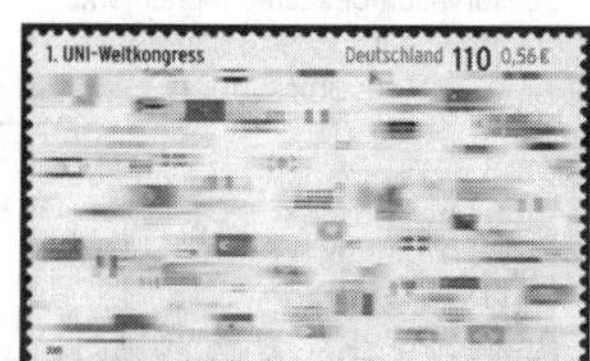

First World Congress of Union Network International — A1048

2001, Sept. 5 *Perf. 13x13½*
2138 A1048 110pf multi 1.00 .50

Opening of Jewish Museum, Berlin — A1049

2001, Sept. 5 Photo. *Perf. 13¾*
2139 A1049 110pf multi 1.00 .50

Souvenir Sheet

For Children — A1050

2001, Sept. 5 Litho. *Perf. 13¾x14*
2140 A1050 110pf multi 1.00 .50

"For You" — A1051

2001, Oct. 11 *Perf. 13x13¼*
2141 A1051 110pf multi 1.00 .50

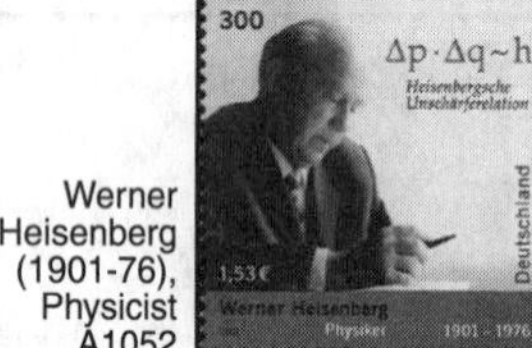

Werner Heisenberg (1901-76), Physicist A1052

2001, Nov. 8 Litho. *Perf. 13¾*
2142 A1052 300pf multi 2.75 1.40

Souvenir Sheet

German Antarctic Expeditions, Cent. — A1053

Expedition vessels: a, Gauss. b, Polarstern.

2001, Nov. 8 *Perf. 13¾x14*
2143 A1053 Sheet of 2, #a-b 3.00 1.50
a. 110pf multi 1.00 .50
b. 220pf multi 2.00 1.00

Introduction of the Euro, Jan. 1 — A1054

2002, Jan. 10 Litho. *Perf. 13¾*
2144 A1054 56c multi 1.00 .50

Coil Stamp
Self-Adhesive
2144A A1054 56c multi 1.00 .50

Hans von Dohnanyi (1902-45), Documenter of Nazi Atrocities A1055

2002, Jan. 10 Photo.
2145 A1055 56c multi 1.00 .50
2145A A1055 56c multi — —

No. 2145A has "2002" in upper right corner and colored face and name.

Bautzen, 1000th Anniv. A1056

2002, Jan. 10 Litho.
2146 A1056 56c multi 1.00 .50
Die Cut Perf. 11
Litho.
Booklet Stamp
Self-Adhesive
2146A A1056 56c multi 1.00 .50
b. Booklet of 10 10.00

More Tolerance — A1057

2002, Jan. 10 *Perf. 13¾x14*
2147 A1057 56c multi 1.00 .50

Adolph Freiherr Knigge (1762-96), Writer — A1058

2002, Feb. 7 Litho. *Perf. 13¾*
2148 A1058 56c multi 1.00 .50

Berlin Subway System, Cent. — A1059

2002, Feb. 7 *Perf. 13¼*
2149 A1059 56c multi 1.00 .50

Johann Christoph Schuster's Mechanical Calculator — A1060

2002, Mar. 7 Litho. *Perf. 14*
2150 A1060 56c multi 1.00 .50

Cultural Foundation of the Federal States.

Deggendorf, 1000th Anniv. — A1061

2002, Mar. 7
2151 A1061 56c multi 1.00 .50

Ecksberg Foundation for the Mentally Handicapped, 150th Anniv. — A1062

Litho. & Engr.
2002, Apr. 4 *Perf. 14x13¾*
2152 A1062 56c multi 1.00 .50

Freemason's Museum, Cent. — A1063

2002, Apr. 4 Litho. *Perf. 14*
2153 A1063 56c multi 1.00 .50

Baden-Württemberg, 50th Anniv. — A1064

2002, Apr. 4 *Perf. 13¼*
2154 A1064 56c multi 1.00 .50

"Post" — A1065

2002, Apr. 4 *Perf. 13x13½*
2155 A1065 56c multi 1.00 .50

Federal Employment Services, 50th Anniv. — A1066

2002, Apr. 4 *Perf. 14*
2156 A1066 153c black & red 2.75 1.40

Voss Type of 2001
Die Cut Perf. 10¼

2002, Apr. 4 **Litho.**

Coil Stamp
Self-Adhesive

2157 A1029 " 1.53 multi 2.75 1.40

Dated 2001. No. 2157 was sold only for euro currency.

Europa
A1067

2002 **Litho.** ***Perf. 13¼***

2158 A1067 56c multi 1.00 .50

Self-Adhesive Coil Stamp
Die Cut Perf. 10¼

2158A A1067 56c multi 1.10 .55

Issued: No. 2158, 5/2; No. 2158A, 7/4.

Garden Kingdom of Dessau-Wörlitz, UNESCO World Heritage Site — A1068

2002 ***Perf. 13¾x14***

2159 A1068 56c multi 1.00 .50

Booklet Stamp
Self-Adhesive

2159A A1068 56c multi 1.10 .55
b. Booklet of 20 22.50

Issued: No. 2159, 5/2; No. 2159A, 8/8.

2002, May 2 ***Perf. 14***

2160 A1069 56c multi 1.00 .50

Children's Church, 150th Anniv.
A1070

2002, May 2 ***Perf. 13¼***

2161 A1070 56c multi 1.00 .50

Souvenir Sheet

Documenta 11 Art Exhibition — A1071

2002, May 2 ***Perf. 13¾x14***

2162 A1071 56c multi 1.00 .50

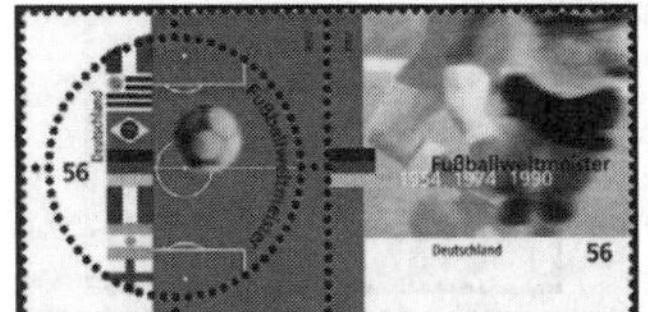

2002 World Cup Soccer Championships, Japan and Korea — A1072

No. 2163: a, Flags, soccer ball and field (28mm diameter). b, Soccer players, years of German championships.
Illustration reduced.

2002, May 2 ***Perf. 13¾***

2163 A1072 Horiz. pair 2.00 1.00
a.-b. 56c Any single 1.00 .50

Issued: No. 2159, 5/2; No. 2159A, 8/8.

Albrecht Daniel Thaer (1752-1828), Agronomist

A1073

2002, May 2 ***Perf. 13x13½***

2164 A1073 225c multi 4.00 2.00

Yellow Feather in Red, by Ernst Wilhelm Nay (1902-68) — A1074

2002, June 6 **Litho.** ***Perf. 13¾x14***

2165 A1074 56c multi 1.00 .50

Endangered Species — A1075

Designs: 51c, Desmoulins whorl snail. 56c, Freshwater pearl mussel.

2002, June 6 ***Perf. 14x14¼***

2166 A1075 51c multi .95 .45
2167 A1075 56c multi 1.00 .50

Issued: No. 2159, 5/2; No. 2159A, 8/8.

World Hunger Help

A1076

2002, July 4 **Litho.** ***Perf. 13¾x14***

2168 A1076 51c multi 1.00 .50

Natl. Germanic Museum, 150th Anniv. — A1077

2002, July 4

2169 A1077 56c multi 1.10 .55

Hermann Hesse (1877-1962), Writer — A1078

2002, July 4 ***Perf. 14***

2170 A1078 56c multi 1.10 .55

Souvenir Sheet

Hochharz Natl. Park — A1079

2002, July 4 ***Perf. 13¾x14***

2171 A1079 56c multi 1.10 .55

Josef Felder (1900-2000), Politician, Journalist
A1080

2002, Aug. 8 **Litho.** ***Perf. 13***

2172 A1080 56c multi 1.10 .55

Volunteer Fire Brigades
A1081

2002, Aug. 8 ***Perf. 14***

2173 A1081 56c multi 1.10 .55

Museum Island, Berlin, UNESCO World Heritage Site
A1082

Litho. & Engr.

2002, Aug. 8 ***Perf. 13¾x14***

2174 A1082 56c blk & Prus blue 1.10 .55

Communications Museum, Berlin — A1083

2002, Aug. 8 **Litho.** ***Perf. 14***

2175 A1083 153c multi 3.00 1.50

Foundation Walls of Roman Villa Bathhouse, Wurmlingen — A1084

2002, Sept. 5 **Litho.** ***Perf. 13¾x14***

2176 A1084 51c multi 1.00 .50

Rotes Elisabeth-Ufer, by Ernst Ludwig Kirchner (1880-1938) — A1085

2002, Sept. 5

2177 A1085 112c multi 2.25 1.10

Souvenir Sheet

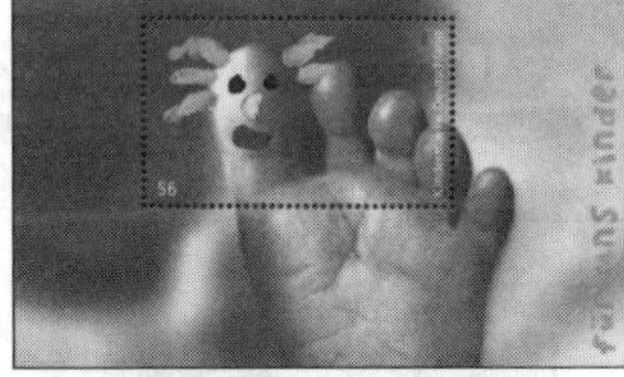

For Children — A1086

2002, Sept. 5 ***Perf. 13x13½***

2178 A1086 56c multi 1.10 .55

Heinrich von Kleist (1777-1811), Writer — A1087

2002, Oct. 10 **Litho.** ***Perf. 13***

2179 A1087 56c multi 1.10 .55

Eugen Jochum (1902-87), Conductor
A1088

2002, Oct. 10 ***Perf. 14x14¼***

2180 A1088 56c multi 1.10 .55

Otto von Guericke (1602-86), Physicist — A1089

2002, Oct. 10 *Perf. 14*
2181 A1089 153c multi 3.00 1.50

Halle Market Church, by Lyonel Feininger (1871-1956) — A1092

2002, Dec. 5 Litho. *Perf. 13¾x14*
2184 A1092 55c multi 1.10 .55

Famous Women Type of 1986 With Euro Denominations Only

Designs: 45c, Annette von Droste-Hülshoff (1797-1848), poet. 55c, Hildegard Knef (1925-2002), actress. "1, Marie Juhacz (1879-1956), politician. "1.44, Esther von Kirchbach (1894-1946), writer.

2002-03 Engr. *Perf. 14*
2188 A602 45c ol grn & Prus bl .95 .45
2190 A602 55c car & blk 1.10 .55
2195 A602 "1 dk bl & claret 2.10 1.10
2197 A602 "1.44 dk bl & ocher 3.00 1.50
Nos. 2188-2197 (4) 7.15 3.60

Issued: No. 2159, 5/2; No. 2159A, 8/8.

Designs: 44c, Berlin Philharmonic Hall. 45c, Tönninger Packhaus (Warehouse, Tönning). 55c, Old Opera House, Frankfurt. "1, Porta Nigra, Trier. "1.44, Birthplace of Ludwig van Beethoven, Bonn. "1.60, Bauhaus, Dessau. "2.20, Monument to Theodor Fontane, Neuruppin.

Typo., Litho. (#2209, 2213)

2002-03 *Perf. 14*
2202 A623 44c blk & yel .90 .45
2203 A623 45c gray blk & brick red .95 .45
2205 A623 55c blk & yel 1.10 .55
2207 A623 "1 blk & green-ish gray 2.10 1.10
2209 A623 "1.44 gray grn & pink 3.00 1.50
2210 A623 "1.60 slate & org 3.25 1.60
2213 A623 "2.20 blue blk & gray bl 4.75 2.40

Litho.
Self-Adhesive
Coil Stamp
Die Cut Perf. 10¼x11

2216 A623 55c blk & yel 1.10 .55

Booklet Stamps
Die Cut Perf. 10¼x11 on 3 Sides

2217 A623 45c gray blk & brick red .95 .45
2218 A623 55c blk & yel 1.10 .55
a. Booklet 4 #2217, 8 #2218 13.00
Nos. 2202-2218 (10) 19.20 9.60

Issued: 44c, 45c, 55c, "1, "1.60, 12/27/02; "1.44, "2.20, 1/16/03.

This is an expanding set. Numbers may change.

Kronach, 1000th Anniv. — A1093

2003, Jan. 16 Litho. *Perf. 14*
2222 A1093 45c multi .95 .50

Georg Elser (1903-45), Failed Assassin of Hitler — A1094

2003, Jan. 16 *Perf. 13¼*
2223 A1094 55c multi 1.25 .60

Treaty for German-French Cooperation, 40th Anniv. A1095

2003, Jan. 16 *Perf. 13¾*
2224 A1095 55c multi 1.25 .60

Bible Year A1096

2003, Jan. 16 *Perf. 14x14¼*
2225 A1096 55c mulit 1.25 .60

Proun 30t, by El Lissitzky (1890-1941) — A1097

2003, Jan. 16
2226 A1097 144c multi 3.00 1.50

Cultural Foundation of the Federal States.

SEMI-POSTAL STAMPS

Issues of the Republic

Regular Issue of 1906-17 Surcharged

1919, May 1 Wmk. 125 *Perf. 14*
B1 A16 10pf + 5pf car red .35 *4.25*
B2 A22 15pf + 5pf dk vio .35 *4.25*
Set, never hinged 1.60

The surtax was for the war wounded.

"Planting Charity" — SP1

Feeding the Hungry — SP2

1922, Dec. 11 Litho. Wmk. 126
B3 SP1 6m + 4m ultra & brn .20 *20.00*
B4 SP1 12m + 8m red org & bl gray .20 *20.00*
Set, never hinged 1.25

Nos. 221, 225 and 196 Surcharged

1923, Feb. 19
B5 A34 5m + 100m .20 *7.75*
B6 A29 25m + 500m .20 *21.00*
a. Inverted surcharge 87.50
Never hinged 150.00
B7 A32 20m + 1000m 1.90 *80.00*
a. Inverted surcharge 625.00 *3,150.*
Never hinged 1,600.
b. Green background inverted 160.00 1,050.
Never hinged 375.00
Nos. B5-B7 (3) 2.30 *108.75*
Set, never hinged 5.25

Note following No. 160 applies to #B1-B7.

1924, Feb. 25 Typo. ***Perf. 14½x15***

Designs: 10pf+30pf, Giving drink to the thirsty. 20pf+60pf, Clothing the naked. 50pf+1.50m, Healing the sick.

B8 SP2 5pf + 15pf dk green 1.00 2.00
B9 SP2 10pf + 30pf vermilion 1.00 2.00
B10 SP2 20pf + 60pf dk blue 5.25 5.75
B11 SP2 50pf + 1.50m red brn 20.00 47.50
Nos. B8-B11 (4) 27.25 57.25
Set, never hinged 97.50

The surtax was used for emergency aid. See No. B58.

Prussia — SP6

1925, Dec. 15 *Perf. 14*

Inscribed: "1925"

B12 SP6 5pf + 5pf shown .40 1.10
B13 SP6 10pf + 10pf Bavaria .90 1.10
B14 SP6 20pf + 20pf Saxony 5.25 11.00
a. Bklt. pane of 2 + 2 labels 160.00 500.00
Never hinged 400.00
Nos. B12-B14 (3) 6.55 13.20
Set, never hinged 30.00

1926, Dec. 1

Inscribed: "1926"

B15 SP6 5pf + 5pf Wurttemberg .90 1.10
B16 SP6 10pf + 10pf Baden 1.25 1.90
a. Bklt. pane of 6 + 2 labels 65.00 160.00
Never hinged 160.00
B17 SP6 25pf + 25pf Thuringia 9.75 16.00
B18 SP6 50pf + 50pf Hesse 37.50 65.00
Nos. B15-B18 (4) 49.40 84.00
Set, never hinged 140.00

See Nos. B23-B32.

Pres. Paul von Hindenburg — SP13

1927, Sept. 26 **Photo.**

B19 SP13 8pf dark green .70 1.10
- *a.* Bklt. pane, 4 #B19, 3 #B20 + label 37.50 92.50
- Never hinged 92.50

B20 SP13 15pf scarlet .70 1.75
B21 SP13 25pf deep blue 5.25 16.00
B22 SP13 50pf bister brown 8.50 21.00
Nos. B19-B22 (4) 15.15 39.85
Set, never hinged 65.00

80th birthday of Pres. Hindenburg. The stamps were sold at double face value. The surtax was given to a fund for War Invalids.

Arms Type of 1925

Design: 8pf+7pf, Mecklenberg-Schwerin.

1928, Nov. 15 **Typo.**

Inscribed: "1928"

B23 SP6 5pf + 5pf Hamburg .45 *2.50*
B24 SP6 8pf + 7pf multi .45 *2.50*
- *a.* Bklt. pane, 4 #B24, 3 #B25 + label 92.50 225.00
- Never hinged 225.00

B25 SP6 15pf + 15pf Oldenburg .65 *2.50*
B26 SP6 25pf + 25pf Brunswick 8.00 *26.00*
B27 SP6 50pf + 50pf Anhalt 40.00 *70.00*
Nos. B23-B27 (5) 49.55 103.50
Set, never hinged 160.00

1929, Nov. 4

Coats of Arms: 8pf+4pf, Lippe-Detmold. 25pf+10pf, Mecklenburg-Strelitz. 50pf+40pf, Schaumburg-Lippe.

Inscribed: "1929"

B28 SP6 5pf + 2pf Bremen .50 *1.10*
- *a.* Bklt. pane of 6 + 2 labels 10.50 26.00
- Never hinged 26.00

B29 SP6 8pf + 4pf multi .50 *1.10*
- *a.* Bklt. pane, 4 #B29, 3 #B30 + label 32.50 80.00
- Never hinged 80.00

B30 SP6 15pf + 5pf Lubeck .60 *1.10*
B31 SP6 25pf + 10pf multi 10.00 *26.00*
B32 SP6 50pf + 40pf choc, ocher & red 35.00 *65.00*
- *a.* "PE" for "PF" 100.00 450.00
- Never hinged 125.00

Nos. B28-B32 (5) 46.60 94.30
Set, never hinged 140.00

Cathedral of Aachen — SP24

Brandenburg Gate, Berlin — SP25

Castle of Marienwerder SP26

Statue of St. Kilian and Marienburg Fortress at Würzburg SP27

Souvenir Sheet

Wmk. 223

1930, Sept. 12 **Engr.** ***Perf. 14***

B33 Sheet of 4 300.00 *1,150.*
- Never hinged 875.00
- *a.* SP24 8pf + 4pf dark green 22.50 *62.50*
- Never hinged 52.50
- *b.* SP25 15pf + 5pf carmine 22.50 62.50
- Never hinged 52.50
- *c.* SP26 25pf + 10p dark blue 22.50 *62.50*
- Never hinged 52.50
- *d.* SP27 50pf + 40pf dark brown 22.50 *62.50*
- Never hinged 52.50

Intl. Phil. Exhib., Berlin, Sept. 12-21, 1930.

No. B33 is watermarked Eagle on each stamp and "IPOSTA"-"1930" in the margins. Size: approximately 105x150. Each holder of an admission ticket was entitled to purchase one sheet. The ticket cost 1m and the sheet 1.70m (face value 98pf, charity 59pf, special paper 13pf).

The margin of the souvenir sheet is ungummed.

Types of International Philatelic Exhibition Issue

1930, Nov. 1 **Wmk. 126**

B34 SP24 8 + 4pf dp green .30 *.45*
- *a.* Bklt. pane of 7 + label 16.00 40.00
- Never hinged 40.00
- *b.* Bklt. pane, 3 #B34, 4 #B35 + label 20.00 50.00
- Never hinged 50.00

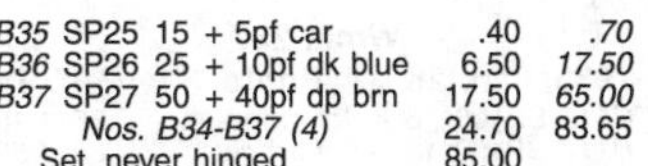

B35 SP25 15 + 5pf car .40 *.70*
B36 SP26 25 + 10pf dk blue 6.50 *17.50*
B37 SP27 50 + 40pf dp brn 17.50 *65.00*
Nos. B34-B37 (4) 24.70 83.65
Set, never hinged 85.00

The surtax was for charity.

The Zwinger at Dresden SP28

Breslau City Hall SP29

Heidelberg Castle SP30

Holsten Gate, Lübeck SP31

1931, Nov. 1

B38 SP28 8 + 4pf dk green .25 *.75*
- *a.* Bklt. pane of 7 + label 13.00 32.50
- Never hinged 32.50
- *b.* Bklt. pane, 3 #B38, 4 #B39 + label 20.00 50.00
- Never hinged 50.00

B39 SP29 15 + 5pf carmine .40 *.75*
B40 SP30 25 + 10pf dk blue 6.50 *17.50*
B41 SP31 50 + 40pf dp brown 30.00 *57.50*
Nos. B38-B41 (4) 37.15 76.50
Set, never hinged 125.00

The surtax was for charity.

Nos. B38-B39 Surcharged

1932, Feb. 2

B42 SP28 6 + 4pf on 8+4pf 4.00 *8.00*
B43 SP29 12 + 3pf on 15+5pf 4.50 *9.75*
Set, never hinged 35.00

Wartburg Castle — SP32

Stolzenfels Castle — SP33

Nuremberg Castle — SP34

Lichtenstein Castle — SP35

Marburg Castle — SP36

1932, Nov. 1 **Engr.**

B44 SP32 4 + 2pf lt blue .25 *.40*
- *a.* Bklt. pane, 5 #B44, 5 #B45 9.25 22.50
- Never hinged 22.50

B45 SP33 6 + 4pf olive grn .25 *.40*
B46 SP34 12 + 3pf lt red .45 *.75*
- *b.* Bklt. pane of 8 + 2 labels 9.25 22.50
- Never hinged 22.50

B47 SP35 25 + 10pf dp blue 6.50 *13.00*
B48 SP36 40 + 40pf brown vio 25.00 *47.50*
Nos. B44-B48 (5) 32.45 62.05
Set, never hinged 125.00

The surtax was for charity.

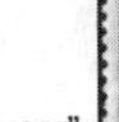

"Tannhäuser" SP37

Designs: 4pf+2pf, "Der Fliegende Hollander." 5pf+2pf, "Das Rheingold." 6pf+4pf, "Die Meistersinger." 8pf+4pf, "Die Walkure." 12pf+3pf, "Siegfried." 20pf+10pf, "Tristan und Isolde." 25pf+15pf, "Lohengrin." 40pf+35pf, "Parsifal."

Wmk. Swastikas (237)

1933, Nov. 1 ***Perf. 13½x13***

B49 SP37 3 + 2pf bister brn 1.60 *3.75*
B50 SP37 4 + 2pf dk blue 1.10 *1.50*
- *b.* Bklt. pane, 5 #B50, 5 #B52 52.50 125.00
- Never hinged 125.00

B51 SP37 5 + 2pf brt green 3.00 *4.50*
B52 SP37 6 + 4pf gray grn 1.10 *1.10*
B53 SP37 8 + 4pf dp orange 1.50 *2.50*
- *b.* Bklt. pane, 5 #B53, 4 #B54 + label 65.00 160.00
- Never hinged 160.00

B54 SP37 12 + 3pf brown red 1.50 *1.40*
B55 SP37 20 + 10pf blue 125.00 125.00
B56 SP37 25 + 15pf ultra 21.00 *29.00*
B57 SP37 40 + 35pf magenta 92.50 92.50
Nos. B49-B57 (9) 248.30 261.25
Set, never hinged 1,300.

Perf. 13½x14

B50a SP37 4 + 2pf dark blue .90 *2.40*
B52a SP37 6 + 4pf gray green .90 *3.75*
B53a SP37 8 + 4pf deep orange 1.75 *3.00*
B54a SP37 12 + 3pf brown red 2.00 *5.00*
B55a SP37 20 + 10pf blue 92.50 75.00
Nos. B50a-B55a (5) 98.05 89.15
Set, never hinged 575.00

Types of Semi-Postal Stamps of 1924 Issue Overprinted "1923-1933"

Souvenir Sheet

1933, Nov. 29 **Typo.** ***Perf. 14½***

B58 Sheet of 4 1,050. *6,750.*
- Never hinged 4,100.
- *a.* SP2 5 + 15pf dark green 65.00 *225.00*
- *b.* SP2 10 + 30pf vermilion 65.00 *225.00*
- *c.* SP2 20 + 60pf dark blue 65.00 *225.00*
- *d.* SP2 50pf + 1.50m dk brown 65.00 *225.00*
- Any single, never hinged 160.00

The Swastika watermark covers the four stamps and above them appears a further watermark "10 Jahre Deutsche Nothilfe" and "1923-1933" below. Sheet size: 208x148mm.

The margin of the souvenir sheet is ungummed.

Businessman SP46

Judge SP54

Designs: 4pf+2pf, Blacksmith. 5pf+2pf, Mason. 6pf+4f, Miner. 8pf+4pf, Architect. 12pf+3pf, Farmer. 20pf+10pf, Agricultural Chemist. 25pf+15pf, Sculptor.

1934, Nov. 5 **Engr.** ***Perf. 13x13½***

B59 SP46 3 + 2pf brown .65 .80
B60 SP46 4 + 2pf black .65 .80
- *a.* Bklt. pane, 5 #B60, 5 #B62 13.00 32.50
- Never hinged 32.50

B61 SP46 5 + 2pf green 5.25 5.25
B62 SP46 6 + 4pf dull grn .40 .40
B63 SP46 8 + 4pf org brn .65 .80
- *a.* Bklt. pane, 5 #B63, 4 #B64 + label 24.00 60.00
- Never hinged 60.00

B64 SP46 12 + 3pf henna brn .40 .40
B65 SP46 20 + 10pf Prus blue 13.00 16.00
B66 SP46 25 + 15pf ultra 13.00 16.00
B67 SP54 40 + 35pf plum 40.00 50.00
Nos. B59-B67 (9) 74.00 90.45
Set, never hinged 350.00

Souvenir Sheet

SP55

1935, June 23 **Wmk. 241** ***Perf. 14***

B68 SP55 Sheet of 4 650.00 650.00
- *a.* 3pf red brown 26.00 29.00
- *b.* 6pf dark green 26.00 29.00
- *c.* 12pf dark carmine 26.00 29.00
- *d.* 25pf dark blue 26.00 29.00

Watermarked cross on each stamp and "OSTROPA 1935" in the margins of the sheet. Size: 148x104mm. 1.70m was the price of a ticket of admission to the Intl. Exhib., Königsberg, June 23-July 3, 1935.

Because the gum on No. B68 contains sulphuric acid and tends to damage the sheet, most collectors prefer to remove it. **Catalogue unused values are for sheet and singles without gum.**

East Prussia SP59

Skating SP69

Designs (Costumes of Various Sections of Germany): 4pf+3pf, Silesia. 5pf+3pf, Rhineland. 6pf+4pf, Lower Saxony. 8pf+4pf, Brandenburg. 12pf+6pf, Black Forest. 15pf+10pf, Hesse. 25pf+15pf, Upper Bavaria. 30pf+20pf, Friesland. 40pf+35pf, Franconia.

Wmk. Swastikas (237)

1935, Oct. 4 ***Perf. 14x13½***

B69 SP59 3 + 2pf dk brown .20 .25
- *a.* Bklt. pane, 4 #B69, 5 #B74 + label 10.50 26.00
- Never hinged 26.00

B70 SP59 4 + 3pf gray .90 *1.10*
B71 SP59 5 + 3pf emerald .20 .60
- *a.* Bklt. pane, 5 #B71, 5 #B72 2.75 6.50
- Never hinged 6.50

B72 SP59 6 + 4pf dk green .20 .25
B73 SP59 8 + 4pf yel brn 1.60 1.00
B74 SP59 12 + 6pf dk car .20 .25
B75 SP59 15 + 10pf red brn 3.75 4.50
B76 SP59 25 + 15pf ultra 6.50 4.50
B77 SP59 30 + 20pf olive brn 8.00 *15.00*
B78 SP59 40 + 35p plum 7.25 *11.00*
Nos. B69-B78 (10) 28.80 38.45
Set, never hinged 125.00

1935, Nov. 25 ***Perf. 13½***

12+6pf, Ski jump. 25+15pf, Bobsledding.

B79 SP69 6 + 4pf green .60 .40
B80 SP69 12 + 6pf carmine 1.10 .75
B81 SP69 25 + 15pf ultra 4.75 *6.50*
Nos. B79-B81 (3) 6.45 7.65
Set, never hinged 42.50

Winter Olympic Games held in Bavaria, Feb. 6-16, 1936.

1936, May 8

Designs: 3pf+2pf, Horizontal bar. 4pf+3pf, Diving. 6pf+4pf, Soccer. 8pf+4pf, Throwing javelin. 12pf+6pf, Torch runner. 15pf+10pf, Fencing. 25pf+15pf, Sculling. 40pf+35pf, Equestrian.

B82 SP69 3 + 2pf brown .20 .25
- *a.* Bklt. pane, 5 #B82, 5 #B86 6.50 16.00
- Never hinged 16.00

B83 SP69 4 + 3pf indigo .20 *.45*
- *a.* Bklt. pane, 5 #B83, 5 #B84 6.50 16.00
- Never hinged 16.00

B84 SP69 6 + 4pf green .20 .25
B85 SP69 8 + 4pf red org 2.75 1.10
B86 SP69 12 + 6pf carmine .25 .25
B87 SP69 15 + 10pf brn vio 4.00 2.75
B88 SP69 25 + 15pf ultra 2.75 3.00
B89 SP69 40 + 35pf violet 4.75 6.50
Nos. B82-B89 (8) 15.10 14.55
Set, never hinged 85.00

Summer Olympic Games, Berlin, 8/1-16/36. See Nos. B91-B92.

Souvenir Sheet

Horse Race — SP80

1936, June 22 Wmk. 237 *Perf. 14*

B90 SP80 42pf brown 6.50 12.00
Never hinged 19.00

A surtax of 1.08m was to provide a 100,000m sweepstakes prize. Wmk. 237 appears on the stamp, with "Munchen Riem 1936" watermarked on sheet margin.

For overprint see No. B105.

Type of 1935
Souvenir Sheets

1936, Aug. 1 *Perf. 14x13½*

B91 SP69 Sheet of 4 22.50 *40.00*
B92 SP69 Sheet of 4 22.50 *40.00*
Set, never hinged 175.00

11th Olympic Games, Berlin. No. B91 contains Nos. B82-B84, B89. No. B92 contains Nos. B85-B88.

Wmk. 237 appears on each stamp with "XI Olympische Spiele-Berlin 1936" watermarked on sheet margin. Sold for 1m each.

Frontier Highway, Munich — SP81

Designs: 4pf+3pf, Ministry of Aviation. 5pf+3pf, Nuremberg Memorial. 6pf+4pf, Bridge over the Saale, Saxony. 8pf+4pf, Germany Hall, Berlin. 12pf+6pf, German Alpine highway. 15pf+10pf, Fuhrer House, Munich. 25pf+15pf, Bridge over the Mangfall. 40pf+35pf, Museum of German Art, Munich.

Perf. 13½x14

1936, Sept. 21 Unwmk.

B93	SP81	3pf + 2pf blk brn	.20	.25
a.		Bklt. pane, 4 #B93 + 5 #B98 + label	8.50	21.00
		Never hinged	21.00	
B94	SP81	4pf + 3pf black	.20	.50
B95	SP81	5pf + 3pf brt grn	.20	.25
a.		Bklt. pane, 5 #B95, 5 #B96)	3.25	8.50
		Never hinged	8.50	
B96	SP81	6pf + 4pf dk grn	.20	.25
B97	SP81	8pf + 4pf brown	.65	1.10
B98	SP81	12pf + 6pf brn car	.20	.25
B99	SP81	15pf + 10pf vio brn	2.50	3.00
B100	SP81	25pf + 15pf indigo	1.75	3.00
B101	SP81	40pf + 35pf rose vio	2.75	4.50
		Nos. B93-B101 (9)	8.65	13.10
		Set, never hinged	52.50	

Souvenir Sheets

Adolf Hitler — SP90

Wmk. 237

1937, Apr. 5 Photo. *Perf. 14*

B102 SP90 Sheet of 4 14.00 8.50
Never hinged 45.00
a. 6pf dark green .90 .85
Never hinged 3.25

48th birthday of Adolf Hitler. Sold for 1m. See #B103-B104. For overprint see #B106.

1937, Apr. 16 *Imperf.*

B103 SP90 Sheet of 4 32.50 20.00
Never hinged 140.00
a. 6pf dark green 2.00 2.75
Never hinged 6.50

German Natl. Phil. Exhib., Berlin, June 16-18, 1937 and the Phil. Exhib. of the Stamp Collectors Group of the Strength Through Joy Organization at Hamburg, Apr. 17-20, 1937. Sold at the Exhib. post offices for 1.50m.

No. B102 with Marginal Inscriptions

Perf. 14 and Rouletted

1937, June 10 Wmk. 237

B104 SP90 Sheet of 4 32.50 *57.50*
Never hinged 160.00
a. 6pf dark grn + 25pf label 2.75 4.50
Never hinged 6.50

No. B104 inscribed in the margin beside each stamp "25 Rpf. einschliesslich Kulturspende" in three lines.

The sheets were rouletted to allow for separation of each stamp with its component label. Sold at the post office as individual stamps with labels attached or in complete sheets.

Souvenir Sheet No. B90 Overprinted in Red

1937, Aug. 1 *Perf. 14*

B105 SP80 42pf brown 52.50 85.00
Never hinged 125.00

4th running of the "Brown Ribbon" horse race at the Munich-Riem Race Course, Aug. 1, 1937.

Souvenir Sheet No. B104 Overprinted in Black on Each Stamp

Perf. 14 and Rouletted

1937, Sept. 3 Wmk. 237

B106 SP90 Sheet of 4 45.00 37.50
Never hinged 160.00
a. 6pf dark grn + 25pf label 3.00 3.25
Never hinged 8.50

1937 Nazi Congress at Nuremburg.

Lifeboat — SP91

Designs: 4pf+3pf, Lightship "Elbe I." 5pf+3pf, Fishing smacks. 6pf+4pf, Steamer. 8pf+4pf, Sailing vessel. 12pf+6pf, The "Tannenberg." 15pf+10pf, Sea-Train "Schwerin." 25pf+15pf, S. S. Hamburg. 40pf+35pf, S. S. Bremen.

Perf. 13½

1937, Nov. 4 Engr. Unwmk.

B107	SP91	3pf + 2pf dk brwn	.20	.25
a.		Bklt. pane, 4 #B107 + 5 #B112 + label	11.00	
B108	SP91	4pf + 3pf black	.90	.65
B109	SP91	5pf + 3pf yel grn	.20	.25
a.		Bklt. pane, 5 #B109, 5 #B110	4.50	
B110	SP91	6pf + 4pf bl grn	.20	.25
B111	SP91	8pf + 4pf orange	.55	*1.00*
B112	SP91	12pf + 6pf car lake	.20	.20
B113	SP91	15pf + 10pf vio brn	1.10	*3.25*
B114	SP91	25pf + 15pf ultra	2.75	3.25
B115	SP91	40pf + 35pf red vio	4.50	*6.50*
		Nos. B107-B115 (9)	10.60	15.60
		Set, never hinged	72.50	

No. B115 actually pictures the S.S. Europa.

Youth Carrying Torch and Laurel — SP100

Adolf Hitler — SP101

Wmk. 237

1938, Jan. 28 Photo. *Perf. 14*

B116 SP100 6 + 4pf dk green .65 *1.10*
B117 SP100 12 + 8pf brt car .80 *1.50*
Set, never hinged 10.50

Assumption of power by the Nazis, 5th anniv.

1938, Apr. 13 Engr. Unwmk.

B118 SP101 12 + 38pf copper red 1.25 1.60
Never hinged 8.50

Hitler's 49th birthday.

Horsewoman SP102

1938, July 20

B119 SP102 42 + 108pf dp brn 18.00 *40.00*
Never hinged 92.50

5th "Brown Ribbon" at Munich.

Adolf Hitler SP103

Theater at Saarbrücken SP104

1938, Sept. 1

B120 SP103 6 + 19pf deep grn 2.00 2.75
Never hinged 13.00

1938 Nazi Congress at Nuremberg. The surtax was for Hitler's National Culture Fund.

1938, Oct. 9 Photo. Wmk. 237

B121 SP104 6 + 4pf blue grn .80 1.10
B122 SP104 12 + 8pf dk car 1.60 2.00
Set, never hinged 14.50

Inauguration of the theater of the District of Saarpfalz at Saarbrücken. The surtax was for Hitler's National Culture Fund.

Castle of Forchtenstein SP105

Designs (scenes in Austria and various flowers): 4pf+3pf, Flexenstrasse in Vorarlberg. 5pf+3pf, Zell am See, Salzburg. 6pf+4pf, Grossglockner. 8pf+4pf, Ruins of Aggstein. 12pf+6pf, Prince Eugene Monument, Vienna. 15pf+10pf, Erzberg. 25pf+15pf, Hall, Tyrol. 40pf+35pf, Braunau.

Unwmk.

1938, Nov. 18 Engr. *Perf. 14*

B123	SP105	3 + 2pf olive brn	.20	.25
a.		Bklt. pane, 4 #B123, 5 #B128 + label	8.00	20.00
		Never hinged	20.00	
B124	SP105	4 + 3pf indigo	1.40	1.00
B125	SP105	5 + 3pf emerald	.20	.30
a.		Bklt. pane, 5 #B125, 5 #B126	2.75	6.50
		Never hinged	6.50	
B126	SP105	6 + 4pf dk grn	.20	.20
B127	SP105	8 + 4pf red org	1.40	1.00
B128	SP105	12 + 6pf dk car	.20	.25
B129	SP105	15 + 10pf dp cl	2.60	3.50
B130	SP105	25 + 15pf dk blue	2.25	3.50
B131	SP105	40 + 35pf plum	5.25	6.00
		Nos. B123-B131 (9)	13.70	16.00
		Set, never hinged	65.00	

The surtax was for "Winter Help."

Sudeten Couple — SP114

1938, Dec. 2 Photo. Wmk. 237

B132 SP114 6 + 4pf blue grn .85 *2.00*
B133 SP114 12 + 8pf dk car 2.00 *2.75*
Set, never hinged 17.00

Annexation of the Sudeten Territory. The surtax was for Hitler's National Culture Fund.

Early Types of Automobiles SP115

1939

Designs: 12pf+8pf, Racing cars. 25pf+10pf, Modern automobile.

B134	SP115	6 + 4pf dk grn	2.75	2.75
B135	SP115	12 + 8pf brt car	2.75	2.75
B136	SP115	25 + 10pf dp blue	4.50	4.75
		Nos. B134-B136 (3)	10.00	10.25
		Set, never hinged	65.00	

Berlin Automobile and Motorcycle Exhibition. The surtax was for Hitler's National Culture Fund. For overprints see #B141-B143.

Adolf Hitler SP118

Exhibition Building SP119

Unwmk.

1939, Apr. 13 Engr. *Perf. 14*

B137 SP118 12 + 38pf carmine 1.25 *3.25*
Never hinged 7.25

Hitler's 50th birthday. The surtax was for Hitler's National Culture Fund.

1939, Apr. 22 Photo. *Perf. 12½*

B138 SP119 6 + 4pf dk green .95 *2.00*
B139 SP119 15 + 5pf dp plum .95 *2.00*
Set, never hinged 11.00

Horticultural Exhib. held at Stuttgart. Surtax for Hitler's National Culture Fund.

Adolf Hitler — SP120

Perf. 14x13½

1939, Apr. 28 Wmk. 237

B140 SP120 6 + 19pf black brn 1.60 *3.25*
Never hinged 8.00

Day of National Labor. The surtax was for Hitler's National Culture Fund.

See No. B147.

Nos. B134-B136 Overprinted in Black

Nürburgring-Rennen

1939, May 18 *Perf. 14*

B141	SP115	6 + 4pf dk green	15.00	20.00
B142	SP115	12 + 8pf brt car	15.00	20.00
B143	SP115	25 + 10pf dp blue	15.00	20.00
		Nos. B141-B143 (3)	45.00	60.00
		Set, never hinged	190.00	

Nurburgring Auto Races, 5/21, 7/23/39.

Racehorse "Investment" and Jockey
SP121

1939, June 18 Engr. Unwmk.

B144 SP121 25 + 50pf ultra 12.00 10.50
Never hinged 50.00

70th anniv. of the German Derby. The surtax was divided between Hitler's National Culture Fund and the race promoters.

Man Holding Rearing Horse — SP122

"Venetian Woman" by Albrecht Dürer — SP123

1939, July 12

B145 SP122 42 + 108pf dp brown 12.50 *21.00*
Never hinged 52.50

6th "Brown Ribbon" at Munich.

1939, July 12 Photo. Wmk. 237

B146 SP123 6 + 19pf dk green 4.50 *6.50*
Never hinged 22.50

Day of German Art. The surtax was used for Hitler's National Culture Fund.

Hitler Type of 1939
Inscribed "Reichsparteitag 1939"

1939, Aug. 25 *Perf. 14x13½*

B147 SP120 6 + 19pf black brn 3.00 *6.50*
Never hinged 14.50

1939 Nazi Congress at Nuremberg.

Meeting in German Hall, Berlin
SP124

Designs: 4pf+3pf, Meeting of postal and telegraph employees. 5pf+3pf, Professional competitions. 6pf+4pf, 6pf+9pf, Professional camp. 8pf+4pf, 8pf+12pf, Gold flag competitions. 10pf+5pf, Awarding prizes. 12&f+6pf, 12pf+18pf, Automobile race. 15pf+10pf, Sports. 16pf+10pf, 16pf+24pf, Postal police. 20pf+10pf, 20pf+30pf, Glider workshops. 24pf+10pf, 24pf+36pf, Mail coach. 25pf+15pf, Convalescent home, Konigstein.

Perf. 13½x14

1939-41 Unwmk. Photo.

B148	SP124	3 + 2pf bister brn	1.40	*4.00*
B149	SP124	4 + 3pf slate blue	1.40	*4.00*
B150	SP124	5 + 3pf brt bl grn	.40	*1.10*
B151	SP124	6 + 4pf myrtle grn	.50	*1.00*
B151A	SP124	6 + 9pf dk grn ('41)	.50	*1.10*
B152	SP124	8 + 4pf dp orange	.50	*1.10*
B152A	SP124	8 + 12pf hn brn ('41)	.75	*.90*
B153	SP124	10 + 5pf dk brown	.40	*1.50*
B154	SP124	12 + 6pf rose brown	.55	*1.50*
B154A	SP124	12 + 18pf dk car rose ('41)	.75	*.90*
B155	SP124	15 + 10pf dp red lilac	.40	*1.50*
B156	SP124	16 + 10pf slate grn	.40	*1.50*
B156A	SP124	16 + 24pf black ('41)	.75	*3.00*
B157	SP124	20 + 10pf ultra	.55	*1.50*
B157A	SP124	20 + 30pf ultra ('41)	.75	*3.00*
B158	SP124	24 + 10pf ol grn	1.40	*3.00*
B158A	SP124	24 + 36pf pur ('41)	2.40	*8.25*
B159	SP124	25 + 15pf dk blue	1.40	*2.40*
		Nos. B148-B159 (18)	15.20	41.25
		Set, never hinged	85.00	

The surtax was used for Hitler's National Culture Fund and the Postal Employees' Fund. See Nos. B273, B275-B277.

Elbogen Castle — SP136

Buildings: 4pf+3pf, Drachenfels on the Rhine. 5pf+3pf, Kaiserpfalz at Goslar. 6pf+4pf, Clocktower at Graz. 8pf+4pf, Town Hall, Frankfurt. 12pf+6pf, Guild House, Klagenfurt. 15pf+10pf, Ruins of Schreckenstein Castle. 25pf+15pf, Fortress of Salzburg. 40pf+35pf, Castle of Hohentwiel.

1939 Unwmk. Engr. *Perf. 14*

B160	SP136	3 + 2pf dk brn	.20	*.35*
a.		Bklt. pane, 4 #B160, 5 #B165 + label	8.00	20.00
		Never hinged	20.00	
B161	SP136	4 + 3pf gray blk	1.25	*1.50*
B162	SP136	5 + 3pf emerald	.20	*.45*
a.		Bklt. pane, 5 #B162, 5 #B163	3.50	8.50
		Never hinged	8.50	
B163	SP136	6 + 4pf slate grn	.20	.30
B164	SP136	8 + 4pf red org	1.25	1.25
B165	SP136	12 + 6pf dk car	.20	*.30*
B166	SP136	15 + 10pf brn vio	1.90	*3.75*
B167	SP136	25 + 15pf ultra	1.50	*3.75*
B168	SP136	40 + 35pf rose vio	2.10	4.75
		Nos. B160-B168 (9)	8.80	16.40
		Set, never hinged	40.00	

Hall of Honor at Chancellery, Berlin — SP145

1940, Mar. 28

B169 SP145 24 + 76pf dk grn 5.25 *11.00*
Never hinged 22.50

2nd National Stamp Exposition, Berlin.

Child Greeting Hitler — SP146

Perf. 14x13½

1940, Apr. 10 Photo. Wmk. 237

B170 SP146 12 + 38pf cop red 1.25 *4.50*
Never hinged 9.75

51st birthday of Adolf Hitler.

Armed Warrior
SP147

Horseman
SP148

1940, Apr. 30 Unwmk. *Perf. 14*

B171 SP147 6 + 4pf sl grn & lt grn .25 *.70*
Never hinged .85

Issued to commemorate May Day.

Perf. 14x13½

1940, June 22 Wmk. 237

B172 SP148 25 + 100pf dp ultra 3.00 *7.50*
Never hinged 14.00

Blue Ribbon race, Hamburg, June 30, 1940. Surtax for Hitler's National Culture Fund.

Chariot
SP149

Unwmk.

1940, July 20 Engr. *Perf. 14*

B173 SP149 42 + 108pf brown 13.00 *22.50*
Never hinged 80.00

7th "Brown Ribbon" at Munich.
The surtax was for Hitler's National Culture Fund and the promoters of the race.

View of Malmedy
SP150

Design: 12pf+8pf, View of Eupen.

Perf. 14x13½

1940, July 25 Photo. Wmk. 237

B174 SP150 6 + 4pf dk green .55 *2.00*
B175 SP150 12 + 8pf org red .55 *2.00*
Set, never hinged 6.50

Issued on the occasion of the reunion of Eupen-Malmedy with the Reich.

Rocky Cliffs of Heligoland
SP152

Artushof in Danzig — SP153

1940, Aug. 9 Unwmk.

B176 SP152 6 + 94pf brt bl grn & red org 3.25 *6.50*
Never hinged 18.00

Heligoland's 50th year as part of Germany.

1940, Nov. 5 Engr. *Perf. 14*

Buildings: 4pf+3pf, Town Hall, Thorn. 5pf+3pf, Castle at Kaub. 6pf+4pf, City Theater, Poznan. 8pf+4pf, Castle at Heidelberg. 12pf+6pf, Porta Nigra Trier. 15pf+10pf, New German Theater, Prague. 25pf+15pf, Town Hall, Bremen. 40pf+35pf, Town Hall, Munster.

B177	SP153	3 + 2pf dk brn	.20	.30
a.		Bklt. pane, 4 #B177 + 5 #B182 + label	6.50	16.00
		Never hinged	16.00	
B178	SP153	4 + 3pf bluish blk	.40	.65
B179	SP153	5 + 3pf yel grn	.20	*.40*
a.		Bklt. pane, 5 #B179, 5 #B180	3.50	8.50
		Never hinged	8.50	
B180	SP153	6 + 4pf dk grn	.20	.25
B181	SP153	8 + 4pf dp org	.80	.70
B182	SP153	12 + 6pf carmine	.20	.25
B183	SP153	15 + 10pf dk vio brn	.80	*2.00*
B184	SP153	25 + 15pf dp ultra	1.10	*2.10*
B185	SP153	40 + 35pf red lil	2.25	*5.00*
		Nos. B177-B185 (9)	6.15	11.65
		Set, never hinged	26.00	

von Behring
SP162

Postilion
SP163

1940, Nov. 26 Photo.

B186 SP162 6 + 4pf dp green .40 *1.25*
B187 SP162 25 + 10pf brt ultra .80 *2.00*
Set, never hinged 9.75

Dr. Emil von Behring (1854-1917), bacteriologist.

1941, Jan. 12 *Perf. 14x13½*

B188 SP163 6 + 24pf dp green .45 1.40
Never hinged 4.00

Postage Stamp Day. The surtax was for Hitler's National Culture Fund.

Benito Mussolini and Adolf Hitler
SP164

Perf. 13½x14

1941, Jan. 30 Wmk. 237

B189 SP164 12 + 38pf rose brn .45 *1.90*
Never hinged 4.50

Issued as propaganda for the Rome-Berlin Axis. The surtax was for Hitler's National Culture Fund.

Adolf Hitler — SP165

Race Horse — SP166

1941, Apr. 17 *Perf. 14x13½*

B190 SP165 12 + 38pf dk red 1.00 *2.40*
Never hinged 6.00

52nd birthday of Adolf Hitler. The surtax was for Hitler's National Culture Fund.

Perf. 13½x14

1941, June 20 Engr. Unwmk.

B191 SP166 25 + 100pf sapphire 2.50 *6.50*
Never hinged 11.00

Issued in commemoration of the Blue Ribbon race held at Hamburg, June 29, 1941.

Amazons
SP167

1941, July 20 *Perf. 14*

B192 SP167 42 + 108pf brown 1.60 *4.00*
Never hinged 7.25

8th "Brown Ribbon" at Munich.

Brandenburg Gate, Berlin — SP168

1941, Sept. 9
B193 SP168 25 + 50pf dp ultra 1.60 *4.25*
Never hinged 8.25

Issued in honor of the Berlin races.

Marburg SP169

Veldes SP170

Pettau — SP171

Triglav — SP172

1941, Sept. 29 **Photo.**
B194 SP169 3 + 7pf brown .60 *1.75*
B195 SP170 6 + 9pf purple .45 *1.75*
B196 SP171 12 + 13pf rose brn .60 *2.10*
B197 SP172 25 + 15pf dk blue 1.25 *1.50*
Nos. B194-B197 (4) 2.90 7.10
Set, never hinged 13.00

Annexation of Styria and Carinthia.

View from Belvedere Palace, Vienna — SP173

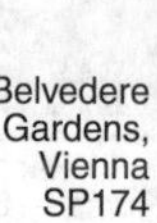

Belvedere Gardens, Vienna SP174

1941, Sept. 16 **Engr.**
B198 SP173 12 + 8pf dp red .60 *1.75*
B199 SP174 15 + 10pf violet .60 *2.00*
Set, never hinged 7.75

Issued to commemorate the Vienna Fair.

Mozart — SP175

1941, Nov. 28
B200 SP175 6 + 4pf dk rose vio .20 *.40*
Never hinged .60

Wolfgang Amadeus Mozart (1756-91).

Philatelist SP176

1942, Jan. 11 **Photo.**
B201 SP176 6 + 24pf dp purple .45 *2.00*
Never hinged 2.50

To commemorate Stamp Day.

Soldier's Head — SP177

1942, Mar. 10 ***Perf. 14x13½***
B202 SP177 12 + 38pf slate blk .25 *1.10*
Never hinged 1.10

To commemorate Hero Memorial Day.

Adolf Hitler — SP178

1942, Apr. 13
B203 SP178 12 + 38pf lake 1.25 *4.75*
Never hinged 9.75

To commemorate Hitler's 53rd birthday.

Racing Three-year-old SP179

1942, June 16 **Engr.** ***Perf. 14***
B204 SP179 25 + 100pf dk bl 4.00 *9.75*
Never hinged 13.00

73rd Hamburg Derby.

Race Horses SP180

1942, July 14
B205 SP180 42 + 108pf brown 1.25 *4.25*
Never hinged 6.00

9th "Brown Ribbon" at Munich.

Lüneburg Lion and Nuremberg Betrothal Cup — SP181

1942, Aug. 8 **Photo.** ***Perf. 14x13½***
B206 SP181 6 + 4pf copper red .20 *.75*
B207 SP181 12 + 88pf green .45 *1.75*
Set, never hinged 2.25

10th anniv. of the German Goldsmiths' Society and the 1st Goldsmiths' Day in Germany.

Henlein Monument, Nuremberg — SP182

1942, Aug. 29 ***Perf. 14***
B208 SP182 6 + 24pf rose vio .40 *1.00*
Never hinged 1.40

400th anniversary of the death of Peter Henlein, inventor of the pocket watch.

Postilion and Map of Europe SP183

Postilion and Globe — SP184

Postilion SP185

Perf. 13½x14, 14x13½

1942, Oct. 12 **Photo.**
B209 SP183 3 + 7pf dull blue .25 *1.10*

Engr.
B210 SP184 6 + 14pf ultra & dp brn .30 *1.10*
B211 SP185 12 + 38pf rose red & dp brn .45 *1.60*
Nos. B209-B211 (3) 1.00 3.80
Set, never hinged 3.00

European Postal Congress, Vienna.

Nos. B209 to B211 Overprinted in Black

1942, Oct. 19
B212 SP183 3 + 7pf .60 *1.75*
B213 SP184 6 + 14pf .60 *1.75*
B214 SP185 12 + 38pf .80 *3.50*
Nos. B212-B214 (3) 2.00 7.00
Set, never hinged 6.50

To commemorate the signing of the European postal-telegraph agreement at Vienna.

Mail Coach SP186

1943, Jan. 10 **Engr.**
B215 SP186 6 + 24pf gray, brn & yel .20 *.65*
Never hinged .55

To commemorate Stamp Day. The surtax went to Hitler's National Culture Fund.

Brandenburg Gate SP187

Nazi Emblem SP188

1943, Jan. 26 **Photo.**
B216 SP187 54 + 96pf cop red .40 *1.40*
Never hinged 1.60

10th anniversary of the assumption of power by the Nazis.

1943, Jan. 26
B217 SP188 3 + 2pf olive bister .20 *.55*
Never hinged .50

Used to secure special philatelic cancellations.

Submarine SP189

Designs: 4pf+3pf, Schutz-Staffel Troops. 5pf+4pf, Motorized marksmen. 6pf+9pf, Signal Corps. 8pf+7pf, Engineer Corps. 12pf+8pf, Grenade assault. 15pf+10pf, Heavy artillery. 20pf+14pf, Anti-aircraft units in action. 25pf+15pf, Dive bombers. 30pf+30pf, Paratroops. 40pf+40pf, Tank. 50pf+50pf, Speed boat.

1943, Mar. 21 **Engr.**
B218 SP189 3 + 2pf dk brn .30 *.80*
B219 SP189 4 + 3pf brown .30 *.80*
B220 SP189 5 + 4pf dk grn .30 *.80*
B221 SP189 6 + 9pf dp violet .30 *.80*
B222 SP189 8 + 7pf brn org .35 *.80*
B223 SP189 12 + 8pf car lake .35 *.80*
B224 SP189 15 + 10pf vio brn .35 *.80*
B225 SP189 20 + 14pf slate bl .35 *.80*
B226 SP189 25 + 15pf indigo .35 *.80*
B227 SP189 30 + 30pf green .50 *1.40*
B228 SP189 40 + 40pf red lil .50 *1.40*
B229 SP189 50 50pf grnsh blk .70 *2.00*
Nos. B218-B229 (12) 4.65 12.00
Set, never hinged 13.00

Army Day and Hero Memorial Day.
Nos. B220 and B224 exist imperf. Value, each $67.50.

Nazi Flag and Children SP201

1943, Mar. 26 **Photo.**
B230 SP201 6 + 4pf dk green .20 *.75*
Never hinged .75

To commemorate the Day of Youth Obligation when all German boys and girls had to take an oath of allegiance to Hitler.

Adolf Hitler SP202

1943, Apr. 13
B231 SP202 3 + 7pf brown blk .30 *.90*
B232 SP202 6 + 14pf dk grn .30 *.90*
B233 SP202 8 + 22pf dk chlky bl .30 *.90*
B234 SP202 12 + 38pf cop red .30 *.90*
B235 SP202 24 + 76pf vio brn .70 *2.50*
B236 SP202 40 + 160pf dk ol grn .70 *2.50*
Nos. B231-B236 (6) 2.60 8.60
Set, never hinged 8.50

Hitler's 54th birthday. No. B231 exists imperf. Value $100.

Reich Labor Service Corpsmen
SP203 SP204

Designs: 6pf+14pf, Corpsman chopping. 12pf+18pf, Corpsman with implements.

1943, June 26 **Engr.**
B237 SP203 3 + 7pf bis brn .20 *.30*
B238 SP204 5 + 10pf pale ol grn .20 *.30*

B239 SP204 6 + 14pf dp blue .20 *.30*
B240 SP204 12 + 18pf dk red .20 *.90*
Nos. B237-B240 (4) 1.80
Set, never hinged 1.75

Anniversary of Reich Labor Service. Nos. B237-B238, B240 exist imperf.

Rosegger's Birthplace, Upper Styria — SP207

Peter Rosegger SP208

Perf. 13½x14, 14x13½

1943, July 27 **Photo.**
B241 SP207 6 + 4pf green .20 *.60*
B242 SP208 12 + 8pf copper red .20 *.60*
Set, never hinged 1.10

Centenary of the birth of Peter Rosegger, Austrian writer.

Hunter SP209

1943, July 27 **Engr.**
B243 SP209 42 + 108pf brown .20 *.80*
Never hinged .65

10th "Brown Ribbon" at Munich. No. B243 exists imperf. Value $300.

Race Horse — SP210

1943, Aug. 14
B244 SP210 6 + 4pf vio blk .20 *.90*
B245 SP210 12 + 88pf dk car .20 *.90*
Set, never hinged 1.10

Grand Prize of the Freudenau, the Vienna race track, Aug. 15, 1943.

Mother and Children — SP211

1943, Sept. 1
B246 SP211 12 + 38pf dark red .20 *.80*
Never hinged .70

10th anniversary of Winter Relief.

St. George in Gold — SP212

1943, Oct. 1
B247 SP212 6 + 4pf dk ol grn .20 *.45*
B248 SP212 12 + 88pf vio brn .20 *.65*
Set, never hinged .90

German Goldsmiths' Society.

Ancient Lübeck — SP213

1943, Oct. 24 **Photo.**
B249 SP213 12 + 8pf copper red .20 *.70*
Never hinged .55

Hanseatic town of Lubeck, 800th anniv. No. B249 exists imperf. Value, $75.

"And Despite All, You Were Victorious" SP214

1943, Nov. 5
B250 SP214 24 + 26pf henna .20 *.70*
Never hinged .55

20th anniv. of the Nazis' Munich beer-hall putsch and to honor those who died for the Nazi movement. #B250 exists imperf.

Dr. Robert Koch — SP215

1944, Jan. 25 **Engr.** **Unwmk.**
B251 SP215 12 + 38pf sepia .20 *.70*
Never hinged .55

Centenary of the birth of the bacteriologist, Robert Koch (1843-1910).

Hitler and Nazi Emblems SP216

1944, Jan. 29 **Photo.**
B252 SP216 54 + 96pf yel brn .20 *.80*
Never hinged .65

Assumption of power by the Nazis, 11th anniv.

Airport Scene — SP217

Seaplane SP218

Plane Seen from Above — SP219

Perf. 14x13½, 13½x14

1944, Feb. 11 **Photo.** **Unwmk.**
B252A SP217 6 + 4pf dk grn .20 *.60*
B252B SP218 12 + 8pf maroon .20 *.70*
B252C SP219 42 + 108pf dp slate bl .25 *1.40*
Nos. B252A-B252C (3) .65 2.70
Set, never hinged 1.75

25th anniv. of German air mail. The surtax was for the National Culture Fund.

Infant's Crib — SP220

6pf+4pf, Public nurse. 12pf+8pf, "Mother & Child" clinic. 15pf+10pf, Expectant mothers.

1944, Mar. 2
B253 SP220 3 + 2pf dk brn .20 *.35*
B254 SP220 6 + 4pf dk grn .20 *.35*
B255 SP220 12 + 8pf dp car .20 *.35*
B256 SP220 15 + 10pf vio brn .20 *.45*
Nos. B253-B256 (4) 1.50
Set, never hinged .95

10th anniv. of "Mother and Child" aid.

Assault Boat — SP221

1944, Mar. 11

Designs: 4pf+3pf, Chain-wheel vehicle. 5pf+3pf, Paratroops. 6pf+4pf, Submarine officer. 8pf+4pf, Schutz-Staffel grenade throwers. 10pf+5pf, Searchlight. 12pf+6pf, Infantry. 15pf+10pf, Self-propelled gun. 16pf+10pf, Speed boat. 20pf+10pf, Sea raider. 24pf+10pf, Railway artillery. 25pf+15pf, Rockets. 30pf+20pf, Mountain trooper.

Inscribed: "Grossdeutsches Reich"
B257 SP221 3 + 2pf yel brn .20 *.75*
B258 SP221 4 + 3pf royal bl .20 *.40*
B259 SP221 5 + 3pf dp yel grn .20 *.35*
B260 SP221 6 + 4pf dp vio .20 *.35*
B261 SP221 8 + 4pf org ver .20 *.40*
B262 SP221 10 + 5pf chocolate .20 *.35*
B263 SP221 12 + 6pf carmine .20 *.35*
B264 SP221 15 + 10pf dp claret .20 *.40*
B265 SP221 16 + 10pf dk bl grn .20 *.80*
B266 SP221 20 + 10pf brt bl .20 *.85*
B267 SP221 24 + 10pf dl org brn .20 *.85*
B268 SP221 25 + 15pf vio bl .35 *2.25*
B269 SP221 30 + 20pf olive grn 35 *2.25*
Nos. B257-B269 (13) 2.90 10.35
Set, never hinged 11.00

To commemorate Hero Memorial Day.

Flora Statue in Fulda's Schloss Garden — SP234

1944, Mar. 11
B270 SP234 12 + 38pf dp brown .20 *.60*
Never hinged .50

1,200th anniversary of town of Fulda.

Adolf Hitler — SP235

1944, Apr. 14 **Engr.** **Unwmk.**
B271 SP235 54 + 96pf rose car .25 *.85*
Never hinged 1.00

To commemorate Hitler's 55th birthday.

Type of 1939-41 and

Woman Mail Carrier SP236

Field Post in the East — SP237

Designs: 8pf+12pf, Mail coach. 16pf+24pf, Automobile race. 20pf+30pf, Postal police. 24pf+36pf, Glider workshops.

1944, May 3 **Photo.**
Designs measure 29½x24½mm
B272 SP236 6 + 9pf vio bl .20 *.35*
B273 SP124 8 + 12pf gray blk .20 *.35*
B274 SP237 12 + 18pf dp plum .20 *.35*
B275 SP124 16 + 24pf dk grn .20 *.35*
B276 SP124 20 + 30pf blue .20 *.90*
B277 SP124 24 + 36pf dk pur .20 *.90*
Nos. B272-B277 (6) 1.20 3.20
Set, never hinged 2.00

Surtax for the Postal Employees' Fund.

Soldier and Tirolese Rifleman — SP238

1944, July
B278 SP238 6 + 4pf dp grn .20 *.40*
B279 SP238 12 + 8pf brn lake .20 *.60*
Set, never hinged .65

7th National Shooting Matches at Innsbruck.

Albert I, Duke of Prussia — SP239

1944, July
B280 SP239 6 + 4pf dk bl grn .20 *.75*
Set, never hinged .70

400th anniv. of Albert University, Königsberg.

Labor Corps Girl SP240

Labor Corpsman SP241

1944, June **Engr.**
B281 SP240 6 + 4pf green .20 *.35*
B282 SP241 12 + 8pf carmine .20 *.50*
Set, never hinged .65

Issued to honor an exhibit of the Reich Labor Service.

Race Horse and Foal — SP242

1944, July 23 ***Perf. 14x13½***
B283 SP242 42 + 108pf brown .20 *1.10*
Never hinged .80

11th "Brown Ribbon" at Munich.

Race Horse's Head in Oak Wreath — SP243

1944, Aug. **Photo.** ***Perf. 14***
B284 SP243 6 + 4pf Prus green .20 *.70*
B285 SP243 12 + 88pf car lake .20 *.80*
Set, never hinged .80

Vienna Grand Prize Race.

Nautilus Cup in Green Vault, Dresden — SP244

1944, Sept. 11
B286 SP244 6 + 4pf dk green .20 *.70*
B287 SP244 12 + 88pf car brn .20 *.80*
Set, never hinged .70

German Goldsmiths' Society.
No. B287 exists imperf. Value $175.

Post Horn and Letter — SP245

1944, Oct. 2
B288 SP245 6 + 24pf dk green .20 *.80*
Never hinged .50

To commemorate Stamp Day.

Eagle and Serpent — SP246

1944, Nov. 9
B289 SP246 12 + 8pf rose red .20 *.75*
Never hinged .50

21st anniv. of the Munich putsch.

Count Anton Günther — SP247

1945, Jan. 6 **Typo.** ***Perf. 13½x14***
B290 SP247 6 + 14pf brown vio .20 *.75*
Never hinged .50

600th anniv. of municipal law in Oldenburg.

People's Army — SP248

1945, Feb. **Photo.** ***Perf. 14x13½***
B291 SP248 12 + 8pf rose car .25 *1.50*
Never hinged 1.00

Proclamation of the People's Army (Volkssturm) in East Prussia to fight the Russians.

Elite Storm Trooper (S. S.) — SP249

Storm Trooper (S. A.) — SP250

1945, Apr. 21 ***Perf. 13½x14***
B292 SP249 12 + 38pf brt car 6.50 *700.00*
B293 SP250 12 + 38pf brt car 6.50 *700.00*
Set, never hinged 52.50

12th anniv. of the assumption of power by the Nazis. Nos. B292-B293 were on sale in Berlin briefly before the collapse of that city.
Exist imperf unused. Value same as perf.
Forged cancels abound. Certificates of authenticity mandatory for used examples.

Souvenir Sheets

SP251

Wmk. 284

1946, Dec. 8 **Typo.** ***Perf. 14***
B294 SP251 Sheet of 3 16.00 *110.00*
Never hinged 32.50

Imperf
B295 SP251 Sheet of 3 16.00 *125.00*
Never hinged 32.50
a. A119 20pf light blue 3.25 *11.00*
b. A119 24pf orange brown 3.25 *11.00*
c. A119 40pf red violet 3.25 *11.00*

No. B294 contains Nos. 543, 544 and 548.
Nos. B294-B295 sold for 5m each. Surtax for refugees and the aged.

Leipzig Proclaimed Market Place, 1160 — SP252

Design: 60pf+40pf, Foreign merchants displaying their wares, 1268.

Wmk. 48

1947, Mar. 5 **Engr.** ***Perf. 13***
B296 SP252 24 +26pf chestnut brn .20 *.80*
B297 SP252 60 + 40pf dp vio blue .20 *1.25*
Set, never hinged .60

1947 Leipzig Fairs.
No. B296 exists imperf. Value $150.
See Nos. 580-583, 10NB1-10NB2, 10NB4-10NB5, 10NB12-10NB13 and German Democratic Republic Nos. B15-B16.

Madonna SP254

Cathedral Towers SP255

Designs: 12pf+8pf, Three Kings. 24pf+16pf, Cologne Cathedral.

Wmk. 286

1948, Aug. 15 **Typo.** ***Perf. 11***
B298 SP254 6 + 4pf org brn .25 *.60*
a. "1948-1248" 3.75 *14.50*
Never hinged 8.75
B299 SP254 12 + 8pf grnsh blue .45 *1.10*
a. "1948-1948" 5.00 *17.50*
Never hinged 11.50
B300 SP254 24 + 16pf car 1.00 *2.40*
B301 SP255 50 + 50pf blue 2.25 *6.25*
Nos. B298-B301 (4) 3.95 10.35
Set, never hinged 9.25

700th anniv. of the laying of the cornerstone of Cologne Cathedral. The surtax was to aid in its reconstruction.
Specialists collect Nos. B298-B301 with watermark in four positions: upright, D's facing left; upright, D's facing right; sideways, D's facing up; sideways, D's facing down. Two types of perforation: line and comb.

Brandenburg Gate, Berlin SP256

Bicycle Racers SP257

Perf. 10½x11½, 11

1948, Dec. **Litho.**
B302 SP256 10 + 5pf green 2.10 *5.25*
B303 SP256 20 + 10pf rose car 2.10 *5.25*
Set, never hinged 9.75

The surtax was for aid to Berlin.

Wmk. 116

1949, May 15 **Engr.** ***Perf. 14***
B304 SP257 10 + 5pf green 1.60 3.50
B305 SP257 20 + 10pf brn org 4.00 *13.00*
Set, never hinged 14.50

1949 Bicycle Tour of Germany.

Goethe at Rome — SP258

Goethe — SP259

30pf+15pf, Goethe portrait facing left.

1949, Aug. 15
B306 SP258 10 + 5pf green .80 2.40
B307 SP259 20 + 10pf red 1.25 4.00
B308 SP259 30 + 15pf blue 6.50 *17.00*
Nos. B306-B308 (3) 8.55 *23.40*
Set, never hinged 25.00

Bicentenary of the birth of Johann Wolfgang von Goethe.
The surtax was for the reconstruction of Goethe House, Frankfurt-on-Main.

Federal Republic

Bavaria Stamp of 1849 SP260

St. Elisabeth SP261

1949, Sept. 30 **Litho.** **Wmk. 285**
B309 SP260 10 + 2pf grn & blk 5.75 *14.50*
Never hinged 9.75

Centenary of German postage stamps.

1949, Dec. 14 **Engr.** **Wmk. 286**

Designs: 10pf+5pf, Paracelsus. 20pf+10pf, F. W. A. Froebel. 30pf+15pf, J. H. Wichern.

B310 SP261 8 + 2pf brn vio 6.25 *17.50*
B311 SP261 10 + 5pf yel grn 6.25 *8.75*
B312 SP261 20 + 10pf red 6.25 *8.75*
B313 SP261 30 + 15pf vio bl 30.00 *82.50*
Nos. B310-B313 (4) 48.75 117.50
Set, never hinged 110.00

The surtax was for welfare organizations.

Seal of Johann Sebastian Bach — SP262

Frescoes from Marienkirche SP263

1950, July 28 ***Perf. 14***
B314 SP262 10 + 2pf dk grn 20.00 *37.50*
B315 SP262 20 + 3pf dk car 22.50 *42.50*
Set, never hinged 110.00

Bicentenary of the death of Bach.

1951, Aug. 30 **Photo.** **Wmk. 286**
Center in Gray
B316 SP263 10 + 5pf green 26.00 *52.50*
B317 SP263 20 + 5pf brn lake 30.00 *65.00*
Set, never hinged 160.00

Construction of Marienkirche, Lübeck, 700th anniv.
The surtax aided in its reconstruction.

Stamps Under Magnifying Glass — SP264

St. Vincent de Paul — SP265

Wmk. 295

1951, Sept. 14 **Typo.** ***Perf. 14***
B318 SP264 10 + 2pf multi 13.00 *37.50*
B319 SP264 20 + 3pf multi 13.00 *37.50*
Set, never hinged 72.50

Natl. Philatelic Exposition, Wuppertal, 1951.

1951, Oct. 23 **Engr.**

Portraits: 10pf+3pf, Friedrich von Bodelschwingh. 20pf+5pf, Elsa Brandstrom. 30pf+10pf, Johann Heinrich Pestalozzi.

B320 SP265	4 + 2pf brown	3.25	*8.00*
B321 SP265	10 + 3pf green	5.00	*6.50*
B322 SP265	20 + 5pf rose red	5.00	*6.50*
B323 SP265	30 + 10pf dp blue	42.50	*92.50*
	Nos. B320-B323 (4)	55.75	113.50
	Set, never hinged	110.00	

The surtax was for charitable purposes.

Nuremberg Madonna SP266

Boy Hikers and Youth Hostel SP267

1952, Aug. 9

B324 SP266	10 + 5pf green	6.50	*14.00*
	Never hinged	14.50	

Centenary of the founding of the Germanic National Museum, Nuremberg. The surtax was for the museum.

1952, Sept. 17 ***Perf. 13½x14***

Design: 20pf+3pf, Girls and Hostel.

B325 SP267	10 + 2pf green	8.25	*16.50*
B326 SP267	20 + 3pf dp car	8.25	*16.50*
	Set, never hinged	32.50	

The surtax was to aid the youth program of the Federal Republic.

Elizabeth Fry SP268

Owl and Cogwheel SP269

10pf+5pf, Dr. Carl Sonnenschein. 20pf+10pf, Theodor Fliedner. 30pf+10pf, Henri Dunant.

1952, Oct. 1

B327 SP268	4 + 2pf org brn	3.00	*5.00*
B328 SP268	10 + 5pf green	3.00	*5.00*
B329 SP268	20 + 10pf brn car	6.00	*9.75*
B330 SP268	30 + 10pf dp blue	30.00	*65.00*
	Nos. B327-B330 (4)	42.00	84.75
	Set, never hinged	92.50	

The surtax was for welfare organizations.

1953, May 7 **Wmk. 295** ***Perf. 14***

B331 SP269	10 + 5pf dp grn	11.00	*24.00*
	Never hinged	22.50	

50th anniv. of the founding of the German Museum in Munich.

Thurn and Taxis Palace Gate — SP270

August Hermann Francke — SP271

Design: 20pf+3pf, Telecommunications Bldg., Frankfurt-on-Main.

Wmk. 285

1953, July 29 **Litho.** ***Perf. 13½***

B332 SP270	10 + 2pf yel grn, bl & fawn	7.25	*22.50*
B333 SP270	20 + 3pf fawn, blk & gray	7.25	*22.50*
	Set, never hinged	40.00	

The surtax was for the International Stamp Exhibition, Frankfurt-on-Main, 1953.

Wmk. 295

1953, Nov. 2 **Engr.** ***Perf. 14***

Designs: 10pf+5pf, Sebastian Kneipp. 20pf+10pf, Dr. Johann Christian Senckenberg. 30pf+10pf, Fridtjof Nansen.

B334 SP271	4 + 2pf choc	1.25	*5.00*
B335 SP271	10 + 5pf bl grn	2.75	*5.00*
B336 SP271	20 + 10pf red	4.00	*6.50*
B337 SP271	30 + 10pf blue	19.00	*50.00*
	Nos. B334-B337 (4)	27.00	66.50
	Set, never hinged	65.00	

The surtax was for welfare organizations.

Catalogue values for unused stamps in this section, from this point to the end of the section, are for Never Hinged items.

Käthe Kollwitz — SP272

Carrier Pigeon and Magnifying Glass — SP273

Portraits: 10pf+5pf, Lorenz Werthmann. 20pf+10pf, Johann Friedrich Oberlin. 40pf+10pf, Bertha Pappenheim.

1954, Dec. 28 ***Perf. 13½x14***

B338 SP272	7pf + 3pf brown	2.75	2.75
B339 SP272	10pf + 5pf green	1.25	1.25
B340 SP272	20pf + 10pf red	8.00	3.50
B341 SP272	40pf + 10pf blue	27.50	35.00
	Nos. B338-B341 (4)	39.50	42.50

The surtax was for welfare organizations.

1955, Sept. 14 **Wmk. 304** ***Perf. 14***

20pf+3pf, Post horn and stamp tongs.

B342 SP273	10pf + 2pf green	4.00	*5.00*
B343 SP273	20pf + 3pf red	9.25	*10.50*

WESTROPA, 1955, philatelic exhibition at Dusseldorf. The surtax aided the Society of German Philatelists.

Amalie Sieveking — SP274

Portraits: 10pf+5pf, Adolph Kolping. 20pf+10pf, Dr. Samuel Hahnemann. 40pf+10pf, Florence Nightingale.

1955, Nov. 15 **Photo. & Litho.**

B344 SP274	7 + 3pf olive bis	2.75	2.25
B345 SP274	10 + 5pf dk green	1.60	1.10
B346 SP274	20 + 10pf red org	1.60	1.10
B347 SP274	40 + 10pf grnsh blue	27.50	32.50
	Nos. B344-B347 (4)	33.45	36.95

Surtax for independent welfare organizations.

Boy and Geometrical Designs SP275

Design: 10pf+5pf, Girl playing flute.

Unwmk.

1956, July 21 **Litho.** ***Perf. 14***

B348 SP275	7pf + 3pf multi	1.60	*2.60*
B349 SP275	10pf + 5pf multi	5.50	*6.50*

The surtax was for the Youth Hostel Organization.

The Midwife SP276

10+5pf, Ignaz Philipp Semmelweis. 20+10pf, The mother. 40+10pf, The children's nurse.

1956, Oct. 1 **Photo.**

Design and Inscription in Black

B350 SP276	7pf + 3pf org brn	1.00	1.75
B351 SP276	10pf + 5pf green	.65	.60
B352 SP276	20pf + 10pf brt red	.65	.60
B353 SP276	40pf + 10pf brt blue	14.50	13.00
	Nos. B350-B353 (4)	16.80	15.95

Issued to honor Ignaz Philipp Semmelweis, the discoverer of the cause of puerperal fever. Surtax for independent welfare organizations.

Children Leaving SP277

Design: 20pf+10pf, Child arriving.

1957, Feb. 1 **Litho.** ***Perf. 13½x13***

B354 SP277	10pf + 5pf gray grn & red org	1.00	*1.60*
B355 SP277	20pf + 10pf red org & lt bl	2.25	*3.25*

The surtax was for vacations for the children of Berlin.

Young Miner SP278

"The Fox who Stole the Goose" SP279

10+5pf, Miner with drill. 20+10pf, Miner & conveyor. 40+10pf, Miner & coal elevator.

1957, Oct. 1 **Wmk. 304** ***Perf. 14***

B356 SP278	7pf + 3pf bis brn & blk	1.00	1.25
B357 SP278	10pf + 5pf blk & yel grn	.65	.65
B358 SP278	20pf + 10pf black & red	1.00	.65
B359 SP278	40pf + 10pf black & blue	14.50	16.00
	Nos. B356-B359 (4)	17.15	18.55

Surtax for independent welfare organizations.

1958, Apr. 1 **Litho.**

20pf+10pf, "A Hunter from the Palatinate."

B360 SP279	10pf + 5pf brn red, grn & blk	1.10	*1.50*
B361 SP279	20pf + 10pf multi	2.25	*2.50*

The surtax was to finance young peoples' study trips to Berlin.

Friedrich Wilhelm Raiffeisen SP280

Dairy Maid SP281

Designs: 20pf+10pf, Girl picking grapes. 40pf+10pf, Farmer with pitchfork.

1958, Oct. 1 **Wmk. 304** ***Perf. 14***

B362 SP280	7pf + 3pf brn & dk brn	.35	.35
B363 SP281	10pf + 5pf grn, red & yel	.30	.30
B364 SP281	20pf + 10pf red, yel & bl	.35	.30
B365 SP281	40pf + 10pf blue & ocher	5.25	5.50
	Nos. B362-B365 (4)	6.25	6.45

Surtax for independent welfare organizations.

Stamp of Hamburg, 1859 — SP282

Design: 20pf+10pf, Stamp of Lübeck, 1859.

1959 **Engr.** **Wmk. 304**

B366 SP282	10pf + 5pf yel green & brown	.20	.30
a.	10pf + 5pf green & brown	.65	1.60
B367 SP282	20pf + 10pf red org & red brn	.20	.40
a.	20pf + 10pf maroon & red brown	1.00	1.60

"Interposta" Philatelic Exhibition, Hamburg, May 22-31, 1959 for the cent. of the 1st stamps of Hamburg and Lübeck.

The surtax on #B366, B367 was for vacations for the children of Berlin.

Issued: #B366-B367, 8/22; #B366a-B367a, 5/22.

Girl Giving Bread to Beggar SP283

Jacob and Wilhelm Grimm SP284

Designs (from "Star Dollars" fairy tale): 10pf+5pf, Girl giving coat to boy, 20pf+10pf, Star-Money from Heaven.

1959, Oct. 1 **Litho.** ***Perf. 14***

B368 SP283	7pf + 3pf brown & yel	.20	.25
B369 SP283	10pf + 5pf green & yel	.20	.25
B370 SP283	20pf + 10pf brick red & yel	.25	.25
B371 SP284	40pf + 10pf bl, blk, ocher & emer	2.50	3.50
	Nos. B368-B371 (4)	3.15	4.25

Surtax for independent welfare organizations.

Little Red Riding Hood and the Wolf — SP285

Various Scenes from Little Red Riding Hood.

1960, Oct. 1 Wmk. 304 *Perf. 14*

B372 SP285 7pf + 3pf brn ol, red & blk .30 .40
B373 SP285 10pf + 5pf grn, red & blk .30 .20
B374 SP285 20pf + 10pf brick red, emer & blk .30 .20
B375 SP285 40pf + 20pf brt bl, red & blk 2.00 3.00
Nos. B372-B375 (4) 2.90 3.80

Surtax for independent welfare organizations.

1961, Oct. 2

Various Scenes from Hansel and Gretel.

B376 SP285 7pf + 3pf multi .20 .20
B377 SP285 10pf + 5pf multi .20 .20
B378 SP285 20pf + 10pf multi .20 .20
B379 SP285 40pf + 20pf multi .90 1.25
Nos. B376-B379 (4) 1.50 1.85

Surtax for independent welfare organizations.
See B384-B387, B392-B395, B400-B403.

Fluorescent Paper was introduced for semipostal stamps, starting with No. B380.

Apollo — SP286

Hoopoe — SP287

10pf+5pf, Camberwell beauty. 20pf+10pf, Tortoise-shell. 40pf+20pf, Tiger swallowtail.

Wmk. 304

1962, May 25 Litho. *Perf. 14*

Butterflies in Natural Colors, Black Inscriptions

B380 SP286 7pf + 3pf bis brn .30 .30
B381 SP286 10pf + 5pf brt green .30 .30
B382 SP286 20pf + 10pf dp crim .60 .90
B383 SP286 40pf + 20pf brt blue .90 1.50
Nos. B380-B383 (4) 2.10 3.00

Issued for the benefit of young people.
Nos. B381-B383 exist without watermark. Value, each $900 unused, $750 used.

Fairy Tale Type of 1960

Scenes from Snow White (Schneewittchen).

1962, Oct. 10 *Perf. 14*

B384 SP285 7pf + 3pf multi .20 .20
B385 SP285 10pf + 5pf multi .20 .20
B386 SP285 20pf + 10pf multi .20 .20
B387 SP285 40pf + 20pf multi .65 .80
Nos. B384-B387 (4) 1.25 1.40

Surtax for independent welfare organizations.

1963, June 12 Unwmk. *Perf. 14*

Birds: 15pf+5pf, European golden oriole. 20pf+10pf, Bullfinch. 40pf+20pf, European kingfisher.

B388 SP287 10pf + 5pf multi .35 .30
B389 SP287 15pf + 5pf multi .30 .45
B390 SP287 20pf + 10pf multi .30 .40
B391 SP287 40pf + 20pf multi 1.25 1.75
Nos. B388-B391 (4) 2.20 2.90

Issued for the benefit of young people.

Fairy Tale Type of 1960

Various Scenes from the Grimm Brothers' "The Wolf and the Seven Kids."

1963, Sept. 23 Litho.

B392 SP285 10pf + 5pf multi .20 .20
B393 SP285 15pf + 5pf multi .20 .20
B394 SP285 20pf + 10pf multi .20 .20
B395 SP285 40pf + 20pf multi .45 .70
Nos. B392-B395 (4) 1.05 1.30

Surtax for independent welfare organizations.

Herring SP288

Fish: 15pf+5pf, Rosefish. 20pf+10pf, Carp. 40pf+20pf, Cod.

1964, Apr. 10 Unwmk. *Perf. 14*

B396 SP288 10pf + 5pf multi .20 .25
B397 SP288 15pf + 5pf multi .20 .20
B398 SP288 20pf + 10pf multi .30 .25
B399 SP288 40pf + 20pf multi .75 1.25
Nos. B396-B399 (4) 1.45 1.95

Issued for the benefit of young people.

Fairy Tale Type of 1960

Various Scenes from Sleeping Beauty (Dornroschen).

1964, Oct. 6 Litho. *Perf. 14*

B400 SP285 10pf + 5pf multi .20 .20
B401 SP285 15pf + 5pf multi .20 .20
B402 SP285 20pf + 10pf multi .20 .20
B403 SP285 40pf + 20pf multi .30 .60
Nos. B400-B403 (4) .90 1.20

Surtax for independent welfare organizations.

Woodcock SP289

1965, Apr. 1 Unwmk. *Perf. 14*

Birds: 15pf+5pf, Ring-necked pheasant. 20pf+10pf, Black grouse. 40pf+20pf, Capercaillie.

B404 SP289 10pf + 5pf multi .20 .20
B405 SP289 15pf + 5pf multi .20 .20
B406 SP289 20pf + 10pf multi .20 .20
B407 SP289 40pf + 20pf multi .25 .70
Nos. B404-B407 (4) .85 1.30

Issued for the benefit of young people.

Cinderella Feeding Pigeons SP290

Various Scenes from Cinderella.

1965, Oct. 6 Litho. *Perf. 14*

B408 SP290 10pf + 5pf multi .20 .20
B409 SP290 15pf + 5pf multi .20 .20
B410 SP290 20pf + 10pf multi .20 .20
B411 SP290 40pf + 20pf multi .35 .50
Nos. B408-B411 (4) .95 1.10

Surtax for independent welfare organizations.
See Nos. B418-B421, B426-B429.

Roe Deer — SP291

1966, Apr. 22 Litho. *Perf. 14*

Designs: 20pf+10pf, Chamois. 30pf+15pf, Fallow deer. 50pf+25pf, Red deer.

B412 SP291 10pf + 5pf multi .20 .20
B413 SP291 20pf + 10pf multi .20 .20
B414 SP291 30pf + 15pf multi .20 .20
B415 SP291 50pf + 25pf multi .50 .70
Nos. B412-B415 (4) 1.10 1.30

Issued for the benefit of young people.
See Nos. B422-B425.

Prussian Letter Carrier — SP292

Design: 30pf+15pf, Bavarian mail coach.

1966 Litho. *Perf. 14*

B416 SP292 30pf + 15pf multi .30 .50
B417 SP292 50pf + 25pf multi .40 .50

Meeting of the Federation Internationale de Philatélie (FIP), Munich, Sept. 26-29, and stamp exhibition, Municipal Museum, Sept. 24-Oct. 1. The surcharge was for the Foundation for the Promotion of Philately and Postal History.
Issued: #B416, 9/24; #B417, 7/13.

Fairy Tale Type of 1965

Various Scenes from The Princess and the Frog.

1966, Oct. 5 Litho. *Perf. 14*

B418 SP290 10pf + 5pf multi .20 .20
B419 SP290 20pf + 10pf multi .20 .20
B420 SP290 30pf + 15pf multi .20 .20
B421 SP290 50pf + 25pf multi .35 .60
Nos. B418-B421 (4) .95 1.20

Surtax for independent welfare organizations.

Animal Type of 1966

10pf+5pf, Rabbit. 20pf+10pf, Ermine. 30pf+15pf, Hamster. 50pf+25pf, Red fox.

1967, Apr. 4 Litho. *Perf. 14*

B422 SP291 10pf + 5pf multi .20 *.20*
B423 SP291 20pf + 10pf multi .20 *.25*
B424 SP291 30pf + 15pf multi .35 *.35*
B425 SP291 50pf + 25pf multi .75 *1.00*
Nos. B422-B425 (4) 1.50 *1.80*

Issued for the benefit of young people.

Fairy Tale Type of 1965

Various Scenes from Frau Holle.

1967, Oct. 3 Litho. *Perf. 14*

B426 SP290 10pf + 5pf multi .20 .20
B427 SP290 20pf + 10pf multi .20 .20
B428 SP290 30pf + 15pf multi .20 .20
B429 SP290 50pf + 25pf multi .50 .80
Nos. B426-B429 (4) 1.10 1.40

Surtax for independent welfare organizations.

Wildcat SP293

Animals: 20pf+10pf, Otter. 30pf+15pf, Badger. 50pf+25pf, Beaver.

1968, Feb. 2 Photo. Unwmk.

B430 SP293 10pf + 5pf multi .20 *.35*
B431 SP293 20pf + 15pf multi .30 *.55*
B432 SP293 30pf + 15pf multi .45 *.80*
B433 SP293 50pf + 25pf multi 1.60 *2.25*
Nos. B430-B433 (4) 2.55 *3.95*

The surtax was for the benefit of young people.

Olympic Games Type of Regular Issue

10pf+5pf, Karl-Friedrich Freiherr von Langen, equestrian. 20pf+10pf, Rudolf Harbig, runner. 30pf+15pf, Helene Mayer, fencer. 50pf+25pf, Carl Diem, sports organizer.

Lithographed and Engraved

1968, June 6 Unwmk. *Perf. 14*

B434 A285 10 + 5pf olive & dk brn .20 .20
B435 A285 20 + 10pf dp emer & dk grn .20 .20
B436 A285 30 + 15pf dp rose & dk red .35 .35
B437 A285 50 + 25pf brt bl & dk bl .60 .60
Nos. B434-B437 (4) 1.35 1.35

The surtax was for the Foundation for the Promotion of the 1972 Olympic Games in Munich.

Doll, c. 1878 — SP294

Pony — SP295

Various 19th Cent. Dolls. #B438-B440 are from Germanic Natl. Museum, Nuremberg; #B441 is from Altona Museum, Hamburg.

1968, Oct. 3 Litho. *Perf. 14*

B438 SP294 10pf + 5pf multi .20 .20
B439 SP294 20pf + 10pf multi .20 .20
B440 SP294 30pf + 15pf multi .20 .20
B441 SP294 50pf + 25pf multi .50 .70
Nos. B438-B441 (4) 1.10 1.30

Surtax for independent welfare organizations.

1969, Feb. 6 Litho. *Perf. 14*

Horses: 20pf+10pf, Work horse. 30pf+15pf, Hotblood. 50pf+25pf, Thoroughbred.

B442 SP295 10pf + 5pf multi .25 .20
B443 SP295 20pf + 10pf multi .25 .20
B444 SP295 30pf + 15pf multi .45 .40
B445 SP295 50pf + 25pf multi 1.40 1.25
Nos. B442-B445 (4) 2.35 2.05

Surtax for the benefit of young people.

SP296

SP297

Olympic Rings and: 10pf+5pf, Track. 20pf+10pf, Hockey. 30pf+15pf, Archery. 50pf+25pf, Sailing.

1969, June 4 Photo. *Perf. 14*

B446 SP296 10pf + 5pf dk brn & lem .20 .20
B447 SP296 20pf + 10pf bl grn & emer .25 .25
B448 SP296 30pf + 15pf mag & dp lil rose .35 .30
B449 SP296 50pf + 25pf dp bl & brt bl .80 .65
Nos. B446-B449 (4) 1.60 1.40

1972 Olympic Games in Munich. The surtax was for the German Olympic Committee.

1969, Oct. 2 Litho. *Perf. 13½x14*

Tin Toys: 10pf+5pf, Locomotive. 20pf+10pf, Gardener. 30pf+15pf, Bird seller. 50pf+25pf, Knight on horseback.

B450 SP297 10pf + 5pf multi .20 .20
B451 SP297 20pf + 10pf multi .20 .20
B452 SP297 30pf + 15pf multi .25 .25
B453 SP297 50pf + 25pf multi .70 .65
Nos. B450-B453 (4) 1.35 1.30

Surtax for independent welfare organizations.

Tin Toy Type of 1969 Inscribed: "Weihnachtsmarke 1969"

Christmas: 10pf+5pf, Jesus in Manger.

1969, Nov. 13 *Perf. 13½x14*

B454 SP297 10pf + 5pf multi .25 .20

Heinrich von Rugge — SP298

Minnesingers: 20pf+10pf, Wolfram von Eschenbach. 30pf+15pf, Walther von Metz. 50pf+25pf, Walther von der Vogelweide.

1970, Feb. 5 Photo. *Perf. 13½x14*

B455	SP298	10pf + 5pf multi	.30	.25
B456	SP298	20pf + 10pf multi	.50	.25
B457	SP298	30pf + 15pf multi	.60	.50
B458	SP298	50pf + 25pf multi	1.25	.95
		Nos. B455-B458 (4)	2.65	1.95

Surtax was for benefit of young people.

Residenz (Palace), Munich SP299

Munich Buildings: 20pf+10pf, Propylaea. 30pf+15pf, Glyptothek. 50pf+25pf, Bavaria Statue and Colonnade.

1970, June 5 Engr. *Perf. 14*

B459	SP299	10pf + 5pf olive bis	.20	.20
B460	SP299	20pf + 10pf dk bl grn	.35	.25
B461	SP299	30pf + 15pf carmine	.40	.30
B462	SP299	50pf + 25pf dk blue	.80	.65
		Nos. B459-B462 (4)	1.75	1.40

The surtax was for the Foundation for the Promotion of the 1972 Olympic Games in Munich.

Jester — SP300

King Caspar — SP301

Puppets: 20pf+10pf, "Hanswurst." 30pf+15pf, Clown. 50pf+25pf, Harlequin.

1970, Oct. 6 Litho. *Perf. 13½x14*

B463	SP300	10pf + 5pf multi	.20	.20
B464	SP300	20pf + 10pf multi	.20	.20
B465	SP300	30pf + 15pf multi	.30	.25
B466	SP300	50pf + 25pf multi	.70	.65
		Nos. B463-B466 (4)	1.40	1.30

Surtax for independent welfare organizations.

1970, Nov. 12

Christmas: 10pf+5pf, Rococo Angel, from Ursuline Sisters' Convent, Innsbruck.

B467	SP300	10pf + 5pf multi	.20	.20

1971, Feb. 5 Litho. *Perf. 14*

Children's Drawings: 20pf+10pf, Flea. 30pf+15pf, Puss-in-Boots. 50pf+25pf, Snake.

B468	SP301	10pf + 5pf multi	.25	.20
B469	SP301	20pf + 10pf multi	.30	.25
B470	SP301	30pf + 15pf multi	.40	.30
B471	SP301	50pf + 25pf multi	.70	.65
		Nos. B468-B471 (4)	1.65	1.40

Surtax for the benefit of young people.

Ski Jump — SP302

Women Churning Butter — SP303

20pf+10pf, Figure skating. 30pf+15pf, Downhill skiing. 50pf+25pf, Ice hockey.

"1971" at Lower Right

1971, June 4 Litho. *Perf. 14*

B472	SP302	10pf + 5pf brn org & blk	.20	.20
B473	SP302	20pf + 10pf green & blk	.35	.25
B474	SP302	30pf + 15pf rose red & blk	.65	.55
B475	SP302	50pf + 25pf blue & blk	1.25	1.10
a.		Souvenir sheet of 4	2.25	2.00
b.		10pf + 5pf brown org & blk	.20	.20
c.		20pf + 10pf green & black	.30	.25
d.		30pf + 15pf rose red & black	.55	.40
e.		50pf + 25pf blue & black	.90	.80
		Nos. B472-B475 (4)	2.45	2.10

Olympic Games 1972.

#B475a contains #B475b-B475e which lack the minute date ("1971") at lower right.

1971, Oct. 5 Litho. *Perf. 14*

Wooden Toys: 25pf+10pf, Horseback rider. 30pf+15pf, Nutcracker. 60pf+30pf, Dovecot.

B476	SP303	20pf + 10pf multi	.20	.20
B477	SP303	25pf + 10pf multi	.20	.20
B478	SP303	30pf + 15pf multi	.30	.25
B479	SP303	60pf + 30pf multi	.90	.70
		Nos. B476-B479 (4)	1.60	1.35

Surtax for independent welfare organizations.

1971, Nov. 11

Christmas: Christmas angel with lights.

B480	SP303	20pf + 10pf multi	.30	.25

Ducks Crossing Road — SP304

Olympic Rings and Wrestling — SP305

Designs: 25pf+10pf, Hunter chasing deer and rabbits. 30pf+15pf, Girl protecting birds from cat. 60pf+30pf, Boy annoying swans.

1972, Feb. 4 Litho. *Perf. 14*

B481	SP304	20pf + 10pf multi	.45	.40
B482	SP304	25pf + 10pf multi	.35	.25
B483	SP304	30pf + 15pf multi	.65	.60
B484	SP304	60pf + 30pf multi	1.25	1.25
		Nos. B481-B484 (4)	2.70	2.50

Animal protection. Surtax for the benefit of young people.

1972, June 5 Photo. *Perf. 14*

25pf+10pf, Sailing. 30pf+15pf, Gymnastics. 60pf+30pf, Swimming.

B485	SP305	20pf + 10pf multi	.30	.25
B486	SP305	25pf + 10pf multi	.30	.25
B487	SP305	30pf + 15pf multi	.30	.25
B488	SP305	60pf + 30pf multi	1.25	1.25
		Nos. B485-B488 (4)	2.15	2.00

20th Olympic Games, Munich, Aug. 26 Sept. 10. See No. B490.

Souvenir Sheet

Olympic Games Site, Munich — SP306

1972, July 5 Litho. *Perf. 14*

B489	SP306	Sheet of 4	3.50	3.50
a.		25pf + 10pf Gymnastics stadium	.80	.80
b.		30pf + 15pf Soccer stadium	.80	.80
c.		40pf + 20pf Tent and lake	.80	.80
d.		70pf + 35pf Television tower, vert.	.80	.80

20th Olympic Games, Munich. Surcharge was for the Foundation for the Promotion of the Munich Olympic Games.

Olympic Games Type of 1972
Souvenir Sheet

1972, Aug. 18 Litho. *Perf. 14*

B490		Sheet of 4	3.50	3.50
a.	SP305	25pf + 5pf Long jump, women's	.35	.35
b.	SP305	30pf + 10pf Basketball	1.00	1.00
c.	SP305	40pf + 10pf Discus, men's	1.25	1.25
d.	SP305	70pf + 10pf Canoeing	.65	.65
e.		Bklt. pane of 4, #B490a-B490d	7.25	7.25

20th Olympic Games, Munich.

Knight — SP307

Adoration of the Kings — SP308

1972, Oct. 5

B491	SP307	25pf + 10pf shown	.25	.20
B492	SP307	30pf + 15pf Rook	.25	.20
B493	SP307	40pf + 20pf Queen	.45	.20
B494	SP307	70pf + 35pf King	1.60	1.40
		Nos. B491-B494 (4)	2.55	2.00

19th cent. chess pieces made by Faience Works, Gien, France; now in Hamburg Museum. Surtax for independent welfare organizations.

1972, Nov. 10 Litho.

B495	SP308	30pf + 15pf multi	.50	.40

Christmas 1972.

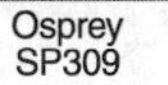
Osprey SP309

Hesse-Kassel SP310

Birds of Prey: 30pf+15pf, Buzzard. 40pf+20pf, Red kite. 70pf+35pf, Montagu's harrier.

1973, Feb. 6 Photo. *Perf. 14*

B496	SP309	25pf + 10pf multi	.80	.65
B497	SP309	30pf + 15pf multi	1.00	.80
B498	SP309	40pf + 20pf multi	1.25	1.25
B499	SP309	70pf + 35pf multi	3.00	2.75
		Nos. B496-B499 (4)	6.05	5.45

Surtax was for benefit of young people.

1973, Apr. 5 Litho. *Perf. 14*

Posthouse Signs: No. B501, Prussia. No. B502a, Württemberg. No. B502b, Bavaria.

B500	SP310	40pf + 20pf multi	.60	.60
B501	SP310	70pf + 35pf multi	1.10	1.10

Souvenir Sheet

B502		Sheet of 2	3.00	3.00
a.		SP310 40pf + 20pf multi	.65	.65
b.		SP310 70pf + 35pf multi	1.00	1.00

IBRA München 1973 International Philatelic Exhibition, Munich, May 11-20. No. B502 sold for 2.20 mark.

French Horn, 19th Century — SP311

Christmas Star — SP312

Musical Instruments: 30pf+15pf, Pedal piano, 18th century. 40pf+20pf, Violin, 18th century. 70pf+35pf, Pedal harp, 18th century.

1973, Oct. 5 Litho. *Perf. 14*

B503	SP311	25pf + 10pf multi	.45	.25
B504	SP311	30pf + 15pf multi	.50	.25
B505	SP311	40pf + 20pf multi	.65	.40
B506	SP311	70pf + 35pf multi	1.60	1.25
		Nos. B503-B506 (4)	3.20	2.15

Surtax was for independent welfare organizations.

1973, Nov. 9 Litho. & Engr.

B507	SP312	30pf + 15pf multi	.45	.35

Christmas 1973.

Young Builder — SP313

30+15pf, Girl in national costume. 40+20pf, Boy studying. 70+35pf, Girl with microscope.

1974, Apr. 17 Photo. *Perf. 14*

B508	SP313	25pf + 10pf multi	.45	.40
B509	SP313	30pf + 15pf multi	.80	.65
B510	SP313	40pf + 20pf multi	1.25	1.25
B511	SP313	70pf + 35pf multi	2.40	2.10
		Nos. B508-B511 (4)	4.90	4.40

Surtax was for benefit of young people.

Campion — SP314

1974, Oct. 15 Litho. *Perf. 14*

Flowers: 40pf+20pf, Foxglove. 50pf+25pf, Mallow. 70pf+35pf, Bellflower.

B512	SP314	30pf + 15pf multi	.25	.20
B513	SP314	40pf + 20pf multi	.35	.25
B514	SP314	50pf + 25pf multi	.40	.35
B515	SP314	70pf + 35pf multi	1.10	1.10
		Nos. B512-B515 (4)	2.10	1.90

Surtax was for independent welfare organizations.

1974, Oct. 29

Christmas: 40pf+20pf, Advent decoration.

B516	SP314	40pf + 20pf multi	.60	.45

Diesel Locomotive Class 218 — SP315

Locomotives: 40pf+20pf, Electric engine Class 103. 50pf+25pf, Electric rail motor train Class 403. 70pf+35pf, Magnetic suspension train "Transrapid" (model).

1975, Apr. 15 Litho. *Perf. 14*

B517	SP315	30pf + 15pf multi	.40	.35
B518	SP315	40pf + 20pf multi	.60	.55
B519	SP315	50pf + 25pf multi	.85	.80
B520	SP315	70pf + 35pf multi	1.40	1.25
		Nos. B517-B520 (4)	3.25	2.95

Surtax was for benefit of young people.

Edelweiss
SP316

Basketball
SP317

Alpine Flowers: 40pf+20pf, Trollflower. 50pf+25pf, Alpine rose. 70pf+35pf, Pasqueflower.

1975, Oct. 15 Litho. *Perf. 14*

B521 SP316 30pf + 15pf multi .35 .25
B522 SP316 40pf + 20pf multi .35 .25
B523 SP316 50pf + 25pf multi .55 .40
B524 SP316 70pf + 35pf multi 1.25 1.00
Nos. B521-B524 (4) 2.50 1.90

Surtax was for independent welfare organizations.

1975, Nov. 14

Christmas: Snow rose.

B525 SP316 40pf + 20pf multi .65 .55

1976, Apr. 6 Litho. *Perf. 14*

Designs: 40pf+20pf, Rowing. 50pf+25pf, Gymnastics, women's. 70pf+35pf, Volleyball.

B526 SP317 30pf + 15pf multi .40 .35
B527 SP317 40pf + 20pf multi .60 .55
B528 SP317 50pf + 25pf multi .80 .65
B529 SP317 70pf + 35pf multi 1.10 1.00
Nos. B526-B529 (4) 2.90 2.55

Youth training for Olympic Games. Surtax was for benefit of young people.

Swimmer and Olympic Rings — SP318

30pf+15pf, Hockey. 50pf+25pf, High jump. 70pf+35pf, Rowing, coxed four.

1976, Apr. 6

B530 SP318 40pf + 20pf multi .45 .40
B531 SP318 50pf + 25pf multi .65 .65

Souvenir Sheet

B532 Sheet of 2 1.25 1.25
a. SP318 30pf + 15pf multi .45 .45
b. SP318 70pf + 35pf multi .70 .70

21st Olympic Games, Montreal, Canada, July 17-Aug. 1. The surtax was for the German Sports Aid Foundation.

Phlox
SP319

Flowers: 40pf+20pf, Marigolds. 50pf+25pf, Dahlias. 70pf+35pf, Pansies.

1976, Oct. 14 Litho. *Perf. 14*

B533 SP319 30pf + 15pf multi .35 .30
B534 SP319 40pf + 20pf multi .45 .40
B535 SP319 50pf + 25pf multi .55 .45
B536 SP319 70pf + 35pf multi .90 .80
Nos. B533-B536 (4) 2.25 1.95

Surtax was for independent welfare organizations.

Souvenir Sheet

Nativity, Window, Frauenkirche, Esslingen — SP320

1976, Nov. 16 Litho. & Engr.

B537 SP320 50pf + 25pf multi .60 .55

Christmas 1976.

Wapen von Hamburg, c. 1730
SP321

Historic Ships: 40pf+20pf, Preussen, 5-master, 1902. 50pf+25pf, Bremen, 1929. 70pf+35pf, Freighter Sturmfels, 1972.

1977, Apr. 14 Litho. *Perf. 14*

B538 SP321 30pf + 15pf multi .45 .40
B539 SP321 40pf + 20pf multi .60 .55
B540 SP321 50pf + 25pf multi .80 .70
B541 SP321 70pf + 35pf multi 1.10 1.00
Nos. B538-B541 (4) 2.95 2.65

Surtax was for benefit of young people.

Caraway — SP322

Meadow Flowers: 40pf+20pf, Dandelion. 50pf+25pf, Red clover. 70pf+35pf, Meadow sage.

1977, Oct. 13 Litho. *Perf. 14*

B542 SP322 30pf + 15pf multi .35 .25
B543 SP322 40pf + 20pf multi .40 .35
B544 SP322 50pf + 25pf multi .45 .40
B545 SP322 70pf + 35pf multi .90 .85
Nos. B542-B545 (4) 2.10 1.85

Surtax was for independent welfare organizations.

See Nos. B553-B556.

Souvenir Sheet

King Caspar Offering Gold, Window, St. Gereon's, Cologne — SP323

1977, Nov. 10

B546 SP323 50pf + 25pf multi .65 .60

Christmas 1977.

Giant Slalom
SP324

Design: No. B548, Steeplechase.

1978 Litho. *Perf. 14*

B547 SP324 50pf + 25pf multi 1.25 1.00
B548 SP324 70pf + 35pf multi 2.50 2.25

Issued: #B547, Jan. 12, #B548, Apr. 13.

Surtax was for the German Sports Foundation.

Balloon Ascent, Oktoberfest, Munich, 1820 — SP325

Designs: 40pf+20pf, Airship LZ 1, 1900. 50pf+25pf, Bleriot monoplane, 1909. 70pf+35pf, Grade monoplane, 1909.

1978, Apr. 13 Litho. *Perf. 14*

B549 SP325 30pf + 15pf multi .45 .40
B550 SP325 40pf + 20pf multi .60 .55
B551 SP325 50pf + 25pf multi .80 .70
B552 SP325 70pf + 35pf multi 1.00 1.00
Nos. B549-B552 (4) 2.85 2.65

Surtax was for benefit of young people.

Flower Type of 1977

Woodland Flowers: 30pf+15pf, Arum. 40pf+20pf, Weaselsnout. 50pf+25pf, Turk's-cap lily. 70pf+35pf, Liverwort.

1978, Oct. 12 Litho. *Perf. 14*

B553 SP322 30pf + 15pf multi .35 .25
B554 SP322 40pf + 20pf multi .45 .40
B555 SP322 50pf + 25pf multi .60 .55
B556 SP322 70pf + 35pf multi .85 .85
Nos. B553-B556 (4) 2.25 2.05

Surtax was for independent welfare organizations.

Souvenir Sheet

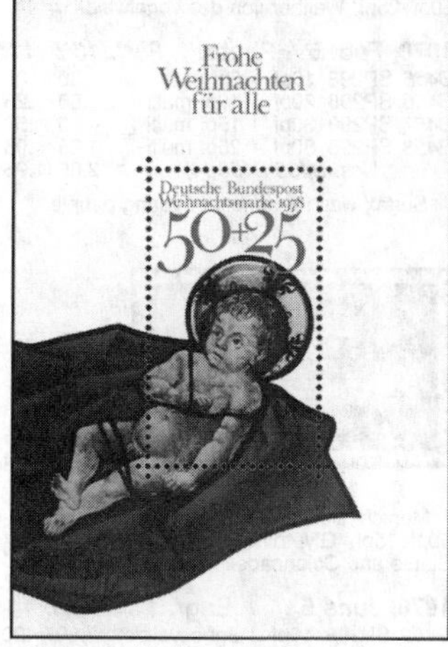

Christ Child, Window, Frauenkirche, Munich — SP326

1978, Nov. 16 Litho. *Perf. 14*

B557 SP326 50pf + 25pf multi .65 .60

Christmas 1978.

Dornier Wal, 1922
SP327

Airplanes: 50pf+25pf, Heinkel HE70, 1932. 60pf+30pf, Junkers W33 Bremen, 1928. 90pf+45pf, Focke-Wulf FW61, 1936.

1979, Apr. 5 Litho. *Perf. 14*

B558 SP327 40pf + 20pf multi .45 .40
B559 SP327 50pf + 25pf multi .65 .60
B560 SP327 60pf + 30pf multi .80 .75
B561 SP327 90pf + 45pf multi 1.00 1.00
Nos. B558-B561 (4) 2.90 2.75

Surtax was for benefit of young people.

See Nos. B570-B573.

Handball
SP328

Design: 90pf+45pf, Canoeing.

1979, Apr. 5

B562 SP328 60pf + 30pf multi .80 .70
B563 SP328 90pf + 45pf multi 1.25 .90

Surtax was for German Sports Foundation.

Post House Sign, Altheim, Saar, 1754 — SP329

1979, Oct. 11 Litho. *Perf. 14*

B564 SP329 60pf + 30pf multi .90 .90

Stamp Day. Surtax was for Foundation of Promotion of Philately and Postal History.

Issued in sheet of 10.

Red Beech
SP330

Woodland Plants: 50pf+25pf, English oak. 60pf+30pf, Hawthorn. 90pf+45pf, Mountain pine.

1979, Oct. 11 Litho. *Perf. 14*

B565	SP330	40pf + 20pf multi	.40	.35
B566	SP330	50pf + 25pf multi	.55	.45
B567	SP330	60pf + 30pf multi	.60	.55
B568	SP330	90pf + 45pf multi	1.00	.90
		Nos. B565-B568 (4)	2.55	2.25

Surtax was for independent welfare organizations.

Nativity, Medieval Manuscript SP331

1979, Nov. 14 Litho. *Perf. 13½*

B569	SP331	60pf + 30pf multi	.80	.70

Christmas 1979.

Aviation Type of 1979

40+20pf, FS 24 Phoenix, 1957. 50+25pf, Lockheed Super Constellation, 1950. 60+30pf, Airbus A300, 1972. 90+45pf, Boeing 747, 1969.

1980, Apr. 10 Litho. *Perf. 14*

B570	SP327	40 + 20pf multi	.35	.25
B571	SP327	50 + 25pf multi	.55	.45
B572	SP327	60 + 30pf multi	.70	.65
B573	SP327	90 + 45pf multi	1.00	1.00
		Nos. B570-B573 (4)	2.60	2.35

Surtax was for benefit of young people.

Soccer SP332

Designs: 60pf+30pf, Equestrian. 90pf+45pf, Cross-country skiing.

1980, May 8 Photo. *Perf. 14*

B574	SP332	50 + 25pf multi	.45	.35
B575	SP332	60 + 30pf multi	.65	.50
B576	SP332	90 + 45pf multi	1.25	1.10
		Nos. B574-B576 (3)	2.35	1.95

Surtax was for German Sports Foundation.

Ceratocephalus — SP333

Wildflowers: 50pf+25pf, Climbing meadow pea. 60pf+30pf, Corn cockle. 90pf+45pf, Grape hyacinth.

1980, Oct. 9 Litho. *Perf. 14*

B577	SP333	40 + 20pf multi	.45	.40
B578	SP333	50 + 25pf multi	.60	.55
B579	SP333	60 + 30pf multi	.65	.55
B580	SP333	90 + 45pf multi	1.10	1.00
		Nos. B577-B580 (4)	2.80	2.50

Surtax was for independent welfare organizations.

Post House Sign, 1754, Altheim, Saar — SP334

1980, Nov. 13 Litho. *Perf. 14*

B581	SP334	60 + 30pf multi	.65	.50

49th FIP Congress (Federation Internationale de Philatelie), Essen, Nov. 12-13.

Nativity, Altomunster Manuscript, 12th Century SP335

1980, Nov. 13 *Perf. 14x13½*

B582	SP335	60 + 30pf multi	.80	.70

Christmas 1980.

Borda Circle, 1800 — SP336

Historic Optical Instruments: 50pf+25pf, Reflecting telescope, 1770. 60pf+30pf, Binocular microscope, 1860. 90pf+45pf, Octant, 1775.

1981, Apr. 10 Litho. *Perf. 13½*

B583	SP336	40 + 20pf multi	.45	.30
B584	SP336	50 + 25pf multi	.80	.65
B585	SP336	60 + 30pf multi	.80	.65
B586	SP336	90 + 45pf multi	1.10	1.00
		Nos. B583-B586 (4)	3.15	2.60

Surtax was for benefit of young people.

Rowing SP337

1981, Apr. 10 *Perf. 14*

B587	SP337	60 + 30pf shown	.80	.60
B588	SP337	90 + 45pf Gliding	1.25	1.10

Surtax was for the German Sports Foundation.

Water Nut — SP338

Endangered Species: 50pf+25pf, Floating heart. 60pf+30pf, Water gillyflower. 90pf+45pf, Water lobelia.

1981, Oct. 8 Litho.

B589	SP338	40 + 20pf multi	.40	.35
B590	SP338	50 + 25pf multi	.55	.45
B591	SP338	60 + 30pf multi	.65	.60
B592	SP338	90 + 45pf multi	1.25	1.10
		Nos. B589-B592 (4)	2.85	2.50

Surtax was for independent welfare organizations.

Nativity, 19th Cent. Painting SP339

1981, Nov. 12 Litho.

B593	SP339	60 + 30pf multi	.80	.65

Christmas 1981.

Antique Cars SP340

Designs: 40+20pf, Benz, 1886. 50+25pf, Mercedes, 1913. 60+30pf, Hanomag, 1925. 90+45pf, Opel Olympia, 1937.

1982, Apr. 15 Litho.

B594	SP340	40 + 20pf multi	.45	.40
B595	SP340	50 + 25pf multi	.60	.55
B596	SP340	60 + 30pf multi	.80	.65
B597	SP340	90 + 45pf multi	1.25	1.25
		Nos. B594-B597 (4)	3.10	2.85

Surtax was for benefit of young people.

Jogging SP341

1982, Apr. 15 Litho.

B598	SP341	60 + 30pf shown	.80	.65
B599	SP341	90 + 45pf Archery	1.25	1.00

Surtax was for the German Sports Foundation.

Tea-rose Hybrid — SP342

60+30pf, Floribunda. 80f+40pf, Bourbon rose. 120+60pf, Polyantha hybrid.

1982, Oct. 14 Litho. *Perf. 14*

B600	SP342	50 + 20pf multi	.45	.40
B601	SP342	60 + 30pf multi	.60	.55
B602	SP342	80 + 40pf multi	.90	.80
B603	SP342	120 + 60pf multi	1.25	1.10
		Nos. B600-B603 (4)	3.20	2.85

Surtax was for independent welfare organizations.

Christmas SP343

1982, Nov. 10

Designs: Nativity, Oak altar, St. Peter's Church, Hamburg, 1380.

B604	SP343	80 + 40pf multi	.95	.70

Historic Motorcycles — SP344

Designs: 50pf+20pf, Daimler-Maybach, 1885. 60pf+30pf, NSU, 1901. 80pf+40pf, Megola-Sport, 1922. 120pf+60pf, BMW, 1936.

1983, Apr. 12 Litho. *Perf. 14*

B605	SP344	50 + 20pf multi	.45	.40
B606	SP344	60 + 30pf multi	.60	.55
B607	SP344	80 + 40pf multi	1.10	1.00
B608	SP344	120 + 60pf multi	1.60	1.40
		Nos. B605-B608 (4)	3.75	3.35

Surtax was for benefit of young people.

1983 Sports Championships — SP345

80+40pf, Gymnastics Festival. 120+60pf, Modern Pentathlon World Championships.

1983, Apr. 12

B609	SP345	80 + 40pf multi	1.00	.85
B610	SP345	120 + 60pf multi	1.50	1.25

Surtax was for German Sports Foundation.

Swiss Androsace SP346

60+30pf, Krain groundsel. 80+40pf, Fleischer's willow herb. 120+60pf, Alpine sow-thistle.

1983, Oct. 13 Litho. *Perf. 14*

B611	SP346	50 + 20pf multi	.45	.40
B612	SP346	60 + 30pf multi	.60	.55
B613	SP346	80 + 40pf multi	1.10	1.00
B614	SP346	120 + 60pf multi	1.60	1.40
		Nos. B611-B614 (4)	3.75	3.35

Surtax was for welfare organizations.

Christmas SP347

1983, Nov. 10 Litho.

B615	SP347	80 + 40pf Carolers	1.25	1.10

Surtax was for free welfare work.

Insects — SP348

1984, Apr. 12 Litho.

Designs: 50pf+20pf, Trichodes apoarius. 60pf+30pf, Vanessa atalanta. 80pf+40pf, Apis mellifera. 120pf+60pf, Chrysotoxum festivum.

B616	SP348	50 + 20pf multi	.45	.40
B617	SP348	60 + 30pf multi	.90	.85
B618	SP348	80 + 40pf multi	1.25	1.10
B619	SP348	120 + 60pf multi	1.75	1.60
		Nos. B616-B619 (4)	4.35	3.95

Surtax was for German Youth Stamp Foundation.

Women's Discus SP349

Olympic Sports: 80pf+40pf, Rhythmic gymnastics. 120pf+60pf, Wind surfing.

1984, Apr. 12

B620	SP349	60 + 30pf multi	.80	.65
B621	SP349	80 + 40pf multi	1.10	1.00
B622	SP349	120 + 60pf multi	2.10	2.00
		Nos. B620-B622 (3)	4.00	3.65

Surtax was for German Sports Foundation.

Orchids
SP350

Designs: 50pf+20pf, Aceras anthropophorum. 60pf+30pf, Orchis ustulata. 80pf+40pf, Limodorum abortivum. 120+60pf, Dactylorhiza sambucina.

1984, Oct. 18 Litho. *Perf. 14*

B623 SP350 50 + 20pf multi .60 .55
B624 SP350 60 + 30pf multi .60 .55
B625 SP350 80 + 40pf multi .90 .85
B626 SP350 120 + 60pf multi 1.90 1.75
Nos. B623-B626 (4) 4.00 3.70

Surtax was for welfare organizations.

Christmas 1984 — SP351

1984, Nov. 8 Litho.

B627 SP351 80pf + 40pf St. Martin 1.10 .90

Surtax was for welfare organizations.

Bowling
SP352

1985, Feb. 21 Photo.

B628 SP352 80pf + 40pf multi 1.10 .90
B629 SP352 120pf + 60pf Kayaking 1.75 1.60

Surtax was for German Sports Foundation.

Antique Bicycles
SP353

50pf+20pf, Draisienne, 1817. 60pf+30pf, NSU Germania, 1886. 80pf+40pf, Crossframe, 1887. 120pf+60pf, Adler tricycle, 1888.

1985, Apr. 16 Litho.

B630 SP353 50pf + 20pf multi .65 .55
B631 SP353 60pf + 30pf multi .75 .70
B632 SP353 80pf + 40pf multi 1.10 1.00
B633 SP353 120pf + 60pf multi 2.10 2.00
Nos. B630-B633 (4) 4.60 4.25

Surtax was for benefit of young people. Each stamp shows the Intl. Youth Year emblem.

MOPHILA '85, Hamburg, Sept. 11-15
SP354

1985, Aug. 13 Litho. *Perf. 14x14½*

B634 SP354 60 + 20pf Coach-man, horses 2.00 1.60
B635 SP354 80 + 20pf Stage-coach 2.00 1.60
a. Pair, #B634-B635 5.00 4.25

Surtax for the benefit of the Philatelic & Postal History Foundation. No. B635a has continuous design.

SP355

Various ornamental borders, medieval prayer book, Prussian State Library, Berlin.

1985, Oct. 15 Litho. *Perf. 14*

B636 SP355 50pf + 20pf multi .55 .45
B637 SP355 60pf + 30pf multi .65 .60
B638 SP355 80pf + 40pf multi .85 .80
B639 SP355 120pf + 60pf multi 1.60 1.50
Nos. B636-B639 (4) 3.65 3.35

Surtax for welfare organizations.

Christmas 1985 — SP356

Woodcut: The Birth of Christ, by Hans Baldung Grien (1485-1545), Freiburg Cathedral High Altar.

1985, Nov. 12 Litho. *Perf. 14*

B640 SP356 80pf + 40pf multi 1.10 1.00

Surtax for welfare organizations.

European World Sports Championships — SP357

1986, Feb. 13 Litho. *Perf. 14*

B641 SP357 80 + 40pf Running 1.25 1.10
B642 SP357 120 + 55pf Bobsledding 2.00 1.90

Surtax for the Natl. Sports Promotion Foundation.

Vocational Training — SP358

1986, Apr. 10

B643 SP358 50 + 25pf Optician .80 .70
B644 SP358 60 + 30pf Mason .90 .85
B645 SP358 70 + 35pf Beautician 1.10 1.00
B646 SP358 80 + 40pf Baker 1.60 1.40
Nos. B643-B646 (4) 4.40 3.95

Surtax for German Youth Stamp Foundation.

Glassware in German Museums — SP359

1986, Oct. 16 Litho.

B647 SP359 50 + 25pf Ornamental flask, c. 300 .60 .50
B648 SP359 60 + 30pf Goblet, c. 1650 .80 .70
B649 SP359 70 + 35pf Imperial eagle tankard, c. 1662 .90 .80
B650 SP359 80 + 40pf Engraved goblet, c. 1720 1.10 1.00
Nos. B647-B650 (4) 3.40 3.00

Surtax for public welfare organizations.

Christmas
SP360

Adoration of the Infant Jesus, Ortenberg Altarpiece, c. 1430, Hesse Museum, Darmstadt.

1986, Nov. 13 Litho. *Perf. 14*

B651 SP360 80 + 40pf multi 1.10 1.00

Surtax for public welfare organizations.

World Championships — SP361

1987, Feb. 12 Litho.

B652 SP361 80 + 40pf Sailing 1.10 .90
B653 SP361 120 + 55pf Cross-country skiing 1.75 1.60

Surtax for the benefit of the national Sports Promotion Foundation.

Youth in Industry
SP362

1987, Apr. 9 Litho.

B654 SP362 50 + 25pf Plumber .90 .85
B655 SP362 60 + 30pf Dental technician 1.10 1.10
B656 SP362 70 + 35pf Butcher 1.25 1.10
B657 SP362 80 + 40pf Bookbinder 1.75 1.60
Nos. B654-B657 (4) 5.00 4.65

Surtax for youth organizations.

Gold and Silver Artifacts
SP363

1987, Oct. 15

B658 SP363 50 + 25pf Roman bracelet, 4th cent. .80 .70
B659 SP363 60 + 30pf Gothic buckle, 6th cent. .90 .85
B660 SP363 70 + 35pf Merovingian disk fibula, 7th cent. .90 .85
B661 SP363 80 + 40pf Purse-shaped reliquary, 8th cent. 1.25 1.25
Nos. B658-B661 (4) 3.85 3.65

Surtax for welfare organizations sonsoring free museum exhibitions.

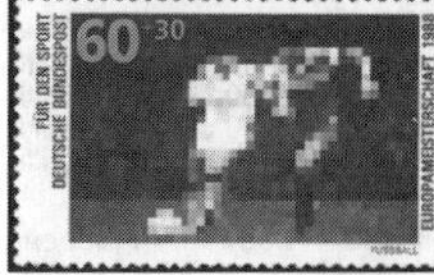

Christmas
SP364

Illustration from Book of Psalms, 13th cent., Bavarian Natl. Museum: Birth of Christ.

1987, Nov. 6

B662 SP364 80 + 40pf multi 1.10 .90

Surtax for public welfare organizations.

Sports
SP365

1988, Feb. 18 Litho.

B663 SP365 60 + 30pf Soccer .75 .65
B664 SP365 80 + 40pf Tennis 1.10 .90
B665 SP365 120 + 55pf Diving 1.60 1.40
Nos. B663-B665 (3) 3.45 2.95

Surtax for Stiftung Deutsche Sporthilfe, a foundation for the promotion of sports in Germany.

Rock Stars
SP366

#B666, Buddy Holly (1936-59). #B667, Elvis Presley (1935-77). #B668, Jim Morrison (1943-71). #B669, John Lennon (1940-80).

1988, Apr. 14 Litho. *Perf. 14*

B666 SP366 50 + 25pf multi .90 .80
B667 SP366 60 + 30pf multi 1.75 1.60
B668 SP366 70 + 35pf multi 1.10 .90
B669 SP366 80 + 40pf multi 1.90 1.60
Nos. B666-B669 (4) 5.65 4.90

Surtax for German Youth Stamp Foundation.

Gold and Rock Crystal Reliquary, c. 1200, Schnutgen Museum, Cologne
SP367

Gold and silver artifacts: No. B671, Bust of Charlemagne, 14th cent., Aachen cathedral. No. B672, Crown of Otto III, 10th cent., Essen cathedral. No. B673, Flower bouquet, c. 1620, Schmuck Museum, Pforzheim.

1988, Oct. 13 Litho.

B670 SP367 50 + 25pf multi .45 .40
B671 SP367 60 + 30pf multi .80 .80
B672 SP367 70 + 35pf multi .80 .80
B673 SP367 80 + 40pf multi 1.10 1.10
Nos. B670-B673 (4) 3.15 3.10

Surtax for welfare organizations.

Christmas
SP368

Illumination from *The Gospel Book of Henry the Lion*, Helmarshausen, 1188, Prussian Cultural Museum, Bavaria: Adoration of the Magi.

1988, Nov. 10 Litho.

B674 SP368 80 + 40pf multi 1.10 1.00

Surtax for public welfare organizations.

World Championship Sporting Events Hosted by Germany — SP369

1989, Feb. 9 Litho.

B675 SP369 100pf + 50pf Table tennis 1.60 1.40
B676 SP369 140pf + 60pf Gymnastics 2.25 2.25

Surtax for the Natl. Sports Promotion Foundation.

IPHLA Philatelic Literature Exhibition, Frankfurt, Apr. 19-23 — SP370

1989, Apr. 20 **Litho.**
B677 SP370 100 + 50pf multi 2.25 1.60

Surtax benefited the Foundation for the Promotion of Philately and Postal History.

Circus SP371

1989, Apr. 20

B678 SP371	60 + 30pf Elephants		1.25	1.00
B679 SP371	70 + 30pf Bareback rider		1.60	1.25
B680 SP371	80 + 35pf Clown		2.25	1.60
B681 SP371	100 + 50pf Caravans, big top		3.25	2.00
	Nos. B678-B681 (4)		8.35	5.85

Surtax for natl. youth welfare organizations.

Mounted Courier of Thurn and Taxis, 18th Cent. SP372

History of mail carrying: No. B683, Hamburg postal service messenger, 1808. No. B684, Bavarian mail coach, c. 1900.

1989, Oct. 12 **Litho.**

B682 SP372	60 + 30pf multi	.80	.70
B683 SP372	80 + 35pf multi	1.25	1.10
B684 SP372	100 + 50pf multi	2.00	1.90
	Nos. B682-B684 (3)	4.05	3.70

Surtax for the benefit of Free Welfare Work.

Christmas SP373

Wood carvings by Veit Stoss in St. Lawrence's Church, Nuremburg, 1517-18.

1989, Nov. 16 **Litho.**

B685 SP373	60 + 30pf Angel	.90	.80
B686 SP373	100 + 50pf Adoration of the Kings	1.25	1.10

Surtax for benefit of the Federal Working Assoc. of Free Welfare Work.

Popular Sports SP374

1990, Feb. 15 **Litho.**

B687 SP374	100 + 50pf Handball	2.10	1.25
B688 SP374	140 + 60pf Physical fitness	2.50	2.00

Surtax for the Natl. Sports Promotion Foundation.

Max and Moritz, by Wilhelm Busch, 125th Anniv. SP375

1990, Apr. 19 **Litho.**

B689 SP375	60 + 30pf Widow Bolte	.65	.65
B690 SP375	70 + 30pf Max	1.00	1.00
B691 SP375	80 + 35pf Max and Moritz	1.25	1.00
B692 SP375	100 + 50pf Max and Moritz, diff.	1.60	1.25
	Nos. B689-B692 (4)	4.50	3.90

Surcharge for the German Youth Stamp Foundation.

Souvenir Sheet

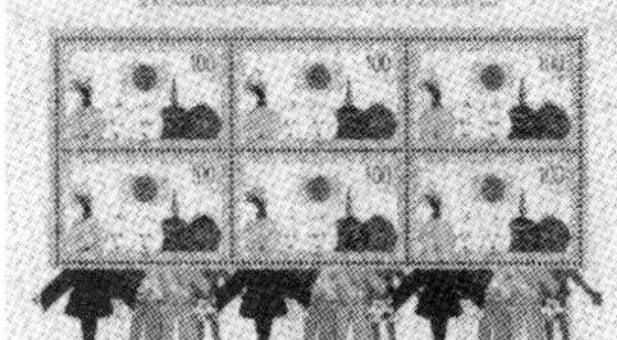

Dusseldorf '90 — SP376

Illustration reduced.

1990, June 21 **Litho.**

B693 SP376	Sheet of 6	12.50	12.50
a.	100pf + 50pf multi	2.00	2.00

Surtax for the Foundation for Promotion of Philately and Postal History. 10th Intl. Philatelic Exhibition of Youth and 11th Natl. Philatelic Exhibition of Youth.

Post and Telecommunications — SP377

Designs: 60pf+30pf, Postal vehicle, 1900. 80pf+35pf, Telephone exchange, 1890. 100pf+50pf, Post office, 1900.

1990, Sept. 27 **Litho.** ***Perf. 13½x14***

B694 SP377	60pf + 30pf multi	.70	.70
B695 SP377	80pf + 35pf multi	1.25	1.25
B696 SP377	100pf + 50pf multi	1.75	1.75
	Nos. B694-B696 (3)	3.70	3.70

Surtax for welfare organizations.

Christmas SP378

1990, Nov. 6 **Litho.** ***Perf. 14***

B697 SP378	50pf + 20pf shown	.65	.65
B698 SP378	60pf + 30pf Smoking manikin	.80	.80
B699 SP378	70pf + 30pf Nutcracker	1.10	1.10
B700 SP378	100pf + 50pf Angel, diff.	1.60	1.60
	Nos. B697-B700 (4)	4.15	4.15

Surtax for welfare organizations.

Sports SP379

1991, Feb. 14 **Litho.** ***Perf. 14***

B701 SP379	70 +30pf Weight lifting	1.00	1.00
B702 SP379	100 +50pf Cycling	1.25	1.25
B703 SP379	140 +60pf Basketball	1.60	1.60
B704 SP379	170 +80pf Wrestling	2.00	2.00
	Nos. B701-B704 (4)	5.85	5.85

Surtax for the Foundation for the Promotion of Sports.

Endangered Butterflies SP380

#B705, Alpen gelbling, alpine sulphur. #B706, Grosser eisvogel, Viceroy. #B707, Grosser schillerfalter, purple emperor. #B708, Blauschillernder beuerfalter, bluish copper. #B709,Schwalben-schwanz, swallowtail. #B710, Alpen apollo, alpine apollo. #B711, Hochmoor gelbling, moor sulphur. #B712, Grosser feuerfalter, large copper.

1991, Apr. 9 **Litho.** ***Perf. 13½***

B705 SP380	30 +15pf multi	.35	.35
B706 SP380	50 +25pf multi	.40	.40
B707 SP380	60 +30pf multi	.80	.80
B708 SP380	70 +30pf multi	.85	.85
B709 SP380	80 +35pf multi	1.10	1.10
B710 SP380	90 +45pf multi	1.25	1.25
B711 SP380	100 +50pf multi	1.60	1.60
B712 SP380	140 +60pf multi	2.00	2.00
	Nos. B705-B712 (8)	8.35	8.35

Surtax for German Youth Stamp Foundation. See Nos. B728-B732.

Souvenir Sheet

Otto Lilienthal's First Glider Flight, Cent. — SP381

1991, July 9 **Litho.** ***Perf. 14***
B713 SP381 100pf +50pf multi 2.50 2.10

Surtax benefited Foundation of Philately and Postal History.

Post Offices SP382

30pf+15pf, Bethel. 60pf+30pf, Budingen postal station. 70pf+30pf, Stralsund. 80pf+35pf, Lauscha. 100pf+50pf, Bonn. 140pf+60pf, Weilburg.

1991, Oct. 10 **Litho.** ***Perf. 14***

B714 SP382	30pf +15pf multi	.40	.40
B715 SP382	60pf +30pf multi	.80	.80
B716 SP382	70pf +30pf multi	1.00	1.00
B717 SP382	80pf +35pf multi	1.25	1.25
B718 SP382	100pf +50pf multi	1.60	1.60
B719 SP382	140pf +60pf multi	2.00	2.00
	Nos. B714-B719 (6)	7.05	7.05

Christmas SP383

Paintings by Martin Schongauer (c. 1450-1491): 60pf+30pf, Angel of the Annunciation. 70pf+30pf, The Annunciation. 80pf+35pf, Angel. 100pf+50pf, Nativity.

1991, Nov. 5 **Litho.** ***Perf. 14***

B720 SP383	60pf +30pf multi	.80	.80
B721 SP383	70pf +30pf multi	1.00	1.00
B722 SP383	80pf +35pf multi	1.60	1.60
B723 SP383	100pf +50pf multi	1.90	1.90
	Nos. B720-B723 (4)	5.30	5.30

Surtax for Federal Working Association of Free Welfare Work.

Olympic Sports SP384

1992, Feb. 6 **Litho.** ***Perf. 14***

B724 SP384	60pf +30pf Women's fencing	.65	.65
B725 SP384	80pf +40pf Rowing coxed eights	.80	.80
B726 SP384	100pf +50pf Dressage	1.60	1.60
B727 SP384	170pf +80pf Men's slalom skiing	2.50	2.50
	Nos. B724-B727 (4)	5.55	5.55

Endangered Butterfly Type of 1991

60+30pf, Purpurbar. 70+30pf, Labkraut schwarmer. 80+40pf, Silbermonch. 100+50pf, Schwarzer bar. 170+80pf, Rauschbeeren-fleckenspanner.

1992, Apr. 9 **Litho.** ***Perf. 13½***

B728 SP380	60pf +30pf multi	.95	.95
B729 SP380	70pf +30pf multi	1.00	1.00
B730 SP380	80pf +40pf multi	1.40	1.40
B731 SP380	100pf +50pf multi	1.50	1.50
B732 SP380	170pf +80pf multi	1.75	1.75
	Nos. B728-B732 (5)	6.60	6.60

Surtax for German Youth Stamp Foundation.

Preservation of Tropical Rain Forests SP385

1992, June 11 **Litho.** ***Perf. 13***
B733 SP385 100pf +50pf multi 1.40 1.40

Antique Clocks SP386

Antique clocks: 60pf+30pf, Turret, c. 1400. 70pf+30pf, Astronomical geographical mantelpiece, 1738. 80pf+40pf, Fluted, c. 1790. 100fpf+50pf, Figurine, c. 1580. 170pf+80pf, Table, c. 1550.

1992, Oct. 15 Litho. *Perf. 14*

B734	SP386	60pf +30pf multi	.80	.80
B735	SP386	70pf +30pf multi	1.00	1.00
B736	SP386	80pf +40pf multi	1.10	1.10
B737	SP386	100pf +50pf multi	1.25	1.25
B738	SP386	170pf +80pf multi	1.90	1.90
		Nos. B734-B738 (5)	6.05	6.05

Surtax for welfare organizations.

Christmas SP387

Carvings from Church of St. Anne, Annaberg-Buchholz, by Franz Maidburg: 60pf + 30pf, Adoration of the Magi. 100pf + 50pf, The Nativity.

1992, Nov. 5

B739	SP387	60pf +30pf multi	.80	.80
B740	SP387	100pf +50pf multi	1.25	1.25

Surtax for benefit of free welfare work.

Sports SP388

Designs: 60pf+30pf, Olympic ski jump, Garmisch-Partenkirchen. 80pf+40pf, Olympic Park, Munich. 100pf+50pf, Olympic Stadium, Berlin. 170pf+80pf, Olympic harbor, Kiel.

1993, Feb. 11 Litho. *Perf. 13½*

B741	SP388	60pf +30pf multi	1.00	1.00
B742	SP388	80pf +40pf multi	1.25	1.25
B743	SP388	100pf +50pf multi	1.60	1.60
B744	SP388	170pf +80pf multi	2.00	2.00
		Nos. B741-B744 (4)	5.85	5.85

Surtax for Natl. Sports Promotion Foundation.

Beetles SP389

Designs: No. B745, Alpenbock (Alpine sawyer). No. B746, Rosenkafer (rose chafer). No. B747, Hirschkafer (stag beetle). No. B748, Sandlaufkafer (tiger beetle). 200pf + 50pf, Maikafer (cockchafer).

1993, Apr. 15 Litho. *Perf. 14*

B745	SP389	80pf +40pf multi	1.25	1.25
B746	SP389	80pf +40pf multi	1.25	1.25
B747	SP389	100pf +50pf multi	1.40	1.40
B748	SP389	100pf +50pf multi	1.40	1.40
B749	SP389	200pf +50pf multi	2.25	2.25
		Nos. B745-B749 (5)	7.55	7.55

Surtax for German Youth Stamp Foundation.

Stamp Day — SP390

1993, Sept. 16 Litho. *Perf. 13½x14*

B750	SP390	100pf +50pf multi	1.10	1.10

Surtax for the Foundation for Promotion of Philately and Postal History.

Traditional Costumes SP391

Costumes from: No. B751, Rugen, Mecklenburg, Western Pomerania. No. B752, Fohr, Schleswig-Holstein. No. B753, Schwalm, Hesse. No. B754, Oberndorf, Bavaria. 200pf + 40pf, Ernstroda, Thuringia.

1993, Oct. 14 *Perf. 14*

B751	SP391	80pf +40pf multi	1.00	1.00
B752	SP391	80pf +40pf multi	1.00	1.00
B753	SP391	100pf +50pf multi	1.25	1.25
B754	SP391	100pf +50pf multi	1.25	1.25
B755	SP391	200pf +40pf multi	2.25	2.25
		Nos. B751-B755 (5)	6.75	6.75

Surtax for welfare organizations. See Nos. B768-B772.

Christmas SP392

Wings of high altar in choir of Blaubeuren Monastery: 80pf+40pf, Adoraration of Magi. 100pf+50pf, Nativity.

1993, Nov. 10 Litho. *Perf. 14*

B756	SP392	80pf +40pf multi	.80	.80
B757	SP392	100pf +50pf multi	1.40	1.40

Surtax for welfare organizations.

Figure Skating SP393

Sports: #B759, Olympic Flame. #B760, Soccer ball, World Cup Trophy. 200pf+80pf, Skiier.

1994, Feb. 10 Litho. *Perf. 14x13½*

B758	SP393	80pf +40pf multi	1.00	1.00
B759	SP393	100pf +50pf multi	1.25	1.25
B760	SP393	100pf +50pf multi	1.25	1.25
B761	SP393	200pf +80pf multi	2.00	2.00
		Nos. B758-B761 (4)	5.50	5.50

1994 Winter Olympics, Lillehammer (#B758). Intl. Olympic Committee, Cent. (#B759). 1994 World Cup Soccer Championships, US (#B760). 1994 Paralympics, Lillehammer (#B761).

Heinrich Hoffmann (1809-94), Physician, Writer of Children's Books SP394

Characters from "Slovenly Peter:" No. B762, Little Pauline. No. B763, Johnny Head-in-the-air. No. B764, Slovenly Peter. No. B765, Naughty Frederick. 200pf+80pf, The Fidget.

1994, Apr. 14 Litho. *Perf. 13½*

B762	SP394	80pf +40pf multi	.90	.90
B763	SP394	80pf +40pf multi	.90	.90
B764	SP394	100pf +50pf multi	1.25	1.25
B765	SP394	100pf +50pf multi	1.25	1.25
B766	SP394	200pf +80pf multi	2.00	2.00
		Nos. B762-B766 (5)	6.30	6.30

Surtax for German Youth Stamp Foundation.

Environmental Protection SP395

1994, June 16 Litho. *Perf. 13*

B767	SP395	100pf +50pf blk & grn	1.40	1.40

Traditional Costume Type 1993

Costumes from: No. B768, Buckeburg. No. B769, Halle an der Saale. No. B770, Hoyerswerda. No. B771, Minden. 200pf+70pf, Betzingen.

1994, Oct. 13 Litho. *Perf. 13½*

B768	SP391	80pf +40pf multi	.90	.90
B769	SP391	80pf +40pf multi	.90	.90
B770	SP391	100pf +50pf multi	1.40	1.40
B771	SP391	100pf +50pf multi	1.40	1.40
B772	SP391	200pf +70pf multi	2.00	2.00
		Nos. B768-B772 (5)	6.60	6.60

Surtax for welfare organizations.

Christmas SP396

Paintings by Hans Memling: 80pf+40pf, Adoration of the Magi. 100pf+50pf, Nativity Scene.

1994, Nov. 9 Litho. *Perf. 13½*

B773	SP396	80pf +40pf multi	1.00	1.00
B774	SP396	100pf +50pf multi	1.25	1.25

Sports SP397

1995, Feb. 9 Photo. *Perf. 13½*

B775	SP397	80pf +40pf Rowing	.70	.70
B776	SP397	100pf +50pf Gymnastics	.90	.90
B777	SP397	100pf +50pf Boxing	.90	.90
B778	SP397	200pf +80pf Volleyball	1.75	1.75
		Nos. B775-B778 (4)	4.25	4.25

World Kayaking Championships, Duisburg (#B775). Intl. Gymnastics Festival, Berlin (#B776). World Amateur Boxing Championships, Berlin (#B777). Volleyball, cent. (#B778).

Dogs SP398

#B779, Munsterlander. #B780, Schnauzer. #B781, German shepherd. #B782, Wire haired dachshund. 200pf+80pf, Wolf spitz.

1995, June 8 Litho. *Perf. 13½*

B779	SP398	80pf +40pf multi	.65	.65
B780	SP398	80pf +40pf multi	.65	.65
B781	SP398	100pf +50pf multi	.90	.90
B782	SP398	100pf +50pf multi	.90	.90
B783	SP398	200pf +80pf multi	1.60	1.60
		Nos. B779-B783 (5)	4.70	4.70

Surtax for benefit of German Youth Stamp Foundation.

See Nos. B792-B796.

Stamp Day — SP399

1995, Sept. 6 Litho. *Perf. 13*

B784	SP399	200pf +100pf multi	2.00	1.75

Surtax for Foundation for Promotion of Philately and Postal History.

Farmhouses — SP400

#B785, Eifel region. #B786, Saxony. #B787, Lower Germany. #B788, Upper Bavaria. 200pf+70pf, Mecklenburg.

1995, Oct. 12 Litho. *Perf. 14*

B785	SP400	80pf +40pf multi	.65	.65
B786	SP400	80pf +40pf multi	.65	.65
B787	SP400	100pf +50pf multi	.90	.90
B788	SP400	100pf +50pf multi	.90	.90
B789	SP400	200pf +70pf multi	1.60	1.60
		Nos. B785-B789 (5)	4.70	4.70

Surtax for welfare organizations.

See Nos. B802-B806.

Christmas SP401

Stained glass windows, Augsburg Cathedral: 80pf+40pf, Annunciation. 100pf+50pf, Nativity.

1995, Nov. 9 Litho. *Perf. 14*

B790	SP401	80pf +40pf multi	.90	.90
B791	SP401	100pf +50pf multi	1.25	1.25

Surtax for welfare organizations.

Dog Type of 1995

#B792, Borzoi. #B793, Chow chow. #B794, St. Bernard. #B795, Collie. 200pf+80pf, Briard.

1996, Feb. 8 Litho. *Perf. 13½*

B792	SP398	80pf +40pf multi	1.00	1.00
B793	SP398	80pf +40pf multi	1.00	1.00
B794	SP398	100pf +50pf multi	1.25	1.25
B795	SP398	100pf +50pf multi	1.25	1.25
B796	SP398	200pf +80pf multi	1.60	1.60
		Nos. B792-B796 (5)	6.10	6.10

Surtax for benefit of German Youth Stamp Foundation.

Modern Olympic Games, Cent. SP402

Olympic champions: 80pf+40pf, Carl Schuhmann (1869-1946), pommel horse. No. B798, Annie Hübler Horn (1885-1976), pairs figure skating. No. B799, Josef Neckermann (1912-92), equestrian. 200pf+80pf, Alfred Flatow (1869-1942), Gustav Felix Flatow (1875-1945), gymnastics.

1996, June 13 Photo. *Perf. 13½*

B797 SP402 80pf +40pf multi 1.10 1.10
B798 SP402 100pf +50pf multi 1.40 1.40
B799 SP402 100pf +50pf multi 1.40 1.40
B800 SP402 200pf +80pf multi 2.50 2.50
Nos. B797-B800 (4) 6.40 6.40

Preservation of Tropical Habitats — SP403

1996, July 18 Photo. *Perf. 14*

B801 SP403 100pf +50pf multi 1.50 1.50

Farmhouse Type of 1995

Location: No. B802, Spree Forest. No. B803, Thuringia. No. B804, Black Forest. No. B805, Westphalia. 200pf+70pf, Schleswig-Holstein.

1996, Oct. 9 Litho. *Perf. 14*

B802 SP400 80pf +40pf multi .95 .70
B803 SP400 80pf +40pf multi .95 .70
B804 SP400 100pf +50pf multi 1.25 .95
B805 SP400 100pf +50pf multi 1.25 .95
B806 SP400 200pf +70pf multi 2.10 1.90
Nos. B802-B806 (5) 6.50 5.20

Christmas SP404

Illuminated pages from Henry II's book of pericopes (Gospels), 11th cent.: 80pf+40pf, Adoration of the Magi. 100pf+50pf, Nativity.

1996, Nov. 14 Litho. *Perf. 14*

B807 SP404 80pf +40pf multi 1.00 1.00
B808 SP404 100pf +50pf multi 1.25 1.25

Surtax for welfare organizations.

Sports SP405

1997, Feb. 4 Litho. *Perf. 14x13½*

B809 SP405 80pf +40pf Aerobics 1.10 1.10
B810 SP405 100pf +50pf Inline skating 1.40 1.40
B811 SP405 100pf +50pf Streetball 1.40 1.40
B812 SP405 200pf +80pf Free climbing 2.50 2.50
Nos. B809-B812 (4) 6.40 6.40

Horses SP406

1997, June 9 Litho. *Perf. 14*

B813 SP406 80pf + 40pf Rheno-German draft 1.00 1.00
B814 SP406 80pf + 40pf Shetland pony 1.00 1.00
B815 SP406 100pf + 50pf Friesian 1.25 1.25
B816 SP406 100pf + 50pf Haflinger 1.25 1.25
B817 SP406 200pf + 80pf Hanoverian 2.75 2.75
Nos. B813-B817 (5) 7.25 7.25

Arms Type of 1992 Redrawn and Inscribed "Hochwasserhilfe 1997" and "DEUTSCHLAND"

1997, Aug. 19 Litho. *Perf. 13½*

B818 A739 110pf +90pf like #1702 1.90 1.90

Souvenir Sheet

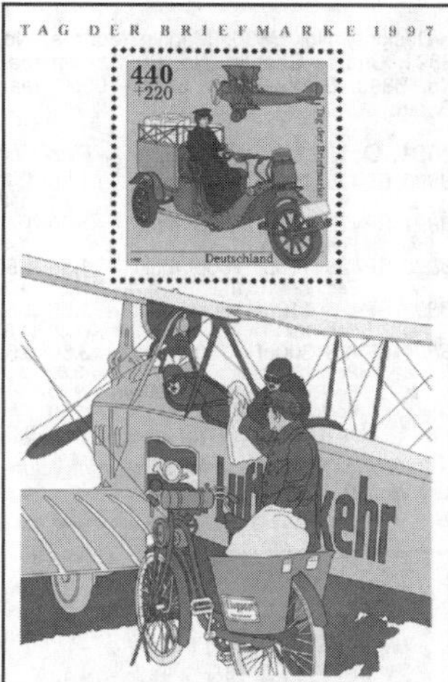

Stamp Day — SP407

Illustration reduced.

1997, Sept. 17 Litho. *Perf. 14*

B819 SP407 440pf +220pf multi 6.50 6.50

Mills — SP408

Designs: 100pf+50pf, Black Forest. No. B821, Hesse. No. B822, Windmill, lower Rhine. No. B823, Scoop windmill, Schleswig-Holstein. 220pf+80pf, Dutch windmill.

1997, Oct. 9 Litho. *Perf. 13½x14*
Background Color

B820 SP408 100pf +50pf grn 1.40 1.40
B821 SP409 110pf +50pf brn 1.50 1.50
B822 SP408 110pf +50pf blue 1.50 1.50
B823 SP408 110pf +50pf yel 1.50 1.50
B824 SP408 220pf +80pf pink 2.25 2.25
Nos. B820-B824 (5) 8.15 8.15

Christmas SP409

1997, Nov. 6 Litho. *Perf. 14*

B825 SP409 100pf +50pf Magi 1.40 1.40
B826 SP409 110pf +50pf Nativity 1.60 1.60

Surtax for Federal Assoc. of Free Welfare Work in Bonn.

Sports SP410

1998 Sporting events: 100pf+50pf, World Cup Soccer Championships, France. No. B828, Winter Olympic Games, Nagano. No. B829, Rowing Championships, Cologne. 300pf+100pf, Winter Paralympics, Nagano.

1998, Feb. 5 Photo. *Perf. 14*

B827 SP410 100pf +50pf multi 1.25 1.25
B828 SP410 110pf +50pf multi 1.40 1.40
B829 SP410 110pf +50pf multi 1.40 1.40
B830 SP410 300pf +100pf multi 3.25 3.25
Nos. B827-B830 (4) 7.30 7.30

Environmental Protection — SP411

1998, May 7 Litho. *Perf. 14*

B831 SP411 110pf +50pf multi 1.40 1.40

Cartoon Figures SP412

#B832, Mouse, Little Yellow Duck, Elephant. #833, Sandman. #834, Maja the Bee. #835, Captain Bluebear. #836, Pumuckl.

1998, June 10 Litho. *Perf. 14*

B832 SP412 100pf +50pf multi 1.25 1.25
B833 SP412 100pf +50pf multi 1.25 1.25
B834 SP412 110pf +50pf multi 1.40 1.40
B835 SP412 110pf +50pf multi 1.40 1.40
B836 SP412 220pf +50pf multi 2.75 2.75
Nos. B832-B836 (5) 8.05 8.05

Surtax for the German Youth Stamp Foundation.

Welfare Stamps SP413

Birds: 100pf+50pf, Hen-harrier. No. B838, Great bustard. No. B839, White-eyed duck. No. B840, Sedge warbler. 220pf+80pf, Wood-chat shrike.

1998, Oct. 8 Litho. *Perf. 14*
Background Colors

B837 SP413 100pf +50pf tan 1.25 1.25
B838 SP413 110pf +50pf gray grn 1.25 1.25
B839 SP413 110pf +50pf gray blue 1.40 1.40
B840 SP413 110pf +50pf blue grn 1.40 1.40
B841 SP413 220pf +80pf lilac 2.75 2.75
Nos. B837-B841 (5) 8.05 8.05

Christmas SP414

1998, Nov. 12

B842 SP414 100pf +50pf Shepherds 1.50 1.50
B843 SP414 110pf +50pf Holy Child 1.60 1.60

Racing Sports SP415

1999, Feb. 18 Photo. *Perf. 14*

B844 SP415 100pf +50pf Bicycles 1.50 1.50
B845 SP415 110pf +50pf Cars 1.60 1.60
B846 SP415 110pf +50pf Horses 1.60 1.60
B847 SP415 300pf +100pf Motorcycles 3.75 3.75
Nos. B844-B847 (4) 8.45 8.45

Declaration of Human Rights Type of 1998

Inscribed "KOSOVO-HILFE 1999"

1999, Apr. 27 Litho. *Perf. 14*

B848 A958 110pf +100pf multi 1.90 1.90

Sutax for aid to refugees from Kosovo.

Souvenir Sheet

IBRA '99, Intl. Stamp Exhibition, Nuremberg — SP416

Design: Bavaria #1 & Saxony #1. Illustration reduced.

1999, Apr. 27 *Perf. 13½*

B849 SP416 300pf +110pf multi 3.75 3.75

German postage stamps, 150th anniv.

Cartoons SP417

#B850, The Little Polar Bear. #B851, Rudi the Crow. #B852, Mecki (hedgehog). #B853, Twipsy, mascot of Expo 2000, Hanover. 220pf+80pf, Tabaluga (green dragon).

1999, June 10 Litho. *Perf. 13¾*

B850 SP417 100pf +50pf multi 1.25 1.25
B851 SP417 100pf +50pf multi 1.25 1.25
B852 SP417 110pf +50pf multi 1.50 1.50
B853 SP417 110pf +50pf multi 1.50 1.50
B854 SP417 220pf +80pf multi 2.50 2.50
Nos. B850-B854 (5) 8.00 8.00

Surtax for the German Youth Stamp Foundation.

The Cosmos — SP418

#B855, Andromeda galaxy. #B856, Cygnus constellation. #B857, X-ray image of exploding star. #B858, Collision of Comet Shoemaker-Levy 9 and Jupiter. 300pf + 100pf, Gamma ray image of entire sky, satellite.

1999, Oct. 14 Litho. *Perf. 14*

B855	SP418	100pf +50pf multi	1.40	1.40
B856	SP418	100pf +50pf multi	1.40	1.40
B857	SP418	110pf +50pf multi	1.50	1.50
B858	SP418	110pf +50pf multi	1.50	1.50
B859	SP418	300pf +100pf multi	3.50	3.50
		Nos. B855-B859 (5)	9.30	9.30

Surtax for the Federal Association of Free Welfare Work. Nos. B858-B859 have a holographic image. Soaking in water may affect hologram.

Christmas SP419

1999, Nov. 4 Litho. *Perf. 13¾*

B860	SP419	100pf +50pf Angel	1.40	1.40
B861	SP419	110pf +50pf Manger	1.50	1.50

Sports — SP420

Ancient art and: 100pf + 50pf, Swimmer. No. B863, Gymnast. No. B864, Sprinters. 300pf + 100pf, Hands.

2000, Feb. 17 Litho. *Perf. 13¾x14*

B862	SP420	100pf + 50pf multi	1.25	1.25
B863	SP420	110pf + 50pf multi	1.40	1.40
B864	SP420	110pf + 50pf multi	1.40	1.40
B865	SP420	300pf + 100pf multi	3.50	3.50
		Nos. B862-B865 (4)	7.55	7.55

Surtax was for German Sports Federation.

Environmental Protection — SP421

2000, May 12 Litho. *Perf. 13¾x14*

B866	SP421	110pf +50pf multi	1.40	1.40

Expo 2000, Hanover — SP422

#B867, 4 backpackers. #B868, Crowd. #B869, Map of Africa, words "see, come, hear, feel." #B870, Eye. #B871, Abstract with Chinese characters. #B872, Abstract.

2000, June 8 Litho. *Perf. 13¾x14*

B867	SP422	100pf +50pf multi	1.00	1.00
B868	SP422	100pf +50pf multi	1.00	1.00
B869	SP422	110pf +50pf multi	1.25	1.25
B870	SP422	110pf +50pf multi	1.25	1.25
B871	SP422	110pf +50pf multi	1.25	1.25
B872	SP422	300pf +100pf multi	2.75	2.75
		Nos. B867-B872 (6)	8.50	8.50

Surtax for German Youth Stamp Foundation.

Actors and Actresses — SP423

#B873, Curd Jürgens (1915-82). #B874, Lilli Palmer (1914-86). #B875, Heinz Rühmann (1902-94). #B876, Romy Schneider (1938-82). #B877, Gert Fröbe (1913-88).

2000, Oct. 12 Litho. *Perf. 14*

B873	SP423	100pf +50pf multi	1.10	1.10
B874	SP423	100pf +50pf multi	1.10	1.10
B875	SP423	110pf +50pf multi	1.25	1.25
B876	SP423	110pf +50pf multi	1.25	1.25
B877	SP423	300pf +100pf multi	2.75	2.75
		Nos. B873-B877 (5)	7.45	7.45

Surtax was for Federal Association of Welfare Work.

Christmas SP424

Designs: 100pf+50pf, Birth of Christ, by Conrad von Soest. 110pf+50pf, Nativity scene.

2000, Nov. 9 Litho. *Perf. 13¾*

B878	SP424	100pf +50pf multi	1.10	1.10
B879	SP424	110pf +50pf multi	1.40	1.40

Surtax for the Federal Association of Voluntary Welfare Work.

See Spain Nos. 3071-3072.

Sports — SP425

Designs: 100pf+50pf, Sports for schools. No. B881, Sports for the disabled. No. B882, Popular and leisure sports. 300pf+100pf, Sports for senior citizens.

2001, Feb. 8 Litho. *Perf. 13¾x14*

B880	SP425	100pf +50pf multi	1.25	1.25
B881	SP425	110pf +50pf multi	1.40	1.40
B882	SP425	110pf +50pf multi	1.40	1.40
B883	SP425	300pf +100pf multi	3.25	3.25
		Nos. B880-B883 (4)	7.30	7.30

Surtax for German Sports Federation.

Wuppertal Suspension Railway — SP426

2001, Mar. 8

B884	SP426	110pf +50pf multi	1.50	1.50

Surtax for the Foundation for Promotion of Philately and Postal History.

Characters from Children's Stories SP427

Designs: No. B885, Pinocchio. No. B886, Pippi Longstockings. No. B887, Jim Knopf. No. B888, Heidi. 300pf +100pf, Tom Sawyer and Huckleberry Finn.

2001, June 13 Litho. *Perf. 13¾*

B885	SP427	100pf +50pf multi	1.40	1.40
B886	SP427	100pf +50pf multi	1.40	1.40
B887	SP427	110pf +50pf multi	1.50	1.50
B888	SP427	110pf +50pf multi	1.50	1.50
B889	SP427	300pf +100pf multi	3.50	3.50
		Nos. B885-B889 (5)	9.30	9.30

Surtax for the German Youth Stamp Foundation.

Film Stars SP428

Designs: No. B890, Marilyn Monroe. No. B891, Charlie Chaplin. No. B892, Film reel. No. B893, Greta Garbo. 300pf+100pf, Jean Gabin.

2001, Oct. 11 Litho. *Perf. 14*

B890	SP428	100pf +50pf multi	1.40	1.40
a.		Perf. 13x13¼x13½x13¼	1.40	1.40
B891	SP428	100pf +50pf multi	1.40	1.40
a.		Perf. 13½x13¼	1.40	1.40
B892	SP428	110pf +50pf multi	1.50	1.50
a.		Perf. 13½x13¼	1.50	1.50
B893	SP428	110pf +50pf multi	1.50	1.50
a.		Perf. 13x13¼	1.50	1.50
B894	SP428	300pf +100pf multi	3.50	3.50
a.		Perf. 13x13¼	3.50	3.50
b.		Booklet pane, #B890a-B894a	9.50	
		Booklet, #B894b	9.50	
		Nos. B890-B894 (5)	9.30	9.30

Surtax for the Federal Association of Voluntary Welfare Work.

Christmas SP429

Designs: 100pf+50pf, Madonna and Child, by Alfredo Roldán. 110pf+50pf, Adoration of the Shepherds, by José de Ribera.

2001, Nov. 8 Litho. *Perf. 13¼*

B895	SP429	100pf +50pf multi	1.40	1.40
B896	SP429	110pf +50pf multi	1.50	1.50
a.		Souvenir sheet (see footnote)	4.25	4.25

No. B896a contains Nos. B895-B896 and lithographed and perf. 13¼ examples of Spain Nos. 3123-3124. No. B896a sold for 4.45m.

See Spain Nos. 3123-3124.

Intl. Year of Mountains — SP430

2002, Jan. 10 Litho. *Perf. 14*

B897	SP430	56c +26c multi	1.50	1.50

Winter Olympic Sports — SP431

Designs: 51c+26c, Biathlon. No. B899, 56c+26c, Ski jumping. No. B900, 56c+26c, Speed skating. 153c+51c, Luge.

2002, Feb. 7 Litho. *Perf. 13¾x14*

B898	SP431	51c +26c multi	1.40	1.40
B899	SP431	56c +26c multi	1.40	1.40
B900	SP431	56c +26c multi	1.40	1.40
B901	SP431	153c +51c multi	3.50	3.50
a.		Booklet pane, #B898-B901	7.75	—
		Booklet, #B901a	7.75	
		Nos. B898-B901 (4)	7.70	7.70

Surtax for German Sports Promotion Foundation.

Toys and Games SP432

Designs: No. B902, Chess pieces. No. B903, Toy truck. No. B904, Doll. No. B905, Teddy bear. 153c+51c, Toy train.

2002, June 6 Litho. *Perf. 13¾*

B902	SP432	51c +26c multi	1.40	1.40
B903	SP432	51c +26c multi	1.40	1.40
B904	SP432	56c +26c multi	1.50	1.50
B905	SP432	56c +26c multi	1.50	1.50
B906	SP432	153c +51c multi	3.75	3.75
		Nos. B902-B906 (5)	9.55	9.55

Surtax for German Youth Stamp Foundation.

Environmental Protection Type of 1998 Inscribed "Hochwasserhilfe 2002"

2002, Aug. 30 Litho. *Perf. 13x13½*

B907	SP411	56c +44c multi	2.00	2.00

Surtax for flood victims relief.

Christmas SP433

Details from paintings by Rogier van der Weyden: 51c+26c, Annunciation to the Virgin. 56c+26c, Miraflores Altarpiece.

2002, Nov. 7 Litho. *Perf. 13¾*

B908	SP433	51c +26c multi	1.60	1.60
B909	SP433	56c +26c multi	1.60	1.60

Surtax for Federal Working Party on Independent Welfare.

Automobiles — SP434

Designs: 45c+20c, 1960 BMW Isetta 300. No. B911, 55c+25c, 1961 VEB Sachsenring Trabant P50. No. B912, 55c+25c, 1949 Volkswagen Beetle. No. B913, 55c+25c, 1954 Mercedes-Benz 300 SL. 144c+56c, 1957 Borgward Isabella Coupe.

2002, Dec. 5 Litho. *Perf. 14*

B910	SP434	45c +20c multi	1.40	1.40
B911	SP434	55c +25c multi	1.60	1.60
B912	SP434	55c +25c multi	1.60	1.60

B913 SP434 55c +25c multi 1.60 1.60
B914 SP434 144c +56c multi 4.00 4.00
Nos. B910-B914 (5) 10.20 10.20

Surtax for Federal Working Party on Independent Welfare.

AIR POST STAMPS

Issues of the Republic

Post Horn with Wings — AP1

Biplane AP2

Perf. 15x14½

1919, Nov. 10 Typo. Unwmk.

C1 AP1 10pf orange .20 *2.00*
C2 AP2 40pf dark green .20 *2.50*
a. Imperf. 1,450.
Set, never hinged .80

No. C2a is ungummed.

Carrier Pigeon AP3

German Eagle AP4

1922-23 Wmk. 126 *Perf. 14, 14½*
Size: 19x23mm

C3 AP3 25(pf) chocolate .30 *14.50*
C4 AP3 40(pf) orange .30 *20.00*
C5 AP3 50(pf) violet .20 *7.00*
C6 AP3 60(pf) carmine .40 *16.00*
C7 AP3 80(pf) blue grn .30 *16.00*

Perf. 13x13½
Size: 22x28mm

C8 AP3 1m dk grn & pale grn .20 *3.00*
C9 AP3 2m lake & gray .20 *3.00*
C10 AP3 3m dk blue & gray .20 *3.50*
C11 AP3 5m red org & yel .20 *3.00*
C12 AP3 10m vio & rose ('23) .20 *9.25*
C13 AP3 25m brn & yel ('23) .20 *7.75*
C14 AP3 100m ol grn & rose ('23) .20 *6.50*
Nos. C3-C14 (12) 2.90 *109.50*
Set, never hinged 7.75

1923

C15 AP3 5m vermilion .20 *40.00*
C16 AP3 10m violet .20 *9.25*
C17 AP3 25m dark brown .20 *9.25*
C18 AP3 100m olive grn .20 *9.75*
C19 AP3 200m deep blue .20 *32.50*
a. Imperf. 42.50
Nos. C15-C19 (5) 1.00 *100.75*
Set, never hinged 1.60

Issued: #C15-C18, June 1. #C19, July 25.
Note following #160 applies to #C1-C19.

1924, Jan. 11 *Perf. 14*
Size: 19x23mm

C20 AP3 5(pf) yellow grn 1.10 1.10
C21 AP3 10(pf) carmine 1.10 1.40
C22 AP3 20(pf) violet blue 4.75 *4.00*
C23 AP3 50(pf) orange 10.00 *19.00*
C24 AP3 100(pf) dull violet 26.00 *42.50*
C25 AP3 200(pf) grnsh blue 50.00 57.50
C26 AP3 300(pf) gray 85.00 82.50
a. Imperf. *1,300.*
Nos. C20-C26 (7) 177.95 208.00
Set, never hinged 1,000.

1926-27

C27 AP4 5pf green .60 .70
C28 AP4 10pf rose red .60 .70
b. Tête bêche pair 80.00 175.00
Never hinged 160.00
d. Bklt. pane 10 (6 No. C28 + 4 No. C29) 47.50 125.00
Never hinged 125.00
C29 AP4 15pf lilac rose ('27) 1.25 1.10
a. Double impression *1,250.*
C30 AP4 20pf dull blue 1.25 1.40
a. Tête bêche pair 80.00 175.00
Never hinged 160.00
b. Bklt. pane 4 (4 No. C30 + 6 labels) 42.50 100.00
Never hinged 100.00
c. Bklt. pane 5 (5 No. C30 + 5 labels) 175.00 425.00
Never hinged 425.00
C31 AP4 50pf brown org 14.00 4.00
C32 AP4 1m black & salmon 14.00 4.75
C33 AP4 2m black & blue 14.00 17.50
C34 AP4 3m black & ol grn 45.00 62.50
Nos. C27-C34 (8) 90.70 92.65
Set, never hinged 725.00

"Graf Zeppelin" Crossing Ocean — AP5

1928-31 Photo.

C35 AP5 1m carmine ('31) 22.50 *30.00*
C36 AP5 2m ultra 35.00 *47.50*
C37 AP5 4m black brown 25.00 *32.50*
Nos. C35-C37 (3) 82.50 110.00
Set, never hinged 325.00

Issued: 2m, 4m, Sept. 20. 1m, May 8.
For overprints see Nos. C40-C45.

AP6

1930, Apr. 19 Wmk. 126

C38 AP6 2m ultra 210.00 260.00
C39 AP6 4m black brown 210.00 260.00
Set, never hinged 2,300.

First flight of Graf Zeppelin to South America. Nos. C38-C39 exist with watermark vertical or horizontal.
Counterfeits exist of Nos. C38-C45.

Nos. C35-C37 Overprinted in Brown

1931, July 15

C40 AP5 1m carmine 97.50 92.50
C41 AP5 2m ultra 140.00 175.00
C42 AP5 4m black brown 350.00 *600.00*
Nos. C40-C42 (3) 587.50 867.50
Set, never hinged 2,600.

Polar flight of Graf Zeppelin.

Nos. C35-C37 Overprinted

1933, Sept. 25

C43 AP5 1m carmine 600.00 *300.00*
C44 AP5 2m ultra 60.00 *160.00*
C45 AP5 4m black brown 60.00 *160.00*
Nos. C43-C45 (3) 720.00 *620.00*
Set, never hinged 2,600.

Graf Zeppelin flight to Century of Progress International Exhibition, Chicago.

Swastika Sun, Globe and Eagle — AP7

Otto Lilienthal — AP8

Design: 3m, Count Ferdinand von Zeppelin.

Perf. 14, 13½x13

1934, Jan. 21 Typo. Wmk. 237

C46 AP7 5(pf) brt green .65 .45
C47 AP7 10(pf) brt carmine .65 .60
C48 AP7 15(pf) ultra 1.00 1.00
C49 AP7 20(pf) dull blue 2.00 1.40
C50 AP7 25(pf) brown 3.00 1.25
C51 AP7 40(pf) red violet 5.50 .90
C52 AP7 50(pf) dk green 8.50 .65
C53 AP7 80(pf) orange yel 3.25 3.25
C54 AP7 100(pf) black 5.25 5.25
C55 AP8 2m green & blk 14.50 16.00
C56 AP8 3m blue & blk 26.00 35.00
Nos. C46-C56 (11) 70.30 65.75
Set, never hinged 400.00

"Hindenburg" — AP10

Perf. 14, 14½x14

1936, Mar. 16 Engr.

C57 AP10 50pf dark blue 14.00 .45
C58 AP10 75pf dull green 15.00 .70

The note concerning gum after No. B68 also applies to Nos. C57-C58.
Unused values are for stamps without gum.

Count Zeppelin — AP11

Airship Gondola — AP12

1938, July 5 Unwmk. *Perf. 13½*

C59 AP11 25pf dull blue 2.00 .70
C60 AP12 50pf green 3.00 .70
Set, never hinged 35.00

Count Ferdinand von Zeppelin (1838-1917), airship inventor and builder.

Catalogue values for unused stamps in this section, from this point to the end of the section, are for Never Hinged items.

Federal Republic

Lufthansa Emblem AP13

Perf. 13½x13

1955, Mar. 31 Litho. Wmk. 295

C61 AP13 5pf lilac rose & blk .65 .65
C62 AP13 10pf green & blk 1.00 1.00
C63 AP13 15pf blue & blk 6.50 5.00
C64 AP13 20pf red & blk 17.50 6.50
Nos. C61-C64 (4) 25.65 13.15

Re-opening of German air service, Apr. 1.

MILITARY AIR POST STAMP

Junkers 52 Transport MAP1

1942 Unwmk. Typo. *Perf. 13½*

MC1 MAP1 ultramarine .20 .25
Never hinged .25
a. Rouletted .20 .35
Never hinged .25

MILITARY PARCEL POST STAMPS

Nazi Emblem — MPP1

1942 Unwmk. Typo. *Perf. 13½*
Size: 28x23mm

MQ1 MPP1 red brown .20 .25
Never hinged .25
a. Rouletted .20 .25
Never hinged .25

1944 Size: 22½x18mm *Perf. 14*

MQ2 MPP1 bright green .40 *125.00*
Never hinged .75

See note "Postally Used vs. CTO" after #160.

No. 520 Overprinted in Black

1944 **Engr.**

MQ3 A115 on 40pf brt red vio .40 175.00
Never hinged .75

Forged surcharges exist.
See postally used note after No. O13.

OFFICIAL STAMPS

Issues of the Republic

In 1920 the Official Stamps of Bavaria and Wurttemberg then current were overprinted "Deutsches Reich" and made available for official use in all parts of Germany. They were, however, used almost exclusively in the two states where they originated and we have listed them among the issues of those states.

O1

O2

O3

O4

O5

O6

O7

O8

O9

O10

O11

O12

1920-21 Typo. Wmk. 125 Perf. 14

O1 O1 5pf deep green .70 *6.50*
O2 O2 10pf car rose .20 .95
O3 O2 10pf orange ('21) .40 *350.00*
O4 O3 15pf violet brn .20 1.00
a. Imperf. ('21) 60.00
O5 O4 20pf deep ultra .20 .95
O6 O5 30pf org, *buff* .20 .95
O7 O6 40pf carmine .20 .95
O8 O7 50pf violet, *buff* .20 .95
O9 O8 60pf red brown ('21) .20 .95
O10 O9 1m red, *buff* .20 .95
O11 O10 1.25m dk bl, *yel* .20 .95
O12 O11 2m dark blue 3.50 1.75
O13 O12 5m brown, *yel* .20 .95
Nos. O1-O13 (13) 6.60
Set, never hinged 21.00

The value of No. O4a is for a copy postmarked at Bautzen.

See No. O15. For surcharges see Nos. O29-O33, O35-O36, O38.

Postally Used vs. CTO
Values quoted for canceled copies of Nos. O1-O46) are for postally used stamps. See note after No. 160.

O13

O14

O15

Wmk. 126, 125 (#O16-O17)

1922-23

O14 O13 75pf dark blue .20 *4.75*
O15 O11 2m dark blue .20 .90
a. Imperf. 85.00
O16 O14 3m brown, *rose* .20 .95
O17 O15 10m dk grn, *rose* .20 .95
O18 O15 10m dk grn, *rose* .20 *6.50*
O19 O15 20m dk bl, *rose* .20 .90
O20 O15 50m vio, *rose* .20 .90
O21 O15 100m rose red, *rose* .20 .90
Nos. O14-O21 (8) 1.60 *16.75*
Set, never hinged 2.50

Issue date: #O18-O21, 1923. Nos. O20-O21 exist imperf.

For surcharges see Nos. O34, O37, O39.

Regular Issue of 1923 Overprinted

a

1923

O22 A34 20m red lilac .20 *6.50*
O23 A34 30m olive grn .20 *22.50*
O24 A29 40m green .20 *2.50*
O25 A35 200m car rose .20 *.95*
O26 A35 300m green .20 *.95*
O27 A35 400m dk brn .20 *.95*
O28 A35 500m red orange .20 *.95*
Nos. O22-O28 (7) 1.40
Set, never hinged 2.50

Official Stamps of 1920-23 Surcharged with New Values
Abbreviations:
Th=(Tausend) Thousand
Mil=(Million) Million
Mlrd=(Milliarde) Billion

1923 **Wmk. 125**

O29 O12 5th m on 5m .20 *2.50*
a. Inverted surcharge 40.00
Never hinged 75.00
O30 O5 20th m on 30pf .20 *2.50*
a. Inverted surcharge 45.00
Never hinged 100.00
b. Imperf. 52.50
Never hinged 100.00
O31 O3 100th m on 15pf .20 *2.50*
a. Imperf. 52.50
Never hinged 92.50
b. Inverted surcharge 40.00
Never hinged 75.00
O32 O2 250th m on 10pf car rose .20 *2.50*
a. Double surcharge 35.00
Never hinged 70.00
O33 O5 800th m on 30pf .25 *210.00*

Official Stamps and Types of 1920-23 Surcharged with New Values

Wmk. 126

O34 O15 75th m on 50m .20 *2.50*
a. Inverted surcharge 40.00
Never hinged 75.00
O35 O3 400th m on 15pf brn .20 *24.00*
O36 O5 800th m on 30pf org, *buff* .20 *3.00*
O37 O13 1 mil m on 75pf .20 *26.00*
O38 O2 2 mil m on 10pf car rose .20 *3.00*
a. Imperf. 77.50
Never hinged 140.00
O39 O15 5 mil m on 100m .20 *5.00*
Nos. O29-O39 (11) 2.55
Set, never hinged 3.50

The 10, 15 and 30 pfennig are not known with this watermark and without surcharge.

#290-291, 295-299 Overprinted Type "a"

1923

O40 A39 100 mil m .20 *125.00*
O41 A39 200 mil m .20 *125.00*
O42 A39a 2 mlrd m .20 *97.50*
O43 A39a 5 mlrd m .20 *72.50*
O44 A39a 10 mlrd m 2.50 *110.00*
O45 A39a 20 mlrd m 3.25 *125.00*
O46 A39a 50 mlrd m 1.60 *175.00*
Nos. O40-O46 (7) 8.15
Set, never hinged 26.00

Same Overprint on Nos, 323-328, Values in Rentenpfennig

1923

O47 A40 3pf brown .20 .25
O48 A40 5pf dk green .20 .25
a. Inverted overprint 77.50 150.00
Never hinged 150.00
O49 A40 10pf carmine .20 .25
a. Inverted overprint 65.00 150.00
Never hinged 125.00
b. Imperf. 24.00
Never hinged 47.50
O50 A40 20pf dp ultra .50 .30
O51 A40 50pf orange .50 .65
O52 A40 100pf brown vio 3.00 6.50
Nos. O47-O52 (6) 4.60 8.20
Set, never hinged 20.00

Same Overprint On Issues of 1924

1924

O53 A41 3pf lt brown .30 .75
a. Inverted overprint 50.00 125.00
Never hinged 97.50
O54 A41 5pf lt green .20 .25
a. Imperf. 62.50
Never hinged 125.00
b. Inverted overprint 82.50
Never hinged 160.00
O55 A41 10pf vermilion .20 .25
O56 A41 20pf blue .20 .25
O57 A41 30pf rose lilac .65 .30
O58 A41 40pf olive green .65 .35
O59 A41 50pf orange 4.50 2.00
O60 A47 60pf red brown 1.25 2.40
O61 A47 80pf slate 6.00 *30.00*
Nos. O53-O61 (9) 13.95 *36.55*
Set, never hinged 45.00

O16

Swastika — O17

1927-33 ***Perf. 14***

O62 O16 3pf bister .25 .20
O63 O16 4pf lt bl ('31) .25 .30
O64 O16 4pf blue ('33) 4.75 5.25
O65 O16 5pf green .20 .20
O66 O16 6pf pale ol grn ('32) .25 .30
O67 O16 8pf dk grn .25 .20
O68 O16 10pf carmine 6.50 5.25
O69 O16 10pf ver ('29) 12.00 14.50
O70 O16 10pf red vio ('30) .25 .30
a. Imperf. 87.50
Never hinged 175.00
O71 O16 10pf choc ('33) 1.90 4.00
O72 O16 12pf org ('32) .25 .30
O73 O16 15pf vermilion 1.60 .30
O74 O16 15pf car ('29) .35 .30
O75 O16 20pf Prus grn 3.50 1.75
O76 O16 20pf gray ('30) .85 .45
O77 O16 30pf olive grn .75 .30
O78 O16 40pf violet .65 .25
O79 O16 60pf red brn ('28) .95 1.00
Nos. O62-O79 (18) 35.50 35.15
Set, never hinged 125.00

1934, Jan. 18 **Wmk. 237**

O80 O17 3pf bister .25 *.80*
O81 O17 4pf dull blue .25 *.60*
O82 O17 5pf brt green .20 *.40*
O83 O17 6pf dk green .20 *.40*
a. Imperf. 100.00
Never hinged 210.00
O84 O17 8pf vermilion 1.00 *.40*
O85 O17 10pf chocolate .25 *.90*
O86 O17 12pf brt carmine 1.50 *1.00*
a. Unwmkd. 3.25 *4.50*
O87 O17 15pf claret .75 *4.00*
O88 O17 20pf light blue .30 *.75*
O89 O17 30pf olive grn .60 *.75*
O90 O17 40pf red violet .60 *.75*
O91 O17 50pf orange yel .70 *.90*
Nos. O80-O91 (12) 6.60 *11.65*
Set, never hinged 21.00

O83 exists imperf.

1942 **Unwmk.** ***Perf. 14***

O92 O17 3pf bister brn .20 *.45*
O93 O17 4pf dull blue .20 *.45*
O94 O17 5pf deep olive .20 *2.10*
O95 O17 6pf deep violet .20 *.45*
O96 O17 8pf vermilion .20 *.45*
O97 O17 10pf chocolate .20 *.40*
O98 O17 12pf rose car .20 *.90*
a. Wmk. 237 1.10 *10.00*
O99 O17 15pf brown car 1.40 *8.75*
O100 O17 20pf light blue .20 *.95*
O101 O17 30pf olive grn .20 *.95*
O102 O17 40pf red violet .20 *.95*
O103 O17 50pf dk green 1.25 *5.25*
Nos. O92-O103 (12) 4.65 *22.05*
Set, never hinged 24.00

LOCAL OFFICIAL STAMPS

For Use in Prussia

("Nr. 21" refers to the district of Prussia) — LO1

1903 Unwmk. Typo. *Perf. 14, 14½*

OL1 LO1 2pf slate .75 3.50
OL2 LO1 3pf bister brn .75 3.50
OL3 LO1 5pf green .25 .30
OL4 LO1 10pf carmine .25 .30
OL5 LO1 20pf ultra .25 .30
OL6 LO1 25pf org & blk, *yel* .25 .30
OL7 LO1 40pf lake & blk .30 1.40
OL8 LO1 50pf pur & blk, *sal* .30 1.40
Nos. OL1-OL8 (8) 3.10 11.00
Set, never hinged 7.75

LO2

LO3

LO4

LO5

LO6

LO7

LO8

1920 Typo. Wmk. 125 *Perf. 14*

OL9 LO2 5pf green .20 2.25
OL10 LO3 10pf carmine .55 1.25
OL11 LO4 15pf vio brn .20 .95
OL12 LO5 20pf dp ultra .20 1.00
OL13 LO6 30pf org, *buff* .20 .95

OL14 LO7 50pf brn lil, *buff* .25 1.00
OL15 LO8 1m red, *buff* 6.00 3.25
Nos. OL9-OL15 (7) 7.60 10.65
Set, never hinged 25.00

For Use in Baden

LO9

1905 Unwmk. Typo. ***Perf. 14, 14½***

OL16 LO9 2pf gray blue 45.00 55.00
OL17 LO9 3pf brown 5.25 6.75
OL18 LO9 5pf green 3.25 5.25
OL19 LO9 10pf rose .65 1.60
OL20 LO9 20pf blue 1.25 2.25
OL21 LO9 25pf org & blk, *yel* 32.50 45.00
Nos. OL16-OL21 (6) 87.90 115.85
Set, never hinged 725.00

NEWSPAPER STAMPS

Newsboy and Globe — N1

Wmk. Swastikas (237)

1939, Nov. 1 Photo. ***Perf. 14***

P1 N1 5pf green .25 2.10
P2 N1 10pf red brown .25 2.10
Set, never hinged 2.75

FRANCHISE STAMPS

For use by the National Socialist German Workers' Party

Party Emblem — F1

1938 Typo. Wmk. 237 ***Perf. 14***

S1 F1 1pf black .55 2.10
S2 F1 3pf bister .55 1.25
S3 F1 4pf dull blue .55 .80
S4 F1 5pf brt green .25 .80
S5 F1 6pf dk green .25 .80
S6 F1 8pf vermilion 2.25 1.00
S7 F1 12pf brt car 3.75 1.00
S8 F1 16pf gray .50 *7.75*
S9 F1 24pf citron .80 3.75
S10 F1 30pf olive grn .80 3.75
S11 F1 40pf red violet .80 7.75
Nos. S1-S11 (11) 11.05 30.75
Set, never hinged 82.50

1942 Unwmk.

S12 F1 1pf gray blk .40 *2.50*
S13 F1 3pf bister brn .20 *.40*
S14 F1 4pf dk gray blue .20 *.40*
S15 F1 5pf gray green .20 *2.50*
S16 F1 6pf violet .20 *.40*
S17 F1 8pf deep orange .20 *.40*
a. Imperf. 70.00
Never hinged 140.00
S18 F1 12pf carmine .20 *.40*
S19 F1 16pf blue green 2.25 *11.50*
S20 F1 24pf yellow brn .25 *.75*
S21 F1 30pf dp olive grn .25 *1.25*
S22 F1 40pf light rose vio .30 *1.60*
Nos. S12-S22 (11) 4.65 *22.10*
Set, never hinged 22.50

GERMAN OCCUPATION STAMPS

100 Centimes = 1 Franc
100 Pfennig = 1 Mark

Issued under Belgian Occupation

Belgian Stamps of 1915-20 Overprinted

Perf. 11½, 14, 14½

1919-21 Unwmk.

1N1 A46 1c orange .25 *.40*
1N2 A46 2c chocolate .25 *.40*
1N3 A46 3c gray blk ('21) .25 *1.60*
1N4 A46 5c green .50 *.80*
1N5 A46 10c carmine 1.00 *1.60*
1N6 A46 15c purple .50 *.80*
1N7 A46 20c red violet .75 *1.00*
1N8 A46 25c blue 1.00 *1.40*
1N9 A54 25c dp blue ('21) 2.75 *5.25*

Overprinted

1N10 A47 35c brn org & blk 1.00 *1.00*
1N11 A48 40c green & blk 1.00 *1.60*
1N12 A49 50c car rose & blk 5.25 *7.75*
1N13 A56 65c cl & blk ('21) 2.40 *7.75*
1N14 A50 1fr violet 20.00 16.00
1N15 A51 2fr slate 40.00 35.00
1N16 A52 5fr deep blue 7.00 *7.75*
1N17 A53 10fr brown 50.00 47.50
Nos. 1N1-1N17 (17) 133.90 137.60
Set, never hinged 325.00

Belgian Stamps of 1915 Surcharged

Nos. 1N18-1N22

Nos. 1N23-1N24

Black Surcharge

1920

1N18 A46 5pf on 5c green .35 *.30*
1N19 A46 10pf on 10c car .45 *.40*
1N20 A46 15pf on 15c pur .60 .60
1N21 A46 20pf on 20c red vio .60 *.90*
1N22 A46 30pf on 25c blue .95 *1.10*

Red Surcharge

1N23 A49 75pf on 50c car rose & blk 11.50 *14.00*
1N24 A50 1m25pf on 1fr violet 17.50 *14.00*
Nos. 1N18-1N24 (7) 31.95 *31.30*
Set, never hinged 85.00

EUPEN ISSUE

Belgian Stamps of 1915-20 Overprinted:

Nos. 1N25-1N36

Nos. 1N37-1N41

1920-21 ***Perf. 11½, 14, 14½***

1N25 A46 1c orange .25 .30
1N26 A46 2c chocolate .25 .30
1N27 A46 3c gray blk ('21) .35 *1.10*
1N28 A46 5c green .35 *.70*
1N29 A46 10c carmine .60 *1.00*
1N30 A46 15c purple .80 *1.00*
1N31 A46 20c red violet .95 *1.10*
1N32 A46 25c blue .80 *1.50*
1N33 A54 25c dp blue ('21) 2.75 *7.50*
1N34 A47 35c brn org & blk 1.10 1.50
1N35 A48 40c green & blk 1.40 1.75
1N36 A49 50c car rose & blk 4.00 *5.75*
1N37 A56 65c cl & blk ('21) 2.10 *8.75*
1N38 A50 1fr violet 15.00 14.50
1N39 A51 2fr slate 26.00 24.00
1N40 A52 5fr deep blue 8.25 8.75
1N41 A53 10fr brown 35.00 37.50
Nos. 1N25-1N41 (17) 99.95 117.00
Set, never hinged 250.00

MALMEDY ISSUE

Belgian Stamps of 1915-20 Overprinted:

Nos. 1N42-1N50

Nos. 1N51-1N53

Nos. 1N54-1N58

1920-21

1N42 A46 1c orange .20 .30
1N43 A46 2c chocolate .20 .30
1N44 A46 3c gray blk ('21) .30 *1.25*
1N45 A46 5c green .40 *.70*
1N46 A46 10c carmine .60 *1.00*
1N47 A46 15c purple .95 *1.10*
1N48 A46 20c red violet 1.10 *1.50*
1N49 A46 25c blue .95 *1.50*
1N50 A54 25c dp blue ('21) 2.75 *7.00*
1N51 A47 35c brn org & blk 1.10 *1.75*
1N52 A48 40c grn & blk 1.10 1.75
1N53 A49 50c car rose & blk 4.75 *5.75*
1N54 A56 65c cl & blk ('21) 2.10 *8.75*
1N55 A50 1fr violet 15.00 13.00
1N56 A51 2fr slate 26.00 24.00
1N57 A52 5fr deep blue 8.25 *13.00*
1N58 A53 10fr brown 35.00 42.50
Nos. 1N42-1N58 (17) 100.75 125.15
Set, never hinged 250.00

OCCUPATION POSTAGE DUE STAMPS

Belgian Postage Due Stamps of 1919-20, Overprinted

1920 Unwmk. ***Perf. 14½***

1NJ1 D3 5c green .60 *.90*
1NJ2 D3 10c carmine 1.10 1.50
1NJ3 D3 20c gray green 2.40 3.50
1NJ4 D3 30c bright blue 2.40 *3.50*
1NJ5 D3 50c gray 11.50 *11.50*
Nos. 1NJ1-1NJ5 (5) 18.00 *20.90*
Set, never hinged 45.00

Belgian Postage Due Stamps of 1919-20, Overprinted

1NJ6 D3 5c green 1.10 .90
1NJ7 D3 10c carmine 2.40 1.50
1NJ8 D3 20c gray green 8.25 8.75
1NJ9 D3 30c bright blue 4.75 *6.50*
1NJ10 D3 50c gray 9.25 8.75
Nos. 1NJ6-1NJ10 (5) 25.75 26.40
Set, never hinged 65.00

A. M. G. ISSUE

Issued jointly by the Allied Military Government of the US and Great Britain, for civilian use in areas under Allied occupation.

OS1

Type I. Thick paper, white gum.
Type II. Medium paper, yellow gum.
Type III. Medium paper, white gum.

Perf. 11, 11½ and Compound

1945-46 Litho. Unwmk.

Type III, Brunswick Printing

Size: 19-19½x22-22½mm

3N1 OS1 1pf slate gray .20 3.25
3N2 OS1 3pf dull lilac .20 .80
3N3 OS1 4pf lt gray .20 .80
3N4 OS1 5pf emerald .20 2.10
3N5 OS1 6pf yellow .20 .80
3N6 OS1 8pf orange 1.10 20.00
3N7 OS1 10pf yel brn .20 .80
3N8 OS1 12pf rose vio .20 .65
3N9 OS1 15pf rose car .20 1.60
3N10 OS1 16pf dp Prus grn .20 9.50
3N11 OS1 20pf blue .20 1.60
3N12 OS1 24pf chocolate .20 8.00
3N13 OS1 25pf brt ultra .20 9.50

Size: 21½x25mm

3N14 OS1 30pf olive .20 1.10
3N15 OS1 40pf dp mag .20 1.50
3N16 OS1 42pf green .20 .90
3N17 OS1 50pf slate grn .20 7.50
3N18 OS1 60pf vio brn .25 11.00
3N19 OS1 80pf bl blk 6.50 175.00

Size: 25x29½mm

3N20 OS1 1m dk ol grn ('46) 5.00 275.00
Nos. 3N1-3N20 (20) 16.05 *531.40*
Set, never hinged 32.50

Most of Nos. 3N1-3N20 exist imperforate and part-perforate.

Type I, Washington Printing

Size: 19-19½x22-22½mm

Perf. 11

3N2a OS1 3pf lilac .20 .80
3N3a OS1 4pf light gray .20 .65
3N4a OS1 5pf emerald .20 .25
3N5a OS1 6pf yellow .20 .25
3N6a OS1 8pf deep orange .20 .25
3N7a OS1 10pf brown .20 .25
3N8a OS1 12pf rose violet .25 .25
3N9a OS1 15pf cerise .20 .65
3N13a OS1 25pf bright ultra .20 .65
Nos. 3N2a-3N13a (9) 4.00
Set, never hinged 1.60

Type II, London Printing

Size: 19-19½x22-22½mm

Photo.

Perf. 14, 14½ and Compound

3N2b OS1 3pf lilac .20 .35
3N3b OS1 4pf light gray .20 .35
3N4b OS1 5pf deep emerald .20 5.75
3N5b OS1 6pf orange yellow .20 .35
3N6b OS1 8pf dark orange .20 2.10
3N8b OS1 12pf rose violet .20 .35
Nos. 3N2b-3N8b (6) 1.20 9.25
Set, never hinged 1.60

ISSUED UNDER FRENCH OCCUPATION

Coats of Arms

Rhine Province OS3

Palatinate District OS4

Saarland OS5

Württemberg OS6

Baden OS7

Johann Wolfgang von Goethe OS8

Friedrich von Schiller — OS9

Heinrich Heine — OS10

Perf. 14x13½

1945-46 Unwmk. Typo.

4N1	OS3	1pf blk, grn & lem	.20	.20
4N2	OS4	3pf dk red, blk & dl yel	.20	.20
4N3	OS6	5pf brn, blk & org yel	.20	.20
4N4	OS7	8pf brn, yel & red	.20	.20
4N5	OS3	10pf brn, grn & lem	2.75	*40.00*
4N6	OS4	12pf red, blk & org yel	.20	.20
4N7	OS5	15pf blk, ultra & red ('46)	.20	.20
4N8	OS6	20pf red, org yel & blk	.20	.20
4N9	OS5	24pf blk, dp ultra & red ('46)	.20	.20
4N10	OS7	30pf blk, org yel & red	.20	.20

Perf. 13

Engr.

4N11	OS8	1m lilac brn	.45	*13.00*
4N12	OS9	2m dp bl ('46)	.30	*40.00*
4N13	OS10	5m dl red brn ('46)	.45	*40.00*
		Nos. 4N1-4N13 (13)	5.75	
		Set, never hinged	12.00	

Exist imperf. Value for set of 13, $300.

BADEN

Johann Peter Hebel OS1

Girl of Constance OS2

Hans Baldung Grien — OS3

Rastatt Castle — OS4

Black Forest Scene OS5

Cathedral of Freiburg — OS6

1947 Unwmk. Photo. *Perf. 14*

5N1	OS1	2pf gray	.20	.25
5N2	OS2	3pf brown	.20	.20
5N3	OS3	10pf slate blue	.20	.20
5N4	OS1	12pf dk green	.20	.20
5N5	OS2	15pf purple	.20	.30
5N6	OS4	16pf olive green	.20	*.80*
5N7	OS3	20pf blue	.20	*.30*
5N8	OS4	24pf crimson	.20	.20
5N9	OS2	45pf cerise	.20	*.55*
5N10	OS1	60pf deep orange	.20	.20
5N11	OS3	75pf brt blue	.20	*.80*
5N12	OS5	84pf blue green	.20	*.95*
5N13	OS6	1m dark brown	.20	*.55*
		Nos. 5N1-5N13 (13)		*5.50*
		Set, never hinged	1.40	

Festival Headdress OS7

Grand Duchess Stephanie OS8

1948

5N14	OS1	2pf dp orange	.20	*.25*
5N15	OS2	6pf violet brn	.20	.20
5N16	OS7	8pf blue green	.20	*.85*
5N17	OS3	10pf dark brown	.20	.20
5N18	OS1	12pf crimson	.20	.20
5N19	OS2	15pf blue	.20	*.45*
5N20	OS4	16pf violet	.30	*1.50*
5N21	OS3	20pf brown	1.25	.75
5N22	OS4	24pf dark green	.20	.20
5N23	OS7	30pf cerise	.45	.85
5N24	OS8	50pf brt blue	.45	.20
5N25	OS1	60pf gray	1.60	.45
5N26	OS5	84pf rose brn	2.25	*3.50*
5N27	OS6	1dm brt blue	2.25	*3.50*
		Nos. 5N14-5N27 (14)	9.95	*13.10*
		Set, never hinged	22.50	

Without "PF"

1948-49

5N28	OS1	2(pf) dp orange	.30	*.45*
5N29	OS4	4(pf) violet	.20	*.35*
5N30	OS2	5(pf) blue	.30	*.55*
5N31	OS2	6(pf) violet brn	9.75	*11.50*
5N32	OS7	8(pf) rose brn	.30	*.90*
5N33	OS3	10(pf) dark green	1.60	1.10
5N37	OS3	20(pf) cerise	.65	.30
5N38	OS4	40(pf) brown	26.00	*52.50*
5N39	OS1	80(pf) red	3.25	*5.75*
5N40	OS5	90(pf) rose brn	26.00	*65.00*
		Nos. 5N28-5N40 (10)	68.35	*138.40*
		Set, never hinged	125.00	

Constance Cathedral and Insel Hotel — OS9

Type I. Frameline thick and straight. Inscriptions thick. Shading dark. Upper part of "B" narrow.

Type II. Frameline thin and zigzag. Inscriptions fine. Shading light. Upper part of "B" wide.

1949, June 22

5N41	OS9	30pf dark blue (I)	8.50	*60.00*
		Never hinged	18.00	
	a.	Type II	*240.00*	*1,250.*
		Never hinged	425.00	

Issued to publicize the International Engineering Congress, Constance, 1949.

Conradin Kreutzer — OS10

1949, Aug. 27

5N42	OS10	10pf dark green	1.00	*5.75*
		Never hinged	2.75	

Conradin Kreutzer (1780-1849), composer.

Stagecoach — OS11

Design: 20pf, Post bus, trailer and plane.

1949, Sept. 17

5N43	OS11	10pf green	2.00	*9.25*
5N44	OS11	20pf red brown	2.00	*9.25*
		Set, never hinged	8.00	

Centenary of German postage stamps.

Globe, Olive Branch and Post Horn — OS12

1949, Oct. 4

5N45	OS12	20pf dark red	2.25	*9.25*
5N46	OS12	30pf deep blue	2.25	*8.00*
		Set, never hinged	10.00	

75th anniv. of the UPU.

OCCUPATION SEMI-POSTAL STAMPS

Arms of Baden OSP1

Cornhouse, Freiburg OSP2

Perf. 13½x14

1949, Feb. 25 Photo. Unwmk.

Cross in Red

5NB1	OSP1	10 + 20pf green	8.50	*65.00*
5NB2	OSP1	20 + 40pf lilac	8.50	*65.00*
5NB3	OSP1	30 + 60pf blue	8.50	*65.00*
5NB4	OSP1	40 + 80pf gray	8.50	*65.00*
	a.	Sheet of 4, #5NB1-5NB4, imperf.	72.50	*925.00*
		Nos. 5NB1-5NB4 (4)	34.00	*260.00*
		Set, never hinged	55.00	

The surtax was for the Red Cross.

No. 5NB4a measures 90x101mm. and has no gum.

1949, Feb. 24 *Perf. 14*

10pf+20pf, Cathedral tower. 20pf+30pf, Trumpeting angel. 30pf+50pf, Fish pool.

5NB5	OSP2	4 + 16pf dk vio	4.50	*29.00*
5NB6	OSP2	10 + 20pf dk grn	4.50	*29.00*
5NB7	OSP2	20 + 30pf car	4.50	*29.00*
5NB8	OSP2	30 + 50pf blue	6.00	*35.00*
	a.	Sheet of 4, #5NB5-5NB8	26.00	*160.00*
		Never hinged	45.00	
	b.	As "a," imperf.	26.00	*160.00*
		Never hinged	45.00	
		Nos. 5NB5-5NB8 (4)	19.50	*122.00*
		Set, never hinged	40.00	

The surtax was for the reconstruction of historical monuments in Freiburg.

Carl Schurz at Rastatt OSP3

Goethe OSP4

1949, Aug. 23

5NB9	OSP3	10 + 5pf green	4.25	*26.00*
5NB10	OSP3	20 + 10pf cer	4.25	*26.00*
5NB11	OSP3	30 + 15pf blue	4.75	*26.00*
		Nos. 5NB9-5NB11 (3)	13.25	*78.00*
		Set, never hinged	25.00	

Centenary of the surrender of Rastatt.

1949, Aug. 12

Various Portraits.

5NB12	OSP4	10 + 5pf green	3.00	*16.00*
5NB13	OSP4	20 + 10pf cer	3.00	*16.00*
5NB14	OSP4	30 + 15pf blue	4.50	*40.00*
		Nos. 5NB12-5NB14 (3)	10.50	*72.00*
		Set, never hinged	21.00	

Johann Wolfgang von Goethe (1749-1832).

RHINE PALATINATE

Beethoven OS1

Wilhelm E. F. von Ketteler OS2

Girl Carrying Grapes OS3

Porta Nigra, Trier OS4

Karl Marx OS5

"Devil's Table", Near Pirmasens OS6

Street Corner, St. Martin OS7

Cathedral of Worms OS8

Cathedral of Mainz OS9

Statue of Johann Gutenberg OS10

Gutenfels and Pfalzgrafenstein Castles on Rhine — OS11

Statue of Charlemagne OS12

1947-48 Unwmk. Photo. Perf. 14

6N1	OS1	2pf gray	.20	.20
6N2	OS2	3pf dk brown	.20	.20
6N3	OS3	10pf slate blue	.20	.20
6N4	OS4	12pf green	.20	.20
6N5	OS5	15pf purple	.20	.20
6N6	OS6	16pf lt ol grn	.20	.55
6N7	OS7	20pf brt blue	.20	.25
6N8	OS8	24pf crimson	.20	.20
6N9	OS10	30pf cerise ('48)	.20	1.00
6N10	OS9	45pf cerise	.20	.50
6N11	OS9	50pf blue ('48)	.20	1.00
6N12	OS1	60pf dp orange	.20	.20
6N13	OS10	75pf blue	.20	.50
6N14	OS11	84pf green	.20	.75
6N15	OS12	1m brown	.20	.55
		Nos. 6N1-6N15 (15)		6.50
		Set, never hinged	1.40	

Exist imperf. Value for set, $600.

1948

6N16	OS1	2pf dp orange	.20	.25
6N17	OS2	6pf violet brn	.20	.25
6N18	OS4	8dpf blue green	.20	.90
6N19	OS3	10pf dk brown	.20	.20
6N20	OS4	12pf crim rose	.20	.20
6N21	OS5	15pf blue	.50	.60
6N22	OS6	16dpf dk violet	.25	1.10
6N23	OS7	20dpf brown	.95	.60
6N24	OS8	24pf green	.20	.20
6N25	OS9	30pf cerise	.40	.30
6N26	OS10	50pf brt blue	.65	.30
6N27	OS1	60dpf gray	3.25	.30
6N28	OS11	84dpf rose brown	1.60	4.00
6N29	OS12	1dm brt blue	2.75	4.00
		Nos. 6N16-6N29 (14)	11.55	13.20
		Set, never hinged	21.00	

Exist imperf. Value for set, $600.

Types of 1947 Without "PF"

1948-49

6N30	OS1	2(pf) dp org	.25	.30
6N31	OS6	4(pf) vio ('49)	.25	.30
6N32	OS5	5(pf) blue ('49)	.30	.50
6N33	OS2	6(pf) vio brn	12.00	11.50
6N33A	OS4	8(pf) rose brn ('49)	26.00	240.00
6N34	OS3	10(pf) dk grn	.30	.30
a.		Imperf.	50.00	160.00
		Never hinged	100.00	
6N35	OS7	20(pf) cerise	.30	.30
6N36	OS8	40(pf) brn ('49)	1.25	2.75
6N37	OS4	80(pf) red ('49)	1.25	3.50
6N38	OS11	90(pf) rose brn ('49)	2.00	11.50
		Nos. 6N30-6N38 (10)	43.90	270.95
		Set, never hinged	92.50	

Type of Baden, 1949

Designs as in Baden.

1949, Sept. 17

6N39	OS11	10pf green	3.50	16.00
6N40	OS11	20pf red brown	3.50	16.00
		Set, never hinged	14.50	

UPU Type of Baden, 1949

1949, Oct. 4

6N41	OS12	20pf dark red	2.75	9.75
6N42	OS12	30pf deep blue	2.75	7.50
		Set, never hinged	9.25	

OCCUPATION SEMI-POSTAL STAMPS

St. Martin — OSP1

Design: 30pf+50pf, St. Christopher.

1948 Unwmk. Photo. Perf. 14

6NB1	OSP1	20pf + 30pf dp cl	.55	40.00
6NB2	OSP1	30pf + 50pf dp bl	.55	40.00
		Set, never hinged	2.75	

The surtax was to aid victims of an explosion at Ludwigshafen.

Type of Baden, 1949, Showing Arms of Rhine Palatinate

1949, Feb. 25 Perf. 13½x14

Cross in Red

6NB3	OSP1	10pf + 20pf grn	7.25	72.50
6NB4	OSP1	20pf + 40pf lil	7.25	72.50
6NB5	OSP1	30pf + 60pf bl	7.25	72.50
6NB6	OSP1	40pf + 80pf gray	7.25	72.50
a.		Sheet of 4, #6NB3-6NB6, imperf.	72.50	1,050.
		Nos. 6NB3-6NB6 (4)	29.00	290.00
		Set, never hinged	52.50	

The surtax was for the Red Cross. #6NB6a measures 90x100mm and has no gum.

Goethe Type of Baden, 1949

Various Portraits.

1949, Aug. 12

6NB7	OSP4	10pf + 5pf green	2.00	16.00
6NB8	OSP4	20pf + 10pf cerise	2.00	16.00
6NB9	OSP4	30pf + 15pf blue	4.00	35.00
		Nos. 6NB7-6NB9 (3)	8.00	67.00
		Set, never hinged	18.00	

WURTTEMBERG

Friedrich von Schiller OS1

Castle of Bebenhausen OS2

Friedrich Hölderlin OS3

Town Gate of Wangen (Allgäu) OS4

Lichtenstein Castle — OS5

Zwiefalten Church — OS6

1947-48 Unwmk. Photo. Perf. 14

8N1	OS1	2pf gray ('48)	.20	.50
8N2	OS3	3pf brown ('48)	.20	.20
8N3	OS4	10pf slate bl ('48)	.20	.30
8N4	OS1	12pf dk green	.20	.20
8N5	OS3	15pf purple ('48)	.20	.30
8N6	OS2	16pf ol grn ('48)	.20	.55
8N7	OS4	20pf blue ('48)	.20	.55
8N8	OS2	24pf crimson	.20	.20
8N9	OS3	45pf cerise	.20	.55
8N10	OS1	60pf dp org ('48)	.20	.45
8N11	OS4	75pf brt blue	.20	.80
8N12	OS5	84pf blue grn	.20	.95
8N13	OS6	1m dk brown	.20	.70
		Nos. 8N1-8N13 (13)		6.25
		Set, never hinged	1.50	

The 12pf and 60pf exist imperf. Value, each $35.

Waldsee OS7

Ludwig Uhland OS8

1948

8N14	OS1	2pf dp orange	.20	.30
8N15	OS3	6pf violet brn	.20	.25
8N16	OS7	8dpf blue grn	.30	1.60
8N17	OS4	10pf dk brown	.20	.30
8N18	OS1	12pf crimson	.20	.25
8N19	OS3	15pf blue	.25	.30
8N20	OS2	16dpf dk violet	.30	1.60
8N21	OS4	20dpf brown	.65	.65
8N22	OS2	24dpf dk green	.35	.45
8N23	OS7	30pf cerise	.50	.45
8N24	OS8	50pf dull blue	.85	.45
8N25	OS1	60dpf gray	5.00	.45
8N26	OS5	84dpf rose brn	1.25	3.00
8N27	OS6	1dm brt blue	1.25	3.00
		Nos. 8N14-8N27 (14)	11.50	13.05
		Set, never hinged	20.00	

The 2pf, 10pf, 24pf and 30pf exist imperf. Value, each $35.

Without "PF"

1948-49

8N28	OS1	2(pf) dp orange	.30	.45
8N29	OS2	4(pf) violet	.80	.30
8N30	OS3	5(pf) blue	2.75	1.60
8N31	OS3	6(pf) vio brown	2.75	4.00
8N32	OS7	8(pf) rose brn	2.75	1.60
8N33	OS4	10(pf) dk green	2.75	.20
8N34	OS4	20(pf) cerise	2.75	.20
8N35	OS2	40(pf) brown	8.50	32.50
8N36	OS1	80(pf) red	16.00	32.50
8N37	OS5	90(pf) rose brn	26.00	75.00
		Nos. 8N28-8N37 (10)	65.35	148.35
		Set, never hinged	125.00	

The 4pf and 6pf exist imperf. Value, respectively $100 and $37.50.

Type of Baden, 1949

Designs as in Baden.

1949, Sept. 17

8N38	OS11	10pf green	3.00	9.75
8N39	OS11	20pf red brown	3.00	9.75
		Set, never hinged	9.75	

UPU Type of Baden, 1949

1949, Oct. 4

8N40	OS12	20pf dark red	2.10	9.75
8N41	OS12	30pf deep blue	2.10	6.75
		Set, never hinged	8.50	

OCCUPATION SEMI-POSTAL STAMPS

Type of Baden, 1949

Design: Arms of Württemberg.

Perf. 13½x14

1949, Feb. 25 Photo. Unwmk.

Cross in Red

8NB1	OSP1	10 + 20pf grn	13.00	85.00
8NB2	OSP1	20 + 40pf lilac	13.00	85.00
8NB3	OSP1	30 + 60pf blue	13.00	85.00
8NB4	OSP1	40 + 80pf gray	13.00	85.00
a.		Sheet of 4, imperf.	100.00	1,200.
		Nos. 8NB1-8NB4 (4)	52.00	340.00
		Set, never hinged	110.00	

The surtax was for the Red Cross.

No. 8NB4a measures 90x100mm and contains one each of Nos. 8NB1 to 8NB4, with red inscription in upper margin and no gum.

View of Isny OSP1

Design: 20pf+6pf, Skier and village.

Wmk. 116

1949, Feb. 11 Typo. Perf. 14

8NB5	OSP1	10 + 4pf dull green	2.25	14.50
8NB6	OSP1	20 + 6pf red brown	2.25	14.50
		Set, never hinged	8.25	

Issued to commemorate the 1948-49 German Ski Championship at Isny im Allgau.

Gustav Werner — OSP2

1949, Sept. 4

8NB7	OSP2	10 + 5pf bl grn	2.00	10.50
8NB8	OSP2	20 + 10pf claret	2.00	10.50
		Set, never hinged	8.00	

Cent. of the founding of Gustav Werner's "Christianity in Action" and "House of Brotherhood."

Goethe Type of Baden, 1949

Various Portraits.

1949, Aug. 12

8NB9	OSP4	10 + 5pf green	3.25	16.00
8NB10	OSP4	20 + 10pf cerise	4.75	22.50
8NB11	OSP4	30 + 15pf blue	4.75	32.50
		Nos. 8NB9-8NB11 (3)	12.75	71.00
		Set, never hinged	21.00	

BERLIN

Issued for Use in the American, British and French Occupation Sectors of Berlin

Germany Nos. 557-569, 571-573 Overprinted Diagonally in Black

a

Wmk. 284

1948, Sept. 1 Typo. Perf. 14

9N1	A120	2pf brown blk	.30	3.50
9N2	A120	6pf purple	.25	3.50
9N3	A121	8pf red	.25	3.50
9N4	A121	10pf yellow grn	.35	.70
9N5	A122	12pf gray	.35	.50
9N6	A120	15pf chocolate	4.50	52.50
9N7	A123	16pf dk blue grn	.30	1.25
9N8	A121	20pf blue	1.75	5.25
9N9	A123	24pf brown org	.20	.30
9N10	A120	25pf orange yel	6.50	42.50
9N11	A122	30pf red	1.00	5.75
9N12	A121	40pf red violet	1.00	5.75
9N13	A123	50pf ultra	2.40	24.00
9N14	A122	60pf red brown	.65	.20
9N15	A122	80pf dark blue	2.00	20.00
9N16	A123	84pf emerald	5.00	75.00

Germany Nos. 574-577 Overprinted Diagonally in Black

b

Engr.

9N17	A124	1m olive	20.00	125.00
9N18	A124	2m dk brown vio	22.50	425.00
9N19	A124	3m copper red	26.00	575.00
9N20	A124	5m dark blue	30.00	575.00
		Nos. 9N1-9N20 (20)	125.30	
		Set, never hinged	300.00	

Forged overprints and cancellations are found on Nos. 9N1-9N20.

Stamps of Germany 1947-48 with "a" Overprint in Red

1948-49 Wmk. 284 Typo. Perf. 14

9N21	A120	2pf brn blk ('49)	.65	1.50
9N22	A120	6pf purple ('49)	4.00	1.50
9N23	A121	8pf red ('49)	16.00	3.50
9N24	A121	10pf yellow grn	.65	.30
9N25	A120	15pf chocolate	1.60	1.50
9N26	A121	20pf blue	.65	.60
9N27	A120	25pf org yel ('49)	32.50	37.50
9N28	A122	30pf red ('49)	26.00	4.50
9N29	A121	40pf red vio ('49)	26.00	11.50
9N30	A123	50pf ultra ('49)	26.00	6.00
9N31	A122	60pf red brown	3.25	.30
9N32	A122	80pf dk bl ('49)	40.00	7.00

With "b" Overprint in Red

Engr.

9N33	A124	1m olive	200.00	375.00
9N34	A124	2m dk brn vio	100.00	190.00
		Nos. 9N21-9N34 (14)	477.30	640.70
		Set, never hinged	1,100.	

Forgeries exist of the overprints on Nos. 9N21-9N34. No. 9N33 exists imperf.

Statue of Heinrich von Stephan
A1 A2

1949, Apr. 9 Litho. *Perf. 14*

9N35 A1 12pf gray 5.00 *6.75*
9N36 A1 16pf blue green 9.75 *13.00*
9N37 A1 24pf orange brn 6.50 .60
9N38 A1 50pf brown olive 50.00 32.50
9N39 A1 60pf brown red 60.00 29.00
9N40 A2 1m olive 26.00 *110.00*
9N41 A2 2m brown violet 32.50 *57.50*
Nos. 9N35-9N41 (7) 189.75 *249.35*
Set, never hinged 650.00

75th anniv. of the UPU.

Brandenburg Gate, Berlin — A3

Tempelhof Airport — A4

Designs: 4pf, 8pf, 40pf, Schoeneberg, Rudolf Wilde Square. 5pf, 25pf, 5m, Tegel Castle. 6pf, 50pf, Reichstag Building. 10pf, 30pf, Cloisters, Kleist Park. 15pf, Tempelhof Airport. 20pf, 80pf, 90pf, Polytechnic College, Charlottenburg. 60pf, National Gallery. 2m, Gendarmen Square. 3m, Brandenburg Gate.

1949 Typo. Wmk. 284
Size: 22x18mm

9N42 A3 1pf black .20 .20
a. Bklt. pane 5 + label 7.75 *20.00*
Never hinged 16.00
b. Tête bêche .30 *.90*
Never hinged .75
9N43 A3 4pf yellow brn .20 .20
a. Bklt. pane 5 + label 7.75 *20.00*
Never hinged 16.00
b. Tête bêche .75 *1.75*
Never hinged 1.50
9N44 A3 5pf blue green .20 .20
9N45 A3 6pf red violet .30 *.80*
9N46 A3 8pf red orange .30 *1.10*
9N47 A3 10pf yellow grn .30 .20
a. Bklt. pane 5 + label 52.50 *140.00*
Never hinged 100.00
9N48 A4 15pf chocolate 3.25 .55
9N49 A3 20pf red 1.25 .20
a. Bklt. pane 5 + label 52.50 *140.00*
Never hinged 100.00
9N50 A3 25pf orange 6.50 .80
9N51 A3 30pf violet bl 2.75 .80
a. Imperf. *600.00*
Never hinged 1,200.
9N52 A3 40pf lake 4.00 .80
9N53 A3 50pf olive 4.00 .20
9N54 A3 60pf red brown 13.00 .20
9N55 A3 80pf dark blue 2.75 .80
9N56 A3 90pf emerald 2.75 .80

Engr.
Size: 29¼-29¾x24-24½mm

9N57 A4 1m olive 5.00 .80
9N58 A4 2m brown vio 13.00 1.10
9N59 A4 3m henna brn 60.00 11.50
9N60 A4 5m deep blue 40.00 11.50
Nos. 9N42-9N60 (19) 159.75 32.75
Set, never hinged 625.00

See Nos. 9N101-9N102, 9N108-9N110.

Goethe and "Iphigenie" — A5

Statue of Atlas, New York — A6

Designs (Goethe and scenes from his works): 20pf, "Reineke Fuchs." 30pf, "Faust."

1949, July 29 Litho. *Perf. 14*

9N61 A5 10pf green 40.00 *52.50*
9N62 A5 20pf carmine 40.00 *57.50*
9N63 A5 30pf ultra 6.50 *40.00*
Nos. 9N61-9N63 (3) 86.50 *150.00*
Set, never hinged 275.00

Bicentenary of the birth of Johann Wolfgang von Goethe.

Germany Nos. 550, 565, 572 and 576 Surcharged "BERLIN" and New Value in Dark Green

1949, Aug. 1 Typo.

9N64 A119 5pf on 45pf 1.00 .20
9N65 A123 10pf on 24pf 3.25 .20
9N66 A122 20pf on 80pf 17.50 13.00

Engr.

9N67 A124 1m on 3m 42.50 13.00
Nos. 9N64-9N67 (4) 64.25 26.40
Set, never hinged 200.00

1950, Oct. 1 Engr. Wmk. 116

9N68 A6 20pf dk carmine 32.50 32.50
Never hinged 80.00

European Recovery Plan.

Albert Lortzing — A7 Freedom Bell, Berlin — A8

1951, Apr. 22

9N69 A7 20pf red brown 20.00 *40.00*
Never hinged 50.00

Centenary of the death of Albert Lortzing, composer.

1951 *Perf. 14*

9N70 A8 5pf chocolate .65 *5.25*
9N71 A8 10pf deep green 3.25 *16.00*
9N72 A8 20pf rose red 1.75 *13.00*
9N73 A8 30pf blue 13.00 *50.00*
9N74 A8 40pf rose violet 5.00 *29.00*
Nos. 9N70-9N74 (5) 23.65 *113.25*
Set, never hinged 72.50

Re-engraved

1951-52

9N75 A8 5pf olive bis ('52) .65 *1.40*
9N76 A8 10pf yellow grn 2.25 *3.25*
9N77 A8 20pf brt red 9.95 *13.00*
9N78 A8 30pf blue ('52) 20.00 *37.50*
9N79 A8 40pf dp car ('52) 9.75 *13.00*
Nos. 9N75-9N79 (5) 42.60 *68.15*
Set, never hinged 92.50

Bell clapper moved from left to right. Imprint "L. Schnell" in lower margin.
No. 9N76 exists imperf. Value $575.
See Nos. 9N94-9N98.

Ludwig van Beethoven — A9 Olympic Symbols — A10

1952, Mar. 26 Engr. Unwmk.

9N80 A9 30pf blue 16.00 *26.00*
Never hinged 35.00

125th anniversary of the death of Ludwig van Beethoven.

1952, June 20 Litho. Wmk. 116

9N81 A10 4pf yellow brown .30 *1.25*
9N82 A10 10pf green 3.25 *11.50*
9N83 A10 20pf rose red 6.50 *20.00*
Nos. 9N81-9N83 (3) 10.05 *32.75*
Set, never hinged 25.00

Pre-Olympic Festival Day, June 20, 1952.

Carl Friedrich Zelter — A11 Arms Breaking Chains — A12

Portraits: 5pf, Otto Lilienthal. 6pf, Walter Rathenau. 8pf, Theodor Fontane. 10pf, Adolph von Menzel. 15pf, Rudolf Virchow. 20pf, Werner von Siemens. 25pf, Karl Friedrich Schinkel. 30pf, Max Planck. 40pf, Wilhelm von Humboldt.

1952-53 Engr. Wmk. 284

9N84 A11 4pf brown .20 .30
9N85 A11 5pf dp blue ('53) .30 .30
9N86 A11 6pf choc ('53) 2.00 *7.00*
9N87 A11 8pf henna brn ('53) .65 *1.75*
9N88 A11 10pf deep green 1.00 .30
9N89 A11 15pf purple ('53) 5.00 *11.50*
9N90 A11 20pf brown red .65 .65
9N91 A11 25pf dp olive ('53) 16.00 4.75
9N92 A11 30pf brn vio ('53) 5.25 *7.00*
9N93 A11 40pf black ('53) 6.50 2.40
Nos. 9N84-9N93 (10) 37.55 35.95
Set, never hinged 110.00

Bell Type of 1951-1952 Second Re-engraving

1953 Wmk. 284 *Perf. 14*

9N94 A8 5pf brown .30 *.60*
9N95 A8 10pf deep green 1.00 *1.25*
9N96 A8 20pf brt red 2.75 2.75
9N97 A8 30pf blue 4.25 *10.50*
9N98 A8 40pf rose violet 18.00 *29.00*
Nos. 9N94-9N98 (5) 26.30 *44.10*
Set, never hinged 65.00

Bell clapper hangs straight down. Marginal imprint omitted.
For overprint & surcharge see #9N106, 9NB17.

1953, Aug. 17 Typo.

Design: 30pf, Brandenburg Gate.

9N99 A12 20pf black 2.00 1.40
9N100 A12 30pf dp carmine 11.00 *24.00*
Set, never hinged 35.00

Strike of East German workers, 6/17/53.

Similar to Type of 1949

Designs: 4pf, Exposition halls. 20pf, Olympic Stadium, Berlin.

1953-54 Wmk. 284 *Perf. 14*

9N101 A3 4pf yellow brn ('54) 1.75 *2.75*
9N102 A3 20pf red 21.00 .55
Set, never hinged 62.50

Catalogue values for unused stamps in this section, from this point to the end of the section, are for Never Hinged items.

Allied Council Building — A13

1954, Jan. 25 Litho.

9N103 A13 20pf red 7.25 4.00

Four Power Conference, Berlin, 1954.

Prof. Ernst Reuter (1889-1953), Mayor of Berlin (1948-53) A14

1954, Jan. 18 Engr. Wmk. 284

9N104 A14 20pf chocolate 7.25 1.40

See No. 9N174.

Ottmar Mergenthaler and Linotype — A15

1954, May 11

9N105 A15 10pf dk blue grn 2.25 2.00

Cent. of the birth of Ottmar Mergenthaler.

No. 9N96 Overprinted in Black

1954, July 17 *Perf. 13½x14*

9N106 A8 20pf bright red 3.50 3.75

Issued to publicize the West German presidential election held in Berlin July 17, 1954.

Germany in Bondage — A16 Richard Strauss — A17

1954, July 20 Typo.

9N107 A16 20pf car & gray 4.25 3.75

10th anniv. of the attempted assassination of Adolf Hitler.

Similar to Type of 1949

Designs: 7pf, Exposition halls. 40pf, Memorial library. 70pf, Hunting lodge, Grunewald.

1954 Wmk. 284 *Perf. 14*

9N108 A3 7pf aqua 5.00 .55
9N109 A3 40pf rose lilac 8.00 2.50
9N110 A3 70pf olive green 92.50 18.00
Nos. 9N108-9N110 (3) 105.50 21.05
Set, hinged 45.00

1954, Sept. 18 Engr.

9N111 A17 40pf violet blue 9.75 3.00

5th anniv. of the death of Richard Strauss, composer.

Early Forge — A18

1954, Sept. 25

9N112 A18 20pf reddish brown 6.50 1.40

Centenary of the death of August Borsig, industrial leader.

M. S. Berlin and Arms of Berlin — A19

1955, Mar. 12 Wmk. 284

9N113 A19 10pf Prus green 1.00 .30
9N114 A19 25pf violet blue 5.50 3.25

Issued to publicize the resumption of shipping under West German ownership.

Wilhelm Furtwängler — A20

Perf. 13½x14

1955, Sept. 17 Unwmk.

9N115 A20 40pf ultra	18.00	16.00

Issued to honor the conductor Wilhelm Furtwangler and to publicize the Berlin Music Festival, September 1955.

Arms of Berlin
A21 A22

1955, Oct. 17 Litho. Wmk. 304

9N116 A21 10pf red, org yel & blk	.35	.30
9N117 A21 20pf red, org yel & blk	4.50	6.25

Meeting of the German Bundestag in Berlin, Oct. 17-22, 1955.

1956, Mar. 16

9N118 A22 10pf red, ocher & blk	1.00	.35
9N119 A22 25pf red, ocher & blk	3.50	3.25

Meeting of the German Bundesrat in Berlin Mar. 16, 1956.

Radio Station, Berlin (A23 has no top inscription. A24 has top inscription.)
A23 A24

Free University
A25

Monument of the Great Elector Frederick William
A26

Designs: 1pf, 3pf, Brandenburg Gate. 5pf, General Post Office. 8pf, City Hall, Neukölln. 10pf, Kaiser Wilhelm Memorial Church. 15pf, Airlift memorial. 25pf, Lilienthal Monument. 30pf, Pfaueninsel Castle. 40pf, Charlottenburg Castle. 50pf, Reuter power plant. 60pf, Chamber of Commerce and Industry and Stock Exchange. 70pf, Schiller Theater. 3m, Congress Hall.

Typo.; Litho. (3pf, #9N122)

1956-63 Wmk. 304 *Perf. 14*

9N120	A25	1pf gray ('57)		.20	.20
9N120A	A25	3pf brt pur ('63)		.20	.20
9N121	A25	5pf rose lil ('57)		.20	.20
9N122	A23	7pf blue green		7.25	1.75
9N123	A24	7pf blue green		.20	.20
9N124	A24	8pf gray		.40	.30
9N125	A24	8pf red org ('59)		.25	.25
9N126	A24	10pf emerald		.20	.20
9N127	A24	15pf chlky blue		.25	.20
9N128	A25	20pf rose car		.20	.20
9N129	A24	25pf dull red brn		.30	.40

Engr.

9N130	A24	30pf gray grn ('57)		.50	.60
9N131	A25	40pf lt ultra ('57)		8.50	5.75
9N132	A24	50pf olive		.50	.65
9N133	A25	60pf lt brn ('57)		.35	.80
9N134	A25	70pf violet		20.00	10.50
9N135	A26	1m olive		1.60	1.60

Size: 29x24½mm

9N136 A25 3m rose cl ('58)	4.50	*9.75*
Nos. 9N120-9N136 (18)	45.60	33.75

No. 9N120 exists on both ordinary and fluorescent paper; No. 9N120A on fluorescent paper only; others on ordinary paper.

Engineers' Society Emblem — A27

Paul Lincke — A28

1956, May 12 Engr. *Perf. 14*

9N140 A27 10pf dark green	1.60	1.25
9N141 A27 20pf dark red	4.00	3.75

Cent. of Soc. of German Civil Engineers.

1956, Sept. 3

9N142 A28 20pf dark red	2.00	2.25

Death of Paul Lincke, composer, 10th anniv.

Radio Station, Berlin-Nikolassee
A29

Spandau, 1850 — A30

1956, Sept. 15

9N143 A29 25pf brown	5.25	6.25

German Industrial Fair, Berlin, Sept. 15-30.

1957, Mar. 7

9N144 A30 20pf gray ol & brn red	.40	.50

725th anniversary of Spandau.

Hansa Model Town and "B" — A31

Designs: 20pf, View of exposition grounds and "B." 40pf, Auditorium and "B."

1957 Engr.

9N145 A31 7pf violet brown	.20	.20
9N146 A31 20pf carmine	.60	.60
9N147 A31 40pf violet blue	1.50	1.75
Nos. 9N145-9N147 (3)	2.30	2.55

Intl. Building Show, Berlin, 7/6-9/29/57.

Friedrich Karl von Savigny, Law Teacher — A32

Uta Statue, Naumburg Cathedral — A33

Portraits: 7pf, Theodor Mommsen, historian. 8pf, Heinrich Zille, painter. 10pf, Ernst Reuter, mayor of Berlin. 15pf, Fritz Haber, chemist. 20pf, Friedrich Schleiermacher, theologian. 25pf, Max Reinhardt, theatrical director. 40pf, Alexander von Humboldt, naturalist and geographer. 50pf, Christian Daniel Rauch, sculptor.

1957-59 Wmk. 304 *Perf. 14*

Portraits in Brown

9N148 A32 7pf blue grn ('58)	.20	.20
9N149 A32 8pf gray ('58)	.20	.20
9N150 A32 10pf green ('58)	.20	.20
9N151 A32 15pf dark blue	.30	.60
9N152 A32 20pf carmine ('58)	.20	.20
9N153 A32 25pf magenta	.65	.70
9N154 A32 30pf olive green	1.60	1.75
9N155 A32 40pf blue ('59)	.65	.70
9N156 A32 50pf olive	3.00	*4.75*
Nos. 9N148-9N156 (9)	7.00	9.30

Issued to honor famous men of Berlin. See No. 9NB19.

1957, Aug. 6

9N157 A33 25pf brown red	.70	.75

Issued to publicize the annual meeting of the East German Culture Society in Berlin.

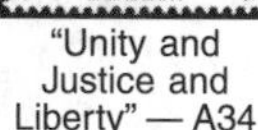

"Unity and Justice and Liberty" — A34

Postilion 1897-1925 — A35

1957, Oct. 15 Litho.

9N158 A34 10pf multicolored	.25	.55
9N159 A34 20pf multicolored	1.75	*2.25*

1st meeting of the 3rd German Bundesrat, Berlin, 10/15.

1957, Oct. 23 Wmk. 304 *Perf. 14*

9N160 A35 20pf multicolored	.60	.65

Issued for Stamp Day and BEPHILA stamp exhibition, Berlin, Oct. 23-27.

World Veterans' Federation Emblem — A36

Christ and the Cosmos — A37

1957, Oct. 28

9N161 A36 20pf bl grn, ol grn & yel	.65	.50

7th General Assembly of the World Veterans' Federation, Berlin, Oct. 24-Nov. 1.

1958, Aug. 13

9N162 A37 10pf lt bl grn & blk	.30	.30
9N163 A37 20pf rose lilac & blk	.75	1.10

Issued in honor of the 78th German Catholics Meeting, Berlin, Aug. 13-17.

Prof. Otto Suhr (1894-1957), Mayor of Berlin (1955-57)
A38

1958, Aug. 30 Engr. *Perf. 14*

9N164 A38 20pf rose red	.80	1.00

Pres. Heuss Type of Germany, 1959

Litho., Engraved (40pf, 70pf)

1959

9N165 A208 7pf blue green	.20	*.30*
9N166 A208 10pf green	.20	*.30*
9N167 A208 20pf dk car rose	.45	.30
9N168 A208 40pf blue	2.00	*3.50*
9N169 A208 70pf dull purple	6.50	*8.25*
Nos. 9N165-9N169 (5)	9.35	*12.65*

Nos. 9N168-9N169 were issued in sheets of 100 and in coils. Every fifth coil stamp has a control number on the back.

Aerial Bridge to Berlin — A39

Globe and Brandenburg Gate — A40

1959, May 12 Engr.

9N170 A39 25pf maroon & blk	.35	.30

10th anniversary of Berlin Airlift.

1959, June 18 Litho. *Perf. 14*

9N171 A40 20pf lt blue & red	.65	.30

Issued to publicize the 14th International Municipal Congress, Berlin, June 18-23.

Friedrich von Schiller (1759-1805), Poet — A41

1959, Nov. 10 Engr. Wmk. 304

9N172 A41 20pf dull red & brn	.30	.25

Dr. Robert Koch (1843-1910), Bacteriologist
A42

Hans Böckler (1875-1951), Labor Leader — A43

1960, May 27 *Perf. 14*

9N173 A42 20pf rose lake	.30	.30

Mayor Type of 1954

Portrait: Dr. Walther Carl Rudolf Schreiber, Mayor of Berlin, 1953-54.

1960, June 30 Wmk. 304 *Perf. 14*

9N174 A14 20pf brown car .30 .40

1961, Feb. 16 Litho. *Perf. 14*

9N175 A43 20pf dk brick red & blk .25 .20

Hans Böckler (1875-1951), labor leader.

Fluorescent Paper was introduced for all stamps, starting with No. 9N176, and including Nos. 9N120 and 9N120A.

Albrecht Dürer — A44

Portraits: 5pf, Albertus Magnus. 7pf, St. Elizabeth of Thuringia. 8pf, Johann Gutenberg. 15pf, Martin Luther. 20pf, Johann Sebastian Bach. 25pf, Balthasar Neumann. 30pf, Immanuel Kant. 40pf, Gotthold Ephraim Lessing. 50pf, Johann Wolfgang von Goethe. 60pf, Friedrich von Schiller. 70pf, Ludwig van Beethoven. 80pf, Heinrich von Kleist. 1m, Annette von Droste-Hülshoff. 2m, Gerhart Hauptmann.

1961-62 Typo. Wmk. 304

9N176 A44 5pf olive .20 .20
9N177 A44 7pf dk bister .20 .30
9N178 A44 8pf lilac .20 *.30*
9N179 A44 10pf olive green .20 .20
b. Tête bêche pair .70 *1.40*
9N180 A44 15pf blue .20 .30
9N181 A44 20pf dark red .20 .20
9N182 A44 25pf orange brn .20 .30

Engr.

9N183 A44 30pf gray .20 *.40*
9N184 A44 40pf blue .40 *.75*
9N185 A44 50pf red brown .30 *.75*
9N186 A44 60pf dk car rose ('62) .30 *.75*
9N187 A44 70pf green .40 *.75*
9N188 A44 80pf brown 2.75 *5.25*
9N189 A44 1m violet blue 1.25 *2.10*
9N190 A44 2m yel grn ('62) 1.40 *3.25*
Nos. 9N176-9N190 (15) 8.40 *15.80*

Nos. 9N176-9N182, 9N184 and 9N187 were issued in sheets and in coils. Every fifth coil stamp has a black control number on the back.

Louise Schroeder A45

1961, June 3 Engr. *Perf. 14*

9N192 A45 20pf dark brown .30 .20

Issued to honor Louise Schroeder, acting mayor of Berlin (1947-1948).

Synod Emblem & St. Mary's Church — A46

Design: 20pf, Emblem and Kaiser Wilhelm Memorial Church.

1961, July 19 Litho. Wmk. 304

9N193 A46 10pf green & vio .20 .20
9N194 A46 20pf rose claret & vio .20 .20

10th meeting of German Protestants (Evangelical Synod), Berlin, July 19-23.

Berlin Bear with Record, TV Set & Radio Tower — A47

1961, Aug. 3 Engr.

9N195 A47 20pf brn red & dk brn .25 .20

German Radio, Television and Phonograph Exhibition, Berlin, Aug. 25-Sept. 3.

Berlin, 1650 — A48

Views of Old Berlin: 10pf, Spree and Waisenbrücke (Orphans' Bridge). 15pf, Mauer Street, 1780. 20pf, Berlin Palace, 1703. 25pf, Potsdam Square, 1825. 40pf, Bellevue Palace, 1800. 50pf, Fischer Bridge, 1830. 60pf, Halle Gate, 1880. 70pf, Parochial Church, 1780. 80pf, University, 1825. 90pf, Opera House, 1780. 1m, Grunewald Lake, 1790.

1962-63 Wmk. 304 *Perf. 14*

9N196 A48 7pf dk gray & gldn brn .20 .20
9N197 A48 10pf grn & dk gray .20 .20
9N198 A48 15pf bluish gray & dk bl ('63) .20 .20
9N199 A48 20pf org brn & sep .20 .20
9N200 A48 25pf ol & gray ('63) .20 .20
9N201 A48 40pf bluish gray & ultra .20 .30
9N202 A48 50pf gray & dk brn ('63) .30 .30
9N203 A48 60pf gray & car rose ('63) .35 .35
9N204 A48 70pf dk gray & lilac .35 .35
9N205 A48 80pf dk gray & dk red ('63) .40 .55
9N206 A48 90pf sep & brn org ('63) .45 .60
9N207 A48 1m ol gray & dp grn .55 .90
Nos. 9N196-9N207 (12) 3.60 4.35

Gelber Hund, 1912, and Boeing 707 — A49

Berlin Bear and Radio Tower — A50

1962, Sept. 12 Litho.

9N208 A49 60pf brt blue & blk .40 .40

50th anniv. of German airmail service.

1963, July 24 Unwmk. *Perf. 14*

9N209 A50 20pf bl, vio bl & gray .25 .20

German Radio, Television and Phonograph Exhibition, Berlin, Aug. 30-Sept. 8.

Schöneberg City Hall, John F. Kennedy Place, Berlin — A51

1964, May 30 Engr. Wmk. 304

9N210 A51 20pf dk brn, *cr* .25 .20

700th anniv. of the Schöneberg district of Berlin. The Senate and House of Representatives of West Berlin meet at Schöneberg City Hall.

Lübke Type of Germany, 1964

1964, July 1 Litho. Unwmk.

9N211 A247 20pf carmine .20 .20
9N212 A247 40pf ultra .30 .25

See Nos. 9N263-9N264.

Capitals Type of Germany

Design: Reichstag Building, Berlin.

1964, Sept. 14 Litho. *Perf. 14*

9N213 A245 20pf blue, blk & grn .30 .25

Kennedy Type of Germany

1964, Nov. 21 Engr. Wmk. 304

9N214 A255 40pf dark blue .40 .30

Castle Gate, Ellwangen — A52

Designs (German buildings through 12 centuries): 10pf, Wall pavilion, Zwinger, Dresden. 15pf, Tegel Castle, Berlin. 20pf, Portico, Lorsch. 40pf, Trifels Fortress, Palatinate. 60pf, Treptow Gate, Neubrandenburg. 70pf, Osthofen Gate, Soest. 80pf, Elling Gate, Weissenburg.

1964-65 Typo. Unwmk.

9N215 A52 10pf brown ('65) .20 .20
b. Tête bêche pair .30 .60
9N216 A52 15pf dk green ('65) .20 .20
9N217 A52 20pf brn red ('65) .20 .20

Engr.

9N218 A52 40pf vio bl ('65) .50 .75
9N219 A52 50pf olive bis 1.10 1.00
9N220 A52 60pf rose red .75 .75
9N221 A52 70pf dk green ('65) 1.75 2.10
9N222 A52 80pf chocolate 1.50 1.10
Nos. 9N215-9N222 (8) 6.20 6.30

Nos. 9N215-9N218, 9N221 were issued in sheets of 100 and in coils. Every fifth coil stamp has a black control number on the back.

Kaiser Wilhelm Memorial Church A53

Nordertor, Flensburg A54

The New Berlin: 15pf, German Opera House, horiz. 20pf, Philharmonic Hall, horiz. 30pf, Jewish Community Center, horiz. 40pf, Regina Martyrum Memorial, horiz. 50pf, Ernst Reuter Square, horiz. 60pf, Europa Center. 70pf, School of Engineering, horiz. 80pf, City Highway. 90pf, Planetarium and observatory, horiz. 1m, Schaeferberg radio tower, Wannsee. 1.10m, University clinic, Steglitz, horiz.

Engraved and Lithographed

1965-66 Unwmk. *Perf. 14*

9N223 A53 10pf multi .20 .20
9N224 A53 15pf multi .20 .20
9N225 A53 20pf multi .20 .20
9N226 A53 30pf multi ('66) .20 .20
9N227 A53 40pf multi ('66) .20 .20
9N228 A53 50pf multi .20 .20
9N229 A53 60pf multi ('66) .25 .30
9N230 A53 70pf multi ('66) .35 .30
9N231 A53 80pf multi .40 .30
9N232 A53 90pf multi ('66) .45 .45
9N233 A53 1m multi ('66) .60 .60
9N234 A53 1.10m multi ('66) .60 .75
Nos. 9N223-9N234 (12) 3.85 3.90

1966-69 Engr. *Perf. 14*

5pf, Berlin Gate, Stettin. 8pf, Castle, Kaub on the Rhine. 10pf, Wall Pavilion, Zwinger, Dresden. 20pf, Portico, Lorsch. 40pf, Trifels Fortress, Palatinate. 50pf, Castle Gate, Ellwangen. 60pf, Treptow Gate, Neubrandenburg. 70pf, Osthofen Gate, Soest. 80pf, Elling Gate, Weissenburg. 90pf, Zschocke Ladies' Home, Königsberg. 1m, Melanchthon House, Wittenberg. 1.10m, Trinity Hospital, Hildesheim. 1.30m, Tegel Castle, Berlin. 2m, Löwenberg Town Hall, interior view.

9N235 A54 5pf olive .20 .20
9N236 A54 8pf car rose .20 .20
9N237 A54 10pf dk brn ('67) .20 .20
9N238 A54 20pf dk grn ('67) .20 .20
9N239 A54 30pf yellow grn .20 .20
9N240 A54 30pf red ('67) .20 .20
9N241 A54 40pf ol bis ('67) .40 .60
9N242 A54 50pf blue ('67) .30 .35
9N243 A54 60pf dp org ('67) 1.25 1.50
9N244 A54 70pf sl grn ('67) .60 .60
9N245 A54 80pf red brn ('67) .75 1.25
9N246 A54 90pf black .40 .60
9N247 A54 1m dull blue .40 .60
9N248 A54 1.10m red brn 1.10 1.00
9N249 A54 1.30m green ('69) 1.90 1.50
9N250 A54 2m purple 1.90 1.40
Nos. 9N235-9N250 (16) 10.20 10.60

Brandenburg Gate Type of Germany

1966-70 Typo. *Perf. 14*

9N251 A268 10pf chocolate .20 .20
a. Bklt. pane of 10 (4 #9N251, 2 #9N252, 4 #9N253) 4.50 9.25
b. Tête bêche pair .50 .75
c. Bklt. pane of 6 (4 #9N251, 2 #9N253) ('70) 2.00 *3.25*
9N252 A268 20pf dp green .20 .20
a. Bklt. pane of 4 (2 #9N252, 2 #9N253) ('70) 1.60 *2.00*
9N253 A268 30pf red .20 .20
a. Tête bêche pair .80 1.10
9N254 A268 50pf dk blue .40 .30
9N255 A268 100pf dk blue ('67) 3.50 3.00
Nos. 9N251-9N255 (5) 4.50 3.90

Nos. 9N251-9N255 were issued in sheets of 100 and in coils. Every fifth coil stamp has a black control number on the back.

A55 A56

Designs: 10pf, Young Man, by Conrat Meit, 1520. 20pf, The Great Elector Friedrich Wilhelm (1640-88), head from monument by Andreas Schlüter. 30pf, The Evangelist Mark, by Tilman Riemenschneider. 50pf, Head of "Victory" from Brandenburg Gate, by Gottfried Schadow, 1793. 1m, Madonna, by Joseph Anton Feuchtmayer. 1.10m, Jesus and John, wood sculpture, anonymous, c. 1320.

1967 Engr. *Perf. 14*

9N256 A55 10pf sepia & lemon .20 .20
9N257 A55 20pf sl grn & bluish gray .20 .20
9N258 A55 30pf brown & olive .20 .20
9N259 A55 50pf black & gray .30 .30
9N260 A55 1m blue & chlky blue .55 .55

Size: 22x40mm

9N261 A55 1.10m brown & buff .75 .90
Nos. 9N256-9N261 (6) 2.20 2.35

Issued to publicize Berlin art treasures.

1967, July 19 Litho. and Engr.

Berlin Radio Tower and Television Screens

9N262 A56 30pf multicolored .25 .20

25th German Radio, Television and Phonograph Exhibition, Berlin, Aug. 25-Sept. 3.

Lübke Type of Germany, 1964

1967, Oct. 14 Litho.

9N263 A247 30pf carmine .20 .20
9N264 A247 50pf ultra .30 .25

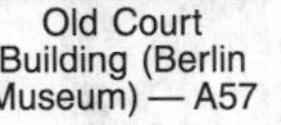

Old Court Building (Berlin Museum) — A57

Turners' Emblem — A58

1968, Mar. 16 Engr. *Perf. 14*
9N265 A57 30pf black .25 .20

500th anniv. of the Berlin Court of Appeal.

1968, Apr. 29 Litho. *Perf. 14*
9N266 A58 20pf gray, blk & red .25 .20

Issued to publicize the German Turner Festival, Berlin, May 28-June 3.

Newspaper Vendor by Christian Wilhelm Allers — A59

19th Century Berliners: 5pf, Hack, by Heinrich Zille, horiz. No. 9N269, Horse omnibus, coachman and passengers, 1890, by C. W. Allers. No. 9N270, Cobbler's apprentice, by Franz Kruger. No. 9N271, Cobbler, by Adolph von Menzel. No. 9N272, Blacksmiths, by Paul Meyerheim. No. 9N273, Three Ladies, by Franz Kruger. 50pf, Strollers at Brandenburg Gate, by Christian W. Allers.

1969 Engr. *Perf. 14*
9N267 A59 5pf black .20 .20
9N268 A59 10pf dp brown .20 .20
9N269 A59 10pf brown .20 .20
9N270 A59 20pf dk olive grn .20 .20
9N271 A59 20pf green .20 .20
9N272 A59 30pf dk red brown .45 .35
9N273 A59 30pf red brown .45 .35
9N274 A59 50pf ultra 1.40 1.25
Nos. 9N267-9N274 (8) 3.30 2.95

Souvenir Sheet

Berlin Zoo Animals — A60

Designs: 10pf, Orangutan family. 20pf, White pelicans. 30pf, Gaur and calf. 50pf, Zebra and foal.

Engraved and Lithographed

1969, June 4 *Perf. 14*
9N275 A60 Sheet of 4 1.60 1.60
a. 10pf bister & black .20 .20
b. 20pf light green & black .20 .20
c. 30pf lilac rose & black .30 .30
d. 50pf blue & black .45 .45

125th anniversary of the Berlin Zoo. The sheet was sold with a 20pf surtax for the benefit of the Zoo.

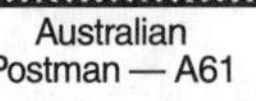

Australian Postman — A61

Joseph Joachim — A62

Designs: 20pf, African telephone operator. 30pf, Middle East telecommunications engineer. 50pf, Loading mail on plane.

1969, July 21 Litho. *Perf. 14*
9N276 A61 10pf olive & apple grn .20 .20
9N277 A61 20pf dk brn, bis & brn .20 .20
9N278 A61 30pf vio blk & bis .35 .35
9N279 A61 50pf dk blue & blue .70 .70
Nos. 9N276-9N279 (4) 1.45 1.45

20th Congress of the Post Office Trade Union Federation, Berlin, July 7-11.

1969, Sept. 12 Photo. *Perf. 14*

Design: 50pf, Alexander von Humboldt, painting by Joseph Stieler.

9N280 A62 30pf multicolored .40 .30
9N281 A62 50pf multicolored .60 .90

Cent. of the Berlin Music School and honoring its 1st director, Joseph Joachim (1831-1907), violinist, conductor and composer; Alexander von Humboldt (1769-1859), naturalist and explorer.

1970, Jan. 7

Theodor Fontane, painting by Hanns Fechner.

9N282 A62 20pf multicolored .30 .25

150th anniv. of the birth of Theodor Fontane (1819-1898), poet and writer.
See No. 9N303.

Film Frame — A63

Symbols of Dance, Theater & Art — A64

1970, June 18 Photo. *Perf. 14*
9N283 A63 30pf multicolored .30 .30

20th International Film Festival.

President Heinemann Type of Germany Inscribed "Berlin"

1970-73 Engr. *Perf. 14*
9N284 A312 5pf dk gray .20 .20
9N285 A312 8pf olive bis .60 .75
9N286 A312 10pf brown .20 .20
9N286A A312 15pf olive .20 .20
9N287 A312 20pf green .20 .20
9N288 A312 25pf dp yel grn .75 .35
9N289 A312 30pf red brown .85 .30
9N290 A312 40pf brown org .45 .20
9N291 A312 50pf dark blue .45 .20
9N292 A312 60pf blue .75 .35
9N293 A312 70pf dk brown .60 .45
9N294 A312 80pf slate grn .75 .65
9N295 A312 90pf magenta 1.60 1.75
9N296 A312 1m olive .75 .50
9N296A A312 110pf olive gray .95 .95
9N297 A312 120pf ocher .95 .80
9N298 A312 130pf ocher 1.40 1.25
9N298A A312 140pf dk blue grn 1.40 1.40
9N299 A312 150pf purple 1.40 .55
9N300 A312 160pf orange 1.90 1.60
9N300A A312 170pf orange 1.40 1.10
9N300B A312 190pf dp claret 1.60 1.10
9N301 A312 2m dp violet 1.60 1.00
Nos. 9N284-9N301 (23) 20.95 16.05

Issued: 5pf, 1m, 7/23; 10, 20pf, 10/23; 30, 90pf, 2m, 1/7/71; 8, 40, 50, 70, 80pf, 4/8/71; 60pf, 6/25/71; 25pf, 8/27/71; 120, 160pf, 3/8/72; 15, 130pf, 6/20/72; 150pf, 7/5/72; 170pf, 9/11/72; 110, 140, 190pf, 1/16/73.

1970, Sept. 4 Litho. *Perf. 13½x14*
9N302 A64 30pf gray & multi .40 .35

20th Berlin Festival Weeks.

Portrait Type of 1969

30pf, Leopold von Ranke, by Julius Schrage.

1970, Oct. 23 Photo. *Perf. 13½x14*
9N303 A62 30pf multicolored .35 .30

175th anniversary of the birth of Leopold von Ranke (1795-1886), historian.

Imperial Eagle Type of Germany

1971, Jan. 18 Litho. *Perf. 13½x14*
9N304 A317 30pf org, red, gray & blk .40 .40

Metropolitan Train, 1932 — A65

5pf, Suburban train, 1925. 10pf, Street cars, 1890. 20pf, Horsedrawn trolley. 50pf, Strect car, 1950. 1m, Subway train, 1971.

1971 Litho. *Perf. 14*
9N305 A65 5pf multicolored .20 .20
9N306 A65 10pf multicolored .20 .20
9N307 A65 20pf multicolored .20 .20
9N308 A65 30pf multicolored .35 .30
9N309 A65 50pf multicolored 1.25 1.00
9N310 A65 1m multicolored 1.40 1.40
Nos. 9N305-9N310 (6) 3.60 3.30

Issued: 30pf, 1m, Jan. 18; others, May 3.

Bagpipe Player, by Dürer — A66

1971, May 21 Engr. *Perf. 14*
9N311 A66 10pf black & brown .30 .25

500th anniversary of the birth of Albrecht Dürer (1471-1528), painter and engraver.

Score from 2nd Brandenburg Concerto and Bach — A67

1971, July 14 Litho. *Perf. 14*
9N312 A67 30pf buff, brn & slate .50 .40

250th anniv. of 1st performance of Johann Sebastian Bach's 2nd Brandenburg Concerto.

A68 A69

1971, July 14 Photo.

Telecommunications tower, Berlin.

9N313 A68 30pf dk blue, blk & car .55 .40

Intl. Broadcasting Exhibition, Berlin.

1971, Aug. 27
9N314 A69 25pf multicolored .40 .30

Hermann von Helmholtz (1821-94), scientist. See Nos. 9N332-9N333, 9N341.

Souvenir Sheet

Racing Cars — A70

1971, Aug. 27 Litho. *Perf. 14*
9N315 A70 Sheet of 4 1.25 1.00
a. 10pf Opel racer .20 .20
b. 25pf Auto Union racer .20 .20
c. 30pf Mercedes-Benz SSKL, 1931 .30 .20
d. 60pf Mercedes and Auto Union cars racing on North embankment .45 .45

50th anniversary of Avus Race Track.

Accident Prevention Type of Germany

5pf, "Matches cause fires." 10pf, Broken ladder. 20pf, Hand & circular saw. 25pf, "Alcohol & automobile." 30pf, Safety helmets prevent injury. 40pf, Defective plug. 50pf, Nail sticking from board. 60pf, 70pf, Traffic safety (ball rolling before car). 100pf, Hoisted cargo. 150pf, Fenced-in open manhole.

1971-73 Typo. *Perf. 14*
9N316 A328 5pf orange .20 .25
9N317 A328 10pf dk brown .20 .20
a. Bklt. pane, 2 each #9N317-9N318, 9N320-9N321 ('74) 6.50
9N318 A328 20pf purple .20 .20
9N319 A328 25pf green .30 .45
9N320 A328 30pf dark red .30 .25
9N321 A328 40pf rose cl .30 .35
9N322 A328 50pf Prus blue 1.60 .80
9N323 A328 60pf violet blue 1.60 1.50
9N323A A328 70pf green & vio bl 1.10 .75
9N324 A328 100pf olive 1.60 .80
9N325 A328 150pf red brown 5.00 4.50
Nos. 9N316-9N325 (11) 12.40 10.05

Issued in sheets of 100 and coils. Every fifth coil stamp has a control number on the back.
Issued: 25pf, 60pf, 9/10; 5pf, 10/29; 10pf, 30pf, 3/8/72; 40pf, 6/20/72; 20pf, 100pf, 7/5/72; 150pf, 9/11/72; 50pf, 1/16/73; 70pf, 6/5/73.

Microscope and Metal Slide — A71

Friedrich Gilly, by Gottfried Schadow — A72

1971, Oct. 26 Photo. *Perf. 14*
9N326 A71 30pf multicolored .35 .30

Materials Testing Laboratory centenary.

1972, Feb. 4 Engr. *Perf. 14*
9N327 A72 30pf black & blue .40 .25

Friedrich Gilly (1772-1800), sculptor.

Grunewaldsee, by Alexander von Riesen — A73

Paintings of Berlin Lakes: 25pf, Wannsee, by Max Liebermann. 30pf, Schlachtensee, by Walter Leistikow.

1972, Apr. 14 Photo. *Perf. 14*
9N328 A73 10pf blue & multi .20 .20
9N329 A73 25pf green & multi .40 .40
9N330 A73 30pf black & multi .60 .50
Nos. 9N328-9N330 (3) 1.20 1.10

A74 A75

1972, May 18
9N331 A74 60pf violet & blk .80 .80

E. T. A. Hoffmann (1776-1822), writer and composer. (Portrait by Wilhelm Hensel.)

Portrait Type of 1971

Designs: No. 9N332, Max Liebermann (1847-1935), self-portrait. No. 9N333, Karl August, Duke of Hardenberg (1750-1822), Prussian statesman, by J. H. W. Tischbein.

1972 Photo. *Perf. 14*
9N332 A69 40pf multicolored .50 .35
9N333 A69 40pf multicolored .45 .35

Issued: #9N332, July 18; #9N333, Nov. 10.

1972, Oct. 20 Engr. & Litho.
9N334 A75 20pf Stamp-printing press .35 .25

Stamp Day 1972, and for the 5th National Youth Philatelic Exhib., Berlin, Oct. 26-29.

Streetcar, 1907 A76

#9N336, Double-decker bus, 1919. #9N337, Double-decker bus, 1925. #9N338, Electrobus, 1933. #9N339, Double-decker bus, 1970. #9N340, Elongated bus, 1973.

1973, Apr. 30 Litho. *Perf. 14*
9N335 A76 20pf gray & multi .30 .25
9N336 A76 30pf gray & multi .55 .35
9N337 A76 40pf gray & multi .80 .50

1973, Sept. 14
9N338 A76 20pf gray & multi .30 .25
9N339 A76 30pf gray & multi .80 .35
9N340 A76 40pf gray & multi .80 .50
Nos. 9N335-9N340 (6) 3.55 2.20

Public transportation in Berlin.

Portrait Type of 1971

Design: 40pf, Ludwig Tieck (1773-1853), poet and writer, by Carl Christian Vogel von Vogelstein.

1973, May 25 Photo. *Perf. 14*
9N341 A69 40pf multicolored .50 .35

Johann Joachim Quantz (1697-1773), Flutist and Composer — A77

1973, June 12 Engr. *Perf. 14*
9N342 A77 40pf black .65 .50

Souvenir Sheet

50 Years of Broadcasting — A78

1973, Aug. 23 Litho. *Perf. 14*
9N343 A78 Sheet of 4 3.25 3.25
a. A78 20pf Speaker, set, 1926 .40 .30
b. A78 30pf Hans Bredow .65 .40
c. A78 40pf Girl, TV, tape recorder .75 .65
d. A78 70pf TV camera .90 .80

50 years of German broadcasting. Sold for 1.80m.

Georg W. von Knobelsdorff A79

Gustav R. Kirchhoff — A80

1974, Feb. 15 Engr. *Perf. 14*
9N344 A79 20pf chocolate .30 .25

275th anniversary of the birth of Georg Wenzelslaus von Knobelsdorff (1699-1753), architect.

1974, Feb. 15 Litho. & Engr.
9N345 A80 30pf gray & dk grn .30 .30

Sesquicentennial of the birth of Gustav Robert Kirchhoff (1824-1887), physicist.

Airlift Memorial, Allied Flags — A81

1974, Apr. 17 Photo. *Perf. 14*
9N346 A81 90pf multicolored 1.40 1.00

End of the Allied airlift into Berlin, 25th anniv.

Adolf Slaby and Waves — A82

1974, Apr. 17 Litho. *Perf. 14*
9N347 A82 40pf black & red .45 .35

125th anniversary of the birth of Adolf Slaby (1849-1913), radio pioneer.

School Seal Showing Athena and Hermes — A83

1974, July 13 Photo. *Perf. 14*
9N348 A83 50pf multicolored .55 .35

400th anniversary of the Gray Brothers' School, a secondary Franciscan school.

0

Berlin-Tegel Airport — A84

Lithographed and Engraved

1974, Oct. 15 *Perf. 14*
9N349 A84 50pf multicolored .75 .50

Opening of Berlin-Tegel Airport and Terminal, Nov. 1, 1974.

Venus, by F. E. Meyer, c. 1775 — A85

Gottfried Schadow — A86

Berlin Porcelain: 40pf, "Astronomy," by W. C. Meyer, c. 1772. 50pf, "Justice," by J. G. Müller, c. 1785.

1974, Oct. 29 Litho. *Perf. 14*
9N350 A85 30pf carmine & multi .40 .30
9N351 A85 40pf carmine & multi .45 .40
9N352 A85 50pf carmine & multi .55 .50
Nos. 9N350-9N352 (3) 1.40 1.20

1975, Jan. 15 Engr. *Perf. 14*
9N353 A86 50pf maroon .65 .40

Johann Gottfried Schadow (1764-1850), sculptor.

S.S. Princess Charlotte A87

Ships: 40pf, S.S. Siegfried. 50pf, S.S. Sperber. 60pf, M.S. Vaterland. 70pf, M.S. Moby Dick.

1975, Feb. 14 Litho. *Perf. 14*
9N354 A87 30pf gray & multi .45 .25
9N355 A87 40pf olive & multi .45 .25
9N356 A87 50pf ultra & multi .85 .50
9N357 A87 60pf red brn & multi .85 .50
9N358 A87 70pf dk blue & multi 1.10 1.00
Nos. 9N354-9N358 (5) 3.70 2.50

Berlin passenger ships

Industry Type of Germany

1975-82 Engr. *Perf. 14*

Design A380

9N359	5pf	Symphonie satellite	.20	.20
9N360	10pf	Electric train	.20	.20
9N361	20pf	Old Weser lighthouse	.20	.20
9N362	30pf	Rescue helicopter	.25	.20
9N363	40pf	Space shuttle	.35	.20
9N364	50pf	Radar station	.35	.20
9N365	60pf	X-ray machine	.65	.30
9N366	70pf	Shipbuilding	.70	.30
9N367	80pf	Tractor	.70	.20
9N368	100pf	Coal excavator	.70	.35
9N368A	110pf	TV camera	1.10	.75
9N369	120pf	Chemical plant	1.00	.65
9N369A	130pf	Brewery	1.75	.75
9N370	140pf	Heating plant	1.00	.90
9N371	150pf	Power shovel	2.25	.75
9N372	160pf	Blast furnace	2.00	.90
9N373	180pf	Payloader	2.25	1.25
9N373A	190pf	As #9N371	2.25	1.40
9N374	200pf	Oil drill platform	1.25	.35
9N375	230pf	Frankfurt airport	2.00	1.25
9N375A	250pf	Airport	3.75	1.40
9N375B	300pf	Electric railroad	3.75	1.25
9N376	500pf	Radio telescope	4.50	2.50
		Nos. 9N359-9N376 (23)	33.15	16.45

Issued: 40, 50, 100pf, 5/15; 10, 30, 70pf, 8/14; 80, 120, 160pf, 10/15; 5, 140, 200pf, 11/14; 20, 500pf, 2/17/76; 60pf, 11/16/78; 230pf, 5/17/79; 150, 180pf, 7/12/79; 110, 130, 300pf, 6/16/82; 190, 250pf, 7/15/82.

Ferdinand Sauerbruch — A88

Lithographed and Engraved

1975, May 15 *Perf. 13½x14*
9N379 A88 50pf dull red & dk brn .60 .40

Ferdinand Sauerbruch (1875-1951) surgeon, birth centenary.

Gymnasts' Emblem — A89

1975, May 15 Photo. *Perf. 14*
9N380 A89 40pf green, gold & blk .40 .30

6th Gymnaestrada, Berlin, July 1-5.

Lovis Corinth (1858-1925), Self-portrait, 1900 — A90

1975, July 15 Photo. *Perf. 14*
9N381 A90 50pf multicolored .65 .45

Architecture Type of Germany

Houses, Naunynstrasse, Berlin-Kreuzberg.

1975, July 15 Litho. & Engr.
9N382 A381 50pf multicolored .65 .45

European Architectural Heritage Year.

Paul Löbe and Reichstag A92

1975, Nov. 14 Engr. *Perf. 14*
9N383 A92 50pf copper red .60 .45

Paul Löbe (1875-1967), president of German Parliament 1920-1932, birth centenary.

Grain — A93

1976, Jan. 5 Photo. *Perf. 14*
9N384 A93 70pf green & yellow .65 .55

Green Week International Agricultural Exhibition, Berlin, 50th anniversary.

Hockey A94

1976, May 13 Engr. *Perf. 14*
9N385 A94 30pf green .50 .30

Women's World Hockey Championships.

Treble Clef — A95

1976, May 13 **Photo.**

9N386	A95	40pf multicolored	.65	.40

German Choir Festival.

Berlin Fire Brigade Emblem — A96

1976, May 13 **Litho.**

9N387	A96	50pf red & multi	.90	.60

Berlin Fire Brigade, 125th anniversary.

Sailboat on Havel River — A97

Berlin Views: 40pf, Spandau Castle. 50pf, Tiergarten.

1976, Nov. 16 **Engr.** ***Perf. 14***

9N388	A97	30pf blue & blk	.40	.30
9N389	A97	40pf brown & blk	.55	.30
9N390	A97	50pf green & blk	.65	.30
		Nos. 9N388-9N390 (3)	1.60	.90

See Nos. 9N422-9N424.

Castle Type of Germany

1977-79 **Typo.** ***Perf. 14***

10pf, Glücksburg. 20pf, 190pf, Pfaueninsel. 25pf, Gemen. 30pf, Ludwigstein. 40pf, Eltz. 50pf, Neuschwanstein. 60pf, Marksburg. 70pf, Mespelbrunn. 90pf, Vischering. 200pf, Bürresheim. 210pf, Schwanenburg. 230pf, Lichtenberg.

9N391	A406	10pf gray blue	.20	.20
a.		Bklt. pane, 4 #9N391, 2 each #9N394, 9N396	5.25	*7.25*
b.		Bklt. pane, 4 #9N391, 2 #9N394, 2 #9N440	2.50	*4.00*
c.		Bklt. pane, 4 #9N391, 2 #9N440, 2 #9N442	9.50	*16.00*
d.		Bklt. pane, 2 each #9N391, 9N394, 9N440-9N441	6.25	*11.50*
9N392	A406	20pf orange	.20	.20
9N393	A406	25pf crimson	.20	.25
9N394	A406	30pf olive	.20	.20
9N395	A406	40pf blue green	.20	.20
9N396	A406	50pf rose car	.45	.20
9N397	A406	60pf brown	.60	.35
9N398	A406	70pf blue	.60	.35
9N399	A406	90pf dark blue	.75	.55
9N400	A406	190pf red brown	1.25	1.10
9N401	A406	200pf green	1.25	1.10
9N402	A406	210pf red brown	1.60	.95
9N403	A406	230pf dark green	1.60	.95
		Nos. 9N391-9N403 (13)	9.10	6.60

Issued in sheets of 100 and coils. Every fifth coil stamp has a control number on the back.

Issued: 60pf, 200pf, 1/13; 40pf, 190pf, 2/16; 10pf, 20pf, 30pf, 4/14; 50pf, 70pf, 5/17; 230pf, 11/16/78; 25pf, 90pf, 1/11/79; 210pf, 2/14/79.

See Nos. 9N438-9N445.

Eugenie d'Alton, by Rausch — A98

1977, Jan. 13 **Photo.** ***Perf. 14***

9N404	A98	50pf violet black	.65	.40

Christian Daniel Rausch (1777-1857), sculptor, birth bicentenary.

Eduard Gaertner (1801-77), Painter — A99

1977, Feb. 16 **Litho. & Engr.**

9N405	A99	40pf lt grn, grn & blk	.40	.30

Fountain, by Georg Kolbe — A100

1977, Apr. 14 **Photo.** ***Perf. 14***

9N406	A100	30pf dark olive	.40	.30

Georg Kolbe (1877-1947), sculptor.

"Bear each other's burdens" A101

1977, May 17 **Litho.** ***Perf. 14***

9N407	A101	40pf green blk & yel	.40	.30

17th meeting of German Protestants (Evangelical Synod), Berlin.

Patent Office, Berlin-Kreuzberg — A102

1977, July 13 **Litho. & Engr.**

9N408	A102	60pf gray & red	1.00	.50

Centenary of German patent laws.

Telephones, 1905 and 1977 A103

Painting by George Grosz (1893-1959) A104

1977, July 13 **Litho.**

9N409	A103	50pf multicolored	1.25	.65

International Broadcasting Exhibition, Berlin, Aug. 26-Sept. 4, and centenary of telephone in Germany.

1977, July 13

9N410	A104	70pf multicolored	.75	.60

15th European Art Exhibition, Berlin, Aug. 14-Oct. 16.

Rhinecanthus Aculeatus — A105

Designs: 30pf, Paddlefish. 40pf, Tortoise. 50pf, Rhinoceros iguana. Designs include statue of iguanodon from Aquarium entrance.

1977, Aug. 16 **Photo.** ***Perf. 14***

9N411	A105	20pf multicolored	.35	.30
9N412	A105	30pf multicolored	.50	.40
9N413	A105	40pf multicolored	.75	.50
9N414	A105	50pf multicolored	1.00	.60
		Nos. 9N411-9N414 (4)	2.60	1.80

25th anniv. of the reopening of Berlin Aquarium.

Walter Kollo (1878-1940), Composer — A106

1978, Jan. 12 **Engr.** ***Perf. 14***

9N415	A106	50pf brn, red & dk brn	.75	.50

Chamber of Commerce Emblem — A107

1978, Apr. 13 **Engr.** ***Perf. 14***

9N416	A107	90pf dk blue & red	1.10	.75

American Chamber of Commerce in Germany, 75th anniversary.

Albrecht von Graefe — A108

1978, May 22 **Engr.** ***Perf. 14***

9N417	A108	30pf red brn & blk	.40	.30

Dr. von Graefe (1828-70) ophthalmologist.

Friedrich Ludwig Jahn — A109

1978, July 13 **Engr.** ***Perf. 14***

9N418	A109	50pf dk carmine	.65	.40

Friedrich Ludwig Jahn (1778-1852), founder of organized gymnastics.

Swimmers — A110

1978, Aug. 17 **Litho.** ***Perf. 14***

9N419	A110	40pf multicolored	.90	.55

3rd World Swimming Championships, Berlin, Aug. 18-28.

The Boat, by Karl Hofer — A111

1978, Oct. 12 **Photo.** ***Perf. 14***

9N420	A111	50pf multicolored	.55	.40

Karl Hofer (1878-1955), painter.

National Library A112

1978, Nov. 16 **Engr.** ***Perf. 14***

9N421	A112	90pf red & olive	1.10	.85

Opening of new National Library building.

Views Type of 1976

Berlin Views: 40pf, Belvedere, Charlottenburg Castle. 50pf, Shell House on Landwehr Canal. 60pf, Village Church, Alt-Lichtenrade.

1978, Nov. 16

9N422	A97	40pf green & blk	.45	.30
9N423	A97	50pf lilac & blk	.55	.45
9N424	A97	60pf brown & blk	.70	.50
		Nos. 9N422-9N424 (3)	1.70	1.25

International Conference Center — A113

Photogravure and Engraved

1979, Feb. 14 ***Perf. 14***

9N425	A113	60pf multicolored	.90	.60

Opening of Intl. Conference Center in Berlin.

A114

60 DEUTSCHE BUNDESPOST BERLIN
Text-kommunikation ueber Bildschirm
INTERNATIONALE FUNKAUSSTELLUNG BERLIN 1979

A115

1979, May 17 **Litho.** ***Perf. 14***

9N426	A114	60pf German eagles	1.10	.75

Cent. of German Natl. Printing Bureau.

1979, July 12 **Photo.** ***Perf. 14***

9N427	A115	60pf TV screen, emblem	.90	.60

Intl. Broadcasting Exhibition, Berlin.

Target and Arrows A116

1979, July 12

9N428	A116	50pf multicolored	.65	.40

World Archery Championships, Berlin.

Moses Mendelssohn
A117

1979, Aug. 9 Engr. *Perf. 14*
9N429 A117 90pf black 1.00 .60

Mendelssohn (1729-86), philosopher.

Gas Lamp — A118

Historic Street Lanterns: 40pf, Carbon arc lamp. 50pf, Hanging gas lamps. 60pf, 5-armed candelabra.

1979, Aug. 9 Litho.
9N430 A118 10pf multicolored .30 .20
9N431 A118 40pf multicolored .55 .45
9N432 A118 50pf multicolored .85 .45
9N433 A118 60pf multicolored .85 .80
Nos. 9N430-9N433 (4) 2.55 1.90

300 years of street lighting in Berlin.

Orchid
A119

1979, Aug. 9
9N434 A119 50pf multicolored .65 .40

Botanical Gardens, Berlin, 300th anniv.

Berlin Poster Columns, 125th Anniversary
A120

Lithographed and Engraved

1979, Nov. 14 *Perf. 14*
9N435 A120 50pf multicolored 1.10 .60

Castle Type of Germany

1979-82 Typo. *Perf. 14*
9N438 A406 35pf Lichtenstein .25 .25
9N439 A406 40pf Wolfsburg .40 .25
9N440 A406 50pf Inzlingen .40 .25
9N441 A406 60pf Rheydt .70 .25
9N442 A406 80pf Wilhelmsthal .50 .20
9N443 A406 120pf Charlottenburg .85 .60
9N444 A406 280pf Ahrensburg 3.00 1.25
9N445 A406 300pf Herrenhausen 3.00 1.00
Nos. 9N438-9N445 (8) 9.10 4.05

Issued: 60pf, 11/14; 40pf, 50pf, 2/14/80; 35pf, 80pf, 30pf, 6/16/82; 120pf, 280pf, 7/15/82.

World Map Showing Continental Drift — A121

1980, Feb. 14 Litho. *Perf. 14*
9N451 A121 60pf multicolored .90 .75

Alfred Wegener (1880-1930), geophysicist and meteorologist; founded theory of continental drift.

German Catholics Day — A122

Cardinal Count Preysing (1880-1950).

1980, May 8 Engr. *Perf. 14*
9N452 A122 50pf blk & car rose .65 .40

Prussian Museum, Berlin, 150th Anniv. — A123

Designs: 40pf, Angel, enamel medallion, 12th cent. 60pf, Monks Reading, oak sculpture, by Ernest Barlach (1870-1938).

1980, July 10 Litho. *Perf. 14*
9N453 A123 40pf multicolored .65 .35
9N454 A123 60pf multicolored .90 .60

Von Steuben Leading Troops — A124

1980, Aug. 14 Litho. *Perf. 14*
9N455 A124 40pf multicolored .75 .40

Friedrich Wilhelm von Steuben (1730-94).

Robert Stolz (1880-1975), Composer
A125

1980, Aug. 14
9N456 A125 60pf dk blue & bis .75 .60

Lilienthal Memorial — A126

Designs: 50pf, Grosse Neugierde Memorial, 1835. 60pf, Lookout tower, Grunewald Memorial to Kaiser Wilhelm I.

1980, Nov. 13 Engr. *Perf. 14*
9N457 A126 40pf dk green & blk .60 .25
9N458 A126 50pf brown & blk .65 .50
9N459 A126 60pf dk blue & blk .95 .50
Nos. 9N457-9N459 (3) 2.20 1.25

Von Gontard and Kleist Park Colonnades, Berlin — A127

1981, Jan. 15 Litho. *Perf. 14*
9N460 A127 50pf multicolored .75 .45

Karl Philipp von Gontard (1731-91), architect.

Achim von Arnim (1781-1831), Poet — A128

1981, Jan. 15 Engr.
9N461 A128 60pf dark green .70 .45

Adelbert von Chamisso (1781-1838), Poet — A129

1981, Jan. 15 Litho.
9N462 A129 60pf brn & gldn brn .70 .45

Berlin-Kreuzberg, Liberation Monument, 1813 — A130

1981, Feb. 12 Engr. *Perf. 14*
9N463 A130 40pf brown .80 .50

Karl Friedrich Schinkel (1781-1841), architect, 400th anniversary of birth.

Arts and Science Medal, Awarded 1842-1933 — A131

1981, July 16 Litho. *Perf. 14*
9N464 A131 40pf multicolored .65 .40

"Prussia—an attempt at a balance" exhibition.

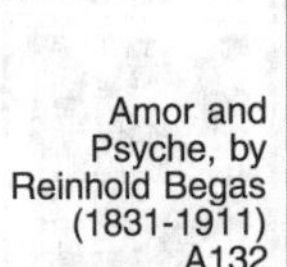

Amor and Psyche, by Reinhold Begas (1831-1911)
A132

1981, July 16 Photo.
9N465 A132 50pf multicolored .65 .40

Intl. Telecommunications Exhibition — A133

1981, July 16 Litho.
9N466 A133 60pf multicolored .90 .60

Peter Beuth (1781-1853), Constitutional Law Expert — A134

Lithographed and Engraved

1981, Nov. 12 *Perf. 14*
9N467 A134 60pf gold & black .65 .50

Nijinsky, by Georg Kolbe, 1914 — A135

20th Century Sculptures: 60pf, Mother Earth II, by Ernst Barlach, 1920. 90pf, Flora Kneeling, by Richard Scheibe, 1930.

1981, Nov. 12 Photo.
9N468 A135 40pf multicolored .40 .55
9N469 A135 60pf multicolored .70 .40
9N470 A135 90pf multicolored .90 .75
Nos. 9N468-9N470 (3) 2.00 1.70

750th Anniv. of Spandau
A136

Lithographed and Engraved

1982, Feb. 18 *Perf. 14*
9N471 A136 60pf multicolored .90 .75

Berlin Philharmonic Centenary — A137

Lithographed and Embossed

1982, Apr. 15 *Perf. 14*
9N472 A137 60pf multicolored .90 .50

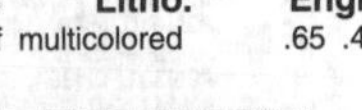

Salzburg Emigration to Prussia, 250th Anniv. — A138

& 1982, May 5 Litho. Engr.
9N473 A138 50pf multicolored .65 .40

Italian Stone Carriers, by Max Pechstein — A139

80pf, Two Girls Bathing, by Otto Mueller.

1982, July 15 Litho. *Perf. 14*
9N474 A139 50pf multicolored .70 .50
9N475 A139 80pf multicolored 1.00 .80

Villa Borsig — A140

1982, Nov. 10 Engr. *Perf. 14*
9N476 A140 50pf shown .95 .60
9N477 A140 60pf Sts. Peter and Paul Church .95 .70
9N478 A140 80pf Villa von der Heydt 1.25 .75
Nos. 9N476-9N478 (3) 3.15 2.05

State Theater, Charlottenburg, 1790 — A141

1982, Nov. 10 **Litho. & Engr.**

9N479 A141 80pf multicolored 1.40 .95

Carl Gotthard Langhans (1732-1808), architect.

A142 A142a

Various street pumps and fire hydrants, 1900.

1983, Jan. 13 **Litho.** ***Perf. 14***

9N480 A142 50pf multi .85 .45
9N481 A142 60pf multi 1.00 .45
9N482 A142 80pf multi 1.25 .95
9N483 A142 120pf multi 1.75 1.60
Nos. 9N480-9N483 (4) 4.85 3.45

1983, Feb. 8 **Engr.** ***Perf. 14***

9N484 A142a 80pf dark brown 1.50 1.25

Berlin-Koblenz Telegraph Service sesquicentennial.

Portrait of Barbara Campanini, 1745, by Antoine Pesne (1683-1757) A143

1983, May 5 **Photo.** ***Perf. 14***

9N485 A143 50pf multicolored .75 .60

Joachim Ringelnatz (1883-1934), Painter and Writer — A144

1983, July 14 **Litho.** ***Perf. 14***

9N486 A144 50pf Silhouette .90 .65

Intl. Radio Exhibition, Sept. 2-11 — A145

1983, July 14

9N487 A145 80pf Nipkow's phototelegraphy diagram 1.40 1.10

Ancient Artwork, Berlin Museum A146

30pf, Bust of Queen Cleopatra VII, 69-30 B.C. 50pf, Statue of Egyptian Couple, Giza, 2400 B.C. 60pf, Stone God with Beaded Turban, Mexico, 300 B.C. 80pf, Enamel Plate, 16th cent.

1984, Jan. 12 **Litho.** ***Perf. 14***

9N488 A146 30pf multicolored .85 .60
9N489 A146 50pf multicolored 1.10 .95
9N490 A146 60pf multicolored 1.40 1.10
9N491 A146 80pf multicolored 1.75 1.40
Nos. 9N488-9N491 (4) 5.10 4.05

Electricity Centenary — A147

Design: Allegorical figure holding light bulb (symbol of electric power).

1984, May 8 **Litho.** ***Perf. 14***

9N492 A147 50pf black & org .70 .50

Conference Emblem — A148

1984, May 8

9N493 A148 60pf multicolored .90 .60

European Ministers of Culture, 4th Conf.

Erich Klausener (1885-1934), Chairman of Catholic Action — A149

1984, May 8 **Engr.** ***Perf. 14x13½***

9N494 A149 80pf dark green .90 .75

Alfred Brehm (1829-1884), Zoologist — A150

Lithographed and Engraved

1984, Apr. 18 ***Perf. 14***

9N495 A150 80pf Brehm, white stork 1.40 .95

Ernst Ludwig Heim (1747-1834), Botanist — A151

1984, Aug. 21 **Engr.** ***Perf. 14***

9N496 A151 50pf brown & blk .90 .70

Sunflowers, by Karl Schmidt-Rottluff (1884-1976) A152

1984, Nov. 8 **Litho.** ***Perf. 14***

9N497 A152 60pf multi .90 .70

Bettina von Arnim (1785-1859), Writer — A153

1985, Feb. 21 **Litho. & Engr.**

9N498 A153 50pf multicolored .75 .70

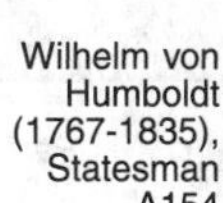

Wilhelm von Humboldt (1767-1835), Statesman A154

1985, Feb. 21 **Engr.**

9N499 A154 80pf blue, blk & red 1.10 .95

1985 Berlin Horticultural Show — A155

1985, Apr. 16 **Litho.** ***Perf. 14***

9N500 A155 80pf Symbolic flower .95 .85

Berlin Bourse, 300th Anniv. A156

1985, May 7 **Litho. & Engr.**

9N501 A156 50pf multicolored .90 .70

Otto Klemperer (1885-1973), Conductor — A157

1985, May 7 **Engr.**

9N502 A157 60pf dp blue violet .95 .85

Telefunken Camera, 1936 — A158

1985, July 16 **Litho.** ***Perf. 14***

9N503 A158 80pf multicolored 1.50 1.10

German Television, 50th anniv., Intl. Telecommunications Exhibition, Berlin.

9th World Gynecological Congress — A159

Design: Emblem of the Intl. Federation for Gynecology and birth aid.

1985, July 16 **Photo.** ***Perf. 13½x14***

9N504 A159 60pf pale yel, ap grn & dp grn .90 .70

Edict of Potsdam, 300th Anniv. A160

Lithographed and Engraved

1985, Oct. 15 ***Perf. 14***

9N505 A160 50pf dk bluish lilac .75 .55

Kurt Tucholsky (1890-1935), Novelist, Journalist — A161

1985, Nov. 12 **Litho.** ***Perf. 14***

9N506 A161 80pf multi 1.40 1.00

Wilhelm Furtwangler (1886-1954), Composer — A162

Score from Sonata in D Sharp.

Lithographed and Engraved

1986, Jan. 16 ***Perf. 14***

9N507 A162 80pf multi 1.50 1.25

Ludwig Mies van der Rohe (1886-1969), Architect — A163

1986, Feb. 13

9N508 A163 50pf multi .80 .80

New Natl. Gallery, Berlin.

16th European Communities Day — A164

1986, Apr. 10 **Litho.** ***Perf. 14***

9N509 A164 60pf Flags .75 .70

Leopold von Ranke (1795-1886), Historian — A165

Gottfried Benn (1886-1956), Writer and Physician — A166

1986, May 5 **Litho.**

9N510 A165 80pf brn blk & tan 1.40 1.10

Engr.

9N511 A166 80pf brt blue 1.40 1.10

Portals and Gateways
A167

1986, June 20 **Litho. & Engr.**

9N512 A167 50pf Charlotteburg Gate 1.10 .90
9N513 A167 60pf Gryphon Gate, Glienicke Castle 1.10 1.10
9N514 A167 80pf Elephant Gate, Berlin Zoo 1.25 1.10
Nos. 9N512-9N514 (3) 3.45 3.10

King Frederick the Great — A168

Painting: The Flute Concert (detail), by Adolph von Menzel.

1986, Aug. 14 **Litho.** ***Perf. 14***

9N515 A168 80pf multicolored 1.25 1.00

Famous Women Type of Germany

Designs: 5pf, Emma Ihrer (1857-1911), politician, labor leader. 10pf, Paula Modersohn-Becker (1876-1907), painter. 20pf, Cilly Aussem (1909-63), tennis champion. 40pf, Maria Sibylla Merian. 50pf, Christine Teusch. 60pf, Dorothea Erxleben (1715-62), physician. 80pf, Clara Schumann. 100pf, Therese Giehse (1898-1975), actress. 130pf, Lise Meitner (1878-1968), physicist. 140pf, Cecile Vogt (1875-1962), neurologist. 170pf, Hannah Arendt (1906-75), American political scientist. 180pf, Lotte Lehmann (1888-1976), soprano. 240pf, Mathilde Franziska Anneke, (1817-84), American author. 250pf, Queen Louise of Prussia (1776-1810). 300pf, Fanny Hensel (1805-1847), composer-conductor. 350pf, Hedwig Dransfeld (1871-1925), women's rights activist. 500pf, Alice Salomon (1872-1948), feminist and social activist.

1986-89 **Engr.** ***Perf. 14***

Type A602

9N516 5pf bluish gray & org brn .25 *.95*
9N517 10pf vio & yel brn .25 *.85*
9N518 20pf lake & Prus bl 1.00 *2.10*
9N519 40pf dp bl & dk lil rose .80 *2.10*
9N520 50pf gray ol & Prus bl 1.25 *1.50*
9N521 60pf dp vio & grnsh blk .65 *2.10*
9N522 80pf dk grn & lt red brn .95 *1.25*
9N523 100pf dk red & grnsh blk 1.10 .85
9N524 130pf Prus bl & dk vio 2.40 *6.50*
9N525 140pf blk & dk ol bis 2.75 *6.50*
9N526 170pf gray grn & dk brn 2.00 *5.25*
9N527 180pf bl & brn vio 2.50 *6.50*
9N528 240pf Prus bl & yel brn 2.50 *7.25*
9N529 250pf dp lil rose & dp bl 5.50 *11.00*
9N530 300pf dk vio & sage grn 5.75 *11.00*
9N531 350pf gray grn & lake 4.50 *8.75*
9N532 500pf slate grn & brt ver 7.25 *18.00*
Nos. 9N516-9N532 (17) 41.40 *92.45*

Issued: 50pf, 80pf, 11/1/86; 40pf, 9/17/87; 10pf, 4/4/88; 20pf, 130pf, 5/5/88; 60pf, 100pf, 170pf, 240pf, 350pf, 11/10/88; 500pf, 1/12/89; 5pf, 2/9/89; 180pf, 250pf, 7/13/89; 140pf, 300pf, 8/10/89.

Berlin 750th Anniv. Type of Germany

Designs: a, Berlin, 1650, engraving by Caspar Merian. b, Charlottenburg Castle, c. 1830. c, AEG Company turbine construction building, by architect Walter Behrens, 1909. d, Philharmonic Concert Hall and Chamber Music Rooms on the Kemperplatz, 1987.

1987, Jan. 15 **Litho.** ***Perf. 14***

9N536 A604 80pf like #1496 1.50 1.10

Souvenir Sheet

Perf. 14x14½

9N537 Sheet of 4 3.25 3.25
a. A604 40pf multicolored .45 .45
b. A604 50pf multicolored .45 .45
c. A604 60pf multicolored .65 .65
d. A604 80pf multicolored 1.00 1.00

No. 9N537 contains four 43x25mm stamps.

Louise Schroeder (1887-1957), Politican — A169

1987, Feb. 12 **Engr.** ***Perf. 14***

9N538 A169 50pf sep & dk red .90 .85

Settlement of Bohemians at Rixdorf, 250th Anniv. — A170

Bohemian refugees, bas-relief detail from monument to King Friedrich Wilhelm I of Prussia, 1912.

1987, May 5 **Litho. & Engr.**

9N539 A170 50pf sep & pale gray grn .65 .55

1987 Intl. Architecture Exhibition — A171

1987, May 5 **Litho.** ***Perf. 14x14½***

9N540 A171 80pf lt ultra, sil & blk 1.00 .75

14th Int'l. Botanical Congress — A172

1987, July 16 **Litho.** ***Perf. 14***

9N541 A172 60pf multicolored .70 .65

Int'l. Radio Exhibition A173

1987, Aug. 20

9N542 A173 80pf Gramophone, compact disc .90 .75

Historic Sites and Objects Type of Germany

Designs: 5pf, Brunswick Lion. 10pf, Frankfurt Airport. 20pf, No. 9N550, Queen Nefertiti, bust, Egyptian Museum, Berlin. 30pf, Corner tower, Celle Castle, 14th cent. 40pf, Chile House, Hamburg. 50pf, Filigree tracery on spires, Freiburg Cathedral. 60pf, Bavaria Munich, bronze statue above the Theresienwiese, Hall of Fame. No. 9N551, Heligoland. 80pf, Entrance to Zollern II, coal mine, Dortmund. 100pf, Altotting Chapel, Bavaria. 120pf, Schleswig Cathedral. 140pf, Bronze flagon from Reinheim. 300pf, Hambach Castle. 350pf, Externsteine Bridge near Horn-Bad Meinberg.

1987-90 **Typo.** ***Perf. 14***

Type A623

9N543 5pf Prus bl & gray .20 .25
9N544 10pf lt chalky bl & slate bl .25 .25
9N545 20pf dull blue & tan .30 .50
9N546 30pf aqua & org brn .65 .40
9N547 40pf ultra, dk red brn & org red .70 1.00
9N548 50pf ultra & yel brn .90 .40
9N549 60pf cob & pale gray .90 .45
9N550 70pf dull bl & fawn 1.10 1.10
9N551 70pf vio bl & henna brn 1.40 3.00
9N552 80pf cob & pale gray 1.10 .50
a. Bklt. pane of 8 (4 10pf, 2 50pf, 2 80pf) ('89) 15.00 *32.50*
9N553 100pf brt bluish grn & olive bis .95 .35
a. Bklt. pane of 8 (2 each 10pf, 60pf, 80pf, 100pf) 30.00 *62.50*
9N554 120pf brn org & lt grnsh bl 1.75 2.10
9N555 140pf tan & lt grn 1.75 1.50
9N556 300pf dk red brn & tan 3.75 2.00
9N557 350pf brt ultra & ol bis 3.75 3.50
Nos. 9N543-9N557 (15) 19.45 17.30

Issued: 30pf, 50pf, 60pf, 80pf, 11/6/87; 10pf, 300pf, 1/14/88; #9N550, 120pf, 7/14/88; 20pf, 140pf, 1/12/89; 100pf, 350pf, 2/9/89; 5pf, 2/15/90; #9N551, 6/21/90.

European Culture — A175

1988, Jan. 14 **Litho.** ***Perf. 14***

9N568 A175 80pf Berlin Bear 1.25 1.00

Urania Science Museum, Cent. A176

1988, Feb. 18

9N569 A176 50pf multicolored .85 .75

A177

Design: Thoroughbred Foal, bronze sculpture by Renee Sintenis (1888-1965).

1988, Feb. 18

9N570 A177 60pf multicolored .70 .50

A178

Design: The Great Elector with Family in Berlin Castle Gardens.

1988, May 5 **Litho. & Engr.**

9N571 A178 50pf multicolored .70 .65

The Great Elector of Brandenburg (d. 1688), founder of the Hohenzollern Dynasty.

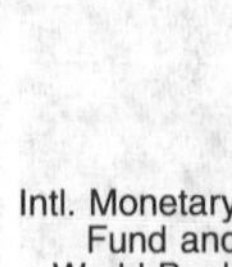

Intl. Monetary Fund and World Bank Congress, Berlin — A179

1988, Aug. 11 **Litho.**

9N572 A179 70pf multicolored .80 .60

Berlin-Potsdam Railway, 150th Anniv. — A180

1988, Oct. 13 **Litho.**

9N573 A180 10pf multicolored .40 .25

The Collector, 1913, by Ernst Barlach (1870-1938)
A181

1988, Oct. 13

9N574 A181 40pf multicolored .50 .40

Berlin Airlift, 40th Anniv. — A182

1989, May 5 **Photo.** ***Perf. 14***

9N575 A182 60pf multicolored .80 .60

13th Intl. Congress of the Supreme Audit Office, Berlin
A183

1989, May 5 **Litho.**

9N576 A183 80pf multicolored .90 .80

Ernst Reuter (1889-1953), Mayor of Berlin — A184

Litho. & Engr.

1989, July 13 ***Perf. 14x14½***

9N577 A184 100pf multicolored 1.40 1.10

Intl. Radio Exhibition, Berlin — A185

1989, July 13 **Litho.**

9N578 A185 100pf multicolored 1.25 .95

Plans of the Zoological Gardens, Berlin, and Designer Peter Joseph Lenne (1789-1866) — A186

Litho. & Engr.

1989, Aug. 10 ***Perf. 14***

9N579 A186 60pf multicolored 1.25 .85

Carl von Ossietzky (1889-1938), Awarded Nobel Peace Prize of 1935 — A187

1989, Aug. 10 **Photo.**
9N580 A187 100pf multicolored 1.25 1.10

450th Anniv. of the Reformation A188

Design: Nikolai Church, Spandau District.

1989, Oct. 12 **Litho.**
9N581 A188 60pf multicolored .75 .70

French Gymnasium, 300th Anniv. — A189

School from 1701 to 1873 and frontispiece of *Leges Gymnasie Gallici,* published in 1689.

1989, Oct. 12 **Litho. & Engr.**
9N582 A189 40pf multicolored .75 .60

Journalists, 1925, by Hannah Hoch (1889-1978) A190

1989, Oct. 12 **Litho.** ***Perf. 13½***
9N583 A190 100pf multicolored 1.40 .95

European Postal Service 500th Anniv. Type

Litho. & Engr.

1990, Jan. 12 ***Perf. 14***
9N584 A673 100pf *The Young Post Rider* 1.75 1.10

Public Transportation, 250th Anniv. — A191

1990, Jan. 12 **Litho.**
9N585 A191 60pf multicolored 1.40 .95

Ernst Rudorff (1840-1916), Conservationist — A192

1990, Jan. 12
9N586 A192 60pf multicolored 1.40 .95

People's Free Theater Organization, Cent. — A193

1990, Feb. 15 ***Perf. 13½***
9N587 A193 100pf multicolored 1.50 1.10

Parliament House, 40th Anniv. — A194

1990, Feb. 15 ***Perf. 14x14½***
9N588 A194 100pf multicolored 1.90 1.40

Bicent. of the Invention of the Barrel Organ — A195

1990, May 3 **Litho.** ***Perf. 14***
9N589 A195 100pf multicolored 1.60 1.10

90th German Catholics Day — A196

1990, May 3
9N590 A196 60pf multicolored 1.40 1.00

German Pharmaceutical Society, Cent. — A197

1990, Aug. 9 **Litho.** ***Perf. 14***
9N591 A197 100pf multicolored 2.75 1.75

Adolph Diesterweg (1790-1866), Educator — A198

1990, Sept. 27
9N592 A198 60pf multicolored 1.90 1.75

Stamps for Berlin were discontinued Oct. 3, 1990, when Germany and the German Democratic Republic merged. The stamps remained valid until Dec. 31, 1991.

OCCUPATION SEMI-POSTAL STAMPS

Offering Plate and Berlin Bear — SP1

Wmk. 284

1949, Dec. 1 **Litho.** ***Perf. 14***

9NB1	SP1	10 + 5pf grn	30.00	*140.00*
9NB2	SP1	20 + 5pf car	30.00	*140.00*
9NB3	SP1	30 + 5pf blue	32.50	*190.00*
a.		Souv. sheet of 3, #9NB1-9NB3	325.00	*2,000.*
		Never hinged	725.00	
		Nos. 9NB1-9NB3 (3)	92.50	*470.00*
		Set, never hinged	300.00	

The surtax was for Berlin victims of currency devaluation.

Harp and Laurel Branch — SP2

"Singing Angels" — SP3

1950, Oct. 29 **Engr.** **Wmk. 116**

9NB4	SP2	10 + 5pf grn	16.00	*30.00*
9NB5	SP3	30 + 5pf dk sl bl	32.50	*77.50*
		Set, never hinged	110.00	

The surtax was to aid in reestablishing the Berlin Philharmonic Orchestra.

Young Stamp Collectors — SP4

Kaiser Wilhelm Memorial Church — SP5

1951, Oct. 7 ***Perf. 14***

9NB6	SP4	10 + 3pf grn	9.75	*22.50*
9NB7	SP4	20 + 2pf brn red	13.00	*29.00*
		Set, never hinged	50.00	

Stamp Day, Berlin, Oct. 7, 1951.

1953, Aug. 9 **Wmk. 284**

Design: 20pf+10pf, 30pf+15pf, Ruins of Kaiser Wilhelm Memorial Church.

9NB8	SP5	4 + 1pf choc	.20	*11.50*
9NB9	SP5	10 + 5pf green	.65	*35.00*
9NB10	SP5	20 + 10pf car	1.25	*35.00*
9NB11	SP5	30 + 15pf dp bl	5.75	*80.00*
		Nos. 9NB8-9NB11 (4)	7.85	*161.50*
		Set, never hinged	20.00	

The surtax was to aid in reconstructing the church.

Catalogue values for unused stamps in this section, from this point to the end of the section, are for Never Hinged items.

Prussian Postilion — SP6

Prussian Field Postilion — SP7

1954, Aug. 4 **Litho.** **Wmk. 284**
9NB12 SP6 20 + 10pf multi 13.00 *24.00*

National Stamp Exhibition, Berlin, Aug. 4-8.

Perf. 13½x14

1955, Oct. 27 **Wmk. 304**
9NB13 SP7 25 + 10pf multi 5.50 *11.00*

The surtax was for the benefit of philately.

St. Otto, Bishop of Bamberg — SP8

Statues: 10pf+5pf, St. Hedwig, Duchess of Silesia. 20pf+10pf, St. Peter.

1955, Nov. 26 **Engr.** ***Perf. 14***

9NB14	SP8	7 + 3pf brown	.65	*2.10*
9NB15	SP8	10 + 5pf gray grn	.95	*2.10*
9NB16	SP8	20 + 10pf rose lil	1.50	*2.75*
		Nos. 9NB14-9NB16 (3)	3.10	*6.95*

25th anniv. of the Bishopric of Berlin.

The surtax was for the reconstruction of destroyed churches throughout the bishopric.

Bell Type of 1951 Surcharged

Perf. 13½x14

1956, Aug. 9 **Wmk. 284**
9NB17 OS8 20pf + 10pf citron 2.10 2.40

The surtax was for help for flood victims.

Postrider of Brandenburg, 1700 — SP9

Ludwig Heck — SP10

Wmk. 304

1956, Oct. 26 **Litho.** ***Perf. 14***
9NB18 SP9 25pf + 10pf multi 2.00 2.50

The surtax was for the benefit of philately.

1957, Sept. 7 **Engr.** ***Perf. 13½x14***
9NB19 SP10 20pf + 10pf red & dk brn .60 .70

Dr. Ludwig Heck, zoologist and long-time director of the Berlin Zoo. The surtax was for the Zoo.

Elly Heuss-Knapp and Relaxing Mothers SP11

Boy at Window — SP12

1957, Nov. 30 *Perf. 14*

9NB20 SP11 20pf + 10pf dk red 1.10 1.60

The surtax was for welfare work among mothers.

1960, Sept. 15 Litho. Wmk. 304

Designs: 10pf+5pf, Girl going to school. 20pf+10pf, Girl with flower and mountains. 40pf+20pf, Boy at seashore.

9NB21 SP12 7pf + 3pf dk brn & brn .20 .25
9NB22 SP12 10pf + 5pf ol grn & slate grn .20 .25
9NB23 SP12 20pf + 10pf dk car & brn blk .45 .40
9NB24 SP12 40pf + 20pf bl & ind 1.00 2.25
Nos. 9NB21-9NB24 (4) 1.85 3.15

The surtax was for vacations for the children of Berlin.

Fluorescent Paper was introduced for semipostal stamps, starting with Nos. 9NB25-9NB28.

Fairy Tale Type of 1960

Various Scenes from Sleeping Beauty.

1964, Oct. 6 Unwmk. *Perf. 14*

9NB25 SP285 10pf + 5pf multi .20 .20
9NB26 SP285 15pf + 5pf multi .20 .20
9NB27 SP285 20pf + 10pf multi .30 .20
9NB28 SP285 40pf + 20pf multi .40 .70
Nos. 9NB25-9NB28 (4) 1.10 1.30

The surtax was for independent welfare organizations.

Beginning with 9NB25-9NB28 semi-postals are types of Germany inscribed "Berlin" except Nos. 9NB129-9NB131.

Bird Type of 1965

Birds: 10pf+5pf, Woodcock. 15pf+5pf, Ring-necked pheasant. 20pf+10pf, Black grouse. 40pf+20pf, Capercaillie.

1965, Apr. 1 Litho. *Perf. 14*

9NB29 SP289 10pf + 5pf multi .20 .20
9NB30 SP289 15pf + 5pf multi .20 .20
9NB31 SP289 20pf + 10pf multi .20 .20
9NB32 SP289 40pf + 20pf multi .45 .60
Nos. 9NB29-9NB32 (4) 1.05 1.20

Issued for the benefit of young people.

Fairy Tale Type of 1965

Various Scenes from Cinderella.

1965, Oct. 6 Litho. *Perf. 14*

9NB33 SP290 10pf + 5pf multi .20 .20
9NB34 SP290 15pf + 5pf multi .20 .20
9NB35 SP290 20pf + 10pf multi .20 .20
9NB36 SP290 40pf + 20pf multi .35 .50
Nos. 9NB33-9NB36 (4) .95 1.10

The surtax was for independent welfare organizations.

Animal Type of 1966

10pf+5pf, Roe deer. 20pf+10pf, Chamois. 30pf+15pf, Fallow deer. 50pf+25pf, Red deer.

1966, Apr. 22 Litho. *Perf. 14*

9NB37 SP291 10pf + 5pf multi .20 .20
9NB38 SP291 20pf + 10pf multi .20 .20
9NB39 SP291 30pf + 15pf multi .20 .20
9NB40 SP291 50pf + 25pf multi .40 .55
Nos. 9NB37-9NB40 (4) 1.00 1.15

Issued for the benefit of young people.

Fairy Tale Type of 1965

Various Scenes from The Princess and the Frog.

1966, Oct. 5 Litho. *Perf. 14*

9NB41 SP290 10pf + 5pf multi .20 .20
9NB42 SP290 20pf + 10pf multi .20 .20
9NB43 SP290 30pf + 15pf multi .30 .20
9NB44 SP290 50pf + 25pf multi .35 .50
Nos. 9NB41-9NB44 (4) 1.05 1.10

Surtax for independent welfare organizations.

Animal Type of 1966

10pf+5pf, Rabbit. 20pf+10pf, Ermine. 30pf+15pf, Hamster. 50pf+25pf, Red fox.

1967, Apr. 4 Unwmk.

9NB45 SP291 10pf + 5pf multi .20 .20
9NB46 SP291 20pf + 10pf multi .20 .20
9NB47 SP291 30pf + 15pf multi .30 .25
9NB48 SP291 50pf + 25pf multi .70 .90
Nos. 9NB45-9NB48 (4) 1.40 1.55

Issued for the benefit of young people.

Fairy Tale Type of 1965

Various Scenes from Frau Holle.

1967, Oct. 3 Litho. *Perf. 14*

9NB49 SP290 10pf + 5pf multi .20 .20
9NB50 SP290 20pf + 10pf multi .20 .20
9NB51 SP290 30pf + 15pf multi .20 .30
9NB52 SP290 50pf + 25pf multi .40 .55
Nos. 9NB49-9NB52 (4) 1.00 1.25

The surtax was for independent welfare organizations.

Animal Type of 1968

Animals: 10pf+5pf, Wildcat. 20pf+10pf, Otter. 30pf+15pf, Badger. 50pf+25pf, Beaver.

1968, Feb. 2 Photo. *Perf. 14*

9NB53 SP293 10pf + 5pf multi .20 .30
9NB54 SP293 20pf + 10pf multi .25 .30
9NB55 SP293 30pf + 15pf multi .40 .55
9NB56 SP293 50pf + 25pf multi 1.25 1.75
Nos. 9NB53-9NB56 (4) 2.10 2.90

Surtax for benefit of young people.

Doll Type of 1968

Various 19th century dolls in sitting position.

1968, Oct. 3 Litho. *Perf. 14*

9NB57 SP294 10pf + 5pf multi .20 .20
9NB58 SP294 20pf + 10pf multi .20 .20
9NB59 SP294 30pf + 15pf multi .20 .20
9NB60 SP294 50pf + 25pf multi .45 .55
Nos. 9NB57-9NB60 (4) 1.05 1.15

The surtax was for independent welfare organizations.

Horse Type of 1969

Horses: 10pf+5pf, Pony. 20pf+10pf, Work horse. 30pf+15pf, Hotblood. 50pf+25pf, Thoroughbred.

1969, Feb. 6 Litho. *Perf. 14*

9NB61 SP295 10pf + 5pf multi .20 .20
9NB62 SP295 20pf + 10pf multi .25 .30
9NB63 SP295 30pf + 15pf multi .35 .40
9NB64 SP295 50pf + 25pf multi .90 1.10
Nos. 9NB61-9NB64 (4) 1.70 2.00

Surtax for benefit of young people.

Tin Toy Type of 1969

Tin Toys: 10pf+5pf, Coach. 20pf+10pf, Woman feeding chickens. 30pf+15pf, Woman grocer. 50pf+25pf, Postilion on horseback.

1969, Oct. 2 Litho. *Perf. 13½x14*

9NB65 SP297 10pf + 5pf multi .20 .20
9NB66 SP297 20pf + 10pf multi .20 .20
9NB67 SP297 30pf + 15pf multi .30 .30
9NB68 SP297 50pf + 25pf multi .75 .75
Nos. 9NB65-9NB68 (4) 1.45 1.45

The surtax was for independent welfare organizations.

1969, Nov. 13 Litho. *Perf. 13½x14*

Christmas: 10pf+5pf, The Three Kings.

9NB69 SP297 10pf + 5pf multi .30 .25

Minnesinger Type of 1970

Minnesingers (and their Ladies): 10pf+5pf, Heinrich von Stretlingen. 20pf+10pf, Meinloh von Sevelingen. 30pf+15pf, Burkhart von Hohenfels. 50pf+25pf, Albrecht von Johansdorf.

1970, Feb. 5 Photo. *Perf. 13½x14*

9NB70 SP298 10pf + 5pf multi .20 .20
9NB71 SP298 20pf + 10pf multi .30 .30
9NB72 SP298 30pf + 15pf multi .40 .40
9NB73 SP298 50pf + 25pf multi .90 .90
Nos. 9NB70-9NB73 (4) 1.80 1.80

Surtax for benefit of young people.

Puppet Type of 1970

10pf+5pf, "Kasperl." 20pf+10pf, Polichinelle. 30pf+5pf, Punch. 50pf+25pf, Pulcinella.

1970, Oct. 6 Litho. *Perf. 13½x14*

9NB74 SP300 10pf + 5pf multi .20 .20
9NB75 SP300 20pf + 10pf multi .20 .20
9NB76 SP300 30pf + 15pf multi .40 .35
9NB77 SP300 50pf + 25pf multi .70 .80
Nos. 9NB74-9NB77 (4) 1.50 1.55

Surtax for independent welfare organizations.

1970, Nov. 12

Christmas: 10pf+5pf, Rococo angel, from Ursuline Sisters' Convent, Innsbruck.

9NB78 SP300 10pf + 5pf multi .25 .20

Drawings Type of 1971

Children's Drawings: 10pf+5pf, Fly. 20pf+10pf, Fish. 30pf+15pf, Porcupine. 50pf+25pf, Cock. All stamps horizontal.

1971, Feb. 5 Litho. *Perf. 14*

9NB79 SP301 10pf + 5pf multi .25 .25
9NB80 SP301 20pf + 10pf multi .20 .20
9NB81 SP301 30pf + 15pf multi .30 .30
9NB82 SP301 50pf + 25pf multi .90 .90
Nos. 9NB79-9NB82 (4) 1.65 1.65

Surtax for the benefit of young people.

Wooden Toy Type of 1971

Wooden Toys: 10pf+5pf, Movable dolls in box. 25pf+10pf, Knight on horseback. 30pf+15pf, Jumping jack. 60pf+30pf, Nurse rocking babies.

1971, Oct. 5

9NB83 SP303 10pf + 5pf multi .20 .20
9NB84 SP303 25pf + 10pf multi .20 .25
9NB85 SP303 30pf + 15pf multi .40 .40
9NB86 SP303 60pf + 30pf multi .75 .75
Nos. 9NB83-9NB86 (4) 1.55 1.60

1971, Nov. 11

Christmas: Christmas angel with candles.

9NB87 SP303 10pf + 5pf multi .30 .25

Animal Protection Type of 1972

10pf+5pf, Boy trying to rob bird's nest. 25pf+10pf, Girl with kittens to be drowned. 30pf+15pf, Watch dog & man with whip. 60pf+30pf, Hedgehog & deer passing before car at night.

1972, Feb. 4

9NB88 SP304 10pf + 5pf multi .20 .20
9NB89 SP304 25pf + 10pf multi .25 .25
9NB90 SP304 30pf + 15pf multi .45 .45
9NB91 SP304 60pf + 30pf multi 1.10 1.10
Nos. 9NB88-9NB91 (4) 2.00 2.00

Surtax for the benefit of young people.

Chess Type of 1972

1972, Oct. 5 Litho. *Perf. 14*

9NB92 SP307 20pf + 10 Knight .25 .25
9NB93 SP307 30pf + 15 Rook .40 .40
9NB94 SP307 40pf + 20 Queen 1.10 1.10
9NB95 SP307 70pf + 35 King 1.50 1.50
Nos. 9NB92-9NB95 (4) 3.25 3.25

Surtax for independent welfare organizations.

Christmas Type of 1972

Design: 20pf+10pf, Holy Family.

1972, Nov. 10 Litho. *Perf. 14*

9NB96 SP308 20pf + 10pf multi .45 .40

Bird Type of 1973

Birds of Prey: 20pf+10pf, Goshawk. 30pf+15pf, Peregrine falcon. 40pf+20pf, Sparrow hawk. 70pf+35pf, Golden eagle.

1973, Feb. 6 Photo. *Perf. 14*

9NB97 SP309 20pf + 10pf multi .40 .40
9NB98 SP309 30pf + 15pf multi .60 .60
9NB99 SP309 40pf + 20pf multi .85 .85
9NB100 SP309 70pf + 35pf multi 1.40 1.40
Nos. 9NB97-9NB100 (4) 3.25 3.25

Surtax was for benefit of young people.

Instrument Type of 1973

Musical Instruments: 20+10pf, Hurdygurdy, 17th cent. 30+15pf, Drum, 16th cent. 40+20pf, Archlute, 18th cent. 70+35pf, Organ, 16th cent.

1973, Oct. 5 Litho. *Perf. 14*

9NB101 SP311 20pf + 10pf multi .30 .30
9NB102 SP311 30pf + 15pf multi .65 .65
9NB103 SP311 40pf + 20pf multi .75 .75
9NB104 SP311 70pf + 35pf multi 1.10 1.10
Nos. 9NB101-9NB104 (4) 2.80 2.80

Surtax was for independent welfare organizations.

Star Type of 1973

Christmas: 20pf+10pf, Christmas star.

1973, Nov. 9 Litho. & Engr.

9NB105 SP312 20pf + 10pf multi .45 .40

Youth Type of 1974

Designs: 20pf+10pf, Boy photographing. 30pf+15pf, Boy athlete. 40pf+20pf, Girl violinist. 70pf+35pf, Nurse's aid.

1974, Apr. 17 Photo. *Perf. 14*

9NB106 SP313 20pf + 10pf multi .30 .30
9NB107 SP313 30pf + 15pf multi .30 .30
9NB108 SP313 40pf + 20pf multi .75 .75
9NB109 SP313 70pf + 35pf multi 1.10 1.10
Nos. 9NB106-9NB109 (4) 2.45 2.45

Surtax was for benefit of young people.

Flower Type of 1974

Designs: 30pf+15pf, Spring bouquet. 40pf+20pf, Autumn bouquet. 50pf+25pf, Roses. 70pf+35pf, Winter flowers. All horiz.

1974, Oct. 15 Litho. *Perf. 14*

9NB110 SP314 30pf + 15pf multi .30 .30
9NB111 SP314 40pf + 20pf multi .65 .65
9NB112 SP314 50pf + 25pf multi .65 .65
9NB113 SP314 70pf + 35pf multi .95 .95
Nos. 9NB110-9NB113 (4) 2.55 2.55

Surtax was for independent welfare organizations.

1974, Oct. 29

Christmas: Christmas bouquet, horiz.

9NB114 SP314 30pf + 15pf multi .60 .60

Locomotive Type of 1975

Steam Locomotives: 30pf+15pf, Dragon. 40pf+20pf, Class 89 (70-75). 50pf+25pf, Class O50. 70pf+35pf, Class O10.

1975, Apr. 15 Litho. *Perf. 14*

9NB115 SP315 30pf + 15pf multi .65 .50
9NB116 SP315 40pf + 20pf multi .65 .65
9NB117 SP315 50pf + 25pf multi 1.25 1.10
9NB118 SP315 70pf + 35pf multi 2.00 2.00
Nos. 9NB115-9NB118 (4) 4.55 4.25

Surtax was for benefit of young people.

Flower Type of 1975

Alpine Flowers: 30pf+15pf, Yellow gentian. 40pf+20pf, Arnica. 50pf+25pf, Cyclamen. 70pf+35pf, Blue gentian.

1975, Oct. 15 Litho. *Perf. 14*

9NB119 SP316 30pf + 15pf multi .45 .45
9NB120 SP316 40pf + 20pf multi .40 .40
9NB121 SP316 50pf + 25pf multi .50 .50
9NB122 SP316 70pf + 35pf multi .90 .90
Nos. 9NB119-9NB122 (4) 2.25 2.25

Surtax was for independent welfare organizations.

1975, Nov. 14

Christmas: 30pf+15pf, Snow heather.

9NB123 SP316 30pf + 15pf multi .65 .65

Sports Type of 1976

30+15pf, Shot put, women's. 40+20pf, Hockey. 50+25pf, Handball. 70+35pf, Swimming.

1976, Apr. 6 Litho. *Perf. 14*

9NB124 SP317 30pf + 15pf multi .45 .45
9NB125 SP317 40pf + 20pf multi .45 .45
9NB126 SP317 50pf + 25pf multi .65 .65
9NB127 SP317 70pf + 35pf multi 1.25 1.25
Nos. 9NB124-9NB127 (4) 2.80 2.80

Youth training for Olympic Games. The surtax was for the benefit of young people.

Iris — SP13

Flowers: 40pf+20pf, Wallflower. 50pf+25pf, Dahlia. 70pf+35pf, Larkspur.

1976, Oct. 14 Litho. *Perf. 14*

9NB128 SP13 30pf + 15pf .30 .30
9NB129 SP13 40pf + 20pf .30 .30
9NB130 SP13 50pf + 25pf .65 .65
9NB131 SP13 70pf + 35pf .90 .90
Nos. 9NB128-9NB131 (4) 2.15 2.15

Surtax was for independent welfare organizations.

Souvenir Sheet
Christmas Type of 1976

Christmas: 30pf+15pf, Annunciation to the Shepherds, stained-glass window, Frauenkirche, Esslingen.

1976, Nov. 16 Litho. & Engr.

9NB132 SP320 30pf + 15pf multi .60 .45

Ship Type of 1977

Historic Ships: 30pf+15pf, Bremer Kogge, c. 1380. 40pf+20pf, Helena Sloman, 1850. 50pf+25pf, Passenger ship, Cap Polonio, 1914. 70pf+35pf, Freighter Widar, 1971.

1977, Apr. 14 Litho. *Perf. 14*

9NB133 SP321 30pf + 15pf .40 .40
9NB134 SP321 40pf + 20pf .45 .45
9NB135 SP321 50pf + 25pf .75 .75
9NB136 SP321 70pf + 35pf 1.00 1.00
Nos. 9NB133-9NB136 (4) 2.60 2.60

Surtax was for benefit of young people.

Flower Type of 1977

Meadow Flowers: 30pf+15pf, Daisy. 40pf+20pf, Cowslip. 50pf+25pf, Sainfoin. 70pf+35pf, Forget-me-not.

1977, Oct. 13 Litho. *Perf. 14*

9NB137 SP322 30pf + 15pf .25 .25
9NB138 SP322 40pf + 20pf .45 .45
9NB139 SP322 50pf + 25pf .65 .65
9NB140 SP322 70pf + 35pf 1.00 1.00
Nos. 9NB137-9NB140 (4) 2.35 2.35

Surtax was for independent welfare organizations.

See Nos. 9NB148-9NB151.

Souvenir Sheet
Christmas Type of 1977

30pf+15pf, Virgin and Child, stained-glass window, Sacristy of St. Gereon Basilica, Cologne.

1977, Nov. 10

9NB141 SP323 30pf + 15pf multi .60 .60

Aviation Type of 1978

Designs: 30pf+15pf, Montgolfier balloon, 1783. 40pf+20pf, Lilienthal's glider, 1891. 50pf+25pf, Wright brothers' plane, 1909. 70pf+35pf, Etrich/Rumpler Taube, 1910.

1978, Apr. 13 Litho. *Perf. 14*

9NB142 SP325 30pf + 15pf .30 .30
9NB143 SP325 40pf + 20pf .45 .45
9NB144 SP325 50pf + 25pf .50 .50
9NB145 SP325 70pf + 35pf 1.00 1.00
Nos. 9NB142-9NB145 (4) 2.25 2.25

Surtax was for benefit of young people.

Sports Type of 1978

50+25pf, Bicycling. 70+35pf, Fencing.

1978, Apr. 13 Litho. *Perf. 14*

9NB146 SP324 50pf + 25pf .75 .50
9NB147 SP324 70pf + 35pf 1.00 .90

Surtax was for German Sports Foundation.

Flower Type of 1977

Woodland Flowers: 30pf+15pf, Solomon's-seal. 40pf+20pf, Wood primrose. 50pf+25pf, Cephalanthera rubra (orchid). 70pf+35pf, Bugle.

1978, Oct. 12 Litho. *Perf. 14*

9NB148 SP322 30pf + 15pf .40 .40
9NB149 SP322 40pf + 20pf .45 .45
9NB150 SP322 50pf + 25pf .65 .65
9NB151 SP322 70pf + 35pf .95 .95
Nos. 9NB148-9NB151 (4) 2.45 2.45

Surtax was for independent welfare organizations.

Souvenir Sheet
Christmas Type of 1978

Christmas: 30pf+15pf, Adoration of the Kings, stained glass window, Frauenkirche, Munich.

1978, Nov. 16 Litho. *Perf. 14*

9NB152 SP326 30pf + 15pf multi .60 .60

Aviation Type of 1979

Airplanes: 40pf+20pf, Vampyr, 1921. 50pf+25pf, Junkers JU52/3M, 1932. 60pf+30pf, Messerschmitt BF/ME 108, 1934. 90pf+45pf, Douglas DC3, 1935.

1979, Apr. 5 Litho. *Perf. 14*

9NB153 SP327 40pf + 20pf .45 .45
9NB154 SP327 50pf + 25pf .65 .65
9NB155 SP327 60pf + 30pf .85 .85
9NB156 SP327 90pf + 45pf 1.25 1.25
Nos. 9NB153-9NB156 (4) 3.20 3.20

Surtax was for benefit of young people.

Sports Type of 1979

60pf+30pf, Runners. 90pf+45pf, Archers.

1979, Apr. 5

9NB157 SP328 60pf + 30pf .75 .75
9NB158 SP328 90pf + 45pf 1.00 1.00

Surtax was for German Sports Foundation.

Plant Type of 1979

Woodland Plants: 40pf+20pf, Larch. 50pf+25pf, Hazelnut. 60pf+30pf, Horse chestnut. 90pf+45pf, Blackthorn.

1979, Oct. 11 Litho. *Perf. 14*

9NB159 SP330 40pf + 20pf .50 .30
9NB160 SP330 50pf + 25pf .65 .50
9NB161 SP330 60pf + 30pf .90 .80
9NB162 SP330 90pf + 45pf 1.10 1.10
Nos. 9NB159-9NB162 (4) 3.15 2.70

Surtax was for independent welfare organizations.

Christmas Type of 1979

Christmas: Nativity, medieval manuscript, Cistercian Abby, Altenberg.

1979, Nov. 14 Litho. *Perf. 13½*

9NB163 SP331 40pf + 20pf multi .75 .65

Aviation Type of 1979

Designs: 40pf+20pf, Vickers Viscount, 1950. 50pf+25pf, Fokker 27 Friendship, 1955. 60pf+30pf, Sud Aviation Caravelle, 1955. 90pf+45pf, Sikorsky-55, 1949.

1980, Apr. 10 Litho. *Perf. 14*

9NB164 SP327 40 + 20pf multi .60 .60
9NB165 SP327 50 + 25pf multi .65 .65
9NB166 SP327 60 + 30pf multi .85 .85
9NB167 SP327 90 + 45pf multi 1.10 1.10
Nos. 9NB164-9NB167 (4) 3.20 3.20

Surtax was for benefit of young people.

Sports Type of 1980

Designs: 50pf+25pf, Javelin. 60pf+30pf, Weight lifting. 90pf+45pf, Water polo.

1980, May 8 Photo. *Perf. 14*

9NB168 SP332 50 + 25pf multi .65 .65
9NB169 SP332 60 + 30pf multi .65 .65
9NB170 SP332 90 + 45pf multi 1.00 1.00
Nos. 9NB168-9NB170 (3) 2.30 2.30

Surtax was for German Sports Foundation.

Wildflower Type of 1980

Wildflowers: 40pf+20pf, Orlaya. 50pf+25pf, Yellow gagea. 60pf+30pf, Summer pheasant's eye. 90pf+45pf, Small-flowered Venus' looking-glass.

1980, Oct. 9 Litho. *Perf. 14*

9NB171 SP333 40 + 20pf multi .60 .60
9NB172 SP333 50 + 25pf multi .75 .75
9NB173 SP333 60 + 30pf multi .75 .75
9NB174 SP333 90 + 45pf multi 1.25 1.25
Nos. 9NB171-9NB174 (4) 3.35 3.35

Surtax was for independent welfare organizations.

Christmas Type of 1980

Christmas: 40pf+20pf, Annunciation to the Shepherds, from Altomunster manuscript, 12th century.

1980, Nov. 13 Litho. *Perf. 14x13½*

9NB175 SP335 40 + 20pf multi .75 .70

Optical Instrument Type of 1981

40pf+20pf, Theodolite, 1810. 50pf+25pf, Equatorial telescope, 1820. 60pf +30pf, Microscope, 1790. 90pf+45pf, Sextant, 1830.

1981, Apr. 10 Litho. *Perf. 13½*

9NB176 SP336 40 + 20pf multi .45 .45
9NB177 SP336 50 + 25pf multi .65 .65
9NB178 SP336 60 + 30pf multi .85 .85
9NB179 SP336 90 + 45pf multi 1.25 1.25
Nos. 9NB176-9NB179 (4) 3.20 3.20

Surtax for benefit of young people.

Sports Type of 1981

Designs: 60pf+30pf, Women's gymnastics. 90pf+45pf, Cross-county running.

1981, Apr. 10 *Perf. 14*

9NB180 SP337 60 + 30pf multi .75 .65
9NB181 SP337 90 + 45pf multi 1.10 1.00

Surtax for the German Sports Foundation.

Plant Type of 1981

40pf+20pf, Common bistort. 50pf+25pf, Pedicularis sceptrum-carolinum. 60pf+30pf, Gladiolus palustris. 90pf+45pf, Iris sibirica.

1981, Oct. 8 Litho.

9NB182 SP338 40 + 20pf multi .60 .60
9NB183 SP338 50 + 25pf multi .70 .60
9NB184 SP338 60 + 30pf multi .80 .60
9NB185 SP338 90 + 45pf multi 1.40 1.25
Nos. 9NB182-9NB185 (4) 3.50 3.05

Surtax was for independent welfare organizations.

Christmas Type of 1981

Adoration of the Kings, 19th cent. painting.

1981, Nov. 12 Litho.

9NB186 SP339 40 + 20pf multi .75 .60

Antique Car Type of 1982

Designs: 40pf+20pf, Daimler, 1889. 50pf+25pf, Wanderer, 1911. 60pf+30pf, Adler limousine, 1913. 90pf+45pf, DKW-F, 1931.

1982, Apr. 15 Litho.

9NB187 SP340 40 + 20pf multi .60 .60
9NB188 SP340 50 + 25pf multi .65 .65
9NB189 SP340 60 + 30pf multi .75 .75
9NB190 SP340 90 + 45pf multi 1.25 1.25
Nos. 9NB187-9NB190 (4) 3.25 3.25

Surtax was for benefit of young people.

Sports Type of 1982

60pf+30pf, Sprinting. 90pf+45pf, Volleyball.

1982, Apr. 15 Litho.

9NB191 SP341 60 + 30pf multi .85 .65
9NB192 SP341 90 + 45pf multi 1.25 .90

Surtax was for the German Sports Foundation.

Flower Type of 1982

Designs: 50pf+20pf, Floribunda grandiflora. 60pf+30pf, Tea-rose hybrid, diff. 80pf+40pf, Floribunda, diff. 120pf+60pf, Miniature rose.

1982, Oct. 14 Litho. *Perf. 14*

9NB193 SP342 50 + 20pf multi .85 .65
9NB194 SP342 60 + 30pf multi .95 .85
9NB195 SP342 80 + 40pf multi 1.25 1.25
9NB196 SP342 120 + 60pf multi 2.10 2.10
Nos. 9NB193-9NB196 (4) 5.15 4.85

Surtax was for independent welfare organizations.

Christmas Type of 1982

Christmas: Adoration of the Kings, Oak altar, St. Peter's Church, Hamburg, 1380.

1982, Nov. 10

9NB197 SP343 50 + 20pf multi .75 .70

Motorcycle Type of 1983

Designs: 50pf+20pf, Hildebrand & Wolfmuller, 1894. 60pf+30pf, Wanderer, 1908. 80pf+40pf, DKW-Lomos, 1922. 120pf+60pf, Mars, 1925.

1983, Apr. 12 Litho. *Perf. 14*

9NB198 SP344 50 + 20pf multi .65 .45
9NB199 SP344 60 + 30pf multi .95 .80
9NB200 SP344 80 + 40pf multi 1.10 .875
9NB201 SP344 120 + 60pf multi 2.50 1.75
Nos. 9NB198-9NB201 (4) 5.20 11.75

Surtax was for benefit of young people.

Sports Type of 1983

Designs: 80pf+40pf, European Latin American Dance Championship. 120pf+60pf, World Hockey Championship.

1983, Apr. 12

9NB202 SP345 80 + 40pf multi 1.25 .95
9NB203 SP345 120 + 60pf multi 2.00 1.60

Surtax was for German Sports Foundation.

Flower Type of Germany

Designs: 50pf+20pf, Mountain wildflower. 60pf+30pf, Alpine auricula. 80pf+40pf, Little primrose. 120pf+60pf, Einsele's aquilegia.

1983, Oct. 13 Litho. *Perf. 14*

9NB204 SP346 50 + 20pf multi .50 .50
9NB205 SP346 60 + 30pf multi .75 .75
9NB206 SP346 80 + 40pf multi 1.40 1.40
9NB207 SP346 120 + 60pf multi 2.25 2.25
Nos. 9NB204-9NB207 (4) 4.90 4.90

Surtax was for welfare organizations.

Christmas Type of Germany

1983, Nov. 10 Litho.

9NB208 SP347 50 + 20pf Nativity .75 .75

Surtax was for free welfare work.

Insect Type of 1984

Designs: 50pf+20pf, Trichius fasciatus. 60pf+30pf, Agrumenia carniolica. 80pf+40pf, Bombus terrestris. 120pf+60pf, Eristalis tenax.

1984, Apr. 12 Litho.

9NB209 SP348 50 + 20pf multi .80 .50
9NB210 SP348 60 + 30pf multi .80 .75
9NB211 SP348 80 + 40pf multi 1.60 .95
9NB212 SP348 120 + 60pf multi 2.00 2.00
Nos. 9NB209-9NB212 (4) 5.20 4.20

Surtax was for German Youth Stamp Foundation.

Olympic Type of 1984

Women's Events: 60pf+30pf, Hurdles. 80pf+40pf, Cycling. 120pf+60pf, Kayak.

1984, Apr. 12

9NB213 SP349 60 + 30pf multi 1.25 .95
9NB214 SP349 80 + 40pf multi 1.60 .95
9NB215 SP349 120 + 60pf multi 2.25 2.25
Nos. 9NB213-9NB215 (3) 5.10 4.15

Surtax was for German Sports Foundation.

Orchid Type of 1984

50+20pf, Listera cordata. 60pf+30pf, Ophrys insectifera. 80pf+40pf, Epipactis palustris. 120pf+60pf, Ophrys coriophora.

1984, Oct. 18 Litho. *Perf. 14*

9NB216 SP350 50 + 20pf multi 1.40 .95
9NB217 SP350 60 + 30pf multi 1.40 .95
9NB218 SP350 80 + 40pf multi 2.25 1.50
9NB219 SP350 120 + 60pf multi 3.50 2.50
Nos. 9NB216-9NB219 (4) 8.55 5.90

Surtax was for welfare organizations.

Christmas Type of 1984

1984, Nov. 8 Litho.

9NB220 SP351 50 + 20pf St. Nicholas .90 .90

Surtax was for welfare organizations.

Sport Type of 1985

1985, Feb. 21 Photo.

9NB221 SP352 80 + 40pf Basketball 1.10 1.25
9NB222 SP352 120 + 60pf Table Tennis 2.00 2.00

Surtax was for German Sport Foundation.

Bicycle Type of 1985

50pf+20pf, Bussing bicycle, 1868. 60pf+30pf, Child's tricycle, 1885. 80pf+40pf, Jaray bicycle, 1925. 120pf+60pf, Opel racer, 1925.

1985, Apr. 16 **Litho.**

9NB223 SP353 50 + 20pf multi .95 .95
9NB224 SP353 60 + 30pf multi .95 .95
9NB225 SP353 80 + 40pf multi 1.25 1.25
9NB226 SP353 120 + 60pf multi 2.75 2.50
Nos. 9NB223-9NB226 (4) 5.90 5.65

Surtax was for benefit of young people. Each stamp also shows the International Youth Year emblem.

Prayer Book Type of 1985

1985, Oct. 15 **Litho.** ***Perf. 14***

9NB227 SP355 50 + 20pf multi .95 .95
9NB228 SP355 60 + 30pf multi 1.25 1.25
9NB229 SP355 80 + 40pf multi 1.25 1.25
9NB230 SP355 120 + 60pf multi 2.00 2.00
Nos. 9NB227-9NB230 (4) 5.45 5.45

Surtax for welfare organizations.

Christmas Type of 1985

Woodcut: Worship of the Kings, Epiphany Altar, Frieburg Cathedral, by Hans Baldung Grien (1485-1545).

1985, Nov. 12 **Litho.** ***Perf. 14***

9NB231 SP356 50 + 20pf multi 1.00 .95

Surtax for welfare organizations.

European Sports Championships Type of 1986

1986, Feb. 13 **Litho.** ***Perf. 14***

9NB232 SP357 80 + 40pf Swimming 1.40 1.40
9NB233 SP357 120 + 55pf Show jumping 1.75 1.75

Surtax for the Natl. Sports Promotion Foundation.

Vocational Training Type of 1986

1986, Apr. 10

9NB234 SP358 50 + 25pf Glazier .95 .95
9NB235 SP358 60 + 30pf Mechanic 1.25 1.25
9NB236 SP358 70 + 35pf Tailor 1.25 1.25
9NB237 SP358 80 + 40pf Carpenter 1.60 1.60
Nos. 9NB234-9NB237 (4) 5.05 5.05

Surtax for German Youth Stamp Foundation.

Glassware Type of 1986

1986, Oct. 16 **Litho.** ***Perf. 13x13½***

9NB238 SP359 50 + 25pf Cantharus, 1st cent. .85 .85
9NB239 SP359 60 + 30pf Tumbler, c. 200 1.10 1.10
9NB240 SP359 70 + 35pf Jug, 3rd cent. 1.10 1.10
9NB241 SP359 80 + 40pf Diatreta, 4th cent. 1.40 1.40
Nos. 9NB238-9NB241 (4) 4.45 4.45

Surtax for public welfare organizations.

Christmas Type of 1986

Christmas: Adoration of the Magi, Ortenberg Altarpiece, c. 1420.

1986, Nov. 13 **Litho.** ***Perf. 14***

9NB242 SP360 50 + 25pf multi .75 .75

Surtax for public welfare organizations.

Sports Championships Type of 1987

1987, Feb. 12 **Litho.**

9NB243 SP361 80 + 40pf Gymnastics 1.25 1.25
9NB244 SP361 120 + 55pf Judo 2.00 1.90

Surtax for the benefit of the national Sports Promotion Foundation.

Industry Type of 1987

1987, Apr. 9 **Litho.**

9NB245 SP362 50 + 25pf Cooper .95 .95
9NB246 SP362 60 + 30pf Stonemason .95 .95
9NB247 SP362 70 + 35pf Furrier 1.25 1.25
9NB248 SP362 80 + 40pf Painter 1.25 1.25
Nos. 9NB245-9NB248 (4) 4.40 4.40

Surtax for youth organizations.

Gold and Silver Artifacts Type of 1987

1987, Oct. 15

9NB249 SP363 50 + 25pf Bonnet ornament, 5th cent. .65 .65
9NB250 SP363 60 + 30pf Athena plate, 1st cent. B.C. .95 .95
9NB251 SP363 70 + 35pf Armilla armlet, c. 1180 1.10 1.10
9NB252 SP363 80 + 40pf Snake bracelet, 300 B.C. 1.40 1.40
Nos. 9NB249-9NB252 (4) 4.10 4.10

Surtax for welfare organizations sponsoring free museum exhibitions.

Christmas Type of 1987

Illustration from Book of Psalms, 13th cent., Bavarian Natl. Museum: Adoration of the Magi.

1987, Nov. 6

9NB253 SP364 50 + 25pf multi .75 .65

Surtax for public welfare ogrganizations.

Sports Type of 1988

1988, Feb. 18 **Litho.**

9NB254 SP365 60 + 30pf Trapshooting 1.25 .95
9NB255 SP365 80 + 40pf Figure skating 1.25 .95
9NB256 SP365 120 + 55pf Hammer throw 1.60 1.60
Nos. 9NB254-9NB256 (3) 4.10 3.50

Music Type of 1988

No. 9NB257, Piano terzet. No. 9NB258, Wind quintet. No. 9NB259, Guitar, mandolin, recorder. No. 9NB260, Children's choir.

1988, Apr. 14 **Litho.** ***Perf. 14***

9NB257 SP366 50 +25pf multi .95 .95
9NB258 SP366 60 +30pf multi 1.25 1.25
9NB259 SP366 70 +35pf multi 1.25 1.25
9NB260 SP366 80 +40pf multi 1.75 1.60
Nos. 9NB257-9NB260 (4) 5.20 5.05

Surtax for German Youth Stamp Foundation.

Artifacts Type of 1988

#9NB261, Brooch, c. 1700, Schmuck Jewelry Museum, Pforzheim. #9NB262, Lion, 1540, Kunstgewerbe Museum, Berlin. #9NB263, Lidded goblet, 1536, Kunstgewerbe Museum. #9NB264, Cope clasp, c. 1400, Aachen cathedral.

1988, Oct. 13 **Litho.**

9NB261 SP367 50 +25pf multi .85 .85
9NB262 SP367 60 +30pf multi .95 .95
9NB263 SP367 70 +35pf multi 1.10 1.10
9NB264 SP367 80 +40pf multi 1.25 1.25
Nos. 9NB261-9NB264 (4) 4.15 4.15

Surtax for welfare organizations.

Christmas Type of 1988

Illumination from *The Gospel Book of Henry the Lion,* Helmarshausen, 1188, Prussian Cultural Museum, Bavaria: Angels announce the birth of Christ to the shepherds.

1988, Nov. 10 **Litho.**

9NB265 SP368 50 +25pf multi .90 .65

Surtax for public welfare organizations.

Sports Type of 1989

1989, Feb. 9 **Litho.**

9NB266 SP369 100 +50pf Volleyball 2.00 2.00
9NB267 SP369 140 +60pf Hockey 2.50 2.50

Surtax for the Natl. Sports Promotion Foundation.

Circus Type of 1989

1989, Apr. 20 **Litho.**

9NB268 SP371 60 +30pf Tamer and tigers 1.10 1.10
9NB269 SP371 70 +30pf Trapeze artists 1.40 1.40
9NB270 SP371 80 +35pf Seals 2.00 2.00
9NB271 SP371 100 +50pf Jugglers 2.25 2.25
Nos. 9NB268-9NB271 (4) 6.75 6.75

Surtax for natl. youth welfare organizations.

Mail Carrying Type of 1989

#9NB272, Messenger, 15th cent. #9NB273, Brandenburg mail wagon, c. 1700. #9NB274, Prussian postal workers, 19th cent.

1989, Oct. 12 **Litho.**

9NB272 SP372 60 +30pf multi 1.75 1.75
9NB273 SP372 80 +35pf multi 2.25 2.00
9NB274 SP372 100 +50pf multi 2.75 2.75
Nos. 9NB272-9NB274 (3) 6.75 6.50

Surtax for the benefit of Free Welfare Work.

Christmas Type of 1989

1989, Nov. 16 **Litho.**

9NB275 SP373 40 +20pf Angel .85 .85
9NB276 SP373 60 +30pf Nativity 1.40 1.40

Surtax for the benefit of the Federal Working Assoc. of Free Welfare Work.

Sports Type of 1990

Designs: No. 9NB277, Water polo. No. 9NB278, Wheelchair basketball.

1990, Feb. 15 **Litho.**

9NB277 SP374 100 +50pf multi 2.25 2.25
9NB278 SP374 140 +60pf multi 4.00 4.50

Surtax for the Natl. Sports Promotion Foundation.

Max and Moritz Type of 1990

1990, Apr. 19 **Litho.**

9NB279 SP375 60 +30pf Max, Moritz 1.25 1.25
9NB280 SP375 70 +30pf Max, Moritz, diff. 1.90 1.90
9NB281 SP375 80 +35pf Moritz 2.00 2.00
9NB282 SP375 100 +50pf Bug, Uncle 2.00 2.00
Nos. 9NB279-9NB282 (4) 7.15 7.15

Surcharge for the German Youth Stamp Foundation.

Post and Telecommunications Type

Designs: 60pf + 30pf, Railway mail car, 1900. 80pf + 35pf, Telephone installation, 1900. 100pf + 50pf, Mail truck, 1900.

1990, Sept. 27 **Litho.** ***Perf. 13½x14***

9NB283 SP377 60 +30pf multi 1.40 1.40
9NB284 SP377 80 +35pf multi 2.00 2.00
9NB285 SP377 100 +50pf multi 2.75 2.75
Nos. 9NB283-9NB285 (3) 6.15 6.15

Surtax for welfare organizations.

GERMAN OFFICES ABROAD

OFFICES IN CHINA

100 Pfennings = 1 Mark
100 Cents = 1 Dollar (1905)

Stamps of Germany, 1889-90, Overprinted in Black at 56 degree Angle

1898 **Unwmk.** ***Perf. 13½x14½***

1 A9 3pf dark brown 5.00 5.50
a. 3pf yellow brown 10.00 *12.50*
b. 3pf reddish ocher 20.00 *52.50*
2 A9 5pf green 2.00 *2.25*
3 A10 10pf carmine 5.00 *5.50*
4 A10 20pf ultramarine 14.50 *14.00*
5 A10 25pf orange 27.50 26.00
6 A10 50pf red brown 14.00 11.00
Nos. 1-6 (6) 68.00 64.25

Overprinted at 45 degree Angle

1c A9 3pf yellow brown 110.00 *20,000.*
1d A9 3pf reddish ocher 150.00
e. 3pf gray brown *1,200.*
2a A9 5pf green 10.00 *11.00*
3a A10 10pf carmine 12.50 9.00
4a A10 20pf ultramarine 11.00 9.00
5a A10 25pf orange 45.00 *50.00*
6a A10 50pf red brown 17.50 14.00

Value for No. 1c used is for a copy with small 1898 Shanghai cancel. Examples with other cancellations or later Shanghai cancels sell for about half the value quoted.

Foochow Issue

Nos. 3 and 3a Handstamp Surcharged **5 pf**

1900

16 A10 5pf on 10pf, #3 425.00 *600.00*
a. On No. 3a 475.00 *750.00*

For similar 5pf surcharges on 10pf carmine, see Tsingtau Issue, Kiauchau.

Tientsin Issue

German Stamps of 1900 Issue Handstamped

1900

17 A11 3pf brown 475. 550.
18 A11 5pf green 300. 275.
19 A11 10pf carmine 675. 625.
20 A11 20pf ultra 600. 650.
21 A11 30pf org & blk, *sal* *5,750.* *5,750.*
22 A11 50pf pur & blk, *sal* *26,000.* *14,000.*
23 A11 80pf lake & blk, *rose* *3,500.* *3,250.*

This handstamp is known inverted and double on most values.

Excellent faked handstamps are plentiful.

Regular Issue

German Stamps of 1900 Overprinted

A14

A15

Overprinted Horizontally in Black

1901 ***Perf. 14, 14½***

24 A11 3pf brown 1.25 1.25
a. 3pf light red brown 55.00 65.00
25 A11 5pf green 1.25 .90
26 A11 10pf carmine 2.10 .75
27 A11 20pf ultra 2.50 1.25
28 A11 25pf org & blk, *yel* 10.00 13.50
29 A11 30pf org & blk, *sal* 9.00 10.50
30 A11 40pf lake & blk 9.50 7.00
31 A11 50pf pur & blk, *sal* 8.75 7.00
32 A11 80pf lake & blk, *rose* 10.50 10.00

Overprinted in Black or Red

33 A12 1m car rose 26.00 26.00
34 A13 2m gray blue 22.50 24.00
35 A14 3m blk vio (R) 37.50 *55.00*
36 A15 5m slate & car, I 375.00 *475.00*
b. Red and/or white retouched 175.00 *250.00*
36A A15 5m slate & car, II 275.00 *350.00*
Nos. 24-36A (14) 790.85 *982.15*

See note after Germany No. 65A for information on retouches on No. 36. For description of the 5m Type I and Type II, see note above Germany No. 62.

Surcharged on German Stamps of 1902 in Black or Red

a

b

c

1905

37 A16(a) 1c on 3pf 2.50 2.75
38 A16(a) 2c on 5pf 2.50 1.00
39 A16(a) 4c on 10pf 5.50 1.00
40 A16(a) 10c on 20pf 2.50 1.50
41 A16(a) 20c on 40pf 17.50 6.50
42 A16(a) 40c on 80pf 29.00 11.50

No.	Type	Description	Unused	Used
43	A17(b)	½d on 1m	12.50	13.50
44	A21(b)	1d on 2m	15.00	17.00
45	A19(c)	1½d on 3m (R)	30.00	40.00
46	A20(b)	2½d on 5m	95.00	250.00
		Nos. 37-46 (10)	212.00	344.75

Surcharged on German Stamps of 1905 in Black or Red

1906-13 **Wmk. 125**

No.	Type	Description	Unused	Used
47	A16(a)	1c on 3pf	.35	.60
48	A16(a)	2c on 5pf	.35	.60
49	A16(a)	4c on 10pf	.35	.60
50	A16(a)	10c on 20pf	.75	4.25
51	A16(a)	20c on 40pf	1.00	2.25
52	A16(a)	40c on 80pf	1.00	30.00
53	A17(b)	½d on 1m	4.75	26.00
54	A21(b)	1d on 2m	5.25	30.00
55	A19(c)	1½d on 3m (R)	6.00	67.50
56	A20(b)	2½d on 5m	24.00	37.50
		Nos. 47-56 (10)	43.80	199.30

Forged cancellations exist.

OFFICES IN MOROCCO

100 Centimos = 1 Peseta

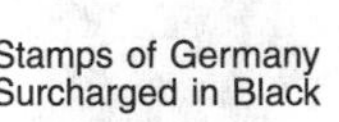
Stamps of Germany Surcharged in Black

1899 **Unwmk.** ***Perf. 13½x14½***

No.	Type	Description	Unused	Used
1	A9	3c on 3pf dk brn	2.75	2.25
2	A9	5c on 5pf green	2.75	2.25
3	A10	10c on 10pf car	6.25	5.50
4	A10	25c on 20pf ultra	13.00	14.00
5	A10	30c on 25pf orange	22.50	27.50
6	A10	60c on 50pf red brn	17.00	35.00
		Nos. 1-6 (6)	64.25	86.50

Before Nos. 1-6 were issued, the same six basic stamps of Germany's 1889-1900 issue were overprinted "Marocco" diagonally without the currency-changing surcharge line, but were not issued. Value, $1,200.

German Stamps of 1900 Surcharged

A12

A13

A14

A15

Black or Red Surcharge

1900 ***Perf. 14, 14½***

No.	Type	Description	Unused	Used
7	A11	3c on 3pf brn	1.10	1.50
8	A11	5c on 5pf grn	1.25	1.00
9	A11	10c on 10pf car	1.75	1.00
10	A11	25c on 20pf ultra	2.25	2.25
11	A11	30c on 25pf org & blk, *yel*	9.00	12.00
12	A11	35c on 30pf org & blk, *sal*	6.50	5.50
13	A11	50c on 40pf lake & blk	6.50	5.50
14	A11	60c on 50pf pur & blk, *sal*	14.50	26.00
15	A11	1p on 80pf lake & blk, *rose*	10.00	10.00
16	A12	1p25c on 1m car rose	27.50	37.50
17	A13	2p50c on 2m gray bl	30.00	47.50
18	A14	3p75c on 3m blk vio (R)	35.00	55.00
19	A15	6p25c on 5m sl & car, type I	300.00	400.00
b.		Red and/or white retouched	150.00	250.00
19A	A15	6p25c on 5m sl & car, type II	190.00	250.00
		Nos. 7-19A (14)	635.35	854.75

A 1903 printing of Nos. 8, 16-18 and 19A differs in the "M" and "t" of the surcharge. Values are for 1900 printing: Nos. 8, 16-18. 1903 printing: No. 19A.

See note after Germany No. 65A for information on retouches on No. 19. For description of the 5m Type I and Type II, see note above Germany No. 62.

German Stamps of 1902 Surcharged in Black or Red

a

b

c

1905

No.	Type	Description	Unused	Used
20	A16(a)	3c on 3pf	2.50	2.40
21	A16(a)	5c on 5pf	4.00	.85
22	A16(a)	10c on 10pf	8.00	.70
23	A16(a)	25c on 20pf	17.50	2.50
24	A16(a)	30c on 25pf	5.75	4.50
25	A16(a)	35c on 30pf	8.50	4.50
26	A16(a)	50c on 40pf	8.00	7.50
27	A16(a)	60c on 50pf	25.00	20.00
28	A16(a)	1p on 80pf	25.00	17.50
29	A17(b)	1p25c on 1m	42.50	30.00
30	A21(b)	2p50c on 2m	75.00	110.00
31	A19(c)	3p75c on 3m (R)	40.00	45.00
32	A20(b)	6p25c on 5m	110.00	160.00
		Nos. 20-32 (13)	371.75	405.45

Surcharged on Germany No. 54

No.	Type	Description	Unused	Used
32A	A11(a)	5c on 5pf	6.75	20.00

German Stamps of 1905 Surcharged

1906-11 **Wmk. 125**

No.	Type	Description	Unused	Used
33	A16(a)	3c on 3pf	7.50	1.75
34	A16(a)	5c on 5pf	7.50	.90
35	A16(a)	10c on 10pf	7.50	.90
36	A16(a)	25c on 20pf	15.00	3.75
37	A16(a)	30c on 25pf	17.50	9.00
38	A16(a)	35c on 30pf	15.00	9.00
39	A16(a)	50c on 40pf	32.50	140.00
40	A16(a)	60c on 50pf	22.50	12.50
41	A16(a)	1p on 80pf	125.00	250.00
42	A17(b)	1p25c on 1m	57.50	160.00
43	A21(b)	2p50c on 2m	57.50	160.00
44	A20(b)	6p25c on 5m	95.00	240.00
		Nos. 33-44 (12)	460.00	987.80

Excellent forgeries exist of No. 41.

Surcharge Spelled "Marokko" in Black or Red

1911

No.	Type	Description	Unused	Used
45	A16(a)	3c on 3pf	.40	.55
46	A16(a)	5c on 5pf	.40	.75
47	A16(a)	10c on 10pf	.40	.85
48	A16(a)	25c on 20pf	.50	.90
49	A16(a)	30c on 25pf	1.00	13.00
50	A16(a)	35c on 30pf	1.00	7.50
51	A16(a)	50c on 40pf	1.00	4.00
52	A16(a)	60c on 50pf	1.50	30.00
53	A16(a)	1p on 80pf	1.40	24.00
54	A17(b)	1p25c on 1m	2.75	55.00
55	A21(b)	2p50c on 2m	4.50	42.50
56	A19(c)	3p75c on 3m (R)	8.50	150.00
57	A20(b)	6p25c on 5m	16.00	225.00
		Nos. 45-57 (13)	39.35	554.05

Forged cancellations exist.

OFFICES IN THE TURKISH EMPIRE

Unused values for Nos. 1-6 are for stamps with original gum. Copies without gum sell for about one-third of the figures quoted.

40 Paras = 1 Piaster

A1

A2

German Stamps of 1880-83 Surcharged in Black or Blue

1884 **Unwmk.** ***Perf. 13½x14½***

No.	Type	Description	Unused	Used
1	A1	10pa on 5pf dull vio	27.50	25.00
2	A2	20pa on 10pf rose	55.00	65.00
3	A2	1pi on 20pf ultra (Bk)	47.50	3.75
4	A2	1pi on 20pf ultra (Bl)	1,350.	47.50
5	A2	1¼pi on 25pf brn	150.00	190.00
6	A2	2½pi on 50pf gray grn	95.00	57.50
a.		2½pi on 50pf deep olive grn	225.00	160.00
		Nos. 1-6 (6)	1,725.	388.75

There are two types of the surcharge on the 1¼pi and 2½pi stamps, the difference being in the spacing between the figures and the word "PIASTER."

There are re-issues of these stamps which vary only slightly from the originals in overprint measurements.

A3

A4

A5

German Stamps of 1889-1900 Surcharged in Black

1889

No.	Type	Description	Unused	Used
8	A3	10pa on 5pf grn	3.00	3.00
9	A4	20pa on 10pf car	6.00	1.90
10	A4	1pi on 20pf ultra	4.50	1.75
11	A5	1¼pi on 25pf org	24.00	15.00
12	A5	2½pi on 50pf choc	30.00	21.00
a.		2½pi on 50pf copper brown	150.00	87.50
		Nos. 8-12 (5)	67.50	42.65

German Stamps of 1900 Surcharged

A12

A13

A14

A15

1900 ***Perf. 14, 14½***

Black or Red Surcharge

No.	Type	Description	Unused	Used
13	A11	10pa on 5pf grn	1.50	1.50
14	A11	20pa on 10pf car	2.00	1.90
15	A11	1pi on 20pf ultra	4.00	1.50
16	A11	1¼pi on 25pf org & blk, *yel*	6.00	3.50
17	A11	1½pi on 30pf org & blk, *sal*	6.00	3.75
18	A11	2pi on 40pf lake & blk	6.00	4.00
19	A11	2½pi on 50pf pur & blk, *sal*	11.00	11.00
20	A11	4pi on 80pf lake & blk, *rose*	13.00	11.00
21	A12	5pi on 1m car rose	29.00	30.00
22	A13	10pi on 2m gray bl	27.50	35.00
23	A14	15pi on 3m blk vio (R)	47.50	80.00
24	A15	25pi on 5m sl & car, type I	275.00	550.00
a.		Double surcharge		9,500.
d.		Red and/or white retouched	140.00	
24B	A15	25pi on 5m sl & car, type II	160.00	300.00
c.		Double surcharge	8,500.	—
		Nos. 13-24B (13)	588.50	1,033.

See note after Germany #65A for information on retouches on #24. For description of the 5m Type I & Type II, see note above Germany #62.

German Stamps of 1900 Surcharged in Black

1903-05

No.	Type	Description	Unused	Used
25	A11	10pa on 5pf green	12.00	14.00
26	A11	20pa on 10pf car	29.00	17.50
27	A11	1pi on 20pf ultra	9.00	7.25

No.	Type	Description	Unused	Used
28	A12	5pi on 1m car rose	80.00	70.00
29	A13	10pi on 2m bl ('05)	125.00	210.00
30	A15	25pi on 5m sl & car	210.00	525.00
a.		Double surcharge	4,250.	
		Nos. 25-30 (6)	465.00	843.75

The 1903-05 surcharges may be easily distinguished from those of 1900 by the added bar at the top of the letter "A."

German Stamps of 1902 Surcharged in Black or Red

a

b

1905			**Unwmk.**
31 A16(a)	10pa on 5pf	3.25	2.00
32 A16(a)	20pa on 10pf	7.50	2.50
33 A16(a)	1pi on 20pf	15.00	1.75
34 A16(a)	1¼pi on 25pf	8.50	6.00
35 A16(a)	1½pi on 30pf	16.00	15.00
36 A16(a)	2pi on 40pf	25.00	15.00
37 A16(a)	2½pi on 50pf	9.50	*22.50*
38 A16(a)	4pi on 80pf	27.50	14.00
39 A17(b)	5pi on 1m	32.50	30.00
40 A21(b)	10pi on 2m	32.50	*37.50*
41 A19(b)	15pi on 3m (R)	42.50	*45.00*
42 A20(b)	25pi on 5m	190.00	*375.00*
	Nos. 31-42 (12)	409.75	*566.25*

German Stamps of 1905 Surcharged in Black or Red

1906-12			**Wmk. 125**
43 A16(a)	10pa on 5pf	1.60	.55
44 A16(a)	20pa on 10pf	2.00	.55
45 A16(a)	1pi on 20pf	3.00	.45
46 A16(a)	1¼pi on 25pf	12.50	10.00
47 A16(a)	1½pi on 30pf	11.00	8.00
48 A16(a)	2pi on 40pf	4.00	1.25
49 A16(a)	2½pi on 50pf	9.00	7.50
50 A16(a)	4pi on 80pf	8.50	*18.00*
51 A17(b)	5pi on 1m	17.00	*27.50*
52 A21(b)	10pi on 2m	17.50	*40.00*
53 A19(b)	15pi on 3m (R)	21.00	*300.00*
54 A20(b)	25pi on 5m	21.00	*55.00*
	Nos. 43-54 (12)	128.10	468.80

German Stamps of 1905 Surcharged Diagonally in Black

1908			
55 A16	5c on 5pf	1.25	*1.40*
56 A16	10c on 10pf	2.75	*3.00*
57 A16	25c on 20pf	6.25	*25.00*
58 A16	50c on 40pf	29.00	*60.00*
59 A16	100c on 80pf	52.50	*65.00*
	Nos. 55-59 (5)	91.75	*154.40*

Forged cancellations exist on #37, 53-54, 57-59.

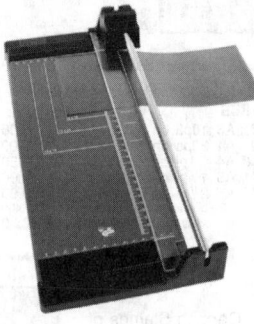

GERMAN DEMOCRATIC REPUBLIC

LOCATION — Eastern Germany
GOVT. — Republic
AREA — 41,659 sq. mi.
POP. — 16,701,500 (1983)
CAPITAL — Berlin (Soviet sector)

100 Pfennigs = 1 Deutsche Mark (East)
100 Pfennigs = 1 Mark of the Deutsche Notenbank (MDN) (1965)
100 Pfennigs = 1 Mark of the National Bank (M) (1969)
100 Pfennigs = 1 Deutsche Mark (West) (1990)

Catalogue values for unused stamps in this country are for Never Hinged items, beginning with Scott 48 in the regular postage section, Scott B14 in the semi-postal section, Scott C1 in the air-post section, and Scott O1 official section.

Watermarks

Watermark 292, see Germany.

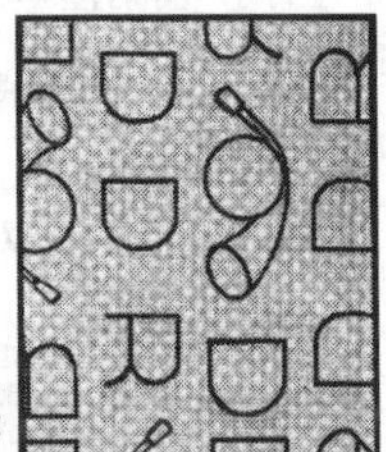

Wmk. 297-DDR and Post Horn

Wmk. 313-Quatrefoil and DDR

FOR USE IN ALL PROVINCES IN THE RUSSIAN ZONE

When the mark was revalued in June, 1948, a provisional overprint, consisting of various city and town names and post office or zone numerals, was applied by hand in black, violet or blue at innumerable post offices to their stocks.

Germany Nos. 557 to 573 Overprinted in Black

1948, July 3 Wmk. 284 *Perf. 14*

10N1 A120 2pf brown blk .20 .20
10N2 A120 6pf purple .20 .20
10N3 A121 8pf red .20 .20
10N4 A121 10pf yellow grn .20 .20
10N5 A122 12pf gray .20 .20
10N6 A120 15pf chocolate .20 .20
10N7 A123 16pf dk blue grn .20 .25
10N8 A121 20pf blue .20 .20
10N9 A123 24pf brown org .20 .20
10N10 A120 25pf orange yel .20 .20
10N11 A122 30pf red .25 .20
10N12 A121 40pf red violet .20 .20
10N13 A123 50pf ultra .20 .40
10N14 A122 60pf red brown .25 .40
 a. 60pf brown red 20.00 *65.00*
10N15 A122 80pf dark blue .50 .50
10N16 A122 84pf emerald .50 .70
 Nos. 10N1-10N16 (16) 3.90 4.45
 Set, never hinged 5.50

Same Overprint on Numeral Stamps of Germany, 1946

1948, Sept.

10N17 A119 5pf yellow grn .20 .45
10N18 A119 30pf olive .25 1.25
10N19 A119 45pf brt red .20 .45
10N20 A119 75pf deep ultra .20 .50
10N21 A119 84pf emerald .25 1.00
 Nos. 10N17-10N21 (5) 1.10 3.65
 Set, never hinged 2.10

Nos 10N1-10N21 all exist with inverted overprint, and majority with double overprint.

Same Overprint on Berlin-Brandenburg Nos. 11N1-11N7

Unwmk.

1948, Sept. Litho. *Perf. 14*

10N22 OS1 5pf green .20 .40
 a. Serrate roulette .20 .40
10N23 OS1 6pf violet .20 .40
10N24 OS1 8pf red .20 .40
10N25 OS1 10pf brown .20 .40
10N26 OS1 12pf rose .20 .75
10N27 OS1 20pf blue .20 .65
10N28 OS1 30pf olive .20 .75
 Nos. 10N22-10N28 (7) 1.40 3.75
 Set, never hinged 2.00

The overprint made #10N22-10N28 valid for postage throughout the Russian Zone.

Gerhard Hauptmann — OS2

Designs: 2pf, 20pf, Käthe Kollwitz. 40pf, Gerhard Hauptmann. 8pf, 50pf, Karl Marx. 10pf, 84pf, August Bebel. 12pf, 30pf, Friedrich Engels. 15pf, 60pf, G. W. F. Hegel. 16pf, 25pf, Rudolf Virchow. 2pf, 20pf, Käthe Kollwitz. 24pf, 80pf, Ernst Thälmann.

Perf. 13x12½

1948 Typo. Wmk. 292

10N29 OS2 2pf gray .20 .20
10N30 OS2 6pf violet .20 .20
10N31 OS2 8pf red brn .20 .25
10N32 OS2 10pf blue grn .20 .25
10N33 OS2 12pf blue 1.40 .25
10N34 OS2 15pf brown .20 1.00
10N35 OS2 16pf turquoise .20 .40
10N36 OS2 20pf maroon .20 .60
10N37 OS2 24pf carmine 1.40 .25
10N38 OS2 25pf olive grn .30 1.10
10N39 OS2 30pf red 1.00 1.00
10N40 OS2 40pf red violet 1.00 .60
10N41 OS2 50pf dk ultra .20 .35
10N42 OS2 60pf dull green .85 .35
10N43 OS2 80pf dark blue .40 .35
10N44 OS2 84pf brown lake .85 1.75
 Nos. 10N29-10N44 (16) 8.80 8.90
 Set, never hinged 21.00

See German Democratic Republic #122-136.

Karl Liebknecht and Rosa Luxemburg OS3

Perf. 13½x13

1949, Jan. 15 Litho. Wmk. 292

10N45 OS3 24pf rose .20 .45
 Never hinged .25

30th anniv. of the death of Karl Liebknecht and Rosa Luxemburg, German socialists.

Dove and Laurel — OS4

1949

10N46 OS4 24pf carmine rose .30 1.25
 Never hinged .90

Overprinted in Black: "3. Deutscher Volkskongress 29.-30. Mai 1949"

1949, May 29

10N47 OS4 24pf carmine rose .40 1.75
 Never hinged 1.00

Nos. 10N46 and 10N47 were issued for the 3rd German People's Congress.

GERMAN DEMOCRATIC REPUBLIC

Catalogue values for unused stamps in this section, from this point to the end of the section, are for Never Hinged items.

Canceled to Order

The government stamp agency started in 1949 to sell canceled sets of new issues.

Used values are for CTO's for Nos. 48-2831, except for souvenir sheets, which are valued as postally used.

Pigeon, Letter and Globe A5

Wmk. Flowers Multiple (292)

1949, Oct. 9 Litho. *Perf. 13½*

48 A5 50pf lt blue & dk blue 7.00 7.50

75th anniv. of the UPU.

Letter Carriers — A6

Skier — A7

1949, Oct. 27 *Perf. 13*

49 A6 12pf blue 5.75 5.75
50 A6 30pf red 9.25 10.50

"Day of the International Postal Workers' Trade Union," October 27-29, 1949.

1950, Mar. 2 *Perf. 13*

51 A7 12pf shown 5.00 3.00
52 A7 24pf Skater 6.00 5.00

1st German Winter Sport Championship Matches, Schierke, 1950.

Globe and Sun — A8

1950, May 1 Typo.

53 A8 30pf deep carmine 16.00 11.50

60th anniv. of Labor Day.

A9

Pres. Wilhelm Pieck — A10

1950-51 Wmk. 292 *Perf. 13x12½*

54 A9 12pf dark blue 19.00 1.25
55 A9 24pf red brown 24.00 .60

Perf. 13x13½

56 A10 1m olive green 22.50 3.25

Litho.

57 A10 2m red brown 14.00 2.75

Engr.

57A A10 5m deep blue ('51) 5.75 1.00
 Nos. 54-57A (5) 85.25 8.85

See Nos. 113-117, 120-121.

Leonhard Euler — A11

Miner — A12

Portraits: 5pf, Alexander von Humboldt. 6pf, Theodor Mommsen. 8pf, Wilhelm von Humboldt. 10pf, H. L. F. von Helmholtz. 12pf, Max Planck. 16pf, Jacob Grimm. 20pf, W. H. Nernst. 24pf, Gottfried von Leibnitz. 50pf, Adolf von Harnack.

Wmk. 292

1950, July 10 Litho. *Perf. 12½*

58 A11 1pf gray 3.00 1.00
59 A11 5pf dp green 4.00 3.25
60 A11 6pf purple 8.50 3.25
61 A11 8pf orange brn 13.50 7.50
62 A11 10pf dk gray grn 12.00 7.50
63 A11 12pf dk blue 10.00 2.25
64 A11 16pf Prus blue 15.00 15.00
65 A11 20pf violet brn 13.50 13.00
66 A11 24pf red 15.00 2.25
67 A11 50pf dp ultra 22.50 16.00
 Nos. 58-67 (10) 117.00 71.00
 Set, hinged 40.00

250th anniv. of the founding of the Academy of Science, Berlin.

See Nos. 352-354.

1950, Sept. 1 *Perf. 13*

Design: 24pf, Smelting copper.

68 A12 12pf blue 4.00 *5.50*
69 A12 24pf dark red 6.50 6.00

750th anniv. of the opening of the Mannsfeld copper mines.

Symbols of a Democratic Vote — A13

Hand Between Dove and Tank — A14

1950, Sept. 28

70 A13 24pf brown red 12.00 3.25

Publicizing the election of Oct. 15, 1950.

1950, Dec. 15 Litho. *Perf. 13*

Designs show hand shielding dove from: 8pf, Exploding shell. 12pf, Atomic explosion. 24pf, Cemetery.

71 A14 6pf violet blue 3.00 2.50
72 A14 8pf brown 3.00 1.10
73 A14 12pf blue 4.25 2.50
74 A14 24pf red 4.25 1.10
 Nos. 71-74 (4) 14.50 7.20

Issued to publicize the "Fight for Peace."

Tobogganing A15

Design: 24pf, Ski jump.

1951, Feb. 3 Litho. *Perf. 13*

76 A15 12pf blue 6.50 5.50
77 A15 24pf rose 8.25 6.50

Issued to publicize the second Winter Sports Championship Matches at Oberhof.

A16

1951, Mar. 4 Wmk. 292 *Perf. 13*

78 A16 24pf rose carmine 13.00 11.00
79 A16 50pf violet blue 13.00 11.00

Issued to publicize the 1951 Leipzig Fair.

Pres. Wilhelm Pieck and Pres. Boleslaw Bierut Shaking Hands Across Oder-Neisse Frontier — A17

1951, Apr. 22 *Perf. 13*

80 A17 24pf scarlet 15.00 12.50
81 A17 50pf blue 15.00 12.50

Visit of Pres. Boleslaw Bierut of Poland to the Russian Zone of Germany.

Mao Tse-tung A18

Redistribution of Chinese Land — A19

1951, June 27 *Perf. 13*

82 A18 12pf dark green *67.50* 17.00
83 A19 24pf deep carmine *85.00* 21.00
84 A18 50pf violet blue *67.50* 21.00
Nos. 82-84 (3) *220.00* 59.00
Set, hinged *110.00*

Issued to publicize East Germany's friendship toward Communist China.

Boy Raising Flag A20

5-Year Plan Symbolism A21

Design: 24pf, 50pf, Girls dancing.

1951, Aug. 3
Grayish Paper, Except 30pf

85 A20 12pf choc & org brn 9.25 4.50
86 A20 24pf dk car & yel grn 9.25 2.75
87 A20 30pf dk bl grn & org brn, *cit* 11.00 5.50
88 A20 50pf vio bl & dk car 11.00 5.50
Nos. 85-88 (4) 40.50 18.25

3rd World Youth Festival, Berlin, 1951.

1951, Sept. 2 Typo. Wmk. 292

89 A21 24pf multicolored 3.75 1.60

East Germany's Five-Year Plan.

Karl Liebknecht — A22

Father and Children with Stamp Collection A23

1951, Oct. 7 Litho. *Perf. 13½x13*

90 A22 24pf red & blue gray 4.00 1.75

Karl Liebknecht, socialist, 80th birth anniv.

1951, Oct. 28 *Perf. 13*

91 A23 12pf deep blue 3.75 1.75

Stamp Day, Oct. 28, 1951.

Stalin and Wilhelm Pieck A24

Design: 12pf, Pavel Bykov and Erich Wirth.

1951

92 A24 12pf deep blue 3.00 2.75
93 A24 24pf red 3.75 3.75

Month of East German-Soviet friendship. Issue dates: 12pf, Dec. 15, 24pf, Dec. 1.

Winter Sports Championship Matches, Oberhof, 1952 — A25

Design: 12pf, Skier. 24pf, Ski jump.

1952, Jan. 12 Wmk. 292

94 A25 12pf blue green 4.00 2.50
95 A25 24pf deep blue 4.00 2.50

Ludwig van Beethoven, 125th Death Anniv. — A26

1952, Mar. 26 *Perf. 13½*

Design: 12pf, Beethoven full face.

96 A26 12pf bl gray & vio bl 1.50 .40
97 A26 24pf gray & red brn 2.10 .65

See Nos. 100-102.

Cyclists — A27

Klement Gottwald — A28

1952, May 5 Photo. *Perf. 13x13½*

98 A27 12pf blue 2.50 1.00

5th International Bicycle Peace Race, Warsaw-Berlin-Prague.

1952, May 1

99 A28 24pf violet blue 2.00 1.10

Friendship between German Democratic Republic and Czechoslovakia.

Type of 1952

Portraits: 6pf, G. F. Handel. 8pf, Albert Lortzing. 50pf, C. M. von Weber.

1952, July 5 Litho. Wmk. 297

100 A26 6pf brn buff & choc 1.75 1.00
101 A26 8pf pink & dp rose pink 1.75 1.60
102 A26 50pf bl gray & dp bl 2.50 2.10
Nos. 100-102 (3) 6.00 4.70

Victor Hugo — A29

Portraits: 20pf, Leonardo da Vinci. 24pf, Nicolai Gogol. 35pf, Avicenna.

Wmk. 292

1952, Aug. 11 Photo. *Perf. 13*

103 A29 12pf brown 2.50 3.00
104 A29 20pf green 2.50 3.00
105 A29 24pf rose 2.50 3.00
106 A29 35pf blue 3.50 4.25
Nos. 103-106 (4) 11.00 13.25

Machine, Globe and Dove — A30

1952, Sept. 7 Wmk. 297 *Perf. 13*

108 A30 24pf red 1.60 .50
109 A30 35pf deep blue 1.60 1.10

Issued to publicize the 1952 Leipzig Fair.

Friedrich Ludwig Jahn — A31

1952, Oct. 15 Litho.

110 A31 12pf blue 1.50 .65

Jahn (1778-1852), introduced gymnastics to Germany, and was a politician.

Halle University — A32

1952, Oct. 18 Photo.

111 A32 24pf green 1.50 .65

450th anniv. of the founding of Halle University, Wittenberg.

Stamp, Flags, Wreath, Dove and Hammer — A33

1952, Oct. 26

112 A33 24pf red brown 1.75 .75

Stamp Day, Oct. 26, 1952.

Pieck Types of 1950

Perf. 13x12½

1952-53 Wmk. 297 Typo.

113 A9 5pf blue green 7.00 2.25
114 A9 12pf dark blue 17.50 1.25
115 A9 24pf red brown 14.00 1.00

Perf. 13x13½

116 A10 1m olive green 22.50 13.00

Litho. *Perf. 13*

117 A10 2m red brown ('53) 19.00 2.50
Nos. 113-117 (5) 80.00 20.00
Set, hinged 27.50

Globe, Dove and St. Stephen's Cathedral — A34

Pres. Wilhelm Pieck — A35

1952, Dec. 8 Photo. *Perf. 13*

118 A34 24pf brt carmine 1.25 1.60
119 A34 35pf deep blue 1.25 2.50

Issued to publicize the Congress of Nations for Peace, Vienna, Dec. 12-19, 1952.

1953 *Perf. 13x13½*

120 A35 1m olive 10.50 .35
a. 1m dark olive 15.00 1.60
121 A35 2m red brown 7.50 .35

See Nos. 339-340, 532.

Portrait Types of Russian Occupation, 1948

Designs as before.

Perf. 13x12½

1953 Typo. Wmk. 297

122 OS2 2pf gray 2.00 1.75
123 OS2 6pf purple 2.00 1.10
124 OS2 8pf red brown 1.40 1.10
125 OS2 10pf blue grn 2.40 2.25
126 OS2 15pf brown 8.75 9.25
127 OS2 16pf turquoise 3.50 2.25
128 OS2 20pf maroon 3.75 1.10
129 OS2 25pf olive grn 140.00 160.00
130 OS2 30pf red 11.00 5.25
131 OS2 40pf red violet 2.00 1.75
132 OS2 50pf dk ultra 17.50 13.00
133 OS2 60pf dull green 3.50 1.75
134 OS2 80pf dark blue 4.50 1.40
a. Varnish coating, dark ultramarine 8.00 *7.50*
135 OS2 80pf crimson 8.00 7.50
136 OS2 84pf brown lake 42.50 47.50
Nos. 122-136 (15) 252.80 256.95
Set, hinged 85.00

"Industry" and Red Flag — A36

Marx and Engels — A37

Karl Marx Speaking — A38

Karl Marx Medallion — A39

Designs: 12pf, Spasski tower and communist flag. 16pf, Marching workers. 24pf, Portrait of Karl Marx. 35pf, Marx addressing audience. 48pf, Karl Marx and Friedrich Engels. 60pf. Red banner above heads and shoulders of workers.

1953 Photo. *Perf. 13*

137 A36 6pf grnsh gray & red .55 .30
138 A37 10pf grnsh gray & dk brn 3.25 .50
139 A36 12pf grn, dp plum & dk grn .55 .35
140 A37 16pf vio bl & dk car 2.00 1.25
141 A38 20pf brown & buff .80 .50
142 A38 24pf brown & red 2.00 .50
143 A36 35pf dp pur & cr 2.00 1.75
144 A36 48pf dk ol grn & red brn 1.25 .50
a. Souvenir sheet of 6 67.50 110.00
Hinged 25.00
145 A37 60pf vio brn & red 3.00 1.75
146 A39 84pf blue & brown 2.50 1.25
a. Souvenir sheet of 4 67.50 110.00
Hinged 25.00
Nos. 137-146 (10) 17.90 8.65

No. 144a contains one each of the denominations in types A36 and A38. Perf. and imperf.

No. 146a contains one each of the denominations in types A37 and A39. Perf. and imperf.

Maxim Gorky — A40

Bicycle Racers — A41

1953, Mar. 28

147 A40 35pf brown .30 .25

1953, May 2 Wmk. 297 *Perf. 13*

24pf, 60pf, Different views of bicycle race.

148 A41 24pf bluish green 1.60 1.25
149 A41 35pf deep ultra .90 .80
150 A41 60pf chocolate 1.25 1.10
Nos. 148-150 (3) 3.75 3.15

6th International Bicycle Peace Race.

Heinrich von Kleist A42

Woman Mariner A43

20pf, Evangelical Marienkirche. 24pf, Sailboat on Oder River. 35pf, City Hall, Frankfurt-on-Oder.

1953, July 6 Litho.

151 A42 16pf chocolate 1.10 1.25
152 A42 20pf blue green .70 1.10
153 A42 24pf rose red 1.10 1.25
154 A42 35pf violet blue 1.10 1.60
Nos. 151-154 (4) 4.00 5.20

700th anniversary of the founding of Frankfurt-on-Oder.

1953 Litho. *Perf. 13x12½*

Designs: 1pf, Coal miner. 6pf, German and Soviet workers. 8pf, Mother teaching Marxist principles. 10pf, Machinists. 12pf, Worker, peasant and intellectual. 15pf, Teletype operator. 16pf, Steel worker. 20pf, Bad Elster. 24pf, Stalin Boulevard. 25pf, Locomotive building. 30pf, Dancing couple. 35pf, Sports Hall, Berlin. 40pf, Laboratory worker. 48pf, Zwinger Castle, Dresden. 60pf, Launching ship. 80pf, Agricultural workers. 84pf, Dove and East German family.

155 A43 1pf black brown 1.10 .20
156 A43 5pf emerald 1.40 .20
157 A43 6pf violet 1.40 .20
158 A43 8pf orange brn 2.00 .20
159 A43 10pf blue green 1.40 .20
160 A43 12pf blue 1.40 .20
161 A43 15pf purple 2.40 .20
162 A43 16pf dk violet 3.25 .20
163 A43 20pf olive 3.25 .20
163A A43 24pf carmine 6.50 .20
164 A43 25pf dk green 4.75 .20
165 A43 30pf dp car 4.75 .20
166 A43 35pf violet bl 10.50 .20
167 A43 40pf rose red 10.50 .20
168 A43 48pf rose red 10.50 .20
169 A43 60pf deep blue 10.50 .20
170 A43 80pf aqua 13.00 .20
171 A43 84pf chocolate 10.50 .20
Nos. 155-171 (18) 99.10 3.60
Set, hinged 32.50

See Nos. 187-204, 227-230A, 330-338, 476-482. For surcharges see #216-223A.

Used values of Nos. 155-171 are for cto reprints with printed cancellations. The reprints differ slightly from originals in design and shade.

Power Shovel — A44

Design: 35pf, Road-building machine.

1953, Aug. 29 Photo. *Perf. 13*

172 A44 24pf red brown 1.25 1.25
173 A44 35pf deep green 2.40 1.75

The 1953 Leipzig Fair.

G. W. von Knobelsdorff and Berlin State Opera House — A45

Design: 35pf, Balthasar Neumann and Wurzburg bishop's palace.

1953, Sept. 16 *Perf. 13x12½*

174 A45 24pf cerise 1.10 .50
175 A45 35pf dk slate blue 1.60 .95

200th anniv. of the deaths of G. W. von Knobelsdorff and Balthasar Neumann, architects.

Lucas Cranach — A46

Nurse Applying Bandage — A47

1953, Oct. 16 *Perf. 13x13½*

176 A46 24pf brown 2.50 .80

400th anniversary of the death of Lucas Cranach (1472-1553), painter.

Perf. 13½x13

1953, Oct. 23 Wmk. 297

177 A47 24pf brown & red 2.00 1.00

Issued to honor the Red Cross.

Mail Delivery — A48

Lion and Lioness — A49

1953, Oct. 25 Photo.

178 A48 24pf blue gray 2.00 .40

Stamp Day, Oct. 24, 1953.

1953, Nov. 2 *Perf. 13x13½*

179 A49 24pf olive brown 1.40 .40

75th anniversary of Leipzig Zoo.

Thomas Muntzer and Attackers A50

16pf, H. F. K. vom Stein. 20pf, Ferdinand von Schill leading cavalry. 24pf, G. L. Blucher and battle scene. 35pf, Students fighting for National Unity. 48pf, Revolution of 1848.

1953, Nov. Photo. *Perf. 13x12½*

180 A50 12pf brown 1.00 .40
181 A50 16pf dp brown 1.00 .40
182 A50 20pf dk car rose 1.00 .30
183 A50 24pf deep blue 1.00 .30
184 A50 35pf dk green 1.75 1.00
185 A50 48pf dk brown 1.75 .85
Nos. 180-185 (6) 7.50 3.25

Issued to honor German patriots.

Franz Schubert — A51

Gotthold E. Lessing — A52

1953, Nov. 13 *Perf. 13½x13*

186 A51 48pf brt orange brn 2.10 1.00

Death of Franz Schubert, 125th anniv.

Types of 1953 Redrawn

Designs as before.

1953-54 Typo. *Perf. 13x12½*

187 A43 1pf black brn .65 .20
188 A43 5pf emerald 1.40 .20
a. Bklt. pane, 3 #188 + 3 #227 11.50 11.50
b. Bklt. pane, 3 #188 + 3 #228 11.50 11.50
189 A43 6pf purple 2.75 .20
190 A43 8pf orange brn 3.50 .20
191 A43 10pf blue grn 21.00 .20
192 A43 12pf grnsh blue 4.25 .20
193 A43 15pf brt vio ('54) 13.00 .20
194 A43 16pf dk purple 3.75 .20
195 A43 20pf olive ('54) 60.00 .20
196 A43 24pf carmine 4.75 .20
197 A43 25pf dk bl grn 2.50 .20
198 A43 30pf dp carmine 3.25 .20
199 A43 35pf dp vio bl 3.25 .20
200 A43 40pf rose red ('54) 8.00 .20
201 A43 48pf rose vio 7.50 .20
202 A43 60pf blue 12.00 .20
203 A43 80pf aqua 2.75 .20
204 A43 84pf chocolate 14.00 .20
Nos. 187-204 (18) 168.30 3.60
Set, hinged 50.00

Nos. 155-171 were printed from screened halftones, and shading consists of dots. Shading in lines without screen on Nos. 187-204. Designers' and engravers' names added below design on all values except 6, 12, 16 and 35pf. There are many other minor differences.

See note on used values after No. 171.

1954, Jan. 20 Photo. *Perf. 13*

205 A52 20pf dark green 1.50 .60

225th anniversary of the birth of G. E. Lessing, dramatist.

Dove Over Conference Table — A53

Joseph V. Stalin — A54

1954, Jan. 25 *Perf. 12½x13*

206 A53 12pf blue 1.25 .50

Four Power Conference, Berlin, 1954.

1954, Mar. 5 Typo. *Perf. 13x12½*

207 A54 20pf gray, dk brn & red org 2.00 .50

1st anniv. of the death of Joseph V. Stalin.

Cyclists A55

Design: 24pf, Cyclists passing farm.

1954, Apr. 30 Photo.

208 A55 12pf brown 1.00 .50
209 A55 24pf dull green 1.40 .75

7th International Bicycle Peace Race.

Dancers — A56

Fritz Reuter — A57

Design: 24pf, Boy, two girls and flag.

1954, June 3 *Perf. 13*

210 A56 12pf emerald .85 .55
211 A56 24pf rose brown .85 .55

Issued to publicize the 2nd German youth meeting for peace, unity and freedom.

1954, July 12

212 A57 24pf sepia 1.40 .65

Death of Fritz Reuter, writer, 80th anniv.

Ernst Thälmann — A58

1954, Aug. 18 *Perf. 13½x13*

213 A58 24pf red org & indigo .75 .45

10th anniv. of the death of Ernst Thälmann (1886-1944), Communist leader.

Hall of Commerce, Leipzig Fair — A59

1954, Sept. 4 *Perf. 13x13½*

214 A59 24pf dark red .45 .30
215 A59 35pf gray blue .55 .40

Issued to publicize the 1954 Leipzig Fair.

Redrawn Types of 1953-54 Surcharged with New Value and "X" in Black

1954 **Typo.** *Perf. 13x12½*

216 A43 5pf on 6pf purple .70 .20
217 A43 5pf on 8pf org brn .85 .30
218 A43 10pf on 12pf grnsh bl .50 .30
219 A43 15pf on 16pf dk pur .70 .20
220 A43 20pf on 24pf car 1.10 .50
221 A43 40pf on 48pf rose vio 2.10 .50
222 A43 50pf on 60pf blue 2.25 .50
223 A43 70pf on 84pf choc 7.00 .50
Nos. 216-223 (8) 15.20 3.00

See note on used values after No. 171.

No. 163A Surcharged with New Value and "X" in Black

1955 **Litho.**

223A A43 20pf on 24pf car .80 .25

Counterfeit surcharges exist on other values of the lithographed set (Nos. 155-171).

Pres. Wilhelm Pieck and Flags A60

1954, Oct. 6 **Photo.**

224 A60 20pf brown 1.60 .60
225 A60 35pf greenish blue 1.60 .75

5th anniv. of the founding of the German Democratic Republic.

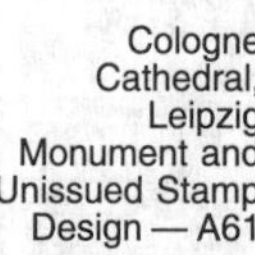

Cologne Cathedral, Leipzig Monument and Unissued Stamp Design — A61

1954, Oct. 23 *Perf. 13x13½*

226 A61 20pf brt car rose 1.10 .45
a. Souvenir sheet, imperf. 35.00 35.00

Stamp Day. No. 226a has frame and inscription in blue. Size: 60x80mm.

Redrawn Types of 1953-54

Designs: 10pf, Worker, peasant and intellectual. 15pf, Steelworker. 20pf, Stalin Boulevard. 40pf, Zwinger Castle, Dresden. 50pf, Launching ship. 70pf, Dove and East German family.

1955 **Typo.** *Perf. 13x12½*

227 A43 10pf blue 2.00 .20
a. Bklt. pane, 4 #227 + 2 #228
227B A43 15pf violet 2.40 .20
228 A43 20pf carmine 1.75 .20
229 A43 40pf rose violet 3.75 .20
230 A43 50pf deep blue 6.25 .20
230A A43 70pf chocolate 8.50 .20
Nos. 227-230A (6) 24.65 1.20

See note on used values after No. 171.

Soviet Pavilion, Leipzig Spring Fair — A62

Women of Three Nations — A63

Design: 35pf, Chinese pavilion.

Perf. 13x13½

1955, Feb. 21 **Photo.** **Wmk. 297**

231 A62 20pf rose violet .50 .40
232 A62 35pf violet blue 1.10 .50

Issued to publicize the Leipzig Spring Fair.

1955, Mar. 1 *Perf. 13x13½*

233 A63 10pf green .70 .25
234 A63 20pf red .70 .25

International Women's Day, 45th year.

Workers' Demonstration — A64

1955, Mar. 15 *Perf. 13x12½*

235 A64 10pf black & red .70 .50

Intl. Trade Union Conference, Apr., 1955.

A65 A66

Monument to the Victims of Fascism.

1955, Apr. 9 *Perf. 13½x13*

236 A65 10pf violet blue .60 .50
237 A65 20pf cerise .80 .85
a. Souv. sheet of 2, #236-237, imperf. 15.00 19.00

No. 237a sold for 50pf.

1955, Apr. 15 *Perf. 12½x13*

Russian War Memorial, Berlin.

238 A66 20pf lilac rose 1.00 .40

Nos. 236-238 issued for 10th anniv. of liberation, No. 237a for reconstruction of natl. memorial sites.

Cyclists — A67

Friedrich von Schiller — A68

1955 **Wmk. 297** *Perf. 13½x13*

239 A67 10pf blue green .55 .30
240 A67 20pf car rose .65 .35

8th International Bicycle Peace Race, Prague-Berlin-Warsaw.

Starting with the 1955 issues, commemorative stamps which are valued in italics were sold on a restricted basis.

1955, Apr. 20

Various Portraits of Schiller.

241 A68 5pf dk gray grn *2.00 1.60*
242 A68 10pf brt blue .25 .20
243 A68 20pf chocolate .25 .20
a. Souv. sheet, #241-243, imperf. *18.00 24.00*
Nos. 241-243 (3) *2.50 2.00*

150th anniv. of the death of Friedrich von Schiller, poet.
No. 243a sold for 50pf.

Karl Liebknecht — A69

Portraits: 10pf, August Bebel. 15pf, Franz Mehring. 20pf, Ernst Thalmann. 25pf, Clara Zetkin. 40pf, Wilhelm Liebknecht. 60pf, Rosa Luxemburg.

1955, June 20 **Photo.** *Perf. 13x12½*

244 A69 5pf blue green .25 .20
245 A69 10pf deep blue .30 .20
246 A69 15pf violet *4.25 2.00*
247 A69 20pf red .30 .20
248 A69 25pf slate .30 .20
249 A69 40pf rose carmine 1.50 .20
250 A69 60pf dk brown .30 .20
Nos. 244-250 (7) *7.20 3.20*

Issued to honor German communists.

Optical Goods — A70

Design: 20pf, Pottery and china.

1955, Aug. 29 **Photo.** *Perf. 13x13½*

253 A70 10pf dark blue .45 .25
254 A70 20pf slate green .45 .25

Issued to publicize the 1955 Leipzig Fair.

Farmer Receiving Deed — A71

Harvesters A72

10pf, Construction of new farm community.

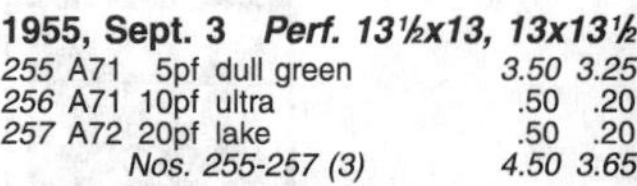

1955, Sept. 3 *Perf. 13½x13, 13x13½*

255 A71 5pf dull green *3.50 3.25*
256 A71 10pf ultra .50 .20
257 A72 20pf lake .50 .20
Nos. 255-257 (3) *4.50 3.65*

10th anniv. of the Land-Reform Program.

Man Holding Badge of Peoples' Solidarity — A73

Engels at "First International," 1864 — A74

Perf. 13½x13

1955, Oct. 10 **Wmk. 297**

258 A73 10pf dark blue .50 .25

10th anniv. of the "Peoples' Solidarity."

1955, Nov. 7 *Perf. 13½x13*

Designs: 10pf, Marx and Engels writing the Communist Manifesto. 15pf, Engels as newspaper editor. 20pf, Friedrich Engels. 30pf, Friedrich Engels. 70pf, Engels on the barricades in 1848.

259 A74 5pf Prus blue & olive .25 .20
260 A74 10pf dk blue & yel .50 .20
261 A74 15pf dk green & ol .50 .20
262 A74 20pf brn vio & org .90 .20
263 A74 30pf org brn & lt bl *5.75 5.25*
264 A74 70pf gray grn & rose car 1.75 .25
a. Souvenir sheet of 6, #259-264 *47.50 57.50*
Nos. 259-264 (6) *9.65 6.30*

Friedrich Engels, 135th birth anniv.

Cathedral at Magdeburg A75

Georgius Agricola A76

German Buildings: 10pf, German State Opera. 15pf, Old City Hall, Leipzig. 20pf, City Hall, Berlin. 30pf, Cathedral at Erfurt. 40pf, Zwinger at Dresden.

1955, Nov. 14

265 A75 5pf black brown .40 .25
266 A75 10pf gray green .40 .25
267 A75 15pf purple .40 .25
268 A75 20pf carmine .40 .50
269 A75 30pf dk red brown *8.25 9.00*
270 A75 40pf indigo 1.10 .50
Nos. 265-270 (6) *10.95 10.75*

For surcharges see Nos. B29-B30.

1955, Nov. 21 **Wmk. 297**

271 A76 10pf brown .50 .30

400th anniv. of the death of Georgius Agricola, mineralogist and scholar.

Portrait of a Young Man, by Dürer — A77

Mozart — A78

Famous Paintings: 10pf, Chocolate Girl, Liotard. 15pf, Portrait of a Boy, Pinturicchio. 20pf, Self-portrait with Saskia, Rembrandt. 40pf, Girl with Letter, Vermeer. 70pf, Sistine Madonna, Raphael.

1955, Dec. 15 *Perf. 13½x13*

272 A77 5pf dk red brown .55 .20
273 A77 10pf chestnut .55 .20
274 A77 15pf pale purple *21.00 16.00*

275 A77 20pf brown .55 .20
276 A77 40pf olive green .55 .25
277 A77 70pf deep blue 1.25 .50
Nos. 272-277 (6) *24.45 17.35*

Issued to publicize the return of famous art works to the Dresden Art Gallery.
See Nos. 355-360, 439-443.

1956, Jan. 27 **Photo.**

Designs: 20pf, Portrait facing left.

278 A78 10pf gray green *8.50 5.50*
279 A78 20pf copper brown 2.50 1.00

200th anniv. of the birth of Wolfgang Amadeus Mozart, composer.

Flag and Schoenefeld Airport, Berlin — A79

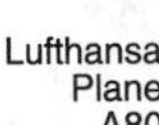
Lufthansa Plane A80

Designs: 15pf, Plane facing right. 20pf, Plane facing down and left.

1956, Feb. 1 ***Perf. 13x12½***

280 A79 5pf multicolored *9.00 6.25*
281 A80 10pf gray green .60 .20
282 A80 15pf dull blue .60 .20
283 A80 20pf brown red .60 .20
Nos. 280-283 (4) *10.80 6.85*

Issued to commemorate the opening of passenger service of the German Lufthansa.

Heinrich Heine — A81

Railroad Cranes — A82

Design: 20pf, Heine (different portrait.)

1956, Feb. 17 ***Perf. 13½x13***

284 A81 10pf Prus green *8.25 4.25*
285 A81 20pf dark red 1.75 .40

Cent. of the death of Heinrich Heine, poet.

1956, Feb. 26 ***Perf. 13x13½***

286 A82 20pf brown red .50 .25
287 A82 35pf violet blue .75 .45

Issued to publicize the Leipzig Spring Fair.

Ernst Thälmann A83

1956, Apr. 16 **Litho.** ***Perf. 13x13½***

288 A83 20pf black olive & red .40 .25
a. Souvenir sheet of 1, imperf *7.50 18.00*

Birth of Ernst Thälmann, 70th anniv.
No. 288a was sold at double face value. The proceeds were used for national memorials at former concentration camps.

Wheel, Hand and Olive Branch — A84

City Hall and Old Market — A85

Design: 20pf, Wheel and coats of arms of Warsaw, Berlin, Prague.

Perf. 13½x13

1956, Apr. 30 **Wmk. 297**

289 A84 10pf lt green .45 .25
290 A84 20pf brt carmine .45 .25

9th International Bicycle Peace Race, Warsaw-Berlin-Prague, May 1-15, 1956.

1956, June 1

Designs: 20pf, Hofkirche and Elbe Bridge. 40pf, Technical College.

291 A85 10pf green .20 .20
292 A85 20pf carmine rose .20 .20
293 A85 40pf brt purple *1.40 1.40*
Nos. 291-293 (3) *1.80 1.80*

750th anniversary of Dresden.

Worker Holding Cogwheel Emblem — A86

1956, June 30 ***Perf. 13½x13***

294 A86 20pf rose red .30 .20

10th anniversary of nationalized industry.

Robert Schumann (Music by Schubert) A87

1956, July 20 ***Perf. 13x13½***

295 A87 10pf brt green *1.40 .95*
296 A87 20pf rose red .50 .20

Centenary of the death of Robert Schumann, composer. See Nos. 303-304.

Soccer Players — A88

Thomas Mann — A89

Designs: 10pf, Javelin Thrower. 15pf, Women Hurdlers. 20pf, Gymnast.

1956, July 25 ***Perf. 13½x13***

297 A88 5pf green .20 .20
298 A88 10pf dk vio blue .20 .20
299 A88 15pf red violet *1.40 .70*
300 A88 20pf rose red .20 .20
Nos. 297-300 (4) *2.00 1.30*

Second Sports Festival, Leipzig, Aug. 2-5.

1956, Aug. 13 **Wmk. 297**

301 A89 20pf bluish black .70 .35

Death of Thomas Mann, novelist, 1st anniv.

Jakub Bart Cisinski — A90

Robert Schumann (Music by Schumann) A91

1956, Aug. 20 **Photo.**

302 A90 50pf claret .70 .35

Birth centenary of Jakub Bart Cisinski, poet.

1956, Oct. 8 ***Perf. 13x13½***

303 A91 10pf brt green *4.00 1.10*
304 A91 20pf rose red 1.75 .25

See Nos. 295, 296.

Lace — A92

Olympic Rings, Laurel and Torch — A93

Design: 20pf, Sailboat.

1956, Sept. 1 **Typo.** ***Perf. 13½x13***

305 A92 10pf green & blk .25 .25
306 A92 20pf rose red & blk .25 .25

Leipzig Fair, Sept. 2-9.

1956, Sept. 28 **Litho.**

Design: 35pf, Classic javelin thrower.

307 A93 20pf brown red .30 .20
308 A93 35pf slate blue .45 .25

16th Olympic Games at Melbourne, Nov. 22-Dec. 8, 1956.

Post Runner of 1450 — A94

Greifswald University Seal — A95

1956, Oct. 27

309 A94 20pf red .30 .20

Issued to publicize the Day of the Stamp.

1956, Oct. 17 ***Perf. 13x13½***

310 A95 20pf magenta .30 .20

500th anniv. of Greifswald University.

Ernst Abbe — A96

Zeiss Works, Jena A97

Portrait: 25pf, Carl Zeiss.

Perf. 12½x13, 13x12½

1956, Nov. 9 **Photo.** **Wmk. 297**

311 A96 10pf dark green .20 .20
312 A97 20pf brown red .20 .20
313 A96 25pf bluish black .30 .25
Nos. 311-313 (3) .70 .65

Carl Zeiss Optical Works, Jena, 110th anniv.

Chinese Girl with Flowers — A98

Designs: 10pf, Negro woman and child. 25pf, European man and dove.

1956, Dec. 10 **Litho.** ***Perf. 13***

314 A98 5pf ol, *pale lem* .90 .70
315 A98 10pf brown, *pink* .20 .20
316 A98 25pf vio bl, *pale vio bl* .20 .20
Nos. 314-316 (3) *1.30 1.10*

Issued for Human Rights Day.

Elephants A99

1956, Dec. 17 **Photo.** ***Perf. 13x12½***

Design in Gray

317 A99 5pf shown .20 .20
318 A99 10pf Flamingoes .20 .20
319 A99 15pf White rhinoceros *3.00 2.10*
320 A99 20pf Mouflon .20 .20
321 A99 25pf Bison .20 .20
322 A99 30pf Polar bear .20 .20
Nos. 317-322 (6) *4.00 3.10*

Issued to publicize the Berlin Zoo.

Freighter A100

Design: 25pf, Electric Locomotive.

1957, Mar. 1 **Litho.** **Wmk. 313**

323 A100 20pf rose red .20 .20
324 A100 25pf bright blue .20 .20

Leipzig Spring Fair.

Silver Thistle A101

10pf, Emerald lizard. 20pf, Lady's-slipper.

1957, Apr. 12 **Photo.** **Wmk. 313**

325 A101 5pf chocolate .20 .20
326 A101 10pf dk slate grn *1.75 1.60*
327 A101 20pf red brown .20 .20
Nos. 325-327 (3) *2.15 2.00*

Nature Conservation Week, Apr. 14-20.

Children at Play — A102

20pf, Friedrich Froebel and Children.

1957, Apr. 18 Litho. *Perf. 13*

328 A102 10pf dk slate grn & ol *.85* *.70*
329 A102 20pf black & brown red .20 .20

175th anniv. of the birth of Friedrich Froebel, educator.

Redrawn Types of 1953

Designs: 5pf, Woman mariner. 10pf, Worker, peasant and intellectual. 15pf, Steel worker. 20pf, Stalin Boulevard. 25pf, Locomotive building. 30pf, Dancing couple. 40pf, Zwinger Castle, Dresden. 50pf, Launching ship. 70pf, Dove and East German family.

Imprint: "E. Gruner K. Wolf"
No imprint on 10pf, 15pf

Perf. 13x12½, 14

1957-58 Typo. Wmk. 313

330 A43 5pf emerald .20 .20
 a. Bklt. pane, 3 #330 + 3 #331b
 b. Bklt. pane, 3 #330 + 3 #333
 c. Booklet pane of 6 .85
331 A43 10pf blue ('58) .20 .20
 a. Bklt. pane, 4 #331b + 2 #333
 b. Perf. 13x12½ 3.00 .20
332 A43 15pf violet ('58) .20 .20
 a. Perf. 13x12½ .25 .20
333 A43 20pf carmine .20 .20
 a. Bklt. pane, 5 #333 + 1 #477
334 A43 25pf bluish green .25 .20
335 A43 30pf dull red .75 .20
336 A43 40pf rose violet 1.10 .20
337 A43 50pf bright blue 1.40 .20
338 A43 70pf chocolate 1.60 .20

See Nos. 476-482.

Pieck Type of 1953

Photo. *Perf. 13x13½*

339 A35 1m dk olive grn ('58) 1.60 .25
340 A35 2m red brown ('58) 3.50 .30
 Nos. 330-340 (11) 11.00 2.35

No. 334 comes only perf 13x12½. Nos 330-333 and 335-338 come both perf 13x12½ and perf 14.

Bicycle Race Route — A103

Perf. 13x13½

1957, Apr. 30 Litho. Wmk. 313

346 A103 5pf orange .30 .20

Issued to publicize the 10th International Bicycle Peace Race, Prague-Berlin-Warsaw.

Steam Shovel A104

Miner — A105

Design: 20pf, Coal conveyor.

Perf. 13x12½, 13½x13 (25pf)

1957, May 3

347 A104 10pf green .20 .20
348 A104 20pf redsh brown .20 .20
349 A105 25pf blue violet *1.60* *.60*
 Nos. 347-349 (3) *2.00* *1.00*

Issued in honor of the coal mining industry.

Henri Dunant and Globe A106

25pf, Henri Dunant facing right and globe.

1957, May 7 Photo. *Perf. 13x12½*

350 A106 10pf green, red & blk .20 .20
351 A106 25pf brt blue, red & blk .20 .20

Tenth Red Cross world conference.

Portrait Type of 1950, Redrawn

Portraits: 5pf, Joachim Jungius. 10pf, Leonhard Euler. 20pf, Heinrich Hertz.

1957, June 7 Litho.

352 A11 5pf brown 1.00 .50
353 A11 10pf green .20 .20
354 A11 20pf henna brown .20 .20
 Nos. 352-354 (3) 1.40 .90

Issued to honor famous German scientists.

Painting Type of 1955.

Famous Paintings: 5pf, Holy Family, Mantegna. 10pf, The Dancer Campani, Carriera. 15pf, Portrait of Morette, Holbein. 20pf, The Tribute Money, Titian. 25pf, Saskia with Red Flower, Rembrandt. 40pf, Young Standard Bearer, Piazetta.

Perf. 13½x13

1957, June 26 Photo. Wmk. 313

355 A77 5pf dk brown .20 .20
356 A77 10pf lt yellow grn .20 .20
357 A77 15pf brown olive .20 .20
358 A77 20pf rose brown .20 .20
359 A77 25pf deep claret .25 .20
360 A77 40pf dk blue gray *3.00* *1.40*
 Nos. 355-360 (6) *4.05* *2.40*

Clara Zetkin — A107

Bertolt Brecht — A108

1957, July 5 *Perf. 13x13½*

361 A107 10pf dk green & red .50 .25

Centenary of the birth of Clara Zetkin, politician and founder of the socialist women's movement.

1957, Aug. 14 *Perf. 13½x13*

362 A108 10pf dark green .25 .20
363 A108 25pf deep blue .35 .20

Brecht (1898-1956), playwright and poet.

Congress Emblem — A109

Fair Emblem — A110

1957, Aug. 23 Litho.

364 A109 20pf brt red & black .40 .25

4th Intl. Trade Union Congress, Leipzig, Oct. 4-15.

1957, Aug. 30 Wmk. 313

365 A110 20pf crimson & ver .20 .20
366 A110 25pf brt blue & lt blue .25 .20

Issued to publicize the 1957 Leipzig Fair.

Savings Book — A111

Postrider, 1563 — A112

1957, Oct. 10 *Perf. 13½x13*

367 A111 10pf grn & blk, *gray* .60 .40
368 A111 20pf rose car & blk, *gray* .25 .25

Issued to publicize "Savings Weeks."

1957, Oct. 25 Wmk. 313

369 A112 5pf black, *pale sepia* .40 .20

Issued for the Day of the Stamp.

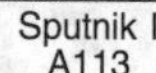

Sputnik I A113

Storming of the Winter Palace A114

20pf, Stratospheric balloon above clouds. 25pf, Ship with plumb line exploring deep sea.

1957-58 *Perf. 12½x13*

370 A113 10pf blue black .30 .20
371 A113 20pf car rose ('58) .40 .20
372 A113 25pf brt blue ('58) *1.40* *.95*
 Nos. 370-372 (3) *2.10* *1.35*

IGY. The 10pf also for the launching of the 1st artificial satellite.

1957, Nov. 7 Photo.

373 A114 10pf yellow grn & red .20 .20
374 A114 25pf brt blue & red .20 .20

40th anniv. of the Russian Revolution.

Guenther Ramin — A115

Dove and Globe — A116

Portrait: 20pf, Hermann Abendroth.

Perf. 13½x13

1957, Nov. 22 Litho. Wmk. 313

375 A115 10pf yellow grn & blk *.70* *.60*
376 A115 20pf red orange & blk .20 .20

Ramin (1898-1956) and Abendroth (1883-1956), musicians, on the 1st anniv. of their death.

1958, Feb. 27 *Perf. 13x13½*

377 A116 20pf rose red .20 .20
378 A116 25pf blue .25 .20

Issued to publicize the 1958 Leipzig Fair.

Radio Tower, Morse Code and Post Horn A117

Design: 20pf, Radio tower and small post horn.

1958, Mar. 6 *Perf. 13x12½*

379 A117 5pf gray & blk *.60* *.40*
380 A117 20pf crim rose & dk red .25 .20

Conf. of Postal Ministers of Communist countries, Moscow, Dec. 3-17, 1957.

Sketch by Zille — A118

Symbolizing Quantum Theory — A119

Design: 20pf, Self-portrait of Zille.

1958, Mar. 20 *Perf. 13½x13*

381 A118 10pf green & gray *1.90* *.90*
382 A118 20pf dp car & gray .45 .20

Centenary of the birth of Heinrich Zille, artist.

1958, Apr. 23 Litho.

Design: 20pf, Max Planck.

383 A119 10pf gray green *.90* *.75*
384 A119 20pf magenta .30 .20

Centenary of the birth of Max Planck, physicist.

Prize Cow — A120

10pf, Mowing machine. 20pf, Beet harvester.

Perf. 13x13½

1958, June 4 Wmk. 313

Size: 28x23mm

385 A120 5pf gray & blk *1.25* *.90*

Size: 39x22mm

Perf. 13x12½

386 A120 10pf brt green .25 .20
387 A120 20pf rose red .25 .20
 Nos. 385-387 (3) *1.75* *1.30*

6th Agricultural Show, Markkleeberg.

Charles Darwin — A121

1958, June 19 *Perf. 13x13½*

Portrait: 20pf, Carl von Linné.

388 A121 10pf green & black *.90* *.70*
389 A121 20pf dk red & black .20 .20

Cent. of Darwin's theory of evolution and the bicent. of Linné's botanical system.

Seven Towers of Rostock and Ships — A122

Congress Emblem — A123

10pf, Ship at pier. 25pf, Ships in harbor.

1958 ***Perf. 13½x13***
390 A122 10pf emerald .20 .20
391 A122 20pf red orange .30 .25
392 A122 25pf lt blue .80 .80
Nos. 390-392 (3) *1.30 1.25*

Establishment of Rostock as a seaport.
Issue dates: 20pf, July 5; 10pf and 25pf, Nov. 24.
For overprint see No. 500.

1958, June 25 ***Perf. 13x13½***
393 A123 10pf rose red .25 .20

5th congress of the Socialist Party of the German Democratic Republic (SED).

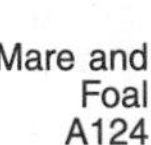
Mare and Foal A124

Designs: 10pf, Trotter. 20pf, Horse race.

1958, July 22 Photo. ***Perf. 13x12½***
394 A124 5pf black brown *1.75 1.60*
395 A124 10pf dark olive green .20 .20
396 A124 20pf dark red brown .20 .20
Nos. 394-396 (3) *2.15 2.00*

Grand Prize of the DDR, 1958.

Jan Amos Komensky (Comenius) A125

Design: 20pf, Teacher and pupils, 17th cent.

1958, Aug. 7 Litho. ***Perf. 13x13½***
397 A125 10pf brt bl grn & blk *1.10* *.70*
398 A125 20pf org brn & blk .20 .20

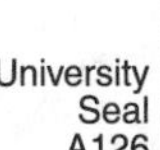
University Seal A126

Design: 20pf, Schiller University, Jena.

1958, Aug. 19 ***Perf. 13x12½***
399 A126 5pf gray & black *1.00* *.70*
400 A126 20pf dark red & gray .25 .20

Friedrich Schiller University in Jena, 400th anniv.

Soldier on Obstacle Course — A127

Arms Breaking A-Bomb — A128

Design: 20pf, Spartacist emblem. 25pf, Marching athletes, map and flag.

Perf. 13½x13

1958, Sept. 19 Litho. Wmk. 313
401 A127 10pf emerald & brn *1.00* *.70*
402 A127 20pf brown red & yel .20 .20
403 A127 25pf lt blue & red .20 .20
Nos. 401-403 (3) *1.40 1.10*

1st Spartacist Sports Meet of Friendly Armies, Leipzig, Sept. 20-28.

1958, Sept. 19 ***Perf. 13x13½***
404 A128 20pf rose red .20 .20
405 A128 25pf blue .30 .20

People's fight against atomic death.

Woman and Leipzig Railroad Station A129

Design: 25pf, Woman in Persian lamb coat and old City Hall, Leipzig.

1958, Aug. 29 ***Perf. 13x12½***
406 A129 10pf green, brn & blk .20 .20
407 A129 25pf blue & black .20 .20

Issued to publicize the 1958 Leipzig Fair.

Post Wagon, 17th Century A130

Design: 20pf, Mail train and plane.

1958, Oct. 23 **Wmk. 313**
408 A130 10pf green *1.40* *.80*
409 A130 20pf lake .30 .20

Issued for the Day of the Stamp.

Brandenburg Gate, Berlin — A131

Head from Greek Tomb — A132

1958, Nov. 29 ***Perf. 13x13½***
410 A131 20pf rose red .30 .20
411 A131 25pf dark blue *1.75 1.00*

Issued to commemorate 10 years of democratic city administration of Berlin.

1958, Dec. 2 ***Perf. 13½x13***

20pf, Giant's head from Pergamum frieze.

412 A132 10pf blue grn & blk *1.10* *.70*
413 A132 20pf dp rose & black .20 .20

Return of art treasures from Russia. See #484-486.

Negro and Caucasian Men — A133

Design: 25pf, Chinese and Caucasian girls.

1958, Dec. 10 ***Perf. 13x12½***
414 A133 10pf brt blue grn & blk .20 .20
415 A133 25pf blue & black *1.10* *.75*

10th anniv. of the signing of the Universal Declaration of Human Rights.

Worker and Soldier — A134

Otto Nuschke — A135

1958, Nov. 7 ***Perf. 12½x13***
416 A134 20pf blk, ver & dl pur *7.25 10.00*

40th anniv. of the Revolution of Nov. 7. (Stamp inscribed Nov. 9.) Withdrawn from sale on day of issue.

Perf. 13½x13

1958, Dec. 27 **Wmk. 313**
417 A135 20pf red .25 .20

First anniversary of the death of Otto Nuschke, vice president of the republic.

Communist Newspaper, "The Red Flag" — A136

1958, Dec. 30 ***Perf. 13x12½***
418 A136 20pf red .30 .25

German Communist Party, 40th anniv.

Rosa Luxemburg Addressing Crowd — A137

20pf, Karl Liebknecht addressing crowd.

Perf. 13x13½

1959, Jan. 15 **Wmk. 313**
419 A137 10pf blue green *1.40* *.85*
420 A137 20pf henna brn & blk .20 .20

40th anniversary of the death of Rosa Luxemburg and Karl Liebknecht.

Gewandhaus, Leipzig — A138

President Wilhelm Pieck — A139

Design: 25pf, Opening theme of Mendelssohn's A Major symphony.

1959, Feb. 28 Engr. ***Perf. 14***
421 A138 10pf green, *grnsh* .30 .25
422 A138 25pf blue, *bluish* *1.25 1.75*

150th anniversary of the birth of Felix Mendelssohn-Bartholdy, composer.

1959, Jan. 3 Photo. ***Perf. 13½x13***
423 A139 20pf henna brown .35 .20

83rd birthday of President Wilhelm Pieck. See No. 511.

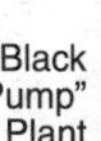
"Black Pump" Plant A140

Design: 25pf, Photographic equipment.

1959, Feb. 28 Litho. ***Perf. 13x12½***
424 A140 20pf carmine rose .20 .20
425 A140 25pf lt ultra .25 .20

1959 Leipzig Spring Fair.

Boy and Girl — A141

Statue of Handel, Halle — A142

1959, Apr. 2 ***Perf. 13½x13***
426 A141 10pf blk, *lt grn* *1.10* *.70*
427 A141 20pf blk, *salmon* .20 .20

5 years of the Youth Consecration ceremony.

1959, Apr. 27 **Wmk. 313**

20pf, Handel by Thomas Hudson, 1749.

428 A142 10pf bluish grn & blk *1.25* *.70*
429 A142 20pf rose & blk .20 .20

Bicentenary of the death of George Frederick Handel, composer.

Alexander von Humboldt and Central American View — A143

Post Horn — A144

Design: 20pf, Portrait and Siberian view.

1959, May 6
430 A143 10pf bluish grn *1.10* *.75*
431 A143 20pf rose .25 .20

Centenary of the death of Alexander von Humboldt, naturalist and geographer.

1959, May 30 ***Perf. 13½x13***
432 A144 20pf scar, yel & blk .20 .20
433 A144 25pf lt bl, yel & blk *.55 .45*

Conference of socialist postal ministers.

Gray Heron A145

10pf, Bittern. 20pf, Lily of the valley & butterfly. 25pf, Beaver. 40pf, Pussy willows and bee.

1959, June 26 ***Perf. 13x12½***
434 A145 5pf lt bl, blk & lil .20 .20
435 A145 10pf grnsh bl, dk brn & org .20 .20
436 A145 20pf org red, grn & vio .20 .20
437 A145 25pf lilac, yel & blk .25 .20
438 A145 40pf gray bl, yel & blk *4.25 2.40*
Nos. 434-438 (5) *5.10 3.20*

Issued to publicize wildlife protection.

Painting Type of 1955.

Famous Paintings: 5pf, Portrait, Angelica Kauffmann. 10pf, The Lady Lace Maker, Gabriel Metsu. 20pf, Mademoiselle Lavergne, Liotard. 25pf, Old Woman with Brazier, Rubens. 40pf, Young Man in Black Coat, Hals.

1959, June 29 Photo. ***Perf. 13½x13***

439 A77 5pf olive .20 .20
440 A77 10pf green .20 .20
441 A77 20pf dp org .20 .20
442 A77 25pf chestnut .25 .20
443 A77 40pf dp magenta *3.75 1.90*
Nos. 439-443 (5) *4.60 2.70*

Great Cormorant — A146

Youths of Three Races — A147

Birds: 10pf, Black Stork. 15pf, Eagle owl. 20pf, Black grouse. 25pf, Hoopoe. 40pf, Peregrine falcon.

Perf. 13x13½

1959, July 2 Litho. Wmk. 313

Designs in Black

444 A146 5pf yellow .20 .20
445 A146 10pf lt green .20 .20
446 A146 15pf pale violet *3.50 2.10*
447 A146 20pf deep pink .20 .20
448 A146 25pf blue .20 .20
449 A146 40pf vermilion .20 .20
Nos. 444-449 (6) *4.50 3.10*

Protection of native birds.

1959, July 25 ***Perf. 12½x13, 13x12½***

25pf, Swedish girl kissing African girl, horiz.

450 A147 20pf crimson .20 .20
451 A147 25pf bright blue *.50 .40*

7th World Youth Festival, Vienna, 7/26-8/14.

Glass Tea Service A148

Design: 25pf, Distilling apparatus, vert.

1959, Sept. 1 ***Perf. 13x12½, 12½x13***

452 A148 10pf bluish brown .20 .20
453 A148 25pf bright blue *1.25 .70*

75 years of Jena glassware.

Lunik 2 Hitting Moon — A149

1959, Sept. 21 ***Perf. 13½x13***

454 A149 20pf rose red .45 .30

Landing of the Soviet rocket Lunik 2 on the moon, Sept. 13, 1959.

New Buildings, Leipzig, Globe and Fair Emblem A150

1959, Aug. 17 ***Perf. 13x12½***

455 A150 20pf gray & rose .30 .25

1959 Leipzig Fall Fair.

Flag and Harvester — A151

Johannes R. Becher — A152

10pf, Fritz Heckert rest home. 15pf, Zwinger, Dresden. 20pf, Steelworker. 25pf, Chemist. 40pf, Central Stadium, Leipzig. 50pf, Woman tractor driver. 60pf, Airplane. 70pf, Merchant ship. 1m, 1st atomic reactor of the DDR.

1959, Oct. 6 ***Perf. 13½x13***

Flag in Black, Red & Orange Yellow Inscription and Design in Black & Red

456 A151 5pf yellow .20 .20
457 A151 10pf gray .20 .20
458 A151 15pf citron .20 .20
459 A151 20pf gray .20 .20
460 A151 25pf lt gray olive .20 .20
461 A151 40pf citron .20 .20
462 A151 50pf salmon .20 .20
463 A151 60pf pale bluish grn .20 .20
464 A151 70pf pale grnsh yel .20 .20
465 A151 1m bister brn .30 .25
Nos. 456-465 (10) 2.10 2.05

German Democratic Republic, 10th anniv.

1959, Oct. 28 Litho. ***Perf. 13x13½***

466 A152 20pf red & slate .90 .20

1st anniversary of the death of Johannes R. Becher, writer.

Printed with alternating yellow labels. The label carries in blue a verse from the national anthem and Becher's signature.

Schiller's Home, Weimar — A153

Post Rider and Mile Stone, 18th Century — A154

Design: 20pf, Friedrich von Schiller.

1959, Nov. 10 Engr. ***Perf. 14***

467 A153 10pf dull green, *grnsh* *1.10 .70*
468 A153 20pf lake, *pink* .40 .20

Birth of Friedrich von Schiller, 200th anniv.

1959, Nov. 17 Litho. ***Perf. 13½x13***

Design: 20pf, Motorized mailman.

469 A154 10pf green *1.00 .65*
470 A154 20pf dk car rose .20 .20

Issued for the Day of the Stamp.

Red Squirrels A155

1959, Nov. 27 ***Perf. 13x12½***

471 A155 5pf shown .25 .20
472 A155 10pf Hares .30 .20
473 A155 20pf Roe deer .30 .20
474 A155 25pf Red deer .40 .20
475 A155 40pf Lynx *5.75 2.10*
Nos. 471-475 (5) *7.00 2.90*

Redrawn Types of 1953 Without Imprint

Perf. 14, 13x12½ (#477)

1959-60 Wmk. 313 Typo.

476 A43 5pf emerald .20 .20
477 A43 10pf lt bl grn *(Machinists)* .20 .20
a. Perf. 14 .60 .20
b. Bklt. pane of 6 #477b 3.00
478 A43 20pf carmine .25 .20
a. Se-tenant with DEBRIA label .95 .20
479 A43 30pf dull red .20 .20
480 A43 40pf rose violet .20 .20
481 A43 50pf brt blue .25 .20
482 A43 70pf choc ('60) .25 .20
Nos. 476-482 (7) 1.55 1.40

No. 478a was issued Sept. 3, 1959, to commemorate the 2nd German Stamp Exhibition, Berlin. Sheet contains 60 stamps, 40 labels.

Two other stamps without imprint are Nos. 331-332.

Type of 1958 and

Pergamum Altar of Zeus — A156

Designs: 5pf, Head of an Attic goddess, 580 B.C. 10pf, Head of a princess from Tell el Amarna, 1360 B.C. 20pf, Bronze figure from Toprak-Kale (Armenia), 7th century B.C.

1959, Dec. 29 Litho. ***Perf. 13½x13***

484 A132 5pf yellow & black .20 .20
485 A132 10pf bluish grn & blk .20 .20
486 A132 20pf rose & black .20 .20
487 A156 25pf lt blue & blk *.70 .50*
Nos. 484-487 (4) *1.30 1.10*

Boxing — A157

10pf, Sprinters. 20pf, Ski jump. 25pf, Sailboat.

Perf. 13x13½

1960, Jan. 27 Wmk. 313

488 A157 5pf brown & ocher *3.25 1.75*
489 A157 10pf green & ocher .20 .20
490 A157 20pf car & ocher .20 .20
491 A157 25pf ultra & ocher .20 .20
Nos. 488-491 (4) *3.85 2.35*

1960 Winter and Summer Olympic Games.

Technical Fair, North Entrance A158

Design: 25pf, "Ring" Fair building.

1960, Feb. 17 ***Perf. 13x12½***

492 A158 20pf red & gray .20 .20
493 A158 25pf lt blue & gray .20 .20

1960 Leipzig Spring Fair.

Purple Foxglove A159

Lenin A160

Medicinal Plants: 10pf, Camomile. 15pf, Peppermint. 20pf, Poppy. 40pf, Dog rose.

1960, Apr. 7 ***Perf. 12½x13***

494 A159 5pf grn, gray & car rose .20 .20
495 A159 10pf citron, gray & grn .20 .20
496 A159 15pf fawn, gray & grn .20 .20
497 A159 20pf grnsh bl, gray & vio .20 .20
498 A159 40pf brn, gray, grn & red *3.75 1.50*
Nos. 494-498 (5) *4.55 2.30*

1960, Apr. 22 Engr. ***Perf. 14***

499 A160 20pf lake .30 .20

90th anniversary of the birth of Lenin.

No. 390 Overprinted: "Inbetriebnahme des Hochseehafens 1.Mai 1960"

1960, Apr. 28 Litho. ***Perf. 13½x13***

500 A122 10pf emerald .30 .25

Inauguration of the seaport Rostock.

Russian Soldier and Liberated Prisoner — A161

1960, May 5 Litho. ***Perf. 13x13½***

501 A161 20pf rose red .25 .25

15th anniv. of Germany's liberation from fascism.

Model of Vacation Ship — A162

Designs: 25pf, Ship before Leningrad.

Perf. 13½x13

1960, June 23 Wmk. 313

502 A162 5pf slate, cit & blk .20 .20
503 A162 25pf blk, yel & ultra *3.25 2.75*
Nos. 502-503,B58-B59 (4) *3.85 3.35*

Launching of the trade union (FDGB) vacation ship, June 25, 1960.

Masked Dancer in Porcelain A163

Lenin Monument, Eisleben A164

Meissen porcelain: 10pf, Plate with Meissen mark and date. 15pf, Otter. 20pf, Potter. 25pf, Coffee pot.

1960, July 28 ***Perf. 12½x13***

504 A163 5pf blue & orange .20 .20
505 A163 10pf blue & emerald .20 .20
506 A163 15pf blue & purple *2.50 2.25*
507 A163 20pf blue & orange red .20 .20
508 A163 25pf blue & apple grn .20 .20
Nos. 504-508 (5) *3.30 3.05*

Meissen porcelain works, 250th anniv.

Perf. 13x13½

1960, July 2 Wmk. 313

Design: 20pf, Thälmann monument, gift for Pushkin, USSR.

509 A164 10pf dark green .20 .20
510 A164 20pf bright red .20 .20

Pieck Type of 1959

1960, Sept. 10 Litho. *Perf. 13½x13*

511 A139 20pf black .25 .25
a. Souv. sheet of 1, imperf. 1.00 1.50

Pres. Wilhelm Pieck (1876-1960).

Modern Postal Trucks A165

Design: 25pf, Railroad mail car, 19th cent.

1960, Oct. 6 *Perf. 13x12½*

512 A165 20pf car rose, blk & yel .20 .20
513 A165 25pf blue, gray & blk *1.75 1.00*

Issued for the Day of the Stamp, 1960.

New Opera House, Leipzig A166

Design: 25pf, Car, sailboat, tent, campers.

1960, Aug. 29 Wmk. 313

514 A166 20pf rose brn & gray .20 .20
515 A166 25pf blue & grysh brn .25 .25

1960 Leipzig Fall Fair.

Hans Burkmair Medal, 1518 A167

Neidhardt von Gneisenau A168

25pf, Dancing Peasants by Albrecht Dürer.

1960, Oct. 20 Litho. *Perf. 12½x13*

516 A167 20pf buff, grn & ocher .20 .20
517 A167 25pf lt blue & blk *1.10 1.10*

400th anniv. of the Dresden Art Gallery.

1960, Oct. 27 *Perf. 13x12½, 12½x13*

20pf, Neidhardt von Gneisenau, horiz.

518 A168 20pf dk car & blk .20 .20
519 A168 25pf ultra *.90 .80*

200th anniversary of the birth of Count August Neidhardt von Gneisenau, Prussian Field Marshal.

Rudolf Virchow A169

Humboldt University, Berlin — A170

10pf, Robert Koch. 25pf, Wilheim & Alexander von Humboldt medal. 40pf, Wilheim Griesinger.

1960, Nov. 4 Litho. *Perf. 13x12½*

520 A169 5pf ocher & blk .20 .20
521 A169 10pf green & blk .20 .20
522 A170 20pf cop red, gray & blk .20 .20
523 A170 25pf brt blue & blk .20 .20
524 A169 40pf car rose & blk *1.75 1.00*
Nos. 520-524 (5) *2.55 1.80*

Nos. 520, 521, 524 for the 250th anniv. of the Charité (hospital), Berlin; Nos. 522-523 the 150th anniv. of Humboldt University, Berlin.

Nos. 520 and 523, and Nos. 521 and 522 are printed se-tenant.

Scientist and Chemical Formula — A171

Designs: 10pf, Chemistry worker (fertilizer). 20pf, Woman worker (automobile). 25pf, Laboratory assistant (synthetic fabrics).

Perf. 13x13½

1960, Nov. 10 Wmk. 313

525 A171 5pf dk red & gray .20 .20
526 A171 10pf orange & brt grn .20 .20
527 A171 20pf blue & red .20 .20
528 A171 25pf yellow & ultra *1.25 1.50*
Nos. 525-528 (4) *1.85 2.10*

Day of the Chemistry Worker.

"Young Socialists' Express" A172

20pf, Sassnitz Harbor station & ferry. 25pf, Diesel locomotive & 1835 "Adler."

Perf. 13x13½; 13x12½ (20pf)

1960, Dec. 5

Sizes: 10pf, 25pf, 28x23mm; 20pf, 38½x22mm

529 A172 10pf emerald & blk .20 .20
530 A172 20pf red & blk .20 .20
531 A172 25pf blue & blk *3.25 2.75*
Nos. 529-531 (3) *3.65 3.15*

125th anniv. of German railroads. No. 530 exists imperf. Value $3.50.

Pieck Type of 1953 with Dates Added

1961, Jan. 3 Photo. *Perf. 13x13½*

532 A35 20pf henna brn & blk .30 .25

Issued on the 85th anniversary of the birth of Pres. Wilhelm Pieck (1876-1960).

380 Kilovolt Switch A173

Lilienstein A174

Design: 25pf, Leipzig Press Center.

1961, Mar. 3 Litho. *Perf. 13½x13*

533 A173 10pf brt grn & dk gray .25 .20
534 A173 25pf vio blue & dk gray .25 .20

Leipzig Spring Fair of 1961.

1961 Typo. *Perf. 14*

Designs: 5pf, Rudelsburg on Saale. 10pf, Wartburg. No. 538, City Hall, Wernigerode. 25pf, Brocken, Harz Mts., horiz.

535 A174 5pf gray .20 .20
536 A174 10pf blue green .20 .20
537 A174 20pf red brown .20 .20
538 A174 20pf dull red .20 .20
539 A174 25pf dark blue .20 .20
Nos. 535-539 (5) 1.00 1.00

Issued: #538, 25pf, 3/14; 5pf, 10pf, #537, 6/22.

Trawler — A176

Designs: 20pf, Fishermen. 25pf, S.S. Robert Koch. 40pf, Cannery worker.

1961, Apr. 4 Engr. Wmk. 313

545 A176 10pf gray green .20 .20
546 A176 20pf claret .20 .20
547 A176 25pf slate .20 .20
548 A176 40pf dull violet *1.60 1.10*
Nos. 545-548 (4) *2.20 1.70*

Deep-sea fishing industry.

Vostok 1 Leaving Earth A177

Designs: 20pf, Cosmonaut in capsule. 25pf, Parachute landing of capsule.

1961, Apr. Litho. *Perf. 13x12½*

549 A177 10pf lt blue grn & red .50 .40
550 A177 20pf red .50 .40
551 A177 25pf lt blue *3.00 2.75*
Nos. 549-551 (3) *4.00 3.55*

1st man in space, Yuri A. Gagarin, 4/12/61. Issue dates: 10pf, Apr. 18; others, Apr. 20.

Zebra A178

Dresden Zoo cent.: 20pf, Black-and-white colobus monkeys.

1961, May 9

552 A178 10pf green & blk *3.50 2.75*
553 A178 20pf lilac rose & blk .30 .25

Engels, Marx, Lenin and Crowd — A179

1961, Apr. 20 Litho. *Perf. 13½x13*

554 A179 20pf red .35 .25

15th anniversary of Socialist Unity Party of Germany (SED).

Stag Leap — A180

Designs: 20pf, Arabesque. 25pf, Exercise on parallel bars, horiz.

1961, June 3 *Perf. 13½x13, 13x13½*

555 A180 10pf blue green .20 .20
556 A180 20pf rose pink .20 .20
557 A180 25pf brt blue *3.75 3.00*
Nos. 555-557 (3) *4.15 3.40*

3rd Europa Cup for Women's Gymnastics.

Salt Miners and Castle Giebichenstein — A181

20pf, Chemist and "Five Towers" of Halle.

1961, June 22 *Perf. 13x12½*

558 A181 10pf blk, grn & yel *1.75 .90*
559 A181 20pf blk, dk red & yel .20 .20

1000th anniv. of the founding of Halle.

Kayak Slalom A182

10pf, Canoe. 20pf, Two seater canoe.

1961, July 6 Litho. Wmk. 313

560 A182 5pf gray & Prus bl *2.00 1.75*
561 A182 10pf gray & slate grn .20 .20
562 A182 20pf gray & dk car rose .20 .20
Nos. 560-562 (3) *2.40 2.15*

Canoe Slalom and Rapids World Championships.

Target Line Casting A183

Design: 20pf, River fishing.

1961, July 21

563 A183 10pf green & blue *1.75 1.40*
564 A183 20pf dk red brn & blue .25 .20

World Fishing Championships, Dresden.

Tulip — A184

"Alte Waage," Historical Building, Leipzig — A185

1961, Sept. 13 Photo. *Perf. 14*

565 A184 10pf shown .20 .20
566 A184 20pf Dahlia .20 .20
567 A184 40pf Rose *5.50 5.75*
Nos. 565-567 (3) *5.90 6.15*

Intl. Horticulture Exhibition, Erfurt.

Perf. 13½x13

1961, Aug. 23 Litho. Wmk. 313

Design: 25pf, Old Exchange Building.

568 A185 10pf citron & bl grn .20 .20
569 A185 25pf lt blue & ultra .65 .25

1961 Leipzig Fall Fair. See Nos. 595-597.

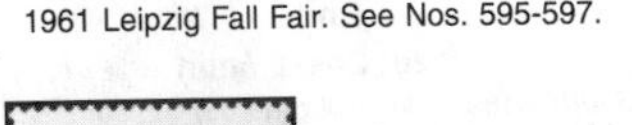

Liszt's Hand, French Sculpture — A186

Television Camera and Screen — A187

Designs: 5pf, Liszt and Hector Berlioz. 20pf, Franz Liszt, medallion by Ernst Rietschel, 1852. 25pf, Liszt and Frederic Chopin.

1961, Oct.-Nov. Engr. *Perf. 14*

570 A186 5pf gray .20 .20
571 A186 10pf blue green *1.50 1.40*
572 A186 20pf dull red .20 .20
573 A186 25pf chalky blue *1.75 1.75*
Nos. 570-573 (4) *3.65 3.55*

150th anniversary of the birth of Franz Liszt, composer.

1961, Oct. 25 *Perf. 13x13½*

Design: 20pf, Microphone and radio dial.

574 A187 10pf brt green & blk *1.10 1.50*
575 A187 20pf brick red & blk .20 .20

Issued for Stamp Day, 1961.

Maj. Gherman Titov and Young Pioneers — A188

10pf, Titov in Leipzig, vert. 15pf, Titov in spaceship. 20pf, Titov & Walter Ulbricht. 25pf, Spaceship Vostok 2. 40pf, Titov & Ulbricht in Berlin.

1961, Dec. 11 Litho. *Perf. 13½*

576 A188 5pf carmine & vio .20 .20
577 A188 10pf olive grn & car .20 .20
578 A188 15pf blue & lilac *5.00 5.25*
579 A188 20pf blue & car rose .20 .20
580 A188 25pf carmine & blue .20 .20
581 A188 40pf car & dk blue .85 .30
Nos. 576-581 (6) *6.65 6.35*

Visit of Russian Maj. Gherman Titov to the German Democratic Republic.

Chairman Walter Ulbricht — A189

1961-67 Wmk. 313 Typo. *Perf. 14*
Size: 17x21mm

582 A189 5pf slate .20 .20
 a. Booklet pane of 8 9.25 13.00
583 A189 10pf brt green .20 .20
 a. Booklet pane of 8 5.25 8.75
584 A189 15pf red lilac .25 .20
585 A189 20pf dark red .30 .20
586 A189 25pf dull bl ('63) .25 .20
587 A189 30pf car rose ('63) .20 .20
588 A189 40pf brt vio ('63) .20 .20
589 A189 50pf ultra ('63) .20 .20
589A A189 60pf dp yel grn ('64) .25 .20
590 A189 70pf red brn ('63) .25 .20
590A A189 80pf brt blue ('67) .40 .40

Engr.
Size: 24x28½mm

590B A189 1dm dull grn ('63) .60 .25
590C A189 2dm brown ('63) 1.10 .40
Nos. 582-590C (13) 4.40 3.05

See #751-752, 1112A-1114A, 1483. Currency abbreviation is "DM" on #590B-590C, "MDN" on #751-752, "M" on #1113-1114A.

Red Ants A190

1962, Feb. 16 Photo.

591 A190 5pf shown *2.25 3.75*
592 A190 10pf Weasels .20 .20
593 A190 20pf Shrews .20 .20
594 A190 40pf Bat .40 .30
Nos. 591-594 (4) *3.05 4.45*

See Nos. 663-667.

Type of 1961

Buildings: 10pf, "Coffee Tree House." 20pf, Gohlis Castle. 25pf, Romanus House.

1962, Feb. 22 Litho. *Perf. 13x13½*

595 A185 10pf olive grn & brn .20 .20
596 A185 20pf orange red & blk .25 .20
597 A185 25pf brt blue & brn .50 .50
Nos. 595-597 (3) .95 .90

Leipzig Spring Fair of 1962.

Air Defense A191

Designs: 10pf, Motorized infantry. 20pf, Soldier and worker as protectors. 25pf, Sailor and destroyer escort. 40pf, Tank and tankman.

1962, Mar. 1 *Perf. 13x12½*

598 A191 5pf light blue .20 .20
599 A191 10pf bright green .20 .20
600 A191 20pf red .20 .20
601 A191 25pf ultra .20 .25
602 A191 40pf brown *1.00 .90*
Nos. 598-602 (5) *1.80 1.75*

National People's Army, 6th anniv.

Cyclists and Hradcany, Prague — A192

25pf, Cyclist, East Berlin City Hall and dove.

1962, Apr. 26 Litho. Wmk. 313

603 A192 10pf multicolored .20 .20
604 A192 25pf multicolored *1.10 .85*
Nos. 603-604,B89 (3) *1.50 1.25*

15th International Bicycle Peace Race, Berlin-Warsaw-Prague.

Johann Gottlieb Fichte — A193

10pf, Fichte's birthplace in Rammenau.

1962, May 17 *Perf. 13x13½*

605 A193 10pf brt green & blk *1.10 1.25*
606 A193 20pf vermilion & blk .20 .20

Bicentenary of the birth of Johann Gottlieb Fichte, philosopher.

Cross, Crown of Thorns and Rose — A194

George Dimitrov at Reichstag Trial, Leipzig — A195

1962, June 7 *Perf. 12½x13*

607 A194 20pf red & black .20 .20
608 A194 25pf brt blue & blk *.90 .65*

20th anniversary of the destruction of Lidice in Czechoslovakia by the Nazis.

1962, June 18 Photo. *Perf. 14*

20pf, Dimitrov as Premier of Bulgaria.

609 A195 5pf blue grn & blk *.45 .25*
610 A195 20pf car rose & blk .20 .20
 a. Pair, #609-610, + label 4.50 *25.00*

George Dimitrov, (1882-1949), communist leader and premier of the Bulgarian Peoples' Republic.

Nos. 609-610 also printed se-tenant, divided by a label inscribed with a Dimitrov quotation.

Corn Planter A196

20pf, Milking machine. 40pf, Combine harvester.

1962, June 26 Litho. *Perf. 13x12½*

611 A196 10pf multicolored .20 .20
612 A196 20pf multicolored .20 .20
613 A196 40pf yel, grn & dk red *1.25 1.00*
Nos. 611-613 (3) *1.65 1.40*

10th Agricultural Exhibition, Markkleeberg.

Map of Baltic Sea and Emblem — A197

Designs: 20pf, Hotel, Rostock, vert. 25pf, Cargo ship "Frieden" in Rostock harbor.

Perf. 13x13½, 13½x13 (20pf)
1962, July 2 Wmk. 313

614 A197 10pf bluish grn & ultra .20 .20
615 A197 20pf dk red & yellow .20 .20
616 A197 25pf blue & bister *1.60 1.25*
Nos. 614-616 (3) *2.00 1.65*

5th Baltic Sea Week, Rostock, July 7-15.

Brandenburg Gate, Berlin — A198

1962, July 17 *Perf. 13½x13*

#618 Heads of youths of three races. #619, Peace dove. #620, National Theater, Helsinki.

617 A198 5pf multicolored *1.60 1.50*
618 A198 5pf multicolored *1.60 1.50*
619 A198 20pf multicolored *1.60 1.50*
620 A198 20pf multicolored *1.60 1.50*
 a. Block of 4, #617-620 *8.50 5.75*
Nos. 617-620,B90-B91 (6) *6.90 6.40*

8th Youth Festival for Peace and Friendship, Helsinki, July 28-Aug. 6, 1962.

No. 620a forms the festival flower emblem.

Free Style Swimming A199

Designs: 10pf, Back stroke. 25pf, Butterfly stroke. 40pf, Breast stroke. 70pf, Water polo.

1962, Aug. 7 Litho. *Perf. 13x13½*
Design in Greenish Blue

621 A199 5pf orange .20 .20
622 A199 10pf grnsh blue .20 .20
623 A199 25pf ultra .20 .20
624 A199 40pf brt violet *1.00 1.00*
625 A199 70pf red brown .20 .20
 a. Block of 6, #621-625, B92 *1.50 1.50*
Nos. 621-625,B92 (6) *2.00 2.00*

10th European Swimming Championships. Leipzig, Aug. 18-25.

Nos. 621-625, B92 each printed in sheets of 50, No. 625a in sheet of 60.

Municipal Store, Leipzig — A200

Engr. & Photo.
1962, Aug. 28 Wmk. 313 *Perf. 14*

Buildings: 20pf, Mädler Passage. 25pf, Leipzig Air Terminal and plane.

626 A200 10pf black & emerald .20 .20
627 A200 20pf black & red .25 .20
628 A200 25pf black & blue .55 .40
Nos. 626-628 (3) 1.00 .80

Leipzig Fall Fair of 1962.

"Transportation and Communication" — A201

1962, Oct. 3 Litho. *Perf. 13½x13*

629 A201 5pf light blue & black .25 .20

10th anniv. of the Friedrich List Transportation College.

Souvenir Sheet

ERSTER GRUPPENFLUG IM KOSMOS

WOSTOK III 11.8.1962. 9.30 Uhr. bis 15.8.1962. 7.55 Uhr (MEZ)
WOSTOK IV 12.8.1962. 9.02 Uhr. bis 15.8.1962. 8.01 Uhr (MEZ)

Pavel R. Popovich, Andrian G. Nikolayev and Space Capsules — A202

1962, Sept. 13 Wmk. 313 *Imperf.*

630 A202 70pf dk blue, lt grn & yel *1.50 3.50*

1st Russian group space flight of Vostoks III and IV, Aug. 11-13, 1962.

DDR Television Signal A203

Young Collectors and World Map — A204

1962, Oct. 25 *Perf. 13½x13*

631 A203 20pf green & gray .20 .20
632 A204 40pf brt pink & blk *1.25 1.25*

No. 631 for the 10th anniv. of television in the German Democratic Republic; No. 632 is for Stamp Day.

Gerhart Hauptmann A205

1962, Nov. 15 *Perf. 13x13½*

633 A205 20pf red & black .30 .20

Centenary of the birth of Gerhart Hauptmann, playwright.

Souvenir Sheet

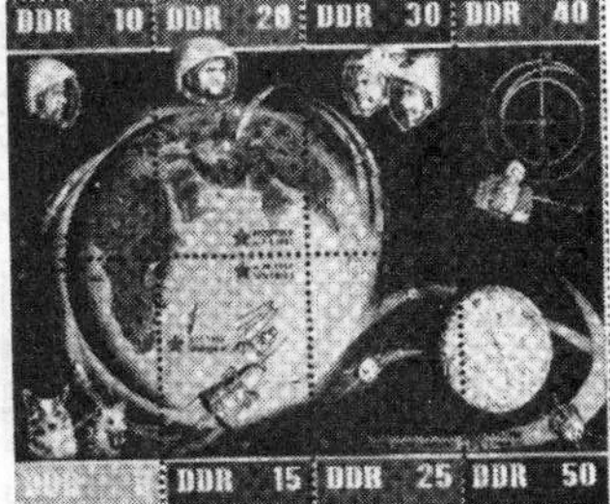

Russian Space Flights and Astronauts — A206

1962, Dec. 28 **Litho.** *Perf. 12½x13*

634 A206 Sheet of 8 24.00 29.00
- *a.* 5pf yellow 1.25 1.40
- *b.* 10pf emerald 1.25 1.40
- *c.* 15pf magenta 2.10 2.40
- *d.* 20pf red 2.10 2.40
- *e.* 25pf greenish blue 2.10 2.40
- *f.* 30pf red brown 2.10 2.40
- *g.* 40pf crimson 1.25 1.40
- *h.* 50pf ultramarine 1.25 1.40

Issued to show the development of Russian space flights from Sputnik 1 to Vostoks 3 and 4, and to honor the Russian astronauts Gagarin, Titov, Nikolayev and Popovich.

Pierre de Coubertin — A207

Design: 25pf, Stadium and Olympic rings.

1963, Jan. 2 *Perf. 13½x13*

635 A207 20pf carmine & gray .20 .20
636 A207 25pf blue & bister 1.25 1.50

Baron Pierre de Coubertin, organizer of the modern Olympic Games, birth cent.

Congress Emblem, Flag with Marx, Engels and Lenin — A208

1963, Jan. 15 *Perf. 13x13½*

637 A208 10pf yel, org, red & blk .25 .20

6th congress of Socialist Unity Party of Germany (SED).

World Map and Exterminator — A209

Designs: 25pf, Map, cross and staff of Aesculapius. 50pf, Map, cross, mosquito.

1963, Feb. 6 *Perf. 13x12½*

638 A209 20pf dp org, dk red & blk .20 .20
639 A209 25pf multicolored .20 .20
640 A209 50pf multicolored .95 .75
Nos. 638-640 (3) 1.35 1.15

WHO drive to eradicate malaria.

Silver Fox A210

Design: 25pf, Karakul.

1963, Feb. 14 **Photo.** *Perf. 14*

641 A210 20pf rose & black .20 .20
642 A210 25pf blue & black 1.10 1.40

Intl. Fur Auctions, Leipzig, 2/14-15, 4/21-24.

Barthels House, Leipzig — A211

Designs: 20pf, New Leipzig City Hall. 25pf, Belltower Building.

1963, Feb. 26 **Wmk. 313** *Perf. 14*

Engr. & Photo.

643 A211 10pf black & citron .20 .20
644 A211 20pf black & red org .25 .20
645 A211 25pf black & blue .80 .70
Nos. 643-645 (3) 1.25 1.10

1963 Leipzig Spring Fair.

Souvenir Sheet

On March 12, 1963, a souvenir sheet publicizing "Chemistry for Peace and Socialism" was issued. It contains two imperforate stamps, 50pf and 70pf, printed on ungummed synthetic tissue. Size: 105x74mm. Value $2.75.

Richard Wagner and "The Flying Dutchman" — A213

Portrait & Scene from Play: 5pf, Johann Gottfried Seume (1763-1810). 10pf, Friedrich Hebbel (1813-63). 20pf, Georg Büchner (1813-37).

1963, Apr. 9 **Litho.** *Perf. 13x12½*

647 A213 5pf brt citron & blk .20 .20
648 A213 10pf brt green & blk .20 .20
649 A213 20pf orange & blk .20 .20
650 A213 25pf dull blue & blk 1.25 1.00
Nos. 647-650 (4) 1.85 1.60

Anniversaries of German dramatists and the 150th anniv. of the birth of Richard Wagner, composer.

First Aid Station A214

Design: 20pf, Ambulance and hospital.

1963, May 14 **Wmk. 313**

651 A214 10pf multicolored .90 .70
652 A214 20pf red, blk & gray .20 .20

Centenary of International Red Cross.

Eugene Pottier, Writer — A215

25pf, Pierre-Chretien Degeyter, composer.

1963, June 18 *Perf. 13x13½*

653 A215 20pf vermilion & blk .20 .20
654 A215 25pf vio blue & blk .90 .80

75th anniv. of the communist song "The International."

A216

No. 655, Valentina Tereshkova, Vostok 6. No. 656, Valeri Bykovski, Vostok 5.

1963, July 18 **Photo.** *Perf. 13½*

655 20pf blue, blk & gray bl .65 .20
656 20pf blue, blk & gray bl .65 .20
- *a.* A216 Pair, #655-656 1.50 .30

Space flights of Valeri Bykovski, June 14-19, and Valentina Tereshkova, 1st woman cosmonaut, June 16-19, 1963.

Motorcyclist in "Motocross" at Apolda — A217

Engr. & Photo.

1963, July 30 *Perf. 14*

20pf, Motorcyclist at Sachsenring, horiz. 25pf, 2 motorcyclists at Sachsenring, horiz.

Size: 23x28mm

657 A217 10pf lt grn & dk grn 3.00 2.50

Size: 48½x21mm

658 A217 20pf rose & dk red .20 .20
659 A217 25pf lt blue & dk blue .20 .20
Nos. 657-659 (3) 3.40 2.90

Motorcycle World Championships.

Monument at Treblinka A218

Perf. 13x13½

1963, Aug. 20 **Litho.** **Wmk. 313**

660 A218 20pf brick red & dk blue .25 .20

Erection of a memorial at Treblinka (Poland) concentration camp.

Globe, Car and Train — A219

1963, Aug. 27 *Perf. 13½x13*

Design: No. 662, Globe, plane and bus.

661 A219 10pf multicolored .60 .20
662 A219 10pf multicolored .60 .20
- *a.* Pair, #661-662 1.75 .25

Issued to publicize the 1963 Leipzig Fall Fair.

Fauna Type of 1962

10pf, Stag beetle. 20pf, Fire salamander. 30pf, Pond turtle. 50pf, Green toad. 70pf, Hedgehogs.

1963, Sept. 10 **Photo.** *Perf. 14*

663 A190 10pf emer, brn & blk .20 .20
664 A190 20pf crimson, blk & yel .20 .20
665 A190 30pf multicolored .20 .20
666 A190 50pf multicolored 2.50 2.10
667 A190 70pf claret brn, brn & bis .45 .35
Nos. 663-667 (5) 3.55 3.05

Neidhardt von Gneisenau and Gebhard Leberecht von Blücher — A220

Designs: 10pf, Cossacks and home guard, Berlin. 20pf, Ernst Moritz Arndt and Baron Heinrich vom Stein. 25pf, Lützow's volunteers before battle. 40pf, Gerhard von Scharnhorst and Prince Mikhail I. Kutuzov.

1963, Oct. 10 **Litho.** *Perf. 13½x13*

Center in Tan and Black

668 A220 5pf brt yellow .20 .20
669 A220 10pf emerald .20 .20
670 A220 20pf dp orange .20 .20
671 A220 25pf dp ultra .20 .20
672 A220 40pf dark red 1.60 .60
Nos. 668-672 (5) 2.40 1.40

150th anniversary of War of Liberation.

Valentina Tereshkova and Space Craft — A221

Burning Synagogue and Star of David in Chains — A222

#674, Tereshkova and map of DDR, vert. #675, Yuri A. Gagarin and map of DDR, vert. 25pf, Tereshkova in space capsule.

1963 *Perf. 13½x13, 13x13½*

Size: 28x28mm (10pf, 25pf); 28x37mm (20pf)

673 A221 10pf ultra & green .20 .20
674 A221 20pf red, blk & ocher .20 .20
675 A221 20pf red, grn & ocher .20 .20
676 A221 25pf orange & blue 2.75 1.60
Nos. 673-676 (4) 3.35 2.20

Visit of astronauts Valentina Tereshkova & Yuri A. Gagarin to the German Democratic Republic.

Perf. 13½x13

1963, Nov. 8 **Wmk. 313**

677 A222 10pf multicolored .25 .20

25th anniv. of the "Crystal Night," the start of the systematic persecution of the Jews in Germany. Inscribed: "Never again Crystal Night."

Letter Sorting Machine A223

Design: 20pf, Mechanized mail loading.

1963, Nov. 25 *Perf. 13x12½*

678 A223 10pf multicolored 1.10 1.25
679 A223 20pf multicolored .20 .20

Issued for Stamp Day.

Ski Jump and Olympic Rings A224

1963, Dec. 16 Litho. ***Perf. 13½x13***

680 A224 5pf shown .20 .20
681 A224 10pf Start .20 .20
682 A224 25pf Landing *1.50 1.60*
Nos. 680-682,B111 (4) *2.10 2.20*

9th Winter Olympic Games, Innsbruck, Jan. 29-Feb. 9, 1964.

Admiral — A225

Butterflies: 15pf, Alpine Apollo. 20pf, Swallowtail. 25pf, Postilion. 40pf, Great fox.

Wmk. 313

1964, Jan. 15 Photo. ***Perf. 14***

Butterflies in Natural Colors

683 A225 10pf citron & blk .30 .20
684 A225 15pf pale violet & blk .30 .20
685 A225 20pf lt brick red & blk .30 .20
686 A225 25pf lt blue & dk brn .30 .20
687 A225 40pf lt ultra & blk *3.50 1.50*
Nos. 683-687 (5) *4.70 2.30*

William Shakespeare — A226

20pf, Quadriga, Brandenburg Gate, Berlin. 25pf, Keystone, History Museum (Zeughaus), Berlin.

1964, Feb. 6 Litho. ***Perf. 13x12½***

688 A226 20pf rose & dk blue .20 .20
689 A226 25pf lt blue & mag .20 .20
690 A226 40pf lt vio & dk bl grn *1.00 .70*
Nos. 688-690 (3) *1.40 1.10*

200th anniv. of the birth of the sculptor Johann Gottfried Schadow (20pf); 300th anniv. of the birth of the sculptor Andreas Schlüter (25pf); 400th anniv. of the birth of William Shakespeare, dramatist (40pf).

Electrical Engineering Exhibit — A227

20pf, Bräunigkes Court, exhibition hall, 1700.

Perf. 13x13½

1964, Feb. 26 Wmk. 313

691 A227 10pf brt green & blk 2.00 .20
692 A227 20pf red & black 2.00 .20
a. Block, 1 each #661-662 + 2 labels 12.50 .75

Leipzig Spring Fair, Mar. 1-10, 1964.

Khrushchev and Inventors — A228

Youth Training for Leadership A229

40pf, Khrushchev, Tereshkova & Gagarin.

1964, May 15 ***Perf. 13x13½***

693 A228 25pf blue .20 .20
694 A228 40pf lilac & grnsh blk *2.10 1.40*

Issued in honor of Premier Nikita S. Khrushchev of the Soviet Union.

1964, May 13 Litho.

Designs: 20pf, Young athletes. 25pf, Accordion player and girl with flowers.

Center in Black

695 A229 10pf ultra, mag & emer .20 .20
696 A229 20pf emer, ultra & mag .20 .20
697 A229 25pf magenta, emer & ultra *1.00 .55*
Nos. 695-697 (3) *1.40 .95*

German Youth Meeting, Berlin.

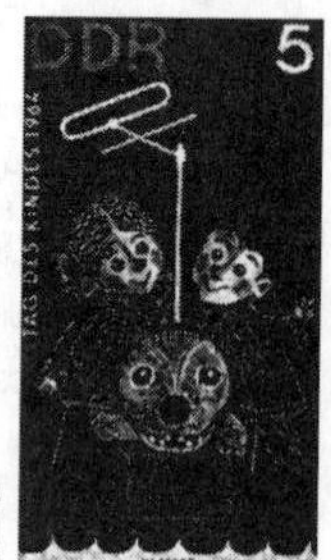

Television Antenna and Puppets — A230

Children's Day: Various characters from children's television programs.

1964, June 1 ***Perf. 13x13½***

698 A230 5pf multicolored .20 .20
699 A230 10pf multicolored .20 .20
700 A230 15pf multicolored .20 .20
701 A230 20pf multicolored .20 .20
702 A230 40pf multicolored *1.10 1.10*
Nos. 698-702 (5) *1.90 1.90*

Woman as Educator and Portrait of Jenny Marx — A231

Designs: 25pf, Women in industry and transistor diagram. 70pf, Women in agriculture.

Perf. 13½x13

1964, June 26 Litho. Wmk. 313

703 A231 20pf crimson, gray & yel .20 .20
704 A231 25pf lt blue, gray & red *.75 .60*
705 A231 70pf emerald, gray & yel .25 .20
Nos. 703-705 (3) *1.20 1.00*

Congress of Women of the German Democratic Republic, June 25-27.

Bicycling A232

Diving — A233

Litho. & Engr.

1964, July 15 ***Perf. 14***

706 A232 5pf shown .20 .20
707 A232 10pf Volleyball .20 .20
708 A232 20pf Judo .20 .20
709 A232 25pf Woman diver .20 .20
710 A232 70pf Equestrian *1.25 1.00*
Nos. 706-710,B118 (6) *2.30 2.00*

Litho.

Perf. 13x13½

711 A233 10pf shown 2.00 1.75
712 A233 10pf Volleyball 2.00 1.75
713 A233 10pf Bicycling 2.00 1.75
714 A233 10pf Judo 2.00 1.75
a. Block of 6, #711-714, B119-B120 17.00 16.00

18th Olympic Games, Tokyo, Oct. 10-25, 1964. See Nos. B118-B120. No. 714a printed in 2 horiz. rows: (1st: #711, #B119, #712. 2nd: #713, #B120, #714). The Olympic rings extend over the 6 stamps.

Monument, Leningrad A234

1964, Aug. 8 Litho. ***Perf. 13x13½***

715 A234 25pf brt blue, blk & yel .60 .20

Issued to honor the victims of the siege of Leningrad, Sept. 1941-Jan. 1943.

Bertha von Suttner — A235

Medieval Glazier and Goblet — A236

Designs: 20pf, Frederic Joliot Curie. 50pf, Carl von Ossietzky.

1964, Sept. 1 ***Perf. 14***

716 A235 20pf red & black .20 .20
717 A235 25pf ultra & black .20 .20
718 A235 50pf lilac & black *.90 .50*
Nos. 716-718 (3) *1.30 .90*

Issued to promote World Peace.

1964, Sept. 3 ***Perf. 14***

15pf, Jena glass for chemical industry.

719 A236 10pf lt ultra & multi .45 .20
720 A236 15pf red & multi .45 .20
a. Pair, #719-720 + label 1.60 .40

Issued for the Leipzig Fall Fair, 1964.

Handstamp of First Socialist International, 1864 — A237

1964, Sept. 16 Photo. Wmk. 313

721 A237 20pf orange red & blk .20 .20
722 A237 25pf dull blue & blk *.50 .45*

Centenary of First Socialist International.

Stamp of 1955 (Dürer's Portrait of Young Man) — A238

1964, Sept. 23 Litho. ***Perf. 13x13½***

723 A238 50pf gray & dk red brn *1.50 .90*
Nos. 723,B124-B125 (3) *1.95 1.30*

Natl. Stamp Exhibition, Berlin, Oct. 3-18.

Coal Transport A239

#724, Navigation. #725, Flag & new Berlin buildings. #727, Chemist. #728, Soldier. #729, Farm woman & cows. #730, Steel worker. #731, Woman scientist & lecture hall. #732, Heavy industry. #733, Optical industry. #734, Consumer goods (woman examining cloth). #735, Foreign trade, Leipzig fair emblem. #736, Buildings industry. #737, Sculptor. #738, Woman skier.

Perf. 13½x13

1964, Oct. 6 Litho. Wmk. 313

724 A239 10pf blue & multi .20 .20
725 A239 10pf blue & multi .20 .20
726 A239 10pf gray & multi .20 .20
727 A239 10pf red & multi .20 .20
728 A239 10pf red & multi .20 .20
729 A239 10pf yel grn & multi .20 .20
730 A239 10pf red & multi .20 .20
731 A239 10pf red & multi .20 .20
732 A239 10pf gray & multi .20 .20
733 A239 10pf gray & multi .20 .20
734 A239 10pf blue & multi .20 .20
735 A239 10pf blue & multi .20 .20
736 A239 10pf yel grn & multi .20 .20
737 A239 10pf yel grn & multi .20 .20
738 A239 10pf blue & multi .20 .20
Nos. 724-738 (15) *3.00 3.00*

German Democratic Republic, 15th anniv.

A souvenir sheet contains 15 imperf. stamps similar to #724-738. Size: 210x287mm. Value, $25.

For surcharge see No. B134.

Man from Mönchgut, Rügen — A240

1964, Nov. 25 Photo. ***Perf. 14***

Regional Costumes: No. 740, Woman from Mönchgut, Rügen. No. 741, Man from Spreewald. No. 742, Woman from Spreewald. No. 743, Man from Thuringia. No. 744, Woman from Thuringia.

739 A240 5pf multicolored *7.00 4.25*
740 A240 5pf multicolored *7.00 4.25*
a. Pair, #739-740 *15.00 9.00*
741 A240 10pf multicolored .25 .20
742 A240 10pf multicolored .25 .20
a. Pair, #741-742 .60 .40
743 A240 20pf multicolored .25 .20
744 A240 20pf multicolored .25 .20
a. Pair, #739-740 .60 .40
Nos. 739-744 (6) *15.00 9.30*

Printed in checkerboard arrangement.

See Nos. 859-864.

Souvenir Sheets

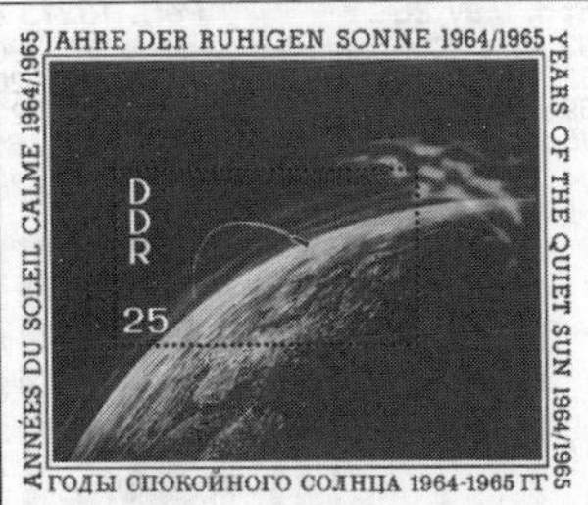

Exploration of Ionosphere — A241

Designs: 40pf, Exploration of sun activities. 70pf, Exploration of radiation belt.

1964, Dec. 29 Litho. *Perf. 13½x13*

745 A241 25pf vio bl & yel *4.00 6.00*
746 A241 40pf vio bl, yel & red *1.60 3.00*
747 A241 70pf dp grn, vio bl & yel *1.60 3.00*
Nos. 745-747 (3) 7.20 12.00

Intl. Quiet Sun Year, 1964-65.

Albert Schweitzer as Physician A242

August Bebel — A243

Designs (Schweitzer): 20pf, As fighter against war and atom bomb. 25pf, At the organ with score of Organ Prelude by Bach.

Wmk. 313

1965, Jan. 14 Photo. *Perf. 14*

748 A242 10pf emerald, blk & bis .20 .20
749 A242 20pf crimson, blk & bis .20 .20
750 A242 25pf blue, blk & bis *2.50 1.25*
Nos. 748-750 (3) 2.90 1.65

90th birthday of Dr. Albert Schweitzer, medical missionary.

Ulbricht Type of 1961-63

Currency in "Mark of the Deutsche Notenbank" (MDN)

1965, Feb. 10 Engr.

Size: 24x28½mm

751 A189 1mdn dull green .40 .30
752 A189 2mdn brown .45 .35

See note below Nos. 590B-590C.

1965 Photo. *Perf. 14*

10pf, Wilhelm Conrad Roentgen. #753A, Adolph von Menzel. 25pf, Wilhelm Külz. 40pf, Erich Weinert. 50pf, Dante Alighieri.

753 A243 10pf dk brn, yel & emer .30 .20
753A A243 10pf dk brn, yel & org .45 .20
754 A243 20pf ol brn, red & buff .30 .20
754A A243 25pf ol brn, yel & bl .55 .20
754B A243 40pf ol brn, buff & car rose .35 .20
755 A243 50pf dk brn, yel & org .85 .20
Nos. 753-755 (6) 2.80 1.20

Roentgen (1845-1923), physicist, discoverer of X-rays. Sesquicentennial of the birth of Adolph von Menzel, painter and graphic artist. Bebel, labor leader (1840-1913). 90th anniv. of the birth of Wilhelm Külz, politician. 75th anniv. of the birth of Erich Weinert, poet. Alighieri (1265-1321), Italian poet.

Issued: #753, 3/24; #753A, 12/8; 20pf, 2/22; 25pf, 7/5; 40pf, 7/28; 50pf, 4/15.

A244

A245

Designs: 10pf, Gold Medal, Leipzig Fair. 15pf, Obverse of medal, arms of German Democratic Republic. 25pf, Chemical plant.

1965, Feb. 25 Wmk. 313

756 A244 10pf lilac rose & gold .20 .20
757 A244 15pf lilac rose & gold .20 .20
758 A244 25pf brt blue, yel & gold .45 .20
Nos. 756-758 (3) .85 .60

1965 Leipzig Spring Fair; 800th anniv. of the Fair.

1965, Mar. 24

Designs: 10pf, Giraffe. 25pf, Common iguana, horiz. 30pf, White-tailed gnu.

759 A245 10pf green & gray .20 .20
760 A245 25pf dk vio bl & gray .20 .20
761 A245 30pf brown & gray *1.60 .90*
Nos. 759-761 (3) 2.00 1.30

10th anniversary of Berlin Zoo.

Col. Pavel Belyayev and Lt. Col. Alexei Leonov A246

25pf, Lt. Col. Leonov floating in space.

Perf. 13½x13

1965, Apr. 15 Litho. Wmk. 313

762 A246 10pf red .25 .20
763 A246 25pf dk ultra *1.75 1.00*

Space flight of Voskhod 2 and the first man walking in space, Lt. Col. Alexei Leonov.

Boxing Glove and Laurel Wreath — A247

1965, Apr. 27 Photo. *Perf. 14*

764 A247 20pf blk, red & gold *.70 .45*

16th European Boxing Championship, Berlin, May, 1965. See No. B126.

Walter Ulbricht and Erich Weinert Distributing "Free Germany" Leaflets on the Eastern Front — A248

50pf, Liberation of concentration camps. 60pf, Russian soldiers raising flag on Reichstag, Berlin. 70pf, Political demonstration.

1965, May 5 Photo. *Perf. 14*

Flags in Red, Black & Yellow

765 A248 40pf blue grn & red .20 .20
766 A248 50pf dull blue & red .20 .20
767 A248 60pf brown & red *1.60 1.25*
768 A248 70pf vio blue & red .20 .20
Nos. 765-768,B127-B131 (9) 3.20 2.85

20th anniv. of liberation from fascism.

Radio Tower and Globe A249

ITU Emblem and Frequency Diagram A250

40pf, Workers & broadcasting equipment.

1965, May 12 Litho. *Perf. 12½x13*

769 A249 20pf dk car rose & blk .25 .20
770 A249 40pf vio bl & blk *.90 .35*

20th anniv. of the German Democratic broadcasting system.

1965, May 17

25pf, ITU emblem & telephone diagram.

771 A250 20pf olive, yel & blk .25 .20
772 A250 25pf vio, pale vio & blk *1.40 .35*

Cent. of the ITU.

Emblem of Free German Trade Union — A251

Hemispheres with Crowd of Workers — A252

1965, June 10 Photo. *Perf. 14*

773 A251 20pf red & gold .20 .20
774 A252 25pf gold, blue & blk *.75 .30*

20th anniv. of the Free German Trade Union (FDGB) and of the World Organization of Trade Unions.

Symbols of Industry — A253

Marx and Lenin — A254

Designs: 20pf, Red Tower. 25pf, City Hall.

1965, June 16

775 A253 10pf gold & emerald .20 .20
776 A253 20pf gold & crimson .20 .20
777 A253 25pf gold & brt blue *.70 .30*
Nos. 775-777 (3) 1.10 .70

800th anniv. of Chemnitz (Karl Marx City).

1965, June 21 Litho. *Perf. 13½x13*

778 A254 20pf red, black & buff .25 .20

6th Conference of Postal Ministers of Communist Countries, Peking, June 21-July 15.

"Alte Waage" and New Building, Leipzig — A255

25pf, Old City Hall. 40pf, Opera House & General Post Office. 70pf, Hotel "Stadt Leipzig."

Unwmk.

1965, Aug. 25 Photo. *Perf. 14*

781 A255 10pf gold, cl brn & ultra .20 .20
a. Souv. sheet of 2, #781, 784 *2.10 3.00*
782 A255 25pf gold, brn, & ocher .20 .20
a. Souv. sheet of 2, #782-783 *1.10 2.50*
783 A255 40pf gold, brn, ocher & yel grn .20 .20
784 A255 70pf gold & ultra *1.40 .60*
Nos. 781-784 (4) 2.00 1.20

800th anniv. of the City of Leipzig. No. 781a sold for 90pf; No. 782a for 80pf. The souvenir sheets were issued Sept. 4, 1965.

Cameras A256

Equestrian A257

Leipzig Fall Fair: 15pf, Electric guitar and organ. 25pf, Microscope.

1965, Sept. 9 *Perf. 14*

785 A256 10pf green, blk & gold .20 .20
786 A256 15pf multicolored .20 .20
787 A256 25pf multicolored .45 .20
Nos. 785-787 (3) .85 .60

Perf. 13½x13

1965, Sept. 15 Litho. Unwmk.

789 A257 10pf shown .20 .20
790 A257 10pf Swimmer .20 .20
791 A257 10pf Runner *2.00 1.60*
Nos. 789-791,B135-B136 (5) 2.80 2.40

Intl. Modern Pentathlon Championships, Leipzig.

Alexei Leonov and Brandenburg Gate — A258

Memorial Monument, Putten — A259

Designs: No. 793, Pavel Belyayev and Berlin City Hall. 25pf, Leonov floating in space and space ship.

Wmk. 313

1965, Nov. 1 Litho. *Perf. 14*

Size: 23½x28½mm

792 A258 20pf blue, sil & red .40 .40
793 A258 20pf blue, sil & red .40 .40

Size: 51x28½mm

794 A258 25pf blue, sil & red .40 .40
a. Strip of 3, #792-794 *2.50 1.25*

Visit of the Russian astronauts to the German Democratic Republic.

1965, Nov. 19 ***Perf. 13x13½***
795 A259 25pf brt bl, pale yel & blk .50 .20

Issued in memory of the victims of a Nazi attack on Putten, Netherlands, Sept. 30, 1944.

Furnace A260

After old woodcuts: 15pf, Ore miners. 20pf, Proustite crystals. 25pf, Sulphur crystals.

Perf. 13x12½

1965, Nov. 11 Litho. Unwmk.
796 A260 10pf black & multi .20 .20
797 A260 15pf black & multi *.45 .45*
798 A260 20pf black & multi .20 .20
799 A260 25pf black & multi .20 .20
Nos. 796-799 (4) 1.05 1.05

Mining Academy in Freiberg, bicent.

Red Kite A261

Otto Grotewohl A262

Birds: 10pf, Lammergeier. 20pf, Buzzard. 25pf, Kestrel. 40pf, Northern goshawk. 70pf, Golden eagle.

1965, Dec. 8 Photo. ***Perf. 14***
Gold Frame
800 A261 5pf orange & blk .20 .20
801 A261 10pf emer, brn & blk .20 .20
802 A261 20pf car, red brn & blk .20 .20
803 A261 25pf blue, red brn & blk .20 .20
804 A261 40pf lilac, blk & dk red .25 .20
805 A261 70pf brn, blk & yel *3.25 1.50*
Nos. 800-805 (6) 4.30 2.50

1965, Dec. 14 Photo. Wmk. 313
806 A262 20pf black .55 .20

Issued in memory of Otto Grotewohl (1894-1964), prime minister (1949-1964).

Souvenir Sheet

Spartacus Letter, Karl Liebknecht and Rosa Luxemburg — A263

1966, Jan. 3 Unwmk.
807 A263 Sheet of 2 1.10 3.50
a. 20pf red & black .30 .25
b. 50pf red & black .30 .25

50th anniv. of the natl. conf. of the Spartacus organization.

Tobogganing, Women's Singles A264

20pf, Men's doubles. 25pf, Men's singles.

Perf. 13½x13

1966, Jan. 25 Litho. Unwmk.
808 A264 10pf citron & dp grn .20 .20
809 A264 20pf car rose & dk vio bl .20 .20
810 A264 25pf blue & dk blue *.95 .50*
Nos. 808-810 (3) 1.35 .90

10th Intl. Tobogganing Championships, Friedrichroda, Feb. 8-13.

Electronic Computer A265

Design: 15pf, Drill and milling machine.

1966, Feb. 24 ***Perf. 13x12½***
811 A265 10pf multicolored .20 .20
812 A265 15pf multicolored .55 .20

Leipzig Spring Fair, 1966.

Jan Arnost Smoler and Linden Leaf — A266

Soldier and National Gallery, Berlin — A267

25pf, House of the Sorbs, Bautzen, Saxony.

1966, Mar. 1 ***Perf. 13x13½***
813 A266 20pf brt bl, blk & brt red .20 .20
814 A266 25pf brt red, blk & brt bl *.45 .30*

Smoler (1816-84), philologist of the Sorbian language. The Sorbs are a small group of slavic people in Saxony.

Wmk. 313

1966, Mar. 1 Photo. ***Perf. 14***

Designs (Soldier and): 10pf, Brandenburg Gate. 20pf, Factory. 25pf, Combine.

815 A267 5pf ol gray, blk & yel .20 .20
816 A267 10pf ol gray, blk & yel .20 .20
817 A267 20pf ol gray, blk & yel .20 .20
818 A267 25pf ol gray, blk & yel *1.00 .50*
Nos. 815-818 (4) 1.60 1.10

National People's Army, 10th anniversary.

Luna 9 on Moon — A268

Medal for Scholarship — A269

1966, Mar. 7 Unwmk.
819 A268 20pf multicolored 1.25 .25

1st soft landing on the moon by Luna 9, 2/3/66.

1966, Mar. 7 Litho. ***Perf. 13½x13***
820 A269 20pf multicolored .35 .20

20th anniv. of the State Youth Organization.

Traffic Signs — A270

Traffic safety: 15pf, Automobile and child with scooter. 25pf, Bicyclist and signaling hand. 50pf, Motorcyclist, ambulance and glass of beer.

1966, Mar. 28 Litho. ***Perf. 13***
821 A270 10pf dk & lt bl, red & blk .20 .20
822 A270 15pf brt grn, citron & blk .20 .20
823 A270 25pf ol bis, brt bl & blk .20 .20
824 A270 50pf car, yel, gray & blk *.75 .50*
Nos. 821-824 (4) 1.35 1.10

Marx, Lenin and Crowd — A271

Designs: 5pf, Party emblem and crowd, vert. 15pf, Marx, Engels and title page of Communist Manifesto, vert. 20pf, Otto Grotewohl and Wilhelm Pieck shaking hands, and Party emblem, vert. 25pf, Chairman Walter Ulbricht receiving flowers.

1966, Mar. 31 Photo. ***Perf. 14***
825 A271 5pf multicolored .20 .20
826 A271 10pf multicolored .20 .20
827 A271 15pf green & blk .20 .20
828 A271 20pf dk carmine & blk .20 .20
829 A271 25pf multicolored *1.10 .75*
Nos. 825-829 (5) 1.90 1.55

20th anniversary of Socialist Unity Party of Germany (SED).

WHO Headquarters, Geneva — A272

Perf. 13x12½

1966, Apr. 26 Litho. Unwmk.
830 A272 20pf multicolored .30 .25

Inauguration of WHO Headquarters, Geneva.

Rügen Island, Königsstuhl — A273

National Parks: 10pf, Spree River woodland. 20pf, Saxon Switzerland. 25pf, Dunes at Westdarss. 30pf, Thale in Harz, Devil's Wall. 50pf, Feldberg Lakes, Mecklenburg.

Perf. 13x12½

1966, May 17 Litho. Unwmk.
831 A273 10pf multicolored .20 .20
832 A273 15pf multicolored .20 .20
833 A273 20pf multicolored .20 .20
834 A273 25pf multicolored .20 .20
835 A273 30pf multicolored .20 .20
836 A273 50pf multicolored *1.25 .75*
Nos. 831-836 (6) 2.25 1.75

Plauen Lace — A274

Various Lace Designs.

1966, May 26 ***Perf. 13x13½***
837 A274 10pf green & lt green .20 .20
838 A274 20pf dk blue & lt blue .20 .20
839 A274 25pf brown red & ver .20 .20
840 A274 50pf dk vio & bluish lil *1.50 .85*
Nos. 837-840 (4) 2.10 1.45

Rhododendron A275

Parachutist Landing on Target — A276

Flowers: 20pf, Lilies of the Valley. 40pf, Dahlias. 50pf, Cyclamen.

Photo. & Engr.

1966 Unwmk. ***Perf. 14x13½***
841 A275 20pf multicolored .20 .20
842 A275 25pf multicolored .20 .20
843 A275 40pf multicolored .25 .20
844 A275 50pf multicolored *3.00 2.10*
Nos. 841-844 (4) 3.65 2.70

Intl. Flower Show, Erfurt.
Issued: 20pf, Aug. 16; others, June 28.

1966, July 12 Litho. ***Perf. 12½x13***

15pf, Group parachute jump. 20pf, Free fall.

845 A276 10pf blue, blk & ol .20 .20
846 A276 15pf multicolored *.45 .40*
847 A276 20pf sky blue, blk & ol .20 .20
Nos. 845-847 (3) .85 .80

8th Intl. Parachute Championships, Leipzig.

Hans Kahle, Song of German Fighters and Medal of Spanish Republic — A277

15pf, Hans Beimler and street fighting in Madrid.

1966, July 15 Photo. ***Perf. 14***
848 A277 5pf multicolored .20 .20
849 A277 15pf multicolored .20 .20
Nos. 848-849,B137-B140 (6) 2.10 1.75

German fighters in the Spanish Civil War.

Television Set — A278

Design: 15pf, Electric typewriter.

Perf. 13x12½

1966, Aug. 29 Litho. Unwmk.
850 A278 10pf brt grn, blk & gray .30 .20
851 A278 15pf red, blk & gray .70 .20

1966 Leipzig Fall Fair.

Women's Doubles Kayak Race — A279

1966, Aug. 16

852 A279 15pf brt blue & multi *.90 .60*

7th Canoe World Championships, Berlin. See No. B141.

Oradour sur Glane Memorial and French Flag A280

Emblem of the Committee for Health Education A281

Perf. 13x13½

1966, Sept. 9 **Wmk. 313**

853 A280 25pf ultra, blk & red .25 .20

Issued in memory of the victims of the Nazi attack on Oradour, France, June 10, 1944.

1966, Sept. 13 ***Perf. 14***

5pf, Symbolic blood donor & recipient, horiz.

854 A281 5pf brt brown & red .20 .20
855 A281 40pf brt blue & red *.90 .40*
Nos. 854-855,B142 (3) *1.35 .80*

Blood donations and health education.

Weight Lifter — A282

Perf. 13½x13

1966, Sept. 22 **Litho.** **Unwmk.**

856 A282 15pf lt brown & blk *1.10 .90*

Intl. and European Weight Lifting Championships, Berlin. See No. B143.

Congress Hall — A283

Emblem — A284

1966, Oct. 10 ***Perf. 13***

857 A283 10pf multicolored *.35 .30*
858 A284 20pf dk blue & yellow .20 .20

6th Cong. of the Intl. Organ. of Journalists, Berlin.

Costume Type of 1964

Regional Costumes: 5pf, Woman from Altenburg. No. 860, Man from Altenburg. No. 861, Woman from Mecklenburg. 15pf, Man from Mecklenburg. 20pf, Woman from Magdeburg area. 30pf, Man from Magdeburg area.

1966, Oct. 25 **Photo.** ***Perf. 14***

859 A240 5pf multicolored .25 .20
860 A240 10pf multicolored .25 .20
a. Pair, #859-860 .60 .50
861 A240 10pf lt green & multi .25 .20
862 A240 15pf lt green & multi .25 .20
a. Pair, #861-862 .60 .50
863 A240 20pf yellow & multi *1.60 1.10*
864 A240 30pf yellow & multi *1.60 1.10*
a. Pair, #863-864 *4.00 2.75*
Nos. 859-864 (6) *4.20 3.00*

Printed in checkerboard arrangement.

Megalamphodus Megalopterus — A285

Various Tropical Fish in Natural Colors.

1966, Nov. 8 **Litho.** ***Perf. 13x12½***

865 A285 5pf lt blue & gray .20 .20
866 A285 10pf blue & indigo .20 .20
867 A285 15pf citron & blk *1.75 1.25*
868 A285 20pf green & blk .20 .20
869 A285 25pf ultra & blk .20 .20
870 A285 40pf emerald & blk .25 .20
Nos. 865-870 (6) *2.80 2.25*

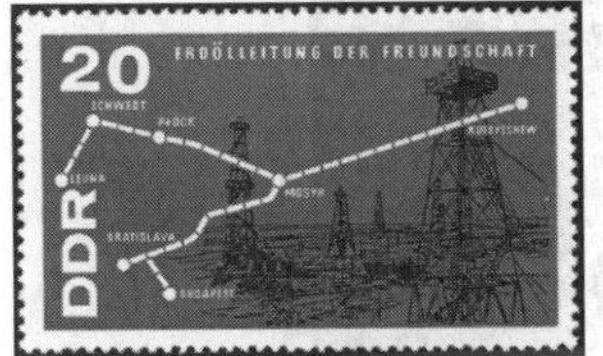

Map of Oil Pipeline and Oil Field — A286

Design: 25pf, Map of oil pipelines and "Walter Ulbricht" Leuna chemical factory.

1966, Nov. 8 ***Perf. 13½x13***

871 A286 20pf red & black .20 .20
872 A286 25pf blue & black *.50 .25*

Chemical industry.

Detail from Ishtar Gate, Babylon, 580 B.C. — A287

Designs from Babylon c. 580 B.C.: 20pf, Mythological animal from Ishtar Gate. 25pf, Lion facing right and ornaments, vert. 50pf, Lion facing left and ornaments, vert.

Perf. 13½x14, 14x13½

1966, Nov. 23 **Photo.**

873 A287 10pf multicolored .20 .20
874 A287 20pf multicolored .20 .20
875 A287 25pf multicolored .20 .20
876 A287 50pf multicolored *.45 .70*
Nos. 873-876 (4) *1.05 1.30*

Near East Museum, Berlin.

Wartburg, Thuringia — A288

Gentian — A289

Design: 25pf, Wartburg, Palace.

1966, Nov. 23 **Litho.** ***Perf. 13x13½***

877 A288 20pf olive .20 .20
878 A288 25pf violet brown *.45 .25*
Nos. 877-878,B145 (3) *.85 .65*

900th anniv. (in 1967) of the Wartburg (castle) near Eisenach, Thuringia.

1966, Dec. 8 **Litho.** ***Perf. 12½x13***

Protected Flowers: 20pf, Cephalanthera rubra (orchid). 25pf, Mountain arnica.

Black Background

879 A289 10pf yel, grn & bl .20 .20
880 A289 20pf yel, grn & red .20 .20
881 A289 25pf red, yel & grn *1.10 .55*
Nos. 879-881 (3) *1.50 .95*

Son Leaving Home — A290

City Hall, Stralsund — A291

Various Scenes from Fairy Tale "The Table, the Ass and the Stick."

1966, Dec. 8 ***Perf. 13½x13***

882 A290 5pf multicolored .20 .20
883 A290 10pf multicolored .20 .20
884 A290 20pf multicolored .45 .40
885 A290 25pf multicolored .45 .40
886 A290 30pf multicolored .20 .20
887 A290 50pf multicolored .20 .20
a. Sheet of 6, #882-887 2.25 2.75

See Nos. 968-973, 1063-1068, 1087-1092, 1176-1181, 1339-1344.

Perf. 14x13½, 13½x14

1967, Jan. 24 **Photo.**

Buildings: 5pf, Wörlitz Castle, horiz. 15pf, Chorin Convent. 20pf, Ribbeck House, Berlin, horiz. 25pf, Moritzburg, Zeitz. 40pf, Old City Hall, Potsdam.

888 A291 5pf multicolored .20 .20
889 A291 10pf multicolored .20 .20
890 A291 15pf multicolored .20 .20
891 A291 20pf multicolored .20 .20
892 A291 25pf multicolored .20 .20
893 A291 40pf multicolored *.85 .55*
Nos. 888-893 (6) *1.85 1.55*

See Nos. 1018, 1020, 1071-1076.

Rifle Shooting, Prone — A292

Designs: 20pf, Shooting on skis. 25pf, Relay race with rifles on skis.

1967, Feb. 15 **Litho.** ***Perf. 13x12½***

894 A292 10pf Prus bl gray & brt pink .20 .20
895 A292 20pf sl grn, brt bl & grn .20 .20
896 A292 25pf ol grn, ol & grnsh bl *.55 .35*
Nos. 894-896 (3) *.95 .75*

World Biathlon Championships (skiing and shooting), Altenberg, Feb. 15-19.

Circular Knitting Machine — A293

Mother and Child — A294

Design: 15pf, Zeiss telescope and galaxy.

1967, Mar. 2 ***Perf. 13½x13***

897 A293 10pf dull mag & brt grn .20 .20
898 A293 15pf ultra & gray .50 .25

Leipzig Spring Fair of 1967.

1967, Mar. 7 ***Perf. 13x13½***

Design: 25pf, Working women.

899 A294 20pf rose brn, red & gray .20 .20
900 A294 25pf dk bl, brt bl & brn *.50 .45*

20th anniv. of the Democratic Women's Federation of Germany.

Marx, Engels, Lenin and Electronic Control Center — A295

Designs (Portraits and): 5pf, Farmer driving combine. No. 903, Students and teacher. 15pf, Family. No. 905, Soldier, sailor and aviator. No. 906, Ulbricht among workers. 25pf, Soldier, sailor, aviator and factories. 40pf, Farmers with modern equipment. Nos. 901, 903-905 are vertical.

1967 **Photo.** ***Perf. 14***

901 A295 5pf multicolored .20 .20
902 A295 10pf multicolored .20 .20
903 A295 10pf multicolored .20 .20
904 A295 15pf multicolored *.30 .30*
905 A295 20pf multicolored .20 .20
906 A295 20pf multicolored .20 .20
907 A295 25pf multicolored .20 .20
908 A295 40pf multicolored *.40 .45*
Nos. 901-908 (8) *1.90 1.95*

7th congress of Socialist Unity Party of Germany (SED), Apr. 17.

Issued: #902, 906-908 3/22; #901, 903-905, 4/6.

Tahitian Women, by Paul Gauguin — A296

Paintings from Dresden Gallery: 20pf, Young Woman, by Ferdinand Hodler. 25pf, Peter in the Zoo, by H. Hakenbeck. 30pf, Venetian Episode (woman feeding pigeons), by R. Bergander. 50pf, Grandmother and Granddaughter, by J. Scholtz. 70pf, Cairn in the Snow, by Caspar David Friedrich.

1967, Mar. 29

909 A296 20pf multi, vert. .20 .20
910 A296 25pf multi, vert. .20 .20
911 A296 30pf multi, vert. .20 .20
912 A296 40pf multi .20 .20
913 A296 50pf multi, vert. *1.25 1.10*
914 A296 70pf multi .25 .20
Nos. 909-914 (6) *2.30 2.10*

Barn Owl — A297

Protected Birds: 10pf, Eurasian crane. 20pf, Peregrine falcon. 25pf, Bullfinches. 30pf, European kingfisher. 40pf, European roller.

1967, Apr. 27 Photo. *Perf. 14*

Birds in Natural Colors

915 A297 5pf gray blue .20 .20
916 A297 10pf gray blue .20 .20
917 A297 20pf gray blue .20 .20
918 A297 25pf gray blue .20 .20
919 A297 30pf gray blue 2.50 1.50
920 A297 40pf gray blue .25 .20
Nos. 915-920 (6) 3.55 2.50

Arms of Warsaw, Berlin and Prague A298

Design: 25pf, Bicyclists and doves.

Perf. 13x12½

1967, May 10 Litho. Wmk. 313

921 A298 10pf org, blk & lil .20 .20
922 A298 25pf lt bl & dk car .35 .30

20th Intl. Bicycle Peace Race, Berlin-Warsaw-Prague.

Cat A299

Children's Drawings: 10pf, Snow White and the Seven Dwarfs. 15pf, Fire truck. 20pf, Cock. 25pf, Flowers in vase. 30pf, Children playing ball.

1967, June 1 Unwmk.

923 A299 5pf multicolored .20 .20
924 A299 10pf black & multi .20 .20
925 A299 15pf dk blue & multi .20 .20
926 A299 20pf orange & multi .20 .20
927 A299 25pf multicolored .20 .20
928 A299 30pf multicolored .85 .50
Nos. 923-928 (6) 1.85 1.50

Issued for International Children's Day.

Girl with Straw Hat, by Salomon Bray — A300

Exhibition Emblem and Map of DDR — A301

Paintings: 5pf, Three Horsemen, by Rubens, horiz. 10pf, Girl Gathering Grapes, by Gerard Dou. 20pf, Spring Idyl, by Hans Thoma, horiz. 25pf, Wilhelmine Schroder-Devrient, by Karl Begas. 50pf, The Four Evangelists, by Jacob Jordaens.

1967, June 7 Photo. *Perf. 14*

929 A300 5pf lt & dk blue .20 .20
930 A300 10pf lt red brn & red brn .20 .20
931 A300 20pf lt & dp yel grn .20 .20
932 A300 25pf pale rose & rose lil .20 .20
933 A300 40pf pale grn & ol grn .20 .20
934 A300 50pf tan & sepia 1.25 .85
Nos. 929-934 (6) 2.25 1.85

Issued to publicize paintings missing from museums since World War II.

Perf. 12½x13

1967, June 14 Litho. Unwmk.

935 A301 20pf dk grn, ocher & red .25 .20

15th Agricultural Exhib., Markkleeberg.

Marie Curie — A302

German Playing Cards — A303

Portraits: 5pf, Georg Herwegh, poet. 20pf, Käthe Kollwitz. 25pf, Johann J. Winckelmann, archaeologist. 40pf, Theodor Storm, writer.

1967 Engr. *Perf. 14*

936 A302 5pf brown .20 .20
937 A302 10pf dark blue .20 .20
938 A302 20pf dull red .20 .20
939 A302 25pf gray .20 .20
940 A302 40pf slate green .60 .45
Nos. 936-940 (5) 1.40 1.25

150th anniv. of the birth of Herwegh, Winckelmann and Storm, and the birth centenaries of Curie and Kollwitz.

1967, July 18 Photo.

Designs: Various German playing cards.

941 A303 5pf red & multi .20 .20
942 A303 10pf green & multi .20 .20
943 A303 20pf multicolored .25 .20
944 A303 25pf multicolored 3.50 2.00
Nos. 941-944 (4) 4.15 2.60

Mare and Foal A304

Horses: 10pf, Stallion. 20pf, Horse race finish. 50pf, Colts, vert.

Perf. 13½x13, 13x13½

1967, Aug. 15 Litho. Unwmk.

945 A304 5pf multicolored .20 .20
946 A304 10pf org, blk & dk brn .20 .20
947 A304 20pf blue & multi .20 .20
948 A304 50pf multicolored 2.25 1.40
Nos. 945-948 (4) 2.85 2.00

Thoroughbred Horse Show of Socialist Countries, Hoppegarten, Berlin.

Small Electrical Appliances A305

Leipzig Fall Fair: 15pf, Woman's fur coat and furrier's trademark.

Perf. 14x13½

1967, Aug. 8 Photo. Unwmk.

949 A305 10pf brt bl, blk & yel .25 .20
950 A305 15pf yellow, brn & blk .55 .25

Max Reichpietsch and Warship — A306

15pf, Albin Köbis, warship. 20pf, Sailors marching with red flag, warship.

1967, Sept. 5 Litho. *Perf. 13½x13*

Bluish Paper

951 A306 10pf dk blue, gray & red .20 .20
952 A306 15pf dk blue, gray & red .75 .35
953 A306 20pf dk blue, gray & red .25 .20
Nos. 951-953 (3) 1.20 .75

50th anniv. of the sailors' uprising at Kiel.

Monument at Kragujevac A307

1967, Sept. 20 *Perf. 13x13½*

954 A307 25pf dk red, yel & blk .50 .25

Issued in memory of the victims of the Nazis at Kragujevac, Yugoslavia, Oct. 21, 1941.

Worker and Symbols of Electrification — A308

Communist Emblem and: 5pf, Worker, Communist newspaper masthead. 15pf, Russian War Memorial, Berlin-Treptow. 20pf, Russian and German soldiers, coat of arms. 40pf, Lenin, cruiser Aurora.

1967, Oct. 6 Photo. *Perf. 14x14½*

955 A308 5pf multicolored .20 .20
956 A308 10pf multicolored .20 .20
957 A308 15pf multicolored .20 .20
958 A308 20pf multicolored .25 .20
959 A308 40pf multicolored 2.00 1.25
a. Souvenir sheet of 2 .85 2.50
Nos. 955-959 (5) 2.85 2.05

50th anniv. of the Russian October Revolution. No. 959a contains 2 imperf. stamps similar to Nos. 958-959 with simulated perforations. It commemorates the Red October Jubilee Stamp Exhibition, Karl-Marx-Stadt, Oct. 6-15. Sold for 85pf.

Martin Luther, by Lucas Cranach — A309

Young Inventors and Fair Emblem — A310

Designs: 25pf, Luther's House, Wittenberg, horiz. 40pf, Castle Church, Wittenberg.

Engraved and Photogravure

1967, Oct. 17 *Perf. 14*

960 A309 20pf black & rose lilac .20 .20
961 A309 25pf black & blue .20 .20
962 A309 40pf black & lemon 1.40 .55
Nos. 960-962 (3) 1.80 .95

450th anniversary of the Reformation.

1967, Nov. 15 Unwmk. *Perf. 14*

Designs: No. 964, Boy's and girl's heads and emblem of the Free German Youth Organization. 25pf, Young workers receiving awards, and medal.

Size: 23x28½mm

963 A310 20pf multicolored .35 .30
964 A310 20pf multicolored .35 .30

Size: 51x28½mm

965 A310 25pf multicolored .35 .30
a. Strip of 3, #963-965 2.75 2.50

Issued to publicize the 10th Masters of Tomorrow Fair, Leipzig, Nov. 15-26.

Goethe House, Weimar A311

Design: 25pf, Schiller House, Weimar.

1967, Nov. 27 Litho. *Perf. 13x12½*

966 A311 20pf gray, blk & brn .20 .20
967 A311 25pf citron, dk grn & brn 1.00 .35

Honoring German classical humanism.

Fairy Tale Type of 1966

Various Scenes from King Drosselbart.

1967, Nov. 27 *Perf. 13½x13*

968 A290 5pf multicolored .20 .20
969 A290 10pf multicolored .20 .20
970 A290 15pf multicolored .60 .50
971 A290 20pf multicolored .60 .50
972 A290 25pf multicolored .20 .20
973 A290 30pf multicolored .20 .20
a. Sheet of 6, #968-973 3.50 3.00

Farmers, Stables and Silos — A312

Perf. 13x12½

1967, Dec. 6 Litho. Unwmk.

974 A312 10pf multicolored .25 .20

1st agricultural co-operatives, 15th anniv.

Nutcracker and Figurines — A313

Speed Skating — A314

20pf, Candle holders: angel and miner.

1967, Dec. 6 Photo. *Perf. 13½x14*

975 A313 10pf green & multi .45 .25
976 A313 20pf red & multi .20 .20

Issued to publicize local handicrafts of the Erzgebirge in Saxony (Ore Mountains).

Perf. 13½x13

1968, Jan. 17 Litho. Unwmk.

Sport and Olympic Rings: 15pf, Slalom. 20pf, Ice hockey. 25pf, Figure skating, pair. 30pf, Long-distance skiing.

977 A314 5pf blue, dk bl & red .20 .20
978 A314 15pf multicolored .20 .20
979 A314 20pf grnsh bl, dk bl & red .20 .20
980 A314 25pf multicolored .20 .20

981 A314 30pf grnsh bl, vio bl & red 2.10 .85
Nos. 977-981,B146 (6) 3.10 1.85

10th Winter Olympic Games, Grenoble, France, Feb. 6-18.

Actinometer, Sun and Potsdam Meteorological Observatory A315

Designs: 20pf, Antenna, Cloud Formation and Map of Europe. 25pf, Weather influence on farming (fields by day and night, produce).

1968, Jan. 24 ***Perf. 13½x13***

Size: 23x28mm

982 A315 10pf brt mag, org & blk .35 .25

Size: 50x28mm

983 A315 20pf multicolored .35 .25

Size: 23x28mm

984 A315 25pf olive, blk & yel .35 .25
a. Strip of 3, #982-984 3.25 2.75

75th anniversary of the Meteorological Observatory in Potsdam.

Venus 4 Interplanetary Station — A316

Design: 25pf, Earth satellites Kosmos 186 and 188 orbiting earth.

1968, Jan. 24 **Photo.** ***Perf. 14***

985 A316 20pf multicolored .20 .20
986 A316 25pf multicolored .65 .35

Russian space explorations.

Fighters of The Underground A317

20pf, "The Liberation." 25pf, "The Partisans."

1968, Feb. 21 **Photo.** ***Perf. 14x13½***

987 A317 10pf black & multi .20 .20
988 A317 20pf black & multi .20 .20
989 A317 25pf black & multi .40 .20
Nos. 987-989 (3) .80 .60

The designs are from the stained glass window triptych by Walter Womacka in the Sachsenhausen Memorial Museum.

Diesel Locomotive — A318

Design: 15pf, Refrigerator fishing ship.

1968, Feb. 29 ***Perf. 14***

990 A318 10pf multicolored .25 .20
991 A318 15pf multicolored .55 .30

The 1968 Leipzig Spring Fair.

Woman from Hoyerswerda A319

Maxim Gorky and View of Gorky A320

Sorbian Regional Costumes: 20pf, Woman from Schleife. 40pf, Woman from Crostwitz. 50pf, Woman from Spreewald.

1968, Mar. 14

992 A319 10pf citron & multi .20 .20
993 A319 20pf fawn & multi .20 .20
994 A319 40pf blue grn & multi .20 .20
995 A319 50pf green & multi 1.60 .75
Nos. 992-995 (4) 2.20 1.35

1968, Mar. 14 **Engr.**

25pf, Stormy petrel and toppling towers.

996 A320 20pf brown & rose car .20 .20
997 A320 25pf brown & rose car .45 .25

Maxim Gorky (1868-1936), Russian writer.

Ring-necked Pheasants A321

15pf, Gray partridges. 20pf, Mallards. 25pf, Graylag geese. 30pf, Wood pigeons. 40pf, Hares.

1968, Mar. 26 **Litho.** ***Perf. 13½x13***

998 A321 10pf gray & multi .20 .20
999 A321 15pf gray & multi .20 .20
1000 A321 20pf gray & multi .20 .20
1001 A321 25pf gray & multi .25 .20
1002 A321 30pf gray & multi .30 .20
1003 A321 40pf gray & multi 2.25 3.25
Nos. 998-1003 (6) 3.40 4.25

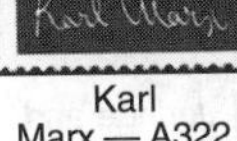

Karl Marx — A322

Fritz Heckert — A323

Designs: 10pf, Title page of the "Communist Manifesto." 25pf, Title page of "Das Kapital."

1968, Apr. 25 **Photo.** ***Perf. 14***

1004 A322 10pf yel grn & blk .20 .20
1005 A322 20pf mag, yel & blk .20 .20
1006 A322 25pf lem, blk & red brn .20 .20
a. Strip of three 1.00 2.25
b. Souvenir sheet of 3 .85 2.50

Karl Marx (1818-83). Nos. 1004-1006 are printed se-tenant. No. 1006a contains 3 imperf. stamps similar to Nos. 1004-1006 with simulated perforations.

1968, Apr. 25

Design: 20pf, Young workers, new apartment buildings and Congress emblem.

1007 A323 10pf multicolored .20 .20
1008 A323 20pf multicolored .20 .20

7th Congress of the Free German Trade Unions.

"Right to Work" — A324

Designs: 10pf, "Right to Live," tree and globe. 25pf, "Right for Peace," dove and sun.

1968, May 8 **Litho.** ***Perf. 13½x13***

1009 A324 5pf maroon & pink .20 .20
1010 A324 10pf brn ol & ol bister .20 .20
1011 A324 25pf Prus bl & lt bl .55 .35
Nos. 1009-1011 (3) .95 .75

International Human Rights Year.

Angler A325

Designs: No. 1013, Rowing (woman). No. 1014, High jump (woman).

Unwmk.

1968, June 6 **Photo.** ***Perf. 14***

1012 A325 20pf ol grn, sl bl & dk red .65 .50
1013 A325 20pf Prus bl, dk bl & ol .20 .20
1014 A325 20pf cop red, dp cl & bl .20 .20
Nos. 1012-1014 (3) 1.05 .90

World angling championships, Gustrow (#1012); European women's rowing championships, Berlin (#1013); 2nd European youth athletic competition, Leipzig (#1014).

Brandenburg Gate, Torch — A326

Youth Festival Emblem — A327

Design: 25pf, Stadium and torch.

1968, June 20 **Litho.** ***Perf. 13½x13***

1015 A326 10pf multicolored .20 .20
1016 A326 25pf multicolored .70 .35

2nd Children's and Youths' Spartakiad, Berlin.

1968, June 20

1017 A327 25pf multicolored .55 .30

9th Youth Festival for Peace & Friendship, Sofia.

See No. B148.

Type of 1967 and

Moritzburg Castle, Dresden — A328

Buildings: 10pf, City Hall, Wernigerode. 25pf, City Hall, Greifswald. 30pf, Sanssouci Palace, Potsdam.

1968, June 25 **Photo.** ***Perf. 13½x14***

1018 A291 10pf multicolored .20 .20
1019 A328 20pf multicolored .20 .20
1020 A291 25pf multicolored .20 .20
1021 A328 30pf multicolored .50 .60
Nos. 1018-1021 (4) 1.10 1.20

Walter Ulbricht and Arms of Republic A329

Photo. & Engr.

1968, June 27 ***Perf. 14***

1022 A329 20pf org, dp car & blk .25 .20

75th birthday of Walter Ulbricht, chairman of the Council of State, Communist party secretary and deputy prime minister.

Old Rostock and Arms A330

Design: 25pf, Historic and modern buildings, 1968, and arms of Rostock.

1968, July 9 **Photo.**

1023 A330 20pf multicolored .20 .20
1024 A330 25pf multicolored .50 .35

750th anniv. of Rostock and to publicize the 11th Baltic Sea Week.

Karl Landsteiner, M.D. (1868-1943) A331

"Trener" Stunt Plane — A332

Portraits: 15pf, Emanuel Lasker (1868-1941), chess champion and writer. 20pf, Hanns Eisler (1898-1962), composer. 25pf, Ignaz Semmelweis, M.D. (1818-1865). 40pf, Max von Pettenkofer (1818-1901), hygienist.

1968, July 17 **Engr.** ***Perf. 14***

1025 A331 10pf gray green .20 .20
1026 A331 15pf black .20 .20
1027 A331 20pf brown .20 .20
1028 A331 25pf gray blue .20 .20
1029 A331 40pf rose lake .55 .50
Nos. 1025-1029 (5) 1.35 1.30

1968, Aug. 13 **Litho.** ***Perf. 12½x13***

25pf, 2 "Trener" stunt planes in parallel flight.

1030 A332 10pf multicolored .20 .20
1031 A332 25pf blue & multi .35 .30

Peasant Woman, by Wilhelm Leibl — A333

Paintings from Dresden Gallery: 10pf, "On the Beach," by Walter Womacka, horiz. 15pf, Mountain Farmers Mowing, by Albin Egger-Lienz, horiz. 40pf, The Artist's daughter, by Venturelli. 50pf, High School Girl, by Michaelis. 70pf, Girl with Guitar, by Castelli.

Perf. 14x13½, 13½x14

1968, Aug. 20 **Photo.**

1032 A333 10pf multicolored .20 .20
1033 A333 15pf multicolored .20 .20
1034 A333 20pf multicolored .20 .20
1035 A333 40pf multicolored .30 .20

1036 A333 50pf multicolored .30 .20
1037 A333 70pf multicolored *1.60 .95*
Nos. 1032-1037 (6) *2.80 1.95*

Model Trains — A334

1968, Aug. 29 ***Perf. 14x13½***
1038 A334 10pf lt ultra, red & blk .25 .20

The 1968 Leipzig Fall Fair.

Spremberg Dam — A335

Designs: 10pf, Pöhl Dam, vert. 15pf, Ohra Dam, vert. 20pf, Rappbode Dam.

Perf. 13x12½, 12½x13
1968, Sept. 11 **Litho.**
1039 A335 5pf multicolored .20 .20
1040 A335 10pf multicolored .20 .20
1041 A335 15pf multicolored *.30 .30*
1042 A335 20pf multicolored .20 .20
Nos. 1039-1042 (4) *.90 .90*

Issued to publicize dams built since 1945.

Runner A336

Designs: 25pf, Woman gymnast, vert. 40pf, Water polo, vert. 70pf, Sculling.

1968, Sept. 18 **Photo.** ***Perf. 14***
1043 A336 5pf multicolored .20 .20
1044 A336 25pf multicolored .20 .20
1045 A336 40pf multicolored .20 .20
1046 A336 70pf blue & multi *1.10 .80*
Nos. 1043-1046,B149-B150 (6) *2.10 1.80*

19th Olympic Games, Mexico City, 10/12-27.

Monument, Fort Breendonk, Belgium — A337

Tiger Beetle — A338

1968, Oct. 10 **Litho.** ***Perf. 13x13½***
1047 A337 25pf multicolored .30 .20

Issued in memory of the victims of the Nazis at the Fort Breendonk Concentration Camp.

1968, Oct. 16 ***Perf. 13½x13***

Insects: 15pf, Ground beetle (Cychrus caraboides). 20pf, Ladybug. 25pf, Ground beetle (Carabus arcensis hrbst.). 30pf, Hister beetle. 40pf, Checkered beetle.

1048 A338 10pf yellow & multi .20 .20
1049 A338 15pf bluish lil & blk .20 .20
1050 A338 20pf multicolored .20 .20
1051 A338 25pf lt lilac & blk *1.60 1.10*
1052 A338 30pf lt green, blk & red .20 .20
1053 A338 40pf pink & black .20 .20
Nos. 1048-1053 (6) *2.60 2.10*

Lenin and Letter to Spartacists — A339

Designs: 20pf, Workers, soldiers and sailors with masthead and slogans. 25pf, Karl Liebknecht and Rosa Luxemburg.

1968, Oct. 29 **Litho.** ***Perf. 13x12½***
1054 A339 10pf lemon, red & blk .20 .20
1055 A339 20pf lemon, red & blk .20 .20
1056 A339 25pf lemon, red & blk *.30 .30*
Nos. 1054-1056 (3) *.70 .70*

November Revolution in Germany, 50th anniv.

Cattleya — A340

Orchids: 10pf, Paphiopedilum albertianum. 15pf, Cattleya fabia. 20pf, Cattleya aclandiae. 40pf, Sobralia macrantha. 50pf, Dendrobium alpha.

1968, Nov. 12 **Photo.** ***Perf. 13***
Flowers in Natural Colors
1057 A340 5pf bluish lilac .20 .20
1058 A340 10pf green .20 .20
1059 A340 15pf bister .20 .20
1060 A340 20pf green .20 .20
1061 A340 40pf light brown .20 .20
1062 A340 50pf gray *1.40 1.00*
Nos. 1057-1062 (6) *2.40 2.00*

Fairy Tale Type of 1966

Various Scenes from Puss in Boots.

1968, Nov. 27 **Litho.** ***Perf. 13½x13***
1063 A290 5pf multicolored .20 .20
1064 A290 10pf multicolored .20 .20
1065 A290 15pf multicolored .70 .60
1066 A290 20pf multicolored .70 .60
1067 A290 25pf multicolored .20 .20
1068 A290 30pf multicolored .20 .20
a. Sheet of 6, #1063-1068 3.75 4.25

Young Pioneers A341

Design: 15pf, Five Young Pioneers.

1968, Dec. 3 ***Perf. 13x13½***
1069 A341 10pf blue & multi .20 .20
1070 A341 15pf multicolored *.40 .25*

20th anniv. of the founding of the Ernst Thalmann Young Pioneers' organization.

Buildings Type of 1967

Buildings: 5pf, City Hall, Tangermunde. 10pf, German State Opera, Berlin. 20pf, Wall Pavilion, Dresden. 25pf, Burgher's House, Luckau. 30pf, Rococo Palace, Dornburg. 40pf, "Stockfish" House, Erfurt.

1969, Jan. 1 **Photo.** ***Perf. 14***
1071 A291 5pf multi .20 .20
1072 A291 10pf multi, horiz. .20 .20
1073 A291 20pf multi .20 .20
1074 A291 25pf multi *.65 .55*
1075 A291 30pf multi, horiz. .20 .20
1076 A291 40pf multi .20 .20
Nos. 1071-1076 (6) *1.65 1.55*

Martin Andersen Nexö, Danish Writer — A342

Portraits: 20pf, Otto Nagel (1894-1967), painter. 25pf, Alexander von Humboldt (1769-1859), naturalist, traveler, statesman. 40pf, Theodor Fontane (1819-1898), writer.

1969, Feb. 5 **Engr.** ***Perf. 14***
1077 A342 10pf grnsh black .20 .20
1078 A342 20pf deep brown .20 .20
1079 A342 25pf violet blue *.65 .30*
1080 A342 40pf brown .20 .20
Nos. 1077-1080 (4) *1.25 .90*

Issued to honor famous men.

Be Attentive and Considerate! A343

10pf, Watch ahead! (car, truck & traffic signal). 20pf, Watch railroad crossings! (train & car at crossing). 25pf, If in doubt don't pass! (cars & truck).

1969, Feb. 18 **Litho.** ***Perf. 13x13½***
1081 A343 5pf lt blue & multi .20 .20
1082 A343 10pf yellow & multi .20 .20
1083 A343 20pf pink & multi .20 .20
1084 A343 25pf multicolored *.30 .30*
Nos. 1081-1084 (4) *.90 .90*

Traffic safety campaign.

Combine A344

Leipzig Spring Fair: 15pf, Planeta-Variant offset printing press.

1969, Feb. 26 **Photo.** ***Perf. 14***
1085 A344 10pf multicolored .20 .20
1086 A344 15pf crimson, blk & bl .20 .20

Spring Snowflake A346

Red Cross, Crescent, Lion and Sun Emblems A347

5 DDR Jorinde and Joringel A345

Various Scenes from Fairy Tale "Jorinde and Joringel."

1969, Mar. 18 **Litho.** ***Perf. 13½x13***
1087 A345 5pf black & multi .20 .20
1088 A345 10pf black & multi .20 .20
1089 A345 15pf black & multi .35 .35
1090 A345 20pf black & multi .35 .35
1091 A345 25pf black & multi .20 .20
1092 A345 30pf black & multi .20 .20
a. Sheet of 6, #1087-1092 2.00 2.00

See Nos. 1176-1181.

Protected Plants: 10pf, Adonis. 15pf, Globe-flowers. 20pf, Garden Turk's-cap. 25pf, Button snakeroot. 30pf, Dactylorchis latifolia.

1969, Apr. 4 **Photo.** ***Perf. 14***
1093 A346 5pf green & multi .20 .20
1094 A346 10pf green & multi .20 .20
1095 A346 15pf green & multi .20 .20
1096 A346 20pf green & multi .20 .20
1097 A346 25pf green & multi *2.10 1.10*
1098 A346 30pf green & multi .25 .20
Nos. 1093-1098 (6) *3.15 2.10*

1969, Apr. 23 **Litho.** ***Perf. 12½x13***

Design: 15pf, Large Red Cross, Red Crescent and Lion and Sun Emblems.

1099 A347 10pf gray, red & yel .20 .20
1100 A347 15pf multicolored *.95 .30*

League of Red Cross Societies, 50th anniv.

Conifer Nursery A348

Erythrite from Schneeberg A349

10pf, Forests as natural resources (timber & resin). 20pf, Forests as regulators of climate. 25pf, Forests as recreation areas (tents along lake).

1969, Apr. 23
1101 A348 5pf multicolored .20 .20
1102 A348 10pf multicolored .20 .20
1103 A348 20pf multicolored .20 .20
1104 A348 25pf multicolored *.90 .55*
Nos. 1101-1104 (4) *1.50 1.15*

Prevention of forest fires.

1969, May 21 **Photo.** ***Perf. 13½x14***

Minerals: 10pf, Fluorite from Halsbrücke. 15pf, Galena from Neudorf. 20pf, Smoky quartz from Lichtenberg. 25pf, Calcite from Niederrabenstein. 50pf, Silver from Freiberg.

1105 A349 5pf tan & multi .20 .20
1106 A349 10pf multicolored .20 .20
1107 A349 15pf gray & multi .20 .20
1108 A349 20pf lemon & multi .20 .20
1109 A349 25pf multicolored *.65 .50*
1110 A349 50pf lt blue & multi .20 .20
Nos. 1105-1110 (6) *1.65 1.50*

Women and Symbols of Agriculture, Science and Industry — A350

Design: 25pf, Woman's head and symbols.

1969, May 28 **Engr.** ***Perf. 14***
1111 A350 20pf dk red & blue .20 .20
1112 A350 25pf blue & dk red *.60 .30*

2nd Women's Congress of the German Democratic Republic.

Ulbricht Type of 1961-67

1969-71 Wmk. 313 Typo. ***Perf. 14***

Size: 17x21mm

1112A A189 35pf Prus blue ('71) .25 .25

Unwmk.

Engr.

Size: 24x28½mm

1113 A189 1m dull green .30 .35
1114 A189 2m brown .35 .40
Nos. 1112A-1114 (3) .90 1.00

See note below Nos. 590B-590C.

Coil Stamp

1970, Jan. 20 Typo. Wmk. 313

Size: 17x21mm

1114A A189 1m olive .45 1.50

Emblem of DDR Philatelic Society — A351

Worker Protecting Children — A352

1969, June 4 Photo. Unwmk.

1115 A351 10pf red, gold & ultra .25 .20

National Philatelic Exhibition "20 Years DDR," Magdeburg, Oct. 31-Nov. 9.

1969, June 4 Litho. ***Perf. 13***

25pf, Workers of various races. 20pf+5pf, Berlin buildings: Brandenburg Gate, Council of State, Soviet Cenotaph, Town Hall Tower, Television Tower, Teachers' Building & Hall.

Size: 23x28mm

1116 A352 10pf lemon & multi .45 .50

Size: 50x28mm

1117 A352 20pf + 5pf multi .45 .50

Size: 23x28mm

1118 A352 25pf lemon & multi .45 .50
a. Strip of 3, #1116-1118 2.75 2.75

Intl. Peace Meeting, Berlin. The surtax on No. 1117 was for the Peace Council of the German Democratic Republic.

Opening Ceremony before Battle of Leipzig Monument — A353

15pf, Parading athletes & stadium. 25pf, Running, hurdling, javelin & flag waving. 30pf, Presentation of colors before old Leipzig Town Hall.

Photo. & Engr.

1969, June 18 ***Perf. 14***

1119 A353 5pf multi & black .20 .20
1120 A353 15pf multi & black .20 .20
1121 A353 25pf multi & black *.90* *.45*
1122 A353 30pf multi & black .20 .20
Nos. 1119-1122,B152-B153 (6) *1.90* *1.45*

5th German Gymnastic and Sports Festival, Leipzig.

Pierre de Coubertin, by Wieland Forster — A354

Knight — A355

Design: 25pf, Coubertin column, Memorial Grove, Olympia.

1969, June 6 ***Perf. 14x13½***

1123 A354 10pf black & lt blue .20 .20
1124 A354 25pf black & sal pink *.55* *.40*

Revival of the Olympic Games, 75th anniv.

1969, July 29 Photo. ***Perf. 14***

#1126, Bicycle wheel. #1127, Volleyball.

1125 A355 20pf red, gold & dk brn .20 .20
1126 A355 20pf green, gold & red .20 .20
1127 A355 20pf multicolored .20 .20
Nos. 1125-1127 (3) .60 .60

16th Students' Chess World Championships, Dresden (No. 1125); Indoor Bicycle World Championships, Erfurt (No. 1126); 2nd Volleyball World Cup (No. 1127).

Merchandise A356

1969, Aug. 27 Litho. ***Perf. 12½x13***

1128 A356 10pf multicolored .20 .20

Leipzig Fall Fair, Aug. 31-Sept. 7, 1969.

Arms of Republic and View of Rostock A357

1m, DDR Arms, Town Hall, Marienkirche and Television Tower, Berlin, vert.

1969, Sept. 23 Photo. ***Perf. 14***

1129 A357 10pf Rostock .20 .20
1130 A357 10pf Neubrandenburg .20 .20
1131 A357 10pf Potsdam .20 .20
1132 A357 10pf Eisenhüttenstadt .20 .20
1133 A357 10pf Hoyerswerda .20 .20
1134 A357 10pf Magdeburg .20 .20
1135 A357 10pf Halle-Neustadt .20 .20
1136 A357 10pf Suhl .20 .20
1137 A357 10pf Dresden .20 .20
1138 A357 10pf Leipzig .20 .20
1139 A357 10pf Karl-Marx-Stadt .20 .20
1140 A357 10pf Berlin .20 .20
Nos. 1129-1140 (12) 2.40 2.40

Souvenir Sheet

1141 A357 1m multicolored 1.25 *3.00*

#1129-1141, 1142-1145 for 20th anniv. of the German Democratic Republic.

No. 1141 contains one 29x52mm stamp.

Television Tower, Berlin — A358

People and Flags — A359

Designs: 20pf, Sphere of Television Tower and TV test picture. No. 1144, Television Tower and TV test picture.

1969, Oct. 6 ***Perf. 14***

1142 A358 10pf multicolored .20 .20
1143 A358 20pf multicolored .20 .20

Souvenir Sheets

1144 A358 1m dk blue & multi 1.10 3.00

Perf. 13x12½

1145 A359 1m red & multi .95 2.10

No. 1144 contains one 21½x60mm stamp.

Cathedral, Otto von Guericke Monument and Hotel International, Magdeburg — A360

1969, Oct. 28 Litho. ***Perf. 13x12½***

1146 A360 20pf multicolored .20 .20

Natl. Postage Stamp Exhibition in honor of the 20th anniv. of the German Democratic Republic, Magdeburg. Oct. 31-Nov. 9. See No. B154.

UFI Emblem — A361

1969, Oct. 28 ***Perf. 13x13½***

1147 A361 10pf multicolored .20 .20
1148 A361 15pf multicolored *.90* *.25*

36th UFI Congress (Union des Foires Internationales), Leipzig, Oct. 28-30.

Memorial Monument, Copenhagen-Ryvangen — A362

Rostock University Seal and Building — A363

1969, Oct. 28 ***Perf. 13***

1149 A362 25pf multicolored .40 .20

Issued in memory of the victims of the Nazis in Denmark.

1969, Nov. 12 ***Perf. 12½x13***

Design: 15pf, Steam turbine, curve and Rostock University emblem.

1150 A363 10pf brt blue & multi .20 .20
1151 A363 15pf violet & multi *.65* *.20*

550th anniversary of Rostock University.

ILO Emblem — A364

Mold for Christmas Cookies — A365

1969, Nov. 12 ***Perf. 13½x14***

1152 A364 20pf dp green & silver .20 .20
1153 A364 25pf lil rose & silver *.90* *.25*

50th anniv. of the ILO.

1969, Nov. 25 Litho. ***Perf. 13½x13***

50pf, Negro couple, shaped spice cookie.

1154 A365 10pf dull org, bl & red brn .75 .65
1155 A365 50pf lt blue & multi 1.25 1.00
a. Pair, #1154-1155 4.25 2.75
Nos. 1154-1155,B155 (3) 2.25 1.90

Folk art of Lusatia.

Antonov An-24 A366

Planes: 25pf, Ilyushin Il-18. 30pf, Tupolev Tu-134. 50pf, Mi-8 helicopter.

1969, Dec. 2 ***Perf. 13x12½***

1156 A366 20pf blue, red & blk .20 .20
1157 A366 25pf vio, red & blk *.80* *.70*
1158 A366 30pf ultra, red & blk .20 .20
1159 A366 50pf olive, red & blk .20 .20
Nos. 1156-1159 (4) *1.40* *1.30*

Siberian Teacher, by D. K. Sveshnikov
A367

Russian Paintings from Dresden Gallery of Modern Masters: 10pf, Steelworker, by V. A. Serov. 20pf, Still Life, by E. A. Aslamasjan. 25pf, Hot Day (boats on river), by J. D. Romas. 40pf, Spring is Coming (young woman and snow-covered street), by L. V. Kabatchek. 50pf, Man on River Bank, by V. J. Makovskij.

1969, Dec. 10 Photo. *Perf. 13*

1160 A367 5pf gray & multi .20 .20
1161 A367 10pf gray & multi .20 .20
1162 A367 20pf gray & multi .20 .20
1163 A367 25pf gray & multi *.75* *.75*
1164 A367 40pf gray & multi .20 .20
1165 A367 50pf gray & multi .20 .20
Nos. 1160-1165 (6) *1.75* *1.75*

Ernst Barlach (1870-1938), Sculptor and Writer — A368

Portraits: 10pf, Johann Gutenberg (1400-68). 15pf, Kurt Tucholsky (1890-1935), writer. 20pf, Ludwig van Beethoven. 25pf, Friedrich Hölderlin (1770-1843), poet. 40pf, Georg Wilhelm Friedrich Hegel (1770-1831), philosopher.

1970, Jan. 20 Engr. *Perf. 14*

1166 A368 5pf blue violet .20 .20
1167 A368 10pf gray brown .20 .20
1168 A368 15pf violet blue .20 .20
1169 A368 20pf rose lilac .25 .20
1170 A368 25pf blue green *1.40* *.45*
1171 A368 40pf rose claret .25 .20
Nos. 1166-1171 (6) *2.50* *1.45*

Rabbit — A369

1970, Feb. 5 Photo. *Perf. 13½x14*

1172 A369 10pf shown .20 .20
1173 A369 20pf Red fox .20 .20
1174 A369 25pf Mink *2.10* *1.40*
1175 A369 40pf Hamster .25 .20
Nos. 1172-1175 (4) *2.75* *2.00*

525th International Fur Auctions, Leipzig.

Fairy Tale Type of 1969

Various Scenes from Fairy Tale "Little Brother and Sister."

1970, Feb. 17 Litho. *Perf. 13½x13*

1176 A345 5pf lilac & multi .20 .20
1177 A345 10pf lilac & multi .20 .20
1178 A345 15pf lilac & multi .40 .35
1179 A345 20pf lilac & multi .40 .35
1180 A345 25pf lilac & multi .20 .20
1181 A345 30pf lilac & multi .20 .20
a. Sheet of 6, #1176-1181 2.75 2.25

Telephone Coordinating Station — A370

15pf, High voltage testing transformer, vert.

1970, Feb. 24 *Perf. 13x12½, 12½x13*

1182 A370 10pf multicolored .20 .20
1183 A370 15pf multicolored .30 .20

Leipzig Spring Fair, Mar. 1-10, 1970.

Horseman's Tombstone (700 A.D.) — A371

Treasures from the Halle Museum: 20pf, Helmet (500 A.D.). 25pf, Bronze basin (1000 B.C.). 40pf, Clay drum (2500 B.C.).

1970, Mar. 3 Photo. *Perf. 13*

1184 A371 10pf dp grn, gray & dk brn .20 .20
1185 A371 20pf multicolored .20 .20
1186 A371 25pf yellow & multi *.50* *.65*
1187 A371 40pf multicolored .20 .20
Nos. 1184-1187 (4) *1.10* *1.25*

Lenin and Clara Zetkin — A372

Designs: 10pf, Lenin, "ISKRA" (newspaper's name), composing frame and printing press. 25pf, Lenin and title page of German edition of "State and Revolution." 40pf, Lenin statue, Eisleben. 70pf, Lenin monument and Lenin Square, Berlin. 1m, Lenin portrait, vert.

Photogravure and Engraved

1970, Apr. 16 *Perf. 14*

1188 A372 10pf multicolored .20 .20
1189 A372 20pf multicolored .20 .20
1190 A372 25pf multicolored *1.10* *.75*
1191 A372 40pf multicolored .20 .20
1192 A372 70pf multicolored .25 .20
Nos. 1188-1192 (5) *1.95* *1.55*

Souvenir Sheet

1193 A372 1m dk carmine & multi 1.25 5.50

Sea Kale — A373

Red Army Soldier Raising Flag over Berlin Reichstag
A374

Protected Plants: 20pf, European pasque-flower. 25pf, Fringed gentian. 30pf, Galeate orchis. 40pf, Marsh tea. 70pf, Round-leaved wintergreen.

1970, Apr. 28 Photo.

1194 A373 10pf multicolored .20 .20
1195 A373 20pf violet & multi .20 .20
1196 A373 25pf multicolored *1.25* *1.25*
1197 A373 30pf multicolored .20 .20
1198 A373 40pf multicolored .20 .20
1199 A373 70pf multicolored .25 .20
Nos. 1194-1199 (6) *2.30* *2.25*

1970, May 5 Litho. *Perf. 13x13½*

20pf, Spasski Tower, Kremlin; State Council Building, Berlin; coats of arms of USSR and DDR, newspaper clipping about friendship treaty with USSR. 25pf, Mutual Economic Aid Building, Moscow, flags of member countries. 70pf, Memorial monument, Buchenwald.

1200 A374 10pf multi .20 .20
1201 A374 20pf multi .20 .20
1202 A374 25pf multi *.65* *.35*
Nos. 1200-1202 (3) *1.05* *.75*

Souvenir Sheet

1203 A374 70pf multi, horiz. 1.25 3.50

25th anniv. of liberation from Fascism.

Shortwave Antenna, RBI Emblem and Globe — A375

Grain and Globe — A376

15pf, Berlin Radio Station, emblems of Radio Berlin Intl. (RBI), Radio DDR & Radio Germany.

1970, May 13 Litho. *Perf. 13½x13*

Size: 23x28mm

1204 A375 10pf ap grn, vio bl & bl .40 .40

Size: 50x28mm

1205 A375 15pf vio bl, dp rose & ap grn .60 .60
a. Pair, #1204-1205 2.25 1.75

DDR broadcasting system, 25th anniv.

1970, May 19

25pf, House of Culture, Dresden, and grain.

1206 A376 20pf vio bl, yel & bl .60 .60
1207 A376 25pf vio bl, yel & bl .60 .60
a. Strip of 2, #1206-1207 + label 3.25 2.75

Issued to publicize the 5th World Cereal and Bread Congress, Dresden, May 24-29.

Fritz Heckert Medal
A377

Design: 25pf, Globes and "FSM."

1970, June 9 *Perf. 13x12½*

1208 A377 20pf red, yel & brn .20 .20
1209 A377 25pf red, bl & yel *.40* *.35*

25th anniv. of the Free German Trade Union and of the World Organization of Trade Unions.

Traffic Policeman — A378

Designs: 10pf, Young Pioneers congratulating police woman. 15pf, Volga police car. 20pf, Railroad policeman with radio-telephone. 25pf, River police in Volga wing-type boat.

1970, June 23 Litho. *Perf. 13x12½*

1210 A378 5pf ocher & multi .20 .20
1211 A378 10pf green & multi .20 .20
1212 A378 15pf ultra & multi .20 .20
1213 A378 20pf multicolored .20 .20
1214 A378 25pf multicolored *1.00* *.30*
Nos. 1210-1214 (5) *1.80* *1.10*

25th anniversary of the People's Police.

Gods Amon, Shu and Tefnut — A379

Designs from Lion Temple in Musawwarat: 15pf, Head of King Arnekhamani. 20pf, Cow from cattle frieze. 25pf, Head of Prince Arka. 30pf, Head of God Arensnuphis, vert. 40pf, Elephants and prisoners of war. 50pf, Lion God Apedemak.

Perf. 13½x14, 14x13½

1970, June 23 Photo.

1215 A379 10pf multicolored .20 .20
1216 A379 15pf multicolored .20 .20
1217 A379 20pf multicolored .20 .20
1218 A379 25pf multicolored *.60* *.65*
1219 A379 30pf multicolored .20 .20
1220 A379 40pf multicolored .20 .20
1221 A379 50pf multicolored .20 .20
Nos. 1215-1221 (7) *1.80* *1.85*

Archaeological work in the Sudan by the Humboldt University, Berlin.

Arms and Flags of DDR and Poland — A380

1970, July 1 Litho. *Perf. 13x12½*

1222 A380 20pf multicolored .25 .20

20th anniversary of the Görlitz Agreement concerning the Oder-Neisse border.

Culture Association Emblem — A381

Athlete on Pommel Horse — A382

Design: 25pf, Johannes R. Becher medal.

1970, July 1 Photo. *Perf. 14*

1223 A381 10pf ultra, sil & brn 1.40 1.50
1224 A381 25pf ultra, gold & brn 1.40 1.50
a. Strip of 2, #1223-1224 + label 7.25 6.50

25th anniv. of the German Kulturbund.

1970, July 1 *Perf. 14x13½*

1225 A382 10pf blk, yel & brn red .20 .20

Issued to publicize the 3rd Children's and Youths' Spartakiad. See No. B156.

Meeting of the American, British and Russian Delegations — A383

10pf, Cecilienhof Castle. 20pf, "Potsdam Agreement" in German, English, French & Russian.

1970, July 28 Litho. *Perf. 13*

Size: 23x28mm

1226 A383 10pf blk, cit & red .20 .20
1227 A383 20pf blk, cit & red .20 .20

Size: 77x28mm

1228 A383 25pf red & blk .20 .20
a. Strip of 3, #1226-1228 .75 1.50

25th anniv. of the Potsdam Agreement among the Allies concerning Germany at the end of WWII.

Men's Pocket and Wrist Watches — A384

1970, Aug. 25 Photo. *Perf. 13½x14*
1229 A384 10pf ultra, blk & gold .25 .20

Leipzig Fall Fair, 1970.

Theodor Neubauer and Magnus Poser — A385

"Homeland" from Soviet Cenotaph, Berlin-Treptow A386

1970, Sept. 2 *Perf. 13x12½, 12½x13*
1230 A385 20pf dk bl, car & pale grn .20 .20
1231 A386 25pf dp car, pale bl .20 .20

Issued in memory of fighters against "fascism and imperialistic wars."

Competition Map and Compass — A387

Design: 25pf, Competition map and runner at 3 different stations.

1970, Sept. 15 Litho. *Perf. 13x12½*
1232 A387 10pf yellow & multi .20 .20
1233 A387 25pf yellow & multi *.70 .25*

World Orienting Championships.

Mother and Child, by Käthe Kollwitz — A388

Works of Art: 10pf, Forest Worker Scharf's Birthday, by Otto Nagel. 20pf, Portrait of a Girl, by Otto Nagel. 25pf, No More War, (Woman with raised arm) by Käthe Kollwitz. 40pf, Head from Gustrow Memorial, by Ernst Barlach. 50pf, The Flutist, by Ernst Barlach.

Photo.; Litho. (25pf, 30pf)
1970, Sept. 22 *Perf. 14x13½*
1234 A388 10pf multicolored .20 .20
1235 A388 20pf multicolored .20 .20
1236 A388 25pf pink & dk brn *.65 .85*
1237 A388 30pf sal & blk .20 .20
1238 A388 40pf yel & blk .20 .20
1239 A388 50pf yel & blk .20 .20
Nos. 1234-1239 (6) 1.65 1.85

Issued in memory of the artists Otto Nagel, Käthe Kollwitz and Ernst Barlach.

The Little Trumpeter A389

1970, Oct. 1 Photo.
1240 A389 10pf dp ultra, brn & org .20 .25

2nd Natl. Youth Stamp Exhib., Karl-Marx-Stadt, Oct. 4-11. The design shows the memorial in Halle for Fritz Weineck, trumpeter for the Red War Veterans' Organization. See No. B160.

Emblem with Flags of East Block Nations — A390

1970, Oct. 1 Litho. *Perf. 13x12½*
1241 A390 10pf carmine & multi .20 .20
1242 A390 20pf multicolored .20 .20

Issued to publicize the Brothers in Arms maneuvers of the East Bloc countries in the territory of the German Democratic Republic.

Musk Ox — A391

Berlin Zoo: 15pf, Shoebill. 20pf, Addax. 25pf, Malayan sun bear.

1970, Oct. 6 Photo. *Perf. 14*
1243 A391 10pf blue & multi .25 .20
1244 A391 15pf green & multi .25 .20
1245 A391 20pf org & multi .40 .25
1246 A391 25pf multicolored *3.75 3.00*
Nos. 1243-1246 (4) 4.65 3.65

UN Headquarters and Emblem — A392

1970, Oct. 20 Photo. *Perf. 13*
1247 A392 20pf ultra & multi .40 .20

25th anniversary of the United Nations.

Friedrich Engels A393

Epiphyllum A394

20pf, Friedrich Engels and Karl Marx. 25pf, Engels and title page of his polemic against Dühring.

Photogravure and Engraved
1970, Nov. 24 *Perf. 14*
1248 A393 10pf ver, gray & blk .20 .20
1249 A393 20pf ver, dk grn & blk .20 .20
1250 A393 25pf ver, dk car rose & blk *.75 .45*
Nos. 1248-1250 (3) 1.15 .85

Friedrich Engels (1820-1895), socialist, collaborator with Karl Marx.

1970, Dec. 2 Photo. *Perf. 14*

Flowering Cactus Plants: 10pf, Astrophytum myriostigma. 15pf, Echinocereus salm-dyckianus. 20pf, Selenicereus grandiflorus. 25pf, Hamatocactus setispinus. 30pf, Mamillaria boolii.

1251 A394 5pf multicolored .20 .20
1252 A394 10pf dk blue & multi .20 .20
1253 A394 15pf multicolored .20 .20
1254 A394 20pf multicolored .20 .20
1255 A394 25pf dk blue & multi *1.25 1.00*
1256 A394 30pf purple & multi .20 .20
Nos. 1251-1256 (6) 2.25 2.00

Souvenir Sheet

Ludwig van Beethoven — A395

1970, Dec. 10 Engr. *Perf. 14*
1257 A395 1m gray 1.25 2.00

Bicentenary of the birth of Ludwig van Beethoven (1770-1827), composer.

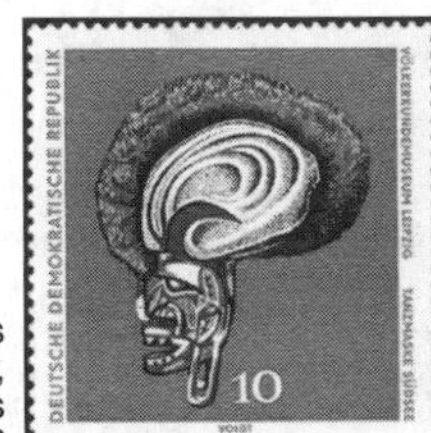

Dancer's Mask, South Seas A396

Works from Ethnological Museum, Leipzig: 20pf, Bronze head, Africa. 25pf, Tea pot, Asia. 40pf, Clay figure (jaguar), Mexico.

1971, Jan. 12 Photo. *Perf. 13*
1258 A396 10pf multicolored .20 .20
1259 A396 20pf multicolored .20 .20
1260 A396 25pf multicolored *.50 .50*
1261 A396 40pf multicolored .20 .20
Nos. 1258-1261 (4) 1.10 1.10

Venus 5, Soft-landing on Moon — A397

#1263, Model of space station. #1264, Luna 16 and Luna 10 satellites. #1265, Group flight of Sojuz 6, 7 and 8. #1266, Proton 1, radiation measuring satellite. #1267, Communications satellite Molniya 1. #1268, Yuri A. Gagarin, first flight of Vostok 1. #1269, Alexei Leonov walking in space, Voskhod 2.

1971, Feb. 11 Litho. *Perf. 13x12½*
1262 A397 20pf dk blue & multi .20 .20
1263 A397 20pf dk blue & multi .20 .20
1264 A397 20pf dk blue & multi .35 .35
1265 A397 20pf dk blue & multi .35 .35
1266 A397 20pf dk blue & multi .35 .35
1267 A397 20pf dk blue & multi .35 .35
1268 A397 20pf dk blue & multi .20 .20
1269 A397 20pf dk blue & multi .20 .20
a. Sheet of 8, #1262-1269 2.50 2.50

Soviet space research.

Johannes R. Becher A398

Karl Liebknecht A399

Portraits: 10pf, Heinrich Mann. 15pf, John Heartfield. 20pf, Willi Bredel. 25pf, Franz Mehring. 40pf, Rudolf Virchow. 50pf, Johannes Kepler.

1971 Engr. *Perf. 14*
1270 A398 5pf brown .20 .20
1271 A398 10pf vio blue .20 .20
1272 A398 15pf black .20 .20
1273 A398 20pf rose lake .20 .20
1274 A398 25pf green *.40 .45*
1274A A398 40pf pale purple .30 .20
1275 A398 50pf dp black .20 .20
Nos. 1270-1275 (7) 1.70 1.65

Honoring prominent Germans. See Nos. 1349-1353.

1971, Feb. 23 Photo.

Design: 25pf, Rosa Luxemburg.

1276 A399 20pf gold, mag & blk .30 .30
1277 A399 25pf gold, mag & blk .30 .30
a. Pair, #1276-1277 .85 .65

Karl Liebknecht (1871-1919) and Rosa Luxemburg (1871-1919), leaders of Spartacist Movement.

Soldier and Army Emblem — A400

1971, Mar. 1 *Perf. 13½x14*
1278 A400 20pf gray & multi .25 .20

15th anniv. of the National People's Army.

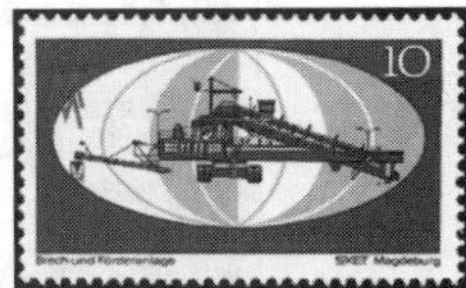

Crushing and Conveyor Plant, Magdeburg — A401

Leipzig Spring Fair: 15pf, Dredger for low temperature work.

1971, Mar. 9 Litho. *Perf. 13x12½*
1279 A401 10pf green & multi .20 .20
1280 A401 15pf multicolored .20 .20

Proclamation of the Commune, Town Hall, Paris — A402

Designs: 20pf, Barricade at Place Blanche, defended by women. 25pf, Illustration by Theophile A. Steinlen for the International. 30pf, Title page for "The Civil War in France," by Karl Marx.

1971, Mar. 9 *Perf. 13*

1281 A402 10pf red, bis & blk .20 .20
1282 A402 20pf red, bis & blk .20 .20
1283 A402 25pf red, buff & blk *.40 .45*
1284 A402 30pf red, gray & blk .20 .20
Nos. 1281-1284 (4) *1.00 1.05*

Centenary of the Paris Commune.

Lunokhod 1 on Moon — A403

1971, Mar. 30 **Photo.** *Perf. 14*

1285 A403 20pf multicolored .40 .25

Luna 17 unmanned, automated moon mission, Nov. 10-17, and the 24th Communist Party Congress of the Soviet Union.

Discobolus — A404

1971, Apr. 6 **Litho.** *Perf. 13½x13*

1286 A404 20pf dull bl, lt bl & buff .45 .20

20th anniversary of the Olympic Committee of German Democratic Republic.

Köpenick Castle — A405

Clasped Hands — A406

Berlin Buildings: 10pf, St. Mary's Church, vert. 20pf, Old Library. 25pf, Ermeler House, vert. 50pf, New Guard Memorial. 70pf, Natl. Gallery of Art.

Perf. 13½x14, 14x13½

1971, Apr. 6 **Photo.**

1287 A405 10pf multicolored .20 .20
1288 A405 15pf multicolored .20 .20
1289 A405 20pf multicolored .20 .20
1290 A405 25pf multicolored *2.10 1.50*
1291 A405 50pf multicolored .20 .20
1292 A405 70pf multicolored .25 .20
Nos. 1287-1292 (6) *3.15 2.50*

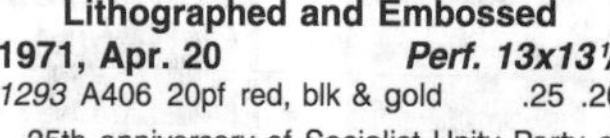

Lithographed and Embossed

1971, Apr. 20 *Perf. 13x13½*

1293 A406 20pf red, blk & gold .25 .20

25th anniversary of Socialist Unity Party of Germany (SED).

Dance Costume, Schleife — A407

Self-Portrait, by Dürer — A408

Sorbian Dance Costumes from: 20pf, Hoyerswerda. 25pf, Cottbus. 40pf, Kamenz.

1971, May 4 **Litho.** *Perf. 13½x13*

Size: 33x42mm

1294 A407 10pf multicolored .20 .20
1295 A407 20pf green & multi .20 .20
1296 A407 25pf blue & multi *.45 .45*
1297 A407 40pf multicolored .20 .20
Nos. 1294-1297 (4) *1.05 1.05*

1971, Nov. 23 *Perf. 13½x13*

Booklet Stamps

Size: 23x28mm

1297A A407 10pf multicolored .20 .20
c. Booklet pane of 4 .90 .90
d. Booklet pane, 2 #1297A, 2 #1297B 2.00 1.90
1297B A407 20pf multicolored .50 .30

1971, May 18 *Perf. 12½x13*

Art Works by Dürer: 40pf, Three Peasants. 70pf, Portrait of Philipp Melanchthon.

1298 A408 10pf multicolored .20 .20
1299 A408 40pf brown & multi .20 .20
1300 A408 70pf gray & multi *1.25 .60*
Nos. 1298-1300 (3) *1.65 1.00*

500th anniversary of the birth of Albrecht Dürer (1471-1528), painter and engraver.

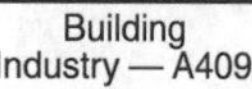

Building Industry — A409

Congress Emblem — A410

Designs: 10pf, Science and technology. No. 1303, Farming. 25pf, Civilian defense.

1971, June 9 **Photo.** *Perf. 14*

1301 A409 5pf cream, red & blk .20 .20
1302 A409 10pf cream, red & blk .20 .20
1303 A409 20pf cream, red, bl & blk .20 .20
1304 A410 20pf gold, dp car & red .25 .20
1305 A409 25pf cream, red & blk *.25 .30*
Nos. 1301-1305 (5) *1.10 1.10*

8th Congress of Socialist Unity Party of Germany (SED).

Golden Fleece, 1730 — A411

Treasures from the Green Vault, Dresden: 5pf, Cherry stone with 180 heads carved on it, 1590. 15pf, Tankard, Nuremberg, 1530. 20pf, Moor with drums on horseback, 1720. 25pf, Decorated writing box, 1562. 30pf, St. George pendant, 1570.

1971, June 22 *Perf. 13*

1306 A411 5pf dp car & multi .20 .20
1307 A411 10pf green & multi .20 .20
1308 A411 15pf violet & multi .20 .20
1309 A411 20pf multicolored .20 .20
1310 A411 25pf multicolored *.45 .70*
1311 A411 30pf multicolored .20 .20
Nos. 1306-1311 (6) *1.45 1.70*

Prisoners, by Fritz Cremer — A412

Design: 25pf, Brutality in Buchenwald Concentration Camp, by Fritz Cremer.

1971, June 22 **Litho.** *Perf. 13*

1312 A412 20pf bister & blk .35 .35
1313 A412 25pf lt blue & blk .35 .35
a. Pair, #1312-1313 with label between 1.10 1.25

Intl. Federation of Resistance Fighters (FIR), 20th anniv.

Coat of Arms of Mongolia — A413

1971, July 6 **Litho.** *Perf. 13*

1314 A413 20pf dk red, yel & blk .25 .20

50th anniv. of the Mongolian People's Revolution.

Child's Head, UNICEF Emblem — A414

1971, July 13 **Photo.**

1315 A414 20pf multicolored .25 .20

25th anniv. of UNICEF.

Militiaman, Soldier and Brandenburg Gate — A415

Design: 35pf, Brandenburg Gate and new buildings in East Berlin.

1971, Aug. 12

1316 A415 20pf red & multi .50 .20
1317 A415 35pf yel & multi 1.10 .55

10 years of Berlin Wall.

Passenger Ship Iwan Franko — A416

Ships: 15pf, Freighter, type 17. 20pf, Freighter Rostock, type XD. 25pf, Fish processing ship "Junge Welt." 40pf, Container cargo ship. 50pf, Explorer ship Akademik Kurtschatow.

1971, Aug. 24 **Engr.**

1318 A416 10pf pale purple .20 .20
1319 A416 15pf pale brn & ind .20 .20
1320 A416 20pf gray green .20 .20
1321 A416 25pf slate *.85 .80*
1322 A416 40pf maroon .20 .20
1323 A416 50pf grysh blue .20 .20
Nos. 1318-1323 (6) *1.85 1.80*

Shipbuilding industry.

Butadiene Plant — A417

Leipzig Fall Fair: 25pf, Refinery.

1971, Sept. 2 **Photo.** *Perf. 13*

1324 A417 10pf olive, vio & mag .20 .20
1325 A417 25pf blue, vio & ol .20 .20

Raised Fists, Photo Montage by John Heartfield, 1937 — A418

1971, Sept. 23

1326 A418 35pf grnsh bl, blk & sil .25 .20

Intl. Year Against Racial Discrimination.

Karl Marx Monument — A419

1971, Oct. 5 **Photo.** *Perf. 14x13½*

1327 A419 35pf vio brn, pink & buff .30 .20

Unveiling of Karl Marx memorial at Karl-Marx-Stadt (Chemnitz).

Wiltz Memorial, Flag of Luxembourg — A420

1971, Oct. 5

1328 A420 25pf multicolored .20 .20

Memorial for Nazi victims, Wiltz, Luxembourg.

Postal Milestones, Saxony, and Zürner's Surveyor Carriage — A421

Photo. & Engr.

1971, Oct. 5 ***Perf. 14***
1329 A421 25pf blue, olive & lilac *.30 .30*

Philatelists' Day 1971. See No. B162.

Darbuka, North Africa — A422

Geodetic Apparatus — A423

Musical Instruments: 15pf, Two morin chuur, Mongolia. 20pf, Violin, Germany. 25pf, Mandolin, Italy. 40pf, Bagpipes, Bohemia. 50pf, Kasso, Sudan.

1971, Oct. 26 Photo. ***Perf. 14x13½***
1330 A422 10pf multicolored .20 .20
1331 A422 15pf multicolored .20 .20
1332 A422 20pf ocher & multi .20 .20
1333 A422 25pf blue & multi .20 .20
1334 A422 40pf gray & multi .20 .20
1335 A422 50pf multicolored .70 .70
Nos. 1330-1335 (6) 1.70 1.70

Instruments from the Music Museum in Markneukirchen.

1971, Nov. 9 Photo. ***Perf. 13½x14***

20pf, Ergaval microscope. 25pf, Planetarium.

Size: 23½x28½mm

1336 A423 10pf blue, blk & red .30 .30
1337 A423 20pf blue, blk & red .30 .30

Size: 50½x28½mm

1338 A423 25pf blue, vio bl & yel .30 .30
a. Strip of 3, #1336-1338 2.25 2.25

Carl Zeiss optical works in Jena, 125th anniv.

Fairy Tale Type of 1966

Designs: Various Scenes from Fairy Tale "The Bremen Town Musicians."

1971, Nov. 23 Litho. ***Perf. 13½x13***
1339 A290 5pf multicolored .20 .20
1340 A290 10pf ocher & multi .20 .20
1341 A290 15pf gray & multi .40 .50
1342 A290 20pf ver & multi .40 .50
1343 A290 25pf violet & multi .20 .20
1344 A290 30pf yellow & multi .20 .20
a. Sheet of 6, #1339-1344 2.50 5.50

Olympic Rings and Sledding — A424

Olympic Rings and: 20pf, Long-distance skiing. 25pf, Biathlon. 70pf, Ski jump.

1971, Dec. 7 Photo. ***Perf. 13½x14***
1345 A424 5pf green, car & blk .20 .20
1346 A424 20pf car rose, vio & blk .20 .20
1347 A424 25pf vio, car & blk *1.10 .95*
1348 A424 70pf vio bl, vio & blk .20 .20
Nos. 1345-1348,B163-B164 (6) 2.10 1.95

11th Winter Olympic Games, Sapporo, Japan, Feb. 3-13, 1972.

Portrait Type of 1971

Portraits: 10pf, Johannes Tralow (1882-1968), playwright. 20pf, Leonhard Frank (1882-1961), writer. 25pf, K. A. Kocor (1822-1904), composer. 35pf, Heinrich Schliemann (1822-1890), archaeologist. 50pf, F. Caroline Neuber (1697-1760), actress.

1972, Jan. 25 Engr. ***Perf. 14***
1349 A398 10pf green .20 .20
1350 A398 20pf rose claret .20 .20
1351 A398 25pf dk blue .20 .20
1352 A398 35pf brown .20 .20
1353 A398 50pf rose violet *.65 .90*
Nos. 1349-1353 (5) 1.45 1.70

Honoring famous personalities.

Gypsum, Eisleben A425

Minerals found in East Germany: 10pf, Zinnwaldite, Zinnwald. 20pf, Malachite, Ullersreuth. 25pf, Amethyst, Wiesenbad. 35pf, Halite, Merkers. 50pf, Proustite, Schneeberg.

1972, Feb. 22 Photo. ***Perf. 13***
1354 A425 5pf grnsh bl & brn blk .20 .20
1355 A425 10pf citron, brn & blk .20 .20
1356 A425 20pf multicolored .20 .20
1357 A425 25pf multicolored .20 .20
1358 A425 35pf lt green, ind & blk .20 .20
1359 A425 50pf gray & multi *.75 .80*
Nos. 1354-1359 (6) 1.75 1.80

Russian Pavilion and Fair Emblem A426

Design: 25pf, Flags of East Germany and Russia, and Fair emblem.

1972, Mar. 3 Photo. ***Perf. 14***
1360 A426 10pf vio blue & multi .20 .20
1361 A426 25pf claret & multi .20 .20

50 years of Russian participation in the Leipzig Fair.

Miniature Sheets

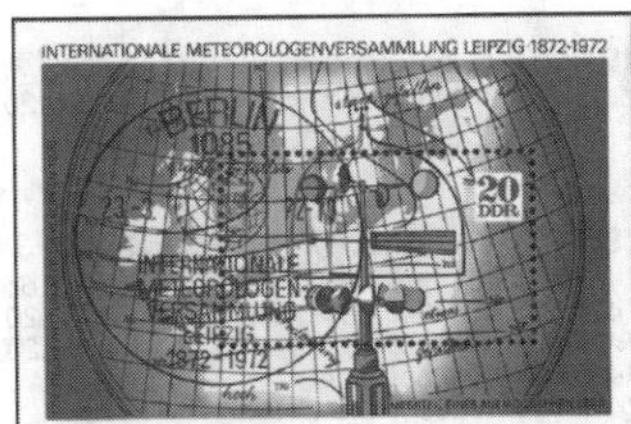

Anemometer, 1896, and Meteorological Chart, 1876 — A427

Designs: 35pf, Dipole and cloud photograph taken by satellite. 70pf, Meteor weather satellite and weather map.

1972, Mar. 23 Litho. ***Perf. 13x12½***
1362 A427 20pf multicolored .50 .60
1363 A427 35pf multicolored .50 .60
1364 A427 70pf green & multi .50 .60
Nos. 1362-1364 (3) 1.50 1.80

Intl. Meteorologists' Cent. Meeting, Leipzig.

World Health Organization Emblem — A428

1972, Apr. 4 Photo. ***Perf. 13***
1365 A428 35pf lt bl, vio bl & sil .25 .20

World Health Day.

Kamov Helicopter A429

Aircraft: 10pf, Agricultural spray plane. 35pf, Ilyushin jet. 1m, Jet and tail with Interflug emblem.

1972, Apr. 25 ***Perf. 14***
1366 A429 5pf blue & multi .20 .20
1367 A429 10pf multicolored .20 .20
1368 A429 35pf blue grn & multi .20 .20
1369 A429 1m multicolored *.90 1.10*
Nos. 1366-1369 (4) 1.50 1.70

Wrestling and Olympic Rings — A430

Sport and Olympic Rings: 20pf, Pole vault. 35pf, Volleyball. 70pf, Women's gymnastics.

1972, May 16 Photo. ***Perf. 13½x14***
1370 A430 5pf blue, gold & blk .20 .20
1371 A430 20pf mag, gold & blk .20 .20
1372 A430 35pf ol bis, gold & blk .20 .20
1373 A430 70pf yel grn, gold & blk *1.90 1.25*
Nos. 1370-1373,B166-B167 (6) 2.90 2.25

20th Olympic Games, Munich, 8/26-9/11.

Flags of USSR and German Democratic Republic — A431

20pf, Flags, Leonid Brezhnev & Erich Honecker.

1972, May 24 Engr. & Photo.
1374 A431 10pf red, yel & blk .35 .25
1375 A431 20pf red, yel & blk .35 .50

Soc. for German-Soviet Friendship, 25th anniv.

Workers — A432

Design: 35pf, Students.

1972, May 24 Litho. ***Perf. 13***
1376 A432 10pf dull yel, org & mag .20 .20
1377 A432 35pf dull yel & ultra .20 .20
a. Strip of 2, #1376-1377 + label .75 .60

8th Congress of Free German Trade Unions, Berlin.

Karneol Rose A433

1972, June 13 Photo. ***Perf. 13***

Size: 36x36mm

1378 A433 5pf shown .20 .20
1379 A433 10pf Berger's Erfurt Rose .20 .20
1380 A433 15pf Charme *1.10 1.10*
1381 A433 20pf Izetka Spree-Athens .20 .20
1382 A433 25pf Kopenick summer .20 .20
1383 A433 35pf Prof. Knoll .20 .20
Nos. 1378-1383 (6) 2.10 2.10

International Rose Exhibition.

Redrawn

1972, Aug. 22 ***Perf. 13½x13***

Booklet Stamps

Size: 23x28mm

1383A A433 10pf multicolored .20 .20
d. Booklet pane of 4 .60 .60
1383B A433 25pf multicolored .80 .30
e. Booklet pane of 4 (2 #1383B, 2 #1383C) 3.50 3.75
1383C A433 35pf multicolored .80 .30
Nos. 1383A-1383C (3) 1.80 .80

Young Mother and Child, by Cranach A434

Paintings by Lucas Cranach: 5pf, Young man. 35pf, Margarete Luther (Martin's mother). 70pf, Reclining nymph, horiz.

1972, July 4 ***Perf. 14x13½, 13½x14***
1384 A434 5pf gold & multi .20 .20
1385 A434 20pf gold & multi .20 .20
1386 A434 35pf gold & multi .20 .20
1387 A434 70pf gold & multi *1.40 1.90*
Nos. 1384-1387 (4) 2.00 2.50

Lucas Cranach (1472-1553), painter.

Compass and Motorcyclist — A435

Designs: 10pf, Parachute and light plane. 20pf, Target and military obstacle race. 25pf, Amateur radio transmitter, Morse key and tape. 35pf, Propeller and sailing ship.

1972, Aug. 8 Photo. ***Perf. 14***
1388 A435 5pf multicolored .20 .20
1389 A435 10pf multicolored .20 .20
1390 A435 20pf multicolored .20 .20
1391 A435 25pf multicolored *.40 .60*
1392 A435 35pf multicolored .20 .20
Nos. 1388-1392 (5) 1.20 1.40

Society for Sport and Technology.

Young Worker Reading, by Jutta Damme — A436

1972, Aug. 22 Photo. *Perf. 13½x14*
1393 A436 50pf multicolored .40 .25

International Book Year 1972.

Polylux Writing Projector — A437

George Dimitrov — A438

25pf, Pentacon-audiovision projector, horiz.

Perf. 12½x13, 13x12½
1972, Aug. 29 Litho.
1394 A437 10pf crimson & blk .20 .20
1395 A437 25pf brt green & blk .20 .20

Leipzig Fall Fair, 1972.

1972, Sept. 19 *Perf. 13x13½*
1396 A438 20pf rose red & blk .30 .20

George Dimitrov (1882-1949), Bulgarian Communist party leader.

Bird Catchers, Egypt, c. 2400 B.C. — A439

Design: 20pf, Tapestry with animal design, Anatolia, c. 1400 A.D.

1972, Sept. 19 Photo. *Perf. 14*
1397 A439 10pf multicolored .20 .20
1398 A439 20pf multicolored .20 .20
Nos. 1397-1398,B168-B169 (4) *1.25 1.25*

Interartes Philatelic Exhib., Berlin, Oct. 4-Nov. 11.

Red Cross Trainees and Red Cross — A440

1972, Oct. 3 Litho. *Perf. 13*

Designs: 15pf, Red Cross rescue launch in the Baltic. 35pf, Red Cross with world map, ship, plane and vehicles.

Size: 23x28mm
1399 A440 10pf grnsh bl, dk bl & red .20 .20
1400 A440 15pf grnsh bl, dk bl & red .20 .20

Size: 50x28mm
1401 A440 35pf grnsh bl, dk bl & red .20 .20
a. Strip of 3, #1399-1401 1.10 1.00

Red Cross at work in the DDR.

Arab Celestial Globe, 1279 — A441

Anti-Fascists Monument — A442

10pf, Globe, by Joachim R. Praetorius, 1568. 15pf, Globe clock, by Reinhold & Roll, 1586. 20pf, Globe clock, by J. Bürgi, c. 1590. 25pf, Armillary sphere, by J. Moeller, 1687. 35pf, Heraldic celestial globe, 1690.

1972, Oct. 17 Photo. *Perf. 14x13½*
1402 A441 5pf gray & multi .20 .20
1403 A441 10pf gray & multi .20 .20
1404 A441 15pf gray & multi *1.60 1.40*
1405 A441 20pf gray & multi .20 .20
1406 A441 25pf gray & multi .20 .20
1407 A441 35pf gray & multi .20 .20
Nos. 1402-1407 (6) *2.60 2.40*

Celestial and terrestrial globes from the National Mathematical and Physics Collection, Dresden.

1972, Oct. 24 Litho. *Perf. 12½x13*
1408 A442 25pf multicolored .30 .20

Monument for Polish soldiers and German anti-Fascists, unveiled in Berlin, May 14, 1972.

Young Workers Receiving Technical Education — A443

25pf, Workers with modern welding machine.

1972, Nov. 2 Photo. *Perf. 13½x14*
1409 A443 10pf blue & multi .20 .20
1410 A443 25pf blue & multi .20 .20
a. Strip of 2, #1409-1410 + label .60 .70

15th Central Fair of Masters of Tomorrow.

Mauz and Hoppel — A444

Designs: Children's television characters.

1972, Nov. 28 Litho. *Perf. 13½x13*
1411 A444 5pf shown .20 .20
1412 A444 10pf Fox and magpie .20 .20
1413 A444 15pf Mr. Owl .50 .50
1414 A444 20pf Mrs. Hedgehog and Borstel .50 .50
1415 A444 25pf Schnuffel and Peips .20 .20
1416 A444 35pf Paul from the Library .20 .20
a. Sheet of 6, #1411-1416 2.25 1.75

Grandmother, Children, Magic Mirror — A445

Scenes from Hans Christian Andersen's "Snow Queen": 10pf, Kay and Snow Queen. 15pf, Gerda in magic garden. 20pf, Gerda and crows at palace. 25pf, Gerda and reindeer in Lapland. 35pf, Gerda and Kay at Snow Queen's palace.

1972, Nov. 28 *Perf. 13x13½*
1417 A445 5pf multicolored .20 .25
1418 A445 10pf multicolored .40 .60
1419 A445 15pf multicolored .20 .25
1420 A445 20pf multicolored .20 .25
1421 A445 25pf multicolored .40 .60
1422 A445 35pf multicolored .20 .25
a. Sheet of 6, #1417-1422 2.50 5.50

See designs A469, A490.

Souvenir Sheet

Heinrich Heine — A446

1972, Dec. 5 *Perf. 12½x13*
1423 A446 1m brn ol, blk & red 1.25 2.50

150th anniversary of the birth of Heinrich Heine (1797-1856), poet.

Coat of Arms of USSR A447

Michelangelo da Caravaggio A448

1972, Dec. 5 Photo. *Perf. 13½x14*
1424 A447 20pf red & multi .30 .20

50th anniversary of the Soviet Union.

1973 Litho. *Perf. 13½x13*
1425 A448 5pf brown *.50 .65*
1426 A448 10pf dull green .20 .20
1427 A448 20pf rose lilac .20 .20
1428 A448 25pf blue .20 .20
1429 A448 35pf brown red .20 .20
1429A A448 40pf rose claret .30 .20
Nos. 1425-1429A (6) *1.60 1.65*

Michelangelo da Caravaggio (1565(?)-1609), Italian painter (5pf). Friedrich Wolf (1888-1953), writer (10pf). Max Reger (1873-1916), composer (20pf). Max Reinhardt (1873-1943), Austrian theatrical director (25pf). Johannes Dieckmann (1893-1969), member and president of People's Chamber (35pf). Hermann Matern (1893-1971), vice-president of DDR (40pf).

Lenin Square, Berlin — A449

Coat of Arms of DDR — A449a

Designs: 5pf, Pelican, Berlin Zoo. 10pf, Neptune Fountain, City Hall Street. 15pf, Fisherman's Island, Berlin. 25pf, World clock, Alexander Square, Berlin. 30pf, Workers' Memorial, Halle. 35pf, Marx monument, Karl-Marx-Stadt. 40pf, Brandenburg Gate, Berlin. 50pf, New Guardhouse, Berlin. 60pf, Zwinger, Dresden. 70pf, Old Town Hall, Office Building, Leipzig. 80pf, Old and new buildings, Rostock-Warnemunde. 1m, Soviet War Memorial, Treptow.

1973-74 Engr. *Perf. 14x14*
Size: 29x23½mm
1430 A449 5pf blue green .20 .20
1431 A449 10pf emerald .30 .20
1432 A449 15pf rose lilac .25 .20
1433 A449 20pf rose magenta .60 .20
1434 A449 25pf grnsh blue .60 .20
1435 A449 30pf orange .20 .20
1436 A449 35pf grnsh blue .60 .20
1437 A449 40pf dull violet .25 .20
1438 A449 50pf blue, *bluish* .30 .20
1439 A449 60pf lilac ('74) .60 .20
1440 A449 70pf redsh brown .60 .20
1441 A449 80pf vio blue ('74) .60 .20
1442 A449 1m olive .95 .20
1443 A449a 2m lake 1.50 .20
1443A A449a 3m rose lilac ('74) 2.00 .50
Nos. 1430-1443A (15) 9.55 3.30

See Nos. 1610-1617, 2071-2085.

Lebachia Speciosa (Oldest Conifer) A450

Fossils from Natural History Museum, Berlin: 15pf, Sphenopteris hollandica (carbon fern). 20pf, Pterodactylus kochi (flying reptile). 25pf, Botryopteris (permian fern). 35pf, Archaeopteryx lithographica (primitive reptile-like bird). 70pf, Odontopieura ovata (trilobite).

1973, Feb. 6 Photo. *Perf. 13*
1444 A450 10pf multicolored .20 .20
1445 A450 15pf ultra, gray & blk .20 .20
1446 A450 20pf yellow & multi .20 .20
1447 A450 25pf emerald, blk & brn .20 .20
1448 A450 35pf ocher & multi .20 .20
1449 A450 70pf ind, blk & yel *1.00 1.25*
Nos. 1444-1449 (6) *2.00 2.25*

Bobsled Track, Oberhof — A451

1973, Feb. 13 Litho. *Perf. 12½x13*
1450 A451 35pf dk bl, bl & org .30 .25

15th Bobsledding Championships, Oberhof.

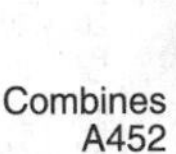

Combines A452

Leipzig Spring Fair: 25pf, Computerized threshing and silage producing machine.

1973, Mar. 6 Litho. *Perf. 13x12½*

1451 A452 10pf olive & multi .20 .20
1452 A452 25pf blue & multi .25 .25

Firecrests A453

Songbirds: 10pf, White-winged crossbill. 15pf, Waxwing. 20pf, White-spotted and red-spotted bluethroats. 25pf, Goldfinch. 35pf, Golden oriole. 40pf, Gray wagtail. 50pf, Wall creeper.

1973, Mar. 20 Photo. *Perf. 14x13½*

1453 A453 5pf multicolored .20 .20
1454 A453 10pf multicolored .20 .20
1455 A453 15pf multicolored .20 .20
1456 A453 20pf multicolored .20 .20
1457 A453 25pf multicolored .20 .20
1458 A453 35pf multicolored .20 .20
1459 A453 40pf multicolored .20 .20
1460 A453 50pf ocher & multi 2.00 2.00
Nos. 1453-1460 (8) 3.40 3.40

Copernicus and Title Page — A454

1973, Feb. 13 Litho. *Perf. 13½x13*

1461 A454 70pf multicolored .50 .30

500th anniversary of the birth of Nicolaus Copernicus (1473-1543), astronomer.

Electric Locomotive — A455

Railroad Cars Manufactured in DDR: 10pf, Refrigerator car. 20pf, Long-distance coach. 25pf, Multiple tank car with pneumatic filling device. 35pf, Two-story coach. 85pf, International coaches.

1973, May 22 Litho. *Perf. 13x12½*

1462 A455 5pf gray & multi .20 .20
1463 A455 10pf brt blue & multi .20 .20
1464 A455 20pf dk blue & multi .20 .20
1465 A455 25pf gray & multi .20 .20
1466 A455 35pf multicolored .20 .20
1467 A455 85pf green & multi 1.60 1.60
Nos. 1462-1467 (6) 2.60 2.60

King Lear, Staged by Wolfgang Langhoff A456

Great Theatrical Productions: 25pf, Midsummer Marriage, staged by Walter Felsenstein. 35pf, Mother Courage, staged by Bertolt Brecht.

1973, May 29 Photo. *Perf. 13*

1468 A456 10pf maroon, rose & yel .20 .20
1469 A456 25pf vio bl, lt bl & rose .20 .20
1470 A456 35pf dk gray, bis & bl .60 .60
Nos. 1468-1470 (3) 1.00 1.00

Goethe and his Home in Weimar — A457

Fireworks, TV Tower, World Clock — A458

Designs (Portraits and Houses): 15pf, Christoph Martin Wieland. 20pf, Friedrich von Schiller. 25pf, Johann Gottfried Herder. 35pf, Lucas Cranach, the Elder. 50pf, Franz Liszt.

1973, June 26 Litho. *Perf. 12½x13*

1471 A457 10pf blue & multi .20 .20
1472 A457 15pf multicolored .20 .20
1473 A457 20pf multicolored .20 .20
1474 A457 25pf multicolored .20 .20
1475 A457 35pf green & multi .20 .20
1476 A457 50pf multicolored 1.50 1.00
Nos. 1471-1476 (6) 2.50 2.00

Famous men and their homes in Weimar.

1973

Designs (Festival Emblem and): 15pf, Vietnamese and European men, book and girder. 20pf, Construction workers and valve. 30pf, Negro and European students, dam and retort. 35pf, Emblems of World Federation of Democratic Youth and International Students Union. 50pf, Brandenburg Gate.

1477 A458 5pf vio blue & multi .20 .20
a. Booklet pane of 4 .75 .75
1478 A458 15pf olive & multi .20 .20
1479 A458 20pf multicolored .20 .20
a. Booklet pane of 4 .75 .75
1480 A458 30pf blue & multi .70 .50
1481 A458 35pf green & multi .20 .20
Nos. 1477-1481 (5) 1.50 1.30

Souvenir Sheet

1482 A458 50pf aqua & multi .70 1.25

10th Festival of Youths and Students, Berlin, July 1973.

Issued: #1477-1481, July 3; #1482, July 26.

Ulbricht Type of 1961-67

1973, Aug. 8 Engr. *Perf. 14*

Size: 24x28½mm

1483 A189 20pf black .40 .25

In memory of Walter Ulbricht (1893-1973), chairman of Council of State.

Pylon, Map of Electric Power System — A459

1973, Aug. 14 Photo. *Perf. 14*

1484 A459 35pf magenta, org & lt bl .30 .25

10th anniversary of the united East European electric power system "Peace."

Sports Equipment — A460

Design: 25pf, Sailboat, guitar, electric drill.

1973, Aug. 28 Photo. *Perf. 14*

1485 A460 10pf multicolored .20 .20
1486 A460 25pf multicolored .25 .20

Leipzig Fall Fair and EXPOVITA exhibition for leisure time equipment.

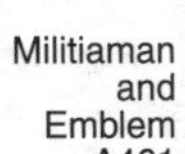

Militiaman and Emblem A461

Designs: 20pf, Militia guarding border at Brandenburg Gate. 50pf, Representatives of Red Veterans' League, International Brigade in Spain and Workers' Militia in DDR, vert.

1973, Sept. 11 Litho. *Perf. 13x12½*

1487 A461 10pf multicolored .20 .20
1488 A461 20pf tan, red & blk .20 .20

Souvenir Sheet

Perf. 12½x13

1489 A461 50pf multicolored .55 1.25

20th anniversary of Workers' Militia of the German Democratic Republic.

Globe and Red Flag Emblem A462

1973, Sept. 11 Photo. *Perf. 13½x14*

1490 A462 20pf gold & red .30 .20

15th anniversary of the review "Problems of Peace and Socialism," published in Prague in 28 languages.

Memorial, Langenstein-Zwieberge — A463

1973, Sept. 18 *Perf. 14x13½*

1491 A463 25pf multicolored .30 .20

In memory of the workers who perished in the subterranean munitions works at Langenstein-Zwieberge.

UN Headquarters, NY, UN and DDR Emblems — A464

1973, Sept. 21 *Perf. 13*

1492 A464 35pf multicolored .30 .20

Admission of the DDR to the UN.

Union Emblem A465

Rocket Launching — A466

1973, Oct. 11 Photo. *Perf. 14x13½*

1493 A465 35pf silver & multi .30 .25

8th Congress of the World Federation of Trade Unions, Varna, Bulgaria.

1973, Oct. 23 *Perf. 14*

20pf, Emblem with map of Russia & hammer & sickle, horiz. 25pf, Oil refinery, Ryazan.

1494 A466 10pf violet bl & multi .20 .20
1495 A466 20pf vio bl, red & sil .20 .20
1496 A466 25pf multicolored .65 .60
Nos. 1494-1496 (3) 1.05 1.00

Soviet Science & Technology Days in DDR.

Madonna with the Rose, by Parmigianino A467

Paintings: 10pf Child with Doll, by Christian L. Vogel. 20pf, Woman with Plaited Blond Hair, by Rubens. 25pf, Lady in White, by Titian. 35pf, Archimedes, by Domenico Fetti. 70pf, Bouquet with Blue Iris, by Jan D. de Heem.

1973, Nov. 13 Photo. *Perf. 14*

1497 A467 10pf gold & multi .20 .20
1498 A467 15pf gold & multi .20 .20
1499 A467 20pf gold & multi .20 .20
1500 A467 25pf gold & multi .20 .20
1501 A467 35pf gold & multi .20 .20
1502 A467 70pf gold & multi 1.75 1.25
Nos. 1497-1502 (6) 2.75 2.25

Human Rights Flame A468

1973, Nov. 20 *Perf. 13*

1503 A468 35pf dp rose, dk car & sil .35 .25

25th anniv. of the Universal Declaration of Human Rights.

Boy Holding Pike — A469

Designs: Various scenes from Russian Folktale "At the Bidding of the Pike."

1973, Dec. 4 Litho. *Perf. 13x13½*
1504 A469 5pf multicolored .20 .40
1505 A469 10pf multicolored .60 .40
1506 A469 15pf multicolored .20 .40
1507 A469 20pf multicolored .20 .40
1508 A469 25pf multicolored .60 .40
1509 A469 35pf multicolored .20 .40
a. Sheet of 6, #1504-1509 2.25 3.50

Edwin Hoernle — A470

1974 Litho. *Perf. 13½x13*

#1511, Etkar Andre. #1512, Paul Merker. #1513, Hermann Duncker. #1514, Fritz Heckert. #1515, Otto Grotewohl. #1516, Wilhelm Florin. #1517, Georg Handke. #1518, Rudolf Breitscheid. #1519, Kurt Bürger. #1519A Carl Moltmann.

1510 A470 10pf gray green .20 .20
1511 A470 10pf rose violet .20 .20
1512 A470 10pf dark blue .20 .20
1513 A470 10pf brown .20 .20
1514 A470 10pf dull green .20 .20
1515 A470 10pf red brown .20 .20
1516 A470 10pf vio blue .20 .20
1517 A470 10pf olive brown .20 .20
1518 A470 10pf slate green .20 .20
1519 A470 10pf dull violet .20 .20
1519A A470 10pf brown .20 .20
Nos. 1510-1519A (11) 2.20 2.20

Leaders of German labor movement.
Issued: #1510-1517, Jan. 8; others July 9.

Flags of Comecon Members A471

1974, Jan. 22 Photo. *Perf. 13*
1520 A471 20pf red & multi .30 .20

25th anniversary of the Council of Mutual Economic Assistance (Comecon).

Pablo Neruda and Chilean Flag A472

1974, Jan. 22 *Perf. 14*
1521 A472 20pf multicolored .30 .20

Pablo Neruda (Neftali Ricardo Reyes, 1904-1973), Chilean poet.

Echinopsis Multiplex A473

Fieldball A474

Various Flowering Cacti: 10pf, Lobivia haageana. 15pf, Parodia sanguiniflora. 20pf, Gymnocal. monvillei. 25pf, Neoporteria rapifera. 35pf, Notocactus concinnus.

1974, Feb. 12 Photo. *Perf. 14*
1522 A473 5pf multicolored .20 .20
1523 A473 10pf tan & multi .20 .20
1524 A473 15pf green & multi 1.60 1.40
1525 A473 20pf multicolored .20 .20
1526 A473 25pf violet & multi .20 .20
1527 A473 35pf multicolored .20 .20
Nos. 1522-1527 (6) 2.60 2.40

1974, Feb. 26 Litho. *Perf. 13*

Design: Various fieldball scenes.

1528 A474 5pf green & multi .25 .25
1529 A474 10pf green & multi .25 .25
1530 A474 35pf green & multi .25 .25
a. Strip of 3, #1528-1530 .90 .90

8th World Fieldball Championships for Men.

Power Testing Station — A475

Leipzig Spring Fair: 25pf, Robotron EC 2040 data processer, horiz.

1974, Mar. 5 Photo. *Perf. 14*
1531 A475 10pf multicolored .20 .20
1532 A475 25pf multicolored .25 .20

Poisonous European Mushrooms A476

1974, Mar. 19 Litho. *Perf. 13x13½*

Designs: 5pf, Rhodophyllus Sinuatus. 10pf, Boletus satanas. 15pf, Amanita pantherina. 20pf, Amanita muscaria. 25pf, Gyromitra esculenta. 30pf, Inocybe patouillardii. 35pf, Amanita phalloides. 40pf, Clitocybe dealbata.

1533 A476 5pf buff & multi .20 .20
1534 A476 10pf buff & multi .20 .20
1535 A476 15pf buff & multi .20 .20
1536 A476 20pf buff & multi .20 .20
1537 A476 25pf buff & multi .20 .20
1538 A476 30pf buff & multi .20 .20
1539 A476 35pf buff & multi .20 .20
1540 A476 40pf buff & multi 1.10 1.00
Nos. 1533-1540 (8) 2.50 2.40

Gustav Robert Kirchhoff — A477

Portraits: 10pf, Immanuel Kant. 20pf, Ehm Welk. 25pf, Johann Gottfried Herder. 35pf, Lion Feuchtwanger.

1974, Mar. 26 Litho. *Perf. 13½x13*
1541 A477 5pf black & gray .20 .20
1542 A477 10pf vio bl & dull bl .20 .20
1543 A477 20pf maroon & rose .20 .20
1544 A477 25pf slate grn & grn .20 .20
1545 A477 35pf brn & lt brn .50 .45
Nos. 1541-1545 (5) 1.30 1.25

"Peace" A477a

1974, Apr. 16 *Perf. 13*
1548 A477a 35pf silver & multi .30 .25

1st World Peace Congress, 25th anniv.

Truck Driver and Arms of DDR A477b

1974, Apr. 30 Photo. *Perf. 13*
1549 A477b 10pf shown .20 .20
1550 A477b 20pf Students .20 .20
1551 A477b 25pf Woman worker .20 .20
1552 A477b 35pf Family .70 .70
Nos. 1549-1552 (4) 1.30 1.30

25th anniv. of the DDR.

Buk Lighthouse, 1878, and Map — A478

Lighthouses, Maps and Nautical Charts: 15pf, Warnemünde, 1898. 20pf, Darsser Ort, 1848. 35pf, Arkona, 1827 and 1902. 40pf, Greifswalder Oie, 1855.

1974, May 7 Litho. *Perf. 14*
1553 A478 10pf multicolored .20 .20
1554 A478 15pf multicolored .20 .20
1555 A478 20pf multicolored .20 .20
1556 A478 35pf multicolored .20 .20
1557 A478 40pf multicolored .90 .75
Nos. 1553-1557 (5) 1.70 1.55

Hydrographic Service of German Democratic Republic. See Nos. 1645-1649.

The Ages of Man, by C. D. Friedrich — A479

C. D. Friedrich, Self-portrait — A480

Paintings by Friedrich: 10pf, Two Men Observing Moon. 25pf, The Heath near Dresden. 35pf, View of Elbe Valley.

1974, May 21 Photo. *Perf. 13½*
1558 A479 10pf gold & multi .20 .20
1559 A479 20pf gold & multi .20 .20
1560 A479 25pf gold & multi 1.25 1.10
1561 A479 35pf gold & multi .20 .20
Nos. 1558-1561 (4) 1.85 1.70

Souvenir Sheet

Engr.

Perf. 14x13½

1562 A480 70pf sepia 1.00 1.50

Caspar David Friedrich (1774-1840), German Romantic painter.

Plauen Lace — A481

Designs: Various Plauen lace patterns.

1974, June 11 Litho. *Perf. 13*
1563 A481 10pf violet, lil & blk .20 .20
1564 A481 20pf brown ol & blk .20 .20
1565 A481 25pf bl, lt bl & blk .95 .85
1566 A481 35pf lil rose, rose & blk .20 .20
Nos. 1563-1566 (4) 1.55 1.45

Trotter — A482

Designs: 10pf, Thoroughbred hurdling, vert. 25pf, Haflinger breed horses. 35pf, British thoroughbred race horse.

Perf. 14x13½, 13½x14
1974, Aug. 13 Photo.
1570 A482 10pf olive & multi .20 .20
1571 A482 20pf multicolored .20 .20
1572 A482 25pf lt blue & multi 1.10 1.10
1573 A482 35pf ocher & multi .20 .20
Nos. 1570-1573 (4) 1.70 1.70

International Horse Breeders' of Socialist Countries Congress, Berlin.

Crane Lifting Diesel Locomotive — A483

Leipzig Fall Fair: 25pf, Sugar beet harvester, type KS6.

1974, Aug. 27 Litho. *Perf. 13x12½*
1574 A483 10pf multicolored .20 .20
1575 A483 25pf orange & multi .25 .20

Miniature China and Mirror Exhibits — A484

Designs: Scenes from 18th century Thuringia, Dolls' Village, Arnstadt Castle Museum.

1974, Sept. 10 Photo. *Perf. 14x13½*
1576 A484 5pf shown .20 .20
1577 A484 10pf Harlequin barker at Fair .20 .20
1578 A484 15pf Wine tasters .20 .20
1579 A484 20pf Cooper and apprentice .20 .20
1580 A484 25pf Bagpiper .95 1.00
1581 A484 35pf Butcher and beggar, women .20 .20
Nos. 1576-1581 (6) 1.95 2.00

Bound Guerrillas, Ardeatine Caves, Rome — A485

Design: No. 1583, Resistance Fighters, monument near Chateaubriant, France.

1974, Sept. 24 ***Perf. 13½x14***

1582 A485 35pf green, blk & red .25 .25
1583 A485 35pf blue, blk & red .25 .25

International war memorials.

Souvenir Sheet

Family and Flag — A486

1974, Oct. 3 **Photo.** ***Perf. 13***

1584 A486 1m multicolored 1.10 2.50

25th anniv. of the DDR.

Freighter and Paddle Steamer — A487

Cent. of the UPU: 20pf, Old steam locomotive and modern Diesel. 25pf, Bi-plane and jet. 35pf, Mail coach and truck.

1974, Oct. 9 ***Perf. 14***

1585 A487 10pf green & multi .20 .20
1586 A487 20pf multicolored .20 .20
1587 A487 25pf blue & multi .20 .20
1588 A487 35pf multicolored .65 .65
Nos. 1585-1588 (4) 1.25 1.25

"In Praise of Dialectics" A488

1974, Oct. 24 **Litho.** ***Perf. 13x13½***

Designs: 10pf+5pf, "Praise to the Revolutionaries." 25pf, "Praise to the Party." Designs are from bas-reliefs by Rossdeutscher, Jastram and Wetzel, illustrating poems by Bertholt Brecht.

1589 A488 10pf + 5pf multi .20 .20
1590 A488 20pf multicolored .20 .20
1591 A488 25pf multicolored .20 .20
a. Strip of 3, #1589-1591 .85 .75

DDR '74 Natl. Stamp Exhib., Karl-Marx-Stadt.

Souvenir Sheet

Drawings by Young Pioneers — A489

1974, Nov. 26 **Litho.** ***Perf. 14***

1592 A489 Sheet of 4 1.25 1.10
a. 20pf Sun shines on everybody .25 .25
b. 20pf My Friend Sascha .25 .25
c. 20pf Carsten, the Best Swimmer .25 .25
d. 20pf Me at the Blackboard .25 .25

Young Pioneers' drawings (7-10 years old).

Man Cutting Tree, and Bird — A490

Designs: Various scenes from Russian folktale "Twittering To and Fro."

1974, Dec. 3 ***Perf. 13x13½***

1593 A490 10pf multicolored .20 .20
1594 A490 15pf multicolored .60 .60
1595 A490 20pf multicolored .20 .20
1596 A490 30pf multicolored .20 .20
1597 A490 35pf multicolored .60 .60
1598 A490 40pf multicolored .20 .20
a. Sheet of 6, #1593-1598 2.50 3.00

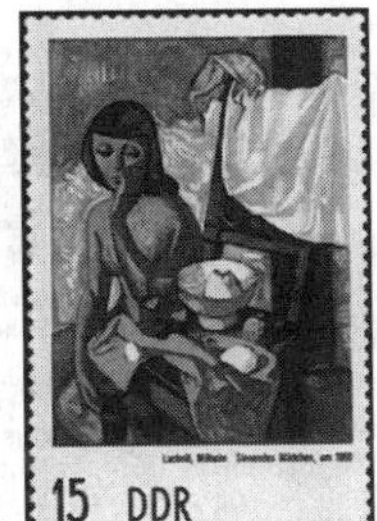

Meditating Girl, by Wilhelm Lachnit — A491

1974, Dec. 10 ***Perf. 13½x14, 14x13½***

Paintings: 10pf, Still Life, by Ronald Paris, horiz. 20pf, Fisherman's House, Vitte, by Harald Hakenbeck. 35pf, Girl in Red, by Rudolf Bergander, horiz. 70pf, The Artist's Parents, by Willi Sitte.

1599 A491 10pf multicolored .20 .20
1600 A491 15pf multicolored .20 .20
1601 A491 20pf multicolored .20 .20
1602 A491 35pf multicolored .20 .20
1603 A491 70pf multicolored 1.25 1.25
Nos. 1599-1603 (5) 2.05 2.05

Paintings in Berlin Museums.

Banded Jasper — A492

Minerals from the collection of the Mining Academy in Freiberg: 15pf, Smoky quartz. 20pf, Topaz. 25pf, Amethyst. 35pf, Aquamarine. 70pf, Agate.

1974, Dec. 17 **Photo.** ***Perf. 14***

1604 A492 10pf lt yellow & multi .20 .20
1605 A492 15pf lt yellow & multi .20 .20
1606 A492 20pf lt yellow & multi .20 .20
1607 A492 25pf lt yellow & multi .20 .20
1608 A492 35pf lt yellow & multi .20 .20
1609 A492 70pf lt yellow & multi 1.25 1.25
Nos. 1604-1609 (6) 2.25 2.25

Type of 1973

Coil Stamps

1974-75 **Photo.** ***Perf. 14***

Size: 21x17½mm

1610 A449 5pf blue grn ('74) .30 .50
1611 A449 10pf emerald .20 .20
1612 A449 20pf rose magenta .35 .20
1613 A449 25pf green ('75) .30 .20
1615 A449 50pf blue ('74) 1.00 1.75
1617 A449 1m olive ('74) 1.25 1.75
Nos. 1610-1617 (6) 3.40 4.60

Black control number on back of every fifth stamp.

The 20pf was issued in sheets of 100 in 1975.

Martha Arendsee (1885-1953), Communist Politician — A493

1975, Jan. 14 **Litho.** ***Perf. 13½x13***

1618 A493 10pf dull red .25 .20

Souvenir Sheet

Peasants' War, Contemporary Woodcuts — A494

1975, Feb. 11 ***Perf. 12½x13***

1619 A494 Sheet of 6 + label 2.50 5.00
a. 5pf Forced labor .25 .25
b. 10pf Peasant paying tithe .25 .25
c. 20pf Thomas Munzer .25 .25
d. 25pf Armed peasants .45 .35
e. 35pf Peasant, "Liberty" flag .45 .35
f. 50pf Peasant on trial .25 .25

Peasants' War, 450th anniversary.

Black Women — A495

Designs: 20pf, Caucasian women. 25pf, Indian woman and child.

1975, Feb. 25 **Litho.** ***Perf. 13***

1620 A495 10pf red & multi .20 .20
1621 A495 20pf red & multi .20 .20
1622 A495 25pf red & multi .20 .20
a. Strip of 3, Nos. 1620-1622 .85 .70

International Women's Year 1975.

Microfilm Pentakta Camera A496

Leipzig Spring Fair: 25pf, Sket cement plant.

1975, Mar. 4 **Photo.** ***Perf. 14***

1623 A496 10pf ultra & multi .20 .20
1624 A496 25pf orange & multi .20 .20

A497

Portraits: 5pf, Hans Otto (1900-33), actor. 10pf, Thomas Mann (1875-1955), writer. 20pf, Albert Schweitzer (1875-1965), medical missionary. 25pf, Michelangelo (1475-1564), painter and sculptor. 35pf, André Marie Ampère (1775-1836), scientist.

1975, Mar. 18 **Litho.** ***Perf. 13½x13***

1625 A497 5pf dk blue .20 .20
1626 A497 10pf dk car rose .20 .20
1627 A497 20pf dk green .20 .20
1628 A497 25pf sepia .20 .20
1629 A497 35pf vio blue .55 .60
Nos. 1625-1629 (5) 1.35 1.40

Famous men, birth anniversaries.

A498

German Zoological Gardens: 5pf, Blue and yellow macaws, Magdeburg Zoo. 10pf, Orangutan family, Dresden. 15pf, Siberian chamois, Halle. 20pf, Rhinoceros, Berlin. 25pf, Dwarf hippopotamus, Erfurt. 30pf, Baltic seal and pup, Rostock. 35pf, Siberian tiger, Leipzig. 50pf, Boehm's zebra, Cottbus. 20pf, 25pf, 30pf, 35pf are horiz.

1975, Mar. 25 ***Perf. 13½x13, 13x13½***

1630 A498 5pf multicolored .20 .20
1631 A498 10pf multicolored .20 .20
1632 A498 15pf multicolored .20 .20
1633 A498 20pf multicolored .20 .20
1634 A498 25pf multicolored .20 .20
1635 A498 30pf multicolored .20 .20
1636 A498 35pf multicolored .20 .20
1637 A498 50pf multicolored 1.10 1.00
Nos. 1630-1637 (8) 2.50 2.40

Soldiers, Industry and Agriculture — A499

1975, May 6 **Photo.** ***Perf. 13½x14***

1638 A499 20pf multicolored .65 .20

20th anniv. of the signing of the Warsaw Treaty (Bulgaria, Czechoslovakia, DDR, Hungary, Poland, Romania, USSR).

Soviet War Memorial, Berlin-Treptow A500

Designs (Arms of German Democratic Rep. and): 20pf, Buchenwald Memorial (detail). 25pf, Woman reconstruction worker. 35pf, Skyscraper and statue at Orenburg (economic integration). 50pf, Soldier raising Red Flag on Reichstag Building, Berlin.

1975, May 6 ***Perf. 14x13½***

1639 A500 10pf red & multi .20 .20
1640 A500 20pf red & multi .20 .20
1641 A500 25pf red & multi .20 .20
1642 A500 35pf red & multi .50 .50
Nos. 1639-1642 (4) 1.10 1.10

Souvenir Sheet

Imperf

1643 A500 50pf red & multi .60 1.25

30th anniversary of liberation from fascism.

Ribbons, Youth Organization Emblems of DDR and USSR — A501

1975, May 13 ***Perf. 14***

1644 A501 10pf multicolored .25 .20

Third Friendship Festival of Russian and German Youths, Halle, 1975.

Lighthouse Type of 1974

Lighthouses, Maps and Nautical Charts: 5pf, Timmendorf, 1872. 10pf, Gellen, 1905. 20pf, Sassnitz, 1904. 25pf, Dornbush, 1888. 35pf, Peenemünde, 1954.

1975, May 13 **Litho.** ***Perf. 14***

1645 A478 5pf multicolored .20 .20
1646 A478 10pf multicolored .20 .20
1647 A478 20pf multicolored .20 .20
1648 A478 25pf multicolored .20 .20
1649 A478 35pf multicolored *.65 .65*
Nos. 1645-1649 (5) *1.45 1.45*

Hydrographic Service of the DDR.

Wilhelm Liebknecht, August Bebel — A502

20pf, Tivoli House & front page of Protocol of Gotha. 25pf, Karl Marx & Friedrich Engels.

1975, May 21 **Photo.**

1650 A502 10pf buff, brn & red *.20 .20*
1651 A502 20pf salmon, brn & red *.20 .20*
1652 A502 25pf buff, brn & red *.20 .20*
a. Strip of 3, #1650-1652 *.80 .55*

Centenary of the Congress of Gotha, the beginning of German Socialist Workers' Party.

Construction Workers, Union Emblem — A503

1975, June 10 **Photo.** ***Perf. 14***

1653 A503 20pf red & multi .25 .20

Free German Association of Trade Unions (FDGB), 30th anniversary.

"Socialist Scientific Cooperation" Mosaic by Walter Womacka A504

1975, June 10 **Litho.** ***Perf. 13***

1654 A504 20pf multicolored .25 .20

Eisenhüttenstadt, first socialist city of DDR, 25th anniversary.

Automatic Clock by Paulus Schuster, 1585 — A505

Clocks, Dresden Museums: 10pf, Astronomical table clock, Augsburg, c. 1560. 15pf, Automatic clock, Hans Schlottheim, c. 1600. 20pf, Table clock, Johann Heinrich Köhler, c. 1720. 25pf, Table clock, Köhler, c. 1700. 35pf, Astronomical clock, Johannes Klein, 1738.

1975, June 24 **Photo.** ***Perf. 14***

1655 A505 5pf multicolored .20 .20
1656 A505 10pf ultra & multi .20 .20
1657 A505 15pf red & multi *.95 1.00*
1658 A505 20pf olive & multi .20 .20
1659 A505 25pf multicolored .20 .20
1660 A505 35pf ocher & multi .20 .20
Nos. 1655-1660 (6) *1.95 2.00*

Dictionary, Compiled by Jacob and Wilhelm Grimm — A506

20pf, Karl-Schwarzschild Observatory, Tautenburg near Jena. 25pf, Electron microscope & chemical plant (scientific & practical cooperation). 35pf, Intercosmos 10 satellite.

1975, July 2 **Litho.** ***Perf. 13½x13***

1661 A506 10pf plum, ol & blk .20 .20
1662 A506 20pf vio bl & blk .20 .20
1663 A506 25pf green, yel & blk .20 .20
1664 A506 35pf blue & multi *.65 .70*
Nos. 1661-1664 (4) *1.25 1.30*

German Academy of Sciences, 275th anniv.

Torch Bearer — A507

1975, July 15 ***Perf. 13½x13***

1665 A507 10pf shown .20 .20
1666 A507 20pf Hurdling .20 .20
1667 A507 25pf Diving .20 .20
1668 A507 35pf Gymnast on bar *.65 .75*
Nos. 1665-1668 (4) *1.25 1.35*

5th Children and Youths Spartakiad.

Map of Europe A508

1975, July 30 **Photo.** ***Perf. 13***

1669 A508 20pf multicolored .25 .20

European Security and Cooperation Conference, Helsinki, July 30-Aug. 1.

China Aster — A509

Medimorph Anesthesia Unit — A510

1975, Aug. 19 **Photo.** ***Perf. 13½x14***

1670 A509 5pf shown .20 .20
1671 A509 10pf Geranium .20 .20
1672 A509 20pf Transvaal daisies .20 .20
1673 A509 25pf Carnation .20 .20
1674 A509 35pf Chrysanthemum .20 .20
1675 A509 70pf Pansies *1.75 1.40*
Nos. 1670-1675 (6) *2.75 2.40*

1975, Aug. 28 ***Perf. 14***

Leipzig Fall Fair: 25pf, Motorcycle, type MZ TS 250, horiz.

1676 A510 10pf multicolored .20 .20
1677 A510 25pf yellow & multi .30 .20

Children and Child Crossing Guard A511

Designs: 15pf, Traffic policewoman. 20pf, Policeman helping, motorist. 25pf, Motor vehicle inspection. 35pf, Volunteer instructor.

1975, Sept. 9 **Litho.** ***Perf. 13x12½***

1678 A511 10pf multicolored .20 .20
1679 A511 15pf green & multi *1.00 .65*
1680 A511 20pf brown & multi .20 .20
1681 A511 25pf violet & multi .20 .20
1682 A511 35pf multicolored .20 .20
Nos. 1678-1682 (5) *1.80 1.45*

Traffic police serving and instructing the public.

Soyuz Take-off — A512

Designs: 20pf, Soyuz and Apollo in space. 70pf, Spacecraft after link-up, horiz., 79x28mm.

Perf. 14x13½, 13½x14

1975, Sept. 15 **Photo.**

1683 A512 10pf multicolored .20 .20
1684 A512 20pf multicolored .20 .20
1685 A512 70pf multicolored *1.25 1.00*
Nos. 1683-1685 (3) *1.65 1.40*

Apollo Soyuz space test project (Russo-American space cooperation), launching July 15; link-up, July 17.

Weimar, 1630, after Merian — A513

Designs: 20pf, Buchenwald Liberation Monument, vert. 35pf, Composite view of old and new buildings in Weimar.

1975, Sept. 23 **Litho.** ***Perf. 13½x13***

1686 A513 10pf green, gray & blk .20 .20
1687 A513 20pf red & multi .20 .20
1688 A513 35pf ultra & multi *.40 .40*
Nos. 1686-1688 (3) *.80 .80*

Millennium of Weimar.

Monument, Vienna — A514

1975, Oct. 14 **Photo.** ***Perf. 14x13½***

1689 A514 35pf red & multi .30 .20

Memorial for the victims of the struggle for a free Austria, 1934-1945.

Louis Braille and Dots — A515

Designs: 35pf, Hands reading Braille. 50pf, Eyeball and protective glasses.

1975, Oct. 14

1690 A515 20pf gray & multi .20 .20
1691 A515 35pf multicolored .20 .20
1692 A515 50pf multicolored *1.00 .85*
Nos. 1690-1692 (3) *1.40 1.25*

World Braille Year 1975. Sesquicentennial of the invention of Braille system of writing for the blind, by Louis Braille (1809-1852).

Post Office Bärenfels A516

1975, Oct. 21 **Photo.** ***Perf. 14***

1693 A516 20pf multicolored .20 .20

Philatelists' Day 1975. See No. B177.

Emperor Ordering Clothes — A517

Designs: Scenes from "The Emperor's New Clothes," by Hans Christian Andersen and Andersen portrait.

1975, Nov. 18 **Litho.** ***Perf. 14x13***

1694 A517 20pf ocher & multi *.30 .30*
1695 A517 35pf ocher & multi *.50 .50*
1696 A517 50pf ocher & multi *.30 .30*
a. Sheet of 3, #1694-1696 *1.60 1.50*

Tobogganing and Olympic Rings — A518

Olympic Rings and: 20pf, Speed-skating Rink, Berlin. 35pf, Figure-skating Hall, Karl-

Marx Stadt. 70pf, Mass skiing at Schmiedefeld. 1m, Innsbruck & surrounding mountains.

1975, Dec. 2 Photo. *Perf. 14*

1697 A518 5pf multicolored .20 .20
1698 A518 20pf olive & multi .20 .20
1699 A518 35pf multicolored .20 .20
1700 A518 70pf multicolored *1.40 1.10*
Nos. 1697-1700,B178-B179 (6) 2.40 2.10

Souvenir Sheet

1701 A518 1m ultra & multi *1.40 2.50*

12th Winter Olympic Games, Innsbruck, Austria, Feb. 4-15, 1976.
No. 1701 contains one 32x27mm stamp.

Pres. Wilhelm Pieck (1876-1960) A519

1975, Dec. 30 Litho. *Perf. 13½x13*

1702 A519 10pf lt ultra & blk .20 .20

Ernst Thälmann (1886-1944) A520

Labor Leaders: No. 1704, Georg Schumann (1886-1945). No. 1705, Wilhelm Koenen (1886-1963). No. 1706, John Schehr (1896-1934).

1976, Jan. 13 *Perf. 13½x13*

1703 A520 10pf rose & blk .20 .20
1704 A520 10pf emerald & blk .20 .20
1705 A520 10pf ocher & blk .20 .20
1706 A520 10pf violet & blk .20 .20
Nos. 1703-1706 (4) .80 .80

See Nos. 1852-1854.

Silbermann Organ, Rötha — A521

Silbermann Organs: 20pf, Freiberg. 35pf, Fraureuth. 50pf, Dresden.

1976, Jan. 27 Photo. *Perf. 14*

1707 A521 10pf green & multi .20 .20
1708 A521 20pf red & multi .20 .20
1709 A521 35pf multicolored .20 .20
1710 A521 50pf brown & multi *.95 .80*
Nos. 1707-1710 (4) 1.55 1.40

Organs built by Gottfried Silbermann (1683-1753).

Souvenir Sheet

Richard Sorge — A522

1976, Feb. 3 Litho. *Imperf.*

1711 A522 1m multicolored *1.40 2.50*

Dr. Richard Sorge (1895-1944), Soviet intelligence agent. No. 1711 contains one stamp with simulated perforations.

Military Flag, Sailor, Soldier, Aviator — A523

20pf, Military flag, ships, tanks, missile & planes.

1976, Feb. 24 Litho. *Perf. 13½x14*

1712 A523 10pf multicolored .20 .20
1713 A523 20pf multicolored .25 .20

National People's Army, 20th anniversary.

Telephone A524

Apartment House, Leipzig A525

1976, Mar. 2 *Perf. 13*

1714 A524 20pf light blue .25 .20

Centenary of first telephone call by Alexander Graham Bell, March 10, 1876.

1976, Mar. 9 Photo. *Perf. 14*

Design: 25pf, Ocean super trawler, horiz.

1715 A525 10pf green & multi .20 .20
1716 A525 25pf vio blue, blk & grn .30 .20

Leipzig Spring Fair.

Palace of the Republic — A526

1976, Apr. 22 Photo. *Perf. 14*

1717 A526 10pf vio blue & multi .50 .20

Inauguration of Palace of the Republic, Berlin. See No. 1721.

Post Office Radar Station — A527

1976, Apr. 27 Photo. *Perf. 13½x14*

1718 A527 20pf multicolored .25 .20

Intersputnik 1976.

Marx, Engels, Lenin and Party Flag — A528

20pf, New factories & apartment houses, party flag, horiz. 1m, Palace of the Republic.

1976, May 11 *Perf. 14x13½, 13½x14*

1719 A528 10pf dp mag, gold & red .20 .20
1720 A528 20pf multicolored .20 .20

Souvenir Sheet

Perf. 14

1721 A526 1m multicolored *1.10 2.00*

9th Congress of Unity Party (SED).

Peace Bicycle Race and Olympic Rings — A529

Designs: 20pf, Town and sport halls, Suhl. 25pf, Regatta course, Brandenburg. 70pf, 1500-meter race. 1m, Central Stadium, Leipzig.

1976, May 18 Photo. *Perf. 13½x14*

1722 A529 5pf green & multi .20 .20
1723 A529 20pf blue & multi .20 .20
1724 A529 25pf multicolored .20 .20
1725 A529 70pf ultra & multi *1.60 1.40*
Nos. 1722-1725,B180-B181 (6) 2.60 2.40

Souvenir Sheet

Perf. 14

1726 A529 1m multicolored *1.25 2.00*

21st Olympic Games, Montreal, Canada, July 17-Aug. 1. No. 1726 contains one stamp (32x27mm).

Ribbons and Emblem A530

Design: 20pf, Young man and woman, industrial installations.

1976, May 25 *Perf. 14*

1727 A530 10pf blue & multi .20 .20
1728 A530 20pf multicolored .20 .20

10th Parliamentary Meeting of the Free German Youth Organization.

Himantoglossum Hircinum — A531

Designs: European orchids.

1976, June 15 Litho. *Perf. 12½x13*

1729 A531 10pf *shown* .20 .20
1730 A531 20pf *Dactylorhiza incarnata* .20 .20
1731 A531 25pf *Anacamptis pyramidalis* .20 .20
1732 A531 35pf *Dactylorhiza sambucina* .20 .20
1733 A531 40pf *Orchis coriophora* .20 .20
1734 A531 50pf *Cypripedium calceolus* *1.75 1.50*
Nos. 1729-1734 (6) 2.75 2.50

Dancer at Rest, by Walter Arnold — A532

Small Sculptures: 10pf, Shetland Pony, by Heinrich Drake, horiz. 25pf, "At the Beach," by Ludwig Engelhardt. 35pf, Hermann Duncker, by Walter Howard. 50pf, "The Conversation," by Gustav Weidanz.

1976, June 22 Photo. *Perf. 14*

1735 A532 10pf blk & bl grn .20 .20
1736 A532 20pf ocher & blk .20 .20
1737 A532 25pf ocher & blk .20 .20
1738 A532 35pf yel grn & blk .20 .20
1739 A532 50pf brick red & blk *1.25 1.10*
Nos. 1735-1739 (5) 2.05 1.90

Marx, Engels, Lenin, Red Flags, Berlin Buildings A533

1976, June 29 Photo. *Perf. 14*

1740 A533 20pf blue, red & dk red .25 .20

European Communist Workers' Congress, Berlin.

Coronation Coach, 1790 — A534

Historic Coaches: 20pf, Open carriage, Russia, 1800. 25pf, Court landau, Saxony, 1840. 35pf, State carriage, Saxony, 1860. 40pf, Mail coach, 1850. 50pf, Town carriage, Saxony, 1889.

1976, July 27

1741 A534 10pf multicolored .20 .20
1742 A534 20pf multicolored .20 .20
1743 A534 25pf multicolored .20 .20
1744 A534 35pf multicolored .20 .20
1745 A534 40pf multicolored .20 .20
1746 A534 50pf multicolored *2.00 1.75*
Nos. 1741-1746 (6) 3.00 2.75

View of Gera A535

Design: 10pf+5pf, View of Gera, c. 1652.

1976, Aug. 5 Litho. *Perf. 13*

1747 A535 10pf + 5pf multi .20 .20
1748 A535 20pf multicolored .20 .20
a. Pair, #1747-1748 + label .55 .50

4th German Youth Philatelic Exhib., Gera.

Boxer — A536

Dogs: 10pf, Airedale terrier. 20pf, German shepherd. 25pf, Collie. 35pf, Giant schnauzer. 70pf, Great Dane.

1976, Aug. 17 ***Perf. 14***

1749 A536 5pf multicolored .20 .20
1750 A536 10pf multicolored .20 .20
1751 A536 20pf multicolored .20 .20
1752 A536 25pf multicolored .20 .20
1753 A536 35pf multicolored .20 .20
1754 A536 70pf multicolored *1.60 1.50*
Nos. 1749-1754 (6) *2.60 2.50*

Oil Distillery A537

Design: 25pf, German Library, Leipzig.

1976, Sept. 1 ***Perf. 13x12½***

1755 A537 10pf multicolored .20 .20
1756 A537 25pf multicolored .25 .20

Leipzig Fall Fair.

Templin Lake Bridge — A538

Designs: 15pf, Overpass, Berlin-Adlergestell. 20pf, Elbe River Bridge, Rosslau. 25pf, Göltzschtal Viaduct. 35pf, Elbe River Bridge, Magdeburg. 50pf, Grosser Dreesch Overpass, Schwerin.

1976, Sept. 21 **Photo.** ***Perf. 14***

1757 A538 10pf multicolored .20 .20
1758 A538 15pf multicolored .20 .20
1759 A538 20pf multicolored .20 .20
1760 A538 25pf multicolored .20 .20
1761 A538 35pf multicolored .20 .20
1762 A538 50pf multicolored *1.25 1.50*
Nos. 1757-1762 (6) *2.25 2.50*

Memorial Monument (detail), Budapest — A539

1976, Oct. 5 **Photo.** ***Perf. 14***

1763 A539 35pf tan & multi .30 .20

Memorial to World War II victims.

Brass Jug, c. 1500 — A540

Artistic Handicraft Works: 20pf, Faience vase with lid, c. 1710. 25pf, Porcelain centerpiece (woman carrying bowl), c. 1768. 35pf, Porter, gilded silver, c. 1700. 70pf, Art Nouveau glass vase, c. 1900.

1976, Oct. 19

1764 A540 10pf dk car & multi .20 .20
1765 A540 20pf ultra & multi .20 .20
1766 A540 25pf green & multi .20 .20
1767 A540 35pf vio blue & multi .20 .20
1768 A540 70pf red brn & multi *1.40 1.40*
Nos. 1764-1768 (5) *2.20 2.20*

Guppy A541

Designs: Various guppies.

1976, Nov. 9 **Litho.** ***Perf. 13½x13***

1769 A541 10pf multicolored .20 .20
1770 A541 15pf multicolored .20 .20
1771 A541 20pf multicolored .20 .20
1772 A541 25pf multicolored .20 .20
1773 A541 35pf multicolored .20 .20
1774 A541 70pf multicolored *1.50 1.50*
Nos. 1769-1774 (6) *2.50 2.50*

Vessels, c. 3000 B.C. — A542

20pf, Cult cart, c. 1300 B.C. 25pf, Roman gold coin, 270-273 A.D. 35pf, Gold pendant, 950 A.D. 70pf, Glass cup, 3rd cent. A.D.

1976, Nov. 23 **Photo.** ***Perf. 13***

1775 A542 10pf multicolored .20 .20
1776 A542 20pf multicolored .20 .20
1777 A542 25pf multicolored .20 .20
1778 A542 35pf multicolored .20 .20
1779 A542 70pf multicolored *1.40 1.40*
Nos. 1775-1779 (5) *2.20 2.20*

Archaeological finds in DDR.

"Air," by Rosalba Carriera — A543

Paintings, Dresden Museum: 15pf, Virgin and Child, by Murillo. 20pf, Woman Viola da Gamba Player, by Bernardo Strozzi. 25pf, Ariadne Forsaken, by Angelica Kauffmann. 35pf, Old Man with Black Cap, by Bartolomeo Nazzari. 70pf, Officer Reading a Letter, by Gerard Terborch.

1976, Dec. 14 **Photo.** ***Perf. 13½x14***

1780 A543 10pf multicolored .20 .20
1781 A543 15pf multicolored .20 .20
1782 A543 20pf multicolored .20 .20
1783 A543 25pf multicolored .20 .20
1784 A543 35pf multicolored .20 .20
1785 A543 70pf multicolored *1.60 1.50*
Nos. 1780-1785 (6) *2.60 2.50*

Rumpelstiltskin and King — A544

Scenes from fairy tale "Rumpel-stiltskin."

1976, Dec. 14 **Litho.** ***Perf. 13***

1786 A544 5pf multicolored .20 .20
1787 A544 10pf multicolored .40 .35
1788 A544 15pf multicolored .20 .20
1789 A544 20pf multicolored .20 .20
1790 A544 25pf multicolored .40 .35
1791 A544 30pf multicolored .20 .20
a. Sheet of 6, #1786-1791 2.25 2.00

Arnold Zweig and Quotation A545

Designs: 20pf, Otto von Guericke and Magdeburg hemispheres. 35pf, Albrecht D. Thaer, wheat, plow and sheep. 40pf, Gustav Hertz and diagram of separation of isotopes.

1977, Feb. 8 **Litho.** ***Perf. 13x12½***

1792 A545 10pf rose & blk .20 .20
1793 A545 20pf gray & blk .20 .20
1794 A545 35pf lt green & blk .20 .20
1795 A545 40pf blue & blk *.65 .65*
Nos. 1792-1795 (4) *1.25 1.25*

Zweig (1887-1968), novelist; von Guericke (1602-86), physicist; Thaer (1752-1828), agronomist & physician; Hertz (1887-1975), physicist.

Spring near Plaue — A546

Natural Monuments: 20pf, Small Organ, Johnsdorf. 25pf, Ivenacker Oaks, Reuterstadt. 35pf, Stone Rose, Saalburg. 50pf, Rauenscher Stein (boulder), Furstenwalde.

1977, Feb. 24 **Litho.** ***Perf. 12½x13***

1796 A546 10pf multicolored .20 .20
1797 A546 20pf multicolored .20 .20
1798 A546 25pf multicolored .20 .20
1799 A546 35pf multicolored .20 .20
1800 A546 50pf multicolored *1.00 1.00*
Nos. 1796-1800 (5) *1.80 1.80*

Fair Building, Book Fair A547

Leipzig Spring Fair: 25pf, Wide aluminum roll casting machine, Nachterstedt factory.

1977, Mar. 8 **Photo.** ***Perf. 14***

1801 A547 10pf multicolored .20 .20
1802 A547 25pf multicolored .20 .20

Costume Senftenberg A548

Start after Wheel Change A549

Sorbian Costumes from: 20pf, Bautzen. 25pf, Klitten. 35pf, Nochten. 70pf, Muskau.

1977, Mar. 22

1803 A548 10pf multicolored .20 .20
1804 A548 20pf multicolored .20 .20
1805 A548 25pf multicolored .20 .20
1806 A548 35pf multicolored .20 .20
1807 A548 70pf multicolored *1.60 1.40*
Nos. 1803-1807 (5) *2.40 2.20*

1977, Apr. 19 **Photo.** ***Perf. 14***

Designs: 20pf, Sprint. 35pf, At finish line.

1808 A549 10pf multicolored *.20 .20*
1809 A549 20pf multicolored *.20 .20*
1810 A549 35pf multicolored *.20 .20*
a. Strip of 3, #1808-1810 *.95 .85*

30th International Peace Bicycling Race.

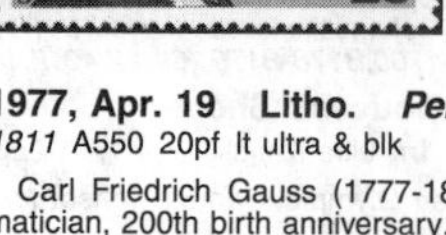

Carl Friedrich Gauss A550

1977, Apr. 19 **Litho.** ***Perf. 13x12½***

1811 A550 20pf lt ultra & blk .35 .20

Carl Friedrich Gauss (1777-1855), mathematician, 200th birth anniversary.

Flags and Handshake A551

1977, May 3 **Photo.** ***Perf. 13***

1812 A551 20pf vio bl & multi .25 .20

9th German Trade Union Congress, Berlin.

VKM Channel Converter, Filter and ITU Emblem — A552

1977, May 17 **Litho.** ***Perf. 14***

1813 A552 20pf multicolored .25 .20

International Telecommunications Day.

Pistol Shooting A553

Designs: 20pf, Deep-sea diver. 35pf, Radio controlled model boat.

1977, May 17 **Photo.**

1814 A553 10pf lt green & multi .20 .20
1815 A553 20pf lt blue & multi .20 .20
1816 A553 35pf salmon & multi *.55 .55*
Nos. 1814-1816 (3) *.95 .95*

Organization for Physical and Technical Training.

Accordion, c. 1900 — A554

Designs: 20pf, Treble viola da gamba, 1747. 25pf, Oboe, 1785, Clarinet, 1830 and flute, 1817. 35pf, Concert zither, 1891. 70pf, Trumpet, 1860.

1977, June 14

1817 A554 10pf multicolored .20 .20
1818 A554 20pf multicolored .20 .20
1819 A554 25pf multicolored .20 .20
1820 A554 35pf multicolored .20 .20
1821 A554 70pf multicolored *1.60 1.60*
Nos. 1817-1821 (5) *2.40 2.40*

Vogtland musical instruments from Markneukirchen Museum.

Mercury and Argus, by Rubens — A555

Rubens Paintings in Dresden Gallery: 10pf, Bath of Bathsheba, vert. 20pf, The Drunk Hercules, vert. 25pf, Diana Returning from the Hunt. 35pf, Old Woman with Brazier, vert. 50pf, Leda and the Swan.

1977, June 28 Photo. *Perf. 14*

1822	A555	10pf multicolored	.20	.20
1823	A555	15pf multicolored	.20	.20
1824	A555	20pf multicolored	.20	.20
1825	A555	25pf multicolored	.20	.20
1826	A555	35pf multicolored	.20	.20
1827	A555	50pf multicolored	*2.10*	*1.50*
		Nos. 1822-1827 (6)	*3.10*	*2.50*

Peter Paul Rubens (1577-1640), Flemish painter, 400th birth anniversary.

Souvenir Sheet

Wreath, Flags of USSR and DDR — A556

1977, June 28

1828	A556	50pf multicolored	*.85*	*1.25*

Soc. for German-Soviet Friendship, 30th anniv.

Tractor with Plow — A557

Designs: 20pf, Fertilizer-spreader. 25pf, Potato digger and loader. 35pf, High-pressure harvester. 50pf, Rotating milking machine.

1977, July 12 Litho. *Perf. 13x12½*

1829	A557	10pf multicolored	.20	.20
1830	A557	20pf multicolored	.20	.20
1831	A557	25pf multicolored	.20	.20
1832	A557	35pf multicolored	.20	.20
1833	A557	50pf multicolored	*1.40*	*1.40*
		Nos. 1829-1833 (5)	*2.20*	*2.20*

Motorized modern agriculture.

High Jump A558

Designs: 20pf, Hurdles, girls. 35pf, Dancing. 40pf, Torch bearer and flags.

1977, July 19

1834	A558	5pf red & multi	.20	.20
1835	A558	20pf lt green & multi	.20	.20
1836	A558	35pf green & multi	.20	.20
1837	A558	40pf blue & multi	*1.25*	*1.10*
		Nos. 1834-1837,B183-B184 (6)	*4.60*	*3.00*

6th Gymnastics and Sports Festival and 6th Children's and Youth Spartacist Games.

"Bread for all" by Wolfram Schubert A559

Konsument Department Store, Leipzig A560

Design: 25pf, "When Communists Dream," by Walter Womacka (detail) and Sozphilex emblem.

1977, Aug. 16 Photo. *Perf. 14*

1838	A559	10pf multicolored	.20	.20
	a.	Souvenir sheet of 4	.90	1.00
1839	A559	25pf multicolored	.35	.30
	a.	Souvenir sheet of 4	1.60	2.00

SOZPHILEX '77 Philatelic Exhibition, Berlin, Aug. 19-28. See No. B185.

1977, Aug. 30

Design: 25pf, Glasses and wooden plate.

1840	A560	10pf blue & multi	.20	.20
1841	A560	25pf multicolored	.25	.20

Leipzig Fall Fair.

Souvenir Sheet

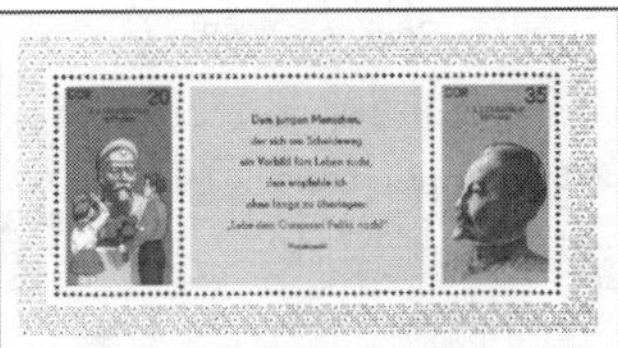

Dzerzhinski and Quotation from Mayakovsky — A561

1977, Sept. 6 Litho. *Perf. 12½x13*

1842	A561	Sheet of 2	*.85*	*2.00*
	a.	20pf multicolored	*.30*	*.30*
	b.	35pf multicolored	*.35*	*.35*

Feliks E. Dzerzhinski (1877-1926), organizer and head of Russian Secret Police (Cheka), birth centenary.

Muldenthal Locomotive, 1861 — A562

Designs: 10pf, Trolley car, Dresden, 1896. 20pf, First successful German plane, 1909. 25pf, 3-wheel car "Phäno-mobile," 1924. 35pf, Passenger steamship on the Elbe, 1837.

1977, Sept. 13 Photo. *Perf. 14*

1843	A562	5pf green & multi	.20	.20
1844	A562	10pf green & multi	.20	.20
1845	A562	20pf green & multi	.20	.20
1846	A562	25pf green & multi	.25	.20
1847	A562	35pf green & multi	*1.60*	*1.10*
		Nos. 1843-1847 (5)	*2.45*	*1.90*

Transportation Museum, Dresden.

Cruiser "Aurora" A563

Designs: 25pf, Storming of the Winter Palace. 1m, Lenin, vert.

1977, Sept. 20

1848	A563	10pf multicolored	*.20*	*.20*
1849	A563	25pf multicolored	*.35*	*.25*

Souvenir Sheet

Perf. 12½x13

1850	A563	1m carmine & blk	*1.50*	*2.00*

60th anniversary of the Russian Revolution.

Mother Russia and Obelisk — A564

1977, Sept. 20 Litho. *Perf. 14*

1851	A564	35pf multicolored	.30	.20

Soviet soldiers' memorial, Berlin-Schönholz.

Labor Leaders Type of 1976

Portraits: No. 1852, Ernst Meyer (1887-1930). No. 1853, August Fröhlich (1877-1966). No. 1854, Gerhart Eisler (1897-1968).

1977, Oct. 18 Litho. *Perf. 14*

1852	A520	10pf olive & brown	.20	.20
1853	A520	10pf rose & brown	.20	.20
1854	A520	10pf lt blue & blk brn	.20	.20
		Nos. 1852-1854 (3)	.60	.60

Souvenir Sheet

Heinrich von Kleist, by Peter Friedl, 1801 — A565

1977, Oct. 18

1855	A565	1m multicolored	*2.10*	*2.00*

Heinrich von Kleist (1777-1811), poet and playwright, birth bicentenary.

Rocket A566

Design: 20pf, as 10pf, design reversed.

1977, Nov. 8 Photo. *Perf. 14*

1856	A566	10pf red, blk & sil	*.20*	*.20*
1857	A566	20pf ultra, blk & gold	*.20*	*.20*
	a.	Pair, #1856-1857 + label	*.65*	*.50*

20th Central Young Craftsmen's Exhibition (Masters of Tomorrow).

A567 A568

Hunting in East Germany: 10pf, Mouflons. 15pf, Red deer. 20pf, Retriever with pheasant, hunter. 25pf, Red fox, wild duck. 35pf, Tractor driver saving fawn. 70pf, Wild boars.

1977, Nov. 15

1858	A567	10pf multicolored	.20	.20
1859	A567	15pf multicolored	*1.60*	*1.40*
1860	A567	20pf multicolored	.20	.20
1861	A567	25pf multicolored	.20	.20
1862	A567	35pf multicolored	.20	.20
1863	A567	70pf multicolored	.25	.20
		Nos. 1858-1863 (6)	*2.65*	*2.40*

1977, Nov. 22 Litho. *Perf. 14*

Firemen's Activities: 10pf, Firemen racing with ladders. 20pf, Children Visiting Firehouse. 25pf, Fire engines fighting forest and brush fires. 35pf, Artificial respiration. 50pf, Fireboat alongside freighter.

1864	A568	10pf multi, horiz.	.20	.20
1865	A568	20pf multi	.20	.20
1866	A568	25pf multi, horiz.	.20	.20
1867	A568	35pf multi	.20	.20
1868	A568	50pf multi, horiz.	*1.60*	*1.50*
		Nos. 1864-1868 (5)	*2.40*	*2.30*

Knight and King — A569

Designs: Various scenes from fairytale: "Six Men Around the World."

1977, Nov. 22 *Perf. 13x13½*

1869	A569	5pf black & multi	.20	.20
1870	A569	10pf black & multi	.55	.45
1871	A569	20pf black & multi	.20	.20
1872	A569	25pf black & multi	.20	.20
1873	A569	35pf black & multi	.55	.45
1874	A569	60pf black & multi	.20	.20
	a.	Sheet of 6, #1869-1874	2.75	2.50

Hips and Dog Rose A570

Medicinal Plants: 15pf, Birch. 20pf, Chamomile. 25pf, Coltsfoot. 35pf, Linden. 50pf, Elder.

1978, Jan. 10 Photo. *Perf. 14*

1875	A570	10pf multicolored	.20	.20
1876	A570	15pf multicolored	.20	.20
1877	A570	20pf multicolored	.20	.20
1878	A570	25pf multicolored	.20	.20
1879	A570	35pf multicolored	.25	.20
1880	A570	50pf multicolored	*1.60*	*1.50*
		Nos. 1875-1880 (6)	*2.65*	*2.50*

Amilcar Cabral — A571

1978, Jan. 17 Litho. *Perf. 14*

1881	A571	20pf multicolored	.30	.20

Amilcar Cabral (1924-1973), freedom movement leader from Guinea-Bissau.

Town Hall, Suhl-Heinrichs A572

Half-timbered Buildings, 17th-18th Centuries: 20pf, Farmhouse, Niederoderwitz. 25pf, Farmhouse, Strassen. 35pf, Townhouse, Quedlinburg. 40pf, Townhouse, Eisenach.

1978, Jan. 24 Photo. *Perf. 14*

1882	A572	10pf multicolored	.20	.20
1883	A572	20pf multicolored	.20	.20
1884	A572	25pf multicolored	.20	.20
1885	A572	35pf multicolored	.20	.20
1886	A572	40pf multicolored	*1.50*	*1.40*
		Nos. 1882-1886 (5)	*2.30*	*2.20*

Mail Truck, 1921 A573

Past and Present Mail Transport: 20pf, Mail truck, 1978. 25pf, Railroad mail car, 1896. 35pf, Railroad mail car, 1978.

1978, Feb. 9 Litho. *Perf. 13x12½*

1887	A573 10pf brown & multi	.20	.20
1888	A573 20pf brown & multi	.30	.30
1889	A573 25pf brown & multi	.35	.35
1890	A573 35pf brown & multi	.50	.50
a.	Block of 4, #1887-1890	1.75	1.60

Earring, 11th Century — A574

Archaeological Artifacts: 20pf, Earring, 10th century. 25pf, Bronze sheath, 10th century. 35pf, Bronze horse, 12th century. 70pf, Arabian coin, 8th century.

1978, Feb. 21 Photo. *Perf. 14*

1891	A574 10pf multicolored	.20	.20
1892	A574 20pf multicolored	.20	.20
1893	A574 25pf multicolored	.20	.20
1894	A574 35pf multicolored	.20	.20
1895	A574 70pf multicolored	*1.25*	*1.25*
	Nos. 1891-1895 (5)	*2.05*	*2.05*

Treasures found on Slavic sites.

Royal House, Leipzig — A575

Leipzig Spring Fair: 25pf, Universal measuring instrument by Carl Zeiss.

1978, Mar. 7

1896	A575 10pf multicolored	.20	.20
1897	A575 25pf multicolored	.30	.25

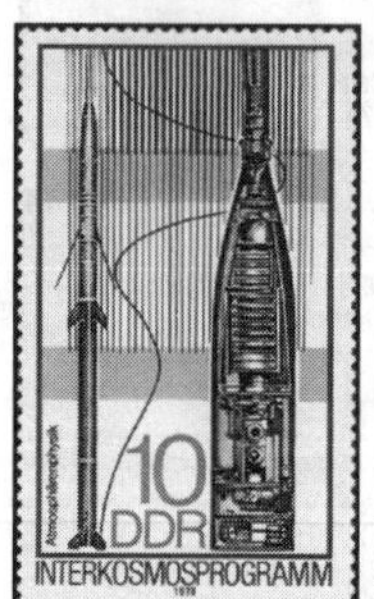

M-100 Meteorological Rocket — A576

Designs: 20pf, Intercosmos I satellite. 35pf, Meteor satellite with spectrometric complex. 1m, MFK-6 multi-spectral camera over city.

1978, Mar. 21 Photo. *Perf. 14x13½*

1898	A576 10pf multicolored	.20	.20
1899	A576 20pf multicolored	.20	.20
1900	A576 35pf multicolored	*.75*	*.75*
	Nos. 1898-1900 (3)	*1.15*	*1.15*

Souvenir Sheet

1901	A576 1m multicolored	*2.00*	*2.50*

Achievements in atmospheric and space research.

Samuel Heinicke, Leipzig, c. 1800 A577

25pf, Deaf child learning sign language.

1978, Apr. 4 Litho. *Perf. 13x12½*

1902	A577 20pf multicolored	.20	.20
1903	A577 25pf multicolored	*.50*	*.45*

National Institute for the Education of the Deaf, established by Samuel Heinicke, 200th anniversary.

Radio Tower, Dequede, TV Truck — A578

Design: 20pf, TV equipment and tower, vert.

1978, Apr. 25 *Perf. 13½x14, 14x13½*

1904	A578 10pf multicolored	.20	.20
1905	A578 20pf multicolored	*.20*	*.25*

World Telecommunications Day.

Saxon Miner, 19th Century — A579

Dress Uniforms, 19th Century: 20pf, Foundry worker, Freiberg. 25pf, Mining Academy student. 35pf, Chief Inspector of Mines.

1978, May 9 *Perf. 12½x13*

1906	A579 10pf silver & multi	.20	.20
1907	A579 20pf silver & multi	.20	.20
1908	A579 25pf silver & multi	.20	.20
1909	A579 35pf silver & multi	*.95*	*.80*
	Nos. 1906-1909 (4)	*1.55*	*1.40*

Lion Cub — A580

Young Animals: 20pf, Leopard. 35pf, Tiger. 50pf, Snow leopard.

1978, May 23 Photo. *Perf. 14*

1910	A580 10pf multicolored	.20	.20
1911	A580 20pf multicolored	.20	.20
1912	A580 35pf multicolored	.20	.20
1913	A580 50pf multicolored	*.95*	*.90*
	Nos. 1910-1913 (4)	*1.55*	*1.50*

Centenary of Leipzig Zoo.

Loading Container — A581

Designs: 20pf, Loading container on flatbed truck. 35pf, Container trains in terminal. 70pf, Loading container on ship.

1978, June 13 Litho. *Perf. 12½x13*

1914	A581 10pf multicolored	.20	.20
1915	A581 20pf multicolored	.20	.20
1916	A581 35pf multicolored	.20	.20
1917	A581 70pf multicolored	*1.40*	*1.25*
	Nos. 1914-1917 (4)	*2.00*	*1.85*

Ceramic Bull — A582

Designs: 10pf, Woman's head, ceramic. 20pf, Gold armband, horiz. 25pf, Animal head, gold ring. 35pf, Seated family from signet ring. 40pf, Necklace, horiz.

Perf. 14x13½, 13½x14

1978, June 20 Photo.

1918	A582 5pf multicolored	.20	.20
1919	A582 10pf multicolored	.20	.20
1920	A582 20pf multicolored	.20	.20
1921	A582 25pf multicolored	.20	.20
1922	A582 35pf multicolored	.20	.20
1923	A582 40pf multicolored	*.95*	*1.00*
	Nos. 1918-1923 (6)	*1.95*	*2.00*

African art from 1st and 2nd centuries in Berlin and Leipzig Egyptian museums.

Old and New Buildings, Cottbus — A583

Design: 10pf + 5pf, View of Cottbus, 1730.

1978, July 18 Litho. *Perf. 13x12½*

1924	10pf + 5pf multi	*.20*	*.20*
1925	20pf multicolored	*.20*	*.20*
a.	A583 Pair, #1924-1925 + label	*.55*	*.55*

5th Youth Philatelic Exhibition, Cottbus.

Justus von Liebig, Wheat and Retort A584

Famous Germans: 10pf, Joseph Dietzgen (1828-1888) and title page. 15pf, Alfred Döblin (1878-1957) and title page. 20pf, Hans Loch (1898-1960) and signature, president of Liberal Democratic Party. 25pf, Dr. Theodor Brugsch (1878-1963), and blood circulation. 35pf, Friedrich Ludwig Jahn (1778-1852) and gymnast. 70pf, Dr. Albrecht von Graefe (1828-1870) and ophthalmological instruments.

1978, July 18

1926	A584 5pf yellow & blk	.20	.20
1927	A584 10pf gray & blk	.20	.20
1928	A584 15pf yel grn & blk	.20	.20
1929	A584 20pf ultra & blk	.20	.20
1930	A584 25pf salmon & blk	.20	.20
1931	A584 35pf lt green & blk	.20	.20
1932	A584 70pf ol & blk	*1.10*	*1.10*
	Nos. 1926-1932 (7)	*2.30*	*2.30*

Festival Emblem and New Buildings, Havana A585

35pf, Balloons and new buildings, Berlin.

1978, July 25 Litho. *Perf. 13x12½*

1933	A585 20pf multicolored	*.25*	*.25*
1934	A585 35pf multicolored	*.25*	*.25*
a.	Strip of 2, #1933-1934 + label	*1.00*	*.90*

11th World Youth Festival, Havana, 7/28-8/5.

Foot Soldier, by Hans Schäufelein — A586

Etchings: 20pf, Woman Reading Letter, by Jean Antoine Watteau. 25pf, Seated Boy, by Gabriel Metsu. 30pf, Seated Young Man, by Cornelis Saftleven. 35pf, St. Anthony, by Mathias Grunewald. 50pf, Seated Man, by Abraham van Diepenbeeck.

1978, July 25 *Perf. 13½x14*

1935	A586 10pf lemon & black	.20	.20
1936	A586 20pf lemon & black	.55	.50
1937	A586 25pf lemon & black	.20	.20
1938	A586 30pf lemon & black	.20	.20
1939	A586 35pf lemon & black	.55	.50
1940	A586 50pf lemon & black	.20	.20
a.	Sheet of 6, #1935-1940	2.25	2.25

Etchings from Berlin Museums.

Fair Building "Three Kings," Leipzig — A587

Leipzig Fall Fair: 10pf, IFA Multicar 25 truck, horiz.

1978, Aug. 29 Photo. *Perf. 14*

1941	A587 10pf multicolored	.20	.20
1942	A587 25pf multicolored	.30	.25

Mauthausen Memorial — A588

1978, Sept. 5 *Perf. 13½x14*

1943	A588 35pf multicolored	.30	.20

International war memorials.

Soyuz, Intercosmos and German-Soviet Space Flight Emblems — A589

Soyuz, Camera and Space Complex A590

Designs: 10pf, Soyuz and Albert Einstein. 20pf, Sigmund Jähn, 1st German cosmonaut, vert. 35pf, Salyut-Soyuz space station, Otto Lilienthal and his glider. 1m, Cosmonauts Bykovsky and Jähn and space ships.

1978, Sept. Photo. *Perf. 14*

1944	A589 20pf multicolored	.30	.20

Litho.

Perf. 13½x13

1945	A590 5pf multicolored	.20	.20
1946	A590 10pf multicolored	.20	.20
1947	A590 20pf multicolored	.20	.20
1948	A590 35pf multicolored	*.65*	*.65*
	Nos. 1944-1948 (5)	*1.55*	*1.45*

Souvenir Sheet

Perf. 13½x14

1949 A590 1m multicolored 1.50 2.50

1st German cosmonaut on Russian space mission. #1949 contains 1 54x33mm stamp. Issued: #1944, Sept. 4; others, Sept. 21.

Marching Soldiers, Tractor, Factory A591

Design: 35pf, Russian and German Soldiers, Communist war veteran, 1933.

1978, Sept. 19 Photo. *Perf. 14*

1950 A591 20pf multicolored .25 .25
1951 A591 35pf multicolored .25 .25
a. Strip of 2, #1950-1951 + label .85 .75

Workers' military units, 25th anniv.

Seven-person Pyramid — A592

10pf, Elephant on tricycle. 20pf, Dressage. 35pf, Polar bear kissing woman trainer.

1978, Sept. 26 Photo. *Perf. 14*

1952 A592 5pf black & multi .25 .35
1953 A592 10pf black & multi .45 .50
1954 A592 20pf black & multi .85 .90
1955 A592 35pf black & multi 1.25 1.75
a. Block of 4, #1952-1955 *4.50 6.50*

Circus in German Democratic Republic.

Construction of Gas Pipe Line, Drushba Section — A593

1978, Oct. 3 Litho. *Perf. 13x12½*

1956 A593 20pf multicolored .30 .20

German youth helping to build gas pipe line from Orenburg to Russian border.

African Behind Barbed Wire — A594

Papilio Hahneli — A595

1978, Oct. 3 Litho. *Perf. 12½x13*

1957 A594 20pf multicolored .30 .20

Anti-Apartheid Year.

1978, Oct. 24 Photo. *Perf. 14*

20pf, Agama lehmanni (lizards). 25pf, Agate from Wiederau. 35pf, Paleobatrachus diluvianus. 40pf, Clock, 1720. 50pf, Table telescope, 1750.

1958 A595 10pf multicolored .20 .20
1959 A595 20pf multicolored .20 .20
1960 A595 25pf multicolored .20 .20
1961 A595 35pf multicolored .20 .20
1962 A595 40pf multicolored .20 .20
1963 A595 50pf multicolored *1.60 1.60*
Nos. 1958-1963 (6) *2.60 2.60*

Dresden Museum of Natural History, 250th anniversary.

Wheel Lock Gun, 1630 — A596

Hunting Guns: 10pf, Double-barreled gun, 1978. 20pf, Spring-cock gun, 1780. 25pf, Superimposed double-barreled gun, 1978. 35pf, Percussion gun, 1850. 70pf, Three-barreled gun, 1978.

1978, Nov. 21 Photo. *Perf. 14*

1964 A596 5pf silver & multi .20 .20
1965 A596 10pf silver & multi .20 .20
1966 A596 20pf silver & multi .20 .20
1967 A596 25pf silver & multi .25 .25
1968 A596 35pf silver & multi .35 .35
a. Vert. strip of 3, 5, 20, 35pf 1.00 .90
1969 A596 70pf silver & multi .75 .75
a. Vert. strip of 3, 10, 25, 70pf 1.75 1.60
Nos. 1964-1969 (6) 1.95 1.95

Printed in sheets of 9.

Rapunzel's Father and Witch — A597

Designs: Scenes from fairy tale "Rapunzel."

1978, Nov. 21 Litho. *Perf. 13*

1970 A597 10pf multicolored .20 .20
1971 A597 15pf multicolored .70 .55
1972 A597 20pf multicolored .20 .20
1973 A597 25pf multicolored .20 .20
1974 A597 35pf multicolored .70 .55
1975 A597 50pf multicolored .20 .20
a. Sheet of 6, #1970-1975 2.50 2.25

Chaffinches A598

Song Birds: 10pf, Nuthatch. 20pf, Robin. 25pf, Bullfinches. 35pf, Blue tit. 50pf, Red linnets.

1979, Jan. 9 Photo. *Perf. 13½x14*

1976 A598 5pf multicolored .20 .20
1977 A598 10pf multicolored .20 .20
1978 A598 20pf multicolored .20 .20
1979 A598 25pf multicolored .20 .20
1980 A598 35pf multicolored .20 .20
1981 A598 50pf multicolored *1.75 1.25*
Nos. 1976-1981 (6) *2.75 2.25*

Chabo Cock — A599

German Cocks: 15pf, Kraienkopp. 20pf, Porcelain-colored bantam. 25pf, Saxonian. 35pf, Phoenix. 50pf, Striped Italian.

1979, Jan. 23 *Perf. 14x13½*

1982 A599 10pf multicolored .20 .20
1983 A599 15pf multicolored .20 .20
1984 A599 20pf multicolored .20 .20
1985 A599 25pf multicolored .20 .20
1986 A599 35pf multicolored .20 .20
1987 A599 50pf multicolored *1.60 1.50*
Nos. 1982-1987 (6) *2.60 2.50*

Telephone Operators, 1900 and 1979 — A600

35pf, Telegraph operators, 1880 and 1979.

1979, Feb. 6 Photo. *Perf. 13½x14*

1988 A600 20pf multicolored .20 .20
1989 A600 35pf multicolored *.55 .45*

Development of German postal telephone and telegraph service.

Souvenir Sheet

Albert Einstein (1879-1955), Theoretical Physicist — A601

1979, Feb. 20 Litho. *Perf. 14*

1990 A601 1m multicolored *1.60 1.50*

Max Klinger House, Leipzig — A602

Leipzig Spring Fair: 25pf, Horizontal drilling and milling machine, horiz.

1979, Mar. 6 Litho. *Perf. 14*

1991 A602 10pf multicolored .20 .20
1992 A602 25pf multicolored .25 .20

Container Ship, Tug, World Map and IMCO Emblem — A603

1979, Mar. 20 Photo.

1993 A603 20pf multicolored .30 .20

World Navigation Day.

Otto Hahn and Equation of Nuclear Fission A604

Famous Germans: 10pf, Max von Laue (1879-1969) and diagram of sulphide zinc. 20pf, Arthur Scheunert (1879-1957), symbol of nutrition and health. 25pf, Friedrich August Kekulé (1829-1896), and benzene ring. 35pf, George Forster (1754-1794) and Capt. Cook's ship Resolution. 70pf, Gotthold Ephraim Lessing (1729-1781) and title page for Nathan the Wise.

1979, Mar. 20 Litho. *Perf. 13x12½*

1994 A604 5pf pale salmon & blk .20 .20
1995 A604 10pf blue gray & blk .20 .20
1996 A604 20pf lemon & blk .20 .20
1997 A604 25pf lt green & blk .20 .20
1998 A604 35pf lt blue & blk .20 .20
1999 A604 70pf pink & blk *1.60 1.25*
Nos. 1994-1999 (6) *2.60 2.25*

See Nos. 2088-2093.

Miniature Sheet

Horch 8, 1911 — A605

Design: 35pf, Trabant 601S de luxe, 1978.

1979, Apr. 3 Litho. *Perf. 14*

2000 Sheet of 2 + label *1.10 1.10*
a. A605 20pf multicolored *.25 .25*
b. A605 35pf multicolored *.65 .65*

Sachsenring automobile plant, Zwickau.

Self-Propelled Car — A606

DDR Railroad Cars: 10pf, Self-unloading freight car Us-y. 20pf, Diesel locomotive BR 110. 35pf, Laaes automobile carrier.

1979, Apr. 17 Litho. *Perf. 13*

2001 A606 5pf multicolored .20 .20
2002 A606 10pf multicolored .20 .20
2003 A606 20pf multicolored .20 .20
2004 A606 35pf multicolored *.65 .65*
Nos. 2001-2004 (4) *1.25 1.25*

Durga, 18th Century — A607

Indian Miniatures in Berlin Museums: 35pf, Mahavira, 15th-16th cents. 50pf, Todi Ragini, 17th cent. 70pf, Asavari Ragini, 17th cent.

1979, May 8 Photo. *Perf. 14x13½*

2005 A607 20pf multicolored .20 .20
2006 A607 35pf multicolored .20 .20
2007 A607 50pf multicolored .20 .20
2008 A607 70pf multicolored *1.75 1.60*
Nos. 2005-2008 (4) *2.35 2.20*

Youth Gathering A608

Design: 10pf+5pf, Torchlight parade of German youth, Oct. 7, 1949.

1979, May 22 Photo. *Perf. 14*

2009 A608 10pf + 5pf multi .20 .20
2010 A608 20pf multicolored .20 .20
a. Strip of 2, #2009-2010 + label .50 .50

National Youth Festival, Berlin.

Housing Project, Berlin A609

20pf, Berlin-Marzahn building site & surveyors.

1979, May 22 Litho. *Perf. 13x12½*

2011 A609 10pf multicolored .20 .20
2012 A609 20pf multicolored .25 .25

Berlin Project of Free German Youth.

Children Playing and Reading — A610

Exhibition Emblem — A611

20pf, Doctor with black & white children.

1979, May 22 Photo. *Perf. 14*

2013 A610 10pf multicolored .20 .20
2014 A610 20pf multicolored .30 .35

International Year of the Child.

1979, June 5

2015 A611 10pf multicolored .30 .20

Agra '79 Agricultural Exhib., Markkleeberg.

Ferry Boats A612

1979, June 26 Photo. *Perf. 14*

2016 A612 20pf Rostock .25 .25
2017 A612 35pf Rugen .25 .25
a. Strip of 2, #2016-2017 + label .90 .80

Railroad ferry from Sassnitz, DDR, to Trelleborg, Sweden, 70th anniversary.

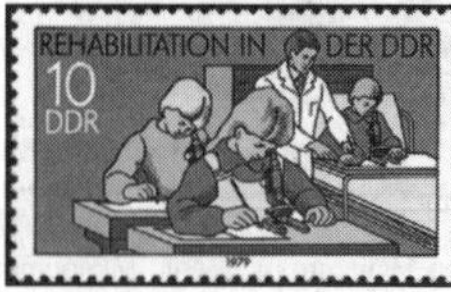

Hospital Classroom — A613

Design: 35pf, Handicapped workers.

1979, June 26 Litho. *Perf. 13x12½*

2018 A163 10pf multicolored .20 .20
2019 A163 35pf multicolored .35 .30

Rehabilitation in DDR.

Bicyclists A614

Design: 20pf, Roller skating.

1979, July 3

2020 A614 10pf multicolored .20 .20
2021 A614 20pf multicolored .30 .30

7th Children's and Youth Spartakiad, Berlin.

Dahlia "Rubens" A615

Dahlias: 20pf, Rosalie. 25pf, Corinna. 35pf, Enzett-Dolli. 50pf, Enzett-Carola. 70pf, Don Lorenzo.

1979, July 17 Photo. *Perf. 13*

2022 A615 10pf multicolored .20 .20
2023 A615 20pf multicolored .20 .20
2024 A615 25pf multicolored .20 .20
2025 A615 35pf multicolored .20 .20
2026 A615 50pf multicolored .20 .20
2027 A615 70pf multicolored 2.00 1.90
Nos. 2022-2027 (6) 3.00 2.90

Dahlias shown at International Garden Exhibition, Erfurt.

Russian Alphabet Around Congress Emblem A616

1979, Aug. 7 Photo. *Perf. 13*

2028 A616 20pf multicolored .25 .20

4th International Congress of Teachers of Russian Language and Literature, Berlin.

Dandelion Fountain, Dresden — A617

Composite of Dresden Buildings — A618

The A618 illustration is reduced.

1979, Aug. 7 *Perf. 14*

2029 A617 20pf multicolored .20 .20

Souvenir Sheet

Litho. *Perf. 13x12½*

2030 A618 1m multicolored 1.60 1.40

DDR '79, Natl. Stamp Exhib., Dresden. See No. B187.

Italian Lira da Gamba, 1592 — A619

Musical Instruments, Leipzig Museum: 25pf, French "serpent," 17th-18th centuries. 40pf, French barrel lyre, 18th century. 85pf, German tenor trumpet, 19th century.

1979, Aug. 21 *Perf. 14*

2031 A619 20pf multicolored .20 .20
2032 A619 25pf multicolored .20 .20
2033 A619 40pf multicolored .20 .20
2034 A619 85pf multicolored 1.75 1.60
Nos. 2031-2034 (4) 2.35 2.20

Galloping — A620

1979, Aug. 21

2035 A620 10pf shown .20 .20
2036 A620 25pf Dressage .65 .55

30th International Horse-breeding Congress of Socialist Countries, Berlin.

Memorial Monument, Nordhausen A621

1979, Aug. 28 Photo. *Perf. 14*

2037 A621 35pf dull vio & blk .35 .25

Memorial to World War II victims.

Teddy Bear — A622

Leipzig Autumn Fair: 25pf, Grosser Blumenberg (building), Leipzig, horiz.

1979, Aug. 28

2038 A622 10pf multicolored .20 .20
2039 A622 25pf multicolored .20 .20

Philipp Dengel (1888-1948) A623

Working-Class Movement Leaders: No. 2041, Heinrich Rau (1899-1961). No. 2042, Otto Buchwitz (1879-1964). No. 2043, Bernard Koenen (1889-1964).

1979, Sept. 11 Litho.

2040 A623 10pf multicolored .20 .20
2041 A623 10pf multicolored .20 .20
2042 A623 10pf multicolored .20 .20
2043 A623 10pf multicolored .20 .20
Nos. 2040-2043 (4) .80 .80

See Nos. 2166-2169, 2249-2253, 2314-2318, 2390-2392, 2452-2454.

DDR Arms and Flag, Worker A624

DDR Arms, Flag and: 10pf, Young man and woman. 15pf, Soldiers. 20pf, Workers.

1979, Oct. 2 Photo. *Perf. 13*

2044 A624 5pf multicolored .20 .20
2045 A624 10pf multicolored .20 .20
2046 A624 15pf multicolored .30 .30
2047 A624 20pf multicolored .20 .20
Nos. 2044-2047 (4) .90 .90

Souvenir Sheet

2048 A624 1m multicolored 1.25 1.10

DDR, 30th anniv. No. 2048 contains one stamp (33x55mm).

Altozier Porcelain Coffee Pot — A625

Meissen Porcelain and Hallmark, 18th-20th Centuries: 5pf, Woman applying make-up, 1967. 15pf, "Grosser Ausschnitt" coffee pot, 1974. 20pf, Covered vase. 25pf, Parrot. 35pf, Harlequin drinking. 50pf, Woman selling flowers. 70pf, Sake bottle.

1979, Nov. 6 Photo. *Perf. 14*

2049 A625 5pf multicolored .20 .20
2050 A625 10pf multicolored .20 .20
2051 A625 15pf multicolored .20 .20
2052 A625 20pf multicolored .25 .25
a. Block of 4, #2049-2052 1.25 .90
2053 A625 25pf multicolored .30 .30
2054 A625 35pf multicolored .50 .50
2055 A625 50pf multicolored .70 .70
2056 A625 70pf multicolored .95 .95
a. Block of 4, #2053-2056 4.00 3.75

Rag Doll, 1800 — A626

Historic Dolls: 15pf, Ceramic, 1960. 20pf, Wooden, 1780. 35pf, Straw, 1900. 50pf, Jointed, 1800. 70pf, Tumbler, 1820.

1979, Nov. 20 Litho.

2057 A626 10pf multicolored .20 .20
2058 A626 15pf multicolored .70 .60
2059 A626 20pf multicolored .20 .20
2060 A626 35pf multicolored .20 .20
2061 A626 50pf multicolored .70 .60
2062 A626 70pf multicolored .20 .20
a. Sheet of 6, #2057-2062 2.75 2.50

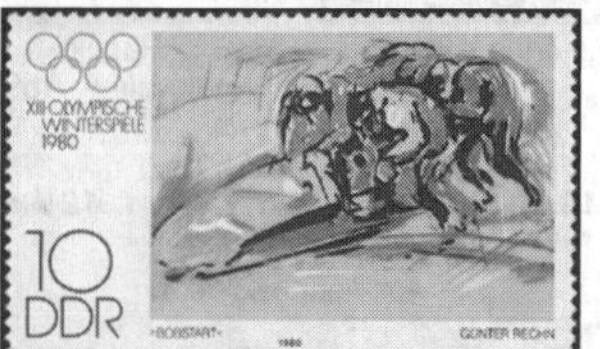

Bobsledding, by Gunter Rechn, Olympic Rings — A627

Olympic Rings and: 20pf, Figure Skating, by Johanna Stake, vert. 35pf, Speed Skating, by Axel Wunsch, vert. 1m, Cross-country Skiing, by Lothar Zitzmann.

1980, Jan. 15 Photo. *Perf. 14*

2063 A627 10pf multicolored .20 .20
2064 A627 20pf multicolored .20 .20
2065 A627 35pf multicolored *.95* .80
Nos. 2063-2065,B189 (4) *1.55* *1.40*

Souvenir Sheet

2066 A627 1m multicolored *1.60* *2.50*

13th Winter Olympic Games, Lake Placid, NY, Feb. 12-24. No. 2066 contains one 29x23½mm stamp. See Nos. 2098-2099, 2119-2121, B190, B192.

"Quiet Music," Grossedlitz — A628

Baroque Gardens: 20pf, Orange grove, Belvedere, Weimar. 50pf, Flower garden, Dornburg Castle. 70pf, Park, Rheinsberg Castle.

1980, Jan. 29

2067 A628 10pf multicolored .20 .20
2068 A628 20pf multicolored .20 .20
2069 A628 50pf multicolored .20 .20
2070 A628 70pf multicolored *1.10* *1.40*
Nos. 2067-2070 (4) *1.70* *2.00*

Type of 1973

Designs as before and: 10pf, Palace of the Republic, Berlin.

1980-81 Engr. *Perf. 14*
Size: 22x17mm

2071 A449 5pf blue green .20 .20
2072 A449 10pf emerald .20 .20
2073 A449 15pf rose lilac .25 .25
2074 A449 20pf rose mag .35 .20
2075 A449 25pf grnsh bl .25 .25
2076 A449 30pf org ('81) .35 .25
2077 A449 35pf blue .35 .25
2078 A449 40pf dull vio .75 .50
2079 A449 50pf blue .45 .25
2080 A449 60pf lilac ('81) .60 .25
2081 A449 70pf redsh brn ('81) .55 .40
2082 A449 80pf vio bl ('81) .70 .35
2083 A449 1m olive .85 .60
2084 A449 2m red 1.40 .70
2085 A449a 3m rose lil ('81) 2.25 1.00
Nos. 2071-2085 (15) 9.50 5.65

Cable-Laying Vehicle, Dish Antenna — A629

20pf, Radio tower, television screen.

1980, Feb. 5 Photo.

2086 A629 10pf multicolored .20 .20
2087 A629 20pf multicolored .20 .20

Famous Germans Type of 1979

Designs: 5pf, Johann Wolfgang Dobereiner (1780-1849), chemist. 10pf, Frederic Joliot-Curie (1900-1958), French physicist. 20pf, Johann Friedrich Naumann (1780-1857), ornithologist. 25pf, Alfred Wegener (1880-1930), geophysicist and meteorologist. 35pf, Carl von Clausewitz (1780-1831), Prussian major general. 70pf, Helene Weigel (1900-1971), actress.

1980, Feb. 26 Litho. *Perf. 13x12½*

2088 A604 5pf pale yel & blk .20 .20
2089 A604 10pf multicolored .20 .20
2090 A604 20pf lt yel grn & blk .20 .20
2091 A604 25pf multicolored .20 .20
2092 A604 35pf lt blue & blk .20 .20
2093 A604 70pf lt red brn & blk *1.00* *.95*
Nos. 2088-2093 (6) *2.00* *1.95*

Type ZT-303 Tractor A630

1980 Leipzig Spring Fair: 10pf, Karl Marx University, Leipzig, vert.

1980, Mar. 4 Photo. *Perf. 14*

2094 A630 10pf multicolored .20 .20
2095 A630 25pf multicolored .25 .20

Werner Eggerath (1900-1977), Labor Leader — A631

1980, Mar. 18 Litho.

2096 A631 10pf brick red & blk .35 .20

Souvenir Sheet

Cosmonauts, Salyut 6 and Soyuz — A632

1980, Apr. 11 Litho. *Perf. 14*

2097 A632 1m multicolored *1.60* *1.40*

Intercosmos cooperative space program.

Olympic Type of 1980

Designs: 10pf, On the Bars, by Erich Wurzer. 50pf, Scull's Crew, by Wilfried Falkenthal.

1980, Apr. 22 Photo. *Perf. 14*

2098 A627 10pf multicolored .20 .20
2099 A627 50pf multicolored *.95* *.80*
Nos. 2098-2099,B190 (3) *1.35* *1.20*

22nd Summer Olympic Games, Moscow, July 19-Aug. 3. See No. B190.

Flags of Member Countries A633

Bauhaus Cooperative Society Building, 1928, Gropius A634

1980, May 13 Photo.

2100 A633 20pf multicolored .35 .20

Signing of Warsaw Pact (Bulgaria, Czechoslovakia, DDR, Hungary, Poland, Romania, USSR), 25th anniv.

1980, May 27

Bauhaus Architecture: 10pf, Socialists' Memorial, 1926, by Mies van der Rohe, horiz. 15pf, Monument, 1922, by William Gropius. 20pf, Steel building, 1926, by Muche and Paulick, horiz. 50pf, Trade-Union School, 1928, by Meyer. 70pf, Bauhaus Building, 1926, by Gropius, horiz.

2101 A634 5pf multicolored .20 .20
2102 A634 10pf multicolored .20 .20
2103 A634 15pf multicolored .20 .20
2104 A634 20pf multicolored .20 .20
2105 A634 50pf multicolored .25 .20
2106 A634 70pf multicolored *1.60* *1.40*
Nos. 2101-2106 (6) *2.65* *2.40*

Rostock View A635

1980, June 10 Photo. *Perf. 14*

2107 A635 10pf shown .20 .20
2108 A635 20pf Dancers .25 .20

18th Workers' Festival, Rostock, June 27-29.

Dish Antenna, Interflug Airlines A636

1980, June 10 Litho. *Perf. 13x12½*

2109 A636 20pf shown *.25* *.25*
2110 A636 25pf Jet *.25* *.25*
2111 A636 35pf Agricultural plane *.35* *.35*
2112 A636 70pf Aerial photography *.75* *.75*
a. Block of 4, #2109-2112 *2.25* *2.00*

Interflug Airlines. See No. B191

Okapi — A637

1980, June 24 *Perf. 14*

2113 A637 5pf shown .20 .20
2114 A637 10pf Wild cats .20 .20
2115 A637 15pf Prairie wolf .20 .20
2116 A637 20pf Arabian oryx .20 .20
2117 A637 25pf White-eared pheasant .20 .20
2118 A637 35pf Musk oxen *1.40* *1.10*
Nos. 2113-2118 (6) *2.40* *2.10*

Olympic Type of 1980

Designs: 10pf, Judo, by Erhard Schmidt. 50pf, Final Spurt, by Siegfried Schreiber. 1m, Spinnaker Yachts, by Karl Raetsch.

1980, July 8 Photo. *Perf. 14*

2119 A627 10pf multicolored .20 .20
2120 A627 50pf multicolored *1.10* *.85*
Nos. 2119-2120,B192 (3) *1.50* *1.25*

Souvenir Sheet

2121 A627 1m multicolored *1.75* *2.00*

22nd Summer Olympic Games, Moscow, 7/19-8/3. #2121 contains one 29x24mm stamp.

Old and New Buildings, Suhl A638

Design: 10pf + 5pf, View of Suhl, 1700.

1980, July 22 Litho. *Perf. 13x12½*

2122 A638 10pf + 5pf multi *.25* *.25*
2123 A638 20pf multicolored *.25* *.25*
a. Pair, #2122-2123 + label *.80* *.60*

6th National Youth Philatelic Exhibition, Suhl. Surtax for East German Association of Philatelists.

Huntley Microscope, London, 1740 — A639

Optical Museum, Karl Zeiss Foundation, Jena: 25pf, Magny microscope, Paris, 1751. 35pf, Amici microscope, Modena, 1845. 70pf, Zeiss microscope, Jena, 1873.

1980, Aug. 12 Photo. *Perf. 14*

2124 A639 20pf multicolored .25 .25
2125 A639 25pf multicolored .25 .25
2126 A639 35pf multicolored .45 .45
2127 A639 70pf multicolored .65 .65
a. Block of 4, #2124-2127 2.50 2.25

Maidenek Memorial — A640

1980, Aug. 26

2128 A640 35pf multicolored .35 .25

Leipzig 1980 Autumn Fair, Information Center — A641

1980, Aug. 26

2129 A641 10pf shown .20 .20
2130 A641 25pf Carpet loom .35 .20

67th Interparliamentary Conference, Berlin — A642

1980, Sept. 9 Photo. *Perf. 14*

2131 A642 20pf Republic Palace, Berlin .55 .20

Paintings by Frans Hals (1580-1666) A643

1980, Sept. 23

2132 A643 10pf *Laughing Boy with Flute* .20 .20
2133 A643 20pf *Man in Gray Coat* .20 .20
2134 A643 25pf *The Mulatto* .20 .20
2135 A643 35pf *Man in Black Coat* *.75* *.75*
Nos. 2132-2135 (4) *1.35* *1.35*

Souvenir Sheet

2136 A643 1m *Self-portrait, horiz.* *1.60* *2.50*

A644

Edible Mushrooms: 5pf, Leccinum Testaceo Scabrum. 10pf, Boletus erythropus. 15pf, Agaricus campester. 20pf, Xerocomus badius. 35pf, Boletus edulis. 70pf, Cantharellus cibarius.

1980, Oct. 28 Litho. *Perf. 13x13½*

2137 A644	5pf multicolored	.20	.20
2138 A644	10pf multicolored	.20	.20
2139 A644	15pf multicolored	.20	.20
2140 A644	20pf multicolored	.20	.20
2141 A644	35pf multicolored	.20	.20
2142 A644	70pf multicolored	1.50	1.50
	Nos. 2137-2142 (6)	2.50	2.50

Exploration of Lignite Deposits (Gravimetry) — A645

Geophysical Exploration: 25pf, Bore-hole measuring (water). 35pf, Seismic geology. (mineral oil, natural gas). 50pf, Seismology.

1980, Nov. 11 Litho. *Perf. 13*

2143 A645	20pf multicolored	.25	.20
2144 A645	25pf multicolored	.30	.25
2145 A645	35pf multicolored	.35	.35
2146 A645	50pf multicolored	.65	.65
a.	Block of 4, #2143-2146	2.25	3.00

Radebeul-Radeburg Railroad Locomotive — A646

1980, Nov. 25 *Perf. 13x12½*

2147	Strip of 2 + label	1.10	.75
a.	A646 20pf shown	.25	.25
b.	A646 25pf Passenger car	.25	.25
2148	Strip of 2 + label	1.10	.75
a.	A646 20pf Bad Doberan-Osteebad Kuhlungsborn Locomotive	.25	.25
b.	A646 35pf Passenger car	.25	.25

Labels show maps of routes and Moritzburg Castle (No. 2147), Bad Doberan Street (No. 2148).

See Nos. 2205-2206.

Toy Locomotive, 1850 — A647

1980, Dec. 9 *Perf. 14*

2149	Sheet of 6	2.75	2.25
a.	A647 10pf shown	.20	.20
b.	A647 20pf Airplane, 1914	.75	.60
c.	A647 25pf Steam roller, 1920	.20	.20
d.	A647 35pf Ship, 1825	.20	.20
e.	A647 40pf Car, 1900	.75	.60
f.	A647 50pf Balloon, 1920	.20	.20

Souvenir Sheet

Wolfgang Amadeus Mozart, 225th Birth Anniv. — A648

1981, Jan. 13 Litho.

2150 A648	1m multicolored	1.60	2.00

St. John's Apple — A649

1981, Jan. 13 Photo.

2151 A649	5pf shown	.20	.20
2152 A649	10pf Snow drop, horiz.	.20	.20
2153 A649	20pf Bladder bush	.20	.20
2154 A649	25pf Paulownia tomentose	.20	.20
2155 A649	35pf German honeysuckle, horiz.	.20	.20
2156 A649	50pf Genuine spice bush	1.60	1.40
	Nos. 2151-2156 (6)	2.60	2.40

Heinrich von Stephan (1831-97), Founder of UPU — A650

1981, Jan. 20 Litho. *Perf. 13x13½*

2157 A650	10pf lt lemon & blk	.30	.20

Dedication of National Commemorative Plaza, Sachsenhausen — A651

1981, Jan. 27 Photo. *Perf. 14*

2158 A651	10pf shown	.20	.20
2159 A651	20pf Changing of guard	.25	.20

National People's Forces, 25th anniversary.

Socialist Union Party, 10th Congress — A652

1981, Feb. 10

2160 A652	10pf multicolored	.25	.20

Postal and Newspaper Apprentice Training — A653

1981, Feb. 10 Litho.

2161 A653	5pf shown	.20	.20
2162 A653	10pf Telephone and telex service	.20	.20
2163 A653	15pf Radio communications	.20	.20
2164 A653	20pf School of Engineering, Leipzig	.20	.20
2165 A653	25pf Communications Academy, Dresden	.90	.70
	Nos. 2161-2165 (5)	1.70	1.50

Working-class Leader Type of 1979

Designs: No. 2166, Erich Baron (1881-1933). No. 2167, Conrad Blenkle (1901-1943). No. 2168, Arthur Ewert (1890-1959). No. 2169, Walter Stoecker (1891-1939).

1981, Feb. 24 Litho. *Perf. 14*

2166 A623	10pf gray grn & blk	.20	.20
2167 A623	10pf lemon & blk	.20	.20
2168 A623	10pf bl vio & blk	.20	.20
2169 A623	10pf lt red brn & blk	.20	.20
	Nos. 2166-2169 (4)	.80	.80

Merkur Hotel, Leipzig — A654

1981 Leipzig Spring Fair: 25pf, Takraf mining conveyor system, horiz.

1981, Mar. 10 Photo. *Perf. 14*

2170 A654	10pf multicolored	.20	.20
2171 A654	25pf multicolored	.30	.20

Ernst Thälmann, by Willi Sitte — A655

10th Communist Party Congress (Paintings): 20pf, Worker, by Bernhard Heising, 25pf, Festivities, by Rudolf Bergander. 35pf, Brotherhood in Arms, by Paul Michaelis. 1m, When Communists Dream, by Walter Womacka.

1981, Mar. 24

2172 A655	10pf multicolored	.20	.20
2173 A655	20pf multicolored	.20	.20
2174 A655	25pf multicolored	.65	.65
2175 A655	35pf multicolored	.20	.20
	Nos. 2172-2175 (4)	1.25	1.25

Souvenir Sheet

2176 A655	1m multicolored	1.10	1.50

Souvenir Sheet

Opening of Sport and Recreation Center, Berlin — A656

1981, Mar. 24 Litho.

2177 A656	1m multicolored	1.75	1.40

Energy Conservation A657

1981, Apr. 21 Litho. *Perf. 12½x13*

2178 A657	10pf orange & blk	.20	.20

Heinrich Barkhausen (1881-1956), Physicist — A658

Famous Men: 20pf, Johannes R. Becher (1891-1958), poet. 25pf, Richard Dedekind (1831-1916), mathematician. 35pf, Georg Philipp Telemann (1681-1767), composer. 50pf, Adelbert V. Chamisso (1781-1838), botanist. 70pf, Wilhelm Raabe (1831-1910), writer.

1981, May 5 *Perf. 13x12½*

2179 A658	10pf dull bl & blk	.20	.20
2180 A658	20pf brick red & blk	.20	.20
2181 A658	25pf dull brn & blk	1.75	1.10
2182 A658	35pf lt vio & blk	.20	.20
2183 A658	50pf yel grn & blk	.25	.20
2184 A658	70pf ol bis & blk	.35	.20
	Nos. 2179-2184 (6)	2.95	2.10

Free German Youth Members A659

1981, May 19

2185 A659	10pf shown	*.20*	*.20*
2186 A659	20pf Youths, diff.	*.20*	*.20*
a.	Pair, #2185-2186 + label	*.75*	*.55*

Free German Youth, 11th Parliament, Berlin.

View and Map of Worlitz Park — A660

1981, June 9 Litho. *Perf. 12½x13*

2187 A660	5pf shown	.20	.20
2188 A660	10pf Tiefurt	.20	.20
2189 A660	15pf Marxwalde	.20	.20
2190 A660	20pf Branitz	.20	.20
2191 A660	25pf Treptow	1.25	1.10
2192 A660	35pf Wiesenburg	.25	.20
	Nos. 2187-2192 (6)	2.30	2.10

Artistic Gymnastics — A661

8th Children's and Youth Spartacist Games: No. 2193, children and youths.

1981, June 23 Photo. *Perf. 14*

2193 A661	10pf + 5pf multi	.45	.30
2194 A661	20pf multicolored	.20	.20

Javelin Throwers A662

1981, June 23 Litho. *Perf. 13x12½*

2195 A662	5pf shown	.20	.20
2196 A662	15pf Men at museum	.20	.20
a.	Pair, #2195-2196 + label	.50	.35

Intl. Year of the Disabled.

Schinkel's Berlin Playhouse — A663

Karl Friedrich Schinkel, (1781-1841), Architect: 25pf, Old Museum, Berlin.

1981, June 23 Litho. & Engr.

2197 A663 10pf tan & blk .60 .20
2198 A663 25pf tan & blk *1.60 .55*

Sugar Loaf House, Gross Zicker — A664

Frame Houses: 10pf, Zaulsdorf, 19th cent., vert. 25pf, Farmhouse, stable, Weckersdorf, vert. 35pf, Restaurant (former farmhouse), Pillgram. 50pf, Eschenbach, vert. 70pf, Farmhouse, Lüdersdorf.

1981, July 7 Photo.

2199 A664 10pf multicolored .20 .20
2200 A664 20pf multicolored .20 .20
2201 A664 25pf multicolored .20 .20
2202 A664 35pf multicolored .20 .20
2203 A664 50pf multicolored .25 .20
2204 A664 70pf multicolored *2.10 1.75*
Nos. 2199-2204 (6) *3.15 2.75*

Railroad Type of 1980

1981, July 21 Litho. *Perf. 13x12½*

2205 Strip of 2 + label *.45 .45*
a. A646 5pf Locomotive, Freital-Kurort-Kipsdorf line .20 .20
b. A646 15pf Luggage car .20 .20
2206 Strip of 2 + label *.45 .45*
a. A646 5pf Locomotive, Putbus-Gohren line .20 .20
b. A646 20pf Passenger car .20 .20

Labels show maps of train routes.

Ebers Papyrus (Egyptian Medical Text, 1600 B.C.), Leipzig — A665

Chemical Plant — A666

Literary Treasures in DDR Libraries: 35pf, Maya manuscript, 12th cent., Dresden. 50pf, Petrarch sonnet illustration, 16th century French manuscript, Berlin.

1981, Aug. 18 Photo. *Perf. 14*

2207 A665 20pf multicolored .20 .20
2208 A665 35pf multicolored .20 .20
2209 A665 50pf multicolored *1.10 1.00*
Nos. 2207-2209 (3) *1.50 1.40*

1981, Aug. 18

Leipzig 1981 Autumn Fair: 25pf, Concert Hall, Leipzig, horiz.

2210 A666 10pf multicolored .20 .20
2211 A666 25pf multicolored .30 .25

Anti-Fascist Resistance Monument, Sassnitz A667

1981, Sept. 8 Photo. *Perf. 14*

2212 A667 35pf multicolored .35 .25

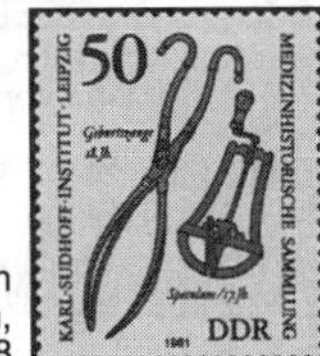

Forceps, 18th Cent., Speculum, 17th Cent. — A668

Historic Medical Instruments, Karl Sudhoff Institute, Leipzig: 10pf, Henbana, censer, 16th cent. 20pf, Pelican, dental elevator and extractors, 17th cent. 25pf, Seton forceps, 17th cent. 35pf, Lithotomy knife, 18th cent., hernia scissors, 17th cent. 85pf, Elevators, 17th cent. 10pf, 20pf, 25pf, 35pf horiz.

1981, Sept. 22

2213 A668 10pf multicolored .20 .20
2214 A668 20pf multicolored .20 .20
2215 A668 25pf multicolored .20 .20
2216 A668 35pf multicolored .20 .20
2217 A668 50pf multicolored *2.00 1.75*
2218 A668 85pf multicolored .35 .25
Nos. 2213-2218 (6) *3.15 2.80*

Philatelists' Day — A669

1981, Oct. 6 Photo. *Perf. 14*

2219 A669 10pf + 5pf Letter by Engels, 1840 *.65 .40*
2220 A669 20pf Postcard by Marx, 1878 .20 .20

River Boat A670

1981, Oct. 20

2221 A670 10pf Tugboat .20 .20
2222 A670 20pf Tugboat, diff. .20 .20
2223 A670 25pf Diesel paddle liner .20 .20
2224 A670 35pf Ice breaker .20 .20
2225 A670 50pf Motor freighter .25 .20
2226 A670 85pf Bucket dredger *2.10 1.75*
Nos. 2221-2226 (6) *3.15 2.75*

Windmill, Dabel — A671

1981, Nov. 10 Photo. *Perf. 14*

2227 A671 10pf shown .20 .20
2228 A671 20pf Pahrenz .20 .20
2229 A671 25pf Dresden-Gohlis .20 .20
2230 A671 70pf Ballstadt *1.25 1.10*
Nos. 2227-2230 (4) *1.85 1.70*

Toys — A672

1981, Nov. 24 Litho. *Perf. 13½*

2231 Sheet of 6 *2.75 2.50*
a. A672 10pf Jointed snake, 1850 *.20 .20*
b. A672 20pf Teddy bear, 1910 *.20 .20*
c. A672 25pf Fish, 1935 *.70 .60*
d. A672 35pf Hobby horse, 1850 *.70 .60*
e. A672 40pf Cuckoo, 1800 *.20 .20*
f. A672 70pf Frog, 1930 *.20 .20*

Meissen Porcelain Teapot, 1715 — A673

1982, Jan. 26 Photo. *Perf. 14*

2232 A673 10pf shown .20 .20
2233 A673 20pf Vase, 1715 .25 .25
2234 A673 25pf Oberon figurine, 1969 .35 .35
2235 A673 35pf Day and Night vase, 1979 .50 .50
a. Block of 4, #2232-2235 1.75 1.50

Souvenir Sheet

2236 Sheet of 2 *1.75 2.50*
a. A673 50pf Portrait *.65 .90*
b. A673 50pf Emblem *.65 .90*

Johann Friedrich Bottger (1682-1719), inventor of Dresden china. No. 2236 contains two 24x29mm stamps.

Post Offices — A674

1982, Feb. 9

2237 A674 20pf Liebenstein .20 .20
2238 A674 25pf Berlin .20 .20
2239 A674 35pf Erfurt .20 .20
2240 A674 50pf Dresden *1.25 1.10*
Nos. 2237-2240 (4) *1.85 1.70*

Intl. Fur Auction, Leipzig A675

1982, Feb. 23 Photo. *Perf. 14*

2241 A675 10pf Marmot, vert. .20 .20
2242 A675 20pf Polecat .20 .20
2243 A675 25pf Mink .20 .20
2244 A675 35pf Stone marten *.95 .95*
Nos. 2241-2244 (4) *1.55 1.55*

Souvenir Sheet

Goethe-Schiller Awards, 1980-1984 — A676

1982, Mar. 9 Litho.

2245 A676 Sheet of 2 *2.00 2.50*
a. 50pf Goethe *.65 .90*
b. 50pf Schiller *.65 .90*

1982 Leipzig Spring Fair A677

1982, Mar. 9 *Perf. 13x12½*

2246 A677 10pf Entrance .20 .20
2247 A677 25pf Exhibit .25 .20

Souvenir Sheet

TB Bacillus Centenary — A678

1982, Mar. 23 *Perf. 14*

2248 A678 1m multi *1.60 2.00*

Working-class Leader Type of 1979

#2249, Max Fechner (1892-1973). #2250, Ottomar Greschke (1882-1957). #2251, Helmut Lehmann (1882-1959). #2252, Herbert Warnke (1902-75). #2253, Otto Winzer (1902-75).

1982, Mar. 23 Engr.

2249 A623 10pf dk red brn .20 .20
2250 A623 10pf green .20 .20
2251 A623 10pf violet .20 .20
2252 A623 10pf dull blue .20 .20
2253 A623 10pf gray olive .20 .20
Nos. 2249-2253 (5) 1.00 1.00

Poisonous Plants — A679

1982, Apr. 6 Litho. *Perf. 14*

2254 A679 10pf Meadow saffron .20 .20
2255 A679 15pf Water arum .20 .20
2256 A679 20pf Marsh tea .20 .20
2257 A679 25pf White bryony .20 .20
2258 A679 35pf Common monkshood .20 .20
2259 A679 50pf Henbane *1.10 1.25*
Nos. 2254-2259 (6) *2.10 2.25*

Free Federation of German Trade Unions, 10th Congress A680

Paintings: 10pf, Mother and Child, by Walter Womacka. 20pf, Discussion at the Innovator Collective, by Willi Neubert, horiz. 25pf, Young Couple, by Karl-Heinz Jacob.

1982, Apr. 20 Photo.

2260 A680 10pf multi .20 .20
2261 A680 20pf multi .20 .20
2262 A680 25pf multi *.45 .45*
Nos. 2260-2262 (3) *.85 .85*

Intl. Book Art Exhibition, Leipzig — A681

1982, Apr. 20

2263 A681 15pf "I" *.30 .30*
2264 A681 35pf Emblem *.30 .30*
a. Pair, #2263-2264 + label *1.10 .90*

A682

Protected species. 10pf, 25pf, 35pf vert.

Perf. 13½x14, 14x13½

1982, May 18 Photo.

2265 A682 10pf Fish hawk .20 .20
2266 A682 20pf Sea eagle .20 .20
2267 A682 25pf Tawny eagle .20 .20
2268 A682 35pf Eagle owl *1.10 .90*
Nos. 2265-2268 (4) 1.70 1.50

19th Workers' Festival, Neubrandenburg — A683

1982, June 8 Photo. *Perf. 14*

2269 A683 10pf View of Neubrandenburg .20 .20
2270 A683 20pf Traditional costumes .30 .25

Souvenir Sheet

Dimitrov Memorial Medal — A684

1982, June 8

2271 A684 1m multi *2.00 2.00*

George Dimitrov (1882-1947), first prime minister of Bulgaria.

Cargo Ship Frieden — A685

1982, June 22

2272 A685 5pf shown .20 .20
2273 A685 10pf Fichtelberg .20 .20
2274 A685 15pf Brocken .20 .20
2275 A685 20pf Weimar .20 .20
2276 A685 25pf Vorwarts .25 .20
2277 A685 35pf Berlin *1.10 1.10*
Nos. 2272-2277 (6) 2.15 2.10

Technology — A686

1982, June 22 Litho. *Perf. 13x12½*

2278 A686 20pf multi .30 .20

Bird Wedding — A687

Sorbian Folklore: 20pf, Zampern masqueraders. 25pf, Easter egg game. 35pf, Painting Easter eggs. 40pf, St. John's Day parade. 50pf, Christmas celebration.

1982, July 6 Litho. *Perf. 13x12½*

2279 A687 Block of 6 *3.25 2.75*
a. 10pf multi .20 .20
b. 20pf multi .20 .20
c. 25pf multi .25 .25
d. 35pf multi .45 .45
e. 40pf multi .50 .50
f. 50pf multi .65 .65

View of Schwerin A688

7th Youth Stamp Exhibition, Schwerin: 10pf + 5pf, View, 1640.

1982, July 6

2280 A688 10pf + 5pf multi .25 .25
2281 A688 20pf multi .25 .25
a. Pair, #2280-2281 + label .90 .80

7th Pioneer Meeting, Dresden A689

1982, July 20 Photo. *Perf. 14x13½*

2282 A689 10pf + 5pf Pioneers, banner .35 .35
2283 A689 20pf Bugle, pennant .20 .20

Seascape, by Ludolf Backhuysen (1631-1708) — A690

17th Cent. Paintings in Natl. Museum, Schwerin: 10pf, Music Making at Home, by Frans van Mieris (1635-1681), vert. 20pf, The Gate Guard, by Carel Fabritius (1622-1654), vert. 25pf, Farmers Company, by Adriaen Brouwer (1606-1638). 35pf, Breakfast Table with Ham, by Willem Clacsz Heda (1593-1680). 70pf, River Landscape, by Jan van Goyen (1596-1656).

1982, Aug. 10 *Perf. 14*

2284 A690 5pf multi .20 .20
2285 A690 10pf multi .20 .20
2286 A690 20pf multi .20 .20
2287 A690 25pf multi .20 .20
2288 A690 35pf multi .20 .20
2289 A690 70pf multi *1.25 1.25*
Nos. 2284-2289 (6) 2.25 2.25

1982 Leipzig Autumn Fair A691

1982, Aug. 24 Litho. *Perf. 13x12½*

2290 A691 10pf Exhibition Hall .20 .20
2291 A691 25pf Decorative box, ring .20 .20

Karl-Marx-Stadt Buildings and Monument — A692

1982, Aug. 24 Photo. *Perf. 14*

2292 A692 10pf multi + label .20 .20

Org. for the Cooperation of Socialist Countries and Posts and Telecommunications Dept., 13th Conference, Karl-Marx-Stadt, Sept. 6-11.

Intl. Federation of Resistance Fighters, 9th Congress, Berlin — A693

1982, Sept. 7 Litho. *Perf. 14*

2293 A693 10pf Emblem .30 .20

Auschwitz-Birkenau Intl. Memorial A694

1982, Sept. 7 Photo.

2294 A694 35pf multi .30 .25

Autumn Flowers — A695

1982, Sept. 21

2295 A695 5pf Autumn anemones .20 .20
2296 A695 10pf Student flowers .20 .20
2297 A695 15pf Hybrid gazanias .20 .20
2298 A695 20pf Sunflowers .20 .20
2299 A695 25pf Chrysanthemums .20 .20
2300 A695 35pf Cosmos bipinnatus *1.50 1.10*
Nos. 2295-2301 (7) 2.70 2.30

Ambulance — A696

1982, Oct. 5 Litho. *Perf. 13x12½*

2301 A696 5pf shown .20 .20
2302 A696 10pf Street cleaner .20 .20
2303 A696 20pf Bus .20 .20
2304 A696 25pf Platform truck .20 .20
2305 A696 35pf Platform truck, diff. .20 .20
2306 A696 85pf Milk truck *1.75 1.40*
Nos. 2301-2306 (6) 2.75 2.40

25th Masters of Tomorrow Central Fair — A697

1982, Oct. 19 *Perf. 14*

2307 A697 20pf multicolored .25 .20

Martin Luther (1483-1546) A698

Designs: 10pf, Seal of Eisleben (town of birth and death). 20pf, Portrait, Eisenach, 1521. 35pf, Wittenberg seal, 1500. 85pf, Portrait, after Cranach, 1528.

1982, Nov. 23 Photo. *Perf. 14x13½*

2308 A698 10pf multi .20 .20
2309 A698 20pf multi .20 .20
a. Miniature sheet of 10 5.00 5.00
2310 A698 35pf multi .30 .20
2311 A698 85pf multi *2.25 1.40*
Nos. 2308-2311 (4) 2.95 2.00

Toy Carpenter, 1830 — A699

1982, Nov. 23 Litho. *Perf. 14*

2312 Sheet of 6 *2.75 2.50*
a. A699 10pf shown .20 .20
b. A699 20pf Cobbler .70 .70
c. A699 25pf Baker .20 .20
d. A699 35pf Cooper .20 .20
e. A699 40pf Tanner .70 .70
f. A699 70pf Carter .20 .20

Souvenir Sheet

Johannes Brahms (1833-1897), Composer — A700

1983, Jan. 11 Litho. *Perf. 14*

2313 A700 1.15m multi *2.50 3.00*

Working-class Leader Type of 1979

#2314, Franz Dahlem (1892-1981). #2315, Karl Maron (1903-75). #2316, Josef Miller (1883-1964). #2317, Fred Oelsser (1903-77). #2318, Siegfried Radel (1893-1943).

1983, Jan. 25 **Photo.**

2314 A623 10pf dark brown .20 .20
2315 A623 10pf dark green .20 .20
2316 A623 10pf dark olive grn .20 .20
2317 A623 10pf deep plum .20 .20
2318 A623 10pf dark blue .20 .20
Nos. 2314-2318 (5) 1.00 1.00

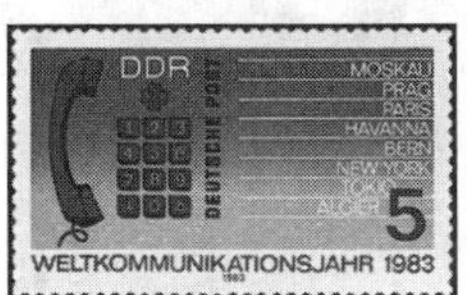

World Communications Year — A701

1983, Feb. 8 **Photo.** ***Perf. 14***

2319 A701 5pf Telephone receiver, buttons .20 .20
2320 A701 10pf Rugen radio .20 .20
2321 A701 20pf Surface and air mail .20 .20
2322 A701 35pf Optical conductors *.95 .75*
Nos. 2319-2322 (4) *1.55 1.35*

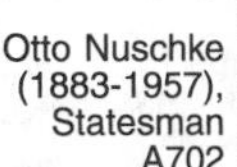

Otto Nuschke (1883-1957), Statesman A702

1983, Feb. 8

2323 A702 20pf red brn, bl & blk .20 .20

Town Hall, Gera, 1576 — A703

1983, Feb. 22 **Photo.** ***Perf. 14***

2324 A703 10pf Stolberg, 1482, horiz. .20 .20
2325 A703 20pf shown .20 .20
2326 A703 25pf Possneck, 1486 .20 .20
2327 A703 35pf Berlin, 1869, horiz. *1.10 1.00*
Nos. 2324-2327 (4) *1.70 1.60*

1983 Leipzig Spring Fair — A704

1983, Mar. 8

2328 A704 10pf Fair building .20 .20
2329 A704 25pf Robotron microcomputer .25 .20

Paul Robeson (1898-1976), Singer — A705

1983, Mar. 22 **Litho.** ***Perf. 13x12½***

2330 A705 20pf multicolored .25 .20

Souvenir Sheet

Schulze-Boysen/Harnack Resistance Org. — A706

Arvid Harnack (1901-42), Harro Schulze-Boysen (1909-42), John Sieg (1903-42).

1983, Mar. 22

2331 A706 85pf multicolored 1.10 1.50

Karl Marx (1818-1883), and Newspaper Mastheads — A707

Portraits and: 20pf, Lyons silk weavers' revolt, 1831, French-German Yearbook. 35pf, Engels, Communist Manifesto. 50pf, Das Kapital titlepage. 70pf, Program of German Workers' Movement text. 85pf, Engels, Lenin, globe. 1.15m Portrait (24x29mm).

1983, Apr. 11 **Photo.** ***Perf. 13x12½***

2332 A707 10pf multicolored .20 .20
2333 A707 20pf multicolored .20 .20
2334 A707 35pf multicolored .20 .20
2335 A707 50pf multicolored .20 .20
2336 A707 70pf multicolored .30 .20
2337 A707 85pf multicolored *1.75 1.75*
Nos. 2332-2337 (6) *2.85 2.75*

Souvenir Sheet

Litho. ***Perf. 14***

2338 A707 1.15m multi *2.00 2.50*

Works of Art from Berlin State Museums — A708

1983, Apr. 19 **Photo.** ***Perf. 14***

2339 A708 10pf Athena .20 .20
2340 A708 20pf Amazon, bronze, 430 BC .30 .20

Narrow-Gauge Railroads — A709

1983, May 17 **Litho.** ***Perf. 13x12½***

2341 Pair, Wernigerode-Nordhausen line *1.25 .85*
a. A709 15pf Locomotive *.30 .30*
b. A709 20pf Passenger car *.30 .30*
2342 Pair, Zittau-Oybin/Johnsdorf line *1.25 .85*
a. A709 20pf Locomotive *.30 .30*
b. A709 50pf Freight car *.30 .30*

Nos. 2341 and 2342 se-tenant with labels showing maps. See Nos. 2405-2406.

Sand Glasses and Sundials A710

Cacti A711

1983, June 7 **Photo.** ***Perf. 14***

2343 A710 5pf Sand glass, 1674 .20 .20
2344 A710 10pf Sand glass, 1700 .20 .20
2345 A710 20pf Sundial, 1611 .20 .20
a. Sheet of 8 *2.00 1.90*
2346 A710 30pf Sundial, 1750 .20 .20
2347 A710 50pf Sundial, 1760 .30 .20
2348 A710 85pf Sundial, 1800 *2.00 1.60*
Nos. 2343-2348 (6) *3.10 2.60*

1983, June 21

2349 A711 5pf Coryphantha elephantidens .20 .20
2350 A711 10pf Thelocactus schwarzii .20 .20
2351 A711 20pf Leuchtenbergia principis .20 .20
2352 A711 25pf Submatucana madisoniorum .20 .20
2353 A711 35pf Oroya peruviana .20 .20
2354 A711 50pf Copiapoa cinerea *1.25 1.25*
Nos. 2349-2354 (6) *2.25 2.25*

Naumberg Cathedral Statues, 15th Cent. A712

1983, July 5 **Photo.** ***Perf. 13***

2355 A712 20pf Thimo and Wilhelm .30 .30
2356 A712 25pf Gepa and Gerburg .35 .35
2357 A712 35pf Hermann and Reglindis .45 .45
2358 A712 85pf Eckehard and Uta 1.10 1.10
a. Block of 4, #2355-2358 2.50 2.50

Technical Training, by Harald Metzkes (b. 1929) A713

SOZPHILEX '83 Junior Stamp Exhibition, Berlin: 10pf+5pf, Glasewaldt and Zinna Defending the Barricade-18th March, 1848, by Theodor Hosemann, vert. Surtax was for exhibition.

1983, July 5 **Litho.** ***Perf. 13x12½***

2359 A713 10pf + 5pf multi *.50 .45*
2360 A713 20pf multi .20 .20

Volleyball A714

1983, July 19 **Photo.** ***Perf. 14***

2361 A714 10pf + 5pf Passing beach balls *.40 .30*
2362 A714 20pf shown .20 .20

7th Gymnastic and Sports Meeting; 9th Children's and Youth Spartikiade, Leipzig.

Simon Bolivar (1783-1830) — A715

1983, July 19

2363 A715 35pf Bolivar, Alexander von Humboldt .45 .25

City Arms — A716

1983, Aug. 9

2364 A716 50pf Berlin *.65 .45*
2365 A716 50pf Cottbus *.65 .45*
2366 A716 50pf Dresden *.65 .45*
2367 A716 50pf Erfurt *.65 .45*
2368 A716 50pf Frankfurt *.65 .45*
Nos. 2364-2368 (5) *3.25 2.25*

See Nos. 2398-2402, 2464-2468.

1983 Leipzig Autumn Fair — A717

1983, Aug. 30

2369 A717 10pf Central Palace .20 .20
2370 A717 25pf Microelectronic pattern .35 .20

Leonhard Euler (1707-1783), Mathematician — A718

1983, Sept. 6

2371 A718 20pf multi .35 .20

Souvenir Sheet

30th Anniv. of Working-Class Brigade Groups — A719

1983, Sept. 6 **Litho.** ***Perf. 12½x13***

2372 A719 1m multicolored *1.60 1.75*

Governmental Palaces, Potsdam Gardens — A720

1983, Sept. 20 ***Perf. 13x12½***

2373 A720 10pf Sanssouci Palace .20 .20

2374 A720 20pf Chinese teahouse .20 .20

2375 A720 40pf Charlottenhof Palace .30 .20

2376 A720 50pf Royal Stables, Film Museum *2.00 1.60*

Nos. 2373-2376 (4) *2.70 2.20*

Monument, Mamajew-Kurgan Hill — A721

1983, Oct. 4 ***Perf. 14***

2377 A721 35pf Mother Home .35 .20

Souvenir Sheet

Martin Luther — A722

1983, Oct. 18 **Litho.** ***Perf. 14***

2378 A722 1m multi *2.25 3.00*

Margin shows title page from Luther Bible, 1541.

Thuringian Glass — A723

1983, Nov. 8 **Photo.** ***Perf. 13½x14***

2379 A723 10pf Cock .20 .20

2380 A723 20pf Cup .20 .20

2381 A723 25pf Vase .20 .20

2382 A723 70pf Ornamental Glass *1.40 1.10*

Nos. 2379-2382 (4) *2.00 1.70*

Souvenir Sheet

New Year 1984 — A724

1983, Nov. 22 **Litho.** ***Perf. 14***

2383 Sheet of 4 *1.40 2.00*

a. A724 10pf multi *.20 .20*

b. A724 20pf multi *.20 .20*

c. A724 25pf multi *.30 .25*

d. A724 35pf multi *.40 .35*

Winter Olympics 1984, Sarajevo A725

1983, Nov. 22 **Photo.** ***Perf. 14***

2384 A725 10pf + 5pf 2-man luge .20 .20

2385 A725 20pf + 10pf Ski jump .20 .20

2386 A725 25pf Skiing .20 .20

2387 A725 35pf Biathlon *1.10 .95*

Nos. 2384-2387 (4) *1.70 1.55*

Souvenir Sheet

2388 A725 85pf Olympic Center *1.40* 2.00

Jena Glass Centenary — A726

1984, Jan. 10 **Litho.** ***Perf. 12½x13***

2389 A726 20pf Otto Schott .30 .20

Working-class Leader Type of 1979

Designs: No. 2390, Friedrich Ebert (1894-1979). No. 2391, Fritz Grosse (1904-1957). No. 2392, Albert Norden (1904-1982).

1984, Jan. 24 **Engr.** ***Perf. 14***

2390 A623 10pf black .20 .20

2391 A623 10pf dark green .20 .20

2392 A623 10pf dark blue .20 .20

Nos. 2390-2392 (3) .60 .60

Souvenir Sheet

Felix Mendelssohn (1809-1847), Composer — A727

1984, Jan. 24 **Litho.**

2393 A727 85pf multi .75 1.25

Margin shows Song Without Words score.

Postal Milestones — A728

Designs: 10pf, Muhlau, 1725; Oederan, 1722. 20pf, Johanngeorgenstadt, 1723; Schonbrunn, 1724. 35pf, Freiberg, 1723. 85pf, Pegau, 1723.

1984, Feb. 7 **Photo.** ***Perf. 14***

2394 A728 10pf multi .20 .20

2395 A728 20pf multi .25 .20

2396 A728 35pf multi .30 .25

2397 A728 85pf multi .65 .60

Nos. 2394-2397 (4) 1.40 1.25

City Arms Type of 1983

1984, Feb. 21

2398 A716 50pf Gera .45 .30

2399 A716 50pf Halle .45 .30

2400 A716 50pf Karl-Marx-Stadt .45 .30

2401 A716 50pf Leipzig .45 .30

2402 A716 50pf Magdeburg .45 .30

Nos. 2398-2402 (5) 2.25 1.50

1984 Leipzig Spring Fair A729

1984, Mar. 6 ***Perf. 14***

2403 A729 10pf Old Town Hall .20 .20

2404 A729 25pf Factory .25 .20

Railroad Type of 1983

1984, Mar. 20 **Litho.** ***Perf. 13x12½***

2405 Pair, Cranzahl Oberwiesenthal line 1.10 .90

a. A709 30pf Locomotive .20 .20

b. A709 80pf Passenger car .50 .50

2406 Pair, Selke Valley line 1.10 .80

a. A709 40pf Locomotive .25 .25

b. A709 60pf Passenger car .30 .30

Labels show maps of routes.

Stone Door, Rostock — A730

Council Building — A731

Intl. Society of Monument Preservation 7th General Meeting: 10pf, Town Hall, Rostock. 15pf, Albrecht Castle, Meissen. 85pf, Stable Courtyard, Dresden. 10pf, 15pf, 85pf horiz.

1984, Apr. 24 **Photo.** ***Perf. 14***

2407 A730 10pf multi .20 .20

2408 A730 15pf multi .20 .20

2409 A730 40pf multi .35 .30

2410 A730 85pf multi .85 .75

Nos. 2407-2410 (4) 1.60 1.45

1984, May 8

2411 A731 70pf multi .55 .25

Standing Commission of Posts and Telecommunications of Council of Mutual Economic Aid, 25th meeting.

Cast-iron Bowl, 19th Cent. A732

Marionette A733

Cast-Iron, Lauchhammer: 85pf, Ascending Man, by Fritz Cremer, 1967.

1984, May 22

2412 A732 20pf multi .20 .20

2413 A732 85pf multi .70 .60

1984, June 5

2414 A733 50pf shown .45 .40

2415 A733 80pf Puppet .75 .65

Natl. Youth Festival A734

1984, June 5 **Litho.** ***Perf. 13x12½***

2416 A734 10pf + 5pf Demonstration .20 .20

2417 A734 20pf Construction workers .20 .20

a. Pair, #2416-2417 + label .55 .35

20th Workers' Festival A735

1984, June 19

2418 A735 10pf View of Gera .20 .20

2419 A735 20pf Traditional costumes .20 .20

a. Pair, #2418-2419 + label .45 .30

Natl. Stamp Exhib., Halle — A736

1984, July 3 ***Perf. 13½x14***

2420 A736 10pf + 5pf Salt carrier .20 .20

2421 A736 20pf Wedding couple .25 .20

Historic Seals, 1442 — A737

1984, Aug. 7 **Litho.** ***Perf. 14***

2422 A737 5pf Baker, Berlin *.25* .20

2423 A737 10pf Wool weaver, Berlin *.40* .25

2424 A737 20pf Wool weaver, Cologne *.85* .25

2425 A737 35pf Shoemaker, Cologne *1.40* 1.00

a. Block of 4, #2422-2425 *4.25* 2.50

Building Renovation and Construction A738

Ironwork Collective Combine East — A739

Litho., Photo. (#2427, 2429, 25pf)

1984 ***Perf. 14x13½***

2426 A738 10pf shown .20 .20

2427 A739 10pf shown .20 .20

2428 A738 20pf Surface mining .25 .25

2429 A739 20pf Armed forces .20 .20

2430 A739 25pf Petro-chemical Collective Combine, Schwedt .25 .25

Nos. 2426-2430 (5) 1.10 1.10

Souvenir Sheets

2431 A738 1m Privy Council Building .85 1.50

2432 A739 1m Family .85 1.50

DDR, 35th anniv. Issued: A738, 8/21; A739, 9/11.

1984 Leipzig Autumn Fair — A740

1984, Aug. 28 **Photo.** ***Perf. 14***

2433 A740 10pf Frege House, Katharine St. .20 .20

2434 A740 25pf Crystal bowl, Olbernhau .25 .20

Members of the Resistance, Sculpture by Arno Wittig — A741

1984, Sept. 18 Photo. *Perf. 14*

2435 A741 35pf multi .60 .25

View of Magdeburg — A742

1984, Oct. 4 Litho. *Perf. 13x12½*

2436 A742 10pf + 5pf shown .20 .20
2437 A742 20pf Old & modern buildings .20 .20
a. Pair, #2436-2437 + label .40 .30

8th Youth Stamp Exhibition, Magdeburg.

35th Anniv. of Republic — A743

1984, Oct. 4 Photo. *Perf. 14*

2438 A743 10pf Construction .20 .20
2439 A743 20pf Military .20 .20
2440 A743 25pf Heavy industry .25 .25
2441 A743 35pf Agriculture .30 .30
Nos. 2438-2441 (4) .95 .95

Souvenir Sheet

2442 A743 1m Arms, dove, vert. .90 1.50

Figurines, Green Vault of Dresden — A744

1984, Oct. 23

2443 A744 10pf Spring .20 .20
2444 A744 20pf Summer .20 .20
a. Miniature sheet of 8, litho., perf. 12½x13 2.00 1.50
2445 A744 35pf Autumn .25 .25
2446 A744 70pf Winter .30 .30
Nos. 2443-2446 (4) .95 .95

Falkenstein Castle — A745

1984, Nov. 6 Litho. *Perf. 14*

2447 A745 10pf shown .20 .20
2448 A745 20pf Kriebstein .20 .20
2449 A745 35pf Ranis .35 .30
2450 A745 80pf Neuenburg .65 .35
Nos. 2447-2450 (4) 1.40 1.05

See Nos. 2504-2507.

Dead Tsar's Daughter and the Seven Warriors A746

Various scenes from the fairytale.

1984, Nov. 27 Litho. *Perf. 13*

2451 Sheet of 6 *8.50* 3.00
a. A746 5pf multi *.20* .20
b. A746 10pf multi *.20* .20
c. A746 15pf multi *1.75* 1.00
d. A746 20pf multi *1.75* 1.00
e. A746 35pf multi *.20* .20
f. A746 50pf multi *.20* .20

Working-class Leader Type of 1979

Designs: No. 2452, Anton Ackermann (1905-1973). No. 2453, Alfred Kurella (1895-1975). No. 2454, Otto Schon (1905-1968).

1985, Jan. 8 Engr. *Perf. 14*

2452 A623 10pf blk brn .20 .20
2453 A623 10pf red brn .20 .20
2454 A623 10pf gray vio .20 .20
Nos. 2452-2454 (3) .60 .60

24th World Luge Championship — A747

1985, Jan. 22 Photo.

2455 A747 10pf Single seat luge .25 .20

Antique Mailboxes — A748

1985, Feb. 5 Litho. *Perf. 14*

2456 A748 10pf 1850 .20 .20
2457 A748 20pf 1860 .20 .20
2458 A748 35pf 1900 .25 .25
2459 A748 50pf 1920 .30 .30
a. Block of 4, Nos. 2456-2459 1.00 .90

Souvenir Sheet

Dresden Opera House Reopening — A749

Litho. & Engr.

1985, Feb. 12 *Perf. 13*

2460 A749 85pf multicolored .85 1.25

1985 Leipzig Spring Fair A750

Bach, Handel and Schutz Tribute A751

1985, Mar. 5 Photo. *Perf. 14*

2461 A750 10pf Statue of Bach, Leipzig .20 .20
2462 A750 25pf Porcelain pot, Meissen .25 .20

Souvenir Sheet

1985, Mar. 19 Litho.

2463 Sheet of 3 1.25 1.75
a. A751 10pf Bach .20 .20
b. A751 20pf Handel .20 .20
c. A751 85pf Heinrich Schutz (1585-1672) .65 .65

City Arms Type of 1983

1985, Apr. 9 Photo. *Perf. 14*

2464 A716 50pf Neubrandenburg .45 .35
2465 A716 50pf Potsdam .45 .35
2466 A716 50pf Rostock .45 .35
2467 A716 50pf Schwerin .45 .35
2468 A716 50pf Suhl .45 .35
Nos. 2464-2468 (5) 2.25 1.75

Seelow Heights Memorial — A752

1985, Apr. 16 Photo. *Perf. 14*

2469 A752 35pf multi .35 .25

Egon Erwin Kisch, Journalist (1885-1948) — A753

1985, Apr. 23 Photo. *Perf. 14*

2470 A753 35pf multi .25 .20

No. 2470 was printed se-tenant with label showing the house where Kisch was born.

Liberation from Fascism, 40th Anniv. — A754

Designs: 10pf, German and Soviet astronauts. 20pf, Coal miner Adolf Hennecke, symbols of industry and energy. 25pf, farm workers, symbols of socialist agriculture. 50pf, Technicians manufacturing microchips, science and technology.

1985, May 7 Photo. *Perf. 14x13½*

2471 A754 10pf multi .20 .20
2472 A754 20pf multi .20 .20
2473 A754 25pf multi .20 .20
2474 A754 50pf multi .40 .40
Nos. 2471-2474 (4) 1.00 1.00

Souvenir Sheet

Perf. 12½x13

2475 A754 1m Berlin-Treptow Soviet Heroes Monument .95 1.50

Warsaw Treaty, 30th Anniv. — A755

1985, May 14 Litho. *Perf. 13x12½*

2476 A755 20pf Flags of pact nations .30 .20

Historical and Modern Buildings A756

12th Youth Parliament, Berlin: 20pf, Ernst Thalmann, flags.

1985, May 21 Litho.

2477 A756 10pf + 5pf multi .20 .20
2478 A756 20pf multi .20 .20
a. Pair, #2477-2478 + label .35 .35

Intl. Olympic Committee 90th Meeting — A757

1985, May 28 Litho. *Perf. 14*

2479 A757 35pf Flag+ label .40 .35

Free German Trade Unions, 40th Anniv. — A758

1985, June 11 Photo.

2480 A758 20pf Red flags .25 .20

Wildlife Preservation A759

1985, June 25 Photo.

2481 A759 5pf Harpy eagle, vert. .20 .20
2482 A759 10pf Red-necked goose .20 .20
2483 A759 20pf Spectacled bear .20 .20
2484 A759 50pf Banteng (Javanese) buffalo .40 .35
2485 A759 85pf Sunda Straits crocodile .80 .70
Nos. 2481-2485 (5) 1.80 1.65

19th Century Steam Engines A760

1985, July 9 Photo.

2486 A760 10pf Bock engine, vert. .20 .20
2487 A760 85pf Beam engine .70 .55

12th World Youth and Student Festival, Moscow A761

1985, July 23 Litho. *Perf. 13x12½*

2488 A761 20pf + 5pf Students reading .20 .20
2489 A761 50pf Student demonstration .30 .30
a. Pair, #2488-2489 + label .85 .70

2nd World Orienteering and Deep-sea Diving Championship — A762

1985, Aug. 13 Photo. *Perf. 14*

2490 A762 10pf Diver at turning buoy .20 .20
2491 A762 70pf Long-distance divers .65 .50

Bose House Fair Building, St. Thomas Churchyard — A763

1985, Apr. 27 Photo.

2492 A763 10pf shown .20 .20
2493 A763 25pf Bach trumpet .30 .20

Leipzig Autumn Fair.

A764

SOZPHILEX '85: 19th century coach and team, 1878, bas-relief by Hermann Steinemann, in the court of the former Berlin Post Office.

1985, Sept. 10 Litho. *Perf. 13x12½*

2494 5pf multi .20 .20
2495 20pf + 5pf multi .20 .20
a. Miniature sheet of 4 #2495b .60 .60
b. A764 Pair, #2494-2495 .30 .30

No. 2495b has a continuous design.

German Railways 150th Anniv. — A765

Socialist Railway Org.: 20pf, GS II signal box, track diagram. 25pf, 1838 Saxonia, first German locomotive, designer Johann Andreas Schubert (1808-1870), Model 250 electric locomotive. 50pf, Helicopter lifting cable drum, section electrification. 85pf, Leipzig Central Station.

Litho.

Perf. 12½x13

1985, Sept. 24

2496 A765 20pf multi .20 .20
2497 A765 25pf multi .25 .20
2498 A765 50pf multi .50 .40
2499 A765 85pf multi .75 .70
Nos. 2496-2499 (4) 1.70 1.50

Bridges in East Berlin A766

Photo.; Litho. (#2501a)

1985, Oct. 8 *Perf. 14*

2500 A766 10pf Gertrauden .20 .20
2501 A766 20pf Jungfern .20 .20
a. Min. sheet of 8, perf. 13x12½ 2.10 2.00
2502 A766 35pf Weidendammer .30 .30
2503 A766 70pf Marx-Engels .50 .50
Nos. 2500-2503 (4) 1.20 1.20

Castles Type of 1984

1985, Oct. 15 Litho.

2504 A745 10pf Hohnstein .20 .20
2505 A745 20pf Rochsburg .20 .20
2506 A745 35pf Schwarzenberg .25 .25
2507 A745 80pf Stein .75 .65
Nos. 2504-2507 (4) 1.40 1.30

Humboldt University, 175th Anniv. — A767

85pf, Charity Hospital, Berlin, 275th anniv.

1985, Oct. 22 *Perf. 14*

2508 A767 20pf Administration bldg. .20 .20
2509 A767 85pf Buildings, 1897, 1982 .75 .65

Castle Cacilienhof, UN Emblem A768

1985, Oct. 22 Photo. *Perf. 13*

2510 A768 85pf multi .75 .35

UN, 40th Anniv.

Circus Art — A769

1985, Nov. 12 *Perf. 14*

2511 A769 10pf Elephant training .20 .20
2512 A769 20pf Trapeze artist .35 .30
2513 A769 35pf Acrobats on unicycles .75 .60
2514 A769 50pf Tiger training 1.10 .90
a. Block of 4, #2511-2514 4.75 7.00

Souvenir Sheet

Brothers Grimm, Fabulists & Philologists A770

Fairy tales compiled by Wilhelm (1786-1859) and Jacob (1785-1863) Grimm.

1985, Nov. 26 Litho. *Perf. 13½x13*

2515 Sheet of 6 2.00 3.50
a. A770 5pf multi .20 .20
b. A770 10pf Valiant Tailor .20 .20
c. A770 20pf Lucky John .40 .85
d. A770 25pf Puss-in-Boots .40 .85
e. A770 35pf Seven Ravens .20 .20
f. A770 85pf Sweet Porridge .20 .20

Monuments to Water Power — A772

Designs: 10pf, Cast iron hand pump, c. 1900. 35pf, Berlin-Altglienicke water tower, c. 1900. 50pf, Berlin-Friedrichshagen waterworks, 1893. 70pf, Rapphoden Hydro-electric Dam, 1959.

Engr., Photo. & Engr. (35pf)

1986, Jan. 21 *Perf. 14*

2516 A772 10pf dk grn & lake .20 .20
2517 A772 35pf buff, blk & dk grn .25 .25
2518 A772 50pf dk red brn & lt ol grn .45 .40
2519 A772 70pf dk bl & brn .55 .50
Nos. 2516-2519 (4) 1.45 1.35

Postal Uniforms, c. 1850 — A773

1986, Feb. 4 Photo. *Perf. 14½x14*

2520 A773 10pf Saxon postillion .20 .20
a. Litho., perf. 12½x13 .20 .20
2521 A773 20pf Prussian postman .25 .20
a. Litho., perf. 12½x13 .25 .20
2522 A773 85pf Prussian P.O. clerk .90 .75
a. Litho., perf. 12½x13 .90 .75
2523 A773 1m Mecklenburg clerk 1.10 .90
a. Litho., perf. 12½x13 1.10 .90
b. Block of 4, #2520a-2523a 2.10 2.00

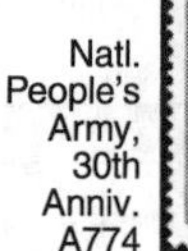

Natl. People's Army, 30th Anniv. A774

1986, Feb. 18 *Perf. 14*

2524 A774 20pf multi .30 .20

No. 2524 printed se-tenant with gold and red inscribed label.

Free German Youth Org., 40th Anniv. — A775

1986, Feb. 18

2525 A775 20pf multi .30 .25

Leipzig Spring Fair A776

1986, Mar. 11 Litho. *Perf. 13x12½*

2526 A776 35pf Fair grounds entrance, 1946 .25 .20
2527 A776 50pf Trawler Atlantik 488 .35 .30

Manned Space Flight, 25th Anniv. — A777

Designs: 40pf, Yuri Gagarin, Soviet cosomonaut, Vostok rocket, 1961. 50pf, Cosmonauts V. Bykowski, USSR, and S. Jahn, DDR, Vega probe, 1986, Intercosmos emblem. 70pf, Venera probe, Venus, spectrometer. 85pf, MKF-6 multi-spectral reconnaissance camera.

1986, Mar. 25 *Perf. 14*

2528 A777 40pf multi .25 .25
2529 A777 50pf multi .30 .30
2530 A777 70pf multi .45 .45
2531 A777 85pf multi .60 .55
a. Block of 4, #2528-2531 2.10 2.25

Socialist Unity 11th Party Day — A778

10pf, Marx, Engels & Lenin. 20pf, Ernst Thalmann. 50pf, Wilhelm Pieck & Otto Grotewohl, Uniting Party Day, 1946. 85pf,Family, motto. 1m, Construction worker, key to economic progress.

1986, Apr. 8 *Perf. 13½x13*

2532 A778 10pf multi .20 .20
2533 A778 20pf multi .20 .20
2534 A778 50pf multi .35 .35
2535 A778 85pf multi .75 .70
Nos. 2532-2535 (4) 1.50 1.45

Souvenir Sheet

Perf. 13x14

2536 A778 1m multi .90 1.50

Ernst Thalmann Park Opening, Berlin — A779

1986, Apr. 15 Photo. *Perf. 14*

2537 A779 20pf Memorial statue .30 .25

Trams and Streetcars — A780

Designs: 10pf, Dresden horse-drawn tram, 1886. 20pf, Leipzig streetcar, 1896. 40pf, Berlin streetcar, 1919. 70pf, Halle streetcar, 1928.

1986, May 20 Photo. *Perf. 14*

2538 A780 10pf multicolored .20 .20
2539 A780 20pf multicolored .20 .20
2540 A780 40pf multicolored .45 .40
2541 A780 70pf multicolored .60 .55
Nos. 2538-2541 (4) 1.45 1.35

Dresden Zoo, 125th Anniv. — A781

Berlin, 750th Anniv. — A782

1986, May 27 Litho. Perf. 14

2542 A781 10pf Orangutan .20 .20
2543 A781 20pf Colobus monkey .30 .25
2544 A781 50pf Mandrill .65 .50
2545 A781 70pf Lemur .75 .65
Nos. 2542-2545 (4) 1.90 1.60

Litho. & Engr., Engr. (70pf, 1m)

1986, June 3 Perf. 12½x13, 13x12½

20pf, 50pf are horiz.

2546 A782 10pf City seal, 1253 .20 .20
2547 A782 20pf Map, 1648 .35 .20
2548 A782 50pf City arms, 1253 .75 .50
2549 A782 70pf Nicholas Church, 1832 1.25 .65
Nos. 2546-2549 (4) 2.55 1.55

Souvenir Sheet

2550 A782 1m Royal Palace, 1986 1.00 1.25

21st Workers' Games, Magdeburg — A783

20pf, Couple in folk dress, house construction. 50pf, Magdeburg Port, River Elbe.

1986, June 17 Litho. Perf. 13x12½

2551 A783 20pf multi .20 .20
2552 A783 50pf multi .25 .25
a. Pair, #2551-2552 + label .70 .75

9th Youth Stamp Exhibition, Berlin — A784

1986, July 22 Litho. Perf. 13x12½

2553 A784 10pf + 5pf Berlin, c. 1652 .20 .20
2554 A784 20pf Art, architecture, 1986 .20 .20
a. Pair, #2553-2554 + label .35 .40

Castles A785

1986, July 29 Perf. 13x12½

2555 A785 10pf Schwerin .20 .20
a. Miniature sheet of 4 .45 .45
2556 A785 20pf Gustrow .20 .20
a. Miniature sheet of 4 .80 .80
2557 A785 85pf Rheinsberg .70 .60
2558 A785 1m Ludwigslust .95 .85
Nos. 2555-2558 (4) 2.05 1.85

Intl. Peace Year A786

1986, Aug. 5 Photo. Perf. 13

2559 A786 35pf multi .40 .30

Berlin Wall, 25th Anniv. — A787

1986, Aug. 5 Litho. Perf. 14

2560 A787 20pf Soldiers, Brandenburg Gate .40 .30

Souvenir Sheet

Leipzig Autumn Fair — A788

1986, Aug. 19

2561 A788 Sheet of 2 1.00 .90
a. 25pf Fair building .20 .20
b. 85pf Cloth merchants, 15th cent. .65 .65

City Coins A789

1986, Sept. 2 Photo. Perf. 13

2562 A789 10pf Rostock, 1637 .20 .20
2563 A789 35pf Nordhausen, 1660 .25 .25
2564 A789 50pf Erfurt, 1633 .35 .30
2565 A789 85pf Magdeburg, 1638 .65 .65
2566 A789 1m Stralsund, 1622 .90 .85
Nos. 2562-2566 (5) 2.35 2.25

44th World Sports Shooting Championships, Suhl — A790

1986, Sept. 2 Perf. 14

2567 A790 20pf Rifle shooting .20 .20
2568 A790 70pf Woman firing handgun .65 .50
2569 A790 85pf Skeet-shooting .75 .60
Nos. 2567-2569 (3) 1.60 1.30

11th World Trade Unions Congress, Berlin — A791

1986, Sept. 9

2570 A791 70pf multi+label .70 .55

Border Guards, 40th Anniv. — A792

1986, Sept. 9

2571 A792 20pf multi .30 .25

Intl. Brigades in Spain, 50th Anniv. — A793

1986, Sept. 11

2572 A793 20pf Memorial, Friedrichshain .30 .25

Natl. Memorial for Concentration Camp Victims, Sachsenhausem, 25th Anniv. — A794

1986, Sept. 23

2573 A794 35pf multi .30 .25

Mukran-Klaipeda Train-Ferry, Inauguration — A795

1986, Sept. 23

2574 A795 50pf Pier, Mukran .30 .30
2575 A795 50pf Ferry .30 .30
a. Pair, #2574-2575 .95 .95

Souvenir Sheet

Carl Maria von Weber (1786-1826), Composer — A796

1986, Nov. 4 Litho. Perf. 14

2576 A796 85pf multi .85 1.25

Indira Gandhi (1917-1984), Prime Minister of India — A797

1986, Nov. 18 Photo.

2577 A797 10pf multi .25 .20

Miniature Sheet

Chandeliers from the Ore Mountains A798

Wrought iron candle-carrying chandeliers presented to Johann Georgenstadt miners annually by the mine blacksmith.

1986, Nov. 18 Photo. Perf. 14

2578 Sheet of 6 2.00 1.75
a. A798 10pf 1778 .20 .20
b. A798 20pf 1796 .20 .20
c. A798 25pf 1810 .40 .35
d. A798 35pf 1821 .40 .35
e. A798 40pf 1830 .20 .20
f. A798 85pf 1925 .20 .20

Statues of Roland, Medieval Hero — A799

1987, Jan. 20 Photo. Perf. 14½x14

2579 A799 10pf Stendal, 1525 .20 .20
2580 A799 20pf Halle, 1719 .20 .20
2581 A799 35pf Brandenburg, 1474 .25 .25
2582 A799 50pf Quedlinburg, 1460 .45 .45
Nos. 2579-2582 (4) 1.10 1.10

See Nos. 2782-2785.

Historic Post Offices A800

1987, Feb. 3 Photo. Perf. 14x14½

2583 A800 10pf Freiberg, 1889 .20 .20
2584 A800 20pf Perleberg, 1897 .20 .20
2585 A800 70pf Weimar, 1889 .45 .45
2586 A800 1.20m Kirschau, 1926 .90 .90
a. Block of 4, #2583-2586 2.00 1.75

Nos. 2583-2586 printed in sheets of fifty and se-tenant in sheets of 40.

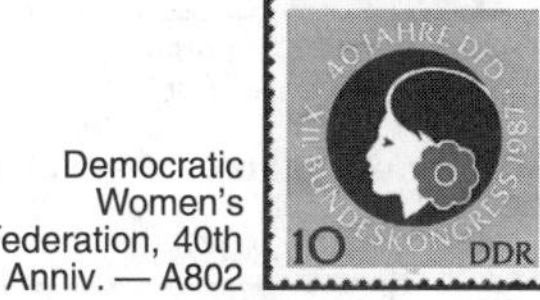

Berlin, 750th Anniv. A801

Architecture: 20pf, Reconstructed Palais Ephraim, Nikolai Quarter, demolished 1936, reopened 1987, vert. 35pf, Old Marzahn Village, modern housing. 70pf, Marx-Engels Forum, Central Berlin. 85pf, Reconstructed Friedrichstadt Palace Theater, reopened 1984.

Perf. 12½x13, 13x12½

1987, Feb. 17 Engr.

2587 A801 20pf vio brn & bluish grn .20 .20
2588 A801 35pf sage grn & dk rose brn .25 .20
2589 A801 70pf org & dk bl .55 .55
2590 A801 85pf dk ol grn & yel grn .85 .75
Nos. 2587-2590 (4) 1.85 1.70

See Nos. 2628-2631.

Democratic Women's Federation, 40th Anniv. — A802

1987, Mar. 3 Litho. Perf. 13½

2591 A802 10pf sil, dk bl & brt red .25 .20

Leipzig Spring Fair A803

1987, Mar. 10 *Perf. 13x12½*
2592 A803 35pf New Fair Hall No. 20 .25 .20
2593 A803 50pf Traders at market, c. 1804 .50 .45

Leaders of the German Workers' Movement — A804

#2594, Fritz Gabler (1897-1974). #2595, Robert Siewert (1887-1973). #2596, Walter Vesper (1897-1978). #2597, Clara Zetkin (1857-1933).

1987, Mar. 24 **Engr.** *Perf. 14*
2594 A804 10pf dark gray .20 .20
2595 A804 10pf dark green .20 .20
2596 A804 10pf black .20 .20
2597 A804 10pf vio black .20 .20
Nos. 2594-2597 (4) .80 .80

See Nos. 2721-2724.

K.A. Lingner (1861-1916), Museum A805

1987, Apr. 7 **Photo.** *Perf. 14*
2598 A805 85pf multi .70 .65

German Hygiene Museum, Dresden, 75th anniv.

Free German Trade Unions 11th Congress A806

1987, Apr. 7 **Litho.** *Perf. 13x12½*
2599 A806 20pf Construction .20 .20
2600 A806 50pf Computer, ship .35 .35
a. Pair, #2599-2600 + label .70 .70

German Red Cross 10th Congress A807

1987, Apr. 7 **Photo.** *Perf. 14*
2601 A807 35pf multi .30 .20

Agricultural Cooperative, 35th Anniv. — A808

1987, Apr. 21 **Litho.** *Perf. 13x12½*
2602 A808 20pf multi .30 .25

Famous Men A809

Designs: 10pf, Ludwig Uhland (1787-1862), poet, philologist. 20pf, Arnold Zweig (1887-1968), novelist. 35pf, Gerhart Hauptmann (1862-1946), 1912 Nobel laureate for literature, and scene from The Weavers. 50pf, Gustav Hertz (1887-1975), physicist, and atomic energy transmission diagram.

1987, May 5
2603 A809 10pf multi .20 .20
2604 A809 20pf multi .20 .20
2605 A809 35pf multi .30 .30
2606 A809 50pf multi .50 .45
Nos. 2603-2606 (4) 1.20 1.15

Freshwater Fish — A810

1987, May 19 **Litho.** *Perf. 13x12½*
2607 A810 5pf Abramis brama .20 .20
2608 A810 10pf Salmo trutta fario .20 .20
2609 A810 20pf Silurus glanis .20 .20
2610 A810 35pf Thymallus thymallus .30 .30
2611 A810 50pf Barbus barbus .45 .30
2612 A810 70pf Esox lucius .65 .65
Nos. 2607-2612 (6) 2.00 1.85

Nos. 2608-2609 exist in sheets of 4.

Fire Engines A811

1987, June 16
2613 A811 10pf Hand-operated, 1756 .20 .20
2614 A811 25pf Steam, 1903 .20 .20
2615 A811 40pf LF 15, 1919 .35 .35
2616 A811 70pf LF 16-TS 8, 1971 .65 .65
a. Block of 4, Nos. 2613-2616 1.60 1.40

Souvenir Sheet

Esperanto Movement, Cent. — A812

1987, July 7 **Litho.** *Perf. 14*
2617 A812 85pf L.L. Zamenhof, globe .75 1.25

World Wildlife Fund A813

1987, July 7 **Photo.**
2618 A813 10pf Two otters .20 .20
2619 A813 25pf Otter swimming .20 .20
2620 A813 35pf Otter .30 .30
2621 A813 60pf Close-up of head .70 .70
Nos. 2618-2621 (4) 1.40 1.40

8th Sports Festival and 11th Youth Sports Championships, Leipzig — A814

1987, July 21
2622 A814 5pf Tug-of-war .20 .20
2623 A814 10pf Handball .20 .20
2624 A814 20pf + 5pf Girls' long jump .20 .20
2625 A814 35pf Table tennis .25 .25
2626 A814 40pf Bowling .35 .35
2627 A814 70pf Running .55 .55
Nos. 2622-2627 (6) 1.75 1.75

Berlin Anniversary Type of 1987

Perf. 12½x13, 13x12½

1987, Feb. 17 **Engr.**
2628 A801 10pf like No. 2587 .20 .20
a. Miniature sheet of 4 .50 .50
2629 A801 10pf like No. 2588 .20 .20
a. Miniature sheet of 4 .50 .50
2630 A801 20pf like No. 2589 .20 .20
a. Miniature sheet of 4 .95 1.00
2631 A801 20pf like No. 2590 .20 .20
a. Miniature sheet of 4 .95 1.00
Nos. 2628-2631 (4) .80 .80

Assoc. of Sports and Science, 35th Anniv. A815

1987, Aug. 4 **Litho.** *Perf. 13x12½*
2632 A815 10pf multi .25 .20

Stamp Day A816

Designs: 10pf+5pf, Court Post Office, Berlin, 1760. 20pf, Wartenberg Palace, former Prussian General Post Office, 1770.

1987, Aug. 11 **Photo.** *Perf. 14*
2633 A816 10pf +5pf multi .20 .20
2634 A816 20pf multi .20 .20
a. Pair, #2633-2634 + label .40 .45

Souvenir Sheet

Leipzig Autumn Fair — A817

Illustration reduced.

1987, Aug. 25 **Litho.** *Perf. 13½*
2635 A817 Sheet of 2 1.00 1.25
a. 40pf multi .30 .30
b. 50pf multi .45 .45

Intl. War Victims' Memorial, Budapest A818

1987, Sept. 8 **Photo.** *Perf. 14*
2636 A818 35pf Statue of Jozsef Somogyi .30 .20

Souvenir Sheet

Thalmann Memorial — A819

Illustration reduced.

Litho. & Engr.

1987, Sept. 8 *Perf. 14*
2637 A819 1.35m buff, ver & blk 1.25 1.75

City of Berlin, 750th anniv.

10th Natl. Art Exhibition, Berlin — A820

Designs: 10pf, Weidendamm Bridge, Berlin, 1986, by Arno Mohr. 50pf, They Only Wanted to Learn How to Read and Write, Nicaragua, 1985-86, by Willi Sitte. 70pf, Large Figure of a Man in Mourning, 1983, scupture by Wieland Forster. 1m, Ceramic bowl, 1986, by Gerd Lucke. Nos. 2638-2640, vert.

1987, Sept. 28 **Litho.**
2638 A820 10pf multi .20 .20
2639 A820 50pf multi .35 .35
2640 A820 70pf multi .50 .50
2641 A820 1m multi .75 .75
Nos. 2638-2641 (4) 1.80 1.80

Lenin, Flag, Smolny Institute, Cruiser Aurora A821

1987, Oct. 27 **Photo.** *Perf. 14*
2642 A821 10pf shown .20 .20
2643 A821 20pf Spasski Tower .20 .20

October Revolution, Russia, 70th anniv.

Robot ZIM 10-S Welding A822

1987, Nov. 3 **Litho.** *Perf. 13x12½*
2644 A822 10pf Personal computer .20 .20
2645 A822 20pf shown .20 .20

30th MMM Science Fair and 10th Central Industrial Fair for Students and Youth Scientists, Leipzig.

Miniature Sheet

Christmas Candle Carousels from the Ore Mountains — A823

Designs: 10pf, Annaberg, c. 1810. 20pf, Freiberg, c. 1830. 25pf, Neustadtel, c. 1870. 35pf, Schneeberg, c. 1870. 40pf, Lossnitz, c. 1880. 85pf, Seiffen, c. 1910.

1987, Nov. 3 Litho. *Perf. 12½x13*

2646 Sheet of 6 2.00 2.10
- ***a.*** A823 10pf multi .20 .20
- ***b.*** A823 20pf multi .40 .40
- ***c.*** A823 25pf multi .20 .20
- ***d.*** A823 35pf multi .20 .20
- ***e.*** A823 40pf multi .40 .40
- ***f.*** A823 85pf multi .20 .20

1988 Winter Olympics, Calgary — A824

1988, Jan. 19 Photo. *Perf. 14½x14*

2647 A824 5pf Ski jumping .20 .20
2648 A824 10pf Speed skating .20 .20
2649 A824 20pf +10pf 4-Man bobsled .25 .25
2650 A824 35pf Biathlon .35 .30
Nos. 2647-2650 (4) 1.00 .95

Souvenir Sheet

Perf. 13x12½

2651 A824 1.20m Single and double luge 1.25 1.50

No. 2649 surtaxed for the Olympic Promotion Society.

Postal Buildings, East Berlin A825

1988, Feb. 2 *Perf. 14*

2652 A825 15pf Berlin-Buch post office .20 .20
2653 A825 20pf Natl. Postal Museum .30 .20
2654 A825 50pf General post office, Berlin-Marzahn .65 .50
Nos. 2652-2654 (3) 1.15 .90

Souvenir Sheet

Bertolt Brecht (1898-1956), Playwright — A826

1988, Feb. 2 Litho. *Perf. 13x12½*

2655 A826 70pf multi .75 1.00

Flowering Plants — A827

Leipzig Spring Fair — A828

1988, Feb. 16 Photo. *Perf. 14*

2656 A827 10pf Tillandsia macrochlamys .20 .20
2657 A827 25pf Tillandsia bulbosa .20 .20
2658 A827 40pf Tillandsia kalmbacheri .30 .30
2659 A827 70pf Guzmania blassii .65 .65
Nos. 2656-2659 (4) 1.35 1.35

1988, Mar. 8 Litho. *Perf. 12½x13*

20pf, Entrance #8. 70pf, Faust & Mephistopheles, bronze statue by Matthieu Molitor.

2660 A828 20pf multi .20 .20
2661 A828 70pf multi .65 .50

Madler Passage (arcade), 75th anniv.

A829

Souvenir Sheet

1988, Mar. 8 *Perf. 14*

2662 A829 70pf multi .95 1.25

Joseph von Eichendorff (1788-1857), poet.

Seals — A830

1988, Mar. 22 Photo. *Perf. 14*

2663 A830 10pf Muhlhausen saddler, 1565 .20 .20
2664 A830 25pf Dresden butcher, 1564 .20 .20
2665 A830 35pf Nauen smith, 16th cent. .25 .25
2666 A830 50pf Frankfurt-Oder clothier, 16th cent. .30 .30
- ***a.*** Block of 4, #2663-2666 1.10 1.10

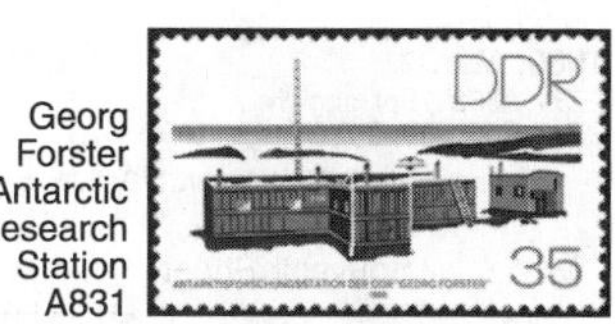

Georg Forster Antarctic Research Station A831

1988, Mar. 22 Litho. *Perf. 13x12½*

2667 A831 35pf multi .35 .20

District Capitals A832

1988, Apr. 5 Photo. *Perf. 14*

2668 A832 5pf Wismar .20 .20
2669 A832 10pf Anklam .20 .20
2670 A832 25pf Ribnitz-Damgarten .20 .20
2671 A832 60pf Stralsund .40 .40
2672 A832 90pf Bergen .65 .65
2673 A832 1.20m Greifswald .95 .95
Nos. 2668-2673 (6) 2.60 2.60

Souvenir Sheet

Ulrich von Hutten (1488-1523), Promulgator of the Lutheran Movement — A833

1988, Apr. 5 Litho. *Perf. 12½x13*

2674 A833 70pf multi .75 1.00

USSR-DDR Manned Space Flight, 10th Anniv. — A834

Designs: 5pf, Cosmonauts S. Jahn and Valery Bykowski, Soyuz-29 landing, Sept. 3, 1978. 10pf, MKS-M multi-channel spectrometer. 20pf, MIR space station.

1988, June 21 Litho. *Perf. 14*

2675 A834 5pf multi .20 .20
2676 A834 10pf multi .20 .20
2677 A834 20pf multi .20 .20
Nos. 2675-2677 (3) .60 .60

See Nos. 2698-2700.

10th Youth Stamp Exhibitions in Erfurt and Karl-Marx-Stadt — A835

Designs: 10pf+5pf, Erfurt. c. 1520. 20+5pf, Chemnitz, c. 1620. 25pf, Historic and modern buildings of Erfurt. 50pf, Historic and modern buildings of Karl-Marx-Stadt.

1988, June 21 Photo.

2678 A835 10pf +5pf multi .20 .20
2679 A835 20pf +5pf multi .20 .20
2680 A835 25pf multi .20 .20
- ***a.*** Pair, #2678, 2680 + label .40 .40

2681 A835 50pf multi .40 .40
- ***a.*** Pair, #2679, 2681 + label .70 .70

Nos. 2678-2679 surtaxed to benefit the Philatelists' League of the DDR Cultural Union.

22nd Workers' Games, Frankfurt-on-Oder — A836

1988, July 7 Litho. *Perf. 13x12½*

2682 20pf multi .20 .20
2683 50pf multi, diff. .35 .35
- ***a.*** A836 Pair, #2682-2683 + label .65 .65

Workers' Militia, 35th Anniv. — A837

1988, July 5 Photo. *Perf. 14*

2684 A837 5pf Oath .20 .20
2685 A837 10pf Ernst Thalmann tribute .20 .20
2686 A837 15pf Roll call .20 .20
2687 A837 20pf Weapons exchange .20 .20
Nos. 2684-2687 (4) .80 .80

8th Young Pioneers' Congress, Karl-Marx-Stadt — A838

1988, July 19 Litho. *Perf. 13x12½*

2688 A838 10pf shown .20 .20
2689 A838 10pf +5pf Youths playing musical instruments .20 .20
- ***a.*** Pair, #2688-2689 + label .30 .25

Surtax financed the congress.

1988 Summer Olympics, Seoul A839

1988, Aug. 9 Photo. *Perf. 14*

2690 A839 5pf Swimming .20 .20
2691 A839 10pf Handball .20 .20
2692 A839 20pf +10pf Hurdles .25 .25
2693 A839 25pf Rowing .25 .25
2694 A839 35pf Boxing .25 .25
2695 A839 50pf +20pf Cycling .55 .55
Nos. 2690-2695 (6) 1.70 1.70

Souvenir Sheet

Litho.

Perf. 13x12½

2696 A839 85pf Relay race 1.40 2.00

Souvenir Sheet

Leipzig Autumn Fair — A840

1988, Aug. 30 Litho. *Perf. 14*

2697 A840 Sheet of 3 1.10 1.60
- ***a.*** 5pf Fair, c. 1810 .20 .20
- ***b.*** 15pf Battle of Leipzig Memorial .20 .30
- ***c.*** 1m Fair, c. 1820 .65 1.10

DDR-USSR Manned Space Flight Type

1988, Aug. 30 Litho. *Perf. 14*

2698 A834 10pf like No. 2675 .20 .20
- ***a.*** Sheet of 4 .60 .60

2699 A834 20pf like No. 2676 .20 .20
- ***a.*** Sheet of 4 .75 .75

2700 A834 35pf like No. 2677 .35 .35
- ***a.*** Sheet of 4 1.60 1.40

Nos. 2698-2700 (3) .75 .75

Fascism Resistance Memorial, Como, Italy — A841

1988, Sept. 13 Photo.

2701 A841 35pf multi .30 .25

Memorial at Buchenwald, 30th Anniv. — A842

1988, Sept. 13 *Perf. 14*

2702 A842 10pf multi .20 .20

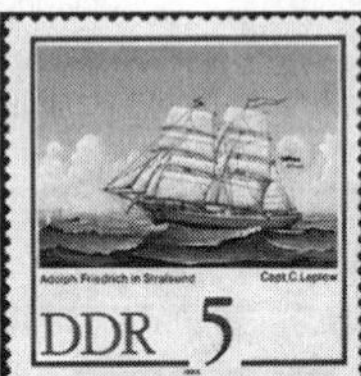

Mariner's Soc., Stralsund, 500th Anniv. — A843

Paintings: 5pf, *Adolph Friedrich* at Stralsund, by C. Leplow. 10pf, *Die Gartenlaube* (built in 1872) at Stralsund, by J.F. Kruger. 70pf, Brigantine *Auguste Mathilde* (built in 1830) at Stralsund, by I.C. Grunwaldt. 1.20m, Brig *Hoffnung* at Cologne, by G.A. Luther.

1988, Sept. 20 Litho. *Perf. 13½x13*

2703 A843 5pf multi .20 .20
2704 A843 10pf multi .20 .20
2705 A843 70pf multi .65 .55
2706 A843 1.20m multi .95 .95
Nos. 2703-2706 (4) 2.00 1.90

Ship Lifts and Bridges A844

1988, Oct. 18 Photo. *Perf. 14x14½*

2707 A844 5pf Magdeburg .20 .20
2708 A844 10pf Magdeburg-Rothensee .20 .20
2709 A844 35pf Niederfinow .25 .20
2710 A844 70pf Altfriesack .50 .50
2711 A844 90pf Rugendamm .65 .65
Nos. 2707-2711 (5) 1.80 1.75

1st Nazi Pogrom (Kristallnacht), Nov. 9, 1938 — A845

1988, Nov. 8 *Perf. 14*

2712 A845 35pf Menorah .35 .20

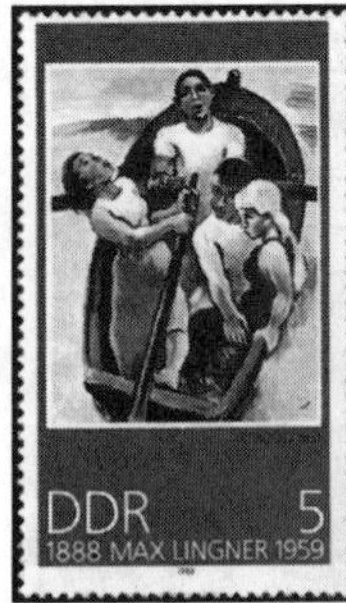

Paintings by Max Lingner (1888-1959) A846

1988, Nov. 8

2713 A846 5pf *In the Boat, 1931* .20 .20
2714 A846 10pf *Yvonne,* 1939 .20 .20
2715 A846 20pf *Free, Strong and Happy,* 1944 .20 .20
2716 A846 85pf *New Harvest,* 1951 .65 .65
Nos. 2713-2716 (4) 1.25 1.25

Souvenir Sheet

Friedrich Wolf (1888-1953), Playwright — A847

1988, Nov. 22 Litho.

2717 A847 1.10m multi .95 1.50

WHO, 40th Anniv. A848

Bone Lace from Erzgebirge A849

1988, Nov. 22 Photo.

2718 A848 85pf multi .75 .35

Miniature Sheet

Various lace designs.

1988, Nov. 22 Litho. *Perf. 12½x13*

2719 Sheet of 6 2.00 2.00
a. A849 20pf multi .20 .20
b. A849 25pf multi .40 .40
c. A849 35pf multi .20 .20
d. A849 40pf multi .20 .20
e. A849 50pf multi .40 .40
f. A849 85pf multi .20 .20

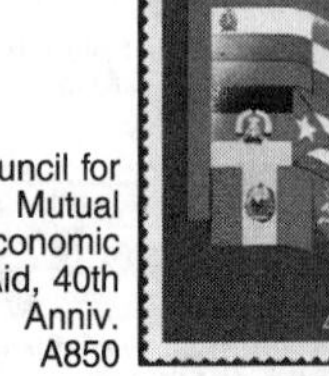

Council for Mutual Economic Aid, 40th Anniv. A850

1989, Jan. 10 Photo. *Perf. 13*

2720 A850 20pf multi .25 .20

Labor Leaders Type of 1987

Portraits: No. 2721, Edith Baumann (1909-1973). No. 2722, Otto Meier (1889-1962). No. 2723, Fritz Selbmann (1899-1975). No. 2724, Alfred Oelssner (1879-1962).

1989, Jan. 24 Engr. *Perf. 14*

2721 A804 10pf dark vio brn .20 .20
2722 A804 10pf dark grn .20 .20
2723 A804 10pf dark blue .20 .20
2724 A804 10pf brn blk .20 .20
Nos. 2721-2724 (4) .80 .80

Telephones A851

Designs: 10pf, Philipp Reis, 1861. 20pf, Siemens & Halske wall model, 1882. 50pf, Wall model OB 03, 1903. 85pf, Table model OB 05, 1905.

1989, Feb. 7 Litho.

2725 A851 10pf shown .20 .20
2726 A851 20pf multi .20 .20
2727 A851 50pf multi .35 .30
2728 A851 85pf multi .65 .55
a. Block of 4, #2725-2728 1.60 1.25

Famous Men A852

1989, Feb. 28 Photo.

2729 A852 10pf Ludwig Renn (1889-1979) .20 .20
2730 A852 10pf Carl von Ossietzky (1889-1938) .20 .20
2731 A852 10pf Adam Scharrer (1889-1948) .20 .20
2732 A852 10pf Rudolf Mauersberger (1889-1971) .20 .20
2733 A852 10pf Johann Beckmann (1739-1811) .20 .20
Nos. 2729-2733 (5) 1.00 1.00

Leipzig Spring Fair — A853

1989, Mar. 7 Litho.

2734 A853 70pf shown .55 .50
2735 A853 85pf Buildings, 1690 .70 .75

Handelshof, 80th anniv. (70pf).

Souvenir Sheet

Thomas Munzer (c. 1468-1525), Religious Reformer — A854

1989, Mar. 21 *Perf. 13x12½*

2736 A854 1.10m multi .95 1.75

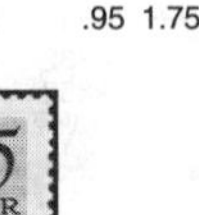

1st Long-distance German Railway, Leipzig-Dresden, Sesquicentennial — A855

15pf, Georg Friedrich List (1789-1846), industrialist, economist. 20pf, Dresden Station in Leipzig, 1839. 50pf, Leipzig Station in Dresden, 1839.

1989, Apr. 4 *Perf. 14*

2737 A855 15pf multi .20 .20
2738 A855 20pf multi .20 .20
2739 A855 50pf multi .40 .40
Nos. 2737-2739 (3) .80 .80

A856 A857

Designs: Meissen Onion-pattern Porcelain, 250th anniv., and sword emblem.

1989, Apr. 18 Litho. *Perf. 12½x13*

2740 A856 10pf Tea caddy .20 .20
2741 A856 20pf Vase .20 .20
2742 A856 35pf Breadboard .30 .30
2743 A856 70pf Teapot .65 .65
Nos. 2740-2743 (4) 1.35 1.35

Size: 33x56mm

Perf. 14

2744 Block of 4 1.60 1.50
a. A856 10pf like No. 2740 .20 .20
b. A856 20pf like No. 2741 .20 .20
c. A856 35pf like No. 2742 .30 .30
d. A856 70pf like No. 2743 .65 .65

1989, May 2 Photo. *Perf. 14½x14*

2745 A857 20pf "I" .20 .20
2746 A857 50pf "B" .35 .30
2747 A857 1.35m "A" 1.10 1.10
Nos. 2745-2747 (3) 1.65 1.60

Intl. Book Fair (IBA), Leipzig.

Student Government — A858

1989, May 9 Litho. *Perf. 13½x12½*

2748 A858 20pf 8th World Youth Festival, Pyongyang .20 .20
2749 A858 20pf +5pf Whitsun meeting of Free German Youth .20 .20
a. Pair, #2748-2749 + label .40 .40

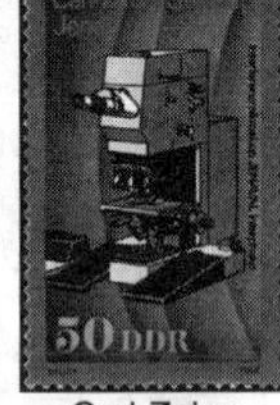

Princess Luise — A859

Carl Zeiss Foundation, Jena, Cent. — A860

Sculptures by Johann Gottfried Schadow (1764-1850), Prussian Court Sculptor.

1989, May 16 Photo. *Perf. 14½x14*

2750 A859 50pf shown .50 .35
2751 A859 85pf Princess Friederike .90 .70

1989, May 16

Modern medical technology: 50pf, Interference microscope Jenaval. 85pf, Bicoordinate measuring instrument ZKM 01-250C.

2752 A860 50pf multi .30 .30
2753 A860 85pf multi .90 .70
a. Pair, #2752-2753 + label 1.40 1.10

Label pictures founder Ernst Abbe (1840-1905).

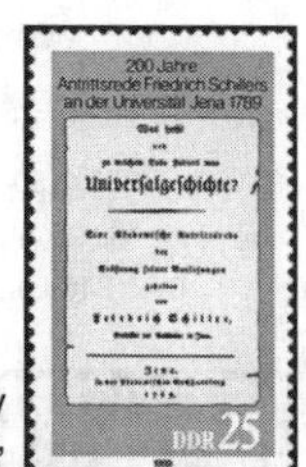

Jena University Inaugural Address, Bicent. — A861

1989, May 23 Photo. Perf. 14

2754 A861 25pf Frontispiece .20 .20
2755 A861 85pf Excerpt .55 .55
a. Pair, #2754-2755 + label .90 .90

Label pictures bust of Friedrich Schiller, author of the address.

Souvenir Sheet

Zoologists — A862

1989, June 13 Litho.

2756 A862 Sheet of 2 1.25 7.50
a. 50pf Alfred Brehm (1829-1884) .35 2.00
b. 85pf Christian Brehm (1787-1864) .70 3.00

French Revolution, Bicent. A863

5pf, Storming of the Bastille, July 14, 1789. 20pf, Revolutionaries, flag bearer. 90pf, Storming Tuileries Palace, Aug. 10, 1792.

1989, July 4 Photo. Perf. 13

2757 A863 5pf multi .20 .20
2758 A863 20pf multi .20 .20
2759 A863 90pf multi .65 .65
Nos. 2757-2759 (3) 1.05 1.05

Intl. Congress of Horse Breeders from Socialist States — A864

1989, July 18 Litho. Perf. 13½

2760 A864 10pf Haflinger .20 .20
2761 A864 20pf English thoroughbred .20 .20
2762 A864 70pf Cold blood .50 .50
2763 A864 110pf Noble warm blood .85 .85
Nos. 2760-2763 (4) 1.75 1.75

Natl. Stamp Exhibition, Magdeburg — A865

1989, Aug. 8 Litho. Perf. 13x12½

2764 A865 20pf Owlglass Fountain .20 .20
2765 A865 70pf +5pf Demons Fountain .65 .65

No. 2765 surtaxed for the philatelic unit of the Kulturbund.

Souvenir Sheet

Leipzig Autumn Fair — A866

1989, Aug. 22 Perf. 14

2766 A866 Sheet of 2 1.25 2.00
a. 50pf Fairground .35 .35
b. 85pf Fairground, diff. .70 .70

Thomas Munzer (1489-1525), Religious Reformer A867

Various details of the painting *Early Bourgeois Revolution in Germany in 1525,* by W. Tubke.

1989, Aug. 22

2767 A867 5pf Globe .20 .20
2768 A867 10pf Fountain .20 .20
2769 A867 20pf Battle scene .20 .20
a. Souvenir sheet of 4 .90 .75
2770 A867 50pf Ark .35 .35
2771 A867 85pf Rainbow, battle .80 .80
Nos. 2767-2771 (5) 1.75 1.75

Muttergruppe, 1965, Bronze Statue in the Natl. Memorial, Ravensbruck A868

1989, Sept. 5 Photo. Perf. 14

2772 A868 35pf multi .30 .25

Natl. Memorial, Ravensbruck, 30th anniv.

Flowering Cacti (*Epiphyllum*) A869

1989, Sept. 19 Litho. Perf. 13

2773 A869 10m Adriana .20 .20
2774 A869 35m Feuerzauber .30 .25
2775 A869 50m Franzisko .50 .45
Nos. 2773-2775 (3) 1.00 .90

DDR, 40th Anniv. — A870

1989, Oct. 3 Perf. 14

2776 A870 5pf Education .20 .20
2777 A870 10pf Agriculture .20 .20
2778 A870 20pf Construction .25 .20
2779 A870 25pf Machinist, computer user .25 .25
Nos. 2776-2779 (4) .90 .85

Souvenir Sheet

2780 A870 135pf Two workers 2.25 2.00

Jawaharlal Nehru, 1st Prime Minister of Independent India — A871

1989, Nov. 7 Photo. Perf. 14

2781 A871 35pf multicolored .30 .25

Statues of Roland Type of 1987

1989, Nov. 7 Perf. 14½x14

2782 A799 5pf Zerbst, 1445 .20 .20
2783 A799 10pf Halberstadt, 1433 .20 .20
2784 A799 20pf Buch-Altmark, 1611 .20 .20
2785 A799 50pf Perleberg, 1546 .35 .35
Nos. 2782-2785 (4) .95 .95

Miniature Sheet

Chandeliers from Erzgebirge — A872

Designs: a, Schneeburg, circa 1860. b, Schwarzenberg, circa 1850. c, Annaberg, circa 1880. d, Seiffen, circa 1900. e, Seiffen, circa 1930. f, Annaberg, circa 1925.

Litho. & Engr.

1989, Nov. 28 Perf. 14

2786 Sheet of 6 2.00 2.00
a. A872 10pf multicolored .20 .20
b. A872 20pf multicolored .40 .40
c. A872 25pf multicolored .20 .20
d. A872 35pf multicolored .20 .20
e. A872 50pf multicolored .40 .40
f. A872 70pf multicolored .20 .20

Bees Collecting Nectar — A873

1990, Jan. 9 Litho.

2787 A873 5pf Apple blossom .20 .20
2788 A873 10pf Blooming heather .20 .20
2789 A873 20pf Rape blossom .20 .20
2790 A873 50pf Red clover .50 .50
Nos. 2787-2790 (4) 1.10 1.10

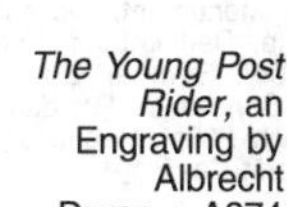

The Young Post Rider, an Engraving by Albrecht Durer — A874

1990, Jan. 12 Litho. Perf. 13

2791 A874 35pf multi .35 .30

Postal communications in Europe, 500th anniv.

See Austria No. 1486, Belgium No. 1332, Germany No. 1592 and Berlin No. 9N584.

Labor Leaders — A875

Portraits: #2792, Bruno Leuschner (1910-65). #2793, Erich Weinert (1890-1953).

1990, Jan. 16 Perf. 14

2792 A875 10pf gray brown .20 .20
2793 A875 10pf deep blue .20 .20

Coats of Arms — A876

Early postal agency insignia: 10pf, Schwarzburg-Rudolstadt and Thurn & Taxis. 20pf, Royal Saxon letter collection. 50pf, Imperial Postal Agency. 1.10pf, Auxiliary post office.

1990, Feb. 6 Photo. Perf. 14

2794 A876 10pf multicolored .20 .20
2795 A876 20pf multicolored .20 .20
2796 A876 50pf multicolored .50 .45
2797 A876 110pf multicolored 1.10 1.00
Nos. 2794-2797 (4) 2.00 1.85

Size: 32x42mm

Perf. 13½

Litho.

2798 Block of 4 3.00 2.00
a. A876 10pf like No. 2794 .20 .20
b. A876 20pf like No. 2795 .20 .20
c. A876 50pf like No. 2796 .50 .45
d. A876 110pf like No. 2797 1.10 1.00

Posts & Telecommunications Workers' Day.

August Bebel (1840-1913), Co-founder of the Social Democratic Party — A877

1990, Feb. 20 Photo.

2799 A877 20pf multicolored .30 .25

Flying Machine Designed by Leonardo da Vinci — A878

1990, Feb. 20 Litho. Perf. 13½x13

2800 A878 20pf shown .20 .20
2801 A878 35pf +5pf Melchior Bauer .35 .35
2802 A878 50pf Albrecht Berblinger .50 .40
2803 A878 90pf Otto Lilienthal .90 .80
Nos. 2800-2803 (4) 1.95 1.75

LILIENTHAL '91 airmail exhibition. No. 2801 surtaxed for philatelic promotion.

Leipzig Spring Fair Seals — A879

Dying Warriors — A880

1990, Mar. 6 ***Perf. 12½x13***

2804 A879 70pf Seal, 1268 .85 .45
2805 A879 85pf Seal, 1497 1.00 .70

City of Leipzig and the Leipzig Spring Fair, 825th annivs.

1990, Mar. 6 Photo. ***Perf. 13½x14***

Sculptures by Andreas Schluter.

2806 A880 40pf shown .40 .30
2807 A880 70pf multi, diff. .75 .70

Museum of German History in the Zeughaus of Berlin.

Famous Men A881

Portraits: No. 2808, Friedrich Diesterweg (1790-1866), educator. No. 2809, Kurt Tucholsky (1890-1935), novelist, journalist.

1990, Mar. 20 Photo. ***Perf. 14***

2808 A881 10pf multicolored .25 .25
2809 A881 10pf multicolored .25 .25

Labor Day, Cent. — A882

1990, Apr. 3

2810 A882 10pf shown .25 .20
2811 A882 20pf Flower, "1890/1990" .55 .30

Dicraeosaurus — A883

Perf. 13x12½, 12½x13

1990, Apr. 17 Litho.

2812 A883 10pf shown .20 .20
2813 A883 25pf Kentrurosaurus .20 .20
a. Miniature sheet of 4 1.10 1.00
2814 A883 35pf Dysalotosaurus .25 .25
2815 A883 50pf Brachiosaurus .35 .35
2816 A883 85pf Brachiosaurus skull .85 .85
Nos. 2812-2816 (5) 1.85 1.85

Natural History Museum of Berlin, cent. Nos. 2815-2816 vert.

Penny Black, 150th Anniv. — A884

1990, May 8 ***Perf. 14***

2817 A884 20pf shown .30 .25
2818 A884 35pf +15pf Saxony #1 .55 .50
2819 A884 110pf No. 48 1.50 1.25
Nos. 2817-2819 (3) 2.35 2.00

A885

Intl. Telecommunications Union, 125th Anniv.: 10pf, David Edward Hughes (1831-1900), type-printing telegraph, 1855. 20pf, Distribution linkage, Berlin-Kopenick post office. 25pf, TV and microwave tower. 50pf, Molniya news satellite, globe. 70pf, Philipp Reis (1834-1874), physicist, designed sound transmission equipment.

1990, May 15

2820 A885 10pf multicolored .20 .20
2821 A885 20pf multicolored .25 .25
2822 A885 25pf multicolored .25 .25
2823 A885 50pf multicolored .65 .55
Nos. 2820-2823 (4) 1.35 1.25

Souvenir Sheet

2824 A885 70pf multicolored 1.75 2.00

Pope John Paul II, 70th Birthday — A886

1990, May 15

2825 A886 35pf multicolored .40 .30

11th Youth Stamp Exhibition, Halle A887

1990, June 5 ***Perf. 13x12½***

2826 A887 10pf +5pf 18th cent. Halle .20 .20
2827 A887 20pf 20th cent. Halle .25 .20
a. Pair, #2826-2827 + label .45 .40

Treasures in the German State Library, Berlin A888

Designs: 20pf, Rules of an order, 1264. 25pf, Rudimentum novitiorum, 1475. 50pf, Chosrou wa Schirin, 18th cent. 110pf, Book-cover of Amalienbibliothek, 18th cent.

1990, June 19

2828 A888 20pf multicolored .30 .20
2829 A888 25pf multicolored .30 .20
2830 A888 50pf multicolored .75 .50
2831 A888 110pf multicolored 1.60 1.25
Nos. 2828-2831 (4) 2.95 2.15

Castle Albrechtsburg and Cathedral, Meissen — A889

30pf, Goethe-Schiller Monument, Weimar. 50pf, Brandenburg Gate, Berlin. 60pf, Kyffhauser Monument. 70pf, Semper Opera, Dresden. 80pf, Castle Sanssouci, Potsdam. 100pf, Wartburg, Eisenach. 200pf, Magdeburg Cathedral. 500pf, Schwerin Castle.

1990, July 2 Photo. ***Perf. 14***

2832 A889 10pf ultramarine .20 .20
2833 A889 30pf olive green .25 .20
2834 A889 50pf bluish green .35 .30
2835 A889 60pf violet brown .45 .30
2836 A889 70pf dark brown .50 .40
2837 A889 80pf red brown .65 .50
2838 A889 100pf dark carmine .95 .55
2839 A889 200pf dark violet 1.25 1.10
2840 A889 500pf green 3.50 2.75
Nos. 2832-2840 (9) 8.10 6.30

Nos. 2832-2852 have face values based on the Federal Republic's Deutsche mark and were valid for postage in both countries.

Postal System, 500th Anniv. A890

30pf, 15th cent. postman. 50pf, 16th cent. postrider. 70pf, Post carriages c. 1595, 1750. 100pf, Railway mail carriages 1842, 1900.

1990, Aug. 28 Litho. ***Perf. 13x13½***

2841 A890 30pf multicolored .30 .30
2842 A890 50pf multicolored .40 .35
2843 A890 70pf multicolored .55 .50
2844 A890 100pf multicolored 1.00 .85
Nos. 2841-2844 (4) 2.25 2.00

Louis Lewandowski (1821-94), Composer — A891

50pf+15pf, New Synagogue, Berlin.

1990, Sept. 18 ***Perf. 14***

2845 A891 30pf multicolored .25 .25
2846 A891 50pf +15pf multi .50 .45

Heinrich Schliemann (1822-1890), Archaeologist A892

1990, Oct. 2 Photo.

Design: 30pf, shown. 50pf, Schliemann, double pot c. 2600-1900 B.C., horiz.

2847 A892 30pf multicolored .25 .25
2848 A892 50pf multicolored .50 .40

Intl. Astronautics Federation, 41st Congress, Dresden A893

1990, Oct. 2

2849 A893 30pf Dresden skyline .20 .20
2850 A893 50pf Globe .35 .30
2851 A893 70pf Moon .65 .50
2852 A893 100pf Mars .85 .75
Nos. 2849-2852 (4) 2.05 1.75

Stamps of the German Democratic Republic were replaced starting Oct. 3, 1990 by those of the Federal Republic of Germany. #2832-2852 remained valid until Dec. 31, 1991.

FOR USE IN ALL PROVINCES IN THE RUSSIAN ZONE

SEMI-POSTALS

Leipzig Fair Issue

Type of German Semi-Postal Stamps

16pf+9pf, 1st New Year's Fair, 1459. 50pf+25pf, Arrival of clothmakers from abroad, 1469.

Wmk. 292

1948, Aug. 29 Litho. ***Perf. 13½***

10NB1 SP252 16 + 9pf dk vio brn .20 .40
10NB2 SP252 50 + 25pf dl vio bl .20 .40
Set, never hinged .50

The 1948 Leipzig Autumn Fair.

Emblem of Philatelic Institute — OSP1

Goethe — OSP2

1948, Oct. 23 ***Perf. 13x13½***

10NB3 OSP1 12 + 3pf red .20 .40
Never hinged .30

Stamp Day, Oct. 26, 1948.

Type of German Semi-Postal Stamps of 1947

30pf+15pf, First fair in newly built Town Hall, 1556. 50pf+25pf, Italians at the Fair, 1536.

1949, Mar. 6 Litho. ***Perf. 13½***

10NB4 SP252 30 + 15pf red 1.00 3.25
10NB5 SP252 50 + 25pf blue 1.25 3.75
Set, never hinged 5.25

1949 Leipzig Spring Fair.

1949, July 20 Wmk. 292 ***Perf. 13***

Designs: Different Goethe portraits.

10NB6 OSP2 6 + 4pf dl vio .80 2.00
10NB7 OSP2 12 + 8pf dl brn .80 2.00
10NB8 OSP2 24 + 16pf red brn .65 1.75
10NB9 OSP2 50 + 25pf dk bl .65 1.75
10NB10 OSP2 84 + 36pf ol gray 1.00 3.50
Nos. 10NB6-10NB10 (5) 1.00 1.05
Set, never hinged 9.25

Johann Wolfgang von Goethe, birth bicent.

Souvenir Sheet

Profile of Goethe — OSP3

1949, Aug. 22 Engr. ***Perf. 14***

10NB11 OSP3 50pf + 4.50m blue 97.50 250.00
Never hinged 175.00

The sheet measures 106x105mm. The surtax was for the reconstruction of Weimar.

Type of German Semi-Postal Stamps

12pf+8pf, Russian merchants at the Fair, 1650. 24pf+16pf, Young Goethe at the Fair, 1765.

1949, Aug. 30 Litho. ***Perf. 13½***

10NB12 SP252 12 + 8pf gray 1.25 5.25
10NB13 SP252 24 + 16pf lake brn 1.60 6.25
Set, never hinged 6.50

1949 Leipzig Autumn Fair.

GERMAN DEMOCRATIC REPUBLIC SEMI-POSTAL STAMPS

Catalogue values for unused stamps in this section, from this point to the end of the section, are for Never Hinged items.

Canceled to Order
Used values are for CTO's from No. B14 to No. B203.

Some se-tenants include a semi-postal stamp. To avoid splitting the se-tenant piece the semi-postal is listed with the regular issue.

Bavaria No. 1 and Magnifier — SP4

Wmk. 292

1949, Oct. 30 Litho. *Perf. 14*
B14 SP4 12pf + 3pf gray blk 5.75 3.75

Stamp Day, 1949. See No. B21a.

Leipzig Fair Issue.
German Type of 1947
Inscribed: "Deutsche Demokratische Republik"

Leipzig Spring Fair: 24pf+12pf, First porcelain at Fair, 1710. 30pf+14pf, First Fair at Municipal Store, 1894.

1950, Mar. 5 *Perf. 13*
B15 SP252 24 + 12pf red vio 7.00 7.00
B16 SP252 30 + 14pf rose car 8.00 8.00

Shepherd Boy with Double Flute — SP5

"Bach Year": 24pf+6pf, Girl with hand organ. 30pf+8pf, Johann Sebastian Bach. 50pf+16pf, Chorus.

1950, June 14 *Perf. 14*
B17 SP5 12pf + 4pf bl grn 4.50 3.75
B18 SP5 24pf + 6pf olive 4.50 3.75
B19 SP5 30pf + 8pf dk red 8.75 8.50
B20 SP5 50pf + 16pf blue 14.00 12.50
Nos. B17-B20 (4) 31.75 28.50

Saxony No. 1, Globe and Dove — SP6

1950, July 1 Photo. Wmk. 292
B21 SP6 84 + 41pf brn red 40.00 11.00
a. Souv. sheet of 2, #B14, B21, imperf. *125.00 125.00*
No. B21a hinged 45.00

German Stamp Exhib. (DEBRIA) held at Leipzig for the cent. of Saxony's 1st postage stamp.

Clearing Land — SP7

Reconstruction program: 24pf+6pf, Bricklaying. 30pf+10pf, Carpentry. 50pf+10pf, Inspecting plans.

1952, May 1 Litho.
B22 SP7 12pf + 3pf brt vio 1.10 .30
B23 SP7 24pf + 6pf henna brn 1.00 .50
B24 SP7 30pf + 10pf dp grn 1.25 .50
B25 SP7 50pf + 10pf vio bl 1.75 1.00
Nos. B22-B25 (4) 5.10 2.30

Dam — SP8

1954, Aug. 16 Unwmk.
B26 SP8 24pf + 6pf green .45 .50

The surtax was for flood victims.

Surcharged with New Value and "X"

1955, Feb. 25
B27 SP8 20 +5pf on 24+6pf .55 .35

The surtax was for flood victims.

Buchenwald Memorial — SP9

Perf. 13½x13

1956, Sept. 8 Wmk. 297
B28 SP9 20pf + 80pf rose red *.90 2.00*

The surtax was for the erection of national memorials at the concentration camps of Buchenwald, Ravensbruck and Sachsenhausen. See No. B43.

Type of 1955 Surcharged "HELFT AGYPTEN +10" (#B29) or "HELFT DEM SOZIALISTISCHEN UNGARN +10" (#B30)

Perf. 13½x13

1956, Dec. 20 Wmk. 313
B29 A75 20pf + 10pf carmine .35 .25
B30 A75 20pf + 10pf carmine .35 .25

Monument to Ravensbrück SP10

Memorial Park and Lake — SP11

Perf. 13x13½, 13½x13

1957, Apr. 25 Litho.
B31 SP10 5pf + 5pf grn *.20 .20*
B32 SP11 20pf + 10pf rose red *.25 .25*

Intl. Day of Liberation. See Nos. B54, B70.

Ernst Thälmann SP12

Bugler, Flag and Camp SP13

Portraits: 25pf+15pf, Rudolf Breitscheid. 40pf+20pf, Rev. Paul Schneider.

1957, Dec. 3 Photo. *Perf. 13*
Portraits in Gray
B33 SP12 20pf + 10pf dp plum .20 .20
B34 SP12 25pf + 15pf dk blue .20 .20
B35 SP12 40pf + 20pf violet .25 .30
a. Souv. sheet of 3, #B33-B35, imperf. 35.00 55.00
Nos. B33-B35 (3) .65 .70

No. B35a issued Sept. 15, 1958.

1958, July 11 Wmk. 313 *Perf. 13*

Portraits: 5pf+5pf, Albert Kuntz. 10pf+5pf, Rudi Arndt. 15pf+10pf, Kurt Adams. 20pf+10pf, Rudolf Renner. 25pf+15pf, Walter Stoecker.

Portraits in Gray
B36 SP12 5pf + 5pf brn blk .20 .50
B37 SP12 10pf + 5pf dk sl grn .20 .50
B38 SP12 15pf + 10pf dp vio .20 2.00
B39 SP12 20pf + 10pf dk red brn .20 .50
B40 SP12 25pf + 15pf bl blk *.40 7.50*
Nos. B36-B40 (5) *1.20 11.00*

Issued to honor the murdered victims of the Nazis at Buchenwald. The surtax was for the erection of national memorials.
See Nos. B49-B53, B55-B57, B60-B64, B71-B75, B79-B81.

1958, Aug. 7 Litho. *Perf. 12½*

Design: 20pf+10pf, Pioneers and flag.

B41 SP13 10pf + 5pf green .20 .20
B42 SP13 20pf + 10pf red .25 .20

Pioneer organization, 10th anniversary.

Type of 1956 Overprinted in Black "14. September 1958"

Perf. 13½x13

1958, Sept. 15 Unwmk.
B43 SP9 20pf + 20pf rose red *.40 .35*

Dedication of the memorial at Buchenwald concentration camp, Sept. 14, 1958.

Exercises with Hoops — SP14

Designs: 10pf+5pf, High jump. 20pf+10pf Vaulting. 25pf+10pf, Girl gymnasts. 40pf+20pf, Leipzig stadium and fireworks.

Perf. 13x13½

1959, Aug. 10 Litho. Wmk. 313
B44 SP14 5pf + 5pf org .20 .20
B45 SP14 10pf + 5pf grn .20 .20
B46 SP14 20pf + 10pf brt car .20 .20
B47 SP14 25pf + 10pf brt bl .20 .20
B48 SP14 40pf + 20pf red vio *1.40 .55*
Nos. B44-B48 (5) *2.20 1.35*

3rd German Sports Festival, Leipzig.

Portrait Type of 1957-58

Portraits: 5pf+5pf, Tilde Klose. 10pf+5pf, Kathe Niederkirchner. 15pf+10pf, Charlotte Eisenblatter. 20pf+10pf, Olga Benario-Prestes. 25pf+15pf, Maria Grollmuss.

1959, Sept. 3 Photo. *Perf. 13*
Portraits in Gray
B49 SP12 5pf + 5pf sep .20 .20
B50 SP12 10pf + 5pf dp grn .20 .20
B51 SP12 15pf + 10pf dp vio .20 .20
B52 SP12 20pf + 10pf mag .20 .20
B53 SP12 25pf + 15pf dk bl *.30 .60*
Nos. B49-B53 (5) *1.10 1.40*

Issued to honor women murdered by the Nazis at Buchenwald.

Ravensbrück Type of 1957 Dated: "12. September 1959"

Perf. 13½x13

1959, Sept. 11 Litho. Wmk. 313
B54 SP11 20pf + 10pf dp car & blk .40 .25

Portrait Type of 1957-58

5pf+5pf, Lothar Erdmann. 10pf+5pf, Ernst Schneller. 20pf+10pf, Lambert Horn.

1960, Feb. 25 Photo. *Perf. 13½x13*
Portraits in Gray
B55 SP12 5pf + 5pf ol bis .20 .20
B56 SP12 10pf + 5pf dk grn .20 .20
B57 SP12 20pf + 10pf dl mag .20 .20
Nos. B55-B57 (3) .60 .60

Issued to honor murdered victims of the Nazis at Sachsenhausen.

Type of Regular Issue, 1960

Designs: 10pf+5pf, Vacation ship under construction, Wismar. 20pf+10pf, Ship before Stubbenkammer and sailboat.

Wmk. 313

1960, June 23 Litho. *Perf. 13*
B58 A162 10pf + 5pf blk, yel & red .20 .20
B59 A162 20pf + 10pf blk, red & bl .20 .20

Portrait Type of 1957-58

Portraits: 10pf+5pf, Max Lademann. 15pf+5pf, Lorenz Breunig. 20pf+10pf, Mathias Thesen. 25pf+10pf, Gustl Sandtner. 40pf+20pf, Hans Rothbarth.

1960 Wmk. 313 *Perf. 13½x13*
Portraits in Gray
B60 SP12 10pf + 5pf grn .20 .20
B61 SP12 15pf + 5pf dp vio *.65 .45*
B62 SP12 20pf + 10pf maroon .20 .20
B63 SP12 25pf + 10pf dk bl .20 .20
B64 SP12 40pf + 20pf lt red brn *1.60 1.00*
Nos. B60-B64 (5) *2.85 2.05*

Issued to honor the murdered victims of the Nazis at Sachsenhausen.

Bicyclist — SP15

25pf+10pf, Bicyclists and spectators.

1960, Aug. 3 *Perf. 13x13½, 13x12½*
Size: 28x23mm
B65 SP15 20pf + 10pf multi .20 .20
Size: 38½x21mm
B66 SP15 25pf + 10pf bl, gray & brn *1.10 1.60*

Bicycling World Championships, Aug. 3-14.

Rook and Congress Emblem SP16

20pf+10pf, Knight. 25pf+10pf, Bishop.

Perf. 14x13½

1960, Sept. 19 Engr. Wmk. 313
B67 SP16 10pf + 5pf blue green .20 .20
B68 SP16 20pf + 10pf rose claret .20 .20
B69 SP16 25pf + 10pf blue *.75 1.60*
Nos. B67-B69 (3) *1.15 2.00*

14th Chess Championships, Leipzig.

Type of 1957

Design: Monument and memorial wall of Sachsenhausen National Memorial.

1960, Sept. 8 Litho. *Perf. 13x13½*
B70 SP10 20pf + 10pf dp car .30 .20

No. B70 was re-issued Apr. 20, 1961, with gray label adjoining each stamp in sheet, to commemorate the dedication of Sachsenhausen National Memorial.

Type of 1957

Portraits: 5pf+5pf, Werner Kube. 10pf+5pf, Hanno Gunther. 15pf+5pf, Elvira Eisenschneider. 20pf+10pf, Hertha Lindner. 25pf+10pf, Herbert Tschäpe.

1961, Feb. 6 *Perf. 13½x13*
Portraits in Black
B71 SP12 5pf + 5pf brt brn .20 .20
B72 SP12 10pf + 5pf bl grn .20 .20
B73 SP12 15pf + 5pf brt lilac *.90 1.40*

B74 SP12 20pf + 10pf dp rose .20 .20
B75 SP12 25pf + 10pf brt bl .20 .20
Nos. B71-B75 (5) *1.70 2.20*

Surtax for the erection of natl. memorials.

Pioneers Playing Volleyball SP17

Designs: 20pf+10pf, Folk dancing. 25pf+10pf, Building model airplanes.

1961, May 25 ***Perf. 13x12½***

B76 SP17 10pf + 5pf multi .20 .20
B77 SP17 20pf + 10pf multi .20 .20
B78 SP17 25pf + 10pf multi *2.10 1.60*
Nos. B76-B78 (3) *2.50 2.00*

Young Pioneers' meeting, Erfurt.

Type of 1957 and

Sophie and Hans Scholl SP18

Portraits: 5pf+5pf, Carlo Schönhaar. 10pf+5pf, Herbert Baum. 20pf+10pf, Liselotte Herrmann. 40pf+20pf, Hilde and Hans Coppi.

Perf. 13½x13, 13x13½

1961, Sept. 7 Litho. Wmk. 313

Portraits in Black

B79 SP12 5pf + 5pf green .20 .20
B80 SP12 10pf + 5pf bl grn .20 .20
B81 SP12 20pf + 10pf rose car .20 .20
B82 SP18 25pf + 10pf blue .20 .20
B83 SP18 40pf + 20pf rose brn *1.60 3.25*
Nos. B79-B83 (5) *2.40 4.05*

Surtax was the support of natl. memorials at Buchenwald, Ravensbrück & Sachsenhausen.

Danielle Casanova of France — SP19

Portraits: 10pf+5pf, Julius Fucik, Czechoslovakia. 20pf+10pf, Johanna Jannetje Schaft, Netherlands. 25pf+10pf, Pawel Finder, Poland. 40pf+20pf, Soya Anatolyevna Kosmodemyanskaya, Russia.

1962, Mar. 22 Engr. *Perf. 13½*

B84 SP19 5pf + 5pf gray .20 .20
B85 SP19 10pf + 5pf green .20 .20
B86 SP19 20pf + 10pf maroon .20 .20
B87 SP19 25pf + 10pf deep blue .25 .20
B88 SP19 40pf + 20pf sepia *1.25 1.50*
Nos. B84-B88 (5) *2.10 2.30*

Issued in memory of foreign victims of the Nazis.

Type of Regular Issue, 1962

Design: 20pf+10pf, Three cyclists and Warsaw Palace of Culture and Science.

Perf. 13x12½

1962, Apr. 26 Litho. Wmk. 313

B89 A192 20pf + 10pf ver, bl, blk & yel .20 .20

Folk Dance — SP20

15pf+5pf, Youths of three nations parading.

1962, July 17 Wmk. 313 *Perf. 14*

B90 SP20 10pf + 5pf multi .25 .20
B91 SP20 15pf + 5pf multi .25 .20
a. Pair, #B90-B91 .90 .70

Issued to publicize the 8th Youth Festival for Peace and Friendship, Helsinki, July 28-Aug. 6, 1962.
No. B91a forms the festival emblem.

Type of Regular Issue, 1962

Design: 20pf+10pf, Springboard diving.

1962, Aug. 7 Wmk. 313 *Perf. 13*

B92 A199 20pf + 10pf lil rose & grnsh bl .20 .20

René Blieck of Belgium — SP21

Seven Cervi Brothers of Italy SP22

Portraits: 10pf+5pf, Dr. Alfred Klahr, Austria. 15pf+5pf, José Diaz, Spain. 20pf+10pf, Julius Alpari, Hungary.

1962, Oct. 4 Engr. *Perf. 14*

B93 SP21 5pf + 5pf dk bl gray .20 .20
B94 SP21 10pf + 5pf green .20 .20
B95 SP21 15pf + 5pf brt vio .20 .20
B96 SP21 20pf + 10pf dl red brn .20 .20
B97 SP22 70pf + 30pf sepia *1.40 1.75*
Nos. B93-B97 (5) *2.20 2.55*

Issued to commemorate foreign victims of the Nazis.

Walter Bohne, Runner SP23

Gymnasts SP24

Portraits: 10pf+5pf, Werner Seelenbinder, wrestler. 15pf+5pf, Albert Richter, bicyclist. 20pf+10pf, Heinz Steyer, soccer player. 25pf+10pf, Kurt Schlosser, mountaineer.

Engr. & Photo.

1963, May 27 Wmk. 313 *Perf. 14*

B98 SP23 5pf + 5pf yel & blk .20 .20
B99 SP23 10pf + 5pf pale yel grn & blk .20 .20
B100 SP23 15pf + 5pf rose lil & blk .20 .20
B101 SP23 20pf + 10pf pink & blk .20 .20
B102 SP23 25pf + 10pf pale bl & blk *1.50 3.00*
Nos. B98-B102 (5) *2.30 3.80*

Issued to commemorate sportsmen victims of the Nazis. Each stamp printed with alternating label showing sporting events connected with each person honored. The surtax went for the maintenance of national memorials. See Nos. B106-B110.

1963, June 13 Litho. *Perf. 12½x13*

Designs: 20pf+10pf, Women gymnasts. 25pf+10pf, Relay race.

B103 SP24 10pf + 5pf blk, yel grn & lem .20 .20
B104 SP24 20pf + 10pf blk, red & vio .20 .20
B105 SP24 25pf + 10pf blk, bl, & gray *2.10 1.90*
Nos. B103-B105 (3) *2.50 2.30*

4th German Gymnastic and Sports Festival, Leipzig. The surtax went to the festival committee.

Type of 1963

Portraits: 5pf+5pf, Hermann Tops, gymnastics instructor. 10pf+5pf, Käte Tucholla, field hockey players. 15pf+5pf, Rudolph Seiffert, long-distance swimmers. 20pf+10pf, Ernst Grube, sportsmen demonstrating for peace. 40pf+20pf, Kurt Biedermann, kayak in rapids.

Engraved and Photogravure

1963, Sept. 24 Wmk. 313 *Perf. 14*

B106 SP23 5pf + 5pf yel & blk .20 .20
B107 SP23 10pf + 5pf grn & blk .20 .20
B108 SP23 15pf + 5pf lil & blk .20 .20
B109 SP23 20pf + 10pf pale pink & blk .20 .20
B110 SP23 40pf + 20pf lt bl & blk *1.75 1.75*
Nos. B106-B110 (5) *2.55 2.55*

See note after No. B102.

Type of Regular Issue, 1963

Design: 20pf+10pf, Ski jumper in mid-air.

Perf. 13½x13

1963, Dec. 16 Litho. Wmk. 313

B111 A224 20pf + 10pf multi .20 .20

Surtax for the Natl. Olympic Committee.

Anton Saefkow SP25

Designs: 10pf+5pf, Franz Jacob. 15pf+5pf, Bernhard Bästlein. 20pf+5pf, Harro Schulze-Boysen. 25pf+10pf, Adam Kuckhoff. 40pf+10pf, Mildred and Arvid Harnack. Nos. B112-B114 show group posting anti-Hitler and pacifist posters. Nos. B115-B117 show production of anti-fascist pamphlets.

1964, Mar. 24 Wmk. 313 *Perf. 13*

Size: 41x32mm

B112 SP25 5pf + 5pf .20 .20
B113 SP25 10pf + 5pf .20 .20
B114 SP25 15pf + 5pf .20 .20
B115 SP25 20pf + 5pf .20 .20
B116 SP25 25pf + 10pf .25 .20

Size: 48½x28mm

B117 SP25 40pf + 10pf *.95 1.00*
Nos. B112-B117 (6) *2.00 2.00*

The surtax was for the support of national memorials for victims of the Nazis.

Olympic Types of Regular Issues

Designs: 40pf+20pf, Two runners. #B119, Equestrian. #B120, Three runners.

Lithographed and Engraved

1964, July 15 Wmk. 313 *Perf. 14*

B118 A232 40pf + 20pf multi .25 .20

Litho.

Perf. 13

B119 A233 10pf + 5pf multi 2.00 1.75
B120 A233 10pf + 5pf multi 2.00 1.75
Nos. B118-B120 (3) 4.25 3.70

See note after No. 714.

Pioneers Studying — SP26

Designs: 20pf+10pf, Pioneers planting tree. 25pf+10pf, Pioneers playing.

1964, July 29

B121 SP26 10pf + 5pf multi .50 .20
B122 SP26 20pf + 10pf multi .50 .20
B123 SP26 25pf + 10pf multi *2.00 1.40*
Nos. B121-B123 (3) *3.00 1.80*

Fifth Young Pioneers Meeting, Karl-Marx-Stadt.

Stamp Exhibition Type of 1964

Designs: 10pf+5pf, Stamp of 1958 (No. 390). 20pf+10pf, Stamp of 1950 (No. 73).

Perf. 13x13½

1964, Sept. 23 Litho. Wmk. 313

B124 A238 10pf + 5pf org & emer .20 .20
B125 A238 20pf + 10pf brt pink & bl .25 .20

Boxing Type of Regular Issue

10pf+5pf, Two boxing gloves and laurel.

Perf. 13½x14

1965, Apr. 27 Photo. Wmk. 313

B126 A247 10pf + 5pf blk, gold, red & blue .20 .20

The surtax went to the German Turner and Sport Organization.

Type of Regular Issue, 1965

5pf+5pf, George Dimitrov at Leipzig trial & communist newspaper. 10pf+5pf, Anti-fascists clandestinely distributing leaflets. 15pf+5pf, Fighting in Spanish Civil War. 20pf+10pf, Ernst Thalman behind bars & demonstration for his release. 25pf+10pf, Founding of Natl. Committee for Free Germany & signatures.

Wmk. 313

1965, May 5 Photo. *Perf. 14*

Flags in Red, Black and Yellow

B127 A248 5pf + 5pf blk, org & red .20 .20
B128 A248 10pf + 5pf grn & red .20 .20
B129 A248 15pf + 5pf lil, red & yel .20 .20
B130 A248 20pf + 10pf blk & red .20 .20
B131 A248 25pf + 10pf ol grn, yel & blk .20 .20
Nos. B127-B131 (5) 1.00 1.00

The surtax went for the maintenance of national memorials.

Doves, Globe and Finnish Flag — SP27

1965, July 5 Litho. *Perf. 13x13½*

B132 SP27 10pf + 5pf vio bl & emer .20 .20
B133 SP27 20pf + 5pf red & vio bl *.40 .25*

World Peace Congress, Helsinki, July 10-17. The surtax went to the peace council of the DDR.

No. 725 Surcharged

Perf. 13½x13

1965, Aug. 23 Wmk. 313

B134 A239 10pf + 10pf multi .30 .20

Surtax was for North Viet Nam.

Sports Type of Regular Issue

Perf. 13½x13

1965, Sept. 15 Litho. Unwmk.

B135 A257 10pf + 5pf Fencer .20 .20
B136 A257 10pf + 5pf Pistol shooter .20 .20

International Modern Pentathlon Championships, Leipzig.

Type of Regular Issue

Designs: 10pf+5pf, Willi Bredel and instruction of International Brigade. 20pf+10pf, Heinrich Rau and parade after battle of Brunete. 25pf+10pf, Hans Marchwitza, international fighters and globe. 40pf+10pf, Artur Becker and battle on the Ebro.

1966, July 15 Photo. *Perf. 14*

B137 A277 10pf + 5pf multi .20 .20
B138 A277 20pf + 10pf multi .20 .20
B139 A277 25pf + 10pf multi .20 .20
B140 A277 40pf + 10pf multi *1.10 .75*
Nos. B137-B140 (4) *1.70 1.35*

The surtax was for the maintenance of national memorials.

Canoe Type of Regular Issue

Design: 10pf+5pf, Men's single canoe race.

Perf. 13x12½

1966, Aug. 16 Litho. Unwmk.
B141 A279 10pf + 5pf multi .20 .20

Red Cross Type of Regular Issue

Design: ICY Red Crescent, Red Cross, and Red Lion and Sun emblems, horiz.

1966, Sept. 13 Wmk. 313 *Perf. 14*
B142 A281 20pf + 10pf vio & red .25 .20

International health cooperation. Surtax for German Red Cross.

Sports Type of Regular Issue

Design: 20pf+5pf, Weight lifter.

Perf. 13½x13

1966, Sept. 22 Litho. Unwmk.
B143 A282 20pf + 5pf ultra & blk .30 .20

Armed Woman Planting Flower — SP28

1966, Oct. 25 *Perf. 13½x13*
B144 SP28 20pf + 5pf blk & pink .30 .20

Surtax was for North Viet Nam.

Wartburg Type of Regular Issue

Design: Wartburg, view from the East.

1966, Nov. 23 *Perf. 13x13½*
B145 A288 10pf + 5pf slate .20 .20

See note after No. 878.

Olympic Type of Regular Issue

Design: 10pf+5pf, Tobogganing.

1968, Jan. 17 Litho. *Perf. 13½x13*
B146 A314 10pf + 5pf grnsh bl, vio bl & red .20 .20

The surtax was for the Olympic Committee of the German Democratic Republic.

Armed Mother and Child — SP29

Armed Vietnamese Couple — SP30

1968, May 8 *Perf. 13½x13*
B147 SP29 10pf + 5pf yel & multi .20 .20

Surtax was for North Viet Nam.

Festival Type of Regular Issue

1968, June 20 Litho. *Perf. 13½x13*
B148 A327 20pf + 5pf multi .25 .20

Olympic Games Type of Regular Issue, 1968

Designs: 10pf+5pf, Pole vault, vert. 20pf+10pf, Soccer, vert.

1968, Sept. 18 Photo. *Perf. 14*
B149 A336 10pf + 5pf multi .20 .20
B150 A336 20pf + 10pf multi .20 .20

The surtax was for the Olympic Committee.

1969, June 4
B151 SP30 10pf + 5pf multi .25 .20

Surtax was for North Viet Nam.

Sports Type of Regular Issue, 1969

Designs: 10pf+5pf, Gymnastics. 20pf+5pf, Art Exhibition with sports motifs.

Photo. & Engr.

1969, June 18 *Perf. 14*
B152 A353 10pf + 5pf multi .20 .20
B153 A353 20pf + 5pf multi .20 .20

The surtax was for the German Gymnastic and Sports League.

Otto von Guericke's Vacuum Test with Magdeburg Hemispheres — SP31

1969, Oct. 28 Litho. *Perf. 13x12½*
B154 SP31 40pf + 10pf multi *.75 .35*

See note after No. 1146.

Folk Art Type of Regular Issue

Design: 20pf+5pf, Decorative plate.

1969, Nov. 25 Litho. *Perf. 13½x13*
B155 A365 20pf + 5pf yel blk & ultra .25 .25

Sports Type of Regular Issue

Design: 20pf+5pf, Children hurdling.

1970, July 1 Photo. *Perf. 14x13½*
B156 A382 20pf + 5pf multi .30 .20

Pioneer Waving Kerchief, and Pioneer Activities — SP32

Design: 25pf+5pf, Girl Pioneer holding kerchief, and Pioneer activities.

1970, July 28 Litho. *Perf. 13x12½*
B157 SP32 10pf + 5pf multi .20 .20
B158 SP32 25pf + 5pf multi .20 .20
a. Pair, #B157-B158 .75 *1.50*

6th Youth Pioneer Meeting, Cottbus. No. B158a has continuous design.

Ho Chi Minh — SP33

1970, Sept. 2 *Perf. 13x13½*
B159 SP33 20pf + 5pf rose, blk & red .50 .20

Surtax was for North Viet Nam.

German Democratic Republic No. 460 — SP34

1970, Oct. 1 Photo. *Perf. 14x13½*
B160 SP34 15pf + 5pf multi .20 *.25*

2nd National Youth Philatelic Exhibition, Karl-Marx-Stadt, Oct. 4-11.

Mother and Child — SP35

Vietnamese Farm Woman — SP36

Photo. & Engr.

1971, Sept. 2 *Perf. 14*
B161 SP35 10pf + 5pf multi .25 .20

Surtax was for North Viet Nam.

Type of Regular Issue

10pf+5pf, Loading & unloading mail at airport.

Photo. & Engr.

1971, Oct. 5 *Perf. 14*
B162 A421 10pf + 5pf multi .20 .20

Olympic Games Type of Regular Issue

Olympic Rings and: 10pf+5pf, Figure skating, pairs. 15pf+5pf, Speed skating.

1971, Dec. 7 Photo. *Perf. 13½x14*
B163 A424 10pf + 5pf bl, car & blk .20 .20
B164 A424 15pf + 5pf grn, blk & bl .20 .20

1972, Feb. 22 Litho. *Perf. 13½x13*
B165 SP36 10pf + 5pf multi .25 .20

Surtax was for North Viet Nam.

Olympic Games Type of Regular Issue

Sport and Olympic Rings: 10pf+5pf, Diving. 25pf+10pf, Rowing.

1972, May 16 Photo. *Perf. 13½x14*
B166 A430 10pf + 5pf grnsh bl, gold & blk .20 .20
B167 A430 25pf + 10pf multi .20 .20

Interartes Type of Regular Issue

Designs: 15pf+5pf, Spear carrier, Persia, 500 B.C. 35pf+5pf, Grape Sellers, by Max Lingner, 1949, horiz.

1972, Sept. 19 Photo. *Perf. 14*
B168 A439 15pf + 5pf multi *.65 .65*
B169 A439 35pf + 5pf multi .20 .20

Flags and World Time Clock SP37

Young Couple, by Günter Glombitza SP38

25pf+5pf, Youth group with guitar and dove.

1973, Feb. 13 Litho. *Perf. 12½x13*
B170 SP37 10pf + 5pf multi .20 .20
B171 SP37 25pf + 5pf multi .20 .20

10th World Youth Festival, Berlin.

1973, Oct. 4 Photo. *Perf. 13½x14*
B172 SP38 20pf + 5pf multi .25 .20

Philatelists' Day and for the 3rd National Youth Philatelic Exhibition, Halle.

Child, Symbols of Reconstruction SP39

Luis Corvalan, Red Flag — SP40

1973, Oct. 11 *Perf. 14x13½*
B173 SP39 10pf + 5pf multi .25 .20

Surtax was for North Viet Nam.

1973, Nov. 5 *Perf. 13½x14*

25pf+5pf, Salvador Allende, Chilean flag.

B174 SP40 10pf + 5pf multi *.20 .20*
B175 SP40 25pf + 5pf multi *.30 .30*

Solidarity with the people of Chile.

Raised Fist and Star — SP41

1975, Sept. 23 Litho. *Perf. 13x13½*
B176 SP41 10pf + 5pf multi .25 .20

Surtax was for the Solidarity Committee of the German Democratic Republic.

Restored Post Gate, Wurzen, 1734 — SP42

1975, Oct. 21 Photo. *Perf. 14*
B177 SP42 10pf + 5pf multi *.30 .30*

Philatelists' Day 1975.

Olympic Games Type of 1975

Designs: 10pf+5pf, Luge run, Oberhof. 25pf+5pf, Ski jump, Rennsteig at Oberhof.

1975, Dec. 2 Photo. *Perf. 14*
B178 A518 10pf + 5pf multi .20 .20
B179 A518 25pf + 5pf multi .20 .20

Olympic Games Type of 1976

Designs: 10pf+5pf, Swimming pool, High School for Physical Education, Leipzig. 35pf+10pf, Rifle range, Suhl.

1976, May 18 Photo. *Perf. 13½x14*
B180 A529 10pf + 5pf multi .20 .20
B181 A529 35pf + 10pf multi .20 .20

TV Tower, Berlin, and Perforations SP43

1976, Oct. 19 Litho. *Perf. 13*
B182 SP43 10pf + 5pf org & bl .25 .20

Surtax was for Sozphilex 77, Philatelic Exhibition of Socialist Countries, in connection with 60th anniversary of October Revolution.

Sports Type of 1977

10pf+5pf, Young milers. 25pf+5pf, Girls artistic gymnastic performance.

1977, July 19 Litho. *Perf. 13x12½*
B183 A558 10pf + 5pf multi .20 .20
B184 A558 25pf + 5pf multi .20 .20

Sozphilex Type of 1977
Souvenir Sheet

Design: 50pf+20pf, World Youth Song, by Lothar Zitzmann, horiz.

1977, Aug. 16 Photo. ***Perf. 13***
B185 A559 50pf + 20pf multi *1.10 2.00*

Hand Holding Torch — SP44

1977, Oct. 18 Litho. ***Perf. 14***
B186 SP44 10pf + 5pf multi .25 .20

Surtax was for East German Solidarity Committee.

Fountain Type of 1979

Design: 10pf+5pf, Goose Boy Fountain.

1979, Aug. 7 Photo. ***Perf. 14***
B187 A617 10pf + 5pf multi *.35 .30*

Vietnamese Soldier, Mother and Child — SP45

1979, Nov. 6 Litho. ***Perf. 14***
B188 SP45 10pf + 5pf red org & blk .30 .20

Surtax was for Vietnam.

Olympic Type of 1980

Ski Jump, sculpture by Gunther Schutz.

1980, Jan. 15 Photo.
B189 A627 25pf + 10pf multi .20 .20

1980, Apr. 22 Photo. ***Perf. 14***

Design: 20pf+5pf, Runners at the Finish, by Lothar Zitzmann.

B190 A627 20 + 5pf multi .20 .20

Interflug Type of 1980
Souvenir Sheet

1980, June 10 Litho. ***Perf. 13x12½***
B191 A636 1m + 10pf Jet, globe *1.75 3.00*

AEROSOZPHILEX 1980 International Airpost Exhibition, Berlin, Aug. 1-10.

Olympic Type of 1980

Design: Swimmer, by Willi Sitte, vert.

1980, July 8 Photo. ***Perf. 14***
B192 A627 20pf + 10pf multi .20 .20

22nd Summer Olympic Games, Moscow, July 19-Aug. 3.

International Solidarity
SP46 SP47

1980, Oct. 14 Photo. ***Perf. 14***
B193 SP46 10pf + 5pf multi .30 .20

1981, Oct. 6 Photo. ***Perf. 14***
B194 SP47 10pf + 5pf multi .25 .20

Palestinian Solidarity — SP48

Palestinian family, Tree of Life.

1982, Sept. 21 Litho. ***Perf. 14***
B195 SP48 10pf + 5pf multi .30 .20

Nicaraguan Solidarity SP49

1983, Nov. 8 Litho. ***Perf. 14x13½***

Literacy, home defense.

B196 SP49 10pf + 5pf multi .25 .20

Solidarity — SP50

1984, Oct. 23 Photo. ***Perf. 14***
B197 SP50 10pf + 5pf Knot .30 .20

Solidarity SP51

1985, May 28 Photo.
B198 SP51 10pf + 5pf Globe, peace dove .25 .20

Surtax for the Solidarity Committee.

Technical Assistance to Developing Nations — SP52

1986, Nov. 4 Photo.
B199 SP52 10pf + 5pf multi .25 .20

Surtax for the Solidarity Committee.

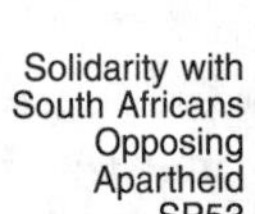

Solidarity with South Africans Opposing Apartheid SP53

1987, June 16 Litho. ***Perf. 14***
B200 SP53 10pf +5pf multi .25 .20

Solidarity SP54

1988, Oct. 4 Photo. ***Perf. 14***
B201 SP54 10pf +5pf multi .35 .30

Surtax for the Solidarity Committee. No. B201 printed se-tenant with label containing a Wilhelm Pieck quote.

UNICEF Emblem and Children of Africa — SP55

1989, Sept. 5 Photo. ***Perf. 14½x14***
B202 SP55 10pf +5pf multi .20 .20

Surtax for the Solidarity Committee.

Leipzig Church, Municipal Arms SP56

1990, Feb. 28 Photo. ***Perf. 13***
B203 SP56 35pf +15pf multicolored .50 .40

We are the People.

Intl. Literacy Year — SP57

1990, July 24 Photo. ***Perf. 14***
B204 SP57 30pf+5pf on 10pf+5pf .85 .75

Not issued without surcharge.

AIR POST STAMPS

Catalogue values for unused stamps in this section, from this point to the end of the section, are for Never Hinged items.

Canceled to Order
Used values are for CTO's.

Stylized Plane
AP1 AP2

Perf. 13x12½, 13x13½ (AP2)

1957, Dec. 13 Litho. Wmk. 313

C1	AP1	5pf	gray & blk	1.50	.20
C2	AP1	20pf	brt car & blk	.20	.20
C3	AP1	35pf	violet & blk	.20	.20
C4	AP1	50pf	maroon & blk	.25	.20
C5	AP2	1m	olive & yel	.80	.20
C6	AP2	3m	choc & yel	1.25	.30
C7	AP2	5m	dk bl & yel	3.00	.50
			Nos. C1-C7 (7)	7.20	1.80

Plane and Envelope — AP3

1982-87 Photo. ***Perf. 14***

C8	AP3	5pf	lt bl & blk	.20	.20
C9	AP3	15pf	brt rose lil & blk	.20	.20
C10	AP3	20pf	ocher & blk	.20	.20
C11	AP3	25pf	ol bis & blk	.25	.20
C12	AP3	30pf	brt grn & blk	.20	.20
C13	AP3	40pf	ol grn & blk	.25	.20
C14	AP3	1m	blue & blk	.75	.35
C15	AP3	3m	brown & blk	2.25	1.10
C16	AP3	5m	dk red & blk	3.50	1.10
			Nos. C8-C16 (9)	7.80	3.75

Issued: 30, 40pf, 1m, 10/26; 5, 20pf, 10/4/83; 3m, 4/10/84; 5m, 9/10/85; 15, 25pf, 10/6/87.

OFFICIAL STAMPS

While valid, these Official stamps were not sold to the public unused. After their period of use, some sets were sold abroad by the government stamp sales agency. Used values of Official stamps are for canceled-to-order copies. Reprints of type O1 stamps have printed cancellations.

Catalogue values for unused stamps in this section, from this point to the end of the section, are for Never Hinged items.

Arms of Republic — O1

Perf. 13x12½

1954 Wmk. 297 Litho.

O1	O1	5pf	emerald	12.00	.20
O2	O1	6pf	violet	6.50	.20
O3	O1	8pf	org brown	12.00	.20
O4	O1	10pf	lt bl grn	12.00	.20
O5	O1	12pf	blue	32.50	.20
O6	O1	15pf	dark violet	12.00	.20
O7	O1	16pf	dark violet	6.50	.20
O8	O1	20pf	olive	7.75	.20
O9	O1	24pf	brown red	6.50	.20
O10	O1	25pf	sage green	7.75	.20
O11	O1	30pf	brown red	4.25	.20
O12	O1	40pf	red	6.75	.20
O13	O1	48pf	rose lilac	3.50	.95
O14	O1	50pf	rose lilac	3.00	.20
O15	O1	60pf	bright blue	3.00	.20
O16	O1	70pf	brown	3.00	.20
O17	O1	84pf	brown	6.50	2.25
			Nos. O1-O17 (17)	145.50	6.20

Type of 1954 Redrawn

Arc of compass projects at right except on No. O22.

1954-56 Typo.

O18	O1	5pf	emer ('54)	3.25	.20
O19	O1	10pf	bl grn	2.00	.20
O20	O1	12pf	dk bl ('54)	2.00	.20
O21	O1	15pf	dk vio	2.25	.20
O22	O1	20pf	ol, arc at left ('55)	*37.50*	.20
a.			Arc of compass projects at right ('56)	450.00	.20
O23	O1	25pf	dark green	2.00	.20
O24	O1	30pf	brown red	3.75	.20
O25	O1	40pf	red	3.75	.20
O26	O1	50pf	rose lilac	2.00	.20
O27	O1	70pf	brown	2.00	.20
			Nos. O18-O27 (10)	60.50	2.00

Shaded background of emblem consists of vertical lines; on Nos. O1-O17 it consists of dots.

Granite paper was used for a 1956 printing of the 5pf, 10pf, 15pf, 20pf and 40pf. Value for set unused $300, used 30 cents.

See Nos. O37-O43.

O2

O3

1956 Wmk. 297 *Perf. 13x12½*

O28 O2	5pf black	.20	.20
O29 O2	10pf black	.20	.20
O30 O2	20pf black	.25	.20
O31 O2	40pf black	.30	.20
O32 O2	70pf black	.35	.20
	Nos. O28-O32 (5)	1.30	1.00

1956 Litho. Wmk. 297

O33 O3	10pf lilac & black	.75	.40
O34 O3	20pf lilac & black	*90.00*	.95
O35 O3	40pf lilac & black	1.25	.40
O36 O3	70pf lilac & black	2.00	1.75
	Nos. O33-O36 (4)	*94.00*	3.50

Nos. O33-O36 exist also with black or violet overprint of 4-digit control number.

See Nos. O44-O45.

No. O34 was reprinted with watermark sideways ("DDR" vertical). Value $4.

Redrawn Type of 1954-56

Perf. 13x12½, 14

1957-60 Typo. Wmk. 313

Granite Paper

O37 O1	5pf emerald	.20	.20
O38 O1	10pf blue green	.20	.20
O39 O1	15pf dark vio	.25	.20
O40 O1	20pf olive	.25	.20
O41 O1	30pf dark red ('58)	.65	.20
O42 O1	40pf red	.40	.20
O42A O1	50pf rose lilac ('60)	1.40	.20
O43 O1	70pf brown ('58)	1.40	.20
	Nos. O37-O43 (8)	4.75	1.60

Nos. O37-O43 were all issued in perf. 13x12½. Nos. O37-O40 were also issued perf. 14. Values are the same.

Type of 1956

1957 Litho. *Perf. 13x12½*

O44 O3	10pf lilac & black	.65	1.50
O45 O3	20pf lilac & black	.65	1.25

Nos. O44-O45 have black or violet overprint of four-digit control number.

Stamps similar to type O3 were issued later, with denomination expressed in dashes: one for 10pf, two for 20pf.

ISSUED UNDER RUSSIAN OCCUPATION

BERLIN-BRANDENBURG

Berlin Bear — OS1

1945 Litho. *Perf. 14*

11N1 OS1	5pf shown	.20	*.30*
11N2 OS1	6pf Bear holding spade	.20	*.30*
11N3 OS1	8pf Bear on shield	.20	*.30*
11N4 OS1	10pf Bear holding brick	.20	*.30*
11N5 OS1	12pf Bear carrying board	.20	*.30*
11N6 OS1	20pf Bear on small shield	.20	*.30*
11N7 OS1	30pf Oak sapling, ruins	.20	*.40*
	Nos. 11N1-11N7 (7)		*2.20*
	Set, never hinged	1.10	

Issued: 5pf, 8pf, 6/9; 12pf, 7/5; others, 7/18.

1945, Dec. 6 *Serrate Roulette 13½*

11N1a	OS1	5pf	.20	*.30*
11N2a	OS1	6pf	3.25	*70.00*
11N3a	OS1	8pf	2.00	*70.00*
11N4a	OS1	10pf	3.25	*70.00*
11N5a	OS1	12pf	4.00	*75.00*
11N6a	OS1	20pf	2.50	*75.00*
11N7a	OS1	30pf	3.25	*87.50*
	Nos. 11N1a-11N7a (7)		18.45	*447.80*
	Set, never hinged		45.00	

No. 11N1a comes with two different roulettes. The roulette that matches Nos. 11N2a-11N7a is valued at $2. No. 11N5a in the second roulette is rare.

MECKLENBURG-VORPOMMERN

OS1

Plowman — OS2

Design: 12pf, Wheat.

1945-46 Typo. *Perf. 10½*

12N1 OS1	6pf black, *green*	.20	*1.10*
12N2 OS1	6pf purple	.45	*2.25*
12N3 OS1	6pf purple, *green*	.30	*2.25*
12N4 OS2	8pf red, *rose*	.25	*1.40*
a.	8pf red lilac, *rose*	.35	*8.75*
12N5 OS2	8pf black, *rose*	1.40	*7.50*
12N6 OS2	8pf red lilac, *green*	.45	*2.75*
12N7 OS2	8pf black, *green*	1.40	*9.25*
12N8 OS2	8pf brown	.35	*2.75*
12N9 OS2	12pf black, *rose*	.25	*1.10*
12N10 OS2	12pf brown lilac	.25	*1.40*
12N11 OS2	12pf red	1.40	*7.00*
12N12 OS2	12pf red, *rose*	.25	*2.00*
	Nos. 12N1-12N12 (12)	6.95	*40.75*
	Set, never hinged	17.50	

Many shades.

Issued: #12N1, 12N9, 8/28; #12N4, 10/6; #12N5, 10/19; #12N7, 11/2; #12N6, 11/3; #12N10, 11/9; #12N2, 11/16; #12N11, 12/20; #12N8, 1/7/46; #12N3, 1/11/46; #12N12, 1/30/46.

Buildings — OS3

Designs: 4pf, Deer. 5pf, Fishing boats. 6pf, Harvesting grain. 8pf, Windmill. 10pf, Two-horse plow. 12pf, Bricklayer on scaffolding. 15pf, Tractor plowing field. 20pf, Ship, warehouse. 30pf, Factory. 40pf, Woman spinning.

1946 Typo. *Imperf.*

12N13 OS3	3pf brown	.95	*26.00*
12N14 OS3	4pf blue	12.00	*37.50*
12N15 OS3	4pf red brown	.95	*24.00*
12N16 OS3	5pf green	.95	*26.00*
12N17 OS3	8pf orange	.95	*26.00*
12N18 OS3	10pf brown	.75	*26.00*

Perf. 10½

12N19 OS3	6pf purple	.55	*4.50*
12N20 OS3	6pf blue	1.75	*14.00*
12N21 OS3	12pf red	.35	*2.25*
12N22 OS3	15pf brown	.35	*3.50*
12N23 OS3	20pf blue	.75	*2.25*
12N24 OS3	30pf blue green	.50	*5.75*
12N25 OS3	40pf red violet	.50	*5.75*
	Nos. 12N13-12N25 (13)	21.30	*203.50*
	Set, never hinged	45.00	

Issued: 3pf, #12N14, 5pf, 6pf, 8pf, 1/17; 10pf, 12pf, 40pf, 1/22; 15pf, 1/24; 30pf, 1/26; 20pf, 1/29; #12N15, 2/25.

Nos. 12N13-12N21 exist on both white and toned paper.

MECKLENBURG-VORPOMMERN SEMI-POSTAL STAMPS

Rudolf Breitscheid (1874-1944), Politician OSP1

Designs: 8pf+22pf, Dr. Erich Klausener (1885-1934), theologian. 12pf+28pf, Ernst Thalmann (1886-1944), politician.

1945, Oct. 21 Typo. *Perf. 10½x11*

12NB1 OSP1	6 +14pf green	8.00	*35.00*
12NB2 OSP1	8 +22pf purple	8.00	*35.00*
12NB3 OSP1	12 +28pf red	8.00	*35.00*
	Nos. 12NB1-12NB3 (3)	24.00	*105.00*
	Set, never hinged	52.50	

Sower OSP2

Child Welfare OSP3

6pf+14pf, Horsedrawn Plow. 12pf+28pf, Reaper.

1945

12NB4 OSP2	6 +14pf bl grn	2.00	*20.00*
12NB5 OSP2	6 +14pf grn	2.00	*20.00*
12NB6 OSP2	8 +22pf brn	2.00	*20.00*
12NB7 OSP2	8 +22pf yel brn	2.00	*20.00*
12NB8 OSP2	12 +28pf red	2.00	*20.00*
12NB9 OSP2	12 +28pf org	2.00	*20.00*
	Nos. 12NB4-12NB9 (6)	12.00	*120.00*
	Set, never hinged	27.50	

Issued: #12NB4, 12NB6, 12NB8, Dec. 8; others Dec. 31.

1945, Dec. 31 *Perf. 11*

12NB10 OSP3	6 +14pf Child in hand	1.10	*26.00*
12NB11 OSP3	8 +22pf Girl in winter	1.10	*26.00*
12NB12 OSP3	12 +28pf Boy	1.10	*26.00*
	Nos. 12NB10-12NB12 (3)	3.30	*78.00*
	Set, never hinged	7.50	

SAXONY PROVINCE

Coat of Arms — OS1

Land Reform — OS2

Perf. 13x12½

1945-46 Typo. Wmk. 48

13N1 OS1	1pf slate	.20	*1.10*
a.	Imperf.	.20	*3.50*
	Never hinged	.45	
13N2 OS1	3pf yellow brown	.20	*1.10*
a.	Imperf.	.20	*2.25*
	Never hinged	.45	
13N3 OS1	5pf green	.20	*1.10*
a.	Imperf.	.30	*4.25*
	Never hinged	.55	
13N4 OS1	6pf purple	.20	*1.10*
a.	Imperf.	.30	*1.40*
	Never hinged	.55	
13N5 OS1	8pf orange	.20	*1.10*
a.	Imperf.	.20	*2.00*
	Never hinged	.45	
13N6 OS1	10pf brown	.20	*1.10*
a.	Imperf.	2.00	*65.00*
	Never hinged	4.50	
13N7 OS1	12pf red	.20	*1.10*
a.	Imperf.	.20	*1.40*
	Never hinged	.45	
13N8 OS1	15pf red brown	.20	*1.10*
13N9 OS1	20pf blue	.20	*1.10*
13N10 OS1	24pf orange brown	.20	*1.10*
13N11 OS1	30pf olive green	.20	*1.10*
13N12 OS1	40pf lake	.45	*4.50*
	Nos. 13N1-13N12 (12)	2.65	*16.60*
	Set, never hinged	2.75	

Issued: #13N1-13N12, 12/1945; #13N1a-13N5a, 13N7a, 10/10/45; #13N6a, 1/1946.

1945-46 Unwmk. *Imperf.*

13N13 OS2	6pf green	.20	*.85*
13N14 OS2	12pf red	.20	*.85*

On Thin Transparent Paper

Wmk. 397

Perf. 13x13½

13N15 OS2	6pf green	.20	*2.75*
13N16 OS2	12pf red	.20	*2.75*
	Nos. 13N13-13N16 (4)		*7.20*
	Set, never hinged	.80	

Issued: #13N13-13N14, 12/17/45; others 2/21/46.

SAXONY PROVINCE SEMI-POSTAL STAMPS

Reconstruction OSP1

Designs: 6+4pf, Housing construction. 12+8pf, Bridge repair. 42+28pf, Locomotives.

1946, Jan. 19 Typo. *Perf. 13*

13NB1 OSP1	6pf +4pf green	.20	*1.10*
a.	Imperf.	.20	*8.75*
13NB2 OSP1	12pf +8pf red	.20	*1.10*
a.	Imperf.	.20	*8.75*
13NB3 OSP1	42pf +28pf violet	.20	*1.10*
a.	Imperf.	.20	*8.75*
	Nos. 13NB1-13NB3 (3)		*3.30*
	Set, never hinged	.50	
	Set, 13NB1a-13NB3a, never hinged	1.10	

Nos. 13NB1a-13NB3a issued Feb. 21.

WEST SAXONY

OS1

Leipzig Fair — OS2

1945 Typo. Wmk. 48 *Perf. 13x12½*

14N1 OS1	3pf brown	.20	*1.10*
14N2 OS1	4pf slate	.20	*1.40*
14N3 OS1	5pf green	.20	*1.40*
a.	Imperf.	.20	*1.40*
	Never hinged	.20	
14N4 OS1	6pf violet	.20	*1.40*
a.	Imperf.	.20	*1.10*
	Never hinged	.20	
14N5 OS1	8pf orange	.20	*1.40*
a.	Imperf.	.20	*1.10*
	Never hinged	.20	
14N6 OS1	10pf gray	.20	*1.40*
14N7 OS1	12pf red	.20	*.75*
a.	Imperf.	.20	*1.10*
	Never hinged	.20	
14N8 OS1	15pf red brown	.30	*4.25*
14N9 OS1	20pf blue	.20	*1.40*
14N10 OS1	30pf olive green	.30	*1.40*
14N11 OS1	40pf red lilac	.30	*3.50*
14N12 OS1	60pf maroon	.30	*5.75*
	Nos. 14N1-14N12 (12)	2.80	*25.15*
	Set, never hinged	12.00	

Issued: 3-4, 20-30pf, 11/9; 5-8, 12pf, 11/12; 10, 15, 40-60pf, 11/15; imperfs., 9/28.

1945, Oct. 18

14N13 OS2	6pf green	.20	*2.00*
14N14 OS2	12pf red	.20	*2.00*
	Set, never hinged	.80	

Leipzig Arms — OS3

Designs: 5pf, 6pf, St. Nicholas Church. 8pf, 12pf, Leipzig Town Hall.

1946, Feb. 12

14N15 OS3	3pf brown	.20	*3.50*
a.	Unwatermarked	.20	*7.00*
14N16 OS3	4pf slate	.20	*3.50*
a.	Unwatermarked	.20	*7.00*
14N17 OS3	5pf green	.20	*3.50*
a.	Unwatermarked	.20	*7.00*
14N18 OS3	6pf violet	.20	*3.50*
a.	Unwatermarked	.20	*7.00*

14N19	OS3	8pf orange	.20	*3.50*
a.		Unwatermarked	.20	*7.00*
14N20	OS3	12pf red	.20	*3.50*
a.		Unwatermarked	.20	*7.00*
		Nos. 14N15-14N20 (6)		*21.00*
		Set, never hinged	1.10	
		Set, 14NB15a-14NB20a, never hinged	1.10	

Nos. 14N15a-14N20a issued Mar. 15.

WEST SAXONY SEMI-POSTAL STAMPS

OSP1

Market, Old Town Hall — OSP2

1946 Typo. Wmk. 48 *Perf. 13x12½*

14NB1	OSP1	3 +2pf yel brn	.20	*1.40*
14NB2	OSP1	4 +3pf slate	.20	*1.40*
14NB3	OSP1	5 +3pf green	.20	*1.40*
14NB4	OSP1	6 +4pf violet	.20	*1.40*
14NB5	OSP1	8 +4pf orange	.20	*1.40*
14NB6	OSP1	10 +5pf gray	.20	*1.40*
14NB7	OSP1	12 +6pf red	.20	*1.40*
14NB8	OSP1	15 +10pf red brn	.20	*1.40*
14NB9	OSP1	20 +10pf blue	.20	*1.40*
14NB10	OSP1	30 +20pf olive grn	.20	*1.40*
14NB11	OSP1	40 +30pf red lilac	.20	*1.40*
14NB12	OSP1	60 +40pf lake	.20	*2.00*
		Nos. 14NB1-14NB12 (12)	2.40	*17.40*
		Set, never hinged	3.50	

Issue dates: Nos. 14NB1, 14NB4, 14NB7, 14NB11, Jan. 7; others, Jan. 28.

1946, May 8 *Perf. 13*

14NB13	OSP2	6 +14pf violet	.20	*1.25*
a.		Imperf.	.30	*4.25*
b.		Unwatermarked	.30	2.25
14NB14	OSP2	12 +18pf bl gray	.20	*2.25*
a.		Imperf.	.30	*4.25*
b.		Unwatermarked	.20	3.50
14NB15	OSP2	24 +26pf org brn	.20	*1.25*
a.		Imperf.	.30	*4.25*
b.		Unwatermarked	.20	1.40
14NB16	OSP2	84 +66pf green	.20	*1.75*
a.		Imperf.	.30	*4.25*
c.		Sheet of 4, #14NB13a-14NB16a	*72.50*	*175.00*
		Never hinged	125.00	
		Nos. 14NB13-14NB16 (4)	.80	*6.50*
		Set, never hinged	.80	
		Set, 14NB13a-14NB16a, never hinged	2.75	
		Set, 14NB13b-14NB16b, never hinged	1.60	

Issue date: Imperf., May 20.

EAST SAXONY

OS1

OS2

1945, June 23 Photo. *Imperf.*

15N1	OS1	12pf red	*150.00*	*475.00*
		Never hinged	275.00	

Withdrawn on day of issue.

Litho. (3pf, #15N9), Photo.

1945-46

15N2	OS2	3pf sepia	.20	*1.40*
15N3	OS2	4pf blue gray	.20	*.70*
a.		4pf gray	.20	*.45*
15N4	OS2	5pf brown	.25	*.85*
15N5	OS2	6pf green	1.25	*4.25*
15N6	OS2	6pf violet	.20	*.50*
15N7	OS2	8pf dark violet	.30	*1.40*
15N8	OS2	10pf dark brown	.35	*2.25*
15N9	OS2	10pf gray	.25	*1.40*
15N10	OS2	12pf red	.20	*.45*
15N11	OS2	15pf lemon	.35	*1.75*
15N12	OS2	20pf blue	.20	*.55*
a.		20pf gray blue	.40	*1.75*
		Never hinged	.75	
15N13	OS2	25pf blue	.35	*2.00*
15N14	OS2	30pf yellow	.20	*.55*
15N15	OS2	40pf lilac	.35	*2.00*

Typo.

Perf. 13x12½

15N16	OS2	3pf brown	.20	*.55*
15N17	OS2	5pf green	.20	*.55*
15N18	OS2	6pf violet	.20	*.55*
15N19	OS2	8pf orange	.20	*.55*
15N20	OS2	12pf vermilion	.20	*.55*
		Nos. 15N2-15N20 (19)	5.65	*22.80*
		Set, never hinged	11.00	

Issued: 12pf, 6/28; #15N5, 6/30; 8pf, #15N8, 7/3; 25pf, 7/5; 5pf, 6/6; 40pf, 7/7; 15pf, 7/10; #15N12a, 7/26; #15N9, 15N12, 15N17-15N20, 11/3; #15N3, 30pf, 11/5; 3pf, 12/5; #15N15, 12/21; #15N6, 1/22/46.

EAST SAXONY SEMI-POSTAL STAMPS

Zwinger, Dresden — OSP1

Design: 12pf+88pf, Rathaus, Dresden.

1946, Feb. 6 Photo. *Perf. 11*

15NB1	OSP1	6pf +44pf green	.20	*2.50*
15NB2	OSP1	12pf +88pf red	.20	*2.50*
		Set, never hinged	.50	

THURINGIA

Fir Trees — OS1

Designs: 6pf, 8pf, Posthorn. 12pf, Schiller. 20pf, 30pf, Goethe.

1945-46 Typo. *Perf. 11*

16N1	OS1	3pf brown	.20	*2.00*
16N2	OS1	4pf black	.20	*1.75*
16N3	OS1	5pf green	.20	*1.40*
a.		Souvenir sheet of 3, #16N1-16N3	*125.00*	*575.00*
		Never hinged	210.00	
16N4	OS1	6pf dark green	.20	*1.00*
16N5	OS1	8pf orange	.20	*1.40*
16N6	OS1	12pf red	.20	*1.00*
16N7	OS1	20pf blue	.20	*1.10*
a.		Imperf.	.20	*1.75*
		Never hinged	.30	
b.		Souv. sheet of 4, #16N2, 16N4, 16N6-16N7, rouletted x imperf. btwn.	*475.00*	1,750.
		Never hinged	975.00	
16N8	OS1	30pf gray	.40	*2.25*
a.		Imperf.	1.10	*7.00*
		Never hinged	2.25	
		Nos. 16N1-16N8 (8)	1.80	11.90
		Set, never hinged	2.50	

#16N3a sold for 2m, #16N7b for 10m.
Issued: 6pf, 10/1; 12pf, 10/19; 5pf, 10/20; 8pf, 11/3; 20pf, 11/24; #16N3a, 16N7b, 12/18; 30pf, 12/22; 3pf, 4pf, 1/4/46.

Souvenir Sheet

Rebuilding of German Natl. Theater, Weimar — OS2

a, 6pf, Schiller. b, 10pf, Goethe. c, 12pf, Liszt. d, 16pf, Wieland. e, 40pf, Natl. Theater.

1946, Mar. 27 Wmk. 48 *Imperf.*

16N9	OS2	Sheet of 5, #a.-e.	13.00	*52.50*
f.		Sheet, unwatermarked, rouletted	20.00	*125.00*
		Never hinged	42.50	

No. 16N9 was issued without gum. Sold for 7.50 marks.

THURINGIA SEMI-POSTAL STAMPS

Bridge Reconstruction OSP1

Designs: 10pf+60pf, Saalburg Bridge. 12pf+68pf, Camsdorf Bridge, Jena. 16pf+74pf, Goschwitz Bridge. 24pf+76pf, Ilm Bridge, Mellingen.

1946, Mar. 30 Typo. *Imperf.*

16NB1	OSP1	10 +60pf red brn	.20	*5.25*
16NB2	OSP1	12 +68pf red	.20	*5.25*
16NB3	OSP1	16 +74pf dark grn	.20	*5.25*
16NB4	OSP1	24 +76pf brown	.20	*5.25*
a.		Souv. sheet of 4, #16NB1-16NB4	*125.00*	*1,050.*
		Never hinged	250.00	
		Nos. 16NB1-16NB4 (4)		*21.00*
		Set, never hinged	.85	

GHANA

'gä-nə

LOCATION — West Africa between Benin and Ivory Coast
GOVT. — Republic
AREA — 92,010 sq. mi.
POP. — 18,101,000 (1997 est.)
CAPITAL — Accra

Ghana is the former British colony of Gold Coast, which achieved independence March 6, 1957. It includes the former trusteeship territory of British Togoland.

12 Pence = 1 Shilling
20 Shillings = 1 Pound
100 Pesewas = 1 Cedi (1965, 1972)
100 New Pesewas = 1 New Cedi (1967)

Used Values in Italics
In 1961 the government canceled all remainder stocks, using cancellations which closely resemble genuine postmarks. Catalogue values in italics (in Ghana) are for canceled-to-order stamps. Postally used copies are worth more.

Catalogue values for all unused stamps in this country are for Never Hinged items.

Watermark

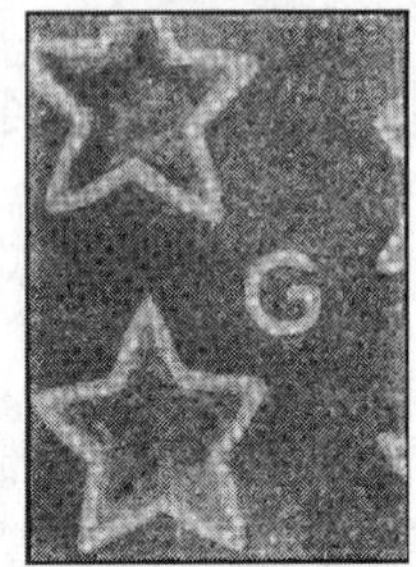
Wmk. 325- Stars and G Multiple

Kwame Nkrumah, Map and Palm-nut Vulture — A1

Perf. 14x14½

1957, Mar. 6 Wmk. 4 Photo.

1	A1	2p rose red	.20	*.20*
2	A1	2½p green	.20	*.20*
3	A1	4p brown	.20	*.20*
4	A1	1sh3p dark blue	.20	*.20*
		Nos. 1-4 (4)	.80	*.80*

Independence, Mar. 6, 1957.
For overprints see Nos. 28-31.

Stamps of Gold Coast, 1952-54, Overprinted in Black or Red

Perf. 11½x12, 12x11½

1957, Mar. 6 Engr.

5	A14	½p yel brown & car	.20	*.20*
6	A14	1p deep blue (R)	.20	*.20*
7	A14	1½p green	.20	*.20*
8	A14	3p rose	.20	*.20*
9	A15	6p org & black (R)	.20	*.20*
10	A14	1sh red org & black	.20	*.20*
11	A14	2sh rose car & ol brn	.25	*.20*
12	A14	5sh gray & red vio	.60	*.25*
13	A15	10sh olive grn & black	1.25	*.35*
		Nos. 5-13 (9)	3.30	*2.00*

Nos. 5-6 exist in vertical coils.
See Nos. 25-27.

Viking Ship and Angelfish A2

1sh3p, Medieval galleon and swordfish. 5sh, Modern cargo ship and flyingfish.

Perf. 12x11½

1957, Dec. 27 Engr. Unwmk.

14 A2 2½p emerald .20 .20
15 A2 1sh3p dark blue .45 .45
16 A2 5sh red lilac 1.75 1.75
Nos. 14-16 (3) 2.40 2.40

Black Star Line inauguration.

Ambassador Hotel — A3

Coat of Arms — A4

Design: 2½p, Opening of Parliament. 1sh3p, National monument.

Perf. 14x14½, 14½x14

1958, Mar. 6 Photo. Wmk. 4

Flags in Original Colors

17 A3 ½p car rose & black .20 .20
18 A3 2½p org yel, red & blk .20 .20
19 A3 1sh3p blue & black .20 .20
20 A4 2sh multicolored .20 .20
Nos. 17-20 (4) .80 .80

First anniversary of Independence.

Map of Africa — A5

Map and Torch — A6

1958, Apr. 15 ***Perf. 13½x14½***

21 A5 2½p multicolored .20 .20
22 A5 3p multicolored .20 .20
23 A6 1sh multicolored .20 .20
24 A6 2sh6p multicolored .20 .20
Nos. 21-24 (4) .80 .80

1st conf. of Independent African States, Accra, Apr. 15-22.

Gold Coast Nos. 151-152 and 154 Overprinted Like Nos. 5-13

Perf. 11½x12, 12x11½

1958, May 26 Engr. Wmk. 4

25 A15 2p chocolate .20 .20
26 A15 2½p red .20 .20
27 A14 4p deep blue .20 .20
Nos. 25-27 (3) .60 .60

Nos. 25-27 were prepared in 1957 and some were sold without authorization. The set was officially released in 1958.

Nos. 1-4 Overprinted: "Prime Minister's Visit U. S. A. and Canada"

1958, July 18 Photo. ***Perf. 14x14½***

28 A1 2p rose red .20 .20
29 A1 2½p green .20 .20
30 A1 4p brown .20 .20
31 A1 1sh3p dark blue .20 .20
Nos. 28-31 (4) .80 .80

Prime Minister Kwame Nkrumah's visit to the US and Canada, July, 1958.

Palm-nut Vulture over Globe — A7

"Britannia" Plane — A8

Designs: 2sh, Stratocruiser and albatross. 2sh6p, Palm-nut vulture and jet plane, horiz.

1958, July 15 ***Perf. 14x14½, 14½x14***

32 A7 2½p multicolored .20 .20
33 A8 1sh3p multicolored .20 .20
34 A8 2sh multicolored .25 .20
35 A7 2sh6p olive bister & blk .35 .30
Nos. 32-35 (4) 1.00 .90

Inauguration of Ghana Airways.

A9

Perf. 14x14½

1958, Oct. 24 Wmk. 4 Litho.

36 A9 2½p multicolored .20 .20
37 A9 1sh3p multicolored .20 .20
38 A9 2sh6p multicolored .20 .20
Nos. 36-38 (3) .60 .60

United Nations Day, Oct. 24.

A10

Perf. 14x14½

1959, Feb. 12 Photo. Wmk. 325

Lincoln Memorial and Kwame Nkrumah.

39 A10 2½p dp plum & brt pink .20 .20
40 A10 1sh3p dp blue & lt bl .20 .20
41 A10 2sh6p ol gray & org yel .20 .20
a. Souv. sheet of 3, #39-41, imperf. 1.25 1.25
Nos. 39-41 (3) .60 .60

Lincoln's birth sesquicentennial.

Kente Cloth with Traditional Symbols A11

Symbol of Greeting — A12

2½p, Talking drums and elephant horn-blower. 2sh, Map of Africa, flag and palm tree.

Perf. 14½x14, 14x14½

1959, Mar. 6 Photo. Wmk. 325

42 A11 ½p multicolored .20 .20
43 A11 2½p multicolored .20 .20
44 A12 1sh3p multicolored .20 .20
45 A11 2sh multicolored .30 .25
Nos. 42-45 (4) .90 .85

Independence, 2nd anniversary.

Flags of Independent States of Africa and Globe — A13

1959, Apr. 15 ***Perf. 14½x14***

46 A13 2½p multicolored .20 .20
47 A13 8½p multicolored .20 .20

Africa Freedom Day, Apr. 15.

Kente Cloth and "God's Omnipotence" Symbol — A13a

Nkrumah Statue, Accra — A14

Shell Ginger — A15

Cacao A16

"God's Omnipotence" Symbol — A16a

Blackwinged Red Bishop — A17

1½p, Ghana timber. 2p, Volta river. 4p, Diamond and mine. 11p, Golden spider lily. 2sh6p, Great blue turaco. 5sh, Tiger orchid. 10sh, Jewelfish (tropical African cichlid).

Perf. 11½x12, 12x11½, 14x14½, 14½x14

1959, Oct. 5 Photo. Wmk. 325

Size: 30½x21mm, 21x30½mm

48 A13a ½p multi *(God's Omnipotence)* .20 .20
49 A14 1p multicolored .20 .20

Size: 26½x37mm, 37x26½mm

50 A15 1½p multicolored .20 .20
51 A16 2p multicolored .20 .20
52 A16 2½p multicolored .20 .20
53 A16a 3p multi *(God's Omnipotence)* .20 .20
54 A16 4p multicolored .20 .20
55 A17 6p multicolored .20 .20
a. Booklet pane of 4 .90
56 A15 11p multicolored .30 .20
57 A15 1sh multicolored .25 .20
58 A17 2sh6p multicolored .60 .30
59 A15 5sh multicolored 1.25 .60

Size: 45x26mm

60 A16 10sh multicolored 2.40 1.50
Nos. 48-60,C1-C2 (15) 7.35 5.05

Nos. 48 and 53 inscribed "God's Omnipotence." Nos. 95-96 inscribed "Gye Nyame."

For surcharges see Nos. 216-217, 219-225, 277-283.

Map and Gold Cup — A18

1p, Soccer players, vert. 3p, Flags and goalkeeper in stadium. 8p, Soccer player at goal. 2sh6p, Kwame Nkrumah Gold Cup, vert.

1959, Oct. 15 ***Perf. 14½x14, 14x14½***

61 A18 ½p multicolored .20 *.20*
62 A18 1p multicolored .20 *.20*
63 A18 3p multicolored .20 *.20*
64 A18 8p multicolored .20 *.20*
65 A18 2sh6p multicolored .35 *.30*
Nos. 61-65 (5) 1.15 *1.10*

West African Soccer Competitions.

Prince Philip A19

Perf. 14½x14

1959, Nov. 24 Photo. Wmk. 325

66 A19 3p brt pink & black .20 *.20*

Visit of Prince Philip.

Talking Drums A20

Designs: 6p, 1sh3p, Ghana flag and UN emblem, vert. 2sh6p, Pile of Ceremonial Stools and "UNTC," vert.

1959, Dec. 10 ***Perf. 14½x14, 14x14½***

Flag in Original Colors

67 A20 3p violet & org yel .20 *.20*
68 A20 6p Prus green & blk .20 *.20*
69 A20 1sh3p grnsh bl, blk & vio .20 *.20*
70 A20 2sh6p dark blue & black .25 *.20*
Nos. 67-70 (4) .85 *.80*

United Nations Trusteeship Council.

Three Flying Eagles — A21

Designs: 3p, Three clusters of fireworks. 1sh3p, Ghana flag forming "3" and dove. 2sh, Ghana flag forming triple sail of symbolic ship.

Perf. 13½x14½

1960, Mar. 6 **Wmk. 325**

No.	Type	Denom.	Description	Unused	Used
71	A21	½p	multicolored	.20	.20
72	A21	3p	multicolored	.20	.20
73	A21	1sh3p	multicolored	.25	.20
74	A21	2sh	multicolored	.35	.20
			Nos. 71-74 (4)	1.00	.80

Independence, 3rd anniversary.

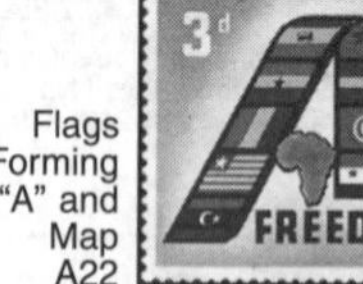

Flags Forming "A" and Map A22

Designs: 6p, Letter "F." 1sh, "D."

1960, Apr. 15 **Photo.** **Wmk. 325**

Flags in Original Colors

No.	Type	Denom.	Description	Unused	Used
75	A22	3p	green, red & black	.20	.20
76	A22	6p	rose & black	.20	.20
77	A22	1sh	blue, black & red	.20	.20
			Nos. 75-77 (3)	.60	.60

Africa Freedom Day, Apr. 15.

President Kwame Nkrumah — A23

Olympic Rings and Hand Holding Torch — A24

Designs: 1sh3p, Flag and star. 2sh, Hand holding torch. 10sh, Coat of Arms and flag of Ghana, horiz.

Perf. 14x14½, 14½x14

1960, July 1 **Litho.**

No.	Type	Denom.	Description	Unused	Used
78	A23	3p	multicolored	.20	.20
79	A23	1sh3p	multicolored	.30	.25
80	A23	2sh	multicolored	.45	.35
81	A23	10sh	multicolored	1.00	.75
a.			Souv. sheet of 4, #78-81, imperf.	1.00	1.00
			Nos. 78-81 (4)	1.95	1.55

Declaration of the Republic, July 1, 1960.

1960, Aug. 15 **Photo.** **Wmk. 325**

Design: 1sh3p, 2sh6p, Runner, Map of Africa and Olympic Rings, horiz.

No.	Type	Denom.	Description	Unused	Used
82	A24	3p	multicolored	.20	.20
83	A24	6p	multicolored	.20	.20
84	A24	1sh3p	multicolored	.20	.20
85	A24	2sh6p	multicolored	.30	.25
			Nos. 82-85 (4)	.90	.85

17th Olympic Games, Rome, Aug. 25-Sept. 11.

Map and Arch — A25

UN Emblem and Ghana Flag — A26

Designs: 3p, Flag and Kwame Nkrumah, horiz. 6p, Star and Nkrumah.

1960, Sept. 21 **Photo.**

No.	Type	Denom.	Description	Unused	Used
86	A25	3p	multicolored	.20	.20
87	A25	6p	multicolored	.20	.20
88	A25	1sh3p	multicolored	.20	.20
			Nos. 86-88 (3)	.60	.60

Founder's Day, Sept. 21, birthday of Dr. Kwame Nkrumah.

1960, Dec. 10 ***Perf. 14x14½***

6p, Flame & emblem. 1sh3p, UN Emblem.

No.	Type	Denom.	Description	Unused	Used
89	A26	3p	multicolored	.20	.20
90	A26	6p	multicolored	.20	.20
91	A26	1sh3p	multicolored	.20	.20
			Nos. 89-91 (3)	.60	.60

Human Rights Day, Dec. 10, 1960.

Talking Drums and Map — A27

Designs: 6p, Map of Africa showing 25 independent states. 2sh, Map of Africa and flags of independent nations in 1958, horiz.

Perf. 14x14½, 14½x14

1961, Apr. 15 **Wmk. 325**

No.	Type	Denom.	Description	Unused	Used
92	A27	3p	multicolored	.20	.20
93	A27	6p	multicolored	.20	.20
94	A27	2sh	multicolored	.40	.25
			Nos. 92-94 (3)	.80	.65

Africa Freedom Day, Apr. 15, 1961.

Types of 1959 Redrawn and

Red-fronted Gazelle — A28

Perf. 11½x12, 14½x14

1961, Apr. 29 **Photo.** **Wmk. 325**

No.	Type	Denom.	Description	Unused	Used
95	A13a	½p	"Gye Nyame"	.20	.20
96	A16a	3p	"Gye Nyame"	.20	.20
a.			Booklet pane of 4	.35	

Perf. 14x14½

No.	Type	Denom.	Description	Unused	Used
97	A28	£1	multicolored	4.50	2.75
			Nos. 95-97 (3)	4.90	3.15

Nos. 95-96 are the same sizes as Nos. 48 and 53 which are inscribed "God's Omnipotence."

For surcharges see Nos. 218, 226, 284.

Column, Eagle and Star — A29

Dove with Olive Branch — A30

World Map, Chain and Olive Branch A31

Designs: 1sh3p, Symbolic flower and star. 2sh, Star and 3 Ghana flags.

1961, July 1 ***Perf. 14x14½***

No.	Type	Denom.	Description	Unused	Used
98	A29	3p	multicolored	.20	.20
99	A29	1sh3p	multicolored	.20	.20
100	A29	2sh	multicolored	.25	.20
			Nos. 98-100 (3)	.65	.60

First anniversary of the Republic.

1961, Sept. 1 ***Perf. 14x14½, 14½x14***

Design: 5sh, Rostrum and olive branch.

No.	Type	Denom.	Description	Unused	Used
101	A30	3p	green	.20	.20
102	A31	1sh3p	dark blue	.25	.20
103	A31	5sh	rose carmine	.40	.30
			Nos. 101-103 (3)	.85	.70

Conference of Non-aligned Nations, Belgrade, Sept. 1961.

Kwame Nkrumah and Globe A32

Designs: 1sh3p, Kente cloth and Nkrumah, vert. 5sh, Kwame Nkrumah, vert.

Perf. 14½x14, 14x14½

1961, Sept. 21 **Wmk. 325**

No.	Type	Denom.	Description	Unused	Used
104	A32	3p	multicolored	.20	.20
a.			Souvenir sheet of 4, imperf.	.60	.60
105	A32	1sh3p	multicolored	.35	.25
a.			Souvenir sheet of 4, imperf.	1.75	1.75
106	A32	5sh	multicolored	1.00	1.00
a.			Souvenir sheet of 4, imperf.	10.00	10.00
			Nos. 104-106 (3)	1.55	1.45

Founder's Day.

The souvenir sheets contain four imperf. stamps each with simulated perforations.

Elizabeth II and Map of Africa A33

1961, Nov. 10 ***Perf. 14½x14***

Gold Inscriptions: Design in Black, Red, Yellow & Green

No.	Type	Denom.	Description	Unused	Used
107	A33	3p	claret	.20	.20
108	A33	1sh3p	Prussian blue	.25	.20
109	A33	5sh	violet blue	1.10	.90
a.			Souvenir sheet of 4	6.00	6.00
			Nos. 107-109 (3)	1.55	1.30

Visit of Queen Elizabeth II to Ghana, Nov. 10-22.

No. 109a contains four imperf. copies of No. 109 with simulated perforations.

Map of Tema Harbor and Ships A34

Perf. 14x13

1962, Feb. 10 **Litho.** **Unwmk.**

No.	Type	Denom.	Description	Unused	Used
110	A34	3p	multicolored	.20	.20
			Nos. 110,C3-C4 (3)	2.10	2.10

Opening of Tema Harbor, as part of Volta River Project.

Dove Flying over Map of Africa — A35

1962, Mar. 6 ***Perf. 13x14***

No.	Type	Denom.	Description	Unused	Used
111	A35	3p	multicolored	.20	.20
			Nos. 111,C5-C6 (3)	1.70	1.25

Conference of African heads of state at Casablanca, 1st anniv.

"Freedom" Illuminating Africa — A36

"Five Continents at Peace" — A37

Perf. 14x14½

1962, Apr. 15 **Photo.** **Wmk. 325**

No.	Type	Denom.	Description	Unused	Used
112	A36	3p	multicolored	.20	.20
113	A36	6p	multicolored	.20	.20
114	A36	1sh3p	multicolored	.20	.20
			Nos. 112-114 (3)	.60	.60

Africa Freedom Day, Apr. 15.

1962, June 21 **Wmk. 325**

Designs: 6p, Atom bomb blast in shape of skull. 1sh3p, Peace dove and globe.

No.	Type	Denom.	Description	Unused	Used
115	A37	3p	deep rose & black	.20	.20
116	A37	6p	black & dk red	.20	.20
117	A37	1sh3p	greenish blue	.35	.30
			Nos. 115-117 (3)	.75	.70

Accra Assembly of Africans for a "World Without Bomb," June 21-28.

Patrice Lumumba A38

1962, June 30 ***Perf. 14½x14***

No.	Type	Denom.	Description	Unused	Used
118	A38	3p	black & orange	.20	.20
119	A38	6p	mar, grn & blk	.20	.20
120	A38	1sh3p	dk grn, pink & blk	.20	.20
			Nos. 118-120 (3)	.60	.60

1st anniv. (on Feb. 12) of the death of Patrice Lumumba, premier of Congo.

Arch and Star — A39

Designs: 6p, Torch in flag colors and globe. 1sh3p, Palm-nut vulture trailing flag, horiz.

Perf. 13x13½, 13½x13

1962, July 1 **Unwmk.**

121 A39	3p	multicolored	.20	.20
122 A39	6p	multicolored	.20	.20
123 A39	1sh3p	multicolored	.30	.25
		Nos. 121-123 (3)	.70	.65

Second anniversary of the republic.

Kwame Nkrumah — A40

1962, Sept. 21 **Litho.** ***Perf. 13x14***

3p, Nkrumah medal. 1sh3p, Nkrumah's head & stars. 2sh, Hands with trowel & building block.

124 A40	1p	multicolored	.20	.20
125 A40	3p	multicolored	.20	.20
126 A40	1sh3p	ultra & black	.20	.20
127 A40	2sh	multicolored	.30	.25
		Nos. 124-127 (4)	.90	.85

Founder's Day, Nkrumah's 53rd birthday.

Malaria Eradication Emblem — A41

Wheat Emblem and Globe — A42

Perf. 14x14½

1962, Dec. 1 **Photo.** **Wmk. 325**

128 A41	1p	carmine rose	.20	.20
129 A41	4p	yellow green	.20	.20
130 A41	6p	olive bister	.20	.20
131 A41	1sh3p	violet	.30	.25
a.		Souvenir sheet of 4, imperf.	.75	.75
		Nos. 128-131 (4)	.90	.85

WHO drive to eradicate malaria.

No. 131a contains one each of Nos. 128-131, with simulated perforation.

Perf. 14x14½, 14½x14

1963, Mar. 21 **Wmk. 325**

Designs: 4p, Hands holding Wheat Emblem, horiz. 1sh3p, Globe, horiz.

132 A42	1p	multicolored	.20	.20
133 A42	4p	multicolored	.20	.20
134 A42	1sh3p	multicolored	.25	.20
		Nos. 132-134 (3)	.65	.60

FAO "Freedom from Hunger" campaign.

Map of Africa in Sun — A43

Cross, Flag and Centenary Emblem — A44

Designs: 4p, Symbolic wood carving, horiz. 1sh3p, Map of Africa and ceremonial fire. 2sh6p, Gazelle and flag.

1963, Apr. 15 **Photo.**

135 A43	1p	crimson & gold	.20	.20
136 A43	4p	orange, blk & red	.20	.20
137 A43	1sh3p	multicolored	.20	.20
138 A43	2sh6p	multicolored	.25	.20
		Nos. 135-138 (4)	.85	.80

Africa Freedom Day, Apr. 15.

Perf. 14x14½, 14½x14

1963, May 28 **Wmk. 325**

1½p, Centenary emblem, horiz. 4p, Family & emblem, horiz. 1sh3p, Emblem & globe.

139 A44	1p	multicolored	.20	.20
140 A44	1½p	multicolored	.20	.20
141 A44	4p	multicolored	.20	.20
142 A44	1sh3p	multicolored	.25	.20
a.		Souvenir sheet of 4, imperf.	.50	.50
		Nos. 139-142 (4)	.85	.80

Cent. of the founding of the Intl. Red Cross.

No. 142a contains one each of Nos. 139-142, with simulated perforation.

A45

Designs: 4p, Three flags. 1sh3p, Map of Africa with Ghana, vert. 2sh6p, Torch, vert.

Perf. 14½x14, 14x14½

1963, July 1 **Photo.**

143 A45	1p	multicolored	.20	.20
144 A45	4p	multicolored	.20	.20
145 A45	1sh3p	multicolored	.20	.20
146 A45	2sh6p	multicolored	.25	.25
		Nos. 143-146 (4)	.85	.85

The 3rd anniversary of the republic.

Dancers, Fireworks and Nkrumah A46

1p, Nkrumah & streamer. 4p, Nkrumah & flag. 5sh, Wisdom symbol.

Perf. 14x14½, 14½x14

1963, Sept. 21

147 A46	1p	multi, vert.	.20	.20
148 A46	4p	multi, vert.	.20	.20
149 A46	1sh3p	multi	.20	.20
150 A46	5sh	multi	.25	.25
		Nos. 147-150 (4)	.85	.85

Founder's Day, Nkrumah's 54th birthday.

Ramses II at Abu Simbel — A47

Designs: 1½p, Rock painting, bird and fish, horiz. 2p, Queen Nefertari, horiz. 4p, Sphinx of Wadi es-Sebua. 1sh3p, Statues of Ramses II at Abu Simbel, horiz.

1963, Nov. 1 **Unwmk.** ***Perf. 11½x11***

151 A47	1p	multicolored	.20	.20
152 A47	1½p	multicolored	.20	.20
153 A47	2p	multicolored	.20	.20
154 A47	4p	multicolored	.20	.20
155 A47	1sh3p	multicolored	.55	.40
		Nos. 151-155 (5)	1.35	1.20

UNESCO world campaign to save historic monuments in Nubia.

Steam and Diesel Engines A48

Perf. 14½x14

1963, Nov. 1 **Wmk. 325**

156 A48	1p	multicolored	.20	.20
157 A48	6p	multicolored	.25	.20
158 A48	1sh3p	multicolored	.60	.50
159 A48	2sh6p	multicolored	1.50	1.25
		Nos. 156-159 (4)	2.55	2.15

The 60th anniversary of Ghana's railroads.

Eleanor Roosevelt and Flame — A49

IQSY Emblem and Satellites — A50

6p, Mrs. Roosevelt & flag. 1sh3p, Mrs. Roosevelt, flag, flame & Ghanaian symbols, horiz.

Perf. 11½x11, 11x11½

1963, Dec. 10 **Unwmk.**

160 A49	1p	multicolored	.20	.20
161 A49	4p	multicolored	.20	.20
162 A49	6p	multicolored	.20	.20
163 A49	1sh3p	multicolored	.30	.25
		Nos. 160-163 (4)	.90	.85

Eleanor Roosevelt; 15th anniv. of the Universal Declaration of Human Rights.

Imperforates

Starting in 1964, certain sets of Ghana exist imperf.

1964, June 1 **Photo.** ***Perf. 14***

164 A50	3p	multicolored	.20	.20
165 A50	6p	multicolored	.20	.20
166 A50	1sh3p	multicolored	.35	.25
a.		Souvenir sheet of 4	1.00	1.00
		Nos. 164-166 (3)	.75	.65

Intl. Quiet Sun Year, 1964-65. No. 166a contains 4 imperf. stamps similar to No. 166 with simulated perforations.

See Nos. 186-188.

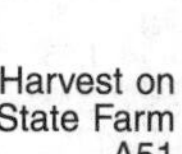

Harvest on State Farm A51

Designs: 6p, Oil refinery, Tema. 1sh3p, Communal labor. 5sh, Ghana flag and people.

1964, July 1 ***Perf. 13x14***

167 A51	3p	multicolored	.20	.20
168 A51	6p	multicolored	.20	.20
169 A51	1sh3p	multicolored	.20	.20
170 A51	5sh	multicolored	.30	.30
a.		Souvenir sheet of 4	1.00	1.00
		Nos. 167-170 (4)	.90	.90

4th anniv. of the Republic. No. 170a contains four stamps similar to Nos. 167-170 with simulated perforations.

Dove, Globe, Olive Branch and Flag — A52

Designs: 6p, Map of Africa and quill pen, vert. 1sh3p, Knotted rope and map of Africa. 5sh, Hands planting symbolic tree, vert.

1964, July 6 ***Perf. 14***

171 A52	3p	multicolored	.20	.20
172 A52	6p	black & red	.20	.20
173 A52	1sh3p	blue & multi	.20	.20
174 A52	5sh	yel & multi	.25	.25
		Nos. 171-174 (4)	.85	.85

Signing of the African Unity Charter, 1st anniv.

Nkrumah and Hibiscus — A53

Boxing — A54

Perf. 14x14½

1964, Sept. 21 **Photo.** **Wmk. 325**

Design in Brown, Green and Rose Red

175 A53	3p	light blue	.20	.20
176 A53	6p	yellow	.20	.20
177 A53	1sh3p	gray	.20	.20
178 A53	2sh6p	emerald	.30	.30
a.		Souvenir sheet of 4	1.25	1.25
		Nos. 175-178 (4)	.90	.90

Founder's Day, Nkrumah's 55th birthday.

No. 178a contains four of No. 178 with simulated perforation.

1964, Oct. 25 ***Perf. 14½x14***

Sport: 1p, Hurdling, horiz. 2½p, Running, horiz. 4p, Broad jump. 6p, Soccer. 1sh3p, Athlete with Olympic torch. 5sh, Banners and Tokyo Olympic emblem, horiz.

179 A54	1p	yellow & multi	.20	.20
180 A54	2½p	multicolored	.20	.20
181 A54	3p	red & multi	.20	.20
182 A54	4p	blue & multi	.20	.20
183 A54	6p	multicolored	.20	.20
184 A54	1sh3p	blue & multi	.25	.20
185 A54	5sh	gray & multi	.30	.25
a.		Souvenir sheet of 3	1.50	1.50
		Nos. 179-185 (7)	1.55	1.45

18th Olympic Games, Tokyo, Oct. 10-25.

No. 185a contains stamps similar to Nos. 183-185 with simulated perforation.

Quiet Sun Year Type of 1964

Unwmk.

1964, Oct. Photo. *Perf. 14*

186 A50 3p gray, bl, grn, yel & red 1.25 1.25
187 A50 6p pink, bl, grn, yel & red 2.50 2.50
188 A50 1sh3p tan, bl, grn, yel, & red 4.00 4.00
Nos. 186-188 (3) 7.75 7.75

Each issued in sheets of 12, with star-strewn blue border inscribed "Ghana International Quiet Sun Year." Stamps arranged in square surrounding vignette of New York World's Fair Unisphere in blue.

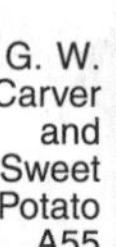

G. W. Carver and Sweet Potato A55

Design: 1sh3p, Albert Einstein, theory of relativity formula and atom symbol.

1964, Dec. 7 Wmk. 325 *Perf. 14½*

189 A55 6p grn & dk blue .20 .20
190 A55 1sh3p Prus bl & claret .30 .25
191 A55 5sh org ver & brn blk 1.50 1.25
a. Souvenir sheet of 3 1.50 1.50
Nos. 189-191 (3) 2.00 1.70

Human Rights Day; Albert Einstein (1878-1955) and George Washington Carver (1864-1943), scientists.

No. 191a commemorates UNESCO Week and contains one each of Nos. 189-191 with simulated perforations.

Secretary Bird — A56

Designs: 1p, Elephant, vert. 2½p, Purple wreath, vert. 3p, Gray parrot, vert. 4p, Blue-naped mousebird. 6p, African tulip tree flowers. 1sh3p, Amethyst starling. 2sh6p, Hippopotamuses.

Perf. 11½x11, 11x11½

1964, Dec. 14 Photo. Unwmk.

192 A56 1p blue & multi .20 .20
193 A56 1½p org & multi .20 .20
194 A56 2½p lt green & multi .25 .20
a. Souv. sheet of 3, #192-194, imperf. 1.40 1.40
195 A56 3p lt green & multi .25 .20
196 A56 4p multicolored .35 .25
197 A56 6p multicolored .35 .20
198 A56 1sh3p multicolored .65 .40
199 A56 2sh6p multicolored 1.40 .85
a. Souv. sheet of 5, #195-199, imperf. 3.75 3.75
Nos. 192-199 (8) 3.65 2.50

ICY Emblem A57

1965, Feb. 15 Litho. *Perf. 14x13*

Design in Black, Red and Green

200 A57 1p gray .20 .20
201 A57 4p bister .20 .20
202 A57 6p tan .20 .20
203 A57 1sh3p light green .40 .30
a. Souvenir sheet of 4 1.75 1.75
Nos. 200-203 (4) 1.00 .90

Intl. Cooperation Year. No. 203a contains 4 imperf. stamps similar to No. 203.

ITU Emblem, Old and New Communication Equipment — A58

1965, Apr. 12 *Perf. 13½*

204 A58 1p multicolored .20 .20
205 A58 6p multicolored .20 .20
206 A58 1sh3p multicolored .30 .20
207 A58 5sh multicolored 1.10 .90
a. Souvenir sheet of 4 1.75 1.75
Nos. 204-207 (4) 1.80 1.50

Cent. of the ITU. No. 207a contains 4 imperf. stamps similar to Nos. 204-207 with simulated perforations.

Lincoln's Home, Springfield, Ill. — A59

1sh3p, Inaugural Address and Lincoln. 2sh, Lincoln and his signature. 5sh, Adaptation of 1869 US Lincoln stamp (No. 122).

Wmk. 325

1965, Apr. Photo. *Perf. 12½*

208 A59 6p multicolored .20 .20
209 A59 1sh3p multicolored .30 .20
210 A59 2sh multicolored .40 .35
211 A59 5sh red & black .75 .50
a. Souvenir sheet of 4 2.00 1.50
Nos. 208-211 (4) 1.65 1.25

Centenary of death of Abraham Lincoln.

No. 211a contains one each of Nos. 208-211 with simulated perforation.

5-Pesewa Coin, Nkrumah's Head — A60

Coins: 10pa, 10 pesewas. 25pa, 25 pesewas. 50pa, 50 pesewas.

Perf. 11x13

1965, July 19 Unwmk. Litho.

Coin in Silver and Black

Size: 45x32mm

212 A60 5pa red, grn, & lt grn .20 .20
213 A60 10pa red, grn, & pink .25 .20

Size: 62x39mm

214 A60 25pa red, grn, & pink .70 .50

Size: 71x43½mm

215 A60 50pa red, grn & lt grn 1.40 1.10
Nos. 212-215 (4) 2.55 2.00

Introduction of decimal currency.

Regular Issue of 1959-61 Surcharged in Red, Blue, Brown, Black or White with New Value and: "Ghana New Currency / 19th July, 1965"

Perf. 12x11½, 14½x14, 14x14½

1965, July 19 Photo. Wmk. 325

216 A14 1pa on 1p (R) .20 .20
217 A16 2pa on 2p (Bl) .20 .20
218 A16a 3pa on 3p (#96, Br) .20 .20
219 A16 4pa on 4p (Bl) .20 .20
220 A17 6pa on 6p (Bk) .20 .20
221 A15 11pa on 11p (W) .25 .20
222 A15 12pa on 1sh (Bl) .30 .20
223 A17 30pa on 2sh6p (Bl) 1.00 .45
224 A15 60pa on 5sh (Bl) 1.75 .90
225 A16 1.20c on 10s (Bl) 3.25 2.25
226 A28 2.40c on £1 (Bl) 7.25 5.75
Nos. 216-226,C7-C8 (13) 15.85 11.35

The two lines of the overprint are diagonal on the 1pa, 11pa, 12pa, 60pa, 1.20c and 2.40c.

The surcharge exists double or inverted on six or more denominations.

Summit Conference, Accra — A61

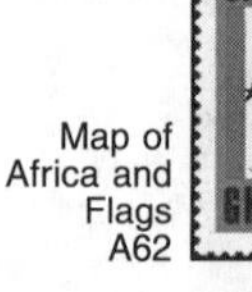
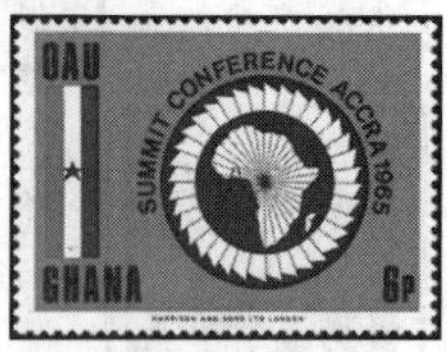

Map of Africa and Flags A62

Designs: 2pa, "OAU" and three heads (triangle pointing up). 5pa, Symbol of African Unity. 15pa, Sunburst and map of Africa. 24pa, Map of Africa.

Perf. 14, 14½x14

1965, Oct. 21 Photo.

Ghana Flag in Red, Black & Green

227 A61 1pa multicolored .20 .20
228 A61 2pa multicolored .20 .20
229 A61 5pa multicolored .20 .20
230 A62 6pa orange & black .20 .20
231 A62 15pa light blue & blk .25 .25
232 A62 24pa lt ultra & green .45 .40
Nos. 227-232 (6) 1.50 1.45

Summit Conference of the Organization for African Unity, Accra, Oct. 1965.

Soccer Goalkeeper — A63

Designs: 15pa, Soccer player and cup, vert. 24pa, Two soccer players and cup.

Perf. 14x13, 13x14

1965, Nov. 15 Unwmk.

233 A63 6pa ocher & multi .20 .20
234 A63 15pa multicolored .25 .20
235 A63 24pa lt blue & multi .40 .30
Nos. 233-235 (3) .85 .70

African Soccer Cup competition.

For overprints see Nos. 244-246.

John F. Kennedy and Eternal Flame — A64

Various Kennedy portraits.

1965, Dec. 15 Wmk. 325 *Perf. 12½*

236 A64 6pa blk, yel, gold & grn .20 .20
237 A64 15pa vio, crim & brt grn .25 .25
238 A64 24pa dp pur & blk .40 .40
239 A64 30pa vio brn & blk .50 .50
a. Souvenir sheet of 4 ('66) 4.00 3.50
Nos. 236-239 (4) 1.35 1.35

President John F. Kennedy (1917-1963).

No. 239a contains four imperf. stamps similar to Nos. 236-239.

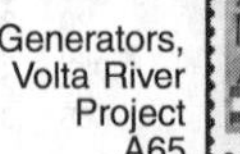

Generators, Volta River Project A65

Designs: 15pa, Dam and Lake Volta. 24pa, "Ghana" forming dam. 30pa, Grain.

Perf. 11x11½

1966, Jan. 22 Unwmk.

240 A65 6pa sepia & multi .20 .20
241 A65 15pa multicolored .20 .20
242 A65 24pa multicolored .25 .25
243 A65 30pa brt blue & blk .35 .35
Nos. 240-243 (4) 1.00 1.00

Opening of the Volta River dam and electric power station at Akosombo.

Nos. 233-235 Overprinted Diagonally: "Black Stars Retain Africa Cup / 21st Nov. 1965"

1966, Feb. 7 *Perf. 14x13, 13x14*

244 A63 6pa ocher & multi .20 .20
245 A63 15pa multicolored .30 .30
246 A63 24pa lt bl & multi .50 .50
Nos. 244-246 (3) 1.00 1.00

Ghana's soccer victory, Nov. 21, 1965.

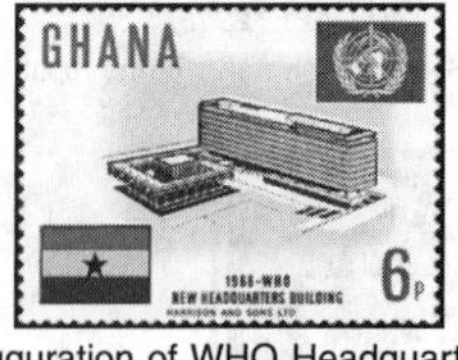

Inauguration of WHO Headquarters, Geneva — A66

Designs: 24pa, 30pa, WHO Headquarters from the west and WHO emblem.

Perf. 14x14½

1966, July 1 Photo. Wmk. 325

247 A66 6pa multicolored .20 .20
248 A66 15pa multicolored .35 .25
249 A66 24pa multicolored .55 .35
250 A66 30pa multicolored .70 .50
a. Souvenir sheet of 4 2.00 1.75
Nos. 247-250 (4) 1.80 1.30

No. 250a contains 4 imperf. stamps similar to Nos. 247-250 with simulated perforations.

Herring, Fishermen and Flag A67

Designs: 15pa, Flatfish and canoes. 24pa, Spadefish and schooner. 30pa, Red snapper and fishing trawler "Shama." 60pa, Mackerel and steamer.

1966, Aug. 10 Unwmk. *Perf. 14x13*

251 A67 6pa ocher & multi .20 .20
252 A67 15pa yel grn & multi .40 .25
253 A67 24pa ver & multi .65 .30
254 A67 30pa blue & multi 1.00 .40
a. Souvenir sheet of 4 3.50 2.00
255 A67 60pa green & multi 1.40 .85
Nos. 251-255 (5) 3.65 2.00

1966 Freedom from Hunger campaign "Young World Against Hunger."

No. 254a contains 4 imperf. stamps similar to No. 254.

Flags of African Unity Charter Signers, Map and Diamond A68

Designs: 6p, Ghana flag and links enclosing map of Africa, vert. 24p, Ship's wheel enclosing map of Africa, and cacao pod.

1966, Sept. Unwmk. *Perf. 13x13½*

256 A68 6pa brt blue & multi .20 .20
257 A68 15pa blue & multi .25 .25
258 A68 24pa dp green & multi .35 .35
Nos. 256-258 (3) .80 .80

Signing of the African Unity Charter, 3rd anniv.

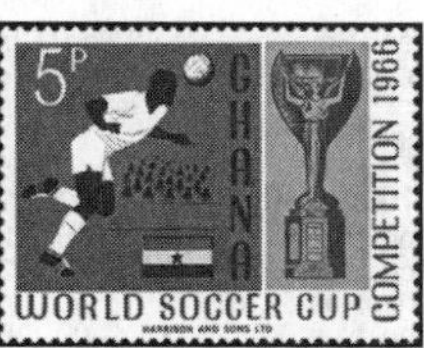

Soccer Player and Rimet Cup — A69

Various Soccer Scenes.

Perf. 14½x14

1966, Nov. 14 Photo. Wmk. 325

259 A69	5pa brown & multi	.20	.20
260 A69	15pa blue & multi	.45	.30
261 A69	24pa green & multi	.70	.40
262 A69	30pa brt rose & multi	.85	.60
263 A69	60pa lilac & multi	1.90	1.25
a.	Souvenir sheet of 4	7.50	7.50
	Nos. 259-263 (5)	4.10	2.75

World Cup Soccer Championship, Wembley, England, July 11-30.

No. 263a contains 4 imperf. stamps similar to No. 263 with simulated perforations.

UNESCO Emblem A70

1966, Dec. 23 Wmk. 325 *Perf. 14½*

264 A70	5pa multicolored	.20	.20
265 A70	15pa multicolored	.35	.20
266 A70	24pa multicolored	.55	.45
267 A70	30pa multicolored	.70	.50
268 A70	60pa multicolored	1.40	1.00
a.	Souvenir sheet of 5	3.25	2.25
	Nos. 264-268 (5)	3.20	2.35

UNESCO, 20th anniv. No. 268a contains 5 imperf. stamps similar to Nos. 264-268 with simulated perforations.

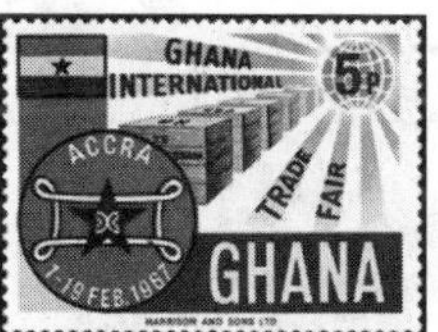

Packing Cases and Fair Emblem A71

Fair Emblem and: 15pa, World map and trade routes to Accra. 24pa, Freighters and loading crane, vert. 36pa, Hand holding cargo net.

1967, Feb. 1 *Perf. 14½x14, 14x14½*

269 A71	5pa multicolored	.20	.20
270 A71	15pa multicolored	.20	.20
271 A71	24pa multicolored	.30	.30
272 A71	36pa multicolored	.50	.50
	Nos. 269-272 (4)	1.20	1.20

International Trade Fair, Accra, Feb. 1-19.

Eagle and Flag — A72

1967, Feb. 24 Photo. *Perf. 14x14½*

Flag in Red, Yellow, Black and Green

273 A72	1np gray bl & dk brn	.20	.20
274 A72	4np ocher & dk brn	.20	.20
275 A72	12½np ol grn & dk brn	.60	.60
276 A72	25np dl cl & dk brn	1.00	1.00
a.	Souvenir sheet of 4, #273-276	3.25	2.50
	Nos. 273-276 (4)	2.00	2.00

1st anniv. of the revolution which overthrew the regime of Kwame Nkrumah.

No. 276a has dull claret marginal inscriptions. An imperf. sheet similar to No. 276a has solid margins of dull claret, colorless inscriptions. Value $2.

Nos. 51, 54-58, 60 and 97 Surcharged in Black, Red or White

1967, Feb. 27 *Perf. 14½x14, 14x14½*

Size: 30½x21mm, 21x30½mm

277 A16	1½np on 2p (B)	9.00	3.00
278 A16	3½np on 4p (R)	.20	.20
279 A17	5np on 6p (R)	.20	.20
280 A15	9np on 11p (W)	.30	.20
281 A15	10np on 1sh (W)	.35	.25
282 A17	25np on 2sh6p (R)	2.50	1.50

Size: 45x26mm

283 A16	1nc on 10sh (R)	9.00	7.25
284 A28	2nc on £1 (R)	16.00	14.00
	Nos. 277-284,C9-C10 (10)	41.15	29.15

Corn — A73

Forest Kingfisher — A74

African Lungfish A75

Designs: 2np, Ghana Mace (golden staff). 2½np, Commelina flower. 4np, Rufous-crowned roller, vert. 6np, Akosombo Dam, Volta River. 8np, Adomi Bridge, Volta River. 9np, Chemeleon. 10np, Quay No. 2, Tema Harbor. 20np, Cape hare. 50np, Black-winged stilt. 1nc, Chief's ceremonial stool. 2nc, Frangipani. 2.50nc, State Chair.

Perf. 11½x12, 12x11½ (A73), 14x14½, 14½x14 (A74-A75)

1967 Photo. Wmk. 325

286 A73	1np multicolored	.20	.20
287 A74	1½np multicolored	.20	.20
288 A74	2np multicolored	.20	.20
289 A74	2½np multicolored	.20	.20
290 A75	3np multicolored	.20	.20
291 A73	4np multicolored	.20	.20
292 A75	6np multicolored	.20	.20
293 A73	8np multicolored	.20	.20
294 A75	9np multicolored	.20	.20
295 A75	10np multicolored	.20	.20
296 A74	20np blue	.35	.25
297 A74	50np multicolored	1.10	.85
298 A74	1nc multicolored	2.25	1.50
299 A74	2nc multicolored	4.50	3.00
300 A74	2.50nc multicolored	5.50	3.50
	Nos. 286-300 (15)	15.70	11.10

For overprints & surcharges see #356-370, 858, 1091, 1092A-1092C, 1092E-1093, 1095, 1096B.

Kumasi Fort, 1896 A76

Castles on Ghana Coast: 12½np, Christiansborg Castle, 1659, and British galleon. 20np, Elmina Castle, 1482, and Portuguese galleon. 25np, Cape Coast Castle, 1664, and Spanish galleon.

1967, June 12 *Perf. 14½*

301 A76	4np grnsh bl & multi	.20	.20
302 A76	12½np red org & multi	.55	.40
303 A76	20np brt grn & multi	1.10	.60
304 A76	25np lt red brn & multi	1.50	.80
	Nos. 301-304 (4)	3.35	2.00

Orbiter 1 Landing on Moon — A77

Designs: 4np, Luna 10 on the moon, and globe. 12½np, Astronaut walking in space.

1967, Aug. 16 Unwmk. *Perf. 13½*

305 A77	4np multicolored	.20	.20
306 A77	10np multicolored	.30	.20
307 A77	12½np multicolored	.40	.30
a.	Souvenir sheet of 3	1.50	1.50
	Nos. 305-307 (3)	.90	.70

Achievements in space. Issued in Ghana in sheets of 30. Sheets of 12 with ornamented, inscribed border also exist; these were sold in Ghana in 1968.

No. 307a contains 3 imperf. stamps similar to Nos. 305-307.

Boy Scouts at Campfire A78

Designs: 10np, Hiking Boy Scout. 12½np, Lord Baden-Powell.

1967, Sept. 18 Photo. *Perf. 14x13½*

308 A78	4np multicolored	.20	.20
309 A78	10np multicolored	.40	.30
310 A78	12½np multicolored	.50	.40
a.	Souvenir sheet of 3	1.10	.90
	Nos. 308-310 (3)	1.10	.90

50th anniv. of the Ghana (Gold Coast) Boy Scouts. Issued in Ghana in sheets of 30. Sheets of 12 with ornamented, inscribed border also exist; these were sold in Ghana in 1968.

No. 310a contains 3 imperf. stamps similar to Nos. 308-310 with simulated perforations.

UN Secretariat Building — A79

Design: 50np, 2.50nc, UN Headquarters.

1967, Oct. 24 Litho. *Perf. 13½x13*

311 A79	4np multicolored	.20	.20
312 A79	10np multicolored	.25	.20
313 A79	50np multicolored	.65	.65
314 A79	2.50nc multicolored	5.50	5.50
a.	Souvenir sheet	6.75	6.75
	Nos. 311-314 (4)	6.60	6.55

United Nations Day. No. 314a contains one imperf. stamp similar to No. 314 with simulated perforations.

Leopard — A80

Designs: 12½np, Christmas butterfly. 20np, Nubian carmine bee-eaters. 50np, Waterbuck.

Wmk. 325

1967, Dec. 28 Photo. *Perf. 12½*

315 A80	4np multicolored	.20	.20
316 A80	12½np multicolored	.30	.20
317 A80	20np multicolored	.75	.40
318 A80	50np multicolored	1.75	1.10
a.	Souvenir sheet of 3	3.00	2.00
	Nos. 315-318 (4)	3.00	1.90

Intl. Tourist Year. No. 318a contains 3 imperf. stamps similar to Nos. 316-318 with simulated perforations.

Convoy Entering Accra A81

12½np, Victory parade. 20np, Waving crowd. 40np, Singing and dancing crowd.

Unwmk.

1968, Feb. 24 Litho. *Perf. 14*

319 A81	4np sal & multi	.20	.20
320 A81	12½np multicolored	.40	.30
321 A81	20np multicolored	.65	.50
322 A81	40np yel & multi	1.40	1.10
	Nos. 319-322 (4)	2.65	2.10

2nd anniversary of Feb. 24th Revolution.

Cacao Beans and Microscope A82

4np, 25np, Cacao tree & beans, microscope.

Perf. 14½x14

1968, Mar. 18 Photo. Wmk. 325

323 A82	2½np grn & multi	.20	.20
324 A82	4np gray & multi	.20	.20
325 A82	10np scar & multi	.20	.20
326 A82	25np multicolored	.50	.50
a.	Souvenir sheet of 4	1.10	1.10
	Nos. 323-326 (4)	1.10	1.10

Issued to publicize Ghana's cocoa production. Sheets of 30.

No. 326a contains four imperf. stamps similar to Nos. 323-326 with simulated perforations.

Nos. 323-326 also exist in sheets of 12 believed not to have been on sale in Ghana.

Lt. Gen. E. K. Kotoka A83

Various portraits of Lt. Gen. Kotoka. 40np vert.

1968, Apr. 17 Unwmk. *Perf. 14*

327 A83	4np pur & multi	.20	.20
328 A83	12½np grn & multi	.45	.45
329 A83	20np multicolored	.90	.90
330 A83	40np gray & multi	1.75	1.75
	Nos. 327-330 (4)	3.30	3.30

Lt. Gen. Emmanuel Kwasi Kotoka (1926-967), leader of the Revolution of 1966 against Nkrumah.

Tobacco — A84

Designs: 5np, Crested porcupine. 12½np, Tapped rubber tree. 20np, Cymothoe sangaris butterfly. 40np, Charaxes ameliae butterfly.

1968, Aug. Photo. *Perf. 14x14½*

331 A84 4np multicolored .20 .20
332 A84 5np multicolored .20 .20
333 A84 12½np multicolored .45 .45
334 A84 20np multicolored .75 .75
335 A84 40np multicolored 1.50 1.50
a. Souvenir sheet of 4 3.00 3.00
Nos. 331-335 (5) 3.10 3.10

No. 335a contains 4 stamps similar to Nos. 331, 332-335 with simulated perforations.

20TH ANNIVERSARY OF THE WORLD HEALTH ORGANIZATION 1968
4NP
GHANA

Surgical Team A85

1968, Nov. 11 *Perf. 14x13*

336 A85 4np grn & multi .20 .20
337 A85 12½np multicolored .45 .30
338 A85 20np pur & multi .70 .65
339 A85 40np bl & multi 1.75 1.50
a. Souvenir sheet of 4 3.25 3.25
Nos. 336-339 (4) 3.10 2.65

WHO, 20th anniv. No. 339a contains 4 imperf. stamps similar to Nos. 336-339.

Hurdling — A86

12½np, Boxing. 20np, Torch bearer, flags & Olympic rings. 40np, Soccer.

1968, Dec. Unwmk. *Perf. 14x14½*

340 A86 4np gray & multi .20 .20
341 A86 12½np gray & multi .35 .25
342 A86 20np ultra & multi .70 .60
343 A86 40np gray & multi 1.40 1.25
a. Souvenir sheet of 4 3.50 3.50
Nos. 340-343 (4) 2.65 2.30

19th Olympic Games, Mexico City, Oct. 12-27, 1968. No. 343a contains 4 imperf. stamps with simulated perforations similar to Nos. 340-343.

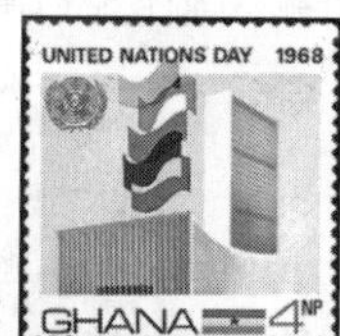

UN Headquarters and Flags — A87

UN Day, 1968: 12np, UN emblem and Ghanaian staff and stool. 20np, UN Headquarters, New York, UN emblem and Ghana flag. 40np, UN emblem surrounded by flags.

1969, Feb. 1 Litho. *Perf. 13x13½*

344 A87 4np multicolored .20 .20
345 A87 12½np pink & multi .35 .20
346 A87 20np blk & multi .75 .50
347 A87 40np lt bl & multi 1.40 1.25
a. Souvenir sheet of 4 3.50 3.00
Nos. 344-347 (4) 2.70 2.15

No. 347a contains 4 imperf. stamps with simulated perforations similar to #344-347.

Joseph Boakye Danquah A88

12½np, 20np, Dr. Martin Luther King, Jr., Human Rights flame & flag of Ghana.

1969, Mar. 7 Photo. *Perf. 14½x14*

348 A88 4np gray & multi .20 .20
349 A88 12½np multicolored .45 .30
350 A88 20np blue & multi .85 .80
351 A88 40np grn & multi 1.50 1.50
a. Souvenir sheet of 4 3.25 3.25
Nos. 348-351 (4) 3.00 2.80

Intl. Human Rights Year, Rev. Martin Luther King, Jr. (1929-1968), American civil rights leader, and Joseph Boakye Danquah (1895-1965), lawyer, writer and Ghanaian political leader.

No. 351a contains 4 imperf. stamps with simulated perforations similar to #348-351.

Parliament A89

Design: 12½np, 40np, Coat of Arms.

Perf. 14½x14

1969, Sept. Wmk. 325

352 A89 4np multicolored .20 .20
353 A89 12½p multicolored .45 .30
354 A89 20np multicolored .75 .70
355 A89 40np multicolored 1.50 1.40
a. Souvenir sheet of 4 3.00 3.00
Nos. 352-355 (4) 2.90 2.60

3rd anniv. of the revolution. No. 355a contains 4 imperf. stamps with simulated perforations similar to Nos. 352-355.

Nos. 286-300 Overprinted in Black, Yellow or Red

Perf. 11½x12, 12x11½ (A73), 14x14½, 14½x14 (A74-A75)

1969, Oct. 1 Photo. Wmk. 325

356 A73 1np multicolored .20 .20
357 A74 1½np multicolored .20 .20
358 A73 2np multicolored .20 .20
359 A73 2½np multicolored .20 .20
360 A75 3np multicolored .20 .20
361 A73 4np multi (Y) .20 .20
362 A75 6np multicolored .20 .20
363 A73 8np multicolored .20 .20
364 A75 9np multicolored .20 .20
365 A75 10np multicolored .20 .20
366 A74 20np blue .45 .45
367 A74 50np multicolored 1.75 1.25
368 A74 1nc multicolored 2.25 1.90
369 A74 2nc multi (R) 5.25 4.50
370 A74 2.50nc multicolored 6.75 5.25
Nos. 356-370 (15) 18.45 15.35

Overprint vertical on vertical stamps.
The 4np also exists with overprint in black and in red.

Map of Africa, Two Ghana Flags Rising from Ghana — A90

Designs: 12½np, "2" with laurel and star. 20np, Three hands and egg (symbol of rebirth) and Kente cloth. 40np, like 4np.

Unwmk.

1969, Dec. 4 Litho. *Perf. 14*

371 A90 4np multicolored .20 .20
372 A90 12½np bl & multi .40 .30
373 A90 20np multicolored .75 .70
374 A90 40np bl & multi 1.50 1.40
Nos. 371-374 (4) 2.85 2.60

Inauguration of the 2nd Republic, Oct. 1969.

Cogwheels and ILO Emblem A91

Perf. 14½x14

1970, Jan. 5 Photo. Wmk. 325

375 A91 4np rose red & multi .20 .20
376 A91 12½np multicolored .45 .30
377 A91 20np multicolored .75 .65
a. Souvenir sheet of 3 1.75 1.10
Nos. 375-377 (3) 1.40 1.15

ILO, 50th anniv. No. 377a contains 3 imperf. stamps similar to Nos. 375-377 with simulated perforations.

Nos. 375-377 printed in sheets of 12.

Red Cross Helping Wounded A92

4np, Red Cross & globe, vert. 12½np, Henri Dunant, Red Cross, Red Crescent, Lion & Sun emblems. 40np, Red Cross and first aid.

1970, Feb. 2 *Perf. 14x14½, 14½x14*

378 A92 4np gold & multi .20 .20
379 A92 12½np gold & multi .30 .20
380 A92 20np blue & multi .60 .25
381 A92 40np multicolored 1.25 .50
a. Souvenir sheet of 4 2.25 2.00
Nos. 378-381 (4) 2.35 1.15

League of Red Cross Societies, 50th anniv. No. 381a contains 4 imperf. stamps similar to Nos. 378-381 with simulated perforations.

Kotoka Airport, Gen. Kotoka and VC10 — A93

12½np, Control tower & tail section of VC10. 20np, Bird's eye view of airport and runway. 40np, Flags in front of Kotoka Airport.

Perf. 13x14

1970, Apr. Unwmk. Litho.

382 A93 4np multicolored .20 .20
383 A93 12½np multicolored .35 .20
384 A93 20np multicolored .65 .50
385 A93 40np multicolored 1.25 1.00
Nos. 382-385 (4) 2.45 1.90

Inauguration of Kotoka Airport.

Lunar Landing Module and Spacecraft — A94

Designs: 12½np, Neil A. Armstrong stepping onto the moon. 20np, Scientific experiments on the moon, horiz. 40np, Neil A. Armstrong, Michael Collins and Edwin E. Aldrin, Jr., after return to earth, horiz.

1970, June 15 Litho. *Perf. 12½*

386 A94 4np multicolored .30 .25
387 A94 12½np multicolored 1.50 1.25
388 A94 20np multicolored 1.75 1.50
389 A94 40np multicolored 6.00 5.00
a. Souvenir sheet of 4 9.00 8.00
Nos. 386-389 (4) 9.55 8.00

See note after US No. C76. No. 389a contains 4 imperf. stamps similar to Nos. 386-389. Exists with and without simulated perfs.

Nos. 386-389 and 389a were overprinted "PHILYMPIA/LONDON 1970" in black or silver in Sept. 1970. They are believed not to have been regularly issued.

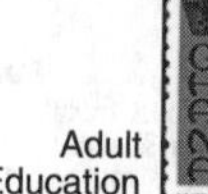

Adult Education A95

Education Year Emblem and: 12½np, Children of various races studying together. 20np, "Ntesie" symbol of wisdom and knowledge. 40np, Nursery school children.

1970, Aug. 10 Litho. *Perf. 13x12½*

390 A95 4np blue & multi .20 .20
391 A95 12½np blue & multi .30 .25
392 A95 20np blue & multi .50 .40
393 A95 40np blue & multi 1.00 .80
Nos. 390-393 (4) 2.00 1.65

Issued for International Education Year.

Inauguration of Second Republic A96

Designs: 12½np, Mace and words of proclamation by K. A. Busia. 20np, Mace and globe with doves. 40np, Opening of Parliament of Second Republic.

1970, Oct. 1 Litho. *Perf. 13*

398 A96 4np multicolored .20 .20
399 A96 12½np multicolored .40 .30
400 A96 20np multicolored .65 .50
401 A96 40np lt bl & multi 1.25 1.10
Nos. 398-401 (4) 2.50 2.10

First anniversary of the Second Republic.

Amaryllis A97

Perf. 14½x14

1970 Photo. Wmk. 325

402 A97 4np shown .20 .20
403 A97 12½np Lioness .30 .20
404 A97 20np African orchid .75 .30
405 A97 40np Elephant 1.50 .75
Nos. 402-405 (4) 2.75 1.45

Kuduo Brass Casket A98

Designs: 12½np, Akan traditional house, Danmum. 20np, Larabanga Mosque. 40np, Akan funerary clay head.

1970, Dec. 7 Litho. *Perf. 14½x14*

406 A98 4np gray & multi .20 .20
407 A98 12½np blue & multi .30 .25
408 A98 20np multicolored .50 .40
a. Souvenir sheet of 4 2.25 2.25
409 A98 40np blue & multi 1.00 .90
Nos. 406-409 (4) 2.00 1.75

No. 408a contains 4 stamps similar to Nos. 406 and 408, a 12½np (Pompeii Basilica) and a 40np (Pompeii scene). Simulated perforation.

Fair Building and Emblem A99

Fair Emblem and: 12½np, Drugstore merchandise. 20np, Automotives and tools. 40np, Cranes and trucks. 50np, Cargo, ship and plane, vert.

Perf. 14½x14, 14x14½

1971, Feb. 5 Photo. Wmk. 325

410 A99 4np multicolored .20 .20
411 A99 12½np lilac & multi .30 .30
412 A99 20np blue & multi .50 .50
413 A99 40np multicolored .90 .90
414 A99 50np multicolored 1.10 1.10
Nos. 410-414 (5) 3.00 3.00

2nd Ghana International Trade Fair, Accra, Feb. 1-14, 1971.

Crucifixion A100

Easter: 12½np, Jesus and disciples. 20np, Resurrection.

Perf. 13½

1971, May 19 Litho. Unwmk.

415 A100 4np multicolored .20 .20
416 A100 12½np multicolored .40 .35
417 A100 20np multicolored .75 .70
Nos. 415-417 (3) 1.35 1.25

Corn and FAO Emblem — A101

Perf. 14x14½

1971, June Wmk. 325 Photo.

418 A101 4np lilac & multi .25 .20
419 A101 12½np lt bl & multi 1.10 .65
420 A101 20np multicolored 2.00 1.25
Nos. 418-420 (3) 3.35 2.10

Freedom from Hunger, second development decade, 1970-1980.

The overprint "In Memoriam / Lord Boyd ORR / 1880-1971" was applied to Nos. 418-420 in October, 1971. The 4np was also surcharged "60NP."

Girl Guide Emblem on Flag of Ghana A102

12½np, Mrs. Elsie Ofuatey-Kodjoe, national founder. 20np, Girl Guides at play. 40np, Campfire and tent. 50np, Girl Guides signalling.

Unwmk.

1971, July 22 Litho. *Perf. 14*

421 A102 4np multicolored .20 .20
422 A102 12½np yel & multi .30 .30
423 A102 20np sal & multi .50 .50
424 A102 40np multicolored 1.00 1.00
425 A102 50np lilac & multi 1.25 1.10
a. Souvenir sheet of 5 3.00 2.75
Nos. 421-425 (5) 3.25 3.10

50th anniversary of the Girl Guides of Ghana. No. 425a contains 5 imperf. stamps similar to Nos. 421-425.

Child Care Center — A103

YWCA Emblem and: 12½np, World Council Meeting and map of Ghana. 20np, Typing class. 40np, Building fund day.

1971, Aug. 5 *Perf. 13*

426 A103 4np multicolored .20 .20
427 A103 12½np ultra & multi .30 .30
428 A103 20np blue & multi .50 .50
429 A103 40np yel & multi .90 .90
a. Souvenir sheet of 4 2.50 2.50
Nos. 426-429 (4) 1.90 1.90

World Council Meeting of Young Women's Christian Association, Accra, Aug. 5. No. 429a contains 4 stamps similar to Nos. 426-429 with simulated perforations.

African Nativity Scene A104

Christmas: 1np, Fireworks, vert. 6np, Flight into Egypt.

Perf. 14x14½, 14½x14

1971, Nov. Photo. Wmk. 325

433 A104 1np multicolored .20 .20
434 A104 3np orange & multi .20 .20
435 A104 6np blue & multi .20 .20
Nos. 433-435 (3) .60 .60

UNICEF Emblem, and Child A105

UNICEF Emblem and: 5np, Infant weighed in net scale, vert. 30np, Student midwife, vert. 50np, Boy in day care center.

Perf. 13½x13, 13x13½

1971, Dec. 20 Litho. Unwmk.

436 A105 5np grn & multi .20 .20
437 A105 15np yel & multi .45 .40
438 A105 30np pink & multi .85 .70
439 A105 50np blue & multi 1.60 1.50
a. Souvenir sheet of 4 4.00 4.00
Nos. 436-439 (4) 3.10 2.80

25th anniv. of UNICEF. No. 439a contains 4 stamps with simulated perforations similar to Nos. 436-439.

Fair Emblem, Map of Africa, Symbol of Unity A106

Fair Emblem and: 15np, Horn of Plenty. 30np, Fireworks over Africa. 60np, 1nc, Names of participating nations over map of Africa.

1972, Feb. 23 Litho. *Perf. 14*

440 A106 5np lt brn & multi .20 .20
441 A106 15np lt bl & multi .65 .50
442 A106 30np green & multi 1.40 1.25
443 A106 60np yel & multi 2.00 1.90
444 A106 1nc lt bl & multi 3.50 3.25
Nos. 440-444 (5) 7.75 7.10

First All-Africa Trade Fair, Nairobi, Kenya, Feb. 23-Mar. 5.

Nos. 440-444 were overprinted "BELGICA 72" in red for release June 24, 1972. The regularity of this issue has been questioned.

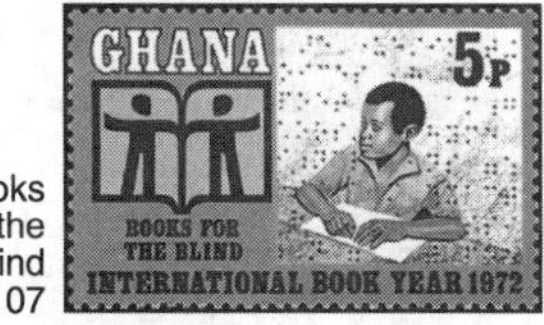

Books for the Blind A107

Book and Flame of Knowledge A108

Book Year Emblem and: 15p, Books for Children ("Anansi and Snake the Postman"). 30p, Books for Recreation (Accra Central Library). 50p, Books for Students (2 students).

1972, Apr. 21 *Perf. 13½*

445 A107 5p blue & multi .20 .20
446 A107 15p yel & multi .35 .35
447 A107 30p lilac & multi .75 .75
448 A107 50p green & multi 1.10 1.10
449 A108 1ce blue & multi 1.75 1.75
a. Souvenir sheet of 5 5.00 5.00
Nos. 445-449 (5) 4.15 4.15

Intl. Book Year. No. 449a contains one each of Nos. 445-449 with simulated perforations.

Star Grass A109

1972, July 3 Litho. *Perf. 13½*

450 A109 5p shown .20 .20
451 A109 15p Mona monkey .50 .30
452 A109 30p Amaryllis 1.50 .60
453 A109 1ce Side-striped squirrel 4.50 2.00
Nos. 450-453 (4) 6.70 3.10

Olympic Emblems, Soccer A110

1972, Sept. 5 Litho. *Perf. 13½x13*

454 A110 5p shown .20 .20
455 A110 15p Running .25 .20
456 A110 30p Boxing .50 .35
457 A110 50p Long jump .80 .65
458 A110 1ce High jump 1.75 1.50
Nos. 454-458 (5) 3.50 2.90

Souvenir Sheet

459 Sheet of 2 3.00 1.60
a. A110 40p like 30p .45 .30
b. A110 60p like 5p .70 .50

20th Olympic Games, Munich, 8/26-9/11.

Senior and Cub Scouts, Badge A111

Designs: 15p, Scout in front of tent. 30p, 40p, Sea Scouts in canoe. 50p, Cub Scouts with den mother. 60p, 1ce, Scouts studying.

1972, Oct. Litho. *Perf. 14*

460 A111 5p blue grn & multi .20 .20
461 A111 15p ocher & multi .50 .40
462 A111 30p lilac & multi 1.00 .75
463 A111 50p multicolored 1.60 1.25
464 A111 1ce blue & multi 3.00 2.50
Nos. 460-464 (5) 6.30 5.10

Souvenir Sheet

Perf. 13½

465 Sheet of 2 3.75 3.75
a. A111 40p brown & multi .60 .40
b. A111 60p green & multi .90 .55

Boy Scout Movement, 65th anniversary. For overprints see Nos. 484-489.

Virgin and Child, by Holbein the Younger — A112

Paintings: 1p, Holy Night, by Correggio. 15p, Virgin and Child, by Andrea Rico. 30p, Melchior. 60p, Virgin and Child with Caspar. 1ce, Balthasar. 30p, 60p, 1ce, are from early 16th century stained glass windows.

1972, Dec. 2 *Perf. 14x13½*

466 A112 1p black & multi .20 .20
467 A112 3p black & multi .20 .20
468 A112 15p black & multi .30 .20
469 A112 30p black & multi .55 .45
470 A112 60p black & multi 1.25 .90
471 A112 1ce black & multi 2.25 1.50
a. Souvenir sheet of 3 5.00 4.00
Nos. 466-471 (6) 4.75 3.45

Christmas. No. 471a contains one each of Nos. 469-471 with simulated perforations.

Market A113

Designs: 1p, Unity Declaration at Kumasi Durbar. 5p, Woman with child selling bananas, vert. 15p, Farmer at rest and produce, vert. 30p, Market. 40p, 1ce, Farmer cutting palm nuts with cutlass. 60p, Miners.

Perf. 14x13½, 13½x14

1973, Apr. Litho.

472 A113 1p multicolored .20 .20
473 A113 3p multicolored .20 .20
474 A113 5p multicolored .20 .20
475 A113 15p multicolored .30 .20
476 A113 30p multicolored .50 .45
477 A113 1ce multicolored 1.60 1.50
Nos. 472-477 (6) 3.00 2.75

Souvenir Sheet

478 Sheet of 2 2.25 2.00
a. A113 40p multicolored .60 .40
b. A113 60p multicolored .90 .55

Operation "Feed Yourself" and for 1st anniv. of the Oct. 13 Revolution.

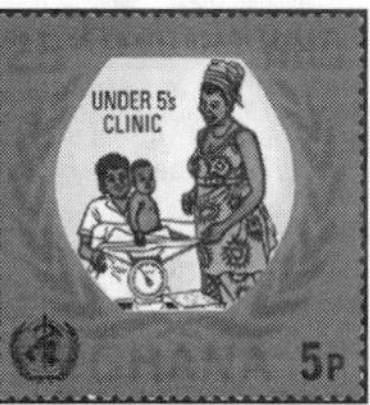

Children's Clinic — A114

WHO Emblem and: 15p, Radiology. 30p, Immunization. 50p, Fight against malnutrition (starving child). 1ce, WHO Headquarters, Geneva.

1973, July *Perf. 14x13½*

479 A114 5p rose red & multi .20 .20
480 A114 15p blue & multi .20 .20
481 A114 30p bister & multi .40 .35
482 A114 50p green & multi .65 .60
483 A114 1ce multicolored 1.25 1.10
Nos. 479-483 (5) 2.70 2.45

WHO, 25th anniversary.

Nos. 460-465 Overprinted: "1st WORLD SCOUTING CONFERENCE IN AFRICA"

1973, July Litho. *Perf. 14*

484 A111 5p green & multi .20 .20
485 A111 15p ocher & multi .25 .25
486 A111 30p lilac & multi .55 .50
487 A111 50p multicolored .90 .80
488 A111 1ce blue & multi 1.90 1.60
Nos. 484-488 (5) 3.80 3.35

Souvenir Sheet

Perf. 13½

489 Sheet of 2 3.50 3.25
a. A111 40p brown & multi 1.00 .70
b. A111 60p green & multi 1.50 1.00

24th Boy Scout World Conference (1st in Africa), Nairobi, Kenya, July 16-21.

Poultry Farming A115

FAO/UN Emblem and: 15p, 40p, Tractor. 50p, Cacao harvest. 60p, 1ce, FAO Headquarters, Rome.

1973 Litho. *Perf. 14½x14*

490 A115 5p blue & multi .20 .20
491 A115 15p blue & multi .50 .45
492 A115 50p blue & multi 1.50 1.40
493 A115 1ce blue & multi 3.00 2.75
Nos. 490-493 (4) 5.20 4.80

Souvenir Sheet

494 Sheet of 2 3.00 2.75
a. A115 40p blue & multi .80 .50
b. A115 60p blue & multi 1.25 .75

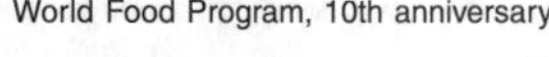
World Food Program, 10th anniversary.

INTERPOL Emblem, Observer A116

INTERPOL Emblem and: 30p, Judge's wig, poison bottle, handcuffs. 50p, photograph and fingerprint. 1ce, Corpse and question mark.

1973 *Perf. 13x13½*

495 A116 5p emerald & multi .20 .20
496 A116 30p rose red & multi .75 .60
497 A116 50p ultra & multi 1.10 .90
498 A116 1ce gray & multi 2.50 2.00
Nos. 495-498 (4) 4.55 3.70

50th anniv. the Intl. Criminal Police Org. (INTERPOL).

Handclasp and "OAU" A117

"OAU" and: 30p, Africa Hall, Addis Ababa. 50p, OAU emblem (map of Africa). 1ce, "X" in Ghana flag colors.

1973, Oct. 22 Litho. *Perf. 14x14½*

499 A117 5p lt bl, blk & brn .20 .20
500 A117 30p bluish grn, blk & brn .40 .40
501 A117 50p pink, black & ol .65 .60
502 A117 1ce multicolored 1.50 1.25
Nos. 499-502 (4) 2.75 2.45

Org. for African Unity, 10th anniv.

Weather Balloon, WMO Emblem A118

WMO Emblem and: 15p, 40p, Tiros weather satellite. 30p, 60p, Computer weather map. 1ce, Radar cloud scanner.

1973, Nov. 16

503 A118 5p multicolored .20 .20
504 A118 15p multicolored .30 .25
505 A118 30p multicolored .60 .50
506 A118 1ce multicolored 1.75 1.50
Nos. 503-506 (4) 2.85 2.45

Souvenir Sheet

507 Sheet of 2 2.50 2.25
a. A118 40p multicolored .75 .40
b. A118 60p multicolored 1.10 .60

Intl. meteorological cooperation, cent. #507 exists imperf.

Adoration of the Kings — A119

Christmas: 3p, 40p, Madonna and Child (contemporary). Nos. 510, 511d, Madonna and Child, by Murillo. No. 511, 60p, Adoration of the Kings, by Tiepolo. No. 511b as 1p.

1973, Dec. 10 *Perf. 14*

508 A119 1p black & multi .20 .20
509 A119 3p gray & multi .20 .20
510 A119 30p multicolored .85 .85
511 A119 50p multicolored 1.75 1.75
Nos. 508-511 (4) 3.00 3.00

Souvenir Sheet

Imperf

511A Sheet of 4 2.75 2.75
b. A119 30p black & multi .45 .45
c. A119 40p gray & multi .60 .60
d. A119 50p multicolored .75 .75
e. A119 60p multicolored .90 .90

No. 511A has simulated perforations.

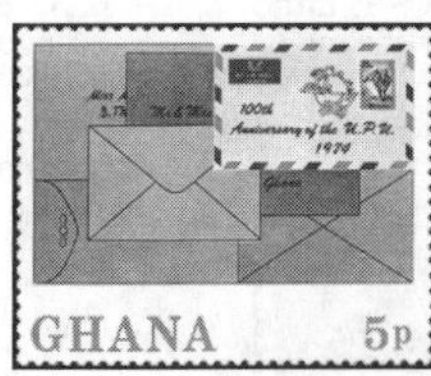

Various Envelopes A120

UPU Emblem and: 9p, 30p, UPU Headquarters, Bern. 40p, 50p, Airmail envelope with Ghana No. 296. 60p, 1ce, Ghana No. 296.

1974, May Litho. *Perf. 14½*

512 A120 5p blue, blk & org .20 .20
513 A120 9p blue, blk & org .20 .20
514 A120 30p blue, blk & org .60 .50
515 A120 1ce blue, blk & org 1.25 1.10
Nos. 512-515 (4) 2.25 2.00

Souvenir Sheet

515A Sheet of 4 2.00 1.75
b. A120 20p blue, blk & org .20 .20
c. A120 30p blue, blk & org .30 .30
d. A120 40p blue, blk & org .50 .50
e. A120 50p blue, blk & org .60 .60

Centenary of Universal Postal Union. For overprints see Nos. 521-524A.

The Betrayal — A121

Designs: 5p, 15p, Jesus Carrying Cross, painting by Thomas de Coloswar, 1427. 20p, 30p, The Betrayal. 25p, 50p, The Deposition. 40p, 1ce, Risen Christ and Mary Magdalene. The designs (except 5p, 15p) are from 15th century English ivory carvings.

1974, Apr. Litho. *Perf. 14*

516 A121 5p black & multi .20 .20
517 A121 30p sil, ultra & brn .45 .45
518 A121 50p sil, red & brn .75 .75
519 A121 1ce silver, ol & brn 1.60 1.60
Nos. 516-519 (4) 3.00 3.00

Souvenir Sheet

Imperf

520 Sheet of 4 1.60 1.60
a. A121 15p black & multi .20
b. A121 20p silver, ultra & brn .30
c. A121 25p silver, red & brn .40
d. A121 40p silver, olive & brn .60

Easter. No. 520 contains 4 stamps with simulated perforations.

Nos. 512-515A Overprinted "INTERNABA 1974"

1974, June 7 *Perf. 14½*

521 A120 5p blue, blk & org .20 .20
522 A120 9p blue, blk & org .25 .20
523 A120 50p blue, blk & org .80 .80
524 A120 1ce blue, blk & org 1.75 1.60
Nos. 521-524 (4) 3.00 2.80

Souvenir Sheet

524A Sheet of 4 2.50 2.25
b. A120 20p blue, blk & org .20 .20
c. A120 30p blue, blk & org .35 .35
d. A120 40p blue, blk & org .50 .50
e. A120 60p blue, blk & org .60 .60

INTERNABA 1974 International Philatelic Exhibition, Basel, June 7-16.
Overprint is applied to individual stamps of No. 524A.

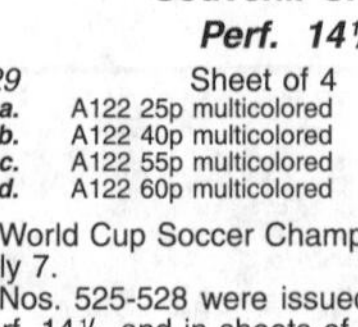

Soccer and World Cup Emblem A122

Designs: Various soccer scenes and world cup emblem.

1974, June 17 Litho. *Perf. 14½, 13*

525 A122 5p multicolored .20 .20
526 A122 30p multicolored .35 .35
527 A122 50p multicolored .60 .60
528 A122 1ce multicolored 1.10 1.10
Nos. 525-528 (4) 2.25 2.25

Souvenir Sheet

Perf. 14½

529 Sheet of 4 2.50 2.50
a. A122 25p multicolored .25
b. A122 40p multicolored .40
c. A122 55p multicolored .60
d. A122 60p multicolored .70

World Cup Soccer Championship, June 13-July 7.
Nos. 525-528 were issued in sheets of 30, perf. 14½, and in sheets of 5 plus label, perf. 13.
For overprints, see Nos. 535-539, 549-553.

Traffic Diagram at Traffic Circle A123

Designs: 15p, Traffic sign "Two-way traffic." 30p, "Change to right hand drive!," vert. 50p, Warning hands sign, vert. 1ce, 2 hands and car symbolizing traffic change, vert.

1974, July 16 *Perf. 13½*

Size: 35x28½mm

530 A123 5p yel grn, red & blk .20 .20
531 A123 15p lilac, red & blk .20 .20

Size: 28½x41mm

Perf. 14½

532 A123 30p multicolored .35 .35
533 A123 50p multicolored .60 .60
534 A123 1ce red, green & blk 1.40 1.40
Nos. 530-534 (5) 2.75 2.75

Publicity for change to right-hand driving, Aug. 4, 1974.

Nos. 525-529 Overprinted: "WEST GERMANY WINNERS"

1974, Aug. 30 Litho. *Perf. 14½, 13*

535 A122 5p multicolored .20 .20
536 A122 30p multicolored .45 .45
537 A122 50p multicolored .75 .75
538 A122 1ce multicolored 1.40 1.40
Nos. 535-538 (4) 2.80 2.80

Souvenir Sheet

539 Sheet of 4 2.50 2.10
a. A122 25p multicolored .25
b. A122 40p multicolored .45
c. A122 55p multicolored .60
d. A122 60p multicolored .65

World Cup Soccer Championship, 1974, victory of German Federal Republic. Overprint is applied to individual stamps of No. 539.

Family and WPY Emblem A124

1974, Sept. 27 *Perf. 12½*

540 A124 5p shown .20 .20
541 A124 30p Clinic .35 .30
542 A124 50p Immunization of children .55 .50
543 A124 1ce Census 1.10 1.10
Nos. 540-543 (4) 2.20 2.10

World Population Year.

Angel — A125 Nativity — A127

Three Kings, Candles — A126

Design: 60p, 1ce, Annunciation.

Perf. 13½, 14 (7p)

1974, Dec. 19 Litho.

544 A125 5p red & multi .20 .20
545 A126 7p blue & multi .20 .20
546 A127 9p orange & multi .20 .20
547 A127 1ce orange & multi 2.50 2.50
Nos. 544-547 (4) 3.10 3.10

Souvenir Sheet

Imperf

548 Sheet of 4 2.75 2.75
a. A125 15p red & multi .20
b. A126 30p blue & multi .45
c. A127 45p orange & multi .70
d. A127 60p orange & multi .90

Christmas. No. 548 contains 4 stamps with simulated perforations.

Nos. 525-529 Overprinted "APOLLO / SOYUZ / JULY 15, 1975"

1975, Aug. 15 Litho. *Perf. 14½, 13*

549 A122 5p multicolored .20 .20
550 A122 30p multicolored .35 .30
551 A122 50p multicolored .65 .50
552 A122 1ce multicolored 1.25 1.00
Nos. 549-552 (4) 2.45 2.00

Souvenir Sheet

Perf. 14½

553 Sheet of 4 2.40 2.40
a. A122 25p multicolored .25
b. A122 40p multicolored .40
c. A122 55p multicolored .60
d. A122 60p multicolored .65

Apollo Soyuz space test project (Russo-American cooperation), launching July 15, link-up, July 17.
Overprint is applied to individual stamps of No. 553.
Nos. 549-552 with perf. 13 are from the sheets of 5 plus label.

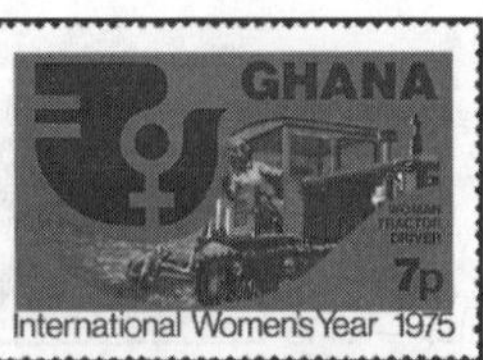

IWY Emblem, Woman Tractor Driver — A128

Intl. Women's Year Emblem and: 15p, like 7p. 30p, 40p, Automobile mechanic. 60p, 65p, Factory workers. 80p, 1ce, Cocoa research.

1975, Sept. 3 Litho. *Perf. 14*

554 A128 7p multicolored .20 .20
555 A128 30p lt violet & multi .50 .50
556 A128 60p multicolored 1.00 1.00
557 A128 1ce lilac & multi 1.60 1.60
Nos. 554-557 (4) 3.30 3.30

Souvenir Sheet

Imperf

558 Sheet of 4 3.50 3.50
a. A128 15p Prus green & multi .20
b. A128 40p light violet & multi .55
c. A128 65p dull green & multi .90
d. A128 80p lilac & multi 1.10

Intl. Women's Year. No. 558 contains 4 stamps with simulated perforations.

Angel over Child in Crib A129

Angel with Harp A130

Designs: 7p, 40p, Angels with lute and bell. 30p, 65p, Angel with viol. 1ce, 80p, Angels with trumpets. 15p, like 5p.

1975, Dec. 31 Litho. ***Perf. 14x13½***
559 A129 2p org & multi .20 .20
560 A130 5p yel, brown & grn .20 .20
561 A130 7p yel, brown & grn .20 .20
562 A130 30p yel, brown & grn .30 .20
563 A130 1ce yel, brown & grn 1.00 .65
Nos. 559-563 (5) 1.90 1.45

Souvenir Sheet

Imperf

564 Sheet of 4 2.25 2.25
a. A130 15p yellow, green & brown .20
b. A130 40p yellow, green & brown .20
c. A130 65p yellow, green & brown .70
d. A130 80p yellow, green & brown .80

Christmas. No. 564 has simulated perforations.

Boy Scouts Reading Map — A131

30p, 40p, Sailing. 60p, 65p, Hiking. 80p, 1ce, Life saving (swimmers). 15p, like 7p.

1976, Jan. 5 ***Perf. 13½x14***
565 A131 7p ocher & multi .20 .20
566 A131 30p blue & multi .65 .25
567 A131 60p green & multi 1.40 .55
568 A131 1ce multicolored 2.25 1.10
Nos. 565-568 (4) 4.50 2.10

Souvenir Sheet

569 Sheet of 4 4.00 4.00
a. A131 15p ocher & multi .25
b. A131 40p blue & multi .65
c. A131 65p green & multi 1.10
d. A131 80p rose claret & multi 1.25

Nordjamb 75, 14th World Boy Scout Jamboree, Lillehammer, Norway, July 29-Aug. 7.
For overprints, see Nos. 578-582.

1¾ Pints Equal 1 Liter A132

Map of Ghana and: 30p, "2¼ lbs of jam a little more than a kilogram." 60p, "A meter of cloth will be a little more than 3 foot 3." 1ce, Thermometer, ice and boiling tea kettle.

1976, Jan. 5 Litho. ***Perf. 14x13½***
570 A132 7p bluish gray & blk .20 .20
571 A132 30p vio blue & multi .45 .25
572 A132 60p ocher & multi .85 .45
573 A132 1ce multicolored 1.50 .90
Nos. 570-573 (4) 3.00 1.80

Introduction of metric system, Sept. 1975.

Fair Grounds — A133

Designs: Various exhibition halls.

1976, Apr. 6 Litho. ***Perf. 14***
574 A133 7p multicolored .20 .20
575 A133 30p yellow & multi .45 .20
576 A133 60p multicolored .85 .45
577 A133 1ce salmon & multi 1.50 .90
Nos. 574-577 (4) 3.00 1.75

International Trade Fair, Accra, Feb. 1-15.

Nos. 565-569 Overprinted in Violet Blue: 'INTERPHIL' 76 BICENTENNIAL EXHIBITION

1976, May 29 Litho. ***Perf. 13½x14***
578 A131 7p ocher & multi .20 .20
579 A131 30p blue & multi .50 .20
580 A131 60p green & multi 1.00 .40
581 A131 1ce multicolored 1.40 .80
Nos. 578-581 (4) 3.10 1.60

Souvenir Sheet

582 Sheet of 4 3.25 2.00
a. A131 15p ocher & multi .20
b. A131 40p blue & multi .60
c. A131 65p green & multi 1.00
d. A131 80p rose claret & multi 1.10

Interphil 76 International Philatelic Exhibition, Philadelphia, Pa., May 29-June 6. Overprint applied to individual stamps of No. 582.

Shot Put — A134

Olympic Rings, Map of Ghana and: 15p, like 7p. 30p, 40p, Soccer. 60p, 65p, Women's 1500 meters. 80p, 1ce, Boxing.

1976, Aug. 9 Litho. ***Perf. 14x13½***
583 A134 7p lt blue & multi .20 .20
584 A134 30p yellow & multi .30 .20
585 A134 60p multicolored .65 .30
586 A134 1ce yellow & multi 1.10 .65
Nos. 583-586 (4) 2.25 1.35

Souvenir Sheet

587 Sheet of 4 2.25 2.25
a. A134 15p light blue & multi .20
b. A134 40p yellow & multi .40
c. A134 65p emerald & multi .65
d. A134 80p yellow & multi .80

21st Olympic Games, Montreal, Canada, July 17-Aug. 1.
For overprints see Nos. 606-610.

Supreme Court, Accra A135

Designs: Various views of Supreme Court Building, Scales of Justice, law book.

1976, Sept. 7 Litho. ***Perf. 14***
588 A135 8p lilac & multi .20 .20
589 A135 30p blue & multi .35 .35
590 A135 60p ver & multi .65 .65
591 A135 1ce multicolored 1.10 1.10
Nos. 588-591 (4) 2.30 2.30

Ghana Supreme Court, centenary.

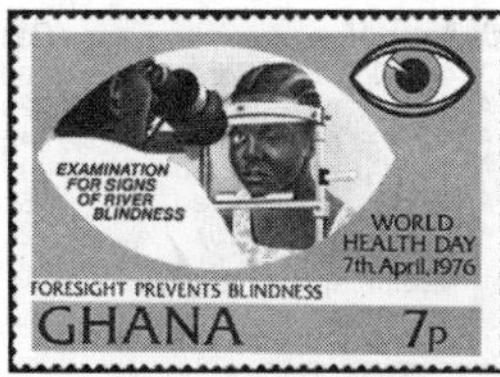

Examination for River Blindness — A136

Designs: 30p, Ghanaian entomologist with microscope. 60p, Flowers. 1ce, Boatmen checking effectiveness of black fly larvae insecticide.

1976, Oct. 28 Litho. ***Perf. 14½x14***
592 A136 7p multicolored .20 .20
593 A136 30p multicolored .50 .50
594 A136 60p multicolored 1.00 1.00
595 A136 1ce multicolored 1.75 1.75
Nos. 592-595 (4) 3.45 3.45

World Health Day. Prevention of blindness.

Children with Gifts and Christmas Tree — A137

Designs: 6p, 15p, Children with firecrackers. 30p, 65p, Family at Christmas dinner. 40p, 80p, 1ce, like 8p.

1976, Dec. 15 Litho. ***Perf. 13½***
596 A137 6p multicolored .20 .20
597 A137 8p multicolored .20 .20
598 A137 30p multicolored .55 .55
599 A137 1ce multicolored 1.75 1.75
Nos. 596-599 (4) 2.70 2.70

Souvenir Sheet

Imperf

600 Sheet of 4 3.25 3.25
a. A137 15p multicolored .20
b. A137 40p multicolored .55
c. A137 65p multicolored .90
d. A137 80p multicolored 1.10

Christmas. No. 600 has simulated perfs.

1876 Gallows Frame Telephone and A. G. Bell — A138

A. G. Bell and: 15p, like 8p. 30p, 40p, 1895 telephone. 60p, 65p, 1929 telephone. 80p, 1ce, 1976 telephone.

1976, Dec. 17 ***Perf. 14½***
601 A138 8p multicolored .20 .20
602 A138 30p multicolored .45 .20
603 A138 60p multicolored 1.00 .45
604 A138 1ce multicolored 1.60 .80
Nos. 601-604 (4) 3.25 1.65

Souvenir Sheet

Perf. 13

605 Sheet of 4 3.00 3.00
a. A138 15p multicolored .20
b. A138 40p multicolored .50
c. A138 65p multicolored .85
d. A138 80p multicolored 1.00

Centenary of first telephone call by Alexander Graham Bell, Mar. 10, 1876.
For overprints, see Nos. 616-620.

Nos. 583-587 Overprinted:
a. EAST GERMANY / WINNERS
b. U.S.S.R. WINNERS
c. U.S.A. WINNERS

1977, Feb. 22 Litho. ***Perf. 14x13½***
606 A134(a) 7p multicolored .20 .20
607 A134(a) 30p multicolored .30 .20
608 A134(b) 60p multicolored .65 .30
609 A134(c) 1ce multicolored 1.40 .55
Nos. 606-609 (4) 2.55 1.25

Souvenir Sheet

610 Sheet of 4 3.25 2.25
a. A134(a) 15p multicolored .30
b. A134(a) 40p multicolored .70
c. A134(b) 65p multicolored 1.00
d. A134(c) 80p multicolored 1.10

1976 Montreal Olympic Games' winners.

Klama Dance, Dipo Tribe — A139

Festival Emblem and: 15p, like 8p. 30p, 40p, African artifacts. 60p, 65p, Acon dance. 80p, 1ce, Mud, straw and wooden huts.

1977, Mar. 24 Litho. ***Perf. 14x13½***
611 A139 8p multicolored .20 .20
612 A139 30p multicolored .55 .25
613 A139 60p multicolored 1.25 .45
614 A139 1ce multicolored 2.00 .75
Nos. 611-614 (4) 4.00 1.65

Souvenir Sheet

615 Sheet of 4 3.50 2.50
a. A139 15p multicolored .35
b. A139 40p multicolored .75
c. A139 65p multicolored 1.10
d. A139 80p multicolored 1.25

2nd World Black and African Festival of Arts and Culture, Lagos, Nigeria, Jan. 15-Feb. 12.

Nos. 601-605 Overprinted: "PRINCE CHARLES / VISITS GHANA / 17th TO 25th / MARCH, 1977"

1977, June 2 Litho. ***Perf. 14½***
616 A138 8p multicolored .20 .20
617 A138 30p multicolored .40 .20
618 A138 60p multicolored .90 .35
619 A138 1ce multicolored 1.40 .60
Nos. 616-619 (4) 2.90 1.35

Souvenir Sheet

Perf. 13

620 Sheet of 4 3.50 2.50
a. A138 15p multicolored .35
b. A138 40p multicolored .75
c. A138 65p multicolored 1.10
d. A138 80p multicolored 1.25

Visit of Prince Charles, Mar. 17-25. Overprint applied to individual stamps of No. 620.

Olive Colobus — A140

Wildlife Fund Emblem and: 15p, like 8p. 20p, 40p, Ebien palm squirrel. 30p, 65p, African wild dog. 60p, 80p, West African manatee.

1977, June 22 Litho. ***Perf. 13½x14***
621 A140 8p multicolored *2.25 .20*
622 A140 20p multicolored *6.50 .25*
623 A140 30p multicolored *7.75 .40*
624 A140 60p multicolored *13.50 .80*
Nos. 621-624 (4) *30.00 1.65*

Souvenir Sheet

625 Sheet of 4 13.00 2.50
a. A140 15p multicolored 1.25
b. A140 40p multicolored 2.75
c. A140 65p multicolored 4.00
d. A140 80p multicolored 4.75

Wildlife protection.

Suzanne Fourment in Velvet Hat, by Rubens — A141

Paintings: 15p, like 8p. 30p, 40p, Isabella of Portugal, by Titian. 60p, 65p, Duke and Duchess of Cumberland, by Gainsborough. 80p, 1ce, Rubens and his wife Isabella, by Rubens.

1977, Sept. Litho. *Perf. 14x13½*

626 A141 8p lt blue & multi .20 .20
627 A141 30p lt blue & multi .55 .55
628 A141 60p lt blue & multi 1.10 1.10
629 A141 1ce lt blue & multi 1.75 1.75
Nos. 626-629 (4) 3.60 3.60

Souvenir Sheet

630 Sheet of 4 4.00 4.00
a. A141 15p light blue & multi .25
b. A141 40p light blue & multi .75
c. A141 65p light blue & multi 1.25
d. A141 80p light blue & multi 1.50

Painters, birth annivs.: Peter Paul Rubens (1577-1640); Titian (1477-1576); Thomas Gainsborough (1727-1788).

Adoration of the Kings — A142

Guild of the Good Shepherd, Abossey Okai — A143

Designs: 6p, 40p, Methodist Church, Wesley, Accra. 8p, Virgin and Child, and Star. 15p, like 2p. 30p, 65p, Holy Spirit Cathedral, Accra. 80p, 1ce, Ebenezer Presbyterian Church, Osu, Accra. Type A143 designs include score of "Hark the Herald Angels Sing."

Perf. 14x14½, 14

1977, Dec. 30 Litho.

631 A142 1p multicolored .20 .20
632 A143 2p multicolored .20 .20
633 A143 6p multicolored .20 .20
634 A142 8p multicolored .20 .20
635 A143 30p multicolored .45 .25
636 A143 1ce multicolored 1.60 .80
Nos. 631-636 (6) 2.85 1.85

Souvenir Sheet

Imperf

637 Sheet of 4 3.75 3.75
a. A143 15p multicolored .25
b. A143 40p multicolored .65
c. A143 65p multicolored 1.00
d. A143 80p multicolored 1.40

Christmas. No. 637 has simulated perfs.

No. 631-637 Overprinted: "REFERENDUM 1978 VOTE EARLY"

Perf. 14x14½, 14

1978, Mar. 28 Litho.

638 A142 1p multicolored .20 .20
639 A143 2p multicolored .20 .20
640 A143 6p multicolored .20 .20
641 A142 8p multicolored .20 .20
642 A143 30p multicolored .45 .25
643 A143 1ce multicolored 1.60 .80
Nos. 638-643 (6) 2.85 1.85

Souvenir Sheet

Imperf

644 Sheet of 4 *30.00*
a. A143 15p multicolored *1.50*
b. A143 40p multicolored *3.75*
c. A143 65p multicolored *6.00*
d. A143 80p multicolored *7.50*

Banana Harvest — A144

Designs: 8p, Vegetable garden. 30p, Produce market. 60p, Fishing. 1ce, Tractor.

1978, May 15 *Perf. 14*

645 A144 2p multicolored .20 .20
646 A144 8p multicolored .20 .20
647 A144 30p multicolored .45 .20
648 A144 60p multicolored .90 .45
649 A144 1ce multicolored 1.50 .75
Nos. 645-649 (5) 3.25 1.80

Operation feed yourself.

Wright Biplane and Crowd — A145

Planes and Crowd: 15p, like 8p. 30p, 40p, Heracles, 1st practical airliner. 60p, 65p, D. H. Comet, 1st jet airliner. 80p, 1ce, Concorde, 1st supersonic airliner.

1978, June 6 Litho. *Perf. 14x13½*

650 A145 8p multicolored .20 .20
651 A145 30p multicolored .45 .20
652 A145 60p multicolored .85 .45
653 A145 1ce multicolored 1.50 .75
Nos. 650-653 (4) 3.00 1.60

Souvenir Sheet

654 Sheet of 4 3.00 3.00
a. A145 15p multicolored .20
b. A145 40p multicolored .60
c. A145 65p multicolored 1.00
d. A145 80p multicolored 1.10

75th anniversary of first powered flight. The cheering crowd forms a continuing design on Nos. 650-654.

Nos. 650-653, 654a-654d Overprinted: "CAPEX 78 / JUNE 9-18 1978"

1978, June 9

655 A145 8p multicolored .20 .20
656 A145 30p multicolored .50 .25
657 A145 60p multicolored 1.00 .50
658 A145 1ce multicolored 1.60 .80
Nos. 655-658 (4) 3.30 1.75

Souvenir Sheet

659 Sheet of 4 3.00 3.00
a. A145 15p multicolored .20
b. A145 40p multicolored .60
c. A145 65p multicolored .90
d. A145 80p multicolored 1.10

CAPEX, Canadian International Philatelic Exhibition, Toronto, Ont., June 9-18.

Soccer, Africa Cup Emblem and Ghana Flag — A146

15p, like 8p. 30p, 40p, Three soccer players, Africa Cup emblem, Ghana flag. 60p, 65p, Two soccer players. Argentina '78 emblem, Argentine flag. 80p, 1ce, Goalkeeper, Argentina '78 emblem and Argentine flag.

1978, July 1 Litho. *Perf. 13½x14*

660 A146 8p multicolored .20 .20
661 A146 30p multicolored .45 .20
662 A146 60p multicolored .85 .45
663 A146 1ce multicolored 1.40 .75
Nos. 660-663 (4) 2.90 1.60

Souvenir Sheet

664 Sheet of 4 2.40 2.40
a. A146 15p multicolored .20
b. A146 40p multicolored .50
c. A146 65p multicolored .70
d. A146 80p multicolored .90

11th African Cup of Nations, Ghana, Mar. 5-19, and 11th World Cup Soccer Championship, Argentina, June 1-25.

Nos. 660-661, 664a-664b Overprinted: "GHANA WINNERS"

Nos. 662-663, 664c-664d Overprinted: "ARGENTINA WINS"

1978, Aug. 21 Litho. *Perf. 13½x14*

665 A146 8p multicolored .20 .20
666 A146 30p multicolored .40 .20
667 A146 60p multicolored .80 .40
668 A146 1ce multicolored 1.40 .65
Nos. 665-668 (4) 2.80 1.45

Souvenir Sheet

669 Sheet of 4 2.00 2.00
a. A146 15p multicolored .20
b. A146 40p multicolored .40
c. A146 65p multicolored .60
d. A146 80p multicolored .70

Winners, 11th African Cup and 11th World Cup Soccer Championships.
Overprint on 60p and 65p is in two lines.

The Betrayal, by Dürer — A147

Etchings by Albrecht Dürer: 39p, The Crucifixion. 60p, The Deposition. 1ce, The Resurrection.

1978, Sept. 1 Litho. *Perf. 14x13½*

670 A147 11p lilac & black .20 .20
671 A147 39p salmon & black .30 .30
672 A147 60p orange & black .40 .40
673 A147 1ce yel green & black .65 .65
Nos. 670-673 (4) 1.55 1.55

Easter.

Bauhinia Purpurea A148

Flowers: 39p, Cassia fistula. 60p, Frangipani. 1ce, Jacaranda mimosifolia.

1978, Nov. 20 Litho. *Perf. 14x13½*

674 A148 11p multicolored .20 .20
675 A148 39p multicolored .25 .20
676 A148 60p multicolored .50 .30
677 A148 1ce multicolored .75 .50
Nos. 674-677 (4) 1.70 1.20

Mail Railroad Car — A149

Ghana railroad, 75th Anniv.: 39p, Pay and bank car. 60p, Locomotive, 1922. 1ce, Diesel locomotive, 1960.

1978, Dec. 4 Litho. *Perf. 13½*

678 A149 11p multicolored .20 .20
679 A149 39p multicolored .50 .40
680 A149 60p multicolored 1.00 .60
681 A149 1ce multicolored 1.50 1.00
Nos. 678-681 (4) 3.20 2.20

Orbiter Spacecraft — A150

15p, like 11p. 39p, 40p, Multiprobe spacecraft. 60p, 65p, Orbiter and Multiprobe circling Venus. 2ce, 3ce, Radar chart of Venus.

1979, July 5 Litho. *Perf. 14x13½*

682 A150 11p multicolored .20 .20
683 A150 39p multicolored .30 .30
684 A150 60p multicolored .45 .45
685 A150 3ce multicolored 2.40 2.40
Nos. 682-685 (4) 3.35 3.35

Souvenir Sheet

Imperf

686 Sheet of 4 3.00 3.00
a. A150 15p multicolored .20
b. A150 40p multicolored .35
c. A150 65p multicolored .60
d. A150 2ce multicolored 1.90

Pioneer Venus Space Project.

O Come All Ye Faithful A152

Christmas Carols: 10p, O Little Town of Bethlehem. 15p, 65p, We Three Kings of Orient Are. 20p, I Saw Three Ships Come Sailing By. 25p, like 8p. No. 696, 1ce, Away in a Manger. 4ce, No. 698d, Ding Dong Merrily on High.

1979, Dec. 20 *Perf. 14½*

692 A152 8p multicolored .20 .20
693 A152 10p multicolored .20 .20
694 A152 15p multicolored .20 .20
695 A152 20p multicolored .20 .20
696 A152 2ce multicolored .75 .35
697 A152 4ce multicolored 1.25 .65
Nos. 692-697 (6) 2.80 1.80

Souvenir Sheet

698 Sheet of 4 2.50 1.25
a. A152 25p multicolored .20 .20
b. A152 65p multicolored .35 .20
c. A152 1ce multicolored .60 .30
d. A152 2ce multicolored 1.25 .60

Christmas.

J.B. Danquah (1895-1965) A153

National Leaders: 65p, John Mensah Sarbah (1864-1910). 80p, J.E.K. Aggrey (1875-1925). 2ce, Kwame Nkrumah (1909-1972). 4ce, G.E. Grant (1878-1956).

1980, Jan. 21 Litho. *Perf. 13½x14*

699 A153 20p multicolored .30 .20
700 A153 65p multicolored .45 .20
701 A153 80p multicolored .45 .20
702 A153 2ce multicolored .90 .55
703 A153 4ce multicolored 1.75 1.00
Nos. 699-703 (5) 3.85 2.15

Man with Clack Bells, Hill A154

Hill and: 25p, Man with clack bells. 50p, 65p, Chief, elephant staff. 1ce, 2ce, Drummer. 4ce, 5ce, Chief, ivory staff.

1980, Mar. 12 Litho. *Perf. 14½*
704 A154 20p multicolored .20 .20
705 A154 65p multicolored .30 .20
706 A154 2ce multicolored 1.00 .50
707 A154 4ce multicolored 1.75 1.00
Nos. 704-707 (4) 3.25 1.90

Souvenir Sheet

708 Sheet of 4 3.25 2.00
a. A154 25p multicolored .20 .20
b. A154 50p multicolored .25 .20
c. A154 1ce multicolored .50 .35
d. A154 5ce multicolored 1.75 1.25

Sir Rowland Hill (1795-1879), originator of penny postage.
Nos. 708a-708d also exist perf 13½, issued in small individual sheetlets. Values slightly more than perf 14½.
For overprints see Nos. 714-718.

Students, IYC Emblem — A155

IYC Emblem and: 25p like 20p. 50p, 65p, Boys playing soccer. 1ce, 2ce, Boys in canoe. 3ce, 4ce, Mother and child.

1980, Apr. 2 Litho. *Perf. 15*
709 A155 20p multicolored .30 .20
710 A155 65p multicolored .50 .20
711 A155 2ce multicolored .90 .50
712 A155 4ce multicolored 1.50 1.00
Nos. 709-712 (4) 3.20 1.90

Souvenir Sheet

713 Sheet of 4 3.25 2.00
a. A155 25p multicolored .25 .20
b. A155 50p multicolored .40 .25
c. A155 1ce multicolored .80 .35
d. A155 3ce multicolored 1.75 1.25

Intl. Year of the Child (in 1979).
For overprints see Nos. 719-723.

Nos. 704-708 Overprinted: "LONDON 1980" / 6th-14th May 1980

1980, May 6 Litho. *Perf. 14½*
714 A154 20p multicolored .20 .20
715 A154 65p multicolored .30 .20
716 A154 2ce multicolored 1.00 .50
717 A154 4ce multicolored 1.90 1.00
Nos. 714-717 (4) 3.40 1.90

Souvenir Sheet

718 Sheet of 4 3.50 2.00
a. A154 25p multicolored .20 .20
b. A154 50p multicolored .30 .20
c. A154 1ce multicolored .55 .30
d. A154 5ce multicolored 2.25 1.25

London 1980 Intl. Stamp Exhib., May 6-14. #718a-718d also exist perf 13½, issued in small individual sheetlets. Value, unused or used, $10.00.

Nos. 709-713 Overprinted: "PAPAL VISIT" / 8th-9th May / 1980

1980, May 8 *Perf. 15*
719 A155 20p multicolored .65 .20
720 A155 65p multicolored 1.25 .35
721 A155 2ce multicolored 2.10 1.00
722 A155 4ce multicolored 3.00 2.00
Nos. 719-722 (4) 7.00 3.55

Souvenir Sheet

723 Sheet of 4 10.50 8.00
a. A155 25p multicolored .45 .25
b. A155 50p multicolored .95 .50
c. A155 1ce multicolored 1.90 1.00
d. A155 3ce multicolored 6.25 3.00

Visit of Pope John Paul II to Ghana, 5/8-9.

Parliament House A156

1980, Aug. 4 Litho. *Perf. 14*
724 A156 20p shown .20 .20
725 A156 65p Supreme Court .25 .30
726 A156 2ce The Castle .40 .60
Nos. 724-726 (3) .85 1.10

Souvenir Sheet

727 Sheet of 3 .85 1.25
a. A156 25p like #724 .20 .20
b. A156 1ce like #725 .25 .35
c. A156 3ce like #726 .40 .70

Third Republic.

Map of West African Member Countries, Flag of Ghana, Jet — A157

1980, Nov. 5 Litho. *Perf. 14½*
728 A157 20p shown .20 .20
729 A157 65p Dish antenna .20 .20
730 A157 80p Cogwheels .25 .25
731 A157 2ce Corn .35 .35
Nos. 728-731 (4) 1.00 1.00

5th Anniversary of ECOWAS (Economic Community of West African States).

A158

A159

1980, Nov. 26
732 A158 20p "OAU" .20 .20
733 A158 65p OAU Banner, Maps .25 .20
734 A158 80p Waves on map of Africa .30 .25
735 A158 2ce Flag, banner, map .50 .50
Nos. 732-735 (4) 1.25 1.15

Org. for African Unity summit conference, Lagos, Nigeria, Apr. 28-29.

1980, Dec. 10 *Perf. 14*

Christmas (Fra Angelico Paintings): 15p, 25p, Adoration of the Magi. 20p, 50p, Virgin and Child Enthroned with Four Angels. 1ce, 2ce, Virgin and Child Enthroned with Eight Angels. 3ce, 4ce, Annunciation.

736 A159 15p multicolored .20 .20
737 A159 20p multicolored .20 .20
738 A159 2ce multicolored .60 .50
739 A159 4ce multicolored 1.00 1.00
Nos. 736-739 (4) 2.00 1.90

Souvenir Sheet

740 Sheet of 4 1.50 1.50
a. A159 25p multicolored .20 .20
b. A159 50p multicolored .25 .20
c. A159 1ce multicolored .30 .30
d. A159 3ce multicolored .40 .90

Nurse Weighing Newborn, Rotary Emblem A160

1980, Dec. 18
741 A160 20p shown .20 .20
742 A160 65p Map of Ghana and world .30 .20
743 A160 2ce Helping hands, world map .70 .55
744 A160 4ce Food distribution 1.25 1.00
Nos. 741-744 (4) 2.45 1.95

Souvenir Sheet

745 Sheet of 4 2.00 1.50
a. A160 25p like #741 .20 .20
b. A160 50p like #742 .25 .20
c. A160 1ce like #743 .30 .25
d. A160 3ce like #744 1.00 .90

Rotary International, 75th anniv.

Narina Trogon — A161

1981, Jan. 12 Litho. *Perf. 14*
746 A161 20p shown 1.10 .20
747 A161 65p White-crowned robin-chat 1.90 .35
748 A161 2ce Swallow-tailed bee-eater 2.50 1.25
749 A161 4ce Long-tailed parakeet 3.50 2.50
Nos. 746-749 (4) 9.00 4.30

Souvenir Sheet

750 Sheet of 4 6.00 3.50
a. A161 25p like #746 .30 .20
b. A161 50p like #747 .75 .30
c. A161 1ce like #748 1.25 .55
d. A161 3ce like #749 3.50 1.60

Pope John Paul II, Pres. Limann, Archbishop of Canterbury — A162

1981, Mar. 3 Litho. *Perf. 14*
751 A162 20p multicolored .20 .20
752 A162 65p multicolored .60 .30
753 A162 80p multicolored .75 .35
754 A162 2ce multicolored 1.75 .90
Nos. 751-754 (4) 3.30 1.75

Visit of Pope John Paul II, May 8-10, 1980.

Earth Satellite Station — A163

1981, Sept. 28 Litho. *Perf. 14*
755 A163 20p shown .20 .20
756 A163 65p Satellites orbiting earth .30 .30
757 A163 80p Satellite .35 .35
758 A163 4ce Satellite, earth 1.60 1.60
Nos. 755-758 (4) 2.45 2.45

Souvenir Sheet

758A Sheet of 4 2.10 2.10
b. A163 25p like #755 .20 .20
c. A163 50p like #756 .20 .20
d. A163 1ce like #757 .45 .45
e. A163 3ce like #758 1.10 1.10

Earth Satellite Station commission.

Common Design Types pictured following the introduction.

Royal Wedding Issue
Common Design Type

1981 Litho. *Perf. 14*
759 CD331 20p Couple .20 .20
759A CD331 65p like 20p .20 .20
760 CD331 80p Charles .25 .25
760A CD331 1ce like 80p .60 .75
760B CD331 3ce like 4ce 1.00 1.00
761 CD331 4ce Royal yacht Britannia 1.00 1.00
Nos. 759-761 (6) 3.25 3.40

Souvenir Sheet

762 CD331 7ce St. Paul's Cathedral 1.25 1.50

Nos. 759-761 each printed se-tenant with label showing heraldic design.
Issued: 20p, 80p, 4ce, 7ce, 7/8; 65p, 1ce, 3ce, 9/16.
For surcharges see Nos. 859, 866, 871, 880, 1168-1169, 1195-1197.

1981, Sept. 16 Litho. *Perf. 14*
763 CD331 2ce like 4ce .50 .50
764 CD331 5ce like 20p 1.25 1.25
a. Bklt. pane, 2 each #763-764 3.50 3.50

Nos. 763-764 issued only in booklets.

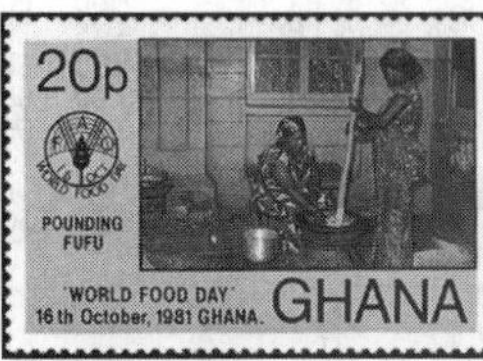

World Food Day A164

1981, Oct. 16 Litho. *Perf. 14*
765 A164 20p Women pounding fufu .20 .20
766 A164 65p Plucking cocoa .30 .30
767 A164 80p Preparing banku .40 .40
768 A164 2ce Processing garri .85 .85
Nos. 765-768 (4) 1.75 1.75

Souvenir Sheet

769 Sheet of 4 1.50 1.50
a. A164 25p like #765 .20 .20
b. A164 50p like #766 .20 .20
c. A164 1ce like #767 .35 .35
d. A164 3ce like #768 1.00 1.00

Angelic Musicians Play for Mary and Child, by Aachener Altares (1480-1520) A165

Christmas (Paintings): 15p, The Betrothal of St. Catherine of Alexandria, by Lucas Cranach (1472-1553). 65p, Child Jesus Embracing His Mother, by Gabriel Metsu (1629-1667). 80p, Virgin and Child, by Fra Filippo Lippi (1406-1469). $2, The Virgin with Infant Jesus, by Barnaba da Modena (1361-1383). $4, The Immaculate Conception, by Bartolome Murillo (1618-1682). $6, Virgin and Child, by Hans Memling (1430-1494).

1981, Nov. 26 *Perf. 14*
770 A165 15p multicolored .30 .30
771 A165 20p multicolored .30 .30
772 A165 65p multicolored .40 .40
773 A165 80p multicolored .40 .40
774 A165 $2 multicolored .75 .75
775 A165 $4 multicolored .85 .85
Nos. 770-775 (6) 3.00 3.00

Souvenir Sheet

776 A165 $6 multicolored 2.00 2.00

Intl. Year of the Disabled A166

1982, Feb. 8 Litho. *Perf. 14*
777 A166 20p Blind man .20 .20
778 A166 65p Woman, crutch .30 .30
779 A166 80p Girl reading Braille .40 .40
780 A166 4ce Couple 1.75 1.75
Nos. 777-780 (4) 2.65 2.65

Souvenir Sheet

781 A166 6ce Group 2.25 2.25

Clawless Otter — A167

1982, Feb. 22

782 A167 20p shown .20 .20
783 A167 65p Bushbuck .50 .50
784 A167 80p Aardvark .60 .60
785 A167 1ce Scarlet bell tree .75 .75
786 A167 2ce Glory lilies 1.50 1.50
787 A167 4ce Blue peas 3.00 3.00
Nos. 782-787 (6) 6.55 6.55

Souvenir Sheet

788 A167 5ce Chimpanzees 3.50 3.50

Blue-spot Commodore A168

1982, Apr. 27 Litho. *Perf. 14*

789 A168 20p shown .85 .85
790 A168 65p Emperor swallow-tail 1.40 1.40
791 A168 2ce Orange admiral 2.25 2.25
792 A168 4ce Giant charaxes 3.00 3.00
Nos. 789-792 (4) 7.50 7.50

Souvenir Sheet

Perf. 14½

793 Sheet of 4 8.00 8.00
a. A168 25p like #789 .40 .40
b. A168 50p like #790 .70 .70
c. A168 1ce like #791 1.50 1.50
d. A168 3ce like #792 4.50 4.50

Scouting Year A169

1982, June 1 Litho. *Perf. 15*

794 A169 20p Tree planting .20 .20
795 A169 65p Camping .50 .50
796 A169 80p Sailing .60 .60
797 A169 3ce Watching elephant 2.25 2.25
Nos. 794-797 (4) 3.55 3.55

Souvenir Sheet

798 A169 5ce Baden-Powell, vert. 3.75 3.75

For surcharges see Nos. 867, 870, 875, 877.

Kpong Hydroelectric Dam Opening — A170

1982, June 28 Litho. *Perf. 14*

799 A170 20p Cranes, lifts .50 .20
800 A170 65p Construction 1.00 .50
801 A170 80p Turbines 1.25 .60
802 A170 2ce Aerial view 2.25 1.50
Nos. 799-802 (4) 5.00 2.80

1982 World Cup A171

Perf. 15, 14½x15 (30p, No. 807, 1ce, 3ce)

1982, July 19 Litho.

803 A171 20p multi .20 .20
804 A171 30p multi, like 20p .30 .30
805 A171 65p multi .50 .50
806 A171 80p multi, like 65p .70 .70
807 A171 80p multi, diff. .60 .60
808 A171 1ce multi, like #807 .60 .60
809 A171 3ce multi 1.10 1.10
810 A171 4ce multi, like 3ce 1.75 1.75
Nos. 803-810 (8) 5.75 5.75

Souvenir Sheet

811 A171 6ce multi 3.00 3.00

Nos. 804, 806, 808-809 in sheets of 5 plus label.

For overprints & surcharges see #826-834, 861-862, 864-865, 868-869, 872-873, 878-879, 912-917.

TB Bacillus Centenary A172

1982, Aug. 9 *Perf. 14*

812 A172 20p Child immunization .50 .50
813 A172 65p Koch, Berlin 1.25 1.25
814 A172 80p Koch, Africa 1.50 1.50
815 A172 1ce Looking through microscope 1.75 1.75
816 A172 2ce Koch, 1905 Nobel medal 2.50 2.50
Nos. 812-816 (5) 7.50 7.50

Christmas — A173

1982, Dec. Litho. *Perf. 15*

817 A173 15p Angel with banner .20 .20
818 A173 20p Holy Family .20 .20
819 A173 65p Three Kings .30 .30
820 A173 4ce Nativity 1.10 1.10
Nos. 817-820 (4) 1.80 1.80

Souvenir Sheet

821 A173 6ce Nativity, diff. 2.00 2.00

A173a

1983, Mar. 10 Litho. *Perf. 15*

822 A173a 20p Flags .30 .30
823 A173a 55p Aerial view .55 .55
824 A173a 80p Minerals 1.25 1.25
825 A173a 3ce Eagle 1.90 1.90
Nos. 822-825 (4) 4.00 4.00

Commonwealth Day. For surcharges see Nos. 860, 863, 874, 876.

Nos. 803-811 Overprinted in Gold: "WINNER ITALY / 3-1"

1983, June Litho.

826 A171 20p multicolored .20 .20
827 A171 30p multicolored .20 .20
828 A171 65p multicolored .25 .25
829 A171 80p multi, on #806 .25 .25
830 A171 80p multi, on #807 .65 .65
831 A171 1ce multicolored .75 .75
832 A171 3ce multicolored 1.60 1.60
833 A171 4ce multicolored 1.50 1.50
Nos. 826-833 (8) 5.40 5.40

Souvenir Sheet

834 A171 6ce multicolored 3.50 3.50

Italy's victory in 1982 World Cup.

For surcharges see Nos. 862, 865, 869, 873, 879, 913, 915, 917.

World Communications Year — A173b

1983, Dec. 13 Litho. *Perf. 14*

835 A173b 1ce shown .20 .20
836 A173b 1.40ce Dish antenna .20 .20
837 A173b 2.30ce Cable ship .35 .35
838 A173b 3ce Switchboard .40 .40
839 A173b 5ce Control tower .60 .60
Nos. 835-839 (5) 1.75 1.75

Souvenir Sheet

840 A173b 6ce Satellite .75 .75

For surcharges see Nos. 1107-1111.

Coastal Marine Mammals A173c

1983, Nov. 15 Litho. *Perf. 15*

841 A173c 1ce Short fin pilot whale 1.10 1.10
842 A173c 1.40ce Gray dolphin 1.25 1.25
843 A173c 2.30ce False killer whale 1.40 1.40
844 A173c 3ce Spinner dolphin 1.75 1.75
845 A173c 5ce Atlantic humpback dolphin 2.25 2.25
Nos. 841-845 (5) 7.75 7.75

Souvenir Sheet

846 A173c 6ce White Alantic humpback dolphin 1.50 1.50

For surcharges see Nos. 918-920.

A174

Christmas A175

1983, Dec. 28 *Perf. 14x13½, 14½x14*

852 A174 70p Children receiving gifts .20 .20
853 A175 1ce Nativity .20 .20
854 A175 1.40ce Children playing .25 .25
855 A175 2.30ce Family praying .30 .30
856 A174 3ce Bongo drums, festivities .35 .35
Nos. 852-856 (5) 1.30 1.30

Souvenir Sheet

857 A175 6ce like #855 .40 .40

Surcharges

Many inverts, doubles, etc., exist on the surcharged stamps that follow.

Previous Issues Surcharged

1984, Feb. 8

858 A74 1ce on 20np #296 .20 .20
859 CD331 1ce on 20p #759 .20 .20
860 A173a 1ce on 20p #822 .20 .20
861 A171 1ce on 20p #803 .20 .20
862 A171 1ce on 20p #826 .20 .20
863 A173a 9ce on 55p #823 .65 .65
864 A171 9ce on 65p #805 .65 .65
865 A171 9ce on 65p #828 .65 .65
866 CD331 9ce on 80p #760 .65 .65
867 A169 10ce on 20p #794 .70 .70
868 A171 10ce on 80p #806 .70 .70
869 A171 10ce on 80p #830 .70 .70
870 A169 19ce on 65p #795 1.40 1.40
871 CD331 20ce on 4ce #761 1.40 1.40
872 A171 20ce on 4ce #810 1.40 1.40
873 A171 20ce on 4ce #833 1.40 1.40
874 A173a 30ce on 80p #824 2.00 2.00
875 A169 30ce on 3ce #797 2.00 2.00
876 A173a 50ce on 3ce #825 3.50 3.50
Nos. 858-876 (19) 18.80 18.80

Souvenir Sheets

877 A169 60ce on 5ce #798 2.50 2.50
878 A171 60ce on 6ce #811 2.50 2.50
879 A171 60ce on 6ce #834 2.25 2.25
880 CD331 60ce on 7ce #762 3.25 3.25

For surcharges on this issue see #1092A-1092C.

Namibia Day A176

Scorpion Weight A177

1984, Jan. 26 *Perf. 14*

881 A176 50p Soldiers raising rifles .20 .20
882 A176 1ce Soldiers, tank .20 .20
883 A176 1.40ce Machete cutting chains .20 .20
884 A176 2.30ce Namibian woman .20 .20
885 A176 3ce Soldiers in combat .20 .20
Nos. 881-885 (5) 1.00 1.00

1983, Dec. 12 Litho. *Perf. 14*

886 A177 5p Banded Jewelfish, horiz. .20 .20
887 A177 10p Banded Jewelfish, map, horiz. .30 .20
888 A177 20p Blood lily .40 .20
889 A177 50p Mounted warrior (gold statuette) .40 .20
890 A177 1ce shown .50 .20
891 A177 2ce Jet, horiz. .50 .30
892 A177 3ce White-collared mangabey .90 .30
893 A177 4ce Pigmy bush baby .40 .30
894 A177 5ce Nigerian iris .50 .45
895 A177 10ce Gray-backed warbler .65 *.90*
Nos. 886-895 (10) 4.75 3.25

For surcharges see Nos. 1089A-1090, 1092, 1092D, 1093A-1094A, 1096-1096A.

Easter — A178

Local Flowers — A179

1984, Apr. Litho. *Perf. 14½*

906 A178 1ce Cross, crown of thorns .20 .20
907 A178 1.40ce Jesus praying .20 .20
908 A178 2.30ce Jesus going to Jerusalem .20 .20
909 A178 3ce Jesus entering Jerusalem .20 .20
910 A178 50ce Jesus with Disciples 1.25 *2.50*
Nos. 906-910 (5) 2.05 3.30

Souvenir Sheet

911 A178 60ce Cross, crown of thorns 1.75 1.75

Nos. 804, 806, 809, 827, 829, 832 Surcharged

1984, Feb. 8 **Litho.**

912 A171 9ce on 3ce #809 .70 .70
913 A171 9ce on 3ce #832 .70 .70
914 A171 10ce on 30p #804 .80 .80
915 A171 10ce on 30p #827 .80 .80
916 A171 20ce on 80p #806 1.60 1.60
917 A171 20ce on 80p #829 1.60 1.60
Nos. 912-917 (6) 6.20 6.20

Nos. 844-846 Surcharged and Overprinted in Red with UPU Emblem and: "19th U.P.U. CONGRESS-HAMBURG"

1984 **Litho.** ***Perf. 14½***

918 A173c 10ce on 3ce multi .55 .55
919 A173c 50ce on 5ce multi 2.75 2.75

Souvenir Sheet

920 A173c 60ce on 6ce multi 3.25 3.25

1984, July **Litho.** ***Perf. 14***

921 A179 1ce Amorphophallus johnsonii .20 .20
922 A179 1.40ce Pancratium trianthum .20 .20
923 A179 2.30ce Eulophia cucullata .20 .20
924 A179 3ce Amorphophallus abyssinicus .20 .20
925 A179 50ce Chlorophytum togoense 3.00 *4.00*
Nos. 921-925 (5) 3.80 4.80

Souvenir Sheet

926 A179 60ce like 1ce 3.00 3.00

Endangered Species — A180

1984, Aug. ***Perf. 14***

927 A180 1ce Bongo .40 .40
928 A180 2.30ce Males locking horns .75 .75
929 A180 3ce Family .85 .85
930 A180 20ce Herd 3.00 3.00
Nos. 927-930 (4) 5.00 5.00

Souvenir Sheets

931 A180 70ce Kob 5.50 5.50
932 A180 70ce Bushbuck 5.50 5.50

1984 Summer Olympics — A181

Native Dancers — A182

1984, Aug. ***Perf. 15***

933 A181 1ce Running .20 .20
934 A181 1.40ce Boxing .20 .20
935 A181 2.30ce Field hockey .20 .20
936 A181 3ce Hurdles .20 .20
937 A181 50ce Rhythmic gymnastics 2.50 *4.00*
Nos. 933-937 (5) 3.30 4.80

Souvenir Sheet

938 A181 70ce Soccer 2.50 2.50

For surcharges see #945-950, 1112-1116.

1984, Sept. ***Perf. 14***

939 A182 1ce Dipo .20 .20
940 A182 1.40ce Adowa .20 .20
941 A182 2.30ce Agbadza .20 .20
942 A182 3ce Damba .20 .20
943 A182 50ce Dipo, diff. 1.50 *3.00*
Nos. 939-943 (5) 2.30 3.80

Souvenir Sheet

944 A182 70ce Mandolin player 2.00 2.00

Nos. 933-938 Ovptd. in Gold with Winner and Country

1984, Dec. 3 **Litho.** ***Perf. 15***

945 A181 1ce Valerie Brisco-Hooks, US .20 .20
946 A181 1.40ce US winners .20 .20
947 A181 2.30ce Pakistan, (field hockey) .20 .20
948 A181 3ce Edwin Moses, US .20 .20
949 A181 50ce Lauri Fung, Canada 2.00 2.00
Nos. 945-949 (5) 2.80 2.80

Souvenir Sheet

950 A181 70ce France 2.75 2.75

Christmas A183

Queen Mother, 85th Birthday A184

1984, Nov. 19 ***Perf. 12x12½***

951 A183 70p Adoration of the Magi .20 .20
952 A183 1ce Chorus of angels .20 .20
953 A183 1.40ce Adoration of the shepherds .20 .20
954 A183 2.30ce Flight into Egypt .20 .20
955 A183 3ce King holding Christ .20 .20
956 A183 50ce Adoration of the angels 1.50 2.00
Nos. 951-956 (6) 2.50 3.00

Souvenir Sheet

957 A183 70ce like 70p 2.75 2.75

1985 ***Perf. 14***

Portraits.

958 A184 5ce multicolored .20 .20
959 A184 8ce like 5ce .20 .20
960 A184 12ce multicolored .25 .25
961 A184 20ce like 12ce .30 .30
962 A184 70ce multicolored 1.60 1.60
963 A184 100ce like 70ce 1.75 1.75
Nos. 958-963 (6) 4.30 4.30

Souvenir Sheet

964 A184 110ce multicolored 2.50 2.50

Issue dates: 5ce, 12ce, 100ce, 110ce, July 29. 8ce, 20ce, 70ce, Dec.

Nos. 959, 961-962 issued in sheets of 5 + label.

For surcharges see Nos. 1117-1119A, 1198-1200, 1311-1317.

Id-El-Fitr Islamic Festival — A185

1985, Aug. 1

965 A185 5ce Entering mosque .20 .20
966 A185 8ce Prayer rug .30 .30
967 A185 12ce Mosque .50 .50
968 A185 18ce Public Koran reading .75 .75
969 A185 50ce Map, Banda Nkwanta Mosque 2.00 2.00
Nos. 965-969 (5) 3.75 3.75

Intl. Youth Year — A186

1985, Aug. 9

970 A186 5ce Street clean-up .20 .20
971 A186 8ce Tree planting .25 .25
972 A186 12ce Food production .30 .30
973 A186 100ce Education 2.00 *3.50*
Nos. 970-973 (4) 2.75 4.25

Souvenir Sheet

974 A186 110ce like 8ce 2.00 2.00

Motorcycle Centenary — A187

1985, Sept. 9

975 A187 5ce 1984 Honda Interceptor .55 .25
976 A187 8ce 1938 DKW .70 .35
977 A187 12ce 1923 BMW R 32 1.00 .55
978 A187 100ce 1900 NSU 5.75 5.75
Nos. 975-978 (4) 8.00 6.90

Souvenir Sheet

979 A187 110ce 1973 Zundapp 5.00 5.00

Audubon Birth Bicent. — A188

1985, Oct. 16

980 A188 5ce York-tailed fly-catcher .80 .80
981 A188 8ce Barred owl 1.60 1.60
982 A188 12ce Black-throated mango 1.60 1.60
983 A188 100ce White-crowned pigeon 4.75 4.75
Nos. 980-983 (4) 8.75 8.75

Souvenir Sheet

984 A188 110ce Downy woodpecker 5.25 5.25

For surcharges see Nos. 1124-1127.

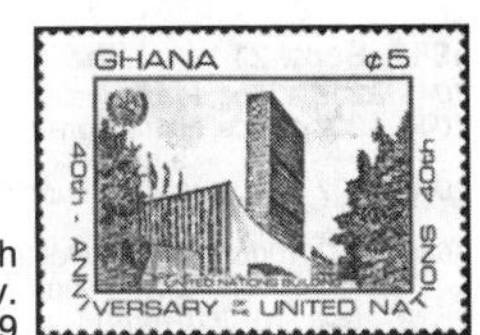

UN, 40th Anniv. A189

1985, Oct. 24 ***Perf. 14½x14***

985 A189 5ce UN building .20 .20
986 A189 8ce UN building, diff. .20 .20
987 A189 12ce Dove .20 *.30*
988 A189 18ce General Assembly .25 *.40*
989 A189 100ce Flags 1.75 *2.25*
Nos. 985-989 (5) 2.60 3.35

Souvenir Sheet

990 A189 110ce UN No. 36 2.00 2.00

UNCTAD, 20th Anniv. A190

1985, Nov. 4 ***Perf. 14***

991 A190 5ce Coffee .20 .20
992 A190 8ce Cocoa .20 .20
993 A190 12ce Lumber .25 .25
994 A190 18ce Bauxite mining 1.10 1.10
995 A190 100ce Gold mining 6.25 6.25
Nos. 991-995 (5) 8.00 8.00

Souvenir Sheet

Perf. 15x14

996 A190 110ce Produce 4.00 4.00

UN Child Survival Campaign A191

1985, Dec. 16 ***Perf. 14***

997 A191 5ce Weighing .20 .20
998 A191 8ce Oral rehydration therapy .30 .30
999 A191 12ce Breast-feeding .50 .50
1000 A191 100ce Immunization 4.00 4.00
Nos. 997-1000 (4) 5.00 5.00

Souvenir Sheet

Perf. 15x14

1001 A191 110ce Emblem, pinwheel 3.50 3.50

AMERIPEX '86 — A192

Perf. 14½x14, 14x14½

1986, Oct. 27 **Litho.**

1002 A192 5ce Young collectors .25 .25
1003 A192 25ce Earth, jet .75 .75
1004 A192 100ce Stewardess, vert. 2.50 2.50
Nos. 1002-1004 (3) 3.50 3.50

Souvenir Sheet

1005 A192 150ce Young collectors, diff. 3.50 3.50

INTER-TOURISM '86, Nov. 8-17 — A193

Designs: 5ce, Kejetia Roundabout, Jumasi. 15ce, Fort St. Jago, Elmina. 25ce, Warriors. 100ce, Chief, retinue. 150ce, Elephants.

1986, Nov. 10 ***Perf. 14***

1006 A193 5ce multi .20 .20
1007 A193 15ce multi .35 .35
1008 A193 25ce multi .55 .55
1009 A193 100ce multi 2.40 2.40
Nos. 1006-1009 (4) 3.50 3.50

Souvenir Sheet

Perf. 15x14

1010 A193 150ce multi 4.25 4.25

1986 World Cup Soccer Championships, Mexico — A194

Fertility Dolls — A195

Various soccer plays.

1987, Jan. 16 **Litho.** ***Perf. 14x14½***

1011 A194 5ce multi .30 .30
1012 A194 15ce multi .45 .45
1013 A194 25ce multi .75 .75
1014 A194 100ce multi 2.25 2.25
Nos. 1011-1014 (4) 3.75 3.75

Souvenir Sheet

1015 A194 150ce multi 3.50 3.50

For surcharges see Nos. 1120-1123D.

1987, Jan. 22

Various dolls.

1016	A195	5ce	multi	.25	.25
1017	A195	15ce	multi	.35	.35
1018	A195	25ce	multi	.65	.65
1019	A195	100ce	multi	2.25	2.25
			Nos. 1016-1019 (4)	3.50	3.50

Souvenir Sheet

1020	A195	150ce	like #1016	3.50	3.50

Intl. Peace Year A196

Perf. 14½x14, 14x14½

1987, Mar. 2 **Litho.**

1021	A196	5ce	Children playing	.25	.25
1022	A196	25ce	Plow	.75	.75
1023	A196	100ce	Earth, doves, vert.	3.00	3.00
			Nos. 1021-1023 (3)	4.00	4.00

Souvenir Sheet

1024	A196	150ce	Dove, plow, vert.	4.00	4.00

GIFEX '87 A197

1987, Mar. 10 ***Perf. 14***

1025	A197	5ce	Lumber, house construction	.20	.20
1026	A197	15ce	Furniture	.30	.30
1027	A197	25ce	Tree stumps	.50	.50
1028	A197	200ce	Logs, art objects	3.00	3.00
			Nos. 1025-1028 (4)	4.00	4.00

Ghana Intl. Forestry Exposition, Accra.

A198

Halley's Comet — A199

Designs: 5ce, Mikhail Vasilyevich Lomonosov (1711-1765), Russian scientist, and the Chamber of Curiosities. 25ce, Landing of the US probe Surveyor on the Moon's surface, 1966. 200ce, Wedgewood memorial to Sir Isaac Newton, the appearance of Halley's Comet in 1790 and US astronauts Armstrong and Aldrin landing Eagle on the Moon in 1969. 250ce, Comet over Fishermen near Christianborg Castle,

1987, Apr. 8 ***Perf. 14½x14***

1029	A198	5ce	multi	.20	.20
1030	A198	25ce	multi	.50	.50
1031	A198	200ce	multi	4.00	4.00
			Nos. 1029-1031 (3)	4.70	4.70

Souvenir Sheet

1032	A199	250ce	multi	5.00	5.00

For surcharges see Nos. 1128-1131,

Solidarity with South Africans for Abolition of Apartheid — A200

1987, May 18 ***Perf. 14x14½***

1033	A200	5ce	Liberated prisoner	.20	.20
1034	A200	15ce	Miner, gold ingots	.30	.30
1035	A200	25ce	Zulu warrior	.50	.50
1036	A200	100ce	Nelson Mandela, shackles	2.00	2.00
			Nos. 1033-1036 (4)	3.00	3.00

Souvenir Sheet

1037	A200	150ce	Mandela, map, star	3.00	3.00

Traditional Musical Instruments — A201

1987, July 13 ***Perf. 14½x14***

1038	A201	5ce	Horns	.20	.20
1039	A201	15ce	Xylophone	.30	.30
1040	A201	25ce	String instruments	.50	.50
1041	A201	100ce	Drums	2.00	2.00
			Nos. 1038-1041 (4)	3.00	3.00

Souvenir Sheet

1042	A201	200ce	Percussion instruments	3.00	3.00

Intl. Year of Shelter for the Homeless A202

1987, Sept. 21 **Litho.** ***Perf. 14***

1043	A202	5ce	Public well	.20	.20
1044	A202	15ce	Home construction	.25	.25
1045	A202	25ce	Village, bridge, car	.40	.40
1046	A202	100ce	Village, electric power lines	1.40	1.40
			Nos. 1043-1046 (4)	2.25	2.25

Festivals — A203

Designs: Preparation of Kpokpoi, Homowo Festival. 15ce, Hunters with catch, Aboakyir Festival. 25ce, Chief dancing, Odwira Festival. 100ce, Chief held aloft in a palanquin, Yam Festival.

1988, Jan. 6 **Litho.** ***Perf. 15***

1047	A203	5ce	multi	.20	.20
1048	A203	15ce	multi	.25	.25
1049	A203	25ce	multi	.40	.40
1050	A203	100ce	multi	1.40	1.40
			Nos. 1047-1050 (4)	2.25	2.25

December 31, 1981 Revolution — A203a

1988, Jan. 26 **Litho.** ***Perf. 13***

1050A	A203a	5ce	Ports	1.50	.50
1050B	A203a	15ce	Railways	12.50	2.50
1050C	A203a	25ce	Cocoa industry	2.50	.75
1050D	A203a	100ce	Mining industry	13.50	*15.00*
			Nos. 1050A-1050D (4)	30.00	18.75

UN Universal Immunization Campaign — A204

Child Survival Campaign emblem and: 5ce, Nurse immunizing woman. 15ce, Child receiving intramuscular vaccine. 25ce, Youth crippled by polio. 100ce, Nurse handing infant to mother.

1988, Feb. 1 ***Perf. 15***

1051	A204	5ce	multi	.20	.20
1052	A204	15ce	multi	.30	.30
1053	A204	25ce	multi	.50	.50
1054	A204	100ce	multi	2.00	2.00
			Nos. 1051-1054 (4)	3.00	3.00

Intl. Fund for Agricultural Development — A204a

1988, Apr. 14 ***Perf. 13***

1054A	A204a	5ce	Fishing	.60	.60
1054B	A204a	15ce	Harvesting	1.00	1.00
1054C	A204a	25ce	Cattle	1.40	1.40
1054D	A204a	100ce	Granary	3.50	3.50
			Nos. 1054A-1054D (4)	6.50	6.50

Tribal Costumes — A205

1988, May 9 **Litho.** ***Perf. 14***

1055	A205	5ce	Akwadjan	.20	.20
1056	A205	25ce	Banaa	.55	.55
1057	A205	250ce	Agwasen	2.75	2.75
			Nos. 1055-1057 (3)	3.50	3.50

1988 Summer Olympics, Seoul A206

1988, Oct. 10

1058	A206	20ce	Boxing	.20	.20
1059	A206	60ce	Running	.60	.60
1060	A206	80ce	Discus	.80	.80
1061	A206	100ce	Javelin	1.00	1.00
1062	A206	350ce	Weight lifting	3.50	3.50
			Nos. 1058-1062 (5)	6.10	6.10

Souvenir Sheet

1063	A206	500ce	like 80ce	5.00	5.00

For overprints see Nos. 1084-1089.

Intl. Red Cross, 125th Anniv. — A207

1988, Dec. 14 **Litho.** ***Perf. 14***

1064	A207	20ce	Nutrition	.50	.50
1065	A207	50ce	Voluntary service	1.00	1.00
1066	A207	60ce	Disaster relief (flood)	1.25	1.25
1067	A207	200ce	Medical assistance	3.25	3.25
			Nos. 1064-1067 (4)	6.00	6.00

Christmas Symbolism — A208

1988, Dec. 19 **Litho.** ***Perf. 14***

1068	A208	20ce	shown	.20	.20
1069	A208	60ce	Mother and child, vert.	.50	.50
1070	A208	80ce	Mother, child, tree, vert.	.70	.70
1071	A208	100ce	Magi follow star	.85	.85
1072	A208	350ce	Abstract, diff., vert.	3.00	3.00
			Nos. 1068-1072 (5)	5.25	5.25

Souvenir Sheet

1073	A208	500ce	Mother and child, diff., vert.	5.00	5.00

Organization of African Unity, 25th Anniv. — A209

Titian, 500th Birth Anniv. (in 1988) — A210

1989, Jan. 3

1074	A209	20ce	Solidarity	.20	.20
1075	A209	50ce	OAU, Addis Ababa	.30	.30
1076	A209	60ce	Haile Selassie, Ethiopia	.65	.65
1077	A209	200ce	Kwame Nkrumah, Ghana	1.10	1.10
			Nos. 1074-1077 (4)	2.25	2.25

"Selassie" is spelled incorrectly on No. 1076. Nos. 1076-1077 horiz.

1989, Jan. 16

1078	A210	20ce	Amor, 1515	.20	.20
1079	A210	60ce	The Appeal	.60	.60
1080	A210	80ce	Bacchus and Ariadne, c. 1523	.80	.80
1081	A210	100ce	Portrait of a Musician, c. 1518	1.00	1.00
1082	A210	350ce	Philip II Seated	3.50	3.50
			Nos. 1078-1082 (5)	6.10	6.10

Souvenir Sheet

1083	A210	500ce	Portrait of a Gentleman, c. 1550	5.00	5.00

Nos. 1058-1063 Ovptd. with Winners' Names

1989, Jan. 23

1084 A206 20ce "A. ZUELOW / DDR / 60 KG" .30 .30
1085 A206 60ce "G. BORDIN / ITALY / MARATHON" .45 .45
1086 A206 80ce "J. SCHULT / DDR" .55 .55
1087 A206 100ce "T. KORJUS / FINLAND" .60 .60
1088 A206 350ce "B. GUIDIKOV / BULGARIA / 75 KG" 1.60 1.60
Nos. 1084-1088 (5) 3.50 3.50

Souvenir Sheet

1089 A206 500ce multi 3.50 3.50

1988 Summer Olympics, Seoul. Margin of No. 1089 ovptd. "GOLD / J. SCHULT DDR / SILVER / R. OUBARTAS USSR / BRONZE / R. DANNEBERG W. GERMANY."

Stamps of 1967-1984 Surcharged

1988-91

1089A A177 20ce on 50p #889 .20 .20
1090 A177 20ce on 1ce #890 .20 .20
1091 A75 50ce on 10np #295 .20 .20
1092 A177 50ce on 10p #887 .20 .20
1092A A74 50ce on 1ce #858 4.00 .50
1092B A74 50ce on 1ce #858 4.00 .50
1092C A74 50ce on 1ce #858 4.00 .50
1092D A177 50ce on 1ce #890
1092E A73 60ce on 1np #286 4.00 .50
1093 A73 60ce on 4np #291 4.00 .50
1093A A177 60ce on 3ce #892 .50 .25
b. Decimal point omitted
1094 A177 80ce on 5p #886 .80 .80
1094A A177 80ce on 5ce #894 5.00 5.00
1095 A74 100ce on 20np #296 .50 .50
1096 A177 100ce on 20p #888 .50 .50
1096A A177 100ce on 3ce #892 .50 .50
1096B A75 200ce on 6np #292 .60 .60

Surcharge has no decimal on No. 1092A, is vertical on No. 1092B and horizontal on No. 1092C.

No. 1090 also exists with 5mm spacing between block and $20.00.

Surcharge on No. 1093A has decimal point.

Unauthorized surchages exist.

Issued: #1089A, 1096B, 7/1/88; #1092A, 1092B, 1092D, 1092E, 1094A, 1096A, 1990; #1092C, 1991; others, 1989.

Minamoto-no-Yoritomo, by Fujiwara-no-Takanobu (1142-1205) — A211

Paintings: 50ce, Takami Senseki, by Watanabe Kazan (1793-1841). 60ce, Ikkyu Sojum, by Bokusai, Muromachi period. 75ce, Nakamura Kuranosuka, by Ogata Korin (1658-1716). 125ce, Portrait of a Lady, Kyoto branch of Kano school, Momoyama period. 150ce, Portrait of Zemmui, anonymous, 12th cent. 200ce, Ono no Komachi, the Poetess, by Hokusai. No. 1104, Kobo Daisi as a Child, anonymous, Kamakura period. No. 1105, Portrait of Kodai-no-Kimi, attributed to Fujiwara-no-Nobuzane, 12th cent. No. 1106, Portrait of Emperor Hanazono, by Fujiwara-no-Goshin, 14th cent.

1989, Aug. 21 Litho. *Perf. 13½x14*

1097 A211 20ce shown .20 .20
1098 A211 50ce multi .45 .45
1099 A211 60ce multi .50 .50
1100 A211 75ce multi .70 .70
1101 A211 125ce multi 1.10 1.10
1102 A211 150ce multi 1.40 1.40
1103 A211 200ce multi 1.75 1.75
1104 A211 500ce multi 2.60 2.60
Nos. 1097-1104 (8) 8.70 8.70

Souvenir Sheets

1105 A211 500ce multi 4.50 4.50
1106 A211 500ce multi 4.50 4.50

Hirohito (1901-1989) and enthronement of Akihito as emperor of Japan.

Nos. 835-838 and 840 Surcharged

1989, July 3 Litho. *Perf. 14*

1107 A173b 60ce on 1ce .70 .70
1108 A173b 80ce on 1.40ce .80 .80
1109 A173b 200ce on 2.30ce 2.10 2.10
1110 A173b 300ce on 3ce 2.40 2.40
Nos. 1107-1110 (4) 6.00 6.00

Souvenir Sheet

1111 A173b 500ce on 6ce 4.00 4.00

Nos. 933-936 and 938 Surcharged

1989, July 3 *Perf. 15*

1112 A181 60ce on 1ce .40 .40
1113 A181 80ce on 1.40ce .60 .60
1114 A181 200ce on 2.30ce 1.50 1.50
1115 A181 300ce on 3ce 2.10 2.10
Nos. 1112-1115 (4) 4.60 4.60

Souvenir Sheet

1116 A181 600ce on 70ce 4.25 4.25

Nos. 958, 960 and 963-964 Surcharged

1989, Nov. 20 Litho. *Perf. 14*

1117 A184 80ce on 5ce #958 .60 .60
1118 A184 250ce on 12ce #960 2.00 2.00
1119 A184 300ce on 100ce #963 2.40 2.40
Nos. 1117-1119 (3) 5.00 5.00

Souvenir Sheet

1119A A184 500ce on 110ce #964 4.00 4.00

Nos. 1011-1013 and 1015 Surcharged

1989 Litho. *Perf. 14x14½*

1120 A194 60ce on 5ce #1011 .50 .50
1121 A194 200ce on 15ce #1012 1.75 1.75
1122 A194 300ce on 25ce #1013 2.50 2.50
Nos. 1120-1122 (3) 4.75 4.75

Souvenir Sheet

1123 A194 600ce on 150ce #1015 4.75 4.75

Nos. 1120-1123 Surcharged

1989 Litho. *Perf. 14x14½*

1123A A194 60ce on 5ce .50 .50
1123B A194 200ce on 15ce 1.60 1.60
1123C A194 300ce on 25ce 2.40 2.40
Nos. 1123A-1123C (3) 4.50 4.50

Souvenir Sheet

1123D A194 600ce on 150ce 4.50 4.50

Nos. 980-982 and 984 Surcharged

1989, Nov. 20 Litho. *Perf. 14*

1124 A188 80ce on 5ce #980 1.75 1.75
1125 A188 100ce on 8ce #981 3.00 3.00
1126 A188 300ce on 12ce #982 3.50 3.50
Nos. 1124-1126 (3) 8.25 8.25

Souvenir Sheet

1127 A188 500ce on 110ce #984 4.00 4.00

Nos. 1029-1032 Surcharged

1989, Nov. 20 *Perf. 14½x14*

1128 A198 60ce on 5ce #1029 .90 .90
a. With comet logo .35 .35
1129 A198 80ce on 25ce #1030 1.10 1.10
a. With comet logo .50 .50
1130 A198 500ce on 200ce #1031 4.00 4.00
a. With comet logo 3.00 3.00
Nos. 1128-1130 (3) 6.00 6.00
Nos. 1128a-1130a (3) 3.85 3.85

Souvenir Sheet

1131 A199 750ce on 250ce #1032 6.00 6.00
a. With comet logo 5.00 5.00

PHILEXFRANCE '89, French Revolution Bicent. — A212

Emblems, French arms and flags: 20ce, Tube-mounted field carriage, flag of 1643 to 1790. 60ce, Infantryman, flag of 1789. 80ce, Handgun, flag of 1789, diff. 350ce, Musket, flag of 1794 to 1814 and 1848 to present. 600ce, Map of Paris.

1989, Sept. 22 Litho. *Perf. 14*

1132 A212 20ce shown .65 .65
1133 A212 60ce multi 1.10 1.10
1134 A212 80ce multi 1.50 1.50
1135 A212 350ce multi 3.75 3.75
Nos. 1132-1135 (4) 7.00 7.00

Souvenir Sheet

1136 A212 600ce multi 4.50 4.50

Mushrooms

A213 A214

1989, Oct. 2 Litho. *Perf. 14*

1137 A213 20ce Collybia .20 .20
1138 A213 50ce Lawyer's wig .40 .40
1139 A214 60ce *Xerocomus subtomentosus* .50 .50
1140 A213 80ce Wood belwits .65 .65
1141 A214 150ce *Suillus placidus* 1.25 1.25
1142 A214 200ce *Lepista nuda* 1.60 1.60
1143 A213 300ce Fairy rings 2.40 2.40
1144 A213 500ce Field mushroom 4.00 4.00
Nos. 1137-1144 (8) 11.00 11.00

Souvenir Sheets

1145 A213 600ce Three *Amanita* species 4.75 4.75
1146 A214 600ce Three *Boletus* species 4.75 4.75

Souvenir Sheet

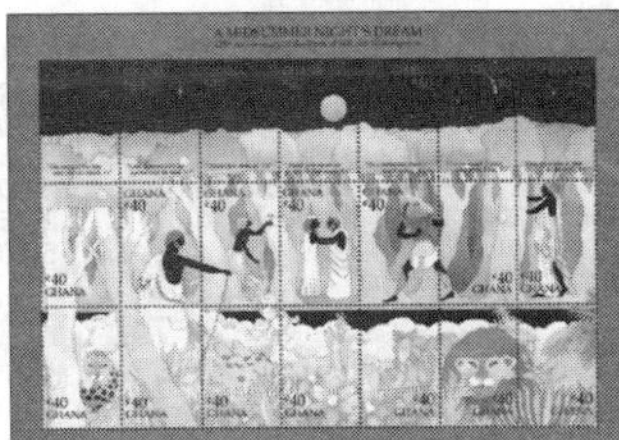

A Midsummer Night's Dream, by Shakespeare — A215

Designs: a, "The course of true love never did run smooth." b, "Love looks not with the eye but with the mind." c, "Nature here shows art." d, "Things growing are not ripe till their season." e, "He is defiled that draws a sword on thee." f, "It is not enough to speak but to speak true." g, "Thou art wise as thou art beautiful." h, Leopard behind trees. i, Theseus. j, Boy holding flower, trees. k, Oberon and Titania among trees. l, Bottom wearing head of a jackass. m, Bottom's leg, leopard behind trees. n, Hippolyta. o, Leopard, tree trunk. p, Tree trunk, foliage, lower portion of Theseus's robe. q, Wisps of fragrance, clouds, hills, foliage. r, Wisps of fragrance, flowering plants. s, Flowering plants. t, Lion, foliage. u, Lion's mane, foliage.

1989, Oct. 9 *Perf. 13½x13*

1147 A215 Sheet of 21 13.00 13.00
a.-u. 40ce any single .60 .60

425th Birth anniv. of William Shakespeare, playwright.

Birds A216

1989, Oct. 16 *Perf. 14*

1148 A216 20ce *Spermestes cuculatus* .35 .35
1149 A216 50ce *Motacilla aguimp* .55 .55
1150 A216 60ce *Halcyon malimbicus* 1.60 1.60
1151 A216 80ce *Ispidina picta* 2.25 2.25
1152 A216 150ce Striped kingfisher 1.40 1.40
1153 A216 200ce Shikra 1.60 1.60
1154 A216 300ce Gray parrot 2.00 2.00
1155 A216 500ce Black kite 3.25 3.25
Nos. 1148-1155 (8) 13.00 13.00

Souvenir Sheets

1156 A216 600ce Four birds 6.00 6.00
1157 A216 600ce Three birds 6.00 6.00

Nos. 1152-1156 vert.

1st Moon Landing, 20th Anniv. A217

Highlights of the Apollo 11 mission.

1989, Nov. 6 *Perf. 14*

1158 A217 20ce *Columbia* .20 .20
1159 A217 80ce Footprint .65 .65
1160 A217 200ce Aldrin on Moon 1.60 1.60
1161 A217 300ce Splashdown 2.40 2.40
Nos. 1158-1161 (4) 4.85 4.85

Souvenir Sheets

1162 A217 500ce Liftoff, vert. 4.00 4.00
1163 A217 500ce Earth, vert. 4.00 4.00

World Environment Day — A218

1989, Nov. 20 Litho. *Perf. 14*

1164 A218 20ce Desertification .20 .20
1165 A218 60ce Bush fires .55 .55
1166 A218 400ce Industrial pollution 3.25 3.25
1167 A218 500ce Soil erosion 4.00 4.00
Nos. 1164-1167 (4) 8.00 8.00

Nos. 760 and 761 Surcharged

1989, Nov. 20 Litho. *Perf. 14*

1168 CD331 100ce on 80p .80 .80
1169 CD331 500ce on 4ce 4.75 4.75

French Revolution, Bicent. — A219

Designs: 20ce, Storming of the Bastille, vert. 60ce, Declaration of Human Rights and Citizenship, vert. 80ce, Storming of the Bastille, diff. 200ce, *Departure of the Volunteers in 1792*, high relief on the Arc de Triomphe, 1833-35, by Francis Rude. 350ce, Planting the Liberty Tree.

Perf. 14x13½, 13½x14

1989, Sept. 22

1170 A219 20ce multicolored .50 .50
1171 A219 60ce multicolored 1.00 1.00
1172 A219 80ce multicolored 1.25 1.25
1173 A219 200ce multicolored 2.25 2.25
1174 A219 350ce multicolored 3.00 3.00
Nos. 1170-1174 (5) 8.00 8.00

Butterflies A220

1990, Feb. 15 Litho. *Perf. 14*

1175 A220 20ce *Bebearia arcadius* .50 .50
1176 A220 60ce *Charaxes laodice* .70 .70
1177 A220 80ce *Euryphura porphyrion* .80 .80
1178 A220 100ce *Neptis nicomedes* .90 .90
1179 A220 150ce *Citrinophila erastus* 1.10 1.10
1180 A220 200ce *Epitola honorius* 1.60 1.60
1181 A220 300ce *Precis wes-termanni* 1.90 1.90
1182 A220 500ce *Cymothoe hypatha* 2.50 2.50
Nos. 1175-1182 (8) 10.00 10.00

Souvenir Sheets

1183 A220 600ce *Telipna bimacula* 5.00 5.00
1184 A220 600ce *Pentila phidia* 5.00 5.00

Seashells — A221

1990, Feb. 20 *Perf. 14x14½*

1185 A221 20ce *Cymbium glans* .60 .60
1186 A221 60ce *Cardium costatum* .75 .75
1187 A221 80ce *Conus genuanus* .90 .90
1188 A221 200ce *Ancilla tankervillei* 2.25 2.25
1189 A221 350ce *Tectarius coronatus* 3.25 3.25
Nos. 1185-1189 (5) 7.75 7.75

Jawaharlal Nehru, 1st Prime Minister of Independent India — A222

Designs: 20ce, Greeting Pres. Kwame Nkrumah of Ghana. 60ce, Addressing Afro-Asian conference. 80ce, Return from tour of China, vert. 200ce, Releasing dove during a children's celebration in New Delhi, vert. 350ce, Portrait, vert.

Perf. 14½x14, 14x14½

1990, Mar. 27 Litho.

1190 A222 20ce shown .65 .65
1191 A222 60ce multicolored .75 .75
1192 A222 80ce multicolored .85 .85
1193 A222 200ce multicolored 1.25 1.25
1194 A222 350ce multicolored 1.75 1.75
Nos. 1190-1194 (5) 5.25 5.25

Nos. 759A and 760A-760B Surcharged

1990 *Perf. 14*

1195 CD331 80ce on 65p .80 .80
1196 CD331 100ce on 1ce 1.00 1.00
1197 CD331 300ce on 3ce 3.00 3.00
Nos. 1195-1197 (3) 4.80 4.80

Nos. 961, 959 and 962 Surcharged

1990

1198 A184 80ce on 20ce .80 .80
1199 A184 200ce on 8ce 2.00 2.00
1200 A184 250ce on 70ce 2.50 2.50
Nos. 1198-1200 (3) 5.30 5.30

Penny Black, 150th Anniv. A223

Great Britain No. 1 and: 20ce, City Medal containing portrait of Victoria by William Wyon adapted for use on the Penny Black. 60ce, No. 1208, Bath mail coach. 80ce, Leeds Mail coach. 200ce, Heath's engraving, based on the Wyon portrait. 350ce, Penny Black master die. 400ce, London mail coach. No. 1207, Printers and flat-bed presses of Perkins, Bacon & Petch, 1840.

1990, May 3 *Perf. 13½x14*

1201 A223 20ce shown .35 .35
1202 A223 60ce multicolored .60 .60
1203 A223 80ce multicolored .80 .80
1204 A223 200ce multicolored 1.75 1.75
1205 A223 350ce multicolored 2.25 2.25
1206 A223 400ce multicolored 2.25 2.25
Nos. 1201-1206 (6) 8.00 8.00

Souvenir Sheets

1207 A223 600ce multicolored 4.75 4.75
1208 A223 600ce multicolored 4.75 4.75

June 4, Revolution, 10th Anniv. (in 1989) — A224

1990, June 5 Litho. *Perf. 14½x14*

1209 A224 20ce shown .20 .20
1210 A224 60ce Pineapple, lobsters .50 .50
1211 A224 80ce Corn, cacao beans .65 .65
1212 A224 200ce Mining 1.60 1.60
1213 A224 350ce Scales, sword 2.75 2.75
Nos. 1209-1213 (5) 5.70 5.70

Intelsat, 25th Anniv. A225

Satellites over: 60ce, Pacific Ocean. 80ce, Pacific, diff. 200ce, South Atlantic. 350ce, Pacific, Indian Oceans.

1990, July 12 *Perf. 14x14½*

1214 A225 20ce multicolored .20 .20
1215 A225 60ce multicolored .50 .50
1216 A225 80ce multicolored .65 .65
1217 A225 200ce multicolored 1.60 1.60
1218 A225 350ce multicolored 2.75 2.75
Nos. 1214-1218 (5) 5.70 5.70

Introduction of Intl. Direct Dialing Service (in 1988) — A226

1990, July 16

1219 A226 20ce shown .20 .20
1220 A226 60ce Man using telephone .50 .50
1221 A226 80ce Man using pay telephone .65 .65
1222 A226 200ce Telephone booths 1.60 1.60
1223 A226 350ce Satellite dish 2.75 2.75
Nos. 1219-1223 (5) 5.70 5.70

Miniature Sheet

African Tropical Rain Forest A227

Designs: No. 1224a, Blue fairy flycatcher. b, Boomslang. c, Superb sunbird. d, Bateleur eagle. e, Yellow-casqued hornbill. f, Salamis temora. g, Potto. h, Leopard. i, Bongo. j, Gray parrot. k, Okapi. l, Gorilla. m, Flap-necked chameleon. n, West African dwarf crocodile. o, Python. p, Giant pangolin. q, Pseudacraea boisduvali. r, African crested porcupine. s, Rosy-columned aerangis. t, Cymothoe sangaris.

No. 1225, Leopard, vert.

1990, Oct. 25 Litho. *Perf. 14x14½*

1224 Sheet of 20 12.50 12.50
a.-t. A227 40ce any single .65 .65

Souvenir Sheet

1225 A227 600ce multicolored 14.00 14.00

Miniature Sheet

Voyager 2 — A228

Photographs from Voyager 2: No. 1226a, Jupiter. b, Neptune, Triton. c, Ariel, moon of Uranus. d, Saturn, Mimas. e, Saturn. f, Rings of Saturn. g, Neptune. h, Uranus, Miranda. i, Volcano on Io.

1990, Dec. 13 Litho. *Perf. 14*

1226 A228 100ce Sheet of 9, #1226a-1226i 8.00 8.00

Souvenir Sheets

1227 A228 600ce Voyager 2 liftoff, vert. 4.25 4.25
1228 A228 600ce Voyager 2, vert. 4.25 4.25

Orchids — A229

Designs: 20ce, Eulophia guineensis. 40ce, Eurychone rothschildiana. 60ce, Bulbophyllum barbigerum. 80ce, Polystachya galeata. 200ce, Diaphananthe kamerunensis. 300ce, Podangis dactyloceras. 400ce, Ancistrochilus rothschildianus. 500ce, Rangaeris muscicola. No. 1237, Bolusiella imbricata. No. 1238, Diaphananthe rutila.

1990, Dec. 17

1229 A229 20ce multicolored .20 .20
1230 A229 40ce multicolored .30 .30
1231 A229 60ce multicolored .50 .50
1232 A229 80ce multicolored .65 .65
1233 A229 200ce multicolored 1.60 1.60
1234 A229 300ce multicolored 2.40 2.40
1235 A229 400ce multicolored 3.25 3.25
1236 A229 500ce multicolored 4.00 4.00
Nos. 1229-1236 (8) 12.90 12.90

Souvenir Sheets

1237 A229 600ce multicolored 5.50 5.50
1238 A229 600ce multicolored 5.50 5.50

Mushrooms — A230

Designs: 20ce, Coprinus atramentarius. 50ce, Marasmius oreades. 60ce, Oudemansiella radicata. 80ce, Cep. 150ce, Hebeloma crustuliniforme. 200ce, Coprinus micaceus. 300ce, Lepiota procera. 500ce, Amanita phalloides.

1990, Dec. 18

1239 A230 20ce multicolored .20 .20
1240 A230 50ce multicolored .40 .40
1241 A230 60ce multicolored .50 .50
1242 A230 80ce multicolored .65 .65
1243 A230 150ce multicolored 1.25 1.25
1244 A230 200ce multicolored 1.60 1.60
1245 A230 300ce multicolored 2.40 2.40
a. Min. sheet of 4, #1240, 1243-1245 5.00 5.00
1246 A230 500ce multicolored 4.00 4.00
a. Min. sheet of 4, #1239, 1241-1242, 1246 5.00 5.00
Nos. 1239-1246 (8) 11.00 11.00

World Cup Soccer Championships, Italy — A231

Players from participating countries.

1990, Dec. 18 Litho. *Perf. 14*

1247 A231 20ce Italy .45 .45
1248 A231 50ce Egypt .60 .60
1249 A231 60ce Cameroun .65 .65
1250 A231 80ce Romania .75 .75
1251 A231 100ce Yugoslavia .90 .90
1252 A231 150ce Cameroun, vert. 1.50 1.50
1253 A231 400ce South Korea 2.40 2.40
1254 A231 600ce West Germany 2.75 2.75
Nos. 1247-1254 (8) 10.00 10.00

Souvenir Sheets

1255 A231 800ce UAE 5.75 5.75
1256 A231 800ce Colombia 5.75 5.75

Peter Paul Rubens (1577-1640), Painter A232

Portraits by Rubens: 20ce, Duke of Mantua. 50ce, Jan Brant. 60ce, Young man. 80ce, Michel Ophovius. 100ce, Caspar Gevaerts. 200ce, Head of a warrior (detail). 300ce, Bearded man. 400ce, Paracelsus. No. 1265, Archduke Ferdinand. No. 1266, Warrior with Two Pages.

1990, Dec. 24 Litho. *Perf. 14*

1257 A232 20ce multicolored .20 .20
1258 A232 50ce multicolored .40 .40
1259 A232 60ce multicolored .50 .50
1260 A232 80ce multicolored .65 .65
1261 A232 100ce multicolored .75 .75
1262 A232 200ce multicolored 1.75 1.75
1263 A232 300ce multicolored 2.50 2.50
1264 A232 400ce multicolored 3.25 3.25
Nos. 1257-1264 (8) 10.00 10.00

Souvenir Sheets

1265 A232 600ce multicolored 4.75 4.75
1266 A232 600ce multicolored 4.75 4.75

Minerals — A233

1991, May 2 Litho. *Perf. 14½x14*

1267 A233 20ce Manganese ore .55 .55
1268 A233 60ce Iron ore .70 .70
1269 A233 80ce Bauxite ore 1.00 1.00
1270 A233 200ce Gold ore 2.25 2.25
1271 A233 350ce Diamond 3.25 3.25
Nos. 1267-1271 (5) 7.75 7.75

Souvenir Sheet

1272 A233 600ce Diamonds 6.75 6.75

Tribal Drums — A234

1991, May 9

1273 A234 20ce Damba .20 .20
1274 A234 60ce Atumpan .50 .50
1275 A234 80ce Kroboto .65 .65
1276 A234 200ce Asafo 1.60 1.60
1277 A234 350ce Obonu 2.75 2.75
Nos. 1273-1277 (5) 5.70 5.70

Souvenir Sheet

1278 A234 600ce Single drum 5.50 5.50

Flowers — A235 A236

1991, May 15

1279 A235 20ce Amorphophallus dracontioides .65 .65
1280 A235 60ce Anchomanes difformis .95 .95
1281 A235 80ce Kaemferia nigerica 1.25 1.25
1282 A235 200ce Aframomum sceptrum 2.25 2.25
1283 A235 350ce Amorphophallus flavovirens 2.40 2.40
Nos. 1279-1283 (5) 7.50 7.50

Souvenir Sheet

1284 A235 600ce White flowers 5.00 5.00

1991, May 17 Litho. *Perf. 14½x14*

1285 A235 20ce Urginea indica .45 .45
1286 A235 60ce Hymenocallis littoralis .85 .85
1287 A235 80ce Crinum jagus 1.40 1.40
1288 A235 200ce Dipcadi tacazzeanum 1.90 1.90
1289 A235 350ce Haemanthus rupestris 2.40 2.40
Nos. 1285-1289 (5) 7.00 7.00

Souvenir Sheet

1290 A235 600ce Red flowers 4.75 4.75

1991, June 21 Litho. *Perf. 13½x14*

Designs: 20ce, Satellite transmissions, airplane. 60ce, Scientific research, honey bee. 80ce, Literacy instruction. 200ce, Agricultural development. 350ce, Industry.

1291 A236 20ce multicolored .20 .20
1292 A236 60ce multicolored .50 .50
1293 A236 80ce multicolored .65 .65
1294 A236 200ce multicolored 1.60 1.60
1295 A236 350ce multicolored 2.75 2.75
Nos. 1291-1295 (5) 5.70 5.70

UN Development Program, 40th anniv.

Lord Robert Baden-Powell (1857-1941), Founder of Boy Scouts — A237

Designs: 20ce, Sketch by Baden-Powell used in first scouting handbook, vert. 50ce, Portrait, vert. 80ce, Scout handbook illustration by Norman Rockwell. 100ce, Native runner, Cape of Good Hope #178. 200ce, Scouts aiding victims after V-1 attack, London, 1944. 500ce, Scout praying, vert. 600ce, Emblem, Cape of Good Hope #178 used. No. 1304, Cover with Cape of Good Hope #178 from Mafeking, 1900. No. 1305, Campsites, 17th World Scout Jamboree, Korea, 1991.

1991, July 16 Litho. *Perf. 14*

1296 A237 20ce buff & black .20 .20
1297 A237 50ce multicolored .40 .40
1298 A237 60ce multicolored .50 .50
1299 A237 80ce black & buff .65 .65
1300 A237 100ce multicolored .80 .80
1301 A237 200ce multicolored 1.60 1.60
1302 A237 500ce multicolored 4.00 4.00
1303 A237 600ce multicolored 4.75 4.75
Nos. 1296-1303 (8) 12.90 12.90

Souvenir Sheets

1304 A237 800ce multicolored 5.50 5.50
1305 A237 800ce multicolored 5.50 5.50

For overprints see Nos. 1567-1572.

Chorkor Smoker A238

Designs: 20ce, Placing fish on racks. 60ce, Preparing smokers. 80ce, Preparing fish. 200ce, Preparing racks for smoker. 350ce, Placing racks in smoker.

1991, July 22 Litho. *Perf. 14x14½*

1306 A238 20ce multicolored .35 .35
1307 A238 60ce multicolored .65 .65
1308 A238 80ce multicolored .75 .75
1309 A238 200ce multicolored 1.50 1.50
1310 A238 350ce multicolored 2.00 2.00
Nos. 1306-1310 (5) 5.25 5.25

Nos. 958-964 Overprinted "90th Birthday / 4th August 1990" and Surcharged

Perf. 14, 12½x12 (#1312-1313, 1315)

1991, July 22

1311 A184 20ce on 5ce #958 .20 .20
1312 A184 20ce on 8ce #959 .20 .20
1313 A184 40ce on 20ce #961 .30 .30
1314 A184 60ce on 12ce #960 .50 .50
1315 A184 80ce on 70ce #962 .65 .65
1316 A184 150ce on 100ce #963 1.25 1.25
Nos. 1311-1316 (6) 3.10 3.10

Souvenir Sheet

1317 A184 200ce on 110ce #964 1.60 1.60

Nos. 1312-1313, 1315 issued in sheets of 5 + label. Overprint is vertical on stamp in No. 1317, horizontal on sheet margin.
The status of this issue is uncertain.

Fish A239

1991, July 29 Litho. *Perf. 14*

1318 A239 20ce Cephalopholis taeniops .20 .20
1319 A239 50ce Synodontis sorex .40 .40
1320 A239 80ce Balistes forcipatus .40 .40
1321 A239 100ce Petrocephalus bane .50 .50
1322 A239 200ce Syngnathus rastellatus 1.00 1.00
1323 A239 300ce Gymnarchus niloticus 2.40 2.40
1324 A239 400ce Hemichromis bimaculatus 3.25 3.25
1325 A239 500ce Sphyrna zygaena 2.50 2.50
Nos. 1318-1325 (8) 10.65 10.65

Souvenir Sheets

1326 A239 800ce Bagrus bayad 6.50 6.50
1327 A239 800ce Dactyloptena orientalis 4.00 4.00

While Nos. 1320-1322, 1325, 1327 have the same issue date as Nos. 1318-1319, 1323-1324, 1326, the value of Nos. 1320-1322, 1325, 1327 was lower when they were released.
For overprints see Nos. 1573-1578.

Paintings by Vincent Van Gogh A240

Designs: 20ce, Reaper with Sickle. 50ce, The Thresher. 60ce, The Sheaf Binder. 80ce, The Sheep Shearers. 100ce, Peasant Woman Cutting Straw. 200ce, The Sower. 500ce, The Plow and the Harrow, horiz. 600ce, The Woodcutter. No. 1336, Evening: The Watch. No. 1337, Evening: The End of the Day.

Perf. 13x13½, 13½x13

1991, Aug. 12 Litho.

1328 A240 20ce multicolored .20 .20
1329 A240 50ce multicolored .40 .40
1330 A240 60ce multicolored .50 .50
1331 A240 80ce multicolored .65 .65
1332 A240 100ce multicolored .80 .80
1333 A240 200ce multicolored 1.60 1.60
1334 A240 500ce multicolored 4.00 4.00
1335 A240 600ce multicolored 4.75 4.75
Nos. 1328-1335 (8) 12.90 12.90

Size: 106x80mm

Imperf

1336 A240 800ce multicolored 6.50 6.50
1337 A240 800ce multicolored 6.50 6.50

10th Non-aligned Ministers Conference, Accra — A241

Natl. Leaders: 20ce, Nasser, Egypt (1952-1970). 60ce, Tito, Yugoslavia (1945-1980). 80ce, Nehru, India (1947-1964). 200ce, Nkrumah, Ghana (1957-1966). 350ce, Sukarno, Indonesia (1945-1967).

1991, Sept. 2 *Perf. 13½x14*

1338 A241 20ce multicolored .20 .20
1339 A241 60ce multicolored .50 .50
1340 A241 80ce multicolored .65 .65
1341 A241 200ce multicolored 1.60 1.60
1342 A241 350ce multicolored 2.75 2.75
Nos. 1338-1342 (5) 5.70 5.70

Birds of Ghana — A242

Designs: No. 1343a, Melba finch. b, Orange-cheeked waxbill. c, Paradise flycatcher. d, Blue plantain-eater, e, Red bishop. f, Splendid glossy starling. g, Red-headed lovebird. h, Palm swift. i, Narina trogon. j, Tawny eagle. k, Bateleur eagle. l, Hoopoe. m, Secretary bird. n, White-backed vulture. o, Bare-headed rockfowl. p, Ground hornbill.

No. 1344a, Openbilled stork. b, African spoonbill. c, Pink-backed pelican. d, Little bittern. e, King reed-hen. f, Saddlebill stork. g, Glossy ibis. h, White-faced tree duck. i, Black-headed heron. j, Hammerkop. k, African darter. l, Woolly-necked stork. m, Yellow-billed stork. n, Black-winged stilt. o, Goliath heron. p, Lily trotter.

No. 1345a, Shikra. b, Abyssinian roller (c, g). c, Carmine bee-eater (g). d, Pintailed whydah (h). e, Purple glossy starling. f, Yellow-backed whydah (j). g, Pel's fishing owl. h, Verreaux's touraco (l). i, Red-cheeked cordon-bleu. j, Olive-bellied sunbird. k, Red-billed hornbill. l, Red-billed quelea. m, Crowned crane (i). n, Blue quail. o, Egyptian vulture (p). p, Helmeted guineafowl.

No. 1346, Marabou stork. No. 1347, Saddlebill stork, diff. No. 1348, African river eagle.

1991, Oct. 14 Litho. *Perf. 14½x14*

Sheets of 16

1343 A242 80ce #a.-p. 7.25 7.25
1344 A242 100ce #a.-p. 10.00 10.00
1345 A242 100ce #a.-p. 12.50 12.50
Nos. 1343-1345 (3) 29.75 29.75

Souvenir Sheets

1346 A242 800ce multicolored 5.00 5.00
1347 A242 800ce multicolored 5.00 5.00
1348 A242 800ce multicolored 5.00 5.00

While No. 1344 has the same issue date as No. 1345, the value of No. 1344 was lower when it was released.

Insects A243

1991, Oct. 25 *Perf. 14x13½*

1349 A243 20ce Nularda .20 .20
1350 A243 50ce Zonocrus .40 .40
1351 A243 60ce Gryllotalpa africana .50 .50
1352 A243 80ce Weevil .65 .65
1353 A243 100ce Coenagrion .80 .80
1354 A243 150ce Sahlbergella 1.25 1.25
1355 A243 200ce Anthia 1.60 1.60
1356 A243 350ce Megacephala 2.75 2.75
Nos. 1349-1356 (8) 8.15 8.15

Souvenir Sheet

Perf. 13x12

1357 A243 600ce Lacetus 4.75 4.75

Landmarks and Shells - A243a

Designs: 50ce, Boti Falls, vert. 60ce, Larabanga Mosque. 80ce, Fort Sebastian, Shama. 100ce, Cape Coast Castle. 200ce, Leucodon cowrie. 400ce, Achatina achatina.

100ce exists in three types:
Type I, "G" has angled curve, bars in "A"s slope down to left, "c" has straight line, bottom inscription 10mm.
Type II, "G" is rounded, bars in "A"s slope down to right, "c" has slanted line, bottom inscription 13mm.
Type III, "G" is rounded, bars in "A"s slope down to right, "c" has straight line, bottom inscription 10mm.

200ce, 400ce
Nos. 1357E, 1357Ej, 1357F, Type I: "G" has angled curve, bar in "A"s" slope down to left.
Nos. 1357Ek, 1357Fl, Type II: "G" is rounded, bars in "A's" slope down to right.

Perf. 13¾x13½, 13½x13¾

1991 Litho.

1357A A243a 50ce multi
1357B A243a 60ce multi
1357C A243a 80ce multi
1357D A243a 100ce multi (I)
g. Type II
h. Type I, perf 14¼x13¾
i. Type III, perf 14¼x13¾
1357E A243a 200ce multi (I)
j. Type I, perf. 14¼x13¾ — —
k. Type II, perf. 14¼x13¾ — —
1357F A243a 400ce multi (I)
l. Type II, perf. 14¼x13¾ — —

This set was printed locally. Shades exist.
Issue dates: 50ce, Nov. 21; others, Dec. 12.

Adoration of the Magi by Hieronymus Bosch A244

Details or entire paintings: 50ce, The Annunciation by Robert Campin. 60ce, Virgin and Child by Dirk Bouts. 80ce, Presentation in the Temple by Hans Memling. 100ce, The Virgin and Child Enthroned with an Angel and a Donor by Memling. 200ce, The Virgin and Child with Saints and a Donor by Jan van Eyck. 400ce, St. Luke Painting the Virgin by Rogier van der Weyden. 700ce, Virgin and Child by Bouts, diff. No. 1366, The Annunciation by Memling. No. 1367, The Virgin and Child Standing in a Niche by van der Weyden.

1991, Dec. 23 *Perf. 12*

1358 A244 20ce multicolored .20 .20
1359 A244 50ce multicolored .40 .40
1360 A244 60ce multicolored .50 .50
1361 A244 80ce multicolored .65 .65
1362 A244 100ce multicolored .80 .80
1363 A244 200ce multicolored 1.60 1.60
1364 A244 400ce multicolored 3.25 3.25
1365 A244 700ce multicolored 5.50 5.50
Nos. 1358-1365 (8) 12.90 12.90

Souvenir Sheets

Perf. 14½

1366 A244 800ce multicolored 6.50 6.50
1367 A244 800ce multicolored 6.50 6.50

Christmas.

Reunification of Germany — A245

Designs: 20ce, Opening of German border, Nov. 9, 1989. 60ce, Signing of Two Plus Four Treaty, Sept. 12, 1990. 80ce, Opening of Brandenburg Gate, Dec. 22, 1989. 800ce, German leaders, Unity Day, Oct. 3, 1990.

No. 1371b, USSR Pres. Mikhail Gorbachev, vert. c, Chancellor Helmut Kohl, vert. d, Map of West Germany, vert. e, Map of East Germany, vert. 1000ce, Currency union, July 1, 1990.

No. 1371g, Doves. h, German Chancellor Helmut Kohl, Foreign Minister Hans-Dietrich Genscher.

1992, Feb. 17 Litho. *Perf. 14*

1368 A245 20ce multicolored .20 .20
1369 A245 60ce multicolored .45 .45
1370 A245 80ce multicolored .50 .50
1371 A245 1000ce multicolored 6.85 6.85
Nos. 1368-1371 (4) 8.00 8.00

Souvenir Sheets

1371A A245 300ce Sheet of 4, #b.-e. 7.50 7.50
1371F A245 400ce Sheet of 2, #g.-h. 2.50 2.50
1372 A245 800ce multicolored 5.50 5.50

While No. 1371F has the same issue date as No. 1371A, the dollar value of No. 1371F was lower when it was released.

1992 Summer Olympics, Barcelona A246

Map and: 20ce, Eddie Blay, boxing, Ghana, 1964. 60ce, Mike Ahey, track, Ghana, 1964-1972. 80ce, T. Wilson, ski jumping, US, 1988. 100ce, East German 4-Man bobsled, 1988. 200ce, Greg Louganis, diving, US, 1984. 300ce, L. Visser, speed skating, Netherlands, 1988. 350ce, J. Passler, biathlon, Italy, 1988. 400ce, Mary Lou Retton, gymnastics, US, 1984. 500ce, Jurgen Hingsen, decathlon, Germany, 1984. 600ce, R. Neubert, heptathlon, West Germany, 1984. No. 1380, Jai alai player, vert. No. 1381, Windmill.

1992, Mar. 3 Litho. *Perf. 14*

1373 A246 20ce multi .20 .20
1373A A246 60ce multi .20 .20
1374 A246 80ce multi .50 .50
1375 A246 100ce multi .60 .60
1376 A246 200ce multi 1.25 1.25
1377 A246 300ce multi 1.90 1.90
1378 A246 350ce multi 2.10 2.10
1378A A246 400ce multi 1.25 1.25
1378B A246 500ce multi 1.50 1.50
1379 A246 600ce multi 3.75 3.75
Nos. 1373-1379 (10) 13.25 13.25

Souvenir Sheets

1380 A246 800ce multi 5.00 5.00
1381 A246 800ce multi 5.00 5.00

While Nos. 1373A, 1378A-1378B have the same issue date as rest of the set the dollar value of Nos. 1373A, 1378A-1378B were lower when they were released.

Phila Nippon '91 A247

1992, Feb. 16 Litho. *Perf. 14*

1382 A247 20ce shown .20 .20
1383 A247 60ce Torii of Itsukushima Jingu shrine .35 .35
1384 A247 80ce Geisha .45 .45
1385 A247 100ce Samurai residence .60 .60
1386 A247 200ce Bonsai tree 1.25 1.25
1387 A247 400ce Olympic sports hall 2.40 2.40
1388 A247 500ce Great Buddha 3.00 3.00
1389 A247 600ce Nagoya castle 3.75 3.75
Nos. 1382-1389 (8) 12.00 12.00

Souvenir Sheets

1390 A247 800ce Takamatsu castle 5.00 5.00
1391 A247 800ce Heian shrine 5.00 5.00

Ghana Natl. Railways A248

Designs: 20c, Engine, 1903, Gold Coast Railway. 50c, Diesel passenger locomotive, Ghana Railways Corp. 60ce, First class coach, 1931 Gold Coast Railway. 80ce, Official inspection coach, Gold Coast Railway. 100ce, Engine No. 401 on turntable. 200c, Twin-bogie cocoa wagon, 1921, Gold Coast Railway. 500ce, Engine No. 223, "Prince of Wales." 600c, Twin-bogie cattle wagon, Gold Coast Railway. No. 1400, German-made locomotive, Gold Coast Railway. No. 1401, Beyer-Garratt #301, 1943, Gold Coast Railway.

1992, Mar. 2

1392 A248 20ce multicolored .20 .20
1393 A248 50ce multicolored .30 .30
1394 A248 60ce multicolored .40 .40
1395 A248 80ce multicolored .50 .50
1396 A248 100ce multicolored .60 .60
1397 A248 200ce multicolored 1.25 1.25
1398 A248 500ce multicolored 3.00 3.00
1399 A248 600ce multicolored 3.75 3.75
Nos. 1392-1399 (8) 10.00 10.00

Souvenir Sheets

1400 A248 800ce multicolored 5.00 5.00
1401 A248 800ce multicolored 5.00 5.00

Decade of Revolutionary Progress A249

1992, Feb. 2 Litho. *Perf. 14x13½*

1402 A249 20ce Bore hole water .20 .20
1403 A249 50ce Mining industry .30 .30
1404 A249 60ce Small scale industry .40 .40
1405 A249 80ce Timber industry .50 .50
1406 A249 200ce Cocoa rehabilitation 1.25 1.25
1407 A249 350ce Rural electrification 2.10 2.10
Nos. 1402-1407 (6) 4.75 4.75

Reptiles A251

1992, Mar. 30 Litho. *Perf. 14*

1414 A251 20ce Angides lugubris .20 .20
1415 A251 50ce Kinixys erosa .30 .30
1416 A251 60ce Agama agama .40 .40
1417 A251 80ce Chameleo gracilis .50 .50
1418 A251 100ce Naja melanleuca .60 .60
1419 A251 200ce Crocodylus niloticus 1.25 1.25
1420 A251 400ce Chelonia mydas 2.40 2.40
1421 A251 500ce Varanus exanthematicus 3.00 3.00
Nos. 1414-1421 (8) 8.65 8.65

Souvenir Sheet

1422 A251 600ce Snake & tortoise 3.50 3.50

Numbers have been reserved for additional values in this set.

Easter A252

Details from paintings: 20ce, The Four Apostles: Sts. John, Peter, Paul & Mark, by Durer. 50ce, The Last Judgment, by Rubens. 60ce, The Four Apostles: Sts. John, Peter, Paul and Mark, diff. by Durer. 80ce, The Last Judgment, diff. by Rubens. 100ce, Crucifixion, by Rubens. 200ce, The Last Judgment, diff. by Rubens. 500ce, Christum Videre, by Rubens. 600ce, The Last Judgment, diff. by Rubens. No. 1432, Last Communion of St. Francis of Assisi, by Rubens. No. 1432A, Scourging the Money Changers from the Temple, by El Greco, horiz.

1992, Mar. 13 *Perf. 13½x14*

1424 A252 20ce multi .20 .20
1425 A252 50ce multi .30 .30
1426 A252 60ce multi .40 .40
1427 A252 80ce multi .50 .50
1428 A252 100ce multi .60 .60
1429 A252 200ce multi 1.25 1.25
1430 A252 500ce multi 3.00 3.00
1431 A252 600ce multi 3.50 3.50
Nos. 1424-1431 (8) 9.75 9.75

Souvenir Sheets

1432 A252 800ce multi 4.75 4.75

Perf. 14x13½

1432A A252 800ce multi 4.75 4.75

Spanish Art — A253

Paintings by Velazquez: 20ce, Two Men at Table. 60ce, Christ in the House of Mary and Martha (detail). 80ce, The Supper at Emmaus. 100ce, Three Muscians. 200ce, Old Woman Cooking Eggs, vert. 400ce, Old Woman Cooking Eggs (detail), vert. 500ce, The Surrender of Breda (detail) diff., vert. 700ce, The Surrender of Breda (detail), vert.

No. 1441, They Still Say that Fish is Expensive, by Joaquin Sorolla y Bastida. No. 1442, The Waterseller of Seville.

1992, May 4 *Perf. 13½*

1433 A253 20ce multicolored .20 .20
1434 A253 60ce multicolored .30 .30
1435 A253 80ce multicolored .40 .40
1436 A253 100ce multicolored .60 .60
1437 A253 200ce multicolored 1.25 1.25
1438 A253 400ce multicolored 2.00 2.00
1439 A253 500ce multicolored 2.50 2.50
1440 A253 700ce multicolored 4.25 4.25

Size: 120x95mm

Imperf

1441 A253 900ce multicolored 5.50 5.50
1442 A253 900ce multicolored 4.50 4.50
Nos. 1433-1442 (10) 21.50 21.50

Granada '92. While Nos. 1434-1435, 1438-1439, 1442 have the same issue date as Nos. 1433, 1436-1437, 1440-1441, the value in relation to the dollar of Nos. 1434-1435, 1438-1439, 1442 was lower when they were released.

Butterflies — A254

Dinosaurs — A255

1992, May 25 Litho. *Perf. 14*

1443 A254 20ce African monarch .20 .20
1444 A254 60ce Mocker swallowtail .35 .35
1445 A254 80ce Painted lady .50 .50
1446 A254 100ce Mountain beauty .60 .60
1447 A254 200ce Blue temora 1.25 1.25
1448 A254 400ce Foxy charaxes 2.40 2.40
1449 A254 500ce Blue pansy 3.00 3.00
1450 A254 700ce Golden pansy 4.25 4.25
Nos. 1443-1450 (8) 12.55 12.55

Souvenir Sheets

1451 A254 900ce Gaudy commodore 5.50 5.50
1452 A254 900ce Christmas butterfly 5.50 5.50

Genoa '92. For overprints see Nos. 1471-1480.

1992, June 1 Litho. *Perf. 14*

1453 A255 20ce Iguanodon .20 .20
1454 A255 50ce Anchisaurus .30 .30
1455 A255 60ce Heterodontosaurus .40 .40
1456 A255 80ce Ouranosaurus .40 .40
1457 A255 100ce Anatosaurus .60 .60
1458 A255 200ce Elaphrosaurus 1.00 1.00
1459 A255 500ce Coelophysis 2.50 2.50
1460 A255 600ce Rhamphorynchus 3.50 3.50
Nos. 1453-1460 (8) 8.90 8.90

Souvenir Sheets

1461 A255 1500ce like #1459 9.00 9.00
1462 A255 1500ce like #1458 7.50 7.50

While Nos. 1453, 1456, 1458-1459 and 1462 have the same issue date as Nos. 1454-1455, 1457, 1460-1461, their value in relation to the dollar was lower when they were released.

Miniature Sheet

Discovery of America, 500th Anniv. — A256

Designs: No. 1463a, Capt. Martin Alonzo Pinzon, Pinta. b, Capt. Vicente Yanez Pinzon, Nina. c, Columbus, Fr. Marchena in La Rabida, 1485. d, Columbus in cabin. e, Land sighted, Oct. 12, 1492. f, Columbus lands on Samana Cay. g, Shipwreck of Santa Maria. h, Columbus returns to Spanish Court, 1493. No. 1464, Columbus, ship.

1992, July Litho. *Perf. 14*

1463 A256 200ce Sheet of 8, #a.-h. 9.50 9.50

Souvenir Sheet

1464 A256 500ce multicolored 3.00 3.00

World Columbian Stamp Expo '92, Chicago.

Shells — A257

1992, Oct. 5 Litho. *Perf. 14*

1465 A257 20ce Olivancillaria hiatula .20 .20
1465A A257 20ce Tympanotonus fuscatus .20 .20
1466 A257 60ce Donax rugosus .30 .30
1466A A257 60ce Murex cornutus .30 .30
1467 A257 80ce Sigaretus concavus .40 .40
1467A A257 80ce Tivela tripla .40 .40
1468 A257 200ce Pila africana 1.00 1.00
1468A A257 200ce Cypraea stercoraria 1.00 1.00
1469 A257 350ce Thais hiatula 1.75 1.75

1469A	A257	350ce Cassis tesselata	1.75	1.75
		Nos. 1465-1469A (10)	7.30	7.30

Souvenir Sheet

1470	A257	600ce Natica favel	3.00	3.00
1470A	A257	600ce Semifusos morio	3.00	3.00

Nos. 1443-1452 Ovptd. "40th / Anniversary / of the / Accession / of / HM Queen / Elizabeth II / 1952-1992" in Silver

1992, Aug. 10 Litho. Perf. 14

1471	A254	20ce on #1443	.20	.20
1472	A254	60ce on #1444	.30	.30
1473	A254	80ce on #1445	.40	.40
1474	A254	100ce on #1446	.50	.50
1475	A254	200ce on #1447	1.00	1.00
1476	A254	400ce on #1448	2.00	2.00
1477	A254	500ce on #1449	2.50	2.50
1478	A254	700ce on #1450	3.50	3.50
		Nos. 1471-1478 (8)	10.40	10.40

Souvenir Sheets

1479	A254	900ce on #1451	4.50	4.50
1480	A254	900ce on #1452	4.50	4.50

Christmas A259

Details or entire paintings: 20ce, Presentation in the Temple, by Master of Brunswick. 50ce, Presentation in the Temple, by Master of St. Severin. 60ce, The Visitation, by Sebastiano del Piombo. 80ce, The Visitation, by Giotto. 100ce, The Circumcision, by Studio of Giovanni Bellini. 200ce, The Circumcision, by Workshop of Benvenuto Garofalo. 500ce, The Visitation, by Workshop of Rogier van der Weyden. 800ce, The Circumcision, by Workshop of Rogier Van der Weyden. No. 1491, The Visitation, by Giotto. No. 1492, The Presentation in the Temple, by Bartolo di Fredi.

1992 Litho. Perf. 13½x14

1483	A259	20ce multicolored	.20	.20
1484	A259	50ce multicolored	.25	.25
1485	A259	60ce multicolored	.30	.30
1486	A259	80ce multicolored	.35	.35
1487	A259	100ce multicolored	.45	.45
1488	A259	200ce multicolored	.90	.90
1489	A259	500ce multicolored	2.25	2.25
1490	A259	800ce multicolored	3.75	3.75
		Nos. 1483-1490 (8)	8.45	8.45

Souvenir Sheet

1491	A259	900ce multicolored	4.50	4.50
1492	A259	900ce multicolored	4.50	4.50

No. 1492 exists imperf.

Anniversaries and Events
A260 A261

Designs: 20ce, LZ3, floating hangar at Lake Constance, horiz. 100ce, Lift-off of Ariane 4 rocket, horiz. 200ce, Leopard in tree, horiz. 300ce, Roman Colosseum, fruits and vegetables, horiz. 400ce, Wolfgang Amadeus Mozart. 600ce, Lift-off of H-1 rocket, Japan. 800ce, LZ10, Schwaben, horiz. No. 1501, Scene from "The Marriage of Figaro." No. 1502, Space shuttle, US. No. 1503, Count Ferdinand von Zeppelin. No. 1504, Bongo, horiz.

1992, Dec. Litho. Perf. 14

1493	A260	20ce multicolored	.20	.20
1494	A260	100ce multicolored	.50	.50
1495	A260	200ce multicolored	1.00	1.00
1496	A260	300ce multicolored	1.50	1.50
1497	A261	400ce multicolored	2.00	2.00
1499	A260	600ce multicolored	3.00	3.00
1500	A260	800ce multicolored	4.00	4.00
		Nos. 1493-1500 (7)	12.20	12.20

Souvenir Sheets

1501	A261	900ce multicolored	4.50	4.50
1502	A260	900ce multicolored	4.50	4.50
1503	A260	900ce multicolored	4.50	4.50
1504	A260	900ce multicolored	4.50	4.50

Count Ferdinand von Zeppelin, 75th anniv. of death (#1493, 1500, 1503). Intl. Space Year (#1494, 1499, 1502). UN Earth Summit, Rio de Janeiro (#1495, 1504). WHO, Intl. Conference on Nutrition, Rome (1496). Mozart, bicent. of death (in 1991) (#1497, 1501).

Flowers — A262

#1505, 1514d (100ce), Lagerstroemia flos-reginae. #1506, Clerodendrum thomsoniae. #1507, 1514c (50ce), Spathodea campanulata. #1508 (60ce), Cassia fistula. #1509, 1514e (150ce), Mellitea ferrugenea. #1510, 1514j (300ce), Hildegardia barteri. #1511, 1514i (150ce), Ipomoea asarifolia. #1512, Petrea volubilis. #1513, 1514f (300ce), Ritchiea reflexa. #1514, 1514h (100ce), Bryphyllum pinnatum.

1993, Mar. 1 Litho. Perf. 14

1505	A262	20ce multicolored	.20	.20
1506	A262	20ce multicolored	.20	.20
1507	A262	60ce multicolored	.30	.30
1508	A262	60ce multicolored	.30	.30
1509	A262	80ce multicolored	.40	.40
1510	A262	80ce multicolored	.40	.40
1511	A262	200ce multicolored	1.00	1.00
1512	A262	200ce multicolored	1.00	1.00
1513	A262	350ce multicolored	1.75	1.75
1514	A262	350ce multicolored	1.75	1.75
		Nos. 1505-1514 (10)	7.30	7.30

Souvenir Sheets

1514A	A262	Sheet of 4, #c.-f.	3.00	3.00
1514B	A262	Sheet of 4, #g.-j.	3.00	3.00

Intl. Conference on Nutrition, Rome — A263

1993, Jan. Litho. Perf. 14

1515	A263	20ce Energy foods	.20	.20
1516	A263	60ce Body-building foods	.30	.30
1517	A263	80ce Protective foods	.40	.40
1518	A263	200ce Disease prevention	1.00	1.00
1519	A263	400ce Food quality control, preservation	2.00	2.00
		Nos. 1515-1519 (5)	3.90	3.90

Crabs A264

Designs: 20ce, Clappa rubroguttata. 60ce, Cardisoma amatum. 80ce, Maia squinado. 400ce, Ocypoda cursor. 800ce, Grapus grapus.

1993, Feb. Perf. 14x13½

1520	A264	20ce multicolored	.20	.20
1521	A264	60ce multicolored	.30	.30
1522	A264	80ce multicolored	.40	.40
1523	A264	400ce multicolored	2.00	2.00
a.		Souv. sheet of 4, #1520-1523	2.75	2.75
1524	A264	800ce multicolored	4.00	4.00
		Nos. 1520-1524 (5)	6.90	6.90

Miniature Sheet of 8

Louvre Museum, Bicent. A265

Details or entire paintings, by Giovanni Domenico Tiepolo (1727-1804) (a-e) and Giovanni Battista Tiepolo (1696-1770) (f-h). No. 1525: a-c, Carnival Scene, (left, center, right). d-e, Tooth Puller, (left, right). f, Rebecca at the Well. g-h, Presenting Christ to the People, (left, right).

700ce, Chancellor Seguier, by Le Brun, horiz.

1993, Mar. 1 Litho. Perf. 12

1525	A265	200ce #a.-h. + label	8.25	8.25

Souvenir Sheet
Perf. 14½

1526	A265	700ce multicolored	3.75	3.75

No. 1526 contains one 55x88mm stamp.

Faberge Eggs — A266 4th Republic — A268

Wild Animals A267

Easter: 50ce, Resurrection Egg. 80ce, Imperial Red Cross Egg with Resurrection Triptych. 100ce, Imperial Uspensky Cathedral Egg. 150ce, Imperial Red Cross Egg with portraits. 200ce, Orange Tree Egg. 250ce, Rabbit Egg. 400ce, Imperial Coronation Egg. 900ce, Silver-gilt enamel Easter Egg. No. 1535, Spring Flower Egg. No. 1536, Egg charms, horiz.

1993, Apr. 26 Perf. 14

1527	A266	50ce multi	.25	.25
1528	A266	80ce multi	.40	.40
1529	A266	100ce multi	.50	.50
1530	A266	150ce multi	.75	.75
1531	A266	200ce multi	1.00	1.00
1532	A266	250ce multi	1.25	1.25
1533	A266	400ce multi	2.00	2.00
1534	A266	900ce multi	4.50	4.50
		Nos. 1527-1534 (8)	10.65	10.65

Souvenir Sheets

1535	A266	1000ce multi	5.00	5.00
1536	A266	1000ce multi	5.00	5.00

1993, May 24 Litho. Perf. 14

1537	A267	20ce African buffalo	.20	.20
1538	A267	50ce Giant forest hog	.25	.25
1539	A267	60ce Potto	.30	.30
1540	A267	80ce Bay duiker	.40	.40
1541	A267	100ce Royal antelope	.50	.50
1542	A267	200ce Serval	1.00	1.00
1543	A267	500ce Golden cat	2.50	2.50
1544	A267	800ce Megaloglossus woermanni	4.00	4.00
		Nos. 1537-1544 (8)	9.15	9.15

Souvenir Sheets

1545	A267	900ce Dormouse	4.50	4.50
1546	A267	900ce White collared mangabey	4.50	4.50

1993, May Litho. Perf. 14

50ce, Kwame Nkrumah Mausoleum, horiz. 100ce, Kwame Nkrumah Conference Center, horiz. 200ce, Constitution book. 350ce, Independence Square. 400ce, Christiansborg Castle.

1547	A268	50ce multicolored	.25	.25
1548	A268	100ce multicolored	.50	.50
1549	A268	200ce multicolored	1.00	1.00
1550	A268	350ce multicolored	1.75	1.75
1551	A268	400ce multicolored	2.00	2.00
		Nos. 1547-1551 (5)	5.50	5.50

A269

Aviation and Automotive Anniversaries — A270

Designs: 50ce, Graf Zeppelin over Alps, vert. No. 1552, Mercedes Benz 300 SLR in 1955 Mille Miglia. No. 1553, LZ7 Deutschland. No. 1554, Vulcan bomber. No. 1555, Ford Trimotor. No. 1556, 1920 Ford Depot Wagon. No. 1557, Nieuport 27, vert. No. 1558, Graf Zeppelin taking aboard letters, vert. No. 1559, 1970 Ford Mach 1 Mustang.

No. 1560, LZ10 Schwaben. No. 1561, Mercedes wins 1937 Monaco Grand Prix. No. 1562, Graf Zeppelin over Rome. No. 1563, 1955 Mercedes Benz Type 196. No. 1564, Early US air mail flight. No. 1565, S.E.5A, 1918. No. 1566, 1910 Ford Super T, 999.

1993 Litho. Perf. 14

1551A	A269	50ce multi	.25	.25
1552	A270	150ce multi	.75	.75
1553	A269	150ce multi	.75	.75
1554	A269	400ce multi	2.00	2.00
1555	A269	400ce multi	2.00	2.00
1556	A270	400ce multi	2.00	2.00
1557	A269	600ce multi	3.00	3.00
1558	A269	600ce multi	3.00	3.00
1559	A270	600ce multi	3.00	3.00
1560	A269	800ce multi	4.00	4.00
1561	A270	800ce multi	4.00	4.00
		Nos. 1551A-1561 (11)	24.75	24.75

Souvenir Sheets

1562	A269	1000ce multi	5.00	5.00
1563	A270	1000ce multi	5.00	5.00
1564	A269	1000ce multi	5.00	5.00
1565	A269	1000ce multi	5.00	5.00
1566	A270	1000ce multi	5.00	5.00

Capt. Hugo Eckener, 125th birth anniv. (#1551A, 1553-1554, 1562). Benz's first four-wheeled vehicle, cent. (#1552, 1561, 1563). Royal Air Force, 75th anniv. (#1554, 1557, 1564). Henry Ford's first gasoline powered engine, cent. (#1556, 1559, 1566).

No. 1564 contains one 57x42mm stamp. Nos. 1563, 1566 contains one 85x28mm stamp.

Issued: #1555-1556, 1558-1559, 1565-1566, May. #1551A-1554, 1557, 1560-1564, June.

Nos. 1300-1305 Ovptd.

1993 Litho. Perf. 14

1567	A237	100ce multicolored	.50	.50
1568	A237	200ce multicolored	1.00	1.00
1569	A237	500ce multicolored	2.50	2.50
1570	A237	600ce multicolored	3.00	3.00
		Nos. 1567-1570 (4)	7.00	7.00

Souvenir Sheet

1571	A237	800ce on #1304	4.00	4.00
1572	A237	800ce on #1305	4.00	4.00

Nos. 1321, 1323-1327 Ovptd. a. in Black "35 YEARS OF / ROTARY INTERNATIONAL / GHANA 1958" or b. in Red "GHANA / RED CROSS SOCIETY / FOUNDED 1932"

1993

1573 A239(a) 100ce multi	.50	.50
1574 A239(b) 300ce multi	1.50	1.50
1575 A239(b) 400ce multi	2.00	2.00
1576 A239(a) 500ce multi	2.50	2.50
Nos. 1573-1576 (4)	6.50	6.50

Souvenir Sheets

1577 A239(a) 800ce on #1326	4.00	4.00
1578 A239(b) 800ce on #1327	4.00	4.00

A271

Mushrooms A272

Designs: 20ce, Cantharellus cibarius. 50ce, Russula cyanoxantha. 60ce, Clitocybe rivulosa. No. 1581, Boletus chrysenteron. No. 1582, Cortinarius elatior. No. 1583, Mycena galericulata. No. 1584, Boletus edulis. No. 1585, Tricholoma gambosum. No. 1586, Lepista saeva. 250ce, Gyroporus castaneus. No. 1589, Nolanea sericea. No. 1590, Hygrophorus puiceus. 500ce, Gomphidius glutinosus. No. 1592, Russula olivacea. 1000ce, Russula aurata.

No. 1594a, 100ce, Cantharellus cibarius. b, 150ce, Cortinarius elatior. c, 300ce, Tricholoma gambosum. d, 600ce, Hygrophorus puiceus.

No. 1595: a, 50ce, like #1581. b, 100ce, like #1583. c, 150ce, like #1584. d, 1000ce, like #1589.

1993, July 30 Litho. *Perf. 14*

1579 A271	20ce multi	.20	.20
1580 A271	50ce multi	.25	.25
1581 A271	60ce multi	.30	.30
1582 A271	80ce multi	.40	.40
1583 A271	80ce multi	.40	.40
1584 A271	200ce multi	1.00	1.00
1585 A271	200ce multi	1.00	1.00
1586 A272	200ce multi	1.00	1.00
1587 A272	250ce multi	1.25	1.25
1588 A271	300ce multi	1.50	1.50
1589 A271	350ce multi	1.75	1.75
1590 A271	350ce multi	1.75	1.75
1591 A272	500ce multi	2.50	2.50
1592 A271	600ce multi	3.00	3.00
1593 A272	1000ce multi	5.00	5.00
	Nos. 1579-1593 (15)	21.30	21.30

Souvenir Sheets

1594 A271	Sheet of 4, #a.-d.	6.00	6.00
1595 A271	Sheet of 4, #a.-d.	6.50	6.50

Copernicus (1473-1543) A273

Designs: 20ce, Early astronomical instrument. 200ce, Telescope. No. 1598, Copernicus, long hair. No. 1599, Copernicus, shorter hair.

1993, Oct. 19 Litho. *Perf. 13½x14*

1596 A273 20ce multicolored	.20	.20
1597 A273 200ce multicolored	1.00	1.00

Souvenir Sheets

Perf. 12x13

1598 A273 1000ce multicolored	5.00	5.00
1599 A273 1000ce multicolored	5.00	5.00

Picasso (1881-1973) A274

1993, Oct. 19 *Perf. 14*

Paintings: 20ce, The Actor, 1905. 80ce, Portrait of Allen Stein, 1906. 800ce, Seated Male Nude, 1908-09.

1600-1602 A274 Set of 3	4.75	4.75

Souvenir Sheet

1603 A274 900ce Guernica, 1937	4.75	4.75

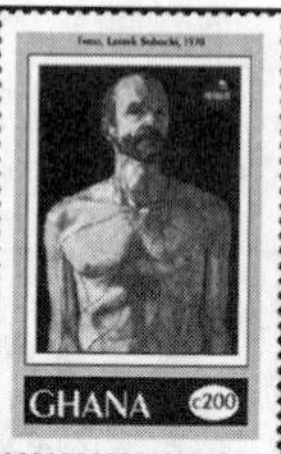
Polska '93 — A275

1994 World Cup Soccer, US — A276

Paintings: 200ce, Tatoo, by Sobocki, 1978. 600ce, Prison, by Blonder, 1934. 1000ce, Baijka o Czlowieku Szczesliwym, by Mickalak, 1925, horiz.

1993, Oct. 19

1604-1605 A275 Set of 2	4.00	4.00

Souvenir Sheet

1606 A275 1000ce multicolored	5.00	5.00

1993, Dec. 1 *Perf. 13½x14*

Designs: 50ce, Abedi Pele, Ghana. 80ce, Pedro Troglio, Argentina. 100ce, Fernando Alvez, Uruguay. 200ce, Franco Baresi, Italy. 250ce, Gomez, Colombia; Katanec, Yugoslavia. 600ce, Diego Maradona, Argentina. 800ce, Hasek, Czech Republic; Wynalda, US. 1000ce, Lothar Matthaeus, Germany.

No. 1615, Giuseppe Giannini, Italy. No. 1616, Rabie Yassein, Egypt; Ruud Gullit, Holland.

1607 A276	50ce multi	.25	.25
1608 A276	80ce multi	.40	.40
1609 A276	100ce multi	.50	.50
1610 A276	200ce multi	1.00	1.00
1611 A276	250ce multi	1.25	1.25
1612 A276	600ce multi	3.00	3.00
1613 A276	800ce multi	4.25	4.25
1614 A276	1000ce multi	5.25	5.25
	Nos. 1607-1614 (8)	15.90	15.90

Souvenir Sheets

Perf. 13

1615 A276	1200ce multi	6.00	6.00
1616 A276	1200ce multi	6.00	6.00

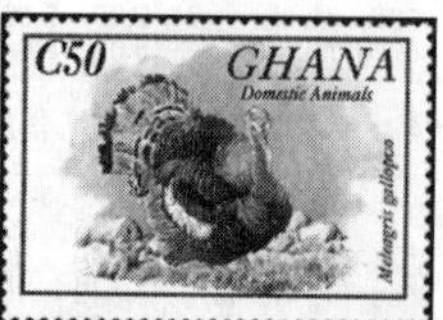
Domestic Animals A277

Designs: 50ce, Meleagris gallopvo. 100ce, Capra hircus. 150ce, Carina moschata. 200ce, Eguus asinus. 250ce, Male gallus gallus. 300ce, Sus vittatus. 400ce, Numida meleagris. 600ce, Canis domesticus. 800ce, Female gallus gallus. 1000ce, Ovis aries.

#1627a, 100ce, like #1618. b, 250ce, like #1624. c, 350ce, like #1622. d, 500ce, like #1626.

#1628a, 100ce, like #1623. b, 250ce, like #1621. c, 350ce, like #1625. d, 500ce, like #1617.

1993, Dec. 8 *Perf. 14*

1617-1626 A277 Set of 10	15.00	15.00

Souvenir Sheets

1627	A277	multicolored	5.00	5.00
1628	A277	multicolored	5.00	5.00

Arts and Crafts — A278

Designs: No. 1629, 50ce, Doll. No. 1630, 50ce, Pot and lid. No. 1631, 200ce, Beads. No. 1632, 200ce, Snake charmers. No. 1633, 250ce, Hoe. No. 1634, 250ce, Scabbard. No. 1635, 600ce, Pipe. No. 1636, 600ce, Deer. No. 1637, 1000ce, Mask. No. 1638, 1000ce, Doll with baby.

No. 1639a, 100ce, like #1629. b, 250ce, like #1631. c, 350ce, like #1633. d, 500ce, like #1635.

No. 1640a, 100ce, like #1630. b, 250ce, like #1632. c, 350ce, like #1634. d, 500ce, like #1636.

1994, Jan. 24 Litho. *Perf. 14*

1629-1638 A278 Set of 10	12.50	12.50

Souvenir Sheets

1639	A278	multicolored	5.00	5.00
1640	A278	multicolored	5.00	5.00

Christmas A279

Paintings and Woodcuts:aintings and Woodcuts: 50ce, Adoration of the Magi. 100ce, The Virgin and Child with Saint John and an Angel, by Botticelli. 150ce, Mary as Queen of Heaven. 200ce, Saint Anne. 250ce, The Madonna of the Magnificat, by Botticelli. 400ce, The Madonna of the Goldfinch, by Tiepolo. 600ce, The Virgin and the Child with the Young St. John the Baptist, by Correggio. 1000ce, Adoration of the Shepherds.

No. 1649, Mystic Nativity (detail), by Botticelli, horiz. No. 1650, Madonna in a Circle, by Durer.

Woodcuts (50ce, 150ce, 200ce, 1000ce) are from Nuremberg Prayer Books, by Durer.

Perf. 13½x14, 14x13½

1993, Dec. 20 Litho.

1641-1648 A279 Set of 8	14.00	14.00

Souvenir Sheets

1649 A279 1000ce multicolored	5.00	5.00
1650 A279 1000ce multicolored	5.00	5.00

A280

Hong Kong '94 — A281

Stamps, tram from Kennedy Town to Shau Kei: No. 1651, Hong Kong #470, back of tram. No. 1652, Front of tram, #1392.

Imperial Palace clocks: No. 1653a, Windmill. b, Horse. c, Balloon. d, Zodiac. e, Shar-Pei dog. f, Cat.

1994, Feb. 18 Litho. *Perf. 14*

1651 A280 200ce multicolored	1.00	1.00
1652 A280 200ce multicolored	1.00	1.00
a. Pair, #1651-1652	2.00	2.00

Miniature Sheet

1653 A281 100ce Sheet of 6, #a.-f.	3.00	3.00

Nos. 1651-1652 issued in sheets of 5 pairs. No. 1652a is a continuous design.

New Year 1994 (Year of the Dog) (#1653e).

Mickey Mouse, 65th Birthday A282

Mickey's films: 50ce, Steamboat Willie, 1928. 100ce, The Band Concert, 1937. 150ce, Moose Hunters, 1937. 200ce, Brave Little Taylor, 1938. 250ce, Fantasia, 1940. 400ce, The Nifty Nineties, 1941. 600ce, Canne Caddy, 1944. 1000ce, Mickey's Christmas Carol, 1983.

No. 1662, Mickey's Elephant, 1936. No. 1663, Mickey's Amateurs, 1937.

1994, Mar. 1 Litho. *Perf. 13½x14*

1654-1661 A282 Set of 8	8.25	8.25

Souvenir Sheets

1662-1663 A282 1200ce each	3.50	3.50

A283

Hummel Figurines: 50ce, Boy with backpack, walking stick. 100ce, Girl holding basket behind back. 150ce, Boy with rabbits. 200ce, Boy carrying chicks in basket. 250ce, Girl with chicks. 400ce, Girl petting lamb. 600ce, Lamb, girl waving handkerchief. 1000ce, Girl with basket, flowers.

No. 1672a, 500ce, like #1665; b, 150ce, like #1671; c, 1200ce, like #1667.

No. 1673a, 300ce, like #1668; b, 200ce, like #1669; c, 500ce, like #1670; d, 1000ce, like #1666.

1994, Apr. 6 *Perf. 14*

1664-1671 A283 Set of 8	8.25	8.25

Souvenir Sheets

1672 A283 Sheet of 4, #a.-c., #1664	5.75	5.75
1673 A283 Sheet of 4, #a.-d.	6.00	6.00

A284

1994, May 16 Litho. *Perf. 14*

Diana Monkeys: 50ce, Adult, young. 200ce, Sitting in tree. 500ce, Holding food. 800ce, Close-up of face.

1674-1677 A284 Set of 4	5.00	5.00
1677a Min. sheet, 3 each #1674-1677	17.00	17.00

World Wildlife Fund.

Wild Animals A285

Designs: 100ce, Bushbuck. 150ce, Spotted hyena. 1000ce, Aardvark. No. 1681, Leopard, vert. No. 1682, Waterbuck, vert.

1994, May 16

1678-1680 A285 Set of 3 3.50 3.50

Souvenir Sheets

1681-1682 A285 2000ce each 5.50 5.50

Miniature Sheets of 12

Cats A286

Designs: No. 1683a, Sorrel Abyssinian. b, Silver classic tabby. c, Chocolate-point Siamese. d, Brown tortie Burmese. e, Exotic shorthair. f, Havana brown. g, Devon rex. h, Black manx. i, British blue shorthair. j, Calico American wirehair. k, Spotted oriental Siamese. l, Red classic tabby.

No. 1684: a, Norwegian forest cat. b, Blue longhair. c, Red self longhair. d, Black longhair. e, Chinchilla. f, Dilut calico longhair. g, Blue tabby-&-white longhair. h, Ruby somali. i, Blue smoke longhair. j, Calico longhair. k, Brown tabby longhair. l, Balinese.

No. 1685, Brown mackeral tabby Scottish fold. No. 1686, Seal-point colorpoint.

1994, June 6 Litho. *Perf. 14*

1683-1684 A286 200ce #a.-l. each 6.50 6.50

Souvenir Sheets

1685-1686 A286 2000ce each 5.50 5.50

Miniature Sheets of 12

Birds A287

Designs: No. 1687a, Red-bellied paradise flycatcher (b, e). b, Many-colored bush-shrike. c, Broad-tailed paradise whydah (b, e). d, White-crowned robin-chat. e, Violet plantain-eater. f, Village weaver. g, Fire-crowned bishop. h, Shoveler. i, Spur-winged goose (l). j, African crake. k, King reed-hen. l, Tiger bittern.

No. 1688: a, Moho. b, Superb sunbird. c, Blue-breasted kingfisher. d, Blue cuckoo-shrike. e, Blue plantain-eater (d, g). f, Greater flamingo (i). g, Lily-trotter (j). h, Night heron. i, Black-winged stilt (l). j, White-spotted pigmy rail. k, Pigmy goose. k, Angola pitta.

No. 1689, Goliath heron. No. 1690, African spoonbill.

1994, June 13

1687-1688 A287 200ce #a.-l, each 6.50 6.50

Souvenir Sheets

1689-1690 A287 2000ce each 5.50 5.50

4th Republic, 1st Anniv. A288

Designs: 50ce, Rural water projects. 100ce, Honoring farmers. 200ce, Rural electrification. 600ce, Rural bridge construction. 800ce, Natl. Theater. 1000ce, Lighting Perpetual Flame.

1994, July 11 Litho. *Perf. 14*

1691-1696 A288 Set of 6 7.50 7.50

D-Day, 50th Anniv. A289

Designs: 60ce, 15-inch Monitor HMS Roberts fires on Houlgate Battery. 100ce, HMS Warspite hits Villerville. 200ce, Flagship USS Augusta.

1500ce, USS Nevada bombards Utah Beach.

1994, July 4 Litho. *Perf. 14*

1697-1699 A289 Set of 3 1.00 1.00

Souvenir Sheet

1700 A289 1500ce multicolored 4.00 4.00

Miniature Sheet of 9

First Manned Moon Landing, 25th Anniv. A290

German, Japanese, scientist-astronauts: a, Sigmund Jahn. b, Ulf Merbold. c, Hans Wilhelm Schlegal. d, Ulrich Walter. e, Reinhard Furrer. f, Ernst Messerschmid. g, Mamoru Mohri. h, Klaus-Dietrich Flade. i, Chaiki Naito-Mukai.

2000ce, "Frau im Mond."

1994, July 4

1701 A290 300ce #a.-i. 7.25 7.25

Souvenir Sheet

1702 A290 2000ce multicolored 5.50 5.50

Duiker Antelopes A291

Designs: 50ce, Crowned. 100ce, Red-flanked. 200ce, Yellow-backed. 400ce, Ogilby's. 600ce, Bay. 800ce, Jentink's.

No. 1709, Cephalophus natalensis. No. 1710, Cephalophus niger.

1994, May 16 Litho. *Perf. 14*

1703-1708 A291 Set of 6 5.50 5.50

Souvenir Sheets

1709-1710 A291 2000ce each 5.00 5.00

A292

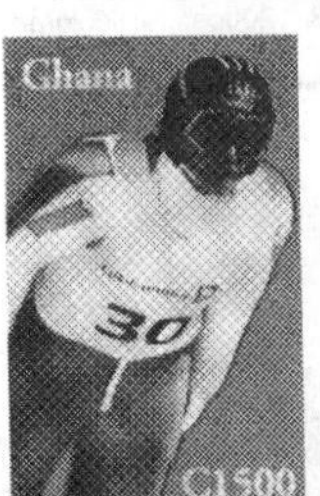

Intl. Olympic Committee, Cent. — A293

300ce, Dieter Modenburg, Germany, high jump, 1984. 400ce, Ruth Fuchs, German Democratic Republic, javelin, 1972, 1976.

1500ce, Jans Weissflog, Germany, large hill ski jump, 1994.

1994, July 4 Litho. *Perf. 14*

1711 A292 300ce multicolored .75 .75

1712 A292 400ce multicolored 1.00 1.00

Souvenir Sheet

1713 A293 1500ce multicolored 3.75 3.75

PHILAKOREA '94 — A294

Designs: 20ce, Ch'unghak-dong village elder in traditional clothes. 150ce, Stone pagoda, Punhwangsa, Korea. 300ce, Traditional country house, Andong region.

Letter pictures, eight-panel screen, Choson Dynasty, 20th cent: Nos. 1717b, f, Birds. c, Rooster. d, Animal with antennae. e, g, Flowers. h, Fish.

1500ce, Temple judges determine final afterlife judgments, horiz.

1994, July 4 *Perf. 14, 13 (#1717)*

1714-1716 A294 Set of 3 1.25 1.25

PHILAKOREA '94 — A295

Miniature Sheet of 8

1717 A295 250ce #a.-h. 5.00 5.00

Souvenir Sheet

1718 A294 1500ce multicolored 3.75 3.75

Miniature Sheet of 6

1994 World Cup Soccer Championships, US — A296

Designs: No. 1719a, Dennis Bergkamp, Netherlands. b, Lothar Matthaus, Germany. c, Giuseppe Signori, Italy. d, Carlos Valderama, Colombia. e, Jorge Campos, Mexico. f, Tony Meola, US.

No. 1720, Citrus Bowl, Orlando, FL, vert. No. 1721, Giants Stadium, Meadowlands, NJ, vert.

1994, July 25 *Perf. 14*

1719 A296 200ce #a.-f. 3.00 3.00

Souvenir Sheets

1720-1721 A296 1200ce each 3.00 3.00

Christmas A297

Italian art: 100ce, Madonna of the Annunciation, by Simone Martini. 200ce, Madonna and Child, by Niccolo di Pietro Gerini. 250ce, Virgin and Child on the Throne with Angels and Saints, by Raffaello Botticelli. 300ce, Madonna and Child with Saints, by Antonio Fiorentino. 400ce, Adoration of the Magi, by Bartolo di Fredi. 500ce, The Annunciation, by Cima da Congeliano. 600ce, Virgin and Child with the Young St. John the Baptist, by Workshop of Botticelli. 1000ce, The Holy Family, by Giorgione.

Details from Adoration of the Kings, by Giorgione: No. 1730, Presenting gifts. No. 1731, Madonna & Child.

1994, Dec. 5 Litho. *Perf. 13½x14*

1722-1729 A297 Set of 8 7.50 7.50

Souvenir Sheets

1730-1731 A297 2000ce each 4.50 4.50

Intl. Year of the Family — A298

Designs: 50ce, Family. 100ce, Technical training. 200ce, Child care. 400ce, Care for the aged. 600ce, Vocational training. 1000ce, Adult education.

1994, Dec. 20 *Perf. 14*

1732-1737 A298 Set of 6 6.00 6.00

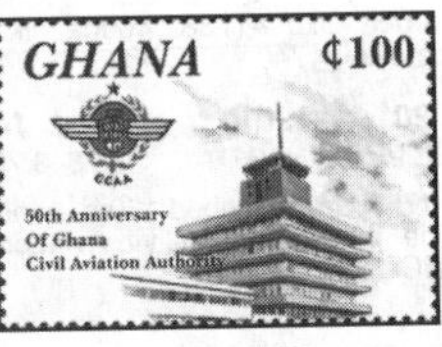

Ghana Civil Aviation Authority, 50th Anniv. A299

Designs: 100ce, Control tower. 400ce, Insignia, marker light. 1000ce, Airplane leaving runway.

1994, Dec. 20

1738-1740 A299 Set of 3 3.75 3.75

See Nos. 1766-1768.

Red Cross & Red Crescent Societies in Ghana, 75th Anniv. A300

Designs: 50ce, Transporting victim. 200ce, Aiding mother, children. 600ce, Erecting tents.

1994, Dec. 20 Litho. *Perf. 14*

1741-1743 A300 Set of 3 2.25 2.25

Souvenir Sheet

1744 Sheet of 3, #1741-1742, 1744a 6.25 6.25

a. A300 1000ce like #1743 5.00 5.00

Fertility Dolls — A301

Various carvings. Denominations: 50ce, 100ce, 150ce, 200ce, 400ce, 600ce, 800ce, 1000ce.

1994, Dec. 20

1745-1752 A301 Set of 8 5.75 5.75

Souvenir Sheet

1753 Sheet of 4, #1745, 1748-1749, 1753a 6.75 6.75

a. A301 250ce like #1752 1.25 1.25

Donald Duck, 60th Birthday (in 1994) — A302

Designs: 40ce, Pluto, Donald, Chip 'n Dale. 50ce, Mickey, pup. 60ce, Daisy. 100ce, Goofy. 150ce, Goofy, diff. 250ce, Donald, Goofy. 400ce, Ludwig Von Drake, Pluto. 500ce, Gramdma Duck, pups. 1000ce, Mickey, Minnie. 1500ce, Pluto.

No. 1764, Daisy, Donald, cake, Mickey, vert. No. 1765, Donald holding fork, spoon, vert.

1995, Feb. 2 Litho. *Perf. 14x13½*

1754-1763 A302 Set of 10 8.50 8.50

Souvenir Sheets

Perf. 13½x14

1764-1765 A302 2000ce each 4.25 4.25

Civil Aviation Authority Type of 1994 with ICAO Emblem and New Inscription

Designs: 100ce, like #1738. 400ce, like #1739. 1000ce, like #1740.

1994, Dec. 20 Litho. *Perf. 14*

1766-1768 A299 Set of 3 3.75 3.75

Nos. 1766-1768 are inscribed "50th Anniversary of The International Civil Aviation Organization (ICAO)."

Panafest '94 — A303

Designs: 50ce, Northern region dancer. 100ce, Relics with landmark. 200ce, Chief sitting in state. 400ce, Royalist ceremonial dress. 600ce, Cape Coast Castle. 800ce, Clay figurines of West Africa.

1994, Dec. 9 Litho. *Perf. 13½*

1769-1774 A303 Set of 6 4.50 4.50

Pan African Historical Theatre Festival, Dec. 1994.

Forts A304

Castles A305

Forts: 50ce, Appolonia, Beyin. 200ce, Patience, Apam. 250ce, Amsterdam, Kormantin. 300ce, St. Jago, Elmina. 400ce, William, Anomabo. 600ce, Kumasi.

Castles: 150ce, Cochem, Germany. 600ce, Hohenzollern, Germany. 800ce, Uwajima, Japan. 100ce, Hohenschwangau, Germany.

Castles: No. 1785a, Windsor, England. b, Osaka, Japan. c, Vaj Dahunyad, Hungary. d, Karlstejn, Czech Republic. e, Kronborg, Denmark. f, Alcazar of Segovia, Spain. g, Chambourd, France. h, Linderhof, Bavaria. i, Red Fort, India.

No. 1786, Elmira Castle. No. 1787, Fort St. Antonio, Axim. No. 1788, Himeji Castle, Japan. No. 1789, Neuschwanstein Castle, Germany.

1995, Apr. 3 *Perf. 14*

1775-1780 A304 Set of 6 3.75 3.75

1781-1784 A305 Set of 4 5.00 5.00

Miniature Sheet of 9

1785 A305 500ce #a.-i. 9.00 9.00

Souvenir Sheets

1786 A304 800ce multi 1.60 1.60

1787 A304 1000ce multi 2.00 2.00

1788-1789 A305 2500ce each 5.00 5.00

Water Birds A306

Designs: 200ce, Eurasian pochard. 500ce, Maccoa duck. 800ce, Cape shoveler. 1000ce, Red-crested pochard.

No. 1794: a, African pygmy goose. b, Southern pochard. c, Cape teal. d, Ruddy shelduck. e, Fulvous whistling duck. f, White-faced whistling geese. g, Ferruginous white-eye. h, Hottentot teal. i, African black duck. j, Yellow-billed duck. k, White-checked pintail duck. l, Hartlaub's duck.

No. 1795, Roseate tern. No. 1796, Northern shoveler.

1995, Apr. 28

1790-1793 A306 Set of 4 5.00 5.00

Miniature Sheet of 12

1794 A306 400ce #a.-l. 9.50 9.50

Souvenir Sheets

1795-1796 A306 2500ce each 5.00 5.00

Nos. 1794-1796 have a continuous design. Nos. 1790-1793 have a white border.

1996 Summer Olympics, Atlanta
A307 A308

Athletes: 500ce, Carl Lewis. 800ce, Eric Liddell. 900ce, Runner. 1000ce, Jim Thorpe.

Sports: No. 1801a, Cycling. b, Archery. c, Diving. d, Swimming. e, Gymnastics-Floor Exercise. f, Fencing. g, Boxing. h, Gymnastics-Rings. i, Javelin. j, Tennis. k, Soccer. l, Equestrian.

No. 1802, John Akii Bua. No. 1803, Pierre de Cobertin.

1995, May 2

1797-1800 A307 Set of 4 6.50 6.50

Miniature Sheet of 12

1801 A308 300ce #a.-l. 7.50 7.50

Souvenir Sheets

1802-1803 A308 1200ce each 2.50 2.50

Miniature Sheet of 6

UN, 50th Anniv. — A309

Secretaries General: No. 1804a, 200ce, Trygve Lie, Norway, 1946-52. b, 300ce, Dag Hammarskjold, Sweden, 1953-61. c, 400ce, U Thant, Burma, 1961-71. d, 500ce, Kurt Waldheim, Austria, 1972-81. e, 600ce, Javier Perez de Cuellar, Peru, 1982-91. f, 800ce, Boutros Boutros-Ghali, Egypt, 1992-.

No. 1805, UN flag, horiz.

1995, July 6 Litho. *Perf. 14*

1804 A309 #a.-f. 5.75 5.75

Souvenir Sheet

1805 A309 1200ce multicolored 2.50 2.50

Miniature Sheets of 6 or 8

A310

End of World War II, 50th Anniv. A311

Military decorations: No. 1806a, US Navy Cross, US Purple Heart. b, UK Air Force Cross, UK Distinguished Flying Cross. c, US Navy and Marine Corps Medal, US Distinguished Service Cross. d, UK Distinguished Service Medal, UK Distinguished Conduct Medal. e, UK Military Medal, UK Military Cross. f, UK Distinguished Service Cross, UK Distinguished Service Order.

No. 1807: a, Churchill. b, Eisenhower. c, Air Chief Marshall Sir Arthur Tedder. d, Montgomery. e, Bradley. f, de Gaulle. g, French Resistance Organization. h, Patton.

No. 1808, US Medal of Honor. No. 1809, Fuhrer's promise.

1995, July 6 Litho. *Perf. 14*

1806 A310 500ce #a.-f. + label 6.00 6.00

1807 A311 400ce #a.-h. + label 6.50 6.50

Souvenir Sheets

1808-1809 A310 1200ce each 2.50 2.50

No. 1809 contains one 42x56mm stamp.

FAO, 50th Anniv. A312

Designs: 200ce, Fish preservation. 300ce, Fishing. 400ce, Ox-drawn plow. 600ce, Harvesting. 800ce, Aforestation.

2000ce, Boat, shoreline, oxen, fruit.

1995, July 6 Litho. *Perf. 14*

1810-1814 A312 Set of 5 4.50 4.50

Souvenir Sheet

1815 A312 2000ce multicolored 4.00 4.00

Rotary Intl., 90th Anniv. A313

Designs: 600ce, Natl. flag, Rotary emblem. 1200ce, Rotary emblem on banner, vert.

1995, July 6

1816 A313 600ce multicolored 1.25 1.25

Souvenir Sheet

1817 A313 1200ce multicolored 2.50 2.50

1995 Boy Scout Jamboree, Holland — A314

No. 1818: a, 400ce, Two boys. 800ce, Two boys, one wearing glasses. c, 1000ce, Two boys facing left.

1200ce, Boy with bamboo poles.

1995, July 6

1818 A314 Strip of 3, #a.-c. 4.50 4.50

Souvenir Sheet

1819 A314 1200ce multicolored 4.00 4.00

No. 1818 is a continuous design.

Queen Mother, 95th Birthday A315

No. 1820: a, Drawing. b, Bright green blue hat. c, Formal portrait. d, Coral outfit.

2500ce, Pale blue outfit.

1995, July 6 *Perf. 13½x14*

1820 A315 600ce Strip or block of 4, #a.-d. 4.75 4.75

Souvenir Sheet

1821 A315 2500ce multicolored 5.00 5.00

No. 1820 was issued in sheets of 8 stamps.

Miniature Sheets of 9

Singapore '95 — A316

Dinosaurs: No. 1822a, Seismosaurus (d-f). b, Supersaurus (a, d). c, Ultrasaurus (f). d, Saurolophus (e). e, Lambeosaurus (d, g-h). f, Parasaurolophus (e, i). g, Triceratops (h). h, Styracosaurus (e, g i). i, Pachyrhinosaurus (h).

No. 1823a, Peteinosaurus (b, d-e). b, Quetzalcoatlus (a, c, e). c, Eudimorphodon (b). d, Allosaurus (e-f, h-i). e, Daspletosaurus (f). f, Tarbosaurus (i). g, Velociraptor (h-i). h, Herrerasaurus (i). i, Coelophysis.

No. 1824, Albertosaur. No. 1825, Tyrannosaurus rex.

1995, Aug. 8 Litho. *Perf. 14*

1822-1823 A316 400ce #a.-i., each 7.25 7.25

Souvenir Sheet

1824-1825 A316 2500ce each 4.00 4.00

Nobel Prize Recipients — A317

Designs: a, Nelson Mandela, peace, 1993. b, Albert Schweitzer, peace, 1952. c, Wole Soyinka, literature, 1986. d, Emil Fischer, chemistry, 1902. e, Rudolf Mossbauer, physics, 1961. f, Archbishop Desmond Tutu, peace, 1984. g, Max Born, physics, 1954. h, Max Planck, physics, 1918. i, Hermann Hesse, literature, 1946.

1200ce, Paul Ehrlich, medicine, 1908.

1995, Oct. 2 Litho. *Perf. 14*

Miniature Sheet of 9

1826 A317 400ce #a.-i. 7.25 7.25

Souvenir Sheet

1827 A317 1200ce multicolored 2.50 2.50

Asantehene, 25th Anniv. — A318

1995 ***Perf. 13½x13***

Designs: 50ce, Emblem. 100ce, Silver casket. 200ce, Golden stool. 400ce, Busummuru sword bearer. 600ce, 800ce, Diff. portraits of Otumfuo Opoku Ware II. 1000ce, Mponponsuo sword bearer.

1828-1834 A318 Set of 7 6.25 6.25

Fauna — A319

Designs: 400ce, Cymothoe beckeri. 500ce, Graphium policene. 1000ce, Urotriorchis macrourus, vert. 2000ce, Xiphias gladius. 3000ce, Monodoctylus sabee. 5000ce, Ardea purpurea, vert.

Perf. 14¼x13¾, 13¾x14¼

1995, June 19 **Litho.**

1835 A319 400ce multi .80 .80
1836 A319 500ce multi 1.00 1.00
1837 A319 1000ce multi 2.00 2.00
a. Perf. 11½
1838 A319 2000ce multi 4.25 4.25
1839 A319 3000ce multi 6.25 6.25
1840 A319 5000ce multi 10.50 10.50
Nos. 1835-1840 (6) 24.80 24.80

Christmas A320

Details or entire paintings: 50ce, The Infant Jesus and the Young St. John, by Murillo. 80ce, Rest on Flight to Egypt, by Memling. 300ce, Sacred Family, by Van Dyck. 600ce, The Virgin and the Infant, by Uccello. 800ce, The Virgin and the Infant, by Van Eyck. 1000ce, Head of Christ, by Rembrandt.

No. 1847, Madonna, by Montagna. No. 1848, The Holy Family, by Pulzone.

1995, Dec. 1 **Litho.** ***Perf. 13½x14***

1841-1846 A320 Set of 6 4.75 4.75

Souvenir Sheets

1847-1848 A320 2500ce each 4.25 4.25

Miniature Sheet

Motion Pictures, Cent. A321

No. 1849: a, 1903 H. Ernmann camera. b, Charles Chaplin. c, Rudolph Valentino. d, Will Rogers. e, Greta Garbo. f, Jackie Cooper. g, Bette Davis. h, John Barrymore. i, Shirley Temple.

No. 1850, Laurel and Hardy.

1995, Dec. 8

1849 A321 400ce Sheet of 9, #a.-i. 6.00 6.00

Souvenir Sheet

1850 A321 2500ce multicolored 4.25 4.25

A322

John Lennon (1940-80) A323

Nos. 1852a-1852g, 1852i, various portraits. No. 1852h, like No. 1851.

No. 1853, Lennon playing guitar, water in background.

1995, Dec. 8 ***Perf. 14***

1851 A322 400ce multicolored .65 .65

Miniature Sheet

Perf. 13½x14

1852 A323 400ce Sheet of 9, #a.-i. 6.50 6.50

Souvenir Sheet

1853 A323 2000ce multicolored 3.50 3.50

No. 1851 was issued in sheets of 16.

Miniature Sheet

Louis Pasteur (1822-95) — A324

Designs: a, In laboratory. b, Discovery of rabies virus and vaccine. c, Pneumococcus discovery, 1880. d, Development of first vaccine with birds. e, Perfection of brewer's yeast culture.

1995, Dec. 13 ***Perf. 14***

1854 A324 600ce Sheet of 5, #a.-e. 6.00 6.00

Miniatures Sheets of 8 + Label

Paintings from the Metropolitan Museum of Art — A325

No. 1855: a, Portrait of a Man, by Van Der Goes. b, Paradise, by Giovanni di Paolo. c, Portrait of a Young Man, by Antonello da Messina. d, Tommaso Portinari, by Memling. e, Wife Maria Portinari, by Memling. f, Portrait of a Lady, by Ghirlandaio. g, St. Christopher & Infant Christ, by Ghirlandaio. h, Francesco D'Este, by van der Weyden.

No. 1856: a, The Interrupted Sleep, by Boucher. b, Diana and Cupid, by Batoni. c, Boy Blowing Bubbles, by Chardin. d, Ancient Rome, by Pannini. e, Modern Rome, by Pannini. f, The Calmady Children, by Lawrence. g, The Triumph of Marius, by G.B. Tiepolo. h, Garden at Vaucression, by E. Vuillard.

No. 1857, The Epiphany, by Giotto. No. 1858, The Calling of Matthew, by Hemessen.

1996, Feb. 12 **Litho.** ***Perf. 13½x14***

1855-1856 A325 400ce #a.-h. + label, each 5.50 5.50

Souvenir Sheets

Perf. 14

1857-1858 A325 2500ce each 4.25 4.25

Nos. 1857-1858 each contain one 85x57mm stamp.

New Year 1996 (Year of the Rat) — A326

Stylized rats, denomination, country name in white: No. 1859: a, With musical instruments, on horseback. b, Holding banners. c, Carrying rat in palanquin. d, Carrying box, holding fish.

No. 1860: Like #1859 with denomination, country name in red.

1000ce, Four rats transporting rat in palanquin, horiz.

1996, Jan. 28 **Litho.** ***Perf. 14***

1859 A326 250ce Strip of 4, #a.-d. 1.75 1.75

Miniature Sheet

1860 A325 250ce Sheet of 4, #a.-d. 1.75 1.75

Souvenir Sheet

1861 A325 1000ce red, pink & yellow 1.75 1.75

No. 1859 was issued in sheets of 12 stamps.

Miniature Sheets of 12

Fauna of the Rainforest — A327

#1862: a, Ramphastos toco. b, Choloepus didactylus. c, Pongo pygmaeus. d, Spiaetus cirrhatus. e, Panthera tigris. f, Ibis leucocephallus. g, Ara chloroptera. h, Saimiri sciureus. i, Macaca fascicularis. j, Cithaerias menander, ithomiidae. k, Coryptophanes cristatus, gekkonidae. l, Boa caninus.

#1863: a, Opisthoccomus hoazin. b, Tarsius bancanus. c, Leontopithecus rosalia. d, Pteropus gouldii. e, Rupicola rupicola. f, Pharomachrus mocino. g, Hyla boans, dendrobates leucomeles. h, Lemur catta. i, Iguana iguana. j, Heliconius burneyi. k, Mellisuga minima. l, Propithecus verreauxi.

No. 1864, Sarcoramphus papa. No. 1865, Pteridophora alberti.

1996, Apr. 15

1862-1863 A327 400ce #a.-l., each 8.25 8.25

Souvenir Sheets

1864-1865 A327 3000ce each 5.00 5.00

China '96 — A328

Pagodas: a, Kaiyuan Si Temple, Fujian. b, Kaiyuan Si Temple, Hebei. c, Fogong Si Temple, Shanxi. d, Xiangshan, Beijing.

1000ce, Baima Si Temple, Henan.

1996, May 13 **Litho.** ***Perf. 14***

1866 A328 400ce Strip of 4, #a.-d. 2.75 2.75

Souvenir Sheet

1867 A328 1000ce multicolored 1.75 1.75

No. 1866 was issued in sheets of 8 stamps.

Queen Elizabeth II, 70th Birthday A329

Designs: a, Portrait. b, Wearing blue hat, coat. c, Wearing printed dress, wide-brim hat.

2500ce, Riding in horse-drawn carriage, horiz.

1996, June 10 **Litho.** ***Perf. 13½x14***

1868 A329 1000ce Strip of 3, #a.-c. 5.00 5.00

Souvenir Sheet

Perf. 14x13½

1869 A329 2500ce multicolored 4.25 4.25

No. 1868 was issued in sheets of 9 stamps.

1996 Summer Olympics, Atlanta A330

Designs: 300ce, Two wrestlers, javelin thrower, Bas Relief, 500BC. 500ce, Wilma Rudolph, gold medalist in track and field, Rome, 1960, Olympic torch. 600ce, The Forum, St. Peter's Basilica, Colosseum, Olympic Stadium, Rome, 1960. 800ce, Soviet flag, ladies' kayak pairs gold medal winners, Rome, 1960.

Medalists in swimming, diving: No. 1874: a, Aileen Riggin, springboard, 1920. b, Pat McCormick, platform, 1952. c, Dawn Fraser, 100m freestyle, 1956. d, Chris Von Saltza, 400m freestyle, 1960. e, Anita Lonsbrough, 200m breaststroke, 1960. f, Debbie Meyer, 400m freestyle, 1968. g, Shane Gould, 400m freestyle, 1972. h, Petra Thuemer, 800m freestyle, 1976. i, Marjorie Gestring, springboard, 1936.

Soccer players, vert: No. 1875a, Abedi Pele, Ghana. b, Quico Navarez, Spain. c, Heino Hanson, Denmark. d, Mostafa Ismail, Egypt. e, Anthony Yeboah, Ghana. f, Jurgen Klinsmann, Germany. g, Cobi Jones, US. h, Franco Baresi, Italy. i, Igor Dobrovolski, Russia.

No. 1876, Kornella Ender, 200m freestyle gold medalist, 1976. No. 1877, Tracy Caulkins, 200m individual medlay gold medalist, 1984.

1996, June 27 ***Perf. 14***

1870-1873 A330 Set of 4 3.75 3.75

Sheets of 9

1874-1875 A330 400ce #a.-i., each 6.00 6.00

Souvenir Sheets

1876-1877 A330 2000ce each 3.50 3.50

Intl.Amateur Boxing Assoc., 50th Anniv. — A331

Boxers: 300ce, Serafim Todorow, Bulgaria. 400ce, Oscar de La Hoya, US. 800ce, Ariel Hernandez, Cuba. 1500ce, Arnolda Mesa, Cuba.

3000ce, Tadahiro Sasaki, Japan.

1996, July 31

1878-1881 A331 Set of 4 5.00 5.00

Souvenir Sheet

1882 A331 3000ce multicolored 5.00 5.00

UNESCO, 50th Anniv. — A332

Designs: 400ce, The Citadel, Haiti, vert. 800ce, Ait-Ben-Haddou (Fortified Village), Morocco, vert. 1000ce, Spissky Hrad (exterior of castle), Slovakia.
2000ce, Cape Coast, Ghana.

1996, July 31 Litho. *Perf. 14*

1883-1885 A332 Set of 3 3.75 3.75

Souvenir Sheet

1886 A332 2000ce multicolored 3.50 3.50

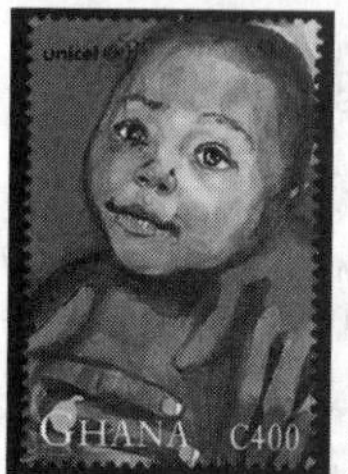

UNICEF, 50th Anniv. — A333

Designs: 400ce, Baby. 500ce, Mother, baby. 600ce, Mother, child drinking from glass.
1000ce, Child, diff.

1996, July 31

1887-1889 A333 Set of 3 2.50 2.50

Souvenir Sheet

1890 A333 1000ce multicolored 1.75 1.75

Jerusalem, 3000th Anniv. — A334

Landmark, flower: 400ce, St. Stephen's (Lion) Gate, Jasminum mesnyi. 600ce, Citadel and Tower of David, nerium oleander. 800ce, Chapel of the Ascension, romulea bulbocodium.
2000ce, Russian Church of St. Mary Magdalene.

1996, July 31

1891-1893 A334 Set of 3 2.10 2.10

Souvenir Sheet

1894 A334 2000ce multicolored 3.50 3.50

For overprints see Nos. 2032-2035.

Musical Instruments A335

a, Fiddles. b, Proverbial drum. c, Double clapless bell & castanet. d, Gourd rattle. e, Horns.

1996, Aug. 5

1895 A335 500ce Sheet of 5, #a.-e. 4.25 4.25

Disney's Best Friends — A336

#1896, Ariel, Flounder, Sebastian. #1897, Pinocchio, Jiminy Cricket. #1898, Cogsworth, Lumiere. #1899, Copper, Tod. #1900, Pocahontas, Meeko, Flit. #1901, Bambi, Flower, Thumper.
#1902: a, 450ce, Pocahontas, Meeko, Flit. b, 150ce, Pinocchio, Jiminy Cricket. c, 200ce, Copper, Tod. d, 600ce, Aladdin, Abu. e, 700ce, Penny, Rufus. f, 350ce, Cogsworth, Lumiere. g, 800ce, Mowgli, Baloo. h, 200ce, Ariel, Flounder, Sebastian, i, 300ce, Bambi, Flower, Thumper.
#1903, Winnie the Pooh, vert. #1904, Simba, Pumbaa.

Perf. 14x13½, 13½x14

1996, Aug. 25

1896-1901 A336 60ce Set of 6 .60 .60
1902 A336 Sheet of 9, #a.-i. 6.00 6.00

Souvenir Sheets

1903 A336 3000ce multicolored 5.00 5.00
1904 A336 3000ce multicolored 5.00 5.00

Stampshow '96 (#1902).

E.W. Agyare (1937-72), Ghana Broadcasting Corp. Technician — A337

1996, July 31 *Perf. 14*

1905 A337 100ce multicolored .20 .20

Radio, Cent. A338

Entertainers: #1906, 500ce, Frank Sinatra. #1907, 600ce, Judy Garland. #1908, 600ce, Bing Crosby. #1909, 800ce, Dean Martin, Jerry Lewis.
2000ce, Edgar Bergen, Charlie McCarthy.

1996, July 31 *Perf. 13½x14*

1906-1909 A338 Set of 4 4.25 4.25

Souvenir Sheet

1910 A338 2000ce multicolored 3.50 3.50

Sylvester Stallone in Movie, "Rocky II" — A339

1996, Nov. 21 Litho. *Perf. 14*

1911 A339 2000ce Sheet of 3 7.00 7.00

New Year 1997 (Year of the Ox) — A340

Various scenes from Chinese story, "Herd Boy and Girl Weaver."

1997, Jan. 22 Litho. *Perf. 14*

1912 A340 500ce Sheet of 9, #a.-i. 5.50 5.50

Souvenir Sheet

China '96 — A341

Statue of the Devil. Illustration reduced.

1996, May 13 Litho. *Perf. 14*

1913 A341 1000ce multicolored 1.75 1.75

No. 1913 was not available until March 1997.

A342

African Hair Styles: No. 1914: a, Dipo. b, Oduku. c, Dansinkran. d, Mbobom. e, Oduku 2.
No. 1915: a, African corn row. b, Chinese raster. c, Chinese raster 2. d, Corn row. e, Mbakaa.

1997, Mar. 3

Sheets of 5

1914-1915 A342 1000ce #a.-e., each 6.00 6.00

A343

1997, Mar. 3

Dr. Hideyo Noguchi (1876-1928), Pathologist: No. 1916: a, Tomb. b, Portrait. c, Birth place. d, Noguchi Institute, Legon. e, Noguchi Gardens, Accra.
No. 1917, Dr. Noguchi in laboratory. No. 1918, Statue.

1916 A343 1000ce Sheet of 5, #a.-e. 6.00 6.00

Souvenir Sheets

1917-1918 A343 3000ce each 3.50 3.50

Independence, 40th Anniv. — A344

200ce, Emblem. 550ce, Dr. Kwame Nkrumah, first president of Ghana, vert. 800ce, Achievement in education. 1100ce, Akosombo Dam.
2000ce, Declaration of independence, Old Polo Grounds, vert. 3000ce, Kofi Annan, UN Secretary General, vert.

1997, Mar. 6 Litho. *Perf. 14*

1919-1922 A344 Set of 4 3.25 3.25

Souvenir Sheets

1923 A344 2000ce multicolored 2.50 2.50
1924 A344 3000ce multicolored 3.75 3.75

Deng Xiaoping (1904-97), Chinese Leader — A345

Various portraits: No. 1925: a, 300ce, Smiling. b, 600ce, Wearing glasses. c, 800ce, like #1925b. d, 1000ce, like #1925a.
No. 1926: a, 500ce, Lips pursed. b, 600ce, Teeth showing. c, 800ce, like #1926b. d, 1000ce, like #1926a.
No. 1927, Reading. No. 1928, Hand in air.

1997, Apr. 28 *Perf. 14x13½*

1925 A345 Sheet of 4, #a.-d. 3.25 3.25
1926 A345 Sheet of 4, #a.-d. 3.50 3.50

Souvenir Sheets

Perf. 13½

1927 A345 3000ce multicolored 3.75 3.75
1928 A345 4000ce multicolored 5.00 5.00

Nos. 1927-1928 each contain one 51x38mm stamp.

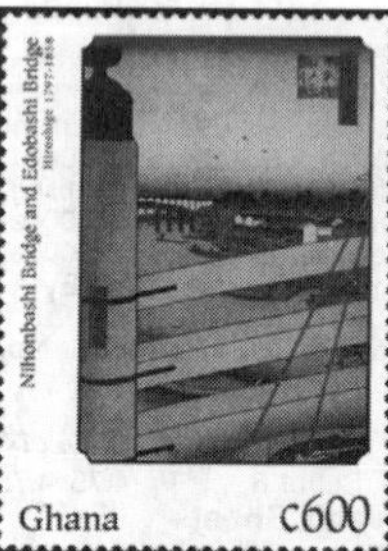

Paintings by Hiroshige (1797-1858) A346

No. 1929: a, Nihonbashi Bridge and Edobashi Bridge. b, View of Nihonbashi Tori 1-chome. c, Open Garden at Fukagawa Hachiman Shrine. d, Inari Bridge and Minato Shrine, Teppozu. e, Bamboo Yards, Kyobashi Bridge. f, Hall of Thirty-Three Bays, Fukagawa.
No. 1930, Teppozu and Tsukiji Honganji Temple. No. 1931, Sumiyoshi Festival, Tsukudajima.

1997, May 29 Litho. *Perf. 13½x14*

1929 A346 600ce Sheet of 6, #a.-f. 4.25 4.25

Souvenir Sheets

1930-1931 A346 3000ce each 3.75 3.75

Queen Elizabeth II, Prince Philip, 50th Wedding Anniv. A347

No. 1932: a, Queen. b, Royal Arms. c, Queen, Prince waving. d, Queen, Prince. e, Royal carriage. f, Portrait of Prince Philip.

3000ce, Portrait of Queen Elizabeth II.

1997, May 29 ***Perf. 14***

1932 A347 800ce Sheet of 6, #a.-f. 5.75 5.75

Souvenir Sheet

1933 A347 3000ce multicolored 2.70 2.70

Heinrich von Stephan (1831-97), Founder of UPU A348

Portrait of Von Stephan and: No. 1934: a, Automobile used for postal delivery. b, UPU emblem. c, First airmail flight, Pierre Blanchard, 1784.
3000ce, African messenger with cleft stick.

1997, May 29 Litho. ***Perf. 14***

1934 A348 1000ce Sheet of 3, #a.-c. 3.50 3.50

Souvenir Sheet

1935 A348 3000ce multicolored 3.50 3.50

PACIFIC 97.

Paul P. Harris (1868-1947), Founder of Rotary Intl. — A349

Portrait of Harris, Rotary emblem and: 2000ce, PolioPlus oral vaccine administration, Egypt. 3000ce, Emblem for PolioPlus vaccine, "A world free of disease."

1997, May 29

1936 A349 2000ce multicolored 2.40 2.40

Souvenir Sheet

1937 A349 3000ce multicolored 3.50 3.50

Ajumpan Drums—A350a

Chernobyl, 10th Anniv. A350

Designs: 800ce, UNESCO. 1000ce, Chabad's Children of Chernobyl.

1997, May 29 ***Perf. 13½x14***

1938 A350 800ce multicolored .95 .95
1939 A350 1000ce multicolored 1.25 1.25

Designs: 800ce, Cyrestis camillus. 1100ce Kente cloth.

1997 Litho. ***Perf. 13½x14¼***

1939A-1939C A350a Set of 3 — —

Issued: 550ce, 5/30; 800ce, 6/4. 1100ce, 6/7.
For surcharge see No. 2360.

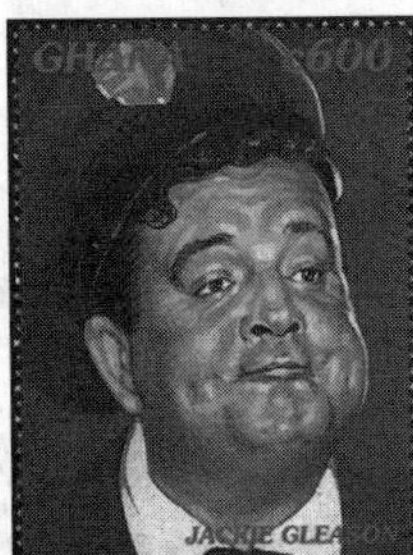

A351

Entertainers — A352

No. 1940: a, Jackie Gleason. b, Danny Kaye. c, John Cleese. d, Lucille Ball. e, Jerry Lewis. f, Sidney James. g, Louis Defuenes. h, Mae West. i, Bob Hope.
2000ce, Professor Ajax Bukana. 3000ce, Groucho Marx.

1997, July 1 ***Perf. 13½x14***

1940 A351 600ce Sheet of 9, #a.-i. 6.50 6.50

Souvenir Sheets

Perf. 14

1941 A352 2000ce Sheet of 2 2.40 2.40

Perf. 13½x14

1942 A351 3000ce multicolored 1.75 1.75

Mushrooms A353

Designs: 200ce, Galerina calyptrata. 300ce, Lepiota ignivolvata. 400ce, Omphalotus olearius. 550ce, Amanita phalloides. 600ce, Entoloma conferendum. 800ce, Entoloma nitidum.
No. 1949: a, Coprinus picaceus. b, Stropharia aurantiaca. c, Cortinarius splendens. d, Gomphidius roseus. e, Russula sardonia. f, Geastrum schmidelia.
No. 1950, Mycena crocata. No. 1951, Craterellus cornucopioides.

1997, July 9 ***Perf. 14***

1943-1948 A353 Set of 6 3.50 3.50
1949 A353 800ce Sheet of 6, #a.-f. 5.75 5.75

Souvenir Sheets

1950-1951 A353 3000ce each 3.50 3.50

Fish A354

Seabirds, Marine Life A355

Designs: 400ce, African pygmy angelfish. 600ce, Angelfish. 800ce, Broomtail wrasse. 1000ce, Indian butterfly fish.
No. 1956: a, Violet crested turaco. b, Pied avocet. c, Bottle-nosed dolphin. d, Bottle-nosed dolphin, long-toed lapwing. e, Longfined spadefish (i). f, Imperial angelfish, manta ray. g, Raccoon butterfly fish, African pompano (h, k). h, Silvertip shark (g, l). i, Longfin banner fish (e, j). j, Longfin banner fish, manta ray (f, i). k, Rusty parrot fish (j). l, Coral trout.
No. 1957, Crown butterfly fish. No. 1958, King angelfish.

1997, July 15

1952-1955 A354 Set of 4 3.50 3.50
1956 A355 500ce Sheet of 12, #a.-l. 7.25 7.25

Souvenir Sheets

1957-1958 A355 3000ce each 3.50 3.50

Flowers A356

Designs: 200ce, Eurychone rothschildiana. 550ce, Bulbophyllum lepidum. 800ce, Ansellia africana. 1100ce, Combretum grandiflorum.
No. 1963, vert: a, Strophanthus preusii. b, Ancistrochilus rothchildianus. c, Mussaendra arcuata. d, Microcoelia guyoniana. e, Gloriosa simplex. f, Brachycorythis kalbreyeri. g, Aframomum sceptrum. h, Thunbergia alata. i, Clerodendrum thomsoniae.
No. 1964, Kigelia africana. No. 1965, Spathodea campanulata.

1997, Aug. 1 Litho. ***Perf. 14½***

1959-1962 A356 Set of 4 2.75 2.75
1963 A356 800ce Sheet of 9, #a.-i. 7.25 7.25

Souvenir Sheets

1964-1965 A356 3000ce each 3.00 3.00

1998 World Cup Soccer Championships, France — A357

Stadiums: 200ce, Azteca, Mexico, 1970, 1986. 300ce, Rose Bowl, US, 1994. 400ce, Giuseppe Meazza, Italy, 1990. 500ce, Olympic, Germany, 1974. 1000ce, Maracana, Brazil, 1950. 2000ce, Bernabeu, Spain, 1982.
Soccer players: No. 1972: a, Patrick Kluvert, Holland. b, Roy Deane, Ireland. c, Abedi Pele Ayew, Ghana. d, Peter Schmeichel, Denmark. e, Roberto di Matteo, Italy. f, Bebeto, Brazil. g, Steve McManaman, England. h, George Appong Weah, Liberia.
#1973, Juninho, Brazil. #1974, Seaman, England.

1997, July 12 ***Perf. 14x13½***

1966-1971 A357 Set of 6 4.50 4.50

Sheet of 8

1972 A357 600ce #a.-h. + label 4.75 4.75

Souvenir Sheets

1973-1974 A357 3000ce each 3.00 3.00

Nos. 1966-1971 were issued in sheets of 10 each.

Birds — A358

200ce, Eurasian goldfinch. 300ce, Cape batis. 400ce, Bearded barbet. 500ce, White-necked raven. 600ce, Purple grenadier. 1000ce, Zebra waxbill.
No. 1981: a, Black bustard. b, Northern lapwing. c, Sandgrouse. d, Red-crested turaco. e, White-browed coucal. f, Lilac-breasted roller. g, Golden pipet. h, Crimson-breasted gonolek. i, Blackcap.
#1982, Nectarina famosa. #1983, Vidua regia.

1997, Oct. 20 Litho. ***Perf. 14***

1975-1980 A358 Set of 6 3.00 3.00
1981 A358 800ce Sheet of 9, #a.-i. 7.25 7.25

Souvenir Sheets

1982-1983 A358 3000ce each 3.00 3.00

Cats and Dogs A359

Cats, #1984-1989: 20ce, Havana. 50ce, Singapura. 100ce, Sphinx. 150ce, British white. 300ce, Snowshoe. 600ce, Persian.
Dogs, #1989A-1989F: 80ce, Papillon. 200ce, Bulldog. 400ce, Shetland sheepdog. 500ce, Schnauzer. 800ce, Shih tzu. 2000ce, Chow chow.
Dogs and cats: No. 1990: a, Russian wolfhound. b, Birman. c, Basset hound. d, Silver tabby. e, Afghan. f, Burmilla.
#1991: a, Abyssinian. b, Border terrier. c, Scottish fold. d, Boston terrier. e, Oriental. f, Keeshond.
#1992, Ragdoll. #1992A, Alaskan malamute.

1997, Oct. 20

1984-1989 A359 Set of 6 1.25 1.25
1989A-1989F A359 Set of 6 4.00 4.00

Sheets of 6

1990-1991 A359 1000ce #a.-f., each 9.25 9.25

Souvenir Sheets

1992-1992A A359 3000ce each 3.00 3.00

Return of Hong Kong to China — A360

Designs: a, Lin Tsi-Hsu (1785-1850). b, Gwan Tian-Pei. Illustration reduced.

1997, Nov. 10

1993 A360 1000ce Sheet of 4, 2 each #a.-b. 4.00 4.00

Huang Binhong (1865-1955) — A361

Various details of "Color Landscape:" No. 1994: a, 200ce. b, 300ce. c, 400ce. d, 500ce. e, 600ce. f, 800ce. g, 1000ce. h, 2000ce.
No. 1995: a, Detail with Chinese inscription. b, Detail without inscription.

1997, Nov. 10

1994 A361 Sheet of 8, #a.-h. 5.75 5.75

Souvenir Sheet

1995 A361 2000ce Sheet of 2, #a.-b. 4.00 4.00

Nos. 1994a-1994h are each 28x90mm.

Christmas A362

Entire paintings or details: 200ce, Cupid by Botticelli. 550ce, Zephyr and Chloris, by Botticelli. 800ce, Trumphant Cupid, by Caravaggio. 1100ce, The Seven Works of Mercy, by Caravaggio. 1500ce, The Toilet of Venus, by Diego Velazquez. 2000ce, Freeing of Saint Peter, by Raphael.

Sculptures: No. 2002, The Cavalcant Annunciation, by Donatello. No. 2003, Isis and Nepthys Protecting the Cartouches of Tutankhamen with their Wings.

1997, Dec. 8 Litho. *Perf. 14*

1996-2001 A362 Set of 6 5.25 5.25

Souvenir Sheets

2002-2003 A362 5000ce each 5.00 5.00

Diana, Princess of Wales (1961-97) — A363

Various portraits, background color of sheet margin: No. 2004, Pink. No. 2005, Blue.

Portraits with (in margin): No. 2006, Elizabeth Taylor. No. 2007, Henry Kissinger.

1997, Dec. 22 Sheets of 6

2004-2005 A363 1200ce #a.-f., each 7.25 7.25

Souvenir Sheets

2006-2007 A363 3000ce each 3.00 3.00

Mickey and Friends A364

Characters, month: No. 2008: a, Mortie and Ferdie, Jan. b, Minnie, Feb. c, Goofy, Mar. d, Mickey, Minnie, & Pluto, Apr. e, Minnie, May. f, Daisy, June.

No. 2009: a, Donald, July. b, Donald and Daisy, Aug. c, Morty and Ferdie, Sept. d, Huey, Dewey, & Louie, Oct. e, Mickey, Nov. f, Mickey & Minnie, Dec.

Characters, season: No. 2010, Daisy, nephews, winter, horiz. No. 2011, Goofy, fall. No. 2012, Mickey, spring, horiz. No. 2013, Minnie, summer.

Perf. 13½x14, 14x13½

1998, Jan. 29 Litho.

Sheets of 6

2008-2009 A364 1000ce #a.-f., each 6.00 6.00

2008g-2009g With added inscription, each 6.00 6.00

Souvenir Sheets

2010-2013 A364 5000ce each 5.00 5.00

2011a-2012a With added inscription, each 5.00 5.00

Nos. 2008g, 2009g, 2011a, 2012a have added inscription in sheet margin showing "Happy Birthday," Mickey Mouse, and "1998" in emblem.

Issued: #2008g, 2009g, 2011a, 2012a, 8/4/98.

Trains A365

Designs: 300ce, Union Pacific SD60M, US. 500ce, ETR 450, Italy. 800ce, X200 Sweden. 1000ce, TGV Duplex, France. 2000ce, El Class Co-Co, Australia. 3000ce, Eurostar, Britain.

#2020: a, SPS 4-4-0, Pakistan. b, Class WP 4-6-2, India. c, Class QI 2-10-2, China. d, Class 12 4-4-2, Belgium. e, Class P8 4-6-0, Germany. f, Castle Class 4-6-0, Britain. g, Tank engine 2-6-0, Austria. h, Class P36 4-8-4, Russia. i, William Mason 4-4-0, US.

#2021: a, AVE, Spain. b, Class 1600, Luxembourg. c, Bullet train, Japan. d, GM F7 Warbonnet, US. e, Class E1500, Morocco. f, Deltic, Great Britain. g, XPT, Australia. h, Le Shuttle, France/Britain. i, Class 201, Ireland.

#2022, Duchess Class 4-6-2, Britain. #2023, TGV, France.

1998, Feb. 26 Litho. *Perf. 14*

2014-2019 A365 Set of 6 7.75 7.75

Sheets of 9

2020-2021 A365 800ce #a.-i., each 7.25 7.25

Souvenir Sheets

2022-2023 A365 5500ce each 5.50 5.50

#2022-2023 each contain one 57x42mm stamp.

Lunar New Year — A366

Signs of Chinese zodiac - #2025: a, Horse. b, Monkey. c, Ram. d, Rooster. e, Dog. f, Ox. g, Rabbit. h, Boar. i, Snake. j, Dragon. k, Tiger. l, Rat.

1998 Litho. *Perf. 13½*

2025 A366 400ce Sheet of 12, #a.-l. 5.00 5.00

Numbers have been reserved for additional values in this set.

Great Black Writers of the 20th Century — A368

Designs: a, Maya Angelou. b, Alex Haley. c, Charles Johnson. d, Richard Wright. e, Toni Cade Bambara. f, Henry Louis Gates, Jr.

1998, Mar. 25 Litho. *Perf. 14*

2027 A368 350ce Sheet of 6, #a.-f. 2.25 2.25

Aircraft A369

No. 2028: a, Messerschmitt Bf 109 E-7. b, Lockheed PV-2 Harpoon. c, Airspeed Oxford MK1. d, Junkers Ju87D-1. e, Yakovlev Yak-9D. f, North American P-51D Mustang. g, Douglas A-20 Havoc. h, Supermarine Attacker F1. i, Mikoyan-Gurevich MIG-15.

No. 2029: a, Breguet 14 B2. b, Curtiss BF2C-1 Goshawk. c, Supermarine Spitfire MK IX. d, Fiat G.50. e, Douglas B-18A. f, Boeing FB-5. g, Bristol F.2B. h, Hawker Fury 1. i, Fiat CR42.

No. 2030, Mitsubishi AGM8 Reisen. No. 2031, Supermarine Spitfire MK XIV, Supermarine Spitfire MK 1.

1998, May 5

Sheets of 9

2028-2029 A369 800ce #a.-i., each 7.25 7.25

Souvenir Sheets

2030-2031 A369 3000ce each 3.00 3.00

#2030-2031 each contain one 57x42mm stamp.

Nos. 1891-1894 Ovptd.

1998, May 13

2032-2034 A334 Set of 3 1.75 1.75

Souvenir Sheet

2035 A334 2000ce multicolored 2.00 2.00

No. 2035 contains additional inscription in sheet margin: "ISRAEL 98 - WORLD STAMP EXHIBITION / TEL-AVIV 13-21 MAY 1998."

Ships A370

Ocean liners - #2036: a, Empress of Ireland. b, Transylvania. c, Mauritania. d, Reliance. e, Aquitania. f, Lapland. g, Cap Polonio. h, France. i, Imperator.

Warships - #2037: a, HMS Rodney. b, USS Alabama. c, HMS Nelson. d, SS Ormonde. e, USS Radford. f, SS Empress of Russia. g, Type XIV, Germany. h, Type A Midget, Japan. i, Brin, Italy.

No. 2038, Titanic. No. 2039, Amistad.

1998, May 5 Litho. *Perf. 14*

Sheets of 9

2036-2037 A370 800ce #a.-i., each 7.25 7.25

Souvenir Sheets

2038-2039 A370 5500ce each 5.50 5.50

#2038-2039 each contain one 42x56mm stamp.

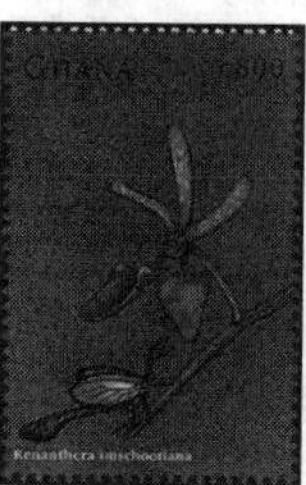

Orchids — A371

No. 2040: a, Renanthera imschootiana. b, Arachnis flosaeris. c, Restrepia lansbergi. d, Paphiopedilum tonsum. e, Phalaenopsis ebauche. f, Pleione limprichti.

No. 2041: a, Phragmipedium schroderae. b, Zygopetalum clayii. c, Vanda coerulea. d, Odontonia boussole. e, Disa uniflora. f, Dendrobium bigibbum.

No. 2042, Cypripedium calceolus. No. 2043, Sobralia candida.

1998, June 2

Sheets of 6

2040-2041 A371 800ce #a.-f., each 4.75 4.75

Souvenir Sheets

2042-2043 A371 5500ce each 5.50 5.50

Elvis Presley (1935-77), Television Comeback Special, 30th Anniv. A372

Various portraits during performance.

1998, June 16 *Perf. 13½*

2044 A372 800ce Sheet of 6, #a.-f. 4.75 4.75

Japanese Flowers — A373

Predominant color of flowers, location of denomination - #2045: a, Green (bamboo), UR. b, Red, LR. c, Yellow, LR. d, Pale green & pink, UR.

No. 2046: a, Pale green, yellow & pink, LR. b, Red, UR. c, Pink, LR. d, White, LR.

No. 2047, Small pink & yellow, LR. No. 2048, Pink, UL.

1998, June 2 Litho. *Perf. 14*

Sheets of 4

2045-2046 A373 2000ce #a.-d., each 8.00 8.00

Souvenir Sheets

2047-2048 A373 5500ce each 5.50 5.50

Ghana Cocoa Board, 50th Anniv. A374

Designs: 200ce, Tetteh Quarshie, pioneer of Ghana Cocoa industry. 550ce, Ripe hybrid cocoa pods. 800ce, Opening of cocoa pods. 1100ce, Fermenting cocoa beans. 1500ce, Shipment of cocoa.

1998, July 8 *Perf. 13x13½*

2049-2053 A374 Set of 5 4.25 4.25

Metropolitan Assembly, Cent. — A375

Designs: 200ce, AMA Centennial emblem. 550ce, King Tackie Tawiah I (1862-1902). 800ce, Achimota School, Accra. 1100ce, Korle Bu Hospital, Accra. 1500ce, Christianborg Castle, Accra.

1998, July 8

2054-2058 A375 Set of 5 4.25 4.25

Intl. Year of the Ocean A376

#2059: a, Dolphins. b, Dolphin (f). c, Seagull. d, Least tern, seagulls. e, Emperor angelfish (i). f, Whit ear. g, Blue shark, diver (k). h, Parrotfish. i, Dottyback. j, Blue-spotted stingray (m, n). k, Masked butterfly fish. l, Jack knife fish (h). m, Octopus (i). n, Turkeyfish (lionfish) (j, k, o). o, Seadragon. p, Rock cod.
#2060, Devil ray. #2061, Great white shark.

1998, Aug. 18 ***Perf. 14***
2059 A376 500ce Sheet of 16, #a.-p. 8.00 8.00

Souvenir Sheets
2060-2061 A376 3000ce each 3.00 3.00

A377

Twentieth Cent. Inventors and Their Inventions - #2062: a, Edison, light bulb. b, Peephole kinetoscope, Edison. c, Tesla coil, Tesla. d, Nikola Tesla (1856-1943). e, Gottlieb Wilhelm Daimler (1834-1900). f, Motorcycle, Daimler. g, Transmitter circuit for telescope, Marconi. h, Guglielmo Marconi.
#2063: a, Orville & Wright. b, 1st Flyer, Wright Brothers. c, Neon lighting and signs, Claude. d, Georges Claude (1870-1960). e, Alexander Graham Bell. f, The telephone, transmitter, Bell. g, Various uses of lasers, Townes. h, Charles Townes (b. 1915).
No. 2064, Robert Goddard (1882-1945), physicist. No. 2065, Paul Ehrlich (1854-1915), chemist, bacteriologist.

1998, Sept. 1 ***Perf. 14***

Sheets of 8
2062-2063 A377 1000ce #a.-h., each 8.00 8.00

Souenir Sheets
2064-2065 A377 1000ce each 5.50 5.50

Nos. 2062b-2062c, 2062f-2062g, 2063b-2063c, 2063f-2063g are each 53x38mm.

A378

Cats and Dogs in Christmas Scenes: 500ce, British colorpoint. 600ce, American shorthair-Dilute calico. 800ce, Peke-faced Persian. 1000ce, Small German spitz. 2000ce, British shorthair blue. 3000ce, Persian Dilute calico.
#2072, English pointer. #2073, Rumpy max.

1998, Dec. 1 **Litho.** ***Perf. 14***
2066-2071 A378 Set of 6 8.00 8.00

Souvenir Sheets
2072-2073 A378 5500ce each 5.50 5.50

Ferrari Automobiles — A378a

No. 2073A: c, : Lampredi. d, 250 GT Cabriolet. e, 121 LM.
3000ce, 365 GTS/4 Spyder.
Illustration reduced.

1998, Dec. 24 **Litho.** ***Perf. 14***
2073A A378a 2000ce Sheet of 3, #c-e 5.25 5.25

Souvenir Sheet

Perf. 13¾x14¼
2073B A378a 3000ce multi 2.60 2.60

No. 2073A contains three 39x25mm stamps.

Diana, Princess of Wales (1961-97) A379

1998, Dec. 24 **Litho.** ***Perf. 14½***
2074 A379 1000ce multicolored 1.00 1.00

No. 2074 was issued in sheets of 6.

Gandhi — A380

No. 2075: a, After 8 month prison term in Poona, 1931. b, On Salt March, 1930. c, Picking up natural salt at end of Salt March, 1930. d, After graduating from high school in Rajkot, 1887.
5500ce, At age 61, 1931.

1998, Dec. 24
2075 A380 2000ce Sheet of 4, #a.-d. 8.00 8.00

Souvenir Sheet
2076 A380 5500ce multicolored 5.50 5.50

Nos. 2075b-2075c are each 53x38mm.

Pablo Picasso A381

#2077, Collage, Composition with Butterfly, 1932. #2078, Sculpture, Mandolin and Clarinet, 1913, vert. #2079, Painting, Ballplayers on the Beach, 1931.
5500ce, Tomato Plant, 1944, vert.

1998, Dec. 24 ***Perf. 14x14½***
2077-2079 A381 Set of 3 4.00 4.00

Souenir Sheet
2080 A381 5500ce multicolored 5.50 5.50

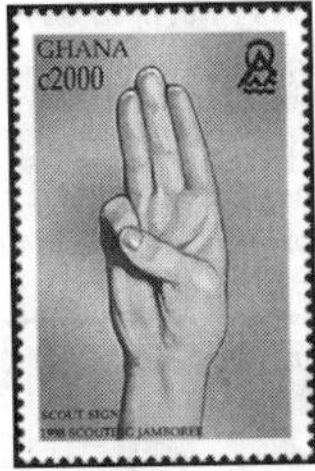
19th World Scouting Jamboree, Chile — A382

No. 2081: a, Scout sign. b, Camping. c, Tying a bowline.
5000ce, Robert Baden-Powell.

1998, Dec. 24 ***Perf. 14***

Sheet of 3
2081 A382 2000ce #a.-c. 6.00 6.00

Souvenir Sheet
2082 A382 5000ce multicolored 5.00 5.00

Royal Air Force, 80th Anniv. A383

No. 2083: a, C130 Hercules. b, Chinook HC2. c, C130 Hercules W2. d, Panavia Tornado F3ADV.
No. 2084, Eurofighter 2000, Chipmunk. No. 2085, Hawk's head, biplane.

1998, Dec. 24

Sheet of 4
2083 A383 2000ce #a.-d. 8.00 8.00

Souvenir Sheets
2084-2085 A383 5500ce each 5.50 5.50

New Year 1999 (Year of the Rabbit) A384

Scenes showing farmer from "Farmer and Rabbit," by Han Fei Tzu: a, Working in field. b, Watching rabbit run into tree. c, Holding rabbit. d, Dreaming of rabbit.

1999, Jan. 4
2086 A384 1400ce Sheet of 4, #a.-d. 5.50 5.50

Dinosaurs A385

Designs: 400ce, Corythosaurus. 600ce, Struthiomimus. 1000ce, Lambeosaurus. 2000ce, Hesperosuchus.
No. 2090: a, Ankylosaurus. b, Anatosaurus. c, Diplodocus. d, Monoclonius. e, Tyrannosaurus. f, Camptosaurus. g, Ornitholestes. h, Archaeopteryx. i, Allosaurus.
No. 2091: a, Pterodactylus. b, Scelidosaurus. c, Pteranodon. d, Plateosaurus. e, Ornithosuchus. f, Kentrosaurus. g, Hypsognathus. h, Erythrosuchus. i, Stegoceros.
No. 2092, Dimorphodon, vert. No. 2093, Apatosaurus.

1999, Mar. 1 **Litho.** ***Perf. 13½***
2087-2089A A385 Set of 4 4.00 4.00

Sheets of 9
2090-2091 A385 800ce #a.-i., each 7.25 7.25

Souvenir Sheets
2092-2093 A385 5000ce each 5.00 5.00

Australia '99, World Stamp Expo A386

Butterflies: 300ce, California sister. 500ce, Red-splashed sulphur. 600ce, Checked white. 800ce, Blue emperor.
No. 2098, vert: a, Red admiral. b, Buckeye. c, Desert checkered skipper. d, Orange sulphur. e, Tiger swallowtail. f, Orange-bordered blue. g, Agraulis vanillae. h, Monarch.
No. 2099, vert: a, Small tortoiseshell. b, Brimstone. c, Camberwell beauty. d, Marbled white. e, Purple emperor. f, Clouded yellow. g, Ladoga camilla. h, Marsh fritillary.
No. 2100, Papilio homerus, vert. No. 2101, Blue copper.

1999, Apr. 26 **Litho.** ***Perf. 14***
2094-2097 A386 Set of 4 2.25 2.25

Sheets of 8
2098-2099 A386 1000ce #a.-h., each 8.00 8.00

Souvenir Sheets
2100-2101 A386 5000ce each 5.00 5.00

Shirley Temple as "Curly Top" — A387

Scenes from film, vert. - #2102: a, Saying prayers. b, Actor John Boles looking at portrait. c, Taking Boles' hand. d, Dressed as old woman.
No. 2103: a, Hugging older sister. b, Dressed as a man. c, Looking at stuffed animals. d, Pulling Boles' tie. e, With family. f, Looking at sister and Boles together.
5000ce, In pink dress, vert.

Perf. 13½x14, 14x13½

1999, Mar. 1 **Litho.**
2102 A387 1000ce Sheet of 4, #a.-d. 3.50 3.50
2103 A387 1000ce Sheet of 6, #a.-f. 5.50 5.50

Souvenir Sheet
2104 A387 5000ce multicolored 5.50 5.50

Amorphophallus Flavovirens - A387a

1999, May 6 **Litho.** ***Perf. 14x14¼***
2104A A387a 200ce multi

Trains A388

Designs: 400ce, ICE 2, Germany, 1966. 500ce, M41, Hungary, 1982. 600ce, DVR, Finland, 1963. 1000ce, AVE 100 class, Spain, 1982.
No. 2109: a, EMD GP7 Illinois Terminal RR, 1949-54. b, EMD SD 38-2, 1972-79. c, EMD SD 60M Soo Line, 1989-96. d, GE U25C, 1963-65. e, EMD GP 28, 1961-63. f, EMD SD 9, 1954-59.
No. 2110: a, Conrail EMD SD80, 1993-99. b, Columbus & Greenville RR EMD SDP35, 1964-66. c, Providence & Worcester RR, MLW M420 Loc. Works, 1973-77. d, Missouri Pacific C36-7, 1978-85. e, Alco C-420 Virginia & Maryland RR, 1963-68. f, Reading RR EMD GP30, 1961-63.
No. 2111, Swiss Federal RR Class RE 6/6 Co-Co, 1972. No. 2112, AGP44, ABB Traction, Inc. 1990-91.

1999, May 10 ***Perf. 14***
2105-2108 A388 Set of 4 2.25 2.25

Sheets of 6
2109-2110 A388 1300ce #a.-f., each 7.00 7.00

Souvenir Sheets
2111-2112 A388 5000ce each 5.00 5.00

Paintings by Hokusai (1760-1849) — A389

Details or entire paintings - #2113: a, Girl Picking Plum Blossoms. b, Surveying a Region. c, Sumo Wrestlers (rear view). d, Sumo Wrestlers (front view). e, Landscape with Seaside Village. f, Courtiers Crossing a Bridge.

No. 2114: a, Climbing the Mountain. b, Nakahara in Sagami Province. c, Sumo Wrestlers (2 fighting). d, An Oiran and Maid by a Fence. e. Fujiwara Yoshitaka.

No. 2115, Palanquin Bearers on a Steep Hill, vert. No. 2116, Three Ladies by a Well, vert.

1999, Aug. 3 Litho. *Perf. 13¾*

2113 A389 1300ce Sheet of 6, #a.-f. 7.00 7.00
2114 A389 1300ce Sheet of 6, #a.-e., 2113c 7.00 7.00

Souvenir Sheets

2115-2116 A389 5000ce each 4.50 4.50

IBRA '99, World Philatelic Exhibition, Nuremberg — A390

Exhibition emblem, sailing ship Schomberg and: #2117, 500ce, Hanover #1. #2119, 1000ce, Lubeck #1.

Emblem, Class P8 4-6-0 locomotive and: #2118, 800ce, Hamburg #1. #2120, 2000ce, Heligoland #1A.

5000ce, Germany #66 tied to airmail label on cover, vert.

Illustration reduced.

1999, Aug. 3 *Perf. 14x14½*

2117-2120 A390 Set of 4 3.75 3.75

Souvenir Sheet

Perf. 14½x14

2121 A390 5000ce multicolored 4.50 4.50

A391

1st Manned Moon Landing, 30th Anniv.: No. 2122: a, Command Module. b, Lunar Module ascension. c, Giant moon rock. d, Lunar module signals home. e, Neil Armstrong. f, One small step.

5000ce, Earth rise, horiz.

1999, Aug. 3 *Perf. 14*

2122 A391 1300ce Sheet of 6, #a.-f. 7.00 7.00

Souvenir Sheet

2123 A391 5000ce multicolored 4.50 4.50

A392

1999, Aug. 4

Queen Mother, 100th Birthday (in 2000) - No. 2124: a, Lady Elizabeth Bowles-Lyon with brother David, 1904. b, Queen Elizabeth, 1957. c, Queen Mother, 1970. d, Queen Mother, 1992.

5000ce, Queen Mother, 1970, diff.

2124 A392 2000ce Sheet of 4, #a.-d. + label 7.25 7.25

Souvenir Sheet

2125 A392 5000ce multicolored 5.00 5.00

No. 2125 contains one 38x50mm stamp. Margins of sheets are embossed.

Fauna A393

200ce, Meles meles. 800ce, Vulpes vulpes.

No. 2128: a, Martes martes. b, Strix aluco. c, Sus scrofa. d, Accipiter gentilis. e, Eliomys quercinus. f, Lucanus cervus.

No. 2129: a, Merops apiaster. b, Upupa epops. c, Cervus elaphus. d, Circaetus gallicus. e, Lacerta ocellata. f, Lynx pardellus.

5000ce, Canis lupus, vert.

1999, Mar. 29 Litho. *Perf. 14*

2126-2127 A393 Set of 2 .90 .90

Sheets of 6

2129 A393 1000ce #a.-f. 5.50 5.50
2128 A393 1000ce #a.-f. 5.50 5.50

Souvenir Sheet

2130 A393 5000ce multicolored 5.00 5.00

1999

Birds: 400ce, Cyanopica cyana. 600ce, Ciconia ciconia. 2000ce, Aegypius monachus, vert. 3000ce, Garrulus glandarius, vert.

5000ce, Aquila heliaca adalberti.

2131-2134 A393 Set of 4 5.50 5.50

Souvenir Sheet

2135 A393 5000ce multicolored 4.75 4.75

Rights of the Child — A394

No. 2136: a, Child, UN building. b, Dove, earth. c, Mother, child.

5000ce, Child.

1999, Aug. 3 Litho. *Perf. 14*

2136 A394 3000ce Sheet of 3, #a.-c. 8.50 8.50

Souvenir Sheet

2137 A394 5000ce multicolored 4.75 4.75

Souvenir Sheets

PhilexFrance 99 — A395

Locomotives: No. 2138, 232-U1 Four cylinder compound 4-6-4. No. 2139, 0-6-0 Suburban tank engine.

1999, Aug. 3 *Perf. 14x13¾*

2138-2139 A395 5000ce each 5.00 5.00

Johann Wolfgang von Goethe (1749-1832), German Poet — A396

No. 2140: a, Wagner entreats Faust in his study. b, Goethe and Friedrich von Schiller. c, Mephistopheles disguised as the fool.

5000ce, Faust attended by spirits.

1999, Aug. 3 Litho. *Perf. 14*

2140 A396 2000ce Sheet of 3, #a.-c. 5.50 5.50

Souvenir Sheet

2141 A396 5000ce multicolored 4.75 4.75

A397

1999, Aug. 20 Litho. *Perf. 14x13¾*

2142 A397 1000ce multicolored .95 .95

1999 Return of Macao to People's Republic of China. Issued in sheets of 4.

A398

1999 Litho. *Perf. 13½x13*

Save the Ozone Layer: 200ce, Fish. 550ce, Earth surrounded by ozone layer, man. 800ce, Crying Earth. 1100ce, People holding up shield against sunlight. 1500ce, Objects with ozone-depleting and non-harmful chemicals.

2143-2147 A398 Set of 5 2.40 2.40

SOS Children's Villages, 50th Anniv. A399

Designs: 200ce, Grandma Alice. 550ce, Kindergarten. 800ce, SOS Children's Village founder Herrmann Gmeiner (1919-86), Asikawa SOS building. 1100ce, Food preparation.

1999 *Perf. 13x13½*

2148-2151 A399 Set of 4 1.50 1.50

Dr. Ephraim Apu, Musician, Birth Cent. — A400

Designs: 200ce, Apu, clef, note. 800ce, Apu playing Odurugya flute. 1100ce, Apu, indigenous flutes.

1999 *Perf. 13½x13*

2152-2154 A400 Set of 3 1.25 1.25

Millennium — A401

Designs: 300ce, Millennium emblem, vert. 700ce, Emblem, Kwame Nkrumah. 1200ce, Emblem, University of Ghana, vert.

1999, Dec. 28 Litho. *Perf. 13¼*

2155-2157 A401 Set of 3 1.25 1.25

New Year 2000 — A402

Various scenes from Chinese story, "Daughter of the Dragon King." Stamps from the two sheets are numbered 1-12 in Chinese characters. The numerals are at the bottom of the top group of Chinese characters.

2000, Feb. 5 *Perf. 14½x14¼*

Sheets of 6

2158 A402 1600ce #a.-f. 5.50 5.50
2159 A402 1700ce #a.-f. 5.75 5.75

Wildlife A403

Designs: 300ce, Black-faced impala. 500ce, Cheetah. 1000ce, Wildebeest. 3000ce, Hippopotamus.

No. 2164, vert.: a, Chimpanzee. b, Boomslang. c, Vulture. d, Leopard. e, Rhinoceros. f, Zebra. g, Crowned crane. h, Lesser kudu.

No. 2165, vert.: a, Purple roller. b, Pelicans. c, Egrets. d, Orange-breasted waxbill. e, Giraffe, f, African buffalo. g, African elephant. h, African lion.

No. 2166, Waterbuck. No. 2167, Ostrich.

2000, Feb. 28 Litho. *Perf. 14*

2160-2163 A403 Set of 4 2.75 2.75

Sheets of 8

2164 A403 1100ce #a.-h. 5.25 5.25
2165 A403 1200ce #a.-h. 5.75 5.75

Souvenir Sheets

2166-2167 A403 7000ce each 4.00 4.00

Tourism A404

a, 300ce, Building, palm trees. b, 300ce, Mud building, natives. c, 300ce, Elephants. d, 1100ce, Natives. e, 1200ce, Natives carrying animal. f, 1800ce, Natives, diff.

2000 Litho. *Perf. 13x13¼*

2168 A404 Booklet pane of 6, #a.-h. 2.25 2.25
Complete booklet, 4 #2168 9.00

There are 2 types of #2168, which differ only by the arrangement of the stamps on the pane. The booklet contains 2 of each type.

Wildlife A405

Designs: 500ce, Zebra duiker. 600ce, Leopard. 2000ce, Bush buck. 3000ce, African wood owl.

No. 2173: a, Blotted genet. b, Tree pangolin. c, Bongo. d, Elephant. e, Flap-necked chameleon. f, West African dwarf crocodile.

No. 2174: a, Lowe's monkey. b, Diana monkey. c, Potto. d, Moustached monkey. e, Thomas's galago. f, Chimpanzee.

No. 2175: a, Gray parrot. b, Hoopoe. c, European roller. d, European bee-eater. e, Blue-breasted kingfisher. f, White-throated bee-eater.

No. 2176, Hippopotamus, vert. No. 2177, Great blue turaco, vert.

2000, May 1 Litho. *Perf. 14*

2169-2172 A405 Set of 4 2.75 2.75

Sheets of 6, #a.-f.

2173-2175 A405 1600ce each 4.25 4.25

Souvenir Sheets

2176-2177 A405 6000ce each 2.75 2.75

Mushrooms—A406

No. 2178, horiz.: a, Slippery jack. b, Violet deceiver. c, Fairy stool. d, Honey fungus. e, Shaggy parasol. f, Russula sp.

No. 2179, horiz.: a, Grisette. b, Common puffball. c, Fan. d, Gray chanterelle. e, Fairies' bonnets. f, Russula sp., diff.

5000ce, Great orange elf-cup. 8000ce, Bitter boletus.

2000, May 15

Sheets of 6

2178 A406 1500ce #a.-f. 4.00 4.00
2179 A406 2000ce #a.-f. 5.50 5.50

Souvenir Sheets

2180 A406 5000ce multi 2.25 2.25
2181 A406 8000ce multi 3.50 3.50

The Stamp Show 2000, London.

Eurasian Goldfinch — A406a

2000, June 1 Litho. *Perf. 13¾x13¼*

2181A A406a 300ce multi — —

Prince William, 18th Birthday — A407

No. 2182: a, In ski gear. b, With ribbons wrapped around fingers. c, With jacket, no tie. d, Close-up.

8000ce, In sweater.

Illustration reduced.

2000, June 26 Litho. *Perf. 14*

2182 A407 2000ce Sheet of 4, #a-d 2.50 2.50

Souvenir Sheet

Perf. 13¾

2183 A407 8000ce multi 2.50 2.50

No. 2182 contains four 28x42mm stamps.

First Zeppelin Flight, Cent. — A408

No. 2184: a, LZ-129. b, LZ-9. c, LZ-4.

5000ce, LZ-11.

Illustration reduced.

2000, June 26 *Perf. 13¾*

2184 A408 1600ce Sheet of 3, #a-c 1.50 1.50

Souvenir Sheet

2185 A408 5000ce multi 1.60 1.60

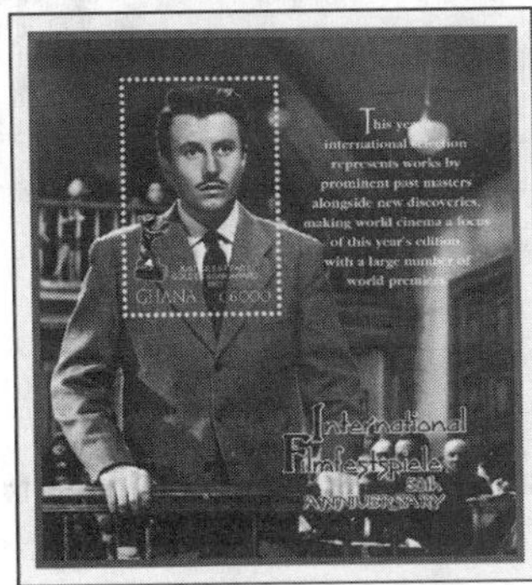

Berlin Film Festival, 50th Anniv. — A409

No. 2186: a, Wetherby. b, Die Frau und der Fremde. c, Hong Gao Liang (Red Sorghum). d, Skriváncí na Niti. e, Music Box. f, Tema.

6000ce, Justice Est Faite.

Illustration reduced.

2000, June 26 *Perf. 14*

2186 A409 2000ce Sheet of 6, #a-f 3.75 3.75

Souvenir Sheet

2187 A409 6000ce multi 1.90 1.90

Apollo-Soyuz Mission, 25th Anniv. — A410

No. 2188: a, Apollo 18. b, Docked spacecraft. c, Soyuz 19.

8000ce, Soyuz, Earth.

Illustration reduced.

2000, June 26

2188 A410 4000ce Sheet of 3, #a-c 3.75 3.75

Souvenir Sheet

2189 A410 8000ce multi 2.50 2.50

Souvenir Sheets

2000 Summer Olympics, Sydney — A411

No. 2190: a, Gymnastics. b, Long jump. c, Los Angeles Coliseum, and US flag. d, Ancient Greek chariot racer.

Illustration reduced.

2000, June 26

2190 A411 1300ce Sheet of 4, #a-d 1.60 1.60

Public Railways, 175th Anniv. — A412

No. 2191: a, Marc Seguin. b, Blenkinsop locomotive. c, Pumping station, Dawlish.

Illustration reduced.

2000, June 26

2191 A412 4000ce Sheet of 3, #a-c 3.75 3.75

Albert Einstein (1879-1955) — A413

Illustration reduced.

2000, June 26 *Perf. 13¾*

2192 A413 8000ce multi 2.50 2.50

Ghana Home Economics Assoc. — A414

Gold Frames

Designs: 300ce, Women, cooking pots. 700ce, Woman with home economics textbook, vert. 1200ce, Emblem, Alberta Ollennu, Patience A. Adow. 1800ce, Emblems, vert.

2000 *Perf. 13x13¼, 13¼x13*

2193-2196 A414 Set of 4 1.25 1.25

See Nos. 2273-2274.

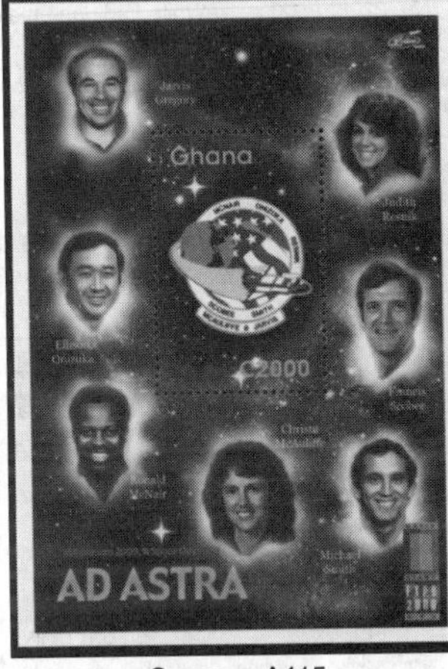

Space — A415

No. 2197, horiz.: a, Mercury. b, Gemini. c, Apollo. d, Vostok. e, Voskhod 2. f, Soyuz.

Illustration reduced.

2000, June 26 Litho. *Perf. 14*

2197 A415 2000ce Sheet of 6, #a-f 3.50 3.50

Souvenir Sheet

2198 A415 2000ce Challenger 51-L patch .60 .60

World Stamp Expo 2000, Anaheim.

Cats and Dogs — A416

Designs: 1100ce, African shorthair. 1200ce, Russian Blue. 1800ce, Basenji. 2000ce, Basset hound.

No. 2203, horiz. a, 1600ce, Weimaraner. b, 1800ce, Keeshond. c, 1800ce, Fox terrier. d, 1800ce, Saluki. e, 1800ce, Dalmatian. f, 1800ce, English setter.

No. 2204, 1800ce, horiz.: a, Silver Persian. b, Creampoint Himalayan. c, British tortoiseshell shorthair. d, American shorthair tabby. e, Black Persian. f, Turkish Van.

No. 2205, 8000ce, Cocker spaniels. No. 2206, 8000ce, Lilac Persian.

2000, Aug. 21

2199-2202 A416 Set of 4 1.90 1.90

Sheets of 6, #a-f

2203-2204 A416 Set of 2 6.50 6.50

Souvenir Sheets

2205-2206 A416 Set of 2 4.75 4.75

Scenes from Tale of the White Snake — A417

No. 2207, 2500ce: a, Xu Xian offers umbrella to White Lady and maid. b, White Lady (with basket) helps husband Xu Xian with business. c, Monk Fa Hai (with necklace) talks to Xu Xian. d, Xu Xian gives wine to wife. e, White Lady becomes snake, Xu Xian has heart attack. f, White Lady (with swords) trying to get medicinal herbs.

No. 2208, 2500ce: a, White Lady and maid at Fa Hai's temple. b, Maid threatens to kill Xu Xian. c, Fa Hai captures White Lady in bowl. d, Maid, Xu Xian at pagoda. e, Maid with sword attacks Fa Hai. f, Maid turns Fa Hai into crab.

Illustration reduced.

2001, Jan. 2 Litho. *Perf. 14*

Sheets of 6, #a-f

2207-2208 A417 Set of 2 8.75 8.75

New Year 2001 (Year of the snake).

Edward G. Robinson — A418

Color of photograph: a, Gray green. b, Lilac. c, Red violet (with hat). d, Brown (with cigar). e, Orange brown (with pipe). f, Blue green.

2001, Apr. 16 Litho. *Perf. 14*

2209 A418 4000ce Sheet of 6, #a-f 6.50 6.50

James Cagney — A419

Color of photograph: a, Olive green. b, Emerald. c, Blue. d, Brown. e, Red violet. f, Orange.

2001, Apr. 16

2210 A419 4000ce Sheet of 6, #a-f 6.50 6.50

Millennium — A420

No. 2211, 2500ce - Architects: a, Walter Gropius. b, Aldo Rossi. c, Le Corbusier. d, Antonio Gaudi. e, Paolo Soleri. f, Ludwig Mies van de Rohe.

No. 2212, 2500ce - Artists: a, Wassily Kandinsky. b, Henry Moore. c, Marc Chagall. d, Norman Rockwell. e, Antonio López García. f, Frida Kahlo.

No. 2213, 14,000ce, Frank Lloyd Wright. No. 2214, 14,000ce, Pablo Picasso. No. 2215, 14,000ce, Human Genome Project.

2001, Apr. 16

Sheets of 6, #a-f

2211-2212 A420 Set of 2 8.25 8.25

Souvenir Sheets

2213-2215 A420 Set of 3 11.50 11.50

Jazz Musicians — A421

No. 2216, 4000ce: a, Scott Joplin. b, Clarence Williams. c, Sidney Bechet. d, Willie "The Lion" Smith. e, Ferdinand "Jelly Roll" Morton. f, Coleman "Bean" Hawkins.

No. 2217, 4000ce: a, Kid Ory. b, Earl "Fatha" Hines. c, Lil Hardin Armstrong. d, John Philip Sousa. e, James P. Johnson. f, Johnny St. Cyr.

No. 2218, 14,000ce, Joe "King" Oliver. No. 2219, 14,000ce, Louis "Satchmo" Armstrong.

2001, Apr. 16

Sheets of 6, #a-f

2216-2217 A421 Set of 2 13.00 13.00

Souvenir Sheets

2218-2219 A421 Set of 2 7.75 7.75

Oriental Art A422

Designs: 500ce, Cranes, by Kano Eisenin Michinobu. 800ce, Flowers and Trees in Chen Chun's Style, by Tsubaki Chinzan. 1200ce, A Poetry Contest of 42 Matches, by unknown artist. 2000ce, Cranes, by Kano, diff. 5000ce, A Poetry Contest of 42 Matches, diff. 12,000ce, Plum Trees, by Tani Buncho.

No. 2226, 3000ce, vert. - The Tales of Ise, by Sumiyoshi Jokei: a, Chapter 1. b, Chapter 4. c, Chapter 6. d, Chapter 9 (Eastbound Trip, Mt. Utsu). e, Chapter 9, (Eastbound Trip, Mt. Fuji). f, Chapter 9, (Eastbound Trip, Black-headed Gulls). g, Chapter 23, (Crossing Kawachi). h, Chapter 23, (By the Well Wall).

No. 2227, 4000ce, vert. - The Story of Sakyamuni, by unknown artist: a, Siddhartha's Excursion Through the South Gate. b, Siddhartha's Excursion Through the East Gate. c, Siddhartha's Excursion Through the North Gate. d, Siddhartha's Excursion Through the West Gate. e, Sakyamuni Entering Nirvana. f, Untitled.

No. 2228, 14,000ce, Cranes, by Kano (red denomination), diff. No. 2229, 14,000ce, Cranes, by Kano (yellow denomination), diff. No. 2230, 14,000ce, Chapter 1, by Sumiyoshi. No. 2231, Chapter 12, by Sumiyoshi.

2001, Apr. 30

2220-2225 A422 Set of 6 6.00 6.00

2226 A422 3000ce Sheet of 8, #a-h 6.50 6.50

2227 A422 4000ce Sheet of 6, #a-f 6.50 6.50

Souvenir Sheets

2228-2231 A422 Set of 4 15.00 15.00

Phila Nippon '01, Japan.

Automobiles — A423

Designs: 2000ce, 1950 Bentley S Series convertible. 3000ce, 1948 Chrysler Town and Country. 5000ce, 1957 Lotus Elite. 6000ce, 1966 Chevrolet Corvette Sting Ray.

No. 2236, 4000ce: a, 1956-59 BMW 507. b, 1934 Bentley English Tourer. c, 1948 Morris Minor MM. d, 1954 Daimler SP-250 Dart. e, 1950 DeSoto custom convertible. f, 1955-60, Ford Thunderbird.

No. 2237, 4000ce: a,1959-63 Porshe 356B. b, 1962 Rolls-Royce Silver Cloud. c, 1958 Austin Healey Sprite MK-1. d, 1954-57 Mercedes 300SL. e, 1949 Citroen 2CV. f, 1949 Cadillac Series 62.

No. 2238, 14,000ce: a, 1933 Mercedes-Benz. No. 2239, 1953-55 Triumph TR-2.

2001, June 18

2232-2235 A423 Set of 4 4.50 4.50

Sheets of 6, #a-f

2236-2237 A423 Set of 2 13.00 13.00

Souvenir Sheets

2238-2239 A423 Set of 2 7.75 7.75

Belgica 2001 Intl. Stamp Exhibition, Brussels. No. 2238-2239 each contain one 85x28mm stamp.

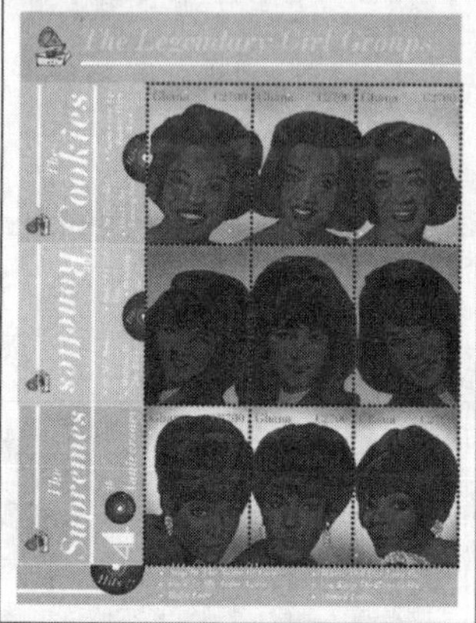

Female Recording Groups of the 1960s — A424

No. 2240 - Various members of: a-c, The Cookies. d-f, The Ronettes. g-i, The Supremes.

2001, Apr. 16 Litho. *Perf. 14*

2240 A424 2700ce Sheet of 9, #a-i 6.75 6.75

Mao Zedong (1893-1976) — A425

No. 2241: a, With arm raised, orange and light orange background. b, Portrait. c, With arm raised, tan gray and blue background.

12,000ce, With flag.

2001, Aug. 27

2241 A425 7000ce Sheet of 3, #a-c 6.00 6.00

Souvenir Sheet

2242 A425 12,000ce multi 3.50 3.50

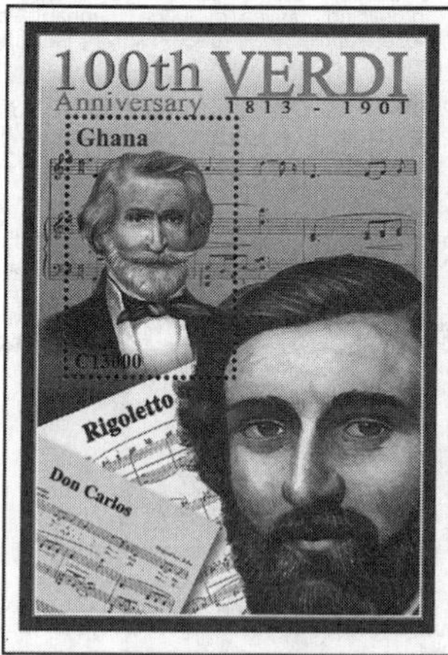

Giuseppe Verdi (1813-1901), Opera Composer — A426

No. 2243: a, Verdi. b, Scores for Aida and Rigoletto. c, Verdi's birthplace. d, Map of Italy.

13,000ce, Verdi and score.

2001, Aug. 27

2243 A426 5000ce Sheet of 4, #a-d 5.75 5.75

Souvenir Sheet

2244 A426 13,000ce multi 3.75 3.75

Toulouse-Lautrec Paintings — A427

No. 2245: a, Jane Avril Leaving the Moulin Rouge. b, Jane Avril Dancing. c, Jane Avril Entering the Moulin Rouge.

2001, Aug. 27 *Perf. 13¾*

2245 A427 6700ce Sheet of 3, #a-c 5.75 5.75

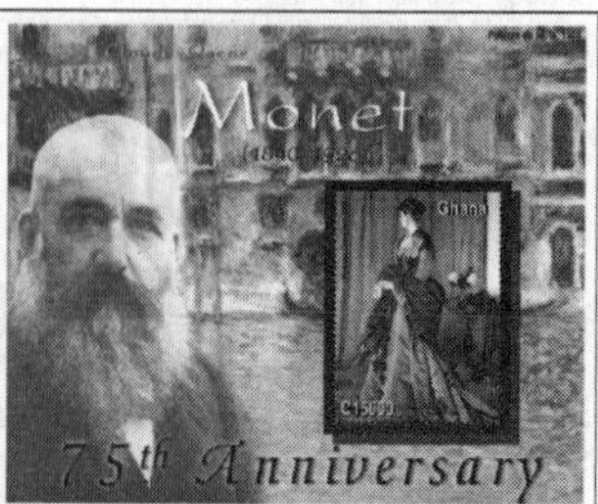

Monet Paintings — A428

No. 2246, horiz.: a, Zaandam. b, On the Seine at Bennecourt. c, The Studio Boat. d, Houses on the Waterfront, Zaandam.

15,000ce, Madame Gaudibert.

2001, Aug. 27
2246 A428 5000ce Sheet of 4, #a-d 5.75 5.75

Souvenir Sheet

2247 A428 15,000ce multi 4.25 4.25

Queen Victoria (1819-1901) — A429

No. 2248: a, Victoria. b, Prince Albert. c, Albert and Victoria. d, Victoria and Albert on wedding day.
12,000ce, Victoria with green and white headpiece.

2001, Aug. 27 ***Perf. 14***
2248 A429 5000ce Sheet of 4, #a-d 5.75 5.75

Souvenir Sheet

2249 A429 12,000ce multi 3.50 3.50

Queen Elizabeth II, 75th Birthday — A430

No. 2250, vert.: a, Bright pink hat. b, White hat. c, Peach hat. d, Crown. e, Blue and pink hat. f, In uniform.
15,000ce, with Prince Philip.

2001, Aug. 27
2250 A430 4000ce Sheet of 6, #a-f 6.75 6.75

Souvenir Sheet

2251 A430 15,000ce multi 4.25 4.25

Whales A431

Designs: 1000ce, Killer whale. 3000ce, Narwhal. 5000ce, Beluga. 6000ce, Bowhead whale.
No. 2256, 4000ce: a, Blue whale. b, Killer whale, diff. c, Northern bottlenose whale. d, Sperm whale. e, Southern right whale. f, Pygmy right whale.
No. 2257, 4000ce: a, Humpback whale. b, Fin whale. c, Bowhead whale, diff. d, Gray whale. e, Narwhal, diff. f, Beluga, diff.
No. 2258, 14,000ce, Sperm whale. No. 2259, 14,000ce, Blue whales.

2001, Oct. 1
2252-2255 A431 Set of 4 4.25 4.25

Sheets of 6, #a-f

2256-2257 A431 Set of 2 13.50 13.50

Souvenir Sheets

2258-2259 A431 Set of 2 8.00 8.00

Rotary Intl. In Ghana, 40th Anniv. (in 1998) A432

Rotary Intl. emblem and: 300ce, Polio victim. 1100ce, Clean water. 1200ce, Founder Paul Harris. 1800ce, Blood donation.

2001 ? ***Perf. 13¼***
2260-2263 A432 Set of 4 1.25 1.25

Orchids — A433

Designs: 1100ce, Paphiopedilum hennisianum. 1200ce, Vuylstekeara cambria Plush. 1800ce, Cymbidium ormoulu. 2000ce, Phalaenopsis Barbara Moler.
No. 2268, 4500ce: a, Cattleya capra. b, Odontoglossum rossii. c, Epidendrum pseudepidendrum. d, Encyclia cochleata. e, Cymbidium baldoyle Melbury. f, Phalaenopsis asean.
No. 2269, 4500ce: a, Odontocidium Tiger-sun. b, Miltonia Emotion. c, Odontonia sappho Excul. d, Cymbidium Bulbarrow. e, Dendrobium nobile. f, Paphiopedilum insigne.
No. 2270, 15,000ce, Calanthe vestita. No. 2271, 15,000ce, Angraecum eburneum.

2001, Oct. 30 **Litho.** ***Perf. 14***
2264-2267 A433 Set of 4 1.75 1.75

Sheets of 6, #a-f

2268-2269 A433 Set of 2 15.00 15.00

Souvenir Sheets

2270-2271 A433 Set of 2 8.25 8.25

Musical Instruments — A434

No. 2272: a, Bamboo orchestra. b, Mmensuon. c, Fontomfrom. d, Pati.

2001, Dec. 3 ***Perf. 14¼***
2272 A434 4000ce Sheet of 4, #a-d 4.50 4.50

Queen Mother Type of 1999 Redrawn

No. 2273: a, Lady Elizabeth Bowles-Lyon with brother David, 1904. b, In Rhodesia, 1957. c, In 1970. d, In 1992.
5000ce, In 1970, diff.

2001, Dec. ***Perf. 14***

Yellow Orange Frames

2273 A392 2000ce Sheet of 4, #a-d, + label 2.25 2.25

Souvenir Sheet

Perf. 13¾

2274 A392 5000ce multi 1.40 1.40

Queen Mother's 101st birthday. No. 2274 contains one 38x50mm stamp with a darker background than on No. 2125. Sheet margins of Nos. 2273-2274 lack embossing and gold arms and frames found on Nos. 2124-2125.

Kwame Nkrumah University of Science and Technology, Kumasi, 50th Anniv. A435

Designs: 300ce, Emblem. No. 2276, 700ce, No. 2280a, 4000ce, Main gate. No. 2277, 1100ce, No. 2280b, 4000ce, Dairy production. No. 2278, 1200ce, No. 2280c, 4000ce, Pharmacy Department. No. 2279, 1800ce, No. 2280d, 4000ce, Residence hall.

2001 ***Perf. 13x13¼***
2275-2279 A435 Set of 5 1.40 1.40

Souvenir Sheet

2280 A435 4000ce Sheet of 4, #a-d 4.50 4.50

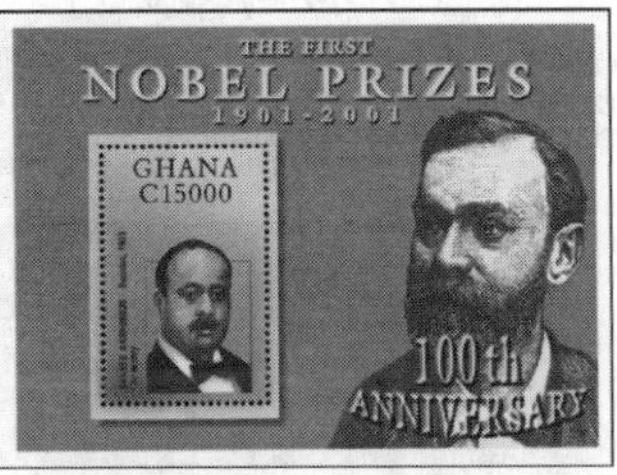

Nobel Prizes, Cent. (In 2001) — A436

No. 2281, 4000ce - Chemistry laureates: a, George A. Olah, 1994. b, Kary Mullis, 1993. c, Sir Harold W. Kroto, 1996. d, Richard R. Ernst, 1991. e, Ahmed H. Zewail, 1999. f, Paul Crutzen, 1995.
No. 2282, 4000ce - Chemistry laureates: a, John E. Walker, 1997. b, Jens C. Skou, 1997. c, Alan G. MacDiarmid, 2000. d, Thomas Robert Cech, 1989. e, John Pole, 1998. f, Rudolph A. Marcus, 1992.
No. 2283, 4000ce - Chemistry laureates: a, Walter Kohn, 1998. b, F. Sherwood Rowland, 1995. c, Mario Molina, 1995. d, Hideki Shirakawa, 2000. e, Paul D. Boyer, 1997. f, Richard Smalley, 1996.
No. 2284, 15,000ce, Svante Arrhenius, Chemistry, 1903. No. 2285, 15,000ce, Alfred Werner, Chemistry, 1913. No. 2286, 15,000ce, Peter Debye, Chemistry, 1936. No. 2287, 15,000ce, Wole Soyinka, Literature, 1986. No. 2288, 15,000ce, Nelson Mandela, Peace, 1993.

2002, Jan. 9 ***Perf. 14***

Sheets of 6, #a-f

2281-2283 A436 Set of 3 20.00 20.00

Souvenir Sheets

2284-2288 A436 Set of 5 21.00 21.00

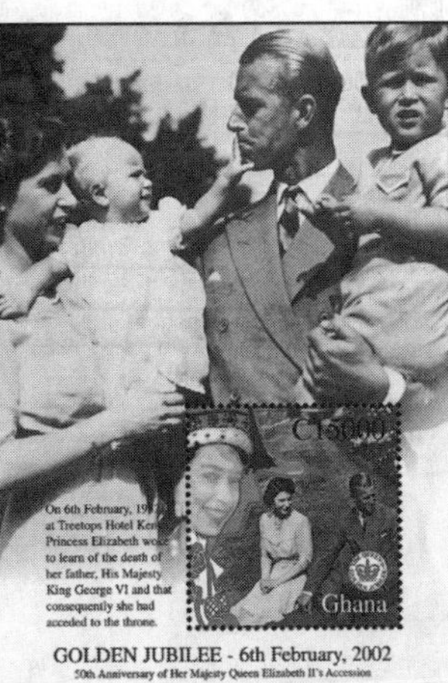

Reign of Queen Elizabeth II, 50th Anniv. — A437

No. 2289: a, Wearing pink dress. b, Sitting on horse. c. Looking at horses. d, In carriage with Prince Philip.
15,000ce, Sitting with Prince Philip (black and white photograph).

2002, Feb. 6 **Litho.** ***Perf. 14¼***
2289 A437 6500ce Sheet of 4, #a-d 7.25 7.25

Souvenir Sheet

2290 A437 15,000ce multi 4.25 4.25

Intl. Copyright Conference, Accra — A438

Designs: 300ce, Conference emblem, vert. 700ce, Person reading. 1100ce, Spider, web, map of Ghana. 1200ce, Map of Ghana, Kente cloth. 1800ce, Drummer.

2002, Feb. 20 ***Perf. 14¼x14, 14x14¼***
2291-2295 A438 Set of 5 1.40 1.40

2002 World Cup Soccer Championships, Japan and Korea — A439

World Cup trophy and: 100ce, Jay Jay Okacha, flag of Nigeria. 150ce, South African player and flag. 300ce, Pele, flag of Brazil. 400ce, Roger Milla, flag of Cameroun. 500ce, Bobby Charlton, flag of England. 800ce, Michel Platini, flag of France. 1000ce, Franz Beckenbauer, flag of West Germany. 1500ce, Ulsan Munsu Stadium, Korea, horiz. 2000ce, German player and flag. 3000ce, Brazilian player and flag. 4000ce, Korean player and flag. 5000ce, Yokohama Intl. Sports Stadium, Japan, horiz. 6000ce, Italian player and flag. 11,000ce, 1950 World Cup poster. 12,000ce, 1934 World Cup poster.
No. 2311, 15,000ce, Geoff Hurst's hat trick for England, 1966. No. 2312, 15,000ce, Gordon Banks making save on Pele, 1970.

2002, Mar. 4 ***Perf. 14***
2296-2310 A439 Set of 15 13.00 13.00

Souvenir Sheets

2311-2312 A439 Set of 2 8.25 8.25

Souvenir Sheet

New Year 2002 (Year of the Horse) — A440

No. 2313: a, Brown panel at L, country name at LR. b, Brown panel at R, country name at UR. c, Brown panel at L, country name at LL. d, Brown panel at R, country name at LR.

2002, Mar. 4 ***Perf. 13¾***

2313 A440 4000ce Sheet of 4, #a-d 4.50 4.50

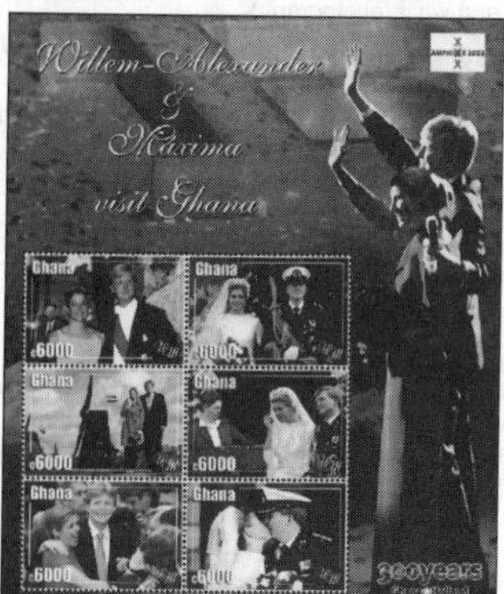

Visit of Netherlands Prince Willem-Alexander and Princess Máxima to Ghana — A441

Couple: a, With Prince wearing sash. b, Holding hands, Prince wearing hat. c, With windmills and flags. d, At wedding ceremony, with another man. e, In crowd. f, Kissing.

2002 ***Perf. 14***

2314 A441 6000ce Sheet of 6, #a-f 8.75 8.75

Amphilex 2002 Intl. Stamp Show, Amsterdam.

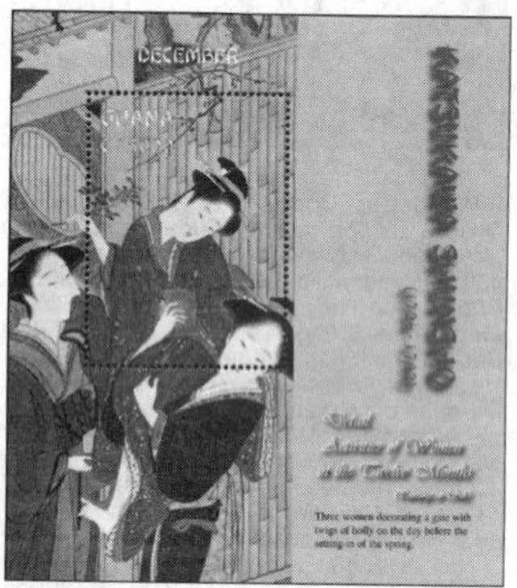

Paintings of Shunsho Katsukawa — A442

No. 2315, 9000ce - Activities of Women in the Twelve Months: a, Trying to retrieve a ball caught in a tree (March). b, Listening to a cuckoo in the bedroom (April). c, Holding a cage filled with fireflies for a woman to read a book (May).

No. 2316, 9000ce - Activities of Women in the Twelve Months: a, Mother and child taking a tub bath while woman holds a revolving lantern (June). b, Strips of paper with wishes and poems are tied on bamboo (July). c, Women enjoying the cool air on a boat (August).

No. 2317, 9000ce - Activities of Women in the Twelve Months: a, Celebrating Feast of the Chrysanthemum (September). b, Looking out for colored leaves (October). c, Mother reading picture book while sitting at a foot warmer (November).

No. 2318, 15,000ce, Three women decorating a gate (woman in blue kimono), from Activities of Women in the Twelve Months. No. 2319, 15,000ce, Part 1 (woman in red kimono) from Snow, Moonlight and Flowers. No. 2320, 15,000ce, Part 2 (woman in black kimono) from Snow, Moonlight and Flowers. No. 2321, 15,000ce, Part 3 (woman in gray kimono) from Snow, Moonlight and Flowers.

2002, July 29 **Litho.** ***Perf. 14¼***

Sheets of 3, *#a-c*

2315-2317 A442 Set of 3 20.00 20.00

Souvenir Sheets

2318-2321 A442 Set of 4 14.50 14.50

United We Stand — A443

2002, Aug. 15 ***Perf. 14***

2322 A443 7000ce multi 1.75 1.75

Printed in sheets of 4.

2002 Winter Olympics, Salt Lake City — A444

Designs: No. 2323, 7000ce, Figure skaters. No. 2324, 7000ce, Freestyle skier.

2002, Aug. 15

2323-2324 A444 Set of 2 3.50 3.50

2324a Souvenir sheet, #2323-2324 3.50 3.50

Intl. Year of Mountains — A445

No. 2325: a, Tateyama, Japan. b, Mt. Shivling, India. c, Wong Leng, Hong Kong. d, Mt. Blanc, France.

15,000ce, Mt. Fuji, Japan.

2002, Aug. 15

2325 A445 6000ce Sheet of 4, #a-d 6.00 6.00

Souvenir Sheet

2326 A445 15,000ce multi 3.75 3.75

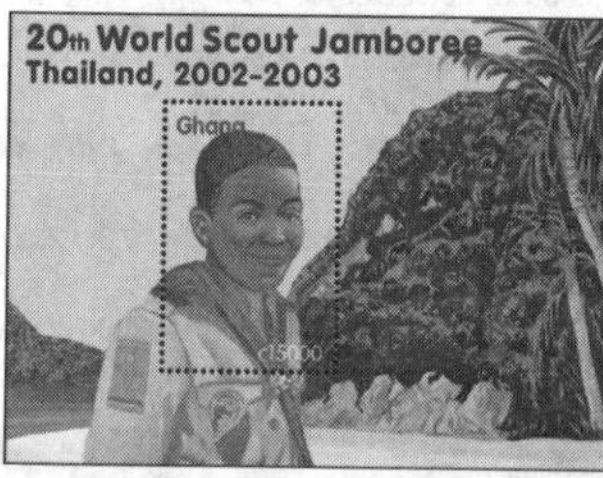

20th World Scout Jamboree, Thailand — A446

No. 2327, horiz.: a, Scout with walking stick. b, Scout with backpack. c, Tent and campfire. d, Tent and scout tying knots.

15,000ce, Scout with red neckerchief.

2002, Aug. 15

2327 A446 6500ce Sheet of 4, #a-d 6.25 6.25

Souvenir Sheet

2328 A446 15,000ce multi 3.75 3.75

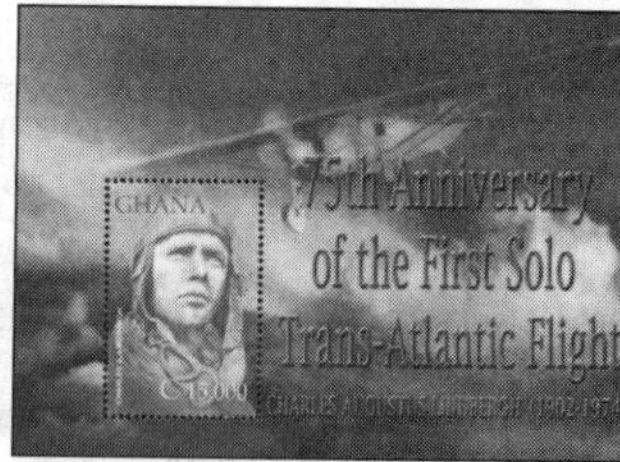

First Solo Transatlantic Flight, 75th Anniv. — A447

No. 2329, 8500ce, horiz.: a, Charles Lindbergh and Spirit of St. Louis. b, Charles and Anne Morrow Lindbergh in airplane.

15,000ce, Lindbergh wearing flying gear.

2002, Aug. 15

2329 A447 8500ce Sheet of 2, #a-b 4.25 4.25

Souvenir Sheet

2330 A447 15,000ce multi 3.75 3.75

Intl. Year of Ecotourism — A448

No. 2331: a, Nectarinia venusta. b, Panthera pardus. c, Kobus kob. d, Syncerus caffer. e, Pan troglodytes. f, Galago.

12,000ce, Loxodonta africana.

2002, Aug. 15

2331 A448 4000ce Sheet of 6, #a-f 6.00 6.00

Souvenir Sheet

2332 A448 12,000ce multi 3.00 3.00

Nos. 1820-1821 Surcharged

2002, Aug. 15 ***Perf. 13½x14***

2333	Strip or block of 4	3.00	3.00
a.	A315 3000ce on 600ce #1820a	.75	.75
b.	A315 3000ce on 600ce #1820b	.75	.75
c.	A315 3000ce on 600ce #1820c	.75	.75
d.	A315 3000ce on 600ce #1820d	.75	.75

Souvenir Sheet

2334 A315 20,000ce on 2500ce #1821 5.00 5.00

No. 2334 and sheets of No. 2333 are additionally overprinted in margin with black border and inscription "In Memoriam / 1900-2002."

Butterflies, Moths, Insects and Birds — A449

No. 2335, 4500ce - Butterflies: a, Iolaus menas. b, Neptis melicerta. c, Cymothoe lucasi. d, Euphaedra francina. e, Lilac nymph. f, Mocker swallowtail.

No. 2336, 4500ce - Moths: a, Phiala cunina. b, Mazuca strigicincta. c, Steindachner's emperor. d, Amphicallia pactolicus. e, Verdant sphinx. f, Oleander hawkmoth.

No. 2337, 4500ce - Insects: a, Bush hopper. b, Ant lion. c, Digger bee. d, Stag beetle. e, Mantis. f, Longhorn beetle.

No. 2338, 4500ce - Birds: a, Malachite kingfisher. b, Brown harrier eagle. c, Heuglin's masked weaver. d, Egyptian plover. e, Swallow-tailed bee-eater. f, Black-faced fire finch.

No. 2339, 15,000ce, Giant blue swallowtail butterfly. No. 2340, 15,000ce, African moon moth. No. 2341, 15,000ce, Mantis nymph. No. 2342, 15,000ce, Rufous fishing owl.

2002, Aug. 26 ***Perf. 14***

Sheets of 6, *#a-f*

2335-2338 A449 Set of 4 26.00 26.00

Souvenir Sheets

2339-2342 A449 Set of 4 14.50 14.50

Edina Bakatue Festival A450

Designs: No. 2343, 1000ce, No. 2349e, 4000ce, Casting of net. No. 2344, 2000ce, No. 2349b, 4000ce, Chief in palanquin. No. 2345, 2500ce, No. 2349c, 4000ce, Regatta. No. 2346, 3000ce, No. 2349d, 4000ce, Festival boat. No. 2347, 4000ce, Opening ritual. No. 2348, 5000ce, No. 2349a, 4000ce, Priestesses.

2002, Oct. 21 ***Perf. 14x13½***

2343-2348 A450 Set of 5 4.25 4.25

2349 A450 4000ce Sheet of 6, #2347, 2349a-2349e 6.00 6.00

Japan Overseas Cooperation Volunteers, 25th Anniv. in Ghana — A451

Designs: No. 2350, 1000ce, Health. No. 2351, 1000ce, Education (Home economics). 2000ce, Education (Science and math). 2500ce, Education (Computer technology). 3000ce, Sports.

No. 2355 (without white inscriptions): a, Like 2000ce. b, Like No. 2350. c, Like 3000ce. d, Like 2500ce. e, Like No. 2351.

2002, Oct. 23 ***Perf. 14***

2350-2354 A451 Set of 5 2.40 2.40

2355 A451 4000ce Sheet of 5, #a-e 5.00 5.00

Awarding of Nobel Peace Prize to UN Secretary General Kofi Annan — A452

Designs: 1000ce, With Ghana Pres. J. A. Kufuor at award ceremony. 2000ce, With Nobel medal and citation. 2500ce, Portrait. 3000ce, In academic procession at Kwame Nkrumah University.

2002, Oct. 28

2356-2359 A452 Set of 4 2.10 2.10

No. 1939C Surcharged

2002, Mar. 7 Litho. *Perf. 14¼x14*

2360 A350b 1000ce on 1100ce multi — —

SEMI-POSTAL STAMPS

Starlets, 1995 Under-17 World Soccer Champions — SP1

200ce+50ce, Holding gold cup won at Ecuador, vert. 550ce+50ce, Starlets '95 team photo. 800ce+50ce, Abu Idorisu, vert. 1100ce+50ce, Emmanuel Bentil, vert. 1500ce+50ce, Bashiru Gambo, vert.

Perf. 13½x13, 13x13½

1997, Aug. 12 Litho.

B1-B5 SP1 Set of 5 4.50 4.50

AIR POST STAMPS

Type of Regular Issue

Designs: 1sh3p, Pennant-winged nightjar. 2sh, Crowned cranes, vert.

Perf. 14½x14, 14x14½

1959, Oct. 5 Photo. Wmk. 325

C1 A17 1sh3p multicolored .40 .20
a. Booklet pane of 4 1.75
C2 A17 2sh multicolored .55 .45

For surcharges see Nos. C7-C10.

Ships, Tema Harbor and Jet — AP1

Perf. 14x13

1962, Feb. 10 Litho. Unwmk.

C3 AP1 1sh3p multicolored .65 .65
C4 AP1 2sh6p multicolored 1.25 1.25
Nos. C3-C4,110 (3) 2.10 2.10

Opening of Tema Harbor, as part of the Volta River Project.

Type of Regular Issue, 1962

1962, Mar. 6 *Perf. 13x14*

C5 A35 1sh3p multicolored .50 .35
C6 A35 2sh6p multicolored 1.00 .70

Nos. C1-C2 Surcharged in White or Green with New Value and: "Ghana New Currency / 19th July, 1965"

Perf. 14½x14, 14x14½

1965, July 19 Photo. Wmk. 325

C7 A17 15pa on 1sh3p multi (W) .35 .25
C8 A17 24pa on 2sh multi (G) .70 .35

The two lines of the overprint are diagonal on No. C8.

Nos. C1, C8 Surcharged in White or Red

1967, Feb. 27 Photo. Wmk. 325

C9 A17 12½np on 1sh3p (W) 1.10 .80
C10 A17 20np on 24pa on 2sh 2.50 1.75

POSTAGE DUE STAMPS

Gold Coast Nos. J2-J6 Overprinted "GHANA" and Bar in Red

Perf. 14

1958, June 25 Wmk. 4 Typo.

J1 D1 1p black .20 .20
J2 D1 2p black .20 .20
J3 D1 3p black .20 *.25*
J4 D1 6p black .20 *.30*
J5 D1 1sh black .20 *.50*
Nos. J1-J5 (5) 1.00 *1.45*

Type of Gold Coast Inscribed "Ghana"

1958, Dec. 1 *Perf. 14*

J6 D1 1p carmine rose .20 .20
J7 D1 2p green .20 .20
J8 D1 3p orange .20 .20
J9 D1 6p ultramarine .20 .20
J10 D1 1sh purple .20 .20
Nos. J6-J10 (5) 1.00 1.00

Nos. J6-J10 Surcharged in Black, Blue or Red with New Value and "Ghana New Currency / 19th July, 1965."

1965, July 19

J11 D1 1pa on 1p car rose .20 .20
J12 D1 2pa on 2p grn (Bl) .20 .20
J13 D1 3pa on 3p org (Bl) .20 .20
J14 D1 6pa on 6p ultra (R) .30 .30
J15 D1 12pa on 1sh pur (Bl) .50 .50
Nos. J11-J15 (5) 1.40 1.40

Surcharge diagonal on Nos. J11 and J15.

No. J12 with additional surcharge, "1½Np" in red, was reported to have been used at one branch post office (Burma Camp) despite official intention. Four similar added surcharges were prepared: 1np on 1pa, 2½np on 3pa, 5np on 6pa, and 10np on 12pa.

D2

1970 Unwmk. Litho. *Perf. 14½x14*

J16 D2 1np carmine rose .40 *.75*
J17 D2 1½np green .40 *.75*
J18 D2 2½np orange .55 *1.00*
J19 D2 5np ultramarine .80 *1.25*
J20 D2 10np dull purple 1.25 *2.50*
Nos. J16-J20 (5) 3.40 *6.25*

1981 Litho. *Perf. 14½x14*

J21 D2 2p red orange .50 *1.00*
J22 D2 3p brown .50 *1.00*

GIBRALTAR

jə-'brol-tər

LOCATION — A fortified promontory, including the Rock, extending from Spain's southeast coast at the entrance to the Mediterranean Sea

GOVT. — British Crown Colony

AREA — 2.5 sq. mi.

POP. — 29,165 (1999 est.)

CAPITAL — Gibraltar

12 Pence = 1 Shilling
20 Shillings = 1 Pound
100 Centimos = 1 Peseta (1889-95)
100 Pence = 1 Pound (1971)

Catalogue values for unused stamps in this country are for Never Hinged items, beginning with Scott 119 in the regular postage section and Scott J1 in the postage due section.

Types of Bermuda Overprinted in Black

1886, Jan. 1 Wmk. 2 *Perf. 14*

1 A6 ½p green 10.00 6.00
2 A1 1p rose 42.50 4.50
3 A2 2p violet brown 87.50 55.00
4 A8 2½p ultra 110.00 3.25
5 A7 4p orange brn 100.00 85.00
6 A4 6p violet 175.00 175.00
7 A5 1sh bister brn 375.00 350.00
Nos. 1-7 (7) 900.00 678.75

Forged overprints of No. 7 are plentiful.

Victoria

A6 A7

A8

A9

1886-98 Typo.

8 A6 ½p dull green 8.50 3.75
9 A6 ½p gray grn ('98) 5.00 1.75
10 A7 1p rose 37.50 4.50
11 A7 1p car rose ('98) 5.50 .50
12 A8 2p brn violet 27.50 17.50
13 A8 2p brn vio & ultra ('98) 20.00 1.75
14 A9 2½p brt ultra ('98) 24.00 .50
a. 2½p ultramarine 75.00 3.00
16 A8 4p orange brn 75.00 75.00
17 A8 4p org brn & grn ('98) 17.00 6.75
18 A8 6p violet 95.00 95.00
19 A8 6p vio & car rose ('98) 37.50 21.00
20 A8 1sh bister 190.00 190.00
21 A8 1sh bis & car rose ('98) 32.50 17.00
Nos. 8-14,16-21 (13) 575.00 435.00

Stamps of 1886 Issue Surcharged in Black

1889, July

22 A6 5c on ½p green 8.00 *12.00*
23 A7 10c on 1p rose 8.00 6.50
24 A8 25c on 2p brn vio 3.00 3.00
a. Small "I" in "CENTIMOS" 125.00 *160.00*
b. Broken "N" 125.00 *160.00*
25 A9 25c on 2½p ultra 16.00 2.50
a. Small "I" in "CENTIMOS" 325.00 110.00
b. Broken "N" 325.00 110.00
26 A8 40c on 4p org brn 52.50 *65.00*
27 A8 50c on 6p violet 52.50 *65.00*
28 A8 75c on 1sh bister 60.00 *70.00*
Nos. 22-28 (7) 200.00 *224.00*

There are two varieties of the figure "5" in the 5c, 25c, 50c and 75c.

A11

1889-95

29 A11 5c green 4.25 .65
30 A11 10c rose 4.25 .40
a. Value omitted *4,750.*
31 A11 20c ol green ('95) 10.00 *50.00*
31A A11 20c ol grn & brn ('95) 35.00 15.00
32 A11 25c ultra 14.00 .60
33 A11 40c orange brn 3.50 2.00
34 A11 50c violet 3.00 *1.60*
35 A11 75c olive green 30.00 26.00
36 A11 1p bister 67.50 16.00
36A A11 1p bis & bl ('95) 4.50 3.75
37 A11 2p blk & car rose ('95) 9.00 *24.00*
38 A11 5p steel blue 40.00 *85.00*
Nos. 29-38 (12) 225.00 *225.00*

King Edward VII

A12 A13

1903, May 1

39 A12 ½p grn & bl grn 7.50 7.00
40 A12 1p violet, *red* 25.00 .50
41 A12 2p grn & car rose 12.50 *21.00*
42 A12 2½p vio & blk, *bl* 2.50 .50
43 A12 6p violet & pur 12.50 *16.00*
44 A12 1sh blk & car rose 25.00 *30.00*
45 A13 2sh green & ultra 100.00 *140.00*
46 A13 4sh vio & green 75.00 *125.00*
47 A13 8sh vio & blk, *bl* 100.00 *125.00*
48 A13 £1 vio & blk, *red* 500.00 *540.00*
Nos. 39-48 (10) 860.00 *1,005.*

1904-12 Wmk. 3

Ordinary or Chalky Paper

49 A12 ½p blue green ('07) 3.50 1.10
a. ½p gray green ('04) 8.00 2.25
50 A12 1p violet, *red* 8.00 .45
51 A12 1p car ('07) 5.50 .55
52 A12 2p grn & car rose 12.50 3.50
53 A12 2p gray ('10) 8.00 *8.75*
54 A12 2½p vio & blk, *bl* 35.00 *77.50*
55 A12 2½p ultra ('07) 5.00 1.40
56 A12 6p vio & pur ('06) 30.00 17.00
a. 6p vio & red violet ('12) 125.00 *350.00*
57 A12 1sh blk & car rose 50.00 9.75
58 A12 1sh blk, *grn* ('10) 22.50 17.50
59 A13 2sh grn & ultra ('05) 72.50 *77.50*
60 A13 2sh vio & bl, *bl* ('10) 47.50 *40.00*
61 A13 4sh vio & grn 200.00 *225.00*
62 A13 4sh blk & red ('10) 100.00 *110.00*
63 A13 8sh vio & grn ('11) 175.00 *160.00*
64 A12 £1 vio & blk, *red* 475.00 475.00
Nos. 49-64 (16) 1,250. *1,225.*

Nos. 49a, 51, 53, 55 are on ordinary paper. Nos. 54, 58, 60-64 are on chalky paper. Others come on both papers.

No. 56a, used, must have a 1912 cancellation. Stamps used later sell for about the same as unused.

A14

King George V — A15

1912, July 17 Ordinary Paper

66 A14 ½p green 1.40 .40
67 A14 1p carmine 2.00 .40
a. 1p scarlet ('16) 3.50 1.00
68 A14 2p gray 3.50 1.25
69 A14 2½p ultra 3.75 1.25

Chalky Paper

70 A14 6p dl vio & red vio 6.50 *8.50*
71 A14 1sh black, *green* 5.00 3.50
a. 1sh black, *emerald* ('24) 12.00 *40.00*
b. 1sh blk, *bl grn, ol back* ('19) 12.00 *25.00*
c. 1sh blk, *emer, ol back* ('23) 24.00 *75.00*
72 A15 2sh vio & ultra, *bl* 20.00 2.50
73 A15 4sh black & scar 25.00 *50.00*
74 A15 8sh vio & green 65.00 *70.00*
75 A15 £1 vio & blk, *red* 125.00 *190.00*
Nos. 66-75 (10) 257.15 *327.80*

1921-32 Ordinary Paper Wmk. 4

76 A14 ½p green .50 *1.25*
77 A14 1p rose red 1.00 .85
78 A14 1½p red brown .75 .40
79 A14 2p gray .75 .75
80 A14 2½p ultra 10.00 *25.00*
81 A14 3p ultra 1.75 1.25

Chalky Paper

82 A14 6p dl vio & red vio 1.25 *3.00*
a. 6p gray lilac & red violet 6.50 3.00
83 A14 1sh black, *emer* 8.00 *12.50*
84 A14 1sh ol grn & blk 7.50 *19.00*
a. 1sh brn olive & black ('32) 15.00 11.00
85 A15 2sh vio & ultra, *blue* 5.00 *35.00*
86 A15 2sh red brn & black 10.00 *24.00*
87 A15 2sh6p green & blk 7.00 *14.50*
88 A15 4sh black & scar 52.50 *95.00*
89 A15 5sh car & black 13.00 *45.00*
90 A15 8sh vio & green 160.00 *310.00*
91 A15 10sh ultra & black 25.00 *62.50*
92 A15 £1 org & black 125.00 *150.00*
93 A15 £5 dl vio & blk 1,750. *3,500.*
Nos. 76-92 (17) 429.00 *800.00*

Years issued: 1½p, 1922. 6p, 1923. Nos. 83, 85, 4sh, 8sh, 1924. 2sh6p, 5sh, 10sh, £5, 1925. ½p, £1, 1927. Nos. 84, 86, 1929.

Type of 1912 Issue
Inscribed: "THREE PENCE"

1930, Apr. 12 Ordinary Paper

94 A14 3p ultramarine 9.50 2.25

Rock of Gibraltar A16

1931-33 Engr. *Perf. 14*

96 A16 1p red 2.00 *2.10*
a. Perf. 13½x14 13.50 4.25
97 A16 1½p red brown 1.50 *1.90*
a. Perf. 13½x14 10.50 3.00
98 A16 2p gray ('32) 4.75 1.25
a. Perf. 13½x14 12.50 1.75
99 A16 3p dk blue ('33) 4.75 2.75
a. Perf. 13½x14 21.00 *21.00*
Nos. 96-99 (4) 13.00 8.00
Set, never hinged 25.00
Nos. 96a-99a (4) 57.50 30.00
Set, never hinged 75.00

Common Design Types pictured following the introduction.

Silver Jubilee Issue
Common Design Type

1935, May 6 *Perf. 11x12*

100 CD301 2p black & ultra 1.50 *2.25*
101 CD301 3p ultra & brown 3.25 3.25
102 CD301 6p indigo & green 9.00 *11.00*
103 CD301 1sh brown vio & ind 9.00 8.50
Nos. 100-103 (4) 22.75 25.00
Set, never hinged 40.00

Coronation Issue
Common Design Type

1937, May 12 *Perf. 11x11½*

104 CD302 ½p deep green .20 .20
105 CD302 2p gray black .65 *1.90*
106 CD302 3p deep ultra 1.40 1.90
Nos. 104-106 (3) 2.25 4.00
Set, never hinged 3.75

George VI — A17

Rock of Gibraltar A18

Designs: 2p, Rock from north side. 3p, 5p, Europa Point. 6p, Moorish Castle. 1sh, Southport Gate. 2sh, Eliott Memorial. 5sh, Government House. 10sh, Catalan Bay.

Perf. 13, 13½x14 (½p, No. 118), 14 (1½p)

1938-49 Engr. Wmk. 4

107 A17 ½p gray green .20 .30
108 A18 1p red brn ('42) .35 *.50*
a. 1p chestnut, perf. 14 19.00 2.50
b. 1p chestnut, perf. 13½ 21.00 2.00
c. Perf. 13½, wmk. sideways ('41) *5.00* *5.00*
109 A18 1½p carmine rose 24.00 .55
b. Perf. 13½ 200.00 40.00
109A A18 1½p gray vio ('43) .20 1.25
110 A18 2p dk gray ('42) .25 1.00
a. Perf. 14 20.00 .50
c. Perf. 13½ 1.00 .40
d. Perf. 13½, wmk. sideways ('41) 475.00 40.00
110B A18 2p car rose ('44) .30 .50
111 A18 3p blue ('42) .25 .25
a. Perf. 14 100.00 5.00
b. Perf. 13½ 14.00 1.00
112 A18 5p red org ('47) .60 1.00
113 A18 6p dl vio & car rose 3.25 1.40
a. Perf. 14 100.00 1.50
b. Perf. 13½ 35.00 3.50
114 A18 1sh grn & blk ('42) 2.25 *3.25*
a. Perf. 14 29.00 20.00
b. Perf. 13½ 50.00 7.50
115 A18 2sh org brn & blk ('42) 2.25 5.50
a. Perf. 14 50.00 22.50
b. Perf. 13½ 90.00 30.00
116 A18 5sh dk car & blk ('44) 8.00 *13.50*
a. Perf 14 ('38) 75.00 *140.00*
b. Perf. 13½ 29.00 17.00
117 A18 10sh bl & blk ('43) 24.00 21.00
a. Perf. 14 50.00 *100.00*
118 A17 £1 orange 27.50 *35.00*
Nos. 107-118 (14) 93.40 85.00
Set, never hinged 140.00

Nos. 108c and 110d were issued in coils.
No. 108 (1p, perf. 13) exists with watermark both normal and sideways. Nos. 110 and 110B (both 2p, perf. 13) have watermark sideways.
For overprints see Nos. 127-130.

Catalogue values for unused stamps in this section, from this point to the end of the section, are for Never Hinged items.

Peace Issue
Common Design Type

1946, Oct. 12 *Perf. 13½x14*

119 CD303 ½p bright green .20 .20
120 CD303 3p bright ultra .25 .20

Silver Wedding Issue
Common Design Types

1948, Dec. 1 Photo. *Perf. 14x14½*

121 CD304 ½p dark green .75 .65

Engr.; Name Typo.
Perf. 11½x11

122 CD305 £1 brown orange 65.00 60.00
Set, hinged 50.00

UPU Issue
Common Design Types
Engr.; Name Typo. on 3p, 6p
Perf. 13½, 11x11½

1949, Oct. 10 Wmk. 4

123 CD306 2p rose carmine 1.00 1.00
124 CD307 3p indigo 2.50 1.10
125 CD308 6p rose violet 2.00 2.00
126 CD309 1sh blue green 1.25 4.00
Nos. 123-126 (4) 6.75 8.10

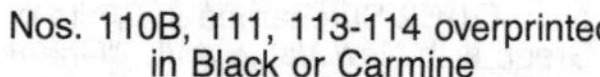
Nos. 110B, 111, 113-114 overprinted in Black or Carmine

1950, Aug. 1 *Perf. 13x12½*

127 A18 2p carmine rose .30 *.75*
128 A18 3p blue .60 *.75*
129 A18 6p dl vio & car rose .75 *1.10*
a. Double overprint 700.00 *850.00*
130 A18 1sh grn & blk (C) .75 *1.10*
Nos. 127-130 (4) 2.40 *3.70*

Adoption of Constitution of 1950.

Coronation Issue
Common Design Type

1953, June 2 Engr. *Perf. 13½x13*

131 CD312 ½p olive green & black .25 .30

Wharves A26

Moorish Castle — A27

Designs: 1p, South view. 1½p, Tunny fishing industry. 2p, Southport Gate. 2½p, Sailing in the bay. 3p, Ocean liner. 4p, Coaling wharf. 5p, Airport. 6p, Europa Point. 1sh, Strait from Buena Vista. 2sh, Rosia Bay. 5sh, Government House. £1, Arms of Gibraltar.

1953, Oct. 19 *Perf. 12½*

132 A26 ½p dk grn & ind .20 .25
133 A26 1p blue green 1.40 .25
134 A26 1½p dark gray .85 .75
135 A26 2p sepia 1.40 .75
136 A26 2½p car lake 2.50 .50
137 A26 3p grnsh blue 3.50 .20
138 A26 4p ultra 2.40 1.25
139 A26 5p deep plum .65 .65
140 A26 6p blue & black .60 .40
141 A26 1sh red brn & bl .30 .50
142 A26 2sh vio & org 18.00 3.00
143 A26 5sh dark brown 24.00 10.00
144 A27 10sh ultra & brn 47.50 27.50
145 A27 £1 yellow & red 47.50 30.00
Nos. 132-145 (14) 150.80 76.00
Set, hinged 85.00

Inscribed: "ROYAL VISIT 1954"

1954, May 10

146 A26 3p greenish blue .30 .30

Candytuft — A28

Rock and Badge of Gibraltar Regiment — A30

Moorish Castle A29

Designs: 2p, St. George's Hall and cannons. 2½p, The keys. 3p, Rock by moonlight. 4p, Catalan Bay. 6p, Map. 7p, Air terminal. 9p, American war memorial. 1sh, Barbary ape. 2sh, Barbary partridge. 5sh, Blue rock thrush. 10sh, Narcissus.

Wmk. 314

1960, Oct. 29 Photo. *Perf. 12½*

147 A28 ½p brt green & lil .20 .25
148 A29 1p black & yel grn .20 .20
149 A29 2p org brn & sl .20 .20
150 A28 2½p blue & black .50 .50
151 A29 3p dk blue & ver .20 .20
152 A29 4p choc & grnsh bl 2.75 .50
a. Wmkd. sideways ('66) .25 .20
153 A28 6p brown & emer .75 .35
154 A28 7p gray & car .75 .60
155 A28 9p grnsh blue & bluish gray .50 .40
156 A29 1sh brown & green .90 .30
157 A29 2sh dark red brn & ultra 13.00 1.90
158 A29 5sh ol & Prus grn 8.00 4.50
159 A28 10sh blue, yel & grn 14.00 8.00

Perf. 14
Engr.

160 A30 £1 org red & slate 17.50 9.00
Nos. 147-160 (14) 59.45 26.90

For overprints see Nos. 165-166.

Freedom from Hunger Issue
Common Design Type

1963, June 4 *Perf. 14x14½*

161 CD314 9p sepia 12.00 3.00

Red Cross Centenary Issue
Common Design Type

1963, Sept. 2 Litho. *Perf. 13*

162 CD315 1p black & red .50 *1.25*
163 CD315 9p ultra & red 13.00 5.00

Shakespeare Issue
Common Design Type

1964, Apr. 23 Photo. *Perf. 14x14½*

164 CD316 7p brown .70 .50

Nos. 151 and 153 Overprinted: "NEW / CONSTITUTION / 1964."

1964, Oct. 16 *Perf. 12½*

165 A29 3p dk blue & ver .20 .20
166 A28 6p brown & emer .30 *.40*
a. No period in overprint 15.00 *17.50*

ITU Issue
Common Design Type
Perf. 11x11½

1965, May 17 Litho. Wmk. 314

167 CD317 4p emerald & yel 2.50 .40
168 CD317 2sh ap grn & dk bl 15.00 5.00

Intl. Cooperation Year Issue
Common Design Type

1965, Oct. 25 *Perf. 14½*

169 CD318 ½p lt violet & grn .20 *.75*
170 CD318 4p blue green & cl 1.25 .85

Churchill Memorial Issue
Common Design Type

1966, Jan. 24 Photo. *Perf. 14*
Design in Black, Gold and Carmine Rose

171 CD319 ½p bright blue .20 *.75*
172 CD319 1p green .20 .20
173 CD319 4p brown .75 .40
174 CD319 9p violet 1.75 1.75
Nos. 171-174 (4) 2.90 3.10

World Cup Soccer Issue
Common Design Type

1966, July 1 Litho. *Perf. 14*

175 CD321 2½p multicolored .70 .30
176 CD321 6p multicolored 1.25 .75

Sea Bream A30a

7p, Orange scorpionfish. 1sh, Stone bass, vert.

Perf. 14x13½, 13½x14

1966, Aug. 27 Photo. Wmk. 314

177 A30a	4p ultra, rose red & black	.20	.20
178 A30a	7p ol, rose red & blk	.25	.20
a.	Value omitted	*625.00*	
179 A30a	1sh brt grn, brn & blk	.35	.30
	Nos. 177-179 (3)	.80	.70

European Sea Angling Championships, Gibraltar, Aug. 28-Sept. 3.

WHO Headquarters Issue

Common Design Type

1966, Sept. 20 Litho. *Perf. 14*

180 CD322	6p multicolored	2.00	1.00
181 CD322	9p multicolored	3.25	1.75

"Our Lady of Europa" A31

Perf. 14x14½

1966, Nov. 15 Photo. Wmk. 314

182 A31	2sh ultra & black	.75	*1.00*

Enthronement of the recovered statue of the Madonna in its new shrine, cent.

UNESCO Anniversary Issue

Common Design Type

1966, Dec. 1 Litho. *Perf. 14*

183 CD323	2p "Education"	.20	.20
184 CD323	7p "Science"	.55	.20
185 CD323	5sh "Culture"	3.25	2.50
	Nos. 183-185 (3)	4.00	2.90

Cable Ship Mirror — A32

Ships and Arms of Gibraltar: ½p Victory, Nelson's flagship. 1p, S.S. Arab. 2p, H.M.S. Carmania. 2½p, M.V. Mons Calpe. 3p, S.S. Canberra. 4p, H.M.S. Hood. 6p, Xebec, Moorish vessel. 7p, Amerigo Vespucci, Italian training ship (sails). 9p, Raffaello, Italian liner. 1sh, H.M.S. Royal Katherine, 17th century British warship. 2sh, H.M.S. Ark Royal, aircraft carrier. 5sh, H.M.S. Dreadnought, atomic submarine. 10sh, S.S. Neuralia, troopship. £1, Mary Celeste, 19th century mystery ship (sails).

Perf. 14x14½

1967-69 Photo. Wmk. 314

Design in Black, Red and Gold; Background as Indicated

186	A32	½p deep rose	.20	.20
187	A32	1p yellow	.20	.20
188	A32	2p ultra	.20	.20
189	A32	2½p orange	.30	.25
190	A32	3p violet	.20	.20
191	A32	4p rose	.30	.20
191A	A32	5p brn & multi ('69)	3.25	.55
192	A32	6p gray	.30	.40
193	A32	7p yellow grn	.30	.35
194	A32	9p green	.30	.50
195	A32	1sh rose brown	.30	.25
196	A32	2sh brt yellow	3.50	2.00
197	A32	5sh brick red	3.50	*5.00*
198	A32	10sh emerald	14.00	*17.50*
199	A32	£1 lt ultra	14.00	*17.50*
		Nos. 186-199 (15)	40.85	*45.30*

Cable Car and ITY Emblem — A33

ITY emblem and: 9p, Bull shark, horiz. 1sh, Skin diver, horiz.

Perf. 14½x14, 14x14½

1967, June 15 Photo. Wmk. 314

200 A33	7p red brn, red & blk	.20	.20
201 A33	9p brt blue, blk & slate	.20	.20
202 A33	1sh emer, blk & org brn	.30	.25
	Nos. 200-202 (3)	.70	.65

International Tourist Year.

Holy Family A34

Christmas: 6p, Church window, vert.

1967, Nov. 1 *Perf. 14½*

203 A34	2p dark red & multi	.20	.20
204 A34	6p dark green & multi	.20	.20

General Eliott and Map of Europe and Great Britain A35

Designs: 9p, Eliott Memorial and tower. 1sh, Gen. Eliott and map of Gibraltar, vert. 2sh, Gen. Eliott directing rescue operations for enemy sailors during Great Siege 1779-83.

Perf. 14½x14, 14x14½

1967, Dec. 11 Photo. Wmk. 314

Size: 37x21mm, 21x37mm

205 A35	4p multicolored	.20	.20
206 A35	9p multicolored	.20	.20
207 A35	1sh multicolored	.20	.20

Size: 58x21½mm

208 A35	2sh multicolored	.40	.25
	Nos. 205-208 (4)	1.00	.85

250th anniv. of the birth of General George Augustus Eliott (1717-1790), Governor of Gibraltar during Great Siege.

Lord Baden-Powell — A36

Designs: 7p, Scout flag, Rock of Gibraltar and globe with map of Europe. 9p, Symbolic tents, heads and Scout salute. 1sh, Three Scout badges.

Perf. 14x14½

1968, Mar. 27 Photo. Wmk. 314

209 A36	4p dull yellow & pur	.20	.20
210 A36	7p brown org, brn & grn	.20	.20
211 A36	9p ultra, black & org	.20	.25
212 A36	1sh yellow & emerald	.20	.25
	Nos. 209-212 (4)	.80	.90

60th anniv. of the Gibraltar Scout Assoc.

Nurse and WHO Emblem A37

20th anniv. of WHO: 4p, Physician with microscope and WHO emblem.

1968, July 1 Photo. Wmk. 314

213 A37	2p yellow, ultra & blk	.20	.20
214 A37	4p pink, black & slate	.20	.20

King John Signing Magna Carta — A38

Shepherd, Lamb and Star — A39

Design: 2sh, Rock of Gibraltar, "Freedom" and Human Rights flame.

1968, Aug. 26 *Perf. 13½x14½*

215 A38	1sh org, gold & dk brn	.20	.20
216 A38	2sh brt green & gold	.25	.25

International Human Rights Year.

1968, Nov. 1 *Perf. 14x13½*

Christmas: 9p, Mary, Jesus and lamb.

217 A39	4p lt brown & multi	.20	.20
218 A39	9p rose & multi	.20	.20

Government House, Gibraltar — A40

9p, Rock of Gibraltar, Commonwealth Parliamentary Association emblem. 2sh, Big Ben, London, arms of Gibraltar.

Perf. 14½x14, 14x14½

1969, May 26 Photo. Wmk. 314

219 A40	4p green & gold	.20	.20
220 A40	9p brt violet & gold	.20	.20
221 A40	2sh lt ultra, gold & red	.30	.20
	Nos. 219-221 (3)	.70	.60

Meeting of the Executive Committee of the General Council of the Commonwealth Parliamentary Assoc., Gibraltar, May 1969.

Rock of Gibraltar A41

1969, July 30 *Perf. 14½x13½*

222 A41	½p orange & gold	.20	.20
223 A41	5p emerald & silver	.20	.20
224 A41	7p brt rose lil & silver	.20	.20
225 A41	5sh ultra & gold	1.25	1.10
	Nos. 222-225 (4)	1.85	1.70

Gibraltar's new constitution.

#222-225 are valued with surrounding selvage.

Royal Artillery Officer, 1758 — A42

Madonna della Seggiola, by Raphael — A43

Uniforms: 6p, Contemporary soldier of the Royal Anglian Regiment. 9p, Soldier, Royal Engineers, 1786. 2sh, Private of Fox's Marines, 1704.

1969, Nov. 6 Photo. *Perf. 14*

226 A42	1p gold & multi	.20	.20
227 A42	6p silver, gold & multi	.55	.30
228 A42	9p silver, gold & multi	.75	.50
229 A42	2sh gold & multi	3.00	2.00
	Nos. 226-229 (4)	4.50	3.00

Descriptions are printed on back on top of gum.

See Nos. 234-237, 276-279, 286-289, 299-302, 310-313, 318-321, 330-333.

1969, Dec. 1 *Perf. 13½x Roulette 9*

Christmas (Paintings): 7p, Madonna and Child, by Luis Morales. 1sh, Virgin of the Rocks, by Leonardo da Vinci.

230 A43	5p gold & multi	.20	.20
231 A43	7p gold & multi	.30	.30
232 A43	1sh gold & multi	.50	.50
a.	Triptych, Nos. 230, 232, 231	1.00	1.00

Europa Issue

Europa Point — A44

1970, June 8 *Perf. 13½*

233 A44	2sh multicolored	.45	.40

Uniform Type of 1969

Uniforms: 2p, Royal Scots officer, 1839. 5p, Private of South Wales Borderers. 7p, Private of Queen's Royal Regiment, 1742. 2sh, Piper of Royal Irish Rangers, 1969.

1970, Aug. 28 Photo. *Perf. 14*

234 A42	2p gold & multi	.35	.20
235 A42	5p gold & multi	.70	.40
236 A42	7p gold & multi	.70	.50
237 A42	2sh gold & multi	2.50	1.50
	Nos. 234-237 (4)	4.25	2.60

Descriptions are printed on back on top of gum.

No. 178a and Rock of Gibraltar A45

Design: 2sh, No. 30a and Moorish Castle.

1970, Sept. 18 *Perf. 13*

238 A45	1sh red & olive	.20	.20
239 A45	2sh ultra & rose	.35	.50

Philympia, London Phil. Exhib., Sept. 18-26.

Virgin Mary by Gabriel Loire A46

1970, Dec. 1 Photo. *Perf. 13x14*

240 A46	2sh multicolored	.30	.30

Christmas. The design is after a stained glass window in the Church of Our Lady of Perpetual Succour, Glasgow.

Decimal Currency Issue

Prince George of Cambridge Quarters, and Trinity Church — A47

Designs show for each denomination a 19th century print and a contemporary photograph of the same view: ½p Battery Rosia. 1½p, Wellington Monument, Alameda Gardens. 2p, View from North Bastion. 2½p, Catalan Bay. 3p, Convent, seen from garden. 4p, The

Exchange and Spanish Chapel. 5p, Commercial Square, Library and Main Guard. 7p, South Barracks and Rosia Magazine. 8p, Moorish Mosque and Castle. 9p, Europa Pass. 10p, South Barracks, from Rosia Bay. 12½p, Southport Gates. 25p, Guards on Alameda. 50p, Europa Pass Gorge, vert. £1 Prince Edward Gate, vert.

In the listing the 1st number is for the 19th cent. design, the 2nd for the 20th cent. design.

Wmk. 314 Sideways

1971, Feb. 15 Litho. *Perf. 14*

Multicolored and:

241 ½p brown red .20 .20
242 ½p brown red .20 .20
a. A47 Pair, Nos. 241-242 .30 *.35*
243 1p light blue .65 .25
244 1p light blue .65 .25
b. A47 Pair, Nos. 243-244 1.30 .50
245 1½p emerald .20 *.30*
246 1½p emerald .20 *.30*
a. A47 Pair, Nos. 245-246 .40 *.75*
247 2p dark brown 1.10 1.10
248 2p dark brown 1.10 1.10
b. A47 Pair, Nos. 247-248 2.25 2.25
249 2½p vermilion .20 *.30*
250 2½p vermilion .20 *.30*
a. A47 Pair, Nos. 249-250 .30 *.50*
251 3p pale green .20 .20
252 3p pale green .20 .20
a. A47 Pair, Nos. 251-252 .30 .30
253 4p gray 1.50 1.25
254 4p gray 1.50 1.25
b. A47 Pair, Nos. 253-254 3.00 2.50
255 5p dark green .25 .25
256 5p dark green .25 .25
a. A47 Pair, Nos. 255-256 .50 .50
257 7p orange .50 .35
258 7p orange .50 .35
a. A47 Pair, Nos. 257-258 1.00 .75
259 8p dark blue .55 .45
260 8p dark blue .55 .45
a. A47 Pair, Nos. 259-260 1.10 .90
261 9p brick red .55 .40
262 9p brick red .55 .40
a. A47 Pair, Nos. 261-262 1.10 .80
263 10p black .65 .55
264 10p black .65 .55
a. A47 Pair, Nos. 263-264 1.30 1.10
265 12½p bister .80 *1.25*
266 12½p bister .80 *1.25*
a. A47 Pair, Nos. 265-266 1.60 *2.50*
267 25p deep purple .85 *1.10*
268 25p deep purple .85 *1.10*
a. A47 Pair, Nos. 267-268 1.75 *2.25*
269 50p blue 1.00 *1.75*
270 50p blue 1.00 *1.75*
a. A47 Pair, Nos. 269-270 2.00 *3.50*
271 £1 sepia 1.50 *2.25*
272 £1 sepia 1.50 *2.25*
a. A47 Pair, Nos. 271-272 3.00 *4.50*
Nos. 241-272 (32) 21.40 *23.90*

Se-tenant both horizontally and vertically.

1973, Sept. 12 Wmk. 314 Upright

247a A47 2p dark brown & multi .70 *1.00*
248a A47 2p dark brown & multi .70 *1.00*
c. Pair, Nos. 247a-248a 1.40 *2.00*
253a A47 4p gray & multi .80 *1.00*
254a A47 4p gray & multi .80 *1.00*
c. Pair, Nos. 253a-254a 1.60 *2.00*
Nos. 247a-254a (4) 3.00 *4.00*

1975, July 9 Wmk. 373

243a A47 1p blue & multi .80 *1.00*
244a A47 1p blue & multi .80 *1.00*
c. Pair, Nos. 243a-244a 1.60 *2.00*

Elizabeth II — A48

Regimental Coat of Arms — A49

Coil Stamps

Perf. 14½x14

1971, Feb. 15 Photo. Wmk. 314

273 A48 ½p red orange .20 *.25*
274 A48 1p bright blue .30 *.25*
275 A48 2p lt yellow green .50 *.75*
a. Strip of 5 (½p, ½p, 1p, 1p, 2p) 1.50 *2.00*
Nos. 273-275 (3) 1.00 *1.25*

Uniform Type of 1969

Uniforms: 1p, Soldier, Black Watch, 1845. 2p, Drum Major with antelope mascot, Royal Fusiliers, 1971. 4p, Soldier, Kings Own Royal Border Regiment, 1704. 10p, Soldier, Devonshire and Dorset Regiment, 1801.

1971, Sept. 6 Litho. *Perf. 14*

276 A42 1p silver & multi .30 .25
277 A42 2p gold & multi .60 .25
278 A42 4p gold & multi 1.10 .40
279 A42 10p sil, gold & multi 3.50 2.00
Nos. 276-279 (4) 5.50 2.90

Descriptions are printed on back on top of gum.

1971, Sept. 25 *Perf. 13x12*

280 A49 3p red, bister & black .40 .35

Presentation of colors to Gibraltar Regiment, Sept. 25, 1971.

Nativity — A50

Christmas: 5p, Journey to Bethlehem.

1971, Dec. 1 Photo. *Perf. 13x13½*

281 A50 3p silver & multi .45 .45
282 A50 5p gold & multi .65 .65

Artificer, 1773 — A51

"Our Lady of Europa" — A52

3p, Tunneler with drill, 1969. 5p, Royal Engineers, 1772 and 1972, and regimental crest, horiz.

1972, Mar. 6 *Perf. 14x13½, 13½x14*

283 A51 1p dk blue & multi .45 *.50*
284 A51 3p red & multi .55 *.60*
285 A51 5p green & multi .75 *.90*
Nos. 283-285 (3) 1.75 2.00

Bicent. of the Royal Engineers in Gibraltar.

Uniform Type of 1969

Uniforms: 1p, Soldier, Duke of Cornwall's Light Infantry, 1704. 3p, Officer, King's Royal Rifle Corps, 1830. 7p, Officer, 37th North Hampshire Regiment, 1825. 10p, Sailor, Royal Navy, 1972.

1972, July 19 Litho. *Perf. 14*

286 A42 1p silver & multi .50 .20
287 A42 3p slate & multi 1.50 .35
288 A42 7p silver & multi 2.25 .75
289 A42 10p gold & multi 2.75 1.50
Nos. 286-289 (4) 7.00 2.80

Design descriptions printed on back on top of gum.

1972, Oct. 1 *Perf. 14½x14*

290 A52 3p brown & multi .20 .20
291 A52 5p green & multi .20 .35

Christmas. Design description printed on back.

Silver Wedding Issue, 1972

Common Design Type

Design: Queen Elizabeth II, Prince Philip, keys of Gibraltar and white narcissus.

1972, Nov. 20 Photo. *Perf. 14x14½*

292 CD324 5p car rose & multi .25 .20
293 CD324 7p slate green & multi .25 .20

Flags of EEC Members and EEC Emblem — A53

Perf. 14½x14

1973, Feb. 22 Litho. Unwmk.

294 A53 5p red & multi .45 .35
295 A53 10p ultra & multi .75 .75

Entry into European Economic Community.

Gibraltar Skull — A54

Designs: 6p, Head of Neanderthal man. 10p, Neanderthal family.

1973, May 22 Wmk. 314 *Perf. 13½*

296 A54 4p lilac rose & multi 1.10 .40
297 A54 6p lt ultra & multi 1.10 .60
298 A54 10p yel green & multi 1.50 1.00
Nos. 296-298 (3) 3.70 2.00

125th anniv. of the discovery of the Gibraltar skull.

Uniform Type of 1969

Uniforms: 1p, Fifer, King's Own Scottish Borderers, 1770. 4p, Officer, Royal Welsh Fusiliers, 1800. 6p, Soldier, Royal Northumberland Fusiliers, 1736. 10p, Private, Grenadier Guards, 1898.

1973, Aug. 22 Litho. *Perf. 14*

299 A42 1p multicolored .45 .30
300 A42 4p multicolored 1.40 .75
301 A42 6p multicolored 2.00 1.50
302 A42 10p multicolored 2.75 *3.25*
Nos. 299-302 (4) 6.60 *5.80*

Descriptions printed on back on top of gum.

Nativity, by Justus Danckerts — A55

1973, Oct. 17 Litho. *Perf. 12½x12*

303 A55 4p brown org & blue .35 .20
304 A55 6p green & claret .55 *.75*

Christmas.

Princess Anne's Wedding Issue

Common Design Type

1973, Nov. 14 *Perf. 14*

305 CD325 6p bl grn & multi .20 .20
306 CD325 14p brt grn & multi .40 .40

Wedding of Princess Anne and Capt. Mark Phillips, Nov. 14, 1973.

V.R. (Queen Victoria) Pillar Box — A56

Virgin with Green Cushion, Andrea Solario — A57

Pillar Boxes: 6p, G.R. (King George). 14p, E.R. (Queen Elizabeth).

1974, May 2 Litho. *Perf. 14*

307 A56 2p yel green & multi .20 *.25*
308 A56 6p gray & multi .30 .30
309 A56 14p dull yel & multi .60 .60
a. Souvenir booklet 8.50
Nos. 307-309 (3) 1.10 1.15

UPU, cent.

No. 309a contains 2 self-adhesive panes printed on peelable paper backing with multicolored advertising on back. One pane of 6 contains 3 each similar to Nos. 307-308; the other pane of 3 contains one each similar to Nos. 307-309. Stamps are imperf. x roulette.

Uniform Type of 1969

Uniforms: 4p, Officer, East Lancashire Regiment, 1742. 6p, Sergeant, Somerset Light Infantry, 1833. 10p, Company man, Royal Sussex Regiment, 1790. 16p, Officer, Royal Air Force, 1974.

1974, Aug. 21 *Perf. 14*

310 A42 4p silver & multi .45 .45
311 A42 6p silver & multi .65 .65
312 A42 10p silver & multi .90 *1.10*
313 A42 16p silver & multi 2.00 *3.00*
Nos. 310-313 (4) 4.00 *5.20*

Descriptions are printed on back on top of gum.

1974, Nov. 5 Litho.

Christmas (Painting): 6p, Madonna of the Meadow, by Giovanni Bellini.

314 A57 4p gold & multi .30 .30
315 A57 6p gold & multi .70 *.90*

Churchill, Parliament and Big Ben A58

20p, Churchill & George V-class battleship.

1974, Nov. 30 *Perf. 14x14½*

316 A58 6p violet & multi .20 .20
317 A58 20p multicolored .55 .55
a. Souvenir sheet of 2, #316-317 4.50 *5.50*

Sir Winston Churchill (1874-1965).

Uniform Type of 1969

Uniforms: 4p, Officer, East Surrey Regiment, 1846. 6p, Private, Highland Light Infantry, 1777. 10p, Officer, Coldstream Guards, 1704. 20p, Sergeant, Gibraltar Regiment, 1974.

1975, Mar. 14 Wmk. 373 *Perf. 14*

318 A42 4p multicolored .25 .25
319 A42 6p multicolored .40 *.45*
320 A42 10p multicolored .75 *.80*
321 A42 20p multicolored 1.60 *2.00*
Nos. 318-321 (4) 3.00 *3.50*

Descriptions are printed on back on top of gum.

Girl Guides Emblem A59

1975, Oct. 10 *Perf. 13½x13*

322 A59 5p violet, gold & blue .30 *.40*
323 A59 7p red brn, gold & blk .40 *.45*
324 A59 15p ocher, silver & blk .70 *.90*
Nos. 322-324 (3) 1.40 1.75

Girl Guides, 50th anniversary.

Child and Bird — A60

Bruges Madonna, by Michelangelo A61

b, Angel playing lute. c, Singing boy. d, Mother & children. e, Praying child. f, Child & lamb.

1975, Nov. 25 ***Perf. 14x14½***

325	Block of 6	2.25	*3.00*
a.-f.	A60 6p any single	.40	*.50*

Christmas. No. 325 printed in sheets of 60 containing 10 blocks of 6 (3x2) stamps with horizontal and vertical gutters between blocks.

1975, Dec. 17 Litho. ***Perf. 14x13½***

Sculptures by Michelangelo: 9p, Traddei Madonna. 15p, Pietà.

326 A61	6p violet blk & multi	.25	.25
327 A61	9p black brn & multi	.30	*.40*
328 A61	15p dk purple & multi	.35	*.70*
a.	Souvenir booklet	4.50	
	Nos. 326-328 (3)	.90	*1.35*

500th birth anniv. of Michelangelo Buonarroti (1475-1564), Italian sculptor, painter and architect.

No. 328a contains 2 self-adhesive panes printed on peelable paper backing with stamp dealer's advertisements on back. One pane of 6 contains 2 each similar to Nos. 326-328; the other pane of 3 contains one each similar to Nos. 326-328. Stamps are imperf. x roulette.

American Bicentennial Emblem, Arms of Gibraltar — A62

Holy Family — A63

1976, May 28 ***Perf. 14x14½***

329 A62	25p multicolored	.75	.65
a.	Souvenir sheet of 4	4.00	*6.00*

American Bicentennial. No. 329a is rouletted all around.

Uniform Type of 1969

Uniforms: 1p, Suffolk Regiment, 1795. 6p, Northamptonshire Regiment, 1779. 12p, Lancashire Fusiliers, 1793. 25p, Royal Army Ordinance Corps. 1896.

1976, July 21 ***Perf. 14***

330 A42	1p multicolored	.25	.20
331 A42	6p multicolored	.45	.25
332 A42	12p multicolored	.65	.45
333 A42	25p multicolored	.90	*1.00*
	Nos. 330-333 (4)	2.25	1.90

Descriptions printed on back on top of gum.

1976, Nov. 3 Litho. Wmk. 373

Stained Glass Windows: 9p, St. Bernard of Clairvaux. 12p, St. John the Evangelist. 20p, Archangel Michael.

334 A63	6p ultra & multi	.25	.20
335 A63	9p brt green & multi	.30	.20
336 A63	12p orange & multi	.45	.50
337 A63	20p dk carmine & multi	.85	*1.10*
	Nos. 334-337 (4)	1.85	2.00

Christmas.

Elizabeth II and Royal Crest — A64

1977, Feb. 7 Litho. ***Perf. 14x13½***

338 A64	6p multicolored	.20	.20
339 A64	£1 multicolored	1.25	*1.75*
a.	Souv. sheet of 2, #338-339, perf. 13	2.00	*2.50*

25th anniv. of the reign of Queen Elizabeth II. #338-339 issued in sheets of 9.

Red Mullet A65

Designs: ½p, 3p, 9p, 15p, 25p, Flowers. 1p, 4p, 10p, 50p, Fish. 2p, 5p, 12p, £1, Butterflies. 2½p, 6p, 20p, £2, Birds. ½p, 2½p, 3p, 6p, 9p, 15p, 20p, 25p, £2, £5, vertical.

1977-80 ***Perf. 14½x14, 14x14½***

340	A65	½p Toothed orchid	.40	*1.25*
341	A65	1p shown	.20	*.40*
342	A65	2p Large blue	.20	*.75*
343	A65	2½p Sardinian warbler	.70	*1.25*
344	A65	3p Giant squill	.20	.20
345	A65	4p Gray wrasse	.20	.20
346	A65	5p Red admiral	.35	*.75*
347	A65	6p Black kite	1.25	.40
348	A65	9p Scorpion vetch	.50	.50
349	A65	10p John Dory	.30	.20
350	A65	12p Clouded yellow	.70	.30
350A	A65	15p Winged asparagus pea	1.10	.40
351	A65	20p Andouin's gull	1.10	*1.90*
352	A65	25p Barbary nut	.90	*1.50*
353	A65	50p Swordfish	1.40	.75
354	A65	£1 Swallowtail	3.00	*3.50*
355	A65	£2 Hoopoe	6.25	*7.50*
355A	A65	£5 Coat of Arms	7.00	*8.25*
		Nos. 340-355A (18)	25.75	*30.00*

½p also comes inscribed 1982, the 4p, 10p, 12p, 25p & 50p inscribed 1981, 9p inscribed 1978.

Issued: £5, 5/16/79; 15p, 11/12/80; others, 4/1/77.

Gibraltar No. 182 — A66

12p, Gibraltar #233. 25p, Gibraltar #294.

1977, May 27 Litho. ***Perf. 14***

356 A66	6p multi	.20	.20
357 A66	12p multi, vert.	.20	*.30*
358 A66	25p multi, vert.	.20	*.40*
	Nos. 356-358 (3)	.60	.90

Amphilex 77 Intl. Phil. Exhib., Amsterdam, May 26-June 5. Issued in sheets of 6.

Annunciation, by Rubens — A67

Rubens Paintings: 9p, Nativity. 12p, Adoration of the Kings. 15p, Holy Family under Apple Tree.

Perf. 14x13½, 13½x14

1977, Nov. 2 Litho.

359 A67	3p multi	.20	.20
360 A67	9p multi	.20	.20
361 A67	12p multi, horiz.	.30	.30
362 A67	15p multi	.30	.30
a.	Souvenir sheet of 4, #359-362	2.75	*3.50*
	Nos. 359-362 (4)	1.00	1.00

Christmas and 400th birth anniv. of Peter Paul Rubens.

Gibraltar from Space A68

Design: 25p, Strait of Gibraltar, aerial view.

1978, May 3 Litho. ***Perf. 13½***

363 A68	12p multicolored	.30	*.45*

Souvenir Sheet

364 A68	25p multicolored	.80	.80

No. 363 issued in sheets of 10.
No. 364 contains one stamp.

Holyroodhouse — A69

Royal Houses: 9p, St. James Palace. 12p, Sandringham House. 18p, Balmoral.

1978, June 12 Litho. ***Perf. 13½***

365 A69	6p multicolored	.20	.20
366 A69	9p multicolored	.25	.20
367 A69	12p multicolored	.35	.30
368 A69	18p multicolored	.45	.45
a.	Souvenir booklet	2.75	
	Nos. 365-368 (4)	1.25	1.15

25th anniv. of coronation of Queen Elizabeth II. No. 368a contains 2 panes printed on peelable paper backing with pictures of castles. One pane contains 6 rouletted stamps, 3 each similar to Nos. 367-368; the other pane contains one 25p (Windsor Castle) rouletted stamp.

Sunderland Seaplane Landing — A70

Gibraltar and: 9p, Two-tiered Caudron taking off, 1918. 12p, Shackleton, 1953-1966. 16p, Hunter warplane, 1954-1966. 18p, Nimrod, 1969-1978.

1978, Sept. 6 Litho. ***Perf. 14***

369 A70	3p multicolored	.20	.20
370 A70	9p multicolored	.25	*.30*
371 A70	12p multicolored	.35	*.40*
372 A70	16p multicolored	.50	*.60*
373 A70	18p multicolored	.70	*.75*
	Nos. 369-373 (5)	2.00	*2.25*

Royal Air Force, 60th anniversary.

Madonna with Goldfinch, by Dürer — A71

Christmas (Paintings by Albrecht Dürer): 5p, Madonna with Animals. 9p, Nativity. 15p, Adoration of the Kings.

1978, Nov. 1 Litho. ***Perf. 14***

374 A71	5p multicolored	.20	.20
375 A71	9p multicolored	.25	.25
376 A71	12p multicolored	.30	.35
377 A71	15p multicolored	.35	.40
	Nos. 374-377 (4)	1.10	1.20

Rowland Hill and Gibraltar No. 10 — A72

Sir Rowland Hill (1795-1879), originator of penny postage and: 9p, Gibraltar No. 274. 12p, Parchment scroll with early postal regulations. 25p, "Barred G" cancellation used on British stamps in Gibraltar.

1979, Feb. 7 Litho. ***Perf. 13½***

378 A72	3p multicolored	.20	.20
379 A72	9p multicolored	.20	.20
380 A72	12p yellow grn & black	.20	.20
381 A72	25p yellow & black	.30	*.50*
	Nos. 378-381 (4)	.90	1.10

Satellite Earth Station, Post Horn, Telephone — A73

1979, May 16 ***Perf. 13½x14***

382 A73	3p lt green & green	.20	.20
383 A73	9p lt brown & brown	.25	*.60*
384 A73	12p gray & ultra	.35	*1.00*
	Nos. 382-384 (3)	.80	*1.80*

European telecommunications system.

Children, IYC Emblem, Nativity — A74

a, African girl. b, Chinese girl. c, Pacific islands girl. d, American Indian girl. e, Shown. f, Scandinavian boy.

Litho.; Silver Embossed

1979, Nov. 14 ***Perf. 14***

385	Block of 6	1.50	1.50
a.-f.	A74 12p any single	.25	.25

Christmas; IYC. No. 385 printed in sheets of 12 containing 2 No. 385 with vertical rouletted gutter between.

Officers, Exchange and Commercial Library, 1830 — A75

Gibraltar Police Force, 150th anniv.: 6p, Early and modern uniforms, Rock of Gibraltar. 12p, Traffic Officer, ambulance. 37p, Policeman and woman, Police Station, Irish Town.

Perf. 14x14½

1980, Feb. 5 Litho. Wmk. 373

386 A75	3p multicolored	.20	.20
387 A75	6p multicolored	.20	.20
388 A75	12p multicolored	.30	.30
389 A75	37p multicolored	.50	.75
	Nos. 386-389 (4)	1.20	1.45

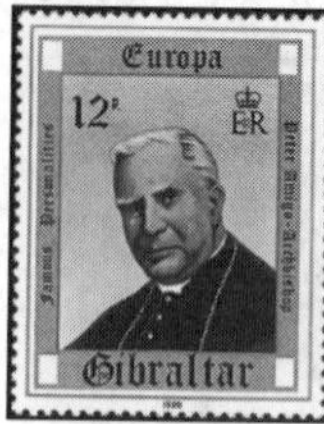

Archbishop Peter Amigo (1864-1949) A76

Europa: No. 391, Gustavo Charles Bacarisas (1872-1971), artist. No. 392, John Mackintosh (1865-1940), philanthropist.

1980, May 6 Wmk. 373 *Perf. 14½*

390 A76	12p multicolored	.20	*.25*
391 A76	12p multicolored	.20	*.25*
392 A76	12p multicolored	.20	*.25*
	Nos. 390-392 (3)	.60	.75

Queen Mother Elizabeth Birthday Issue

Common Design Type

1980, Aug. 4 Litho. *Perf. 14*

393 CD330 15p multicolored .30 .30

"Victory" and Rock of Gibraltar, by Monamy Swaine A77

Paintings: 3p, Lord Nelson, by John Francis Rigaud, 1781, vert. 15p, Lord Nelson, by William Beechey, vert. 40p, Victory Towed into Gibraltar by Clarkson Stanfield.

1980, Aug. 20 Litho. *Perf. 14*

394 A77	3p multicolored	.20	.20
395 A77	9p multicolored	.25	.25
396 A77	15p multicolored	.30	.30
a.	Souvenir sheet	.90	*1.00*
397 A77	40p multicolored	.75	.75
	Nos. 394-397 (4)	1.50	1.50

Horatio Nelson (1758-1805).

Holy Family A78

1980, Nov. 12

398 A78	15p shown	.25	*.35*
399 A78	15p Three kings	.25	*.35*
a.	Pair, #398-399	.50	*.70*

Christmas. No. 399a has continuous design.

Hercules Separating Africa and Europe — A79

Dining Room, The Convent — A80

Europa: 15p, Hercules standing on Rock of Gibraltar and Morocco.

Perf. 14x13½

1981, Feb. 24 Wmk. 373

400 A79	9p multicolored	.20	.20
401 A79	15p multicolored	.30	.35

1981, May 22 Litho. *Perf. 14½x14*

402 A80	4p shown	.20	.20
403 A80	14p King's Chapel	.25	.20
404 A80	15p Aerial view	.35	.20
405 A80	55p Cloister	.75	.75
	Nos. 402-405 (4)	1.55	1.35

450th anniv. of The Convent (Governor's residence, originally Franciscan monastery).

Prince Charles and Lady Diana A81

1981, July 27 Litho. *Perf. 14½*

406 A81 £1 multicolored 1.50 1.50

Royal wedding. Se-tenant with decorative label.

Queen Elizabeth II — A82

1981, Sept. 29 *Perf. 14½*

Booklet Stamps

407 A82	1p black	.40	.40
a.	Bklt. pane of 10 + 2 labels (2 #407, 2 #408, 6 #409)	2.00	
b.	Bklt. pane of 5 + label (#407, #408, 3 #409)	1.50	
408 A82	4p dark blue	.40	.40
409 A82	15p green	.40	.40
	Nos. 407-409 (3)	1.20	1.20

Airmail Service, 50th Anniv. A83

1981, Sept. 29 *Perf. 14½*

410 A83	14p Paper plane	.30	.30
411 A83	15p Envelopes, aerogram	.30	.30
412 A83	55p Airplane circling globe	.90	.90
	Nos. 410-412 (3)	1.50	1.50

Intl. Year of the Disabled A84

1981, Nov. 19 Litho. Wmk. 373

413 A84 14p multicolored .30 .30

Christmas A85

1981, Nov. 19 *Perf. 14*

414 A85	15p Children singing carols	.30	.20
415 A85	55p Decorated mailbox, vert.	1.10	.75

Douglas DC-3 — A86

1982, Feb. 10 Litho. *Perf. 14*

416 A86	1p shown	.20	.20
417 A86	2p Vickers Viking	.20	.20
a.	Wmk. 384, dated 1986 ('87)	2.25	3.00
418 A86	3p Airspeed Ambassador	.20	.20
419 A86	4p Vickers Viscount	.20	.20
420 A86	5p Boeing 727	.20	.20
a.	Wmk. 384, dated 1986 ('87)	2.25	3.00
421 A86	10p Vickers Vanguard	.40	.40
422 A86	14p Short Solent	.50	.50
423 A86	15p Fokker F-27 Friendship	1.00	.60
424 A86	17p Boeing 737	.65	.65
425 A86	20p BAC One-eleven	.80	.80
426 A86	25p Lockheed Constellation	2.00	1.25
427 A86	50p De Havilland Comet 4B	3.00	2.00
428 A86	£1 Saro Windhover	4.50	2.50
429 A86	£2 Hawker Siddeley Trident 2	6.50	5.50
430 A86	£5 DH-89A Dragon Rapide	9.00	*12.50*
	Nos. 416-430 (15)	29.35	27.70

No. 425 exists with 1985 imprint.

Royal Navy Ship Crests — A87

1982, Apr. 14 Litho. *Perf. 14*

431 A87	½p Opossum	.20	.20
432 A87	15½p Norfolk	.45	.45
433 A87	17p Fearless	.60	.60
434 A87	60p Rooke	1.60	*2.25*
	Nos. 431-434 (4)	2.85	*3.50*

See Nos. 449-452, 465-468, 474-477, 492-495, 501-504, 528-531, 552-555, 574-577, 587-590.

Europa A88

1982, June 11 Litho. *Perf. 14*

435 A88	14p Planes preparing for takeoff	.25	*.60*
436 A88	17p Generals Eisenhower and Giraud	.35	*.70*

Operation Torch, 1943.

Chamber of Commerce Centenary — A89

Anniversaries: 15½p, British Forces Postal Service centenary. 60p, Scouting year.

1982, Sept. 22

437 A89	½p multicolored	.20	.20
438 A89	15½p multicolored	.30	.30
439 A89	60p multicolored	1.10	1.10
	Nos. 437-439 (3)	1.60	1.60

Intl. Direct Telephone Dialing System Inauguration — A90

1982, Oct. 1 *Perf. 14½*

440 A90 17p Map .40 .40

Christmas A91

Perf. 14x14½

1982, Nov. 18 Litho. Wmk. 373

441 A91	14p Holly	.35	.30
442 A91	17p Mistletoe	.50	.35

A92

1983, Mar. 14 Litho. *Perf. 14*

443 A92	4p Local street	.20	.20
444 A92	14p Scouts on parade	.30	.30
445 A92	17p Flag, vert.	.40	.40
446 A92	60p Queen Elizabeth II, vert.	1.00	*1.25*
	Nos. 443-446 (4)	1.90	*2.15*

Commonwealth Day.

Europa A93

1983, May 21 *Perf. 14x13½*

447 A93	16p St. George's Hall	.30	.30
448 A93	19p Water catchments	.40	.40

Royal Navy Crest Type of 1982

1983, July 1 Litho. *Perf. 14*

449 A87	4p Faulknor	.20	.20
450 A87	14p Renown	.70	.30
451 A87	17p Ark Royal	.75	.35
452 A87	60p Sheffield	1.25	1.25
	Nos. 449-452 (4)	2.90	2.10

Fortresses — A94

1983, Sept. 13 *Perf. 13½x14*

453 A94	4p Landport Gate, 1729	.20	.20
454 A94	17p Koehler gun, 1782	.40	.40
455 A94	77p King's Bastion, 1799	1.40	1.40
a.	Souvenir sheet of 3, #453-455	2.75	2.75
	Nos. 453-455 (3)	2.00	2.00

Christmas A95

Raphael Paintings.

1983, Nov. 17 Litho. *Perf. 14*

456 A95 4p Adoration of the Magi .20 .20
457 A95 17p Madonna of Foligno, vert. .50 .45
458 A95 60p Sistine Madonna, vert. 1.75 1.75
Nos. 456-458 (3) 2.45 2.40

Europa (1959-1984) A96

Intl. Postal and Telecommunication Links.

1984, Mar. 6 Litho. *Perf. 14½*

459 A96 17p No. 98 .35 *.45*
460 A96 23p Communications circuit .45 *.75*

Field Hockey A97

1984, May 25 Litho. *Perf. 14*

461 A97 20p shown .50 *.65*
462 A97 21p Basketball .60 *.70*
463 A97 26p Rowing .65 *.80*
464 A97 29p Soccer .75 *.90*
Nos. 461-464 (4) 2.50 *3.05*

Royal Navy Crest Type of 1982

1984, Sept. 21 Litho. *Perf. 13½x13*

465 A87 20p Active 1.25 *1.50*
466 A87 21p Foxhound 1.25 *1.75*
467 A87 26p Valiant 1.40 *1.75*
468 A87 29p Hood 1.50 *2.00*
Nos. 465-468 (4) 5.40 *7.00*

Christmas A98

Perf. 14x14½

1984, Nov. 7 Litho. Wmk. 373

469 A98 20p Parade float .50 .50
470 A98 80p Float, diff. 2.00 2.00

Europa Issue

Musical Symbols — A99

1985, Feb. 26 Photo. *Perf. 12½*
Granite Paper

471 A99 20p multi, diff. .40 .35
472 A99 29p shown .60 *1.50*

Save the Children Fund A100

Globe and legend in various positions.

1985, May 3 Litho. *Perf. 13x13½*

473 Strip of 4 3.25 *4.00*
a.-d. A100 26p any single .80 *1.00*

Royal Navy Crests Type of 1982

1985, July 3 Litho. *Perf. 14*

474 A87 4p Duncan 1.25 .60
475 A87 9p Fury 1.50 1.10
476 A87 21p Firedrake 1.75 *2.25*
477 A87 80p Malaya 2.00 *3.00*
Nos. 474-477 (4) 6.50 *6.95*

Intl. Youth Year — A101

1985, Sept. 6 *Perf. 14½*

478 A101 4p Emblem .30 .20
479 A101 20p Hands, diamond 1.10 1.10
480 A101 80p Girl Guides anniv. emblem 2.50 *3.00*
Nos. 478-480 (3) 3.90 *4.30*

St. Joseph's Parish Church, Cent. — A102

Creche, Detail — A103

Perf. 13½xRoulette 7 Between, 13½

1985, Oct. 25 Wmk. 373 Litho.

481 A102 Pair 1.00 *1.10*
a. 4p Centenary seal .50 *.55*
b. 4p Church .50 *.55*
c. No. 481a, perf. 13½ on 4 sides .50 *.55*
482 A103 80p multicolored 3.00 *3.50*

Christmas. Nos. 481a-481b rouletted between. Printed in sheets of 10 pairs with the bottom row containing 5 No. 481c. Strips of 3, Nos. 481a-481c exist.

Europa A104

1986, Feb. 10 Litho. *Perf. 13x13½*

483 A104 22p Butterfly, house .75 .50
484 A104 29p Seagull, hotel 1.25 *2.50*

Postage Stamp Cent. — A105

Elizabeth II, 60th Birthday — A106

1986, Mar. 25 *Perf. 13½x13*

485 A105 4p No. 18 .30 .20
486 A105 22p No. 42 1.00 .80
487 A105 32p No. 67 1.50 *1.60*
488 A105 36p No. 118 1.60 *2.00*

Size: 32x48mm

Perf. 14

489 A105 44p No. 131 2.00 *2.50*
Nos. 485-489 (5) 6.40 *7.10*

Souvenir Sheet

490 A105 29p No. 2 2.25 2.25

1986, May 22 Litho. *Perf. 14*

491 A106 £1 multicolored 2.25 *3.00*

Royal Naval Crests Type of 1982

1986, Aug. 28 Litho. *Perf. 14*

492 A87 22p Lightning 1.60 .80
493 A87 29p Hermione 1.75 1.40
494 A87 32p Laforey 1.90 *2.50*
495 A87 44p Nelson 2.25 *3.25*
Nos. 492-495 (4) 7.50 *7.95*

Christmas, Intl. Peace Year — A107

1986, Oct. 14 Litho. *Perf. 14½x14*

496 A107 18p St. Mary the Crowned Cathedral 1.00 .40
497 A107 32p St. Andrew's Church 1.40 *2.00*

Souvenir Sheet

Wedding of Prince Andrew and Sarah Ferguson — A108

1986, Aug. 28 Litho. *Perf. 15*

498 A108 44p multicolored 1.10 *1.60*

Europa — A109

1987, Feb. 17 Wmk. 384 *Perf. 15*

499 A109 22p Neptune House 1.25 .40
500 A109 29p Ocean Heights 1.75 *3.00*

Royal Navy Crests Type of 1982

1987, Apr. 2 *Perf. 13½x13*

501 A87 18p Wishart 1.25 .60
502 A87 22p Charybdis 1.40 .90
503 A87 32p Antelope 1.90 *2.25*
504 A87 44p Eagle 2.50 *3.00*
Nos. 501-504 (4) 7.05 *6.75*

Warrant Granted to the Royal Engineers, 200th Anniv. — A110

1987, Apr. 25 Wmk. 373 *Perf. 14½*

505 A110 18p Victoria Stadium 1.10 .50
506 A110 32p Casket, Freedom Scroll 1.50 *2.40*
507 A110 44p Monogram 2.25 *3.00*
Nos. 505-507 (3) 4.85 *5.90*

Guns and Artillery A111

Designs: 1p, 13-inch mortar, 1783. 2p, 6-inch Coast, 1909. 3p, 8-inch Howitzer, 1783. 4p, Bofors L40/70, 1951. 5p, 100-ton RML, 1882. 10p, 5.25 HAA, 1953. 18p, 25-pounder Gun-howitzer, 1943. 19p, 64-pounder RML, 1873. 22p, 12-pounder, 1758. 50p, 10-inch RML, 1870. £1, Russian 24-pounder, 1854. £3, 9.2-inch Coast Mk. 10, 1935. £5, 24-pounder, 1779.

1987, June 1 Wmk. 373 *Perf. 12½*

508 A111 1p multicolored .20 *.35*
509 A111 2p multicolored .30 *.35*
510 A111 3p multicolored .30 *.35*
511 A111 4p multicolored .40 .20
512 A111 5p multicolored .40 .35
513 A111 10p multicolored .40 .40
514 A111 18p multicolored .60 *.65*
515 A111 19p multicolored .65 *.75*
516 A111 22p multicolored .65 .35
517 A111 50p multicolored 1.25 *2.50*
518 A111 £1 multicolored 2.25 2.75
519 A111 £3 multicolored 6.00 11.00
520 A111 £5 multicolored 9.50 12.50
Nos. 508-520 (13) 22.90 *32.50*

For surcharge see No. 595.

Christmas — A112

1987, Nov. 12 Wmk. 384 *Perf. 14½*

521 A112 4p Three Wise Men .20 .20
522 A112 22p Holy Family .90 .75
523 A112 44p Shepherds 1.60 *2.50*
Nos. 521-523 (3) 2.70 *3.45*

Europa — A113

Transport and communication: No. 524, Rock of Gibraltar, Cruise Ship. No. 525, Passenger jet, yacht, dish aerial. No. 526, Bus, buggy. No. 527, Rock of Gibraltar, automobile, telephone.

Perf. 14½x14 on 3 Sides; Rouletted Between

1988, Feb. 16 Litho. Wmk. 373

524 0 22p multicolored 1.25 *1.50*
525 0 22p multicolored 1.25 *1.50*
a. A113 Pair, #524-525 2.50 *3.00*
526 0 32p multicolored 1.75 *2.00*
527 0 32p multicolored 1.75 *2.00*
a. A113 Pair, #526-527 3.50 *4.00*
Nos. 524-527 (4) 6.00 *7.00*

Nos. 525a, 527a have continuous design.

Royal Navy Crests Type of 1982

Perf. 13½x13

1988, Apr. 7 **Wmk. 384**
528 A87 18p Clyde 1.25 .50
529 A87 22p Foresight 1.60 1.00
530 A87 32p Severn 1.75 2.25
531 A87 44p Rodney 2.40 3.50
Nos. 528-531 (4) 7.00 7.25

Birds
A114

1988, June 15 **Wmk. 373** ***Perf. 14***
532 A114 4p Bee eater .50 .20
533 A114 22p Common puffin 1.25 .75
534 A114 32p Honey buzzard 1.75 2.25
535 A114 44p Blue rock thrush 2.25 3.00
Nos. 532-535 (4) 5.75 6.20

Operation Raleigh, 1984-88
A115

Designs: 19p, Square-rigger. 22p, Sir Walter Raleigh and expedition emblem. 32p, Maps and modern transport ship Sir Walter Raleigh. 44p, Ship Sir Walter Raleigh.

Perf. 13x13½

1988, Sept. 14 **Litho.** **Wmk. 373**
536 A115 19p multicolored .60 .60
537 A115 22p multicolored .70 .70
538 A115 32p multicolored 1.00 1.00
Nos. 536-538 (3) 2.30 2.30

Souvenir Sheet

539 Sheet of 2, #537, 539a 3.50 3.50
a. A115 44p multicolored 1.50 1.50

400th anniv. of Sir Walter Raleigh's voyage to the New World to establish the 1st English-speaking colony, in what is now North Carolina.

Christmas
A116

Children's drawings: 4p, Snowman, by Rebecca Falero. 22p, Nativity, by Dennis Penalver. 44p, Santa Claus, by Gavin Key.

1988, Nov. 2 **Wmk. 384** ***Perf. 14***
540 A116 4p multicolored .20 .20
541 A116 22p multicolored .55 .70

Size: 25x33mm

542 A116 44p multicolored 1.25 1.75
Nos. 540-542 (3) 2.00 2.65

Europa
A117

Toys: 32p, Doll, doll house, puppy, ball, boat.

Perf. 13x13½

1989, Feb. 15 **Wmk. 384**
543 A117 25p shown 1.25 .60
544 A117 32p multicolored 1.50 2.00

Gibraltar Regiment, 50th Anniv. — A118

Perf. 13½x13

1989, Apr. 28 **Wmk. 373**
545 A118 4p The Port Sergeant .40 .20
546 A118 22p Regimental colors, Queen's colors 1.25 .75
547 A118 32p Drum Major 1.75 1.75
Nos. 545-547 (3) 3.40 2.70

Souvenir Sheet

548 Sheet of 2, Nos. 546, 548a 3.50 3.00
a. A118 44p Regimental arms 1.75 1.75

Intl. Red Cross, 125th Anniv. — A119

Perf. 15x14½

1989, July 7 **Wmk. 384**
549 A119 25p Mother and child .75 .50
550 A119 32p Malnourished children 1.00 1.25
551 A119 44p Accident victims 1.50 2.00
Nos. 549-551 (3) 3.25 3.75

Royal Navy Crests Type of 1982

1989, Sept. 7 **Litho.** ***Perf. 14***
552 A87 22p Blankney 1.50 .60
553 A87 25p Deptford 1.50 1.25
554 A87 32p Exmoor 2.00 1.75
555 A87 44p Stork 3.00 3.00
Nos. 552-555 (4) 8.00 6.60

Souvenir Sheets

Coins — A120

No. 556: a, 1p Barbary Partridge. b, 2p Lighthouse at Europa Point. c, 10p Tower of Homage. d, 5p Barbary Ape.

No. 557: a, 50p Gibraltar Candytuft. b, £5 Pillars of Hercules. c, £2 Cannon from the Great Siege Period, 1779-1783. d, £1 Natl. coat of arms. e, Common obverse side of coins picturing Maklouf head of Queen Elizabeth II. f, 20p Our Lady of Europa.

1989, Oct. 10 ***Perf. 14½x15***
556 Sheet of 4 1.25 1.25
a.-d. A120 4p any single .30 .30
557 Sheet of 6 4.75 4.75
a.-f. A120 22p any single .75 .75

Christmas
A121

Wmk. 384

1989, Oct. 11 **Litho.** ***Perf. 14½***
558 A121 4p Santa's sleigh .20 .20
559 A121 22p Shepherds see star .75 .50
560 A121 32p Holy family 1.10 1.25
561 A121 44p Adoration of the Magi 1.75 2.25
Nos. 558-561 (4) 3.80 4.20

Europa 1990 — A122

Post offices: No. 562, G.P.O. exterior. No. 563, Carved crown and "VR" from p.o. archway and G.P.O. interior. No. 564, South District P.O. interior. No. 565, South District P.O. exterior.

Perf. 14½, Rouletted 9½ Between

1990, Mar. 6 **Litho.** **Unwmk.**
562 22p multicolored 1.00 1.10
563 22p multicolored 1.00 1.10
a. A122 Pair, #562-563 2.00 2.25
564 32p multicolored 1.50 1.75
565 32p multicolored 1.50 1.75
a. A122 Pair, #564-565 3.00 3.50
Nos. 562-565 (4) 5.00 5.70

Pairs are rouletted between.

Early Fire Truck
A123

1990, Apr. 2 ***Perf. 14½x14***
566 A123 4p Early firemen, hose, vert. .75 .20
567 A123 20p shown 1.50 .75
568 A123 42p Modern truck 1.75 2.00
569 A123 44p Modern fireman, vert. 2.00 2.00
Nos. 566-569 (4) 6.00 4.95

Fire Service, 125th anniv.

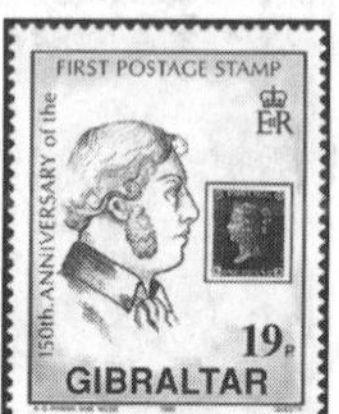

Penny Black, 150th Anniv. — A124

19p, Henry Corbould, Great Britain No. 1. 22p, 1st Royal Mail coach, Bristol-London. 32p, Sir Rowland Hill, Great Britain No. 1. 44p, Great Britain No. 1, Maltese Cross cancel.

1990, May 3 ***Perf. 13½x14***
570 A124 19p multicolored .75 .65
571 A124 22p multicolored 1.00 .75
572 A124 32p multicolored 2.00 2.50
Nos. 570-572 (3) 3.75 3.90

Souvenir Sheet

573 A124 44p multicolored 3.50 3.50

Royal Navy Crest Type of 1982

1990, July 10 **Litho.** ***Perf. 14***
574 A87 22p Calpe 1.50 .60
575 A87 25p Gallant 1.60 1.50
576 A87 32p Wrestler 2.00 2.25
577 A87 44p Greyhound 2.50 3.00
Nos. 574-577 (4) 7.60 7.35

Europort Model
A125

1990, Oct. 10 **Litho.** ***Perf. 14½***
578 A125 22p shown .80 .75
579 A125 23p Building components .80 1.10
580 A125 25p Land reclamation 1.00 1.10
Nos. 578-580 (3) 2.60 2.95

Christmas — A126

Europa
A127

1990, Oct. 10 ***Perf. 13½***
581 A126 4p shown .20 .20
582 A126 22p Santa Claus .70 .50
583 A126 42p Christmas tree 1.50 1.75
584 A126 44p Creche 1.50 1.75
Nos. 581-584 (4) 3.90 4.20

1991, Feb. 26 **Litho.** ***Perf. 13½***
585 A127 25p Spaceplane, satellite .90 .75
586 A127 32p ERS-1 satellite 1.10 1.40

Royal Navy Crest Type of 1982

1991, Apr. 9 **Litho.** ***Perf. 13½x13***
587 A87 4p Hesperus .35 .20
588 A87 21p Forester 1.40 1.25
589 A87 22p Furious 1.40 1.25
590 A87 62p Scylla 3.50 4.50
Nos. 587-590 (4) 6.65 7.20

Birds
A128

1991, May 30 **Litho.** ***Perf. 13½***
591 A128 13p Black stork .75 .90
592 A128 13p Egyptian vulture .75 .90
593 A128 13p Barbary partridge .75 .90
594 A128 13p Shag .75 .90
a. Block of 4, #591-594 3.00 3.75

World Wildlife Fund.

No. 519 Surcharged

Wmk. 373

1991, May 30 **Litho.** ***Perf. 12½***
595 A111 £1.05 on £3 multi 3.25 1.50

Views of Gibraltar
A129

Paintings: 22p, North View of Gibraltar, by Gustavo Bacarisas (1873-1971). 26p, Parson's Lodge, by Elena Mifsud (1906-1989). 32p, Governor's Parade, by Jacobo Azabury, OBE (1890-1980). 42p, Waterport Wharf, by Rudesindo Mannia (1899-1982), vert.

1991, Sept. 10 **Litho.** ***Perf. 15x14***
596 A129 22p multicolored .75 .40
597 A129 26p multicolored .90 .75
598 A129 32p multicolored 1.40 1.75

Perf. 14x15

599 A129 42p multicolored 2.00 2.50
Nos. 596-599 (4) 5.05 5.40

Christmas
A130

Christmas carols: 4p, Once in Royal David's City. 24p, Silent Night. 25p, Angels We Have Heard on High. 49p, O Come All Ye Faithful.

1991, Oct. 15 Litho. *Perf. 14½*

600 A130 4p multicolored .25 .20
601 A130 24p multicolored 1.00 .50
602 A130 25p multicolored 1.00 1.00
603 A130 49p multicolored 1.75 *2.25*
Nos. 600-603 (4) 4.00 *3.95*

Souvenir Sheet

Phila Nippon '91 — A131

1991, Nov. 15

604 A131 £1.05 Plain tiger 4.25 4.25

Queen Elizabeth II's Accession to the Throne, 40th Anniv.

Common Design Type

Wmk. 373

1992, Feb. 6 Litho. *Perf. 14*

605 CD349 4p multicolored .20 .20
606 CD349 20p multicolored .60 .60
607 CD349 24p multicolored .75 *.80*
608 CD349 44p multicolored 1.40 *1.50*
609 CD349 54p multicolored 1.75 *1.90*
Nos. 605-609 (5) 4.70 *5.00*

Discovery of America, 500th Anniv. — A132

1992, Feb. 6 Unwmk. *Perf. 14½*

610 A132 24p Columbus, Santa Maria 1.10 *1.25*
611 A132 24p Map, Nina 1.10 *1.25*
a. Pair, #610-611 2.25 *2.50*
612 A132 34p Map, Pinta 1.25 *1.50*
613 A132 34p Map, sailor 1.25 *1.50*
a. Pair, #612-613 2.50 *3.00*
Nos. 610-613 (4) 4.70 *5.50*

Europa. Printed in sheets containing 4 pairs.

Around the World Yacht Rally, 1991-92
A133

Compass rose, sail and maps of routes through: 21p, Atlantic Ocean, vert. 24p, Malay Archipelago. 25p, Indian Ocean. 49p, Mediterranean and Red Seas, vert.

1992, Apr. 15 Litho. *Perf. 13½*

614 A133 21p multicolored .75 .75
615 A133 24p multicolored 1.00 *1.25*
616 A133 25p multicolored 1.00 *1.40*
Nos. 614-616 (3) 2.75 *3.40*

Souvenir Sheet

617 A133 Sheet of 2, #614 & 617a 2.50 2.50
a. A133 49p multicolored 1.75 1.75

Anglican Diocese of Gibraltar, 150th Anniv.
A134

4p, Holy Trinity Cathedral, vert. 24p, Crest and map. 44p, Construction work on Cathedral during 1800's. 54p, Bishop Tomlinson, first Bishop of Diocese (1842-1863), vert.

1992, Aug. 21 Litho. *Perf. 14*

618 A134 4p multicolored .25 .20
619 A134 24p multicolored 1.25 .50
620 A134 44p multicolored 2.10 *2.25*
621 A134 54p multicolored 2.40 *2.50*
Nos. 618-621 (4) 6.00 *5.45*

Christmas
A135

Designs: 4p, Church of the Sacred Heart of Jesus. 24p, Cathedral of St. Mary the Crowned. 34p, St. Andrew's Church. 49p, St. Joseph's Church.

1992, Nov. 10 Litho. *Perf. 14*

622 A135 4p multicolored .20 .20
623 A135 24p multicolored .95 .45
624 A135 34p multicolored 1.60 *1.75*
625 A135 49p multicolored 2.25 *3.00*
Nos. 622-625 (4) 5.00 *5.40*

Contemporary Art — A136

Europa: No. 626, Masks of Comedy and Tragedy, record. No. 627, Painting, dancer, pottery. No. 628, Architecture, sculpture. No. 629, Video camera, 35mm film.

1993, Mar. 2 Litho. *Perf. 14½*

626 A136 24p multicolored 1.10 1.10
627 A136 24p multicolored 1.10 1.10
a. Pair, #626-627 2.25 2.25
628 A136 34p multicolored 1.40 1.75
629 A136 34p multicolored 1.40 1.75
a. Pair, #628-629 2.75 3.50
Nos. 626-629 (4) 5.00 5.70

Souvenir Sheet

World War II Warships
A137

Designs: a, HMS Hood. b, HMS Ark Royal c, HMAS Waterhen. d, USS Gleaves.

1993, Apr. 27 Litho. *Perf. 14*

630 A137 24p Sheet of 4, #a.-d. 6.00 6.00

See Nos. 660, 684, 714, 732.

Architectural Heritage
A138

1993-94 Litho. *Perf. 13*

631 A138 1p Landport Gate .20 .20
632 A138 2p St. Mary the Crowned .20 .20
633 A138 3p Parsons Lodge Battery .20 .20
634 A138 4p Moorish Castle .20 .20
635 A138 5p General Post Office .20 .20
636 A138 10p South Barracks .25 .25
637 A138 21p American War Memorial .60 .60
638 A138 24p Garrison Library .70 .70
639 A138 25p Southport Gates .70 .70
640 A138 26p Casemates Gate .75 .75
641 A138 50p Central Police Station 1.25 1.25
642 A138 £1 Prince Edward's Gate 2.25 2.25
643 A138 £3 Lighthouse 7.50 7.50
644 A138 £5 Coat of arms, keys to fortress, vert. 11.00 11.00
Nos. 631-644 (14) 26.00 26.00

Nos. 631, 635, 637, 639, 642-643 are vert.

Portions of the design on No. 644 were applied by a thermographic process producing a shiny, raised effect.

Issued: £5, 6/6/94; others, 6/28/93.

See Nos. 686-693.

Anniversaries — A139

1993, Sept. 21 Litho. *Perf. 13*

645 A139 21p Coins .60 .50
646 A139 24p Jet, biplane fighters .80 .65
647 A139 34p Garrison Library 1.10 *1.50*
648 A139 49p Churchill, searchlights 1.60 *2.25*
Nos. 645-648 (4) 4.10 *4.90*

First decimal coins, 25th anniv. Royal Air Force, 75th anniv. Garrison Library, bicent. Churchill's visit to Gibraltar, 50th anniv.

Christmas
A140

Mice and: 5p, Christmas tree. 24p, Christmas cracker. 44p, Singing carols. 49p, Snowman.

1993, Nov. 16 Litho. *Perf. 13½*

649 A140 5p multicolored .20 .20
650 A140 24p multicolored .90 .65
651 A140 44p multicolored 1.75 1.60
652 A140 49p multicolored 1.90 2.00
Nos. 649-652 (4) 4.75 4.45

European Discoveries — A141

Europa: No. 653, Atoms exploding, Lord Penney (1909-91). No. 654, Chemistry flasks, polonium, radium, Marie Curie. No. 655, Diesel engine, Rudolf Diesel. No. 656, Telescope, Galileo.

1994, Mar. 1 Litho. *Perf. 13½*

653 A141 24p multicolored 1.00 1.00
654 A141 24p multicolored 1.00 1.00
a. Pair, #653-654 2.00 2.00
655 A141 34p multicolored 1.25 *1.40*
656 A141 34p multicolored 1.25 *1.40*
a. Pair, #655-656 2.50 *2.75*
Nos. 653-656 (4) 4.50 *4.80*

1994 World Cup Soccer Championships, US — A142

26p, FIFA cup, US map, flag. 39p, Players, US map as playing field. 49p, Leg action.

1994, Apr. 19 Litho. *Perf. 13½*

657 A142 26p multi .85 .45
658 A142 39p multi 1.40 1.40
659 A142 49p multi, vert. 1.75 *2.00*
Nos. 657-659 (3) 4.00 *3.85*

Souvenir Sheet

World War II Warships Type of 1993

Designs: a, 5p, HMS Penelope. b, 25p, HMS Warspite. c, 44p, USS McLanahan. d, 49p, HNLMS Isaac Sweers.

1994, June 6 Litho. *Perf. 13½x13*

660 A137 Sheet of 4, #a.-d. 5.00 *5.50*

Souvenir Sheet

PHILAKOREA '94 — A143

1994, Aug. 16 Litho. *Perf. 13*

661 A143 £1.05 multicolored 3.75 3.75

Marine Life — A144

1994, Sept. 27 Litho. *Perf. 14*

662 A144 21p Golden star coral .65 .65
663 A144 24p Star fish .75 .75
664 A144 34p Gorgonian sea fan 1.00 1.00
665 A144 49p Turkish wrasse 1.50 1.50
Nos. 662-665 (4) 3.90 3.90

Intl. Olympic Committee, Cent. — A145

1994, Nov. 22 Litho. *Perf. 14*

666 A145 49p Discus 1.50 *1.60*
667 A145 54p Javelin 1.75 1.75

Christmas Songbirds
A146

1994, Nov. 22 *Perf. 13½*

668 A146 5p Great tit, vert. .20 .20
669 A146 24p Robin .75 .75
670 A146 34p Blue tit 1.00 *1.10*
671 A146 54p Goldfinch, vert. 1.60 *1.75*
Nos. 668-671 (4) 3.55 3.80

New Members in European Union
A147

Flags: 24p, Austria. 26p, Finland. 34p, Sweden. 49p, Sweden, Finland, Austria, emblem of European Union.

1995, Jan. 3 Litho. *Perf. 14*

672 A147	24p multicolored	.75	.75
673 A147	26p multicolored	.85	.85
674 A147	34p multicolored	1.00	*1.10*
675 A147	49p multicolored	1.50	*1.60*
	Nos. 672-675 (4)	4.10	*4.30*

Peace & Freedom — A148

Europa: No. 676, Cross, barbed wire, text. No. 677, Rainbow, dove, hands. No. 678, Shackles, text. No. 679, Doves, hands.

1995, Feb. 28 Litho. *Perf. 13½*

676	24p multicolored	.70	*.75*
677	24p multicolored	.70	*.75*
a.	A148 Pair, #676-677	1.40	*1.60*
678	34p multicolored	1.00	*1.10*
679	34p multicolored	1.00	*1.10*
a.	A148 Pair, #678-679	2.00	*2.40*
	Nos. 676-679 (4)	3.40	*3.70*

Island Games — A149

1995, May 8 Litho. *Perf. 14x13½*

680 A149	24p Sailing	.65	*.70*
681 A149	44p Running	1.40	*1.50*
682 A149	49p Swimming	1.50	*1.60*
	Nos. 680-682 (3)	3.55	*3.80*
680a	Booklet pane of 3	2.00	
681a	Booklet pane of 3	4.50	
682a	Booklet pane of 3	5.00	
682b	Bklt. pane, 1 ea. #680-682	3.25	
	Commemorative booklet, 1 each #680a-682b	15.00	

Souvenir Sheet

VE Day, 50th Anniv. — A150

Illustration reduced.

1995, May 8

683 A150	£1.05 multicolored	3.25	*3.50*

World War II Warships Type of 1993
Souvenir Sheet

Designs: a, 5p, HMS Calpe. b, 24p, HMS Victorious. c, 44p, USS Weehawken. d, 49p, FFS Savorgnan de Brazza.

1995, June 6 Litho. *Perf. 13½x14*

684 A137	Sheet of 4, #a.-d.	3.75	*4.00*

Singapore '95 — A151

Orchids: a, 22p, Bee. b, 23p, Brown bee. c, 24p, Pyramidal. d, 25p, Mirror. e, 26p, Sawfly.

1995, Sept. 1 Litho. *Perf. 14x14½*

685 A151	Strip of 5, #a.-e.	3.50	*3.75*

Architectural Heritage Type of 1993

1995, Sept. 1 Litho. *Perf. 13*

686 A138	6p House of Assembly	.20	.20
687 A138	7p Bleak House	.20	.20
688 A138	8p Bust of Gen. Eliott	.25	.25
689 A138	9p Supreme Court Bldg.	.30	.30
690 A138	20p Convent	.60	.60
691 A138	30p St. Bernard's Hospital	.85	.85
692 A138	40p City Hall	1.10	1.10
693 A138	£2 Church of Sacred Heart of Jesus	5.50	5.50
	Nos. 686-693 (8)	9.00	9.00

Nos. 686, 688, 691, 693 are vert.

UN, 50th Anniv. A152

1995, Oct. 24 Litho. *Perf. 13½*

694 A152	34p shown	1.10	1.10
695 A152	49p Peace dove	1.50	1.50

Miniature Sheets of 4 + 4 Labels

Motion Pictures, Cent. — A153

Designs: No. 696: a, Ingrid Bergman. b, Vittorio De Sica. c, Marlene Dietrich. d, Laurence Olivier.

No. 697: a, 38p, Audrey Hepburn. b, 25p, Romy Schneider. c, 28p, Yves Montand. d, 5p, Marilyn Monroe.

1995, Nov. 13 Litho. *Perf. 14½x14*

696 A153	24p #a.-d.	3.00	3.00
697 A153	#a.-d.	3.00	3.00

Christmas A154

Designs: 5p, Santa Claus. 24p, Sack of toys. 34p, Reindeer. 54p, Santa with sleigh, reindeer flying over rooftops.

1995, Nov. 27 *Perf. 14*

698 A154	5p multicolored	.20	.20
699 A154	24p multicolored	.75	.75
700 A154	34p multicolored	1.10	1.10
701 A154	54p multicolored	1.75	1.75
	Nos. 698-701 (4)	3.80	3.80

Miniature Sheet

Puppies A155

#702: a, 5p, Shih tzu. b, 21p, Dalmatian. c, Cocker spaniel. d, 25p, West Highland white terrier. e, 34p, Labrador. f, 35p, Boxer.

1996, Jan. 24 Litho. *Perf. 14*

702 A155	Sheet of 6, #a.-f.	3.75	3.75

No. 702 is a continuous design.

Women of the British Royal Family A156

1996, Feb. 9 Litho. *Perf. 13½*

703 A156	24p Princess Anne	.75	.75
704 A156	24p Princess Diana	.75	.75
705 A156	34p Queen Mother	1.10	1.10
706 A156	34p Queen Elizabeth II	1.10	1.10
	Nos. 703-706 (4)	3.70	3.70

Europa.

European Soccer — A157

Team members in action scenes: 21p, West Germany, 1980. 24p, France, 1964. 34p, Holland, 1988. £1.20, Denmark, 1992.

1996, Apr. 2 Litho. *Perf. 13*

707 A157	21p multicolored	.60	.60
708 A157	24p multicolored	.70	.70
709 A157	34p multicolored	.95	.95
710 A157	£1.20 multicolored	3.50	3.50
a.	Souvenir sheet, Nos. 707-710	5.75	5.75
	Nos. 707-710 (4)	5.75	5.75

Modern Olympic Games, Cent. A158

1996, May 2 Litho. *Perf. 13½*

711 A158	34p Ancient athletes	1.00	1.00
712 A158	49p Athletes, 1896	1.40	1.40
713 A158	£1.05 Athletes, 1990s	3.00	3.00
	Nos. 711-713 (3)	5.40	5.40

World War II Type of 1993
Souvenir Sheet

a, 5p, HMS Starling. b, 25p, HMS Royalist. c, 49p, USS Philadelphia. d, 54p, HMCS Prescott.

1996, June 8 Litho. *Perf. 13½x14*

714 A137	Sheet of 4, #a.-d.	4.25	4.25

UNICEF, 50th Anniv. A159

a, 21p, Girl, boy. b, 24p, Three children. c, 49p, Three children, diff. d, 54p, Girl, boy, diff.

1996, June 8 *Perf. 13½x13*

715 A159	Strip of 4, #a.-d.	4.50	4.50

World Wildlife Fund A160

Red kite: a, In flight. b, One adult. c, One on rock, one in flight. d, Adults, young in nest.

1996, July 12 Litho. *Perf. 14½*

716 A160	34p Block or strip of 4, #a.-d.	4.25	4.25

Christmas Images Formed with "Lego" Blocks — A161

1996, Nov. 27 Litho. *Perf. 14*

717 A161	5p Pudding	.20	.20
718 A161	21p Snowman	.70	.70
719 A161	24p Present	.80	.80
720 A161	34p Santa Claus	1.10	1.10
721 A161	54p Candle	1.75	1.75
	Nos. 717-721 (5)	4.55	4.55

Sailing Ship "Mary Celeste" — A162

Europa: No. 722, "Mary Celeste" in rough seas. No. 723, Men on board ship. No. 724, Boat approaching "Mary Celeste." No. 725, In full sail.

1997, Feb. 12 Litho. *Perf. 14*

722 A162	28p multicolored	.95	.95
723 A162	28p multicolored	.95	.95
724 A162	30p multicolored	1.00	1.00
725 A162	30p multicolored	1.00	1.00
	Nos. 722-725 (4)	3.90	3.90

Kittens A163

Designs: a, 5p, Silver tabby American shorthair. b, 24p, "Rumpy" Manx red tabby. c, 26p, Blue point Birmans. d, 28p, Red self longhair. e, 30p, British shorthair, tortoiseshell & white. f, 35p, British bicolor shorthairs.

1997, Feb. 12

726 A163	Sheet of 6, #a.-f.	5.00	5.00
g.	Bklt. pane of 3, #726a, 726c, 726e	2.00	
h.	Bklt. pane of 3, #726b, 726c, 726d	2.60	
i.	Bklt. pane of 4, #726a, 726b, 726e, 726f	3.25	
j.	Bklt. pane of 4, #726c, 726d, 726e, 726f	4.00	
k.	Booklet pane, #726	5.00	
	Complete booklet, #726g-726k	17.00	

Hong Kong '97. No. 726k is rouletted at left and does not have Hong Kong '97 emblem and inscription in bottom selvage.

Gibraltar 23p

Butterflies — A164

Designs: 23p, Anthocharis belia euphenoides. 26p, Charaxes jasius. 30p, Vanessa cardui. £1.20, Iphiclides podalirius.

1997, Apr. 7 Litho. *Perf. 14x13½*

728 A164	23p multicolored	.75	.75
729 A164	26p multicolored	.85	.85
730 A164	30p multicolored	1.00	1.00
731 A164	£1.20 multicolored	4.00	4.00
a.	Souvenir sheet of 4, #728-731	6.60	6.60
	Nos. 728-731 (4)	6.60	6.60

Warships Type of 1993

a, 24p, HMS Enterprise. b, 26p, HMS Cleopatra. c, 38p, USS Iowa. d, 50p, Polish Warship Orkan.

1997, June 9 Litho. *Perf. 13½*

732 A137	Sheet of 4, #a.-d.	4.50	4.50

Queen Elizabeth II and Prince Philip, 50th Wedding Anniv. — A165

Designs: £1.20, Prince Philip driving a four-in-hand, Queen beside him. £1.40, Queen, Prince Philip at Royal Ascot, Queen "Trooping the Color."

1997, July 10 Litho. *Perf. 14x13½*

733 A165 £1.20 multicolored 4.00 4.00
734 A165 £1.40 multicolored 4.50 4.50
a. Pair, #733-734 8.50 8.50

1997 Dior Fashion Designs, by John Galliano — A166

30p, Long black dress, hat. 35p, Mini skirt, lace top. 50p, Formal gown. 62p, Suit, hat. £1.20, Formal gown, diff.

1997, Sept. 9 Litho. *Perf. 13½x13*

735 A166 30p multicolored 1.00 1.00
736 A166 35p multicolored 1.25 1.25
737 A166 50p multicolored 1.75 1.75
a. Pair, #735, 737 2.75 2.75
738 A166 62p multicolored 2.00 2.00
a. Pair, #736, 738 3.25 3.25
Nos. 735-738 (4) 6.00 6.00

Souvenir Sheet

739 A166 £1.20 multicolored 4.00 4.00

Christmas A167

Stained glass windows: 5p, Our Lady and St. Bernard. 26p, The Epiphany of the Lord. 38p, St. Joseph holding Jesus. 50p, The Holy Family. 62p, The Miraculous Medal Madonna.

1997, Nov. 18 Litho. *Perf. 13½*

740 A167 5p multicolored .20 .20
741 A167 26p multicolored .90 .90
742 A167 38p multicolored 1.25 1.25
743 A167 50p multicolored 1.75 1.75
744 A167 62p multicolored 2.00 2.00
Nos. 740-744 (5) 6.10 6.10

A168

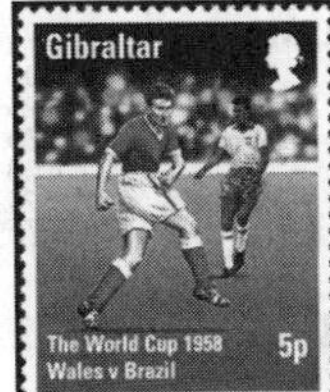

A169

1997, Dec. 15 Litho. *Perf. 13*

745 A168 26p multicolored .90 .90

Sir Joshua Hassan (1915-97), government leader.

1998, Jan. 23

Scenes from previous World Cup Championships: 5p, Wales v. Brazil, 1958. 26p, N. Ireland v. France, 1958. 38p, Scotland v. Holland, 1978. £1.20, England v. W. Germany, 1966.

746 A169 5p multicolored .25 .25
747 A169 26p multicolored .95 .95
748 A169 38p multicolored 1.25 1.25
749 A169 £1.20 multicolored 4.00 4.00
a. Souvenir sheet, #746-749 6.50 6.50
Nos. 746-749 (4) 6.45 6.45

1998 World Cup Soccer Championships, France.

Diana, Princess of Wales (1961-97)
Common Design Type

Various portraits: a, 26p, Wearing black & white outfit. b, 26p, Wearing pink & white outfit. c, 38p, In black dress. d, 38p, In blue & gold jacket.

1998, Mar. 31 Litho. *Perf. 14½x14*

754 CD355 Sheet of 4, #a.-d. 5.00 5.00

The 20p surtax from international sales was donated to the Princess Diana Memorial Fund and the surtax from national sales was donated to a designated local charity.

Royal Air Force, 80th Anniv.
Common Design Type of 1993 Re-inscribed

Designs: 24p, Saro London. 26p, Fairey Fox. 38p, Handley Page Halifax GR.VI. 50p, Hawker Siddeley Buccaneer S.2B.

No. 759: a, 24p, Sopwith 1½ Strutter. b, 26p, Bristol M.1B. c, 38p, Supermarine Spitfire XII. d, 50p, Avro York.

1998, Apr. 1 *Perf. 14*

755 CD350 24p multicolored .80 .80
756 CD350 26p multicolored .85 .85
757 CD350 38p multicolored 1.25 1.25
758 CD350 50p multicolored 1.60 1.60
Nos. 755-758 (4) 4.50 4.50

Souvenir Sheet of 4

759 CD350 #a.-d. 4.50 4.50

Europa — A170

Costumes worn by Miss Gibraltar for National Day: No. 760, Military style. No. 761, Long skirt, long-sleeved top. No. 762, Short skirt, long cape. No. 763, Black lace scarf, ruffled petticoat.

1998, May 22 Litho. *Perf. 13*

760 A170 26p multicolored .85 .85
761 A170 26p multicolored .85 .85
762 A170 38p multicolored 1.25 1.25
763 A170 38p multicolored 1.25 1.25
Nos. 760-763 (4) 4.20 4.20

UNESCO 1998 Intl. Year of the Ocean A171

Marine life: a, 5p, Striped dolphin. b, 26p, Killer whale, vert. c, £1.20, Blue whale. d, 5p, Common dolphin, vert.

1998, May 22 *Perf. 14*

764 A171 Sheet of 4, #a.-d. 5.00 5.00

Italia '98 and Portugal '98.

Battle of the Nile — A172

1998, Aug. 1 Litho. *Perf. 13½*

765 A172 12p Nileus .40 .40
766 A172 26p Lord Nelson .85 .85
a. Booklet pane of 1 .85
767 A172 28p Frances Nisbet .90 .90
a. Bklt. pane, #765-767 2.25
768 A172 35p HMS Vanguard 1.10 1.10

Size: 45x27mm

769 A172 50p Battle of the Nile 1.60 1.60
a. Bklt. pane, #768-769, 2 #768 4.75
b. Bklt. pane, #766, 768-769 3.75
c. Bklt. pane, #765-769 5.00
Complete booklet, #766a, 767a, 769a-769c 16.50
Nos. 765-769 (5) 4.85 4.85

Quotations From Famous People A173

#770, "Love comforts like sunshine after rain," Shakespeare. #771, "The price of greatness is responsibility," Churchill. #772, "Hate the sin, love the sinner," Gandhi. #773, "Imagination is more important than knowledge," Einstein.

1998, Oct. 6 Litho. *Perf. 14½*

770 A173 26p multicolored .85 .85
771 A173 26p multicolored .85 .85
772 A173 38p multicolored 1.25 1.25
773 A173 38p multicolored 1.25 1.25
Nos. 770-773 (4) 4.20 4.20

Nos. 770-773 were each printed in sheets of 6 with se-tenant labels.

A174 A175

1998, Nov. 10 Litho. *Perf. 13*

774 A174 5p Nativity .20 .20
775 A174 26p Star over manger .30 .30
776 A174 30p Balthasar .35 .35
777 A174 35p Melchoir .45 .45
778 A174 50p Caspar .60 .60
Nos. 774-778 (5) 1.90 1.90

Christmas.

1999, Mar. 4 Litho. *Perf. 13½*

779 A175 1p claret .20 .20
780 A175 2p brown .20 .20
781 A175 4p blue .20 .20
782 A175 5p green .20 .20
783 A175 10p brown orange .35 .35
784 A175 12p red .40 .40
785 A175 20p blue green .70 .70
786 A175 28p lilac rose .95 .95
787 A175 30p vermilion 1.00 1.00
788 A175 40p gray olive 1.40 1.40
789 A175 42p slate 1.50 1.50

Size: 22½x28mm
Perf. 14½

790 A175 50p olive bister 1.75 1.75
791 A175 £1 black 3.50 3.50
792 A175 £3 ultramarine 10.00 10.00

Self-Adhesive
Die Cut Perf. 9x9½

793 A175 1st vermilion .90 .90
Nos. 779-793 (15) 23.25 23.25

No. 793 was valued at 26p on day of issue.

Nature Reserves — A176

1999, Mar. 4 *Perf. 13½x13*

794 A176 30p Barbary macaque 1.00 1.00
795 A176 30p Dartford warbler 1.00 1.00
796 A176 42p Kingfisher 1.40 1.40
797 A176 42p Dusky perch 1.40 1.40
Nos. 794-797 (4) 4.80 4.80

Europa.

Maritime Heritage — A177

Designs: 5p, Roman Anchorage. 30p, Medieval galley house. 42p, British relief ships. £1.20, HMS Berwick.

1999, Mar. 19 *Perf. 12½*

798 A177 5p multicolored .20 .20
799 A177 30p multicolored 1.00 1.00
800 A177 42p multicolored 1.40 1.40
801 A177 £1.20 multicolored 4.00 4.00
a. Souvenir sheet, #798-801 6.60 6.60
Nos. 798-801 (4) 6.60 6.60

John Lennon (1940-80) A178

Portraits: 20p, With flower over one eye. 30p, Black and white photo. 40p, Wearing glasses.

No. 805, Holding marriage license in front of Rock of Gibraltar. No. 806, Standing in front of airplane.

1999, Mar. 20 *Perf. 13*

802 A178 20p multicolored .70 .70
803 A178 30p multicolored 1.00 1.00
804 A178 40p multicolored 1.40 1.40
Nos. 802-804 (3) 3.10 3.10

Souvenir Sheets

805 A178 £1 multicolored 3.50 3.50
806 A178 £1 multicolored 3.50 3.50

UPU, 125th Anniv. — A179

1999, June 7 Litho. *Perf. 12½*

807 A179 5p Postal van .20 .20
808 A179 30p Space station 1.00 1.00

Fighter Planes and Raptors A180

Designs: No. 809, RAF Eurofighter 2000 Typhoon. No. 810, RAF F3 Tornado. No. 811, RAF GR7 Harrier II. No. 812, Lesser kestrel. No. 813, Peregrine falcon. No. 814, Kestrel.

1999, June 7 ***Perf. 13x13¼***

809 A180 30p multicolored 1.00 1.00
810 A180 30p multicolored 1.00 1.00
811 A180 30p multicolored 1.00 1.00
a. Sheet of 3, #809-811 3.00 3.00
812 A180 42p multicolored 1.40 1.40
a. Pair, #809, 812 2.40 2.40
813 A180 42p multicolored 1.40 1.40
a. Pair, #810, 813 2.40 2.40
814 A180 42p multicolored 1.40 1.40
a. Pair, #811, 814 2.40 2.40
b. Sheet of 3, #812-814 7.25 7.25

See Nos. 851-853.

Wedding of Prince Edward and Sophie Rhys-Jones A181

Perf. 13x13¼, 13¼x13

1999, June 19 **Litho.**

815 A181 30p shown 1.00 1.00
816 A181 42p Couple, vert. 1.40 1.40

Sports in Gibraltar, Cent. — A182

1999, July 2 ***Perf. 13***

817 A182 30p Soccer 1.00 1.00
818 A182 42p Rowing 1.40 1.40
819 A182 £1.20 Cricket 4.00 4.00
Nos. 817-819 (3) 6.40 6.40

Wedding of Prince Edward to Sophie Rhys-Jones A183

Perf. 13x13¼, 13¼x13

1999, Oct. 11 **Litho.**

820 A183 54p shown 1.75 1.75
821 A183 66p Couple standing, vert. 2.25 2.25

Christmas and New Year's Greetings A184

Designs: No. 822, "Happy Christmas," Santa, sleigh. No. 823, "Season's Greetings." No. 824, "Happy Millennium." No. 825, "Happy Christmas," Santa, reindeer. 42p, "Yo ho ho." 54p, Santa, tree, fireplace.

1999, Nov. 11 **Litho.** ***Perf. 14***

822 A184 5p multicolored .20 .20
823 A184 5p multicolored .20 .20
824 A184 30p multicolored 1.00 1.00
825 A184 30p multicolored 1.00 1.00
826 A184 42p multicolored 1.40 1.40
827 A184 54p multicolored 1.75 1.75
Nos. 822-827 (6) 5.55 5.55

Stampin' the Future Children's Stamp Design Contest Winners A185

Artwork by: 30p, Colin Grech. 42p, Kim Barea. 54p, Stephan Williamson-Fa. 66p, Michael Podesta.

2000. Jan. 28 **Litho.** ***Perf. 14½x14***

828 A185 30p multi 1.00 1.00
829 A185 42p multi 1.40 1.40
830 A185 54p multi 1.75 1.75
831 A185 66p multi 2.10 2.10
a. Block or strip of 4, #828-831 6.25 6.25

European Soccer — A186

2000, Apr. 17 **Litho.** ***Perf. 12½***

832 A186 30p France .90 .90
833 A186 30p Holland .90 .90
834 A186 42p Denmark 1.25 1.25
835 A186 42p Germany 1.25 1.25
a. Souvenir sheet, #832-835 4.50 4.50
836 A186 54p England 1.60 1.60
a. Souvenir sheet of 4 6.50 6.50
Nos. 832-836 (5) 5.90 5.90

The Stamp Show 2000, London (#836a).

Europa — A187

2000, Apr. 17 ***Perf. 13¼x13***

837 A187 30p Fountain .90 .90
838 A187 40p Hands 1.10 1.10
839 A187 42p Airplane 1.25 1.25
840 A187 54p Rainbow 1.60 1.60
Nos. 837-840 (4) 4.85 4.85

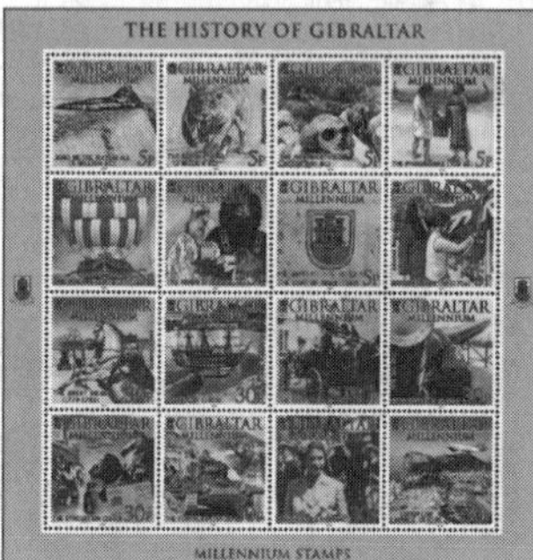

Millennium — A188

History of Gibraltar: a, 3000-meter waterfall. b, The sandy plains. c, The Neanderthals. d, The Phoenicians. e, The Romans. f, The Arabs. g, Coat of arms, 1502. h, British Gibraltar. i, The great siege. j, Trafalgar. k, The city. l, Fortifications. m, The evacuation. n, The fortress. o, Queen Elizabeth II. p, European finance center.

Illustration reduced.

2000, May 9 ***Perf. 14***

841 A188 Sheet of 16 8.50 8.50
a.-h. 5p Any single .20 .20
i.-p. 30p Any single .90 .90
q. Souvenir booklet 22.50

No. 841q contains a pane of 2 of each of Nos. 841a-841j and a pane of 3 of each of Nos. 841k-841p.

Prince William, 18th Birthday — A189

Designs: 30p, With Princess Diana. 42p, As child. 54p, With Prince Charles. 66p, In suit.

2000, June 21 **Litho.** ***Perf. 12½***

842 A189 30p multi .90 .90
843 A189 42p multi 1.25 1.25
844 A189 54p multi 1.60 1.60
845 A189 66p multi 2.00 2.00
a. Souvenir sheet, #842-845 5.75 5.75
Nos. 842-845 (4) 5.75 5.75

Queen Mother, 100th Birthday — A190

Designs: 30p, As young woman. 42p, With King George VI. 54p, With blue hat. 66p, With orange hat.

2000, Aug. 4

846 A190 30p multi .90 .90
847 A190 42p multi 1.25 1.25
848 A190 54p multi 1.60 1.60
849 A190 66p multi 2.00 2.00
a. Souvenir sheet, #846-849 5.75 5.75
Nos. 846-849 (4) 5.75 5.75

Moorish Castle A191

Photo. & Engr.

2000, Sept. 15 ***Perf. 11½x11¾***

850 A191 £5 multi 15.00 15.00

Fighter Planes and Raptors Type

No. 851: a, RAF "Gibraltar" Supermarine Spitfire. b, Male merlin.
No. 852: a, RAF "City of Lincoln" Avro Lancaster B1-3. b, Bonelli's eagle.
No. 853: a, RAF Hawker Hurricane MK IIC. b, Female merlin.

2000, Sept. 15 **Litho.** ***Perf. 14½x14***

851 Pair 2.10 2.10
a. A180 30p multi .85 .85
b. A180 42p multi 1.25 1.25
852 Pair 2.10 2.10
a. A180 30p multi .85 .85
b. A180 42p multi 1.25 1.25
853 Pair 2.10 2.10
a. A180 30p multi .85 .85
b. A180 42p multi 1.25 1.25
c. Souvenir sheet, #851a, 852a, 853a 2.60 2.60
d. Souvenir sheet, #851b, 852b, 853b 3.75 3.75
Nos. 851-853 (3) 6.30 6.30

Christmas A192

5p, Baby Jesus. No. 855, 30p, Joseph, Mary, donkey. No. 856, 30p, Mary, Jesus. 40p, Joseph, Mary, innkeeper. 42p, Holy Family, donkey. 54p, Holy Family, Magi.

2000, Nov. 13 ***Perf. 14***

854-859 A192 Set of 6 6.00 6.00

Queen Victoria (1819-1901) A193

Designs: 30p, On wedding day. 42p, Portrait. 54p, In carriage. 66p, Jubilee portrait.

2001, Jan. 22 ***Perf. 12¾***

860-863 A193 Set of 4 5.75 5.75

New Year 2001 (Year of the Snake) — A194

Snakes: No. 864, 5p, Grass. No. 865, 5p, Ladder. No. 866, 5p, Montpelier. No. 867, 30p, Viperine. No. 868, 30p, Southern smooth. No. 869, 30p, False smooth. 66p, Horseshoe whip.

2001, Feb. 1 **Litho.** ***Perf. 13¾***

864-870 A194 Set of 7 5.00 5.00
870a Souvenir sheet, #864-870 5.00 5.00

Size of No. 870: 31x62mm. Hong Kong 2001 Stamp Exhibition (No. 870a).

Europa — A195

Designs: 30p, Long-snouted seahorse. 40p, Snapdragon. 42p, Yellow-legged gull. 54p, Goldfish.

2001, Feb. 1 ***Perf. 13¼x13***

871-874 A195 Set of 4 5.00 5.00

Queen Elizabeth II, 75th Birthday A196

Designs: No. 875, 30p, As child. No. 876, 30p, As young woman. No. 877, 42p, In wedding dress. No. 878, 42p, At coronation. 54p, Wearing hat.
£2, In blue dress.

2001, Apr. 21 **Litho.** ***Perf. 14***

875-879 A196 Set of 5 5.50 5.50

Souvenir Sheet

Perf. 13¾

880 A196 £2 multi 5.75 5.75

No. 880 contains one 35x48mm stamp.

Gibraltar Chronicle, Bicent. — A197

Designs: 30p, Battle of Trafalgar. 42p, Invention of the telephone. 54p, The end of World War II. 66p, First man on the Moon.

2001, May 21 ***Perf. 14x14½***

881-884 A197 Set of 4 5.50 5.50

Queen Type of 1999

2001, June 1 **Litho.** ***Perf. 14x14¼***

Size: 22x28mm

885 A175 £1.20 carmine 3.50 3.50
886 A175 £1.40 blue 4.00 4.00

Fighter Planes and Raptors Type of 1999

No. 887: a, 40p, RAF Jaguar GR1B. b, 40p, Hobby.
No. 888: a, 40p, Royal Navy Sea Harrier FA MK 2. b, 40p, Marsh harrier.
No. 889: a, 40p, RAF Hawk T MK 1. b, 40p, Sparrowhawk.

2001, Sept. 3 Litho. *Perf. 14½x14*
Pairs, #a-b

887-889 A180 Set of 3 7.00 7.00
889c Souvenir sheet, #887a, 888a, 889a 3.50 3.50
889d Souvenir sheet, #887b, 888b, 889b 3.50 3.50

Christmas A198

Snoopy, from Peanuts comic strip: 5p, In Santa Claus suit ringing bell, Woodstock. 30p, Charlie Brown, Christmas tree. 40p, Wreath. 42p, In Santa Claus suit carrying cookies, Woodstock. 54p, On dog house.

2001, Nov. 12 *Perf. 14*
890-894 A198 Set of 5 5.00 5.00
894a Souvenir sheet, #890-894 5.00 5.00

Souvenir Sheet

Introduction of Euro Coinage to Europe — A199

Coins in denominations of: a, 5p, 1 cent. b, 12p, 2 cents. c, 30p, 5 cents. d, 35p, 10 cents. e, 40p, 20 cents. f, 42p, 50 cents. g, 54p, 1 euro. h, 66p, 2 euro.

2002, Jan. 1 Litho. *Perf. 13¼x13*
895 A199 Sheet of 8, #a-h 8.00 8.00

A clear varnish was applied by a thermographic process producing a shiny, raised effect.

Reign Of Queen Elizabeth II, 50th Anniv. Issue
Common Design Type

Designs: No. 896, 30p, Princess Elizabeth in field, 1942. No. 897, 30p, Wearing tiara, 1961. No. 898, 30p, With Princess Margaret, microphones. No. 899, 30p, Wearing hat, 1993. 75p, 1955 portrait by Annigoni (38x50mm).

Perf. 14¼x14½, 13¾ (75p)
2002, Feb. 6 Litho. Wmk. 373
896-900 CD360 Set of 5 5.75 5.75
a. Souvenir sheet, #896-900 5.75 5.75

Europa — A200

Famous clowns: 30p, Joseph Grimaldi (1778-1831). 40p, Karl Adrien Wettach (1880-1959). 42p, Nicholai Polakovs (1900-74). 54p, Hubert Jean Charles Cairoli (1910-80).

Perf. 13¼x13
2002, Mar. 4 Litho. Unwmk.
901-904 A200 Set of 4 4.75 4.75

Bobby Moore, English Soccer Player — A201

Moore in 1966: 30p, Holding up World Cup. 42p, Kissing World Cup. 54p, With Queen Elizabeth II. 66p, In action.

Perf. 13¼x13
2002, May 1 Litho. Unwmk.
905-908 A201 Set of 4 5.75 5.75
a. Souvenir sheet, #905-908 5.75 5.75

Wildlife A202

Designs: No. 909, 30p, Red fox. No. 910, 30p, Barbary macaque, vert. 40p, White tooth shrew. £1, Rabbit, vert.

Perf. 14¼x14, 14x14¼
2002, June 6 Litho. Unwmk.
909-912 A202 Set of 4 6.00 6.00
a. Souvenir sheet, #909-912 6.00 6.00

Prince Harry, 18th Birthday — A203

Designs: 30p, As child in Princess Diana's arms. 42p, Waving. 54p, Wearing baseball cap. 66p, In suit and tie.

2002, Sept. 15 Litho. *Perf. 12½*
913-916 A203 Set of 4 6.00 6.00
a. Souvenir sheet, #913-916 6.00 6.00

Rock of Gibraltar — A204

View of Rock from: a, North. b, South. c, East (46x38mm). d, West (46x38mm).

2002, Sept. 15 Litho. *Perf. 13¼x13*
917 Horiz. strip of 4 8.00 8.00
a.-b. A204 30p Either single .95 .95
c.-d. A204 £1 Either single 3.00 3.00

Particles of the Rock of Gibraltar were applied to portions of the designs by a thermographic process.

Christmas — A205

Creche scenes from: 5p, Cathedral of St. Mary the Crowned. 30p, St. Joseph's Parish Church. 40p, St. Theresa's Parish Church. 42p, Our Lady of Sorrows Church, Catalan Bay. 52p, St. Bernard's Church. 54p, Cathedral of the Holy Trinity.

2002, Nov. 13 *Perf. 13*
918-923 A205 Set of 6 7.00 7.00

POSTAGE DUE STAMPS

Catalogue values for unused stamps in this section are for Never Hinged items.

D1 D2

Perf. 14
1956, Dec. 1 Wmk. 4 Typo.
Chalky Paper

J1 D1 1p green 2.75 *3.00*
J2 D1 2p brown 4.00 *5.00*
J3 D1 4p ultramarine 5.00 *5.50*
Nos. J1-J3 (3) 11.75 *13.50*

"p" instead of "d"
Perf. 17½x18
1971, Feb. 15 Typo. Wmk. 314
Chalky Paper

J4 D1 ½p green .45 *.55*
J5 D1 1p dark brown .45 *.50*
J6 D1 2p dark blue .55 *.55*
Nos. J4-J6 (3) 1.45 *1.60*

Perf. 14x13½
1976, Oct. 13 Litho. Wmk. 373

J7 D2 1p orange .20 .20
J8 D2 3p bright ultra .20 .20
J9 D2 5p vermilion .20 .20
J10 D2 7p bright red lilac .25 *.30*
J11 D2 10p gray .40 *.45*
J12 D2 20p green .75 *.80*
Nos. J7-J12 (6) 2.00 *2.15*

D3

D4

1984, July 2 *Perf. 14½x14*

J13 D3 1p black .20 .20
J14 D3 3p red .20 .20
J15 D3 5p blue .20 .20
J16 D3 10p sky blue .25 .25
J17 D3 25p lilac .65 .65
J18 D3 50p orange 1.25 1.25
J19 D3 £1 green 2.50 2.50
Nos. J13-J19 (7) 5.25 5.25

1996, Sept. 30 Litho. *Perf. 14½x14*

Landmarks: 1p, Water Port Gates. 10p, HM Dockyard. 25p, Military Hospital. 50p, Governor's Cottage. £1, Laguna. £2, Catalan Bay.

J20 D4 1p multicolored .20 .20
J21 D4 10p multicolored .30 .30
J22 D4 25p multicolored .75 .75
J23 D4 50p multicolored 1.50 1.50
J24 D4 £1 multicolored 3.00 3.00
J25 D4 £2 multicolored 6.25 6.25
Nos. J20-J25 (6) 12.00 12.00

Finches — D5

Designs: 5p, Greenfinch. 10p, Serin. 20p, Siskin. 50p, Linnet. £1, Chaffinch. £2, Goldfinch.

Perf. 13x13¼
2002, June 6 Litho. Unwmk.
J26-J31 D5 Set of 6 11.50 11.50

WAR TAX STAMP

No. 66 Overprinted

1918, Apr. Wmk. 3 *Perf. 14*
MR1 A14 ½p green .30 *.75*
a. Double overprint 750.00

GILBERT AND ELLICE ISLANDS

'gil-bərt ən,d, 'e-ləs 'ī-ləndz

LOCATION — Groups of islands in the Pacific Ocean northeast of Australia
GOVT. — British Crown Colony
AREA — 375 sq. mi.
POP. — 57,816 (est. 1973)
CAPITAL — Tarawa

The Gilbert group of which Butaritari, Tarawa and Tamana are the more important, is on the Equator. Ellice Islands, Phoenix Islands, Line Islands (Fanning, Washington and Christmas), and Ocean Island are included in the Colony. The islands were annexed by Great Britain in 1892 and formed into the Gilbert and Ellice Islands Colony in 1915 on request of the native governments.

The colony divided into the Gilbert Islands and Tuvalu, Jan. 1, 1976.

12 Pence = 1 Shilling
20 Shillings = 1 Pound
100 Cents = 1 Dollar (1966)

Catalogue values for unused stamps in this country are for Never Hinged items, beginning with Scott 52.

Stamps and Type of Fiji Overprinted in Black or Red

1911, Jan. 1 Wmk. 3 *Perf. 14*
Ordinary Paper

1 A22 ½p green 7.50 *27.50*
2 A22 1p carmine 32.50 35.00
a. Pair, one without overprint
3 A22 2p gray 7.50 *11.00*
4 A22 2½p ultramarine 15.00 *22.50*

Chalky Paper

5 A22 5p violet & ol grn 27.50 *50.00*
6 A22 6p violet 22.50 *40.00*
7 A22 1sh black, *green* 21.00 37.50
Nos. 1-7 (7) 133.50 *223.50*

Pandanus — A2

1911, Mar. Engr.
Ordinary Paper

8 A2 ½p green 3.50 *11.00*
9 A2 1p carmine 1.60 *5.25*
10 A2 2p gray 1.25 *5.25*
11 A2 2½p ultramarine 3.75 *8.25*
Nos. 8-11 (4) 10.10 *29.75*

King George V — A3

For description of Dies I and II, see back of this section of the Catalogue.

Die I

1912-24 Typo.

14 A3 ½p deep green .35 *3.50*
15 A3 1p carmine 2.00 *3.50*
a. 1p scarlet 3.50 *7.50*
16 A3 2p gray ('16) 13.50 *19.00*
17 A3 2½p ultra ('16) 1.60 *8.50*

Chalky Paper

18 A3 3p vio, *yel* ('19) 2.25 *6.50*
19 A3 4p blk & red, *yel* .70 *5.00*
20 A3 5p vio & ol grn 1.40 *5.50*
21 A3 6p vio & red vio 1.10 *5.75*
22 A3 1sh black, *green* 1.10 *4.25*
23 A3 2sh vio & ultra, *bl* 13.00 *22.50*
24 A3 2sh6p blk & red, *bl* 13.50 *19.00*
25 A3 5sh grn & red, *yel* 29.00 *47.50*

Die II

26 A3 £1 vio & blk, *red* ('24) 600.00 *1,400.*
Nos. 14-25 (12) 79.50 *150.50*

Die II

1921-27 Ordinary Paper Wmk. 4

27 A3 ½p green .75 *1.50*
28 A3 1p deep vio ('27) 1.25 *2.50*
29 A3 1½p scarlet ('24) 1.90 *3.50*
30 A3 2p gray 4.00 *12.50*

Chalky Paper

31 A3 10sh green & red, *emer* ('24) 175.00 *325.00*
Nos. 27-31 (5) 182.90 *345.00*

Common Design Types pictured following the introduction.

Silver Jubilee Issue
Common Design Type

1935, May 6 Engr. *Perf. 11x12*

33 CD301 1p black & ultra 2.00 *7.50*
34 CD301 1½p car & blue 1.50 *3.00*
35 CD301 3p ultra & brn 4.50 *9.50*
36 CD301 1sh brn vio & indigo 25.00 *20.00*
Nos. 33-36 (4) 33.00 *40.00*
Set, never hinged 57.50

Coronation Issue
Common Design Type

1937, May 12 *Perf. 13½x14*

37 CD302 1p dark purple .20 .20
38 CD302 1½p carmine .25 .25
39 CD302 3p bright ultra .45 .45
Nos. 37-39 (3) .90 .90
Set, never hinged 1.25

Great Frigate Bird — A4

Pandanus — A5

Designs: 1½p, Canoe crossing reef. 2p, Canoe and boat house. 2½p, Islander's house. 3p, Seascape. 5p, Ellice Islands canoe. 6p, Coconut trees. 1sh, Phosphate loading jetty, Ocean Island. 2sh, Cutter "Nimanoa." 2sh6p, Gilbert Islands canoe. 5sh, Coat of arms of colony.

Perf. 11½x11 (Nos. 40, 43, 50), 12½ (Type A5), 13½ (Nos. 42, 44, 45, 48)

1939, Jan. 14 Engr. Wmk. 4

40 A4 ½p dk grn & sl bl .20 *.60*
41 A5 1p dk vio & brt bl green .20 *1.25*
42 A4 1½p car & black .20 *.75*
43 A4 2p black & brn .25 *.85*
44 A4 2½p ol grn & blk .20 *.60*
45 A4 3p ultra & black .20 *.85*
a. Perf. 12 ('55) .25 *1.90*
46 A5 5p dk brn & ultra 2.10 1.00
47 A5 6p dl vio & olive .20 *.40*
48 A4 1sh gray bl & blk 2.25 1.50
a. Perf. 12 ('51) 2.25 *11.00*
49 A5 2sh red org & ultra 8.00 8.00
50 A4 2sh6p brt bl grn & bl 8.50 *12.00*
51 A5 5sh dp blue & red 9.00 *13.50*
Nos. 40-51 (12) 31.30 *41.30*
Set, never hinged 55.00

Catalogue values for unused stamps in this section, from this point to the end of the section, are for Never Hinged items.

Peace Issue
Common Design Type

1946, Dec. 16 *Perf. 13½x14*

52 CD303 1p deep magenta .20 .20
53 CD303 3p deep blue .25 .25

Silver Wedding Issue
Common Design Types

1949, Aug. 29 Photo. *Perf. 14x14½*

54 CD304 1p violet .20 .20

Engraved; Name Typographed

Perf. 11½x11

55 CD305 £1 red 19.00 *20.00*

UPU Issue
Common Design Types

Engr.; Name Typo. on 2p, 3p

1949, Oct. 1 *Perf. 13½, 11x11½*

56 CD306 1p rose violet .60 *.75*
57 CD307 2p gray black 3.00 1.90
58 CD308 3p indigo .75 *1.75*
59 CD309 1sh blue .75 *1.75*
Nos. 56-59 (4) 5.10 6.15

Coronation Issue
Common Design Type

1953, June 2 Engr. *Perf. 13½x13*

60 CD312 2p gray & black .75 2.00

Types of 1939-42 with Portrait of Queen Elizabeth II, and

Canoe Crossing Reef — A6

Perf. 11½x11 (Nos. 61, 63, 70), 12½ (Type A5), 12 (Nos. 64-65, 68, 72)

1956, Aug. 1

61 A4 ½p brt ultra & blk .20 *.40*
62 A5 1p violet & olive .25 .25
63 A4 2p dull pur & brt green .40 *.70*
64 A4 2½p green & black .30 .30
65 A4 3p dk car & black .35 .35
66 A5 5p red orange & brt ultra 3.50 1.50
67 A5 6p dk gray & red brown 1.00 .80
68 A4 1sh ol green & blk 1.50 .80
69 A5 2sh dk brown & brt ultra 6.00 3.75
70 A4 2sh6p dp ultra & rose red 9.00 4.25
71 A5 5sh green & blue 13.00 10.00
72 A6 10sh turq blue & blk 27.50 22.50
Nos. 61-72 (12) 63.00 45.60

See Nos. 84-85.

Loading Phosphate on Freighter A7

2½p, Original lump of phosphate. 1sh, Loading phosphate on truck, Ocean Island.

Wmk. 314

1960, May 1 Photo. *Perf. 12*

73 A7 2p rose lilac & green .70 *.80*
74 A7 2½p olive & black .70 *.80*
75 A7 1sh grnsh blue & blk .70 *.80*
Nos. 73-75 (3) 2.10 2.40

60th anniversary of the discovery of phosphate deposits at Ocean Island.

Freedom from Hunger Issue
Common Design Type

1963, June 4 *Perf. 14x14½*

76 CD314 10p ultramarine 2.00 .50

Red Cross Centenary Issue
Common Design Type

1963, Sept. 2 Litho. *Perf. 13*

77 CD315 2p black & red 1.00 .40
78 CD315 10p ultra & red 3.25 2.75

Plane and Fiji-Ellice-Gilbert Route — A8

Designs: 1sh, Eastern reef heron in flight, horiz. 3sh7p, Plane and Tarawa sailboat.

1964, July 20 *Perf. 11½x11, 11x11½*

79 A8 3p lt blue, bl & blk .60 .20
80 A8 1sh dk blue, bl & blk .75 .30
81 A8 3sh7p lt green, grn & blk 1.40 1.25
Nos. 79-81 (3) 2.75 1.75

Inauguration of air service between Fiji and Gilbert and Ellice Islands.

Queen Types of 1956

Perf. 11½x11, 12½

1964-65 Engr. Wmk. 314

84 A4 2p dull pur & brt green .90 1.50
85 A5 6p dk gray & red brown 1.75 1.75

Issue dates: 2p, Oct. 30. 6p, Apr. 1965.

ITU Issue
Common Design Type

1965, June 4 Litho. *Perf. 11x11½*

87 CD317 3p dp org & turq blue .20 .20
88 CD317 2sh6p grnsh bl & red lilac 1.25 1.25

Village Elder Blowing Conch and Meeting House (Maneaba) — A9

Designs: 1p, Ellice Islanders torch fishing. 2p, Gilbertese girl weaving frangipani garland. 3p, Gilbertese woman dancing The Ruoia. 4p, Gilbertese man dancing. 5p, Gilbertese woman drawing water. 6p, Ellice kosu dance. 7p, Fatele taua dance, Ellice men. 1sh, Gilbertese woman harvesting taro roots (babai). 1sh6p, Ellice man and woman dancing fatele toka. 2sh, Ellice Islanders pounding taro roots. 3sh7p, Gilbertese sitting dance, ruoia, horiz. 5sh, Gilbertese boys playing stick game, horiz. 10sh, Ellice men beating box-drum, horiz. £1, Coat of arms, horiz.

Perf. 12x11, 11x12

1965, Aug. 16 Litho. Wmk. 314

89 A9 ½p blue grn & multi .20 .20
90 A9 1p vio bl & multi .20 .20
91 A9 2p lt olive & multi .20 .20
92 A9 3p red & multi .20 .20
93 A9 4p purple & multi .20 .20
94 A9 5p car rose & multi .25 .20
95 A9 6p multicolored .25 .20
96 A9 7p brown & multi .35 .20
97 A9 1sh bl vio & multi .65 .20
98 A9 1sh6p yel & multi 1.25 .60
99 A9 2sh multicolored 1.25 1.10
100 A9 3sh7p ultra & multi 2.25 .65
101 A9 5sh multicolored 2.25 .80
102 A9 10sh green & multi 3.00 1.25
103 A9 £1 blue & multi 3.50 2.50
Nos. 89-103 (15) 16.00 8.70

See #135-149. For surcharges see #110-124.

Intl. Cooperation Year Issue
Common Design Type

1965, Oct. 25 Litho. *Perf. 14½*

104 CD318 ½p blue grn & cl .20 .20
105 CD318 3sh7p lt violet & grn .80 .30

Churchill Memorial Issue
Common Design Type

1966, Jan. 24 Photo. *Perf. 14*

Design in Black, Gold and Carmine Rose

106 CD319 ½p brt blue .20 .20
107 CD319 3p green .30 .20
108 CD319 3sh brown .60 .40
109 CD319 3sh7p violet .70 .40
Nos. 106-109 (4) 1.80 1.20

Nos. 89-103 Surcharged with New Value and Three Bars

Perf. 12x11, 11x12

1966, Feb. 14 Litho.

110 A9 1c on 1p multi .20 .20
111 A9 2c on 2p multi .20 .20
112 A9 3c on 3p multi .20 .20
113 A9 4c on ½p multi .20 .20
114 A9 5c on 6p multi .20 .20
115 A9 6c on 4p multi .20 .20
116 A9 8c on 5p multi .20 .20
117 A9 10c on 1sh multi .20 .20
118 A9 15c on 7p multi 1.25 .50
119 A9 20c on 1sh6p multi .70 .35
120 A9 25c on 2sh multi .70 .30
121 A9 35c on 3sh7p multi 2.00 .25
122 A9 50c on 5sh multi 1.25 .50
123 A9 $1 on 10sh multi 1.25 .60
124 A9 $2 on £1 multi 2.40 1.90
Nos. 110-124 (15) 11.15 6.00

World Cup Soccer Issue
Common Design Type

1966, July 1 Litho. *Perf. 14*

125 CD321 3c multicolored .20 .20
126 CD321 35c multicolored .60 .30

WHO Headquarters Issue
Common Design Type

1966, Sept. 20 Litho. *Perf. 14*

127 CD322 3c multicolored .20 .20
128 CD322 12c multicolored .50 .40

UNESCO Anniversary Issue
Common Design Type

1966, Dec. 1 Litho. *Perf. 14*

129 CD323 5c "Education" .60 *.80*
130 CD323 10c "Science" .90 .20
131 CD323 20c "Culture" 1.50 1.00
Nos. 129-131 (3) 3.00 2.00

H.M.S. Royalist, 1892, and Union Jack A10

10c, Cutter & canoe at trading post. 35c, Family.

Perf. 14½x14

1967, Sept. 1 Photo. Wmk. 314

132 A10 3c green, blue & red .25 .30
133 A10 10c multicolored .20 .20
134 A10 35c multicolored .45 .40
Nos. 132-134 (3) .90 .90

75th anniv. as a British Protectorate.

Type of 1965

Perf. 12x11, 11x12

1968, Jan. 1 Litho. Wmk. 314

135 A9 1c like 1p .20 .20
136 A9 2c like 2p .20 .20
137 A9 3c like 3p .20 .20
138 A9 4c like ½p .20 .20
139 A9 5c like 6p .20 .20
140 A9 6c like 4p .20 .20
141 A9 8c like 5p .20 .20
142 A9 10c like 1sh .20 .20
143 A9 15c like 7p .65 .20
144 A9 20c like 1sh6p .90 .20
145 A9 25c like 2sh 1.75 .20
146 A9 35c like 3sh7p 2.10 .20
147 A9 50c like 5sh 2.10 1.75
148 A9 $1 like 10sh 2.10 2.50
149 A9 $2 like £1 5.50 2.75
Nos. 135-149 (15) 16.70 9.40

Map of Tarawa Atoll — A11

Designs: 10c, US Marines wading ashore at Betio. 15c, Battle scene on Betio. 35c, Raising US and British flags on Betio.

1968, Nov. 21 Photo. *Perf. 14*

150 A11 3c multicolored .20 .20
151 A11 10c multicolored .20 .20
152 A11 15c multicolored .30 .30
153 A11 35c multicolored .50 .50
Nos. 150-153 (4) 1.20 1.20

Battle of Tarawa against Japan, 25th anniv.

School Boy and Map of Abemama Atoll A12

Designs: 10c, Secondary school boy and girl on map of Tarawa, with rest of Gilbert and Ellice Islands. 35c, Student in cap and grown on main Fiji island (Viti Levu) and map of South Pacific Islands.

1969, June 2 Litho. *Perf. 12½*

154 A12 3c dull org & multi .20 .20
155 A12 10c black & multi .20 .20
156 A12 35c dull grn & multi .40 .40
Nos. 154-156 (3) .80 .80

1st anniv. of the University of the South Pacific in Fiji, and to show the progress of education in the area it serves.

Polynesian Madonna A13

1969, Oct. 20 *Perf. 11½*

157 A13 2c multicolored .20 .20
158 A13 10c multicolored .40 .25

Christmas.

Canceled to Order

The Philatelic Bureau of Gilbert and Ellice Islands began in 1970 to sell canceled sets of new issues. Values in the second ("used") column are for these canceled-to-order stamps.

Mouth-to-Mouth Resuscitation — A14

1970, Mar. 9 Litho. *Perf. 14½*

159 A14 10c multi .20 .20
160 A14 15c multi, diff. .35 .30
161 A14 35c multi, diff. .75 .75
Nos. 159-161 (3) 1.30 1.25

Centenary of the British Red Cross.

Mother and Child Care A15

Designs: 10c, Woman physician and laboratory equipment. 15c, Chest X-ray and technician. 35c, Map of Gilbert and Ellice Islands and UN emblem.

Perf. 12½x13

1970, June 26 Litho. Wmk. 314

162 A15 5c lilac & multi .20 .20
163 A15 10c black, gray & red .20 .20
164 A15 15c yellow & multi .35 .35
165 A15 35c blue grn, bl & blk .50 .50
Nos. 162-165 (4) 1.25 1.25

25th anniv. of the United Nations.

Map of Onotoa, Beru, Tamana and Arorae Islands A16

Designs: 10c, Sailing ship "John Williams III," vert. 25c, Rev. Samuel James Whitmee, vert. 35c, Map of Islands and steamship "John Williams VII."

Perf. 14x14½, 14½x14

1970, Sept. 1 Litho. Wmk. 314

166 A16 2c blue & multi .20 .20
167 A16 10c brt green & black .30 .30
168 A16 25c lt ultra & red brn .50 .50
169 A16 35c ver, blk & lt gray .75 .75
Nos. 166-169 (4) 1.75 1.75

Centenary of the landing in the Southern Gilbert Islands by the first missionaries of the London Missionary Society.

Island Child with Halo on Pandanus Mat — A17

Christmas: 10c, Sanctuary of New Tarawa Cathedral. 35c, Three Gilbertese sailing canoes within Star of Bethlehem.

1970, Oct. 3 *Perf. 14½*

170 A17 2c ocher & multi .20 .20
171 A17 10c ocher & multi .20 .20
172 A17 35c pink & multi .40 .40
Nos. 170-172 (3) .80 .80

Harvesting Copra — A18

Lagoon Fishing A19

3c, Women cleaning pandanus leaves. 4c, Fishermen casting nets. 5c, Gilbertese canoes. 6c, Dehusking coconuts. 8c, Woman weaving pandanus fronds. 10c, Basket weaving. 15c, Tiger shark. 20c, Beating rolled pandanus leaf. 25c, Loading copra. 35c, Night fishing. 50c, Local handicraft. $1, Woman weaving coconut screen. $2, Coat of arms.

Wmk. 314 Upright (A18), Sideways (A19)

1971, May 31 Litho. *Perf. 14*

173 A18 1c multicolored .20 .20
174 A19 2c multicolored .20 .20
175 A19 3c multicolored .20 .20
176 A19 4c multicolored .30 .20
177 A19 5c multicolored .65 .25
178 A18 6c multicolored .40 .30
179 A18 8c multicolored .50 .30
180 A18 10c multicolored .55 .40
181 A18 15c multicolored 3.50 .80
182 A19 20c multicolored 2.10 1.60
183 A19 25c multicolored 2.75 1.25
184 A19 35c multicolored 3.25 .95
185 A18 50c multicolored 1.75 2.10
186 A18 $1 multicolored 2.50 4.25
187 A18 $2 multicolored 7.00 8.50
Nos. 173-187 (15) 25.85 21.50

Wmk. 314 Upright (A19), Sideways (A18)

1972-73

174a A19 2c multicolored 10.00 *11.50*
177a A19 5c multicolored 3.75 3.75
178a A18 6c multicolored 10.00 *12.50*
181a A18 15c multicolored 4.25 3.75
182a A19 20c multicolored 4.25 3.75
Nos. 174a-182a (5) 32.25 35.25

Issue dates: Sept. 7, 1972, June 13, 1973.

Legislative Council, 1971 (former House of Representatives) — A20

New Constitution: 10c, Meeting House.

1971, Aug. 1 Wmk. 314 *Perf. 14*

188 A20 3c orange & multi .20 .20
189 A20 10c green & multi .35 .35

Nativity Scene — A21

Christmas: 10c, Star of Bethlehem and palm fronds. 35c, Fishermen in outrigger canoe looking at Star.

1971, Oct. 1

190 A21 3c vio blue, blk & yel .20 .50
191 A21 10c grnsh bl, blk & gold .30 .30
192 A21 35c car rose, blk & rose .50 .50
Nos. 190-192 (3) 1.00 1.30

Children and UNICEF Emblem A22

25th Anniv. of UNICEF: 10c, Seated child. 35c, Child's head.

1971, Dec. 11

193 A22 3c brt pink & multi .20 .40
194 A22 10c black & multi .20 .20
195 A22 35c blue & multi .60 .75
Nos. 193-195 (3) 1.00 1.35

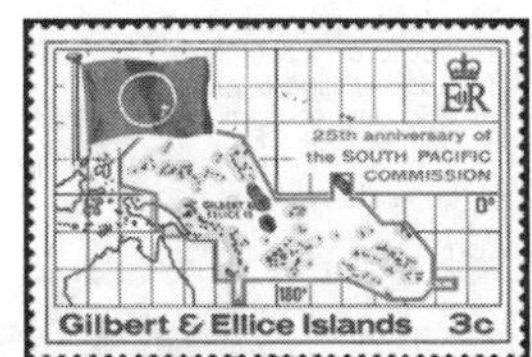

Commission Flag, Map of South Pacific — A23

South Pacific Commission, 25th Anniv.: 10c, Island boats. 35c, Flags of 8 member nations plus Tonga, a non-member.

1972, Feb. 21 *Perf. 13½x14*

196 A23 3c gray & multi .20 .50
197 A23 10c tan, ultra & brown .30 .25
198 A23 35c ultra & multi .30 .75
Nos. 196-198 (3) .80 1.50

Corals A24

1972, May 26 *Perf. 14x14½*

199 A24 3c Alveopora .20 .30
200 A24 10c Euphyllia .45 .20
201 A24 15c Melithea .60 .30
202 A24 35c Spongodes 1.75 1.00
Nos. 199-202 (4) 3.00 1.80

"Peace" on Star of Bethlehem A25

Christmas: 10c, Holy Family, made of shells. 35c, Christ child sleeping in giant clam and covered with dawn cowrie, horiz.

1972, Sept. 15 *Perf. 13½*

203 A25 3c gold & multi .20 .20
204 A25 10c gold & multi .20 .20
205 A25 35c gold & multi .45 .45
Nos. 203-205 (3) .85 .85

Silver Wedding Issue, 1972

Common Design Type

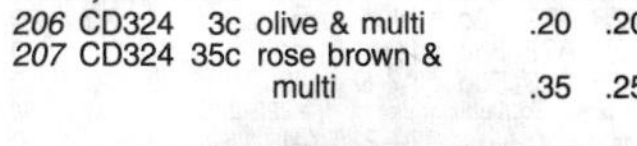

Design: Queen Elizabeth II, Prince Philip and kaue floral headdress.

1972, Nov. 20 Photo. *Perf. 14x14½*

206 CD324 3c olive & multi .20 .20
207 CD324 35c rose brown & multi .35 .25

Funafuti, Land of Bananas A26

Designs: 10c, Butaritari, the smell of the sea. 25c, Tarawa, the center of the world. 35c, Abemama, the land of the moon.

1973, Mar. 5 Litho. *Perf. 14½x14*

208 A26 3c yellow & multi .20 *.40*
209 A26 10c brt green & multi .30 .30
210 A26 25c dull blue & multi .45 .60
211 A26 35c orange & multi .50 .70
Nos. 208-211 (4) 1.45 2.00

Legends of island names.

Ellice Dancer — A27

Christmas (Within Outline of Nautilus Shell): 10c, Outrigger canoe in lagoon. 35c, Evening on the lagoon. 50c, Map of Christmas Island, Pacific Ocean.

1973, Sept. 24 *Perf. 14*

212 A27 3c vio blue & multi .20 .20
213 A27 10c multicolored .20 .20
214 A27 35c multicolored .40 .20
215 A27 50c vio blue & multi .50 *.90*
Nos. 212-215 (4) 1.30 1.50

Princess Anne's Wedding Issue

Common Design Type

1973, Nov. 14 *Perf. 14*

216 CD325 3c brt green & multi .20 .20
217 CD325 35c slate & multi .40 .30

Meteorological Observation — A28

WMO Emblem and: 10c, Island observation station. 35c, Wind finding radar. 50c, Map of Gilbert and Ellice Islands world weather watch stations.

1973, Nov. 26 Litho. *Perf. 14½*

218	A28	3c orange & multi	.85	.50
219	A28	10c dp bister & multi	.90	.35
220	A28	35c gray & multi	1.25	.50
221	A28	50c dk blue & multi	2.00	2.00
		Nos. 218-221 (4)	5.00	3.35

Cent. of intl. meteorological cooperation.

Te-Mataaua Crest and Canoe — A29

Designs: Various family crests and canoes.

1974, Mar. 4 Litho. *Perf. 13½*

222	A29	3c tan & multi	.20	.20
223	A29	10c lt blue & multi	.20	.20
224	A29	35c yellow & multi	.30	.20
225	A29	50c pink & multi	.30	.60
a.		Souvenir sheet of 4, #222-225	4.00	*4.50*
		Nos. 222-225 (4)	1.00	1.20

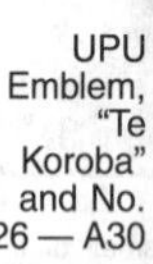

UPU Emblem, "Te Koroba" and No. 26 — A30

UPU cent.: 10c, Sailing ship "Kiakia" and No. 51. 25c, BAC 111 jet and No. 187. 35c, UPU emblem.

1974, June 10 *Perf. 14*

226	A30	4c blue green & multi	.20	.20
227	A30	10c orange & multi	.20	.20
228	A30	25c dp blue & multi	.35	.30
229	A30	35c red orange & black	.50	.40
		Nos. 226-229 (4)	1.25	1.10

Toy Canoe, Star and Boat A31

Star of Bethlehem and: 10c, Pinwheel and boat. 25c, Coconut ball (crate) and boat. 35c, Three boats (Wise Men) and stars.

1974, Sept. 23

230	A31	4c yel green & multi	.20	.25
231	A31	10c red brown & multi	.20	.20
232	A31	25c multicolored	.25	.40
233	A31	35c red brown & multi	.35	.45
		Nos. 230-233 (4)	1.00	1.30

Christmas.

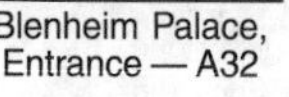

Blenheim Palace, Entrance — A32 Churchill Painting — A33

Design: 35c, Churchill Statue, London.

1974, Nov. 30 Litho. *Perf. 14*

234	A32	4c multicolored	.20	.20
235	A33	10c ultra & black	.20	.20
236	A33	35c blue, ocher & blk	.30	.30
		Nos. 234-236 (3)	.70	.70

Sir Winston Churchill (1874-1965).

Carpilius Maculatus — A34

Crabs: 10c, Ranina ranina. 25c, Portunus pelagicus. 35c, Ocypode ceratophthalma.

1975, Jan. 27 Litho. *Perf. 14*

237	A34	4c violet & multi	.20	.20
238	A34	10c green & multi	.50	.50
239	A34	25c buff & multi	1.25	1.25
240	A34	35c lt blue & multi	1.75	1.75
		Nos. 237-240 (4)	3.70	3.70

Living Cowries and Empty Shells — A35

1975, May 26 Wmk. 314 *Perf. 14*

241	A35	4c Cypraea argus	.50	.40
242	A35	10c Cypraea cribraria	.75	.20
243	A35	25c Cypraea talpa	1.75	1.25
244	A35	35c Cypraea mappa	2.50	2.25
a.		Souvenir sheet of 4, #241-244	15.00	15.00
		Nos. 241-244 (4)	5.50	4.10

Map of Beru (The Bud) A36

Designs: 10c, Map of Onotoa (Six Giants). 25c, Map of Abaiang (Land to the North). 35c, Map of Marakei (Floating fish trap).

Wmk. 314

1975, Aug. 1 Litho. *Perf. 14*

245	A36	4c brt green & multi	.20	.20
246	A36	10c brown & multi	.20	.20
247	A36	25c vio blue & multi	.40	.40
248	A36	35c org red & multi	.60	.60
		Nos. 245-248 (4)	1.40	1.40

Legends of island names.

Christ Child Within Coconut — A37

Christmas: 10c, Sadd Memorial Chapel (Protestant), Tarawa. 25c, R.C. Church, Ocean Island. 35c, Fishermen in outrigger canoes seeing star.

1975, Sept. 22 *Perf. 14*

249	A37	4c brown & multi	.20	*.35*
250	A37	10c brt blue & multi	.20	.20
251	A37	25c violet & multi	.40	*.50*
252	A37	35c green & multi	.50	*.75*
		Nos. 249-252 (4)	1.30	*1.80*

POSTAGE DUE STAMPS

D1

1940, Aug. Typo. Wmk. 4 *Perf. 12*

J1	D1	1p emerald	5.00	*15.00*
J2	D1	2p dark red	5.50	*15.00*
J3	D1	3p chocolate	7.50	*16.00*
J4	D1	4p deep blue	9.00	*20.00*
J5	D1	5p deep green	12.00	*20.00*
J6	D1	6p brt red vio	12.00	*20.00*
J7	D1	1sh dull violet	15.00	*30.00*
J8	D1	1sh6p turq green	25.00	*50.00*
		Nos. J1-J8 (8)	91.00	*186.00*
		Set, never hinged	135.00	

WAR TAX STAMP

No. 15a Overprinted

1918 Wmk. 3 *Perf. 14*

MR1	A3	1p scarlet	.60	.60

GILBERT ISLANDS

'gil-bərt 'ī-ləndᵴ

LOCATION — A group of islands in the Pacific Ocean northeast of Australia.
GOVT. — British Crown Colony
AREA — 270 sq. mi.
POP. — 52,000 (1973)
CAPITAL — Tarawa

The Gilbert Islands Colony consists of the Gilbert Islands, Phoenix, Ocean and Line Islands. They were part of the Gilbert and Ellice Islands colony until 1976. See Tuvalu.

Catalogue values for all unused stamps in this country are for Never Hinged items.

Stamps and Types of Gilbert and Ellice Islands 1971 Overprinted in Red, Black or Gold

Wmk. 373; 314 (2c, 4c)

1976, Jan. 2 Litho. *Perf. 14*

253	A18	1c multi (R)	.20	.25
a.		Watermark 314	.20	.20
254	A19	2c multi (R)	.20	1.75
a.		Watermark upright	.20	.20
255	A19	3c multi (R)	.20	1.00
a.		Watermark 314	17.50	10.00
256	A19	4c multi (R)	.20	.85
257	A19	5c multi (R)	.20	.85
258	A18	6c multi (B)	.20	.85
259	A18	8c multi (R)	.20	.85
260	A18	10c multi (B)	.25	.85
261	A18	15c multi (B)	1.75	1.00
262	A19	20c multi (R)	1.50	1.50
a.		Watermark 314 sideways	2.00	1.75
b.		Watermark 314 upright	70.00	70.00
263	A19	25c multi (B)	1.75	1.10
a.		Watermark 314	42.50	42.50
264	A19	35c multi (G)	1.75	1.50
a.		Watermark 314	850.00	950.00
265	A18	50c multi (B)	3.25	1.90
a.		Watermark 314	*850.00*	*900.00*
266	A18	$1 multi (R)	15.00	6.75
		Nos. 253-266 (14)	26.65	21.00

Location of overprint varies.

Maps of Tarawa and Funafuti A38

4c, Charts of Gilbert and Tuvalu Islands.

1976, Jan. 2 Wmk. 373

267	A38	4c multicolored	.20	*.50*
268	A38	35c multicolored	1.25	1.50

Separation of the Gilbert and Ellice Islands.

M.V. Teraaka A39

3c, M.V. Tautunu. 4c, Moorish idol. 5c, Hibiscus. 6c, Reef egret. 7c, Roman Catholic Cathedral, Tarawa. 8c, Frangipani. 10c, Maneaba meeting house. 12c, Betio Harbor. 15c, Sunset. 20c, Marakei Atoll. 35c, Chapel, Tangintebu. 40c, Flamboyant tree. 50c, Hypolimnas bolina elliciana (butterfly). $1, Landing craft, Tabakea. $2, Gilbert Islands flag.

1976, July 1 Litho. *Perf. 14*

269	A39	1c multicolored	.40	*.55*
270	A39	3c multicolored	.60	*.65*
271	A39	4c multicolored	.30	*.55*
272	A39	5c multicolored	.30	.25
273	A39	6c multicolored	1.50	.70
274	A39	7c multicolored	.20	*.25*
275	A39	8c multicolored	.20	*.25*
276	A39	10c multicolored	.20	*.25*
277	A39	12c multicolored	.35	.35
278	A39	15c multicolored	.40	.35
279	A39	20c multicolored	.35	.30
280	A39	35c multicolored	.35	.30
281	A39	40c multicolored	.40	.35
282	A39	50c multicolored	1.75	1.40
283	A39	$1 multicolored	1.10	*2.00*
284	A39	$2 multicolored	1.10	*2.00*
		Nos. 269-284 (16)	9.50	10.50

Church A40

Children's Drawings: 15c, Feasting (vegetables, fish, pig, chicken), vert. 20c, Communal meeting house, vert. 35c, Children watching dancer.

1976, Sept. 15 Litho. *Perf. 14*

285	A40	5c blue & multi	.45	.20
286	A40	15c green & multi	.65	.20
287	A40	20c rose & multi	.65	.65
288	A40	35c salmon & multi	.65	.65
		Nos. 285-288 (4)	2.40	1.70

Christmas.

Porcupine Fish Helmet — A41

Artifacts: 15c, Shark's teeth dagger. 20c, Fighting gauntlet. 35c, Coconut body armor.

1976, Dec. 6 Litho. *Perf. 13½x13*

289	A41	5c multicolored	.25	.20
290	A41	15c multicolored	.50	.30
291	A41	20c multicolored	.50	.40

292 A41 35c multicolored .75 .80
a. Souvenir sheet of 4, #289-292 10.00 10.00
Nos. 289-292 (4) 2.00 1.70

Prince Charles, 1970 Visit — A42

1977, Feb. 7 ***Perf. 14***

Designs: 20c, Prince Philip, 1959 visit. 40c, Queen in coronation robes.

293 A42 8c multicolored .25 .20
294 A42 20c multicolored .45 .20
295 A42 40c multicolored .55 .35
Nos. 293-295 (3) 1.25 .75

Reign of Queen Elizabeth II, 25th anniv.

John Byron and Dolphin, 1765 A43

Explorers: 15c, Edmund Fanning, 1798, and "Betsey." 20c, Fabian Gottlieb von Bellingshausen, 1820, and "Vostok." 35c, Charles Wilkes, 1838-42, and "Vincennes."

1977, June 1 Wmk. 373 ***Perf. 14***

296 A43 5c multicolored 1.10 *1.25*
297 A43 15c multicolored 1.40 2.50
298 A43 20c multicolored 1.40 *2.50*
299 A43 35c multicolored 1.60 *3.75*
Nos. 296-299 (4) 5.50 *10.00*

Resolution and Discovery off Christmas Island — A44

15c, Capt. Cook's logbook entry, 1777. 20c, Capt. Cook on board ship. 40c, Capt. Cook landing on Christmas Island.

1977, Sept. 12 Litho. ***Perf. 14***

300 A44 8c multi .55 .20
301 A44 15c multi, horiz .55 .20
302 A44 20c multi .75 .40
303 A44 40c multi, horiz. .75 .75
a. Souvenir sheet of 4, #300-303 9.00 9.00
Nos. 300-303 (4) 2.60 1.55

Christmas; bicentenary of Capt. Cook's discovery of Christmas Island.

Scout Emblem, Beach Scene — A45

15c, Patrol meeting. 20c, Scout weaving mat. 40c, Canoeing.

1977, Dec. 5 Litho. ***Perf. 13***

304 A45 8c gold & multi .20 .20
305 A45 15c gold & multi, horiz. .25 .25
306 A45 20c gold & multi, horiz. .45 .40
307 A45 40c gold & multi 1.00 .80
Nos. 304-307 (4) 1.90 1.65

50th anniversary of Gilbert Islands Scouting.

Taurus with Aldebaran — A46

1978, Feb. 20 Litho. ***Perf. 14***

Night Sky over Gilbert Islands: 20c, Canis Major with Sirius. 25c, Scorpio with Antares. 45c, Orion with Betelgeuse and Rigel.

308 A46 10c blue & black .20 .20
309 A46 20c dp rose & black .50 .25
310 A46 25c olive grn & black .50 .50
311 A46 45c orange & black .90 .95
Nos. 308-311 (4) 2.10 1.90

Common Design Types pictured following the introduction.

Elizabeth II Coronation Anniversary

Common Design Types

Souvenir Sheet

1978, Apr. 21 Unwmk.

312 Sheet of 6 1.40 1.40
a. CD326 45c Unicorn of Scotland .25 .25
b. CD327 45c Elizabeth II .25 .25
c. CD328 45c Great frigate bird .25 .25

Arrows, Tarawa and Abemama Islands, School Insignia A47

10c, Birds inscribed Bikenibeu, Abemama, Bairiki (school locations). 25c, Children greeting each other from maps of Islands. 45c, Abemama & Tarawa school buildings.

Perf. 14x13½

1978, June 5 Wmk. 373

313 A47 10c multicolored .20 .20
314 A47 20c multicolored .25 .25
315 A47 25c multicolored .25 .25
316 A47 45c multicolored .40 .40
Nos. 313-316 (4) 1.10 1.10

King George V School, 25th anniversary of return from Abemama to Tarawa.

Garland A48

Christmas: Various garlands.

1978, Sept. 4 Litho. ***Perf. 14***

317 A48 10c multicolored .20 .20
318 A48 20c multicolored .20 .20
319 A48 25c multicolored .20 .20
320 A48 45c multicolored .30 .30
a. Souvenir sheet of 4, #317-320, perf. 13x13½ 2.50 3.00
Nos. 317-320 (4) .90 .90

Endeavour A49

Designs: 20c, Green turtle. 25c, Quadrant. 45c, Capt. Cook after Flaxman/Wedgwood medallion.

1979, Jan. 15 Litho. ***Perf. 11***

321 A49 10c multicolored .20 .30
322 A49 20c multicolored .45 .35
323 A49 25c multicolored .45 .50

Litho.; Embossed

324 A49 45c multicolored .45 .75
Nos. 321-324 (4) 1.55 1.90

Capt. Cook's voyages.

Gilbert Islands stamps were replaced in 1979 by those of Kiribati.

GOLD COAST

'gōld 'kōst

LOCATION — West Africa between Dahomey and Ivory Coast
GOVT. — Former British Crown Colony
AREA — 91,843 sq. mi.
POP. — 3,089,000 (1952)
CAPITAL — Accra

Attached to the colony were Ashanti and Northern Territories (protectorate). Togoland, under British mandate, was also included for administrative purposes.

Gold Coast became the independent state of Ghana in 1957.

See Ghana.

12 Pence = 1 Shilling
20 Shillings = 1 Pound

Catalogue values for unused stamps in this country are for Never Hinged items, beginning with Scott 128.

Queen Victoria
A1 A3

Perf. 12½

1875, July Typo. Wmk. 1

1 A1 1p blue 450.00 80.00
2 A1 4p red violet 425.00 100.00
3 A1 6p orange 625.00 70.00
Nos. 1-3 (3) 1,500. 250.00

1876-79 ***Perf. 14***

4 A1 ½p bister ('79) 55.00 22.50
5 A1 1p blue 16.00 6.50
a. Half used as ½p on cover *3,000.*
6 A1 2p green ('79) 75.00 10.50
a. Half used as 1p on cover *2,500.*
b. Quarter used as ½p on cover *4,000.*
7 A1 4p red violet 175.00 6.75
a. Quarter used as 1p on cover *6,000.*
b. Half used as 2p on cover *4,750.*
8 A1 6p orange 100.00 17.50
a. One sixth used as 1p on cover *7,000.*
b. Half used as 3p on cover *5,500.*
Nos. 4-8 (5) 421.00 63.75

Handstamp Surcharged "1D" in Black

1883, May

9 A1 1p on 4p red violet

Some experts question the status of No. 9. One canceled copy is in the British Museum. Another copy is supposed to exist (Ferrari).

1883-91 Wmk. 2

10 A1 ½p bister ('83) 145.00 50.00
11 A1 ½p green ('84) 2.75 .75
12 A1 1p blue ('83) 850.00 65.00
13 A1 1p rose ('84) 3.00 .50
a. Half used as ½p on cover *3,250.*
14 A1 2p gray ('84) 2.75 .60
b. Half used as 1p on cover *4,000.*
15 A1 2½p bl & org ('91) 3.75 .75
16 A1 3p ol green ('89) 8.00 4.50
a. 3p olive bister 8.00 4.50
17 A1 4p dull vio ('84) 9.00 1.50
a. 4p claret 10.00 3.00
b. Half used as 2p on cover —
18 A1 6p orange ('89) 7.00 5.00
a. One sixth used as 1p on cover —
19 A1 1sh purple ('88) 4.25 1.25
a. 1sh violet 35.00 12.50
20 A1 2sh brown ('84) 42.50 14.00
a. 2sh yellow brown 75.00 37.50

No. 18 Surcharged in Black

1889, Mar.

21 A1 1p on 6p orange 100.00 50.00

The surcharge exists in two spacings between "PENNY" and bar: 7mm and 8mm.

1889

22 A3 5sh lilac & ultra 70.00 13.00
23 A3 10sh lilac & red 85.00 17.00
24 A3 20sh green & red 3,250.

1894

25 A3 20sh vio & blk, *red* 175.00 37.50

1898-1902

26 A3 ½p lilac & green 1.00 .85
27 A3 1p lil & car rose 1.00 .40
28 A3 2p lil & red ('02) 25.00 *100.00*
29 A3 2½p lilac & ultra 4.00 *4.25*
30 A3 3p lilac & yel 3.00 1.25
31 A3 6p lilac & purple 5.00 1.25
32 A3 1sh gray grn & blk 6.00 *11.50*
33 A3 2sh gray grn & car rose 12.50 *14.00*
34 A3 5sh grn & lil ('00) 42.50 24.00
35 A3 10sh grn & brn ('00) 125.00 42.50
Nos. 26-35 (10) 225.00 *200.00*

Numerals of 2p, 3p and 6p of type A3 are in color on colorless tablet.

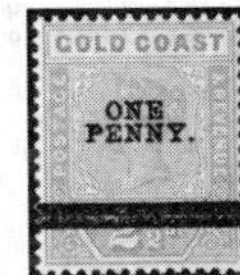

Nos. 29 and 31 Surcharged in Black

1901, Oct. 6

36 A3 1p on 2½p lil & ultra 2.50 3.50
37 A3 1p on 6p lilac & pur 2.50 3.50
a. "ONE" omitted 275.00 *475.00*

Beware of copies offered as No. 37a that have part of "ONE" showing.

King Edward VII
A5 A6

1902 Wmk. 2

38 A5 ½p violet & green .75 *.45*
39 A5 1p vio & car rose .90 .25
40 A5 2p vio & red org 12.50 *4.00*
41 A5 2½p vio & ultra 3.25 *3.50*
42 A5 3p vio & orange 2.10 1.10
43 A5 6p violet & pur 2.25 1.10
44 A5 1sh green & blk 7.50 2.50
45 A5 2sh grn & car rose 9.75 15.00
46 A5 5sh green & violet 26.00 *65.00*
47 A5 10sh green & brn 37.50 *100.00*
48 A5 20sh vio & blk, *red* 97.50 *150.00*
Nos. 38-48 (11) 200.00 *342.90*

Numerals of 2p, 3p, 6p and 2sh6p of type A5 are in color on colorless tablet.

1904-07 Wmk. 3

49 A5 ½p vio & grn ('07) 2.00 *5.00*
50 A5 1p vio & car rose 6.50 .30
51 A5 2p vio & red org 4.00 .45
52 A5 2½p vio & ultra ('06) 42.50 40.00
53 A5 3p vio & org ('05) 11.00 .50
54 A5 6p vio & pur ('06) 35.00 1.25
55 A5 2sh6p grn & yel ('06) 24.00 *87.50*
Nos. 49-55 (7) 125.00 *135.00*

Nos. 49 and 52 are on ordinary paper. Nos. 50, 51, 53 and 54 are on both ordinary and chalky paper. No. 55 is on chalky paper.

1907-13 Ordinary Paper

56 A5 ½p green 1.50 .25
57 A5 1p carmine 3.00 .20
58 A5 2p gray ('09) 1.60 .50
59 A5 2½p ultramarine 2.75 1.25

Chalky Paper

60 A5 3p violet, *yel* ('09) 4.50 .40
61 A5 6p dull violet ('08) 9.50 .40
a. 6p dull violet & red violet 2.75 2.50

62 A5 1sh blk, *grn* ('09) 4.50 .75
63 A5 2sh violet & bl, *bl* ('10) 6.00 12.50
64 A5 2sh6p blk & red, *blue* ('11) 18.00 *45.00*
65 A5 5sh grn & red, *yel* ('13) 45.00 *85.00*
Nos. 56-65 (10) 96.35 *146.25*

#63 is on both ordinary and chalky paper.

1908, Nov. Ordinary Paper
66 A6 1p carmine 1.50 .20

King George V
A7 A8

For description of Dies I and II, see front of this section of the Catalogue.

Die I

1913-21 Ordinary Paper
69 A7 ½p green .30 .20
70 A8 1p carmine .20 .20
a. 1p scarlet .35 .20
71 A7 2p gray 2.00 .70
72 A7 2½p ultramarine .85 .55

Chalky Paper
73 A7 3p vio, *yel* ('15) .85 .20
a. Die II ('19) 6.75 5.75
74 A7 6p dull vio & red vio 1.25 1.10
75 A7 1sh black, *green* 1.25 .85
a. 1sh black, *emerald* 2.25 .95
b. 1sh black, *bl grn*, ol back 1.20 .85
c. Die II ('21) 2.25 .95
76 A7 2sh vio & bl, *bl* 6.75 2.00
a. Die II ('21) 200.00 60.00
77 A7 2sh6p blk & red, *bl* 6.75 5.00
a. Die II ('21) 22.50 22.50
78 A7 5sh grn & red, *yel* 11.00 12.50
a. Die II ('21) 19.00 *42.50*
79 A7 10sh grn & red, *grn* ('16) 16.00 21.00
a. 10sh grn & red, *emer* 21.00 21.00
b. 10sh grn & red, *bl grn*, ol back 19.00 21.00
80 A7 20sh vio & blk, *red* ('16) 95.00 55.00

Surface-colored Paper
81 A7 3p violet, *yel* .55 .45
82 A7 5sh grn & red, *yel* 8.50 *17.50*
Nos. 69-82 (14) 151.25 117.25

Numerals of 2p, 3p, 6p and 2sh6p of type A7 are in color on plain tablet.

Die II

1921-25 Ordinary Paper Wmk. 4
83 A7 ½p green ('22) .25 .25
84 A8 1p brown ('22) .20 .20
85 A7 1½p carmine ('22) .40 .20
86 A7 2p gray .45 .25
87 A7 2½p orange ('23) .40 *7.25*
88 A7 3p ultra ('22) .55 .50

Chalky Paper
89 A7 6p dl vio & red vio ('22) .65 *2.50*
90 A7 1sh blk, *emer* ('25) 2.00 *2.50*
91 A7 2sh vio & bl, *bl* ('24) 2.25 *2.75*
92 A7 2sh6p blk & red, *bl* ('25) 3.75 *15.00*
93 A7 5sh grn & red, *yel* ('25) 8.75 *35.00*

Die I
94 A7 15sh dl vio & grn ('21) 125.00 *260.00*
a. Die II ('25) 110.00 *260.00*
95 A7 £2 grn & org 350.00 *800.00*
Nos. 83-95 (13) 494.65 *1,126.*

Christiansborg Castle — A9

1928, Aug. 1 Photo. *Perf. 13½x14½*
98 A9 ½p green .55 .35
99 A9 1p red brown .55 .20
100 A9 1½p scarlet .65 *1.25*
101 A9 2p slate .55 .20
102 A9 2½p yellow 1.00 *3.00*
103 A9 3p ultramarine .55 .35
104 A9 6p dull vio & blk 1.00 .35
105 A9 1sh red org & blk 1.90 .55
106 A9 2sh purple & black 11.50 3.75
107 A9 5sh ol green & car 37.50 35.00
Nos. 98-107 (10) 55.75 45.00

Common Design Types pictured following the introduction.

Silver Jubilee Issue
Common Design Type

1935, May 6 Engr. *Perf. 11x12*
108 CD301 1p black & ultra .55 .35
109 CD301 3p ultra & brown 2.75 *4.25*
110 CD301 6p indigo & green 3.00 *8.25*
111 CD301 1sh brn vio & indigo 3.00 *8.25*
Nos. 108-111 (4) 9.30 *21.10*
Set, never hinged 17.50

Coronation Issue
Common Design Type

1937, May 12 *Perf. 11x11½*
112 CD302 1p brown .30 *.50*
113 CD302 2p dark gray .40 *1.50*
114 CD302 3p deep ultra .50 *.60*
Nos. 112-114 (3) 1.20 *2.60*
Set, never hinged 3.00

A10

George VI and Christiansborg Castle — A11

1938-41 Wmk. 4 *Perf. 12*
115 A10 ½p green .25 *.30*
116 A10 1p red brown .25 .20
117 A10 1½p rose red .25 *.30*
118 A10 2p gray black .25 .20
119 A10 3p ultramarine .25 .25
120 A10 4p rose lilac .50 *.80*
121 A10 6p rose violet .50 .20
122 A10 9p red orange .60 .35
123 A11 1sh gray grn & blk .60 .30
124 A11 1sh3p turq grn & red brown 1.25 .25
125 A11 2sh dk vio & dp bl 2.75 *6.50*
126 A11 5sh rose car & ol green 5.50 *8.25*
127 A11 10sh purple & black 4.25 *12.50*
Nos. 115-127 (13) 17.20 30.40
Set, never hinged 24.00

Issued: 10sh, July, 1940; 1sh3p, Apr. 12, 1941; others, Apr. 1.

Catalogue values for unused stamps in this section, from this point to the end of the section, are for Never Hinged items.

Peace Issue
Common Design Type

1946, Oct. 14 *Perf. 13½*
128 CD303 2p purple .20 .20
a. Perf. 13½x14 5.00 1.50
129 CD303 4p deep red violet .55 *1.50*
a. Perf. 13½x14 2.50 2.00

A12

A13

½p, Mounted Constable. 1p, Christiansborg Castle. 1½p, Emblem of Joint Provincial Council. 2p, Talking Drums. 2½p, Map. 3p, Manganese mine. 4p, Lake Bosumtwi. 6p, Cacao farmer. 1sh, Breaking cacao pods. 2sh, Trooping the colors. 5sh, Surfboats. 10sh, Forest.

1948, July 1 Engr. *Perf. 12*
130 A12 ½p emerald .20 .25
131 A13 1p deep blue .20 .20
132 A13 1½p red 1.25 .60
133 A12 2p chocolate .50 .20
134 A13 2½p lt brown & red 1.90 2.25
135 A13 3p blue 3.75 .40
136 A13 4p dk car rose 3.25 1.10
137 A12 6p org & black .25 .25
138 A13 1sh red org & blk .55 .25
139 A13 2sh rose car & ol brn 2.90 1.75
140 A13 5sh gray & red vio 19.00 4.00
141 A12 10sh ol grn & black 7.50 4.00
Nos. 130-141 (12) 41.25 15.25

Silver Wedding Issue
Common Design Types

1948, Dec. 20 Photo. *Perf. 14x14½*
142 CD304 1½p scarlet .20 .20

Engraved; Name Typographed
Perf. 11½x11
143 CD305 10sh dk brn olive 11.00 10.00

UPU Issue
Common Design Types

Engr.; Name Typo. on 2½p and 3p
1949, Oct. 10 *Perf. 13½, 11x11½*
144 CD306 2p red brown .25 .25
145 CD307 2½p deep orange 1.75 1.50
146 CD308 3p indigo .40 .60
147 CD309 1sh blue green .40 .40
Nos. 144-147 (4) 2.80 2.75

Map of West Africa — A14

Mounted Constable — A15

Designs: 1p, Christiansborg Castle. 1½p, Emblem of Joint Provincial Council. 2p, Talking drums. 3p, Manganese mine. 4p, Lake Bosumtwi. 6p, Cacao farmer. 1sh, Breaking cacao pods. 2sh, Trooping the colors. 5sh, Surfboats. 10sh, Forest.

Perf. 11½x12, 12x11½
1952-54 Engr.
148 A14 ½p yel brn & car .20 .20
149 A14 1p deep blue .20 .20
150 A14 1½p green .20 .70
151 A15 2p chocolate .20 .20
152 A15 2½p red .20 .25
153 A14 3p rose .30 .20
154 A14 4p deep blue .25 .25
155 A15 6p orange & black .30 .20
156 A14 1sh red org & black .60 .20
157 A14 2sh rose car & ol brn 5.50 .50
158 A14 5sh gray & red vio 8.50 2.75
159 A15 10sh olive grn & blk 7.00 7.00
Nos. 148-159 (12) 23.45 12.65

Nos. 148-149 exist in vertical coils.
Issued: 2½p, 12/19/52; ½p, 1½p, 3p, 4p, 4/1/53; 1p, 2p, 6p, 1sh-10sh, 3/1/54.
For overprints see Ghana #5-13, 25-27.

Coronation Issue
Common Design Type

1953, June 2 *Perf. 13½x13*
160 CD312 2p dk brown & black .50 .20

POSTAGE DUE STAMPS

D1

1923-52 Typo. Wmk. 4 *Perf. 14*
J1 D1 ½p black 20.00 *80.00*
J2 D1 1p black .65 *.85*
J3 D1 2p black 1.25 *4.50*
a. Wmk. 4a (error) 85.00
J4 D1 3p black .65 *3.00*
a. Wmk. 4a (error) 85.00
J5 D1 6p black ('52) .75 *3.50*
a. Wmk. 4a (error) 125.00
J6 D1 1sh black ('52) .75 *22.50*
a. Wmk. 4a (error) 175.00
Nos. J1-J6 (6) 24.05 *114.35*

Issue date: 6p, 1sh, Oct. 1.

WAR TAX STAMP

Regular Issue of 1913 Surcharged

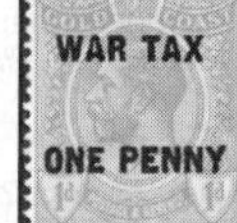

1918, June Wmk. 3 *Perf. 14*
MR1 A8 1p on 1p scarlet .25 .30

GRAND COMORO

'grand 'kä-mə-,rō

LOCATION — One of the Comoro Islands in the Mozambique Channel between Madagascar and Mozambique.
GOVT. — French Colony
AREA — 385 sq. mi. (approx.)
POP. — 50,000 (approx.)
CAPITAL — Moroni

100 Centimes = 1 Franc

See Comoro Islands.

Navigation and Commerce — A1

Perf. 14x13½
1897-1907 Typo. Unwmk.
Name of Colony in Blue or Carmine
1 A1 1c blk, *lil bl* .75 .65
2 A1 2c brn, *buff* 1.00 .80
3 A1 4c claret, *lav* 1.50 .85
4 A1 5c grn, *grnsh* 2.75 2.00
5 A1 10c blk, *lavender* 5.75 3.50
6 A1 10c red ('00) 6.50 5.75
7 A1 15c blue, quadrille paper 12.00 5.75
8 A1 15c gray, *lt gray* ('00) 6.50 5.75
9 A1 20c red, *grn* 7.75 6.75
10 A1 25c blk, *rose* 10.50 8.50
11 A1 25c blue ('00) 13.00 9.00
12 A1 30c brn, *bister* 14.00 10.00
13 A1 35c blk, *yel* ('06) 13.00 9.00
14 A1 40c red, *straw* 14.00 10.00
15 A1 45c blk, *gray grn* ('07) 50.00 37.50
16 A1 50c car, *rose* 26.00 13.50
17 A1 50c brn, *bluish* ('00) 27.50 22.50
18 A1 75c dp vio, *org* 40.00 22.50
19 A1 1fr brnz grn, *straw* 22.50 16.00
Nos. 1-19 (19) 275.00 190.30

Perf. 13½x14 stamps are counterfeits.

Issues of 1897-1907 Surcharged in Black or Carmine

1912
20 A1 5c on 2c brn, *buff* .70 .70
a. Inverted surcharge 200.00
21 A1 5c on 4c cl, *lav* (C) .70 .70
22 A1 5c on 15c blue (C) .65 .65
23 A1 5c on 20c red, *grn* .65 .65
24 A1 5c on 25c blk, *rose* (C) .70 .70
25 A1 5c on 30c brn, *bis* (C) .90 .90
26 A1 10c on 40c red, *straw* .90 .90

27	A1	10c on 45c blk, *gray grn* (C)	1.00	1.00
28	A1	10c on 50c car, *rose*	1.00	1.00
29	A1	10c on 75c dp vio, *org*	1.25	1.25
		Nos. 20-29 (10)	8.45	8.45

Two spacings between the surcharged numerals are found on Nos. 20-29.

Nos. 20-29 were available for use in Madagascar and the entire Comoro archipelago.

Stamps of Grand Comoro were superseded by those of Madagascar, and in 1950 by those of Comoro Islands.

GREAT BRITAIN

'grāt 'bri-tən

(United Kingdom)

LOCATION — Northwest of the continent of Europe and separated from it by the English Channel
GOVT. — Constitutional monarchy
AREA — 94,511 sq. mi.
POP. — 59,128,000 (1998 est.)
CAPITAL — London

12 Pence = 1 Shilling
20 Shillings = 1 Pound
100 Pence = 1 Pound (1970)

Catalogue values for unused stamps in this country are for Never Hinged items, beginning with Scott 264 in the regular postage section, Scott B1 in the semi-postal section. Scott J34 in the postage due section, and Scott 93, Scott 246 and Scott 521 in British Offices in Morocco. All of the listings in British Offices -- Middle East Forces, for Use in Eritrea, for Use in Somalia and for Use in Tripolitania are valued as never-hinged.

The letters in the corners of the early postage issues indicate position in the horizontal and vertical rows in which that particular specimen was placed.

In the case of illustration A1, this stamp came from the 14th horizontal row (N) and was the 12th stamp (L) from the left in that row. The left corner refers to the horizontal row and the right corner to the vertical row. Thus no two stamps on the plate bore the same combination of letters.

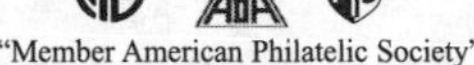

When four corner letters are used (starting in 1858), the lower ones indicate the stamp's position in the sheet and the top ones are the same letters reversed.

Watermarks

Wmk. 18- Small Crown

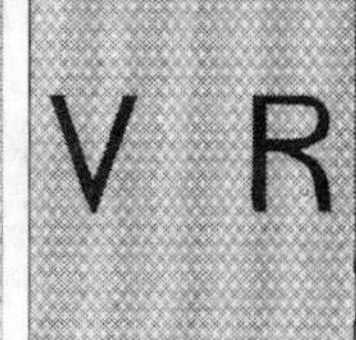
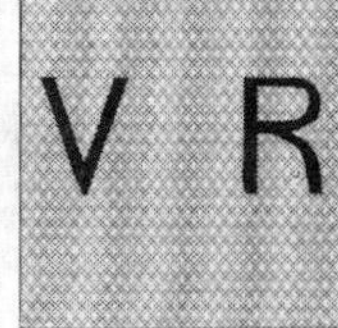
Wmk. 19- V R

Wmk. 20- Large Crown

Wmk. 21- Small Garter

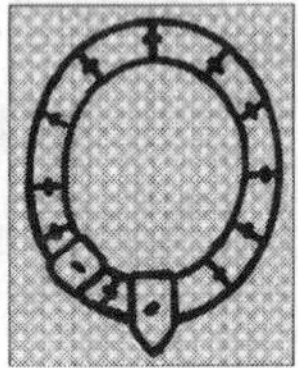
Wmk. 22- Medium Garter

Wmk. 23- Large Garter

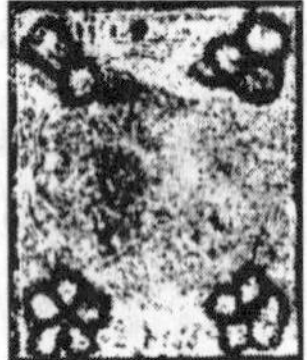

Wmk. 24- Heraldic Emblems

Wmk. 25- Spray of Rose

Wmk. 26- Maltese Cross

Wmk. 27- "Half Penny" in Script

Wmk. 28- Anchor

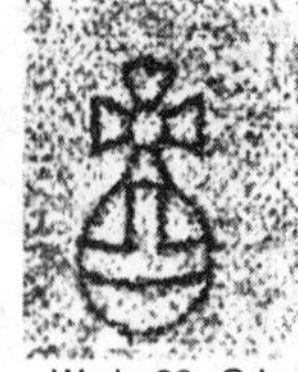
Wmk. 29- Orb

Wmk. 30- Imperial Crown

Wmk. 31- Anchor

Wmk. 32- Crown and GvR Multiple

Wmk. 33- Crown and GvR

Wmk. 33 - In the normal watermark (sometimes termed the "repeated" watermark) the letters "GvR" are extended. The royal cyphers are placed one above the other and usually two appear on each stamp. In the multiple watermark the letters "GvR" are condensed, the cyphers are smaller and are so placed that those in each succeeding row are below the spaces between the cyphers in the row above.

Wmk. 34- Large Crown and GvR

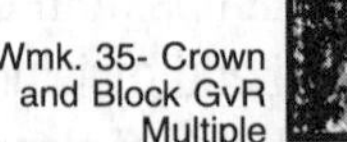
Wmk. 35- Crown and Block GvR Multiple

Wmk. 219- Large Crown and GvR

Wmk. 250- Crown and E8R Multiple

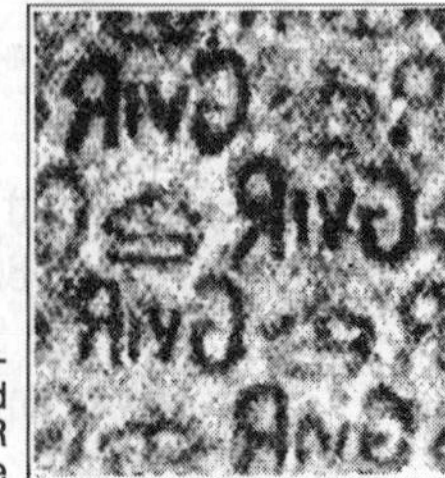
Wmk. 251- Crown and GviR Multiple

Wmk. 259- Crown and Large G VI R

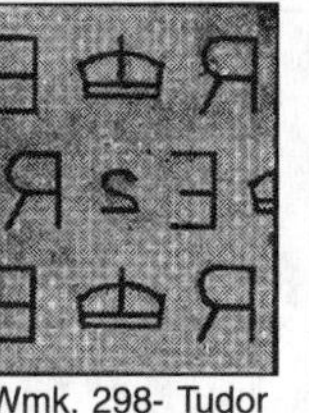
Wmk. 298- Tudor Crown and E 2 R Multiple

Wmk. 308- St. Edward's Crown and E 2 R Multiple

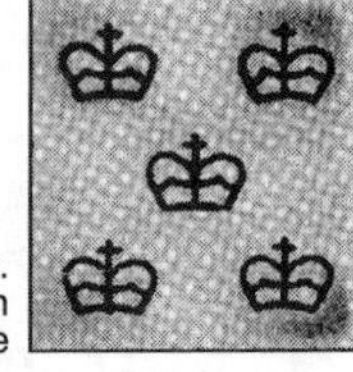
Wmk. 322- St. Edward's Crown Multiple

Values for unused stamps are for examples with original gum as defined in the catalogue introduction. Very fine examples of Nos. 8-56, 58-73, 78-89, 94-95, and the Official overprints on these designs, will have perforations touching the design on at least one side due to the narrow spacing of the stamps on the plates. Stamps with perfs well clear of the design on all four sides range from scarce to rare and command substantially higher prices.

Cancellations on stamps from the 1847 issue to the 1864 issue, and in many cases beyond, are usually heavy. Values quoted are for stamps with better than average cancellations. Stamps with circular date stamps range from scarce to rare and command higher prices.

Queen Victoria
A1 A2

1840, May Wmk. 18 Engr. *Imperf.*
White Paper

1	A1 1p black	3,250.	190.
2	A2 2p blue	7,000.	400.

No. 1 was printed from 11 plates; No. 2 from 2 plates. The 1p plates 1, 2, 5, 6, 8 and 9 can be found in two or more states. Stamp values are for the most common plates.

Issue dates: 1p, May 6; 2p, May 7.

See Nos. 3, 8-9, 11-12, 14, 16, 18, 20, O1.

Compare designs A1-A2 with A8, A10.

For shades, see the *Scott Classic Catalogue.*

1841 Bluish Paper

3	A1 1p red brown	160.00	12.00
	c. Rouletted 12	*4,500.*	
	d. "A" missing in lower right corner (position BA, P77)	—	*5,500.*
4	A2 2p blue	1,400.	55.00
	c. 2p violet blue	*7,500.*	60.00

No. 3 exists on silk thread paper, but was not regularly issued.

No. 4 was printed from two plates.

See Nos. 10, 13, 15, 17, 19, 21.

For shades, see the *Scott Classic Catalogue.*

During the reigns of Victoria and Edward VII, many color trials were produced on perfed, gummed and watermarked papers.

A3

A4

With Vertical Silk Threads

1847 Embossed Unwmk.

5 A3 1sh pale green 4,750. 475.00
a. 1sh green 4,750. 500.00
Cut to shape 10.00

Die numbers (on base of bust): 1 and 2.

Nos. 5-7 were printed one stamp at a time on the sheet. Space between the stamps usually is very small. Impressions that touch, or even overlap, are numerous.

Values for Nos. 5-6 are for examples with complete frames and clear white margins on all four sides. Values for No. 7 are for examples with complete design but not necessarily clear margins around the design.

1848

6 A3 10p red brown 3,500. 675.00
Cut to shape 10.00

Die numbers (on base of bust): 1, 2, 3, 4; also without die number.

1854 Wmk. 19

7 A4 6p red violet 4,000. 500.00
a. 6p dull violet 4,000. 500.00
b. 6p deep violet 5,000. 1,400.
Cut to shape 8.00

1854-55 Wmk. 18 Engr. *Perf. 16*

Bluish Paper

8 A1 1p red brown 175.00 16.50
a. 1p yellow brown 250.00 27.50
9 A1 1p red brown, re-engraved ('55) 250.00 45.00
a. Imperf. —
10 A2 2p blue 1,700. 80.00
a. 2p pale blue 1,750. 85.00

In the re-engraved 1p stamps, the lines of the features are deeper and stronger, the fillet behind the ear more distinct, the shading about the eye heavier, the line of the nostril is turned downward at right and an indentation of color appears between lower lip and chin.

Perf. 14

11 A1 1p red brown ('55) 400.00 55.00
a. Imperf.
12 A1 1p red brown, re-engraved ('55) 325.00 42.50
a. 1p org brn, re-engraved 800.00 100.00
13 A2 2p blue ('55) 2,100. 160.00
a. Imperf. (P5) —

Wmk. 20 exists in two types. The first includes two vertical prongs, rising from the top of the crown's headband and extending into each of the two balancing midsections. The second type (illustrated), introduced in 1861, omits these prongs.

1855 Wmk. 20 *Perf. 16*

Bluish Paper

14 A1 1p red brown, re-engraved 650.00 75.00
15 A2 2p blue 3,250. 225.00
a. Imperf. (P5) *2,750.*

1855 Bluish Paper *Perf. 14*

16 A1 1p red brown, re-engraved 160.00 9.00
a. 1p orange brn, re-engraved 350.00 37.50
b. 1p brown rose, re-engraved 225.00 32.50
c. Imperf. 1,200. 950.00
17 A2 2p blue 1,400. 47.50

1856-58 White Paper *Perf. 16*

18 A1 1p rose red, re-engraved ('57) 825.00 45.00
19 A2 2p blue, thin lines ('58) 3,500. 190.00

Perf. 14

20 A1 1p rose red, re-engraved ('56) 37.50 8.50
a. Imperf. 675.00 550.00
b. 1p red brown, re-engraved 350.00 92.50
21 A2 2p blue, thin lines ('57) 1,500. 47.50
a. Imperf. — *3,750.*
b. Vertical pair, imperf horiz. —

Queen Victoria — A5

1855 Typo. Wmk. 21

22 A5 4p rose, *bluish* 3,000. 300.00
23 A5 4p rose, *white* 4,500. 550.00

Compare design A5 with A11, A16, A31.

1856 Wmk. 22

24 A5 4p rose, *bluish* 3,750. 350.00
25 A5 4p rose, *white* 2,500. 275.00

1857 Wmk. 23

26 A5 4p rose, *white* 925.00 82.50

A6

A7

1856 Wmk. 24

27 A6 6p lilac 625.00 75.00
a. 6p deep lilac 700.00 100.00
b. Wmk. 3 roses and shamrock
28 A7 1sh green 925.00 200.00
a. 1sh pale green 925.00 200.00
b. 1sh deep green 1,850. 250.00
e. Imperf —

Compare design A6 with A13, A18, A22. Compare A7 with A15, A21, A29.

A8

A9

1858-69 Engr. Wmk. 20 *Perf. 14*

29 A8 2p blue (P9) 200.00 9.00
Plate 7 600.00 40.00
Plate 8 550.00 30.00
Plate 12 925.00 100.00
b. Imperf. (P9) *3,500.*

Plate numbers are contained in the scroll work at the sides of the stamp.

Lines Above and Below Head Thinner

30 A8 2p blue ('69) (P13) 240.00 18.00
Plate 14 275.00 24.00
Plate 15 250.00 24.00
a. Imperf. (P13) *2,600.*

1860-70

31 A9 1½p lilac rose, *bluish* (P1) ('60) 2,500.
32 A9 1½p dull rose (P3) ('70) 240.00 42.50
a. 1½p lake red 240.00 37.50
Plate 1 240.00 37.50
c. Imperf (P1, 3) *2,500.*

The 1½p stamps from Plate 1 carry no plate number. The Plate 3 number is in the border at each side above the lower corner letters.

No. 31 was prepared but not issued.

The "OP-PC" variety is a broken letter.

Queen Victoria — A10

1864

33 A10 1p rose red 14.00 1.90
a. 1p brick red 14.00 1.90
b. 1p lake red 14.00 1.90
c. Imperf. (P116, see footnote) 1,550. 1,100.

Plate 71	32.50	2.75
Plate 72	37.50	3.75
Plate 73	37.50	2.75
Plate 74	37.50	1.90
Plate 76	32.50	1.90
Plate 77	*120,000.*	*100,000.*
Plate 78	82.50	1.90
Plate 79	27.50	1.90
Plate 80	42.50	1.90
Plate 81	42.50	2.10
Plate 82	82.50	3.75
Plate 83	110.00	6.50
Plate 84	55.00	2.10
Plate 85	37.50	2.10
Plate 86	47.50	3.75
Plate 87	27.50	1.90
Plate 88	125.00	7.50
Plate 89	37.50	1.90
Plate 90	37.50	1.90
Plate 91	50.00	5.75
Plate 92	32.50	1.90
Plate 93	47.50	1.90
Plate 94	42.50	4.75
Plate 95	37.50	1.90
Plate 96	42.50	1.90
Plate 97	37.50	3.25
Plate 98	47.50	5.75
Plate 99	50.00	4.75
Plate 100	55.00	2.10
Plate 101	55.00	8.50
Plate 102	42.50	1.90
Plate 103	47.50	3.25
Plate 104	70.00	4.75
Plate 105	82.50	6.50
Plate 106	50.00	1.90
Plate 107	55.00	6.50
Plate 108	75.00	2.10
Plate 109	80.00	3.25
Plate 110	55.00	8.25
Plate 111	47.50	2.10
Plate 112	65.00	2.10
Plate 113	47.50	11.00
Plate 114	225.00	11.00
Plate 115	82.50	2.10
Plate 116	70.00	8.50
Plate 117	42.50	1.90
Plate 118	47.50	1.90
Plate 119	42.50	1.90
Plate 120	14.00	1.90
Plate 121	37.50	9.00
Plate 122	14.00	1.90
Plate 123	37.50	1.90
Plate 124	26.00	1.90
Plate 125	37.50	1.90
Plate 127	50.00	2.10
Plate 129	37.50	7.50
Plate 130	50.00	2.10
Plate 131	60.00	15.00
Plate 132	125.00	20.00
Plate 133	100.00	8.25
Plate 134	14.00	1.90
Plate 135	87.50	24.00
Plate 136	82.50	19.00
Plate 137	26.00	2.10
Plate 138	17.00	1.90
Plate 139	55.00	15.00
Plate 140	17.00	1.90
Plate 141	100.00	8.50
Plate 142	65.00	22.50
Plate 143	55.00	14.00
Plate 144	87.50	19.00
Plate 145	27.50	2.10
Plate 146	37.50	5.75
Plate 147	47.50	2.75
Plate 148	37.50	2.75
Plate 149	37.50	5.75
Plate 150	14.00	1.90
Plate 151	55.00	8.50
Plate 152	55.00	5.00
Plate 153	92.50	8.50
Plate 154	47.50	1.90
Plate 155	47.50	2.10
Plate 156	42.50	1.90
Plate 157	47.50	1.90
Plates 158-159	27.50	1.90
Plate 160	27.50	1.90
Plate 161	55.00	6.50
Plate 162	47.50	6.50
Plates 163-164	47.50	2.75
Plate 165	42.50	1.90
Plate 166	42.50	5.50
Plate 167	42.50	1.90
Plate 168	47.50	7.50
Plate 169	55.00	6.50
Plate 170	32.50	1.90
Plate 171	14.00	1.90
Plate 172	27.50	1.90
Plate 173	65.00	8.25
Plate 174	27.50	1.90
Plate 175	55.00	3.25
Plate 176	55.00	2.10
Plate 177	37.50	1.90
Plate 178	55.00	3.25
Plate 179	47.50	2.10
Plate 180	55.00	4.75
Plate 181	42.50	1.90
Plate 182	82.50	4.75
Plate 183	50.00	2.75
Plate 184	27.50	2.10
Plate 185	47.50	2.75
Plate 186	60.00	2.10
Plate 187	47.50	1.90
Plate 188	65.00	9.25
Plate 189	65.00	6.50
Plate 190	47.50	5.50
Plate 191	27.50	6.50
Plate 192	47.50	1.90
Plate 193	27.50	1.90
Plates 194-195	47.50	7.50
Plate 196	47.50	4.75
Plate 197	50.00	8.25
Plate 198	37.50	5.50
Plate 199	50.00	5.50
Plate 200	55.00	1.90
Plate 201	27.50	4.75
Plate 202	55.00	7.50
Plate 203	27.50	*15.00*
Plate 204	50.00	2.10
Plate 205	50.00	2.75
Plates 206-207	55.00	8.25
Plate 208	50.00	15.00
Plate 209	47.50	8.25
Plate 210	60.00	11.00
Plate 211	65.00	19.00
Plate 212	55.00	10.00
Plate 213	55.00	10.00
Plates 214-216	60.00	17.00
Plate 217	65.00	6.50
Plate 218	60.00	7.50
Plate 219	85.00	65.00
Plate 220	37.50	6.50
Plate 221	65.00	15.00
Plate 222	75.00	37.50
Plate 223	82.50	55.00
Plate 224	92.50	45.00
Plate 225	1,200.	375.00

Plate numbers are contained in the scroll work at the sides of the stamp.

No. 33 was printed from 1864 to 1879.

Thirty-nine plate numbers besides Plate 116 (No. 33c) are also known imperforate. Values for used copies start at $450.

Stamps from plate 177 have been altered and offered as plate 77.

A11

1862 Typo. Wmk. 23

34 A11 4p vermilion (P3) 925.00 75.00
b. Hair lines (P4) 825.00 65.00
d. Imperf. (P4) 2,100.

Hair lines on No. 34a are fine colorless lines drawn diagonally across the corners of the stamp.

A12

A13

A14

A15

1862 **Wmk. 24**

37 A12 3p pale rose 925.00 210.00
- *a.* 3p deep rose 1,750. 250.00
- *b.* With white dots under side ornaments 14,000. *3,000.*
- *c.* Wmk. 3 roses & shamrock

39 A13 6p lilac 1,000. 75.00
- *a.* 6p deep lilac 1,100. 92.50
- *b.* Hair lines 1,500. 150.00
- *c.* As "b," imperf. (P4) 1,600.
- *d.* Wmk. 3 roses & shamrock
- *e.* As "d," hair lines

40 A14 9p straw 2,400. 225.00
- *a.* 9p bister 2,400. 250.00
- *b.* Hair lines *8,500.* *3,000.*

42 A15 1sh green 1,200. 125.00
- *a.* 1sh deep green (P1) 1,400. 225.00
- *b.* As "c," imperf. 1,500.
- *c.* 1sh deep green, with hair lines (P2) 14,000.

Hair lines on Nos. 39b, 40b, 42c are fine colorless lines drawn diagonally across the corners of the stamp.

Compare design A14 with A19.

A16

1865 **Wmk. 23**

43 A16 4p vermilion (P12) 350.00 47.50
- Plate 10 475.00 82.50
- Plate 11 375.00 47.50
- Plate 14 425.00 75.00
- *a.* 4p dull vermilion (P8) 375.00 47.50
- Plate 7 425.00 75.00
- Plates 9,13 375.00 47.50
- *b.* Imperf. (P11, 12) 700.00

A17

(Hyphen after SIX) — A18

A19

A20

A21

1865 **Wmk. 24**

44 A17 3p rose (P4) 700.00 82.50
- *a.* Wmk. 3 roses & shamrock 1,600. 425.00

45 A18 6p lilac (P5) 450.00 65.00
- *a.* 6p deep lilac 550.00 82.50
- Plate 6 1,400. 125.00
- *b.* Double impression *6,500.*
- *c.* Wmk. 3 roses & shamrock (P5) 475.00
- As "c," plate 6 750.00

46 A19 9p straw (P4) 1,400. 325.00
- Plate 5 *13,500.*
- *a.* Wmk. 3 roses & shamrock (P4) *2,500.* *550.00*

47 A20 10p red brn (P1) *21,500.*

48 A21 1sh green (P4) 1,000. 140.00
- *b.* Wmk. 3 roses & shamrock *475.00*
- *c.* Vert. pair, imperf. btwn. *6,250.*

No. 46, plate 5, is from a proof sheet.

See Nos. 49-50, 52-54. Compare design A17 with A27.

(No hyphen after SIX) — A22

A23

1867-80 **Wmk. 25**

49 A17 3p rose (P5) 325.00 37.50
- *a.* 3p deep rose 325.00 47.50
- Plate 4 600.00 140.00
- Plate 6 300.00 37.50
- Plate 7 400.00 42.50
- Plate 8 375.00 42.50
- Plate 9 375.00 47.50
- Plate 10 400.00 82.50
- *b.* Imperf. (P5,6,8,9) 1,000.

50 A18 6p dull violet (P6) 700.00 70.00
- *a.* bright violet (P6) 700.00 75.00

51 A22 6p red violet (P8, 9) ('69) 425.00 60.00
- Plate 10 *20,000.*
- *a.* 6p violet (P8) 475.00 60.00
- *b.* Imperf. (P8, 9) 1,400. 1,100.

52 A19 9p bister (P4) ('67) 925.00 175.00
- *a.* Imperf. (P4) 3,250.

53 A20 10p red brown (P1) 1,600. 225.00
- Plate 2 *20,000.* *4,000.*
- *a.* 10p deep red brown 1,850. 275.00
- *b.* Imperf. (P1) 3,250.

54 A21 1sh green (P4) 500.00 27.50
- Plate 5 550.00 27.50
- Plate 6 700.00 27.50
- Plate 7 700.00 55.00
- *a.* 1sh deep green 650.00 32.50
- *b.* Imperf. (P4) 1,600. 825.00

55 A23 2sh blue (P1) 1,500. 110.00
- *a.* 2sh pale blue 2,100. 160.00
- Plate 3 5,500.
- *b.* Imperf. (P1) 3,250.

56 A23 2sh pale brn (P1) ('80) *8,500.* 1,800.
- *a.* Imperf. (P1) 6,000.

No. 51, plate 10 and No. 53, plate 2, are from proof sheets.

A24

1867 **Wmk. 26** ***Perf. 15½x15***

57 A24 5sh rose (P1) 3,750. 375.00
- Plate 2 4,750. 500.00
- *a.* 5sh pale rose 3,750. 375.00
- *b.* Imperf. (P1) 5,250.

See No. 90. Compare design A24 with A51.

A25

1870 **Engr.** **Wmk. 27** ***Perf. 14***

58 A25 ½p rose (P5) 70.00 14.00
- Plate 1 140.00 65.00
- Plate 3 110.00 32.50
- Plate 4 100.00 24.00
- Plate 6 75.00 14.00
- Plate 8 175.00 82.50
- Plate 9 2,400. 425.00
- Plate 10 90.00 14.00
- Plate 11-14 75.00 14.00
- Plate 15 110.00 32.50
- Plate 19 125.00 47.50
- Plate 20 150.00 65.00
- *a.* Imperf (see footnote) — —

Plates 1, 3-6, 8, 10, 14 are known imperf. Values: from $1,000 unused, $675 used.

A26

A27

A28

A29

Type A28 has a lined background.

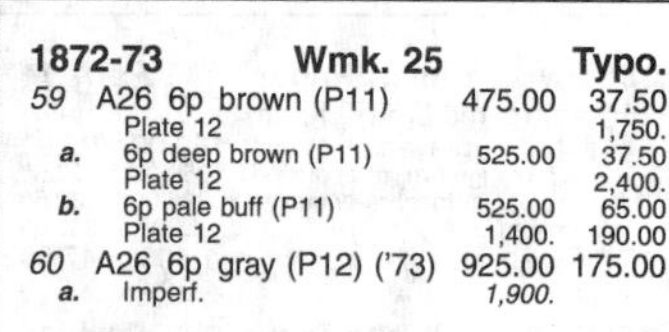

1872-73 **Wmk. 25** **Typo.**

59 A26 6p brown (P11) 475.00 37.50
- Plate 12 1,750.
- *a.* 6p deep brown (P11) 525.00 37.50
- Plate 12 2,400.
- *b.* 6p pale buff (P11) 525.00 65.00
- Plate 12 1,400. 190.00

60 A26 6p gray (P12) ('73) 925.00 175.00
- *a.* Imperf. *1,900.*

1873-80

61 A27 3p rose (shades) (P11, 15-16, 19) 250.00 32.50
- Plates 12, 17, 18 300.00 32.50
- Plate 14 325.00 32.50
- Plate 20 350.00 55.00

62 A28 6p gray (P15, 16) 325.00 47.50
- Plates 13, 14 325.00 47.50
- Plate 17 475.00 92.50

63 A28 6p buff (P13) 10,000.

64 A29 1sh pale green (P12, 13) 375.00 55.00
- Plates 10, 11 450.00 75.00
- Plate 14 *15,000.*
- *a.* 1sh deep green (P8, 9) 450.00 70.00

65 A29 1sh salmon (P13) ('80) 2,100. 375.00

No. 64, plate 14, is from a proof sheet.

See Nos. 83, 86-87. For surcharges see Nos. 94-95. For overprints see Nos. O6, O30.

A30

1875 **Wmk. 28**

66 A30 2½p claret (P1, 2) 375.00 70.00
- Plate 3 600.00 100.00
- *a.* Bluish paper (P1) 525.00 82.50
- As "a," P2 3,500. 750.00
- As "a," P3 2,750.
- *b.* Lettered "LH-FL" *9,250.* 1,100.

1876-80 **Wmk. 29**

67 A30 2½p claret (P4-9, 11-16) 325.00 37.50
- Plate 3 625.00 75.00
- Plate 10 350.00 47.50
- Plate 17 925.00 190.00

68 A30 2½p ultra (P19) ('80) 250.00 27.50
- Plate 17 325.00 47.50
- Plate 18, 20 300.00 32.50

A31

A32

1876-80 **Wmk. 23**

69 A31 4p vermilion (P15) 1,100. 300.00
- Plate 16 *18,500.*

70 A31 4p pale ol grn ('77) (P16) 525.00 160.00
- Plate 15 575.00 190.00
- Plate 17 *10,000.*
- *a.* Imperf (P15) *675.00*

71 A31 4p gray brn (P17) ('80) 1,000. 275.00

72 A32 8p brn lilac (P1) ('76) 4,250.

73 A32 8p org (P1) ('76) 750.00 240.00

No. 72 was never placed in use.

No. 69, plate 16, is from proof sheets.

A33

A34

1878 **Wmk. 26** ***Perf. 15½x15***

74 A33 10sh slate (P1) 27,500. 1,350.

75 A34 £1 brn lil (P1) 32,500. 1,950.

See Nos. 91-92. Compare design A34 with A52.

A35

A36

A37

A38

A39

A40

1880-81 **Wmk. 30** ***Perf. 14***

78 A35 ½p green 37.50 9.25
- *a.* Imperf. 825.00
- *b.* No watermark 3,750.

79 A36 1p red brown 14.00 9.25
- *a.* Imperf. 825.00
- *b.* Wmk. 29, error

80 A37 1½p red brown 125.00 32.50

81 A38 2p lilac rose 160.00 65.00

82 A30 2½p ultra (P23) ('81) 250.00 24.00
- Plate 21 300.00 27.50
- Plate 22 250.00 24.00
- *a.* Imperf. (P23) *300.00*

83 A27 3p rose (P21) ('81) 300.00 55.00
- Plate 20 400.00 100.00

84 A31 4p gray brown (P17, 18) 250.00 42.50

85 A39 5p dp indigo ('81) 450.00 82.50
- *a.* Imperf. *1,900.* *1,400.*

86 A28 6p gray (P18) 240.00 47.50
- Plate 17 250.00 47.50

87 A29 1sh sal (P14) ('81) 325.00 95.00
- Plate 13 375.00 95.00

The 1sh in purple was not issued. Value, unused, $4,500.

See No. 98. For overprints see Nos. O2-O3, O37, O45, O55.

Compare design A35 with A54.

1881

88 A40 1p lilac (14 dots in each angle) 110.00 17.00

89 A40 1p lilac (16 dots in each angle) 2.40 .75
- *a.* Printed on both sides 550.00
- *b.* Imperf., pair 1,250.
- *c.* No watermark 925.00
- *d.* Bluish paper 2,400.
- *e.* Printed on the gummed side 550.00

For overprint see No. O4.

1882-83 **Wmk. 31**

90 A24 5sh rose, *bluish* (P4) 7,500. 1,700.
- *a.* White paper 7,500. 1,700.

91 A33 10sh slate, *bluish* (P1) 32,500. 2,450.
- *a.* White paper 32,500. 2,100.

92 A34 £1 brown lilac, *bluish* (P1) 40,000. 4,250.
- *a.* White paper 42,500. 3,100.

A41

1882 **Wmk. Two Anchors (31)**

93 A41 £5 brt orange (P1) 6,500. 2,350.
- *a.* £5 pale dull orange, *bluish* 21,000. 5,500.
- *b.* £5 bright orange, *bluish* 22,500. 5,500.

The paper of No. 93b is less bluish than that of No. 93a, and it is a later printing.

Types of 1873-80 Surcharged in Carmine **3d**

1883 **Wmk. 30**

94 A27 3p on 3p violet 300.00 110.00

95 A28 6p on 6p violet 325.00 110.00
- *a.* Double surcharge *7,750.*

A44

1883 **Wmk. 31**

96 A44	2sh6p lilac	325.00	100.00
a.	Bluish paper	3,000.	750.00

See British Offices Abroad for overprints on types A44-A133.
These overprints include "M.E.F.," "B.A.," "B.M.A.," "E.A.F.," "CHINA," "Morocco Agencies," "TANGIER," "LEVANT," "PARAS," and "PIASTRE(S)."

A45

A46

A47

A48

A49

A50

1883-84 **Wmk. 30**

98 A35	½p slate blue ('84)	18.50	6.50
99 A45	1½p lilac ('84)	80.00	32.50
100 A46	2p lilac ('84)	125.00	60.00
101 A47	2½p lilac ('84)	65.00	11.00
102 A48	3p lilac ('84)	160.00	80.00
103 A49	4p green ('84)	375.00	160.00
104 A45	5p green ('84)	375.00	160.00
105 A46	6p green ('84)	400.00	190.00
106 A50	9p green	700.00	350.00
107 A48	1sh green ('84)	525.00	190.00
	Nos. 98-107 (10)	2,823.	1,240.

Values are for copies of good color. Faded copies sell for much less.

No. 104 with line instead of period under "d" was not regularly issued. Value, $6,500.

Nos. 98-105 and 107 exist imperf. Values from $750 to $900 each for Nos. 98-105, $1,800 for No. 107.

For overprints see Nos. O5, O7, O27-O29.

A51

A52

1884 **Wmk. 31**

108 A51	5sh carmine rose	525.00	125.00
a.	Bluish paper	4,750.	1,600.
109 A52	10sh ultra	1,200.	350.
a.	10sh cobalt	16,750.	4,900.
b.	Bluish paper	16,750.	4,250.
c.	As "a," bluish paper	24,000.	7,500.

For overprints see Nos. O8-O9.

A53

1884 **Wmk. 30**

110 A53	£1 brown violet	17,500.	1,500.

See Nos. 123-124. For overprints see Nos. O10, O13, O15.

Queen Victoria Jubilee Issue

A54

A55

A56

A57

A58

A59

A60

A61

A62

A63

A64

A65

Two types of 5p:
I - Squarish dots beside "d."
II - Tiny vertical dashes beside "d."

1887-92 **Wmk. 30**

111 A54	½p vermilion	1.40	.95
a.	Printed on both sides		
b.	Double impression	7,500.	
112 A55	1½p violet & grn	14.00	6.50
113 A56	2p grn & car rose	26.00	11.00
a.	2p green & vermilion	325.00	190.00
114 A57	2½p violet, *blue*	20.00	2.75
115 A58	3p violet, *yellow*	20.00	3.00
a.	3p violet, *orange*	425.00	175.00
116 A59	4p brown & grn	27.50	12.00
117 A60	4½p car rose & grn ('92)	9.25	*37.50*
118 A61	5p lilac & bl, II	32.50	10.00
a.	Type I	450.00	47.50
119 A62	6p violet, *rose*	27.50	9.25
120 A63	9p blue & lilac	55.00	37.50
121 A64	10p car rose & lilac ('90)	42.50	35.00
122 A65	1sh green	190.00	55.00
	Nos. 111-122 (12)	465.65	220.45

See Nos. 125-126. For overprints see Nos. O11-O12, O14, O16-O18, O31-O36, O38, O44, O46-O48, O54, O56-O58, O65-O66.

1888 **Wmk. Three Orbs (29)**

123 A53	£1 brown violet	32,500.	2,600.

1891 **Wmk. 30**

124 A53	£1 green	2,600.	425.

1900 **Wmk. 30**

125 A54	½p blue green	1.60	*1.90*
a.	Imperf	2,400.	
126 A65	1sh car rose & green	47.50	*110.00*

No. 125 in bright blue is a color changeling.

King Edward VII — A66

A67

A68

A69

A70

A71

A72

A73

A74

A75

A76

A77

A78

1902-11 **Wmk. 30** ***Perf. 14***

Ordinary Paper

127 A66	½p gray green	1.90	1.40
128 A66	1p scarlet	1.90	1.40
c.	1p aniline rose ('11)	160.00	125.00
e.	Booklet pane of 6	40.00	
f.	No watermark	37.50	*40.00*
g.	Imperf., pair	9,500.	
129 A67	1½p vio & green	32.50	17.00
130 A68	2p yel grn & car	40.00	17.00
b.	2p deep grn & red	24.00	19.00
131 A66	2½p ultra	19.00	9.25

132 A69 3p dull pur, *org yel* 37.50 19.00
133 A70 4p gray brn & grn 47.50 27.50
134 A71 5p dull pur & ultra 50.00 19.00
135 A66 6p pale dull vio 32.50 17.00
a. 6p slate purple 32.50 15.00
b. 6p red violet 27.50 24.00
c. 6p dark violet 27.50 *32.50*
136 A72 9p ultra & dull vio 72.50 55.00
137 A73 10p car & dull pur 75.00 55.00
a. 10p scarlet & dull purple 75.00 70.00
138 A74 1sh car & dull grn 75.00 32.50
a. 1sh scarlet & dark green 82.50 55.00

Wmk. 31

139 A75 2sh6p lilac 160.00 125.00
a. 2sh6p dark violet 140.00 140.00
140 A76 5sh car rose 200.00 150.00
b. 5sh carmine 200.00 110.00
141 A77 10sh ultra 500.00 300.00

Wmk. Three Imperial Crowns (30)

142 A78 £1 blue green 1,200. 450.00
Nos. 127-138 (12) 485.30 271.05

Nos. 129, 130 and 132 to 139 inclusive exist on both ordinary and chalky paper.

See Nos. 143, 144, 146-150. For overprints see Nos. O19-O26, O39-O43, O49-O53, O59-O64, O67-O83.

See British Offices Abroad for overprints on types A44-A133.
These overprints include "M.E.F.," "B.A.," "B.M.A.," "E.A.F.," "CHINA," "Morocco Agencies," "TANGIER," "LEVANT," "PARAS," and "PIASTRE(S)."

1904 **Wmk. 30**

143 A66 ½p pale yellow green 1.90 1.40
b. Booklet pane of 5 + label 275.00
c. Booklet pane of 6 30.00
d. Double impression *17,500.*
e. Imperf., pair *15,000.*

Edward VII — A79

1909-10

144 A70 4p pale orange ('10) 19.00 14.00
145 A79 7p gray ('10) 9.25 *17.00*

1911 ***Perf. 15x14***

146 A66 ½p dull yel green 37.50 *42.50*
147 A66 1p carmine rose 14.00 14.00
148 A66 2½p brt ultra 20.00 14.00
149 A69 3p violet, *yellow* 37.50 14.00
a. 3p gray, *lemon* *3,000.*
150 A70 4p orange 27.50 14.00
Nos. 146-150 (5) 136.50 98.50

King George V
A80 A81

1911 **Wmk. 30** ***Perf. 15x14***

151 A80 ½p yellow green 4.50 3.75
a. Booklet pane of 6 50.00
b. Perf. 14 (error) *9,000.* 375.00
152 A81 1p carmine 4.25 2.25
a. Booklet pane of 6 50.00
b. Perf. 14 (error) — —
c. 1p scarlet 13.00 2.75
d. As "c," booklet pane of 6 100.00

1912, Jan. 1 **Re-engraved**

153 A80 ½p yellow green 14.00 7.50
154 A81 1p scarlet 4.75 1.90
a. 1p aniline scarlet 140.00 82.50

In the re-engraved stamps the lines of the hair and beard are clearer. The re-engraved ½p has 3 lines of shading instead of 4 between the point of neck and frame; in the 1p the body of the lion is nearly covered by lines of shading.

1912, Aug. **Wmk. 33** ***Perf. 15x14***
Die I (Before Re-engraving)

155 A80 ½p yellow green 37.50 37.50
a. Booklet pane of 6 175.00

156 A81 1p scarlet 27.50 27.50
a. Booklet pane of 6 110.00

Die II (Re-engraved)

157 A80 ½p yellow green 5.00 2.75
158 A81 1p scarlet 7.50 2.75

1912, Oct. **Wmk. 32**

158A A80 ½p yellow green 14.00 7.50
c. Imperf., pair 225.00
158B A81 1p scarlet 14.00 7.50
d. Imperf., pair 210.00

A82

A83

A84

A85

A86

A87

A88 A89

King George V — A90

"Britannia Rules the Waves" A91

TWO PENCE:

Die I - Four horizontal lines above the head. Heavy colored lines above and below the bottom tablet. The inner frame line is closer to the central design than it is to the outer frame line.

Die II - Three lines above the head. Thinner lines above and below the bottom tablet. The inner frame line is midway between the central design and the outer frame line.

1912-13 **Wmk. 33** ***Perf. 15x14***

159 A82 ½p green .90 *.90*
a. Double impression *22,500.*
b. Booklet pane of 6 12.00
160 A83 1p scarlet .95 *.95*
a. Booklet pane of 6 10.00
b. Tete beche pair 67,500.
161 A84 1½p red brown 3.75 1.40
a. 1½p orange brown 19.00 15.00
b. "PENCF" 125.00 75.00
c. Unwmkd. 150.00 100.00
d. Booklet pane of 6 22.50
e. Booklet pane of 4 + 2 labels 350.00
162 A85 2p deep orange (I) 5.50 2.75
a. 2p deep orange (II) 4.75 3.25
b. Booklet pane of 6 (I) 50.00
c. Booklet pane of 6 (II) 85.00
163 A86 2½p ultra 11.00 3.75
164 A87 3p bluish violet 6.50 1.90
165 A88 4p slate green 14.00 1.90
166 A89 5p yellow brown 14.00 4.75
a. Unwmkd. 500.00
167 A89 6p rose lilac 14.00 6.50
a. 6p dull violet 24.00 9.25
b. Perf. 14 82.50 *100.00*
168 A89 7p olive green 19.00 9.25
169 A89 8p black, *yellow* 30.00 10.00
170 A90 9p black brown 19.00 5.50
171 A90 10p light blue 20.00 19.00
172 A90 1sh bister 19.00 3.75
Nos. 159-172 (14) 177.60 72.30

No. 167 is on chalky paper.

Nos. 159-172 were printed in a variety of shades.

See #177-178, 183, 187-200, 210, 212-220.

Compare design A83 with A97.

See British Offices Abroad for overprints on types A44-A133.
These overprints include "M.E.F.," "B.A.," "B.M.A.," "E.A.F.," "CHINA," "Morocco Agencies," "TANGIER," "LEVANT," "PARAS," and "PIASTRE(S)."

Perf. 11x12

1913-18 **Engr.** **Wmk. 34**

173 A91 2sh6p dark brown 190.00 110.00
a. 2sh6p light brown 190.00 160.00
174 A91 5sh rose car 275.00 225.00
a. 5sh carmine 300.00 250.00
175 A91 10sh indigo blue 425.00 325.00
a. 10sh blue 1,000. 600.00
176 A91 £1 green 1,200. 750.00
Nos. 173-176 (4) 2,090. 1,410.

Nos. 173-176 were printed in 1913 by Waterlow Bros. & Layton; Nos. 173a-175a were printed in 1915-18 by Thomas De La Rue & Co.

See Nos. 179-181, 222-224.

1913 **Wmk. 32** **Typo.** ***Perf. 15x14***
Coil Stamps

177 A82 ½p green 140.00 *160.00*
178 A83 1p scarlet 200.00 *210.00*

Type of 1913-18 Retouched

1919 **Engr.** **Wmk. 34** ***Perf. 11x12***

179 A91 2sh6p pale brown 92.50 55.00
180 A91 5sh car rose 200.00 82.50
181 A91 10sh blue 275.00 125.00
Nos. 179-181 (3) 567.50 262.50

The retouched stamps usually have a dot above the middle of the top frame. They are 22¾mm high, whereas Nos. 173-176 are 22mm high.

Nos. 179-181 were printed by Bradbury, Wilkinson & Co.

Type of 1912-13

1922 **Typo.** **Wmk. 33** ***Perf. 15x14***

183 A90 9p olive green 92.50 27.50

British Empire Exhibition Issue

British Lion and George V A92

Wmk. 35

1924, Apr. 23 **Engr.** ***Perf. 14***

185 A92 1p vermilion 9.00 10.00
Never hinged 13.50
186 A92 1½p dark brown 14.00 14.00
Never hinged 21.00

See Nos. 203-204.

Types of 1912-13 Issue

1924 **Typo.** ***Perf. 15x14***

187 A82 ½p green .95 .95
Never hinged 1.25
a. Wmk. sideways 6.50 3.25
Never hinged 12.00
b. Booklet pane of 6 10.00
Never hinged 15.00
c. Double impression *7,500.*
188 A83 1p scarlet .95 .95
Never hinged 1.25
a. Wmk. sideways 17.00 14.00
Never hinged 32.50
b. Booklet pane of 6 10.00
Never hinged 15.00
189 A84 1½p red brown .95 .95
Never hinged 1.25
a. Tête bêche pair 350.00 *575.00*
Never hinged 500.00
b. Wmk. sideways 6.50 3.50
Never hinged 14.50
c. Booklet pane of 6 10.00
Never hinged 15.00
d. Bklt. pane of 4 + 2 labels 92.50
Never hinged 150.00
e. Double impression 8,500.
190 A85 2p dp orange (II) 2.25 2.25
Never hinged 3.00
a. Wmk. sideways 70.00 *75.00*
Never hinged 125.00
b. Unwatermarked 525.00
Never hinged 750.00
191 A86 2½p ultra 4.50 2.75
Never hinged 8.00
a. Unwatermarked *1,000.*
Never hinged *1,250.*
192 A87 3p violet 9.25 2.25
Never hinged 15.00
193 A88 4p slate green 11.00 2.25
Never hinged 20.00
194 A89 5p yel brown 19.00 2.75
Never hinged 40.00
195 A89 6p dull violet 2.75 1.40
Never hinged 4.00
198 A90 9p olive green 11.00 3.25
Never hinged 17.50
199 A90 10p dull blue 35.00 37.50
Never hinged 90.00
200 A90 1sh bister 20.00 2.75
Never hinged 40.00
Nos. 187-200 (12) 117.60 60.00

Nos. 187a, 188a, 189b, 190a issued in coils.

Inverted watermarks on the three lowest values are usually from booklet panes.

Nos. 188-189 were issued also on experimental paper with variety of Wmk. 35: closer spacing; letters shorter, rounder.

British Empire Exhibition Issue
Type of 1924, Dated "1925"

1925, May 9 **Engr.** ***Perf. 14***

203 A92 1p vermilion 14.00 *22.50*
Never hinged 21.00
204 A92 1½p brown 40.00 *60.00*
Never hinged 60.00

A93

A94

A95

St. George Slaying the Dragon A96

1929, May 10 **Typo.** ***Perf. 15x14***

205 A93 ½p green 2.00 *2.00*
Never hinged 3.00
a. Wmk. sideways 27.50 *32.50*
Never hinged 85.00
b. Booklet pane of 6 22.50
206 A94 1p scarlet 2.00 2.00
Never hinged 3.00
a. Wmk. sideways 65.00 *60.00*
Never hinged 95.00
b. Booklet pane of 6 22.50
207 A94 1½p dark brown 2.00 1.60
Never hinged 3.00
a. Wmk. sideways 27.50 22.50
Never hinged 60.00
b. Booklet pane of 6 16.00
c. Booklet pane of 4 + 2 labels 175.00
208 A95 2½p deep blue 9.25 9.25
Never hinged 20.00
Nos. 205-208 (4) 15.25 14.85

Nos. 205a, 206a and 207a were issued in coils.

Wmk. 219

Engr. ***Perf. 12***

209 A96 £1 black 700.00 600.00
Never hinged 1,150.

Universal Postal Union, 9th Congress.

Types of 1924 and

A97

The backgrounds appear to be solid, but under a magnifying glass show the photoengraving screen.

Perf. 14½x14

1934-36 **Photo.** **Wmk. 35**

210 A82 ½p dark green .45 .45
Never hinged .85
a. Wmk. sideways 6.50 3.25
Never hinged 14.00
b. Booklet pane of 6 11.00
211 A97 1p carmine .45 .45
Never hinged .85
a. Wmk. sideways 11.50 11.50
Never hinged 22.50
b. Booklet pane of 6 11.00

No.	Description	Unused	Used
c.	Imperf., pair	1,200.	
d.	Pair, imperf. btwn.	2,000.	
212	A84 1½p red brown	.45	.45
	Never hinged	.85	
a.	Imperf., pair	300.00	
b.	Wmk. sideways	6.00	3.75
	Never hinged	8.50	
c.	Booklet pane of 6	5.50	
d.	Booklet pane of 4 + 2 labels	60.00	
213	A85 2p red org ('35)	.70	.70
	Never hinged	1.00	
a.	Imperf., pair	1,750.	
b.	Wmk. sideways	90.00	65.00
	Never hinged	160.00	
214	A97 2½p ultra ('35)	1.40	1.10
	Never hinged	2.00	
215	A87 3p dk violet ('35)	1.40	1.10
	Never hinged	2.00	
216	A88 4p dk sl grn ('35)	1.90	1.10
	Never hinged	3.00	
217	A89 5p yel brown ('36)	5.50	2.50
	Never hinged	8.50	
218	A90 9p dk ol grn ('35)	11.00	2.50
	Never hinged	16.00	
219	A90 10p Prus blue ('36)	14.00	10.00
	Never hinged	24.00	
220	A90 1sh bister brn ('36)	14.00	1.25
	Never hinged	27.50	
	Nos. 210-220 (11)	51.25	21.60

The designs in this set are slightly smaller than the 1912-13 issue.

Nos. 210a, 211a, 212b and 213b were issued in coils.

Britannia Type of 1913-18

1934 Engr. Wmk. 34 *Perf. 11x12*

No.	Description	Unused	Used
222	A91 2sh6p brown	60.00	32.50
	Never hinged	100.00	
223	A91 5sh carmine	140.00	72.50
	Never hinged	250.00	
224	A91 10sh dark blue	300.00	70.00
	Never hinged	500.00	
	Nos. 222-224 (3)	500.00	175.00

Waterlow & Sons. Can be distinguished by the crossed lines in background of portrait. Previous issues have horizontal lines only.

Silver Jubilee Issue

A98

Perf. 14½x14

1935, May 7 Photo. Wmk. 35

No.	Description	Unused	Used
226	A98 ½p dark green	.70	.20
	Never hinged	1.00	
a.	Booklet pane of 4	13.00	
227	A98 1p carmine	1.10	.80
	Never hinged	1.60	
a.	Booklet pane of 4	13.00	
228	A98 1½p red brown	.70	.35
	Never hinged	1.00	
a.	Booklet pane of 4	6.50	
229	A98 2½p ultramarine	4.25	3.00
	Never hinged	6.00	
a.	2½p Prussian blue	4,750.	4,750.
	Never hinged	5,500.	
	Nos. 226-229 (4)	6.75	4.35

25th anniv. of the reign of George V. Device at right differs on 1½p and 2½p.

Edward VIII — A99

1936 Wmk. 250

No.	Description	Unused	Used
230	A99 ½p dark green	.25	.25
	Never hinged	.50	
a.	Booklet pane of 6	1.50	
	Never hinged	2.00	
231	A99 1p crimson	.55	.45
	Never hinged	.75	
a.	Booklet pane of 6	1.50	
	Never hinged	2.00	
232	A99 1½p red brown	.25	.25
	Never hinged	.35	
a.	Booklet pane of 6	1.50	
	Never hinged	2.00	
b.	Booklet pane of 4 + 2 labels	55.00	
	Never hinged	75.00	
c.	Booklet pane of 2	1.50	
	Never hinged	2.50	
233	A99 2½p bright ultra	.25	.75
	Never hinged	.35	
	Nos. 230-233 (4)	1.30	1.70

King George VI and Queen Elizabeth A100

Perf. 14½x14

1937, May 13 Wmk. 251

No.	Description	Unused	Used
234	A100 1½p purple brown	.25	.25
	Never hinged	.35	

Coronation of George VI and Elizabeth.

See British Offices Abroad for overprints on types A44-A133. These overprints include "M.E.F.," "B.A.," "B.M.A.," "E.A.F.," "CHINA," "Morocco Agencies," "TANGIER," "LEVANT," "PARAS," and "PIASTRE(S)."

A101

A102

King George VI — A103

Nos. 235-240 show face and neck highlighted, background solid.

1937-39

No.	Description	Unused	Used
235	A101 ½p deep green	.20	.25
	Never hinged	.25	
a.	Wmk. sideways	.35	.45
	Never hinged	.45	
b.	Booklet pane of 6	2.00	
	Never hinged	2.75	
c.	Booklet pane of 4	17.50	25.00
	Never hinged	35.00	
d.	Booklet pane of 2	3.00	
	Never hinged	4.50	
236	A101 1p scarlet	.20	.20
	Never hinged	.25	
a.	Wmk. sideways	7.50	8.25
	Never hinged	19.00	
b.	Booklet pane of 6	4.50	
	Never hinged	6.00	
c.	Booklet pane of 4	45.00	42.50
	Never hinged	87.50	
d.	Booklet pane of 2	3.00	
	Never hinged	4.50	
237	A101 1½p red brown	.20	.20
	Never hinged	.20	
a.	Wmk. sideways	.75	1.10
	Never hinged	1.00	
b.	Booklet pane of 6	3.00	
	Never hinged	4.50	
c.	Booklet pane of 4 + 2 labels	35.00	
	Never hinged	50.00	
d.	Booklet pane of 2	2.00	
	Never hinged	2.75	
238	A101 2p orange ('38)	.45	.45
	Never hinged	.70	
a.	Wmk. sideways	40.00	35.00
	Never hinged	65.00	
b.	Booklet pane of 6	15.00	
	Never hinged	22.50	
239	A101 2½p bright ultra	.20	.20
	Never hinged	.25	
a.	Wmk. sideways	35.00	19.00
	Never hinged	60.00	
b.	Booklet pane of 6	15.00	
	Never hinged	20.00	
c.	Tête bêche pair	—	
240	A101 3p dk purple ('38)	2.00	.90
	Never hinged	3.50	
241	A102 4p gray green ('38)	.40	.70
	Never hinged	.60	
a.	Imperf., pair	2,000.	
	Never hinged	2,500.	
b.	Horiz. pair, imperf. on 3 sides	2,400.	
	Never hinged	3,000.	
242	A102 5p lt brown ('38)	1.25	.80
	Never hinged	2.25	
a.	Imperf., pair	2,250.	
	Never hinged	3,000.	
b.	Horiz. pair, imperf. on 3 sides	2,000.	
	Never hinged	2,500.	
243	A102 6p rose lilac ('39)	.90	.55
	Never hinged	1.10	
244	A103 7p emerald ('39)	2.10	.55
	Never hinged	4.00	
a.	Horiz. pair, imperf. on 3 sides	2,000.	
	Never hinged	2,500.	
245	A103 8p brt rose ('39)	2.50	.75
	Never hinged	3.50	
246	A103 9p dp ol green ('39)	2.75	.75
	Never hinged	5.00	
247	A103 10p royal bl ('39)	2.75	.75
	Never hinged	5.25	
a.	Imperf., pair	3,750.	
	Never hinged	4,500.	
248	A103 1sh brown ('39)	2.75	.70
	Never hinged	5.50	
	Nos. 235-248 (14)	18.65	7.75

Nos. 235a, 236a, 237a, 238a and 239a were issued in coils.

Nos. 235c and 236c are watermarked sideways.

The 1½p, 1p, 1½p, 2p and 2½p with watermark inverted are from booklet panes.

No. 238 bisects were used in Guernsey from 12/27/40 to 2/24/41.

See Nos. 258-263, 266, 280-285.

Oman Surcharges

Various definitive and commemorative stamps between Nos. 243 and 372 were surcharged in annas (a), new paisa (np) and rupees (r) for use in Oman. The surcharges do not indicate where the stamps were used.

King George VI and Royal Arms — A104

King George VI — A105

1939-42 Engr. Wmk. 259 *Perf. 14*

No.	Description	Unused	Used
249	A104 2sh6p chestnut	15.00	5.50
	Never hinged	32.50	
249A	A104 2sh6p yel green ('42)	3.25	1.40
	Never hinged	4.25	
250	A104 5sh dull red	6.00	1.90
	Never hinged	8.50	
251	A105 10sh indigo	75.00	19.00
	Never hinged	210.00	
251A	A105 10sh ultra ('42)	13.50	4.75
	Never hinged	19.00	
	Nos. 249-251A (5)	112.75	32.55

See No. 275.

Victoria and George VI A106

Perf. 14½x14

1940, May 6 Photo. Wmk. 251

No.	Description	Unused	Used
252	A106 ½p deep green	.20	.25
	Never hinged	.30	
253	A106 1p scarlet	.45	.35
	Never hinged	.90	
254	A106 1½p red brown	.20	.70
	Never hinged	.45	
255	A106 2p orange	.25	.35
	Never hinged	.45	
256	A106 2½p brt ultra	1.00	.45
	Never hinged	2.00	
257	A106 3p dark purple	1.50	3.25
	Never hinged	2.75	
	Nos. 252-257 (6)	3.60	5.35

Centenary of the postage stamp.

No. 255 bisects were used in Guernsey from 12/27/40 to 2/24/41.

Type of 1937-39, with Background Lightened

1941-42

No.	Description	Unused	Used
258	A101 ½p green	.20	.20
	Never hinged	.25	
a.	Booklet pane of 6	2.50	
	Never hinged	3.50	
b.	Booklet pane of 2	1.00	
	Never hinged	1.25	
c.	Imperf., pair	1,650.	
	Never hinged	2,350.	
d.	Tete beche pair	2,750.	
	Never hinged	3,750.	
e.	Booklet pane of 4		
259	A101 1p vermilion	.20	.25
	Never hinged	.25	
a.	Wmk. sideways ('42)	2.50	4.75
	Never hinged	3.75	
b.	Booklet pane of 2	1.00	
	Never hinged	1.25	
c.	Imperf., pair	2,250.	
	Never hinged	3,000.	
d.	Booklet pane of 4		
260	A101 1½p lt red brn ('42)	.25	.75
	Never hinged	.50	
a.	Booklet pane of 2	2.25	
	Never hinged	3.25	
b.	Booklet pane of 4		
261	A101 2p light orange	.25	.45
	Never hinged	.50	
a.	Wmk. sideways ('42)	13.00	17.50
	Never hinged	26.00	
b.	Booklet pane of 6	5.50	
	Never hinged	8.00	
c.	Imperf., pair	1,900.	
	Never hinged	2,500.	
d.	Tete beche pair	2,400.	
	Never hinged	3,250.	
262	A101 2½p ultra	.20	.25
	Never hinged	.25	
a.	Wmk. sideways ('42)	7.50	11.00
	Never hinged	14.00	
b.	Booklet pane of 6	3.00	
	Never hinged	4.00	
c.	Imperf., pair	2,000.	
	Never hinged	2,750.	
d.	Tete beche pair	2,350.	
	Never hinged	3,250.	
263	A101 3p violet	1.10	.90
	Never hinged	1.90	
	Nos. 258-263 (6)	2.20	2.80

Nos. 259a, 261a and 262a were issued in coils.

Nos. 258b, 258e, 259b, 259d, 260a-260b are made from sheets.

Catalogue values for unused stamps in this section, from this point to the end of the section, are for Never Hinged items.

Peace Issue

A107

King George VI and Symbols of Peace and Industry A108

Perf. 14½x14

1946, June 11 Photo. Wmk. 251

No.	Description	Unused	Used
264	A107 2½p bright ultra	.20	.20
265	A108 3p violet	.20	.20

Return to peace at the close of WW II.

George VI Type of 1939

1947, Dec. 29

No.	Description	Unused	Used
266	A103 11p violet brown	2.00	2.25

A109

King George VI and Queen Elizabeth A110

1948, Apr. 26 *Perf. 14½x14, 14x14½*

No.	Description	Unused	Used
267	A109 2½p brt ultra	.20	.20
268	A110 £1 dp chalky blue	37.50	32.50

25th anniv. of the marriage of King George VI and Queen Elizabeth.

A111

Vraicking (Gathering Seaweed) A112

1948, May 10 *Perf. 14½x14*

No.	Description	Unused	Used
269	A111 1p red	.20	.20
270	A112 2½p bright ultra	.20	.20

3rd anniversary of the liberation of the Channel Islands from German occupation.

Sold at post offices in the Channel Islands, but valid for postage throughout Great Britain.

A113

A114

A115

A116

1948, July 29

271 A113 2½p bright ultra .20 .20
272 A114 3p deep violet .30 .20
273 A115 6p red violet .55 .35
274 A116 1sh dark brown .90 .60
Nos. 271-274 (4) 1.95 1.35

1948 Olympic Games held at Wembley during July and August.

George VI Type of 1939

Wmk. 259

1948, Oct. 1 Engr. *Perf. 14*

275 A105 £1 red brown 12.50 *15.00*

A117

A118

A119

A120

Perf. 14½x14

1949, Oct. 10 Photo. Wmk. 251

276 A117 2½p bright ultra .20 .20
277 A118 3p brt violet .20 .30
278 A119 6p red violet .25 .30
279 A120 1sh brown .65 .80
Nos. 276-279 (4) 1.30 1.60

UPU, 75th anniversary.

Types of 1937

1950-51 Wmk. 251 *Perf. 14½x14*

280 A101 ½p light orange .20 .20
 a. Booklet pane of 2 1.00
 b. Booklet pane of 4 1.75
 c. Booklet pane of 6 2.50
 d. Imperf., pair *650.00*
 e. Tete beche pair *2,750.*
281 A101 1p ultramarine .20 .20
 a. Wmk. sideways .60 .20
 b. Booklet pane of 2 1.20
 c. Booklet pane of 4 1.75
 d. Booklet pane of 6 2.50
 e. Booklet pane of 3 + 3 labels 12.00
 f. Imperf., pair *1,750.*
282 A101 1½p green .35 .20
 a. Wmk. sideways 2.00 *2.50*
 b. Booklet pane of 2 1.50
 c. Booklet pane of 4 3.00
 d. Booklet pane of 6 3.75
283 A101 2p lt red brown .45 .20
 a. Wmk. sideways 1.40 *1.75*
 b. Booklet pane of 6 7.00
 c. Tete beche pair *2,750.*
284 A101 2½p vermilion .30 .20
 a. Wmk. sideways 1.40 1.40
 b. Booklet pane of 6 3.25
 c. Tete beche pair
285 A102 4p ultra ('50) 1.40 1.00
Nos. 280-285 (6) 2.90 2.00

Nos. 281a, 282a, 283a and 284a were issued in coils.

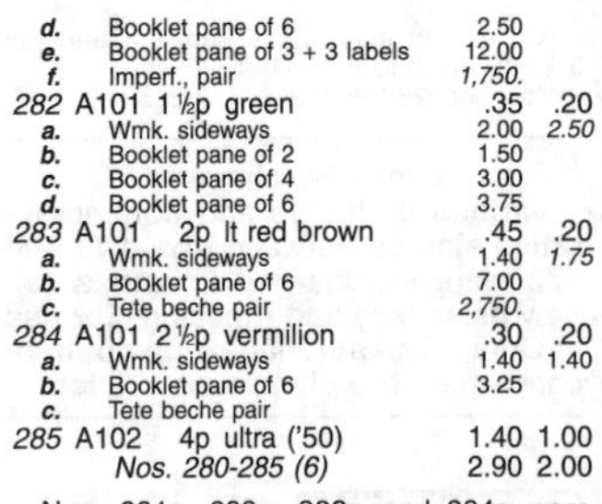

H.M.S. Victory
A121

St. George Slaying the Dragon
A122

Royal Arms
A123

Design: 5sh, White Cliffs, Dover.

Perf. 11x12

1951, May 3 Engr. Wmk. 259

286 A121 2sh6p green 2.25 .90
287 A121 5sh dull red 27.50 1.50
288 A122 10sh ultra 8.50 8.00
289 A123 £1 lt red brown 32.50 15.00
Nos. 286-289 (4) 70.75 25.40

Britannia, Symbols of Commerce and Prosperity, King George VI — A124

Festival Symbol
A125

Perf. 14½x14

1951, May 3 Photo. Wmk. 251

290 A124 2½p scarlet .20 .25
291 A125 4p bright ultra .25 .35

Festival of Britain, 1951.

Queen Elizabeth
A126 A127

A128 A129

A130 A131

A132

The 2½d exists in two types: Type I, in the front cross of the diadem, the top line extends half the width of the cross; Type II, the top line extends across the full width of the top of the cross.

Perf. 14½x14

1952-54 Photo. Wmk. 298

292 A126 ½p red orange ('53) .20 .20
 a. Booklet pane of 2 .70
 b. Booklet pane of 4 1.25
 c. Booklet pane of 6 1.50
293 A126 1p ultra ('53) .20 .20
 a. Booklet pane of 2 .90
 b. Booklet pane of 4 1.75
 c. Booklet pane of 6 2.25
 d. Booklet pane 3 + 3 labels 25.00
294 A126 1½p green ('52) .20 .20
 a. Booklet pane of 2 .70
 b. Booklet pane of 4 1.25
 c. Booklet pane of 6 ('53) 1.50
 d. Wmk. sideways .35 *.50*
 e. As "c," imperf. (error) *750.00*
295 A126 2p red brn ('53) .20 .20
 a. Booklet pane of 6 2.50
 b. Wmk. sideways 1.00 *1.50*
296 A127 2½p scarlet, Type I ('52) .20 .20
 a. Booklet pane of 6, Type II ('53) 7.00
 b. Wmk. sideways, Type I ('54) 7.50 *8.50*
 c. Type II .60 .55
297 A127 3p dk purple .65 .50
298 A128 4p ultra ('53) 2.75 .80
299 A129 5p lt brn ('53) .65 2.10
300 A129 6p lilac rose 3.25 .75
301 A129 7p emerald 8.50 4.00
302 A130 8p brt rose ('53) .65 .60
303 A130 9p dp ol grn 21.00 2.50
304 A130 10p royal blue 12.00 2.50
305 A130 11p vio brown 25.00 10.00
306 A131 1sh brown ('53) .80 .50
307 A132 1sh3p dk grn ('53) 3.75 2.25
308 A131 1sh6p dk bl ('53) 10.00 2.50
Nos. 292-308 (17) 90.00 30.00

Nos. 294d, 295b, 296b issued in coils.

Nos. 292-296 with watermark inverted are from booklets.

Type II stamps of No. 296 come only from booklet panes.

See Nos. 317-333, 353-369.

Compare design A128 with A139.

See regional issues, Guernsey, Jersey and Isle of Man for other stamps showing this portrait of the Queen, which have different frames or devices added to the design.

See British Offices Abroad for overprints on types A44-A133.
These overprints include "M.E.F.," "B.A.," "B.M.A.," "E.A.F.," "CHINA," "Morocco Agencies," "TANGIER," "LEVANT," "PARAS," and "PIASTRE(S)."

Caernarfon Castle, Wales — A133

Castles: 2sh6p, Carrickfergus, Ireland. 10sh, Edinburgh, Scotland. £1, Windsor, England.

1955 Engr. Wmk. 308 *Perf. 11x12*

309 A133 2sh6p dark brown 10.00 2.00
310 A133 5sh crimson 35.00 3.25
311 A133 10sh brt ultra 70.00 11.00
312 A133 £1 intense blk 110.00 32.50
Nos. 309-312 (4) 225.00 48.75

See Nos. 371-374, 525-528.

A134

A135

A136

A137

Perf. 14½x14

1953, June 3 Photo. Wmk. 298

313 A134 2½p scarlet .20 .20
314 A135 4p ultra .45 *1.75*
315 A136 1sh3p dark green 3.25 2.75
316 A137 1sh6p dark blue 6.25 3.50
Nos. 313-316 (4) 10.15 8.20

Types of 1952-54

1955-57 Wmk. 308 *Perf. 14½x14*

317 A126 ½p red orange ('56) .20 .20
 a. Booklet pane of 6 1.50
 b. Booklet pane of 4 1.25
 d. Booklet pane of 2 .60
318 A126 1p ultra ('56) .20 .20
 a. Bklt. pane of 3 + 3 labels 15.00
 b. Booklet pane of 6 1.75
 c. Booklet pane of 4 1.25
 e. Tete Beche pair 300.00
 f. Booklet pane of 2 .70
319 A126 1½p green ('56) .25 .25
 a. Booklet pane of 6 7.00
 b. Booklet pane of 4 5.50
 c. Wmk. sideways ('56) .25 .50
 e. Tete beche pair *1,000.*
 f. Booklet pane of 2 1.25
320 A126 2p red brown ('56) .20 *.25*
 a. Wmk. sideways ('56) .25 .50
 b. Booklet pane of 6 2.50
 d. Tete beche pair *500.00*
 e. Vert. pair, imperf. between *1,500.*
 f. As "a," horiz. pair, imperf. between *1,500.*
 h. Imperf., pair 250.00
321 A127 2½p scar, Type I ('56) .20 *.25*
 a. Booklet pane of 6, Type II 4.00
 b. Wmk. sideways, Type I ('56) 1.50 1.00
 d. Type II .30 .25
 e. Tete beche pair 200.00
 f. Imperf., pair
322 A127 3p dk purple ('56) .20 *.25*
 a. Booklet pane of 6 4.00
 b. Booklet pane of 4 5.50
 c. Wmk. sideways 15.00 12.50
 e. Tete beche pair *700.00*
323 A128 4p ultra 1.10 .40
324 A129 5p lt brn ('56) 4.50 4.25
325 A129 6p lilac rose ('56) 3.25 .95
326 A129 7p emerald 37.50 7.50
327 A130 8p brt rose ('56) 4.50 .95
328 A130 9p dp ol grn ('56) 16.00 2.40
329 A130 10p royal bl ('56) 14.50 2.40
330 A130 11p vio brown .40 *1.40*
331 A131 1sh brown 14.50 .55
332 A132 1sh3p dk grn ('56) 25.00 1.40
333 A131 1sh6p dark blue 17.50 1.40
Nos. 317-333 (17) 140.00 25.00

Nos. 319c, 320a, 321b, 322c issued in coils.

Nos. 317-322 with watermark inverted are from booklets. See Nos. 353-369.

Black Graphite Lines on Back

1957-59 Wmk. 308

317c A126 ½p red orange .25 .20
 p. Phosphor. ('59) 4.00 *4.50*
318d A126 1p ultra .25 .25
 p. Phosphor. ('59) 9.00 8.00
319d A126 1½p green .25 *1.10*
 p. Phosphor. ('59) 3.25 3.25
320c A126 2p red brown 1.25 *1.60*
 p. Phosphor. ('59) 175.00 125.00

321c A127 2½p scarlet (II) 6.75 4.00
322d A127 3p dark purple .25 .20
Nos. 317c-322d (6) 9.00 7.35

The vertical black graphite lines were applied to facilitate mail sorting by an electronic machine. The 2p has one line (at right, seen from back), the others two.

Phosphorescent bands were overprinted vertically in Nov. 1959 on the face of the preceding ½p, 1p, 1½p and 2p graphite-lined stamps, plus the 2p, 2½p, 3p, 4p and 4½p graphite-lined stamps with Wmk. 322, in a letter-sorting experiment. These faint bands can be seen best with an ultraviolet lamp; without it they can be seen best on unused stamps.

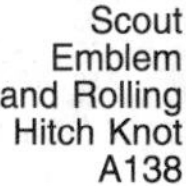

Scout Emblem and Rolling Hitch Knot A138

4p, Swallows. 1sh3p, Globe encircled by compass.

Perf. 14½x14

1957, Aug. 1 **Wmk. 308**
334 A138 2½p scarlet .20 .20
335 A138 4p ultra .30 *1.00*
336 A138 1sh3p dk green 3.50 3.25
Nos. 334-336 (3) 4.00 4.45

50th anniv. of the Boy Scout movement and the World Scout Jubilee Jamboree, Sutton Coldfield, Aug. 1-12.

A139

1957, Sept. 12 **Photo.**
337 A139 4p ultra .65 *.75*

46th Conf. of the Inter-Parliamentary Union, London, Sept. 12-19.

Welsh Dragon A140

Designs: 6p, Flag with British Empire and Commonwealth Games Emblem. 1sh3p, Welsh dragon holding laurel.

1958, July 18 ***Perf. 14½x14***
338 A140 3p dk purple .20 .20
339 A140 6p red lilac .20 .30
340 A140 1sh3p green 1.50 1.50
Nos. 338-340 (3) 1.90 2.00

6th British Empire and Commonwealth Games, Cardiff, July 18-26.

Regional Issues of Great Britain for Guernsey, Jersey, Isle of Man, Northern Ireland, Scotland and Wales-Monmouthshire are listed in separate sections following Great Britain Envelopes.

Types of 1952-55

Perf. 14½x14

1958-65 **Photo.** **Wmk. 322**
353 A126 ½p red orange .20 .20
a. Booklet pane of 6 .70
b. Booklet pane of 4 .55
e. Booklet pane of 4 (3 No. 353 + No. 357) ('63) 7.50 7.50
f. Tete beche pair *850.00*
g. Booklet pane of 4 (2 Nos. 353 + 2 No. 357) ('64) 2.25 2.25
354 A126 1p ultra ('59) .20 .20
a. Booklet pane of 6 ('59) 1.00
b. Booklet pane of 4 .75
e. Imperf., pair
f. Bklt. pane, #2 #354, 2 #358 ('65) 2.25 2.25
355 A126 1½p green .20 .20
a. Booklet pane of 6 1.00
b. Booklet pane of 4 .75
356 A126 2p red brown .20 .20
a. Wmk. sideways .20 .20
b. Booklet pane of 6 6.00
357 A127 2½p scarlet, type II ('59) .20 .20
a. Type I ('61) .50 .50
b. Wmk. sideways, type I .30 *.40*
c. Booklet pane of 6, Type II ('59) 1.00
f. Tete beche pair, type II
g. Booklet pane of 4, type II ('64) 2.50
h. Imperf., pair
358 A127 3p dark purple .20 .20
a. Booklet pane of 6 1.75
b. Booklet pane of 4 1.25
e. Imperf., pair 90.00
g. Wmk. sideways .20 .20
359 A128 4p ultra .35 .20
b. Booklet pane of 6 ('65) 3.00
c. Booklet pane of 4 ('65) 1.50
d. Wmk. sideways .60 .50
360 A128 4½p henna brn .20 .20
361 A129 5p light brown .20 .20
362 A129 6p lil rose ('59) .30 .20
363 A129 7p emerald .35 .20
364 A130 8p brt rose ('60) .35 .20
365 A130 9p dp ol grn ('59) .35 .20
366 A130 10p royal blue .75 .20
367 A131 1sh brown .35 .20
368 A132 1sh3p dk grn ('59) .30 .20
369 A131 1sh6p dark blue 3.00 .25
Nos. 353-369 (17) 7.70 3.45

Nos. 356a and 357b were issued in coils. The 3p and 4p watermarked sideways may be from a coil or booklet pane of 4.

Booklet panes of this issue have watermarks normal, inverted or sideways.

Part perf. booklet panes exist of No. 353a and No. 354a.

Black Graphite Lines on Back

1958-59 **Wmk. 322**
353c A126 ½p red orange ('59) 6.50 6.50
d. Booklet pane of 6 25.00
354c A126 1p ultra 1.50 1.10
d. Booklet pane of 6 15.00
355c A126 1½p green ('59) 60.00 55.00
d. Booklet pane of 6 300.00
356c A126 2p red brown 8.75 2.50
cp. Phosphor. ('59) 4.50 4.50
357d A127 2½p scarlet (II) ('59) 10.00 8.00
dp. Phosphor. ('59) 19.00 17.50
e. Booklet pane of 6 100.00
358c A127 3p dark purple .75 .40
cp. Phosphor. ('59) 10.00 7.50
d. Booklet pane of 6 5.50
359a A128 4p ultra ('59) 5.00 3.50
ap. Phosphor. ('59) 14.00 12.50
360a A128 4½p henna brn ('59) 7.50 3.00
ap. Phosphor. ('59) 25.00 17.50
Nos. 353c-360a (8) 100.00 80.00

The vertical black graphite lines were applied to facilitate mail sorting by an electronic machine. The 2p has one line; the others two. Missing or misplaced lines occur on 1p, 3p and 4p.

Nos. 353c and 354c were issued only in booklets or coils; No. 355c only in booklets.

Phosphorescent Stamps of 1958-65

1960-67 **Wmk. 322**
353p A126 ½p red orange .20 .20
ap. Booklet pane of 6 4.00
bp. Booklet pane of 4 50.00
354p A126 1p ultra .20 .20
ap. Booklet pane of 6 5.00
bp. Booklet pane of 4 12.00
fp. Booklet pane of 2 each #354p, 358p 40.00
355p A126 1½p green .20 .20
ap. Booklet pane of 6 5.00
bp. Booklet pane of 4 50.00
356p A126 2p red brown .20 .20
ap. Watermark sideways .20 .20
357p A127 2½p scarlet (II) .20 *.40*
ap. Type I ('61) 37.50 27.50
cp. Booklet pane of 6 60.00
358p A127 3p dark purple .40 *.80*
ap. Booklet pane of 6 7.50
bp. Booklet pane of 4 12.50
gp. Watermark sideways 1.25 .50
359p A128 4p ultramarine .25 .25
bp. Booklet pane of 6 6.25
cp. Booklet pane of 4 5.00
dp. Watermark sideways .20 .20
360p A128 4½p henna brown ('61) .25 .25
361p A129 5p lt brown ('67) .25 .25
362p A129 6p lilac rose .40 .25
363p A129 7p emerald ('67) .45 .30
364p A130 8p brt rose ('67) .40 .30
365p A130 9p dp ol grn ('67) .45 .30
366p A130 10p royal blue ('67) .60 .40
367p A131 1sh brown ('67) .30 *.40*
368p A132 1sh3p dark green 1.50 *2.25*
369p A131 1sh6p dark blue ('66) 1.50 1.40
Nos. 353p-369p (17) 7.75 8.35

The 2p, 2½p (II) and 3p were issued with both one and two phosphorescent bands. The less expensive is valued here.

Watermarked sideways, the 2p is from a coil; the 3p and 4p from booklet pane or coil; the ½p, 1p and 1½p from booklet panes (hence unlisted in this state).

Booklet panes of 4 with phosphorescent bands; ½p, 1p, 1½p, 3p (2 bands), 4p, and 1p se-tenant with 3p (1 or 2 bands). Booklet panes of 6 with phosphorescent bands: ½p, 1p, 1½p, 2½p (II) (1 or 2 bands), 3p (1 or 2 bands), 4p.

1959 **Engr.** **Wmk. 322** ***Perf. 11x12***
371 A133 2sh6p dark brown .40 .20
372 A133 5sh crimson .75 .40
373 A133 10sh bright ultra 2.50 1.75
374 A133 £1 intense blk 7.50 4.25
Nos. 371-374 (4) 11.15 6.60

Postboy on Horseback A147

Queen Elizabeth II, Oak Leaves and 1660 Post Horn — A148

Perf. 14½x14, 14x14½

1960, July 7 **Photo.** **Wmk. 322**
375 A147 3p bright violet .40 .40
376 A148 1sh3p dark green 3.00 3.00

Tercentenary of the act establishing the General Letter Office (General Post Office).

Symbolic Wheel CD3

Perf. 14½x14

1960, Sept. 19 **Wmk. 322**
377 CD3 6p red lilac & grn 1.50 .25
378 CD3 1sh6p dk bl & red brn 6.00 4.25

1st anniv. of the establishment of CEPT.

Symbolic Thrift Plant — A150

Nut Tree, Nest, Squirrel, Owl A151

Thrift Plant A152

Perf. 14x14½, 14½x14

1961, Aug. 28 **Photo.** **Wmk. 322**
379 A150 2½p scar & blk .20 .20
a. Black omitted *7,500.*
380 A151 3p pur & org .20 .20
a. Orange omitted 125.00 75.00
381 A152 1sh6p dk bl & ver 2.00 1.50
Nos. 379-381 (3) 2.40 1.90

Centenary of Post Office Savings Bank.

CEPT Emblem A153

Nineteen Doves Flying as One CD4

Design: 10p, Queen at right.

1961, Sept. 18 ***Perf. 14½x14***
382 A153 2p red brn, yel & rose .20 .20
383 CD4 4p ultra, pink & buff .20 .20
384 CD4 10p dk bl, yel grn & Prus blue .20 *.40*
a. Yellow green omitted *4,000.*
b. Dark blue omitted *3,000.*
Nos. 382-384 (3) .60 .80

Hammer Beam Roof of Westminster Hall — A155

Parliament — A156

Perf. 14½x14, 14x14½

1961, Sept. 25 **Wmk. 322**
385 A155 6p red lil & gold .30 .20
a. Gold omitted *425.00*
386 A156 1sh3p green & slate 2.00 1.75
a. Slate (Queen's head) omitted *4,000.*

7th Commonwealth Parliamentary Conf.

National Productivity Symbol — A157

Designs: 3p, Two arrows and map of the British Isles. 1sh3p, Five arrows pointing up.

Perf. 14½x14

1962, Nov. 14 **Photo.** **Wmk. 322**
387 A157 2½p car rose & dk grn .20 .20
388 A157 3p violet & blue .20 .20
a. Queen's head omitted *800.00*
389 A157 1sh3p dk grn, car rose & bl 1.40 *1.90*
a. Queen's head omitted *3,500.*
Nos. 387-389 (3) 1.80 2.30

Phosphorescent

387p A157 2½p car rose & dk grn 1.25 1.25
388p A157 3p violet & blue 2.75 2.50
389p A157 1sh3p dk grn, car rose & bl 25.00 13.00
Nos. 387p-389p (3) 29.00 16.75

National Productivity Year. The watermark on Nos. 387-388 is inverted.

Phosphorescent Commemorative stamps between Nos. 387-493 were issued both with and without phosphorescence on the front unless otherwise noted with the issue.

Starting with No. 514, commemorative stamps were issued only with phosphorescence on the front unless otherwise noted.

Phosphorescent Regulars: Starting in 1967, all small stamps (lower values) of the regular series were issued only with phosphorescence.

Wheat Emblem and People A158

1sh3p, Children of different races.

1963, Mar. 21 **Wmk. 322**

390 A158 2½p pink & dp car .20 .20
p. Phosphor. 1.60 1.20
391 A158 1sh3p yellow & brn 1.75 *2.00*
p. Phosphor. 25.00 17.50

FAO "Freedom from Hunger" campaign.

Paris Postal Conference A159

1963, May 7 **Wmk. 322**

392 A159 6p purple & green .35 .35
a. Green omitted *1,750.*
p. Phosphor. 7.00 6.00

Cent. of the 1st Intl. Postal Conf., Paris, 1863, and Paris Postal Conf., May 7-9, 1963.

Buttercups, Daisies and Bee A160

Design: 4½p, Badger, Fawn, woodpecker, lark, titmouse, butterfly, mouse and wild plants.

1963, May 16 ***Perf. 14½x14***

393 A160 3p multicolored .20 .20
p. Phosphor. .50 .60
394 A160 4½p multicolored .20 *.30*
p. Phosphor. 2.50 *2.75*

Natl. Nature Week, May 18-25, and the importance of wildlife conservation.

Helicopter Lifting Man from Lifeboat A161

Lifeboat Men A162

Design: 4p, 19th cent. lifeboat under sail.

1963, May 31 **Photo.**

395 A161 2½p multicolored .20 .20
396 A161 4p multicolored .35 *.65*
397 A162 1sh6p multicolored 2.25 *2.50*
Nos. 395-397 (3) 2.80 3.35

Phosphorescent

395p A161 2½p multicolored 1.25 .55
396p A161 4p multicolored 2.25 1.25
397p A162 1sh6p multicolored 42.50 27.50
Nos. 395p-397p (3) 46.00 29.30

9th Intl. Life-Boat Conf., Edinburgh, 6/3-5.

Red Cross and Elizabeth II — A163

1sh3p, Cross at UL. 1sh6p, Cross in center.

1963, Aug. 15 **Wmk. 322**

Cross in Red

398 A163 3p purple .20 .20
a. Red cross omitted *3,000.*
399 A163 1sh3p gray & blue 2.40 2.50
400 A163 1sh6p dl bl & ol bister 2.50 2.75
Nos. 398-400 (3) 5.10 5.45

Phosphorescent

398p A163 3p purple .50 .50
399p A163 1sh3p gray & blue 35.00 27.50
400p A163 1sh6p dull blue & ol bister 30.00 22.50
Nos. 398p-400p (3) 65.50 50.50

Red Cross Cent. Cong., Geneva, Sept. 2.

Cable Around World and Under Sea A164

1963, Dec. 3 ***Perf. 14½x14***

401 A164 1sh6p blue & blk 2.50 *2.75*
a. Black omitted *3,000.*
p. Phosphor. 16.00 14.00

Opening of the Commonwealth Pacific (telephone) cable service, COMPAC.

Puck and Bottom from "A Midsummer Night's Dream," Shakespeare — A165

Hamlet Holding Yorick's Skull A166

First Folio Portrait of Shakespeare and: 6p, Feste the Clown, from "Twelfth Night." 1sh3p, Romeo and Juliet. 1sh6p, Henry V praying at Agincourt.

Perf. 14½x14

1964, Apr. 23 **Photo.** **Wmk. 322**

402 A165 3p multicolored .20 .20
403 A165 6p multicolored .30 .30
404 A165 1sh3p multicolored .65 .75
405 A165 1sh6p multicolored 1.25 1.25

Perf. 11x12

Engr.

406 A166 2sh6p dark gray 1.60 1.50
Nos. 402-406 (5) 4.00 4.00

Phosphorescent

402p A165 3p multicolored .20 *.30*
403p A165 6p multicolored .45 *.70*
404p A165 1sh3p multicolored 3.00 *5.00*
405p A165 1sh6p multicolored 8.75 5.25
Nos. 402p-405p (4) 12.40 11.25

400th anniv. of the birth of William Shakespeare. No. 406 was not issued with phosphorescence.

Apartment Buildings, London A170

Designs: 4p, Shipyards, Belfast. 8p, Beddgelert Forest Park, Snowdonia. 1sh6p, Dounreay nuclear reactor and sheaves of wheat.

1964, July 1 **Photo.** ***Perf. 14½x14***

410 A170 2½p multicolored .20 .20
411 A170 4p multicolored .25 .25
a. Violet ("4d") omitted *175.00*
b. Ocher omitted *275.00*
c. Violet & ocher omitted *175.00*
412 A170 8p multicolored .55 .55
a. Green omitted *4,500.*
413 A170 1sh6p multicolored 3.00 3.00
Nos. 410-413 (4) 4.00 4.00

Phosphorescent

410p A170 2½p multicolored .30 .25
411p A170 4p multicolored .80 .75
412p A170 8p multicolored 6.50 5.00
413p A170 1sh6p multicolored 18.00 11.00
Nos. 410p-413p (4) 25.60 17.00

20th Intl. Geographical Cong., London, July 20-28.

Spring Gentian A171

1964, Aug. 5 **Wmk. 322**

414 A171 3p shown .20 .20
a. Blue omitted *4,500.*
415 A171 6p Dog rose .25 .25
416 A171 9p Honeysuckle 1.40 1.40
a. Light green omitted *4,500.*
417 A171 1sh3p Fringed water lily 1.90 1.25
Nos. 414-417 (4) 3.75 3.10

Phosphorescent

414p A171 3p shown .25 .20
415p A171 6p Dog rose 1.50 1.10
416p A171 9p Honeysuckle 4.50 2.25
417p A171 1sh3p Fringed water lily 21.00 17.00
Nos. 414p-417p (4) 27.25 20.55

10th Intl. Botanical Cong., Edinburgh, Aug. 3-12.

Forth Road Bridge A172

Design: 6p, Bridge and railroad bridge.

1964, Sept. 4 ***Perf. 14½x14***

418 A172 3p blk, lil & blue .20 .20
p. Phosphor. .85 .85
419 A172 6p vio blk, grnsh bl & car lake .30 .25
a. Greenish blue omitted *2,750.* *1,500.*
p. Phosphor. 4.25 4.25

Opening of Forth Road Bridge, Scotland.

Winston Churchill A173

Design: 1sh3p, Large portrait.

1965, July 8 **Photo.** **Wmk. 322**

420 A173 4p dk brown & blk .20 .20
p. Phosphor. .30 .25
421 A173 1sh3p gray & black .30 .30
p. Phosphor. 2.50 *3.25*

Sir Winston Spencer Churchill (1874-1965), statesman and WWII leader.

Seal of Simon de Montfort A174

St. Stephen's Hall, Westminster Hall and Abbey, Engraving by Wenceslaus Hollar, 1647 — A175

1965, July 19 ***Perf. 14½x14***

422 A174 6p dark olive .20 .20
p. Phosphor. .65 .65
423 A175 2sh6p brown black .80 .80

700th anniv. of Parliament. No. 423 was not issued with phosphorescence; size: 58x21mm.

Salvation Army Band and "Blood and Fire" Flag A176

1sh6p, Salvation Army officers and flag.

1965, Aug. 9

424 A176 3p dk bl, yel & brt car .20 .20
p. Phosphor. .50 .40
425 A176 1sh6p red, yel & brt bl .70 *.90*
p. Phosphor. 2.50 *3.00*

Centenary of the Salvation Army.

Lister's Carbolic Spray A177

1sh, Joseph Lister & carbolic acid formula.

1965, Sept. 1

426 A177 4p gray, bluish blk & red brn .20 .20
a. Red brown (tubing) omitted *250.00*
b. Bluish black omitted *2,000.*
p. Phosphor. .25 .25
427 A177 1sh blk, blue & pur .65 *.80*
p. Phosphor. 2.50 1.50

Introduction of antiseptic surgery by Joseph Lister, cent.

Trinidad Folk Dancers, Shrove Monday Carnival A178

Design: 1sh6p, French Canadian folk dancers, Les Feux Follets.

Perf. 14½x14

1965, Sept. 1 **Photo.** **Wmk. 322**

428 A178 6p orange & blk .20 .20
p. Phosphor. .25 .25
429 A178 1sh6p brt vio & blk .80 .90
p. Phosphor. 2.25 2.25

1st Commonwealth Arts Festival, 9/16-10/2.

Supermarine Spitfire Fighters — A179

Anti-Aircraft Gun Battery in Action A180

Designs: No. 431, Pilot in cockpit of Hawker Hurricane fighter. No. 432, Wing tips of Messerschmitt ME-109 and Spitfire. No. 433, Two Spitfires attacking Heinkel HE-111 bomber. No. 434, Spitfire attacking Junkers JU-187B Stuka dive bomber. No. 435, Hurricanes returning over wreckage of Dornier DO-17 Z bomber. 1sh3p, Vapor trails over St. Paul's Cathedral, London.

Perf. 14½x14

1965, Sept. 13 **Photo.** **Wmk. 322**

430 A179 4p slate & dk ol .45 .45
431 A179 4p slate & dk ol .45 .45
432 A179 4p sl, dk ol, brt bl & red .45 .45
433 A179 4p slate & dk ol .45 .45
434 A179 4p slate & dk ol .45 .45
435 A179 4p sl, dk ol & brt blue .45 .45
a. Bright blue omitted
b. Block of 6, #430-435 2.75 1.50
436 A180 9p vio bl, org & vio black 1.90 1.90
437 A180 1sh3p brt bl, sl & grnsh gray 1.90 1.90
Nos. 430-437 (8) 6.50 6.50

Phosphorescent

430p A179 4p slate & dark ol .80 .80
431p A179 4p slate & dark ol .80 .80
432p A179 4p sl, dk ol, brt bl & red .80 .80
433p A179 4p slate & dark ol .80 .80
434p A179 4p slate & dark ol .80 .80
435p A179 4p sl, dk ol & brt bl .80 .80
a. Block of 6, #430p-435p 3.30 2.10
436p A180 9p vio bl, org & vio black 2.50 2.50

437p	A180	1sh3p brt bl, slate & grnsh gray	2.50	2.50
		Nos. 430p-437p (8)	9.80	9.80

25th anniv. of the Battle of Britain. Nos. 430-435 printed in blocks of 6 (3x2) in sheets of 120.

Post Office Tower and Georgian Buildings — A181

Design: 1sh3p, Post Office Tower and Nash Terrace, Regents Park, horiz.

1965, Oct. 8 ***Perf. 14x14½, 14½x14***

438 A181	3p brt bl, lem & ol green		.20	.20
p.	Phosphor.		.20	.20
439 A181	1sh3p grn, ol grn & bl		.35	.40
p.	Phosphor.		.30	.40

Opening of the Post Office Tower, London.

UN Emblem A182

ICY Emblem A183

1965, Oct. 25 ***Perf. 14½x14***

440 A182	3p multicolored	.20	.20
p.	Phosphor.	.35	.35
441 A183	1sh6p multicolored	.40	.50
p.	Phosphor.	2.75	2.75

20th anniv. of the UN and Intl. Cooperation Year, 1965.

"World Telecommunication Stations" — A184

ITU Cent.: 1sh6p, "Radio waves & switchboard."

1965, Nov. 15 **Photo.** **Wmk. 322**

442 A184	9p multicolored	.25	.25
p.	Phosphor.	1.50	1.50
443 A184	1sh6p bl, red, blk, ind & pink	.50	.60
a.	Pink omitted	750.00	
p.	Phosphor.	5.50	5.75

Robert Burns and Saltier Cross of St. Andrew A185

Design: 1sh3p, Alexander Nasmyth portrait of Burns, his signature and symbols of his life. Portrait of Burns on 4p stamp is adaptation of Archibald Skirvings', chalk drawing, 1798.

1966, Jan. 25 ***Perf. 14½x14***

444 A185	4p blue, blk & dk sl	.20	.20
p.	Phosphor.	.25	.30
445 A185	1sh3p org, blk & Prus blue	.30	.40
p.	Phosphor.	2.00	2.25

Robert Burns (1759-1796), Scottish national poet.

Westminster Abbey — A186

Fan Vaulting, Chapel of Henry VII A187

1966, Feb. 28 **Photo.** ***Perf. 14½x14***

452 A186	3p blue, blk, & red brn	.20	.20
p.	Phosphor.	.20	.20

Perf. 11x12

Engr.

453 A187	2sh6p black	.35	.45

900th anniv. of Westminster Abbey. No. 453 issued only without phosphor.

Landscape near Hassock, Sussex A188

Views: 6p, Antrim, Northern Ireland. 1sh3p, Harlech Castle, Wales. 1sh6p, The Cairngorms (mountains), Scotland.

Perf. 14½x14

1966, May 2 **Photo.** **Wmk. 322**

454	A188	4p multicolored	.20	.20
455	A188	6p multicolored	.20	.20
456	A188	1sh3p multicolored	.25	.30
457	A188	1sh6p multicolored	.30	.35
		Nos. 454-457 (4)	.95	1.05

Phosphorescent

454p	A188	4p multicolored	.20	.20
455p	A188	6p multicolored	.20	.20
456p	A188	1sh3p multicolored	.25	.30
457p	A188	1sh6p multicolored	.30	.35
		Nos. 454p-457p (4)	.95	1.05

Soccer Players — A189

Players and Crowd A190

1sh3p, Goalkeeper and two players.

Perf. 14x14½, 14½x14

1966, June 1 **Photo.** **Wmk. 322**

458	A189	4p multicolored	.20	.20
459	A190	6p multicolored	.20	.20
a.		Black omitted	75.00	
b.		Yellow green omitted	1,500.	
c.		Red omitted	1,750.	
460	A190	1sh3p multicolored	.25	.25
a.		Blue omitted	140.00	
		Nos. 458-460 (3)	.65	.65

Phosphorescent

458p	A189	4p multicolored	.20	.20
459p	A190	6p multicolored	.20	.20
460p	A190	1sh3p multicolored	.25	.25
		Nos. 458p-460p (3)	.65	.65

Final games of the 1965-66 World Soccer Championship for the Jules Rimet Cup, Wembley, July 11-30.

See No. 465.

Blackheaded Gull — A191

Perf. 14½x14

1966, Aug. 8 **Photo.** **Wmk. 322**

Birds in Natural Colors

461	A191	4p shown	.20	.20
p.		Phosphor.	.20	.20
462	A191	4p Blue tit	.20	.20
p.		Phosphor.	.20	.20
463	A191	4p European robin	.20	.20
p.		Phosphor.	.20	.20
464	A191	4p European blackbird	.20	.20
p.		Phosphor.	.20	.20
a.		Block of 4, #461-464	.80	.50
b.		Block of 4, #461p-464p	.80	.75

Seven colors have been found omitted (singly or in combinations) on Nos. 461-464; green, red, ultramarine, brown, red brown, yellow and black.

No. 458 Inscribed: "ENGLAND WINNERS"

1966, Aug. 18 ***Perf. 14x14½***

465 A189	4p multicolored	.20	.20

England's victory in the World Soccer Cup Championship.

Jodrell Bank Radio Telescope A192

Designs: 6p, Automobiles (Jaguar and 3 Mini-Minors). 1sh3p, SR N6 Hovercraft. 1sh6p, Windscale atomic reactor.

1966, Sept. 19 ***Perf. 14½x14***

466	A192	4p yellow & blk	.20	.20
467	A192	6p org, red & dk bl	.20	.20
a.		Red (Mini-Minors) omitted	3,500.	
b.		Dark blue (Jaguar & imprint) omitted	3,000.	
468	A192	1sh3p sl, blk, org & bl	.30	.30
469	A192	1sh6p multicolored	.35	.35
		Nos. 466-469 (4)	1.05	1.05

Phosphorescent

466p	A192	4p yellow & black	.20	.20
467p	A192	6p org, red & dk bl	.20	.20
468p	A192	1sh3p slate, blk, org & bl	.35	.35
469p	A192	1sh6p multicolored	.45	.45
		Nos. 466p-469p (4)	1.20	1.20

British technology.

Battle of Hastings A193

Battle of Hastings from Bayeux Tapestry: No. 471, Two knights on horseback, one killed, one attacking. No. 472, Slain Harold on horseback and knight with shield. No. 473, Knight with shield and axe fighting horseman. No. 474, Knight on foot killing man, and horseman attacking with lance. No. 475, Four knights and two horses in battle scene. 6p, Norman ship. 1sh3p, King Harold's housecarls (body guard) battling Normans.

Photo.; Gold Impressed on 6p, 1sh3p

Perf. 14½x14

1966, Oct. 14 **Wmk. 322**

Size: 38½x22mm

470	A193	4p multicolored	.20	.20
471	A193	4p multicolored	.20	.20
472	A193	4p multicolored	.20	.20
473	A193	4p multicolored	.20	.20
474	A193	4p multicolored	.20	.20
475	A193	4p multicolored	.20	.20
a.		Strip of 6, #470-475	.75	
476	A193	6p multi & gold	.30	.30

Size: 58x22mm

477	A193	1sh3p multi & gold	.75	.65
		Nos. 470-477 (8)	2.25	2.15

Phosphorescent

470p	A193	4p multicolored	.20	.20
471p	A193	4p multicolored	.20	.20
472p	A193	4p multicolored	.20	.20
473p	A193	4p multicolored	.20	.20
474p	A193	4p multicolored	.20	.20
475p	A193	4p multicolored	.20	.20
b.		Strip of 6, #470p-475p	.75	
476p	A193	6p multi & gold	.30	.30
477p	A193	1sh3p multi & gold	.85	.85
		Nos. 470p-477p (8)	2.35	2.35

900th anniv. of the Battle of Hastings.

Eight colors have been found omitted (singly or in pair) on Nos. 470-475 and 470p-477p: gray, orange, blue, dark blue, bright green, olive green, brown and magenta. Also violet on 1sh3p.

Gold Omitted

The variety "Gold (Queen's head) omitted" can be counterfeited by chemically removing the gold.

Christmas — A194

Photo.; Gold Impressed

1966, Dec. 1 ***Perf. 14x14½***

478	A194	3p King	.20	.20
b.		Green omitted		250.00
p.		Phosphor.	.20	.20
479	A194	1sh6p Snowman	.25	.25
b.		Pink omitted	700.00	
p.		Phosphor.	.25	.25

Loading Ship at Dock and Train A195

Design: 1sh6p, Loading plane from trucks and flags of EFTA members.

Perf. 14½x14

1967, Feb. 20 **Photo.** **Wmk. 322**

480 A195	9p blue & multi	.20	.20
p.	Phosphor.	.20	.20
481 A195	1sh6p violet & multi	.20	.20
p.	Phosphor.	.20	.20

European Free Trade Assoc. Tariffs were abolished Dec. 31, 1966, among EFTA members (Austria, Denmark, Finland, Great Britain, Norway, Portugal, Sweden, Switzerland).

Colors omitted include: 9p—yellow, brown, light blue, light violet and green singly; black, brown, light blue and yellow simultaneously. 1sh6p—dark blue, bister, yellow, red, ultramarine and gray. Value range for one-color omissions, $17.50 to $35.

Hawthorn and Wild Blackberry A196

Flowers: No. 489, Morning-glory and viper's bugloss. No. 490, Ox-eye daisy, coltsfoot and buttercup. No. 491, Bluebell, red campion and wood anemone. 9p, Dog violet. 1sh9p, Primrose.

Perf. 14½x14

1967, Apr. 24 **Photo.** **Wmk. 322**

488	A196	4p multicolored	.20	.20
489	A196	4p multicolored	.20	.20
490	A196	4p multicolored	.20	.20
491	A196	4p multicolored	.20	.20
a.		Block of 4, #488-491	.45	
492	A196	9p multicolored	.30	.25
493	A196	1sh9p multicolored	.40	.35
		Nos. 488-493 (6)	1.50	1.40

Phosphorescent

488p	A196	4p multicolored	.20	.20
489p	A196	4p multicolored	.20	.20
490p	A196	4p multicolored	.20	.20
491p	A196	4p multicolored	.20	.20
a.		Block of 4, #488p-491p	.45	

492p A196 9p multicolored .25 .25
493p A196 1sh9p multicolored .35 .35
Nos. 488p-493p (6) 1.40 1.40

Four colors have been found omitted on Nos. 488-491 and three on 488p-491p: dark brown, red, violet and dull purple.

Master Lambton, by Thomas Lawrence — A198

Mares and Foals, by George Stubbs A199

Design: 1sh6p, Children Coming out of School, by Laurence Stephen Lowry.

Photo.; Gold Impressed on 4p, 1sh6p
Perf. 14x14½, 14½x14

1967, July 10 Unwmk.
514 A198 4p multicolored .20 .20
a. Gold (Queen's head & value) omitted 125.00
515 A199 9p multicolored .20 .20
a. Black (Queen's head & value) omitted 350.00
b. Yellow omitted 1,000.
516 A199 1sh6p multicolored .20 .20
a. Blue omitted 150.00
b. Gray omitted 75.00
c. Gold (Queen's head) omitted 800.00
Nos. 514-516 (3) .60 .60

See Nos. 568-571.

Gipsy Moth IV — A200

1967, July 24 Photo. *Perf. 14½x14*
517 A200 1sh9p multicolored .20 .20

Sir Francis Chichester's one-man voyage around the world, Aug. 27, 1966-May 28, 1967.

Radar Screen A201

British Discoveries: 1sh, Penicillin mold. 1sh6p, Vickers 10 twin jet engines. 1sh9p, Television camera, vert.

Perf. 14½x14, 14x14½
1967, Sept. 19 Photo. Wmk. 322
518 A201 4p multicolored .20 .20
519 A201 1sh multicolored .20 .20
520 A201 1sh6p multicolored .20 .20
521 A201 1sh9p multicolored .20 .20
a. Gray omitted 250.00
Nos. 518-521 (4) .80 .80

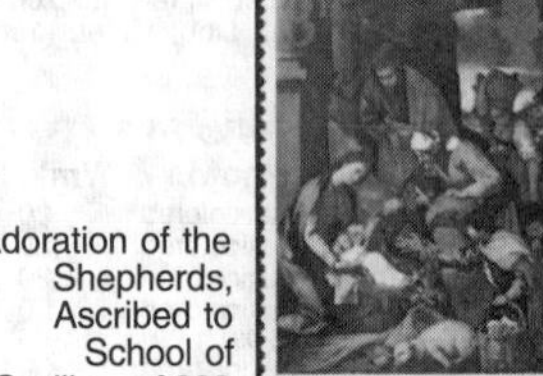

Adoration of the Shepherds, Ascribed to School of Seville — A202

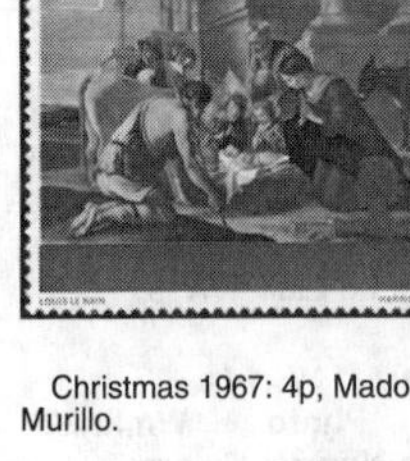

Adoration of the Shepherds, by Le Nain A203

Christmas 1967: 4p, Madonna and Child, by Murillo.

Photo.; Gold Impressed
Perf. 14x14½, 14½x14

1967 Unwmk.
522 A202 3p multicolored .20 .20
a. Gold (Queen's head & value) omitted 55.00
b. Pink omitted 750.00
523 A202 4p multicolored .20 .20
a. Gold (Queen's head & value) omitted 50.00
524 A203 1sh6p multicolored .20 .20
a. Gold (Queen's head & value) omitted 3,000.
b. Blue omitted 325.00
Nos. 522-524 (3) .60 .60

Issue dates: 4p, Oct. 18; 3p, 1sh6p, Nov. 27.

Castle Type of 1955
Perf. 11x12

1967-68 Engr. Unwmk.
525 A133 2sh6p dk brown ('68) .30 .30
526 A133 5sh crimson ('68) .70 .60
527 A133 10sh brt ultra ('68) 3.75 *5.00*
528 A133 £1 intense black 3.25 *4.00*
Nos. 525-528 (4) 8.00 9.90

Aberfeldy Bridge, Perthshire A204

Designs: 4p, Prehistoric Tarr Steps, Exmoor. 1sh6p, Menai Bridge, North Wales, 1826. 1sh9p, Viaduct, Highway M4.

Perf. 14½x14
1968, Apr. 29 Photo. Unwmk.
560 A204 4p gold & multi .20 .20
561 A204 9p gold & multi .20 .20
a. Blue omitted
b. Gold (Queen's head) omitted 125.00
562 A204 1sh6p gold & multi .20 *.30*
a. Gold (Queen's head) omitted 125.00
b. Red omitted
563 A204 1sh9p gold & multi .20 *.35*
a. Gold (Queen's head) omitted 150.00
Nos. 560-563 (4) .80 1.05

Emmeline Pankhurst Statue A205

Designs: 4p, Letters "TUC" and faces. 1sh, Sopwith Camel 1914-1918 fighter plane and formation of Lightning jets. 1sh9p, Capt. Cook's "Endeavour" and signature.

1968, May 29
564 A205 4p brt grn, blk, ol & bl .20 .20
565 A205 9p gray, violet & blk .20 .20
566 A205 1sh gray, ol, red, bl & blk .20 .20
567 A205 1sh9p blk & bister .20 .20
Nos. 564-567 (4) .80 .80

Cent. of Trades Union Congress (4p); 50th anniv. of women's suffrage (9p); 50th anniv. of the Royal Air Force (1sh); bicent. of Captain Cook's first discovery voyage (1sh9p).

Paintings Types of 1967

Paintings: 4p, Elizabeth I, c. 1575, artist unknown. 1sh, Pinkie (Miss Sarah Moulton-Barrett) by Sir Thomas Lawrence. 1sh6p, St. Mary le Port, by John Piper. 1sh9p, The Hay Wain (landscape), by John Constable.

Photo.; Gold Impressed
Perf. 14x14½, 14½x14

1968, Aug. 12
568 A198 4p multicolored .20 .20
a. Gold (Queen's head & value) omitted 100.00
569 A198 1sh multicolored .20 .25
a. Gold (Queen's head & value) omitted 150.00
570 A198 1sh6p multicolored .20 .30
a. Gold (Queen's head & value) omitted 75.00
571 A199 1sh9p multicolored .20 .35
a. Gold (Queen's head & value) omitted 350.00
Nos. 568-571 (4) .80 1.10

Sizes: 4p, 27x37½mm; 1sh, 25½x37½mm; 1sh6p, 31x37½mm; 1sh9p, 38x28mm.

Boy and Girl with Rocking Horse A206

Girl Playing with Dolls and Dollhouse A207

Christmas: 1sh6p, Boy with toy train and building blocks.

Perf. 14½x14, 14x14½
1968, Nov. 25 Photo.
572 A206 4p gold & multi .20 .20
a. Gold omitted 2,000.
573 A207 9p gold & multi .20 .20
a. Yellow omitted 60.00
574 A207 1sh6p gold & multi .20 .20
Nos. 572-574 (3) .60 .60

British Ships A208

Designs: 5p, R.M.S. Queen Elizabeth 2. No. 576, Elizabethan Galleon. No. 577, East Indiaman. No. 578, Cutty Sark. No. 579, S.S. Great Britain. No. 580, R.M.S. Mauretania.

1969, Jan. 15 *Perf. 14½x14*
Size: 58x22mm
575 A208 5p multicolored .20 .20
a. Black omitted 1,000.
b. Gray omitted 75.00
c. Red omitted 37.50

Size: 38½x22mm
576 A208 9p multicolored .20 .20
a. Red & blue omitted 1,500.
577 A208 9p multicolored .20 .20
578 A208 9p multicolored .20 .20
a. Strip of 3, #576-578 .60

Size: 58x22mm
579 A208 1sh multicolored .20 .30
580 A208 1sh multicolored .20 .30
a. Pair, #579-580 .75
Nos. 575-580 (6) 1.20 1.40

British seamen and shipbuilders.

Concorde over Great Britain and France A209

Designs: 9p, Concorde seen from above and from side, flags of France and Great Britain. 1sh6p, Outlines of plane's nose and tail superimposed.

1969, Mar. 3 Photo. *Perf. 14½x14*
581 A209 4p multicolored .20 .20
a. Violet omitted 200.00
b. Orange omitted 100.00
582 A209 9p multicolored .20 .20
583 A209 1sh6p multicolored .20 .20
a. Silver omitted 175.00
Nos. 581-583 (3) .60 .60

First flight of the prototype Concorde plane at Toulouse, France, Mar. 1, 1969.

Alcock, Brown, Daily Mail and Vickers Vimy Plane A210

"EUROPA" and "CEPT" CD12

Hand Holding Wrench A212

Flags of NATO Nations Forming one Flag A213

Vickers-Vimy Plane and Globe — A214

1969, Apr. 2
584 A210 5p multicolored .20 .20
585 CD12 9p multicolored .20 .25
586 A212 1sh multicolored .20 .25
587 A213 1sh6p multicolored .20 .30
a. Black omitted 50.00
b. Green omitted 50.00
588 A214 1sh9p multicolored .20 .30
Nos. 584-588 (5) 1.00 1.30

50th anniv. of the 1st non-stop Atlantic flight from Newfoundland to Ireland of Capt. John Alcock and Lt. Arthur Whitten Brown; 10th anniv. of the Conference of European Postal and Telecommunications Administrations; 50th anniv. of the ILO (1sh); 20th anniv. of NATO; 50th anniv. of the first England to Australia flight (1sh9p).

Durham Cathedral A215

British Cathedrals: No. 590, York Minster. No. 591, St. Giles', Edinburgh. No. 592, Canterbury. 9p, St. Paul's. 1sh6p, Liverpool Metropolitan.

Perf. 14½x14
1969, May 28 Photo. Unwmk.
589 A215 5p multicolored .20 .20
590 A215 5p multicolored .20 .20
591 A215 5p multicolored .20 .20
592 A215 5p multicolored .20 .20
a. Block of 4, #589-592 .25 .25
593 A215 9p multicolored .25 .25
a. Black (9d) omitted 80.00
594 A215 1sh6p multicolored .40 .40
Nos. 589-594 (6) 1.45 1.45

King's Gate, Caernarvon Castle, Wales — A216

Celtic Cross, Margam Abbey, Glamorgan A217

Prince of Wales — A218

Designs: No. 596, Eagle Tower, Caernarvon Castle (2 flags). No. 597, Queen Eleanor's Gate, Caernarvon Castle.

Perf. 14x14½

1969, July 1 Photo. Unwmk.

595	A216	5p silver & multi	.20	.20
596	A216	5p silver & multi	.20	.20
597	A216	5p silver & multi	.20	.20
a.		Strip of 3, #595-597	.25	.25
598	A217	9p gold, gray & black	.20	.20
599	A218	1sh black & gold	.20	.20
		Nos. 595-599 (5)	1.00	1.00

Investiture of Prince Charles as Prince of Wales, July 1.

Mahatma Gandhi and Flag of India A219

1969, Aug. 13 *Perf. 14½x14*

600	A219	1sh6p orange, blk & grn	.20	.20

Mohandas K. Gandhi (1869-1948), leader in India's fight for independence.

Emblem of Post Office Bank A220

International Subscriber Dialing — A221

Automatic Letter Sorting A222

Design: 1sh, Telecommunications (pulse code modulation graph).

Perf. 13½x14

1969, Oct. 1 Litho. Unwmk.

601	A220	5p blue & multi	.20	.20
602	A221	9p ultra & multi	.20	.20
603	A221	1sh green & multi	.20	.20
604	A222	1sh6p multicolored	.20	.20
		Nos. 601-604 (4)	.80	.80

Technological advancements of the British Post Office, transfer of responsibility from the government to the Post Office Corporation.

Angel A223

Christmas: 5p, Three shepherds. 1sh6p, The Three Kings.

Photo.; Gold Embossed

1969, Nov. 26 *Perf. 14x15*

605	A223	4p multicolored	.20	.20
606	A223	5p multicolored	.20	.20
607	A223	1sh6p multicolored	.20	.20
		Nos. 605-607 (3)	.60	.60

Fife Harling House, Scotland A224

British Rural Architecture: 9p, Cotswold limestone house, Gloucestershire, England. 1sh, Aberaeron town house, Wales. 1sh6p, Irish cottage with Ulster thatching.

Perf. 14x15

1970, Feb. 11 Photo. Unwmk.

Size: 38½x22mm

608	A224	5p multicolored	.20	.20
609	A224	9p multicolored	.20	.20

Size: 38½x27mm

610	A224	1sh multicolored	.20	.20
611	A224	1sh6p multicolored	.25	.25
		Nos. 608-611 (4)	.85	.85

Mayflower Leaving Plymouth, England A225

Designs: 5p, Signing of the Declaration of Arbroath. 9p, Florence Nightingale and soldiers in Scutari Hospital. 1sh, Earl Grey, Great Britain; Charles Robert, France; Victor Bohmert, Germany; De Keussler, Russia, and document in 4 languages. 1sh9p, Sir William Herschel, Francis Bailey, Sir John Herschel and telescope.

Photo.; Gold Embossed

1970, Apr. 1 *Perf. 14x15*

612	A225	5p red & multi	.20	.20
613	A225	9p blue & multi	.20	.20
614	A225	1sh lt blue & multi	.25	.25
615	A225	1sh6p olive & multi	.30	.30
616	A225	1sh9p brt pink & multi	.30	.30
		Nos. 612-616 (5)	1.25	1.25

650th anniv. of the Declaration of Arbroath (5p); Florence Nightingale (1820-1910), nurse and hospital reformer (9p); Intl.Cooperative Alliance, 75th anniv. (1sh); 350th anniv. of Mayflower sailing (1sh6p); sesquicentennial of the Royal Astronomical Soc. (1sh9p).

Missing colors or embossing occur on each denomination.

"The Pickwick Papers," by Dickens A226

Wordsworth's Grasmere, Lake District A227

Designs: No. 618, Mr. and Mrs. Micawber ("David Copperfield"). No. 619, David Copperfield and Betsy Trotwood ("David Copperfield"). No. 620, "Oliver Twist."

Perf. 14x14½

1970, June 3 Photo. Unwmk.

617	A226	5p orange & multi	.20	.20
618	A226	5p lil rose & multi	.20	.20
619	A226	5p grnsh blue & multi	.20	.20
620	A226	5p lemon & multi	.20	.20
a.		Block of 4, #617-620	.40	.30
621	A227	1sh6p citron & multi	.30	.30
		Nos. 617-621 (5)	1.10	1.10

Charles Dickens (1812-70), novelist. William Wordsworth (1770-1850), poet, No. 621.

Athletics A228

1970, July 15 Litho. *Perf. 14x14½*

639	A228	5p shown	.20	.20
640	A228	1sh6p Swimming	.30	.30
641	A228	1sh9p Bicycling	.30	.30
		Nos. 639-641 (3)	.80	.80

9th British Commonwealth Games, Edinburgh, July 16-25.

Philympia, London Phil. Exhib., Sept. 18-26 — A229

5p, Penny black. 9p, 1847 1-shilling stamp, #5. 1sh6p, 1855 4-pence stamp, #22.

1970, Sept. 18 Photo. *Perf. 14x14½*

642	A229	5p multicolored	.20	.20
643	A229	9p multicolored	.20	.20
644	A229	1sh6p multicolored	.20	.20
		Nos. 642-644 (3)	.60	.60

Christmas (Illuminations from 14th Century de Lisle Psalter) — A230

Designs: 4p, Angel and Shepherds. 5p, Nativity. 1sh6p, Adoration of the Kings.

1970, Nov. 25 Photo. *Perf. 14x14½*

645	A230	4p red & multi	.20	.20
646	A230	5p violet & multi	.20	.20
a.		Imperf., pair	250.00	
647	A230	1sh6p olive & multi	.25	.25
		Nos. 645-647 (3)	.65	.65

Decimal Currency Issue

"P" instead of "D"

Mountain Road, by T.P. Flanagan A231

Paintings from Northern Ireland: 7½p, Deer's Meadow, by Thomas Carr. 9p, Tolymore Forest Park, by Colin Middleton.

1971, June 16 Photo. *Perf. 14½x14*

648	A231	3p multicolored	.20	.20
649	A231	7½p multicolored	.35	.35
650	A231	9p multicolored	.45	.45
		Nos. 648-650 (3)	1.00	1.00

Ulster '71 Festival, Belfast, May-Oct.

John Keats (1795-1821) — A232

Writers and their signatures: 5p, Thomas Gray (1716-71). 7½p, Sir Walter Scott (1771-1832).

1971, July 28 Photo. *Perf. 14½x14*

651	A232	3p dull bl, blk & gold	.20	.20
652	A232	5p olive, blk & gold	.35	.35
653	A232	7½p yel brn, blk & gold	.45	.45
		Nos. 651-653 (3)	1.00	1.00

Soldier, Sailor, Airman, Nurse, 1921, and Poppy A233

Designs: 7½p, Roman centurion on horseback, York Castle and coat of arms. 9p, Rugby players 100 years ago, and rose.

1971, Aug. 25

654	A233	3p ultra & multi	.20	.20
655	A233	7½p ocher & multi	.40	.40
656	A233	9p olive & multi	.40	.40
		Nos. 654-656 (3)	1.00	1.00

50th anniv. of the British Legion (3p); 1900th anniv. of the founding of York (7½p); cent. of the Rugby Football Union (9p).

Physical Sciences Building, University College of Wales, Aberystwyth — A234

Modern University Buildings: 5p, Faraday Building, Engineering Faculty, University of Southampton. 7½p, Engineering Building, University of Leicester. 9p, Hexagon Restaurant, University of Essex.

1971, Sept. 22 Photo. *Perf. 14½x14*

657	A234	3p citron & multi	.20	.20
658	A234	5p rose vio & multi	.20	.20
659	A234	7½p dp brn & multi	.45	.45
660	A234	9p dk blue & multi	.75	.75
		Nos. 657-660 (4)	1.60	1.60

No. 658 exists with large "p" in "5p." These are from plate combination 1A1B1C1D and were not officially issued.

Dream of the Kings A235

Christmas (from Stained Glass Windows, Canterbury Cathedral): 3p, Adoration of the Kings. 7½p, Journey of the Kings.

1971, Oct. 13

661	A235	2½p scarlet & multi	.20	.20
662	A235	3p ultra & multi	.20	.20
663	A235	7½p green & multi	.85	.85
		Nos. 661-663 (3)	1.25	1.25

James Clark Ross (1800-1862) and Map of South Polar Sea — A236

British Polar Explorers: 5p, Martin Frobisher (1535-1594), and Desceliers map, 1550. 7½p, Henry Hudson (c. 1560-1611) and Petrus Plancius map, 1592. 9p, Robert Falcon Scott (1868-1912) and map of Antarctica.

1972, Feb. 16 *Perf. 14x14½*

664	A236	3p dp bister & multi	.20	.20
665	A236	5p brick red & multi	.20	.20
666	A236	7½p violet & multi	.40	.40
667	A236	9p blue & multi	.50	.50
		Nos. 664-667 (4)	1.30	1.30

See Nos. 689-693.

Head of Tutankhamen as Fisherman — A237

Coast Guard A238

Ralph Vaughan Williams and "Sea Symphony" A239

1972, Apr. 26 Photo. *Perf. 14½x14*
668 A237 3p gold & multi .20 .20

Photo.; Queen's Head Gold Embossed

669 A238 7½p blue & multi .35 .35
670 A239 9p multicolored .70 .70
Nos. 668-670 (3) 1.25 1.25

50th anniv. of the discovery of the tomb of Tutankhamen by Howard Carter and Lord Carnarvon; sesquicentennial of the British Coast guard; Ralph Vaughan Williams (1872-1958), composer.

St. Andrew's, Greensted-Juxta-Ongar — A240

Old Village Churches: 4p, All Saints, Earls Barton. 5p, St. Andrew's, Letheringsett. 7½p, St. Andrew's, Helpringham. 9p, St. Mary the Virgin, Huish Episcopi.

Photo.; Queen's Head Gold Embossed

1972, June 21 *Perf. 14x14½*
671 A240 3p dull blue & multi .20 .20
672 A240 4p olive & multi .20 .20
673 A240 5p dp grn & multi .20 .20
674 A240 7½p red & multi .70 .70
675 A240 9p blue & multi .70 .70
Nos. 671-675 (5) 2.00 2.00

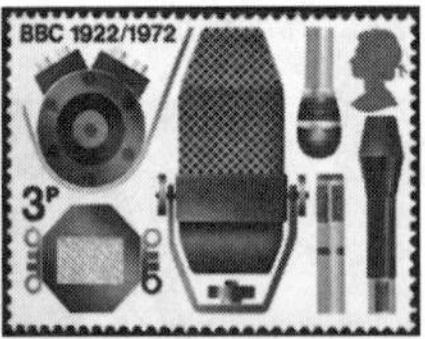

Various BBC Microphones — A241

Designs: 5p, Wooden horn loudspeaker 1925. 7½p, Color TV camera, 1972. 9p, Marconi's oscillator and spark transmitter, 1897.

1972, Sept. 13 Photo. *Perf. 14½x14*
676 A241 3p black, brn & yel .20 .20
677 A241 5p henna brn & blk .20 .20
678 A241 7½p black & magenta .45 .45
679 A241 9p black & yel .50 .50
Nos. 676-679 (4) 1.35 1.35

Daily broadcasting in the United Kingdom, 50th anniv. (British Broadcasting Corp., #676-678), Marconi-Kemp experiments resulting in the 1st radio transmission across water, 75th anniv. (#679).

Angel with Trumpet — A242

Photo.; Gold Embossed

1972, Oct. 18 *Perf. 14x14½*
680 A242 2½p shown .20 .20
681 A242 3p Angel with lute .20 .20
682 A242 7½p Angel with harp .30 .30
Nos. 680-682 (3) .70 .70

Christmas.

Queen Elizabeth II, Prince Philip — A243

1972, Nov. 20 Photo. *Perf. 14x14½*
683 A243 3p dk bl, sep & sil .25 .25
684 A243 20p dk pur, sepia & sil .75 .75

25th anniv. of the marriage of Queen Elizabeth II and Prince Philip. No. 684 is without phosphor.

Britain as Part of European Community A244

1973, Jan. 3
685 A244 3p brown org & multi .20 .20
686 A244 5p blue & multi .30 .30
687 A244 5p emerald & multi .50 .50
a. Pair, #686-687 .75 1.50
Nos. 685-687 (3) 1.00 1.00

Britain's entry into the European Community.

Oak A245

1973, Feb. 28 Photo. *Perf. 14½x14*
688 A245 9p multicolored .40 .40

Tree Planting Year.

Explorer Type of 1972

British Explorers: No. 689, David Livingstone and map of Africa. No. 690, Henry Stanley and map of Africa. 5p, Sir Francis Drake and world map. 7½p, Sir Walter Raleigh and world map. 9p, Charles Sturt and map of Australia.

1973, Apr. 8 Photo. *Perf. 14x14½*
689 A236 3p multicolored .20 .20
690 A236 3p multicolored .20 .20
a. Pair, #689-690 .75 1.00
691 A236 5p multicolored .30 .30
692 A236 7½p multicolored .35 .35
693 A236 9p multicolored 1.00 .90
Nos. 689-693 (5) 2.05 1.95

William Gilbert Grace — A246

Designs: Caricatures of William Gilbert Grace, the Great Cricketer, by Harry Furniss.

1973, May 16 Photo. *Perf. 14x14½*
694 A246 3p brown & black .20 .20
695 A246 7½p green & black .55 .55
696 A246 9p blue & black .75 .75
Nos. 694-696 (3) 1.50 1.50

Centenary of British County Cricket.

Sir Joshua Reynolds, Self-portrait A247

1973, July 4 Photo. *Perf. 14x14½*

Paintings: 5p, Sir Henry Raeburn (1756-1823), self-portrait. 7½p, Nelly O'Brien, by Reynolds (1723-92). 9p, Rev. R. Walker (The Skater), by Raeburn.

697 A247 3p multicolored .20 .20
698 A247 5p multicolored .20 .20
699 A247 7½p multicolored .40 .40
700 A247 9p gray & multi .45 .45
Nos. 697-700 (4) 1.25 1.25

Tuscan Portico, St. Paul's Church, Covent Garden A248

Designs: No. 701, Costumes for Oberon and Titania. No. 703, Prince's Lodging, Newmarket. No. 704, Stage scenery for Oberon.

Litho. and Typo.

1973, Aug. 15 *Perf. 14½x14*
701 A248 3p black, pur & gold .20 .20
702 A248 3p gold, brn & blk .20 .20
a. Pair, #701-702 .45 .30
703 A248 5p black, blue & gold .50 .50
704 A248 5p gold, olive & blk .50 .50
a. Pair, #703-704 1.25 1.25
Nos. 701-704 (4) 1.40 1.40

400th birth anniv. of Inigo Jones (1573-1652), architect and designer.

Parliament, from Millbank A249

Design: 8p, Parliament, from Whitehall.

1973, Sept. 12 Engr. and Typo.
705 A249 8p buff, gray & blk .30 .30
706 A249 10p black & gold .40 .35

Opening by the Queen of the 19th Commonwealth Parliamentary Assoc. Conf., Westminster Hall.

Princess Anne and Mark Phillips A250

1973, Nov. 14 Photo. *Perf. 14½x14*
707 A250 3½p violet & silver .20 .20
708 A250 20p brown & silver .55 .55

Wedding of Princess Anne and Captain Mark Phillips, Nov. 14, 1973.

Good King Wenceslas A251

Christmas: Illustrations for Christmas carol "Good King Wenceslas" showing king and page.

1973, Nov. 28
709 A251 3p shown .40 .30
710 A251 3p Page looking out of window .40 .30
711 A251 3p Page leaving castle .40 .30
712 A251 3p Page in storm .40 .30
713 A251 3p Page bringing gifts .40 .30
a. Strip of 5, #709-713 2.50 2.50
714 A251 3½p Page and peasant .40 .30
Nos. 709-714 (6) 2.40 1.80

Horse Chestnut A252

1974, Feb. 27 Photo. *Perf. 14½x14*
715 A252 10p green & multi .35 .35

Fire Engine, 1766 A253

Designs: 3½p, First motorized fire engine, 1904. 5½p, Prize winning Sutherland fire engine, 1863. 8p, First steam engine, 1830.

1974, Apr. 24
716 A253 3½p multicolored .20 .20
717 A253 5½p multicolored .25 .25
718 A253 8p multicolored .30 .30
719 A253 10p multicolored .35 .35
Nos. 716-719 (4) 1.10 1.10

Fire Prevention (Metropolis) Act, bicent.

Packet "Peninsular," 1888, and "Southampton Packet Letter" Postmark — A254

Development of Overseas Mail Transport: 5½p, Farnham Biplane and "Aerial Post" postmark. 8p, Truck and pillar box for airmail and "London F.S. Air Mail" postmark. 10p, Imperial Airways flying boat and "Southampton Airport" postmark.

1974, June 12 *Perf. 14½x14*
720 A254 3½p multicolored .20 .20
721 A254 5½p multicolored .20 .20
722 A254 8p multicolored .25 .25
723 A254 10p multicolored .35 .35
Nos. 720-723 (4) 1.00 1.00

UPU, Cent.

Robert the Bruce A255

"Great Britons" on caparisoned chargers.

1974, July 10 ***Perf. 14½x14***

724 A255	4½p	shown	.20	.20
725 A255	5½p	Owain Glyndwr	.20	.20
726 A255	8p	King Henry V	.35	.35
727 A255	10p	Black Prince	.40	.40
		Nos. 724-727 (4)	1.15	1.15

Churchill, Lord Warden of the Cinque Ports, 1942 — A256

Designs (Churchill): 5½p, with bowler and cigar, 1940. 8p, with top hat, as Secretary of War and Air, 1919. 10p, in uniform of South African Light Horse Regiment, 1899.

1974, Oct. 9 Photo. ***Perf. 14x14½***

728 A256	4½p	silver & multi	.20	.20
729 A256	5½p	silver & multi	.25	.25
730 A256	8p	silver & multi	.35	.35
731 A256	10p	silver & multi	.50	.50
		Nos. 728-731 (4)	1.30	1.30

Sir Winston Spencer Churchill (1874-1965).

Adoration of the Kings, York Minster, c. 1355 A257

Christmas (Roof Bosses): 4½p, Nativity, St. Helen's, Norwich, c. 1480. 8p, Virgin and Child, Church of Ottery St. Mary, Devonshire, c. 1350. 10p, Virgin and Child, Lady Chapel, Worcester Cathedral, c. 1224.

1974, Nov. 27 ***Perf. 14½x14***

732 A257	3½p	gold & multi	.20	.20
733 A257	4½p	gold & multi	.20	.20
734 A257	8p	gold & multi	.25	.25
735 A257	10p	gold & multi	.35	.35
		Nos. 732-735 (4)	1.00	1.00

"Peace-Burial at Sea," by Turner — A258

Paintings: 5½p, "Snowstorm-Steamer off a Harbour's Mouth." 8p, "Arsenal, Venice." 10p, "View of St. Laurent."

1975, Feb. 19 Photo. ***Perf. 14½x14***

736 A258	4½p	multicolored	.20	.20
737 A258	5½p	multicolored	.20	.20
738 A258	8p	multicolored	.20	.20
739 A258	10p	multicolored	.25	.20
		Nos. 736-739 (4)	.85	.80

Birth bicent. of Joseph Mallord William Turner (1775-1851), painter.

Charlotte Square, Edinburgh A259

National Theater, London A260

Designs: No. 740, The Rows, Chester (double-storied medieval shopping streets). 8p, Sir Christopher Wren's Flamsteed House, Royal Observatory, Greenwich. 10p, St. George's Chapel, Windsor.

1975, Apr. 23 ***Perf. 14½x14***

740 A259	7p	multicolored	.20	.20
741 A259	7p	multicolored	.20	.20
742 A259	8p	multicolored	.20	.20
743 A259	10p	multicolored	.30	.30
744 A260	12p	multicolored	.35	.35
		Nos. 740-744 (5)	1.25	1.25

European Architectural Heritage Year 1975. Nos. 740-741 printed se-tenant in sheets of 100. 300th anniv. of Royal Observatory, (No. 742) and 500th anniv. of St. George's Chapel (No. 743).

Dinghies A261

1975, June 11 **Photo. & Engr.**

745 A261	7p	shown	.20	.20
746 A261	8p	Racing keelboats	.20	.20
747 A261	10p	Cruising yachts	.20	.20
748 A261	12p	Multihulls	.40	.40
		Nos. 745-748 (4)	1.00	1.00

Royal Thames Yacht Club bicent. and other sailing club anniversaries.

Stephenson's Locomotion, 1825 — A262

Locomotives: 8p, Abbotsford, Waverley Class, 1876. 10p, Caerphilly Castle, 1923. 12p, High-speed train, 1975.

1975, Aug. 13 Photo. ***Perf. 14½x14***

749 A262	7p	multicolored	.25	.20
750 A262	8p	multicolored	.25	.20
751 A262	10p	multicolored	.45	.40
752 A262	12p	multicolored	.55	.45
		Nos. 749-752 (4)	1.50	1.25

Sesquicentennial of public railroads in Great Britain.

Parliament A263

1975, Sept. 3

753 A263	12p	multicolored	.30	.30

62nd Inter-Parliamentary Conference, London, Sept. 1975.

Emma and Mr. Woodhouse from "Emma" — A264

Designs (Illustrations by Barbara Brown of Characters from Jane Austen's Novels): 10p, Catherine Morland from "Northanger Abbey." 11p, Mr. Darcy from "Pride and Prejudice." 13p, Mary and Henry Crawford from "Mansfield Park."

1975, Oct. 22 Photo. ***Perf. 14x14½***

754 A264	8½p	multicolored	.20	.20
755 A264	10p	multicolored	.30	.30
756 A264	11p	multicolored	.35	.35
757 A264	13p	multicolored	.40	.40
		Nos. 754-757 (4)	1.25	1.25

Jane Austen (1775-1817), novelist.

Angels with Lute and Harp A265

Christmas: 8½p, Angel with mandolin. 11p, Angel with horn. 13p, Angel with trumpet.

1975, Nov. 26 Photo. ***Perf. 14½x14***

758 A265	6½p	violet & multi	.20	.20
759 A265	8½p	multicolored	.25	.25
760 A265	11p	multicolored	.30	.30
761 A265	13p	ocher & multi	.35	.35
		Nos. 758-761 (4)	1.10	1.10

Woman Making Social Call A266

Designs: 10p, Policeman making emergency call. 11p, District nurse making social welfare call. 13p, Refinery worker making field call.

1976, Mar. 10 Photo. ***Perf. 14½x14***

777 A266	8½p	multicolored	.20	.20
778 A266	10p	multicolored	.25	.25
779 A266	11p	multicolored	.30	.30
780 A266	13p	multicolored	.35	.35
		Nos. 777-780 (4)	1.10	1.10

1st telephone call by Alexander Graham Bell, Mar. 10, 1876.

Coal Miner's Hands (Thomas Hepburn) A267

Designs: 10p, Child's hands, textile mill (Robert Owen). 11p, Boy's hand sweeping chimney (Lord Shaftesbury). 13p, Woman's hands holding prison bars (Elizabeth Frey).

1976, Apr. 28 Photo. ***Perf. 14½x14***

781 A267	8½p	gray & black	.20	.20
782 A267	10p	multicolored	.30	.30
783 A267	11p	multicolored	.35	.35
784 A267	13p	multicolored	.40	.40
		Nos. 781-784 (4)	1.25	1.25

19th cent. industrial & social reformers: Hepburn formed 1st miners' union in 1831; Owen, improved working conditions in his mill and established schools; Lord Shaftesbury, philanthropist and sponsor of reform work laws; Frey, pioneer of women's prison reforms.

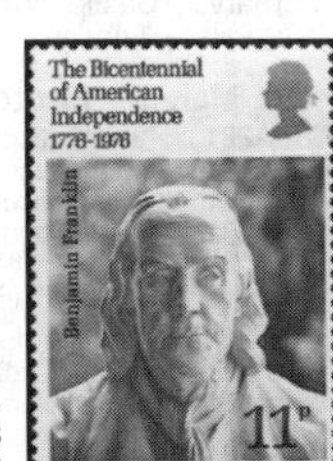

Benjamin Franklin, by Jean-Jacques Caffieri — A268

1976, June 2 ***Perf. 14x14½***

785 A268	11p	multicolored	.30	.30

American Bicentennial.

Royal National Rose Society, Centenary A269

Roses Painted by Kristin Rosenberg.

1976, June 30 Photo. ***Perf. 14x14½***

786 A269	8½p	Elizabeth of Glamis Rose	.20	.20
787 A269	10p	Grandpa Dickson	.30	.30
788 A269	11p	Rosa Mundi	.30	.30
789 A269	13p	Sweet Briar	.45	.45
		Nos. 786-789 (4)	1.25	1.25

Archdruid, Eisteddfod A270

Morris Dancing — A271

British Cultural Traditions: 11p, Piper and dancers, Highland gathering. 13p, Woman playing Welsh harp (telyn), Eisteddfod.

1976, Aug. 4 Photo. ***Perf. 14x14½***

790 A270	8½p	multicolored	.20	.20
791 A271	10p	multicolored	.25	.25
792 A271	11p	multicolored	.30	.30
793 A270	13p	multicolored	.35	.35
		Nos. 790-793 (4)	1.10	1.10

Squire, from Canterbury Tales — A272

Designs: 10p, Page from Tretyse of Love, c. 1493, set in Caxton typeface. 11p, Philosopher, from The Game and Playe of Chesse, c. 1483. 13p, Printing press and printers, early 16th century woodcut.

Photo.; Queen's Head Gold Embossed

1976, Sept. 29 ***Perf. 14x14½***

794 A272	8½p	blue & indigo	.20	.20
795 A272	10p	olive & dk grn	.25	.25
796 A272	11p	gray & black	.30	.30
797 A272	13p	ocher & red brn	.35	.35
		Nos. 794-797 (4)	1.10	1.10

500 years of British printing, introduced by William Caxton (1422-1491).

Virgin and Child, Clare Chasuble A273

Christmas (English medieval embroideries): 8½p, Angel with crown. 11p, Angel appearing to the shepherds. 13p, Three Kings bringing gifts, Butler-Bowden cope.

1976, Nov. 24 Photo. ***Perf. 14½x14***
798 A273 6½p multicolored .20 .20
799 A273 8½p multicolored .25 .25
800 A273 11p multicolored .35 .35
801 A273 13p multicolored .35 .35
Nos. 798-801 (4) 1.15 1.15

Racket Sports A274

1977, Jan. 12 Photo. ***Perf. 14½x14***
802 A274 8½p Tennis .20 .20
803 A274 10p Table tennis .25 .25
804 A274 11p Squash .35 .35
805 A274 13p Badminton .40 .40
Nos. 802-805 (4) 1.20 1.20

Wimbledon Tennis Championships, cent. and 1977 World Table Tennis Championships, Birmingham.

Steroids Conformational Analysis — A275

Designs: 10p, Vitamin C synthesis (formula and orange). 11p, Starch chromatography. 13p, Salt crystallography.

1977, Mar. 2 Photo. ***Perf. 14½x14***
806 A275 8½p multicolored .25 .20
807 A275 10p multicolored .30 .30
808 A275 11p multicolored .35 .35
809 A275 13p multicolored .40 .40
Nos. 806-809 (4) 1.30 1.25

British chemists who won Nobel prize. Derek Barton, 1969 (8½p); Walter Norman Haworth, 1937 (10p); Archer J. P. Martin and Richard L. M. Synge, 1952 (11p); William and Lawrence Bragg, 1915 (13p).

Queen Elizabeth II — A276

1977 Photo. ***Perf. 14½x14***
810 A276 8½p silver & multi .25 .20
811 A276 9p silver & multi .30 .25
812 A276 10p silver & multi .30 .30
813 A276 11p silver & multi .35 .35
814 A276 13p silver & multi .45 .45
Nos. 810-814 (5) 1.65 1.55

25th anniv. of the reign of Elizabeth II. Issue dates: 9p, June 15;.others, May 11.

Pentagons, Symbolic of Continents and Nations — A277

1977, June 8 Photo. ***Perf. 14x14½***
815 A277 13p multicolored .40 .40

Summit Conference of Commonwealth Heads of Government, London, June 1977.

Wildlife Protection — A278

1977, Oct. 5 Photo. ***Perf. 14x14½***
816 A278 9p Hedgehog .35 .25
817 A278 9p Brown hare .40 .25
818 A278 9p Red squirrel .50 .25
819 A278 9p Otter .35 .25
820 A278 9p Badger .35 .25
a. Strip of 5, #816-820 2.00

"Two Turtle Doves, Three French Hens. . ." — A279

The Twelve Days of Christmas: No. 822, 4 colly birds, 5 gold rings, 6 geese a-laying. No. 823, 7 swans a-swimming, 8 maids a-milking. No. 824, 9 drummers drumming, 10 pipers piping. No. 825, 11 ladies dancing, 12 lords a-leaping. 9p, A partridge in a pear tree.

1977, Nov. 23 Photo. ***Perf. 14½x14***
821 A279 7p multicolored .20 .20
822 A279 7p multicolored .20 .20
823 A279 7p multicolored .20 .20
824 A279 7p multicolored .20 .20
825 A279 7p multicolored .20 .20
a. Strip of 5, #821-825 1.00
826 A279 9p multicolored .25 .20
Nos. 821-826 (6) 1.25 1.20

Oil Production Platform, North Sea — A280

Designs: 10½p, Coal, pithead. 11p, Natural gas, flame. 13p, Electricity-producing nuclear power plant and uranium atom diagram.

1978, Jan. 25 Photo. ***Perf. 14x14½***
827 A280 9p multicolored .30 .20
828 A280 10½p multicolored .35 .20
829 A280 11p multicolored .40 .20
830 A280 13p multicolored .45 .25
Nos. 827-830 (4) 1.50 .85

Great Britain's wealth of energy resources.

Tower of London A281

British Architecture: 10½p, Abbey and Palace, Holyrood House, Edinburgh. 11p, Caernarvon Castle, Wales. 13p, Hampton Court Palace, London.

1978, Mar. 1 Photo. ***Perf. 14½x14***
831 A281 9p multicolored .25 .20
832 A281 10½p multicolored .30 .20
833 A281 11p multicolored .35 .20
834 A281 13p multicolored .45 .20
a. Souv. sheet of 4, #831-834 1.50
Nos. 831-834 (4) 1.35 .80

No. 834a issued to publicize London 1980 Intl. Stamp Exhib. and sold for 53½p. The surtax went to exhibition fund.

Gold State Coach — A282

Designs: 10½p, St. Edward's crown. 11p, Orb. 13p, Imperial State crown.

1978, May 31 Photo. ***Perf. 14x14½***
835 A282 9p vio blue & gold .25 .20
836 A282 10½p car lake & gold .30 .20
837 A282 11p dp green & gold .35 .20
838 A282 13p purple & gold .40 .20
Nos. 835-838 (4) 1.30 .80

25th anniv. of coronation of Elizabeth II.

Shire Horse A283

British Horses: 10½p, Shetland pony. 11p, Merlyn Cymreig Welsh pony. 13p, Thoroughbred.

1978, July 5 Photo. ***Perf. 14½x14***
839 A283 9p multicolored .25 .20
840 A283 10½p multicolored .30 .20
841 A283 11p multicolored .40 .20
842 A283 13p multicolored .45 .25
Nos. 839-842 (4) 1.40 .85

"Penny-farthing," 19th Century — A284

British bicycles: 10½p, 1920 touring bicycles. 11p, Modern small-wheel bicycles. 13p, Road racers.

1978, Aug. 2 Photo. ***Perf. 14½x14***
843 A284 9p multicolored .30 .20
844 A284 10½p multicolored .35 .20
845 A284 11p multicolored .35 .25
846 A284 13p multicolored .40 .25
Nos. 843-846 (4) 1.40 .90

Cent. of 1st natl. cycling organizations: British Cycling Fed. and Cyclists Touring Club.

Carolers Around Christmas Tree A285

Christmas: 9p, Christmas waits (watchmen). 11p, 18th century carolers. 13p, Boar's head carol.

1978, Nov. 22 Photo. ***Perf. 14½x14***
847 A285 7p multicolored .20 .20
848 A285 9p multicolored .25 .20
849 A285 11p multicolored .35 .20
850 A285 13p multicolored .45 .20
Nos. 847-850 (4) 1.25 .80

Old English Sheepdog A286

British dogs: 10½p, Welsh springer spaniel. 11p, West Highland white terrier. 13p, Irish setter.

1979, Feb. 7 Photo. ***Perf. 14½x14***
851 A286 9p multicolored .25 .20
852 A286 10½p multicolored .30 .20
853 A286 11p multicolored .30 .20
854 A286 13p multicolored .35 .20
Nos. 851-854 (4) 1.20 .80

British Wild Flowers — A287

1979, Mar. 21 Photo. ***Perf. 14x14½***
855 A287 9p Primroses .25 .20
856 A287 10½p Daffodils .30 .20
857 A287 11p Bluebells .30 .20
858 A287 13p Snowdrops .35 .20
Nos. 855-858 (4) 1.20 .80

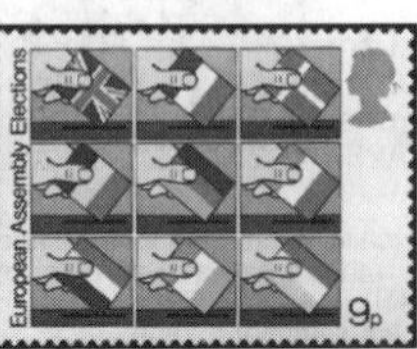

Flags of Member Nations as Ballots A288

Flags of European Community Members: United Kingdom, Italy, Denmark, Belgium, Fed. Rep. of Germany, France, Netherlands, Ireland, Luxembourg. Positions of hands and flags different on each denomination.

1979, May 9 Photo. ***Perf. 14½x14***
859 A288 9p multicolored .25 .20
860 A288 10½p multicolored .30 .20
861 A288 11p multicolored .30 .20
862 A288 13p multicolored .35 .20
Nos. 859-862 (4) 1.20 .80

European Parliament, 1st direct elections, 6/7-10.

Saddling of Mahmoud, 1936 Derby, by Alfred Munnings A289

200th Anniv. of the Derby: 10½p, Liverpool Great National Steeple Chase, 1839, aquatint by F. C. Turner. 11p, First Spring Meeting, Newmarket, 1793, by J. N. Sartorius. 13p, Charles II watching racing at Dorsett Ferry, Windsor, 1684, by Francis Barlow.

1979, June 6 Photo. ***Perf. 14½x14***
863 A289 9p multicolored .25 .20
864 A289 10½p multicolored .30 .20
865 A289 11p multicolored .30 .20
866 A289 13p multicolored .35 .20
Nos. 863-866 (4) 1.20 .80

Peter Rabbit — A290

Children's books: 10½p, The Wind in the Willows. 11p, Winnie the Pooh. 13p, Alice's Adventures in Wonderland.

1979, July 11 Photo. ***Perf. 14x14½***
867 A290 9p multicolored .35 .20
868 A290 10½p multicolored .40 .20
869 A290 11p multicolored .40 .25
870 A290 13p multicolored .50 .25
Nos. 867-870 (4) 1.65 .90

International Year of the Child.

Rowland Hill — A291

Designs: 11½p, Bellman, early 19th cent. 13p, London post office and mailman, early 19th cent. 15p, Victorian woman and child mailing letter.

1979, Aug. 22 Photo. *Perf. 14x14½*

871 A291	10p multicolored		.25	.20
872 A291	11½p multicolored		.30	.20
873 A291	13p multicolored		.35	.20
874 A291	15p multicolored		.40	.25
a.	Souvenir sheet of 4, #871-874		1.40	.90
	Nos. 871-874 (4)		1.30	.85

Sir Rowland Hill (1795-1879), originator of penny postage.

No. 874a issued to publicize London 1980 Intl. Stamp Exhib. and sold for 59½p. The surtax went to exhibition fund.

Police Constable and Children A292

Designs: 11½p, Police constable directing traffic. 13p, Police woman on horseback. 15p, River patrol boat.

1979, Sept. 26 Photo. *Perf. 14½x14*

875 A292	10p multicolored	.30	.20
876 A292	11½p multicolored	.35	.20
877 A292	13p multicolored	.40	.20
878 A292	15p multicolored	.45	.25
	Nos. 875-878 (4)	1.50	.85

London Metropolitan Police, 150th anniv.

Three Kings Following Star A293

Christmas: 10p, Angel appearing before the shepherds. 11½p, Nativity. 13p, Joseph and Mary traveling to Bethlehem. 15p, Annunciation.

1979, Nov. 21 Photo. *Perf. 14½x14*

879 A293	8p multicolored	.25	.20
880 A293	10p multicolored	.30	.20
881 A293	11½p multicolored	.30	.20
882 A293	13p multicolored	.35	.20
883 A293	15p multicolored	.45	.20
	Nos. 879-883 (5)	1.65	1.00

Kingfisher — A294

1980, Jan. 16 Photo. *Perf. 14x14½*

884 A294	10p shown	.30	.20
885 A294	11½p Dipper	.35	.20
886 A294	13p Moorhen	.40	.20
887 A294	15p Yellow wagtail	.45	.25
	Nos. 884-887 (4)	1.50	.85

"Rocket" Locomotive A295

1980, Mar. 12 Photo. *Perf. 14½x14*

904 A295	12p shown	.35	.20
905 A295	12p 1st, 2nd class cars	.35	.20
906 A295	12p 3rd class and sheep cars	.35	.20
907 A295	12p Flat cars	.35	.20
908 A295	12p Flat car, mail coach	.35	.20
a.	Strip of 5, #904-908	1.75	1.00

Liverpool-Manchester Railroad, 150th anniv. No. 908a has a continuous design.

London View A296

1980, Apr. 9 Engr. *Perf. 14½*

909 A296	50p multicolored	1.40	.70
a.	Souvenir sheet	1.65	1.50

London 1980, Intl. Stamp Exhib., May 6-14. No. 909a, issued May 7, sold for 75p.

Buckingham Palace — A297

1980, May 7 Photo. *Perf. 14x14½*

910 A297	10½p shown	.30	.20
911 A297	12p Albert Memorial	.35	.20
912 A297	13½p Royal Opera House	.40	.20
913 A297	15p Hampton Court	.45	.20
914 A297	17½p Kensington Palace	.50	.25
	Nos. 910-914 (5)	2.00	1.05

Emily Bronte and "Wuthering Heights" A298

Victorian novelists and scenes from their novels: 12p, Charlotte Bronte, "Jane Eyre." 13½p, George Eliot, "The Mill on the Floss." 17½p, Mrs. Gaskell, "North and South." 12p and 13½p show CEPT (Europa) emblem.

1980, July 9 Photo. *Perf. 15x14*

915 A298	12p multicolored	.25	.20
916 A298	13½p multicolored	.25	.20
917 A298	15p multicolored	.30	.30
918 A298	17½p multicolored	.60	.60
	Nos. 915-918 (4)	1.40	1.30

Queen Mother Elizabeth, 80th Birthday — A299

1980, Aug. 4 Photo. *Perf. 14x14½*

919 A299	12p multicolored	.45	.20

English Conductors A300

Designs: 12p, Henry Wood, (1869-1944) Conductor. 13½p, Thomas Beecham (1879-1961). 15p, Malcolm Sargent (1895-1967). 17½p, John Barbirolli (1899-1970).

1980, Sept. 10

920 A300	12p multicolored	.35	.20
921 A300	13½p multicolored	.40	.20
922 A300	15p multicolored	.45	.20
923 A300	17½p multicolored	.50	.25
	Nos. 920-923 (4)	1.70	.85

Running — A301

1980, Oct. 10 Litho. *Perf. 14x14½*

924 A301	12p shown	.35	.20
925 A301	13½p Rugby	.40	.20
926 A301	15p Boxing	.45	.20
927 A301	17½p Cricket	.50	.25
	Nos. 924-927 (4)	1.70	.85

Centenaries: Amateur Athletics Assoc.; Welsh Rugby Union; Amateur Boxing Assoc.; 1st cricket test match against Australia.

Christmas Tree with Candles A302

Christmas (Traditional Decorations): 12p, Candles, ivy, ribbons. 13½p, Mistletoe, apples. 15p, Paper chain and bell. 17½p, Holly wreath.

1980, Nov. 19 Photo. *Perf. 14½x14*

928 A302	10p multicolored	.30	.20
929 A302	12p multicolored	.35	.20
930 A302	13½p multicolored	.40	.20
931 A302	15p multicolored	.45	.20
932 A302	17½ multicolored	.50	.25
	Nos. 928-932 (5)	2.00	1.05

Lovebirds, Angels and Heart (Valentine's Day) A303

Folklore: 18p, Morris Dancers, 16th century window, Shropshire. 22p, Wheat, fruit, farm couple dancing (Lammastide). 25p, Medieval mummers, 14th century manuscript illustration. 14p and 18p show CEPT (Europa) emblem.

1981, Feb. 6 Photo. *Perf. 14½x14*

933 A303	14p multicolored	.45	.20
934 A303	18p multicolored	.55	.70
935 A303	22p multicolored	.70	.70
936 A303	25p multicolored	.80	.80
	Nos. 933-936 (4)	2.50	2.40

Guide Dog Leading Blind Man A304

1981, Mar. 25 Photo.

937 A304	14p shown	.40	.20
938 A304	18p Sign language	.50	.25
939 A304	22p Man in wheelchair	.60	.30
940 A304	25p Foot painting	.70	.35
	Nos. 937-940 (4)	2.20	1.10

International Year of the Disabled.

Small Tortoiseshell A305

1981, May 13 *Perf. 14x14½*

941 A305	14p shown	.45	.25
942 A305	18p Large blue	.55	.30
943 A305	22p Peacock	.70	.35
944 A305	25p Checkered skipper	.80	.40
	Nos. 941-944 (4)	2.50	1.30

Glenfinnan, Highlands, Scotland A306

50th anniv. of National Trust for Scotland: 18p, Derwentwater, Lake District, England. 20p, Stackpole Head, Dyfed, Wales. 22p, Giant's Causeway, County Antrim, Northern Ireland. 25p, St. Kilda, Scotland.

1981, June 24 Photo. *Perf. 14½x14*

945 A306	14p multicolored	.40	.20
946 A306	18p multicolored	.50	.25
947 A306	20p multicolored	.60	.30
948 A306	22p multicolored	.65	.35
949 A306	25p multicolored	.75	.40
	Nos. 945-949 (5)	2.90	1.50

Prince Charles and Lady Diana — A307

1981, July 22 Photo. *Perf. 14x14½*

950 A307	14p multicolored	1.00	.25
951 A307	25p multicolored	1.50	.45

Wedding of Charles, Prince of Wales, and Lady Diana Spencer, St. Paul's Cathedral, July 29.

Hikers Reading Map A308

1981, Aug. 12 Litho. *Perf. 14*

952 A308 14p shown .45 .25
953 A308 18p Girl at potter's wheel .55 .30
954 A308 22p Woman administering artificial respiration .70 .35
955 A308 25p Hurdler .80 .40
Nos. 952-955 (4) 2.50 1.30

The Duke of Edinburgh's Awards (expeditions, skills, service, recreation), 25th anniv.

Cockle Dredging A309

1981, Sept. 23 Photo. *Perf. 14½x14*

956 A309 14p shown .40 .20
957 A309 18p Hauling trawl net .50 .25
958 A309 22p Lobster potting .65 .35
959 A309 25p Hauling seine net .75 .40
Nos. 956-959 (4) 2.30 1.20

Fishermen's Year and Royal Natl. Mission to Deep Sea Fishermen centenary.

Joseph and Mary Arriving at Bethlehem A310

Christmas: Children's Drawings.

1981, Nov. 18 Photo.

960 A310 11½p Santa Claus .35 .20
961 A310 14p Jesus .40 .20
962 A310 18p Angel .50 .25
963 A310 22p shown .65 .35
964 A310 25p Three Kings .75 .40
Nos. 960-964 (5) 2.65 1.40

Death Centenary of Charles Darwin (1809-1882) — A311

1982, Feb. 10 Photo.

965 A311 15½p Giant tortoises .45 .25
966 A311 19½p Iguanas .55 .30
967 A311 26p Darwin's finches .80 .40
968 A311 29p Skulls .85 .45
Nos. 965-968 (4) 2.65 1.40

Youth Organizations A312

1982, Mar. 24 Photo. *Perf. 14x14½*

983 A312 15½p Boy's Brigade .50 .25
984 A312 19½p Girl's Brigade .65 .35
985 A312 26p Boy Scouts .85 .45
986 A312 29p Girl Guides 1.00 .50
Nos. 983-986 (4) 3.00 1.55

75th anniv. of scouting and 125th birth anniv. of founder Robert Baden-Powell (26p).

Performing Arts — A313

1982, Apr. 28 Photo. *Perf. 14x14½*

987 A313 15½p Ballet .50 .20
988 A313 19½p Pantomime .65 .65
989 A313 26p Shakespearean drama .85 .85
990 A313 29p Opera 1.00 1.00
Nos. 987-990 (4) 3.00 2.70

Nos. 987-990 show CEPT (Europa) emblem.

King Henry VIII and the Mary Rose A314

1982, June 16 *Perf. 14½x14*

991 A314 15½p shown .50 .25
992 A314 19½p Admiral Blake, Triumph .65 .35
993 A314 24p Lord Nelson, Victory .75 .40
994 A314 26p Lord Fisher, Dreadnought .85 .45
995 A314 29p Viscount Cunningham, Warspite 1.00 .50
Nos. 991-995 (5) 3.75 1.95

Textile Designs — A315

1982, July 23 Photo. *Perf. 14x14½*

996 A315 15½p Strawberry Thief, 1883 .45 .20
997 A315 19½p Tulips, 1906 .60 .30
998 A315 26p Cherry Orchard, 1930 .80 .40
999 A315 29p Chevron, 1973 .95 .45
Nos. 996-999 (4) 2.80 1.35

Information Technology — A316

15½p, Hieroglyphics, library, word processor. 26p, Viewdata set, satellite, laser pen.

1982, Sept. 8 Photo.

1000 A316 15½p multicolored .50 .25
1001 A316 26p multicolored .85 .45

Austin's Seven (1922) and Metro A317

Cars: 19½p, Ford Model T (1913) and Escort. 26p, Jaguar SS (1931) and XJ6 (1967). 29p, Rolls-Royce Silver Ghost (1907) and Silver Spirit (1982).

1982, Oct. 13 Litho. *Perf. 14½x14*

1002 A317 15½p multicolored .45 .40
1003 A317 19½p multicolored .65 .50
1004 A317 26p multicolored .75 .65
1005 A317 29p multicolored 1.00 .75
Nos. 1002-1005 (4) 2.85 2.30

Christmas 1982 A318

Designs: Christmas carols.

1982, Nov. 17 Photo.

1006 A318 12½p While Shepherds Watched .40 .20
1007 A318 15½p The Holly and the Ivy .45 .25
1008 A318 19½p I Saw Three Ships .60 .30
1009 A318 26p We Three Kings .80 .40
1010 A318 29p Good King Wenceslas .95 .45
Nos. 1006-1010 (5) 3.20 1.60

River Fish A319

1983, Jan. 26 Photo. *Perf. 15x14*

1011 A319 15½p Salmon .40 .25
1012 A319 19½p Pike .55 .35
1013 A319 26p Trout .70 .45
1014 A319 29p Perch .90 .50
Nos. 1011-1014 (4) 2.55 1.55

Commonwealth Day — A320

Landscapes by Donald Hamilton Fraser.

1983, Mar. 9 Photo. *Perf. 14x14½*

1015 A320 15½p Tropical island .45 .30
1016 A320 19½p Desert .55 .35
1017 A320 26p Farmland .75 .50
1018 A320 29p Mountains .80 .55
Nos. 1015-1018 (4) 2.55 1.70

Engineering Achievements (Europa) — A321

1983, May 25 Photo. *Perf. 15x14*

1019 A321 16p Humber Bridge .50 .20
1020 A321 20½p Thames Flood Barrier 1.40 1.25
1021 A321 28p Emergency oil rig support vessel Lolair 1.60 1.25
Nos. 1019-1021 (3) 3.50 2.70

A322

Designs: 16p, The Royal Scots (Royal Regiment). 20½p, Royal Welsh Fusiliers. 26p, Royal Green Jackets. 28p, Irish Guards. 31p, Parachute Regiment.

1983, July 6 *Perf. 14x14½*

1022 A322 16p multicolored .55 .30
1023 A322 20½p multicolored .40 .35
1024 A322 26p multicolored .90 .45
1025 A322 28p multicolored .95 .50
1026 A322 31p multicolored 1.10 .55
Nos. 1022-1026 (5) 3.90 2.15

A323

Designs: 16p, 20th cent. garden, Sissinghurst. 20½p, Biddulph Grange, 19th cent. 28p, Blenheim, 18th cent. 31p, Pitmeeden, 17th cent.

1983, Aug. 24 Litho. *Perf. 14*

1027 A323 16p multicolored .55 .30
1028 A323 20½p multicolored .70 .35
1029 A323 28p multicolored .95 .50
1030 A323 31p multicolored 1.10 .50
Nos. 1027-1030 (4) 3.30 1.65

British Fairs A324

1983, Oct. 5 Photo. *Perf. 14½x14*

1031 A324 16p Merry-go-round .55 .30
1032 A324 20½p Animals, rides .70 .35
1033 A324 28p Games .95 .50
1034 A324 31p Ancient market fair 1.00 .50
Nos. 1031-1034 (4) 3.20 1.65

850th anniv. of St. Bartholomew's Fair.

Christmas A325

1983, Nov. 16 Photo.

1035 A325 12½p Birds mailing cards .35 .25
1036 A325 16p Three Kings chimney pots .50 .30
1037 A325 20½p Birds under umbrella .55 .35
1038 A325 28p Birds under street lamp .80 .50
1039 A325 31p Topiary dove .90 .50
Nos. 1035-1039 (5) 3.10 1.90

Heraldry A326

Designs: 16p, Arms of The College of Arms. 20½p, Arms of Richard III, founder. 28p, Arms of The Earl Marshal. 31p, Arms of The City of London.

1984, Jan. 17 Photo. *Perf. 14½*

1040 A326 16p multicolored .55 .30
1041 A326 20½p multicolored .70 .35
1042 A326 28p multicolored .95 .50
1043 A326 31p multicolored 1.00 .50
Nos. 1040-1043 (4) 3.20 1.65

National Cattle Breeders' Association A327

1984, Mar. 6 Litho. *Perf. 15x14½*

1044 A327 16p Highland Cow .50 .25
1045 A327 20½p Chillingham Wild Bull .60 .30
1046 A327 26p Hereford Bull .80 .40
1047 A327 28p Welsh Black Bull .85 .45
1048 A327 31p Irish Moiled Cow .95 .50
Nos. 1044-1048 (5) 3.70 1.90

Royal Institute of British Architects Sesquicentennial — A328

Urban renewal projects and plans.

1984, Apr. 3 Photo.

1049 A328 16p Liverpool .55 .35
1050 A328 20½p Durham .70 .40
1051 A328 28p Bristol .95 .55
1052 A328 31p Perth 1.10 .60
Nos. 1049-1052 (4) 3.30 1.90

Europa (1959-1984) — A329

1984, May 9 Photo. *Perf. 14½x14*

1053 A329 16p Bridge .80 .25
1054 A329 16p Abduction of Europa .80 .25
1055 A329 20½p like No. 1053 1.90 1.75
1056 A329 20½p like No. 1054 1.90 1.75
Nos. 1053-1056 (4) 5.40 4.00

Nos. 1054, 1056 also for 2nd Election of the European Parliament.

London Economic Summit, June 7-9 — A330

1984, June 5 Photo. *Perf. 14x15*

1057 A330 31p Lancaster House 1.00 .50

Greenwich Meridian, Cent. — A331

1984, June 26 Litho. *Perf. 14x14½*

1058 A331 16p View from Apollo 11 .55 .30
1059 A331 20½p English Channel map .70 .35
1060 A331 28p Greenwich Observatory .95 .50
1061 A331 31p Airy's transit telescope, 1850 1.10 .55
Nos. 1058-1061 (4) 3.30 1.70

Bath-Bristol-London Mail Coach Bicentenary — A332

18th century drawings by James Pollard.

Photo. & Engr.

1984, July 31 *Perf. 14½x14*

1062 A332 16p Bath, 1784 .55 .25
1063 A332 16p Exeter, 1816 .55 .25
1064 A332 16p Norwich, 1827 .55 .25
1065 A332 16p Holyhead & Liverpool .55 .25
1066 A332 16p Edinburgh, 1831 .55 .25
a. Strip of 5, #1062-1066 3.00

50th Anniv. of British Council A333

1984, Sept. 25 Photo.

1067 A333 17p Education for development .60 .30
1068 A333 22p Promoting the arts .80 .40
1069 A333 31p Technical training 1.10 .55
1070 A333 34p Language & libraries 1.10 .60
Nos. 1067-1070 (4) 3.60 1.85

Christmas 1984 A334

Crayon Sketches by Yvonne Gilbert.

1984, Nov. 20 Photo. *Perf. 15x14*

1088 A334 13p Holy Family .45 .20
1089 A334 17p Arrival in Bethlehem .55 .25
1090 A334 22p Shephard and Lamb .70 .35
1091 A334 31p Virgin and child 1.00 .50
1092 A334 34p Offering Frankincense 1.10 .55
Nos. 1088-1092 (5) 3.80 1.85

Bklt. of 20 13p sold at 30p discount. Stamps have blue stars printed on the back.

Great Western Railway Sesquicentennial — A335

1985, Jan. 22 Photo. *Perf. 15x14*

1093 A335 17p Flying Scotsman .60 .40
1094 A335 22p Golden Arrow .70 .55
1095 A335 29p Cheltenham Flyer .80 .65
1096 A335 31p Royal Scot 1.25 .75
1097 A335 34p Cornish Riviera 1.25 .95
Nos. 1093-1097 (5) 4.60 3.30

Insects — A336

1985, Mar. 12 Photo. *Perf. 15x14½*

1098 A336 17p Buff tailed bumble bee .55 .30
1099 A336 22p Seven spotted ladybird .65 .45
1100 A336 29p Wart-biter bush-cricket .80 .50
1101 A336 31p Stag beetle .90 .50
1102 A336 34p Emperor dragonfly 1.10 .60
Nos. 1098-1102 (5) 4.00 2.35

Music Year (Europa) A337

British Composers: 17p, Water Music, by George Frideric Handel. 22p, The Planets Suite, by Gustav Holst. 31p, The First Cuckoo, by Frederick Delius. 34p, Sea Pictures, by Edward Elgar.

1985, May 14 *Perf. 14½*

1103 A337 17p Reflections in pool .90 .20
1104 A337 22p View of planets 1.25 *1.40*
1105 A337 31p Roosting cuckoo 2.00 1.90
1106 A337 34p Waves, wing 2.10 2.00
Nos. 1103-1106 (4) 6.25 5.50

Safety at Sea A338

1985, June 18 Litho. *Perf. 14*

1107 A338 17p Lifeboat .60 .30
1108 A338 22p Beachy Head Lighthouse, chart .80 .45
1109 A338 31p Marecs-A satellite 1.10 .60
1110 A338 34p Signal buoy, yacht 1.25 .65
Nos. 1107-1110 (4) 3.75 2.00

Royal Mail Service, 350th Anniv. — A339

Designs: 17p, Royal Mail Datapost motorcyclist and plane. 22p, Postbus on country road. 31p, Parcel service delivery. 34p, Postman delivering mail.

1985, July 30 Photo. *Perf. 14x14½*

1111 A339 17p multicolored .60 .35
1112 A339 22p multicolored .80 .45
1113 A339 31p multicolored 1.00 .50
1114 A339 34p multicolored 1.25 .65
Nos. 1111-1114 (4) 3.65 1.95

Arthurian Legends A340

Designs: 17p, Arthur consulting with Merlin. 22p, The Lady of the Lake with the sword "Excalibur." 31p, Guinevere and Lancelot fleeing from Camelot. 34p, Sir Galahad praying during his quest for the Holy Grail.

1985, Sept. 3 Photo. *Perf. 15x14*

1115 A340 17p multicolored .55 .30
1116 A340 22p multicolored .70 .45
1117 A340 31p multicolored 1.00 .60
1118 A340 34p multicolored 1.10 .65
Nos. 1115-1118 (4) 3.35 2.00

500th anniv. of William Caxton's edition of Le Morte D'Arthur, by Sir Thomas Mallory.

20th Cent. Stars and Directors of Film — A341

Photographs: 17p, Peter Sellers (1925-80). 22p, David Niven (1910-83). 29p, Charlie Chaplin (1889-1977). 31p, Vivien Leigh (1913-67). 34p, Sir Alfred Hitchcock (1899-1980), director.

1985, Oct. 8 Photo. *Perf. 14½*

1119 A341 17p multicolored .60 .35
1120 A341 22p multicolored .80 .45
1121 A341 29p multicolored 1.10 .70
1122 A341 31p multicolored 1.25 .75
1123 A341 34p multicolored 1.40 .80
Nos. 1119-1123 (5) 5.15 3.05

Christmas Pantomime A342

1985, Nov. 19 Photo. *Perf. 15x14½*

1124 A342 12p Principal boy .35 .20
a. Booklet pane of 20 7.00
1125 A342 17p Genie .50 .30
1126 A342 22p Grande dame .65 .35
1127 A342 31p Good fairy .90 .50
1128 A342 34p Cat 1.00 .55
Nos. 1124-1128 (5) 3.40 1.90

No. 1124a has random star design printed on back.

Industry Year A343

1986, Jan. 14 Litho. *Perf. 15x14*

1129 A343 17p North Sea oil rig, light bulb .55 .35
1130 A343 22p Medical research lab, thermometer .70 .40
1131 A343 31p Steel mill, garden hoe 1.00 .55
1132 A343 34p Cornfield, bread 1.10 .60
Nos. 1129-1132 (4) 3.35 1.90

Halley's Comet A344

Designs: 17p, Caricature, Edmond Halley (1656-1742), astronomer. 22p, European Space Agency Giotto spacecraft pursuing comet. 31p, Comet and legend, Maybe Twice in a Lifetime. 34p, Comet orbiting sun.

1986, Feb. 18 Photo.

1133 A344 17p multicolored .55 .35
1134 A344 22p multicolored .70 .40
1135 A344 31p multicolored 1.00 .55
1136 A344 34p multicolored 1.10 .60
Nos. 1133-1136 (4) 3.35 1.90

A345

Queen Elizabeth II, 60th Birthday A346

1986, Apr. 21 Photo.

1137 A345 17p multicolored .60 .35
1138 A346 17p multicolored .60 .35
a. Pair, #1137-1138 1.25 .70
1139 A345 34p multicolored 1.25 .70
1140 A346 34p multicolored 1.25 .70
a. Pair, #1139-1140 2.50 1.40

Europa A347

1986, May 20 Photo. *Perf. 14½*

1141 A347 17p Barn owl .50 .50
1142 A347 22p Pine marten 1.00 1.00
1143 A347 31p Wild cat 1.50 1.50
1144 A347 34p Natterjack toad 1.75 1.75
Nos. 1141-1144 (4) 4.75 4.75

Domesday Book, 900th Anniv. A348

1986, June 17 Photo.

1145 A348 17p Peasant .45 .35
1146 A348 22p Freeman .85 .45
1147 A348 31p Knight 1.25 .65
1148 A348 34p Lord 1.40 .70
Nos. 1145-1148 (4) 3.95 2.15

Domesday Book, first nationwide survey in British history.

Sports A349

1986, July 15 Photo. *Perf. 15x14*

1149 A349 17p Track and field .60 .35
1150 A349 22p Rowing .75 .50
1151 A349 29p Weight lifting 1.00 .65
1152 A349 31p Shooting 1.05 .70
1153 A349 34p Field hockey 1.15 .80
Nos. 1149-1153 (5) 4.55 3.00

1986 Commonwealth Games, Edinburgh. World Hockey Cup, London.

Wedding of Prince Andrew and Sarah Ferguson — A350

1986, July 22 *Perf. 14x15*

1154 A350 12p multicolored .50 .25
1155 A350 17p multicolored .75 .30

Commonwealth Parliamentary Assoc. Conf., London — A351

1986, Aug. 19 Litho. *Perf. 14x14½*

1156 A351 34p multicolored 1.25 .75

Royal Air Force Commanders and Aircraft A352

Designs: 17p, Lord Dowding (1882-1970), Hurricane. 22p, Lord Tedder (1890-1967), Hawker Typhoon. 29p, Lord Trenchard (1873-1956), De Havilland 9A World War I bomber. 31p, Sir Arthur Harris (1892-1984), Avro Lancaster. 34p, Lord Portal (1893-1971), De Havilland Mosquito.

1986, Sept. 16 Photo. *Perf. 14½*

1157 A352 17p multicolored .55 .35
1158 A352 22p multicolored .70 .50
1159 A352 29p multicolored .95 .65
1160 A352 31p multicolored 1.00 .70
1161 A352 34p multicolored 1.10 .80
Nos. 1157-1161 (5) 4.30 3.00

Christmas A353

Customs: 12p, 13p, Glastonbury Thorn. 18p, Tanad Valley Plygain. 22p, Hebrides Tribute. 31p, Dewsbury Church Knell. 34p, Hereford Boy Bishop.

1986, Nov. 18 Photo. *Perf. 15x14½*

1162 A353 12p multicolored .40 .20
1163 A353 13p multicolored .40 .20
a. Pane of 36 14.50
1164 A353 18p multicolored .60 .30
1165 A353 22p multicolored .70 .35
1166 A353 31p multicolored 1.00 .45
1167 A353 34p multicolored 1.10 .50
Nos. 1162-1167 (6) 4.20 2.00

No. 1163a printed in two panes of 18 with gutter between, stars on back; folded and sold in discount booklet for £4.30.

Flora — A354

Photographs by Alfred Lammer.

1987, Jan. 20 Photo. *Perf. 14½*

1168 A354 18p Gaillardia .60 .30
1169 A354 22p Echinops .70 .40
1170 A354 31p Echeveria 1.00 .55
1171 A354 34p Colchicum 1.10 .60
Nos. 1168-1171 (4) 3.40 1.85

Sir Isaac Newton (1642-1727), Physicist, Mathematician A355

Manuscripts and principles: 18p, Philosophiae Naturalis Principia Mathematica, 1687. 22p, Motion of bodies in ellipses. 31p, Opticks Treatise of the Refraction, Reflections and Colors of Light. 34p, The System of the World.

1987, Mar. 24 Photo. *Perf. 14*

1172 A355 18p multicolored .60 .35
1173 A355 22p multicolored .75 .45
1174 A355 31p multicolored 1.10 .55
1175 A355 34p multicolored 1.25 .65
Nos. 1172-1175 (4) 3.70 2.00

Europa A356

Modern architecture: 18p, Willis Faber & Dumas Building, Ipswich, designed by Norman Foster. 22p, Pompidou Centre, Paris, designed by Richard Rogers and Renzo Piano. 31p, Staatsgalerie, Stuttgart, designed by James Stirling and Michael Wilford. 34p, European Investment Bank, Luxembourg, designed by Sir Denys Lasdun.

1987, May 12 Photo. *Perf. 15x14*

1176 A356 18p multicolored .60 .20
1177 A356 22p multicolored .90 .80
1178 A356 31p multicolored 1.50 1.25
1179 A356 34p multicolored 1.75 1.25
Nos. 1176-1179 (4) 4.75 3.50

St. John Ambulance, Cent. — A357

First aid.

1987, June 16 Litho. *Perf. 14x14½*

1180 A357 18p Ambulance, 1887 .60 .35
1181 A357 22p War victims, 1940 .75 .45
1182 A357 31p Public event, 1965 1.05 .60
1183 A357 34p Transplant organ flight, 1987 1.15 .70
Nos. 1180-1183 (4) 3.55 2.10

Order of the Thistle, Scotland, 300th Anniv. of Revival A358

Coats of arms: 18p, Lord Lyon, King of Arms, 1687. 22p, Duke of Rothesay, bestowed on Prince Charles in 1974. 31p, Royal Scottish Academy of Painting, Sculpture & Architecture, 1826. 34p, The Royal Society of Edinburgh, 1783.

1987, July 21 Photo. *Perf. 14½*

1184 A358 18p multicolored .60 .35
1185 A358 22p multicolored .75 .45
1186 A358 31p multicolored 1.00 .60
1187 A358 34p multicolored 1.15 .70
Nos. 1184-1187 (4) 3.50 2.10

Accession of Queen Victoria, 150th Anniv. A359

Portraits of Victoria and: 18p, Great Exhibition (1851) at the Crystal Palace, Grace Darling's rescue (1838) of the Forfashire's survivors, and Monarch of the Glen, by Sir Edwin Henry Landseer. 22p, Launching of Brunel's ship Great Eastern, portrait of Prince Consort Albert, Mrs. Beeton's Book of Household Management (1889). 31p, The Albert Memorial, Prime Minister Disraeli and 1st ballot box. 34p, The Boer War, Guglielmo Marconi's wireless telegraph communications linking Paris and London (1898), and diamond jubilee emblem.

Photo. & Engr.

1987, Sept. 8 *Perf. 15x14*

1188 A359 18p multicolored .60 .35
1189 A359 22p multicolored .75 .45
1190 A359 31p multicolored 1.05 .60
1191 A359 34p multicolored 1.15 .70
Nos. 1188-1191 (4) 3.55 2.10

Studio Pottery A360

1987, Oct. 13 Photo. *Perf. 14½*

1192 A360 18p Bernard Leach .60 .35
1193 A360 26p Elizabeth Fritsch .85 .45
1194 A360 31p Lucie Rie 1.05 .60
1195 A360 34p Hans Coper 1.15 .70
Nos. 1192-1195 (4) 3.65 2.10

Christmas A361

Childhood memories: 13p, Decorating tree. 18p, Looking out window, Christmas eve. 26p, Sweet dreams. 31p, Reading new book to toys, Christmas morning. 34p, Playing horn, snowman.

1987, Nov. 17 Photo. *Perf. 15x14*

1196 A361 13p multicolored .45 .25
a. Pane of 36 16.25
1197 A361 18p multicolored .60 .30
1198 A361 26p multicolored .90 .45
1199 A361 31p multicolored 1.05 .50
1200 A361 34p multicolored 1.15 .60
Nos. 1196-1200 (5) 4.15 2.10

No. 1196a printed in two panes of 18 with gutter between, stars on back; folded and sold in discount booklets for £4.30.

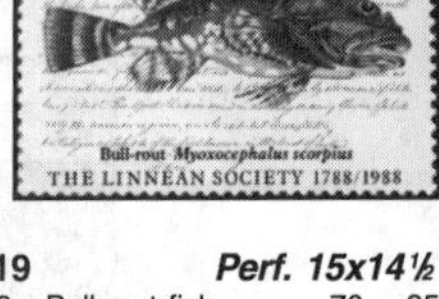

Linnean Society of London, 200th Anniv. A362

1988, Jan. 19 *Perf. 15x14½*

1201 A362 18p Bull-rout fish .70 .35
1202 A362 26p Yellow waterlily 1.00 .45
1203 A362 31p Bewick's swan 1.15 .60
1204 A362 34p Morel 1.25 .65
Nos. 1201-1204 (4) 4.10 2.05

Linnaeus (Carl von Linne, 1707-78), inventor of system of taxonomic nomenclature.

Welsh Bible, 400th Anniv. — A363

1988, Mar. 1 Photo. *Perf. 14½*

1205 A363 18p William Morgan .60 .35
1206 A363 26p William Salesbury .85 .50
1207 A363 31p Richard Davies 1.00 .60
1208 A363 34p Richard Parry 1.15 .65
Nos. 1205-1208 (4) 3.60 2.10

Sports — A364

1988, Mar. 22 Photo. *Perf. 14½*

1209 A364 18p Balance beam .60 .35
1210 A364 26p Downhill skiing .85 .50
1211 A364 31p Tennis 1.10 .60
1212 A364 34p Soccer 1.15 .65
Nos. 1209-1212 (4) 3.70 2.10

Ski Club of Great Britain and centenaries of the British Amateur Gymnastics Assoc., Lawn Tennis Assoc. and the Soccer League.

Europa 1988 A365

Transportation and communication, 1938.

1988, May 10 *Perf. 15x14*

1213 A365 18p Mallard locomotive .70 .45
1214 A365 26p Queen Elizabeth ocean liner 1.00 .60
1215 A365 31p Tram No. 1173, Glasgow 1.15 .70
1216 A365 34p Handley Page aircraft, Croydon Airport 1.25 .80
Nos. 1213-1216 (4) 4.10 2.55

Defeat of the Spanish Armada by the Royal Navy, 400th Anniv. A366

Designs: No. 1217, Armada approaching The Lizard, July 19, 1588. No. 1218, Royal Navy vessels sailing from Plymouth to engage Spaniards in battle, July 21. No. 1219, Battle scene off the Isle of Wight, July 25. No. 1220, Battle scene off Calais, France, July 28-29. No. 1221, Spanish ships foundering in the North Sea storms, July 30-Aug. 2. Printed in a continuous design.

1988, July 19

1217 A366 18p multicolored .60 .35
1218 A366 18p multicolored .60 .35
1219 A366 18p multicolored .60 .35
1220 A366 18p multicolored .60 .35
1221 A366 18p multicolored .60 .35
a. Strip of 5, Nos. 1217-1221 3.00 1.75

Australia Bicentennial A367

Designs: No. 1222, Colonist, First Fleet vessel. No. 1223, British and Australian parliaments, Queen Elizabeth II. No. 1224, Cricketer W.G. Grace. No. 1225, John Lennon (1940-1980), William Shakespeare (1564-1616) and Sydney Opera House. Flag of Australia appears on #1223a, 1225a.

1988, June 21 Litho. *Perf. 14½*

1222 A367 18p multicolored .70 .40
1223 A367 18p multicolored .70 .40
a. Pair, #1222-1223 1.40 .80
1224 A367 34p multicolored 1.30 .75
1225 A367 34p multicolored 1.30 .75
a. Pair, #1224-1225 2.60 1.50
Nos. 1222-1225 (4) 4.00 2.30

See Australia Nos. 1082-1085.

Nonsensical Drawings by Edward Lear (1812-1888) — A368

Illustrations and text: 19p, *The Owl and the Pussycat,* 1867. 27p, Self-portrait as a bird, pen-and-ink sketch from a letter. 32p, "C" is for Cat, alphabet book character. 35p, Girl, birds and part of a limerick.

1988, Sept. 6 Photo. *Perf. 15x14*

1226 A368 19p multicolored .70 .35
1227 A368 27p multicolored .95 .50
1228 A368 32p multicolored 1.15 .70
1229 A368 35p multicolored 1.25 .70
a. Souv. sheet of 4, #1226-1229 9.00
Nos. 1226-1229 (4) 4.05 2.25

No. 1229a sold for £1.35. The surtax benefited Stamp World London '90.

Photographs of Castles by Prince Andrew — A369

1988, Oct 18 Engr.

1230 A369 £1 Carrickfergus 2.75 1.75
1231 A369 £1.50 Caernarfon 4.00 2.65
1232 A369 £2 Edinburgh 5.50 3.50
1233 A369 £5 Windsor 13.00 8.75
Nos. 1230-1233 (4) 25.25 16.65

See Nos. 1445-1448.

Christmas Cards A370

1988, Nov. 15 Photo. *Perf. 15x14½*

1234 A370 14p Journey to Bethlehem .40 .25
1235 A370 19p Shepherds see star .60 .35
1236 A370 27p Magi follow star .80 .55
1237 A370 32p Nativity .95 .65
1238 A370 35p The Annunciation 1.10 .70
Nos. 1234-1238 (5) 3.85 2.50

Birds — A371

1989, Jan. 17 *Perf. 14x15*

1239 A371 19p Puffin .70 .45
1240 A371 27p Avocet 1.00 .60
1241 A371 32p Oystercatcher 1.15 .70
1242 A371 35p Gannet 1.25 .80
Nos. 1239-1242 (4) 4.10 2.55

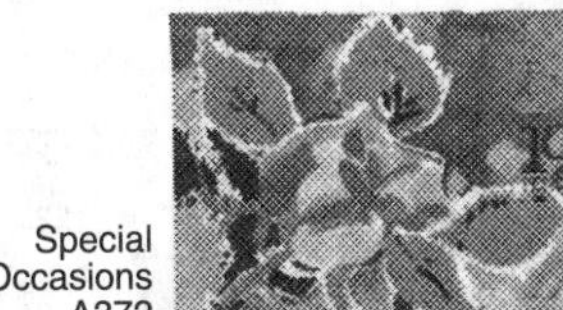
Special Occasions A372

1989, Jan. 31 Photo. *Perf. 15x14*
Booklet Stamps

1243 A372 19p Rose 2.50 .35
1244 A372 19p Cupid 2.50 .35
1245 A372 19p Ships 2.50 .35
1246 A372 19p Fruit bowl 2.50 .35
1247 A372 19p Teddy Bear 2.50 .35
a. Bklt. pane of 10 (2 each #1243-1247) +12 labels 25.00
Nos. 1243-1247 (5) 12.50 1.75

Labels inscribed "CONGRATULATIONS," "BEST WISHES," "HAPPY BIRTHDAY," "HAPPY ANNIVERSARY," "WITH LOVE," or "THANK YOU."

No. 1247a is valued with perfs guillotined. Full perfs sell for more.

Food and Farming Year — A373

Foods and tile mosaics in agricultural motifs.

1989, Mar. 7 Photo. *Perf. 14½*

1248 A373 19p Fruit and vegetables .55 .40
1249 A373 27p Meat, fish, fruit .80 .55
1250 A373 32p Dairy products 1.10 .65
1251 A373 35p Breads, cake, cereal 1.10 .70
Nos. 1248-1251 (4) 3.55 2.30

Fireworks — A374

1989, Apr. 11 Photo. *Perf. 14x14½*

1252 A374 19p Mortarboard 1.00 .70
1253 A374 19p "X" on ballot 1.00 .70
a. Pair, #1252-1253 2.00 1.40
1254 A374 35p Posthorn 1.75 1.25
1255 A374 35p Globe 1.75 1.25
a. Pair, #1254-1255 3.50 2.50
Nos. 1252-1255 (4) 5.50 3.90

Public education in England and Wales, 150th anniv. (#1252); European Parliament 3rd elections (#1253); 26th world congress of Postal Telegraph and Telephone Intl., Brighton, Sept. 18-23 (#1254); Interparliamentary Union Cent. Conf., 82nd session, Sept. 4-9 (#1255).

Europa 1989 — A375

1989, May 16 *Perf. 14x15*

Children's toys.

1256 A375 19p Airplane, locomotive .70 .40
1257 A375 27p Building-block tower .90 .55
1258 A375 32p Checkerboard, die, ladder, chips 1.15 .65
1259 A375 35p Doll house, boat, robot 1.25 .70
Nos. 1256-1259 (4) 4.00 2.30

Industrial Archaeology A376

1989, July 4 Photo. *Perf. 14x15*

1280 A376 19p Ironbridge .70 .45
1281 A376 27p Tin Mine .95 .60
1282 A376 32p Mills 1.15 .70
1283 A376 35p Pontcysyllte Aqueduct 1.25 .80
Nos. 1280-1283 (4) 4.05 2.55

1989, July 25 Souvenir Sheet

1284 Sheet of 4 7.00
a. A376 19p like #1280, horiz. .85
b. A376 27p like #1281, horiz. 1.20
c. A376 32p like #1282, horiz. 1.40
d. A376 35p like #1283, horiz. 1.50

No. 1284 sold for £1.40.

Microscopy A377

Specimens under magnification: 19p, Snowflake, the soc. emblem. 27p, Blue fly. 32p, Blood cells. 35p, Microchip.

1989, Sept. 5 Litho. *Perf. 14½x14*

1285 A377 19p multicolored .55 .45
1286 A377 27p multicolored .80 .60
1287 A377 32p multicolored 1.00 .70
1288 A377 35p multicolored 1.10 .80
Nos. 1285-1288 (4) 3.45 2.55

Royal Microscopical Soc., 150th anniv.

The Lord Mayor's Show, London — A378

Procession of the Lord Mayor's coach from Guildhall to the Law Courts in the Strand: No. 1289, Royal mail coach and The Guildhall. No. 1290, Drummer, cavalrymen and Mansion House. No. 1291, Gold coach, 1757, and The Royal Exchange. No. 1292, Coachman and St. Paul's Cathedral. No. 1293, Drummer, cavalryman and the Law Courts.

1989, Oct. 17 Litho. *Perf. 14x15*

1289 A378 20p multicolored .70 .45
1290 A378 20p multicolored .70 .45
1291 A378 20p multicolored .70 .45
1292 A378 20p multicolored .70 .45
1293 A378 20p multicolored .70 .45
a. Strip of 5, #1289-1293 3.50 2.25

Ely Cathedral, Cambridgeshire, 800th Anniv. — A379

1989, Nov. 14 Photo. *Perf. 15x14*

1294 A379 15p Gothic arches, 4 peasants .50 .25
Nos. 1294,B2-B5 (5) 4.00 2.85

Christmas.

Royal Soc. for the Prevention of Cruelty to Animals, 150th Anniv. — A381

1990, Jan. 23 Litho. *Perf. 14x15*

1300 A381 20p Kitten .75 .55
1301 A381 29p Rabbit 1.10 .85
1302 A381 34p Duckling 1.25 1.00
1303 A381 37p Puppy 1.40 1.10
Nos. 1300-1303 (4) 4.50 3.50

Miniature Sheet

Famous Smiles A382

1990, Feb. 6 Photo. *Perf. 15x14*

1304 A382 20p Teddy bear 2.00 1.00
1305 A382 20p Dennis the Menace 2.00 1.00
1306 A382 20p Mr. Punch 2.00 1.00
1307 A382 20p Cheshire Cat 2.00 1.00
1308 A382 20p Man in the Moon 2.00 1.00
1309 A382 20p The Laughing Policeman 2.00 1.00
1310 A382 20p Clown 2.00 1.00
1311 A382 20p Mona Lisa 2.00 1.00
1312 A382 20p Queen of Hearts 2.00 1.00
1313 A382 20p Stan Laurel 2.00 1.00
a. Pane of 10, #1304-1313 25.00 15.00
Nos. 1304-1313 (10) 10.00

No. 1313a sold folded and unattached in booklet cover.

See Nos. 1364-1373.

A383

Europa 1990: No. 1314, Alexandra Palace. No. 1315, School of Art, Glasgow. 29p, British Philatelic Bureau, Edinburgh. 37p, Templeton Carpet Factory, Glasgow.

1990, Mar. 6 Photo. *Perf. 14x15*

1314 A383 20p multicolored .70 .50
a. Bklt. pane of 4 + printed margin 2.00
1315 A383 20p multicolored .70 .50
1316 A383 29p multicolored 1.00 .70
1317 A383 37p multicolored 1.25 .90
Nos. 1314-1317 (4) 3.65 2.60

Stamp World '90, London (No. 1314); Glasgow, European City of Culture (Nos. 1315, 1317).

For Prestige booklet containing pane #1314a, see listings in the Booklets section.

Queen's Awards for Export and Technological Achievement, 25th Anniv. — A384

1990, Apr. 10 Litho.

1318 A384 20p Export .70 .45
1319 A384 20p Technology .70 .45
a. Pair, #1318-1319 1.40
1320 A384 37p like No. 1318 1.25 .75
1321 A384 37p like No. 1319 1.25 .75
a. Pair, #1320-1321 2.50
Nos. 1318-1321 (4) 3.90 2.40

Se-tenant pairs have continuous designs.

Kew Gardens, 150th Anniv. — A385

1990, June 5 Photo.

1322 A385 20p Cycad .70 .45
1323 A385 29p Stone pine 1.00 .60
1324 A385 34p Willow tree 1.15 .65
1325 A385 37p Cedar 1.25 .80
Nos. 1322-1325 (4) 4.10 2.50

Thomas Hardy (1840-1928), Writer and Clyffe Clump, Dorset — A386

1990, July 10 Photo. *Perf. 14x15*

1326 A386 20p multicolored .70 .40

Queen Mother, 90th Birthday — A387

Designs: Portraits of Queen Elizabeth, The Queen Mother.

1990, Aug. 2 *Perf. 14x15, 14½*

1327 A387 20p Recent portrait .70 .45
1328 A387 29p As Queen Consort, 1937 1.00 .65
1329 A387 34p As Duchess of York 1.15 .75
1330 A387 37p As Lady Elizabeth Bowes-Lyon 1.25 .80
Nos. 1327-1330 (4) 4.10 2.65

Gallantry Awards — A388

Designs: No. 1331, Victoria Cross. No. 1332, George Cross. No. 1333, Military Cross, Military Medal. No. 1334, Distinguished Flying Cross, Distinguished Flying Medal. No. 1335, Distinguished Service Cross, Distinguished Service Medal. Nos. 1333-1335 horiz.

1990, Sept. 11 *Perf. 14x15, 15x14*

1331 A388 20p multicolored .70 .55
1332 A388 20p multicolored .70 .55
1333 A388 20p multicolored .70 .55
1334 A388 20p multicolored .70 .55
1335 A388 20p multicolored .70 .55
Nos. 1331-1335 (5) 3.50 2.75

Astronomy A389

Designs: 22p, Armagh Observatory, Jodrell Bank and La Palma telescopes. 26p, Early telescope, celestial diagram. 31p, Greenwich Old Observatory, sextant, chronometer. 37p, Stonehenge, celestial navigation.

1990, Oct. 16 *Perf. 14*

1336 A389 22p multicolored .75 .45
1337 A389 26p multicolored .90 .55
1338 A389 31p multicolored 1.10 .70
1339 A389 37p multicolored 1.30 .80
Nos. 1336-1339 (4) 4.05 2.50

Christmas A390

1990, Nov. 13 Litho. *Perf. 15x14*

1340 A390 17p Building snowman .55 .30
a. Booklet pane of 20 13.00
1341 A390 22p Carrying Christmas tree .70 .40
1342 A390 26p Caroling .85 .50
1343 A390 31p Sledding 1.10 .60
1344 A390 37p Ice skating 1.25 .75
Nos. 1340-1344 (5) 4.45 2.55

Dogs — A391

Paintings by George Stubbs: 22p, King Charles Spaniel. 26p, A Pointer. 31p, Two Hounds in a Landscape. 33p, A Rough Dog. 37p, Fino and Tiny.

1991, Jan. 8 Photo. *Perf. 14x14½*

1345 A391 22p multicolored .70 .40
1346 A391 26p multicolored .80 .50
1347 A391 31p multicolored 1.00 .60
1348 A391 33p multicolored 1.10 .65
1349 A391 37p multicolored 1.25 .75
Nos. 1345-1349 (5) 4.85 2.90

Royal Veterinary College bicentennial, National Canine Defense League and Cruft's Dog Show, centennial.

Symbols of Good Luck A392

1991, Feb. 5 Photo. *Perf. 15x14*
Booklet Stamps

1350 A392 1st shown 1.25 .60
1351 A392 1st Shooting star, rainbow 1.25 .60
1352 A392 1st Bird, charm bracelet 1.25 .60
1353 A392 1st Black cat 1.25 .60
1354 A392 1st Bluebird, key 1.25 .60
1355 A392 1st Duck, frog 1.25 .60
1356 A392 1st Black boot, shamrocks 1.25 .60
1357 A392 1st Rainbow, pot of gold 1.25 .60
1358 A392 1st Peacock moths 1.25 .60
1359 A392 1st Wishing well, sixpence 1.25 .60
a. Bklt. pane of 10, #1350-1359 15.00

No. 1359a printed se-tenant with 12 greetings labels. No. 1359a sold for £2.20 at date of issue.

Scientists & Their Technology A393

Designs: No. 1360, Michael Faraday, electricity. No. 1361, Charles Babbage, computers. 31p, Radar, developed by Robert Watson-Watt. 37p, Jet engine developed by Frank Whittle.

1991, Mar. 5 *Perf. 14x15*

1360 A393 22p multicolored .65 .50
1361 A393 22p multicolored .65 .50
1362 A393 31p multicolored 1.10 .75
1363 A393 37p multicolored 1.25 .85
Nos. 1360-1363 (4) 3.65 2.60

Famous Smiles Type of 1990

1991, Mar. 26 Photo. *Perf. 15x14*
Booklet Stamps

1364 A382 1st Teddy bear .90 .50
1365 A382 1st Dennis the Menace .90 .50
1366 A382 1st Mr. Punch .90 .50
1367 A382 1st Cheshire Cat .90 .50
1368 A382 1st Man in the Moon .90 .50
1369 A382 1st The Laughing Policeman .90 .50
1370 A382 1st Clown .90 .50
1371 A382 1st Mona Lisa .90 .50
1372 A382 1st Queen of Hearts .90 .50
1373 A382 1st Stan Laurel .90 .50
a. Booklet pane of 10 10.00
b. Sheet, #1364-1373 + 10 labels 8.50

No. 1373a sold for £2.20 at date of issue. No. 1373a was affixed to booklet cover and was printed se-tenant with 12 greetings labels.

No. 1373b issued 5/22/00. Labels depict ribbons and are inscribed "The Stamp Show / 2000". The sheet with ribbon labels sold for £2.95, while the sheet with personalized labels sold for £5.95.

A394

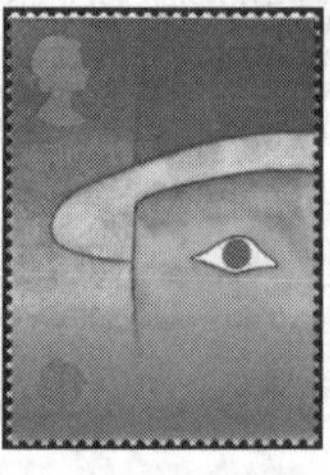

Europa — A395

Illustrations reduced.

1991, Apr. 23 Photo. *Perf. 14x15*

1374 A394 22p Planets .70 .45
1375 A394 22p Stars .70 .45
a. Pair, #1374-1375 1.40 .90
1376 A395 37p shown 1.25 .75
1377 A395 37p Crescent eye 1.25 .75
a. Pair, #1376-1377 2.50 1.50
Nos. 1374-1377 (4) 3.90 2.40

Sports — A396

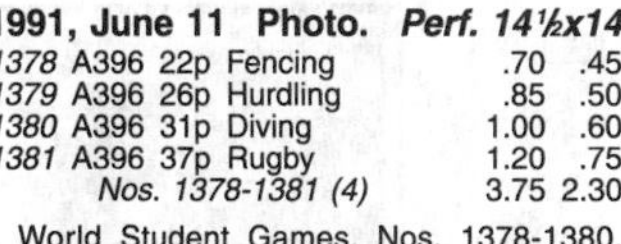

1991, June 11 Photo. *Perf. 14½x14*
1378 A396 22p Fencing .70 .45
1379 A396 26p Hurdling .85 .50
1380 A396 31p Diving 1.00 .60
1381 A396 37p Rugby 1.20 .75
Nos. 1378-1381 (4) 3.75 2.30

World Student Games, Nos. 1378-1380. Rugby World Cup, No. 1381.

Roses — A397

1991, July 16 Litho. *Perf. 14½x14*
1382 A397 22p Silver Jubilee .65 .35
1383 A397 26p Mme. Alfred Carriere .80 .40
1384 A397 31p Rosa moyesii .95 .45
1385 A397 33p Harvest Fayre 1.00 .55
1386 A397 37p Mutabilis 1.15 .65
Nos. 1382-1386 (5) 4.55 2.40

Dinosaurs A398

1991, Aug. 20 Photo. *Perf. 14½x14*
1387 A398 22p Iguanodon .70 .50
1388 A398 26p Stegosaurus .85 .60
1389 A398 31p Tyrannosaurus 1.00 .70
1390 A398 33p Protoceratops 1.05 .70
1391 A398 37p Triceratops 1.20 .85
Nos. 1387-1391 (5) 4.80 3.35

First use of word "dinosaur" by Sir Richard Owen, 150th anniv.

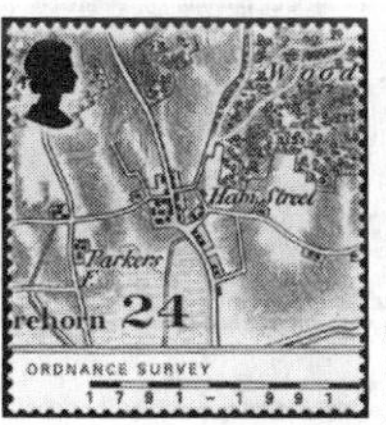

Ordnance Survey Maps, Bicent. — A399

Maps of village of Hamstreet, Kent.

1991, Sept. 17 Litho. & Engr.
1392 A399 24p 1816 .80 .50

Litho.

1393 A399 28p 1906 .90 .55
1394 A399 33p 1959 1.05 .65
1395 A399 39p 1991 1.25 .75
Nos. 1392-1395 (4) 4.00 2.45

Christmas A400

Illuminated leters from Venetian manuscript "Acts of Mary and Jesus": 18p, "P," Adoration of the Magi. 24p, "M," Mary placing Jesus in manger. 28p, "A," Angel warning Joseph. 33p, "Q," The Annunciation. 39p, "N," Flight into Egypt.

1991, Nov. 12 Photo. *Perf. 15x14*
1416 A400 18p multicolored .60 .45
a. Booklet pane of 20 12.00
1417 A400 24p multicolored .80 .60
1418 A400 28p multicolored .95 .75
1419 A400 33p multicolored 1.15 .80
1420 A400 39p multicolored 1.35 1.00
Nos. 1416-1420 (5) 4.85 3.60

Animals in Winter A401

1992, Jan. 14 Photo. *Perf. 15x14*
1421 A401 18p Fallow deer .60 .45
1422 A401 24p Brown hare .80 .55
1423 A401 28p Fox .95 .70
1424 A401 33p Redwing 1.15 .80
1425 A401 39p Welsh mountain sheep 1.35 .90
a. Booklet pane of 4 5.40
Nos. 1421-1425 (5) 4.85 3.40

For Prestige booklet containing pane #1425a, see listings in the Booklets section.
Issue date: No. 1425a, Mar. 1.

Memories A402

1992, Jan. 28 Litho. *Perf. 15x14*
Booklet Stamps
1426 A402 1st Flowers .80 .40
1427 A402 1st Locket .80 .40
1428 A402 1st Key .80 .40
1429 A402 1st Model car .80 .40
1430 A402 1st Compass, 4-leaf clover .80 .40
1431 A402 1st Pocket watch .80 .40
1432 A402 1st Envelope, fountain pen .80 .40
1433 A402 1st Buttons, pearls .80 .40
1434 A402 1st Marbles .80 .40
1435 A402 1st Starfish, shovel and bucket .80 .40
a. Bklt. pane of 10, #1426-1435 8.00

No. 1435a printed se-tenant with 12 greeting labels and sold for £2.40 at date of issue.

Queen Elizabeth II's Accession to the Throne, 40th Anniv. A403

Queen Elizabeth II: No. 1436, In coronation regalia. No. 1437, Facing right, wearing garter robes as head of Church of England. No. 1438, Holding infant Prince Andrew. No. 1439, Wearing military uniform at Trooping of the Color. No. 1440, Wearing purple hat.

1992, Feb. 6 Litho. *Perf. 14½x14*
1436 A403 24p multicolored .80 .60
1437 A403 24p multicolored .80 .60
1438 A403 24p multicolored .80 .60
1439 A403 24p multicolored .80 .60
1440 A403 24p multicolored .80 .60
a. Strip of 5, #1436-1440 4.00 3.00

Alfred, Lord Tennyson, Death Cent. — A404

Portraits and illustrations for poems: 24p, The Beguiling of Merlin by Sir Edward Burne-Jones. 28p, April Love by Arthur Hughes. 33p, The Lady of Shalott by John William Waterhouse. 39p, Mariana by Dante Gabriel Rossetti.

1992, Mar. 10 Photo.
1441 A404 24p multicolored .80 .55
1442 A404 28p multicolored .95 .65
1443 A404 33p multicolored 1.15 .80
1444 A404 39p multicolored 1.35 .90
Nos. 1441-1444 (4) 4.25 2.90

Castle Type of 1988

Nos. 1445-1448 have been re-engraved to show greater detail than on Nos. 1230-1233. The silhouette of the Queen's head on Nos. 1445-1448 is printed in a special ink that changes color from green to gold.

Perf. 15x14 Syncopated

1992-95 Engr.
1445 A369 £1 like #1230 2.50 .55
1446 A369 £1.50 like #1231 3.75 1.00
1447 A369 £2 like #1232 4.75 1.00
1447A A369 £3 like #1230 9.50 3.50
1448 A369 £5 like #1233 12.00 4.00
Nos. 1445-1448 (5) 32.50 10.05

Nos. 1445-1447, 1448 were re-issued 12/6/94 with lines strengthened. Castles appear darker than on original issue.
Issued: £3, 8/22/95; others, 3/24/92.

Castle Type Re-engraved

1997, July 29
1446a A369 £1.50 Caernarfon 3.75 1.00
1447b A369 £2 Edinburgh 4.75 1.00
1447Ac A369 £3 Carrickfergus 9.50 3.00
1448a A369 £5 Windsor 12.00 4.00

Queen's head is silkscreened and feels smooth on Nos. 1446a, 1447b, 1447Ac, 1448a. Letters "C" and "S" in Castle do not have serifs. Letters in castle names also differ from the 1992 and 1995 printings. The elliptical perforation begins one perf hole higher than on the earlier printings.

Discovery of America, 500th Anniv. A405

Design: 39p, Sailing ship, Operation Raleigh Grand Regatta.

Litho. & Engr.

1992, Apr. 7 *Perf. 14½*
1449 A405 24p multicolored 1.50 .50
1450 A405 39p multicolored 2.25 1.00

Europa.

Events A406

Designs: No. 1451, British Olympic Assoc. flag. No. 1452, Flying torch flag of British Paralympic Assoc. No. 1453, British pavilion.

1992, Apr. 7 Litho.
1451 A406 24p multicolored .80 .40
1452 A406 24p multicolored .80 .40
a. Pair, #1451-1452 1.60 .80
1453 A406 39p multicolored 1.35 .65
Nos. 1451-1453 (3) 2.95 1.45

1992 Summer Olympics (No. 1451) and Paralympics (No. 1452), Barcelona. Expo '92, Seville (No. 1453).

English Civil War, 350th Anniv. — A407

1992, June 16 Photo. *Perf. 14½*
1454 A407 24p Pikeman .80 .55
1455 A407 28p Drummer .95 .65
1456 A407 33p Musketeer 1.15 .80
1457 A407 39p Standard bearer 1.35 .90
Nos. 1454-1457 (4) 4.25 2.90

Yeoman of the Guard, by Gilbert & Sullivan A408

Scenes from comic operas: 24p, The Gondoliers. 28p, The Mikado. 33p, The Pirates of Penzance. 39p, Iolanthe.

1992, July 21 Photo. *Perf. 14½x14*
1458 A408 18p multicolored .50 .50
1459 A408 24p multicolored .80 .65
1460 A408 28p multicolored .95 .75
1461 A408 33p multicolored 1.15 .90
1462 A408 39p multicolored 1.35 1.10
Nos. 1458-1462 (5) 4.75 3.90

Sir Arthur Sullivan, 150th anniv. of birth.

Protect the Environment A409

Children's drawings: 24p, Acid rain kills. 28p, Ozone layer. 33p, Greenhouse effect. 39p, Bird of hope.

1992, Sept. 15 Photo. *Perf. 14½*
1463 A409 24p multicolored .70 .55
1464 A409 28p multicolored .85 .60
1465 A409 33p multicolored .95 .75
1466 A409 39p multicolored 1.25 .90
Nos. 1463-1466 (4) 3.75 2.80

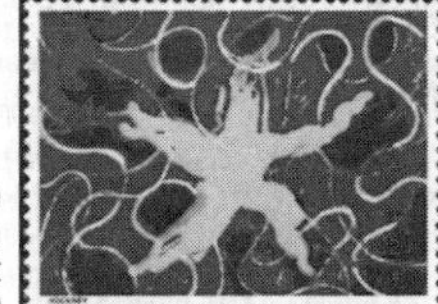

Single European Market A410

1992, Oct. 13 Photo. *Perf. 15x14*
1467 A410 24p multicolored .80 .80

Christmas A411

Stained glass windows: 18p, Angel Gabriel. 24p, Madonna and Child. 28p, King offering gold crown. 33p, Shepherds. 39p, Kings offering frankincense and myrrh.

1992, Nov. 10 Photo. *Perf. 15x14*
1468 A411 18p multicolored .55 .45
a. Booklet pane of 20 11.00
1469 A411 24p multicolored .70 .55
1470 A411 28p multicolored .85 .65
1471 A411 33p multicolored 1.00 .80
1472 A411 39p multicolored 1.20 .95
Nos. 1468-1472 (5) 4.30 3.40

Mute Swans — A412

Designs: 18p, Male, St. Catherine's Chapel, Abbotsbury. 24p, Cygnet, reed bed, Abbotsbury Swannery. 28p, Pair, cygnet. 33p, Eggs in nest, Tithe Barn. 39p, Head of young swan.

1993, Jan. 19 Photo. *Perf. 14x15*

1473 A412 18p multicolored .75 .35
1474 A412 24p multicolored 1.00 .50
1475 A412 28p multicolored 1.25 .60
1476 A412 33p multicolored 1.50 .70
1477 A412 39p multicolored 1.60 .85
Nos. 1473-1477 (5) 6.10 3.00

Abbotsbury Swannery, 600th anniv.

Britannia — A413

Litho., Typo. and Embossed
Perf. 14x14½ Syncopated
1993, Mar. 2
Granite Paper

1478 A413 £10 multicolored 22.50 12.00
a. Silver (Queen's head, security crosses) omitted 4,000.

Soaking may damage these stamps.

Greetings Stamps A414

Children's Characters: No. 1479, Long John Silver, parrot. No. 1480, Tweedledum, Tweedledee. No. 1481, Just William, Violet Elizabeth. No. 1482, Toad, Mole. No. 1483, Bash Street Kids, teacher. No. 1484, Peter Rabbit, Mrs. Rabbit. No. 1485, Father Christmas, Snowman. No. 1486, Big Friendly Giant, Sophie. No. 1487, Rupert Bear, Bill Badger. No. 1488, Aladdin, Genie.

Perf. 15x14 Syncopated
1993, Feb. 2 Litho.

1479 A414 (1st) multicolored .80 .35
1480 A414 (1st) multicolored .80 .35
1481 A414 (1st) multicolored .80 .35
1482 A414 (1st) multicolored .80 .35
1483 A414 (1st) multicolored .80 .35
1484 A414 (1st) multicolored .80 .35
a. Booklet pane of 4 3.25
1485 A414 (1st) multicolored .80 .35
1486 A414 (1st) multicolored .80 .35
1487 A414 (1st) multicolored .80 .35
1488 A414 (1st) multicolored .80 .35
a. Bklt. pane of 10, #1479-1488 8.00

No. 1479-1488 sold for 24p on day of issue. No. 1488a printed se-tenant with 20 greetings labels. See note above No. 1445.

Issue date: No. 1484a, Aug. 10.

For Prestige booklet containing pane #1484a, see listings in the Booklets section.

Marine Chronometer No. 4 — A415

Designs: 24p, Face. 28p, Escapement, remontoire and fusee. 33p, Balance spring, temperature compensator. 39p, Back of movement.

1993, Feb. 16 Litho. *Perf. 14½*

1489 A415 24p multicolored .65 .45
1490 A415 28p multicolored .75 .55
1491 A415 33p multicolored .90 .60
1492 A415 39p multicolored 1.10 .75
Nos. 1489-1492 (4) 3.40 2.35

John Harrison (1693-1776), inventor of marine chronometer.

Orchids A416

14th World Orchid Conf., Glasgow: 18p, Dendrobium hellwigianum. 24p, Paphiopedilum Maudiae "Magnificum." 28p, Cymbidium lowianum. 33p, Vanda Rothschildiana. 39p, Dendrobium vexillarius.

1993, Mar. 16 Litho. *Perf. 15x14*

1493 A416 18p multicolored .50 .35
1494 A416 24p multicolored .65 .45
1495 A416 28p multicolored .75 .55
1496 A416 33p multicolored .90 .60
1497 A416 39p multicolored 1.10 .75
Nos. 1493-1497 (5) 3.90 2.70

Contemporary Art — A417

Europa: 24p, Sculpture, Family Group, by Henry Moore. 28p, Print, Kew Gardens, by Edward Bawden. 33p, Painting, St. Francis and the Birds, by Stanley Spencer. 39p, Painting, Still Life, Odyssey 1, by Ben Nicholson.

1993, May 11 Photo. *Perf. 14x14½*

1498 A417 24p multicolored .70 .20
1499 A417 28p multicolored .85 .85
1500 A417 33p multicolored 1.00 1.00
1501 A417 39p multicolored 1.25 .75
Nos. 1498-1501 (4) 3.80 2.80

Roman Artifacts A418

24p, Gold aureus of Claudius. 28p, Bronze bust of Hadrian. 33p, Gemstone carved with head of Roma. 39p, Mosaic of Christ.

1993, June 15 Photo. *Perf. 14½x14*

1502 A418 24p multicolored .70 .45
1503 A418 28p multicolored .85 .55
1504 A418 33p multicolored 1.10 .60
1505 A418 39p multicolored 1.15 .75
Nos. 1502-1505 (4) 3.80 2.35

British Canals, Bicent. A419

Designs: 24p, Grand Junction Canal boats. 28p, Stainforth and Keadby Canal. 33p, Brecknock and Abergavenny Canal boats, horse. 39p, Crinan Canal, steamers and fishing boats.

1993, July 20 Litho. *Perf. 14½x14*

1506 A419 24p multicolored .70 .50
1507 A419 28p multicolored .85 .60
1508 A419 33p multicolored 1.00 .70
1509 A419 39p multicolored 1.15 .80
Nos. 1506-1509 (4) 3.70 2.60

Autumn Fruits A420

1993, Sept. 14 Photo. *Perf. 15x14*

1510 A420 18p Horse chestnut .50 .30
1511 A420 24p Blackberries .70 .45
1512 A420 28p Filbert .85 .55
1513 A420 33p Rowanberries 1.00 .65
1514 A420 39p Pears 1.15 .75
Nos. 1510-1514 (5) 4.20 2.70

Sherlock Holmes — A421

Holmes and: No. 1515, Dr. Watson, The Reigate Squire. No. 1516, Sir Henry, The Hound of the Baskervilles. No. 1517, Lestrade, The Six Napoleons. No. 1518, Mycroft, The Greek Interpreter. No. 1519, Moriarty, The Final Problem.

1993, Oct. 12 Litho. *Perf. 14x14½*

1515 A421 24p multicolored .90 .50
1516 A421 24p multicolored .90 .50
1517 A421 24p multicolored .90 .50
1518 A421 24p multicolored .90 .50
1519 A421 24p multicolored .90 .50
a. Strip of 5, #1515-1519 4.50 2.50

"A Christmas Carol," by Charles Dickens, 150th Anniv. A423

Designs: 19p, Tiny Tim, Bob Cratchit. 25p, Mr. & Mrs. Fezziwig. 30p, Scrooge. 35p, Prize Turkey. 41p, Mr. Scrooge's Nephew.

1993, Nov. 9 Photo. *Perf. 15x14*

1528 A423 19p multicolored .55 .35
a. Booklet pane of 20 11.00
1529 A423 25p multicolored .75 .50
1530 A423 30p multicolored .90 .60
1531 A423 35p multicolored 1.00 .65
1532 A423 41p multicolored 1.25 .80
Nos. 1528-1532 (5) 4.45 2.90

Age of Steam — A424

Designs: 19p, Tandem locomotives, West Highland Line, North British Railway. 25p, Locomotive #60149, Kings Cross Station, London. 30p, Locomotive #43000 on turntable, Blyth North engine shed. 35p, Locomotive entering station. 41p, Locomotive on bridge over Worcester & Birmingham Canal.

1994, Jan. 18 Photo. *Perf. 14½*

1533 A424 19p black & green .55 .35
1534 A424 25p black & purple .75 .50
1535 A424 30p black & red brn .90 .60
1536 A424 35p black & red violet 1.00 .65
1537 A424 41p black & dark blue 1.25 .80
Nos. 1533-1537 (5) 4.45 2.90

Dan Dare A425

The Three Bears A426

Rupert the Bear A427

Alice in Wonderland — A428

Noggin the Nog A429

Peter Rabbit A430

Little Red Riding Hood A431

Orlando, the Marmalade Cat A432

Biggles A433

Paddington A434

Perf. 15x14 Syncopated
1994, Feb. 1 Photo.
Booklet Stamps

1538 A425 (1st) multicolored .75 .40
1539 A426 (1st) multicolored .75 .40
1540 A427 (1st) multicolored .75 .40
1541 A428 (1st) multicolored .75 .40
1542 A429 (1st) multicolored .75 .40
1543 A430 (1st) multicolored .75 .40
1544 A431 (1st) multicolored .75 .40
1545 A432 (1st) multicolored .75 .40

1546	A433	(1st) multicolored	.75	.40
1547	A434	(1st) multicolored	.75	.40
a.		Bklt. pane of 10, #1538-1547	7.50	

Nos. 1538-1547 sold for 25p on day of issue. No. 1547a was printed se-tenant with 20 greetings labels.

Investiture of Prince of Wales, 25th Anniv. A435

Watercolor landscapes, by Prince Charles: 19p, Chirk Castle, Clwyd, Wales. 25p, Ben Arkle, Sutherland, Scotland. 30p, Mourne Mountains, County Down, Northern Ireland. 35p, Dersingham, Norfolk, England. 41p, Dolwyddelan, Gwynedd, Wales.

1994, Mar. 1 Photo. *Perf. 15x14*

1548	A435	19p multicolored	.55	.35
1549	A435	25p multicolored	.75	.50
1550	A435	30p multicolored	.90	.60
a.		Booklet pane of 4	3.60	
1551	A435	35p multicolored	1.00	.65
1552	A435	41p multicolored	1.25	.80
		Nos. 1548-1552 (5)	4.45	2.90

For Prestige booklet containing pane #1550a, see listings in the Booklets section.

British Picture Postcards, Cent. — A436

Seaside characters: 19p, "Bather at Blackpool." 25p, "Where's my Little Lad." 30p, "Wish You Were Here." 35p, "Punch and Judy Show." 41p, "The Tower Crane."

1994, Apr. 12 Litho. *Perf. 14x14½*

1553	A436	19p multicolored	.55	.35
1554	A436	25p multicolored	.75	.50
1555	A436	30p multicolored	.90	.60
1556	A436	35p multicolored	1.00	.65
1557	A436	41p multicolored	1.25	.80
		Nos. 1553-1557 (5)	4.45	2.90

Blackpool Tower, cent. (#1553). Tower Bridge, cent. (#1557).

Opening of Channel Tunnel — A437

Nos. 1558, 1560, British lion, French rooster, meeting over Channel. Nos. 1559, 1561, Joined hands above speeding train.

1994, May 3 Photo. *Perf. 14x14½*

1558	A437	25p dk blue & multi	.75	.55
1559	A437	25p dk blue & multi	.75	.55
a.		Pair, #1558-1559	1.50	1.10
1560	A437	41p lt blue & multi	1.25	.90
1561	A437	41p multicolored	1.25	.90
a.		Pair, #1560-1561	2.50	1.80
		Nos. 1558-1561 (4)	4.00	2.90

See France Nos. 2421-2424.

D-Day, 50th Anniv. — A438

Photographs from Imperial War Museum's archives: No. 1562, Ground crew reloading FAF Bostons. No. 1563, Coastal bombardment by HMS Warspite. No. 1564, Commandos landing on Gold Beach. No. 1565, Infantry regrouping on Sword Beach. No. 1566, Advancing inland from Ouistreham.

1994, June 6 Litho. *Perf. 14*

1562	A438	25p multicolored	.90	.60
1563	A438	25p multicolored	.90	.60
1564	A438	25p multicolored	.90	.60
1565	A438	25p multicolored	.90	.60
1566	A438	25p multicolored	.90	.60
a.		Strip of 5, #1562-1566	4.50	2.50

Honorable Company of Edinburgh Golfers, 250th Anniv. — A439

Golf courses: 19p, St. Andrews, old course. 25p, Muirfield, 18th hole. 30p, Carnoustie, 15th hole. 35p, Royal Troon, "postage stamp" 8th hole. 41p, Turnberry, 9th hole.

1994, July 5 Photo. *Perf. 14*

1567	A439	19p multicolored	.55	.35
1568	A439	25p multicolored	.75	.50
1569	A439	30p multicolored	.90	.60
1570	A439	35p multicolored	1.00	.65
1571	A439	41p multicolored	1.25	.80
		Nos. 1567-1571 (5)	4.45	2.90

Summertime Events — A440

Designs: 19p, Royal Welsh Agricultural Show, Llanelwedd. 25p, Wimbledon. 30p, Yachts on Solent during Cowes Week. 35p, Cricket at Lord's. 41p, Scottish Highland Games, Braemar.

1994, Aug. 2 *Perf. 14½x14*

1572	A440	19p multicolored	.55	.35
1573	A440	25p multicolored	.75	.50
1574	A440	30p multicolored	.90	.60
1575	A440	35p multicolored	1.00	.65
1576	A440	41p multicolored	1.25	.80
		Nos. 1572-1576 (5)	4.45	2.90

Medical Discoveries — A441

Europa: 25p, Ultrasonic imaging. 30p, Scanning electron microscopy. 35p, Magnetic resonance imaging. 41p, Computed tomography.

1994, Sept. 27 Photo. *Perf. 14x14½*

1577	A441	25p multicolored	.75	.20
1578	A441	30p multicolored	.90	.90
1579	A441	35p multicolored	1.00	1.00
1580	A441	41p multicolored	1.10	1.10
		Nos. 1577-1580 (4)	3.75	3.20

Christmas A442

School children portraying: 19p, Mary, Joseph, with infant Jesus. 25p, Magi. 30p, Mary holding Jesus. 35p, Shepherds. 41p, Angels.

1994, Nov. 1 Photo. *Perf. 15x14*

1581	A442	19p multicolored	.60	.40
a.		Booklet pane of 20	12.00	
1582	A442	25p multicolored	.80	.50
1583	A442	30p multicolored	.95	.60
1584	A442	35p multicolored	1.10	.70
1585	A442	41p multicolored	1.25	.85
		Nos. 1581-1585 (5)	4.70	3.05

Cats A443

Designs: 19p, Black cat. 25p, Siamese, tabby cats. 30p, Yellow cat. 35p, Calico, Abyssinian cats. 41p, Black & white cat.

1995, Jan. 17 Litho. *Perf. 15x14*

1586	A443	19p multicolored	.60	.35
1587	A443	25p multicolored	.80	.50
1588	A443	30p multicolored	.95	.60
1589	A443	35p multicolored	1.10	.65
1590	A443	41p multicolored	1.25	.80
		Nos. 1586-1590 (5)	4.70	2.90

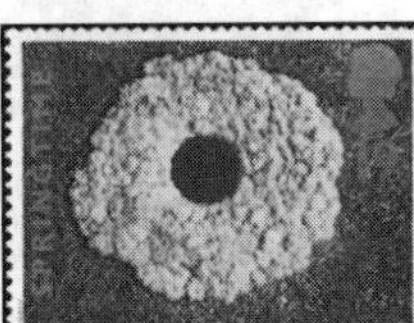

Springtime A444

Sculptures from natural materials, by Andy Goldsworthy: 19p, Dandelions. 25p, Chestnut leaves. 30p, Garlic leaves. 35p, Hazel leaves. 41p, Spring grass.

1995, Mar. 14 Photo. *Perf. 15x14*

1591	A444	19p multicolored	.60	.35
1592	A444	25p multicolored	.80	.50
1593	A444	30p multicolored	.95	.60
1594	A444	35p multicolored	1.10	.65
1595	A444	41p multicolored	1.25	.80
		Nos. 1591-1595 (5)	4.70	2.90

'La Danse a la Campagne,' by Renoir — A445

'Troilus and Criseyde,' by Peter Brooks A446

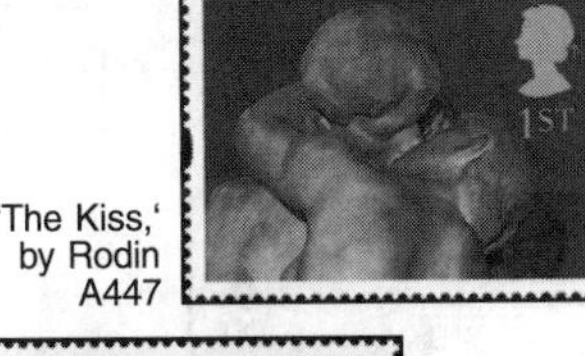

'The Kiss,' by Rodin A447

'Girls on the Town,' by Beryl Cook A448

'Jazz,' by Andrew Mockett A449

'Girls Performing aKathal Dance' (Aurangzeb Period) A450

'Alice Keppel with her Daughter,' by Alice Hughes A451

'Children Playing,' by L.S. Lowry A452

'Circus Clowns,' by Emily Fitmin and Justin Mitchell A453

Decoration from 'All the Love Poems of Shakespeare,' by Eric Gill — A454

Perf. 14 Syncopated

1995, Mar. 21 Litho.

1596	A445	1st multicolored	.80	.40
1597	A446	1st multicolored	.80	.40
1598	A447	1st multicolored	.80	.40
1599	A448	1st multicolored	.80	.40
1600	A449	1st multicolored	.80	.40
1601	A450	1st multicolored	.80	.40
1602	A451	1st multicolored	.80	.40
1603	A452	1st multicolored	.80	.40
1604	A453	1st multicolored	.80	.40
1605	A454	1st multicolored	.80	.40
a.		Bklt. pane of 10, #1596-1605	8.00	

Complete booklet sold for £2.50 on day of issue.

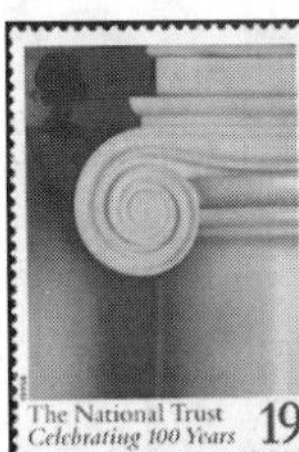

National Trust, Cent. — A455

Designs: 19p, Celebrating 100 years. 25p, Protecting land. 30p, Conserving art. 35p, Saving coast. 41p, Repairing buildings.

1995, Apr. 11 Photo. *Perf. 14x15*

1606	A455	19p multicolored	.60	.35
1607	A455	25p multicolored	.80	.50
a.		Booklet pane of 6	4.80	
1608	A455	30p multicolored	.95	.60
1609	A455	35p multicolored	1.10	.65
1610	A455	41p multicolored	1.25	.80
		Nos. 1606-1610 (5)	4.70	2.90

For Prestige booklet containing panes #1607a, see listings in the Booklets section. Issued: #1607a, 4/25/95.

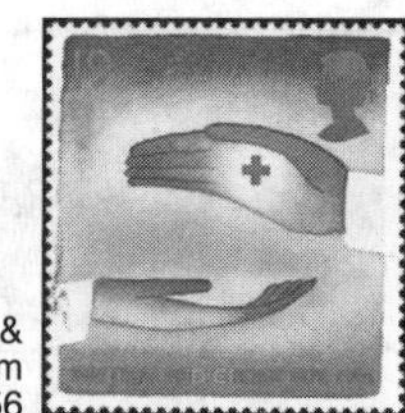
Peace & Freedom A456

Designs: No. 1611, Hands, British Red Cross 1870-1995. No. 1612, British troops, people celebrating liberation of Paris. No. 1613, Dove, outstretched hand, UN, 1945-95. No. 1614, St. Paul's Cathedral, floodlights forming Victory V. 30p, Hands above earth, UN 1945-95.

1995, May 2 Photo. *Perf. 14½x14*

1611 A456 19p multicolored .60 .40
1612 A456 19p multicolored .60 .40
1613 A456 25p multicolored .80 .50
1614 A456 25p multicolored .80 .50
1615 A456 30p multicolored .95 .60
Nos. 1611-1615 (5) 3.75 2.40

End of World War II, 50th anniv. (#1612, 1614), Europa (#1613, 1615).

H. G. Wells (1866-1946), Science Fiction Writer — A457

Novels: 25p, The Time Machine. 30p, The First Men on the Moon. 35p, The War of the Worlds. 41p, The Shape of Things to Come.

1995, June 6 Litho. *Perf. 14½x14*

1616 A457 25p multicolored .80 .45
1617 A457 30p multicolored .95 .55
1618 A457 35p multicolored 1.10 .65
1619 A457 41p multicolored 1.25 .80
Nos. 1616-1619 (4) 4.10 2.45

Opening of Shakespeare's New Globe Theatre A458

Bankside theatres: No. 1620, Swan, 1595. No. 1621, The Rose, 1595. No. 1622, The Globe, 1599. No. 1623, The Hope, 1613. No. 1624, The Globe, 1614.

1995, Aug. 8 Litho. *Perf. 14½x14*

1620 A458 25p multicolored .80 .45
1621 A458 25p multicolored .80 .45
1622 A458 25p multicolored .80 .45
1623 A458 25p multicolored .80 .45
1624 A458 25p multicolored .80 .45
a. Strip of 5, #1620-1624 4.00 2.25

Pioneers of Communication — A459

Designs: 19p, Sir Rowland Hill, introduction of uniform penny postage. 25p, Hill as older man, design A1. 41p, Guglielmo Marconi, early wireless equipment. 60p, Marconi as older man using radiophone, sinking *Titanic.*

Litho. & Engr.

1995, Sept. 5 *Perf. 14½*

1625 A459 19p multicolored .60 .35
1626 A459 25p multicolored .80 .45
1627 A459 41p multicolored 1.25 .70
1628 A459 60p multicolored 1.90 1.10
Nos. 1625-1628 (4) 4.55 2.60

Rugby League, Cent. — A460

1995, Oct. 3 Photo. *Perf. 14x14½*

1629 A460 19p Harold Wagstaff .60 .35
1630 A460 25p Gus Risman .80 .45
1631 A460 30p Jim Sullivan .95 .55
1632 A460 35p Billy Batten 1.10 .60
1633 A460 41p Brian Bevan 1.25 .70
Nos. 1629-1633 (5) 4.70 2.65

Christmas — A461

Designs showing robin in winter scene: 19p, In pillar box. 25p, On fence rail, holly bush. 30p, Standing on snow covered milk bottle. 41p, Sitting on snow covered road sign, blue fence. 60p, Sitting on door knob, Christmas decoration on door.

1995, Oct. 30 Photo. *Perf. 14¾x14*

1634 A461 19p multicolored .60 .35
a. Booklet pane of 20 12.00
b. Sheet of 20 + 20 labels 11.50
1635 A461 25p multicolored .80 .45
1636 A461 30p multicolored .95 .55
1637 A461 41p multicolored 1.25 .70
1638 A461 60p multicolored 1.90 1.10
a. Booklet pane of 4 7.75
Nos. 1634-1638 (5) 5.50 3.15

No. 1634b was issued 10/3/00. It sold for £3.99 and has labels that read "Seasons Greetings" and "Glad Tidings." Sheets with personalized labels were made available only to select Royal Post customers via mail order purchases, and sold for more.

Robert Burns (1759-1796), Poet — A462

Lines from poems: 19p, "Wee sleeket, cowran, tim'rous beastie." 25p, "O my luve's like a red, red rose." 41p, "Scots, wha hae wi Wallace bled." 60p, "Should auld acquaintance be forgot."

1996, Jan. 25 Litho. *Perf. 14½*

1639 A462 19p multicolored .60 .35
1640 A462 25p multicolored .75 .40
1641 A462 41p multicolored 1.25 .70
1642 A462 60p multicolored 1.80 1.00
Nos. 1639-1642 (4) 4.40 2.45

Greetings Cartoons A463

#1643, More Love. #1644, Sincerely. #1645, Human condition. #1646, Mental Floss. #1647, Don't ring. #1648, Dear lottery prize winner. #1649, I'm writing to you... #1650, Fetch this... #1651, My day starts... #1652, The check in the post.

Perf. 14½ Syncopated

1996-2001 Litho.

1643 A463 1st black & lilac .75 .40
1644 A463 1st black & green .75 .40
1645 A463 1st black & blue .75 .40
1646 A463 1st black & purple .75 .40
1647 A463 1st black & red .75 .40
1648 A463 1st black & blue .75 .40
1649 A463 1st black & red .75 .40
1650 A463 1st black & purple .75 .40
1651 A463 1st black & green .75 .40
1652 A463 1st black & lilac .75 .40
a. Booklet pane, #1643-1652+20 labels 7.50
b. Sheet of 10, #1643-1652, + 10 labels, perf. 14½x14 8.50 —

Issued: No. 1652b, 12/18/01. Others, 2/26/96.

No. 1652b lacks perforation syncopation. Labels could be personalized for an additional amount.

Wildfowl and Wetlands Trust, 50th Anniv. A464

Paintings by Charles Tunnicliffe RA (1901-79): 19p, Muscovy duck. 25p, Lapwing. 30p, White-fronted goose. 35p, Bittern. 41p, Whooper swan.

1996, Mar. 12 Photo. *Perf. 14x14½*

1653 A464 19p multicolored .60 .35
1654 A464 25p multicolored .75 .50
1655 A464 30p multicolored .95 .60
1656 A464 35p multicolored 1.10 .65
1657 A464 41p multicolored 1.25 .80
Nos. 1653-1657 (5) 4.65 2.90

Motion Pictures, Cent. — A465

Designs: 19p, Exterior of Odeon at Harrogate, 1930s theater. 25p, Laurance Olivier, Vivien Leigh in scene from "That Hamilton Woman." 30p, Cinema ticket from "The Picture House." 35p, Rooster emblem of Pathe News, motion picture newsreels. 41p, Theater marquee.

1996, Apr. 16 Photo. *Perf. 14x14½*

1658 A465 19p multicolored .60 .35
1659 A465 25p multicolored .75 .50
1660 A465 30p multicolored .90 .55
1661 A465 35p multicolored 1.10 .65
1662 A465 41p multicolored 1.25 .80
Nos. 1658-1662 (5) 4.60 2.85

1996 European Soccer Championships — A466

Lengendary players: 19p, Dixie Dean (1907-80). 25p, Bobby Moore (1941-93). 35p, Duncan Edwards (1936-58). 41p, Billy Wright (1924-94). 60p, Danny Blanchflower (1926-93).

1996, May 14 Litho. *Perf. 15x14*

1663 A466 19p gray, red & blk .60 .35
a. Bklt. pane of 4 + printed margin 2.40
1664 A466 25p gray, grn & blk .80 .50
a. Bklt. pane of 4 + printed margin 3.25
1665 A466 35p gray, yel & blk 1.10 .65
1666 A466 41p blk, blue & gray 1.25 .80
1667 A466 60p gray, org & blk 1.90 1.15
a. Bklt. pane, 2 ea #1665-1667 8.50
Nos. 1663-1667 (5) 5.65 3.45

Issued: No. 1652b, 12/18/01. Others, 2/26/96. For Prestige booklet containing panes #1663a, 1664a, 1667a, see listings in the Booklets section.

1996 Summer Olympic, Paralympic Games, Atlanta A467

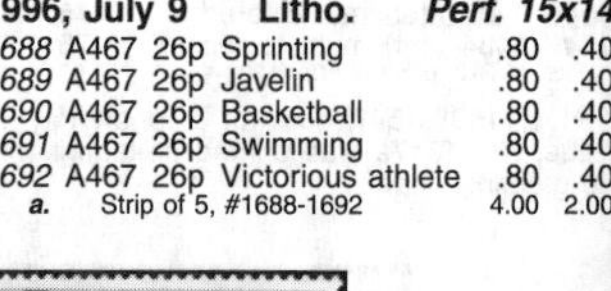

1996, July 9 Litho. *Perf. 15x14*

1688 A467 26p Sprinting .80 .40
1689 A467 26p Javelin .80 .40
1690 A467 26p Basketball .80 .40
1691 A467 26p Swimming .80 .40
1692 A467 26p Victorious athlete .80 .40
a. Strip of 5, #1688-1692 4.00 2.00

20th Century Women of Achievement A468

Europa: 20p, Dorothy Hodgkin (1910-94), chemist. 26p, Margot Fonteyn (1919-91), ballerina. 31p, Elisabeth Frink (1930-93), sculptor. 37p, Daphne du Maurier (1907-89), novelist. 43p, Marea Hartman (1920-94), sports administrator.

1996, Aug. 6 Photo. *Perf. 14½*

1693 A468 20p multicolored .60 .25
1694 A468 26p multicolored .80 .25
1695 A468 31p multicolored .95 *1.25*
1696 A468 37p multicolored 1.00 1.00
1697 A468 43p multicolored 1.40 1.40
Nos. 1693-1697 (5) 4.75 4.15

British Television Programs for Children, 50th Anniv. A469

Designs: 20p, Annette Mills, "Muffin the Mule." 26p, Sooty. 31p, String puppets Troy Tempest and Lord Titan. 37p, The Clangers. 43p, Dangermouse.

1996, Sept. 3 *Perf. 14½x14*

1698 A469 20p multicolored .65 .30
a. Pane of 4 #1698b + printed margin 2.60
b. Perf. 15x14 .65 .30
1699 A469 26p multicolored .80 .40
1700 A469 31p multicolored .95 .50
1701 A469 37p multicolored 1.10 .55
1702 A469 43p multicolored 1.35 .70
Nos. 1698-1702 (5) 4.85 2.45

For Prestige booklet containing pane #1698a, see listings in the Booklet section.

Issued: #1698a, 9/23/97.

Classic British Sports Cars — A470

Designs: 20p, 1955 Triumph TR3. 26p, MG TD. 37p, Austin-Healy 100. 43p, 1948 Jaguar XK 120. 63p, Morgan Plus Four.

1996, Oct. 1 Photo. *Perf. 14½*

1703 A470 20p multicolored .65 .30
1704 A470 26p multicolored .80 .40
1705 A470 37p multicolored 1.10 .55
1706 A470 43p multicolored 1.35 .70
1707 A470 63p multicolored 2.00 1.00
Nos. 1703-1707 (5) 5.90 2.95

Christmas A471

Designs: 2nd, Three kings, star. 1st, The Annunciation. 31p, Mary, Joseph on journey to Bethlehem. 43p, Madonna and Child. 63p, Angel telling shepherds of Christ's birth.

1996, Oct. 28 Photo. *Perf. 14½x14*

1708 A471 2nd multicolored .65 .40
a. Booklet pane of 20 13.00
1709 A471 1st multicolored .85 .50
1710 A471 31p multicolored 1.00 .65

1711 A471 43p multicolored 1.40 .90
1712 A471 63p multicolored 2.00 1.25
Nos. 1708-1712 (5) 5.90 3.70

Gentiana Acaulis A472

Magnolia Altissima A473

Camellia Japonica A474

Tulip A475

Fuchsia "Princess of Wales" A476

Le Perroquet Rouge A477

Gazania Splendens A478

Iris Latifolia A479

Amaryllis Bresiliensis A480

Granadilla A481

Perf. 14½x14 Syncopated

1997, Jan. 6 Litho.

Booklet Stamps

1713 A472 1st multicolored .85 .40
1714 A473 1st multicolored .85 .40
1715 A474 1st multicolored .85 .40
1716 A475 1st multicolored .85 .40
1717 A476 1st multicolored .85 .40
1718 A477 1st multicolored .85 .40
1719 A478 1st multicolored .85 .40
1720 A479 1st multicolored .85 .40
1721 A480 1st multicolored .85 .40
1722 A481 1st multicolored .85 .40
a. Bklt. pane of 10, #1713-1722 8.50

#1722a sold for £2.50 on day of issue.

King Henry VIII and His Six Wives A482

1997, Jan. 21 Photo. *Perf. 15*

1723 A482 26p shown .90 .50

Size: 27x38mm

Perf. 14x15

1724 A482 26p Catherine of Aragon .90 .50
1725 A482 26p Anne Boleyn .90 .50
1726 A482 26p Jane Seymour .90 .50
1727 A482 26p Anne of Cleves .90 .50
1728 A482 26p Catherine Howard .90 .50
1729 A482 26p Catherine Parr .90 .50
a. Strip of 6, #1724-1729 5.40 3.00
Nos. 1723-1729 (7) 6.30 3.50

St. Augustine of Canterbury & St. Columba of Iona — A483

Designs: 26p, Columba's journey across Irish Sea to Iona. 37p, St. Columba at work, Ionian Sea. 43p, St. Augustine baptizing King Ethelbert. 63p, St. Augustine outside Cathedral at Canterbury, Kent coastline.

1997, Mar. 11 Photo. *Perf. 14½x14*

1730 A483 26p multicolored .90 .45
1731 A483 37p multicolored 1.30 .65
1732 A483 43p multicolored 1.50 .75
1733 A483 63p multicolored 2.20 1.10
Nos. 1730-1733 (4) 5.90 2.95

Stories and Legends — A484

Europa: 26p, Dracula. 31p, Frankenstein. 37p, Dr. Jekyll and Mr. Hyde. 43p, The Hound of the Baskervilles.

1997, May 13 Photo. *Perf. 14x15*

1754 A484 26p multicolored .90 .50
1755 A484 31p multicolored 1.10 *1.25*
1756 A484 37p multicolored 1.25 1.25
1757 A484 43p multicolored 1.50 1.50
Nos. 1754-1757 (4) 4.75 4.50

Aircraft, Designers A485

20p, Supermarine Spitfire, R.J. Mitchell. 26p, Avro Lancaster, Roy Chadwick. 37p, DeHavilland Mosquito, R.E. Bishop. 43p, Gloster Meteor, George Carter. 63p, Hawker Hunter, Sidney Camm.

1997, June 10 Photo. *Perf. 15x14*

1758 A485 20p multicolored .60 .30
1759 A485 26p multicolored .90 .45
1760 A485 37p multicolored 1.25 .65
1761 A485 43p multicolored 1.50 .75
1762 A485 63p multicolored 2.00 1.00
Nos. 1758-1762 (5) 6.25 3.15

All the Queen's Horses A486

20p, 43p, Carriage horses from Royal Mews. 26p, 63p, Mount horses from Household Cavalry.

1997, July 9 Litho. *Perf. 14x14½*

1763 A486 20p multicolored .60 .30
1764 A486 26p multicolored .90 .45
1765 A486 43p multicolored 1.50 .75
1766 A486 63p multicolored 2.00 1.00
Nos. 1763-1766 (4) 5.00 2.50

British Horse Society, 50th anniv.

Post Offices A487

Designs: 20p, Haroldswick, Shetland Islands, Scotland. 26p, Painswick, Gloucestershire, England. 43p, Beddgelert, Gwynedd, Wales. 63p, Ballyroney, County Down, Northern Ireland.

1997, Aug. 12 Litho. *Perf. 14½x14*

1767 A487 20p multicolored .60 .30
1768 A487 26p multicolored .80 .40
1769 A487 43p multicolored 1.30 .65
1770 A487 63p multicolored 1.90 .95
Nos. 1767-1770 (4) 4.60 2.30

Enid Blyton, Author of Children's Stories, Birth Cent. — A488

Characters from books: 20p, "Noddy." 26p, "Famous Five." 37p, "Secret Seven." 43p, "Faraway Tree." 63p, "Malory Towers."

1997, Sept. 9 Litho. *Perf. 14x14½*

1771 A488 20p multicolored .65 .30
1772 A488 26p multicolored .85 .40
1773 A488 37p multicolored 1.20 .60
1774 A488 43p multicolored 1.40 .70
1775 A488 63p multicolored 2.00 1.00
Nos. 1771-1775 (5) 6.10 3.00

Christmas Crackers A489

Designs: 2nd, Santa as Man in Moon sharing cracker with two children. 1st, Santa bursting through wrapping paper with cracker. 31p, Santa riding across sky on giant cracker. 43p, Santa on giant snowball holding cracker. 63p, Santa climbing into chimney with sack full of crackers.

1997, Oct. 27 Photo. *Perf. 15x14*

1776 A489 2nd multicolored .65 .30
a. Booklet pane of 20 13.00
1777 A489 1st multicolored .85 .40
b. Sheet of 10 + 10 labels 8.50
1778 A489 31p multicolored 1.00 .50
1779 A489 43p multicolored 1.40 .70
1780 A489 63p multicolored 2.00 1.00
Nos. 1776-1780 (5) 5.90 2.90

Nos. 1776-1777 were sold for 20p and 26p, respectively, on day of issue.

No. 1777b issued 10/3/00. It sold for £2.95 and has labels that read "Seasons Greetings" and "Ho Ho Ho." Sheets with personalized labels were made available only to select Royal Post customers via mail order purchases, and sold for more.

Queen Elizabeth II, Prince Philip, 50th Wedding Anniv. A490

Designs: 20p, 43p, Wedding portrait, 1947. 26p, 63p, Anniversary portrait, 1997.

1997, Nov. 13 Photo. *Perf. 15*

1781 A490 20p multicolored .65 .30
1782 A490 26p multicolored .85 .40
1783 A490 43p multicolored 1.40 .70
1784 A490 63p multicolored 2.00 1.00
Nos. 1781-1784 (4) 4.90 2.40

Endangered Species — A491

Designs: 20p, Common dormouse. 26p, Lady's slipper orchid. 31p, Song thrush. 37p, Shining ram's horn snail. 43p, Mole cricket. 63p, Devil's bolete.

1998, Jan. 20 Litho. *Perf. 14x14½*

1785 A491 20p multicolored .65 .30
1786 A491 26p multicolored .85 .40
1787 A491 31p multicolored 1.00 .50
1788 A491 37p multicolored 1.20 .60
1789 A491 43p multicolored 1.40 .70
1790 A491 63p multicolored 2.00 1.00
Nos. 1785-1790 (6) 7.10 3.50

Diana, Princess of Wales (1961-97) — A492

Portraits of Diana wearing: No. 1791, Choker. No. 1792, Blue dress. No. 1793, Tiara. No. 1794, Checked dress. No. 1795, Black dress.

1998, Feb. 3 Photo. *Perf. 14x15*

1791 A492 26p multicolored .85 .40
1792 A492 26p multicolored .85 .40
1793 A492 26p multicolored .85 .40
1794 A492 26p multicolored .85 .40
1795 A492 26p multicolored .85 .40
a. Strip of 5, #1791-1795 4.25
b. As "a," imperf. —

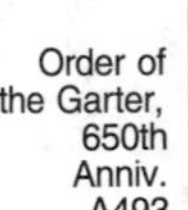

Order of the Garter, 650th Anniv. A493

Queen's Beasts (supporters of Royal Arms created for Queen Elizabeth II's coronation in 1953): No. 1796, Lion of England, Griffin of Edward III. No. 1797, Falcon of Plantagenet, Bull of Clarence. No. 1798, Lion of Mortimer, Yale of Beaufort. No. 1799, Greyhound of Richmond, Dragon of Wales. No. 1800, Unicorn of Scotland, Horse of Hanover.

Litho. & Engr.

1998, Feb. 24 ***Perf. 15x14***

1796 A493 26p multicolored	.85	.60
1797 A493 26p multicolored	.85	.60
1798 A493 26p multicolored	.85	.60
1799 A493 26p multicolored	.85	.60
1800 A493 26p multicolored	.85	.60
a. Strip of 5, #1796-1800	4.25	3.00

Queen Type of 1952 with Face Values in Decimal Currency

Perf. 14 Syncopated

1998, Mar. 10 **Litho.**

1801 A129 20p dk grn & lt grn	.65	.30
a. Booklet pane of 6 + printed margin	4.00	
1802 A129 26p dk brn & lt brn	.85	.60
a. Booklet pane of 9 + printed margin	7.75	
1803 A129 37p dk red lil & lt lil	1.20	.60
a. Booklet pane 3 each #1802-1803 + printed margin	6.25	
b. Booklet pane, 4 #1801, 2 ea #1802-1803 + printed margin	6.75	

Lighthouses A494

1998, Mar. 24 ***Perf. 14x14½***

1804 A494 20p St. John's Point	.65	.30
1805 A494 26p The Smalls	.85	.40
1806 A494 37p Needles Rocks	1.20	.60
1807 A494 43p Bell Rock	1.40	.70
1808 A494 63p Eddystone	2.00	1.00
Nos. 1804-1808 (5)	6.10	3.00

Comedians A495

20p, Tommy Cooper (1922-84). 26p, Eric Morecambe (1926-84). 37p, Joyce Grenfell (1910-79). 43p, Les Dawson (1933-93). 63p, Peter Cook (1937-95).

1998, Apr. 23 Litho. ***Perf. 14½x14***

1809 A495 20p multicolored	.70	.35
1810 A495 26p multicolored	.90	.45
1811 A495 37p multicolored	1.25	.60
1812 A495 43p multicolored	1.45	.70
1813 A495 63p multicolored	2.15	1.10
Nos. 1809-1813 (5)	6.45	3.20

National Health Service, 50th Anniv. — A496

Designs: 20p, Hands forming heart, "10,000 donors give blood every day." 26p, Adult hand clasping child's, "1,700,000 prescriptions dispensed every day." 43p, Hands forming cradle, "2,000 babies delivered every day." 63p, Taking pulse, "130,000 hospital outpatients seen every day."

1998, June 23 Litho. ***Perf. 14x14½***

1814 A496 20p multicolored	.70	.35
1815 A496 26p multicolored	.90	.45
1816 A496 43p multicolored	1.40	.70
1817 A496 63p multicolored	2.25	1.10
Nos. 1814-1817 (4)	5.25	2.60

Magical World of Children's Literature A496a

Stories depicted: 20p, "The Hobbit," by J.R.R. Tolkien. 26p, "The Lion, The Witch and the Wardrobe," by C.S. Lewis. 37p, "The Phoenix and the Carpet," by E. Nesbit. 43p, "The Borrowers," by Mary Norton. 63p, "Through the Looking Glass," by Lewis Carroll.

1998, July 21 Photo. ***Perf. 15x14***

1820 A496a 20p multicolored	.70	.35
1821 A496a 26p multicolored	.90	.45
1822 A496a 37p multicolored	1.25	.60
1823 A496a 43p multicolored	1.40	.70
1824 A496a 63p multicolored	2.25	1.10
Nos. 1820-1824 (5)	6.50	3.20

Notting Hill Carnival A497

Expressionist photographic images of dancers, color of costumes: 20p, Yellow. 26p, Blue. 43p, Gold and white. 63p, Green.

1998, Aug. 25 ***Perf. 14x14½***

1825 A497 20p multicolored	.70	.35
1826 A497 26p multicolored	.90	.45
1827 A497 43p multicolored	1.40	.70
1828 A497 63p multicolored	2.25	1.10
Nos. 1825-1828 (4)	5.25	2.60

Europa (#1825-1826).

Land Speed Records A498

Car, driver, year, record speed: 20p, Bluebird, Sir Malcolm Campbell, 1925, 151 mph. 26p, Red Sunbeam, Sir Henry Segrave, 1926, 152 mph. 30p, Babs, John G. Parry Thomas, 1926, 171 mph. 43p, Railton Mobil Special, John R. Cobb, 1947, 394 mph. 63p, Bluebird CN7, Donald Campbell, 1964, 403 mph.

1998, Sept. 29 Photo. ***Perf. 15x14***

1829 A498 20p multicolored	.70	.35
a. Perf. 14½x13½	.70	.35
b. As "a," booklet pane of 4 + printed margin (BK164)	2.75	
1830 A498 26p multicolored	.90	.45
1831 A498 30p multicolored	1.00	.50
1832 A498 43p multicolored	1.40	.70
1833 A498 63p multicolored	2.25	1.10
Nos. 1829-1833 (5)	6.25	3.10

Christmas Angels A499

1998, Nov. 2 Photo. ***Perf. 15x14***

1834 A499 20p shown	.70	.35
a. Booklet pane of 20	14.00	
1835 A499 26p Praying	.90	.45
1836 A499 30p Playing flute	1.00	.50
1837 A499 43p Playing lute	1.40	.70
1838 A499 63p Praying, diff.	2.25	1.10
Nos. 1834-1838 (5)	6.25	3.10

British Achievements During Past 1000 Years — A500

Inventions: 20p, Timekeeping, John Harrison's chronometer. 26p, Development of steam power. 43p, William Henry Fox Talbot's use of negatives to create photographs. 63p, Development of computers.

Transportation: 20p, Jet travel. 26p, Development of bicycle. 43p, Isambard Kingdom Brunel's Clifton Suspension Bridge, Great Western Railway. 63p, Capt. Cook's expeditions.

Health care: 20p, First smallpox vaccination, by Edward Jenner. 26p, Development of nursing care. 43p, Discovery of penicillin, by Alexander Fleming. 63p, First "test tube" baby (in-vitro fertilization), pioneered by Patrick Steptoe and Robert Edwards.

Emigration: 20p, Migration to Scotland. 26p, Pilgrim fathers. 43p, Destination Australia. 63p, Migration to UK.

Workers: 19p, Weavers. 26p, Mill towns. 44p, Ship building. 64p, City finance.

Entertainment and sports: 19p, Freddie Mercury, lead singer of Queen. 26p, Bobby Moore, 1966 World Cup Soccer Champions. 44p, Dalek from "Dr. Who" television series. 64p, Charlie Chaplin.

Citizens' Rights: 19p, Equal rights. 26p, Right to health. 44p, Right to learn. 64p, First rights.

Scientists: 19p, Decoding DNA. 26p, Darwin's theory. 44p, Faraday's electricity. 64p, Newton, Hubble Telescope.

Farmers: 19p, Strip farming (Europa). 26p, Mechanical farming. 44p, Food from afar. 64p, Satellite agriculture.

Soldiers: 19p, Battle of Bannockburn. 26p, Civil War. 44p, World Wars, cemetery. 64p, Peace keeping.

Christians: 19p, John Wesley (1703-91), founder of Methodism, and "Hark, The Herald Angels Sing," hymn by brother Charles (1707-88). 26p, King James Bible. 44p, St. Andrews Pilgrimage. 64p, First Christmas.

Artists: 19p, World of the stage. 26p, World of music. 44p, World of literature. 64p, New worlds.

1999 Photo. ***Perf. 14¼x14½***

Inventions

1839 A500 20p multi (48)	.70	.35
1840 A500 26p multi (47)	.90	.45
1841 A500 43p multi (46)	1.40	.70
1842 A500 63p multi (45)	2.25	1.10
a. Perf. 13¾	2.25	
b. Booklet pane, 4 #1842a (BK165)	9.00	

Transportation

1843 A500 20p multi (44)	.70	.35
1844 A500 26p multi (43)	.90	.45
1845 A500 43p multi (42)	1.40	.70
1846 A500 63p multi (41)	2.25	1.10

Health Care

Perf. 13¾x14

1847 A500 20p multi (40)	.70	.35
a. Booklet pane of 4 (BK165)	3.00	
1848 A500 26p multi (39)	.90	.45
1849 A500 43p multi (38)	1.40	.70
1850 A500 63p multi (37)	2.25	1.10

Emigration

Perf. 14¼x14½

1851 A500 20p multi (36)	.70	.35
1852 A500 26p multi (35)	.90	.45
1853 A500 43p multi (34)	1.40	.70
1854 A500 63p multi (33)	2.25	1.10

Workers

Perf. 14¼x14½

1855 A500 19p multi (32)	.60	.30
1856 A500 26p multi (31)	.85	.40
a. Booklet pane #1852, 1856 (BK1141)	1.75	
1857 A500 44p multi (30)	1.40	.70
1858 A500 64p multi (29)	2.00	1.00

Entertainment & Sports

Perf. 14¼x14½

1859 A500 19p multi (28)	.60	.30
1860 A500 26p multi (27)	.85	.40
1861 A500 44p multi (26)	1.40	.70
1862 A500 64p multi (25)	2.00	1.00

Citizen's Rights

Perf. 14¼x14½

1863 A500 19p multi (24)	.60	.30
1864 A500 26p multi (23)	.85	.40
1865 A500 44p multi (22)	1.40	.70
1866 A500 64p multi (21)	2.00	1.00

Scientists

Perf. 14¼ (#1868-1869), 13¾ (#1867, 1870)

1867 A500 19p multi (20)	.60	.30
1868 A500 26p multi (19)	.85	.40
a. Perf. 14¼x14	.85	
b. Booklet pane, 4 #1868a (BK165)	3.50	
1869 A500 44p multi (18)	1.40	.70
a. Perf. 14¼x14	1.40	
b. Booklet pane, 4 #1869a (BK165)	5.75	
1870 A500 64p multi (17)	2.00	1.00
a. Perf. 14¼	2.00	2.00
b. Souvenir sheet, 4 #1870a	8.00	8.00

Farmers

Perf. 14¼x14½

1871 A500 19p multi (16)	.60	.30
1872 A500 26p multi (15)	.85	.40
a. Booklet pane of 2 (BK1142)	1.75	
1873 A500 44p multi (14)	1.40	.70
1874 A500 64p multi (13)	2.00	1.00

Soldiers

Perf. 14¼x14½

1875 A500 19p multi (12)	.60	.30
1876 A500 26p multi (11)	.85	.40
1877 A500 44p multi (10)	1.40	.70
1878 A500 64p multi (9)	2.00	1.00

Christians

1879 A500 19p multi (8)	.60	.30
a. Booklet pane of 20	12.00	
1880 A500 26p multi (7)	.85	.40
1881 A500 44p multi (6)	1.40	.70
1882 A500 64p multi (5)	2.00	1.00

Artists

Perf. 14¼x14½

1883 A500 19p multi (4)	.60	.30
1884 A500 26p multi (3)	.85	.40
1885 A500 44p multi (2)	1.40	.70
1886 A500 64p multi (1)	2.00	1.00
Nos. 1839-1886 (48)	59.80	29.60

Issued: #1839-1842, 1/12; #1843-1846, 2/2; #1847-1850, 3/2; #1851-1854, 4/6; #1855-1858, 5/4; #1859-1862, 6/1; #1863-1866, 7/6; #1867-1870, 8/3; #1871-1874, 9/7; #1870b, 8/11; #1875-1878, 10/5; #1879-1882, 11/2; #1883-1886, 12/7.

See #1889, 1890-1929, 1938, 1942-1943.

Marriage of Prince Edward and Sophie Rhys-Jones — A501

1999, June 15 Photo. ***Perf. 15x14***

1887 A501 26p shown	.85	.40
1888 A501 64p Profile portrait	2.00	1.00

Souvenir Sheet

Millennium A502

Clock and globe showing: a, North America. b, Southeast Asia. c, Middle East. d, Europe.

Perf. 14¼x14½

1999, Dec. 14 **Photo.**

1889 Sheet of 4	8.25	4.25
a.-d. A502 64p any single	2.00	1.00

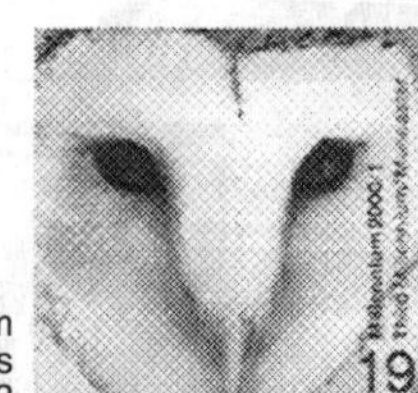

Millennium Projects A503

Above and Beyond: 19p, Barn owl's head, 3rd Millennium conservation projects, Muncaster. 26p, Night sky, National Space Center, Leicester. 44p, Buildings and waterfall, Torrs Walkway project, Derbyshire. 64p, Sea birds, Scottish Sea Bird Center.

Fire & Light: 19p, Beacon, Beacon Millennium project. 26p, Rheilffordd Eryri / Snowdonia, Welsh Highland Railway rebuilding project. 44p, Lightning bolt, Dynamic Earth project. 64p, Lights, Croydon Skyline project.

Water & Coast: 19p, Stones, Durham Coast restoration project. 26p, Frog, flowers, National Pondlife Center, conservation project. 44p, Parc Arfordirol project. 64p, Portsmouth Harbor project.

Life & Earth: 2nd, Wetlands, ECOS/Ballymena Project. 1st, Ants, Web of Life Exhibition at London Zoo. 44p, Solar cells, Earth Center, Doncaster. 64p, Plant leaves in water, Project SUZY, Teeside.

Art & Craft: 2nd, Ceramica project, Stoke-on-Trent. 1st, Tate Gallery of Modern Art,

London. 45p, Cycle Network Artworks Project. 65p, The Lowry Arts Complex, Balford.

People & Place: 2nd, Millennium Greens project. 1st, Gateshead Millennium Bridge, Newcastle. 45p, Mile End Park, London. 65p, On the Line project.

Stone & Soil: 2nd, Raising of Strangford Stone, Killyleagh, Northern Ireland. 1st, Trans Pennine Trail project. 45p, Kingdom of Fife Cycle Ways project, Scotland. 65p, Changing Places project of Groundwork Foundation.

Tree & Leaf: 2nd, Yews for the Millennium project. 1st, Eden Project, St. Austell. 45p, Millennium Seed Bank project, Ardingly. 65p, Forest for Scotland project.

Mind & Matter: 2nd, Ant's head, Wildscreen at Bristol Project. 1st, People in rowboat, Norfolk and Norwich Project, Newport. 45p, X-ray image of hand and computer mouse, Millennium Point Project, Birmingham. 65p, Plaid globe, Scottish Cultural Resources Access Network.

Body & Bone: 2nd, Dancers, Millennium Dome project, Greenwich. 1st, Soccer players, Hampden Park project, Glasgow. 45p, Bath Spa project. 65p, Center for Life, Newcastle.

Spirit & Faith: 2nd, Stained glass window, St. Edmundsbury Cathedral project. 1st, Church floodlighting project. 45p, St. Patrick Center project, Downpatrick. 65p, York mystery plays.

Sound & Vision: 2nd, Bells, Ringing in the Millennium project. 1st, Eye, Year of the Artist. 45p, Harp, Camofym Millennium Center, Cardiff. 65p, TS2K Talent and Skills project.

Photo., Litho. (#1892, 1900, 1911, 1913)

2000

Above & Beyond

Perf. 13¾x14, 14¼x14½ (#1892)

1890 A503 19p multi (1) .60 .30
1891 A503 26p multi (2) .85 .40
1892 A503 44p multi (3) 1.40 .70
1893 A503 64p multi (4) 2.10 1.00

Perf. 14¼x14½

Fire & Light

1894 A503 19p multi (5) .60 .30
1895 A503 26p multi (6) .85 .40
1896 A503 44p multi (7) 1.40 .70
1897 A503 64p multi (8) 2.00 1.00

Water & Coast

1898 A503 19p multi (9) .60 .30
1899 A503 26p multi (10) .85 .40
1900 A503 44p multi (11) 1.40 .70
1901 A503 64p multi (12) 2.00 1.00

Life & Earth

1902 A503 2nd multi (13) .60 .30
1903 A503 1st multi (14) .85 .40
1904 A503 44p multi (15) 1.40 .70
1905 A503 64p multi (16) 2.00 1.00

Art & Craft

1906 A503 2nd multi (17) .60 .30
1907 A503 1st multi (18) .80 .40
1908 A503 45p multi (19) 1.40 .70
1909 A503 65p multi (20) 1.90 .95

People & Place

1910 A503 2nd multi (21) .60 .30
1911 A503 1st multi (22) .80 .40
1912 A503 45p multi (23) 1.40 .70
1913 A503 65p multi (24) 1.90 .95

Stone & Soil

1914 A503 2nd multi (25) .60 .30
1915 A503 1st multi (26) .80 .40
1916 A503 45p multi (27) 1.40 .70
1917 A503 65p multi (28) 1.90 .95
a. Booklet pane of 2 (BK169) 3.80

Tree & Leaf

1918 A503 2nd multi (29) .60 .30
a. Bklt. pane of 4 (BK169) 2.40
1919 A503 1st multi (30) .80 .40
a. Bklt. pane, #1915, 1919 (BK1202) 1.60
1920 A503 45p multi (31) 1.40 .70
a. Bklt. pane of 4 (BK169) 5.60
1921 A503 65p multi (32) 1.90 .95
a. Bklt. pane of 2 (BK169) 3.80

Mind & Matter

Litho.

1922 A503 2nd multi (33) .55 .30
1923 A503 1st multi (34) .80 .40
1924 A503 45p multi (35) 1.40 .70
1925 A503 65p multi (36) 1.90 .95

Body & Bone

1926 A503 2nd multi (37) .55 .30

Photo.

Perf. 13¾

1927 A503 1st multi (38) .80 .40
1928 A503 45p multi (39) 1.40 .70
1929 A503 65p multi (40) 1.90 .95

Perf. 14¼

Spirit & Faith

1930 A503 2nd multi (41) .55 .30
a. Bklt. pane of 20 (BK1211) 11.00
1931 A503 1st multi (42) .80 .40
1932 A503 45p multi (43) 1.40 .70
1933 A503 65p multi (44) 1.90 .95

Sound & Vision

1934 A503 2nd multi (45) .55 .30
1935 A503 1st multi (46) .80 .40
1936 A503 45p multi (47) 1.40 .70
1937 A503 65p multi (48) 1.90 .95
Nos. 1890-1937 (48) 56.90 28.40

#1902, 1906, 1910, 1914, 1918, 1922, 1926, 1930, 1934 sold for 19p; #1903, sold for 26p; #1907, 1911, 1915, 1919, 1923, 1927, 1931, 1935 sold for 27p on day of issue.

Issued: #1890-1893, 1/18; #1894-1897, 2/1; #1898-1901, 3/7; #1902-1905, 4/4; #1906-1909, 5/2; #1910-1913, 6/6; #1914-1917, 7/4; #1918-1921, 8/1; #1917a-1921a, 9/18; #1922-1925, 9/5; #1926-1929, 10/3; #1930-1933, 11/7; #1934-1937, 12/5.

2000 Photo. *Perf. 14¼x14½*

1938 A503 (1st) Like #1891 .80 .40
a. Booklet pane, #1903, 1938 (BK1201) 1.75
1939 A503 (1st) Like #1891 .85 .40
a. Booklet pane of 4 (BK172) 3.50

Issued: No. 1938, 5/26. No. 1939, 9/24.

Nos. 1938 and 1939 each sold for 27p on day of issue, and were issued only in booklets.

Types of 1953 and 2000

Souvenir Sheet

2000, May 23 Photo. *Perf. 14¾x14*

1942 Sheet, #1942a, 4 #MH335 6.50 3.25
a. A136 £1 dark green 3.00 1.50

The Stamp Show 2000, London.

Souvenir Sheet

Queen Mother's 100th Birthday — A504

Designs: a, Queen Elizabeth II. b, Prince William. c, Queen Mother. d, Prince Charles. Illustration reduced.

2000, Aug. 4 Photo. *Perf. 14½*

1943 A504 Sheet of 4 3.25 1.60
a.-d. 27p Any single .80 .40
e. Booklet pane, #1943 with silver border (BK168) 3.25
f. Booklet pane, 4 #1943c (BK168) 3.25

Millennium 2001 A505

Painted faces of children: 2nd, Flower. 1st, Tiger. 45p, Owl. 65p, Butterfly.

Perf. 14¼x14½

2001, Jan. 16 Photo.

1944 A505 2nd multi .55 .30
1945 A505 1st multi .80 .40
1946 A505 45p multi 1.40 .70
1947 A505 65p multi 1.90 .95
Nos. 1944-1947 (4) 4.65 2.35

Stamps inscribed "2nd" and "1st" sold for 19p and 27p respectively on day of issue.

Greetings A506

2001, Feb. 6 Photo. *Perf. 14¼*

1948 A506 1st shown .80 .40
1949 A506 1st Cheers .80 .40
1950 A506 1st Love .80 .40
1951 A506 1st Thanks .80 .40
1952 A506 1st Welcome .80 .40
a. Sheet, 4 vert. strips #1948-1952 + 20 labels 17.00 17.00
Nos. 1948-1952 (5) 4.00 2.00

Nos. 1948-1952 each sold for 27p on day of issue.

No. 1952a issued 6/5/01. No. 1952a sold for £5.95.

Dogs and Cats A507

Designs: No. 1953, Dog and man on park bench. No. 1954, Dog in bathtub. No. 1955, Dog looking over carrel. No. 1956, Cat in handbag. No. 1957, Cat on fence. No. 1958, Dog in automobile. No. 1959, Cat in curtained window. No. 1960, Dog looking over fence. No. 1961, Cat looking at bird through window. No. 1962, Cat in sink.

2001, Feb. 13 *Die Cut Perf. 14½x14*

Self- Adhesive

Booklet Stamps

1953 A507 1st blk & sil .80 .40
1954 A507 1st blk & sil .80 .40
1955 A507 1st blk & sil .80 .40
1956 A507 1st blk & sil .80 .40
1957 A507 1st blk & sil .80 .40
1958 A507 1st blk & sil .80 .40
1959 A507 1st blk & sil .80 .40
1960 A507 1st blk & sil .80 .40
1961 A507 1st blk & sil .80 .40
1962 A507 1st blk & sil .80 .40
a. Booklet, #1953-1962 8.00
b. Booklet, #1953-1962, 2 #MH297 9.50
Nos. 1953-1962 (10) 8.00 4.00

Nos. 1953-1962 each sold for 27p on day of issue.

The Weather A508

Designs: 19p, Rain. 27p, Fair. 45p, Much rain, storms. 65p, Very dry, set fair.

Perf. 14¼x14½

2001, Mar. 13 Photo.

1963 A508 19p multi .55 .25
1964 A508 27p multi .80 .40
1965 A508 45p multi 1.25 .65
1966 A508 65p multi 1.90 .95
a. Souvenir sheet, #1963-1966 4.50 2.25
Nos. 1963-1966 (4) 4.50 2.25

Purple cloud at bottom of No. 1964 is printed with thermochromic ink and changes color to blue when warmed.

Submarines — A509

Designs: 2nd, Vanguard Class, 1992. 1st, Swiftsure Class, 1973. 45p, Unity Class, 1939. 65p, Holland Class, 1901.

2001 Photo. *Perf. 14¾x14*

1967 A509 2nd multi .55 .25
a. Perf. 15¼x14¾ .55 .25
1968 A509 1st multi .80 .40
a. Perf. 15¼x14¾ .80 .40
1969 A509 45p multi 1.25 .65
a. Perf. 15¼x14¾ 1.25 .65
b. Booklet pane, 2 each #1967a, 1969a (BK170) 3.60
1970 A509 65p multi 1.90 .95
a. Perf. 15¼x14¾ 1.90 .95
b. Booklet pane, 2 each #1968a, 1970a (BK170) 5.40

Self-Adhesive

Die Cut Perf. 15½x14¼

1971 A509 1st multi .80 .40
a. Booklet, 2 #1971, 4 #MH298 5.00
Nos. 1967-1971 (5) 5.30 2.65

Issued: Nos. 1967-1970, 4/10; No. 1971, 4/17; Nos. 1967a, 1968a, 1969a, 1970a, 10/22/01.

On day of issue No. 1967 sold for 19p and Nos. 1968 and 1971 sold for 27p.

Buses A510

Designs: No. 1972, Blue and red Leyland X-type (half), London General (#11), yellow green and orange Leyland Titan, dark green and yellow AEC Regent I (half). No. 1973, AEC Regent I (half), Daimler COG5 (#8), Guy Arab Mk II (#51), green and yellow AEC Regent (half). No. 1974, AEC Regent (half), Bristol KSW 5G (#68), AEC Routemaster (#21), red and yellow Bristol Lodekka (half). No. 1975, Bristol Lodekka (half), Leyland Titan (#12B), Leyland Atlantean (#53X), red and yellow Daimler Fleetline (half). No. 1976, Daimler Fleetline (half), MCW Metrobus (#770), Leyland Olympian (#12), red and blue Dennis Trident (half).

2001, May 15 Photo. *Perf. 14¼x14*

1972 A510 1st multi .80 .40
1973 A510 1st multi .80 .40
1974 A510 1st multi .80 .40
1975 A510 1st multi .80 .40
1976 A510 1st multi .80 .40
a. Horiz. strip, #1972-1976 4.00 2.00
b. Souvenir sheet, #1972-1976 4.00 2.00

Nos. 1972-1976 each sold for 27p on day of issue.

Women's Hats — A511

Hats designed by: 1st, Pip Hackett. E, Dai Rees. 45p, Stephen Jones. 65p, Philip Treacy.

Perf. 14½x14¼

2001, June 19 Litho.

1977 A511 1st multi .80 .40
1978 A511 E multi 1.00 .50
1979 A511 45p multi 1.25 .65
1980 A511 65p multi 1.90 .90
Nos. 1977-1980 (4) 4.95 2.45

Nos. 1977 and 1978 sold for 27p and 36p respectively on day of issue.

Europa A512

2001, July 10 Photo. *Perf. 14¾x14*

1981 A512 1st Frog .75 .40
1982 A512 E Great diving beetle 1.00 .50
1983 A512 45p Stickleback 1.25 .65
1984 A512 65p Dragonfly 1.90 .95
Nos. 1981-1984 (4) 4.90 2.50

Nos. 1981 and 1982 sold for 27p and 36p respectively on day of issue.

Puppets — A513

2001, Sept. 4 Photo. *Perf. 14x15*

1985	A513 1st Policeman		.80	.40
1986	A513 1st Clown		.80	.40
1987	A513 1st Punch		.80	.40
1988	A513 1st Judy		.80	.40
1989	A513 1st Beadle		.80	.40
1990	A513 1st Crocodile		.80	.40
a.	Horiz. strip of 6, #1985-1990		4.80	2.40

Booklet Stamps
Self-Adhesive
Die Cut Perf. 14x15½

1991	A513 1st Punch	.80	.40
1992	A513 1st Judy	.80	.40
a.	Booklet, Nos. 1991-1992, 4 #MH298	5.00	
	Nos. 1985-1992 (8)	6.40	3.20

Nos. 1985-1992 sold for 27p on day of issue.

Nobel Prizes, Cent. — A514

Items symbolic of prize categories: 2nd, Carbon 60 molecule (Chemistry). 1st, Globe (Economics). E, Dove (Peace). 40p, Crosses (Physiology or Medicine). 45p, The Addressing of Cats, by T.S. Eliot (Literature). 65p, Boron atom (Physics)

2001, Oct. 2 Photo. *Perf. 14½x14¼*

1993	A514 2nd multi	.55	.25

Photo. & Engr.

1994	A514 1st multi	.80	.40

Photo. & Embossed

1995	A514 E multi	1.10	.55

Photo.

1996	A514 40p multi	1.10	.55
1997	A514 45p multi	1.25	.65

Photo. With Hologram Affixed

1998	A514 65p multi	1.90	.95
	Nos. 1993-1998 (6)	6.70	3.35

Nos. 1993-1995 each sold for 19p, 27p and 37p respectively on day of issue. Molecule on No. 1993 is covered with a thermochromic film that changes color when warmed. No. 1996 has a scrach and sniff coating with a eucalyptus odor. Soaking in water may affect holographic images.

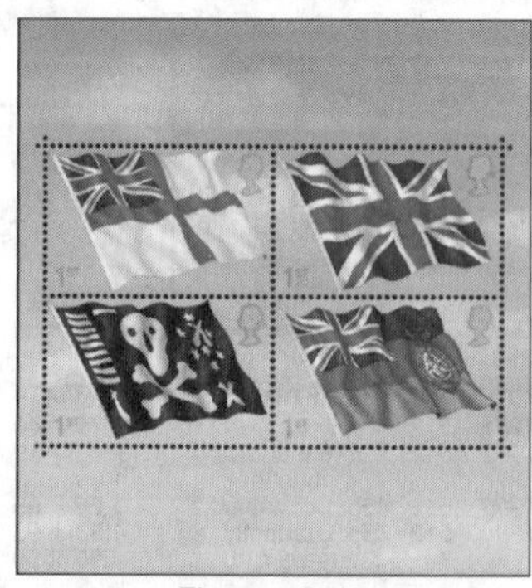
Flags — A515

Designs: Nos. 1999a, 2001, White ensign. No. 1999b, Union flag. Nos. 1999c, 2000, Jolly Roger. No. 1999d, Flag of the Chief of the Defense Staff.

2001, Oct. 22 Photo. *Perf. 14¾*
Miniature Sheet

1999	A515 Sheet of 4	3.25	1.60
a.-d.	1st Any single	.80	.40
e.	Booklet pane, #1999 + selvage at L (BK170)	3.25	

Booklet Stamps
Self-Adhesive
Die Cut Perf. 14¾

2000	A515 1st multi	.80	.40
2001	A515 1st multi	.80	.40
a.	Booklet, #2000-2001, 4 #MH298	4.80	

Nos. 1999a-1999d, 2000-2001 each sold for 27p on day of issue. The left edge of No. 1999 is straight while rouletting separates the selvage from the sheet on No. 1999e.

Christmas A516

Robins and: 2nd, Snowman. 1st, Birdhouse. E, Birdbath. 45p, Suet ball. 65b, Nest.

Die Cut Perf. 14¼x14½
2001, Nov. 6 Photo.
Self-Adhesive

2002	A516 2nd multi	.55	.25
a.	Booklet of 24	13.50	
2003	A516 1st multi	.80	.40
a.	Booklet of 12	9.75	
2004	A516 E multi	1.10	.55
2005	A516 45p multi	1.25	.65
2006	A516 65p multi	1.90	.95
	Nos. 2002-2006 (5)	5.60	2.80

Nos. 2002-2004 each sold for 19p, 27p, and 37p respectively on day of issue.

Just So Stories, by Rudyard Kipling, Cent. A517

Designs: No. 2007, How the Whale Got His Throat (whale in bed). No. 2008, How the Camel Got His Hump (genie, camel). No. 2009, How the Rhinoceros Got His Skin (man in palm tree, rhinoceros). No. 2010, How the Leopard Got His Spots (man putting spots on leopard). No. 2011, The Elephant's Child (crocodile, elephant, snake). No. 2012, The Sing-song of Old Man Kangaroo (dog chasing kangaroo). No. 2013, The Beginning of the Armadilloes (jaguar, armadillo). No. 2014, The Crab That Played With the Sea (people in boat, giant crab). No. 2015, The Cat That Walked by Himself (people, dog, cat and shadow in cave). No. 2016, The Butterfly That Stamped (castle, giant butterfly).

Serpentine Die Cut 14½x14
2002, Jan. 15 Photo.
Booklet Stamps
Self-Adhesive

2007	A517 1st multi	.80	.40
2008	A517 1st multi	.80	.40
2009	A517 1st multi	.80	.40
2010	A517 1st multi	.80	.40
2011	A517 1st multi	.80	.40
2012	A517 1st multi	.80	.40
2013	A517 1st multi	.80	.40
2014	A517 1st multi	.80	.40
2015	A517 1st multi	.80	.40
2016	A517 1st multi	.80	.40
a.	Booklet, #2007-2016	8.00	

Nos. 2007-2016 each sold for 27p on day of issue. Titles of stories are not on stamps, but in margin.

Reign of Queen Elizabeth II, 50th Anniv. — A518

Photographs of Queen by: 2nd, Dorothy Wilding, 1952. 1st, Cecil Beaton, 1968. E, Lord Snowdon, 1978, 45p, Yousef Karsh, 1984. 65p, Tim Graham, 1996.

Perf. 14½x14¼
2002, Feb. 6 Photo. Wmk. 401

2017	A518 2nd blk & sil	.55	.25
2018	A518 1st blk & sil	.80	.40
2019	A518 E blk & sil	1.10	.55
2020	A518 45p blk & sil	1.25	.65
a.	Booklet pane, #2017-2020 (BK171)	3.75	—
2021	A518 65p blk & sil	1.90	.95
a.	Booklet pane, #2018-2021 (BK171)	5.25	—
	Nos. 2017-2021 (5)	5.60	2.80

Nos. 2017-2019 each sold for 19p, 27p, and 37p respectively on day of issue.

Queen Types of 1952

Wmk. 401

Perf. 14¾x14 Syncopated
2002, Feb. 6 Photo. Wmk. 401

2022	A127 2nd red	.55	.25
2023	A126 1st green	.80	.40
a.	Booklet pane, 5 #2022, 4 #2023, + label (BK171)	6.00	—

Nos. 2022 and 2023 sold for 19p and 27p respectively on day of issue.

A New Baby A519

Hello A520

Moving A521

Best Wishes A522

Love A523

Perf. 14¾x14
2002, Mar. 5 Litho. Unwmk.

2024	A519 1st multi	.80	.40
2025	A520 1st multi	.80	.40
2026	A521 1st multi	.80	.40
2027	A522 1st multi	.80	.40
2028	A523 1st multi	.80	.40
	Nos. 2024-2028 (5)	4.00	2.00

Nos. 2024-2028 each sold for 27p on day of issue.

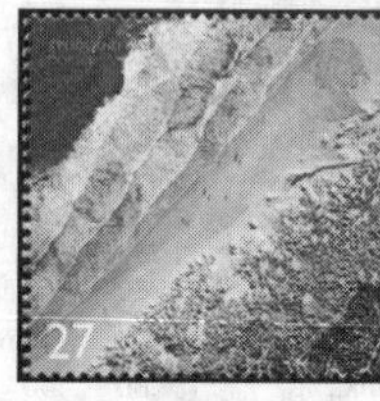
Aerial Photographs of Coastline A524

2002, Mar. 19 *Perf. 14¼x14½*

2029	A524 27p Studland Bay	.80	.40
2030	A524 27p Luskentyre	.80	.40
2031	A524 27p Dover	.80	.40
2032	A524 27p Padstow	.80	.40
2033	A524 27p Broadstairs	.80	.40
2034	A524 27p St. Abb's Head	.80	.40
2035	A524 27p Dunster Beach	.80	.40
2036	A524 27p Newquay	.80	.40
2037	A524 27p Portrush	.80	.40
2038	A524 27p Conwy	.80	.40
a.	Block of 10, #2029-2038	8.00	4.00

Circus — A525

Designs: 2nd, High wire performer. 1st, Lion tamer. E, Trick tricyclists. 45p, Krazy kar. 65p, Equestrienne.

2002, Apr. 9 Photo. *Perf. 14¼x14½*

2039	A525 2nd multi	.55	.25
2040	A525 1st multi	.80	.40
2041	A525 E multi	1.10	.55
2042	A525 45p multi	1.25	.65
2043	A525 65p multi	1.90	.95
	Nos. 2039-2043 (5)	5.60	2.80

Europa (Nos. 2040-2041). Nos. 2039-2041 sold for 19p, 27p and 37p respectively on day of issue.

Queen Mother (1900-2002) A526

2002, Apr. 25 *Perf. 14x14¾*

2044	A526 1st 1990 photo	.80	.40
2045	A526 E 1948 photo	1.10	.55
2046	A526 45p 1930 photo	1.25	.65
2047	A526 65p 1907 photo	1.90	.95
	Nos. 2044-2047 (4)	5.05	2.55

Nos. 2044-2045 sold for 27p and 37p respectively on day of issue. Compare with Type A387.

Jet Aircraft — A527

Designs: 2nd, Airbus A340-600, 2002. 1st, Concorde, 1976. E, Trident, 1964. 45p, VC10, 1964. 65p, Comet, 1952.

2002, May 2 *Perf. 14½*

2048	A527 2nd multi	.55	.25
2049	A527 1st multi	.80	.40
2050	A527 E multi	1.10	.55
2051	A527 45p multi	1.25	.65
2052	A527 65p multi	1.90	.95
a.	Souvenir sheet, #2048-2052	5.75	2.75

Booklet Stamp
Self-Adhesive
Die Cut Perf. 14½

2053	A527 1st multi	.80	.40
a.	Booklet, 2 #2053, 4 #MH297	4.80	
	Nos. 2048-2053 (6)	6.40	3.20

Nos. 2048-2052 sold for 19p, 27p and 37p respectively on day of issue.

A528

2002 World Cup Soccer Championships, Japan and Korea — A529

Soccer ball and: Nos. 2056a, 2057, Upper left portion of English flag. Nos. 2056b, 2058, Upper right portion of English flag. No. 2056c, Lower left portion of English flag. Nos. 2055, 2056c, Lower right portion of English flag.

2002, May 21 Photo. *Perf. 14¼*

2054	A528 1st multi	.80	.40
2055	A529 1st dull blue & multi	.85	.40

Souvenir Sheet

2056	Sheet, #2054, #2056a-2056d	4.00	4.00
a.-d.	A529 1st deep blue & multi, perf. 14¾x14, any single	.80	.40

Booklet Stamps

Die Cut Perf. 14¾x14

Self-Adhesive

2057	A529 1st deep blue & multi	.80	.40
2058	A529 1st deep blue & multi	.80	.40
a.	Booklet, #2057, 2058, 4 #MH298	4.80	

Nos. 2054, 2056a-2056d, 2057-2058 sold for 27p on day of sale. No. 2055 was issued only in sheets of 20 stamps + 16 labels that sold for £5.95, and which could have the labels personalized for an additional fee.

17th Commonwealth Games, Manchester — A530

Designs: 2nd, Swimming. 1st, Running. E, Cycling. 47p, Long jump. 68p, Wheelchair racing.

Perf. 14¾x14¼

2002, July 16 Photo.

2059	A530 2nd multi	.60	.30
2060	A530 1st multi	.85	.40
2061	A530 E multi	1.10	.55
2062	A530 47p multi	1.50	.75
2063	A530 68p multi	2.10	1.10
	Nos. 2059-2063 (5)	6.15	3.10

Nos. 2059-2061 each sold for 19p, 27p and 37p respectively on day of issue.

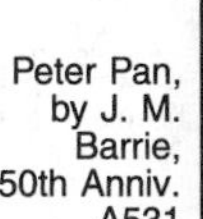

Peter Pan, by J. M. Barrie, 150th Anniv. A531

Designs: 2nd, Tinkerbell. 1st, Darling children. E, Crocodile and clock. 47p, Captain Hook. 68p, Peter Pan.

Perf. 14¾x14¼

2002, Aug. 20 Photo.

2064	A531 2nd multi	.60	.30
2065	A531 1st multi	.85	.40
2066	A531 E multi	1.10	.55
2067	A531 47p multi	1.40	.70
2068	A531 68p multi	2.10	1.10
	Nos. 2064-2068 (5)	6.05	3.05

Nos. 2064-2066 each sold for 19p, 27p and 37p respectively on day of issue.

Thames River Bridges in London A532

2002, Sept. 10 Litho. *Perf. 14¾x14*

2069	A532 2nd Millennium	.60	.30
2070	A532 1st Tower	.85	.40
2071	A532 E Westminster	1.10	.55
2072	A532 47p Blackfriars	1.50	.75
2073	A532 68p London	2.10	1.10

Booklet Stamp

Serpentine Die Cut 14¾x14

2074	A532 1st Tower	.85	.40
a.	Booklet, 2 #2074, 4 #MH300	5.00	
	Nos. 2069-2074 (6)	7.00	3.50

Nos. 2070 and 2074 sold for 27p; Nos. 2069, 2071 sold for 19p and 37p respectively on day of sale.

Pillar Boxes, 150th Anniv. — A534

Designs: 2nd, Decorative box, 1857. 1st, Mainland box, 1874. E, Airmail box, 1934. 47p, Oval dual-aperture box, 1939. 68p, Modern box, 1980.

Litho. & Engr.

2002, Oct. 8 *Perf. 14x14¼*

2076	A534 2nd multi	.60	.30
2077	A534 1st multi	.85	.40
2078	A534 E multi	1.10	.55
2079	A534 47p multi	1.50	.75
2080	A534 68p multi	2.10	1.10
	Nos. 2076-2080 (5)	6.15	3.10

Nos. 2076-2078 each sold for 19p, 27p and 37p on day of issue.

Christmas A535

Die Cut Perf. 14½x14

2002, Nov. 5 Photo.

Self-Adhesive

2081	A535 2nd Spruce branches	.60	.30
a.	Booklet pane of 24	14.50	
2082	A535 1st Holly	.85	.40
a.	Booklet pane of 12	10.50	
2083	A535 E Ivy	1.25	.60
2084	A535 47p Mistletoe	1.50	.75
2085	A535 68p Pine cone	2.10	1.10
	Nos. 2081-2085 (5)	6.30	3.15

Nos. 2081-2085 each sold for 19p, 27p and 37p on day of issue.

Types of 1952-54

Souvenir Sheet

Perf. 15x14¼ Syncopated

2002, Dec. 5 Photo. Wmk. 401

2086	Sheet of 9 + label	7.00	3.50
a.	A126 1p red orange	.20	.20
b.	A126 2p ultramarine	.20	.20
c.	A126 5p brown	.20	.20
d.	A127 2nd scarlet	.60	.30
e.	A126 1st green	.85	.40
f.	A129 33p light brown	1.00	.50
g.	A130 37p bright rose	1.10	.55
h.	A131 47p brown	1.50	.20
i.	A132 50p dark green	1.60	.80

Nos. 2086d and 2086e sold for 19p and 27p respectively on day of issue.

Barn Owl in Flight — A536

Barn Owl in Flight — A537

Barn Owl in Flight — A538

Barn Owl in Flight — A539

Barn Owl in Flight — A540

Kestrel in Flight — A541

Kestrel in Flight — A542

Kestrel in Flight — A543

Kestrel in Flight — A544

Kestrel in Flight — A545

2003, Jan. 14 Litho. *Perf. 14¼x14½*

2087	A536 1st multi	.85	.40
2088	A537 1st multi	.85	.40
2089	A538 1st multi	.85	.40
2090	A539 1st multi	.85	.40
2091	A540 1st multi	.85	.40
2092	A541 1st multi	.85	.40
2093	A542 1st multi	.85	.40
2094	A543 1st multi	.85	.40
2095	A544 1st multi	.85	.40
2096	A545 1st multi	.85	.40
a.	Block of 10, #2087-2096	8.50	4.00

Nos. 2087-2096 each sold for 27p on day of issue.

Check-off Slogans A546

Designs: No. 2097, Gold star, See me, Playtime. No. 2098, I love you, XXXX, S.W.A.L.K. No. 2099, Angel, Poppet, Little terror. No. 2100, Yes, No, Maybe. No. 2101, Oops!, Sorry, Will try harder. No. 2102, I did it!, You did it!, We did it!

2003, Feb. 4 Litho. *Perf. 14¼x14*

2097	A546 1st multi	.90	.45
2098	A546 1st multi	.90	.45
2099	A546 1st multi	.90	.45
2100	A546 1st multi	.90	.45
2101	A546 1st multi	.90	.45
2102	A546 1st multi	.90	.45
a.	Block of 6, #2097-2102	5.40	2.70

SEMI-POSTAL STAMPS

Catalogue values for unused stamps in this section are for Never Hinged items.

Handicapped Person — SP1

Perf. 14½x14

1975, Jan. 22 Photo. Unwmk.

B1	SP1 4½p +1½p blue & lt blue	.25	.25

For the benefit of health and handicap charities. No. B1 is phosphorescent.

Christmas Type of 1989

Ely Cathedral, Cambridgeshire: No. B2, Romanesque arches, west front. No. B3, Central tower. No. B4, Interlocking arches, Romanesque arcades, west transept. No. B5, Peasant, stained-glass window in triple arch, west front.

1989, Nov. 14 Photo. *Perf. 15x14*

B2	A379 15p +1p multicolored	.50	.40
B3	A379 20p +1p multicolored	.70	.50
B4	A379 34p +1p multicolored	1.10	.80
B5	A379 37p +1p multicolored	1.20	.90
	Nos. B2-B5 (4)	3.50	2.60

POSTAGE DUE STAMPS

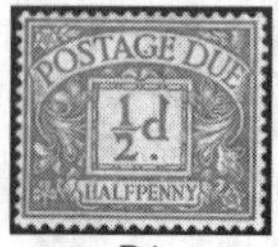
D1

D2

Perf. 14x14½

1914-22 Typo. Wmk. 33

J1 D1 ½p emerald .50 .25
Never hinged 1.00
J2 D1 1p rose .50 .25
Never hinged 1.00
J3 D1 1½p red brown ('22) 45.00 19.00
Never hinged 100.00
J4 D1 2p brown black .50 .25
Never hinged 1.25
J5 D1 3p violet ('18) 4.75 .75
Never hinged 8.00
J6 D1 4p gray green ('21) 17.00 12.00
Never hinged 30.00
J7 D1 5p org brown 5.50 3.25
Never hinged 10.00
J8 D1 1sh blue 37.50 13.50
Never hinged 70.00
Nos. J1-J8 (8) 111.25 49.25

1924-30 Wmk. 35

J9 D1 ½p emerald 1.10 .70
Never hinged 2.00
J10 D1 1p car rose .55 .25
Never hinged 2.50
J11 D1 1½p red brown 42.50 17.50
Never hinged 70.00
J12 D1 2p black brown 1.00 .25
Never hinged 6.00
J13 D1 3p violet 1.50 .25
Never hinged 7.00
a. Experimental wmk. 35.00 32.50
Never hinged 50.00
b. Printed on the gummed side 70.00
Never hinged 130.00
J14 D1 4p deep green 14.00 2.75
Never hinged 30.00
J15 D1 5p org brown ('30) 30.00 26.00
Never hinged 50.00
J16 D1 1sh blue 9.25 .95
Never hinged 16.00
J17 D2 2sh6p brown, *yellow* 42.50 1.90
Never hinged 90.00
Nos. J9-J17 (9) 142.40 50.55

The experimental watermark of No. J13a resembles Wmk. 35 but is spaced more closely, with letters short and rounded, crown with flat arch and sides high, lines thicker.

1936-37 Wmk. 250

J18 D1 ½p emerald ('37) 3.50 *7.50*
Never hinged 7.00
J19 D1 1p car rose ('37) 1.00 *1.90*
Never hinged 1.40
J20 D1 2p blk brown ('37) 3.75 *10.00*
Never hinged 6.50
J21 D1 3p violet ('37) .90 *2.00*
Never hinged 1.50
J22 D1 4p slate green 10.00 *32.50*
Never hinged 21.00
J23 D1 5p bister 7.50 *21.00*
Never hinged 15.00
a. 5p orange brown ('37) 27.50 *22.50*
Never hinged 52.50
J24 D1 1sh blue ('36) 5.25 *8.25*
Never hinged 10.00
J25 D2 2sh6p brn, *yel* ('37) 140.00 8.25
Never hinged 260.00
Nos. J18-J25 (8) 171.90 91.40

1938-39 Wmk. 251

J26 D1 ½p emerald 4.00 4.50
Never hinged 8.25
J27 D1 1p carmine rose 1.25 .70
Never hinged 2.75
J28 D1 2p black brown 1.25 .70
Never hinged 2.40
J29 D1 3p violet 5.00 .95
Never hinged 11.00
J30 D1 4p slate green 35.00 12.00
Never hinged 70.00
J31 D1 5p bister ('39) 6.50 .70
Never hinged 13.00
J32 D1 1sh blue 35.00 1.90
Never hinged 70.00
J33 D2 2sh6p brown, *yel* ('39) 35.00 2.50
Never hinged 70.00
Nos. J26-J33 (8) 123.00 23.95

Catalogue values for unused stamps in this section, from this point to the end of the section, are for Never Hinged items.

1951-52

J34 D1 ½p orange 1.00 *2.00*
J35 D1 1p violet blue 1.40 1.00
J36 D1 1½p green ('52) 1.75 2.00
J37 D1 4p bright blue 30.00 10.00
J38 D1 1sh olive bister 35.00 12.00
Nos. J34-J38 (5) 69.15 27.00

1954-55 Wmk. 298

J39 D1 ½p orange ('55) 3.25 3.25
J40 D1 2p brn black ('55) 3.25 1.50
J41 D1 3p purple ('55) 50.00 21.00
J42 D1 4p brt blue ('55) 16.00 8.50
a. Imperf., pair 200.00
J43 D1 5p bister brn ('55) 14.00 10.00
J44 D2 2sh6p dk pur brn, *yel* 110.00 8.00
Nos. J39-J44 (6) 196.50 52.25

1955-57 Wmk. 308 *Perf. 14x14½*

J45 D1 ½p orange ('56) 2.00 2.75
J46 D1 1p ultra ('56) 3.50 .85
J47 D1 1½p green ('56) 3.50 2.00
J48 D1 2p brown blk ('56) 32.50 5.75
J49 D1 3p purple ('56) 5.75 2.00
J50 D1 4p brt blue ('56) 20.00 4.75
J51 D1 5p bister brn ('56) 27.50 2.75
J52 D1 1sh dp olive bister 65.00 2.75
J53 D2 2sh6p dk red brn, *yel* ('57) 150.00 9.50
J54 D2 5sh red, *yellow* 95.00 18.00
Nos. J45-J54 (10) 404.75 51.10

1959-63 Wmk. 322 *Perf. 14x14½*

J55 D1 ½p orange ('61) .20 .50
J56 D1 1p ultra ('60) .20 .20
J57 D1 1½p green ('60) 1.00 1.90
J58 D1 2p brown black .70 .20
J59 D1 3p purple .40 .20
J60 D1 4p brt blue ('60) .40 .20
J61 D1 5p bister brn ('62) .40 .35
J62 D1 6p dp mag ('62) .40 .25
J63 D1 1sh dp ol bis ('60) .60 .25
J64 D2 2sh6p dark red brown, *yellow* ('61) 3.50 .45
J65 D2 5sh red, *yellow* ('61) 6.50 .80
J66 D2 10sh ultra, *yel* ('63) 7.50 3.50
J67 D2 £1 blk, *yellow* ('63) 42.50 7.00
Nos. J55-J67 (13) 64.30 15.80

Nos. J1-J67 are watermarked sideways.

Perf. 14x14½

1968-69 Unwmk. Typo.

J68 D1 2p greenish black .50 .25
J69 D1 3p purple .50 .20
J70 D1 4p bright blue .60 .25
J71 D1 5p brown org ('69) 6.00 8.00
J72 D1 6p deep magenta 1.00 .40
J73 D1 1sh bister ('69) 2.00 .35
Nos. J68-J73 (6) 10.60 9.45

1968-69 Photo.

J74 D1 4p bright blue ('69) 6.00 4.00
J75 D1 8p bright red 1.25 .75

D3

D4

Perf. 14x14½

1970-75 Photo. Unwmk.

J79 D3 ½p grnsh blue ('71) .20 .20
J80 D3 1p magenta ('71) .20 .20
J81 D3 2p green ('71) .20 .20
J82 D3 3p ultra ('71) .20 .20
J83 D3 4p olive bister ('71) .20 .20
J84 D3 5p bluish lilac ('71) .20 .20
J85 D3 7p brown red ('74) .30 .25
J86 D4 10p carmine rose .40 .25
J87 D4 11p slate ('75) .45 .25
J88 D4 20p olive .75 .50
J89 D4 50p ultramarine 2.00 1.00
J90 D4 £1 black 4.00 2.25
J91 D4 £5 org & black ('73) 30.00 3.50
Nos. J79-J91 (13) 39.10 9.20

D5

D6

1982, June 9 Photo. *Perf. 14x14½*

J92 D5 1p rose carmine .20 .20
J93 D5 2p ultramarine .20 .20
J94 D5 3p deep rose lilac .20 .20
J95 D5 4p dark blue .20 .20
J96 D5 5p sepia .20 .20
J97 D5 10p brown .30 .20
J98 D5 20p dark ol green .45 .30
J99 D5 25p slate blue .60 .35
J100 D5 50p black 1.25 .70
J101 D5 £1 vermilion 2.25 1.25
J102 D5 £2 greenish blue 4.25 1.25
J103 D5 £5 yellow bister 11.00 1.25
Nos. J92-J103 (12) 21.10 6.30

Perf. 15x14 Syncopated, Type C (2 Sides)

1994, Feb. 15 Photo. & Embossed

J104 D6 1p vermilion & org .20 .20
J105 D6 2p red lilac & red .20 .20
J106 D6 5p yel & brn .20 .20
J107 D6 10p yel & grn .25 .25
J108 D6 20p green & blue .60 .60
J109 D6 25p red .70 .70
J110 D6 £1 vio & red lilac 2.50 2.50
J111 D6 £1.20 blue & green 2.75 2.75
J112 D6 £5 green & black 11.00 11.00
Nos. J104-J112 (9) 18.40 18.40

OFFICIAL STAMPS

Type of Regular Issue of 1840 "V R" in Upper Corners

1840 Wmk. 18 *Imperf.*

O1 A1 1p black *6,500.* 11,500.

No. O1 was never placed in use.

Postage stamps perforated with a crown and initials "H.M.O.W.," "O.W.," "B.T." or "S.O.," or with only the initials "H.M.S.O." or "D.S.I.R.," were used for official purposes.

Counterfeits exist of Nos. O2-O83.

Inland Revenue

Regular Issues Overprinted in Black:

I.R. OFFICIAL
a

I. R. OFFICIAL
b

Type "a" is overprinted on the stamps of ½ penny to 1 shilling, type "b" on the higher values.

1882-85 Wmk. 30 *Perf. 14*

O2 A35 ½p green 47.50 19.00
O3 A35 ½p slate bl ('85) 47.50 20.00
O4 A40 1p lilac 3.75 1.90
a. "OFFICIAL" omitted *3,750.*
b. Ovpt. lines transposed
O5 A47 2½p lilac ('85) 150.00 52.50
O6 A28 6p gray 175.00 47.50
O7 A48 1sh green ('85) *3,000.* 550.00

Wmk. 31

O8 A51 5sh car rose ('85) 1,500. 475.00
a. Bluish paper ('85) *3,000.* 850.00
O9 A52 10sh ultramarine *3,000.* 600.00
a. 10sh cobalt *5,750.* 950.00
b. Bluish paper *6,000.* 1,750.

Wmk. Three Imperial Crowns (30)

O10 A53 £1 brown vio *22,500.* *7,500.*

1888-89 Wmk. 30

O11 A54 ½p vermilion 2.40 1.40
a. "I.R." omitted *2,350.*
O12 A65 1sh green ('89) 250.00 95.00

1890 Wmk. Three Orbs (29)

O13 A53 £1 brown vio *30,000.* *8,500.*

1891 Wmk. 30

O14 A57 2½p violet, *blue* 65.00 5.50

Wmk. Three Imperial Crowns (30)

1892

O15 A53 £1 green *3,750.* 575.
a. No period after "R" *10,000.* *1,000.*

1901 Wmk. 30

O16 A54 ½p blue green 5.50 4.25
O17 A62 6p violet, *rose* 160.00 42.50
O18 A65 1sh car rose & green 850.00 325.00

1902-04

O19 A66 ½p gray green 20.00 2.75
O20 A66 1p carmine 14.00 1.90
O21 A66 2½p ultra 450.00 100.00
O22 A66 6p dull vio ('04) *100,000.* *75,000.*
O23 A74 1sh car rose & green 575.00 140.00

Wmk. 31

O24 A76 5sh car rose *4,500.* *1,900.*
O25 A77 10sh ultra *22,500.* *15,000.*

Wmk. Three Imperial Crowns (30)

O26 A78 £1 green *13,500.* *7,500.*

Nos. O4, O8, O9 and O15 also exist with overprint in blue black.

Government Parcels

Overprinted GOVT PARCELS

1883-86 Wmk. 30

O27 A45 1½p lilac ('86) 125.00 40.00
O28 A46 6p green ('86) 775.00 400.00
O29 A50 9p green 650.00 275.00
O30 A29 1sh salmon (P13) 450.00 110.00
Plate 14 750.00 165.00
Nos. O27-O30 (4) 2,000. 825.00

1887-92

O31 A55 1½p violet & green 24.00 3.00
O32 A56 2p green & car rose ('91) 60.00 10.00
O33 A60 4½p car rose & grn ('92) 125.00 100.00
O34 A62 6p violet, *rose* 57.50 15.00
O35 A63 9p blue & lil ('88) 80.00 20.00
O36 A65 1sh green 175.00 100.00
Nos. O31-O36 (6) 521.50 248.00

1897

O37 A40 1p lilac 30.00 10.00
a. Inverted overprint 1,500. 850.00

1900

O38 A65 1sh car rose & grn 175.00 70.00
a. Inverted overprint *6,000.*

1902

O39 A66 1p carmine 16.00 7.00
O40 A68 2p green & car 70.00 20.00
O41 A66 6p dull violet 110.00 20.00
O42 A72 9p ultra & violet 240.00 65.00
O43 A74 1sh car rose & grn 375.00 100.00
Nos. O39-O43 (5) 811.00 212.00

Office of Works

Overprinted O.W. OFFICIAL

1896

O44 A54 ½p vermilion 100.00 57.50
O45 A40 1p lilac 175.00 57.50

1901-02

O46 A54 ½p blue green 175.00 90.00
O47 A61 5p lilac & ultra 875.00 200.00
O48 A64 10p car rose & lil 1,450. 300.00

1902

O49 A66 ½p gray green 400.00 110.00
O50 A66 1p carmine 400.00 110.00
O51 A68 2p green & car 750.00 240.00
O52 A66 2½p ultramarine 800.00 300.00
O53 A73 10p car rose & vio *5,750.* 2,250.

Army

Overprinted:

a

ARMY OFFICIAL
b

1896

O54 A54(a) ½p vermilion 2.40 1.40
a. "OFFICIAI" 57.50 27.50
O55 A40(a) 1p lilac 2.40 1.40
a. "OFFICIAI" 57.50 24.00
O56 A57(b) 2½p violet, *blue* 5.75 3.50
Nos. O54-O56 (3) 10.55 6.30

1900

O57 A54(a) ½p blue green 2.40 *4.25*

1901

O58 A62(b) 6p violet, *rose* 17.00 *19.00*

1902

O59 A66(a) ½p gray green 3.00 1.40
O60 A66(a) 1p carmine 3.00 1.40
a. "ARMY" omitted —
O61 A66(a) 6p dull violet 80.00 37.50
Nos. O59-O61 (3) 86.00 40.30

Overprinted **ARMY** **OFFICIAL**

1903

O62	A66	6p dull violet	950.00	450.00

Royal Household

Overprinted

1902

O63	A66	½p gray green	160.00	110.00
O64	A66	1p carmine	140.00	100.00

Board of Education

Overprinted

1902

O65	A61	5p lilac & ultra	550.00	110.00
O66	A65	1sh car rose & grn	1,000.	400.00

1902-04

O67	A66	½p gray green	21.00	7.75
O68	A66	1p carmine	20.00	6.75
O69	A66	2½p ultramarine	525.00	60.00
O70	A71	5p lilac & ultra ('04)	2,250.	1,000.
O71	A74	1sh car rose & grn	*42,500.*	*32,500.*

Admiralty

Overprinted

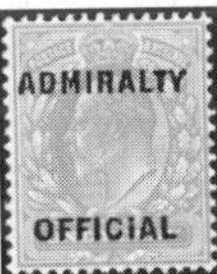

1903

O72	A66	½p gray green	12.00	9.25
O73	A66	1p carmine	6.50	4.00
O74	A67	1½p vio & green	65.00	52.50
O75	A68	2p green & car	125.00	65.00
O76	A66	2½p ultra	140.00	52.50
O77	A69	3p violet, *yel*	125.00	52.50
		Nos. O72-O77 (6)	473.50	235.75

Overprinted **ADMIRALTY** **OFFICIAL**

1903

O78	A66	½p gray green	12.00	6.50
O79	A66	1p carmine	11.00	5.75
O80	A67	1½p vio & green	300.00	190.00
O81	A68	2p green & car	450.00	225.00
O82	A66	2½p ultramarine	550.00	325.00
O83	A69	3p violet, *yel*	375.00	95.00

The two types of the "Admiralty Official" overprint differ principally in the shape of the letter "M."

ENVELOPES

Britannia Sending Letters to World (William Mulready, Designer) — E1

Illustration reduced.

1840

U1	E1	1p black	240.00	*300.00*
U2	E1	2p blue	325.00	*800.00*

LETTER SHEETS

U3	E1	1p black	225.00	*275.00*
U4	E1	2p blue	300.00	*750.00*

REGIONAL ISSUES

Sold only at post offices within the respective regions, but valid for postage throughout Great Britain. Issues for Guernsey, Jersey and Isle of Man are listed with the Bailiwick issues that follow.

Starting in 1967, all Regional stamps were issued only with phosphorescence.

Catalogue values for unused stamps in this section are for Never Hinged items.

ENGLAND

Three Lions — A1

Perf. 15x14 Syncopated

2001, Apr. 23 **Photo.**

1	A1	2nd shown	.55	.25
2	A1	1st Crowned Lion	.80	.40
3	A1	E Oak tree	1.00	.50
4	A1	65p Tudor rose	1.90	.95
5	A1	68p Tudor rose	2.10	1.10
		Nos. 1-5 (5)	6.35	3.20

Issued: Nos. 1-4, 4/23/01. No. 5, 7/4/02.

Nos. 1-3 sold for 19p, 27p and 36p respectively on day of issue.

NORTHERN IRELAND

A1

A2

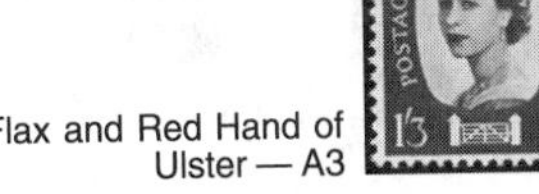

Flax and Red Hand of Ulster — A3

Perf. 15x14

1958-67 **Photo.** **Wmk. 322**

1	A1	3p dark purple	.20	.20
	p.	Phosphor. ('67)	.20	.20
2	A1	4p ultra ('66)	.20	.20
	p.	Phosphor. ('67)	.20	.20
3	A2	6p rose lilac	.30	.20
4	A2	9p dk green ('67)	.35	.20
5	A3	1sh3p dark green	.35	.20
6	A3	1sh6p dark blue ('67)	.35	.20
		Nos. 1-6 (6)	1.75	1.20

Nos. 4, 6 and following are phosphorescent.

1968-69 **Unwmk.**

Design: 1sh6p, Flax plant, Red Right Hand of Ulster and Ulster field gate.

7	A1	4p ultramarine	.20	.20
8	A1	4p olive brown	.20	.20
9	A1	4p bright red ('69)	.30	.20
10	A1	5p dark blue	.20	.20
11	A3	1sh6p dark blue ('69)	3.50	2.00
		Nos. 7-11 (5)	4.40	2.80

Giants Causeway — A4

Perf. 14¾x14 Syncopated

2001-02 **Litho.**

12	A4	2nd shown	.55	.25
13	A4	1st Farm fields	.80	.40
14	A4	E Linen	1.00	.50
15	A4	65p Parian China	1.90	.95
16	A4	68p Parian China	2.10	1.10
		Nos. 12-16 (5)	6.35	3.20

Issued: Nos. 12-15, 3/6/01; No. 16, 7/4/02.

Nos. 12-14 sold for 19p, 27p and 36p respectively on day of issue.

SCOTLAND

St. Andrew's Cross and Thistle — A1

A2

A3

Perf. 15x14

1958-67 **Photo.** **Wmk. 322**

1	A1	3p dark purple	.20	.20
	p.	Phosphor.	.20	.20
2	A1	4p ultra ('66)	.20	.20
	p.	Phosphor. ('67)	.20	.20
3	A2	6p rose lilac	.25	.20
	p.	Phosphor. ('63)	.25	.20
4	A2	9p dark green ('67)	.35	.20
5	A3	1sh3p dark green	.35	.20
	p.	Phosphor. ('63)	.35	.20
6	A3	1sh6p dark blue ('67)	.35	.20
		Nos. 1-6 (6)	1.70	1.20

The 3p with two phosphorescent bands was issued in 1963; with one side band in 1965, and one center band in 1967. The value of No. 1p is for one center band. Nos. 4, 6 and following are phosphorescent.

1967-70 **Unwmk.**

7	A1	3p purple ('68)	.20	.20
8	A1	4p ultramarine	.20	.20
9	A1	4p olive brown ('68)	.20	.20
10	A1	4p brt red ('69)	.20	.20
11	A1	5p dark blue ('68)	.25	.20
12	A2	9p dark green ('70)	7.50	4.75
13	A3	1sh6p dark blue ('68)	1.40	.85
		Nos. 7-13 (7)	9.95	6.60

Natl. Flag (St. Andrew's Cross) — A4

Perf. 14¾x14 Syncopated

1999-2002 **Photo.**

14	A4	(2nd) shown	.60	.30
15	A4	(1st) Lion Rampant	.85	.40
	a.	Booklet pane, #15, 4 England #1, 4 England #2 (BK172)	6.50	
16	A4	(E) Thistle	.95	.50
	a.	Booklet pane, 4 each #15-16, + label (BK170)	7.20	
17	A4	64p Tartan	2.00	1.00
18	A4	65p As #17	2.10	1.00
	a.	Booklet pane, 6 #14, 2 #18 + label (BK168)	7.50	
19	A4	68p Tartan	2.10	1.10
		Nos. 14-19 (6)	8.60	4.30

#14-16 sold for 19p, 26p, & 30p, respectively, on day of issue.

Issued: #14-17, 6/8; #18, 4/25/00; #18a, 8/4/00; #16a, 10/22/01. #19, 7/4/02. #15a, 9/24/02.

WALES & MONMOUTHSHIRE

A1

A2

Welsh Dragon — A3

Designs: 6p, 9p, Dragon in rectangular panel at bottom. 1sh3p, 1sh6p, Dragon and leek.

Perf. 15x14

1958-67 **Photo.** **Wmk. 322**

1	A1	3p dark purple	.20	.20
	p.	Phosphor. band ('67)	.20	.20
2	A1	4p ultra ('66)	.20	.20
	p.	Phosphor. bands ('67)	.20	.20
3	A2	6p rose lilac	.40	.30
4	A2	9p dark green ('67)	.30	.20
5	A3	1sh3p dark green	.30	.20
6	A3	1sh6p dark blue ('67)	.30	.20
		Nos. 1-6 (6)	1.70	1.30

Nos. 4, 6 and following are phosphorescent.

1967-69 **Unwmk.**

7	A1	3p dark purple	.20	.20
8	A1	4p ultra ('68)	.20	.20
9	A1	4p olive brown ('68)	.20	.20
10	A1	4p brt red ('69)	.20	.20
11	A1	5p dark blue ('68)	.20	.20
12	A3	1sh6p dark blue ('69)	3.25	2.50
		Nos. 7-12 (6)	4.25	3.50

Leek — A4

Perf. 15x14 Syncopated

1999-2000 **Photo.**

13	A4	2nd shown	.60	.30
14	A4	1st Dragon	.85	.40
15	A4	E Daffodil	.95	.50
16	A4	64p Prince of Wales feathers	2.00	1.00
17	A4	65p Prince of Wales feathers	2.10	1.00
		Nos. 13-17 (5)	6.50	3.20

Booklet Stamps

Perf. 13¾x14¼

18	A2	2nd Leek	.55	.30
	a.	Booklet pane, 4 each #18, MH336 + label (BK169)	5.75	
19	A4	68p Prince of Wales Feathers	2.10	1.10

#13, 18 sold for 19p; #14, 26p; & #15, 30p, on day of issue.

Issued: #13-16, 6/8; #17, 4/25/00. #19, 7/4/02.

MACHINS

MACHIN DEFINITIVE STAMPS

Sterling Currency Issue

MA1

Type I

Type II

Two types of 2p:
Type I- Head off-center to right. Foot of "2" 1mm from left margin.
Type II- Head centered. Foot of "2" ½mm from left margin.

MH21

MH168

Two types of "£" symbol:
No. MH21 has a loop at the bottom and the numeral is a figure "1."
No. MH168 has no loop and numeral is like a capital "I."

Perf. 15x14

1967-69 Photo. Unwmk.

Size: 17½x21½mm

MH1 ½ brown orange .20 .20
MH2 1p olive .20 .20
a. Booklet pane of 6 (BK101-BK104, BK121) 1.00
MH3 2p maroon (I) .20 .20
MH4 2p maroon (II) .20 .20
MH5 3p dark violet .20 .20
a. Booklet pane of 6 (BK121) 12.00
b. Booklet pane, 2 ea #MH2, MH5 (BK83) 2.00
c. imperf, pair 700.00
MH6 4p brown black .20 .20
a. Bklt. pane of 2 + 2 labels (BK84) 1.00
b. Bklt. pane of 4 (BK83-BK84) 1.00
c. Booklet pane of 6 (BK101-BK102, BK114-BK115, BK121-BK122) 1.50
d. Booklet pane, 4 #MH2, 2 #MH6 (BK122) 4.00
MH7 4p bright red .20 .20
a. Bklt. pane of 2 + 2 labels (BK85) 1.00
b. Booklet pane of 4 (BK85) 1.00
c. Booklet pane of 6 (BK103-BK104, BK116-BK117, BK123-BK124) 1.00
d. Booklet pane of 15 + recipe (BK125-BK126) 5.00
e. Booklet pane, 4 #MH2, 2 #MH7 (BK123-BK124) 3.75
f. Coil strip of 5, #MH2, #MH5, #MH7, 2 #MH4 3.00
MH8 5p dark blue .20 .20
a. Booklet pane of 6 (BK110-BK112, BK122-BK124) 1.50
b. Booklet pane, 6 each #MH2, #MH7, 3 #MH8 + recipe (BK125-BK126) 14.00
c. Booklet pane of 15 + recipe (BK125-BK126) 5.00
MH9 6p magenta .30 .20
MH10 7p bright green .40 .20
MH11 8p scarlet .20 .25
MH12 8p lt greenish blue .50 .25
MH13 9p dark green .40 .20
MH14 10p gray .50 .40
MH15 1sh light violet .45 .20
MH16 1sh6p indigo & greenish bl .60 .20
a. Greenish blue omitted 110.00
MH17 1sh9p black & orange .50 .20

Perf. 12

Engr.

Size: 27x31mm

MH18 2sh6p brown .90 .20
MH19 5sh dark carmine 2.25 .55
MH20 10sh ultramarine 7.00 5.00
MH21 £1 bluish black 3.25 1.25
Nos. MH1-MH21 (21) 18.85 10.70

Nos. MH10-MH13 have denomination at right. Many of Nos. MH1-MH17 exist with phosphor bands omitted in error.

Issued: ½p, 1p, #MH3, 6p, 2/5/68; #MH4, 8/27/69; 3p, 4/6/68; #MH6, 6/16/68; #MH7, #MH12, 1/6/69; 5p, 7p, #MH11, 10p, 7/1/68; 9p, 1sh6p, 8/8/67; 1sh, 1sh9p, 6/5/67; #MH18-MH21, 3/5/69.

Decimal Currency Issues
(P Instead of D)

MA2

Nos. MH22-MH189, MH199-MH243 are Type MA2. Specialized illustrations are shown for identification purposes.

Two types of 1p: Type I: Thick numeral and "p," which are 2½mm from bottom of design. Type II: Thinner numeral and "p," which are 3mm from bottom of design.

Perf. 15x14

1970-95 Photo. Unwmk.

Size: 17½x21½mm

MH22 ½p greenish blue .20 .20
a. Booklet pane of 5 + label (BK129-BK130, BK132, BK138, BK143) 4.50
MH23 1p magenta, Type I .20 .20
MH23A 1p magenta, Type II .60 .60
MH24 1½p black .20 .20
a. Booklet pane, 2 each #MH23-MH24 (BK127-BK128) 2.00

Issued: ½p, #MH23, 1½p, 2/15/71. #MH23A, 8/4/80.

a

b

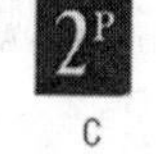
c

Three types of 2p:
a, Wide "2," thick at bottom of curve.
b, Wide "2," thin at bottom of curve.
c, Narrow "2."

MH25 2p dark green (a) .20 .20
a. Coil strip, 2 ea #MH22-MH23, 1 #MH25 .60
MH26 2p dark green (b) .20 .20
a. Booklet pane, 2 each #MH22, MH26(BK127-BK128) 4.00
b. Booklet pane of 6 + printed margin (BK145) .60
MH27 2p dark green (c) 3.00 3.00
MH28 2p light green (c) .20 .20

Litho.

MH29 2p dk grn, perf 14 (a) .20 .20
MH30 2p dark green (a) .30 .20
MH31 2p dark green (c) .80 .25
MH31A 2p dk grn, perf 14 (c) 2.00 .20

Nos. MH24a, MH26a exist with with stamps se-tenant vertically or horizontally.

Issued: #MH25, 12/12/79; #MH26, 2/15/71; #MH27, 9/5/88; #MH28, 7/26/88; #MH29, 5/21/80; #MH30, 7/10/84; #MH31, 2/23/88; MH31A, 2/9/93.

No. MH31A comes from #MH128a (BK420) only.

a

b

c

Three types of 2½p:
a, Thick numerals & "P," end of curve of small "2" is thick.
b, Thinner numerals & "P," end of curve of small "2" is thin.
c, Very thin numerals & "P," end of curve of small "2" is pointy.

MH32 2½p pink (a) .20 .20
a. Booklet pane of 4 + 2 labels (BK129-BK130, BK132) 5.50
b. Booklet pane of 5 + label (BK129-BK130, BK132, BK138, BK143) 5.50
MH33 2½p pink (b) .20 .20
MH34 2½p pink (c) 2.00 3.00
a. Booklet pane, 3 #MH22, 9 #MH34 + printed margin (BK144) 25.00
b. Booklet pane, 4 #MH22, 2 #MH34 + printed margin (BK144) 75.00

#MH34a, MH34b valued in F-VF condition.

MH35 2½p vermilion (b) .20 .20

Issued: #MH32 2/15/71; MH33, 5/21/75; #MH34, 5/24/72; MH35, 1/14/81.
#MH34 issued only in booklets.

a

b

Two types of 3p:
a, Thick numeral with top serif.
b, Thin numeral without serif.

MH36 3p ultramarine (a) .20 .20
a. Booklet pane, 2 #MH32, 4 #MH36 (BK138, BK143) 8.00
b. Booklet pane, 5 + label (BK131, BK133-BK136, BK139) 5.00
c. Bklt. pane of 6 (BK138, BK143) 5.00
d. Booklet pane of 12, 6 each #MH34, #MH36 + printed margin (BK144) 18.00
e. Booklet pane of 12 + printed margin (BK144) 10.00
MH37 3p deep lilac rose (a) .20 .20
a. Coil strip, #MH35, 3 #MH37 .75 .35
MH38 3p deep lilac rose (b) 1.50 .75

Issued: #MH36, 9/10/73; #MH37, 10/22/80; #MH38, 1/21/92.

a

b

Two types of 3½p:
a, Numerals in fraction aligned diagonally.
b, Numerals in fraction aligned vertically.

MH39 3½p gray green (a) .40 .20
a. Booklet pane of 5 + label (BK137, BK139-BK141) 6.00
MH40 3½p violet brown (b) .50 .20

Issued: #MH39, 6/24/74; #MH40, 3/30/83.

a

b

c

Three types of 4p:
a, Wide "4" with large serif and thick crossbar.
b, Wide "4" with small serif and thin crossbar.
c, Narrow "4."

MH41 4p olive bister (a) .30 .20
a. Imperf., pair
MH42 4p greenish blue (a) 1.25 .20
a. Coil strip, #MH22, 3 MH42 4.00 .50
MH43 4p brt greenish bl (a) .20 .20
a. Coil strip, #MH23, 3 MH43 3.25
b. Coil strip, #MH28, 3 MH43 3.25
MH44 4p greenish blue (b) 2.25 .20
MH45 4p brt greenish bl (c) 1.75 .20
MH46 4p bright blue (c) 1.25 .20
a. Coil strip, #MH38, 3 MH46 5.25
MH47 4p Prussian blue, litho., perf 13½x14 (b) .25 .20
MH48 4p Prus blue, litho. (c) .60 .20
MH49 4½p grayish blue .50 .20
a. Booklet pane of 5 + label (BK140, BK142) 6.00

Issued: #MH41, unknown; #MH42-MH42a, 12/30/81; #MH43-MH43a, 8/14/84; #MH43b, 9/5/88. #MH44, 8/26/81; #MH45, 9/3/84; #MH46, 7/26/88; #MH46a, 9/19/89. #MH47, 1/30/80; #MH48, 5/13/86; 4 1/2p, 10/24/73.
#MH43 issued only in strips.

a

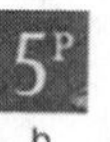
b

Two types of 5p:
a, 5p is 3.25mm wide.
b, 5p is 2.75mm wide.

MH50 5p bluish lilac (a) .30 .20
MH51 5p lilac, litho., perf 13½x14 (a) .40 .20
MH52 5p red brown, litho., perf 13½x14 (a) .60 .20
MH53 5p red brown, litho. (a) .70 .20
MH54 5p red brown (b) 2.00 .90
MH55 5p brown (b) .20 .20
a. Coil strip, #MH55, 3 #MH46 4.00
b. Coil strip, 2 ea #MH46, MH55 2.75
c. Coil strip, #MH46, 3 MH55 1.75
MH56 5½p dark violet .35 .20

Issued: #MH50, 2/15/71; #MH51, 5/21/80; #MH52, 1/27/82; #MH53, 2/21/84; #MH54, 10/20/86; #MH55, 7/26/88; #MH55a, 11/27/90; #MH55b, 10/1/91. #MH55c, 1/31/95. 5 1/2p, 10/24/73.

a

b

c

Three types of 6p:
a, Thick numeral and "P."
b, Thinner numeral and "P," numeral is pointed at top and very thin where loop joins.
c, Narrow numeral.

MH57 6p light emerald (a) .30 .20
MH58 6p light emerald (b) .50 .20
a. Booklet pane, #MH58, 2 MH22, 3 MH23 (BK225) 1.40
b. Coil strip, #MH23, MH26, MH58, 2 #MH22 .95
MH59 6p brt olive green (c) .25 .20
MH60 6½p Prussian blue .30 .20

Issued: #MH57, 2/15/71; #MH58, 6/9/76; #MH58b, 12/3/75. #MH59, 9/10/91; 6 1/2p, 9/4/74.
#MH58 issued only in booklets and strips.

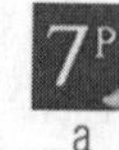
a

b

Two types of 7p:
a, Wide numeral.
b, Narrow numeral.

MH61 7p dark red brown (a) .30 .20
a. Coil strip, #MH61, 2 ea MH22-MH23 .60
b. Booklet pane, #MH61, 2 ea MH22-MH23 + label (BK226) .75
MH62 7p henna brown (b) 1.25 *1.50*
MH63 7½p lt red brown .40 .20
MH64 8p red .35 .20
a. Coil strip, #MH64, 2 MH23 + 2 labels .60
b. Booklet pane, #MH64, 2 MH23 + label (BK227) .75
MH65 8½p yellow green .35 .20
a. Bklt. pane, 2 ea #MH22-MH23, MH60, 4 MH65 (BK228) 5.25

No. MH65a exists with the four 8 1/2p stamps se-tenant on either the left or right side of the pane.

MH66 9p black & ocher .65 .25
MH67 9p violet blue .45 .20
a. Booklet pane, 2 #MH23, 3 ea MH61, MH67 (BK229-BK230) 3.50
b. Booklet pane, 10 ea #MH61, MH67 (BK672) 6.50

No. MH67a exists with the three 9p stamps se-tenant on either the left or right side of the pane.

MH68 9½p bright lilac .35 .20

Issued: #MH61, 1/15/75; #MH61a, 12/14/77. #MH62, 10/29/85; 7 1/2p, 2/15/71; 8p, 10/24/73; #MH64a, 1/16/80. 8½p, 9/24/75; #MH66, 2/15/71; #MH67, 9 1/2p, 2/25/76.

a

b

c

Three types of 10p:
a, Round "0."
b, Thin part of "0" at upper left, lower right.
c, Thin part of "0" at top, bottom.

MH69 10p org brn & lt org (a) .65 .25
MH70 10p light org brn (b) .45 .20
a. Bklt. pane of 9 + printed margin (BK145) 2.50
b. Booklet pane, 2 ea #MH26, MH64, 3 #MH70 + label (BK231-BK232) 2.50
c. Booklet pane, 10 ea #MH64, MH70 (BK709) 6.25
MH70D 10p light org brn (c) 35.00 20.00

No. MH70b exists with the three 10p stamps se-tenant on either the left or right side of the pane.

MH71 10p brn orange (c) .60 .20
MH72 10½p yellow .50 .25
MH73 10½p steel blue .80 .50
MH74 11p pink .50 .20

Issued: #MH69, 8/11/71; #MH70, MH72, 11p, 2/25/76; #MH71, 9/4/90; #MH73, 4/26/78; #MH70D, 9/4/84.

a

b

Two types of 11½p:
a, Thin numerals in fraction.

b, Thick numerals in fraction.

MH75 11½p olive bister (a) .60 .40
MH76 11½p gray brown (a) .50 .20
a. Booklet pane, 2 #MH42, 3 each MH35, MH76 (BK236) 4.50
MH77 11½p gray brown (b) .60 .20

#MH77 comes from #MH86c (BK826), only.
Issued: #MH75, 8/15/79; #MH76, 1/14/81; #MH77, 11/11/81;

a b

Two types of 12p:
a, Wide numerals.
b, Narrow, thin numerals.

MH78 12p yellow green (a) .55 .30
a. Booklet pane of 9 + printed margin (BK145) 3.00
b. Booklet pane of 9 (#MH26, 4 each #MH70, MH78) + printed margin (BK145) 13.50
c. Booklet pane of 10 each #MH70, MH78 (BK759) 9.00
d. Booklet pane, 3 #MH26, 2 each MH70, MH78 + label (BK233) 2.25
MH79 12p bright green (b) .60 .35
a. Booklet pane of 9 + printed margin (BK140) 6.00
b. Booklet pane, 2 #MH23, 4 MH79 (BK245) 8.00

Issued: #MH78, 1/30/80; #MH79, 10/29/85.

a b

Two types of 12½p:
a, Thin, narrow numerals.
b, Thick, wider numerals.

MH80 12½p light emerald (a) .50 .25
a. Booklet pane of 6 + printed margin (BK146-BK147) 5.00
b. Booklet pane of 9, #MH25, MH37, 7 MH80 + printed margin (BK146) 6.00
c. Booklet pane, #MH22, 4 MH37, 3 MH80 (BK237-BK238) 3.00
d. Booklet pane, 2 #MH23, 3 each MH40, MH80 (BK239) 7.50

No. MH80c exists with the three 12½p stamps se-tenant on either the left or right side of the pane. Booklets with 20 #MH80 were sold at a discount. Stamps in these booklets had 5-point double-lined stars printed on the reverse.

MH81 12½p green (b) .80 .25

No. MH81 comes from #MH93d (BK572).
Issued: #MH80, 1/27/82; #MH81, 2/1/82.

a b

Two types of 13p:
a, "3" with serif.
b, "3" without serif.

MH82 13p gray green (a) .60 .40
MH83 13p lt red brown (b) .50 .20
a. Booklet pane of 6 + printed margin (BK148, BK151) 3.50
b. Booklet pane of 9 + printed margin (BK149, BK151) 5.00
c. Booklet pane, 2 #MH45, 3 each MH23, MH83 (BK240) 4.75
d. Booklet pane, #MH23, 2 MH54, 3 MH83 (BK244, BK248) 5.00
e. Booklet pane of 4, margins all around (BK285) 3.00
f. Booklet pane of 10, margins all around (BK534) 6.00
g. As "d," imperf edges (BK250-BK251) 5.00

Panes of #MH83 with stars printed on the reverse were sold at a discount.

MH84 13p lt red brn, litho. (b) .80 .60
a. Booklet pane of 6 + printed margin (BK152) 5.00
MH85 13½p brown purple .60 .60

Issued: #MH82, 8/15/79; #MH83, 8/28/84; #MH84, 2/9/88; 13½p, 1/30/80.

a b

Two types of 14p:
a, Wide "4."
b, Narrow "4."

MH86 14p gray blue (a) .70 .35
a. Bklt. pane, #MH22-MH23, MH86, 3 MH77 (BK234-BK235) 2.25
b. Booklet pane, 4 #MH76, 6 MH86 (BK524) 5.25
c. Booklet pane, 10 each #MH77, MH86 (BK826) 12.50
MH87 14p dark blue (b) .60 .40
a. Booklet pane of 4, margins all around (BK295) 5.00
b. Booklet pane of 4, imperf on T, B (BK296) 5.00
c. Booklet pane of 4, imperf on T, B, R (BK297) 19.00
d. Boolet pane of 10, margins all around (BK558) 5.50
e. Booklet pane of 10, imperf on T, B (BK560) 8.00
MH88 14p dark blue, litho. (b) 1.75 .75
MH89 14p dark blue, litho., perf 14 (b) 4.00 .90

No. MH89 comes from #MH108a (BK412), only.

MH90 15p deep ultramarine .70 .35
MH91 15p bright blue .75 .25

Issued: #MH86, 1/14/81; #MH87, 9/5/88; #MH88, 10/11/88; #MH89, 4/25/89; #MH90, 8/15/79; #MH91, 9/26/89.

a b

Two types of 15½p:
a, Thin numerals in fraction, top bar of "5" thin.
b, Thick numerals in fraction, top bar of "5" thick.

MH92 15½p light violet (a) .70 .35
MH93 15½p light violet (b) .70 .35
a. Booklet pane of 6 + printed margin (BK146) 4.25
b. Booklet pane of 9 + printed margin (BK146) 6.50
c. Booklet pane, 4 #MH80, 6 MH93 (BK573-BK574) 6.75
d. Booklet pane, 4 #MH81, 6 MH93 (BK572) 8.25
e. Booklet pane, 10 each #MH80, MH93 (BK802) 11.00

No. MH93e was printed with 10-point single-line blue stars on the reverse over the gum.

MH94 16p brownish gray .55 .25
a. Booklet pane, #MH37, 2 MH40 6 MH94 + printed margin (BK147) 4.50
b. Booklet pane of 9 + printed margin (BK147) 5.50
c. Booklet pane, 4 #MH81, 6 MH94 (BK594) 12.00

Panes of #MH94 with double-line D printed on reverse were sold at a discount in BK584.

MH95 16½p fawn 1.00 .75

Issued: #MH92, 1/14/81; #MH93, 2/1/82; 16p, 3/30/83; 16½p, 1/27/82.
#MH93 issued only in booklets.

a b

Two types of 17p:
a, Wide "7."
b, Narrow "7."

MH96 17p light green (a) .85 .35
MH97 17p blue gray (b) .55 .30
a. Booklet pane of 3 + label (star printed on reverse-BK241-BK242) 2.50
b. Booklet pane of 9 + printed margin (BK149-BK150) 5.50
c. Booklet pane of 6 + printed margin (BK148-BK150) 20.00
d. Booklet pane, #MH70D, MH83, 7 MH97 + printed margin (BK148) 45.00
e. Booklet pane, 4 #MH79, 6 MH97 (BK616-BK618) 7.00
f. Booklet pane, 4 #MH83, 6 MH97 (BK641) 6.00
g. Booklet pane of 10 (double-lined "D" printed on reverse-BK652) 6.00
MH98 17p dark blue (b) 1.25 .35
a. Bklt. pane of 3 + label (BK256) 3.00
MH99 17p dk bl, litho. (b) 1.00 .35
a. Booklet pane of 6 + printed margin (BK155) 6.50
MH100 17½p lt red brown .90 .80
MH101 18p violet blue .80 .70
MH102 18p olive green .75 .30
a. Booklet pane of 9 + printed margin (BK151) 6.75
b. Booklet pane, #MH23, MH83, 2 MH102 (BK246-BK247, BK249) 3.00
c. Booklet pane of 4, margins all around (BK328) 3.50
d. Booklet pane, #MH83, 5 MH102 (BK406-BK407) 6.00
e. Booklet pane of 10, margins all around (BK714) 8.50
f. As "d," imperf edges (BK408-BK410) 6.00
MH103 18p ol grn, litho. .90 .60
a. Booklet pane of 6 + printed margin (BK152) 5.50
b. Booklet pane of 9 + printed margin (BK152) 7.75
MH104 18p brt yel grn .75 .40
MH105 18p brt yel grn, litho. 1.25 .30
a. Booklet pane of 6 + printed margin (BK157) 7.75
MH106 19p brt orange 1.25 .35
a. Bklt. pane, #MH87, 2 #MH106 + label (BK252-BK253) 3.75
b. Booklet pane, 2 #MH87, 4 MH106 (BK411, BK413) 8.00
c. Booklet pane of 4, margins all around (BK348) 6.00
d. Booklet pane of 4, imperf on T, B (BK349) 6.00
e. Booklet pane of 4, imperf on T, B, R (BK350) 19.00
f. Booklet pane of 10, margins all around (BK729) 7.50
g. Booklet pane of 10, imperf on T, B (BK730) 10.00
MH107 19p red org, litho. 2.25 .90
MH108 19p red org, litho., perf 14 2.50 1.00
a. Booklet pane, 2#MH89, 4 #MH108 (BK412) 17.00
MH110 19½p olive gray 1.75 1.50

Issued: #MH96, 1/30/80; #MH97, 3/30/80; #MH98, 9/4/90; #MH99, 3/19/91; 17½p, 1/30/80; #MH101, 1/14/81; #MH102, 8/28/84; #MH103, 2/9/88; #MH104, 9/10/91; #MH105, 10/27/92; #MH106, 8/3/88; #MH107, 10/11/88; #MH108, 4/25/89; 19½p, 1/27/82.
#MH99, MH103, MH105, MH108 issued only in booklets.

a b

Two types of 20p:
a, Thin part of "0" at upper left, lower right.
b, Thin part of "0" at top, bottom.

MH111 20p dp pur brn (a) 1.25 .20
MH112 20p dp pur brn, litho., perf 13¾x14 (a) 1.25 .40
MH113 20p dp pur brn, litho., perf 15x14 (b) 1.40 .40
MH114 20p greenish bl (b) 1.00 .40
MH115 20p brown black (b) 1.00 .35
a. Booklet pane, 2 #MH91, MH115 + label (BK254) 5.00
b. Booklet pane of 5 + label (BK414) 8.00
MH116 20½p ultramarine 1.50 .50
MH117 22p dark blue .90 .45
MH118 22p yellow green .90 .55
MH119 22p yel grn, litho. (MH150a) 9.50 3.00
MH120 22p orange red 1.00 .40
a. Booklet pane, 2 #MH98, 3 MH120 + 3 labels (BK417) 3.75
MH121 22p org red, litho. 1.00 .40
a. Booklet pane of 9 + printed margin (BK155) 10.00
MH122 23p rose pink 1.50 .50
MH123 23p brt yel grn 1.00 .40
MH124 24p violet 1.75 .80
MH125 24p brown red 1.75 .40
MH126 24p brown 1.00 .40
a. Booklet pane, 2 each #MH23, MH126 (BK257-BK259) 1.75
b. Booklet pane, 2 #MH27, 4 MH126 + 2 labels (BK418-BK419) 3.50
MH127 24p brown, litho. 1.25 .35
a. Booklet pane of 6 + printed margin (BK157) 8.00
MH128 24p brn, litho. perf 14 1.50 .35
a. Booklet pane, 2 #MH31A, 4 MH128 + 2 labels (BK420) 9.50
MH129 25p lilac 1.00 .80

Issued: #MH111, 2/25/76; #MH112, 5/21/80; #MH113, 5/13/86; #MH114, 8/23/88; #MH115, 9/26/89; 20½p, 3/30/83; #MH117, 10/22/80; #MH118, 8/28/84; #MH119, 2/9/88; #MH120, 9/4/90; #MH121, 3/19/91; #MH122, 3/30/83; #MH123, 8/3/88; #MH124, 8/28/84; MH125, 9/26/89; #MH126, 9/10/91; #MH127, 10/27/92; #MH128, 2/9/93; 25p, 1/14/81.
#MH119, MH121, MH127 issued only in booklets.

a b

Two types of 26p:
a, Wide numerals.
b, Narrow numerals.

MH130 26p red (a) 1.25 .55
a. Booklet pane, #MH23, MH130, 2 MH83, 5 MH102 + printed margin (BK151) 17.50
MH131 26p red (b) 6.00 6.00
a. Booklet pane of 4, margins all around (BK446) 24.00
MH132 26p olive gray (b) 1.25 .50
MH133 27p brown 1.25 .75
a. Booklet pane of 4, margins all around (BK456) 5.00
b. Booklet pane of 4, horiz. edges imperf (BK457) 27.50
MH134 27p violet 1.25 .50
MH135 28p deep violet blue 1.00 .60
MH136 28p dk olive bister 1.25 .50
MH137 28p dull blue green 1.25 .50

Issued: #MH130, 1/27/82; #MH131, 8/4/87; #MH132, 9/4/90; #MH133, 8/3/88; #MH134, 9/4/90; #MH135, 3/30/83; #MH136, 8/23/88; #MH137, 9/10/91.
#MH131 issued only in booklets.

a b

Two types of 29p:
a, Wide numerals.
b, Narrow numerals.

MH138 29p brown olive (a) 2.00 1.40
MH139 29p dp rose lilac (b) 2.00 .45
MH140 29p dp rose lilac, litho., perf 14 (b) 4.75 3.00
a. Booklet pane of 4, imperf edges (BK478) 20.00
MH141 30p dk olive green 1.25 .50
MH142 31p brt rose lilac 1.25 .60
a. Bklt. pane, #MH142, 6 MH79, 2 MH97 + printed margin (BK150) 17.00
MH143 31p ultramarine 1.50 .60
MH144 31p ultra, litho., perf 14 1.75 .60
a. Booklet pane of 4, imperf on T, B (BK503) 7.25
MH145 32p Prussian blue 1.25 .75
MH146 33p emerald 1.50 .65
MH147 33p emerald, litho. 3.00 .65
a. Bklt. pane, 6 #MH121, 2 MH147 + label, printed margin (BK155) 15.00
MH148 33p emer, litho. perf 14 1.50 .45
a. Booklet pane of 4, margins all around (BK544) 6.00
MH149 34p dark brown 1.50 1.00
a. Bklt. pane, #MN149, 2 MH45, 4 MH83, 2 MH97 + printed margin (BK149) 17.00
MH150 34p dark brn, litho. 8.00 2.00
a. Bklt. pane, 6 #MH84, 1 ea MH103, MH119, MH150 + printed margin (BK152) 25.00
MH151 34p dull blue green 1.75 .80
MH152 34p brt rose lilac 1.50 .80
MH153 35p dark brown 1.50 1.00
MH154 35p orange yellow 1.90 .80
MH155 37p scarlet 1.90 .75
MH156 39p brt rose lilac 1.75 .80
MH157 39p brt rose lil, litho. perf 14 1.90 .80
a. Booklet pane of 4, imperf on T, B (BK662) 7.00
MH158 39p brt rose lil, litho. (MH178a, MH187b) 2.00 .80

Issued: #MH138, 1/27/82; #MH139, 9/26/89; #MH140, 10/2/89; #MH141, 9/26/89; #MH142, 3/30/83; #MH143, 9/4/90; #MH144, 9/17/90; #MH145, 8/23/88; #MH146, 9/4/90; #MH147, 3/19/91; #MN148, 9/16/91; #MH149, 8/28/84; #MH150, 2/9/88; #MH151, 9/26/89; #MH152, 9/10/91; #MH153, 8/23/88; #MH154, 9/10/91; #MH155, 9/26/89; #MH156, 9/10/91; #MH157, 9/16/91; #MH158, 10/27/92.
#MH144, MH147-MH148, MH150 issued only in booklets.

 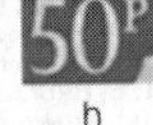

a b

Two types of 50p:
a, Wide numerals.
b, Narrow numerals.

MH159 50p bister brown (a) 2.25 .35
MH160 50p ocher (b) 2.00 .80

Issued: #MH159, 2/2/77; #MH160, 5/21/80.

 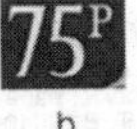

a b

Two types of 75p:
a, Wide numerals.

b, Narrow numerals.

MH161 75p black, litho., perf 13½x14 (a) 3.50 1.50
MH162 75p black, litho. (a) 4.00 1.50
MH163 75p black, litho. (b) 11.00 3.50
MH164 75p black (b) 2.50 1.10

Issued: #MH161, 3/1/80; #MH162, 2/21/84; #MH163, 2/23/88; #MH164, 7/26/88.

Engr.

Perf. 12

Size: 27x31mm

MH165 10p carmine rose .50 .75
MH166 20p olive 1.00 .15
MH167 50p ultramarine 1.25 .60
p. Phosphor 2.50 .60
MH168 £1 bluish black 4.25 1.25

For illustration of £1, see above #MH1.

No. MH168, imperf, are from printers' waste.

Issued: #MH165-MH167, 6/17/70; £1, 12/6/72.

Photo.

Perf. 14x15

Size: 27x38mm

MH169 £1 olive grn & yel 3.25 .60
MH170 £1.30 slate bl & buff 5.50 *6.00*
MH171 £1.33 black & pale rose lilac 8.25 6.00
MH172 £1.41 indigo & buff 9.00 7.50
MH173 £1.50 blk & lt pink 7.00 3.50
MH174 £1.60 indigo & buff 7.00 3.50
MH175 £2 mar & lt grn 6.00 1.50
MH176 £5 dk bl & pink 14.00 4.00

Issued: £1, 2/2/77; £1.30, 8/3/83; £1.33, 8/28/84; £1.41, 9/17/85; £1.50, 9/2/86; £1.60, 9/15/87; £2, £5, 2/2/77.

2nd or 1st Class (Non-Denominated)

2nd and 1st class stamps sell for the current rates and remain valid indefinitely for the indicated service

Perf. 15x14

MH177 2nd bright blue 1.25 .40
a. Booklet pane of 4, imperf on T, B, R (BK961) 25.00
b. Booklet pane of 10, imperf on T, B (BK1028, BK1078) 15.00
MH178 2nd bright blue, litho. 1.25 .40
a. Booklet pane, 2 each #MH105, MH147, MH158, MH178 + label, printed margin (BK158) 15.00
MH179 2nd bright blue, litho., perf 14 1.25 .40
a. Booklet pane of 4, imperf on T, B, R (BK960) 5.00
b. Booklet pane of 4, imperf on T, B (BK963-BK964) 5.00
c. Booklet pane of 10, imperf on T, B (BK1034-BK1035) 12.50

Nos. MH177-MH179 each sold for 14p on day of issue.

MH180 2nd dark blue 1.40 .30
a. Booklet pane of 10, imperf on T, B (BK1030) 8.50
MH181 2nd dark blue, litho. 2.00 .30
MH182 2nd dark blue, litho., perf 14 .75 .30
a. Booklet pane of 4, imperf on T, B (BK962) 3.00
b. Booklet pane of 10, imperf on T, B (BK1032) 7.50

Nos. MH180-MH182 each sold for 15p on day of issue.

MH183 1st brown black 2.00 .65
a. Booklet pane of 4, imperf on T, B, R (BK995) 25.00
b. Booklet pane of 10, imperf on T, B (BK1041) 20.00
MH184 1st brown black, litho., perf 14 2.25 .65
a. Booklet pane of 4, imperf on T, B, R (BK994) 9.50
MH185 1st brown black, litho. 2.50 .65

Nos. MH183-MH185 each sold for 19p on day of issue.

MH186 1st orange red 1.00 .40
a. Booklet pane of 10, imperf on T, B (BK1068, BK1091) 10.50
MH187 1st orange red, litho. .80 .40
a. Booklet pane, 3 each #MH178, MH187 + printed margin (BK158) 5.50
b. Booklet pane, #MH178, MH187, 2 ea MH105, MH127, MH158 + label, printed margin (BK157) *15.00*
c. Booklet pane of 8+ label, printed margin (see footnote) (BK156) 6.75
d. Booklet pane of 10, imperf on T, B (BK1092-BK1093) 8.00

No. MH187c contains #MH178, MH187, 2 each MH147, WMMH34, WMMH45.

MH188 1st orange red, litho., perf 14 .80 .40
a. Booklet pane of 4, imperf on T, B (BK996-BK997) 3.25

b. Booklet pane of 10, imperf on T, B (BK1070) 8.00
MH189 1st orange red, litho., perf 13x13½ 2.50 1.50

Nos. MH186-MH189 each sold for 20p on day of issue.

Distance of denomination to the margin and bust may vary on different printings of the same stamp.

Issued: #MH177, 8/22/89; #MH178, 9/18/89; #MH179, 8/22/89; #MH180-MH182, 8/7/90; #MH183-MH184, 8/22/89; #MH185, 9/19/89; #MH186-MH188, 8/7/90; #MH189, 10/90.

#MH177-MH189 issued only in booklets.

Victoria and Elizabeth II — MA3

1990-2000 Photo. *Perf. 15x14*

MH190 15p bright blue .75 .35
a. Booklet pane of 10, imperf on T, B (BK619) 7.50
MH191 15p brt bl, litho., perf 14 1.50 .50
a. Booklet pane of 4 with imperf on T, B, R (BK307) 7.50
b. Booklet pane of 10 with imperf on T, B, R (BK620) 12.00
MH192 15p bright blue, litho. 2.25 .55
a. Booklet pane of 10 (BK621) 22.50
MH193 20p black & brown black .65 .50
a. Booklet pane, #MH193, 2 MH190 + label (BK255) 3.00
b. Booklet pane of 4 with imperf on T, B, R (BK371) 6.00
c. Bklt. pane of 5 + label (BK415) 4.00
d. Booklet pane of 6 + printed margin (BK154) 4.00
e. Booklet pane of 10 with imperf on T, B (BK743) 12.00
f. Souvenir sheet of 1 5.00
MH194 20p black & brn blk, litho., perf 14 1.00 .65
a. Booklet pane of 4 with imperf on T, B, R (BK372) 7.50
b. Bklt. pane of 5 + label (BK416) 5.00
c. Booklet pane of 10 with imperf on T, B, R (BK744) 12.00
MH195 20p black & brn blk, litho. 2.25 .65
a. Booklet pane of 10 (BK745) 22.50
MH196 29p deep rose lilac 1.50 .70
a. Booklet pane, #MH91, MH115, MH160, MH177, MH183, MH190, MH193, MH196 + label, printed margin (BK154) 22.50
MH197 34p dull blue green 1.60 1.00
MH198 37p scarlet 1.75 1.00

Perf. 13¾x14¼ Syncopated

MH198A 1st blk & yel .85 .40
b. Booklet pane of 6 (BK167) 5.25

Nos. MH191-MH192, MH194-MH195, MH198A were issued only in booklets.

No. MH198A sold for 26p on day of issue.

Issued: #MH190, MH193, MH196-MH198, 1/10; #MH191, MH194, 1/30; #MH192, MH195, 4/17; #MH198A, 2/15/00.

Syncopated Perf. 15x14

1993-97 Type MA2

MH199 1p magenta .20 .20
MH200 1p mag, litho. (MH216b) .75 .20
MH201 2p dark green .20 .20
MH202 4p Prussian blue .20 .20
MH203 5p rose brown .20 .20
MH204 6p bright olive green .25 .20
MH205 6p bright olive green, litho. (MH214a) 13.00 .20
MH206 10p brown orange .35 .20
MH207 10p brown orange, litho. (MH231a) 5.00 2.00
MH208 19p olive green .75 .30
MH209 19p ol grn, litho. (MH214a, MH231a) 1.25 1.25
a. Booklet pane of 6 + printed margin (BK160) 6.00
MH210 20p greenish blue .70 .30
MH211 20p bright yel grn .60 .30
MH212 20p brt yel grn, litho. (MH216a-MH216b) 1.10 .30
MH213 25p salmon .85 .40
a. Booklet pane of 2 + 2 labels (BK260-BK262) 1.75
MH214 25p sal, litho. (MH231a) .90 .40
a. Bklt. pane, #MH205, MH209, 4 MH214 + printed margin (BK159) 12.50
b. Booklet pane of 8 + label, printed margin (see footnote) (BK161) 6.50

No. MH214b contains 2 each #MH214, NIMH59, SMH65, WMMH60.

MH215 26p brown .85 .40
MH216 26p brown, litho. 1.00 .40
a. Bklt. pane, #MH212, 7 MH216 (BK749) 7.00
b. Bklt. pane, #MH212, 2 MH200, 3 MH216 + 2 labels (BK426) 4.00
MH218 29p gray 1.00 .45
MH219 30p olive green 1.00 .75
MH220 30p olive green, litho. (MH231a) 4.00 .75
MH221 31p deep rose lilac .95 .50
MH222 35p orange yellow 1.10 .50
MH223 35p org yel, litho. 1.50 .50
a. Booklet pane of 4 (BK562-BK563) 6.00
MH224 36p blue 1.10 .55
MH225 37p bright rose lilac 1.25 .55
MH226 37p brt rose lilac, litho. 1.75 .55
a. Booklet pane of 4 (BK605) 7.00
MH227 38p red 1.25 .65
MH228 39p bright pink 1.50 .65
MH230 41p drab 1.75 .65
MH231 41p drab, litho. 2.00 .65
a. Booklet pane, #MH207, MH220, MH223, MH231, 2 each MH209, MH214 + label, printed margin (BK160) 10.00
b. Booklet pane of 4 (BK685-BK686) 10.00
MH232 43p dark brown 1.75 .70
MH233 50p ocher 1.50 .75
MH234 60p slate blue, litho. 2.50 .85
a. Booklet pane of 4 (BK790-BK791) 10.00
MH235 63p bright green 2.00 1.00
MH236 63p brt grn, litho. 2.50 1.00
a. Bklt. pane of 4 (BK815-BK816) 10.00
MH237 £1 violet 3.25 3.25

No. MH237 is printed with Iriodin ink, giving stamp design a three dimensional appearance.

MH238 2nd bright blue .65 .50
MH239 2nd bright blue, litho. .80 .50
MH240 1st orange red 1.00 .80
MH241 1st orange red, litho. 1.00 .80
a. Miniature sheet of 1 6.50 6.50
b. Booklet pane of 4 + label (BK1000, BK1002, BK1004) 6.50
c. Booklet pane of 9 + printed margin (BK165) 9.00

No. MH241a was sold for £1 on day of issue in pre-packaged greeting cards at Boots pharmacy. Unfolded examples were later sold by British Philatelic Bureau. Value indicated is for unfolded example.

Size: 21½x17½mm

Self-Adhesive

Die Cut 14x15 Syncopated

MH243 1st orange red 1.10 .35
a. Booklet pane of 20 (BK1251) 22.00

#MH238-MH239 each sold for 18p on day of issue; #MH240-MH241, MH243 each for 24p.

Issued: #MH201, 4/11/95; #MH204, 4/27/93; #MH219, 7/27/93; #MH222, 8/17/93; #MH234, 8/9/94; #MH237, 8/22/95; #MH238, 9/7/93; #MH241, 9/6/93. #MH241c, 2/16/99.

Nos. MH239, MH240, 4/6/93.

Nos. MH199, MH203, MH212, MH206, 6/8/93.

Nos. MH208, MH213, MH218, MH224, MH227, MH230, 10/26/93.

Nos. MH214, MH223, MH222, 11/1/93.

Nos. MH202, MH210, MH233, 12/14/93.

Nos. MH205, MH209, 7/26/94.

Nos. MH207, MH220, 4/25/95.

Nos. MH215, MH221, MH225, MH228, MH232, MH235, 6/25/96.

Nos. MH200, MH203, MH216, MH226, MH236, 7/8/96.

Nos. MH200, MH205, MH207, MH209, MH212, MH216, MH219, MH226, MH231, MH236 issued only in booklets.

No. MH243a is a complete booklet.

Queen Type of 1970 with Redrawn Portrait

Type MA2: Upper lip not defined by sharp line, nostril is incomplete, hairlines not sharply defined, upper corners of cross formeé are widely separated.

Redrawn portrait: Upper lip sharply outlined, nostril is complete and defined by two lines, hairlines are sharply defined, upper corners of cross formeé are close together so they nearly complete a square.

Perf. 15x14 Syncopated, 13¾x14¼ Syncopated (#MH254A, MH264B)

1997-2002 Photo.

MH245 1p magenta .20 .20
MH246 2p dark green .20 .20
MH247 4p Prussian blue .20 .20
MH248 5p rose brown .20 .20
MH249 6p bright olive green .20 .20
MH249A 7p gray .20 .20
MH249B 8p dk olive bister .25 .20
MH250 10p brown orange .30 .20
MH251 10p brn org, perf 14 2.00 .20
MH254 19p bister .60 .30
MH254A 19p bister (MH264c) 1.25 .30
MH255 20p bright yellow green .60 .30
MH256 26p gold .85 .40
MH257 26p brown .85 .40
a. Booklet pane, 3 each #MH255, MH257 + printed margin (BK162) 4.50
b. Bklt. pane, #MH255, 2 MH245, 3 MH257 + 2 labels (BK427) 4.00
c. Booklet pane, #MH255, 7 MH257 (BK751) 6.50
d. Booklet pane, #MH245-MH246, MH254, 3 #MH257 + 2 labels (BK428) 3.50
e. Booklet pane, #MH254, 7 #MH257 (BK752) 6.50
f. Booklet pane, 4 #MH245, 3 #MH254, 1 #MH257 + label (BK165) 3.00
MH259 30p olive green .90 .45
MH260 31p deep rose lil 1.00 .50
MH261 33p dk blue green 1.00 .50
MH262 37p brt rose lilac 1.10 .55
MH263 37p black 1.10 .55
MH264 38p dark blue 1.25 1.00
MH264B 38p dk blue 3.00 1.00
c. Booklet pane, 4 #MH254A, 2 #MH264B (BK167) 7.50
MH265 39p brt pink 1.25 .30
MH266 40p chalky blue 1.25 .60
a. Booklet pane of 4 (BK676) 5.00
MH267 41p carmine rose 1.25 .65
MH267A 42p olive 1.25 .65
MH268 43p dark brown 1.40 .70
MH269 43p dk brn, perf 14 2.25 2.25
a. Booklet pane, #NIMH70, SMH76, WMMH71, 3 MH269 + printed margin (BK164) 5.25
MH270 44p brown 1.60 .70
MH270A 45p brt rose lilac 1.40 .70
MH270B 47p blue green 1.40 .70
MH271 50p ocher 1.50 .30
MH275 63p bright green 2.00 1.25
MH276 64p greenish blue 2.00 1.40
MH277 65p Prussian blue 1.75 1.00
a. Booklet pane of 4 (BK830) 7.50
MH278 68p drab 2.10 1.10
MH279 £1 violet 2.50 .40
a. Souv. sheet, see footnote 8.00 4.00

No. MH279 is printed with Iriodin ink, giving stamp design a three dimensional appearance.

No. MH279a contains #MH247-MH249, MH250, MH260, MH265, MH276, MH279 + 2 labels.

MH280 £1.50 red, engr. 3.50 2.25
MH281 £2 slate blue, engr. 6.50 3.25
MH282 £3 purple, engr. 9.00 4.75
MH283 £5 brown, engr. 14.00 8.00
MH284 2nd bright blue .60 .30
MH285 2nd bright blue, perf 14 .60 .30
a. Booklet pane, #NIMH74, SMH80, WMMH75, 3 MH285 + printed margin (BK164) 5.00
b. Booklet pane, 2 #MH251, 3 each MH269, MH285 + label, printed margin (BK164) 6.75
MH287 1st gold .85 .40
a. Bklt. pane, 4 ea #MH256, MH287 + label, printed margin (BK162) 8.50
MH288 1st orange red (BK1005, BK1140) .60 .40
a. Booklet pane of 8, label + printed margin (BK165) 5.00
b. Booklet pane of 8 (BK1141-BK1142) 5.00
c. Booklet pane of 4 + label (BK1006) 2.50
d. Booklet pane, #MH284, 3 #MH288 + 4 labels (BK429) 2.25
e. Bklt. pane, 2 #MH284, 4 #MH288 (BK753) 4.00
MH289 1st org red, perf 14 1.25 .40
a. Booklet pane of 10 (BK1139A) 12.50
MH290 E dark blue 1.00 .40
a. Booklet pane of 4 (BK1010) 4.00
b. Booklet pane, 4 each #MH284, MH290, + label (BK171) 6.50 —

c. Booklet pane, 4 #MH287, 4 #MH290 + label (BK172, BK173) 8.00

#MH284-MH285 sold for 20p on day of issue; #MH287-MH289 for 26p; #MH290 for 30p. #MH284-MH285 were later sold for 19p. Selling prices for booklets containing these stamps will be considered to have 20p stamps.

Queen Type of 1970 with Redrawn Portrait

MH292

MH294

MH297

MH299

MH300

MH301

On Nos. MH292 and MH297, the numeral and letters are thinner, and perf tips are flat with distinct corners, while on MH294 and MH299, numeral and letters are thicker and bolder, and perf tips have a slight arc and are rounded at the corners.

On No. MH300 the numeral and letters are thick and bold and perf tips have a slight arc and are rounded at the corners, while on No. MH301, the numeral and letters are thin and perf tips are distinctly serpentine with little flatness on the peaks or valleys.

Die Cut Perf. 14¾x14 Sync., Die Cut Perf. 15x14¼Sync. (MH 293, MH298)

Self-Adhesive Stamps

Booklet Stamps (MH293, MH298)

MH292 2nd bright blue .70 .35
a. Booklet pane of 6 3.50
MH293 2nd bright blue .55 .30
a. Booklet pane of 10 5.50
b. Booklet pane of 12 6.75
c. Booklet of 6 3.50
MH294 2nd bright blue .60 .30
a. Booklet of 12 7.25
MH297 1st vermilion .90 .45
a. Booklet pane of 6 5.00
b. Booklet pane of 12 9.75
MH298 1st vermilion .80 .40
a. Booklet pane of 10 8.00
b. Booklet pane of 12 9.75
c. Booklet of 6 5.00
MH299 1st vermilion .85 .40
a. Booklet of 6 5.25
MH300 1st gold .80 .40
a. Booklet of 6 5.00
MH301 1st gold .80 .40
a. Booklet of 6 5.00
b. Booklet of 12 9.75
MH302 E dark blue 1.10 .55
a. Booklet of 6 6.75
MH304 42p olive 1.25 .65
a. Booklet of 6 7.50
MH306 68p drab 2.10 1.10
a. Booklet of 6 13.00

Nos. MH292, MH293, MH297 and MH298 were also issued as coils, which have no selvage surrounding stamps.

No. MH293 & single stamps from No. MH292a sold for 19p on day of issue; #MH292, 20p; #MH297, 26p; #MH298 & single stamps from #MH297a, MH297b, 27p.

Nos. MH292a, MH293a, MH293b, MH297a, MH297b, MH298a, and MH298b are complete booklets.

No. MH297a exists with self-adhesive label depicting Queen Victoria.

Die Cut Perf. 14x15 Syncopated

Self-Adhesive Coil Stamps

Size: 21x17mm

MH308 2nd bright blue 2.75 .30
MH309 1st orange red 3.00 .40

Size: 30x40mm

Perf. 14x14½

MH310 1st black, engr. 2.00 .40
a. Booklet pane of 4 + printed margin (BK165) 8.00
MH311 1st black, typo. 2.00 .40
a. Booklet pane of 4 + printed margin (BK165) 8.00

Self-Adhesive

Die Cut Perf. 14x14½

MH312 1st gray, litho. & embossed 2.00 .40
a. Booklet pane of 4 + printed margin (BK165) 8.00

#MH312 is valued in used condition on piece. Soaking and pressing #MH312 removes the embossed image of the Queen.

No. MH300 sold for 20p on day of issue. Nos. MH305, MH310-MH312 sold for 26p on day of issue.

Issued: #MH245, MH249, MH268, MH271, MH279, 4/1/97; #MH256, MH287, 4/21/97. #MH255, MH284, MH300, MH305, 4/29/97; #MH246-MH248, MH250, MH259, MH265, 5/27/97; #MH260, MH264, MH275, MH288, 8/26/97; #MH257, 11/18/97; #MH292, MH297, 4/6/98; #MH251, MH269, MH285, 10/13/98; #MH289, 12/1/98; #MH290, 1/12/99; #MH288c, 5/12/99; #MH280-MH283, 3/9/99; #MH310-MH312, 2/16/99; #MH289, 3/16/99; #MH249A, MH254, MH264A, MH270, MH276, 4/20/99; #MH254A, MH264B, 2/15/00; 8p, 33p, 40p, 41p, 45p, 65p, #MH288d, MH288e, 4/25/00; #MH279a, 5/22/00; #MH292a, MH293, MH297a, MH297b, MH298, 1/29/01.

Nos. MH293c, MH298c issued 1/29/01.

Nos. MH251, MH254A, MH264B, MH269, MH285 (BK164), MH289 (BK1139A), MH290 (BK1010) issued only in booklets.

No. MH290b issued 2/6/02. E stamps from MH 290b sold for 37p on day of issue.

No. MH290c issued 9/24/02.

Issued: Nos. MH263, MH267A, MH278, MH270B, MH294, MH299, MH302, MH304, MH306, 7/4/02; Nos. MH300-MH301, 6/5/02. No. MH294 sold for 19p, Nos. MH299, MH300 and MH301 sold for 27p, and No. MH302 sold for 37p on day of issue.

This is an expanding set. Nos. MH245-MH312 may change.

Queen Elizabeth II (No Frame, Perforations Touch Vignette) — MA4

Perf. 14¾x14 Syncopated

2000 Photo. Design MA4

MH335 1st olive green .85 .40
a. Bklt. pane of 8 (BK1201) 7.00
b. Bklt. pane of 9 (BK168) 7.25

Perf. 13¾x14¼ Syncopated

MH336 1st olive green .85 .40
a. Booklet pane of 10 (BK1144) 8.50
b. Booklet pane of 8 + label (BK167) 7.00

Issued: #MH335, MH336, 1/6; #MH336b, 2/15; #MH335a, 5/26; #MH335b, 8/4.

No. MH336 issued only in booklets. Perforations are Syncopated.

No. MH335 and MH336 sold for 26p on day of issue.

This is an expanding set, numbers may change.

MACHINS REGIONAL ISSUES

NORTHERN IRELAND

All stamps are Design MA2 unless noted.

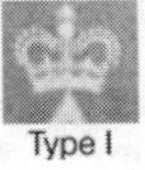
Type I

Type II

Two types of crown:

Type I: All pearls individually drawn, screened background.

Type II: Large pearls with strong white line below them.

First three pearls at left joined together. Solid background.

1971-93 Photo. *Perf. 15x14*

NIMH1 2½p bright pink .75 .20
NIMH2 3p ultramarine .40 .20
NIMH3 3½p slate .30 .20
NIMH4 4½p dark blue .30 .20
NIMH5 5p bright violet 1.25 1.25
NIMH6 5½p dark violet .30 .20
NIMH7 6½p Prussian blue .30 .20
NIMH8 7p dark red brn .30 .20
NIMH9 7½p chestnut 2.25 1.90
NIMH10 8p red .35 .25
NIMH11 8½p yellow green .30 .20
NIMH12 9p violet blue .40 .25
NIMH13 10p orange brown .40 .30
NIMH14 10½p steel blue .55 .30
NIMH15 11p red .55 .35
NIMH16 11½p gray brn, litho,, perf 13½x14 .95 .75
NIMH17 12p yellow green .70 .25
NIMH18 12p brt grn, litho. .95 .50
NIMH19 12½p lt emer, litho., perf 13½x14 .60 .40
NIMH20 12½p lt emer, litho. 6.00 4.00
NIMH21 13p lt red brown, litho., type II 1.00 .35
a. Type I 1.25 .50
NIMH22 13½p brown purple .80 .30
NIMH23 14p gray bl, litho. .90 .50
NIMH24 14p dark bl, litho. 1.00 .35
NIMH25 15p deep ultra .70 .30

Litho.

NIMH26 15p bright blue 1.00 .35
NIMH27 15½p light violet, perf 13½x14 .75 .75
NIMH28 16p brownish gray, perf 13½x14 1.10 1.25
NIMH29 16p brownish gray 8.00 6.00
NIMH30 17p blue gray, type I .95 .50
a. Type II 150.00
NIMH31 17p dark blue 1.00 .40
NIMH32 18p violet blue, perf 13½x14 1.00 1.00
NIMH33 18p olive green 1.00 .50
NIMH34 18p bright yel grn 1.00 .30
NIMH35 18p bright yel grn, perf 13½x14 2.50 .50
NIMH36 19p red orange .75 .50
NIMH37 19½p olive gray, perf 13½x14 2.25 2.50
NIMH38 20p brown black .85 .50
NIMH39 20½p ultramarine, perf 13½x14 4.75 2.75
NIMH40 22p dark blue, perf 13½x14 1.25 1.00
NIMH41 22p yellow green 1.25 .60
NIMH42 22p red orange 1.25 .60
NIMH43 23p bright yel grn 1.25 .60
NIMH44 24p brown red 1.50 .60
NIMH45 24p brown 1.25 .40
a. Bklt. pane, see footnote (BK158) 4.25

#NIMH45a contains NIMH34, NIMH45, SMH35, SMH47, WMMH34, WMMH45.

NIMH46 26p red, perf 13½x14, type I 1.25 .90
NIMH47 26p red, type II 4.00 1.00
NIMH48 26p olive gray 1.25 .70
NIMH49 28p deep viol bl, perf 13½x14, type I 1.25 .90
NIMH50 28p deep viol bl, type II 1.25 .90
NIMH51 28p dull blue green 1.25 .50
NIMH52 31p brt rose lil, type I 1.25 1.00
a. Type II 2.25 1.10
NIMH53 32p Prussian blue 1.25 .80
NIMH54 34p dull blue green 1.50 .90
NIMH55 37p scarlet 1.75 .90
NIMH56 39p brt rose lilac 1.75 .65

Issued: #NIMH1, 3p, 5p, NIMH9, 7/7/71; #NIMH3, NIMH6, 8p, 1/23/74; #NIMH4, 11/6/74;

#NIMH7, NIMH11, 1/14/76; 10p, 11p, 10/20/76; 7p, 9p, NIMH14, 1/18/78.

#NIMH17, NIMH22, #NIMH25, 7/23/80; #NIMH16, #NIMH23, NIMH32, NIMH40, 4/8/81; #NIMH19, 1/24/82; #NIMH27, #NIMH28, NIMH37, NIMH46, 2/24/82; NIMH39, #NIMH49, 4/27/83;

#NIMH20, #NIMH29, 2/28/84; 13p, #NIMH30, NIMH41, 31p, 10/23/84; #NIMH18, 1/7/86; #NIMH33, 1/6/87; #NIMH50, 1/27/87; #NIMH24, 19p, 23p, 32p, 11/8/88; #NIMH26, 30p, NIMH44, 34p, 11/28/89; #NIMH31, NIMH42, NIMH48, 37p, 12/4/90; #NIMH34, NIMH45, NIMH51, 39p, 12/3/91; #NIMH35, NIMH45a, 8/10/93; #NIMH47, 12/7/93.

Perf. 15x14 Syncopated

1993-96 Litho.

NIMH57 19p olive green .75 .30
NIMH58 20p brt yel green 1.00 .30
NIMH59 25p salmon .75 .40
a. Bklt. pane, see footnote (BK160) 4.25

No. NIMH59a contains #NIMH57, NIMH59, SMH63, SMH65, WMMH58, WMMH60 + label, printed margin.

NIMH60 26p brown 1.25 .40
NIMH61 30p olive green 1.25 .45
NIMH62 37p bright rose lilac 2.00 .55
NIMH63 41p drab 2.00 .60
a. Bklt. pane, #NIMH61, NIMH63, 2 #NIMH57, 4 #NIMH59 + label, printed margin (BK159) 6.25
b. Bklt. pane, #NIMH57, NIMH59, NIMH61, NIMH63 + printed margin (BK159) 3.50
NIMH64 63p bright green 2.50 1.00

Issued: 19p, 25p, 30p, 41p, 12/7/93; #NIMH59a, 4/25/95; 20p, 26, 37p, 63p, 7/23/96.

Queen Design of 1970 with Redrawn Portrait

Perf. 15x14 Syncopated

1997-2000 Photo.

NIMH68 19p olive green .60 .30
NIMH69 20p brt yel grn .75 .30
NIMH70 20p brt yel grn, perf 14 2.00 .30
NIMH73 26p brown .90 .45
NIMH74 26p brown, perf 14 2.00 .45
NIMH81 37p bright rose lilac 1.25 .65
a. Bklt. pane, see footnote (BK162) 6.50

No. NIMH81a contains #NIMH73, NIMH81, SMH79, SMH87, WMMH74, WMMH82 + printed margin.

NIMH82 38p dark blue 1.25 .60
NIMH83 40p chalky blue 1.00 .60
NIMH91 63p bright green 2.50 1.00
NIMH92 64p greenish blue 2.50 1.00
NIMH93 65p Prussian blue 2.10 1.00

Issued: #NIMH69, NIMH73, 37p, 63p, 7/9/97; #NIMH81a, 9/24/97; #NIMH70, NIMH74, 10/13/98; #NIMH68, NIMH82, NIMH92, 6/8/99; 40p, 65p, 4/25/00.

Nos. NIMH70, NIMH74 issued only in booklets (BK164).

This is an expanding set, numbers may change.

Perf. 13¾x14¼ Syncopated

2000 Photo.

NIMH96 1st orange red (WM-MH96a) .85 .40

Perf. 15x14 Syncopated

NIMH99 1st org red .85 .40

#NIMH96, NIMH99 sold for 26p on day of issue. #NIMH96 issued only in booklets.

Issued: #NIMH96, 2/15/00; #NIMH99, 4/25/00.

SCOTLAND

All stamps are Design MA2 unless noted.

Type I

Type II

Two types of lion:

Type I: Thin tongue, no line across bridge of nose, three "feathers" on left of tail are widely separated.

Type II: Thick tongue where it enters mouth, eye connected to background by solid line, three "feathers" on left of tail are close together.

1971-93 Photo. *Perf. 15x14*

SMH1 2½p bright pink .30 .20
SMH2 3p ultramarine .40 .20
SMH3 3½p slate .30 .20
SMH4 4½p dark blue .30 .20
SMH5 5p brt violet 1.50 1.25
SMH6 5½p dark violet .30 .20
SMH7 6½p Prussian blue .30 .20
SMH8 7p dark red brn .30 .20
SMH9 7½p chestnut 1.50 1.50
SMH10 8p red .50 .25
SMH11 8½p yellow green .50 .25
SMH12 9p violet blue .50 .25
SMH13 10p orange brown .50 .20
SMH14 10½p steel blue .50 .40
SMH15 11p red .50 .40
SMH16 11½p gray brn, litho., perf 13½x14 1.00 .65
SMH17 12p yellow green .50 .40
SMH18 12p brt green, litho., perf 13½x14 2.00 .75
SMH19 12p green, litho. 2.00 .65

SMH20 12½p lt emer, litho., perf 13½x14 .60 .35

SMH21 13p lt red brown, litho., perf 13½x14, type I .80 .35

a. Type II 7.50 3.75

SMH22 13p lt red brn, litho. .75 .35

SMH23 13½p brown purple .75 .30

SMH24 14p gray blue, litho., perf 13½x14 .75 .40

SMH25 14p dk bl, litho. .55 .35

a. Booklet pane of 6 + printed margin (BK153) 3.50

SMH26 15p deep ultra .60 .50

Litho.

SMH27 15p bright blue .60 .35

Perf. 13½x14

SMH28 15½p light violet .85 .75

SMH29 16p brownish gray .80 .45

SMH30 17p blue gray, type II 1.50 1.00

a. Type I 4.00 3.00

Perf. 15x14

SMH31 17p blue gray 4.50 3.50

SMH32 17p dark blue 1.00 .40

SMH33 18p violet blue, perf 13½x14 1.00 .75

SMH34 18p olive green 1.00 .40

SMH35 18p bright yel grn .60 .30

SMH36 18p brt yel grn, perf 13½x14 1.25 .50

SMH37 19p red orange .70 .50

a. Booklet pane of 6 + printed margin (BK153) 4.25

b. Booklet pane of 9 + printed margin (BK153) 6.50

SMH38 19½p olive gray, perf 13½x14 2.00 2.00

SMH39 20p brown black 1.00 .50

Perf. 13½x14

SMH40 20½p ultra 4.75 .75

SMH41 22p dk blue 1.10 1.00

SMH42 22p yel grn, type I 2.75 2.00

a. Type II 50.00 40.00

Perf. 15x14

SMH43 22p yellow green 1.25 .50

SMH44 22p red orange 1.25 .60

SMH45 23p bright yel grn 1.50 .60

a. Booklet pane #SMH45, 2 #SMH37, 5 #SMH25 + printed margin (BK153) 5.25

SMH46 24p brown red 1.50 .70

SMH47 24p brown 1.00 .40

SMH48 24p chestnut, perf 13½x14 2.50 .65

SMH49 26p red, perf 13½x14, type I 1.10 .90

SMH50 26p red 3.00 2.00

SMH51 26p olive gray 1.25 .70

SMH52 28p dp vio bl, perf 13½x14 1.10 .90

SMH53 28p deep violet blue 1.25 .90

SMH54 28p dull bl grn 1.10 .50

SMH55 28p dull bl grn, perf 13½x14 5.00 4.00

SMH56 31p brt rose lilac, perf 13½x14 2.00 .90

a. Type II 100.00 90.00

SMH57 31p brt rose lilac 2.50 .90

SMH58 32p Prussian blue 1.75 .90

SMH59 34p dull bl grn 1.75 .90

SMH60 37p scarlet 2.00 .90

SMH61 39p brt rose lilac 2.00 .65

SMH62 39p brt rose lilac, perf 13½x14 3.00 2.00

Issued: #SMH1, 3p, 5p, #SMH9, 7/7/71; #SMH3, SMH6, 8p, 1/23/74; #SMH4, 11/6/74; #SMH7, SMH11, 1/14/76; 10p, 11p, 10/20/76; 7p, 9p, #SMH14, 1/18/78; #SMH17, SMH23, #SMH26, 7/23/80.

#SMH16, #SMH24, SMH33, SMH41, 4/8/81; #SMH20, SMH28, SMH38, #SMH49, 2/24/82;

16p, #SMH40, #SMH52, 4/27/83; #SMH21, SMH30, SMH42, SMH56, 10/23/84; #SMH18, 1/7/86; #SMH19, 1/24/86; #SMH31, SMH57, 4/29/86; #SMH22, 11/4/86; #SMH34, 1/6/87.

#SMH43, SMH50, SMH53, 1/27/87; #SMH25, 19p, 23p, 32p, 11/8/88; #SMH27, 20p, SMH46, 34p, 1/28/89; #SMH32, SMH44, SMH51, 37p, 12/4/90;

#SMH35, SMH47, SMH54, SMH61, 12/3/91; #SMH36, 9/26/92; #SMH48, 10/92; #SMH62, 11/92; #SMH55, 2/18/93.

Perf. 15x14 Syncopated

1993-96 Litho.

SMH63 19p olive green .90 .30

SMH64 20p brt yel green 1.00 .30

SMH65 25p salmon .90 .40

SMH66 26p brown 1.10 .40

SMH67 30p olive green 2.00 .45

SMH68 37p bright rose lilac 2.00 .55

SMH69 41p drab 1.50 .60

SMH70 63p bright green 3.50 1.00

Issued: 19p, 20p, 30p, 41p, 12/7/93; 20p, 26p, 37p, 63p, 7/23/96.

Queen Design of 1970 with Redrawn Portrait

Perf. 15x14 Syncopated

1997-98 Photo.

SMH75 20p brt yel green .60 .30

SMH76 20p brt yel grn, perf 14 1.75 1.00

SMH79 26p brown .90 .45

SMH80 26p brown, perf 14 2.00 .45

SMH87 37p bright rose lilac 1.50 .65

SMH97 63p bright green 2.00 1.00

Issued: #SMH75, SMH79, 37p, 63p, 7/1/97; #SMH76, SMH80, 10/13/98.

Nos. SMH76, SMH80 issued only in booklets (BK164).

This is an expanding set, numbers may change.

Perf. 13¾x14¼ Syncopated

2000 Photo.

SMH101 1st org red (WMMH96a) .85 .40

Issued: No. SMH96, 2/15/00. No. SMH96 sold for 26p on day of issue and was issued only in booklets.

WALES & MONMOUTHSHIRE

All stamps are Design MA2 unless noted.

Type I

Type II

Two types of dragon:

Type I: Eye is complete with white dot in center. Wing tips, tail and tongue are thin.

Type II: Eye is joined to nose by solid line. Wing tips, tail and tongue are thick.

1971-93 Photo. *Perf. 15x14*

WMMH1 2½p bright pink .20 .20

WMMH2 3p ultra .30 .20

WMMH3 3½p slate .30 .20

WMMH4 4½p dark blue .30 .20

WMMH5 5p brt violet 1.25 1.25

WMMH6 5½p dark violet .30 .20

WMMH7 6½p Prussian blue .30 .20

WMMH8 7p dark red brn .30 .20

WMMH9 7½p chestnut 1.75 2.00

WMMH10 8p red .40 .25

WMMH11 8½p yel grn .40 .25

WMMH12 9p violet blue .40 .25

WMMH13 10p orange brn .40 .30

WMMH14 10½p steel blue .55 .40

WMMH15 11p red .55 .40

WMMH16 11½p gray brn, litho., perf 13½x14 .95 .50

WMMH17 12p yel grn .60 .40

Litho.

WMMH18 12p brt grn 1.50 1.00

WMMH19 12½p lt emer, perf 13½x14 .70 .35

WMMH20 12½p lt emer 5.00 4.00

WMMH21 13p lt red brn, type I .50 .30

a. Type II 2.25

Photo.

WMMH22 13½p brown pur .85 .75

WMMH23 14p gray blue, litho., perf 13½x14 .85 .40

WMMH24 14p dark blue .70 .35

WMMH25 15p deep ultra .70 .50

Litho.

WMMH26 15p bright blue .70 .40

WMMH27 15½p light violet .95 .50

WMMH28 16p brownish gray, perf 13½x14 1.60 1.00

WMMH29 16p brownish gray 1.75 .80

WMMH30 17p blue gray, type I .95 .40

a. Type II 35.00 30.00

WMMH31 17p dark blue .70 .40

WMMH32 18p vio bl, perf 13½x14 1.00 .90

WMMH33 18p olive green 1.00 .40

WMMH34 18p brt yel grn .60 .30

a. Booklet pane of 6 + printed margin (BK156) 3.60

WMMH35 18p brt yel grn, perf 13½x14 5.00 4.00

WMMH36 19p red orange .70 .40

WMMH37 19½p ol gray, perf 13½x14 2.00 2.00

WMMH38 20p brown black .70 .50

WMMH39 20½p ultra 3.50 3.50

WMMH40 22p dk bl, perf 13½x14 1.10 1.00

WMMH41 22p yel grn .95 .60

WMMH42 22p orange red .85 .60

WMMH43 23p brt yel grn 1.00 .60

WMMH44 24p brown red .95 .70

WMMH45 24p brown .90 .40

a. Booklet pane of 6 + printed margin (BK156) 5.50

WMMH46 24p brown, perf 13½x14 3.25 3.25

WMMH47 26p red, type I, perf 13½x14 1.00 .80

WMMH48 26p red, type II 4.75 2.50

WMMH49 26p olive gray 1.25 .70

WMMH50 28p dp vio bl, type I, perf 13½x14 1.40 .80

WMMH51 28p dp vio bl, type II 1.25 .70

WMMH52 28p dull bl grn 1.40 .50

WMMH53 31p brt rose lil 1.25 .90

WMMH54 32p Prus blue 1.50 .90

WMMH55 34p dull bl grn 1.50 .90

WMMH56 37p scarlet 1.75 .90

WMMH57 39p brt rose lil 1.75 .65

Issued: #WMMH1, 3p, 5p, WMMH9, 7/7/71; #WMMH3, WMMH6, 8p, 1/23/74; #WMMH4, 11/6/74; #WMMH7, WMMH11, 1/14/76; 10p, 11p, 10/20/76.

7p, 9p, #WMMH14, 1/18/78; #WMMH17, WMMH22, WMMH25, 7/23/80; #WMMH16, #WMMH23, WMMH32, WMMH40, 4/8/81; #WMMH19, WMMH27, WMMH37, WMMH47, 2/24/82; #WMMH28, WMMH39, WMMH50, 4/27/83; #WMMH20, WMMH29, 1/10/84.

139, #WMMH30, WMMH41, 31p, 10/23/84; #WMMH18, 1/7/86; #WMMH33, 1/6/87; #WMMH48, WMMH51, 1/27/87; #WMMH24, 19p, 23p, 32p, 8/11/88; #WMMH26, 20p, WMMH44, 34p, 11/28/89.

#WMMH31, WMMH42, WMMH49, 37p, 12/4/90; #WMMH34, WMMH45, WMMH52, 39p, 12/3/91; #WMMH46, 9/14/92; #WMMH35, 1/12/93.

Perf. 15x14 Syncopated

1993-96 Litho.

WMMH58 19p olive green .75 .30

WMMH59 20p brt yel grn 1.10 .30

WMMH60 25p salmon .75 .40

WMMH61 26p brown 1.25 .40

WMMH62 30p olive green .90 .45

WMMH63 37p bright rose lilac 1.50 .55

WMMH64 41p drab 1.50 .65

WMMH65 63p bright green 3.00 1.00

Issued: 19p, 25p, 30p, 41p, 12/7/93. 20p, 26p, 37p, 63p, 7/23/96.

Queen Design of 1970 with Redrawn Portrait

"P" Removed

Perf. 15x14 Syncopated

1997-98 Photo.

WMMH70 20p brt yel grn .75 .30

WMMH71 20p brt yel grn, perf 14 2.00 .30

WMMH74 26p brown .90 .45

WMMH75 26p brown, perf 14 2.00 .45

WMMH82 37p bright rose lilac 1.50 .65

WMMH92 63p brt yel grn 2.00 1.00

Issued: #WMMH70, WMMH74, 37p, 63p, 7/1/97; #WMMH71, WMMH75, 10/13/98.

Nos. WMMH71, WMMH75 issued only in booklets (BK164).

This is an expanding set, numbers may change.

Perf. 13¾x14¼ Syncopated

2000 Photo.

WMMH96 1st orange red .85 .40

a. Bklt. pane, 3 ea #NIMH96, SMH101, WMMH96 (BK167) 7.75

Issued: No. WMMH96, 2/15/00. No. WMMH96 sold for 26p on day of issue and was issued only in booklets.

See Isle of Man #8-11 for additional Machin Head definitives.

BOOKLETS

Booklets are listed in denomination sequence by reign. Numbers in parenthesis following each listing reflect the number of cover varieties or edition numbers that apply to each cover style.

Values shown for complete booklets are for examples containing most panes having full perforations on two edges of the pane only. Booklets containing most or all panes with very fine, full perforations on all sides are scarce and will sell for more. Also, in booklets where most of the value is contained in only one pane of several, it is assumed that this pane has full perforations on two sides only. If this pane is very fine, the booklet will be worth a considerable premium over the value given.

This section does not contain complete booklets consisting solely of self-adhesive stamps. These are catalogued as minors under stamp listings.

Sterling Currency

BC1

1904

BK1 BC1 2sh ½p *red*, 4 #128e 160.00

1906-11

BK2 BC1 2sh *red*, 2 #128e, 3 #143c, #143b 650.00

BK3 BC1 2sh *red*, 3 #128e, 1 each #143b-143c (4) 750.00

Cover inscription on Nos. BK2-BK3 revised to reflect changed contents.

1911

BK4 BC1 2sh *red*, 2#151a, 3 #152a 350.00

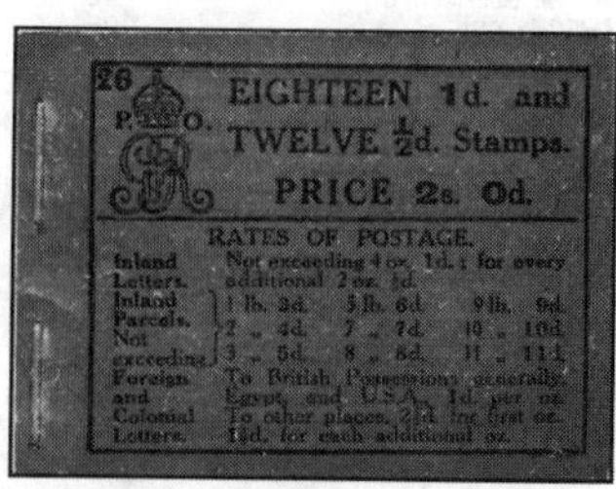

BC2

1912-13

BK5 BC2 2sh *red*, 2 #151a, 3 #152a 450.00

BK6 BC2 2sh *red*, 2 #155a, 3 #156a (4) 600.00

Cover inscription on Nos. BK5-BK6 shows only Inland Postage Rates.

1913

BK7 BC2 2sh *red*, 2 #159b, 3 #160a (35) 225.00

BK8 BC2 2sh *org*, 2 #159b,3 #160a (20) 275.00

BC3

1917

BK9 BC3 2sh *org,* 2 #159b, 3 #160a (17) 290.00

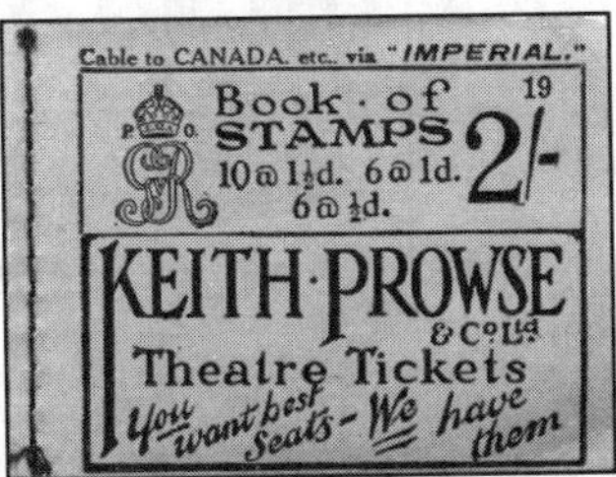

BC4

1924-34

BK10 BC4 2sh *blue,* #159b, 160a, 161d-161e (2) 725.00
BK11 BC4 2sh *blue,* #187b, 188b, 189c-189d (277) 225.00

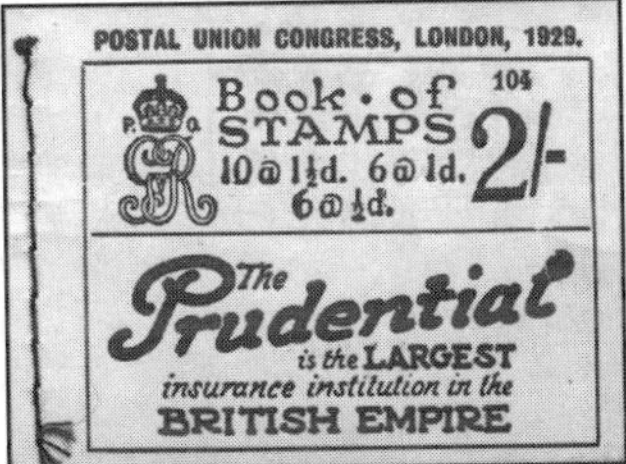

BC5

1929

BK12 BC5 2sh blue, *buff,* #205b-207b, 207c 250.00

1935

BK13 BC4 2sh *blue,* #210b-211b, 212c-212d (58) 160.00

BC6

1935

BK14 BC6 2sh blue, *buff,* #226a-227a, 3 #228a 45.00

1918-19

BK15 BC4 3sh *org,* 2 each #159b, 160a, 161d (11) 325.00
BK16 BC4 3sh *org,* #159b, 160a, 3 #161d (15) 325.00

Cover used for Nos. BK15-BK16 does not have inscription above top line.

1921

BK17 BC4 3sh *blue,* 3 #162b (3) 425.00
BK18 BC4 3sh *blue,* 3 #162c (3) 375.00

1922

BK19 BC4 3sh *scar,* #159b, 160a, 3 #161d (33) 325.00
BK20 BC4 3sh *blue,* 4 #161d (2) 375.00

1924-34

BK21 BC4 3sh *scar,* #187b-188b, 3 #189c (237) 110.00

1929

BK22 BC5 3sh blue, *buff,* #205b-206b, 3 #207b (5) 300.00

1935

BK23 BC4 3sh *scar,* #210b-211b, 3 #212c (27) 175.00
BK24 BC6 3sh red, *buff,* #226a-227a, 5 #228a (4) 50.00

1920

BK25 BC4 3sh6p *org,* #160a, 3 #162b (6) 375.00

Cover used for No. BK25 does not have inscription above top line.

1921

BK26 BC4 3sh6p *org red,* #159b, 160a, 161d, 2 #162b (7) 375.00
BK27 BC4 3sh6p *org red,* #159b, 160a, 161d, 2 #162c (13) 375.00

1931-35

BK28 BC4 5sh *grn,* #187b-188b, 189d, 5 #189c 1,650.
BK29 BC4 5sh *buff,* #187b-188b, 189d, 5 #189c (7) 525.00
BK30 BC4 5sh *buff,* #210b-211b, 212d, 5 #212c (7) 125.00

BC7

1936

BK31 BC7 6p *buff,* 2 #232c 35.00

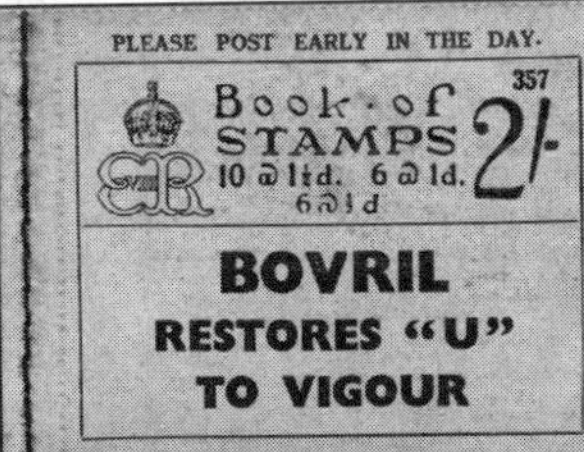

BC8

BK32 BC8 2sh *blue,* #230a-231a, #232a-232b (31) 60.00
BK33 BC8 3sh *scar,* #230a-231a, 3 #232a (12) 50.00
BK34 BC8 5sh *buff,* #230a-231a, 6 #232a (2) 125.00

1938-40

BK35 BC7 6p *buff,* 2 #237d 25.00
BK36 BC7 6p *pink,* #235d-237d 150.00
BK37 BC7 6p *pale grn,* #235c-236c 65.00

No. BK37 is 53x41mm.

1947-51

BK38 BC7 1sh *buff,* 2 ea #258b-259b, 260a 15.00
BK39 BC7 1sh *buff,* 2 ea #280a, 281b-282b 15.00
BK40 BC7 1sh *buff,* #258e, 259d, 260b 3,000.
BK41 BC7 1sh *buff,* #280b-282b 15.00

Nos. BK40-BK41 are 53x41mm.

Round GPO Emblem — BC9

1952-53

BK42 BC9 1sh *buff,* #280b, 281c-282c 11.00
a. Inland postage rate corrected in ink on inside booklet cover 13.00

Oval GPO Emblem — BC10

1954

BK43 BC10 1sh *buff,* #280b, 281c-282c 17.50

1937

BK44 BC8 2sh *blue,* #235b-236b, #237b-237c (26) 225.00

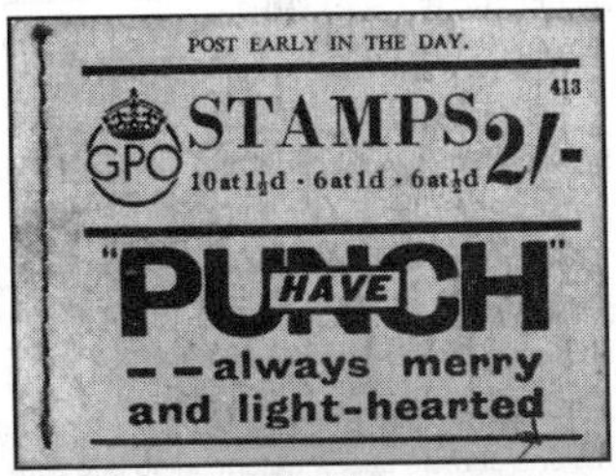

BC11

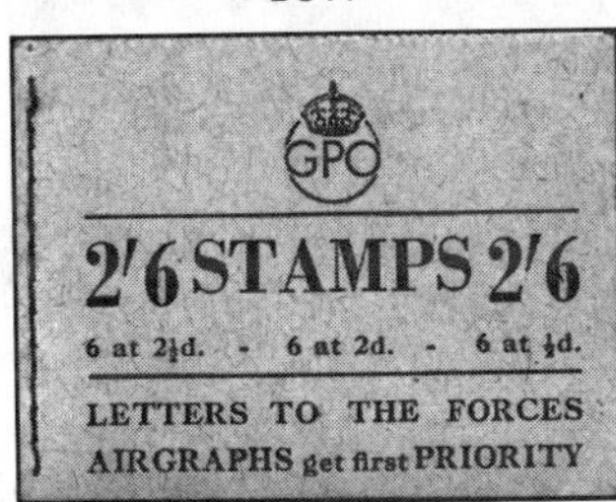

BC12

1938

BK45 BC11 2sh *blue,* #235b-236b, #237b-237c (95) 225.00

1940-42

2sh6p Booklets

BK46 BC11 *scar,* #235b, #238b-239b (7) 550.00
BK47 BC11 *blue,* #235b, #238b-239b (6) 550.00

Denomination part of cover of Nos. BK46-BK47 is printed in white on black background.

BK48 BC11 *grn,* #235b, #238b-239b (80) 225.00
BK49 BC11 *grn,* #258a, #261b-262b (120) 275.00

1943

BK50 BC12 *grn,* #258a, #261b-262b (90) 25.00

With booklets issued in August and September 1943, commercial advertising on British booklets was discontinued. Covers and interleaving were used for Post Office slogans. Booklets were no longer numbered, but carried the month and year of issue.

1951-52

BK51 BC12 *grn,* #280c, #283b-284b (10) 20.00
BK52 BC12 *grn,* #280c, 281e, #282d, 284b (15) 20.00

1937-38

3sh Booklets

BK53 BC8 *scar,* #235a-236a, 3 #237b (10) 400.00
BK54 BC11 *scar,* #235a-236a, 3 #237b (34) 400.00

1937-43

5sh Booklets

BK55 BC8 *buff,* #235b-236b, 237c, 5 #237b (3) 450.00
BK56 BC11 *buff,* #235b-236b, 237c, 5 #237b (9) 425.00
BK57 BC11 *buff,* #235b, 238b, 3 #239b (16) 425.00
BK58 BC11 *buff,* #258a, 261b, 3 #262b (20) 425.00

1943-53

BK59 BC12 *tan,* #258a, 261b, 3 #262b (49) 50.00
BK60 BC12 *tan,* #258a, 261b, 3 #262b (20) 500.00

Cover on No. BK60 has thick horizontal lines separating the GPO emblem and the various inscriptions.

BK61 BC12 *tan,* #280a, 283b, 3 #284b (5) 30.00
BK62 BC12 *tan,* #280c, 281e, 282d, 3 #284b (5) 22.50
BK63 BC12 *tan,* #280c, 281d-282d, 283b, 2 #284b (2) 30.00

BC13

1953-54

2sh6p Booklets

BK64 BC12 *grn,* #280c, 281e, 294c, #296a (6) 15.00
BK65 BC13 *grn,* #280c, 281e, 294c, 296a (7) 22.50
BK66 BC13 *grn,* #281e, 292c, 294c, 296a 425.00

5sh Booklets

BK67 BC12 *brn,* #280c, 281d, 283b, 294c, 2 #296a (3) 18.00
BK68 BC13 *brn,* #280c, 281d, 283b, 294c, 2 #296a (2) 20.00
BK69 BC13 *brn,* #281d, 283b, 292c, 294c, 2 #296a 150.00
BK70 BC13 *brn,* #283b, 292c-294c, 2 #296a 70.00

1953-57

1sh Booklets

BK71 BC7 *buff,* 2 each #292a-294a 3.25
BK72 BC7 *buff,* 2 each #317d, 318f, 319f 9.00

1954-59

BK73 BC10 *buff,* #292b-294b (2) 4.50
BK74 BC10 *buff,* #317b, 318c, 319b (3) 4.00
BK75 BC10 *buff,* #353b-355b (2) 4.75

1959

2sh Booklets

BK76 BC10 *salmon,* #317b, 318c, 319b, 322b 5.00

BC14

1960-65

2sh Booklets

BK77 BC14 *sal,* #353b-355b, 358b 3.50
BK77A BC14 *pale yel,* 353b-355b, 358b 4.75
BK78 BC14 red, *pale yel,* #353e, 2 #357g 4.00
a. White stiching 4.00
BK79 BC14 *pale yel,* #353b-355b, 358b (17) 17.00
a. #353bp-355bp, 358bp (13) 40.00

BK80 BC14 red, *pale yel,* 4 #353g 1.50
BK81 BC14 *org yel,* #354f, 359c (7) 3.00
a. #354fp, 359cp (12) 10.50
BK82 BC14 red, *org yel,* 2 #358b .60

1968-69

BK83 BC14 *org yel,* #MH5b, MH6b (3) 1.00
BK84 BC14 *gray,* #MH6a-MH6b (5) 1.00
BK85 BC14 *gray,* #MH7a-MH7b (12) 1.25

1954, Mar.

2sh6p Booklets

BK86 BC13 *grn,* #292c, 293d, 294c, 296a (19) 16.00

No. BK86 inscribed Apr. 1954 through Aug. 1955 are valued. Booklet inscribed Mar. 1954 is valued at $200.

No. BK86 inscribed Aug. 1955 through Nov. 1955, may contain one or more panes watermarked 308 substituted for those listed. Value $50.

1955, Dec.

BK87 BC13 *grn,* #317a, 318b, 319a, 321a (16) 16.00

No. BK87 inscribed Dec. 1955 through June 1956 may contain one or more panes watermarked 298 substituted for those listed. Value $15.

1957

BK88 BC13 *grn,* #317a, 320b, 321a (9) 15.00

3sh Booklets

1958, Jan.

BK89 BC13 *red,* #317a, 318b, 319a, 322a (9) 13.50

No. BK89 inscribed Nov. 1958, may contain one or more panes watermarked 322 substituted for those listed. Value $13.

1958, Dec.-59

BK90 BC13 *red,* #353a-355a, 358a (5) 14.00
a. #353d, 354d, 355d, 358d (2) 150.00

No. BK90 dated Dec. 1958, may contain one or more panes watermarked 308 substituted for those listed. Value $14.

BK91 BC13 *brick red,* #353a-355a, 358a (14) 13.00
a. #353d, 354d, 355d, 358d (4) 200.00
b. #353ap, 354ap, 355ap, 358ap (2) 28.00

BC15

1960

BK92 BC15 *brick red,* #353a-355a, 358a (46) 14.00
a. #353ap-355ap, 358ap (35) 30.00

3sh9p Booklets

1953, Nov.

BK93 BC13 *red,* 3 #296a (10) 15.00

No. BK93 inscribed Oct. or Dec. 1955 may contain one or more panes watermarked 308 substituted for those listed. Value $16.

1956, Feb.

BK94 BC13 *red,* 3 #321a (10) 9.00

1957, Oct.-Dec. 1960

4sh6p Booklets

BK95 BC13 *dull mauve,* 3 #322a (7) 10.00
BK96 BC13 *dull mauve,* 3 #358a 25.00
BK97 BC14 *dull mauve,* 3 #358a (4) 10.00
a. 3 #358d 12.00
BK98 BC14 *pale reddish lil,* 3 #358a (9) 10.00
a. 3 #358d (4) 11.00
b. 3 #358ap 22.00
BK99 BC15 *pale reddish lil,* 3 #358a (36) 12.50
a. 3 #358ap (31) 35.00

1965

BK100 BC15 *slate bl,* #354a, 2 #359b (7) 7.50
a. #354ap, 2 #359bp (13) 10.00

1968

BK101 BC15 *slate bl,* #MH2a, 2 #MH6c 6.50

Ship with GPO Emblem — BC16

1968-70

4sh6p Booklets

BK102 BC16 *blue,* #MH2a, 2 #MH6c (3) 2.00
BK103 BC16 *blue,* #MH2a, 2 #MH7c (9) 2.00

Ship Type with St. Edward's Crown instead of GPO emblem

BK104 BC16 *blue,* #MH2a, 2 #MH7c (2) 4.50

5sh Booklets

1954, Mar.

BK105 BC13 *brn,* #292c-294c, 295a-296a (10) 26.00

No. BK105 inscribed Sept. 1955 may contain one or more panes watermarked 308 substituted for those listed. Value $16.

1955, Nov.

BK106 BC13 *brn,* #317a, 318b, 319a, 320b, 321a (14) 15.00

No. BK106 inscribed Nov. 1955, Jan. 1956 or May 1956 may contain one or more panes watermarked 298 substituted for those listed. Value $17.

1958

BK107 BC13 *brn,* #317a, 318b, 321a, 2 #322a (5) 15.00

No. BK107 inscribed July or Nov. 1958 may contain one or more panes watermarked 322 substituted for those listed. Value $15.

1959, Jan.

BK108 BC14 *bl,* #353a-354a, 357c, 2 #358a (11) 15.00
a. #353d-354d, 357e, 2 #358d (3) 60.00
b. #353ap-354ap, 357cp, 2 #358ap 40.00

No. BK108 inscribed Jan. 1959 may contain one or more panes watermarked 308 substituted for those listed. Value $15.

1961, Jan.

BK109 BC15 *bl,* #353a-354a, 357c, 2 #358a (27) 16.00
a. #353ap-354ap, 357cp, 2 #358ap (24) 57.50

House with GPO Emblem — BC17

1968-70

BK110 BC17 *org brn,* 2 #MH8a (5) 2.50

House Type with St. Edward's Crown instead of GPO Emblem

BK111 BC17 5sh *org brn,* 2 #MH8a (7) 1.75

BC18

1970

BK112 BC18 *org brn,* 2 #MH8a 1.75

6sh Booklets

1965

BK113 BC15 *claret,* 3 #359b (23) 13.00
a. 3 #359bp (27) 16.00

1967

BK114 BC15 *claret,* 3 #MH6c (10) 27.50

Bird with GPO Emblem — BC19

1968-70

BK115 BC19 *org,* 3 #MH6c (8) 2.00
BK116 BC19 *org,* 3 #MH7c (5) 2.00

Bird Type with St. Edward's Crown instead of GPO Emblem

BK117 BC19 *org,* 3 #MH7c (5) 4.00

1961-67

10sh Booklets

BK118 BC15 *grn,* #353a-355a, 356b, 5 #358a (2) 40.00
BK119 BC15 *gray grn,* #354a-355a, 357c, 5 #358a (7) 30.00
BK120 BC15 *tan,* #354a, 358a, 4 #359b (5) 12.00
a. #354ap, 358ap, 4 #359bp (3) 6.00

Explorers with GPO Emblem — BC20

1968-70

BK121 BC20 *pur,* #MH2a, MH5a, 4 #MH6c (2) 6.00

Explorer Type with clear GPO Emblem

BK122 BC20 *yel grn,* #MH6d, 2 ea #MH6c, #MH8a 6.00
BK123 BC20 *yel grn,* #MH7c, MH7e, MH8a (4) 3.50

Explorer Type with St. Edward's Cross instead of GPO Emblem

BK124 BC20 *yel grn,* #MH7e, 2 ea #MH7c, MH8a (2) 7.50

BC21

£1 Booklets

1969

BK125 BC21 multi, 2 #MH7d, MH8b-MH8c 17.50
BK126 BC21 2 #MH7d, MH8b-MH8c, stapled 110.00

Decimal Currency Booklets (Stitched)

BC22

1971-74

BK127 BC22 10p *org yel,* #MH24a, MH26a (21) 2.50

BC23

1974-76

BK128 BC23 10p *org yel,* #MH24a, MH26a (9) 2.50

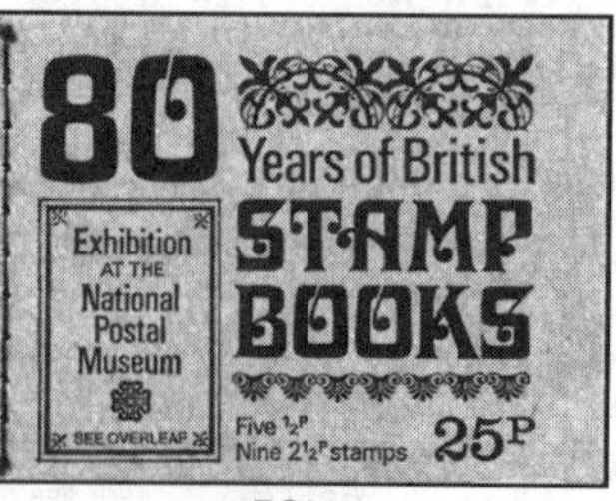

BC24

1971-73

BK129 BC24 25p *dull purple* (12) 5.00

Contents: #MH22a, MH32a-MH32b.

BC25

1971

BK130 BC25 25p *dull purple* 8.25

Contents: #MH22a, MH32a-MH32b.

BK131 BC25 30p *bright pur,* #MH36b 5.75

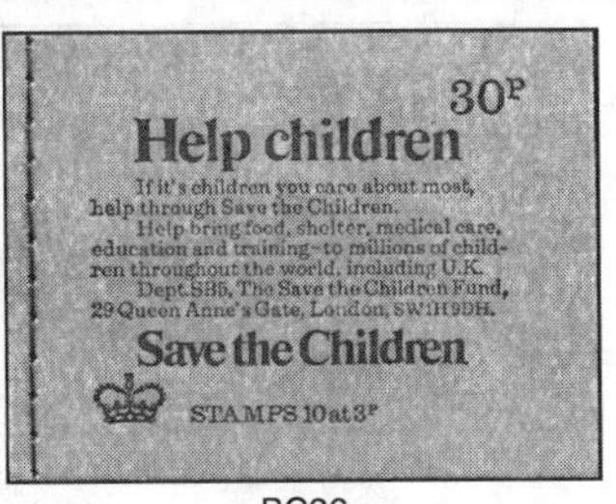

BC26

1973-74
BK132 BC26 25p *dull mauve* 8.00
Contents: #MH22a, MH32a-MH32b.
BK133 BC26 30p *vermilion,* 2 #MH36b 6.00

Bird Type with St. Edward's Crown instead of GPO Emblem

1971-73
BK134 BC19 30p *pur,* 2 #MH36b (16) 5.50
BK135 BC19 30p *buff,* 2 #MH36b 8.25

BC27

1973-74
BK136 BC27 30p *red,* 2 #MH36b 6.00
BK137 BC27 35p *blue,* 2 #MH39a 4.00
BK138 BC27 50p *pale bluish grn* 12.00
Contents: #MH22a, MH32b, MH36a, MH36c (4).
BK139 BC27 50p *pale grn,* MH36b, 2 #MH39a (2) 6.75
BK140 BC27 85p *purple,* #MH39a, 3 #MH49a 10.00

BC28

1973-74
BK141 BC28 35p *bl,* 2 #MH39a (3) 4.25
BK142 BC28 45p *yel brn,* 2 #MH49a (3) 6.75

BC29

1971-72
BK143 BC29 50p *pale bluish green* 11.50
Contents: #MH22a, MH32b, MH36a, MH36c (8).

Prestige Booklets

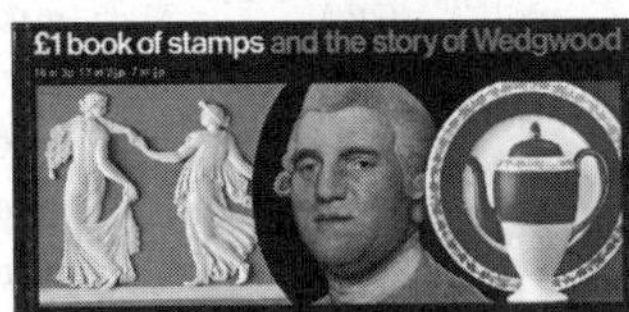

BC30

1972, May 24
BK144 BC30 £1 *Wedgewood* 150.00
Contents: #MH34a-MH34b, #MH36d-MH36e. Valued with a F-VF 1/2p stamp.

BC31

1980, Apr. 16
BK145 BC31 £3 *Wedgwood* 20.00
Contents: #MH26b, MH70a, MH78a-MH78b.

1982, May 19
BK146 £4 *Stanley Gibbons* 20.00
Contents: #MH80a-MH80b, MH93a-MH93b.

1983, Sept. 14
BK147 £4 *Royal Mint* 19.00
Contents: #MH94a-MH94b, 2 #MH80a.

1984, Sept. 4
BK148 £4 *Christian Heritage* 55.00
Contents: #MH97c-MH97d, 2 #MH83a.

1985, Jan. 8
BK149 £5 *The Times* 50.00
Contents: #MH83b, MH97b-MH97c, MH149a.

1986, Mar. 18
BK150 £5 *British Rail* 50.00
Contents: #MH79a, MH97b-MH97c, MH142a.

1987, Mar. 3
BK151 £5 *P &O* 32.50
Contents: #MH83a-MH83b, MH102a, MH130a.

1988, Feb. 9
BK152 £5 *The Financial Times* 40.00
Contents: #MH84a, MH103a-MH103b, MH150a.

1989, Mar. 21
BK153 £5 *Scots Connection* 22.50
Contents: #SMH25a,SMH37a-SMH37b, SMH45a.

1990, Mar. 20
BK154 £5 *London Life* 37.50
Contents: #1314a, MH196a, 2 #MH193d.

1991, Mar. 19
BK155 £6 *Agatha Christie* 37.50
Contents: #MH121a, MH147a, 2 #MH99a.

1992, Feb. 25
BK156 £6 *Cymru-Wales* 27.50
Contents: #1425a, MH187c, WMMH34a, WMMH45a.

1992, Oct. 27
BK157 £6 *J.R.R. Tolkien* 32.50
Contents: #MH105a, MH187b, 2 #MH127a.

1993, Aug. 10
BK158 £5.64 *Beatrix Potter* 30.00
Although inscribed £6 on the cover, No. BK158 was sold for £5.64, the face value of its contents, which were #1484a, MH178a, MH187a, NIMH45a.

1994, July 26
BK159 £6.04 *N. Ireland* 27.50
Contents: #1550a, MH214a, NIMH63a-NIMH63b, 2 postal cards.

1995, Apr. 25
BK160 £6 *National Trust* 24.00
Contents: #1607a, MH209a, MH231a, NIMH59a.

1996, May 14
BK161 £6.48 *European Soccer Championships* 21.50
Contents: #1663a, 1664a, 1667a, MH214b.

1997, Sept. 23
BK162 £6.15 *75th Anniv. of BBC* 22.50
Contents: #1689a, MH287a, MH257a, NIMH81a.

1998, Mar. 10
BK163 £7.49 *Definitive Portrait* 25.00
Contents: #1801a, 1802a, 1803a-1803b.

1998, Oct. 13
BK164 £6.16 *Breaking Barriers* 20.00
Contents: #1829b, MH269a, MH285a-MH285b.

1999, Feb. 16
BK165 (£7.54) *Profile on Print* 29.00
Contents: #MH241c, MH288a, MH310a-MH312a.

1999, Sept. 21
BK166 (£6.99) *World Changers* 25.00
Contents: #1842b, 1847a, 1868b, 1869b, MH257f.

2000, Feb. 15
BK167 (£7.50) *Special by Design* 25.00
Contents: #MH198b, MH264Bc, MH336b, WMMH96a.

2000, Aug. 4
BK168 (£7.03) *The Life of the Century* 22.50
Contents: #1943e, 1943f, Scotland 18a, MH335b.

2000, Sept. 18
BK169 (£7) *A Treasury of Trees* 22.00
Contents: #1917a, 1918a, 1920a, 1921a, Wales and Monmouthshire 18a.

2001, Oct. 22
BK170 (£6.76) *Unseen and Unheard* 20.00
Contents: #1969b, 1970b, 1999e, Scotland 16a.

2002, Feb. 6
BK171 (£7.23) *A Gracious Accession* 21.50
Contents: #2020a, 2021a, 2023a, MH290b.

2002, Sept. 24
BK172 (£6.83) *Across the Universe* 21.50
Contents: 1939a, 2075e, Scotland 15a, MH290c.

Numbers have been reserved for future prestige booklets.

Decimal Currency Booklets (Folded)

Booklets are listed in denomination sequence in chronological order in this section.

BC32

1976-77
BK225 BC32 10p red, *gray,* #MH58a (3) 1.25

BC33

1978
BK226 BC33 10p brn, *bl,* #MH61b (6) 1.25

1979-80
BK227 BC33 10p *London '80,* #MH64b (2) .75

BC34

1977
BK228 BC34 50p #MH65a 5.25
BK229 BC34 50p #MH67a 3.50

Nos. BK228-BK229, BK230-BK231, BK237-BK238 exist with either version of #MH65a, MH67a, MH70b, MH80c. See the notes following the listings for these panes.

Commercial Vehicles — BC35

1978-95

50p Booklets, Cover BC35

BK230 Commercial Vehicles, #MH67a (6) 3.50
BK231 Commercial Vehicles, #MH70b 2.50
BK232 Veteran Cars, #MH70b 2.50
BK233 Veteran Cars, #MH78d (3) 2.25
BK234 Veteran Cars, #MH86a (2) 2.25
BK235 Follies, #MH86a 2.25
BK236 Follies, #MH76a (2) 7.00
BK237 Follies, #MH80c (4) 3.00
BK238 Rare Farm Animals, #MH80c 3.00
BK239 Rare Farm Animals, #MH80d (4) 7.50
BK240 Orchids, #MH83c (4) 4.75
BK241 Pillar Box, #MH97a 2.50
BK242 Pond Life, #MH97a (2) 2.50

Nos. BK241-BK242 sold for a 1p discount. Some panes have stars on reverse.

BK244 Pond Life, #MH83d (2) 5.00
BK245 Roman Britain, #MH79b 10.00
BK246 Roman Britain, #MH102b (2) 3.50
BK247 Marylebone Cricket Club, #MH102b (4) 3.50
BK248 Botanical Gardens, #MH83d (2) 5.00
BK248A Botanical Gardens, #MH83g (2) 5.00
BK249 London Zoo, #MH102b (2) 3.50
BK250 London Zoo, #MH83g 5.00
BK251 Marine Life, #MH83g 5.00
BK252 Marine Life, #MH106a 3.75
BK253 Gilbert & Sullivan Operas, #MH106a (3) 3.75
BK254 Aircraft, #MH115a 7.00
BK255 Aircraft, #MH193a 7.00
BK256 Aircraft, #MH98a (2) 5.00
BK257 Archaeology, #MH126a (4) 3.00
BK258 Sheriff's Millennium, #MH126a 2.50
BK259 Postal History, #MH126a (3) 2.00
BK260 Postal History, #MH213a 2.00
BK261 Coaching Inns, #MH213a (4) 2.00
BK262 Sea Charts, #MH213a (4) 2.00

With Window — BC36

Without Window — BC37

1987

BK285 BC36 52p #MH83e 3.00

1988-89

BK295 BC36 56p #MH87a (2) 5.00
BK296 BC37 56p #MH87b 5.00
BK297 BC37 56p #MH87c 30.00

1990

BK307 BC37 60p #MH191a 7.50

1976-77

BK317 BC34 65p 10 #MH60 7.00
BK325 BC34 70p 10 #MH61 5.00

Nos. BK317, BK325-BK327, BK370, BK394, BK404-BK405, BK467-BK468, BK488-BK492, BK513-BK514, BK524-BK533, BK554-BK557, BK573-BK574, BK584, BK594, BK616-BK618, BK631, BK641, BK651-BK652, BK673-BK675, BK696-BK699, BK709-BK713, BK715-BK718, BK728, BK732-BK733 exist with stamps affixed to cover by selvage at either right or left edges of block or pane of stamps.

BC38

1978-79

70p Booklets

BK326 BC38 Country Crafts, 10 #MH61 (6) 5.00
BK327 BC38 Derby Mechanized Letter Office, 10 #MH61 7.00

1987

BK338 BC36 72p red, yel & blk, #MH102c 3.50

1988-89

BK348 BC36 76p #MH106c (2) 6.00
BK349 BC37 76p #MH106d 6.00
BK350 BC37 76p #MH106e 30.00

BC39

1992

BK360 BC39 78p 2 #MH157 4.00

Cover of #BK360 does not show the numeral four. Contents of #BK360 is 1/2 of #MH157a, the right hand vertical pair of stamps being removed.

1979

BK370 BC38 80p Military Aircraft, 10 #MH64 3.00

1990

BK371 BC37 80p red, yel & blk, #MH193b 10.00
BK372 BC37 80p red, yel & blk, #MH194a 7.50

1976-79

BK382 BC34 85p gray & ol grn, 10 #MH65 7.00
BK392 BC34 90p lt & dk bl, 10 #MH67 5.00
BK393 BC38 90p British Canals, 10 #MH67 (6) 6.00
BK394 BC38 90p Derby Letter Office, 10 #MH67 10.00

1979-95

£1 Booklets

BK403 BC38 Industrial Archaeology, 10 #MH70 4.00
BK404 BC38 Military Aircraft, 10 #MH70 (3) 4.00
BK405 BC35 Violin, 6 #MH97 5.00
BK406 BC35 Musical Instruments, #MH102d (2) 6.00
BK407 BC35 Sherlock Holmes, #MH102d (2) 6.00
BK408 BC35 Sherlock Holmes, #MH102f (2) 6.00
BK409 BC35 London Zoo, #MH102f 6.00
BK410 BC35 Oliver Twist, #MH102f 8.00
BK411 BC35 Nicholas Nickleby, #MH106b (2) 8.00
BK412 BC35 Great Expectations, #MH108a 10.00
BK413 BC35 Marine Life, #MH106b 8.00
BK414 BC35 Wicken Fen, #MH115b 8.00
BK415 BC35 Click Mill, #MH193c 8.00
BK416 BC35 Wicken Fen, #MH194b 8.00
BK417 BC35 Jack & Jill Mills, #MH120a (2) 5.00
BK418 BC35 Punch Magazine, #MH126b (4) 4.00
BK419 BC35 Sheriff's Millennium, #MH126b 4.25
BK420 BC35 Educational Institutions, #MH128a (3) 4.25
BK421 BC35 Educational Institutions, 4 #MH214 3.75
BK422 BC35 Prime Ministers, 4 #MH214 3.75
BK423 BC35 Prime Ministers, 4 #MH213 (3) 3.50
BK424 BC35 End of World War II, 4 #MH213 (4) 3.50

BC40

1996-2000

BK425 BC40 £1 multi, 4 #MH214 3.75
BK426 BC40 £1 multi, #MH216b 3.25
BK427 BC40 £1 multi, #MH257b 4.00
BK428 BC40 £1 multi, #MH257d 3.50
BK429 BC40 £1 #MH288d 3.25

1987-88

£1.04 Booklet

BK446 BC36 #MH131a 24.00

£1.08 Booklets

BK456 BC36 #MH133a 15.00
BK457 BC37 #MH133b 30.00

1981

£1.15 Booklets

BK467 BC38 Military Aircraft, 10 #MH76 (2) 4.50
BK468 BC38 Museums, 10 #MH76 (2) 4.50

1989

£1.16 Booklet

BK478 BC37 multi, #MH140a 25.00

1980-86

£1.20 Booklets

BK488 BC38 Industrial Archaeology, 10 #MH78 (3) 4.00
BK489 BC38 Pillar Box, 10 #MH79 6.00
BK490 BC38 National Gallery, 10 #MH79 6.00
BK491 BC38 Handwriting, 10 #MH79 6.00
BK492 BC38 Christmas, 10 #MH83 10.00

No. BK492 was sold at a discount. Each stamp has a blue double-line star printed on reverse.

BC41

1998

£1.20 Booklet

BK493 BC41 multi, 4 #MH259 3.75

1990

£1.24 Booklet

BK503 BC39 multi, #MH144a 7.00

1982-83

£1.25 Booklets

BK513 BC38 Museums, 10 #MH81 (4) 4.00
BK514 BC38 Railway Engines, 10 #MH81 (5) 5.00

1981-88

£1.30 Booklets

BK524 BC38 Postal History, #MH86b (2) 7.00
BK525 BC38 Trams, 10 #MH83 (4) 5.00
BK526 BC38 Books for Children, 10 #MH83 5.00
BK527 BC38 Keep in Touch, 10 #MH83 5.00
BK528 BC38 Ideas for your Garden, 10 #MH83 5.00
BK529 BC38 Brighter Writer, 10 #MH83 5.00
BK530 BC38 Jolly Postman, 10 #MH83 5.00
BK531 BC38 Linnean Society, 10 #MH83 5.00
BK532 BC38 Recipe Cards, 10 #MH83 5.00
BK533 BC38 Party Pack, 10 #MH83 5.00
BK534 BC36 red, yel & blk, #MH83f 6.00

1991

£1.32 Booklet

BK544 BC39 multi, #MH148a 5.00

1981-89

£1.40 Booklets

BK554 BC38 Industrial Archaeology, 10 #MH86 (2) 5.50
BK555 BC38 Women's Costumes, 10 #MH86 (2) 5.50
BK556 BC38 Pocket Planner, 10 #MH87 4.50
BK557 BC38 William Henry Fox Talbot, 10 #MH87 4.50

1988-95

£1.40 Booklets

BK558 BC36 #MH87d 5.50
BK559 BC36 10 #MH88 16.50
BK560 BC37 #MH87e 10.00
BK561 BC37 10 #MH88 16.50
BK562 BC39 4 #MH223 6.00
BK563 BC41 4 #MH223 (2) 6.00

1982

£1.43 Booklets

BK572 BC38 James Chalmers, #MH93d 6.00
BK573 BC38 Postal History, #MH93c (4) 6.00
BK574 BC38 Holiday Postcard Stamp Book, #MH93c 6.00

1983

£1.45 Booklet

BK584 BC38 Britain's Countryside, 10 #MH94 5.50

Stamps in #BK584 have double-lined D printed on reverse.

1983

£1.46 Booklet

BK594 BC38 Postal History, #MH94c (4) 12.00

BC42

1996-97

£1.48 Booklets

BK605	BC41	#MH226a (2)	4.50
BK606	BC42	4 #MH264	4.50

1986-90

£1.50 Booklets

BK616	BC38	*Pillar Box*, #MH97e	7.00
BK617	BC38	*National Gallery*, #MH97e	7.00
BK618	BC38	*Handwriting*, #MH97e	7.00
BK619	BC37	#MH190a	7.50
BK620	BC37	#MH191b	12.00
BK621	BC37	#MH192a	11.00

1999

£1.52 Booklet

BK630	BC41	4 #MH264A	5.00

1985

£1.53 Booklet

BK631	BC38	*Royal Mail, 350th Anniv.*, 10 #1111	6.00

1984

£1.54 Booklet

BK641	BC38	*Postal History*, #MH97f (4)	6.00

1982-85

£1.55 Booklets

BK651	BC38	*Women's Costumes*, 10 #MH93 (4)	6.00
BK652	BC38	*Social Letter Writing*, 10 #MH97	6.00

No. BK652 sold for a 15p discount. Panes have double-lined "D" printed on reverse.

1991

£1.56 Booklet

BK662	BC39	#MH157a	6.50

1978-2000

£1.60 Booklets

BK672	BC38	*Christmas*, #MH67b	6.50
BK673	BC38	*Birthday Box*, 10 #MH97 (2)	5.50
BK674	BC38	*Britain's Countryside*, 10 #MH94	5.50
BK675	BC38	*Write It*, 10 #MH97	5.50
BK676	BC41	#MH266a	5.00

1993-96

£1.64 Booklets

BK685	BC39	#MH231b	10.00
BK686	BC41	#MH231b (2)	10.00

1984-86

£1.70 Booklets

BK696	BC38	*Love Letters*, 10 #MH97 (2)	5.50
BK697	BC38	*Pillar Box*, 10 #MH97 (2)	5.50
BK698	BC38	*National Gallery*, 10 #MH97	5.50
BK699	BC38	*Handwriting*, 10 #MH97	5.50

1979-88

£1.80 Booklets

BK709	BC38	*Christmas*, #MH70c	6.25
BK710	BC38	*Books for Children*, 10 #MH102	7.50
BK711	BC38	*Keep in Touch*, 10 #MH102	7.50
BK712	BC38	*Ideas for your Garden*, 10 #MH102	7.50
BK713	BC38	*Brighter Writer*, 10 #MH102	7.50
BK714	BC36	red, yel & blk, #MH102e	8.50
BK715	BC38	*Jolly Postman*, 10 #MH102	7.50
BK716	BC38	*Linnean Society*, 10 #MH102	7.50
BK717	BC38	*Recipe Cards*, 10 #MH102	7.50
BK718	BC38	*Party Pack*, 10 #MH102	7.50

1988-89

£1.90 Booklets

BK728	BC38	*Pocket Planner*, 10 #MH106	8.00
BK729	BC36	red, yel & blk, #MH106f	6.50
BK730	BC37	#MH106g	10.00
BK731	BC37	10 #MH107	12.00
BK732	BC38	*William Henry Fox Talbot*, 10 #MH106	6.50

BC43

1989

£1.90 Booklet

BK733	BC43	*Greetings*, #1247a	25.00

Artwork for #BC43 spanned six booklet covers. Only portions of the design appear on each cover.

Value is for pane with perfs guillotined. Value for booklet with pane having full perfs is approximately 60% more.

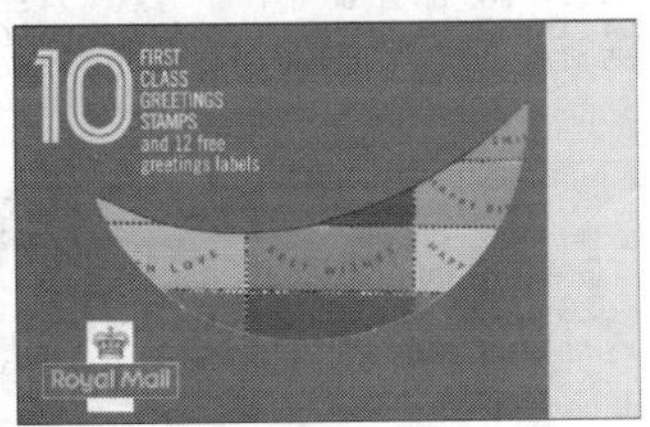

BC44

1990

£2 Booklets

BK742	BC44	#1313a	30.00
BK743	BC37	#MH193e	12.00
BK744	BC37	#MH194c	12.00
BK745	BC37	#MH195a	20.00
BK746	BC35	*Postal Vehicles*, 8 #MH213 (3)	7.00
BK747	BC35	*Rowland Hill*, 8 #MH213 (4)	7.00
BK748	BC40	8 #MH214	7.00
BK749	BC40	#MH216a	6.25

1998-2000

BK751	BC40	#MH257c	6.50
BK752	BC40	#MH257e	6.50
BK753	BC40	#MH288e	6.25

1980-93

£2.20 Booklets

BK759	BC38	*Christmas*, #MH78c	9.00
BK760	BC38	*Christmas*, 20 #MH80	8.00

£2.30 Booklet

BK770	BC38	*Christmas*, 20 #1088	8.00

£2.40 Booklet

BK780	BC38	*Christmas*, 20 #1124	7.00

Stamps in #BK760, BK770, BK780 have double-line star printed on reverse over gum.

BC45

1994-95

£2.40 Booklets

BK790	BC39	#MH234a (2)	7.00
BK791	BC41	#MH234a (2)	7.00
BK792	BC45	#1638a	7.75

1981-94

£2.50 Booklets

BK802	BC38	*Christmas*, #MH93e	10.00

No. BK802 was sold for a 30p discount. Stamps in #BK802 have a 10-point single-line blue star printed on reverse over gum.

BK803	BC45	*Santa, Reindeer*, 10 #1529	7.50
BK804	BC45	*Christmas Play Props*, 10 #1582	8.00
BK805	BC45	*Christmas Robin*, 10 #1635	8.00

1996-97

£2.52 Booklet

BK815	BC41	#MH236a (3)	8.00

1981

£2.55 Booklet

BK826	BC38	*Christmas*, #MH86c	11.00

1999

£2.56 Booklet

BK827	BC41	4 #MH276	8.00

2000

£2.60 Booklet

BK830	BC41	#MH277a	8.50

1990-95

£3.40 Booklet

BK836	BC45	*Snowman*, #1340a	13.00

£3.60 Booklets

BK846	BC45	*Holly*, #1416a	12.00
BK847	BC45	*Santa, Reindeer*, #1468a	11.00

£3.80 Booklets

BK857	BC45	*Santa, Reindeer*, #1528a	11.00
BK858	BC45	*Christmas Play Props*, #1581a	12.00
BK859	BC45	*Christmas Robin*, #1634a	12.00

No-Value Indicated Booklets

BC46

1989-2000

BK960	BC37	(56p)	#MH179a	10.00
BK961	BC37	(60p)	#MH177a	30.00
BK962	BC39	(60p)	#MH182a	4.00
BK963	BC39	(68p)	#MH179b	5.00
BK964	BC46	(72p)	#MH179b	4.00
BK965	BC39	(72p)	4 #MH238	4.00
BK966	BC39	(72p)	4#MH239	4.00
BK967	BC41	(76p)	4 #MH238	4.00
BK968	BC41	(76p)	4 #MH239 (2)	4.00
BK969	BC41	(80p)	4 #MH284 (2)	2.50
BK994	BC37	(76p)	#MH184a	10.00
BK995	BC37	(80p)	#MH183a	40.00
BK996	BC39	(80p)	#MH188a (2)	4.00
BK997	BC46	(96p)	#MH188a	4.00
BK998	BC39	(96p)	4 #MH240	2.75
BK999	BC39	(96p)	4 #MH241	2.75
BK1000	BC39	(£1)	#MH241b	6.50
BK1001	BC41	(£1)	4 #MH241 (4)	4.00
BK1002	BC41	(£1)	#MH241b (4)	6.50

(£1.04) Booklets

BK1003	BC41	4 #MH288	4.00
BK1004	BC41	#MH241b	6.50
BK1005	BC41	4 #MH288	4.00
BK1006	BC41	4 #MH288+label	4.00

(£1.20) Booklet

BK1010	BC41	#MH290a	4.00

(£1.40) Booklets

BK1028	BC37	#MH177b	15.00
BK1029	BC37	10 #MH178	10.00

(£1.50) Booklets

BK1030	BC39	#MH180a	8.50
BK1031	BC39	10 #MH181	20.00
BK1032	BC39	#MH182b	7.50

(£1.70) Booklets

BK1033	BC39	10 #MH178	10.00
BK1034	BC39	#MH179c	12.50

(£1.80) Booklets

BK1035	BC46	#MH179c	12.50
BK1036	BC46	10 #MH178	10.00
BK1037	BC39	#MH177b	15.00
BK1038	BC39	10 #MH239 (3)	10.00

(£1.90) Booklets

BK1039	BC41	10 #MH239 (5)	10.00
BK1040	BC41	10 #MH238 (4)	10.00
BK1041	BC37	#MH183b	20.00

(£2) Booklets

BK1068	BC39	#MH186a (2)	10.50
BK1069	BC39	10 #MH187 (3)	8.00
BK1070	BC39	#MH188b (3)	8.00
BK1071	BC41	10 #MH284	6.00
BK1072	BC41	10 #MH285	6.00

(£2.40) Booklets

BK1091	BC46	#MH186a	10.50
BK1092	BC46	#MH187d	8.00
BK1093	BC39	#MH187d	8.00
BK1094	BC39	10 #MH240	6.50
BK1095	BC39	10 #MH241 (11)	6.50

(£2.50) Booklets

BK1116	BC41	10 #MH240 (11)	6.50
BK1117	BC41	10 #MH241 (12)	6.50

(£2.60) Booklets

BK1137	BC41	10 #MH287	8.50
BK1139	BC41	10 #MH288	10.00
BK1139A	BC41	#MH289a	10.00
BK1140	BC41	10 #MH288	10.00
BK1141	BC41	#1856a, MH288b	9.75
BK1142	BC41	#1872a, MH288b	10.00
BK1143	BC41	10 #MH335	8.50
BK1144	BC41	#MH336a	8.50

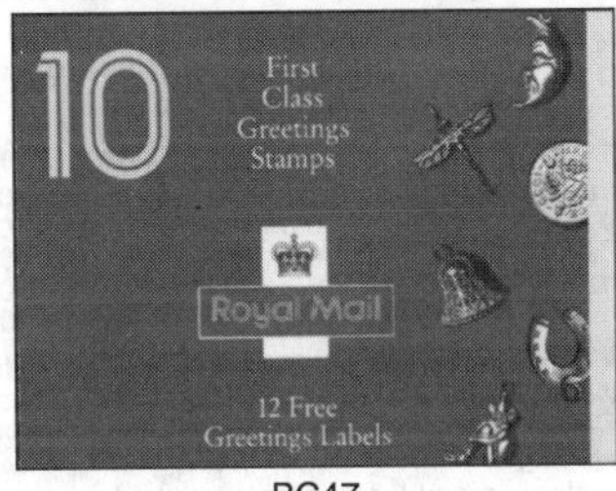

BC47

1991-2000

(£2.20) Booklets

BK1160	BC47	#1359a	10.00
BK1161	BC47	*Laughing Pillar Box*, #1373a	10.00

(£2.40) Booklets

BK1171	BC47	*Memories*, #1435a	8.00
BK1172	BC47	*Rupert Bear*, #1488a (3)	8.00

(£2.50) Booklets

BK1182	BC47	*Rupert Bear, Paddington Bear*, #1547a	7.50
BK1183	BC47	*Clown*, #1605a	8.00
BK1184	BC47	*More Love*, #1652a	7.50

(£2.60) Booklets

BK1194	BC47	*Christmas*, 10 #1709	6.50
BK1195	BC47	*Flower*, #1722a (4)	8.50
BK1196	BC47	*Chocolates*, #1722a	8.50
BK1197	BC47	*Memorable Post*, #1722a	8.50
BK1198	BC47	*Santa Claus*, 10 #1777	8.50
BK1199	BC47	*Christmas*, 10 #1835	9.00
BK1200	BC47	10 #1880	8.50

(£2.70) Booklets

BK1201	BC41	#1938a, MH335a	8.75
BK1202	BC47	#1919a, MH335a	8.75
BK1203	BC47	10 #1931	8.00

(£3.80) Booklet

BK1210	BC47	#1879a	12.00
BK1211	BC47	#1930a	11.00

(£4) Booklets

BK1220	BC47	*Magi*, #1708a	17.00
BK1221	BC47	*Santa Claus, Children*, #1776a	13.00
BK1222	BC47	*Christmas*, #1834a	14.00

BRITISH OFFICES ABROAD

Catalogue values for unused stamps in this section are for Never Hinged items.

OFFICES IN AFRICA
MIDDLE EAST FORCES

For use in Ethiopia, Cyrenaica, Eritrea, the Dodecanese and Somalia

Stamps of Great Britain, 1937-42 Overprinted in Black or Blue Black

1942-43 Wmk. 251 *Perf. 14½x14*

1 A101 1p scarlet .70 *1.50*
2 A101 2p orange .30 *2.25*
3 A101 2½p bright ultra .30 .40
4 A101 3p dark purple .30 .20
a. Double overprint
5 A102 5p lt brn (Blk) .30 .20
a. Blue black overprint ('43) 1.00 .20
6 A102 6p rose lilac ('43) .35 .20
7 A103 9p dp olive grn ('43) .80 .20
8 A103 1sh brown ('43) .45 .20

Wmk. 259
Perf. 14

9 A104 2sh6p yel green ('43) 6.50 .90
Nos. 1-9 (9) 10.00 6.05

Same Overprint in Blue Black on Nos. 259, 261, 262 and 263

1943, Jan. 1 Wmk. 251

10 A101 1p vermilion 1.40 .20
11 A101 2p light orange 1.40 1.10
12 A101 2½p ultramarine .30 .20
13 A101 3p violet 1.40 .20
Nos. 10-13 (4) 4.50 1.70

There were two printings of Nos. 1-5, both issued Mar. 2, 1942, and both black. The Cairo printing measures 13½mm, the London printing 14mm.

Nos. 5a and 6-13 compose a third printing, also made in London. On these stamps, issued Jan. 1, 1943, the overprint is 13½mm wide. The 2sh6p overprint is black, the others blue black.

Same Ovpt. in Black on #250, 251A

1947 Wmk. 259 *Perf. 14*

14 A104 5sh dull red 12.50 *16.00*
15 A105 10sh ultramarine 13.00 10.00

In 1950 Nos. 1-15 were declared valid for use in Great Britain. Used values are for copies postmarked in territory of issue. Others sell for about 25 percent less.

POSTAGE DUE STAMPS

Postage Due Stamps of Great Britain Overprinted in Blue

1942 Wmk. 251 *Perf. 14x14½*

J1 D1 ½p emerald .25 *8.75*
J2 D1 1p carmine rose .25 *1.50*
J3 D1 2p black brown 1.25 1.25
J4 D1 3p violet .50 *3.75*
J5 D1 1sh blue 3.25 *9.75*
Nos. J1-J5 (5) 5.50 *25.00*

No. J1-J5 were used in Eritrea.

FOR USE IN ERITREA

Catalogue values for unused stamps in this section are for Never Hinged items.

100 Cents = 1 Shilling

Stamps of Great Britain 1937-42 Surcharged

a

1948, June Wmk. 251 *Perf. 14½x14*

1 A101 5c on ½p green (II) .50 *.75*
2 A101 10c on 1p vermilion (II) .60 *2.50*
3 A101 20c on 2p light org (II) .45 *2.40*
4 A101 25c on 2½p ultra (II) .45 *.65*
5 A101 30c on 3p violet (II) 1.10 *4.75*
6 A101 40c on 5p light brown .25 *4.50*
7 A101 50c on 6p rose lilac .25 *1.00*
8 A103 75c on 9p deep ol grn .45 *.85*
9 A103 1sh on 1sh brown .45 .50

"B. M. A." stands for British Military Administration.

Great Britain Nos. 249A, 250 and 251A Surcharged

1948, June Wmk. 259 *Perf. 14*

10 A104 2sh50c on 2sh6p yel grn 6.00 *10.50*
11 A104 5sh on 5sh dl red 6.00 *17.00*
12 A105 10sh on 10sh ultra 17.50 *22.50*

Great Britain No. 245 Surcharged Type "a"

1949 Wmk. 251 *Perf. 14½x14*

13 A103 65c on 8p brt rose 6.00 2.10
Nos. 1-13 (13) 40.00 *70.00*

Stamps of Great Britain 1937-42 Surcharged

c

1950, Feb. 6

14 A101 5c on ½p green (II) .55 *6.00*
15 A101 10c on 1p ver (II) .25 *2.50*
16 A101 20c on 2p lt orange (II) .25 *.60*
17 A101 25c on 2½p ultra (II) .25 *.50*
18 A101 30c on 3p violet (II) .25 *1.50*
19 A102 40c on 5p light brown .35 *1.25*
20 A102 50c on 6p rose lilac .25 .25
21 A103 65c on 8p bright rose 1.10 *1.25*
22 A103 75c on 9p dp ol grn .25 .20
23 A103 1sh on 1sh brown .25 .20

Great Britain Nos. 249A, 250, 251A Surcharged

Wmk. 259 *Perf. 14*

24 A104 2sh50c on 2sh6p yel grn 3.75 *4.25*
25 A104 5sh on 5sh dl red 5.25 *9.00*
26 A105 10sh on 10sh ultra 47.50 47.50
Nos. 14-26 (13) 60.25 *75.00*

Great Britain Nos. 280, 281, 283 and 284 Surcharged Type "c"

Perf. 14½x14

1951, May 3 Wmk. 251

27 A101 5c on ½p lt orange .25 *.50*
28 A101 10c on 1p ultra .25 *.50*
29 A101 20c on 2p lt red brown .25 .25
30 A101 25c on 2½p vermilion .25 .25

Great Britain Nos. 286-288 Surcharged

B.A.
ERITREA
2 SH. 50 CTS.

Perf. 11x12

1951, May 31 Wmk. 259

31 A121 2sh50c on 2sh6p grn 6.50 *18.00*
32 A121 5sh on 5sh dl red 20.00 18.00
33 A122 10sh on 10sh ultra 20.00 18.00
Nos. 27-33 (7) 47.50 55.50

Surcharge arranged to fit the design on #33.

POSTAGE DUE STAMPS

Catalogue values for unused stamps in this section are for Never Hinged items.

Great Britain Nos. J26-J29, J32 Surcharged

1948 Wmk. 251 *Perf. 14x14½*

J1 D1 5c on ½p emer 10.00 *19.00*
J2 D1 10c on 1p car rose 10.00 *21.00*
J3 D1 20c on 2p blk brn 7.00 *14.50*
J4 D1 30c on 3p violet 10.00 *13.00*
J5 D1 1sh on 1sh blue 18.00 *27.50*
Nos. J1-J5 (5) 55.00 *95.00*

Great Britain Nos. J26 to J29 and J32 Surcharged

1950, Feb. 6

J6 D1 5c on ½p emer 11.00 *45.00*
J7 D1 10c on 1p car rose 9.00 *15.00*
a. "C" of CENTS omitted *1,700.*
J8 D1 20c on 2p blk brn 9.50 *13.00*
J9 D1 30c on 3p violet 11.00 *16.00*
J10 D1 1sh on 1sh blue 14.50 *21.00*
Nos. J6-J10 (5) 55.00 *110.00*

EAST AFRICA FORCES

FOR USE IN SOMALIA (ITALIAN SOMALILAND)

12 Pence = 1 Shilling
100 Cents = 1 Shilling

Catalogue values for unused stamps in this section, from this point to the end of the section, are for Never Hinged items.

Stamps of Great Britain 1938-42 Overprinted in Blue

Perf. 14½x14

1943, Jan. 15 Wmk. 251

1 A101 1p vermilion .60 .40
2 A101 2p light orange 1.60 1.25
3 A101 2½p ultramarine .30 3.25
4 A101 3p violet .50 .20
5 A101 5p light brown .50 .40
6 A101 6p rose lilac .30 .85
7 A103 9p dp olive green .85 2.00
8 A103 1sh brown 1.60 .30

On Great Britain No. 249A

1946 Wmk. 259 *Perf. 14*

9 A104 2sh6p yellow green 7.75 *6.00*
Nos. 1-9 (9) 14.00 *14.65*

Stamps of Great Britain, 1937-42 Surcharged

Perf. 14½x14

1948, May 27 Wmk. 251

10 A101 5c on ½p grn (II) 1.00 *1.60*
11 A101 15c on 1½p lt red brn (II) 1.40 *13.00*
12 A101 20c on 2p lt org (II) 2.50 *3.50*
13 A101 25c on 2½p ultra (II) 2.10 *4.00*
14 A101 30c on 3p vio (II) 2.10 *8.25*
15 A102 40c on 5p lt brown .80 .20
16 A102 50c on 6p rose lilac .45 *1.75*
17 A103 75c on 9p dp ol grn 1.90 *15.00*
18 A103 1sh on 1sh brown 1.25 .20

Great Britain Nos. 249A and 250 Surcharged

Wmk. 259 *Perf. 14*

19 A104 2sh50c on 2sh6p yel grn 3.50 *22.50*
20 A104 5sh on 5sh dl red 8.00 *30.00*
Nos. 10-20 (11) 25.00 *100.00*

Stamps of Great Britain 1937-42 Surcharged

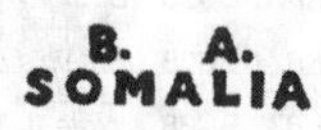

Perf. 14½x14

1950, Jan. 2 Wmk. 251

21 A101 5c on ½p grn (II) .20 *2.75*
22 A101 15c on 1½p lt red brn (II) .55 *14.00*
23 A101 20c on 2p lt org (II) .55 *5.75*
24 A101 25c on 2½p ultra (II) .45 *6.50*
25 A101 30c on 3p violet (II) .90 *3.75*
26 A102 40c on 5p light brn .50 *.75*
27 A102 50c on 6p rose lilac .45 *1.00*
28 A103 75c on 9p deep ol grn 1.10 *5.75*
29 A103 1sh on 1sh brown .55 *1.25*

Great Britain Nos. 249A and 250 Surcharged

B. A.
SOMALIA
2 SH. 50 CTS.

Wmk. 259 *Perf. 14*

30 A104 2sh50c on 2sh 6p yel grn 3.75 *21.00*
31 A104 5sh on 5sh dull red 8.50 *25.00*
Nos. 21-31 (11) 17.50 *87.50*

FOR USE IN TRIPOLITANIA

Catalogue values for unused stamps in this section are for Never Hinged items.

Stamps of Great Britain, 1937-42, Surcharged

M.A.L.=Military Authority Lire

Perf. 14½x14

1948, July 1 Wmk. 251

1 A101 1 l on ½p green (II) .50 *.95*
2 A101 2 l on 1p ver (II) .30 .20
3 A101 3 l on 1½p lt red brn (II) .30 *.45*
4 A101 4 l on 2p lt org (II) .30 *.45*
5 A101 5 l on 2½p ultra (II) .30 .20
6 A101 6 l on 3p violet (II) .30 *.35*
7 A102 10 l on 5p lt brown .30 .20
8 A102 12 l on 6p rose lilac .30 .20
9 A103 18 l on 9p dp ol grn .50 *.60*
10 A103 24 l on 1sh brown .50 *.90*

Great Britain Nos. 249A, 250 and 251A Surcharged

Wmk. 259 ***Perf. 14***

11 A104 60 l on 2sh6p yel grn 2.40 *7.00*
12 A104 120 l on 5sh dl red 12.50 *16.00*
13 A105 240 l on 10sh ultra 19.00 *82.50*
Nos. 1-13 (13) 37.50 *110.00*

Stamps of Great Britain 1937-42 Surcharged

Perf. 14½x14

1950, Feb. 6 Wmk. 251

14 A101 1 l on ½p green (II) 1.40 *9.50*
15 A101 2 l on 1p ver (II) 1.50 *.35*
16 A101 3 l on 1½p lt red brn (II) .45 *9.50*
17 A101 4 l on 2p lt org (II) .35 *4.00*
18 A101 5 l on 2½p ultra (II) .25 *.60*
19 A101 6 l on 3p violet (II) 1.10 *3.00*
20 A102 10 l on 5p lt brown .30 *3.50*
21 A102 12 l on 6p rose lilac 1.10 .45
22 A103 18 l on 9p dp ol grn 1.40 *2.10*
23 A103 24 l on 1sh brown 1.40 *3.00*

Great Britain Nos. 249A, 250 and 251A Surcharged

Wmk. 259 ***Perf. 14***

24 A104 60 l on 2sh6p yel grn 3.75 *10.50*
25 A104 120 l on 5sh dl red 16.00 *21.00*
26 A105 240 l on 10sh ultra 26.00 *52.50*
Nos. 14-26 (13) 55.00 *120.00*

Great Britain Nos. 280-284 Surcharged like Nos. 14-23

Perf. 14½x14

1951, May 3 Wmk. 251

27 A101 1 l on ½p lt org .20 *4.25*
28 A101 2 l on 1p ultra .20 *.75*
29 A101 3 l on 1½p green .35 *6.50*
30 A101 4 l on 2p lt red brown .20 *1.00*
31 A101 5 l on 2½p ver .30 *6.50*

Great Britain Nos. 286-288 Surcharged

1951, May 3 Wmk. 259 ***Perf. 11x12***

32 A121 60 l on 2sh6p grn 4.25 *17.50*
33 A121 120 l on 5sh dl red 7.00 *21.00*
34 A122 240 l on 10sh ultra 32.50 *37.50*
Nos. 27-34 (8) 45.00 *95.00*

Surcharge arranged to fit the design on #34.

POSTAGE DUE STAMPS

Catalogue values for unused stamps in this section are for Never Hinged items.

Great Britain Nos. J26-J29, J32 Surcharged

1948 Wmk. 251 ***Perf. 14x14½***

J1 D1 1 l on ½p emer 5.50 *42.50*
J2 D1 2 l on 1p car rose 2.50 *27.50*
J3 D1 4 l on 2p blk brn 7.25 *25.00*
J4 D1 6 l on 3p violet 7.25 *17.50*
J5 D1 24 l on 1sh blue 27.50 *87.50*
Nos. J1-J5 (5) 50.00 *200.00*

Great Britain Nos. J26-J29, J32 Surcharged

1950, Feb. 6

J6 D1 1 l on ½p emer 10.75 *70.00*
J7 D1 2 l on 1p car rose 2.25 *24.00*
J8 D1 4 l on 2p blk brn 2.50 *26.00*
J9 D1 6 l on 3p violet 17.00 *55.00*
J10 D1 24 l on 1sh blue 42.50 *125.00*
Nos. J6-J10 (5) 75.00 *300.00*

CHINA

100 Cents = 1 Dollar

Stamps of Hong Kong, 1912-14, Overprinted

1917 Wmk. 3 ***Perf. 14***

Ordinary Paper

1 A11 1c brown 2.40 1.40
2 A11 2c deep green 1.90 .30
3 A12 4c scarlet 2.10 .30
4 A13 6c orange 3.00 .55
5 A12 8c gray 6.50 1.25
6 A11 10c ultramarine 6.50 .30

Chalky Paper

7 A14 12c violet, *yel* 4.50 2.40
8 A14 20c olive grn & vio 9.00 .55
9 A15 25c red vio & dl vio (on #117) 7.00 *14.00*
10 A13 30c orange & violet 19.00 4.75
11 A14 50c black, *emerald* 24.00 8.00
a. 50c blk, *blue green*, ol back 37.50 1.50
b. 50c blk, *emerald*, ol back 16.00 5.50
12 A11 $1 blue & vio, *bl* 65.00 2.50
13 A14 $2 black & red 150.00 55.00
14 A13 $3 violet & grn 250.00 150.00
15 A14 $5 red & grn, *bl grn*, ol back 300.00 190.00
16 A13 $10 blk & vio, *red* 675.00 325.00
Nos. 1-16 (16) 1,525. 756.30

Stamps of Hong Kong, 1921-26, Overprinted

1922-27 Wmk. 4

Ordinary Paper

17 A11 1c brown 1.60 *3.25*
18 A11 2c green 2.40 2.10
19 A12 4c scarlet 3.00 1.90
20 A13 6c orange 3.00 *4.00*
21 A12 8c gray 3.50 *12.50*
22 A11 10c ultramarine 4.50 1.90

Chalky Paper

23 A14 20c ol grn & vio 6.50 4.75
24 A15 25c red violet & dull vio 12.50 *55.00*
25 A14 50c blk, *emerald* ('27) 45.00 *140.00*
26 A11 $1 ultra & vio, *bl* 55.00 32.50
27 A14 $2 black & red 190.00 *250.00*
Nos. 17-27 (11) 327.00 *507.90*

MOROCCO

100 Centimos = 1 Peseta
12 Pence = 1 Shilling
20 Shillings = 1 Pound
100 Centimes = 1 Franc

These stamps were issued for various purposes:

a- For general use at the British Post Offices throughout Morocco.
b- For use in the Spanish Zone of Northern Morocco.
c- For use in the French Zone of Southern Morocco.
d- For use in the International Zone of Tangier.

For convenience these stamps are listed in four groups according to the coinage expressed or surcharged on the stamps, namely:

#1-108: Value expressed in Spanish currency.
#201-280: Value in British currency.
#401-440: Value in French currency.
#501-611: Stamps overprinted "Tangier."

Spanish Currency

Gibraltar Stamps of 1889-95 Overprinted

1898 Wmk. 2 ***Perf. 14***

Black Overprint

1 A11 5c green 1.00 *1.25*
2 A11 10c carmine rose 1.40 .20
b. Double overprint 500.00
3 A11 20c olive green 3.75 *4.50*
4 A11 25c ultramarine 1.90 .40
5 A11 40c orange brown 3.00 2.25
6 A11 50c violet 22.50 16.00
7 A11 1pe bister & blue 9.00 *19.00*
8 A11 2pe blk & car rose 9.00 *19.00*
Nos. 1-8 (8) 51.55 *62.60*

Dark Blue Overprint

9 A11 40c orange brown *50.00* *32.50*
10 A11 50c violet 9.00 14.00
11 A11 1pe bister & blue *125.00* *175.00*

Inverted "V" for "A"

1a A11 5c 20.00 *24.00*
2a A11 10c 225.00 *275.00*
3a A11 20c 37.50 *45.00*
4a A11 25c 100.00 *125.00*
5a A11 40c 150.00 *175.00*
6a A11 50c 250.00 *275.00*
7a A11 1pe 190.00 *250.00*
8a A11 2pe 225.00 *250.00*

Overprinted in Black

(Narrower "M," ear of "g" horiz.)

1899

12 A11 5c green .30 .20
13 A11 10c carmine rose .35 .20
14 A11 20c olive green 3.00 .70
15 A11 25c ultramarine 4.50 .90
16 A11 40c orange brown 30.00 19.00
17 A11 50c violet 5.50 3.50
18 A11 1pe bister & blue 18.00 *25.00*
19 A11 2pe blk & car rose 27.50 *42.50*
Nos. 12-19 (8) 89.15 *92.00*

"M" with long serif

12a A11 5c 8.00 8.00
13a A11 10c 8.00 8.00
14a A11 20c 22.50 22.50
15a A11 25c 27.50 27.50
16a A11 40c 175.00 150.00
17a A11 50c 90.00 *110.00*
18a A11 1pe *125.00* *150.00*
19a A11 2pe 225.00 *300.00*

Type of Gibraltar, 1903, with Value in Spanish Currency, Overprinted

1903-05

20 A12 5c gray grn & bl grn 4.25 1.50
21 A12 10c violet, *red* 3.75 .20
22 A12 20c gray grn & car rose ('04) 8.00 *37.50*
23 A12 25c vio & blk, *bl* 3.25 .20
24 A12 50c violet 67.50 *140.00*
25 A12 1pe blk & car rose 40.00 *140.00*
26 A12 2pe black & ultra 45.00 *110.00*
Nos. 20-26 (7) 171.75 *429.40*

"M" with long serif

20a A12 5c 35.00 32.50
21a A12 10c 30.00 27.50
22a A12 20c 60.00 *125.00*
23a A12 25c 37.50 37.50
24a A12 50c 275.00 *425.00*
25a A12 1pe 250.00 *400.00*
26a A12 2pe 275.00 *375.00*

1905-06 Wmk. 3 Chalky Paper

27 A12 5c gray grn & bl grn 3.25 2.25
28 A12 10c violet, *red* 1.40 .60
29 A12 20c gray grn & car rose ('06) 2.25 *22.50*
30 A12 25c violet & blk, *bl* ('06) 22.50 5.00
31 A12 50c violet 5.50 *26.00*
32 A12 1pe blk & car rose 21.00 *67.50*
33 A12 2pe black & ultra 13.00 *30.00*
Nos. 27-33 (7) 68.90 *153.85*

No. 29 is on ordinary paper. Nos. 27 and 28 are on both ordinary and chalky paper.

"M" with long serif

27a A12 5c 32.50 32.50
28a A12 10c 32.50 19.00
29a A12 20c 32.50 *85.00*
30a A12 25c 175.00 110.00
31a A12 50c 125.00 *175.00*
32a A12 1pe 175.00 *250.00*
33a A12 2pe 150.00 *200.00*

Numerous other minor overprint varieties exist of Nos. 1-33.

British Stamps of 1902-10 Surcharged in Spanish Currency:

a: #34-42, 46-48, 49, 63, 71

b: #43-45

1907-10 Wmk. 30

34 A66 5c on ½p pale grn .45 .20
35 A66 10c on 1p car .45 .20
36 A67 15c on 1½p vio & grn .65 .35
a. "1" of "15" omitted 3,250.
37 A68 20c on 2p grn & car .55 .35
38 A66 25c on 2½p ultra 1.50 .75
39 A70 40c on 4p brn & grn 1.10 *2.00*
40 A70 40c on 4p org ('10) .45 .90
41 A71 50c on 5p lil & ultra 1.75 1.75
42 A73 1pe on 10p car rose & vio 5.50 *7.50*

Wmk. 31

43 A75 3pe on 2sh6p vio 21.00 21.00
44 A76 6pe on 5sh car rose 37.50 37.50
45 A77 12pe on 10sh ultra 60.00 60.00
Nos. 34-45 (12) 130.90 132.50

Nos. 36-37, 39-43 are on chalky paper.

Great Britain Nos. 153, 154 and 148 Surcharged

1912 Wmk. 30 ***Perf. 15x14***

46 A80 5c on ½p yel grn 1.60 .20
47 A81 10c on 1p scarlet .40 .20
48 A66 25c on 2½p ultra 19.00 19.00
Nos. 46-48 (3) 21.00 19.40

British Stamps of 1912-18 Surcharged in Black or Carmine:

c

d

e

1914-18 **Wmk. 33**

49 A82(a) 5c on ½p grn .50 .20
50 A83(d) 10c on 1p scar .70 .20
51 A84(c) 15c on 1½p red brn ('15) .70 .20
52 A85(d) 20c on 2p org (I) .60 .20
53 A86(d) 25c on 2½p ultra 1.25 .20
54 A90(d) 1pe on 10p lt bl 1.75 *4.00*

Wmk. 34

Perf. 11x12

55 A91(e) 3pe on 2sh6p lt brn 24.00 *87.50*
a. 3pe on 2sh6p dark brown 30.00 *87.50*
56 A91(e) 6pe on 5sh car 25.00 *42.50*
a. 6pe on 5sh light carmine 110.00 *160.00*
57 A91(e) 12pe on 10sh dk bl (C) 95.00 *140.00*
a. 12pe on 10sh blue 95.00 *140.00*
Nos. 49-57 (9) 149.50 *275.00*

Great Britain Nos. 159, 165 Surcharged in Spanish Currency

f

g

1917-23 **Wmk. 33** ***Perf. 15x14***

58 A82(f) 3c on ½p green .50 *3.00*
59 A88(g) 40c on 4p sl green 3.50 *6.50*

Great Britain Nos. 189, 191, 179 Surcharged in Spanish Currency

1926 **Wmk. 35**

60 A84(c) 15c on 1½p red brn 7.00 *19.00*
61 A86(d) 25c on 2½p ultra 1.10 1.40

Wmk. 34

Perf. 11x12

62 A91(e) 3pe on 2sh6p brn 24.00 *65.00*
Nos. 60-62 (3) 32.10 *85.40*

British Stamps of 1924 Surcharged in Spanish Currency

1929-31 **Wmk. 35** ***Perf. 15x14***

63 A82(a) 5c on ½p grn ('31) 1.50 *10.00*
64 A83(d) 10c on 1p scar 14.00 *20.00*
65 A85(d) 20c on 2p org (II) ('31) 4.00 *5.50*
66 A88(g) 40c on 4p sl grn ('30) 1.25 *1.50*
Nos. 63-66 (4) 20.75 *37.00*

Silver Jubilee Issue

Great Britain Nos. 226-229 Surcharged in Blue or Red

1935, May 8 ***Perf. 14½x14***

67 A98 5c on ½p dk grn .80 .70
68 A98 10c on 1p car 2.25 1.90
a. Pair, one reading "CEN-TIMES" 1,200.
69 A98 15c on 1½p red brn 4.00 *13.00*
70 A98 25c on 2½p ultra (R) 3.25 1.90
Nos. 67-70 (4) 10.30 17.50

25th anniv. of the reign of King George V.

Great Britain Nos. 210-214, 216, 219 Surcharged in Spanish Currency

1935-37 **Photo.**

71 A82(a) 5c on ½p dk grn ('36) .60 *11.50*
72 A97(d) 10c on 1p car 2.00 *5.00*
73 A84(c) 15c on 1½p red brn 3.50 2.50
74 A85(d) 20c on 2p red org ('36) .30 .20
75 A97(d) 25c on 2½p ultra ('36) 1.00 *3.00*
76 A88(d) 40c on 4p dk sl grn ('37) .35 *2.50*
77 A90(d) 1pe on 10p Prus bl ('37) 3.25 .30
Nos. 71-77 (7) 11.00 *25.00*

Great Britain Nos. 230-233 Surcharged

"MOROCCO" 14mm

1936 **Wmk. 250**

78 A99 5c on ½p dk green .20 .20
79 A99 10c on 1p crimson .30 .50
a. "Morocco" 15mm long 2.75 *8.00*
80 A99 15c on 1½p red brown .20 .20
81 A99 25c on 2½p brt ultra .20 .20
Nos. 78-81 (4) .90 1.10

Great Britain #234 Surcharged in Blue

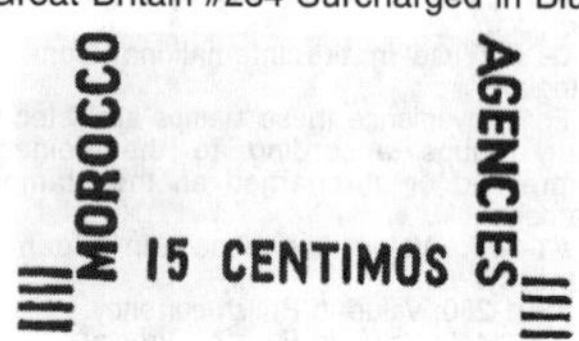

Perf. 14½x14

1937, May 13 **Wmk. 251**

82 A100 15c on 1½p purple brn .20 .20

Coronation of George VI and Elizabeth.

Great Britain Nos. 235-237, 239, 241, 244 Surcharged in Blue or Black

h

1937-40

83 A101 5c on ½p dp grn (Bl) .25 .20
84 A101 10c on 1p scarlet .20 .20
85 A101 15c on 1½p red brown (Bl) .25 .20
86 A101 25c on 2½p brt ultra .30 *.40*
87 A102 40c on 4p gray green ('40) 11.50 8.75
88 A103 70c on 7p emer ('40) .25 *7.25*
Nos. 83-88 (6) 12.75 17.00

Great Britain Nos. 252-254, 256 Surcharged in Blue or Black

1940, May 6

89 A106 5c on ½p deep grn (Bl) .20 .80
90 A106 10c on 1p scarlet .30 .95
91 A106 15c on 1½p red brn (Bl) .45 .95
92 A106 25c on 2½p brt ultra .50 .30
Nos. 89-92 (4) 1.45 3.00

Centenary of the postage stamp.

Catalogue values for unused stamps in this section, from this point to the end of the section, are for Never Hinged items.

Great Britain Nos. 267 and 268 Surcharged in Black:

i

j

Perf. 14½x14, 14x14½

1948, Apr. 26 **Wmk. 251**

93 A109(i) 25c on 2½p .20 .20
94 A110(j) 45pe on £1 17.50 *22.50*

25th anniv. of the marriage of King George VI and Queen Elizabeth.

Great Britain Nos. 271-274 Surcharged "MOROCCO AGENCIES" and New Value

1948, July 29 ***Perf. 14½x14***

95 A113 25c on 2½p brt ultra .20 .20
96 A114 30c on 3p dp vio .20 .20
97 A115 60c on 6p red vio .30 .30
98 A116 1.20pe on 1sh dk brn .60 .60
a. Double surcharge 600.00
Nos. 95-98 (4) 1.30 1.30

1948 Olympic Games, Wembley, July-Aug. A square of dots obliterates the original denomination on No. 98.

Great Britain Nos. 280-282, 284-285, 247 Surcharged Type "h"

1951-52 **Wmk. 251** ***Perf. 14½x14***

99 A101 5c on ½p lt orange 1.40 2.00
100 A101 10c on 1p ultra 2.25 3.50
101 A101 15c on 1½p green 1.75 9.50
102 A101 25c on 2½p ver 1.75 3.50
103 A102 40c on 4p ultra ('52) 1.40 6.50
104 A103 1pe on 10p ryl bl ('52) .45 *2.50*
Nos. 99-104 (6) 9.00 *27.50*

Great Britain Nos. 292-293 Surcharged Type "h"

1954-55 **Wmk. 298**

105 A126 5c on ½p red org .20 .20
106 A126 10c on 1p ultra ('55) .20 .20

Great Britain Nos. 317 and 323 Surcharged Type "h"

1956 **Wmk. 308** ***Perf. 14x14½***

107 A126 5c on ½p red org .20 .20
108 A128 40c on 4p ultra 1.00 1.00

BRITISH CURRENCY

Stamps of Morocco Agencies were accepted for postage in Great Britain, starting in mid-1950. Copies with contemporaneous Morocco cancellations sell for more.

British Stamps of 1902-11 Overprinted

a

b

Overprint "a" 14½mm long

1907-12 **Wmk. 30** ***Perf. 14***

Ordinary Paper

201 A66 ½p pale yel grn 1.00 .65
202 A66 1p carmine 3.50 1.40

Chalky Paper

203 A68 2p green & car 3.25 1.40
204 A70 4p brown & grn 3.75 2.00
205 A70 4p orange ('12) 4.50 *3.75*
a. Perf. 15x14 9.00 *17.00*
206 A66 6p dull vio 7.00 3.75
207 A74 1sh car rose & grn 16.00 12.50

Overprinted Type "b"

Wmk. 31

208 A75 2sh6p violet 50.00 *57.50*
Nos. 201-208 (8) 89.00 *82.95*

British Stamps of 1912-18 Overprinted Type "a"

Perf. 14½x14, 15x14

1914-21 **Wmk. 33**

209 A82 ½p green ('18) .20 .20
210 A83 1p scarlet ('17) .55 .20
211 A84 1½p red brn ('21) 1.65 *8.00*
212 A85 2p orange ('18) .80 .20
213 A87 3p violet ('21) 1.75 .30
214 A88 4p slate grn ('21) .70 .50
215 A89 6p dull vio ('21) 4.75 *12.00*
216 A90 1sh bister ('17) 8.25 1.65

c

Wmk. 34 ***Perf. 11x12***

217 A91 2sh6p lt brown 30.00 32.50
a. 2sh6p brown 30.00 30.00
b. 2sh6p black brown 30.00 32.50
c. Double overprint 2,250. 1,400.
Nos. 209-217 (9) 48.65 55.55

Same Overprint on Great Britain Nos. 179-180

1925-31

218 A91 2sh6p gray brown 32.50 30.00
219 A91 5sh car rose ('31) 55.00 55.00

British Stamps of 1924 Overprinted Type "a" (14½mm long)

1925-31 **Wmk. 35** ***Perf. 15x14***

220 A82 ½p green .70 .55
221 A84 1½p red brn ('31) 8.25 11.00
222 A85 2p dp org (Die II) 1.10 1.10
223 A86 2½p ultra 1.25 *2.75*
224 A89 6p red vio ('31) 4.50 *5.50*
225 A90 1sh bister 12.50 4.00
Nos. 220-225 (6) 28.30 24.90

Silver Jubilee Issue

Great Britain Nos. 226-229 Overprinted in Blue or Red

1935, May 8 ***Perf. 14½x14***

226 A98 ½p dark green (Bl) .45 .45
227 A98 1p carmine (Bl) .45 .55
228 A98 1½p red brown (Bl) 2.00 *3.75*
229 A98 2½p ultramarine (R) 2.25 2.50
Nos. 226-229 (4) 5.15 *7.25*

25th anniversary of the reign of King George V.

British Stamps of 1924 Overprinted Type "a" (15½mm long)

1935-36

230 A82 ½p green 3.25 *6.50*
231 A86 2½p ultra *125.00* 30.00
232 A88 4p slate green 5.50 *16.00*
233 A89 6p red violet .55 .80
234 A90 1sh bister 50.00 50.00
Nos. 230-234 (5) 184.30 103.30

British Stamps of 1934-36 Overprinted "MOROCCO AGENCIES"

1935-36

235 A97 1p carmine .20 .25
236 A84 1½p red brn ('36) .75 *10.00*
237 A85 2p red org ('36) .20 .20
238 A97 2½p ultra ('36) .80 *4.00*
239 A87 3p dk violet ('36) .20 .20
240 A88 4p dk slate grn ('36) .20 .20
241 A90 1sh bis brn ('36) .55 .60

Overprinted Type "c"

Wmk. 34

Perf. 11x12

242 A91 2sh6p brown 42.50 24.00
243 A91 5sh carmine ('37) 27.50 30.00
Nos. 235-243 (9) 72.90 69.45

Great Britain Nos. 231, 233 Overprinted

"MOROCCO" 14mm

1936 Wmk. 250 *Perf. 14½x14*

244 A99 1p crimson .20 .20
a. "Morocco" 15mm long .75 .75
245 A99 2½p bright ultra .20 .20
a. "Morocco" 15mm long .75 .75

Catalogue values for unused stamps in this section, from this point to the end of the section, are for Never Hinged items.

Great Britain Nos. 258-263, 241-248, 266, 249A-250 Overprinted "MOROCCO AGENCIES" (14½mm long)

1949, Aug. 16 Wmk. 251

246 A101 ½p green .25 .25
247 A101 1p vermilion .40 .40
248 A101 1½p lt red brown .60 .60
249 A101 2p lt orange .60 .60
250 A101 2½p ultra .60 .60
251 A101 3p violet .60 .60
252 A102 4p gray green .75 .75
253 A102 5p lt brown 1.10 1.10
254 A102 6p rose lilac 1.00 1.00
255 A103 7p emerald 1.25 1.25
256 A103 8p brt rose 1.65 1.65
257 A103 9p dp olive grn 1.40 1.40
258 A103 10p royal blue 1.65 1.65
259 A103 11p violet brn 1.90 1.90
260 A103 1sh brown 1.90 1.90

"MOROCCO AGENCIES" 17½mm long
Wmk. 259
Perf. 14

261 A104 2sh6p yellow grn 13.00 13.00
262 A104 5sh dull red 25.00 25.00
Nos. 246-262 (17) 53.65 53.65

Great Britain Nos. 280-284, 286-287 Overprinted "MOROCCO AGENCIES" (14½mm long)

Perf. 14½x14

1951, May 3 Wmk. 251

263 A101 ½p lt orange .20 .20
264 A101 1p ultra .20 .20
265 A101 1½p green .30 .30
266 A101 2p lt red brown .30 .30
267 A101 2½p vermilion .45 .45

"MOROCCO AGENCIES" 17½mm long
Wmk. 259
Perf. 11x12

268 A121 2sh6p green 11.00 14.00
269 A121 5sh dull red 16.00 20.00
Nos. 263-269 (7) 28.45 35.45

Great Britain Nos. 292-296, 299, 302 and 306 Overprinted "MOROCCO AGENCIES" (14½mm long)

1952-55 Wmk. 298 *Perf. 14½x14*

270 A126 ½p red orange .20 .20
271 A126 1p ultramarine .20 .20
272 A126 1½p green ('52) .20 .20
273 A126 2p red brown .20 .20
274 A127 2½p scarlet ('52) .30 .30
275 A128 4p ultra ('55) .50 .50
276 A129 5p light brown .60 .60
277 A129 6p lilac rose ('55) .65 .65
278 A130 8p bright rose 1.40 1.40
279 A131 1sh brown 1.10 1.10
Nos. 270-279 (10) 5.35 5.35

Same Ovpt. on Great Britain No. 321

1956 Wmk. 308 *Perf. 14½x14*

280 A127 2½p scarlet 1.00 1.00

French Currency

British Stamps of 1912-22 Surcharged in French Currency in Red or Black:

h

i

Perf. 14½x14, 15x14

1917-24 Wmk. 33

401 A82(h) 3c on ½p green (R) .35 2.25
402 A82(h) 5c on ½p green .20 .20
403 A83(h) 10c on 1p scarlet 1.40 .20
404 A84(h) 15c on 1½p red brn 1.25 .20
405 A86(h) 25c on 2½p ultra .70 .20
406 A88(h) 40c on 4p slate green 1.25 .55
407 A89(h) 50c on 5p yel brn ('23) .50 2.50
408 A90(h) 75c on 9p ol grn ('24) .35 .65
409 A90(i) 1fr on 10p lt blue 3.00 1.10
Nos. 401-409 (9) 9.00 7.85

Great Britain No. 179 Surcharged:

k

1924 Wmk. 34 *Perf. 11x12*

410 A91(k) 3fr on 2sh6p brn 13.00 4.00

British Stamps of 1924 Surcharged in French Currency as in 1917-24

1925-26 Wmk. 35 *Perf. 15x14*

411 A82(h) 5c on ½p green .30 4.00
412 A83(h) 10c on 1p scarlet .30 .20
413 A84(h) 15c on 1½p red brn .75 1.25
414 A86(h) 25c on 2½p ultra .30 .20
415 A88(h) 40c on 4p sl green .45 .45
416 A89(h) 50c on 5p yel brown .45 .20
417 A90(h) 75c on 9p ol green 1.40 .20
418 A90(i) 1fr on 10p dl blue .65 .20
Nos. 411-418 (8) 4.60 6.70

Great Britain Nos. 180, 198 and 200 Surcharged type "k"

1932 Wmk. 34 *Perf. 11x12*

419 A91 6fr on 5sh car rose 40.00 40.00

1934 Wmk. 35 *Perf. 14½x14*

420 A90 90c on 9p ol green 7.00 3.75
421 A90 1.50fr on 1sh bister 4.75 2.00

Silver Jubilee Issue

Great Britain Nos. 226-229 Surcharged in Blue or Red

1935, May 8 *Perf. 14½x14*

422 A98 5c on ½p dk green .20 .20
423 A98 10c on 1p carmine 1.25 1.50
424 A98 15c on 1½p red brn .50 .50
425 A98 25c on 2½p ultra (R) .50 .50
Nos. 422-425 (4) 2.45 2.70

25th anniv. of the reign of King George V.

British Stamps of 1934-36 Surcharged Types "h" or "k"

Perf. 14½x14

1935-37 Photo. Wmk. 35

426 A82(h) 5c on ½p dk grn .20 .20
427 A97(h) 10c on 1p car ('36) .20 .20
428 A84(h) 15c on 1½p red brn .60 .60
429 A97(h) 25c on 2½p ultra .20 .20
430 A88(h) 40c on 4p dk sl grn .20 .20
431 A89(h) 50c on 5p yel brn .20 .20
432 A90(h) 90c on 9p dk ol grn .20 .20
433 A90(k) 1fr on 10p Prus bl .20 .20
434 A90(h) 1.50fr on 1sh bister brn ('37) .30 .40

Waterlow Printing

Wmk. 34 *Perf. 11x12*

435 A91(k) 3fr on 2sh6p brn 11.50 8.25
436 A91(k) 6fr on 5sh car ('36) 22.50 18.00
Nos. 426-436 (11) 36.30 28.65

Great Britain Nos. 230, 232 Surcharged

1936 Wmk. 250 *Perf. 14½x14*

437 A99 5c on ½p dark green .20 .20
438 A99 15c on 1½p red brown .20 .20

Great Britain No. 234 Surcharged in Blue

1937, May 13 Wmk. 251

439 A100 15c on 1½p purple brn .20 .20

Coronation of George VI and Elizabeth.

Great Britain No. 235 Surcharged in Blue

1937

440 A101 5c on ½p deep green .20 .20

For Use in the International Zone of Tangier

Great Britain Nos. 187-190 Overprinted in Black

a

1927 Wmk. 35 *Perf. 15x14*

501 A82 ½p green .65 .80
502 A83 1p scarlet .80 .20
503 A84 1½p red brown 2.60 1.65
504 A85 2p orange (II) 2.60 .20
Nos. 501-504 (4) 6.65 2.85

Same Overprint on Great Britain Nos. 210-212

1934-35 Photo. *Perf. 14½x14*

505 A82 ½p dark green .40 .40
506 A97 1p carmine 1.10 1.25
507 A84 1½p red brown .40 .40
Nos. 505-507 (3) 1.90 2.05

Silver Jubilee Issue

Great Britain Nos. 226-228 Overprinted in Blue

b

1935, May 8

508 A98 ½p dark green .60 1.25
509 A98 1p carmine 6.75 5.50
510 A98 1½p red brown .75 .20
Nos. 508-510 (3) 8.10 6.95

25th anniv. of the reign of King George V.

Great Britain Nos. 230-232 Overprinted Type "a"

1936 Wmk. 250

511 A99 ½p dark green .20 .20
512 A99 1p crimson .20 .20
513 A99 1½p red brown .20 .20
Nos. 511-513 (3) .60 .60

Great Britain No. 234 Overprinted Type "b" in Blue

1937, May 13 Wmk. 251

514 A100 1½p purple brown .20 .20

Coronation of George VI and Elizabeth.

Great Britain Nos. 235-237 Overprinted in Blue or Black

c

1937 *Perf. 14½x14*

515 A101 ½p deep green (Bl) .20 .20
516 A101 1p scarlet (Bk) .20 .20
517 A101 1½p red brown (Bl) .20 .20
Nos. 515-517 (3) .60 .60

Great Britain Nos. 252-254 Ovptd. Type "a" in Blue or Black

1940, May 6

518 A106 ½p deep green (Bl) .20 .20
519 A106 1p scarlet (Bk) .25 .25
520 A106 1½p red brown (Bl) .35 .35
Nos. 518-520 (3) .80 .80

Centenary of the postage stamp.

Catalogue values for unused stamps in this section, from this point to the end of the section, are for Never Hinged items.

Great Britain Nos. 258 and 259 Overprinted Type "c" in Blue or Black

1944-45

521 A101 ½p green (Bl) .20 .20
522 A101 1p ver (Bk) ('45) .20 .20

Great Britain Nos. 264-265 Overprinted:

d

e

1946, June 11

523 A107(d) 2½p bright ultra .20 .20
524 A108(e) 3p violet .25 .25

Return to peace at close of World War II.

Great Britain Nos. 267 and 268 Overprinted Type "a"

1948, Apr. 26 *Perf. 14½x14, 14x14½*

525 A109 2½p bright ultra .20 .20
a. Pair, one without overprint *1,750.*
526 A110 £1 dp chalky bl 27.50 32.50

25th anniv. of the marriage of King George VI and Queen Elizabeth.

Great Britain Nos. 271 to 274 Overprinted Type "a"

1948, July 29 *Perf. 14½x14*

527 A113 2½p bright ultra .20 .20
528 A114 3p deep violet .30 .25
529 A115 6p red violet .40 .30
530 A116 1sh dark brown .80 .70
Nos. 527-530 (4) 1.70 1.45

1948 Olympic Games, Wembley, July-Aug.

Stamps of Great Britain, 1937-47, and Nos. 249A, 250 and 251A Overprinted Type "c"

1949, Jan. 1

531 A101 2p lt org (II) .20 .20
532 A101 2½p ultra (II) .20 .20
533 A101 3p violet (II) .20 .20
534 A102 4p gray green .70 .70
535 A102 5p light brown .70 .70
536 A102 6p rose lilac .45 .45
537 A103 7p emerald .55 .55
538 A103 8p bright rose .75 .75
539 A103 9p deep ol grn .75 .75
540 A103 10p royal blue 1.00 1.00
541 A103 11p violet brn 1.20 1.20
542 A103 1sh brown .70 .70

Wmk. 259

Perf. 14

543 A104 2sh6p yellow grn 5.75 5.75
544 A104 5sh dull red 6.25 6.25
545 A105 10sh ultra 32.50 32.50
Nos. 531-545 (15) 51.90 51.90

Great Britain Nos. 276 to 279 Overprinted Type "a"

Perf. 14½x14

1949, Oct. 10 Wmk. 251

546 A117 2½p bright ultra .20 .20
547 A118 3p bright violet .25 .20
548 A119 6p red violet .30 .30
549 A120 1sh brown .60 .60
Nos. 546-549 (4) 1.35 1.30

Great Britain Nos. 280-288 Overprinted Type "c" or "a" (Shilling Values)

1950-51

550 A101 ½p lt orange .20 .20
551 A101 1p ultra .20 .20
552 A101 1½p green .40 .40
553 A101 2p lt red brn .40 .40
554 A101 2½p vermilion .30 .30
555 A102 4p ultra ('50) .85 .85

Wmk. 259

Perf. 11x12

556 A121 2sh6p green 4.25 4.25
557 A121 5sh dull red 9.25 9.25
558 A122 10sh dull ultra 18.00 18.00
Nos. 550-558 (9) 33.85 33.85

Great Britain Nos. 292-308 Overprinted Type "c"

1952-54 Wmk. 298 *Perf. 14½x14*

559 A126 ½p red org ('53) .20 .20
560 A126 1p ultra ('53) .20 .20
561 A126 1½p green ('52) .20 .20
562 A126 2p red brn ('53) .20 .20
563 A127 2½p scarlet ('52) .20 .20
564 A127 3p dk pur (Dk Bl) .25 .20
565 A128 4p ultra ('53) .60 .60
566 A129 5p lt brown ('53) 1.25 1.25
567 A129 6p lilac rose .60 .60
568 A129 7p emerald 1.10 1.25
569 A130 8p brt rose ('53) 1.10 1.25
570 A130 9p dp olive grn 1.10 1.25
571 A130 10p royal blue 1.50 1.50
572 A130 11p violet brn 1.50 1.50
573 A131 1sh brown ('53) .75 .80
574 A132 1sh3p dk grn ('53) 1.10 1.25
575 A131 1sh6p dk blue ('53) 1.50 1.50
Nos. 559-575 (17) 13.35 13.95

Stamp and Type of Great Britain 1955 Overprinted Type "a"

Perf. 11x12

1955, Sept. 23 Engr. Wmk. 308

576 A133 2sh6p dark brown 2.50 3.00
577 A133 5sh crimson 7.50 9.00
578 A133 10sh brt ultra 15.00 18.00
Nos. 576-578 (3) 25.00 30.00

Coronation Issue

Great Britain Nos. 313-316 Overprinted Type "a"

1953, June 3 Photo. Wmk. 298

579 A134 2½p scarlet .50 .40
580 A135 4p brt ultra .90 .65
581 A136 1sh3p dark green 2.75 1.90
582 A137 1sh6p dark blue 3.25 2.25
Nos. 579-582 (4) 7.40 5.20

Great Britain Nos. 317, 323, 325 and 332 Overprinted Type "c"

1956 Wmk. 308 *Perf. 14½x14*

583 A126 ½p red orange .20 .20
584 A126 1p ultramarine .30 .20
585 A126 1½p green .55 .50
586 A126 2p red brown .90 .20
587 A127 2½p scarlet .70 .20
588 A127 3p dark purple .70 .35
589 A128 4p ultra 1.40 1.40
590 A129 6p lilac rose .90 .40
591 A132 1sh3p dark green 1.00 8.50
Nos. 583-591 (9) 6.65 11.95

Great Britain Nos. 317-333 and 309-311 Overprinted "1857-1957 TANGIER"

1957, Apr. 1 Photo. Wmk. 308

592 A126 ½p red orange .20 .20
593 A126 1p ultramarine .20 .20
594 A126 1½p green .20 .20
595 A126 2p red brown .20 .20
596 A127 2½p scarlet .20 .20
597 A127 3p dark purple .20 .20
598 A128 4p ultramarine .20 .20
599 A129 5p lt brown .20 .20
600 A129 6p lilac rose .30 .20
601 A129 7p emerald .40 .25
602 A130 8p brt rose .40 .25
603 A130 9p dp olive grn .40 .25
a. "TANGIER" omitted 5,500.
604 A130 10p royal blue .45 .30
605 A130 11p violet brown .60 .40
606 A131 1sh brown .30 .30
607 A132 1sh3p dark green .60 .40
608 A131 1sh6p dark blue .85 .50

Engr.

Perf. 11x12

609 A133 2sh6p dark brown 2.00 1.25
610 A133 5sh crimson 3.25 2.75
611 A133 10sh ultramarine 6.50 5.25
Nos. 592-611 (20) 17.65 13.70

Centenary of British P.O. in Tangier.

Nos. 609-611 are found with hyphen omitted (one stamp in sheet of 40).

British stamps overprinted "Tangier" were discontinued Apr. 30, 1957.

TURKISH EMPIRE

40 Paras = 1 Piaster
12 Pence = 1 Shilling (1905)

a

b

12 PIASTRES
c

40 PARAS
d

Surcharged on Great Britain Nos. 101, 104, 96

1885, Apr. 1 Wmk. 30 *Perf. 14*

1 A47(a) 40pa on 2½p lil 60.00 1.00
2 A45(b) 80pa on 5p grn 175.00 8.50

Wmk. 31

3 A44(c) 12pi on 2sh6p lilac 35.00 20.00
a. Bluish paper 250.00 125.00
Nos. 1-3 (3) 270.00 29.50

Great Britain Nos. 114, 118 Surcharged

1887 Wmk. 30

4 A57(a) 40pa on 2½p vio, *bl* 1.50 .20
a. Double surcharge 3,000. 2,500.
5 A61(b) 80pa on 5p lil & bl 6.25 .75
a. Small "0" in "80" 85.00 75.00

Great Britain No. 111 Handstamp Surcharged

1893, Feb. 25

6 A54(d) 40pa on ½p ver 500.00 175.00

No. 6 was a provisional, made and used at Constantinople for five days. Excellent forgeries are known.

Great Britain No. 121 Surcharged

e

1896

7 A64(e) 4pi on 10p car rose & lil 25.00 8.00

British Stamps of 1902 Surcharged

1902-05 Wmk. 30

8 A66(a) 40pa on 2½p ultra 5.00 .20
9 A71(b) 80pa on 5p lil & bl 7.00 1.50
a. Small "0" in "80" 275.00 100.00
10 A73(e) 4pi on 10p car rose & vio 3.50 3.25

Wmk. 31

11 A75(c) 12pi on 2sh6p vio ('03) 35.00 30.00
12 A76(c) 24pi on 5sh car rose ('05) 47.50 47.50
Nos. 8-12 (5) 98.00 82.45

Great Britain Nos. 131, 134 Surcharged

f

1906 Wmk. 30

13 A66(f) 1pi on 2½p ultra 3.50 .20
14 A71(f) 2pi on 5p lil & ultra 10.00 1.75

Nos. 10, 11, 14 are on both ordinary and chalky paper.

Great Britain Nos. 127-135, 138 Overprinted

g

1905

15 A66 ½p pale green .90 .20
16 A66 1p carmine .90 .25
17 A67 1½p violet & grn 6.00 5.75
18 A68 2p green & car 1.75 3.75
19 A66 2½p ultra 7.75 16.50
20 A69 3p violet, *yel* 7.75 13.00
21 A70 4p brown & grn 6.50 11.00
22 A71 5p lilac & ultra 12.00 18.00
23 A66 6p dull violet 9.00 18.00
24 A74 1sh car rose & grn 21.00 30.00
Nos. 15-24 (10) 73.55 116.45

Nos. 17, 18 and 24 are on both ordinary and chalky paper.

No. 18 Surcharged 1 Piastre

1906, July 2

25 A68 1pi on 2p grn & car 1,500. 650.

British Stamps of 1902-09 Surcharged:

j

k

1909

26 A67 30pa on 1½p vio & grn 4.00 .85
27 A69 1pi10pa on 3p vio, *yel* 7.00 14.00
28 A70 1pi30pa on 4p brn & grn 5.00 9.50
29 A70 1pi30pa on 4p org 8.25 17.00
30 A66 2pi20pa on 6p dl violet 12.50 27.50
31 A74 5pi on 1sh car rose & grn 3.00 4.50
Nos. 26-31 (6) 39.75 73.35

No. 29 is on ordinary paper, the others are on chalky paper.

Great Britain Nos. 132, 144, 135 Surcharged:

m

n

1910

32 A69(m) 1¼pi on 3p vio, *yel* .35 .35
33 A70(m) 1¾pi on 4p orange .45 .45
34 A66(n) 2½pi on 6p dl vio .80 .80
Nos. 32-34 (3) 1.60 1.60

There are three different varieties of "4" in the fraction of the 1¾ piastre.

Great Britain Nos. 151-154 Overprinted Type "g"

1911-12 *Perf. 15x14*

35 A80 ½p yellow green .50 .60
36 A81 1p carmine .75 .90

Re-engraved

37 A80 ½p yel grn ('12) .20 .20
38 A81 1p scarlet ('12) .25 .25

Great Britain No. 148 Surcharged

o

39 A66(o) 1pi on 2½p ultra 1.75 1.50
Nos. 35-39 (5) 3.45 3.45

The surcharge on No. 39 exists in two types with the letters 2½ and 3mm high respectively. The stamp also differs from No. 13 in the perforation.

British Stamps of 1912-13 Surcharged with New Values

1913-14 Wmk. 33

40 A84(j) 30pa on 1½p red brown 2.50 5.25
41 A86(o) 1pi on 2½p ultra 1.00 .20
42 A87(m) 1¼pi on 3p vio 1.75 2.75
43 A88(m) 1¾pi on 4p sl grn 2.50 3.25
44 A90(o) 4pi on 10p lt bl 4.00 7.75
45 A90(o) 5pi on 1sh bis 17.50 32.50
Nos. 40-45 (6) 29.25 51.70

British Stamps of 1912-19 Overprinted Type "g"

1913-21

46 A82 ½p green .20 .20
47 A83 1p scarlet .20 1.25
48 A85 2p orange ('21) 1.00 11.00
49 A87 3p violet ('21) 6.25 6.00
50 A88 4p sl grn ('21) 3.75 7.75
51 A89 5p yel brn ('21) 7.50 14.00
52 A89 6p dl vio ('21) 14.00 5.25
53 A90 1sh bister ('21) 8.25 4.25

Wmk. 34

Perf. 11x12

54 A91 2sh6p brn ('21) 30.00 40.00
Nos. 46-54 (9) 71.15 89.70

British Stamps of 1912-19 Surcharged as in 1909-10 and

p

q

1921 Wmk. 33 *Perf. 14½x14*

55 A82(j) 30pa on ½p grn .20 .20
a. Inverted surcharge 100.00
56 A83(p) 1½pi on 1p scar .20 .20
57 A86(p) 3¾pi on 2½p ultra .20 .20
58 A87(p) 4½pi on 3p vio .20 .20
59 A89(p) 7½p on 5p yel brn .20 .20
60 A90(p) 15pi on 10p lt bl .45 .35
61 A90(p) 18¾pi on 1sh bis 4.25 3.00

Wmk. 34

Perf. 11x12

62 A91(q) 45pi on 2sh6p brown 17.50 24.00
63 A91(q) 90pi on 5sh car rose 30.00 32.50
64 A91(q) 180pi on 10sh blue 45.00 35.00
Nos. 55-64 (10) 98.20 95.85

GUERNSEY

'gərn-zē

LOCATION — A group of islands in the English Channel
GOVT. — Dependent territory (bailiwick) of the British Crown
AREA — 30 sq. mi.

POP. — 58,681 (1996)
CAPITAL — St. Peter Port

The bailiwick includes the islands of Guernsey, Alderney, Sark, Herm, Jethou and Lithou.

Following the establishment of the British General Post Office as a public corporation on October 1, 1969, the post office of the Bailiwick of Guernsey became a separate entity and British postage stamps ceased to be valid.

Catalogue values for unused stamps in this country are for Never Hinged items.

Watermark

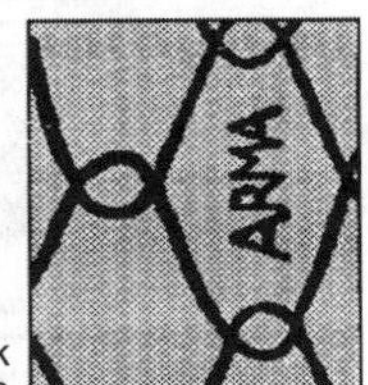

Wmk. 396- Link Fence

British Regional Issue

Guernsey Lily and Crown of William the Conqueror
A1 A2

Perf. 15x14

1958-69 Photo. Wmk. 322

1 A1 2½p rose red ('64) .30 .25
2 A2 3p light purple .30 .20
p. Phoshor. ('67) .20 .20
3 A2 4p ultra ('66) .30 .20
p. Phosphor. ('67) .20 .20

Unwmk.

4 A2 4p ultra ('68) .20 .20
5 A2 4p olive brown ('68) .20 .20
6 A2 4p bright red ('69) .20 .20
7 A2 5p dark blue ('68) .20 .20
Nos. 1-7 (7) 1.70 1.45

Nos. 4-7 are phosphorescent.

Sold to the general public only at post offices within Guernsey, but valid for postage throughout Great Britain.

See also Great Britain Nos. 269-270.

Bailiwick Issues

William the Conqueror, Queen Elizabeth II and Map of Bailiwick — A3

Creux Harbor, Sark — A4

Designs (Queen Elizabeth II and): ½p, Castle Cornet and Edward the Confessor. 1½p, Martello Tower and Henry II. 2p, Arms of Sark and King John. 3p, Arms of Alderney and Edward III. 4p, Guernsey lily and Henry V. 5p, Arms of Guernsey and Queen Elizabeth I. 6p, Arms of Alderney and Charles II. 9p, Arms of Sark and George III. 1sh, Arms of Guernsey and Queen Victoria. 1sh6p, Map of Bailiwick and William I. 1sh9p, Guernsey lily and Queen Elizabeth I. 2sh6p, Martello Tower and King John. 10sh, Braye Harbor, Alderney. £1, St. Peter Port, Guernsey.

Perf. 14½x14

1969-70 Photo. Unwmk.

8 A3 ½p magenta & blk .20 .20
9 A3 1p ultra & black .20 .20
10 A3 1½p bister & blk .20 .20
11 A3 2p dk blue & multi .20 .20
12 A3 3p deep org & multi .25 .20
13 A3 4p yel green & multi .35 .35
a. Booklet pane of 1 .85 .85
14 A3 5p vio blue & multi .30 .20
a. Booklet pane of 1 1.40 1.40
15 A3 6p ol green & multi .35 *.45*
16 A3 9p plum & multi .35 *.45*
17 A3 1sh dk olive & multi .35 *.45*
18 A3 1sh6p blue grn & blk .35 *.45*
19 A3 1sh9p magenta & multi .80 .75
20 A3 2sh6p purple & blk 4.00 3.00

Perf. 12½

21 A4 5sh multicolored 3.25 2.25
22 A4 10sh multicolored 24.00 22.50
a. Perf. 13½x13 52.50 45.00

Perf. 13½x13

23 A4 £1 multicolored 3.25 3.00
a. Perf. 12½ 4.50 4.50
Nos. 8-23 (16) 38.40 34.85

Issued: #22, 23a, 3/5/70; others, 10/1/69.
Nos. 9 and 18 are inscribed "40o 30' N."
See Nos. 28-29, 41-55.

Col. Isaac Brock — A5

Designs: 5p, Sir Isaac Brock as major general. 1sh9p, as ensign, flags of 1789 and 1969. 2sh6p, Regimental coat of arms and flags, horiz.

Perf. 14x13½, 13½x14

1969, Dec. 1 Litho. Unwmk.

24 A5 4p multicolored .25 .20
25 A5 5p black & multi .25 .20
26 A5 1sh9p dp blue & multi 1.10 .90
27 A5 2sh6p purple & multi 1.10 .90
Nos. 24-27 (4) 2.70 2.20

Sir Isaac Brock (1769-1812), born on Guernsey, commander of Quebec garrison.

Map Type of 1969 Redrawn

1969-70 Photo. *Perf. 14½x14*

28 A3 1p "49o 30'N" .25 .25
a. Booklet pane of 1 .45 .45
29 A3 1sh6p "49o 30'N" 3.00 2.00

No. 28a was issued Dec. 12, 1969, in booklets containing Nos. 13a, 14a, 28a. No. 70 issued 2/4/70.

Nos. 9 and 18 are inscribed "40o 30' N."

Destroyer "Bulldog" near Castle Cornet — A6

Designs: 5p, Liberation fleet in roadsteads between Guernsey, Herm and Jethou. 1sh6p, Brigadier A. E. Snow reading proclamation of King George VI on steps of Elizabeth College in Guernsey, vert.

1970, May 9 Photo. *Perf. 11½*

30 A6 4p vio blue & lt blue .25 .20
31 A6 5p dp plum & gray .25 .20
32 A6 1sh6p dk brown & bis 2.00 1.90
Nos. 30-32 (3) 2.50 2.30

25th anniv. of Guernsey's liberation from the Germans.

Guernsey Cow — A7

1970, Aug. 12 Photo. *Perf. 11½*

33 A7 4p Tomatoes 1.25 .50
34 A7 5p shown 1.25 .50
35 A7 9p Guernsey bull 6.00 2.50
36 A7 1sh6p Freesias 6.75 5.00
Nos. 33-36 (4) 15.25 8.50

For similar design see No. 68.

St. Anne, Alderney A8

Christmas (Churches): 5p, St. Peter, Town Church, Guernsey. 9p, St. Peter, Sark, vert. 1sh6p, St. Tugual Chapel, Herm, vert.

1970, Nov. 11 Photo. *Perf. 11½*

37 A8 4p blue, gold & brn .35 .20
38 A8 5p brt grn, gold & brn .45 .20
39 A8 9p rose red, gold & brown 1.25 1.10
40 A8 1sh6p brt purple, gold & brown 2.40 1.75
Nos. 37-40 (4) 4.45 3.25

Decimal Currency Issue
Types of 1969
"p" instead of "d"

Designs: ½p, Castle Cornet and Edward the Confessor. 1p, 5p, Map of Bailiwick and William the Conqueror. 1½p, Martello Tower and Henry II. 2p, Guernsey lily and Henry V. 2½p, Arms of Guernsey and Elizabeth I. 3p, Arms of Alderney and Edward III. 3½p, Guernsey lily and Elizabeth I. 4p, Arms of Sark and King John. 6p, Arms of Alderney and Charles II. 7½p, Arms of Guernsey and Queen Victoria. 9p, Arms of Sark and George III. 10p, Martello Tower and King John. 20p, Creux Harbor. 50p, Braye Harbor.

1971 Photo. *Perf. 14½x14*

41 A3 ½p magenta & blk .20 .20
a. Booklet pane of 1 .20
42 A3 1p ultra & black .20 .20
43 A3 1½p bister & blk .25 .25
44 A3 2p yel green & multi .25 .25
a. Booklet pane of 1 .35
45 A3 2½p vio blue & multi .25 .25
a. Booklet pane of 1 .35
46 A3 3p dp orange & multi .30 .30
47 A3 3½p magenta & multi .30 .30
48 A3 4p dk blue & multi .30 .30
49 A3 5p brt green & multi .30 .30
50 A3 6p dk green & multi .30 .30
51 A3 7½p brn olive & multi .40 .40
52 A3 9p plum & multi .45 .45
53 A3 10p purple & black 1.50 1.50

Perf. 13

54 A4 20p dk red & multi .75 .75
55 A4 50p multicolored 1.25 1.25
Nos. 41-55 (15) 7.00 7.00

Issue dates: #53-55, Jan. 6; others Feb. 15.

Thomas de la Rue, Hong Kong No. 1 — A9

Thomas de la Rue and: 2½p, GB No. 22. 4p, Italy No. 26. 7½p, US Confederate States No. 6.

1971, June 2 Engr. *Perf. 14x13½*

56 A9 2p brown .70 .20
57 A9 2½p carmine .70 .20
58 A9 4p dark green 2.10 1.75
59 A9 7½p violet blue 2.50 1.75
Nos. 56-59 (4) 6.00 3.90

Thomas de la Rue (1793-1866), founder of Thomas de la Rue & Co., Ltd., security printers.

Ebenezer Methodist Church — A10

Historic Churches of Guernsey: 2½p, St. Pierre du Bois. 5p, St. Joseph's, vert. 7½p, St. Philippe de Torteval, vert.

1971, Oct. 27 Photo. *Perf. 11½*

60 A10 2p green, sil & blk .40 .35
61 A10 2½p blue, sil & blk .45 .40
62 A10 5p pur, silver & blk 1.60 1.50
63 A10 7½p red, silver & blk 2.75 2.50
Nos. 60-63 (4) 5.20 4.75

Christmas 1971.

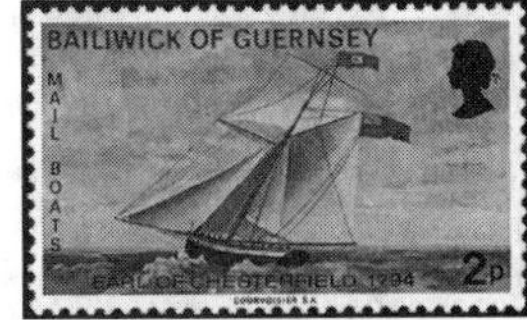

Mail Boat, Earl of Chesterfield, 1794 — A11

1972, Feb. 10 Photo. *Perf. 11½*

64 A11 2p shown .20 .20
65 A11 2½p *Dasher, 1827* .20 .20
66 A11 7½p *Ibex, 1891* .40 .40
67 A11 9p *Alberta, 1900* .60 .60
Nos. 64-67 (4) 1.40 1.40

See Nos. 77-80.

Guernsey Bull — A12

1972, May 22 Photo. *Perf. 11½*

68 A12 5p brown & multi .75 .60

Guernsey Breeders, 2nd World Conf. For similar designs see Nos. 33-36.

Wild Flowers A13

1972, May 24

69 A13 2p Sorrel .20 .20
70 A13 2½p Orchis maculata, vert. .20 .20
71 A13 7½p Carpobrotus edulis .45 .45
72 A13 9p Pimpernel, vert. .55 .55
Nos. 69-72 (4) 1.40 1.40

Angels, St. Martin's Church — A14

Stained Glass Windows from Guernsey Churches: 2½p, Virgin and Child, St. André's. 7½p, Virgin Mary, St. Sampson's. 9p, Christ Victorious, St. Pierre's.

1972, Nov. 20 Photo. *Perf. 11½*

73 A14 2p brick red & multi .20 .20
74 A14 2½p lt violet & multi .20 .20
75 A14 7½p yellow & multi .35 .35
76 A14 9p lt green & multi .35 .35
Nos. 73-76 (4) 1.10 1.10

Christmas 1972 and for the 25th anniv. of the marriage of Queen Elizabeth II and Prince Philip.

Mail Boat Type of 1972

1973, Mar. 9 Photo. *Perf. 11½*

77 A11 2½p *St. Julien, 1925* .20 .20
78 A11 3p *Isle of Sark, 1932* .25 .25
79 A11 7½p *St. Patrick, 1947* .45 .45
80 A11 9p *Sarnia, 1961* .45 .45
Nos. 77-80 (4) 1.35 1.35

No. 78 is incorrectly inscribed "Isle of Guernsey 1930."

Supermarine Sea Eagle — A15

Airplanes: 3p, Westland Wessex. 5p, De Havilland Rapide. 7½p, Douglas Dakota. 9p, Vickers Viscount.

1973, July 4 Photo. *Perf. 11½*

81 A15 2½p multicolored .20 .20
82 A15 3p multicolored .20 .20
83 A15 5p multicolored .20 .20
84 A15 7½p multicolored .45 .45
85 A15 9p multicolored .55 .55
Nos. 81-85 (5) 1.60 1.60

50th anniversary of air service to Guernsey.

The Good Shepherd, St. Michel du Valle — A16

Stained-glass Windows from Guernsey Churches: 3p, Jesus preaching, St. Marie du Castel. 7½p, St. Dominic, Notre Dame du Rosaire. 20p, Virgin and Child, St. Sauveur.

1973, Oct. 24 Photo. *Perf. 11½*

86 A16 2½p salmon & multi .20 .20
87 A16 3p blue & multi .20 .20
88 A16 7½p yellow & multi .20 .20
89 A16 20p multicolored .55 .55
Nos. 86-89 (4) 1.15 1.15

Christmas 1973.

Princess Anne and Mark Phillips — A17

1973, Nov. 14

90 A17 25p blue & multi .70 .70

Wedding of Princess Anne and Capt. Mark Phillips, Nov. 14, 1973.

"John Lockett," 1875 — A18

Guernsey Lifeboats: 3p, "Arthur Lionel," 1875. 8p, "Euphrosyne Kendal," 1954. 10p, "Arum," 1972.

1974, Jan. 15 Photo. *Perf. 11½*
Granite Paper

91 A18 2½p multicolored .20 .20
92 A18 3p multicolored .20 .20
93 A18 8p multicolored .25 .25
94 A18 10p multicolored .25 .25
Nos. 91-94 (4) .90 .90

Sesqui. of Royal Natl. Lifeboat Institution.

A19

Militia — A20

1974-78 Photo. *Perf. 11½*
Granite Paper (Nos. 95-107)

95 A19 ½p 1815 .20 .20
 a. Bklt. pane of 8 (5 #95, 3 #99) .35
 b. Bklt. pane of 16 (4 #95, 6 #99 and 6 #100) 1.10
96 A19 1p 1825 .20 .20
 a. Bklt. pane of 8 (4 #96, #100, 2 #102, #102A) ('77) .85
 b. Pane of 4 (#96, 2 #98, #102A) ('78) .55
97 A19 1½p 1787 .20 .20
98 A19 2p 1815 .20 .20
99 A19 2½p Royal, 1868 .20 .20
100 A19 3p Royal, 1895 .20 .20
101 A19 3½p Royal, 1867 .20 .20
102 A19 4p 1822 .20 .20
102A A19 5p Royal, 1895 .25 .25
103 A19 5½p Royal. 1833 .20 .20
104 A19 6p Royal. 1832 .20 .20
104A A19 7p 1822 .35 .35
105 A19 8p Royal, 1868 .20 .20
106 A19 9p 1785 .20 .20
107 A19 10p 1824 .20 .20

Perf. 13x13½, 13½x13

108 A20 20p Royal, 1848, vert. .40 .25
109 A20 50p Royal, 1868, vert. 1.00 .80
110 A20 £1 1814 2.40 1.25
Nos. 95-110 (18) 7.00 5.50

Issued: #95-107, 4/2/74; #108-110, 4/1/75; #102A, 104A, 5/2976; #96a, 2/8/77; #96b, 2/7/78.

Stamps in booklet panes are from special sheets of 80 (two 8x5 panes) which were sold separately.

Bailiwick Seal and UPU Emblem — A21

UPU Cent.: 3p, Map of Guernsey. 8p, UPU Headquarters, Bern, flag of Guernsey. 10p, Legislative Chamber, Parliament.

1974, June 11 Photo. *Perf. 11½*
Granite Paper

111 A21 2½p multicolored .20 .20
112 A21 3p ultra & multi .20 .20
113 A21 8p multicolored .25 .25
114 A21 10p multicolored .25 .25
Nos. 111-114 (4) .90 .90

Cradle Rock, by Renoir A22

Paintings by Renoir: 5½p, Moulin-Huet Bay. 8p, Woman at the Shore, vert. 10p, Self-portrait, vert.

1974, Sept. 21 Photo. *Perf. 13¼*

115 A22 3p multicolored .20 .20
116 A22 5½p multicolored .20 .20
117 A22 8p multicolored .25 .25
118 A22 10p multicolored .25 .25
Nos. 115-118 (4) .90 .90

Pierre Auguste Renoir (1841-1919), who painted pictures shown on Nos. 115-117 while visiting Guernsey.

Guernsey Spleenwort — A23

Designs: Guernsey ferns.

1975, Jan. 7 Photo. *Perf. 11½*

119 A23 3½p shown .20 .20
120 A23 4p Sand quillwort .20 .20
121 A23 8p Guernsey fern .20 .20
122 A23 10p Least adder's tongue .25 .25
Nos. 119-122 (4) .85 .85

Hauteville, Hugo's House A24

Victor Hugo Statue, Candie Gardens — A25

Designs: 8p, United Europe Oak, Hauteville (planted by Hugo). 10p, Departure for the Hunt, Aubusson tapestry, Hauteville.

1975, June 6 Photo. *Perf. 11½*
Granite Paper

123 A24 3½p dull yel & multi .20 .20
124 A25 4p lt blue & multi .20 .20
125 A25 8p yel green & multi .20 .20
126 A24 10p multicolored .25 .25
 a. Souvenir sheet of 4, #123-126 .80 .80
Nos. 123-126 (4) .85 .85

Victor Hugo (1802-85), French writer, political exile in Guernsey (1855-70).

Arms and Map of Guernsey — A26

Designs (Globe with Map of Bailiwick): 6p, Flag of Guernsey. 10p, Flag of Guernsey and arms of Alderney, horiz. 12p, Flag of Guernsey and arms of Sark, horiz.

1975, Oct. 7 Photo. *Perf. 13½*

127 A26 4p olive green & multi .20 .20
128 A26 6p rose lilac & multi .20 .20
129 A26 10p brt green & multi .25 .25
130 A26 12p orange & multi .25 .25
Nos. 127-130 (4) .90 .90

Christmas 1975.

Lighthouses — A27

1976, Feb. 10 Photo. *Perf. 11½*
Granite Paper

131 A27 4p Les Hanois .20 .20
132 A27 6p Les Casquets .20 .20
133 A27 11p Quesnard, Alderney .25 .25
134 A27 13p Point Robert, Sark .35 .35
Nos. 131-134 (4) 1.00 1.00

Guernsey Milk Can — A28

Europa: 25p, Silver christening cup.

1976, May 29 Photo. *Perf. 11½*
Granite Paper

135 A28 10p multicolored .40 .35
136 A28 25p multicolored .85 .65

Sheets of 9.

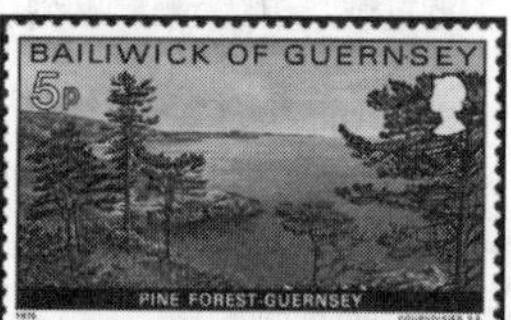

Pine Forest, Guernsey — A29

Guernsey Views: 7p, Herm Harbor and Jethou. 11p, Grande Grave Bay, Sark Cliffs, vert. 13p, Trois Vaux Bay, Alderney Cliffs, vert.

1976, Aug. 3 Photo. *Perf. 11½*
Granite Paper

137 A29 5p multicolored .20 .20
138 A29 7p multicolored .20 .20
139 A29 11p multicolored .30 .30
140 A29 13p multicolored .30 .30
Nos. 137-140 (4) 1.00 1.00

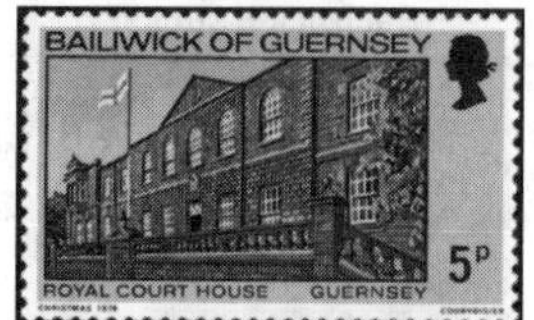

Royal Court House, Guernsey — A30

Christmas (Buildings in the Bailiwick): 7p, Elizabeth College, Guernsey. 11p, La Seigneurie, Sark. 13p, Island Hall, Alderney.

1976, Oct. 14 Photo. *Perf. 11½*
Granite Paper

141 A30 5p multicolored .20 .20
142 A30 7p multicolored .20 .20
143 A30 11p multicolored .30 .30
144 A30 13p multicolored .30 .30
Nos. 141-144 (4) 1.00 1.00

Elizabeth II with Order of the Garter — A31

Design: 7p, Queen Elizabeth II.

1977, Feb. 8 Photo. *Perf. 12x11½*

145 A31 7p blue & multi .20 .20
146 A31 35p purple & multi .80 .80

25th anniv. of the reign of Elizabeth II.

Talbots Valley — A32

25p, Fields and hedges, Talbots Valley.

1977, May 17 Photo. *Perf. 11½*
Granite Paper

147 A32 7p multicolored .20 .20
148 A32 25p multicolored .60 .60

Megalithic Tomb, Le Catioroc — A33

Prehistoric monuments: 5p, Menhir (statue), Castel, vert. 11p, Cist (tomb), Alderney. 13p, Menhir, St. Martin, vert.

1977, Aug. 2 Photo. *Perf. 11½*

149 A33 5p multicolored .20 .20
150 A33 7p multicolored .20 .20
151 A33 11p multicolored .30 .30
152 A33 13p multicolored .30 .30
Nos. 149-152 (4) 1.00 1.00

Mobile First Aid Unit A34

7p, Mobile radar & rescue coordination unit, for ships in distress. 11p, Marine ambulance "Flying Christine II," vert. 13p, Cliff rescue, vert.

1977, Oct. 25 Photo. *Perf. 11½*

153 A34 5p multicolored .20 .20
154 A34 7p multicolored .20 .20
155 A34 11p multicolored .25 .25
156 A34 13p multicolored .25 .25
Nos. 153-156 (4) .90 .90

St. John Ambulance Assoc. cent. (in GB).

View from Clifton, c. 1830 A35

19th Century Prints, Guernsey: 7p, Market Square, c. 1838. 11p, Petit-Bo Bay, c. 1839. 13p, The Quay, c. 1830.

1978, Feb. 7 Litho. *Perf. 14x13½*

157 A35 5p pale green & black .20 .20
158 A35 7p buff & black .20 .20
159 A35 11p pink & black .25 .25
160 A35 13p lt violet & black .35 .35
Nos. 157-160 (4) 1.00 1.00

See Nos. 236-239.

Memorial to Seamen of Ship Prosperity; Sark 1974 — A36

Europa: 7p, Victoria monument, vert.

1978, May 2 Litho. *Perf. 14½*

161 A36 5p multicolored .20 .20
162 A36 7p multicolored .25 .25

Elizabeth II — A37

1978, May 2 Photo. *Perf. 11½*

163 A37 20p ultra & black .60 .60

25th anniv. of coronation of Elizabeth II.

Inscribed: "VISIT OF/H.M. THE QUEEN AND/H.R.H. THE DUKE OF EDINBURGH/JUNE 28-29, 1978"

1978, June 28

164 A37 7p emerald & black .30 .30

Gannet A38

Birds: 7p, Firecrest. 11p, Dartford warbler. 13p, Spotted redshank.

1978, Aug. 29 Photo. *Perf. 11½*

165 A38 5p multicolored .20 .20
166 A38 7p multicolored .20 .20
167 A38 11p multicolored .30 .30
168 A38 13p multicolored .30 .30
Nos. 165-168 (4) 1.00 1.00

Solanum — A39

Christmas: 7p, Christmas rose. 11p, Holly, vert. 13p, Mistletoe, vert.

1978, Oct. 31 Photo. *Perf. 11½*

169 A39 5p multicolored .20 .20
170 A39 7p multicolored .20 .20
171 A39 11p multicolored .25 .25
172 A39 13p multicolored .25 .25
Nos. 169-172 (4) .90 .90

1 Double, 1930 — A40

1979, Feb. 13
Granite Paper

173 A40 ½p 1 double, 1930 .20 .20
174 A40 1p 2 doubles, 1899 .20 .20
175 A40 2p 4 doubles, 1902 .20 .20
176 A40 4p 8 doubles, 1959 .20 .20
177 A40 5p 3 pence, 1956 .20 .20
178 A40 6p 5 new pence, 1968 .20 .20
179 A40 7p 50 new pence, 1969 .20 .20
180 A40 8p 10 new pence, 1970 .20 .20
181 A40 9p ½ new penny, 1971 .20 .20
182 A40 10p 1 new penny, 1971 .20 .20
183 A40 11p 2 new pence, 1971 .20 .20
184 A40 12p 1 penny, 1977 .20 .20
185 A40 13p 2 pence, 1977 .20 .20
186 A40 14p 5 pence, 1977 .25 .25
187 A40 15p 10 pence, 1977 .25 .25
188 A40 20p 25 pence, 1977 .30 .20
Nos. 173-188 (16) 3.40 3.30

No. 177 is dark brown, No. 182, green & bronze. See Nos. 198B-203A.

Booklets containing 5 each #176, 181, 185 and 2 #176, 3 #181, 5 #185 exist produced from sheets of 30 (two 3x5 panes) and 20 (two 2x5 panes).

Oldest Pillar Box, 1853 Cancel, Truck — A41

Europa: 8p, Telephone, 1897, telex machine.

1979, May 8 Photo. *Perf. 11½*

189 A41 6p multicolored .25 .25
190 A41 8p multicolored .25 .25

Steam Tram, 1879 A42

Public Transportation: 8p, Electric tram, 1896. 11p, Autobus, 1911. 13p, Autobus, 1979.

1979, Aug. 7 Photo. *Perf. 11½*

191 A42 6p multicolored .20 .20
192 A42 8p multicolored .20 .20
193 A42 11p multicolored .25 .25
194 A42 13p multicolored .25 .25
Nos. 191-194 (4) .90 .90

Centenary of public transportation.

Postal Bureau and Headquarters — A43

Designs: 8p, Mail and telegram deliverymen. 13p, Parcel trucks. 15p, Post Office philatelic room.

1979, Oct. 1 Photo. *Perf. 11½*

195 A43 6p multicolored .20 .20
196 A43 8p multicolored .20 .20
197 A43 13p multicolored .25 .25
198 A43 15p multicolored .35 .35
a. Souvenir sheet of 4, Nos. 195-198 1.10 1.10
Nos. 195-198 (4) 1.00 1.00

Guernsey PO, 10th anniv.; Christmas 1979.

Coin Type of 1979

Designs: 10p, like No. 182. 11½p, ½ pence, 1979. 50p, Battle of Hastings coin, 1966. £1, Queen Elizabeth II 25th anniv., 1977, horiz. £2, Queen Elizabeth II 25th wedding anniv., 1972, horiz. £5, Official seal.

1980-81 Photo. *Perf. 11½*

198B A40 5p orange brown & multi .45 .45
199 A40 10p orange & bronze .25 .20
200 A40 11½p red & bronze .30 .20

Size: 26x45, 45x26mm

201 A40 50p red org & sil 1.10 .90
202 A40 £1 green & sil 2.40 2.00
203 A40 £2 blue & silver 5.00 3.25
203A A40 £5 multi ('81) 10.50 10.50
Nos. 198B-203A (7) 20.00 17.50

No. 177 is dark brown. Booklets containing 5 each #180, 198B, 185 and 4 #180, 5 #198B, 1 #185 exist produced from sheets of 30 (three 2x5 panes or two 3x5 panes).

Issue dates: £5, May 22, others, Feb. 5.

Policewoman Helping Child — A44

Guernsey Police Force, 60th Anniv.: 15p, Policeman on motorcycle. 17½p, Police dog and officer.

1980, May 6 Litho. *Perf. 14*

204 A44 7p multicolored .20 .20
205 A44 15p multicolored .45 .45
206 A44 17½p multicolored .50 .50
Nos. 204-206 (3) 1.15 1.15

Major Gen. John Gaspard Le Marchant — A45

Europa: 13½p, Admiral James Lord de Saumarez (1757-1836).

1980, May 6 Photo. *Perf. 11½*
Granite Paper

207 A45 10p multicolored .30 .30
208 A45 13½p multicolored .45 .45

Guernsey Golden Goat — A46

Designs: Various Guernsey golden goats.

1980, Aug. 5 Photo. *Perf. 13*

209 A46 7p multicolored .20 .20
210 A46 10p multicolored .25 .25
211 A46 15p multicolored .35 .35
212 A46 17½p multicolored .45 .45
Nos. 209-212 (4) 1.25 1.25

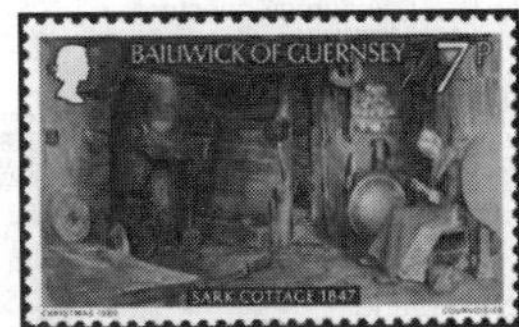

Sark Cottage, by Peter Le Lievre, 1847 — A47

Christmas 1980 (Le Lievre Paintings): 10p, Moulin Huet, 1850. 13½p, Boats at Sea, 1850. 15p, Cow Lane, 1852, vert. 17½p, Portrait, by Le Lievre's sister, vert.

1980, Nov. 15 Photo. *Perf. 12*
Granite Paper

213 A47 7p multicolored .20 .20
214 A47 10p multicolored .25 .25
215 A47 13½p multicolored .35 .35
216 A47 15p multicolored .40 .40
217 A47 17½p multicolored .45 .45
Nos. 213-217 (5) 1.65 1.65

Common Blue A48

1981, Feb. 24 Photo. *Perf. 14½*

218 A48 8p shown .20 .20
219 A48 12p Red Admiral .20 .20
220 A48 22p Small Tortoiseshell .50 .50
221 A48 25p Wall Brown .60 .60
Nos. 218-221 (4) 1.50 1.50

Le Petit Bonhomme Andriou (Head-shaped Rock) — A49

1981, May 22 Litho. *Perf. 14½*

222 A49 12p shown .40 .40
223 A49 18p Guernsey lily .60 .60

Europa.

Prince Charles and Lady Diana — A50

Royal Wedding: a, Charles. c, Diana.

1981, July 29 Litho. *Perf. 14½x15*

224 Strip of 3 .90 .90
a.-c. A50 8p any single .25 .25
225 Strip of 3 1.25 1.25
a.-c. A50 12p any single .40 .40

Size: 49x32mm

226 A50 25p Royal family .90 .90
a. Souv. sheet, #224-226, perf. 14x14½ 3.25 3.25
Nos. 224-226 (3) 3.05 3.05

Sark Launch — A51

Designs: Interisland transportation.

1981, Aug. 25 Photo. *Perf. 11½*

Granite Paper

227 A51 8p shown .20 .20
228 A51 12p Trislander plane .35 .35
229 A51 18p Hydrofoil .50 .50
230 A51 22p Herm catamaran .65 .65
231 A51 25p Alderney coaster .70 .70
Nos. 227-231 (5) 2.40 2.40

Rifle-shooting Competition A52

1981, Nov. 17 Litho. *Perf. 14¾*

232 A52 8p shown .20 .20
233 A52 12p Riding .35 .35
234 A52 22p Swimming .60 .60
235 A52 25p Electronics workers .70 .70
Nos. 232-235 (4) 1.85 1.85

Intl. Year of the Disabled.

Print Type of 1978

1982, Feb. 2 Litho. & Engr.

236 A35 8p Jethou .20 .20
237 A35 12p Fermain Bay .35 .35
238 A35 22p The Terres .60 .60
239 A35 25p St. Pierre Port .70 .70
Nos. 236-239 (4) 1.85 1.85

La Societe Guernesiaise Centenary A53

Society Emblem and Activities: 8p, Sir Edgar MacCulloch, founding president. 13p, William the Conqueror's fleet, Battle at Hastings (history). 20p, Sir James Saumarez's Crescent rescued from French fleet (history). 24p, Dragonfly (entomology). 26p, Vale Parish Church bird sanctuary (ornithology). 29p, Samian bowl, King's Road excavation (archaeology). 13p and 20p show CEPT (Europa) emblem.

1982, Apr. 28 Photo. *Perf. 11½*

Granite Paper

240 A53 8p multicolored .25 .25
241 A53 13p multicolored .40 .40
242 A53 20p multicolored .60 .60
243 A53 24p multicolored .75 .75
244 A53 26p multicolored .75 .75
245 A53 29p multicolored .80 .80
Nos. 240-245 (6) 3.55 3.55

Scouting Year — A54

1982, July 13 Litho. *Perf. 14½*

246 A54 8p Sea scouts, Castle Cornet, St. Peter Port .25 .25
247 A54 13p Boy scouts building bridge .40 .40
248 A54 26p Cub scouts parading .75 .75
249 A54 29p Air scouts reading chart .95 .95
Nos. 246-249 (4) 2.35 2.35

Christmas 1982 — A55

1982, Oct. 12 Photo. *Perf. 14½*

250 A55 8p Midnight mass, St. Peter Port Church .20 .20
251 A55 13p Exchanging presents .35 .35
252 A55 24p Dinner .65 .65
253 A55 26p Exchanging cards .70 .70
254 A55 29p Watching Queen's TV greeting .90 .90
Nos. 250-254 (5) 2.80 2.80

Centenary of Boys' Brigade — A56

Designs: Various brigade activities.

1983, Jan. 18 *Perf. 14*

255 A56 8p multicolored .25 .25
256 A56 13p multicolored .40 .40
257 A56 24p multicolored .70 .70
258 A56 26p multicolored .75 .75
259 A56 29p multicolored 1.00 1.00
Nos. 255-259 (5) 3.10 3.10

Europa 1983 — A57

Views of St. Peter Port Harbor. oldst

1983, Mar. 14 Photo. *Perf. 11½*

Granite Paper

260 A57 13p multicolored .35 .35
261 A57 13p multicolored .35 .35
a. Pair, #260-261 .70 .70
262 A57 20p multicolored .55 .55
263 A57 20p multicolored .55 .55
a. Pair, #262-263 1.10 1.10

View at Guernsey, by Renoir — A58

Centenary of Renoir's Visit: 13p, Children at the Seashore (26x39mm). 26p, Marine Guernsey. 28p, Moulin Huet Bay through the Trees. 31p, Fog in Guernsey.

Perf. 12, 11½x12 (13p)

1983, Sept. 6 Photo.

Granite Paper

264 A58 9p multicolored .25 .25
265 A58 13p multicolored .40 .40
266 A58 26p multicolored .80 .80
267 A58 28p multicolored .85 .85
268 A58 31p multicolored .95 .95
Nos. 264-268 (5) 3.25 3.25

Star of the West, 1869 Merchant Ship, Capt. J.G. Lenfestey — A59

1983, Nov. 15 Photo. *Perf. 14½*

269 A59 9p Launching .25 .25
270 A59 13p Leaving St. Peter Port .40 .40
271 A59 26p Rio Grande Bar .80 .80
272 A59 28p St. Lucia .85 .85
273 A59 31p Voyage Map .95 .95
Nos. 269-273 (5) 3.25 3.25

Dame of Sark (Sibyl Hathaway, 1884-1974) — A60

Biographical Scenes: 9p, Portrait, La Seigneurie (residence). 13p, German occupation, 1940-45. 26p, Royal visit, 1957. 28p, Chief Pleas (parliament). 31p, Dame of Sark rose.

1984, Feb. 7 Litho. *Perf. 14½*

274 A60 9p multicolored .25 .25
275 A60 13p multicolored .40 .40
276 A60 26p multicolored .80 .80
277 A60 28p multicolored .85 .85
278 A60 31p multicolored .95 .95
Nos. 274-278 (5) 3.25 3.25

Links with the Commonwealth — A61

Designs: 9p, Flag of Guernsey, Royal Court. 31p, Union Jack, Castle Cornet.

1984, Apr. 10 Litho. *Perf. 14½*

279 A61 9p multicolored .25 .25
280 A61 31p multicolored 1.10 1.10

Europa (1959-84) — A62

1984, Apr. 10 *Perf. 15*

281 A62 13p multicolored .55 .55
282 A62 20½p multicolored .85 .85

Petit Port — A63

Perf. 15x14½, 14½x15

1984-85 Litho.

283 A63 1p Little Chapel, vert. ('85) .20 .20
284 A63 2p Ft. Grey ('85) .20 .20
285 A63 3p St. Apolline Chapel, vert. .20 .20
286 A63 4p shown .20 .20
287 A63 5p Little Russel ('85) .20 .20
288 A63 6p The Harbour, Herm ('85) .20 .20
289 A63 7p Saints ('85) .20 .20
290 A63 8p St. Saviour, vert. ('85) .20 .20
291 A63 9p Cambridge Berth .20 .20
292 A63 10p Belvoir, Herm .35 .20
a. Min. sheet, 2 2p, 4 4p, 2 5p, 2 10p 2.50
293 A63 11p La Seigneurie, Sark ('85) .20 .20
294 A63 13p St. Saviour's Reservoir .35 .35
a. Min. sheet, 2 4p, 3 9p, 5 13p 3.00
b. Min. sheet, 5 each 4p, 9p, 13p 5.00
295 A63 14p St. Peter Port, vert. .20 .20
a. Min. sheet, 4 9p, 6 14p 4.50
b. Min. sheet, 2 9p, 8 14p 4.75
c. Min. sheet, 5 10p, 5 14p 4.50
296 A63 15p Havelet, vert. ('85) .35 .20
a. Min. sheet, 3p, 2 4p, 4 11p, 3 15p 3.75
b. Min. sheet, 5 each 11p, 15p 4.50
297 A63 20p La Coupee, Sark .60 .20
a. Min. sheet, 4 6p, 4 14p, 2 20p 3.00
b. Min. sheet, 5 14p, 5 20p 3.50
298 A63 30p Grandes Rocques ('85) .70 .70
299 A63 40p St. Torteval Church, vert. .95 .95
300 A63 50p Bordeaux 1.10 1.10
301 A63 £1 Albecq 2.25 2.25
302 A63 £2 L'Ancresse ('85) 5.00 5.00
Nos. 283-302 (20) 13.85 13.15

Issued: 1p, 2p, 5p, 6p, 7p, 8p, 11p, 15p, 30p, £2, 7/23/84; 3p, 4p, 9p, 10p, 13p, 14p, 20p, 40p, 50p, £1, 9/18/84; #292a, 12/2/85; #294a-294b, 9/18/84; #295a-295b, 3/19/85; #295c, 4/1/86; #296a-296b, 3/30/87; #297a-297b, 12/27/89.

Miniature sheets sold folded and unattached in booklet covers.

See Nos. 372-378, 453-454.

Lieutenant-General John Doyle (1756-1834) — A64

Designs: 13p, Portrait by James Ramsey, 1817. 29p, American War of Independence battle. 31p, Land fill, Grand Havre Bay. 34p, Ship approaching Casquets Reef, 1811. 29p, 31p, 34p horiz.

1984, Nov. 20 Photo. *Perf. 11½*

303 A64 13p multicolored .40 .40
304 A64 29p multicolored .90 .90
305 A64 31p multicolored .95 .95
306 A64 34p multicolored 1.00 1.00
Nos. 303-306 (4) 3.25 3.25

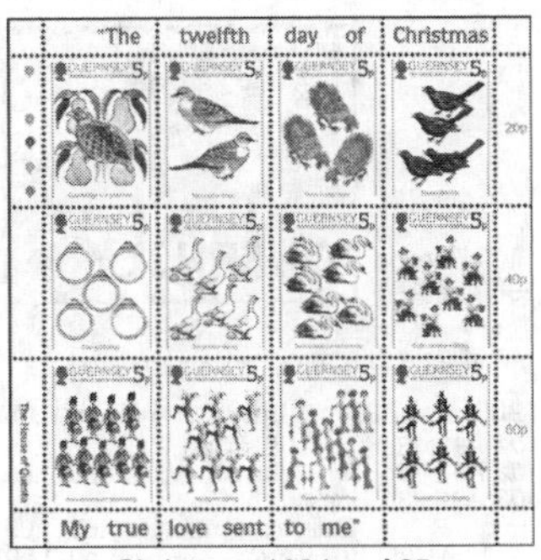

Christmas 1984 — A65

Twelve Days of Christmas: a, Partridge in a Pear Tree. b, 2 Turtle Doves. c, 3 French Hens. d, 4 Colly Birds. e, 5 Golden Rings. f, 6 Geese-a-Laying. g, 7 Swans a-Swimming. h, 8 Maids a-Milking. i, 9 Drummers Drumming. j, 10 Pipers Piping. k, 11 Ladies Dancing. l, 12 Lords a-Leaping. Illustration reduced.

1984, Nov. 20 Litho. *Perf. 14½*

307 A65 Sheet of 12	2.50	2.50
a.-l. 5p any single	.20	.20

Indigenous Fish — A66

1985, Jan. 22 Photo. *Perf. 12*

308 A66 9p Cockoo Wrasse	.35	.35
309 A66 13p Red Gurnard	.55	.55
310 A66 29p Red Mullet	1.10	1.10
311 A66 31p Mackerel	1.40	1.40
312 A66 34p Sunfish	1.60	1.60
Nos. 308-312 (5)	5.00	5.00

Liberation from German Forces, 40th Anniv. A67

1985, May 9 Litho. *Perf. 14x14½*

313 A67 22p Peace dove	.90	.90

Celebrating the end of the war in Europe (VE-Day).

Europa 1985 — A68

Designs: 14p, Musical staff, flags of Great Britain, Netherlands, Germany, Italy, Cross of St. George. 22p, Music, cello, French horn.

1985, May 14 Litho. *Perf. 14½*

314 A68 14p multicolored	.50	.50
315 A68 22p multicolored	.85	.85

Intl. Youth Year — A69

1985, May 14 Litho. *Perf. 14*

316 A69 9p IYY emblem, circle of children	.35	.35
317 A69 31p Girl Guides in camp	1.10	1.10

Children's drawings.

Girl Guides, 75th Anniv. — A70

1985, May 14 Litho. *Perf. 14*

318 A70 34p Leader, guide and brownie	1.40	1.40

Child's drawing.

Christmas 1985 — A71

Religious and folk figures: a, Santa Claus. b, Lussibruden. c, Balthasar. d, St. Nicholas. e, La Befana. f, Julenisse. g, Christkind. h, King Wenceslas. i, Shepherd of Les Baux. j, Caspar. k, Baboushka. l, Melchior.

1985, Nov. 19 Litho. *Perf. 12½*

Granite Paper

319 A71 Sheet of 12	*5.75*	*5.75*
a.-l. 5p any single	.45	.45

Watercolors by Paul Jacob Naftel — A72

1985, Nov. 19 *Perf. 15x14½*

320 A72 9p Vraicing	.30	.30
321 A72 14p Castle Cornet	.50	.50
322 A72 22p Rocquaine Bay	.75	.75
323 A72 31p Little Russel	1.10	1.10
324 A72 34p Seaweed Gatherers	1.40	1.40
Nos. 320-324 (5)	4.05	4.05

Queen Elizabeth II, 60th Birthday — A74

1986, Apr. 21 *Perf. 14*

330 A74 60p multicolored	2.10	2.10

Europa 1986 — A75

1986, May 22 *Perf. 11½*

Granite Paper

331 A75 10p Operation Gannet	.30	.30
332 A75 14p Whitsun orchid	.45	.45
333 A75 22p Guernsey elm	.75	.75
Nos. 331-333 (3)	1.50	1.50

Wedding of Prince Andrew and Sarah Ferguson — A76

1986, July 23 Litho. *Perf. 14*

334 A76 14p Couple	.60	.60

Size: 48x32mm

335 A76 34p Couple, diff.	1.50	1.50

Sports A77

1986, July 24 *Perf. 14½*

336 A77 10p Lawn bowling, vert.	.30	.30
337 A77 14p Cricket, vert.	.45	.45
338 A77 22p Badminton, vert.	.70	.70
339 A77 29p Field hockey, vert.	1.00	1.00
340 A77 31p Swimming	1.10	1.10
341 A77 34p Rifle shooting	1.25	1.25
Nos. 336-341 (6)	4.80	4.80

Museums A78

1986, Nov. 18 Litho. *Perf. 14½*

342 A78 14p Guernsey Museum and Art Gallery	.45	.45
343 A78 29p Ft. Grey Maritime Museum	.90	.90
344 A78 31p Castle Cornet	1.00	1.00
345 A78 34p Natl. Trust of Guernsey Folk Museum	1.10	1.10
Nos. 342-345 (4)	3.45	3.45

Miniature Sheet

Christmas — A79

Carols: a, "While Shepherds Watched Their Flocks by Night." b, "In the Bleak Mid-Winter." c, "O Little Town of Bethlehem." d, "The Holly and the Ivy." e, "O Little Christmas Tree." f, "Away in a Manger." g, "Good King Wenceslas." h, "We Three Kings of Orient Are." i, "Hark the Herald Angels Sing." j, "I Saw Three Ships." k, "Little Donkey." l, "Jingle Bells."

1986, Nov. 18 *Perf. 12½*

346 A79 Sheet of 12	3.00	3.00
a.-l. 6p any single	.25	.25

Souvenir Sheet

Duke of Richmond, 18th Century Map Detail — A80

1987, Feb. 10 Litho. *Perf. 14½*

347 Sheet of 4	3.50	3.50
a. A80 14p shown	.50	.50
b. A80 29p North	.90	.90
c. A80 31p Southwest	.95	.95
d. A80 34p Southeast	1.00	1.00

Duke of Richmond's survey of Guernsey, bicent.

Europa 1987 — A81

Modern architecture.

1987, May 5 Litho. *Perf. 13x13½*

348 A81 15p Postal headquarters	.45	.45
349 A81 15p Headquarters, schematic view	.45	.45
a. Pair, #348-349	.90	.90
350 A81 22p Grammar school entrance	.70	.70
351 A81 22p School, schematic view	.70	.70
a. Pair, #350-351	1.40	1.40

Andros and La Plaiderie Court House, Guernsey A82

Andros and: 29p, Governor's Palace, Virginia. 31p, "Governor Andros and the Boston People," print from Harper's New Monthly Magazine. 34p, Map of New Amsterdam (New York City).

1987, July 7 *Perf. 12*

Granite Paper

352	A82 15p multicolored	.50	.50
353	A82 29p multicolored	.90	.90
354	A82 31p multicolored	.95	.95
355	A82 34p multicolored	1.00	1.00
	Nos. 352-355 (4)	3.35	3.35

Sir Edmund Andros (1637-1714), lieutenant-governor of Guernsey (1704-1706) and statesman of Colonial America (1672-1710).

William the Conqueror (c. 1028-1087), King of England (1066-1087) — A83

11p, Jester warning young William of a plot to murder him. #357, Battle of Hastings. #358, King William, his banner at the Battle of Hastings. #359, William the Conqueror. #360, Abbey at Caen & Queen Matilda of Flanders (d. 1083). 34p, Halley's Comet & regalia of William I.

1987, Sept. 9 *Perf. 13½x14*

356	A83 11p multicolored	.35	.35
357	A83 15p multicolored	.50	.50
358	A83 15p multicolored	.50	.50
a.	Pair, #357-358	1.00	1.00
359	A83 22p multicolored	.75	.75
360	A83 22p multicolored	.75	.75
a.	Pair, #359-360	1.50	1.50
361	A83 34p multicolored	1.10	1.10
	Nos. 356-361 (6)	3.95	3.95

Visit of John Wesley (1703-1791), Religious Reformer, Bicent. — A84

Designs: 7p, Preaching at the quay, Alderney. 15p, Preaching at Mon Plaisir. 29p, Preaching at Assembly Rooms, St. Peter Port. 31p, Wesley and La Ville Baudu, an early Methodist meeting place, Vale Parish. 34p, Wesley and Ebenezer Methodist Church, first Methodist chapel, Union Street, 1816.

1987, Nov. 17 **Litho.** *Perf. 14½*

362	A84 7p multicolored	.25	.25
363	A84 15p multicolored	.55	.55
364	A84 29p multicolored	.95	.95
365	A84 31p multicolored	1.00	1.00
366	A84 34p multicolored	1.10	1.10
	Nos. 362-366 (5)	3.85	3.85

Voyage of the Golden Spur, Apr. 12, 1872-Jan. 4, 1874 — A85

Designs: 11p, Off St. Sampson's Harbor. 15p, Entering Hong Kong Harbor. 29p, Anchored off Macao. 31p, In China Tea Race. 34p, Golden Spur, map of voyage.

1988, Feb. 9 **Litho.** *Perf. 13½x14*

367	A85 11p multicolored	.40	.40
368	A85 15p multicolored	.55	.55
369	A85 29p multicolored	.95	.95
370	A85 31p multicolored	1.00	1.00
371	A85 34p multicolored	1.10	1.10
	Nos. 367-371 (5)	4.00	4.00

Guernsey's Golden Age of Shipping: largest vessel built on Guernsey, the Golden Spur, launched Oct. 15, 1864, wrecked at Haiphong on Feb. 27, 1879.

Landscape Type of 1984

Perf. 14½x15, 15x14½

1988-89 **Litho.**

372	A63 12p Petit Bot beach, vert.	.40	.40
373	A63 16p St. John's Hostel for the Aged	.50	.50
a.	Min. sheet, 5 each 12p, 16p	6.00	
b.	Min. sheet, 4 4p, 3 12p, 3 16p	4.50	
374	A63 18p Le Variouf, vert.	.60	.60
a.	Min. sheet, 4p, 6p, 3 12p, 3 18p	3.75	
b.	Min. sheet, 4 12p, 4 18p	3.25	
	Nos. 372-374 (3)	1.50	1.50

Nos. 373a-373b and 374a-374b sold unattached in booklet covers.

Issued: Nos. 372-373b, 3/28/88; Nos. 374-374b, 2/28/89.

Coil Stamps

Sizes: 21½x17½mm, 17½x21½mm

Perf. 14x14½, 14½x14

375	A63 11p La Seigneurie, Sark	.45	.45
376	A63 12p Petit Bot beach	.50	.50
377	A63 15p Havelet, vert.	.60	.60
378	A63 16p St. John's Hostel for the Aged	.65	.65
	Nos. 375-378 (4)	2.20	2.20

Issued: 11p, 15p, 5/15/87; 12p, 16p, 3/28/88.

Waves, Map — A85a

Perf. 14½x14

1989, Apr. 3 **Photo.** **Coil Stamp**

380	A85a (18p) green	1.00	1.00

Inscribed "MINIMUM FIRST CLASS POSTAGE TO UK PAID." See No. 431.

Europa 1988 A86

Communication and transportation: No. 381, Bedford Rascal postal van, Lihou Is. rowboat. No. 382, Rowboat, Viscount plane. No. 383, Horse and buggy, front wheel of bicycle. No. 384, Back wheel of bicycle, No. 4 coach.

1988, May 10 **Litho.** *Perf. 14½*

381	A86 16p multicolored	.45	.45
382	A86 16p multicolored	.45	.45
a.	Pair, #381-382	.90	.90
383	A86 22p multicolored	.70	.70
384	A86 22p multicolored	.70	.70
a.	Pair, #383-384	1.40	1.40
	Nos. 381-384 (4)	2.30	2.30

#382a, 384a have continuous designs.

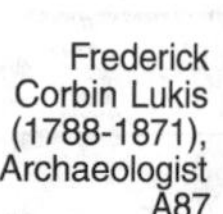

Frederick Corbin Lukis (1788-1871), Archaeologist A87

Designs: 12p, Entrance to Lukis House, St. Peter Port, and portrait. 16p, Bound manuscript containing illustrations painted by Lukis's daughter Mary Anne (born 1822). 29p, Lukis supervising excavation of Le Creux es Faies dolmen at L'Eree, Guernsey. 31p, Rear of Lukis House and garden. 34p, Artifacts recovered by Lukis and preserved as part of the museum collection.

1988, July 12 **Photo.** *Perf. 12½*

Granite Paper

385	A87 12p multicolored	.35	.35
386	A87 16p multicolored	.50	.50
387	A87 29p multicolored	.90	.90
388	A87 31p multicolored	1.00	1.00
389	A87 34p multicolored	1.10	1.10
	Nos. 385-389 (5)	3.85	3.85

1988 World Offshore Powerboat Championships — A88

Designs: 16p, Racing boats, Royal Navy helicopter. 30p, Boats racing through Gouliot Passage (separating Sark from Brecqhou). 32p, Boats, helicopter, St. John's Ambulance rescue ship, vert. 35p, Race course marked in red on Admiralty Chart, vert.

1988, Sept. 6 *Perf. 12*

Granite Paper

390	A88 16p multicolored	.60	.60
391	A88 30p multicolored	.95	.95
392	A88 32p multicolored	1.00	1.00
393	A88 35p multicolored	1.10	1.10
	Nos. 390-393 (4)	3.65	3.65

Publication of *Flora Sarniensis,* Bicent. — A89

Designs: 12p, Joshua Gosselin (1739-1813), botanist, and herbarium made by Rollo Sherwill in 1976. No. 395, *Lagurus ovatus* (pressed specimen). No. 396, *Lagurus ovatus,* diff. No. 397, *Silene gallica quinquevulnera* (pressed specimen). No. 398, *Silene gallica quinquevulnera,* diff. 35p, *Limonium binervosum sarniense serquense.*

1988, Nov. 15 **Litho.** *Perf. 14*

394	A89 12p shown	.40	.40
395	A89 16p multicolored	.50	.50
396	A89 16p multicolored	.50	.50
a.	Pair, #395-396	1.00	1.00
397	A89 23p multicolored	.75	.75
398	A89 23p multicolored	.75	.75
a.	Pair, #397-398	1.50	1.50
399	A89 35p multicolored	1.10	1.10
	Nos. 394-399 (6)	4.00	4.00

Miniature Sheet

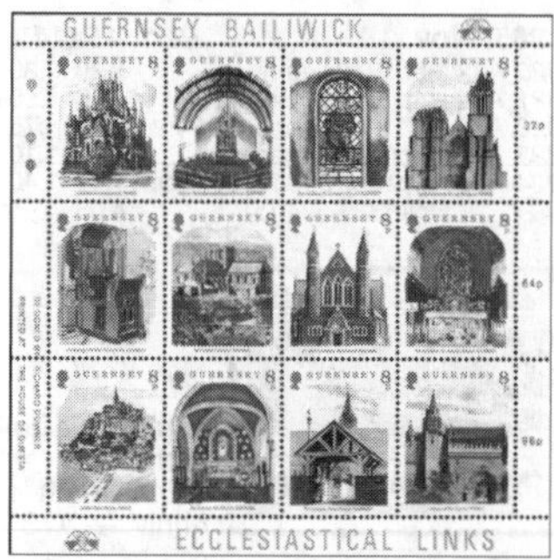

Ecclesiastical Links to France and Great Britain — A90

Church interiors, exteriors and artifacts: a, Coutances Cathedral, France. b, Notre Dame du Rosaire Church interior, Guernsey. c, Stained-glass window, St. Sampson's Church, Guernsey. d, Dol-de-Bretagne Cathedral, France. e, Bishop's Throne, Town Church, Guernsey. f, Winchester Cathedral, England. g, St. John's Cathedral, Portsmouth, England. h, High Altar, St. Joseph's Church, Guernsey. i, Mont Saint-Michel, France. j, Chancel, Vale Church, Guernsey. k, Lich gate, Forest Church, Guernsey. l, Marmoutier Abbey, France.

1988, Nov. 15 *Perf. 14½x15*

400	A90 Sheet of 12	3.50	3.50
a.-l.	8p any single	.25	.25

Christmas 1988.

Europa 1989 — A91

Traditional children's toys and games.

1989, Feb. 28 **Litho.** *Perf. 13½*

401	A91 12p Tip cat (Le Cat)	.35	.35
402	A91 16p Girl, Cobo Alice doll	.50	.50
403	A91 23p Hopscotch (Le Colimachaon)	.65	.65
	Nos. 401-403 (3)	1.50	1.50

Aircraft A92

1989, May 5

404	A92 12p DH86 Express	.40	.40
a.	Booklet pane of 6	2.75	
405	A92 12p Southampton	.40	.40
406	A92 18p DH89 Rapide	.60	.60
a.	Booklet pane of 6	4.25	
407	A92 18p Sunderland	.60	.60
408	A92 35p BAe 146	1.10	1.10
a.	Booklet pane of 6	7.75	
409	A92 35p Shackleton	1.10	1.10
	Nos. 404-409 (6)	4.20	4.20

Guernsey Airport, 50th anniv. (Nos. 404, 406, 408); others, 201st Squadron Affiliation, 50th anniv.

Visit of Queen Elizabeth II, May 23-24 — A93

1989, May 23 *Perf. 15x14*

410	A93 30p Portrait by June Mendoza	1.00	1.00

Great Western Railway Steamer Service Between Weymouth and the Channel Isls., Cent. — A94

1989, Sept. 5 **Litho.** *Perf. 13½*

411	A94 12p S.S. *Ibex,* 1891	.40	.40
412	A94 18p P.S. *Great Western,* 1872	.55	.55
413	A94 29p S.S. *St. Julien,* 1925	.95	.95
414	A94 34p S.S. *Roebuck,* 1925	1.00	1.00
415	A94 37p S.S. *Antelope,* 1889	1.10	1.10
a.	Souvenir sheet of 5, #411-415	4.25	4.25
	Nos. 411-415 (5)	4.00	4.00

Zoological Trust of Guernsey — A95

1989, Nov. 17 Litho. *Perf. 14x13½*

416 A95 18p Two-toed sloth .60 .60
417 A95 29p Capuchin monkey .95 .95
418 A95 32p White-lipped tamarin 1.10 1.10
419 A95 34p Squirrel monkey 1.10 1.10
420 A95 37p Lar gibbon 1.25 1.25
a. Strip of 5, #416-420 5.00 5.00

Animals of the rainforest.

Miniature Sheet

Christmas — A96

Ornaments on tree: a, Star. b, Angel. c, Candles. d, Robin red breast. e, Presents on sled. f, Caroler. g, Santa Claus pictured on wooden ornament. h, Herald and stars pictured on glass ball. i, Presents in stocking. j, Bell. k, Reindeer. l, Chapel.

1989, Nov. 17 *Perf. 13*

421 A96 Sheet of 12 4.00 4.00
a.-l. 10p any single .30 .30

Europa 1990 — A97

Post offices.

1990, Feb. 27 Litho. *Perf. 13½x14*

422 A97 20p Sark, c. 1890 .65 .65
423 A97 20p Sark, 1990 .65 .65
424 A97 24p Arcade, c. 1840 .80 .80
425 A97 24p Arcade, 1990 .80 .80
Nos. 422-425 (4) 2.90 2.90

Penny Black, 150th Anniv. A98

Designs: 14p, Great Britain No. 1, Maltese Cross cancellation in red, mail steamer in St. Peter Port Harbor. 20p, Great Britain No. 3, Maltese Cross cancellation in black, pedestrians, mailbox at Elm Grove and Union Street in 1852. 32p, Great Britain No. 255 bisected, 1940, and military band. 34p, Guernsey No. 2, crown of William the Conqueror, Guernsey lily. 37p, Guernsey No. 10, crowd in line outside Guernsey P.O.

1990, May 3 *Perf. 14*

426 A98 14p multicolored .45 .45
427 A98 20p multicolored .60 .60
428 A98 32p multicolored 1.00 1.00
429 A98 34p multicolored 1.00 1.00
430 A98 37p multicolored 1.10 1.10
a. Souvenir sheet of 5, #426-430 4.25 4.25
b. No. 430a ovptd. "NZ 1990" emblem, "FROM LONDON 90 TO NEW ZEALAND 90" 17.50 17.50
Nos. 426-430 (5) 4.15 4.15

Map and Waves Type of 1989

1989, Dec. 27 Photo. *Perf. 14½x14*

Coil Stamp

431 A85a (14p) ultra & lt ultra .85 .85

Inscribed "MINIMUM BAILIWICK POSTAGE PAID."

Lord Anson's Circumnavigation of the World, 250th Anniv. — A99

Designs: 14p, Philip Saumarez writing ship's log. 20p, *Centurion, Gloucester, Severn, Pearle, Wager* and *Tryal* departing from Portsmouth. 29p, Landfall at St. Catherine's Is. off Brazil, 1740. 34p, *Tryal* rounding Cape Horn, 1741. 37p, Camp at Juan Fernandez, 1741.

1990, July 24 Litho. *Perf. 13½x14*

436 A99 14p multicolored .45 .45
437 A99 20p multicolored .65 .65
438 A99 29p multicolored .95 .95
439 A99 34p multicolored 1.10 1.10
440 A99 37p multicolored 1.25 1.25
Nos. 436-440 (5) 4.40 4.40

Gray Seal A100

1990, Oct. 16 Litho. *Perf. 14½*

441 A100 20p shown .85 .85
442 A100 26p Bottlenose dolphin 1.75 1.75
443 A100 31p Basking shark 2.00 2.00
444 A100 37p Harbor porpoise 2.40 2.40
Nos. 441-444 (4) 7.00 7.00

World Wildlife Fund.

Miniature Sheet

Christmas — A101

Winter birds: a, Blue and Great Tits. b, Snow Bunting. c, Kestrel. d, Starling. e, Greenfinch. f, Robin. g, Wren. h, Barn owl. i, Mistle Thrush. j, Heron. k, Chaffinch. l, Kingfisher.

1990, Oct. 16 *Perf. 13½*

445 A101 Sheet of 12 4.25 4.25
a.-l. 10p any single .35 .35

Occupation Stamp No. N1, 50th Anniv. A102

1991, Feb. 18 Litho. *Perf. 13½*

446 A102 37p shown 1.10 1.10
447 A102 53p No. N2 1.60 1.60
448 A102 57p No. N3 1.75 1.75
a. Booklet pane of 3, #446-448 5.00

No. 448a printed in three formats with Nos. 446-448 in different order.

Europa — A103

Designs: No. 449, Royal Visit to Guernsey, discovery of Neptune, 1846. No. 450, Royal Visit to Sark, launch of Sputnik, 1957. No. 451, Maiden voyage of ferry Sarnia, first manned space flight, 1961. No. 452, Independence of Guernsey Post Office, first man on moon, 1969.

1991, Apr. 1 Litho. *Perf. 13½x14*

449 A103 21p multicolored .65 .65
450 A103 21p multicolored .65 .65
451 A103 26p multicolored .85 .85
452 A103 26p multicolored .85 .85
Nos. 449-452 (4) 3.00 3.00

Landscape Type of 1984

1991 Litho. *Perf. 15x14½, 14½x15*

453 A63 21p King's Mills, St. Saviours .60 .60
a. Min. sheet (3 each #453, #296, 2 each #287, #288) 3.00
b. Min. sheet (5 each #453, #296) 5.00
454 A63 26p Town Church, St. Peter Port .75 .75

Issued: 21p, 26p, 4/1; #453a, 453b, 4/2. #453a, 453b sold unattached in booklet covers.

Guernsey Yacht Club, Cent. — A104

1991, July 2 Litho. *Perf. 14*

459 A104 15p Guernsey Sailing Trust .50 .50
460 A104 21p Guernsey Regatta .70 .70
461 A104 26p Channel Islands Challenge .80 .80
462 A104 31p Rolex Swan Regatta 1.00 1.00
463 A104 37p Old Gaffers Assoc. 1.25 1.25
a. Souvenir sheet of 5, #459-463 4.75 4.75
Nos. 459-463 (5) 4.25 4.25

"Guernsey" and denomination in white on sheet stamps, yellow on souvenir sheet stamps.

Miniature Sheet

Christmas — A105

Children's Paintings: a, Reindeer by Melanie Sharpe. b, Christmas dessert by James Quinn. c, Snowman by Lisa Marie Guille. d, Snowman by Jessica Ede-Golightly. e, Birds by Sharon Le Page. f, Shepherds, sheep, angels by Anna Coquelin. g, Manger scene by Claudine Lihou. h, Three kings by Jonathan Le Noury. i, Children, angels, star by Marcia Mahy. j, Christmas tree, presents by Laurel Garfield. k, Santa Claus by Rebecca Driscoll. l, Snowman by Ian Lowe.

1991, Oct. 15 Litho. *Perf. 13*

464 A105 Sheet of 12 4.25 4.25
a.-l. 12p any single .35 .35

Nature Conservation A106

Birds and plants: No. 465: a, Two oyster catchers. b, Three turnstones. c, Two dunlins, two turnstones. d, Curlew, two turnstones. e, Ringed plover, chicks.

No. 466: a, Violet and white flowers. b, Yellow flowers. c, Small yellow flowers. d, Violet, yellow and white flowers. e, Long-stemmed yellow flowers.

1991, Oct. 15 *Perf. 14½*

465 Strip of 5 2.50 2.50
a.-e. A106 15p any single .50 .50
466 Strip of 5 3.50 3.50
a.-e. A106 21p any single .70 .70

Discovery of America, 500th Anniv. — A107

1992, Feb. 6 Litho. *Perf. 13½x14*

467 A107 23p Columbus .90 .90
468 A107 23p Columbus' signatures .90 .90
469 A107 28p Map of 1st voyage 1.10 1.10
470 A107 28p Santa Maria 1.10 1.10
a. Souvenir sheet, #467-470 7.00 7.00
b. No. 470a overprinted in brown in sheet margin 8.00 8.00
Nos. 467-470 (4) 4.00 4.00

Europa. No. 470b overprint shows emblem of World Columbian Stamp Expo '92.

Issue date: No. 470b, May 22.

Queen Elizabeth II's Accession to Throne, 40th Anniv. — A108

Various portraits of Queen Elizabeth II.

1992, Feb. 6 Litho. *Perf. 14*

471 A108 23p multicolored .70 .70
472 A108 28p multicolored .85 .85
473 A108 33p multicolored 1.00 1.00
474 A108 39p multicolored 1.25 1.25
Nos. 471-474 (4) 3.80 3.80

Souvenir Sheet

Guernsey Cows — A109

1992, May 22 Litho. *Perf. 14*

475 A109 75p multicolored 2.50 2.50

Royal Guernsey Agricultural and Horticultural Society, 150th anniv.

Flowers — A110

1992-96 ***Perf. 13***

476 A110 1p Stephanotis floribunda .20 .20
477 A110 2p Potted hydrangea .20 .20
478 A110 3p Stock .20 .20
479 A110 4p Anemones .20 .20
480 A110 5p Gladiolus .20 .20
481 A110 6p Gypsophila paniculata, asparagus plumosus .20 .20
482 A110 7p Guernsey lily .20 .20
483 A110 8p Enchantment lily .20 .20
484 A110 9p Clematis freckles .20 .20
485 A110 10p Alstroemeria .25 .25
486 A110 16p Standard carnation, horiz. .50 .40
a. Perf. 14 on 3 sides .60 .50
b. Booklet pane of 8 #486a 4.50
487 A110 20p Spray rose .60 .55
488 A110 23p Mixed freesia, horiz. .60 .55
a. Bklt. pane of 5 #486a, 3 #488c 5.00 5.00
b. Booklet pane of 8, #488c 6.25 6.25
c. Perf. 14 on 3 sides .75 .60
489 A110 24p Standard rose, horiz. .70 .55
a. Perf. 14 on 3 sides .80 .60
b. Booklet pane of 8 #489a 6.25
490 A110 25p Iris ideal .70 .55
a. Perf. 14½ on 3 sides .80 .60
b. As "a," booklet pane of 4 3.25
491 A110 28p Lisianthus, horiz. .85 .60
a. Perf. 14 on 3 sides 1.00 .65
b. Booklet pane of 4 #491a 3.75
492 A110 30p Spray chrysanthemum, horiz. 1.00 .85
493 A110 40p Spray carnation 1.25 1.00
494 A110 50p Single freesia, horiz. 1.50 1.10

Size: 39x30mm

Perf. 13½

495 A110 £1 Bouquet, horiz. 2.75 2.00
a. Souv. sheet of 1 + label, perf. 13 3.25 3.25
b. Souv. sheet of 1 + label, perf. 13 3.25 3.25
496 A110 £2 Chelsea flower show, horiz. 4.75 3.50

Size: 39x31mm

497 A110 £3 Floral fantasia, horiz. 6.75 6.00
Nos. 476-497 (22) 24.00 19.70

PHILAKOREA '94 (#495a). Singapore '95 (#495b).

Issued: 3p, 4p, 5p, 10p, 16p, 20p, 23p, 40p, 50p, £1, 5/22/92; 1p, 2p, 6p, 7p, 8p, 9p, 24p, 28p, 30p, £2, #486a, 3/2/93; 25p, 2/18/94; #495a, 8/94; #495b, 9/1/95; £3, 1/24/96.

#495 dated "1992," #495a, 495b "1994, 1995."

Perf 14 or 14½ stamps issued only in booklets.

See Nos. 584-585.

Operation Asterix A111

1992, Sept. 18 **Litho.** ***Perf. 13***

498 A111 16p Ship construction .45 .45
499 A111 23p Loading cargo .65 .65
500 A111 28p Ship at sea .85 .85
501 A111 33p Ship on fire .95 .95
502 A111 39p Ship sinking 1.25 1.25
a. Bklt. pane of #498-502 + label 4.50
Nos. 498-502 (5) 4.15 4.15

No. 502a exists with four different labels.

Historic Trams A112

Designs: 16p, Tram No. 10 decorated for Battle of Flowers. 23p, No. 10 passing Hougue a la Perre. 28p, Tram No. 1 at St. Sampsons. 33p, First steam tram, St. Peter Port, 1879. 39p, Last electric tram, 1934.

1992, Nov. 17 **Litho.** ***Perf. 13½x14***

503 A112 16p multicolored .55 .55
504 A112 23p multicolored .75 .75
505 A112 28p multicolored .95 .95
506 A112 33p multicolored 1.10 1.10
507 A112 39p multicolored 1.25 1.25
Nos. 503-507 (5) 4.60 4.60

Christmas — A113

a, Father dressed as Santa. b, Girl pulling end of cracker. c, Mother. d, Champagne, crumpets. e, Turkey. f, Plum pudding. g, Cake. h, Cookies. i, Wine, blue cheese. j, Nuts. k, Ham. l, Cake roll.

1992, Nov. 17 ***Perf. 13½***

508 A113 Sheet of 12 4.50 4.50
a.-l. 13p any single .35 .35

A114

Rupert Bear and friends, created by Mary Tourtel: No. 509: Rupert Bear, Bingo, and dog. No. 510a, 24p, Bill Badger, Willie Mouse, Reggie Rabbit, and Podgy Pig with snowman. No. 510b, 16p, Airplane above castle tower. No. 510c, 24p, Balloonist leaping away from Gregory on sled. No. 510d, 16p, Professor's servant and Autumn Elf. No. 510e, 16p, Algy Pug. No. 510f, 16p, Baby Badger on sled. No. 510g, 24p, Tiger Lily and Edward Trunk.

1993, Feb. 2 **Litho.** ***Perf. 13½x13***

509 A114 24p multicolored .75 .75
510 A114 Sheet of 8, #a.-g. & #509 4.75 4.75

No. 510 printed in continuous design. Nos. 510b, 510d-510f are 25x26mm.

Contemporary Art — A115

Europa: No. 511, Tapestry, by Kelly Fletcher. No. 512, The Fish Market, by Sally Reed. No. 513, Dress Shop, King's Road, by Damon Bell. No. 514, Red Abstract, by Molly Harris.

1993, May 7 **Litho.** ***Perf. 13½x14***

Size: 45x30mm (#512, 513)

511 A115 24p multicolored .70 .70
512 A115 24p multicolored .70 .70
513 A115 28p multicolored .85 .85
514 A115 28p multicolored .85 .85
Nos. 511-514 (4) 3.10 3.10

Siege of Castle Cornet, 1643-51 — A116

16p, Shipboard arrest of Parliamentarian officials. 24p, Parliamentarian warships firing on castle. 28p, Captured officials fleeing from castle. 33p, Cannon firing from castle into St. Peter Port. 39p, Surrender of castle.

1993, May 7 ***Perf. 15x14***

515 A116 16p multicolored .50 .50
516 A116 24p multicolored .70 .70
517 A116 28p multicolored .85 .85
518 A116 33p multicolored 1.00 1.00
519 A116 39p multicolored 1.10 1.10
a. Souvenir sheet of 5, #515-519 4.25 4.25
Nos. 515-519 (5) 4.15 4.15

Thomas de la Rue, Printer, Birth Bicent. — A117

Designs: 16p, Playing card king, queen and jack. 24p, Swift reservoir fountain pens. 28p, Envelope folding machine. 33p, Great Britain type A5. 39p, £1 Mauritius bank note, portrait of de la Rue.

1993, July 27 **Litho.** ***Perf. 13½***

520 A117 16p multicolored .45 .45
521 A117 24p multicolored .70 .70
522 A117 28p multicolored .85 .85

Engr.

523 A117 33p rose carmine 1.00 1.00
524 A117 39p green 1.10 1.10
Nos. 520-524 (5) 4.10 4.10

520a Booklet pane of 4 2.00
521a Booklet pane of 4 3.00
522a Booklet pane of 4 3.50
523a Booklet pane of 4 4.00
524a Booklet pane of 4 4.75

Miniature Sheet

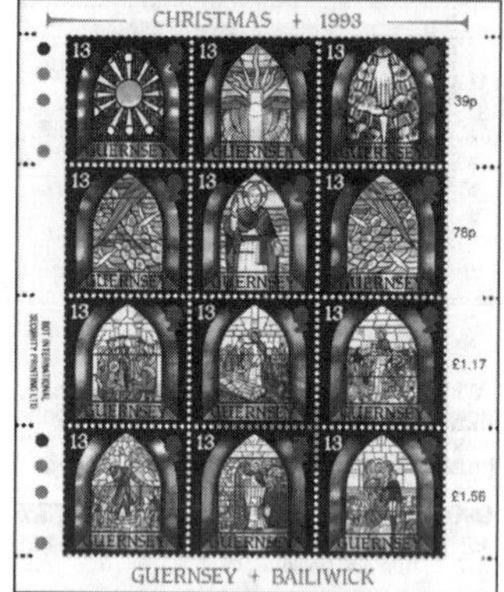

Christmas — A118

Stained glass windows, Chapel of Christ the Healer: a, Sunburst. b, Light from sun. c, Hand of God. d, Doves descending left. e, Christ raising hand. f, Doves descending right. g, Christ Child sitting in temple. h, Christ raising daughter of Jairus from dead. i, "Suffer little children to come unto me." j, Scene from Pilgrim's Progress. k, The Light of the World. l, Archangel of Healing.

1993, Nov. 2 **Litho.** ***Perf. 13x13½***

525 A118 Sheet of 12 4.50 4.50
a.-l. 13p any single .35 .35

Archaeological Discoveries — A119

Europa: No. 526, Warrior on horseback. No. 527, Burial site, Les Fouaillages. No. 528, Sword, scabbard, spear. No. 529, Cerny-style pots, arrowheads, axe.

1994, Feb. 18 **Litho.** ***Perf. 13½***

526 A119 24p multicolored .65 .65
a. Sheet of 10 with added inscription 7.50 7.50
527 A119 24p multicolored .65 .65
528 A119 30p multicolored .85 .85
529 A119 30p multicolored .85 .85
Nos. 526-529 (4) 3.00 3.00

No. 526a inscribed in sheet margin with Hong Kong '94 emblem and "PHILATELIC EXHIBITION / 18-21 FEBRUARY 1994" in English and Chinese.

Souvenir Sheet

D-Day, 50th Anniv. — A120

£2, Canadian Wing Spitfires flying over Normandy coastline.

1994, June 6 **Litho.** ***Perf. 14***

530 A120 £2 multicolored 5.75 5.75

Classic Cars A121

Designs: 16p, 1894 Peugeot Type 3. 24p, 1903 Mercedes Simplex. 35p, 1906 Humber 14.4hp. 41p, 1936 Bentley 4¼ L. 60p, 1948 MG TC.

1994, July 19 **Litho.** ***Perf. 15x14***

531 A121 16p multicolored .45 .45
532 A121 24p multicolored .70 .70
533 A121 35p multicolored 1.00 1.00
534 A121 41p multicolored 1.10 1.10
535 A121 60p multicolored 1.75 1.75
Nos. 531-535 (5) 5.00 5.00

531a Booklet pane of 4 2.10
532a Booklet pane of 4 3.25
533a Booklet pane of 4 5.00
534a Booklet pane of 4 5.50
535a Booklet pane or 4 7.75

Guernsey Post Office, 25th Anniv. A122

Designs: 16p, Trident ferry. 24p, Handley Page Super Dart Herald of Channel Express. 35p, Aurigny Air Services' JOEY. 41p, Bon Marin de Serk ferry. 60p, Map of Guernsey, Herm, Alderney, Sark.

1994, Oct. 1 **Litho.** ***Perf. 14***

536 A122 16p multicolored .45 .45
537 A122 24p multicolored .70 .70
538 A122 35p multicolored 1.00 1.00
539 A122 41p multicolored 1.25 1.25
540 A122 60p multicolored 1.75 1.75
a. Souvenir sheet, #536-540 5.50 5.50
Nos. 536-540 (5) 5.15 5.15

Miniature Sheets

Christmas — A123

Antique toys - #541: a, Doll house. b, Doll. c, Small teddy bear in carriage. d, Cards, post boxes with candy. e, Top. f, Picture puzzle blocks.

#542: a, Rocking horse. b, Large teddy bear. c, Tricycle. d, Wooden pull duck. e, Tin plate locomotive. f, Ludo game.

1994, Oct. 1 ***Perf. 13***

541	A123 Sheet of 6	2.50	2.50
a.-f.	13p any single	.40	.40
542	A123 Sheet of 6	4.50	4.50
a.-f.	24p any single	.75	.75

Greetings — A124

Faces formed by: No. 543, Shrimp, oyster, lobster, fish. No. 544, Sand buckets, shovel, sand. No. 545, Flowers. No. 546, Lettuce, tomatoes, mushroom, squash. No. 547, Seaweed, shells. No. 548, Anchor, life preservers. No. 549, Wine, cork, knife, fork. No. 550, Butterflies, caterpillars.

1995, Feb. 2 Litho. ***Perf. 14***

543	A124 24p multicolored	.70	.70
544	A124 24p multicolored	.70	.70
545	A124 24p multicolored	.70	.70
546	A124 24p multicolored	.70	.70
547	A124 24p multicolored	.70	.70
548	A124 24p multicolored	.70	.70
549	A124 24p multicolored	.70	.70
550	A124 24p multicolored	.70	.70
a.	Miniature sheet of 8, #543-550	6.25	5.75
	Complete booklet, #550a	5.75	
	Nos. 543-550 (8)	5.60	5.60

Doves — A125

Europa: 25p, Doves standing. 30p, Doves in flight. Illustration reduced.

1995, May 9 Litho. ***Perf. 14***

551	A125 25p green	.70	.70
552	A125 30p blue	.80	.80

Nos. 551-552 contain a three-dimensional image hidden in the patterns composed of doves.

Liberation of Guernsey, 50th Anniv. A126

Designs: 16p, Churchill making broadcast, crowd. 24p, St. Peter Port harbor. 35p, Military band. 41p, Red Cross ship Vega. 60p, Soldier kissing civilian woman.

1995, May 9 ***Perf. 13½x14***

553	A126 16p multicolored	.45	.45
554	A126 24p multicolored	.75	.75
555	A126 35p multicolored	1.10	1.10
556	A126 41p multicolored	1.25	1.25
557	A126 60p multicolored	1.90	1.90
a.	Souvenir sheet of 5, #553-557	5.50	5.50
	Nos. 553-557 (5)	5.45	5.45

Visit by Prince of Wales A127

1995, May 9 ***Perf. 14***

558	A127 £1.50 multicolored	4.50	4.50

UN, 50th Anniv. — A128

Portion of UN emblem, denomination: a, UL. b, UR. c, LL. d, LR.

Litho. & Embossed

1995, Oct. 24 ***Perf. 14x13½***

559	A128 Block of 4	6.00	6.00
a.-d.	50p any single	1.50	1.50

Christmas — A129

Designs, with denomination at:
Shops in the city, children playing in snow - #560: a, LL. b, LR.
Homes in winter, children playing in snow - #561: a, LL. b, LR.
Children playing instruments, singing - #562: a, LL. b, LR.
Children of many nations - #563: a, LL. b, LR.

1995, Nov. 16 Litho. ***Perf. 13½x13***

560	A129 Pair	.80	.80
a.-b.	13p any single	.40	.40
561	A129 Pair	.90	.90
a.-b.	13p +1p, any single	.45	.45
562	A129 Pair	1.50	1.50
a.-b.	24p any single	.75	.75
563	A129 Pair	1.75	1.75
a.-b.	24p +2p, any single	.85	.85
	Nos. 560-563 (4)	4.95	4.95

Nos. 560-563 are each continuous designs.
UNICEF, 50th anniv.

Women of Achievement — A130

Europa: 25p, Princess Anne, children of different nations. 30p, Queen Elizabeth II, people of different nations.

1996, Apr. 21 Litho. ***Perf. 14***

564	A130 25p multicolored	.65	.65
565	A130 30p multicolored	.85	.85

Queen Elizabeth II, 70th birthday (#565).
See Isle of Man Nos. 679-680.

1996 European Soccer Championships — A131

Various flags from participating countries and: No. 566a, USSR player kicking ball. No. 566b, English players in white shirts, 1968. No. 567a, Italian player in blue shirt with ball. No. 567b, Belgium player in red, Italian players, 1972. No. 568a, Irish player in green kicking. No. 568b, Dutch player in blue, 1988. No. 569a, German player in white with ball. No. 569b, Danish player in red, 1992.

1996, Apr. 25 ***Perf. 14x13½***

566	A131 Pair	1.00	1.00
a.-b.	16p any single	.50	.50
567	A131 Pair	1.50	1.50
a.-b.	24p any single	.75	.75
568	A131 Pair	2.25	2.25
a.-b.	35p any single	1.10	1.10
569	A131 Pair	2.50	2.50
a.-b.	41p any single	1.25	1.25
	Nos. 566-569 (4)	7.25	7.25

Souvenir Sheet

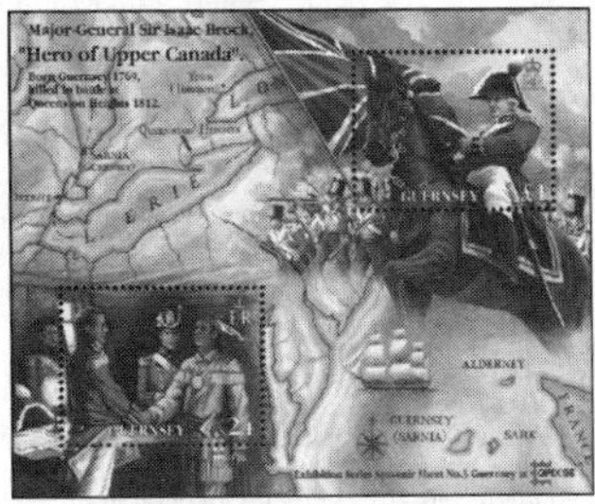

Sir Isaac Brock (1769-1812), British Commander in Upper Canada — A132

Designs: a, 24p, Brock shaking hands with Tecumseh. b, £1, Brock on horse.

1996, June 8 Litho. ***Perf. 14x13½***

570	A132 Sheet of 2, #a.-b.	3.75	3.75

CAPEX '96.

Modern Olympic Games, Cent. — A133

The original pentathlon.

1996, July 19 Litho. ***Perf. 14***

571	A133 16p Running	.45	.45
572	A133 24p Javelin	.60	.60
573	A133 41p Discus	1.10	1.10
574	A133 55p Wrestling	1.60	1.60
575	A133 60p Jumping	1.75	1.75
a.	Souvenir sheet, #571-575	5.50	5.50
	Nos. 571-575 (5)	5.50	5.50

No. 574 is 53x31mm. Olymphilex'96 (#574).

Motion Pictures, Cent. A134

Classic Movie Detectives: 16p, Humphrey Bogart as Philip Marlowe. 24p, Peter Sellers as Inspector Clouseau. 35p, Basil Rathbone as Sherlock Holmes. 41p, Margaret Rutherford as Miss Marple. 60p, Warner Oland as Charlie Chan.

1996, Nov. 6 Litho. ***Perf. 15x14***

576	A134 16p multicolored	.45	.45
577	A134 24p multicolored	.60	.60
578	A134 35p multicolored	1.00	1.00
579	A134 41p multicolored	1.10	1.10
580	A134 60p multicolored	1.75	1.75
	Nos. 576-580 (5)	4.90	4.90

576a	Booklet pane of 3	1.40
577a	Booklet pane of 3	1.90
578a	Booklet pane of 3	3.00
579a	Booklet pane of 3	3.50
580a	Booklet pane of 3	5.25
580b	Bklt. pane of 5, #576-580	5.50
	Complete booklet, #576a-580b	22.50

Christmas A135

Scenes depicting the Christmas story: 24p, Madonna and Child. 25p, Nativity.

No. 583, vert: a, Annuniciation by Angel Gabriel. b, Mary, Joseph on way to Bethlehem. c, Inn keeper turning them away. d, Angel appearing before shepherds. e, Holy Family in stable. f, Adoration of the shepherds. g, Magi following star. h, Magi presenting gifts. i, Prophet's warning to Mary, Joseph. j, Madonna and Child. k, Angel appearing in Joseph's dream. l, Flight into Egypt.

1996, Nov. 6 ***Perf. 13***

581	A135 24p multicolored	.70	.70
582	A135 25p multicolored	.80	.80

Miniature Sheet

583	A135 13p Sheet of 12, #a.-l.	4.75	4.75

Flower Type of 1992

1997 Litho. ***Perf. 13***

584	A110 18p Standard rose	.50	.40
a.	Perf. 14 on 3 Sides	.55	.45
b.	As "a," booklet pane of 8	5.50	
	Complete booklet, #584b	5.50	
585	A110 26p Freesia pink glow, horiz.	.75	.60
a.	Perf. 14 on 3 Sides	.80	.60
b.	As "a," booklet pane of 4	3.75	
	Complete booklet, #585b	3.75	

Butterflies and Moths A136

Designs: 18p, Holly blue. 25p, Hummingbird hawk-moth. 26p, Emperor moth. 37p, Brimstone.
£1, Painted lady.

1997, Feb. 12 Litho. ***Perf. 14***

586	A136 18p multicolored	.85	.85
587	A136 25p multicolored	1.00	1.00
588	A136 26p multicolored	1.40	1.40
589	A136 37p multicolored	1.75	1.75
	Nos. 586-589 (4)	5.00	5.00

Souvenir Sheet

Perf. 13½

590	A136 £1 multicolored	3.25	3.25

World Wildlife Fund (#586-589), Hong Kong '97 (#590).

Stories and Legends — A137

The Toilers of the Sea, by Victor Hugo: 26p, Man fighting sea monster, face in sea, ship. 31p, Ship, man seated on rock visualizing woman.

1997, Apr. 24 Litho. ***Perf. 13½***

591	A137 26p multicolored	.70	.70
592	A137 31p multicolored	.90	.90

Nos. 591-592 each issued in sheets of 10.
Europa.

Island Scenes — A138

18p, Shell Beach, Herm. 25p, La Seigneurie, Sark, vert. 26p, Castle Comet, Guernsey.

1997, Apr. 24 ***Die Cut Perf. 11***
Self-Adhesive

593 A138 18p multicolored .60 .60
a. Booklet pane of 8 5.50
Complete booklet, #593a 5.50
594 A138 25p multicolored .85 .85
a. Booklet pane of 8 7.75
Complete booklet, #594a 7.75
595 A138 26p multicolored .85 .85
a. Booklet pane of 4 3.75
Complete booklet, #595a 3.75
Nos. 593-595 (3) 2.30 2.30

See Nos. 625-628.

Souvenir Sheet

PACIFIC 97 — A139

a, 30p, St. Peter Port, 1868. b, £1, Sailing ships.

1997, May 29 **Litho.** ***Perf. 14***
596 A139 Sheet of 2, #a.-b. 4.25 4.25

Communications — A140

1997, Aug. 21 **Litho.** ***Perf. 13½x13***
597 A140 18p Radio .60 .60
598 A140 25p Television .85 .85
599 A140 26p Telephone .85 .85
600 A140 37p Newspaper 1.25 1.25
601 A140 43p Post system 1.40 1.40
602 A140 63p Computer network 2.00 2.00
Nos. 597-602 (6) 6.95 6.95

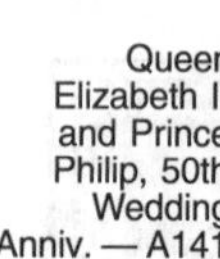

Queen Elizabeth II and Prince Philip, 50th Wedding Anniv. — A141

Designs: 18p, At St. George's Hall, Guernsey, 1957. 25p, Queen being saluted by guardsman, 1953. 26p, Queen, family on horseback, 1957. 37p, Prince, Queen in casual attire, 1972. 43p, Queen saluting, at Trooping of the Color, 1987. 63p, Portrait, 1997.

1997, Nov. 20 **Litho.** ***Perf. 14***
603 A141 18p multicolored .60 .60
604 A141 25p multicolored .85 .85
a. Bklt. pane, 3 each #603-604 5.00
605 A141 26p multicolored .85 .85
606 A141 37p multicolored 1.25 1.25
a. Bklt. pane, 3 each #605-606 7.25
607 A141 43p multicolored 1.40 1.40
608 A141 63p multicolored 2.00 2.00
a. Bklt. pane, 3 each #607-608 11.50
b. Booklet pane, #603-608 7.75
Complete booklet, #604a, 606a, 608a, 608b 32.50
Nos. 603-608 (6) 6.95 6.95

A142

Teddy Bears celebrating Christmas: 15p, Baking in kitchen. 25p, Beside Christmas tree. 26p, Seated in chair reading story. 37p, As Santa Claus. 43p, With presents. 63p, Seated at Christmas dinner.

1997, Nov. 6
609 A142 15p multicolored .50 .50
610 A142 25p multicolored .85 .85
611 A142 26p multicolored .85 .85
612 A142 37p multicolored 1.25 1.25
613 A142 43p multicolored 1.40 1.40
614 A142 63p multicolored 2.00 2.00
a. Souvenir sheet, #609-614 7.00 7.00
Nos. 609-614 (6) 6.85 6.85

A143

1998, Feb. 10 **Litho.** ***Perf. 14½***

Millennium Tapestries: Embroidered panels showing images of Guernsey during last ten centuries, Guernsey-French inscriptions.

615 A143 25p 11th century .85 .85
616 A143 25p 12th century .85 .85
617 A143 25p 13th century .85 .85
618 A143 25p 14th century .85 .85
a. Bklt. pane, 2 each #615-616, 1 each #617-618 5.75
619 A143 25p 15th century .85 .85
620 A143 25p 16th century .85 .85
a. Bklt. pane, 2 each #617-618, 1 each #619-620 5.75
621 A143 25p 17th century .85 .85
622 A143 25p 18th century .85 .85
a. Bklt. pane, 2 each #619-620, 1 each #621-622 5.75
623 A143 25p 19th century .85 .85
624 A143 25p 20th century .85 .85
a. Bklt. pane, 2 each #621-622, 1 each #623-624 5.75
b. Bklt. pane, 2 each #623-624, 1 each #615-616 5.75
Complete booklet, #618a, 620a, 622a, 624a-624b 30.00
c. Strip of 10, #615-624 8.50 8.50

Island Scenes Type of 1997
Die Cut Perf. 9½x9
1998, Mar. 25 **Litho.**
Self-Adhesive

625 A138 (20p) Fort Grey .70 .70
626 A138 (20p) Grand Havre .70 .70
a. Booklet pane, 4 each #625-626 6.25
Complete booklet, #626a 6.25
627 A138 (25p) Little Chapel .85 .85
628 A138 (25p) Guernsey cow .85 .85
a. Booklet pane, 4 each #627-628 7.50
Complete booklet, #628a 7.50
Nos. 625-628 (4) 3.10 3.10

Nos. 625-626 are inscribed "Bailwick Minimum Postage Paid" and were valued at 20p on day of issue. Nos. 627-628 are inscribed "UK Minimum Postage Paid" and were valued at 25p on day of issue.

Aircraft A144

Designs: 20p, Fairey IIIC, Balloon, Sopwith Camel, Avro 504. 25p, Fairey Swordfish, Tiger Moth, Supermarine Walrus, Gloster Gladiator. 30p, Hawker Hurricane, Supermarine Spitfire, Vickers Wellington, Short Sunderland, Westland Lysander, Bristol Blenheim. 37p, De Havilland Mosquito, Avro Lancaster, Auster III, Gloster Meteor, Horsa glider. 43p, Canberra, Hawker Sea Fury, Bristol Sycamore, Hawker Hunter, Handley Page Victor, BAe Lightning. 63p, Pavania Tornado GRI, BAe Hawk, BAe Sea Harrier, Westland Lynx, Hawker Siddeley Nimrod.

1998, May 7 ***Perf. 13½x13***
629 A144 20p multicolored .70 .70
630 A144 25p multicolored .85 .85
631 A144 30p multicolored 1.00 1.00
632 A144 37p multicolored 1.25 1.25
633 A144 43p multicolored 1.50 1.50
634 A144 63p multicolored 2.20 2.20
Nos. 629-634 (6) 7.50 7.50

Royal Air Force, 80th anniv.

Souvenir Sheet

Cambridge Rules for Soccer, 150th Anniv. — A145

a, 30p, Jules Rimet, first president of FIFA. b, £1.75, Bobby Moore, Queen Elizabeth II.

1998, May 7 ***Perf. 13½x14***
635 A145 Sheet of 2, #a.-b. 7.00 7.00

Natl. Holidays and Festivals — A146

Europa: 20p, People in traditional costumes watching animals, West Show. 25p, Band in parade, Battle of Flowers, North Show. 30p, Prince Charles, Liberation Monument under Guernsey flag, tank, Liberation Day. 37p, Goat, equestrian event, flowers, South Show.

1998, Aug. 11 **Litho.** ***Perf. 13½***
636 A146 20p multicolored .55 .55
637 A146 25p multicolored .70 .70
638 A146 30p multicolored .90 .90
639 A146 37p multicolored 1.10 1.10
Nos. 636-639 (4) 3.25 3.25

A147

Royal Yacht Britannia — A148

Designs: 1p, Small fishing boat. 2p, St. Ambulance Inshore Rescue inflatable dinghy. 3p, Pilot boat. 4p, St. John Ambulance boat, Flying Christine III. 5p, Crab boat. 6p, Ferry. 7p, Workboat, Sarnia. 8p, Fisheries Protecton vessel, Leopardess. 9p, Large fishing boat. 10p, Powerboat. 20p, Dart 18 racing catamaran. 30p, Bermudan rigged sloop. 40p, Motor cruiser. 50p, Ocean-going yacht. 75p, Motor cruiser anchored. £1, Cruise ship, Queen Elizabeth II. £3, Cruise ship Oriana

1998-2000 **Litho.** ***Perf. 14***
640 A147 1p multicolored .20 .20
641 A147 2p multicolored .20 .20
642 A147 3p multicolored .20 .20
643 A147 4p multicolored .20 .20
644 A147 5p multicolored .20 .20
645 A147 6p multicolored .20 .20
646 A147 7p multicolored .20 .20
647 A147 8p multicolored .25 .25
648 A147 9p multicolored .30 .30

Size: 27x27mm
Perf. 14½x14¼

649 A147 10p multicolored .30 .30
650 A147 20p multicolored .60 .60
651 A147 30p multicolored .90 .90
652 A147 40p multicolored 1.25 1.25
654 A147 50p multicolored 1.60 1.60
656 A147 75p multicolored 2.50 2.50

Size: 34x26mm
Litho. & Embossed
Perf. 14¼x14½

658 A148 £1 multicolored 3.25 3.25
660 A148 £3 multicolored 9.00 9.00

Size: 48x36mm
Perf. 14¾x14½

663 A148 £5 gold & multi 16.50 16.50
Nos. 640-663 (18) 37.85 37.85

Issued: £5, 8/11; 1p, 2p, 3p, 4p, 5p, 6p, 7p, 8p, 10p, 40p, 50p, 75p, £1, 7/27/99; 20p, 30p, £3, 8/4/00.

Introduction of Christmas Tree to Britain, 150th Anniv. — A149

Christmas tree and toys from past 150 years: 17p, Teletubby "Po," video game machine, 1998. 25p, Doll, double decker bus, c. 1968. 30p, Stuffed panda, toy army tank, c. 1938. 37p, Model of Bluebird race car, doll, c. 1928. 43p, Teddy bear, train pull toy, c. 1908. 63p, Spinning top, wooden doll, c. 1850.

1998, Nov. 10 **Litho.** ***Perf. 13½***
664 A149 17p multicolored .55 .55
665 A149 25p multicolored .85 .85
666 A149 30p multicolored 1.00 1.00
667 A149 37p multicolored 1.25 1.25
668 A149 43p multicolored 1.40 1.40
669 A149 63p multicolored 2.25 2.25
a. Souvenir sheet, #664-669 7.30 7.30
Nos. 664-669 (6) 7.30 7.30

Queen Elizabeth, the Queen Mother — A150

Three strings of pearls and photographs: No. 670, As a child, 1907. No. 671, At wedding, 1923. No. 672, Holding newly-born Princess Elizabeth, 1926. No. 673, Wearing crown at coronation of King George VI, 1937. No. 674, In green hat, 1940. No. 675, Holding fishing pole, 1966. No. 676, Wearing tiara, 1963. No. 677, Holding flowers, 1992. No. 678, Presenting trophy, 1989. No. 679, In blue hat, 1990.

1999, Feb. 4 **Litho.** ***Perf. 13***
Color of LL Corner

670 A150 25p pink .85 .85
671 A150 25p blue .85 .85
672 A150 25p red brown .85 .85
673 A150 25p purple .85 .85
a. Bklt. pane, 2 each #670-671, 1 each #672-673 5.75
674 A150 25p green .85 .85
675 A150 25p green .85 .85
a. Bklt. pane, 2 each #672-673, 1 each #673-674 5.75
676 A150 25p purple .85 .85
677 A150 25p red brown .85 .85
678 A150 25p blue .85 .85
a. Bklt. pane, 2 each #674-675, 1 each #676-677 5.75
679 A150 25p pink .85 .85
a. Bklt. pane, 2 each #676-677, 1 each #678-679 5.75
b. Bklt. pane, 2 each #678-679, 1 each #670-671 5.75
Complete booklet, #673a, 675a, 678a, 679a, 679b 30.00
c. Strip of 10, #670-679 8.50 8.50

Herm Island — A151

Local Carriage Labels and: 20p, Burnet roses, Shell Beach. 25p, Puffins, Belvoir Bay. 30p, Small Heath butterfly. 38p, Various shells, Shell Beach.

1999, Apr. 27 Litho. *Perf. 13½x13*

680 A151 20p multicolored .65 .65
681 A151 25p multicolored .85 .85
682 A151 30p multicolored 1.00 1.00
683 A151 38p multicolored 1.25 1.25
Nos. 680-683 (4) 3.75 3.75

Europa.

Royal Lifeboat Assoc., 175th Anniv. A152

20p, Spirit of Guernsey, 1995. 25p, Sir William Arnold, 1973. 30p, Euphrosyne Kendal, 1954. 38p, Queen Victoria, 1929. 44p, Arthur Lionel, 1912. 64p, Vincent Kirk Ella, 1888.

1999, Apr. 27

684 A152 20p multicolored .65 .65
685 A152 25p multicolored .85 .85
686 A152 30p multicolored 1.00 1.00
687 A152 38p multicolored 1.25 1.25
688 A152 44p multicolored 1.50 1.50
689 A152 64p multicolored 2.25 2.25
Nos. 684-689 (6) 7.50 7.50

Souvenir Sheet

Wedding of Prince Edward and Sophie Rhys-Jones — A153

Illustration reduced.

1999, June 19 Litho. *Perf. 13½*

690 A153 £1 multicolored 3.25 3.25

Royal Military Academy, Sandhurst, Bicent. — A154

20p, Major General Le Marchant, founder, 1799. 25p, Duke of York, sponsor, 1802. 30p, Field Marshal Earl Haig, 1884-85. 38p, Field Marshal Montgomery, 1907-08. 44p, Major David Niven, actor, 1928-30. 64p, Sir Winston Churchill, 1893-95.

1999, July 27 Litho. *Perf. 14*

691 A154 20p multicolored .65 .65
692 A154 25p multicolored .85 .85
693 A154 30p multicolored 1.00 1.00
694 A154 38p multicolored 1.25 1.25
695 A154 44p multicolored 1.40 1.40
696 A154 64p multicolored 2.25 2.25
Nos. 691-696 (6) 7.40 7.40

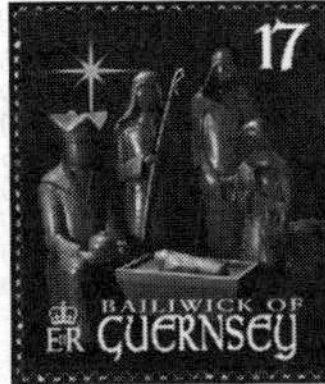

Christmas A155

Creche figures around manger: 17p, Magus, shepherd, Mary, Joseph, donkey. 25p, Mary. 30p, Joseph, Mary. 38p, Donkey, Mary, cow. 44p, Mary, two shepherds. 64p, Three Magi.

1999, Oct. 19 Litho. *Perf. 13¾x14¼*

697 A155 17p multicolored .55 .55
698 A155 25p multicolored .80 .80
699 A155 30p multicolored .90 .90
700 A155 38p multicolored 1.25 1.25
701 A155 44p multicolored 1.40 1.40
702 A155 64p multicolored 2.10 2.10
a. Souvenir sheet, #697-702 7.00 7.00
Nos. 697-702 (6) 7.00 7.00

Millennium A156

Children's drawings by: 20p, Fallon Ephgrave. 25p, Abigail Downing. 30p, Laura Martin. 38p, Sarah Haddow. 44p, Sophie Medland. 64p, Danielle McIver.

2000, Jan. 1 Litho. *Perf. 14¼x14½*

703 A156 20p multi .65 .65
704 A156 25p multi .80 .80
705 A156 30p multi 1.00 1.00
706 A156 38p multi 1.25 1.25
707 A156 44p multi 1.40 1.40
708 A156 64p multi 2.10 2.10
Nos. 703-708 (6) 7.20 7.20

Nos. 703-708 depict the winning designs in the Future Children's Stamp Design Contest.

Europa, 2000

Common Design Type and

A157

Designs: 21p, Kite. 26p, Yacht sails. 65p, Rainbow and doves.

2000, May 9 Litho. *Perf. 13¼*

709 A157 21p multi .65 .65
710 A157 26p multi .75 .75
711 CD17 36p multi 1.10 1.10
712 A157 65p multi 1.90 1.90
Nos. 709-712 (4) 4.40 4.40

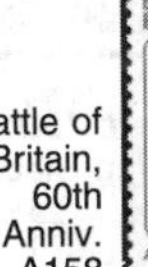

Battle of Britain, 60th Anniv. A158

Designs: 21p, Bristol Blenheim. 26p, Hawker Hurricane. 36p, Boulton Paul Defiant II. 40p, Gloster Gladiator. 45p, Bristol Beaufighter IF. 65p, Supermarine Spitfire IIc.

2000, April 28 Litho. *Perf. 13¼x13*

713 A158 21p multi .65 .65
714 A158 26p multi .75 .75
715 A158 36p multi 1.10 1.10
716 A158 40p multi 1.25 1.25
717 A158 45p multi 1.40 1.40
a. Booklet pane, #713-715, 717 4.50
b. Booklet pane, #713, 715-717 5.00
c. Booklet pane, #714-717 5.00
718 A158 65p multi 1.90 1.90
a. Booklet pane of 2 4.50
b. Bklt. pane, #713-714, 716, 718 5.25
Complete booklet, #717a-717c, 718a-718b 25.00
Nos. 713-718 (6) 7.05 7.05

The Stamp Show 2000, London (Nos. 717a-717c, 718a-718b).

Flowers in Candie Gardens — A159

No. 719: a, Long styled iris. b, Watsonia. c, Arum lily. d, Hoop petticoat daffodil. e, Triteleia laxa. f, Peacock flower. g, African blue lily. h, Corn lily. i, Sea lily. j, Guernsey lily.

2000, Aug. 4 Litho. *Perf. 13½x13*

719 Horiz. strip of 10 7.75 7.75
a.-j. A159 26p Any single .75 .75

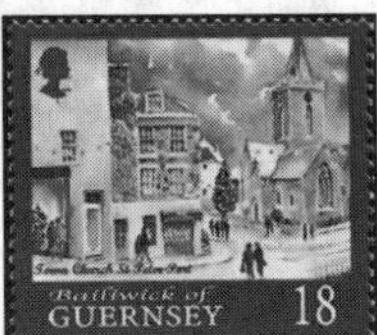

Christmas A160

Snow-covered churches: 18p, Town Church, St. Peter's Port. 26p, St. Sampson's Church. 36p, Vale Church. 40p, St. Pierre du Bois Church. 45p, St. Martin's Church. 65p, St. John's Church, St. Peter's Port.

2000, Oct. 19 Litho. *Perf. 14¼x13¾*

720 A160 18p multi .55 .55
721 A160 26p multi .75 .75
722 A160 36p multi 1.00 1.00
723 A160 40p multi 1.10 1.10
724 A160 45p multi 1.25 1.25
725 A160 65p multi 1.90 1.90
a. Souvenir sheet, #720-725 6.75 6.75
Nos. 720-725 (6) 6.55 6.55

Queen Victoria (1819-1901) — A161

Various portraits and: 21p, Statue of Victoria. 26p, Document. 36p, Statues of Victoria and Prince Albert. 40p, Commemoration stone, St. Peter's Port. 45p, Statue of Prince Albert. 65p, Victoria Tower.

2001, Jan. 22 *Perf. 14¾*

726 A161 21p multi .60 .60
727 A161 26p multi .75 .75
728 A161 36p multi 1.00 1.00
729 A161 40p multi 1.10 1.10
730 A161 45p multi 1.25 1.25
731 A161 65p multi 1.90 1.90
a. Souvenir sheet, #726-731 6.75 6.75
Nos. 726-731 (6) 6.60 6.60

Hong Kong 2001 Stamp Exhibition (No. 731a).

Birds A162

2001, Feb. 1 Litho. *Perf. 14x14¾*

732 A162 21p Kingfisher .60 .60
733 A162 26p Garganey .75 .75
734 A162 36p Little egret 1.00 1.00
735 A162 65p Little ringed plover 1.90 1.90
Nos. 732-735 (4) 4.25 4.25

Europa (26p, 36p).

Guernsey Dog Club, Cent. — A163

Island Views — A164

Designs: 22p, Cavalier King Charles spaniel. 27p, Miniature schnauzer. 36p, German shepherd. 40p, Cocker spaniel. 45p, West Highland white terrier. 65p, Dachshund.

2001, Apr. 26 Litho. *Perf. 13x13¼*

736 A163 22p multi .60 .60
737 A163 27p multi .75 .75
738 A163 36p multi 1.00 1.00
739 A163 40p multi 1.10 1.10
740 A163 45p multi 1.25 1.25
741 A163 65p multi 1.90 1.90
Nos. 736-741 (6) 6.60 6.60

Serpentine Die Cut 14¼x14

2001, Apr. 26 Litho.

No. 742: a, La Corbière sunset. b, Rue des Hougues. c, St. Saviour's Reservoir. d, Shell Beach, Herm. e, Telegraph Bay, Alderney. f, Alderney Railway. g, Vazon Bay. h, La Coupée, Sark. i, Les Hanois. j, Albecq,

Self-Adhesive

742 Sheet of 10 7.00
a.-e. A164 GY Any single .60 .60
f.-j. A164 UK Any single .75 .75
k. Booklet, 2 each #742a-742e 6.50
l. Booklet, 2 each #742f-742j 8.25
m.-q. As "a-e," photo., any single .60 .60
r. Strip, #742m-742q 3.00
s.-w. As "f-j," photo., any single .75 .75
x. Strip, #742s-742w 3.75

The photogravure stamps have a fuzzier appearance overall than the lithographed stamps. This is most noticeable in the crown where under magnification the bumps on the crown's outline are clearly distinct and well-defined as semicircles on the lithographed stamps, while ragged and ill-defined with a pointy appearance, on the photogravure stamps.

Nos. 742a-742e each sold for 22p, and Nos. 742f-742j each sold for 27p on day of issue.

Type of 1969 and

Change of Guernsey Post Office to Guernsey Post Ltd., Oct. 1, 2001 — A165

Designs: 22p, Vision (water droplet on leaf). 27p, Understanding (hummingbird and flower). 36p, Individuality (butterfly's wing). 40p, Strength (nautilus shell cross-section). 45p, Community (honeycomb). 65p, Maturity (Dandelion gone to seed). £1, Like No. 23.

2001, Aug. 1 Litho. *Perf. 13¼x13*

743 A165 22p multi .65 .65
a. Booklet pane of 3 2.10 —
744 A165 27p multi .80 .80
a. Booklet pane of 3 2.75 —
745 A165 36p multi 1.00 1.00
a. Booklet pane of 3 3.25 —
746 A165 40p multi 1.10 1.10
a. Booklet pane of 3 3.75 —
747 A165 45p multi 1.25 1.25
a. Booklet pane of 3 4.25 —
748 A165 65p multi 1.90 1.90
a. Booklet pane of 3 6.25 —

Perf. 14x14¼

749 A4 £1 Booklet pane of 1 3.25 3.25
Booklet, #743a, 744a, 745a, 746a, 747a, 748a, 749 26.00
Nos. 743-749 (7) 9.95 9.95

Panels on the at top and bottom of No. 749 are dark blue and clouds in silver margin are distinct. Never-bound examples of No. 749 with Prussian blue panels and less distinct clouds in the silver margin were given to standing order subscribers at no charge.

Christmas A166

Decorations: 19p, Tree of Joy, St. Peter Port. 27p, Cross, Les Cotils Christian Center. 36p, Les Ruettes Cottage, St. Saviour's. 40p, 17th cent. farmhouse. 45p, Sark Post Office. 65p, High Street, St. Peter Port.

2001, Oct. 16 ***Perf. 14¼x14½***

750	A166 19p multi		.55	.55
751	A166 27p multi		.80	.80
752	A166 36p multi		1.00	1.00
753	A166 40p multi		1.10	1.10
754	A166 45p multi		1.25	1.25
755	A166 65p multi		1.90	1.90
a.	Souvenir sheet, #750-755		6.75	6.75
	Nos. 750-755 (6)		6.60	6.60

Hafnia 01 Philatelic Exhibition, Copenhagen (#755a).

Circus — A167

Designs: 22p, Juggler. 27p, Clowns. 36p, Trapeze artists. 40p, Knife thrower. 45p, Acrobat. 65p, High-wire cyclist.

2002, Feb. 6 Litho. ***Perf. 14¾x14½***

756	A167 22p multi	.65	.65
757	A167 27p multi	.80	.80
758	A167 36p multi	1.00	1.00
759	A167 40p multi	1.10	1.10
760	A167 45p multi	1.25	1.25
761	A167 65p multi	1.90	1.90
	Nos. 756-761 (6)	6.70	6.70

Europa (27p, 36p).

Victor Hugo (1802-85), Writer — A168

Designs: 22p, Hugo and St. Peter Port. 27p, Cosette from Les Misérables. 36p, Valjean from Les Misérables. 40p, Javert from Les Misérables. 45p, Cosette and Marius from Les Misérables. 65p, Les Misérables, score from play based on book.

2002, Feb. 6 ***Perf. 13¼x13***

762	A168 22p multi	.65	.65
763	A168 27p multi	.80	.80
764	A168 36p multi	1.00	1.00
765	A168 40p multi	1.10	1.10
766	A168 45p multi	1.25	1.25
767	A168 65p multi	1.90	1.90
a.	Souvenir sheet of 6, #762-767	6.75	6.75
	Nos. 762-767 (6)	6.70	6.70

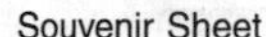
Souvenir Sheet

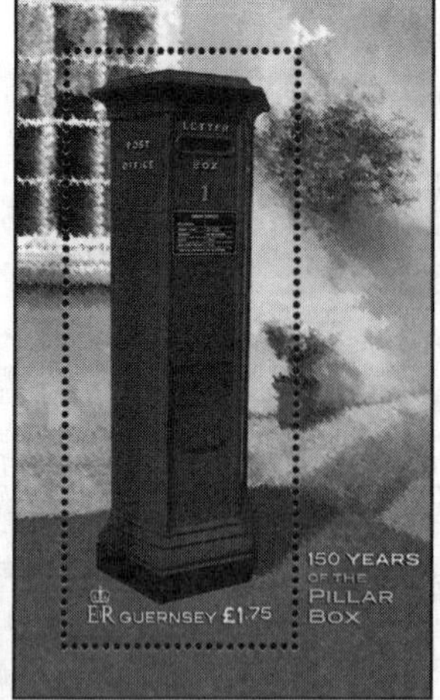

Pillar Boxes, 150th Anniv. — A169

2002, Apr. 30 ***Perf. 14½x14¼***

768	A169 £1.75 multi	5.25	5.25

Reign of Queen Elizabeth II, 50th Anniv. — A170

Various views of Queen.

2002, Apr. 30 ***Perf. 13½***

769	A170 22p multi	.65	.65
770	A170 27p multi	.80	.80
771	A170 36p multi	1.10	1.10
772	A170 40p multi	1.25	1.25
773	A170 45p multi	1.40	1.40
a.	Booklet pane, #770-773	4.75	
774	A170 65p multi	1.90	1.90
a.	Booklet pane, #769, 772-774	5.25	
b.	Booklet pane, #769-771, 774	4.50	
c.	Booklet pane, #769-774	7.25	
	Nos. 769-774 (6)	7.10	7.10

See Alderney No. 184a.

Vacations in Sark — A171

No. 775: a, Family on dock, boat near dock. b, Family disembarking tractor-pulled transport. c, Family at campground. d, Family with bicycles at La Coupée. e, Swimming at Venus Pool.

No. 776: a, Family at La Seigneurie Gardens. b, Family at village pillar box. c, Family in horse-drawn cart. d, Family dining outdoors. e, Family at beach.

2002, July 30 ***Perf. 13¼***

775	Horiz. strip of 5	4.25	4.25
a.-e.	A171 27p Any single	.85	.85
776	Horiz. strip of 5	4.25	4.25
a.-e.	A171 27p Any single	.85	.85

Awarding of Victoria Cross to Major Herbert Wallace Le Patourel, 60th Anniv.
A172

Designs: 22p, Parade of Elizabeth College Combined Cadet Corps, 1934. 27p, In battle, Tunisia, 1942. 36p, As repatriated prisoner of war, 1943. 40p, Presentation of Victoria Cross ribbon, 1943. 45p, Return to Guernsey, 1948. 65p, Carrying King's Colors, 1968.

2002, July 30 ***Perf. 13¼x13***

777	A172 22p multi	.65	.65
778	A172 27p multi	.80	.80
779	A172 36p multi	1.10	1.10
780	A172 40p multi	1.25	1.25
781	A172 45p multi	1.40	1.40
782	A172 65p multi	2.00	2.00
	Nos. 777-782 (6)	7.20	7.20

Souvenir Sheet

Queen Mother Elizabeth (1900-2002) — A173

Litho. With Foil Application

2002, Aug. 4 ***Perf. 13¼***

783	A173 £2 multi	6.25	6.25

POSTAGE DUE STAMPS

Castle Cornet and St. Peter Port — D1

Perf. 12½x12

1969, Oct. 1 Photo. Unwmk.

Black Numeral

J1	D1	1p deep magenta	1.00	.75
J2	D1	2p yellow green	2.25	1.75
J3	D1	3p red	3.00	2.00
J4	D1	4p ultra	4.00	2.25
J5	D1	5p yellow bister	6.25	3.75
J6	D1	6p greenish blue	8.00	4.50
J7	D1	1sh red brown	21.00	13.00
		Nos. J1-J7 (7)	45.50	28.00

Type of 1969
"p" instead of "d"

1971-76

Black Numeral

J8	D1	½p deep magenta	.20	.20
J9	D1	1p yellow green	.20	.20
J10	D1	2p red	.20	.20
J11	D1	3p ultra	.20	.20
J12	D1	4p yellow bister	.20	.20
J13	D1	5p greenish blue	.25	.25
J14	D1	6p purple ('76)	.20	.20
J15	D1	8p orange ('75)	.25	.25
J16	D1	10p red brown	.50	.50
J17	D1	15p gray ('76)	.50	.50
		Nos. J8-J17 (10)	2.70	2.70

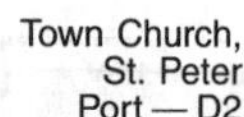
Town Church, St. Peter Port — D2

1977-80 Photo. ***Perf. 13½x13***

Arms and Denomination in Black

J18	D2	½p red brown	.20	.20
J19	D2	1p lilac rose	.20	.20
J20	D2	2p orange	.20	.20
J21	D2	3p red	.20	.20
J22	D2	4p greenish blue	.20	.20
J23	D2	5p olive green	.20	.20
J24	D2	6p greenish blue	.20	.20
J25	D2	8p ocher	.25	.25
J26	D2	10p dark blue	.30	.30
J27	D2	14p green ('80)	.40	.40
J28	D2	15p purple	.40	.40
J29	D2	16p salmon rose ('80)	.50	.50
		Nos. J18-J29 (12)	3.25	3.25

Woman Milking Cow — D3

1982, July 13 Litho. ***Perf. 14½***

J30	D3	1p shown	.20	.20
J31	D3	2p Vale Mill	.20	.20
J32	D3	3p Sark cottage	.20	.20
J33	D3	4p St. Peter Port	.20	.20
J34	D3	5p Well, Moulin Huet	.20	.20
J35	D3	16p Seaweed gathering	.35	.35
J36	D3	18p Upper Walk, White Rock	.40	.40
J37	D3	20p Cobo Bay	.45	.45
J38	D3	25p Saints' Bay	.50	.50
J39	D3	30p La Coupee, Sark	.70	.70
J40	D3	50p Old Harbor, St. Peter Port	1.00	1.00
J41	D3	£1 Greenhouses, Victoria Tower	2.25	2.25
		Nos. J30-J41 (12)	6.65	6.65

OCCUPATION STAMPS

Issued Under German Occupation

OS1

Rouletted 14x7

1941-44 Typo. Unwmk.

N1	OS1	½p yellow green	3.50	2.25
N2	OS1	1p vermilion	2.50	1.75
N3	OS1	2½p ultramarine	6.00	4.00
		Nos. N1-N3 (3)	12.00	8.00

Issued: ½p, 4/7; 1p, 2/18; 2½p, 4/4/44.

Numerous shades and papers exist. The rouletting is very crude and may not be measurable. This is not a defect.

Wmk. 396 Chain Link Fence

1942 ***Rouletted 14x7***

Bluish French Bank Note Paper

N4	OS1	½p green	20.00	20.00
N5	OS1	1p red	16.00	*20.00*

Issue dates: ½p, Mar. 11; 1p, Apr. 9.

Nos. N1-N5 remained valid until 4/13/46.

ALDERNEY

'ol-dər-nē

LOCATION — Northernmost of the Channel Islands in the Guernsey Bailiwick
GOVT. — Dependent territory under Bailiwick of Guernsey.
AREA — 3 sq. mi.
POP. — 2, 373 (1994 est.)
CAPITAL — St. Anne's

Part of the Bailiwick of Guernsey, this island began issuing its own stamps.

Catalogue values for unused stamps in this section are for Never Hinged items.

Map of Alderney, Arms — A1

1983, June 14 Litho. *Perf. 12*

No.	Type	Denom.	Description	Unused	Used
1	A1	1p	shown	.30	.30
2	A1	4p	Hanging Rock	.30	.30
3	A1	9p	States Building	.30	.30
4	A1	10p	St. Anne's Church	.30	.30
5	A1	11p	Yachts, Braye Bay	.35	.35
6	A1	12p	Victoria St., St. Anne	.35	.35
7	A1	13p	Map, arms	.35	.35
8	A1	14p	Ft. Clonque	.40	.40
9	A1	15p	Corblets Bay Port	.40	.40
10	A1	16p	Old Tower, St. Anne	.50	.50
11	A1	17p	Essex Castle Golf Course	.55	.55
12	A1	18p	Ships in Old Harbor	.55	.55
			Nos. 1-12 (12)	4.65	4.65

Oystercatcher, Telegraph Bay — A2

1984, June 12 *Perf. 14½*

No.	Type	Denom.	Description	Unused	Used
13	A2	9p	shown	1.50	1.10
14	A2	13p	Turnstone, Corblets Bay	1.50	1.00
15	A2	26p	Ringed plover, Corblets Bay	4.00	3.00
16	A2	28p	Dunlin, Arch Bay	4.00	3.25
17	A2	31p	Curlew, Old Harbor	4.00	3.25
			Nos. 13-17 (5)	15.00	11.60

Alderney Airport, 50th Anniv. A3

Aircraft: 9p, Wessex helicopter of the Queen's Flight, 1984. 13p, Aurigny Air Joey Britten-Norman Trislander, 1981. 29p, Morton Air Services DeHavilland Heron, 1946. 31p, DeHavilland Dragon Rapide, c. 1930. 34p, Saunders-Roe Saro Windhover, 1935.

1985, Mar. 19 *Perf. 12x11½*

No.	Type	Denom.	Description	Unused	Used
18	A3	9p	multicolored	1.75	1.50
19	A3	13p	multicolored	2.50	1.50
20	A3	29p	multicolored	4.25	3.50
21	A3	31p	multicolored	5.25	3.75
22	A3	34p	multicolored	5.25	3.75
			Nos. 18-22 (5)	19.00	14.00

Regimental Uniforms, Alderney Garrison — A4

1985, Sept. 24 *Perf. 14½*

No.	Type	Denom.	Description	Unused	Used
23	A4	9p	Royal Engineers, 1890	.30	.30
24	A4	14p	Duke of Albany's Own Highlanders, 1856	1.10	.55
25	A4	29p	Royal Artillery, 1855	1.10	1.10
26	A4	31p	South Hampshire Regiment, 1810	1.50	1.25
27	A4	34p	Royal Irish Regiment, 1782	1.75	1.40
			Nos. 23-27 (5)	5.75	4.60

Forts — A5

1986, Sept. 23 Litho. *Perf. 13x13½*

No.	Type	Denom.	Description	Unused	Used
28	A5	10p	Grosnez	1.25	1.25
29	A5	14p	Tourgis	1.50	1.50
30	A5	31p	Clonque	3.50	3.50
31	A5	34p	Albert	3.75	3.75
			Nos. 28-31 (4)	10.00	10.00

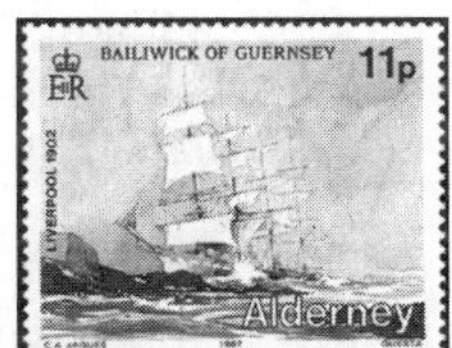

Shipwrecks A6

1987, May 5 Litho. *Perf. 14½*

No.	Type	Denom.	Description	Unused	Used
32	A6	11p	Liverpool, 1902	2.00	.80
33	A6	15p	Petit Raymond, 1906	2.50	.80
34	A6	29p	Maina, 1910	5.00	5.00
35	A6	31p	Burton, 1911	5.25	5.00
36	A6	34p	Point Law, 1975	5.25	5.25
			Nos. 32-36 (5)	20.00	16.85

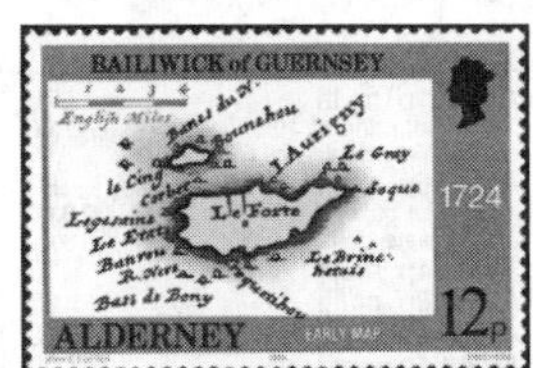

18th-20th Cent. Maps — A7

Designs: 12p, Herman Moll map, 1724. 18p, Survey by I.H. Bastide, 1739. 27p, Land survey by F. Goodwin, 1830. 32p, Wartime occupation map, 1943. 35p, Ordnance survey, 1988.

1989, July 7 Litho. *Perf. 13½x14*

No.	Type	Denom.	Description	Unused	Used
37	A7	12p	multicolored	.50	.50
38	A7	18p	multicolored	.75	.75
39	A7	27p	multicolored	1.10	1.10
40	A7	32p	multicolored	1.25	1.25
41	A7	35p	multicolored	1.40	1.40
			Nos. 37-41 (5)	5.00	5.00

Quesnard Lighthouse A8

Designs: 21p, Inner Harbor, Braye. 23p, The Island Hall, Alderney. 24p, Alderney Railway locomotive, J. T. Daly. 28p, Lifeboat, Louis Marchesi of Round Table.

1989-93 Litho. *Perf. 15x14*

No.	Type	Denom.	Description	Unused	Used
42	A8	20p	multicolored	1.25	1.00
43	A8	21p	multicolored	1.25	1.00
44	A8	23p	multicolored	.85	.75
45	A8	24p	multicolored	2.25	2.00
46	A8	28p	multicolored	2.40	2.00
			Nos. 42-46 (5)	8.00	6.75

Issued: 20p, 12/27; 21p, 4/2/91; 23p, 2/6/92; 24p, 28p, 3/3/93.

Ships Called HMS *Alderney* A9

1990, May 3 Litho. *Perf. 13½*

No.	Type	Denom.	Description	Unused	Used
55	A9	14p	Bomb ketch, 1738	.55	.55
56	A9	20p	Sixth-rate, 1742	.70	.70
57	A9	29p	Sloop, 1755	1.00	1.00
58	A9	34p	A-Class submarine, 1945	1.25	1.25
59	A9	37p	Fishery protection vessel, 1979	1.50	1.50
			Nos. 55-59 (5)	5.00	5.00

Automation of Casquets Lighthouse — A10

1991, Apr. 20 Litho. *Perf. 14x13½*

No.	Type	Denom.	Description	Unused	Used
60	A10	21p	Wreck of HMS Victory, 1744	2.10	2.10
61	A10	26p	Returning by rowboat	2.40	2.40
62	A10	31p	Helicopter relief	3.00	3.00
63	A10	37p	Lighthouse, birds	4.00	4.00
64	A10	50p	MV Patricia	5.00	5.00
			Nos. 60-64 (5)	16.50	16.50

Battle of La Hogue, 300th Anniv. — A11

23p, 28p, and 33p, Various details from painting by unknown artist. 50p, Entire painting.

1992, Sept. 18 Litho. *Perf. 13½*

No.	Type	Denom.	Description	Unused	Used
65	A11	23p	multicolored	2.00	2.00
66	A11	28p	multicolored	2.50	2.50
67	A11	33p	multicolored	3.00	3.00

Size: 45x30mm

Perf. 14x14½

No.	Type	Denom.	Description	Unused	Used
68	A11	50p	multicolored	3.75	3.75
			Nos. 65-68 (4)	11.25	11.25

Marine Life — A12

Designs: a, 24p, Palinurus elephas. b, 28p, Metridium senile. c, 33p, Luidia ciliaris. d, 39p, Psammechinus miliaris.

1993, Nov. 2 Litho. *Perf. 15x14½*

No.	Type	Description	Unused	Used
69	A12	Strip of 4, #a.-d.	7.00	7.00

Flora and Fauna — A13

Designs: 1p, Ischnura elegans, ranunculus trichophyllus, sparganium erectum. 2p, Crocidura russula, hypericum linarifolium. 3p, Fulmarus glacialis, carpobrotus edulis. 4p, Colias croceus, trifolium pratense. 5p, Bombus lucorum, orobanche rapum-genistae, cytisus scoparius. 6p, Sylvia undata, cuscuta epithymum, ulex europaeus. 7p, Inachis io, cirsium acaule. 8p, Talpa europaea, endymion non-scripta. 9p, Tettigonia viridissima, ulex europaeus. 10p, Zygaena filipendulae, echium vulgare. 16p, Polyommatus icarus, anacamptis pyramidalis. 20p, Oryctolagus cuniculus, rannunculus repens, pteridium aquilinum. 24p, Larus marinus, romulea columnae. 30p, Fratercula arctica, sedum anglicum. 40p, Saturnia pavonia, rubus fruticosus. 50p, Erinaceus europaeus, oxalis articulata. £1, Sterna hirundo, cynodon dactylon, horiz. £2, Morus bassanus, fucus vesiculosus.

1994-95 Litho. *Perf. 14*

No.	Type	Denom.	Description	Unused	Used
70	A13	1p	multicolored	.20	.20
71	A13	2p	multicolored	.20	.20
72	A13	3p	multicolored	.20	.20
73	A13	4p	multicolored	.20	.20
74	A13	5p	multicolored	.20	.20
75	A13	6p	multicolored	.20	.20
76	A13	7p	multicolored	.20	.20
77	A13	8p	multicolored	.25	.25
78	A13	9p	multicolored	.30	.30
79	A13	10p	multicolored	.30	.30
80	A13	16p	multicolored	.45	.45
a.			Perf. 14x15 on three sides	.50	.50
b.			As "a," booklet pane of 8	4.50	
81	A13	20p	multicolored	.55	.55
a.			Perf. 14x15 on three sides	.60	.60
b.			As "a," booklet pane of 8	5.50	
82	A13	24p	multicolored	.65	.65
a.			Perf. 14x15 on three sides	.70	.70
b.			As "a," booklet pane of 8	6.25	
83	A13	30p	multicolored	.80	.80
84	A13	40p	multicolored	1.10	1.10
85	A13	50p	multicolored	1.40	1.40
86	A13	£1	multicolored	2.75	2.75

Perf. 14x15

No.	Type	Denom.	Description	Unused	Used
87	A13	£2	multicolored	5.75	5.75
			Nos. 70-87 (18)	15.70	15.70

No. 81 is dated "1994." Nos. 81a-81b are dated "1998."

Issued: £2, 2/28/95; others, 5/5/94.

See Nos. 98-100.

Career of Flt. Lt. Tommy Rose DFC (1895-1968) — A14

No. 88: a, 1917-18 Royal Flying Corps. b, 1939-45 Chief Test Pilot. c, Phillips & Powis (Miles) Aircraft.

No. 89: a, Winner, 1935 King's Cup Air Race. b, Winner, 1947 Manx Air Derby. c, UK-Cape-UK Speed Record, 1936.

1995, Sept. 1 Litho. *Perf. 14x15*

No.	Type	Denom.	Description	Unused	Used
88	A14	35p	Strip of 3, #a.-c.	3.50	3.50
89	A14	41p	Strip of 3, #a.-c.	3.75	3.75

Nos. 88-89 printed in sheets of 12 stamps + 3 labels.

Souvenir Sheet

Return of Islanders, 50th Anniv. — A15

Illustration reduced.

1995, Nov. 16 Litho. *Perf. 13½*
90 A15 £1.65 multicolored 5.00 5.00

30th Signal Regiment Activities in Alderney, 25th Anniv. A16

a, 24p, Training. b, 41p, Natl. contingencies overseas. c, 60p, Strategic communications. d, 75p, UN operations.

1996, Jan. 24 Litho. *Perf. 14*
91 A16 Strip of 4, #a.-d. 6.00 6.00

Domestic Cats — A17

16p, Butterfly, brown & white cat. 24p, Gray cat on table. 25p, Two cats on chair. 35p, Cat pulling on table cloth. 41p, Calico cat in toy cart, white cat. 60p, Siamese cat with yarn.

1996, July 19 Litho. *Perf. 13½*
92 A17 16p multicolored .50 .50
93 A17 24p multicolored .65 .65
94 A17 25p multicolored .75 .75
95 A17 35p multicolored 1.10 1.10
96 A17 41p multicolored 1.25 1.25
97 A17 60p multicolored 6.50 6.50
a. Souvenir sheet, #92-97 5.75 5.75
Nos. 92-97 (6) 10.75 10.75

No. 97a is a continuous design.

Fauna and Flora Type of 1994

Designs: 18p, Aglais urticae, Buddleja davidii. 25p, Anthus petrosus, matthiola incana. 26p, Ammophila sabulosa, calystegia soldanella, horiz.

1997, Jan. 2 Litho. *Perf. 14½*
98 A13 18p multicolored .55 .55
a. Perf. 14x15 on 3 sides .80
b. As "a," booklet pane of 8 5.00
Complete booklet, #98b 5.00
99 A13 25p multicolored .75 .75
a. Perf. 14x15 on 3 sides .75
b. As "a," booklet pane of 8 6.50
Complete booklet, #99b 6.50
100 A13 26p multicolored .80 .80
Nos. 98-100 (3) 2.10 2.10

Alderney Cricket Club, 150th Anniv. — A18

1997, Aug. 21 Litho. *Perf. 13½*
101 A18 18p Harold Larwood .50 .50
102 A18 25p John Arlott .65 .65
103 A18 37p Pelham J. Warner 1.00 1.00
104 A18 43p W.G. Grace 1.10 1.10
105 A18 63p John Wisden 1.75 1.75
a. Souvenir sheet, #101-105 + label 5.25 5.25
Nos. 101-105 (5) 5.00 5.00

Garrison Island — A19

#106, Founding of the harbor. #107, Ariadne at anchor. #108, Quarrying at Mannez. #109, Earliest train ferrying stone. #110, Queen Victoria arrives ashore. #111, Royal yacht at anchor. #112, Railway and quarry workers greet the Queen. #113, Queen Victoria tours the island.

1997, Nov. 20 Litho. *Perf. 14½x14*
106 A19 18p multicolored .50 .50
107 A19 18p multicolored .50 .50
a. Pair, #106-107 1.00 1.00
108 A19 25p multicolored .70 .70
109 A19 25p multicolored .70 .70
a. Pair, #108-109 1.40 1.40
b. Booklet pane, #107a, 109a 2.75
110 A19 26p multicolored .70 .70
111 A19 26p multicolored .70 .70
a. Pair, #110-111 1.40 1.40
b. Booklet pane, #107a, 111a 3.25
112 A19 31p multicolored .85 .85
113 A19 31p multicolored .85 .85
a. Pair, #112-113 1.75 1.75
b. Booklet pane, #111a, 113a 3.50
c. Booklet pane, #109a, 113a 3.50
Nos. 106-113 (8) 5.50 5.50

See Nos. 119-126, 134-141.

Alderney Diving Club, 21st Anniv. — A20

20p, Modern superlite helmet. 30p, Cousteau-Gagnan demand valve, 1943. 37p, Heinke closed helmet, 1845. 43p, Siebe closed helmet, 1840. 63p, Deane open helmet, 1829.

1998, Feb. 10 Litho. *Perf. 13*
114 A20 20p multicolored .60 .60
115 A20 30p multicolored .90 .90
116 A20 37p multicolored 1.10 1.10
117 A20 43p multicolored 1.25 1.25
118 A20 63p multicolored 1.90 1.90
a. Souvenir sheet, #114-118 + label 5.75 5.75
Nos. 114-118 (5) 5.75 5.75

Garrison Island Type of 1997

#119, Alderney Post Office. #120, Traders in Victoria Street. #121, Court House. #122, Police Station and Fire Service. #123, St. Anne's Church. #124, Wedding Party at The Albert Gate. #125, SS Courier unloading. #126, Fishermen at quay.

1998, Nov. 10 Litho. *Perf. 14½x14*
119 A19 20p multicolored .60 .60
120 A19 20p multicolored .60 .60
a. Pair, #119-120 1.25 1.25
121 A19 25p multicolored .85 .85
122 A19 25p multicolored .85 .85
a. Pair, #121-122 1.75 1.75
b. Booklet pane, #120a, 122a 3.25
123 A19 30p multicolored 1.00 1.00
124 A19 30p multicolored 1.00 1.00
a. Pair, #123-124 2.00 2.00
b. Booklet pane, #120a, 124a 3.50
125 A19 37p multicolored 1.50 1.50
126 A19 37p multicolored 1.50 1.50
a. Pair, #125-126 3.00 3.00
b. Booklet pane, #124a, 126a 5.50
c. Booklet pane, #122a, 126a 5.25
Complete booklet, #109b, 111b, 113b, 113c, 122b, 124b, 126b, 126c 32.50
Nos. 119-126 (8) 7.90 7.90

Souvenir Sheet

The Wreck of the SS Stella, Cent. — A21

a, 25p, Stained glass window, Anglican Cathdral, Liverpool, dedicated to Mary Rogers, chief stewardess. b, £1.75, Ship leaving Southampton.

1999, Feb. 4 Litho. *Perf. 14*
127 A21 Sheet of 2, #a.-b. 6.75 6.75

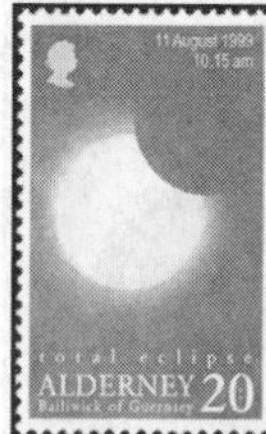

Total Solar Eclipse — A22

Stages of eclipse on 8/11/99: 20p, 10:15. 25p, 10:51. 30p, 11:14. 38p, 11:16. 44p, 11:17. 64p, 11:36.

1999, Apr. 27 Litho. *Perf. 13½x13*
128 A22 20p multicolored .65 .65
129 A22 25p multicolored .85 .85
130 A22 30p multicolored 1.00 1.00
131 A22 38p multicolored 1.25 1.25
132 A22 44p multicolored 1.40 1.40
133 A22 64p multicolored 2.10 2.10
a. Souvenir sheet, #128-133 + label 7.25 7.25
Nos. 128-133 (6) 7.25 7.25

Garrison Island Type of 1997

Designs: No. 134, Fort Grosnez, c. 1855. No. 135, Ninth Battalion, Royal Garrison Artillery. No. 136, Arsenal, Fort Albert. No. 137, Royal Engineer Unit. No. 138, Fort Tourgis, c. 1865. No. 139, Second Battalion, Royal Scots Regiment. No. 140, Fort Houmet Herbé, c. 1870. No. 141, Royal Alderney Artillery Militia.

1999, Oct. 19 Litho. *Perf. 14¼x13¾*
134 A19 20p multicolored .70 .70
135 A19 20p multicolored .70 .70
a. Pair, #134-135 1.40 1.40
136 A19 25p multicolored .80 .80
137 A19 25p multicolored .80 .80
a. Pair, #136-137 1.60 1.60
b. Booklet pane, #135a, 137a 3.25
138 A19 30p multicolored 1.00 1.00
139 A19 30p multicolored 1.00 1.00
a. Pair, #138-139 2.00 2.00
b. Booklet pane, #135a, 139a 3.75
c. Booklet pane, #137a, 139a 4.00
140 A19 38p multicolored 1.25 1.25
141 A19 38p multicolored 1.25 1.25
a. Pair, #140-141 2.50 2.50
b. Booklet pane, #135a, 141a 4.50
c. Booklet pane, #137a, 141a 4.75
d. Booklet pane, #139a, 141a 5.00
Complete booklet, #137b, 139b, 139c, 141b, 141c, 141d 27.50
Nos. 134-141 (8) 7.50 7.50

Peregrine Falcon — A23

Falcons: 21p, Attacking turnstone near lighthouse. 26p, With prey. 34p, With eggs. 38p, With chicks. 44p, With young near Fort Clonque. 64p, Preparing to fly.

2000, Feb. 4 Litho. *Perf. 14½x14*
142 A23 21p multi .70 .70
a. Booklet pane of 10 7.00
Complete booklet 7.00
143 A23 26p multi .80 .80
a. Booklet pane of 10 8.00
Complete booklet 8.00
144 A23 34p multi 1.10 1.10
145 A23 38p multi 1.25 1.25
146 A23 44p multi 1.40 1.40
147 A23 64p multi 2.00 2.00
Nos. 142-147 (6) 7.25 7.25

Worldwide Fund for Nature, Nos. 144-147.

The Wombles on Vacation A24

Wombles: 21p, With map. 26p, On beach. 36p, At lighthouse. 40p, Picnicking. 45p, On golf course. 65p, At airport.

2000, Apr. 28 Litho. *Perf. 14¼x13¾*
148 A24 21p multi .65 .65
149 A24 26p multi .75 .75
150 A24 36p multi 1.10 1.10
151 A24 40p multi 1.25 1.25
152 A24 45p multi 1.40 1.40
153 A24 65p multi 1.90 1.90
a. Souvenir sheet, #148-153 7.25 7.25
Nos. 148-153 (6) 7.05 7.05

The Stamp Show 2000, London (No. 153a).

Souvenir Sheet

Queen Mother, 100th Birthday — A25

Illustration reduced.

Litho. with Foil Application

2000, Aug. 4 *Perf. 13¼*
154 A25 £1.50 multi 4.50 4.50

Garrison Island Type of 1997

#155, Regimental boxing tournament. #156, Sports Day of Alderney Gala Week, 1924. #157, Regimenal Band of 15th entertains. #158, Garrison Ball, 1873, Fort Albert mess room. #159, Garrison assembly for Queen's birthday celebrations, 1859. #160, Demonstration of field guns on the Butes. #161, Inspection of honor guard, 1863. #162, Arrival of Lt. Gov. Major Gen. Marcus Slade.

2000, Oct. 19 Litho. *Perf. 13¼x13*
155 A19 21p multi .60 .60
156 A19 21p multi .60 .60
a. Pair, #155-156 1.20 1.20
157 A19 26p multi .75 .75
158 A19 26p multi .75 .75
a. Pair, #157-158 1.50 1.50
b. Booklet pane, #156a, 158a 3.00
159 A19 36p multi 1.10 1.10
160 A19 36p multi 1.10 1.10
a. Pair, #159-160 2.20 2.20
b. Booklet pane, #158a, 160a 4.00
161 A19 40p multi 1.25 1.25
162 A19 40p multi 1.25 1.25
a. Pair, #161-162 2.50 2.50
b. Booklet pane, #156a, 162a 4.00
c. Booklet pane, #160a, 162a 5.25
Booklet, #158b, 162c, 2 each #160b, 162b 24.00
Nos. 155-162 (8) 7.40 7.40

Each of the two panes of Nos. 160b and 162b in the booklet have different selvages.

Souvenir Sheet

Queen Elizabeth, 75th Birthday — A26

2001, Feb. 1 Litho. *Perf. 14¼*
163 A26 £1.75 multi 5.00 5.00

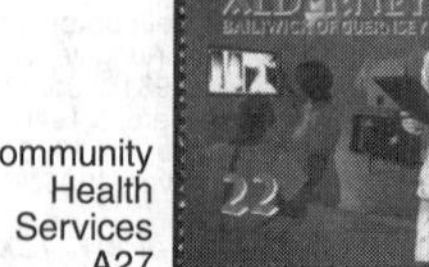

Community Health Services A27

Health care workers and: 22p, Hospital x-ray department. 27p, Mignot Memorial Hospital in 1980s. 36p, Princess Anne visiting hospital, 1972. 40p, Nurse with infant, 1960s. 45p, Queen Elizabeth II laying hospital cornerstone, 1957. 65p, Opening of original hospital, 1920s.

2001, Apr. 26 Litho. *Perf. 14¼x14½*
164 A27 22p multi .60 .60
165 A27 27p multi .75 .75
166 A27 36p multi 1.00 1.00
167 A27 40p multi 1.10 1.10
168 A27 45p multi 1.25 1.25
169 A27 65p multi 1.90 1.90
Nos. 164-169 (6) 6.60 6.60

Alderney Golf Club — A28

Designs: 22p, Golf ball with core of feathers, 1901. 27p, Golfing fashions, 1920s. 36p, Player and ball on Alderney Golf Club green, 1970s. 40p, Modern putter. 45p, Golf accessories. 65p, Modern lofted wood.

2001, Aug. 1 Litho. *Perf. 14¾*

170	A28	22p multi	.65	.65
171	A28	27p multi	.80	.80
172	A28	36p multi	1.00	1.00
173	A28	40p multi	1.10	1.10
174	A28	45p multi	1.25	1.25
175	A28	65p multi	1.90	1.90
a.		Souvenir sheet, #170-175	6.75	6.75
		Nos. 170-175 (6)	6.70	6.70

Phila Nippon '01 (#175a).

Garrison Island Type of 1997

Designs: No. 176, Work continues at the breakwater. No. 177, Officials observe work in progress. No. 178, Steam frigate Emerald grounded. No. 179, Soldiers disembarking Emerald. No. 180, Torpedo boats moored at breakwater. No. 181, Railway provides mobile artillery. No. 182, HMS Majestic at anchor, 1901. No. 183, Torpedo boats maneuver at speed.

2001, Oct. 16 Litho. *Perf. 13¼x13*

176	A19	22p multi	.65	.65
177	A19	22p multi	.65	.65
a.		Pair, #176-177	1.30	1.30
178	A19	27p multi	.80	.80
179	A19	27p multi	.80	.80
a.		Pair, #178-179	1.60	1.60
b.		Booklet pane, #177a, 179a	3.25	—
180	A19	36p multi	1.00	1.00
181	A19	36p multi	1.00	1.00
a.		Pair, #180-181	2.00	2.00
b.		Booklet pane, #179a, 181a	4.00	—
182	A19	40p multi	1.10	1.10
183	A19	40p multi	1.10	1.10
a.		Pair, #182-183	2.20	2.20
b.		Booklet pane, #177a, 183a	3.75	—
c.		Booklet pane, #179a, 183a	4.25	—
d.		Booklet pane, #181a, 183a	4.75	—
		Booklet, #179b, 181b, 183c, 183d, 2 #183b	24.00	
		Nos. 176-183 (8)	7.10	7.10

Booklet sold for £7.50. Each of the two panes of No. 183b in the booklet have different selvages.

Souvenir Sheet

Reign of Queen Elizabeth II, 50th Anniv. — A29

2002, Feb. 6 Litho. *Perf. 13¾x13½*

184	A29	£2 multi	5.75	5.75
a.		Booklet pane of 1	5.75	
		Booklet, #184a, Guernsey #773a, 774a, 774b, 774c	27.50	

No. 184a is sewn into booklets, but is otherwise identical to No. 184.

Issued: #184: 2/6; #184a, 4/30.

Birds — A30

2002, Apr. 30 *Perf. 13¾*

185	A30	22p Hobby	.65	.65
186	A30	27p Black kite	.80	.80
187	A30	36p Merlin	1.10	1.10
188	A30	40p Honey buzzard	1.25	1.25
189	A30	45p Osprey	1.40	1.40
190	A30	65p Marsh harrier	1.90	1.90
a.		Souvenir sheet, #185-190	7.25	7.25
		Nos. 185-190 (6)	7.10	7.10

Lighting at Les Casquets Lighthouse — A31

Designs: 22p, Coal fire, 1725. 27p, Oil lantern, 1779. 36p, Argand lamp, 1790. 45p, Revolving apparatus, 1818. 65p, Electrification, 1952.

2002, July 30 *Perf. 12¾x13¼*

191	A31	22p multi	.65	.65
192	A31	27p multi	.80	.80
193	A31	36p multi	1.10	1.10
194	A31	45p multi	1.40	1.40
195	A31	65p multi	2.00	2.00
		Nos. 191-195 (5)	5.95	5.95

JERSEY

jər-zē

LOCATION — Island in the English Channel
GOVT. — Dependent territory (bailiwick) of the British Crown
AREA — 45 sq. mi.
POP. — 89,721 (1999 est.)
CAPITAL — St. Helier

Following the establishment of the British General Post Office as a public corporation on October 1, 1969, the post office of the Bailiwick of Jersey became a separate entity and British postage stamps ceased to be valid.

Catalogue values for unused stamps in this country are for Never Hinged items.

British Regional Issue

A1

Royal Mace and Arms of Jersey — A2

Perf. 15x14

1958-69 Photo. Wmk. 322

1	A1	2½p rose red ('64)	.35	.25
2	A2	3p light purple	.35	.20
p.		Phosphor. ('67)	.20	.20
3	A2	4p ultra ('66)	.35	.20
p.		Phosphor. ('67)	.20	.20

Unwmk.

4	A2	4p olive brown ('68)	.20	.20
5	A2	4p brt red ('69)	.20	.20
6	A2	5p dark blue ('68)	.20	.20
		Nos. 1-6 (6)	1.65	1.25

Nos. 4-6 are phosphorescent.

Sold to the general public only at post offices within Jersey, but valid for postage throughout Great Britain.

See also Great Britain Nos. 269-270.

Bailiwick Issues

Elizabeth Castle and Queen Elizabeth II — A3

Queen Elizabeth II — A4

Designs (Queen Elizabeth II and): 1p, La Hougue Bie (prehistoric tomb). 2p, Portelet Bay. 3p, La Corbière Lighthouse. 4p, Mont Orgueil by night. 5p, Arms of Jersey and Royal Mace. 6p, Jersey cow. 9p, 1sh6p, Map of English Channel with Jersey. 1sh, Mont Orgueil. 2sh6p, Airport. 5sh, Legislative Chamber. 10sh, Royal Court. £1, Queen Elizabeth II, photograph by Cecil Beaton.

Perf. 14½

1969, Oct. 1 Photo. Unwmk.

7	A3	½p ocher & multi	.20	.20
8	A3	1p brown & multi	.20	.20
a.		Booklet pane of 1	.35	
b.		Booklet pane of 2	.90	
9	A3	2p multicolored	.20	.20
10	A3	3p dp blue & multi	.20	.20
11	A3	4p multicolored	.20	.20
a.		Booklet pane of 1	.60	
b.		Booklet pane of 2	1.10	
12	A3	5p multicolored	.20	.20
a.		Booklet pane of 2	1.75	
13	A3	6p multicolored	.20	.20
14	A3	9p multicolored	.20	*.30*
15	A3	1sh lilac & multi	.55	.50
16	A3	1sh6p green & multi	1.10	1.10

Perf. 12

17	A4	1sh9p multicolored	1.10	1.10
18	A3	2sh6p multicolored	1.25	1.00
19	A3	5sh multicolored	7.50	6.50
20	A3	10sh gray & multi	19.00	11.00
a.		10sh green & multi (error)	*4,000.*	
21	A4	£1 tan & multi	2.40	2.40
		Nos. 7-21 (15)	34.50	25.30

See Nos. 34-48, 107-109.

Jersey Post Office First Day Cover A5

1969, Oct. 1 *Perf. 14½*

22	A5	4p multicolored	.20	.20
23	A5	5p blue & multi	.25	.20
24	A5	1sh6p brown & multi	.80	1.10
25	A5	1sh9p emerald & multi	1.25	1.40
		Nos. 22-25 (4)	2.50	2.90

Inauguration of independent postal service.

Jersey Woman Reaching for Royal Mace, Flags of USSR, US and Great Britain — A6

4p, Lord Coutanche, Bailiff of Jersey, by James Gunn, vert. 5p, Sir Winston Churchill, by D. Van Praag, vert. 1sh9p, Swedish Red Cross ship "Vega."

1970, May 9 Photo. *Perf. 11½*

26	A6	4p gold & multi	.25	.20
27	A6	5p gold & multi	.25	.20
28	A6	1sh6p gold & multi	1.00	1.00
29	A6	1sh9p gold & multi	1.00	1.00
		Nos. 26-29 (4)	2.50	2.40

25th anniv. of Jersey's liberation from the Germans.

"Rags to Riches" Cinderella — A7

Designs (Parade Floats Made of Flowers): 4p, "A Tribute to Enid Blyton," author of children's books. 1sh6p, "Gourmet's Delight." 1sh9p, "We're the Greatest" (ostriches and trees).

1970, July 28 Photo. *Perf. 11½*

30	A7	4p gold & multi	.35	.20
31	A7	5p gold & multi	.35	.30
32	A7	1sh6p gold & multi	5.00	2.75
33	A7	1sh9p gold & multi	5.00	3.50
		Nos. 30-33 (4)	10.70	6.75

"Battle of Flowers" annual parade.

Decimal Currency Issue
Types of 1969
"p" instead of "d"

Designs: ½p, Elizabeth Castle. 1p, La Corbiere Lighthouse. 1½p, Jersey cow. 2p, Mont Orgueil by night. 2½p, Arms of Jersey and Royal Mace. 3p, La Hougue Bie. 3½p, Portelet Bay. 4p, 7½p, Map of English Channel and Jersey. 5p, Mont Orgueil by day. 6p, Martello Tower at Archirondel. 9p, Queen Elizabeth II, by Cecil Beaton. 10p, Airport. 20p, Legislative Chamber. 50p, Royal Court.

1970-75 Photo. *Perf. 14½*

34	A3	½p ocher & multi ('71)	.20	.20
a.		Booklet pane of 1	.20	
35	A3	1p multicolored ('71)	.20	.20
a.		Booklet pane of 2 ('75)	.20	
b.		Booklet pane of 4 ('75)	.35	
36	A3	1½p multicolored ('71)	.20	.20
37	A3	2p multicolored ('71)	.20	.20
a.		Booklet pane of 1	.20	
b.		Booklet pane of 2	.35	
38	A3	2½p multicolored ('71)	.20	.20
a.		Booklet pane of 1	.35	
b.		Booklet pane of 2	.45	
39	A3	3p brn & multicolored ('71)	.20	.20
a.		Booklet pane of 1 ('72)	.35	
b.		Booklet pane of 2 ('72)	.45	
40	A3	3½p multicolored ('71)	.20	.20
a.		Booklet pane of 1 ('74)	.35	
b.		Booklet pane of 2 ('74)	.50	
41	A3	4p multicolored ('71)	.20	.20
a.		Booklet pane of 2 ('75)	.50	
b.		Booklet pane of 4 ('75)	.75	
42	A3	5p lilac & multi ('71)	.20	.20
a.		Booklet pane of 2 ('75)	.55	
b.		Booklet pane of 4 ('75)	.95	
43	A3	6p green & multi ('71)	.20	.20
44	A3	7½p multicolored ('71)	.25	.25
45	A4	9p multicolored ('71)	.35	.35

Perf. 12

46	A3	10p multicolored	.40	.40
47	A3	20p multicolored	.60	.60
48	A3	50p multicolored	1.40	1.40
		Nos. 34-48 (15)	5.00	5.00

See also Nos. 107-109.

White-eared Pheasant — A8

2½p, Thick-billed parrots, vert. 7½p, Ursine colobus monkeys, vert. 9p, Ring-tailed lemurs.

1971, Mar. 9 Photo. *Perf. 11½*

49	A8	2p deep plum & multi	.35	.20
50	A8	2½p dark gray & multi	.40	.20
51	A8	7½p olive & multi	4.50	2.75
52	A8	9p vio blue & multi	5.25	4.00
		Nos. 49-52 (4)	10.50	7.15

Jersey Wildlife Preservation Trust.

See Nos. 65-68.

British Legion Emblem A9

2½p, Poppy field & poppy emblem. 7½p, Jack Counter (1899-1970) & Victoria Cross. 9p, Flags of France & Great Britain.

1971, June 15 Litho. *Perf. 14½*

53	A9	2p multicolored	.25	.20
54	A9	2½p multicolored	.25	.20
55	A9	7½p multicolored	1.40	1.25
56	A9	9p multicolored	1.40	1.40
		Nos. 53-56 (4)	3.30	3.05

50th anniversary of the British Legion.

English Fleet in Channel, by Peter Monamy
A10

Paintings by Jersey Artists: 2p, Tante Elizabeth (women in farm kitchen), by Edmund Blampied, vert. 7½p, Boyhood of Raleigh (man and boys at seashore), by Sir John Millais. 9p, The Blind Beggar (old man and girl), by W. W. Ouless, vert.

1971, Oct. 5 Photo. *Perf. 11½*

57 A10 2p gold & multi .20 .20
58 A10 2½p gold & multi .25 .20
59 A10 7½p gold & multi 1.60 1.40
60 A10 9p gold & multi 1.60 1.40
Nos. 57-60 (4) 3.65 3.20

Jersey Fern — A11

Jersey Royal Artillery Shako — A12

Jersey Wild Flowers: 5p, Thrift. 7½p, Orchid (laxiflora). 9p, Viper's bugloss.

1972, Jan. 18

Flowers in Natural Colors

61 A11 3p brown & blk .25 .20
62 A11 5p lt blue & blk .55 .25
63 A11 7½p lilac & blk 1.60 1.40
64 A11 9p green & blk 1.60 1.50
Nos. 61-64 (4) 4.00 3.35

Wildlife Type of 1971

2½p, Cheetahs. 3p, Rothschild's mynahs, vert. 7½p, Spectacled bear. 9p, Tuatara lizards.

1972, Mar. 17 Photo. *Perf. 11½*

Queen's Head in Gold

65 A8 2½p Prus blue & multi .50 .20
66 A8 3p dk pur & multi .35 .20
67 A8 7½p yel bis & multi 1.00 1.00
68 A8 9p multicolored 1.25 1.00
Nos. 65-68 (4) 3.10 2.40

Jersey Wildlife Preservation Trust.

1972, June 27

69 A12 2½p shown .20 .20
70 A12 3p 2nd North Regiment .20 .20
71 A12 7½p South West Regiment .50 .25
72 A12 9p 3rd (South) Light Infantry .65 .50
Nos. 69-72 (4) 1.55 1.15

Royal Jersey Militia shakos of 19th century.

Princess Anne — A13

Designs: 3p, Queen Elizabeth II and Prince Philip, horiz. 7½p, Prince Charles. 20p, Queen Elizabeth II and family, horiz.

1972, Nov. 1 Photo. *Perf. 11½*

73 A13 2½p citron & multi .20 .20
74 A13 3p rose & multi .20 .20
75 A13 7½p blue & multi .25 .20
76 A13 20p gray & multi .30 .30
Nos. 73-76 (4) .95 .90

25th anniversary of the marriage of Queen Elizabeth II and Prince Philip.

Silver Wine and Christening Cups, 18th Century
A14

Designs: 3p, Gold torque, Bronze Age, vert. 7½p, Seal of Charles II, 1659, vert. 9p, Armorican (Brittany) coins, c. 55 B.C.

1973, Jan. 23 Photo. *Perf. 11½*

77 A14 2½p ultra & multi .20 .20
78 A14 3p dp car & multi .20 .20
79 A14 7½p org & multi .25 .25
80 A14 9p blue & multi .25 .25
Nos. 77-80 (4) .90 .90

Cent. of the Jersey Soc. Designs are from exhibits in the Soc. museum in St. Helier.

Balloon, Letter to Jersey from Siege of Paris, 1870 — A15

5p, Astra seaplane, 1912. 7½p, Supermarine Sea Eagle, 1923. 9p, De Havilland DH86, 1933.

1973, May 16 Photo. *Perf. 11½*

81 A15 3p brt blue & multi .20 .20
82 A15 5p blue grn & multi .20 .20
83 A15 7½p ultra & multi .25 .25
84 A15 9p vio blue & multi .35 .35
Nos. 81-84 (4) 1.00 1.00

Aviation history connected with Jersey before 1939.

19th Century Locomotives
A16

1973, Aug. 6 Photo. *Perf. 11½*

85 A16 2½p North Western .20 .20
86 A16 3p Calvados .20 .20
87 A16 7½p Carteret .25 .20
88 A16 9p Caesarea .30 .25
Nos. 85-88 (4) .95 .85

Centenary of Jersey Eastern Railroad.

Princess Anne and Mark Phillips
A17

1973, Nov. 14 Photo. *Perf. 11½*

89 A17 3p lt blue & multi .20 .20
90 A17 20p pink & multi .80 .80

Wedding of Princess Anne and Capt. Mark Phillips, Nov. 14, 1973.

Spider Crab
A18

1973, Nov. 15 Photo. *Perf. 11½*

91 A18 2½p shown .20 .20
92 A18 3p Conger eel .20 .20
93 A18 7½p Lobster .30 .25
94 A18 20p Ormer .40 .30
Nos. 91-94 (4) 1.10 .95

Jersey Spring Flowers — A19

1974, Feb. 13 Photo. *Perf. 12x11½*

95 A19 3p Freesias .20 .20
96 A19 5½p Anemones .20 .20
97 A19 8p Carnations & gladioli .25 .25
98 A19 10p Daffodils & iris .35 .35
Nos. 95-98 (4) 1.00 1.00

First Letter Box, Letter with 1852 Cancel
A20

UPU Cent.: 3p, Postmen, 1862 and 1969. 5½p, Contemporary pillar box and first day cover of No. 101. 20p, BAC 111 and paddle steamer "Aquila," 1874.

1974, June 7 Photo. *Perf. 11½*

99 A20 2½p multicolored .20 .20
100 A20 3p ultra & multi .20 .20
101 A20 5½p olive & multi .20 .20
102 A20 20p gray & multi .40 .40
Nos. 99-102 (4) 1.00 1.00

John Wesley — A21

Lithographed and Engraved

1974, July 31 *Perf. 13½x14*

103 A21 3p shown .20 .20
104 A21 3½p Hillary .20 .20
105 A21 8p Wace .25 .25
106 A21 20p Churchill .50 .50
Nos. 103-106 (4) 1.15 1.15

Anniversaries: Methodism in Jersey, bicen.; John Wesley, theologian, founder of Methodism. Sesquicentennial of Royal Natl. Lifeboat Institution, Lt. Col. Sir William Hillary, founder. 800th death anniv. of Canon Wace, poet and chronicler. Sir Winston Churchill.

Type of 1969

4½p, Arms of Jersey and Royal Mace. 5½p, Jersey cow. 8p, Mont Orgueil by night.

1974, Oct. 31 Photo. *Perf. 14½*

107 A3 4½p olive & multi .20 .20
108 A3 5½p magenta & multi .20 .20
109 A3 8p yellow & multi .25 .25
Nos. 107-109 (3) .65 .65

English Yacht, 1660, by Peter Monamy
A22

Marine paintings by Peter Monamy (d. 1749): 5½p, French ship. 8p, Dutch ship, horiz. 25p, Naval battle, 1662.

1974, Nov. 22 Photo. *Perf. 11½*

Size: 31x38, 38x31mm

116 A22 3½p gold & multi .20 .20
117 A22 5½p gold & multi .20 .20
118 A22 8p gold & multi .25 .25

Size: 54x25mm

119 A22 25p gold & multi .60 .60
Nos. 116-119 (4) 1.25 1.25

Potato Digger — A23

19th cent. farming tools: 3½p, Cider apple crusher. 8p, Six-horse plow. 10p, Hay cart.

1975, Feb. 25 Photo. *Perf. 11½*

120 A23 3p multicolored .20 .20
121 A23 3½p multicolored .20 .20
122 A23 8p multicolored .25 .25
123 A23 10p multicolored .30 .30
Nos. 120-123 (4) .95 .95

Shell Design as Letter "J" — A24

Posters: 8p, Beach umbrella. 10p, Beach chair. 12p, Sand castle with Union Jacks & Jersey flag.

1975, June 8 Photo. *Perf. 11½*

124 A24 5p multicolored .20 .20
125 A24 8p multicolored .20 .20
126 A24 10p multicolored .25 .25
127 A24 12p multicolored .35 .35
a. Souvenir sheet of 4 1.25 1.25
Nos. 124-127 (4) 1.00 1.00

Tourist publicity. No. 127a contains Nos. 124-127 in continuous design extending into margin.

Queen Mother Elizabeth
A25

1975, May 30 Photo. *Perf. 11½*

128 A25 20p multicolored .75 .50

Visit of Queen Mother Elizabeth to Jersey.

Common Tern — A26

1975, July 28 Photo. *Perf. 11½*

129 A26 4p shown .20 .20
130 A26 5p Storm petrel .20 .20
131 A26 8p Brent geese .40 .20
132 A26 25p Shag .70 .35
Nos. 129-132 (4) 1.50 .95

Siskin 3A, 1925 — A27

R.A.F. Planes: 5p, Southampton 1, 1925. 10p, Spitfire 1, 1931. 25p, Gnat T.1, 1962.

1975, Oct. 30	Photo.	Perf. 11½		
133	A27	4p blue & multi	.20	.20
134	A27	5p lt green & multi	.20	.20
135	A27	10p yellow & multi	.30	.30
136	A27	25p ultra & multi	.65	.65
		Nos. 133-136 (4)	1.35	1.35

Royal Air Force Assoc., Jersey Branch, 50th anniv.

Map of Jersey with 12 Parishes A28

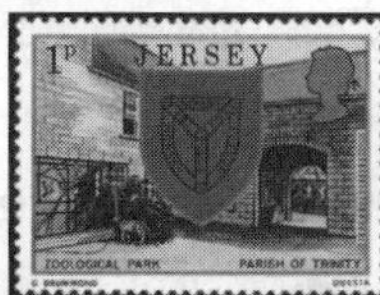

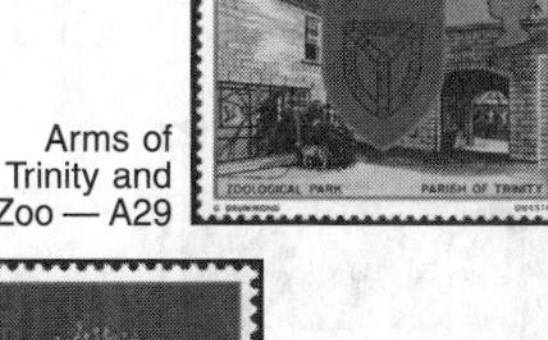

Arms of Trinity and Zoo — A29

Queen Elizabeth II — A30

Arms and scene: 5p, Church of St. Mary. 6p, Grouville, Seymour Tower. 7p, St. Brelade, La Corbière Lighthouse. 8p, Church of St. Saviour. 9p, St. Helier, Elizabeth Castle. 10p, St. Martin, Gorey Harbor. 11p, St. Peter, Jersey Airport. 12p, St. Ouen, Grosnez Castle. 13p, St. John, Bonne Nuit Harbor. 14p, St. Clement and Le Hocq Tower. 15p, St. Lawrence, Morel Farm. 20p, 12 Parishes, view of harbor. 30p, Jersey flag, map of Island. 40p, Postal Administration emblem, PO Headquarters. 50p, Jersey, Parliament and Royal Court. £1, Flag of Lt.-Governor, Government House.

1976-77 Litho. Perf. 14½

Size: 33x23mm

No.	Type	Description	Unused	Used
137	A28	½p lt blue & multi	.20	.20
138	A29	1p bister & multi	.20	.20
a.		Bklt. pane of 2 + 2 labels	.80	
b.		Booklet pane of 4	.80	
139	A29	5p rose & multi	.20	.20
a.		Booklet pane of 4	.80	
140	A29	6p vio blue & multi	.20	.20
a.		Booklet pane of 4 ('78)	.90	
141	A29	7p fawn & multi	.20	.20
a.		Booklet pane of 4	.55	
142	A29	8p yel grn & multi	.20	.20
a.		Booklet pane of 4 ('78)	.80	
143	A29	9p lil rose & multi	.20	.20
a.		Booklet pane of 4 ('80)	1.10	
144	A29	10p ol bis & multi	.25	.25
145	A29	11p bl grn & multi	.30	.30
146	A29	12p org & multi	.30	.30
147	A29	13p blue & multi	.30	.30
148	A29	14p yel org & multi	.45	.45
149	A29	15p vio & multi	.45	.45

Photo.

Perf. 12

Size: 41x26mm, 26x41mm

No.	Type	Description	Unused	Used
150	A29	20p gold & multi	.50	.50
151	A28	30p gold & multi	.65	.65
152	A29	40p gold & multi	.95	.95
153	A29	50p gold & multi	1.10	1.10
154	A29	£1 gold & multi	3.25	3.25
155	A30	£2 multicolored ('77)	3.75	3.75
		Nos. 137-155 (19)	13.65	13.65

Issue dates: Nos. 137-149, Jan. 29; Nos. 150-154, Aug. 20. No. 155, Nov. 16.

Sir Walter Raleigh and Old Map of Virginia — A31

US Bicentennial: 7p, Sir George Carteret and old map of New Jersey. 11p, Philippe Dauvergne and ships landing on Long Island. 13p, John Singleton Copley and his "Death of Major Pierson."

1976, May 29	Photo.	Perf. 11½		
160	A31	5p multicolored	.20	.20
161	A31	7p multicolored	.20	.20
162	A31	11p multicolored	.30	.30
163	A31	13p multicolored	.40	.40
		Nos. 160-163 (4)	1.10	1.10

Dr. Grandin, Central and Southern China Map A32

7p, Yangtze River journey. 11p, On horseback to Chaotung. 13p, Dr. Grandin holding infant.

1976, Nov. 25	Photo.	Perf. 11½		
164	A32	5p multicolored	.20	.20
165	A32	7p multicolored	.20	.20
166	A32	11p multicolored	.30	.30
167	A32	13p multicolored	.40	.40
		Nos. 164-167 (4)	1.10	1.10

Lilian Mary Grandin (1876-1924), Jersey-born missionary doctor in China.

Queen Wearing St. Edward's Crown — A33

7p, Queen with Jersey Bailiff Sir Alexander Coutanche, 1957. 25p, Portrait, 1976.

1977, Feb. 7	Photo.	Perf. 11½		
168	A33	5p multicolored	.20	.20
169	A33	7p multicolored	.20	.20
170	A33	25p multicolored	.50	.50
		Nos. 168-170 (3)	.90	.90

25th anniv. of the reign of Elizabeth II.

1/13th sh, 1871 and 1/12th sh, 1877 A34

Coins: 7p, 1/12th sh, 1949. 11p, Silver crown, 1966. 13p, Silver £2, 1972.

1977, Mar. 25	Litho.	Perf. 14		
171	A34	5p multicolored	.20	.20
172	A34	7p multicolored	.20	.20
173	A34	11p multicolored	.35	.35
174	A34	13p multicolored	.40	.40
		Nos. 171-174 (4)	1.15	1.15

Centenary of Jersey's currency reform.

Sir William Weston and Santa Anna, 1530 A35

Designs: 7p, Sir William Drogo and horse-drawn ambulance, 1877. 11p, Duke of Connaught and Jersey ambulance, 1917. 13p, Richard, Duke of Gloucester and ambulance team, 1977.

1977, June 24	Litho.	Perf. 14x13½		
175	A35	5p multicolored	.20	.20
176	A35	7p multicolored	.20	.20
177	A35	11p multicolored	.25	.25
178	A35	13p multicolored	.35	.35
		Nos. 175-178 (4)	1.00	1.00

St. John Ambulance Assoc. cent. (in GB).

Victoria and Albert Arriving in Jersey, 1846 A36

Designs: 10½p, Victoria College, 1852. 11p, Statue of Sir Galahad near college gate, vert. 13p, College Hall, interior, vert.

1977, Sept. 29	Litho.	Perf. 14½		
179	A36	7p multicolored	.20	.20
180	A36	10½p multicolored	.20	.20
181	A36	11p multicolored	.30	.30
182	A36	13p multicolored	.40	.40
		Nos. 179-182 (4)	1.10	1.10

Jersey Victoria College, 125th anniv.

Harry Vardon Statuette, Layout of Golf Course A37

Designs: 8p, Golf grip and swing perfected by Vardon. 11p, Vardon's putting grip and stance. 13p, Vardon's British and US Open Golf trophies, his book "The Complete Golfer" and biography.

1978, Feb. 28	Litho.	Perf. 14		
183	A37	6p multicolored	.20	.20
184	A37	8p multicolored	.25	.25
185	A37	11p multicolored	.25	.25
186	A37	13p multicolored	.30	.30
		Nos. 183-186 (4)	1.00	1.00

Cent. of Royal Jersey Golf Club and to honor Vardon (1870-1937), Jersey-born golfer.

Mont Orgueil — A38

Europa: 8p, St. Aubin's Fort. 10½p, Elizabeth Castle.

1978, May 1	Photo.	Perf. 11½		
187	A38	6p multicolored	.20	.20
188	A38	8p multicolored	.20	.20
189	A38	10½p multicolored	.30	.30
		Nos. 187-189 (3)	.70	.70

Gaspe Basin, by P. J. Ouless — A39

8p, Early map of Gaspe Peninsula, after Capt. Cook. 10½p, Sailing ship Century. 11p, Early map of Jersey. 13p, St. Aubin's Bay Town & Harbor.

1978, June 9	Litho.	Perf. 14x15		
190	A39	6p multicolored	.20	.20
191	A39	8p multicolored	.20	.20
192	A39	10½p multicolored	.25	.20
193	A39	11p multicolored	.30	.20
194	A39	13p multicolored	.40	.25
		Nos. 190-194 (5)	1.35	1.05

Jersey's links with Canada and for CAPEX, Canadian Intl. Phil. Exhib., Toronto, Ont., June 9-18.

Elizabeth II, Portraits 1953 and 1977 — A40

Design: 8p, Elizabeth II and Prince Philip.

1978, June 27	Photo.	Perf. 11½		
195	A40	8p car, sil & black	.20	.20
196	A40	25p blue, sil & black	.70	.70

25th anniv. of coronation of Queen Elizabeth II and for Royal visit, June 27.

Mail Cutter — A41

Packets: 8p, Flamer, paddle vessel. 10½p, Diana, screw steamer. 11p, Ibex, steamer. 13p, Caesarea, mini-liner.

1978, Oct. 18	Litho.	Perf. 14½x14		
197	A41	6p multicolored	.20	.20
198	A41	8p multicolored	.20	.20
199	A41	10½p multicolored	.25	.20
200	A41	11p multicolored	.30	.20
201	A41	13p multicolored	.40	.25
		Nos. 197-201 (5)	1.35	1.05

First Government packet between Britain and Jersey, bicentenary.

Jersey Pillar Box, 1860 — A42

Europa: No. 203, Mailman emptying 1979 mailbox. No. 204, Telephone switchboard, c. 1900. No. 205, Technician working on contemporary telecommunications system.

Perf. 14, 14½x15

1979, Mar. 1		Litho.		
202	A42	8p yellow & blk	.20	.20
203	A42	8p carmine & blk	.20	.20
a.		Pair, #202-203	.35	.35
204	A42	10½p violet & blk	.40	.40
205	A42	10½p blue & blk	.40	.40
a.		Pair, #204-205	.80	.80
		Nos. 202-205 (4)	1.20	1.20

Nos. 203a, 205a have continuous design. Both exist perf. 14 and 14½x15.

Soft-colored Jersey Heifer — A43

25p, Milk-laden Jersey cow with 1st Prize ribbon.

Perf. 14 (#206), 13¾ (#207)

1979, Mar. 1				
206	A43	6p multicolored	.20	.20

Size: 48x31mm

No.	Type	Description	Unused	Used
207	A43	25p multicolored	.75	.75

30th anniv. of 1st Intl. Conf. of Jersey Breed Societies and 9th Conf. of the World Jersey Cattle Bureau.

Percival Mew Gull — A44

Planes: 8p, De Havilland Chipmunk. 10½p, Druine D-31 Turbulent. 11p, De Havilland Tiger Moth. 13p, North American Harvard Mk. 4.

1979, Apr. 24	Photo.	Perf. 11½		
208	A44	6p multicolored	.20	.20
209	A44	8p multicolored	.20	.20
210	A44	10½p multicolored	.20	.20
211	A44	11p multicolored	.30	.30
212	A44	13p multicolored	.35	.35
		Nos. 208-212 (5)	1.25	1.25

25th International Air Rally.

My First Sermon, by Millais — A45

Paintings by Millais: 10½p, Orphan. 11p, The Princes in the Tower. 25p, Jesus in the Home of His Parents, horiz.

1979, Aug. 13 Photo. *Perf. 11½*

Size: 25x35mm

213 A45 8p multicolored .25 .25
214 A45 10½p multicolored .30 .30
215 A45 11p multicolored .30 .30

Size: 49x30mm

Perf. 12x12½

216 A45 25p multicolored .70 .70
Nos. 213-216 (4) 1.55 1.55

IYC and for John Everett Millais (1829-96).

Waldrapp Ibis — A46

1979, Nov. 8 Photo. *Perf. 11½*

217 A46 6p Pink pigeons .20 .20
218 A46 8p Orangutans .20 .20
219 A46 11½p shown .20 .20
220 A46 13p Lowland gorillas .35 .35
221 A46 15p Rodrigues fruit bats .45 .45
Nos. 217-221 (5) 1.40 1.40

Nos. 217-218, 220-221 vertical.

Mont Orgueil Fortress A47

Fortresses, 300th Anniversary: 11½p, St. Aubin Tower. 13p, Elizabeth. 25p, Map of Jersey showing fortress locations.

1980, Feb. 5 Litho. *Perf. 14½x13½*

222 A47 8p multicolored .20 .20
223 A47 11½p multicolored .25 .25
224 A47 13p multicolored .30 .30

Perf. 13½x14

Size: 37½x26mm

225 A47 25p multicolored .65 .65
Nos. 222-225 (4) 1.40 1.40

Potato Harvest — A48

Royal Jersey Potato Cent.: 7p, Planting potatoes. 17½p, Loading dock, Weighbridge.

1980, May 6 Litho. *Perf. 14*

226 A48 7p multicolored .20 .20
227 A48 15p multicolored .30 .30
228 A48 17½p multicolored .40 .40
Nos. 226-228 (3) .90 .90

A49

Europa (Wax Figures from Mont Orgueil and Elizabeth Castles): No. 230a, Charles II and Sir George Carteret; 230b, Lady Carteret. Pairs in continuous design.

1980, May 6

229 A49 Pair .50 .50
a.-b. 9p any single .25 .25
230 A49 Pair .60 .60
a.-b. 13½p any single .30 .30

Three-lap Motorcycle Race — A51

1980, July 24 Litho. *Perf. 12*

Granite Paper

231 A51 7p shown .20 .20
232 A51 9p Intl. road race .20 .20
233 A51 13½p Motorcycle scrambling .35 .35
234 A51 15p Sand racing, saloon cars .40 .40
235 A51 17½p Natl. Hill climb .45 .45
Nos. 231-235 (5) 1.60 1.60

Jersey Motorcycle and Light Car Club, 60th anniv.

"Eye of the Wind" Leaving St. Helier — A52

Designs: 9p, Medical research, Cuna Indians, Panama. 13½p, Exploration, Papua New Guinea. 14p, Capt. Scott's ship, Antarctica. 15p, Conservation, Sulawesi. 17½p, Marine studies.

1980, Oct. 1 Litho. *Perf. 14½*

236 A52 7p multicolored .20 .20
237 A52 9p multicolored .20 .20
238 A52 13½ multicolored .25 .25
239 A52 14p multicolored .25 .25
240 A52 15p multicolored .35 .35
241 A52 17½p multicolored .40 .40
Nos. 236-241 (6) 1.65 1.65

Operation Drake, a two-year, round-the-world scientific expedition in tribute to Royal Geographic Society sesquicentennial.

Armed Soldiers and Wounded Drummer A53

Designs: Details from The Death of Major Peirson, by John Singleton Copley.

1981, Jan. 6 Photo. *Perf. 12½*

Granite Paper

242 A53 7p multicolored .20 .20
243 A53 10p multicolored .25 .25
244 A53 15p multicolored .35 .35
245 A53 17½p multicolored .45 .45
a. Souvenir sheet of 4, #242-245 1.50 1.50
Nos. 242-245 (4) 1.25 1.25

Battle of Jersey bicentenary. No. 245a has continuous design.

De Bagot Family Arms — A54

Jersey, Channel Map A54a

Queen Elizabeth II, by Norman Hepple — A54b

1981-83 Litho. *Perf. 14*

246 A54 ½p shown .20 .20
247 A54 1p De Carteret .20 .20
a. Booklet pane of 6 .35
248 A54 2p La Cloche .20 .20
a. Booklet pane of 6 .55
249 A54 3p Dumaresq .20 .20
a. Booklet pane of 6 .65
250 A54 4p Payn .20 .20
251 A54 5p Janvrin .20 .20
252 A54 6p Poingdestre .20 .20
253 A54 7p Pipon .25 .20
a. Booklet pane of 6 1.60
254 A54 8p Marett .30 .25
a. Booklet pane of 6 ('83) 2.10
255 A54 9p Le Breton .30 .20
256 A54 10p Le Maistre .35 .20
a. Booklet pane of 6 2.50
257 A54 11p Bisson .40 .20
b. Booklet pane of 6 ('83) 3.00
258 A54 12p Robin .40 .25
259 A54 13p Herault .45 .25
260 A54 14p Messervy .50 .25
261 A54 15p Fiott .55 .30
262 A54 20p Badier .75 .30
263 A54 25p L'Arbalestier .90 .30
264 A54 30p Journeaulx 1.10 .40
265 A54 40p Lempriere 1.25 .55
266 A54 50p D'Auvergne 1.50 .70
267 A54a £1 shown 2.25 1.50

Photo.

Perf. 12½x12

268 A54b £5 multi 11.00 9.25
Nos. 246-268 (23) 23.65 16.50

Issued: #246-256, 2/24; #248a, 12/1; #257-262, 7/28; #263-267, 2/23/82; #254a, 257a, 4/19/83; £5, 11/17/83.

1984-88 *Perf. 15x14*

247b A54 1p ('88) .30 .25
248b A54 2p Bklt. pane of 6 ('86) .55
248c A54 2p ('84) .20 .20
249b A54 3p Bklt. pane of 6 ('84) .65
249c A54 3p ('84) .25 .20
250a A54 4p Bklt. pane of 6 ('87) 1.10
250b A54 4p ('87) .25 .25
251a A54 5p ('86) .30 .30
252a A54 6p ('86) .25 .20
255a A54 9p Bklt. pane of 6 ('84) 1.60
255b A54 9p ('84) .50 .50
256b A54 10p Bklt. pane of 6 ('86) 2.00
256c A54 10p ('86) .40 .35
257a A54 11p Bklt. pane of 6 ('87) 2.50
257c A54 11p ('87) .45 .45
258a A54 12p Bklt. pane of 6 ('84) 2.50
258b A54 12p ('84) .70 .60
259a A54 13p ('84) .40 .25
260a A54 14p Bklt. pane of 6 ('86) 2.75
260b A54 14p ('84) .35 .25
261a A54 15p ('87) .50 .45
261b A54 15p Bklt. pane of 6 ('87) 3.00
262a A54 20p ('86) .75 .60
264a A54 30p ('86) 1.25 1.25
265a A54 40p ('87) 1.75 1.50
266a A54 50p ('87) 2.40 2.25

Issued: #251a, 252a, 262a, 264a, Mar. 4.

No. 247a dated "February 1981," "December 1981" or "April 1983"; No. 248a dated "December 1981" or "April 1983"; Nos. 253a, 256a dated "February 1981" or "December 1981;" No. 250a dated "April 1987" or "May 1988." No. 258a dated "April 1984" or "May 1988."

See Nos. 381-388.

Knight of Hamby Killing the Dragon A55

Europa (Legends): 10p, La Hougue Bie. 18p, Easter Voyage of St. Brelade. No. 272, Servant killing Knight of Hamby. No. 273, Shipwreck of St. Brelade. No. 274, Fish, ships' departure.

1981, Apr. 7 *Perf. 14½*

271 A55 10p multicolored .30 .30
272 A55 10p multicolored .30 .30
a. Pair, #271-272 .60 .60
273 A55 18p multicolored .50 .50
274 A55 18p multicolored .50 .50
a. Pair, #273-274 1.00 1.00
Nos. 271-274 (4) 1.60 1.60

Royal Square by Gaslight A56

1981, May 22 Photo. *Perf. 12*

Granite Paper

275 A56 7p The Harbor .20 .20
276 A56 10p The Quay .25 .25
277 A56 18p shown .40 .40
278 A56 22p Halkett Place .50 .50
279 A56 25p Central Market .60 .60
Nos. 275-279 (5) 1.95 1.95

Gas light sesquicentennial.

Prince Charles and Lady Diana A57

1981, July 28 Photo. *Perf. 12*

Granite Paper

280 A57 10p multicolored .25 .25
281 A57 25p multicolored 1.25 1.25

Royal Wedding.

Christmas Tree, Royal Square, St. Helier — A58

1981, Sept. 29 Litho. *Perf. 14½*

282 A58 7p shown .20 .20
283 A58 10p East window, St. Helier's Church, choir .30 .30
284 A58 18p Boxing Day, Jersey Drag Hunt .50 .50
Nos. 282-284 (3) 1.00 1.00

Christmas 1981.

Europa 1982 — A59

Designs: Maps showing formation of Channel Islands resulting from rise in sea level.

1982, Apr. 20 Litho. *Perf. 14½*

285 A59 11p 16,000 BC .30 .30
286 A59 11p 10,000 BC, vert. .30 .30
287 A59 19½p 7,000 BC, vert. .50 .50
288 A59 19½p 4,000 BC .50 .50
Nos. 285-288 (4) 1.60 1.60

Rollon Duke of Normandy, William the Conqueror, Clameur de Haro (Plea of Injunction) — A60

Links with France: No. 290, Kings John and Philippe Auguste, Siege of Rouen. No. 291, Jean Martxell (1694-1753), brandy merchant. No. 292, Victor Hugo. No. 293, Pierre Teilhard de Chardin (1881-1955), theologian. No. 294, Charles Rey (1897-1981), meteorologist.

1982, June 11 Litho. Perf. 14

289 A60 8p multicolored .20 .20
290 A60 8p multicolored .20 .20
a. Bklt. pane of 4+label, 2 each #289-290 .90 .90
b. Pair, #289-290 .40 .40
291 A60 11p multicolored .30 .30
292 A60 11p multicolored .30 .30
a. Bklt. pane of 4+label, 2 each #291-292 1.40 1.40
b. Pair, #291-292 .60 .60
293 A60 19½p multicolored .55 .55
294 A60 19½p multicolored .55 .55
a. Bklt. pane of 4+label, 2 each #293-294 2.50 2.50
b. Pair, #293-294 1.10 1.10
Nos. 289-294 (6) 2.10 2.10

Issue date: Nos. 290a-294a, Sept. 7. Two versions of Nos. 290a, 292a and 294a exist: the label is inscribed in English or French.

Scouting Year A61

Designs: 8p, Sir William Smith (Boys Brigade founder). 11p, Liberation parade, 1945, vert. 24p, Boys Brigade annual display, 1903. 26p, The Baden-Powells, 1924, vert. 29p, Scouts.

1982, Nov. 18 Photo. Perf. 12
Granite Paper

295 A61 8p multicolored .25 .25
296 A61 11p multicolored .35 .35
297 A61 24p multicolored .70 .70
298 A61 26p multicolored .75 .75
299 A61 29p multicolored .85 .85
Nos. 295-299 (5) 2.90 2.90

Port Egmont A62

250th Birth Anniv. of Capt. Philippe de Carteret (1733-97): 18th cent. engravings.

1983, Feb. 15 Litho. Perf. 14¼

300 A62 8p shown .20 .20
301 A62 11p Dolphin, Swallow .25 .25
302 A62 19½p Discovering Pitcairn Is. .50 .50
303 A62 24p English Cove, New Ireland .65 .65
304 A62 26p Sinking pirate ship .70 .70
305 A62 29p Endymion .80 .80
Nos. 300-305 (6) 3.10 3.10

No. 19 A63

Royal Mace — A64

1983, Apr. 19 Litho.

306 A63 11p shown .40 .40
307 A64 11p shown .40 .40
a. Pair, #306-307 .80 .80
308 A63 19½p No. 20a .60 .60
309 A64 19½p Bailiff's seal .60 .60
a. Pair, #308-309 1.25 1.25
Nos. 306-309 (4) 2.00 2.00

Europa.

World Communications Year — A65

1st Postmaster Charles William LeGeyt (1733-1827): 8p, Commanding Grenadier Co., 25th Foot, Battle of Minden, 1759. 11p, London-Weymouth mail coach. 24p, PO Mail Packet attacked by French privateer. 25p, Hue St. PO. 29p, St. Helier Harbor.

1983, June 21 Litho. Perf. 14

310 A65 8p multicolored .25 .25
311 A65 11p multicolored .30 .30
312 A65 24p multicolored .70 .70
313 A65 26p multicolored .75 .75
314 A65 29p multicolored .85 .85
Nos. 310-314 (5) 2.85 2.85

Intl. Assoc. of French-Speaking Parliamentarians 1983 General Assembly — A66

1983, June 21 Perf. 15

315 A66 19½p multicolored .75 .75

Cardinal Newman, by Walter William Ouless (1848-1933) A67

1983, Sept. 20 Photo. Perf. 11½

316 A67 8p shown .25 .25
317 A67 11p M. De Cazotte and his Daughter .35 .35
318 A67 20½p Thomas Hardy .65 .65

Size: 41x34mm

319 A67 31p David with the Head of Goliath .95 .95
Nos. 316-319 (4) 2.20 2.20

Jersey Wildlife Preservation Trust — A68

1984, Jan. 17 Litho. Perf. 14

320 A68 9p Golden Lion Tamarin .35 .35
321 A68 12p Snow Leopard .40 .40
322 A68 20½p Jamaican Boa .70 .70
323 A68 26p Round Island Gecko .90 .90
324 A68 28p Coscoroba Swan .95 .95
325 A68 31p St. Lucia Parrot 1.00 1.00
Nos. 320-325 (6) 4.30 4.30

Europa 1984 (25th Anniv.) — A69

1984, Mar. 12 Perf. 14½x15

326 A69 9p multicolored .30 .30
327 A69 12p multicolored .35 .35
328 A69 20½p multicolored .65 .65
Nos. 326-328 (3) 1.30 1.30

Souvenir Sheet

Jersey Links with the Commonwealth — A70

1984, Mar. 12 Perf. 15x14½

329 A70 75p multicolored 2.75 2.75

Commonwealth Postal Administrations Conf.

Royal Natl. Lifeboat Institution Centenary A71

Rescue Scenes (Lifeboats and Ships).

1984, June 1 Litho. Perf. 14½

330 A71 9p Sarah Brooshoft, Demie de Pas Light .35 .35
331 A71 9p Hearts of Oak, Maurice Georges .35 .35
332 A71 12p Elizabeth Rippon, Hanna .45 .45
333 A71 12p Elizabeth Rippon, Santa Maria .45 .45
334 A71 20½p Elizabeth Rippon, Bacchus .75 .75
335 A71 20½p Thomas James King, Cythara .75 .75
Nos. 330-335 (6) 3.10 3.10

40th Anniv. of Intl. Civil Aviation Org. A72

1984, July 24 Litho. Perf. 14
Granite Paper

336 A72 9p Bristol Type 170 .35 .35
337 A72 12p Airspeed AS-57 Ambassador 2 .45 .45
338 A72 26p De Havilland Heron 1B .85 .85
339 A72 31p DH-89A Dragon Rapide 1.10 1.10
Nos. 336-339 (4) 2.75 2.75

Robinson Crusoe, by John Alexander Gilfillan (1793-1864) — A73

Gilfillan Paintings.

1984, Sept. 21 Photo. Perf. 11½

340 A73 9p shown .30 .30
341 A73 12p Edinburgh Castle .40 .40
342 A73 20½p Maori Village .65 .65
343 A73 26p Australian Landscape .85 .85
344 A73 28p Waterhouse's Corner, Adelaide .95 .95
345 A73 31p Capt. Cook at Botany Bay 1.00 1.00
Nos. 340-345 (6) 4.15 4.15

Christmas 1984 — A74

1984, Nov. 15 Photo. Perf. 12x11½

346 A74 9p St. Helier orchid .45 .45
347 A74 12p Mt. Bingham orchid .55 .55

Ship Paintings by Philip John Ouless (1817-85) — A75

1985, Feb. 26 Photo. Perf. 14x14½

348 A75 9p Hebe, 1874 .30 .30
349 A75 12p Gaspe .35 .35
350 A75 22p London, 1856 .75 .75
351 A75 31p Rambler 1.10 1.10
352 A75 34p Elizabeth Castle 1.25 1.25
Nos. 348-352 (5) 3.75 3.75

Europa 1985 A76

Performing Arts: 10p, John Ireland, composer (1879-1962). 13p, Ivy St. Helier, actress (1886-1971). 22p, Claude Debussy, composer.

1985, Apr. 23 Litho. Perf. 14

353 A76 10p multicolored .35 .35
354 A76 13p multicolored .45 .45
355 A76 22p multicolored .80 .80
Nos. 353-355 (3) 1.60 1.60

Intl. Youth Year — A77

1985, May 30 Litho. Perf. 14½

356 A77 10p Girls' Brigade .30 .30
357 A77 13p Girl Guides .40 .40
358 A77 29p Jersey Youth Service .85 .85
359 A77 31p Sea Cadet Corps .95 .95
360 A77 34p Air Training Corps 1.00 1.00
Nos. 356-360 (5) 3.50 3.50

Railway History A78

1985, July 16 Photo. ***Perf. 12x11½***

361 A78 10p Duke of Normandy, Cheapside .45 .45
362 A78 13p Saddletank, First Tower .50 .50
363 A78 22p La Moye, Millbrook .90 .90
364 A78 29p St. Helier's, St. Aubin 1.10 1.10
365 A78 34p St. Aubyns, Corbiere 1.40 1.40
Nos. 361-365 (5) 4.35 4.35

Centenary of Jersey's first train from St. Helier to Corbiere.

Huguenot Heritage A79

300th anniv. of revocation of the Edict of Nantes (religious tolerance) by King Louis XIV of France: No. 366, James Hemery (1814-1849), Dean of Jersey, Rector of St. Helier. No. 367, Francis Henry Jeune, Baron St. Helier, law lord and junior counsel in the Tichbourne case. No. 368, Francois Voisin, merchant. No. 369, Pierre Amiraux, silversmith. No. 370, George Henry Ingouville, Victoria Cross recipient. No. 371, Robert Brohier, co-founder of Schweppes soft-drink company.

1985, Sept. 10 Litho. ***Perf. 14***

366 A79 10p Memorial window, St. Helier Town Church .35 .35
a. Booklet pane of 4 1.50
367 A79 10p Houses of Parliament, Westminster .35 .35
a. Booklet pane of 4 1.50
368 A79 13p Great Fair, Nijni-Novgorod, Russia .40 .40
a. Booklet pane of 4 1.75
369 A79 13p Silver coffee pot, pitcher .40 .40
a. Booklet pane of 4 1.75
370 A79 22p Naval Battle of Viborg .65 .65
a. Booklet pane of 4 3.00
371 A79 22p Glass bottles, carbonated water commercial patent .65 .65
a. Booklet pane of 4 3.00
Nos. 366-371 (6) 2.80 2.80

Thomas Benjamin Frederick Davis (1867-1942), Shipping Magnate, Philanthropist — A80

Portrait and endowments: 10p, Howard Davis Hall, Victoria College. 13p, Yacht, racing schooner Westward. 31p, Howard Davis Park, St. Helier. 34p, Howard Davis Agricultural Development Farm, Trinity.

1985, Oct. 25 ***Perf. 13½***

372 A80 10p multicolored .35 .35
373 A80 13p multicolored .40 .40
374 A80 31p multicolored 1.00 1.00
375 A80 34p multicolored 1.10 1.10
Nos. 372-375 (4) 2.85 2.85

50th anniv. of Howard Davis Hall, Victoria College, donated by Davis in memory of his son.

Arms Type of 1981-82 and

Elizabeth II, 60th Birthday — A80a

1985-91 Litho. ***Perf. 15x14***

381 A54 16p Malet .50 .30
a. Booklet pane of 6 ('88) 3.25
382 A54 17p Mabon .50 .40
383 A54 18p De St. Martin ('88) .75 .70
384 A54 19p Hamptonne ('88) .85 .75
386 A54 26p De Bagot ('88) .75 .60
388 A54 75p Remon ('87) 2.40 1.75

Perf. 11½x12

389 A80a £1 multicolored 3.25 3.00

Photo.
Granite Paper

390 A80a £2 multicolored 6.00 3.50
Nos. 381-390 (8) 15.00 11.00

Issued: 16, 17p, 10/25; £1, 4/21/86; 75p, 4/23/87; 18, 19, 26p, 4/26/88; £2, 3/19/91.
No. 381a inscribed "May 1988."

Jersey Lily — A81

Lillie Langtry, by Sir John Millais — A82

1986, Jan. 28 Litho. ***Perf. 15x14½***

391 A81 13p multicolored .50 .50
392 A82 34p multicolored 1.25 1.25
a. Souvenir sheet of 5 (4 13p, 34p) 3.75 3.75

Intl. Flower Gala, June 10-14.

Halley's Comet Sightings A83

Comet and coinciding historic events: 10p, Conquest of England, Bayeux Tapestry, A.D. 912 and 1066 sightings. 22p, Lady Carteret signing New Jersey over to William Penn, Edmond Halley observing comet, comets of 1301 & 1682. 31p, Giotto spacecraft and technology developed in 1910, 1986. Caesarea maiden voyage.

1986, Mar. 4 ***Perf. 13½x13***

393 A83 10p multicolored .35 .35
394 A83 22p multicolored .80 .80
395 A83 31p multicolored 1.10 1.10
Nos. 393-395 (3) 2.25 2.25

Europa 1986 — A84

1986, Apr. 21 ***Perf. 14½***

396 A84 10p Viola kitaibeliana .35 .35
397 A84 14p Matthiola sinuata .50 .50
398 A84 22p Romulea columnae .80 .80
Nos. 396-398 (3) 1.65 1.65

Environmental conservation.

Jersey Natl. Trust, 50th Anniv. A85

1986, June 17 Litho. ***Perf. 13½x13***

399 A85 10p Le Rat cottage .35 .35
400 A85 14p The Elms, headquarters .40 .40
401 A85 22p Morel Farm entrance .65 .65
402 A85 29p Quetivel Mill .90 .90
403 A85 31p La Vallette .95 .95
Nos. 399-403 (5) 3.25 3.25

Wedding of Prince Andrew and Sarah Ferguson — A86

1986, July 23 ***Perf. 13½***

404 A86 14p multicolored .45 .45
405 A86 40p multicolored 1.40 1.40

Paintings by Edmund Blampied (1886-1966), Artist — A87

1986, Aug. 28 Litho. ***Perf. 14***

406 A87 10p Gathering Vraic .35 .35
407 A87 14p Driving Home in the Rain .50 .50
408 A87 29p The Miller .95 .95
409 A87 31p The Joy Ride 1.00 1.00
410 A87 34p Tante Elizabeth 1.10 1.10
Nos. 406-410 (5) 3.90 3.90

Christmas, Intl. Peace Year — A88

1986, Nov. 4 ***Perf. 14½***

411 A88 10p Dove, map, flower .35 .35
412 A88 14p Lovebirds .45 .45
413 A88 34p Dove, noise-maker 1.10 1.10
Nos. 411-413 (3) 1.90 1.90

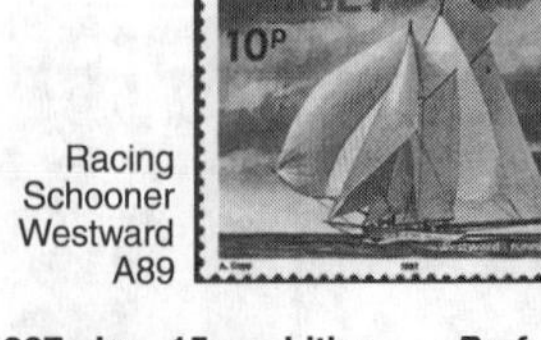

Racing Schooner Westward A89

1987, Jan. 15 Litho. ***Perf. 13½***

414 A89 10p Under full sail .35 .35
415 A89 14p T.B. Davis, owner .45 .45
416 A89 31p Overhauling Britannia 1.00 1.00
417 A89 34p Dry dock, St. Helier 1.25 1.25
Nos. 414-417 (4) 3.05 3.05

Jersey Airport, 50th Anniv. A90

1987, Mar. 3 Litho. ***Perf. 14***

418 A90 10p DH86 Belcroute Bay .35 .35
419 A90 14p Boeing 757, Douglas DC-9 .40 .40
420 A90 22p Britten Norman Trislander, Islander .70 .70
421 A90 29p Short SD330, Vickers Viscount .85 .85
422 A90 31p BAC1-11, HPR.7 Dart Herald .95 .95
Nos. 418-422 (5) 3.25 3.25

Europa 1987 A91

Modern architecture.

1987, Apr. 23 ***Perf. 15x14***

423 A91 11p St. Mary and St. Peter's Church .45 .45
424 A91 15p Villa Devereux .55 .55

Size: 61x31mm

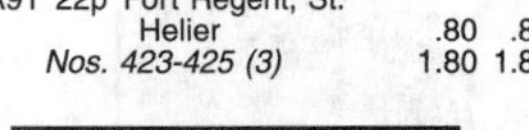

425 A91 22p Fort Regent, St. Helier .80 .80
Nos. 423-425 (3) 1.80 1.80

Adm. Philippe D'Auvergne (1754-1816) — A92

Ships: 11p, Racehorse trapped in the Arctic. 15p, Alarm burned at Rhode Island. 29p, Arethusa wrecked off Ushant, France. 31p, Rattlesnake stranded on Trinidad. 34p, Mont Orgueil Castle.

1987, July 9 ***Perf. 14***

426 A92 11p multicolored .35 .35
427 A92 15p multicolored .45 .45
428 A92 29p multicolored .90 .90
429 A92 31p multicolored .95 .95
430 A92 34p multicolored 1.00 1.00
Nos. 426-430 (5) 3.65 3.65

William the Conqueror (c. 1028-87), King of England (1066-87) — A93

Designs in the style of the Bayeux Tapestry: 11p, King Charles negotiating peace with the Vikings, 911, and cession of Jersey to Rollo's son William, 933. 15p, Duke Robert I and King Edward ashore Jersey after storm, 1030; Edward's succession to the throne of England, 1042. 22p, William the Conqueror's coronation, 1066, and succession of William II, 1087. 29p, Death of King William Rufus, and Henry defeating Duke Robert to unite England and Normandy, 1106. 31p, Death of Henry, battle for the throne and succession of King Stephen, 1135. 34p, Successions of Henry II, 1154, and John Lackland, 1189.

1987 ***Perf. 13½***

431 A93 11p multicolored .30 .30
a. Booklet pane of 4 + label 1.40
432 A93 15p multicolored .40 .40
a. Booklet pane of 4 + label 1.75
433 A93 22p multicolored .60 .60
a. Booklet pane of 4 + label 2.75
434 A93 29p multicolored .80 .80
a. Booklet pane of 4 + label 3.50
435 A93 31p multicolored .85 .85
a. Booklet pane of 4 + label 3.75

436 A93 34p multicolored .95 .95
a. Booklet pane of 4 + label 4.50
Nos. 431-436 (6) 3.90 3.90

Paintings by John Le Capelain (1812-1848) — A94

1987, Nov. 3 Photo. *Perf. 12x11½*
437 A94 11p Grosnez Castle .30 .30
438 A94 15p St. Aubin's Bay .45 .45
439 A94 22p Mt. Orgueil Castle .60 .60
440 A94 31p Town Fort and Harbor, St. Helier .90 .90
441 A94 34p The Hermitage 1.00 1.00
Nos. 437-441 (5) 3.25 3.25

Christmas.

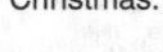

Hybrids, Eric Young Orchid Foundation, Trinity — A95

Nos. 443, 445 are vertical.

1988, Jan. 12 Litho. *Perf. 14*
442 A95 11p Cymbidium pontac .35 .35
443 A95 15p Odontioda Eric Young .45 .45
444 A95 29p Lycaste auburn Seaford and Ditchling .80 .80
445 A95 31p Odontoglossum St. Brelade .90 .90
446 A95 34p Cymbidium mavourneen Jester 1.00 1.00
Nos. 442-446 (5) 3.50 3.50

Jersey Dog Club, Cent. A96

1988, Mar. 2
447 A96 11p Labrador retriever .45 .45
448 A96 15p Wire-haired dachshund .60 .60
449 A96 22p Pekingese .80 .80
450 A96 31p Cavalier King Charles spaniel 1.00 1.00
451 A96 34p Dalmatian 1.10 1.10
Nos. 447-451 (5) 3.95 3.95

Europa 1988 A97

Nos. 453 and 455 vert.

Perf. 14x13½, 13½x14
1988, Apr. 26 Litho.
452 A97 16p Air transport .55 .55
453 A97 16p Air communication .55 .55
454 A97 22p Sea transport .75 .75
455 A97 22p Sea communication .75 .75
Nos. 452-455 (4) 2.60 2.60

Wildlife Preservation Trust, 25th Anniv. — A98

1988, July 6 Litho.
456 A98 12p Rodrigues fody, vert. .40 .40
457 A98 16p Volcano rabbit .55 .55
458 A98 29p White-faced marmoset, vert. .95 .95
459 A98 31p Ploughshare tortoise 1.00 1.00
460 A98 34p Mauritius kestrel, vert. 1.10 1.10
Nos. 456-460 (5) 4.00 4.00

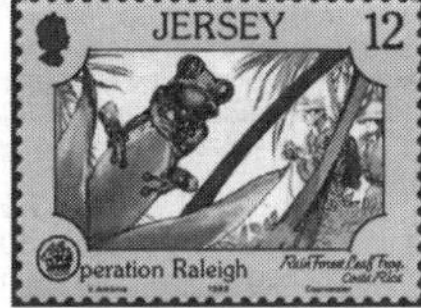

Operation Raleigh A99

Activities: 12p, Rain Forest Leaf Frog, Costa Rica. 16p, Archaeological Survey, Peru. 22p, Glacier Climbing, Chile. 29p, Medical Assistance, Solomon Isls. 31p, Underwater Exploration, Australia. 34p, *Zebu* returns to St. Helier, Jersey.

1988, Sept. 27 Photo. *Perf. 12*
461 A99 12p multicolored .40 .40
462 A99 16p multicolored .50 .50
463 A99 22p multicolored .70 .70
464 A99 29p multicolored .90 .90
465 A99 31p multicolored 1.00 1.00
466 A99 34p multicolored 1.10 1.10
Nos. 461-466 (6) 4.60 4.60

Operation Raleigh: voyage of the *Zebu,* on which youths were trained with the aim of remotivating them and helping them to earn new self-respect.
WHO 40th anniv. (29p).

Parish Churches A100

1988, Nov. 15 Litho. *Perf. 14*
467 A100 12p St. Clement .40 .40
468 A100 16p St. Ouen .50 .50
469 A100 31p St. Brelade 1.00 1.00
470 A100 34p St. Lawrence 1.10 1.10
Nos. 467-470 (4) 3.00 3.00

Christmas. See Nos. 549-552, 610-613.

Classic Cars A101

Designs: 12p, 1912 Talbot Tourer, seaweed harvest at Le Hocq. 16p, 1920 De Dion Bouton, Grosnez Castle ruins. 23p, 1926 Austin Chummy, brick kiln at Mont a l'Abbe. 30p, 1926 Ford Model T, harvest of the Jersey royal potato crop. 32p, 1930 Bentley 8-Litre, Guard House and Gate at Government House. 35p, 1931 Cadillac V16 Fleetwood Sports Phaeton, St. Ouen's Manor.

1989, Jan. 31
471 A101 12p multicolored .40 .40
472 A101 16p multicolored .55 .55
473 A101 23p multicolored .75 .75
474 A101 30p multicolored .95 .95
475 A101 32p multicolored 1.00 1.00
476 A101 35p multicolored 1.10 1.10
Nos. 471-476 (6) 4.75 4.75

See Nos. 604-609, 903-908.

Scenic Views — A102

Coronation of Queen Elizabeth II, 40th Anniv. — A102a

Royal Arms A102b

1989-95 Litho. *Perf. 13½*
477 A102 1p Belcroute Bay .20 .20
478 A102 2p High St., St. Aubin .20 .20
480 A102 4p Royal Jersey Golf Course .20 .20
a. Booklet pane of 6 .80 .80
481 A102 5p Portelet Bay .20 .20
a. Booklet pane of 6 1.40 1.40
485 A102 10p Les Charrieres D'Anneport .30 .30
486 A102 13p St. Helier Marina .40 .40
487 A102 14p St. Ouen's Bay .40 .40
a. Booklet pane of 6 2.75 2.75
b. Booklet pane of 8 3.75 3.75
488 A102 15p Rozel Harbor .45 .45
a. Booklet pane of 6 3.00 3.00
489 A102 16p St. Aubin's Harbor .50 .50
a. Booklet pane of 8 4.50 4.50
490 A102 17p Jersey Airport .50 .50
491 A102 18p Corbiere Lighthouse .55 .55
a. Booklet pane of 6 3.75 3.75
492 A102 19p Val de la Mare .55 .55
493 A102 20p Elizabeth Castle .45 .45
a. Booklet pane of 6 3.00 3.00
494 A102 21p Greve de Lecq .50 .50
495 A102 22p Samares Manor .45 .45
a. Booklet pane of 8 4.00 4.00
496 A102 23p Bonne Nuit Harbor .75 .75
497 A102 24p Grosnez Castle .60 .60
498 A102 25p Augres Manor .70 .70
499 A102 26p Central Market .75 .75
500 A102 27p St. Brelade's Bay .80 .80
501 A102 30p St. Ouen's Manor .85 .85
502 A102 40p La Hougue Bie 1.10 1.10
503 A102 50p Mont Orgueil Castle 1.25 1.25
504 A102 75p Royal Square 2.00 2.00

Perf. 14½
505 A102a £1 multicolored 2.75 2.75

Perf. 15x14
506 A102b £4 multicolored 7.50 7.50
Nos. 477-506 (26) 24.90 24.90

Panes issued for Stamp World London '90. Inscribed May 1990.
Issued: 1p-20p, 3/21/89; 21p-27p, 1/16/90; 30p-75p, 3/13/90; #481a, 488a, 493a, 2/12/91; £1, 6/2/93; £4, 1/2/95. Nos. 487b, 489a, 495a were released on May 22, but were not readily available until September 1992. Other booklets, 1990.

World Wildlife Fund — A103

1989, Apr. 25 Litho. *Perf. 13x13¼*
507 A103 13p Large checkered skipper 1.75 1.75

Perf. 13¼x13
508 A103 13p Agile frog, horiz. 1.75 1.75
509 A103 17p Green lizard, horiz. 1.75 1.75

Perf. 13½x13¾
510 A103 17p Barn owl 1.75 1.75
Nos. 507-510 (4) 7.00 7.00

Europa 1989 — A104

Children's games.

1989, Apr. 25 *Perf. 14*
511 A104 17p Playpen .60 .60
512 A104 17p Playground .60 .60
513 A104 23p Magician, games .70 .70
514 A104 23p Cricket, rugby, soccer, tennis .70 .70
Nos. 511-514 (4) 2.60 2.60

Visit of Queen Elizabeth II — A105

1989, May 24 Litho. *Perf. 14½*
515 A105 £1 Ferry Terminal, St. Helier 3.25 3.25

French Revolution, Bicent. A106

Designs: 13p, D'Auvergne meets Louis XVI, 1786. 17p, Storming the Bastille, 1789. 23p, Marie de Bouillon at the Chateau de Navarre, 1790. 30p, Mission from Mont Orgueil, 1795. 32p, Support for the Chouans, 1796. 35p, The last Chouannerie, 1799.

1989, July 7 *Perf. 13½*
516 A106 13p multicolored .40 .40
517 A106 17p multicolored .50 .50
518 A106 23p multicolored .70 .70
519 A106 30p multicolored .90 .90
520 A106 32p multicolored 1.00 1.00
521 A106 35p multicolored 1.10 1.10
Nos. 516-521 (6) 4.60 4.60

516a Booklet pane of 4 1.75
517a Booklet pane of 4 2.25
518a Booklet pane of 4 3.25
519a Booklet pane of 4 4.00
520a Booklet pane of 4 4.50
521a Booklet pane of 4 5.00

Great Western Railway Steamer Service Between Weymouth and the Channel Isls., Cent. — A107

1989, Sept. 5 Litho. *Perf. 13½x14*
522 A107 13p *St. Helier,* 1925 .40 .40
523 A107 17p *Caesarea II,* 1910 .50 .50
524 A107 27p *Reindeer,* 1897 .85 .85
525 A107 32p *Ibex,* 1891 1.00 1.00
526 A107 35p *Lynx,* 1889 1.10 1.10
Nos. 522-526 (5) 3.85 3.85

Paintings by Sarah Louisa Kilpack (1839-1909) — A108

1989, Oct. 24 Litho. *Perf. 13x12½*

527 A108 13p Gorey Harbour .40 .40
528 A108 17p La Corbiere .50 .50
529 A108 23p Greve de Lecq .70 .70
530 A108 32p Bouley Bay 1.00 1.00
531 A108 35p Mont Orgueil 1.00 1.00
Nos. 527-531 (5) 3.60 3.60

Europa 1990 A109

Post offices.

Perf. 13½x14, 14x13½

1990, Mar. 13 Litho.

532 A109 18p Broad Street, 1969 .55 .55
533 A109 18p Mont Millais, 1990 .55 .55
534 A109 24p Hue Street, 1815 .75 .75
535 A109 24p Halkett Place, 1890 .75 .75
Nos. 532-535 (4) 2.60 2.60

Nos. 532-533 vert.

Festival of Tourism — A110

1990, May 3 Litho. *Perf. 14x13½*

536 A110 18p Battle of Flowers .60 .60
537 A110 24p Recreation .70 .70
538 A110 29p History .90 .90
539 A110 32p Salon Culinaire 1.00 1.00
a. Souvenir sheet of 4, #536-539 3.50 3.50
Nos. 536-539 (4) 3.20 3.20

News Media A111

1990, June 26 Litho. *Perf. 13½*

540 A111 14p Print (newspapers), 1784-1889 .50 .50
541 A111 18p The Evening Post, 1890 .60 .60
542 A111 34p BBC Radio Jersey, 1982 1.10 1.10
543 A111 37p Channel Television, 1962 1.25 1.25
Nos. 540-543 (4) 3.45 3.45

UNESCO World Literacy Year.

Battle of Britain, 50th Anniv. A112

1990, Sept. 4 *Perf. 14*

544 A112 14p Hawk .55 .55
545 A112 18p Spitfire .65 .65
546 A112 24p Hurricane .90 .90
547 A112 34p Wellington 1.25 1.25
548 A112 37p Lancaster 1.40 1.40
Nos. 544-548 (5) 4.75 4.75

Parish Churches Type of 1988

1990, Nov. 13 Litho. *Perf. 13½x14*

549 A100 14p St. Helier .50 .50
550 A100 18p Grouville .60 .60
551 A100 34p St. Saviour 1.10 1.10
552 A100 37p St. John 1.25 1.25
Nos. 549-552 (4) 3.45 3.45

Prince's Tower, La Hougue Bie, 1801 A113

Philippe d'Auvergne: 20p, Arrested in Paris, 1802. 26p, Plotting against Napoleon, 1803. 31p, Execution of Cadoudal, 1804. 37p, H.M. Cutter Surly, 1809. 44p, Prince de Bouillon, 1816.

1991, Jan. 22 Litho. *Perf. 13½*

553 A113 15p multicolored .50 .50
554 A113 20p multicolored .70 .70
555 A113 26p multicolored .85 .85
556 A113 31p multicolored 1.00 1.00
557 A113 37p multicolored 1.25 1.25
558 A113 44p multicolored 1.40 1.40
Nos. 553-558 (6) 5.70 5.70

A114

Europa (Satellites and their functions): No. 559, ERS-1, oceanography. No. 560, Landsat, Earth resources. No. 561, Meteosat, meteorology. No. 562, Olympus, communications.

1991, Mar. 19 Litho. *Perf. 14½x13*

559 A114 20p multicolored .65 .65
560 A114 20p multicolored .65 .65
561 A114 26p multicolored .85 .85
562 A114 26p multicolored .85 .85
Nos. 559-562 (4) 3.00 3.00

A115

15p, German Occupation Stamps for Jersey, 50th anniv. 20p, Eastern Railway extension to Gorey Pier, 100th anniv. 26p, Jersey Herd Book, 125th anniv. 31p, Victoria Harbor, 150th anniv. 53p, Hospital bequest of Marie Bartlett, 250th anniv.

1991, May 16 Litho. *Perf. 13½*

563 A115 15p multicolored .50 .50
564 A115 20p multicolored .65 .65
565 A115 26p multicolored .75 .75
566 A115 31p multicolored .90 .90
567 A115 53p multicolored 1.60 1.60
Nos. 563-567 (5) 4.40 4.40

Butterflies & Moths A116

1991, July 9 Litho. *Perf. 13x12½*

568 A116 15p Glanville fritillary .50 .50
569 A116 20p Jersey tiger .65 .65
570 A116 37p Small elephant hawk-moth 1.10 1.10
571 A116 57p Peacock 1.75 1.75
Nos. 568-571 (4) 4.00 4.00

See Nos. 727-731.

Overseas Aid — A117

Designs: 15p, Water drilling rig, Ethiopia. 20p, Construction work, Rwanda. 26p, Technical school, Kenya. 31p, Leprosy and eye care, Tanzania. 37p, Agriculture and cultivation aid, Zambia. 44p, Health care and immunization, Lesotho.

1991, Sept. 3 Litho. *Perf. 13½*

572 A117 15p multicolored .50 .50
573 A117 20p multicolored .65 .65
574 A117 26p multicolored .80 .80
575 A117 31p multicolored .90 .90
576 A117 37p multicolored 1.00 1.00
577 A117 44p multicolored 1.50 1.50
Nos. 572-577 (6) 5.35 5.35

Christmas — A118

Illustrations by Edmund Blampied from Peter Pan: 15p, This is the place for me. 20p, The Island Come True. 37p, The Never Bird. 53p, The Great White Father.

1991, Nov. 5 Litho. *Perf. 14*

578 A118 15p multicolored .50 .50
579 A118 20p multicolored .70 .70
580 A118 37p multicolored 1.25 1.25
581 A118 53p multicolored 1.75 1.75
Nos. 578-581 (4) 4.20 4.20

Winter Birds — A119

1992, Jan. 7 Litho. *Perf. 13½x14*

582 A119 16p Pied wagtail .55 .55
583 A119 22p Firecrest .75 .75
584 A119 28p Snipe .95 .95
585 A119 39p Lapwing 1.40 1.40
586 A119 57p Fieldfare 1.90 1.90
Nos. 582-586 (5) 5.55 5.55

Shanghai Harbor, 1860 A120

William Mesny, 150th birth anniv: No. 588, Running the Taiping blockade, 1862. No. 589, General Mesny, River Gate, 1874. No. 590, Mesny accompanying Gill to Burma, 1877. No. 591, Mesny advises Governor Chang, 1882. No. 592, Mesny, Mandarin First Class, 1886.

1992, Feb. 25 Litho. *Perf. 13½*

587 A120 16p multicolored .50 .50
588 A120 16p multicolored .50 .50
589 A120 22p multicolored .75 .75
590 A120 22p multicolored .75 .75
591 A120 33p multicolored 1.00 1.00
592 A120 33p multicolored 1.00 1.00
Nos. 587-592 (6) 4.50 4.50

587a Booklet pane of 4 2.25 2.25
588a Booklet pane of 4 2.25 2.25
589a Booklet pane of 4 3.25 3.25
590a Booklet pane of 4 3.25 3.25
591a Booklet pane of 4 4.50 4.50
592a Booklet pane of 4 4.50 4.50

Discovery of America, 500th Anniv. A121

Columbus, ship and: 22p, John Bertram (1796-1882). 28p, Sir George Carteret (1610-1680). 39p, Sir Walter Raleigh (1554-1618).

1992, Apr. 14 Litho. *Perf. 14½*

593 A121 22p multicolored .70 .70
594 A121 28p multicolored .90 .90
595 A121 39p multicolored 1.25 1.25
Nos. 593-595 (3) 2.85 2.85

Europa.

Jersey-Built Sailing Ships — A122

1992, Apr. 14 Litho. *Perf. 14*

596 A122 16p Tickler .50 .50
597 A122 22p Hebe .70 .70
598 A122 50p Gemini 1.65 1.65
599 A122 57p Percy Douglas 1.75 1.75
a. Souvenir sheet of 4, #596-599 4.75 4.75
Nos. 596-599 (4) 4.60 4.60

Batik — A123

16p, Snow leopards. 22p, Three elements. 39p, Three men in a tub. 57p, Cockatoos.

1992, June 23 Litho. *Perf. 14½*

600 A123 16p multicolored .60 .60
601 A123 22p multicolored .80 .80
602 A123 39p multicolored 1.25 1.25
603 A123 57p multicolored 1.75 1.75
Nos. 600-603 (4) 4.40 4.40

Classic Car Type of 1989

Designs: 16p, 1925 Morris Cowley "Bullnose." 22p, 1932 Rolls Royce 20/25. 28p, 1924 Chenard & Walcker T5. 33p, 1932 Packard 900 Series Light Eight. 39p, 1927 Lanchester 21. 50p, 1913 Buick 30 Roadster.

1992, Sept. 8 Litho. *Perf. 13x12½*

604 A101 16p multicolored .45 .45
605 A101 22p multicolored .65 .65
606 A101 28p multicolored .80 .80
607 A101 33p multicolored 1.00 1.00
608 A101 39p multicolored 1.10 1.10
609 A101 50p multicolored 1.50 1.50
Nos. 604-609 (6) 5.50 5.50

Parish Church Type of 1988

1992, Nov. 3 Litho. *Perf. 13½x14*

610 A100 16p Trinity .45 .45
611 A100 22p St. Mary .65 .65
612 A100 39p St. Martin 1.10 1.10
613 A100 57p St. Peter 1.65 1.65
Nos. 610-613 (4) 3.85 3.85

Non-Value Indicator Stamps — A124

Scenic views: No. 614, Building with arches. No. 615, Cemetery, church. No. 616, Flowers, cattle. No. 617, Cattle in pasture.

Beach scenes: No. 618, People lying on beach with umbrella. No. 619, Man with windsurfer. No. 620, Crab facing right. No. 621, Crab, facing left.

Parade floats: No. 622, Smiling face, rainbow. No. 623, Dragon head, Oriental theme. No. 624, Umbrellas, Asian theme. No. 625, Elephant's tusks, African theme.

1993, Jan. 26 Litho. *Perf. 13½*

614 A124 (17p) Bailiwick .50 .50
615 A124 (17p) Bailiwick .50 .50
616 A124 (17p) Bailiwick .50 .50
617 A124 (17p) Bailiwick .50 .50
a. Block of 4, #614-617 2.00 2.00
b. Booklet pane of 8, 2 each #614-617 4.00
618 A124 (23p) UK .65 .65
619 A124 (23p) UK .65 .65
620 A124 (23p) UK .65 .65
621 A124 (23p) UK .65 .65
a. Block of 4, #618-621 2.75 2.75
b. Booklet pane of 8, 2 each #618-621 5.50
622 A124 (28p) European .75 .75
623 A124 (28p) European .75 .75
624 A124 (28p) European .75 .75
625 A124 (28p) European .75 .75
a. Block of 4, #622-625 3.00 3.00
b. Booklet pane of 8, 2 each #622-625 6.00 6.00
Nos. 614-625 (12) 7.60 7.60

The minimum postage rate is represented for each area where mail is delivered.

Orchids — A125

17p, Phragmipedium Eric Young "Jersey." 23p, Odontoglossum Augres "Trinity." 28p, Miltonia Saint Helier "Colomberie." 39p, Phragmipedium pearcei. 57p, Calanthe Grouville "Gorey."

1993, Jan. 26 Litho. *Perf. 14½x13*

626 A125 17p multicolored .55 .55
627 A125 23p multicolored .75 .75
628 A125 28p multicolored .90 .90
629 A125 39p multicolored 1.25 1.25
630 A125 57p multicolored 1.75 1.75
Nos. 626-630 (5) 5.20 5.20

Europa — A126

Contemporary Art: 23p, Jersey Opera House, by Ian Rolls. 28p, The Ham and Tomato Bap, by Jonathan Hubbard. 39p, Vase of Flowers, by Neil MacKenzie.

1993, Apr. 1 Litho. *Perf. 13½x14*

631 A126 23p multicolored .70 .70
632 A126 28p multicolored .85 .85
633 A126 39p multicolored 1.10 1.10
Nos. 631-633 (3) 2.65 2.65

Royal Air Force, 75th Anniv. A127

Designs: 17p, Douglas Dakota. 23p, Wight Seaplane. 28p, Avro Shakleton AEW2. 33p, Gloster Meteor, DeHavilland Vampire. 39p, BAe Harrier GR1A. 57p, Panavia Tornado F3.

1993, Apr. 1 *Perf. 14*

634 A127 17p multicolored .50 .50
635 A127 23p multicolored .70 .70
636 A127 28p multicolored .85 .85
637 A127 33p multicolored 1.00 1.00
638 A127 39p multicolored 1.10 1.10
639 A127 57p multicolored 1.75 1.75
a. Souvenir sheet of 2, #635, 639 5.25 5.25
Nos. 634-639 (6) 5.90 5.90

Stamps from No. 639a do not have white border.

German Occupation Stamps by Edmund Blampied, 50th Anniv. A128

1993, June 2 Litho. *Perf. 13½*

640 A128 17p No. N3 .50 .50
641 A128 23p No. N4 .70 .70
642 A128 28p No. N5 .85 .85
643 A128 33p No. N6 1.00 1.00
644 A128 39p No. N7 1.10 1.10
645 A128 50p No. N8 1.50 1.50
Nos. 640-645 (6) 5.65 5.65

Birds — A129

1993, Sept. 7 Litho. *Perf. 13½x14*

646 A129 17p Short-toed treecreeper .50 .50
647 A129 23p Dartford warbler .70 .70
648 A129 28p Wheatear .85 .85
649 A129 39p Cirl bunting 1.10 1.10
650 A129 57p Jay 1.75 1.75
Nos. 646-650 (5) 4.90 4.90

Christmas — A130

Stained glass windows by Henry Bosdet, from St. Aubin on the Hill.

1993, Nov. 2 Litho. *Perf. 14½x13*

651 A130 17p multicolored .50 .50
652 A130 23p multicolored .65 .65
653 A130 39p multicolored 1.10 1.10
654 A130 57p multicolored 1.65 1.65
Nos. 651-654 (4) 3.90 3.90

Mushrooms A131

1994, Jan. 11 Litho. *Perf. 14½*

655 A131 18p Shaggy ink cap .50 .50
656 A131 23p Fly agaric .65 .65
657 A131 30p Chanterelle .95 .95
658 A131 41p Parasol mushroom 1.25 1.25
659 A131 60p Latticed stinkhorn 1.75 1.75
Nos. 655-659 (5) 5.10 5.10

Souvenir Sheet

New Year 1994 (Year of the Dog) — A132

1994, Feb. 18 Litho. *Perf. 15x14½*

660 A132 £1 multicolored 3.25 3.25

Hong Kong '94.

Cats — A133

1994, Apr. 5 Litho. *Perf. 13½*

661 A133 18p Maine coon, vert. .55 .55
662 A133 23p British shorthair .70 .70
663 A133 35p Persian, vert. 1.00 1.00
664 A133 41p Siamese 1.10 1.10
665 A133 60p Non-pedigree, vert. 1.60 1.60
Nos. 661-665 (5) 4.95 4.95

Jersey Cat Club, 21st anniv., and 4th Championship Show.

Europa A134

Designs: No. 666, Mammoths on cliff, c. 250,000 B.C. No. 667, Paleolithic hunters dragging mammoth by tusks. No. 668, Neolithic dolmen, "La Hougue Bie," c. 4,000 B.C. No. 669, Exterior of "La Hougue Bie," during construction.

1994, Apr. 5 Litho. *Perf. 13½x14*

666 A134 23p multicolored .65 .65
667 A134 23p multicolored .65 .65
a. Pair, #666-667 1.30 1.30
668 A134 30p multicolored .85 .85
669 A134 30p multicolored .85 .85
a. Pair, #668-669 1.70 1.70
Nos. 666-669 (4) 3.00 3.00

D-Day, 50th Anniv. A135

#670, Airborne Forces enroute to drop zones. #671, Allied Fleet of Normandy Coast. #672, Coming ashore, Gold Beach. #673, Coming ashore, Sword Beach. #674, Spitfires on beachead patrol. #675, Normandy invasion map.

1994, June 6 Litho. *Perf. 13½*

670 A135 18p multicolored .55 .55
671 A135 18p multicolored .55 .55
a. Bklt. pane, 3 each #670-671 3.50
672 A135 23p multicolored .70 .70
673 A135 23p multicolored .70 .70
a. Bklt. pane, 3 each #672-673 4.75
674 A135 30p multicolored .90 .90
675 A135 30p multicolored .90 .90
a. Bklt. pane, 3 each #674-675 6.00
b. Bklt. pane of 6, #670-675 5.00
Nos. 670-675 (6) 4.30 4.30

Intl. Olympic Committee, Cent. — A136

1994, June 6 *Perf. 14*

676 A136 18p Sailing .55 .55
677 A136 23p Rifle shooting .70 .70
678 A136 30p Hurdles .90 .90
679 A136 41p Swimming 1.25 1.25
680 A136 60p Field hockey 1.60 1.60
Nos. 676-680 (5) 5.00 5.00

Marine Life A137

Designs: 18p, Strawberry anemone. 23p, Hermit crab, parasitic anemone. 41p, Velvet swimming crab. 60p, Common jellyfish.

1994, Aug. 2 Litho. *Perf. 13½x13*

681 A137 18p multicolored .60 .60
682 A137 23p multicolored .75 .75
683 A137 41p multicolored 1.25 1.25
684 A137 60p multicolored 1.75 1.75
Nos. 681-684 (4) 4.35 4.35

Postal Independence, 25th Anniv. — A138

Designs: 18p, Condor 10 Wavepiercer. 23p, Map of Jersey, postbox. 35p, BEA "Vanguard" aircraft. 41p, Aurigny "Short 360" aircraft. 60p, Sealink vessel "Caesarea."

1994, Oct. 1 Litho. *Perf. 14*

685 A138 18p multicolored .60 .60
686 A138 23p multicolored .75 .75
687 A138 35p multicolored .95 .95
688 A138 41p multicolored 1.10 1.10
689 A138 60p multicolored 1.60 1.60
a. Souvenir sheet, #685-689 + label 5.25 5.25
Nos. 685-689 (5) 5.00 5.00

Christmas A139

Christmas carols: 18p, "Away in the manger..." 23p, "Hark! the herald angels sing..." 41p, "While shepherds watched..." 60p, "We three kings of Orient are..."

1994, Nov. 8

690 A139 18p multicolored .60 .60
691 A139 23p multicolored .70 .70
692 A139 41p multicolored 1.10 1.10
693 A139 60p multicolored 1.60 1.60
Nos. 690-693 (4) 4.00 4.00

Greetings Stamps — A140

Designs: No. 694, Dog, "Good Luck." No. 695, Rose, "With Love." No. 696, Chick, "Congratulations." No. 697, Bouquet of flowers, "Thank You."

No. 698, Dove, "With love." No. 699, Cat, "Good Luck." No. 700, Carnations, "Thank You." No. 701, Parrot, "Congratulations."
60p, Boar, "Happy New Year."

1995, Jan. 24 Litho. *Perf. 13½x13*

694 A140 18p multicolored .55 .55
695 A140 18p multicolored .55 .55
696 A140 18p multicolored .55 .55
697 A140 18p multicolored .55 .55
  a. Strip of 4, #694-697 2.25 2.25
698 A140 23p multicolored .65 .65
699 A140 23p multicolored .65 .65
700 A140 23p multicolored .65 .65
701 A140 23p multicolored .65 .65
  a. Strip of 4, #698-701 2.75 2.75

Size: 25x64mm

702 A140 60p multicolored 1.75 1.75
  a. Booklet pane, #697a, #701a, #702 7.50
  Complete booklet, #702a 7.50
  Nos. 694-702 (9) 6.55 6.55

New Year 1995 (Year of the Boar) (#702).

Camellias A141

1995, Mar. 21 Litho. *Perf. 14*

703 A141 18p Captain Rawes .60 .60
704 A141 23p Brigadoon .75 .75
705 A141 30p Elsie Jury .95 .95
706 A141 35p Augusto L'Gouveia Pinto 1.10 1.10
707 A141 41p Bella Romana 1.40 1.40
  Nos. 703-707 (5) 4.80 4.80

International Camellia Society conference, Jersey, Mar. 30-Apr. 4, 1995.

Liberation, by Philip Jackson A142

1995, May 9 Litho. *Perf. 13½*

708 A142 23p gray & black .65 .65
709 A142 30p pink & black .85 .85

Europa.

Liberation, 50th Anniv. A143

#710, Bailiff, Crown Officers taken to HMS Beagle. #711, Red Cross ship SS Vega. #712, Germans surrender on board HMS Beagle. #713, First troops of task force 135, Ordinance Yard, St. Helier. #714, Royal visitors, June 1945. #715, Supplies come ashore from LSTs, Operation Nestegg.
£1, Princess Elizabeth, Queen Elizabeth, Winston Churchill, King George VI, Princess Margaret at Buckingham Palace, VE Day.

1995, May 9 Litho. *Perf. 14½x14*

710 A143 18p multicolored .60 .60
711 A143 18p multicolored .60 .60
  a. Bklt. pane, 3 each #710-711 4.00
712 A143 23p multicolored .75 .75
713 A143 23p multicolored .75 .75
  a. Bklt. pane, 3 each #712-713 5.00
714 A143 60p multicolored 1.90 1.90
715 A143 60p multicolored 1.90 1.90
  a. Bklt. pane, 3 each #714-715 12.50
  Nos. 711-715 (5) 5.90 5.90

Souvenir Sheet

716 A143 £1 multicolored 3.25 3.25
  a. Booklet pane, #716 3.50
  Complete booklet, #711a, #713a, #715a, #716a 25.00

No. 716 contains one 81x29mm stamp.

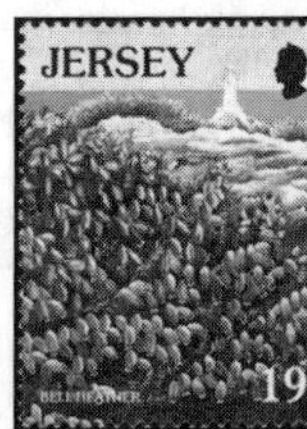

Wild Flowers — A144

1995, July 4 Litho. *Perf. 13½*

717 A144 19p Bell heather .60 .60
718 A144 19p Sea campion .60 .60
719 A144 19p Spotted rock-rose .60 .60
720 A144 19p Thrift .60 .60
721 A144 19p Sheep's-bit .60 .60
  a. Strip of 5, #717-721 3.00 3.00
722 A144 23p Field bind-weed .75 .75
723 A144 23p Common bird's-foot .75 .75
724 A144 23p Sea holly .75 .75
725 A144 23p Common centaury .75 .75
726 A144 23p Dwarf pansy .75 .75
  a. Strip of 5, #722-726 3.75 3.75
  Nos. 717-726 (10) 6.75 6.75

Butterfly & Moth Type of 1991

1995, Sept. 1 Litho. *Perf. 14*

727 A116 19p Peacock pansy .60 .60
728 A116 23p Green-barred swallowtail .75 .75
729 A116 30p Orange emigrant .95 .95
730 A116 41p Scarlet mormon 1.25 1.25
731 A116 60p Common birdwing 1.90 1.90
  a. Souvenir sheet of 2, #730-731 3.25 3.25
  Nos. 727-731 (5) 5.45 5.45

Singapore '95 (#731a).
Stamps from No. 731a do not have border around the designs or inscriptions at bottom.

Christmas A145

Childrens' stories: 19p, Puss in Boots. 23p, Cinderella. 41p, Sleeping Beauty. 60p, Aladdin.

1995, Oct. 24 Litho. *Perf. 13½*

732 A145 19p multicolored .60 .60
733 A145 23p multicolored .75 .75
734 A145 41p multicolored 1.25 1.25
735 A145 60p multicolored 1.90 1.90
  Nos. 732-735 (4) 4.50 4.50

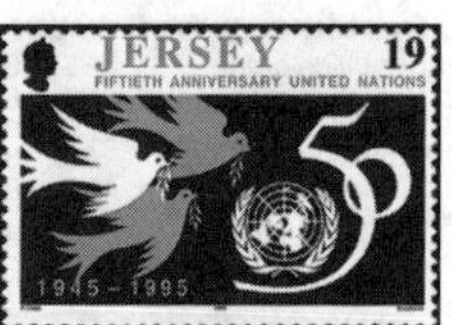

UN, 50th Anniv. A146

1995, Oct. 24 Litho. *Perf. 13x14*

736 A146 19p Doves, emblem .60 .60
737 A146 23p Olive branch, emblem .75 .75
738 A146 41p As 23p 1.25 1.25
739 A146 60p As 19p 1.90 1.90
  Nos. 736-739 (4) 4.50 4.50

UNICEF, 50th Anniv. A147

Children, map areas of UNICEF activities: 19p, Africa. 23p, Globe. 30p, Europe, Balkans. 35p, South America, Caribbean. 41p, South Asia. 60p, Australia, South Pacific.

1996, Feb. 19 Litho. *Perf. 14½*

740 A147 19p multicolored .55 .55
741 A147 23p multicolored .70 .70
742 A147 30p multicolored .90 .90
743 A147 35p multicolored 1.00 1.00
744 A147 41p multicolored 1.10 1.10
745 A147 60p multicolored 1.75 1.75
  Nos. 740-745 (6) 6.00 6.00

Souvenir Sheet

New Year 1996 (Year of the Rat) — A148

Illustration reduced.

1996, Feb. 19 *Perf. 14*

746 A148 £1 multicolored 3.25 3.25

Queen Elizabeth II, 70th Birthday — A149

1996, Apr. 21 Litho. *Perf. 14x15*

747 A149 £5 multicolored 12.00 12.00

Women of Achievement A150

Europa: 23p, Elizabeth Garrett, first British woman physician. 30p, Emmeline Pankhurst (1858-1928), suffragist.

1996, Apr. 25 *Perf. 14*

748 A150 23p multicolored .65 .65
749 A150 30p multicolored .85 .85

1996 European Soccer Championships — A151

Various soccer plays.

1996, Apr. 25

750 A151 19p multicolored .55 .55
751 A151 23p multicolored .70 .70
752 A151 35p multicolored 1.00 1.00
753 A151 41p multicolored 1.10 1.10
754 A151 60p multicolored 1.75 1.75
  Nos. 750-754 (5) 5.10 5.10

Modern Olympic Games, Cent. A152

1996, June 8 Litho. *Perf. 14*

755 A152 19p Rowing .60 .60
756 A152 23p Judo .65 .65
757 A152 35p Fencing .95 .95
758 A152 41p Boxing 1.10 1.10
759 A152 60p Basketball 1.75 1.75
  Nos. 755-759 (5) 5.05 5.05

Souvenir Sheet

760 A152 £1 Olympic torch, flame 3.25 3.25

Intl. Amateur Boxing Assoc., 50th anniv. (#758). CAPEX '96 (#760). No. 760 contains one 50x38mm stamp.

Tourism A153

1996, June 8 Litho. *Perf. 14*

761 A153 19p North Coast .60 .60
762 A153 23p Portelet Bay .70 .70
  a. Bklt. pane, 3 each #761-762 4.50
763 A153 30p Greve de Lecq Bay .90 .90
764 A153 35p Beauport Beach .95 .95
  a. Bklt. pane, 3 each #763-764 6.25
765 A153 41p Plemont Bay 1.10 1.10
766 A153 60p St. Brelade's Bay 1.75 1.75
  a. Bklt. pane, 1 each #761-766 6.50
  b. Bklt. pane, 3 each #765-766 9.50
  Complete booklet, #762a, 764a, 766a, 766b 27.50
  Nos. 761-766 (6) 6.00 6.00

Horses A154

1996, Sept. 13 Litho. *Perf. 13½x14*

767 A154 19p Drag hunt .60 .60
768 A154 23p Horse drivig .70 .70
769 A154 30p Race training .85 .85
770 A154 35p Show jumping 1.00 1.00
771 A154 41p Pony club 1.10 1.10
772 A154 60p Shire horses 1.75 1.75
  Nos. 767-772 (6) 6.00 6.00

Christmas A155

19p, Journey to Bethlehem. 23p, Archangel Gabriel visits shepherds. 30p, Nativity. 60p, Magi.

1996, Nov. 12 *Perf. 13x13½*

773 A155 19p multicolored .60 .60
774 A155 23p multicolored .75 .75
775 A155 30p multicolored .95 .95
776 A155 60p multicolored 1.90 1.90
  Nos. 773-776 (4) 4.20 4.20

Souvenir Sheet

New Year 1997 (Year of the Ox) — A156

Illustration reduced.

1997, Feb. 7 Litho. *Perf. 13½*

777 A156 £1 multicolored 3.25 3.25
  a. With added inscription in sheet margin 3.25 3.25

No. 777a inscribed in sheet margin with "JERSEY AT HONG KONG '97" in red and Hong Kong '97 emblem in black.

Birds — A157

1997, Feb. 12 *Perf. 14½*

778 A157 1p Red-breasted merganser .20 .20
779 A157 10p Common tern .25 .25
780 A157 15p Black-headed gull .45 .45

781 A157 20p Dunlin .55 .55
782 A157 24p Puffin .65 .65
783 A157 37p Oystercatcher 1.10 1.10
784 A157 75p Redshank 2.10 2.10
785 A157 £2p Shag 5.75 5.75
a. Souv. sheet of 8, #778-785 11.00 11.00
b. As "a," with added inscription in sheet margin 11.00 11.00

No. 785b contains PACIFIC '97 World Philatelic Exhibition emblem in sheet margin. Issued: 5/29.

Nos. 781-782 exist dated "1998."

See Nos. 825-832, 864-871, 909-916.

Lillie the Cow — A158

Designs: No. 786, Building sand castle. No. 787, Taking photographs. No. 788, Lying on beach. No. 789, In restaurant.

1997, Feb. 12 ***Die Cut Perf 9½x9***

Self-Adhesive

786 A158 (23p) multicolored .75 .75
787 A158 (23p) multicolored .75 .75
788 A158 (23p) multicolored .75 .75
789 A158 (23p) multicolored .75 .75
a. Strip of 4, #786-789 3.00

Peelable backing is rouletted 9 between stamps.

Coil Stamps

786a Die cut perf. 8¾x9, dated "2000" .75 .75
787a Die cut perf. 8¾x9, dated "2000" .75 .75
788a Die cut perf. 8¾x9, dated "2000" .75 .75
789b Die cut perf. 8¾x9, dated "2000" .75 .75
c. Strip of 4, #786a-789b 3.00

Nos. 786-789 are inscribed "U.K. MINIMUM POSTAGE PAID." Stamps dated "1999" were originally sold for 25p. Stamps dated "2000" were originally sold for 26p.

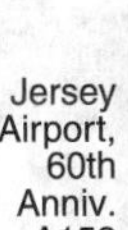

Jersey Airport, 60th Anniv. A159

1997, Mar. 10 **Litho.** ***Perf. 13½x14***

790 A159 20p DH95 Flamingo .65 .65
791 A159 24p HPR1 Marathon .70 .70
792 A159 31p DH114 Heron .90 .90
793 A159 37p Boeing 737-236 1.10 1.10
794 A159 43p BN Trislander 1.25 1.25
795 A159 63p BAe 146-200 1.90 1.90
Nos. 790-795 (6) 6.50 6.50

Stories and Legends A160

Europa: 20p, Bull of St. Clement. 24p, Black Horse of St. Ouen. 31p, Black Dog of Bouley Bay. 63p, Les Fontaines des Mittes.

1997, Apr. 15 **Litho.** ***Perf. 14½x14***

796 A160 20p multicolored .60 .60
797 A160 24p multicolored .70 .70
798 A160 31p multicolored .95 .95
799 A160 63p multicolored 1.50 1.50
Nos. 796-799 (4) 3.75 3.75

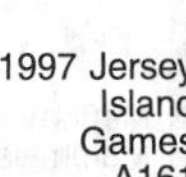

1997 Jersey Island Games A161

1997, June 28 **Litho.** ***Perf. 13½x14***

800 A161 20p Cycling .60 .60
801 A161 24p Archery .70 .70
802 A161 31p Windsurfing .90 .90
803 A161 37p Gymnastics 1.10 1.10
804 A161 43p Volleyball 1.25 1.25
805 A161 63p Running 1.90 1.90
Nos. 800-805 (6) 6.45 6.45

Jesey Wildlife Preservation Trust A162

Endangered species: 20p, Mallorcan midwife toad. 24p, Aye-aye. 31p, Echo parakeet. 37p, Pigmy hog. 43p, St. Lucia whip-tail. 63p, Madagascar teal.

1997, Sept. 2 **Litho.** ***Perf. 13***

806 A162 20p multicolored .60 .60
807 A162 24p multicolored .70 .70
808 A162 31p multicolored .90 .90
809 A162 37p multicolored 1.10 1.10
810 A162 43p multicolored 1.25 1.25
811 A162 63p multicolored 1.90 1.90
Nos. 806-811 (6) 6.45 6.45

Trees — A163

1997, Sept. 2 ***Perf. 14½***

812 A163 20p Ash .60 .60
813 A163 24p Elder .70 .70
814 A163 31p Beech .90 .90
815 A163 37p Sweet chestnut 1.10 1.10
816 A163 43p Hawthorn 1.25 1.25
817 A163 63p Common oak 1.90 1.90
Nos. 812-817 (6) 6.45 6.45

Christmas A164

Santa Claus at various Jersey landmarks: 20p, Jersey Airport. 24p, St. Aubin's Harbor. 31p, Mont Orgueil Castle. 63p, Royal Square, St. Helier.

1997, Nov. 11 **Litho.** ***Perf. 14***

818 A164 20p multicolored .65 .65
819 A164 24p multicolored .80 .80
820 A164 31p multicolored 1.00 1.00
821 A164 63p multicolored 2.00 2.00
Nos. 818-821 (4) 4.45 4.45

Queen Elizabeth II and Prince Philip, 50th Wedding Anniv. A165

Designs: No. 822, Wedding portrait. No. 823, Anniversary portrait.

£1.50, Full length wedding portrait, vert.

1997, Nov. 20 **Litho.** ***Perf. 14½***

822 A165 50p multicolored 1.60 1.60
823 A165 50p multicolored 1.60 1.60
a. Pair, #822-823 3.25 3.25

Souvenir Sheet

Perf. 13½x14

824 A165 £1.50 multicolored 4.25 4.25

No. 824 contains one 38x51mm stamp.

Bird Type of 1997

1998, Jan. 28 **Litho.** ***Perf. 14½***

825 A157 2p Sanderling .20 .20
826 A157 5p Great crested grebe .20 .20
827 A157 21p Sandwich tern .70 .70
828 A157 25p Brent goose .75 .75
829 A157 30p Fulmar .90 .90
830 A157 40p Turnstone 1.25 1.25
831 A157 60p Avocet 1.90 1.90
832 A157 £1 Razorbill 3.30 3.30
a. Souvenir sheet of 8, #825-832 9.50 9.50
Nos. 825-832 (8) 9.20 9.20

Souvenir Sheet

New Year 1998 (Year of the Tiger) — A166

Illustration reduced.

1998, Jan. 28 ***Perf. 14***

833 A166 £1 multicolored 3.00 3.00

Buses A167

Designs: 20p, JMT Bristol 4 Tonner, 1923. 24p, SCS Regent Double Decker, 1934. 31p, Slade's Dennis Lancet, 1936. 37p, Tantivy Leyland PLSC Lion, 1947. 43p, JBS Morris Bus, 1958. 63p, JMT Leyland Titan TD4 Double Decker, 1961.

1998, Apr. 2 **Litho.** ***Perf. 14***

834 A167 20p multicolored .70 .70
835 A167 24p multicolored .70 .70
a. Bklt. pane, 3 each #834-835 4.75
836 A167 31p multicolored .90 .90
837 A167 37p multicolored 1.25 1.25
a. Bklt. pane, 3 each #836-837 7.00
838 A167 43p multicolored 1.40 1.40
839 A167 63p multicolored 2.00 2.00
a. Bklt. pane, 3 each #838-839 11.00
b. Bklt. pane, 1 each, #834-839 7.75
Complete booklet, #835a, 837a, 839a, 839b 30.00
Nos. 834-839 (6) 6.95 6.95

National Festivals — A168

Europa: 20p, Creative Arts Festival. 24p, Jazz Festival. 31p, Good Food Festival. 63p, Floral Festival.

1998, Apr. 2 ***Perf. 14x13½***

840 A168 20p multicolored .60 .60
841 A168 24p multicolored .70 .70
842 A168 31p multicolored .85 .85
843 A168 63p multicolored 1.60 1.60
Nos. 840-843 (4) 3.75 3.75

Yachting — A169

Nos. 844-848: Various Hobie Cats sailing in St. Aubin's Bay.

Nos. 849-853: Various yachts racing in annual "Lombard Challenge."

1998, May 18 **Litho.** ***Perf. 13***

844 A169 20p multicolored .70 .70
845 A169 20p multicolored .70 .70
846 A169 20p multicolored .70 .70
847 A169 20p multicolored .70 .70
848 A169 20p multicolored .70 .70
a. Strip of 5, #844-848 3.50 3.50
849 A169 24p multicolored .75 .75
850 A169 24p multicolored .75 .75
851 A169 24p multicolored .75 .75
852 A169 24p multicolored .75 .75
853 A169 24p multicolored .75 .75
a. Strip of 5, #849-853 3.75 3.75

"Days Gone By" — A170

Jersey lily and: No. 854, Cider making. No. 855, Potato barrels transported by horse and cart. No. 856, Gathering seaweed for fertilizer. No. 857, Milking Jersey cows by hand.

Serpentine Die Cut Perf. 11¼

1998, Aug. 11 **Litho.**

Self-Adhesive

854 A170 (20p) multicolored .70 .70
855 A170 (20p) multicolored .70 .70
856 A170 (20p) multicolored .70 .70
857 A170 (20p) multicolored .70 .70
a. Strip of 4, #854-857 2.80 2.80

Nos. 854-857 are inscribed "Bailiwick / Minimum Postage Paid." They were sold for 22p. Stamps from the first printing are dated "1998." Stamps from subsequent printings are dated "1999," "2000" and "2001."

Marine Life A171

1998, Aug. 11 **Litho.** ***Perf. 15x14½***

858 A171 20p Bass .60 .60
859 A171 24p Red gurnard .70 .70
860 A171 31p Skate .90 .90
861 A171 37p Mackerel 1.25 1.25
862 A171 43p Tope 1.25 1.25
863 A171 63p Cuckoo wrasse 1.90 1.90
Nos. 858-863 (6) 6.60 6.60

Intl. Year of the Ocean.

Bird Type of 1997

1998, Aug. 11 ***Perf. 14½***

864 A157 4p Gannet .20 .20
865 A157 22p Ringed plover .70 .70
866 A157 26p Grey plover .75 .75
867 A157 31p Golden plover .90 .90
868 A157 32p Greenshank .90 .90
869 A157 35p Curlew 1.25 1.25
870 A157 44p Herring gull 1.25 1.25
871 A157 50p Great black-backed gull 1.50 1.50
a. Souvenir sheet of 8, #864-871 7.50 7.50
Nos. 864-871 (8) 7.45 7.45

Jersey Autumn Flowers A172

1998, Oct. 23 **Litho.** ***Perf. 14½***

872 A172 20p Iris .60 .60
873 A172 24p Carnations .70 .70
874 A172 31p Chrysanthemums .90 .90
875 A172 37p Pinks 1.25 1.25
876 A172 43p Roses 1.25 1.25
877 A172 63p Lilies 2.00 2.00
Nos. 872-877 (6) 6.70 6.70

Souvenir Sheet

Perf. 14

878 A172 £1.50 Lilium star gazer 4.50 4.50

No. 878 contains one 50x38mm stamp. Italia '98 (#878).

Christmas A173

Island manger (crib), service club sponsor: 20p, Central Market, Jersey Round Table. 24p, St. Thomas' Church, Soroptimist Intl. of Jersey. 31p, Trinity Parish Church, Rotary Club of Jersey. 63p, Royal Square, Lions Club of Jersey.

1998, Nov. 10 ***Perf. 13x13½***

879 A173 20p multicolored .60 .60
880 A173 24p multicolored .70 .70
881 A173 31p multicolored .90 .90
882 A173 63p multicolored 2.00 2.00
Nos. 879-882 (4) 4.20 4.20

Souvenir Sheet

New Year 1999 (Year of the Rabbit) — A174

Illustration reduced.

1999, Feb. 16 **Litho.** ***Perf. 13½***

883 A174 £1 multicolored 3.25 3.25

UPU, 125th Anniv. A175

Jersey mail transport: 20p, Eastern Railway train. 24p, Mail steamer, "Brighton." 43p, DH 86A, first airmail arrival. 63p, Morris Minor P.O. van.

1999, Feb. 16 ***Perf. 14***

884 A175 20p multicolored .65 .65
885 A175 24p multicolored .80 .80
886 A175 43p multicolored 1.40 1.40
887 A175 63p multicolored 2.00 2.00
Nos. 884-887 (4) 4.85 4.85

Royal Natl. Lifeboat Institution, 175th Anniv. A176

1999, Feb. 16 ***Perf. 14½***

888 A176 75p St. Catherine 2.50 2.50
889 A176 £1 St. Helier 3.25 3.25
a. Pair, #888-889 5.75 5.75

Orchids — A177

Designs: 21p, Cymbidium Maufant "Jersey." 25p, Miltonia Millbrook "Jersey." 31p, Paphiopedilum Transvaal. 37p, Paphiopedilum Elizabeth Castle. 43p, Calanthe Five Oaks. 63p, Cymbidium Icho Tower "Trinity."
£1.50, Miltonia Portelet.

Perf. 14¼x13¼

1999, Mar. 19 **Litho.**

890 A177 21p multicolored .70 .70
891 A177 25p multicolored .85 .85
892 A177 31p multicolored 1.00 1.00
893 A177 37p multicolored 1.25 1.25
894 A177 43p multicolored 1.40 1.40
895 A177 63p multicolored 2.00 2.00
Nos. 890-895 (6) 7.20 7.20

Souvenir Sheet

Perf. 13½

896 A177 £1.50 multicolored 4.75 4.75

Australia '99 World Stamp Expo (#896).

IBRA'99 Intl. Philatelic Exhibition, Nuremberg A178

National Parks: 21p, Howard Davis Park. 25p, Sir Winston Churchill Memorial Park. 31p, Coronation Park. 63p, La Collette Gardens.

1999, Apr. 27 ***Perf. 13x13½***

897 A178 21p multicolored .55 .55
898 A178 25p multicolored .65 .65
899 A178 31p multicolored .80 .80
900 A178 63p multicolored 1.75 1.75
Nos. 897-900 (4) 3.75 3.75

Europa (#898-899).

Wedding of Prince Edward and Sophie Rhys-Jones — A179

1999, June 19 **Litho.** ***Perf. 14½***

901 A179 35p yellow & multi 1.10 1.10
902 A179 35p blue & multi 1.10 1.10
a. Pair, #901-902 2.25 2.25

Classic Car Type of 1989

Designs: 21p, 1899 Jersey-built Benz. 25p, 1910 Star Tourer. 31p, 1938 Citroen "Traction Avant." 37p, 1937 Talbot BG110 Tourer. 43p, 1934 Morris Cowley Six Special Coupé. 63p, 1946 Ford Anglia E04A Saloon.

1999, July 2 **Litho.** ***Perf. 14***

903 A101 21p multicolored .70 .70
904 A101 25p multicolored .80 .80
a. Bklt. pane, 3 each #903-904 5.00
905 A101 31p multicolored 1.00 1.00
906 A101 37p multicolored 1.25 1.25
a. Bklt. pane, 3 each #905-906 7.50
907 A101 43p multicolored 1.40 1.40
908 A101 63p multicolored 2.00 2.00
a. Bklt. pane, 3 each #907-908 11.50
b. Booklet pane, #903-908 8.00
Complete booklet, #904a, 906a, 908a, 908b 32.50
Nos. 903-908 (6) 7.15 7.15

PhilexFrance '99 (#904a, 906a, 908a-908b).

Bird Type of 1997

1999, Aug. 21 **Litho.** ***Perf. 14¾***

909 A157 23p Bar-tailed godwit .75 .75
910 A157 27p Common scoter .85 .85
911 A157 28p Lesser black-backed gull .90 .90
912 A157 29p Little egret .90 .90
913 A157 33p Little grebe 1.00 1.00
914 A157 34p Cormorant 1.10 1.10
915 A157 45p Rock pipit 1.40 1.40
916 A157 65p Gray heron 2.10 2.10
a. Souvenir sheet of 8, #909-916 9.00 9.00
Nos. 909-916 (8) 9.00 9.00

Small Mammals A180

Designs: 21p, Hedgehog. 25p, Red squirrel. 31p, Nathusius pipestrelle. 37p, Jersey bank vole. 43p, Lesser white-toothed shrew. 63p, Common mole.

1999, Aug. 21 **Litho.** ***Perf. 13¼x13***

917 A180 21p multicolored .65 .65
918 A180 25p multicolored .80 .80
919 A180 31p multicolored 1.00 1.00
920 A180 37p multicolored 1.25 1.25
921 A180 43p multicolored 1.40 1.40
922 A180 63p multicolored 2.00 2.00
Nos. 917-922 (6) 7.10 7.10

Lighthouses A181

1999, Oct. 5 **Litho.** ***Perf. 14***

923 A181 21p Gorey Pierhead .65 .65
924 A181 25p La Corbiere .80 .80
925 A181 34p Noirmont Point 1.10 1.10
926 A181 38p Deme de Pas 1.25 1.25
927 A181 44p Greve d'Azette 1.40 1.40
928 A181 64p Sorel Point 2.00 2.00
Nos. 923-928 (6) 7.20 7.20

Christmas A182

Poinsettias and: 21p, Mistletoe. 25p, Holly. 34p, Ivy. 64p, Christmas rose.

1999, Nov. 9 **Litho.** ***Perf. 13¾***

929 A182 21p multi .65 .65
930 A182 25p multi .80 .80
931 A182 34p multi 1.10 1.10
932 A182 64p multi 2.10 2.10
Nos. 929-932 (4) 4.65 4.65

Coat of Arms A183

Litho. & Embossed with Foil Application

2000, Jan. 1 ***Perf. 13¼***

933 A183 £10 gold & multi 30.00 30.00

Millennium.

Souvenir Sheet

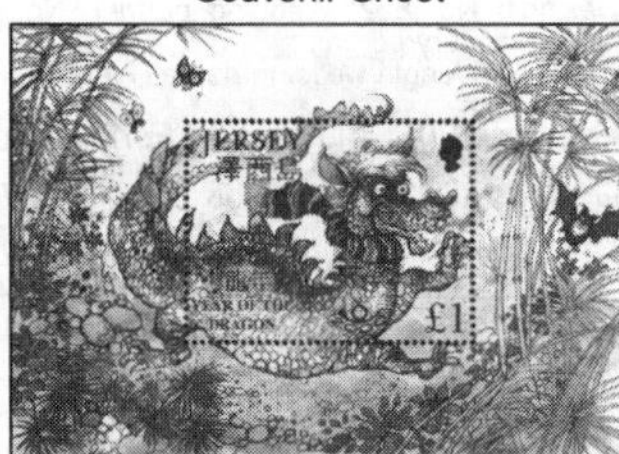

New Year 2000 (Year of the Dragon) — A184

Illustration reduced.

2000, Feb. 5 **Litho.** ***Perf. 13¾***

934 A184 £1 multi 3.00 3.00

Europa, 2000

Common Design Type and

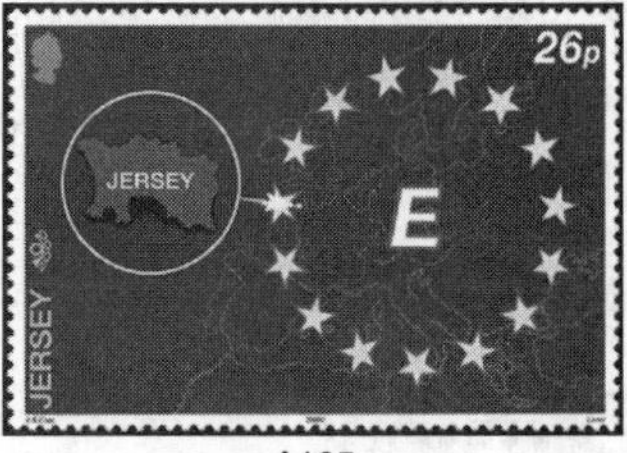

A185

2000, May 9 ***Perf. 13¼x13***

935 A185 26p multi .75 .75
936 CD17 34p multi 1.10 1.10

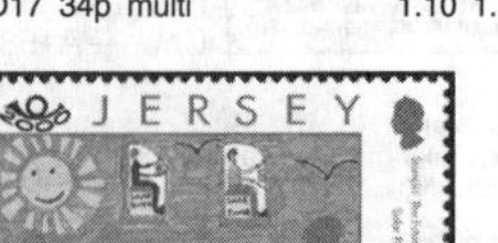

Stampin' the Future — A186

Children's Stamp Design Contest Winners: No. 937, Ocean Adventure, by Gemma Carré. No. 938, Solar Power, by Chantal Varley-Best. No. 939, Floating City and Space Cars, by Nicola Singleton. No. 940, Conservation, by Carly Logan.

2000, May 9 **Litho.** ***Perf. 14***

937 A186 22p multi .65 .65
938 A186 22p multi .65 .65
939 A186 22p multi .65 .65
940 A186 22p multi .65 .65
a. Souvenir sheet, #937-940 2.60 2.60
Nos. 937-940 (4) 2.60 2.60

Ships — A187

#941, Roman merchant ship. #942, Viking long boat. #943, Warship, 13th cent. #944, Merchant ship, 14th-15th cent. #945, Tudor warship, 16th cent.

#946, Warship, 17th cent. #947, Navy cutter, 18th cent. #948, Barque, 19th cent. #949, Oyster cutter, 19th cent. #950, Ketch, 20th cent.

2000, May 22 ***Perf. 13¾***

941 A187 22p multi .65 .65
942 A187 22p multi .65 .65
943 A187 22p multi .65 .65
944 A187 22p multi .65 .65
945 A187 22p multi .65 .65
a. Strip of 5, #941-945 3.25 3.25
946 A187 26p multi .80 .80
947 A187 26p multi .80 .80
948 A187 26p multi .80 .80
949 A187 26p multi .80 .80
a. Booklet pane, #941-944, 946-949 6.50
950 A187 26p multi .80 .80
a. Strip of 5, #946-950 4.00 4.00
b. Souvenir sheet, #941-950 7.25 7.25
c. Booklet pane, #941-942, 944-946, 948-950 6.50
d. Booklet pane, #941, 943-947, 949-950 6.50
e. Booklet pane, #941-943, 945-948, 950 6.50
f. Bklt. pane, #942-945, 947-950 6.50
Booklet, #949a, 950c-950f 32.50

Marine Mammals A188

Designs: 22p, Bottle-nosed dolphin. 26p, Long-finned pilot whale. 34p, Harbor porpoise. 38p, Atlantic gray seal. 44p, Risso's dolphin. 64p, White-beaked dolphin.
£1.50, Common dolphin.

2000, June 5 *Perf. 14¾x14*

951 A188 22p multi .65 .65
952 A188 26p multi .80 .80
953 A188 34p multi 1.00 1.00
954 A188 38p multi 1.10 1.10
955 A188 44p multi 1.25 1.25
956 A188 64p multi 1.90 1.90
Nos. 951-956 (6) 6.70 6.70

Souvenir Sheet

957 A188 £1.50 multi 4.50*As #957, with World Stamp Expo 2000 emblem in 4.50 margin 4.5

No. 957 contains one 81x29mm stamp.
Issued: No. 957a, 7/7/00.

Prince William, 18th Birthday A189

William &: #958, Mountain. #959, Polo player. #960, Fireworks. #961, Castle.

2000, June 21 *Perf. 14¼x14½*

958 A189 75p multi 2.25 2.25
959 A189 75p multi 2.25 2.25
960 A189 75p multi 2.25 2.25
961 A189 75p multi 2.25 2.25
Nos. 958-961 (4) 9.00 9.00

Queen Mother, 100th Birthday A190

Litho. with Foil Application

2000, Aug. 4 *Perf. 14½x14¼*

962 A190 50p Purple hat 1.50 1.50
963 A190 50p Pink hat 1.50 1.50
a. Souvenir sheet, #962-963 3.00 3.00

Battle of Britain, 60th Anniv. A191

Designs: 22p, Supermarine Spitfire Mk. Ia. 26p, Hawker Hurricane Mk. I. 36p, Bristol Blenheim Mk. IV. 40p, Vickers Wellington Mk. Ic. 45p, Boulton Paul Defiant Mk. I. 65p, Short Sunderland Mk. I.

2000, Sept. 15 **Litho.** *Perf. 14¼x14*

964 A191 22p multi .65 .65
965 A191 26p multi .75 .75
966 A191 36p multi 1.10 1.10
967 A191 40p multi 1.25 1.25
968 A191 45p multi 1.40 1.40
969 A191 65p multi 1.90 1.90
Nos. 964-969 (6) 7.05 7.05

Christmas A192

2000, Nov. 7 *Perf. 13*

970 A192 22p Virgin Mary .65 .65
971 A192 26p Shepherd .75 .75
972 A192 36p Angel 1.00 1.00
973 A192 65p Magus 1.90 1.90
Nos. 970-973 (4) 4.30 4.30

Souvenir Sheet

New Year 2001 (Year of the Snake) — A193

2001, Jan. 24 **Litho.** *Perf. 13¾*

974 A193 £1 multi 3.00 3.00

Steamships on Jersey-France Route — A194

2001, Jan. 24 *Perf. 13x13¼*

975 A194 22p Rose .65 .65
976 A194 26p Comete .75 .75
977 A194 36p Cygne 1.00 1.00
978 A194 40p Victoria 1.10 1.10
979 A194 45p Attala 1.25 1.25
980 A194 65p Brittany 1.90 1.90
Nos. 975-980 (6) 6.65 6.65

Agricultural Products — A195

No. 981: a, Jersey cows. b, Royal potatoes. c, Tomatoes. d, Cauliflower and purple broccoli. e, Zucchini and peppers.

Serpentine Die Cut 11¼

2001, Apr. 3

Self-Adhesive

981 Strip of 5 3.75
a.-e. A195 (26p) Any single .75 .75

No. 981 exists dated "2002."

Navy Ships Named Jersey A196

Ships in service from: 23p, 1654-91. 26p, 1694-98. 37p, 1698-1731. 41p, 1736-83. 46p, 1860-73. 66p, 1938-41.

2001, Apr. 3 *Perf. 14*

982 A196 23p multi .65 .65
983 A196 26p multi .75 .75
984 A196 37p multi 1.00 1.00
985 A196 41p multi 1.10 1.10
986 A196 46p multi 1.40 1.40
987 A196 66p multi 1.90 1.90
Nos. 982-987 (6) 6.80 6.80

Queen Elizabeth II, 75th Birthday — A197

2001, Apr. 21 *Perf. 14x14¾*

988 A197 £3 multi 8.50 8.50

Pond Life A198

Designs: 23p, Agile frog. 26p, Trout. 37p, White water lily. 41p, Common blue damselfly. 46p, Palmate newt. 66p, Tufted duck.

2001, May 22 *Perf. 14¾x14*

989 A198 23p multi .65 .65
990 A198 26p multi .70 .70
991 A198 37p multi .95 .95
992 A198 41p multi 1.00 1.00
993 A198 46p multi 1.10 1.10
994 A198 66p multi 1.60 1.60
Nos. 989-994 (6) 6.00 6.00

Souvenir Sheet

Perf. 14¼

995 A198 £1.50 Kingfisher 3.75 3.75
a. As #995, with Belgica 2001 emblem in margin 4.25 4.25

Europa (#990-991). No. 995 contains one 38x50mm stamp.
Issued: No. 995a, 6/9/01.

Birds of Prey — A199

Designs: 23p, Long-eared owl. 26p, Peregrine falcon. 37p, Short-eared owl. 41p, Marsh harrier. 46p, Sparrowhawk. 66p, Tawny owl. £1.50, Barn owl.

2001, July 3 **Litho.** *Perf. 13½*

996 A199 23p multi .65 .65
997 A199 26p multi .75 .75
998 A199 37p multi 1.00 1.00
999 A199 41p multi 1.10 1.10
1000 A199 46p multi 1.25 1.25
a. Booklet pane, #997, 998, 2 each #996, 1000 6.25 —
1001 A199 66p multi 1.90 1.90
a. Booklet pane, #996-1001 7.50 —
b. Booklet pane, 2 each #996, 998, 1001 8.00 —
c. Booklet pane, #996-998, 1001, 2 #999 7.00 —
Nos. 996-1001 (6) 6.65 6.65
1002 A199 £1.50 Booklet pane of 1 4.75 4.75
Booklet, #1000a, 1001a, 1001b, 1001c, 1002 35.00

Souvenir Sheet

1003 A199 £1.50 multi 4.25 4.25
a. Like #1003, with Hafnia 01 emblem 4.25 4.25

Issued: No. 1003a, 10/16/01.

On No. 1002, "Tyto" is 4mm from the owl's head (owl is in center of stamp), while on No. 1003, it is 9mm from the head (owl is at right of stamp). The size of No. 1002 is 154x100mm, while the size of No. 1003 is 110x75.

Souvenir Sheet

Racing Yacht Jersey Clipper — A200

2001, Sept. 17 *Perf. 13¾*

1004 A200 £1.50 multi 4.50 4.50

Fire Engines A201

Designs: 23p, Tilley 26 manual, c. 1845. 26p, Albion Merryweather, c. 1935. 37p, Dennis Ace, c. 1940. 41p, Dennis F8 pump escape, c. 1952. 46p, Land Rover Merryweather, c. 1968. 66p, Dennis Carmichael, c. 1989.

2001, Sept. 25 *Perf. 13x13¼*

1005 A201 23p multi .65 .65
1006 A201 26p multi .75 .75
1007 A201 37p multi 1.10 1.10
1008 A201 41p multi 1.25 1.25
1009 A201 46p multi 1.40 1.40
1010 A201 66p multi 1.90 1.90
Nos. 1005-1010 (6) 7.05 7.05

Christmas A202

No. 1011: a, Nativity. b, Street decorations. c, Carolers. d, Santa Claus. e, Bells and other ornaments on Christmas tree.

No. 1012: a, Adoration of the Shepherds. b, Carolers, Santa Claus, reindeer. c, Bell ornament, Christmas tree with candles. d, Church bells. e, Cracker with bells on wrapper.

Serpentine Die Cut 11x11¼

2001, Nov. 6

Coil Stamps

Self-Adhesive

1011 Horiz. strip of 5 3.50 —
a.-e. A202 (23p) green & multi, any single .70 .70
1012 Horiz. strip of 5 4.25 —
a.-e. A202 (29p) red & multi, any single .85 .85
f. Booklet pane of 16, 2 each #1011a, 1011c-1011e, 1012a-1012b, 1012d-1012e 12.50

Jersey State Vessels A203

Designs: 23p, Launch "Duchess of Normandy." 29p, Tugboat "Duke of Normandy." 38p, Customs patrol boat "Challenger." 47p, Pilot boat "Le Fret." 68p, Sea fisheries protection boat "Norman Le Brocq."

2002, Jan. 22 **Litho.** *Perf. 13x13¼*

1013 A203 23p multi .65 .65
1014 A203 29p multi .80 .80
1015 A203 38p multi 1.10 1.10
1016 A203 47p multi 1.40 1.40
1017 A203 68p multi 1.90 1.90
Nos. 1013-1017 (5) 5.85 5.85

Reign of Queen Elizabeth II, 50th Anniv. — A204

Litho. & Embossed With Foil Application

2002, Feb. 6 *Perf. 13¼*
1018 A204 £3 multi 8.50 8.50

Souvenir Sheet

New Year 2002 (Year of the Horse) — A205

2002, Feb. 12 Litho. *Perf. 13¾*
1019 A205 £1 multi 3.00 3.00

Battle of Flowers Depictions of Circus Figures — A206

2002, Mar. 12 Litho. *Perf. 13¾*
1020 A206 23p Elephant, cats .65 .65
1021 A206 29p Clown .85 .85
1022 A206 38p Clown, diff. 1.10 1.10
1023 A206 68p Seal 1.90 1.90
Nos. 1020-1023 (4) 4.50 4.50

Europa (#1021-1022).

La Moye Golf Club, Cent. A207

Designs: 23p, Aubrey Boomer. 29p, Harry Vardon. 38p, Sir Henry Cotton. 47p, Golfer's swing. 68p, Golfer addressing ball.

2002, Apr. 16 *Perf. 14*
1024 A207 23p multi .65 .65
1025 A207 29p multi .85 .85
1026 A207 38p multi 1.10 1.10
1027 A207 47p multi 1.40 1.40
1028 A207 68p multi 1.90 1.90
Nos. 1024-1028 (5) 5.90 5.90

Police Vehicles A208

Designs: 23p, Vauxhall 12, c. 1952. 29p, 1959-60 Jaguar 2.4 MkII. 38p, 1972-73 Austin 1800. 40p, Ford Cortina MkIV, c. 1978. 47p, 1995-2000 Honda motorcycle. 68p, 1998-2000 Vauxhall Vectra.

2002, May 24 Litho. *Perf. 13x13¼*
1029 A208 23p multi .65 .65
1030 A208 29p multi .85 .85
1031 A208 38p multi 1.10 1.10
1032 A208 40p multi 1.25 1.25
1033 A208 47p multi 1.40 1.40
1034 A208 68p multi 2.00 2.00
Nos. 1029-1034 (6) 7.25 7.25

Insects A209

Designs: 23p, Honeybee. 29p, Seven-spot ladybug. 38p, Great green bush cricket. 40p, Greater horntail. 47p, Emperor dragonfly. 68p, Hawthorn shield bug.

2002, June 18 *Perf. 14¾x14*
1035 A209 23p multi .70 .70
1036 A209 29p multi .85 .85
1037 A209 38p multi 1.10 1.10
1038 A209 40p multi 1.25 1.25
1039 A209 47p multi 1.40 1.40
1040 A209 68p multi 2.10 2.10
Nos. 1035-1040 (6) 7.40 7.40

Queen Mother Elizabeth (1900-2002) — A210

Litho. with Foil Application

2002, Aug. 4 *Perf. 14x14¾*
1041 A210 £2 multi 6.25 6.25

Battle of Flowers, Cent. A211

Designs: 23p, Hydrangeas. 29p, Chrysanthemums. 38p, Hare's tails, pampas grass. 40p, Asters. 47p, Carnations. 68p, Gladioli. £2, Float "Zanzibar."

2002, Aug. 8 Litho. *Perf. 13x13¼*
1042 A211 23p multi .70 .70
1043 A211 29p multi .90 .90
1044 A211 38p multi 1.10 1.10
1045 A211 40p multi 1.25 1.25
1046 A211 47p multi 1.40 1.40
1047 A211 68p multi 2.10 2.10
a. Booklet pane, #1042-1047 7.50
Nos. 1042-1047 (6) 7.45 7.45

Souvenir Sheet

Perf. 13

1048 A211 £2 multi 6.25 6.25
a. Booklet pane of 1 6.25
Booklet, #1048a, 3 #1047a 30.00

No. 1047a has three different layouts of stamps on pane. No. 1048 contains one 76x39mm stamp. No. 1048a is sewn into booklet but is otherwise identical to No. 1048.

Cats A212

Designs: 23p, British dilute tortoiseshell. 29p, Cream Persian. 38p, Blue exotic shorthair. 40p, Black smoke Devon Rex. 47p, British silver tabby. 68p, Usual Abyssinian.
£2, British cream and white bi-color, vert.

2002, Oct. 12 *Perf. 14¾x14¼*
1049 A212 23p multi .70 .70
1050 A212 29p multi .90 .90
1051 A212 38p multi 1.10 1.10
1052 A212 40p multi 1.25 1.25
1053 A212 47p multi 1.50 1.50
1054 A212 68p multi 2.10 2.10
Nos. 1049-1054 (6) 7.55 7.55

Souvenir Sheet

Perf. 14¼

1055 A212 £2 multi 6.25 6.25

No. 1055 contains one 38x50mm stamp.

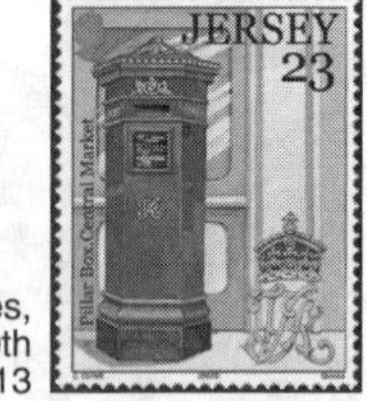

Letter Boxes, 150th Anniv. — A213

Designs: 23p, Pillar box, Central Market. 29p, Wall box, Colomberie. 38p, Wall box, St. Clement's Inner Road. 40p, Ship box. 47p, Pillar box, Parade, 1952. 68p, Pillar box, La Collette, 2000.
£2, First letter box, David Place, 1852.

2002, Nov. 23 *Perf. 14½x14¼*
1056 A213 23p multi .70 .70
1057 A213 29p multi .90 .90
1058 A213 38p multi 1.25 1.25
1059 A213 40p multi 1.25 1.25
1060 A213 47p multi 1.50 1.50
1061 A213 68p multi 2.10 2.10
Nos. 1056-1061 (6) 7.70 7.70

Souvenir Sheet

Perf. 14¾

1062 A213 £2 multi 6.25 6.25

No. 1062 contains one 39x76mm stamp.

POSTAGE DUE STAMPS

Numeral — D1

Map of Jersey — D2

Unwmk.

1969, Oct. 1 Litho. *Perf. 14*
J1 D1 1p violet blue .90 .70
J2 D1 2p sepia .90 .70
J3 D1 3p brt carmine 3.00 1.75
J4 D2 1sh emerald 8.75 7.00
J5 D2 2sh6p gray green 14.00 13.50
J6 D2 5sh red orange 27.50 27.50
Nos. J1-J6 (6) 55.05 51.15

Type of 1969
Decimal Currency

1971-75 Litho. *Perf. 14*
J7 D2 ½p black .20 .20
J8 D2 1p pale violet .20 .20
J9 D2 2p brown .20 .20
J10 D2 3p bright pink .20 .20
J11 D2 4p orange .20 .20
J12 D2 5p emerald .20 .20
J13 D2 6p orange ('74) .20 .20
J14 D2 7p brt yellow ('74) .20 .20
J15 D2 8p grnsh blue ('75) .25 .25
J16 D2 10p gray .30 .30
J17 D2 11p bister ('75) .35 .35
J18 D2 14p lilac .40 .40
J19 D2 25p dull green ('74) .80 .80
J20 D2 50p plum ('75) 1.50 1.50
Nos. J7-J20 (14) 5.20 5.20

St. Clement Arms, Dovecote, Samares — D3

Arms and Scenes from Jersey Parishes: 2p, St. Lawrence and Handois Reservoir. 3p, St. John and Sorel Point. 4p, St. Ouen and Pinnacle Rock. 5p, St. Peter and Quetivel Mill. 10p, St. Martin and St. Catherine's Breakwater. 12p, St. Helier and St. Helier Harbor. 14p, St. Saviour and Highlands College. 15p, St. Brelade and Beauport Bay. 20p, Grouville and La Hougue Bie. 50p, St. Mary and Perry Farm. £1, Trinity and Bouley Bay.

1978, Jan. 17 Litho. *Perf. 14*
J21 D3 1p brt green & blk .20 .20
J22 D3 2p orange & blk .20 .20
J23 D3 3p maroon & blk .20 .20
J24 D3 4p vermilion & blk .20 .20
J25 D3 5p dp ultra & blk .20 .20
J26 D3 10p olive & blk .20 .20
J27 D3 12p blue & blk .25 .25
J28 D3 14p red org & blk .30 .30
J29 D3 15p lilac rose & blk .35 .35
J30 D3 20p yel green & blk .40 .40
J31 D3 50p brown & blk 1.00 1.00
J32 D3 £1 violet & blk 2.10 2.10
Nos. J21-J32 (12) 5.60 5.60

St. Brelade — D4

1982, Sept. 4 Litho. *Perf. 13½x14*
J33 D4 1p shown .20 .20
J34 D4 2p St. Aubin .20 .20
J35 D4 3p Rozel .20 .20
J36 D4 4p Greve de Lecq .20 .20
J37 D4 5p Bouley Bay .20 .20
J38 D4 6p St. Catherine .20 .20
J39 D4 7p Gorey .20 .20
J40 D4 8p Bonne Nuit .20 .20
J41 D4 9p La Rocque .25 .25
J42 D4 10p St. Helier .25 .25
J43 D4 20p Ronez .50 .50
J44 D4 30p La Collette .70 .70
J45 D4 40p Elizabeth Castle .90 .90
J46 D4 £1 Upper Harbor Marina 2.00 2.00
Nos. J33-J46 (14) 6.20 6.20

OCCUPATION STAMPS

Issued Under German Occupation

OS1

1941-42 Typo. Unwmk. *Perf. 11*
N1 OS1 ½p green 4.50 3.25
N2 OS1 1p vermilion 4.25 2.50

Numerous shades and papers exist.
Issue dates: 1p, Apr. 1; ½p, Jan. 29, 1942.

OS2

1943-44 *Perf. 13½*
N3 OS2 ½p Old Jersey farm 10.00 5.75
N4 OS2 1p Portelet Bay 1.50 .75
a. On newsprint 2.25 1.25
N5 OS2 1½p Corbiere Lighthouse 2.00 *3.25*
N6 OS2 2p Elizabeth Castle 4.50 3.50
N7 OS2 2½p Mont Orgueil Castle 1.75 1.00
a. On newsprint 1.00 1.00
N8 OS2 3p Gathering seaweed 1.25 *2.75*
Nos. N3-N8 (6) 21.00 *17.00*

Issued: ½p, 1p, 6/1/43; 1½p, 2p, 6/8/43; 2½p, 3p, 6/29/43; #N4a, 2/28/44; #N7a, 2/25/44.
Nos. N1-N8 remained valid until 4/13/46.

ISLE OF MAN

ˈīˌəl əv ˈman

LOCATION — In the Irish Sea, off Northwest coast of England
GOVT. — Semi-autonomous within the British Commonwealth
AREA — 221 sq. mi.
POP. — 75,686 (1999 est.)
CAPITAL — Douglas

Catalogue values for unused stamps in this section are for Never Hinged items, beginning with Scott 1 in the regular postage section and Scott J1 in the postage due section.

British Regional Issues

A1

A2

Manx Emblem — A3

Perf. 15x14

1958-69 Photo. Wmk. 322

No.	Type	Denomination	Unused	Used
1	A1	2½p rose red ('64)	.50	.40
2	A2	3p purple	.20	.20
p.		Phosphor. ('68)	.20	.20
3	A2	4p ultra ('66)	1.10	.20
p.		Phosphor. ('67)	.20	.20
		Unwmk.		
4	A2	4p ultra ('68)	.20	.20
5	A2	4p olive brown ('68)	.20	.20
6	A2	4p bright red ('69)	.55	.25
7	A2	5p dark blue ('68)	.55	.20
		Nos. 1-7 (7)	3.30	1.65

Nos. 4-7 are phosphorescent.

A 1963 printing of No. 2 is on chalky paper.

1971, July 7 Photo. Unwmk.

No.	Type	Denomination	Unused	Used
8	A3	2½p bright pink	.30	.20
9	A3	3p ultramarine	.30	.20
10	A3	5p bluish lilac	.55	.50
11	A3	7½p light red brown	.55	.60
		Nos. 8-11 (4)	1.70	1.50

Sold to the general public only at post offices within the Isle of Man, but valid for postage throughout Great Britain.

Bailiwick Issues

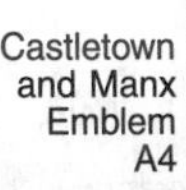

Castletown and Manx Emblem A4

Manx Cat — A5

Perf. 11½

1973, July 5 Photo. Unwmk.

No.	Type	Denomination	Unused	Used
12	A4	½p shown	.20	.20
a.		Booklet pane of 2	2.75	
b.		Booklet pane of 4 ('74)	.90	
13	A4	1p Port Erin	.20	.20
14	A4	1½p Mt. Snaefell	.20	.20
15	A4	2p Laxey Village	.20	.20
a.		Booklet pane of 2	2.75	
16	A4	2½p Tynwald Hill	.20	.20
a.		Booklet pane of 2	.75	
17	A4	3p Douglas Promenade	.20	.20
a.		Booklet pane of 2	.70	
b.		Booklet pane of 4 ('74)	.90	
18	A4	3½p Port St. Mary	.20	.20
a.		Booklet pane of 4 ('74)	1.40	
19	A4	4p Fairy Bridge	.20	.20
20	A4	5p Peel, Castle and shore	.20	.20
21	A4	6p Cregneish Village	.35	.35
22	A4	7½p Ramsey Bay	.35	.35
23	A4	9p Douglas Bay	.35	.35
24	A5	10p shown	.45	.45
25	A5	20p Manx ram	.60	.60
26	A5	50p Manx shearwaters	1.60	1.60
27	A5	£1 Viking longship	2.75	2.75
		Nos. 12-27 (16)	8.25	8.25

See Nos. 52-59.

Vikings Landing on Man, 938 — A6

1973, July 5 *Perf. 14*

No.	Type	Denomination	Unused	Used
28	A6	15p multicolored	.60	.60

Inauguration of postal independence.

Engine No. 1, Sutherland, 1873 — A7

1973, Aug. 4 *Perf. 14½x14*

No.	Type	Denomination	Unused	Used
29	A7	2½p shown	.20	.20
30	A7	3p Caledonia, 1885	.20	.20
31	A7	7½p Kissack, 1910	.50	.50
32	A7	9p Pender, 1873	.60	.60
		Nos. 29-32 (4)	1.50	1.50

Centenary of Manx steam railroad.

Leslie Randles, 1923 Winner A8

3½p, Alan Holmes, 1957 double winner.

1973, Sept. 4 Litho. *Perf. 14*

No.	Type	Denomination	Unused	Used
33	A8	3p multicolored	.20	.20
34	A8	3½p multicolored	.20	.20

Manx Grand Prix Motorcycle Race, 50th anniversary.

Princess Anne and Mark Phillips — A9

Litho. & Engr.

1973 Nov. 14 *Perf. 14x13½*

No.	Type	Denomination	Unused	Used
35	A9	25p lt blue & multi	.85	.85

Wedding of Princess Anne and Capt. Mark Phillips, Nov. 14, 1973.

William Hillary, R.N.L.I. Badge A10

Wreck of "St. George" A11

Designs: 8p, Tower of Refuge and lifeboat "Manchester & Salford." 10p, "Osman Gabriel" at Port Erin. 3½p and 8p are from paintings.

1974, Mar. 4 Photo. *Perf. 11½*

No.	Type	Denomination	Unused	Used
36	A10	3p black & multi	.20	.20
37	A11	3½ black & multi	.20	.20
38	A11	8p black & multi	.45	.45
39	A11	10p black & multi	.55	.55
		Nos. 36-39 (4)	1.40	1.40

Sesqui. of the founding of the Royal Natl. Lifeboat Institution by Sir William Hillary.

Stanley Woods on Moto Guzzi Motorcycle — A12

Designs: 3½p, Freddie Frith on Norton. 8p, Max Deubel on BMW with sidecar. 10p, Mike Hailwood on Honda.

1974, May 29 Litho. *Perf. 13*

No.	Type	Denomination	Unused	Used
40	A12	3p yellow grn & multi	.20	.20
41	A12	3½p crimson & multi	.20	.20
42	A12	8p yellow & multi	.30	.25
43	A12	10p ultra & multi	.30	.25
		Nos. 40-43 (4)	1.00	.90

Tourist Trophy Motorcycle Races on the Isle of Man.

Arms and Ruins of Rushen Abbey A13

Designs: 4½p, King Edgar of England visiting Chester in boat rowed by 8 kings including King Magnus Haraldson. 8p, Fleet under King Magnus' command and arms he gave to Isle of Man. 10p, Bridge at Avignon, Bishop's mitre and Three Legs of Man.

1974, Sept. 18 Litho. *Perf. 14*

No.	Type	Denomination	Unused	Used
44	A13	3½p multicolored	.20	.20
45	A13	4½p multicolored	.20	.20
46	A13	8p multicolored	.30	.30
47	A13	10p multicolored	.40	.40
		Nos. 44-47 (4)	1.10	1.10

1,000th death anniv. of Magnus Haraldson, King of Many Islands (Nos. 45-46), and 600th death anniv. of William Russell, Bishop of Sodor and Mann (Nos. 44, 47).

Churchill and "Bugler Dunne at Colenso, 1899" — A14

Sir Winston Churchill: 4½p, Government Buildings, Douglas, and Warrant of Appointment. 8p, Manx A.A. Regiment in action. 20p, Freedom of Douglas Scroll, and casket.

1974, Nov. 22 Photo. *Perf. 11½*

No.	Type	Denomination	Unused	Used
48	A14	3½p multicolored	.20	.20
49	A14	4½p multicolored	.20	.20
50	A14	8p multicolored	.20	.20
51	A14	20p multicolored	.55	.55
a.		Souvenir sheet of 4, #48-51	1.25	1.25
		Nos. 48-51 (4)	1.15	1.15

Type of 1973

1975 Unwmk. *Perf. 11½*

No.	Type	Denomination	Unused	Used
52	A4	4½p Tynwald Hill	.20	.20
53	A4	5½p Douglas Promenade	.20	.20
54	A4	7p Laxey Village	.40	.40
55	A4	8p Ramsey Bay	.40	.40
58	A4	11p Monk's Bridge	.45	.45
59	A4	13p Derbyhaven	.60	.60
		Nos. 52-59 (6)	2.25	2.25

Issued: #52, 55, 1/8; #53-54, 5/28; #58-59, 10/29.

Log Cabin School, Cleveland Medal, Names of Settlers A15

Designs: 5½p, Terminal Tower Building, Cleveland, John Gill and Robert Carran. 8p, Clague House Museum, Margaret and Robert Clague. 10p, Thomas Quayle and S. S. William T. Graves.

1975, Mar. 14 Photo. *Perf. 11½*

No.	Type	Denomination	Unused	Used
62	A15	4½p multicolored	.20	.20
63	A15	5½p multicolored	.20	.20
64	A15	8p multicolored	.30	.30
65	A15	10p multicolored	.35	.35
		Nos. 62-65 (4)	1.05	1.05

Sesquicentennial of arrival of Manx settlers in Cleveland, Ohio area.

Tom Sheard and "Douglas" — A16

Designs: 7p, Walter L. Handley and "Rex-Acme." 10p, Geoffrey Duke and "Gilera." 12p, Peter Williams and "Norton."

1975, May 28 Litho. *Perf. 13½*

No.	Type	Denomination	Unused	Used
66	A16	5½p bister & multi	.20	.20
67	A16	7p salmon & multi	.20	.20
68	A16	10p lt green & multi	.30	.30
69	A16	12p ultra & multi	.35	.35
		Nos. 66-69 (4)	1.05	1.05

Tourist Trophy Motorcycle races on Isle of Man.

Sir George Goldie and his Birthplace A17

Designs (Sir George Goldie and): 7p, Map of Africa with Niger River basin, vert. 10p, Goldie as president of Royal Geographical Society and Society emblem, vert. 12p, River boats: trading hulk, native canoe, sternwheeler.

1975, Sept. 9 Photo. *Perf. 11½*

No.	Type	Denomination	Unused	Used
70	A17	5½p multicolored	.20	.20
71	A17	7p multicolored	.20	.20
72	A17	10p multicolored	.30	.30
73	A17	12p multicolored	.35	.35
		Nos. 70-73 (4)	1.05	1.05

Sir George Dashwood Goldie-Taubman (1846-1925), founder of Royal Niger Company.

Manx Bible — A18

Bicentenary of Manx Bible and Christmas 1975: 7p, Rev. Philip Moore and Old Ballaugh Church. 11p, Bishop Mark Hildesley and Bishops Court. 13p, Shipwreck off Cumberland Coast with John Kelly holding manuscript above water.

1975, Oct. 29 Litho. *Perf. 14*

No.	Type	Denomination	Unused	Used
74	A18	5½p multicolored	.20	.20
75	A18	7p multicolored	.20	.20
76	A18	11p multicolored	.25	.25
77	A18	13p multicolored	.35	.35
		Nos. 74-77 (4)	1.00	1.00

William Christian Listening to Patrick Henry — A19

Designs: 7p, Christian carrying Fincastle Resolutions to Williamsburg. 13p, Col. Patrick Henry and Lt. Col. William Christian of 1st Virginia Regiment. 20p, Christian as frontiersman and Indians.

1976, Mar. 12 Litho. *Perf. 13½*

78	A19	5½p multicolored	.20	.20
79	A19	7p multicolored	.20	.20
80	A19	13p multicolored	.35	.35
81	A19	20p multicolored	.40	.40
a.		Souv. sheet of 4, #78-81, perf. 14	1.60	1.60
		Nos. 78-81 (4)	1.15	1.15

American Bicentennial. William Christian (1743-1786), patriot, son of a Manx-man and Patrick Henry's brother-in-law.

First Double-decker Tram Car — A20

Designs: 7p, Toast-rack tram, 1890. 11p, Horse bus, 1895. 13p, Decorated tram with Queen Elizabeth II and Prince Philip.

1976, May 26 Photo. *Perf. 11½*

82	A20	5½p multicolored	.20	.20
83	A20	7p multicolored	.25	.25
84	A20	11p multicolored	.40	.40
85	A20	13p multicolored	.40	.40
		Nos. 82-85 (4)	1.25	1.25

Douglas horse trams, centenary.

Barroose Beaker, Bronze Age — A21

Virgin and Child, on Sodor and Man Banner — A22

Europa (Manx Ceramic Art): No. 87, Souvenir teapot (3-legged man), 19th cent. No. 88, Laxey jug, 1854. No. 89, Cronk Aust food vessel, early Bronze Age. No. 90, Sansbury bowl, 1851. No. 91, Knox urn, 20th cent. Nos. 89-91, horiz.

1976, July 28 Photo. *Perf. 11½*

86	A21	5p multicolored	.25	.25
87	A21	5p multicolored	.25	.25
88	A21	5p multicolored	.25	.25
a.		Strip of 3, #86-88	.80	.80
89	A21	10p multicolored	.25	.25
90	A21	10p multicolored	.25	.25
91	A21	10p multicolored	.25	.25
a.		Strip of 3, #89-91	.80	.80
		Nos. 86-91 (6)	1.50	1.50

Printed in sheets of 9 (3x3).

1976, Oct. 14 Litho. *Perf. 14¾x14½*

Virgin and Child on Embroidered Church Banners: 7p, St. Peter's, Onchan, Mothers' Union. 11p, Castletown. 13p, St. Olav's, Ramsey.

92	A22	6p multicolored	.20	.20
93	A22	7p multicolored	.20	.20
94	A22	11p multicolored	.30	.30
95	A22	13p multicolored	.40	.40
		Nos. 92-95 (4)	1.10	1.10

Christmas 1976 & cent. of Mothers' Union.

Elizabeth II and Arms of Man A23

Designs: 7p, Queen Elizabeth II and Prince Philip, vert. 25p, Queen, 1976 portrait.

Perf. 13½x14, 14x13½

1977, Mar. 1 Litho. & Engr.

96	A23	6p multicolored	.20	.20
97	A23	7p multicolored	.20	.20
98	A23	25p multicolored	.70	.70
		Nos. 96-98 (3)	1.10	1.10

25th anniv. of the reign of Elizabeth II.

Carrick Bay from Tom-the-Dipper's — A24

Europa: 10p, Looking south from Mooragh Park, Ramsey.

1977, May 25 Litho. *Perf. 14*

99	A24	6p multicolored	.25	.25
100	A24	10p multicolored	.35	.35

"Pa" Applebee at Ballig Bridge, 1912 — A25

Designs: 7p, Hairpin curve at Governor's Bridge and ambulance attendants. 11p, Boy Scouts tending scoreboards. 13p, John Willams at Windy Corner on Snaefell Mountain, winner of 1976 Open Classic Race.

1977, May 25 *Perf. 13½*

101	A25	6p multicolored	.20	.20
102	A25	7p multicolored	.25	.25
103	A25	11p multicolored	.35	.35
104	A25	13p multicolored	.40	.40
		Nos. 101-104 (4)	1.20	1.20

Tourist Trophy Motorcycle Races, and Boy Scouts, 70th anniv.; St. John Ambulance Assoc. cent. (in GB).

Meeting House, Mt. Morrison — A26

Designs: 7p, John Wesley preaching at Castletown, 1777. 11p, Wesley preaching outside Braddan Church. 13p, Methodist Church on Douglas Promenade, 1976.

1977, Oct. 19 Photo. *Perf. 11½*

Size: 30x24mm

105	A26	6p multicolored	.20	.20

Size: 37½x24mm

106	A26	7p multicolored	.25	.25
107	A26	11p multicolored	.35	.35

Size: 30x24mm

108	A26	13p multicolored	.40	.40
		Nos. 105-108 (4)	1.20	1.20

Bicentenary of John Wesley's first visit to the Isle of Man.

Seaplane and Carrier Ben My Chree — A27

Royal Air Force, 60th Anniv.: 7p, Bristol Scout and carrier Vindex, 1915. 11p, Boulton Paul Defiant over Douglas Bay, 1941. 13p, RAF Jaguar over Ramsey, 1977.

1978, Feb. 28 Litho. *Perf. 13½x14*

109	A27	6p multicolored	.20	.20
110	A27	7p multicolored	.25	.25
111	A27	11p multicolored	.35	.35
112	A27	13p multicolored	.40	.40
		Nos. 109-112 (4)	1.20	1.20

Watch Tower, Langness — A28

Jurby Church — A29

Fuchsia — A30

Landmarks: 6p, Government buildings. 7p, Tynwald Hill. 8p, Milner's Tower. 9p, Laxey Wheel. 10p, Castle Rushen. 11p, St. Ninian's Church. 12p, Tower of Refuge. 13p, St. German's Cathedral. 14p, Point of Ayre Lighthouse. 15p, Corrin's Tower. 16p, Douglas Head Lighthouse. 25p, Manx cat. 50p, Chough (crows). £1, Viking warrior.

1978 Litho. *Perf. 14, 14½*

113	A28	½p multicolored	.20	.20
114	A29	1p multicolored	.20	.20
115	A28	6p multicolored	.20	.20
116	A29	7p multicolored	.20	.20
a.		Perf. 14½	*8.00*	*6.50*
117	A28	8p multicolored	.20	.20
118	A28	9p multicolored	.20	.20
119	A29	10p multicolored	.25	.25
120	A28	11p multicolored	.25	.25
121	A29	12p multicolored	.30	.30
122	A29	13p multicolored	.35	.35
123	A29	14p multicolored	.35	.35
124	A29	15p multicolored	.40	.40
125	A29	16p multicolored	.40	.40
a.		Perf. 14½	*27.50*	*22.50*

Photo.

Perf. 11½

126	A30	20p multicolored	.55	.55
127	A30	25p multicolored	.80	.80
128	A30	50p multicolored	1.50	1.50
129	A30	£1 multicolored	3.25	3.25
		Nos. 113-129 (17)	9.60	9.60

6p exists only perf. 14. ½p-11p, 16p values are for perf. 14, 12p-15p for perf. 14½.

Issued: #113-125, 2/28; #126-129, 10/18.

Elizabeth II — A31

1978, May 24 Litho. *Perf. 14½x14¼*

130	A31	25p blue & multi	.75	.75

25th anniv. of coronation of Elizabeth II.

Keeil Chiggyrt Stone — A32

Europa (Carved Gravestones): No. 132, Wheel-headed cross slab. No. 133, Celtic Wheel cross. No. 134, Thor cross. No. 135, Olaf Liotulfson cross. No. 136, Odd's and Thorleif's crosses.

1978, May 24 *Perf. 11½*

131	A32	6p multicolored	.20	.20
132	A32	6p multicolored	.20	.20
133	A32	6p multicolored	.20	.20
a.		Strip of 3, #131-133	.45	.45
134	A32	11p multicolored	.30	.30
135	A32	11p multicolored	.30	.30
136	A32	11p multicolored	.30	.30
a.		Strip of 3, #134-136	.90	.90
		Nos. 131-136 (6)	1.50	1.50

Printed se-tenant in sheets of 9 (3x3).

J. K. Ward, Ward Library, Peel — A33

13p, Lumber camp at Three Rivers & J. K. Ward.

1978, June 10 Litho. *Perf. 13½*

137	A33	6p multicolored	.20	.20
138	A33	13p multicolored	.30	.30

James K. Ward (1819-1910), Manx pioneer in Canada.

Athletes, Games' Emblem and Manx Arms A34

Eagle, Manx Arms, Maple Leaf A35

1978, June 10

139	A34	7p multicolored	.20	.20
140	A35	11p multicolored	.30	.30

11th Commonwealth Games, Edmonton, Aug. 3-12 (7p); North American Manx Soc., 50th anniv. (11p).

"Hunt the Wren" — A36

1978, Oct. 18 Litho. *Perf. 13*

141 A36 5p multicolored .30 .25

Christmas 1978.

Philip M. C. Kermode and Nassa Kermodei A37

7p, Peregrine falcons. 11p, Fulmars. 13p, Asilid fly.

1979, Feb. 27 Litho. *Perf. 14*

142 A37 6p multicolored .20 .20
143 A37 7p multicolored .25 .25
144 A37 11p multicolored .30 .30
145 A37 13p multicolored .40 .40
Nos. 142-145 (4) 1.15 1.15

Isle of Man Natural History and Antiquarian Society.

Viking Ship — A38

A39

Viking Raid at Garwick A40

Designs (Tynwald Emblem and): 7p, 10th century meeting at Tynwald. 11p, Tynwald Hill and St. John's Church. 13p, Contemporary Tynwald Day parade.

Perf. 14½x14 (#146-147), 13¼ (#148-151)

1979, May 16 Litho.

146 A38 3p *Insularem* .20 .20
a. Bklt. pane, 4 #146, 2 #147 .60
b. *Insularum* ("1980") .20 .20
c. Bklt. pane, 4 #146b, 2 #147 1.10
147 A39 4p multicolored .20 .20
148 A40 6p multicolored .20 .20
149 A40 7p multicolored .20 .20
150 A40 11p multicolored .25 .25
151 A40 13p multicolored .30 .30
Nos. 146-151 (6) 1.35 1.35

Millennium of Tynwald, Legislative Council. #146-147 printed se-tenant in sheets of 80.
No. 146a comes in two arrangements.
#147 from #146c, 190a are dated "1980."

19th Century Mailman — A41

Europa: 11p, Contemporary mailman.

1979, May 16 *Perf. 14½*

152 A41 6p multicolored .20 .20
153 A41 11p multicolored .40 .40

Ceremony on Tynwald Hill — A42

Design: 13p, Procession from St. John's Church to Tynwald Hill.

1979, July 5 Litho. *Perf. 14½*

154 A42 7p multicolored .20 .20
155 A42 13p multicolored .40 .40

Visit of Queen Elizabeth II for the celebration of millennium of Tynwald.

Girl Holding Teddy Bear — A43

Christmas and IYC: 7p, Children with Santa.

1979, Oct. 19 Litho. *Perf. 13¼x13½*

156 A43 5p multicolored .20 .20
157 A43 7p multicolored .30 .30

Capt. John Quilliam and Spencer A44

Capt. Quilliam: 6p, Seized by press gang. 8p, Battle of Trafalgar. 15p, Castle Rushen.

1979, Oct. 19 *Perf. 14*

158 A44 6p multicolored .20 .20
159 A44 8p multicolored .20 .20
160 A44 13p multicolored .30 .30
161 A44 15p multicolored .40 .40
Nos. 158-161 (4) 1.10 1.10

Capt. John Quilliam (1771-1829), British naval hero and member of House of Keys.

"Odin's Raven" A45

1979, Oct. 19 *Perf. 14x14½*

162 A45 15p multicolored .65 .65

Voyage of replica Viking longboat across North Sea (Trondheim to Peel), May 27-July 4.
See No. 176a.

Conglomerate Arch and Emblem — A46

Langness Emblem and: 8p, Braaid Circle. 12p, Cashtal yn Ard (Neolithic burial ground). 13p, Volcanic rocks, Scarlett. 15p, Sugar-loaf Rock.

1980, Feb. 5 Litho. *Perf. 14½*

163 A46 7p multicolored .20 .20
164 A46 8p multicolored .25 .25
165 A46 12p multicolored .35 .35
166 A46 13p multicolored .35 .35
167 A46 15p multicolored .35 .35
Nos. 163-167 (5) 1.50 1.50

Royal Geographical Soc., 150th anniv.

"Mona's Isle I" A47

1980, May 6 Photo. *Perf. 11½*

Granite Paper

168 A47 7p *shown* .20 .20
169 A47 8p *Douglas I* .20 .20
170 A47 11½p *Mona's Queen II, sinking U-boat* .25 .25
171 A47 12p *King Orry III* .30 .30
172 A47 13p *Ben-My-Chree IV* .35 .35
173 A47 15p *Lady of Mann II* .45 .45
a. Souvenir sheet of 6, #168-173 2.00 2.00
Nos. 168-173 (6) 1.75 1.75

Isle of Man Steam Packet Co. sesqui.; London 80 Intl. Stamp Exhib., May 6-14.

Thomas Edward Brown and Characters from his Poems — A48

Europa (Brown (1830-1897), Poet and Scholar): 13½p, Cricket game, Clifton College Bristol.

1980, May 6

174 A48 7p multicolored .25 .25
175 A48 13½p multicolored .35 .35

Visit of King Olav V of Norway A49

1980, June 13 Litho. *Perf. 14½*

176 A49 12p multicolored .40 .40
a. Souv. sheet of 2, #162, 176 .95 .95

Visit of King Olav V of Norway, Aug. 2-7, 1979, and NORWEX 80 stamp exhibition, Oslo, June 13-22.

William Kermode and "Robert Quayle" A50

Kermode Family (First Manx Pioneers in Tasmania): 9p, First homestead, Mona Vale, Merino sheep, 1834. 13½p, Ross Bridge, W. Kermode. 15p, Calendar House, 1868. 17½p, Parliament Buildings, Hobart, Robert Quayle Kermode.

1980, Sept. 29 Litho.

177 A50 7p multicolored .20 .20
178 A50 9p multicolored .25 .25
179 A50 13½p multicolored .40 .40
180 A50 15p multicolored .45 .45
181 A50 17½p multicolored .50 .50
Nos. 177-181 (5) 1.80 1.80

Wren A51

1980, Sept. 29 Litho. *Perf. 13½x14*

182 A51 6p shown .20 .20
183 A51 8p Robin .20 .20

Wildlife conservation and Christmas 1980.

Luggers, Red Pier, Douglas A52

1981, Feb. 24 Litho. *Perf. 14*

184 A52 8p shown .20 .20
185 A52 9p Wanderer saving Lusitania Survivors .20 .20
186 A52 18p Nickey, Port St. Mary .45 .45
187 A52 20p Nobby, Ramsey Harbor .55 .55
188 A52 22p Sunbeam and Zebra, Port Erin .60 .60
Nos. 184-188 (5) 2.00 2.00

Royal National Mission to Deep Sea Fishermen centenary.

Peregrine Falcon — A53

1980, Sept. 29 Litho. *Perf. 14½x14*

Booklet Stamps

189 A53 1p shown .35 .35
190 A53 5p Loaghtyn ram .35 .35
a. Bklt. pane, 2 each #147, 189, 190 1.25

Crosh Cuirn (Cross of Mountain Ash Twigs, Harvest Charm) — A54

Europa: 18p, Bollan fish cross-bone (fishermen's charm).

1981, May 22 Litho. *Perf. 14½*

191 A54 8p multicolored .25 .25
192 A54 18p multicolored .60 .60

Col. Mark Wilks, Peel Castle A55

1981, May 22 *Perf. 14*

193 A55 8p shown .25 .25
194 A55 20p Wilks, Fort. St. George, Madras .45 .45
195 A55 22p Wilks, Napoleon .60 .60
196 A55 25p Wilks at Kirby estate .70 .70
Nos. 193-196 (4) 2.00 2.00

Wilks (d. 1831), governor of St. Helena.

Suffragettes Emmeline Goulden Pankhurst and Sophia Jane Goulden — A56

1981, May 22 *Perf. 14*

197 A56 9p multicolored .35 .35

Centenary of women's suffrage and of House of Keys Election Act (granting widows and unmarried women voting rights).

Prince Charles and Lady Diana
A57

1981, July 29 Litho. *Perf. 14*

198 A57 9p multicolored .25 .25
199 A57 25p multicolored 1.00 1.00
a. Souv. sheet, 2 each #198-199 2.75 2.75

Royal Wedding.

Queen Elizabeth II — A58

1981, Sept. 29 Photo. *Perf. 11½*
Granite paper

200 A58 £2 multicolored 4.75 4.75

Douglas War Memorial, Poppies, Quote from Laurence Binyon's For the Fallen — A59

1981, Sept. 29
Granite Paper

201 A59 8p shown .20 .20
202 A59 10p Maj. R.H. Cain, Battle of Arnhem, 1944 .25 .25
203 A59 18p Festival of Remembrance .55 .55
204 A59 20p Tynwald and Spitfire, Dunkirk, 1940 .65 .65
Nos. 201-204 (4) 1.65 1.65

Royal British Legion, 60th anniv.

Nativity Stained-glass Window, 1865, St. George's Church, Douglas — A60

9p: Christmas pageant, Glencrutchery Special School, Douglas.

1981, Sept. 29 Litho. *Perf. 14½x14*

205 A60 7p multicolored .25 .25

Size: 47x28mm

206 A60 9p multicolored .35 .35

Christmas and St. George's Church bicen. (7p), IYD (9p).

Scouting Year — A61

Designs: 9p, Cunningham House (Man Scout Headquarters). 10p, Baden-Powell's visit, 1911. 19½p, Portrait (32x41mm., Perf. 14½). 24p, Baden-Powell with scouts, message. 29p, Sign, handshake, globe, emblem.

1982, Feb. 23 Litho. *Perf. 13½x14*

207 A61 9p multicolored .20 .20
208 A61 10p multicolored .20 .20
209 A61 19½p multicolored .55 .55
210 A61 24p multicolored .70 .70
211 A61 29p multicolored .85 .85
Nos. 207-211 (5) 2.50 2.50

Europa 1982 — A62

Designs: 9p, Bishop Thomas Wilson (1663-1755) and his "The Principles and Duties of Christianity," first book printed in Manx, 1707. 19½p, Visit of Thomas, 2nd Earl of Derby, 1507.

1982, June 1 Photo. *Perf. 12½*
Granite Paper

212 A62 9p multicolored .25 .25
213 A62 19½p multicolored .55 .55

75th Anniv. of Tourist Trophy Motorcycle Races — A63

Designs: Winners on their bikes.

1982, June 1 Litho. *Perf. 14*

214 A63 9p Charlie Collier, 431 Matchless, 1907 .20 .20
215 A63 10p Freddie Dixon, Douglas, 1923 .20 .20
216 A63 24p Jimmie Simpson, Norton, 1932 .80 .80
217 A63 26p Mike Hailwood, Norton, 1961 .80 .80
218 A63 29p Jock Taylor, 700 Fowler Yamaha, '80 .80 .80
Nos. 214-218 (5) 2.80 2.80

Isle of Man Steam Packet Co. Mail Contract Sesquicentennial — A64

1982, Oct. 5 Litho. *Perf. 13½x14*

219 A64 12p Mona I .50 .50
220 A64 19½p Manx Maid II .75 .75

Christmas 1982
A65

Perf. 13¼x13½, 13½x13¼
1982, Oct. 5

221 A65 8p Three Kings .25 .25
222 A65 11p Robin, Christmas tree, vert. .45 .45

Souvenir Sheet

Princess Diana and Prince William — A66

1982, Oct. 12 *Perf. 14½x14¼*

223 A66 50p multicolored 2.00 2.00

Birth of Prince William of Wales (June 21) and 21st birthday of Princess Diana (July 1).

Marine Birds
A67

1983, Feb. 15 Litho. *Perf. 14½*

224 A67 1p Puffins, Cranstal .20 .20
225 A67 2p Gannets, Point of Ayre .20 .20
226 A67 5p Lesser black-backed gulls, Santon .20 .20
227 A67 8p Cormorants, Maughold Head .30 .30
228 A67 10p Kittiwakes, White Strand .40 .40
229 A67 11p Shags, Calf of Man .45 .45
230 A67 12p Herons, Douglas Foreshore .50 .50
231 A67 13p Herring gulls, Peel .55 .55
232 A67 14p Razorbills, Calf of Man .55 .55
233 A67 15p Great black-backed gulls, Calf of Man .60 .60
234 A67 16p Shelducks, Poyll Vaaish .65 .65
235 A67 18p Oystercatchers, Langness .70 .70

1983, Sept. 14 *Perf. 14*
Size: 39x25mm

236 A67 20p Arctic terns, Blue Point .80 .80
237 A67 25p Guillemots, Calf of Man 1.00 1.00
238 A67 50p Redshanks, Langness 1.75 1.75
239 A67 £1 Mute swans, Port St. Mary Bay 3.50 3.50
Nos. 224-239 (16) 12.35 12.35

Centenary of Salvation Army in Isle of Man — A68

Designs: 10p, Citadel opening ceremony, 1932, T.H. Cannell. 12p, Founder William Booth, early meeting place (former Unitarian Church, Douglas). 19½p, Band, Bandmaster Gordon Cowley, 1981. 26p, Lt.-Col. Thomas Bridson, treating lepers in Dutch East Indies.

1983, Feb. 15 Photo. *Perf. 11½*
Granite Paper

240 A68 10p multicolored .25 .25
241 A68 12p multicolored .35 .35
242 A68 19½ multicolored .60 .60
243 A68 26p multicolored .80 .80
Nos. 240-243 (4) 2.00 2.00

Europa 1983 — A69

1983, May 18 *Perf. 14*

244 A69 10p Laxey Wheel .40 .40
245 A69 20½p Designer Robert Casement .70 .70

King William's College Sesquicentennial — A70

Graduates: 10p, Nick Keig, Yachtsman. 12p, College, arms. 28p, William Bragg, 1915 Nobel Prize winner in physics, ionization spectrometer. 31p, Gen. George Stuart White, Defense of Ladysmith, Boer War.

1983, May 18 Photo. *Perf. 11½*
Granite Paper

246 A70 10p multicolored .20 .20
247 A70 12p multicolored .30 .30
248 A70 28p multicolored .80 .80
249 A70 31p multicolored .95 .95
Nos. 246-249 (4) 2.25 2.25

World Communications Year and 10th Anniv. of Post Office — A71

1983, July 5 Litho. *Perf. 15*

250 A71 10p New P.O. Headquarters .40 .40
251 A71 15p Viking landing, 938 .65 .65

Christmas 1983
A72

1983, Sept. 14 Litho. *Perf. 13x13½*

252 A72 9p Shepherds .40 .40
253 A72 12p Three Kings .50 .50

Karran Fleet
A73

Links with Falkland Islands — A74

1984, Feb. 14 Litho. *Perf. 14*

254 A73 10p Manx King, 1884 .30 .30
255 A73 13p Hope, 1858 .45 .45
256 A73 20½p Rio Grande, 1868 .65 .65
257 A73 28p Lady Elizabeth, 1879 1.10 1.10
258 A73 31p Sumatra, 1858 1.25 1.25
Nos. 254-258 (5) 3.75 3.75

1984, Feb. 14
259 Sheet of 2, #257, 259a 2.75 2.75
a. A74 31p multicolored 1.50 1.50

Europa (1959-1984) A75

1984, Apr. 27 Photo. Perf. 11½
260 A75 10p dk yel org, dk brn & buff .40 .40
261 A75 20½p blue, dk bl & lt bl .75 .75

DH-48, Ronaldsway Airport — A76

1984, Apr. 27 Litho. Perf. 14
262 A76 11p shown .35 .35
263 A76 13p DH-86, Calf of Man .40 .40
264 A76 26p DC-3, Ronaldsway Airport .75 .75
265 A76 28p Vickers Viscount, Douglas .75 .75
266 A76 31p Islander, Ronaldsway Airport .75 .75
Nos. 262-266 (5) 3.00 3.00

50th Anniv. of official airmail service and 40th anniv. of Intl. Civil Aviation Org.

William Cain as Mayor of Melbourne, 1886-87 — A77

1984, Sept. 21 Litho. Perf. 14½
267 A77 11p Ballasalla (birthplace) .35 .35
268 A77 22p Voyage to Australia .65 .65
269 A77 28p Railway, Victoria .80 .80
270 A77 30p shown .85 .85
271 A77 33p Royal Exhibition Buildings, Melbourne .95 .95
Nos. 267-271 (5) 3.60 3.60

William Cain (1831-1914), building contractor and public servant in Australia.

Queen Elizabeth II, CPA Emblem A78

1984, Sept. 21 Perf. 14
272 A78 14p shown .45 .45
273 A78 33p Arms, Elizabeth II 1.10 1.10

30th Conference of Commonwealth Parliamentary Assoc., Sept. 28-Oct. 5.

Christmas — A79

Stained-glass windows.

1984, Sept. 21
274 A79 10p Birds, Glencrutchery House .40 .40
275 A79 13p Arms, Lonan Old Church .50 .50

75th Anniv. of Girl Guides — A80

Designs: 11p, Cunningham House (headquarters), Mrs. W. and J. Cunningham (early Island Commissioners). 14p, Princess Margaret (president), color guard. 29p, Lady Olave Baden-Powell, headquarters opening. 31p, Uniforms, 1910-85. 34p, Sign, handclasp, trefoil.

1985, Jan. 31 Photo. Perf. 12
276 A80 11p multicolored .40 .40
277 A80 14p multicolored .50 .50
278 A80 29p multicolored .85 .85
279 A80 31p multicolored 1.00 1.00
280 A80 34p multicolored 1.25 1.25
Nos. 276-280 (5) 4.00 4.00

Elizabeth II A81

1985, Jan. 31 Litho. Perf. 14
281 A81 £5 multicolored 13.50 13.50

Europa 1985 — A82

Manx composers and excerpts from their works: No. 282a, "O'Land of our Birth." No. 282b, William H. Gill (1839-1922). No. 283a, Hymn "Crofton;" No. 283b, Dr. John Clague (1842-1908).

1985, Apr. 24 Photo. Perf. 12
282 A82 Pair 1.25 1.25
a.-b. 12p any single .65 .65
283 A82 Pair 1.50 1.50
a.-b. 22p any single .75 .75

Motoring — A83

Motor races and winning vehicles: No. 284a, 1906 Tourist Trophy Race. No. 284b, 1922 Tourist Trophy Race. No. 285a, 1950 British Empire Trophy Race. No. 285b, 1934 Manin Moar Race. No. 286a, 1984 Tourist Trophy Motorcycle Race (official car). No. 286b, 1981 Rothmans Manx Intl. Rally.

1985, May 25 Litho. Perf. 14
284 A83 Pair .90 .90
a.-b. 12p any single .45 .45
285 A83 Pair 1.25 1.25
a.-b. 14p any single .60 .60
286 A83 Pair 2.50 2.50
a.-b. 31p any single 1.25 1.25
Nos. 284-286 (3) 4.65 4.65

H.R.H. Alexandra (1885-1925), Princess of Wales — A84

SSA presidents: 15p, Queen Mary (1925-1953). 29p, Earl Mountbatten of Burma (1953-1979). 34p, Prince Michael of Kent (1982-).

1985, Sept. 4 Litho. Perf. 14
287 A84 12p multicolored .45 .45
288 A84 15p multicolored .60 .60
289 A84 29p multicolored 1.10 1.10
290 A84 34p multicolored 1.40 1.40
Nos. 287-290 (4) 3.55 3.55

Soldier's, Sailors' & Airmen's Families Assoc., cent.

Lt.-Gen. Sir Mark Cubbon, K.C.B. (1785-1861), Commissioner of Mysore — A85

1985, Oct. 2 Litho. Perf. 14
291 A85 12p Kirk Maughold Parish Church, 14th century .50 .50
292 A85 22p Portrait, vert. .90 .90
293 A85 45p Equestrian monument, 1866 Bangalore, India, vert. 1.75 1.75
Nos. 291-293 (3) 3.15 3.15

Christmas 1985 A86

1985, Oct. 2 Litho. Perf. 13½
294 A86 11p Onchan Parish Church, 1833 .40 .40
295 A86 14p St. John's Church .65 .65
296 A86 31p Bride Parish Church, 1876 1.50 1.50
Nos. 294-296 (3) 2.55 2.55

1986 Commonwealth Games, Edinburgh — A87

1986, Feb. 5 Litho. Perf. 14
297 A87 12p Women's swimming .40 .40
298 A87 15p Walking .50 .50
299 A87 31p Rifle shooting .95 .95
300 A87 34p Bicycling 1.25 1.25
Nos. 297-300 (4) 3.10 3.10

Viking Necklace, Peel Castle A88

Artifacts, architecture: 15p, Meayll Circle burial ground, Rushen. 22p, Prehistoric Cervus giganteus skeleton, Glose-y-Garey, vert. 26p, Norwegian viking longship, vert. 29p, Open-air Museum, Cregneash.

1986, Feb. 5 Perf. 14½x14, 14x14½
301 A88 12p multicolored .40 .40
302 A88 15p multicolored .45 .45
303 A88 22p multicolored .70 .70
304 A88 26p multicolored .85 .85
305 A88 29p multicolored 1.10 1.10
Nos. 301-305 (5) 3.50 3.50

Centenaries of Manx Museum and Ancient Monuments Act.

Europa 1986, Manx National Trust — A89

Designs: No. 306a, Bride hills and the Ayres. No. 306b, Calf of Man. No. 307a, Eary Cushlin. No. 307b, St. Michael's Isle.

1986, Apr. 10 Litho. Perf. 12
306 A89 Pair .90 .90
a.-b. 12p any single .45 .45
307 A89 Pair 1.60 1.60
a.-b. 22p any single .80 .80

Settling of Plymouth — A90

Designs: 12p, Ellanbane, Isle of Man, Myles Standish's home. 15p, The Mayflower. 31p, Pilgrims landing, 1620. 34p, Capt. Myles Standish (c. 1584-1656).

1986, May 22 Perf. 13½
308 A90 12p multicolored .40 .40
309 A90 15p multicolored .50 .50
310 A90 31p multicolored 1.10 1.10
311 A90 34p multicolored 1.25 1.25
a. Souvenir sheet of 2, #310-311, perf. 13x12½ 2.75 2.75
Nos. 308-311 (4) 3.25 3.25

AMERIPEX '86, Chicago, May 22-June 1.

Heritage Year — A91

1986, Apr. 10 Litho. Perf. 15x14
312 A91 2p Viking longship bow .20 .20
a. Bklt. pane of 6, 2 #312, 4 #313 4.50
313 A91 10p Celtic cross .90 .90
a. Bklt. pane of 3 + 3 labels 2.75

Issued in booklets only.

Wedding of Prince Andrew and Sarah Ferguson A92

1986, July 23
314 A92 15p Wedding date .70 .70
315 A92 40p Engagement date 1.60 1.60

Royal Birthdays — A93

No. 316: a, Prince Philip, 65. #b, Elizabeth II, 60. No. 317 is the same size as No. 316.

1986, Aug. 28 **Perf. 11½**

316 A93 Pair 1.40 1.40
a.-b. 15p any single .70 .70
317 A93 34p Royal couple 1.40 1.40

STOCKHOLMIA '86, Swedish Post Office 350th anniv. Stamps issued in sheets of 6.

Intl. Peace Year — A94

1986, Sept. 25 **Litho.** **Perf. 14**

318 A94 11p Robins, globe, Braille .45 .45
319 A94 14p Hands, dove .50 .50
320 A94 31p Hand-holding, sign language 1.00 1.00
Nos. 318-320 (3) 1.95 1.95

Accession of Queen Victoria to the British Throne, 150th Anniv. A95

Photographs of Victorian Douglas, by John Miller Nicholson.

1987, Jan. 21 **Litho.** **Perf. 14½**

321 A95 2p North Quay .20 .20
322 A95 3p The Old Fish Market .20 .20
323 A95 10p Breakwater .35 .35
a. Bklt. pane of 8 (2 2p, 2 3p, 4 10p) ('87) 1.90
324 A95 15p Jubilee Clock .55 .55
a. Bklt. pane of 8 (2 2p, 2 3p, 2 10p, 2 15p) ('87) 2.25
325 A95 31p Loch Promenade 1.25 1.25
326 A95 34p Beach 1.40 1.40
Nos. 321-326 (6) 3.95 3.95

No. 323a comes in two arrangements.

19th Century Paintings by John Miller Nicholson (1840-1913) — A96

Harbor scenes: 12p, The Old Fish Market and Harbor, Douglas. 26p, Red Sails at Douglas. 29p, The Double Corner. 34p, Peel Harbor.

1987, Feb. 18 **Perf. 13½**

327 A96 12p multicolored .45 .45
328 A96 26p multicolored .95 .95
329 A96 29p multicolored 1.00 1.00
330 A96 34p multicolored 1.25 1.25
Nos. 327-330 (4) 3.65 3.65

Promenade, Douglas — A97

1987, Apr. 29 **Litho.** **Perf. 13½**

331 A97 12p Sea Terminal, 1965 .65 .65
332 A97 12p Tower of Refuge, 1832 .65 .65
a. Pair, #331-332 1.25 1.25
333 A97 22p Gaiety Theater, c. 1900 1.00 1.00
334 A97 22p Villa Marina 1.00 1.00
a. Pair, #333-334 2.00 2.00
Nos. 331-334 (4) 3.30 3.30

Europa 1987.

Tourist Trophy Motorcycle Races, 80th Anniv. — A98

1987, May 27 **Perf. 13½x13**

335 A98 12p 1939 Supercharged BMW 500CC .45 .45
336 A98 15p 1953 Manx "Kneeler" Norton 350CC .60 .60
337 A98 29p 1956 MV Agusta 500CC 4 1.10 1.10
338 A98 31p 1957 Guzzi 500CC V8 1.25 1.25
339 A98 34p 1967 Honda 250CC 6 1.40 1.40
a. Souv. sheet of 5, #335-339 + 7 labels, perf 14x13½ 5.00 5.00
Nos. 335-339 (5) 4.80 4.80

Wildflowers — A99

1987, Sept. 9 **Litho.** **Perf. 14½x13½**

340 A99 16p Fuchsia, wild roses .55 .55
341 A99 29p Field scabius, ragwort 1.00 1.00
342 A99 31p Wood anemone, celandine 1.00 1.00
343 A99 34p Violets, primroses 1.10 1.10
Nos. 340-343 (4) 3.65 3.65

Christmas — A100

Victorian family scenes based on drawings by Alfred Hunt for The Illustrated London News, c. 1870-1890.

1987, Oct. 16 **Perf. 14**

344 A100 12p Stirring the pudding .45 .45
345 A100 15p Christmas tree selection .55 .55
346 A100 31p Decorating tree 1.25 1.25
Nos. 344-346 (3) 2.25 2.25

Railways & Tramways A101

Designs: 1p, Horse-drawn "Toast Rack" tram, Douglas Bay, 1884. 2p, No. 5 electric tram, Snaefell Mountain Railway, 1895. 3p, No. 3 open-top double-deck electric tram, Marine Drive-Port Soderick line, Douglas Southern Electric Tramway, 1896. 5p, Tower of Refuge and open tram, Douglas Head Incline Railway. 10p, Electric tram at Maughold Head, 1893, Douglas and Laxey Coast Electric Tramway. 13p, Douglas Cable Car No. 72, 1896. 14p, Manx Northern Railway No. 4 Caledonia, a Dubs 0-6-0T, 1885, at Gob-y-Deigan. 15p, Great Laxey Mine Railway Lewin steam engine Ant pulling coal cars. 16p, Henry B. Loch, first locomotive on the island, Port Erin Breakwater Railway, 1864. 17p, Locomotive No. 1, Ramsey Harbor Tramway. 18p, Engine No. 7 Tynwald, 1880, Foxdale Railway. 19p, Douglas Corp. engine, Baldwin Reservoir Railway. 20p, "Kissack" leaving St. John's for Peel. 25p, "Hutchinson" leaving Douglas Station. 50p, "Polar Bear" of Groudle Glen Railway. £1, The Royal Train.

1988 **Litho.** **Perf. 13½**

347 A101 1p multicolored .20 .20
348 A101 2p multicolored .20 .20
349 A101 3p multicolored .20 .20
350 A101 5p multicolored .20 .20
351 A101 10p multicolored .35 .35
352 A101 13p multicolored .50 .50
353 A101 14p multicolored .55 .55
354 A101 15p multicolored .55 .55
355 A101 16p multicolored .60 .60
a. Bklt. pane, 2 3p, 13p, 2 16p 1.90
b. Bklt. pane, 4 13p, 6 16p 5.75
356 A101 17p multicolored .60 .60
a. Bklt. pane, 2 3p, 2 14p, 17p 2.00
b. Booklet pane, 4 14p, 6 17p 5.75
357 A101 18p multicolored .65 .65
358 A101 19p multicolored .65 .65
e. Bklt. pane, 4 15p, 6 19p 6.00

Perf. 15

358A A101 20p multicolored .75 .75
358B A101 25p multicolored .85 .85
358C A101 50p multicolored 1.75 1.75
358D A101 £1 multicolored 3.50 3.50
Nos. 347-358D (16) 12.10 12.10

Stamps in Nos. 356a, 356b inscribed 1989. No. 358e inscribed 1990. Nos. 358C-358D exist inscribed "1992;" Nos. 349, 353 "1989;" No. 356 "1991."

Nos. 356a and 356b also exist in special booklet sheets of 50 stamps containing either 10 #356a or 5 #356b.

Issued: 1p-19p, 2/10; #355a-355b, 3/16; 20p-£1, 9/21; #356a, 356b, 10/16/89; #358e, 2/14/90.

See Nos. 448-459.

Car Racing — A102

Winning automobiles, drivers: 13p, Vauxhall Opel, Russell Brookes, 1985. 26p, Ford Escort, Ari Vatanen of Finland, 1976. 31p, Repco March 761, Terry Smith, 1980. 34p, Williams/Honda Nigel Mansell, 1986-87.

1988, Feb. 10 **Perf. 13½x14½**

359 A102 13p multicolored .60 .60
360 A102 26p multicolored 1.25 1.25
361 A102 31p multicolored 1.40 1.40
362 A102 34p multicolored 1.50 1.50
Nos. 359-362 (4) 4.75 4.75

Europa 1988 A103

Telecommunications: No. 363, IOM-UK optical fiber cable-laying plow. No. 364, Cable-laying ship. No. 365, 1st IOM Earth station, Braddan, established by Manx Telecom. No. 366, Intelsat V satellite.

1988, Apr. 14 **Litho.** **Perf. 14x13½**

363 A103 13p multicolored .60 .60
364 A103 13p multicolored .60 .60
a. Pair, #363-364 1.25 1.25
365 A103 22p multicolored 1.00 1.00
366 A103 22p multicolored 1.00 1.00
a. Pair, #365-366 2.00 2.00
Nos. 363-366 (4) 3.20 3.20

Submarine cable linking the Isle of Man and Silecroft in Cumbria, 1987 (13p). Nos. 364a, 366a have continuous designs.

Historic Ships Built on the Isle A104

Isle of Man flag, Australia bicen. emblem or US flag and: 16p, Euterpe, 1863, built in Ramsey. 29p, Vixen leaving Peel for Australia, 1853. 31p, Ramsey, an immigrant ship in Brisbane, 1870. 34p, Star of India (renamed in 1906, was the Euterpe), restored 1960-1976, Maritime Museum at San Diego.

1988, May 11 **Litho.** **Perf. 14**

367 A104 16p multicolored .60 .60
368 A104 29p multicolored 1.10 1.10
369 A104 31p multicolored 1.10 1.10
370 A104 34p multicolored 1.25 1.25
a. Souvenir sheet of 2 (16p, 34p) 2.75 2.75
Nos. 367-370 (4) 4.05 4.05

Fuchsia Blossoms — A105

1988, Sept. 21 **Litho.** **Perf. 13½x14**

371 A105 13p Magellanica .45 .45
372 A105 16p Pink cloud .55 .55
373 A105 22p Leonora .80 .80
374 A105 29p Satellite 1.00 1.00
375 A105 31p Preston Guild 1.10 1.10
376 A105 34p Thalia 1.25 1.25
Nos. 371-376 (6) 5.15 5.15

British Fuchsia Society, 50th anniv.

Christmas A106

1988, Oct. 12 **Perf. 14**

377 A106 12p Long-earred owl .75 .75
378 A106 15p Robin .90 .90
379 A106 31p Partridge 1.75 1.75
Nos. 377-379 (3) 3.40 3.40

Manx Cats A107

Various cats.

1989, Feb. 8

380 A107 16p multicolored .65 .65
381 A107 27p multicolored 1.10 1.10
382 A107 30p multicolored 1.40 1.40
383 A107 40p multicolored 1.60 1.60
Nos. 380-383 (4) 4.75 4.75

Celtic Works of Art by Archibald Knox (1864-1933) — A108

Designs: 13p, Tudric pewter and enamel clock, 1903, vert. 16p, Cross, a watercolor, vert. 23p, Silver tankard, 1902, vert. 32p, Liberty silver and Cymric gold brooches. 35p, Silver jewel box with inlaid turquoise, mother-of-pearl and enamel, 1900.

1989, Feb. 8 **Litho.** **Perf. 13**

384 A108 13p multicolored .50 .50
385 A108 16p multicolored .60 .60
386 A108 23p multicolored .85 .85
387 A108 32p multicolored 1.10 1.10
388 A108 35p multicolored 1.25 1.25
Nos. 384-388 (5) 4.30 4.30

Mutiny on the *Bounty* A109

Designs: 13p, William Bligh, Old Onchan Church. 16p, Bligh and crewmen cast adrift. 30p, Peter Heywood on Tahiti, 1770. 32p, *Bounty* off Pitcairn. 35p, Fletcher Christian on Pitcairn.

1989, Apr. 28 Litho. *Perf. 14*

389 A109 13p multicolored .45 .45
390 A109 16p multicolored .60 .60
391 A109 30p multicolored 1.00 1.00
392 A109 32p multicolored 1.10 1.10
393 A109 35p multicolored 1.25 1.25
Nos. 389-393 (5) 4.40 4.40

Souvenir Sheet

394 Sheet of 3 + label 4.50 4.50
a. A109 23p Pitcairn Isls. No. 321d .80 .80
b. A109 27p Norfolk Is. No. 453 .95 .95
c. Booklet pane, #394 4.50
d. Booklet pane, 1 each #389-394a 5.50
e. Bklt. pane of 6, #389-393, #394b 5.50
f. Booklet pane, 3 each #394a, #394b 5.25

See Norfolk Is. Nos. 452-456 and Pitcairn Isls. Nos. 320-322.

No. 394 contains Nos. 393, 394a-394b.

No. 394c is 145x101mm and is rouletted at left.

Europa 1989 A110

Children's games: No. 395, Jumping rope, hopscotch, London Bridge is falling down. No. 396, Running, wheelbarrow race, leap frog, piggyback ride. No. 397, Boy building fort, girl blowing soap bubbles, puzzle. No. 398, Doll house, blocks, girl playing with rag doll and puzzle.

1989, May 17 *Perf. 13½*

395 A110 13p multicolored .50 .50
396 A110 13p multicolored .50 .50
a. Pair, #395-396 1.00 1.00
397 A110 23p multicolored 1.00 1.00
398 A110 23p multicolored 1.00 1.00
a. Pair, #397-398 2.00 2.00
Nos. 395-398 (4) 3.00 3.00

Nos. 396a, 398a have continuous designs.

World Wildlife Fund — A111

1989, Sept. 20 Litho. *Perf. 14*

399 A111 13p Puffin .75 .75
400 A111 13p Black guillemot .75 .75
401 A111 13p Cormorant .75 .75
402 A111 13p Kittiwake .75 .75
a. Block or strip of 4, #399-402 3.00 3.00
Nos. 399-402 (4) 3.00 3.00

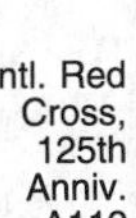

Intl. Red Cross, 125th Anniv. A112

1989, Oct. 16 Litho. *Perf. 14*

403 A112 14p Training youths .50 .50
404 A112 17p Emblems .60 .60
405 A112 23p Signing 1st Geneva convention, 1864 .85 .85
406 A112 30p Ambulance services 1.00 1.00
407 A112 35p Henri Dunant, founder 1.25 1.25
Nos. 403-407 (5) 4.20 4.20

Noble's Hospital, Douglas, cent.

Christmas — A113

1989, Oct. 16 *Perf. 14½x15*

408 A113 13p Maternity home .45 .45
409 A113 16p Mother and child .55 .55
410 A113 34p Madonna and child, scripture 1.25 1.25
411 A113 37p Church, baptismal ceremony 1.40 1.40
Nos. 408-411 (4) 3.65 3.65

Jane Crookall Maternity Home 50th anniv. (13p) and 75th anniv. of the consecration of St. Ninian's Church (37p).

Queen Elizabeth II, Lord of Man, Trooping the Colors — A114

1990, Feb. 14 Litho. *Perf. 14½*

412 A114 £2 multicolored 5.25 5.25

Humorous Edwardian Postcards — A115

15p, The Isle of Man Express Going Up a Gradient. 19p, A Way We Have in the Isle of Man. 32p, Douglas -- Waiting for the Male Boat. 34p, The Last Toast Rack Home Douglas Parade. 37p, The Last Isle of Man Boat.

1990, Feb. 14 *Perf. 14*

413 A115 15p multicolored .50 .50
414 A115 19p multicolored .65 .65
415 A115 32p multicolored 1.10 1.10
416 A115 34p multicolored 1.25 1.25
417 A115 37p multicolored 1.40 1.40
Nos. 413-417 (5) 4.90 4.90

Europa 1990 — A116

Mailmen and post offices.

1990, Apr. 18 Litho. *Perf. 13½*
Size of Nos. 419, 421: 42x28mm

418 A116 15p Mailman, 1990 .60 .60
419 A116 15p Ramsey P.O., 1990 .60 .60
a. Pair, #418-419 1.25 1.25
420 A116 24p Mailman, c. 1890 .95 .95
421 A116 24p Douglas P.O., c. 1890 .95 .95
a. Pair, #420-421 1.90 1.90
Nos. 418-421 (4) 3.10 3.10

Great Britain No. 1 — A117

Designs: 19p, Wyon Medal. 32p, William Wyon's essay. 34p, Perkins Bacon engine-turned essay of 1839. 37p, Great Britain No. 2.

No. 423 (various Penny Blacks and text): a.-e. Positions AA-AE. f.-j. Positions BA-BE. k.-n. Positions CA-CE. p.-t. Positions DA-DE. u.-y. Positions EA-EE.

Note that A-A top of square on No. 423a, centered on No. 422a.

1990, May 3 Litho. *Perf. 14x13½*

422 Pane of 5 4.75 4.75
a. A117 1p shown .20 .20
b. A117 19p multicolored .70 .70
c. A117 32p multicolored 1.25 1.25
d. A117 34p multicolored 1.25 1.25
e. A117 37p multicolored 1.40 1.40
g. Bklt. pane, 2 each #422b-422e 9.50
h. No. 422 ovptd. "From STAMP WORLD LONDON '90 / To NEW ZEALAND '90" 14.00 14.00

Miniature Sheet

423 Sheet of 25 2.50 2.50
a.-y. A117 1p like #422a, any single .20 .20
z. Pane of 8, #a.-d., f.-i. .55

Souvenir Sheet
Litho. & Engr.

424 A117 £1 4 Great Britain #1 3.50 3.50
a. Booklet pane of 1 3.50 3.50

Left margin of #422g, 423z and 424a rouletted.

Queen Mother, 90th Birthday — A118

1990, Aug. 4 Litho. *Perf. 13x13½*

425 A118 90p multicolored 3.00 3.00

Sheets of 10 alternating with 10 labels.

Battle of Britain, 50th Anniv. A119

1990, Sept. 5 Litho. *Perf. 14*

426 A119 15p Home defense .70 .70
427 A119 15p Air sea rescue .70 .70
a. Pair, #426-427 1.40 1.40
428 A119 24p Rearming fighters 1.00 1.00
429 A119 24p Height of battle 1.00 1.00
a. Pair, #428-429 2.00 2.00
430 A119 29p Civil defense 1.25 1.25
431 A119 29p Anti-aircraft defense 1.25 1.25
a. Pair, #430-431 2.50 2.50
Nos. 426-431 (6) 5.90 5.90

Sir Winston Churchill (1874-1965) — A120

1990, Sept. 5 *Perf. 13½*

432 A120 19p multicolored .65 .65
433 A120 32p multicolored 1.10 1.10
434 A120 34p multicolored 1.25 1.25
435 A120 37p multicolored 1.25 1.25
Nos. 432-435 (4) 4.25 4.25

Christmas — A121

1990, Oct. 10 *Perf. 13x13½*

436 A121 14p Mailing letters .50 .50
437 A121 18p Sledding, skating .65 .65
438 A121 34p Snowman 1.10 1.10
439 A121 37p Throwing snowball 1.25 1.25
a. Souvenir sheet of 4, #436-439 4.00 4.00
Nos. 436-439 (4) 3.50 3.50

Denominations on stamps in No. 439a are black.

Manx Photographers A122

Designs: 17p, Henry Bloom Noble, by Marshall Wane. 21p, Douglas, by Frederic Frith & Co. 26p, Studio Portrait, by Hilda Newby. 31p, Cashtal yn Ard, by Christopher Killip. 40p, Peel, by Colleen Corlett.

1991, Jan. 6 Litho. *Perf. 14x14½*

440 A122 17p multicolored .60 .60
441 A122 21p multicolored .70 .70
442 A122 26p multicolored .90 .90
443 A122 31p multicolored 1.10 1.10
444 A122 40p multicolored 1.40 1.40
Nos. 440-444 (5) 4.70 4.70

Railways and Tramways Type of 1988 with Queen's Head in White (#448, 458-459)

Designs: 18p, TPO Special leaving Douglas Station, 1991. 23p, Double decker horse tram.

1991-92 Litho. *Perf. 13½*

448 A101 4p like No. 352 .20 .20
456 A101 18p multicolored .65 .65
458 A101 21p like No. 353 .85 .85
a. Souv. sheet, 2 each #448, #458 2.25 2.25
b. Bklt. pane, #458, 3 #448, 4 #356 3.75
c. Booklet pane, 3 #448, 1 each #356, #458 1.90
459 A101 23p multicolored .80 .80
a. Bklt. pane, 6 #456, 4 #459 7.25
Nos. 448-459 (4) 2.50 2.50

No. 458a for Ninth Conf. of Commonwealth Postal Administrations, Douglas, Isle of Man.

Issued: 4p, 21p, #458b, 458c, 1/9; #458a, 7/1; 18p, 23p, #459a, 1/8/92.

No. 458b exists in special booklet sheets containing 5 #458b and 5 each #448, #458.

No. 458b dated 1991.

Manx Lifeboats A123

1991, Feb. 13 *Perf. 14*

463 A123 17p Sir William Hillary .60 .60
464 A123 21p Osman Gabriel .75 .75
465 A123 26p James & Ann Ritchie .90 .90
466 A123 31p The Gough Ritchie 1.10 1.10
467 A123 37p John Batstone 1.25 1.25
Nos. 463-467 (5) 4.60 4.60

Europa — A124

1991, Apr. 24 Litho. *Perf. 14*

468 A124 17p Satellites .75 .75
469 A124 17p Boats, Ariane rocket .75 .75
a. Vert. pair, #468-469 1.50 1.50
470 A124 26p Satellites, diff. 1.10 1.10
471 A124 26p Space shuttle, jet 1.10 1.10
a. Vert. pair, #470-471 2.25 2.25
Nos. 468-471 (4) 3.70 3.70

Tourist Trophy Mountain Course, 80th Anniv. A125

Designs: 17p, Oliver Godfrey, Indian 500cc, Bray Hill, 1911. 21p, Freddie Dixon, Douglas banking sidecar, Ballacraine, 1923. 26p, Bill Ivy, Yamaha 125cc, Waterworks, 1968. 31p, Giacomo Agostini, MV Agusta 500cc, Creg-ny-Baa, 1972. 37p, Joey Dunlop, RVF Honda 750cc, Ballaugh Bridge, 1985.

1991, May 30 Litho. *Perf. 14½x13*

472 A125 17p multicolored .60 .60
473 A125 21p multicolored .75 .75
474 A125 26p multicolored .90 .90
475 A125 31p multicolored 1.10 1.10
476 A125 37p multicolored 1.25 1.25
a. Souv. sheet of 5, #472-476 + 7 labels 4.75 4.75

b. As "a," ovptd. in black & red in sheet margin 6.50 6.50
Nos. 472-476 (5) 4.60 4.60

No. 476b overprint includes show emblem and "PHILA / NIPPON '91."

Issue date: No. 476b, Nov. 16.

Fire Engines A126

Designs: 17p, Laxey hand cart. 21p, Douglas horse drawn steamer. 30p, Merryweather Hatfield pump. 33p, Dennis F8 pumping appliance. 37p, Volvo turntable ladder.

1991, Sept. 18 Litho. *Perf. 14½*

477 A126 17p multicolored .55 .55
478 A126 21p multicolored .75 .75
479 A126 30p multicolored 1.00 1.00
480 A126 33p multicolored 1.10 1.10
481 A126 37p multicolored 1.25 1.25
Nos. 477-481 (5) 4.65 4.65

Swans A127

Designs: No. 482, Mute swans, Douglas Harbor. No. 483, Black swans, Curraghs Wildlife Park. No. 484, Whooper swans, Bishops Dub, Ballaugh. No. 485, Bewick's swans, Eairy Dam, Foxdale. No. 486, Coscaroba swans, Curraghs Wildlife Park. No. 487, Trumpeter swans.

1991, Sept. 18 *Perf. 13*

482 A127 17p multicolored .55 .55
483 A127 17p multicolored .55 .55
a. Pair, #482-483 1.10 1.10
484 A127 26p multicolored .85 .85
485 A127 26p multicolored .85 .85
a. Pair, #484-485 1.75 1.75
486 A127 37p multicolored 1.25 1.25
487 A127 37p multicolored 1.25 1.25
a. Pair, #486-487 2.50 2.50
Nos. 482-487 (6) 5.30 5.30

Pairs have continuous designs.

Christmas — A128

1991, Oct. 14 *Perf. 14x14½*

488 A128 16p Three kings .55 .55
489 A128 20p Jesus in manger, Mary .70 .70
490 A128 26p Shepherds .90 .90
491 A128 37p Angels 1.25 1.25
Nos. 488-491 (4) 3.40 3.40

Litho.

Die Cut

Self-Adhesive Booklet Stamps

492 A128 16p like #488 1.00 1.00
493 A128 20p like #489 1.25 1.25
a. Bklt. pane, 8 #492, 4 #493 13.50 13.50

Queen Elizabeth II's Accession to the Throne, 40th Anniv. — A129

Various portraits of Queen Elizabeth II.

1992, Feb. 6 Litho. *Perf. 14*

494 A129 18p multicolored .60 .60
495 A129 23p multicolored .80 .80
496 A129 28p multicolored 1.00 1.00
497 A129 33p multicolored 1.10 1.10
498 A129 39p multicolored 1.40 1.40
Nos. 494-498 (5) 4.90 4.90

Parachute Regiment, 50th Anniv. A130

Designs: No. 499, North Africa & Italy, 1942-43. No. 500, Operation Overlord, Normandy, 1944. No. 501, Operation Market Garden, Arnhem, 1944. No. 502, Operation Varsity, Rhine, 1945. No. 503, Near, Middle and Far East, 1945-68. No. 504, Operation Corporate, Falkland Islands, 1982, and Utrinque Paratus, 1992.

1992, Feb. 6 *Perf. 14*

499 A130 23p multicolored .80 .80
500 A130 23p multicolored .80 .80
a. Pair, #499-500 1.60 1.60
501 A130 28p multicolored 1.00 1.00
502 A130 28p multicolored 1.00 1.00
a. Pair, #501-502 2.00 2.00
503 A130 39p multicolored 1.50 1.50
504 A130 39p multicolored 1.50 1.50
a. Pair, #503-504 3.00 3.00
Nos. 499-504 (6) 6.60 6.60

Printed in sheets of 8.

Pilgrims' Voyage to America, 1620 — A131

Europa: No. 505, Pilgrims in longboats. No. 506, Speedwell, Delfshaven, Holland. No. 507, Mayflower. No. 508, Speedwell, Dartmouth, England.

1992, Apr. 16 Litho. *Perf. 14x13½*

505 A131 18p multicolored .75 .75
506 A131 18p multicolored .75 .75
a. Pair, #505-506 1.50 1.50
507 A131 28p multicolored 1.50 1.50
508 A131 28p multicolored 1.50 1.50
a. Pair, #507-508 3.00 3.00
Nos. 505-508 (4) 4.50 4.50

Nos. 506a, 508a have continuous design.

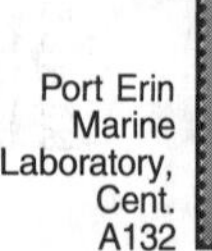

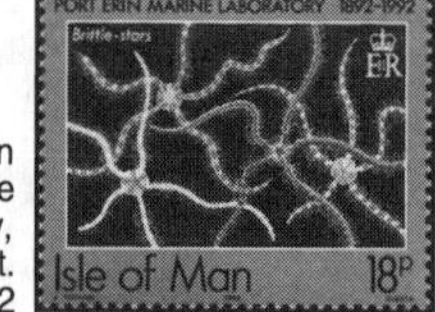

Port Erin Marine Laboratory, Cent. A132

1992, Apr. 16 *Perf. 14½*

509 A132 18p Brittle stars .65 .65
510 A132 23p Phytoplankton .85 .85
511 A132 28p Herring 1.00 1.00
512 A132 33p Great scallop 1.10 1.10
513 A132 39p Dahlia anemone, delesseria 1.40 1.40
Nos. 509-513 (5) 5.00 5.00

Union Pacific, First Transcontinental Railroad — A133

#514, "Jupiter," 1869. #515, "#119," 1869. #516, "#844," 1992. #517, "#3985," 1992. £1.50, Golden Spike Ceremony, Union Pacific and Central Pacific Railroads, 1869.

1992, May 22 Litho. *Perf. 13½x14*

514 A133 33p multicolored 1.10 1.10
515 A133 33p multicolored 1.10 1.10
a. Pair, #514-515 + label 2.25 2.25
516 A133 39p multicolored 1.40 1.40
517 A133 39p multicolored 1.40 1.40
a. Pair, #516-517 + label 3.00 3.00
b. Bklt. pane, 1 ea #515a, 517a 5.25

Souvenir Sheet

518 A133 £1.50 multicolored 5.25 5.25
a. Booklet pane, #518 5.25
b. Bklt. pane, #518a, 2 #517b 16.00

World Columbian Stamp Expo '92. No. 518 contains one 60x50mm stamp.

Nos. 514-515 and 516-517 issued in sheets of 10.

Nos. 515a, 517a have 3 different labels. No. 517b exists with two different pairs of labels. No. 518a has a rouletted white border at left and right.

Manx Harbors — A134

#519, King Orry, Douglas Harbor. 23p, Castletown Harbor. 37p, Port St. Mary Harbor. 40p, Ramsey Harbor. a, King Orry. b, St. Eloi. Illustration reduced.

1992, Sept. 18 Litho. *Perf. 14½x14*

519 A134 18p multicolored .60 .60
520 A134 23p multicolored .75 .75
521 A134 37p multicolored 1.25 1.25
522 A134 40p multicolored 1.40 1.40
Nos. 519-522 (4) 4.00 4.00

Souvenir Sheet

523 Sheet of 2 4.00 4.00
a. A134 18p multicolored .60 .60
b. A134 £1 multicolored 3.25 3.25

Genoa '92. #523 contains 30x24mm stamps.

Christmas — A135

Designs: 17p, Nativity window, St. German's Cathedral, Peel. 22p, Adoration of the Magi panel, St. Matthew's Church, Douglas. 28p, Nativity window, St. George's Church, Douglas. 37p, Reredos of The Annunciation, St. Mary of the Isle, Douglas. 40p, Good Shepherd window, Trinity Methodist Church, Douglas.

1992, Oct. 13 Litho. *Perf. 14½*

524 A135 17p multicolored .50 .50
525 A135 22p multicolored .70 .70
526 A135 28p multicolored .90 .90
527 A135 37p multicolored 1.10 1.10
528 A135 40p multicolored 1.25 1.25
Nos. 524-528 (5) 4.45 4.45

Nigel Mansell, Formula I World Champion, 1992 A136

Williams Renault FW 14B at: 20p, British Grand Prix, 1992. 24p, French Grand Prix, 1992.

1992, Nov. 8 *Perf. 13½*

529 A136 20p multicolored .80 .80
530 A136 24p multicolored .95 .95

Ships A137

British Red Ensign A137a

Queen Elizabeth II — A137b

1993-96 Litho. *Perf. 13½*

531 A137 1p HMS Amazon .20 .20
532 A137 2p Fingal .20 .20
533 A137 4p Sir Winston Churchill .20 .20
534 A137 5p Dar Mlodziezy .20 .20
543 A137 20p Tynwald I .40 .40
544 A137 21p Ben Veg .50 .50
545 A137 22p Waverley .50 .50
546 A137 23p HMY Britannia .55 .55
a. Souv. sheet of 1, Perf. 13 .90 .90
547 A137 24p Francis Drake .50 .50
a. Bklt. pane, 4 #543, 6 #547 5.00
b. Bklt. pane, 2 #543, 3 #547 2.50
548 A137 25p Royal Viking Sky .60 .60
a. Booklet pane, 2 #533, 2 #544, 2 #548 3.75
Complete booklet, #548a 3.75
549 A137 26p Lord Nelson .65 .65
550 A137 27p Europa .65 .65
551 A137 30p Snaefell V .75 .75
551A A137 35p Sea Cat .85 .85
552 A137 40p Lady of Man 1.00 1.00
553 A137 50p Mona's Queen II 1.25 1.25
553A A137 £1 QE2, Mona's Queen V 2.50 2.50

Perf. 14½

553B A137a £2 multicolored 3.50 3.50
553C A137b £5 multicolored 15.00 15.00
Nos. 531-553C (19) 30.00 30.00

#546a, for return of Hong Kong to China, is wmk. 373.

No. 553C has a holographic image. Soaking in water may affect the hologram.

Issued: 1p-5p, 20p-27p, 1/4/93; 30p, 40p-£1, 9/15/93; £2, 1/24/94; £5, 7/5/94; 35p, 1/11/96; #546a, 7/1/97; #548a, 1997.

Nos. 533, 543, 547 exist dated "1995;" Nos. 544, 546, 548, 548a, 553A dated "1997."

See Nos. 683-697.

Manx Electric Railway, Cent. — A138

20p, #13 trailer, #1 motor car. 24p, #19 trailer, #9 tunnel car. 28p, #59 Royal trailer special saloon car, #19 motor car. 39p, #33 motor car, #45 trailer, #13 small van.

Illustration reduced.

1993, Feb. 3 *Perf. 14*

554 A138 20p multicolored .65 .65
555 A138 24p multicolored .75 .75
556 A138 28p multicolored .95 .95
557 A138 39p multicolored 1.00 1.00
a. Booklet pane of #554-557 3.50 3.50
Nos. 554-557 (4) 3.35 3.35

No. 557a exists with four different marginal inscriptions and in four different arrangements.

Contemporary Art by Bryan Kneale — A139

Europa: No. 558, Statue of Sir Hall Caine. No. 559, Painting, The Brass Bedstead. No. 560, Abstract bronze. No. 561, Drawing of polar bear skeleton.

1993, Apr. 14 Litho. *Perf. 14*

558 A139 20p multicolored .70 .70
559 A139 20p multicolored .70 .70
a. Pair, #558-559 1.40 1.40
560 A139 28p multicolored .80 .80
561 A139 28p multicolored .80 .80
a. Pair, #560-561 1.60 1.60
Nos. 558-561 (4) 3.00 3.00

Motorcycling Events — A140

Riders and events: 20p, Gold Medalists Graham Oates, Bill Marshall, Intl. Six-Day Trial, 1933, Ariel Square Four. 24p, Geoff Duke, Team Sergeant, Royal Signals Display Team, 1947, Triumph Twin. 28p, Denis Parkinson, winner of Senior Manx Grand Prix, 1953, Manx Norton. 33p, Richard Swallow, winner of Junior Classic Manx Grand Prix, 1991, Aermacchi. 39p, Steve Colley, winner of Scottish Six-Day Trial, 1992, Beta Zero.

1993, June 3 Litho. *Perf. 13½x14*

562 A140 20p multicolored .65 .65
563 A140 24p multicolored .70 .70
564 A140 28p multicolored .85 .85
565 A140 33p multicolored 1.00 1.00
566 A140 39p multicolored 1.10 1.10
a. Souv. sheet of 5, #562-566 + 4 labels 4.50 4.50
Nos. 562-566 (5) 4.30 4.30

Butterflies A141

1993, Sept. 15 Litho. *Perf. 14½*

567 A141 24p Dark green fritillary .70 .70
568 A141 24p Painted lady .70 .70
569 A141 24p Holly blue .70 .70
570 A141 24p Red admiral .70 .70
571 A141 24p Peacock .70 .70
a. Strip of 5, #567-571 3.50 3.50

Christmas — A142

Designs: 19p, Children decorating Christmas tree. 23p, Snowman, girl. 28p, Boy unwrapping presents. 39p, Girl, teddy bear. 40p, Girl with holly basket, boy on sled.

1993, Oct. 12 *Perf. 14*

572 A142 19p multicolored .55 .55
573 A142 23p multicolored .65 .65
574 A142 28p multicolored .80 .80
575 A142 39p multicolored 1.10 1.10
576 A142 40p multicolored 1.10 1.10
Nos. 572-576 (5) 4.20 4.20

Tourism A143

No. 577, Gaiety Theatre, Douglas. No. 578, Field hockey, golf, soccer (#577). No. 579, Yacht racing, artist's hand painting picture of castle (#580). No. 580, TT Motorcycle Races, Red Arrows demonstration squadron. (#581). No. 581, Musical instruments. No. 582, Laxey Wheel, Manx cat. No. 583, Tower of Refuge, beach, sand bucket (#584). No. 584, Cyclist. No. 585, Tynwald Day, classic racing car (#579, 580, 584, 586). No. 586, Santa Claus riding Mince Pie Train, Groudle Glen.

1994, Feb, 18 Litho. *Perf. 13½*

Booklet Stamps

577 A143 24p multicolored .65 .65
578 A143 24p multicolored .65 .65
579 A143 24p multicolored .65 .65
580 A143 24p multicolored .65 .65
581 A143 24p multicolored .65 .65
582 A143 24p multicolored .65 .65
583 A143 24p multicolored .65 .65
584 A143 24p multicolored .65 .65
585 A143 24p multicolored .65 .65
586 A143 24p multicolored .65 .65
a. Booklet pane of 10, #577-586 6.50

Birds A144

Magpie, Calf of Man Bird Observatory — A145

1994, Feb. 18 *Perf. 14*

587 A144 20p White-throated robin .60 .60
588 A144 20p Black-eared wheatear .60 .60
a. Pair, #587-588 1.25 1.25
589 A144 24p Goldcrest .70 .70
590 A144 24p Northern oriole .70 .70
a. Pair, #589-590 1.40 1.40
591 A144 30p Kingfisher .95 .95
592 A144 30p Hoopoe .95 .95
a. Pair, #591-592 1.90 1.90
Nos. 587-592 (6) 4.50 4.50

Souvenir Sheet

Perf. 13½x13

593 A145 £1 shown 2.75 2.75

Hong Kong '94 (#593).

Europa A146

Designs: No. 594, Eubranchus tricolor. No. 595, Loligo forbesii. No. 596, Edward Forbes (1815-54), naturalist. No. 597, Solaster moretonis. No. 598, Adamsia carciniopados on hermit crab. No. 599, Solaster endeca.

1994, May 5 Litho. *Perf. 13¼x14½*

594 A146 20p multicolored .55 .55
595 A146 20p multicolored .55 .55
596 A146 20p multicolored .55 .55
a. Strip of 3, #594-596 1.75 1.75
597 A146 30p multicolored .90 .90
598 A146 30p multicolored .90 .90
599 A146 30p multicolored .90 .90
a. Strip of 3, #597-599 2.75 2.75

D-Day, 50th Anniv. A147

Designs: No. 600, Transport Ben-My-Chree IV, landing ships, US Maj. Gen. Walter Bedell Smith. No. 601, Transports Victoria, Lady of Mann I, Adm. Sir Bertram Ramsay, RN, Naval Commander. No. 602, Infantry, tanks on Gold, Juno, Sword Beaches, Gen. Montgomery, Commander, 21st Army Group. No. 603, Tanks, landing craft on Gold, Juno, Sword Beaches, Lt. Gen. Sir Miles C. Dempsey, Commander, British 2nd Army. No. 604, US 8th, 9th Air Forces, Air Chief Marshal Sir Trafford Leigh-Mallory, RAF, Air Force Commander. No. 605, Air Chief Marshall Sir Arthur Tedder, RAF, Deputy Supreme Allied Commander, RAF 2nd Tactical Air Force & Bomber Command. No. 606, Landing craft, Omaha, Utah Beaches, Lt. Gen. Omar N. Bradley, Commander, US 1st Army. No. 607, Infantry, tanks on Omaha, Utah Beaches, Gen. Eisenhower, Supreme Allied Commander.

1994, June 6 Litho. *Perf. 14*

600 A147 4p multicolored .20 .20
601 A147 4p multicolored .20 .20
a. Pair, #600-601 .25 .25
602 A147 20p multicolored .60 .60
603 A147 20p multicolored .60 .60
a. Pair, #602-603 1.25 1.25
604 A147 30p multicolored .95 .95
605 A147 30p multicolored .95 .95
a. Pair, #604-605 1.90 1.90
606 A147 41p multicolored 1.25 1.25
607 A147 41p multicolored 1.25 1.25
a. Pair, #606-607 2.50 2.50
Nos. 600-607 (8) 6.00 6.00

Nos. 601a, 603a, 605a, 607a are continuous designs.

Postman Pat A148

Postman Pat at: 1p, Sea Terminal, Douglas. 20p, Laxey Wheel. 24p, Cregneash. 30p, Manx Electric Railway. 36p, Peel Harbor. 41p, Tourist office, Douglas Promenade.
£1, Postman Pat.

1994, Sept. 14 Litho. *Perf. 14½x14*

608 A148 1p multicolored .20 .20
a. Booklet pane of 2 .20
609 A148 20p multicolored .60 .60
a. Booklet pane of 2 1.25
610 A148 24p multicolored .75 .75
a. Booklet pane of 2 1.50
611 A148 30p multicolored .90 .90
a. Booklet pane of 2 1.90
612 A148 36p multicolored 1.10 1.10
a. Booklet pane of 2 2.25
613 A148 41p multicolored 1.25 1.25
a. Booklet pane of 2 2.50
Nos. 608-613 (6) 4.80 4.80

Souvenir Sheet

614 A148 £1 multicolored 3.00 3.00
a. Booklet pane of 1 3.00 3.00

No. 614a is rouletted 9 at left.

Intl. Olympic Committee, Cent. — A149

1994, Oct. 11 *Perf. 14*

615 A149 10p Cycling .30 .30
616 A149 20p Alpine skiing .60 .60
617 A149 24p Swimming .75 .75
618 A149 35p Steeplechase 1.10 1.10
619 A149 48p Emblem 1.40 1.40
Nos. 615-619 (5) 4.15 4.15

A150

1994, Oct. 11

Christmas: 19p, Santa, Mrs. Claus greeting children on Santa Train to Santon, horiz. 23p, Santa Claus on tractor, Postman Pat. 60p, Santa Claus arriving by boat, Port St. Mary, horiz.

620 A150 19p multicolored .65 .65
621 A150 23p multicolored .85 .85
622 A150 60p multicolored 1.50 1.50
Nos. 620-622 (3) 3.00 3.00

Snaefell Mountain Electric Railway, Cent. — A151

Designs: 20p, Opening day, Car No. 2. 24p, Car 3 ascending Laxey Valley, Car 4 in green livery. 35p, Car 5, Car 6. 42p, Caledonia on construction duty, Goods Car 7.
£1, Bungalow Hotel & Station, Snaefell.
Illustration reduced.

1995, Feb. 8 Litho. *Perf. 14*

623 A151 20p multicolored .65 .65
624 A151 24p multicolored .80 .80
625 A151 35p multicolored 1.10 1.10
626 A151 42p multicolored 1.40 1.40
Nos. 623-626 (4) 3.95 3.95

Souvenir Sheet

Perf. 14x13½

627 A151 £1 multicolored 3.25 3.25
a. Sheet from souvenir booklet 3.25 3.25

No. 627 contains one 61x38mm stamp.

No. 627a is rouletted in margin at left with additional vertical sheet margin inscriptions. At left is a description of the design. At right is "1895-Centenary Snaefell Mountain Railway-1995."

Steam-Powered Vehicles — A152

Designs: 20p, Foden Wagon, 5 ton. 24p, Clayton & Shuttleworth, 7hp, Fowler, 6hp. 30p, Wallis & Steevens, 6hp. 35p, Marshall, 6hp. 41p, Marshall Convertible, 5hp.

1995, Feb. 8 *Perf. 13½*

628 A152 20p multicolored .65 .65
629 A152 24p multicolored .80 .80
630 A152 30p multicolored .95 .95
631 A152 35p multicolored 1.10 1.10
632 A152 41p multicolored 1.25 1.25
Nos. 628-632 (5) 4.75 4.75

Peace & Freedom — A153

Europa: 20p, Flight of doves forming tidal wave, Tower of Refuge, Douglas Bay. 30p, Dove with olive branch breaking barbed wire.

1995, Apr. 28 Litho. *Perf. 13½*
633 A153 20p multicolored .65 .65
634 A153 30p multicolored .95 .95

VE Day, 50th Anniv. A154

Designs: No. 635, Spitfire, tank, 1939-45 Star, African Star. No. 636, France and Germany Star, Italy Star, Hawker Typhoon, artillery. No. 637, Lancaster bomber, aircraft carrier, Air Crew Europe Star, Atlantic Star. No. 638, Pacific Star, Burma Star, Avenger torpedo bomber, soldiers. No. 639, Parliament, Manx flag. No. 640, British flag, crowd celebrating. No. 641, Children celebrating at street party, Manx flag. No. 642, British flag, visit of Queen Elizabeth, King George VI, 1945.

1995, May 8 *Perf. 14*
635 A154 10p multicolored .35 .35
636 A154 10p multicolored .35 .35
a. Pair, #635-636 .65 .65
637 A154 20p multicolored .65 .65
638 A154 20p multicolored .65 .65
a. Pair, #637-638 1.25 1.25
639 A154 24p multicolored .75 .75
640 A154 24p multicolored .75 .75
a. Pair, #639-640 1.50 1.50
641 A154 40p multicolored 1.25 1.25
642 A154 40p multicolored 1.25 1.25
a. Pair, #641-642 2.50 2.50
Nos. 635-642 (8) 6.00 6.00

British Motor Car Racing, 90th Anniv. A155

Tourist Trophy Race drivers, cars: 20p, R. Parnell, 1951 Maserati 4 CLT. 24p, S. Moss, 1951 Frazer Nash. 30p, R.J.B. Seaman, 1936 Delage. 36p, Prince Bira, 1937 ERA R2B Romulus. 41p, K. Lee Guinness, 1914 Sunbeam 1. 42p, F. Dixon, 1934 Riley.
£1, John S. Napier, 1905 Arrol Johnston.

1995, May 8
643 A155 20p multicolored .65 .65
644 A155 24p multicolored .75 .75
645 A155 30p multicolored .95 .95
646 A155 36p multicolored 1.10 1.10
647 A155 41p multicolored 1.25 1.25
648 A155 42p multicolored 1.40 1.40
Nos. 643-648 (6) 6.10 6.10

Souvenir Sheet

649 A155 £1 multicolored 3.25 3.25

No. 649 contains one 47x58mm stamp.

Mushrooms A156

Designs: 20p, Amanita muscaria. 24p, Boletus edulis. 30p, Coprinus disseminatus. 35p, Pleurotus ostreatus. 45p, Geastrum triplex.
£1, Shaggy ink cap, bee orchid.

1995, Sept. 1 Litho. *Perf. 13½x14*
650 A156 20p multicolored .65 .65
651 A156 24p multicolored .75 .75
652 A156 30p multicolored .95 .95
653 A156 35p multicolored 1.10 1.10
654 A156 45p multicolored 1.40 1.40
Nos. 650-654 (5) 4.85 4.85

Souvenir Sheet

Perf. 14x13½

655 A156 £1 multicolored 3.25 3.25

No. 655 contains one 51x60mm stamp. Singapore '95 (#655).

Thomas the Tank Engine A157

Designs: 20p, Bertie arrives on the quayside. 24p, Mail train and Thomas. 30p, Bertie and trains at Ballasalla. 36p, Viking and Thomas at Port Erin. 41p, The mail gets through. 45p, Race at Laxey Wheel.

1995, Sept. 1 *Perf. 14*
656 A157 20p multicolored .65 .65
657 A157 24p multicolored .75 .75
a. Booklet pane of 2, #656-657 1.40
658 A157 30p multicolored .95 .95
a. Booklet pane of 2, #657-658 1.75
659 A157 36p multicolored 1.10 1.10
a. Booklet pane of 2, #658-659 2.05
660 A157 41p multicolored 1.25 1.25
a. Booklet pane of 2, #659-660 2.35
661 A157 45p multicolored 1.40 1.40
a. Booklet pane of 2, #656, 661 2.05
b. Booklet pane of 2, #660-661 2.75
Complete booklet, #657a, 658a, 659a, 660a, 661a-661b 12.50
Nos. 656-661 (6) 6.10 6.10

Christmas A158

Designs: 19p, Church, holly. 23p, Bird on holly branch. 42p, Snow crocuses, church. 50p, Antique farming equipment in snow.

1995, Oct. 10 Litho. *Perf. 14x14½*
662 A158 19p multicolored .60 .60
663 A158 23p multicolored .70 .70
664 A158 42p multicolored 1.25 1.25
665 A158 50p multicolored 1.50 1.50
Nos. 662-665 (4) 4.05 4.05

Lighthouses — A159

Location, year opened: 20p, Langness, 1880, vert. 24p, Point of Ayre, 1818. 30p, Chicken Rock, 1873, vert. 36p, Calf of Man, 1818. 41p, Douglas Head, 1832. vert. 42p, Maughold Head, 1914.

1996, Feb. 27 Litho. *Perf. 14*
666 A159 20p multicolored .65 .65
a. Booklet pane of 4 + 4 labels 2.60
667 A159 24p multicolored .75 .75
a. Booklet pane of 4 3.00
668 A159 30p multicolored .95 .95
669 A159 36p multicolored 1.10 1.10
670 A159 41p multicolored 1.25 1.25
a. Booklet pane, 2 each #668, 670 + 4 labels 4.50
671 A159 42p multicolored 1.25 1.25
a. Bklt. pane, 2 ea #669, 671 4.75
Complete booklet, #666a, 667a, 670a, 671a 15.00
Nos. 666-671 (6) 5.95 5.95

Manx Cats A160

Various cats and: 20p, Arms of Man. 24p, British Union Flag as of ball yarn. 36p, Brandenburg Gate. 42p, US flag, Statue of Liberty. 48p, Australian flag, map.
£1.50, Gray adult cat, gray and yellow kittens.

1996, Mar. 14
672 A160 20p multicolored .65 .65
673 A160 24p multicolored .75 .75
674 A160 36p multicolored 1.10 1.10
675 A160 42p multicolored 1.25 1.25
676 A160 48p multicolored 1.50 1.50
Nos. 672-676 (5) 5.25 5.25

Souvenir Sheet

677 A160 £1.50 multicolored 4.50 4.50
a. With additional inscription 5.00 5.00

No. 677 contains one 51x60mm stamp. No. 677a contains CAPEX '96 exhibition emblem in sheet margin. Issued 7/8/96.

Douglas Borough, Cent. — A161

Die Cut Perf. 9x9½
1996, Mar. 14 Litho.
Self-Adhesive

678 A161 (40p) multicolored 1.25 1.25

The backing of No. 678 is rouletted 13.

Women of Achievement — A162

Europa: 24p, Princess Anne, children of different nations. 30p, Queen Elizabeth II, people of different nations.

1996 *Perf. 14*
679 A162 24p multicolored .75 .75
680 A162 30p multicolored .95 .95

Queen Elizabeth II, 70th birthday (#680). See Guernsey Nos. 564-565.

Ship Type of 1993

1996 Litho. *Perf. 14*
Size: 21x19mm
683 A137 4p like #533 .20 .20
693 A137 20p like #543 .65 .65
697 A137 24p like #547 .75 .75
Nos. 683-697 (3) 1.60 1.60
a. Bklt. pane, 2 ea 4p, 20p, 24p 3.25
Complete booklet, No. 697a 3.25

Irish Winners of Tourist Trophy Motorcycle Races — A163

20p, Alec Bennett. 24p, Stanley Woods. 45p, Artie Bell. 60p, Robert & Joey Dunlop.
£1, Demonstration squadron Hawks flying over motorcycles, vert.

1996, May 30 Litho. *Perf. 14*
701 A163 20p multicolored .60 .60
702 A163 24p multicolored .70 .70
703 A163 45p multicolored 1.25 1.25
704 A163 60p multicolored 1.75 1.75
Nos. 701-704 (4) 4.30 4.30

Souvenir Sheet

705 A163 £1 multicolored 3.25 3.25

See Ireland Nos. 1010-1014.

Royal British Legion, 75th Anniv. — A164

Poppies and: 20p, National poppy appeal trophy. 24p, Manx war memorial. 42p, Poppy appeal. 75p, Crest.

1996, June 8
706 A164 20p multicolored .60 .60
707 A164 24p multicolored .70 .70
708 A164 42p multicolored 1.25 1.25
709 A164 75p multicolored 2.25 2.25
Nos. 706-709 (4) 4.80 4.80

UNICEF, 50th Anniv. A165

Children receiving aid, map of country: #710, Mexico. #711, Sri Lanka. #712, Colombia. #713, Zambia. #714, Afghanistan. #715, Viet Nam.

1996, Sept. 18 Litho. *Perf. 13½x14*
710 A165 24p multicolored .75 .75
711 A165 24p multicolored .75 .75
a. Pair, #710-711 1.50 1.50
712 A165 30p multicolored .95 .95
713 A165 30p multicolored .95 .95
a. Pair, #712-713 1.90 1.90
714 A165 42p multicolored 1.25 1.25
715 A165 42p multicolored 1.25 1.25
a. Pair, #714-715 2.50 2.50
Nos. 710-715 (6) 5.90 5.90

Dogs — A166

1996, Sept. 18 *Perf. 14½*
716 A166 20p Labrador .60 .60
a. Booklet pane of 4 2.40
717 A166 24p Border collie .65 .65
a. Booklet pane of 4 2.60
718 A166 31p Dalmatian .90 .90
719 A166 38p Mongrel 1.10 1.10
720 A166 43p English setter 1.25 1.25
721 A166 63p Alsatian 1.90 1.90
a. Booklet pane, 1 each #718-721 5.25
Nos. 716-721 (6) 6.40 6.40

Souvenir Sheet

Perf. 13½x14

722 A166 £1.20 Border collie, labrador 3.75 3.75
a. Booklet pane of 1 3.75
Complete booklet, #716a, 717a, 721a, 722a 15.00

Nos. 716-721 are each printed with se-tenant label. No. 722 contains one 38x50mm stamp. No. 722a is rouletted around margin of sheet.

Christmas A167

Children's drawings: 19p, Snowman. 23p, Santa, "Happy Christmas" in Manx. 50p, Family, Christmas tree, presents. 75p, Santa in sleigh flying over rooftops.

1996, Nov. 2 Litho. *Perf. 14x14½*
723 A167 19p multicolored .60 .60
724 A167 23p multicolored .70 .70
725 A167 50p multicolored 1.45 1.45
726 A167 75p multicolored 2.25 2.25
Nos. 723-726 (4) 5.00 5.00

Owls — A168

1997, Feb. 12 Litho. *Perf. 14*
727 A168 20p Barn owl .55 .55
a. Booklet pane of 4 2.25

728 A168 24p Short-eared owl .65 .65
a. Booklet pane of 4 2.60
729 A168 31p Long-eared owl .80 .80
730 A168 36p Little owl 1.00 1.00
731 A168 43p Snowy owl 1.10 1.10
732 A168 56p Tawny owl 1.60 1.60
a. Booklet pane of 4, #729-732 4.50
Nos. 727-732 (6) 5.70 5.70

Souvenir Sheet

Perf. 13

733 A168 £1.20 Long-eared owl 3.50 3.50
a. Booklet pane of 1 3.50
Complete booklet, #727a, 728a, 732a, 733a 13.00

No. 733, 733a each contain one 56x60mm stamp. No. 733a is rouletted at left. Hong Kong '97 (#733, 733a).

Springtime A169

1997, Feb. 12 ***Perf. 14***

734 A169 20p Spring flowers .60 .60
735 A169 24p Sheep .70 .70
736 A169 43p Waterfowl 1.25 1.25
737 A169 63p Frog, ducks 1.90 1.90
Nos. 734-737 (4) 4.45 4.45

Stories and Legends A170

21p, Moddey Dhoo. 25p, The Trammen Tree. 31p, Fairy Bridge. 36p, Fin Macooil. 37p, The Buggane of St. Trinian's. 43p, Fynoderee.

1997, Apr. 24 Litho. ***Perf. 13½x14***

738 A170 21p multicolored .60 .60
739 A170 25p multicolored .75 .75
740 A170 31p multicolored .90 .90
741 A170 36p multicolored 1.10 1.10
742 A170 37p multicolored 1.10 1.10
743 A170 43p multicolored 1.25 1.25
Nos. 738-743 (6) 5.70 5.70

Europa (#739-740).

Aircraft A171

Designs: No. 744, Sopwith Tabloid. No. 745, Grumman Tiger. No. 746, Manx Airlines BAe ATP. No. 747, Manx Airlines BAe 146-200. No. 748 Boeing 757-200. No. 749, Farman biplane. No. 750, Spitfire. No. 751, Hurricane.

1997, Apr. 24 ***Perf. 14***

744 A171 21p multicolored .55 .55
745 A171 21p multicolored .55 .55
a. Pair, #744-745 1.10 1.10
746 A171 25p multicolored .70 .70
747 A171 25p multicolored .70 .70
a. Pair, #746-747 1.40 1.40
748 A171 31p multicolored .80 .80
749 A171 31p multicolored .80 .80
a. Pair, #748-749 1.60 1.60
750 A171 36p multicolored 1.00 1.00
751 A171 36p multicolored 1.00 1.00
a. Pair, #750-751 2.00 2.00
Nos. 744-751 (8) 6.10 6.10

Golf Courses A172

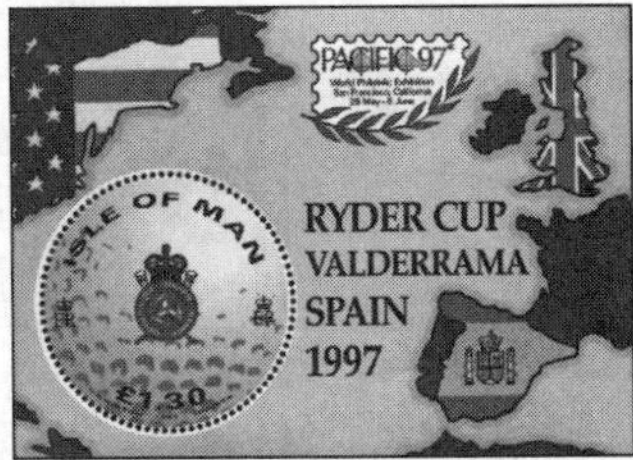

1997 Ryder Cup, Valderrama, Spain — A173

21p, 14th Hole, Ramsey Golf Club. 25p, 15th Hole, King Edward Bay Golf and Country Club. 43p, 17th Hole, Rowany Golf Club. 50p, 8th Hole, Casteltown Golf Links.

1997, May 29 Litho. ***Perf. 14***

752 A172 21p multicolored .55 .55
a. Booklet pane of 3 1.75
753 A172 25p multicolored .70 .70
a. Booklet pane of 3 2.10
754 A172 43p multicolored 1.10 1.10
755 A172 50p multicolored 1.40 1.40
a. Bklt. pane, 2 ea #754-755 5.00
Nos. 752-755 (4) 3.75 3.75

Souvenir Sheet

756 A173 £1.30 multicolored 3.50 3.50
a. Booklet pane of 1 3.50
Complete booklet, #752a, 753a, 755a, 756a 12.50

PACIFIC 97 (#756). No. 756 contains one 40mm diameter stamp.

No. 756a has a large white border, is 155x96mm and is sewn into booklet.

Trial of Nations Motorcycle Competition — A174

Various motorcyclists.

1997, Sept. 29 Litho. ***Perf. 13½***

757 A174 21p multicolored .60 .60
758 A174 25p multi, vert. .75 .75
759 A174 37p multi, vert. 1.10 1.10
760 A174 44p multicolored 1.40 1.40
Nos. 757-760 (4) 3.85 3.85

Queen Elizabeth II and Prince Philip, 50th Wedding Anniv. — A175

Designs: a, Early drawing of couple. b, Wedding portrait. c, Drawing of Queen waving, Prince in top hat. d, Portrait, 1997.

£1, Queen, Prince touring Isle of Man, 1989.

1997, Nov. 3 Litho. ***Perf. 14x14½***

761 A175 50p Strip of 4, #a.-d. 5.75 5.75

Souvenir Sheet

Perf. 14

762 A175 £1 multicolored 3.00 3.00

No. 761 was issued in sheets of 16 stamps. No. 762 contains one 48x58mm stamp.

Christmas — A176

1997, Nov. 3 ***Perf. 14***

763 A176 20p Angel, shepherd .65 .65
764 A176 24p Wise man, angel .75 .75

Size: 54x39mm

765 A176 63p Nativity 1.90 1.90
Nos. 763-765 (3) 3.30 3.30

Flowers — A177

1998, Feb. 12 Litho. ***Perf. 13x13½***

766 A177 4p Shamrocks .20 .20
767 A177 21p Cushag .70 .70
768 A177 25p Princess of Wales Rose .85 .85
769 A177 50p Daffodil 1.75 1.75
770 A177 £1 Spear thistle 3.25 3.25
Nos. 766-770 (5) 6.75 6.75

Nos. 766-768 also exist in special booklet sheets containing 10 of each denomination.

See Nos. 794-801.

A178

Viking Longships: 21p, Dragon's head figurehead. 25p, Ship under full sail. 31p, Ship with sail furled. 75p Ship's stern.

£1, Man on ship pointing, fortress.

1998, Feb. 14 ***Perf. 14***

771 A178 21p multicolored .70 .70
772 A178 25p multicolored .85 .85
773 A178 31p multicolored 1.00 1.00
774 A178 75p multicolored 2.50 2.50
Nos. 771-774 (4) 5.05 5.05

Souvenir Sheet

775 A178 £1 multicolored 3.30 3.30

Marine Life A179

Designs: 10p, Bottle-nosed dolphin. 21p, Basking shark swimming right. 25p, Basking shark swimming forward. 31p, Minke whale. 63p, Killer whale.

1998, Mar. 14 Litho. ***Perf. 14***

776 A179 10p multicolored .35 .35
777 A179 21p multicolored .70 .70
a. Booklet pane of 6, 3 each #776-777 + 3 labels 3.25
778 A179 25p multicolored .85 .85
779 A179 31p multicolored 1.00 1.00
780 A179 63p multicolored 2.10 2.10
a. Bklt. pane of 8, #776-777, 2 ea #778-780 + label 9.00
Souvenir booklet, #777a, 780a 12.25
Nos. 776-780 (5) 5.00 5.00

Trains A180

Designs: 21p, Hutchinson 2-4-0. 25p, G.H. Wood 2-4-0. 31p, Maitland 2-4-0. 63p, Loch 2-4-0.

1998, May 2 Litho. ***Perf. 14½x14***

781 A180 21p multicolored .70 .70
782 A180 25p multicolored .85 .85
783 A180 31p multicolored 1.00 1.00
784 A180 63p multicolored 2.20 2.20
a. Bklt. pane of 4, #781-784 4.75 4.75
Nos. 781-784 (4) 4.75 4.75

Souvenir Sheet

785 A180 Sheet of 2 4.25 4.25
a. £1 Engine 4.00 4.00
b. 25p Passenger cars .25 .25
c. Booklet pane of 1 4.25 4.25
Complete bklt., #785c, 2 #784a 14.00
d. As #785, inscribed in sheet margin 4.25 4.25

No. 784a exists with two different backgrounds and stamps in different order. Complete booklets contain one of each pane.

No. 785d is inscribed in sheet margin with PhilexFrance '99, World Philatelic Exhibition emblem and was issued 7/2/99.

Europa A181

National Days celebration: 25p, People under tent, seated in stand, watching ceremony. 30p, Women dancing in traditional costumes.

1998, July 2 ***Perf. 13x13½***

786 A181 25p multicolored .85 .85
787 A181 30p multicolored 1.00 1.00

1998 Tourist Trophy Motorcycle Races — A182

Designs: 21p, Eight-man pyramid. 25p, Joey Dunlop rounding curve. 31p, Dave Molyneux with side car. 43p, Naomi Taniguchi racing. 63p, Mike Hailwood racing.

1998, June 1 Litho. ***Perf. 14***

788 A182 21p multicolored .70 .70
789 A182 25p multicolored .85 .85
790 A182 31p multicolored 1.00 1.00
791 A182 43p multicolored 1.40 1.40
792 A182 63p multicolored 2.25 2.25
Nos. 788-792 (5) 6.20 6.20

A183

Diana, Princess of Wales (1961-97): a, In black evening dress. b, Accepting flowers. c, Holding hand to face. d, In protective clothing.

1998, June 19 ***Perf. 13***

793 A183 25p Strip of 4, #a.-d. 3.50 3.50

Flower Type

Perf. 13, 13x13½ (5p, 22p, 26p)

1998-99 Litho.

Flowers: 1p, Bearded iris. 2p, Daisy. 5p, Silver jubilee rose. 10p, Oriental poppy. 20p, Heath spotted orchid. 22p, Gorse. 26p, Dog rose. 30p, Fuchsia-lady thumb.

794 A177 1p multicolored .20 .20
795 A177 2p multicolored .20 .20
796 A177 5p multicolored .20 .20
797 A177 10p multicolored .35 .35
798 A177 20p multicolored .65 .65
799 A177 22p multicolored .75 .75
800 A177 26p multicolored .85 .85
a. Bklt. pane, #800, 2 #766, 3 #799 3.50
Complete booklet, #800a 3.50
801 A177 30p multicolored 1.00 1.00
Nos. 794-801 (8) 4.20 4.20

Issued: 5p, 22p, 26p, 4/26/99; others, 7/2/98.

Queen Mother and Queen Elizabeth II
A185

1998, July 2 Litho. *Perf. 13*
802 A185 £2.50 multicolored 8.50 8.50

Christmas
A186

Santa Claus: 20p, Loading sleigh at North Pole. 24p, With list, reindeer standing in clouds, Isle of Man below. 30p, Going over Spring Valley Sorting Office. 43p, Passing through Baldrine. 63p, Leaving presents, children inside house.

1998, Sept. 25 Litho. *Perf. 14½x14*
803 A186 20p multicolored .65 .65
804 A186 24p multicolored .80 .80
805 A186 30p multicolored 1.00 1.00
806 A186 43p multicolored 1.40 1.40
807 A186 63p multicolored 2.25 2.25
Nos. 803-807 (5) 6.10 6.10

Manx Nature Reserve and Parks (Europa) — A187

Designs: 25p, Cottage, Ballaglass Glen. 30p, Glen Maye Waterfall.

1999, Mar. 4 Litho. *Perf. 14*
808 A187 25p multicolored .75 .75
809 A187 30p multicolored 1.00 1.00

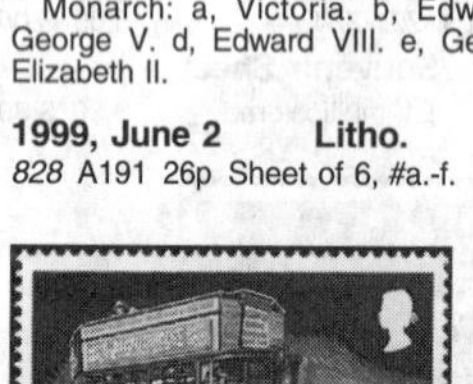

Post Boxes — A188

10p, Oval box, Kirk Onchan Post Office. 20p, Wall box, Ballaterson, Ballaugh. 21p, Cylindrical box, Laxey Station. 25p, Wall box, Spaldrick, Port Erin. 44p, Oval box, Derby Road, Douglas. 63p, Wall box, Baldrine Station.

1999, Mar. 4
810 A188 10p multicolored .35 .35
811 A188 20p multicolored .65 .65
812 A188 21p multicolored .70 .70
813 A188 25p multicolored .80 .80
814 A188 44p multicolored 1.40 1.40
815 A188 63p multicolored 2.00 2.00
Nos. 810-815 (6) 5.90 5.90

Royal Natl. Lifeboat Institution, 175th Anniv. — A189

1999, Mar. 4
816 A189 21p Ramsey lifeboat .70 .70
817 A189 25p Douglas lifeboat .85 .85
818 A189 37p Peel lifeboat 1.25 1.25
819 A189 43p Port Erin lifeboat 1.40 1.40
820 A189 56p Port St. Mary lifeboat 1.90 1.90
a. Bklt. pane, #816-820 + 4 labels 6.25
Nos. 816-820 (5) 6.10 6.10

Booklet Stamps

821 A189 43p #38 1.50 1.50
822 A189 56p #464 1.90 1.90
a. Booklet pane, #816-818, #821-822 + 4 labels 6.25

Souvenir Sheet

823 A189 £1 William Hillary (1771-1847) 3.50 3.50
a. Booklet pane of 1 3.50
Complete booklet, #820a, #822a, #823a 16.00

IBRA '99 (#822a), Australia '99, World Stamp Expo. (#823). No. 823 contains one 38x50mm stamp.

Celtic Jewelry Depicting Seasons — A190

1999, May 14 *Perf. 14½x14*
824 A190 22p Winter .75 .75
825 A190 26p Spring .85 .85
826 A190 50p Summer 1.60 1.60
827 A190 63p Autumn 2.10 2.10
Nos. 824-827 (4) 5.30 5.30

20th Century British Monarchs
A191

Monarch: a, Victoria. b, Edward VII. c, George V. d, Edward VIII. e, George VI. f, Elizabeth II.

1999, June 2 Litho. *Perf. 14*
828 A191 26p Sheet of 6, #a.-f. 5.25 5.25

Manx Buses
A192

22p, 1922 Tilling Stevens 46 double-decker. 26p, 1928 Thornycroft BC 28-seat. 28p, 1927 ADC 416 28-seat. 37p, 1914 Staker Squire 25-seat. 38p, 1927 Thornycroft A2 20-seat. 40p, 1938 Leyland Lion LT9 34-seat.

1999, June 18
829 A192 22p multicolored .75 .75
830 A192 26p multicolored .85 .85
831 A192 28p multicolored .90 .90
832 A192 37p multicolored 1.25 1.25
833 A192 38p multicolored 1.25 1.25
834 A192 40p multicolored 1.40 1.40
Nos. 829-834 (6) 6.40 6.40

831a Bklt. pane, #829-830, 2 #831 3.50
832a Bklt. pane, #829-830, 2 #832 4.25
833a Bklt. pane, #829-830, 2 #833 4.25
834a Bklt. pane, #829-830, 2 #834 4.50
Complete booklet, #831a-834a 17.00

Wedding of Prince Edward and Sophie Rhys-Jones — A193

1999, June 19
835 A193 22p Sophie, vert. .75 .75
836 A193 39p Prince Edward, vert. 1.00 1.00
837 A193 44p Couple 1.40 1.40
Nos. 835-837 (3) 3.15 3.15

Royal Wedding Photos - A193a

Designs: 26p, Couple standing, vert. 53p, Couple seated in carriage.

1999, Sept. 1 Litho. *Perf. 14¼*
837A A193a 26p multi .85 .85
837B A193a 53p multi 1.75 1.75

Churches — A194

Illustration reduced.

Perf. 13¼x13½

1999, Sept. 22 Litho.
838 A194 21p St. Luke's .65 .65
839 A194 25p St. Mark's .80 .80
840 A194 30p Cathedral Peel .95 .95
841 A194 64p Malew 2.10 2.10
Nos. 838-841 (4) 4.50 4.50

Bee Gees Songs
A195

Designs: 22p, "Massachusetts." 26p, "Words." 29p, "I've Gotta Get a Message to You." 37p, "Ellan Vannin." 38p, "You Win Again." 66p, "Night Fever."
60p, "Immortality." 90p, "Stayin' Alive."

1999, Oct. 12 Litho. *Perf. 13¼x13½*
842 A195 22p multicolored .70 .70
843 A195 26p multicolored .85 .85
844 A195 29p multicolored .90 .90
845 A195 37p multicolored 1.10 1.10
846 A195 38p multicolored 1.25 1.25
847 A195 66p multicolored 2.25 2.25
Nos. 842-847 (6) 7.05 7.05

Souvenir Sheets

848 A195 60p multicolored 2.00 2.00
849 A195 90p multicolored 3.00 3.00

Nos. 848-849 each contain one 40mm diameter stamp. Nos. 842-847 each issued in sheets of 9 stamps and 3 labels.

Souvenir Sheet

Millennium
A196

Objects in the night sky: a, 50p, Mars, stars Deneb, Altair, Vega. b, £2, Constellations Lynx, Draco, Ursa Minor, Ursa Major. c, 50p, Mercury, Venus, Deneb, Vega, Altair, orbit of International Space Station (ISS).

Perf. 14¼x14½

1999, Dec. 31 Litho.
850 A196 Sheet of 3, #a.-c. 10.00 10.00

History of Time — A197

Clock escapements of: 22p, 1735 by John Harrison. 26p, 2000 by George Daniels. 29p, 1767 by Harrison. 34p, 1769 by Thomas Mudge. 38p, 1779 by John Arnold. 44p, 1780 by Thomas Earnshaw.

2000, Jan. 24 Litho. *Perf. 13x13½*
851 A197 22p multi .70 .70
852 A197 26p multi .80 .80
853 A197 29p multi .95 .95
854 A197 34p multi 1.10 1.10
855 A197 38p multi 1.25 1.25
856 A197 44p multi 1.40 1.40
Nos. 851-856 (6) 6.20 6.20

Queen Mother (b. 1900) — A198

Pictures of Queen Mother from - No. 857: a, 1923. b, 1940. c, 1944.
No. 858: a, 1954. b, 1985. c, 1988.
No. 859, 1984.
£1, Queen Mother on Isle of Man.
Illustration reduced.

2000, Feb. 29 Litho. *Perf. 14*
857 Strip of 3 2.40 2.40
a. A198 22p multi .65 .65
b. A198 26p multi .80 .80
c. A198 30p multi .90 .90
858 Strip of 3 5.00 5.00
a. A198 44p multi 1.40 1.40
b. A198 52p multi 1.60 1.60
c. A198 64p multi 2.00 2.00

Souvenir Sheet

Perf. 14¼

859 A198 £1 multi 3.00 3.00
a. With emblem of The Stamp Show 2000 in margin 3.00 3.00

Size of Nos. 857a-857c, 858a-858c, 42x28mm.
Issued: No. 859a, 5/22/00.

Song Birds — A199

2000, May 5 *Perf. 14½x14¼*
860 Strip of 4 5.50 5.50
a. A199 22p Swallow .60 .60
b. A199 26p Spotted flycatcher .75 .75
c. A199 64p Skylark 1.90 1.90
d. A199 77p Yellowhammer 2.25 2.25

Military Leaders and Isle of Man Military Personnel
A200

Battle of Britain, 60th Anniv. — A201

#861: a, John Quilliam (1771-1829), Admiral Lord Nelson (1758-1805). b, Caesar Bacon (1791-1876), Duke of Wellington (1769-1852).
#862: a, Thomas Leigh Goldie (1807-54), Earl of Cardigan (1797-1868). b, John Dunne (1884-1950), Sir Robert Baden-Powell (1857-1941).
#863: a, George Kneale (1896-1917), Viscount Kitchener (1850-1916). b, Alan Watterson (1910-42), Sir Winston Churchill (1874-1965).
#864: a, Planes in air. b, Plane on ground.
Illustration A201 reduced.

2000, May 22 Litho. *Perf. 13¼*

861 Pair, #a-b, + central label 1.50 1.50
a. A200 22p multi .65 .65
b. A200 26p multi .80 .80
862 Pair, #a-b, + central label 2.60 2.60
a. A200 36p multi 1.10 1.10
b. A200 48p multi 1.50 1.50
863 Pair, #a-b, + central label 3.75 3.75
a. A200 50p multi 1.50 1.50
b. A200 77p multi 2.25 2.25
c. Booklet pane, #861a, 861b, 862a, 862b, 863a 5.75
d. Booklet pane, #861a, 862b, 863a, 863b 6.00
Nos. 861-863 (3) 7.85 7.85

Souvenir Sheet

Perf. 14¾x14¼

864 A201 60p Sheet of 2, #a-b 3.75 3.75
c. Booklet pane, #864 3.75
Booklet, #863c, 863d, 864c 16.00

No. 864c has stitched margin at left.

Souvenir Sheet

Prince William, 18th Birthday — A202

2000, June 21 Litho. *Perf. 14*

865 Sheet of 5 6.00 6.00
a. A202 22p As toddler .65 .65
b. A202 26p With Queen Mother .80 .80
c. A202 45p In checked shirt 1.40 1.40
d. A202 52p With Princes Charles, Harry 1.50 1.50
e. A202 56p In ski gear 1.60 1.60

Gaiety Theater, Cent. A203

2000, July 16

866 A203 22p Ballet .65 .65
867 A203 26p Comedy .80 .80
868 A203 36p Drama 1.10 1.10
869 A203 45p Pantomime 1.40 1.40
870 A203 52p Opera 1.50 1.50
871 A203 65p Musicals 1.90 1.90
Nos. 866-871 (6) 7.35 7.35

Global Challenge Yacht Race — A204

Sail from yacht "Isle of Man," and ports of call: 22p, Southampton. 26p, Sydney. 36p, Wellington. 40p, Buenos Aires. 44p, Boston. 65p, Cape Town.

Perf. 13¼x13¾

2000, Sept. 10 Litho.

872 A204 22p multi .65 .65
873 A204 26p multi .80 .80
874 A204 36p multi 1.10 1.10
875 A204 40p multi 1.25 1.25
876 A204 44p multi 1.40 1.40
877 A204 65p multi 1.90 1.90
Nos. 872-877 (6) 7.10 7.10

Travel Poster Art of Isle of Man Steam Packet Co. — A205

Designs: 22p, Three legs of Man, ship. 26p, Cliffs and sailboats. 36p, Woman and Isle of Man. 45p, Woman, ship, flag. 65p, Ship.

2000, Oct. 16 *Perf. 13½x13¼*

878 A205 22p multi .65 .65
879 A205 26p multi .80 .80
880 A205 36p multi 1.10 1.10
881 A205 45p multi 1.40 1.40
882 A205 65p multi 1.90 1.90
Nos. 878-882 (5) 5.85 5.85

Europa, 2000

Common Design Type

2000, Nov. 7 *Perf. 14*

883 CD17 36p multi 1.10 1.10

Christmas A206

2000, Nov. 7

884 A206 21p Peace .65 .65
885 A206 25p Hope .75 .75
886 A206 45p Love 1.40 1.40
887 A206 65p Faith 1.90 1.90
Nos. 884-887 (4) 4.70 4.70

Souvenir Sheet

New Year 2001 (Year of the Snake) — A207

Litho. with Foil Application

2001, Jan. 22 *Perf. 13¾*

888 A207 £1 St. Patrick 3.00 3.00

Hong Kong 2001 Stamp Exhibition.

Queen Victoria (1819-1901) — A208

Designs: 22p, Wyon medal, Queen Victoria, Great Britain Type A1. 26p, Great Exhibition medal, Albert Tower. 34p, Coin, Steamship Great Britain. 39p, Coin, scene from Oliver Twist, St. Thomas' Church, Douglas. 40p, Coin, first train to arrive in Vancouver, Canada and Jubilee streetlamp standard. 52p, Coin, Foxdale Clock Tower, family of diamond magnate Joe Mylchreest.

2001, Jan. 22 Litho. *Perf. 13½*

889 A208 22p multi .65 .65
890 A208 26p multi .75 .75
891 A208 34p multi 1.00 1.00
892 A208 39p multi 1.10 1.10
893 A208 40p multi 1.10 1.10
894 A208 52p multi 1.50 1.50
Nos. 889-894 (6) 6.10 6.10

Insects A209

Designs: 22p, White-tailed bumblebee. 26p, Seven-spot ladybug. 29p, Lesser mottled grasshopper. 58p, Manx robber fly. 66p, Elephant hawkmoth.

2001, Feb. 1 *Perf. 14½*

895 A209 22p multi .65 .65
896 A209 26p multi .75 .75
897 A209 29p multi .85 .85
898 A209 58p multi 1.60 1.60
899 A209 66p multi 1.90 1.90
Nos. 895-899 (5) 5.75 5.75

Souvenir Sheet

Queen Elizabeth II, 75th Birthday — A210

Stamps: 29p, Great Britain #MH1. 34p, Great Britain #300. 37p, Isle of Man #8. 50p, Isle of Man #3.

2001, Apr. 18 Litho. *Perf. 14*

900 A210 Sheet of 4, #a-d 4.25 4.25

Manx Postmen and Cancels — A211

2001, Apr. 18

901 A211 22p 1805 .60 .60
902 A211 26p 1859 .75 .75
903 A211 36p 1910 1.00 1.00
904 A211 39p 1933 1.10 1.10
905 A211 40p 1983 1.10 1.10
906 A211 66p 2001 1.90 1.90
Nos. 901-906 (6) 6.45 6.45

William Joseph Dunlop (1952-2001), Motorcycle Racer — A212

Various photographs.

2001, May 17

907 A212 22p multi .60 .60
908 A212 26p multi .75 .75
909 A212 36p multi 1.00 1.00
910 A212 45p multi 1.25 1.25
911 A212 65p multi 1.90 1.90
912 A212 77p multi 2.25 2.25
Nos. 907-912 (6) 7.75 7.75

Horse Racing A213

Designs: 22p, Manx Derby. 26p, Post Haste. 36p, Red Rum. 52p, Hyperion. 63p, Isle of Man.

2001, May 18 *Perf. 13¼x13½*

913 A213 22p multi .60 .60
914 A213 26p multi .75 .75
915 A213 36p multi 1.00 1.00
916 A213 52p multi 1.50 1.50
917 A213 63p multi 1.75 1.75
Nos. 913-917 (5) 5.60 5.60

Gourmet Food — A214

2001, Aug. 10 Litho. *Perf. 14¼*

918 A214 22p Beef .65 .65
919 A214 26p Queenies .75 .75
a. Sheet of 10 7.50 —
920 A214 36p Seafood 1.00 1.00
a. Sheet of 10 10.00 —
921 A214 45p Lamb 1.25 1.25
922 A214 50p Kippers 1.50 1.50
923 A214 66p Dairy 1.90 1.90
Nos. 918-923 (6) 7.05 7.05

Europa (#919, 920).

Architecture of Mackay Hugh Baillie Scott — A215

Designs: 22p, Castletown Police Station, 1901. 26p, Leafield/Braeside, 1897. 37p, Red House, 1893. 40p, Ivydene, 1893. 80p, Onchan Village Hall, 1898.

2001, Sept. 3 *Perf. 13¼x13½*

924 A215 22p multi .65 .65
925 A215 26p multi .75 .75
926 A215 37p multi 1.10 1.10
927 A215 40p multi 1.25 1.25
928 A215 80p multi 2.40 2.40
Nos. 924-928 (5) 6.15 6.15

Reign of Queen Elizabeth II, 50th Anniv. (in 2002) — A216

Drawings of Queen: 22p, At dining table. 26p, With crowd, holding flower bouquet. 39p, With dogs. 40p, With men wearing hats. 45p, With correspondence. 65p, Alone, holding flower bouquet.

Litho. With Foil Application

2001-02 *Perf. 14¼*

929 A216 22p multi .65 .65
930 A216 26p multi .75 .75
931 A216 39p multi 1.10 1.10
a. Booklet pane of 3, #929-931 2.50 —
932 A216 40p multi 1.25 1.25
933 A216 45p multi 1.25 1.25
934 A216 65p multi 1.90 1.90
a. Booklet pane of 3, #932-934 4.50 —
Nos. 929-934 (6) 6.90 6.90

Issued: Nos. 929-934, 10/29/01. Nos. 931a, 934a, 2/6/02.

Christmas A217

Floral arrangements: 21p, Holly on Christmas tree-shaped frame. 25p, Wreath. 37p, Table decoration with candles. 45p, Topiary tree. 65p, Wreath, diff.

2001, Nov. 5 Litho. *Perf. 14x14½*

Stamp + Label

Background Color

No.	Type	Description	Unused	Used
935	A217	21p green	.60	.60
936	A217	25p red	.75	.75
937	A217	37p gold	1.10	1.10
938	A217	45p silver	1.25	1.25
939	A217	65p violet	1.90	1.90
		Nos. 935-939 (5)	5.60	5.60

Reign of Queen Elizabeth II, 50th Anniv. — A218

No. 940 - Paintings: a, The Coronation, by Terence Cuneo. b, Her Majesty the Queen as Colonel in Chief, Grenadier Guards on Imperial, by Cuneo (Queen on horse). c, Her Majesty in Evening Dress, by June Mendoza. d, Her Majesty the Queen, by Chen Yan Ning. e, The Royal Family, by John Wonnacott.

£1, Her Majesty Queen Elizabeth II Lord of Mann, sculpture by David Cregeen.

Litho. with Foil Application

2002, Feb. 6 *Perf. 14*

No.	Description	Unused	Used
940	Vert. strip of 5	7.00	7.00
a.-e.	A218 50p Any single	1.40	1.40
f.	Booklet pane of 3, #940a-940c	4.20	—
g.	Booklet pane of 2, #940d-940e	2.80	—

Souvenir Sheet

Perf. 14½x14

No.	Description	Unused	Used
941	A218 £1 multi	3.00	3.00
a.	Booklet pane of 1 with larger margin	3.00	—
	Booklet, #931a, 934a, 940f, 940g, 941a	17.00	

No. 941 contains one 60x40mm stamp.

No. 941 exists with purple inscription in sheet margin, "The Isle of Man Celebrates The Jubilee / 4th June 2002."

17th Commonwealth Games, Manchester, England — A219

Designs: 22p, Cycling. 26p, Running. 29p, Javelin, women's high jump. 34p, Swimming. 40p, Hurdles, pole vault. 45p, Wheelchair racing.

2002, Mar. 11 Litho. *Perf. 14*

No.	Type	Description	Unused	Used
942	A219	22p multi	.65	.65
943	A219	26p multi	.75	.75
944	A219	29p multi	.85	.85
945	A219	34p multi	.95	.95
946	A219	40p multi	1.10	1.10
947	A219	45p multi	1.25	1.25
		Nos. 942-947 (6)	5.55	5.55

Queen Mother Elizabeth (1900-2002) A220

2002, Apr. 23 *Perf. 13x13¼*

No.	Type	Description	Unused	Used
948	A220	£3 multi	8.75	8.75

Paintings by Toni Onley A221

Designs: 22p, Monks' Bridge, Ballasalla. 26p, Laxey. 37p, Langness Lighthouse. 45p, King William's College. 65p, The Mull Circle & Bradda Head.

2002, May 1 *Perf. 13¼x13½*

No.	Type	Description	Unused	Used
949	A221	22p multi	.65	.65
950	A221	26p multi	.75	.75
951	A221	37p multi	1.10	1.10
952	A221	45p multi	1.40	1.40
953	A221	65p multi	1.90	1.90
		Nos. 949-953 (5)	5.80	5.80

2002 World Cup Soccer Championships, Japan and Korea — A222

Various players.

2002, May 1 *Perf. 13½*

No.	Type	Description	Unused	Used
954	A222	22p multi	.65	.65
955	A222	26p multi	.75	.75
956	A222	39p multi	1.10	1.10
957	A222	40p multi	1.25	1.25
958	A222	66p multi	1.90	1.90
959	A222	68p multi	2.00	2.00
		Nos. 954-959 (6)	7.65	7.65

Flower Sketches by Sir Paul McCartney A223

Various sketches.

2002, July 1 Litho. *Perf. 13¼x12¾*

No.	Type	Description	Unused	Used
960	A223	22p multi	.65	.65
961	A223	26p multi	.80	.80
962	A223	29p multi	.90	.90
963	A223	52p multi	1.60	1.60
964	A223	63p multi	1.90	1.90
965	A223	77p multi	2.40	2.40
		Nos. 960-965 (6)	8.25	8.25

Photographs of Local Scenes — A224

Designs: a, Laxey Wheel, by Kathy Brown. b, Sheep at Druidale, by John Hall. c, Carousel at Silverdale, by Colin Edwards. d, Grandma, by Stephanie Corkill. e, Manx Rock, by Ruth Nicholls. f, TT Riders at Signpost, by Neil Brew. g, Groudle Railway, by Albert Lowe. h, Royal Cascade, by Brian Speedie. i, St. Johns, by John Hall. j, Niarbyl Cottages with Poppies, by Cathy Galbraith.

2002, Aug. 30 Litho. *Perf. 14*

No.	Description	Unused	Used
966	Block of 10	8.50	8.50
a.-j.	A224 27p Any single	.85	.85

Photography Type of 2002

Designs like No. 966.

Serpentine Die Cut 6¼

2002, Aug. 30 Litho.

Self-Adhesive

No.	Description	Unused	Used
967	Booklet of 10	8.50	
a.-j.	A224 27p Any single	.85	.85

Photography Type of 2002

Designs: a, Manx Milestone, by Mrs. B. J. Trimble. b, Plow Horses, by Miss D. Flint. c, Manx Emblem, by Ruth Nicholls. d, Loaghtan Sheep, by Diana Buford. e, Fishing Fleet at Port St. Mary, by Phil Thomas. f, Peel, by Michael Thompson. g, Daffodils, by Thompson. h, Millennium Sword, by Mr. F. K. Smith. i, Peel Castle, by Kathy Brown. j, Snaefell Railway, by Joan Burgess.

2002, Oct. 1 Litho. *Perf. 14*

No.	Description	Unused	Used
968	Block of 10	7.25	7.25
a.-j.	A224 23p Any single	.70	.70

Self-Adhesive

Serpentine Die Cut 6¼

No.	Description	Unused	Used
969	Booklet of 10	7.25	
a.-j.	A224 23p Any single	.70	.70

Christmas and Europa — A225

Designs: 22p, Santa Claus. 26p, Madonna and Child. 37p, Clown. 47p, Cymbal player. 68p, Fairy.

£1.30, "Christmas."

2002, Nov. 5 *Perf. 14x14½*

No.	Type	Description	Unused	Used
970	A225	22p multi	.70	.70
971	A225	26p multi	.80	.80
972	A225	37p multi	1.25	1.25
973	A225	47p multi	1.50	1.50
974	A225	68p multi	2.10	2.10
		Nos. 970-974 (5)	6.35	6.35

Miniature Sheet

Perf. 14¾

No.	Type	Description	Unused	Used
975	A225	£1.30 multi	4.25	4.25

Europa (#972). No. 975 contains one 99x38mm stamp.

Post Office Vehicles A226

Designs: 23p, Handcart. 27p, Morris Z van. 37p, Morris LD van. 42p, DI BSA Bantam motorcycle. 89p, Ford Escort 55 delivery van.

2003, Feb. 14 *Perf. 14¼*

No.	Type	Description	Unused	Used
976	A226	23p multi	.75	.75
977	A226	27p multi	.85	.85
978	A226	37p multi	1.25	1.25
979	A226	42p multi	1.40	1.40
980	A226	89p multi	3.00	3.00
		Nos. 976-980 (5)	7.25	7.25

Space Exploration — A227

No. 981: a, Tromode Teleport. b, Satellite earth station.

No. 982: a, Pioneering the space frontier (denomination at left). b, Pioneering the space frontier (denomination at right).

No. 983: a, Sea Launch Odyssey launch platform. b, Sea Launch Commander.

No. 984: a, Loral Skynet Telstar 1. b, Loral Skynet Telstar 8.

No. 985: a, Space station, Phobos. b, Astronauts, Mars.

Illustration reduced.

2002, Feb. 14 *Perf. 13¼x13½*

No.	Type	Description	Unused	Used
981	A227	Horiz. pair	1.50	1.50
a.-b.		23p Either single	.75	.75
982	A227	Horiz. pair	1.75	1.75
a.-b.		27p Either single	.85	.85
983	A227	Horiz. pair	2.50	2.50
a.-b.		37p Either single	1.25	1.25
984	A227	Horiz. pair	2.80	2.80
a.-b.		42p Either single	1.40	1.40
		Nos. 981-984 (4)	8.55	8.55

Souvenir Sheet

Perf. 13¼x13

No.	Type	Description	Unused	Used
985	A227	Horiz. pair	5.00	5.00
a.-b.		75p Either single	2.50	2.50

No. 985 contains two 29x38mm stamps.

POSTAGE DUE STAMPS

Catalogue values for unused stamps in this section are for Never Hinged items.

D1

D2

Imprint: "1973 Questa"

Perf. 13½

1973, July 5 Litho. Unwmk.

Inscriptions and Coat of Arms in Black and Red

No.	Type	Description	Unused	Used
J1	D1	½p yellow	.20	.20
J2	D1	1p buff	.30	.30
J3	D1	2p lt yellow grn	1.00	1.00
J4	D1	3p gray	1.75	1.75
J5	D1	4p dull rose	2.75	2.75
J6	D1	5p light blue	3.00	3.00
J7	D1	10p light violet	6.75	6.75
J8	D1	20p lt grnsh blue	16.00	16.00
		Nos. J1-J8 (8)	31.75	31.75

Imprint: "1973 A Questa"

1973, Sept.

No.	Type	Description	Unused	Used
J1a	D1	½p	1.60	1.40
J2a	D1	1p	.85	.40
J3a	D1	2p	.25	.20
J4a	D1	3p	.20	.20
J5a	D1	4p	.25	.20
J6a	D1	5p	.25	.20
J7a	D1	10p	.40	.35
J8a	D1	20p	.85	.60
		Nos. J1a-J8a (8)	4.65	3.55

1975, Jan. 8 Litho. *Perf. 14*

Inscriptions and Coat of Arms in Black and Red

No.	Type	Description	Unused	Used
J9	D2	½p yellow	.20	.20
J10	D2	1p buff	.20	.20
J11	D2	4p lilac rose	.20	.20
J12	D2	7p blue	.25	.25
J13	D2	9p sepia	.30	.30
J14	D2	10p lilac	.35	.35
J15	D2	50p orange	1.10	1.10
J16	D2	£1 bright green	2.25	2.25
		Nos. J9-J16 (8)	4.85	4.85

D3

D4

1982-92 Litho. *Perf. 15x14*

No.	Type	Description	Unused	Used
J17	D3	1p light green	.20	.20
J18	D3	2p bright pink	.20	.20
J19	D3	5p grnsh blue	.20	.20
J20	D3	10p bright lilac	.35	.35
J21	D3	20p gray	.65	.65
J22	D3	50p dull yellow	1.60	1.60
J23	D3	£1 brick red	2.25	2.25
J24	D3	£2 blue	5.00	5.00

Litho.

Perf. 13x13½

No.	Type	Description	Unused	Used
J25	D4	£5 multicolored	11.50	11.50
		Nos. J17-J25 (9)	21.95	21.95

Issued: £5, 9/16/92; others, 10/5/82.

GREECE

'grēs

(Hellas)

LOCATION — Southern part of the Balkan Peninsula in southeastern Europe, bordering on the Ionian, Aegean and Mediterranean Seas
GOVT. — Republic
AREA — 50,949 sq. mi.
POP. — 10,511,000 (1997 est.)
CAPITAL — Athens

In 1923 the reigning king was forced to abdicate and the following year Greece was declared a republic. In 1935, the king was recalled by a "plebiscite" of the people. Greece became a republic in June 1973. The country today includes the Aegean Islands of Chios, Mytilene (Lesbos), Samos, Icaria (Nicaria) and Lemnos, the Ionian Islands (Corfu, etc.) Crete, Macedonia, Western Thrace and part of Eastern Thrace, the Mount Athos District, Epirus and the Dodecanese Islands.

100 Lepta = 1 Drachma
100 Cents = 1 Euro (2002)

Catalogue values for unused stamps in this country are for Never Hinged items, beginning with Scott 472 in the regular postage section, Scott B1 in the semi-postal section, Scott C48 in the airpost section, Scott CB1 in the airpost semi-postal section, Scott RA69 in the postal tax section, and Scott N239 in the occupation and annexation section.

Values for unused stamps are for examples with original gum as defined in the catalogue introduction. Any exceptions will be noted.

Values for Large Hermes Head stamps with double control numbers on the back, Nos. 20e, 21c, 27a, et al, are for examples with two distinct and separate impressions, not for blurred or "slide doubles" caused by paper slippage on the press.

Watermarks

Wmk. 129- Crown and ET

Wmk. 252- Crowns

Paris Print

Hermes (Mercury) — A1

Paris Print, Fine Impression

The enlarged illustrations show the head in various states of the plates. The differences are best seen in the shading lines on the cheek and neck.

1861 Unwmk. Typo. *Imperf.*

Without Figures on Back

No.	Type	Description	Unused	Used
1	A1	1 l choc, *brnish*	275.00	275.00
a.		1 l red brown, *brnish*	300.00	300.00
2	A1	2 l ol bis, *straw*	25.00	*37.50*
a.		2 l brown buff, *buff*	27.50	*37.50*
3	A1	5 l yel grn, *grnsh*	450.00	85.00
4	A1	20 l bl, *bluish*	700.00	57.50
a.		20 l deep blue, *bluish*	1,000.	160.00
b.		On pelure paper	1,100.	*200.00*
5	A1	40 l vio, *bl*	200.00	85.00
6	A1	80 l rose, *pink*	175.00	80.00
a.		80 l carmine, *pink*	175.00	80.00

Large Figures, 8mm high, on Back

No.	Type	Description	Unused	Used
7	A1	10 l red org, *bl*	550.00	325.00
a.		"10" on back inverted	—	—
c.		"0" of "10" invtd. on back	—	*1,250.*
d.		"1" of "10" invtd. on back	—	*1,250.*

No. 7 without "10" on back is a proof.

Trial impressions of Paris prints exist in many shades, some being close to those of the issued stamps. The gum used was thin and smooth instead of thick, brownish and crackly as on the issued stamps.

See #8-58. For surcharges see #130, 132-133, 137-139, 141-143, 147-149, 153-154, 157-158.

Faint quadrille, horizontal or vertical lines are visible in the background of some Athens print large Hermes head stamps.

Nos. 16, 16a, 16b are the only 1 l stamps that have these lines.

Athens Prints

Athens Print, Typical Clear Impression

Athens Print, Typical Coarse Impression

Figures on Back

5 l:

5

#11

#18-45

Fine Printing (F)
Fine Printing (F, '62) see footnote
Coarse Printing (C)

1861-62

Without Figures on Back

No.	Type	Description	Unused	Used
8	A1	1 l choc, *brnish* (F, '62)	35.00	*50.00*
a.		1 l dk chocolate, *brnish* (F)	1,000.	1,000.
b.		1 l chocolate, *brnish* (F)	450.00	450.00
9	A1	2 l bis brn, *bister* (F)	35.00	*50.00*
a.		2 l dark brown, *straw*, (C)	*4,000.*	—
b.		2 l bister brown, *bister* (C)	40.00	*57.50*
c.		2 l bis brn, *bister* (F, '62)	42.50	*57.50*
10	A1	20 l dk bl, *bluish* (C)		*9,000.*

With Figures on Back

No.	Type	Description	Unused	Used
11	A1	5 l grn, *grnsh* (F)	175.00	72.50
a.		5 l green, *greenish* (C)	190.00	75.00
b.		As "a," double "5" on back (F, C)		*1,250.*
c.		5 l green, *greenish,* bl grn figures on back (F, '62)	200.00	42.50
12	A1	10 l org, *grnsh* (F, '62)	225.00	32.50
a.		10 l orange, *greenish* (C)	575.00	80.00
c.		10 l orange, *greenish* (F)	400.00	75.00
13	A1	20 l blue, *bluish* (F, '62)	*350.00*	42.50
a.		20 l dull blue, *bluish* (C)	*4,500.*	125.00
b.		20 l dark blue, *bluish,* (F)	*2,500.*	62.50
14	A1	40 l red vio, *pale bl* (F, '62)	*1,750.*	100.00
a.		40 l red violet, *blue* (C)	*4,750.*	325.00
b.		40 l red violet, *blue,* (F)	*3,000.*	225.00
15	A1	80 l carmine, *pink* (F, '62)	70.00	55.00
a.		80 l carmine, *pink* (F)	625.00	82.50
b.		80 l dl rose, *pink* (F)	575.00	80.00

Nos. 8-15 are known as the "Athens Provisionals." The first printings were not very successful, producing the "coarse printings." Later printings used an altered printing method that gave better results (the "fine printings"). All these were issued in the normal manner by the Post Office.

Nos. 8, 9c, 11c, 12, 13, 14, 15 have uninterrupted and even shading lines that do not taper off at the ends. They were produced in May 1862 (F, '62). Other fine printing stamps were produced in Feb.-Apr. 1862 (F).

The numerals on the back are strongly shaded in the right lines with the corresponding left lines being quite thin. The colors of the numerals are generally strong and often show clumps of ink.

Nos. 15a and 15b have vermilion figures on the back, while those of all later printings are carmine.

1862-67

With Figures on Back, Except 1 l and 2 l

No.	Type	Description	Unused	Used
16	A1	1 l brn, *brnish* (poor print)	30.00	30.00
a.		1 l red brn, *brnish* (poor print)	60.00	60.00
b.		1 l choc, *brnish*	42.50	42.50
17	A1	2 l bister, *bister*	5.75	*8.50*
a.		2 l brnsh bis, *bister*	8.50	*11.00*
18	A1	5 l grn, *grnsh*	150.00	8.50
a.		5 l yellowish green, *grnsh*	150.00	8.50
19	A1	10 l org, *blue* ('64)	200.00	10.00
a.		10 l yel org, *bluish*	250.00	37.50
b.		As "b," "10" inverted on front of stamp		*10,000.*
c.		10 l red org, *bl* (Dec. '65)	*200.00*	10.00
d.		"01" on back		*100.00*
20	A1	20 l bl, *bluish*	160.00	5.50
a.		20 l lt bl, *bluish* (fine print)	190.00	11.00
b.		20 l dark blue, *bluish*	275.00	17.50
c.		20 l blue, *greenish*	*800.00*	11.00
d.		"80" on back		*1,000.*
e.		Double "20" on back		*750.00*
f.		Without "20" on back		*4,000.*
21	A1	40 l lilac, *bl*	225.00	17.00
a.		40 l grayish lilac, *blue*	1,150.	20.00
b.		40 l lilac brown, *lil gray*	*800.00*	14.00
c.		Double "40" on back		1,000.
22	A1	80 l car, *pale rose*	50.00	10.00
a.		80 l rose, *pale rose*	55.00	10.00
b.		"8" on back inverted	—	225.00
c.		"80" on back inverted		—
d.		"8" only on back		500.00
e.		"0" only on back		500.00

Nos. 16-22 represent a series of printings for each value, from 1862 through 1867, until a major cleaning of the plates was done in 1868. **Impressions range from very fine and clear to coarse and blotchy.**

Some printings of Nos. 16, 16a, 16b show faint vertical, horizontal or quadrilled lines in the background. Later 1 l stamps do not show these lines.

Many stamps of this and succeeding issues which are normally imperforate are known privately rouletted, pin-perforated, percé en scie, etc.

1868

From Cleaned Plates

With Figures on Back, Except 1 l and 2 l

No.	Type	Description	Unused	Used
23	A1	1 l gray brn, *brnish*	32.50	*40.00*
a.		1 l brown, *brownish*	32.50	*40.00*
24	A1	2 l gray bis, *bister*	12.00	*14.00*
25	A1	5 l grn, *grnsh*	*1,400.*	50.00
26	A1	10 l pale org, *bluish*	*900.00*	16.00
a.		"01" on back		—
27	A1	20 l pale bl, *bluish*	*900.00*	7.00
a.		Double "20" on back		*725.00*
28	A1	40 l rose vio, *bl*	200.00	17.00
a.		"20" on back, corrected to "40"	*1,750.*	*1,250.*
29	A1	80 l rose car, *pale rose*	125.00	125.00

The "0" on the back of No. 29 is printed more heavily than the "8."

1870

With Figures on Back, Except 1 l

No.	Type	Description	Unused	Used
30	A1	1 l deep reddish brn, *brnish*	60.00	*70.00*
a.		1 l redsh brn, *brnish*	100.00	*125.00*
31	A1	20 l lt bl, *bluish*	*1,100.*	7.50
a.		20 l blue, *bluish*	*1,200.*	7.50
b.		"02" on back		425.00
c.		"20" on back inverted		425.00

Nos. 30 and 30a have short lines of shading on cheek. The spandrels of No. 31 are very pale with the lines often broken or missing.

This was an Athens Printing made under supervision of German workmen.

1870

Medium to Thin Paper
Without Mesh
With Figures on Back, Except 1 l and 2 l

32 A1 1 l brn, *brnish* 80.00 80.00
a. 1 l purple brown, *brnish* 125.00 125.00
33 A1 2 l sal bis, *bister* 8.00 *15.00*
34 A1 5 l grn, *grnsh* *1,600.* 42.50
35 A1 10 l lt red org, *grnsh* *1,100.* 42.50
a. "01" on back —
b. "10" on back inverted — 550.00
36 A1 20 l bl, *bluish* *725.00* 7.00
a. "02" on back 275.00
b. Double "20" on back 700.00
37 A1 40 l sal, *grnsh* 425.00 35.00
a. 40 l lilac, *greenish* —

The stamps of this issue have rather coarse figures on back.

No. 37a is printed in the exact shade of the numerals on the back of No. 37.

1872

Thin Transparent Paper
Showing Mesh
With Figures on Back, Except 1 l

38 A1 1 l grayish brown, *straw* 35.00 *40.00*
a. 1 l red brn, *yelsh* 45.00 *55.00*
39 A1 5 l grn, *greenish* 375.00 17.50
a. 5 l dark green, *grnsh* 400.00 20.00
b. Double "5" on back 100.00
40 A1 10 l red org, *grnsh* *600.00* 6.00
a. 10 l red orange, *pale lilac* *2,750.* 95.00
b. As #40, "10" on back inverted — 45.00
c. Double "10" on back 625.00
d. "0" on back 325.00
e. "01" on back — *1,250.*
41 A1 20 l dp bl, *bluish* 700.00 6.50
a. 20 l blue, *bluish* 700.00 10.00
b. 20 l dark blue, *blue* 900.00 17.00
42 A1 40 l brn, *bl* 20.00 *30.00*
a. 40 l olive brown, *blue* 22.50 *30.00*
b. 40 l red violet, *blue* 450.00 45.00
c. 40 l gray violet, *blue* 450.00 40.00
d. Figures on back bister (#42b, 42c) — 60.00

The mesh is not apparent on Nos. 38, 38a.

1875

On Cream Paper Unless Otherwise Stated
With Figures on Back, Except 1 l and 2 l

43 A1 1 l gray brn 5.75 4.25
a. 1 l dark gray brown 32.50 32.50
b. 1 l black brown 42.50 *50.00*
c. 1 l red brown 22.50 *27.50*
d. 1 l dark red brown 22.50 *32.50*
e. 1 l purple brown 35.00 *42.50*
44 A1 2 l bister 10.00 *25.00*
45 A1 5 l pale yel grn 125.00 12.00
a. 5 l dk yel grn 150.00 21.00
46 A1 10 l orange 140.00 12.00
a. 10 l orange, *yellow* 150.00 12.00
c. "00" on back 750.00 72.50
d. "1" on back — 110.00
e. "0" on back — 72.50
f. "01" on back — 200.00
g. Double "10" on back — 275.00
47 A1 20 l ultra 85.00 4.00
a. 20 l blue 150.00 7.25
b. 20 l deep Prussian blue 1,300. 35.00
c. "02" on back — 240.00
d. "20" on back inverted — *5,250.*
e. As "c," inverted — *750.00*
f. Double "20" on back — 300.00
48 A1 40 l salmon 21.00 *37.50*

The back figures are found in many varieties, including "1" and "0" inverted in "10."

Value for No. 47e is for example with "2" of "02" broken (deformed). Also known with unbroken "2"; value used about $600.

1876

Without Figures on Back
Paris Print, Clear Impression

49 A1 30 l ol brn, *yelsh* 150.00 30.00
a. 30 l brown, *yellowish* 250.00 65.00
50 A1 60 l grn, *grnsh* 25.00 *60.00*

Athens Print, Coarse Impression, Yellowish Paper

51 A1 30 l dark brown 42.50 4.00
a. 30 l black brown 42.50 4.00
52 A1 60 l green 275.00 35.00

1880-82 **Cream Paper**
Without Figures on Back

53 A1 5 l green 17.50 2.25
54 A1 10 l orange 17.50 2.25
a. 10 l yellow 17.50 2.25
b. 10 l red orange *2,100.* 35.00
55 A1 20 l ultra 250.00 100.00
56 A1 20 l pale rose (aniline ink) ('82) 3.00 1.75
a. 20 l rose (aniline ink) ('82) 4.25 2.75
b. 20 l deep carmine 160.00 7.50
57 A1 30 l ultra ('82) 125.00 7.25
a. 30 l slate blue 125.00 7.25
58 A1 40 l lilac 42.50 7.25
a. 40 l violet 42.50 15.00

Stamps of type A1 were not regularly issued with perf. 11½ but were freely used on mail.

Hermes — A2

Lepta denominations have white numeral tablets.

Belgian Print, Clear Impression

1886-88 ***Imperf.***

64 A2 1 l brown ('88) 1.00 1.00
65 A2 2 l bister ('88) 2.00 *72.50*
66 A2 5 l yel grn ('88) 3.50 1.25
67 A2 10 l yellow ('88) 6.00 1.00
68 A2 20 l car rose ('88) 22.50 1.00
69 A2 25 l blue 65.00 1.00
70 A2 40 l violet ('88) 32.50 15.00
71 A2 50 l gray grn 3.00 1.00
72 A2 1d gray 40.00 1.00
Nos. 64-72 (9) 175.50 94.75

See Nos. 81-116. For surcharges see Nos. 129, 134, 140, 144, 150, 151-152, 155-156.

1891 ***Perf. 11½***

81 A2 1 l brown 2.00 2.00
82 A2 2 l bister 6.00 —
83 A2 5 l yel grn 12.50 9.00
84 A2 10 l yellow 18.00 9.00
85 A2 20 l car rose 32.50 12.50
86 A2 25 l blue 100.00 17.50
87 A2 40 l violet 90.00 50.00
88 A2 50 l gray grn 15.00 4.50
89 A2 1d gray 100.00 5.00
Nos. 81-89 (9) 376.00

The Belgian Printings perf. 13½ and most of the values perf. 11½ (Nos. 82-86) were perforated on request of philatelists at the main post office in Athens. While not regularly issued they were freely used for postage.

Athens Print, Poor Impression

Wmk. Greek Words in Some Sheets

1889-95 ***Imperf.***

90 A2 1 l black brn 1.40 1.00
a. 1 l brown 1.50 1.00
91 A2 2 l pale bister 1.25 *1.50*
a. 2 l buff 1.75 *2.00*
92 A2 5 l green 2.50 1.00
a. Double impression *125.00* *250.00*
b. 5 l deep green 5.00 1.25
93 A2 10 l yellow 10.00 1.00
a. 10 l orange 20.00 3.00
b. 10 l dull yellow 30.00 2.00
94 A2 20 l carmine 3.25 1.00
a. 20 l rose 16.00 1.25
95 A2 25 l dull blue 40.00 1.00
a. 25 l indigo 85.00 4.50
b. 25 l ultra 75.00 2.50
c. 25 l brt blue 40.00 2.25
96 A2 25 l lilac 3.00 1.00
a. 25 l red vio ('93) 9.00 2.25
97 A2 40 l red vio ('91) 40.00 22.50
98 A2 40 l blue ('93) 5.25 1.25
99 A2 1d gray ('95) 225.00 4.75

Perf. 13½

100 A2 1 l brown 20.00 20.00
101 A2 2 l buff 1.50 1.50
104 A2 20 l carmine 12.50 4.75
a. 20 l rose 22.50 5.75
105 A2 40 l red violet 70.00 42.50

Other denominations of type A2 were not officially issued with perf. 13½.

Perf. 11½

107 A2 1 l brown 1.50 1.10
a. 1 l black brown 5.75 4.50
108 A2 2 l pale bister 2.00 1.60
a. 2 l buff 2.25 2.25
109 A2 5 l pale green 3.00 .90
a. 5 l deep green 5.00 1.25
110 A2 10 l yellow 10.00 1.00
a. 10 l dull yellow 27.50 2.00
b. 10 l orange 40.00 4.50
111 A2 20 l carmine 4.00 .60
a. 20 l rose 20.00 1.25
112 A2 25 l dull blue 47.50 3.00
a. 25 l indigo 95.00 17.50
b. 25 l ultra 65.00 42.50
c. 25 l bright blue 47.50 7.25
113 A2 25 l lilac 4.00 1.25
a. 25 l red violet 9.00 2.25
114 A2 40 l red violet 45.00 30.00
115 A2 40 l blue 7.50 1.50
116 A2 1d gray 225.00 8.00

Partly-perforated varieties sell for about twice as much as normal copies.

The watermark on Nos. 90-116 consists of three Greek words meaning Paper for Public Service. It is in double-lined capitals, measures 270x35mm, and extends across three panes.

Boxers — A3

Discobolus by Myron — A4

Vase Depicting Pallas Athene (Minerva) — A5

Chariot Driving A6

Stadium and Acropolis A7

Statue of Hermes by Praxiteles — A8

Statue of Victory by Paeonius — A9

Acropolis and Parthenon A10

Perf. 14x13½, 13½x14

1896 **Unwmk.**

117 A3 1 l ocher .90 .45
118 A3 2 l rose 1.40 .45
a. Without engraver's name 10.50 9.50
119 A4 5 l lilac 1.75 .90
120 A4 10 l slate gray 2.25 1.40
121 A5 20 l red brn 11.00 2.25
122 A6 25 l red 11.00 2.25
123 A5 40 l violet 10.00 5.75
124 A6 60 l black 20.00 11.00
125 A7 1d blue 45.00 9.00
126 A8 2d bister 160.00 55.00
a. Horiz. pair, imperf. btwn.
127 A9 5d green 290.00 250.00
128 A10 10d brown 350.00 *290.00*
Nos. 117-128 (12) 903.30 628.45

1st intl. Olympic Games of the modern era, held at Athens. Counterfeits of Nos. 123-124 and 126-128 exist.

For surcharges see Nos. 159-164.

Preceding Issues Surcharged

1900 ***Imperf.***

129 A2 20 l on 25 l dl bl, #95c 2.50 .75
a. 20 l on 25 l indigo, #95a 35.00 30.00
b. 20 l on 25 l ultra, #95b 50.00 40.00
c. Double surcharge 40.00 —
d. Triple surcharge 50.00 —
e. Inverted surcharge 40.00 —
f. "20" above word 90.00 —
g. Pair, one without surcharge 150.00 —
h. "20" without word 90.00 —
130 A1 30 l on 40 l vio, *cr*, #58a 2.50 2.50
a. 30 l on 40 l lilac, #58 5.25 4.50
b. Broad "0" in "30" 8.00 5.00
c. First letter of word is "A" 60.00 37.50
d. Double surcharge *250.00* *200.00*
132 A1 40 l on 2 l bis, *cr*, #44 4.50 4.00
a. Broad "0" in "40" 8.00 6.00
b. First letter of word is "A" 60.00 45.00
133 A1 50 l on 40 l sal, *cr*, #48 4.50 3.50
a. Broad "0" in "50" 8.00 5.25
b. First letter of word is "A" 60.00 45.00
c. "50" without word 175.00 125.00
d. "50" above word 175.00 125.00
134 A2 1d on 40 l red vio (No. 97) 10.00 3.00
137 A1 3d on 10 l org, *cr*, #54 40.00 40.00
a. 3d on 10 l yellow, #54a 40.00 40.00
138 A1 5d on 40 l red vio, *bl*, #21 80.00 80.00
a. 5d on 40 l red vio, *bl*, #28 90.00 *100.00*
b. "20" on back corrected to "40" *1,000.*
139 A1 5d on 40 l red vio, *bl*, #42b 300.00

Perf. 11½

140 A2 20 l on 25 l dl bl, #112 2.50 .75
a. 20 l on 25 l indigo, #112a 75.00 45.00
b. 20 l on 25 l ultra, #112b 60.00 40.00
c. Double surcharge 37.50 —
d. Triple surcharge 50.00 —
e. Inverted surcharge 37.50 —
f. "20" above word 90.00 —
141 A1 30 l on 40 l vio, *cr*, #58a 2.50 2.50
a. 30 l on 40 l lilac, #58 7.50 7.00
b. Broad "0" in "30" 7.00 7.00
c. First letter of word "A" 70.00 60.00
d. Double surcharge
142 A1 40 l on 2 l bis, *cr*, #44 5.00 3.50
a. Broad "0" in "40" 7.50 7.50
b. First letter of word "A" 77.50 77.50
143 A1 50 l on 40 l sal, *cr*, #48 5.00 3.50
a. Broad "0" in "50" 9.00 7.50
b. First letter of word "A" 80.00 80.00
c. "50" without word 175.00
144 A2 1d on 40 l red vio, #114 15.00 11.00
147 A1 3d on 10 l yel, *cream*, #54a 37.50 37.50
a. 3d on 10 l org, *cr*, #54 50.00 *55.00*
148 A1 5d on 40 l red vio, *bl*, #21 100.00 100.00
a. 5d on 40 l red vio, *bl*, #28 110.00 *125.00*
149 A1 5d on 40 l red vio, *bl*, #42 300.00

Perf. 13½

150 A2 2d on 40 l red vio, #105 7.50 *8.75*

The 1d on 40 l perf. 13½ and the 2d on 40 l, both imperf. and perf. 13½, were not officially issued.

Surcharge Including "A M"

"A M" = "Axia Metalliki" or "Value in Metal (gold)."

1900 ***Imperf.***

151 A2 25 l on 40 l vio, #70 5.00 5.00
152 A2 50 l on 25 l bl, #69 20.00 20.00
153 A1 1d on 40 l brn, *bl*, #42b 80.00 80.00
154 A1 2d on 5 l grn, *cr*, #53 12.50 12.50

Perf. 11½

155 A2 25 l on 40 l vio, #87 7.50 7.50
156 A2 50 l on 25 l bl, #86 27.50 *27.50*
157 A1 1d on 40 l brn, *bl*, #42b 110.00 110.00
158 A1 2d on 5 l grn, *cr*, #53 15.00 15.00
Nos. 151-158 (8) 277.50 277.50

Partly-perforated varieties of Nos. 129-158 sell for about two to three times as much as normal copies.

Surcharge Including "A M" on Olympic Issue in Red

1900-01 ***Perf. 14x13½***

159 A7 5 l on 1d blue 7.50 4.75
a. Wrong font "M" with serifs 50.00 *60.00*
b. Double surcharge 175.00 175.00
160 A5 25 l on 40 l vio 50.00 40.00
161 A8 50 l on 2d bister 45.00 35.00
a. Broad "0" in "50" 57.50 40.00
162 A9 1d on 5d grn ('01) 160.00 125.00
a. Greek "D" instead of "A" as 3rd letter 525.00 *600.00*
163 A10 2d on 10d brn ('01) 37.50 *52.50*
a. Greek "D" instead of "A" as 3rd letter 225.00 210.00
Nos. 159-163 (5) 300.00 257.25

Black Surcharge on No. 160

164 A5 50 l on 25 l on 40 l vio (R + Bk) 450.00 425.00
a. Broad "0" in "50" 425.00 *525.00*

Nos. 151-164 and 179-183, gold currency stamps, were generally used for parcel post and foreign money orders. They were also available for use on letters, but cost about 20 per cent more than the regular stamps of the same denomination.

Counterfeit surcharges exist of #159-164.

Giovanni da Bologna's Hermes
A11 A12

A13

FIVE LEPTA.

Type I - Letters of "ELLAS" not outlined at top and left. Only a few faint horizontal lines between the outer vertical lines at sides.

Type II - Letters of "ELLAS" fully outlined. Heavy horizontal lines between the vertical frame lines.

Perf. 11½, 12½, 13½

1901 Engr. Wmk. 129

165	A11	1 l yellow brn	.25	.20
166	A11	2 l gray	.30	.20
167	A11	3 l orange	.45	.25
168	A12	5 l grn, type I	.45	.20
a.		5 l yellow green, type I	.45	.20
b.		5 l yellow green, type II	.45	.20
169	A12	10 l rose	1.25	.20
170	A11	20 l red lilac	1.40	.20
171	A12	25 l ultra	1.75	.20
172	A11	30 l dl vio	8.50	1.50
173	A11	40 l dk brn	1.50	1.10
174	A11	50 l brn lake	11.00	.75

Perf. 12½, 14 and Compound

175	A13	1d black	26.00	2.00
a.		Horiz. pair, imperf. btwn.	275.00	
c.		Horiz. pair, imperf. vert.	250.00	
d.		Vert. pair, imperf. horiz.	250.00	

Litho.

Perf. 12½

176	A13	2d bronze	7.25	5.00
177	A13	3d silver	7.25	*8.50*
a.		Horiz. pair, imperf. btwn.	800.00	
178	A13	5d gold	9.00	9.00
		Nos. 165-178 (14)	76.35	29.30
		Set, never hinged	200.00	

All values1 l through 1d issued on both thick and thin paper. Nos. 173-174 are values for thin paper - values for thick paper are higher.

For overprints and surcharges see Nos. RA3-RA13, N16, N109.

Imperf., Pairs

165a	A11	1 l	10.00
166a	A11	2 l	13.00
167a	A11	3 l	13.00
168c	A12	5 l	10.00
169a	A12	10 l	15.00
170a	A11	20 l	13.00
171a	A12	25 l	13.00
172a	A11	30 l	200.00
173a	A11	40 l	240.00
174a	A11	50 l	50.00
175b	A13	1d	200.00

Nos. 165a-175a were issued on both thick and thin paper. Values are for the less expensive thin paper.

Hermes — A14

1902, Jan. 1 Engr. *Perf. 13½*

179	A14	5 l deep orange	1.10	1.00
a.		Imperf., pair	75.00	
180	A14	25 l emerald	21.00	2.00
181	A14	50 l ultra	21.00	2.50
a.		Imperf., pair	500.00	
182	A14	1d rose red	21.00	5.50
183	A14	2d orange brn	30.00	30.00
		Nos. 179-183 (5)	94.10	41.00
		Set, never hinged	275.00	

See note after No. 164. In 1913 remainders of Nos. 179-183 were used as postage dues.

Apollo Throwing Discus A15

Jumper, with Jumping Weights A16

Victory — A17

Atlas and Hercules A18

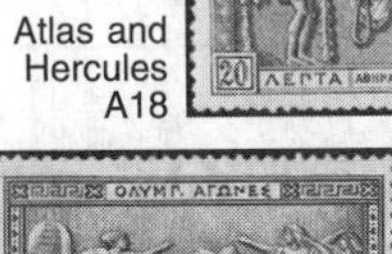

Struggle of Hercules and Antaeus A19

Wrestlers A20

Daemon of the Games A21

Foot Race A22

Nike, Priest and Athletes in Pre-Games Offering to Zeus — A23

Wmk. Crown and ET (129)

1906, Mar. Engr. *Perf. 13½, 14*

184	A15	1 l brown	.40	.35
a.		Imperf., pair	*275.00*	
185	A15	2 l gray	.40	.35
a.		Imperf., pair	*275.00*	
186	A16	3 l orange	.40	.35
a.		Imperf., pair	275.00	
187	A16	5 l green	.55	.35
a.		Imperf., pair	100.00	
188	A17	10 l rose red	1.25	.55
a.		Imperf., pair	*275.00*	
189	A18	20 l magenta	2.75	.55
a.		Imperf., pair	*525.00*	
190	A19	25 l ultra	2.75	.70
a.		Imperf., pair	*525.00*	
191	A20	30 l dl pur	3.00	2.25
a.		Double impression	*1,000.*	
192	A21	40 l dk brown	3.00	2.25
193	A18	50 l brn lake	5.50	2.75
194	A22	1d gray blk	50.00	9.00
a.		Imperf., pair	*1,000.*	
195	A22	2d rose	70.00	25.00
196	A22	3d olive yel	125.00	100.00
197	A23	5d dull blue	140.00	110.00
		Nos. 184-197 (14)	405.00	254.45
		Set, never hinged	900.00	

Greek Special Olympic Games of 1906 at Athens, celebrating the 10th anniv. of the modern Olympic Games.

Surcharged stamps of this issue are revenues.

A24

Iris Holding Caduceus A25

Hermes Donning Sandals A26

Hermes Carrying Infant Arcas — A27

Hermes, from Old Cretan Coin — A28

Designs A24 to A28 are from Cretan and Arcadian coins of the 4th Century, B.C.

Serrate Roulette 13½

1911-21 Engr. Unwmk.

198	A24	1 l green	.25	.20
199	A25	2 l car rose	.25	.20
200	A24	3 l vermilion	.40	.20
201	A26	5 l green	.75	.20
202	A24	10 l car rose	3.75	.20
203	A25	20 l gray lilac	1.50	.35
204	A25	25 l ultra	6.25	.20
a.		Rouletted in black	175.00	125.00
205	A26	30 l car rose	1.25	.75
206	A25	40 l deep blue	4.50	2.25
207	A26	50 l dl vio	7.50	1.50
208	A27	1d ultra	7.50	.60
209	A27	2d vermilion	12.50	.60
210	A27	3d car rose	10.00	.75
a.		Size 20¼x25½mm ('21)	50.00	27.50
211	A27	5d ultra	25.00	2.00
a.		Size 20¼x25½mm ('21)	150.00	22.50
212	A27	10d dp bl ('21)	125.00	62.50
a.		Size 20x26½mm ('11)	200.00	110.00
213	A28	25d deep blue	45.00	27.50
		Nos. 198-213 (16)	251.40	100.00
		Set, never hinged	425.00	

The 1921 reissues of the 3d, 5d and 10d measure 20¼x25½mm instead of 20x26½mm.

See Nos. 214-231. For overprints see Nos. 233-248B, N1, N10-N15, N17-N52A, N110-N148, Thrace 22-30, N26-N75.

Imperf., Pairs

198a	A24	1 l	70.00	70.00
200a	A24	3 l	*200.00*	190.00
201a	A26	5 l	20.00	21.00
202a	A24	10 l	40.00	40.00
203a	A25	20 l	175.00	175.00
204b	A25	25 l	225.00	240.00
206a	A25	40 l	275.00	

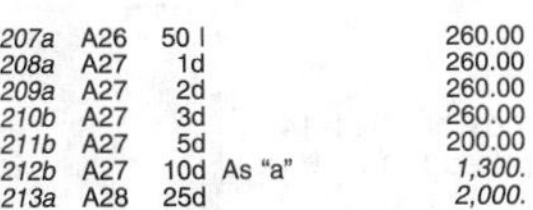

207a	A26	50 l	260.00
208a	A27	1d	260.00
209a	A27	2d	260.00
210b	A27	3d	260.00
211b	A27	5d	200.00
212b	A27	10d As "a"	*1,300.*
213a	A28	25d	*2,000.*

Serrate Roulette 10½x13½, 13½

1913-23 Litho.

214	A24	1 l green	.20	.20
a.		Without period after "Ellas"	70.00	—
215	A25	2 l rose	.20	.20
216	A24	3 l vermilion	.20	.20
217	A26	5 l green	.20	.20
218	A24	10 l carmine	.20	.20
219	A25	15 l dl bl ('18)	.25	.20
220	A25	20 l slate	.25	.20
221	A25	25 l ultra	2.50	.20
a.		25 l blue	.20	
c.		Double impression	—	
222	A26	30 l rose ('14)	.55	.20
223	A25	40 l indigo ('14)	1.50	.50
224	A26	50 l vio brn ('14)	2.90	.25
225	A26	80 l vio brn ('23)	3.75	1.00
226	A27	1d ultra ('19)	5.00	.50
227	A27	2d ver ('19)	4.50	.50
228	A27	3d car rose ('20)	6.00	.60
229	A27	5d ultra ('22)	8.00	.70
230	A27	10d dp bl ('22)	6.50	.90
231	A28	25d indigo ('22)	8.00	2.50
		Nos. 214-231 (18)	50.70	9.25
		Set, never hinged	175.00	

Nos. 221, 223 and 226 were re-issued in 1926, printed in Vienna from new plates. There are slight differences in minor details.

The 10 lepta brown, on thick paper, type A28, is not a postage stamp. It was issued in 1922 to replace coins of this denomination during a shortage of copper.

Imperf., Pairs

214b	A24	1 l	60.00
215a	A25	2 l	100.00
216a	A24	3 l	160.00
217a	A26	5 l	60.00
218a	A24	10 l	75.00
220a	A25	20 l	75.00
221b	A25	25 l	160.00
222a	A26	30 l	160.00
223a	A25	40 l	140.00
224a	A26	50 l	275.00
225b	A26	80 l	85.00
227a	A27	2d	95.00
228b	A27	3d	275.00
229a	A27	5d	325.00

Raising Greek Flag at Suda Bay, Crete A29

1913, Dec. 1 Engr. *Perf. 14½*

232	A29	25 l blue & black	4.50	3.00
		Never hinged	9.00	
a.		Imperf., pair	*1,000.*	

Union of Crete with Greece. Used only in Crete.

Stamps of 1911-14 Overprinted in Red or Black

Serrate Roulette 13½

1916, Nov. 1 **Litho.**

233	A24	1 l green (R)	.20	.20
234	A25	2 l rose	.20	.20
235	A24	3 l vermilion	.20	.20
236	A26	5 l green (R)	.45	.35
237	A24	10 l carmine	.50	.35
238	A25	20 l slate (R)	1.00	.35
239	A25	25 l blue (R)	1.00	.35
a.		25 l ultra	90.00	20.00
240	A26	30 l rose	1.00	.75
a.		Pair, one without ovpt.		
241	A25	40 l indigo (R)	8.50	2.25
242	A26	50 l vio brn (R)	27.50	2.00

Engr.

243	A24	3 l vermilion	.45	.45
244	A26	30 l car rose	1.00	1.00
245	A27	1d ultra (R)	20.00	.60
a.		Rouletted in black	300.00	200.00
246	A27	2d vermilion	17.50	2.75
247	A27	3d car rose	10.50	2.75
248	A27	5d ultra (R)	67.50	6.00
248B	A27	10d dp bl (R)	17.50	15.00
		Nos. 233-248B (17)	175.00	35.55
		Set, never hinged	350.00	

Most of Nos. 233-248B exist with overprint double, inverted, etc. Minimum value of errors $16. Excellent counterfeits of the overprint varieties exist.

Issued by the Venizelist Provisional Government

Iris — A32

1917, Feb. 5 **Litho.** *Perf. 14*

249	A32	1 l dp green	.25	.20
250	A32	5 l yel grn	.25	.20
251	A32	10 l rose	.60	.25
252	A32	25 l lt blue	.85	.25
253	A32	50 l gray vio	6.00	1.75
254	A32	1d ultra	1.50	.50
255	A32	2d lt red	3.00	1.00
256	A32	3d claret	12.00	5.00
257	A32	5d gray bl	3.75	2.00
258	A32	10d dk blue	45.00	12.50
259	A32	25d slate	70.00	70.00
		Nos. 249-259 (11)	143.20	93.65
		Set, never hinged	300.00	

The 4d was used only as a revenue stamp.

Imperf., Pairs

249a	A32	1 l	8.50
250a	A32	5 l	8.50
251a	A32	10 l	8.50
252a	A32	25 l	16.00
253a	A32	50 l	22.50
254a	A32	1d	20.00
255a	A32	2d	27.50
256a	A32	3d	60.00
257a	A32	5d	60.00
258a	A32	10d	100.00
259a	A32	25d	110.00

Stamps of 1917 Surcharged

1923

260	A32	5 l on 10 l rose	.25	.25
a.		Inverted surcharge	17.50	*25.00*
261	A32	50 l on 50 l gray vio	.25	.25
262	A32	1d on 1d ultra	.25	.25
a.		1d on 1d gray	.25	.25
263	A32	2d on 2d lt red	.50	.50
264	A32	3d on 3d claret	1.40	1.40
265	A32	5d on 5d dk bl	1.60	1.60
266	A32	25d on 25d slate	17.50	17.50
		Nos. 260-266 (7)	21.75	21.75
		Set, never hinged	37.50	

Same Surcharge on Occupation of Turkey Stamps, 1913

Perf. 13½

267	O2	5 l on 3 l org	.20	.20
a.		Inverted surcharge	17.50	
268	O1	10 l on 20 l vio	1.00	1.00
a.		Inverted surcharge	75.00	
269	O2	10 l on 25 l pale bl	.25	.25
270	O1	10 l on 30 l gray grn	.25	.25
271	O2	10 l on 40 l ind	.90	.90
272	O1	50 l on 50 l dk bl	.25	.25
a.		Inverted surcharge	65.00	35.00
273	O1	2d on 2d gray brn	40.00	40.00
274	O2	3d on 3d dl bl	3.00	3.00
a.		Imperf., pair	450.00	
275	O1	5d on 5d gray	2.75	2.75
276	O2	10d on 1d vio brn	7.50	7.50
276A	O2	10d on 10d car	650.00	
		Never hinged	900.00	
		Nos. 267-276 (10)	56.10	56.10
		Set, never hinged	110.00	

Dangerous counterfeits of No. 276A exist.

Same Surcharge on Stamps of Crete

Perf. 14

On Crete #50, 52, 59

276B	A6	5 l on 1 l red brn	17.00	17.00
277	A8	10 l on 10 l red	.20	.20
277B	A8	10 l on 25 l bl	80.00	80.00

On Crete #66-69, 71

278	A8	10 l on 25 l blue	.20	.20
279	A6	50 l on 50 l lilac	.40	*.65*
279A	A6	50 l on 50 l ultra	5.00	*7.50*
280	A9	50 l on 1d gray vio	2.00	*3.00*
280A	A11	50 l on 5d grn & blk	17.00	17.00

On Crete #77-82

281	A15	10 l on 20 l bl grn	90.00	90.00
282	A16	10 l on 25 l ultra	.40	.40
a.		Double surcharge	45.00	
283	A17	50 l on 50 l yel brn	.20	.30
284	A18	50 l on 1d rose car & brn	1.75	1.50
a.		Imperf., pair	350.00	
285	A19	3d on 3d org & blk	8.00	8.00
286	A20	5d on 5d ol grn & blk	7.00	7.00

On Crete #83-84

287	A21	10 l on 25 l bl & blk	.50	.50
a.		Imperf., pair		
287B	A22	50 l on 1d grn & blk	3.00	3.00

On Crete #96

288	A23	10 l on 10 l brn red	.20	.20
a.		Inverted surcharge	25.00	

On Crete #91

288B	A17	50 l on 50 l yel brn	*650.00*	

Dangerous counterfeits of the overprint on No. 288B are plentiful.

On Crete #109

289	A19	3d on 3d org & blk	14.00	14.00

On Crete #111, 113-120

290	A6	5 l on 1 l vio brn	.20	.20
a.		Inverted surcharge	20.00	
291	A13	5 l on 5 l grn	.20	.20
a.		Inverted surcharge	40.00	
292	A23	10 l on 10 l brn red	.20	.20
a.		Inverted surcharge	40.00	
293	A15	10 l on 20 l bl grn	.25	.25
a.		Inverted surcharge	40.00	
294	A16	10 l on 25 l ultra	.30	.30
a.		Inverted surcharge	40.00	
295	A17	50 l on 50 l yel brn	.35	.35
296	A18	50 l on 1d rose car & brn	3.00	3.00
a.		Inverted surcharge		
b.		Double surcharge	150.00	
c.		Double surch., one invtd.		
d.		Imperf., pair		
297	A19	3d on 3d org & blk	7.50	7.50
298	A20	5d on 5d ol grn & blk	125.00	125.00

Dangerous counterfeits of No. 298 exist.

Crete #J2-J9

299	D1	5 l on 5 l red	.20	.20
a.		Inverted surcharge	35.00	5.00
300	D1	5 l on 10 l red	.30	.30
301	D1	10 l on 20 l red	10.00	10.00
a.		Inverted surcharge		
302	D1	10 l on 40 l red	.30	.30
303	D1	50 l on 50 l red	.30	*.50*
304	D1	50 l on 1d red	.30	.50
a.		Double surcharge		
305	D1	50 l on 1d on 1d red	6.75	6.75
306	D1	2d on 2d red	.75	.75

On Crete #J11-J13

307	D1	5 l on 5 l red	2.50	2.50
308	D1	5 l on 10 l red	.90	.90
a.		"Ellas" inverted	5.00	
309	D1	10 l on 20 l red	32.50	32.50

On Crete #J20-J22, J24-J26

310	D1	5 l on 5 l red	.20	.20
311	D1	5 l on 10 l red	.20	.20
a.		Inverted surcharge	10.00	
312	D1	10 l on 20 l red	.20	.20
313	D1	50 l on 50 l red	.40	.40
314	D1	50 l on 1d red	3.00	3.00
315	D1	2d on 2d red	5.00	5.00

These surcharged Postage Due stamps were intended for the payment of ordinary postage.

Nos. 260 to 315 were surcharged in commemoration of the revolution of 1922.

Nos. 59, 91, 109, 111, 113-120, J11-J13, J20-J22, J24-J26 are on stamps previously overprinted by Crete.

Issues of the Republic

Lord Byron — A33

Byron at Missolonghi — A34

1924, Apr. 16 **Engr.** *Perf. 12*

316	A33	80 l dark blue	.50	.20
317	A34	2d dk vio & blk	1.10	.60
		Set, never hinged	2.25	

Death of Lord Byron (1788-1824) at Missolonghi.

Tomb of Markos Botsaris — A35

Serrate Roulette 13½

1926, Apr. 24 **Litho.**

318	A35	25 l lilac	.75	.45
		Never hinged	1.25	

Centenary of the defense of Missolonghi against the Turks.

Corinth Canal A36

Dodecanese Costume A37

Macedonian Costume A38

Monastery of Simon Peter on Mt. Athos A39

White Tower of Salonika A40

Temple of Hephaestus A41

The Acropolis — A42

Cruiser "Georgios Averof" — A43

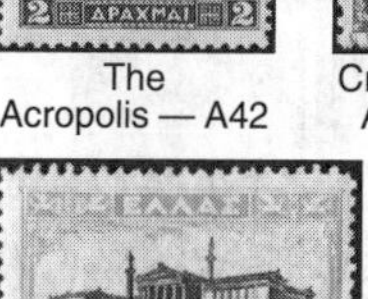
Academy of Sciences, Athens — A44

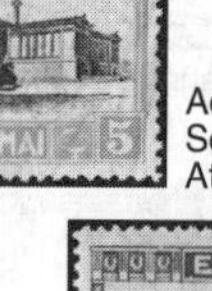
Temple of Hephaestus A45

Acropolis A46

Perf. 12½x13, 13, 13x12½, 13½, 13½x13

1927, Apr. 1 **Engr.**

321	A36	5 l dark green	.20	.20
a.		Vert. pair, imperf. horiz.	125.00	85.00
322	A37	10 l orange red	.20	.20
a.		Horiz. pair, imperf. between	125.00	85.00
c.		Double impression	70.00	
323	A38	20 l violet	.20	.20
324	A39	25 l slate blue	.25	.20
a.		Imperf., pair	125.00	125.00
b.		Vert. pair, imperf. between	140.00	100.00
325	A40	40 l slate blue	.25	.20
326	A36	50 l violet	.65	.20
327	A36	80 l dk bl & blk	.55	.20
a.		Imperf., pair	750.00	
328	A41	1d dk bl & bis brn (I)	.70	.20
a.		Imperf., pair	140.00	110.00
b.		Center inverted		*5,000.*
c.		Double impression of center	300.00	200.00
d.		Double impression of frame	300.00	200.00
329	A42	2d dk green & blk	5.50	.30
a.		Imperf., pair	450.00	*625.00*
330	A43	3d dp violet & blk	4.75	.30
a.		Double impression of center	150.00	*190.00*
b.		Center inverted		*7,000.*
331	A44	5d yellow & blk	9.25	1.25
a.		Imperf., pair	750.00	750.00
b.		Center inverted	9,000.	*3,250.*
c.		5d yellow & green	100.00	35.00
332	A45	10d brn car & blk	22.50	8.50
333	A44	15d brt yel grn & blk	27.50	12.50
334	A46	25d green & blk	52.50	14.00
a.		Double impression of center		—
		Nos. 321-334 (14)	125.00	38.45
		Set, never hinged	400.00	

See Nos. 364-371 and notes preceding No. 364. For overprints see Nos. RA55, RA57, RA60, RA66, RA70-RA71.

This series as prepared, included a 1 lepton dark brown, type A37, but that value was never issued. Most copies were burned. Value $250.

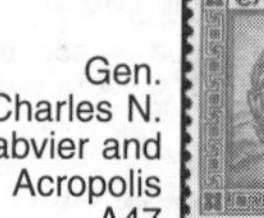

Gen. Charles N. Fabvier and Acropolis A47

1927, Aug. 1 *Perf. 12*

335	A47	1d red	.20	.20
336	A47	3d dark blue	1.25	.55
337	A47	6d green	8.50	8.25
		Nos. 335-337 (3)	9.95	9.00
		Set, never hinged	27.50	

Cent. of the liberation of Athens from the Turks in 1826.

For surcharges see Nos. 376-377.

Bay of Navarino and Pylos A48

Battle of Navarino A49

"Edward" omitted — A50

"Edward" added — A51

Admiral de Rigny — A52

Admiral van der Heyden — A53

Designs: #340-341, Sir Edward Codrington.

Perf. 13½x12½, 12½x13½, 13x12½, 12½x13

1927-28 Litho.

338	A48	1.50d gray green	1.50	.25
a.		Imperf., pair	250.00	
b.		Horiz. pair, imperf. btwn.	800.00	
c.		Horiz. pair, imperf. vert.	225.00	
339	A49	4d dk gray bl ('28)	4.75	.75
340	A50	5d dk brn & gray	2.75	*3.25*
a.		5d blk brn & blk ('28)	11.50	6.00
341	A51	5d dk brn & blk ('28)	17.50	8.25
342	A52	5d vio bl & blk ('28)	17.50	8.25
343	A53	5d lake & blk ('28)	11.00	4.25
		Nos. 338-343 (6)	55.00	25.00
		Set, never hinged	175.00	

Centenary of the naval battle of Navarino. For surcharges see Nos. 372-375.

Admiral Lascarina Bouboulina A54

Athanasios Diakos A55

Map of Greece in 1830 and 1930 — A56

Sortie from Missolonghi A58

Patriots Declaring Independence — A57

Portraits: 10 l, Constantine Rhigas Ferreos. 20 l, Gregorios V. 40 l, Prince Alexandros Ypsilantis. No. 345, Bouboulina. No. 355, Diakos. No. 346, Theodoros Kolokotronis. No. 356, Konstantinos Kanaris. No.347, Georgios Karaiskakis. No. 357, Markos Botsaris. 2d, Andreas Miaoulis. 3d, Lazaros Koundouriotis. 5d, Count John Capo d'Istria (Capodistria), statesman and doctor. 10d, Petros Mavromichalis. 15d, Dionysios Solomos. 20d, Adamantios Korais.

Various Frames

1930, Apr. 1 Engr. *Perf. 13½, 14*

Imprint of Perkins, Bacon & Co.

344	A55	10 l brown	.20	.20
345	A54	50 l red	.20	.20
346	A54	1d car rose	.20	.20
347	A55	1.50d lt blue	.30	.30
348	A55	2d orange	.40	.40
349	A55	5d purple	1.10	1.10
350	A54	10d gray blk	5.25	5.25
351	A54	15d yellow grn	9.50	9.50
352	A55	20d blue blk	13.50	13.50

Imprint of Bradbury, Wilkinson & Co.

Perf. 12

353	A55	20 l black	.20	.20
354	A55	40 l blue grn	.20	.20
355	A55	50 l brt blue	.20	.20
356	A55	1d brown org	.20	.20
357	A55	1.50d dk red	.30	.30
358	A55	3d dk brown	.50	.50
359	A56	4d dk blue	2.25	2.25
360	A57	25d black	13.50	13.50
361	A58	50d red brn	22.50	*22.50*
		Nos. 344-361 (18)	70.50	*70.50*
		Set, never hinged	175.00	

Greek independence, cent. Some exist imperf.

Arcadi Monastery and Abbot Gabriel (Mt. Ida in Background) A60

1930, Nov. 8 *Perf. 12*

363	A60	8d deep violet	12.00	1.00
		Never hinged	40.00	

Issue of 1927 Re-engraved

50 l, Design is clearer, especially "50" and the 10 letters.

Type I

Type II

1d. Type I - Greek letters "L," "A," "D" have sharp pointed tops; numerals "1" are 1½mm wide at the foot, and have a straight slanting serif at top.

1d. Type II - Greek letters "L," "A," "D" have flat tops; numerals "1" are 2mm wide at foot and the serif at top is slightly curved. Perf. 14.

There are many minor differences in the lines of the two designs.

1d. Type III - The "1" in lower left corner has no serif at left of foot. Lines of temple have been deepened, so details stand out more clearly.

2d. On 1927 stamp the Parthenon is indistinct and blurred. On 1933 stamp it is strongly outlined and clear. Between the two pillars at lower right are four blocks of marble. These blocks are clear and distinct on the 1933 stamp but run together on the 1927 issue.

3d. Design is clearer, especially vertical lines of shading in smoke stacks and reflections in the water. Two or more sides perf. 11½.

10d. Background and shading of entire stamp have been lightened. Detail of frame is clearer and more distinct.

15d. Many more lines of shading in sky and foreground. Engraving is sharp and clear, particularly in frame. Two or more sides perf. 11½.

25d. Background has been lightened and foreground reduced until base of larger upright column is removed and fallen column appears nearly submerged.

Sizes in millimeters:

50 l, 1927, 18x24¾. 1933, 18½x24½.

1d, 1927, 24¾x17¾. 1931, 24¾x17¼. 1933, 24½x18¼.

2d, 1927, 24½x17¾. 1933, 24½x18½.

Perf. 11½, 11½x12½, 12½x10, 13, 13x12½, 14

1931-35

364	A36	50 l dk vio ('33)	3.75	.90
365	A41	1d dk bl & org brn, type II	9.00	.90
366	A41	1d dk bl & org brn, type III ('33)	5.25	.20
367	A42	2d dk grn & blk ('33)	2.50	.45
368	A43	3d red vio & blk ('34)	3.00	.25
a.		Imperf., pair		
369	A45	10d brn car & blk ('35)	42.50	1.25
370	A44	15d pale yel grn & blk ('34)	75.00	16.00
a.		Imperf., pair	*1,000.*	
371	A46	25d dk grn & blk ('35)	22.50	15.00
		Nos. 364-371 (8)	163.50	34.95
		Set, never hinged	400.00	

Nos. 336-337, 340-343 Surcharged in Red

1932 *Perf. 12½x13½, 12½x13*

372	A52	1.50d on 5d	1.75	.20
373	A53	1.50d on 5d	1.65	.20
a.		Double surcharge	100.00	
374	A50	2d on 5d	4.50	.20
375	A51	2d on 5d	6.25	.20

Perf. 12

376	A47	2d on 3d	2.00	.20
a.		Double surcharge	120.00	
377	A47	4d on 6d	2.25	1.00
		Nos. 372-377 (6)	18.40	2.00
		Set, never hinged	40.00	

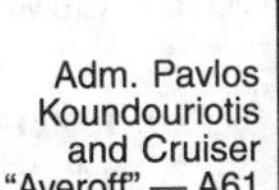

Adm. Pavlos Koundouriotis and Cruiser "Averoff" — A61

Pallas Athene — A62

Youth of Marathon — A63

1933 *Perf. 13½x13, 13x13½*

378	A61	50d black & ind	40.00	1.50
a.		Imperf., pair	2,000.	
379	A62	75d blk & vio brn	85.00	*140.00*
a.		Imperf., pair	750.00	
		Never hinged	1,500.	
380	A63	100d brn & dull grn	350.00	20.00
a.		Imperf., pair	2,500.	
		Nos. 378-380 (3)	475.00	*161.50*
		Set, never hinged	1,100.	

The imperf pairs are without gum. For surcharges see Nos. 386-387.

Approach to Athens Stadium A64

Perf. 11½, 11½x10, 13½x11½

1934, Dec. 10

381	A64	8d blue	52.50	2.00
		Never hinged	125.00	

Perforations on No. 381 range from 10½ to 13, including compounds.

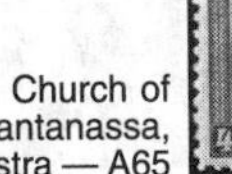

Church of Pantanassa, Mistra — A65

1935, Nov. 1 *Perf. 13x12½*

382	A65	4d brown	15.00	1.50
		Never hinged	35.00	
a.		Horiz. pair, imperf. between	600.00	
b.		Imperf., pair	600.00	

Issues of the Monarchy

J71, J76, J82, 380, 379 Surcharged in Red or Blue

Nos. 383-385

Nos. 386-387

Serrate Roulette 13½

1935, Nov. 24 Litho.

383	D3	50 l on 40 l indigo (R)	.20	.20
a.		Double surcharge		25.00
384	D3	3d on 3d car (Bl)	.50	.35

Perf. 13

385	D3	3d on 3d rose red (Bl)	2.50	1.90

Perf. 13x13½

386	A63	5d on 100d (R)	2.00	1.90
387	A62	15d on 75d (Bl)	6.00	5.50
		Nos. 383-387 (5)	11.20	9.85
		Set, never hinged	24.00	

King Constantine — A66

Center Engr., Frame Litho.

Perf. 12x13½

1936, Nov. 18 Wmk. 252

389	A66	3d black & brown	.50	.35
a.		Pair, printer's name in Greek	20.00	
b.		Pair, printer's name in English	20.00	
390	A66	8d black & blue	1.00	.80
a.		Pair, printer's name in Greek	20.00	
b.		Pair, printer's name in English	20.00	
		Set, never hinged	3.00	

Re-burial of the remains of King Constantine and Queen Sophia.

Two printings exist, the first containing varieties "a" and "b" with gray border; second with black border.

King George II — A67

Pallas Athene — A68

1937, Jan. 24 Engr. *Perf. 12½x12*

391	A67	1d green	.20	.20
392	A67	3d red brown	.25	.20
393	A67	8d dp blue	.80	.35
394	A67	100d carmine lake	11.00	11.00
		Nos. 391-394 (4)	12.25	11.75
		Set, never hinged	25.00	

For surcharges see Nos. 484-487, 498-500, RA86-RA87, N241-N242.

1937, Apr. 17 Unwmk. *Perf. 11½*

395	A68	3d yellow brown	.50	.25
		Never hinged	1.00	

Centenary of the University of Athens.

Contest with Bull — A69

Lady of Tiryns — A70

Zeus of Dodona — A71

Coin of Amphictyonic League A72

Diagoras of Rhodes, Victor at Olympics A73

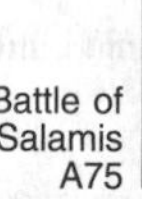

Venus of Melos — A74

Battle of Salamis A75

Chariot of Panathenaic Festival A76

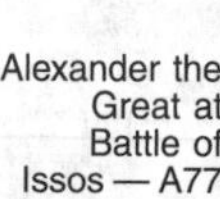

Alexander the Great at Battle of Issos — A77

St. Paul Preaching to Athenians A78

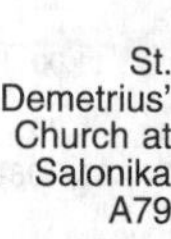

St. Demetrius' Church at Salonika A79

Leo III Victory over Arabs — A80

Allegorical Figure of Glory — A81

Perf. 13½x12, 12x13½

1937, Nov. 1 Litho. Wmk. 252

396	A69	5 l	brn red & bl	.20	.20
a.			Double impression of frame	55.00	
397	A70	10 l	bl & brn red	.20	.20
a.			Double impression of frame	55.00	
398	A71	20 l	black & grn	.20	.20
399	A72	40 l	green & blk	.20	.20
a.			Green impression doubled	55.00	
400	A73	50 l	brown & blk	.20	.20
401	A74	80 l	ind & yel brn	.20	.20
			Engr.		
402	A75	2d	ultra	.20	.20
403	A76	5d	red	.20	.20
a.			Printer's name omitted	5.00	
404	A77	6d	olive brn	.20	.20
405	A78	7d	dk brown	.50	.45
406	A79	10d	red brown	.20	.20
407	A80	15d	green	.20	.20
408	A81	25d	dk blue	.20	.20
			Nos. 396-408 (13)	2.90	2.85
			Set, never hinged	3.25	

See Nos. 413, 459-466. For overprints and surcharges see Nos. 455-458, 476-477, RA75-RA78, RA83-RA85, N202-N217, N246-N247.

Cerigo, Paxos, Lefkas

Greek stamps with Italian overprints for the islands of Cerigo (Kithyra), Paxos and Lefkas (Santa Maura) are fraudulent.

Royal Wedding Issue

Princess Frederika-Louise and Crown Prince Paul — A82

1938 Wmk. 252 *Perf. 13½x12*

409	A82	1d	green	.20	.20
410	A82	3d	orange brn	.30	.20
411	A82	8d	dark blue	.50	.60
			Nos. 409-411 (3)	1.00	1.00
			Set, never hinged	1.75	

Arms of Greece, Romania, Yugoslavia and Turkey A83

Statue of King Constantine A84

Perf. 12x12½

1938, Feb. 8 Litho. Unwmk.

412	A83	6d	blue	5.00	1.60
			Never hinged	12.50	

Balkan Entente.

Tiryns Lady Type of 1937 Corrected Inscription

1938 Wmk. 252 *Perf. 12x13½*

413	A70	10 l	blue & brn red	.45	*.65*
			Never hinged	.75	

The first four letters of the third word of the inscription read "TIPY" instead of "TYPI."

Perf. 12x13½

1938, Oct. 8 Engr. Unwmk.

414	A84	1.50d	green	.40	.20
415	A84	30d	orange brn	2.10	*2.60*
			Set, never hinged	5.00	

For overprint see No. N218.

Coats of Arms of Ionian Islands — A85

Fort at Corfu — A86

King George I of Greece and Queen Victoria of England A87

Perf. 12½x12, 13½x12

1939, May 21 Engr. Unwmk.

416	A85	1d	dk blue	.75	.25
417	A86	4d	green	2.60	.90
418	A87	20d	yellow org	15.00	15.00
419	A87	20d	dull blue	15.00	15.00
420	A87	20d	car lake	15.00	15.00
			Nos. 416-420 (5)	48.35	46.15
			Set, never hinged	100.00	

75th anniv. of the union of the Ionian Islands with Greece.

Runner with Shield — A88

10th Pan-Balkan Games: 3d, Javelin thrower. 6d, Discus thrower. 8d, Jumper.

Perf. 12x13½

1939, Oct. 1 Litho. Unwmk.

421	A88	50 l	slate grn & grn	.25	.20
422	A88	3d	henna brn & dl rose	.90	.50
423	A88	6d	cop brn & dl org	2.50	2.00
424	A88	8d	ultra & gray	2.50	2.25
			Nos. 421-424 (4)	6.15	4.95
			Set, never hinged	13.00	

Arms of Greece, Romania, Turkey and Yugoslavia — A92

Perf. 13x12½

1940, May 27 Wmk. 252

425	A92	6d	blue	7.25	2.00
426	A92	8d	blue gray	5.00	2.00
			Set, never hinged	25.00	

Balkan Entente.

Emblem of Youth Organization A93

Boy Member — A94

Designs: 3d, 100d, Emblem of Greek Youth Organization. 10d, Girl member. 15d, Javelin Thrower. 20d, Column of members. 25d, Flag bearers and buglers. 30d, Three youths. 50d, Line formation. 75d, Coat of arms.

Perf. 12½, 13½x12½

1940, Aug. 3 Litho. Wmk. 252

427	A93	3d	sil, dp ultra & red	.75	1.10
428	A94	5d	dk bl & blk	6.00	6.75
429	A94	10d	red org & blk	6.75	*9.25*
430	A94	15d	dk grn & blk	27.50	*30.00*
431	A94	20d	lake & blk	22.50	22.50
432	A94	25d	dk bl & blk	22.50	22.50
433	A94	30d	rose vio & blk	22.50	22.50
434	A94	50d	lake & blk	27.50	27.50
435	A94	75d	dk bl, brn & gold	27.50	30.00
436	A93	100d	sil, dp ultra & red	32.50	*35.00*
			Nos. 427-436,C38-C47 (20)	422.10	413.55
			Set, never hinged	725.00	

4th anniv. of the founding of the Greek Youth Organization. The stamps were good for postal duty Aug. 3-5, 1940, only. They remained on sale until Feb. 3, 1941.

For overprints see Nos. N219-N238.

Windmills on Mykonos A103

Bourtzi Fort — A104

Aspropotamos River — A105

Candia Harbor, Crete — A106

Houses at Hydra — A107

Meteora Monasteries A108

Edessa A109

Pantokratoros Monastery and Port — A110

Bridge at Konitsa A111

Ekatontapiliani Church, Paros — A112

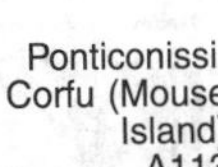

Ponticonissi, Corfu (Mouse Island) A113

Perf. 12½, 13½x12½

1942-44 Litho. Wmk. 252

437 A103 2d red brown .20 .20
438 A104 5d lt bl grn .20 .20
a. "NAYO . . ." 7.50 7.50
439 A105 10d lt blue .20 .20
440 A106 15d red vio .20 .20
441 A107 25d org red .20 .20
442 A108 50d sapphire .20 .20
443 A109 75d dp rose .20 .20
444 A110 100d black .20 .20
445 A110 200d ultra .20 .20
a. Imprint omitted 3.50 3.50
446 A111 500d dk olive .20 .20
447 A112 1000d org brn .20 .20
448 A113 2000d dp blue .20 .20
449 A111 5000d rose red .20 .20
450 A112 15,000d rose lil .20 .20
451 A113 25,000d green .20 .20
452 A105 500,000d blue .20 .20
453 A103 2,000,000d turq grn .20 .20
454 A104 5,000,000d rose brn .20 .20
Nos. 437-454 (18) 3.60 3.60

Double impressions exist of 10d, 25d, 50d, 100d, 200d, 1,000d and 2,000d. Value, each $30.

Issued: #439-442, 9/1; 200d, 12/1; #446-448, 3/15/44; #449-451, 7/1/44; #452-454, 9/15/44.

For surcharges and overprint see Nos. 472C, 473B-475, 478-481, 501-505, B1-B5, B11-B15, RA72-RA74, N239-N240, N243-N245, N248.

Imperf., Pairs

439a	A105	10d	52.50
440a	A106	15d	52.50
441a	A107	25d	40.00
442a	A108	50d	40.00
446a	A111	500d	40.00
447a	A112	1000d	40.00
448a	A113	2000d	40.00
449a	A111	5000d	40.00
450a	A112	15,000d	40.00
451a	A113	25,000d	40.00
452a	A105	500,000d	40.00
454a	A104	5,000,000d	40.00

Nos. 400, 402-404 Surcharged in Blue Black

1944-45 *Perf. 13½x12*

455 A73 50 l brn & blk .20 .20
a. Double surcharge 30.00 30.00
456 A75 2d ultra .20 .20
457 A76 5d red .20 .20
a. Inverted surcharge 40.00
b. Double surcharge 40.00
c. Printer's name omitted (403a) 10.00 10.00
d. Pair, one without surcharge 15.00
458 A77 6d olive brn ('45) .25 .25
Nos. 455-458 (4) .85 .85

Glory Type of 1937

Perf. 12½x13½

1945 Litho. Wmk. 252

459 A81 1d dull rose vio .20 .20
460 A81 3d rose brown .20 .20
a. Imperf., pair 150.00
461 A81 5d ultra .20 .20
a. Imperf., pair 150.00
462 A81 10d dull brown .20 .20
463 A81 20d dull violet .20 .20
464 A81 50d olive black .20 .25
465 A81 100d pale blue 3.25 3.25
a. Imperf., pair 175.00
466 A81 200d slate 2.75 2.50
Nos. 459-466 (8) 7.20 7.00
Set, never hinged 11.00

Doric Column and Greek Flag A114

Franklin D. Roosevelt A115

1945, Oct. 28 Unwmk.

467 A114 20d orange brown .20 .20
468 A114 40d blue .20 .20
a. Double impression 20.00
Set, never hinged .40

Vote of Oct. 28, 1940, refusing Italy's ultimatum. "OXI" means "No."
Exist imperf.

1945, Dec. 21 Unwmk.

469 A115 30d blk & red brn .20 .20
a. Center double 25.00
c. Inverted frame 65.00
d. Imperf., pair 40.00
470 A115 60d blk & sl gray .20 .20
a. Center double 25.00
b. 60d black & blue gray 10.00 10.00
c. Imperf., pair 25.00
d. Inverted frame 60.00
471 A115 200d blk & vio brn .20 .20
a. Center double 25.00 *70.00*
b. Imperf., pair 40.00
Nos. 469-471 (3) .60 .60
Set, never hinged .50

Death of Pres. Franklin D. Roosevelt.

Catalogue values for unused stamps in this section, from this point to the end of the section, are for Never Hinged items.

Nos. C61, C63, 447-451, 453, 398, 401, 454 and 452 Surcharged in Black or Carmine

Perf. 12½, 12x13½, 13½x12½

1946 Wmk. 252

472 AP35 10d on 10d .25 .20
a. Inverted surcharge 90.00 —
b. Double surcharge 20.00
472C A113 10d on 2000d (C) .25 .20
473 AP35 20d on 50d (C) .25 .20
a. Inverted surcharge 100.00
473B A112 20d on 1000d .25 .20
474 A113 50d on 25,000d (C) .35 .20
475 A103 100d on 2,000,000d (C) .75 .25
476 A71 130d on 20 l (C) .85 .20
b. Double surcharge 25.00
476A A71 250d on 20 l (C) 1.00 .20
c. Double surcharge 85.00
477 A74 300d on 80 l .85 .20
a. Purple brown surcharge 15.00 15.00
b. Double surcharge 77.50
478 A104 500d on 5,000,000d 2.25 .60
a. Inverted surcharge 77.50
b. Double surcharge 77.50
479 A105 1000d on 500,000d (C) 10.50 1.25
a. Double surcharge 40.00
480 A111 2000d on 5000d 42.50 2.75
481 A112 5000d on 15,000d 100.00 27.50
a. Blue surcharge 100.00 80.00
Nos. 472-481 (13) 160.05 33.95

The surcharge exists in various shades on most denominations. A 150d on 20 l is fraudulent.

Eleutherios K. Venizelos A116

Panaghiotis Tsaldaris A117

Perf. 12x13½

1946, Mar. 25 Litho. Wmk. 252

482 A116 130d brn ol & buff .20 .20
a. Double impression of brn olive 6.50
483 A116 300d red brn & pale brn .20 .20
a. Double impression of red brown 12.50

Venizelos (1864-1936), statesman.

Nos. 391 to 394 Surcharged in Blue Black

1946, Sept. 28 *Perf. 12½x12*

484 A67 50d on 1d .35 .20
485 A67 250d on 3d .85 .20
a. Date omitted 25.00
b. Inverted surcharge 25.00 —
486 A67 600d on 8d 5.00 .75
a. Additional surcharge on back, inverted 65.00
b. Carmine surcharge 140.00
487 A67 3000d on 100d 13.00 .90
Nos. 484-487 (4) 19.20 2.05

Plebiscite of Sept. 1, 1946, which resulted in the return of King George II to Greece.

Perf. 12½x13½

1946, Nov. 15 Litho. Unwmk.

488 A117 250d red brn & buff 1.75 .45
489 A117 600d dp bl & pale bl 1.75 .70
a. Double impression 20.00

Naval Convoy A118

Torpedoing of Cruiser Helle — A119

Women Carrying Ammunition in Pindus Mountains A120

Troops in Albania A121

Campaign of Greek Troops in Italy — A122

Allegory of Flight — A123

Greek Torpedo Boat Towing Captive Submarine A124

Design: 5000d, Memorial Tomb, El Alamein.

1946-47 Unwmk. Engr. *Perf. 13*

490 A118 50d dk bl grn .25 .20
491 A119 100d dp ultra .35 .20
492 A120 250d yel grn ('46) .45 .20
493 A121 500d yel brn .85 .20
494 A122 600d dk brown 1.00 .35
495 A123 1000d dull lil 3.25 .25
496 A124 2000d dp ultra 13.50 1.75
497 A119 5000d dk car 21.00 1.40
a. Imperf., pair 1,300.
Nos. 490-497 (8) 40.65 4.55

1947 stamps issued May 1.

King George II Memorial Issue

Nos. 391-393 Surcharged in Black

Perf. 12½x12

1947, Apr. 15 Wmk. 252

498 A67 50d on 1d grn .35 .20
a. Double surcharge 65.00
499 A67 250d on 3d red brn .85 .20
a. Double surcharge 65.00
b. Pair, one without surcharge 65.00
500 A67 600d on 8d dp bl 2.60 .50
a. Double surcharge 65.00
Nos. 498-500 (3) 3.80 .90

Nos. 446, 438, 442, 439 and 443 Surcharged in Carmine or Black

1947 *Perf. 12½*

501 A111 20d on 500d .25 .20
a. Double surcharge 25.00
502 A104 30d on 5d .75 .35
503 A108 50d on 50d .35 .20
504 A105 100d on 10d 1.25 .20
505 A109 450d on 75d (Bk) 2.00 .25
Nos. 501-505 (5) 4.60 1.20

Castellorizo Castle A126

Dodecanese Vase A127

Dodecanese Costume A128

Monastery where St. John Preached, Patmos A129

Emanuel Xanthos — A130

Sailing Vessel of 1824 — A131

Revolutionary Stamp of 1912 — A132

Statue of Hippocrates A133

Colossus of Rhodes A134

Perf. 12½x13½, 13½x12½

1947-48 Litho. Wmk. 252

No.	Type	Denom.	Color	Unused	Used
506	A126	20d	ultra	.20	.20
507	A127	30d	blk brn & buff	.20	.20
508	A128	50d	chlky bl	.25	.20
509	A129	100d	blk grn & pale grn	.25	.20
510	A130	250d	gray grn & pale grn	.50	.20
511	A132	450d	dp bl ('48)	1.25	.20
512	A131	450d	dp bl & pale bl ('48)	1.00	.20
a.			Imperf., pair	250.00	
513	A132	500d	red	.60	.20
514	A133	600d	vio brn & pale pink	.60	.20
515	A134	1000d	brn & cream	.50	.20
a.			Imperf., pair	225.00	
			Nos. 506-515 (10)	5.35	2.00

Return of the Dodecanese to Greece. See Nos. 520-522, 525-534.

Battle of Crete — A135

1948, Sept. 15 Engr. *Perf. 13x13½*

No.	Type	Denom.	Color	Unused	Used
516	A135	1000d	dark green	3.50	.35

Battle of Crete, 7th anniversary.

Abduction of Children A136

Concentration Camp — A137

Protective Mother — A138

Perf. 13½x12½, 12½x13½

1949, Feb. 1 Litho. Wmk. 252

No.	Type	Denom.	Color	Unused	Used
517	A136	450d	dk & lt violet	1.75	.35
518	A137	1000d	dk & lt brown	5.00	.25
519	A138	1800d	dk red & cream	4.50	.25
			Nos. 517-519 (3)	11.25	.85

Types of 1947

1950, Apr. 5 *Perf. 12½x13½*

No.	Type	Denom.	Color	Unused	Used
520	A127	2000d	org brn & sal	25.00	.25
a.			Imperf., pair	125.00	
521	A133	5000d	rose vio	27.50	.25
522	A134	10,000d	ultra	40.00	.60
			Nos. 520-522 (3)	92.50	1.10

Map of Crete and Flags A139

Perf. 13½x13

1950, Apr. 28 Engr. Wmk. 252

No.	Type	Denom.	Color	Unused	Used
523	A139	1000d	deep blue	6.00	.25
a.			Imperf., pair	*425.00*	

Battle of Crete, 9th anniversary.

Youth of Marathon — A140

Engraved and Lithographed

1950, May 21 *Perf. 13x13½*

No.	Type	Denom.	Color	Unused	Used
524	A140	1000d	cream & dp grn	1.25	.25
a.			Without dates	375.00	
b.			"1949" only	375.00	
c.			Dates inverted	375.00	
d.			Dates doubled	375.00	

75th anniv. (in 1949) of the UPU. Exists imperf., used only.

Types of 1947-48

Perf. 12½x13½, 13½x12½

1950 Litho. Wmk. 252

No.	Type	Denom.	Color	Unused	Used
525	A130	200d	orange	.35	.20
526	A128	300d	orange	.50	.20
527	A129	400d	blue	.85	.20
528	A133	700d	lilac rose	1.25	.20
529	A133	700d	blue green	12.00	.25
a.			Imperf., pair	260.00	
530	A131	800d	pur & pale grn	1.75	.20
531	A132	1300d	carmine	7.50	.20
532	A126	1500d	brn org	42.50	1.00
533	A127	1600d	ultra & bl gray	4.50	.25
534	A134	2600d	emer & pale grn	5.50	.75
			Nos. 525-534 (10)	76.70	3.45

Altar and Sword A141

St. Paul — A142

St. Paul by El Greco — A143

Preaching to Athenians — A144

Perf. 13½x12, 12x13½

1951, June 15 Engr. Unwmk.

No.	Type	Denom.	Color	Unused	Used
535	A141	700d	red vio	2.50	.25
536	A142	1600d	lt blue	7.50	.90
537	A143	2600d	dk ol bis	9.75	1.10
538	A144	10,000d	red brn	97.50	55.00
			Nos. 535-538 (4)	117.25	57.25

1900th anniv. of St. Paul's visit to Athens.

Industrialization A145

Designs: 800d, Fishing. 1300d, Rebuilding. 1600d, Farming. 2600d, Home Industries. 5000d, Electrification and map of Greece.

Perf. 12½x13½

1951, Sept. 20 Wmk. 252

No.	Type	Denom.	Color	Unused	Used
539	A145	700d	red org	2.50	.20
540	A145	800d	aqua	6.00	.20
541	A145	1300d	grnsh bl	6.00	.20
542	A145	1600d	olive grn	20.00	.25
543	A145	2600d	vio gray	45.00	.90
544	A145	5000d	dp plum	60.00	.25
			Nos. 539-544 (6)	139.50	2.00

Issued to publicize Greek recovery under the Marshall Plan.

King Paul I — A146

Allegorical Figure and Medal — A147

1952, Dec. 14 Engr. *Perf. 12½x12*

No.	Type	Denom.	Color	Unused	Used
545	A146	200d	deep green	1.25	.20
546	A146	1000d	red	3.75	.25
547	A147	1400d	blue	10.00	1.10
548	A146	10,000d	dk red lil	35.00	10.00
			Nos. 545-548 (4)	50.00	11.55

50th birthday of King Paul I.

Oranges A148

Tobacco — A149

National Products: 1000d, Olive oil, Pallas Athene. 1300d, Wine. 2000d, Figs. 2600d, Grapes and bread. 5000d, Bacchus holding grapes.

1953, July 1 *Perf. 13½x13, 13x13½*

No.	Type	Denom.	Color	Unused	Used
549	A148	500d	dp car & org	1.25	.20
550	A149	700d	dk brn & org yel	1.25	.20
551	A148	1000d	bl & lt ol grn	2.50	.20
a.			Imperf., pair	400.00	
552	A149	1300d	dp plum & org brn	3.75	.20
553	A149	2000d	dk brn & lt grn	8.50	.25
554	A149	2600d	vio & ol bis	22.50	.70
555	A149	5000d	dk brn & yel grn	22.50	.25
			Nos. 549-555 (7)	62.25	2.00

Pericles A150

Homer A151

Hunting Wild Boar — A152

Shepherd Carrying Calf — A152a

Designs: 200d, Mycenaean oxhead vase. 500d, Zeus of Istiaea. 600d, Head of a youth. 1000d, Alexander the Great. 1200d, Charioteer of Delphi. 2000d, Vase of Dipylon. 4000d, Voyage of Dionysus. 20,000d, Pitcher bearers.

Perf. 13½x13, 12½x12, 13x13½

1954, Jan. 15 Litho.

No.	Type	Denom.	Color	Unused	Used
556	A150	100d	red brn	.35	.20
557	A150	200d	black	.35	.20
558	A151	300d	blue vio	.85	.20
559	A151	500d	green	1.25	.20
560	A151	600d	rose pink	1.40	.20
561	A151	1000d	dl bl & blk	1.75	.20
562	A150	1200d	ol grn	1.75	.20
563	A150	2000d	red brn	5.75	.20
564	A152	2400d	grnsh bl	5.75	.25
a.			Double impression	100.00	
565	A152a	2500d	dk bl grn	7.25	.25
566	A151	4000d	dk car	18.00	.25
567	A150	20,000d	rose lilac	125.00	1.10
			Nos. 556-567 (12)	169.45	3.45

See Nos. 574-581, 632-638, and 689.

British Parliamentary Debate and Ink Blot — A153

1954, Sept. *Perf. 12½*

Center in Black

No.	Type	Denom.	Color	Unused	Used
568	A153	1.20d	cream	2.50	.20
569	A153	2d	orange	9.75	2.00
570	A153	2d	lt bl	9.75	2.00
571	A153	2.40d	lilac	9.75	2.00
572	A153	2.50d	pink	9.75	.70
573	A153	4d	citron	25.00	2.50
			Nos. 568-573 (6)	66.50	9.40

Document in English on Nos. 569, 572, 573; in French on Nos. 570, 571 and in Greek on No. 568.

Issued to promote the proposed union between Cyprus and Greece.

Types of 1954

Perf. 13½x13, 12½x12, 13x13½

1955 Litho. Wmk. 252

Designs: 20 l, Mycenaean oxhead vase. 30 l, Pericles. 50 l, Zeus of Istiaea. 1d, Head of a youth. 2d, Alexander the Great. 3d, Hunting wild boar. 3.50d, Homer. 4d, Voyage of Dionysus.

No.	Type	Denom.	Color	Unused	Used
574	A150	20 l	dk green	.25	.20
575	A150	30 l	yellow brn	.35	.20
576	A151	50 l	car lake	.60	.20
577	A151	1d	blue grn	1.25	.20
578	A151	2d	brown & blk	7.50	.20
579	A152	3d	red org	5.00	.20
580	A151	3.50d	rose crim	5.00	.35
581	A151	4d	violet bl	45.00	.30
			Nos. 574-581 (8)	64.95	1.85

Samos Coin Picturing Pythagoras A154

Pythagorean Theorem A155

Samos Mapped in Antique Style — A156

1955, Aug. 20 *Perf. 12x13½*

582	A154	2d	green	2.50	.20
583	A155	3.50d	intense blk	7.50	1.10
584	A154	5d	plum	27.50	1.00
585	A156	6d	blue	27.50	*25.00*
			Nos. 582-585 (4)	65.00	*27.30*

2500th anniv. of the founding of the 1st School of Philosophy by Pythagoras on Samos.

Globe and Rotary Emblem — A157

Perf. 12x13½

1956, May 15 Litho. Wmk. 252

586	A157	2d	ultra	7.50	.25

50th anniv. of Rotary Intl. (in 1955).

King Alexander A158

Crown Prince Constantine — A159

Portraits: 30 l, George I. 50 l, Queen Olga. 70 l, King Otto. 1d, Queen Amalia. 1.50d, King Constantine. 2d, 7.50d, King Paul. 3d, George II. 3.50d, Queen Sophia. 4d, Queen Frederica. 5d, King Paul and Queen Frederica. 10d, King, Queen and Crown Prince.

Perf. 13½x12, 12x13½

1956, May 21 Engr.

587	A158	10 l	blue vio	.20	.20
588	A159	20 l	dull pur	.20	.20
589	A159	30 l	sepia	.20	.20
590	A159	50 l	red brn	.30	.20
591	A159	70 l	lt ultra	.35	.20
592	A159	1d	grnsh bl	.65	.20
593	A159	1.50d	gray bl	1.50	.20
594	A159	2d	black	2.00	.20
595	A159	3d	brown	1.10	.20
596	A159	3.50d	copper brn	5.75	.25
597	A159	4d	gray green	6.00	.20
598	A158	5d	rose car	3.75	.20
599	A159	7.50d	ultra	5.00	.90
600	A158	10d	dk blue	14.50	.45
			Nos. 587-600 (14)	41.50	3.80

See Nos. 604-617.

Dionysios Solomos and Nicolaos Mantzaros A160

Dionysios Solomos — A161

5d, View on Zante and bust of Solomos.

Perf. 13½x12, 12x13½

1957, Mar. 26 Litho. Wmk. 252

601	A160	2d	red brn & ocher	2.00	.25
602	A161	3.50d	bl & gray	5.00	2.50
603	A160	5d	dk grn & ol bis	5.00	3.50
			Nos. 601-603 (3)	12.00	6.25

Centenary of the death of Dionysios Solomos, composer of the Greek national anthem.

Types of 1956

Designs as before.

Perf. 13½x12

1957 Wmk. 252 Engr.

604	A158	10 l	rose lake	.45	.20
605	A159	20 l	orange	.45	.20
606	A159	30 l	gray blk	.45	.20
607	A159	50 l	grnsh blk	.45	.20
608	A159	70 l	rose lil	1.25	.60
609	A159	1d	rose red	.95	.20
610	A159	1.50d	lt ol grn	1.60	.20
611	A159	2d	carmine	1.60	.20
612	A159	3d	dk blue	2.25	.20
613	A159	3.50d	blk vio	6.00	.20
a.			Imperf., pair		
614	A159	4d	red brn	6.00	.20
615	A158	5d	gray blue	6.00	.20
616	A159	7.50d	yel org	15.00	.75
617	A158	10d	green	19.00	.60
			Nos. 604-617 (14)	61.45	4.15

Oil Tanker A162

Ships: 1d, Ocean liner. 1.50d, Sailing ship, 1820. 2d, Byzantine vessel. 3.50d, Ship from 6th century B. C. 5d, "Argo."

1958, Jan. 30 Litho. *Perf. 13½x12*

618	A162	50 l	multi	.20	.20
619	A162	1d	ultra, blk & bis	.20	.20
620	A162	1.50d	blk & car	.20	.20
a.			Double impression of blk	150.00	
621	A162	2d	vio bl, blk & red brn	.30	.30
622	A162	3.50d	lt bl, blk & red	.85	1.00
a.			Double impression of blk	150.00	120.00
623	A162	5d	bl grn, blk & car	8.25	6.00
			Nos. 618-623 (6)	10.00	7.90

Issued to honor the Greek merchant marine.

Narcissus — A163

Designs: 30 l, Daphne (laurel) and Apollo. 50 l, Adonis (hibiscus) and Aphrodite. 70 l, Pitys (pine) and Pan. 1d, Crocus. 2d, Iris. 3.50d, Tulips. 5d, Cyclamen.

1958, Sept. 15 Wmk. 252 *Perf. 13*

Size: 22½x38mm

624	A163	20 l	multi	.20	.20
625	A163	30 l	multi	.20	.20
626	A163	50 l	multi	.20	.20
627	A163	70 l	multi	.20	.20

Perf. 12½x12

Size: 21½x26mm

628	A163	1d	multi	.30	.25

Perf. 12x13½

Size: 22x32mm

629	A163	2d	multi	.20	.20
630	A163	3.50d	multi	1.00	1.00
a.			Imperf., pair	300.00	
631	A163	5d	multi	1.40	1.40
			Nos. 624-631 (8)	3.70	3.65

International Congress for the Protection of Nature, held in Athens.

Types of 1954

Designs: 10 l, Pericles. 20 l, Mycenaean oxhead vase. 50 l, Zeus of Istiaea. 70 l, Charioteer of Delphi. 1d, Head of a youth. 1.50d, Pitcher bearers. 2.50d, Alexander the Great.

Two types of 2.50d:

I- 9 dots in upper half of right border.

II- 10 dots.

Perf. 13½x13, 12½x12

1959 Litho. Wmk. 252

632	A150	10 l	emerald	.20	.20
633	A150	20 l	magenta	.40	.20
634	A151	50 l	lt bl grn	1.40	.20
635	A150	70 l	red org	.40	.20
636	A151	1d	reddish brn	3.50	.20
637	A150	1.50d	brt bl	6.25	.20
638	A151	2.50d	mag & blk (II)	10.50	.20
a.			Type I	55.00	.50
			Nos. 632-638 (7)	22.65	1.40

Zeus-Eagle Coin — A164

Helios-Rose Coin — A165

Ancient Greek Coins: 20 l, Athena & Owl. 50 l, Nymph Arethusa & Chariot. 70 l, Hercules & Zeus. 1.50d, Griffin & Square. 2.50d, Apollo & Lyre. 4.50d, Apollo & Labyrinth. 6d, Aphrodite & Apollo. 8.50d, Ram's Head & Incuse Squares.

1959, Mar. 24 Wmk. 252 *Perf. 14*

Coins in Various Shades of Gray

639	A164	10 l	red brn & blk	.40	.20
640	A164	20 l	dp bl & blk	.40	.20
641	A164	50 l	plum & blk	1.00	.20
642	A164	70 l	ultra & blk	1.00	.20
643	A165	1d	dk car rose & blk	2.25	.20
644	A164	1.50d	ocher & blk	2.25	.20
645	A164	2.50d	dp mag & blk	2.75	.20
646	A165	4.50d	Prus grn & blk	3.75	.20
647	A165	6d	ol grn & blk	4.25	.20
648	A165	8.50d	dp car & blk	3.75	1.00
			Nos. 639-648 (10)	21.80	2.80

See Nos. 750-758.

Audience, Vase 580 B. C. — A166

Theater, Delphi A167

Designs: 50 l, Clay tragedy mask, 3rd cent. B.C. 1d, Flute, drum and lyre. 2.50d, Clay statue of an actor, 3rd cent. B.C. 4.50d, Andromeda, vase, 4th cent. B.C. 6d, Actors, bowl 410 B.C.

Perf. 13x13½, 13½x13

1959, June 20 Litho. Wmk. 252

649	A166	20 l	blk, fawn & gray	.20	.20
650	A166	50 l	dk red brn & ol bis	.20	.20
651	A166	1d	grn, brn & ocher	.20	.20
652	A166	2.50d	brn & bl	.35	.30
653	A167	3.50d	red brn, grn & sep	8.75	6.50
654	A167	4.50d	blk & fawn	1.25	.90
655	A166	6d	blk, fawn & gray	1.25	.90
			Nos. 649-655 (7)	12.20	9.20

Ancient Greek theater.

"Victory" and Soldiers — A168

Perf. 13x13½

1959, Aug. 29 Wmk. 252

656	A168	2.50d	red brn, ultra & blk	1.50	.25

10th anniversary of civil war.

St. Basil — A169

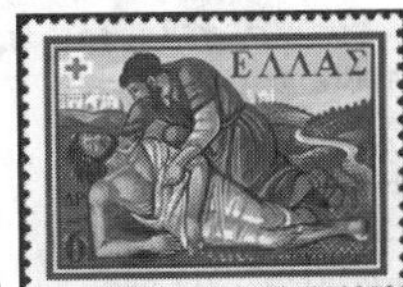

The Good Samaritan A170

Designs: 20 l, Plane tree of Hippocrates. 50 l, Aesculapius. 2.50d, Achilles and Patroclus. 3d, Globe and Red Cross over people receiving help. 4.50d, Henri Dunant.

Perf. 13½x12, 12x13½

1959, Sept. 21 Litho.

657	A170	20 l	multi	.20	.20
658	A169	50 l	multi	.20	.20
659	A169	70 l	multi	.20	.20
660	A169	2.50d	multi	.20	.20
661	A169	3d	multi	8.00	6.50
662	A169	4.50d	multi	.35	.35
663	A170	6d	multi	.45	.45
			Nos. 657-663 (7)	9.60	8.10

Cent. of the Red Cross idea. Sizes: Nos. 658-660, 662 24½x32mm, No. 661 32x47mm.

Imre Nagy — A171

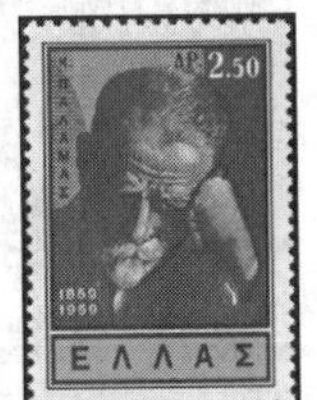

Costis Palamas — A172

Perf. 13x13½

1959, Dec. 8 **Wmk. 252**

664 A171 4.50d	org brn & dk brn	.85	.85
665 A171 6d	brt bl, bl & blk	.85	.85

3rd anniv. of the crushing of the 1956 Hungarian Revolution, and to honor Premier Imre Nagy, its leader.

1960, Jan. 25 ***Perf. 12x13½***

666 A172 2.50d	multi	2.00	.20

Centenary of the birth of Costis Palamas (1859-1943), poet.

Ship Battling Storm A173

4.50d, Ship in calm sea and rainbow.

Perf. 13½x13

1960, Apr. 7 **Wmk. 252**

667 A173 2.50d	multi	.25	.20
668 A173 4.50d	multi	.75	.85

Issued to publicize World Refugee Year, July 1, 1959-June 30, 1960.

Boy Scout on Horseback, St. George and Dragon — A174

Scouts Planting Tree A175

30 l, Scout taking oath & boy of ancient Athens. 40 l, Scouts helping in disaster. 70 l, Scouts reading map & tent. 1d, Boy Scout, Sea Scout & Air Scout. 2.50d, Crown Prince Constantine. 6d, Scout flag of Greece & Military Merit medal.

Perf. 13x13½, 13½x13

1960, Apr. 23 **Litho.**

669 A174 20 l	multi	.20	.20
670 A174 30 l	multi	.20	.20
671 A174 40 l	multi	.20	.20
672 A175 50 l	multi	.20	.20
673 A175 70 l	multi	.20	.20
674 A175 1d	multi	.20	.20
675 A174 2.50d	multi	.40	.20
676 A175 6d	multi	2.25	1.10
Nos. 669-676 (8)		3.85	2.50

Greek Boy Scout Organization, 50th anniv.

Greek Holding Sacred Disk Proclaiming Armistice During Games — A176

Lighting Olympic Flame A177

Designs: 70 l, Youth taking oath. 80 l, Boy cutting olive branches for Olympic prizes. 1d, Judges entering stadium. 1.50d, Long jump. 2.50d, Discus thrower. 4.50d, Sprinters. 5d, Javelin thrower. 6d, Crowning the victors. 12.50d, Victor in chariot entering home town.

Perf. 13x13½, 13½x13

1960, Aug. 12 **Wmk. 252**

677 A176 20 l	multi	.20	.20
678 A177 50 l	multi	.20	.20
679 A176 70 l	multi	.20	.20
680 A177 80 l	multi	.20	.20
a. Imperf., pair		400.00	
681 A177 1d	multi	.20	.20
682 A177 1.50d	multi	.20	.20
683 A176 2.50d	multi	.40	.20
684 A177 4.50d	multi	.85	.65
a. Dbl. impression of black		300.00	160.00
685 A176 5d	multi	.45	.50
686 A177 6d	multi	.60	.65
687 A177 12.50d	multi	6.50	6.00
Nos. 677-687 (11)		10.00	9.20

17th Olympic Games, Rome, 8/25-9/11.

Common Design Types pictured following the introduction.

Europa Issue, 1960

Common Design Type

Perf. 13½x12

1960, Sept. 19 **Litho.** **Wmk. 252**

Size: 33x23mm

688 CD3 4.50d	ultra	*2.75*	1.40
a. Double impression		165.00	

Shepherd Type of 1954

1960, Sept. 1 **Wmk. 252** ***Perf. 13***

689 A152a 3d	ultra	1.25	.20

Crown Prince Constantine and Yacht — A178

1961, Jan. 18 ***Perf. 13½x13***

690 A178 2.50d	multi	.45	.25

Victory of Crown Prince Constantine and his crew at the 17th Olympic Games, Rome (Gold medal, Yachting, Dragon class).

Castoria A179

Delphi — A180

Landscapes and Ancient Monuments: 20 l, Meteora. 50 l, Hydra harbor. 70 l, Acropolis, Athens. 80 l, Mykonos. 1d, St. Catherine's Church, Salonika. 1.50d, Olympia. 2.50d, Knossos. 3.50d, Rhodes. 4d, Epidauros amphitheater. 4.50d, Temple of Poseidon, Sounion. 5d, Temple of Zeus, Athens. 7.50d, Aslan's mosque, Ioannina. 8d, Mount Athos. 8.50d, Santorini. 12.50d, Marble lions, Delos.

Perf. 13½x12½, 12½x13½

1961, Feb. 15 **Engr.** **Wmk. 252**

691 A179 10 l	dk gray bl	.20	.20
692 A179 20 l	dk purple	.20	.20
693 A179 50 l	blue	.20	.20
694 A179 70 l	dk purple	.20	.20
695 A179 80 l	brt ultra	.35	.20
696 A179 1d	red brn	.50	.20
697 A179 1.50d	brt grn	.65	.25
698 A179 2.50d	carmine	2.00	.20
699 A179 3.50d	purple	.75	.20
700 A179 4d	sl grn	5.50	.20
701 A179 4.50d	dk blue	.90	.20
702 A179 5d	claret	5.50	.25
703 A180 6d	slate grn	1.25	.20
704 A179 7.50d	black	.50	.25
705 A180 8d	dk vio bl	2.50	.25
706 A180 8.50d	org ver	3.25	.65
707 A179 12.50d	dk brn	1.00	.50
Nos. 691-707 (17)		25.45	4.35

Issued for tourist publicity.

Lily Vase — A181

Partridge and Fig Pecker A182

Minoan Art: 1d, Fruit dish. 1.50d, Rhyton bearer. 2.50d, Ladies of Knossos Palace. 4.50d, Sarcophagus of Hagia Trias. 6d, Dancer. 10d, Two vessels with spouts.

Perf. 13x13½, 13½x13

1961, June 30 **Litho.**

708 A181 20 l	multi	.20	.20
709 A182 50 l	multi	.30	.20
710 A182 1d	multi	.40	.20
711 A181 1.50d	multi	.60	.25
712 A182 2.50d	multi	4.50	.20
713 A181 4.50d	multi	1.50	1.00
714 A182 6d	multi	5.00	1.10
715 A182 10d	multi	5.50	5.50
Nos. 708-715 (8)		18.00	8.65

Democritus Nuclear Research Center — A183

Democritus — A184

1961, July 31 ***Perf. 13½x13***

716 A183 2.50d	dp lil rose & rose lil	.50	.20
717 A184 4.50d	vio bl & pale vio bl	.75	.60

Inauguration of the Democritus Nuclear Research Center at Aghia Paraskevi.

Europa Issue, 1961

Common Design Type

1961, Sept. 18 ***Perf. 13½x12***

Size: 32½x22mm

718 CD4 2.50d	ver & pink	.20	.20
a. Pink omitted (inscriptions white)		*7.25*	*6.50*
719 CD4 4.50d	ultra & lt ultra	.20	.20

Nicephoros Phocas — A185

1961, Sept. 22 **Wmk. 252**

720 A185 2.50d	multi	.50	.35

1000th anniv. of the liberation of Crete from the Saracens by the Byzantine general (later emperor) Phocas.

Hermes Head of 1861 — A186

1961, Dec. 20 **Litho.** ***Perf. 13x13½***

Each denomination shows a different stamp of 1861 issue.

721 A186 20 l	brn, red brn & cream	.20	.20
722 A186 50 l	brn, bis & straw	.20	.20
723 A186 1.50d	emer & gray	.20	.25
724 A186 2.50d	red org & ol bis	.20	.20
725 A186 4.50d	dk bl, bl & gray	.40	.30
726 A186 6d	rose lil, pale rose & bl	.55	.30
727 A186 10d	car, rose & cr	1.25	1.25
Nos. 721-727 (7)		3.00	2.70

Centenary of Greek postage stamps.

Tauropos Dam and Lake — A187

Ptolemais Power Station A188

Designs: 50 l, Ladhon river hydroelectric plant. 1.50d, Louros river dam. 2.50d, Aliverion power plant. 4.50d, Salonika hydroelectric sub-station. 6d, Agra river hydroelectric station, interior.

Perf. 13x13½, 13½x13

1962, Apr. 14 **Wmk. 252**

728 A187 20 l	multi	.20	.20
729 A187 50 l	multi	.20	.20
730 A188 1d	multi	.20	.20
731 A188 1.50d	multi	.20	.20
732 A188 2.50d	multi	1.00	.20
733 A188 4.50d	multi	.80	.60
734 A188 6d	multi	2.40	2.40
Nos. 728-734 (7)		5.00	4.00

National electrification project.

Youth with Shield and Helmet from Ancient Vase — A189

Designs: 2.50d, Zappion hall, horiz. 4.50d, Kneeling soldier from Temple of Aphaea, Aegina. 6d, Standing soldier from stele of Ariston.

Perf. 13½x12, 12x13½

1962, May 3 **Litho.** **Wmk. 252**

Sizes: 22x33mm, 33x22mm

735 A189 2.50d	grn, bl, red & brn	.20	.20
736 A189 3d	brn, buff & red brn	.20	.20
737 A189 4.50d	bl & gray	.30	.30

Size: 21x37mm

738 A189 6d	brn red & blk	.30	.20
Nos. 735-738 (4)		1.00	.90

Ministerial congress of NATO countries, Athens, May 3-5.

Europa Issue, 1962
Common Design Type

1962, Sept. 17 *Perf. 13½x12*
Size: 33x23mm

739 CD5 2.50d ver & blk *.40* .25
740 CD5 4.50d ultra & blk *1.00* .50

Hands and Grain — A190

Demeter — A191

1962, Oct. 30 *Perf. 13x13½*
741 A190 1.50d dp car, blk & brn .40 .20
742 A190 2.50d brt grn, blk & brn .60 .25

Agricultural Insurance Program.

Perf. 12x13½
1963, Apr. 25 **Wmk. 252**

Design: 4.50d, Wheat and globe.

743 A191 2.50d brn car, gray & blk .30 .20
744 A191 4.50d multicolored .60 .25

FAO "Freedom from Hunger" campaign.

George I, Constantine XII, Alexander I, George II and Paul I — A192

Perf. 13½x12½
1963, June 29 **Engr.**
745 A192 50 l rose car .20 .20
746 A192 1.50d green .35 .20
747 A192 2.50d redsh brn .80 .20
748 A192 4.50d dk blue 1.40 .60
749 A192 6d violet 1.90 .25
Nos. 745-749 (5) 4.65 1.45

Centenary of the Greek dynasty.

Coin Types of 1959

Ancient Greek Coins: 50 l, Nymph Arethusa & Chariot. 80 l, Hercules & Zeus. 1d, Helios & Rose. 1.50d, Griffin & Square. 3d, Zeus & Eagle. 3.50d, Athena & Owl. 4.50d, Apollo & Labyrinth. 6d, Aphrodite & Apollo. 8.50d, Ram's head & Incuse Squares.

Perf. 13½x13, 13x13½
1963, July 5 **Litho.** **Wmk. 252**
Coins in Various Shades of Gray

750 A164 50 l violet bl .20 .20
751 A164 80 l dp magenta .20 .20
752 A165 1d emerald .20 .20
753 A164 1.50d lilac rose .50 .20
754 A164 3d olive .35 .20
755 A164 3.50d vermilion .25 .20
756 A165 4.50d redsh brn .35 .30
757 A165 6d blue grn .35 .20
758 A165 8.50d brt blue 1.10 .50
Nos. 750-758 (9) 3.50 2.20

"Acropolis at Dawn" by Lord Baden-Powell — A193

Jamboree Badge (Boeotian Shield) — A194

Athenian Treasury, Delphi — A195

Designs: 2.50d, Crown Prince Constantine, Chief Scout. 3d, Athanassios Lefkadites (founder of Greek Scouts) and Lord Baden-Powell. 4.50d, Scout bugling with conch shell.

1963, Aug. 1
759 A193 1d bl, sal & ol .20 .20
760 A194 1.50d dk bl, org brn & brn .20 .20
761 A194 2.50d multi .65 .20
762 A193 3d multi .20 .20
763 A194 4.50d multi .50 .20
Nos. 759-763 (5) 1.75 1.00

11th Boy Scout Jamboree, Marathon, July 29-Aug. 16, 1963.

1963, Sept. 16 *Perf. 12x13½*

2d, Centenary emblem. 2.50d, Queen Olga, founder of Greek Red Cross. 4.50d, Henri Dunant.

764 A195 1d multi .25 .20
765 A195 2d multi .20 .20
766 A195 2.50d multi .20 .20
767 A195 4.50d multi .35 .35
Nos. 764-767 (4) 1.00 .95

International Red Cross Centenary.

Europa Issue, 1963
Common Design Type

1963, Sept. 16 *Perf. 13½x12*
Size: 33x23mm

768 CD6 2.50d green *2.00* .20
769 CD6 4.50d brt magenta *2.75* 2.00

Vatopethion Monastery A196

King Paul I (1901-1964) A197

Designs: 80 l, St. Denys' Monastery. 1d, "Protaton" (Founder's) Church, horiz. 2d, Stavronikita Monastery. 2.50d, Jeweled cover of Nicephoros Phocas Gospel. 3.50d, Fresco of St. Athanassios, founder of community. 4.50d, Presentation of Christ, 11th century manuscript. 6d, Great Lavra Church, horiz.

Perf. 13x13½, 13½x13
1963, Dec. 5 **Litho.** **Wmk. 252**
770 A196 30 l multi .20 .20
771 A196 80 l multi .20 .20
772 A196 1d multi .20 .20
773 A196 2d multi .40 .20
774 A196 2.50d multi 1.25 .20
775 A196 3.50d multi .50 .35
776 A196 4.50d multi .40 .25
777 A196 6d multi .60 .20
Nos. 770-777 (8) 3.75 1.80

Millennium of the founding of the monastic community on Mt. Athos.

1964, May 6 *Perf. 12x13½*
778 A197 30 l brown .20 .20
779 A197 50 l purple .20 .20
780 A197 1d green .55 .20
781 A197 1.50d orange .20 .20
782 A197 2d blue .40 .20
783 A197 2.50d chocolate .50 .20
784 A197 3.50d red brn .40 .20
785 A197 4d ultra .85 .20
786 A197 4.50d bluish blk .90 .35
787 A197 6d rose pink 1.25 .20
Nos. 778-787 (10) 5.45 2.15

Archangel Michael — A198

Designs: 1d, Bulgaroctonus coin of Emperor Basil II. 1.50d, Two armed saints from ivory triptych by Harbaville, Louvre. 2.50d, Lady, fresco by Panselinos, Protaton Church, Mt. Athos. 4.50d, Angel, mosaic, Daphni Church, Athens.

1964, June 10 *Perf. 12x13½*
788 A198 1d multi .20 .20
789 A198 1.50d multi .20 .20
790 A198 2d multi .20 .20
791 A198 2.50d multi .20 .20
792 A198 4.50d multi .50 .50
Nos. 788-792 (5) 1.30 1.30

Byzantine Art and for the Byzantine Art Exhibition, Athens, Apr.-June, 1964.
Exist imperf.

Birth of Aphrodite, Emblem of Kythera A199

Designs (emblems of islands): 20 l, Trident, Paxos. 1d, Head of Ulysses, Ithaca. 2d, St. George slaying dragon, Lefkas. 2.50d, Zakyntnos, Zante. 4.50d, Cephalus, dog and spear, Cephalonia. 6d, Trireme, Corfu.

Perf. 13½x12
1964, July 20 **Litho.** **Wmk. 252**
793 A199 20 l multi .20 .20
794 A199 30 l multi .20 .20
795 A199 1d multi .20 .20
796 A199 2d multi .20 .20
797 A199 2.50d sl grn & dl grn .25 .20
798 A199 4.50d multi .60 .45
799 A199 6d multi .35 .20
Nos. 793-799 (7) 2.00 1.65

Centenary of the union of the Ionian Islands with Greece.

Child and Sun — A200

1964, Sept. 10 **Wmk. 252**
800 A200 2.50d multi .50 .20

50th anniv. of the Natl. Institute of Social Welfare for the Protection of Children and Mothers (P.I.K.P.A.).

Europa Issue, 1964
Common Design Type

1964, Sept. 14 **Litho.** *Perf. 13x13½*
Size: 23x39mm

801 CD7 2.50d lt grn & dk red *2.00* .25
802 CD7 4.50d gray & brn *3.00* 1.00

King Constantine II and Queen Anne-Marie A201

Peleus and Atalante Fighting, 6th Cent. B.C. Vase A202

1964, Sept. 18 **Engr.** *Perf. 13½x14*
803 A201 1.50d green .20 .20
804 A201 2.50d rose car .20 .20
805 A201 4.50d brt ultra .30 .25
Nos. 803-805 (3) .70 .65

Wedding of King Constantine II and Princess Anne-Marie of Denmark, Sept. 18, 1964.

Perf. 12x13½, 13½x12
1964, Oct. 24 **Litho.** **Wmk. 252**

Designs: 1d, Runners on amphora, horiz. 2d, Athlete on vase, horiz. 2.50d, Discus thrower and judge, pitcher. 4.50d, Charioteer, sculpture, horiz. 6d, Boxers, vase, horiz. 10d, Apollo, frieze from Zeus Temple at Olympia.

806 A202 10 l multi .20 .20
807 A202 1d multi .20 .20
808 A202 2d multi .20 .20
809 A202 2.50d multi .20 .20
810 A202 4.50d multi .40 .30
811 A202 6d multi .20 .20
812 A202 10d multi .30 .20
Nos. 806-812 (7) 1.70 1.50

18th Olympic Games, Tokyo, Oct. 10-25.

Detail from "Christ Stripped of His Garments" by El Greco A203

Aesculapius Theatre, Epidauros A204

Paintings by El Greco: 1d, Concert of the Angels. 1.50d, El Greco's painted signature, horiz. 2.50d, Self-portrait. 4.50d, Storm-lashed Toledo.

Perf. 12x13½, 13½x12
1965, Mar. 6 **Litho.** **Wmk. 252**
813 A203 50 l sepia & multi .20 .20
814 A203 1d gray & multi .20 .20
a. Double impression of black *45.00*
815 A203 1.50d multi .20 .20
816 A203 2.50d slate & multi .20 .20
817 A203 4.50d multi .30 .25
Nos. 813-817 (5) 1.10 1.05

350th anniv. of the death of Domenico Theotocopoulos, El Greco (1541-1614).

1965, Apr. 30 **Litho.** *Perf. 12x13½*

Design: 4.50d, Herod Atticus Theatre, and Acropolis, Athens.

818 A204 1.50d multi .20 .20
819 A204 4.50d multi .25 .25

Epidauros and Athens theatrical festivals.

ITU Emblem, Old and New Telecommunication Equipment — A205

1965, Apr. 30 *Perf. 13½x12*
820 A205 2.50d multi .30 .20

Cent. of the ITU.

Swearing-in Ceremony A206

Flag of Philiki Hetaeria, the Friends' Society A207

Perf. 13½x12

1965, May 31 Litho. Wmk. 252

821 A206 1.50d multi .20 .20
822 A207 4.50d gray & multi .20 .20

150th anniv. of the Friends' Society, a secret organization for the liberation of Greece from Turkey.

Emblem of A.H.E.P.A. A208

1965, June 30

823 A208 6d lt bl, blk & ol .30 .20

Congress of the American Hellenic Educational Progressive Association, Athens.

Eleutherios Venizelos, Therissos, 1905 — A209

Designs: 2d, Venizelos signing Treaty of Sevres, 1920. 2.50d, Venizelos portrait.

1965, June 30 Engr. ***Perf. 12½x13***

824 A209 1.50d green .20 .20
825 A209 2d dark blue .20 .20
826 A209 2.50d brown .20 .20
Nos. 824-826 (3) .60 .60

Cent. of the birth of Eleutherios Venizelos (1864-1936), statesman and prime minister.

Symbols of Planets — A210

Astronaut in Space — A211

Design: 6d, Two space ships over globe.

Perf. 12½x13½

1965, Sept. 11 Litho. Wmk. 252

827 A210 50 l multi .20 .20
828 A211 2.50d multi .20 .20
829 A211 6d multi .20 .20
Nos. 827-829 (3) .60 .60

16th Astronautical Cong., Athens, 9/12-18.

Victory Medal — A212

Stadium, Phaleron A213

Design: 1d, Games' emblem and "JBA."

Perf. 13½x13, 13x13½

1965, Sept. 11

830 A213 1d multicolored .20 .20
831 A212 2d multicolored .20 .20
832 A213 6d multicolored .20 .20
Nos. 830-832 (3) .60 .60

24th Balkan Games, Sept. 1-10.

Europa Issue, 1965

Common Design Type

1965, Oct. 21 ***Perf. 13½x12***

Size: 33x23mm

833 CD8 2.50d bl gray, blk & dk bl *.60* .20
834 CD8 4.50d olive, blk & grn *1.10* .35

Hipparchus and Astrolabe A214

1965, Oct. 21 Litho. Wmk. 252

835 A214 2.50d bl grn, blk & dk red .25 .20

Opening of the Evghenides Planetarium, Athens.

St. Andrew's Church, Patras — A215

St. Andrew — A216

1965, Nov. 30 ***Perf. 12x13½***

836 A215 1d multicolored .20 .20
837 A216 5d multicolored .20 .20

Return of the head of St. Andrew from St. Peter's, Rome to St. Andrew's, Patras. The design of the 5d is from an 11th cent. mosaic at St. Luke's Monastery, Boeotia.

Ants and Anthill — A217

Savings Bank and Book — A218

1965, Nov. 30 Litho. Wmk. 252

838 A217 10 l grn, blk & bis .20 .20
839 A218 2.50d multi .20 .20

50th anniv. of the Post Office Savings Bank.

Theodore Brysakes A219

Jean Gabriel Eynard A220

Banknote of 1867 — A221

Greek Painters: 1d, Nikeforus Lytras. 2.50d, Constantin Volonakes. 4d, Nicolas Gyses. 5d, George Jacobides.

Perf. 13x13½

1966, Feb. 28 Litho. Wmk. 252

840 A219 80 l multi .20 .20
841 A219 1d multi .20 .20
842 A219 2.50d multi .20 .20
843 A219 4d multi .20 .20
844 A219 5d multi .20 .20
Nos. 840-844 (5) 1.00 1.00

Perf. 12x13½

1966, Mar. 30 Engr. Wmk. 252

2.50d, Georgios Stavros. 4d, Bank's 1st headquarters, etching by Yannis Kefallinos.

845 A220 1.50d gray grn .20 .20
846 A220 2.50d brown .20 .20
847 A221 4d ultra .20 .20
848 A221 6d black .20 .20
Nos. 845-848 (4) .80 .80

National Bank of Greece, 125th anniv.

Symbolic Water Cycle — A222

UNESCO Emblem — A223

WHO Headquarters, Geneva — A224

Perf. 12x13½, 13½x12

1966, Apr. 18 Litho.

849 A222 1d multicolored .20 .20
850 A223 3d multicolored .20 .20
851 A224 5d multicolored .20 .20
Nos. 849-851 (3) .60 .60

Hydrological Decade (UNESCO), 1965-74, (1d); 20th anniv. of UNESCO (3d); inauguration of the WHO Headquarters, Geneva (5d).

Geannares Michael (Hatzes) — A225

Explosion at Arkadi Monastery A226

Map of Crete — A227

1966, Apr. 18

852 A225 2d multi .20 .20
853 A226 2.50d multi .20 .20
854 A227 4.50d multi .25 .20
Nos. 852-854 (3) .65 .60

Cent. of the Cretan revolt against the Turks. Geannares Michael (Hatzes), the leader of the revolt, was a member of Cretan government and a writer.

Copper Mask, 4th Century, B.C. — A228

Dionysus on a Thespian Ship-Chariot A229

Designs: 2.50d, Old Theater of Dionysus, Athens, 6th Century B.C. 4.50d, Dancing Dionysus, from vase by Kleophrades, c. 500 B.C.

Perf. 12x13½, 13½x12

1966, May 26 Litho. Wmk. 252

855 A228 1d multi .20 .20
856 A229 1.50d multi .20 .20
857 A229 2.50d multi .20 .20
858 A228 4.50d multi .20 .20
Nos. 855-858 (4) .80 .80

2500th anniversary of Greek theater.

Boeing 707-320 over New York Buildings and Greek Column A230

1966, May 26 ***Perf. 13x12½***

859 A230 6d blue & dark blue .30 .20

Inauguration of transatlantic flights of Olympic Airways.

Tobacco Worker — A231

Design: 5d, Woman sorting tobacco leaves.

Perf. 12½x13½

1966, Sept. 19 Litho. Wmk. 252

860 A231 1d multicolored .20 .20
861 A231 5d multicolored .35 .20

Greek tobacco industry, and 4th Intl. Scientific Tobacco Congress, Athens, Sept. 19-26.

Europa Issue, 1966

Common Design Type

1966, Sept. 19 Litho. Wmk. 252

Size: 23x33mm

862 CD9 1.50d olive .60 .20
863 CD9 4.50d lt red brown 1.25 .50

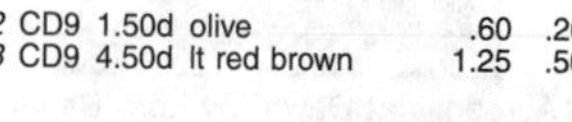

Carved Cases for Knitting Needles — A232

Bridegroom, Embroidery from Epirus A233

Designs (Popular Art): 50 l, Lyre, Crete. 1d, Massa (stringed instrument). 1.50d, Bas-relief (cross and angels). 2d, Icon (Sts. Constantine and Helena). 2.50d, Virgin (wood carving, Church of St. Nicholas, Galaxeidon). 3d, Embroidery (sailing ship from Skyros). 4d, Embroidery (wedding parade). 4.50d, Carved wooden distaff (Sts. George and Barbara). 5d, Silver and agate necklace and earrings. 20d, Handwoven cloth, Cyprus.

Perf. 12x13½, 13½x12

1966, Nov. 21 Litho. Wmk. 252

864 A232	10 l	multi	.20	.20
865 A233	30 l	multi	.20	.20
866 A232	50 l	multi	.20	.20
867 A232	1d	multi	.20	.20
868 A232	1.50d	multi	.20	.20
869 A232	2d	multi	.50	.20
870 A232	2.50d	multi	.20	.20
871 A233	3d	multi	.20	.20
872 A233	4d	multi	.45	.20
873 A232	4.50d	multi	.20	.20
874 A232	5d	multi	.35	.20
875 A233	20d	multi	.45	.50
		Nos. 864-875 (12)	3.35	2.70

King Constantine II, Queen Anne-Marie and Princess Alexia — A234

Designs: 2d, Princess Alexia. 3.50d, Queen Anne-Marie and Princess Alexia.

Perf. 13½x14

1966, Dec. 19 Engr. Wmk. 252

876 A234	2d	green	.20	.20
877 A234	2.50d	brown	.20	.20
878 A234	3.50d	ultra	.20	.20
		Nos. 876-878 (3)	.60	.60

Princess Alexia, successor to the throne of Greece.

"Night" by John Cossos (1830-73) — A235

Sculptures: 50 l, Penelope by Leonides Drosses (1836-1882). 80 l, Shepherd by George Fytales. 2d, Woman's torso by Constantine Demetriades (1881-1943). 2.50d, "Colocotrones" (equestrian statue) by Lazarus Sochos (1862-1911). 3d, Sleeping Young Lady by John Halepas (1851-1938), horiz. 10d, Woodcutter by George Filippotes (1839-1919), horiz.

Perf. 12x13½, 13½x12

1967, Feb. 28 Litho. Wmk. 252

879 A235	20 l	Prus bl, gray & blk	.20	.20
880 A235	50 l	brn, gray & blk	.20	.20
881 A235	80 l	brn red, gray & blk	.20	.20
882 A235	2d	vio bl, gray & blk	.20	.20
883 A235	2.50d	ultra, blk & grn	.20	.20
884 A235	3d	bl, lt bl, gray & blk	.20	.20
885 A235	10d	bl & multi	.20	.20
		Nos. 879-885 (7)	1.40	1.40

Issued to honor modern Greek sculptors.

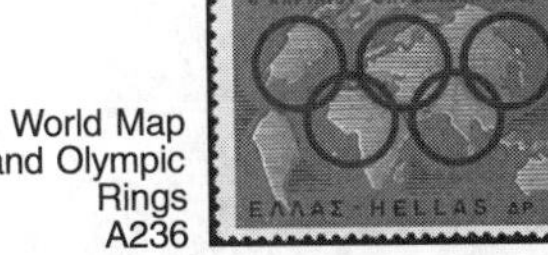

World Map and Olympic Rings A236

Discus Thrower by C. Demetriades A237

Designs: 1.50d, Runners on ancient clay vessel. 2.50d, Hurdler and map of Europe and Near East. 6d, Rising sun over Altis ruins at Olympia.

Perf. 13½x12, 12x13½

1967, Apr. 6 Litho. Wmk. 252

886 A236	1d	multi	.20	.20
887 A236	1.50d	multi	.20	.20
888 A236	2.50d	multi	.20	.20
889 A237	5d	multi	.30	.20
890 A236	6d	multi	.35	.20
		Nos. 886-890 (5)	1.25	1.00

Olympic Games Day, Apr. 6 (1d); Classic Marathon Race, Apr. 6 (1.5d); athletic qualifying rounds for the Cup of Europe, June 24-25 (2.50d); 9th contest for the European Athletic Championships, 1969 (5d); founding of the Intl. Academy at Olympia and the 7th meeting of the Academy, July 29-Aug. 14, 1967 (6d).

Europa Issue, 1967

Common Design Type

Perf. 12x13½

1967, May 2 Litho. Wmk. 252

Size: 23x33½mm

891 CD10	2.50d	buff, lt & dk brn	*.45*	.20
892 CD10	4.50d	grn, lt & dk grn	*.80*	.50

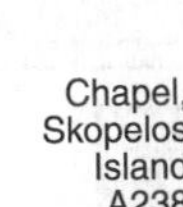

Chapel, Skopelos Island A238

Plaka District, Athens — A239

Intl. Tourist Year: 4.50d, Doric Temple of Epicurean Apollo, by Itkinus, c. 430 B.C.

Perf. 13½x12, 12x13½

1967, June 26 Litho. Wmk. 252

893 A238	2.50d	multi	.20	.20
894 A238	4.50d	multi	.30	.30
a.		Double impression of black		
895 A239	6d	multi	.25	.20
		Nos. 893-895 (3)	.75	.70

Destroyer and Sailor A240

Training Ship, Merchant Marine Academy — A241

Maritime Week: 2.50d, Merchant Marine Academy, Aspropyrgos, Attica, and rowing crew. 3d, Cruiser Georgios Averoff and Naval School, Poros. 6d, Merchant ship and bearded figurehead.

1967, June 26

896 A240	20 l	multi	.20	.20
897 A241	1d	multi	.20	.20
898 A240	2.50d	multi	.20	.20
899 A240	3d	multi	.30	.20
900 A240	6d	multi	.20	.20
		Nos. 896-900 (5)	1.10	1.00

Soldier and Rising Phoenix A242

Blast Furnaces A243

Perf. 12x13½

1967, Aug. 30 Litho. Wmk. 252

901 A242	2.50d	blue & multi	.20	.20
902 A242	3d	orange & multi	.20	.20
903 A242	4.50d	multi	.20	.20
		Nos. 901-903 (3)	.60	.60

Revolution of Apr. 21, 1967.

1967, Nov. 29 ***Perf. 13x14***

904 A243	4.50d	brt bl & dk vio bl	.20	.20

1st meeting of the UN Industrial Development Organization, Athens, Nov. 29-Dec. 20.

Sailboats A244

Children's Drawings: 1.50d, Steamship and island. 3.50d, Farmhouse. 6d, Church on hill.

1967, Dec. 20 ***Perf. 13½x12½***

905 A244	20 l	multi	.20	.20
906 A244	1.50d	grn, dk bl & blk	.20	.20
907 A244	3.50d	multi	.25	.25
908 A244	6d	multi	.20	.20
		Nos. 905-908 (4)	.85	.85

Javelin A245

Apollo, Olympic Academy Seal A246

Discus Thrower by Demetriades A247

Designs: 1d, Jumping. 2.50d, Attic vase showing lighting of Olympic torch. 4d, Olympic rings and world map, horiz. 6d, Long-distance runners, vert.

Wmk. 252

1968, Feb. 28 Litho. ***Perf. 12½***

909 A245	50 l	ultra & bis	.20	.20
910 A245	1d	grn, yel, blk & gray	.20	.20
911 A246	1.50d	blk, bl & buff	.20	.20
912 A246	2.50d	ol grn, blk & org brn	.20	.20
913 A246	4d	gray & multi	.35	.20
914 A247	4.50d	bl, grn, yel & blk	.55	.35
915 A245	6d	brn, red & bl	.30	.20
		Nos. 909-915 (7)	2.00	1.55

50 l, 1d, 6d, 27th Balkan Games, Athens, Aug. 29-Sept. 1; 1.50d, Meeting of the Intl. Olympic Academy; 2.50d, Lighting of the Olympic torch for 19th Olympic Games, Mexico City; 4d, Olympic Day, Apr. 6; 4.50d, 9th European Athletic Championships, 1969.

Europa Issue, 1968

Common Design Type

Perf. 13½x12

1968, Mar. 29 Litho. Wmk. 252

Size: 33x23mm

916 CD11	2.50d	cop red, bis & blk	*.40*	.35
917 CD11	4.50d	vio, bister & blk	*1.10*	1.00

Emblems of Greek and International Automobile Clubs — A248

1968, Mar. 29 ***Perf. 13x14***

918 A248	5d	ultra & org brn	.50	.35

General Assembly of the International Automobile Federation, Athens, Apr. 8-14.

Athena Defeating Alkyoneus, from Pergamos Altar, 180 B.C. — A249

Athena, 2nd Century, B.C. — A250

Winged Victory of Samothrace, c. 190 B.C. — A251

Designs: 50 l, Alexander the Great on horseback, from sarcophagus, c. 310 B.C. 1.50d, Emperors Constantine and Justinian bringing offerings to Virgin Mary, Byzantine mosaic. 2.50d, Emperor Constantine Paleologos, lithograph by D. Tsokos, 1859. 3d, Greece in Missolonghi, by Delacroix. 4.50d, Greek Soldier (evzone), by G. B. Scott.

Perf. 13½x13, 13x13½, 13½x14 (A249)

1968, Apr. 27

919 A249	10 l	gray & multi	.20	.20
920 A250	20 l	grn & multi	.20	.20
921 A250	50 l	pur & multi	.20	.20
922 A249	1.50d	gray & multi	.20	.20
923 A250	2.50d	multi	.20	.20
924 A251	3d	multi	.20	.20
925 A251	4.50d	multi	.25	.20
926 A251	6d	multi	.35	.30
		Nos. 919-926 (8)	1.80	1.70

"The Hellenic Fight for Civilization" exhibition

Monument to the Unknown Priest and Teacher, Rhodes A252

Map & Flag of Greece — A253

Cross and Globe — A254

Perf. 14x13½, 13½x14

1968, July 11 Litho. Wmk. 252

927	A252	2d multicolored	.30	.20
928	A253	5d multicolored	.40	.40

20th anniv. of the union of the Dodecanese Islands with Greece.

1968, July 11 ***Perf. 13½x14***

929	A254	6d multicolored	.45	.35

19th Biennial Congress of the Greek Orthodox Archdiocese of North and South America.

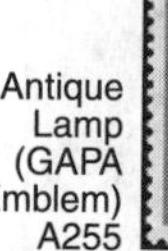

Antique Lamp (GAPA Emblem) A255

1968, July 11 ***Perf. 14x13½***

930	A255	6d multicolored	.35	.30

Regional Congress of the Greek-American Progressive Association, G.A.P.A.

Fragment of Bas-relief, Temple of Aesculapius, Athens — A256

Perf. 13½x14

1968, Sept. 8 Litho. Wmk. 252

931	A256	4.50d multicolored	1.00	.90

Issued to publicize the 5th European Cardiology Congress, Athens, Sept. 8-14.

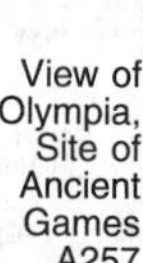

View of Olympia, Site of Ancient Games A257

Pindar and Olympic Ode — A258

Hygeia and WHO Emblem — A259

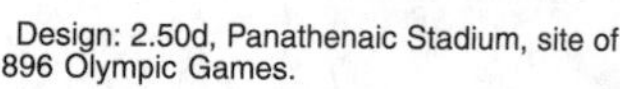

Design: 2.50d, Panathenaic Stadium, site of 1896 Olympic Games.

Perf. 14x13½, 13x13½

1968, Sept. 25 Litho. Wmk. 252

932	A257	2.50d multicolored	.20	.20
933	A257	5d green & multi	.20	.20
934	A258	10d bl, yel & brn	.90	.70
		Nos. 932-934 (3)	1.30	1.10

19th Olympic Games, Mexico City, 10/12-27.

On 10d, hyphen is omitted at end of 5th line of ode on 5 of 50 stamps in each sheet.

1968, Nov. 8 ***Perf. 13½x14***

935	A259	5d gray & multi	.55	.30

20th anniv. of WHO.

Mediterranean, Breguet 19 and Flight Route, 1928 — A260

Farman, 1912, Plane and F-104G Jet — A261

St. Zeno, The Letter Bearer — A262

Design: 2.50d, Greek air force pilot ramming enemy plane over Langada.

1968, Nov. 8 ***Perf. 14x13½, 13½x14***

936	A260	2.50d ultra, blk & yel	.20	.20
937	A260	3.50d multicolored	.20	.20
938	A261	8d multicolored	1.25	.90
		Nos. 936-938 (3)	1.65	1.30

Exploits of Royal Hellenic Air Force.

Perf. 13½x14

1969, Feb. 10 Litho. Wmk. 252

939	A262	2.50d multicolored	.45	.20

Establishment of the feast day of St. Zeno as the day of Greek p.o. personnel.

Hephaestus and Cyclops, Bas-relief A263

Parade of Harvesters, Minoan Vase — A264

1969, Feb. 10 ***Perf. 13½x12½***

940	A263	1.50d multicolored	.35	.20
941	A264	10d multicolored	.90	.65

50th anniv. of the ILO.

Yachts in Vouliagmeni Harbor — A265

Athens Festival, Chorus of Elders — A266

View of Astypalaia — A267

Perf. 13½x12½, 12½x13½

1969, Mar. 3

942	A265	1d multicolored	.20	.20
943	A266	5d multicolored	.80	.70
944	A267	6d multicolored	.40	.20
		Nos. 942-944 (3)	1.40	1.10

Issued for tourist publicity.

Attic Shield and Helmet on Greek Coin, 461-450 B.C. — A268

Hoplites and Flutist, from Proto-Corinthian Pitcher, 640-630 B.C. — A269

Perf. 12½x13½, 13½x12½

1969, Apr. 4 Litho. Wmk. 252

945	A268	2.50d rose red, blk & sl	.35	.20
946	A269	4.50d multi	.85	.65

20th anniv. of NATO.

Europa Issue, 1969

Common Design Type

1969, May 5 ***Perf. 13½x12½***

Size: 33x23mm

947	CD12	2.50d multi	*1.25*	.20
948	CD12	4.50d multi	*2.00*	.90

Victory Medal A270

Pole Vault and Pentathlon (from Panathenaic Amphora) A271

5d, Relay race and runners from amphora, 525 B.C., horiz. 8d, Modern and ancient (Panathenaic amphora, c. 480 B.C.) discus throwers.

Perf. 12½x13½, 13½x12½

1969, May 5

949	A270	20 l red & multi	.20	.20
950	A271	3d gray & multi	.20	.20
951	A271	5d multicolored	.20	.20
952	A271	8d multicolored	1.40	.75
		Nos. 949-952 (4)	2.00	1.35

Issued to publicize the 9th European Athletic Championships, Athens, Sept. 16-21.

Greece and the Sea Issue

Oil Tanker A272

Merchant Vessels and Warships, 1821 — A273

Designs: 80 l, Brig and steamship, painting by Ioannis Poulakas, vert. 4.50d, Warships on maneuvers. 6d, Battle of Salamis, 480 B.C., painting by Constantine Volonakis.

Perf. 12½x13½, 13½x12½, 13½x13

1969, June 28 Litho. Wmk. 252

953	A272	80 l multicolored	.20	.20
954	A272	2d blk, bl & gray	.20	.20
955	A273	2.50d dk bl & multi	.20	.20
956	A272	4.50d brn, gray & bl	.75	.35
957	A273	6d multicolored	.90	.45
		Nos. 953-957 (5)	2.25	1.40

Raising Greek Flag — A274

1969, Aug. 31 ***Perf. 13x13½***

958	A274	2.50d blue & multi	.55	.20

20th anniv. of the Grammos-Vitsi victory.

Athena Promachos and Map of Greece A275

"National Resistance" A276

Greek Participation in World War II — A277

Perf. 13x13½, 13½x14

1969, Oct. 12 Litho. Wmk. 252

959	A275	4d multicolored	.20	.20
960	A276	5d multicolored	.60	.50
961	A277	6d multicolored	.45	.20
		Nos. 959-961 (3)	1.25	.90

25th anniv. of the liberation of Greece in WW II.

No. 960 exists imperf.

Demetrius Tsames Karatasios, by G. Demetriades A278

Pavlos Melas, by P. Mathiopoulos A279

2.50d, Emmanuel Pappas, statue by Nicholas Perantinos. 4.50d, Capetan Kotas.

Perf. 12x13½

1969, Nov. 12 Litho. Wmk. 252

962	A278	1.50d	multicolored	.20	.20
963	A278	2.50d	blue & multi	.20	.20
964	A279	3.50d	gray & multi	.20	.20
965	A279	4.50d	multicolored	.95	.55
			Nos. 962-965 (4)	1.55	1.15

Issued to honor Greek heroes in Macedonia's struggle for liberation.

Angel of the Annunciation, Daphni Church, 11th Century — A280

Dolphins, Delos, 110 B.C. A281

Christ's Descent into Hell, Nea Moni Church, 11th Cent. A282

Greek Mosaics: 1.50d, The Holy Ghost (dove), Hosios Loukas Monastery, 11th cent. 2d, The Hunter, Pella, 4th cent. B.C. 5d, Bird, St. George's Church, Salonica, 5th cent.

Perf. 12x13½, 13½x12 (1d), 13x13½ (6d)

1970, Jan. 16 Litho. Wmk. 252

966	A280	20 l	multicolored	.20	.20
967	A281	1d	multicolored	.20	.20
968	A280	1.50d	blue & multi	.20	.20
969	A280	2d	gray & multi	.30	.20
970	A280	5d	bister & multi	.40	.40
971	A282	6d	multicolored	.70	.60
			Nos. 966-971 (6)	2.00	1.80

Hercules and the Cretan Bull — A283

Hercules and the Erymanthian Boar — A284

Labors of Hercules: 30 l, Capture of Cerberus. 1d, Capture of the golden apples of the Hesperides. 1.50d, Lernean Hydra. 2d, Slaying of Geryon. 3d, Centaur Nessus. 4.50d, Fight with the river god Achelos. 5d, Nemean lion. 6d, Stymphalian birds. 20d, Giant Antaeus. Designs of 20 l and 1d are from Temple of Zeus, Olympia; others from various vessels; all from 7th-5th cent. B.C.

Perf. 13½x12, 12x13½

1970, Mar. 16 Litho. Wmk. 252

972	A283	20 l	gray, blk & yel	.20	.20
973	A283	30 l	ocher & multi	.20	.20
974	A284	1d	bl gray, blk & bl	.20	.20
975	A283	1.50d	dk brn, bis & sl grn	.20	.20
976	A283	2d	ocher & multi	1.00	.20
977	A284	2.50d	ocher, dk brn & dl red	.20	.20
978	A284	3d	multicolored	1.25	.20
979	A283	4.50d	dk bl & multi	.20	.20
980	A283	5d	multicolored	.30	.20
981	A283	6d	multicolored	.30	.20
982	A283	20d	black & multi	1.25	.50
			Nos. 972-982 (11)	5.30	2.50

Satellite, Earth Station and Hemispheres A285

1970, Apr. 21 ***Perf. 13½x12***

983	A285	2.50d	bl, gray & yel	.40	.20
984	A285	4.50d	brn, ol & bl	.75	.75

Opening of the Earth Satellite Telecommunications Station "Thermopylae," Apr. 21, 1970.

Europa Issue, 1970

Common Design Type and

Owl (Post Horns and CEPT) — A287

1970, Apr. 21 ***Perf. 13½x12, 12x13½***

985	CD13	2.50d	rose red & org	*1.90*	.20
986	A287	3d	brt bl, gray & vio bl	*.90*	.20
987	CD13	4.50d	ultra & org	*2.75*	1.25
			Nos. 985-987 (3)	5.55	1.65

St. Demetrius with Cyril and Methodius as Children A288

Emperor Michael III with Sts. Cyril and Methodius A290

A289

Perf. 13½x14 (50 l); 12x13½ (2d, 10d); 13x13½ (5d)

1970, Apr. 17 Litho. Wmk. 252

988	A288	50 l multi	.20	.20
989		2d St. Cyril	.50	.45
990	A290	5d multi	.50	.20
991		10d St. Methodius	1.00	.45
a.		A289 Pair, #989, 991	1.50	.90
		Nos. 988-991 (4)	2.20	1.30

Sts. Cyril and Methodius who translated the Bible into Slavonic.

Greek Fir A292

Jankaea Heldreichii A293

6d, Rock partridge, horiz. 8d, Wild goat.

Perf. 13x14, 14x13, 12x13½ (2.50d)

1970, June 16 Litho. Wmk. 252

992	A292	80 l	multi	.25	.20
993	A293	2.50d	multi	1.10	.20
994	A292	6d	multi	1.75	.30
995	A292	8d	multi	1.90	1.75
			Nos. 992-995 (4)	5.00	2.45

European Nature Conservation Year, 1970.

Map Showing Link Between AHEPA Members and Greece A294

1970, Aug. 1 ***Perf. 13½x13***

996	A294	6d blue & multi	.75	.25

48th annual AHEPA (American Hellenic Educational Progressive Assoc.) Cong., Athens, Aug. 1970.

UPU Headquarters, Bern — A295

Education Year Emblem — A296

Mahatma Gandhi — A297

United Nations Emblem — A298

Ludwig van Beethoven — A299

Perf. 13½x12, 13x14, 12x13½

1970, Oct. 7 Litho. Wmk. 252

997	A295	50 l	bis & multi	.20	.20
998	A296	2.50d	bl & multi	.30	.20
999	A297	3.50d	multi	.75	.20
1000	A298	4d	bl & multi	.75	.20
1001	A299	4.50d	blk & multi	1.25	.90
			Nos. 997-1001 (5)	3.25	1.70

Inauguration of the UPU Headquarters, Bern (50 l); Intl. Education Year (2.50d); cent. of the birth of Mohandas K. Gandhi (1869-1948), leader in India's struggle for independence (3.50d); 25th anniv. of the UN (4d); Ludwig van Beethoven (1770-1827), composer (4.50d).

The Shepherds (Mosaic) — A300

Christmas (from Mosaic in the Monastery of Hosios Loukas, Boetia, 11th cent.): 4.50d, The Three Kings and Angel. 6d, Nativity, horiz.

1970, Dec. 5 ***Perf. 13x14, 14x13***

1002	A300	2d	bister & multi	.20	.20
1003	A300	4.50d	bister & multi	.50	.25
1004	A300	6d	bister & multi	.60	.45
			Nos. 1002-1004 (3)	1.30	.90

"Leonidas" A301

Priest Sworn in as Fighter, from Commemorative Medal — A302

Eugenius Voùlgaris (1716-1806) A303

Battle of Corinth A304

Kaltetsi Monastery, Seal of Peloponnesian Senate — A305

Death of Bishop Isaias, Battle of Alamana — A306

Designs: No. 1009, *Pericles.* No. 1010, Sacrifice of Kapsalis. 1.50d, *Terpsichore.* No. 1012, Patriarch Grigorius IV. No. 1013, Suliot women in battle, horiz. No. 1015, *Karteria*. No. 1016, Adamantios Korias, M.D. No. 1017, Memorial column, provincial administrative seal of Epidaurus. 3d, Naval battle, Samos, horiz. 5d, Battle of Athens. 6d, Naval battle, Yeronda. 6.50d, Battle of Maniaki. 9d, Battle of Karpenisi, death of Marcos Botsaris. 10d, Bishop Germanos blessing flag. 15d, *Secret School*. 20d, John Capodistrias' signature and seal.

1971 Litho. Wmk. 252

1005 A301	20 l multi		.20	.20
1006 A302	50 l multi		.20	.20
1007 A303	50 l multi		.20	.20
1008 A304	50 l multi		.20	.20
1009 A301	1d multi		.20	.20
1010 A304	1d multi		.20	.20
1011 A301	1.50d multi		.20	.20
1012 A302	2d multi		.20	.20
1013 A304	2d multi		.20	.20
1014 A305	2d multi		.20	.20
1015 A301	2.50d multi		.20	.20
1016 A303	2.50d multi		.30	.20
1017 A305	2.50d multi		.20	.20
1018 A304	3d multi		.20	.20
1019 A306	4d multi		.20	.20
1020 A304	5d multi		.30	.20
1021 A301	6d multi		.30	.20
1022 A301	6.50d multi		.40	.20
1023 A301	9d multi		.40	.20
1024 A306	10d multi		.40	.20
1025 A306	15d multi		.50	.30
1026 A305	20d multi		.60	.30
	Nos. 1005-1026 (22)		6.00	4.60

Sesquicentennial of Greece's uprising against the Turks. Emphasize role of Navy (#1005, 1009, 1011, 1015, 1018, 1021), issued 3/15; Church (#1006, 1012, 1019, 1024), 2/8; Instructors (#1007, 1016, 1025), 6/21; Land Forces (#1008, 1010, 1013, 1020, 1022-1023), 9/21; Provincial Administrations (#1014, 1017, 1026), 10/19.

Sizes: 37x24mm: #1005, 1009, 1011, 1015; 40x27½mm, #1021; 48x33mm, #1022, 1023.

Perfs.: 14x13, #1005, 1009, 1011, 1013, 1015, 1018; 13½x14, #1006, 1012; 12x13½, #1007, 1016, 1019, 1022-1025; 13x14, #1008, 1010, 1020; 13½x13, #1014, 1017, 1021, 1026.

Spyridon Louis, Winner of 1896 Marathon Race, Arriving at Stadium A307

Pierre de Coubertin and Memorial Column — A308

Perf. 13½x13, 13x13½

1971, Apr. 10 Litho. Wmk. 252

1027 A307	3d multi	.25	.20
1028 A308	8d multi	.55	.50

Olympic Games revival, 75th anniv.

Europa Issue, 1971

Common Design Type

1971, May 18 *Perf. 13½x12*

Size: 33x22½mm

1029 CD14	2.50d grn, yel & blk	*1.25*	.20
1030 CD14	5d org, yel & blk	*2.25*	1.40

Hosios Lukas Monastery A309

Monasteries and Churches: 1d, Daphni Church. 2d, St. John the Divine, Patmos. 2.50d, Koumbelidiki Church, Kastoria. 4.50d, Chalkeon Church, Thessalonica. 6.50d, Paregoritissa Church, Arta. 8.50d, St. Paul's Monastery, Mt. Athos.

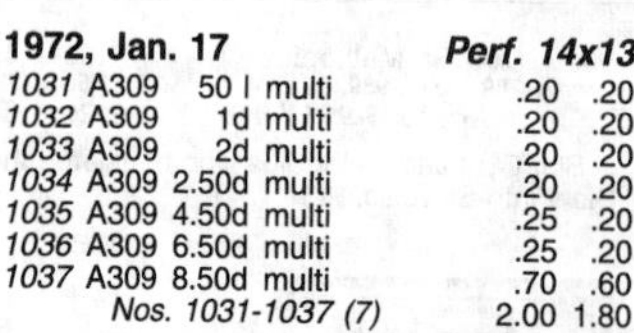

1972, Jan. 17 *Perf. 14x13*

1031 A309	50 l multi	.20	.20
1032 A309	1d multi	.20	.20
1033 A309	2d multi	.20	.20
1034 A309	2.50d multi	.20	.20
1035 A309	4.50d multi	.25	.20
1036 A309	6.50d multi	.25	.20
1037 A309	8.50d multi	.70	.60
	Nos. 1031-1037 (7)	2.00	1.80

Cretan Costume — A310

Designs: Greek regional costumes.

1972, Mar. 1 *Perf. 12½x13½*

1038 A310	50 l	shown	.20	.20
1039 A310	1d	Woman, Pindus	.20	.20
1040 A310	2d	Man, Missolonghi	.20	.20
1041 A310	2.50d	Woman, Sarakatsan, Attica	.20	.20
a.		"1972" omitted	6.00	6.00
1042 A310	3d	Woman, Island of Nisyros	.20	.20
1043 A310	4.50d	Woman, Megara	.30	.20
1044 A310	6.50d	Woman, Trikeri	.50	.20
1045 A310	10d	Woman, Pylaia, Macedonia	1.00	.60
		Nos. 1038-1045 (8)	2.80	2.00

See Nos. 1073-1089, 1121-1135.

Memorial Medal, Science and Industry A311

Flag and Map of Greece — A312

Honeycomb, Transportation and Industry — A313

Perf. 13½x13, 13x13½

1972, Apr. 21 Wmk. 252

1046 A311	2.50d blue & multi	.20	.20
1047 A312	4.50d ocher & multi	.20	.20
1048 A313	5d multi	.25	.20
	Nos. 1046-1048 (3)	.65	.60

5th anniversary of the revolution.

Europa Issue 1972

Common Design Type

1972, May 2 *Perf. 12x13½*

Size: 23x33mm

1049 CD15	3d multi	*.40*	.20
1050 CD15	4.50d blue & multi	*1.40*	.80

Acropolis and Car — A314

Route of Automobile Rally — A315

1972, May 26 *Perf. 13½x12*

1051 A314	4.50d multi	.45	.40
1052 A315	5d bl & multi	.45	.40

20th Acropolis Automobile Rally, May 26-29.

Gaia Handing Erecthonius to Athena, Cecrops A316

Designs: 2d, Uranus, from altar of Zeus at Pergamum. 2.50d, Gods defeating the Giants, Treasury of Siphnos. 5d, Zeus of Dodona.

1972, June 26 Litho. *Perf. 14x13½*

1053 A316	1.50d yel grn & blk	.20	.20
1054 A316	2d dk bl & blk	.20	.20
1055 A316	2.50d org brn & blk	.20	.20
1056 A316	5d dk brn & blk	.35	.25
a.	Strip of 4, #1053-1056	.85	.85

Greek mythology. No. 1056 issued only se-tenant with Nos. 1053-1055 in sheets of 40 (4x10). Nos. 1053-1055 issued also in sheets of 50 each.

Olympic Rings, Wrestlers A317

50 l, Young athlete, crowning himself, c. 480 B.C., vert. 3.50d, Spartan woman running, Archaic period, vert. 4.50d, Episkyros ball game, 6th century B.C. 10d, Running youths, from Panathenaic amphora.

Perf. 13½x14, 14x13½

1972, July 28 Litho. Wmk. 252

1057 A317	50 l mar, blk & gray	.20	.20
1058 A317	1.50d brn, gray & blk	.20	.20
1059 A317	3.50d ocher & multi	.20	.20
1060 A317	4.50d grn, buff & blk	.25	.20
1061 A317	10d blk & fawn	.40	.35
	Nos. 1057-1061 (5)	1.25	1.15

20th Olympic Games, Munich, 8/26-9/11.

Young Stamp Collector — A318

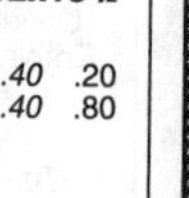

Three Kings and Angels — A319

1972, Nov. 15 *Perf. 13x14*

1062 A318	2.50d multi	.25	.20

Stamp Day.

1972, Nov. 15

1063 A319	2.50d shown	.20	.20
1064 A319	4.50d Nativity	.20	.20
a.	Pair, #1063-1064	.30	.30

Christmas 1972.

Technical University, 1885, by Luigi Lanza — A320

1973, Mar. 30 *Perf. 13½x13*

1065 A320	2.50d multi	.20	.20

Centenary of the Metsovion National Technical University.

"Spring," Fresco — A321

Breast-form Jug — A322

"Wooing and Twittering Swallows" Fresco — A323

Designs: 30 l, "Blue Apes" fresco. 1.50d, Jug decorated with birds. 5d, "Wild Goats" fresco. 6.50d, Wrestlers, fresco.

1973, Mar. 30 *Perf. 13x13½, 13½x13*

1066 A321	10 l multi	.20	.20
1067 A322	20 l multi	.20	.20
1068 A323	30 l multi	.20	.20
1069 A322	1.50d grn & multi	.20	.20
1070 A323	2.50d multi	.20	.20
1071 A323	5d multi	.20	.20
1072 A323	6.50d multi	.65	.65
	Nos. 1066-1072 (7)	1.85	1.85

Archaeological treasures from Santorini Island (Thera).

Costume Type of 1972

Women's costumes except 10 l, 20 l, 50 l, 5d, 15d.

1973, Apr. 18 *Perf. 12½x13½*

1073 A310	10 l	Peloponnesus	.20	.20
1074 A310	20 l	Central Greece	.20	.20
1075 A310	30 l	Locris	.20	.20
1076 A310	50 l	Skyros	.20	.20
1077 A310	1d	Spetsai	.20	.20
1078 A310	1.50d	Almyros	.20	.20
1079 A310	2.50d	Macedonia	.20	.20
1080 A310	3.50d	Salamis	.20	.20
1081 A310	4.50d	Epirus	.20	.20
1082 A310	5d	Lefkas	.20	.20
1083 A310	6.50d	Skyros	.20	.20
1084 A310	8.50d	Corinth	.30	.20
1085 A310	10d	Corfu	.30	.20
1086 A310	15d	Epirus	.40	.20
1087 A310	20d	Thessaly	.75	.20
1088 A310	30d	Macedonia	.90	.50
1089 A310	50d	Thrace	1.40	.65
		Nos. 1073-1089 (17)	6.25	4.15

Europa Issue 1973
Common Design Type

1973, May 2 ***Perf. 13½x12½***
Size: 35x22mm

1090 CD16 2.50d dp bl & lt bl .30 .20
1091 CD16 3d dp car & dp org .30 .20
1092 CD16 4.50d ol grn & yel .80 .40
Nos. 1090-1092 (3) 1.40 .80

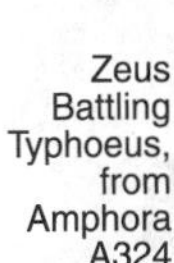

Zeus Battling Typhoeus, from Amphora A324

1d, Mount Olympus, after photograph. 2.50d, Zeus battling Giants, from Pergamum Altar. 4.50d, Punishment of Atlas and Prometheus, from vase.

Perf. 14x13½
1973, June 25 **Wmk. 252**

1093 A324 1d gray & blk .20 .20
1094 A324 2d multi .20 .20
1095 A324 2.50d gray, blk & buff .20 .20
1096 A324 4.50d ocher & multi .25 .20
a. Strip of 4, #1093-1096 1.00 1.00

Greek mythology.

Dr. George Papanicolaou A325

Icon, The Annunciation A326

Perf. 13x13½
1973, Aug. 10 **Litho.** **Wmk. 252**

1097 A325 2.50d multi .20 .20
1098 A325 6.50d multi .20 .20

Dr. George Papanicolaou (1883-1962), cytologist and cancer researcher.

1973, Aug. 10

1099 A326 2.50d multi .20 .20

Miraculous icon of Our Lady of the Annunciation found on Tinos, 1823.

A327

A328

Triptolemus holding wheat on chariot.

Perf. 13x14
1973, Oct. 22 **Litho.** **Wmk. 252**

1100 A327 4.50d buff, dk brn & red .20 .20

5th Symposium of the European Conf. of Transport Ministers, Athens, Oct. 22-25.

1973, Nov. 15 **Engr.**

National Benefactors: 1d, Georgios Averoff. 2d, Apostolos Arsakis. 2.50d, Constantine Zappas. 4d, Andrea Sygros. 6.50d, John Varvakis.

1101 A328 1.50d dk red brn .20 .20
1102 A328 2d car rose .20 .20
1103 A328 2.50d slate green .20 .20
1104 A328 4d purple .20 .20
1105 A328 6.50d black .20 .20
Nos. 1101-1105 (5) 1.00 1.00

Child Examining Stamp — A329

1973, Nov. 15 **Litho.** ***Perf. 14x13***

1106 A329 2.50d multi .20 .20

Stamp Day.

Lord Byron in Souliot Costume — A330

Byron Taking Oath at Grave of Botsaris — A331

Perf. 13x14
1974, Apr. 4 **Wmk. 252** **Litho.**

1107 A330 2.50d multi .20 .20
1108 A331 4.50d multi .20 .20

George Gordon, Lord Byron (1788-1824), English poet involved in Greek struggle for independence.

Harpist of Keros, c. 2800-2200 B.C. — A332

Europa: 4.50d, Statue of Young Women, c. 510 B.C. 6.50d, Charioteer of Delphi, c. 480-450 B.C.

1974, May 10 ***Perf. 13x14***

1109 A332 3d dp bl & multi .20 .20
1110 A332 4.50d dl red & multi .20 .20
1111 A332 6.50d yel & multi .40 .25
Nos. 1109-1111 (3) .80 .65

Zeus and Hera Enthroned, and Iris — A333

Design from Mycenean Vase and UPU Emblem — A334

Greek mythology (from Vases, 5th Cent. B.C.): 2d, Birth of Athena, horiz. 2.50d, Artemis, Apollo, Leto, horiz. 10d, Hermes, the messenger.

1974, June 24 ***Perf. 13x14, 14x13***

1112 A333 1.50d ocher, blk & brn .20 .20
1113 A333 2d blk, ocher & brn .20 .20
1114 A333 2.50d blk, ocher & brn .20 .20
1115 A333 10d blk, ocher & brn .20 .20
Nos. 1112-1115 (4) .80 .80

1974, Sept. 14 ***Perf. 12½x13½***

UPU cent.: 4.50d, Hermes on the Move, horiz. 6.50d, Woman reading letter.

1116 A334 2d vio & blk .20 .20
1117 A334 4.50d vio & blk .20 .20
1118 A334 6.50d vio & blk .20 .20
Nos. 1116-1118 (3) .60 .60

Crete No. 80 A335

1974, Nov. 15 **Litho.** ***Perf. 13½x13***

1119 A335 2.50d multi .20 .20

Stamp Day.

Flight into Egypt — A336

Illustration reduced.

1974, Nov. 15 ***Perf. 13½x14***

1120 A336 Strip of 3 .40 .30
a. 2d ocher & multi .20 .20
b. 4.50d ocher & multi .20 .20
c. 8.50d ocher & multi .20 .20

Christmas 1974. Design is from 11th cent. Codex of Dionysos Monastery on Mount Athos.

Costume Type of 1972

Designs: Women's costumes, except 1.50d.

1974, Dec. 5 ***Perf. 12½x13½***

1121 A310 20 l Megara .20 .20
1122 A310 30 l Salamis .20 .20
1123 A310 50 l Edipsos .20 .20
1124 A310 1d Kyme .20 .20
1125 A310 1.50d Sterea Hellas .20 .20
1126 A310 2d Desfina .20 .20
1127 A310 3d Epirus .20 .20
1128 A310 3.50d Naousa .20 .20
1129 A310 4d Hasia .20 .20
1130 A310 4.50d Thasos .20 .20
1131 A310 5d Skopelos .20 .20
1132 A310 6.50d Epirus .20 .20
1133 A310 10d Pelion .20 .20
1134 A310 25d Kerkyra .40 .20
1135 A310 30d Boeotia .50 .20
Nos. 1121-1135 (15) 3.50 3.00

Secret Vostitsa Assembly, 1821 — A337

Grigorios Dikeos-Papaflessas A338

Aghioi Apostoli Church, Kalamata A339

Perf. 13½x12½, 12½x13½
1975, Mar. 24

1136 A337 4d multi .20 .20
1137 A338 7d multi .20 .20
1138 A339 11d multi .20 .20
Nos. 1136-1138 (3) .60 .60

Grigorios Dikeos-Papaflessas (1788-1825), priest and leader in Greece's uprising against the Turks, sesquicentennial of death.

Vase with Flowers — A340

Erotokritos and Aretussa — A341

11d, Girl with Hat. All designs are after paintings by Theophilos Hatzimichael (d. 1934).

Perf. 12½x13½
1975, May 10 **Litho.** **Wmk. 252**

1139 A340 4d multi *.20* .20
1140 A341 7d multi *.25* .25
1141 A340 11d multi *.75* .40
Nos. 1139-1141 (3) 1.20 .85

House, Kastoria A342

Greek Houses, 18th Cent.: 40 l, Arnea, Halkidiki. 4d, Veria. 6d, Siatista. 11d, Ambelakia, Thessaly.

1975, June 26 ***Perf. 13½x12½***

1142 A342 10 l brt bl & blk .20 .20
1143 A342 40 l red org & blk .20 .20
1144 A342 4d bister & blk .25 .20
1145 A342 6d ultra & multi .20 .20
1146 A342 11d org & blk .45 .30
Nos. 1142-1146 (5) 1.30 1.10

IWY Emblem, Neolithic Goddess — A343

"Looking to the Future" — A344

8.50d, Confrontation between Antigone & Creon.

Perf. 12½x13½

1975, Sept. 29	**Litho.**	**Wmk. 252**	
1147 A343	1.50d lilac & dk brn	.20	.20
1148 A343	8.50d bis, blk & brn	.20	.20
1149 A344	11d bl & blk	.20	.20
	Nos. 1147-1149 (3)	.60	.60

International Women's Year 1975.

Papanastasiou and University Buildings — A345

First University Building A346

University City Plan A347

1975, Sept. 29		***Perf. 14x13½***	
1150 A345	1.50d tan & sepia	.20	.20
1151 A346	4d multi	.20	.20
1152 A347	11d multi	.20	.20
	Nos. 1150-1152 (3)	.60	.60

Thessaloniki University, 50th anniversary. Alexandros Papanastasiou (1876-1936), founded University while Prime Minister.

Evangelos Zappas and Zappeion Building — A348

National Benefactors: 4d, Georgios Rizaris and Rizarios Ecclesiastical School. 6d, Michael Tositsas and Metsovion Technical University. 11d, Nicolaos Zosimas and Zosimea Academy.

Perf. 14x13

1975, Nov. 15	**Litho.**	**Wmk. 252**	
1153 A348	1d blk & grn	.20	.20
1154 A348	4d blk & brn	.20	.20
1155 A348	6d blk & org	.20	.20
1156 A348	11d blk & brick red	.20	.20
	Nos. 1153-1156 (4)	.80	.80

Greece No. 380 — A349

1975, Nov. 15		***Perf. 13x14***	
1157 A349	11d dull grn & brn	.20	.20

Stamp Day 1975.

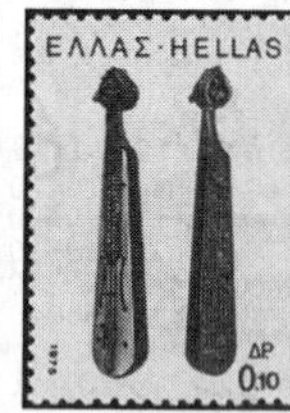

Pontos Lyre — A350

Musicians, Byzantine Mural — A351

Designs: 1d, Cretan lyre. 1.50d, Tambourine. 4d, Guitarist, from amphora, horiz. 6d, Bagpipes. 7d, Lute. 10d, Barrel organ. 11d, Pipes and zournadas. 20d, Musicians and singers praising God, Byzantine mural, horiz. 25d, Drums. 30d, Kanonaki, horiz.

Perf. 12½x13½, 13½x12½

1975, Dec. 15	**Litho.**	**Wmk. 252**	
1158 A350	10 l multi	.20	.20
1159 A351	20 l multi	.20	.20
1160 A350	1d ultra & multi	.20	.20
1161 A350	1.50d multi	.20	.20
1162 A351	4d multi	.20	.20
1163 A350	6d multi	.20	.20
1164 A350	7d multi	.20	.20
1165 A350	10d multi	.25	.20
1166 A350	11d red & multi	.25	.20
1167 A351	20d multi	.25	.20
1168 A350	25d multi	.25	.20
1169 A350	30d multi	.40	.20
	Nos. 1158-1169 (12)	2.80	2.40

Popular musical instruments.

Early Telephone, Globe, Waves A352

11d, Globe, waves, telephone 1976.

Perf. 13½x12½

1976, Mar. 23	**Litho.**	**Wmk. 252**	
1170 A352	7d blk & multi	.20	.20
1171 A352	11d blk & multi	.20	.20
a.	Pair, Nos. 1170-1171	.35	.35

1st telephone call by Alexander Graham Bell, Mar. 10, 1876.

Sortie of Missolonghi — A353

1976, Mar. 23		***Perf. 13½x13***	
1172 A353	4d multi	.20	.20

Sortie of the garrison of Missolonghi, sesquicentennial.

Florina Jugn — A354

Avramidis Plate — A355

Europa: 11d, Egina pitcher with Greek flags.

Perf. 13x14, 12½x12 (A355)

1976, May 10	**Litho.**	**Wmk. 252**	
1173 A354	7d buff & multi	.20	.20
1174 A355	8.50d blk & multi	.20	.20
1175 A354	11d gray & multi	.25	.20
	Nos. 1173-1175 (3)	.65	.60

Lion Attacking Bull — A356

Head of Silenus — A357

Designs: 4.50d, Flying aquatic birds. 7d, Wounded bull. 11d, Cow feeding calf, horiz. Designs from Creto-Mycenaean engraved seals, c. 1400 B.C.

Perf. 13x12½, 13½x14, 14x13½

1976, May 10			
1176 A356	2d bis & multi	.20	.20
1177 A356	4.50d multi	.20	.20
1178 A356	7d multi	.20	.20
1179 A357	8.50d pur & multi	.20	.20
1180 A357	11d brn & multi	.20	.20
	Nos. 1176-1180 (5)	1.00	1.00

Long Jump A358

Montreal and Athens Stadiums — A359

Designs (Classical and Modern Events): 2d, Basketball. 3.50d, Wrestling. 4d, Swimming. 25d, Lighting Olympic flame and Montreal Olympic Games torch.

Perf. 14x13½, 12½x13½ (A359)

1976, June 25	**Litho.**	**Wmk. 252**	
1181 A358	50 l org & multi	.20	.20
1182 A358	2d org & multi	.20	.20
1183 A358	3.50d org & multi	.20	.20
1184 A358	4d bl & multi	.20	.20
1185 A359	11d multi	.20	.20
1186 A358	25d org & multi	.40	.20
	Nos. 1181-1186 (6)	1.40	1.20

21st Olympic Games, Montreal, Canada, July 17-Aug. 1.

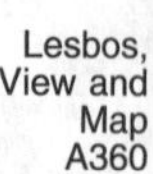

Lesbos, View and Map A360

Perf. 13½x14, 14x13½

1976, July 26	**Litho.**	**Wmk. 252**	
1187 A360	30d Lemnos, vert.	.25	.20
1188 A360	50d shown	.45	.25
1189 A360	75d Chios	.75	.30
1190 A360	100d Samos	1.10	.55
	Nos. 1187-1190 (4)	2.55	1.30

Greek Aegean Islands.

Three Kings Speaking to the Jews — A361

Christmas: 7d, Nativity. Designs from manuscripts in Esfigmenou Monastery, Mount Athos.

1976, Dec. 8		***Perf. 13½x14***	
1191 A361	4d yellow & multi	.20	.20
1192 A361	7d yellow & multi	.20	.20

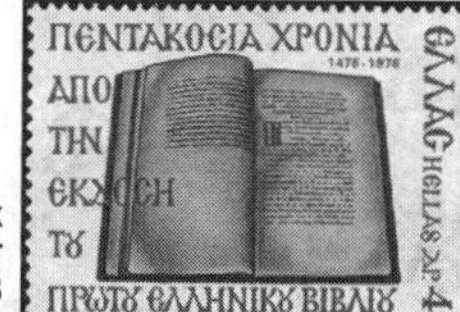

Greek Grammar of 1478 A362

1976, Dec. 8		***Perf. 14x13***	
1193 A362	4d multi	.20	.20

500th anniversary of printing of first Greek book by Constantin Lascaris, Milan.

Heinrich Schliemann A363

Brooch with Figure of Goddess — A364

Designs: 4d, Gold bracelet, horiz. 7d, Gold diadem, horiz. 11d, Gold mask (Agamemnon). Treasures from Mycenaean tombs.

1976, Dec. 8		***Perf. 13x14, 14x13***	
1194 A363	2d multi	.20	.20
1195 A364	4d multi	.20	.20
1196 A364	5d grn & multi	.20	.20
1197 A364	7d multi	.20	.20
1198 A364	11d multi	.20	.20
	Nos. 1194-1198 (5)	1.00	1.00

Cent. of the discovery of the Mycenaean royal shaft graves by Heinrich Schliemann.

Aesculapius with Patients — A365

Patient in Clinic — A366

Designs: 1.50d, Aesculapius curing young man. 2d, Young Hercules with old nurse. 20d, Old man with votive offering of large leg.

Perf. 12½x13½ (A365); 13x12 (A366)

1977, Mar. 15 Litho. Wmk. 252

1199 A365 50 l multi .20 .20
1200 A366 1d multi .20 .20
1201 A366 1.50d multi .20 .20
1202 A366 2d multi .20 .20
1203 A365 20d multi .20 .20
Nos. 1199-1203 (5) 1.00 1.00

International Rheumatism Year.

Winged Wheel, Modern Transportation — A367

1977, May 16 Litho. *Perf. 14x13½*

1204 A367 7d multi .20 .20

European Conference of Ministers of Transport (E.C.M.T.), Athens, June 1-3.

Mani Castle, Vathia A368

Europa: 7d, Santorini, vert. 15d, Windmills on Lasithi plateau.

Perf. 14x13½, 13½x14

1977, May 16 Litho. Wmk. 252

1205 A368 5d multicolored .20 .20
1206 A368 7d multicolored .20 .20
1207 A368 15d multicolored .25 .25
Nos. 1205-1207 (3) .65 .65

Alexandria Lighthouse, from Roman Coin — A369

Designs: 1d, Alexander places Homer's works into Achilles' tomb, fresco by Raphael. 1.50d, Alexander descends to the bottom of the sea, Flemish miniature. 3d, Alexander searching for water of life, Hindu plate. 7d, Alexander on horseback, Coptic carpet. 11d, Alexander hearing oracle that his days are numbered, Byzantine manuscript. 30d, Death of Alexander, Persian miniature. All designs include gold coin of Lysimachus with Alexander's head.

1977, July 23 *Perf. 14x13*

1208 A369 50 l silver & multi .20 .20
1209 A369 1d silver & multi .20 .20
1210 A369 1.50d silver & multi .20 .20
1211 A369 3d silver & multi .20 .20
1212 A369 7d silver & multi .20 .20
1213 A369 11d silver & multi .20 .20
1214 A369 30d silver & multi .25 .20
Nos. 1208-1214 (7) 1.45 1.40

Cultural influence of Alexander the Great (356-323 B.C.), King of Macedonia.

"Greece Rising Again" A370

People in Front of University A371

Greek Flags, Laurel, University A372

Perf. 13½x12½, 12x12½, 12½x12

1977, July 23 Unwmk.

1215 A370 4d multi .20 .20
1216 A371 7d multi .20 .20
1217 A372 20d multi .20 .20
Nos. 1215-1217 (3) .60 .60

Restoration of Democracy in Greece.

Archbishop Makarios, Map of Cyprus — A373

Design: 4d, Archbishop Makarios, vert.

Perf. 13x13½, 13½x13

1977, Sept. 10 Litho. Unwmk.

1218 A373 4d sepia & blk .20 .20
1219 A373 7d buff, brn & blk .20 .20

Archbishop Makarios (1913-1977), President of Cyprus.

Old Athens Post Office A374

Neo-Hellenic architecture: 1d, Institution for the Blind, Salonika. 1.50d, Townhall, Syros. 2d, National Bank of Greece, Piraeus. 5d, Byzantine Museum, Athens. 50d, Municipal Theater, Patras.

1977, Sept. 22 *Perf. 13½x13*

1220 A374 50 l multi .20 .20
1221 A374 1d multi .20 .20
1222 A374 1.50d multi .20 .20
1223 A374 2d multi .20 .20
1224 A374 5d multi .20 .20
1225 A374 50d multi .35 .20
Nos. 1220-1225 (6) 1.35 1.20

Battle of Navarino, Lithograph — A375

Adm. Van Heyden, Sir Edward Codrington, Count de Rigny — A376

1977, Oct. 20 *Perf. 13½x13*

1226 A375 4d brn, buff & blk .20 .20
1227 A376 7d multi .20 .20

150th anniversary of Battle of Navarino.

Parthenon and Refinery — A377

Caryatid and Factories — A379

Fish and Birds Suffering from Pollution A378

Design: 7d, Birds and trees in polluted air.

1977, Oct. 20 *Perf. 13½x14, 14x13½*

1228 A377 3d org & blk .20 .20
1229 A378 4d multi .20 .20
1230 A378 7d multi .20 .20
1231 A379 30d blk, gray & slate .20 .20
Nos. 1228-1231 (4) .80 .80

Protection of the environment.

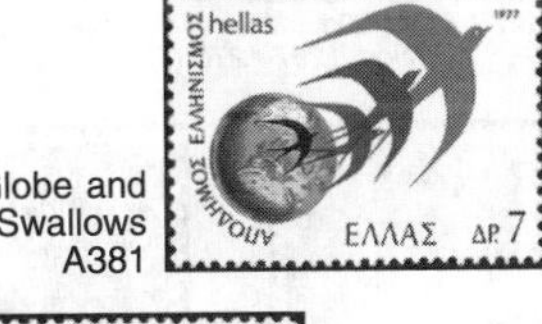

Map of Greece and Ships — A380

Globe and Swallows A381

Letter with Flags, Swallow A382

5d, Globe with Greek flag. 13d, World map showing dispersion of Greeks abroad.

1977, Dec. 15 *Perf. 13½x12½*

1232 A380 4d multi .20 .20
1233 A380 5d multi .20 .20
1234 A381 7d multi .20 .20
1235 A382 11d multi .20 .20
1236 A380 13d multi .20 .20
Nos. 1232-1236 (5) 1.00 1.00

Greeks living abroad.

Kalamata Harbor, by Constantine Parthenis — A383

Greek Paintings: 2.50d, Boats, Arsanas, by Spyros Papaloucas, vert. 4d, Santorini, by Constantine Maleas. 7d, The Engagement, by Nicolaus Gyzis. 11d, Woman with Straw Hat, by Nicolaus Lytras, vert. 15d, "Spring" (nude), by Georgio Iacovidis.

1977, Dec. 15 *Perf. 13½x13, 13x13½*

1237 A383 1.50d yel & multi .20 .20
1238 A383 2.50d yel & multi .20 .20
1239 A383 4d yel & multi .20 .20
1240 A383 7d yel & multi .20 .20
1241 A383 11d yel & multi .20 .20
1242 A383 15d yel & multi .20 .20
Nos. 1237-1242 (6) 1.20 1.20

Ebenus Cretica — A384

Greek Flora: 2.50d, Dwarf lily. 3d, Campanula oreadum. 4d, Tiger lily. 7d, Viola delphinantha. 25d, Paeonia rhodia.

1978, Mar. 30 Litho. *Perf. 13x13½*

1243 A384 1.50d multi .20 .20
1244 A384 2.50d multi .20 .20
1245 A384 3d multi .20 .20
1246 A384 4d multi .20 .20
1247 A384 7d multi .25 .20
1248 A384 25d multi .25 .20
Nos. 1243-1248 (6) 1.30 1.20

Postrider, Cancellation A385

5d, S.S. Maximilianos & Hermes Head. 7d, 19th cent. mail train & #122. 30d, Mailmen on motorcycles & #1062.

1978, May 15 *Perf. 13½x12½*

1249 A385 4d buff & multi .20 .20
1250 A385 5d buff & multi .20 .20
1251 A385 7d buff & multi .20 .20
1252 A385 30d buff & multi .25 .20
a. Souvenir sheet of 4 .65 .65
Nos. 1249-1252 (4) .85 .80

150th anniv. of Greek postal service.

No. 1252a issued Sept. 25, contains Nos. 1249-1252 in slightly changed colors. Sold for 60d.

Lighting Olympic Flame, Olympia — A386

Start of 100-meter Race — A387

1978, May 15 *Perf. 13x14*

1253 A386 7d multi .20 .20
1254 A387 13d multi .20 .20

80th session of International Olympic Committee, Athens, May 10-21.

Europa Issue 1978

St. Sophia, Salonica A388

Lysicrates Monument, Athens — A389

1978, May 15 ***Perf. 13x14, 14x13***

1255	A388	4d multi	.20 .20
1256	A389	7d multi	.20 .20

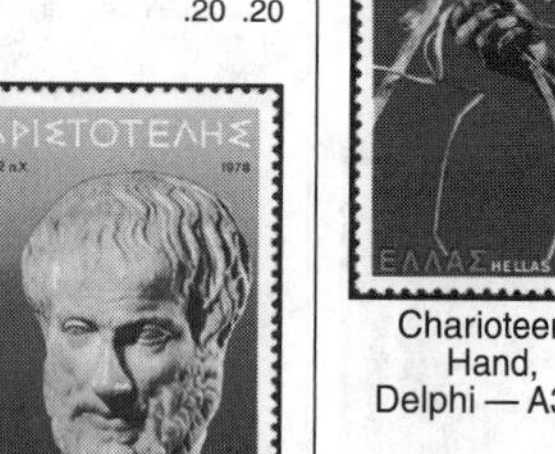

Aristotle, Roman Bust — A390

School of Athens, by Raphael — A391

Map of Chalcidice, Base of Statue from Attalus Arcade A392

Aristotle the Wise, Byzantine Fresco, St. George's Church, Ioannina A393

Perf. 13x13½, 13½x14 (20d)

1978, July 10 **Litho.**

1257	A390	2d multi	.20 .20
1258	A391	4d multi	.20 .20
1259	A392	7d multi	.20 .20
1260	A393	20d multi	.20 .20
		Nos. 1257-1260 (4)	.80 .80

Aristotle (384-322 B.C.), systematic philosopher.

Rotary Emblem A394

Surgeons Operating — A395

Ugo Foscolo, View of Zante — A396

Hellenistic Bronze Head — A397

Charioteer's Hand, Delphi — A398

Wright Brothers' Plane, Daedalus and Icarus — A399

1978, Sept. 21 **Litho.** ***Perf. 12½***

1261	A394	1d multi	.20 .20
1262	A395	1.50d multi	.20 .20
1263	A396	2.50d multi	.20 .20
1264	A397	5d multi	.20 .20
1265	A398	7d multi	.20 .20
1266	A399	13d multi	.20 .20
		Nos. 1261-1266 (6)	1.20 1.20

Rotary in Greece, 50th anniv. (1d); 11th Greek Surgery Cong., Salonica (1.50d); Ugo Foscolo (1778-1827), Italian writer (2.50d); European Convention on Human Rights, 25th anniv. (5d); 2nd Conf. of Ministers of Culture of the Council of Europe member countries, Athens, Oct. 23-27 (7d); 75th anniv. of 1st powered flight (13d).

Poor Woman and her 5 Children A400

Scenes from Fairy Tale "The 12 Months": 3d, The poor woman and the 12 months. 4d, The poor woman and the gold coins. 20d, Punishment of the greedy woman.

1978, Nov. 6 **Litho.** ***Perf. 13½x13***

1267	A400	2d multi	.20 .20
1268	A400	3d multi	.20 .20
1269	A400	4d multi	.20 .20
1270	A400	20d multi	.20 .20
		Nos. 1267-1270 (4)	.80 .80

"Transplants" A401

The Miracle of St. Anarghiri A402

1978, Nov. 6 ***Perf. 12½x13½***

1271	A401	4d multi	.20 .20
1272	A402	10d multi	.20 .20

Advancements in organ transplants.

Cruiser A403

New and Old Greek Naval Ships: 1d, Torpedo boats. 2.50d, Submarine Papanicolis. 4d, Battleship Psara. 5d, Sailing ship "Madonna of Hydra." 7d, Byzantine corvette. 50d, Archaic trireme.

1978, Dec. 15 **Litho.** ***Perf. 13½x12***

1273	A403	50 l multi	.20 .20
1274	A403	1d multi	.20 .20
1275	A403	2.50d multi	.20 .20
1276	A403	4d multi	.20 .20
1277	A403	5d multi	.20 .20
1278	A403	7d multi	.20 .20
1279	A403	50d multi	.45 .35
		Nos. 1273-1279 (7)	1.65 1.55

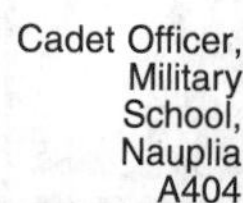

Cadet Officer, Military School, Nauplia A404

Cadet Officers' School Emblem — A405

Design: 10d, Cadet Officers Military School, Athens, Cadet's uniform, 1978.

1978, Dec. 15 ***Perf. 13½x12, 12x13½***

1280	A404	1.50d multi	.20 .20
1281	A405	2d multi	.20 .20
1282	A404	10d multi	.20 .20
		Nos. 1280-1282 (3)	.60 .60

Cadet Officers Military School, 150th anniv.

Virgin and Child — A406

Baptism of Christ — A407

Designs from 16th century icon stands in Stavronikita Monastery.

1978, Dec. 15 ***Perf. 13x13½***

1283	A406	4d multi	.20 .20
1284	A407	7d multi	.20 .20

Christmas 1978.

Map of Greece A408

1978, Dec. 28 ***Perf. 14x13***

1285	A408	7d multi	.20 .20
1286	A408	11d multi	.20 .20
1287	A408	13d multi	.20 .20
		Nos. 1285-1287 (3)	.60 .60

Kitsos Tzavellas — A409

Souli Castle A410

10d, Fighting Souliots. 20d, Fight of Zalongo.

Perf. 12½x13½, 13½x12½

1979, Mar. 12 **Litho.**

1288	A409	1.50d buff, blk & brn	.20 .20
1289	A410	3d multi	.20 .20
1290	A410	10d multi	.20 .20
1291	A409	20d buff, blk & brn	.20 .20
		Nos. 1288-1291 (4)	.80 .80

Struggle of the Souliots, 18th century fighters for freedom from Turkey.

Cycladic Figure from Amorgos — A411

Mailmen from Crete — A412

1979, Apr. 26 **Litho.** ***Perf. 12x13½***

1292	A411	20d multi	.20 .20

Aegean art.

1979, May 11 ***Perf. 13½x14***

Europa: 7d, Rural mailman on horseback, Crete.

1293	A412	4d multi	.20 .20
1294	A412	7d multi	.20 .20
a.		Pair, #1293-1294	.30 .30

Nicolas Scoufas A413

Basketball A415

Locomotives — A414

Mene Psarianosi Symeonidis Fossil A416

Temple of Hephaestus and Byzantine Church A417

Victory of Paeonius Statue, Flags of Balkan Countries A418

1979, May 12 ***Perf. 13x14, 14x13***

1295	A413	1.50d multi	.20 .20
1296	A414	2d multi	.20 .20
1297	A415	3d multi	.20 .20
1298	A416	4d multi	.20 .20
1299	A417	10d multi	.20 .20
1300	A418	20d multi	.20 .20
		Nos. 1295-1300 (6)	1.20 1.20

Nicolas Scoufas (1779-1818), founder of (patriotic) Friendly Society; Piraeus-Athens-to-the-frontier railroad, 75th anniv.; European Basketball Championship; 7th Intl. Cong. for the Study of the Neocene Period in the Mediterranean; Balkan Tourist Year 1979; 50 years of track and field competitions in Balkan countries.

Wheat with Members' Flags, Greek Coins — A419

European Parliament, Strasbourg — A420

Perf. 13x14, 14x13

1979, May 28			**Litho.**
1301 A419	7d multi	.20	.20
1302 A420	30d multi	.25	.25

Greece's entry into European Economic Community and Parliament.

Statue of a Girl, IYC Emblem — A421

Intl. Year of the Child: 8d, Girl & pigeons. 20d, Mother & Children, painting by Iacovides.

1979, June 27 **Litho.**		***Perf. 13x14***	
1303 A421	5d multi	.20	.20
1304 A421	8d multi	.20	.20
1305 A421	20d multi	.20	.20
	Nos. 1303-1305 (3)	.60	.60

Philip II, Bust — A422

Purple Heron — A423

Designs: 8d, Golden wreath. 10d, Copper vessel. 14d, Golden casket, horiz. 18d, Silver ewer. 20d, Golden quiver (detail). 30d, Gold and iron cuirass.

Perf. 13½x14, 14x13½

1979, Sept. 15			**Litho.**
1306 A422	6d multi	.20	.20
1307 A422	8d multi	.20	.20
1308 A422	10d multi	.20	.20
1309 A422	14d multi	.20	.20
1310 A422	18d multi	.20	.20
1311 A422	20d multi	.20	.20
1312 A422	30d multi	.30	.20
	Nos. 1306-1312 (7)	1.50	1.40

Archaeological finds from Vergina, Macedonia.

1979, Oct. 15

Protected Birds: 8d, Gull. 10d, Falcon, horiz. 14d, Kingfisher, horiz. 20d, Pelican. 25d, White-tailed sea eagle.

1313 A423	6d multi	.20	.20
1314 A423	8d multi	.20	.20
1315 A423	10d multi	.20	.20
1316 A423	14d multi	.20	.20
1317 A423	20d multi	.20	.20
1318 A423	25d multi	.25	.20
	Nos. 1313-1318 (6)	1.25	1.20

Council of Europe wildlife and natural habitat protection campaign.

Agricultural Bank A424

St. Cosmas — A425

Basil the Great — A426

Balkan Countries, Magnifier — A427

Aristotelis Valaoritis — A428

Golfer A429

Hippocrates A430

Parliament in Session A431

Perf. 14x13½, 13½x14

1979, Nov. 24			**Litho.**
1319 A424	3d multi	.20	.20
1320 A425	4d multi	.20	.20
1321 A426	6d multi	.20	.20
1322 A427	8d multi	.20	.20
1323 A427	10d multi, horiz.	.20	.20
1324 A428	12d multi	.20	.20
1325 A429	14d multi	.20	.20
1326 A430	18d multi	.20	.20
1327 A431	25d multi	.25	.20
	Nos. 1319-1327 (9)	1.85	1.80

Agricultural Bank of Greece, 50th anniv.; Cosmas the Aetolian (1714-79), Greek missionary and martyr; Basil the Great (330-379), Archbishop of Caesarea; Balkanfila, Balkan Stamp Exhibition, Athens, Nov. 24-Dec. 2; Aristotelis Valaoritis (1824-79), Greek poet; 27th World Golf Championship, Nov. 8-11; Intl. Hippocratic Foundation of Cos; Greek Parliament, 104th anniv.

Parnassus — A432

Tempe Valley A433

Perf. 12½x13½, 13½x12½

1979, Dec. 15			**Litho.**
1328 A432	50 l shown	.20	.20
1329 A433	1d shown	.20	.20
1330 A432	2d Melos	.20	.20
1331 A432	4d Vikos Gorge	.20	.20
1332 A433	5d Missolonghi Salt Lake	.20	.20
1333 A432	6d Louros Aqueduct	.20	.20
1334 A432	7d Samothrace	.20	.20
1335 A433	8d Sithonia-Halkidiki	.20	.20
1336 A433	10d Samarias Gorge, vert	.20	.20
1337 A432	12d Siphnos	.20	.20
1338 A433	14d Kyme	.20	.20
1339 A432	18d Ios	.20	.20
1340 A432	20d Thasos	.20	.20
1341 A433	30d Paros	.30	.20
1342 A432	50d Cephalonia	.30	.20
	Nos. 1328-1342 (15)	3.20	3.00

Byzantine Castle of Thessalonica A434

4d, Aegosthena Castle, vert. 8d, Cave of Perama Ioannina, vert. 10d, Cave of Dyros, Mani, vert. 14d, Arta Bridge. 20d, Kalogiros Bridge, Epirus.

Perf. 12½x14, 14x12½

1980, Mar. 15			**Litho.**
1343 A434	4d multi	.20	.20
1344 A434	6d multi	.20	.20
1345 A434	8d multi	.20	.20
1346 A434	10d multi	.20	.20
1347 A434	14d multi	.20	.20
1348 A434	20d multi	.20	.20
	Nos. 1343-1348 (6)	1.20	1.20

Gate of Galerius A435

1980, Mar. 15

1349 A435 8d multi .20 .20

1st Hellenic Congress of Nephrology, Thessalonica, Mar. 20-22.

Solar System A436

Design: 10d, Temple of Hera, Aristarchus' theory and diagram.

1980, May 5 **Litho.**		***Perf. 13½x12½***	
1350 A436	10d multi	.20	.20
1351 A436	20d multi	.25	.20

Aristarchus of Samos, first astronomer to discover heliocentric theory of universe, 2300th birth anniv.; Intl. Scientific Congress on Aristarchus, Samos, June 17-19.

Maria Callas (1923-1977), Opera Singer A437

Europa: 8d, Georges Seferis (1900-1971), writer and diplomat.

1980, May 5			
1352 A437	8d multi	.20	.20
1353 A437	14d multi	.30	.25

Energy Conservation Manual A438

Perf. 13½x12½, 12½x13½

1980, May 5			
1354 A438	8d shown	.20	.20
1355 A438	20d Candle in bulb, vert.	.25	.25

Firemen A439

St. Demetrius, Angel, Fresco — A440

Soldiers Marching through Crete — A441

Ancient Vase, Olives A442

Federation Emblem, Newspaper A443

Constantinos Ikonomos — A444

1980, July 14 **Litho.**		***Perf. 12½***	
1356 A439	4d multi	.20	.20
1357 A440	6d multi	.20	.20
1358 A441	8d multi	.20	.20
1359 A442	10d multi	.20	.20
1360 A443	14d multi	.20	.20
1361 A444	20d multi	.25	.20
	Nos. 1356-1361 (6)	1.25	1.20

Fire Brigade, 50th anniv.; St. Demetrius, 1700th birth anniv.; Therissos Revolution, 75th anniv.; 2nd Intl. Olive Oil Year; Intl. Federation of Journalists, 15th Cong., Athens, May 12-16; Constantinos Ikonomos (1780-1857), writer and revolutionary.

Olympic Stadium, Temple Coin, Olympia A445

Olympic Rings and: 14d, Stadium and coin of Delphi 18d, Epidaurus theater, coin of Olympia 20d, Rhodes Stadium, Cos coin. 50d, Panathenean Stadium; 1st Olympic Games medal.

1980, Aug. 11 **Litho.**		***Perf. 13½x13***	
1362 A445	8d multi	.20	.20
1363 A445	14d multi	.25	.20
1364 A445	18d multi	.25	.20

1365	A445	20d	multi	.30	.20
1366	A445	50d	multi	.55	.40
			Nos. 1362-1366 (5)	1.55	1.20

22nd Summer Olympic Games, Moscow, July 19-Aug. 3.

Asbestos A446

Perf. 13½x12½

1980, Sept. 22 **Litho.**

1367	A446	6d	shown	.20	.20
1368	A446	8d	Gypsum, vert.	.20	.20
1369	A446	10d	Copper ore	.20	.20
1370	A446	14d	Barite, vert.	.25	.20
1371	A446	18d	Chromite	.25	.20
1372	A446	20d	Mixed sulphides, vert.	.25	.20
1373	A446	30d	Bauxite, vert.	.25	.20
			Nos. 1367-1373 (7)	1.60	1.40

Tow Truck — A447

Air Force Jet — A448

Airplane and Hangar A449

Ships in Port A450

Students' Association Headquarters A451

1980, Oct. 31 **Litho.** ***Perf. 12½***

1374	A447	6d	multi	.20	.20
1375	A448	8d	multi	.20	.20
1376	A449	12d	multi	.20	.20
1377	A450	20d	multi	.20	.20
1378	A451	25d	multi	.20	.20
			Nos. 1374-1378 (5)	1.00	1.00

Road Assistance Service of Automobile and Touring Club of Greece, 20th anniv.; Air Force, 50th anniv.; Flyers' Club of Thessaloniki, 50th anniv.; Piraeus Port Organization, 50th anniv.; Association for Macedon ian Studies, 40th anniv.

Madonna and Child, by Theodore Poulakis — A452

Christmas 1980: He is Happy Thanks to You, by Theodore Poulakis. No. 1381a has continuous design.

1980, Dec. 10 ***Perf. 13½***

1379	6d	multi	.20	.20
1380	14d	multi	.20	.20
1381	20d	multi	.25	.20
a.		A452 Strip of 3, #1379-1381	.60	.55

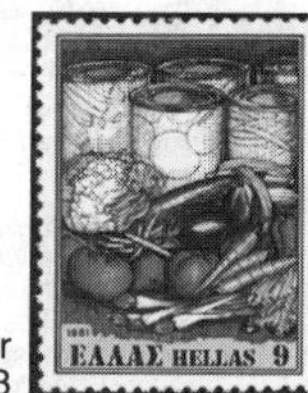

Vegetables for Export — A453

1981, Mar. 16 **Litho.** ***Perf. 12½***

1382	A453	9d	shown	.20	.20
1383	A453	17d	Fruits	.25	.20
1384	A453	20d	Cotton	.25	.20
1385	A453	25d	Marble	.30	.20
			Nos. 1382-1385 (4)	1.00	.80

Europa Issue 1981

Kira Maria Folk Dance, Alexandria — A454

1981, May 4 **Litho.** ***Perf. 14x13***

1386	A454	12d	shown	.25	.20
1387	A454	17d	Cretan Sousta (dance)	.50	.35

Runner, Olympic Stadium, Kalogreza A455

1981, May 4

1388	A455	12d	shown	.25	.20
1389	A455	17d	Runners, Europe	.25	.20

13th European Athletic Championship, Athens, 1982.

Torso Showing Kidneys A456

Sky Diver and Airplanes A457

Views of Thessaly and Epirus — A458

Oil Rig and Map of Thassos Island — A460

Vase with Painted Eyes A459

Globes and Ancient Coin A461

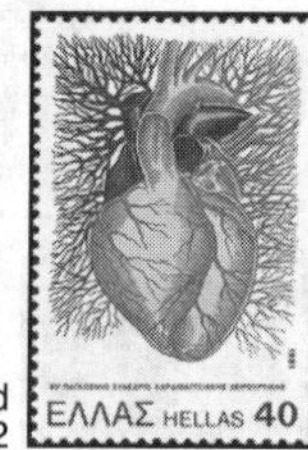

Heart and Vessels — A462

Perf. 13½x14, 14x13½

1981, May 22 **Litho.**

1390	A456	2d	multi	.20	.20
1391	A457	3d	multi	.20	.20
1392	A458	6d	multi	.20	.20
1393	A459	9d	multi	.25	.20
1394	A460	12d	multi	.25	.20
1395	A461	21d	multi	.25	.20
1396	A462	40d	multi	.35	.20
			Nos. 1390-1396 (7)	1.70	1.40

8th Intl. Nephrology Conf., Athens, June 7-12; Greek National Air Club, 50th anniv.; Intl. Historical Symposium, Volos, Sept. 27-30; Greek Ophthalmological Society, 50th anniv.; inauguration of oil production at Thassos Island; World Assoc. for Intl. Relations, Athens, 2nd anniv.; 15th Intl. Cardiovascular Surgery Conference, Athens, Sept. 6-10.

Cockles A463

1981, June 30 **Litho.** ***Perf. 14x13½***

1397	A463	4d	shown	.20	.20
1398	A463	5d	Parrot fish	.20	.20
1399	A463	12d	Painted comber	.30	.20
1400	A463	15d	Common dentex	.30	.25
1401	A463	17d	Parnassius apollo	.40	.25
1402	A463	50d	Colias hyale	1.25	.90
			Nos. 1397-1402 (6)	2.65	2.00

Bell Tower, Epirus — A464

Altar Gate, St. Paraskevi's Church — A465

Bell Towers and Wood Altar Gates (Iconostases): 9d, Pelion, horiz. 12d, Church of Sts. Constantine and Helen, Epirus. 17d, St. Nicolas Church, Velvendos, horiz. 30d, St. Jacob icon, Church Museum, Alexandroupolis. 40d, St. Nicholas Church, Makrinitsa.

1981, Sept. 30 **Litho.**

1403	A464	4d	multi	.20	.20
1404	A465	6d	multi	.20	.20
1405	A465	9d	multi	.25	.20
1406	A464	12d	multi	.30	.20
1407	A465	17d	multi	.35	.20
1408	A465	30d	multi	.35	.20
1409	A465	40d	multi	.35	.20
			Nos. 1403-1409 (7)	2.00	1.40

European Urban Renaissance Year — A466

St. Simeon, Archbishop of Thessalonica A467

Promotion of Breastfeeding A468

Gina Bachauer, Pianist, 5th Death Anniv. A469

Constantine Broumidis, Artist, Death Centenary A470

Sesquicentennial of Greek Banknotes — A471

Perf. 14x13½, 13½x14

1981, Nov. 20 **Litho.**

1410	A466	3d	multi	.20	.20
1411	A467	9d	multi	.20	.20
1412	A468	12d	multi	.25	.20
1413	A469	17d	multi	.40	.20
1414	A470	21d	multi	.45	.20
1415	A471	50d	multi	.50	.25
			Nos. 1410-1415 (6)	2.00	1.25

Old Parliament Building, Athens A472

Angelos Sikelianos (1884-1951), Poet A473

Harilaos Tricoupis, Politician, Birth Sesquicentennial A474

Aegean Islands Exhib., Rhodes, Athens — A475

Petralona Cave and Skull — A477

Olympic Airlines, 25th Anniv. A476

Perf. 13½x12½, 12½x13½

1982, Mar. 15 Litho.

1416 A472 2d multi .20 .20
1417 A473 9d multi .20 .20
1418 A474 15d multi .20 .20
1419 A475 21d multi .20 .20
1420 A476 30d multi .30 .20
1421 A477 50d multi .60 .20
Nos. 1416-1421 (6) 1.70 1.20

Historical and Ethnological Society centennial (2d); 3rd European Anthropology Congress, Halkidiki, Sept. (50d).

Europa 1982 — A478

1982, May 10 Litho. *Perf. 13½x14*

1422 A478 21d Battle of Marathon, 490 BC *.75* .20
1423 A478 30d 1826 Revolution *1.25* .50

13th European Athletic Championships, Athens — A479

1982, May 10 *Perf. 14x13½, 13½x14*

1424 A479 21d Pole vaulting, horiz. .20 .20
1425 A479 25d Running .30 .20
1426 A479 40d Sports, horiz. .50 .40
Nos. 1424-1426 (3) 1.00 .80

Byzantine Book Illustrations A480

Perf. 13½x12½, 12½x13½

1982, June 26 Litho.

1427 A480 4d Gospel book heading .20 .20
1428 A480 6d Illuminated "E," vert. .20 .20
1429 A480 12d Illuminated "T," vert. .20 .20
1430 A480 15d Gospel reading canon table, vert. .20 .20
1431 A480 80d Zoology book heading .85 .60
Nos. 1427-1431 (5) 1.65 1.40

George Caraiskakis (1782-1827), Liberation Hero — A481

Amnesty Intl. — A482

Designs: 12d, Camp in Piraeus, by von Krazeisen. 50d, Meditating.

1982, Sept. 20 Litho. *Perf. 13x13½*

1432 A481 12d multi .20 .20
1433 A481 50d multi .60 .50

1982, Sept. 20 *Perf. 13x14*

1434 A482 15d Vigil .20 .20
1435 A482 75d Prisoners .75 .40

Natl. Resistance Movement, 1941-44 — A483

Designs: 1d, Demonstration of Mar. 24, 1942. 2d, Sacrifice of Inhabitants of Kalavrita, by S. Vasiliou. 5d, Resistance Fighters in Thrace, by A. Tassos. 9d, The Start of Resistance in Crete, by P. Gravalos. 12d, Partisan Men and Women, by P. Gravalos. 21d, Blowing Up a Bridge, by A. Tassos. 30d, Fighters at a Barricade, by G. Sikeliotis. 50d, The Fight in Northern Greece, by B. Katraki, 5d, 9d, 12d, 21d vert.

1982, Nov. 8 Litho. *Perf. 12½*

1436 A483 1d multi .20 .20
1437 A483 2d multi .20 .20
1438 A483 5d multi .20 .20
1439 A483 9d multi .20 .20
1440 A483 12d multi .20 .20
1441 A483 21d multi .20 .20
a. Souv. sheet, 5d, 9d, 12d, 21d 1.40 1.40
1442 A483 30d multi .30 .20
1443 A483 50d multi .50 .25
a. Souv. sheet, 1d, 2d, 30d, 50d 1.40 1.40
Nos. 1436-1443 (8) 2.00 1.65

Christmas 1982 — A484

Designs: Various Byzantine Nativity bas-reliefs, Byzantine Museum.

1982, Dec. 6 Litho. *Perf. 13½x12½*

1444 A484 9d multi .20 .20
1445 A484 21d multi .30 .25
a. Pair, #1444-1445 .45 .40

25th Anniv. of Intl. Maritime Org. A485

Ship Figureheads. 15d, 18d, 25d, 40d vert.

1983, Mar. 14 *Perf. 14x13½, 13½x14*

1446 A485 11d Ares, Tsamados .25 .20
1447 A485 15d Ares, Miaoulis .35 .20
1448 A485 18d Female figure .35 .20
1449 A485 25d Spetses, Boubou-lina .45 .20
1450 A485 40d Epameinondas, K. Babas .45 .20
1451 A485 50d Carteria .90 .40
Nos. 1446-1451 (6) 2.75 1.40

Postal Code Inauguration A486

1983, Mar. 14 Litho. *Perf. 12½*

1452 A486 15d Cover, map .20 .20
1453 A486 25d Hermes, post horn, vert. .35 .20

Rowing A487

1983, Apr. 28 *Perf. 14x13, 13x14*

1454 A487 15d shown .25 .20
1455 A487 18d Water skiing, vert. .35 .20
1456 A487 27d Wind surfing, vert. .55 .35
1457 A487 50d Skiers on chair-lift, vert. .90 .50
1458 A487 80d Skiing 1.25 .75
Nos. 1454-1458 (5) 3.30 2.00

Europa Issue 1983

Acropolis — A488

Archimedes and His Hydrostatic Principle — A489

Perf. 12½x13½, 13x13½

1983, Apr. 28 Litho.

1459 A488 25d multi *1.40* .25
1460 A489 80d multi *2.75* .60

Marinos Antypas (1873-1907), Farmers' Movement Leader — A490

Designs: 9d, Nicholas Plastiras (1883-1953), prime minister. 15d, George Papandreou (1888-1968), statesman. 20d, Constantine Cavafy (1863-1933), poet. 27d, Nikos Kazantzakis (1883-1957), writer. 32d, Manolis Calomiris (1883-1962), composer. 40d, George Papanicolaou (1883-1962), medical researcher. 50d, Despina Achladioti (1890-1982), nationalist.

1983, July 11 Litho. *Perf. 13½x14*

1461 A490 6d multi .20 .20
1462 A490 9d multi .20 .20
1463 A490 15d multi .25 .20
1464 A490 20d multi .35 .20
1465 A490 27d multi .45 .20
1466 A490 32d multi .60 .25
1467 A490 40d multi .70 .25
1468 A490 50d multi .80 .30
Nos. 1461-1468 (8) 3.55 1.80

A491

1983, Sept. 26 Litho. *Perf. 13½x13*

1469 A491 50d Portrait bust .85 .50

1st Intl. Conf. on the Works of Democritus (Philosopher, 460-370 BC), Xanthe, Oct.

A492

1983, Nov. 17 Litho. *Perf. 13*

1470 A492 15d Poster .25 .25
1471 A492 30d Flight from school .40 .30

Polytechnic School Uprising, 1st anniv.

The Deification of Homer — A493

Homer Inspired Artworks: 3d, The Abduction of Helen by Paris, horiz. 4d, The Wooden Horse, horiz. 5d, Achilles Throwing Dice with Ajax, horiz. 6d, Achilles. 10d, Hector Receiving His Arms from His Parents. 14d, Single-handed Battle Between Ajax and Hector, horiz. 15d, Priam Requesting the Body of Hector, horiz. 20d, The Blinding of Polyphemus. 27d, Ulysses Escaping from Polyphemus' Cave, horiz. 30d, Ulysses Meeting with Nausica. 32d, Ulysses on the Island of the Sirens, horiz. 50d, Ulysses Slaying the Suitors, horiz. 75d, The Heroes of the Iliad, horiz. 100d, Homer.

1983, Dec. 19 Litho. *Perf. 13*

1472 A493 2d multi .20 .20
1473 A493 3d multi .20 .20
1474 A493 4d multi .20 .20
1475 A493 5d multi .20 .20
1476 A493 6d multi .20 .20
1477 A493 10d multi .20 .20
1478 A493 14d multi .20 .20
1479 A493 15d multi .20 .20
1480 A493 20d multi .25 .20
1481 A493 27d multi .30 .20
1482 A493 30d multi .40 .20
1483 A493 32d multi .45 .20
1484 A493 50d multi .60 .20
1485 A493 75d multi 1.00 .35
1486 A493 100d multi 1.25 .65
Nos. 1472-1486 (15) 5.85 3.60

Horse's Head from Chariot of Seline A494

Horsemen and Heroes A495

Nos. 1492a-1492b, Equestrian scene. Nos. 1492c-1492d, Athenian Elders.

1984, Mar. 15 Litho. *Perf. 14½x14*

1487 A494 14d shown .20 .20
1488 A494 15d Dionysus .25 .20
1489 A494 20d Hestia, Dione, Aphrodite .45 .20
1490 A494 27d Ilissus .60 .25
1491 A494 32d Lapith, centaur .80 .30
Nos. 1487-1491 (5) 2.30 1.15

Souvenir Sheet

Perf. 13x13½

1492 Sheet of 4 3.75 3.00
a. A495 15d multi .45 .35
b. A495 21d multi .65 .55
c. A495 27d multi .85 .75
d. A495 32d multi 1.00 .85

Marble from the Parthenon. No. 1492 sold for 107d.

Nos. 1492a-1492b and 1492c-1492d have continuous designs.

Europa (1959-84) A496

1984, Apr. 30 Litho. *Perf. 14x13½*
1493 A496 15d multi .40 .25
1494 A496 27d multi *1.00* .75
a. Pair, #1493-1494 *2.25* 2.10

1984 Summer Olympics — A497

Designs: 14d, Ancient Olympic stadium crypt. 15d, Athletes training. 20d, Broad jump, discus thrower. 32d, Athletes, diff. 80d, Stadium, Demetrius Bikelos, poet, organizer of 1896 Athens games.

1984, Apr. 30 *Perf. 13½x14*
1495 A497 14d multi .20 .20
1496 A497 15d multi .25 .20
1497 A497 20d multi .40 .25
1498 A497 32d multi .60 .35
1499 A497 80d multi 1.50 .80
a. Strip of 5, #1495-1499 3.25 1.75

Also issued in booklets.

Turkish Invasion of Cyprus, 10th Anniv. — A498

1984, July 10 Litho. *Perf. 13*
1500 A498 20d Tank, map, vert. .40 .20
1501 A498 32d Map, barbed wire .60 .25

Also issued in booklets.

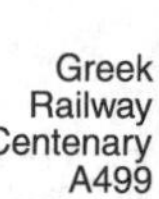

Greek Railway Centenary A499

Perf. 13x13½, 13½x13
1984, July 20 Litho.
1502 A499 15d Pelion .25 .20
1503 A499 20d Papadia Bridge, vert. .35 .20
1504 A499 30d Piraeus-Peloponnese .75 .25
1505 A499 50d Cogwheel Calavryta, vert. 1.25 .35
Nos. 1502-1505 (4) 2.60 1.00

Sesquicentenary of Athens as Capital City — A500

15d, 4d silver coin, 5th cent. BC, city plan, vert. 100d, Views of ancient & modern Athens.

Perf. 13½x13, 13x13½
1984, Oct. 12 Litho.
1506 A500 15d multi .40 .20
1507 A500 100d multi 1.60 .50

10th Anniv. of Democratic Govt. — A501

1984, Oct. 12 Litho. *Perf. 13x13½*
1508 A501 95d "10" on flag 2.00 .50

Christmas 1984 — A502

Scenes from 18th cent. icon by Athanasios Tountas.

1984, Dec. 6 Litho. *Perf. 13½x13*
1509 A502 14d Annunciation .25 .20
1510 A502 20d Nativity .35 .20
1511 A502 25d Presentation in the Temple .50 .20
1512 A502 32d Baptism of Christ .90 .30
a. Block of 4, #1509-1512 2.25 .80

Also issued in booklets.

Runner A503

Palais des Sports A504

Perf. 13, 13x13½ (#1515)
1985, Mar. 1 Litho.
1513 A503 12d shown .20 .20
1514 A503 15d Shot put .30 .20
1515 A504 20d shown .30 .20
1516 A503 25d Hurdles .50 .20
1517 A503 80d Women's high jump 1.50 .75
Nos. 1513-1517 (5) 2.80 1.55

European Indoor Athletics Championships, Palais des Sports, New Phaleron.

Europa 1985 — A505

CEPT emblem and: 27d, Musical contest between Marsyas and Apollo. 80d, Dimitris Mitropoulos (1896-1960) and Nikos Skalkottas (1904-1949), composers.

1985, Apr. 29 *Perf. 14x14½*
1518 A505 27d multi .65 .55
1519 A505 80d multi .85 .65

Exist se-tenant as strip of 3, 27d+80d+27d in booklets.

Melos Catacombs, A.D. 2nd Cent., Trypete A506

1985, Apr. 29 *Perf. 14½x14*
1520 A506 15d Niche .20 .20
1521 A506 20d Altar, Central Gallery .45 .20
1522 A506 100d Catacombs 1.50 .60
Nos. 1520-1522 (3) 2.15 1.00

Republic of Cyprus, 25th Anniv. — A507

1985, June 24 *Perf. 13x13½*
1523 A507 32d Map of Cyprus, urn .60 .30

Coin of King Cassander (315 B.C.), Personification of Salonika, Galerius Era Bas-relief — A508

Sts. Demetrius and Methodius, Mosaics — A509

Designs: 15d, Emperor sacrificing at Altar, Arch of Galerius, Roman era. 20d, Eastern walls of Salonika, Byzantine era. 32d, Houses in the Upper City. 50d, Liberation of Salonika by the Greek Army, 1912. 80d, German occupation, 1941-44, the Old Mosque. 95d, View of city, Trade Fair grounds, Aristotelian University tower.

Perf. 14½x14 (A508), 14x14½ (A509)
1985, June 24
1524 A508 1d multi .20 .20
1525 A509 5d multi .35 .20
1526 A508 15d multi .40 .20
1527 A508 20d multi .40 .20
1528 A508 32d multi .45 .20
1529 A508 50d multi .60 .20
1530 A508 80d multi .80 .30
1531 A509 95d multi 1.10 .30
Nos. 1524-1531 (8) 4.30 1.80

Salonika City, 2300th anniv. Aristotelian University, Trade Fair, 60th annivs.

Athenian Cultural Heritage A510

Ancient art and architecture: 15d, Democracy Crowning the City, bas-relief from a column, Ancient Agora of Athens, vert. 20d, Mosaic pavement of tritons, nereids, dolphins, etc., Roman baths at Hieratus, Isthmia, A.D. 2nd cent. 32d, Angel, fresco, Grotto of Pentheli, A.D. 13th cent., vert. 80d, Capodistrian University, Athens.

1985, Oct. 7 *Perf. 13½x13, 13x13½*
1532 A510 15d multi .20 .20
1533 A510 20d multi .30 .20
1534 A510 32d multi .40 .25
1535 A510 80d multi 1.10 .65
Nos. 1532-1535 (4) 2.00 1.30

Intl. Youth Year — A511

UN 40th Anniv. — A512

#1540, Girl crowned with flowers, Stadium of Peace and Friendship, Athens.

1985, Oct. 7 *Perf. 14x14½*
1536 A511 15d Children, olive wreath .25 .20
1537 A511 25d Children, doves .45 .20
1538 A512 27d UN General Assembly, dove .55 .20
1539 A512 100d UN building, emblem 1.75 .60
Nos. 1536-1539 (4) 3.00 1.20

Souvenir Sheet

1985, Nov. 22 *Perf. 14x13*
1540 A511 100d multi 1.50 .50

No. 1540 contains one 43x47mm stamp.

Pontic Hellenism Cultural Reformation A513

Perf. 14x12½, 12½x14
1985, Dec. 9 Litho.
1541 A513 12d Folk dance .20 .20
1542 A513 15d Our Lady Soumela Monastery .20 .20
1543 A513 27d Folk costumes, vert. .35 .20
1544 A513 32d Trapezus High School .45 .20
1545 A513 80d Sinope Castle 1.10 .50
Nos. 1541-1545 (5) 2.30 1.30

Greek Gods — A514

1986, Feb. 17 Litho. *Perf. 13 Horiz.*
1546 A514 5d Hestia .20 .20
1547 A514 18d Hermes .20 .20
1548 A514 27d Aphrodite .25 .20
1549 A514 32d Ares .25 .20
1550 A514 35d Athena .30 .20
1551 A514 40d Hephaestus .30 .20
1552 A514 50d Artemis .45 .20
1553 A514 110d Apollo 1.00 .30
1554 A514 150d Demeter 1.40 .55
1555 A514 200d Poseidon 1.90 .70
1556 A514 300d Hera 2.75 1.00
1557 A514 500d Zeus 5.00 1.50
Nos. 1546-1557 (12) 14.00 5.45

Each denomination sold in bklts. containing 20 panes of 5 stamps. Also issued perf. 13.

Youth of Antikythera A515

Soccer Players A517

Diadoumenos, by Polycleitus A516

Wrestlers, Hellenic Era Statue — A518

Cyclists — A520

Volleyball Players A519

Commemorative Design for 1st Modern Olympic Games — A521

1986, Mar. 3 ***Perf. 12***

1558 A515	18d multi		.30	.20
1559 A516	27d multi		.45	.20
1560 A517	32d multi		.50	.25
1561 A518	35d multi		.55	.25
1562 A519	40d multi		.65	.30
1563 A520	50d multi		.80	.40
1564 A521	110d multi		2.00	.90
	Nos. 1558-1564 (7)		5.25	2.50

First World Junior Athletic Championships. Pan-European Junior Soccer Championships. Pan-European Free-style and Greco-Roman Wrestling Championships. Men's World Volleyball Championships. Sixth International Round-Europe Cycling Meet. Modern Olympic Games, 90th anniv.

European Traffic Safety Year — A522

1986, Mar. 3 ***Perf. 12½x14***

1565 A522	18d Seat belts	.25	.20
1566 A522	27d Motorcycle	.40	.20
1567 A522	110d Speed limits	1.60	.70
	Nos. 1565-1567 (3)	2.25	1.10

Prevention of Forest Fires A523

1986, Apr. 23 Litho. ***Perf. 14x13½***

1568 A523	35d shown	1.00	.50
1569 A523	110d Prespa Lakes wetlands	3.00	2.50
a.	Bklt. pane, 2 each 35d, 110d	*22.50*	
b.	Pair, 35d, 110d	5.00	4.00

Europa.
No. 1569a is imperf horizontally.

New Postal Services — A524

May Day Strike, Chicago, Cent. — A525

1986, Apr. 23 ***Perf. 13½x14, 14x13½***

1570 A524	18d Intelpost	.40	.20
1571 A524	110d Express mail, horiz.	1.40	.70

1986, Apr. 23 ***Perf. 12½***

1572 A525	40d Strikers, monument	.65	.30

Eleutherios K. Venizelos (1864-1936), Premier A526

18d, Venizelos, Ministers taking oath of office, 1917. 110d, Old Hania Harbor, Crete.

1986, June 30 Litho. ***Perf. 14x12½***

1573 A526	18d multi	.25	.20
1574 A526	110d multi	1.75	.70

6th Intl. Cretological Conference, Crete.

Intl. Peace Year — A527

1986, Oct. 6 Litho. ***Perf. 12½***

1575 A527	18d Dove, sun, vert.	.25	.20
1576 A527	35d Flags, dove, vert.	.50	.20
1577 A527	110d World cage, dove	1.60	.70
	Nos. 1575-1577 (3)	2.35	1.10

Christmas A528

Aesop's Fables A529

Religious art in the Benaki Museum: 22d, Madonna and Child Enthroned, triptych center panel, 15th cent. 46d, Adoration of the Magi, 15th cent. 130d, Christ Enthroned with St. John the Evangelist, triptych panel.

1986, Dec. 1 Litho. ***Perf. 13½x14***

1578 A528	22d multi	.30	.20
1579 A528	46d multi	.65	.25
1580 A528	130d multi	1.75	.70
	Nos. 1578-1580 (3)	2.70	1.15

Size of No. 1579: 27x35mm.

Perf. 12½ Horiz.

1987, Mar. 5 Litho.

1581 A529	2d Fox and the Grapes	.20	.20
1582 A529	5d North Wind and the Sun	.20	.20
1583 A529	10d Stag and the Lion	.20	.20
1584 A529	22d Zeus and the Snake	.35	.20
1585 A529	32d Crow and the Fox	.50	.20
1586 A529	40d Woodcutter and Hermes	.60	.25
1587 A529	46d Ass in a Lion's Skin	.70	.30
1588 A529	130d Tortoise and the Hare	2.00	.80
	Nos. 1581-1588 (8)	4.75	2.35

Each denomination sold in booklets containing 20 panes of 5 stamps. Also issued perf. 12½x13.

Europa 1987 — A530

Modern art: 40d, Composition, by Achilleas Apergis. 130d, Delphic Light, by Gerassimos Sklavos.

1987, May 4 Litho. ***Perf. 12½***

1589 A530	40d multi	.90	.50
1590 A530	130d multi	3.00	1.75
a.	Bklt. pane, 2 each #1589-1590	5.00	
b.	Pair, #1589-1590	4.00	2.25

Stamps in #1590a have straight edges.

25th European Basketball Championships, Stadium of Peace and Friendship — A531

A532

1987, May 4 ***Perf. 13½x14, 12½***

1591 A531	22d Jump shot, stadium, vert.	.35	.20
1592 A532	25d Emblem, spectators	.40	.20
1593 A531	130d Two players, vert.	2.00	.85
	Nos. 1591-1593 (3)	2.75	1.25

Higher Education Sesquicentenary — A533

Perf. 14x13½, 13½x14

1987, May 4 Litho.

1594 A533	3d Students, tapestry	.20	.20
1595 A533	23d Owl, medallion	.40	.20
1596 A533	40d Institute, symbols of science	.70	.30
1597 A533	60d Institute, students	1.00	.40
	Nos. 1594-1597 (4)	2.30	1.10

Capodistrias University of Athens (Nos. 1594-1595); The Natl. Metsovio Polytechnic Institute (Nos. 1596-1597). #1596-1597 vert.

Souvenir Sheet

25th European Men's Basketball Championships A534

1987, June 3 Litho. ***Perf. 13x14***

1598	Sheet of 3	2.50	2.50
a.	A534 40d Jump ball	.45	.45
b.	A534 60d Layup	.65	.65
c.	A534 100d Dunk shot	1.10	1.10

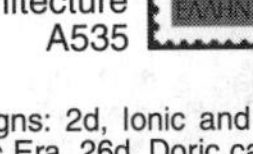

Architecture A535

Designs: 2d, Ionic and Corinthian capitals, Archaic Era. 26d, Doric capital, the Parthenon (detail). 40d, Ionic capital and the Erechteum. 60d, Corinthian capital and the Tholos in Epidaurus.

1987, July 1 Litho. ***Perf. 13½x12½***

1599 A535	2d multi	.20	.20
1600 A535	26d multi	.35	.20
1601 A535	40d multi	.50	.25
1602 A535	60d multi	.80	.35
	Nos. 1599-1602 (4)	1.85	1.00

Engraving by Yiannis Kephalinos — A536

Panteios School A537

Perf. 12½x14, 14x12½

1987, Oct. 1 Litho.

1603 A536	26d multi	.35	.20
1604 A537	60d multi	.85	.35

School of Fine Arts, 150th anniv. (26d), and Panteios School of Political Science, 60th anniv. (60d).

Greek Natl. Team, Winner, 25th European Men's Basketball Championship A538

1987, Oct. 1 ***Perf. 13x14***

1605 A538	40d multi	.65	.25

Traditional and Modern Greek Theater A539

Designs: 2d, Eleni Papadaki in Hecuba, by Euripides, and outdoor theater, Philippi. 4d, Christopher Nezer in The Wasps, by Aristophane, and outdoor theater, Dodona. 7d, Emilios Veakis in Oedipus Rex and theater, Delphi. 26d, Marika Cotopouli in The Shepherdess's Love, by Dimitris Koromilas. 40d, Katina Paxinou in Abraham's Sacrifice, by Vitzentzos Cornaros. 50d, Kyveli in Countess Valeraina's Secret, by Gregory Xenopoulos. 60d, Director Carolos Koun, stage setting. 100d, Dimitris Rontiris teaching ancient dance, Greek National Theater.

1987, Dec. 2 Litho. ***Perf. 14x13½***

1606 A539	2d multi	.20	.20
1607 A539	4d multi	.20	.20
1608 A539	7d multi	.20	.20
1609 A539	26d multi	.35	.20
1610 A539	40d multi	.55	.25
1611 A539	50d multi	.65	.35
1612 A539	60d multi	.80	.45
1613 A539	100d multi	1.40	.75
	Nos. 1606-1613 (8)	4.35	2.60

Christmas — A540

1987, Dec. 2 ***Perf. 13x12½***

1614	26d Angel facing right	.40	.20
1615	26d Angel facing left	.40	.20
a.	Bklt. pane, 5 each #1614-1615	4.00	
b.	A540 Pair, #1614-1615	.80	.40

Marine Life — A541

1988, Mar. 2 ***Perf. 12½ Vert.***

1616 A541 30d Codonellina .50 .20
1617 A541 40d Diaperoecia major .65 .30
1618 A541 50d Artemia .80 .40
1619 A541 60d Posidonia oceanica 1.00 .45
1620 A541 100d Padina pavonica 1.60 .80
Nos. 1616-1620 (5) 4.55 2.15

Each denomination sold in bklts. containing 20 panes of 5 stamps. Also issued perf. 14x12½ in sheets of 50.

Europa 1988 — A542

Communication and transport: 60d, Telecommunications satellite, telephone and facsimile machine. 150d, Passenger trains.

1988, May 6 Litho. ***Perf. 12½***

1621 60d multi *1.75* .75
1622 150d multi *4.25* 1.75
a. Bklt. pane of 4, 2 each #1621-1622, perf. 14 vert. 9.00
b. A542 Pair, 60d, 150d *6.00* 2.75

Single stamps also issued in strips of 5, perf. 14 vert.

1988 Olympics A543

Designs: 4d, Ancient Olympia and Temple of Zeus. 20d, Javelin thrower and and ancient Olympians in open-air gymnasium. 30d, Centenary emblem of the modern Games (cent. in 1996). 60d, Wrestlers, runners and other ancient athletes in training. 170d, Modern torch-bearer.

1988, May 6 ***Perf. 14x12***

1623 A543 4d multi .20 .20
1624 A543 20d multi .50 .25
1625 A543 30d multi .75 .35
1626 A543 60d multi 1.50 .75
1627 A543 170d multi 4.25 2.25
a. Strip of 5, #1623-1627 7.25
b. Bklt. pane of 5, #1623-1627, perf. 12½ vert. 7.25

Each denomination also sold in bklts. containing 20 panes of 5 stamps, perf. 12½ vert.
See Korea No. B53.

A544 A545

Waterfalls: 10d, Catarractis village falls at the foot of the Tzoumerca Mountain Range. 60d, Edessa Waterfalls. 100d, Edessaios River cascades.

1988, July 4 Litho. ***Perf. 12½x14***

1628 A544 10d multi .20 .20
1629 A544 60d multi 1.25 .50
1630 A544 100d multi 2.00 .95
Nos. 1628-1630 (3) 3.45 1.65

Each denomination also sold in booklets containing 20 panes of 5 stamps, perf. 14 vert.

1988, July 4 ***Perf. 13x12½***

1631 A545 60d multi 2.00 .75

20th Pan-European Postal Trade Unions Congress. No. 1631 also sold in booklets containing 20 panes of 5 stamps, perf. 14 vert.

A546

A547

Designs: 30d, Premier Eleutherios Venizelos (1864-1936), natl. flag and map. 70d, Lady liberty, flag and map.

1988, Oct. 7 Litho. ***Perf. 12½x13***

1632 A546 30d shown .55 .25
1633 A546 70d multi 1.40 .65

Union of Crete with Greece and liberation of Epirus and Macedonia from Turkish rule, 75th annivs.

Each denomination also sold in booklets containing 20 panes of 5 stamps, perf. 14 horiz.

1988, Oct. 7 ***Perf. 13 Vert. or Horiz.***

Departmental Seats: 2d, Mytilene-Lesbos Harbor, painting by Theophilos. 3d, Alexandroupolis lighthouse. 4d, St. Nicholas bell tower, Kozane. 5d, Labor Center, Hermoupolis. 7d, Sparta Town Hall. 8d, Pegasus of Leukas. 10d, Castle of the Knights, Rhodes. 20d, The Acropolis, Athens. 25d, Kavalla aqueduct. 30d, Statue of Athanasios Diakos and castle, Lamia. 50d, Preveza cathedral bell tower and Venetian clock. 60d, Corfu promenade. 70d, Harbor view of Hagios Nicolaos. 100d, Poligiros public fountains. 200d, Church of the Apostle Paul, Corinth.

1634 A547 2d multi .20 .20
1635 A547 3d multi .20 .20
1636 A547 4d multi .20 .20
1637 A547 5d multi .20 .20
1638 A547 7d multi .20 .20
1639 A547 8d multi .20 .20
1640 A547 10d multi .20 .20
1641 A547 20d multi .25 .20
a. Bklt. pane, 4 each 3d, 5d, 10d, 20d 2.35
1642 A547 25d multi .35 .20
1643 A547 30d multi .40 .20
1644 A547 50d multi .60 .30
1645 A547 60d multi .75 .35
1646 A547 70d multi .90 .40
1647 A547 100d multi 1.25 .55
1648 A547 200d multi 2.50 1.25
Nos. 1634-1648 (15) 8.40 4.85

3d-5d, 10d-20d, 30d-50d vert. Nos. 1634-1648 issued in panes of 20, perf. 13 vert. or horiz. and in sheets, perf. 13.

Council of Europe, Rhodes, Dec. 2-3 A548

Christmas A549

Designs: 60d, Map and Castle of the Knights, Rhodes. 100d, Head of Helios, Rhodian 2nd-3rd cent. B.C. coin, and flags.

1988, Dec. 2 Litho. ***Perf. 12½***

1649 A548 60d multi 1.00 .45
1650 A548 100d multi 1.75 .75

Nos. 1649-1650 also issued in booklet panes of 5, perf. 14 horiz.

1988, Dec. 2 ***Perf. 12½ on 3 Sides***

Paintings: 30d, *Adoration of the Magi*, by El Greco. 70d, *The Annunciation*, by Costas Parthenis, horiz.

1651 A549 30d multi .45 .20
a. Bklt. pane of 10 4.50

Perf. 14

1652 A549 70d multi 1.10 .50

No. 1651 issued in booklets. No. 1652 also issued in booklets containing 20 panes of 5 stamps, perf. 14 vert.

A550 A551

Athens '96 emblem and: 30d, High jumper and ancient Olympia. 60d, Wrestlers and view of Delphi. 70d, Swimmers and The Acropolis, Athens. 170d, Sports complex.

Perf. 13½ Vert.

1989, Mar. 17 Litho.

1653 A550 30d multi .45 .20
1654 A550 60d multi .95 .40
1655 A550 70d multi 1.10 .50
1656 A550 170d multi 2.75 1.40
a. Strip of 4, Nos. 1653-1656, perf. 14x13½ 5.50
b. Bklt. pane of 4, #1653-1656 5.50

1989, May 22 Litho. ***Perf. 12½x14***

Europa: Children's toys.

1657 A551 60d Whistling bird *1.10* .50
1658 A551 170d Butterfly *3.25* 1.75
a. Bklt. pane, 2 each #1657-1658, perf 14 6.60
b. Pair, #1657-1658 *4.50* 2.50

Printed se-tenant in sheets of 16. Nos. 1657-1658 also issued separately in booklets containing 20 panes of 5 stamps, perf. 14 vert.

Anniversaries — A552

1989, May 22 ***Perf. 14x13½***

1659 A552 30d Flags .40 .20
1660 A552 50d Flag, La Liberte .65 .25
1661 A552 60d Flag, ballot box .75 .30
1662 A552 70d Coin, emblem .90 .40
1663 A552 200d Flag, "40" 2.50 1.25
Nos. 1659-1663 (5) 5.20 2.40

Six-nation Initiative for Peace and Disarmament, 5th anniv. (30d); French revolution, bicent. (50d); European Parliament Elections in Greece, 10th anniv. (60d); Interparliamentary Union, cent. (70d); and Council of Europe, 40th anniv. (200d).

Nos. 1659-1663 also issued in bklts. containing 20 panes of 5 stamps, perf. 13½ horiz.

A553

BALKANFILA XII, Sept. 30-Oct. 8, Salonica — A554

1989, Sept. 25 Litho. ***Perf. 14x12½***

1664 A553 60d shown .70 .30
1665 A553 70d Eye, magnifying glass .80 .35

Souvenir Sheet

Perf. 14x13

1666 A554 200d shown 2.50 2.50

Wildflowers A555

1989, Dec. 8 Litho. ***Perf. 14x12½***

1667 A555 8d Wild rose .20 .20
1668 A555 10d Common myrtle .20 .20
1669 A555 20d Field poppy .25 .20
1670 A555 30d Anemone .35 .20
1671 A555 60d Dandelion, chicory .75 .30
1672 A555 70d Mallow .80 .35
1673 A555 200d Thistle 2.25 1.10
Nos. 1667-1673 (7) 4.80 2.55

Ursus arctos A556

Rare and endangered species.

1990, Mar. 16 Litho. ***Perf. 14x12½***

1674 A556 40d shown .50 .20
1675 A556 70d *Caretta caretta* .90 .40
1676 A556 90d *Monachus monachus* 1.10 .45
1677 A556 100d *Lynx lynx* 1.25 .50
Nos. 1674-1677 (4) 3.75 1.55

Europa 1990 — A557

Post offices: 70d, Old Central P.O. interior. 210d, Contemporary p.o. exterior.

1990, May 11 Litho. ***Perf. 13½x12½***

1678 A557 70d multicolored .85 .35
1679 A557 210d multicolored 2.50 1.00
a. Bklt. pane, 2 each #1678-1679 6.75
b. Pair, #1678-1679 3.50 1.50

Natl. Reconcilation A558

Political Reformers A559

1990, May 11 ***Perf. 12½x13½***

1680 A558 40d Flag, handshake .50 .20
1681 A558 70d Dove, ribbon .85 .35
1682 A558 100d Map, gift of flowers 1.25 .45
Nos. 1680-1682 (3) 2.60 1.00

1990, May 11

1683 A559 40d Gregoris Lambrakis (1912-63) .50 .20
1684 A559 40d Pavlos Bakoyiannis (1935-89) .50 .20

A560 A561

Department Seats: 2d, Karditsa, the commercial-animal fair. 5d, Trikkala fort and clock tower. 8d, Veroia, street with traditional architecture. 10d, Mesolongion, Central Monument of Fallen Heroes in the Exodus. 15d, Chios, view. 20d, Tripolis, street with neoclassical architecture. 25d, Volos, view with town hall, woodcut by A. Tassou. 40d, Kalamata, neoclassical town hall. 50d, Pyrgos, central marketplace. 70d, Ioannina, view of lake and island. 80d, Rethymnon, sculpture at the port. 90d, Argostolion, view before earthquake. 100d, Nauplia, Bourtzi with Palamidi in the background. 200d, Patras, central lighthouse. 250d, Florina, street with neoclassical architecture. Nos. 1685, 1687, 1695, 1698 vert.

Perf. 13½ Horiz. or Vert.

1990, June 20 **Litho.**

1685 A560 2d multicolored .20 .20
1686 A560 5d multicolored .20 .20
1687 A560 8d multicolored .20 .20
1688 A560 10d multicolored .20 .20
1689 A560 15d multicolored .20 .20
1690 A560 20d multicolored .20 .20
1691 A560 25d multicolored .25 .20
1692 A560 40d multicolored .40 .20
1693 A560 50d multicolored .50 .20
1694 A560 70d multicolored .70 .25
1695 A560 80d multicolored .80 .30
1696 A560 90d multicolored .95 .35
1697 A560 100d multicolored 1.00 .40
1698 A560 200d multicolored 2.00 .80
1699 A560 250d multicolored 2.50 1.00
Nos. 1685-1699 (15) 10.30 4.90

Each denomination sold in booklets containing 20 panes of 5 stamps. Also issued perf. 13x12, 12x13.

See Nos. 1749-1760, 1792-1801.

1990, July 13 ***Perf. 12½x13½***

1700 A561 20d Sailing .25 .20
1701 A561 50d Wrestling .60 .25
1702 A561 80d Sprinting .90 .35
1703 A561 100d Basketball 1.25 .50
1704 A561 250d Soccer 3.00 1.25
a. Strip of 5, #1700-1704 6.00

1996 Summer Olympics. Athens, proposed site for centennial Summer Olympic Games. Exists perf. 13½ vert.

Heinrich Schliemann (1822-1890), Archaeologist — A562

1990, Oct. 11 **Litho.** ***Perf. 14x13½***

1705 A562 80d multicolored .95 .40

See Germany No. 1615.

Greco-Italian War, 50th Anniv. — A563

1990, Oct. 11 ***Perf. 12½***

1706 A563 50d Woman knitting .60 .20
1707 A563 80d Virgin Mary, soldier .95 .35
1708 A563 100d Women volunteers 1.25 .45
Nos. 1706-1708 (3) 2.80 1.00

Souvenir Sheet

Stamp Day — A564

1990, Dec. 14 **Litho.** ***Perf. 14x13***

1709 A564 300d multicolored *7.50 7.50*

The Muses — A565

Designs: 50d, Calliope, Euterpe, Erato. 80d, Terpsichore, Polyhymnia, Melpomene. 250d, Thalia, Clio, Urania.

1991, Mar. 11 **Litho.** ***Perf. 12½***

1710 A565 50d multicolored .60 .20
1711 A565 80d multicolored .95 .40
1712 A565 250d multicolored 3.00 1.25
Nos. 1710-1712 (3) 4.55 1.85

Battle of Crete by Ioannis Anousakis — A566

300d, Map, flags of participating allied armies.

1991, May 20 **Litho.** ***Perf. 12½x13½***

1713 A566 60d multicolored .75 .25

Size: 32x24mm

Perf. 12½

1714 A566 300d multicolored 3.50 1.25

Battle of Crete, 50th anniv.

Europa A567

Designs: 80d, Icarus pushing modern satellite. 300d, Chariot of the Sun.

1991, May 20 ***Perf. 12½***

1715 A567 80d multicolored .95 .40
1716 A567 300d multicolored 3.50 1.25
a. Pair, #1715-1716 4.50 1.65
b. Bklt. pane, 2 ea. #1715-1716 9.25 3.50

No. 1716a printed in continuous design.

A568 A569

1991, June 25 **Litho.** ***Perf. 13½x14***

1717 A568 10d Swimming .20 .20
1718 A568 60d Basketball .75 .25
1719 A568 90d Gymnastics 1.10 .40
1720 A568 130d Weight lifting 1.60 .50
1721 A568 300d Hammer throw 3.50 1.25
Nos. 1717-1721 (5) 7.15 2.60

1991 Mediterranean Games, Athens.

1991, Sept. 20 **Litho.** ***Perf. 13½x14***

1722 A569 100d multicolored 1.10 .35

Athenian Democracy, 2500th anniv.

Souvenir Sheet

Greek Presidency of CEPT — A570

Europe with Zeus metmorphosed into a bull, from Attic vase, c. 500 B.C.

1991, Sept. 20 ***Perf. 14x13***

1723 A570 300d multicolored 3.00 1.10

A571 A572

Greek Membership in EEC, 10th anniv.: 50d, Pres. Konstantin Karamanlis signing Treaty of Greek entrance into EEC. 80d, Map showing EEC members, Pres. Karamanlis.

1991, Dec. 9 **Litho.** ***Perf. 13x14***

1724 A571 50d multicolored .55 .20
1725 A571 80d multicolored .90 .30

1991, Dec. 9 ***Perf. 12½x13½***

1726 A572 80d Speed skaters .90 .30
1727 A572 300d Slalom skier 3.25 1.10
a. Pair, #1726-1727 4.25 1.40

16th Winter Olympics, Albertville.

A573

1992 Summer Olympics, Barcelona A574

Perf. 12½, 14x13½ (90d, 340d)

1992, Apr. 3 **Litho.**

1728 A573 10d Javelin .20 .20
1729 A573 60d Equestrian .65 .30
1730 A574 90d Runner .90 .45
1731 A573 120d Gymnastics 1.25 .65
1732 A574 340d Runners 3.50 1.75
Nos. 1728-1732 (5) 6.50 3.35

Health — A575

Designs: 60d, Protection against AIDS. 80d, Diseases of digestive system. 90d, Dying flower symbolizing cancer. 120d, Hephaestus at his forge, 6th century BC. 280d, Alexandros S. Onassis Cardiosurgical Center.

1992, May 22 **Litho.** ***Perf. 12½***

1733 A575 60d multicolored .60 .30
1734 A575 80d multicolored .85 .40
1735 A575 90d multicolored .90 .45
1736 A575 120d multicolored 1.25 .65
1737 A575 280d multicolored 2.90 1.50
Nos. 1733-1737 (5) 6.50 3.30

No. 1734, 1st United European Gastroenterology Week. No. 1736, European Year of Social Security, Hygiene and Health in the Workplace.

Discovery of America, 500th Anniv. A576

Europa: 340d, Map of 15th century Chios, Columbus.

1992, May 22 ***Perf. 13½x12½***

1738 A576 90d shown .90 .45
a. Perf. 12½ vert. .90 .45
1739 A576 340d multicolored 3.50 1.75
a. Pair, #1738-1739 4.50 2.25
b. Perf. 12½ vert. 3.50 1.75
c. Bklt. pane, 2 each #1738a, 1739b 9.00

Souvenir Sheet

European Conference on Transportion — A577

1992, June 8 ***Perf. 14x13***

1740 A577 300d multicolored 3.00 3.00

Macedonian Treasures — A578

Designs: 10d, Head of Hercules wearing lion skin, Vergina treasures. 20d, Bust of Aristotle, map of Macedonia, horiz. 60d, Alexander the Great at Battle of Issus, horiz. 80d, Archaeologist Manolis Andronikos, tomb of King Philip II. 90d, Deer hunt mosaic, Pella. 120d, Macedonian tetradrachm. 340d, St. Paul, 4th century church near Philippi.

1992, July 17 **Litho.** ***Perf. 12½***

1741 A578 10d multicolored .20 .20
1742 A578 20d multicolored .20 .20
1743 A578 60d multicolored .45 .20
1744 A578 80d multicolored .65 .20
1745 A578 90d multicolored .75 .20
1746 A578 120d multicolored 1.00 .45
1747 A578 340d multicolored 2.25 .30
Nos. 1741-1747 (7) 5.50 1.75

European Unification — A579

1992, Oct. 12 Litho. *Perf. 14x13*

1748 A579	90d multicolored	.70	.45

Departmental Seat Type of 1990

Designs: 10d, Piraeus, the old clock. 20d, Amphissa, view of city with citadel. 30d, Samos (Vathy), the Heraion. 40d, Canea, city in 1800s. 50d, Zakinthos (Zante), view in 1800s. 60d, Karpenision, Velouchi and city. 70d, Kilkis, the cave, vert. 80d, Xanthe, door of Town Hall, vert. 90d, Salonika, Macedonian Struggle Museum. 120d, Komotine, Tsanakleous School. 340d, Drama, spring. 400d, Larissa, Pinios bridge.

Perf. 10 Horiz. or Vert.

1992, Oct. 12

1749 A560	10d multicolored	.20	.20
1750 A560	20d multicolored	.20	.20
1751 A560	30d multicolored	.20	.20
1752 A560	40d multicolored	.20	.20
1753 A560	50d multicolored	.25	.20
1754 A560	60d multicolored	.25	.20
1755 A560	70d multicolored	.35	.20
1756 A560	80d multicolored	.35	.20
1757 A560	90d multicolored	.65	.20
1758 A560	120d multicolored	.75	.20
1759 A560	340d multicolored	1.90	.35
1760 A560	400d multicolored	2.10	.50
	Nos. 1749-1760 (12)	7.40	2.85

Each denomination sold in booklets containing 20 panes of 5 stamps. Also issued perf. 13 from sheets.

City of Rhodes, 2400th Anniv. — A580

Designs: 60d, Headstone, 4th cent. B.C. 90d, Bathing Aphrodite, 1st cent. B.C. 120d, St. Irene, Church of St. Catherine, 14th cent. 250d, St. Paul's Gate, 15th cent.

1993, Feb. 26 Litho. *Perf. 13x14*

1761 A580	60d multicolored	.55	.30
1762 A580	90d multicolored	.80	.40
1763 A580	120d multicolored	1.10	.55
1764 A580	250d multicolored	2.25	1.10
	Nos. 1761-1764 (4)	4.70	2.35

Rememberences of Greek Wars — A581

Designs: 10d, Death of Georgakis Olympios, 1821. 30d, Theodore Kolokotronis in battle, 1821. 60d, Pavlos Melas. 90d, Glory lays wreath over graves of dead from Balkan Wars. 120d, Greek soldiers at Battle of El Alamein, 1942, horiz. 150d, Greek troops in Aegean Islands, 1943-45, horiz. 200d, Kalavryta Massacre Memorial.

Perf. 13x14, 14x13

1993, May 25 Litho.

1765 A581	10d multicolored	.20	.20
1766 A581	30d multicolored	.30	.20
1767 A581	60d multicolored	.55	.30
1768 A581	90d multicolored	.85	.40
1769 A581	120d multicolored	1.10	.55
1770 A581	150d multicolored	1.40	.70
1771 A581	200d multicolored	1.75	.90
	Nos. 1765-1771 (7)	6.15	3.25

The Benefits of Transportation, by K. Parthenis — A582

Europa: 90d, Tree, three people, ships. 350d, Woman and children, town.

1993, May 25 *Perf. 13x14*

1772	90d multicolored	.75	.40
a.	Perf. 13½ vert.	.75	.40
1773	350d multicolored	3.25	1.60
a.	A582 Pair, #1772-1773	4.00	2.00
b.	Perf. 13½ vert.	3.25	1.60
c.	Bklt. pane, 2 each #1772a, 1773b	8.25	

No. 1773a has continuous design.

Buildings in Athens A583

Designs: 30d, Concert Hall. 60d, Numismatic Museum (Iliou Melathron). 90d, Natl. Library of Greece. 200d, Opthalmology Hospital.

1993, Oct. 4 Litho. *Perf. 14*

1774 A583	30d multicolored	.25	.20
1775 A583	60d multicolored	.50	.25
1776 A583	90d multicolored	.75	.35
1777 A583	200d multicolored	1.75	.85
	Nos. 1774-1777 (4)	3.25	1.65

Souvenir Sheet

Greek Presidency of the European Community Council of Ministers — A584

1993, Dec. 20 Litho. *Perf. 14*

1778 A584	400d multicolored	3.25	1.60

Chariot of Selene Driven by Hermes A585

1994, Mar. 7 Litho. *Perf. 13x13½*

1779 A585	200d multicolored	1.60	.80

2nd Pan-European Transportation Conference.

Passion of Christ A586

Designs: 30d, Last Supper, 16th cent. icon, St. Catherine's Church, Crete, vert. 60d, Crucifixion, detail from 1552 wall drawing, Great Meteoron, vert. 90d, Burial, 1620-45 icon, Church of the Presentation of the Lord, Patmos. 150d, Resurrection, illustrated manuscript of Mt. Athos, 11th cent.

1994, Apr. 8 Litho. *Perf. 14*

1780 A586	30d multicolored	.25	.25
1781 A586	60d multicolored	.50	.25
1782 A586	90d multicolored	.75	.40
1783 A586	150d multicolored	1.25	.60
	Nos. 1780-1783 (4)	2.75	1.50

European Inventors, Discoverers A587

Europa: 90d, Thales of Miletus (625?-547? B.C.), philospher, mathematician. 350d, Konstantinos Karatheodoris (1873-1950).

1994, May 9 Litho. *Perf. 14x13½*

1784 A587	90d multicolored	.75	.35
a.	Perf. 13½ vert.	.75	.35
1785 A587	350d multicolored	2.75	1.40
a.	Pair, #1784-1785	3.50	1.75
b.	Perf. 13½ vert.	2.75	1.40
c.	Bklt. pane, 2 each #1784a-1785b	7.00	

Athletic Events, Anniversaries A588

Designs: 60d, Demetrios Vikelas (1835-1908), first president Intl. Olympic Committee, vert. 90, Modern, ancient soccer players. 120d, Volleyball, net, vert. 400d, Statue of Liberty, modern, ancient soccer players.

1994, June 6 Litho. *Perf. 14*

1786 A588	60d multicolored	.50	.25
1787 A588	90d multicolored	.75	.35
1788 A588	120d multicolored	1.00	.50
	Nos. 1786-1788 (3)	2.25	1.10

Souvenir Sheet

Perf. 14x13½

1789 A588	400d multicolored	3.25	1.60

Intl. Olympic Committee, cent. (#1786). 1994 World Cup Soccer Championships, US (#1787, #1789). World Volleyball Championships, Piraeus & Salonika (#1788).

No. 1789 contains one 42x52mm stamp.

Greek Presidency of European Community Council of Ministers A589

Designs: 90d, Winged chariot driven by Greece. 120d, Doric columns, European Community flag.

1994, June 21 *Perf. 13*

1790 A589	90d multicolored	.75	.35
1791 A589	120d multicolored	1.00	.50

Departmental Seat Type of 1990

Designs: 10d, Katerine, Tsalopoulou mansion house, vert. 20d, Arta, Byzantine Church Parigoritissas. 30d, Lebadea, medieval bridge, tower of catalanian castle, Krias springs vert. 40d, Kastoria, Church of Panagia Koumbelidkis. 50d, Grevena, outdoor theatre. 60d, Edessa, waterfall. 80d, Chalcis, red house. 90d, Serrai, government house, Merarchias road, Acropolis of Koulas. 120d, Candia (Herakleion), town hall. 150d, Egoumenitsa, Church of Evangelistria, vert.

Perf. 10½ Horiz. or Vert.

1994, Oct. 5 Litho.

1792 A560	10d multicolored	.20	.20
1793 A560	20d multicolored	.20	.20
1794 A560	30d multicolored	.25	.20
1795 A560	40d multicolored	.35	.35
1796 A560	50d multicolored	.45	.45
1797 A560	60d multicolored	.55	.55
1798 A560	80d multicolored	.70	.70
1799 A560	90d multicolored	.75	.75
1800 A560	120d multicolored	1.00	1.00
1801 A560	150d multicolored	1.25	1.25
	Nos. 1792-1801 (10)	5.70	5.65

Each denomination sold in booklets containing 20 panes of 5 stamps. Also issued perf. 13 in sheets of 50.

Constitution, 150th Anniv. — A590

Designs: 60d, People, army demonstrating, by Carl Howpt, vert. 150d, Portraits of Ioannis Makriyannis, Andreas Metaxas, Demetrios Kallergis. 200d, Painting of night of Sept. 3, 1843. 340d, Article 107, seal of Greek Parliament, signature of President.

1994, Nov. 21 Litho. *Perf. 14x13*

1802 A590	60d multicolored	.55	.55
1803 A590	150d multicolored	1.25	1.25
1804 A590	200d multicolored	1.75	1.75
1805 A590	340d multicolored	3.00	3.00
	Nos. 1802-1805 (4)	6.55	6.55

Melina Mercouri (1925-94), Actress, Politician — A591

1995, Mar. 7 Litho. *Perf. 14x13*

1806 A591	60d shown	.55	.55
1807 A591	90d Portrait, Parthenon	.80	.80
1808 A591	100d Portraits as actress	.90	.90
1809 A591	340d Portrait, vert.	3.00	3.00
	Nos. 1806-1809 (4)	5.25	5.25

Liberation of Concentration Camps, 50th Anniv. A592

Europa: 90d, Prisoners. 340d, Peace doves, broken barbed wire fence.

1995, May 3 Litho. *Perf. 14*

1810 A592	90d multicolored	.75	.40
a.	Perf. 13½ vert.	.75	.40
1811 A592	340d multicolored	3.00	1.50
a.	Pair, #1810-1811	3.75	1.90
b.	Perf. 13½ vert.	3.00	1.50
c.	Bklt. pane, 2 each #1810a, 1811b	7.75	
	Complete booklet, #1811c	7.75	

Anniversaries & Events — A593

Designs: 10d, Stylized emblem, basketball, vert. 70d, University building. 90d, Architectural ruins, vert. 100d, Flag, soldier, vert. 120d, Statue of Peace, by Kifissodotos, vert. 150d, Dolphins. 200d, Early telephone, push buttons, vert. 300d, Owl, basketball, vert.

Perf. 13½x13, 13x13½

1995, June 21 Litho.

1812 A593	10d multicolored	.20	.20
1813 A593	70d multicolored	.65	.30
1814 A593	90d multicolored	.80	.40
1815 A593	100d multicolored	.90	.45
1816 A593	120d multicolored	1.10	.55
1817 A593	150d multicolored	1.25	.65
1818 A593	200d multicolored	1.75	.90
1819 A593	300d multicolored	2.75	1.25
	Nos. 1812-1819 (8)	9.40	4.70

5th World Junior Basketball Championships (#1812). Agricultural University of Athens, 75th anniv. (#1813). UN, 50th anniv. (#1814, #1816). End of World War II, 50th anniv. (#1815). European Nature Conservation Year (#1817). Telephone in Greece, cent. (#1818). 29th European Basketball Championships (#1819).

Book of Revelation, 1900th Anniv. — A594

Visions of the Apocalypse: 80d, First vision, Angels of the Seven Churches of Asia Minor, icon by Thomas Bathas, vert. 110d, Apostle John at Cave of the Apocalypse dictating to Prochoros, miniature from manuscript of Four Gospels, vert. 300d, First Angel with trumpet from silver gilded Gospel cover.

1995, Sept. 18 Litho. *Perf. 14*

1820 A594 80d multicolored	.70	.35
1821 A594 110d multicolored	.95	.45
1822 A594 300d multicolored	2.75	1.40
Nos. 1820-1822 (3)	4.40	2.20

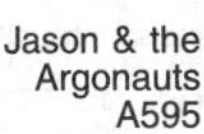

Jason & the Argonauts A595

Designs: 80d, Argonauts, the Argus, goddess Athena setting out for Colchis. 120d, Phineas, Hermes, one of the Voreadae, Harpy. 150d, Jason taming the bull, Medea and Nike. 200d, Jason takes Golden Fleece, kills serpent with Medea's help. 300d, Medea watches, Jason, crowned by Nike, giving Golden Fleece to Pelias.

1995, Nov. 6 Litho. *Perf. 13x13½*

1823 A595 80d multicolored	.70	.35
1824 A595 120d multicolored	1.10	.55
1825 A595 150d multicolored	1.25	.65
1826 A595 200d multicolored	1.75	.90
1827 A595 300d multicolored	2.75	1.25
Nos. 1823-1827 (5)	7.55	3.70

Lighthouses — A596

1995, Dec. 18 Litho. *Perf. 14*

1828 A596 80d Psyttaleia	.70	.35
1829 A596 120d Sapienza	1.00	.50
1830 A596 150d Kastri (Othonoi)	1.25	.65
1831 A596 500d Zourva (Hydra)	4.25	2.00
Nos. 1828-1831 (4)	7.20	3.50

Souvenir Sheets

Modern Olympic Games, Cent. A597

Perf. 13½x13, 13x13½

1996, Mar. 25 Litho.

1832 Sheet of 4	8.50	8.50
a. A597 80d like #117, vert.	.65	.65
b. A597 120d like #118, vert.	1.00	1.00
c. A597 150d like #119, vert.	1.25	1.25
d. A597 650d like #120, vert.	5.50	5.50
1833 Sheet of 4	8.50	8.50
a. A597 80d like #122	.65	.65
b. A597 120d like #124	1.00	1.00
c. A597 150d like #125	1.25	1.25
d. A597 650d like #128	5.50	5.50
1834 Sheet of 4	8.50	8.50
a. A597 80d like #121, vert.	.65	.65
b. A597 120d like #123, vert.	1.00	1.00
c. A597 150d like #126, vert.	1.25	1.25
d. A597 650d like #127, vert.	5.50	5.50

Famous Women — A598

Europa: 120d, Sappho (c.610-580BC), lyric poet. 430d, Amalia Fleming.

1996, Apr. 22 Litho. *Perf. 14x14½*

1835 120d multicolored	1.10	.55
a. Perf. 14½ vert.	1.10	.55
1836 430d multicolored	3.75	1.90
a. A598 Pair, #1835-1836	5.00	2.50
b. Perf. 14½ vert.	3.75	1.90
c. Booklet pane, 2 each #1835a, 1836b	10.00	
Complete booklet, #1836c	10.00	

Modern Olympic Games, Cent. A599

Stylized designs: 10d, Greek runners, vert. 80d, Discus thrower, vert. 120d, Weight lifter, vert. 200d, Wrestlers.

Perf. 13½x14, 14x13½

1996, June 4 Litho.

1837 A599 10d multicolored	.20	.20
1838 A599 80d multicolored	.70	.35
1839 A599 120d multicolored	1.00	.50
1840 A599 200d multicolored	1.75	.85
Nos. 1837-1840 (4)	3.65	1.90

First Intl. Medical Olympiad — A600

1996, July 8 Litho. *Perf. 13½*

1841 A600 80d Hippocrates	.75	.35
1842 A600 120d Galen	1.10	.55

Castles A601

1996, Oct. 7 Litho. *Perf. 13x13½*

1843 A601 10d Mytilene	.20	.20
1844 A601 20d Lindos	.20	.20
1845 A601 30d Rethymnon	.35	.20
1846 A601 70d Assos Cephalonia	.65	.35
1847 A601 80d Serbs	.75	.35
1848 A601 120d Monemvasia	1.10	.55
1849 A601 200d Didimotihon	1.75	.90
1850 A601 430d Vonitsas	4.00	1.90
1851 A601 1000d Nikopolis	9.00	4.50
Nos. 1843-1851 (9)	18.00	9.15

Each denomination sold in booklets containing 20 panes of 5 stamps. Also issued perf. 13 vert.

Figures from Shadow Theatre — A602

100d, Four characters, diff. 120d, Three characters. 200d, Two characters, dragon.

1996, Nov. 15 Litho. *Perf. 14*

1852 A602 80d multicolored	.75	.35
1853 A602 100d multicolored	.90	.45
1854 A602 120d multicolored	1.10	.55
1855 A602 200d multicolored	1.75	.90
Nos. 1852-1855 (4)	4.50	2.25

Hellenic Language A603

Designs: 80d, Oldest Hellenic inscription, wine pitcher, 720BC. 120d, Verse IX, 436-445 from Homer's Iliad, 1st-2nd cent. AD. 150d, Psalm of the Holy Apostles, 6th cent. AD. 350d, Reference to Hellenic language, Dionysios Solomos, 1824.

1996, Dec. 18 Litho. *Perf. 13x13½*

1856 A603 80d multicolored	.75	.35
1857 A603 120d multicolored	1.00	.50
1858 A603 150d multicolored	1.25	.65
1859 A603 350d multicolored	3.00	1.50
Nos. 1856-1859 (4)	6.00	3.00

Andreas G. Papandreou (1919-96), Prime Minister — A604

Papandreou at various ages and: 80d, Graduation cap, books, diploma. 120d, Leaving airplane. 150d, Building. 500d, Greek flag, dove.

1997, Feb. 12 Litho. *Perf. 13*

1860 A604 80d multicolored	.70	.35
1861 A604 120d multicolored	1.00	.50
1862 A604 150d multicolored	1.30	.65
1863 A604 500d multicolored	4.50	2.25
Nos. 1860-1863 (4)	7.50	3.75

Thessaloniki, European Cultural Capital A605

Designs: 80d, Frescoe of St. Dimitrios, patron saint of Thessaloniki, Church of Aghios Nikolaos Orphanos, vert. 100d, Hippocratic Hospital. 120d, Marble pedestal with inscription, medallion with woman's head, vert. 150d, Detail of mosaic from Rotunda cupola, vert. 300d, "Iaspis" chalice, 14th cent., Mt. Athos.

1997, Mar. 26 *Perf. 13½*

1864 A605 80d multicolored	.70	.35
1865 A605 100d multicolored	.90	.45
1866 A605 120d multicolored	1.00	.50
1867 A605 150d multicolored	1.30	.65
1868 A605 300d multicolored	2.60	1.25
Nos. 1864-1868 (5)	6.50	3.20

Bridges of Macedonia A606

1997, Apr. 24 Litho. *Perf. 14*

1869 A606 80d Village of Trikomo	.70	.35
1870 A606 120d Portitsa	1.00	.50
1871 A606 150d Village of Ziakas	1.35	.65
1872 A606 350d Village of Kastro	3.10	1.50
Nos. 1869-1872 (4)	6.15	3.00

Stories and Legends A607

Europa: 120d, Prometheus, the giver of fire. 430d, Digenis Akritas, Greek swordsmen on horseback.

1997, May 19 Litho. *Perf. 14*

1873 A607 120d multicolored	1.00	.50
a. Perf. 13½vert.	1.00	.50
1874 A607 430d multicolored	3.75	1.90
a. Pair, #1873-1874	4.75	2.40
b. Perf. 13½vert.	3.75	1.90
c. Booklet pane, 2 each #1873a, 1874b	9.50	
Complete booklet, #1874c	9.50	

6th IAAF World Track & Field Championships, Athens — A608

Official IAAF emblem, Greek flag and: 20d, Runners. 100d, Nike. 140d, High jump. 170d, Hurdles. 500d, Olympic Stadium, Athens.

1997, July 11 Litho. *Perf. 13x13½*

1875 A608 20d multicolored	.20	.20
1876 A608 100d multicolored	.90	.45
1877 A608 140d multicolored	1.25	.60
1878 A608 170d multicolored	1.50	.75
1879 A608 500d multicolored	4.50	2.25
Nos. 1875-1879 (5)	8.35	4.25

Famous People A609

Designs: 20d, Alexandros Panagoulis (1939-76), resistance leader, vert. 30d, Grigorios Xenopoulos (1867-1951), novelist, vert. 40d, Odysseus Elytis (1911-96), poet. 50d, Panayiotis Kanellopoulos (1902-86), prime minister, vert. 100d, Harilaos Trikoupis (1832-96), politician. 170d, Maria Callas (1923-77), opera singer. 200d, Rigas Vélestinlis-Feraios (1757-98), revolutionary, vert.

Perf. 13½x13, 13x13½

1997, Oct. 31 Litho.

1880 A609 20d multicolored	.20	.20
1881 A609 30d multicolored	.25	.20
1882 A609 40d multicolored	.30	.20
1883 A609 50d multicolored	.45	.20
1884 A609 100d multicolored	.80	.40
1885 A609 170d multicolored	1.40	.70
1886 A609 200d multicolored	1.60	.80
Nos. 1880-1886 (7)	5.00	2.70

Film Comedians A610

Designs: 20d, Vassilis Avlonitis. 30d, Vassilis Argyropoulos. 50d, Georgia Vassileiadou. 70d, Lambros Constantaras. 100d, Vassilis Logothetidis. 140d, Dionysis Papagiannopoulos. 170d, Nikos Stavrides. 200d, Mimis Fotopoulos.

1997, Dec. 17 Litho. *Perf. 13x13½*

1887 A610 20d multicolored	.20	.20
1888 A610 30d multicolored	.25	.25
1889 A610 50d multicolored	.40	.40
1890 A610 70d multicolored	.55	.55
1891 A610 100d multicolored	.80	.80
1892 A610 140d multicolored	1.10	1.10
1893 A610 170d multicolored	1.40	1.40
1894 A610 200d multicolored	1.60	1.60
Nos. 1887-1894 (8)	6.30	6.30

Incorporation of the Dodecanese Islands into Greece, 50th Anniv. — A611

100d, German commander signing treaty turning islands over to English and Greek military, Symi (Simi), May 8, 1945. 140d, Greece and Colossus of Rhodes, Greek flag. 170d, English general turns islands over to Greek military command, Rhodes, 3/31/47. 500d, Greek flag raised over Dodencanese, Kasos (Caso), 3/7/47.

1998, Feb. 27 Litho. *Perf. 13½x13*

1895	A611	100d multicolored	.80	.80
1896	A611	140d multicolored	1.10	1.10
1897	A611	170d multicolored	1.40	1.40
1898	A611	500d multicolored	4.00	4.00
		Nos. 1895-1898 (4)	7.30	7.30

Hagia Sophia General Children's Hospital, Cent. — A612

Holy Monastery of Xenon, 1000th Anniv. A613

4th World Congress of Thracians, Nea Orestiada A614

16th World Congress of Cardiology Research, Athens — A615

European Movement, 50th Anniv. — A616

Perf. 13x13½, 13½x13

1998, Apr. 30 Litho.

1899	A612	20d multicolored	.20	.20
1900	A613	100d multicolored	.80	.80
1901	A614	140d multicolored	1.10	1.10
1902	A615	150d Building, heart, horiz.	1.25	1.25
1903	A615	170d multicolored	1.25	1.25
1904	A616	500d multicolored	4.00	4.00
		Nos. 1899-1904 (6)	8.60	8.60

Souvenir Sheet

1998 FIBA World Basketball Championships, Greece — A617

Illustration reduced.

1998, June 15 Litho. *Perf. 14*

1905	A617	300d multicolored	2.50	2.50

Natl. Festivals A618

Europa: 140d, Culture Festival, Grecian Theatre, Epidaurus. 500d, Culture Festival, Herod Atticus Theatre, Athens.

1998, May 29 Litho. *Perf. 14x13½*

1906	A618	140d multicolored	1.10	1.10
a.		Perf. 13 vert.	1.10	1.10
1907	A618	500d multicolored	4.00	4.00
a.		Pair, #1906-1907	5.25	5.25
b.		Perf. 13 vert.	4.00	4.00
c.		Bklt. pane, 2 ea. #1906a, 1907b	10.50	
		Complete booklet, #1907c	10.50	

Castle Ruins in Greece A619

1998, July 15 Litho. *Perf. 13½*

1908	A619	30d Hierapetra	.25	.25
1909	A619	50d Korfu	.40	.40
1910	A619	70d Limnos	.55	.55
1911	A619	100d Argolis	.80	.80
1912	A619	150d Iraklion	1.25	1.25
1913	A619	170d Navpaktos, vert.	1.40	1.40
1914	A619	200d Ioannina, vert.	1.60	1.60
1915	A619	400d Plataea	3.25	3.25
1916	A619	550d Karitainas, vert.	4.50	4.50
1917	A619	600d Fragkokastello, Crete	4.75	4.75
		Nos. 1908-1917 (10)	18.75	18.75

Each denomination also sold in booklets containing 20 panes of stamps, perf. 13⅓ horiz. or vert.

Greek Orthodox Community of Venice, 500th Anniv. — A620

Designs: 30d, Cathedral. 40d, Icon, vert. 140d, Illuminated manuscript, vert. 230d, Icon of Madonna and Child surrounded by saints.

1998, Oct. 26 Litho. *Perf. 14*

1918	A620	30d multicolored	.40	.40
1919	A620	40d multicolored	.50	.50
1920	A620	140d multicolored	1.75	1.75
1921	A620	230d multicolored	3.00	3.00
		Nos. 1918-1921 (4)	5.65	5.65

Greek Writers of Antiquity — A621

1998 Litho. *Perf. 13½x13*

1922	A621	20d Homer	.20	.20
1923	A621	100d Sophocles	.80	.80
1924	A621	140d Thucydides	1.10	1.10
1925	A621	200d Plato	1.60	1.60
1926	A621	250d Demosthenes	2.00	2.00
		Nos. 1922-1926 (5)	5.70	5.70

Intl. Year of the Ocean A622

Designs: 40d, Ancient ship, map of Mediterranean Sea. 100d, Sailing ship, Neptune. 200d, Modern ship . 500d, Silver tetradrachm of Antigonos Doson, 229-221 B.C.

1999, Feb. 19 Litho. *Perf. 13x13½*

1927	A622	40d multicolored	.30	.30
1928	A622	100d multicolored	.80	.80
1929	A622	200d multicolored	1.60	1.60
1930	A622	500d multicolored	4.00	4.00
		Nos. 1927-1930 (4)	6.70	6.70

Pres. Konstantin Karamanlis (1907-98) — A623

Various portraits of Karamanlis and: 100d, Representations of economic development, 1955-63. 170d, People celebrating. 200d, Emblem of European Union. 500d, National flag, vert.

1999, Apr. 19 Litho. *Perf. 14*

1931	A623	100d multicolored	.80	.80
1932	A623	170d multicolored	1.25	1.25
1933	A623	200d multicolored	1.60	1.60
1934	A623	500d multicolored	4.00	4.00
		Nos. 1931-1934 (4)	7.65	7.65

Europa A624

Various views Mytikas peak (Mt. Olympus) and wildflowers.

1999, May 24 Litho. *Perf. 14*

1935	A624	170d multicolored	1.40	1.40
a.		Perf. 13¼ vert.	1.40	1.40
1936	A624	550d multicolored	4.25	4.25
a.		Pair, #1935-1936	5.75	5.75
b.		Perf. 13¼ vert.	4.25	4.25
c.		Booklet pane, 2 each #1935a, 1936b	11.50	
		Complete booklet, #1936c	11.50	

Greece-Japan Diplomatic Relations, Cent. — A625

1999, June 28 Litho. *Perf. 13¾x14*

1937	A625	120d multicolored	.95	.95

4000 Years of Hellenism — A626

Designs: a, Sanctuary of Apollo Hylates, Kourion. b, Mycenaean "Krater of the Warriors," Athens. c, Mycenaean amphoral krater, Cyprus Museum. d, Sanctuary of Apollo Epikourios, Delphi.

1999, June 28 Litho. *Perf. 13½x13*

1938	A626	120d Block of 4, #a.-d.	3.00	3.00

See Cyprus No. 936.

Community Support Framework, 5th Anniv. A627

Designs: 20d, Modernization of Greek Railway Organization. 120d, Rio-Antirrio Bridge. 140d, Modernization of Greek Post Office. 250d, Athens Metro train. 500d, Eleftherios Venizelos Airport, Athens.

1999, Nov. 8 Litho. *Perf. 13x13¼*

1939	A627	20d multi	.20	.20
1940	A627	120d multi	.75	.75
1941	A627	140d multi	.85	.85
1942	A627	250d multi	1.50	1.50
1943	A627	500d multi	3.00	3.00
		Nos. 1939-1943 (5)	6.30	6.30

Armed Forces A628

20d, Exercise with helicopters, rafts. 30d, Patrol boat. 40d, F-16s in flight. 50d, CL-215 dousing forest fire. 70d, Destroyers. 120d, Distribution of goods in Bosnia. 170d, Mirage 2000 in flight. 250d, Exercise with helicopters, tanks. 600d, Submarine Okeanos.

Perf. 13¾x13½

1999, Dec. 13 Litho.

1944	A628	20d multi	.20	.20
1945	A628	30d multi	.20	.20
1946	A628	40d multi	.25	.25
1947	A628	50d multi	.30	.30
1948	A628	70d multi	.40	.40
1949	A628	120d multi	.70	.70
1950	A628	170d multi	1.00	1.00
1951	A628	250d multi	1.50	1.50
1952	A628	600d multi	3.50	3.50
		Nos. 1944-1952 (9)	8.05	8.05

Christianity, 2000th Anniv. A629

Designs: 20d, Birth of Christ, vert. 50d, Inter-religious dialogue, vert. 120d, Angels with instruments, vert. 170d, Dove. 200d, Communion. 500d, Providence, vert.

2000, Jan. 1 *Perf. 14¼x14*

1953	A629	20d multi	.20	.20
1954	A629	50d multi	.30	.30
1955	A629	120d multi	.70	.70

Perf. 14x14¼

1956	A629	170d multi	1.00	1.00

Size: 35x35mm

Perf. 13¾

1957	A629	200d multi	1.25	1.25

Size: 27x57mm

Perf. 13½x14

1958	A629	500d multi	3.00	3.00
		Nos. 1953-1958 (6)	6.45	6.45

Europa, 2000

Common Design Type

2000, May 9 Litho. *Perf. 13¼x13*

1959	CD17	170d multi	1.00	1.00
a.		Perf. 13 vert.	1.00	1.00
b.		Booklet pane, 4 #1959a	4.00	
		Complete booklet, #1959b	4.00	

Ships — A630

Designs: 10d, Steamship Ilissos. 120d, Destroyer Adrias. 170d, Steamship Ia II. 400d, Destroyer Vas. Olga.

Perf. 14¼x13¾

2000, June 26 **Litho.**

1960	A630	10d multi	.20	.20
1961	A630	120d multi	.65	.65
1962	A630	170d multi	.90	.90
1963	A630	400d multi	2.25	2.25
		Nos. 1960-1963 (4)	4.00	4.00

Stampin' the Future Children's Stamp Design Contest Winners
A631

Art by: 130d, Spyros Dalakos (rainbow). 180d, Ornella Moshovaki-Chaiger (robots). 200d, Zisis Zariotis (building, tree, vehicles). 620d, Athina Limoudi (rocket).

2000, June 26

1964	A631	130d multi	.70	.70
1965	A631	180d multi	.95	.95
1966	A631	200d multi	1.10	1.10
1967	A631	620d multi	3.50	3.50
		Nos. 1964-1967 (4)	6.25	6.25

Sydney and Athens — A632

Olympic torch, flag and: 200d, Parthenon. 650d, Sydney Opera House.

Perf. 13¼x13¾

2000, Sept. 15 **Litho.**

1968-1969 A632 Set of 2 4.50 4.50

See Australia Nos. 1873-1874.

Emblem of 2004 Athens Olympic Games — A633

Various backgrounds. Denominations: 10d, 50d, 130d, 180d, 200d, 650d.

2000, Nov. 7 *Perf. 14x14¼*

1970-1975 A633 Set of 6 6.25 6.25

Souvenir Sheet

Stamps of the Cretan Government, Cent. — A634

No. 1976: a, 200d, Crete #69. b, 650d, Crete #71.
Illustration reduced.

2000, Dec. 18 **Litho.** *Perf. 14x14¼*

1976 A634 Sheet of 2, #a-b 4.50 4.50

Christianity, 2000th Anniv. A635

Designs: 20d, Sculpture of Christ as Orpheus, vert. 30d, Sculpture of The Good Shepherd, vert. 40d, Mosaic of Christ, vert. 100d, Mural of Christ. 130d, Icon of Christ (green frame), vert. 150d, Icon of Christ with open Bible, vert. 180d, Icon of Christ with closed Bible (dark blue frame), vert. 1000d, Byzantine coin depicting Christ.

2000, Dec. 18 *Perf. 14x14¼, 14¼x14*

1977-1984 A635 Set of 8 8.75 8.75

Post Office Savings Bank, Cent. A636

Designs: 20d, Mother and child, vert. 130d, Emblem and 2-euro coin.

Perf. 13¼x13¾, 13¾x13¼

2001, May 15 **Litho.**

1985-1986 A636 Set of 2 .75 .75

UN High Commissioner for Refugees, 50th Anniv. — A637

2001, May 15 *Perf. 13¾x13¼*

1987 A637 140d multi .70 .70

Thessaloniki Intl. Trade Fair, 75th Anniv. — A638

2001, May 15 *Perf. 13¼x13¾*

1988 A638 180d multi .90 .90

Aristotle University, Thessaloniki, 75th Anniv. — A639

2001, May 15 *Perf. 13¾x13¼*

1989 A639 200d multi 1.00 1.00

Academy of Athens, 75th Anniv. A640

2001, May 15

1990 A640 500d multi 2.50 2.50

Ioannis Zigdis (1913-97), Politician — A641

2001, May 15 *Perf. 13¼x13¾*

1991 A641 700d multi 3.50 3.50

Europa — A642

Designs: Nos. 1992a, 1992c, Dry leaf, parched earth. Nos. 1992b, 1992d, Water, fresh leaves.

2001, May 15 *Perf. 14¼x13¾*

1992 A642	Horiz. pair	4.25	4.25
a.	180d multi	1.00	1.00
b.	650d multi	3.25	3.25
c.	Horiz. pair, perf. 13¼ vert.	4.25	4.25
d.	As "a," perf. 13¼ vert.	1.00	1.00
e.	As "b," perf. 13¼ vert.	3.25	3.25
f.	Booklet pane, 2 # 1992c	8.50	
	Booklet, #1992f	8.50	

Birds and Flowers A643

Designs: 20d, Little egret. 50d, White stork. 100d, Bearded vulture. 140d, Orchid, vert. 150d, Dalmatian pelican, vert. 200d, Lily, Plastira Lake. 700d, Egyptian vulture. 850d, Black vulture.

Perf. 13¾x13¼, 13¼x13¾

2001, June 27

1993-2000 A643 Set of 8 11.00 11.00

Symbol of Hellenic Post — A644

Illustration reduced.

2001, Sept. 8 **Litho.** *Perf. 13x12¾*

2001	Pair + 2 labels	2.00	2.00
a.	A644 140d blue & yellow	.85	.85
b.	A644 200d blue	1.10	1.10

Souvenir Sheet

Christianity in Armenia, 1700th Anniv. — A645

2001, Dec. 5 *Perf. 13*

2002 A645 850d multi 4.50 4.50

Souvenir Sheet

2004 Summer Olympics, Athens — A646

2001, Dec. 5 *Perf. 13¾*

2003 A646 1200d multi 6.50 6.50

100 Cents = 1 Euro (€)

Dances A647

Designs: 2c, Kamakaki. 3c, Bride's dowry. 5c, Zagorissios, vert. 10c, Balos. 15c, Synkathistos. 20c, Tsakonikos, vert. 30c, Pyrrichios. 35c, Fourles, vert. 40c, Apokriatikos. 45c, Kotsari. 50c, Pentozalis, vert. 55c, Karagouna. 60c, Hassapiko. 65c, Zalistos. 85c, Pogonissios. €1, Kalamatianos. €2, Maleviziotis. €2.15, Tsamikos. €2.60, Zeibekikos, vert. €3, Nyfiatikos. €4, Paschaliatikos.

Perf. 13x13¼, 13¼x13

2002, Jan. 2 **Litho.**

2004	A647	2c multi	.20	.20
2005	A647	3c multi	.20	.20
2006	A647	5c multi	.20	.20
2007	A647	10c multi	.20	.20
2008	A647	15c multi	.25	.25
2009	A647	20c multi	.35	.35
2010	A647	30c multi	.50	.50
2011	A647	35c multi	.60	.60
2012	A647	40c multi	.70	.70
2013	A647	45c multi	.80	.80
2014	A647	50c multi	.85	.85
2015	A647	55c multi	.95	.95
2016	A647	60c multi	1.00	1.00
2017	A647	65c multi	1.10	1.10
2018	A647	85c multi	1.50	1.50
2019	A647	€1 multi	1.75	1.75
2020	A647	€2 multi	3.50	3.50
2021	A647	€2.15 multi	3.75	3.75
2022	A647	€2.60 multi	4.50	4.50
2023	A647	€3 multi	5.25	5.25
2024	A647	€4 multi	7.00	7.00
		Nos. 2004-2024 (21)	35.15	35.15

2004 Summer Olympics, Athens A648

Ancient Olympics: 41c, Runners. 59c, Sculpture of charioteer, vert. 80c, Javelin thrower. €2.05, Doryphoros of Polycleitos, vert. €2.35, Weight lifter.
€5, Stadium archway.

Perf. 13¾x13¼, 13¼x13¾

2002, Mar. 15 **Litho.**

2025-2029 A648 Set of 5 11.00 11.00

Souvenir Sheet

Perf. 12¾

2030 A648 €5 multi 9.00 9.00

No. 2030 contains one 49x28mm stamp.

Europa — A649

2002, May 9 ***Perf. 13¼x13¾***

2031 A649	Horiz. pair, #a-b	6.00	6.00
a.	60c Elephant	1.25	1.25
b.	€ 2.60 Equestrian act	4.75	4.75
c.	Horiz. pair, perf. 13¼ vert.	6.00	6.00
d.	As "a," perf. 13¼ vert.	1.25	1.25
e.	As "b," perf. 13¼ vert.	4.75	4.75
f.	Booklet pane, 2, #2031c	12.00	—
	Booklet, #2031f	12.00	

Scouting A650

Designs: 45c, Navy Scout, sailboats. 60c, Scout, emblem of World Conference. 70c, Scouts planting tree. € 2.15, Scouts, map and mountain.

2002, June 26 **Litho.** ***Perf. 13x13½***

2032-2035 A650	Set of 4	7.75	7.75

Greek Language A651

Designs: 45c, Hieros Nomos, Athens Acropolis, 5th cent. B.C. 60c, Linear B script, 13th cent. B.C., vert. 90c, The Memoirs of General Makriyiannis. € 2.15, Byzantine script, 11th cent., vert.

Perf. 13¾x13¼, 13¼x13¾

2002, Sept. 23

2036-2039 A651	Set of 4	8.25	8.25

Ancient Olympic Winners With Laurel Wreaths — A652

Head color: 45c, Green. 60c, Dark blue. € 2.15, Pink. € 2.60, Light blue.

2002, Oct. 30 **Litho.** ***Perf. 13¼x13¾***

2040-2043 A652	Set of 4	12.00	12.00

Souvenir Sheet

Stadia of First Olympics — A653

2002, Oct. 30 ***Perf. 12¾***

2044 A653	€ 6 multi	12.00	12.00

Archbishops of Athens A654

Archbishop and years of reign: 10c, Chrystostomos I (1923-38). 45c, Chrysanthos (1938-41). € 2.15, Damaskinos (1941-49). € 2.60, Serapheim (1974-98).

2002, Dec. 10 ***Perf. 13x13½***

2045-2048 A654	Set of 4	11.00	11.00

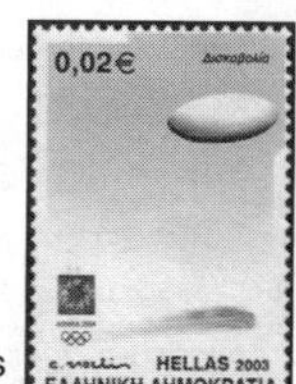

Olympic Sports Equipment — A655

Designs: 2c, Discus. 5c, Hammer. 47c, Javelin. 65c, Pole vault pole and bar. € 2.17, Hurdles. € 2.85, Weights.

2003, Feb. 11 ***Perf. 13¾x14¼***

2049-2054 A655	Set of 6	13.50	13.50

2004 Summer Olympics, Athens.

Souvenir Sheet

Mascots for 2004 Summer Olympics, Athens — A656

No. 2055: a, € 2.50, Mascot with red shirt. b, € 2.85, Mascot with blue shirt.

2003, Feb. 11 ***Perf. 13¼***

2055 A656	Sheet of 2, #a-b	11.50	11.50

SEMI-POSTAL STAMPS

Nos. 440-444 Surcharged in Blue

1944 **Wmk. 252** ***Perf. 12½***

B1	A106 100,000d on 15d	.30	*.75*
B2	A107 100,000d on 25d	.30	*.75*
B3	A108 100,000d on 50d	.30	*.75*
B4	A109 100,000d on 75d	.30	*.75*
B5	A110 100,000d on 100d	.30	*.75*
	Nos. B1-B5,CB1-CB5 (10)	3.00	*7.50*
	Set, never hinged	6.00	

The proceeds aided victims of the Piraeus bombing, Jan. 11, 1944. The exceptionally high face value discouraged the use of these stamps.

Nos. 437-441 Surcharged in Blue

1944, July 20

50,000d + 450,000d

B11	A103	on 2d	.25	*.60*
B12	A104	on 5d	.25	*.60*
B13	A105	on 10d	.25	*.60*
B14	A106	on 15d	.25	*.60*
a.		Pair, one without surcharge	60.00	
B15	A107	on 25d	.25	*.60*
		Nos. B11-B15,CB6-CB10 (10)	2.50	*6.00*
		Set, never hinged	5.00	

The surtax aided children's camps.

AIR POST STAMPS

Italy-Greece-Turkey-Rhodes Service

Flying Boat off Phaleron Bay — AP1

Flying Boat over Acropolis — AP2

Flying Boat over Map of Southern Europe — AP3

Flying Boat Seen through Colonnade — AP4

Perf. 11½

1926, Oct. 20 **Unwmk.** **Litho.**

C1	AP1 2d multicolored	1.50	1.10
a.	Horiz. pair, imperf. vert.	650.00	
C2	AP2 3d multicolored	8.00	7.50
C3	AP3 5d multicolored	1.50	1.10
C4	AP4 10d multicolored	7.50	7.50
	Nos. C1-C4 (4)	18.50	17.20
	Set, never hinged	45.00	

Graf Zeppelin Issue

Zeppelin over Acropolis AP5

1933, May 2 ***Perf. 13½x12½***

C5	AP5 30d rose red	10.00	10.00
C6	AP5 100d deep blue	42.50	42.50
C7	AP5 120d dark brown	42.50	42.50
	Nos. C5-C7 (3)	95.00	95.00
	Set, never hinged	190.00	

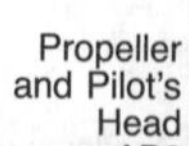

Propeller and Pilot's Head AP6

Temple of Apollo, Corinth AP7

Plane over Hermoupolis, Syros — AP8

Allegory of Flight
AP9 AP12

Map of Italy-Greece-Turkey-Rhodes Airmail Route — AP10

Head of Hermes and Airplane — AP11

1933, Oct. 10 **Engr.** ***Perf. 12***

C8	AP6 50 l green & org	.20	.20
C9	AP7 1d bl & brn org	.30	.25
C10	AP8 3d dk vio & org brn	.45	.45
C11	AP9 5d brn org & dk bl	6.50	4.00
C12	AP10 10d dp red & blk	1.40	1.25
C13	AP11 20d black & grn	6.50	3.75
C14	AP12 50d dp brn & dp bl	40.00	*45.00*
	Nos. C8-C14 (7)	55.35	*54.90*
	Set, never hinged	125.00	

By error the 1d stamp is inscribed in the plural "Draxmai" instead of the singular "Draxmh." This stamp exists bisected, used as a 50 lepta denomination.

All values of this set exist imperforate but were not regularly issued.

For General Air Post Service

Airplane over Map of Greece — AP13

Airplane over Map of Icarian Sea — AP14

Airplane over Acropolis AP15

Perf. 13x13½, 13x12½, 13½x13, 12½x13

1933, Nov. 2

C15	AP13 50 l green	.20	.25
C16	AP13 1d red brown	.30	.50
C17	AP14 2d lt violet	.55	.75
C18	AP15 5d ultra	3.25	3.25
a.	Imperf., pair	600.00	500.00
b.	Horiz. pair, imperf. vert.	600.00	
C19	AP14 10d car rose	6.00	*7.00*
C20	AP13 25d dark blue	27.50	18.00

C21 AP15 50d dark brown 27.50 *37.50*
a. Imperf., pair 700.00 600.00
Nos. C15-C21 (7) 65.30 *67.25*
Set, never hinged 140.00

Helios Driving the Sun Chariot AP16

Iris — AP17

Daedalus Preparing Icarus for Flying — AP18

Pallas Athene Holding Pegasus — AP19

Hermes AP20

Zeus Carrying off Ganymede AP21

Triptolemos, King of Eleusis AP22

Bellerophon and Pegasus — AP23

Phrixos and Helle on the Ram Flying over the Hellespont AP24

Perf. 13x12½, 12½x13

1935, Nov. 10 Engr.

Grayish Paper

Size: 34x23½mm, 23½x34mm

C22 AP16 1d deep red .45 .45
C23 AP17 2d dull blue 1.00 .60
C24 AP18 5d dk violet 9.00 3.00
C25 AP19 7d blue violet 12.00 6.00
C26 AP20 10d bister brown 2.50 2.50
C27 AP21 25d rose 4.25 *4.00*
C28 AP22 30d dark green .50 .50
C29 AP23 50d violet 3.50 *4.00*
C30 AP24 100d brown .75 *1.10*
Nos. C22-C30 (9) 33.95 *22.15*
Set, never hinged 75.00

Re-engraved

1937-39

White Paper

Size: 34¼x24mm, 24x34¼mm

C31 AP16 1d red .20 .20
C32 AP17 2d gray blue .20 .20
C33 AP18 5d violet .20 .20
C34 AP19 7d dp ultra .20 .20
C35 AP20 10d brn org 1.75 *2.50*
Nos. C31-C35 (5) 2.55 *3.30*
Set, never hinged 3.75

Issued: #C35, 3/1/39; others 8/3/37.

Postage Due Stamp, 1913, Overprinted in Red

Serrate Roulette 13½

1938, Aug. 8 Litho. Unwmk.

C36 D3 50 l violet brown .20 .20
Never hinged .25
a. "O" for "P" in word at foot 27.50 27.50

Same Overprint on No. J79 in Red

1939, June 26 ***Perf. 13½x12½***

C37 D3 50 l dark brown .20 .20
Never hinged .20

Meteora Monasteries, near Trikkala — AP25

Designs: 4d, Simon Peter Monastery. 6d, View of Santorin. 8d, Church of Pantanassa. 16d, Santorin view. 32d, Ponticonissi, Corfu. 45d, Acropolis, Athens. 55d, Erechtheum. 65d, Temple of Nike Apteros. 100d, Temple of the Olympian Zeus, Athens.

Wmk. Crowns (252)

1940, Aug. 3 Litho. ***Perf. 12½***

C38 AP25 2d red org & blk .60 .95
C39 AP25 4d dk grn & blk 2.75 2.50
C40 AP25 6d lake & blk 5.00 4.50
C41 AP25 8d dk bl & blk 12.75 11.50
C42 AP25 16d rose vio & blk 20.00 17.00
C43 AP25 32d red org & blk 27.50 *32.50*
C44 AP25 45d dk grn & blk 37.50 32.50
C45 AP25 55d lake & blk 37.50 32.50
C46 AP25 65d dk bl & blk 37.50 32.50
C47 AP25 100d rose vio & blk 45.00 40.00
Nos. C38-C47 (10) 226.10 206.45
Set, never hinged 375.00

4th anniv. of the founding of the Greek Youth Organization. The stamps were good for postal duty on Aug. 3-5, 1940, only. They remained on sale until Feb. 3, 1941.

For overprints see Nos. N229-N238.

Catalogue values for unused stamps in this section, from this point to the end of the section, are for Never Hinged items.

Postage Due Stamps Nos. J81 and J75 Surcharged in Red

1941-42 Unwmk. ***Perf. 13x12½***

C48 D3 1d on 2d lt red .20 .20
a. Inverted surcharge 40.00

Serrate Roulette 13½

C49 D3 1d on 2d ver ('42) .20 .20
a. Inverted surcharge 30.00
b. Double surcharge 20.00

Nos. J83, J84, J86, J87 Overprinted in Red

1941-42 ***Perf. 13, 12½x13***

C50 D3 5d gray bl ('42) .20 .20
a. Inverted overprint 40.00
b. Double overprint 30.00
c. Pair, one without ovpt. 20.00
d. Surcharge on back 20.00
e. On No. J78 ('42) 125.00 *150.00*
C51 D3 10d gray grn .30 .30
a. Inverted overprint 15.00
b. Vert. pair, imperf. btwn. 300.00
C52 D3 25d lt red .75 .75
a. Inverted overprint 100.00
C53 D3 50d orange 1.40 1.40
Nos. C50-C53 (4) 2.65 2.65

Boreas, North Wind — AP35

Winds: 5d, Notus, South. 10d, Apeliotes, East. 20d, Lips, Southwest. 25d, Zephyrus, West. 50d, Kaikias, Northeast.

Wmk. 252

1942, Aug. 15 Litho. ***Perf. 12½***

C55 AP35 2d emerald .20 .20
C56 AP35 5d red org .20 .20
a. Imperf., pair 300.00
b. Double impression 50.00 —
C57 AP35 10d red brown .20 .20
C58 AP35 20d brt blue .20 .20
C59 AP35 25d dk red org .20 .20
C60 AP35 50d gray blk 1.60 1.60
a. Double impression 100.00
Nos. C55-C60 (6) 2.60 2.60

1943, Sept. 15

Winds: 10d, Apeliotes, East. 25d, Zephyrus, West. 50d, Kaikias, Northeast. 100d, Boreas, North. 200d, Eurus, Southeast. 400d, Skiron, Northwest.

C61 AP35 10d rose red .20 .20
C62 AP35 25d Prus green .20 .20
C63 AP35 50d violet blue .20 .20
C64 AP35 100d slate black .20 .20
C65 AP35 200d claret .20 .20
C66 AP35 400d steel blue .20 .20
Nos. C61-C66 (6) 1.20 1.20

Double impressions exist of 10d and 400d. Value, each $30.

For surcharges see #472, 473, CB1-CB10.

Imperf., Pairs

C61a AP35 10d 100.00
C62a AP35 25d 100.00
C63a AP35 50d 100.00
C64a AP35 100d 100.00
C65a AP35 200d 100.00
C66a AP35 400d 100.00

Priest Blessing Troops on Summit of Mt. Grammos AP36

Torchbearer AP37

Designs: 1700d, Victory above Mt. Vitsi. 2700d, Battle Scene. 7000d, Victory leading infantry.

1952, Aug. 29 Engr. ***Perf. 12x13½***

C67 AP36 1000d deep blue .95 .25
C68 AP36 1700d dp blue grn 3.25 1.10
C69 AP36 2700d brown 9.00 3.75
C70 AP36 7000d olive green 27.50 10.00
Nos. C67-C70 (4) 40.70 15.10

Greek army's struggle against communism.

1954, May 15 ***Perf. 13***

Designs: 2400dr, Coin of Amphictyonic League. 4000dr, Pallas Athene.

C71 AP37 1200d dp orange 5.00 .25
C72 AP37 2400d dk green 27.50 1.25
C73 AP37 4000d dp ultra 47.50 2.50
Nos. C71-C73 (3) 80.00 4.00

5th anniv. of the signing of the North Atlantic Treaty.

Piraeus AP38

Harbors: 15d, Salonika. 20d, Patras. 25d, Hermoupolis (Syra). 30d, Volos. 50d, Cavalla. 100d, Herakleion (Candia).

Perf. 13½x13

1958, July 1 Wmk. 252 Litho.

C74 AP38 10d multicolored 8.75 .20
C75 AP38 15d multicolored 1.25 .20
C76 AP38 20d multicolored 8.75 .20
C77 AP38 25d multicolored 1.25 .35
C78 AP38 30d multicolored 1.75 .35
C79 AP38 50d multicolored 4.25 .40
C80 AP38 100d multicolored 24.00 2.10
Nos. C74-C80 (7) 50.00 3.80

AIR POST SEMI-POSTAL STAMPS

#C61-C65 Surcharged in Blue like #B1-B5

1944, June Wmk. 252 ***Perf. 12½***

CB1 AP35 100,000d on 10d .30 *.75*
CB2 AP35 100,000d on 25d .30 *.75*
CB3 AP35 100,000d on 50d .30 *.75*
a. Inverted overprint 30.00
CB4 AP35 100,000d on 100d .30 *.75*
CB5 AP35 100,000d on 200d .30 *.75*
Nos. CB1-CB5 (5) 1.50 *3.75*
Set, never hinged 3.00

The exceptionally high face value discouraged the use of these stamps.

The proceeds aided victims of the Piraeus bombing, January 11, 1944.

#C61-C65 Surcharged in Blue like #B11-B15

1944, July

50,000d + 450,000d

CB6 AP35 on 10d .25 *.60*
CB7 AP35 on 25d .25 *.60*
CB8 AP35 on 50d .25 *.60*
CB9 AP35 on 100d .25 *.60*
CB10 AP35 on 200d .25 *.60*
Nos. CB6-CB10 (5) 1.25 *3.00*
Set, never hinged 2.50

The surtax aided children's camps. Surcharge exists inverted or double. Value, each $55.

POSTAGE DUE STAMPS

D1 D2

Perf. 9, 9½, and 10, 10½ and Compound

1875 Litho. Unwmk.

J1 D1 1 l green & black 1.25 1.25
J2 D1 2 l green & black 1.25 1.25
J3 D1 5 l green & black 1.50 1.00
J4 D1 10 l green & black 1.50 1.00
J5 D1 20 l green & black 30.00 15.00
J6 D1 40 l green & black 7.00 4.50
J7 D1 60 l green & black 30.00 16.00
J8 D1 70 l green & black 7.00 7.00
J9 D1 80 l green & black 15.00 12.00
J10 D1 90 l green & black 9.00 9.00
J11 D1 1d green & black 10.00 9.00
J12 D1 2d green & black 11.00 9.00
Nos. J1-J12 (12) 124.50 86.00

Imperforate and part perforated, double and inverted center varieties of Nos. J1-J12 are believed to be printers' waste.

Perf. 12, 13 and 10½x13

J13 D1 1 l green & black 1.50 1.50
J14 D1 2 l green & black 13.00 11.00
J15 D1 5 l green & black 2.50 2.50
J16 D1 10 l green & black 3.00 3.00
J17 D1 20 l green & black 24.00 21.00
J18 D1 40 l green & black 9.00 7.00
J19 D1 60 l green & black 37.50 24.00
J20 D1 70 l green & black 7.00 7.00
J21 D1 80 l green & black 11.00 11.00
J22 D1 90 l green & black 16.00 11.00
J23 D1 1d green & black 24.00 16.00
J24 D1 2d green & black 21.00 16.00
Nos. J13-J24 (12) 169.50 131.00

Redrawn

"Lepton" or "Lepta" in Larger Greek Letters

1876 ***Perf. 9, 9½, and 10, 10½***

J25 D2 1 l green & black 3.75 3.75
J26 D2 2 l dk grn & blk 5.00 4.75
J27 D2 5 l dk grn & blk 300.00 225.00
J28 D2 10 l green & black 2.50 1.75
J29 D2 20 l green & black 3.25 2.50
J30 D2 40 l green & black 27.50 21.00
J31 D2 60 l green & black 22.50 12.50
J32 D2 70 l green & black 18.00 21.00
J33 D2 80 l green & black 15.00 12.50
J34 D2 90 l green & black 15.00 13.00
J35 D2 100 l green & black 18.00 12.50
J36 D2 200 l green & black 18.00 12.50
Nos. J25-J36 (12) 448.50 342.75

Perf. 11½ to 13

J37 D2 1 l yel grn & blk 1.25 .70
J38 D2 2 l yel grn & blk 1.25 .70
J39 D2 5 l yel grn & blk 3.50 .90
J40 D2 10 l yel grn & blk 2.00 1.55
a. Perf. 10-10½x11½-13 3.00
J41 D2 20 l yel grn & blk 2.00 1.50
J42 D2 40 l yel grn & blk 11.00 8.00
J43 D2 60 l yel grn & blk 7.00 7.00
J47 D2 100 l yel grn & blk 9.00 9.00
J48 D2 200 l yel grn & blk 10.00 8.00
Nos. J37-J48 (9) 47.00 37.30

Footnote below #J12 applies to #J25-J48.

D3

1902 Engr. Wmk. 129 ***Perf. 13½***

J49 D3 1 l chocolate .20 .20
J50 D3 2 l gray .20 .20
J51 D3 3 l orange .20 .20
J52 D3 5 l yel grn .20 .20
J53 D3 10 l scarlet .25 .20
J54 D3 20 l lilac .30 .20
J55 D3 25 l ultra 8.00 4.00
J56 D3 30 l dp vio .30 .30
J57 D3 40 l dk brn .35 .25
J58 D3 50 l red brn .35 .20
J59 D3 1d black .90 .60

Litho.

J60 D3 2d bronze 1.00 1.00
J61 D3 3d silver 2.00 2.00
J62 D3 5d gold 6.00 6.00
Nos. J49-J62 (14) 20.25 15.55

See Nos. J63-J88, J90-J93. For overprints and surcharges see Nos. 383-385, J89, RA56, RA58-RA59, NJ1-NJ31.

Imperf., Pairs

J50a D3 2 l 60.00
J51a D3 3 l 60.00
J52a D3 5 l 60.00
J55a D3 25 l 100.00
J56a D3 30 l 100.00
J58a D3 50 l 100.00
J59a D3 1d 100.00

Serrate Roulette 13½

1913-26 Unwmk.

J63 D3 1 l green .20 .20
J64 D3 2 l carmine .20 .20
J65 D3 3 l vermilion .20 .20
J66 D3 5 l green .20 .20
a. Imperf., pair 150.00
b. Double impression 60.00
c. "o" for "p" in lowest word 3.00 3.00
J67 D3 10 l carmine .20 .20
J68 D3 20 l slate .20 .20
J69 D3 25 l ultra .20 .20
J70 D3 30 l carmine .20 .20
J71 D3 40 l indigo .20 .20
J72 D3 50 l vio brn .30 .25
a. "o" for "p" in lowest word 25.00 20.00
J73 D3 80 l lil brn ('24) .40 .20
J74 D3 1d blue 6.00 .80
a. 1d ultramarine 9.00 3.50
J75 D3 2d vermilion 2.00 1.50
J76 D3 3d carmine 4.50 1.50
J77 D3 5d ultra 25.00 8.00
J78 D3 5d gray bl ('26) 4.00 1.50
Nos. J63-J78 (16) 44.00 15.55

In 1922-23 and 1941-42 some postage due stamps were used for ordinary postage.

In 1916 Nos. J52, and J63 to J75 were surcharged for the Mount Athos District (see note after No. N166) but were never issued there. By error some of them were put in use as ordinary postage due stamps in Dec., 1924. In 1932 the balance of them was burned.

Type of 1902 Issue

Perf. 13, 13½x12½, 13½x13

1930 Litho.

J79 D3 50 l dk brown .30 .30
J80 D3 1d lt blue .30 .30
J81 D3 2d lt red .30 .30
J82 D3 3d rose red 27.50 25.00
J83 D3 5d gray blue .30 .30
J84 D3 10d gray green .30 .30
J85 D3 15d red brown .30 .30
J86 D3 25d light red .70 .65
Nos. J79-J86 (8) 30.00 27.45

Type of 1902 Issue

1935 Engr. ***Perf. 12½x13***

J87 D3 50d orange .30 .30
J88 D3 100d slate green .30 .30

No. J70 Surcharged with New Value in Black

1942

J89 D3 50 (l) on 30 l carmine .90 .90

Type of 1902

1943 Wmk. 252 Litho. ***Perf. 12½***

J90 D3 10d red orange .20 .20
J91 D3 25d ultramarine .20 .20
J92 D3 100d black brown .20 .20
J93 D3 200d violet .20 .20
Nos. J90-J93 (4) .80 .80

POSTAL TAX STAMPS

"The Tragedy of War" — PT1

Red Cross, Nurses, Wounded and Bearers PT1a

Serrate Roulette 13½

1914 Litho. Unwmk.

RA1 PT1 2 l red ('18) .20 .20
a. 2 l carmine .35 .25
b. Imperf., pair 200.00
RA2 PT1 5 l blue .50 *.75*
a. Imperf., pair 250.00

1915 ***Serrate Roulette 13***

RA2B PT1a (5 l) dk bl & red 8.00 1.50

The tax was for the Red Cross.

Women's Patriotic League Badge — PT1b

1915, Nov. ***Perf. 11½***

RA2C PT1b (5 l) dk bl & car 1.00 1.00
d. Horiz. pair, imperf. btwn. 50.00

The tax was for the Greek Women's Patriotic League.

Nos. 165, 167, 170, 172-175 Surcharged in Black or Brown:

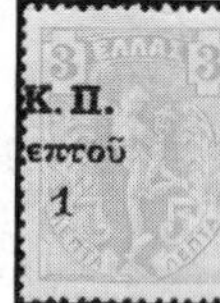

a

b

In type "b" the letters, especially those in the first line, are thinner than in type "a," making them appear taller.

Perf. 11½, 12½, 13½ and Compound

1917 Engr. Wmk. 129

RA3 A11(a) 1 l on 1 l 1.50 1.50
a. Double surcharge 5.00
RA4 A11(a) 1 l on 1 l (Br) 20.00 20.00
RA5 A11(a) 1 l on 3 l .30 .30
RA6 A11(b) 1 l on 3 l .30 .30
a. Triple surcharge 5.00
b. Dbl. surch., one invtd. 5.00
c. "K.M." for "K.II." 20.00
RA7 A11(a) 5 l on 1 l 2.00 2.00
a. Double surcharge 10.00
b. Dbl. surch., one invtd. 10.00
c. Inverted surcharge 10.00
RA8 A11(a) 5 l on 20 l .65 .65
a. Double surcharge 10.00
b. Dbl. surch., one invtd. 10.00
RA9 A11(b) 5 l on 40 l .65 .65
a. Imperf.
RA10 A11(b) 5 l on 50 l .65 .65
a. Double surcharge 25.00
b. Dbl. surch., one invtd. 25.00
RA11 A13(b) 5 l on 1d 2.25 2.25
a. Imperf.
b. Inverted surcharge 50.00
RA12 A11(a) 10 l on 30 l .80 .80
a. Imperf.
b. Double surcharge 20.00
RA13 A11(a) 30 l on 30 l .90 .90
a. Double surcharge 20.00
Nos. RA3-RA13 (11) 30.00 30.00

Same Surcharge On Occupation Stamps of 1912

Serrate Roulette 13½

1917 Litho. Unwmk.

RA14 O2 (b) 5 l on 25 l pale bl .45 .45
a. Triple surch., one invtd. 6.00
b. Double surcharge 6.00
RA15 O2 (b) 5 l on 40 l indigo .45 .45
a. Dbl. surch., one invtd. 6.00
b. Double surcharge 6.00
RA16 O1 (b) 5 l on 50 l dk bl .45 .45
a. Double surcharge 10.00
b. Inverted surcharge 10.00
Nos. RA14-RA16 (3) 1.35 1.35

There are many wrong font, omitted and misplaced letters and punctuation marks and similar varieties in the surcharges on Nos. RA3 to RA16.

Revenue Stamps Surcharged in Brown

"Victory" — R1

K. Π.
λεπτοῦ
1

1917

RA17 R1 1 l on 10 l blue .60 .60
RA18 R1 1 l on 80 l blue .60 .60
RA19 R1 5 l on 10 l blue 12.00 12.00
RA20 R1 5 l on 60 l blue 4.00 3.00
a. Perf. vert. through middle 4.25 2.50
RA21 R1 5 l on 80 l blue 3.00 3.00
a. Perf. vert. through middle 7.50 4.00
b. Inverted surcharge
RA22 R1 10 l on 70 l blue 14.00 5.00
a. Perf. vert. through middle 4.25 2.00
RA23 R1 10 l on 90 l blue 10.00 8.00
a. Perf. vert. through middle 12.50 11.00
RA24 R1 20 l on 20 l blue 650.00 475.00
RA25 R1 20 l on 30 l blue 4.00 4.00
RA26 R1 20 l on 40 l blue 12.00 10.00
RA27 R1 20 l on 50 l blue 5.00 4.00
RA28 R1 20 l on 60 l blue 350.00 150.00
RA29 R1 20 l on 80 l blue 35.00 22.50
RA30 R1 20 l on 90 l blue 3.00 3.00
a. Inverted surcharge 65.00
Nos. RA17-RA30 (14) 1,103. 700.70

No. RA19 is known only with vertical perforation through the middle.

Counterfeits exist of #RA17-RA43, used.

Surcharged in Brown or Black

RA31 R1 1 l on 50 l vio (Bk) .60 .60
RA32 R1 5 l on 10 l bl (Br) .60 .60
a. Inverted surcharge 60.00
b. Left "5" invert. 60.00
RA33 R1 5 l on 10 l vio (Br) .60 .60
RA34 R1 10 l on 50 l vio (Br) 4.00 4.00
RA35 R1 10 l on 50 l vio (Bk) 22.50 20.00
RA36 R1 20 l on 2d bl (Bk) 6.00 4.00
a. Surcharged "20 lept. 30" 60.00 60.00
b. Horiz. pair, imperf. btwn.
Nos. RA31-RA36 (6) 34.30 29.80

The "t," fourth Greek letter of the denomination in the surcharge ("Lept."), is normally omitted on Nos. RA31, RA34-RA36.

Corfu Issue

Surcharged in Black

1917

RA37 R1 1 l on 10 l blue 1.00 1.00
RA38 R1 5 l on 50 l blue 30.00 30.00
RA39 R1 10 l on 50 l blue 400.00 350.00
RA40 R1 20 l on 50 l blue 1,000. 600.00

Surcharged in Black

K.Π.
20 ΛΕΠΤΑ 20

RA41 R1 10 l on 50 l blue 7.00 6.00
RA42 R1 20 l on 50 l blue 18.00 12.00
RA43 R1 30 l on 50 l blue 10.00 8.00

Surcharged in Black

K. Π.
Λεπτὰ

RA44 R1 5 l on 10 l vio & red 6.00 1.00
a. "K" with serifs 10.00 3.50

Counterfeits exist of Nos. RA17-RA44.

Similar stamps with denominations higher than 30 lepta were for revenue use.

Wounded Soldier — PT2

1918 ***Serrate Roulette 13½, 11½***

RA45 PT2 5 l bl, yel & red 7.00 1.50

Overprinted

RA46 PT2 5 l blue, yel & red 8.00 1.50

The letters are the initials of Greek words equivalent to "Patriotic Relief Institution." The proceeds were given to the Patriotic League, for the aid of disabled soldiers.

Counterfeits exist of Nos. RA45-RA46.

PT3

Surcharge in Red

1922 Litho. *Perf. 11½*

Dark Blue & Red

RA46A PT3 5 l on 10 l *275.00* 5.00
RA46B PT3 5 l on 20 l 50.00 25.00
RA46C PT3 5 l on 50 l 250.00 80.00
RA46D PT3 5 l on 1d 3.25 *35.00*

Counterfeit surcharges exist. Copies of Nos. RA46A-RA46C without surcharge, each 50 cents.

Red Cross Help to Soldier and Family
PT3a

St. Demetrius
PT4

1924 *Perf. 11½, 13½ x 12½*

RA47 PT3a 10 l blue, buff & red .70 .25
a. Imperf., pair 40.00
b. Horiz. pair, imperf. btwn. 40.00

Proceeds were given to the Red Cross.

1934 *Perf. 11½*

RA48 PT4 20 l brown .20 .20
a. Horiz. pair, imperf. between 10.00
b. Vertical pair, imperf. between 15.00
c. Imperf., pair 20.00

No. RA48 was obligatory as a tax on all interior mail, including air post, mailed from Salonika.

For surcharge see No. RA69.

"Health"
PT5 PT6

1934, Dec. 28 *Perf. 13, 13x13½*

RA49 PT5 10 l bl grn, org & buff .20 .20
a. Vert. pair, imperf. horiz.
RA50 PT5 20 l ultra, org & buff .45 .20
RA51 PT5 50 l grn, org & buff 1.25 .40
Nos. RA49-RA51 (3) 1.90 .80

For surcharge see No. RA67.

1935

RA52 PT6 10 l yel grn, org & buff .20 .20
RA53 PT6 20 l ultra, org & buff .20 .20
RA54 PT6 50 l grn, org & buff .50 .35
Nos. RA52-RA54 (3) .90 .75

The use of #RA49-RA54 was obligatory on all mail during 4 weeks each year including Christmas, the New Year and Easter, and on parcel post packages at all times. For the benefit of the tubercular clerks and officials of the Post, Telephone and Telegraph Service.

See No. RA64. For surcharge see No. RA68.

No. 364 Overprinted in Red

1937, Jan. 20 Engr. *Perf. 13x12½*

RA55 A36 50 l violet 1.25 .20
a. Inverted overprint .75 .20

No. RA55a first appeared as an error, then was issued deliberately in quantity to avoid speculation.

Same Overprint in Blue on No. J67

Litho.

Serrate Roulette 13½

RA56 D3 10 l carmine .20 .20
a. Inverted overprint 50.00

No. RA56 with blue overprint double exists only with additional black overprint of Ionian Islands No. NRA1a.

Same Overprint in Green on No. 364

1937 Engr. *Perf. 13x12½*

RA57 A36 50 l violet .75 .20

Same Overprint, with Surcharge of New Value, on Nos. J66, J68 and 323 in Blue or Black

Serrate Roulette 13½

1938 Litho. Unwmk.

RA58 D3 50 l on 5 l grn .35 .25
a. "o" for "p" in lowest word 25.00 25.00
b. Vert. pair, imperf. horiz. 50.00
RA59 D3 50 l on 20 l slate .90 .50

Engr. *Perf. 13x12½*

RA60 A38 50 l on 20 l vio (Bk) .75 .20
Nos. RA58-RA60 (3) 2.00 .95

Surcharge on No. RA60 is 14½x16½mm.

Queens Olga and Sophia
PT7

1939, Feb. 1 Litho. *Perf. 13½x12*

RA61 PT7 10 l brt rose, *pale rose* .20 .20
RA62 PT7 50 l gray grn, *pale grn* .20 .20
RA63 PT7 1d dl bl, *lt bl* .20 .20
Nos. RA61-RA63 (3) .60 .60

For overprints and surcharges see Nos. RA65, RA79-RA81A, NRA1-NRA3.

"Health" Type of 1935

1939 *Perf. 12½*

RA64 PT6 50 l brn & buff .40 .30

No. RA62 Overprinted in Red

1940 *Perf. 13½x12*

RA65 PT7 50 l gray grn, *pale grn* .25 .25
a. Inverted overprint 35.00
b. Pair, one without surcharge 20.00

Proceeds of #RA64-RA65 were used for the benefit of tubercular clerks and officials of the Post, Telephone and Telegraph Service. #RA65 was used in Albania during the Greek occupation, 1940-41 without additional overprint.

No. 321 Surcharged in Carmine

1941 Unwmk. Engr. *Perf. 13½x13*

RA66 A36 50 l on 5 l dk grn .20 .20
a. Inverted surcharge 15.00

No. RA49 and Type of 1935 Surcharged with New Value in Black

Perf. 12½x13, 13x13½

Litho.

RA67 PT5 50 l on 10 l 2.00 2.00
RA68 PT6 50 l on 10 l dp bl grn, dl org & buff .20 .20
a. Inverted surcharge 40.00
b. Double surcharge 40.00

Catalogue values for unused stamps in this section, from this point to the end of the section, are for Never Hinged items.

No. RA48 Surcharged in Green

1942 *Perf. 11½*

RA69 PT4 1d on 20 l brn .20 .20
a. Pair, one without surcharge 25.00
b. Imperf., pair 25.00
c. Double surcharge 15.00

Nos. 321, 324 Surcharged In Red or Carmine

1942-43 Engr. *Perf. 13½x13*

RA70 A36 10d on 5 l ('43) .20 .20
a. Double surcharge 25.00
RA71 A39 10d on 25 l (C) .20 .20
a. Inverted surcharge 25.00

No. 444 Overprinted in Red

1944 Wmk. 252 Litho. *Perf. 12½*

RA72 A110 100d black .20 .20
a. Double overprint 9.00
b. Inverted overprint 9.00

No. 443 Surcharged in Blue

RA73 A109 5000d on 75d .20 .20
a. Double surcharge 20.00

No. 437 Surcharged in Blue

RA74 A103 25000d on 2d .20 .20
a. Double surcharge 25.00
b. Additional surcharge on back 17.50

No. 399 Surcharged in Blue or Carmine

1945 *Perf. 13½x12*

RA75 A72 1d on 40 l .20 .20
a. Double surcharge 15.00

RA76 A72 2d on 40 l (C) .20 .20
a. Vert. pair, one without surch. 15.00
b. Surcharged on back 10.00
c. Inverted surcharge 10.00

Tax on Nos. RA67, RA68-RA70 to RA76 aided the postal clerks' tuberculosis fund.

Nos. 396 and 399 Surcharged in Carmine

1946

RA77 A72 20d on 40 l .40 .20
a. Pair, one without surcharge 25.00
RA78 A69 20d on 5 l 1.00 .20

Same Surcharge in Carmine on Nos. RA62 and RA63

1946-47 Unwmk. *Perf. 13½x12*

RA79 PT7 50d on 50 l ('47) .20 .20
a. Inverted surcharge 25.00
RA80 PT7 50d on 1d .20 .20
a. Violet black surcharge 4.00 1.00

The tax on Nos. RA77 to RA80 was for the Postal Clerks' Welfare Fund.

Nos. RA65 and RA62 Surcharged in Carmine

1947

RA81 50d on 50 l (RA65) 1.50 .20
RA81A 50d on 50 l (RA62) 32.50 32.50

Tax for the postal clerks' tuberculosis fund.

St. Demetrius — PT8

1948 Litho. *Perf. 12x13½*

RA82 PT8 50d yellow brown .20 .20

Obligatory on all domestic mail. The tax was for restoration of historical monuments and churches destroyed during World War II.

Nos. 397 and 413 Surcharged in Blue

1950 Wmk. 252

RA83 A70 50d on 10 l (#397) 1.00 .20
a. Stamp with double frame 8.00
b. Surcharge reading down 18.00 18.00
RA84 A70 50d on 10 l (#413) 1.00 .20
a. Surcharge reading down 16.00 16.00

Tax for the Postal Clerks' Welfare Fund.

No. 396 Surcharged in Carmine

1951 *Perf. 13½x12*

RA85 A69 50d on 5 l 2.00 .20

Tax for the Postal Employees' Welfare Fund.

No. 392 Surcharged in Black

1951 Wmk. 252 Perf. 12½x12

RA86	A67	50d on 3d red brn	2.00	.20
a.		Pair, one without surcharge	30.00	
b.		"50" omitted	18.00	

Tax for the postal clerks' tuberculosis fund.

No. 393 Surcharged in Carmine

1952

RA87	A67	100d on 8d deep blue	1.00	.20

The tax was for the State Welfare Fund.

Ruins of Church of Phaneromeni, Zante — PT9

Zeus on Macedonian Coin of Philip II — PT10

500d, Map & scene of destruction, Argostoli.

1953 Wmk. 252 Litho. Perf. 12½

RA88	PT9	300d indigo & pale grn	.80	.20
RA89	PT9	500d dk brn & buff	3.00	.40

The tax was for the reconstruction of Cephalonia, Ithaca, and Zante, Ionian Islands destroyed by earthquake.

1956 Perf. 13½

Design: 1d, Aristotle.

RA90	PT10	50 l dk car rose	.35	.20
a.		Imperf., pair	100.00	
RA91	PT10	1d brt blue	.90	.60

Tax for archaeological research in Macedonia. The coin on No. RA90 portrays Zeus despite inscription of Philip's name.

POSTAL TAX SEMI-POSTAL STAMPS

Child — PTSP1

Mother and Child — PTSP2

Virgin and Christ Child — PTSP3

Perf. 12x13½

1943 Wmk. 252 Litho.

RAB1	PTSP1	25d + 25d bl grn	.20	.20
RAB2	PTSP2	100d + 50d rose vio	.20	.20
RAB3	PTSP3	200d + 100d red brn	.20	.20
		Nos. RAB1-RAB3 (3)	.60	.60

Surtax aided needy children. These stamps were compulsory on domestic mail in Oct. 1943.

OCCUPATION AND ANNEXATION STAMPS

During the Balkan wars, 1912-13, Greece occupied certain of the Aegean Islands and part of Western Turkey. She subsequently acquired these territories and they were known as the New Greece.

Most of the special issues for the Aegean Islands were made by order of the military commanders.

For Use in the Aegean Islands Occupied by Greece

CHIOS

Greece No. 221 Overprinted in Red

Serrate Roulette 13½

1913 Litho. Unwmk.

N1	A25	25 l ultramarine	45.00	45.00
a.		Inverted overprint	200.00	150.00
b.		Greek "L" instead of "D"	200.00	150.00

ICARIA (NICARIA)

Penelope — I1

1912 Unwmk. Litho. Perf. 11½

N2	I1	2 l orange	1.00	1.50
N3	I1	5 l blue green	1.00	1.50
N4	I1	10 l rose	1.00	1.50
N5	I1	25 l ultra	1.00	1.50
N6	I1	50 l gray lilac	1.25	3.00
N7	I1	1d dark brown	2.00	9.00
N8	I1	2d claret	3.00	15.00
N9	I1	5d slate	4.50	22.50
		Nos. N2-N9 (8)	14.75	55.50

Counterfeits of Nos. N1-N15 are plentiful.

Stamps of Greece, 1911-23, Overprinted Reading Up

1913 Engr.

On Issue of 1911-21

N10	A25	2 l car rose	20.00	20.00
N11	A24	3 l vermilion	20.00	20.00

Litho.

On Issue of 1912-23

N12	A24	1 l green	20.00	20.00
N13	A24	3 l vermilion	20.00	20.00
N14	A26	5 l green	20.00	20.00
N15	A24	10 l carmine	20.00	20.00
		Nos. N10-N15 (6)	120.00	120.00

LEMNOS

Regular Issues of Greece Overprinted in Black

On Issue of 1901

1912 Wmk. 129 Engr. Perf. 13½

N16	A11	20 l red lilac	1.40	1.40

On Issue of 1911-21

Unwmk.

Serrate Roulette 13½

N17	A24	1 l green	.70	.70
N18	A25	2 l carmine rose	.70	.70
N19	A24	3 l vermilion	.70	.70
N20	A26	5 l green	.70	.70
N21	A24	10 l car rose	.70	.70
N22	A25	20 l gray lilac	.70	.70
N23	A25	25 l ultra	1.00	1.00
N24	A26	30 l car rose	1.00	1.00
N25	A25	40 l deep blue	2.00	2.00
N26	A26	50 l dl violet	2.00	2.00
N27	A27	1d ultra	3.75	3.75
N28	A27	2d vermilion	15.00	15.00
N29	A27	3d car rose	18.00	18.00
N30	A27	5d ultra	22.50	22.50
N31	A27	10d deep blue	82.50	82.50
N32	A28	25d deep blue	82.50	82.50

On Issue of 1912-23

Litho.

N33	A24	1 l green	.30	.30
a.		Without period after "Ellas"	125.00	125.00
N34	A26	5 l green	.30	.30
N35	A24	10 l carmine	.30	.30
N36	A25	25 l ultra	1.50	1.50
		Nos. N16-N36 (21)	238.25	238.25

Red Overprint

On Issue of 1911-21

Engr.

N37	A25	2 l car rose	.70	.70
N38	A24	3 l vermilion	.70	.70
N39	A25	20 l gray lilac	1.75	1.75
N40	A26	30 l car rose	3.00	3.00
N41	A25	40 l deep blue	3.00	3.00
N42	A26	50 l dull violet	3.00	3.00
N43	A27	1d ultra	3.50	3.50
N44	A27	2d vermilion	30.00	30.00
N45	A27	3d car rose	19.00	19.00
N46	A27	5d ultra	35.00	35.00
N47	A27	10d deep blue	85.00	85.00
N48	A28	25d deep blue	85.00	85.00

On Issue of 1912-23

Litho.

N49	A24	1 l green	.70	.70
a.		Without period after "Ellas"	125.00	125.00
N50	A26	5 l green	.30	.30
N51	A24	10 l carmine	1.40	1.40
N52	A25	25 l ultra	1.75	1.75
		Nos. N37-N52 (16)	273.80	273.80

The overprint is found inverted or double on many of Nos. N16-N52. There are several varieties in the overprint: Greek "D" for "L," large Greek "S" or "O," and small "O."

No. N49 with Added "Greek Administration" Overprint, as on Nos. N109-N148, in Black

1913

N52A	A24	1 l green	22.50	22.50

Counterfeits of #N16-N52A are plentiful.

MYTILENE (LESBOS)

Turkey Nos. 162, 158 Overprinted in Blue

Perf. 12, 13½ and Compound

1912 Typo. Unwmk.

N53	A21	20pa rose	22.50	22.50
N54	A21	10pi dull red	110.00	110.00

On Turkey Nos. P68, 151-155, 137, 157-158 in Black

N55	A21	2pa olive green	2.00	2.00
N56	A21	5pa ocher	2.00	2.00
N57	A21	10pa blue green	2.00	2.00
N58	A21	20pa rose	2.00	2.00
N59	A21	1pi ultra	4.00	4.00
N60	A21	2pi blue black	22.50	22.50
N61	A19	2½pi dk brown	11.00	11.00
N62	A21	5pi dk violet	22.50	22.50
N63	A21	10pi dull red	110.00	110.00
		Nos. N55-N63 (9)	178.00	178.00

On Turkey Nos. 161-163, 145 in Black

N64	A21	10pa blue green	4.00	4.00
a.		Double overprint	35.00	
N65	A21	20pa rose	4.00	4.00
N66	A21	1pi ultra	4.00	4.00
N67	A19	2pi blue black	47.50	47.50

Nos. N55, N58, N65, N59 Surcharged in Blue or Black

N68	A21	25 l on 2pa	7.50	7.50
a.		New value inverted	40.00	
N69	A21	50 l on 20pa	10.00	10.00
b.		New value inverted	45.00	
N70	A21	1d on 20pa (N65) (Bk)	20.00	20.00
a.		New value inverted	45.00	
N71	A21	2d on 1pi (Bk)	22.50	22.50
a.		New value inverted		

Same Overprint on Turkey No. J49

N72	A19	1pi blk, *dp rose*	50.00	50.00

The overprint is found on all values reading up or down with inverted "i" in the first word and inverted "e" in the third word.

No. N72 was only used for postage.

Counterfeits of Nos. N53-N72 are plentiful.

SAMOS

Issues of the Provisional Government

Map of Samos OS1

1912 Unwmk. Typo. Imperf.

N73	OS1	5 l gray green	20.00	5.50
N74	OS1	10 l red	20.00	5.50
N75	OS1	25 l blue	40.00	20.00
a.		25 l green (error)	500.00	600.00
		Nos. N73-N75 (3)	80.00	31.00

Nos. N73-N75 exist in tête bêche pairs. Value per set, $500 unused, $250 used.

Counterfeits exist of Nos. N73 to N75.

Hermes — OS2

1912 Litho. Perf. 11½

Without Overprint

N76	OS2	1 l gray	3.00	1.50
N77	OS2	5 l lt green	3.75	1.50
N78	OS2	10 l rose	4.00	1.50
b.		Half used as 5 l on cover		15.00
N79	OS2	25 l lt blue	7.00	1.50
N80	OS2	50 l violet brn	12.50	10.00

With Overprint

N81	OS2	1 l gray	1.00	1.10
N82	OS2	5 l blue grn	1.00	1.10
N83	OS2	10 l rose	1.75	1.50
b.		Half used as 5 l on cover		20.00
N84	OS2	25 l blue	2.00	2.00
N85	OS2	50 l violet brn	11.00	6.50
N86	OS2	1d orange	10.00	10.00
		Nos. N76-N86 (11)	57.00	38.20

For overprints and surcharge see Nos. N92-N103.

Imperf., Pairs

Without Overprint

N76a	OS2	1 l	40.00	
N77a	OS2	5 l	40.00	
N78a	OS2	10 l	40.00	
N79a	OS2	25 l	40.00	
N80a	OS2	50 l	40.00	

With Overprint

N81a	OS2	1 l	100.00	
N82a	OS2	5 l	100.00	
N83a	OS2	10 l	100.00	
N85a	OS2	50 l	100.00	100.00

Church in Savior's Name and Fort Ruins
OS3

Manuscript Initials in Red or Black

1913

No.	Type	Description	Unused	Used
N87	OS3	1d brown (R)	16.00	14.00
N88	OS3	2d deep blue (R)	16.00	14.00
N89	OS3	5d gray grn (R)	30.00	25.00
N90	OS3	10d yellow grn (R)	90.00	80.00
N91	OS3	25d red (Bk)	80.00	67.50
		Nos. N87-N91 (5)	232.00	200.50

Victory of the Greek fleet in 1824 and the union with Greece of Samos in 1912. The manuscript initials are those of Pres. Themistokles Sofulis.

Values the same for copies without initials.

Exist imperf. Counterfeits of Nos. N87-N91 are plentiful.

For overprints see Nos. N104-N108.

Nos. N76 to N80 Overprinted

1914

No.	Type	Description	Unused	Used
N92	OS2	1 l gray	4.00	4.00
N93	OS2	5 l lt green	4.00	4.00
N94	OS2	10 l rose	4.25	4.00
a.		Double overprint	60.00	
N95	OS2	25 l lt blue	12.00	12.00
N96	OS2	50 l violet brn	8.00	8.00
a.		Double overprint	100.00	
		Nos. N92-N96 (5)	32.25	32.00

Charity Issues of Greek Administration

Nos. N81 to N86 Overprinted in Red or Black

1915

No.	Type	Description	Unused	Used
N97	OS2	1 l gray (R)	20.00	20.00
a.		Black overprint	125.00	
N98	OS2	5 l blue grn (Bk)	.80	.80
a.		Red overprint	125.00	
b.		Double overprint	125.00	
N99	OS2	10 l rose (Bk)	.90	.90
a.		Red overprint	125.00	
b.		Inverted overprint	125.00	
N100	OS2	25 l blue (Bk)	.80	.80
a.		Red overprint	125.00	
N101	OS2	50 l violet brn (Bk)	1.00	1.00
a.		Red overprint	125.00	
N102	OS2	1d orange (R)	2.00	2.00
a.		Inverted overprint	125.00	
b.		Black overprint	100.00	
c.		Double black overprint	150.00	

No. N102 With Additional Surcharge in Black

No.	Type	Description	Unused	Used
N103	OS2	1 l on 1d orange	7.00	7.00
a.		Black surcharge double	150.00	
b.		Black surcharge inverted	150.00	
		Nos. N97-N103 (7)	32.50	32.50

Issue of 1913 Overprinted in Red or Black

1915

No.	Type	Description	Unused	Used
N104	OS3	1d brown (R)	15.00	15.00
N105	OS3	2d dp blue (R)	20.00	20.00
a.		Double overprint		
N106	OS3	5d gray grn (R)	40.00	40.00
N107	OS3	10d yellow grn (Bk)	45.00	45.00
a.		Inverted overprint		
N108	OS3	25d red (Bk)	600.00	600.00
		Nos. N104-N108 (5)	720.00	720.00

Nos. N97 to N108 inclusive have an embossed control mark, consisting of a cross encircled by a Greek inscription.

Most copies of Nos. N104-N108 lack the initials.

Counterfeits of Nos. N104-N108 are plentiful.

FOR USE IN PARTS OF TURKEY OCCUPIED BY GREECE (NEW GREECE)

Regular Issues of Greece Overprinted

Black Overprint Meaning "Greek Administration"

On Issue of 1901

1912 Wmk. 129 Engr. *Perf. 13½*

No.	Type	Description	Unused	Used
N109	A11	20 l red lilac	2.00	2.00

On Issue of 1911-21

Unwmk.

Serrate Roulette 13½

No.	Type	Description	Unused	Used
N110	A24	1 l green	.60	.50
N111	A25	2 l car rose	.60	.50
N112	A24	3 l vermilion	.60	.50
N113	A26	5 l green	.60	.50
N114	A24	10 l car rose	1.00	.80
N115	A25	20 l gray lilac	1.50	.80
N116	A25	25 l ultra	2.00	1.00
N117	A26	30 l car rose	2.25	2.25
N118	A25	40 l deep blue	3.25	2.00
N119	A26	50 l dl violet	3.25	2.00
N120	A27	1d ultra	6.50	2.00
N121	A27	2d vermilion	30.00	25.00
N122	A27	3d car rose	30.00	30.00
N123	A27	5d ultra	12.00	10.00
N124	A27	10d deep blue	200.00	200.00
N125	A28	25d dp bl, ovpt. horiz.	125.00	125.00

On Issue of 1913-23

Litho.

No.	Type	Description	Unused	Used
N126	A24	1 l green	.60	.60
b.		Without period after "Ellas"	100.00	100.00
N127	A26	5 l green	.60	.50
N128	A24	10 l carmine	1.40	.70
N129	A25	25 l blue	3.25	2.00
		Nos. N109-N129 (21)	427.00	408.65

Red Overprint

On Issue of 1911-21

Engr.

No.	Type	Description	Unused	Used
N130	A24	1 l green	.80	.80
N131	A25	2 l car rose	6.00	4.00
N132	A24	3 l vermilion	5.00	4.00
N133	A26	5 l green	.90	.70
N134	A25	20 l gray lilac	6.00	1.50
N135	A25	25 l ultra	45.00	45.00
N136	A26	30 l car rose	20.00	15.00
N137	A25	40 l deep blue	3.00	2.25
N138	A26	50 l dl violet	3.00	3.00
N139	A27	1d ultra	12.00	6.00
N140	A27	2d vermilion	45.00	40.00
N141	A27	3d car rose	20.00	17.00
N142	A27	5d ultra	250.00	225.00
N143	A27	10d deep blue	25.00	20.00
N144	A28	25d dp bl, ovpt. horiz.	50.00	50.00
a.		Vertical overprint	200.00	200.00

On Issue of 1913-23

Litho.

No.	Type	Description	Unused	Used
N145	A24	1 l green	5.00	5.00
a.		Without period after "Ellas"	125.00	
N146	A26	5 l green	.85	.85
N147	A24	10 l carmine	40.00	35.00
N148	A25	25 l blue	2.25	1.75
		Nos. N130-N148 (19)	539.80	476.85

The normal overprint is vertical, reading upward on N109-N124, N126-N143, N145-N148. It is often double or reading downward. There are numerous broken, missing and wrong font letters with a Greek "L" instead of "D" as the first letter of the second word.

Counterfeits exist of Nos. N109-N148.

Cross of Constantine
O1

Eagle of Zeus
O2

1912 Litho.

No.	Type	Description	Unused	Used
N150	O1	1 l brown	.25	.20
N151	O2	2 l red	.25	.20
a.		2 l rose	.30	.20
N153	O2	3 l orange	.30	.20
N154	O1	5 l green	1.25	.20
N155	O1	10 l rose red	5.00	.20
N156	O1	20 l violet	11.00	2.25
N157	O2	25 l pale blue	2.00	.75
N158	O1	30 l gray grn	42.50	2.00
N159	O2	40 l indigo	6.00	4.00
N160	O1	50 l dark blue	3.00	2.50
N161	O2	1d violet brn	4.00	2.50
N162	O1	2d gray brn	40.00	7.00
N163	O2	3d dull blue	100.00	20.00
N164	O1	5d gray	100.00	25.00
N165	O2	10d carmine	100.00	*160.00*
N166	O1	25d gray blk	100.00	*160.00*
		Nos. N150-N166 (16)	515.55	*387.00*

Occupation of Macedonia, Epirus and some of the Aegean Islands.

Sold only in New Greece.

Dangerous forgeries of #N165-N166 exist.

In 1916 some stamps of this issue were overprinted in Greek: "I (era) Koinotis Ag (iou) Orous" for the Mount Athos Monastery District. They were never placed in use and most of them were destroyed.

For surcharges and overprints see Nos. 267-276A, RA14-RA16, Thrace 31-33.

Imperf., Pairs Without Overprint

No.	Type	Description	Value
N150a	O1	1 l	500.00
N151b	O2	2 l	500.00
N153a	O2	3 l	500.00
N154a	O1	5 l	200.00
N155a	O1	10 l	200.00
N156a	O1	20 l	1,750.
N157a	O2	25 l	1,750.
N158a	O1	30 l	1,750.
N159a	O2	40 l	1,750.
N163a	O2	3d	*2,500.*

CAVALLA

ΕΛΛΗΝΙΚΗ
ΔΙΟΙΚΗΣΙΣ

Bulgaria Nos. 89-97 Surcharged in Red

25 ΛΕΠΤΑ 25

1913 Unwmk. Engr. *Perf. 12*

No.	Type	Description	Unused	Used
N167	A20	5 l on 1s	*13.50*	*13.50*
N169	A25	10 l on 15s	*50.00*	*50.00*
N170	A26	10 l on 25s	*15.00*	*15.00*
N171	A21	15 l on 2s	*25.00*	*25.00*
N172	A22	20 l on 3s	*25.00*	*25.00*
N173	A23	25 l on 5s	*10.50*	*8.50*
N174	A24	50 l on 10s	*13.50*	*8.50*
N175	A25	1d on 15s	*80.00*	*60.00*
N176	A27	1d on 30s	*60.00*	*30.00*
N177	A28	1d on 50s	*100.00*	*50.00*

Blue Surcharge

No.	Type	Description	Unused	Used
N178	A24	50 l on 10s	*13.50*	*9.00*
		Nos. N167-N178 (11)	*406.00*	*294.50*

The counterfeits and reprints of Nos. N167-N178 are difficult to distinguish from originals. Many overprint varieties exist.

Some specialists question the status of Nos. N167-N178.

DEDEAGATCH

(Alexandroupolis)

ΕΛΛΗΝΙΚΗ
ΔΙΟΙΚΗΣΙΣ
ΔΕΔΕΑΓΑΤΣ
ΔΕΚΑ ΛΕΠΤΑ

D1-(10 lepta)

1913 Unwmk. Typeset *Perf. 11½*

Control Mark in Red

No.	Type	Description	Unused	Used
N179	D1	5 l black	35.00	30.00
N180	D1	10 l black	4.00	4.00
N181	D1	25 l black	4.00	4.00
a.		Sheet of 8	100.00	100.00
		Nos. N179-N181 (3)	43.00	38.00

Nos. N179-N181 issued without gum in sheets of 8, consisting of one 5 l, three 10 l normal, one 10 l inverted, three 25 l and one blank. The sheet yields se-tenant pairs of 5 l & 10 l, 10 l & 25 l; tete beche pairs of 5 l & 10 l, 10 l & 25 l and 10 l & 10 l.

Also issued imperf., value $175 unused, $125 canceled.

The 5 l reads "PENTE LEPTA" in Greek letters; the 10 l is illustrated; the 25 l carries the numeral "25."

Bulgaria Nos. 89-90, 92-93, 95 Surcharged

Red Surcharge

1913 *Perf. 12*

No.	Type	Description	Unused	Used
N182	A20	5 l on 1s	60.00	42.50
N183	A26	1d on 25s	60.00	42.50

Blue Surcharge

No.	Type	Description	Unused	Used
N184	A24	10 l on 10s	30.00	25.00
N185	A23	25 l on 5s	32.50	25.00
N187	A21	50 l on 2s	60.00	42.50
		Nos. N182-N185,N187 (5)	242.50	177.50

The surcharges on Nos. N182 to N187 are printed from a setting of eight, which was used for all, with the necessary changes of value. No. 6 in the setting has a Greek "L" instead of "D" for the third letter of the third word of the surcharge.

The 25 l surcharge also exists on 8 copies of the 25s, Bulgaria No. 95.

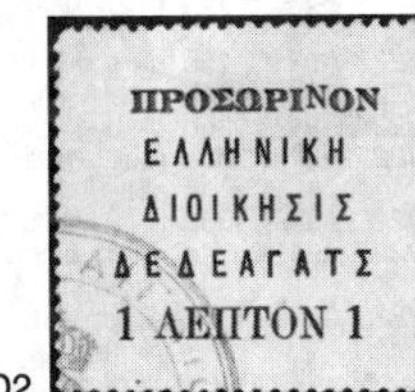

D2

ΠΡΟΣΩΡΙΝΟΝ
ΕΛΛΗΝΙΚΗ
ΔΙΟΙΚΗΣΙΣ
ΔΕΔΕΑΓΑΤΣ
5 ΛΕΠΤΑ 5

D3

1913, Sept. 15 Typeset *Perf. 11½*

Control Mark in Blue

No.	Type	Description	Value
N188	D2	1 l blue	65.00
N189	D2	2 l blue	65.00
N190	D2	3 l blue	65.00
N191	D2	5 l blue	65.00
N192	D2	10 l blue	65.00
N193	D2	25 l blue	65.00
N194	D2	40 l blue	65.00
N195	D2	50 l blue	65.00
		Nos. N188-N195 (8)	520.00

Issued without gum in sheets of 8 containing all values.

1913, Sept. 25 Typeset

Control Mark in Blue

No.	Type	Description	Value
N196	D3	1 l blue, *gray blue*	65.00
N197	D3	5 l blue, *gray blue*	65.00
N198	D3	10 l blue, *gray blue*	65.00
N199	D3	25 l blue, *gray blue*	65.00
N200	D3	30 l blue, *gray blue*	65.00
N201	D3	50 l blue, *gray blue*	65.00
		Nos. N196-N201 (6)	390.00

Nos. N196 to N201 were issued without gum in sheets of six containing all values.

Counterfeits of Nos. N182-N201 are plentiful.

FOR USE IN NORTH EPIRUS (ALBANIA)

Greek Stamps of 1937-38 Overprinted in Black

Perf. 13½x12, 12x13½

1940 Litho. Wmk. 252

N202 A69 5 l brn red & bl .20 .20
a. Inverted overprint 50.00
N203 A70 10 l bl & brn red (No. 413) .20 .20
a. Double impression of frame 10.00
N204 A71 20 l blk & grn .20 .20
a. Inverted overprint 50.00
N205 A72 40 l grn & blk .20 .20
a. Inverted overprint 50.00
N206 A73 50 l brn & blk .20 .20
N207 A74 80 l ind & yel brn .20 .20
N208 A67 1d green .20 .20
a. Inverted overprint 35.00
N209 A75 2d ultra .20 .20
N210 A67 3d red brn .20 .20
N211 A76 5d red .20 .20
N212 A77 6d ol brn .20 .20
N213 A78 7d dk brn .40 .40
N214 A67 8d deep blue .55 .55
N215 A79 10d red brn .55 .55
N216 A80 15d green .95 .95
N217 A81 25d dark blue 1.10 1.10
a. Inverted overprint *90.00*

Engr.

Unwmk.

N218 A84 30d org brn 2.75 2.75
Nos. N202-N218 (17) 8.50 8.50

Same Overprinted in Carmine on National Youth Issue

1941 Litho. *Perf. 12½, 13½x12½*

N219 A93 3d sil, dp ultra & red 1.00 1.00
N220 A94 5d dk bl & blk 1.60 1.60
N221 A94 10d red org & blk 2.00 2.00
N222 A94 15d dk grn & blk 26.00 26.00
N223 A94 20d lake & blk 3.25 3.25
N224 A94 25d dk bl & blk 6.50 6.50
N225 A94 30d rose vio & blk 6.50 6.50
N226 A94 50d lake & blk 6.50 6.50
N227 A94 75d dk bl, brn & gold 6.50 6.50
N228 A93 100d sil, dp ultra & red 6.50 6.50
a. Inverted overprint *175.00*
Nos. N219-N228 (10) 66.35 66.35

Same Overprint in Carmine on National Youth Air Post Stamps

N229 AP25 2d red org & blk .65 .65
a. Inverted overprint *75.00*
N230 AP25 4d dk grn & blk 3.25 3.25
a. Inverted overprint *150.00*
N231 AP25 6d lake & blk 3.25 3.25
a. Inverted overprint *150.00*
N232 AP25 8d dk bl & blk 3.25 3.25
N233 AP25 16d rose vio & blk 5.00 5.00
N234 AP25 32d red org & blk 5.00 5.00
N235 AP25 45d dk grn & blk 6.50 6.50
N236 AP25 55d lake & blk 6.50 6.50
N237 AP25 65d dk bl & blk 6.50 6.50
N238 AP25 100d rose vio & blk 6.50 6.50
Nos. N229-N238 (10) 46.40 46.40

Some specialists have questioned the status of Nos. N230a and N231a.

For other stamps issued by Greece for use in occupied parts of Epirus and Thrace, see the catalogue listings of those countries.

Catalogue values for unused stamps in this section, from this point to the end of the section, are for Never Hinged items.

FOR USE IN THE DODECANESE ISLANDS

Greece, No. 472C, with Additional Overprint in Carmine or Silver

1947 Wmk. 252 Litho. *Perf. 12½*

N239 A113 10d on 2,000d (C) .30 .30
N240 A113 10d on 2,000d (S) .30 .30

These stamps sold for 5 lire (100 drachmas) and paid postage for that amount.

King George II Memorial Issue

Greece, Nos. 484 and 485, With Additional Overprint in Black

1947 Engr. *Perf. 12½x12*

N241 A67 50d on 1d green .75 .75
N242 A67 250d on 3d red brown .75 .75

The letters are initials of the Greek words for "Military Administration of the Dodecanese."

Greece, Nos. 501 and 502 Overprinted in Carmine

1947 Wmk. 252 Litho. *Perf. 12½*

N243 A111 20d on 500d dk ol .40 .40
N244 A104 30d on 5d lt bl grn .60 .60

Greece, Nos. 437, 406, 407 and 445, Surcharged in Black or Carmine

1947 *Perf. 12½, 13½x12*

N245 A103 50d on 2d .70 .70

Engr.

N246 A79 250d on 10d 1.40 1.40
N247 A80 400d on 15d (C) 1.75 1.75
a. Inverted surcharge 150.00

Litho.

N248 A110 1000d on 200 (C) .85 .85
a. Imprint omitted 40.00
Nos. N245-N248 (4) 4.70 4.70

POSTAGE DUE STAMPS

FOR USE IN PARTS OF TURKEY OCCUPIED BY GREECE (NEW GREECE)

Postage Due Stamps of Greece, 1902, Overprinted

1912 Wmk. 129 Engr. *Perf. 13½*

Black Overprint

NJ1 D3 1 l chocolate .40 .40
NJ2 D3 2 l gray .40 .40
NJ3 D3 3 l orange .40 .40
NJ4 D3 5 l yel grn .40 .40
NJ5 D3 10 l scarlet 1.00 1.00
NJ6 D3 20 l lilac 1.00 1.00
NJ7 D3 30 l dp vio 2.00 2.00
NJ8 D3 40 l dk brn 3.50 3.50
NJ9 D3 50 l red brn 5.00 5.00
NJ10 D3 1d black 20.00 20.00
NJ11 D3 2d bronze 15.00 8.00
NJ12 D3 3d silver 42.50 42.50
NJ13 D3 5d gold 85.00 85.00
Nos. NJ1-NJ13 (13) 176.60 169.60

Red Overprint

NJ14 D3 1 l chocolate .60 .60
NJ15 D3 2 l gray .60 .60
NJ16 D3 3 l orange .40 .40
NJ17 D3 5 l yel grn .60 .50
NJ18 D3 10 l scar, down 4.00 4.00
NJ19 D3 20 l lilac .60 .60
NJ20 D3 30 l dp vio 3.50 2.25
NJ21 D3 40 l dk brn .60 .50
NJ22 D3 50 l red brn .60 .50
NJ23 D3 1d black 6.00 4.00
NJ24 D3 2d bronze 6.00 6.00
NJ25 D3 3d silver 12.50 12.50
NJ26 D3 5d gold 25.00 25.00
Nos. NJ14-NJ26 (13) 61.00 57.45

The normal position of the overprint is reading upward but it is often reversed. Some of the varieties of lettering which occur on the postage stamps are also found on the postage due stamps. Double overprints exist on some denominations.

FOR USE IN NORTH EPIRUS (ALBANIA)

Postage Due Stamps of Greece, 1930, Surcharged or Overprinted in Black:

a

b

Perf. 13, 13x12½

1940 Litho. Unwmk.

NJ27 D3(a) 50 l on 25d lt red .80 .80
NJ28 D3(b) 2d light red .80 .80
a. Inverted overprint 40.00
NJ29 D3(b) 5d blue gray .80 .80
NJ30 D3(b) 10d green 1.00 1.00
NJ31 D3(b) 15d red brown .80 .80
Nos. NJ27-NJ31 (5) 4.20 4.20

POSTAL TAX STAMPS

FOR USE IN NORTH EPIRUS (ALBANIA)

Postal Tax Stamps of Greece, Nos. RA61-RA63, Overprinted Type "b" in Black

1940 Unwmk. Litho. *Perf. 13½x12*

NRA1 PT7 10 l .20 .20
NRA2 PT7 50 l .20 .20
a. Inverted overprint 50.00
NRA3 PT7 1d .40 .40
Nos. NRA1-NRA3 (3) .80 .80

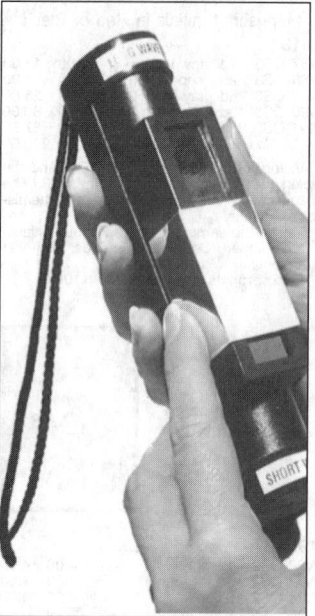

GREENLAND

ˈgrēn-lənd

LOCATION — North Atlantic Ocean
GOVT. — Danish
AREA — 840,000 sq. mi.
POP. — 56,076 (1998)
CAPITAL — Nuuk (Godthaab)

In 1953 the colony of Greenland became an integral part of Denmark.

100 Ore = 1 Krone

Catalogue values for unused stamps in this country are for Never Hinged items, beginning with Scott 28 in the regular postage section, Scott B1 in the semi-postal section.

Christian X — A1

Polar Bear — A2

Perf. 13x12½

1938-46 Unwmk. Engr.

1	A1	1o olive black	.20	.20
2	A1	5o rose lake	1.50	1.10
3	A1	7o yellow green	2.40	2.75
4	A1	10o purple	.70	.55
5	A1	15o red	.70	.55
6	A1	20o red ('46)	1.00	1.10
7	A2	30o blue	4.25	5.50
8	A2	40o blue ('46)	14.50	6.25
9	A2	1k light brown	4.75	7.00
		Nos. 1-9 (9)	30.00	25.00
		Set, never hinged	57.50	

Issue dates: Nov. 1, 1938, Aug. 1, 1946.

For surcharges see Nos. 39-40.

Harp Seal — A3

Christian X — A4

Dog Team — A5

Designs: 1k, Polar bear. 2k, Eskimo in kayak. 5k, Eider duck.

1945, Feb. 1 ***Perf. 12***

10	A3	1o ol blk & vio	15.00	20.00
11	A3	5o rose lake & ol bister	15.00	20.00
12	A3	7o green & blk	15.00	20.00
13	A4	10o purple & olive	15.00	20.00
14	A4	15o red & brt ultra	15.00	20.00
15	A5	30o dk blue & red brn	15.00	20.00
16	A5	1k brown & gray blk	15.00	20.00
17	A5	2k sepia & dp grn	15.00	20.00
18	A5	5k dk pur & dl brn	15.00	20.00
		Nos. 10-18 (9)	135.00	180.00
		Set, never hinged	247.50	

Nos. 10-18 Overprinted in Carmine or Blue

1945

19	A3	1o (C)	30.00	35.00
20	A3	5o (Bl)	30.00	35.00
21	A3	7o (C)	30.00	35.00
22	A4	10o (Bl)	47.50	62.50
a.		Overprint in carmine	210.00	225.00
23	A4	15o (C)	45.00	62.50
a.		Overprint in blue	80.00	110.00
24	A5	30o (Bl)	45.00	62.50
a.		Overprint in carmine	80.00	110.00
25	A5	1k (C)	45.00	62.50
a.		Overprint in blue	80.00	110.00
26	A5	2k (C)	45.00	62.50
a.		Overprint in blue	80.00	110.00
27	A5	5k (Bl)	45.00	62.50
a.		Overprint in carmine	80.00	110.00
		Nos. 19-27 (9)	362.50	480.00
		Set, never hinged	700.00	
		Nos. 22a-27a (6)	610.00	775.00
		Set, never hinged	1,250.	

Liberation of Denmark from the Germans.

Overprint illustrated as on Nos. 19-21. Larger type and different settings used for Types A4 and A5. Overprint often smudged.

Nos. 19-27 exist with overprint inverted. Value, 1k, $700, 30o, $500, others, each $400.

Catalogue values for unused stamps in this section, from this point to the end of the section, are for Never Hinged items.

Frederik IX — A6

Polar Ship "Gustav Holm" — A7

1950-60 Unwmk. Engr. ***Perf. 13***

28	A6	1o dark olive green	.20	.20
29	A6	5o deep carmine	.20	.20
30	A6	10o green	.20	.20
31	A6	15o purple	.30	.30
a.		15o dull purple	2.75	1.10
32	A6	25o vermilion	1.75	.75
33	A6	30o dark blue	21.00	1.50
34	A6	30o vermilion	.30	.20
35	A7	50o deep blue	37.50	9.75
36	A7	1k brown	10.00	2.10
37	A7	2k dull red	5.50	2.10
38	A7	5k gray	1.25	1.00
		Nos. 28-38 (11)	78.20	18.30

Issued: #28-30, 31a, 32, 35-37, 8/15/50; #33, 12/1/53; #38, 8/14/58; #34, 10/29/59; #31, 10/60.

For surcharges see Nos. B1-B2.

Nos. 8 and 9 Surcharged

1956, Mar. 8

39	A2	60o on 40o blue	5.00	1.50
40	A2	60o on 1k lt brown	50.00	6.50

Drum Dancer — A8

Designs: 50o, The Boy and the Fox. 60o, The Mother of the Sea. 80o, The Girl and the Eagle. 90o, The Great Northern Diver and the Raven.

1957-69 Engr. ***Perf. 13***

41	A8	35o gray olive	.90	.75
42	A8	50o brown red	.80	1.00
43	A8	60o blue	2.50	1.00
44	A8	80o light brown	.90	1.00
45	A8	90o dark blue	2.90	2.75
		Nos. 41-45 (5)	8.00	6.50

Issued: 35o, 3/16/61; 50o, 9/22/66; 60o, 5/2/57; 80o, 9/18/69; 90o, 11/23/67.

Hans Egede A9

Knud Rasmussen A10

1958, Nov. 5

46	A9	30o henna brown	7.50	1.50

200th anniv. of death of Hans Egede, missionary to Eskimos in Greenland.

1960, Nov. 24 ***Perf. 13***

47	A10	30o dull red	1.25	.90

50th anniv. of establishment by Rasmussen of the mission and trading station at Thule (Dundas).

Northern Lights and Crossed Anchors — A11

Frederick IX — A12

Polar Bear — A13

1963-68 Engr.

48	A11	1o gray	.20	.20
49	A11	5o rose claret	.20	.20
50	A11	10o green	.20	.20
51	A11	12o yellow grn	.20	.30
52	A11	15o rose vio	.55	.50
53	A12	20o ultra	2.50	2.10
54	A12	25o lt brown	.20	.20
55	A12	30o green	.20	.20
56	A12	35o dull red	.20	.20
57	A12	40o gray	.20	.20
58	A12	50o grnsh blue	6.25	4.50
59	A12	50o dark red	.20	.20
60	A12	60o rose claret	.20	.20
61	A12	80o orange	.55	.50
62	A13	1k brown	.40	.20
63	A13	2k dull red	2.50	.45
64	A13	5k dark blue	2.00	.75
65	A13	10k dull slate grn	2.50	.50
		Nos. 48-65 (18)	19.25	11.60

Issued: #48-52, 3/7/63; #53, 61, 7/25/63; #62-65, 9/17/643; #54, 56-58, 3/11/64; #59, 9/9/65; #60, 2/29/68; #55, 11/21/68.

Niels Bohr (1885-1962) and Atom Diagram — A14

1963, Nov. 21 Unwmk.

66	A14	35o red brown	.25	.25
67	A14	60o dark blue	3.25	3.25

50th anniv. of atom theory of Prof. Bohr.

A15

A16

1964, Nov. 26

68	A15	35o brown red	.50	.50

Samuel Kleinschmidt (1814-1886), philologist.

1967, June 10

69	A16	50o red	3.00	3.00

Wedding of Crown Princess Margrethe and Prince Henri de Monpezat.

Frederik IX and Map of Greenland — A17

1969, Mar. 11 Engr. ***Perf. 13***

70	A17	60o dull red	1.10	1.10

70th birthday of King Frederik IX.

Musk Ox — A18

Liberation Celebration at Jakobshaven A19

Designs: 1k, Right whale diving off Disko Island. 2k, Narwhal. 5k, Polar bear. 10k, Walruses.

1969-76 Engr. *Perf. 13*

71	A18	1k dark blue	.30	.30
72	A18	2k gray green	.55	.40
73	A18	5k blue	1.40	.55
74	A18	10k sepia	2.50	1.25
75	A18	25k greenish gray	6.50	2.50
		Nos. 71-75 (5)	11.25	5.00

Issued: 1k, 3/5/70; 2k, 2/20/75; 5k, 2/19/76; 10k, 2/15/73; 25k, 11/27/69.

1970, May 4

76	A19	60o red brown	1.75	1.75

Hans Egede and Gertrude Rask on the Haabet — A20

1971, May 6 Engr. *Perf. 13*

77	A20	60o brown red	1.50	1.50

250th anniv. of arrival of Hans Egede in Greenland and the beginning of its colonization.

Mail-carrying Kayaks — A21

Designs: 70o, Umiak (women's rowboat). 80o, Catalina seaplane dropping mail by parachute. 90o, Dog sled. 1k, Coaster Kununguak and pilot boat. 1.30k, Schooner Sokongen. 1.50k, Longboat off Greenland coast. 2k, Helicopter over mountains.

1971-77 Engr. *Perf. 13*

78	A21	50o green	.20	.20
79	A21	70o dull red ('72)	.30	.20
80	A21	80o black ('76)	.30	.20
81	A21	90o blue ('72)	.30	.20
82	A21	1k red ('76)	.30	.20
83	A21	1.30k dull bl ('75)	.55	.55
84	A21	1.50k gray grn ('74)	.45	.45
85	A21	2k blue ('77)	.70	.70
		Nos. 78-85 (8)	3.10	2.70

Issued: #78, 11/4; #81, 2/29; #79, 9/21; #84, 2/21; #83, 4/17; #80, 10/11; #85, 2/24.

Queen Margrethe — A22

1973-79 Engr. *Perf. 13*

86	A22	5o car rose ('78)	.20	.20
87	A22	10o gray green	.20	.20
a.		10o emerald ('89)	5.50	5.50
88	A22	60o sepia	.20	.20
89	A22	80o sepia ('79)	.30	.20
90	A22	90o red brown ('74)	.50	.50
91	A22	1k dark red ('77)	.30	.25
a.		Bklt. pane, 4 #87a, 6 #91b	30.00	
b.		1k carmine ('89)	2.00	2.00
92	A22	1.20k dk blue ('74)	.50	.50
93	A22	1.20k maroon ('78)	.40	.35
94	A22	1.30k dk blue ('77)	.40	.40
95	A22	1.30k red ('79)	.40	.35
96	A22	1.60k blue ('79)	.50	.50
97	A22	1.80k dl green ('78)	.50	.50
		Nos. 86-97 (12)	4.40	4.15

#86, 89, 93, 95-97 inscribed "Kalaallit Nunaat."

The background lines on Nos. 87, 91 are sharp and complete. On No. 87a, 91b they are irregular and broken.

Issue dates: Nos. 87-88, Apr. 16. Nos. 90, 92, Oct. 24. Nos. 91, 94, May 26. Nos. 86, 93, 97, Apr. 17. Nos. 89, 95-96, Mar. 29.

Trawler and Kayaks — A23

Falcon and Radar — A24

2k, Old Trade Buildings, Copenhagen, vert.

1974, May 16 Engr. *Perf. 13*

98	A23	1k lt red brown	.50	.40
99	A23	2k sepia	.60	.50

Royal Greenland Trade Dept. Bicentennial.

1975, Sept. 4 Engr. *Perf. 13*

100	A24	90o red	.35	.35

50th anniversary of Greenland's telecommunications system.

Sirius Sled Patrol A25

1975, Oct. 16 Engr. *Perf. 13*

101	A25	1.20k sepia	.35	.35

Sirius sled patrol in northeast Greenland, 25th anniversary.

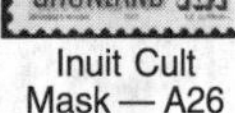

Inuit Cult Mask — A26

Jorgen Bronlund, Jakobshavn, Disko Bay — A27

Designs: 6k, Tupilac, a magical creature, carved whalebone. 7k, Soapstone sculpture. 8k, Eskimo with Family, driftwood sculpture, by Johannes Kreutzmann (1862-1940).

1977-80

102	A26	6k deep rose lilac	1.60	1.25
103	A26	7k gray olive	1.90	1.60
104	A26	8k dark blue	2.10	1.75
105	A26	9k black	2.40	1.90
		Nos. 102-105 (4)	8.00	6.50

Issue dates: 6k, Oct. 5, 1978. 7k, Sept. 6, 1979. 8k, Feb. 29, 1980. 9k, Sept. 6, 1977.

The 6k, 7k, 8k are inscribed "Kalaallit Nunaat."

1977, Oct. 20

106	A27	1k red brown	.30	.25

Jorgen Bronlund, arctic explorer, birth centenary.

Meteorite — A28

1978, Jan. 20 Engr. *Perf. 13*

107	A28	1.20k dull red	.40	.40

Scientific Research Commission, centenary.

Sun Rising over Mountains — A29

1978, June 5 Engr. *Perf. 13*

108	A29	1.50k dark blue	.45	.35

25th anniversary of Constitution.

Hans Egede, Settlers, Troops and Drummer A30

1978, Aug. 29 Engr. *Perf. 13*

109	A30	2.50k red brown	.75	.60

Founding of Godthaab, 250th anniversary.

A31

A32

1979, May 1 Engr.

110	A31	1.10k Navigator	.35	.35

Establishment of home rule, May 1, 1979.

1979, Oct. 18 Engr. *Perf. 13*

Eskimo Boy, aurora borealis, IYC emblem.

111	A32	2k olive green	.60	.50

International Year of the Child.

The Legend of the Reindeer and the Larva, by Jens Kreutzmann, 1860 — A33

Designs: 2.70k, Harpooning a Walrus, Jakob Danielsen. No. 114, Life in Thule, c. 1900, by Aninaaq. No. 115, Landscape, Ammassalik Fjord, Eastern Greenland, Peter Rosing (1892-1965). 3k, Footrace, woodcut by Aron from Kagec (1822-1869). 3.70k, Polar Bear Killing Seal Hunter, K. Andreassen (1890-1934). 9k, Hares Hunting, Gerhard Kleist (1855-1931).

1980-87 Engr. *Perf. 13*

112	A33	1.60k red	.45	.45
113	A33	2.70k deep violet	.75	.75
114	A33	2.80k lake	.60	.60
115	A33	2.80k lake	.75	.65
116	A33	3k black	.95	.95
117	A33	3.70k blue black	1.00	.95
118	A33	9k dark green	2.25	2.00
		Nos. 112-118 (7)	6.75	6.35

Issued: 1.60k, 3/26/81; 2.70k, 6/24/82; #114, 9/4/86; #115, 4/9/87; 3k, 9/4/80; 3.70k, 2/9/84; 9k, 9/5/85.

Queen Margrethe, Map of Greenland A34

1980-89 Engr. *Perf. 13*

120	A34	50o purple ('81)	.25	.25
a.		50o dull purple ('89)	6.00	6.00
121	A34	80o sepia	.25	.25
122	A34	1.30k red	.35	.35
123	A34	1.50k royal blue ('82)	.40	.40
124	A34	1.60k ultra	.45	.45
125	A34	1.80k dull red ('82)	.60	.40
126	A34	2.30k dk grn ('81)	.60	.55
127	A34	2.50k red ('83)	.60	.50
128	A34	2.80k copper red ('85)	1.25	.60
129	A34	3k fawn ('88)	1.40	.80
130	A34	3.20k rose ('89)	1.50	.90
a.		Bklt. pane of 10 (4 #120a, 6 #130)	30.00	
131	A34	3.80k slate blue ('85)	1.25	1.25
132	A34	4.10k brt blue ('88)	1.50	1.50
133	A34	4.40k ultra ('89)	1.75	1.75
		Nos. 120-133 (14)	12.15	9.95

Issued: #121-122, 124, 4/16; #120, 126, 1/29; #123, 125, 5/13; #127, 3/30; #128, 131, 2/7; #129, 132, 2/4; #130, 133, 1/30.

Rasmus Berthelsen (Teacher, Hymnist), in Training College Library, 1830 — A35

1980, May 29 Engr. *Perf. 13*

134	A35	2k brown, *cream*	.60	.50

Greenland Public Library Service, 150th anniv.

Ejnar Mikkelsen on board Gustav Holm, 1934 — A36

1980, Oct. 16 Engr. *Perf. 13*

135	A36	4k slate green	1.10	1.00

Ejnar Mikkelsen, inspector of East Greenland, birth centenary.

Pandalus Borealis — A37

Designs: No. 137, Anarhicas minor. No. 138, Reinhardtius Hippoglossoides. No. 139, Mallotus villosus. 25k, Codfish. 50k, Salmo salar.

1981-86 Engr. *Perf. 13*

136	A37	10k multicolored	2.50	1.25
137	A37	10k dk bl & blk	4.00	2.50
138	A37	10k multicolored	2.75	2.50
139	A37	10k grnsh blk & blk	2.75	2.50
140	A37	25k multicolored	5.75	2.50
141	A37	50k multicolored	13.50	6.25
		Nos. 136-141 (6)	31.25	17.50

Issued: 25k, 5/21; #136, 4/1/82; 50k, 1/27/83; #137, 10/11/84; #138, 10/10/85; #139, 10/16/86.

Saqqaq Eskimo in Kayak, Reindeer — A38

5k, Tunit-Dorset hunters hauling seal.

1981, Oct. 15 Engr. *Perf. 12½*

146	A38	3.50k dark blue	1.00	1.00
147	A38	5k brown	1.50	1.50

Thule District Eskimos Catching Whale, 1000AD — A39

Greenland history: No. 149, Bishop Joen Smyrill's house and staff, 12th cent. No. 150, Wooden dolls, 13th cent. No. 151, Eskimo mummy, sacrificial stones, 14th cent. No. 152, Hans Pothorst, explorer, 15th cent. No. 153, Glass pearls, 16th cent. No. 154, Apostle spoons, 17th cent. No. 155, Key, trading station, 18th cent. No. 156, Trade Ship Hvalfisken, masthead, 19th cent. No. 157, Communications satellite, Earth, 20th cent.

1982, Sept. 30

148	A39	2k brown red	.45	.45
149	A39	2.70k dark blue	.60	.60

1983, Sept. 15

150	A39	2.50k red	.55	.55
151	A39	3.50k brown	.80	.80
152	A39	4.50k blue	1.00	1.00

1984, Mar. 29

153	A39	2.70k red brown	.70	.70
154	A39	3.70k dark blue	.90	.90
155	A39	5.50k brown	1.40	1.40

1985, Mar. 21

156	A39	2.80k violet	.60	.60
157	A39	6k blue black	1.10	1.10
		Nos. 148-157,B10 (11)	9.10	9.10

250th Anniv. of Settlement of New Herrnhut — A40

1983, Nov. 2 Engr.

158	A40	2.50k brown	.80	.80

Henrik Lund, Natl. Anthem Score, Lichtenau Fjord — A41

1984, Sept. 6 **Engr.**

159 A41 5k dark green 1.75 1.75

Henrik Lund (1875-1948), natl. anthem composer, artist, only Greenlander to win Ingenio et Arti medal.

A42 A43

1984, June 6 **Engr.** ***Perf. 13***

160 A42 2.70k dull red 1.10 1.10

Prince Henrik, 50th birthday.

1984, July 25 **Engr.** ***Perf. 13***

161 A43 3.70k Danish grenadier, 1734 1.00 1.00

Town of Christianshab, 250th anniv.

Ingrid, Queen Mother of Denmark, Chrysanthemums — A44

1985, May 21 **Litho. & Engr.**

162 A44 2.80k multi .80 .80

Arrival in Denmark of Princess Ingrid, 50th anniv. See Denmark No. 775.

Intl. Youth Year — A45

1985, June 27 **Litho.**

163 A45 3.80k Emblem, birds nesting, fiord 1.00 1.00

Greenland Port Post Office, Flags — A46

1986, Mar. 6 **Engr.** ***Perf. 13***

164 A46 2.80k dark red .75 .75

Transfer of postal control under Greenland Home Rule, Jan. 1, 1986.

Artifacts — A47

1986-88 **Engr.** ***Perf. 13***

165 A47 2.80k Sewing needles, case .70 .60

165A A47 3k Buckets, bowl, scoop .75 .50

166 A47 3.80k Ulos .95 .85

167 A47 3.80k Masks .95 .85

168 A47 5k Harpoon points 1.40 .85

169 A47 6.50k Lard lamps 1.75 1.50

172 A47 10k Carved faces 2.50 1.75

Nos. 165-172 (7) 9.00 6.90

Issued: #166, 6.50k, May 22. 2.80k, 3.80k, June 11, 1987. 3k, 5k, 10k, Oct. 27, 1988.

This is an expanding set. Numbers will change if necessary.

Souvenir Sheet

HAFNIA '87 — A48

1987, Jan. 23 **Litho.** ***Perf. 13***

175 A48 Sheet of 3 6.00 6.00

a. 2.80k Gull in flight 1.60 1.60

b. 3.80k Mountain 1.90 1.90

c. 6.50k Gulls in water 2.25 2.25

No. 175 sold for 19.50k. See No. 199.

Year of the Fishing, Sealing and Whaling Industries — A49

1987, Apr. 9 **Litho.** ***Perf. 13***

176 A49 3.80k multi 1.00 .90

Lagopus Mutus — A50 Birds of Prey — A51

1987-90 **Litho.** ***Perf. 13***

177 A51 3k Falco rusticolus 1.25 1.10

178 A51 3.20k Clangula hyemalis 1.00 .80

179 A51 4k Anser caerulescens 1.10 .90

180 A51 4.10k Corvus corax 1.50 1.40

181 A51 4.40k Plectrophenax nivalis 1.25 1.25

182 A50 5k shown 1.40 1.25

183 A51 5.50k Haliaeetus albicilla 2.25 1.75

184 A51 5.50k Cepphus grylle 1.50 1.25

185 A51 6.50k Uria lomvia 2.00 1.60

186 A51 7k Gavia immer 2.40 1.75

187 A51 7.50k Stercorarius longicaudus 2.10 2.10

188 A50 10k Nyctea scandiaca 3.00 2.50

Nos. 177-188 (12) 20.75 17.65

Issued: 5k, 10k, 9/3; 3k, 4.10k, #183, 7k, 4/14/88 ; 3.20k, 4.40k, #184, 6.50k, 3/16/89 ; 4k, 7.50k, 1/15/90.

Plants — A52

1989-92 **Litho.** ***Perf. 13***

189 A52 4k *Campanula gieseckiana* 1.25 1.00

190 A52 4k *Pedicularis hirsuta* 1.40 1.00

191 A52 5k *Eriophorum scheuchzeri* 1.40 1.40

192 A52 5.50k *Ledum groenlandicum* 1.75 1.75

193 A52 6.50k *Cassiope tetragona* 2.25 2.10

194 A52 7.25k *Saxifraga oppositifolia* 2.25 2.25

196 A52 10k *Papaver radicatum*, vert. 2.75 2.00

Nos. 189-196 (7) 13.05 11.50

Issued: 5k, 10k, 10/12/89; #189, 5.50k, 6.50k, 6/7/90; #190, 7.25k, 3/26/92. #189-190 vert.

This is an expanding set. Numbers will change if necessary.

HAFNIA Type of 1987

Souvenir Sheet

Uummannaq Mountain in winter, horiz.

1987, Oct. 16 **Litho.** ***Perf. 13x12½***

199 A48 2.80k slate blue & lake 2.50 2.50

No. 199 sold for 4k.

Greenland Home Rule, 10th Anniv.

A53 A54

1989, May 1 **Litho.** ***Perf. 13***

200 A53 3.20k Flag, landscape .90 .80

201 A54 4.40k Coat of arms 1.25 1.25

Queen Margrethe — A55

Nos. 214, 217 Surcharged in Red or Blue

1990-96 **Engr.** ***Perf. 13***

214 A55 25o green .20 .20

217 A55 1k brown .30 .35

a. Bklt. pane, 4 #214, 6 #217 *12.50*

b. Bklt. pane, 4 each #214, 217 2.50

224 A55 4k carmine rose 1.25 1.25

225 A55 4.25k red *1.50* *1.50*

226 A55 4.25k on 25o #214 (R) *1.25* *1.25*

227 A55 4.50k on 1k #217 (Bl) 1.40 1.40

228 A55 6.50k blue 2.00 2.00

229 A55 7k violet 2.25 2.25

Nos. 214-229 (8) *10.15* *10.20*

Issued: #217a, 5/3/90; #217b, 9/9/93; 7k, 2/10/94; #225, 1996; #226-227, 12/31/95; others, 4/5/90.

No. 226 exists with inverted surcharge. Value, $600.

This is an expanding set. Numbers will change if necessary.

Frederik Lynge (1889-1957), Politician — A56

25k, Augo Lynge (1899-1959), politician

1990, Oct. 18 **Engr.** ***Perf. 13x12½***

231 A56 10k rose brn & dk bl 3.00 3.00

232 A56 25k vio & dk bl 7.00 7.00

See Nos. 242-243, 249.

Phoca Hispida — A57

Walrus and Seals.

Litho. & Engr.

1991, Mar. 14 ***Perf. 13***

233 A57 4k shown 1.25 1.25

234 A57 4k Pagophilus groenlandicus 1.25 1.25

235 A57 7.25k Cystophora cristata 2.25 2.25

236 A57 7.25k Odobenus rosmarus 2.25 2.25

237 A57 8.50k Erignatus barbatus 2.75 2.75

238 A57 8.50k Phoca vitulina 2.75 2.75

a. Miniature sheet of 6, #233-238 13.50 15.00

Nos. 233-238 (6) 12.50 12.50

Village of Ilulissat, 250th Anniv. — A58

1991, May 15 **Litho.** ***Perf. 13***

239 A58 4k multicolored 1.50 1.25

Tourism — A59

1991, May 15 ***Perf. 12½x13***

240 A59 4k Iceberg 1.25 1.25

241 A59 8.50k Skiers, sled dogs 2.50 2.75

See Nos. 259-260, 289-290.

Famous Men Type of 1990

10k, Jonathan Petersen (1881-1961), musician. 50k, Hans Lynge (1906-88), artist & writer. 100k, Lars Moller (1842-1926), newspaper editor.

1991-92 **Engr.** ***Perf. 13x12½***

242 A56 10k black & dk blue 2.75 2.50

243 A56 50k red brn & blue 14.00 12.50

249 A56 100k claret & slate 25.00 22.50

Nos. 242-249 (3) 41.75 37.50

Issued: 10k, 50k, 9/5; 100k, 9/15/92.

Settlement of Paamiut, 250th Anniv. A60

1992, May 14 **Engr.** ***Perf. 13***

252 A60 7.25k dk bl & ol brn 2.75 2.50

Denmark's Queen Margrethe and Prince Henrik, Silver Wedding Anniv. — A61

1992, June 10 **Litho.** ***Perf. 12½x13***

253 A61 4k multicolored 2.00 2.00

A62

A63

1992, Nov. 12 Litho. *Perf. 13*
254 A62 4k Christmas 2.25 1.75

1993, Feb. 4 Litho. *Perf. 13*
255 A63 4k multicolored 1.25 1.25

Intl. Year of Indigenous Peoples.

Crabs — A64

4k, Neolithodes grimaldii. 7.25k, Chionoecetes oiliqo. 8.50k, Hyas coarctatus, Hyas araneus.

Litho. & Engr.

1993, Mar. 25 *Perf. 13*
256 A64 4k multicolored 1.25 1.25
257 A64 7.25k multicolored 3.25 3.25
a. Chionoecetes opilio 8.75 *11.00*
b. Booklet pane, 4 each #256, 257a 40.00
258 A64 8.50k multicolored 2.75 2.75

Issue date: No. 257b, Sept. 9.

Tourism Type of 1991

1993, May 6 Litho. *Perf. 12½x13*
259 A57 4k Village in winter 1.25 1.25
260 A57 8.50k Ruins, coastline 2.75 2.75

AIDS Research A66

1993, Sept. 9 Litho. *Perf. 13*
261 A66 4k multicolored 1.25 1.25

Native Animals — A67

Litho. & Engr.

1993, Oct. 14 *Perf. 13*
262 A67 5k Canis lupus 1.50 1.50
263 A67 8.50k Alopex lagopus 2.75 2.75
264 A67 10k Rangifer tarandus 3.25 3.25
Nos. 262-264 (3) 7.50 7.50

See Nos. 270-272, 296-298.

Christmas A68

1993, Nov. 11 Litho. *Perf. 13*
265 A68 4k multicolored 1.25 1.25

Buksefjord Electrical Project — A69

Litho. & Engr.

1994, Mar. 24 *Perf. 13*
266 A69 4k multicolored 1.25 1.25

Ammassalik, Cent. — A70

1994, Mar. 24
267 A70 7.25k multicolored 2.25 2.25

Expedition to North East Greenland, 1906-08 A71

Europa: 4k, Icebound Danmark. 7.25k, Danmark, expedition car, dogs.

1994, May 5 Litho. *Perf. 13*
268 A71 4k multicolored 1.25 1.25
269 A71 7.25k multicolored 2.25 2.25

Native Animal Type of 1993

Designs: 5.50k, Mustela erminea. 7.25k, Dicrostonyx torquatus. 9k, Lepus arcticus.

Litho. & Engr.

1994, Sept. 8 *Perf. 13*
270 A67 5.50k multicolored 1.75 1.75
271 A67 7.25k multicolored 2.50 2.50
272 A67 9k multicolored 3.25 3.25
Nos. 270-272 (3) 7.50 7.50

Ship's Figureheads — A72

Litho. & Engr.

1994, Oct. 13 *Perf. 13*
273 A72 4k Ceres 1.25 1.25
274 A72 8.50k Nordlyset 2.75 2.75

See Nos. 299-300, 309-310.

Christmas Paintings, by Julia Pars — A73

1994, Nov. 10 Litho. *Perf. 12½x13*
275 A73 4k shown 1.40 1.40
276 A73 5k Santa, dogs, igloo 1.75 1.75

Orchids — A74

Litho. & Engr.

1995-96 *Perf. 13x12½*
279 A74 4k Listera cordata 1.40 1.40
280 A74 4.25k Corallorhiza trifida 1.50 1.50
281 A74 4.50k Amerorchis rotundifolia 1.60 1.60
282 A74 7.25k Leucorchis albida 2.50 2.50
283 A74 7.50k Plantanthera hyperborea 2.75 2.75
a. Booklet pane, #281, 283, 2 ea #225, 280 + 4 labels 10.50
Complete booklet, 2 #283a 21.00
Nos. 279-283 (5) 9.75 9.75

No. 283a exists with different labels and stamps in different order. Complete booklet contains one of each type of No. 283a.

Issued: 4k, 7.25k, 2/9/95.

This is an expanding set. Numbers may change.

Ilinniarfissuaq Seminarium, Nuuk (The Greenland Training College), 150th Anniv. — A75

Litho. & Engr.

1995, Mar. 23 *Perf. 13*
287 A75 4k multicolored 1.40 1.40

United Nations, 50th Anniv. — A76

1995, Mar. 23
288 A76 7.25k multicolored 2.50 2.50

Tourism Type of 1991

1995, Apr. 20 Litho. *Perf. 12½x13*
289 A59 4k Iceberg, inlet 1.50 1.50
290 A59 8.50k Mountains 3.25 3.25

Peace & Liberty A77

Europa: 4k, Envelope, simulated stamp. 8.50k, Doves flying over Greenland.

1995, May 5 *Perf. 12½x13*
291 A77 4k multicolored 1.50 1.50
292 A77 8.50k multicolored 3.25 3.25

Souvenir Sheets
Types A3-A5 Surcharged

America Series — A78

Designs: No. 295a, Dog team. b, Polar bear. c, Eskimo in kayak. d, Eider duck.

Illustration reduced.

1995, May 5 Litho. *Perf. 13*
293 A78 Sheet of 2 + 4 labels *5.25 5.25*
a. 5k on 10o pur & ol (Type A4) *2.60 2.60*
b. 5k on 15o red & vio (Type A4) *2.60 2.60*
294 A78 Sheet of 3 *6.50 6.50*
a. 1k on 1o dk ol & vio bl (Type A3) *.50 .50*
b. 5k on 5o rose lake & brn (Type A3) *2.60 2.60*
c. 7k on 7o dk grn & blk (Type A3) *3.50 3.50*
295 A78 Sheet of 4 *8.25 8.25*
a. 4k on 30o dk bl & red brn (Type A5) *2.00 2.00*
b. 4k on 1k brn & gray blk (Type A5) *2.00 2.00*
c. 4k on 2k sep & dp grn (Type A5) *2.00 2.00*
d. 4k on 5k dp pur & dl brn (Type A5) *2.00 2.00*

Native Animal Type of 1993

Litho. & Engr.

1995, Sept. 7 *Perf. 13*
296 A67 4k Ursus maritimus 1.40 1.40
297 A67 7.25k Gulo gulo 2.50 2.50
298 A67 7.50k Ovibus moschatus 2.75 2.75
Nos. 296-298 (3) 6.65 6.65

Ship's Figureheads Type of 1994

Litho. & Engr.

1995, Oct. 12 *Perf. 13*
299 A72 4k Hvalfisken, vert. 1.40 1.40
300 A72 8.50k Tjalfe 3.00 3.00

Christmas A79

1995, Nov. 9 Litho. *Perf. 13*
301 A79 4k Boy running in snow 1.40 1.40
302 A79 5k Girl running in snow 1.75 1.75

Whales A80

Designs: 25o, Orcinus orca. 50o, Megaptera novaeangliae. 1k, Delphinapterus leucas. 4.50k, Physeter catodon. 6.50k, Balaena mysticetus. 9.50k, Balaenoptera acutorostrata.

1996, Apr. 25 Litho. *Perf. 13*
303 A80 25o blue, black & red .20 .20
304 A80 50o blue, black & red .20 .20
305 A80 1k blue, black & red .35 .35
306 A80 4.50k blue, black & red 1.40 1.40
a. Bklt. pane, #304, 2 ea #303, 306 4.00
Complete booklet, 2 #306a 8.00
307 A80 6.50k blue, black & red 2.25 2.25
308 A80 9.50k blue, black & red 3.25 3.25
a. Souvenir sheet, Nos. 303-308 7.75 7.75

No. 306a exists with stamps in different order. Issued: No. 306a, 1/1/97.

See Nos. 319-322, 329-334.

Ship's Figureheads Type of 1994

Litho. & Engr.

1996, Sept. 5 *Perf. 13*
309 A72 15k Blaahejren, vert. 5.25 5.25
310 A72 20k Gertrud Rask 7.00 7.00

Arnarulunnguaq (1896-1933), Member of Thule Expedition — A81

1996, Sept. 5 Engr.
311 A81 4.50k dark blue 1.50 1.50

Europa.

Christmas A82

Designs: 4.25k, Girl looking through frozen window pane, angels scratched in ice. 4.50k, Paper star, children singing.

1996, Nov. 7 Litho. *Perf. 13*
312 A82 4.25k multicolored 1.40 1.40
313 A82 4.50k multicolored 1.50 1.50
a. Booklet pane, 3 each #312-313 8.75
Complete booklet, 2 #313a 17.50

No. 313a was issued in two formats, one with No. 312 at the UL, the other with No. 313 at the UL. The complete booklet contains one of each format.

A83

A84

Litho. & Engr.

1997, Jan. 14 *Perf. 13*

314 A83 4.50k multicolored 1.50 1.50

Coronation of Queen Margrethe II, 25th anniv.

1997, Jan. 14

Butterflies: 2k, Clossiana chariclea. 3k, Colias hecla. 4.75k, Plebejus franklinii. 8k, Lycaena phlaeas.

315 A84 2k multicolored .65 .65
316 A84 3k multicolored 1.00 1.00
317 A84 4.75k multicolored 1.50 1.50
318 A84 8k multicolored 2.60 2.60
a. Booklet pane of 6, 2 #314, 1 ea #315-318 + 2 labels 9.00
Complete booklet, 2 #318a 18.00
Nos. 315-318 (4) 5.75 5.75

Issued: No. 318a, 5/5.

No. 318a exists with stamps in two different orders and with two different backgrounds, one of green plants, the other of red flowers. The complete booklet contains one of each type of pane.

Whale Type of 1996

Designs: 5k, Balaenoptera musculus. 5.75k, Balaenoptera physalus. 6k, Balaenoptera borealis. 8k, Monodon monoceros.

1997, May 5 **Litho.** *Perf. 13*

319 A80 5k blue, black & red 1.50 1.50
320 A80 5.75k blue, black & red 1.75 1.75
321 A80 6k blue, black & red 1.75 1.75
322 A80 8k blue, black & red 2.50 2.50
a. Souvenir sheet of 4, #319-322 7.50 7.50
Nos. 319-322 (4) 7.50 7.50

Story of the "Bear of the Sea" — A85

1997, May 5 **Litho. & Engr.** *Perf. 13*

323 A85 4.75k black & blue black 1.50 1.50

Europa.

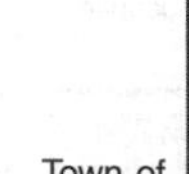

Town of Nanortalik, Bicent. A86

Litho. & Engr.

1997, Aug. 15 *Perf. 13*

324 A86 4.50k multicolored 1.25 1.25

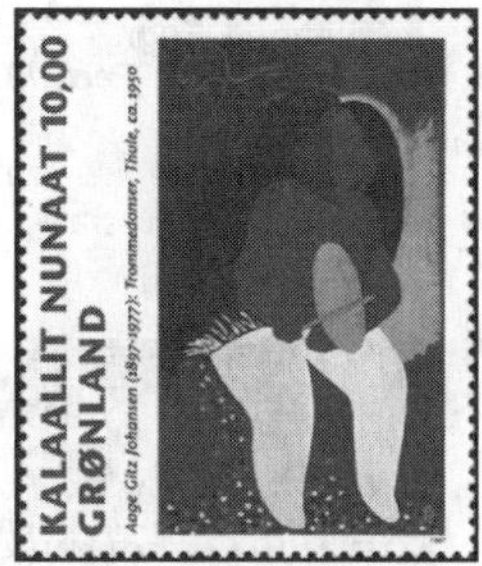
Paintings by Aage Gitz-Johansen (1897-1977) — A87

Designs: 10k, Native dancer, Thule. 16k, Nude woman, Ammassalik.

1997, Aug. 15 **Litho.** *Perf. 13x12½*

325 A87 10k multicolored 2.75 2.75
326 A87 16k multicolored 4.50 4.50

Christmas A88

Designs: 4.50k, Child with dogs in snow. 4.75k, Family in sled with Christmas presents, tree, father preparing harness.

1997, Nov. 6 **Litho.** *Perf. 13x12½*

327 A88 4.50k multicolored 1.25 1.25
328 A88 4.75k multicolored 1.40 1.40
a. Booklet pane, 3 each #327-328 8.00
Complete booklet, 2 #328a 16.00

No. 328a comes in two configurations. One has #327 at UL, the second has #328 at UL. Complete booklet has one of each pane.

Whale Type of 1996

Designs: 2k, Phocoena phocoena. 3k, Lagenorhynchus albirostris. No. 331, Globicephala melaena. No. 332, Hyperoodon ampullatus. No. 333, Lagenorhynchus acutus. No. 334, Eubalaena glacialis.

1998, Feb. 5 **Litho.** *Perf. 13*

329 A80 2k multicolored .60 .60
330 A80 3k multicolored 1.10 1.10
331 A80 4.50k multicolored 1.25 1.25
332 A80 4.50k multicolored 1.25 1.25
333 A80 4.75k multicolored 1.40 1.40
334 A80 4.75k multicolored 1.40 1.40
a. Souvenir sheet of 6, #329-334 7.00 7.00
Nos. 329-334 (6) 7.00 7.00

Intl. Year of the Ocean.

New Order of 1950 — A89

Design: Augo Lynge, Frederik Lynge, first Greenland politicians in Danish Parliament.

1998, Feb. 5 **Engr.** *Perf. 13*

335 A89 4.50k multicolored 1.25 1.25

Europa — A90

Children's drawings of "Children's Day in Greenland:" 4.75k, Happy faces beside lake. 10k, People celebrating across Greenland.

1998, May 29 **Litho.** *Perf. 13*

336 A90 4.75k multicolored 1.40 1.40
337 A90 10k multicolored 3.00 3.00

Ships — A91

Litho. & Engr.

1998, Aug. 20 *Perf. 13*

338 A91 4.50k Gertrud Rask 1.25 1.25
a. Booklet pane of 6 7.50
339 A91 4.75k Hans Egede 1.40 1.40
a. Booklet pane of 6 8.50
Complete booklet, #338a, 339a 16.00

Paintings by Hans Lynge (1906-88) — A92

Designs: 11k, "Brother Gets Breast-fed." 25k, "Refuelling" (men in boat).

1998, Aug. 20 **Litho.** *Perf. 13*

340 A92 11k multicolored 3.25 3.25
341 A92 25k multicolored 7.50 7.50

Christmas A93

1998, Nov. 5 **Litho.** *Perf. 13*

342 A93 4.50k Dickey, kamikker 1.40 1.40
a. Booklet pane of 6 8.50
343 A93 4.75k Kamikker, hat 1.50 1.50
a. Booklet pane of 6 9.00
Complete booklet, #342a, 343a 17.50

World Wildlife Fund — A94

Nyctea scandiaca (snowy owl): 1k, Nesting with young. 4.75k, In flight. 5.50k, Two adults. 5.75k, Perched on rock.

Litho. & Engr.

1999, Feb. 8 *Perf. 13*

344 A94 1k multicolored .25 .25
345 A94 4.75k multicolored 1.40 1.40
a. Booklet pane, 3 each #344-345 5.00
346 A94 5.50k multicolored 1.60 1.60
347 A94 5.75k multicolored 1.60 1.60
a. Booklet pane, 3 each #346-347 9.50
Complete booklet, #345a, 347a 14.50
Nos. 344-347 (4) 4.85 4.85

Europa A95

1999, May 7 **Litho. & Engr.** *Perf. 13*

348 A95 6k Polar bear 1.75 1.75

Paintings, by Peter Rosing (1892-1965) — A96

Designs: 7k, The Man from Aluk, 1944. 20k, Homecoming, 1956.

1999, May 7 **Litho.** *Perf. 12½x13*

349 A96 7k multicolored 2.00 2.00
350 A96 20k multicolored 5.75 5.75

Arctic Vikings A97

1999, Aug. 13 **Engr.** *Perf. 13x13¼*

351 A97 4.50k Viking ship 1.25 1.25
352 A97 4.75k Man on driftwood 1.40 1.40
353 A97 5.75k Arrowhead, coins 1.60 1.60
354 A97 8k Tjodhilde's church 2.25 2.25
a. Souvenir sheet, #351-354 6.50 6.50
Nos. 351-354 (4) 6.50 6.50

See Nos. 358-361.

Christmas A98

1999, Nov. 11 **Litho.** *Perf. 13x13¼*

355 A98 4.50k Writing letter 1.25 1.25
a. Booklet pane of 6 7.50
356 A98 4.75k Handshake 1.40 1.40
a. Booklet pane of 6 8.50
Complete booklet, #355a, 356a 16.00

Millennium A99

1999, Nov. 11 **Litho.** *Perf. 13x13¼*

357 A99 5.75k multicolored 1.60 1.60

Arctic Vikings Type of 1999

Designs: 25o, Hunter, four walruses. 3k, Storyteller. 5.50k, Dog chasing reindeer. 21k, Man, gyrfalcon, polar bear, narwhal tusk, items made from animals.

2000, Feb. 21 **Engr.** *Perf. 13x13¼*

358 A97 25o bl gray & brn .20 .20
359 A97 3k bl gray & brn .80 .80
360 A97 5.50k bl gray 1.50 1.50
361 A97 21k bl gray 5.75 5.75
a. Souvenir sheet, #358-361 8.25 8.25
Nos. 358-361 (4) 8.25 8.25

Navy Dog Sled Patrol A100

Litho. & Engr.

2000, Feb. 21 *Perf. 12¾*

362 A100 10k multi 2.75 2.75

Europa, 2000

Common Design Type

2000, May 9 **Litho.** *Perf. 13¼x13*

363 CD17 4.75k multi 1.40 1.40

Queen Margrethe — A101

2000-01 Engr. *Perf. 13x13¼*

364 A101 25o blk & bl gray .20 .20
365 A101 50o red brn & bl gray .20 .20
367 A101 4.50k red & bl gray 1.25 1.25
368 A101 4.75k bl & bl gray 1.40 1.40
372 A101 8k yel grn & bl gray 2.10 2.10
374 A101 10k grn & bl gray 2.75 2.75
375 A101 12k pur & bl gray 3.00 3.00
Nos. 364-375 (7) 10.90 10.90

Issued: 4.50k, 4.75k, 8k, 10k, 5/9/00. 25o, 12k, 5/9/01. 50o, 10/21/02.
This is an expanding set.

Cultural Heritage — A102

2000, Aug. 18 Litho. *Perf. 13¼x13*

376 A102 4.50k Wooden map 1.10 1.10
a. Booklet pane of 6 + 2 labels 6.75
377 A102 4.75k Sealskin 1.25 1.25
a. Booklet pane of 6 + 2 labels 7.50
Booklet, #376a, 377a 14.50

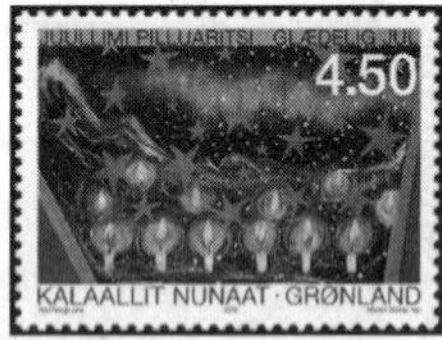
Christmas A103

2000, Nov. 9 Litho. *Perf. 13x13¼*

378 A103 4.50k Stars, candles 1.10 1.10
a. Booklet pane of 6 6.75
379 A103 4.75k Star 1.25 1.25
a. Booklet pane of 6 7.50
Booklet, #378a, 379a 14.50

Arctic Vikings Type of 1999

Designs: 1k, Hunter, dead seals. 4.50k, Mice eating food. 5k, Man and pack animals leaving. 10k, Birds on ruins.

2001, Feb. 5 Engr. *Perf. 13x13¼*

380 A97 1k indigo & red .25 .25
381 A97 4.50k indigo & blue 1.10 1.10
382 A97 5k indigo & blue 1.25 1.25
383 A97 10k indigo & red 2.50 2.50
a. Souvenir sheet, #380-383 5.25 5.25

Cultural Heritage Type of 2000

Designs: 4.50k, Smoked fish. 4.75k, Fishing spear.

2001, May 9 Litho. *Perf. 13¼x13*

384 A102 4.50k multi 1.10 1.10
a. Booklet pane of 6 + 2 labels 6.75
385 A102 4.75k multi 1.10 1.10
a. Booklet pane of 6 + 2 labels 6.75
Booklet, #384a, 385a 13.50

Europa A104

2001, May 9 Litho. & Engr. *Perf. 13*

386 A104 15k Krill 3.50 3.50

Unissued Stamps from the 1930s — A105

Designs: 5.75k, 5o Northern lights. 8k, 10o Seal. 21k, 15o Polar bear.

Litho. & Engr.

2001, Oct. 16 *Perf. 12¾*

387 A105 5.75k blk & brn 1.40 1.40
388 A105 8k blk & brn 2.00 2.00
389 A105 21k blk & brn 5.25 5.25
a. Souvenir sheet, #387-389 + 3 labels 8.75 8.75

Christmas A106

Grouse and: 4.50k, Berries. 4.75k, Mountain.

2001, Oct. 16 Litho. *Perf. 13x13¼*

390 A106 4.50k multi 1.10 1.10
a. Booklet pane of 6 6.75 —
391 A106 4.75k multi 1.10 1.10
a. Booklet pane of 6 6.75 —
Booklet, #390a, 391a 13.50

Cultural Heritage Type of 2000

Designs: 4.50k, Thule drum. 4.75k, Mask.

2002, Mar. 5 Litho. *Perf. 13x13¼*

392 A102 4.50k multi 1.10 1.10
a. Miniature sheet of 8 + label 9.00 —
393 A102 4.75k multi 1.10 1.10
a. Miniature sheet of 8 + label 9.00 —

Sculptures A107

Designs: 1k, Stone and Man, by various sculptors. 31k, Nuuk Snow Festival snow sculpture.

2002, Mar. 5 *Perf. 12¾*

394 A107 1k multi .25 .25
395 A107 31k multi 7.25 7.25

Europa — A108

2002, June 24 Litho. *Perf. 12¾*

396 A108 11k multi 2.75 2.75

Ships A109

2002, June 24 Engr. *Perf. 13x13¼*

397 A109 2k Nordlyset .50 .50
398 A109 4k Hvidbjornen 1.00 1.00
399 A109 6k Staerkodder 1.50 1.50
a. Booklet pane of 4, 2 each #398-399 5.00 —
400 A109 16k Haabet 4.00 4.00
a. Booklet pane of 4, 2 each #397, 400 9.00 —
Booklet, #399a, 400a 14.00
Nos. 397-400 (4) 7.00 7.00

Intl. Council for Exploration of the Seas, Cent. — A110

Designs: 7k, Somniosus microcephalus and iceberg. 19k, Sebastes mentella and exploration ship Paamiut.

Litho. & Engr.

2002, Oct. 21 *Perf. 13¼x13*

401 A110 7k multi 1.90 1.90
402 A110 19k multi 5.25 5.25
a. Souvenir sheet, #401-402 7.25 7.25

See Denmark Nos. 1237-1238, Faroe Islands No. 426.

Christmas — A111

Designs: 4.50k, Man with gifts, children on sled with tree. 4.75k, Family with gifts near fire.
Illustration reduced.

2002, Oct. 21 Litho. *Perf. 12¾*

403 A111 4.50k multi 1.25 1.25
404 A111 4.75k multi 1.25 1.25

Booklet Stamps
Self-Adhesive
Serpentine Die Cut 14

405 A111 4.50k multi 1.25 1.25
406 A111 4.75k multi 1.25 1.25
a. Horiz. pair, #405-406 2.50
b. Booklet, 6 each #405-406 15.00

SEMI-POSTAL STAMPS

Catalogue values for unused stamps in this section are for Never Hinged items.

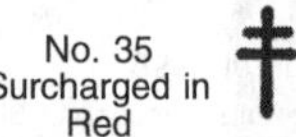
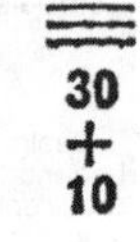
No. 35 Surcharged in Red

1958, May 22 Engr. *Perf. 13*

B1 A7 30o + 10o on 50o 5.00 1.60

The surtax was for the campaign against tuberculosis in Greenland.

No. 32 Surcharged: "Gronlandsfonden 30+10" and Bars

1959, Feb. 23 Unwmk.

B2 A6 30o + 10o on 25o 4.00 3.00

The surtax was for the benefit of the Greenland Fund.

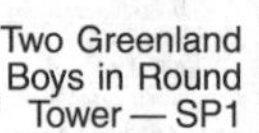
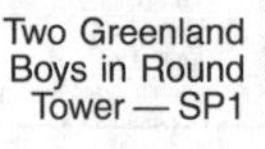
Two Greenland Boys in Round Tower — SP1

1968, Sept. 12 Engr. *Perf. 13*

B3 SP1 60o + 10o dark red 1.00 *1.00*

Surtax for child welfare work in Greenland.

Hans Egede Explaining Bible to Natives — SP2

1971, July 3 Engr. *Perf. 13*

B4 SP2 60o + 10o red brown 2.50 2.50

See footnote after No. 77.

Frederik IX, "Dannebrog" off Umanak — SP3

1972, Apr. 20

B5 SP3 60o + 10o dull red 1.60 1.60

King Frederik IX (1899-1972). The surtax was for humanitarian and charitable purposes.

Heimaey Town and Volcano — SP4

1973, Oct. 18 Engr. *Perf. 13*

B6 SP4 70o + 20o gray & red 1.60 1.60

The surtax was for the victims of the eruption of Heimaey Volcano.

Arm Pulling, by Hans Egede — SP5

1976, Apr. 8 Engr. *Perf. 12½*

B7 SP5 100o + 20o multi .60 .60

Surtax for the Greenland Athletic Union.

Rasmussen and Eskimos — SP6

1979, June 7 Engr. *Perf. 13*

B8 SP6 1.30k + 20o brown red .80 .80

Knud Rasmussen (1879-1933), arctic explorer and ethnologist.

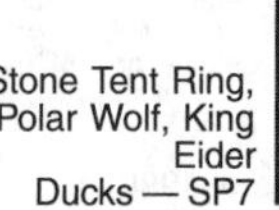

Stone Tent Ring, Polar Wolf, King Eider Ducks — SP7

1981, Sept. 3 Engr. *Perf. 13*

B9 SP7 1.60k + 20o lt red brn .75 .75

Surtax was for Peary Land Expeditions.

History Type of 1982

Design: Eric the Red sailing for Greenland.

1982, Aug. 2 Engr. *Perf. 12½*

B10 A39 2k + 40o dk red brn 1.00 1.00

Surtax was for Cultural House, Julianehab.

Blind Man — SP8

1983, May 19 Engr.

B11 SP8 2.50k + 40o multi 1.10 1.10

Surtax was for the handicapped.

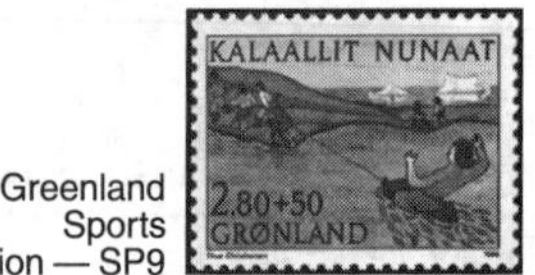
Greenland Sports Union — SP9

1986, Apr. 17 Litho.

B12 SP9 2.80k + 50o Water game 1.25 *1.40*

Surtax for the Sports Union.

Greenland PO, 50th Anniv. — SP10

1988, Sept. 16 Litho. *Perf. 12½x13*
B13 SP10 300o +50o multi 1.60 1.60

Surtax for the purchase of postal artifacts.

Sled Dog, Common Eider — SP11

Litho. & Engr.

1990, Sept. 6 *Perf. 13*
B14 SP11 400o + 50o multi 2.00 2.00

Surtax for the Greenland Environmental Foundation.

SP12

SP13

1991, Sept. 5 Litho. *Perf. 13*
B15 SP12 4k +50o multi *12.50 12.50*

Blue Cross of Greenland, 75th Anniv. Surtax benefits Blue Cross of Greenland.

1992, Oct. 8 Litho. *Perf. 13*
B16 SP13 4k +50o multi 3.25 3.25

Cancer research in Greenland.

Red Cross — SP14

Boy Scouts in Greenland, 50th Anniv. SP15

1993, June 17 Litho. *Perf. 13*
B17 SP14 4k +50o red & blue 1.60 1.60
B18 SP15 4k +50o multi 1.60 1.60
a. Souv. sheet, 2 ea #B17-B18 *18.00 18.00*

1994 Winter Olympics, Lillehammer SP16

1994, Feb. 10 Litho. *Perf. 13*
B19 SP16 4k +50o Skiers 1.50 1.50
a. Souvenir sheet of 4 7.00 7.50

Surtax to support Greenlandic athletes.

Natl. Flag, 10th Anniv. — SP17

1995, June 21 Litho. *Perf. 13*
B20 SP17 4k +50o multi 1.75 1.75
a. Souvenir sheet of 4 7.00 7.00

Surtax for benefit of Greenland Flag Society.

Handicapped and Disabled in Greenland — SP18

1996, Sept. 5 Litho. *Perf. 13*
B21 SP18 4.25k +50o multi 1.60 1.60
a. Souvenir sheet of 4 6.75 6.75

Katuaq Cultural Center, Nuuk SP19

Litho. & Engr.

1997, Jan. 14 *Perf. 13*
B22 SP19 4.50k +50o multi 1.60 1.60
a. Souvenir sheet of 4 6.75 6.75

SP20

SP21

Women's Society of Greenland: Kathrine Chemnitz (1894-1978), first Gen. Secretary.

1998, May 29 Litho. *Perf. 13*
B23 SP20 4.50k +50o multi 1.50 1.50
a. Souvenir sheet of 4 6.00 6.00

1999, May 7 Engr. *Perf. 13*
B24 SP21 4.50k +50o Pincushion, Natl. Museum 1.40 1.40
a. Souvenir sheet of 4 5.75 5.75

Surtax for the benefit of Greenland National Museum & Archives.

Drum Dance — SP22

Litho. & Engr.

2000, Aug. 18 *Perf. 13¼x13*
B25 SP22 4.50k + 1k multi 1.40 1.40
a. Souvenir sheet of 4 5.75 5.75

Surtax to benefit the Hafnia 01 Philatelic Exhibition, Copenhagen.

2002 Arctic Winter Games — SP23

2001, Feb. 5 Litho. *Perf. 13¼x13*
B26 SP23 4.50k +50o multi 1.25 1.25
a. Souvenir sheet of 4 5.00 5.00

SP24

2002, Mar. 5 Litho. *Perf. 12¾*
B27 SP24 4.50k +50o multi 1.25 1.25
a. Souvenir sheet of 4 5.00 5.00

Surtax for "Children Are People, Too" Project of Paarisa.

PARCEL POST STAMPS

Arms of Greenland — PP1

Perf. 11, 11½

1905-37 Unwmk. Typo.
Q1 PP1 1o ol grn ('16) 45.00 *50.00*
a. Perf. 12½ ('05) 600.00 *650.00*
Q2 PP1 2o yellow ('16) 250.00 110.00
Q3 PP1 5o brown ('16) 92.50 *110.00*
a. Perf. 12½ ('05) 575.00 *600.00*
Q4 PP1 10o blue ('37) 30.00 *60.00*
a. Perf. 12½ ('05) 725.00 525.00
b. Perf. 11½ ('16) 40.00 *55.00*
Q5 PP1 15o violet ('16) 140.00 *150.00*
Q6 PP1 20o red ('16) 13.00 11.00
a. Perf. 11 ('37) 30.00 *50.00*
Q7 PP1 70o violet ('37) 30.00 *110.00*
a. Perf. 11½ ('30) 190.00 190.00
Q8 PP1 1k yellow ('37) 30.00 *120.00*
a. Perf. 11½ ('30) 40.00 *55.00*
Q9 PP1 3k brown ('30) 105.00 *150.00*
Nos. Q1-Q9 (9) 735.50 *871.00*

1937 Litho. *Perf. 11*
Q10 PP1 70o pale violet 32.50 *105.00*
Q11 PP1 1k yellow 30.00 *65.00*
Nos. Q10-Q11, never hinged 100.00

On lithographed stamps, PAKKE-PORTO is slightly larger, hyphen has rounded ends and lines in shield are fine, straight and evenly spaced.

On typographed stamps, hyphen has squared ends and shield lines are coarse, uneven and inclined to be slightly wavy.

Used values are for stamps postally used from Denmark. Numeral cancels indicate use as postal savings stamps and are worth less. Greenland village cancels are worth more.

Sheets of 25. Certain printings of Nos. Q1-Q2, Q3a, Q4a and Q5-Q6 were issued without sheet margins. Stamps from the outer rows are straight edged. Some of these sheets were reperfed later.

GRENADA

grə-ˈnā-də

LOCATION — Windward Islands, West Indies
GOVT. — Independent nation in the British Commonwealth
AREA — 133 sq. mi.
POP. — 98,600 (1998 est.)
CAPITAL — St. George's

Grenada consists of Grenada Island and the southern Grenadines, including Carriacou. This colony was granted associated statehood with Great Britain in 1967 and became an independent state Feb. 7, 1974.

12 Pence = 1 Shilling
100 Cents = 1 Dollar (1949)

Catalogue values for unused stamps in this country are for Never Hinged items, beginning with Scott 143 in the regular postage section, Scott B1 in the semi-postal section, Scott C1 in the air post section, Scott J15 in the postage due section, and Scott O1 in the official section.

Watermarks

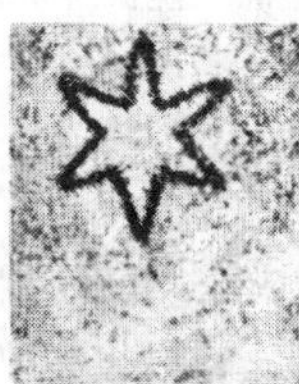

Wmk. 5- Small Star

Wmk. 6- Large Star

Wmk. 7- Large Star with Broad Points

Values for unused stamps are for examples with original gum as defined in the catalogue introduction. Very fine examples of Nos. 1-19, 27-29, and 31-38 will have perforations touching the design on at least one side due to the narrow spacing of the stamps on the plates. Stamps with perfs clear of the design on all four sides are scarce and will command higher prices.

Queen Victoria — A1

Rough Perf. 14 to 16

1861 Engr. Unwmk.
1 A1 1p green 50.00 45.00
a. 1p blue green 4,000. 300.00
b. As No. 1, horiz. pair, imperf. btwn.
2 A1 6p rose 775.00 85.00
b. 6p lake red, perf. 11-12½ 800.00

No. 2b was not issued. No. 2 imperf is a proof.

1863-71 Wmk. 5
3 A1 1p green ('64) 65.00 12.50
a. 1p yellow green 95.00 25.00
4 A1 6p rose 600.00 17.50
5 A1 6p vermilion ('71) 725.00 17.50
a. 6p dull red 2,900. 225.00
g. Double impression 2,000.

No. 5a always has sideways watermark. Other colors sometimes have sideways watermark.

1873-78 *Clean-Cut Perf. about 15*
5B A1 1p deep green 80.00 30.00
c. 1p blue green ('78) 225.00 30.00
h. Half used as ½p on cover 7,500.
5D A1 6p vermilion ('75) 725.00 27.50
e. 6p dull red 750.00 35.00
f. Double impression 1,450.

1873 **Wmk. 6**
6 A1 1p blue green 70.00 18.00
a. Diagonal half used as ½p on cover 7,500.
7 A1 6p vermilion 600.00 27.50

1875 ***Perf. 14***
7A A1 1p yellow green 65.00 12.50
b. Half used as ½p on cover 6,750.
c. Perf. 15 *6,750.* *1,900.*

A2

A2a

Revenue Stamps Surcharged in Black

1875-81 ***Perf. 14, 14½***
8 A2 ½p purple ('81) 11.00 5.00
a. "OSTAGE" 175.00 125.00
b. Imperf., pair 300.00
c. "ALF" *3,000.*
d. "PEN"
e. No hyphen between "HALF" and "PENNY" 175.00 125.00
f. Double surcharge 275.00 275.00
9 A2a 2½p lake ('81) 50.00 10.00
a. Imperf., pair 425.00
b. Imperf. vertically, pair 3,000.
c. "PENCF" 400.00 200.00
d. No period after "PENNY" 225.00 90.00
e. "PENOE" 150.00
10 A2 4p blue ('81) 90.00 20.00

Revenue Stamps Surcharged in Dark Blue

11 A2 1sh purple 625.00 20.00
a. "SHLIIING" *4,000.* 650.00
b. "NE SHILLING" *2,500.*
c. "OSTAGE" *4,750.* *2,000.*
d. Invtd. "S" in "POSTAGE" *3,750.* *750.00*

See Nos. 27-35.

1881 **Wmk. 7**
12 A2 2½p lake 150.00 47.50
a. 2½p claret 425.00 110.00
b. As No. 12, "PENCF" 700.00 250.00
c. As No. 12, No period after "PENNY" 550.00 200.00
d. As "a," "PENCF" 1,450. 575.00
e. As "a," no period after "PENNY" 950.00 450.00
13 A2 4p blue 225.00 175.00

A3

A4

A5

A6

Revenue Stamp Overprinted "POSTAGE" in Black

1883 **Wmk. 5**

Denomination & Crown in 2nd Color

14 A3 ½p orange & grn 750.00 200.00
a. Unsevered pair *4,000.* *1,300.*
15 A4 ½p orange & grn 200.00 125.00
a. Unsevered pair *1,250.* *425.00*
16 A5 1p orange & grn *260.00* 50.00
a. Inverted overprint 1,600. 1,100.
b. Double overprint 1,250. 1,100.
c. Inverted "S" in "Postage" 750.00 525.00
d. Diagonal half used as ½p on cover *2,900.*

"Postage" in Manuscript, Red or Black

18 A6 1p orange & grn (R) — *3,000.*
19 A6 1p orange & green — *2,250.*

On Nos. 14-19 the words "ONE PENNY" measure from 10-11¼mm in length.

On No. 15, the lower "POSTAGE" is always inverted.

It has been claimed that although Nos. 18 and 19 were used, they were not officially issued.

A8

A10

1883 **Wmk. 2** ***Perf. 14***
20 A8 ½p green 1.25 1.25
a. Tete beche pair 3.75 *13.00*
21 A8 1p rose 50.00 4.00
a. Tete beche pair 225.00 225.00
22 A8 2½p ultra 7.00 .75
a. Tete beche pair 24.00 *45.00*
23 A8 4p slate 5.00 3.50
a. Tete beche pair 16.50 *50.00*
24 A8 6p red lilac 5.00 *6.50*
a. Tete beche pair 17.50 *50.00*
25 A8 8p bister 10.00 *12.00*
a. Tete beche pair 30.00 *70.00*
26 A8 1sh violet 100.00 55.00
a. Tete beche pair 1,000. *1,050.*
Nos. 20-26 (7) 178.25 83.00

Stamps of types A8, A10 and D2 were printed with alternate horizontal rows inverted.

For surcharges see Nos. 36-38, J4-J7.

Revenue Stamps Surcharged

d. 1 POSTAGE.

1886 **Wmk. 6**
27 A2 1p on 1½ org 35.00 30.00
a. Inverted surcharge 275.00 275.00
b. Diagonal half used as ½ on cover 1,750.
c. Double surcharge 400.00 275.00
d. "HALH" instead of "HALF" 250.00 200.00
28 A2 1p on 1sh org 32.50 29.00
a. "SHILLNG" instead of "SHILLING" 400.00 350.00
b. No period after "POSTAGE" *350.00*
c. Half used as ½p on cover 1,750.

Wmk. 5
29 A2 1p on 4p org 140.00 85.00

1887 **Wmk. 2**
30 A10 1p rose .90 .70
a. Tete beche pair 2.25 *7.50*

Revenue Stamps Surcharged:

HALF PENNY POSTAGE
h

4d. POSTAGE
i

POSTAGE d. AND 1 REVENUE
k

POSTAGE AND REVENUE 1d.
l

1888-91 **Wmk. 5** ***Perf. 14½***
31 A2 (h) ½p on 2sh org ('89) 14.00 *17.50*
a. Double surcharge 400.00 400.00
b. First "S" in "SHILLINGS" inverted 300.00 300.00
32 A2 (i) 4p on 2sh org 35.00 25.00
a. "4d" and "POSTAGE" 5mm apart 60.00 27.50
b. "S" inverted, as in #31b 500.00 425.00
c. As "a," inverted "S," as in #31b 600.00 525.00

"d" Vertical instead of Slanting

33 A2 (i) 4p on 2sh org 700.00 400.00
34 A2 (k) 1p on 2sh org ('90) 70.00 70.00
a. Inverted surcharge 600.00 —
b. "S" inverted 600.00 600.00
35 A2 (l) 1p on 2sh org ('91) 50.00 50.00
a. Inverted surcharge
b. No period after "d" 300.00 —
c. "S" inverted 500.00 500.00

No. 25 Surcharged in Black:

POSTAGE AND REVENUE 1d.

2½d.

Wmk. 2
36 A8 1p on 8p bister 8.00 *11.00*
a. Tete beche pair 90.00 *125.00*
b. Inverted surcharge 275.00 250.00
c. No period after "d" 325.00 325.00

"2" of "½" Upright

37 A8 2½p on 8p bister 18.00 *20.00*
a. Tete beche pair 125.00 *175.00*
b. Inverted surcharge
c. Double surcharge 700.00 *750.00*
d. Triple surcharge 950.00

e. Double surcharge, one inverted 450.00 450.00

"2" of "½" Italic

38 A8 2½p on 8p bister 18.00 *20.00*
a. Tete beche pair 125.00 *175.00*
b. Tete beche pair, #37, 38 125.00
c. Inverted surcharge
d. Double surcharge 700.00 *750.00*
e. Triple surcharge 950.00
f. Triple surch., two inverted 850.00
g. Double surcharge, one inverted 450.00 450.00

Queen Victoria — A17

1895-99 **Wmk. 2** **Typo.** ***Perf. 14***
39 A17 ½p lilac & green 2.00 1.40
40 A17 1p lilac & car rose 3.75 .60
41 A17 2p lilac & brown 35.00 26.00
42 A17 2½p lilac & ultra 4.25 1.50
43 A17 3p lilac & orange 5.50 *13.00*
44 A17 6p lilac & green 9.50 *20.00*
45 A17 8p lilac & black 10.50 *35.00*
46 A17 1sh green & org 14.50 *27.50*
Nos. 39-46 (8) 85.00 *125.00*

Numerals of ½p, 3p, 8p and 1sh of type A17 are in color on colorless tablet.

Issue dates: 1p, May, 1896; ½p, 2p, Sept. 1899; others, Sept. 5, 1895.

Columbus' Flagship, La Concepcion
A18

King Edward VII
A19

1898, Aug. 15 **Engr.** **Wmk. 1**
47 A18 2½p ultra 12.50 7.00
a. Bluish paper 35.00 *45.00*

Discovery of the island by Columbus, Aug. 15th, 1498.

1902 **Wmk. 2** **Typo.**
48 A19 ½p violet & grn 2.75 1.10
49 A19 1p vio & car rose 3.75 .25
50 A19 2p vio & brown 2.50 *9.00*
51 A19 2½p vio & ultra 3.00 2.40
52 A19 3p vio & org 3.00 *7.75*
53 A19 6p vio & green 2.25 *14.50*
54 A19 1sh green & org 3.25 *22.50*
55 A19 2sh grn & ultra 17.00 *47.50*
56 A19 5sh grn & car rose 37.50 *55.00*
57 A19 10sh green & vio 100.00 *190.00*
Nos. 48-57 (10) 175.00 *350.00*

Numerals of ½p, 3p, 1sh, 2sh and 10sh of type A19 are in color on colorless tablet.

1904-06 **Wmk. 3** ***Perf. 14***
58 A19 ½p vio & green 14.00 *17.50*
59 A19 1p vio & car rose 7.50 2.00
60 A19 2p vio & brown 40.00 *70.00*
61 A19 2½p vio & ultra 40.00 *55.00*
62 A19 3p vio & org 2.00 *5.50*
63 A19 6p vio & green 3.75 *6.75*
64 A19 1sh green & org 5.00 *18.00*
65 A19 2sh grn & ultra 21.00 *57.50*
66 A19 5sh grn & car rose 47.50 *70.00*
67 A19 10sh green & vio 125.00 *190.00*
Nos. 58-67 (10) 305.75 *492.25*

Nos. 62, 63 and 65 are on both ordinary and chalky paper.

Issued: #58, 60-62, 64, 1905; #63, 65-67, 1906.

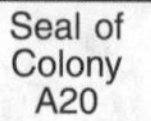
Seal of Colony
A20

King George V
A21

1906-11 **Engr.**
68 A20 ½p green 3.50 .30
69 A20 1p carmine 5.00 .20
70 A20 2p yellow 2.50 2.50
71 A20 2½p blue 5.50 1.50
a. 2½p ultramarine 6.75 3.00

Typo.

Chalky Paper

Numerals white on dark ground

72 A20 3p vio, *yel* ('08) 4.00 1.50
73 A20 6p violet ('08) 18.00 *20.00*
74 A20 1sh blk, *grn* ('11) 6.50 4.00
75 A20 2sh vio & blue, *blue* ('08) 17.50 10.00
76 A20 5sh red & green, *yel* ('08) 47.50 *60.00*
Nos. 68-76 (9) 110.00 *100.00*

1908 **Wmk. 2**
77 A20 1sh black, *green* 25.00 *45.00*
78 A20 10sh red & grn, *grn* 95.00 *150.00*

1913 **Ordinary Paper** **Wmk. 3**
79 A21 ½p green .85 *.95*
80 A21 1p scarlet 2.50 .75
a. 1p carmine 2.50 .30
81 A21 2p orange 1.25 .25
82 A21 2½p ultra 1.25 *3.25*

Chalky Paper

83 A21 3p violet, *yel* .55 *.80*
84 A21 6p dull vio & red vio 1.25 *8.50*
85 A21 1sh black, *green* .85 *9.50*
a. 1sh black, *emerald* 1.75 *10.00*
b. 1sh blk, *bl grn*, olive back 47.50 *75.00*
c. As "a," olive back 1.75 *6.25*
86 A21 2sh vio & ultra, *bl* 5.00 *11.00*
87 A21 5sh grn & red, *yel* 14.00 *55.00*
88 A21 10sh grn & red, *grn* 47.50 *85.00*
a. 10sh grn & red, *emer* 45.00 *110.00*
Nos. 79-88 (10) 75.00 *175.00*

1914 **Surface-colored Paper**
89 A21 3p violet, *yel* .65 *1.50*
90 A21 1sh black, *green* 1.25 *7.00*

1921-29 **Ordinary Paper** **Wmk. 4**
91 A21 ½p green .90 .25
92 A21 1p rose red .50 .50
93 A21 1p brown ('22) 1.00 .25
94 A21 1½p rose red ('22) 1.00 1.00
95 A21 2p orange .80 .25
96 A21 2p gray ('26) 2.10 *2.40*
97 A21 2½p ultramarine 1.75 *7.25*
98 A21 2½p gray ('22) .70 *7.75*
99 A21 3p ultra ('22) 1.75 *8.50*

Chalky Paper

100 A21 3p vio, *yel* ('26) 2.00 *4.25*
101 A21 4p blk & red, *yel* ('26) 1.00 *3.25*
102 A21 5p gray vio & ol grn 1.00 *3.50*
103 A21 6p dl vio & red vio 1.50 *15.00*
104 A21 6p blk & red ('26) 2.00 *2.10*
105 A21 9p gray vio & blk 2.00 *8.00*
106 A21 1sh blk, *emer* 2.50 *35.00*
107 A21 1sh org brn ('26) 4.50 *8.75*
108 A21 2sh vio & ultra, *bl* 5.00 *14.50*
109 A21 2sh6p blk & red, *bl* ('29) 7.00 *15.00*
110 A21 3sh grn & vio 7.00 *22.50*
111 A21 5sh green & red, *yel* 11.00 *30.00*
112 A21 10sh green & red, *emer* 45.00 *110.00*
Nos. 91-112 (22) 102.00 *300.00*

Grand Anse Beach — A22

Seal of the Colony — A23

View of Grand Etang
A24

View of St. George's
A25

1934, Oct. 23 Engr. *Perf. 12½*

114 A22 ½p green .20 *.95*
a. Perf. 12½x13 ('36) 4.00 *35.00*

Perf. 13½x12½

115 A23 1p blk brn & blk .65 *.30*
a. Perf 12½ 1.00 2.50

Perf. 12½x13½

116 A24 1½p car & black .90 .45
a. Perf 12½ ('36) 4.50 3.00

Perf. 12½

117 A23 2p org & black .60 .40
118 A25 2½p deep blue .40 .40
119 A23 3p ol grn & blk 1.00 *2.25*
120 A23 6p claret & blk 1.50 1.50
121 A23 1sh brown & blk 1.25 *3.25*
122 A23 2sh6p ultra & blk 9.00 *22.50*
123 A23 5sh vio & black 25.00 *42.50*
Nos. 114-123 (10) 40.50 *74.50*
Set, never hinged 95.00

Common Design Types pictured following the introduction.

Silver Jubilee Issue
Common Design Type

1935, May 6 *Perf. 11x12*

124 CD301 ½p green & blk .65 *1.00*
125 CD301 1p black & ultra .65 *1.50*
126 CD301 1½p car & blue .65 *1.50*
127 CD301 1sh brn vio & ind 5.50 *14.00*
Nos. 124-127 (4) 7.45 *18.00*
Set, never hinged 12.00

Coronation Issue
Common Design Type

1937, May 12 Wmk. 4 *Perf. 11x11½*

128 CD302 1p dark purple .25 .25
129 CD302 1½p dark carmine .25 .20
130 CD302 2½p deep ultra .50 .35
Nos. 128-130 (3) 1.00 .80
Set, never hinged 1.25

George VI — A26

Seal of the Colony — A28

Grand Anse Beach — A27

View of Grand Etang — A29

View of St. George's A30

Seal of the Colony A31

1937, July 12 Photo. *Perf. 14½x14*

131 A26 ¼p chestnut .75 .25

1938, Mar. 16 Engr. *Perf. 12½*

132 A27 ½p green 2.50 1.10
133 A28 1p blk brn & blk .55 .30
134 A29 1½p scarlet & blk .25 *.95*
135 A28 2p orange & blk .20 *.55*
136 A30 2½p ultramarine .20 *.35*
137 A28 3p olive grn & blk .20 *2.10*
138 A28 6p red vio & blk .70 .45
139 A28 1sh org brn & blk 1.40 .45
140 A28 2sh ultra & black 9.25 2.00
141 A28 5sh purple & blk 2.00 2.00

Perf. 14

142 A31 10sh rose car & gray blue 14.50 9.50
a. 10sh deep car & gray blue, perf. 12 ('43) 260.00 *800.00*
b. Perf. 12x13 42.50 8.00
Nos. 131-142 (12) 32.50 20.00
Set, never hinged 55.00

1938-42 *Perf. 12½x13½, 13½x12½*

132a A27 ½p 2.60 .75
133a A28 1p .30 .20
134a A29 1½p car & blk 1.25 .40
135a A28 2p 1.40 .75
136a A30 2½p *3,000.* *240.00*
137a A28 3p 2.50 *1.00*
138a A28 6p ('42) 1.25 .35
139a A28 1sh ('42) 2.00 1.50
140a A28 2sh ('41) 11.00 2.00
141a A28 5sh ('47) 1.60 *4.50*

Catalogue values for unused stamps in this section, from this point to the end of the section, are for Never Hinged items.

Peace Issue
Common Design Type

1946, Sept. 25 *Perf. 13½x14*

143 CD303 1½p carmine .20 .20
144 CD303 3½p deep blue .20 .20

Silver Wedding Issue
Common Design Types

1948, Oct. 27 Photo. *Perf. 14x14½*

145 CD304 1½p scarlet .20 .20

Engr.; Name Typo.
Perf. 11½x11

146 CD305 10sh gray green 11.00 16.00

UPU Issue
Common Design Types
Engr.; Name Typo. on 6c, 12c
Perf. 13½, 11x11½

1949, Oct. 10 Wmk. 4

147 CD306 5c ultra .25 .25
148 CD307 6c deep olive .35 .35
149 CD308 12c red lilac .65 .65
150 CD309 24c red brown 1.00 1.00
Nos. 147-150 (4) 2.25 2.25

A32

A33

A34

1951, Jan. 8 Engr. *Perf. 11½*
Center in Black

151 A32 ½c chestnut .20 .20
152 A32 1c blue green .20 .20
153 A32 2c dark brown .20 .20
154 A32 3c carmine .25 .20
155 A32 4c deep orange .40 .25
156 A32 5c purple .50 .30
157 A32 6c olive .50 .50
158 A32 7c blue 1.25 .30
159 A32 12c red violet 2.00 .75

Perf. 11½x12½

160 A33 25c dark brown 2.00 .50
161 A33 50c ultra 3.00 .60
162 A33 $1.50 orange 7.50 5.00

Perf. 11½x13
Center in Gray Blue

163 A34 $2.50 deep carmine 7.00 6.00
Nos. 151-163 (13) 25.00 15.00

See #180-183, 202. For overprints see #166-169.

University Issue
Common Design Types

1951, Feb. 16 *Perf. 14x14½*

164 CD310 3c dp car & gray blk .40 .40
165 CD311 6c olive & black .60 .60

NEW CONSTITUTION
1951

Nos. 154-156 and 159 Overprinted in Black or Carmine

1951, Sept. 21 *Perf. 11½*

166 A32 3c carmine & black .20 .25
167 A32 4c dp orange & black .20 .25
168 A32 5c purple & black (C) .20 .25
169 A32 12c red violet & black .20 .25
Nos. 166-169 (4) .80 1.00

Adoption of a new constitution for the Windward Islands.

Coronation Issue
Common Design Type

1953, June 3 *Perf. 13½x13*

170 CD312 3c carmine & black .25 .20

Types of 1951 Inscribed "E II R" and

Queen Elizabeth II — A35

1953-59 Engr. *Perf. 11½*
Center in Black

171 A35 ½c chestnut ('54) .20 .20
172 A35 1c blue green .20 .20
173 A35 2c dark brown .20 .20
174 A35 3c carmine ('54) .20 .20
175 A35 4c dp orange ('54) .20 .20
176 A35 5c purple ('54) .20 .20
177 A35 6c olive .45 1.10
178 A35 7c blue ('55) 1.25 .20
179 A35 12c red violet .20 .20

Perf. 11½x12½

180 A33 25c dark brown ('55) 1.40 .20
181 A33 50c ultra ('55) 5.50 .35
182 A33 $1.50 orange ('55) 11.00 *12.50*

Perf. 11½x13
Center in Gray Blue

183 A34 $2.50 deep car ('59) 17.50 9.25
Nos. 171-183 (13) 38.50 25.00

See Nos. 195-202.

No. 182 was locally surcharged "2" and two black horizontal lines and issued Dec. 23, 1965, for revenue use. It was used postally, though not authorized for postal use. The "2" is found in two type faces.

West Indies Federation
Common Design Type
Perf. 11½x11

1958, Apr. 22 Wmk. 314

184 CD313 3c green .30 .20
185 CD313 6c blue .40 .40
186 CD313 12c carmine rose .50 .20
Nos. 184-186 (3) 1.20 .80

Victoria and Elizabeth II and Mail Truck A36

Queens and: 8c, "La Concepcion" and Dakota plane. 25c, Steam Packet "Solent" and B.O.A.C. plane.

1961, June 1 Photo. *Perf. 14½x14*

187 A36 3c gray & deep car .20 .20
188 A36 8c orange & ultra .50 .25
189 A36 25c blue & maroon .55 .25
Nos. 187-189 (3) 1.25 .70

Centenary of first Grenada postage stamps.

Freedom from Hunger Issue
Common Design Type

1963, June 4 *Perf. 14x14½*

190 CD314 8c green .30 .20

Red Cross Centenary Issue
Common Design Type

1963, Sept. 2 Litho. *Perf. 13*

191 CD315 3c black & red .20 .20
192 CD315 25c ultra & red .45 .20

Types of 1953-55
Wmk. 314

1963-64 Engr. *Perf. 11½*
Center in Black

195 A35 2c dark brown .20 .20
196 A35 3c carmine .20 .20
197 A35 4c dp orange .20 .30
198 A35 5c purple .20 .20
199 A35 6c olive 175.00 60.00
201 A35 12c red violet .30 .20

Perf. 11½x12½

202 A33 25c dark brown 1.50 .90
Nos. 195-198,201-202 (6) 2.60 2.00

Issued: 6c, 1963; others, May 12, 1964.

ITU Issue
Common Design Type

1965, May 17 Litho. *Perf. 11x11½*

205 CD317 2c vermilion & olive .20 .20
206 CD317 50c yellow & ver .25 .20

Intl. Cooperation Year Issue
Common Design Type

1965, Oct. 25 Litho. *Perf. 14½*

207 CD318 1c blue grn & claret .20 .20
208 CD318 25c lt violet & green .20 .20

Churchill Memorial Issue
Common Design Type

1966, Jan. 24 Photo. *Perf. 14*
Design in Black, Gold and Carmine Rose

209 CD319 1c bright blue .20 .20
210 CD319 3c green .20 .20
211 CD319 25c brown .25 .25
212 CD319 35c violet .35 .35
Nos. 209-212 (4) 1.00 1.00

Royal Visit Issue
Common Design Type

1966, Feb. 4 Litho. *Perf. 11x12*

213 CD320 3c violet blue .20 .20
214 CD320 35c dark car rose .60 .20

Careenage, St. George's A37

Queen Elizabeth II — A38

Designs: 1c, Hillsborough, Carriacou. 2c, Bougainvillea. 3c, Flamboyant plant. 5c, Levera Beach. 8c, Annandale Falls. 10c, Cacao pods. 12c, Inner Harbor. 15c, Nutmeg. 25c, St. George's. 35c, Grand Anse Beach. 50c, Bananas. $1, Seal of Colony. $3, Map of Grenada.

Perf. 14½x13½, 14½ (A38)

1966, Apr. 1 Photo. Wmk. 314

215 A37 1c blue, grn & yel .20 .30
216 A37 2c dk grn & dp car rose .20 .20
217 A37 3c multicolored .20 .20
218 A37 5c multicolored .30 .20
219 A37 6c ultra, grn & car rose .30 .20
220 A37 8c dp grn, ind & yel .30 .20
221 A37 10c yel grn, brn & dk car .25 .20
222 A37 12c multicolored .25 .30
223 A37 15c multicolored .25 .30
224 A37 25c dk bl, grn & car rose .25 .20
225 A37 35c multicolored .40 .20
226 A37 50c violet & green .65 *.80*
227 A38 $1 brn, ultra & dull grn 4.75 2.00
228 A38 $2 multicolored 3.50 *5.00*
229 A38 $3 brt grnsh bl, dk bl & dl yel 3.50 *7.50*
Nos. 215-229 (15) 15.30 *17.80*

For overprints and surcharges see Nos. 237-261.

The overprint "Children Need Milk" and surcharges were applied in 1968 in Grenada to Nos. 227-229. The surcharges respectively are 1c+3c, 2c+3c and 3c+3c. The surcharge exists in two sizes on the $2 stamp.

World Cup Soccer Issue
Common Design Type

1966, July 1 Litho. *Perf. 14*
230 CD321 5c multicolored .20 .20
231 CD321 50c multicolored .35 *.50*

WHO Headquarters Issue
Common Design Type

1966, Sept. 20 Litho. *Perf. 14*
232 CD322 8c multicolored .20 .20
233 CD322 25c multicolored .30 .25

UNESCO Anniversary Issue
Common Design Type

1966, Dec. 1 Litho. *Perf. 14*
234 CD323 2c "Education" .20 .20
235 CD323 15c "Science" .20 .20
236 CD323 50c "Culture" .40 *.60*
Nos. 234-236 (3) .80 1.00

Nos. 216-217, 220 and 224 Overprinted "ASSOCIATED STATEHOOD 1967" in Silver

Perf. 14½x13½

1967, Mar. 3 Photo. Wmk. 314
237 A37 2c dk grn & dp car rose .20 .20
238 A37 3c multicolored .20 .20
239 A37 8c dp grn, ind & yel .20 .20
240 A37 25c dk bl, grn & car rose .20 .20
Nos. 237-240 (4) .80 .80

Nos. 216, 221, 223 and 227-228 Surcharged

Perf. 14½x13½, 14½ (A38)

1967, July 1 Photo. Wmk. 314
241 A37 1c on 15c multi .20 .20
242 A37 2c dk grn & dp car rose .20 .20
243 A37 3c on 10c multi .20 .20
244 A38 $1 multicolored .30 .25
245 A38 $2 multicolored .40 .40
Nos. 241-245 (5) 1.30 1.25

EXPO '67 Intl. Exhib., Montreal, Apr. 28-Oct. 27.

Nos. 215-229 Overprinted in Black: "ASSOCIATED STATEHOOD"

1967-68 Photo. Wmk. 314
246 A37 1c multicolored .20 .20
247 A37 2c multicolored .20 .20
248 A37 3c multicolored .20 .20
249 A37 5c multicolored .20 .20
250 A37 6c multicolored .20 .20
251 A37 8c multicolored .20 .20
252 A37 10c multicolored .20 .20
253 A37 12c multicolored .20 .20
254 A37 15c multicolored .20 .20
255 A37 25c multicolored .20 .20
256 A37 35c multicolored .50 .20
257 A37 50c multicolored .70 .30
258 A38 $1 multicolored .80 .50
259 A38 $2 multicolored 1.25 *1.00*
260 A38 $3 multicolored 2.25 *3.00*

Overprinted and Surcharged
261 A38 $5 on $2 multi 1.75 *3.50*
Nos. 246-261 (16) 9.25 *10.50*

Issued: $5, 5/18/68; others, 10/19/67.

Pres. John F. Kennedy A39

Pres. Kennedy and: 25c, 50c, Bird-of-paradise flower. 35c, $1, Roses.

Perf. 14½x14

1968, Jan. 13 Unwmk.
262 A39 1c lt blue & multi .20 .20
263 A39 15c orange & multi .20 .20
264 A39 25c violet & multi .20 .20
265 A39 35c multicolored .20 .20
266 A39 50c blue & multi .25 .25
267 A39 $1 multicolored .35 .35
Nos. 262-267 (6) 1.40 1.40

50th anniv. of the birth of Pres. John F. Kennedy (1917-1963).

Bugler and Jamboree Emblem — A40

Jamboree Emblem and: 2c, 50c, Boy Scouts sitting in tent. 3c, $1, Lord Baden-Powell.

1968, Feb. 1 Photo. *Perf. 13x14*
268 A40 1c orange & multi .20 .20
269 A40 2c emer & multi .20 .20
270 A40 3c yellow & multi .20 .20
271 A40 35c multicolored .20 .20
272 A40 50c blue & multi .30 .30
273 A40 $1 multicolored .40 .40
Nos. 268-273 (6) 1.50 1.50

12th Boy Scout Jamboree, Farragut State Park, Idaho, Aug. 1-9, 1967.

Seascape, by Winston Churchill — A41

Paintings: 12c, Pine at the shore. 15c, 35c, Houses at the shore. 50c, Churchill painting a seascape.

Perf. 14x14½

1968, Mar. 23 Unwmk.
274 A41 10c multicolored .20 .20
275 A41 12c multicolored .20 .20
276 A41 15c multicolored .20 .20
277 A41 25c multicolored .20 .20
278 A41 35c multicolored .25 .20
279 A41 50c multicolored .30 .25
Nos. 274-279 (6) 1.35 1.25

Winston Churchill as a painter.

Edith McGuire, US, 200m. Dash, 1964 A42

Gold Medal Winners: 2c, 50c, Arthur Wint, Jamaica, 400m run, 1948. 3c, 60c, Adhemar Ferreira da Silva, Brazil, hop, step and jump, 1952 & 1956. 10c, Like 1c.

1968, Sept. 24 Photo. *Perf. 12½*
280 A42 1c ultra & multi .20 *.30*
281 A42 2c lilac & multi .20 *.30*
282 A42 3c green & multi .20 *.30*
283 A42 10c red org & multi .20 *.30*
284 A42 50c Prus blue & multi .45 .45
285 A42 60c orange & multi .50 *.65*
Nos. 280-285 (6) 1.75 2.30

19th Olympic Games, Mexico City, Oct. 12-27. Nos. 280-282 and 283-285 are printed in sheets of 9 (3 of each denomination).

For surcharges see Nos. 310-315.

Transplant Operations — A43

Perf. 13x13½

1968, Nov. 25 Photo. Unwmk.
286 A43 5c Kidney .20 .20
287 A43 25c Heart .30 .20
288 A43 35c Lung .40 .20
289 A43 50c Cornea .50 .50
Nos. 286-289 (4) 1.40 1.10

20th anniv. of WHO.

Adoration of the Magi, by Veronese A44

Paintings: 15c, Madonna and Child with St. John and St. Catherine, by Titian. 35c, Adoration of the Magi, by Botticelli. $1, "A Knight Adoring the Infant Christ" by Vincenzo di Biagio Catena.

1968, Dec. 3 *Perf. 12½*
290 A44 5c vio blue & multi .20 .20
291 A44 15c crimson & multi .20 .20
292 A44 35c dk green & multi .20 .20
293 A44 $1 dk blue & multi .25 .25
Nos. 290-293 (4) .85 .85

Christmas. For overprints see Nos. 341-344.

Hibiscus and "La Concepcion" — A45

Yacht in St. George's Harbour — A45a

Designs: 2c, Bird-of-paradise flower. 3c, Bougainvillea. 5c, Rock hind (fish; horiz.). 6c, Sailfish. 8c, Red snapper, horiz. 10c, Giant toad, horiz. 12c, Yellowfoot tortoise. No. 302, Tree boa, horiz. No. 302A, Thunbergia. 25c, Mouse opossum. 35c Armadillo, horiz. 50c, Mona monkey. $1, Bananaquit (bird). $2, Brown pelican. $3, Magnificent frigate bird. $5, Bare-eyed thrush.

Perf. 14x14½, 14½x14; 14x13½ (#302A); 13½x14 (#305A)

Photo.; Litho. (#302A, 305A)

1968-71 Unwmk.
294 A45 1c dl yel & multi .20 .20
295 A45 2c brt pink & multi .20 .20
296 A45 3c blue & multi .20 .20
297 A45 5c violet & multi .20 .20
298 A45 6c emer & multi .20 .20
299 A45 8c multicolored .20 .25
300 A45 10c multicolored .20 .20
301 A45 12c ver & multi .20 .20
302 A45 15c emer & multi .90 .65
302A A45 15c gray & multi 5.00 2.50
303 A45 25c multicolored .30 .20
304 A45 35c multicolored .35 .20
305 A45 50c ultra & multi .45 .25
305A A45a 75c blue & multi 10.00 5.00
306 A45 $1 multicolored 3.00 1.75
307 A45 $2 multicolored 4.25 *6.00*
308 A45 $3 yel & multi 4.25 3.75
309 A45 $5 multicolored 6.00 *12.50*
Nos. 294-309 (18) 36.10 *34.45*

Nos. 294-309 vary in size from 25x44mm to 29x46mm.

The overprint "VOTE/FEB. 28 1972" was applied to the 2c, 3c, 6c and 25c in Feb., 1972.

Issued: 5c, 10c, 25c, $2, 2/4/69; 3c, 8c, 35c, $5, 7/1/69; #302A, 1970; 75c, 10/9/71; others, 10/68.

For surcharges see Nos. 462-464. For overprints see Nos. 528-541, C3-C19.

Nos. 280-285 Surcharged in Carmine

1969, Feb. *Perf. 12½*
310 A42 5c on 1c multi .20 .20
311 A42 8c on 2c multi .20 .20
312 A42 25c on 3c multi .20 .20
313 A42 35c on 10c multi .20 .20
314 A42 $1 on 50c multi .20 .25
315 A42 $2 on 60c multi .30 .40
Nos. 310-315 (6) 1.30 1.45

Gov. Hilda Bynoe and View of St. George's A46

Designs: 15c, Premier Eric M. Gairy, fruits and St. George's. 60c, Emblems of Brussels, New York and Montreal World's Fairs.

1969, May 1 Litho. *Perf. 13x13½*
316 A46 5c multicolored .20 .20
317 A46 15c multicolored .20 .20
318 A46 50c multicolored .20 .20
319 A46 60c multicolored .20 .30
Nos. 316-319 (4) .80 .90

Nos. 310-319 issued to publicize CARIFTA (Caribbean Free Trade Area) Exposition, St. George's, Apr. 5-30.

Gov. Hilda Bynoe — A47

Designs: 25c, Dr. Martin Luther King, Jr. $1, Belshazzar's Feast, by Rembrandt, horiz.

Perf. 13x12½, 12½x13

1969, June 8 Photo. Unwmk.
320 A47 5c multicolored .20 .20
321 A47 25c multicolored .20 .20
322 A47 35c multicolored .20 .20
323 A47 $1 multicolored .30 .40
Nos. 320-323 (4) .90 1.00

International Human Rights Year.

Batsman Playing Off-drive — A48

Cricket: 10c, Batsman playing defensive stroke. 25c, Batsman sweeping ball. 35c, Batsman playing on-drive.

1969, Aug. 1 *Perf. 14x14½*
324 A48 3c dk blue & multi .30 *.95*
325 A48 10c fawn & multi .35 *.40*
326 A48 25c dp green & multi .60 *.80*
327 A48 35c brt purple & multi .75 *.85*
Nos. 324-327 (4) 2.00 *3.00*

Astronaut Collecting Moon Rocks, Landing Module and Earth — A49

Designs: ½c, like $1. 1c, Apollo 11, moon and earth. 2c, Landing module "Eagle." 3c, Memorial tablet left on moon. 8c, Separation of rocket and spaceship. 25c, Take off from Cape Kennedy, vert. 35c, Apollo 11 circling the moon, vert. 50c, Splashdown, vert. ½c, 2c, 25c, 50c, $1 inscribed: "We came in peace for all mankind." 1c, 3c, 8c, 35c inscribed: "Like the moon it shall be established forever" Psalms 89:37.

Perf. 13x13½ (½c), 12½

1969, Sept. 24 Litho. Unwmk.

Size: 56x35mm

328 A49 ½c multicolored .20 .20

Size: 44½x28mm, 28x44½mm

329 A49 1c multicolored .20 .20
330 A49 2c multicolored .20 .20
331 A49 3c multicolored .20 .20
332 A49 8c multicolored .20 .20
333 A49 25c multicolored .20 .20
334 A49 35c multicolored .20 .20
335 A49 50c multicolored .20 .20
336 A49 $1 multicolored .40 .60
a. Souvenir sheet of 2 1.75 1.75
Nos. 328-336 (9) 2.00 2.20

Man's first moonlanding (Apollo 11), July 20, 1969.

No. 336a contains stamps similar to Nos. 331 and 336 with simulated perforations.

For surcharge and overprints see #349, 379-382.

Mahatma Gandhi — A50

Gandhi in various positions. 15c, 25c are vert.

1969, Oct. 8 *Perf. 11½x12, 12x11½*

Queen's Head in Gold

337 A50 6c multicolored .20 .20
338 A50 15c multicolored .25 .20
339 A50 25c multicolored .40 .20
340 A50 $1 multicolored .65 .50
a. Souvenir sheet of 4 3.00 3.00
Nos. 337-340 (4) 1.50 1.10

Mohandas K. Gandhi (1869-1948), leader in India's fight for independence.

No. 340a contains stamps similar to Nos. 337-340 with simulated perforation.

Nos. 290-293 Overprinted in Black or Silver with Bars and "1969"

1969, Dec. 23 Photo. *Perf. 12½*

341 A44 2c on 15c multi .20 *.50*
342 A44 5c multi (S) .20 .20
343 A44 35c multi (S) .20 .20
344 A44 $1 multi (S) .65 *1.10*
Nos. 341-344 (4) 1.25 *2.00*

Christmas.

Edward Teach (Blackbeard) A51

Pirates: 25c, Anne Bonney and sailboats. 50c, Jean Lafitte and sailboats. $1, Mary Read, ships and fighting pirates.

1970, Feb. 1 Engr. *Perf. 13x13½*

345 A51 15c black .40 .20
346 A51 25c emerald .50 .20
347 A51 50c purple 1.10 .20
348 A51 $1 carmine 2.00 .75
Nos. 345-348 (4) 4.00 1.35

No. 328 Surcharged

Type I

Type II

1970, Mar. 18 Litho. *Perf. 13x13½*

349 A49 5c on ½c multi (I) .20 .20
a. Type II .80 .80

Christ, from "The Last Supper," by Andrea del Sarto — A52

Paintings: No. 351 (5c), St. John, from Last Supper by Andrea del Sarto. Nos. 352-353 (15c), Christ Crowned with Thorns, by Anthony Van Dyck. Nos. 354-355 (25c), Passion of Christ, by Hans Memling. Nos. 356-357 (60c), Christ in the Tomb, by Peter Paul Rubens. Nos. 350, 352, 354 and 356 have denomination in lower right corner; others in lower left corner. The stamps of the same denomination are printed se-tenant without separating margin, reproducing continuous picture.

1970, Apr. 13 Litho. *Perf. 11½x11*

350 5c rose car & multi .20 .20
351 5c rose car & multi .20 .20
a A52 Pair, #350-351 .40 .40
352 15c ultra & multi .20 *.25*
353 15c ultra & multi .20 *.25*
a A52 Pair, #352-353 .40 *.50*
354 25c brt vio & multi .20 *.25*
355 25c brt vio & multi .20 *.25*
a A52 Pair, #354-355 .40 .50
356 60c dull org & multi .35 *.55*
357 60c dull org & multi .35 *.55*
b A52 Pair, #354-355 .80 1.10
a. Souvenir sheet of 4, #354-357 1.25 1.25
Nos. 350-357 (8) 1.90 *2.50*

Easter.

Girl Pushing Carriage with Kittens — A53

Designs: 15c, Girl playing with puppy and kitten. 30c, Boy fishing and cat. 60c, Children with pets.

1970, May 27 Litho. *Perf. 11*

358 A53 5c multicolored .20 .20
359 A53 15c multicolored .20 .20
360 A53 30c multicolored .35 .35
a. Souvenir sheet of 2 .65 .65
361 A53 60c multicolored .75 *1.00*
a. Souvenir sheet of 2 1.50 1.50
Nos. 358-361 (4) 1.50 1.75

William Wordsworth (1770-1850). English poet. No. 360a contains stamps similar to Nos. 358 and 360; No. 361a contains stamps similar to Nos. 359 and 361. Sheets have simulated perforations.

Indian Parliament — A54

Commonwealth Parliamentary Association Emblem and: 25c, British Parliament. 50c, Canadian Parliament. 60c, Grenadian Parliament.

1970, June 15 *Perf. 14½x14*

362 A54 5c multicolored .20 .20
363 A54 25c multicolored .20 .20
364 A54 50c multicolored .20 .20
365 A54 60c multicolored .20 .20
a. Souvenir sheet of 4, #362-365 .75 .75
Nos. 362-365 (4) .80 .80

7th Caribbean Regional Conf. of the Commonwealth Parliamentary Assoc., St. George's. June 13-20.

Sun Tower and EXPO Emblem A55

EXPO Emblem and: 2c, Livelihood Industry pavilion, horiz. 3c, Ikenobo, Japanese floral art, vert. 10c, Adam and Eve, by Tintoretto and Italian pavilion, horiz. 25c, UN pavilion and flags reflected in pool, 50c, Peace statue of St. Francis, San Francisco pavilion, cable car and Golden Gate Bridge, $1, Toshiba-Ihi pavilion, horiz.

1970, Aug. 8 Litho. *Perf. 13½*

366 A55 1c brt blue & multi .20 .20
367 A55 2c multicolored .20 .20
368 A55 3c buff & multi .20 .20
369 A55 10c multicolored .20 .20
370 A55 25c gray & multi .20 .20
371 A55 50c gray & multi .25 *1.00*
Nos. 366-371 (6) 1.25 2.00

Souvenir Sheet

372 A55 $1 gold & multi 1.00 *1.75*

EXPO '70 Intl. Exhib., Osaka, Japan, Mar. 15-Sept. 13.

Pres. Roosevelt and Flag-Raising on Iwo Jima — A56

Designs: 5c, Marshal Georgi K. Zhukov and fall of Berlin. 15c, Winston Churchill and evacuation of Dunkirk. 25c, Charles de Gaulle and liberation of Paris. 50c, General Dwight D. Eisenhower and D-Day landing. 60c, Field Marshal Bernard Montgomery and Battle of Alamein.

1970, Sept. 3 *Perf. 11*

373 A56 ½c multicolored .20 *.55*
374 A56 5c multicolored .70 .30
375 A56 15c multicolored 1.40 .45
376 A56 25c multicolored 1.40 .45
377 A56 50c multicolored 1.90 1.50
378 A56 60c multicolored 1.90 *2.75*
a. Souv. sheet of 4 #373, 375, 377-378 5.00 5.00
Nos. 373-378 (6) 7.50 6.00

End of World War II, 25th anniversary.

Nos. 333-336 Overprinted in Black or Silver: "PHILYMPIA / LONDON 1970"

1970, Sept. 18 *Perf. 12½*

379 A49 25c multicolored .20 .20
380 A49 35c multicolored .20 .20
381 A49 50c multicolored .25 .25
382 A49 $1 multi (S) .60 .60
Nos. 379-382 (4) 1.25 1.25

Philympia 1970, London philatelic exhibition, Sept. 18-26. The overprint on No. 382 is vertical, reading up.

This overprint was applied in silver to No. 336a.

UPU Headquarters, Emblem and Old Transportation — A57

UPU Headquarters, emblem and: 25c, Jet plane, ship and diesel train. 50c, Rowland Hill, vert. $1, Abraham Lincoln, vert.

1970, Oct. 17 Litho. *Perf. 14½*

383 A57 15c orange & multi .45 .45
384 A57 25c blue & multi .45 .20
385 A57 50c multicolored .45 .40
386 A57 $1 rose & multi .55 1.00
a. Souvenir sheet of 2 1.75 2.00
Nos. 383-386 (4) 1.90 2.05

Opening of the new UPU Headquarters in Bern. No. 386a contains stamps similar to Nos. 385-386.

Madonna of the Goldfinch, by Tiepolo — A58

Christmas (Paintings): No. 388, 35c, Virgin and Child with Sts. Peter and Paul, by Dirk Bouts. No. 389, $1, Virgin and Child, by Bellini. 3c, Like No. 387. 2c, 50c, Madonna of the Basket, by Correggio.

1970, Dec. 5 *Perf. 14x13½*

387 A58 ½c yel grn & multi .20 .20
388 A58 ½c pink & multi .20 .20
389 A58 ½c yellow & multi .20 .20
390 A58 2c lt blue & multi .20 .20
391 A58 3c dp rose & multi .20 .20
392 A58 35c dk green & multi .35 .40
393 A58 50c brown & multi .50 .50
394 A58 $1 purple & multi .75 1.10
a. Souvenir sheet of 2, #393-394 2.75 2.25
Nos. 387-394 (8) 2.60 3.00

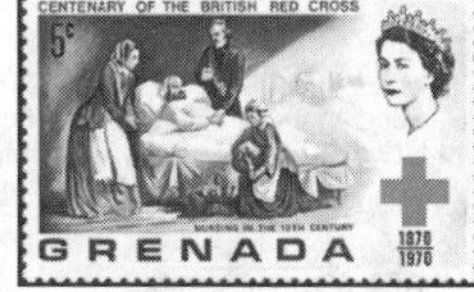

Nursing in 19th Century A59

Designs: 15c, Horse-drawn ambulance, Northern France, 1918. 25c, First aid station, 1941. 60c, Red Cross truck loaded on plane, 1970 emergency aid.

1970, Dec. 12 Litho. *Perf. 14½x14*

395 A59 5c red & multi .20 .20
396 A59 15c red & multi .30 .20
397 A59 25c red & multi .50 .35
398 A59 60c red & multi 1.00 .95
a. Souvenir sheet of 4, #395-398 2.25 2.00
Nos. 395-398 (4) 2.00 1.70

Centenary of the British Red Cross Society.

John Dewey, Children Learning to Paint — A60

Designs: 10c, Jean-Jacques Rousseau and students. 50c, Moses Maimonides and biology student. $1, Bertrand Russell and boys.

1971, May 8 Litho. *Perf. 13½*

399 A60 5c multicolored .20 .20
400 A60 10c multicolored .20 .20
401 A60 50c multicolored .60 .50
402 A60 $1 multicolored 1.25 .75
a. Souvenir sheet of 2, #401-402 2.25 2.50
Nos. 399-402 (4) 2.25 1.65

International Education Year.

Jennifer Hosten and Map of Grenada A61

1971, June 1 Litho. *Perf. 13½*

403 A61 5c vio blue & multi .20 .20
404 A61 10c red lilac & multi .20 .20
405 A61 15c brt rose & multi .40 .20
406 A61 25c violet & multi .50 .30
407 A61 35c blue & multi .60 .60
408 A61 50c red & multi 1.10 1.00
a. Souvenir sheet of 1 2.50 2.75
Nos. 403-408 (6) 3.00 2.50

Honoring Miss Jennifer Hosten of Grenada, Miss World, 1971. No. 408a, printed on silk, contains imperf. stamp similar to No. 408.

Nos. 403-408 and 408a were overprinted "INTERPEX/1972" in Mar. 1972.

For surcharge and overprints #465, C23-C26.

Canadian and French Boy Scouts — A62

Boy Scouts from: 35c, West Germany and US. 50c, Australia and Japan. 75c, Grenada and Great Britain.

1971, Aug. Litho. *Perf. 11*

409 A62 5c multicolored .20 .20
410 A62 35c multicolored .45 .45
411 A62 50c multicolored .60 .70
412 A62 75c multicolored .75 1.00
a. Souvenir sheet of 2, #411-412 2.50 3.00
Nos. 409-412 (4) 2.00 2.35

13th Boy Scout World Jamboree, Asagiri Plain, Japan, Aug. 2-10.

Napoleon, by Edouard Détaille A63

Paintings of Napoleon: 15c, Outside Madrid, by Carle Vernet. 35c, Crossing the Alps, by Jacques Louis David. $2, Portrait, by David.

1971, Sept. *Perf. 13x13½*

413 A63 5c multicolored .20 .20
414 A63 15c multicolored .20 .20
415 A63 35c multicolored .50 .50
a. Souvenir sheet of 1 2.50 2.25
416 A63 $2 multicolored 1.75 2.00
Nos. 413-416 (4) 2.65 2.90

Sesquicentennial of the death of Napoleon Bonaparte (1769-1821).

No. 415a contains stamp similar to No. 415 with simulated perforations.

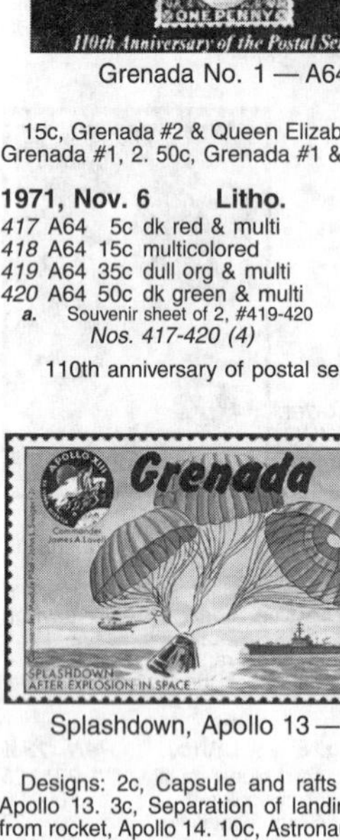

Grenada No. 1 — A64

15c, Grenada #2 & Queen Elizabeth II. 35c, Grenada #1, 2. 50c, Grenada #1 & scroll.

1971, Nov. 6 Litho. *Perf. 11*

417 A64 5c dk red & multi .20 .20
418 A64 15c multicolored .20 .20
419 A64 35c dull org & multi .40 .25
420 A64 50c dk green & multi .60 .90
a. Souvenir sheet of 2, #419-420 1.25 1.25
Nos. 417-420 (4) 1.40 1.55

110th anniversary of postal service.

Splashdown, Apollo 13 — A65

Designs: 2c, Capsule and rafts in ocean, Apollo 13. 3c, Separation of landing module from rocket, Apollo 14. 10c, Astronauts collecting moon rocks, Apollo 14. 25c, Astronauts in moon rover, Apollo 15. 50c, $1, Rocket blast-off, Apollo 15, vert.

1971, Nov.

421 A65 1c multicolored .20 .20
422 A65 2c multicolored .20 .20
423 A65 3c black & multi .20 .20
424 A65 10c black & multi .30 .20
425 A65 25c multicolored 1.10 .35
426 A65 $1 multicolored 2.50 2.50
Nos. 421-426 (6) 4.50 3.65

Souvenir Sheet

427 A65 50c multicolored 2.75 2.75

US moon missions of Apollo 13, 14 and 15.

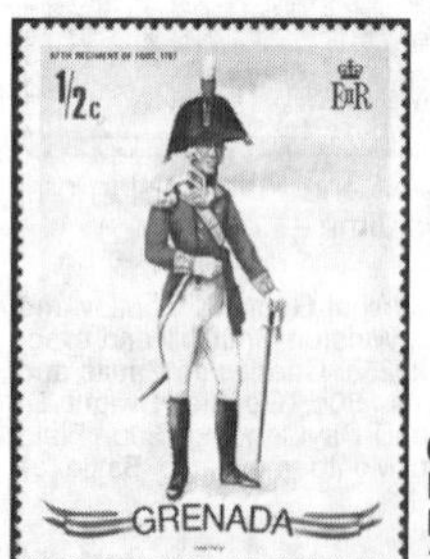

67th Regiment of Foot, 1787 — A66

Designs: 1c, 45th Regiment of Foot, 1792. 2c, 29th Regiment of Foot, 1794. 10c, 9th Regiment of Foot, 1801. 25c, 2nd Regiment of Foot, 1815. $1, 70th Regiment of Foot, 1764.

1971, Dec. *Perf. 13½x14*

428 A66 ½c red & multi .20 .20
429 A66 1c red & multi .20 .20
430 A66 2c red & multi .20 .20
431 A66 10c red & multi .50 .20
432 A66 25c red & multi .90 .30
433 A66 $1 red & multi 2.75 2.75
a. Souv. sheet of 2, #432-433, perf. 15 4.50 4.50
Nos. 428-433 (6) 4.75 3.85

Uniforms of British units stationed in Grenada.

For surcharges see Nos. 439, C1-C2.

Adoration of the Kings, by Memling — A67

Christmas: 25c, Madonna and Child, sculpture by Michelangelo. 35c, Madonna and Child, by Murillo. 50c, Madonna with the Apple, by Memling. $1, Adoration of the Kings, by Jan Mostaert.

1971, Dec. *Perf. 14x13½*

434 A67 15c gold & multi .20 .20
435 A67 25c gold & multi .30 .20
436 A67 35c gold & multi .35 .20
437 A67 50c gold & multi .50 .75
Nos. 434-437 (4) 1.35 1.35

Souvenir Sheet

438 A67 $1 gold & multi 1.25 1.25

No. 430 Surcharged with New Value, Olympic Rings and: "WINTER OLYMPICS / FEB. 3-13, 1972 / SAPPORO, JAPAN"

1972, Feb. 3 *Perf. 13½x14*

439 A66 $2 on 2c red & multi 2.25 2.25
a. Souvenir sheet of 2 2.75 2.75

11th Winter Olympic Games, Sapporo, Japan, Feb. 3-13. See Nos. C1-C2.

No. 439a is overprinted in red on No. 433a (no surcharge); margin inscribed in red: "SAPPORO 1972."

King Arthur, UNICEF Emblem A68

UNICEF Emblem and: 1c, 50c, Robin Hood. 2c, 75c, Robinson Crusoe, vert. 25c, like ½c. $1, Mary and her Little Lamb, vert.

1972, Mar. 4 *Perf. 14½x14, 14x14½*

450 A68 ½c dp blue & multi .20 .20
451 A68 1c yellow & multi .20 .20
452 A68 2c dp yel & multi .20 .20
453 A68 25c salmon & multi .20 .20
454 A68 50c multicolored .30 .35
455 A68 75c blue & multi .40 .60
456 A68 $1 multicolored .50 .85
a. Souvenir sheet of 1 1.25 1.25
Nos. 450-456 (7) 2.00 2.60

25th anniv. (in 1971) of UNICEF.

Yachting A69

1c, 50c, Equestrian. 2c, 35c, Running, vert.

1972, Sept. 8 Litho. *Perf. 14*

457 A69 ½c multicolored .20 .20
458 A69 1c lt blue & multi .20 .20
459 A69 2c orange & multi .20 .20
460 A69 35c yellow & multi .60 .90
461 A69 50c yel grn & multi .80 1.25
Nos. 457-461,C20-C21 (7) 3.25 4.00

20th Olympic Games, Munich, Aug. 26-Sept. 11. See No. C22.

Nos. 294-296, 403 Surcharged with New Value and Two Bars

Perf. 14x14½, 13½

1972, Oct. Photo.

462 A45 12c on 1c multi .55 .55
463 A45 12c on 2c multi .55 .55
464 A45 12c on 3c multi .55 .55
465 A61 12c on 5c multi .55 .55
Nos. 462-465 (4) 2.20 2.20

Silver Wedding Issue, 1972

Common Design Type

Design: Queen Elizabeth II, Prince Philip, seal of Grenada and myristica fragrans.

Perf. 14x14½

1972, Nov. 20 Wmk. 314

466 CD324 8c olive & multi .20 .20
467 CD324 $1 multicolored .50 .50

Boy Scout Saluting A70

Designs: 1c, Two Scouts knotting ropes. 2c, 70c, 75c, Scouts from different nations. 3c, 60c, $1, Lord Baden-Powell.

Unwmk.

1972, Dec. 2 Litho. *Perf. 14*

468 A70 ½c yellow & multi .20 .20
469 A70 1c red & multi .20 .20
470 A70 2c yellow & multi .20 .20
471 A70 3c brt lilac & multi .20 .20
472 A70 75c lt blue & multi 1.25 1.25
473 A70 $1 multicolored 1.75 1.75
Nos. 468-473,C27-C28 (8) 4.90 4.90

Souvenir Sheet

474 Sheet of 2 2.75 2.75
a. A70 60c ocher & multi 1.25 1.25
b. A70 70c pale lilac & multi 1.50 1.50

Boy Scouts, 65th anniversary.

Virgin and Child, Crosier — A71

Christmas: 3c, 35c, 70c, The Three Kings. 5c, $1, Holy Family. 25c, 60c, Like 1c.

1972, Dec. 9 Litho. *Perf. 14x13½*

475 A71 1c blue & multi .20 .20
476 A71 3c gray & multi .20 .20
477 A71 5c multicolored .20 .20
478 A71 25c multicolored .25 .25
479 A71 35c lt blue & multi .35 .35
480 A71 $1 ocher & multi 1.00 1.00
Nos. 475-480 (6) 2.20 2.20

Souvenir Sheet

Perf. 15

481 Sheet of 2 1.50 1.50
a. A71 60c blue & multi .60 .60
b. A71 70c bright pink & multi .80 .80

Flamingos A72

1973, Jan. 5 Litho. *Perf. 14*

482 A72 25c shown .75 .30
483 A72 35c Tapir .75 .30
484 A72 60c Macaws 1.50 1.25
485 A72 70c Ocelot 1.50 1.50
Nos. 482-485 (4) 4.50 3.35

National Zoo of Grenada.

Class II Ocean Racing Yacht A73

1973, Jan. 26 Litho. *Perf. 13½x14*

486 A73 25c shown .35 .35
487 A73 35c Boats in St. George's Harbour .50 .50
488 A73 60c Yacht "Bloodhound" .85 .85

489 A73 70c St. George's Harbour .95 .95
Nos. 486-489 (4) 2.65 2.65

Yachting off Grenada.

Sun God Helios, Equinoxes and Solstices — A74

WMO Emblem and: 1c, Poseidon and Nomad automatic storm detector. 2c, Zeus and radarscope. 3c, Goddess Iris, rainbow, weather balloon. 35c, Hermes, ATS 3 satellite. 50c, Zephyr and circulation of atmosphere. 75c, Demeter, space photograph of storm. $1, Selene, globe showing world rainfall. $2, Computer weather map (42x31mm).

1973, July 6 Litho. *Perf. 13½*

490 A74 ½c multicolored .20 .20
491 A74 1c multicolored .20 .20
492 A74 2c multicolored .20 .20
493 A74 3c multicolored .20 .20
494 A74 35c multicolored .40 .20
495 A74 50c multicolored .60 .30
496 A74 75c multicolored .75 .60
497 A74 $1 multicolored .75 .75
Nos. 490-497 (8) 3.30 2.65

Souvenir Sheet

498 A74 $2 multicolored 2.25 2.25

Intl. meteorological cooperation, cent.

Racing Class Yachts — A75

1973, Aug. 3 Litho. *Perf. 13½*

499 A75 ½c shown .20 .20
500 A75 1c Cruising class .20 .20
501 A75 2c Open-decked sloops .20 .20
502 A75 35c Sloop Mermaid .40 .20
503 A75 50c St. George's Harbour .50 .30
504 A75 75c Map of Carriacou .75 .75
505 A75 $1 Boat building .90 .90
Nos. 499-505 (7) 3.15 2.75

Souvenir Sheet

506 A75 $2 End of race 2.00 2.25

Carriacou Regatta, August 1973.

Ignaz Philipp Semmelweiss A76

Designs: Physicians and scientists.

1973, Sept. 17 Litho. *Perf. 14½*

507 A76 ½c shown .20 .20
508 A76 1c Louis Pasteur .20 .20
509 A76 2c Edward Jenner .20 .20
510 A76 3c Sigmund Freud .20 .20
511 A76 25c Emil von Behring .35 .35
512 A76 35c Carl Jung .50 .50
513 A76 50c Charles Calmette .75 .75
514 A76 $1 William Harvey 1.50 1.50
Nos. 507-514 (8) 3.90 3.90

Souvenir Sheet

515 A76 $2 Marie Curie 2.00 2.00

WHO, 25th anniv.

Princess Anne and Mark Phillips — A77

1973, Nov. 14 Wmk. 314 *Perf. 13½*

516 A77 25c dp orange & multi .30 .80
517 A77 $2 green & multi .30 .80
a. Souv. sheet of 2 (75c, $1) 1.00 1.00

Wedding of Princess Anne and Capt. Mark Phillips.

Nos. 516-517 were issued only in sheets of 5 plus label. Colors of 75c and $1 are as those of 25c and $2.

Virgin and Child, by Carlo Maratti — A78

Christmas (Paintings): 1c, Virgin and Child, by Carlo Crivelli. 2c, Virgin and Child, by Verrocchio. 3c, Adoration of the Shepherds, by Roberti. 25c, Holy Family, by Federigo Baroccio. 35c, Holy Family, by Bronzino. 75c, Mystic Nativity, by Botticelli. $1, Adoration of the Kings, by Geertgen tot Sint Jans. $2, Adoration of the Kings, by Jan Mostaert (30x45mm).

1973, Nov. Unwmk. *Perf. 14½*

519 A78 ½c lt brown & multi .20 .20
520 A78 1c citron & multi .20 .20
521 A78 2c blue & multi .20 .20
522 A78 3c green & multi .20 .20
523 A78 25c multicolored .35 .35
524 A78 35c multicolored .35 .35
525 A78 75c vio blue & multi .45 1.10
526 A78 $1 multicolored .55 1.40
Nos. 519-526 (8) 2.50 4.00

Souvenir Sheet

Perf. 13½x14

527 A78 $2 red & multi 1.75 1.75

Nos. 294-297, 299-301, 303-304, 305A-309 Overprinted

Perf. 14x14½, 14½x14

1974, Feb. 7 Photo.

528 A45 1c multicolored .20 .20
529 A45 2c multicolored .20 .20
530 A45 3c multicolored .20 .20
531 A45 5c multicolored .20 .20
532 A45 8c multicolored .20 .20
533 A45 10c multicolored .20 .20
534 A45 12c multicolored .20 .20
535 A45 25c multicolored .50 .35
536 A45 35c multicolored .75 .50

Litho.

Perf. 13½x14

537 A45a 75c multicolored *2.10 1.25*

Photo.

Perf. 14x14½

538 A45 $1 multicolored *3.75 1.50*
539 A45 $2 multicolored *6.25 6.00*
540 A45 $3 multicolored *8.25 7.50*
541 A45 $5 multicolored *12.50 15.00*
Nos. 528-541 (14) *35.50 33.50*

Grenada's independence, Feb. 7, 1974. Size of overprint on vertical stamps 16x5mm; on horizontal stamps 20x6mm.

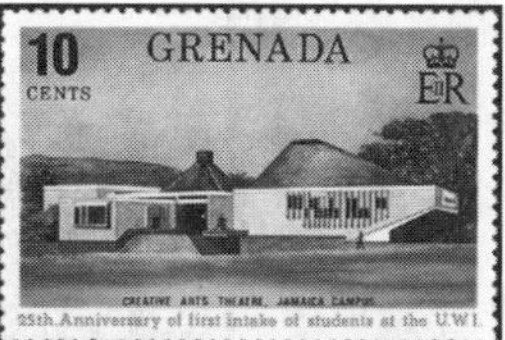

Creative Arts Theater, Jamaica Campus — A79

Designs: 25c, Marryshow House, University Center. 50c, Chapel, vert. $1, $2, University coat of arms, vert.

1974, Apr. 10 Litho. *Perf. 13½*

542 A79 10c multicolored .20 .20
543 A79 25c multicolored .20 .20
544 A79 50c multicolored .35 .35
545 A79 $1 multicolored .50 .50
Nos. 542-545 (4) 1.25 1.25

Souvenir Sheet

546 A79 $2 multicolored 1.00 1.00

25th anniv. of the University of the West Indies.

Prime Minister Eric M. Gairy — A80

1974, Aug. 19 Litho. *Perf. 13½*

547 A80 3c Nutmeg and mace .20 .20
548 A80 8c Map of Grenada .20 .20
549 A80 25c shown .25 .25
550 A80 35c Anse Beach and Flag .25 .25
551 A80 $1 Coat of arms .60 .60
Nos. 547-551 (5) 1.50 1.50

Souvenir Sheet

552 A80 $2 Coat of arms 1.00 1.00

Grenada's independence.

Soccer, Flags of West Germany and Chile — A81

1974, Sept. 3 Litho. *Perf. 14½*

Soccer Games and Flags: 1c, East Germany and Australia. 2c, Yugoslavia and Brazil. 10c, Scotland and Zaire. 25c, Netherlands and Uruguay. 50c, Sweden and Bulgaria. 75c, Italy and Haiti. $1, Poland and Argentina. $2, Flags of participating nations, horiz.

553 A81 ½c multicolored .20 .20
554 A81 1c multicolored .20 .20
555 A81 2c multicolored .20 .20
556 A81 10c multicolored .20 .20
557 A81 25c multicolored .20 .20
558 A81 50c multicolored .25 .25
559 A81 75c multicolored .45 .45
560 A81 $1 multicolored .65 .65
Nos. 553-560 (8) 2.35 2.35

Souvenir Sheet

Perf. 13

561 A81 $2 multicolored 1.50 1.50

World Cup Soccer Championship, Munich, June 13-July 7.

19th Century US Mail Train, Concorde and UPU Emblem — A82

UPU Emblem and: 1c, Sailing ship "Caesar," 1839, and helicopter. 2c, Zeppelin, jet and early planes. 8c, Pigeon post, 1480, telephone dial. 15c, Bellman, 18th cent. and radar. 25c, German Imperial messenger, 1450, satellite. 35c, French pillar box and ocean liner. $1, German mailman, 18th cent., and futuristic mail train. $2, St. Gotthard mail coach, 1735, vert.

1974, Oct. 8 Litho. *Perf. 14½*

562 A82 ½c rose & multi .20 .20
563 A82 1c gray & multi .20 .20
564 A82 2c dull pink & multi .20 .20
565 A82 8c yellow & multi .20 .20
566 A82 15c yel grn & multi .35 .20
567 A82 25c dull yel & multi .40 .20
568 A82 35c lilac & multi .55 .20
569 A82 $1 lt blue & multi 1.60 1.60
Nos. 562-569 (8) 3.70 3.00

Souvenir Sheet

Perf. 13

570 A82 $2 multicolored 1.50 *2.00*

UPU, cent.

Sir Winston Churchill — A83

Design: $2, Churchill, different portrait.

1974, Oct. 28 Litho. *Perf. 13½*

571 A83 35c multicolored .40 .40
572 A83 $2 multicolored 1.10 1.10

Souvenir Sheet

573 Sheet of 2 1.00 1.00
a. A83 75c like 35c .40 .40
b. A83 $1 like $2 .60 .60

Winston Churchill (1874-1965).

Virgin and Child, by Botticelli — A84

Christmas: Paintings of the Virgin and Child.

1974, Nov. 18 *Perf. 14½*

574 A84 ½ shown .20 .20
575 A84 1c Niccolo di Pietro .20 .20
576 A84 2c Van der Weyden .20 .20
577 A84 3c Bastiani .20 .20
578 A84 10c Giovanni .20 .20
579 A84 25c Van der Weyden .25 .20
580 A84 50c Botticelli .30 .30
581 A84 $1 Mantegna .45 .45
Nos. 574-581 (8) 2.00 1.95

Souvenir Sheet

Perf. 13½

582 A84 $2 Niccolo di Pietro 1.00 1.00

Yachts and Point Saline A85

1c, Grenada Yacht Club race, St. George's. 2c, Careenage taxi (boat). 3c, Large working boats. 5c, Deep Water Dock, St. George's. 6c, Cacao beans in drying trays. 8c, Nutmeg branch. 10c, River Antoine Estate rum distillery, c. 1785. 12c, Cacao branch. 15c, Fishermen landing catch at Fontenoy. 20c, Parliament Building, St. George's. 25c, Fort George cannons. 35c, Pearls Airport. 50c, General Post Office. 75c, Carib Leap, Sauteurs Bay. $1, Careenage, St. George's. $2, St. George's harbor at night. $3, Grand Anse Beach. $5, Canoe Bay and Black Bay from Point Saline Lighthouse. $10, Sugar-loaf Island from Levera Beach.

1975 Litho. *Perf. 14½*

Size: 38x25mm

583 A85 ½c multicolored .20 *.55*
584 A85 1c multicolored .20 .20
585 A85 2c multicolored .20 .20
586 A85 3c multicolored .20 .20
587 A85 5c multicolored .25 .20
588 A85 6c multicolored .20 .20
589 A85 8c multicolored 1.25 .20
590 A85 10c multicolored .20 .20
591 A85 12c multicolored .35 .20
592 A85 15c multicolored .20 .20
593 A85 20c multicolored .20 .20
594 A85 25c multicolored .25 .20
595 A85 35c multicolored .25 .20
596 A85 50c multicolored .20 .25

Perf. 13½x14

Size: 45x28mm

597 A85 75c multicolored .55 .40
598 A85 $1 multicolored .60 .60
599 A85 $2 multicolored .60 *1.25*
600 A85 $3 multicolored .65 *1.75*
601 A85 $5 multicolored .80 *2.50*
602 A85 $10 multicolored 2.40 *5.50*
Nos. 583-602 (20) 9.75 15.20

Issue dates: Nos. 583-596, Jan. 13; Nos. 597-601, Jan. 22; No. 602, Mar. 26.

For overprints, see Nos. 965-979.

1978 *Perf. 13*

584a A85 1c .20 .20
585a A85 2c .20 .20
586a A85 3c .20 .20
587a A85 5c .20 .20
588a A85 6c .20 .20
590a A85 10c .20 .20
592a A85 15c .20 .20
593a A85 20c .20 .20
594a A85 25c .20 .20
596a A85 50c .40 .40
Nos. 584a-596a (10) 2.20 2.20

Sailfish A86

Designs: Big game fish.

1975, Feb. 3 *Perf. 14½*

603 A86 ½c shown .20 .20
604 A86 1c Blue marlin .20 .20
605 A86 2c White marlin .20 .20
606 A86 10c Yellowfin tuna .20 .20
607 A86 25c Wahoo .30 .30
608 A86 50c Dolphin .50 .50
609 A86 70c Grouper .75 .75
610 A86 $1 Great barracuda 1.00 1.00
Nos. 603-610 (8) 3.35 3.35

Souvenir Sheet

Perf. 13

611 A86 $2 Mako shark 1.75 1.75

Passiflora Quadrangularis — A87

Designs: Flowers of Grenada.

1975, Feb. 26 Litho. *Perf. 14½*

612 A87 ½c shown .20 .20
613 A87 1c Bleeding heart .20 .20
614 A87 2c Poinsettia .20 .20
615 A87 3c Obroma cacao .20 .20
616 A87 10c Gladioli .20 .20
617 A87 25c Red head-yellow head .35 .20
618 A87 50c Plumbago .50 .25
619 A87 $1 Orange blossoms .90 .50
Nos. 612-619 (8) 2.75 1.95

Souvenir Sheet

Perf. 13½

620 A87 $2 Barbados gooseberry 2.00 2.00

Grenada Flag and UN Emblem — A88

Designs: 1c, UN and Grenada flags. 2c, $1, UN emblem and Grenada coat of arms. 35c, UN emblem over map of Grenada. 50c, Grenada flag in front of UN Headquarters. 75c, like ½c. $2, UN emblem and scroll.

1975, Mar. 19 *Perf. 14½*

621 A88 ½c multicolored .20 .20
622 A88 1c multicolored .20 .20
623 A88 2c multicolored .20 .20
624 A88 35c multicolored .25 .25
625 A88 50c multicolored .35 .35
626 A88 $2 multicolored .80 .80
Nos. 621-626 (6) 2.00 2.00

Souvenir Sheet

Perf. 13½

627 Sheet of 2 1.50 1.50
a. A88 75c multicolored .60 .60
b. A88 $1 multicolored 1.00 1.00

Grenada's admission to the United Nations, Sept. 17, 1974.

Midnight Ride of Paul Revere — A89

1c, Crispus Attucks at Boston Massacre. 2c, Patrick Henry. 3c, Franklin visiting Washington at the front. 5c, Lexington-Concord. 10c, John Paul Jones. #634, Arms of Grenada & US. #635, Flags of Grenada & US.

1975, May 6 Litho. *Perf. 14½, 13*

628 A89 ½c Prus blue & multi .20 .20
629 A89 1c buff & multi .20 .20
630 A89 2c dp org & multi .20 .20
631 A89 3c orange & multi .20 .20
632 A89 5c Prus blue & multi .20 .20
633 A89 10c ultra & multi .20 .20
Nos. 628-633,C29-C32 (10) 3.40 *2.20*

Souvenir Sheets

Perf. 13½

634 A89 $2 tan & multi 1.25 *.40*
635 A89 $2 gray & multi 1.25 *.40*

American Revolution Bicentennial. Size of stamps on Nos. 634-635: 47x34mm.

Nos. 628-633 issued in sheets of 40. Each denomination was also printed in sheets of 5 plus label, perf. 13.

Angel Collecting Jesus' Blood in Grail, by Bellini — A90

Easter (Paintings): 1c, Pieta, by Bellini. 2c, The Deposition, by Rogier van der Weyden. 3c, Pieta, by Bellini. 35c, Descent from the Cross, by Bellini. 75c, Jesus Rising from the Tomb, by Bellini. $1, Descent from the Cross, by Procaccini. $2, Pieta, by Botticelli.

1975, May 21

636 A90 ½c multicolored .20 .20
637 A90 1c multicolored .20 .20
638 A90 2c multicolored .20 .20
639 A90 3c multicolored .20 .20
640 A90 35c multicolored .45 .20
641 A90 75c multicolored .55 .20
642 A90 $1 multicolored .65 .20
Nos. 636-642 (7) 2.45 *1.40*

Souvenir Sheet

Perf. 13½

643 A90 $2 multicolored 2.00 *.70*

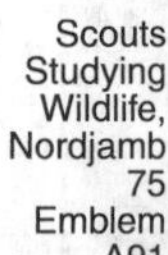

Scouts Studying Wildlife, Nordjamb 75 Emblem A91

Nordjamb 75 Emblem and: 1c, Seamanship; Scouts in sailboat. 2c, Survival; Scouts reading map. 35c, First aid. 40c, Physical fitness; gymnastics. 75c, Mountaineering. $1, Emergency boat building. $2, Scouts singing.

1975, July 2 Litho. *Perf. 14*

644 A91 ½c blue & multi .20 .20
645 A91 1c blue & multi .20 .20
646 A91 2c blue & multi .20 .20
647 A91 35c blue & multi .55 .20
648 A91 40c blue & multi .60 .20
649 A91 75c blue & multi .75 .20
650 A91 $2 blue & multi 1.75 *.40*
Nos. 644-650 (7) 4.25 *1.60*

Souvenir Sheet

651 A91 $1 blue & multi 1.25 *.25*

Nordjamb 75, 14th Boy Scout World Jamboree, Lillehammer, Norway, July 29-Aug. 7.

Leafy Jewel Box — A92

Designs: Sea shells.

1975, Aug. 1 Litho. *Perf. 14*

652 A92 ½c shown .20 .20
653 A92 1c Emerald nerite .20 .20
654 A92 2c Yellow cockle .20 .20
655 A92 25c Purple sea snail .85 .20
656 A92 50c Turkey wing 1.75 *.40*
657 A92 75c West Indian fighting conch 2.25 *.50*
658 A92 $1 Noble wentletrap 2.25 *.50*
Nos. 652-658 (7) 7.70 *2.20*

Souvenir Sheet

659 A92 $2 Music volute 3.00 *.90*

Butterflies — A93

1975, Sept. 22 Litho. *Perf. 14*

660 A93 ½c Large tiger .20 .20
661 A93 1c Five continents .20 .20
662 A93 2c Large striped blue .20 .20
663 A93 35c Gonatryx .50 *.25*
664 A93 45c Spear-winged cattle heart .65 *.30*
665 A93 75c Risty nymula 1.10 *.40*
666 A93 $2 Blue night 3.00 *.75*
Nos. 660-666 (7) 5.85 *2.30*

Souvenir Sheet

667 A93 $1 Lycrophon 2.00 *.50*

Crew Race A94

Young Man, by Michelangelo A95

1975, Oct. 13 Litho. *Perf. 14*

668 A94 ½c shown .20 .20
669 A94 1c Women's swimming .20 .20
670 A94 2c Steeplechase .20 .20
671 A94 35c Gymnastics .25 .20
672 A94 45c Soccer .25 .20
673 A94 75c Boxing .40 *.25*
674 A94 $2 Bicycling 1.10 *.35*
Nos. 668-674 (7) 2.60 *1.60*

Souvenir Sheet

675 A94 $1 Sailing 1.25 *.35*

7th Pan-American Games, Mexico City, Oct. 13-26.

1975, Nov. 3

Works by Michelangelo (except 50c): ½c, David. 2c, Moses. 40c, Zachariah. 50c, St. John the Baptist (sculpture). 75c, Judith and Holofernes (detail). $1, Madonna (head from Pietà). $2, Doni Madonna (detail from Holy Family).

676 A95 ½c black & multi .20 .20
677 A95 1c black & multi .20 .20
678 A95 2c black & multi .20 .20
679 A95 40c black & multi .45 .20
680 A95 50c black & multi .55 .20
681 A95 75c black & multi .85 *.25*
682 A95 $2 black & multi 2.25 *.50*
Nos. 676-682 (7) 4.70 *1.75*

Souvenir Sheet

683 A95 $1 black & multi 1.75 *.30*

Michelangelo Buonarroti (1475-1564), Italian painter, sculptor and architect.

Virgin and Child Paintings — A96 Bananaquit — A97

1975, Dec. 8

684 A96 ½c Filippino Lippi .20 .20
685 A96 1c Mantegna .20 .20
686 A96 2c Luis de Morales .20 .20
687 A96 35c G. M. Morandi .25 .20
688 A96 50c Antonello da Messina .25 .20
689 A96 75c Durer .30 .20
690 A96 $1 Velazquez .35 .20
Nos. 684-690 (7) 1.75 *1.40*

Souvenir Sheet

691 A96 $2 Bellini 1.25 *.50*

Christmas.

1976, Jan. 20 Litho. *Perf. 14*

Designs: 1c, Orange-rumped agouti. 2c, Hawksbill turtle, horiz. 5c, Dwarf poinciana. 35c, Albacores, horiz. 40c, Cardinal's guard flower. $1, Belted kingfisher. $2, Antillean armadillo, horiz.

692 A97 ½c multicolored .20 .20
693 A97 1c multicolored .20 .20
694 A97 2c multicolored .20 .20
695 A97 5c multicolored .20 .20
696 A97 35c multicolored 1.00 .20
697 A97 40c multicolored 1.10 .20
698 A97 $2 multicolored 2.75 *.75*
Nos. 692-698 (7) 5.65 1.95

Souvenir Sheet

699 A97 $1 multicolored 7.00 *1.00*

Carnival Dancers A98

Designs: 1c, Scuba diving. 2c, Cruise ship in St. George's Harbor. 35c, Game fishing. 50c, St. George's Golf Course. 75c, Tennis. $1, Mount Rich rock carvings. $2, Sailboats.

1976, Feb. 25 Litho. *Perf. 14*

700 A98 ½c multicolored .20 .20
701 A98 1c multicolored .20 .20
702 A98 2c multicolored .20 .20
703 A98 35c multicolored .75 .20
704 A98 50c multicolored 2.40 *.25*

705	A98	75c multicolored	2.75	*.35*
706	A98	$1 multicolored	3.00	*.35*
		Nos. 700-706 (7)	9.50	1.75

Souvenir Sheet

707	A98	$2 multicolored	2.25	*.75*

Tourist publicity.

Descent from the Cross, by Master of Okolicsno — A99

Easter (Paintings): 1c, Pieta, by Correggio. 2c, Crucifixion, by van der Weyden. 3c, Burial of Christ, by Dürer. 35c, God the Father Holding Crucified Christ, by unknown master (Florence). 75c, Ascension, by Raphael. $1, Burial of Christ, by Raphael. $2, Pieta, by Crespi.

1976, Mar. 29

708	A99	½c multicolored	.20	*.20*
709	A99	1c multicolored	.20	*.20*
710	A99	2c multicolored	.20	*.20*
711	A99	3c multicolored	.20	*.20*
712	A99	35c multicolored	.20	*.20*
713	A99	75c multicolored	.40	*.20*
714	A99	$1 multicolored	.45	*.25*
		Nos. 708-714 (7)	1.85	1.45

Souvenir Sheet

715	A99	$2 multicolored	1.25	*1.25*

Sharpshooters, 1780 — A100

First Stars and Stripes and: 1c, Defense of Liberty Pole. 2c, Men loading muskets. 35c, 75c, Fight for Liberty. 50c, $2, Peace Treaty, 1783. $1, Drumming march on Breed's Hill. $3, Gunboat, c. 1776.

1976, Apr. 15 Litho. *Perf. 14*

716	A100	½c multicolored	.20	*.20*
717	A100	1c multicolored	.20	*.20*
718	A100	2c multicolored	.20	*.20*
719	A100	35c multicolored	.35	*.20*
720	A100	50c multicolored	.50	*.20*
721	A100	$1 multicolored	1.00	*.20*
722	A100	$3 multicolored	2.75	*.30*
		Nos. 716-722 (7)	5.20	1.50

Souvenir Sheet

723	Sheet of 2	2.50	*1.75*
a.	A100 75c multicolored	.75	*.65*
b.	A100 $2 multicolored	1.75	*1.10*

American Bicentennial.

Girl Guide Emblems, Nature Study — A101

Volleyball — A102

Various Girl Guide Emblems and: 1c, Cooking. 2c, $2, First aid, diff. 50c, Tenting. 75c, Home economics. $1, Drawing.

1976, June 1 Litho. *Perf. 14*

724	A101	½c multicolored	.20	*.20*
725	A101	1c multicolored	.20	*.20*
726	A101	2c multicolored	.20	*.20*
727	A101	50c multicolored	.50	*.20*
728	A101	75c multicolored	.75	*.30*
729	A101	$2 multicolored	2.25	*.50*
		Nos. 724-729 (6)	4.10	1.60

Souvenir Sheet

730	A101	$1 multicolored	1.75	*1.75*

Girl Guides of Grenada, 50th anniv.

1976, June 21 Litho. *Perf. 14*

Olympic Rings and: 1c, Bicycling. 2c, Rowing. 35c, Judo. 45c, Hockey. 75c, Women's gymnastics. $1, High jump. $3, Equestrian.

731	A102	½c multicolored	.20	*.20*
732	A102	1c multicolored	.20	*.20*
733	A102	2c multicolored	.20	*.20*
734	A102	35c multicolored	.25	*.20*
735	A102	45c multicolored	.30	*.20*
736	A102	75c multicolored	.50	*.40*
737	A102	$1 multicolored	.70	*.40*
		Nos. 731-737 (7)	2.35	1.80

Souvenir Sheet

738	A102	$3 multicolored	1.50	*1.25*

21st Olympic Games, Montreal, Canada, July 17-Aug. 1.

Moulin Rouge, by Toulouse-Lautrec A103

Paintings by Toulouse-Lautrec: 1c, Start of the Quadrille. 2c, Woman's Head. 3c, Hall at the Moulin Rouge. 40c, Man Delivering Laundry. 50c, Dancing the Bolero. $1, Lady with Boa. $2, Signor Boileau at the Cafe.

1976, July 20 Litho. *Perf. 14*

739	A103	½c multicolored	.20	*.20*
740	A103	1c multicolored	.20	*.20*
741	A103	2c multicolored	.20	*.20*
742	A103	3c multicolored	.20	*.20*
743	A103	40c multicolored	.70	*.20*
744	A103	50c multicolored	.85	*.20*
745	A103	$2 multicolored	2.40	*.50*
		Nos. 739-745 (7)	4.75	1.70

Souvenir Sheet

746	A103	$1 multicolored	2.75	*1.25*

Henri de Toulouse-Lautrec (1864-1901), painter, 75th death anniv.

Map of West Indies, Bats, Wicket and Ball A103a

Prudential Cup — A103b

1976, July 26

747	A103a	35c lt blue & multi	.70	.70
748	A103b	$1 lilac rose & blk	2.00	2.00

World Cricket Cup, won by West Indies Team, 1975.

Piper Apache A104

Airplanes: 1c, Beech Twin Bonanza. 2c, D.H. Twin Otter. 40c, Britten Norman Islander. 50c, D.H. Heron. $2, Hawker Siddeley Avro 748. $3, B.A.C. One-Eleven.

1976, Aug. 18

749	A104	½c multicolored	.20	*.20*
750	A104	1c multicolored	.20	*.20*
751	A104	2c multicolored	.20	*.20*
752	A104	40c multicolored	.75	*.20*
753	A104	50c multicolored	.80	*.20*
754	A104	$2 multicolored	2.75	*.75*
		Nos. 749-754 (6)	4.90	1.75

Souvenir Sheet

755	A104	$3 multicolored	3.25	*1.25*

Helios Mission, Assembly — A105

Designs: 1c, Helios spacecraft in space 2c, Helios assembled. 15c, Helios, system test and checkout. 45c, Viking nearing Mars, horiz. 75c, Viking on Mars. $2, Viking spacecraft assembled. $3, Helios orbiter and Viking lander.

1976, Sept. 1 Litho. *Perf. 14*

756	A105	½c multicolored	.20	*.20*
757	A105	1c multicolored	.20	*.20*
758	A105	2c multicolored	.20	*.20*
759	A105	15c multicolored	.20	*.20*
760	A105	45c multicolored	.30	*.20*
761	A105	75c multicolored	.45	*.25*
762	A105	$2 multicolored	.90	*.40*
		Nos. 756-762 (7)	2.45	1.65

Souvenir Sheet

763	A105	$3 multicolored	1.50	*1.50*

Helios (solar probe) mission and Viking Mars missions.

S.S. Geestland, Geest Line Flag — A106

Ships: 1c, M.V. Federal Palm, West Indies Shipping Service. 2c, H.M.S. Blake and ship's crest. 25c, M.V. Vistafjord and Norwegian-American Line flag. 75c, S.S. Canberra and P. & O. Line flag. $1, S.S. Regina and Chandris Line flag. $2, Santa Maria and Spanish flag, 1492. $5, S.S. Arandora and Blue Star Line flag.

1976, Nov. 3 Litho. *Perf. 14½*

764	A106	½c blue & multi	.20	*.20*
765	A106	1c blue & multi	.20	*.20*
766	A106	2c blue & multi	.20	*.20*
767	A106	25c blue & multi	.65	*.20*
768	A106	75c blue & multi	1.25	*.25*
769	A106	$1 blue & multi	1.50	*.35*
770	A106	$5 blue & multi	3.00	*.75*
		Nos. 764-770 (7)	7.00	2.15

Souvenir Sheet

771	A106	$2 multicolored	2.50	*2.50*

Ships connected with Grenada's development.

Altarpiece of San Barnaba, by Botticelli A107

Christmas (Paintings): 1c, Annunciation, by Botticelli. 2c, Madonna with Chancellor Rolin, by Jan van Eyck. 35c, Annunciation, by Fra Filippo Lippi. 50c, Madonna of the Magnificat, by Botticelli. 75c, Madonna of the Pomegranate, by Botticelli. $2, Gipsy Madonna, by Titian. $3, Madonna with St. Cosmas and Saints, by Botticelli.

1976, Dec. 8 Litho. *Perf. 14*

772	A107	½c multicolored	.20	*.20*
773	A107	1c multicolored	.20	*.20*
774	A107	2c multicolored	.20	*.20*
775	A107	35c multicolored	.20	*.20*
776	A107	50c multicolored	.30	*.20*
777	A107	75c multicolored	.45	*.25*
778	A107	$3 multicolored	1.10	*.40*
		Nos. 772-778 (7)	2.65	1.65

Souvenir Sheet

779	A107	$2 multicolored	1.25	*.75*

Globe and Telephone Users A108

Designs: ½c, A. G. Bell, 1876 and modern telephones. 2c, Satellites around globe, world map. 18c, Videophone. 40c, Satellite and ground stations. $1, Satellite and telephone communication with ships. $2, British "Trimphone" and radar station. $5, Flags of the world surrounding globe, and telephone.

1976, Dec. 17 Litho. *Perf. 14*

780	A108	½c multicolored	.20	*.20*
781	A108	1c multicolored	.20	*.20*
782	A108	2c multicolored	.20	*.20*
783	A108	18c multicolored	.35	*.20*
784	A108	40c multicolored	.45	*.20*
785	A108	$1 multicolored	.60	*.30*
786	A108	$2 multicolored	1.00	*.50*
		Nos. 780-786 (7)	3.00	1.80

Souvenir Sheet

787	A108	$5 multicolored	2.50	*1.50*

Centenary of first telephone conversation by Alexander Graham Bell, Mar. 10, 1876.

Coronation of Elizabeth II — A109

Designs: ½c, Coronation. 1c, $1, Orb and scepter. 35c, $3, Trooping of the Guards. 50c, $2, Spoon and ampulla. 35c, (bklt.), $2.50, Elizabeth II and Prince Philip. $5, Royal visit to Grenada.

1977, Feb. 8 Litho. *Perf. 14, 12*

788	A109	½c multicolored	.25	*.25*
789	A109	1c multicolored	.25	*.25*
790	A109	35c multicolored	.25	*.25*
791	A109	$2 multicolored	.60	*.40*
792	A109	$2.50 multicolored	.65	*.40*
a.		Booklet pane of 6 (35c)	1.50	
b.		Booklet pane of 3 (50c, $1, $3)	4.75	
		Nos. 788-792 (5)	2.00	1.55

Souvenir Sheet

793	A109	$5 multicolored	2.00	*2.00*

Reign of Queen Elizabeth II, 25th anniv.

Nos. 792a-792b are self-adhesive, roulette x imperf. Marginal inscriptions.

Nos. 788-792 were printed in sheets of 40 (10x4), perf. 14, and sheets of 5 plus label, perf. 12, in changed colors.

For overprints see Nos. 821-826.

Water Skiing, One-ski Slalom A110

Designs: 1c, Speedboat racing around Grand Anse. 2c, Crew racing, St. George's. 22c, Swimming, Grand Anse. 35c, Local work boat races. 75c, Water polo, careenage, St. George's. $2, Game fishing. $3, South Coast yacht race.

1977, Apr. 13 Litho. *Perf. 14*

794	A110	½c multicolored	.20	*.20*
795	A110	1c multicolored	.20	*.20*
796	A110	2c multicolored	.20	*.20*
797	A110	22c multicolored	.20	*.20*
798	A110	35c multicolored	.35	*.20*

799 A110 75c multicolored .55 .20
800 A110 $2 multicolored 1.10 .35
Nos. 794-800 (7) 2.80 1.55

Souvenir Sheet

801 A110 $3 multicolored 1.75 1.25

1977 Easter Water Parade.

Tent, OAS Emblem A111

1977, June 14 Litho. *Perf. 14*

802 A111 35c multicolored .25 .25
803 A111 $1 multicolored .65 .65
804 A111 $2 multicolored 1.10 1.10
Nos. 802-804 (3) 2.00 2.00

7th Regular Session, General Assembly of Organization of American States.

Scouts on Raft A112

Designs: 1c, Tug-of-war. 2c, Boy Scout regatta. 18c, Scouts around camp fire. 40c, Field kitchen. $1, Boy Scouts and Sea Scouts. $2, Hiking and map reading. $3, Semaphore.

1977, Sept. 6 Litho. *Perf. 14*

805 A112 ½c multicolored .20 .20
806 A112 1c multicolored .20 .20
807 A112 2c multicolored .20 .20
808 A112 18c multicolored .20 .20
809 A112 40c multicolored .40 .20
810 A112 $1 multicolored 1.00 .35
811 A112 $2 multicolored 2.00 .55
Nos. 805-811 (7) 4.20 1.90

Souvenir Sheet

812 A112 $3 multicolored 2.25 1.25

6th Caribbean Jamboree, Kingston, Jamaica, Aug. 5-14.

Annunciation to the Shepherds — A113

Ceiling Paintings, St. Martin's Church, Zillis, Switzerland, 12th Century: 1c, Joseph on his way. 2c, Virgin and Child, Flight into Egypt. 22c, Angel leading the way. 35c, King on way to Herod. 75c, Three horses. $2, Virgin and Child. $3, Adoration of the Kings.

1977, Nov. 3 Litho. *Perf. 14*

813 A113 ½c multicolored .20 .20
814 A113 1c multicolored .20 .20
815 A113 2c multicolored .20 .20
816 A113 22c multicolored .20 .20
817 A113 35c multicolored .20 .20
818 A113 75c multicolored .20 .20
819 A113 $2 multicolored .40 .30
Nos. 813-819 (7) 1.60 1.50

Souvenir Sheet

820 A113 $3 multicolored 1.25 1.00

Christmas.

Nos. 788-793 Overprinted "Royal Visit W.I. 1977"

1977, Nov. 10 *Perf. 12, 14*

821 A109 ½c multicolored .20 .20
822 A109 1c multicolored .20 .20
823 A109 35c multicolored .20 .20
824 A109 $2 multicolored .30 .40
825 A109 $2.50 multicolored .35 .50
Nos. 821-825 (5) 1.25 1.50

Souvenir Sheet

Perf. 14

826 A109 $5 multicolored 1.00 1.50

Caribbean visit of Queen Elizabeth II. Nos. 821-822 are perf. 12, others perf. 12 and 14.

Christjaan Eijkman — A114

Portraits: 1c, Winston Churchill, Literature, 1953. 2c, Woodrow Wilson, Peace, 1919. 35c, Frederic Passy, Peace 1901. $1, Albert Einstein, Physics, 1921. $2, Alfred Nobel, founder. $3, Carl Bosch, Chemistry, 1931.

1978, Jan. 25 Litho. *Perf. 14*

827 A114 ½c multicolored .20 .20
828 A114 1c multicolored .20 .20
829 A114 2c multicolored .20 .20
830 A114 35c multicolored .30 .20
831 A114 $1 multicolored .75 .30
832 A114 $3 multicolored 2.25 .55
Nos. 827-832 (6) 3.90 1.65

Souvenir Sheet

833 A114 $2 multicolored 1.25 1.00

Nobel Prize winners.

Early Zeppelin and Count Zeppelin A115

Designs: 1c, Lindbergh and Spirit of St. Louis. 2c, "Deutschland" airship. 22c, Lindbergh landing in Paris. 35c, Lindbergh in cockpit. 75c, Lindbergh and Spirit of St. Louis in flight. $1, Zeppelin over Alps. $2, Count Zeppelin and early airship. $3, Zeppelin over White House.

1978, Feb. 13 Litho. *Perf. 14*

834 A115 ½c multicolored .20 .20
835 A115 1c multicolored .20 .20
836 A115 2c multicolored .20 .20
837 A115 22c multicolored .30 .20
838 A115 75c multicolored .55 .20
839 A115 $1 multicolored .65 .25
840 A115 $3 multicolored 1.40 .50
Nos. 834-840 (7) 3.50 1.75

Souvenir Sheet

841 Sheet of 2 1.75 .75
a. A115 35c multicolored .30
b. A115 $2 multicolored 1.75

Aviation history.

Launching of Space Shuttle — A116

Black- headed Gulls — A117

Space Shuttle: 1c, Booster separation. 2c, External tank separation. 18c, In orbit. 75c, Satellite placement. $2, Landing approach. $3, On landing pad.

1978, Feb. 28

842 A116 ½c multicolored .20 .20
843 A116 1c multicolored .20 .20
844 A116 2c multicolored .20 .20
845 A116 18c multicolored .30 .20
846 A116 75c multicolored .70 .20
847 A116 $2 multicolored 1.40 .40
Nos. 842-847 (6) 3.00 1.40

Souvenir Sheet

848 A116 $3 multicolored 2.00 1.00

US space shuttle.

1978, Mar. 8 Litho. *Perf. 14*

Wild Birds of Grenada and Wildlife Fund Emblem: 1c, Wilson's petrels. 2c, Killdeers. 50c, White-necked jacobin and hibiscus. 75c, Blue-faced booby. $1, Broad-winged hawk. $2, Scaley-necked pigeon. $3, Scarlet ibis.

849 A117 ½c multicolored .20 .20
850 A117 1c multicolored .20 .20
851 A117 2c multicolored .20 .20
852 A117 50c multicolored 1.90 .25
853 A117 75c multicolored 2.25 .40
854 A117 $1 multicolored 3.50 .50
855 A117 $2 multicolored 4.25 .75
Nos. 849-855 (7) 12.50 2.50

Souvenir Sheet

856 A117 $3 multicolored 9.00 1.00

Marquise de Spinola, by Rubens A118

Ludwig van Beethoven A119

Paintings by Peter Paul Rubens (1577-1640): 5c, Reception of Marie de Medicis. 15c, Rubens and Helena Fourment. 25c, Ludovicus Nonnius. 45c, Helena Fourment with her Children. 75c, Child's head. $3, Suzanne Fourment in Velvet Hat.

1978, Mar. 30 Litho. *Perf. 13½x14*

857 A118 5c lt blue & multi .25 .20
858 A118 15c lt blue & multi .25 .20
859 A118 18c lt blue & multi .25 .20
860 A118 25c lt blue & multi .25 .20
861 A118 45c lt blue & multi .40 .20
862 A118 75c lt blue & multi .60 .20
863 A118 $3 lt blue & multi 1.50 .55
Nos. 857-863 (7) 3.50 1.75

Souvenir Sheet

864 A118 $5 lt blue & multi 2.00 1.00

1978, Apr. 24 *Perf. 14*

Designs: 15c, Woman violinist playing concerto. 18c, Various musical instruments. 22c, Piano. 50c, Two violins. 75c, Beethoven's piano and score. $2, Beethoven and score. $3, Beethoven and his house. 15c, 18c, 22c, 75c, $2, $3, horiz.

865 A119 5c multicolored .20 .20
866 A119 15c multicolored .20 .20
867 A119 18c multicolored .30 .20
868 A119 22c multicolored .30 .20
869 A119 50c multicolored .60 .40
870 A119 75c multicolored .90 .55
871 A119 $3 multicolored 2.50 .75
Nos. 865-871 (7) 5.00 2.50

Souvenir Sheet

872 A119 $2 multicolored 2.00 1.25

Ludwig van Beethoven (1770-1827), composer, death sesquicentennial.

Elizabeth II with Crown, Scepter and Orb — A120

Trooping of the Colors — A121

Designs: 35c, Coronation. $2.50, St. Edward's crown. $5, Elizabeth II and Prince Philip.

1978, June 2 Litho. *Perf. 14*

873 A120 35c multicolored .25 .25
874 A120 $2 multicolored .75 .75
875 A120 $2.50 multicolored .75 .75
Nos. 873-875 (3) 1.75 1.75

Souvenir Sheet

876 A120 $5 multicolored 1.50 1.50

Imperf

Self-adhesive

35c, Elizabeth II at Maundy Money distribution ceremony. $5, Elizabeth II and Prince Philip.

877 Souvenir booklet 3.25
a. A121 Bklt. pane, 3 each 25c, 35c 1.00
b. A121 Booklet pane of 1, $5 2.50

Coronation of Queen Elizabeth II, 25th anniv.

Nos. 873-875 were printed in sheets of 40 (10x4), perf. 14, and sheets of 3 plus label, perf. 12, in changed colors. Labels show royal insignia.

No. 877 contains 2 booklet panes printed on peelable paper backing showing coins.

Goalkeeper Reaching for Ball — A122

Designs: Goalkeeper reaching for ball, various stages of motion.

1978, Aug. 1 Litho. *Perf. 15*

878 A122 40c multicolored .20 .20
879 A122 60c multicolored .25 .25
880 A122 90c multicolored .40 .40
881 A122 $2 multicolored .90 .90
Nos. 878-881 (4) 1.75 1.75

Souvenir Sheet

882 A122 $2.50 multicolored 1.75 1.75

11th World Cup Soccer Championship, Argentina, June 1-25.

Flying Objects, 16th Century Drawing and Flying Saucer, 1962 A123

Designs: 35c, Radar probing skies, and Mars surface. $2, Prime Minister Eric Gairy and UN General Assembly Building. $3, Flying saucer with downwards beam, and UFO photograph.

1978, Aug. 17

883 A123 5c multicolored .20 .20
884 A123 35c multicolored .30 .30
885 A123 $3 multicolored 2.50 2.50
Nos. 883-885 (3) 3.00 3.00

Souvenir Sheet

886 A123 $2 multicolored 1.60 1.60

Proposal by Prime Minister Eric Gairy of Grenada to the UN General Assembly to study unidentified flying objects, Oct. 7, 1977.

Wright Glider and Allegory of Flight A124

15c, Flyer I, 1903, & eagle. 18c, Flyer III & allegory of flight. 22c, Flyer III & eagle. 50c, Orville Wright, Flyer & allegory of flight. 75c, Flyer, 1908, & eagle. $2, Flyer & allegory of flight. $3, Wilbur Wright, Flyer & allegory of flight.

1978, Aug. 24 *Perf. 14*

887 A124 5c multicolored .20 .20
888 A124 15c multicolored .20 .20
889 A124 18c multicolored .20 .20
890 A124 22c multicolored .20 .20
891 A124 50c multicolored .30 .30

892 A124 75c multicolored .40 .40
893 A124 $3 multicolored 1.25 1.25
Nos. 887-893 (7) 2.75 2.75

Souvenir Sheet

894 A124 $2 multicolored 1.50 1.50

75th anniversary of first powered flight by Wright brothers, Dec. 17, 1903.

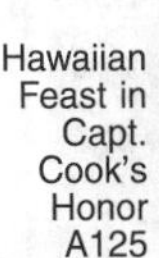

Hawaiian Feast in Capt. Cook's Honor A125

Capt. Cook and: 35c, Hawaiian warriors' dance. 75c, Honolulu harbor. $3, "Resolution." $4, Death scene.

1978, Dec. 5 Litho. *Perf. 14*

895 A125 18c multicolored .65 .65
896 A125 35c multicolored .75 .75
897 A125 75c multicolored 1.50 1.50
898 A125 $3 multicolored 2.10 2.10
Nos. 895-898 (4) 5.00 5.00

Souvenir Sheet

899 A125 $4 multicolored 3.75 3.75

Bicentenary of Capt. Cook's arrival in Hawaii and 250th anniversary of his birth.

Detail from Paumgartner Altar, by Dürer — A126

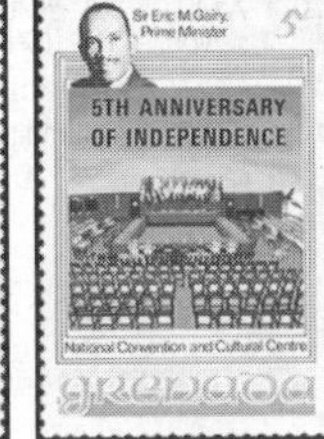

Convention and Cultural Center — A127

Dürer Paintings: 60c, The Three Kings. 90c, Virgin and Child. $2, Head of the Virgin. $4, Virgin and Child.

1978, Dec. 20 Litho. *Perf. 14*

900 A126 40c multicolored .25 .25
901 A126 60c multicolored .35 .35
902 A126 90c multicolored .40 .40
903 A126 $2 multicolored .75 .75
Nos. 900-903 (4) 1.75 1.75

Souvenir Sheet

904 A126 $4 multicolored 2.00 2.00

Christmas and 450th death anniv. of Albrecht Dürer (1471-1528), German painter.

1979, Feb. 8 Litho. *Perf. 14*

18c, Geodesic Dome. 22c, Rowboat race, Easter parade, St. George's. 35c, Prime Minister Eric M. Gairy. $3, Cross at Fort Frederick at night.

905 A127 5c multicolored .20 .20
906 A127 18c multicolored .20 .20
907 A127 22c multicolored .20 .20
908 A127 35c multicolored .20 .20
909 A127 $3 multicolored .80 .80
Nos. 905-909 (5) 1.60 1.60

5th anniversary of independence.

Chenille Plant — A128

Birds in Flight — A129

Native Flowers: 50c, Red hibiscus. $1, Skyflower. $2, Pink pride of India. $3, Rosebay.

1979, Feb. 26

910 A128 18c multicolored .20 .20
911 A128 50c multicolored .30 .30
912 A128 $1 multicolored .50 .50
913 A128 $3 multicolored 1.25 1.25
Nos. 910-913 (4) 2.25 2.25

Souvenir Sheet

914 A128 $2 multicolored 1.50 1.50

1979, Mar. 15

$2, Bird in flight & Human Rights emblem.

915 A129 15c multicolored .20 .20
916 A129 $2 multicolored .80 .80

Universal Declaration of Human Rights, 30th anniversary.

Children Playing Cricket — A130

IYC Emblem and: 22c, Boys playing baseball. $4, Children with model spaceship. $5, Three children.

1979, Apr. 23 Litho. *Perf. 14*

917 A130 18c multicolored .25 .25
918 A130 22c multicolored .25 .25
919 A130 $5 multicolored 4.50 4.50
Nos. 917-919 (3) 5.00 5.00

Souvenir Sheet

920 A130 $4 multicolored 2.50 2.50

Intl. Year of the Child.

Balloon and Space Shuttle A131

Designs: 35c, Octopus holding sailors, nuclear submarine. 75c, Rocket and moon. $3, Imaginary plane and space ship. $4, Multi-propellered ship and US space shuttle.

1979, May 4

921 A131 18c multicolored .20 .20
922 A131 35c multicolored .25 .25
923 A131 75c multicolored .55 .55
924 A131 $3 multicolored 2.00 2.00
Nos. 921-924 (4) 3.00 3.00

Souvenir Sheet

925 A131 $4 multicolored 2.00 2.00

Jules Verne (1828-1905), science fiction writer.

African Mail Runner A132

Sir Rowland Hill (1795-1879), originator of penny postage, and: 40c, American Pony Express. $1, Oriental pigeon post. $3, European mail coach. $5, Tete-beche stamps with revenue surcharge, 1883.

1979, June Litho. *Perf. 14*

926 A132 20c multicolored .20 .20
927 A132 40c multicolored .20 .20
928 A132 $1 multicolored .25 .25
929 A132 $3 multicolored .65 .65
Nos. 926-929 (4) 1.30 1.30

Souvenir Sheet

930 A132 $5 multicolored 1.25 1.25

Nos. 926-929 were printed in sheets of 40, perf. 14, and in sheets of 5 plus label, perf. 12, in changed colors.

For overprints see Nos. 989A-989D.

Boys, Map of Grenada, Vaccination Gun — A133

1979, Aug. 2 Litho. *Perf. 14*

931 A133 5c multicolored .20 .20
932 A133 $1 multicolored .90 .90

Intl. Year of the Child, immunization of children.

Reef Shark A134

Designs: 45c, Spotted eagle ray. 50c, Many-tooth conger. 60c, Golden olive shells. 70c, West Indian murex. 75c, Giant tuns. 90c, Brown boobies. $1, Magnificent frigate bird. $2.50, Sooty tern.

1979, Aug. 22 Litho. *Perf. 14*

933 A134 40c multicolored .35 .35
934 A134 45c multicolored .35 .35
935 A134 50c multicolored .40 .40
936 A134 60c multicolored .60 .60
937 A134 70c multicolored .70 .70
938 A134 75c multicolored .80 .80
939 A134 90c multicolored 1.90 1.90
940 A134 $1 multicolored 1.90 1.90
Nos. 933-940 (8) 7.00 7.00

Souvenir Sheet

941 A134 $2.50 multicolored 3.25 3.25

Flight into Egypt, Tapestry A135

Tapestries: 25c, Virgin and Child. 30c, Angel, vert. 40c, Infant Jesus, by Doge Marino Grimani, vert. 90c, Shepherds, vert. $1, Flight into Egypt, vert. $2, Virgin in Glory, vert. $4, Virgin and Child, by Grimani, vert.

1979, Oct. 16 Litho. *Perf. 14*

942 A135 6c multicolored .20 .20
943 A135 25c multicolored .20 .20
944 A135 30c multicolored .20 .20
945 A135 40c multicolored .20 .20
946 A135 90c multicolored .30 .30
947 A135 $1 multicolored .30 .30
948 A135 $2 multicolored .60 .60
Nos. 942-948 (7) 2.00 2.00

Souvenir Sheet

949 A135 $4 multicolored 1.75 1.75

Christmas.

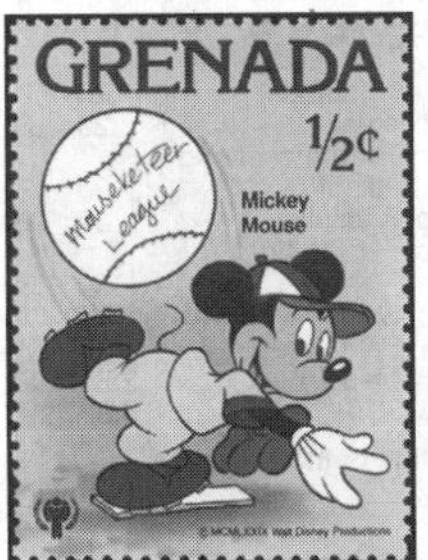

Disney Characters and IYC Emblem A135a

Designs: Sport scenes.

1979, Nov. 2 Litho. *Perf. 11*

950 A135a ½c Mickey Mouse, baseball .20 .20
951 A135a 1c Donald, high jump .20 .20
952 A135a 2c Goofy, basketball .20 .20
953 A135a 3c Goofy, hurdles .20 .20
954 A135a 4c Donald Duck, golf .20 .20
955 A135a 5c Mickey, cricket .20 .20
956 A135a 10c Mickey, soccer .20 .20
957 A135a $2 Mickey, tennis 2.75 2.75
958 A135a $2.50 Minnie, equestrian 2.75 2.75
Nos. 950-958 (9) 6.90 6.90

Souvenir Sheet

Perf. 13½

959 CD329 $3 Goofy in riding habit 3.00 3.00

See Nos. 1031-1032.

Hands, Paul P. Harris, Rotary Emblem — A136

Rotary Emblem and Hands Holding: 30c, Caduceus. 90c, Wheat. $2, Family. $4, Emblem.

1980, Feb. 25 Litho. *Perf. 14*

960 A136 6c multicolored .25 .25
961 A136 30c multicolored .25 .25
962 A136 90c multicolored .35 .35
963 A136 $2 multicolored .90 .90
Nos. 960-963 (4) 1.75 1.75

Souvenir Sheet

964 A136 $4 multicolored 1.75 1.75

Rotary International, 75th anniversary.

Nos. 585-586, 588-591, 593-594, 596-602 Overprinted in Black: PEOPLE'S REVOLUTION / 13 MARCH 1979

1980 *Perf. 15, 13½*

965 A85 2c multicolored .20 .20
966 A85 3c multicolored .20 .20
967 A85 6c multicolored .20 .20
968 A85 8c multicolored .20 .20
969 A85 10c multicolored .20 .20
970 A85 12c multicolored .20 .20
971 A85 20c multicolored .20 .20
972 A85 25c multicolored .40 .40
973 A85 50c multicolored .40 .40
974 A85 75c multicolored .65 .65
975 A85 $1 multicolored .80 .80
976 A85 $2 multicolored 1.60 1.60
977 A85 $3 multicolored 2.00 2.00
978 A85 $5 multicolored 2.50 2.50
979 A85 $10 multicolored 4.25 4.25
Nos. 965-979 (15) 14.00 14.00

Issue dates: 25c, Apr. 7; others, Feb. 28.

Boxing, Kremlin, Olympic Rings A137

1980, Mar. 24 *Perf. 14*

980 A137 25c shown .20 .20
981 A137 40c Bicycling .20 .20
982 A137 90c Equestrian .25 .25
983 A137 $2 Running .60 .60
Nos. 980-983 (4) 1.25 1.25

Souvenir Sheet

984 A137 $4 Yachting 1.00 1.00

22nd Summer Olympic Games, Moscow, July 19-Aug. 3.

Tropical Kingbirds — A138

1980, Apr. 8

985 A138 20c shown .80 .80
986 A138 40c Rufous-breasted hermits 1.10 1.10

987 A138 $1 Troupials 1.60 1.60
988 A138 $2 Ruddy quail doves 2.00 2.00
Nos. 985-988 (4) 5.50 5.50

Souvenir Sheet

989 A138 $3 Prairie warblers 3.75 3.75

Nos. 926-929 Overprinted: "LONDON 1980"

1980, May 6 Litho. *Perf. 12*

989A A132 20c multicolored .20 .20
989B A132 40c multicolored .30 .30
989C A132 $1 multicolored .50 .50
989D A132 $3 multicolored 1.75 1.75
Nos. 989A-989D (4) 2.75 2.75

London '80 Intl. Stamp Exhib., May 6-14.

Free School Hot Lunches A139

1980, May 19 Litho. *Perf. 14*

990 A139 10c shown .20 .20
991 A139 40c Food canning .25 .25
992 A139 $1 Health care .55 .55
993 A139 $2 Housing projects .85 .85
Nos. 990-993 (4) 1.85 1.85

Souvenir Sheet

994 A139 $5 Prime Minister Bishop, vert. 1.50 1.50

People's Revolution, 1st anniv.

Jamb Statues, West Portal, Chartres Cathedral — A140

Masterpieces: 10c, Les Desmoiselles d'Avignon, by Picasso. 40c, Winged Victory of Samothrace. 50c, The Night Watch, by Rembrandt. $1, Edward VI as a Child, by Holbein, the Younger. $3, Queen Nefertiti. $4, Weier Haws, by Dürer, vert.

1980, June Litho. *Perf. 14*

995 A140 8c multicolored .20 .20
996 A140 10c multicolored .20 .20
997 A140 40c multicolored .25 .25
998 A140 50c multicolored .25 .25
999 A140 $1 multicolored .40 .40
1000 A140 $3 multicolored 1.10 1.10
Nos. 995-1000 (6) 2.40 2.40

Souvenir Sheet

1001 A140 $4 multicolored 1.50 1.50

Carib Canoes A141

Designs: 1c, Boat building. 2c, Small workboat. 4c, "Santa Maria." 5c, West India man barque, 1840. 6c, "Orinoco," 1851. 10c, Schooner. 12c, Trimaran. 15c, "Petite Amie," Spice Island cruising yacht. 20c, Fishing pirogue. 25c, Harbor police launch. 30c, Grand Anse speedboat. 40c, "Seimstrand." 50c, "Ariadne," 3-masted schooner. 90c, "Geestide," banana boat. $1, "Cunard Countess," cruise ship. $3, Rumrunner. $5, "Statendam." $10, Coast Guard patrol boat.

1980, Sept. 9 Litho. *Perf. 14*

1002 A141 ½c multicolored .20 .20
1003 A141 1c multicolored .20 .20
1004 A141 2c multicolored .20 .20
1005 A141 4c multicolored .40 .40
1006 A141 5c multicolored .40 .40
1007 A141 6c multicolored .40 .40
1008 A141 10c multicolored .45 .20
1009 A141 12c multicolored 1.00 .50
1010 A141 15c multicolored .50 .20
1011 A141 20c multicolored 1.00 .20
1012 A141 25c multicolored 2.00 .30
1013 A141 30c multicolored 1.50 .30
1014 A141 40c multicolored 2.00 .40
1015 A141 50c multicolored .50 .50
1016 A141 90c multicolored 1.75 .50
1017 A141 $1 multicolored 3.00 .75
1018 A141 $3 multicolored 2.50 2.50
1019 A141 $5 multicolored 3.50 3.50
1020 A141 $10 multicolored 5.00 5.00
Nos. 1002-1020 (19) 26.50 16.65

#1017 reprinted inscribed 1982, #1015, 1984.

For overprints see #O1-O10, O12-O13, O15, O17.

1982-84 *Perf. 12½x12*

1002a A141 ½c .20 .20
1006a A141 5c .60 .60
1008a A141 10c .65 .65
1011a A141 20c 1.00 1.00
1012a A141 25c 2.00 2.00
1013a A141 30c 1.50 1.50
1014a A141 40c 2.00 2.00
1015a A141 50c ('84) .80 .80
1018a A141 $3 3.00 3.00
1019a A141 $5 4.25 4.25
1020a A141 $10 ('84) 9.50 9.50
Nos. 1002a-1020a (11) 25.50 25.50

Snow White at Well — A142

Christmas: Various scenes from Walt Disney's Snow White and the Seven Dwarfs.

1980, Sept. 25 Litho. *Perf. 11*

1021 A142 ½c multicolored .20 .20
1022 A142 1c multicolored .20 .20
1023 A142 2c multicolored .20 .20
1024 A142 3c multicolored .20 .20
1025 A142 4c multicolored .20 .20
1026 A142 5c multicolored .20 .20
1027 A142 10c multicolored .20 .20
1028 A142 $2.50 multicolored 2.75 2.75
1029 A142 $3 multicolored 3.25 3.25
Nos. 1021-1029 (9) 7.40 7.40

Souvenir Sheet

1030 A142 $4 multicolored 5.00 5.00

No. 1030 contains a vertical stamp.

Disney Type of 1980

50th anniversary of Pluto character: $2, Pluto and birthday cake. $4, Pluto.

1981, Jan. 19 Litho. *Perf. 14*

1031 A135a $2 multicolored 2.50 2.50

Souvenir Sheet

1032 A135a $4 multicolored 3.50 3.50

No. 1031 issued in sheets of 8.

Adult Education — A143

1981, Mar. 13 Litho. *Perf. 12½*

1033 A143 5c Flags of the Revolution and Grenada .20 .20
1034 A143 10c shown .20 .20
1035 A143 15c Food processing plant .20 .20
1036 A143 25c Agriculture .20 .20
1037 A143 40c Fishing boat, crawfish .30 .30
1038 A143 90c Ships .70 .70
1039 A143 $1 Palm trees .75 .75
1040 A143 $3 Map 2.25 2.25
Nos. 1033-1040 (8) 4.80 4.80

2nd Festival of the Revolution.

Mickey Mouse and Goofy with Easter Basket A144

Easter: Various Disney characters with Easter baskets.

1981, Apr. 7 *Perf. 11*

1041 A144 35c multi .30 .30
1042 A144 40c multi .35 .35
1043 A144 $2 multi 1.75 1.75
1044 A144 $2.50 multi 2.25 2.25
Nos. 1041-1044 (4) 4.65 4.65

Souvenir Sheet

1045 A144 $4 multi 3.50 3.50

Large Heads, by Picasso — A145

Paintings by Pablo Picasso (1881-1973): 25c, Woman-Flower. 30c, Portrait of Madame. 90c, Cavalier with Pipe. $5, Woman on the Bank of the Seine.

1981, Apr. 28 *Perf. 14*

1046 A145 25c multicolored .20 .20
1047 A145 30c multicolored .25 .25
1048 A145 90c multicolored .70 .70
1049 A145 $4 multicolored 3.25 3.25
Nos. 1046-1049 (4) 4.40 4.40

Souvenir Sheet

1050 A145 $5 multicolored 4.50 4.50

Royal Wedding Issue

Common Design Type

1981, June 16 Litho. *Perf. 15*

1051 CD331 50c Couple .40 .40
1052 CD331 $2 Holyrood House 1.50 1.50
1053 CD331 $4 Charles 3.00 3.00
Nos. 1051-1053 (3) 4.90 4.90

Souvenir Sheet

1054 CD331 $5 Glass coach 3.75 3.75

Souvenir Booklet

1055 CD331 9.00
a. Pane of 6 (3x$1, Lady Diana, 3x$2, Charles) 6.00
b. Pane of 1, $5, Couple 3.00

No. 1055 contains imperf., self-adhesive stamps.

Sheets of 5 plus label contain 30c, 40c or $4 in changed colors, perf. 14x14½.

For overprints see Nos. O11, O14, O16,

The Bath, by Mary Cassatt (1845-1926) A146

Decade for Women (Paintings by Women): 40c, Mademoiselle Charlotte du Val d'Ognes, by Constance Marie Charpentier. 60c, Self-portrait, by Mary Beale. $3, Woman in White Stockings, by Suzanne Valadon. $5, The Artist Hesitating between the Arts of Music and Painting, horiz.

1981, Oct. 13 Litho. *Perf. 14*

1058 A146 15c multicolored .20 .20
1059 A146 40c multicolored .30 .30
1060 A146 60c multicolored .45 .45
1061 A146 $3 multicolored 2.25 2.25
Nos. 1058-1061 (4) 3.20 3.20

Souvenir Sheet

1062 A146 $5 multicolored 3.50 3.50

Cinderella and Prince Charming Dancing at the Ball — A147

Christmas: Scenes from Walt Disney's Cinderella.

1981, Nov. 2 Litho. *Perf. 14x13½*

1063 A147 ½c multi .20 .20
1064 A147 1c multi .20 .20
1065 A147 2c multi .20 .20
1066 A147 3c multi .20 .20
1067 A147 4c multi .20 .20
1068 A147 5c multi .20 .20
1069 A147 10c multi .20 .20
1070 A147 $2.50 multi 2.25 2.25
1071 A147 $3 multi 2.75 2.75
Nos. 1063-1071 (9) 6.40 6.40

Souvenir Sheet

1072 A147 $5 multi 4.75 4.75

Columbia Space Shuttle — A148

Views of the Columbia space shuttle.

1981, Nov. 12

1073 A148 30c multicolored .20 .20
1074 A148 60c multicolored .40 .40
1075 A148 70c multicolored .50 .50
1076 A148 $3 multicolored 2.00 2.00
Nos. 1073-1076 (4) 3.10 3.10

Souvenir Sheet

1077 A148 $5 multicolored 3.75 3.75

UPU Membership Centenary — A149

1981, Dec. 10 Litho. *Perf. 15*

1078 A149 25c St. George's P.O. .20 .20
1079 A149 30c No. 1 .20 .20
1080 A149 90c No. 384 .60 .60
1081 A149 $4 No. 189 2.75 2.75
Nos. 1078-1081 (4) 3.75 3.75

Souvenir Sheet

1082 A149 $5 No. 562 3.75 3.75

Intl. Year of the Disabled (1981) — A150

1982, Feb. 4 *Perf. 14*

1083 A150 30c Artist .20 .20
1084 A150 40c Computer operator .30 .30
1085 A150 70c Teaching Braille .50 .50
1086 A150 $3 Drummer 2.00 2.00
Nos. 1083-1086 (4) 3.00 3.00

Souvenir Sheet

1087 A150 $4 Auto mechanic 3.00 3.00

Scouting Year A151

1982, Feb. 19 *Perf. 15*

1088 A151 70c Gardening .50 .50
1089 A151 90c Map reading .60 .60
1090 A151 $1 Bee keeping .65 .65
1091 A151 $4 Hospital reading 2.00 2.00
Nos. 1088-1091 (4) 3.75 3.75

Souvenir Sheet

1092 A151 $5 Trophy presentation 3.00 3.00

Flambeaux A152

Norman Rockwell A153

1982, Mar. 24 **Litho.** *Perf. 14*

1093 A152 10c shown .20 .20
1094 A152 60c Large orange sulphurs .45 .45
1095 A152 $1 Red anartias .75 .75
1096 A152 $3 Polydamas swallowtails 2.50 2.50
Nos. 1093-1096 (4) 3.90 3.90

Souvenir Sheet

1097 A152 $5 Caribbean buckeyes 4.00 4.00

1982, Apr. 12 **Litho.** *Perf. 14x13½*

1098 A153 15c shown .20 .20
1099 A153 30c Card Tricks .25 .25
1100 A153 60c Pharmacist .45 .45
1101 A153 70c Pals .55 .55
Nos. 1098-1101 (4) 1.45 1.45

Princess Diana Issue

Common Design Type

1982, July 1 **Litho.** *Perf. 14½x14*

1101A CD332 50c Kensington Palace .35 .35
1102 CD332 60c like 50c .40 .40
1102A CD332 $1 Couple in field .65 .65
1103 CD332 $2 like $1 1.40 1.40
1103A CD332 $3 Diana in green dress 2.00 2.00
1104 CD332 $4 like $3 2.75 2.75
Nos. 1101A-1104 (6) 7.55 7.55

Souvenir Sheet

1105 CD332 $5 Diana, diff. 3.50 3.50

For overprints see Nos. 1115A-1119.

Franklin Roosevelt Birth Centenary A154

Designs: 10c, Mary McLeod Bethune, director of Negro Affairs, 1942. 60c, Leadbelly (Huddie Ledbetter, Works Progress Administration). $1.10, Signing Fair Employment Act, 1941. $3, Farm Security Administration.

1982, July 27 **Litho.** *Perf. 14*

1106 A154 10c multi .20 .20
1107 A154 60c multi .40 .40
1108 A154 $1.10 multi .75 .75
1109 A154 $3 multi 2.00 2.00
Nos. 1106-1109 (4) 3.35 3.35

Souvenir Sheet

1110 A154 $5 multi 3.50 3.50

Easter A155

Details from Raphael's "On the Way to Calvary." 70c, $1.10, $4, $5, vert.

1982, Sept. 2 *Perf. 14½*

1111 A155 40c multi .30 .30
1112 A155 70c multi .40 .40
1113 A155 $1.10 multi .65 .65
1114 A155 $4 multi 2.75 2.75
Nos. 1111-1114 (4) 4.10 4.10

Souvenir Sheet

1115 A155 $5 multi 3.50 3.50

Nos. 1101A-1105 Overprinted: "ROYAL BABY / 21.6.82"

1982, Sept. 27 **Litho.** *Perf. 14½x14*

1115A CD332 50c multi .35 .35
1116 CD332 60c multi .40 .40
1116A CD332 $1 multi .65 .65
1117 CD332 $2 multi 1.40 1.40
1117A CD332 $3 multi 2.00 2.00
1118 CD332 $4 multi 2.75 2.75
Nos. 1115A-1118 (6) 7.55 7.55

Souvenir Sheet

1119 CD332 $5 multi 3.50 3.50

Birth of Prince William of Wales, June 21.

Orient Express A156

1982, Oct. 4

1120 A156 30c shown .20 .20
1121 A156 60c Trans-Siberian Express .40 .40
1122 A156 70c Fleche D'or .50 .50
1123 A156 90c Flying Scotsman .60 .60
1124 A156 $1 German Federal Railways .65 .65
1125 A156 $3 German Natl. Railways 2.00 2.00
Nos. 1120-1125 (6) 4.35 4.35

Souvenir Sheet

1126 A156 $5 20th Century Limited, US 3.50 3.50

Christmas — A157

Scenes from Walt Disney's Robin Hood.

1982, Dec. 7 **Litho.** *Perf. 14*

1127 A157 ½c multi .20 .20
1128 A157 1c multi .20 .20
1129 A157 2c multi .20 .20
1130 A157 3c multi .20 .20
1131 A157 4c multi .20 .20
1132 A157 5c multi .20 .20
1133 A157 10c multi .20 .20
1134 A157 $2.50 multi 2.00 2.00
1135 A157 $3 multi 2.75 2.75
Nos. 1127-1135 (9) 6.15 6.15

Souvenir Sheet

1136 A157 $5 multi 5.00 5.00

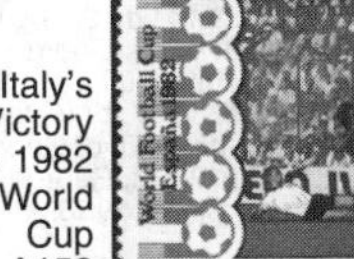

Italy's Victory in 1982 World Cup A158

1982, Dec. 2 *Perf. 14x13½*

1137 A158 60c Stolen ball .45 .45
1138 A158 $4 Captain holding trophy 3.00 3.00

Souvenir Sheet

1139 A158 $5 Flags 3.75 3.75

Killer Whale — A159

1982, Dec. 15 *Perf. 14*

1140 A159 15c shown .20 .20
1141 A159 40c Sperm whale .30 .30
1142 A159 70c Blue whale .50 .50
1143 A159 $3 Common dolphins 2.25 2.25
Nos. 1140-1143 (4) 3.25 3.25

Souvenir Sheet

1144 A159 $5 Humpback whale 3.75 3.75

500th Birth Anniv. of Raphael — A160

1983, Feb. 15 **Litho.** *Perf. 14*

1145 A160 25c Construction of the Ark .20 .20
1146 A160 30c Jacob's Vision .25 .25
1147 A160 90c Joseph Interprets the Dreams .70 .70
1148 A160 $4 Joseph Interprets Pharaoh's Dream 3.00 3.00
Nos. 1145-1148 (4) 4.15 4.15

Souvenir Sheet

1149 A160 $5 Creation of the Animals 3.75 3.75

A161

1983, Mar. 14

1150 A161 10c Dental care .20 .20
1151 A161 70c Airport runway construction .55 .55
1152 A161 $1.10 Beach .85 .85
1153 A161 $3 Boat building 2.25 2.25
Nos. 1150-1153 (4) 3.85 3.85

Commonwealth Day.

World Communication Year — A162

1983, Apr. 18

1154 A162 30c Ship-satellite communication .25 .25
1155 A162 40c Rural telephone installation .30 .30
1156 A162 $2.50 Weather map 1.75 1.75
1157 A162 $3 Airport control tower 2.25 2.25
Nos. 1154-1157 (4) 4.55 4.55

Souvenir Sheet

1158 A162 $5 Satellite 3.75 3.75

For overprints see Nos. 1248-1250.

Franklin Sport Sedan, 1928 A163

1983, May 4 **Litho.** *Perf. 15*

1159 A163 6c shown .20 .20
1160 A163 10c Delage D8, 1933 .20 .20
1161 A163 40c Alvis, 1938 .30 .30
1162 A163 60c Invicta S-type Tourer, 1931 .45 .45
1163 A163 70c Alfa-Romeo 1750 Gran Sport, 1930 .50 .50
1164 A163 90c Isotta Fraschini, 1930 .70 .70
1165 A163 $1 Bugatti Royal Type 41, 1941 .75 .75
1166 A163 $2 BMV 328, 1938 1.50 1.50
1167 A163 $3 Marmon V-16, 1931 2.25 2.25
1168 A163 $4 Lincoln KB Saloon, 1932 3.00 3.00
Nos. 1159-1168 (10) 9.85 9.85

Souvenir Sheet

1169 A163 $5 Cougar XR-7, 1972 3.75 3.75

Manned Flight Bicentenary — A164

1983, July 18 **Litho.** *Perf. 14*

1170 A164 30c Norge blimp .25 .25
1171 A164 60c Gloster-VI sea plane .45 .45
1172 A164 $1.10 Curtiss NC-4 .80 .80
1173 A164 $4 Dornier Do-18 3.00 3.00
Nos. 1170-1173 (4) 4.50 4.50

Souvenir Sheet

1174 A164 $5 Hot air ballooning, vert. 3.75 3.75

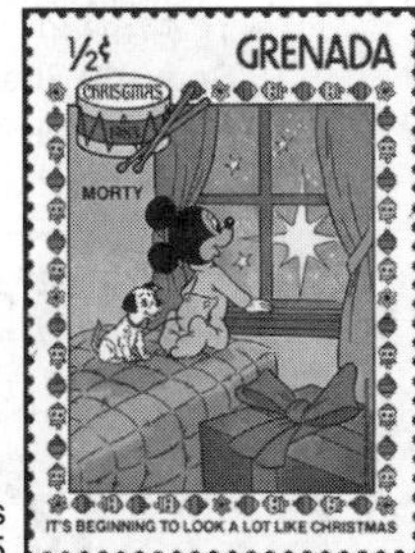

Christmas A165

Designs: Walt Disney's It's Beginning to look a lot like Christmas.

1983, Nov. *Perf. 11*

1175 A165 ½c Morty and Patches .20 .20
1176 A165 1c Ludwig von Drake .20 .20
1177 A165 2c Gyro Gearloose .20 .20
1178 A165 3c Pluto and Figaro .20 .20
1179 A165 4c Morty and Ferdy .20 .20
1180 A165 5c Mickey Mouse and Goofy .20 .20
1181 A165 10c Chip'n'Dale .20 .20
1182 A165 $2.50 Mickey and Minnie 1.75 1.75

1183 A165 $3 Donald and Grandma Duck 2.50 2.50
Nos. 1175-1183 (9) 5.65 5.65

Souvenir Sheet

1184 A165 $5 Goofy 4.00 4.00

1984 Olympics — A166

Designs: Various Disney characters.

1983, Dec. 19 Litho. *Perf. 13½*

1185 A166 ½c Pommel Horse .20 .20
1186 A166 1c Boxing .20 .20
1187 A166 2c Archery .20 .20
1188 A166 3c Uneven bars .20 .20
1189 A166 4c Hurdles .20 .20
1190 A166 5c Weightlifting .20 .20
1191 A166 $1 Kayak .75 .75
1192 A166 $2 Marathon 1.50 1.50
1193 A166 $3 Pole Vault 2.25 2.25
Nos. 1185-1193 (9) 5.70 5.70

Souvenir Sheet

1194 A166 $5 Medley Relay, vert. 4.50 4.50

Inscribed with Olympic Rings Emblem

1984 *Perf. 12½x12*

1185a A166 ½c .20 .20
1186a A166 1c .20 .20
1187a A166 2c .20 .20
1188a A166 3c .20 .20
1189a A166 4c .20 .20
1190a A166 5c .20 .20
1191a A166 $1 .75 .75
1192a A166 $2 1.50 1.50
1193a A166 $3 2.25 2.25
Nos. 1185a-1193a (9) 5.70 5.70

Souvenir Sheet

1194a A166 $5 Olympic rings emblem inscribed 4.50 4.50

Nos. 1185a-1193a printed in sheets of 5.

Banana Boat A167

1984, July 16 Litho. *Perf. 15*

1195 A167 40c shown .30 .30
1196 A167 70c Queen Elizabeth 2 .50 .50
1197 A167 90c Working sailboats .70 .70
1198 A167 $4 Amerikanis 3.00 3.00
Nos. 1195-1198 (4) 4.50 4.50

Souvenir Sheet

1199 A167 $5 Spanish galleon, flotilla 3.75 3.75

King William I, 1066-87 — A168

British Kings or Queens and Years of their reigns: No. 1200b, William II, 1087-1100. c, Henry I, 1100-35. d, Stephen, 1135-54. e, Henry II, 1154-89. f, Richard I, 1189-99. g, John, 1199-1216.

No. 1201a, Henry III, 1216-72. b, Edward I, 1272-1307. c, Edward II, 1307-27. d, Edward III, 1327-77. e, Richard II, 1377-99. f, Henry IV, 1399-1413. g, Henry V, 1413-22.

No. 1202a, Henry VI, 1422-61. b, Edward IV, 1461-83. c, Edward V, 1483. d, Richard III, 1483-85. e, Henry VII, 1485-1509. f, Henry VIII, 1509-47. g, Edward VI, 1547-53.

No. 1203a, Jane Grey, 1553. b, Mary I, 1553-58. c, Elizabeth I, 1558-1603. d, James I, 1603-25. e, Charles I, 1625-49. f, Charles II, 1660-85. g, James II, 1685-88.

No. 1204a, William III, 1688-1702. b, Mary II, 1688-94. c, Anne, 1702-14. d, George I, 1714-27. e, George II, 1727-60. f, George III, 1760-1820. g, George IV, 1820-30.

No. 1205a, William IV, 1830-37. b, Victoria, 1837-1901. c, Edward VII, 1901-10. d, George V, 1910-36. e, Edward VIII, 1936. f, George VI, 1936-52. g, Elizabeth II, since 1952. Size: 141x128mm.

1984, Jan. 25 Litho. *Perf. 14*

1200 Sheet of 7 + label 21.00 21.00
a.-g. A168 $4, any single 3.00 3.00
1201 Sheet of 7 + label 21.00 21.00
a.-g. A168 $4, any single 3.00 3.00
1202 Sheet of 7 + label 21.00 21.00
a.-g. A168 $4, any single 3.00 3.00
1203 Sheet of 7 + label 21.00 21.00
a.-g. A168 $4, any single 3.00 3.00
1204 Sheet of 7 + label 21.00 21.00
a.-g. A168 $4, any single 3.00 3.00
1205 Sheet of 7 + label 21.00 21.00
a.-g. A168 $4, any single 3.00 3.00

Local Flowers A169

1984, May *Perf. 15*

1206 A169 25c Lantana .20 .20
1207 A169 30c Plumbago .25 .25
1208 A169 90c Spider lily .70 .70
1209 A169 $4 Giant alocasia 3.00 3.00
Nos. 1206-1209 (4) 4.15 4.15

Souvenir Sheet

1210 A169 $5 Orange trumpet vine 3.75 3.75

For overprints see Nos. 1216-1218.

Coral Reef Fish, World Wildlife Fund Emblem A170

1984, May Litho. *Perf. 14*

1211 A170 10c Blue parrot fish .40 .40
1212 A170 30c Flame-back cherub fish .90 .90
1213 A170 70c Painted wrasse 2.25 2.25
1214 A170 90c Straight-tailed razorfish 3.00 3.00
Nos. 1211-1214 (4) 6.55 6.55

Souvenir Sheet

1215 A170 $5 Spanish hogfish 3.75 3.75

Nos. 1208-1210 Overprinted: "19th U.P.U CONGRESS—HAMBURG"

1984 Litho. *Perf. 15*

1216 A169 90c multi .70 .70
1217 A169 $4 multi 3.00 3.00

Souvenir Sheet

1218 A169 $5 multi 3.75 3.75

AUSIPEX '84 — A171

Correggio & Degas — A171a

1984, Sept. 21 *Perf. 14*

1219 A171 $1.10 Puffing Billy .80 .80
1220 A171 $4 Australia II 3.00 3.00

Souvenir Sheet

1221 A171 $5 Melbourne tram 3.75 3.75

1984, Aug. Litho. *Perf. 14*

Paintings by Correggio: 10c, The Night (detail). 30c, Virgin Adoring the Child. 90c, Mystical Marriage of St. Catherine with St. Sebastian. $4, Madonna and the Fruit Basket. No. 1230, Madonna at the Spring.

Paintings by Degas: 25c, L'Absinthe. 70c, Pouting, horiz. $1.10, The Millinery Shop. $3, The Bellelli Family. No. 1231, The Cotton Market.

1222 A171a 10c multi .20 .20
1223 A171a 25c multi .20 .20
1224 A171a 30c multi .25 .25
1225 A171a 70c multi .50 .50
1226 A171a 90c multi .70 .70
1227 A171a $1.10 multi .80 .80
1228 A171a $3 multi 2.25 2.25
1229 A171a $4 multi 3.00 3.00
Nos. 1222-1229 (8) 7.90 7.90

Souvenir Sheets

1230 A171a $5 multi 3.75 3.75
1231 A171a $5 multi 3.75 3.75

19th Cent. Locomotives — A172

1984, Oct. *Perf. 14½*

1232 A172 30c Locomotion, 1825 .25 .25
1233 A172 40c Novelty, 1829 .30 .30
1234 A172 60c Washington Farmer, 1836 .45 .45
1235 A172 70c French Crampton, 1859 .50 .50
1236 A172 90c Dutch State, 1873 .70 .70
1237 A172 $1.10 Champion, 1882 .80 .80
1238 A172 $2 Webb Compound, 1893 1.50 1.50
1239 A172 $4 Berlin 74, 1900 3.00 3.00
Nos. 1232-1239 (8) 7.50 7.50

Souvenir Sheets

1240 A172 $5 Crampton Phoenix, 1863 3.75 3.75
1241 A172 $5 2-8-2 Mikado, 1897 3.75 3.75

Christmas and 50th Anniv. of Donald Duck A173

Scenes from various Donald Duck movies.

Perf. 13½x14, 12 ($2)

1984, Nov. Litho.

1242 A173 45c multicolored .35 .35
1243 A173 60c multicolored .50 .50
1244 A173 90c multicolored .80 .80
1245 A173 $2 multicolored 1.75 1.75
1246 A173 $4 multicolored 3.50 3.50
Nos. 1242-1246 (5) 6.90 6.90

Souvenir Sheet

1247 A173 $5 multicolored 4.50 4.50

Nos. 1155. 1157, and 1158 Overprinted: "OPENING OF / POINT SALINE / INT'L AIRPORT"

1984, Oct. 28 Litho. *Perf. 14½x14*

1248 A162 40c on #1155 .30 .30
1249 A162 $3 on #1157 2.25 2.25

Souvenir Sheet

Same Overprint in Margin in 2 Lines

1250 A162 $5 on #1158 3.75 3.75

Audubon Birth Bicentenary A174

1985, Feb. Litho. *Perf. 14*

1251 A174 50c Clapper Rail .35 .35
1252 A174 70c Hooded Warbler .50 .50
1253 A174 90c Flicker .65 .65
1254 A174 $4 Bohemian Waxwing 3.00 3.00
Nos. 1251-1254 (4) 4.50 4.50

Souvenir Sheet

1255 A174 $5 Pigeon Hawk, horiz. 3.75 3.75

See Nos. 1352-1356.

Motorcycle Centenary — A175

1985, Mar. 11 Litho. *Perf. 14*

1256 A175 25c Honda XL500R .20 .20
1257 A175 50c Suzuki GS1100ES .30 .30
1258 A175 90c Kawasaki KZ700 .45 .45
1259 A175 $4 BMW K100 1.75 1.75
Nos. 1256-1259 (4) 2.70 2.70

Souvenir Sheet

1260 A175 $5 Yamaha 500CC 3.75 3.75

Girl Guides, 75th Anniv. A176

1985, Apr. 15

1261 A176 25c Nature hike .20 .20
1262 A176 60c Cookout .45 .45
1263 A176 90c Singing around campfire .65 .65
1264 A176 $3 Public service 2.25 2.25
Nos. 1261-1264 (4) 3.55 3.55

Souvenir Sheet

1265 A176 $5 Flags 3.75 3.75

Opening of Point Saline Intl. Airport, Oct. 28, 1984 A177

Inaugural flights.

1985, Apr. 30

1266 A177 70c From Barbados .60 .60
1267 A177 $1 From New York .85 .85
1268 A177 $4 To Miami 3.25 3.25
Nos. 1266-1268 (3) 4.70 4.70

Souvenir Sheet

1269 A177 $5 Point Saline Intl. Airport 3.75 3.75

Intl. Civil Aviation Org., 40th Anniv. A178

1985, May 15

1270 A178 10c McDonnell Douglas DC-8 .20 .20
1271 A178 50c Super Constellation .40 .40
1272 A178 60c Vickers Vanguard .50 .50
1273 A178 $4 DeHavilland Twin Otter 3.00 3.00
Nos. 1270-1273 (4) 4.10 4.10

Souvenir Sheet

1274 A178 $5 Avro 748 Turboprop 3.75 3.75

Water Sports A179

1985, June 15 ***Perf. 15***

1275 A179 10c Model boat racing .20 .20
1276 A179 50c Snorkeling, Sandy Island carriacou .40 .40
1277 A179 $1.10 Sailing, Grand Anse Beach .90 .90
1278 A179 $4 Windsurfing 3.00 3.00
Nos. 1275-1278 (4) 4.50 4.50

Miniature Sheet

1279 A179 $5 Snorkelers, surfers, sailboats 3.75 3.75

Island Flowers — A180

½c, Strelitzia reginae. 1c, Passiflora coccinea. 2c, Nerium oleander. 4c, Ananas comosus. 5c, Anthurium andraeanum. 6c, Bougainvillea glabra. 10c, Hibiscus rosa-sinensis. 15c, Alpinia purpurata. 25c, Euphorbia pulcherrima. 30c, Antigonon leptopus. 40c, Datura candida. 50c, Hippeastrum puniceum. 60c, Opuntia megacantha. 70c, Acalypha hispida. 75c, Cordia sebestina. $1, Catharan-thus roseus. $1.10, Ixora macrothyrsa. $3, Justicia brandegeeana. $5, Plumbago capensis. $10, Lantana camara. $20, Jatropha integerrima.

1985-88 ***Perf. 14***

1280 A180 ½c multi .20 .20
1281 A180 1c multi .20 .20
1282 A180 2c multi .20 .20
1283 A180 4c multi .20 .20
1284 A180 5c multi .20 .20
1285 A180 6c multi .20 .20
1286 A180 10c multi .20 .20
1287 A180 15c multi .20 .20
1288 A180 25c multi .20 .20
1289 A180 30c multi .20 .20
1290 A180 40c multi .30 .30
1291 A180 50c multi .35 .35
1292 A180 60c multi .40 .40
1293 A180 70c multi .45 .45
1293B A180 75c multi .60 .60
1294 A180 $1 multi .70 .70
1295 A180 $1.10 multi .75 .75
1296 A180 $3 multi 2.00 2.00
1297 A180 $5 multi 3.25 3.25
1297A A180 $10 multi 6.50 6.50
1297B A180 $20 multi 13.00 13.00
Nos. 1280-1297B (21) 30.30 30.30

Issued: #1280-1293, 1294-1297, 7/1; $10, 11/11; $20, 8/1/86; 75c, 1/12/88.

For overprints see #1357-1358, 1558-1560.

1986 ***Perf. 12x12½***

1280a A180 ½c .20 .20
1281a A180 1c .20 .20
1282a A180 2c .20 .20
1283a A180 4c .20 .20
1284a A180 5c .20 .20
1285a A180 6c .20 .20
1286a A180 10c .20 .20
1287a A180 15c .20 .20
1288a A180 25c .20 .20
1289a A180 30c .20 .20
1290a A180 40c .30 .30
1291a A180 50c .35 .35
1292a A180 60c .40 .40
1293a A180 70c .45 .45
1294a A180 $1 .70 .70
1295a A180 $1.10 .75 .75
1296a A180 $3 2.00 2.00
1297c A180 $5 3.25 3.25
1297d A180 $10 6.50 6.50
Nos. 1280a-1297d (19) 16.70 16.70

Issued: #1280a-1285a, 1287a-1292a, 1294a-1296a, Mar.; 10c, 70c, $5, July; $10, Dec.

Nos. 1289, 1291, 1292 and 1294 reprinted with "1987" imprint, No. 1286 with "1988" imprint.

Queen Mother, 85th Birthday A181

Photographs: $1, At the Royal Opera, vert. $1.50, Playing pool, London Press Club. $2.50, At Epsom for the Oaks Day races, vert. $5, In open carriage with Prince Charles, Thanksgiving Day, 1980, vert.

1985, July 5

1298 A181 $1 multicolored .70 .70
1299 A181 $1.50 multicolored 1.10 1.10
1300 A181 $2.50 multicolored 1.75 1.75
Nos. 1298-1300 (3) 3.55 3.55

Souvenir Sheet

1301 A181 $5 multicolored 3.75 3.75

1986, Jan. 20 Litho. ***Perf. 12x12½***

1301A A181 90c like #1298 .65 .65
1301B A181 $1 like #1299 .75 .75
1301C A181 $3 like #1300 2.25 2.25
Nos. 1301A-1301C (3) 3.65 3.65

#1301A-1301C issued in sheets of 5 + label.

Intl. Youth Year — A182

1985, Aug. 21 ***Perf. 15***

1302 A182 25c Gardening .20 .20
1303 A182 50c At the beach .35 .35
1304 A182 $1.10 Education .75 .75
1305 A182 $3 Health care 2.00 2.00
Nos. 1302-1305 (4) 3.30 3.30

Souvenir Sheet

1306 A182 $5 Harmonizing 3.25 3.25

4th Caribbean Cuboree, Aug. 17-23 A183

1985, Sept. 5 ***Perf. 14***

1307 A183 10c Pitching tents .20 .20
1308 A183 50c Swimming .40 .40
1309 A183 $1 Stamp collecting .85 .85
1310 A183 $4 Bird watching 3.25 3.25
Nos. 1307-1310 (4) 4.70 4.70

Souvenir Sheet

1311 A183 $5 Grand Circle ritual 4.00 4.00

Johann Sebastian Bach — A184

Portrait, signature, music from Ciaccona and: 25c, Crumhorn. 70c, Oboe d'amore. $1, Violin. $3, Harpsichord. $5, Portrait.

1985, Sept. 19

1312 A184 25c multicolored .20 .20
1313 A184 70c multicolored .45 .45
1314 A184 $1 multicolored .70 .70
1315 A184 $3 multicolored 2.00 2.00
Nos. 1312-1315 (4) 3.35 3.35

Souvenir Sheet

1316 A184 $5 multicolored 3.50 3.50

The Prince & the Pauper — A185

Walt Disney characters.

1985, Oct. 30

1317 A185 25c Prince & Pauper meet .20 .20
1318 A185 50c Exchange clothes .45 .45
1319 A185 $1.10 Prince as the Pauper .95 .95
1320 A185 $1.50 Prince rescued 1.40 1.40
1321 A185 $2 Pauper as the Prince 1.75 1.75
Nos. 1317-1321 (5) 4.75 4.75

Souvenir Sheet

1322 A185 $5 Prince & Pauper celebrate 4.25 4.25

IYY, Mark Twain (1835-1910), author.

Elizabeth II, Royal Visit to Spice Island — A186

1985, Oct. 31 ***Perf. 14½***

1323 A186 50c Flags of Grenada, U.K. .40 .40
1324 A186 $1 Elizabeth II, vert. .80 .80
1325 A186 $4 HMS Britannia 3.00 3.00
Nos. 1323-1325 (3) 4.20 4.20

Souvenir Sheet

1326 A186 $5 Map 3.75 3.75

The Brothers Grimm — A187

Disney characters in The Fisherman and His Wife.

1985, Nov. 4 Litho. ***Perf. 14***

1327 A187 30c multicolored .25 .25
1328 A187 60c multicolored .55 .55
1329 A187 70c multicolored .60 .60
1330 A187 $1 multicolored .85 .85
1331 A187 $3 multicolored 2.75 2.75
Nos. 1327-1331 (5) 5.00 5.00

Souvenir Sheet

1332 A187 $5 multicolored 4.00 4.00

Indigenous Fish and Coral — A188

1985, Nov. 15

1333 A188 25c Red-spotted hawkfish .20 .20
1334 A188 50c Spotfin butterflyfish .40 .40
1335 A188 $1.10 Fire coral, orange sponge .80 .80
1336 A188 $3 Pillar coral 2.25 2.25
Nos. 1333-1336 (4) 3.65 3.65

Souvenir Sheet

1337 A188 $5 Bigeye 3.75 3.75

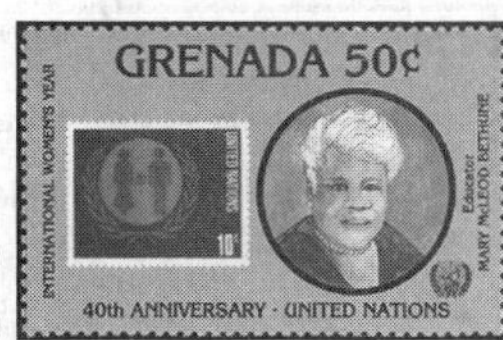

UN, 40th Anniv. A189

UN stamps and famous people: 50c, No. 258, Mary McLeod Bethune (1875-1955), American educator. $2, No. 156, Maimonides (1135-1204), Judaic scholar. $2.50, No. 41, Alexander Graham Bell (1847-1922), inventor of the telephone. $5, Dag Hammarskjold (1905-1961), 2nd UN secretary general.

1985, Nov. 22 ***Perf. 14½***

1338 A189 50c multicolored .40 .40
1339 A189 $2 multicolored 1.50 1.50
1340 A189 $2.50 multicolored 1.75 1.75
Nos. 1338-1340 (3) 3.65 3.65

Souvenir Sheet

1341 A189 $5 multicolored 3.75 3.75

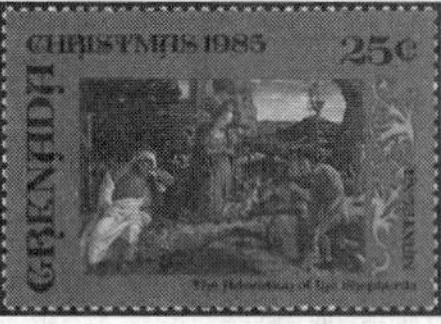

Christmas A190

Religious paintings: 25c, Adoration of the Shepherds, by Andre Mantegna (1431-1506). 60c, Journey of the Magi, by Sassetta (d. 1450). 90c, Madonna and Child Enthroned with Saints, by Raphael (1483-1520). $4, Nativity, by Monaco. $5, Madonna and Child Enthroned with Saints, by Agnolo Gaddi (c. 1350-1396).

1985, Dec. 23 ***Perf. 15***

1342 A190 25c multicolored .20 .20
1343 A190 60c multicolored .45 .45
1344 A190 90c multicolored .65 .65
1345 A190 $4 multicolored 3.00 3.00
Nos. 1342-1345 (4) 4.30 4.30

Souvenir Sheet

1346 A190 $5 multicolored 3.75 3.75

Statue of Liberty, Cent. A191

Views of New York City.

1986, Jan. 6

1347 A191 5c Columbus Circle, 1893 .20 .20
1348 A191 25c Circle, 1986 .20 .20
1349 A191 40c Central Park Mounted Police, 1895 .30 .30
1350 A191 $4 Mounted Police, 1986 3.00 3.00
Nos. 1347-1350 (4) 3.70 3.70

Souvenir Sheet

1351 A191 $5 Statue of Liberty 3.75 3.75

Nos. 1347-1348, 1351 vert.

Audubon Type of 1985

1986, Jan. 20 ***Perf. 12x12½***

1352 A174 50c Snowy egret .40 .40
1353 A174 90c Red flamingo .65 .65
1354 A174 $1.10 Barnacle goose .80 .80
1355 A174 $3 Smew 2.25 2.25
Nos. 1352-1355 (4) 4.10 4.10

Souvenir Sheet

Perf. 14

1356 A174 $5 Brant Goose, horiz. 3.75 3.75

Nos. 1291 and 1297 Overprinted "VISIT OF PRES. REAGAN 20 FEB. 1986"

1986, Feb. 20 ***Perf. 14***

1357 A180 50c multicolored .40 .40
1358 A180 $5 multicolored 3.75 3.75

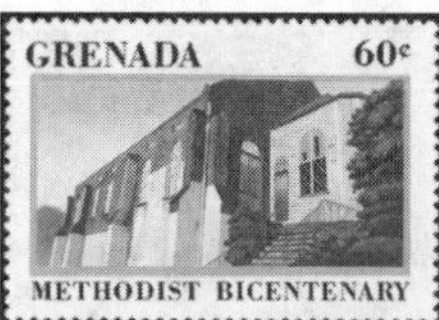

St. George Methodist Church, Bicent. A192

1986, Feb. 24 ***Perf. 15***

1359 A192 60c multicolored .45 .45

Souvenir Sheet

1360 A192 $5 multicolored 3.75 3.75

Heritage Year.

1986 World Cup Soccer Championships, Mexico — A193

Various soccer plays.

1986, Mar. 6 ***Perf. 14***

1361 A193 50c multicolored .40 .40
1362 A193 70c multicolored .50 .50
1363 A193 90c multicolored .65 .65
1364 A193 $4 multicolored 3.00 3.00
Nos. 1361-1364 (4) 4.55 4.55

Souvenir Sheet

1365 A193 $5 multicolored 3.75 3.75

For overprints see Nos. 1399-1403.

Halley's Comet A194

5c, Clyde Tombaugh, discovered Pluto, 1930, & Dudley Observatory. 20c, US X-24B space shuttle prototype, 1973. 40c, Medallic art, Catholic Church, 1618. $4, Lot & his daughters fleeing Sodom & Gomorrah, 1949 B.C. $5, Comet over Grand Anse Beach.

1986, Mar. 20

1366 A194 5c multicolored .20 .20
1367 A194 20c multicolored .20 .20
1368 A194 40c multicolored .30 .30
1369 A194 $4 multicolored 3.00 3.00
Nos. 1366-1369 (4) 3.70 3.70

Souvenir Sheet

1370 A194 $5 multicolored 3.75 3.75

For overprints see Nos. 1416-1420.

Queen Elizabeth II, 60th Birthday
Common Design Type

2c, Signing the log, 1951. $1.50, Presenting polo trophy, Windsor, 1965. $4, Derby Day, 1977. $5, Royal family portrait, 1939.

1986, Apr. 21 ***Perf. 14***

1371 CD339 2c yel & blk .20 .20
1372 CD339 $1.50 pale grn & multi 1.10 1.10
1373 CD339 $4 dl lil & multi 3.00 3.00
Nos. 1371-1373 (3) 4.30 4.30

Souvenir Sheet

1374 CD339 $5 tan & blk 3.75 3.75

AMERIPEX '86 — A195

Walt Disney characters playing baseball.

1986, May 22 Litho. ***Perf. 11***

1375 A195 1c Pitcher .20 .20
1376 A195 2c Catcher .20 .20
1377 A195 3c Strike .20 .20
1378 A195 4c Force out .20 .20
1379 A195 5c Fly ball .20 .20
1380 A195 6c Third base .25 .25
1381 A195 $2 Manager 1.75 1.75
1382 A195 $3 Error 3.00 3.00
Nos. 1375-1382 (8) 6.00 6.00

Souvenir Sheets
Perf. 14

1383 A195 $5 Batter 5.00 5.00
1384 A195 $5 Grand slam 5.00 5.00

Royal Wedding Issue, 1986
Common Design Type

Designs: 2c, Prince Andrew and Sarah Ferguson. $1.10, Andrew. $4, Andrew in flight suit, helicopter. $5, Couple, diff.

1986, July 23 ***Perf. 14***

1385 CD340 2c multicolored .20 .20
1386 CD340 $1.10 multicolored .80 .80
1387 CD340 $4 multicolored 3.00 3.00
Nos. 1385-1387 (3) 4.00 4.00

Souvenir Sheet

1388 CD340 $5 multicolored 3.75 3.75

Seashells A196

Designs: 25c, Gmelin brown-lined latirus. 60c, Lamarck lamellose wentletrap. 70c, Swainson turkey wing. $4, Linne rooster-tail conch. $5, Linne angular triton.

1986, July 15 Litho. ***Perf. 15***

1389 A196 25c multicolored .20 .20
1390 A196 60c multicolored .45 .45
1391 A196 70c multicolored .50 .50
1392 A196 $4 multicolored 3.00 3.00
Nos. 1389-1392 (4) 4.15 4.15

Souvenir Sheet

1393 A196 $5 multicolored 3.75 3.75

Mushrooms A197

1986, Aug. 1 ***Perf. 15***

1394 A197 10c Lepiota rose-lamellata .20 .20
1395 A197 60c Lentinus bertieri .45 .45
1396 A197 $1 Lentinus re-tinervis .75 .75
1397 A197 $4 Eccilia cysti-ophorus 3.00 3.00
Nos. 1394-1397 (4) 4.40 4.40

Souvenir Sheet

1398 A197 $5 Cystolepiota eri-ophora 3.75 3.75

Nos. 1361-1365 Ovptd. "WINNERS Argentina 3 / W. Germany 2" in Gold

1986, Sept. 15 Litho. ***Perf. 14***

1399 A193 50c multicolored .40 .40
1400 A193 70c multicolored .50 .50
1401 A193 90c multicolored .65 .65
1402 A193 $4 multicolored 3.00 3.00
Nos. 1399-1402 (4) 4.55 4.55

Souvenir Sheet

1403 A193 $5 multicolored 3.75 3.75

Disarmament Week and Intl. Peace Year — A198

60c, Mahatma Gandhi, rifles, dove. $4, Martin Luther King, Jr., hands, olive branch.

1986, Sept. 15 ***Perf. 15***

1404 A198 60c multi, vert. .45 .45
1405 A198 $4 multi 3.00 3.00

Christmas — A199

Disney characters. Nos. 1406-1407, 1411-1412 vert.

1986, Nov. 3 ***Perf. 11***

1406 A199 30c Mickey, hearth .30 .30
1407 A199 45c Mickey, Santa .40 .40
1408 A199 60c Donald, Mickey Mouse phone .55 .55
1409 A199 70c Goofy, toy band .65 .65
1410 A199 $1.10 Daisy, dolls 1.00 1.00
1411 A199 $2 Goofy as Santa 1.90 1.90
1412 A199 $2.50 Goofy playing piano 2.25 2.25
1413 A199 $3 Train ride 2.75 2.75
Nos. 1406-1413 (8) 9.80 9.80

Souvenir Sheets

1414 A199 $5 Donald, Goofy, Mickey 4.75 4.75
1415 A199 $5 Dewey 4.75 4.75

Nos. 1366-1370 Ovptd. with Halley's Comet Emblem

1986, Oct. 15 Litho. ***Perf. 14***

1416 A194 5c multicolored .20 .20
1417 A194 20c multicolored .20 .20
1418 A194 40c multicolored .30 .30
1419 A194 $4 multicolored 3.00 3.00
Nos. 1416-1419 (4) 3.70 3.70

Souvenir Sheet

1420 A194 $5 multicolored 3.75 3.75

Fauna and Flora A200

1986, Nov. 17 ***Perf. 14***

1421 A200 10c Chicken, rooster .20 .20
1422 A200 30c Fish-eating bat .25 .25
1423 A200 60c Goat .50 .50
1424 A200 70c Cow .60 .60
1425 A200 $1 Anthurium .80 .80
1426 A200 $1.10 Royal poinciana .90 .90
1427 A200 $2 Frangipani 1.50 1.50
1428 A200 $4 Orchid 3.25 3.25
Nos. 1421-1428 (8) 8.00 8.00

Souvenir Sheets

1429 A200 $5 Horse 4.00 4.00
1430 A200 $5 Trees 4.00 4.00

Automobile, Cent. — A202

1886 Daimler and modern automobiles.

1986, Nov. 20 ***Perf. 15***

1431 A202 10c 1984 Maserati Biturbo .20 .20
1432 A202 30c 1960 AC Cobra .25 .25
1433 A202 60c 1963 Corvette .50 .50
1434 A202 70c 1932 Duesenberg SJ7 .55 .55
1435 A202 90c 1957 Porsche .70 .70
1436 A202 $1.10 1930 Stoewer .90 .90
1437 A202 $2 1957 VW Beetle 1.60 1.60
1438 A202 $3 1963 Mercedes 600 Limo 2.40 2.40
Nos. 1431-1438 (8) 7.10 7.10

Souvenir Sheets

1439 A202 $5 1914 Stutz 4.00 4.00
1440 A202 $5 1941 Packard 4.00 4.00

Song of Songs, by Marc Chagall (1887-1984) — A203

Paintings: No. 1441, The Rooster. No. 1442, Lovers in the Moonlight. No. 1443, Woman and Haystack. No. 1444, Snow-Covered Church. No. 1445, Peasant Life. No. 1446, Moses Receiving the Tablets. No. 1447, Vitebsk: From Mt. Zadunuv. No. 1449, Song of Songs, diff. No. 1450, The Creation of Man. No. 1451, Spring. No. 1452, Jacob's Struggle with the Angel. No. 1453, Song of Songs (wedding detail). No. 1454, The Painter to the Moon, 1917. No. 1455, Moses Striking the Rock. No. 1456, To My Betrothed, 1911. No. 1457, Sacrifice of Isaac. No. 1458, Monkey Acting as Judge Over Dispute Between Wolf and Fox, 1925. No. 1459, Song of Songs (bride riding Pegasus). No. 1460, Lovers in the Lilac, 1930. No. 1461, Song of Songs (sun, spirits). No. 1462, Jacob's Dream. No. 1463, Purim, 1916. No. 1464, Fantastic Horsecart. No. 1465, Listening to the Cock, 1944. No. 1466, Self-portrait, 1914. No. 1467, The Juggler, 1943. No. 1468, Noah and the Rainbow. No. 1469, Moses Before the Burning Bush. No. 1470, Around Her, 1945. No. 1471, The Trough, 1925. No. 1472, The Poet of Half-Past-Three. No. 1473, The Tree of Life, 1948. No. 1474, Woman with the Blue Face, 1932. No. 1475, Chrysanthemums, 1926. No. 1476, Spoonful of Milk, 1912. No. 1477, The Soldier Drinks, 1911. No. 1478, Noah's Ark. No. 1479, Flowers and Fruit. No. 1480, Adam and Eve Expelled fron Paradise. No. 1481. Return from Synagogue. No. 1482, Aleko: A Fantasy of St. Petersburg. No. 1483, The Orchard. No. 1484, Solitude. No. 1485, Paris Through the Window, 1913. No. 1486, The Wedding, 1910. No. 1487, Paradise. No. 1488, The Dream, 1939. No. 1489, Abraham and the Three Angels. No. 1490, Water Carrier Under the Moon, 1914.

1986-87

1441-1480 A203 $1 each .80 .80

Size: 110x95mm
Imperf

1481-1490 A203 $5 each 4.00 4.00

Nos. 1441-1446, 1450-1452 1455-1458, 1464-1467 and 1470-1479 vert.

Issued: #1441-1452, 1481-1483, 1986; #1453-1480, 1484-1490, 1987.

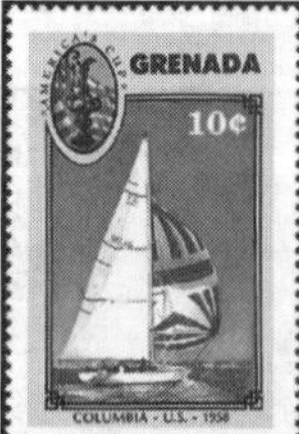

A204

America's Cup — A205

1987, Feb. 5 Litho. *Perf. 15*

1491 A204 10c Columbia, 1958 .20 .20
1492 A204 60c Resolute, 1920 .50 .50
1493 A204 $1.10 Endeavor, 1934 .90 .90
1494 A204 $4 Rainbow, 1934 3.25 3.25
Nos. 1491-1494 (4) 4.85 4.85

Souvenir Sheet

1495 A205 $5 Weatherly, 1962 4.00 4.00

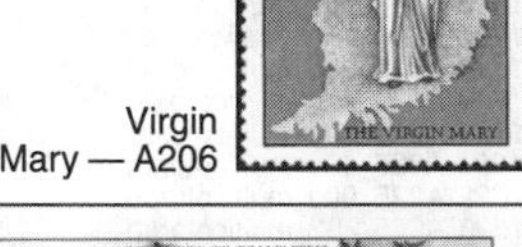

Virgin Mary — A206

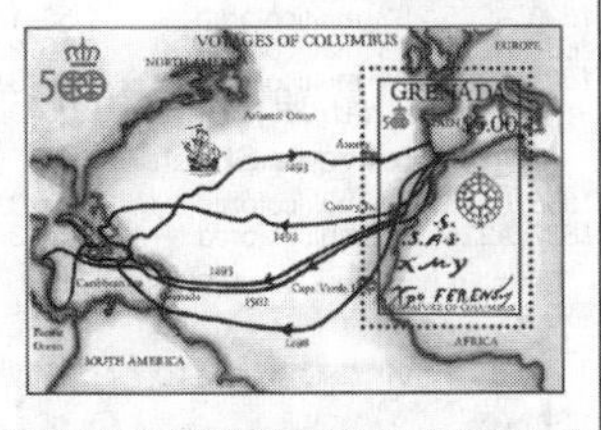

Map of Voyage, Columbus' Signature — A207

1987, Apr. 27 *Perf. 15*

1496 A206 10c shown .20 .20
1497 A206 30c Nina, Pinta, Santa Maria .25 .25
1498 A206 50c Columbus, map .40 .40
1499 A206 60c Columbus .45 .45
1500 A206 90c Isabella, Ferdinand .70 .70
1501 A206 $1.10 Discovering the Antilles .80 .80
1502 A206 $2 Carib Indians 1.50 1.50
a. Souv. sheet of 3, 30c, 90c, $2 2.40 2.40
1503 A206 $3 American Indians, 1493 2.25 2.25
a. Souv. sheet of 5 + label, 10c, 50c, 60c, $1.10, $3 4.00 4.00
Nos. 1496-1503 (8) 6.55 6.55

Souvenir Sheets

1504 A207 $5 shown 3.75 3.75
1505 A207 $5 Columbus, Christ child 3.75 3.75

Discovery of America 500th anniv. (in 1992). Nos. 1497, 1500 and 1502 horiz.

CAPEX '87 A208

Fish. Nos. 1506, 1508 vert.

1987, June 15

1506 A208 10c Black grouper .20 .20
1507 A208 30c Blue marlin .25 .25
1508 A208 60c White marlin .45 .45
1509 A208 70c Big-eye thresher shark .50 .50
1510 A208 $1 Bonefish .75 .75
1511 A208 $1.10 Wahoo .80 .80
1512 A208 $2 Sailfish 1.50 1.50
1513 A208 $4 Albacore 3.00 3.00
Nos. 1506-1513 (8) 7.45 7.45

Souvenir Sheets

1514 A208 $5 Barracuda 3.75 3.75
1515 A208 $5 Yellowfin tuna, vert. 3.75 3.75

Transportation Innovations — A209

1987, May 18 *Perf. 14*

1516 A209 10c Cornu's Helicopter, 1907 .20 .20
1517 A209 15c The Monitor and Merrimack, 1862 .20 .20
1518 A209 30c LZ1 Zeppelin, c. 1900 .25 .25
1519 A209 50c S.S. Sirius, 1838 .40 .40
1520 A209 60c Trans-Siberian Railway .45 .45
1521 A209 70c USS Enterprise, 1960 .50 .50
1522 A209 90c Blanchard's Balloon, 1785 .70 .70
1523 A209 $1.50 USS Holland 1, 1900 1.10 1.10
1524 A209 $2 S.S. Oceanic, 1871 1.50 1.50
1525 A209 $3 1984 Lamborghini Countach 2.25 2.25
Nos. 1516-1525 (10) 7.55 7.55

For overprints see Nos. 1599-1602.

Statue of Liberty, Cent. A210

1987, Aug. 5

1526 A210 10c Computer structural diagrams .20 .20
1527 A210 25c Fireworks around statue .20 .20
1528 A210 50c Fireworks in front of statue .40 .40
1529 A210 60c Statue, boats .45 .45
1530 A210 70c Structural diagram, close-up .50 .50
1531 A210 $1 Rear of statue, close-up .75 .75
1532 A210 $1.10 Liberty and Manhattan Isls. .80 .80
1533 A210 $2 Statue, boats, diff. 1.50 1.50
1534 A210 $4 Ocean liner, New York Harbor 3.00 3.00
Nos. 1526-1534 (9) 7.80 7.80

Nos. 1529, 1531-1534 vert.

Inventors and Innovators A211

Designs: 50c, Sir Isaac Newton (1642-1727), law of gravity. $1.10, Jons Jakob Berzelius (1779-1848), symbols of chemical elements. $2, Robert Boyle (1627-1691), and Boyle's Law of pressure and volume. $3, James Watt (1736-1819), and diagram of steam engine. $5, Wright Flyer, Voyager.

1987, Sept. 9

1535 A211 50c multicolored .40 .40
1536 A211 $1.10 multicolored .85 .85
1537 A211 $2 multicolored 1.50 1.50
1538 A211 $3 multicolored 2.25 2.25
Nos. 1535-1538 (4) 5.00 5.00

Souvenir Sheet

1539 A211 $5 multicolored 3.75 3.75

No. 1536 inscribed with incorrect spelling of inventors name, "John Jacob Berzelius." No. 1538 inscribed with incorrect caption; James Watt and Watt engine are pictured, not Rudolf Diesel and the Diesel engine.

Miniature Sheets

Fairy Tales — A212

Snow White (50th Anniv.): No. 1540a, Snow White scrubs stairs. b, Wicked Queen, looking glass. c, Snow White fleeing. d, Dwarfs, mine. e, Snow White at cottage. f, Snow White, dwarfs. g, Snow White dancing with dwarfs. h, Eating poison apple. i, Prince kissing Snow White.

Sleeping Beauty: No. 1541a, Royal family. b, Maleficent cursing infant (Aurora). c, Merryweather altering curse. d, Three good fairies. e, Briar Rose (Aurora), forest animals. f, Aurora, spinning wheel. g, Sleeping Beauty (Aurora). h, Prince Phillip battling dragon (Maleficent). i, Sleeping Beauty awakes.

Cinderella: No. 1542a, Ella (Cinderella) and father. b, Cinderella sweeping. c, Cinderella, animals in barn. d, Cinderella, stepmother, stepsisters. e, Mice. f, Fairy Godmother. g, Cinderella transformed, coach. h, i, Duke puts glass slipper on Cinderella's foot.

Pinocchio: No. 1543a, Geppetto and puppet. b, Jiminy Cricket. c, Pinocchio, J. Worthington Foulfellow and Gideon. d, Pinocchio, Master Stromboli. e, Blue Fairy rescues Pinocchio. f, Pinocchio, donkeys. g, Pinocchio riding fish. h, Pinocchio and Geppetto at sea. i, Pinocchio transformed into a boy.

Alice in Wonderland: No. 1544a, Alice, rabbit hole. b, Alice in bottle. c, Walrus and Carpenter. d, White Rabbit in pink house. e, Alice, pink butterfly. f, March Hare, Mad Hatter. g, Alice in garden. h, Queen of Hearts. i, Alice on trial.

Peter Pan: No. 1545a, Nana. b, Peter Pan. c, Peter Pan, Tinker Bell, Wendy, John and Michael Darling flying. d, In NeverNever Land. e, Peter Pan and Tiger Lily. f, Captain Hook and First Mate Smee. g, Pater Pan dueling with Captain Hook. h, Tinker Bell, pirate ship. i, Captain Hook, crocodile.

No. 1546, Snow White and Prince riding off into sunset. No. 1547, Aurora and Prince Phillip dancing. No. 1548, Cinderella and Prince Charming marry. No. 1549, Pinocchio, Jiminy Cricket and Gepetto. No. 1550, Alice, cat, mother. No. 1551, Darling children waving goodbye to Peter Pan.

1987, Sept. 9 *Perf. 14x13½*

1540 Sheet of 9 2.00
a.-i. A212 30c any single .25 .25
1541 Sheet of 9 2.00
a.-i. A212 30c any single .25 .25
1542 Sheet of 9 2.00
a.-i. A212 30c any single .25 .25
1543 Sheet of 9 2.00
a.-i. A212 30c any single .25 .25
1544 Sheet of 9 2.00
a.-i. A212 30c any single .25 .25
1545 Sheet of 9 2.00
a.-i. A212 30c any single .25 .25
Nos. 1540-1545 (6) 12.00

Souvenir Sheets

1546-1551 A212 $5 each 3.75 3.75

Souvenir Sheet

Baseball All-Star Game, Oakland, July 14 — A213

Athletes, team emblems: a, Wade Boggs, Boston Red Sox. b, Eric Davis, Cincinnati Reds.

1987, Nov. 2 Litho. *Perf. 14*

1552 A213 Sheet of 2 1.45 1.45
a.-b. $1 any single .70 .70

Massachusetts State Crest — A214

Designs: 15c, Independence Hall, Philadelphia. 50c, Benjamin Franklin. $4, Robert Morris (1734-1806), financier of American Revolution. $5, Pres. James Madison.

1987, Nov. 2

1553 A214 15c multi, vert. .20 .20
1554 A214 50c multi, vert. .35 .35
1555 A214 60c shown .45 .45
1556 A214 $4 multi, vert. 2.90 2.90
Nos. 1553-1556 (4) 3.90 3.90

Souvenir Sheet

1557 A214 $5 multi, vert. 3.60 3.60

US Constitution bicent.

Nos. 1286, 1291 and 1296 Overprinted

1987, Nov. 2

1558 A180 10c multicolored .20 .20
1559 A180 50c multicolored .35 .35
1560 A180 $3 multicolored 2.00 2.00
Nos. 1558-1560 (3) 2.55 2.55

HAFNIA '87 — A215

Disney animated characters in adaptation of fairy tales by Hans Christian Andersen.

1987, Nov. 16 Litho. *Perf. 14*

1561 A215 25c The Shadow .20 .20
1562 A215 30c The Storks .25 .25
1563 A215 50c The Emperor's New Clothes .40 .40
1564 A215 60c The Tinderbox .45 .45
1565 A215 70c The Shepherdess and the Chimney Sweep .55 .55
1566 A215 $1.50 The Little Mermaid 1.10 1.10
1567 A215 $3 The Princess and the Pea 2.25 2.25
1568 A215 $4 The Marsh King's Daughter 3.00 3.00
Nos. 1561-1568 (8) 8.20 8.20

Souvenir Sheets

1569 A215 $5 The Flying Trunk, horiz. 3.75 3.75
1570 A215 $5 The Sandman, horiz. 3.75 3.75

Christmas — A216

Religious paintings: 15c, The Annunciation, by Fra Angelico. 30c, The Annunciation, attributed to Hubert van Eyck (c. 1370-1426). 60c, Adoration of the Magi, by Januarius Zick (1730-1797). $4, The Flight Into Egypt, by David. $5, The Circumcision, produced by artists of the Giovanni Bellini Studio, 14th cent.

1987, Dec. 15

1571 A216 15c multicolored .20 .20
1572 A216 30c multicolored .25 .25
1573 A216 60c multicolored .45 .45
1574 A216 $4 multicolored 3.00 3.00
Nos. 1571-1574 (4) 3.90 3.90

Souvenir Sheet

1575 A216 $5 multicolored 3.75 3.75

T. Albert Marryshow (b. 1887) — A217

1988, Jan. 22 Litho. *Perf. 14*

1576 A217 25c scarlet, red brn & brn blk .20 .20

40th Wedding Anniv. of Queen Elizabeth II and Prince Philip — A218

1988, Feb. 15

1577 A218 15c Wedding portrait, 1947 .20 .20
1578 A218 50c Elizabeth, Charles, Anne .40 .40
1579 A218 $1 Elizabeth, Anne .75 .75
1580 A218 $4 Elizabeth, c. 1980 3.00 3.00
Nos. 1577-1580 (4) 4.35 4.35

Souvenir Sheet

1581 A218 $5 Elizabeth, 1947 3.75 3.75

Disney Animated Characters and 1988 Summer Olympics, Seoul A219

1988, Apr. 13 Litho. *Perf. 13½x14*

1582 A219 1c Lighting torch, Olympia .20 .20
1583 A219 2c Torch bearers .20 .20
1584 A219 3c Flag bearers .20 .20
1585 A219 4c Releasing doves .20 .20
1586 A219 5c Opening ceremony .20 .20
1587 A219 10c Olympic motto .20 .20
1588 A219 $6 Tiger character trademark 3.75 3.75
1589 A219 $7 Oldest Korean p.o. 4.50 4.50
Nos. 1582-1589 (8) 9.45 9.45

Souvenir Sheets

1590 A219 $5 Sportsmanship oath 3.50 3.50
1591 A219 $5 Closing ceremony 3.50 3.50

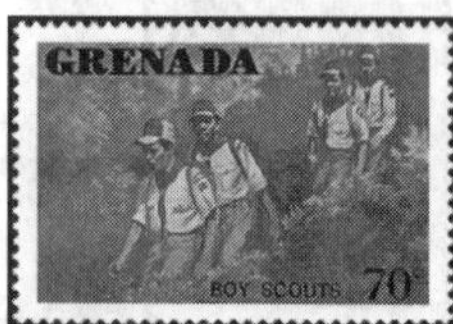

Boy Scouts A220

1988, May 3 Litho. *Perf. 14*

1592 A220 20c Fishing, vert. .20 .20
1593 A220 70c Hiking .55 .55
1594 A220 90c First-aid .70 .70
1595 A220 $3 Canoeing, vert. 2.25 2.25
Nos. 1592-1595 (4) 3.70 3.70

Souvenir Sheet

1596 A220 $5 Scout holding koala, vert. 3.75 3.75

Rotary Conference, District 405, St. George, May 5-7 — A221

Rotary Intl. emblem and: $2, Map of District 405 island nations (Grenada, Guyana, Surinam and French Guiana), 15th cent. Spanish galleon Santa Maria, vert. $10, Motto "Service Above Self."

1988, May 5 *Perf. 13½x14*

1597 A221 $2 multicolored 1.50 1.50

Souvenir Sheet

Perf. 14x13½

1598 A221 $10 shown 7.50 7.50

Nos. 1522-1525 Overprinted for Philatelic Exhibitions

a

b

c

d

1988, Apr. 19 Litho. *Perf. 14*

1599 A209 (a) 90c multi .70 .70
1600 A209 (b) $1.50 multi 1.10 1.10
1601 A209 (c) $2 multi 1.50 1.50
1602 A209 (d) $3 multi 2.25 2.25
Nos. 1599-1602 (4) 5.55 5.55

Birds — A222

1988, May 31

1603 A222 10c Roseate tern .20 .20
1604 A222 25c Laughing gull .20 .20
1605 A222 50c Osprey .40 .40
1606 A222 60c Rose-breasted grosbeak .45 .45
1607 A222 90c Purple gallinule .70 .70
1608 A222 $1.10 White-tailed tropicbird .80 .80
1609 A222 $3 Blue-faced booby 2.25 2.25
1610 A222 $4 Northern shoveler 3.00 3.00
Nos. 1603-1610 (8) 8.00 8.00

Souvenir Sheet

1611 A222 $5 Belted kingfisher 3.75 3.75
1612 A222 $5 Rusty-tailed flycatcher 3.75 3.75

Miniature Sheets

Classic Automobiles A223

Cars (US unless otherwise stated): No. 1613a, 1934 Tatra Type 77, Czechoslovakia. b, 1938 Rolls-Royce Phantom III, Britain. c, 1947 Studebaker Champion Starlight. d, 1948 Porsche Gmund, Germany. e, 1948 Tucker. f, 1931 Peerless V-16. g, 1931 Minerva AL, Belgium. h, 1933 REO Royale. i, 1933 Pierce-Arrow Silver Arrow. j, 1934 Hupmobile Aerodynamic.

No. 1614a, 1925 Vauxhall Type OE30/98, Britain. b, 1926 Wills Sainte Claire. c, 1928 Bucciali, France. d, 1929 Irving Napier Golden Arrow, Britain. e, 1930 Studebaker President. f, 1907 Thomas Flyer. g, 1908 Isotta-Fraschini Tipo J, Italy. h, 1910 Fiat 10/14HP, Italy. i, 1911 Mercer Type 35 Raceabout. j, 1917 Marmon Model 34 Cloverleaf.

No. 1615a, 1965 Peugeot 404, France. b, 1969 Ford Capri, Britain. c, 1975 Ferrari 312T, Italy. d, 1978 Lotus T-79, Britain. e, 1979 Williams-Cosworth FW07, Britain. f, 1948 H.R.G. 1500 Sports, Britain. g, 1949 Crosley Hotshot. h, 1955 Volvo PV444, Sweden. i, 1960 Maserati Tipo 61, Italy. j, 1963 Saab 96, Sweden.

1988, June 1 *Perf. 13x13½*

1613 Sheet of 10 14.50 14.50
a.-j. A223 $2 any single 1.40 1.40
1614 Sheet of 10 14.50 14.50
a.-j. A223 $2 any single 1.40 1.40
1615 Sheet of 10 14.50 14.50
a.-j. A223 $2 any single 1.40 1.40

Paintings by Titian (c. 1488-1576) A224

Paintings by Titian: 10c, Lavinia Vecellio, c. 1546. 20c, Portrait of a Man, c. 1510. 25c, Andrea De Franceschi, 1532. 90c, Head of a Soldier, 1511. $1, Man With a Flute. $2, Lucrezia and Tarquinius, c. 1515. $3, Duke of Mantua with Dog, 1525. $4, La Bella Di Tiziano, 1536. No. 1624, Allegory of Alfonso D'Avalos. No. 1625, Fall of Man, 1570, horiz.

1988, June 15 *Perf. 13½x14*

1616 A224 10c multicolored .20 .20
1617 A224 20c multicolored .20 .20
1618 A224 25c multicolored .20 .20
1619 A224 90c multicolored .70 .70
1620 A224 $1 multicolored .75 .75
1621 A224 $2 multicolored 1.50 1.50
1622 A224 $3 multicolored 2.25 2.25
1623 A224 $4 multicolored 3.00 3.00
Nos. 1616-1623 (8) 8.80 8.80

Souvenir Sheets

1624 A224 $5 multicolored 3.75 3.75

Perf. 14x13½

1625 A224 $5 multicolored 3.75 3.75

Zeppelins A225

Designs: 10c, Graf Zeppelin over the Federal Building, Chicago, 1933 World's Fair, vert. 15c, LZ-1 over Lake Constance, 1900. 25c, Washington aerial balloon lifting off the aircraft carrier USS George Washington Parke Custis off Port Royal, South Carolina, 1862, vert. 45c, Hindenburg over a Maybach Zeppelin automobile, Friedrichshaven, 1936. 50c, Goodyear Blimp over the Statue of Liberty, 1986, vert. 60c, Hindenburg passing over the Statue of Liberty during its final flight, 1937. 90c, Experimental docking of aircraft (piloted by Ernst Udet) with the Hindenburg, 1936. $2, Hindenburg over the Olympic stadium, Berlin, 1936, vert. $3, Hindenburg over Christ of the Andes statue, Rio de Janeiro, 1937, vert. $4, Hindenburg over mail plane catapult ship Bremen, 1936. No. 1636, Zepplin over DLH base, Bathurst, Gambia, 1935. No. 1637, Graf Zeppelin over mosque, Moscow, 1930.

1988, July 1 *Perf. 14*

1626 A225 10c multicolored .20 .20
1627 A225 15c multicolored .20 .20
1628 A225 25c multicolored .20 .20
1629 A225 45c multicolored .35 .35
1630 A225 50c multicolored .40 .40
1631 A225 60c multicolored .45 .45
1632 A225 90c multicolored .70 .70
1633 A225 $2 multicolored 1.50 1.50
1634 A225 $3 multicolored 2.25 2.25
1635 A225 $4 multicolored 3.00 3.00
Nos. 1626-1635 (10) 9.25 9.25

Souvenir Sheets

1636 A225 $5 multicolored 3.75 3.75
1637 A225 $5 multicolored 3.75 3.75

The ship name on No. 1628 is incorrect.

SYDPEX '88, Sydney, Australia — A226

Walt Disney characters in Australian settings: 1c, Camping in the Outback, a howling Tasmanian wolf. 2c, Offering peanuts to wallabies. 3c, With a kangaroo and joey against Ayers Rock. 4c, Riding emus, emu-wrens. 5c, Camp and wombat. 10c, Duck-billed platypuses. No. 1644, Photographing a kookaburra. $6, Koala and Mickey waving flags of Grenada, Australia and the United States, map. No. 1646, Flags and candles atop Cake in the shape of Australia. No. 1647, Mickey, Minnie Pluto and Goofy taking a break during a walkabout.

1988, Aug. 1 Litho. *Perf. 14x13½*

1638 A226 1c multicolored .20 .20
1639 A226 2c multicolored .20 .20
1640 A226 3c multicolored .20 .20
1641 A226 4c multicolored .20 .20
1642 A226 5c multicolored .20 .20
1643 A226 10c multicolored .20 .20
1644 A226 $5 multicolored 3.75 3.75
1645 A226 $6 multicolored 4.50 4.50
Nos. 1638-1645 (8) 9.45 9.45

Souvenir Sheet

1646 A226 $5 multicolored 3.75 3.75
1647 A226 $5 multicolored 3.75 3.75

Mickey Mouse, 60th anniversary.

Intl. Fund for Agricultural Development, 10th Anniv. — A227

1988, Aug. 11 Litho. *Perf. 14*

1648 A227 25c Pineapple, vert. .20 .20
1649 A227 75c Banana, vert. .55 .55
1650 A227 $3 Mace, nutmeg 2.25 2.25
Nos. 1648-1650 (3) 3.00 3.00

Flowering Trees and Shrubs of the Caribbean A228

1988, Sept. 30 Litho.

1651 A228 15c Lignum vitae .20 .20
1652 A228 25c Saman .20 .20
1653 A228 35c Red frangipani .25 .25
1654 A228 45c Flowering maple .30 .30
1655 A228 60c Yellow poui .40 .40
1656 A228 $1 Wild chestnut .70 .70
1657 A228 $3 Mountain immortelle 2.10 2.10
1658 A228 $4 Queen of flowers 2.75 2.75
Nos. 1651-1658 (8) 6.90 6.90

Souvenir Sheets

1659 A228 $5 Flamboyant 3.50 3.50
1660 A228 $5 Orchid tree 3.50 3.50

Miniature Sheet

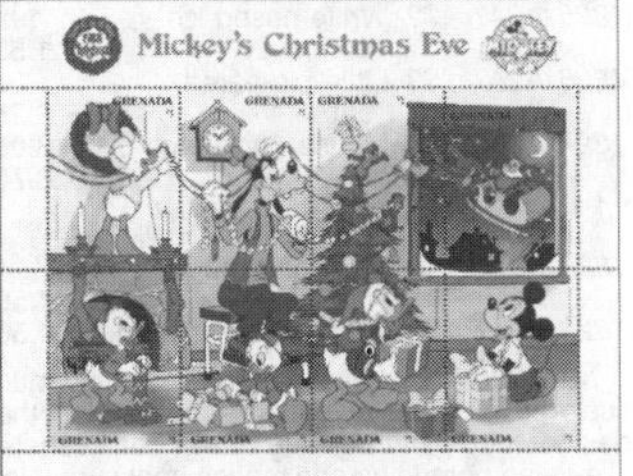

Christmas, Mickey Mouse 60th Anniv. — A229

Designs: a, Huey draping garland. b, Goofy stringing popcorn. c, Chip'n'Dale decorating tree. d, Santa Claus in his sleigh. e, Dewey hanging stockings. f, Louie unpacking decorations. g, Donald Duck. h, Mickey Mouse. No. 1662, Morty and Ferdie leaving milk and cookies for Santa, horiz. No. 1663, Morty and Ferdie dreaming of presents, horiz.
Illustration reduced.

Perf. 13½x14, 14x13½

1988, Dec. 1 Litho.

1661 A229 Sheet of 8 6.00 6.00
a.-h. $1 any single .75 .75

Souvenir Sheets

1662 A229 $5 multicolored 3.75 3.75
1663 A229 $5 multicolored 3.75 3.75

Miniature Sheets

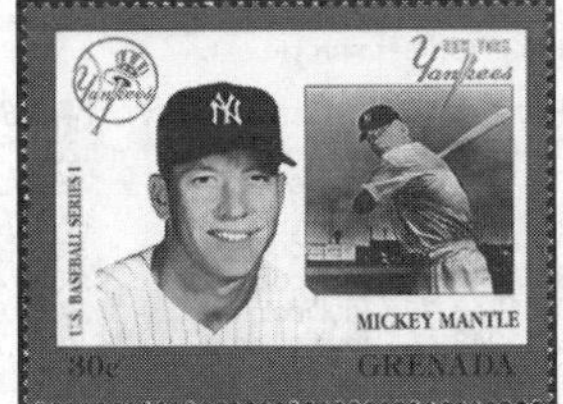

Major League Baseball Players — A230

No. 1664: a, Mickey Mantle. b, Roger Clemens. c, Rod Carew. d, Ryne Sandberg. e, Mike Scott. f, Tim Raines. g, Willie Mays. h, Bret Saberhagen. i, Honus Wagner.
No. 1665: a, Roberto Clemente. b, Cal Ripken, Jr. c, Bob Feller. d, George Bell. e, Mark McGwire. f, Alvin Davis. g, Pete Rose. h, Dan Quisenberry. i, Babe Ruth.
No. 1666: a, Jackie Robinson. b, Dwight Gooden. c, Brooks Robinson, Jr. d, Nolan Ryan. e, Mike Schmidt. f, Gary Gaetti. g, Nellie Fox. h, Tony Gwynn. i, Dizzy Dean.
No. 1667: a, Ernie Banks. b, National League emblem. c, Julio Franco. d, Jack Morris. e, Fernando Valenzuela. f, Lefty Grove. g, Ted Williams. h, Darryl Strawberry. i, Dale Murphy.
No. 1668: a, Johnny Bench. b, Dave Stieb. c, Reggie Jackson. d, Harold Baines. e, Wade Boggs. f, Pete O'Brien. g, Stan Musial. h, Wally Joyner. i, Grover Cleveland Alexander.
No. 1669: a, Jose Cruz. b, American League emblem. c, Al Kaline. d, Chuck Klein. e, Don Mattingly. f, Mike Witt. g, Mark Langston. h, Hubie Brooks. i, Harmon Killebrew.
No. 1670: a, George Brett. b, Joe Carter. c, Frank Robinson. d, Mel Ott. e, Benito Santiago. f, Teddy Higuera. g, Lloyd Moseby. h, Bobby Bonilla. i, Warren Spahn.
No. 1671: a, Gary Carter. b, Hank Aaron. c, Gaylord Perry. d, Ty Cobb. e, Andre Dawson. f, Charlie Hough. g, Kirby Puckett. h, Robin Yount. i, Don Drysdale.
No. 1672: a, Luis Aparicio. b, Paul Molitor. c, Lou Gehrig. d, Jeffrey Leonard. e, Eric Davis. f, Pete Incaviglia. g, Steve Rogers. h, Ozzie Smith. i, Randy Jones.

1988, Nov. 28 Litho. *Perf. 14*

1664 Sheet of 9 1.90
a.-i. A230 30c any single .20 .20
1665 Sheet of 9 1.90
a.-i. A230 30c any single .20 .20
1666 Sheet of 9 1.90
a.-i. A230 30c any single .20 .20
1667 Sheet of 9 1.90
a.-i. A230 30c any single .20 .20
1668 Sheet of 9 1.90
a.-i. A230 30c any single .20 .20
1669 Sheet of 9 1.90
a.-i. A230 30c any single .20 .20
1670 Sheet of 9 1.90
a.-i. A230 30c any single .20 .20
1671 Sheet of 9 1.90
a.-i. A230 30c any single .20 .20
1672 Sheet of 9 1.90
a.-i. A230 30c any single .20 .20
Nos. 1664-1672 (9) 17.10

No. 1665 was reprinted with No. 1665g replaced by a label inscribed "U.S. Baseball Series."

Singers — A231

1988, Dec. 5 Litho. *Perf. 14*

1673 A231 10c Tina Turner .20 .20
1674 A231 25c Lionel Ritchie .20 .20
1675 A231 45c Whitney Houston .35 .35
1676 A231 60c Joan Armatrading .45 .45
1677 A231 75c Madonna .60 .60
1678 A231 $1 Elton John .75 .75
1679 A231 $3 Bruce Springsteen 2.25 2.25
1680 A231 $4 Bob Marley 3.00 3.00
Nos. 1673-1680 (8) 7.80 7.80

Souvenir Sheet

1681 Sheet of 4 (2 55c,2 $1) 2.40 2.40
a. A231 55c Yoko Minamino .40 .40
b. A231 $1 Yoko Minamino, diff. .75 .75

Armatrading is misspelled "Ammertrading."

Car Type of 1988
Miniature Sheets

Locomotives.
No. 1682: a, 1889 Canada Atlantic Railway No. 2 0-6-0, Canada. b, 1875 Virginia & Truckee Railroad J.W. Bowker 2-4-0, US. c, 1872 Philadelphia & Reading Railway Ariel 2-2-2, US. d, 1867 Chicago & Rock Is. Railroad America 4-4-0, US. e, 1866 Lehigh Valley Railroad Consolidation No. 63 2-8-0, US. f, 1860 Great Western Railway Scotia 0-6-0, Canada. g, 1854 Grand Trunk Railway Birkenhead Class 4-4-0, Canada. h, 1837 Camden & Amboy Railroad Monster 0-8-0, US. i, 1834 B&O Railroad Grasshopper Class 0-4-0, US. j, 1829 B&O Railroad Tom Thumb 0-2-2, US.
No. 1683: a, 1925 United Railways of Yucatan Yucatan 4-4-0, Mexico. b, 1924 Canadian Natl. Railways Class T2 2-10-2, Canada. c, 1919 St. Louis-San Francisco Railroad USRA Light Mikado 2-8-2, US. d, 1919 Atlantic Coast Line Railroad USRA Light Pacific 4-6-2, US. e, 1913 Edaville Railroad (Bridgton & Saco River Railroad) No. 7 2-4-4-T, US. f, 1903 Denver & Rio Grande Western Railroad Mudhens Class K27 2-8-2, US. g, 1902 PRR Class E-2 No. 7002 4-4-2, US. h, 1899 PRR Class H6 2-8-0, US. i, 1893 Mohawk & Hudson Railroad De Witt Clinton 0-4-0, US. j, 1891 St. Clair Tunnel Company No. 598 0-10-0, Canada.
No. 1684: a, 1947 Chesapeake & Ohio Railroad M-1 Class No. 500 steam turbine electric, US. b, 1946 Rutland Railroad No. 93 4-8-2, US. c, 1942 PRR Class T1 4-4-4-4, US. d, 1942 Chesapeake & Ohio Railroad Class H-8 2-6-6-6, US. e, 1941 Atchison, Topeka & Santa Fe Railway EMD Model FT Bo-Bo, US. f, 1940 Gulf, Mobile & Ohio Railroad ALCO Models S-1 & S-2 Bo-Bo, US. g, 1937 New York, New Haven & Hartford Railroad Class 15 4-6-4, US. h, 1936 Seaboard Air Line Railroad Class R 2-6-6-4, US. i, 1930 Newfoundland Railway Class R-2 2-8-2, Canada. j, 1928 Canadian Natl. Railway No. 9000 2-Do-1 + 1-Do-2, Canada.

1989, Jan. 23 Litho. *Perf. 13x13½*

1682 Sheet of 10 14.50 14.50
a.-j. A223 $2 any single 1.40 1.40
1683 Sheet of 10 14.50 14.50
a.-j. A223 $2 any single 1.40 1.40
1684 Sheet of 10 14.50 14.50
a.-j. A223 $2 any single 1.40 1.40

Medalists of the 1988 Summer Olympics, Seoul — A232

Designs: 10c, Jackie Joyner-Kersee, US, long jump. 25c, Steffi Graf, Federal Republic of Germany, women's singles tennis. 45c, Peter Rono, Kenya, 1500m run. 75c, Greg Barton, US, kayak singles. $1, Italy, women's team foil. $2, Kristin Otto, German Democratic Republic, women's 100m freestyle swimming. $3, Holger Behrendt, German Democratic Republic, still rings. $4, Japan, duet synchronized swimming. No. 1693, Yukio Iketani, Japan, men's floor exercise. No. 1694, West Germany, 400m relay, and (Olympic) flame over track.

1989, Apr. 6 Litho. *Perf. 14*

1685 A232 10c multicolored .20 .20
1686 A232 25c multicolored .20 .20
1687 A232 45c multicolored .35 .35
1688 A232 75c multicolored .60 .60
1689 A232 $1 multicolored .75 .75
1690 A232 $2 multicolored 1.50 1.50
1691 A232 $3 multicolored 2.25 2.25
1692 A232 $4 multicolored 3.00 3.00
Nos. 1685-1692 (8) 8.85 8.85

Souvenir Sheets

1693 A232 $6 multicolored 4.50 4.50
1694 A232 $6 multicolored 4.50 4.50

"The Fifty-three Stations on the Tokaido" — A233

Prints by Hiroshige (1797-1858): 10c, Shinagawa on Edo Bay. 25c, Pine Trees on the Road to Totsuka. 60c, Kanagawa on Edo Bay. 75c, Crossing Banyu River to Hiratsuka. $1, Windy Shore at Odawara. $2, Snow-covered Post Station of Mishima. $3, Full Moon at Fuchu. $4, Crossing the Stream at Okitsu. No. 1703, Mt. Uzu at Okabe. No. 1704, Mountain Pass at Nissaka.

1989, May 15 Litho. *Perf. 14x13½*

1695 A233 10c multicolored .20 .20
1696 A233 25c multicolored .20 .20
1697 A233 60c multicolored .45 .45
1698 A233 75c multicolored .65 .65
1699 A233 $1 multicolored .75 .75
1700 A233 $2 multicolored 1.50 1.50
1701 A233 $3 multicolored 2.25 2.25
1702 A233 $4 multicolored 3.00 3.00
Nos. 1695-1702 (8) 9.00 9.00

Souvenir Sheets

1703 A233 $5 multicolored 3.75 3.75
1704 A233 $5 multicolored 3.75 3.75

Hirohito (1901-1989) and enthronement of Akihito as emperor of Japan.

Indigenous Birds — A234

1989, June 6 Litho. *Perf. 14*

1705 A234 5c Great blue heron .20 .20
1706 A234 10c Green heron .20 .20
1707 A234 15c Ruddy turnstone .20 .20
1708 A234 25c Blue-winged teal .20 .20
1709 A234 35c Ring-necked plover .30 .30
1710 A234 45c Emerald-throated hummingbird .35 .35
1711 A234 50c Hairy hermit .40 .40
1712 A234 60c Lesser Antillean bullfinch .45 .45
1713 A234 75c Brown pelican .60 .60
1714 A234 $1 Black-crowned night heron .75 .75
1715 A234 $3 Sparrow hawk 2.25 2.25
1716 A234 $5 Barn swallow 3.75 3.75
1717 A234 $10 Red-billed tropicbird 7.50 7.50
1718 A234 $20 Barn owl 15.00 15.00
Nos. 1705-1718 (14) 32.15 32.15

Nos. 1709-1718 vert.

1990-93 Litho. *Perf. 11½x13*

1705a A234 5c .20 .20
1706a A234 10c .20 .20
1707a A234 15c .20 .20
1708a A234 25c .20 .20

Perf. 13x11½

1709a A234 35c .25 .25
1710a A234 45c .35 .35
1711a A234 50c .40 .40
1712a A234 60c .45 .45
1713a A234 75c .55 .55
1714a A234 $1 .70 .70
1715a A234 $3 2.25 2.25
1716a A234 $5 3.75 3.75
1717a A234 $10 7.50 7.50
1718a A234 $20 15.00 15.00
Nos. 1705a-1718a (14) 32.00 32.00

Issued: #1718a, 1/22/90.

1990 World Cup Soccer Championships, Italy — A235

1989, June 12 *Perf. 14*

1719 A235 10c Scotland .20 .20
1720 A235 25c England vs. Brazil .20 .20
1721 A235 60c Paolo Rossi, Italy .50 .50
1722 A235 75c Jairzinho of Brazil .60 .60
1723 A235 $1 Swedish Striker .75 .75
1724 A235 $2 Pele, Brazil 1.50 1.50
1725 A235 $3 Mario Kempes, Argentina 2.25 2.25
1726 A235 $4 Pat Jennings 3.00 3.00
Nos. 1719-1726 (8) 9.00 9.00

Souvenir Sheets

1727 A235 $6 Argentina vs. Holland 4.50 4.50
a. $6 1990 score ovptd. in margin 4.50 4.50
1728 A235 $6 Goalie 4.50 4.50

Issue date: No. 1727a, Nov. 30, 1990.

PHILEXFRANCE '89 — A236

19th Cent. ships and cargo: 25c, Chebeck, sugarcane. 75c, Lugger, cotton. $1, Merchantman, cocoa. $4, Ketch, coffee. $6, Vue du Fort et Ville de St. George dans l'Isle de la Grenade et du Morne, 1779.

1989, July 7 *Perf. 14*

1729 A236 25c multicolored .20 .20
1730 A236 75c multicolored .55 .55
1731 A236 $1 multicolored .75 .75
1732 A236 $4 multicolored 3.00 3.00

Size: 114x71mm

Imperf

1733 A236 $6 multicolored 4.50 4.50
Nos. 1729-1733 (5) 9.00 9.00

First Moon Landing, 20th Anniv. A237

Space achievements: 15c, Alan Shepard, 1st American in space, 1961. 35c, Friendship 7, piloted by John Glenn, 1st manned orbit of the Earth, 1962. 45c, Apollo 8 mission, 1st manned orbit of the Moon, 1968. 70c, Lunar rover on Moon, 1972. $1, Apollo 11 mission emblem and Eagle lunar module on the Moon, 1969. $2, Gemini 8-Agena, 1st space docking, 1969. $3, Edward White, 1st American to walk in space, 1965. $4, Apollo 7 mission emblem. No. 1742, Simple flight plan for the Apollo 11 mission. No. 1743, Raising of the American flag on the Moon.

1989, July 20 **Perf. 14**
1734 A237 15c multicolored .20 .20
1735 A237 35c multicolored .30 .30
1736 A237 45c multicolored .35 .35
1737 A237 70c multicolored .50 .50
1738 A237 $1 multicolored .75 .75
1739 A237 $2 multicolored 1.50 1.50
1740 A237 $3 multicolored 2.25 2.25
1741 A237 $4 multicolored 3.00 3.00
Nos. 1734-1741 (8) 8.85 8.85

Souvenir Sheets
1742 A237 $5 multicolored 3.75 3.75
1743 A237 $5 multicolored 3.75 3.75

Mushrooms A238

YWCA, Cent. A239

15c, *Hygrocybe occidentalis scarletina*. 40c, *Marasmius haemato- cephalus*. 50c, *Hygrocybe hypohaemacta*. 70c, *Lepiota pseudoignicolor*. 90c, *Cookeina tricholoma*. $1.10, *Leucopaxillus gracillimus*. $2.25, *Hygrocybe nigrescens*. $4, *Clathrus crispus*.
#1752, *Mycena holoporphyra*. #1753, *Xeromphalina tenuipes*.

1989, Aug. 17 **Litho.** **Perf. 14**
1744-1751 A238 Set of 8 7.50 7.50

Souvenir Sheets
1752-1753 A238 $6 Set of 2 9.00 9.00

1989, Sept. 11 **Perf. 14**
1754 A239 50c shown .40 .40
1755 A239 75c Emblem, horiz. .60 .60

Butterflies A240

1989, Oct. 2 **Perf. 14**
1756 A240 6c Orion .20 .20
1757 A240 30c Southern daggertail .25 .25
1758 A240 40c Soldier .30 .30
1759 A240 60c Silver spot .45 .45
1760 A240 $1.10 Gulf fritillary .80 .80
1761 A240 $1.25 Monarch .95 .95
1762 A240 $4 Polydamas swallowtail 3.00 3.00
1763 A240 $5 Flambeau 3.75 3.75
Nos. 1756-1763 (8) 9.70 9.70

Souvenir Sheets
1764 A240 $6 St. Christopher hairstreak 4.50 4.50
1765 A240 $6 White peacock 4.50 4.50

Discovery of America, 500th Anniv. (in 1992) — A241

Anniv. and UPAE emblems and various pre-Columbian petroglyphs.

1989, Oct. 16 **Litho.** **Perf. 14**
1766 A241 45c multicolored .35 .35
1767 A241 60c multi, diff. .45 .45
1768 A241 $1 multi, diff. .75 .75
1769 A241 $4 multi, diff. 3.00 3.00
Nos. 1766-1769 (4) 4.55 4.55

Souvenir Sheet
1770 A241 $6 multi, diff. 4.50 4.50

World Stamp Expo '89, Scenes from *Ben and Me* — A242

Walt Disney characters, story of the American Revolution: 1c, Amos leaves home. 2c, Amos meets young Benjamin Franklin. 3c, Invention of the Franklin stove. 4c, Invention of bifocals. 5c, *Pennsylvania azette*. 6c, Franklin at printing press. 10c, Experimenting with electricity. $5, As an American diplomat in England. No. 1779, Amos's "Document of Agreement." No. 1780, Franklin presiding over meeting of the Ben Franklin Stamp Club. No. 1781, 2nd Continental Congress, Philadelphia, 1775.

Perf. 14x13½, 13½x14
1989, Nov. 17 **Litho.**
1771 A242 1c multi .20 .20
1772 A242 2c multi .20 .20
1773 A242 3c multi .20 .20
1774 A242 4c multi .20 .20
1775 A242 5c multi .20 .20
1776 A242 6c multi .20 .20
1777 A242 10c multi .20 .20
1778 A242 $5 multi 3.25 3.25
1779 A242 $6 multi 3.75 3.75
Nos. 1771-1779 (9) 8.40 8.40

Souvenir Sheets
1780 A242 $6 multi, vert. 3.75 3.75
1781 A242 $6 multi 3.75 3.75

Christmas — A243

Paintings by Rubens: 20c, *Christ in the House of Mary and Martha*. 35c, *The Circumcision*. 60c, *Trinity Adored by Duke of Mantua and Family*. $2, *Holy Family with St. Francis*. $3, *The Ildefonso Altarpiece*. $4, *Madonna and Child with Garland and Putti*, by Rubens and Jan Brueghel. No. 1788, *Adoration of the Magi*. No. 1789, *Virgin and Child Adored by Angels*.

1990, Jan. 4 **Litho.** **Perf. 14**
1782 A243 20c multicolored .20 .20
1783 A243 35c multicolored .30 .30
1784 A243 60c multicolored .45 .45
1785 A243 $2 multicolored 1.50 1.50
1786 A243 $3 multicolored 2.25 2.25
1787 A243 $4 multicolored 3.00 3.00
Nos. 1782-1787 (6) 7.70 7.70

Souvenir Sheets
1788 A243 $5 multicolored 3.75 3.75
1789 A243 $5 multicolored 3.75 3.75

Anniversaries and Events (in 1989) — A244

Designs: 10c, Alexander Graham Bell, early telephone, telephone lines. 25c, George Washington, the Capitol Building. 35c, William Shakespeare, birthplace, Stratford-on-Avon. 75c, Jawaharlal Nehru, Mahatma Gandhi. $1, Hugo Eckener, Ferdinand von Zeppelin, zeppelin *Delag*. $2, Charlie Chaplin. $3, Ship in port. $4, Pres. Friedrich Ebert, Heidelberg Gate. No. 1798, Concorde jet. No. 1799, Ship, 13th century, vert.

1990, Feb. 12 **Litho.** **Perf. 14**
1790 A244 10c multicolored .20 .20
1791 A244 25c multicolored .20 .20
1792 A244 35c multicolored .30 .30
1793 A244 75c multicolored .60 .60
1794 A244 $1 multicolored .75 .75
1795 A244 $2 multicolored 1.50 1.50
1796 A244 $3 multicolored 2.25 2.25
1797 A244 $4 multicolored 3.00 3.00
Nos. 1790-1797 (8) 8.80 8.80

Souvenir Sheets
1798 A244 $6 multicolored 4.50 4.50
1799 A244 $6 multicolored 4.50 4.50

Invention of the telephone, 1876 (10c); American presidency, 200th anniv. (25c); 425th birth anniv. of Shakespeare (35c); birth cent. of Nehru (75c); 1st passenger zeppelin, 80th anniv. ($1); birth cent. of Charlie Chaplin ($2); Hamburg, 800th anniv. ($3, No. 1799); Federal Republic of Germany, 40th anniv. ($4); and test flight of the Concorde supersonic jet, 20th anniv. (No. 1798).

Orchids — A245

1990, Mar. 6 **Litho.** **Perf. 14**
1800 A245 1c *Odontoglossum triumphans* .20 .20
1801 A245 25c *Oncidium splendidum* .20 .20
1802 A245 60c *Laelia anceps* .50 .50
1803 A245 75c *Cattleya trianaei* .60 .60
1804 A245 $1 *Odontoglossum rossii* .75 .75
1805 A245 $2 *Brassia gireoudiana* 1.50 1.50
1806 A245 $3 *Cattleya dowiana* 2.25 2.25
1807 A245 $4 *Sobralia macrantha* 3.00 3.00
Nos. 1800-1807 (8) 9.00 9.00

Souvenir Sheets
1808 A245 $6 *Laelia rubescens* 4.50 4.50
1809 A245 $6 *Oncidium lanceanum* 4.50 4.50

EXPO '90 Intl. Garden and Greenery Exposition, Japan.

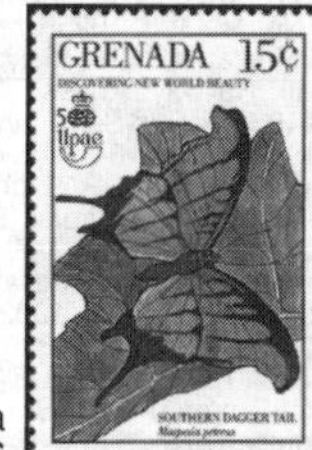

America Issue — A246

Butterflies, UPAE and discovery of America 500th anniv. emblems: 15c, Southern dagger tail. 25c, Caribbean buckeye. 75c, Malachite. 90c, Orion. $1, St. Lucia mestra. $2, Red rim. $3, Flambeau. $4, Red anartia. No. 1818, Giant hairstreak. No. 1819, Orange-barred sulphur.

1990, Mar. 16 **Litho.** **Perf. 14**
1810 A246 15c multicolored .20 .20
1811 A246 25c multicolored .20 .20
1812 A246 75c multicolored .60 .60
1813 A246 90c multicolored .70 .70
1814 A246 $1 multicolored .75 .75
1815 A246 $2 multicolored 1.50 1.50
1816 A246 $3 multicolored 2.25 2.25
1817 A246 $4 multicolored 3.00 3.00
Nos. 1810-1817 (8) 9.20 9.20

Souvenir Sheets
1818 A246 $6 multicolored 4.50 4.50
1819 A246 $6 multicolored 4.50 4.50

Wildlife A247

1990, Apr. 3 **Litho.** **Perf. 14**
1820 A247 10c Caribbean monk seal .20 .20
1821 A247 15c Little brown bat .20 .20
1822 A247 45c Norway rat .35 .35
1823 A247 60c Old-world rabbit .45 .45
1824 A247 $1 Water opossum .75 .75
1825 A247 $2 White-nosed ichneumon 1.50 1.50
1826 A247 $3 Little big-eared bat 2.25 2.25
1827 A247 $4 Mouse opossums 3.00 3.00
Nos. 1820-1827 (8) 8.70 8.70

Souvenir Sheets
1828 A247 $6 Old-world rabbit. diff. 4.50 4.50
1829 A247 $6 Water opossum 4.50 4.50

No. 1826 is vert. Nos. 1828-1829 have multicolored decorative margins contininuing the designs and picturing little brown bat, prehensile-tailed porcupine and mouse opossum (No. 1828) or four-eyed opossum, West Indies manatee and Norway rat (No. 1829).

World War II A248

Designs: 25c, Operation Battleaxe, June 15, 1941. 35c, Allied landing in southern France, Aug. 15, 1944. 45c, US invasion of Guadalcanal, Aug. 7, 1942. 50c, Allied defeat of Japanese army in New Guinea, Jan. 22, 1943. 60c, US forces secure Leyte, Dec. 11, 1944. 75c, US forces enter Cologne, Mar. 5, 1945. $1, Allied offensive to break out of Anzio, May 23, 1944. $2, Battle of the Bismarck Sea, Mar. 3, 1943. $3, US fleet under Adm. Nimitz, Dec. 17, 1941. $4, Allied landing at Salerno, Sept. 9, 1943. $6, German U-boat.

1990, Apr. 30 **Litho.** **Perf. 14x13½**
1830 A248 25c multicolored .20 .20
1831 A248 35c multicolored .25 .25
1832 A248 45c multicolored .30 .30
1833 A248 50c multicolored .40 .40
1834 A248 60c multicolored .45 .45
1835 A248 75c multicolored .60 .60
1836 A248 $1 multicolored .75 .75
1837 A248 $2 multicolored 1.50 1.50
1838 A248 $3 multicolored 2.25 2.25
1839 A248 $4 multicolored 3.00 3.00
Nos. 1830-1839 (10) 9.70 9.70

Souvenir Sheet
1840 A248 $6 multicolored 4.50 4.50

Souvenir Sheet

Penny Black, 150th Anniv. — A249

1990, May 3 **Litho.** **Perf. 14**
1841 A249 $6 violet 4.50 4.50

Stamp World London '90.

Stamp World London '90 — A250

Walt Disney characters and British trains.

1990, June 21 ***Perf. 14***

1844 A250 5c 1925 King Arthur Class .20 .20
1845 A250 10c 1813 Puffing Billy .20 .20
1846 A250 20c 1765 Colliery Tram-wagon .20 .20
1847 A250 45c 1935 No. 2509 Silver Link .40 .40
1848 A250 $1 1948 No. 60149 Amadis .75 .75
1849 A250 $2 1830 Liverpool 1.50 1.50
1850 A250 $4 1870 Flying Scotsman 3.00 3.00
1851 A250 $5 1972 Advanced Passenger Train 3.75 3.75
Nos. 1844-1851 (8) 10.00 10.00

Souvenir Sheets

1852 A250 $6 Stockton & Darlington Railway Opening, 1825, vert. 4.50 4.50
1853 A250 $6 1809 *Catch-Me-Who-Can* 4.50 4.50

Queen Mother, 90th Birthday — A251

1990, July 5 **Litho.** ***Perf. 14***

1854 A251 $2 Wearing black hat 1.50 1.50
1855 A251 $2 shown 1.50 1.50
1856 A251 $2 Wearing crown 1.50 1.50
Nos. 1854-1856 (3) 4.50 4.50

Souvenir Sheet

1857 A251 $6 Like No. 1855 4.50 4.50

1992 Summer Olympics, Barcelona — A252

Character trademark and: 10c, Men's steeplechase. 15c, Equestrian. 45c, Men's 200 meter butterfly. 50c, Field hockey. 65c, Balance beam. 75c, Flying Dutchman Class yachting. $2, Freestyle wrestling. $3, Men's diving. $4, Women's cycling. $5, Men's basketball. No. 1863, Three-day equestrian event. No. 1863A, Men's 10,000 M race.

1990, July 9

1858 A252 10c multicolored .20 .20
1858A A252 15c multicolored .20 .20
1859 A252 45c multicolored .35 .35
1859A A252 50c multicolored .40 .40
1860 A252 65c multicolored .50 .50
1860A A252 75c multicolored .60 .60
1861 A252 $2 multicolored 1.50 1.50
1861A A252 $3 multicolored 2.25 2.25
1862 A252 $4 multicolored 3.00 3.00
1862A A252 $5 multicolored 3.75 3.75
Nos. 1858-1862A (10) 12.75 12.75

Souvenir Sheet

1863 A252 $8 multicolored 6.00 6.00
1863A A252 $8 multicolored 6.00 6.00

Nos. 1858A, 1859A, 1860A, 1861A, 1862A, 1863A were not available until 1991.

US Airborne, 50th Anniv. A253

1990, July 3

1864 A253 75c Mass jump .60 .60

Souvenir Sheets

1865 A253 $2.50 Paratrooper landing 1.90 1.90
1866 A253 $6 Paratroopers 1940, 1990 4.50 4.50

Yellow Goatfish A254

1990, Aug. 8

1867 A254 10c shown .20 .20
1868 A254 25c Black margate .20 .20
1869 A254 65c Bluehead wrasse .50 .50
1870 A254 75c Puddingwife .60 .60
1871 A254 $1 Foureye butterflyfish .80 .80
1872 A254 $2 Honey damselfish 1.60 1.60
1873 A254 $3 Queen angelfish 2.40 2.40
1874 A254 $5 Cherubfish 4.00 4.00
Nos. 1867-1874 (8) 10.30 10.30

Souvenir Sheets

1875 A254 $6 Smooth trunkfish 4.75 4.75
1876 A254 $6 Sergeant major 4.75 4.75

Birds A255

1990, Sept. 10 **Litho.** ***Perf. 14***

1877 A255 15c Tropical mockingbird .20 .20
1878 A255 25c Gray kingbird .20 .20
1879 A255 65c Bare-eyed thrush .50 .50
1880 A255 75c Antillean crested hummingbird .60 .60
1881 A255 $1 House wren .80 .80
1882 A255 $2 Purple martin 1.60 1.60
1883 A255 $4 Hooded tanager 3.25 3.25
1884 A255 $5 Common ground dove 4.00 4.00
Nos. 1877-1884 (8) 11.15 11.15

Souvenir Sheets

1885 A255 $6 Fork-tailed flycatcher 4.75 4.75
1886 A255 $6 Smooth-billed ani 4.75 4.75

Crustaceans — A256

1990, Sept. 17

1887 A256 5c Coral crab .20 .20
1888 A256 10c Smoothtail spiny lobster .20 .20
1889 A256 15c Flamestreaked box crab .20 .20
1890 A256 25c Spotted swimming crab .20 .20
1891 A256 75c Sally lightfoot rock crab .60 .60
1892 A256 $1 Spotted spiny lobster .80 .80
1893 A256 $3 Longarm spiny lobster 2.40 2.40
1894 A256 $20 Caribbean spiny lobster 16.00 16.00
Nos. 1887-1894 (8) 20.60 20.60

Souvenir Sheets

1895 A256 $6 Spanish lobster 4.75 4.75
1896 A256 $6 Copper lobster 4.75 4.75

World Cup Soccer Championships, Italy — A257

Players from participating countries.

1990, Sept. 24

1897 A257 10c Cameroun .20 .20
1898 A257 25c Spain .20 .20
1899 A257 $1 West Germany .80 .80
1900 A257 $5 Scotland 4.00 4.00
Nos. 1897-1900 (4) 5.20 5.20

Souvenir Sheets

1901 A257 $6 Uruguay 4.75 4.75
1902 A257 $6 Italy 4.75 4.75

Christmas A258

Paintings by Raphael: 10c, The Ansidei Madonna. 15c, The Sistine Madonna. $1, Madonna of the Baldacchino. $2, The Large Holy Family. $5, Madonna in the Meadow. No. 1908, Madonna of the Veil. No. 1909, Madonna of the Diadem.

1990, Dec. 31 **Litho.** ***Perf. 14***

1903 A258 10c multicolored .20 .20
1904 A258 15c multicolored .20 .20
1905 A258 $1 multicolored .80 .80
1906 A258 $2 multicolored 1.60 1.60
1907 A258 $5 multicolored 4.00 4.00
Nos. 1903-1907 (5) 6.80 6.80

Souvenir Sheets

1908 A258 $6 multicolored 4.75 4.75
1909 A258 $6 multicolored 4.75 4.75

Peter Paul Rubens (1577-1640), Painter — A259

Entire paintings or different details from: 5c, $1, $4, The Brazen Serpent. 10c, Garden of Love. 25c, Head of Cyrus. 75c, Tournament in Front of a Castle. $2, Judgement of Paris. $5, The Karmesse. No. 1918, The Prodigal Son. No. 1919, Anger of Neptune.

1991, Jan. 31 **Litho.** ***Perf. 14***

1910 A259 5c multicolored .20 .20
1911 A259 10c multicolored .20 .20
1912 A259 25c multicolored .20 .20
1913 A259 75c multicolored .60 .60
1914 A259 $1 multicolored .80 .80
1915 A259 $2 multicolored 1.60 1.60
1916 A259 $4 multicolored 3.25 3.25
1917 A259 $5 multicolored 4.00 4.00
Nos. 1910-1917 (8) 10.85 10.85

Souvenir Sheets

1918 A259 $6 multicolored 4.75 4.75
1919 A259 $6 multicolored 4.75 4.75

Disney Film *Fantasia,* 50th Anniv. — A260

5c, Mickey as Sorcerer's apprentice, walking broom. 10c, Mushroom Dance Ensemble from The Nutcracker Suite. 20c, Pterodactyls from The Rite of Spring. 45c, Centaurs from The Pastoral Symphony. $1, Bacchus & Jacchus from The Pastoral Symphony. $2, Ostrich ballerina in Dance of the Hours. $4, Elephant dance from Dance of the Hours. $5, Diana, Goddess of the Moon from Dance of the Hours. #1928, Mickey as Sorcerer's apprentice. #1929, Mickey, Leopold Stokowski. $12, Mickey as Sorcerer's Apprentice, vert.

1991, Feb. 4 **Litho.** ***Perf. 14***

1920 A260 5c multicolored .20 .20
1921 A260 10c multicolored .20 .20
1922 A260 20c multicolored .20 .20
1923 A260 45c multicolored .35 .35
1924 A260 $1 multicolored .80 .80
1925 A260 $2 multicolored 1.60 1.60
1926 A260 $4 multicolored 3.25 3.25
1927 A260 $5 multicolored 4.00 4.00
Nos. 1920-1927 (8) 10.60 10.60

Souvenir Sheets

1928 A260 $6 multicolored 4.75 4.75
1929 A260 $6 multicolored 4.75 4.75
1930 A260 $12 multicolored 9.50 9.50

Butterflies A261

5c, Adelphia iphicla. 10c, Nymphalidae claudina. 15c, Brassolidae polyxena. 20c, Zebra longwing. 25c, Marpesia corinna. 30c, Morpho hecuba. 45c, Morpho rhetenor. 50c, Dismorphia spio. 60c, Prepona omphale. 70c, Morpho anaxibia. 75c, Marpesia iole. $1, Metalmark. $2, Morpho cisseis. $3, Danaidae plexippus. $4, Morpho achilleana. $5, Calliona argenissa. #1947, Anteos clorinde. #1948, Haetera piera. #1949, Papilio cresphontes. #1950, Prepona pheridames.

1991, Apr. 8 **Litho.** ***Perf. 14***

1931 A261 5c multicolored .20 .20
1932 A261 10c multicolored .20 .20
1933 A261 15c multicolored .20 .20
1934 A261 20c multicolored .20 .20
1935 A261 25c multicolored .20 .20
1936 A261 30c multicolored .25 .25
1937 A261 45c multicolored .35 .35
1938 A261 50c multicolored .40 .40
1939 A261 60c multicolored .50 .50
1940 A261 70c multicolored .60 .60
1941 A261 75c multicolored .60 .60
1942 A261 $1 multicolored .80 .80
1943 A261 $2 multicolored 1.60 1.60
1944 A261 $3 multicolored 2.40 2.40
1945 A261 $4 multicolored 3.25 3.25
1946 A261 $5 multicolored 4.00 4.00
Nos. 1931-1946 (16) 15.75 15.75

Souvenir Sheets

1947 A261 $6 multicolored 4.75 4.75
1948 A261 $6 multicolored 4.75 4.75
1949 A261 $6 multicolored 4.75 4.75
1950 A261 $6 multicolored 4.75 4.75

Voyages of Discovery A262

Explorer's ships: 5c, Vitus Bering, 1728-1729. 10c, Louis de Bougainville, 1766-1769. 25c, Polynesians. 50c, Alvaro de Mendana, 1567-1569. $1, Charles Darwin, 1831-1835. $2, Capt. James Cook, 1768-1771. $4, Capt. Willem Schouten, 1615-1617. $5, Abel Tasman, 1642-1644. No. 1959, Columbus' ship Santa Maria. No. 1960, Loss of Santa Maria.

1991, Apr. 29

1951 A262 5c multicolored .20 .20
1952 A262 10c multicolored .20 .20
1953 A262 25c multicolored .20 .20
1954 A262 50c multicolored .40 .40
1955 A262 $1 multicolored .80 .80
1956 A262 $2 multicolored 1.60 1.60
1957 A262 $4 multicolored 3.25 3.25
1958 A262 $5 multicolored 4.00 4.00
Nos. 1951-1958 (8) 10.65 10.65

Souvenir Sheets

1959 A262 $6 multicolored 4.75 4.75
1960 A262 $6 multicolored 4.75 4.75

Discovery of America, 500th anniv. (in 1992).

PHILANIPPON '91 — A263

Walt Disney characters celebrating festivals of Japan: 5c, Daisy Duck and Minnie Mouse, Peach Fete, Festival of the Dolls. 10c, Morty and Ferdie, Tango Festival, Boys' Day Festival. 20c, Mickey, Minnie Mouse, Hoshi-Matsuri, Star Festival. 45c, Minnie, Daisy folk dancing at Bon-Odori Summer Festival. $1, Huey, Dewey and Louie wearing Eboshi headdresses at Yari-Matsuri, Spear Festival of Ohji. $2, Mickey, Goofy pulling Daisy, Minnie in Yamaboko, Gion Festival of Kyoto. $4, Minnie, Daisy preparing rice broth for Nanakusa, Festival of the Seven Plants. $5, Huey, Dewey floating straw boat at O-Bon, Festival of Lanterns. No. 1969, Goofy, Tori-No-Hichi or Rake Festival, vert. No. 1970, Minnie Mouse, Japanese New Year, vert. No. 1971, Mickey, Snow Festival, vert.

1991, May 6 Litho. *Perf. 13½x14*

1961 A263 5c multicolored .20 .20
1962 A263 10c multicolored .20 .20
1963 A263 20c multicolored .20 .20
1964 A263 45c multicolored .35 .35
1965 A263 $1 multicolored .80 .80
1966 A263 $2 multicolored 1.60 1.60
1967 A263 $4 multicolored 3.25 3.25
1968 A263 $5 multicolored 4.00 4.00
Nos. 1961-1968 (8) 10.60 10.60

Souvenir Sheets

1969 A263 $6 multicolored 4.75 4.75
1970 A263 $6 multicolored 4.75 4.75
1971 A263 $6 multicolored 4.75 4.75

Paintings by Vincent Van Gogh — A264

Designs: 20c, Blossoming Almond Branch in a Glass, vert. 25c, La Mousme, Sitting, vert. 30c, Still Life with Red Cabbages and Onions. 40c, Japonaiserie: Flowering Plum Tree, vert. 45c, Japonaiserie: Bridge in Rain, vert. 60c, Still Life with Basket of Apples. 75c, Italian Woman (Agostina Segatori), vert. $1, The Painter on His Way to Work, vert. $2, Portrait of Pere Tanguy, vert. $3, Still Life with Plaster Statuette, a Rose and Two Novels, vert. $4, Still Life: Bottle, Lemons and Oranges. $5, Orchard with Blossoming Apricot Trees. No. 1984, Farmhouse in a Wheatfield. No. 1985, The "Roubine du Roi" Canal with Washerwoman, vert. No. 1986, Japonaiserie: Oiran, vert. No. 1987, The Gleize Bridge over the Viguerat Canal. No. 1988, Rocks with Oak Tree.

1991, May 13 Litho. *Perf. 13½*

1972 A264 20c multicolored .20 .20
1973 A264 25c multicolored .20 .20
1974 A264 30c multicolored .25 .25
1975 A264 40c multicolored .30 .30
1976 A264 45c multicolored .35 .35
1977 A264 60c multicolored .50 .50
1978 A264 75c multicolored .60 .60
1979 A264 $1 multicolored .80 .80
1980 A264 $2 multicolored 1.60 1.60
1981 A264 $3 multicolored 2.40 2.40
1982 A264 $4 multicolored 3.25 3.25
1983 A264 $5 multicolored 4.00 4.00
Nos. 1972-1983 (12) 14.45 14.45

Size: 100x75mm, 75x100mm

Imperf

1984-1988 A264 $6 each 4.75 4.75

Mushrooms A265

Designs: 15c, Psilocybe cubensis. 25c, Leptonia caeruleocapitata. 65c, Cystolepiota eriophora. 75c, Chlorophyllum molybdites. $1, Xerocomus hypoxanthus. $2, Volvariella cubensis. $4, Xerocomus coccolobae. $5, Pluteus chrysophlebius. No. 1997, Hygrocybe miniata. No. 1998, Psathyrella tuberculata.

1991, June 1 *Perf. 14*

1989 A265 15c multicolored .20 .20
1990 A265 25c multicolored .20 .20
1991 A265 65c multicolored .50 .50
1992 A265 75c multicolored .60 .60
1993 A265 $1 multicolored .80 .80
1994 A265 $2 multicolored 1.60 1.60
1995 A265 $4 multicolored 3.25 3.25
1996 A265 $5 multicolored 4.00 4.00
Nos. 1989-1996 (8) 11.15 11.15

Souvenir Sheet

1997 A265 $6 multicolored 4.75 4.75
1998 A265 $6 multicolored 4.75 4.75

Miniature Sheets

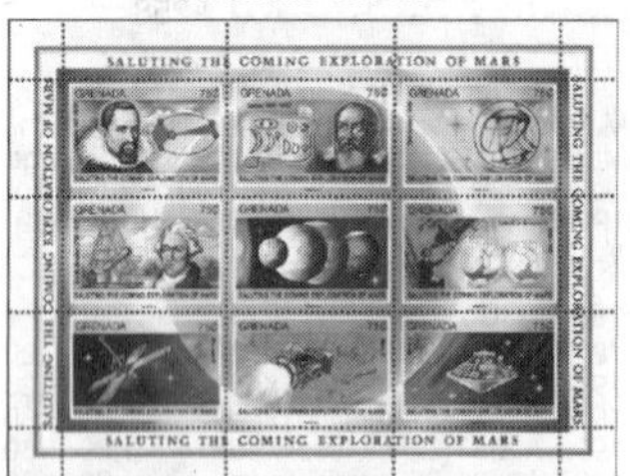

Exploration of Mars — A266

Designs (all different): No. 1999: a, Johannes Kepler, 1571-1630. b, Galileo Galilei, 1564-1642. c, Martian canals drawn by Giovanni Schiaparelli, 1886. d, Sir William Herschel, 1738-1882. e, Mars, planets. f, Percival Lowell at telescope. g, Mariner 4. h, Mars 2. i, Mars 3.

No. 2000: a, e, Profiles of Mars. b, Olympus Mons. c, Dusty face of Mars. d, Martian moon Phobos. f, Martian moon Deimos. g, Nix Olympica. h, Terrain feature resembling human face. i, South Polar Cap.

No. 2001: a, Mars from Thobus. b, Martian dusk. c, "Voyager descent." d, Viking 2 lander on Mars. e, f, Martian landscape. g, h, i, Panorama view from Viking 2 lander.

No. 2002: a, b, Mariner 9. c, Mars. d, Polar cycle. e, Plain of Sinai. f, South pole. g, Nix Olympica. h, Martian surface. i, Outflow channel.

No. 2003, Phobos spacecraft over Mars. No. 2004, Future spacecraft. No. 2005, Future spacecraft, Mars.

1991, June 21 *Perf. 14x13½*

Sheets of 9

1999 A266 75c #a.-i. 5.50 5.50
2000 A266 $1.25 #a.-i. 9.00 9.00
2001 A266 $2 #a.-i. 14.50 14.50
2002 A266 $7 #a.-i. 50.00 50.00

Souvenir Sheets

2003 A266 $6 multicolored 4.75 4.75
2004 A266 $6 multicolored 4.75 4.75
2005 A266 $6 multicolored 4.75 4.75

Royal Family Birthday, Anniversary

Common Design Type

1991, July 5 Litho. *Perf. 14*

2006 CD347 10c multicolored .20 .20
2007 CD347 15c multicolored .20 .20
2008 CD347 40c multicolored .30 .30
2009 CD347 50c multicolored .40 .40
2010 CD347 $1 multicolored .80 .80
2011 CD347 $2 multicolored 1.60 1.60
2012 CD347 $4 multicolored 3.25 3.25
2013 CD347 $5 multicolored 4.00 4.00
Nos. 2006-2013 (8) 10.75 10.75

Souvenir Sheet

2014 CD347 $5 Philip, Elizabeth 4.00 4.00
2015 CD347 $5 Diana, sons, Charles 4.00 4.00

10c, 50c, $1, Nos. 2013, 2015, Charles and Diana, 10th Wedding anniversary. Others, Queen Elizabeth II, 65th birthday.

University of West Indies, 40th Anniv. A266a

Designs: 45c, Marryshow House, Grenada. 50c, Administrative Building, Barbados.

1991, July 19

2016 A266a 45c multicolored .35 .35
2017 A266a 50c multicolored .40 .40

Anglican High School, 75th Anniv. A267

1991, July 29

2018 A267 10c Existing school .20 .20
2019 A267 25c New school design .20 .20

Railways of the World — A269

Railways of Great Britain: No. 2020a, Stephenson's first engine, 1814. b, George Stephenson (1781-1848). c, Stephenson's Killingworth engine, 1816. d, Locomotion No. 1, 1825. e, Locomotion in Darlington, 1825. f, Opening of Stockton & Darlington Railway, 1825. g, Royal George No. 5, 1827. h, Northumbrian Rocket, 1829. i, Planet Class engine, 1830.

No. 2021a, Old Ironsides, US, 1832. b, Wilberforce, Stockton & Darlington Railway, Great Britain, 1832. c, Stephenson's Der Adler, Germany, 1835. d, Stephenson's North Star, Great Britain, 1837. e, London & Birmingham No. 1, Great Britain, 1838. f, Stephenson's 1st Austrian locomotive, 1838. g, Mud Digger, US, 1840. h, Standard Norris, US, 1840. i, Fire Fly Class, Great Britain, 1840.

No. 2022a, Lion, Liverpool and Manchester, Great Britain, 1841. b, Beuth 2-2-2, Berlin-Anhalt Railway, Germany, 1843. c, Derwent No. 25, Stockton & Darlington Railway, Great Britain, 1845. d, MKpV, WCB, Vienna, 1846. e, First railway in Hungary, Budapest to Vac, 1846. f, Stockton & Darlington, 1846. g, Stephenson's long boiler type, Paris, 1847. h, Baldwin 4-4-0, US, 1850. i, 2-4-0, Germany, 1850. No. 2023, Boiler of Locomotion No. 1. No. 2024, Liverpool & Manchester Railway, Great Britain, 1833.

1991-92 Litho. *Perf. 14*

Sheets of 9

2020 A269 75c #a.-i. 5.50 5.50
2021 A269 $1 #a.-i. 7.25 7.25
2022 A269 $2 #a.-i. 14.50 14.50

Souvenir Sheet

2023 A269 $6 multicolored 4.75 4.75
2024 A269 $6 multicolored 4.75 4.75

Issued: 75c, #2023, Dec. 2; others, May 7, 1992.

Miniature Sheet

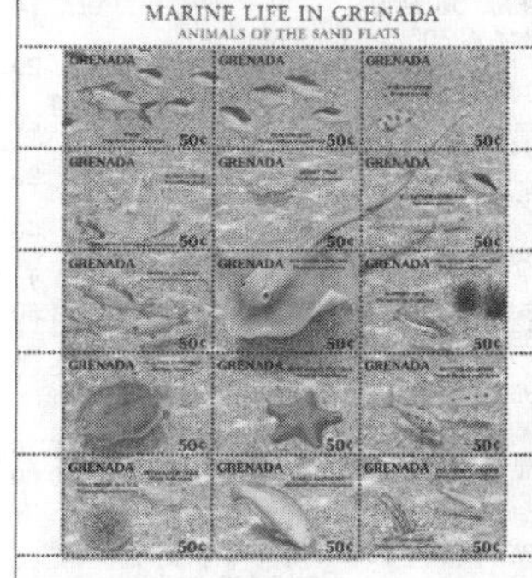

Marine Life in the Sand Flats — A270

Designs: No. 2025a, Barbu. b, Beaugregory. c, Porcupinefish. d, Conchfish, queen conch. e, Hermit crab. f, Bluestripe lizardfish. g, Spotfin mojarra. h, Southern stingray. i, Slippery dick, long-spined sea urchin. j, Peacock flounder. k, West Indian sea star. l, Spotted goatfish. m, West Indian sea egg, reticulated olive. n, Pearly razorfish. o, Mottled and yellowhead jawfish. $6, Shortnose batfish.

1991, Dec. 5 Litho. *Perf. 14*

2025 A270 50c Sheet of 15, #a.-o. 6.00 6.00

Souvenir Sheet

2026 A270 $6 multicolored 4.75 4.75

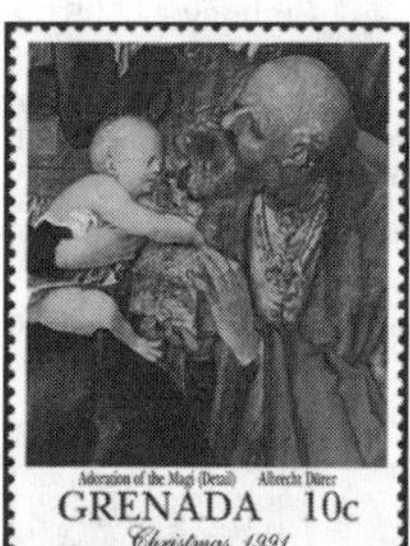

Christmas A271

Details from paintings by Albrecht Durer: 10c, Adoration of the Magi. 35c, The Madonna with the Siskin. 50c, The Feast of the Rose Garlands. 75c, Madonna and Child (Virgin with the Pear). $1, The Virgin in Half-Length. $2, Madonna and Child. $4, Virgin and Child with St. Anne. $5, Virgin and Child, diff. No. 2035, Virgin with a Multitude of Animals. No. 2036, The Nativity.

1991, Dec. 9 *Perf. 12*

2027 A271 10c multicolored .20 .20
2028 A271 35c multicolored .30 .30
2029 A271 50c multicolored .40 .40
2030 A271 75c multicolored .60 .60
2031 A271 $1 multicolored .80 .80
2032 A271 $2 multicolored 1.60 1.60
2033 A271 $4 multicolored 3.25 3.25
2034 A271 $5 multicolored 4.00 4.00
Nos. 2027-2034 (8) 11.15 11.15

Souvenir Sheets

Perf. 14½

2035 A271 $6 multicolored 4.75 4.75
2036 A271 $6 multicolored 4.75 4.75

Thrill Sports — A272

Walt Disney characters enjoying thrill sports.

1992, Feb. 11 Litho. *Perf. 14x13½*

2037 A272 5c Windsurfing .20 .20
2038 A272 10c Skateboarding .20 .20
2039 A272 20c Gliding .20 .20
2040 A272 45c Stunt kite flying .35 .35
2041 A272 $1 Mountain biking .75 .75

2042 A272 $2 Parachuting 1.60 1.60
2043 A272 $4 Go-carting 3.25 3.25
2044 A272 $5 Water skiing 3.75 3.75
Nos. 2037-2044 (8) 10.30 10.30

Souvenir Sheets

2045 A272 $6 Roller blade hockey 4.75 4.75
2046 A272 $6 Bungee jumping 4.75 4.75
2046A A272 $6 Hang gliding 4.75 4.75
2046B A272 $6 River rafting 4.75 4.75

Queen Elizabeth II's Accession to the Throne, 40th Anniv.

Common Design Type

1992, Feb. 6 ***Perf. 14***

2047 CD348 10c multicolored .20 .20
2048 CD348 50c multicolored .40 .40
2049 CD348 $1 multicolored .80 .80
2050 CD348 $5 multicolored 4.00 4.00
Nos. 2047-2050 (4) 5.40 5.40

Souvenir Sheets

2051 CD348 $6 Queen at left 4.75 4.75
2052 CD348 $6 Queen at right 4.75 4.75

Spanish Art — A273

Paintings: 10c, The Corpus Christi Procession in Seville, by Manuel Cabral y Aguado, horiz. 35c, The Mancorbo Channel, by Carlos de Haes. 50c, Countess of Vilches, by Federico de Madrazo y Kuntz. 75c, Countess of Santovenia, by Eduardo Rosales Gallina. $1, Queen Maria Isabel de Braganza, by Bernardo Lopez Piquer. $2, $4, The Presentation of Don John of Austria to Charles V (different details), by Gallina. $5, The Testament of Isabella the Catholic, by Eduardo Rosales Gallina, horiz. No. 2061, Meeting of Poets in Antonio Maria Esquivel's Studio, by Antonio Maria Esquivel y Suarez de Urbina. No. 2062, The Horse Corral in the Old Madrid Bullring, by Manuel Castellano, horiz.

1992, Apr. 30 Litho. ***Perf. 13***

2053 A273 10c multicolored .20 .20
2054 A273 35c multicolored .30 .30
2055 A273 50c multicolored .40 .40
2056 A273 75c multicolored .60 .60
2057 A273 $1 multicolored .80 .80
2058 A273 $2 multicolored 1.60 1.60
2059 A273 $4 multicolored 3.25 3.25
2060 A273 $5 multicolored 4.00 4.00

Size: 120x95mm

Imperf

2061 A273 $6 multicolored 4.75 4.75
2062 A273 $6 multicolored 4.75 4.75
Nos. 2053-2062 (10) 20.65 20.65

Granada '92.

A274

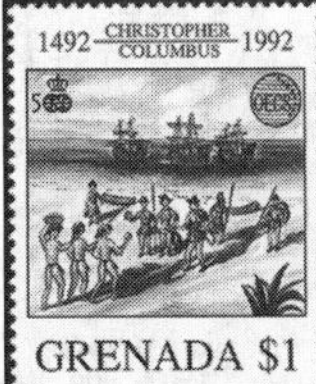

Discovery of America, 500th Anniv. — A275

1992, May 7 Litho. ***Perf. 14***

2063 A274 10c Green-winged parrot .20 .20
2064 A274 25c Santa Maria .20 .20
2065 A274 35c Columbus .30 .30
2066 A274 50c Hourglass .40 .40
2067 A274 75c Queen Isabella .65 .65
2068 A274 $4 Cantino map, 1502 3.25 3.25
Nos. 2063-2068 (6) 5.00 5.00

Souvenir Sheets

2069 A274 $6 Map, ship, fish 4.75 4.75
2070 A274 $6 Map, arms, Genoa 4.75 4.75

World Columbian Stamp Expo '92, Chicago.

1992 ***Perf. 14½***

2071 A275 $1 Coming ashore .80 .80
2072 A275 $2 Native, ships 1.60 1.60

Organization of East Caribbean States.

Hummingbirds A276

1992, May 28

2073 A276 10c Ruby-throated .20 .20
2074 A276 25c Vervain .20 .20
2075 A276 35c Blue-headed .30 .30
2076 A276 50c Cuban Emerald .40 .40
2077 A276 75c Antillean Mango .60 .60
2078 A276 $2 Purple-throated carib 1.60 1.60
2079 A276 $4 Puerto Rican emerald 3.25 3.25
2080 A276 $5 Green-throated carib 4.00 4.00
Nos. 2073-2080 (8) 10.55 10.55

Souvenir Sheets

2081 A276 $6 Rufous-breasted hermit 4.75 4.75
2082 A276 $6 Antillean crested 4.75 4.75

Genoa '92.

USO, 50th Anniv. — A277

1992 Summer Olympics, Barcelona — A278

1992, June 1 ***Perf. 14***

2083 A277 15c Gracie Fields .20 .20
2084 A277 25c Jack Benny .20 .20
2085 A277 35c Jinx Falkenburg .30 .30
2086 A277 50c Frances Langford .40 .40
2087 A277 75c Joe E. Brown .60 .60
2088 A277 $1 Phil Silvers .80 .80
2089 A277 $2 Danny Kaye 1.50 1.50
2090 A277 $5 Frank Sinatra 4.00 4.00
Nos. 2083-2090 (8) 8.00 8.00

Souvenir Sheets

2091 A277 $6 Anna May Wong 4.75 4.75
2092 A277 $6 Bob Hope 4.50 4.50

1992

2093 A278 10c Badminton .20 .20
2094 A278 25c Women's long jump .20 .20
2095 A278 35c Women's 100-meter dash .30 .30
2096 A278 50c Cycling .40 .40
2097 A278 75c Decathlon (pole vault), horiz. .60 .60
2098 A278 $2 Judo, horiz. 1.60 1.60
2099 A278 $4 Women's gymnastics 3.25 3.25
2100 A278 $5 Javelin 4.00 4.00
Nos. 2093-2100 (8) 10.55 10.55

Souvenir Sheets

2101 A278 $6 Men's floor exercise 4.75 4.75
2102 A278 $6 Men's vault 4.75 4.75

Model Trains A279

Designs: 10c, The Blue Comet, standard gauge, US, 1933. 35c, Switching locomotive, 2-inch gauge, 1906. 40c, B & O Tunnel locomotive, 2-inch gauge, 1905. 75c, Grand Canyon, standard gauge, US, 1931. $1, Lithographed tin streamliner, O gauge, 1930's. $2, Switching locomotive #237, No. 1 gauge, US, 1911. $4, Parlor car, standard gauge, US, 1928. $5, Locomotive #4687 of Improved President's Special, standard gauge, 1927. No. 2111, Engine #3239, No. 1 gauge, US, 1912. No. 2112, Ives engine #1132, 1921.

1992, Oct. 22 Litho. ***Perf. 14***

2103 A279 10c multicolored .20 .20
2104 A279 35c multicolored .30 .30
2105 A279 40c multicolored .30 .30
2106 A279 75c multicolored .60 .60
2107 A279 $1 multicolored .75 .75
2108 A279 $2 multicolored 1.50 1.50
2109 A279 $4 multicolored 3.00 3.00
2110 A279 $5 multicolored 3.75 3.75
Nos. 2103-2110 (8) 10.40 10.40

Souvenir Sheet

Perf. 13

2111 A279 $6 multicolored 4.50 4.50
2112 A279 $6 multicolored 4.50 4.50

Nos. 2111-2112 contains one 51x40mm stamp.

Souvenir Sheet

Guggenheim Museum, NYC — A280

1992, Oct. 28 ***Perf. 14***

2113 A280 $6 multicolored 5.25 5.25

Postage Stamp Mega Event '92, NYC.

Christmas A281

Details or entire paintings: 10c, The Adoration of the Magi, by Fra Filippo Lippi. 15c, Madonna Adoring Child in a Wood, by Fra Filippo Lippi. 25c, Adoration of the Magi, by Botticelli. 35c, The Epiphany-Adoration of the Magi, by Hieronymus Bosch. 50c, Adoration of the Magi, by Giovanni de Paolo. 75c, The Adoration of the Magi, by Gentile da Fabriano. 90c, Adoration of the Magi, by Juan Batista Maino. $1, The Adoration of the Child, by Master of Liesborn. $2, The Adoration of the Kings, by Master of Liesborn. $3, The Adoration of the Three Wise Men, by Pedro Berruguete. $4, The Adoration of the Child, by Filippo Lippi. $5, The Adoration of the Child, by Correggio. No. 2126, Adoration of the Magi, by Hans Memling. No. 2127, Adoration of the Magi, by Andrea Mantegna. No. 2128, Adoration of the Shepherds, by De La Tour.

1992, Nov. 16 Litho. ***Perf. 13½x14***

2114 A281 10c multicolored .20 .20
2115 A281 15c multicolored .20 .20
2116 A281 25c multicolored .20 .20
2117 A281 35c multicolored .30 .30
2118 A281 50c multicolored .40 .40
2119 A281 75c multicolored .60 .60
2120 A281 90c multicolored .70 .70
2121 A281 $1 multicolored .75 .75
2122 A281 $2 multicolored 1.50 1.50
2123 A281 $3 multicolored 2.25 2.25
2124 A281 $4 multicolored 3.00 3.00
2125 A281 $5 multicolored 3.75 3.75
Nos. 2114-2125 (12) 13.85 13.85

Souvenir Sheet

2126 A281 $6 multicolored 4.50 4.50
2127 A281 $6 multicolored 4.50 4.50
2128 A281 $6 multicolored 4.50 4.50

Regattas of the World — A282

Yachts, races: 15c, Matador, Newport News Regatta. 25c, Awesome, Antigua Regatta. 35c, Mistress Quickly, Bermuda Regatta. 50c, Emeraude, St. Tropez Regatta. $1, Diva G, German Admirals Cup. $2, Lady Be, French Admirals Cup. $4, Midnight Sun, Admirals Cup Regatta. $5, Carat, Sardinia Cup Regatta. No. 2137, 1979 Fastnet Race, horiz. No. 2138, Grenada Regatta, horiz.

1992, Oct. Litho. ***Perf. 14***

2129 A282 15c multicolored .20 .20
2130 A282 25c multicolored .20 .20
2131 A282 35c multicolored .30 .30
2132 A282 50c multicolored .40 .40
2133 A282 $1 multicolored .75 .75
2134 A282 $2 multicolored 1.40 1.40
2135 A282 $4 multicolored 3.00 3.00
2136 A282 $5 multicolored 3.75 3.75
Nos. 2129-2136 (8) 10.00 10.00

Souvenir Sheets

2137 A282 $6 multicolored 4.50 4.50
2138 A282 $6 multicolored 4.50 4.50

A283

Anniversaries and Events — A284

Designs: 25c, LZ1 on maiden flight, 1900. 50c, Endosat, proposed robot plane. 75c, Konrad Adenauer, factory. $1.50, Golden lion tamarin. No. 2143 Mountain gorilla. No. 2144, WHO emblem and "Heartbeat-the Rhythm of Health." $3, Wolfgang Amadeus Mozart. No. 2146, German flag, map, Adenauer. No. 2147, Voyager 2, Neptune. $5, Count Zeppelin, Graf Zeppelin. $6, Lion's Club emblem, Admiral Richard E. Byrd. No. 2150, Scene from "The Magic Flute." No. 2151, Konrad Adenauer. No. 2152, Earth Summit emblem, northern spotted owl. No. 2153, Count Zeppelin. No. 2154, Satellite rescue, vert.

1992 Litho. ***Perf. 14***

2139 A283 25c multicolored .20 .20
2140 A283 50c multicolored .40 .40
2141 A283 75c multicolored .60 .60
2142 A283 $1.50 multicolored 1.10 1.10
2143 A283 $2 multicolored 1.50 1.50
2144 A283 $2 multicolored 1.50 1.50
2145 A284 $3 multicolored 2.25 2.25
2146 A283 $4 multicolored 3.00 3.00
2147 A283 $4 multicolored 3.00 3.00
2148 A283 $5 multicolored 3.75 3.75
2149 A283 $6 multicolored 4.50 4.50
Nos. 2139-2149 (11) 21.80 21.80

Souvenir Sheets

2150 A284 $6 multicolored 4.50 4.50
2151 A283 $6 multicolored 4.50 4.50
2152 A283 $6 multicolored 4.50 4.50
2153 A283 $6 multicolored 4.50 4.50
2154 A283 $6 multicolored 4.50 4.50

Count Ferdinand von Zeppelin, 75th anniv. of death (#2139, 2148, 2153). Intl. Space Year (#2140, 2147, 2154). Konrad Adenauer, 25th anniv. of death (#2141, 2146, 2151). Earth Summit, Rio de Janeiro (#2142-2143, 2152).

Mozart, bicent. of death (in 1991) (#2145, 2150). Lions Intl., 75th anniv. (#2149).

Issue dates: Nos. 2145, 2150, Oct. Nos. 2140-2141, 2144, 2146-2147, 2149, 2151, 2154, Nov. Nos. 2139, 2142-2143, 2148, 2152-2153, Dec.

Grenada Dove — A285

1992

2155 A285 10c multicolored .20 .20

Entertainers — A286

Gold record award winners: No. 2156a, Cher. b, Michael Jackson. c, Elvis Presley. d, Dolly Parton. e, Johnny Mathis. f, Madonna. g, Nat King Cole. h, Janis Joplin.

No. 2157a, Frank Sinatra. b, Perry Como. No. 2158a, Chuck Berry. b, James Brown.

1992, Nov. 19 Litho. *Perf. 14*

Miniature Sheet

2156 A286 90c Sheet of 8, #a.-h. 5.50 5.50

Souvenir Sheets

2157 A286 $3 Sheet of 2, #a.-b. 4.50 4.50
2158 A286 $3 Sheet of 2, #a.-b. 4.50 4.50

Care Bears Promote Conservation — A287

75c, Bear on uncontaminated beachfront. $2, Bear with parasol, butterfly on flower, vert.

1992, Dec. 15 Litho. *Perf. 14*

2159 A287 75c multicolored .60 .60

Souvenir Sheet

2160 A287 $2 multicolored 1.50 1.50

Dogs A288

Designs: 10c, Samoyed, St. Basil's Cathedral, Moscow. 15c, Chow chow, Ling Yin Monastery, China. 25c, Boxer, Traitor's Gate, United Kingdom. 90c, Basenji, Yamma Mosque, Niger. $1, Golden Labrador Retriever, Parliament, Ottawa, Canada. $3, Saint Bernard, Parsenn, Switzerland. $4, Rhodesian ridgeback, Melrose House, South Africa. $5, Afghan, Mazar-i-Sharif, Afghanistan. No. 2169, Alaskan malamute, Alaska. No. 2170, Australian cattle dog, Australia.

1993, Jan. 20 Litho. *Perf. 14*

2161 A288 10c multicolored .20 .20
2162 A288 15c multicolored .20 .20
2163 A288 25c multicolored .20 .20
2164 A288 90c multicolored .65 .65
2165 A288 $1 multicolored .75 .75
2166 A288 $3 multicolored 2.25 2.25
2167 A288 $4 multicolored 3.00 3.00
2168 A288 $5 multicolored 3.75 3.75
Nos. 2161-2168 (8) 11.00 11.00

Souvenir Sheet

2169 A288 $6 multicolored 4.50 4.50
2170 A288 $6 multicolored 4.50 4.50

Miniature Sheet

Louvre Museum, Bicent. — A289

Paintings by Jean-Antoine Watteau (1684-1721): a, The Faux-Pas. b, A Gentleman. c, Young Lady with Archlute. d, Young Man Dancing. e, Autumn. f, The Judgement of Paris. g-h, Pierrot (diff. details).

No. 2172, The Embarkation for Cythera, horiz.

1993, Mar. 8 Litho. *Perf. 12*

2171 A289 $1 Sheet of 8, #a.-h. + label 6.00 6.00

Souvenir Sheet

Perf. 14½

2172 A289 $6 multicolored 4.50 4.50

No. 2172 contains one 88x55mm stamp.

Moths A290

1993, Apr. 13 Litho. *Perf. 14*

2173 A290 10c Magnificent .20 .20
2174 A290 35c Metzl's io .30 .30
2175 A290 45c Owl .35 .35
2176 A290 75c Pink-spotted hawk .60 .60
2177 A290 $1 Faithful beauty .75 .75
2178 A290 $2 Green geometrid 1.50 1.50
2179 A290 $4 Gaudy sphinx 3.00 3.00
2180 A290 $5 Black witch 3.75 3.75
Nos. 2173-2180 (8) 10.45 10.45

Souvenir Sheets

2181 A290 $6 Titan hawk, vert. 4.50 4.50
2182 A290 $6 Avocado, vert. 4.50 4.50

Flowers — A291

1993, May 17 Litho. *Perf. 14*

2183 A291 10c Heliconia .20 .20
2184 A291 35c Pansy .30 .30
2185 A291 45c Water lily .35 .35
2186 A291 75c Bougainvillea .60 .60
2187 A291 $1 Calla lily .75 .75
2188 A291 $2 California poppy 1.50 1.50
2189 A291 $4 Red ginger 3.00 3.00
2190 A291 $5 Anthurium 3.75 3.75
Nos. 2183-2190 (8) 10.45 10.45

Souvenir Sheet

2191 A291 $6 Christmas rose, horiz. 4.50 4.50
2192 A291 $6 Moth orchids, horiz. 4.50 4.50

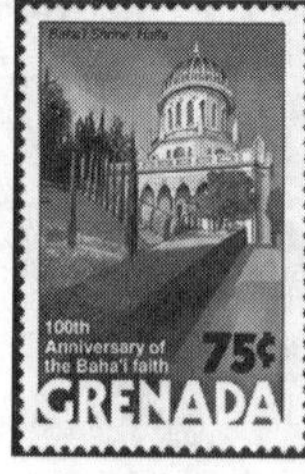

Baha'i Shrine, Haifa, Israel — A292

1993, May Litho. *Perf. 13½x14*

2193 A292 75c multicolored .60 .60

Baha'i faith in Grenada, cent.

Miniature Sheet

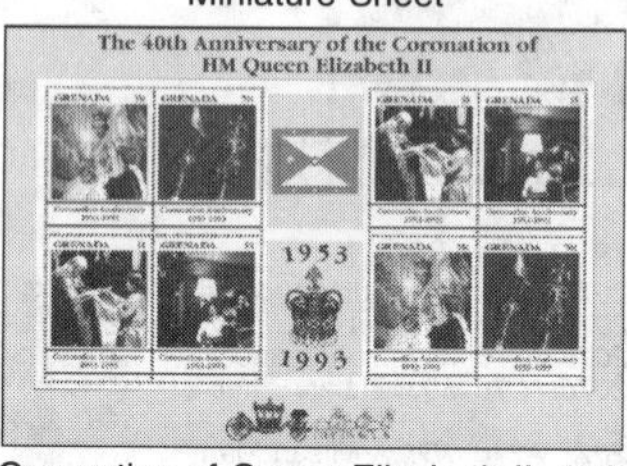

Coronation of Queen Elizabeth II, 40th Anniv. — A293

Designs: a, 35c, Official coronation photograph. b, 70c, Queen Consort's Ivory Rod, Queen Consort's Scepter. c, $1, Elizabeth accepting scepter during ceremony. $5, Queen, family, 1960s.

$6, Portrait, by Peter George Greenham, 1965.

1993, June 2 *Perf. 13½x14*

2194 A293 Sheet, 2 each #a.-d. 10.50 10.50

Souvenir Sheet

Perf. 14

2195 A293 $6 multicolored 4.50 4.50

No. 2195 contains one 28x42mm stamp.

A294

Anniversaries and Events — A295

Designs: 35c, Telescope. 50c, Willy Brandt, Sen. Edward Kennedy, Mrs. Robert Kennedy, 1973. $4, Astronaut standing on moon. No. 2199, Willy Brandt, Kurt Waldheim. No. 2200, Copernicus. $6, Newspaper headline announcing Brandt's resignation.

1993, July 1 Litho. *Perf. 14*

2196 A294 35c multicolored .30 .30
2197 A295 50c black & brown .40 .40
2198 A294 $4 multicolored 3.00 3.00
2199 A295 $5 black & brown 3.75 3.75
Nos. 2196-2199 (4) 7.45 7.45

Souvenir Sheets

2200 A294 $5 multicolored 3.75 3.75
2201 A295 $6 brown & black 4.50 4.50

Nicolaus Copernicus, 450th anniv. of death (#2196, 2198, 2200). Willy Brandt, 1st anniv. of death (#2197, 2199, 2201).

Grenada Carnival, 1992 A296

1993, July 1

2202 A296 35c Public Library, vert. .30 .30
2203 A296 75c Dancers .60 .60

Public Library, cent. (in 1992) (#2202).

Miniature Sheet

Songbirds A297

Designs: No. 2204a, 15c, Red-eyed vireo. b, 25c, Scissor-tailed flycatcher (g). c, 35c, Palmchat. d, 35c, Chaffinch. e, 45c, Yellow wagtail. f, 45c Painted bunting. g, 50c, Short-tailed pygmy flycatcher. h, 65c, Rainbow bunting. i, 75c, Red crossbill. j, 75c, Kauai akialoa. k, $1, Yellow-throated wagtail. l, $4, Barn swallow.

No. 2205, Song thrush. No. 2206, White-crested laughing thrush.

1993, July 13

2204 A297 Sheet of 12, #a.-l. 6.60 6.60

Souvenir Sheets

2205 A297 $6 multicolored 4.50 4.50
2206 A297 $6 multicolored 4.50 4.50

Miniature Sheet

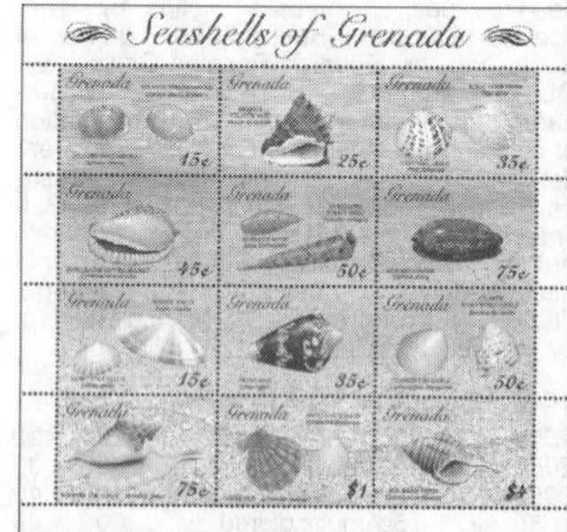

Seashells — A298

Designs: No. 2207a, 15c, Atlantic gray cowrie, Atlantic yellow cowrie. b, 15c, Candy stick tellin, sunrise tellin. c, 25c, Common Atlantic vase. d, 35c, Lightning venus, royal comb venus. e, 35c, Crown cone. f, 45c, Reticulated cowrie-helmet. g, 50c, Barbados miter, variegated turret shell. h, 50c, Common egg cockle, Atlantic strawberry cockle. i, 75c, Measled cowrie. j, 75c, Rooster tail conch. k, $1, Lion's paw, Antillean scallop. l, $4, Dog-head triton.

No. 2208, Dyson's keyhole limpet. No. 2209, Virgin nerite, emerald nerite.

1993, July 19 Litho. *Perf. 14*

2207 A298 Sheet of 12, #a.-l. 7.00 7.00

Souvenir Sheets

2208 A298 $6 multicolored 4.50 4.50
2209 A298 $6 multicolored 4.50 4.50

A299

Picasso (1881-1973): 25c, Woman with Loaves, 1906. 90c, Weeping Woman, 1937. $4, Woman Seated in Armchair, 1947. $6, Three Women at the Spring, 1921.

1993, July 1 Litho. *Perf. 14*

2210 A299	25c	multicolored	.20	.20
2211 A299	90c	multicolored	.70	.70
2212 A299	$4	multicolored	3.00	3.00
		Nos. 2210-2212 (3)	3.90	3.90

Souvenir Sheet

2213 A299 $6 multicolored 4.50 4.50

A300

1993, July 1

1994 Winter Olympics, Lillehammer, Norway: 35c, Gaeten Boucher, speedskating gold medalist, 1984. $5, Norbert Schramm, figure skater. $6, Michela Figini, Sigrid Wolf, Karen Percy, Super G medalists, 1988, horiz.

2214 A300	35c	multicolored	.25	.25
2215 A300	$5	multicolored	3.75	3.75

Souvenir Sheet

2216 A300 $6 multicolored 4.50 4.50

Polska '93 — A301

Paintings: $1, Portrait of Marii Prohaska, by Tytus Czyzewski, 1923. $3, Marysia et Burek a Geylan, by S.I. Wirkiewicz, 1920-21. $6, Parting, by Witold Wojtkiewicz, 1908.

1993, July 1 Litho. *Perf. 14*

2217 A301	$1	multicolored	.75	.75
2218 A301	$3	multicolored	2.25	2.25

Souvenir Sheet

2219 A301 $6 multicolored 4.50 4.50

Taipei '93 — A302

Designs: 35c, Fire-breathing dragon, New Year's Fair, Chongqing. 45c, Stone elephant, Spirit Way to Ming Tomb, Nanjing. $2, Marble peifang, Ming Tombs, Beijing. $4, Stone pillar, Nanjing.

Paintings by Han Meilin: No. 2224a, Ornamental cock. b, Tiger cub. c, Owl. d, Cat. e, Gorillas. f, Leopard.

No. 2225, Orangutan.

1993, Aug. 13 Litho. *Perf. 14*

2220 A302	35c	multicolored	.25	.25
2221 A302	45c	multicolored	.35	.35
2222 A302	$2	multicolored	1.50	1.50
2223 A302	$4	multicolored	3.00	3.00
		Nos. 2220-2223 (4)	5.10	5.10

Miniature Sheet

2224 A302 $1.50 Sheet of 6, #a.-f. 6.75 6.75

Souvenir Sheet

2225 A302 $6 multicolored 4.50 4.50

With Bangkok '93 Emblem

Designs: 35c, Nora Nair, Prasad Phra Thepidon, Wat Phra Kaew. 45c, Stucco deities, Library, Wat Phra Singh. $2, Naga snake, Chiang Mai's Temple. $4, Stucco elephants, Wat Chang Lom.

Thai sculpture: No. 2230a, Horses. b, Wheel of the Law, 7th-8th cent. c, Lanna bronze elephant, 1575. d, Kendi in form of elephant. e, Bronze duck, 14th-15th cent. f, Horseman, 14th-15th cent.

No. 2231, Elephants, horiz.

1993, Aug. 13

2226 A302	35c	multicolored	.25	.25
2227 A302	45c	multicolored	.35	.35
2228 A302	$2	multicolored	1.50	1.50
2229 A302	$4	multicolored	3.00	3.00
		Nos. 2226-2229 (4)	5.10	5.10

Miniature Sheet of 6

2230 A302 $1.50 #a.-f. 6.75 6.75

Souvenir Sheet

2231 A302 $6 multicolored 4.50 4.50

With Indopex '93 Emblem

35c, Megalithic carving, Sumba Island, Indonesia. 45c, Entrance to Gao Gaja (Elephant Cave), Bali. $2, Loving Mother Bridge, Taroko Gorge Natl. Park. $4, Kala head gateway to Balinese Temple, Northern Bali.

Indonesian sculpture - #2236: a, Kris holder and Kris, 19th cent. b, Hanuman protecting Sita, I. Dojotan of Mas. c, Sendi of Visnu mounted on Garuda, 19th cent. d, Wahana (mini vehicle for votive fig.), 20th cent. e, Mercurial monkey warrior Hanuman, Rodja of Mas. f, Singa (polychrome lion).

No. 2237, Loris.

1993, Aug. 13 *Perf. 13½x14*

2232 A302	35c	multicolored	.25	.25
2233 A302	45c	multicolored	.35	.35
2234 A302	$2	multicolored	1.50	1.50
2235 A302	$4	multicolored	3.00	3.00
		Nos. 2232-2235 (4)	5.10	5.10

Miniature Sheet of 6

2236 A302 $1.50 #a.-f. 1.10 1.10

Souvenir Sheet

2237 A302 $6 multicolored 4.50 4.50

Miniature Sheets of 6

Italian Soccer Assoc. and Genoa Soccer Club, Cent. — A303

Players for Genoa Soccer Club: No. 2238a, Vittorio Sardelli. b, Juan Carlos Verdeal. c, Fosco Becattini. d, Julio Cesar Abadie. e, Luigi Meroni. f, Roberto Pruzzo.

No. 2239a, James K. Spensley. b, Renzo de Vecchi. c, Giovanni de Pra. d, Luigi Burlando. e, Felice Levratto. f, Guglielmo Stabile.

No. 2240, 1991 Genoa team photo, horiz.

No. 2241, Genoa team emblem.

1993, Sept. 7 Litho. *Perf. 14*

2238-2239 A303 $3 #a.-f., ea 13.50 13.50

Souvenir Sheets

2240-2241 A303 $15 each 11.00 11.00

No. 2240 contains one 48x35mm stamp. No. 2241 contains one 29x45mm stamp.

1994 World Cup Soccer Championships, US — A304

Designs: 10c, Nikolai Larionov, Russia. 25c, Andrea Carnevale, Italy. 35c, Enzo Scifo, Belgium, Soon-Ho Choi, South Korea. 45c, Gary Lineker, England. $1, Diego Maradona, Argentina. $2, Lothar Matteaus, Germany. $4, Jan Karas, Poland, Julio Cesar Silva, Brazil. $5, Claudio Caniggia, Argentina.

No. 2250, Wlodzimierz, Poland. No. 2251, Jose Basualdo, Argentina.

1993, Sept. 7 Litho. *Perf. 14*

2242-2249 A304 Set of 8 9.00 9.00

Souvenir Sheets

2250-2251 A304 $6 each 4.50 4.50

Mickey Mouse, 65th Birthday — A305

Movie clips: 25c, The Band Concert, 1935. 35c, Mickey's Circus, 1936. 50c, Magician Mickey, 1937. 75c, Moose Hunters, 1937. $1, Mickey's Amateurs, 1937. $2, Tugboat Mickey, 1940. $4, Orphan's Benefit, 1941. $5, Mickey's Christmas, 1983.

No. 2260, Mickey's Birthday Party, 1942. No. 2261, Mickey's Trailer, 1938.

1993, Nov. 11 Litho. *Perf. 14x13½*

2252-2259 A305 Set of 8 9.00 9.00

Souvenir Sheets

2260-2261 A305 $6 each 4.50 4.50

Christmas A306

Woodcuts by Durer: 10c, The Nativity. 25c, "The Annunciation." $1, "Adoration of the Magi." $5, "The Virgin Mary in the Sun."

Paintings by Leonardo Da Vinci: 35c, The Litta Madonna. 60c, Madonna and Child with St. Anne and the Infant St. John. 90c, Madonna with the Carnation. $4, The Benois Madonna.

No. 2270, The Holy Family with Three Hares, by Durer. No. 2271, Adoration of the Magi, by Da Vinci.

The 25c actually shows the Adoration of the Magi. The $1 actually shows The Virgin Mary in the Sun. The $5 actually shows The Annunciation.

1993, Nov. 22 Litho. *Perf. 13½x14*

2262-2269 A306 Set of 8 9.00 9.00

Souvenir Sheets

2270-2271 A306 $6 each 4.50 4.50

Hugo Eckener (1868-1954) — A307

Graf Zeppelin over: 35c, Vienna. 75c, Pyramids at Giza. $5, Rio de Janeiro. #2275, Flensburg.

1993, Dec. 21 *Perf. 14*

2272-2274 A307 Set of 3 4.50 4.50

Souvenir Sheet

2275 A307 $6 multicolored 4.50 4.50

Royal Air Force, 75th Anniv. A308

1993, Dec. 21

2276 A308	50c	Lysander	.40	.40
2277 A308	$3	Hawker Typhoon	2.25	2.25

Souvenir Sheet

2278 A308 $6 Hawker Hurricane 4.50 4.50

Automotive Anniversaries — A309

35c, 1932 Mercedes Benz 370 S Cabriolet. 45c, 1966 Ford Mustang. $3, 1930 Model A Ford Phaeton. $4, Mercedes Benz 300 SL Gullwing.

No. 2283, 1903 Ford Model A. No. 2284, 1934 Mercedes Benz 290.

1993, Dec. 21 Litho. *Perf. 14*

2279-2282 A309 Set of 4 6.00 6.00

Souvenir Sheets

2283-2284 A309 $6 each 4.50 4.50

1st Benz 4-wheel car, cent. 1st Ford engine, cent.

First Gas Balloon Flight in America, Bicent. A310

Designs: 45c, Lift-off from Philadelphia. $2, Balloon in flight, vert. $6, Blanchard's balloon in flight, diff., vert.

1993, Dec. 21 Litho. *Perf. 14*

2285-2286 A310 Set of 2 2.00 2.00

Souvenir Sheet

2287 A310 $6 multicolored 4.50 4.50

Fine Art — A311

Self-portraits, by Matisse: 15c, 1900. 45c, 1918. $2, 1906. $4, 1900, diff.

Self-portraits, by Rembrandt: 35c, 1629. 50c, 1640. 75c, 1652. $5, 1625-31.

No. 2296, The Painter in His Studio, by Matisse. No. 2297, The Sampling Officials of the Draper's Guild, by Rembrandt, horiz.

1993, Dec. 31 Litho. *Perf. 13½x14*

2288 A311	15c	multicolored	.20	.20
2289 A311	35c	multicolored	.25	.25
2290 A311	45c	multicolored	.35	.35
2291 A311	50c	multicolored	.40	.40
2292 A311	75c	multicolored	.55	.55
2293 A311	$2	multicolored	1.50	1.50
2294 A311	$4	multicolored	3.00	3.00
2295 A311	$5	multicolored	3.75	3.75
		Nos. 2288-2295 (8)	10.00	10.00

Souvenir Sheets

2296 A311 $6 multicolored 4.50 4.50

Perf. 14x13½

2297 A311 $6 multicolored 4.50 4.50

Spice Islands Billfish Tournament, 25th Anniv. — A312

15c, Blue marlin. 25c, Sailfish with angler. 35c, Yellowfin tuna with angler. 50c, White marlin with angler. 75c, Catching a sailfish.

1993, Dec. Litho. *Perf. 14*
2302-2306 A312 Set of 5 1.50 1.50

A313

Hong Kong '94 — A314

Stamps, painting, Hong Kong Post Office-1846, by M. Bruce: No. 2307, Hong Kong #263, left detail. No. 2308, Right detail, #1597.
Porcelain ware, Qing Dynasty: No. 2309a, Vase with dragon decor. b, Hat stand. c, Gourd-shaped vase. d, Rotating vase with openwork. e, Candlestick with dogs. f, Hat stand, diff.

1994, Feb. 18 Litho. *Perf. 14*
2307 40c multicolored .30 .30
2308 40c multicolored .30 .30
a. A313 Pair, #2307-2308 .60 .60

Miniature Sheet
2309 A314 45c Sheet of 6, #a.-f. 2.00 2.00

Nos. 2307-2308 issued in sheets of 5 pairs. No. 2308a is a continuous design.
New Year 1994 (Year of the Dog) (#2309e).

Independence, 20th Anniv. — A315

1994, Feb. 8 Litho. *Perf. 14*
2310 A315 35c Natl. flag, boat .25 .25

Souvenir Sheet
2311 A315 $6 Map of Granada 4.50 4.50

Miniature Sheets

Dinosaurs A316

Jurassic: No. 2312a, Germanodactylus. b, Dimorphodon. c, Ramphorhynchus. d, Apatosaurus (h). e, Pterodactylus. f, Stegosaurus. g, Brachiosaurus. h, Allosaurus (l). i, Plesiosaurus. j, Ceratosaurus. k, Compsognathus. l, Elaphosaurus.
Cretaceous: No. 2313a, Quetzalcoatlus. b, Pteranodon ingens (c). c, Tropeognathus. d, Phobetor. e, Alamosaurus (i). f, Triceratops (e). g, Tyrannosaurus rex (h). h, Tyrannosaurus rex (up close) (l). i, Lambeosaurus. j, Spinosaurus. k, Parasaurolophus (l). l, Hadrosaurus.
No. 2314, Plateosaurus, vert. No. 2315, Pteranodon ingens.

1994, Apr. 13
Sheets of 12
2312 A316 75c #a.-l. 6.75 6.75
2313 A316 75c #a.-l. 6.75 6.75

Souvenir Sheets
2314 A316 $6 multicolored 4.50 4.50
2315 A316 $6 multicolored 4.50 4.50

Mushrooms A317

Designs: 35c, Hygrocybe acutoconica. 45c, Leucopaxillus gracillimus. 50c, Leptonia caeruleocapitata. 75c, Leucoprinus birnbaumii. $1, Marasmius atrorubens. $2, Boletellus cubensis. $4, Chlorophyllum molybdites. $5, Psilocybe cubensis.
No. 2324, Mycena pura. No. 2325, Pyrrhoglossum lilaceipes.

1994, Apr. 6
2316 A317 35c multicolored .25 .25
2317 A317 45c multicolored .35 .35
2318 A317 50c multicolored .40 .40
2319 A317 75c multicolored .55 .55
2320 A317 $1 multicolored .75 .75
2321 A317 $2 multicolored 1.50 1.50
2322 A317 $4 multicolored 3.00 3.00
2323 A317 $5 multicolored 3.75 3.75
Nos. 2316-2323 (8) 10.55 10.55

Souvenir Sheets
2324 A317 $6 multicolored 4.50 4.50
2325 A317 $6 multicolored 4.50 4.50

D-Day, 50th Anniv. A318

Designs: 40c, Sherman Dual-Drive swimming tanks. $2, Churchill "Ark" in operation. $3, Churchill "Bobbin" lays path over soft ground.
$6, Churchill "Avre."

1994, Aug. 4 Litho. *Perf. 14*
2326-2328 A318 Set of 3 4.00 4.00

Souvenir Sheet
2329 A318 $6 multicolored 4.50 4.50

Miniature Sheet of 6

First Manned Moon Landing, 25th Anniv. — A319

Tribute to crew of space shuttle Challenger: No. 2330a, Flame erupting before explosion. b, Judith A. Resnick. c, Aircraft flyover in "Missing Man" formation. d, Dick Scobee. e, Challenger 51-L patch. f, Michael J. Smith.
$6, Crew of mission 51-L.

1994, Aug. 4
2330 A319 $2 #a.-f. 5.00 5.00

Souvenir Sheet
2331 A319 $6 multicolored 4.50 4.50

A320

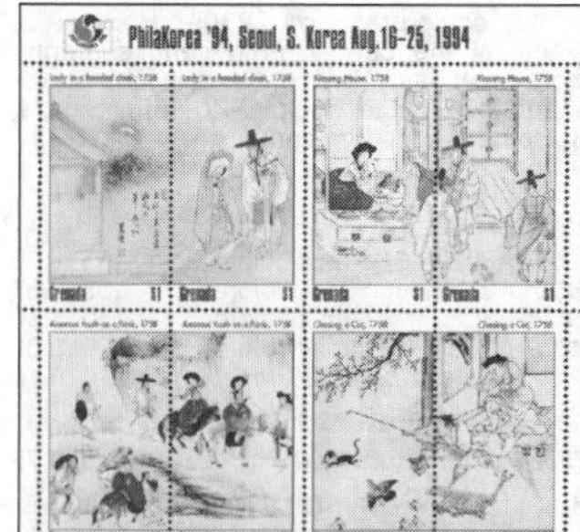
PHILAKOREA '94 — A321

Designs: 40c, Wonson Park & Garden. $1, Port of Pusan. $4, National Theatre, Seoul.
Paintings by Sin Yunbok, Late Choson Dynasty: No. 2335a-2335b, Lady in a Hooded Cloak. c-d, Kiaseng House. e-f, Amorous Youth on a Picnic. g-h, Chasing a Cat.
$6, Roof Tiling, by Kim Hongdo, vert.

1994, Aug. 4 *Perf. 14, 13½ (#2335)*
2332-2334 A320 Set of 3 4.00 4.00

Miniature Sheet of 8
2335 A321 $1 #a.-h. 6.00 6.00

Souvenir Sheet
2336 A320 $6 multicolored 4.50 4.50

A322

Orchids: 15c, Brassavola cuculatta. 25c, Comparettia falcata. 45c, Epidendrum ciliare. 75c, Epidendrum cochleatum. $1, Ionopsis utricularioides. $2, Oncidium cebolleta. $4, Oncidium luridium. $5, Rodriquezia secunda.
No. 2345, Ionopis utriculariodes, diff. No. 2346, Onicium luridum, diff.

1994, Aug. 7 *Perf. 14*
2337-2344 A322 Set of 8 10.00 10.00

Souvenir Sheets
2345-2346 A322 $6 each 4.50 4.50

A323

1994 World Cup Soccer Championships, US: No. 2347a, Tony Meola, US. b, Steve Mark, Grenada. c, Gianluigi Lentini, Italy. d, Belloumi, Algeria. e, Nunoz, Spain. f, Lothar Matthaus, Germany.
#2348, Steve Mark, diff. #2349, Poster from 1st World Cup Championships, Uruguay, 1930.

1994, Aug. 11 *Perf. 14*
Miniature Sheet of 6
2347 A323 75c #a.-f. 3.50 3.50

Souvenir Sheet
2348-2349 A323 $6 each 4.50 4.50

Fish A324

Designs: 15c, Yellowtail snapper. 20c, Blue tang. 25c, Porkfish, vert. 75c, Foureye butterflyfish. $1, Longsnout seahorse, vert. $2, Spotted moray eel, vert. $4, Fairy basslet. $5, Queen triggerfish, vert.
#2358, Queen angelfish. #2359, Squirrelfish.

1994, Sept. 1
2350-2357 A324 Set of 8 10.00 10.00

Souvenir Sheets
2358-2359 A324 $6 each 4.50 4.50

A325

Intl. Olympic Committee, Cent. — A326

Designs: 50c, Heike Dreschler, Germany, long jump, 1992. $1.50, Nadia Comaneci, Romania, Gymnastics, 1976, 1980.
$6, Dan Jansen, US, 1000-meters long track speed skating, 1994.

1994, Aug. 4
2360 A325 50c multicolored .40 .40
2361 A325 $1.50 multicolored 1.10 1.10

Souvenir Sheet
2362 A326 $6 multicolored 4.50 4.50

1994, Year of the Dog — A327

Scenes from Disney's Society Dog Show: 2c, Mickey bathing Pluto. 3c, Using atomizer. 4c, Having tail "set." 5c, Putting on mascara. 10c, Having nails done. 15c, Mickey using flea powder on Pluto. 20c, On judge's stand. $4, Judge looking at Pluto. $5, Pluto in chair with first prize.
No. 2372, Pluto wearing "13," first prize ribbon. No. 2373, Little dog beside judge. No. 2374, Pluto with first prize ribbon.

1994, Sept. 22 Litho. *Perf. 14x13½*
2363-2371 A327 Set of 9 7.25 7.25

Souvenir Sheets
2372-2374 A327 $6 each 4.50 4.50

Butterflies — A328

1994, Sept. 28 *Perf. 14*

2375	A328 10c	Red anartia	.20	.20
2376	A328 15c	Ruddy dag-gerwing	.20	.20
2377	A328 25c	Fiery skipper	.20	.20
2378	A328 35c	Caribbean buckeye	.30	.30
2379	A328 45c	Giant hair-streak	.30	.30
2380	A328 50c	Zebra longw-ing	.40	.40
2381	A328 75c	Diadem	.55	.55
2382	A328 $1	Blue night	.75	.75
2383	A328 $2	Orion	1.50	1.50
2384	A328 $3	Orange-barred sulphur	2.25	2.25
2385	A328 $4	Long-tail skipper	3.00	3.00
2386	A328 $5	Polydamas swallowtail	3.75	3.75
2386A	A328 $10	Bamboo page	7.50	7.50
2386B	A328 $20	Queen cracker	15.00	15.00
	Nos. 2375-2386B (14)		35.90	35.90

#2377-2378 exist dated 1996.
See Nos. 2585-2586.

Intl. Year of the Family A329

1994, Aug. 4
2387 A329 $1 multicolored .75 .75

Order of the Caribbean Community — A330

First award recipients: 15c, Sir Shridath Ramphal, statesman, Guyana. 65c, William Demas, economist, Trinidad & Tobago. $2, Derek Walcott, writer, St. Lucia.

1994, Sept. 1
2388-2390 A330 Set of 3 2.25 2.25

Christmas A331

Paintings, by Zurbaran: 10c, The Virgin and Child with St. John. 15c, The Circumcision. 25c, Adoration of St. Joseph. 35c, Adoration of the Magi. 75c, The Portiuncula. $1, The Virgin and Child with St. John, 1662. $2, The Virgin and Child with St. John, 1658-64. $4, The Flight into Egypt.
No. 2399, Adoration of the Shepherds, horiz. No. 2400, Our Lady of Ransom and Two Mercedarians.

1994, Dec. 5 Litho. *Perf. 13½x14*
2391-2398 A331 Set of 8 6.50 6.50

Souvenir Sheets
2399-2400 A331 $6 each 4.50 4.50

A332

A333

Birds: 25c, Grenada dove, horiz. 35c, Grenada doves, horiz. 45c, Cuban tody. No. 2404, 75c, Grenada dove, diff. No. 2405, 75c, Painted bunting, horiz. No. 2406, $1, Grenada dove, in flight. No. 2407, $1, Red-legged honeycreeper, horiz. $5, Green jay, horiz.
No. 2409, Chestnut-sided shrike-vireo, horiz. No. 2410, Chaffinch, horiz.

1995, Jan. 10 Litho. *Perf. 14*
2401-2408 A332 Set of 8 7.25 7.25

Souvenir Sheet
2409-2410 A332 $6 each 4.50 4.50

World Wildlife Fund (#2401-2402, 2404, 2406).

1995, Jan. 12

Designs: 25c, Junior Murray, Grenada/W. Indies. 35c, R.B. Richardson, Leeward Isl./W. Indies. $2, A.J. Steward, England, horiz.
No. 2414, West Indies team, horiz.

2411-2413 A333 Set of 3 2.00 2.00

Souvenir Sheet
2414 A333 $3 multicolored 2.25 2.25

English Touring Cricket, cent.

Water Birds A334

25c, Hooded merganser. 35c, Teal. $1, Harlequin duck. $3, European wigeon.
No. 2419a, King eider. b, Shoveler. c, Long-tailed duck. d, Chiloe wigeon. e, Red-breasted merganser. f, Falcated teal. g, Vericolor teal. h, Smew. i, Red-crested pochard. j, Northern pintail. k, Barrow's goldeneye. l, Stellar's eider.
No. 2420, European wigeon, diff. No. 2421, Egyptian goose.

1995, Mar. 27 Litho. *Perf. 14*
2415-2418 A334 Set of 4 3.50 3.50

Miniature Sheet of 12
2419 A334 75c #a.-l. 6.75 6.75

Souvenir Sheets
2420 A334 $5 multicolored 3.75 3.75
2421 A334 $6 multicolored 4.50 4.50

New Year 1995 (Year of the Boar) — A335

a, 50c, Pig priest, China. b, 75c, Porcelain pig, Scotland. c, $1, Porcelain pig, Italy.
$2, Jade pig, China.

1995, Apr. 21 Litho. *Perf. 14*
2422 A335 Strip of 3, #a.-c. 1.75 1.75

Souvenir Sheet
2423 A335 $2 multicolored 1.50 1.50

No. 2422 was issued in miniature sheets containing 3 #2422.

Miniature Sheets of 6 and 8

End of World War II, 50th Anniv. A336

No. 2423A: b, Great Marianas Turkey Shoot. c, Battle of Midway. d, Battle of the Bismarck Sea. e, Musashi sinks at Leyte Gulf. f, Henderson Field. g, Battle of Guadalcanal.
Fighter planes: No. 2424a, Lavochkin LA7, Soviet Air Force. b, Hawker Hurricane, Royal Air Force (RAF). c, North American P-51D, US Army Air Force (USAAF). d, Messerschmitt ME 109F, Luftwaffe. e, Bristol Beaufighter, RAF. f, Messerschmitt ME 262, Luftwaffe. g, Republic P-47D, USAAF. h, Hawker Tempest V, RAF.
No. 2425, Nose of P-47D. No. 2425A, B-29 bomber.

1995, May 8
2423A A336 $2 #b.-g. + label 9.25 9.25
2424 A336 $2 #a.-h. + label 12.00 12.00

Souvenir Sheets
2425 A336 $6 multicolored 4.50 4.50
2425A A336 $6 multicolored 4.50 4.50

18th World Scout Jamboree, Holland — A337

Designs: a, 75c, Palm trees, scout. b, $1, Mountain climbing. c, $2, Scout salute, flag.
$6, Canoeing.

1995, May 8
2426 A337 Strip of 3, #a.-c. 2.75 2.75

Souvenir Sheet
2427 A337 $6 multicolored 4.50 4.50

No. 2426 issued in sheets of 9 stamps.

UN, 50th Anniv. — A338

Designs: a, 75c, Man bending sword into plowshare. b, $1, Earth, dove. c, $2, UN Headquarters.
$6, Emblem.

1995, May 8
2428 A338 Strip of 3, #a.-c. 2.75 2.75

Souvenir Sheet
2429 A338 $6 multicolored 4.50 4.50

No. 2428 is a continuous design and was issued in sheets of 9 stamps.

Grenada-Republic of China Friendship — A339

Designs: 75c, Flags of Grenada, Republic of China. $1, Prime Minister Nicholas Brathwaite, Grenada, Pres. Lee Teng-hui, Republic of China.

1995, Apr. 27 Litho. *Perf. 14*
2430 A339 75c multicolored .60 .60
2431 A339 $1 multicolored .75 .75
a. Souvenir sheet, #2430-2431 1.40 1.40

Domesticated Animals — A340

Designs: 10c, Cocker spaniel. 15c, Pinto. 25c, Rottweiler. 35c, German shepherd. 45c, Persian. 50c, Snowshoe. 75c, Percheron. $1, Scottish fold. $2, Arabian. $3, Andalusian. $4, C.P. shorthair. $5, Chihuahua.
No. 2445, Manx. No. 2446, Donkey. No. 2447, Shar pei.

1995, May 3
2432-2443 A340 Set of 12 13.00 13.00

Souvenir Sheets
2444-2445 A340 $5 each 3.75 3.75
2446 A340 $6 multi 4.50 4.50

Miniature Sheets of 9

Sierra Club, Cent. A341

No. 2447, vert: a, Margay, mouth open. b, Margay seated. c, Margay up close. d, Condor facing left. e, Condor facing right. f, Condor looking back. g, White-faced saki on tree limb. h, White-faced saki, face in light. i, Patagonia Region, South America.
No. 2448: a, Darwin's rhea, two facing right. b, Darwin's rhea, two facing left. c, One Darwin's rhea. d, Snow covered mountains, Patagonia Region. e, Mountain peaks, Patagonia Region. f, White-faced saki. g, Crested caracara facing right. h, Two crested caracara. i, Crested caracara facing left.

1995, May 5
2447-2448 A341 $1 #a.-i., each 6.75 6.75

FAO, 50th Anniv. — A342

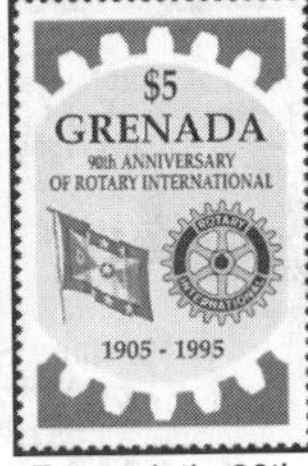
Rotary Intl., 90th Anniv. — A343

No. 2449: a, 75c, Woman with baskets. b, $1, Boy with basket. c, $2, Men working in field.
$6, FAO emblem.

1995, May 8
2449 A342 Strip of 3, #a.-c. 3.00 3.00

Souvenir Sheet
2450 A342 $6 multicolored 4.50 4.50

No. 2449 was issued in sheets of 9 stamps.

1995, May 8
2451 A343 $5 shown 3.75 3.75

Souvenir Sheet
2452 A343 $6 Paul Harris, emblem 4.50 4.50

Queen Mother, 95th Birthday — A344

No. 2453: a, Drawing. b, Holding flower. c, Formal portrait. d, Blue hat, white coat.
$6, As younger woman.

1995, May 8 ***Perf. 13½x14***

2453 A344 $1.50 Strip or block of 4, #a.-d. 4.50 4.50

Souvenir Sheet

2454 A344 $6 multicolored 4.50 4.50

No. 2453 was issued in sheets of 8 stamps.
Sheets of Nos. 2453 and 2454 exist with black border and text "In Memoriam 1900-2002" overprinted in sheet margins.

1996 Summer Olympics, Atlanta — A345

No. 2455: a, Tian Bingyi, China, badminton. b, Waldemar Leigien, Poland, Frank Wieneke, Germany, judo. c, Nelli Kim, USSR, women's gymnastics. d, Allessandro Andri, Italy, shot put.
No. 2456: a, Jackie Joyner, US, heptathlon. b, Mitsuo Tsukahara, Japan, gymnastics. c, Flo Hyman, US, Zhang Rung Fang, China, volleyball. d, Steffi Graf, Germany, tennis.
No. 2457, Sailing. No. 2458, Wilma Rudolph, US, track.

1995, June 23

2455 A345 75c Strip of 4, #a.-d. 2.25 2.25
2456 A345 $2 Strip of 4, #a.-d. 6.00 6.00

Souvenir Sheets

2457-2458 A345 $6 each 4.50 4.50

Anniversaries & Events — A346

25c, Junior Murray, cricket player. 75c, Spices. #2461, $1, Sendall Tunnel, cent. #2462, $1, Caribbean Development Bank, 25th anniv.

1995, Aug. 18 **Litho.** ***Perf. 14***

2459-2462 A346 Set of 4 2.25 2.25

Miniature Sheets of 9

Trains of the World A347

No. 2463: a, ETR 450, Italy. b, Isparta to Bozanonu, Turkey. c, TGV, France. d, ICE Inter-City Express, Germany. e, Nishi Nippon Rail, Japan. f, Bullet Train, Japan. g, Standard 4-4-0, Central Pacific RR, US. h, Amatrak 900 Bo-Bo Electric, US. i, Sir Nigel Gresley LNER, Great Britain.
No. 2464: a, Bi Level Vista Dome, Kinki Nippon Rail, Japan. b, Rolios Rail, South Africa. c, Class 460 Bo-Bo, Switzerland. d, The Central, Peru. e, X2000 Tilt Body Train, Sweden. f, Toronto-Vancouver, Canada. g, Talisman 125 Class 31, Great Britain. h, Flying Scotsman, Great Britain. i, Indian Pacific, Australia.
$5, Diesel Hydraulic, Korea. $6, Trans-Mongolian Beijing to Ulan Bator.

1995, Sept. 5

2463-2464 A347 $1 #a.-i., each 6.75 6.75

Souvenir Sheets

2465 A347 $5 multicolored 3.75 3.75
2466 A347 $6 multicolored 4.50 4.50

Singapore '95 (#2463).

Miniature Sheet of 9

Elvis Presley (1935-77) A348

Various portraits.

1995, Sept. 5 ***Perf. 13½x14***

2467 A348 $1 #a.-i. 6.75 6.75

A349

Motion Picture, Cent. A350

No. 2470: a, Film reel, Oscar statuette. b, "HOLLYWOOD" sign. c, Charlie Chaplin. d, Shirley Temple. e, Spencer Tracy, Katherine Hepburn. f, Marilyn Monroe. g, John Wayne. h, Marlon Brando. i, Tom Cruise.
$5, Orson Wells as Citizen Kane, horiz.

1995, Sept. 5 ***Perf. 14***

2468 A349 75c Marilyn Monroe .60 .60
2469 A349 75c Elvis Presley .60 .60

Miniature Sheet of 9

Perf. 13½x14

2470 A350 $1 #a.-i. 6.75 6.75

Souvenir Sheet

Perf. 14x13½

2471 A350 $5 multicolored 3.75 3.75

Nos. 2468-2469 were each issued in miniature sheets of 16. No. 2470 is a continuous design.

Local Entertainers A351

Designs: No. 2472, 35c, Ajamu, white outfit. No. 2473, 35c, Mighty Sparrow, blue suit. 50c, Mighty Sparrow, black tuxedo. 75c, Ajamu, checkered shirt, sailor hat.

1995, Sept. 5 **Litho.** ***Perf. 14***

2472-2475 A351 Set of 4 1.50 1.50

Miniature Sheets

Marine Life A352

No. 2476: a, Yellowtail damselfish. b, Bluehead wrasse. c, Balloonfish. d, Shy hamlet. e, Orange tube coral. f, Rock beauty.
No. 2477: a, Creole wrasse. b, Queen angelfish. c, Trumpetfish (e, f). d, Barred hamlet. e, Tube sponge (b, f, h, i). f, Porcupine fish. g, Fire coral (d, e, h). h, Fairy basslet. i, Anemone.
No. 2478, Elkhorn coral. No. 2479, Common seahorse, gulfweed.

1995, Apr. 24

2476 A352 $1 Sheet of 6, #a.-f. 4.50 4.50
2477 A352 $1 Sheet of 9, #a.-i. 6.75 6.75

Souvenir Sheets

2478-2479 A352 $6 each 4.50 4.50

Issued: No. 2477, 2478, 4/24/95; Nos. 2476, 2479, 9/19/95.

Mickey's High Sea Adventure A353

Designs: 15c, Mickey sword fighting with pirate. 25c, Mickey with treasure chest. 35c, Minnie trying on jewelry from chest. 75c, Pluto with telescope, Mickey over barrel. $3, Pirate. $5, Mickey holding scarf with Minnie's name.
No. 2486, Pirate fox fighting on ratlines. No. 2487, Minnie lowered from pirate ship to Mickey.

1995, Oct. 2 ***Perf. 13½x14***

2480-2485 A353 Set of 6 5.50 5.50

Souvenir Sheets

2486-2487 A353 $6 each 4.50 4.50

Miniature Sheets of 9

Nobel Prize Fund Established, Cent. — A354

Recipients: No. 2488a, Albert A. Michelson, physics, 1907. b, Ralph Bunche, peace, 1950. c, Edwin Neher, physiology or medicine, 1991. d, Klaus von Klitzing, physics, 1985. e, Johann Deisenhofer, chemistry, 1988. f, Max Delbrück, physiology or medicine, 1969. g, J. Georg Bednorz, physics, 1987. h, Feodor Lynen, physiology or medicine, 1964. i, Walther Bothe, physics, 1954.
No. 2489: a, Hans G. Dehmelt, physics, 1989. b, Heinrich Böll, literature, 1972. c, Georges Köhler, physiology or medicine, 1984. d, Wolfgang Pauli, physics, 1945. e, Sir Bernard Katz, physiology or medicine, 1970. f, Ernest Ruska, physics, 1986. g, William Golding, literature, 1983. h, Hartmut Michel, chemistry, 1988. i, Hans A. Bethe, physics, 1967.
No. 2490: a, James Franck, physics, 1925. b, Gustav Hertz, physics, 1925. c, Friedrich Bergus, chemistry, 1931. d, Otto Loewi, physiology or medicine, 1936. e, Fritz Lipmann, physiology or medicine, 1953. f, Otto Meyerhof, physiology or medicine, 1922. g, Paul Heyse, literature, 1910. h, Jane Addams, peace, 1931. i, Carl F. Braun, physics, 1909.
No. 2491, Winston Churchill, literature, 1953. No. 2492, Woodrow Wilson, peace, 1919. No. 2493, Theodore Roosevelt, peace, 1906.

1995, Oct. 18 **Litho.** ***Perf. 14***

2488-2490 A354 $1 #a.-i., each 6.75 6.75

Souvenir Sheets

2491-2493 A354 $6 each 4.50 4.50

Teresa Teng, Japanese Entertainer A355

Nos. 2495-2496: Various portraits.

1995, Sept. 29

2494 A355 75c shown .60 .60

Miniature Sheets

2495 A355 35c Sheet of 16, #a.-p. 4.25 4.25
2496 A355 75c Sheet of 9, #a.-i. 5.00 5.00

Nos. 2495a-2495p are 24x38mm.

Christmas A356

Details or entire paintings: 15c, The Madonna, by Montagna. 25c, Sacred Conversation Piece, by dei Pitati. 35c, Nativity, by Van Loo. 75c, The Virgin of the Fountain, Van Eyck. $2, Apparition of the Virgin, by Tiepolo. $5, The Holy Family, by Ribera.
No. 1503, Madonna with the Christ Child, by Van Dyck. No. 1504, Vision of St. Anthony, by Van Dyck.

1995, Nov. 28 **Litho.** ***Perf. 13½x14***

2497-2502 A356 Set of 6 6.50 6.50

Souvenir Sheets

2503-2504 A356 $6 each 4.50 4.50

Liberation of Grenada, 12th Anniv. A357

US Pres. Ronald Reagan and: No. 2505: a, Fort George. b, US, Grenada flags. c, St. George. No. 2506, Island scene, map. No. 2507, Waterfall.

1995, Dec. 8 ***Perf. 14***

2505 A357 75c Strip of 3, #a.-c. 1.75 1.75

Souvenir Sheets

2506 A357 $5 multicolored 3.75 3.75
2507 A357 $6 multicolored 4.50 4.50

No. 2505 was issued in sheets of 9 stamps.

Pope John Paul II, 1995 Visit to New York City — A358

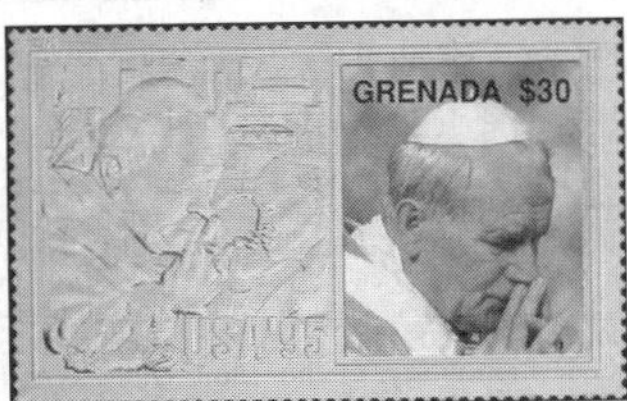

A358a

Pope John Paul II and: No. 2508, Statue of Liberty. No. 2509, St. Patrick's Cathedral. No. 2510, New York skyline.
Illustration A358a reduced.

1995, Dec. 13

2508 A358 $1 multicolored .75 .75
2509 A358 $1 multicolored .75 .75

Souvenir Sheet

2510 A358 $6 multicolored 4.50 4.50

Litho. & Embossed

Perf. 9

2510A A358a $30 gold & multi

Nos. 2508-2509 were each issued in sheets of 9.

New Year 1996 (Year of the Rat) — A359

Stylized rats: a, green & multi. b, red & multi. c, orange brown & multi.
$1, Two rats, horiz.

1996, Jan. 2 Litho. *Perf. 14*

2511 A359 75c Strip of 3, #a.-c. 1.75 1.75

Miniature Sheet

2512 A359 75c Sheet of 1 #2511 1.75 1.75

Souvenir Sheet

2513 A359 $1 multicolored .75 .75

No. 2511 was issued in sheets of 9 stamps.

Woodcuts by Dürer and Paintings by Rubens A360

Details or entire works: 15c, Young Woman, by Dürer. 25c, Four Horsemen from Apocalypse, by Dürer. 35c, Assumption and Coronation of Virgin, by Dürer. 75c, Mulay Ahmed, by Rubens. $1, Anthony Van Dyck Aged 15, by Rubens. $2, Head of a Young Monk, by Rubens. $3, A Scholar Inspired by Nature, by Rubens. $5, Hanns Dürer, by Dürer.
$5, Martrydom of St. Ursula, by Rubens. $6, The Death and Life of a Virgin, by Dürer.

1996. Jan. 29 Litho. *Perf. 13½x14*

2514-2521 A360 Set of 8 9.50 9.50

Souvenir Sheets

2522 A360 $5 multicolored 3.75 3.75
2523 A360 $6 multicolored 4.50 4.50

Disney Dancers — A361

Character, dance: 35c, Goofy, tap dance, vert. 45c, Donald, Mexican hat dance. 75c, Daisy, hula, vert. 90c, Mickey, Minnie, tango. $1, Daisy, Donald, jitterbug, vert. $2, Mickey, Minnie, Ukrainian folk dance. $3, Goofy, Pluto, ballet. $4, Minnie, Mickey, line dancing.
$5, Minnie, the can-can. $6, Scrooge McDuck, Scottish sword dance.

Perf. 13½x14, 14x 13½

1996, Feb. 26 Litho.

2524-2531 A361 Set of 8 9.50 9.50

Souvenir Sheets

2532 A361 $5 multicolored 3.75 3.75
2533 A361 $6 multicolored 4.50 4.50

Queen Elizabeth II, 70th Birthday A362

Designs: No. 2534a, 35c, In blue dress. b, 75c, In white hat. c, $4, In black hat.
$6, Younger picture with Prince Phillip.

1996, May 8 Litho. *Perf. 13½x14*

2534 A362 Strip of 3, #a.-c. 3.75 3.75

Souvenir Sheet

2535 A362 $6 multicolored 4.50 4.50

No. 2534 was issued in sheets of 9 stamps.

Ferrari Race Cars — A363

Designs: a, 125-F1. b, Tipo 625. c, P4. d, 312P. e, 312, Formula 1. f, 312B.
$6, F333 SP.

1996, May 8 *Perf. 14*

2536 A363 $1.50 Sheet of 6, #a.-f. 6.75 6.75

Souvenir Sheet

2537 A363 $6 multicolored 4.50 4.50

China '96, 9th Asian Intl. Philatelic Exhibition (#2536). No. 2537 contains one 85x28mm stamp.

Modern Olympic Games, Cent. A364

Designs: 35c, 1896 Olympic Gold Medal, vert. 75c, Olympic Stadium, Athens, 1896. $2, Ancient Greek Olympic runners. $3, Spiridon Louis, 1896 marathon winner.

1996, May 8 Litho. *Perf. 14*

2538-2541 A364 Set of 4 4.60 4.60

See Nos. 2599-2602.

Jerusalem, 3000th Anniv. — A365

Various city gates: 75c, $2, $3.
$5, Buildings inside city, horiz.

1996, June 26

2542-2544 A365 Set of 3 4.50 4.50

Souvenir Sheet

2545 A365 $5 multicolored 3.75 3.75

UNICEF, 50th Anniv. A366

Designs: 35c, Child writing in book. $2, Child planting seedling. $3, Faces of boy, girl.
$5, Boy, vert.

1996, June 26

2546-2548 A366 Set of 3 4.00 4.00

Souvenir Sheet

2549 A366 $5 multicolored 3.75 3.75

Radio, Cent. A367

Entertainers: 35c, Jack Benny. 75c, Gertrude Berg. $1, Eddie Cantor. $2, Groucho Marx.
$6, George Burns, Gracie Allen, horiz.

Perf. 13½x14, 14x13½

1996, June 26

2550-2553 A367 Set of 4 3.25 3.25

Souvenir Sheet

2554 A367 $6 multicolored 4.50 4.50

Classic Cars A368

No. 2555: a, 1939 Type 57C Atalante. b, 1900 Cannstatt-Daimler. c, 1925 Delage. d, 1899 Coventry Daimler. e, 1900 Vauxhall. f, 1912 T-15 Hispano-Suza.
No. 2556: a, 35c, 1929 Mercedes-Benz. b, 1935 J. Duesenberg. c, 1914 Mercer. d, 1927 Bugatti Type 35. e, 1929 Alfa Romeo. f, 1910 Rolls Royce.
No. 2557, 1915 L-Head Mercer. No. 2558, 1937 Mercedes.

1996, July 25 Litho. *Perf. 14*

2555 A368 $1 Sheet of 6, #a.-f. 4.50 4.50
2556 A368 Sheet of 6, #a.-f. 5.75 5.75

Souvenir Sheets

2557-2558 A368 $6 each 4.50 4.50

Nos. 2557-2558 each contain one 57x43mm stamp.

Ships A369

War ships: No. 2559: a, Bounty, Britain, 1788. b, Bismark, Germany, 1941. c, Chuii Apoo, China, 1849. d, F224 Lubeck, Germany, 1970. e, Barbary Corsair, France, 1655. f, Augsburg, Germany, 1970. g, Henri Grace A Dieu, 1514, France. h, Prince of Wales, Britain, 1941. i, Santa Anna, Spain, 1512.
Sailing ships: No. 2560a, Gorch Fock, Germany, 1916. b, Henry B. Hyde, US, 1886. c, Resolution, Britain, 1652. d, USS Constitution, 1797. e, Nippon Maru, Japan, 1930. f, Preussen, Germany, 1902. g, Taeping, Britain, 1852. h, Chariot of Fame, US, 1853. i, Star of India, US, 1861.
$5, Victory, Britain, 1805. $6, Cutty Sark, Britain, 1869.

1996, Aug. 14

Sheets of 9

2559-2560 A368 $1 #a.-i., each 6.75 6.75

Souvenir Sheets

2561 A369 $5 multicolored 3.75 3.75
2562 A369 $6 multicolored 4.50 4.50

Trains A370

Designs: 35c, C51 Imperial Train, Japan. 75c, Reingold, Germany. $2, Pioneer, US. $3, LA France, France.
Trains of the Orient: No. 2567: a, C62 4-6-4, Japanese Natl. Railways. b, 4-6-0, Shantung Railways, China. c, C57 Light 4-6-2, Japanese Natl. Railways. d, Diesel Express, Japanese Natl. Railways. e, 4-6-2, Shanghai-Nanking Railway, China. f, 051 2-8-2, Japanese Natl. Railways.
Trains of the world: No. 2568a, Atlantic Coast Line, US. b, #1619, Pioneer Smith Compound, England. c, 4-8-4 Trans-Siberian Railway. d, "Atlantic type," Palatinate Railway, Germany. e, 4-6-0 Paris, Lyons and Mediterranean Railway, France. f, 0341 Diesel Electric, Italian State Railways.
$5, Baden State Railways, Germany. $6, C11 2-6-4, Japanese National Railways.

1996, Aug. 28

2563-2566 A370 Set of 4 4.50 4.50

Sheets of 6

2567-2568 A370 $1 #a.-f., each 4.50 4.50

Souvenir Sheets

2569 A370 $5 multicolored 3.75 3.75
2570 A370 $6 multicolored 4.50 4.50

Flowers A371

No. 2571: a, Winter jasmine. b, Chrysanthemum. c, Lilac. d, Japanese iris. e, Hibiscus. f, Sacred lotus. g, Apple blossom. h, Gladiolus. i, Japanese quince.
No. 2572, vert: a, Canterbury bell. b, Rose. c, Nasturtium. d, Daffodil. e, Tulip. f, Snapdragon. g, Zinnia. h, Sweetpea. i, Pansy.
$5, Aster. $6, Peony, vert.

1996, Sept. 9 Litho. *Perf. 14*

Sheets of 9

2571-2572 A371 $1 #a.-i., each 6.75 6.75

Souvenir Sheets

2573 A371 $5 multicolored 3.75 3.75
2574 A371 $6 multicolored 4.50 4.50

Zeppelins A372

No. 2575: a, 30c, L31, Germany. b, 30c, L35, Germany. c, 50c, L30, Germany. d, 75c, LZ10, Germany. e, $3, L3, Germany. f, $3, Beardmore No. 24, British.

No. 2576: a, Zeppelin L21, Germany. b, Zodiac Type 13 Spiess, France. c, NI "Norge." d, D-LZ 127 "Graf Zeppelin," Germany. e, D-LZ 129 "Hindenburg," Germany. f, Zeppelin NT, Germany, 1996.

No. 2577, L13, Germany. No. 2578, Zeppelin ZT, Germany.

1996, Sept. 9

Sheets of 6

2575 A372 #a.-f. 6.00 6.00
2576 A372 $1.50 #a.-f. 6.75 6.75

Souvenir Sheets

2577-2578 A372 $6 each 4.50 4.50

Birds A373

No. 2579: a, Horned guan. b, St. Lucia parrot. c, Black penelopina. d, Grenada dove. e, St. Vincent parrot. f, White-breasted thrasher.

$5, Barbados yellow warbler. $6, Semper's warbler.

1996

2579 A373 $1.50 Sheet of 6, #a.-f. 6.75 6.75

Souvenir Sheets

2580 A373 $5 multicolored 3.75 3.75
2581 A373 $6 multicolored 4.50 4.50

Endangered Species — A374

Designs: a, Blue whale. b, Humpback whale. c, Right whale. d, Hawksbill turtle. e, Leatherback turtle. f, Green turtle.

1996, Sept. 18 Litho. *Perf. 14*

2582 A374 $1.50 Sheet of 6, #a.-f. 6.75 6.75

Jacqueline Kennedy Onassis (1929-94) — A375

Various portraits.

1996, Aug. 26

2583 A375 $1 Sheet of 9, #a.-i. 6.75 6.75

Souvenir Sheet

2584 A375 $6 multicolored 4.50 4.50

Butterfly Type of 1994

90c, Tropical chequered skipper. $1.50, Godman's hairstreak.

1996, Nov. 7 Litho. *Perf. 12*

2585 A328 90c multicolored .70 .70
2586 A328 $1.50 multicolored 1.10 1.10

A376

1996, Nov. 7 *Perf. 14*

Sea Creatures: No. 2587: a, Killer whale. b, Dolphin. c, Dolphins. d, Sea lion, royal angelfish. e, Dolphins, hawksbill turtle. f, Hawksbill turtles (e). g, Royal angelfish. h, Pennant butterflyfish. i, Sea lion, squirrel fish.

No. 2588: a, Brown pelican. b, Killer whale. c, Whale (c). d, Dolphins, sea lion. e, Shortfin pilot whale, blue ringed octopus, sea lion (d, f, h). f, Hammerhead sharks, sea lion. g, Blue striped grunts. h, Stingray, Van Gogh fusiliers (i). i, Van Gogh fusiliers, golden coney, ribbon moray eel (h).

No. 2589, Sea lions, horiz. No. 2590, Dolphins, horiz.

2587-2588 A376 $1 Sheets of 9, #a.-i., each 7.00 7.00

Souvenir Sheets

2589-2590 A376 $6 each 4.50 4.50

Christmas A377

Details or entire paintings: 25c, The Visitation, by Tintoretto. 35c, Virgin with the Child, by Palma Vecchio. 50c, The Adoration of the Magi, by Botticelli. 75c, The Annunciation, by Titian. $1, The Flight into Egypt, by Tintoretto. $3, The Holy Family with the Infant Saint John, by Andrea Del Sarto.

#2597, Adoration of the Magi, by Paolo Schiavo. #2598, Madonna and Child with Saints, by Vincenzo Foppa.

1996, Nov. 18 *Perf. 13½x14*

2591-2596 A377 Set of 6 4.50 4.50

Souvenir Sheets

2597-2598 A377 $6 each 4.50 4.50

Modern Olympic Games Type of 1996

Marathon medalists: No. 2599: a, Boughera El Quafi, 1928. b, Gustav Jansson, 1952. c, Spiridon Louis, 1896. d, Basil Heatley, 1964. e, Emil Zatopek, 1952. f, Frank Shorter, 1972. g, Alain Mimoun, 1956. h, Kokichi Tsuburaya, 1964. i, Delfo Cabrera, 1948.

Weight lifting medalists: No. 2600: a, Harald Sakata, 1948. b, Tom Kono, 1952. c, Naim Suleymanoglu, 1988. d, Lee Hyung Kun, 1988. e, Vassily Alexeyev, 1972. f, Chen Weiqiang, 1984. g, Ye Huanming, 1988. h, Manfred Nerlinger, 1984. i, Joseph Depietro, 1948.

$5, Manfred Nerlinger, vert. $6, Thomas Hicks, 1904, vert.

1996, July 8 Litho. *Perf. 14*

Sheets of 9

2599-2600 A364 $1 #a.-i., each 6.75 6.75

Souvenir Sheets

2601 A364 $5 multicolored 3.75 3.75
2602 A364 $6 multicolored 4.50 4.50

US Pres. Ronald Reagan A378

Various portraits.

1996, Aug. 26 *Perf. 13½*

2603 A378 $1 Sheet of 9, #a.-i. 6.75 6.75

Sylvester Stallone in Movie, "Rocky" — A379

1996, Nov. 21 Litho. *Perf. 14*

2604 A379 $2 Sheet of 3 4.50 4.50

New Year 1997 (Year of the Ox) — A380

Oxen: Nos. 2605a, 2606a, Horns pointed down. Nos. 2605b, 2606b, Horns pointed up. Nos. 2605c, 2606c, Shown.

Illustration reduced.

Serpentine Die Cut 11

1997, Jan. 2 Litho.

Self-Adhesive

Sheets of 3

2605 A380 $2 #a.-c., gold & multi 4.50 4.50
2606 A380 $2 #a.-c., sil & multi 4.50 4.50

Mickey Visits Hong Kong — A381

No. 2607: a, Pet birds. b, Kung-fu tea. c, Chinese Wet Market. d, Handmade grasshopper. e, Mid-Autumn Festival. f, Tai-chi.

No. 2608: a, 35c, Tram. b, 50c, Victoria Harbor. c, 75c, Buddha. d, 90c, Bank of China. e, $2, Bottle gas. f, $3, Seafood restaurant.

No. 2609, Mickey at The Peak, vert. $4, Minnie, Mickey, Hong Kong mail, vert. $5, Mickey pulling rickshaw, vert. $6, Mickey at Peking Noodle Show, vert.

1997, Feb. 12 Litho. *Perf. 14x13½*

2607 A381 $1 Sheet of 6, #a.-f. 4.50 4.50
2608 A381 Sheet of 6, #a.-f. 5.75 5.75

Souvenir Sheets

Perf. 13½x14

2609 A381 $3 multicolored 2.25 2.25
2610 A381 $4 multicolored 3.00 3.00
2611 A381 $5 multicolored 3.75 3.75
2612 A381 $6 multicolored 4.50 4.50

Hong Kong '97.

UNESCO, 50th Anniv. — A382

Designs: 35c, Kyoto, Japan. 75c, Quedlinburg, Germany. 90c, Dubrovnik, Croatia. $1, Ruins, Delphi, Greece. $2, Tomar, Portugal. $3, Palace of Chaillot, Paris, France.

No. 2619, Chinese sites, vert.: a, Entrance to caves, Desert of Taklamakan. b, House, Taklamakan. c, Monument, Taklamakan. d, Palace of Cielos Purpuras, Wudang. e, House, Wudang. f, Stone Guard, Great Wall. g, Ming Dynasty, Wudang. h, Section, Great Wall.

No. 2620, vert.: a, Bryggen Wharf, Bergen, Norway. b, Old City of Bern, Switzerland. c, Warsaw, Poland. d, Fortress Walls, Luxembourg. e, Palace of Drottningholm, Sweden. f, Petäj ävesi Old Church, Finland. g, Vilnius, Lithuania. h, Church of Jelling, Denmark.

No. 2621: a, Cathedral, Segovia, Spain. b, ürzburg, Germany. c, Lakes of Plitvice, Croatia. d, Monastery of Batalha, Portugal. e, River Seine, Paris, France.

No. 2622, Monastery of Popocatepetl, Mexico. No. 2623, Shirakami-Sanchi, Japan. No. 2624, Monastery of the Hieronymites and Tower of Belem, Portugal.

1997, Apr. 3 Litho. *Perf. 14*

2613-2618 A382 Set of 6 6.00 6.00

Sheets of 8 or 5 + Label

2619-2620 A382 $1 #a.-h., each 6.00 6.00
2621 A382 $1.50 #a.-e. 5.75 5.75

Souvenir Sheets

2622-2624 A382 $6 each 4.50 4.50

Cats — A383

Dogs — A384

Cats: 35c, Devon rex. 90c, Japanese bobtail. $2, Cornish rex.

No. 2628: a, Turkish van. b, Ragdoll. c, Siberian. d, Egyptian mau. e, American shorthair. f, Bengal. g, Asian longhair. h, Somali. i, Turkish angora.

1997, Apr. 10

2625-2627 A383 Set of 3 2.50 2.50

Sheet of 9

2628 A383 $1 #a.-i. 6.75 6.75

Souvenir Sheet

2629 A383 $6 Singapura 4.50 4.50

1997, Apr. 10

Dogs: 75c, Cavalier King Charles spaniel. $1, Afghan hound. $3, Pekingese.

No. 2633: a, Lhasa apso. b, Rough collie. c, Norwich terrier. d, America cocker spaniel. e, Chinese crested dog. f, Old English sheepdog. g, Standard poodle. h, German shepherd. i, German shorthaired pointer.

No. 2634, Bernese mountain dog.

2630-2632 A384 Set of 3 3.50 3.50

Sheet of 9

2633 A384 $1 #a.-i. 6.75 6.75

Souvenir Sheet

2634 A384 $6 multicolored 4.50 4.50

Prehistoric Animals — A385

Designs: 35c, Dunkleosteus. 75c, Tyrannosaurus rex. $2, Askeptosaurus, vert. $3, Triceratops, vert.

No. 2639: a, Sordes. b, Dimorphodon. c, Diplodocus. d, Allosaurus. e, Pentaceratops. f, Protoceratops.

No. 2640, Maiasaura, vert. No. 2641, Trystychius, Cladoselache, vert.

1997, Apr. 15

2635-2638 A385 Set of 4 4.50 4.50
2639 A385 $1.50 Sheet of 6, #a.-f. 6.75 6.75

Souvenir Sheets

2640-2641 A385 $6 each 4.50 4.50

Marine Life A386

Designs: 45c, Porcelain crab. 75c, Humpback whale. 90c, Hermit crab. $1, Great white shark. $3, Green sea turtle. $4, Whale shark.
No. 2648, vert: a, Octopus. b, Lei triggerfish. c, Lionfish. d, Harlequin wrasse. e, Clown fish. f, Moray eel.
No. 2649, Pacific barracudas. No. 2650, Scalloped hammerhead shark.

1997, May 2
2642-2647 A386 Set of 6 7.50 7.50
2648 A386 $1.50 Sheet of 6, #a.-f. 6.75 6.75

Souvenir Sheets
2649-2650 A386 $6 each 4.50 4.50

Queen Elizabeth II, Prince Philip, 50th Wedding Anniv. A386a

No. 2651: a, Queen, Prince waving. b, Royal Arms. c, Formal portrait in royal attire. d, Formal portrait in street clothes. e, Windsor Castle. f, Prince Philip.
$6, Formal portrait in royal attire, diff.

1997, May 28 Litho. *Perf. 14*
2651 A386a $1 Sheet of 6, #a.-f. 4.50 4.50

Souvenir Sheet
2652 A386a $6 multicolored 4.50 4.50

Paintings by Hiroshige (1797-1858) A387

No. 2653: a, Nihon Embankment, Yoshiwara. b, Asakusa Ricefields and Torinomachi Festival. c, Senju Great Bridge. d, Dawn Inside the Yoshiwara. e, Tile Kilns and Hasiba Ferry, Sumida River. f, View from Massaki of Suijin Shrine, Uchigawa Inlet and Sekiya.
No. 2654, Kinryuzan Temple, Asakusa. No. 2655, Night View of Saruwaka-machi.

1997, May 28 *Perf. 13½x14*
2653 A387 $1.50 Sheet of 6, #a.-f. 6.75 6.75

Souvenir Sheets
2654-2655 A387 $6 each 4.50 4.50

Heinrich von Stephan (1831-97), Founder of UPU A388

No. 2656: a, Postal delivery on motorcycle. b, UPU emblem. c, Postal delivery on skis and snowshoes, Rockies, 1900. $6, Chinese long distance carrier.

1997, May 28 Litho. *Perf. 14*
2656 A388 $2 Sheet of 3, #a.-c. 4.50 4.50

Souvenir Sheet
2657 A388 $6 multicolored 4.50 4.50

PACIFIC 97.

Paul P. Harris (1868-1947), Founder of Rotary, Intl. — A389

Designs: $3, Rotary emblem, vocational training service program, The Philippines, portrait of Harris.
$6, Doves, hands holding globe inscribed "Act with Integrity, Serve with love, Work for Peace".

1997, May 28
2658 A389 $3 multicolored 2.25 2.25

Souvenir Sheet
2659 A389 $6 multicolored 4.50 4.50

Chernobyl Disaster, 10th Anniv. A390

Designs: No. 2660, Chabad's Children of Chernobyl. No. 2661, UNESCO.

1997, May 28 *Perf. 13½x14*
2660 A390 $2 multicolored 1.50 1.50
2661 A390 $2 multicolored 1.50 1.50

Grimm's Fairy Tales A391

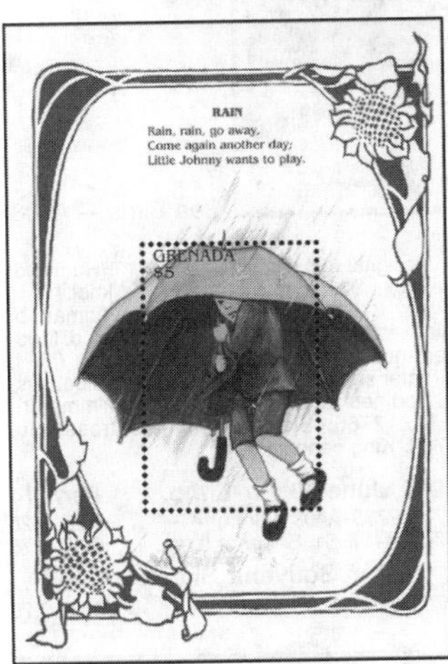
Mother Goose — A392

Scenes from "Snow White and the Seven Dwarfs:" No. 2662: a, Witch as woman looking into mirror. b, Dwarfs looking at Snow White as she sleeps. c, Snow White awakening, Prince. $6, Witch holding out apple for Snow White.
$5, "Little Johnny" walking in rain with umbrella.

1997, May 28 *Perf. 13½x14*
2662 A391 $2 Sheet of 3, #a.-c. 4.50 4.50

Souvenir Sheets
Perf. 14, 13½x14
2663 A392 $5 multicolored 3.75 3.75
2664 A391 $6 multicolored 4.50 4.50

1998 Winter Olympics Games, Nagano A393

Designs: 45c, Luge. 75c, Speed skater in red. $2, Male figure skater. $3, Slalom skier.
No. 2669: a, Luge, diff. b, Ski jumper. c, Downhill skier. d, Speed skater in blue. e, Two-man bobsled. f, Female figure skater. g, Biathlon. h, Hockey. i, Freestyle skier upside down.
No. 2670, Downhill skier in air, vert. No. 2671, 4-Man bobsled.

1997, June 26 *Perf. 14*
2665-2668 A393 Set of 4 4.75 4.75
2669 A393 $1 Sheet of 9, #a.-i. 6.75 6.75

Souvenir Sheets
2670-2671 A393 $6 each 4.50 4.50

Return of Hong Kong to China — A394

Views of city, Chinese flag as Chinese inscription: 90c, Bank of China, night scene. $1, Skyscrapers. $1.75, "Hong Kong," city in lights, horiz. $2, Deng Xiaoping (1904-97), Hong Kong, horiz.

1997, July 1
2672-2675 A394 Set of 4 4.25 4.25

Nos. 2672-2673 were issued in sheets of 4. Nos. 2674-2675 are 59x28mm and were issued in sheets of 3.

Disney's Hercules A395

No. 2676: a, Hercules. b, Pegasus. c, Megara. d, Philoctetes. e, Nessus. f, Hydra. g, Pain and Panic. h, Hades.
No. 2677, Young Hercules. No. 2678, Calliope surrounded by Terpsichore, Melpomene, Clio, Thalia.

1997, Aug. 7 Litho. *Perf. 13½x14*
2676 A395 $1 Sheet of 8, #a.-h. 6.00 6.00

Souvenir Sheets
2677-2678 A396 $6 each 4.50 4.50

Butterflies A396

Designs: 45c, Peacock. 75c, Orange flambeau. 90c, Eastern tailed blue. $2, Black and red. $3, Large white. $4, Oriental swallowtail.
No. 2685: a, Brimstone. b, Mocker swallowtail. c, American painted lady. d, Tiger swallowtail. e, Long wing. f, Sunset moth. g, Australian blue mountain swallowtail. h, Bird wing.
No. 2686, Monarch. No. 2687, Blue morpho.

1997, Aug. 12 *Perf. 14*
2679-2684 A396 Set of 6 8.50 8.50
2685 A396 $1 Sheet of 8, #a.-h. 6.00 6.00

Souvenir Sheets
2686-2687 A396 $5 each 3.75 3.75

1998 World Cup Soccer Championships, France — A397

Various actions scenes from Italy v. West Germany, 1982. 15c, 75c, 90c, $2, $3, $4, vert.
Winning teams: No. 2694: a, Uruguay. b, Brazil, 1958. c, Germany. d, Argentina. e, Italy. f, West Germany. g, Italy. h, Brazil, 1970.
Soccer players: No. 2695: a, Seaman, England. b, Klinsmann, Germany. c, Berger, Czech Rep. d, McCoist, Scotland. e, Gascoigne, England. f, Djorkaeff, France. g, Sammer, Germany. h, Futre, Portugal.
No. 2696, Beckenbauer, Germany, vert. No. 2697, Moore, England.

1997 *Perf. 13½x14*
2688-2693 A397 Set of 6 8.00 8.00

Sheets of 8
Perf. 14x13½
2694-2695 A397 $1 #a.-h. + label 6.00 6.00

Souvenir Sheets
2696-2697 A397 $6 each 4.50 4.50

Minnie Mouse in Hawaiian Holiday — A398

Stamps in flip book sequence showing Minnie doing Hula dance: No. 2698: a, 1. b, 2. c, 3. d, 4. e, 5. f, 6. g, 7. h, 8.
No. 2699: a, 9. b, 10. c, 11. d, 12. e, 13. f, 14. g, 15. h, 16. i, 17.
$6, 18.

1997, Aug. 7 Litho. *Perf. 14x13½*

Sheets of 8 or 9
2698 A398 50c #a.-h. + label 3.00 3.00
2699 A398 50c #a.-i. 3.50 3.50

Souvenir Sheet
2700 A398 $6 multicolored 4.50 4.50

PACIFIC 97.

Mushrooms — A399

Designs: 35c, Boletus erythropus. 75c, Armillariella mellea. 90c, Amanita flavorubens. $1, Indigo milky. $2, Tylopilus balloui. $4, Boletus parasiticus.
No. 2707: a, Boletus parasiticus, diff. b, Frostis bolete. c, Amanita myscara flavilolvata. d, Volvariella volvacea. e, Stuntz's blue legs. f, Orange-latex milky.
No. 2708: a, Agaricus solidipes. b, Salmon waxy cap. c, Fused marasmius. d, Shellfish-scented russula. e, Red-capped scaber stalk. f, Calocybe tricholoma gambosum.
No. 2709, Omphalotus illudens. No. 2710, Agaricus agrenteus.

1997, Sept. 4 *Perf. 14*
2701-2706 A399 Set of 6 6.75 6.75

Sheets of 6
2707-2708 A399 $1.50 #a.-f., ea 6.75 6.75

Souvenir Sheets
2709-2710 A399 $6 each 4.50 4.50

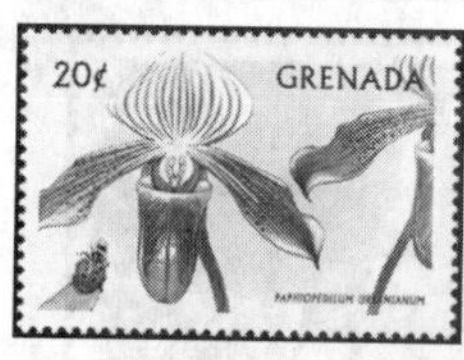
Orchids
A400

Designs: 20c, Paphiopedilum urbanianum. 35c, Trichoceros parviflorus. 45c, Euanthe sanderiana, vert. 75c, Oncidium macranthum, vert. 90c, Psychopsis kramerianum, vert. $1, Oncidium hastatum, vert. $3, Masdevallia saltatrix, vert. $4, Cattleya luteola.

No. 2719, vert: a, Odontoglossum crispum. b, Cattleya brabantiae. c, Cattleya bicolor. d, Trichopilia suavia. e, Encyclia mariae. f, Angraecum leonis.

No. 2720, vert: a, Broughtonia sanguinea. b, Anguloa virginalis. c, Dendrobium Bigibbum. d, T. forcia, L. lucasiana. e, Cymbidium. f, Cymbidium, diff.

No. 2721, Oncidium onustum. No. 2722, Laelia milleri.

1997, Sept. 4

2711-2718 A400 Set of 8 8.00 8.00

Sheets of 6

2719-2720 A400 $2 #a.-f., each 9.00 9.00

Souvenir Sheets

2721-2722 A400 $6 each 4.50 4.50

Diana, Princess of Wales (1961-97) — A401

Various portraits.

1997, Oct. 15 Litho. *Perf. 14½*

2723 A401 $1.50 Sheet of 6, #a.-f. 6.75 6.75

Souvenir Sheet

2724 A401 $5 multicolored 3.75 3.75

Christmas — A402

Works of art, entire paintings, or details: 35c, Angel, by Matthias Grunewald. 50c, Saint Demetrius (icon). 75c, Reliquary in the Form of a Triptych. $1, Angel of the Annunciation, by Jan van Eyck. $3, The Annunciation, by Simone Martini. $4, Saint Michael (mosaic).

No. 2731, The Annunciation, by Titian, horiz. No. 2732, The Coronation of the Virgin, by Fra Angelico.

1997, Dec. 5 Litho. *Perf. 14*

2725-2730 A402 Set of 6 12.00 12.00

Souvenir Sheets

2731-2732 A402 $6 each 4.50 4.50

New Year 1998 (Year of the Tiger) — A403

Designs: a, shown, b, With mouth open. c, With ears rolled back. Illustration reduced.

1998, Jan. 5 Litho. *Die Cut Perf. 9*

Self-Adhesive

Sheets of 3, #a.-c.

2733 A403 $1.50 gold & multi
2734 A403 $1.50 sil & multi

Nos. 2733b, 2734b have point of triangle down.

Fish
A404

65c, Black-tailed humbug. 90c, Yellow sweetlips. $1, Common squrrelfish. $2, Powder blue surgeon.

No. 2739: a, Blue tang. b, Porkfish. c, Banded butterflyfish. d, Threadfin butterflyfish. e, Red-headed. f, Emperor angelfish.

No. 2740: a, Scribbled angelfish. b, Lemonpeel angelfish. c, Bandit angelfish. d, Bicolor cherub. e, Regal tang. f, Yellow tang.

No. 2741, Two-banded anemonefish. No. 2742, Long-nosed butterflyfish.

1998, Feb. 10 Litho. *Perf. 14*

2735-2738 A404 Set of 4 3.50 3.50

Sheets of 6, #a.-f.

2739-2740 A404 $1.50 each 6.75 6.75

Souvenir Sheets

2741-2742 A404 $6 each 4.50 4.50

Orchids
A405

No. 2743: a, Arachnis clarkei. b, Cymbidium eburneum. c, Dendrobium chrysotoxum. d, Paphiopedilum insigne. e, Paphiopedilum venustum. f, Renanthera imschootiana.

No. 2744: a, Sophronitis grandiflora. b, Phalaenopsis amboinensis. c, Zygopetalum intermedium. d, Paphiopedilum purpuratum. e, Miltonia regnellii. f, Dendrobium parishii.

No. 2745, Lycaste aromatica. No. 2746, Pleione maculata.

1998, Apr. 21 Litho. *Perf. 14*

Sheets of 6, #a.-f.

2743-2744 A405 $1.50 each 6.75 6.75

Souvenir Sheets

2745-2746 A405 $6 multicolored 4.50 4.50

Ships
A406

No. 2747: a, Brig. b, Clipper. c, Caique. d, Mississippi Riverboat. e, Luxury liner. f, The Mayflower. g, Frigate. h, Janggolan. i, Junk.

No. 2748: a, Dhow. b, Galleon. c, Felucca. d, Schooner. e, Aircraft carrier. f, Knau. g, Destroyer. h, Longship. i, Queen Elizabeth 2.

#2749, The Lusitania. #2750, Submarine.

1998, Apr. 26 Litho. *Perf. 14*

Sheets of 9

2747-2748 A406 $1 #a.-i., each 6.75 6.75

Souvenir Sheets

2749-2750 A406 $6 each 4.50 4.50

No. 2749 contains one 85x28mm stamp; No. 2750 one 56x42mm stamp.

Disney's Hercules
A407

Hercules grows up - #2751: a, Hercules, Zeus. b, Hercules and Pegasus walking past creature. c, Phil, Hercules. d, Hercules swinging through air. e, Centaur carrying captured Meg. f, Hercules attacking centaur. g, Hercules fighting lion. h, Hercules, Pegasus looking at prints.

Birth and childhood of Hercules - #2752: a, Zeus and Hera with newborn Hercules. b, Hades finds baby. c, Hades in the night. d, Baby sleeping. e, Baby swept away by Pain and Panic. f, Old couple with Baby Hercules. g, Hercules pulling cart. h, Hercules looking into mirror.

Hercules triumphant - #2753: a, Hercules carrying Meg. b, Meg, Hades. c, Hercules being trained by Phil. d, Hercules meeting Hades. e, Monster coming through city. f, Zeus. g, Hercules lifting column off Meg. h, Hercules diving into water.

#2754, Hercules with sword, fighting Hydra. #2755, Hades on fire. #2756, Hercules, Meg on Pegasus, horiz. #2757, Zeus, Hercules, horiz. #2758, Hades. #2759, Zeus with baby Pegasus.

1998, June 16 Litho. *Perf. 13½x14*

Sheets of 8

2751 A407 10c #a.-h. .60 .60
2752-2753 A407 $1 #a.-h., each 6.00 6.00

Souvenir Sheets

2754-2759 A407 $6 each 4.50 4.50

Sea Birds — A408

Designs: 90c, Arctic skua. $1.10, Humboldt penguin. $2, Herring gull. $3, Red knot.

No. 2764, horiz.: a, Northern fulmar. b, Black-legged kittiwake. c, Cape petrel. d, Mediterranean gull. e, Brandt's cormorant (h). f, Greater shearwater. g, Black-footed albatross. h, Red-necked phalarope. i, Black skimmer (f).

No. 2765, Black-browed albatross. No. 2766, King penguin.

1998, June 30 Litho. *Perf. 14*

2760-2763 A408 Set of 4 5.25 5.25
2764 A408 $1 Sheet of 9, #a.-i. 6.75 6.75

Souvenir Sheets

2765-2766 A408 $5 each 3.75 3.75

Diana, Princess of Wales (1961-97) — A409

Portrait of Diana with rose: No. 2767, Wearing hat. No. 2768, Without hat. Illustration reduced.

Litho. & Embossed

1998, July 14 *Die Cut 7½*

2767 A409 $20 gold & multi
2768 A409 $20 gold & multi

Supermarine Spitfires — A410

No. 2769: a, MK IX. b, MK XIV. c, MK XII. d, MK XI. e, H.F. MK VIII. f, MK VB.

No. 2770: a, MK I. b, MK VIII. c, MK III. d, MK XVI. e, MK V. f, MK XIX.

No. 2771, MK IX. No. 2772, MK IA.

1998, July 20 Litho. *Perf. 14*

Sheets of 6, #a.-f.

2769-2770 A410 $1.50 each 6.75 6.75

Souvenir Sheets

2771-2772 A410 $6 each 4.50 4.50

Nos. 2771-2772 each contain one 57x43mm stamp.

Intl. Year of the Ocean
A411

No. 2773: a, Walrus. b, African black footed penguins. c, African black-footed penguin. d, California sea lion. e, Green turtle. f, Redfin anthias. g, Sperm whale. h, French angelfish, Australian sea lion. i, Jellyfish. j, Sawfish. k, Male and female cuckoo wrasse. l, Garibaldi. m, Spinecheek anemonefish. n, Leafy seadragon. o, Blue-spotted goatfish. p, Two-spot gobies.

No. 2774, Atlantic spotted dolphins. No. 2775, Octopus.

1998, Aug. 19

2773 A411 75c Sheet of 16, #a.-p. 9.00 9.00

Souvenir Sheets

2774 A411 $5 multicolored 3.75 3.75
2775 A411 $6 multicolored 4.50 4.50

CARICOM, 25th Anniv. — A412

1998, Sept. 13 Litho. *Perf. 13½*

2776 A412 $1 multicolored .75 .75

Mahatma Gandhi (1869-1948)
A413

Design: $6, Portrait, head down.

1998, Sept. 13 *Perf. 14*

2777 A413 $1 multicolored 1.50 1.50

Souvenir Sheet

2778 A413 $6 multicolored 4.50 4.50

No. 2777 was issued in sheets of 4.

Paintings by Pablo Picasso (1881-1973) — A414

45c, The Bathers, 1918, vert. $2, Luncheon on the Grass, 1960. $3, The Swimmer, 1929. $5, Woman Reading, 1944, vert.

Perf. 14½x14, 14x14½

1998, Sept. 15

2779-2781 A414 Set of 3 4.25 4.25

Souvenir Sheet

2782 A414 $5 multicolored 3.75 3.75

Paintings by Eugéne Delacroix (1798-1863) — A415

No. 2783: a, Horsemen Fighting in the Plain. b, The Assassination of the Bishop of Liege. c, Still-life with Lobsters. d, The Battle of Nancy. e, The Shipwreck of Don Juan. f, The Death of Ophelia. g, Attila and the Barbarians. h, Entertaining the Arabians.

$5, Entry of the Cruaders into Constantinople.

1998, Sept. 15 ***Perf. 14***

Sheet of 8

2783 A415 $1 #a.-h. 6.00 6.00

Souvenir Sheet

2784 A415 $5 multicolored 3.75 3.75

Organization of American States, 50th Anniv. A416

1998, Sept. 15 **Litho.** ***Perf. 14***

2785 A416 $1 multicolored .75 .75

Diana, Princess of Wales (1961-97) A417

1998 ***Perf. 14½***

2786 A417 $1 multicolored .75 .75

Self-Adhesive

Serpentine Die Cut Perf. 11½

Sheet of 1

Size: 52x65mm

2786A A417 $6 Diana, buildings

No. 2786 was issued in sheets of 6.

Soaking in water may affect the multi-layer image of No. 2786A.

Issued: $1, 9/15; $6, 11/5/98.

Enzo Ferrari (1898-1988), Automobile Manufacturer — A418

No. 2787: a, 250 GT Berlinetta Lusso. b, 250 GTO. c, 250 GT Boano/Ellena cabriolet.

$5, Dino 246 GTS.

1998, Sept. 15 ***Perf. 14***

2787 A418 $2 Sheet of 3, #a.-c. 4.50 4.50

Souvenir Sheet

2788 A418 $5 multicolored 3.75 3.75

No. 2786 was issued in sheets of 6. No. 2788 contains one 91x35mm stamp.

1998 World Scouting Jamboree, Chile — A419

Designs: $2, Scout salute. $3, World Scout flag. $4, Scout first aid. $6, World Scout flag.

1998, Sept. 15

2789-2791 A419 Set of 3 6.75 6.75

Souvenir Sheet

2792 A419 $6 multi, horiz. 4.50 4.50

Royal Air Force, 80th Anniv. A420

No. 2793: a, Vickers Supermarine Spitfire Mk2a. b, Vickers Supermarine Spitfire HF Mk1XB flying right. c, Vickers Supermarine Spitfire HF Mk1Xb flying left. d, Hawker Hurricane 11C.

No. 2794: a, EF-2000 Eurofighter prototype. b, Nimrod MR2P. c, Eurofighter 2000, diff. d, C-47 Dakota.

No. 2795, Eurofighter 2000, VC10. No. 2796, Biplane, hawk's head. No. 2797, Biplane, hawk. No. 2798, Eurofighter 2000, Jet Provost.

1998, Sept. 15

Sheets of 4

2793-2794 A420 $2 #a.-d., each 6.00 6.00

Souvenir Sheets

2795-2798 A420 $6 each 4.50 4.50

Tennis Stars A421

45c, Arthur Ashe. 75c, Martina Hingis. 90c, Chris Evert. $1, Steffi Graf. $1.50, Arantxa Sanchez Vicario. $3, Martina Navratilova. $2, Monica Seles. $6, Martina Hingis, diff.

1998, Oct. 28

2799-2805 A421 Set of 7 7.25 7.25

Souvenir Sheet

2806 A421 $6 multicolored 4.50 4.50

Peacekeepers, Beirut, Lebanon, 1982-84 — A422

1998, Nov. 30 **Litho.** ***Perf. 14***

2807 A422 $1 multicolored .80 .80

Christmas A423

Birds: 45c, Blue-hooded Euphonia. 75c, Black-bellied whistling duck. 90c, Purple martin. $1, Imperial parrot. $2, Adelaide's warbler. $3, Roseate flamingo.

$5, Green-throated carib. $6, Purple-throated carib, Canada #85.

1998, Dec. 1

2808-2813 A423 Set of 6 6.25 6.25

Souvenir Sheet

2814 A423 $5 multicolored 3.75 3.75
2815 A423 $6 multicolored 4.50 4.50

No. 2815 contains one 38x61mm stamp.

Christmas — A424

Works of art: 35c, Painting, The Angel's Parting from Tobias, by Jean Bilevelt. 45c, Painting, Allegory of Faith, by Moretto da Brescia. 90c, Sculpture, Cross, with Depiction of the Crucifixion, by Ugolino di Tedice. $1, The Triumphal Entry into Jerusalem, Master of the Thuison Altarpiece.

1998, Dec. 1

2816-2819 A424 Set of 4 2.00 2.00

New Year 1999 (Year of the Rabbit) — A425

Various rabbits, color of country name: a, green. b, orange. c, red. Illustration reduced.

1999, Jan. 4 **Litho.** ***Die Cut Perf. 9***

Self-Adhesive

Sheet of 3

2820 A425 $1 sil & multi, #a.-c. 2.25 2.25

No. 2820b has point of triangle down.

A426

Famous People: No. 2821: a, Martin Luther King, Jr. (1929-68). b, Socrates (470-399BC). c, Thomas Moore (1478-1535). d, Chaim Weizmann (1874-1952). e, Alexander Solzhenitsyn (b. 1918). f, Galileo Galilei (1564-1642). g, Michael Servetus (1511-53). h, Salman Rushdie (b. 1947).

$6, Mother Teresa (1910-97).

1999, Mar. 1 **Litho.** ***Perf. 14***

2821 A426 $1 Sheet of 8, #a.-h. 6.00 6.00

Souvenir Sheet

2822 A426 $6 multicolored 4.50 4.50

Nos. 2821b-2821c, 2821e-2821f are 53x38mm.

A427

Space Exploration - #2823: a, Robert H. Goddard. b, Werner von Braun. c, Yuri Gagarin. d, Freedom 7 rocket. e, Aleksei Leonov. f, Apollo 11 astronauts on moon.

No. 2824: a, Mariner 9. b, Voyager 1. c, Bruce McCandless. d, Giotto probe. e, Space Shuttle. f, Magellan probe.

No. 2825, John H. Glenn, Jr. No. 2826, Neil A. Armstrong.

1999, Mar. 5

Sheets of 6

2823-2824 A427 $1.50 #a.-f., ea 6.75 6.75

Souvenir Sheets

2825-2826 A427 $6 each 4.50 4.50

Mickey's Dream Wedding A428

No. 2827: a, Goofy. b, Mickey. c, Minnie. d, Daisy Duck. e, Donald Duck. f, Pluto. g, Huey, Dewey & Louie. h, Dog.

No. 2828, Mickey eating cake. No. 2829, Mickey, Minnie in back of carriage, horiz.

1999, Mar. 12 ***Perf. 13½x14, 14x13½***

2827 A428 $1 Sheet of 8, #a.-h. 6.00 6.00

Souvenir Sheets

2828-2829 A428 $6 each 4.50 4.50

Mickey Mouse, 70th anniv.

Trains A429

Designs: 25c, Grand Trunk Western. 35c, Louisville & Nashville. 45c, Gulf, Mobile & Ohio. 75c, Missouri Pacific. 90c, RTG, French Natl. Railway. $1, Florida East Coast. $3, Kansas City Southern. $4, New Haven.

No. 2838: a, Western Pacific. b, Union Pacific. c, Chesapeake & Ohio. d, Southern Pacific. e, Baltimore & Ohio. f, Wabash.

No. 2839: a, Burlington Route. b, Texas Special, Missouri, Kansas & Texas. c, City of Los Angeles. d, Northwestern. e, Canadian National. f, Rock Island.

No. 2840: a, Rio Grande. b, Erie Lackawanna. c, New York Central. d, Pennsylvania. e, Milwaukee Road. f, Illinois Central.

No. 2841: a, TGV, French National Railways. b, HST, British Railways. c, TEE, Trans Europe Express. d, Ancona Express Itay. e, XPT, Australia. f, APT-P, British Railways.

No. 2842, Bullet Train, Japan. No. 2843, Inter City Express, Germany. No. 2844, Santa Fe. No. 2845, ELD 4, Netherlands.

1999, Mar. 15 ***Perf. 14***

2830-2837 A429 Set of 8 8.00 8.00

Sheets of 6

2838-2841 A429 $1.50 #a.-f., ea 6.75 6.75

Souvenir Sheets

2842-2845 A429 $6 each 4.50 4.50

Australia '99, World Stamp Expo A430

Flora and fauna: $1, Orangutan. $2, Dourocouli. $3. Black caiman. $4, Black leopard, vert.

No. 2850, vert: a, African binturong. b, Two elephants. c, One elephant. d, Garkulax mitratus. e, Vanda hookeriana (a, f). f, Heron. g, Fur seal (f). h, Pied shag (g). i, Round batfish (e). j, Loggerhead turtle (f, k). k, Three harlequin sweet lips (l). l, Two harlequin sweet lips (k).

No. 2851: a, Papilio blumei (d). b, Egret (e). c, Kumarahou (b, f). d, Javan rhinoceros (g). e, Silver eye. f, Kiore (i). g, Cyclorana novaehollandiae. h, Caterpillar. i, Grey duck (h). j, Honey blue-eye. k, Krefft's tortoise. l, Archer fish.

No. 2852, Impalas. No. 2853, Ring-tailed lemurs.

1999, Apr. 12 Litho. *Perf. 14*

2846-2849 A430 Set of 4 7.50 7.50

Sheets of 12

2850-2851 A430 75c #a.-l., each 6.75 6.75

Souvenir Sheets

2852-2853 A430 $6 each 4.50 4.50

Paintings by Hokusai (1760-1849) A431

Entire paintings or details - #2854: a, The Actor Ichikawa Danjuro as Tomoe Gozen. b, E-Tehon drawings (washing clothes). c, The Prostitute of Eguchi. d, Sudden Shower from a Fine Sky. e, E-tehon drawings (hanging clothes up to dry). f, Shimada.

No. 2855: a, Head of Old Man. b, Horse Drawings (with head down). c, Girl Making Cord for Binding Hats. d, Li Po Admiring the Waterfall of Lo-Shan. e, Horse drawings (with head up). f, Potted Dwarf Pine with Basin.

No. 2856, Women on the Beach at Enoshima. No. 2857, The Guardian God Fudo Myoo and His Two Young Attendants.

1999, May 24 Litho. *Perf. 13½x14*

Sheets of 6

2854-2855 A431 $1.50 #a.-f., ea 6.75 6.75

Souvenir Sheets

2856-2857 A431 $6 each 4.50 4.50

Johann Wolfgang von Goethe (1749-1832), Poet — A432

No. 2858: a, Faust contemplates the moon in his story. b, Portrait of Goethe and Freidrich von Schiller (1759-1805). c, Faust converses with Wagner outside the town gate.

No. 2860, Margaret Muses in "Faust."

1999, May 24 *Perf. 14*

2858 A432 $3 Sheet of 3, #a.-c. 6.75 6.75

Souvenir Sheets

2860 A432 $6 multi 4.50 4.50

IBRA '99, World Philatelic Exhibition, Nuremberg — A433

IBRA'99 emblem, 1893 4-4-0 locomotive and: No. 2862, 75c, Prussia #2. No. 2864, $1, Saxony #1.

Emblem, Humboldt sailing ship and: No. 2863, 90c, Mecklenburg-Schwerin #1. No. 2865, $2, Mecklenburg-Strelitz #1.

$6, Saxony #1. Illustration reduced.

1999, May 24 Litho. *Perf. 14*

2862-2865 A433 Set of 4 3.50 3.50

Souvenir Sheet

2866 A433 $6 multicolored 4.50 4.50

Apollo 11 Moon Landing, 30th Anniv. A434

#2867: a, Footprint on moon. b, V2 Rocket. c, Command module, Columbia. d, Lunar rover. e, Lunar lander, Eagle. f, Command module during re-entry.

#2868: a, Moon. b, Edward H. White during first spacewalk. c, Edwin "Buzz" Aldrin. d, Earth. e, Michael Collins. f, Neal A. Armstrong, first man to walk on moon.

#2869, Launch of Apollo 11, vert. #2870, US flag, Armstrong on Moon.

1999, May 24

Sheets of 6

2867-2868 A434 $1.50 #a.-f., ea 6.75 6.75

Souvenir Sheets

2869-2870 A434 $6 multicolored 4.50 4.50

Souvenir Sheets

PhilexFrance '99, World Philatelic Exhibition — A435

Designs: No. 2871, 2-8-0 Heavy freight locomotive, French State Railways. No. 2872, 4 Cylinder Compound Pacific, Paris-Lyons and Mediterranean Railway.

Illustration reduced.

1999, May 24 *Perf. 13¾*

2871-2872 A435 $6 each 4.50 2.25

A436

Wedding of Prince Edward and Sophie Rhys-Jones - #2873: a, Edward. b, Sophie and Edward. c, Sophie.

$6, Couple, horiz.

1999, June 18 Litho. *Perf. 13½*

2873 A436 $3 Sheet of 3, #a.-c. 6.75 6.75

Souvenir Sheet

2874 A436 $6 multicolored 4.50 4.50

A437

Children: a, Two with fur hats. b, One with pink hat. c, Boy without shirt, girl with shawl.

$6, Wearing white shirt.

1999, May 24 Litho. *Perf. 14*

2875 A437 $3 Sheet of 3, #a.-c. 6.75 6.75

Souvenir Sheet

2876 A437 $6 multicolored 4.50 4.50

UN Rights of the Child, 10th anniv.

British Comedy "Carry On" — A438

a, Dick. b, Doctor. c, England. d, Matron. e, Round the Bend. f, Up the Jungle. g, Loving. h, Up the Khyber.

$6, Various characters.

1999, May 24 *Perf. 13½x14*

2877 A438 $1 Sheet of 8, #a.-h. 6.00 6.00

Perf. 13¾

2877I A438 $6 multicolored 4.50 4.50

Variety Club of Great Britain, 50th anniv.

UPU, 125th Anniv. A439

Mail from space: a, Cosmonaut with letter from home. b, Supply and mail ship, "Progress." c, Postmark of space station Mir. d, Buran shuttle, Mir in space.

$6, Space station Mir.

1999, May 24 *Perf. 14*

2878 A439 $2 Sheet of 4, #a.-d. 6.00 6.00

Souvenir Sheet

2879 A439 $6 multicolored 4.50 4.50

Queen Mother, 100th Birthday (in 2000) — A440

A440a

Gold Frames

No. 2880: a, Queen Mother, Prince Charles, 1948. b, Queen Mother, 1970. c, Queen Mother in Australia, 1958. d, Queen Mother.

$6, Queen Mother, 1953.

1999, Aug. 16

Sheet of 4

2880 A440 $2 #a.-d. + label 6.00 6.00

Souvenir Sheet

2881 A440 $6 multicolored 4.50 4.50

Litho. & Embossed

Die Cut Perf. 8¾

Without Gum

2881A A440a $20 gold & multi

No. 2881 contains one 38x50mm stamp. Margins of sheet are embossed.

See Nos. 3212-3213.

Birth of the Silver Screen A441

Musicians - #2882: a, George Gershwin, 1929. b, Florence Mills, 1928. c, Sam Beckett, 1925. d, Bessie Smith, 1923. e, Billie Holiday, 1933. f, Bert Williams, 1914. g, Cole Porter, 1934. h, Sophie Tucker, 1915.

Actors - #2883: a, Lon Chaney, 1930. b, Buster Keaton, 1930. c, Norma Shearer, 1934. d, James Gagney, 1930. e, Hedda Hopper, 1933. f, Jean Harlow, 1931. g, Marlene Dietrich, 1930. h, Ramon Novarro, 1928.

No. 2884, Louis Armstrong. No. 2885, Clark Gable, 1932,

1999, Aug. 18

Sheets of 8

2882-2883 A441 $1 #a.-h., each 6.00 6.00

Souvenir Sheets

2884-2885 A441 $6 each 4.50 4.50

Star Trek A442

Various starships.

1999, July 20 Litho. *Perf. 13¼*

2886 A442 $1.50 Sheet of 9, #a.-i. 10.00 10.00

Dinosaurs A443

35c, Ouranosaurus. 45c, Struthiomimus, vert. 75c, Parasaurolophus, vert. $2, Triceratops. $3, Stegoceras. $4, Stegosaurus.

No. 2893: a, Agathaumus. b, Camarosaurus. c, Quetzalcoatlus. d, Alioramus. e, Camptosaurus. f, Albertosaurus. g, Anatosaurus. h, Spinosaurus. i, Centrosaurus.

No. 2894: a, Archaeopteryx. b, Brachiosaurus. c, Dilophosaurus. d, Dimetrodon. e, Psittacosaurus. f, Acrocanthosaurus. g, Stenonychosaurus. h, Dryosaurus. i, Compsognathus.

No. 2895, Velociraptor, vert. No. 2896, Tyrannosaurus, vert.

1999, Sept. 1 Litho. *Perf. 14*

2887-2892 A443 Set of 6 7.75 7.75

Sheets of 9

2893-2894 A443 $1 #a.-i, each 6.75 6.75

Souvenir Sheets

2895-2896 A443 $6 each 4.50 4.50

Christmas — A444

Candle and: 20c, Rose. 75c, Tulip. 90c, Pear. $1, Hibiscus. $4, Lily.

$6, The Nativity, by Sandro Botticelli.

1999, Dec. 7 Litho. *Perf. 14*

2897-2901 A444 Set of 5 5.00 5.00

Souvenir Sheet

2902 A444 $6 multi 4.50 4.50

Flowers A445

Various flowers making up a photomosaic of Princess Diana.

1999, Dec. 31 Litho. *Perf. 13¾*

2903 A445 $1 Sheet of 8, #a.-h. 6.00 6.00

See No. 3055.

New Year 2000 (Year of the Dragon) — A446

Inscription color: a, Blue green. b, Red. c, Violet.

2000, Feb. 5 *Perf. 12½x12¾*

2904 A446 $2 Sheet of 3, #a.-c. 4.50 4.50

No. 2904b has point of triangle down.

Birds A447

Designs: 75c, Roseate spoonbill. 90c, Scarlet ibis. $1.50, Sparkling violet-ear. $2, Northern jacana.

No. 2909: a, Blue-headed euphonia. b, Troupial. c, Caribbean parakeet. d, Forest thrush. e, Hooded tanager. f, Stripe-headed tanager. g, Ringed kingfisher. h, Zenaida dove.

No. 2910: a, Adelaide's warbler. b, Hispaniolan trogon. c, Sun parakeet. d, Black-necked stilt. e, Sora rail. f, Fulvous tree duck. g, Blue-headed parrot. h, Tropical mockingbird.

No. 2911, Antillean siskin. No. 2912, Cedar waxwing, vert.

2000, Mar. 1 Litho. *Perf. 14*

2905-2908 A447 Set of 4 3.75 3.75

Sheets of 8, #a.-h.

2909-2910 A447 $1 each 6.00 6.00

Souvenir Sheets

2911-2912 A447 $6 each 4.50 4.50

No. 2911 contains one 50x37mm stamp. No. 2912 contains one 37x50mm stamp.

Mushrooms A448

Designs: 35c, Clitocybe geotropa. 45c, Psalliota augusta. $1, Amanita rubescens. $4, Boletus satanas.

No. 2917: a, Ungulina marginata. b, Pleurotus ostreatus. c, Flammula penetrans. d, Morchella crassipes. e, Lepiota procera. f, Tricholoma aurantium.

No. 2918: a, Pholiota spectabilis. b, Mycena polygramma. c, Collybia iocephala. d, Corinus cornatus. e, Amanita muscaria. f, Boletus aereus.

No. 2919, Lepiota acutesquamosa. No. 2920, Daedala quercina.

2000, May 1 *Perf. 14*

2913-2916 A448 Set of 4 4.25 4.25

Sheets of 6, #a.-f.

2917-2918 A448 $1.50 each 6.75 6.75

Souvenir Sheets

2919-2920 A448 $6 each 4.50 4.50

Paintings of Anthony Van Dyck A449

No. 2921: a, Young Woman Resting Her Head on Her Hand. b, Self-portrait. c, Woman Looking Upwards. d, Head of an Old Man, c. 1621. e, Head of a Boy. f, Head of an Old Man, 1616-18.

No. 2922: a, Charles I on Horseback with Seigneur de St. Antoine. b, St. Martin Dividing His Cloak. c, Giovanni Paolo Balbi on Horseback. d, Marchese Anton Giulio Brignole-Sale on Horseback. e, Study of a Horse. f, An Oriental on Horseback.

No. 2923: a, Portrait of a Man. b, Portrait of a Man Aged Seventy. c, Portrait of a Woman. d, An Elderly Man. e, Portrait of a Young Man. f, Man with a Glove.

No. 2924: a, St. John the Baptist. b, St. Anthony of Padua and the Ass of Rimini. c, The Stoning of St. Stephen. d, The Martyrdom of St. Sebastian. e, St. Sebastian Bound for Martyrdom. f, St. Jerome.

No. 2925: a, Inscribed "Portrait of Anthony Van Dyck," actually a self-portrait of Rubens. b, Inscribed "Self-portrait (after Peter Paul Rubens)." c, Isabella Brant, Wife of Peter Paul Rubens. d, The Penitent Apostle Peter. e, Head of a Robber. f, The Heads of the Apostles, by Rubens.

No. 2926, Prince Thomas-Francis of Savoy-Carignan on Horseback. No. 2927, Charles I on Horseback. No. 2928, The Emperor Theodosius Refused Entry in Milan Cathedral, horiz. No. 2929, St. Jerome (in the Wilderness). No. 2930, St. Martin Dividing His Cloak, horiz. No. 2931, Portrait of a Man and His Wife.

2000, May 1 *Perf. 13¾*

Sheets of 6, #a.-f.

2921-2922 A449 $1 each 4.50 4.50

2923-2925 A449 $1.50 each 6.75 6.75

Souvenir Sheets

2926-2928 A449 $5 each 3.75 3.75

2929-2931 A449 $6 each 4.50 4.50

Millennium A450

Highlights of 1650-1700: a, Painter Jan Vermeer dies. b, Birth of microbiology. c, Salem Witch Trials. d, Sir Isaac Newton builds first reflecting telescope. e, Voltaire born. f, Ivan V and Peter become joint rulers of Russia. g, First Qing Dynasty Emperor, Shun Zhi, dies. h, Christiaan Huygens discovers rings of Saturn. i, Robert Hooke identifies cells. j, Wang Shih-min paints "Verdant Peaks." k, René Descartes dies. l, Canal du Midi completed. m, Glorious Revolution. n, King William's War ends. o, Gian Domenico Cassini observes polar caps on Mars. p, Newton formulates law of gravitation (60x40mm). q, Ole Roemer discovers that light moves at a finite speed.

2000, May 1 *Perf. 12½*

2932 A450 50c Sheet of 17, #a.-q., + label 6.25 6.25

Orchids — A451

Designs: 75c, Brassolaeliocattleya. 90c, Maxilbera. $1, Isochilius. $2, Oncidium.

No. 2937: a, Laeliocattleya. b, Sophrocattleya (red). c, Epidendrum. d, Cattleya. e, Ionopsis. f, Brassoepidendrum.

No. 2938: a, Lycaste. b, Cochleanthes. c, Brassocattleya. d, Brassolaeliacattleya, diff. e, Iwanagaara. f, Sophrocattleya (orange).

No. 2939, Vanilla. No. 2940, Brassocattleya, diff.

2000, May 15 Litho. *Perf. 14*

2933-2936 A451 Set of 4 3.50 3.50

Sheets of 6, #a.-f.

2937-2938 A451 $1.50 each 6.75 6.75

Souvenir Sheets

2939-2940 A451 $6 each 4.50 4.50

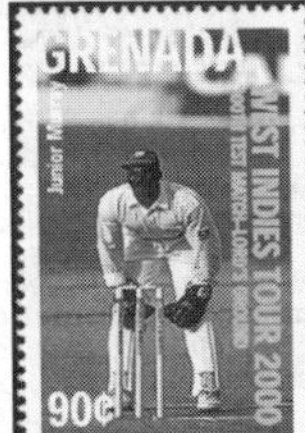

100th Test Match at Lord's Ground — A452

90c, Junior Murray. $5, Rawl Lewis.

$6, Lord's Ground, horiz.

2000, May 15 Litho. *Perf. 14*

2941-2942 A452 Set of 2 4.50 4.50

Souvenir Sheet

2943 A452 $6 multi 4.50 4.50

Prince William, 18th Birthday — A453

No. 2944: a, In suit. b, In suit, with person in tan suit. c, In suit, waving. d, In ski jacket.

$6, In suit, diff.

Illustration reduced.

2000, May 15 *Perf. 14*

2944 A453 $1.50 Sheet of 4, #a-d 4.50 4.50

Souvenir Sheet

Perf. 13¾

2945 A453 $6 multi 4.50 4.50

No. 2944 contains four 28x42mm stamps.

First Zeppelin Flight, Cent. — A454

No. 2946 - Ferdinand von Zeppelin and: a, LZ-130. b, LZ-2. c, LZ-127.

$6, LZ-129.

Illustration reduced.

2000, May 15 *Perf. 14*

2946 A454 $3 Sheet of 3, #a-c 6.75 6.75

Souvenir Sheet

2947 A454 $6 multi 4.50 4.50

No. 2946 contains three 42x28mm stamps.

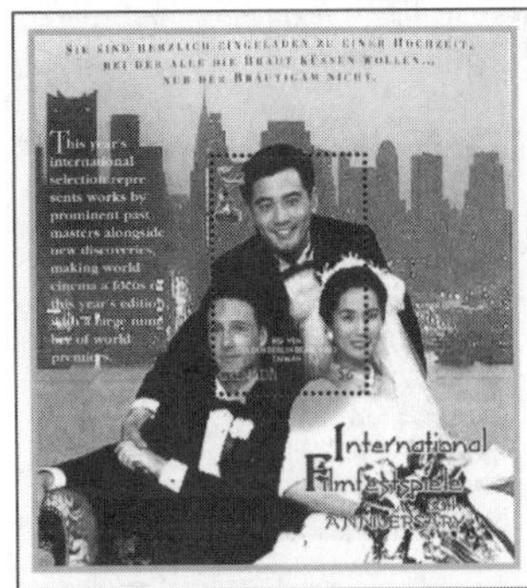

Berlin Film Festival, 50th Anniv. — A455

No. 2948: a, Alphaville. b, Rod Steiger. c, Os Fuzis. d, Jean-Pierre Leaud. e, Cul-de-sac. f, Ikiru.

$6, Hsi Yen.

Illustration reduced.

2000, May 15

2948 A455 $1.50 Sheet of 6, #a-f 6.75 6.75

Souvenir Sheet

2949 A455 $6 multi 4.50 4.50

Apollo-Soyuz Mission, 25th Anniv. — A456

No. 2950, vert.: a, Soyuz launch vehicle. b, Soyuz 19. c, Apollo 18 and Soyuz 19 docked. $6, Valeri Kubasov and Thomas Stafford. Illustration reduced.

2000, May 15

2950 A456 $3 Sheet of 3, *#a-c* 6.75 6.75

Souvenir Sheet

2951 A456 $6 multi 4.50 4.50

Souvenir Sheets

2000 Summer Olympics, Sydney — A457

No. 2952: a, Archibald Hahn. b, Show jumping. c, Sports Palace, Rome, and Italian flag. d, Ancient Greek chariot racing. Illustration reduced.

2000, May 15

2952 A457 $2 Sheet of 4, *#a-d* 6.00 6.00

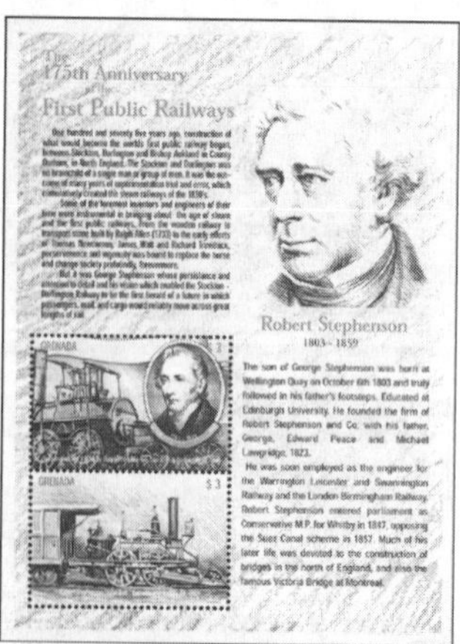

Public Railways, 175th Anniv. — A458

No. 2953: a, Locomotion No. 1, George Stephenson. b, John Bull. Illustration reduced.

2000, May 15

2953 A458 $3 Sheet of 2, *#a-b* 4.50 4.50

Johann Sebastian Bach (1685-1750) — A459

Illustration reduced.

2000, May 15

2954 A459 $6 multi 4.50 4.50

Souvenir Sheet

Albert Einstein (1879-1955) — A460

Illustration reduced.

2000, May 15 Litho. ***Perf. 14¼***

2955 A460 $6 multi 4.50 4.50

Space — A461

No. 2956: a, Luna 4. b, Clementine. c, Luna 12. d, Luna 16. e, Apollo 11 Lunar module. f, Ranger 7.
$6, Apollo command and service modules. Illustration reduced.

2000, May 15 Litho. ***Perf. 14***

2956 A461 $1.50 Sheet of 6, *#a-f* 6.75 6.75

Souvenir Sheet

2957 A461 $6 multi 4.50 4.50

World Stamp Expo 2000, Anaheim

Marine Life A462

Designs: 45c, Porkfish. 75c, Short bigeye. 90c, Red snapper. $1, Creole wrasse. $2, Indigo hamlet. $3, Blue tang.

No. 2964: a, Juvenile French angelfish. b, Beaugregory. c, Queen angelfish. d, Sergeant major. e, Bank butterflyfish. f, Spanish hogfish. g, Porkfish. h, Banded butterflyfish. i, Longsnout seahorse.

No. 2965: a, Hawksbill turtle. b, Foureye butterflyfish. c, Porcupinefish. d, Yellowtail damselfish. e, Adult French angelfish. f, Yellow goatfish. g, Blue-striped grunt. h, Spanish grunt. i, Queen triggerfish.

No. 2966, Queen angelfish. No. 2967, Blue tang.

2000, Aug. 8

2958-2963 A462 Set of 5 6.00 6.00

Sheets of 9, *#a-i*

2964-2965 A462 $1 Set of 2 13.50 13.50

Souvenir Sheets

2966-2967 A462 $6 Set of 2 9.00 9.00

Grenada National Stadium A463

Designs: $2, Aerial view.

No. 2969: a, Cricket team photo. b, Cricketers playing.

2000, Aug. 8

2968 A463 $2 multi 1.50 1.50

Souvenir Sheet

2969 A463 $1 Sheet of 2, *#a-b* 1.50 1.50

European Soccer Championships — A464

No. 2970, horiz. - Belgium: a, Vanderhaege. b, Belgian team. c, Ronny Gaspercic. d, Lorenzo Staelens. e, Stadium Koning Boudewijn. f, Strupar and Mpenza.

No. 2971, horiz. - Spain: a, Sergi Barjuan. b, Spanish team. c, Luis Enrique. d, Hierro. e, De Kuip Stadium. f, Raul Gonzales.

No. 2972, horiz. - Yugoslavia: a, Dejan Savicevic. b, Yugoslavian team. c, Predrag Migatovic. d, Savo Milosevic. e, Jan Breydel Stadium. f, Darko Kovacevic.

No. 2973, Belgian coach Robert Waseige. No. 2974, Spanish coach José Antonio Camacho. No. 2975, Yugoslavian coach Vujadin Boskov. Illustration reduced.

2000, Aug. 8 ***Perf. 13¾***

Sheets of 6, *#a-f*

2970-2972 A464 $1.50 Set of 3 20.00 20.00

Souvenir Sheets

2973-2975 A464 $6 Set of 3 13.50 13.50

Ferrari Automobiles — A465

20c, 1953 500 Mondial. 45c, 1948 166 Inter. 75c, 1953 340 MM. 90c, 1964 500 Superfast. $1, 1948 166 MM. $1.50, 1952 250 S. $2, 1957 250 California. $3, 1966 365 California.

2000, Sept. 5 ***Perf. 14***

2976-2983 A465 Set of 8 7.25 7.25

Antique Automobiles A466

45c, 1921 Marmon Model 34. 75c, 1917 Buick D44. 90c, 1918 Hudson Runabout Landau. $1, 1915 Chevolet Royal Mail. $2, 1925 Kissel Speedster. $3, 1915 Ford Model T.

No. 2990: a, 1925 Cadillac V63. b, 1939 Plymouth. c, 1934 Franklin Club Sedan. d, 1933 Fiat Ardita. e, 1929 Essex Speedabout. f, 1932 Stutz Bearcat.

No. 2991: a, 1929 Rolls Royce. b, 1932 Graham Convertible. c, 1937 Mercedes-Benz 540K. d, 1948 Jaguar MkV. e, 1939 Lagonda Drophead Coupe. f, 1930 Alfa Romeo Gran Sport.

No. 2992, 1915 Dodge Tourer. No. 2993, 1924 Chrysler.

2000, Sept. 5

2984-2989 A466 Set of 6 6.00 6.00

Sheets of 6, *#a-f*

2990-2991 A466 $1.50 Set of 2 13.50 13.50

Souvenir Sheets

2992-2993 A466 $6 Set of 2 9.00 9.00

Popes — A467

No. 2994: a, Stephen VIII, 939-42. b, Theodore I, 642-49. c, Theodore II, 897. d, Valentine, 827. e, Vitalian, 657-72. f, Zacharias, 741-52.
$6, Sylvester II, 999-1003.

2000, Sept. 5 ***Perf. 13¾***

2994 A467 $1.50 Sheet of 6, *#a-f* 6.75 6.75

Souvenir Sheet

2995 A467 $6 multi 4.50 4.50

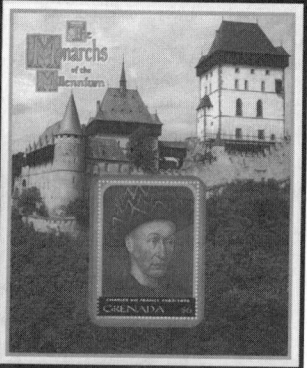

Monarchs — A468

No. 2996: a, George III of Great Britain, 1760-1820. b, George IV of Great Britain, 1820-30. c, Duchess Charlotte of Luxembourg, 1964-present. d, Grand Duke Jean of Luxembourg, 1964-present.
$6, Charles VIII of France, 1483-98.

2000, Sept. 5 ***Perf. 13¾***

2996 A468 $1.50 Sheet of 4, *#a-d* 4.50 4.50

Souvenir Sheet

2997 A468 $6 multi 4.50 4.50

Shirley Temple in "Heidi" — A469

No. 2998, horiz.: a, With woman holding candle. b, With girl in green dress c, On stairs. d, With Christmas gift.

No. 2999, horiz.: a, Walking with woman. b, Touching bearded man. c, Holding goat. d,

With doves. e, With bearded man. f, Seated with woman.
Illustration reduced.

2000, Oct. 6 Litho. *Perf. 13¾*

2998 A469 $1.50 Sheet of 4, #a-d		4.50	4.50
2999 A469 $1.50 Sheet of 6, #a-f		6.75	6.75

Souvenir Sheet

3000 A469	$6 Seated near tree	4.50	4.50

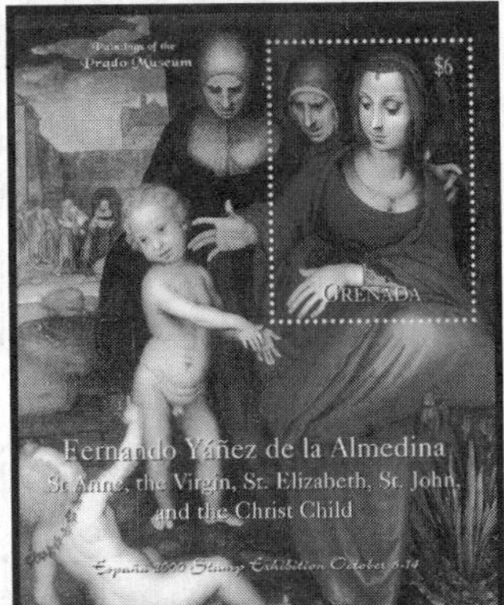

Paintings from the Prado — A470

#3001: a, Monk and king from The Virgin of the Catholic Monarchs, by an Anonymous Castilian. b, Madonna and child from The Virgin of the Catholic Monarchs. c, Monk and queen from The Virgin of the Catholic Monarchs. d, The Flagellation, by Alexo Fernandez. e, The Virgin and Souls in Purgatory, by Pedro Machuca. f, The Holy Trinity, by El Greco.

#3002: a, Playing at Giants, by El Greco. b, The Holy Family Under the Oak Tree, by Raphael. c, Don Gaspar Melchior de Jovellanos, by Francisco de Goya. d, Man with arm on hip from Joseph in the Pharaoh's Palace, by Jacopo Amiconi. e, Man and woman from Joseph in the Pharaoh's Palace. f, Man on bended knee from Joseph in the Pharaoh's Palace.

#3003: a, The Savior Blessing, by Francisco de Zurbarán. b, St. John the Baptist, by Francisco Solimena. c, Noli Me Tangere, by Corregio. d, St. Casilda, by Zurbarán. e, Nicolás Omazur by Bartolomé Esteban Murillo. f, Juan Martínez Montañés, by Diego Velázquez.

#3004, St. Anne, the Virgin, St. Elizabeth, St. John and the Christ child, by Fernando Yáñez de la Almedina. #3005, The Virgin of the Catholic Monarchs. #3006, Joseph in the Pharaoh's Palace, horiz.
Illustration reduced.

2000, Oct. 19 *Perf. 12x12¼, 12¼x12*

Sheets of 6, #a-f

3001-3003 A470 $1.50 Set of 3	20.00	20.00

Souvenir Sheets

3004-3006 A470 $6 Set of 3	13.50	13.50

Espana 2000 Intl. Philatelic Exhibition.

Battle of Britain, 60th Anniv. — A471

No. 3007: a, Messerschmitt BF 109E and bomb blast. b, Supermarine Spitfire MK XI. c, V1 flying bomb. d, U-boat. e, Ack-ack gun unit. f, Bedford field ambulance.

No. 3008: a, Messerschmitt BF 109E. b, German paratrooper. c, Hawker Hurricane HK 1. d, RAF airfield. e, Heinkel HE 111 H. f, Nose of Supermarine Spitfire MK XI.

No. 3009, Line of Hawker Hurricanes. No. 3010, Supermarine Spitfire MK XI.
Illustration reduced.

2000, Oct. 30 *Perf. 14*

Sheets of 6, #a-f

3007-3008 A471 $1.50 Set of 2	13.50	13.50

Souvenir Sheets

3009-3010 A471 $6 Set of 2	9.00	9.00

A472

Shetland Sheepdog, Grenada, $2 — A473

Birds: 25c, Purple gallinule. 40c, Limpkin. 50c, Black-necked stilt. 60c, Painted bunting. 75c, Yellow-breasted warbler. $1, Blackburnian warbler. $1.25, Blue grosbeak. $1.50, Black-and-white warbler. $1.60, Blue whistling thrush. $3, Common yellowthroat. $4, Indigo bunting. $5, Gray catbird. $10, Bananaquit. $20, Blue-gray gnatcatcher.

2000, Oct. 30 *Perf. 14¾x14*

3011-3024 A472 Set of 14	37.50	37.50

2000, June 23 Litho. *Perf. 14*

Dogs: $2, Shetland sheepdog. $3, Central Asian sheepdog.

No. 3027, horiz.: a, Labrador retriever. b, Standard poodle. c, Boxer. d, Rough-coated Jack Russell terrier. e, Tibetan terrier. f, Welsh corgi.

$6, Irish red and white setter, horiz.

3025-3026 A473 Set of 2	3.75	3.75
3027 A473 $1.50 Sheet of 6, #a-f	6.75	6.75

Souvenir Sheet

3028 A473 $6 multi	4.50	4.50

Butterflies A474

45c, Marpesia eleuchea bahamaensis. 75c, Pterourus palamedes. 90c, Dryas julia framptoni. $1, Hypna clytemnestra iphegenia.

No. 3033, $1.50: a, Danaus plexippus. b, Anartia amathea. c, Colobura dirce. d, Parides gundiachianus. e, Spiroeta stelenes. f, Hamadryas feronia.

No. 3034, $1.50: a, Merchantis isthmia. b, Colias eurytheme. c, Papilio troilus d, Junonia coenia. e, Doxocopa laure. f, Pierella hyalinus.

No. 3035, $6, Agraulis vanilae insularis. No. 3036, $6, Danaus gilippus.

2000, June 26

3029-3032 A474 Set of 4	2.40	2.40

Sheets of 6, #a-f

3033-3034 A474 Set of 2	13.50	13.50

Souvenir Sheets

3035-3036 A474 Set of 2	9.00	9.00

A475

Trains — A476

No. 3037, $1.50: a, Diesel-electric locomotive, Royal State Railway of Thailand. b, Diesel-electric locomotive, Danish Railways. c, French-built Turbo train. d, Diesel, Spanish Railways. e, Virgen del Rosario, Spanish Railways. f, 22 Class Co-Co Diesel-electric locomotive, Malayan Railways.

No. 3038, $1.50: a, Class 87 electric locomotive, British Railways. b, Electric-Diesel locomotive, Iraqi Railway. c, Electric locomotive, Austrian Railways. d, 1.4 meter gauge locomotive, South Australia Railways. e, Automated electric locomotive, Black Mesa & Lake Powell Railroad. f, Diesel-electric, Yugoslav Railways.

No. 3039, $1.50: a, Class 10 4-6-2, German Federal Railway. b, Class E.10 Bo-Bo Electric locomotive, German Federal Railways. c, Class 23 2-6-2, German Federal Railway. d, 2-8-4 locomotive, German Federal Railway. e, Rebuilt 01 Class Pacific, East German State Railway. f, High speed Diesel railcar, Deutschen Reichsbahn.

No. 3040, $1.50: a, Borsig Standard 2-2-2. b, Austerity 2-10-0 Series 52, German Federal Railway. c, Adler, facing right, Nuremburg-Furth Railway. d, Bardenia, Baden State Railways. e, Drache. f, Adler, facing left.

No. 3041, $6, Diesel T.E.E. Parsifal. No. 3042, $6, High speed electric, Netherlands Railway. No. 3043, $6, Electric train, Swiss Railways. No. 3044, $6, Silver Fern, New Zealand Railways. No. 3045, $6, Borsig locomotive, Berlin and Anhalt Railway. No. 3046, $6, Krauss-Maffei V.200 Diesel-hydraulic locomotive, German Federal Railway.
Illustrations reduced.

2000, Sept. 5

Sheets of 6, #a-f

3037-3038 A475 Set of 2	13.50	13.50
3039-3040 A476 Set of 2	13.50	13.50

Souvenir Sheets

3041-3044 A475 Set of 4	18.00	18.00
3045-3046 A476 Set of 2	9.00	9.00

Descriptions of trains are in margins on Nos. 3039-3940, 3045-3046.

Nursery Rhymes — A477

No. 3047, Little Bo Peep, $1.50, vert.: a, Crook, tree, dove. b, Little Bo Peep. c, Sheep. d, Geese. e, Goose, Little Bo Peep's leg. f, Dog.

No. 3048, The Old Woman Who Lived in a Shoe, $1.50, vert.: a, Child, roof. b, Child with hat, rainbow. c, Cow, sun, rainbow. d, Child at door. e, Old woman, child. f, Child on shoe.

No. 3049, Little Boy Blue, $1.50, vert.: a, Sheep, house. b, Sun. c, Cow. d, Geese, path. e, Dog, Little Boy Blue's leg. f, Little Boy Blue.

No. 3050, The Cat and the Fiddle, $1.50, vert. a, Bird, house. b, Cow jumping over moon. c, Spoon. d, Dog, house. e, Cat and fiddle. f, Dish.

No. 3051, $6, Little Bo Peep. No. 3052, $6, The Old Woman Who Lived in a Shoe. No. 3053, $6, Little Boy Blue. No. 3054, Cow jumping over the moon.
Illustration reduced.

2000, Sept. 9 *Perf. 13¾x13¼*

Sheets of 6, #a-f

3047-3050 A477 Set of 4	27.50	27.50

Souvenir Sheets

Perf. 13¼x13¾

3051-3054 A477 Set of 4	18.00	18.00

Flower Photomosaic Type of 1999

Queen Mother

Various flowers making up photomosaic.

2000, Nov. 20 *Perf. 13¾*

3055 A445 $1 Sheet of 8, #a-h	6.00	6.00

Cats — A478

75c, Maine Coon cat. 90c, Selkirk Rex.

No. 3058, horiz.: a, Spotted tabby British shorthair. b, Burmilla. c, British blue shorthair. d, Siamese. e, Japanese bobtail. f, Oriental shorthair.

2000, June 23 Litho. *Perf. 14*

3056-3057 A478 Set of 2	1.25	1.25
3058 A478 $1.50 Sheet of 6, #a-f	6.75	6.75

Souvenir Sheet

3059 A478 $6 Scottish Fold	4.50	4.50

Queen Mother, 100th Birthday — A479

2000, Nov. 20

3060 A479 $1.50 multi	1.10	1.10

Printed in sheets of 6.

Christmas — A480

Designs: 15c, 50c, No. 3065b, Angel looking left. 25c, $5, No. 3065a, Angel looking right.

2000, Dec. 4

3061-3064 A480 Set of 4	4.50	4.50
3065 A480 $2 Sheet, 2 ea #a-b	6.00	6.00

Souvenir Sheet

3066 A480 $6 Baby Jesus	4.50	4.50

Souvenir Sheets

Betty Boop — A481

Designs: No. 3067, $6, Wearing lei. No. 3068, $6, Holding fishing pole and fish. No. 3069, $6, Wearing polka dot hat. No. 3070, $6, Holding castanets. No. 3071, $6, At Japanese tea ceremony. No. 3072, $6, Wearing pink hat. No. 3073, $6, In mountains, wearing flowered hat. No. 3074, $6, Wearing beret. No. 3075, $6, As Statue of Liberty. No. 3076, $6, In Hollywood. No. 3077, $6, On horse. No. 3078, $6, On camel's back.
Illustration reduced.

2000, Oct. 11 Litho. *Perf. 13¾*

3067-3078 A481 Set of 12 55.00 55.00

Souvenir Sheet

New Year 2001 (Year of the Snake) — A482

No. 3079: a, Blue green denomination. b, Red denomination. c, Purple denomination.
Illustration reduced.

2001, Jan. 2 *Perf. 12½x13*

3079 A482 $2 Sheet of 3, #a-c 4.50 4.50

Rijksmuseum, Amsterdam, Bicent. — A483

No. 3080, $1.50: a, William I, Prince of Orange, by Adriaen Thomasz Key. b, Rutger Jan Schimmelpennick and Family, by Pierre Paul Prud'hon. c, Johan Rudolf Thorbecke, by Johan Heinrich Neuman. d, St. Sebastian, by Joachim Wtewael. e, St. Sebastian, by Hendrick ter Brugghen. f, Portrait of a Man With a Ring, by Werner Van Den Valckert.

No. 3081, $1.50: a, The Syndics of the Amsterdam Goldsmith's Guild, by Thomas de Keyser. b, Portrait of a Gentleman, by de Keyser. c, Portrait of Eva Wtewael, by Wtewael. d, The Cattle Ferry, by Esaias van de Velde. e, Landscape With the Parable of the Tares Among the Wheat, by Abraham Bloemaert. f, Princess Henrietta Marie Stuart, by Bartholomeus van der Helst.

No. 3082, $1.50: a, The Merry Fiddler, by Gerard van Honthorst. b, The Merry Drinker, by Frans Hals. c, Granida and Daifilo, by van Honthorst. d, Vertumnus and Pomona, by Paulus Moreelse. e, Flutist from The Concert, by ter Brugghen. f, A Young Student at His Desk: Melancholy, by Pieter Codde.

No. 3083, $1.50: a, The Haarlem Painter Abraham Casteleyn and His Wife Margarieta van Bancken, by Jan de Bray. b, Two figures from The Concert. c, The Procuress, by Dirck van Baburen. d, Woman Seated at a Virginal, by Johannes Vermeer. e, Dignified Couples Courting, by Willem Buytewech. f, The Young Flute Player, by Judith Leyster.

No. 3084, $6, Interior of the Portuguese Synagogue in Amsterdam, by Emanuel de Witte. No. 3085, $6, The Denial of St. Peter, by Rembrandt, horiz. No. 3086, $6, Winter Landscape With Skaters, by Hendrick Avercamp, horiz. No. 3087, $6, The Raampoortje, by Wouter Johannes van Troostwijk, horiz.
Illustration reduced.

2001, Jan. 15 *Perf. 13¾*

Sheets of 6, #a-f

3080-3083 A483 Set of 4 27.50 27.50

Souvenir Sheets

3084-3087 A483 Set of 4 18.00 18.00

Pokémon — A484

No. 3088: a, Rattata. b, Sandshrew. c, Wartortle. d, Primeape. e, Golduck. f, Persian.
Illustration reduced.

2001, Feb. 1

3088 A484 $1.50 Sheet of 6, #a-f 6.75 6.75

Souvenir Sheet

3089 A484 $6 Jolteon 4.50 4.50

Waterfowl — A485

No. 3090, $1.25: a, African pygmy goose. b, Silver teal. c, Marbled teal. d, Garganey. e, Wandering whistling duck. f, Northern shoveler.

No. 3091, $1.25: a, Female flightless steamer duck. b, Radjah. c, Cape teal. d, Hartlaub's duck. e, Ruddy shelduck. f, White-cheeked pintail.

No. 3092, $1.25, vert.: a, Fulvous whistling duck. b, African black duck. c, Madagascar white-eye. d, Female pygmy goose. e, Female wood duck. f, Male wood duck.

No. 3093, $6, Flightless steamer duck. No. 3094, $6, Flying steamer duck. No. 3095, $6, Australian shelduck, vert.

Perf. 13¼x13¾, 13¾x13¼

2001, Mar. 5 Litho.

Sheets of 6, #a-f

3090-3092 A485 Set of 3 17.00 17.00

Souvenir Sheets

3093-3095 A485 Set of 3 13.50 13.50

Hong Kong 2001 Stamp Exhibition.

Cricket Players — A486

No. 3096: Various photos of Sir Donald Bradman swinging bat.

No. 3097, Various photos of Shane Warne bowling.

No. 3098, Various photos of Sir Jack Hobbs.

No. 3099, Various photos of Sir Vivian Richards.

No. 3100, Various photos of Sir Garfield Sobers.

No. 3101, oval vignettes: a, Bradman. b, Sobers. c, Hobbs. d, Warne. e, Richards.

2001, May 15 *Perf. 14*

3096 Sheet of 8, #a-h 6.00 6.00
a.-h. A486 $1 Any single .75 .75
3097 Sheet of 8, #a-h 6.00 6.00
a.-h. A486 $1 Any single .75 .75
3098 Sheet of 4, #a-d 6.00 6.00
a.-d. A486 $2 Any single 1.50 1.50
3099 Sheet of 4, #a-d 6.00 6.00
a.-d. A486 $2 Any single 1.50 1.50
3100 Sheet of 4, #a-d 6.00 6.00
a.-d. A486 $2 Any single 1.50 1.50
3101 Sheet of 5, #a-e 7.50 7.50
a.-e. A486 $2 Any single 1.50 1.50
Nos. 3096-3101 (6) 37.50 37.50

A487

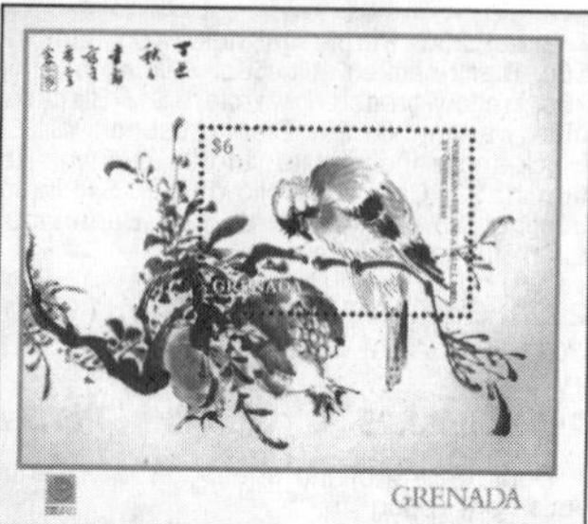

Phila Nippon '01, Japan — A488

Art: 75c, Scenes of Daily Life in Edo, by Miyagawa Choshun. 90c, Twelve Famous Places in Japan, by Kano Isenin Naganobu. $1, After the Rain, by Kawai Gyokudo. $1.25, Ryogoku Bridge Crowded With People, by Kano Kyuei. No. 3106, $2, A Courtesan of Fukagawa, by Katsukawa Shunei. $3, Rite of Bear Killing, by unknown artist.

No. 3108 - Details from the Lotus Sutra, $2, vert.: a, Figure in white at left. b, Figure with flag at lower right. c, Water in center. d, White pagoda at top right.

No. 3109 - Details from the Tale of Genji, $2 (size: 84x28mm): a, Yugao Chapter. b, Suetsumuhana Chapter. c, Wakamurasaki Chapter. d, Momiji-no-ga Chapter.

No. 3110, $6, Pomegranates and a Small Bird, by Onishi Keisai. No. 3111, $6, Bodhisattva from the Lotus Sutra, vert.

2001, May 1 Litho. *Perf. 14*

3102-3107 A487 Set of 6 6.75 6.75

Sheets of 4, #a-d

3108-3109 A488 Set of 2 12.00 12.00

Souvenir Sheets

3110-3111 A488 Set of 2 9.00 9.00

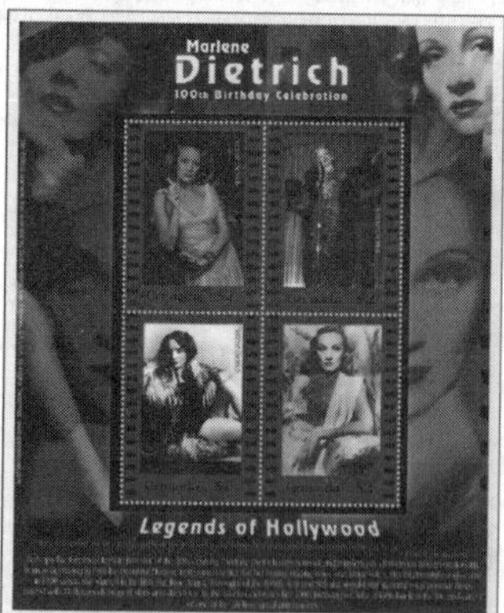

Marlene Dietrich — A489

No. 3112: a, With cigarette. b, Behind microphone. c, Seated, showing legs. d, Seated.

2001, May 15 *Perf. 13¾*

3112 A489 $2 Sheet of 4, #a-d 6.00 6.00

Queen Victoria (1819-1901) — A490

No. 3113: a, In white, as young girl. b, Wearing crown as young woman. c, Wearing crown as old woman.
$6, On throne.

2001, May 15 *Perf. 14*

3113 A490 $3 Sheet of 3, #a-c 6.75 6.75

Souvenir Sheet

3114 A490 $6 multi 4.50 4.50

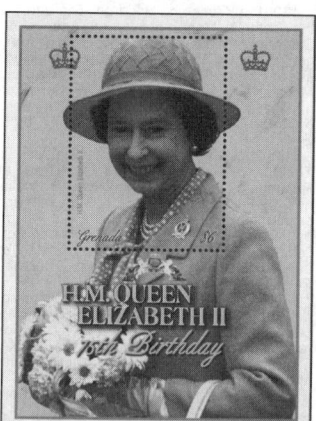

Queen Elizabeth II, 75th Birthday — A491

No. 3115: a, Straw hat. b, Red hat. c, Flowered hat. d, Blue hat.
$6, Blue hat with brim.

2001, May 15 *Perf. 14*

3115 A491 $2 Sheet of 4, #a-d 6.00 6.00

Souvenir Sheet

Perf. 13¾

3116 A491 $6 multi 4.50 4.50

No. 3116 contains one 38x51mm stamp.

UN Women's Human Rights Campaign — A492

Designs: 90c, Woman, bird, torch. $1, Woman.

2001, May 15 Litho. *Perf. 14*

3117-3118 A492 Set of 2 1.40 1.40

Mao Zedong (1893-1976) — A493

No. 3119 - background colors: a, Deep purple. b, Pinkish gray. c, Mottled red violet.
$6, Mao with cap.

2001, May 15 ***Perf. 13¾***

3119 A493 $2 Sheet of 3, #a-c 4.50 4.50

Souvenir Sheet

3120 A493 $3 multi 2.25 2.25

Giuseppe Verdi (1813-1910), Opera Composer — A494

No. 3121: a, Actor with crown. b, Score from Ernani. c, Verdi. d, La Scala Theater, Milan.
$6, Verdi with hat.

2001, May 15 ***Perf. 14***

3121 A494 $2 Sheet of 4, #a-d 6.00 6.00

Souvenir Sheet

3122 A494 $6 multi 4.50 4.50

Toulouse-Lautrec Paintings — A495

No. 3123: a, Alone. b, Two Half-naked Women. c, The Toilette. d, Justine Dieuhl.
$6, Mademoiselle Dihau at the Piano.

2001, May 15 ***Perf. 13¾***

3123 A495 $2 Sheet of 4, #a-d 6.00 6.00

Souvenir Sheet

3124 A495 $6 multi 4.50 4.50

A496

Ships — A497

Designs: 45c, Phoenician trading ship. 75c, Portuguese caravel. 90c, Marblehead schooner. No. 3128, Mala pansi. $1.50, US corvette. $2, Racing schooner.

No. 3131, $1: a, English carrack. b, Mediterranean carrack. c, Spanish galleon. d, Elizabeth Grumster. e, British East Indiaman. f, Clipper ship. g, British gunship. h, British flagship. i, English hoy.

No. 3132, $1: a, English cog. b, Roman merchantman. c, Greek war galley. d, Greek merchantman. e, Norse Oseberg ship. f, Egyptian sailboat. g, Egyptian oared ship. h, 16th cent. galleass. i, Norman sailing ship.

No. 3133, $1: a, Gloucester fishing schooner. b, Racing sloop. c, Chinese junk. d, Sambuk. e, Baltimore clipper schooner. f, Schooner yacht. g, US Clipper ship. h, US frigate. i Steam naval packet.

No. 3134, $6, Gulf Streamer. No. 3135, $6, Suhaili.

Illustration A497 reduced.

2001, June 18 ***Perf. 14***

3125-3130 A496 Set of 6 5.00 5.00

Sheets of 9, #a-i

3131-3133 A496 Set of 3 21.00 21.00

Miniature Sheets

3134-3135 A497 Set of 2 9.00 9.00

Belgica 2001 Intl. Stamp Exhibition, Brussels (Nos. 3131-3133).

A498

Flowers A499

Designs: 25c, Brassavola nodosa. No. 3137, $1, Allamanda cathartica. No. 3138, $2, Aspasia epidendroides. $3, Oncidium splendidum.

35c, Flor de San Miguel. 75c, Red frangipani. No. 3142, $1, Paper flower. No. 3143, $2, Flor de muerto.

No. 3144, $1.50: a, Candlebush. b, Flamingo flower. c, Bush morning glory. d, Laelia anceps. e, Galeandra baueri. f, Chinese hibiscus.

No. 3145, $1.50: a, Red ginger. b, Bird of paradise. c, Psychlis atropurpurea. d, Cattleya velutina. e, Caularthron bicornutum. f, Cattleya warneri.

No. 3146, $1.50, vert.: a, Mandeville. b, Tithonia rotundifolia. c, June rose. d, Columnea argentea. e, Chameleon plant. f, Protlandia albiflora.

No. 3147, $1.50, vert.: a, Wild chestnut. b, Jatropha integerrima. c, Fern tree. d, Geiger tree. e, Golden trumpet. f, Saman.

No. 3148, $6, Ipomoea learii, horiz. No. 3149, $6, Anthurium scherzerianum, horiz.

No. 3150, $6, Ladies eardrops. No. 3151, $6, Heliconia psittacorum, vert.

2001

3136-3139 A498 Set of 4 4.75 4.75

3140-3143 A499 Set of 4 3.25 3.25

Sheets of 6, #a-f

3144-3145 A498 Set of 2 13.50 13.50

3146-3147 A499 Set of 2 13.50 13.50

Souvenir Sheets

3148-3149 A498 Set of 2 9.00 9.00

3150-3151 A499 Set of 2 9.00 9.00

Kane — A500

No. 3152 - Kane: a, In air, above ring ropes. b, On one knee. c, In air. d, With red background. e, With gradiated gray and yellow background. f, Holding up opponent with both hands. g, With spotlight background. h, Holding up shirtless opponent. i, Holding up opponent with one hand.

No. 3153, $5, With red background, diff. No. 3154, $5, With opponent.

2001 ***Perf. 13¾***

3152 A500 $1 Sheet of 9, #a-i 6.75 6.75

Souvenir Sheets

3153-3154 A500 Set of 2 7.50 7.50

The Three Stooges — A501

No. 3155, $1: a, Larry, Moe, two cowboys. b, Moe and Shemp with hats, Larry. c, Shemp and Larry in drag, Moe with mustache. d, Moe with gun, Larry, Shemp, woman. e, Larry, Moe, Shemp with certificate. f, Shemp, Moe. g, Larry, picture. h, Moe, picture. i, Shemp.

No. 3156, $1: a, Larry, Curly, Moe with tool. b, Joe DeRita eating hay, horse, Larry, Moe. c, Shemp, Larry with flowers, Moe. d, Moe, Shemp, Larry, reading paper. e, Larry, Moe, Shemp with pots. f, Moe, Shemp, Larry with money. g, Shemp with knight. h, Joe DeRita, horse, Moe, Larry. i, Larry with knight.

No. 3157, $5, Larry, Moe, Shemp, woman from movie poster. No. 3158, $5, Shemp pulling Moe's arm. No. 3159, $5, Joe DeRita and Larry. No. 3160, $5, Larry and Joe DeRita, jet engine. No. 3161, $5, Moe, Larry holding woman's hand. No. 3162, $5, Larry, Moe listening to jet engine, horiz. No. 3163, $5, Larry, Moe, Shemp and cowboy, horiz. No. 3164, $5, Shemp behind bar, cowboys fighting Larry and Moe, horiz. No. 3165, $5, Curly, Moe, Larry and propeller, horiz. No. 3166, $5, Moe, Larry, woman with drink, horiz. No. 3167, $6, Moe, Larry with knight, horiz. No. 3168, $6, Curly in wringer, Moe, horiz.

2001

Sheets of 9, #a-i

3155-3156 A501 Set of 2 13.50 13.50

Souvenir Sheets

3157-3168 A501 Set of 12 47.50 47.50

Lighthouses A502

Designs: 25c, Montauk Point, NY. 50c, Alcatraz, CA. $1, Barnegat, NJ. $2, St. Augustine, FL.

No. 3173, $1.50: a, Admiralty Head, WA. b, Hooper's Strait, MD. c, Hunting Island, SC. d, Key West Lighthouse Museum, FL. e, Old Point Loma, CA. f, Old Mackinac Moint, MI.

No. 3174, $1.50: a, Point Amour, Canada. b, Inubo-Saki, Japan. c, Belle-Ile. France. d, Faerder, Norway. e, Cape Agulhas, South Africa. f, Minicoy, India.

No. 3175, $1.50: a, Keri, Estonia. b, Anholt, Denmark. c, Porer, Croatia. d, Laotieshan, China. e, Sapientza Methoni, Greece. f, Arkona, Germany.

No. 3176, $6, Boston, MA. No. 3177, $6, Pellworm, Germany. No. 3178, $6, Kvitsoy, Norway. No. 3179, Mahota Pagoda, China.

2001, Aug. 27 **Litho.** ***Perf. 14***

3169-3172 A502 Set of 4 2.75 2.75

Sheets of 6, #a-f

3173-3175 A502 Set of 3 20.00 20.00

Souvenir Sheets

3176-3179 A502 Set of 4 18.00 18.00

Marine Mammals A503

Designs: 25c, Commerson's dolphin. 50c, Pacific white-sided dolphin. $2, Northern bottlenosed whale. $3, Baird's beaked whale.

No. 3184, $1.50: a, Risso's dolphin. b, Fraser's dolphin. c, Dall's porpoise. d, Right whale. e, Gray whale. f, Minke whale.

No. 3185, $1.50: a, Common dolphin. b, Antillean beaked whale. c, Killer whale. d, Bryde's whale. e, Cuvier's beaked whale. f, Sei whale.

No. 3186, $1.50: a, Harbor porpoise. b, Beluga. c, White-beaked dolphin. d, Narwhal. e, Bowhead whale. f, Fin whale.

No. 3187, $6, Sperm whale. No. 3188, $6, Blue whale. No. 3189, $6, Southern right whale. No. 3190, $6, Humpback whale.

2001, Sept. 10

3180-3183 A503 Set of 4 4.25 4.25

Sheets of 6, #a-f

3184-3186 A503 Set of 3 20.00 20.00

Souvenir Sheets

3187-3190 A503 Set of 4 18.00 18.00

Monet Paintings — A504

No. 3191, horiz.: a, Boats in Winter Quarters, Etretat. b, Regatta at Sainte Adresse. c, The Bridge at Bougival. d, The Beach at Sainte Adresse.
$6, Monet's Garden at Vétheuil.

2001, May 15 Litho. *Perf. 13¾*

3191 A504 $2 Sheet of 4, #a-d 6.00 6.00

Souvenir Sheet

3192 A504 $6 multi 4.50 4.50

2002 World Cup Soccer Championships, Japan and Korea — A505

No. 3193, $1.50: a, Poster, 1950. b, West German championship team, 1954. c, Just Fontaine, 1958. d, Garrincha, Brazil, 1962. e, Bobby Moore, England, 1966. f, Pelé, Brazil, 1970.

No. 3194, $1.50: a, Osvaldo Ardiles, Argentina, 1978. b, Lakhdar Belloumi, Algeria, 1982. c, Diego Maradona, Argentina, 1986. d, Matthaüs and Völler, West Germany, 1990. e, Seo Jung Won, South Korea, 1994. f, Ronaldo, Brazil, 1998.

No. 3195, $6, Face from Jules Rimet trophy. No. 3196, $6, Face and globe from World Cup trophy.

2001, Nov. 29 *Perf. 13¾x14¼*

Sheets of 6, #a-f

3193-3194 A505 Set of 2 13.50 13.50

Souvenir Sheet

3195-3196 A505 Set of 2 9.00 9.00

Christmas A506

Santa Claus and: 15c, House, Christmas tree. 50c, Trees, snowman. $1, Tree, ice skates. $4, Children.

$6, Santa eating cookie.

2001, Dec. 3 *Perf. 14*

3197-3200 A506 Set of 4 4.25 4.25

Souvneir Sheet

3201 A506 $6 multi 4.50 4.50

A507

Nobel Prizes, Cent. — A508

1901 Laureates: 75c, Emil A. von Behring, Medicine. 90c, Wilhelm C. Röntgen, Physics. $1, Jacobus H. van't Hoff, Chemistry. No. 3205, $1.50, Frederic Passy, Peace. $2, Jean-Henri Dunant, Peace. $3, René Sully-Prudhomme, Literature.

No. 3208, horiz. - Albert Einstein, 1921 Physics laureate, with: a, Dark hair, black suit. b, Pipe. c, Gray suit. d, Pink sweater. e, Gray hair, black suit. f, Blue sweater.

$6, Einstein wearing hat.

2001, Dec. 13

3202-3207 A507 Set of 6 7.00 7.00

3208 A508 $1.50 Sheet of 6, #a-f 6.75 6.75

Souvenir Sheet

3209 A508 $6 multi 4.50 4.50

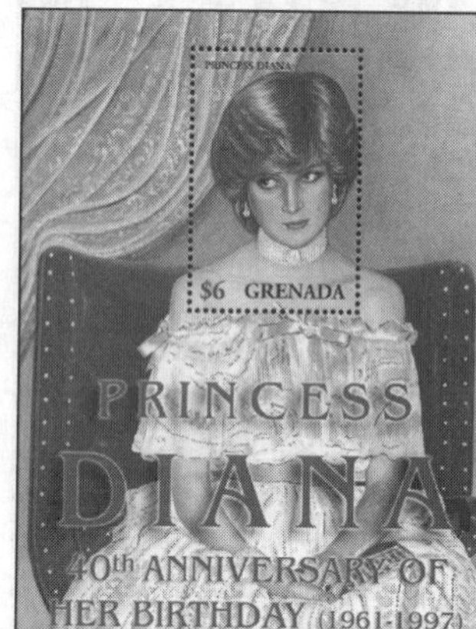

Princess Diana (1961-97) — A509

No. 3210: a, Blue gown. b. White gown. c, Red gown.

$6, With pink curtain.

2001, Dec. 13

3210 A509 $1.50 Sheet, 2 each #a-c 6.75 6.75

Souvenir Sheet

3211 A509 $6 multi 4.50 4.50

Queen Mother Type of 1999

No. 3212: a, Queen Mother, Prince Charles, 1948. b, Queen Mother, 1970. c, Queen Mother in Australia, 1958. d, Queen Mother.

$6, Queen Mother, 1953.

2001, Dec. 13 *Perf. 14*

Yellow Orange Frames

3212 A440 $2 Sheet of 4, #a-d, + label 6.00 6.00

Souvenir Sheet

Perf. 13¾

3213 A440 $6 multi 4.50 4.50

Queen Mother's 101st birthday. No. 3213 contains one 38x50mm stamp with a redder backdrop than that found on No. 2881. Sheet margins of Nos. 3212-3213 lack embossing and gold arms found on Nos. 2880-2881.

New Year 2002 (Year of the Horse) — A510

Ceramic horses of T'ang dynasty - No. 3214: a, Brown horse with long, tan mane. b, Blue horse with pink hooves. c, Black horse with gray mane. d, Tan horse with round ornaments.

$4, Brown horse with gray and green saddle.

2001, Dec. 17 *Perf. 13¾*

3214 A510 $1.50 Sheet of 4, #a-d 4.50 4.50

Souvenir Sheet

3215 A510 $4 multi 3.00 3.00

A511

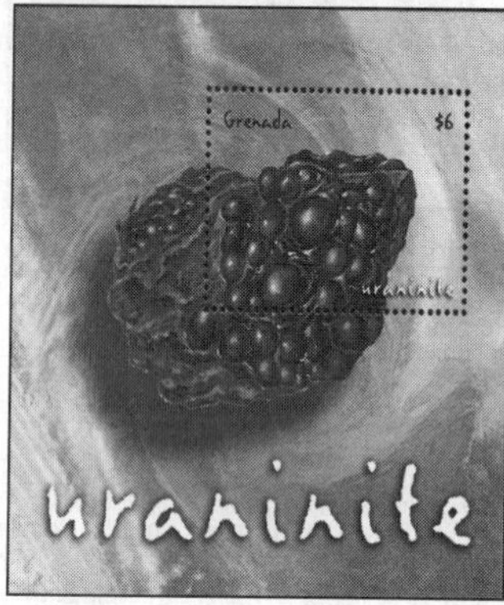

Gemstones and Minerals — A512

Monthly gemstones - No. 3216, $1.50: a, Garnet (January). b, Amethyst (February). c, Aquamarine (March). d, Diamond (April). e, Emerald (May). f, Pearl (June).

No. 3217, $1.50: a, Ruby (July). b, Sardonyx (August). c, Sapphire (September). d, Opal (October). e, Topaz (November). f, Turquoise (December).

Gemstones in mineral form - No. 3218: a, Ruby. b, Diamond. c, Sapphire. d, Opal. e, Turquoise. f, Jade.

No. 3219, $6, Uraninite. No. 3220, $6, Calcite. No. 3221, $6, Quartz, vert.

2001, Dec. 31 *Perf. 14*

Sheets of 6, #a-f

3216-3217 A511 Set of 2 13.50 13.50

3218 A512 $1.50 Sheet of 6, #a-f 6.75 6.75

Souvenir Sheets

3219-3221 A512 Set of 3 13.50 13.50

US Presidents — A513

No. 3222, $1.50 - John F. Kennedy and: a, Field. b, Flag, building, microphone. c, Airplane.

No. 3223, $1.50 - Ronald Reagan: a, In uniform with binoculars. b, With red tie. c, With flag.

No. 3224, $6, Kennedy. No. 3225, $6, Reagan.

2001, Dec. 31

Sheets, 2 each #a-c

3222-3223 A513 Set of 2 13.50 13.50

Souvenir Sheets

3224-3225 A513 Set of 2 9.00 9.00

Souvenir Sheets

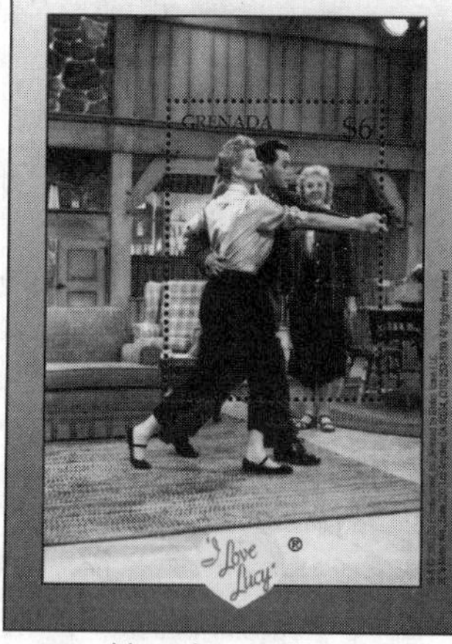

I Love Lucy — A514

Designs: No. 3226, $6, Ethel watching Lucy and Desi dance. No. 3227, $6, Desi, Lucy, Fred and Ethel near door. No. 3228, $6, Desi holding Lucy. No. 3229, $6, Lucy in plaid shirt.

2001 *Perf. 13¾*

3226-3229 A514 Set of 4 18.00 18.00

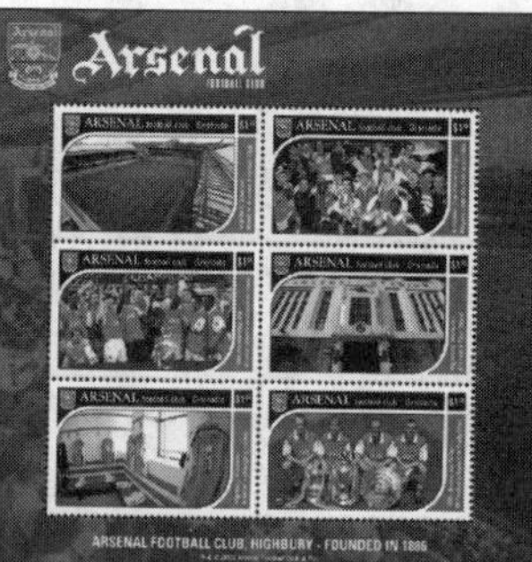

English Soccer Teams — A515

No. 3230, $1.50 - Arsenal: a, Inside of Highbury Stadium. b, Players celebrate 1994 European Cup and Winner's Cup. c, Players celebrate 1998 premiership. d, East stands, Highbury Stadium. e, Locker rooms. f, Four players with trophies, 1998.

No. 3231, $1.50 - Aston Villa: a, Sign on Villa Park. b, Fans watching night game. c, Empty stadium, field at right. d, Empty stadium, field at left. e, Holte End of stadium. f, Fans in stands.

No. 3232, $1.50 - Bolton Wanderers: a, Empty Reebok Stadium. b, Players celebrating 2001 Division 1 playoff win. c, Promotion to Premier League. d, Fans celebrate. e, Players, coaches with trophy. f, Game played in Reebok Stadium.

No. 3233, $1.50 - Everton: a, 2001-02 team. b, Re-signing of Duncan Ferguson. c, Statue of William Ralph "Dixie" Dean. d, Fans. e, Goodison Park. f, 1969-70 league championship team.

No. 3234, $1.50 - Ipswich Town: a, Players holding banner and trophy after 2000 Division 1 playoff final. b, 2001-02 team. c, Manager George Burley and Chairman David Sheepshanks. d, Pablo Counago fights for ball. e, Captain Matt Holland. f, George Burley receives Manager of the Year award.

No. 3235, $1.50 - Liverpool: a, Anfield. b, 2000-01 Worthington Cup winners. c, 2000-01 FA Cup winners. d, Fans. e, 2000-01 UEFA Cup winners. f, Treble Cup parade.

No. 3236, $1.50 - Manchester United: a, Legends Meredith, Law and Charlton. b, Three 1998-99 trophies. c, Views of Old Trafford, 1948, 1956. d, Recent views of Old Trafford. e, Third premiership in three years, 2000-01. f, Heroes, Best, Robson and Beckham.

No. 3237, $1.50 - Rangers: a, View of Ibrox Stadium from street. b, 1972 European Cup and Winner's Cup team. c, Scottish FA Cup, Scottish Premier League Trophy. d, Aerial view of Ibrox Stadium. e, Fans in stadium. f, Nine consecutive Scottish League wins.

2001, Sept. 12 Litho. *Perf. 13¼*

Sheets of 6, #a-f

3230-3237 A515 Set of 8 55.00 55.00

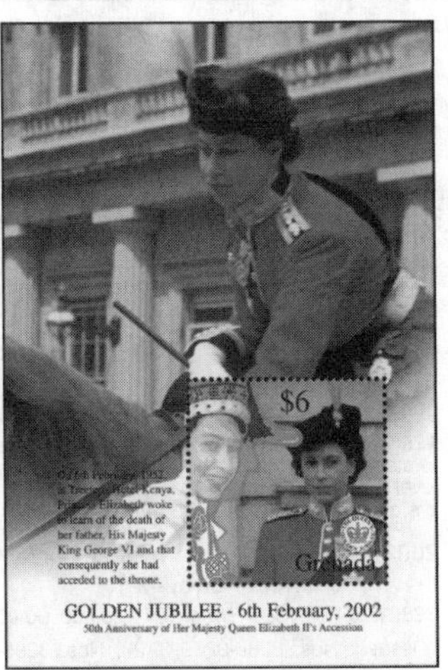

Reign of Queen Elizabeth II, 50th Anniv. — A516

No. 3238: a, With Prince Philip. b, Wearing flowered hat. c, Wearing tiara. d, Wearing gray coat with white collar.
$6, Wearing uniform.

2002, Feb. 6 ***Perf. 14½***

3238 A516 $2 Sheet of 4, #a-d 6.00 6.00

Souvenir Sheet

3239 A516 $6 multi 4.50 4.50

United We Stand — A517

2002, Feb. ***Perf. 13¾x13½***

3240 A517 $2 multi 1.50 1.50

Issued in sheets of 4.

Dale Earnhardt, Race Car Driver — A518

Years of Winston Cup Championships: No. 3241, $2, 1980. No. 3242, $2, 1986. No. 3243, $2, 1987. No. 3244, $2, 1990. No. 3245, $2, 1991. No. 3246, $2, 1993. No. 3247, $2, 1994.

2002, Mar. 4 Litho. ***Perf. 14x13¾***

3241-3247 A518 Set of 7 10.50 10.50

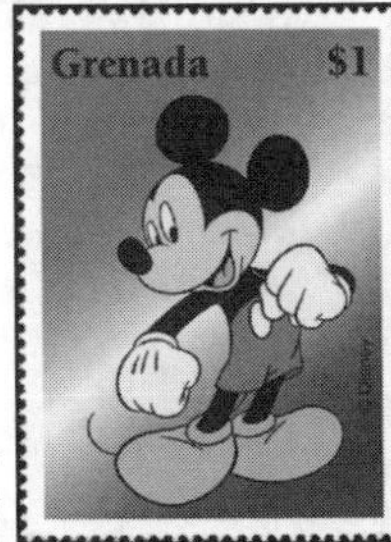

Mickey Mouse A519

No. 3249 - Scenes from: a, The Nifty Nineties, 1941. b, Magician Mickey, 1937. c, Steamboat Willie, 1928. d, Fantasia, 1940. e, Mickey Mouse Club, 1955. f, Cactus Kid, 1930. g, The Prince and the Pauper, 1990. h, Brave Little Tailor, 1938. i, Canine Caddy, 1941.

2002, Apr. 24 ***Perf. 13¾***

3248 A519 $1 shown .75 .75

3249 A519 $1 Sheet of 9, #a-i 6.75 6.75

No. 3248 was printed in sheets of nine.

American Civil War Naval History — A520

No. 3250, $1: a, CSS Teaser. b, US gunboats on the James River. c, USS Tyler. d, USS Maratanza. e, USS Metacomet. f, USS Rattler.

No. 3251, $1.25: a, CSS Tennessee. b, USS Hartford. c, USS Chickasaw. d, USS Ossipee. e, Battle of Mobile Bay. f, USS Chickasaw at Mobile Bay.

No. 3252, $1.50: a, CSS H.L. Hunley. b, USS Cumberland. c, CSS Old Dominion. d, USS Housatonic. e, USS Hartford. f, USS Essex.

No. 3253, $1.50: a, CSS Alabama. b, USS Kearsarge and CSS Alabama. c, USS Hatteras. d, CSS Alabama and decoy. e, CSS Sumter. f, USS Kearsarge.

No. 3254, $6, USS Monitor. No. 3255, $6, CSS Florida. No. 3256, $6, CSS Tennessee. No. 3257, $6, Capt. Raphael Semmes aboard CSS Alabama.

2002, Apr. 8 Litho. ***Perf. 13¼x13½***

Sheets of 6, #a-f

3250-3253 A520 Set of 4 24.00 24.00

Souvenir Sheets

3254-3257 A520 Set of 4 18.00 18.00

Chiune Sugihara, Japanese Diplomat Who Saved Jews in World War II — A521

2002, July 1 ***Perf. 13½x13¾***

3258 A521 $2 multi 1.50 1.50

Printed in sheets of 4.

2002 Winter Olympics, Salt Lake City A522

Skier with: No. 3259, $2, Red skis. No. 3260, $2, Yellow skis.

2002, July 1 ***Perf. 13¼x13½***

3259-3260 A522 Set of 2 3.00 3.00

a. Souvenir sheet, #3259-3260 3.00 3.00

Intl. Year of Mountains — A523

No. 3261: a, Mt. Mawensi, Kenya. b, Mt. Stanley, Uganda. c, Mt. Taweche, Nepal. d, Mt. San Exupery, Argentina.
$6, Mt. Aso, Japan.

2002, July 1

3261 A523 $2 Sheet of 4, #a-d 6.00 6.00

Souvenir Sheet

3262 A523 $6 multi 4.50 4.50

Intl. Year of Ecotourism — A524

No. 3263, horiz.: a, Tower and pennants. b, Bird. c, Flower, vacationer on chair. d, Diver, fish. e, Fish. f, Sailboats.
$6, Map of Grenada, bird.

2002, July 1 ***Perf. 13¼x13½***

3263 A524 $1 Sheet of 6, #a-f 4.50 4.50

Souvenir Sheet

Perf. 13½x13¼

3264 A524 $6 multi 4.50 4.50

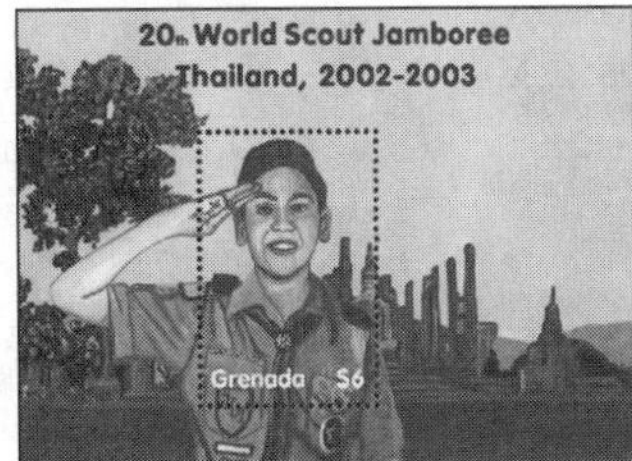

20th World Scout Jamboree, Thailand — A525

No. 3265, horiz.: a, Scout in canoe with oar out of water. b, Scout in canoe with oar in water. c, Bugler. d, Scout making Scout sign.
$6, Scout saluting.

2002, July 1 ***Perf. 13¼x13½***

3265 A525 $2 Sheet of 4, #a-d 6.00 6.00

Souvenir Sheet

Perf. 13½x13¼

3266 A525 $6 multi 4.50 4.50

Model Heidi Klum — A526

No. 3267: a, Arms up. b, Arms down. c, No arms shown.
Illustration reduced.

2002, Aug. 16 ***Perf. 14***

3267 A526 $1.50 Horiz. strip of 3, #a-c 3.50 3.50

Printed in sheets containing two strips.

Elvis Presley (1935-77) A527

2002, Aug. 26 ***Perf. 13½x13¾***

3268 A527 $1 multi .75 .75

Printed in sheets of 9.

Pokémon — A528

No. 3269: a, Mareep. b, Sunkern. c, Teddiursa. d, Swinub. e, Murkrow. f, Snubbull.
$6, Togepi.

2002, Aug. 26 ***Perf. 13¾***

3269 A528 $1.50 Sheet of 6, #a-f 6.75 6.75

Souvenir Sheet

3270 A528 $6 multi 4.50 4.50

A529

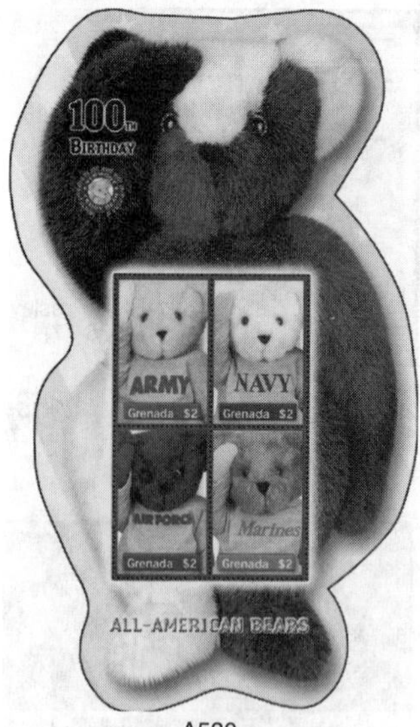

A530

Teddy Bears, Cent. — A531

No. 3271: a, 25c, Bear with red hat, lace collar, cheese wheels. b, $1.25, Bear with black cap. c, $3, Bear with wooden shoes. d, $5, Bear with red hat and ribbon.

No. 3272: a, Army bear. b, Navy bear. c, Air Force bear. d, Marines bear.

No. 3273: a, Basketball bear. b, Martial arts bear. c, Golf bear. d, Baseball bear.

2002, Aug. 26 ***Perf. 14***

3271 A529 Sheet of 4, #a-d 7.25 7.25

Perf. 14¼

3272 A530 $2 Sheet of 4, #a-d 6.00 6.00
3273 A531 $2 Sheet of 4, #a-d 6.00 6.00

Dutch Nobel Prize Winners — A532

Dutch Lighthouses — A533

Traditional Dutch Women's Costumes — A534

No. 3274: a, Jacobus H. van't Hoff, Chemistry, 1901. b, Nobel Peace medal. c, Pieter Zeeman, Physics, 1902. d, Johannes D. van der Waals, Physics, 1910. e, Tobias M. C. Asser, Peace, 1911. f, Heike Kammerlingh-Onnes, Physics, 1913.

No. 3275: a, Schiermonnikoog. b, Texel. c, Egmond. d, Scheveningen. e, Schouwen. f, Hellevoetsluis.

No. 3276: a, Zeeland (woman with red necklace, patterned dress). b, Noord-Brabant (woman with black shawl). c, Noord-Holland (woman with flowered neckpiece).

2002, Aug. 29 ***Perf. 13½x13¼***

3274 A532 $1.50 Sheet of 6, #a-f 6.75 6.75
3275 A533 $1.50 Sheet of 6, #a-f 6.75 6.75

Perf. 13¼

3276 A534 $3 Sheet of 3, #a-c 6.75 6.75

Amphilex 2002 Intl. Stamp Exhibition, Amsterdam.

Shirley Temple — A535

Scenes from "Our Little Girl" - No. 3277, horiz.: a, With man. b, With man and woman. c, With dog and man. d, With woman and two men. e, On seesaw with dog. f, With dog.

No. 3278: a, With woman. b, with man and clown. c, Kneeling beside chair. d, With man and woman.

$6, In pink dress.

2002, Sept. 3 ***Perf. 14¼***

3277 A535 $1.50 Sheet of 6, #a-f 6.75 6.75
3278 A535 $2 Sheet of 4, #a-d 6.00 6.00

Souvenir Sheet

3279 A535 $6 multi 4.50 4.50

Souvenir Sheet

Terrorist Attack on World Trade Center, 1st Anniv. — A536

2002, Sept. 11 ***Perf. 13¾***

3280 A536 $6 multi 4.50 4.50

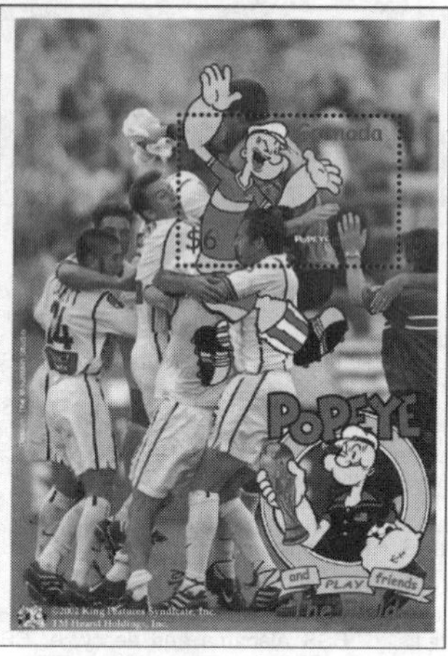

Popeye — A537

No. 3281, vert.: a, Popeye in Florence, Italy. b, Popeye and Brutus in Paris, France. c, Popeye in Athens, Greece. d, Popeye and Olive Oyl in Venice, Italy. e, Popeye in London, England. f, Popeye in Norway.

No. 3282, vert. - At soccer match: a, Swee'Pea. b, Jeep. c, Popeye. d, Brutus.

No. 3283, $6, Popeye playing soccer. No. 3284, $6, Brutus playing soccer. No. 3285, $6, Popeye at Leaning Tower of Pisa, vert.

Perf. 14¼ (#3281, 3285), 14

2002, Sept. 23

3281 A537 $1.50 Sheet of 6, #a-f 6.75 6.75
3282 A537 $2 Sheet of 4, #a-d 6.00 6.00

Souvenir Sheets

3283-3285 A537 Set of 3 13.50 13.50

No. 3218 contains six 38x50mm stamps; No. 3285 contains one 50x75mm stamp.

English Soccer Teams Type of 2001

No. 3286, $1.50 - Tottenham Hotspur: a, Fans watching match in White Hart Lane Stadium. b, Sheringham and Anderton in action against Fulham. c, Poyet scoring against Liverpool. d, Tottenham Hotspur wins UEFA Cup, 1972. e, Celebrations after win against Chelsea. f, Fans in stadium, team insignia.

No. 3287, $1.50 - Manchester City: a, Maine Road Stadium from stands. b, Fans celebrate becoming Division One champions. c, Manager Kevin Keegan and trophy. d, Team with trophy. e, Players wearing medals, with trophy. f, Field level view of Maine Road Stadium.

No. 3288, $1.50 - Norwich City: a, Match at the Nest. b, Promotion to the Top Flight, 1971-72. c, Milk Cup win, 1985. d, Carrow Road Stadium. e, Win against Bayern Munich, 1993. f, Action from 1958-59 Cup run.

No. 3289, $1.50 - Arsenal, Double Winners: a, Tony Adams and Patrick Vieira hold FA Cup. b, Team wearing tan shirts, holding championship bannners. c, Team without banners, at Premiership trophy presentation. d, Photo of 2001-02 Premiership team, standing and wearing red shirts. e, Four players celebrate winning goal against Chelsea. f, Manager Arsene Wenger and Tony Adams at Double Winners Parade.

No. 3290, $1.50 - Arsenal, Premiership Winners: a, Inside of Highbury Stadium, team emblem and name in red panels. b, Celebrations after Gilberto scores winning goal. c, Team with FA Community Shield sign. d, Team photo, empty stands. e, Gilberto with FA Community Shield. f, Highbury Stadium with fans, team emblem.

No. 3291, $1.50 - Manchester United: a, David Beckham after free kick. b, Team photo, empty stands. c, Aerial view of Old Trafford Stadium. d, Celebration after Ole Gunnar Solskjaer's 100th goal for Manchester United. e, Fans at Old Trafford Stadium. f, North stand of Old Trafford Stadium.

No. 3292, $1.50 - Liverpool: a, Anfield's Centenary stand, as seen from Main stand. b, 2002-03 team photo. c, Gerard Houllier and Phil Thompson. d, Milan Baros celebrates goal. e, Vladimir Smicer congratulating Danny Murphy. f, The Kop, as seen from Anfield Road end.

No. 3293, $1.50 - Celtic: a, Interior of Celtic Park. b, Martin O'Neill with SPL Trophy. c, Henrik Larsson celebrating goal. d, 2002-03 team photo. e, Players celebrating a goal. f, Exterior of Celtic Park.

No. 3294, $1.50 - Chelsea: a, Night match at Stamford Bridge Stadium. b, Team with 1998 Cup Winners' Cup Final trophy. c, Fans in stadium. d, Sign for the Shed End. e, Field level view of Stamford Bridge Stadium. f, Players celebrating 2000 FA Cup victory.

2002 ***Perf. 14x13¾***

Sheets of 6, #a-f

3286-3294 A515 Set of 9 60.00 60.00

Issued: Nos. 3286-3289, 9/23; Nos. 3290-3294, 11/14.

Butterflies, Insects, Mushrooms and Whales — A538

No. 3295, $1.50 - Butterflies: a, Common morpho. b, Blue night. c, Small flambeau. d, Grecian shoemaker. e, Orange-barred sulphur. f, Cramer's mesene.

No. 3296, $1.50 - Insects: a, Honeybees. b, Dragonfly. c, Milkweed bug. d, Bumblebee. e, Migratory grasshopper. f, Monarch caterpillar.

No. 3297, $1.50 - Mushrooms: a, Boletus crocipodius. b, King bolete. c, Velvet shank. d, Death cap. e, Golden cavalier. f, Fly agaric.

No. 3298, $1.50 - Whales: a, Blue. b, Pygmy sperm. c, Humpback. d, Killer. e, Bowhead. f, Gray.

No. 3299, $6, Figure-of-eight butterfly. No. 3300, $6, Hercules beetle. No. 3301, $6, Sharp-scaled parasol mushroom. No. 3302, $6, Blue whale, horiz.

2002, Oct. 21 ***Perf. 14***

Sheets of 6, #a-f

3295-3298 A538 Set of 4 27.50 27.50

Souvenir Sheets

3299-3302 A538 Set of 4 18.00 18.00

Sir Norman Wisdom, British Comedian A539

2002, Nov. 3 ***Perf. 13¾***

3303 A539 $1.50 multi 1.10 1.10

Printed in sheets of 6.

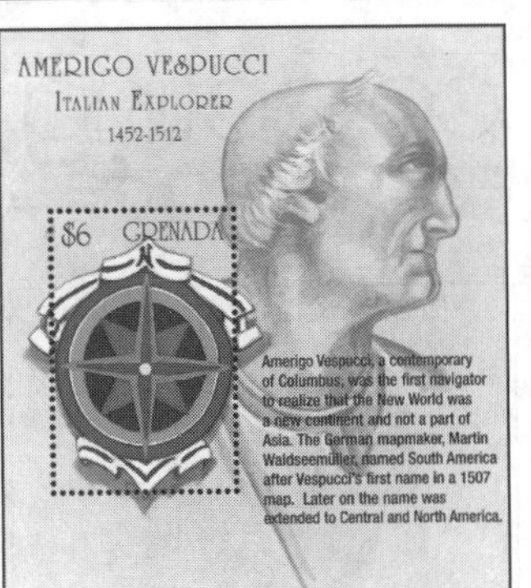

Amerigo Vespucci (1454-1512), Explorer — A540

No. 3304, $3: a, Map of South America, ship. b, Compass rose, ship. c, Map of Europe and Africa.

No. 3305, $3, horiz.: a, Sextant, map of northern South America. b, Vespucci, map of central South America. c, Ship, map of southern South America.

No. 3306, $6, Compass rose. No. 3307, $6, Globe.

2002, Nov. 4 ***Perf. 13¾***

Sheets of 3, #a-c

3304-3305 A540 Set of 2 13.50 13.50

Souvenir Sheets

Perf. 14

3306-3307 A540 Set of 2 9.00 9.00

No. 3304 contains three 38x50mm stamps; No. 3305 contains three 50x38mm stamps.

Christmas A541

Cimabue paintings: 15c, Madonna and Child, Four Angels and St. Francis, entire. 25c, Madonna and Child and Two Angels, vert. 50c, Madonna Enthroned, detail, vert. $1, Madonna Enthroned, entire, vert. $4, Madonna and Child, Four Angels and St. Francis, detail, vert.

$6, Nativity by Perugino, vert.

2002, Nov. 4 ***Perf. 14***

3308-3312 A541 Set of 5 4.50 4.50

Souvenir Sheet

3313 A541 $6 multi 4.50 4.50

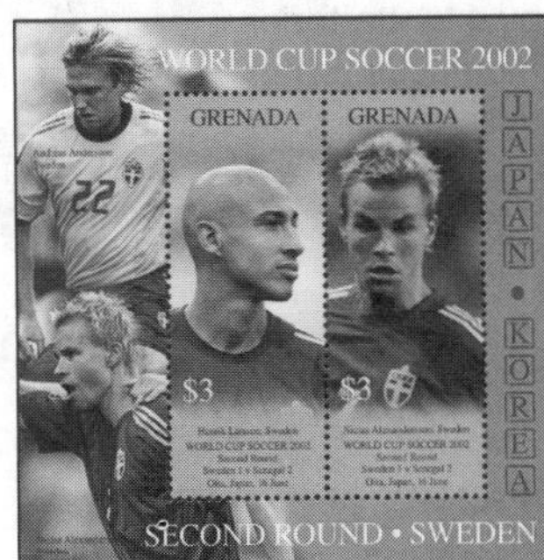

Second Round Matches of 2002 World Cup Soccer Championships, Japan and Korea — A542

No. 3314, $1.50 - Sweden vs. Senegal: a, Johan Mjalby. b, Magnus Hedman. c, Fredrik Ljungberg. d, Khalilou Fadiga. e, El Hadji Diouf. f, Papa Bouba Diop.

No. 3315, $1.50 - Brazil vs. Belgium: a, Roberto Carlos. b, Juninho Paulista. c, Ronaldinho. d, Johan Walem. e, Marc Wilmots. f, Bart Goor.

No. 3316, $3 - Swedish players: a, Henrik Larsson. b, Niclas Alexandersson.

No. 3317, $3 - Senegal players: a, Fadiga. b, Coach Bruno Metsu.

No. 3318, $3 - Brazil players: a, Coach Luiz Felipe Scolari. b, Ronaldo.

No. 3319, $3 - Belgium players: a, Wesley Sonck. b, Coach Robert Waseige.

2002, Nov. 18 ***Perf. 13¼***

Sheets of 6, #a-f

3314-3315 A542 Set of 2 13.50 13.50

Souvenir Sheets of 2, #a-b

3316-3319 A542 Set of 4 18.00 18.00

Souvenir Sheet

United States Natl. Law Enforcement and Firefighters Children's Foundation — A543

2002, Nov. 28 ***Perf. 14¼***

3320 A543 $6 multi 4.50 4.50

Pres. John F. Kennedy (1917-63) — A544

No. 3321, horiz.: a, Meeting with Cabinet. b, Signing bill into law. c, Meeting civil rights leaders. d, With Astronaut John Glenn. e, On campaign trail. f, Arrival in Dallas, Nov. 22, 1963.

$6, At microphone.

2002, Dec. 4 ***Perf. 14***

3321 A544 $1.50 Sheet of 6, #a-f 6.75 6.75

Souvenir Sheet

3322 A544 $6 multi 4.50 4.50

Intl. Federation of Stamp Dealers Associations, 50th Anniv. — A545

2002, Dec. 16 **Litho.**

3323 A545 $2 multi 1.50 1.50

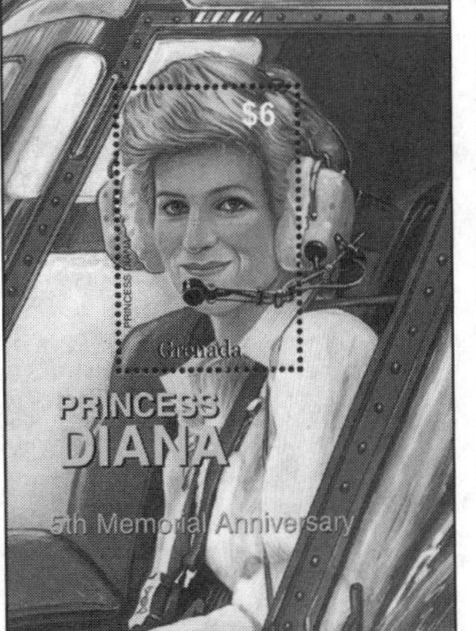

Princess Diana (1961-97) — A546

No. 3324: a, Wearing bow tie. b, Wearing blue dress. c, Wearing red and white hat. d, Holding flowers.

$6, Wearing earphones and microphone.

2002 ***Perf. 14***

3324 A546 $2 Sheet of 4, #a-d 6.00 6.00

Souvenir Sheet

3325 A546 $6 multi 4.50 4.50

I Love Lucy Type of 2001

Souvenir Sheets

No. 3326, $6, Lucy standing near fireplace. No. 3327, $6, Lucy and Ethel at desk. No. 3328, $6, Fred and Desi standing. No. 3329, $6, Fred and Desi at desk, horiz.

2002 ***Perf. 13¾***

3326-3329 A514 Set of 4 18.00 18.00

New Year 2003 (Year of the Ram) A547

2003, Jan. 27 ***Perf. 13¾***

3330 A547 $1.25 multi .95 .95

Printed in sheets of 4.

SEMI-POSTAL STAMPS

Catalogue values for unused stamps in this section are for Never Hinged items.

ESPANA '82 World Cup Soccer SP1

Players and Flags of Winning Countries.

Unwmk.

1981, Nov. 30 **Litho.** ***Perf. 14***

B1	SP1 25c + 10c West Germany, 1974	.35	.35
B2	SP1 40c + 20c Argentina, 1978	.60	.60
B3	SP1 50c + 25c Brazil, 1970	.75	.75
B4	SP1 $1 + 50c Grt. Britain, 1966	1.50	1.50
	Nos. B1-B4 (4)	3.20	3.20

Souvenir Sheet

B5 SP1 $5 + 50c World Cup, ESPANA '82 3.75 3.75

Nos. B1-B4 each issued in sheets of 12 with sheet background showing soccer ball.

1988 Seoul Olympics — SP2

1986, Dec. 1 **Litho.** ***Perf. 15***

B6	SP2 10c + 5c Pole vault	.20	.20
B7	SP2 50c + 20c Balance beam	.30	.30
B8	SP2 70c + 30c Shot put	.40	.40
B9	SP2 $2 + $1 High jump	1.25	1.25
	Nos. B6-B9 (4)	2.15	2.15

Souvenir Sheet

B10 SP2 $3 + $1 Swimming 1.75 1.75

Surtax for natl. Olympic team.

World Philatelic Programs SP3

Halley's Comet or Stamp Collecting emblem and: No. B11, Halley's initial work on nebulae, 1676. No. B12, Experiments at sea (tall ship, manned capsule). No. B13, Halley observes complete lunar cycle, 1720-1738. No. B14, Halley publishes Newton's Principia, 1687. No. B15, Halley charts the southern skies, 1676.

1989, Apr. 25 **Litho.** ***Perf. 14***

B11	SP3 25c +5c multi	.25	.25
B12	SP3 75c +5c multi	.60	.60
B13	SP3 90c +5c multi	.70	.70
B14	SP3 $2 +5c multi	1.50	1.50

Size: 111x78mm

Imperf

B15	SP3 $5 +5c multi	3.75	3.75
	Nos. B11-B15 (5)	6.80	6.80

AIR POST STAMPS

Catalogue values for unused stamps in this section are for Never Hinged items.

Nos. 428-429 Surcharged with New Value, Olympic Rings, "Air Mail" and: "WINTER OLYMPICS / FEB. 3-13, 1972 / SAPPORO, JAPAN"

Perf. 13½x14

1972, Feb. 3 **Litho.** **Unwmk.**

C1	A66 35c on ½c multi	.40	.40
C2	A66 50c on 1c multi	.60	.60

11th Winter Olympic Games, Sapporo, Japan, Feb. 3-13.

Nos. 294-300, 302A, 303-309 Surcharged Type "a" or Overprinted Type "b"

a

b

Perfs. as Before

1972, May 2 — Photo.; Litho.

C3	A45	5c violet & multi	.20	.20
C4	A45	8c multicolored	.20	.20
C5	A45	10c orange & multi	.20	.20
C6	A45	15c gray & multi	.20	.20
C7	A45	25c multicolored	.30	.30
C8	A45	30c on 1c multi	.35	.35
C9	A45	35c multicolored	.40	.40
C10	A45	40c on 2c multi	.45	.45
C11	A45	45c on 3c multi	.50	.50
C12	A45	50c multicolored	.55	.55
C13	A45	60c on 5c multi	.70	.70
C14	A45	70c on 6c multi	.80	.80
C15	A45	$1 multicolored	2.25	.75
C16	A45	$1.35 on 8c multi	2.00	1.60
C17	A45	$2 multicolored	3.50	2.25
C18	A45	$3 multicolored	4.25	3.25
C19	A45	$5 multicolored	6.50	*7.50*
		Nos. C3-C19 (17)	23.35	20.20

"AIR MAIL" reading down on 5c, 15c, 25c, 35c, 60c and $5.

Olympic Type of Regular Issue

Olympic Rings and: 25c, 60c, $1, Boxing. 70c, Equestrian (not inscribed air mail).

1972, Sept. 8 — Litho. — *Perf. 14*

C20	A69	25c blue & multi	.40	.40
C21	A69	$1 green & multi	.85	.85

Souvenir Sheet

C22		Sheet of 2	1.50	1.50
a.		A69 60c blue & multi	.50	.50
b.		A69 70c deep yellow & multi	1.00	1.00

Nos. 409-412 Overprinted Vertically, Reading Up "AIR MAIL"

1972, Oct. — Litho. — *Perf. 11*

C23	A62	5c multicolored	.20	.20
C24	A62	35c multicolored	.60	.60
C25	A62	50c multicolored	1.00	1.00
C26	A62	75c multicolored	2.00	2.00
		Nos. C23-C26 (4)	3.80	3.80

Boy Scout Type of Regular Issue

Designs: 25c, Scout saluting. 35c, Two Scouts knotting ropes.

1972, Nov. — *Perf. 14*

C27	A70	25c dp blue & multi	.45	.45
C28	A70	35c brn org & multi	.65	.65

John Hancock — AP1

Designs: 50c, Benjamin Franklin. 75c, John Adams. $1, Marquis de Lafayette.

1975, May 6 — Litho. — *Perf. 14½, 13*

C29	AP1	40c multicolored	.30	*.20*
C30	AP1	50c multicolored	.50	*.25*
C31	AP1	75c multicolored	.65	*.25*
C32	AP1	$1 multicolored	.75	*.30*
		Nos. C29-C32 (4)	2.20	*1.00*

American Revolution Bicentennial.

Nos. C29-C32 issued in sheets of 40. Each denomination was also printed in sheets of 5 plus label, perf. 13.

POSTAGE DUE STAMPS

D1

D2

1892 — Typo. — Wmk. 2 — *Perf. 14*

J1	D1	1p black	25.00	3.00
J2	D1	2p black	125.00	3.50
J3	D1	3p black	150.00	4.50
		Nos. J1-J3 (3)	300.00	11.00

Black Surcharge

J4	D2	1p on 6p red lilac	60.00	2.50
a.		Tete beche pair	500.00	
b.		Double surcharge		125.00
c.		Same as "b," tete beche pair		
J5	D2	1p on 8p bister	400.00	6.75
a.		Tete beche pair	*1,650.*	*950.00*
J6	D2	2p on 6p red lilac	125.00	5.00
a.		Tete beche pair	*700.00*	
J7	D2	2p on 8p bister	750.00	12.00
a.		Tete beche pair	*3,000.*	
		Nos. J4-J7 (4)	1,335.	26.25

Nos. J4-J7 were printed with alternate horizontal rows inverted.

1906-11 — Wmk. 3

J8	D1	1p black ('11)	2.25	2.25
J9	D1	2p black	4.50	3.75
J10	D1	3p black	9.50	6.00
		Nos. J8-J10 (3)	16.25	12.00

D3

1921-22 — Wmk. 4

J11	D3	1p black	1.00	*1.40*
J12	D3	1½p black	4.25	*6.50*
J13	D3	2p black	3.00	*4.50*
J14	D3	3p black	3.25	*4.75*
		Nos. J11-J14 (4)	11.50	*17.15*

Issued: 1½p, Dec. 15, 1922, others, Dec. 1921.

Catalogue values for unused stamps in this section, from this point to the end of the section, are for Never Hinged items.

1952, Mar. 1

J15	D3	2c black	.30	*3.00*
a.		Wmk. 4a (error)	25.00	
J16	D3	4c black	.30	*3.00*
a.		Wmk. 4a (error)	25.00	
J17	D3	6c black	.40	*5.00*
a.		Wmk. 4a (error)	42.50	
J18	D3	8c black	.30	*5.00*
a.		Wmk. 4a (error)	50.00	
		Nos. J15-J18 (4)	1.30	*16.00*

WAR TAX STAMPS

Nos. 80a, 80 Overprinted — WAR TAX

1916 — Wmk. 3 — *Perf. 14*

MR1	A21	1p carmine	1.75	1.50
a.		1p scarlet	3.00	3.00
b.		Double overprint	225.00	
c.		Inverted overprint	225.00	

No. 80 Overprinted — WAR TAX

MR2	A21	1p scarlet	.30	.20

OFFICIAL STAMPS

Catalogue values for unused stamps in this section are for Never Hinged items.

Nos. 1006-1018, 1020, 1051-1053 Overprinted: "P.R.G."

1982, July 15 — Litho. — *Perf. 14, 15*

O1	A141	5c multicolored	.20	.20
O2	A141	6c multicolored	.20	.20
O3	A141	10c multicolored	.20	.20
O4	A141	12c multicolored	.20	.20
O5	A141	15c multicolored	.20	.20
O6	A141	20c multicolored	.20	.20
O7	A141	25c multicolored	.20	.20
O8	A141	30c multicolored	.25	.25
O9	A141	40c multicolored	.30	.30
O10	A141	50c multicolored	.40	.40
O11	CD331	50c multicolored	.40	.40
O12	A141	90c multicolored	.75	.75
O13	A141	$1 multicolored	.80	.80
O14	CD331	$2 multicolored	2.00	2.00
O15	A141	$3 multicolored	2.50	2.50
O16	CD331	$4 multicolored	4.50	4.50
O17	A141	$10 multicolored	8.00	8.00
		Nos. O1-O17 (17)	21.30	21.30

PRG stands for People's Revolutionary Government.

GRENADA GRENADINES

grə-ˈnā-də ˌgre-nə-ˈdēnz

LOCATION — North of Grenada
GOVT. — Part of Grenada
CAPITAL — None

Main islands are Carriacou and Ronde.

Catalogue values for all unused stamps in this country are for Never Hinged items.

All stamps are a type of Grenada unless otherwise noted or illustrated. Nos. 15-58 have the additional inscription Grenadines.

Grenada Nos. 516-517a Overprinted

Perf. 13½x14

1973, Dec. 23 Litho. Wmk. 314

1 A77 25c dp orange & multi .20 .20
2 A77 $2 green & multi .70 .50
a. Souvenir sheet of 2 (75c, $1) .90 .50

Grenada Nos. 294-297, 299-301, 303, 306-309 Overprinted

Perf. 14x14½, 14½x14

1974, May 29 Photo. Unwmk.

Size: 25x44mm

3 A45 1c multicolored .20 .20
4 A45 2c multicolored .20 .20
5 A45 3c multicolored .20 .20
6 A45 5c multicolored .20 .20
7 A45 8c multicolored .20 .20
8 A45 10c multicolored .20 .20
9 A45 12c multicolored .20 .20
10 A45 25c multicolored .25 .25

Size: 25x47mm

11 A45 $1 multicolored 2.25 .65
12 A45 $2 multicolored 2.50 1.00
13 A45 $3 multicolored 2.50 1.50
14 A45 $5 multicolored 3.75 1.75
Nos. 3-14 (12) 12.65 6.55

World Cup Soccer Type

Designs: Soccer matches and flags. ½c, West Germany-Chile. 1c, East Germany-Australia. 2c, Yugoslavia-Brazil. 10c, Scotland-Zaire. 25c, Netherlands-Uruguay. 50c, Sweden-Bulgaria. 75c, Italy-Haiti. $1, Poland-Argentina. $2, Flags of participating nations.

1974, Sept. 17 Litho. Perf. 14½

15 A81 ½c multicolored .20 .20
16 A81 1c multicolored .20 .20
17 A81 2c multicolored .20 .20
18 A81 10c multicolored .20 .20
19 A81 25c multicolored .20 .20
20 A81 50c multicolored .25 .25
21 A81 75c multicolored .25 .25
22 A81 $1 multicolored .30 .30
Nos. 15-22 (8) 1.80 1.80

Souvenir Sheet

23 A81 $2 multicolored 1.10 1.10

UPU Centenary Type

UPU Emblem and: 8c, Mailboat *Caesar*, 1839, helicopter. 25c, German messenger, 1540, satellite. 35c, Biplanes, zeppelin, jet. No. 27, US Mail train, 19th cent., Concorde. No. 28a, Bellman, 18th cent., radar. $2, German postman, 18th cent., mail train, 1980's.

1974, Oct. 8 Perf. 14½

24 A82 8c multicolored .20 .20
25 A82 25c multicolored .20 .20
26 A82 35c multicolored .20 .20
27 A82 $1 multicolored .65 .40
Nos. 24-27 (4) 1.25 1.00

Souvenir Sheet

Perf. 13

28 Sheet of 2 1.75 1.75
a. A82 $1 multicolored .50 .50
b. A82 $2 multicolored 1.25 1.25

Churchill Type

Design: $2, Churchill, different portrait.

1974, Nov. 11 Perf. 13½

29 A83 35c multicolored .20 .20
30 A83 $2 multicolored .50 .50

Souvenir Sheet

31 Sheet of 2 .65 .65
a. A82 75c like 35c .30 .30
b. A82 $1 like $2 .35 .35

Christmas Type

Paintings of the Virgin and Child.

1974, Nov. 27 Perf. 14½

32 A84 ½c Botticelli .20 .20
33 A84 1c Niccolo di Pietro .20 .20
34 A84 2c Van der Weyden .20 .20
35 A84 3c Bastiani .20 .20
36 A84 10c Giovanni .20 .20
37 A84 25c Van der Weyden, diff. .20 .20
38 A84 50c Botticelli .20 .20
39 A84 $1 Mantegna .30 .25
Nos. 32-39 (8) 1.70 1.65

Souvenir Sheet

Perf. 13½

40 A84 $2 Niccolo di Pietro .75 .75

Big Game Fish Type

1975, Feb. 17 Perf. 14½

41 A86 ½c Sailfish .20 .20
42 A86 1c Blue marlin .20 .20
43 A86 2c White marlin .20 .20
44 A86 10c Yellowfin tuna .20 .20
45 A86 25c Wahoo .20 .20
46 A86 50c Dolphin .30 .20
47 A86 70c Grouper .40 .30
48 A86 $1 Great barracuda .50 .50
Nos. 41-48 (8) 2.20 2.00

Souvenir Sheet

Perf. 13

49 A86 $2 Mako shark 1.00 1.25

Flowers of Grenada Type

1975, Mar. 11 Perf. 14½

50 A87 ½c Grandilla barbadine .20 .20
51 A87 1c Bleeding heart .20 .20
52 A87 2c Poinsettia .20 .20
53 A87 3c Cocoa .20 .20
54 A87 10c Gladioli .20 .20
55 A87 25c Red head-yellow head .20 .20
56 A87 50c Plumbago .30 .30
57 A87 $1 Orange blossoms .50 .50
Nos. 50-57 (8) 2.00 2.00

Souvenir Sheet

Perf. 13½

58 A87 $2 Barbados gooseberry 1.10 1.10

Christ Crowned with Thorns, by Titian — G1

Easter paintings of the Crucifixion by various artists.

1975, June 24 Perf. 14½

59 G1 ½c shown .20 .20
60 G1 1c Giotto .20 .20
61 G1 2c Tintoretto .20 .20
62 G1 3c Cranach .20 .20
63 G1 35c Caravaggio .20 .20
64 G1 75c Tiepolo .20 .20
65 G1 $2 Velasquez .30 .25
Nos. 59-65 (7) 1.50 1.45

Souvenir Sheet

Perf. 13½

66 G1 $1 Titian, diff. .75 .75

Works by Michelangelo (1475-1564) — G2

Butterflies — G3

Designs: ½c, Dawn (sculpture, detail from Medici tomb). 1c, Delphic Sibyl. 2c, Giuliano de Medici (sculpture). 40c, The Creation. 50c, Lorenzo de Medici (sculpture). 75c, Persian Sibyl. $1, The Prophet Jeremiah. $2, Head of Christ (sculpture).

1975, July 16 Perf. 14½

67 G2 ½c violet & multi .20 .20
68 G2 1c multicolored .20 .20
69 G2 2c green & multi .20 .20
70 G2 40c multicolored .20 .20
71 G2 50c brt red & multi .25 .25
72 G2 75c multicolored .35 .35
73 G2 $2 brt blue & multi .50 .50
Nos. 67-73 (7) 1.90 1.90

Souvenir Sheet

Perf. 13½

74 G2 $1 multicolored 1.00 .75

1975, Aug. 12 Perf. 15

75 G3 ½c Emperor .20 .20
76 G3 1c Queen .20 .20
77 G3 2c Tiger pierid .20 .20
78 G3 35c Cracker .35 .35
79 G3 45c Scarlet bamboo page .45 .40
80 G3 75c Apricot .75 .75
81 G3 $2 Purple king shoemaker 1.75 1.75
Nos. 75-81 (7) 3.90 3.85

Souvenir Sheet

Perf. 13½

82 G3 $1 Bamboo page 2.90 2.50

Jamboree Scenes and Badges G4

Nordjamb 75 Emblem and: ½c, Progress badge. 1c, Boating badge. 2c, Coxswain badge. 35c. Interpreter badge. 45c, Ambulance badge. 75c, Chief scout's award. $1, Venture award. $2, Queen's scout award.

1975, Aug. 22 Perf. 15

83 G4 ½c lemon yel & multi .20 .20
84 G4 1c vio blue & multi .20 .20
85 G4 2c green & multi .20 .20
86 G4 35c dull vio & multi .20 .20
87 G4 45c org brown & multi .20 .20
88 G4 75c brown & multi .30 .30
89 G4 $2 green & multi .70 .70
Nos. 83-89 (7) 2.00 2.00

Souvenir Sheet

Perf. 13½

90 G4 $1 dull vio & multi .90 .75

Nordjamb 75, 14th Boy Scout World Jamboree, Lillehammer, Norway, July 29-Aug. 7.

Surrender of Lord Cornwallis G5

Designs: 1c, Minuteman. 2c, Paul Revere's Ride. 3c, Battle of Bunker Hill. 5c, *Spirit of '76*. 45c, Backwoodsman. 75c, Boston Tea Party. No. 98, Naval engagement. No. 99, George Washington. No. 100, White House, flags.

1975, Sept. 30 Perf. 14

Size: 39x25mm

91 G5 ½c multicolored .20 .20
92 G5 1c multicolored .20 .20
93 G5 2c multicolored .20 .20
94 G5 3c multicolored .20 .20
95 G5 5c multicolored .20 .20
96 G5 45c multicolored .20 .20

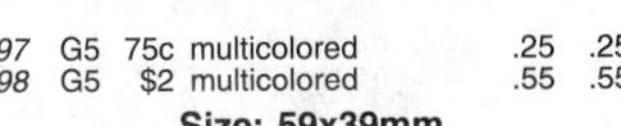

97 G5 75c multicolored .25 .25
98 G5 $2 multicolored .55 .55

Size: 59x39mm

Perf. 11

99 G5 $2 multicolored, vert. .55 .55
a. Souvenir sheet of 1, imperf. 1.10 1.10
100 G4 $2 multicolored .55 .55
a. Souvenir sheet of 1, imperf. 1.10 1.10
Nos. 91-100 (10) 3.10 3.10

American Revolution Bicentennial. Nos. 99a, 100a have simulated perfs.

Fencing G6

1975, Oct. 27 Perf. 15

101 G6 ½c shown .20 .20
102 G6 1c Hurdling .20 .20
103 G6 2c Pole vault .20 .20
104 G6 35c Weightlifting .20 .20
105 G6 45c Javelin .20 .20
106 G6 75c Discus .20 .20
107 G6 $2 Diving .35 .25
Nos. 101-107 (7) 1.55 1.45

Souvenir Sheet

108 G6 $1 Sprinter .60 .60

Pan American Games, Mexico City, Oct. 12-26, 1975.

Type of 1975

Designs: ½c, Cruising Yachts, Point Saline. 1c, Yacht Club race, St. George's. 2c, Careenage Taxi. 3c, Working boats. 5c, Deep water dock, St. George's. 6c, Cocoa beans drying. 8c, Nutmegs. 10c, Rum distillery, River Antoine Estate. 12c, Cocoa tree. 15c, Landing catch at Fontenoy. 20c, Parliament building, St. George's. 25c, Fort George cannons. 35c, Pearls airport. 50c, General Post Office. 75c, Caribs Leap, Sauteurs Bay. $1, Careenage, St. George's. $2, St. George's harbor at night. $3, Grand Anse beach. $5, Canoe and Black Bays from Point Saline lighthouse. $10, Sugar Loaf Island from Levera beach.

1975-76 Perf. 14½

Size: 38x25mm

109 A85 ½c multicolored .20 .25
110 A85 1c multicolored .20 .20
111 A85 2c multicolored .20 .20
112 A85 3c multicolored .20 .20
113 A85 5c multicolored .20 .20
114 A85 6c multicolored .20 .20
115 A85 8c multicolored .20 .20
116 A85 10c multicolored .20 .20
117 A85 12c multicolored .20 .20
118 A85 15c multicolored .20 .20
119 A85 20c multicolored .20 *.35*
120 A85 25c multicolored .20 .20
121 A85 35c multicolored .60 .20
122 A85 50c multicolored .25 *.60*

Perf. 13½x14

Size: 45x28mm

123 A85 75c multicolored .50 .50
124 A85 $1 multicolored .75 .75
125 A85 $2 multicolored 1.10 *1.75*
126 A85 $3 multicolored 1.40 *2.10*
127 A85 $5 multicolored 1.75 *4.75*
128 A85 $10 multicolored 2.75 *4.75*
Nos. 109-128 (20) 11.50 18.00

Issued: #109-127, 11/5/75; #128, 1/1/76.
For overprints see Nos. 360-372.

Madonna and Child by Durer — G8

Christmas: Paintings showing Madonna and Child by various artists.

1975, Dec. 17 Perf. 14

129 G8 ½c shown .20 .20
130 G8 1c Durer, diff. .20 .20
131 G8 2c Correggio .20 .20
132 G8 40c Botticelli .20 .20
133 G8 50c Niccolo da Cremona .20 .20

134 G8 75c Correggio, diff. .20 .20
135 G8 $2 Correggio, diff. .35 .25
Nos. 129-135 (7) 1.55 1.45

Souvenir Sheet

136 G8 $1 Bellini .70 .60

Sea Shells
G9

1976, Jan. 13

137 G9 ½c Bleeding Tooth .20 .20
138 G9 1c Wedge clam .20 .20
139 G9 2c Hawk wing conch .20 .20
140 G9 3c Distorsio clathrata .20 .20
141 G9 25c Scotch bonnet .40 .20
142 G9 50c King helmet .80 .20
143 G9 75c Queen conch 1.25 .25
Nos. 137-143 (7) 3.25 1.45

Souvenir Sheet

144 G9 $2 Atlantic triton 2.00 1.50

Lignum Vitae
G10

Designs: 1c, Cocoa thrush. 2c, Tarantula. 35c, Hooded tanager. 50c, Nyctaginaceae. 75c, Grenada dove. $1, Marine toad. $2, Blue-hooded euphonia.

1976, Feb. 4

145 G10 ½c multicolored .20 .20
146 G10 1c multicolored .20 .20
147 G10 2c multicolored .20 .20
148 G10 35c multicolored .75 .20
149 G10 50c multicolored 1.10 .25
150 G10 75c multicolored 1.60 .30
151 G10 $1 multicolored 2.25 .30
Nos. 145-151 (7) 6.30 1.65

Souvenir Sheet

152 G10 $2 multicolored 4.25 1.25

Hooked Sailfish
G11

Designs: 1c, Careened schooner, Carriacou. 2c, Annual regatta. 18c, Boat building. 22c, Workboat race. 75c, Cruising off Petit Martinique. $1, Water skiing. $2, Yacht racing.

1976, Feb. 17

153 G11 ½c multicolored .20 .20
154 G11 1c multicolored .20 .20
155 G11 2c multicolored .20 .20
156 G11 18c multicolored .30 .20
157 G11 22c multicolored .30 .20
158 G11 75c multicolored .50 .30
159 G11 $1 multicolored .65 .35
Nos. 153-159 (7) 2.35 1.65

Souvenir Sheet

160 G11 $2 multicolored 1.00 1.00

Making a Camp Fire
G12

50th anniv. of Girl Guides of Grenada: 1c, First aid. 2c, Nature study. 50c, Cooking. $1, Drawing. $2, Playing guitar.

1976, Mar. 17

161 G12 ½c multicolored .20 .20
162 G12 1c multicolored .20 .20
163 G12 2c multicolored .20 .20
164 G12 50c multicolored .50 .25
165 G12 $1 multicolored 1.00 .30
Nos. 161-165 (5) 2.10 1.15

Souvenir Sheet

166 G12 $2 multicolored 1.25 1.00

Christ Mocked by Bosch — G13

Easter Paintings: 1c, Christ Crucified by Messina. 2c, Adoration by Durer. 3c, Lamentation of Christ by Durer. 35c, The Entombment by Van Der Weyden. $2, Blood of the Redeemer by Bellini. $3, The Deposition by Raphael.

1976, Apr. 28

167 G13 ½c multicolored .20 .20
168 G13 1c multicolored .20 .20
169 G13 2c multicolored .20 .20
170 G13 3c multicolored .20 .20
171 G13 35c multicolored .20 .20
172 G13 $3 multicolored .50 .30
Nos. 167-172 (6) 1.50 1.30

Souvenir Sheet

173 G13 $2 multicolored .90 .90

Frigate South Carolina
G14

1c, Schooner Lee. 2c, HMS Roebuck. 35c, Andrew Doria. 50c, Sloop Providence. $1, Flagship Alfred. $2, Frigate Confederacy. $3. Cutter Revenge.

1976, May 18

174 G14 ½c multicolored .20 .20
175 G14 1c multicolored .20 .20
176 G14 2c multicolored .20 .20
177 G14 35c multicolored .80 .80
178 G14 50c multicolored .95 .25
179 G14 $1 multicolored 1.40 .35
180 G14 $2 multicolored 2.25 .75
Nos. 174-180 (7) 6.00 2.75

Souvenir Sheet

181 G14 $3 multicolored 2.50 2.50

American Revolution Bicentennial.

Piper Apache
G15

Designs: 1c, Beech Twin Bonanza. 2c, de Havilland Twin Otter. 40c, Britten Norman Islander. 50c, de Havilland Heron. $2, Hawker Siddeley Avro 748. $3, BAC 1-11.

1976, June 10

182 G15 ½c multicolored .20 .20
183 G15 1c multicolored .20 .20
184 G15 2c multicolored .20 .20
185 G15 40c multicolored .25 .20
186 G15 50c multicolored .35 .20
187 G15 $2 multicolored 1.10 .40
Nos. 182-187 (6) 2.30 1.40

Souvenir Sheet

188 G15 $3 multicolored 2.00 2.00

Olympic Games, Montreal
G16

1976, July 1

189 G16 ½c Cycling .20 .20
190 G16 1c Gymnastics .20 .20
191 G16 2c Hurdling .20 .20
192 G16 35c Shot put .20 .20
193 G16 45c Diving .20 .20
194 G16 75c Sprinting .20 .20
195 G16 $2 Rowing .40 .40
Nos. 189-195 (7) 1.60 1.60

Souvenir Sheet

196 G16 $3 Sailing 1.00 1.00

Virgin and Child by Cima — G17

Christmas: 1c, 2c, The Nativity by Romanino. 35c, Adoration of the Kings by Brueghel. 50c, Madonna and Child by Girolamo. 75c, Adoration of the Magi by Giorgione, horiz. $2, The Adoration of the Kings by Angelico, horiz. $3, The Holy Family by Garofalo.

1976, Oct. 19

197 G17 ½c multicolored .20 .20
198 G17 1c multicolored .20 .20
199 G17 2c multicolored .20 .20
200 G17 35c multicolored .20 .20
201 G17 50c multicolored .25 .20
202 G17 75c multicolored .25 .25
203 G17 $2 multicolored .50 .35
Nos. 197-203 (7) 1.80 1.60

Souvenir Sheet

204 G17 $3 multicolored 1.00 1.00

Alexander Graham Bell, First Telephone
G18

Portraits of Bell and Telephone from: 1c, 1895. 2c, 1900. 35c, 1915. 75c, 1920. $1, 1929. $2, 1963. $3, 1976.

1977, Jan. 28

205 G18 ½c multicolored .20 .20
206 G18 1c multicolored .20 .20
207 G18 2c multicolored .20 .20
208 G18 35c multicolored .20 .20
209 G18 75c multicolored .20 .20
210 G18 $1 multicolored .25 .20
211 G18 $2 multicolored .30 .25
Nos. 205-211 (7) 1.55 1.45

Souvenir Sheet

212 G18 $3 multicolored 1.50 1.25

Centenary of 1st telephone conversation, Mar. 10, 1876.

Coronation Coach — G19

Royal Visit — G20

Designs: 50c, Crown of St. Edward. No. 214, Queen entering Abbey. No. 219, Queen and Prince Charles. $4, Queen is crowned. No. 216, Mall on Coronation Night. No. 220, Queen's Flag.

Litho. and Embossed

1977, Feb. 7 ***Perf. 13½***

213 G19 35c multicolored .20 .20
214 G19 $2 multicolored .25 .20
215 G19 $4 multicolored .35 .25
Nos. 213-215 (3) .80 .65

Souvenir Sheet

Perf. 14

216 G19 $5 multicolored 1.00 1.00

Booklet Stamps

Roulette x imperf.

Self-adhesive

217 G20 35c multicolored .20 .20
a. Booklet pane of 6 .75
218 G20 50c multicolored .35 .35
219 G20 $2 multicolored .55 .55
220 G20 $5 multicolored .65 .65
a. Bklt. pane of 3, #218, #219, #220 1.25

Reign of Queen Elizabeth II, 25th anniv.
Nos. 213-215, perf. 11, have different background colors and come from sheetlets of 3 stamps plus label.
For overprints see Nos. 237-240.

Easter — G21

Adoration of Jesus by Correggio — G22

Paintings of the Crucifixion by various artists.

1977, July 5 **Litho.** ***Perf. 14***

221 G21 ½c Fra Angelico .20 .20
222 G21 1c Fra Angelico, diff. .20 .20
223 G21 2c El Greco .20 .20
224 G21 18c El Greco, diff. .20 .20
225 G21 35c Fra Angelico, diff. .20 .20
226 G21 50c Giottino .20 .20
227 G21 $2 da Messina .30 .25
Nos. 221-227 (7) 1.50 1.45

Souvenir Sheet

228 G21 $3 Fra Angelico, diff. .90 .90

1977, Nov. 17 ***Perf. 14***

Christmas: Paintings of the Madonna and Child by various artists.

229 G22 ½c shown .20 .20
230 G22 1c Giorgione .20 .20
231 G22 2c Morales .20 .20
232 G22 18c Raphael .20 .20
233 G22 35c Van Dyck .20 .20
234 G22 50c Filippo Lippi .20 .20
235 G22 $2 Filippo Lippi, diff. .30 .25
Nos. 229-235 (7) 1.50 1.45

Souvenir Sheet

236 G22 $3 Ghirlandaio .90 .90

Nos. 213-216 Overprinted

1977, Nov. 23 ***Perf. 13½***

237 G19 35c multicolored .20 .20
238 G19 $2 multicolored .40 .40
239 G19 $4 multicolored .75 .75
Nos. 237-239 (3) 1.35 1.35

Souvenir Sheet

240 G19 $5 multicolored 1.00 1.00

Caribbean visit of Queen Elizabeth II.
Nos. 237-239 exist perf. 11.

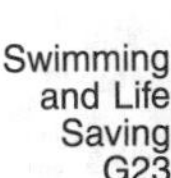

Swimming and Life Saving G23

6th Caribbean Jamboree, Kingston, Jamaica, Aug. 5-14: 1c, Hiking. 2c, Ropes and Knots. 22c, Erecting Tent. 35c, Limbo dance. 75c, Cooking. $2, Pioneer bridge building. $3, Sea Scouts' race.

1977, Dec. 7 *Perf. 14*

241 G23 ½c multicolored .20 .20
242 G23 1c multicolored .20 .20
243 G23 2c multicolored .20 .20
244 G23 22c multicolored .20 .20
245 G23 35c multicolored .35 .20
246 G23 75c multicolored .60 .20
247 G23 $3 multicolored 1.10 .40
Nos. 241-247 (7) 2.85 1.60

Souvenir Sheet

248 G23 $2 multicolored 1.50 1.50

Space Shuttle Blast-off G24

Designs: 1c, Booster separation. 2c, External tank separation. 22c, Working in orbit. 50c, Re-entry. $2, Towing in. $3, Landing.

1978, Feb. 3

249 G24 ½c multicolored .20 .20
250 G24 1c multicolored .20 .20
251 G24 2c multicolored .20 .20
252 G24 22c multicolored .20 .20
253 G24 50c multicolored .20 .20
254 G24 $3 multicolored 1.50 .50
Nos. 249-254 (6) 2.50 1.50

Souvenir Sheet

255 G24 $2 multicolored 1.00 1.00

US Space Shuttle.

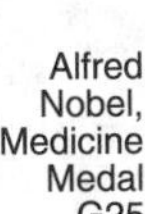

Alfred Nobel, Medicine Medal G25

Alfred Nobel and: 1c, Physics, Chemistry Medal. 2c, Peace Medal. 22c, Nobel Institute, Oslo. 75c, Peace Prize committee. $2, Peace Medal, Nobel's will. $3, Literature Medal.

1978, Feb. 22

256 G25 ½c multicolored .20 .20
257 G25 1c multicolored .20 .20
258 G25 2c multicolored .20 .20
259 G25 22c multicolored .20 .20
260 G25 75c multicolored .45 .25
261 G25 $3 multicolored 1.75 .50
Nos. 256-261 (6) 3.00 1.55

Souvenir Sheet

262 G25 $2 multicolored 1.25 1.25

Nobel Prize awards.

Germany No. C37 — G26

15c, France #C43. 25c, Liechtenstein #C8 specimen. 35c, Panama #257. 50c, Russia #C15. 75c, US #C10. $2, Germany #C57. $3, Spain #C56.

1978, Mar. 15

263 G26 5c multicolored .20 .20
264 G26 15c multicolored .20 .20
265 G26 25c multicolored .20 .20
266 G26 35c multicolored .30 .20
267 G26 50c multicolored .40 .20
268 G26 $3 multicolored 1.25 .50
Nos. 263-268 (6) 2.55 1.50

Souvenir Sheet

269 Sheet of 2 1.60 1.60
a. G26 75c multicolored .40 .40
b. G26 $2 multicolored 1.10 1.10

50th anniv. of Lindbergh's solo trans-Atlantic flight. 75th anniv. of 1st Zeppelin flight.

Coronation Ring — G27

Designs: $2, Queen's Orb. $2.50, Imperial State Crown. $5, Queen Elizabeth II.

1978, Apr. 12 *Perf. 14*

270 G27 50c multicolored .20 .20
271 G27 $2 multicolored .35 .35
272 G27 $2.50 multicolored .45 .45
Nos. 270-272 (3) 1.00 1.00

Souvenir Sheet

273 G27 $5 multicolored 1.00 1.00

Nos. 270-272, perf 12, printed in sheets of 3 + label, have different background colors. Issue date; June 2, 1978.

G28

Designs: 18c, Drummer, Royal Regiment of Fusiliers. 50c, Drummer, Royal Anglian Regiment. $5, Drum Major, Queen's Regiment.

1978, Apr. 12 ***Roulette x imperf.***

Booklet Stamps

Self-Adhesive

274 Souvenir booklet 2.50 *3.00*
a. G28 Pane of 6 (3 ea 18c, 50c) 1.00 1.00
b. G28 Pane of 1 ($5) 2.00 2.00

G29

1978, May 18 *Perf. 14*

Paintings by Rubens: 5c, Le Chapeau de Paille. 15c, Hector Killed by Achilles. 18c, Helene Fourment and Her Children. 22c, Rubens and Isabella Brandt. 35c, Ildefonso Altarpiece. $2, Self-portrait. $3, Four Negro Heads.

275 G29 5c multicolored .20 .20
276 G29 15c multicolored .20 .20
277 G29 18c multicolored .20 .20
278 G29 22c multicolored .20 .20
279 G29 35c multicolored .20 .20
280 G29 $3 multicolored 1.50 1.50
Nos. 275-280 (6) 2.50 2.50

Souvenir Sheet

281 G29 $2 multicolored 1.10 1.10

400th birth anniv. of Rubens.

Wright Flyer G30

Designs: 15c, Orville Wright, vert. 18c, Wilbur Wright, vert. 25c, 35c, 75c, $2, $3, various Wright airplanes.

1978, Aug. 10

282 G30 5c multicolored .20 .20
283 G30 15c multicolored .20 .20
284 G30 18c multicolored .20 .20
285 G30 25c multicolored .20 .20
286 G30 35c multicolored .20 .20
287 G30 75c multicolored .25 .25
288 G30 $3 multicolored .75 .75
Nos. 282-288 (7) 2.00 2.00

Souvenir Sheet

289 G30 $2 multicolored 1.10 1.10

75th anniv. of first powered flight by the Wright brothers, Dec. 17, 1903.

Audubon's Shearwater G31

Players, Soccer Ball G32

10c, Northern ring-necked plover. 18c, Garnet-throated hummingbird. 22c, Black-bellied tree duck. 40c, Purple martin. $1, Yellow-billed tropic bird. $2, Long-billed curlew. $5, Snowy egret.

1978, Sept. 28

290 G31 5c multi *.50* .20
291 G31 10c multi *.80* .20
292 G31 18c multi, horiz. *1.10* .20
293 G31 22c multi, horiz. *1.10* .20
294 G31 40c multi, horiz. *1.75* .30
295 G31 $1 multi *2.50* .45
296 G31 $2 multi *3.75* .70
Nos. 290-296 (7) *11.50* 2.25

Souvenir Sheet

297 G31 $5 multicolored *5.50* 3.00

1978, Nov. 2

Soccer players in action.

298 G32 15c multicolored .20 .20
299 G32 35c multicolored .20 .20
300 G32 50c multicolored .25 .20
301 G32 $3 multicolored .75 .75
Nos. 298-301 (4) 1.40 1.35

Souvenir Sheet

302 G32 $2 multicolored 1.10 1.10

World Cup Soccer Championships, Argentina, June 1-25.

Captain Cook, Kalaniopu (King of Hawaii), 1778 G33

22c, Cook, Hawaiian native. 50c, Cook, death scene, 2/14/79. $3, Cook and offering ceremony. $4, Cook, HMS Resolution.

1978, Dec. 13

303 G33 18c multicolored .20 .20
304 G33 22c multicolored .25 .25
305 G33 50c multicolored .50 .50
306 G33 $3 multicolored 3.25 2.00
Nos. 303-306 (4) 4.20 2.95

Souvenir Sheet

307 G33 $4 multicolored 2.50 2.50

250th birth anniv. of Captain James Cook and Bicentennial of his discovery of the Hawaiian Islands.

Durer Paintings — G34

Christmas: 40c, The Virgin at Prayer. 60c, Dresden Alterpiece. 90c, Madonna and Child. $2, Madonna and Child. $4, Salvator Mundi.

1978, Dec 20

308 G34 40c multicolored .20 .20
309 G34 60c multicolored .25 .25
310 G34 90c multicolored .30 .30
311 G34 $2 multicolored .90 .90
Nos. 308-311 (4) 1.65 1.65

Souvenir Sheet

312 G34 $4 multicolored 1.25 1.25

Strelitzia Reginae — G35

1979, Feb. 15

313 G35 22c shown .20 .20
314 G35 40c Euphorbia pulcherrima .35 .35
315 G35 $1 Heliconia humilis .60 .40
316 G35 $3 Thunbergia alata 1.10 .75
Nos. 313-316 (4) 2.25 1.70

Souvenir Sheet

317 G35 $2 Bougainvillea glabra 1.00 1.00

Children with Pig G36

International Year of the Child: 50c, Children with donkey. $1, Children with goats. $3, Children fishing. $4, Child with coconuts.

1979, Mar. 22

318 G36 18c multicolored .20 .20
319 G36 50c multicolored .20 .20
320 G36 $1 multicolored .70 .70
321 G36 $3 multicolored .90 .90
Nos. 318-321 (4) 2.00 2.00

Souvenir Sheet

322 G36 $4 multicolored 1.25 1.25

Around the World in 80 Days G37

150th birth anniv. of Jules Verne: 18c, 20,000 Leagues Under the Sea. 38c, From the Earth to the Moon. 75c, From the Earth to the Moon, diff. $3, Five Weeks in a Balloon.

1979, Apr. 20

323 G37 18c multicolored .20 .20
324 G37 38c multicolored .20 .20
325 G37 75c multicolored .40 .40
326 G37 $3 multicolored 1.75 1.75
Nos. 323-326 (4) 2.55 2.55

Souvenir Sheet

327 G37 $4 multicolored 1.90 1.90

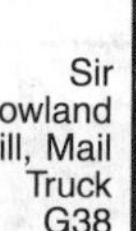

Sir Rowland Hill, Mail Truck G38

Designs: $1, Ocean liner. $2, Mail train. $3, Concorde. $4, Sir Rowland Hill.

1979, July 30 ***Perf. 14***

328 G38 15c multicolored .20 .20
329 G38 $1 multicolored .20 .20
330 G38 $2 multicolored .85 .85
331 G38 $3 multicolored 1.25 1.25
Nos. 328-331 (4) 2.50 2.50

Souvenir Sheet

332 G38 $4 multicolored 1.75 1.75

Death centenary of Sir Rowland Hill.
Nos. 328-331, perf. 12, printed in sheets of 5 + label, have different colored backgrounds.

Virgin and Child Enthroned (Byzantine Era, 11th Cent.) — G39

Christmas sculptures: 25c, Presentation in the Temple by Beauneveu c. 1390. 30c, Flight to Egypt (Utrecht, c. 1510). 40c, Madonna and Child by della Quercia, 1047-48. 90c, Madonna della Mela by della Robbia, c. 1455. $1, Madonna and Child by Rossellino, 1461-66. $2, Madonna (Antwerp, 1700). $4, Virgin (Krumau, c. 1390).

1979, Oct. 23 ***Perf. 14***

333 G39 6c multicolored .20 .20
334 G39 25c multicolored .20 .20
335 G39 30c multicolored .20 .20
336 G39 40c multicolored .20 .20
337 G39 90c multicolored .20 .20
338 G39 $1 multicolored .25 .25
339 G39 $2 multicolored .50 .50
Nos. 333-339 (7) 1.75 1.75

Souvenir Sheet

340 G39 $4 multicolored 1.00 1.00

Great Hammerhead Shark — G40

Designs: 45c, Banded butterflyfish. 50c, Permit. 60c, Threaded turban. 70c, Milk conch. 75c, Great blue heron. 90c, Colored Atlantic natica. $1, Red footed booby. $2.50, Collared plover.

1979, Nov. 9

341 G40 40c multicolored *.55 .55*
342 G40 45c multicolored *.60 .60*
343 G40 50c multicolored *.70 .70*
344 G40 60c multicolored *.80 .80*
345 G40 70c multicolored *1.00 1.00*
346 G40 75c multicolored *1.10 1.10*
347 G40 90c multicolored *1.25 1.25*
348 G40 $1 multicolored *1.40 1.40*
Nos. 341-348 (8) *7.40 7.40*

Souvenir Sheet

349 G40 $2.50 multicolored 2.25 2.25

Doctor Goofy G41

International Year of the Child: 1c, Admiral Mickey Mouse. 2c, Fireman Goofy. 3c, Nurse Minnie Mouse. 4c, Drum Major Mickey Mouse. 5c, Policeman Donald Duck. 10c, Pilot Donald Duck. $2, Mailman Goofy, horiz. $2.50 Engineer Donald Duck, horiz. $3, Fireman Mickey Mouse.

1979, Dec. 12 ***Perf. 11***

350 G41 ½c multicolored .20 .20
351 G41 1c multicolored .20 .20
352 G41 2c multicolored .20 .20
353 G41 3c multicolored .20 .20
354 G41 4c multicolored .20 .20
355 G41 5c multicolored .20 .20
356 G41 10c multicolored .20 .20
357 G41 $2 multicolored 1.75 1.75
358 G41 $2.50 multicolored 2.25 2.25
Nos. 350-358 (9) 5.40 5.40

Souvenir Sheet

Perf. 13½

359 G41 $3 multicolored 2.50 2.50

Nos. 114, 117-128 Overprinted

1980, Mar. 10 ***Perf. 15***

360 A85 6c multicolored .20 .20
361 A85 12c multicolored .20 .20
362 A85 15c multicolored .20 .20
363 A85 20c multicolored .20 .20
364 A85 25c multicolored .20 .20
365 A85 35c multicolored .20 .20
366 A85 50c multicolored .30 .30

Perf. 13½x14

367 A85 75c multicolored .35 .35
368 A85 $1 multicolored .50 .50
369 A85 $2 multicolored .75 .75
370 A85 $3 multicolored 1.40 1.40
371 A85 $5 multicolored 2.00 2.00
372 A85 $10 multicolored 3.25 3.25
Nos. 360-372 (13) 9.75 9.75

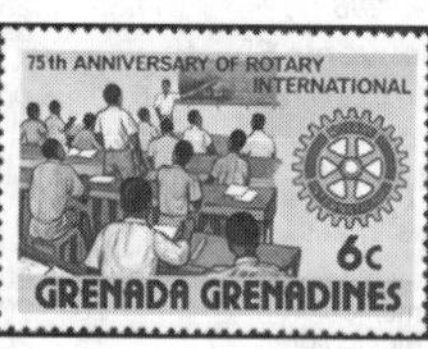

Classroom G42

Rotary Intl., 75th anniv.: 30c, Rotary emblem, people. 60c, Rotary executive making contribution to physician. $3, Young patients, nurses. $4, Paul P. Harris, founder of Rotary.

1980, Mar. 12 ***Perf. 14***

373 G42 6c multicolored .20 .20
374 G42 30c multicolored .25 .25
375 G42 60c multicolored .45 .45
376 G42 $3 multicolored 1.60 1.60
Nos. 373-376 (4) 2.50 2.50

Souvenir Sheet

377 G42 $4 multicolored 1.50 1.50

Yellow-bellied Seedeater — G43

40c, Blue-hooded euphonia. 90c, Yellow warbler. $2, Tropical mockingbird. $3, Barn owl.

1980, Apr. 14

378 G43 25c multicolored *.60 .60*
379 G43 40c multicolored *.65 .65*
380 G43 90c multicolored *1.50 1.50*
381 G43 $2 multicolored *2.00 2.00*
Nos. 378-381 (4) *4.75 4.75*

Souvenir Sheet

382 G43 $3 multicolored *4.25 4.25*

Running G44

Designs: 40c, Soccer. 90c, Boxing. $2, Wrestling. $4, Runners in silhouette.

1980, Apr. 21

383 G44 30c multicolored .20 .20
384 G44 40c multicolored .20 .20
385 G44 90c multicolored .40 .40
386 G44 $2 multicolored .85 .85
Nos. 383-386 (4) 1.65 1.65

Souvenir Sheet

387 G44 $4 multicolored 1.00 1.00

22nd Summer Olympic Games, Moscow, July 19-Aug. 3.

Nos. 328-331 Overprinted

1980, May 6 ***Perf. 12***

388 G38 15c multicolored .20 .20
389 G38 $1 multicolored .80 .80
390 G38 $2 multicolored 1.75 1.75
391 G38 $3 multicolored 2.75 2.75
Nos. 388-391 (4) 5.50 5.50

Issued in sheets of 5 + label.

Longspine Squirrelfish — G45

Designs: 1c, Blue chromis. 2c, Foureye butterflyfish. 4c, Sergeant major. 5c, Yellowtail snapper. 6c, Mutton snapper. 10c, Cocoa damselfish. 12c, Royal gramma. 15c, Cherubfish. 20c, Blackbar soldierfish. 25c, Comb grouper. 30c, Longsnout butterflyfish. 40c, Pudding wife. 50c, Midnight parrotfish. 90c, Redspotted hawkfish. $1, Hogfish. $3, Beau gregory. $5, Rock beauty. $10, Barred hamlet.

1980, Aug. 6 ***Perf. 14***

392 G45 ½c multicolored .20 .20
a. Perf. 12, inscribed 1982
393 G45 1c multicolored .20 .20
394 G45 2c multicolored .20 .20
395 G45 4c multicolored .20 .20
396 G45 5c multicolored .20 .20
397 G45 6c multicolored .20 .20
398 G45 10c multicolored .20 .20
399 G45 12c multicolored .20 .20
400 G45 15c multicolored .20 .20
401 G45 20c multicolored .20 .20
402 G45 25c multicolored .20 .20
403 G45 30c multicolored .20 .20
404 G45 40c multicolored .25 .25
405 G45 50c multicolored .30 .30
406 G45 90c multicolored .45 .45
407 G45 $1 multicolored .55 .55
408 G45 $3 multicolored 1.50 1.50
409 G45 $5 multicolored 2.00 2.00
410 G45 $10 multicolored 3.25 3.25
Nos. 392-410 (19) 10.70 10.70

No. 398 exists with 1984 date below design.

Bambi with Mother — G46

Various scenes from Walt Disney's Bambi.

1980, Oct. 7 ***Perf. 11***

411 G46 ½c multicolored .20 .20
412 G46 1c multicolored .20 .20
413 G46 2c multicolored .20 .20
414 G46 3c multicolored .20 .20
415 G46 4c multicolored .20 .20
416 G46 5c multicolored .20 .20
417 G46 10c multicolored .20 .20
418 G46 $2.50 multicolored 1.60 1.60
419 G46 $3 multicolored 1.60 1.60
Nos. 411-419 (9) 4.60 4.60

Souvenir Sheet

420 G46 $4 multicolored 2.75 2.75

Christmas.

The Unicorn in Captivity by Unknown 15th Cent. Artist — G47

Designs: 10c, The Fighting Temeraire by J.M.W. Turner. 25c, Sunday Afternoon on the Ile De La Grande-Jatte by Seurat. 90c, Max Schmitt in a Single Scull by Eakins. $2, The Burial of the Count of Orgaz by El Greco. $3, George Washington by Stuart. $5, Kaiser Karl the Great by Durer. Nos. 425-427 are vert.

1981, Jan. 25 ***Perf. 14***

421 G47 6c multicolored .20 .20
422 G47 10c multicolored .20 .20
423 G47 25c multicolored .20 .20
424 G47 90c multicolored .50 .50
425 G47 $2 multicolored .90 .90
426 G47 $3 multicolored 1.25 1.25
Nos. 421-426 (6) 3.25 3.25

Souvenir Sheet

427 G47 $5 multicolored 2.50 2.50

Disney Type of 1979

50th anniv. of Pluto character: $2, Mickey Mouse, Pluto and birthday cake. $4, Pluto.

1981, Jan. 26

428 A135a $2 multicolored 1.00 1.00

Souvenir Sheet

429 A135a $4 multicolored 2.75 2.75

No. 428 issued in sheets of 8.

Chip Coloring Easter Eggs — G48

Easter: Various Disney characters coloring Easter eggs.

1981, Apr. 14 ***Perf. 11***

430 G48 35c multicolored .20 .20
431 G48 40c multicolored .20 .20
432 G48 $2 multicolored 1.10 1.10
433 G48 $2.50 multicolored 1.50 1.50
Nos. 430-433 (4) 3.00 3.00

Souvenir Sheet

Perf. 14

434 G48 $4 multicolored 2.75 2.75

Bust of a Woman — G49

Diana — G50

Paintings by Pablo Picasso (1881-1973): 40c, Woman (Study for Les Demoiselles d'Avignon). 90c, Nude with Raised Arms (The Dancer of Avignon). $4, The Dryad. $5, Les Demoiselles d'Avignon.

1981, May 5 ***Perf. 14***

435 G49 6c multicolored .20 .20
436 G49 40c multicolored .20 .20
437 G49 90c multicolored .35 .35
438 G49 $4 multicolored 1.75 1.75

Size: 103x128mm

Imperf

439 G49 $5 multicolored 2.25 2.25
Nos. 435-439 (5) 4.75 4.75

Common Design Types pictured following the introduction.

Royal Wedding Issue

Common Design Type

1981, June 16 ***Perf. 15***

440 CD331 40c Couple .20 .20
441 CD331 $2 Balmoral Castle .60 .60
442 CD331 $4 Charles 1.00 1.00
Nos. 440-442 (3) 1.80 1.80

Souvenir Sheet

443 CD331 $5 Royal Coach 1.50 1.50

Sheets of 5 plus label contain 30c (like No. 440), 40c (like No. 441), or $4 in changed colors, perf 15x14½.

Roulette x imperf. (#444a), Imperf. (#444b)

1981, June 16

$2, Charles. $5, Diana and Charles.

Booklet

Self-Adhesive

444 G50 Souvenir Booklet 3.50
a. Pane of 6 (3 each $1, $2) 2.00
b. Pane of 1, $5 1.50

Royal wedding.

Amy Johnson, Pilot of 1st Britain-Australia Solo Flight by a Woman, May 1930 — G51

Decade for Women: 70c, Mme. la Baronne de Laroche, 1st qualified aviatrix, May 1910. $1.10, Ruth Nichols. $3, Amelia Earhart, 1st Atlantic solo flight by woman, May 1932. $5, Valentina Tereshkova, 1st woman in space, June 1963.

1981, Oct. 13 ***Perf. 14***

445 G51 30c multicolored .45 .45
446 G51 70c multicolored .70 .70
447 G51 $1.10 multicolored .85 .85
448 G51 $3 multicolored 1.75 1.75
Nos. 445-448 (4) 3.75 3.75

Souvenir Sheet

449 G51 $5 multicolored 2.00 2.00

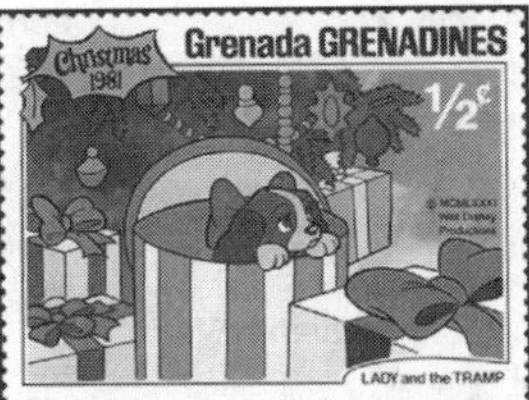

Lady and the Tramp — G52

Christmas. Various scenes from Walt Disney's film Lady and the Tramp.

1981, Nov. 2

450 G52 ½c multicolored .20 .20
451 G52 1c multicolored .20 .20
452 G52 2c multicolored .20 .20
453 G52 3c multicolored .20 .20
454 G52 4c multicolored .20 .20
455 G52 5c multicolored .20 .20
456 G52 10c multicolored .20 .20
457 G52 $2.50 multicolored 2.50 1.75
458 G52 $3 multicolored 3.00 2.25
Nos. 450-458 (9) 6.90 5.40

Souvenir Sheet

459 G52 $5 multicolored 5.00 4.00

747 Carrying Space Shuttle — G53

Designs: 40c, Re-entry. $1.10, External tank separation. $3, Touchdown. $5, Lift-off.

1981, Nov. 2 ***Perf. 14½***

460 G53 10c multicolored .20 .20
461 G53 40c multicolored .40 .30
462 G53 $1.10 multicolored 1.00 .80
463 G53 $3 multicolored 3.00 2.25
Nos. 460-463 (4) 4.60 3.55

Souvenir Sheet

464 G53 $5 multicolored 4.00 4.00

Soccer Player — G54

World Cup Soccer Championships, Spain, 1982: Soccer players in various positions.

1981, Nov. 30 ***Perf. 14***

465 G54 20c multicolored .20 .20
466 G54 40c multicolored .20 .20
467 G54 $1 multicolored .35 .30
468 G54 $2 multicolored .75 .60
Nos. 465-468 (4) 1.50 1.30

Souvenir Sheet

469 G54 $4 multicolored 1.75 1.50

Stagecoach, Mail Truck — G55

UPU Membership Cent.: 40c, UPU Emblem. $2.50, Sailing ship, ocean liner. $4, Biplane, Concorde. $5, Steam train, high-speed trains.

1982, Jan. 13 ***Perf. 15***

470 G55 30c multicolored .20 .20
471 G55 40c multicolored .25 .20
472 G55 $2.50 multicolored 1.60 1.00
473 G55 $4 multicolored 2.50 2.00
Nos. 470-473 (4) 4.55 3.40

Souvenir Sheet

474 G55 $5 multicolored 4.25 3.50

Sprinting G56

90c, Sea scouts sailing. $1.10, Hand crafts. $3, Animal husbandry. $5, Music around campfire.

1982, Feb. 19

475 G56 6c multicolored .20 .20
476 G56 90c multicolored .60 .60
477 G56 $1.10 multicolored .70 .70
478 G56 $3 multicolored 1.75 1.75
Nos. 475-478 (4) 3.25 3.25

Souvenir Sheet

479 G56 $5 multicolored 3.25 3.25

Boy Scouts, 75th anniv. Lord Baden-Powell, 125th birth anniv.

White Peacock G57

Designs: 40c, St. Vincent long-tail skipper. $1.10, Painted lady. $3, Orion. $5, Silver spot.

1982, Mar. 24 ***Perf. 14***

480 G57 30c multicolored .40 .40
481 G57 40c multicolored .60 .60
482 G57 $1.10 multicolored 1.50 1.50
483 G57 $3 multicolored 3.75 3.75
Nos. 480-483 (4) 6.25 6.25

Souvenir Sheet

484 G57 $5 multicolored 4.00 4.00

Princess Diana Issue

Common Design Type

1982, July 1 ***Perf. 14½x14***

485 CD332 50c Blenheim Palace .80 .80
486 CD332 60c Like 50c .70 .70
487 CD332 $1 Couple in field 1.25 1.25
488 CD332 $2 Like $1 1.75 1.75
489 CD332 $3 Diana 2.25 2.25
490 CD332 $4 Like $3 2.25 2.25
Nos. 485-490 (6) 9.00 9.00

Souvenir Sheet

491 CD332 $5 Diana, diff. 6.00 6.00

50c, $1, $3 issued in sheets of 5 plus label.

Overprinted

1982, Aug. 30

492 CD332 50c multicolored .30 .30
493 CD332 60c multicolored .35 .35
494 CD332 $1 multicolored .60 .60
495 CD332 $2 multicolored 1.25 1.25
496 CD332 $3 multicolored 1.75 1.75
497 CD332 $4 multicolored 2.50 2.50
Nos. 492-497 (6) 6.75 6.75

Souvenir Sheet

498 CD332 $5 multicolored 4.00 4.00

Birth of Prince William of Wales, June 21.

Roosevelt Type of 1982

Designs: 30c, New Deal soil conservation. 40c, Roosevelt, George Washington Carver. 70c, Civilian Conservation Corps. $3, Roosevelt, Liberian Pres. Edwin Barclay. $5, Roosevelt addressing Howard University.

1982, July 27 ***Perf. 14***

499 A154 30c multicolored .50 .50
500 A154 40c multicolored .50 .50
501 A154 70c multicolored .60 .60
502 A154 $3 multicolored 1.40 1.40
Nos. 499-502 (4) 3.00 3.00

Souvenir Sheet

503 A154 $5 multicolored 3.50 3.50

Presentation of Christ in the Temple — G58

Easter Paintings by Rembrandt: 60c, Descent from the Cross. $2, Raising of the Cross. $4, Resurrection of Christ. $5, The Risen Christ.

1982, Sept. 2 ***Perf. 14½***

504 G58 30c multicolored .55 .55
505 G58 60c multicolored .70 .70
506 G58 $2 multicolored 1.00 1.00
507 G58 $4 multicolored 1.75 1.75
Nos. 504-507 (4) 4.00 4.00

Souvenir Sheet

508 G58 $5 multicolored 3.50 3.50

G59

1982, Oct. 4 ***Perf. 15***

509 G59 10c Santa Fe .65 .65
510 G59 40c Mistral .85 .85
511 G59 70c Rheingold .90 .90
512 G59 $1 ET 403 1.10 1.10
513 G59 $1.10 Mallard 1.40 1.40
514 G59 $2 Tokaido 1.60 1.60
Nos. 509-514 (6) 6.50 6.50

Souvenir Sheet

515 G59 $5 Settebello 3.75 3.75

Soccer Players G60

Italy, World Cup Soccer Champions: $4, Soccer players, diff. $5, Map of Italy.

1982, Dec. 2 ***Perf. 14***

516 G60 60c multicolored .45 .45
517 G60 $4 multicolored 3.00 3.00

Souvenir Sheet

518 G60 $5 multicolored 2.50 2.50

Christmas Type of 1982

Scenes from Walt Disney's film The Rescuers.

1982, Dec. 14 ***Perf. 13½***

519 A157 ½c multicolored .20 .20
520 A157 1c multicolored .20 .20
521 A157 2c multicolored .20 .20
522 A157 3c multicolored .20 .20
523 A157 4c multicolored .20 .20
524 A157 5c multicolored .20 .20
525 A157 10c multicolored .20 .20
526 A157 $2.50 multicolored 2.75 2.75
527 A157 $3 multicolored 2.75 2.75
Nos. 519-527 (9) 6.90 6.90

Souvenir Sheet

528 A157 $5 multicolored 4.50 4.50

Whales Type of 1982

Designs: 10c, Pilot whale. 60c, Dall porpoise. $1.10, Humpback whale. $3, Bowfin whale. $5, Spotted dolphin.

1983, Jan. 10 ***Perf. 14***

529 A159 10c multicolored .85 .85
530 A159 60c multicolored 1.90 1.90
531 A159 $1.10 multicolored 3.50 3.50
532 A159 $3 multicolored 5.75 5.75
Nos. 529-532 (4) 12.00 12.00

Souvenir Sheet

533 A159 $5 multicolored 5.00 5.00

Raphael Paintings Type

Designs: 25c, David and Goliath. 30c, David Sees Bathsheba. 90c, Triumph of David. $4, Anointing of Solomon. $5, Anointing of David.

1983, Feb. 15 *Perf. 14*

534 A160 25c multicolored .30 .30
535 A160 30c multicolored .30 .30
536 A160 90c multicolored .65 .65
537 A160 $4 multicolored 1.25 1.25
Nos. 534-537 (4) 2.50 2.50

Souvenir Sheet

538 A160 $5 multicolored 2.50 2.50

Audio and Video Communication — G61

World Communications Year: 60c, Ambulance. $1.10, Helicopters. $3, Satellite. $5, Diver, bottle-nose porpoise.

1983, Apr. 7 *Perf. 14*

539 G61 30c multicolored .25 .25
540 G61 60c multicolored .45 .45
541 G61 $1.10 multicolored .80 .80
542 G61 $3 blk, red & blue 1.50 1.50
Nos. 539-542 (4) 3.00 3.00

Souvenir Sheet

543 G61 $5 multicolored 3.00 3.00

For overprints see Nos. 629-630A.

Car Type of 1983

Designs: 10c, 1931 Chrysler Imperial Roadster. 30c, 1925 Doble Steam Car. 40c, 1965 Ford Mustang. 60c, 1930 Packard Tourer. 70c, 1913 Mercer Raceabout. 90c, 1963 Corvette Stingray. $1.10, 1935 Auburn 851 Supercharger Speedster. $2.50, 1933 Pierce Arrow Silver Arrow. $3, 1929 Duesenberg Dual Cowl Phaeton. $4, 1928 Mercedes-Benz SSK. $5, 1923 McFarlan Knickerbocker Cabriolet.

1983, May 4 *Perf. 14½*

544 A163 10c multicolored .20 .20
545 A163 30c multicolored .25 .20
546 A163 40c multicolored .25 .25
547 A163 60c multicolored .35 .35
548 A163 70c multicolored .35 .35
549 A163 90c multicolored .35 .35
550 A163 $1.10 multicolored .35 .35
551 A163 $2.50 multicolored .85 .85
552 A163 $3 multicolored 1.00 1.00
553 A163 $4 multicolored 1.10 1.10
Nos. 544-553 (10) 5.05 5.00

Souvenir Sheet

554 A163 $5 multicolored 3.00 3.00

Anniversary of Manned Flight Type

Designs: 40c, Short Solent flying boat. 70c, Curtiss R3C-2 seaplane. 90c, Hawker Nimrod biplane. $4, Montgolfier balloon. $5, Victoria Luise airship.

1983, July 18 *Perf. 14*

555 A164 40c multicolored .80 .80
556 A164 70c multicolored .95 .95
557 A164 90c multicolored 1.00 1.00
558 A164 $4 multicolored 3.50 3.50
Nos. 555-558 (4) 6.25 6.25

Souvenir Sheet

559 A164 $5 multicolored 3.25 3.25

Christmas G62

Walt Disney characters in scenes from "Jingle Bells."

1983, Nov. 7 *Perf. 11*

560 G62 ½c multicolored .20 .20
561 G62 1c multicolored .20 .20
562 G62 2c multicolored .20 .20
563 G62 3c multicolored .20 .20
564 G62 4c multicolored .20 .20
565 G62 5c multicolored .20 .20
566 G62 10c multicolored .20 .20
567 G62 $2.50 multicolored 4.25 4.25
568 G62 $3 multicolored 4.50 4.50
Nos. 560-568 (9) 10.15 10.15

Souvenir Sheet

Perf. 13½

569 G62 $5 multicolored 4.25 4.25

G63

1984, Jan. 9 *Perf. 14*

570 G63 30c Weightlifting .25 .25
571 G63 60c Gymnastics .50 .50
572 G63 70c Archery .60 .60
573 G63 $4 Sailing 2.40 2.40
Nos. 570-573 (4) 3.75 3.75

Souvenir Sheet

574 G63 $5 Basketball 3.25 3.25

Olympic Games, Los Angeles.

G64

1984, Apr. 9 *Perf. 15*

Designs: 15c, Frangipani. 40c, Dwarf poinciana. 70c, Walking iris. $4, Lady's slipper. $5, Brazilian glory vine.

575 G64 15c multicolored .20 .20
576 G64 40c multicolored .30 .30
577 G64 70c multicolored .55 .55
578 G64 $4 multicolored 2.50 2.50
Nos. 575-578 (4) 3.55 3.55

Souvenir Sheet

579 G64 $5 multicolored 3.25 3.25

For overprints see Nos. 598-600.

Easter G65

Walt Disney characters with Easter hats.

1984, May 1 *Perf. 11*

580 G65 ½c multicolored .20 .20
581 G65 1c multicolored .20 .20
582 G65 2c multicolored .20 .20
583 G65 3c multicolored .20 .20
584 G65 4c multicolored .20 .20
585 G65 5c multicolored .20 .20
586 G65 10c multicolored .20 .20
587 G65 $2 multicolored 1.75 1.75
588 G65 $4 multicolored 2.25 2.25
Nos. 580-588 (9) 5.40 5.40

Souvenir Sheet

589 G65 $5 multicolored 4.00 4.00

Bobolink G66

Birds: 50c, Eastern kingbird. 60c, Barn swallow. 70c, Yellow warbler. $1, Rose-breasted grosbeak. $1.10, Yellowthroat. $2, Catbird. $5, Fork-tailed flycatcher.

1984, May 21 *Perf. 14*

590 G66 40c multicolored 1.75 1.75
591 G66 50c multicolored 2.00 2.00
592 G66 60c multicolored 2.25 2.25
593 G66 70c multicolored 2.25 2.25
594 G66 $1 multicolored 2.50 2.50
595 G66 $1.10 multicolored 3.00 3.00
596 G66 $2 multicolored 3.75 3.75
Nos. 590-596 (7) 17.50 17.50

Souvenir Sheet

597 G66 $5 multicolored 7.00 7.00

Nos. 577-579 Overprinted

1984, June 19 *Perf. 15*

598 G64 70c multicolored 1.00 1.00
599 G64 $4 multicolored 4.25 4.25

Souvenir Sheet

600 G64 $5 multicolored 3.50 3.50

Geeststar G67

1984, July 16 *Perf. 15*

601 G67 30c shown .25 .25
602 G67 60c Daphne .45 .45
603 G67 $1.10 Schooner Southwind .85 .85
604 G67 $4 Oceanic 3.25 3.25
Nos. 601-604 (4) 4.80 4.80

Souvenir Sheet

605 G67 $5 Privateer 4.50 4.50

Correggio Paintings Type

Designs: 10c, The Hunt—Blowing the Horn. 30c, St. John the Evangelist, horiz. 90c, The Hunt—The Deer's Head. $4, The Virgin Crowned by Christ, horiz. $5, Martyrdom of the Four Saints.

1984, Aug. 22 *Perf. 14*

606 A171a 10c multicolored .20 .20
607 A171a 30c multicolored .25 .25
608 A171a 90c multicolored .70 .70
609 A171a $4 multicolored 3.25 3.25
Nos. 606-609 (4) 4.40 4.40

Souvenir Sheet

610 A171a $5 multicolored 4.00 4.00

The Song of the Dog — G68

Paintings by Edgar Degas: 70c, Cafe-Concert. $1.10, The Orchestra of the Opera. $3, The Dance Lesson. $5, Madame Camus at the Piano.

1984, Aug. 22

611 G68 25c multicolored .20 .20
612 G68 70c multicolored .55 .55
613 G68 $1.10 multicolored .85 .85
614 G68 $3 multicolored 2.50 2.50
Nos. 611-614 (4) 4.10 4.10

Souvenir Sheet

615 G68 $5 multicolored 4.00 4.00

150th birth anniv. of Degas.

Queen Victoria Gardens G69

$4, Ayers Rock. $5, Yarra River, Melbourne.

1984, Sept. 21

616 G69 $1.10 multicolored .85 .85
617 G69 $4 multicolored 3.25 3.25

Souvenir Sheet

618 G69 $5 multicolored 4.00 4.00

AUSIPEX International Stamp Exhibition, Melbourne, Australia.

Colonel Steven's Model, "1825" G70

Locomotives: 50c, Royal George, 1827. 60c, Stourbridge Lion, 1829. 70c, Liverpool, 1830. 90c, South Carolina, 1832. $1.10, Monster, 1836. $2, Lafayette, 1837. $4, Lion, 1838.

1984, Oct. 3 *Perf. 15*

619 G70 20c multicolored .20 .20
620 G70 50c multicolored .40 .40
621 G70 60c multicolored .50 .50
622 G70 70c multicolored .60 .60
623 G70 90c multicolored .75 .75
624 G70 $1.10 multicolored .90 .90
625 G70 $2 multicolored 1.60 1.60
626 G70 $4 multicolored 3.50 3.50
Nos. 619-626 (8) 8.45 8.45

Souvenir Sheets

627 G70 $5 Sequin's Engine, 1829 4.25 4.25
628 G70 $5 Der Adler, 1835 4.25 4.25

Nos. 539, 541, 543 Overprinted

1984, Oct. 28 *Perf. 14*

629 G61 30c multicolored .25 .25
630 G61 $1.10 multicolored .95 .95

Souvenir Sheet

630A G61 $5 multicolored 4.00 4.00

Opening of the Point Saline International Airport. No. 630A is overprinted in the margin.

Christmas Type of 1984

Scenes from various Donald Duck movies.

1984, Nov. 26 *Perf. 13½x14*

631 A173 45c multicolored .40 .40
632 A173 60c multicolored .50 .50
633 A173 90c multicolored .75 .75
634 A173 $2 multi, perf. 12 1.75 1.75
635 A173 $4 multicolored 3.50 3.50
Nos. 631-635 (5) 6.90 6.90

Souvenir Sheet

636 A173 $5 multicolored 4.50 4.50

No. 634 issued in sheets of 8.

Audubon Type of 1985

Designs: 50c, Blue-winged teal. 90c, White ibis. $1.10, Swallow-tailed kite. $3, Common Gallinule. $5, Mangrove cuckoo.

1985, Feb. 11 *Perf. 14*

637 A174 50c multicolored .40 .40
638 A174 90c multicolored .75 .75
639 A174 $1.10 multicolored .95 .95
640 A174 $3 multicolored 2.50 2.50
Nos. 637-640 (4) 4.60 4.60

Souvenir Sheet

641 A174 $5 multicolored 4.00 4.00

See Nos. 732-736.

Motorcycle Centenary — G71

Anniv. emblem and: 30c, Kawasaki 750, 1972. 60c, Honda Goldwing GL1000, 1974, horiz. 70c, Kawasaki Z650, 1976, horiz. $4, Honda CBX, 1977. $5, BMW R100RS, 1978.

1985, Mar. 11

642 G71 30c multicolored .25 .25
643 G71 60c multicolored .45 .45
644 G71 70c multicolored .50 .50
645 G71 $4 multicolored 3.00 3.00
Nos. 642-645 (4) 4.20 4.20

Souvenir Sheet

646 G71 $5 multicolored 4.25 4.25

Intl. Youth Year G72

Designs: 50c, Folding bandages (health). 70c, Diver, turtle (environment). $1.10, Sailing (leisure). $3, Boys playing chess (education). $5, Hands touching globe.

1985, Apr. 15

647 G72 50c multicolored .40 .40
648 G72 70c multicolored .50 .50
649 G72 $1.10 multicolored .85 .85
650 G72 $3 multicolored 2.25 2.25
Nos. 647-650 (4) 4.00 4.00

Souvenir Sheet

651 G72 $5 multicolored 4.00 4.00

Intl. Civil Aviation Org., 40th Anniv. G73

Designs: 5c, Lockheed Lodestar. 70c, Avro 748 Turboprop. $1.10, Boeing 727. $4, Boeing 707. $5, Pilatus Britten-Norman Islander.

1985, Apr. 30

652 G73 5c multicolored .20 .20
653 G73 70c multicolored .50 .50
654 G73 $1.10 multicolored .80 .80
655 G73 $4 multicolored 3.00 3.00
Nos. 652-655 (4) 4.50 4.50

Souvenir Sheet

656 G73 $5 multicolored 4.00 4.00

Girl Guides Type

Designs: 30c, Lady Baden-Powell, Guide leaders. 50c, Botany field trip. 70c, Making camp, vert. $4, Sailing, vert. $5, Lord and Lady Baden-Powell, vert.

1985, May 30

657 A176 30c multicolored .25 .25
658 A176 50c multicolored .40 .40
659 A176 70c multicolored .60 .60
660 A176 $4 multicolored 3.25 3.25
Nos. 657-660 (4) 4.50 4.50

Souvenir Sheet

661 A176 $5 multicolored 4.00 4.00

Grenadine Grizzled Skipper G74

Butterflies: 1c, Red anartia. 2c, Lesser Antillean giant hairstreak. 4c, Santa Domingo longtail skipper. 5c, Spotted Manuel's skipper. 6c, Grenada's polydamus swallowtail. 10c, Palmira sulphur. 12c, Pupillated orange sulphur. 15c, Migrant sulphur. 20c, St. Christopher's hairstreak. 25c, St. Lucia mestra. 30c, Insular gulf fritillary. 40c, Michael's Caribbean buckeye. 60c, Frampton's flambeau. 70c, Bamboo page. $1.10, Antillean cracker. $2.50, Red crescent hairstreak. $5, Single colored Antillean white. $10, Lesser whirlabout. $20, Blue night.

1985-86 *Perf. 14*

662 G74 ½c multicolored .20 .20
663 G74 1c multicolored .20 .20
664 G74 2c multicolored .20 .20
665 G74 4c multicolored .20 .20
666 G74 5c multicolored .20 .20
667 G74 6c multicolored .20 .20
668 G74 10c multicolored .20 .20
669 G74 12c multicolored .20 .20
670 G74 15c multicolored .20 .20
671 G74 20c multicolored .20 .20
672 G74 25c multicolored .20 .20
673 G74 30c multicolored .25 .25
674 G74 40c multicolored .30 .30
675 G74 60c multicolored .45 .45
676 G74 70c multicolored .50 .50
677 G74 $1.10 multicolored .80 .80
678 G74 $2.50 multicolored 1.90 1.90
679 G74 $5 multicolored 3.50 3.50
680 G74 $10 multicolored 7.25 7.25
681 G74 $20 multicolored 15.00 15.00
Nos. 662-681 (20) 32.15 32.15

Issued: #662-679, 6/17; #680, 11/11; #681, 1/8/86.

For overprints see Nos. 737-738.

1986 *Perf. 12½x12*

662a G74 ½c multicolored .20 .20
663a G74 1c multicolored .20 .20
664a G74 2c multicolored .20 .20
665a G74 4c multicolored .20 .20
666a G74 5c multicolored .20 .20
667a G74 6c multicolored .20 .20
668a G74 10c multicolored .20 .20
669a G74 12c multicolored .20 .20
670a G74 15c multicolored .20 .20
671a G74 20c multicolored .20 .20
672a G74 25c multicolored .20 .20
673a G74 30c multicolored .25 .25
674a G74 40c multicolored .30 .30
675a G74 60c multicolored .45 .45
676a G74 70c multicolored .50 .50
677a G74 $1.10 multicolored .75 .75
678a G74 $2.50 multicolored 1.80 1.80
679a G74 $5 multicolored 3.50 3.50
680a G74 $10 multicolored 7.25 7.25
681a G74 $20 multicolored 15.00 15.00
Nos. 662a-681a (20) 32.00 32.00

Issued: #662a-677a, 679a, 1986; #678a, 680a, 9/1986 ; #681a, 5/1989.

Queen Mother Birthday Type

$1, Portrait. $1.50, At Ascot, horiz. $2.50, Queen Mother, Prince Charles. $5, Portrait, diff.

1985, July 3 *Perf. 14*

682 A181 $1 multicolored .75 .75
683 A181 $1.50 multicolored 1.25 1.25
684 A181 $2.50 multicolored 2.00 2.00
Nos. 682-684 (3) 4.00 4.00

Souvenir Sheet

685 A181 $5 multicolored 4.00 4.00

1986, Jan. 28 *Perf. 12x12½*

686 A181 70c like #682 .60 .60
687 A181 $1.10 like #683 .75 .75
688 A181 $3 like #684 2.50 2.50
Nos. 686-688 (3) 3.85 3.85

Issued in sheets of 5 plus label.

Water Sports Type

Designs: 15c, Scuba diving. 70c, Playing in waterfall. 90c, Water skiing. $4, Swimming. $5, Skin diver, sailboat.

1985, July 15 *Perf. 15*

689 A179 15c multicolored .20 .20
690 A179 70c multicolored .55 .55
691 A179 90c multicolored .70 .70
692 A179 $4 multicolored 3.00 3.00
Nos. 689-692 (4) 4.45 4.45

Souvenir Sheet

693 A179 $5 multicolored 4.00 4.00

Queen Conch G75

Marine Life: 90c, Porcupine fish, fire coral. $1.10, Ghost crab. $4, West Indies spiny lobster. $5, Long-spined urchin.

1985, Aug. 1 *Perf. 14*

694 G75 60c multicolored .50 .50
695 G75 90c multicolored .75 .75
696 G75 $1.10 multicolored .90 .90
697 G75 $4 multicolored 3.25 3.25
Nos. 694-697 (4) 5.40 5.40

Souvenir Sheet

698 G75 $5 multicolored 4.00 4.00

Bach Anniversary Type

Portrait, signature, music from Invention No. 9 and: 15c, Natural trumpet. 60c, Bass viol. $1.10, Flute. $3, Double flageolet. $5, Portrait.

1985, Sept. 3 *Perf. 14*

699 A184 15c multicolored .20 .20
700 A184 60c multicolored .50 .50
701 A184 $1.10 multicolored .80 .80
702 A184 $3 multicolored 2.50 2.50
Nos. 699-702 (4) 4.00 4.00

Souvenir Sheet

703 A184 $5 multicolored 4.00 4.00

Royal Visit Type

10c, Arms of Great Britain, Grenada. $1, Queen Elizabeth II. $4, HMY Britannia. $5, Map.

1985, Nov. 4 *Perf. 14½*

704 A186 10c multicolored .20 .20
705 A186 $1 multi, vert. .80 .80
706 A186 $4 multicolored 3.25 3.25
Nos. 704-706 (3) 4.25 4.25

Souvenir Sheet

707 A186 $5 multicolored 4.00 4.00

UN Anniversary Type

UN stamps and famous people: $1, #373, Neil Armstrong. $2, #221, Mahatma Gandhi. $2.50, #43, Maimonides. $5, Ralph Bunche.

1985, Nov. 22

708 A189 $1 multicolored .80 .80
709 A189 $2 multicolored 1.50 1.50
710 A189 $2.50 multicolored 2.00 2.00
Nos. 708-710 (3) 4.30 4.30

Souvenir Sheet

711 A189 $5 multicolored 4.00 4.00

Twain & Disney Type

Walt Disney characters in scenes from "Letters From Hawaii": 25c, Mickey, Minnie on beach. 50c, Donald Duck surfing. $1.50, Donald roasting marshmallow. $3, Mickey canoeing. $5, Mickey, cat.

1985, Nov. 27 *Perf. 14x13½*

712 A185 25c multicolored .20 .20
713 A185 50c multicolored .40 .40
714 A185 $1.50 multicolored 1.25 1.25
715 A185 $3 multicolored 2.50 2.50
Nos. 712-715 (4) 4.35 4.35

Souvenir Sheet

716 A185 $5 multicolored 4.25 4.25

Brothers Grimm & Disney Type

Walt Disney characters in scenes from "The Elves and the Shoemaker": 30c, Mickey as shoemaker. 60c, Elves helping. 70c, Mickey, new shoes. $4, Minnie at sewing machine. $5, Minnie & Mickey.

1985, Nov. 27 *Perf. 13½x14*

717 A187 30c multicolored .25 .25
718 A187 60c multicolored .50 .50
719 A187 70c multicolored .55 .55
720 A187 $4 multicolored 3.25 3.25
Nos. 717-720 (4) 4.55 4.55

Souvenir Sheet

721 A187 $5 multicolored 4.25 4.25

Madonna and Child by Titian — G76

Christmas paintings: 70c, Madonna and Child with St. Mary and John the Baptist by Bugiardini. $1.10, Adoration of the Magi by Di Fredi. $3, Madonna and Child with Young St. John the Baptist by Bartolomeo. $5, The Annunciation by Botticelli.

1985, Dec. 23 *Perf. 15*

722 G76 50c multicolored .40 .40
723 G76 70c multicolored .50 .50
724 G76 $1.10 multicolored .85 .85
725 G76 $3 multicolored 2.25 2.25
Nos. 722-725 (4) 4.00 4.00

Souvenir Sheet

726 G76 $5 multicolored 3.75 3.75

Statue of Liberty Type of 1985

Designs: 5c, Croton Reservoir, 1875. 10c, NY Public Library, 1986. 70c, Old Boathouse, Central Park, 1894. $4, Boating, Central Park, 1986. $5, Statue of Liberty, vert.

1986, Jan. 6 *Perf. 15*

727 A191 5c multicolored .20 .20
728 A191 10c multicolored .20 .20
729 A191 70c multicolored .50 .50
730 A191 $4 multicolored 3.00 3.00
Nos. 727-730 (4) 3.90 3.90

Souvenir Sheet

731 A191 $5 multicolored 3.75 3.75

Audubon Type of 1985

Designs: 50c, Louisiana heron. 70c, Black-crowned night heron. 90c, Bittern. $4, Glossy ibis. $5, King eider.

1986, Jan. 28 *Perf. 12½x12*

732 A174 50c multicolored .40 .40
733 A174 70c multicolored .50 .50
734 A174 90c multicolored .70 .70
735 A174 $4 multicolored 3.00 3.00
Nos. 732-735 (4) 4.60 4.60

Souvenir Sheet
Perf. 14

736 A174 $5 multicolored 3.70 3.70

Nos. 732-735 issued in sheets of 5 plus label.

Nos. 676, 679 Overprinted

1986, Feb. 20 *Perf. 14*

737 G74 70c multicolored .50 .50
738 G75 $5 multicolored 3.75 3.75

World Cup Soccer Championships, Mexico — G77

Various soccer plays.

1986, Mar. 18

739 G77 10c multicolored .20 .20
740 G77 70c multicolored .50 .50
741 G77 $1 multicolored .75 .75
742 G77 $4 multicolored 3.00 3.00
Nos. 739-742 (4) 4.45 4.45

Souvenir Sheet

743 G77 $5 multicolored 3.75 3.75

For overprints see Nos. 772-776.

Halley's Comet Type

Designs: 5c, Nicolaus Copernicus, Earl of Rossi's six foot reflector. 20c, Sputnik. 40c, Tycho Brahe's notes, sketch of comet of 1577. $4, Edmond Halley, comet of 1682. $5, Halley's comet. Captions on 40c and $4 are reversed.

1986, Mar. 26

744 A194 5c multicolored .20 .20
745 A194 20c multicolored .20 .20
746 A194 40c multicolored .30 .30
747 A194 $4 multicolored 3.00 3.00
Nos. 744-747 (4) 3.70 3.70

Souvenir Sheet

748 A194 $5 multicolored 3.75 3.75

"Tycho," on 40c, and "Nicolaus" on 5c misspelled.

For overprints see Nos. 787-791. Compare No. 748 with No. 913.

Queen Elizabeth II, 60th Birthday
Common Design Type

Designs: 2c, At Windsor Park, 1933. $1.50, Queen Elizabeth II. $4, In Sydney, Australia, 1970. $5, Family portrait, Coronation Day, 1937.

1986, Apr. 21

749 CD339 2c yel & blk .20 .20
750 CD339 $1.50 pale grn & multi 1.10 1.10
751 CD339 $4 dl lil & multi 3.00 3.00
Nos. 749-751 (3) 4.30 4.30

Souvenir Sheet

752 CD339 $5 tan & blk 3.75 3.75

AMERIPEX '86 Type

Walt Disney characters visiting: 30c, Grand Canyon. 60c, Golden Gate Bridge. $1, Chicago Watertower. $3, The White House. $5, NY Harbor, Statue of Liberty.

1986, May 22 ***Perf. 11***

753 A195 30c multicolored .25 .25
754 A195 60c multicolored .45 .45
755 A195 $1 multicolored .75 .75
756 A195 $3 multicolored 2.25 2.25
Nos. 753-756 (4) 3.70 3.70

Souvenir Sheet
Perf. 14

757 A195 $5 multicolored 3.75 3.75

Royal Wedding Issue, 1986
Common Design Type

Designs: 60c, Prince Andrew and Sarah Ferguson. 70c, Andrew. $4, Andrew in dress uniform, helicopter. $5, Couple, diff.

1986, July 1 ***Perf. 14***

758 CD340 60c multicolored .45 .45
759 CD340 70c multicolored .55 .55
760 CD340 $4 multicolored 3.00 3.00
Nos. 758-760 (3) 4.00 4.00

Souvenir Sheet

761 CD340 $5 multicolored 3.75 3.75

Mushrooms
G78

Seashells
G79

Designs: 15c, Hygrocybe firma. 50c, Xerocomus coccolobae. $2, Volvariella cubensis. $3, Lactarius putidus. $5, Leponia caeruleocapitata.

1986, July 15 ***Perf. 15***

762 G78 15c multicolored .20 .20
763 G78 50c multicolored .40 .40
764 G78 $2 multicolored 1.50 1.50
765 G78 $3 multicolored 2.25 2.25
Nos. 762-765 (4) 4.35 4.35

Souvenir Sheet

766 G78 $5 multicolored 3.75 3.75

1986, Aug. 1

Designs: 15c, Giant Atlantic pyram. 50c, Beau's murex. $1.10, West Indian fighting conch. $4, Alphabet coral. $5, Brown-lined paper bubble.

767 G79 15c multicolored .20 .20
768 G79 50c multicolored .40 .40
769 G79 $1.10 multicolored .85 .85
770 G79 $4 multicolored 3.00 3.00
Nos. 767-770 (4) 4.45 4.45

Souvenir Sheet

771 G79 $5 multicolored 3.75 3.75

Nos. 739-743 Overprinted in Gold: WINNERS / Argentina 3 / W.Germany 2

1986, Sept. 15 ***Perf. 14***

772 G77 10c multicolored .20 .20
773 G77 70c multicolored .50 .50
774 G77 $1 multicolored .75 .75
775 G77 $4 multicolored 3.00 3.00
Nos. 772-775 (4) 4.45 4.45

Souvenir Sheet

776 G77 $5 multicolored 3.75 3.75

Manicou
G80

Wildlife.

1986, Sept. 15 ***Perf. 15***

777 G80 10c shown .20 .20
778 G80 30c Giant toad .25 .25
779 G80 60c Land tortoise .45 .45
780 G80 70c Murine opossum .55 .55
781 G80 90c Burmese mongoose .65 .65
782 G80 $1.10 Antillean armadillo .85 .85
783 G80 $2 Agouti 1.50 1.50
784 G80 $3 Humpback whale 2.25 2.25
Nos. 777-784 (8) 6.70 6.70

Souvenir Sheets

785 G80 $5 Mona monkey 3.75 3.75
786 G80 $5 Iguana 3.75 3.75

Nos. 744-748 Overprinted in Silver or Black

1986, Oct. 15 ***Perf. 14***

787 A194 5c multicolored (Bk) .20 .20
788 A194 20c multicolored .20 .20
789 A194 40c multicolored (Bk) .30 .30
790 A194 $4 multicolored 3.00 3.00
Nos. 787-790 (4) 3.70 3.70

Souvenir Sheet

791 A194 $5 multicolored 3.75 3.75

Christmas Type of 1986

1986 Nov. 3 ***Perf. 11***

792 A199 25c Chip 'n' Dale .20 .20
793 A199 30c Mickey Mouse .25 .25
794 A199 50c Piglet, Pooh, Jose Carioca .35 .35
795 A199 60c Daisy .40 .40
796 A199 70c A kiss under the mistletoe .45 .45
797 A199 $1.50 Huey, Dewey, and Louie 1.10 1.10
798 A199 $3 Mickey Mouse, Morty 2.25 2.25
799 A199 $4 Kittens on the keys 3.00 3.00
Nos. 792-799 (8) 8.00 8.00

Souvenir Sheets

800 A199 $5 Mickey Mouse 3.75 3.75
801 A199 $5 Bambi 3.75 3.75

Nos. 793, 795-796, 799 vert.

Automobile Centenary Type

Designs: 10c, 1984 Aston-Martin Volante. 30c, 1948 Jaguar Mk V. 60c, 1956 Nash Ambassador. 70c, 1984 Toyota Supra. 90c, 1985 Ferrari Testarossa. $1, 1955 BMW 501B. $2, 1968 Mercedes-Benz 280SL. $3, 1932 Austro-Daimler ADR8.

1986, Nov. 20 ***Perf. 15***

802 A202 10c multicolored .20 .20
803 A202 30c multicolored .25 .25
804 A202 60c multicolored .45 .45
805 A202 70c multicolored .50 .50
806 A202 90c multicolored .70 .70
807 A202 $1 multicolored .75 .75
808 A202 $2 multicolored 1.50 1.50
809 A202 $3 multicolored 2.25 2.25
Nos. 802-809 (8) 6.60 6.60

Souvenir Sheets

810 A202 $5 1977 Morgan +8 3.75 3.75
811 A202 $5 Checker Taxi 3.75 3.75

Chagall Type

Paintings: No. 812, The Mirror. No. 813, Dancer with a Fan. No. 814, The Acrobat. No. 815, Abraham's Sacrifice. No. 816, The Fruit Seller. No. 817, The Rooster. No. 818, The Wedding. No. 819, Horsewoman. No. 820, The Aged Lion from Fables of La Fontaine. No. 821, The Fruit Basket. No. 822, The Satyr and the Wayfarer. No. 823, Self-portrait with Seven Fingers. No. 824, Fruit and Flowers. No. 825, Lovers and Flowers. No. 826, The Wedded with an Angel. No. 827, In the Cafe, 1936. No. 828, The Equestrian. No. 829, Blue Violinist, 1947. No. 830, I and the Village. No. 831, Portrait of Vava, 1955. No. 832, To Russia, Asses and Cattle, 1911. No. 833, The Accordion Player. No. 834, The Violinist, 1913. No. 835, Mother and Child, 1968. No. 836. Sunday, 1953. No. 837, Red and Black World, 1951. No. 838, Double Portrait with Wineglass, 1917. No. 839, Homage to Apollinaire. No. 840, Time is a River without Banks, 1930. No. 841, The Rue de La Paix, 1953. No. 842, Bonjour Paris. No. 843, The Blue Home, 1926, horiz. No. 844, Still-life, 1912, horiz. No. 845, Autumn Village. No. 846, Aleko: Scene I (Costume Design). No. 847, The Jew in Pink, 1914. No. 848, The Clown Musician, 1927. No. 849, War, 1943. No. 850, The Artist Angel. No. 851, Woman at Window, 1961. No. 852, Birthday, 1915. No. 853, Wheatfield on a Summer Afternoon, 1942. No. 854, The Nude Above Vitebsk. No. 855, Aleko and Zemphira by Moonlight. No. 856, The Family Dinner. No. 857, Life. No. 858, The Flying Carriage, 1913. No. 859, The Studio. No. 860, Birth. No. 861, Rain.

1986-87 ***Perf. 14x13½***

812-851 A203 $1.10 each .85 .85

Size: 110x95mm
Imperf

852-861 A203 $5 each 3.75 3.75

Issued: Nos. 824-851, 855-861, 1987.

America's Cup Type

1987, Feb. 5 ***Perf. 15***

862 A204 25c Defender, 1895 .20 .20
863 A204 45c Caleta, 1886 .30 .30
864 A204 70c Azzurra, 1981 .50 .50
865 A204 $4 Australia II, 1983 3.00 3.00
Nos. 862-865 (4) 4.00 4.00

Souvenir Sheet

866 A204 $5 Columbia, Shamrock, 1899 3.75 3.75

Discovery of America Type

1987, Apr. 27

867 A206 15c Columbus .20 .20
868 A206 30c Queen Isabella .20 .20
869 A206 50c Santa Maria .35 .35
870 A206 60c Landing in New World .40 .40
871 A206 90c Lesser Antilles .60 .60
872 A206 $1 King Ferdinand .65 .65
873 A206 $2 Fort of La Navidad 1.40 1.40
874 A206 $3 Galley off Hispaniola 2.00 2.00
a. Sheet of 8 6.25 6.25
Nos. 867-874 (8) 5.80 5.80

Souvenir Sheets

875 A207 $5 Native Canoe 3.75 3.75
876 A207 $5 Santa Maria at anchor 3.75 3.75

Transportation Innovations Type

Designs: 10c, Saunders Roe SR-N1 Hovercraft, 1959. 15c, Bugatti Royale, 1931. 30c, Aleksei Leonov, 1st space walk, 1965. 50c, CSS Hunley, submarine, 1864. 60c, Rolls Royce Flying Bedstead, VTOL aircraft, 1954. 70c, Jenny Lind, locomotive, 1854. 90c, Duryea, 1893. $1.50, Steam locomotive, London subway, 1863. $2, SS Great Britain, screw-driven steamship, 1843. $3, Budweiser rocket, 1979.

1987, May 18 ***Perf. 14***

877 A209 10c multicolored .20 .20
878 A209 15c multicolored .20 .20
879 A209 30c multicolored .25 .25
880 A209 50c multicolored .40 .40
881 A209 60c multicolored .45 .45
882 A209 70c multicolored .50 .50
883 A209 90c multicolored .70 .70
884 A209 $1.50 multicolored 1.10 1.10
885 A209 $2 multicolored 1.50 1.50
886 A209 $3 multicolored 2.25 2.25
Nos. 877-886 (10) 7.55 7.55

Capex '87 Type

Fish.

1987, June 15

887 A208 6c Yellow chub .20 .20
888 A208 30c Kingfish .25 .25
889 A208 50c Mako shark .40 .40
890 A208 60c Dolphinfish .45 .45
891 A208 90c Bonito .70 .70
892 A208 $1.10 Cobia .85 .85
893 A208 $3 Great tarpon 2.25 2.25
894 A208 $4 Swordfish 3.00 3.00
Nos. 887-894 (8) 8.10 8.10

Souvenir Sheets

895 A208 $5 Jewfish 3.75 3.75
896 A208 $5 Amberjack 3.75 3.75

Statue of Liberty Type

10c, Washing statue's face. 15c, Commemorative medals. 25c, Band facing right. 30c, Band facing forward. 45c, Liberty's face. 50c, Washing statue's hair, horiz. 60c, Commemorative statuettes, horiz. 70c, Boats in NY Harbor, horiz. $1, Re-opening. $1.10, Blimps, Liberty & Manhattan Islands. $2, Warship. $3, Commemorative flags.

1987, Aug. 5

897 A210 10c multicolored .20 .20
898 A210 15c multicolored .20 .20
899 A210 25c multicolored .20 .20
900 A210 30c multicolored .25 .25
901 A210 45c multicolored .35 .35
902 A210 50c multicolored .40 .40
903 A210 60c multicolored .40 .40
904 A210 70c multicolored .50 .50
905 A210 $1 multicolored .75 .75
906 A210 $1.10 multicolored .85 .85
907 A210 $2 multicolored 1.50 1.50
908 A210 $3 multicolored 2.25 2.25
Nos. 897-908 (12) 7.85 7.85

Inventors Type

Designs: 60c, Isaac Newton, Newton Medal. $1, Louis Daguerre, inventor of Daguerreotype. $2, Antoine Lavoisier, French chemist, apparatus. $3, Rudolf Diesel, German engineer, Diesel engine. $5, Halley's comet.

1987, Sept. 9

909 A211 60c multicolored .40 .40
910 A211 $1 multicolored .75 .75
911 A211 $2 multicolored 1.50 1.50
912 A211 $3 multicolored 2.25 2.25
Nos. 909-912 (4) 4.90 4.90

Souvenir Sheet

913 A211 $5 multicolored 3.75 3.75

No. 913 inscribed "Great Scientific Discoveries" in margin.

No. 912 incorrectly inscribed "James Watt, Steam Engine." See Grenada No. 1538.

US Constitution Bicentennial Type

10c, Constitutional Convention, Philadelphia. 50c, Georgia state flag. 60c, Capitol, vert. $4, Thomas Jefferson, vert. $5, Alexander Hamilton, vert.

1987, Nov. 1

914 A214 10c multicolored .20 .20
915 A214 50c multicolored .40 .40
916 A214 60c multicolored .40 .40
917 A214 $4 multicolored 3.00 3.00
Nos. 914-917 (4) 4.00 4.00

Souvenir Sheet

918 A214 $5 multicolored 3.75 3.75

Hafnia '87 Type

Walt Disney characters in adaptations of Hans Christian Andersen Fairy Tales: 25c, The Swineherd. 30c, What the Good Man Does is Always Right. 50c, Little Tuk. 60c, The World's Fairest Rose. 70c, The Garden of Paradise. $1.50, The Naughty Boy. $3, What the Moon Saw. $4, Thumbelina. No. 927, Hans Clodhopper. No. 928, Elder Tree Mother.

1987, Nov. 16

919 A215 25c multicolored .20 .20
920 A215 30c multicolored .25 .25
921 A215 50c multicolored .40 .40
922 A215 60c multicolored .40 .40
923 A215 70c multicolored .50 .50
924 A215 $1.50 multicolored 1.10 1.10
925 A215 $3 multicolored 2.25 2.25
926 A215 $4 multicolored 3.00 3.00
Nos. 919-926 (8) 8.10 8.10

Souvenir Sheets

927 A215 $5 multicolored 3.75 3.75
928 A215 $5 multicolored 3.75 3.75

Christmas — G81

Paintings by El Greco: 10c, Virgin and Child with Saints Martin and Agnes. 50c, Detail from Virgin and Child with Saints Martin and Agnes. 60c, The Annunciation. $4, Holy Family with St. Anne. $5, Adoration of the Shepherds.

1987, Dec. 15

929 G81 10c multicolored .20 .20
930 G81 50c multicolored .40 .40
931 G81 60c multicolored .45 .45
932 G81 $4 multicolored 2.25 2.25
Nos. 929-932 (4) 3.30 3.30

Souvenir Sheet

933 G81 $5 multicolored 3.75 3.75

Wedding Anniv. Type

1988, Feb. 15

934 A218 20c Elizabeth, Anne .20 .20
935 A218 30c Wedding portrait .25 .25
936 A218 $2 Elizabeth, Charles, Anne 1.50 1.50
937 A218 $3 Elizabeth wearing tiara 2.25 2.25
Nos. 934-937 (4) 4.20 4.20

Souvenir Sheet

938 A218 $5 Elizabeth in wedding gown 3.75 3.75

1988 Summer Olympics Type

Walt Disney characters in modern and ancient events.

1988, Apr. 13 ***Perf. 13½x14, 14x13½***

939 A219 1c Rhythmic gymnastics .20 .20
940 A219 2c Pankration .20 .20
941 A219 3c Synchronized swimming .20 .20
942 A219 4c Hoplite race .20 .20
943 A219 5c Baseball .20 .20
944 A219 10c Horse race .25 .25
945 A219 $6 Windsurfing 4.50 4.50
946 A219 $7 Chariot race 5.25 5.25
Nos. 939-946 (8) 11.00 11.00

Souvenir Sheet

947 A219 $5 Tennis 3.75 3.75
948 A219 $5 Pentathlon 3.75 3.75

Boy Scout Type

1988, May 3 ***Perf. 14***

949 A220 50c Semaphore, vert. .40 .40
950 A220 70c Canoeing, vert. .50 .50
951 A220 $1 Cook-out .75 .75
952 A220 $3 Campfire 2.25 2.25
Nos. 949-952 (4) 3.90 3.90

Souvenir Sheet

953 A220 $5 Pitching tent 3.75 3.75

Bird Type

1988, May 31

954 A222 20c Yellow-crowned night heron .20 .20
955 A222 25c Brown pelican .20 .20
956 A222 45c Audubon's shearwater .35 .35
957 A222 60c Red-footed booby .40 .40
958 A222 70c Bridled tern .50 .50
959 A222 90c Red-billed tropicbird .65 .65
960 A222 $3 Blue-winged teal 2.25 2.25
961 A222 $4 Sora 3.00 3.00
Nos. 954-961 (8) 7.55 7.55

Souvenir Sheets

962 A222 $5 Little blue heron 3.75 3.75
963 A222 $5 Purple-throated carib 3.75 3.75

Titian Type

Paintings by Titian: 15c, Man with Blue Eyes, 1545. 30c, The Three Ages of Man, 1512. 60c, Don Diego Mendoza, 1545. 75c, Emperor Charles V Seated, 1548. $1, A Young Man in a Fur, 1515. $2, Tobias and the Angel, 1543. $3, Pietro Bembo, 1540. $4, Pier Luigi Farnese, 1546. No. 972, Sacred and Profane Love. No. 973, Venus and Adonis.

1988, June 15 ***Perf. 13½x14***

964 A224 15c multicolored .20 .20
965 A224 30c multicolored .25 .25
966 A224 60c multicolored .40 .40
967 A224 75c multicolored .55 .55
968 A224 $1 multicolored .75 .75
969 A224 $2 multicolored 1.50 1.50
970 A224 $3 multicolored 2.25 2.25
971 A224 $4 multicolored 3.00 3.00
Nos. 964-971 (8) 8.90 8.90

Souvenir Sheet

972 A224 $5 multicolored 3.75 3.75
973 A224 $5 multicolored 3.75 3.75

Airship Type

Historic flights: 10c, Hindenburg over Rio de Janeiro, 1937. 20c, Hindenburg over NYC, 1937. 30c, US Navy airships, WWII convoy to Europe, 1944. 40c, Hindenburg docking at Lakehurst, NJ, 1937, vert. 60c, Joint flight, Hindenburg and Graf Zeppelin, 1936, vert. 70c, DC-3, Hindenburg, Los Angeles at Lakehurst, 1936. $1, Graf Zeppelin II over England, 1939, vert. $2, Deutschland, 1st passenger flight, 1912. $3, Graf Zeppelin over Dome of the Rock, Jerusalem, 1931. $4, Hindenburg Olympic flight, 1936. No. 984, Graf Zeppelin over Vatican City, 1933, vert. No. 985, Graf Zeppelin Polar flight, 1931.

1988, July 1 ***Perf. 14***

974 A225 10c multicolored .20 .20
975 A225 20c multicolored .20 .20
976 A225 30c multicolored .25 .25
977 A225 40c multicolored .30 .30
978 A225 60c multicolored .40 .40
979 A225 70c multicolored .50 .50
980 A225 $1 multicolored .75 .75
981 A225 $2 multicolored 1.50 1.50
982 A225 $3 multicolored 2.25 2.25
983 A225 $4 multicolored 3.00 3.00
Nos. 974-983 (10) 9.35 9.35

Souvenir Sheets

984 A225 $5 multicolored 3.75 3.75
985 A225 $5 multicolored 3.75 3.75

Fairy Tales Type
Miniature Sheets

Bambi: No. 986a, Newborn Bambi, mother and forest animals. b, Bambi, Flower and Thumper. c, Bambi and opossum family hanging from tree. d, Bambi, his mother, and Faline, a female fawn. e, Foraging in a snow storm. f, Meeting his father, the Great Stag. g, Competing for Faline's attention. h, The Great Stag leading animals to safety during forest fire. i, Bambi, grown, becomes the Great Stag.

The Fox and the Hound: No. 987a, Big Mama, consoling the orphaned baby fox, Tod. b, Widow Tweed feeding Tod. c, Tod playing with Copper, the hound. d, Copper leashed. e, Copper and Chief. f, Chief barking at Tod, Copper shocked. g, Porcupine. h, Vixey, a female fox. i, Bear attacking Copper.

101 Dalmatians: No. 988a, Pongo, Perdita and their masters. b, Pongo and Perdita, courting. c, Three puppies. d, Cruella de Ville and henchmen. e, Captain the Horse, Colonel the Sheepdog and Tibbs the Cat. f, Dalmatians following Tibbs to freedom. g, Cruella racing car in pursuit. h, Dalmatians disguised in soot. i, Nanny dusting off the soot.

Dumbo: No. 989a, Stork delivering Dumbo. b, Elephant making fun of Dumbo's large ears. c, Dumbo, Mrs. Jumbo performing. d, Timothy the Mouse. e, Timothy and Dumbo. f, Crows pushing Dumbo off a cliff. g, Dumbo flying away from burning building. h, Dumbo flying with the crows. i, Dumbo and Mrs. Jumbo on train.

Lady and the Tramp: No. 990a, Darling holding Lady. b, Lady meets the Tramp. c, Lady looking in bassinet. d, Siamese cats, Lady. e, Lady, Tramp, crocodiles. f, Tramp kisses Lady. g, Lady in dog catcher's carriage. h, Lady and Tramp attacking rat. i, Trusty and Jock overturning dog catcher's carriage where Tramp is imprisoned.

The Aristocats: No. 991a, Edgar driving Madame Mornfamille's carriage. b, Dutchess and kittens. c, Edgar feeding the cats cream spiked with sleeping pills. d, Edgar transporting cats on motorcycle. e, Walter O'Malley discovers the abandoned cats. f, Three geese. g, Scat Cat and friends holding a jam session. h, Edgar attacks O'Malley with a pitch fork. i, Frau-Frau kicking Edgar.

No. 992, Faline and newborn twin fawns. No. 993, Tod and Vixey. No. 994, Pongo, Perdita and puppies. No. 995, Dumbo flying with Timothy the Mouse. No. 996, Lady and Tramp's puppies. No. 997, Walter O'Malley, Dutchess and kittens.

1988, July 25 ***Perf. 14x13½***

986 Sheet of 9 2.00 2.00
a.-i. A212 30c any single .20 .20
987 Sheet of 9 2.00 2.00
a.-i. A212 30c any single .20 .20
988 Sheet of 9 2.00 2.00
a.-i. A212 30c any single .20 .20
989 Sheet of 9 2.00 2.00
a.-i. A212 30c any single .20 .20
990 Sheet of 9 2.00 2.00
a.-i. A212 30c any single .20 .20
991 Sheet of 9 2.00 2.00
a.-i. A212 30c any single .20 .20
Nos. 986-991 (6) 12.00 12.00

Souvenir Sheets

992-997 A212 $5 each 3.75 3.75

SYDPEX '88 Type

Walt Disney characters: 1c, Conducting at Sydney Opera House. 2c, Climbing Ayers Rock. 3c, Working at a sheep station. 4c, Visiting Lone Pine Koala Sanctuary. 5c, Playing Australian football. 10c, Racing camels. No. 1004, Lawn bowling. $6, America's Cup trophy and Australia II. No. 1006, The Great Barrier Reef. No. 1007, Beach party.

1988, Aug. 1 ***Perf. 14x13½***

998 A226 1c multicolored .20 .20
999 A226 2c multicolored .20 .20
1000 A226 3c multicolored .20 .20
1001 A226 4c multicolored .20 .20
1002 A226 5c multicolored .20 .20
1003 A226 10c multicolored .20 .20
1004 A226 $5 multicolored 3.25 3.25
1005 A226 $6 multicolored 3.75 3.75
Nos. 998-1005 (8) 8.20 8.20

Souvenir Sheets

1006 A226 $5 multicolored 3.25 3.25
1007 A226 $5 multicolored 3.25 3.25

Flowering Trees Type

1988, Sept. 30 ***Perf. 14***

1008 A228 10c Potato tree, vert. .20 .20
1009 A228 20c Wild cotton .20 .20
1010 A228 30c Shower of gold, vert. .25 .25
1011 A228 60c Napoleon's button, vert. .45 .45
1012 A228 90c Geiger tree .65 .65
1013 A228 $1 Fern tree .75 .75
1014 A228 $2 French cashew 1.50 1.50
1015 A228 $4 Amherstia, vert. 3.00 3.00
Nos. 1008-1015 (8) 7.00 7.00

Souvenir Sheets

1016 A228 $5 African tulip tree, vert. 3.75 3.75
1017 A228 $5 Swamp immortelle 3.75 3.75

Car Type
Miniature Sheets

Designs: No. 1018a, 1925 Doble Series E, US. b, 1926 Alvis 12/50, United Kingdom. c, 1927 Sunbeam 3-liter, UK. d, 1928 Franklin Airman, US. e, 1929 Delage D8S, France. f, 1897 Mors, France. g, 1904 Peerless Green Dragon, US. h, 1909 Pope-Hartford, US. i, 1920 Daniels Submarine Speedster, US. j, 1922 McFarlan 9.3 liter, US.

No. 1019a, 1949 Frazer Nash Lemans Replica, UK. b, 1953 Pegaso Z102, Spain. No. 1019c, 1953 Siata Spyder V-8, Italy. d, 1953 Kurtis-Offenhauser, US. No. 1019e, 1954 Kaiser-Darrin, US. f, 1930 Tracta, France. g, 1932 Maybach Zeppelin, Germany. h, 1934 Railton Light Sports, UK. i, 1936 Hotchkiss, France. j, 1939 Mercedes-Benz W163, Germany.

No. 1020a, 1982 Aston Martin Vantage V8, UK. b, 1982 Porsche 956, Germany. No. 1020c, 1983 Lotus Esprit Turbo, UK. d, 1984 McLaren MP4/2, UK. e, 1985 Mercedes-Benz 190E 2-3-16, Germany. f, 1963 Ferrari 250 GT Lusso, Italy. g, 1964 Porsche 904, Germany. h, 1967 Volvo P1800, Sweden. i, 1970 McLaren-Chevrolet M8D, US. j, 1981 Jaguar XJ6, UK.

1988, Oct. 7 ***Perf. 13x13½***

1018 Sheet of 10 15.00 15.00
a.-j. A223 $2 any single 1.50 1.50
1019 Sheet of 10 15.00 15.00
a.-j. A223 $2 any single 1.50 1.50
1020 Sheet of 10 15.00 15.00
a.-j. A223 $2 any single 1.50 1.50

Christmas and Mickey Mouse 60th Anniv. Type
Miniature Sheet

"Mickey's Christmas Parade": No. 1021a, Dumbo. b, Goofy. c, Minnie Mouse. d, Morty, Ferdy and Clarabelle Cow. e, Huey, Dewey and Louie. f, Donald Duck. g, Wooden soldiers marching. h, Mickey Mouse leading parade. No. 1022, Capt. Hook on float. No. 1023, Mickey and Donald on float.

1988, Dec. 1 ***Perf. 13½x14***

1021 Sheet of 8 6.00 6.00
a.-h. A229 $1 any single .75 .75

Souvenir Sheets
Perf. 14x13

1022 A229 $7 multicolored 5.25 5.25
1023 A229 $7 multicolored 5.25 5.25

Japanese Painting Type

"The Fifty-three Stations on the Tokaido" by Hiroshige (1979-1858): 15c, Crossing the Oi at Shimada by Ferry. 20c, Daimyo and Entourage at Arai. 45c, Cargo Portage through Goyu. 75c, Snowfall at Fujigawa. $1, Horses for the Emperor at Chirifu. $2, Rainfall at Tsuchiyama. $3, At Inn of Ishibe. $4, On the Shore of Lake Biwa at Otsu. No. 1032, Pilgrimage to Atsuta Shrine at Miya. No. 1033, Fishing Village of Yokkaichi on the Mie.

1989, May 15 ***Perf. 14x13½***

1024 A233 15c multicolored .20 .20
1025 A233 20c multicolored .20 .20
1026 A233 45c multicolored .30 .30
1027 A233 75c multicolored .55 .55
1028 A233 $1 multicolored .75 .75
1029 A233 $2 multicolored 1.50 1.50
1030 A233 $3 multicolored 2.25 2.25
1031 A233 $4 multicolored 3.00 3.00
Nos. 1024-1031 (8) 8.75 8.75

Souvenir Sheets

1032 A233 $5 multicolored 3.75 3.75
1033 A233 $5 multicolored 3.75 3.75

1988 Olympic Medalists Type

Designs: 15c, Henry Maske, East Germany, boxing (165 lbs.). 50c, Andreas Schroeder, East Germany, freestyle wrestling (286 lbs.). 60c, East German team, women's gymnastics. 75c, Greg Louganis, US, men's springboard and platform diving. $1, Mitsuru Sato, Japan, freestyle wrestling (115 lbs.). $2, West German team, 4x200m freestyle relay. $3, Dieter Baumann, West Germany, 5000m race. $4, Jackie Joyner-Kersee, US, heptathlon. No. 1042, Joachim Kunz, East Germany, weight lifting (149 lbs.). No. 1043, West German equestrian team, 3-day event.

1989, Apr. 13 ***Perf. 14***

1034 A232 15c multicolored .20 .20
1035 A232 50c multicolored .35 .35
1036 A232 60c multicolored .40 .40
1037 A232 75c multicolored .55 .55
1038 A232 $1 multicolored .75 .75
1039 A232 $2 multicolored 1.50 1.50
1040 A232 $3 multicolored 2.25 2.25
1041 A232 $4 multicolored 3.00 3.00
Nos. 1034-1041 (8) 9.00 9.00

Souvenir Sheets

1042 A232 $6 multicolored 4.25 4.25
1043 A232 $6 multicolored 4.25 4.25

World Cup Soccer Championships, Italy — G82

Designs: 15c, World Cup, vert. 45c, Kaiser Franz, West Germany, vert. 75c, Like 20c, flag of Italy, 1982 champions. $1, Pele, Brazil, vert. $2, Like 20c, flag of West Germany, 1974 champions. $3, Like 20c, flag of Brazil, 1970 champions. $4, Jules Rimet Cup, vert. No. 1052, Pele, Jules Rimet Cup, vert. No. 1053, Goalie.

1989, June 12

1044 G82 15c multicolored .20 .20
1045 G82 20c multicolored .20 .20
1046 G82 45c multicolored .30 .30
1047 G82 75c multicolored .55 .55
1048 G82 $1 multicolored 1.50 1.50
1049 G82 $2 multicolored 3.00 3.00
1050 G82 $3 multicolored 2.25 2.25
1051 G82 $4 multicolored 3.00 3.00
Nos. 1044-1051 (8) 11.00 11.00

Souvenir Sheets

1052 G82 $6 multicolored 4.25 4.25
1053 G82 $6 multicolored 4.25 4.25

Car Type of 1988
Miniature Sheets

North American locomotives: No. 1054a, Morris & Essex, Dover, 1841. No. 1054b, B&O, Memmon No. 57, 1848. No. 1054c, Camden & Amboy, John Stevens, 1849. No. 1054d, Lawrence Machine Shop, Lawrence, 1853. No. 1054e, South Carolina, James S. Corry, 1859. No. 1054f, Mine Hill & Schuylkill Haven, Flexible Beam No. 3, 1860. No. 1054g, DL&W, Montrose, 1861. No. 1054h, Central Pacific, Pequop No. 68, 1868. No. 1054i, Boston & Providence, Daniel Nason, 1863. No. 1054j, Morris & Essex, Joe Scranton, 1870.

No. 1055a, Central Railroad of New Jersey, No. 124, 1871. No. 1055b, Baldwin Steam Motor for Street Railways, 1876. No. 1055c, Lackawanna & Bloomsburg, Luzerne, 1878. No. 1055d, Central Mexicano, No. 150, 1892. No. 1055e, Denver, South Park & Pacific, Breckenridge No. 15, 1879. No. 1055f, Miles Planting & Manufacturing Co., "Daisy" Plantation locomotive, 1894. No. 1055g, Central of Georgia, Baldwin 854 No. 1136, 1895. No. 1055h, Savannah, Florida & Western, No. 111, 1900. No. 1055i, Douglas, Gilmore, & Co. No. 3, 1902. No. 1055j, Lehigh Valley Coal Co., Compressed Air locomotive No. 900, 1903.

No. 1056a, Morgan's Louisiana & Texas, McKeen Motorcar, 1908. No. 1056b, Clear Lake Lumber Co., Type B Climax, 1910. No. 1056c, Blue Jay Lumber Co., Heisler No. 10, 1912. No. 1056d, Stewartstown, Gasoline Engine No. 6, 1920's. No. 1056e, Bangor & Aroostook, Class G No. 186, 1921. No. 1056f, Hammond Lumber Co., No. 6, 1923. No. 1056g, Central Railroad of New Jersey, No. 1000, 1925. No. 1056h, Atchison, Topeka & Santa Fe, Super Chief No. 1-1A, 1935. No. 1056i, Norfolk & Western, Class Y-6, 1948. No. 1056i, Boston & Maine, Budd Railcar, 1949.

1989, June 28 ***Perf. 13x13½***

1054 Sheet of 10 15.00 15.00
a.-j. A223 $2 any single 1.50 1.50
1055 Sheet of 10 15.00 15.00
a.-j. A223 $2 any single 1.50 1.50
1056 Sheet of 10 15.00 15.00
a.-j. A223 $2 any single 1.50 1.50

PHILEXFRANCE '89 — G83

Walt Disney characters in Paris.

1989, July 7 *Perf. 14x13½, 13½x14*

1057 G83 1c Military school .20 .20
1058 G83 2c Conciergerie .20 .20
1059 G83 3c Hotel de Ville, vert. .20 .20
1060 G83 4c Genie of the Bastille, vert. .20 .20
1061 G83 5c The Opera .20 .20
1062 G83 10c Gardens of Luxembourg .25 .25
1063 G83 $5 Arche de la Defense, vert. 3.25 3.25
1064 G83 $6 Place Vendome, vert. 3.50 3.50
Nos. 1057-1064 (8) 8.00 8.00

Souvenir Sheets

1065 G83 $6 Riding moped 4.00 4.00
1066 G83 $6 Hot air ballooning 4.00 4.00

Moon Landing Anniv. Type

Apollo 11 mission, 1969: 25c, Liftoff, vert. 50c, Splashdown. 60c, Spacecraft approaching moon, vert. 75c, Buzz Aldrin conducting experiment on lunar surface. $1, Leaving Earth orbit. $2, Transport of launch vehicle to pad, vert. $3, Lunar module liftoff. $4, Eagle lands on moon, vert. No. 1075, Footprint on moon. No. 1076, Armstrong stepping onto the moon, vert.

1989, July 20 *Perf. 14*

1067 A237 25c multicolored .20 .20
1068 A237 50c multicolored .35 .35
1069 A237 60c multicolored .40 .40
1070 A237 75c multicolored .55 .55
1071 A237 $1 multicolored .75 .75
1072 A237 $2 multicolored 1.50 1.50
1073 A237 $3 multicolored 2.25 2.25
1074 A237 $4 multicolored 3.00 3.00
Nos. 1067-1074 (8) 9.00 9.00

Souvenir Sheets

1075 A237 $5 multicolored 3.75 3.75
1076 A237 $5 multicolored 3.75 3.75

Mushroom Type

1989, Aug. 17

1078 A238 6c Collybia aurea .20 .20
1079 A238 10c Podaxis pistillaris .20 .20
1080 A238 20c Hygrocybe firma .20 .20
1081 A238 30c Agaricus rufoaurantiacus .25 .25
1082 A238 75c Leptonia howellii .55 .55
1083 A238 $2 Marasmiellus purpureus 1.50 1.50
1084 A238 $3 Marasmius trinitatis 2.25 2.25
1085 A238 $4 Hygrocybe martinicensis 3.00 3.00
Nos. 1078-1085 (8) 8.15 8.15

Souvenir Sheets

1086 A238 $6 Lentinus crinitus 4.25 4.25
1087 A238 $6 Agaricus purpurellus 4.25 4.25

Butterflies Type

1989, Oct. 2 *Perf. 14*

1088 A239 25c Androgeus swallowtail .20 .20
1089 A239 35c Cloudless sulpher .25 .25
1090 A239 45c Cracker .30 .30
1091 A239 50c Painted lady .35 .35
1092 A239 75c Great southern white .50 .50
1093 A239 90c Little sulpher .65 .65
1094 A239 $2 Migrant sulpher 1.50 1.50
1095 A239 $3 Mimic 2.25 2.25
Nos. 1088-1095 (8) 6.00 6.00

Souvenir Sheets

1096 A239 $6 Giant hairstreak 4.25 4.25
1097 A239 $6 Red anartia 4.25 4.25

World Stamp Expo Type

Scenes from Walt Disney animated films and quotes from Poor Richard's Almanack by Benjamin Franklin: 1c, "Beware of little expenses, a small leak will sink a great ship." 2c, "Trust thyself and another shall not betray thee." 3c, "A spoonful of honey will catch more flies than a gallon of vinegar." 4c, "No gain without pain." 5c, "A true friend is the best possession." 6c, "Haste makes waste." 8c, "A quiet conscience sleeps in thunder, but rest and guilt live far asunder." 10c, "The muses love the morning." $5, "An egg today is better than a hen tomorrow." No. 1107, "He that riseth late, must trot all day." No. 1108, "If you'd be belov'd, make yourself amiable." No. 1109, "In Christmas feasting pray take care; let not your table be a snare; but with the poor God's bounty share. Adieu my friends! Till the next year," vert.

1989, Nov. **Litho.** *Perf. 14x13½*

1098 A242 1c multicolored .20 .20
1099 A242 2c multicolored .20 .20
1100 A242 3c multicolored .20 .20
1101 A242 4c multicolored .20 .20
1102 A242 5c multicolored .20 .20
1103 A242 6c multicolored .20 .20
1104 A242 8c multicolored .20 .20
1105 A242 10c multicolored .20 .20
1106 A242 $5 multicolored 3.50 3.50
1107 A242 $6 multicolored 3.75 3.75
Nos. 1098-1107 (10) 8.85 8.85

Souvenir Sheet

1108 A242 $6 multicolored 3.75 3.75
1109 A242 $6 multicolored 3.75 3.75

World Stamp Expo '89, Washington, D.C.

Shakespearean Actors and Theater Masks — G84

15c, Ethel Barrymore (1879-1959). $1.10, Richard Burton (1925-1984). $2, John Barrymore (1882-1942). $3, Paul Robeson (1898-1976). $6, Bando Tamasaburo & Nakamura Kanzaburo.

1989, Oct. 9 **Litho.** *Perf. 14*

1110 G84 15c multicolored .20 .20
1111 G84 $1.10 multicolored .80 .80
1112 G84 $2 multicolored 1.50 1.50
1113 G84 $3 multicolored 2.25 2.25
Nos. 1110-1113 (4) 4.75 4.75

Souvenir Sheet

1114 G84 $6 multicolored 4.50 4.50

20th Century Musicians — G85

1989, Oct. 9

1115 G85 10c Buddy Holly .20 .20
1116 G85 25c Jimi Hendrix .20 .20
1117 G85 75c Mighty Sparrow .60 .60
1118 G85 $4 Katsutoji Kineya 3.00 3.00
Nos. 1115-1118 (4) 4.00 4.00

Souvenir Sheet

1119 G85 $6 Lotte Lenya, Kurt Weill 4.50 4.50

Jimi is spelled incorrectly as "Jimmy."

Discovery of America Type

1989, Oct. 16

1120 A241 15c Canoeing .20 .20
1121 A241 75c Cooking .60 .60
1122 A241 90c Using stone tools .70 .70
1123 A241 $3 Eating 2.25 2.25
Nos. 1120-1123 (4) 3.75 3.75

Souvenir Sheet

1124 A241 $6 Building fire 4.50 4.50

Christmas Type

Religious paintings by Rubens: 10c, The Annunciation. 15c, The Flight of the Holy Family into Egypt. 25c, The Presentation in the Temple. 45c, The Holy Family Under the Apple Tree. $2, Madonna and Child with Saints. $4, The Virgin and Child Enthroned with Saints. No. 1132, The Holy Family. No. 1132, Adoration of the Magi. No. 1133, Adoration of the Magi, diff.

1990, Jan. 4 *Perf. 14*

1125 A243 10c multicolored .20 .20
1126 A243 15c multicolored .20 .20
1127 A243 25c multicolored .20 .20
1128 A243 45c multicolored .35 .35
1129 A243 $2 multicolored 1.50 1.50
1130 A243 $4 multicolored 3.00 3.00
1131 A243 $5 multicolored 3.75 3.75
Nos. 1125-1131 (7) 9.20 9.20

Souvenir Sheets

1132 A243 $5 multicolored 3.75 3.75
1133 A243 $5 multicolored 3.75 3.75

America Issue (Insects) G86

1990, Mar. 16 *Perf. 14*

1134 G86 35c Hercules beetle .30 .30
1135 G86 40c Click beetle .30 .30
1136 G86 50c Harlequin beetle .40 .40
1137 G86 60c Gold rim butterfly .50 .50
1138 G86 $1 Red skimmer dragonfly .75 .75
1139 G86 $2 Buprestid beetle 1.50 1.50
1140 G86 $3 Mimic butterfly 2.25 2.25
1141 G86 $4 Scarab beetle 3.00 3.00
Nos. 1134-1141 (8) 9.00 9.00

Souvenir Sheets

1142 G86 $6 Canna skipper butterfly 4.50 4.50
1143 G86 $6 Monarch butterfly 4.50 4.50

Orchids — G87

1990, Mar. 6 **Litho.** *Perf. 14*

1144 G87 15c Brassocattleya thalie .20 .20
1145 G87 20c Odontocidium tigersun .20 .20
1146 G87 50c Odontioda hambuhren .40 .40
1147 G87 75c Paphiopedium delrosi .55 .55
1148 G87 $1 Vuylstekeara yokara .75 .75
1149 G87 $2 Paphiopedilum geelong 1.50 1.50
1150 G87 $3 Wilsonara tigerwood 2.25 2.25
1151 G87 $4 Cymbidium ormoulu 3.00 3.00
Nos. 1144-1151 (8) 8.85 8.85

Souvenir Sheets

1152 G87 $6 Odontonia sappho 4.50 4.50
1153 G87 $6 Cymbidium vieux rose 4.50 4.50

EXPO '90 Intl. Garden and Greenery Exposition, Osaka, Japan.

Wildlife Type

1990, Apr. 3

1154 A247 5c West Indies giant rice rat .20 .20
1155 A247 25c Agouti .20 .20
1156 A247 30c Humpback whale .25 .25
1157 A247 40c Pilot whale .30 .30
1158 A247 $1 Spotted dolphin .75 .75
1159 A247 $2 Mongoose 1.50 1.50
1160 A247 $3 Prehensile-tailed porcupine 2.25 2.25
1161 A247 $4 West Indies manatee 3.00 3.00
Nos. 1154-1161 (8) 8.45 8.45

Souvenir Sheets

1162 A247 $6 Caribbean monk seal 4.50 4.50
1163 A247 $6 Mongoose 4.50 4.50

World War II Type

Designs: 6c, First British troops arrive in France, Sept. 6, 1939. 10c, British launch "Operation Crusader", Nov. 18, 1941. 20c, Rommel begins retreat from El Alamein, Nov. 4, 1942. 45c, US forces land on Aleutian Islands, May 11, 1943. 50c, US Marines land on Tarawa, Nov. 20, 1943. 60c, US 5th Army enters Rome, June 4, 1944. 75c, US troops reach River Seine, Aug. 19, 1944. $1, Battle of the Bulge, Dec. 16, 1944. $5, Allies launch final phase of Italian Campaign, Apr. 9, 1945. No. 1173, Atom bomb dropped on Hiroshima, Aug. 6, 1945. No. 1174, St. Paul's Catherdral during London blitz, Battle of Britain, 1940.

1990, Apr. 30

1164 A248 6c multicolored .20 .20
1165 A248 10c multicolored .20 .20
1166 A248 20c multicolored .20 .20
1167 A248 45c multicolored .35 .35
1168 A248 50c multicolored .40 .40
1169 A248 60c multicolored .45 .45
1170 A248 75c multicolored .55 .55
1171 A248 $1 multicolored .75 .75
1172 A248 $5 multicolored 3.75 3.75
1173 A248 $6 multicolored 4.50 4.50
Nos. 1164-1173 (10) 11.35 11.35

Souvenir Sheets

1174 A248 $6 multicolored 4.50 4.50

Disney Type

Disney characters portraying Shakespearian characters: 15c, Daisy Duck at Ann Hathaway's Cottage, Shottery. 30c, Minnie Mouse and a young Shakespeare walking in Stratford birthplace, vert. 50c, Minnie as Mary Arden, Shakespeare's mother in Wilmcote, vert. 60c, Mickey in front of New Place, Stratford. $1, Mickey walking in Great Garden of New Place. $2, Mickey at Guild Chapel, Scholars Lane, vert. $4, Mickey at the Royal Shakespeare Theater, Stratford, vert. $5, Ludwig von Drake instructing Shakespeare. No. 1183, Mickey at Edge Hill, Stratford, vert. No. 1184, Mickey and Minnie rowing past Holy Trinity Church, Stratford-Upon-Avon.

1990, May *Perf. 14x13½*

1175 A250 15c multicolored .20 .20
1176 A250 30c multicolored .25 .25
1177 A250 50c multicolored .40 .40
1178 A250 60c multicolored .45 .45
1179 A250 $1 multicolored .75 .75
1180 A250 $2 multicolored 1.25 1.25
1181 A250 $4 multicolored 2.75 2.75
1182 A250 $5 multicolored 3.50 3.50
Nos. 1175-1182 (8) 9.55 9.55

Souvenir Sheets

Perf. 14

1183 A250 $6 multicolored 4.00 4.00
1184 A250 $6 multicolored 4.00 4.00

Penny Black Type
Souvenir Sheet

1990, May 3 **Litho.** *Perf. 14*

1185 A249 $6 Globe with South America 4.50 4.50

Stamp World London '90.

Queen Mother, 90th Birthday Type

1990, July 5

1186 A251 $2 Pink hat 1.50 1.50
1187 A251 $2 With Charles 1.50 1.50
1188 A251 $2 Blue outfit 1.50 1.50
Nos. 1186-1188 (3) 4.50 4.50

Souvenir Sheet

1189 A251 $6 like #1187 4.50 4.50

Bird Type

1990, Sept. 10 **Litho.** *Perf. 14*

1190 A255 25c Yellow-bellied seedeater .20 .20
1191 A255 45c Carib grackle .35 .35
1192 A255 50c Black-whiskered vireo .40 .40
1193 A255 75c Bananaquit .55 .55
1194 A255 $1 Collared swift .75 .75
1195 A255 $2 Yellow-bellied elaenia 1.50 1.50
1196 A255 $3 Blue-hooded euphonia 2.25 2.25
1197 A255 $5 Eared dove 3.75 3.75
Nos. 1190-1197 (8) 9.75 9.75

Souvenir Sheets

1198 A255 $6 Mangrove cuckoo 4.50 4.50
1199 A255 $6 Scaly-breasted thrasher 4.50 4.50

Crustaceans

1990, Sept. 17

1200 A256 10c Slipper lobster .20 .20
1201 A256 25c Green reef crab .20 .20
1202 A256 65c Caribbean lobsterette .50 .50
1203 A256 75c Blind deep sea lobster .60 .60
1204 A256 $1 Flattened crab .75 .75
1205 A256 $2 Ridged slipper lobster 1.50 1.50
1206 A256 $3 Land crab 2.25 2.25
1207 A256 $4 Mountain crab 3.00 3.00
Nos. 1200-1207 (8) 9.00 9.00

Souvenir Sheets

1208 A256 $6 Caribbean king crab 4.50 4.50
1209 A256 $6 Purse crab 4.50 4.50

G88

G89

Players from participating countries.

1990, Sept. 24
1210 G88 15c England .20 .20
1211 G88 45c Argentina .30 .30
1212 G88 $2 Sweden 1.50 1.50
1213 G88 $4 South Korea 3.00 3.00
Nos. 1210-1213 (4) 5.00 5.00

Souvenir Sheets
1214 G88 $6 Yugoslavia 4.50 4.50
1215 G88 $6 United States 4.50 4.50

World Cup Soccer Championships, Italy.

1990, Nov. 11 Litho. *Perf. 14*
1216 G89 10c Boxing .20 .20
1217 G89 25c Olympic flame .20 .20
1218 G89 50c Soccer .40 .40
1219 G89 75c Discus .55 .55
1220 G89 $1 Pole vault .75 .75
1221 G89 $2 Equestrian 3-day event 1.50 1.50
1222 G89 $4 Women's basketball 3.00 3.00
1223 G89 $5 Men's gymnastics 3.75 3.75
Nos. 1216-1223 (8) 10.35 10.35

Souvenir Sheets
1224 G89 $6 Sailboarding 4.50 4.50
1225 G89 $6 Decathlon 4.50 4.50

1992 Summer Olympics, Barcelona.

Rubens Type

Entire paintings or different details from: 5c, 25c, Adam and Eve, vert. 15c, Esther before Ahasuerus. 50c, Expulsion from Eden. $1, Cain Slaying Abel, vert. $2, Lot's Flight. $4, Samson and Delilah. $5, Abraham and Melchizedek. No. 1234, The Meeting of David and Abigail. No. 1235, Daniel in the Lions Den.

1991, Jan. 31 Litho. *Perf. 14*
1226 A259 5c multicolored .20 .20
1227 A259 15c multicolored .20 .20
1228 A259 25c multicolored .20 .20
1229 A259 50c multicolored .40 .40
1230 A259 $1 multicolored .75 .75
1231 A259 $2 multicolored 1.50 1.50
1232 A259 $4 multicolored 3.00 3.00
1233 A259 $5 multicolored 3.75 3.75
Nos. 1226-1233 (8) 10.00 10.00

Souvenir Sheets
1234 A259 $6 multicolored 4.50 4.50
1235 A259 $6 multicolored 4.50 4.50

Fish Type of 1990

1991, Feb. 5
1236 A254 15c Barred hamlet .20 .20
1237 A254 35c Squirrelfish .25 .25
1238 A254 45c Red-spotted hawkfish .35 .35
1239 A254 75c Bigeye .55 .55
1240 A254 $1 Spiny puffer .75 .75
1241 A254 $2 Smallmouth grunt 1.50 1.50
1242 A254 $3 Harlequin bass 2.25 2.25
1243 A254 $4 Creole fish 3.00 3.00
Nos. 1236-1243 (8) 8.85 8.85

Souvenir Sheets
1244 A254 $6 Fairy basslet 4.50 4.50
1245 A254 $6 Copper sweeper 4.50 4.50

Hummel Figurines — G90

Orchids — G91

1991, Mar. 1 Litho. *Perf. 14*
1246 G90 10c Angel, star .20 .20
1247 G90 15c Angel, guitar, Christ Child .20 .20
1248 G90 25c Shepherd .20 .20
1249 G90 50c Angel, lantern, horn .35 .35
1250 G90 $1 Angel, children, Christ Child .70 .70
1251 G90 $2 Angel, candle, Christ Child 1.40 1.40
1252 G90 $4 Angel with baskets 2.90 2.90
1253 G90 $5 Angels singing 3.65 3.65
Nos. 1246-1253 (8) 9.60 9.60

Souvenir Sheets
1254 Sheet of 4 2.90 2.90
a. G90 5c like No. 1247 .20 .20
b. G90 40c like No. 1249 .30 .30
c. G90 60c like No. 1250 .40 .40
d. G90 $3 like No. 1253 2.10 2.10
1255 Sheet of 4 5.25 5.25
a. G90 20c like No. 1246 .20 .20
b. G90 30c like No. 1248 .25 .25
c. G90 75c like No. 1251 .55 .55
d. G90 $6 like No. 1252 4.25 4.25

Christmas 1990.

1991-92 Litho. *Perf. 14*

Designs: 5c, Brassia maculata. 10c, Oncidium lanceanum. 15c, Broughtonia sanguinea. 25c, Diacrium bicornutum. 35c, Cattleya labiata. 45c, Epidendrum fragrans. 50c, Oncidium papilio. 75c, Neocogniauxia monophylla. $1, Epidendrum polybulbon. $2, Spiranthes speciosa. $4, Epidendrum ciliare. $5, Phais tankervilliae. $10, Brassia caudata. $20, Brassavola cordata.

1256 G91 5c multicolored .20 .20
1257 G91 10c multicolored .20 .20
1258 G91 15c multicolored .20 .20
1259 G91 25c multicolored .20 .20
1260 G91 35c multicolored .25 .25
1261 G91 45c multicolored .30 .30
1262 G91 50c multicolored .35 .35
1263 G91 75c multicolored .55 .55
1264 G91 $1 multicolored .70 .70
1265 G91 $2 multicolored 1.40 1.40
1266 G91 $4 multicolored 2.90 2.90
1267 G91 $5 multicolored 3.50 3.50
1268 G91 $10 multicolored 7.25 7.25
1269 G91 $20 multicolored 15.00 15.00
Nos. 1256-1269 (14) 33.00 33.00

Issued: $20, 6/92; others, 4/1/91.

Butterfly Type

Designs: 5c, Crimson-patched longwing. 10c, Morpho helena. 15c, Morpho sulkowskyi. 20c, Dynastor napoleon. 25c, Pieridae callinira. 30c, Anartia amathea. 35c, Heliconiidae dido. 45c, Papilionidae columbus. 50c, Nymphalidae praeneste. 60c, Panacea prola. 75c, Julia. $1, Papilionidae orthosilaus. $2, Pyrrhopyge cometes. $3, Papilionidae paeon. $4, Morpho cypris. $5, Choringa. No. 1286, Caligo idomenides. No. 1287, Monarch. No. 1287A, Nymphalidae amydon. No. 1287B, Papilio childrenae.

1991, Apr. 8 Litho. *Perf. 14*
1270 A261 5c multicolored .20 .20
1271 A261 10c multicolored .20 .20
1272 A261 15c multicolored .20 .20
1273 A261 20c multicolored .20 .20
1274 A261 25c multicolored .20 .20
1275 A261 30c multicolored .25 .25
1276 A261 35c multicolored .25 .25
1277 A261 45c multicolored .30 .30
1278 A261 50c multicolored .35 .35
1279 A261 60c multicolored .45 .45
1280 A261 75c multicolored .55 .55
1281 A261 $1 multicolored .75 .75
1282 A261 $2 multicolored 1.50 1.50
1283 A261 $3 multicolored 2.10 2.10
1284 A261 $4 multicolored 2.90 2.90
1285 A261 $5 multicolored 3.50 3.50
Nos. 1270-1285 (16) 13.90 13.90

Souvenir Sheets
1286 A261 $6 multicolored 4.25 4.25
1287 A261 $6 multicolored 4.25 4.25
1287A A261 $6 multicolored 4.25 4.25
1287B A261 $6 multicolored 4.25 4.25

Save Our Planet — G100

Walt Disney characters and ecology themes: 10c, Daisy and Donald, alternate forms of transportation. 15c, Goofy saving water. 25c, Donald, Daisy camping simply. 45c, Donald protecting birds. $1, Donald holding ascending balloons. $2, Minnie, Daisy using natural coolers. $4, Mickey, nephews cleaning beaches. $5, Scrooge McDuck using pedal power. No. 1296, Little Hiawatha and Iron Eyes Cody viewing destroyed forest. No. 1297, Donald, recycling. No. 1298, Minnie, Mickey planting trees.

1991, Apr. 22 Litho. *Perf. 14*
1288 G100 10c multicolored .20 .20
1289 G100 15c multicolored .20 .20
1290 G100 25c multicolored .20 .20
1291 G100 45c multicolored .30 .30
1292 G100 $1 multicolored .70 .70
1293 G100 $2 multicolored 1.50 1.50
1294 G100 $4 multicolored 2.90 2.90
1295 G100 $5 multicolored 3.50 3.50
Nos. 1288-1295 (8) 9.50 9.50

Souvenir Sheets
1296 G100 $6 multicolored 4.25 4.25
1297 G100 $6 multicolored 4.25 4.25
1298 G100 $6 multicolored 4.25 4.25

Voyages of Discovery Type

Discovery of America, 500th anniv. (in 1992).: 15c, Ferdinand Magellan, 1519-1521. 20c, Sir Francis Drake, 1577-1580. 50c, Capt. James Cook, 1768-1771. 60c, Douglas World Cruiser, 1924. $1, Sputnik, 1957. $2, Yuri Gagarin, 1961. $4, John Glenn, 1962. $5, Space Shuttle, 1981. No. 1307, Columbus' fleet. No. 1308, The Pinta, vert.

1991, Apr. 29 Litho. *Perf. 14*
1299 A262 15c multicolored .20 .20
1300 A262 20c multicolored .20 .20
1301 A262 50c multicolored .35 .35
1302 A262 60c multicolored .45 .45
1303 A262 $1 multicolored .70 .70
1304 A262 $2 multicolored 1.40 1.40
1305 A262 $4 multicolored 2.90 2.90
1306 A262 $5 multicolored 3.50 3.50
Nos. 1299-1306 (8) 9.70 9.70

Souvenir Sheets
1307 A262 $6 multicolored 4.25 4.25
1308 A262 $6 multicolored 4.25 4.25

Disney Phila Nippon '91 Type

Walt Disney characters demonstrating arts, crafts and industries of Japan: 15c, Minnie, silkworms. 30c, Mickey, Minnie, Morty and Ferdie photographing the Torii. 50c, Donald, Mickey, origami. 60c, Mickey, Minnie diving for pearls. $1, Minnie modeling kimono. $2, Mickey making masks. $4, Donald, Mickey making paper. $5, Minnie, Pluto, pottery. #1317, Mickey making prints, vert. #1318, Mickey arranging flowers, vert. #1319, Mickey, tea ceremony, vert. #1320, Mickey carving ivory and wood into netsukes, vert.

1991, May 6
1309 A263 15c multi .20 .20
1310 A263 30c multi .25 .25
1311 A263 50c multi .35 .35
1312 A263 60c multi .45 .45
1313 A263 $1 multi .70 .70
1314 A263 $2 multi 1.40 1.40
1315 A263 $4 multi 2.90 2.90
1316 A263 $5 multi 3.50 3.50
Nos. 1309-1316 (8) 9.75 9.75

Souvenir Sheets
1317 A263 $6 multi 4.25 4.25
1318 A263 $6 multi 4.25 4.25
1319 A263 $6 multi 4.25 4.25
1320 A263 $6 multi 4.25 4.25

Mushrooms Type

1991, June 1 Litho. *Perf. 14*
1321 A265 5c Pyrrhoglossum pyrrhum .20 .20
1322 A265 45c Agaricus purpurellus .30 .30
1323 A265 50c Amanita craseoderma .35 .35
1324 A265 90c Hygrocybe acutoconica .65 .65
1325 A265 $1 Limacella guttata .70 .70
1326 A265 $2 Lactarius hygrophoroides 1.40 1.40
1327 A265 $4 Boletellus cubensis 2.90 2.90
1328 A265 $5 Psilocybe caerulescens 3.50 3.50
Nos. 1321-1328 (8) 10.00 10.00

Souvenir Sheets
1329 A265 $6 Marasmius haematocephalus 4.25 4.25
1330 A265 $6 Lepiota spiculata 4.25 4.25

Royal Family Birthday, Anniversary
Common Design Type

1991, July 5 Litho. *Perf. 14*
1331 CD347 5c multi .20 .20
1332 CD347 20c multi .20 .20
1333 CD347 25c multi .20 .20
1334 CD347 60c multi .45 .45
1335 CD347 $1 multi .70 .70
1336 CD347 $2 multi 1.40 1.40
1337 CD347 $4 multi 2.90 2.90
1338 CD347 $5 multi 3.50 3.50
Nos. 1331-1338 (8) 9.55 9.55

Souvenir Sheet
1339 CD347 $5 Elizabeth, Philip 3.50 3.50
1340 CD347 $5 Diana, Charles, with sons 3.50 3.50

5c, 60c, $1, Nos. 1338, 1340, Charles and Diana, 10th wedding anniversary. Others, Queen Elizabeth II, 65th birthday.

Van Gogh Painting Type

Designs: 5c, Two Thistles, vert. 10c, The Baby Marcelle Roulin, vert. 15c, Still Life: Basket with Six Oranges. 25c, Orchard in Blossom, vert. 45c, Portrait of Armand Roulin, vert. 50c, Wood Gatherers in the Snow (detail). 60c, Almond Tree in Blossom, vert. $1, Portrait of an Old Man, vert. $2, The Seine Bridge at Asnieres. $3, Vase with Lilacs, Daisies & Anemones, vert. $4, Self-portrait, vert. $5, Portrait of Patience Escalier, vert. No. 1353, Les Alyscamps, vert. No. 1354, Quay with Men Unloading Sand Barges. No. 1355, Sunset: Wheat Fields Near Arles.

Perf. 13½x14, 14x13½
1991, Nov. 18 Litho.
1341 A264 5c multicolored .20 .20
1342 A264 10c multicolored .20 .20
1343 A264 15c multicolored .20 .20
1344 A264 25c multicolored .20 .20
1345 A264 45c multicolored .30 .30
1346 A264 50c multicolored .40 .40
1347 A264 60c multicolored .45 .45
1348 A264 $1 multicolored .75 .75
1349 A264 $2 multicolored 1.40 1.40
1350 A264 $3 multicolored 2.10 2.10
1351 A264 $4 multicolored 2.90 2.90
1352 A264 $5 multicolored 3.50 3.50
Nos. 1341-1352 (12) 12.60 12.60

Size: 102x127mm, 127x102mm
Imperf
1353 A264 $6 multicolored 4.25 4.25
1354 A264 $6 multicolored 4.25 4.25
1355 A264 $6 multicolored 4.25 4.25

Marine Life Type
Miniature Sheet

Marine life of the deeper reef: No. 1356a, Sargassum triggerfish. b, Tobaccofish. c, Longsnout butterflyfish. d, Cherubfish. e, Black jack head. f, Black jack tail, masked goby. g, Spotfin hogfish. h, Fairy basslet. i, Orangeback bass. j, Candy basslet. k, Blackcap basslet. l, Longspine squirrelfish. m, Jackknife fish. n, Bigeye. o, Short Bigeye. $6, Caribbean flashlight fish.

1991, Dec. 5 Litho. *Perf. 14*
1356 A270 50c Sheet of 15, #a.-o. 5.50 5.50

Souvenir Sheet
1357 A270 $6 multicolored 4.25 4.25

Christmas Art Type

Details, entire paintings or engravings by Martin Schongauer: 10c, Angel of the Annunciation. 35c, Madonna of the Rose Hedge. 50c, Madonna of the Rose Hedge, diff. 75c, Nativity. $1, Adoration of the Shepherds. $2, Nativity, diff. $4, Nativity, diff. $5, Symbol of St. Matthew. No. 1366, Nativity, diff. No. 1367, Adoration of the Shepherds.

1991, Dec. 9 *Perf. 12*
1358 A271 10c multicolored .20 .20
1359 A271 35c multicolored .25 .25
1360 A271 50c multicolored .35 .35
1361 A271 75c multicolored .55 .55
1362 A271 $1 multicolored .70 .70
1363 A271 $2 multicolored 1.40 1.40
1364 A271 $4 multicolored 2.90 2.90
1365 A271 $5 multicolored 3.50 3.50
Nos. 1358-1365 (8) 9.85 9.85

Souvenir Sheets
Perf. 14½
1366 A271 $6 multicolored 4.25 4.25
1367 A271 $6 multicolored 4.25 4.25

Queen Elizabeth II's Accession to the Throne, 40th Anniv.
Common Design Type

1992, Feb. 6 Litho. *Perf. 14*
1368 CD348 60c multicolored .45 .45
1369 CD348 75c multicolored .55 .55
1370 CD348 $2 multicolored 1.40 1.40
1371 CD348 $4 multicolored 2.90 2.90
Nos. 1368-1371 (4) 5.30 5.30

Souvenir Sheets
1372 CD348 $6 Queen, rural scene 4.25 4.25
1373 CD348 $6 Queen, harbor 4.25 4.25

Railways of the World Type

Steam locomotives: No. 1379a, Medoc Class, Switzerland, 1857. b, Sterling, Great

Britain, 1870. c, No. 90, France, 1877. d, Standard, US, 1880. e, Vittorio Emanuel II, Italy, 1884. f, Johnson Single, Great Britain, 1887. g, No. 999, US, 1893. h, Q1 Class, Great Britain, 1896. i, Claud Hamilton, Great Britain, 1900.

No. 1380a, Class P8, Germany, 1906. b, Class P, Denmark, 1935. c, Class Ps, US, 1926. d, Class 4-4-0, Ireland, 1932. e, Class GS, US, 1937. f, Class 12, Belgium, 1938. g, Class J, US, 1941. h, PA series, US, 1946. i, Class 4E1, South Africa, 1954.

No. 1381a, Tee 4-car train, Europe, 1957. b, FL9B, US, 1960. c, Shin-Kansen 16-car train, Japan, 1964. d, Class 103.1, Germany 1970. e, RTG 4-car train set, France, 1972. f, ETR 401 Pendolino 4-car train, Italy, 1976. g, Class 370, Great Britain, 1981. h, LRC, Canada, 1982. i, Mav BZMOT 601 1B1, Hungary, 1983.

No. 1382, ETR 401 four-car train, Italy, 1976. No. 1382A, Werner von Siemens' first electric locomotive, Germany, 1879.

1992, Feb. 13 Litho. *Perf. 14*

Sheets of 9

1379	A269	75c #a.-i.	5.00	5.00
1380	A269	$1 #a.-i.	6.75	6.75
1381	A269	$2 #a.-i.	13.50	13.50
		Nos. 1379-1381 (3)	25.25	25.25

Souvenir Sheets

1382	A269	$6 multicolored	4.50	4.50
1382A	A269	$6 multicolored	4.50	4.50

1992 Summer Olympics, Barcelona — G101

Designs: 10c, Women's 100-meter backstroke. 15c, Women's handball. 25c, 4x100-meter relay. 35c, Hammer throw. 50c, 110-meter hurdles. 75c, Pole vault. $1, Volleyball. $2, Weight lifting. $5, Stationary rings. $6, Soccer. No. 1393, Baseball. No. 1394, Finn class single-handed dinghy.

1992, Mar. 23 Litho. *Perf. 14*

1383	G101	10c multicolored	.20	.20
1384	G101	15c multicolored	.20	.20
1385	G101	25c multicolored	.20	.20
1386	G101	35c multicolored	.25	.25
1387	G101	50c multicolored	.40	.40
1388	G101	75c multicolored	.55	.55
1389	G101	$1 multicolored	.75	.75
1390	G101	$2 multicolored	1.40	1.40
1391	G101	$5 multicolored	3.50	3.50
1392	G101	$6 multicolored	4.25	4.25
		Nos. 1383-1392 (10)	11.70	11.70

Souvenir Sheets

1393	G101	$15 multicolored	11.50	11.50
1394	G101	$15 multicolored	11.50	11.50

Spanish Art Type

Paintings: 10c, The Surrender of Seville, by Francisco de Zurbaran. 35c, The Liberation of Saint Peter by an Angel, by Antonio de Pereda. 50c, Joseph Explains the Dreams of the Pharaoh, by Antonio del Castillo Saavedra, horiz. 75c, The Flower Vase, by Juan de Arellano. $1, The Duke of Pastrana, by Juan Carreno de Miranda. $2, $4, The Annunciation (diff. details), by Francisco Rizi. $5, Old Woman Seated, attributed to Antonio Puga. No. 1403, The Triumph of Saint Hermenegildo, by Francisco de Herrera, the Younger, vert. No. 1404, Relief of Genoa by the Second Marquis of Santa Cruz, by de Pereda, horiz.

1992, Apr. 30 *Perf. 13*

1395	A273	10c multicolored	.20	.20
1396	A273	35c multicolored	.25	.25
1397	A273	50c multicolored	.40	.40
1398	A273	75c multicolored	.55	.55
1399	A273	$1 multicolored	.75	.75
1400	A273	$2 multicolored	1.50	1.50
1401	A273	$4 multicolored	3.00	3.00
1402	A273	$5 multicolored	3.50	3.50

Size: 95x110mm

Imperf

1403	A273	$6 multicolored	4.25	4.25
1404	A273	$6 multicolored	4.50	4.50
		Nos. 1395-1404 (10)	18.90	18.90

Granada '92.

Discovery of America, 500th Anniv. G102

Designs: 10c, Don Isaac Abarbanel (1437-1508), Spanish Minister of Finance. 25c, Columbus. 35c, Crewman sighting land. 50c, King Ferdinand and Queen Isabella. 60c, Columbus and Queen Isabella. $5, Santa Maria and map. No. 1411, Portrait of Columbus. No. 1412, Columbus at first landfall.

1992, May 7 Litho. *Perf. 14*

1405	G102	10c multicolored	.20	.20
1406	G102	25c multicolored	.20	.20
1407	G102	35c multicolored	.25	.25
1408	G102	50c multicolored	.35	.35
1409	G102	60c multicolored	.50	.50
1410	G102	$5 multicolored	3.50	3.50
		Nos. 1405-1410 (6)	5.00	5.00

Souvenir Sheets

1411	G102	$6 multicolored	4.50	4.50
1412	G102	$6 multicolored	4.50	4.50

World Columbian Expo '92, Chicago.

USO Anniv. Type of 1992

1992, May 7

1413	A277	10c James Cagney	.20	.20
1414	A277	15c Ann Sheridan	.20	.20
1415	A277	35c Jerry Colonna	.30	.30
1416	A277	50c Spike Jones	.40	.40
1417	A277	75c Edgar Bergen, Charlie McCarthy	.55	.55
1418	A277	$1 Andrews Sisters	.75	.75
1419	A277	$2 Dinah Shore	1.50	1.50
1420	A277	$5 Bing Crosby	3.75	3.75
		Nos. 1413-1420 (8)	7.65	7.65

Souvenir Sheets

1421	A277	$6 Marlene Dietrich	4.50	4.50
1422	A277	$6 Fred Astaire	4.50	4.50

Hummingbird Type of 1992

Designs: 5c, Blue-headed male. 10c, Rufous-breasted hermit female. 20c, Blue-headed female. 45c, Green-throated carib male. 90c, Antillean crested male. $2, Purple-throated carib male. $4, Purple-throated carib female. $5, Antillean crested female. No. 1431, Rufous-breated hermit female. No. 1432, Green-throated carib female.

1992, May 7

1423	A276	5c multicolored	.20	.20
1424	A276	10c multicolored	.20	.20
1425	A276	20c multicolored	.20	.20
1426	A276	45c multicolored	.30	.30
1427	A276	90c multicolored	.65	.65
1428	A276	$2 multicolored	1.50	1.50
1429	A276	$4 multicolored	3.00	3.00
1430	A276	$5 multicolored	3.75	3.75
		Nos. 1423-1430 (8)	9.80	9.80

Souvenir Sheets

1431	A276	$6 multicolored	4.50	4.50
1432	A276	$6 multicolored	4.50	4.50

Genoa '92.

Discovery of America Type

1992 *Perf. 14½*

1433	A275	$1 Coming ashore	.75	.75
1434	A275	$2 Natives, ships	1.50	1.50

Walt Disney's Goofy, 60th Anniv. — G103

Scenes from Disney cartoon films: 5c, Father's Day Off, 1953. 10c, Cold War, 1951. 15c, Home Made Home, 1951. 25c, Get Rich Quick, 1951. 50c, Man's Best Friend, 1952. 75c, Aquamania, 1961. 90c, Tomorrow We Diet, 1951. $1, Teachers Are People, 1952. $2, The Goofy Success Story, 1955. $3, Double Dribble, 1946. $4, Hello Aloha, 1952. $5, Father's Lion, 1952. No. 1447, Father's Weekend, 1953, vert. No. 1448, Motor Mania, 1950. No. 1449, Hold That Pose, 1950, vert.

1992, Nov. 24 Litho. *Perf. 14x13½*

1435	G103	5c multicolored	.20	.20
1436	G103	10c multicolored	.20	.20
1437	G103	15c multicolored	.20	.20
1438	G103	25c multicolored	.20	.20
1439	G103	50c multicolored	.40	.40
1440	G103	75c multicolored	.60	.60
1441	G103	90c multicolored	.70	.70
1442	G103	$1 multicolored	.75	.75
1443	G103	$2 multicolored	1.50	1.50
1444	G103	$3 multicolored	2.25	2.25
1445	G103	$4 multicolored	3.00	3.00
1446	G103	$5 multicolored	3.75	3.75
		Nos. 1435-1446 (12)	13.75	13.75

Souvenir Sheets

Perf. 13½x14

1447	G103	$6 multicolored	4.50	4.50
1448	G103	$6 multicolored	4.50	4.50
1449	G103	$6 multicolored	4.50	4.50

Model Trains Type of 1992

Designs: 15c, #2220 Switcher locomotive, 2-inch gauge, US, 1910. 25c, 0-4-0 Engine, Bridge Port Line, O gauge, US, 1907. 50c, First Ives Co. electric toy locomotive, O gauge, US, 1910. 75c, J. C. Penney Special, standard gauge, US, 1920. $1, Cast metal locomotive, O gauge, US, 1916. $2, Copper-plated cast iron locomotive & tender pull toy, US, 1900. $4, Chromium plated locomotive #4689, standard gauge, US, 1928. $5, Ives long cab locomotive of the Olympian set, standard gauge, US, 1929.

No. 1458, Clockwork model, O gauge, US, 1910. No. 1459, American Flyer Statesman passenger train.

1992, Oct. 22 Litho. *Perf. 14*

1450	A279	15c multicolored	.20	.20
1451	A279	25c multicolored	.20	.20
1452	A279	50c multicolored	.40	.40
1453	A279	75c multicolored	.60	.60
1454	A279	$1 multicolored	.75	.75
1455	A279	$2 multicolored	1.50	1.50
1456	A279	$4 multicolored	3.00	3.00
1457	A279	$5 multicolored	3.75	3.75
		Nos. 1450-1457 (8)	10.40	10.40

Souvenir Sheet

Perf. 13

1458	A279	$6 multicolored	4.50	4.50
1459	A279	$6 multicolored	4.50	4.50

Nos. 1458-1459 contain one 51x40mm stamp.

New York City Type
Souvenir Sheet

1992, Oct. 28 *Perf. 14*

1460	A280	$6 Brooklyn Bridge	4.50	4.50

Postage Stamp Mega Event '92, New York City.

Christmas Type of 1992

Details or entire paintings of The Annunciation by: 5c, Robert Campin. 15c, Melchior Broederlam. 25c, The Annunciation (2 panels), by Fra Filippo Lippi. 35c, Simone Martini. 50c, Fra Filippo Lippi, detail of angel. 75c, The Annunciation (Mary), by Fra Filippo Lippi. 90c, Albert Bouts. $1, D. Di Michelino. $2, Van der Weyden. $3, Sandro Botticelli, detail of angel. $4, Botticelli, detail of Mary. $5, Bernardo Daddi, horiz. No. 1472, Rogier Van der Weyden, vert. No. 1473, Hubert Van Eyck. No. 1474, Botticelli.

Perf. 13½x14, 14x13½

1992, Nov. 16

1461	A281	5c multicolored	.20	.20
1462	A281	15c multicolored	.20	.20
1463	A281	25c multicolored	.20	.20
1464	A281	35c multicolored	.30	.30
1464A	A281	50c multicolored	.40	.40
1465	A281	75c multicolored	.60	.60
1466	A281	90c multicolored	.70	.70
1467	A281	$1 multicolored	.75	.75
1468	A281	$2 multicolored	1.50	1.50
1469	A281	$3 multicolored	2.25	2.25
1470	A281	$4 multicolored	3.00	3.00
1471	A281	$5 multicolored	3.75	3.75
		Nos. 1461-1471 (12)	13.85	13.85

Souvenir Sheets

1472	A281	$6 multicolored	4.50	4.50
1473	A281	$6 multicolored	4.50	4.50
1474	A281	$6 multicolored	4.50	4.50

America's Cup Yacht Race — G104

Designs: 15c, Atalanta, Mischief, 1881. 25c, Valkyrie III, Defender. 35c, Shamrock IV, Resolute. 75c, Endeavour II, Ranger, 1937. $1, Sceptre, Columbia, 1958. $2, Australia II, Liberty. $4, Stars and Stripes, Kookaburra III. $5, New Zealand, Stars and Stripes, 1988. No. 1483, America, Aurora, 1851. No. 1484, Emblems of 1992 participants.

1992, Oct. *Perf. 14*

1475	G104	15c multicolored	.20	.20
1476	G104	25c multicolored	.20	.20
1477	G104	35c multicolored	.30	.30
1478	G104	75c multicolored	.60	.60
1479	G104	$1 multicolored	.75	.75
1480	G104	$2 multicolored	1.50	1.50
1481	G104	$4 multicolored	3.00	3.00
1482	G104	$5 multicolored	3.75	3.75
		Nos. 1475-1482 (8)	10.30	10.30

Souvenir Sheets

1483	G104	$6 multicolored	4.50	4.50
1484	G104	$6 multicolored	4.50	4.50

Nos. 1483-1484 contains one 58x43mm stamp.

G105

Anniversaries and Events — G106

Designs: 25c, Zeppelin Viktoria Luise over Kiel Harbor. 50c, Space Shuttle Columbia. 75c, Flag, arms of Germany, Konrad Adenauer. $1.50, Giant anteater. No. 1489, Scarlet macaw, vert. No. 1490, Emblem of Intl. Conf. on Nutrition. $3, Wolfgang Amadeus Mozart. No. 1492, Berlin airlift. No. 1493, Space Shuttle Endeavour crew repairing Intelsat VI. $5, Hindenburg disaster. No. 1495, Adm. Richard E. Byrd's Ford Trimotor flying over North Pole, 1926. No. 1496, Map of Federal Republic of Germany, vert. No. 1497, Zeppelin Z.4 above clouds. No. 1498, First flight of space shuttle Endeavour. No. 1499, Scene from "The Marriage of Figaro." No. 1500, Jaguar.

1992 Litho. *Perf. 14*

1485	G105	25c multicolored	.20	.20
1486	G105	50c multicolored	.35	.35
1487	G105	75c multicolored	.60	.60
1488	G105	$1.50 multicolored	1.10	1.10
1489	G105	$2 multicolored	1.50	1.50
1490	G105	$2 multicolored	1.50	1.50
1491	G106	$3 multicolored	2.25	2.25
1492	G105	$4 multicolored	3.00	3.00
1493	G105	$4 multicolored	3.00	3.00
1494	G105	$5 multicolored	3.75	3.75
1495	G105	$5 multicolored	3.75	3.75
		Nos. 1485-1495 (11)	21.00	21.00

Souvenir Sheets

Perf. 13½

1496	G105	$6 multicolored	4.50	4.50
1497	G105	$6 multicolored	4.50	4.50
1498	G105	$6 multicolored	4.50	4.50

Perf. 14

1499	G106	$6 multicolored	4.50	4.50
1500	G105	$6 multicolored	4.50	4.50

Count Zeppelin, 75th anniv. of death (#1485, 1494, 1497). Intl. Space Year (#1486, 1493). Konrad Adenauer, 25th anniv. of death (#1487, 1492, 1496).Earth Summit, Rio de Janeiro (#1488-1489, 1500). Intl. Conf. on Nutrition, Rome (#1490). Wolfgang Amadeus Mozart, bicent. of death (in 1991) (#1491,

1499). Intl. Lions Intl., 75th anniv. (#1495). Space Year (#1498).
Issue dates: Nos. 1491, 1499, Oct. Nos. 1485-1486, 1490, 1493-1495, 1497, Nov. Nos. 1487-1489, 1492, 1496, 1500, Dec.
No. 1496 contains one 39x50mm stamp, Nos. 1497-1498 one 50x39mm stamp, No. 1500 one 52x40mm stamp.

Miniature Sheet
Entertainers Type of 1992

Grammy award winners: No. 1501a, Leonard Bernstein. b, Ray Charles. c, Bob Dylan. d, Barbra Streisand. e, Frank Sinatra. f, Harry Belafonte. g, Aretha Franklin. h, Garth Brooks.
No. 1502a, Johnny Cash. b, Willie Nelson.
No. 1503a, Charlie Parker. b, Miles Davis.

1992, Nov. 19 *Perf. 14*
1501 A286 90c Sheet of 8, #a.-h. 5.50 5.50

Souvenir Sheets
1502 A286 $3 Sheet of 2, #a.-b. 4.50 4.50
1503 A286 $3 Sheet of 2, #a.-b. 4.50 4.50

Dogs — G107

Butterflies — G108

Designs: 35c, Irish Setter, Glendalough, Ireland. 50c, Boston terrier, State House, Boston, US. 75c, Beagle, Temple to Athena, Greece. $1, Weimaraner, Nesselwang, Germany. $3, Norwegian elkhound, Urnes Stave Church, Norway. $4, Mastiff, Great Sphinx, Egypt. No. 1510, Akita, Kyoto torii, Japan. No. 1511, Saluki, Rub'al Khali, Saudi Arabia. No. 1512, Shar pei, China. No. 1513, Bulldog, United Kingdom.

1993, Jan. 20 Litho. *Perf. 14*
1504 G107 35c multicolored .30 .30
1505 G107 50c multicolored .40 .40
1506 G107 75c multicolored .60 .60
1507 G107 $1 multicolored .75 .75
1508 G107 $3 multicolored 2.25 2.25
1509 G107 $4 multicolored 3.00 3.00
1510 G107 $5 multicolored 3.75 3.75
1511 G107 $5 multicolored 3.75 3.75
Nos. 1504-1511 (8) 14.80 14.80

Souvenir Sheets
1512 G107 $6 multicolored 4.50 4.50
1513 G107 $6 multicolored 4.50 4.50

Louvre Painting Type
Miniature Sheet

Details or entire paintings: No. 1514a, The Virgin and Child with Young St. John the Baptist, by Botticelli. b, The Buffet, by Chardin. c, The Provider, by Chardin. d, Erasmus, by Durer. e, Self-Portrait, by Durer. f, Jeanne of Aragon, by Raphael. g-h, La Belle Jardiniere (diff. details), by Raphael.
$6, Charles I, King of England, Hunting, by Van Dyck.

1993, Mar. 8 Litho. *Perf. 12*
1514 A289 $1 Sheet of 8, #a.-h. + label 6.00 6.00

Souvenir Sheet
Perf. 14½
1515 A289 $6 multicolored 4.50 4.50

No. 1515 contains one 55x88mm stamp.

1993, Apr. 13 Litho. *Perf. 14*
1516 G108 15c Polydamas swallowtail .20 .20
1517 G108 35c Guaraguao skipper .30 .30
1518 G108 45c Giant hair-streak .35 .35
1519 G108 75c Malachite .60 .60
1520 G108 $1 Cloudless sulphur .75 .75
1521 G108 $2 Silver spot 1.50 1.50
1522 G108 $4 St. Christopher's hair-streak 3.00 3.00
1523 G108 $5 Common long-tail skipper 3.75 3.75
Nos. 1516-1523 (8) 10.45 10.45

Souvenir Sheets
1524 G108 $6 Orion 4.50 4.50
1525 G108 $6 Zebra 4.50 4.50

Flowers Type of 1993

1993, May
1526 A291 35c Hibiscus .30 .30
1527 A291 35c Columbine .30 .30
1528 A291 45c Red ginger .35 .35
1529 A291 75c Bougainvillea .60 .60
1530 A291 $1 Crown imperial .75 .75
1531 A291 $2 Fairy orchid 1.50 1.50
1532 A291 $4 Heliconia 3.00 3.00
1533 A291 $5 Tulip 3.75 3.75
Nos. 1526-1533 (8) 10.55 10.55

Souvenir Sheets
1534 A291 $6 Balloonflower, horiz. 5.50 5.50
1535 A291 $6 Blackberry lily, horiz. 4.50 4.50

No. 1536 will not be assigned.

Coronation of Queen Elizabeth II Type of 1993
Miniature Sheet

Designs: a, 35c, Official coronation photograph. b, 50c, Ampulla, spoon. c, $2, Queen, following coronation. d, $4, Queen, Prince Charles and his family, c. 1984.
$6, Portrait, by Pietro Annigoni, 1954.

1993, June 2 Litho. *Perf. 13½x14*
1537 A293 Sheet, 2 each #a.-d. 10.50 10.50

Souvenir Sheet
Perf. 14
1538 A293 $6 multicolored 4.50 4.50

No. 1538 contains one 28x42mm stamp.

Anniversaries and Events Types of 1993

Designs: 50c, Telescope. 75c, Willy Brandt, Lyndon Johnson, 1961. $4, Radio telescope. $5, Willy Brandt, Eleanor Hulles, 1957. No. 1543, Copernicus. No. 1544, Willy, Rut Brandt.

1993, July 1 Litho. *Perf. 14*
1539 A294 50c multicolored .40 .40
1540 A295 75c multicolored .60 .60
1541 A294 $4 multicolored 3.00 3.00
1542 A295 $5 multicolored 3.75 3.75
Nos. 1539-1542 (4) 7.75 7.75

Souvenir Sheets
1543 A294 $6 multicolored 4.50 4.50
1544 A295 $6 multicolored 4.50 4.50

Copernicus, 450th death anniv. (#1539, 1541, 1543). Willy Brandt, 1st death anniv. (#1540, 1542, 1544).

Songbird Type of 1993
Miniature Sheet

Designs: No. 1545a, 15c, Painted bunting. b, 15c, White-throated sparrow. c, 25c, Common grackle. d, 25c, Royal flycatcher. e, 35c, Swallow tanager. f, 35c, Vermilion flycatcher. g, 45c, Black headed bunting. h, 50c, Rosebreasted grosbeak. i, 75c, Corn bunting. j, 75c, Rosebreasted thrush tanager. k, $1, Buff-throated saltator. l, $4, Plush-capped finch.
No. 1546, Bohemian waxwing. No. 1547, Pine grosbeak.

1993, July 13
1545 A297 Sheet of 12, #a.-l. 6.75 6.75

Souvenir Sheets
1546 A297 $6 multicolored 4.50 4.50
1547 A297 $6 multicolored 4.50 4.50

Seashell Type of 1993
Miniature Sheet

Designs: No. 1548a, 15c, Hawk wing conch. b, 15c, Music volute. c, 25c, Globe vase, deltoid rock shell. d, 35c, Spiny vase. e, 35c, Common sundial, common purple snail. f, 45c, Caribbean donax, gaudy asaphis. g, 45c, Mouse cone. h, 50c, Gold-mouthed triton. i, 75c, Tulip mussel, trigonal tivela. j, 75c, Common dove shell, chestnut latirus. k, $1, Widemouthed purpura. l, $4, Atlantic thorny oyster, Atlantic wing oyster.
No. 1549, Turkey wing. No. 1550, Zebra periwinkle.

1993, July 19 Litho. *Perf. 14*
1548 A298 Sheet of 12, #a.-l. 7.00 7.00

Souvenir Sheet
1549 A298 $6 multicolored 4.50 4.50
1550 A298 $6 multicolored 4.50 4.50

Picasso Type of 1993

Paintings: 15c, Painter and Model, 1928. $1, The Artist and His Model, 1963. $4, The Drawing Lession, 1925. $6, Picasso seated in front of canvas, 1956.

1993, July 1 Litho. *Perf. 14*
1551 A299 15c multi, horiz. .20 .20
1552 A299 $1 multi, horiz. .80 .80
1553 A299 $4 multi, horiz. 3.00 3.00
Nos. 1551-1553 (3) 4.00 4.00

Souvenir Sheet
1554 A299 $6 multi, horiz. 4.50 4.50

Olympics Type of 1993

Design: $6, Emil Zogragski, ski jump.

1993, July 1
1555 A300 $6 multicolored 4.50 4.50

Polska '93 Type of 1993

Paintings: 75c, Gra w Gudziki, by Ludomir Slerdinski, 1928. $2, Pocalunek Mongoskiego Ksiecia, by S.I. Witkiewicz, 1915. $6, Allegory, by Jan Wydra, 1929.

1993, July 1
1556 A301 75c multi, horiz. .55 .55
1557 A301 $2 multi, horiz. 1.50 1.50

Souvenir Sheet
1558 A301 $6 multicolored 4.50 4.50

Taipei '93 Type

Designs: 35c, Macao Palace, Hong Kong. 45c, Stone pixie, Ming Tomb, Nanjing. $1, Stone camels, Ming Tomb, Nanjing. $5, Stone lion and elephant, Ming Tomb, Nanjing.
Sculpture: No. 1563a, Nesting quail incense burner. b, Standing quail incense burner. c, Seated qilin incense burner. d, Pottery horse, Han Dynasty. e, Seated caparisoned elephant. f, Cow (imitation delft).
No. 1564, Sumatran tiger.

1993 Litho. *Perf. 14x13½*
1559 A302 35c multi, horiz. .25 .25
1560 A302 45c multi, horiz. .35 .35
1561 A302 $1 multi, horiz. .75 .75
1562 A302 $5 multi, horiz. 3.75 3.75
Nos. 1559-1562 (4) 5.10 5.10

Miniature Sheet
1563 A302 $1.50 Sheet of 6, #a.-f. 6.75 6.75

Souvenir Sheet
Perf. 13½x14
1564 A302 $6 multicolored 4.50 4.50

Nos. 1563a-1563f are horiz.

With Bangkok '93 Emblem

Designs: 35c, Naga snakes, Chiang Mai's Temple, Thailand. 45c, Sri Mariamman Temple, Singapore. $1, Topiary, Hua Hin Resort, Thailand. $5, Pak Tai Temple, Cheung Chau Island.
Thai paintings: No. 1569a, Buddha's victory over Mara. b, Mythological elephant. c, Battle with Mara. d, Untitled work, by Panya Wijinthanasarn, 1984. e, Temple mural. f, Elephants in Pahcekha Buddha's Heaven.
No. 1570, Monkey.

1993 *Perf. 14x13½*
1565 A302 35c multi, horiz. .25 .25
1566 A302 45c multi, horiz. .35 .35
1567 A302 $1 multi, horiz. .75 .75
1568 A302 $5 multi, horiz. 3.75 3.75
Nos. 1565-1568 (4) 5.10 5.10

Miniature Sheet
1569 A302 $1.50 Sheet of 6, #a.-f. 6.75 6.75

Souvenir Sheet
Perf. 13½x14
1570 A302 $6 multicolored 4.50 4.50

Nos. 1569a-1569f are horiz.

Indopex '93 Type

Designs: 35c, Natl. Museum, Central Jakarta, Indonesia. 45c, Sacred Wheel & Deer, Monastery. $1, Ramayana relief, Panataran Temple. $5, Candi Tikus, Trawulan, East Java.
Paintings: No. 1575a, Bullock Carts, bu Batara Lubis, 1951. b, Surat Irsa II, by A.D. Pirous, 1983. c, Self-portrait with Goat, by Kartika, 1987. d, The Cow-est Cow, by Ivan Sagito, 1987. e, Rain Storm, by Sudjana Kerton, 1984. f, Story of Pucuk Flower, by Effendi, 1972.
No. 1576, Banteng cattle.

1993, Aug. 13 Litho. *Perf. 14x13½*
1571 A302 35c multicolored .25 .25
1572 A302 45c multicolored .35 .35
1573 A302 $1 multicolored .75 .75
1574 A302 $5 multicolored 3.75 3.75
Nos. 1571-1574 (4) 5.10 5.10

Miniature Sheet
1575 A302 $1.50 Sheet of 6, #a.-f. 6.75 6.75

Souvenir Sheet
1576 A302 $6 multicolored 4.50 4.50

Nos. 1571-1576 are horiz.

1994 World Cup Soccer Championships, US — G109

Designs: 15c, Stuart McCall, Carlos Verri. 25c, Carlos Verri, Diego Maradona. 35c, S. Schillaci, J.P. Saldana. 45c, Ruud Gullit, Mark Wright. $1, Carlos Verri, Diego Maradona. $2, Zubizarreta, Fernandez, Albert. $4, Gheorghe Hagi, Paul McGrath. $5, Alberto Gorriz, Enzo Scifo. No. 1585, Schaefer Stadium, Foxboro, MA. No. 1586, Rudi Voeller, vert.

1993, Sept. 7 Litho. *Perf. 14*
1577 G109 15c multicolored .20 .20
1578 G109 25c multicolored .20 .20
1579 G109 35c multicolored .20 .20
1580 G109 45c multicolored .40 .40
1581 G109 $1 multicolored .75 .75
1582 G109 $2 multicolored 1.50 1.50
1583 G109 $4 multicolored 3.00 3.00
1584 G109 $5 multicolored 3.75 3.75
Nos. 1577-1584 (8) 10.00 10.00

Souvenir Sheets
1585 G109 $6 multicolored 4.50 4.50
1586 G109 $6 multicolored 4.50 4.50

Mickey Mouse, 65th Anniv. Type

Movie clips: 15c, The Worm Turns, 1937. 35c, Mickey's Rival, 1936. 50c, The Pointer, 1939. 75c, Society Dog Show, 1939. $1, A Gentleman's Gentleman, 1941. $2, The Little Whirlwind, 1941. $4, Mickey Down Under, 1948. $5, R'coon Dawg, 1951.
No. 1595, Mickey's Garden, 1935, vert. No. 1596, Lonesome Ghosts, 1937.

Perf. 13½x14, 14x13½
1993, Nov. 11 Litho.
1587 A305 15c multicolored .20 .20
1588 A305 35c multicolored .30 .30
1589 A305 50c multicolored .40 .40
1590 A305 75c multicolored .55 .55
1591 A305 $1 multicolored .75 .75
1592 A305 $2 multicolored 1.50 1.50
1593 A305 $4 multicolored 3.00 3.00
1594 A305 $5 multicolored 3.75 3.75
Nos. 1587-1594 (8) 10.45 10.45

Souvenir Sheets
1595 A305 $6 multicolored 4.50 4.50
1596 A305 $6 multicolored 4.50 4.50

Christmas Type of 1993

Various details from Adoration of the Shepherds by Durer: 10c, 75c, $1, $4. No. 1605, horiz.
Various details from Oddi Altarpiece by Raphael: 25c, 35c, 50c, $5, No. 1606.

Perf. 13½x14, 14x13½ (#1605)
1993, Nov. 22 Litho.
1597-1602 A306 Set of 8 9.00 9.00

Souvenir Sheets
1603-1604 A306 $6 each 4.50 4.50

Eckener Type of 1993

Designs: 50c, Graf Zeppelin over Rio De Janeiro. 75c, Dr. Hugo Eckener. $5, Eckener commanding Graf Zeppelin. $6, Eckener, Pres. Herbert Hoover.

1993, Dec. 21 Litho. *Perf. 14*
1607-1609 A307 Set of 3 4.75 4.75

Souvenir Sheet
1610 A307 $6 multicolored 4.50 4.50

Royal Air Force Anniv. Type of 1993

Designs: 15c, Avro Lancaster. $5, Short Sunderland. $6, Supermarine Spitfire.

1993, Dec. 21
1611 A308 15c multicolored .20 .20
1612 A308 $5 multicolored 3.75 3.75

Souvenir Sheet
1613 A308 $6 multicolored 4.50 4.50

Automobile Anniv. Type

Designs: 25c, 1955 Mercedes Benz 300SLR. 45c, 1957 Ford Thunderbird. $4,

1929 Ford 150A Station Wagon. $5, Mercedes Benz 540K.
No. 1618, 1929 Mercedes Benz SSK. No. 1619, 1924 Ford Model T.

1993, Dec. 21 Litho. *Perf. 14*
1614-1617 A309 Set of 4 7.25 7.25

Souvenir Sheets

1618-1619 A309 $6 each 4.50 4.50

1st Benz 4-wheel car, 1st Ford engine, cent.

First Gas Balloon Flight in America Type

Designs: 35c, Blanchard's balloon crossing Delaware River. $3, Blanchard delivering Washington's passport of introduction. $6, Balloon in flight, vert.

1993, Dec. 21 Litho. *Perf. 14*
1620-1621 A310 Set of 2 2.50 2.50

Souvenir Sheet

1622 A310 $6 multicolored 4.50 4.50

Fine Art Type

Details or entire paintings by Rembrandt: 15c, Hendrickje Stoffels as Flora. 35c, Lady & Gentlemen in Black. 50c, Aristotle with Bust of Homer. $5, Christ & the Woman of Samaria.
Details or entire paintings by Matisse: 75c, Interior: Flowers and Parakeets. $1, Goldfish. $2, The Girl with Green Eyes. $3, Still Life with a Plaster Figure.
No. 1631, Anna Accused of Stealing the Kid, by Rembrandt. No. 1632, Tea in the Garden by Matisse, horiz.

Perf. 13½x14, 14x13½
1993, Dec. 31 Litho.
1623-1630 A311 Set of 8 10.00 10.00

Souvenir Sheets

1631-1632 A311 $6 each 4.50 4.50

Hong Kong '94 Type

Designs: No. 1633, Hong Kong #426, jet at Kai Tak Airport. No. 1634, Junk, Kwaloon Bay, #975.
Chinese jade: No. 1635a, White jade brush washer. b, Archaic jade brush washer. c, Dark green jade brush washer. d, Green jade alms bowl. e, Archaic jade dog. f, Yellow jade brush washer.

1994, Feb. 18 Litho. *Perf. 14*
1633 A313 40c multicolored .30 .30
1634 A313 40c multicolored .30 .30
a. Pair, #1633-1634 .60 .60

Miniature Sheet

1635 A314 45c Sheet of 6, #a.-f. 2.00 2.00

Nos. 1633-1634 issued in sheets of of 5 pairs. No. 1634a is a continuous design. Nos. 1635a-1635f are horiz.
New Year 1994 (Year of the Dog) (#1635e).

Dinosaurs G110

15c, Spinosaurus. 35c, Apatosaurus. 45c, Tyrannosaurus rex. 55c, Triceratops. $1, Pachycephalosaurus. $2, Pteranodon. $4, Parasaurolophus. $5, Brachiosaurus.
No. 1644, Brachiosaurus, vert. No. 1645, Tyrannosaurus, spinosaurus, vert.

1994 Litho. *Perf. 14*
1636-1643 G110 Set of 8 10.00 10.00

Souvenir Sheets

1644-1645 G110 $6 each 4.50 4.50

Mushrooms G111

Designs: 35c, Hygrocybe hypohaemacta. 45c, Cantherellus cinnabarinus. 50c, Marasmius haematocephalus. 75c, Mycena pura. $1, Gymnopilus russipes. $2, Galocybe cyanocephala. $4, Pleuteus chrysophlebius. $5, Chlorophyllum molybdites.

No. 1654, Collybia fibrosipes. No. 1655, Xeromphalina tenuipes.

1994
1646-1653 G111 Set of 8 10.50 10.50

Souvenir Sheets

1654-1655 G111 $6 each 4.50 4.50

D-Day Type of 1994

40c, Churchill bridgelayer in action. $2, Sherman "Firefly" attacks beach. $3, Churchill Crocodile flame thrower. $6, Sherman "Crab" flail tank.

1994, Aug. 4 Litho. *Perf. 14*
1656-1658 A318 Set of 3 4.00 4.00

Souvenir Sheet

1659 A318 $6 multicolored 4.50 4.50

First Manned Moon Landing, 25th Anniv. Type of 1994
Miniature Sheet of 6

Tribute to Challenger crew: No. 1660a, Slidewire escape training. b, Christa A. McAuliffe. c, Challenger 51-L on pad LC39B. d, Gregory B. Jarvis. e, Ellison S. Onizuka. f, Ronald E. McNair.
$6, Judith A. Resnick, vert.

1994, Aug. 4
1660 A319 $1.10 #a.-f. 5.00 5.00

Souvenir Sheet

1661 A319 $6 multicolored 4.50 4.50

PHILAKOREA '94 Type

Designs: 40c, Onung Tomb, Korea. $1, Stone pogoda, Mt. Nansan, Kyongju. $4, Pusan Port.
Paintings, by Sin Yunbok, late Choson Dynasty, 1758: No. 1665a-1665b, Admiring spring in the Country. c-d, Women on Dano Day. e-f, Enjoying Lotuses While Listening to Music. g-h, Women by a Crystal Stream.
$6, Blacksmith's Shop, by Kim Duksin (1754-1822).

1994, Aug. 4 *Perf. 14, 13½ (#1665)*
1662-1664 A320 Set of 3 4.00 4.00

Miniature Sheet of 8

1665 A321 $1 #a.-h. 6.00 6.00

Souvenir Sheet

1666 A320 $6 multicolored 4.50 4.50

Orchid Type of 1994

15c, Cattleya aurantiaca. 25c, Blettia patula. 45c, Sobralia macrantha. 75c, Encyclia belizensis. $1, Sophrolaeliocattleya. $2, Encyclia frangrans. $4, Schombocattleya. $5, Brassolaeliocattleya.
No. 1675, Brassavola nodosa. No. 1676, Ornithidium coccineum.

1994, Aug. 7 *Perf. 14*
1667-1674 A322 Set of 8 10.00 10.00

Souvenir Sheets

1675-1676 A322 $6 each 4.50 4.50

1994 World Cup Soccer Type
Miniature Sheet of 6

Designs: No. 1677a, Steve Mark, Grenada. b, Jurgen Kohler, Germany. c, Almir, Brazil. d, Michael Windiscmann, US. e, Guiseppe Giannini, Italy. f, Rashidi Yekini, Nigeria.
No. 1678, Kemari. No. 1679, The World Cup.

1994, Aug. 11 *Perf. 14*
1677 A323 75c #a.-f. 3.50 3.50

Souvenir Sheets

1678-1679 A323 $6 each 4.50 4.50

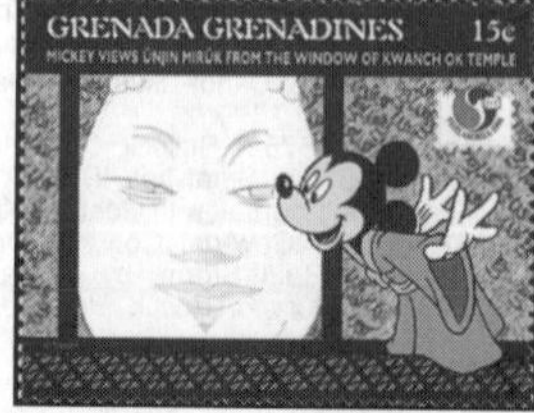

Disney's PHILAKOREA '94 — G112

15c, Mickey, Unjin Miruk, Kwanch Ok Temple. 35c, Goofy, statue of Admiral Yi, Chonju. 50c, Cousin Gus, Donald. 75c, Mickey playing flute. $1, Goofy, Tolharubang Grandfather statue. $2, Mickey, Minnie, Hyang-Wonjong. $4, Mickey, Unsan Pyolshin Festival. $5, Minnie, ceremonial fan.
No. 1688, Minnie, Buk drum, vert. No. 1689, Mickey, Pugok Hawaii, vert.

1994, Aug. 16 Litho. *Perf. 14x13½*
1680-1687 G112 Set of 8 10.50 10.50

Souvenir Sheets

Perf. 13½x14
1688-1689 G112 $6 each 4.50 4.50

This set exists with very low face values.

Fish Type of 1994
Miniature Sheets of 12

Designs: No. 1690a, Yellowtail snapper (b, e). b, Caribbean reef shark (a). c, Great barracuda. d, Redtail parrotfish. e, Blue tang. f, Queen angelfish. g, Red hind (h). h, Rock beauty. i, Queen parrotfish. j, Spanish hogfish. k, Spotted moray. l, Queen triggerfish (i).
No. 1691a, Pork fish (b). b, Blue chromis (a). c, Caribbean reef shark. d, Longspine squirrelfish. e, Foureye butterflyfish. f, Blue head. g, Royal gramma. h, Sharpnose puffer. i, Longsnout seahorse. j, Blackbar soldierfish (g, k). k, Redlip blenny. l, Rainbow wrasse.
No. 1692, Rainbow wrasse, diff. No. 1693, Queen angelfish, diff.

1994, Sept. 1 *Perf. 14*
1690-1691 A324 75c #a.-l, each 6.75 6.75

Souvenir Sheets

1692-1693 A324 $6 each 4.50 4.50

Intl. Olympic Committe Type of 1994

Designs: 50c, Silke Renk, Germany, javelin, 1992. $1.50, Mark Spitz, US, swimming, 1972.
$6, Team Japan, Nordic combined, 1994.

1994 *Perf. 14*
1694 A325 50c multi, horiz. .40 .40
1695 A325 $1.50 multi, horiz. 1.10 1.10

Souvenir Sheet

1696 A326 $6 multicolored 4.50 4.50

Intl. Year of the Family Type of 1994

1994
1697 A329 $1 Family of 5 .75 .75

Order of the Caribbean Community Type

Designs: 25c, Sir Shridath Ramphal, statesman, Guyana. 50c, William Demas, economist, Trinidad & Tobago. $2, Derek Walcott, writer, St. Lucia.

1994, Sept. 1
1698-1700 A330 Set of 3 2.00 2.00

Christmas Type of 1994

Paintings, by Bartolome Murillo: 15c, The Annunciation. 35c, The Adoration of the Shepherds. No. 1703, 50c, Flight into Egypt. No. 1704, 50c, Virgin and Child with St. Rose. 75c, Virgin and Child. $1, Virgin of the Rosary. $4, The Holy Family.
No. 1708, Adoration of the Shepherds. No. 1709, The Holy Family with a Little Bird.

1994, Dec. 5 Litho. *Perf. 13½x14*
1701-1707 A331 Set of 7 5.50 5.50

Souvenir Sheets

1708-1709 A331 $6 each 4.50 4.50

Bird Type of 1995

25c, Ground dove. 50c, White-winged dove, horiz. $2, Inca dove. $4, Mourning dove, horiz.

1995, Jan. 10 *Perf. 14*
1710-1713 A332 Set of 4 5.00 5.00

English Touring Cricket, Cent. Type

Designs: 50c, M.A. Atherton, England, horiz. 75c, C.E.L. Ambrose, Leeward Isl./W. Indies. $1, B.C. Lara, Trinidad/W. Indies. $3, West Indies Team, horiz.

1995, Jan. 12
1714-1717 A333 Set of 3 1.75 1.75

Souvenir Sheet

1718 A333 $3 multicolored 2.25 2.25

Miniature Sheet of 10

Capitals of the World — G113

Designs: a, London. b, Cairo. c, Vienna. d, Paris. e, Rome. f, Budapest. g, Moscow. h, Beijing. i, Tokyo. j, Wasington.

1995, Mar. 10 Litho. *Perf. 14*
1719 G113 $1 #a.-j. 7.75 7.75

New Year 1995 (Year of the Boar) — G114

Various stylized boars with different Chinese inscriptions: a, Smiling, purple legs. b, Smiling, red legs. c, Brown legs. d, Red legs.
$2, Two boars, horiz.

1995, Apr. 21 Litho. *Perf. 14½*
1720 G114 75c Block or horiz. strip of 4, #a.-d. 2.25 2.25
e. Souvenir sheet of 4, #1720a-1720d 2.25 2.25

Souvenir Sheet

1721 G114 $2 multicolored 1.50 1.50

No. 1720 was issued in miniature sheets of 16 stamps.

VE Day Type of 1995
Miniature Sheets of 6 and 8

#1721A: b, Mitsubishi G4M1 "Betty." c, Aircraft carrying submarine I-14. d, Mitsubishi G3M1. e, Destroyer Akizuki. f, Battleship Kirishima. g, Cruiser Asigari.
Bombers: #1722: a, Avro Lancaster, Tallboy bomb. b, Junkers JU-88. c, B-25 Mitchell. d, B-17 Flying Fortress. e, Petlyakov Pe-2. f, Martin B-26 Marauder. g, Henkel He-111. h, Consolidated B-24 Liberator.
#1723, Pres. Truman displaying newspaper headline. #1723A, Aichi D3A1 "Val" dive bomber.

1995, May 8 *Perf. 14*
1721A A336 $2 #b.-g. + label 9.25 9.25
1722 A336 $2 #a.-h. + label 12.00 12.00

Souvenir Sheets

1723 A336 $6 multicolored 4.50 4.50
1723A A336 $6 multicolored 4.50 4.50

Inscription in central label of No. 1721A misidentifies a Yokosuka MXY-7 Okha kamikaze plane.
No. 1723 contains one 57x42mm stamp.

Scout Jamboree Type of 1995

a, 75c, Beach scene, scout. b, $1, Mountains, sea, scout with pole. c, $2, Flag, scout salute.
$6, Snorkeling, fish.

1995, May 8
1724 A337 Strip of 3, #a.-c. 2.75 2.75

Souvenir Sheet

1725 A337 $6 multicolored 4.50 4.50

No. 1724 was issued in sheets of 9 stamps.

UN, 50th Anniv. Type of 1995

Designs: a, 75c, Building, UN flag. b, $1, Trygve Lie (1896-1968), Norway, 1st Secretary General. c, $2, Flag, member of UN peacekeeping force.
$6, Dove, emblem.

1995, May 8
1726 A338 Strip of 3, #a.-c. 2.75 2.75

Souvenir Sheet

1727 A338 $6 multicolored 4.50 4.50

No. 1726 is a continuous design and was issued in sheets of 9 stamps.

Miniature Sheets of 9

Marine Life of the Caribbean G115

No. 1728: a, Dolphins. b, Scorpion fish. c, Sea turtle, rock beauty. d, Butterflyfish, nurse shark. e, Angel fish. f, Grouper coney. g, Rainbow eel, moray eel. h, Sun flower-star, coral crab. i, Octopus.
No. 1729: a, Bull shark. b, Big white shark. c, Octopus. d, Barracuda (e). e, Moray eel (f,

h, i). f, Spotted eagle ray. g, Goldspotted snake. h, Stingray. i, Grouper.

$5, French angelfish. $6, Hammerhead shark.

1995, May 3 Litho. *Perf. 14*

1728-1729 G115 $1 #a.-i., each 6.75 6.75

Souvenir Sheets

1730 G115 $5 multicolored 3.75 3.75
1731 G115 $6 multicolored 4.50 4.50

Domesticated Animals — G116

Horses: 15c, Suffolk punch. 25c, Shetland pony. $1, Arab. $3, Shire horse.

Dogs: No. 1736a, Shetland sheepdog. b, Bull terrier. c, Afghan. d, Scottish terrier. e, Labrador retriever. f, English springer spaniel. g, Samoyed. h, Irish setter. i, Border collie. j, Pekingese. k, Dachshund. l, Weimaraner.

Cats: No. 1737a, Blue persian. b, Sorrel abyssinian. c, White angora. d, Brown burmese. e, Red tabby exotic shorthair. f, Seal-point birman. g, Korat. h, Norwegian forest cat. i, Lilac-point Balinese. j, British shorthair. k, Red self longhair. l, Calico manx.

No. 1738, English setter. No. 1739, Seal-point colorpoint.

1995, May 3

1732-1735 G116 Set of 4 3.50 3.50

Miniature Sheets of 12

1736-1737 G116 75c #a.-l., each 6.75 6.75

Souvenir Sheets

1738-1739 G116 $6 each 4.50 4.50

Miniature Sheets of 9

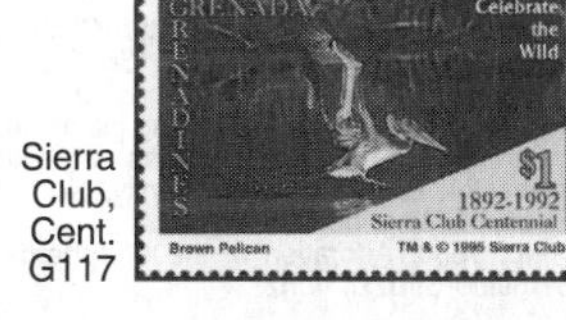

Sierra Club, Cent. G117

No. 1740: a, Brown pelican. b, Northern spotted owl. c, Northern spotted owl in winter. d, Jaguarundi. e, Central American spider monkeys facing forward. f, Two Central American spider monkeys. g, Central American spider monkey. h, Wood stork. i, Maned wolves.

No. 1741, vert: a, Northern spotted owl. b, Brown pelican. c, Brown pelican up close. d, Jaguarundi up close. e, Jaguarundi. f, Maned wolf. g, Wood stork facing right. h, Wood stork facing left. i, Maned wolf up close.

1995, May 5

1740-1741 G117 $1 #a.-i., each 6.75 6.75

FAO, 50th Anniv. — G118

No. 1742: a, 75c, Man working in field. b, $1, Woman working in field. c, $2, Two workers in field.

$6, Child with chopsticks.

1995, May 8

1742 G118 Strip of 3, #a.-c. 3.00 3.00

Souvenir Sheet

1743 G118 $6 multicolored 4.50 4.50

No. 1742 was issued in sheets of 9 stamps.

Rotary Intl., 90th Anniv. G119

1995, May 8

1744 G119 $5 Paul Harris, emblem 3.75 3.75

Souvenir Sheet

1745 G119 $6 Old, new emblems 4.50 4.50

Queen Mother, 95th Anniv. Type of 1995

No. 1746: a, Drawing. b, In black outfit. c, Formal portrait. d, In green outfit.

No. 1747, Speaking at Blitz Memorial.

1995, May 8

1746 A344 $1.50 Strip or block of 4, #a.-d. 4.50 4.50

Souvenir Sheet

1747 A344 $6 multicolored 4.50 4.50

No. 1746 was issued in sheets of 8 stamps.

Sheets of Nos. 1746-1747 exist with black border and text "In Memoriam - 1900-2002" in sheet margins.

1996 Summer Olympics Type

No. 1748, horiz: a, Rosemary Ackerman, East Germany, high jump. b, Li Ning, China, gymnastics. c, Denise Parker, US, archery.

No. 1749, horiz: a, Terry Carlisle, US, skeet shooting. b, Kathleen Nord, East Germany, 200-meter butterfly. c, Brigit Schmidt, East Germany, kayaking.

No. 1750, George Foreman, US, boxing. No. 1751, Dan Gable US, Kikuo Wada, Japan, wrestling.

1995, June 23

1748 A345 15c Strip of 3, #a.-c. .35 .35
1749 A345 $3 Strip of 3, #a.-c. 6.75 6.75

Souvenir Sheets

1750-1751 A345 $6 each 4.50 4.50

G120

Designs: 10c, Brown pelican. 15c, Common stilt. 25c, Cuban trogan. 35c, Flamingo. 75c, Parrot. $1, Pintail duck. $2, Ringed kingfisher. $3, Strip-headed tanager.

No. 1760: a, Great blue heron. b, Jamaican tody. c, Laughing gull. d, Purple-throated carib. e, Red-legged thrush. f, Ruddy duck. g, Shoveler duck. h, West Indian red-bellied woodpecker.

No. 1761, Blue-hooded Euphania. No. 1762, Village weaver.

1995, Sept. 5 Litho. *Perf. 14*

1752-1759 G120 Set of 8 5.75 5.75

Miniature Sheet of 8

1760 G120 $1 #a.-h. 6.00 6.00

Souvenir Sheets

1761-1762 G120 $5 each 3.75 3.75

Singapore '95 (#1760-1762). No. 1760d is mis-spelled.

Mickey's High Sea Adventure — G121

10c, Goofy carrying treasure chests, Donald. 35c, Mickey, Minnie at helm. 75c, Mickey, Donald, Goofy opening treasure chest. $1, Pirates confronting Mickey. $2, Mickey, Goofy, Donald in life boat. $5, Goofy using mop to fight enemy.

No. 1769, Cannonballs being shot at Goofy, vert. No. 1770, Mickey on island, monkey pinching his nose, vert.

1995, Oct. 2 Litho. *Perf. 14x13½*

1763-1768 G121 Set of 6 7.00 7.00

Souvenir Sheets

Perf. 13½x14

1769-1770 G121 $6 each 4.50 4.50

Nobel Prize Recipients Type of 1995

No. 1770A, Derek Walcott, literature, 1992. No. 1770B, W. Arthur Lewis, economics, 1979.

No. 1771: a, Heike Kamerlingh Onnes, physics, 1913. b, Fridtjof Nanson, 1922. c, Sir Ronald Ross, physiology or medicine, 1902. d, Paul Müller, physiology or medicine, 1948. e, Allvar Gullstrand, physiology or medicine, 1911. f, Gerhart Hauptmann, literature, 1912. g, Hans Spemann, physiology or medicine, 1935. h, Cecil F. Powell, physics, 1950. i, Walther Bothe, physics, 1954.

No. 1772: a, Jules Bordet, physiology or medicine, 1919. b, René Cassin, peace, 1968. c, Verner von Heidenstam, literature, 1916. d, Jose Echegaray, literature, 1904. e, Otto Wallach, chemistry, 1910. f, Corneille Heymans, physiology or medicine, 1938. g, Ivar Giaever, physics, 1973. h, Sir William Cremer, peace, 1903. i, John W. Strutt, physics, 1904.

No. 1773: a, James Franck, physics, 1925. b, Tobias M.C. Asser, peace, 1911. c, Carl F.G. Spitteler, literature, 1919. d, Christiaan Eijkman, physiology or medicine, 1929. e, Ragnar Granit, physiology or medicine, 1967. f, Frederic Passy, peace, 1901. g, Louis Neel, physics, 1970. h, Sir William Ramsay, chemistry, 1904. i, Philip Noel-Baker, peace, 1959.

No. 1774, Albert Schweitzer, peace, 1952. No. 1775, Willy Brandt, peace, 1971. No. 1776, Winston Churchill, literature, 1953.

1995, Oct. 18 Litho. *Perf. 14*

1770A A354 75c multicolored .55 .55
1770B A354 75c multicolored .55 .55

Miniature Sheets of 9

1771-1773 A354 $1 #a.-i., each 6.75 6.75

Souvenir Sheets

1774-1776 A354 $6 each 4.50 4.50

Miniature Sheets of 9

Motion Pictures, Cent. G122

Actresses: No. 1777a, Marion Davies. b, Marlene Dietrich. c, Lillian Gish. d, Bette Davis. e, Elizabeth Taylor. f, Veronica Lake. g, Ava Gardner. h, Grace Kelly. i, Kim Novak.

Romantic couples: No. 1778a, Nita Naldi, Rudolph Valentino. b, Ramon Navaro, Alice Terry. c, Frederic March, Joan Crawford. d, Clark Gable, Vivien Leigh. e, Barbara Stanwyck, Burt Lancaster. f, Warren Beatty, Natalie Wood. g, Spencer Tracy, Katharine Hepburn. h, Humphrey Bogart, Lauren Bacall. i, Omar Sharif, Julie Christie.

No. 1779, Sophia Loren. No. 1780, Greta Garbo, John Gilbert, horiz.

1995, Nov. 3 *Perf. 13½x14*

1777-1778 G122 $1 #a.-i., each 6.75 6.75

Souvenir Sheets

Perf. 13½x14, 14x13½

1779-1780 G122 $6 each 4.50 4.50

Classic Racing Cars G123

Designs: 10c, 1990's Williams-Renault Formula 1. 25c, 1980's Le Mans Porsche 956. 35c, 1970's Lotus "John Player Special." 75c, 1960's Ford GT 40. $2, 1950's Mercedes Benz W196. $3, 1920's Mercedes SSK.

$6, 1971 Tyrrell-Ford Fourmula 1.

1995, Nov. 7 *Perf. 14*

1781-1786 G123 Set of 6 4.50 4.50

Souvenir Sheet

1787 G123 $6 multicolored 4.50 4.50

Local Transportation — G124

1995, Nov. 7

1788 G124 35c Donkey .25 .25
1789 G124 75c Bus .55 .55

Miniature Sheet

Sailing Ships G125

Designs: No. 1790a, Preussen. b, Japanese junk. c, Pirate ship. d, Mayflower. e, Chinese junk. f, Santa Maria.

$5, Spanish galleon.

1995, Nov. 7

1790 G125 $1 Sheet of 6, #a.-f. 4.50 4.50

Souvenir Sheet

1791 G125 $5 multicolored 3.75 3.75

No. 1791 contains one 57x42mm stamp.

Christmas Type of 1995

Details or entire paintings: 10c, Immaculate Conception, by De Cosimo. 15c, St. Michel Dedicating Arms to the Madonna, by Le Nain. 35c, Annunciation, by de Credi. 50c, The Holy Family, by Jordaens. $3, Madonna and Child, by Lippi. $5, Madonna and Child with Ten Saints, by Fiorentino.

No. 1798, Adoration of the Shepherds, by Van Oost. No. 1799, Holy Family, by Del Sart.

1995, Nov. 28 *Perf. 13½x14*

1792-1797 A356 Set of 6 6.75 6.75

Souvenir Sheets

1798-1799 A356 $6 each 4.50 4.50

New Year 1996 (Year of the Rat) — G126

Stylized rats: No. 1800: a, blue & multi. b, violet & multi. c, red & multi. d, green & multi.

$2, Two rats, horiz.

1996, Jan. 2 Litho. *Perf. 14½*

1800 G126 75c Block of 4, #a.-d. 2.25 2.25

Miniature Sheet

1801 G126 75c Sheet of 1 #1800 2.25 2.25

Souvenir Sheet

1802 G126 $2 multicolored 1.50 1.50

No. 1800 was issued in sheets of 16 stamps.

Works by Dürer and Rubens Type of 1996

Details or entire work: 15c, The Centaur Family, by Dürer. 35c, Oriental Ruler Seated, by Dürer. 50c, The Entombment, by Dürer. 75c, Man in Armor, by Rubens. $1, Peace Embracing Plenty, by Rubens. $2, Departure of Lot, by Rubens. $3, The Four Evangelists, by Rubens. No. 1810, $5, Knight, Death and Devil, by Dürer.

No. 1811, The Father of the Church, by Rubens. $6, St. Jerome, 1514 engraving, by Dürer.

1996, Jan. 29 Litho. *Perf. 14*
1803-1810 A360 Set of 8 9.50 9.50

Souvenir Sheets
1811 A360 $5 multicolored 3.75 3.75
1812 A360 $6 multicolored 4.50 4.50

Disney Holidays — G127

Disney characters celebrating: 25c, New Year's Day, "Hopping John" Feast. 50c, May Day. 75c, Independence Day. 90c, Halloween. $3, Thanksgiving. $4, Hanukkah.
No. 1819, Caribbean Carnival. No. 1820, St. Patrick's Day Parade, vert.

1996, Apr. 17 Litho. *Perf. 14x13½*
1813-1818 G127 Set of 6 6.75 6.75

Souvenir Sheets
Perf. 14x13½, 13½x14
1819-1820 G127 $6 each 4.50 4.50

Sheets of 4

Sites in China — G128

No. 1821: a, Entryway to hall, Imperial Palace. b, Great Wall's eastern end, Shanhaiguan. c, Fortress in Great Wall, Shanhaiguan. d, Gate of Heavenly Peace, Tiananmen, main entrance to Imperial City.
No. 1822: a, Mausoleum of Dr. Sun Yat-Sen, Nanjing. b, Summer Palance, Beijing. c, Temple of Heaven, Beijing. d, Hall of Supreme Harmony, Forbidden City, Beijing.
No. 1823, Great Wall of China. No. 1824, Marble boat, Summer Palace, Beijing.
Illustration reduced.

1996, May 8 *Perf. 13*
1821-1822 G128 $1 #a.-d., each 3.00 3.00

Souvenir Sheets
1823-1824 G128 $6 each 4.50 4.50

China '96, 9th Asian Intl. Philatelic Exhibition (#1821-1822).
No. 1823 contains one 40x51mm stamp, No. 1824 one 51x40mm stamp.
See No. 1881.

Queen Elizabeth II, 70th Birthday Type of 1996

Designs: a, 35c, Portrait in blue dress. b, $2, Wearing crown. c, $4, Windsor Castle.
$6, Standing in front of palace.

1996, May 8 Litho. *Perf. 13½x14*
1825 A362 Strip of 3, #a.-c. 4.75 4.75

Souvenir Sheet
1826 A362 $6 multicolored 4.50 4.50

No. 1825 was issued in sheets of 9 stamps with each strip in a different order.

Flowers — G129

35c, Camellia "Apple Blossom." 90c, Camellia japonica "Extravaganza." $1, Chrysanthemum "Primrose Dorothy Else." $2, Dahlia "Brandaris."
No. 1831: a, Odontoglossum. b, Cattleya. c, Paphiopedilum "Venus's Slipper." d, Laeliocattleya "Marysville."
No. 1832: a, Fushcia "Citation." b, Fuchsia "Amy Lye." c, Clysonimus butterfly. d, Digitalis purpurea "Foxglove" (h). e, Lilium martagon "Martagon Lily." f, Tulip "Couleur Cardinal." g, Galanthus nivalis "Snowdrop." h, Rose "Superstar." i, Crocus "Dutch Yellow Mammouth." j, Lilium speciosum Japanese lily. k, Lilium "Joan Evans." l, Rose "Rosemary Harkness."
$5, Narcissus "Rembrandt." $6, Gladiollus "Flowersong."

1996, June 12 Litho. *Perf. 14*
1827-1830 G129 Set of 4 3.25 3.25
1831 G129 75c Strip of 4, #a.-d. 2.25 2.25
1832 G129 75c Sheet of 12, #a.-l. 6.75 6.75

Souvenir Sheets
1833 G129 $5 multicolored 3.75 3.75
1834 G129 $6 multicolored 4.50 4.50

No. 1831 issued in sheets of 12 stamps.

UNICEF, 50th Anniv. G130

Letters spelling UNICEF and: 75c, Child smiling. $2, Child eating. $3, Child reading.
$6, Child on mother's back.

1996, June 26
1836-1838 G130 Set of 3 4.50 4.50

Souvenir Sheet
1839 G130 $6 multicolored 4.50 4.50

#1838 is unassigned.

Jerusalem, 3000th Anniv. G131

Flowers and: a, $1, Pool of Bethesda. b, $2, Damascus Gate. c, $3, Church of All Nations, Gethsemane.
$6, Church of the Holy Sepulchre.

1996, June 26
1840 G131 Sheet of 3, #a.-c. 4.50 4.50

Souvenir Sheet
1841 G131 $6 multicolored 4.50 4.50

Radio, Cent. Type of 1996

Entertainers: 35c, Ed Wynn. 75c, Red Skelton. $1, Joe Penner. $3, Jerry Colonna.
$6, Bob Elliot, Ray Goulding, horiz.

1996, June 26 *Perf. 13½x14*
1842-1845 A367 Set of 4 3.75 3.75

Souvenir Sheet
Perf. 14x13½
1846 A367 $6 multicolored 4.50 4.50

Olympics Type of 1996

35c, Memorial Coliseum, Los Angeles, 1994. 75c, Connie Carpenter-Phinney, US. $2, Mohamed Bouchighe, Algeria, vert. $3, Jackie Joyner-Kersee, US.
Gymnasts, vert: No. 1851: a, Julianne McNamara, US. b, Takuti Hayato, Japan. c, Nikolai Adrianov, Russia. d, Mitch Gaylord, US. e, Ludmilla Tourischeva, Russia. f, Karin Janz, Germany. g, Peter Kormann, US. h, Sawao Kato, Japan. i, Nadia Comaneci, Romania.
Equestrian participants, vert: No. 1852a, Josef Neckermann, Germany. b, Harry Boldt, Germany. c, Elena Petouchkova, Russia. d, Alwin Schockemoehle, Germany. e, Hans Winkler, Germany. f, Joe Fargis, US. g, David Broome, Great Britain. h, Reiner Klimke, Germany. i, Richard Meade, Great Britain.
No. 1853, Young Japanese girl, vert. No. 1854, William Steinkraus, US.

1996, July 15 *Perf. 14*
1847-1850 A364 Set of 4 4.50 4.50

Sheets of 9
1851-1852 A364 $1 #a.-i., each 6.75 6.75

Souvenir Sheets
1853 A364 $5 multicolored 3.75 3.75
1854 A364 $6 multicolored 4.50 4.50

Classic Cars — G132

No. 1855: a, Delaunay-Belleville HB6, France. b, Bugatti Type-15, Italy. c, Mazda Type 800, Japan. d, Mercedes 24/100/140 Sport, Germany. e, MG K3 Rover, England. f, Plymouth Fury, US.
No. 1856: a, 35c, Chevrolet Belair Convertible, US. b, 75c, Rolls Royce Torpedo, England. c, $1, Nissan Type "Cepric," Japan. d, VIP car. e, Mercedes Benz 500k, Germany. f, Bugatti Type-13, Italy.
$5, Bugatti "Roadster" Type-55. $6, Lincoln Type-L, US.

1996, July 25 Litho. *Perf. 14*
1855 G132 $1 Sheet of 6, #a.-f. 4.50 4.50
1856 G132 Sheet of 6, #a.-f. 5.75 5.75

Souvenir Sheets
1857 G132 $5 multicolored 3.75 3.75
1858 G132 $6 multicolored 4.50 4.50

Nos. 1857-1858 each contain one 51x39mm stamp.

Ships G133

Traditional Grenada schooners: 35c, Red and white. 75c, Blue and white.
Ancient ships: No. 1861: a, Anthenian war triremes, 1000BC. b, Egyptian Nile trader, 30BC. c, Bangladesh dinghi, 3100BC. d, Queen Hatshepsut warship, 1476BC. e, Chinese junk, 200BC. f, Polynesian voyager, 600BC.
Ocean liners: No. 1862: a, Europa, Germany, 1957. b, Lusitania, England, 1906. c, Queen Mary, England, 1936. d, Bianca C, Italy. e, SS France, 1932. f, Orion, England, 1915.
$5, Queen Elizabeth 2, England, 1969. $6, Viking ship, 610BC.

1996, Aug. 14
1859 G133 35c multicolored .25 .25
1860 G133 75c multicolored .55 .55

Sheets of 6
1861-1862 G133 $1 #a.-f., each 4.50 4.50

Souvenir Sheets
1863 G133 $5 multicolored 3.75 3.75
1864 G133 $6 multicolored 4.50 4.50

No. 1863 contains one 51x42mm stamp, No. 1864 one 42x51mm stamp.

Famous Composers G134

Composer, work illustrated: No. 1865: a, Bèla Bartòk, "Mikrokosmos," 1926. b, Giacomo Puccini, "Madame Butterfly," 1904. c, George Gershwin, "Rhapsody in Blue," 1923. d, Leonard Bernstein, "West Side Story", 1957. e, Kurt Weill, "Three Penny Opera," 1928. f, John Cage, "Music of Changes," 1951. g, Aaron Copland, "El Salón Mexico," 1936. h, Sergei Prokofiev, "Peter and the Wolf," 1936. i, Igor Stravinsky, "Rite of Spring," 1913.
No. 1866: a, Felix Mendelssohn, overture to "Midsummer Night's Dream," 1826. b, Franz Schubert, "Die Forelle" (The Trout) D.550, 1817. c, Franz Joseph Haydn, "String Quartet in D Major," Op. 64 No. 5 (Lark), 1790. d, Robert Schumann, "Spring," Symphony No. 1, Op. 38, 1841. e, Ludwig Van Beethoven, "Moonlight" sonata Op. 27, No. 2. f, Gioacchino Rossini, "William Tell," 1829. g, George Frederick Handel, "Royal Fireworks Music," 1749. h, Peter Ilyich Tchaikovsky, "Swan Lake," Op.20, 1876. i, Frederic Chopin, "Fantasia," in F minor, Op. 49, 1840-41.
$5, Richard Strauss. $6, Mozart, "Jupiter" symphony in C major.

1996, Aug. 26

Sheets of 9
1865-1866 G134 $1 #a.-i., each 6.75 6.75

Souvenir Sheets
1867 G134 $5 multicolored 3.75 3.75
1868 G134 $6 multicolored 4.50 4.50

Trains G135

No. 1869: a, Pacific Blue Peter, British Eastern. b, Class P36 4-8-4, Russia. c, Class OJ 2-10-2, China. d, Class 12 4-4-2, Belgium. e, Challenger Class 4-6-6-4, US. f, Class 25 4-8-4 Condenser, South Africa.
No. 1870: a, Federal Railways Class 38 4-6-0, Germany. b, Duchess of Hamilton Class 4-6-2, London & Glasgow. c, Class WP 4-6-2, Indian State Railways. d, Class 141R "L'Americane" 282, France (American-built). e, Class A4 4-6-2 Mallard, England. f, Deutche Reichsbahn Class 18 4-6-2, Germany.
$5, Cornish Rivera Express, King Class 4-6-2, Britain. $6, Caledonian "Royal Scot Class," 4-6-0, Britain.

1996, Aug. 28

Sheets of 6
1869-1870 G135 $1.50 #a.-f., each 6.75 6.75

Souvenir Sheets
1871 G135 $5 multicolored 3.75 3.75
1872 G135 $6 multicolored 4.50 4.50

Christmas Type of 1996

Details of painting, Suffer Little Children to Come Unto Me, by Van Dyck: 15c, Child with beads over shoulder. 25c, Christ annointing head of child. $1, Mother holding infant, father, children. $1.50, Christ, disciples. $2, Father, infant. $4, Christ, children, family. No. 1879, Entire painting, horiz.
No. 1880, Adoration of the Shepherds, by Bernaldo Strozzi, horiz.

1996, Nov. 18 Litho. *Perf. 13½x14*
1873-1878 A377 Set of 6 7.00 7.00

Souvenir Sheets
1879-1880 A377 $6 each 4.50 4.50

Souvenir Sheet

China '96 — G136

Geisha House. Illustration reduced.

1996, May 8 Litho. *Perf. 13x13½*
1881 G136 $2 multicolored 1.10 1.10

No. 1881 was not available until March 1997.

Hong Kong Past and Present G137

Man Ho Temple: No. 1882: a, 1841. b, 1983.
City of Victoria with view of St. John's Cathedral: No. 1883: a, 1886. b, 1983.
Victoria Harbor, Hong Kong: No. 1884: a, 1858. b, 1983.
No. 1885: a, Treaty of Nanking, 1842. b, Margaret Thatcher signing Joint Declaration, 1984.
Victoria Harbor: No. 1886: a, Older black & white photograph. b, Modern photograph.

1997, Feb. 12 Litho. *Perf. 14*
Sheets of 2

1882-1886 G137 $3 #a.-b., each 4.50 4.50

Hong Kong '97.

UNESCO Type of 1997

Designs: 15c, Kyoto, Japan. 25c, Roman ruins at Trier, Germany. $1, Mount Taishan, China. $1.50, Scandola Nature Reserve, France. $2, Fortress Wall, Dubrovnik, Croatia. $4, Angra Do Heroismo, Portugal.

No. 1893, vert.: a, Sanctuary of Congonhas, Brazil. b, Cartagena, Colombia. c, City of Puebla, Mexico. d, Mayan Ruins, Copan, Honduras. e, Monastery of Popocatepetl, Mexico. f, Galapagos Islands, Ecuador. g, Waterfall, La Amisted Natl. Park, Costa Rica. h, Glaciares Natl. Park, Argentina.

No. 1894, vert.: a, b, c, Kyoto, Japan. d, Ayutthaya, Thailand. e, Temple of Borobudur, Indonesia. f, Monuments, Pattadakal, India. g, Polonnaruwa, Sri Lanka. h, Sagarmatha Natl. Park, Nepal.

No. 1895: a, Cathedral of Notre Dame, France. b, Timbered house, Maulbronn, Germany. c, Himeji-Jo, Japan. d, Ruins, Delphi, Greece. e, Palace of Fontainebleau, France.

No. 1896, Temple, Chengde, China. No. 1897, Pre-hispanic city of Teotihuacan, Mexico. No. 1898, Mont St. Michel, France.

1997, Apr. 3 Litho. *Perf. 14*

1887-1892 A382 Set of 6 6.75 6.75

Sheets of 8 or 5 + Label

1893-1894 A382 $1 #a.-h., each 6.00 6.00
1895 A382 $1.50 #a.-e. 5.75 5.75

Souvenir Sheets

1896-1898 A382 $6 each 4.50 4.50

Dogs and Cats G138

Dogs: 35c, Springer spaniel. 75c, Doberman pinscher. $1, Italian spinone, vert. $2, Cocker spaniel, vert.

No. 1903: a, Leonberger. b, Newfoundland. c, Boxer. d, St. Bernard. e, Silky terrier. f, Miniature schnauzer.

No. 1904, Golden retriever puppy.

1997, Apr. 10

1899-1902 G138 Set of 4 3.00 3.00

Sheet of 6

1903 G138 $1.50 #a.-f. 6.75 6.75

Souvenir Sheet

1904 G138 $6 multicolored 6.75 6.75

1997, Apr. 10

Cats: 45c, Abyssinian blue. 50c, Bermese cream, vert. 90c, Persian tortoiseshell and white. $3, Oriental shorthair red Agouti tabby, vert.

No. 1909: a, Siamese chocolate point. b, Oriental shorthair white. c, Burmese sable. d, Abysinian tabby. e, Persian shaded silver. f, Tonkinese natural mink.

1905-1908 G138 Set of 4 3.75 3.75

Sheet of 6

1909 G138 $1.50 #a.-f. 6.75 6.75

Souvenir Sheet

1910 G138 $6 Sphinx, vert. 6.75 6.75

Prehistoric Animal Type of 1997

Designs: 45c, Stegosaurus. 90c, Diplodocus. $1, Pteranodon, vert. $2, Deinonychus, ankylasaurus, vert.

No. 1915: a, Rhamphorhynchus, brachiosaurus (c, d, e,). b, Archaeopteryx. c, Anurognathus. d, Albertosaurus (f). e, Herrerasaurus. f, Platyhystrix.

No. 1916, Hypacrosaurus. No. 1917, Apatosaurus, allosaurus, vert.

1997, Apr. 15 Litho. *Perf. 14*

1911-1914 A385 Set of 4 3.00 3.00
1915 A385 $1.50 Sheet of 6, #a.-f. 6.75 6.75

Souvenir Sheets

1916-1917 A385 $6 each 4.50 4.50

Queen Elizabeth II, Prince Philip, 50th Wedding Anniv. Type of 1997

No. 1918: a, Colored portrait. b, Royal Arms. c, Black and white portrait. d, Black and white portrait in royal attire. e, Sandringham House. f, Queen in blue dress, Prince in uniform.

$6, Wedding portrait.

1997, May 28 Litho. *Perf. 14*

1918 A386a $1 Sheet of 6, #a.-f. 4.50 4.50

Souvenir Sheet

1919 A386a $6 multicolored 4.50 4.50

Paintings by Hiroshige Type of 1997

No. 1920: a, Koume Embankment. b, Azuma Shrine and the Entwined Camphor. c, Yanagishima. d, Inside Akiba Shrine, Ukeji. e, Distant View of Kinryuzan Temple and Azuma Bridge. f, Night View of Matsuchiyama and the San'ya Canal.

No. 1921, Five Pines, Onagi Canal. No. 1922, Spiral Hall, Five Hundred Rakan Temple.

1997, May 28 *Perf. 13½x14*

1920 A387 $1.50 Sheet of 6, #a.-f. 6.75 6.75

Souvenir Sheets

1921-1922 A387 $6 each 4.50 4.50

Heinrich von Stephan Type of 1997

1997, May 28 Litho. *Perf. 14*

Portrait of Von Stephan and: No. 1923: a, The Pony Express, 1860-61. b, UPU emblem. c, Steam locomotive postal delivery, 1800's.

$6, Camel courier, Baghdad.

1923 A388 $1.50 Sheet of 3, #a.-c. 2.50 2.50

Souvenir Sheet

1924 A388 $6 multicolored 4.50 4.50

PACIFIC 97.

Paul P. Harris Type of 1997

1997, May 28

Designs: $3, Women in Burkina Faso pumping well water, portrait of Harris.

$6, Early Rotary parade float.

1925 A389 $3 multicolored 2.25 2.25

Souvenir Sheet

1926 A389 $6 multicolored 4.50 4.50

Grimm's Fairy Tale and Mother Goose Types of 1997

1997, May 28 *Perf. 13½x14*

Scenes from "The Fox and the Geese:" No. 1927: a, Fox, geese. b, Geese singing as fox waves knife, fork. c, Fox asleep, geese celebrating. No. 1928, Fox lurking in forest, horiz.

No. 1929, Girl with black sheep.

1927 A391 $2 Sheet of 3, #a.-c. 4.50 4.50

Souvenir Sheets

Perf. 14x13½, 14

1928 A391 $6 multicolored 4.50 4.50
1929 A392 $6 multicolored 4.50 4.50

1998 Winter Olympic Games, Nagano G139

Designs: 90c, Downhill skier. $2, Luge. $3, Male figure skater. $5, Speed skater in blue hat.

No. 1934: a, Downhill skier in air. b, Freestyle skier. c, Curling. d, Ski jumper. e, Bobsled. f, Biathlon. g, Speed skater in yellow and red hat. h, Hockey. i, Cross-country skier.

No. 1935, Luge, diff., vert. No. 1936, Female figure skater.

1997, June 26 *Perf. 14*

1930-1933 G139 Set of 4 8.25 8.25
1934 G139 $1 Sheet of 9, #a.-i. 6.75 6.75

Souvenir Sheets

1935-1936 G139 $6 each 4.50 4.50

Return of Hong Kong to China Type

Chinese flag in foreground, "Hong Kong" in English and Chinese with city scene showing through words: $1, Night scene. $1.25, Daytime view of skyscrapers. $1.50, Skyline at night, horiz. $2, View of harbor, horiz.

1997, July 1

1937-1940 A394 Set of 4 4.50 4.50

Nos. 1937-1938 were issued in sheets of 4. Nos. 1939-1940 are 59x28mm and were issued in sheets of 3.

Fish G140

Designs: 10c, Wimplefish. 15c, Clown triggerfish. 25c, Ringed emperor angelfish. 35c, Hooded butterfly fish. 45c, Semicircle angelfish. 75c, Scribbled angelfish. 90c, Threadfin butterfly fish. $1, Clown surgeonfish.

1997, July 22 Litho. *Perf. 14*

1941 G140 10c multicolored .20 .20
1942 G140 15c multicolored .20 .20
1943 G140 25c multicolored .20 .20
1944 G140 35c multicolored .25 .25
1945 G140 45c multicolored .35 .35
1946 G140 75c multicolored .55 .55
1947 G140 90c multicolored .70 .70
1948 G140 $1 multicolored .75 .75
Nos. 1941-1948 (8) 3.20 3.20

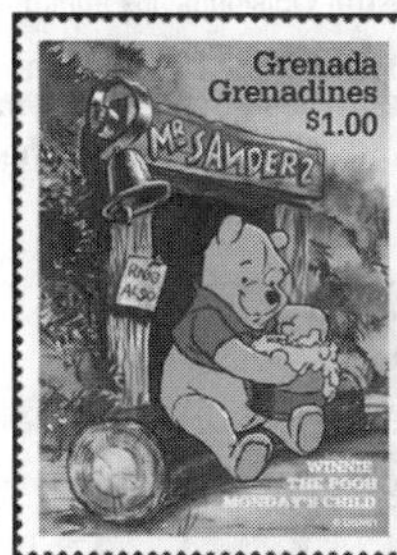

Winnie the Pooh G141

#1949: a, Winnie the Pooh. b, Kanga & Roo. c, Eeyore. d, Tigger. e, Piglet & Gopher. f, Rabbit.

$6, Christopher Robin.

1997, Aug. 7 Litho. *Perf. 13½x14*

1949 G141 $1 Sheet of 6, #a.-f. 4.50 4.50

Souvenir Sheet

1950 G141 $6 multicolored 4.50 4.50

1998 World Cup Soccer Type of 1997

Team pictures: 10c, Italy, 1934. 20c, Angola. 45c, Brazil, 1958. $1, Uruguay, 1950. $1.50, West Germany, 1974. $5, Italy, 1938.

World Cup winners: No. 1951: a, England. b, W. Germany, 1954. c, Uruguay. d, West Germany, 1990. e, Argentina, 1986. f, Brazil. g, Argentina, 1978. h, W. Germany 1974.

Tournament stars, vert.: No. 1952: a, Ademir, Brazil. b, Kocsis, Hungary. c, Leonidas, Brazil. d, Nejedly, Czechoslovakia. e, Schiavio, Italy. f, Stabile, Uruguay. g, Pele, Brazil. h, Fritzwalter, W. Germany.

No. 1953, Shearer, England, vert. No. 1954, Paulao, Angola.

1997, Aug. 11

1950A-1950F A397 Set of 6 6.25 6.25

Sheets of 8

1951-1952 A397 #a.-h, + label 6.00 6.00

Souvenir Sheets

1953-1954 A397 $6 each 4.50 4.50

Fish Type of 1997

$2, Tursiops truncatus. $5, Balistes vetula. $10, Pterois volitans. $20, Equetus lanceolatus.

1997, July 22 Litho. *Perf. 14*

1955 G140 $2 multicolored 1.50 1.50
1956 G140 $5 multicolored 3.75 3.75
1957 G140 $10 multicolored 7.50 7.50
1958 G140 $20 multicolored 15.00 15.00
Nos. 1955-1958 (4) 27.75 27.75

Sealed with a Kiss — G142

Characters from Disney's classic animated films: No. 1959: a, Snow White, 1937. b, Pinocchio, 1940. c, Peter Pan, 1953. d, Cinderella, 1950. e, The Little Mermaid, 1989. f, Beauty and the Beast, 1991. g, Aladdin, 1992. h, Pocahontas, 1995. i, Hunchback of Notre Dame, 1996.

$5, The Artistocats, 1970, vert.

1997, Aug. 7 Litho. *Perf. 14x13½*

1959 G142 $1 Sheet of 9, #a.-i. 6.75 6.75

Souvenir Sheet

Perf. 13½x14

1960 G142 $5 multicolored 3.75 3.75

Butterflies of the World G143

75c, Polyura dehaani. 90c, Polyura dolon. $1, Charaxes candiope. $1.50, Pantaporia punctata. $2, Charaxes etesippe. $3, Charaxes castor.

Euphaedra: No. 1967: a, Francina. b, Eleus. c, Harpalyce. d, Cyparissa. e, Gausape. f, Imperialis.

No. 1968: a, Euthalia confucius. b, Euthalia kardama. c, Limenitis albomaculata. d, Hestina assimilis. e, Kalima inachus. f, Euthalia teutoides.

No. 1969, Charaxes numenes, vert. No. 1970, Charaxes nobilis, vert.

1997, Aug. 12 *Perf. 14*

1961-1966 G143 Set of 6 6.75 6.75

Sheets of 6

1967-1968 G143 $1.50 #a.-f., ea 6.75 6.75

Souvenir Sheets

1969-1970 G143 $6 each 4.50 4.50

James Dean (1931-55), Actor G144

Various portraits.

1997, Aug. 22 *Perf. 14x13½*

1971 G144 $1 Sheet of 9, #a.-i. 6.75 6.75

Mushrooms — G145

Designs: 75c, Clitocybe metachroa. 90c, Clavulinopsis helvola. $1, Lycoperdon pyriforme. $1.50, Auricularia auricula-judae. $2, Clathrus archeri. $3, Lactarius trivialis.

No. 1978: a, Entoloma incanum. b, Coprinus atramentarius. c, Mycena polygramma. d, Lepista nuda. e, Pleurotis cornucopiae. f, Laccaria amethystina.

No. 1979, Amanita muscaria. No. 1980, Morchella esculenta.

1997, Sept. 4 *Perf. 14*

1972-1977 G145 Set of 6 6.75 6.75
1978 G145 $1.50 Sheet of 6, #a.-f. 6.75 6.75

Souvenir Sheets

1979-1980 G145 $6 each 4.50 4.50

G146

Orchids — G147

Designs: 35c, Symphyglossum sanguineum. 45c, Doritaenopsis "Mythic Beauty." 75c, Odontoglossum cervantesii. 90c, Cattleya "Pumpernickel." $1, Vanda "Patricia Law." $1.50, Odontonia "Debutante." $2, Laeliocattleya "Mini Purple." $3, Phragmipedium "Dominiarium."

No. 1989: a, Cymbidium "Showgirl." b, Disa "Blackii." c, Phalaenopsis aphrodite. d, Iwanagaara "Apple Blossum." e, Masdevallia "Copper Angel." f, Paphiopedilum micranthum. g, Paphiopedilum "Claire de Lune." h, Cattleya forbesii. i, Dendrobium "Dawn Maree."

No. 1990: a, Lycaste "Aquila." b, Brassolaeliocattleya "Dorothy Bertsch." c, Phalaenopsis "Zuma Urchin." d, Promenaea xanthina. e, Amesiella philippinensis. f, Brassocattleya "Angel Lace." g, Brassoepidsendrum "Peggy Ann." h, Miltonia seine. i, Sophralaeliocattleya "Precious Stones."

No. 1991: a, Miltoniosis "Jean Sabourin." b, Cymbididium "Red Beauty." c, Brassocattleya "Green Dragon." d, Phalaenopsis hybrid. e, Laelio cattleya "Mary Ellen Carter." f, Disa hybrid.

No. 1992: a, Lycaste macrobulbon. b, Cochleanthes discolor. c, Cymbidium "Nang Carpenter." d, Paphiopedilum "Clair de Lune." e, Masdevallia caudata. f, Cymbidum "Showgirl."

$5, Phalenopsis "Medford Star." $6, Brassolaeliocattleya "Mem. Dorothy Bertsch."

1997, Sept. 4
1981-1988 G146 Set of 8 7.50 7.50
Sheets of 9 and 6
1989-1990 G147 $1 #a.-i., ea 6.75 6.75
1991-1992 G146 $1.50 #a.-f., ea 6.75 6.75
Souvenir Sheets
1993 G146 $5 multicolored 3.75 3.75
1994 G146 $6 multicolored 4.50 4.50

Famous Composers, Musicians G148

No. 1995: a, Beethoven. b, Tchaikovsky. c, J.S. Bach. d, Chopin. e, Stravinsky. f, Haydn. g, Mahler. h, Rossini.

No. 1996, Mozart. No. 1997, Schubert.

1997, Oct. 10 Litho. *Perf. 14½x14*
Sheet of 8
1995 G148 $1 #a.-h. + label 6.00 6.00
Souvenir Sheets
1996-1997 G148 $6 each 4.50 4.50

Diana, Princess of Wales (1961-97) G149

Various portraits of Diana wearing various hats, scenes following her death: No. 1998: a, Buckingham Palace. b, Island, Spencer Estate, Althorp. c, Westminster Abbey. d, Gate, Spencer Estate. e, Gate, Kensington Palace. g, Spencer Estate, Althorp.

$6, Diana smelling flowers in front of Kensington Palace.

1997, Nov. 10 *Perf. 14*
1998 G149 $1.50 Sheet of 6, #a.-f. 6.75 6.75
Souvenir Sheet
1999 G149 $6 multicolored 4.50 4.50

No. 1999 contains one 60x40mm stamp.

Christmas Art Type of 1997

Entire paintings, details, or sculptures: 20c, Choir of Angels, by Simon Marmion. 75c, The Annunciation, by Giotto. 90c, Festival of the Rose Garlands, by Albrecht Durer. $1.50, Madonna with Two Angels, by Hans Memling. $2, The Ognissanti Madonna, by Giotto. $3, Angel with Candlestick, by Michelangelo.

No. 2006, Cupid Commemorating a Marriage by Incising on a Table, by Jean-Baptiste Huet, horiz. No. 2007, The Rising of the Sun, by Francois Boucher, horiz.

1997, Dec. 5 Litho. *Perf. 14*
2000-2005 A402 Set of 6 12.50 12.50
Souvenir Sheets
2006-2007 A402 $6 each 4.50 4.50

Marine Life Type of 1997

No. 2008: a, Holocanthus ciliaris. b, Ballstoides conspicillum. c, Chaetodon quadrimaculatus. d, Microspathodon chrysurus. e, Halichoeres garnoti. f, Gramma loreto. g, Liopropoma carmabi. h, Lactophrys triqueter. i, Cephalopolis miniatus.

No. 2009, Carcharhinus melanopterus. No. 2010, Obistognathus aurifrons, vert.

1997, Dec. 12 Litho. *Perf. 14*
2008 A386 $1 Sheet of 9, #a.-i. 6.75 6.75
Souvenir Sheets
2009-2010 A386 $6 each 4.50 4.50

New Year 1998 (Year of the Tiger) — G150

Die Cut Perf. 11
1998, Feb. 10 Litho.
Self-Adhesive
2011 G150 $1.50 Hologram 1.10
Souvenir Sheet
2012 G150 $3 like #2011 2.25

No. 2011 was issued in sheets of 4. No. 2012 contains one 52x65mm stamp.

Great Ships, Shipwrecks — G151

Ships - #2013: a, CSS Alabama. b, Persia. c, Ariel. d, CSS Florida. e, Great Eastern. f, Jacob Bell. g, Star of India. h, Robert E. Lee. i, US Monitor Passaic. j, Madagascar. k, HMS Devastation. l, General Grant.

"Gone with the Wind," vert. - #2014: a, Clark Gable. b, Blockade runner wrecked on Sullivan's Island, North Carolina, 1863. c, Margaret Mitchell. d, George Alfred Trenholm, model for character Rhett Butler. e, Dock Street Theater, confiscated from Trenholm after Civil War. f, Howlet sinks off Charleston, South Carolina, 1865. g, USS Tecumseh sunk by Confederate gunboats, 1864. h, City jail, where Trenholm was imprisioned, 1865.

No. 2015, Nashville sinks the Union clipper, Harvey Birch, vert. No. 2016, Dr. Lee Spence, expert on shipwrecks and sunken treasures, Alabama sinking Hatteras off Texas coast.

1998, May 7 Litho. *Perf. 14*
2013 G151 75c Sheet of 12, #a.-l. 6.75 6.75
2014 G151 $1 Sheet of 8, #a.-h. 6.00 6.00
Souvenir Sheets
2015-2016 G151 $6 each 4.50 4.50

#2015-2016 contain one 57x43mm stamp.

Modern, Future Aircraft G152

70c, Concept strike fighter. 90c, Concept space shuttle. $2, Concept air & space jet. $3, V Jet II.

#2021: a, Velocity 173 RG Elite. b, Davis DA 9. c, Concorde. d, Voyager. e, Factimobile. f, RAF 2000. g, Boomerang. h, N1M Flying Wing.

#2022, Gee-Bee replica. #2023, Concept Aeropod.

1998, May 13
2017-2020 G152 Set of 4 5.00 5.00
2021 G152 $1 Sheet of 8, #a.-h. 6.00 6.00
Souvenir Sheets
2022-2023 G152 $6 each 4.50 4.50

No. 2022 is inscribed "Delmar."

Orchids — G153

Designs: $1, Laclia tenebrosa. $1.50, Phragmipedium besseae. $2, Pschopsis papilio. $3, Masdevallia coccinea.

No. 2028: a, Lycaste deppei. b, Dendrobium victoriae. c, Dendrobium nobile. d, Cymbidium danyanum. e, Cymbidium starbright. f, Cymbidium giganteum. g, Chysis aurea. h, Broughtonia sanguinea. i, Cattleya guttata.

No. 2029: a, Calanthe vestita. b, Cattleya bicolor. c, Laelia anceps. d, Epidendrum prismatocarpum. e, Coelogyne ochcracea. f, Doritaenopsis eclantant. g, Laelia gouldiana. h, Encyclia vitellina. i, Maxillaria praestans.

No. 2030, Masdevallia ignea. No. 2031, Encyclia brassavolae.

1998, May 19
2024-2027 G153 Set of 4 5.75 5.75
Sheets of 9
2028-2029 G153 $1 #a.-i., each 6.75 6.75
Souvenir Sheets
2030-2031 G153 $6 each 4.50 4.50

Sea Birds Type of 1998

75c, Bonaparte's gull. 90c, Western sandpiper. $2, Great black-backed gull. $3, Dotterell.

No. 2036: a, Terns. b, Brown pelican. c, Black-legged kittiwake. d, Herring gull. e, Lesser noddy. f, Kittiwake.

No. 2037: a, Whimbrels. b, Golden white-tailed tropic bird. c, Arctic tern. d, Ruddy turnstones. e, Imperial shag. f, Magellan gull.

No. 2038, Yellow-nosed albatross, vert. No. 2039, Broad-billed prion.

1998, June 30 Litho. *Perf. 14*
2032-2035 A408 Set of 4 5.00 5.00
Sheets of 6
2036-2037 A408 $1.50 #a.-f., ea 6.75 6.75
Souvenir Sheets
2038-2039 A408 $5 each 3.75 3.75

Diana, Princess of Wales (1961-97) — G155

Diana in front of Kensington Palace: No. 2040, Wearing tiara, ruffled dress. No. 2041, Wearing white dress, pearls.

Litho. & Embossed
1998, July 14 *Die Cut 7½*
2040 G155 $20 gold
2041 G155 $20 gold & multi

Intl. Year of the Ocean Type

No. 2042: a, Great black-backed gull. b, Common dolphin. c, Seal. d, Amazonian catfish. e, Shark. f, Goldfish. g, Cyathopharynx. h, Whale. i, Telmatochromis. j, Crab. k, Octopus. l, Turtle.

No. 2043: a, Dolphins. b, Seal. c, Turtle. d, Leopard shark. e, Flame angelfish. f, Syndontis. g, Lamprologus. h, Kryptopterus bicirrhus. i, Pterophyllum scalare. j, Swimming pancake. k, Cowfish. l, Sea horse.

No. 2044, Tetraodon mbu. No. 2045, Goldfish.

1998, Aug. 19 Litho. *Perf. 14*
Sheets of 12
2042 A411 75c #a.-l. 6.75 6.75
2043 A411 90c #a.-l. 8.00 8.00
Souvenir Sheets
2044-2045 A411 $6 each 4.50 4.50

Gandhi Type of 1998

Portraits of Gandhi.

1998, Sept. 15 Litho. *Perf. 14*
2046 A413 $1 multicolored .75 .75
Souvenir Sheet
2047 A413 $6 multicolored 4.50 4.50

No. 2046 was issued in sheets of 4.

Picasso Type of 1998

Paintings: 45c, Bust of a Woman, 1943, vert. $2, Three Musicians, 1921. $3, Studio at La Californie, 1956.

$5, Woman with a Blue Hat, 1901.

Perf. 14½x14, 14x14½
1998, Sept. 15
2048-2050 A414 Set of 3 4.25 4.25
Souvenir Sheet
2051 A414 $5 multicolored 3.75 3.75

Delacroix Type of 1998

Paintings - #2052: a, The Natchez. b, Christ and His Disciples Crossing the Sea of Galilee. c, Sunset. d, Moroccans Outside the Walls of Tangier. e, The Fireplace. f, Forest View with a Oak Tree. g, View of the Harbor at Dieppe. h, Arabs Skirmishing in the Mountains.

$5, Orphan Girl in a Cemetary, vert.

1998, Sept. 15 Litho. *Perf. 14*
2052 A415 $1 Sheet of 8, #a.-h. 6.00 6.00
Souvenir Sheet
2053 A415 $5 multicolored 4.50 4.50

Organization of American States Type

1998, Sept. 15
2054 A416 $1 multicolored .75 .75

Diana Type of 1998

1998 *Perf. 14½*
2055 A417 $1.50 multicolored 1.10 1.10
Self-Adhesive
Serpentine Die Cut Perf. 11½
Sheet of 1
Size: 53x65mm
2055A A417 $8 Diana, buildings

No. 2055 was issued in sheets of 6.

Soaking in water may affect the multi-layer image of No. 2055A.

Issued: $1.50, 9/15; $8, 11/5/98.

Ferrari Type of 1998

No. 2056: a, 275 GTB. b, 340 MM. c, 250 GT SWB Berlinetta SEFAC "Hot Rod."

$5, First Ferrari Cabriolet (011-S).

1998, Sept. 15 *Perf. 14*
2056 A418 $2 Sheet of 3, #a.-c. 4.50 4.50
Souvenir Sheet
2057 A418 $5 multicolored 4.50 4.50

No. 2057 contains one 91x35mm stamp.

Scout Jamboree Type of 1998

Designs: 90c, Scout sign. $1.50, Lord Baden-Powell. $5, Scout salute.

$6, Lord Baden-Powell, diff., vert.

1998, Sept. 15
2058-2060 A419 Set of 3 5.75 5.75

Souvenir Sheet

2061 A419 $6 multicolored 4.50 4.50

Royal Air Force Type of 1998

No. 2062: a, Chinook. b, BAe Harrier GR5. c, Panavia Tornado F3 ADV. d, Chinook HC2 carrying 105mm light gun.

No. 2063: a, Tornado GR1. b, BAe Hawk TIA. c, Sepecat Jaguar GRI. d, Harrier GR7.

No. 2064, Eurofighter 2000, Hunter. No. 2065, Biplane, hawk in flight. No. 2066, Head of hawk, biplane. No. 2067, Eurofighter 2000, Tornado.

1998, Sept. 15

Sheets of 4

2062-2063 A420 $2 #a.-d., each 6.00 6.00

Souvenir Sheets

2064-2067 A420 $6 each 4.50 4.50

Disney Christmas Trains — G156

Silly Symphony Railroad - #2068: a, Santa in locomotive, rabbit. b, Giraffe, elephant, tiger. c, Wolf, Three Little Pigs. d, Robin Hood blowing horn, Jiminy Cricket, penguins, children. e, Geese, Indian boy, turtle in caboose.

Mickey's Toontown Christmas Train - #2069: a, Mickey in locomotive. b, Pluto, chipmunks in coal car. c, Donald, Daisy Duck in passenger car. d, Goofy leading Huey, Dewey, & Louie in caroling. e, Minnie in caboose.

Pooh's Railroad - #2070: a, Piglet as engineer. b, Winnie the Pooh shoveling honey. c, Rabbit, Owl. d, Kanga, Roo, Christopher Robin. e, Eeyore, Tigger.

No. 2071, Santa setting up toy train under Christmas tree. No. 2072, Mickey as engineer. No. 2073, Winnie the Pooh reading paper, Rabbit, Piglet.

1998, Oct. 15 ***Perf. 14x13½***

Sheets of 5

2068-2070 G156 $1 #a.-e., each 3.75 3.75

Souvenir Sheets

2071-2073 G156 $6 each 4.50 4.50

New Year 1999 (Year of the Rabbit) Type

Various rabbits, color of country name: a, green. b, orange. c, red.

1999, Jan. 4 Litho. ***Die Cut Perf. 9***

Self-Adhesive

Sheet of 3

2074 A425 $1.50 gold & multi, #a.-c. 3.50 3.50

No. 2074b has point of triangle down.

Queen Elizabeth II and Prince Philip, 50th Wedding Anniv. — G157

Litho. & Embossed

1999, Jan. 8 ***Die Cut Perf. 7***

Without Gum

2075 G157 $20 gold & multi

Australia '99, World Stamp Expo G158

Dinosaurs - #2076: a, Troodon. b, Camptosaurus. c, Parasaurolophus. d, Dryosaurus. e, Gallimimus. f, Camarasaurus (all vert.).

#2077: a, Duckbill. b, Lambeosaurus. c, Iguanodon. d, Euoplocephalus. e, Triceratops. f, Brachiosaurus. g, Ponoptosaurus. h, Stegosaurus.

#2078, Edmontosaurus. #2079, Tyrannosaurus, vert. #2080, Halticosaurus, vert.

1999, Mar. 1 Litho. ***Perf. 14***

2076 G158 $1 Sheet of 6, #a.-f. 4.50 4.50
2077 G158 $1.50 Sheet of 8, #a.-h. 9.25 9.25

Souvenir Sheets

2078-2080 G158 $6 each 4.50 4.50

Trains G159

Designs: 15c, India, 4-4-0 express passenger and mail engine. 75c, Ireland, 4-4-0. 90c, Canada, 4-6-0. $1.50, India, 4-4-0 express. $2, Australia, 4-6-2. $3, Great Britain, Stirling 0-4-2.

No. 2087: a, Belgium, type 4-4-0. b, Sweden, class "Cc" type 4-4-0. c, Chile, 0-6-4. d, Bolivia, Fairlie-type double engine.

No. 2088: a, Belgium, 4-cylinder 4-6-0. b, England, 4-cylinder 4-6-0. c, Northern Ireland, 2-cylinder compound 4-4-0. d, Holland, 4-4-0.

No. 2089: a, Switzerland, 0-8-0. b, Ireland, 0-6-0. c, US 4-6-0. d, Great Britain, Prince of Wales class 4-2-2.

No. 2090: a, Ireland, narrow gauge 2-4-2. b, Russia, 0-8-0. c, England, Ivatt large-boilered Atlantic. d, Germany, Atlantic type express.

No. 2091: a, France, 4-6-0. b, New Zealand, 2-6-4. c, Burma, 4-4-4. d, Malaya, 4-6-0.

No. 2092, France, 4-4-0. No. 2093, Italy, 0-6-4.

1999, Apr. 12 Litho. ***Perf. 14***

2081-2086 G159 Set of 6 6.25 6.25

Sheets of 4

2087-2091 G159 $2 #a.-d., each 6.00 6.00

Souvenir Sheets

2092-2093 G159 $6 each 4.50 4.50

Flora and Fauna Type of 1999

Designs: 75c, Porkfish. 90c, Leatherback turtle. $1.50, Ruby-throated hummingbird. $2, Theope eudocia.

No. 2098, vert: a, White-tailed tropicbird. b, Laughing gull. c, Palm tree. d, Humpback whale. e, Painted bunting. f, Common grackle. g, Green anole. h, Morpho peleides. i, Prepoua meandor.

No. 2099, vert: a, Common dolphin. b, Catonephele numiti. c, Sooty tern. d, Vermilion flycatcher. e, Blue grosbeak. f, Great egret. g, Actinote pellenea. h, Anteos clorinade. i, Common iguana.

No. 2100, Bannaquit. No. 2101, Beay gregory.

1999, Apr. 26

2094-2097 A430 Set of 4 3.75 3.75

Sheets of 9

2098-2099 A430 $1 #a.-i., each 6.75 6.75

Souvenir Sheets

2100-2101 A430 $6 each 4.50 4.50

Hokusai Type of 1999

Entire paintings or details, horiz. - #2102: a, A Breeze on a Fine Day. b, Ejiri. c, Horse drawings (kicking up hind legs). d, Horse drawings (with head down). e, View Along the Bank of the Sumida River. f, Thunderstorm Below the Mountain.

No. 2103: a, Fuchû. b. Doll Fair at Fikkendana. c, Sumo Wrestlers (with arms locked). d, Sumo Wrestlers (one head butting). e, Sôjô Henjô. f, Twin Gardens Gateway of the Asakusa Kannon Temple.

No. 2104 Kôbô Daishi Exorcising Demon that Causes Sickness. No. 2105, Stretching Cloth.

1999, May 24 Litho. ***Perf. 14x13½***

Sheets of 6

2102-2103 A431 $1.50 #a.-f., ea 6.75 6.75

Souvenir Sheet

2104-2105 A431 $6 each 4.50 4.50

John H. Glenn's Return to Space G160

Portraits - #2106: a, Thumbs up, 1998 flight. b, Receiving NASA Service Award from Pres. Kennedy, 1962. c, Talking to Ground Control from Discovery, 1998. d, Climbing out of Friendship 7, 1962. e, Being checked for balance, 1998. f, Climbing into Friendship 7, 1962.

No. 2107, vert.: a, Portrait as Ohio Senator, 1974. b, Official portrait, 1962. c, Suit-up test, 1998. d, Suiting up for Discovery, 1998. e, Meeting press after Discovery flight, 1998. f, Smiling aboard Discovery, 1998. g, Medical research, 1998. h, Official portrait, 1998.

1999, May 24 ***Perf. 14x14½***

Sheets of 6 and 8

2106 G160 $1 #a.-f. 4.50 4.50
2107 G160 $1 #a.-h. 6.00 6.00

Hokusai Type of 1999

No. 2108: a, Peasants dancing under the linden tree. b, Faust dreams of soaring above the mortal.

No. 2109, Portrait of Goethe.

1999, May 24 ***Perf. 14***

2108 A432 $3 Sheet of 3, #a.-b., Grenada #2858b 6.75 6.75

Souvenir Sheet

2109 A432 $6 multi 4.50 4.50

IBRA '99 World Stamp Expo Type of 1999

IBRA '99 emblem, Luckenbach sailing ship and: No. 2110, 35c, Thurn and Taxis #1. No. 2113, $3, North German Confederation #1.

Emblem, Leipzig-Dresden Railway and: No. 2111, 45c, Schleswig-Holstein #1. No. 2112, $1.50, Oldenburg #4.

$6, Cover showing pair of Thurn & Taxis #1. Illustration reduced.

1999, May 24 Litho. ***Perf. 14***

2110-2113 A433 Set of 4 4.00 4.00

Souvenir Sheet

2114 A433 $6 multicolored 4.50 4.50

Philexfrance '99 Type

Souvenir Sheets

Designs: No. 2115, Co-co 7000 class high speed electric locomotive. No. 2116, Cha Pelon 4-8-0.

Illustration reduced.

1999, May 24 Litho. ***Perf. 14***

2115-2116 A435 $6 each 3.50 3.50

Beginning with Nos. 2117-2118, stamps from Grenada Grenadines will be inscribed GRENADA / Carriacou & Petite Martinique.

Wedding of Prince Edward and Sophie Rhys-Jones Type

No. 2117: a, Edward. b, Sophie, Edward. c, Sophie.

$6, Couple.

1999, June 18 Litho. ***Perf. 13½***

2117 A436 $3 Sheet of 3, #a.-c. 6.75 6.75

Souvenir Sheet

2118 A436 $6 multicolored 4.50 4.50

UN Rights of the Child Type of 1999

No. 2119: a, Boy. b, Liv Ullman, UNICEF's first woman ambassador. c, Woman.

$6, Maurice Pate, founding director of UNICEF.

1999, May 24 Litho. ***Perf. 14***

2119 A437 $3 Sheet of 3, #a.-c. 6.75 6.75

Souvenir Sheet

2120 A437 $6 multicolored 4.50 4.50

Queen Mother Type of 1999

Gold frames

No. 2121: a, Lady Elizabeth Bowles-Lyon. b, Queen Elizabeth in Rhodesia, 1957. c, Queen Elizabeth, Princess Elizabeth, and Princess Anne, 1950. d, Queen Mother, 1988.

$6, Queen Mother, Berlin.

1999, Aug. 16

Sheet of 4

2121 A440 $2 #a.-d. + label 6.00 6.00

Souvenir Sheet

2122 A440 $6 multicolored 4.50 4.50

No. 2122 contains one 38x50mm stamp. Margins of sheets are embossed.

See Nos. 2369-2370.

Litho. & Embossed

Die Cut Perf. 8¾

Without Gum

2122A A440a $20 gold & multi

Famous People Type of 1999

Actors - #2123: a, George Raft (1895-1980). b, Raft in movie scene. c, Fatty Arbuckle (1887-1933) in movie scene. d, Portrait of Arbuckle. e, Buster Keaton (1895-1966). f, Keaton in movie scene. g, Harold Lloyd (1893-1971) in movie scene. h, Portrait of Lloyd.

No. 2124: a, James Cagney (1899-1986). b, Cagney in movie scene. c, Edward G. Robinson (1893-1973). d, Robinson in movie scene.

$6, Charlie Chaplin (1889-1977).

1999, Aug. 20 Litho. ***Perf. 14***

2123 A426 $1 Sheet of 8, #a.-h. 6.00 6.00
2124 A426 $2 Sheet of 4, #a.-d. 6.00 6.00

Souvenir Sheet

2125 A426 $6 multicolored 4.50 4.50

Space Exploration — G161

No. 2126: a, Sputnik I. b, Explorer I. c, Telstar I. d, Marisat I. e, Long Duration Exposure Facility. f, Hubble Space Telescope.

No. 2127, vert.: a, X-15. b, Mercury Redstone 3 rocket, Freedom 7. c, Mercury Atlas 6 rocket, Friendship 7. d, Gemini 4, Edward H. White II. e, Saturn V rocket, Edwin Aldrin. f, Lunar rover.

No. 2128, Space Shuttle Columbia. No. 2129, Mars Pathfinder.

1999, Oct. 8 Litho. ***Perf. 14***

Sheets of 6, #a.-f.

2126-2127 G161 $1.50 each 6.75 6.75

Souvenir Sheets

2128-2129 G161 $6 each 4.50 4.50

Christmas Type of 1999

Christmas plants: 15c, Poinsettia. 35c, Holly. 75c, Fir tree. $3, Geranium.

$6, The Adoration of the Magi.

1999, Nov. 23 Litho. ***Perf. 13¾***

2130-2134 A444 Set of 5 4.25 4.25

Souvenir Sheet

2135 A444 $6 multicolored 4.50 4.50

Kirk Douglas (b. 1916), Actor G162

Douglas in various poses.

1999 Litho. *Perf. 13¾*

2136 G162 $1.50 Sheet of 6, #a.-f. 6.75 6.75

Souvenir Sheet

2137 G162 $6 multi 4.50 4.50

Elvis Presley G163

Presley in various poses.

1999

Sheet of 6

2138 G163 $1.50 #a.-f. 6.75 6.75

Millennium Type of 2000

Highlights of 1970s - No. 2139: a, Salvador Allende elected Pres. of Chile. b, Earth Day. c, CAT scan introduced. d, Pres. Nixon goes to China. e, Massacre at Olympics. f, Gas shortages. g, Sydney Opera House opens. h, Pres. Nixon resigns. i, New theory of black holes. j, US bicentennial. k, 1st "Test tube" baby. l, Pope John Paul II visits Poland. m, Iran's Islamic Revolution. n, Concorde makes 1st flight. o, Charles de Gaulle dies. p, Camp David agreements (60x40mm). q, Mother Teresa wins Nobel Peace Prize.

Highlights of 1300-1350 - No. 2140: a, Robert the Bruce crowned King of Scotland. b, Giotto paints frescoes. c, Mansa Musa rules Mali. d, Dante completes "The Divine Comedy." e, Noh theater developed in Japan. f, Tenochtitlan founded by Aztecs. g, Ibn Battutah journeys to Africa and Asia. h, Munich fire. i, Ivan I of Russia increases Moscow's importance. j, Hundred Years' War begins. k, First use of cannons in Europe. l, Black Death devastates Europe. m, Boccaccio begins writing "Decameron." n, Eyeglasses developed in Italy. o, Plate armor replaces chain mail. p, Grand Canal of China completed. (60x40mm). q, Migration of Maoris to New Zealand.

Sea Exploration - No. 2141: a, Ferdinand Magellan. b, Restless seas. c, Queen Elizabeth I. d, Albatrosses. e, Penguins. f, Tahiti. g, Breadfruit. h, Easter Island. i, Maori carving. j, Lobster. k, Orchid. l, Walrus. m, Kangaroo. n, The Beagle. o, Frigatebird. p, Strait of Magellan (60x40mm). q, Capt. James Cook.

2000 Litho. *Perf. 12¾x12½*

Sheets of 17

2139 A450 20c #a.-q., + label 2.50 2.50
2140 A450 50c #a.-q. + label 6.25 6.25
2141 A450 50c #a.-q., + label 6.25 6.25

Issued: #2139, 3/28; #2140-2141, 2/1.

Souvenir Sheet

New Year 2000 (Year of the Dragon) — G164

2000, Feb. 5 *Perf. 13¾*

2142 G164 $4 multi 3.00 3.00

G165

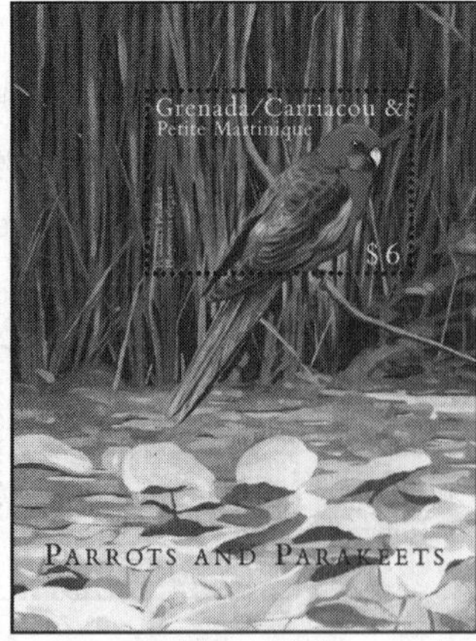

Birds — G166

Designs: 75c, Barn swallow. 90c, Caribbean coot. $2, Common moorhen. $3, Orange-winged parrot.

No. 2147: a, Red-collared lorikeet. b, Citron-crested cockatoo. c, Stella's lorikeet. d, Leadbeater's cockatoo. e, Golden conure. f, Red-spotted parakeet. g, Nobel macaw. h, Goffins cockatoo. i, Sun conure.

No. 2148: a, Turquoise parakeet. b, Scarlet-chested parakeet. c, Red-capped parakeet. d, Eastern rosella. e, Budgerigar. f, Orange-flanked parakeet. g, Mallee ringneck. h, Red-rumped parakeet. i, Yellow-fronted parakeet.

No. 2149: a, Puerto Rican emerald. b, Green mango. c, Red-legged thrush. d, Red-crowned parrot. e, Hispaniolan parrot. f, Yellow-crowned parrot.

No. 2150: a, Yellow-shouldered blackbird. b, Troupial. c, Green-throated Carib. d, Black-hooded parakeet. e, Scarlet tanager. f, Yellow-crowned bishop.

No. 2151, Puerto Rican lizard-cuckoo. No. 2152, Pin-tailed whydah, vert. No. 2153, Pennant's parakeet. No. 2154, Scarlet macaw, vert.

Illustration G166 reduced.

2000, Mar. 1 Litho. *Perf. 14*

2143-2146 G165 Set of 4 5.00 5.00

Sheets of 9, #a.-i.

2147-2148 G166 $1 each 6.75 6.75

Sheets of 6, #a.-f.

2149-2150 G165 $1.50 each 6.75 6.75

Souvenir Sheets

Perf. 13¾

2151-2152 G165 $6 each 4.50 4.50

Perf. 14

2153-2154 G166 $6 each 4.50 4.50

No. 2151 contains one 48x32mm stamp; No. 2152 contains one 32x48mm stamp.

Tropical Fish G167

35c, Slender mbuna. 45c, Pygoplite diacanthus. #2157, 75c, Siamese fighting fish. #2158, 75c, Pomacanthus semicirclatus. 90c, Zanclus canescens. #2160, $1, Dwarf pencilfish. #2161, $1, Xiphophorus maculatus. #2162, $2, Wimplefish. #2163, $2, Gramma loreto. $3, Zebrasoma xanthurum.

#2165: a, Emperor angelfish. b, Strawberryfish. c, Jackknife fish. d, Flame angelfish. e, Clarke's anemonefish. f, Flash-back dottyback. g, Coral trout. h, Foxface.

#2166: a, Bumbelbee goby. b, Black-headed blenny. c, Boarfish. d, Achilles tang. e, Swordtail. f, Moorish idol. g, Banded pipefish. h, Striped sea catfish.

#2167: a, Bodianus rufus. b, Coris aygula. c, Centropyge bicolor. d, Balistoides conspicillum. e, Poecilia reticulata. f, Heniochus acuminatus.

#2168: a, Plectorhynchus chaetodonoids. b, Bodianus puchellus. c, Acanthurus leucosternon. d, Chromileptis altivelis. e, Pterophyllum scalare f, Premnas biaculeatus.

#2169, Equetus punctatus. #2170, Harlequin tuskfish. #2171, Purplequeen. #2172, Pomacanthius imperator, vert.

2000, Mar. 28 *Perf. 14*

2155-2164 G167 Set of 10 9.00 9.00

Sheets of 8, #a.-h.

2165-2166 G167 $1 each 6.00 6.00

Sheets of 6, #a.-f.

2167-2168 G167 $1.65 each 7.50 7.50

Souvenir Sheets

2169-2172 G167 $6 each 4.50 4.50

Van Dyck Painting Type of 2000

No. 2173: a, Cardinal Bentivoglio. b, Cardinal Infante Ferdinand. c, Cesare Alessandro Scaglia. d, A Roman Clergyman. e, Jean-Charles della Faille. f, Cardinal Domenico Rivarola.

No. 2174: a, Portrait of an Elderly Woman. b, Head of a Young Woman. c, Portrait of a Man. d, Jan van den Wouwer. e, Portrait of a Young Man. f, Portrait of Everhard Jabach.

No. 2175: a, A Man in Armor. b, Portrait of a Young General. c, Emanuele Filiberto, Prince of Savoy. d, Donna Polixena Spinola Guzman de Leganes. e, Luigia Cattaneo Gentile. f, Portrait of Giovanni Battista Cattaneo.

No. 2176: a, Marchesa Paolina Adorno Brignole-Sale, 1623-25. b, Marchesa Geronima Spinola. c, Marchesa Paolina Adorno Broignole-Sale, 1627. d, Marcello Durazzo. e, Marchesa Grimaldi Cattaneo with a Black Page. f, Young Man of the House of Spinola.

No. 2176G: h, A Man in Armor. i, Portrait of a Young General. j, Emanuele Filiberto, Prince of Savoy. k, Donna Polixena Spinola Guzman de Leganes. l, Luigia Cattaneo Gentile. m, Giovanni Battista Cattaneo.

#2177, Portrait of Jacques le Roy. #2178, Hendrik van der Bergh. #2179, Frederik Hendrik, Prince of Orange. #2180, Justus van Meerstraeten. #2181, The Abbot Scaglia Adoring the Virgin and Child, horiz. #2182, Maria Louisa de Tassis, horiz.

2000, May 1 *Perf. 13¾*

Sheets of 6, #a.-f.

2173-2176 A449 $1.50 each 6.75 6.75
2176G A449 $1.50 Sheet of 6, #a-f 6.75 6.75

Souvenir Sheets

2177-2178 A449 $5 each 3.75 3.75
2179-2182 A449 $6 each 4.50 4.50

Prince William Type of 2000

No. 2183: a, Wearing scarf. b, Wearing suit with vest. c, Wearing casual shirt. d, Wearing gray suit.

$6, Wearing sweater.

2000, May 15 Litho. *Perf. 14*

2183 A453 $1.50 Sheet of 4, #a-d 4.50 4.50

Souvenir Sheet

Perf. 13¾

2184 A453 $6 multi 4.50 4.50

No. 2183 contains four 28x42mm stamps.

Zeppelin Type of 2000

No. 2185 - Ferdinand von Zeppelin and: a, LZ-3. b, LZ-56. c, LZ-88.

$6, LZ-1.

2000, May 15 *Perf. 14*

2185 A454 $3 Sheet of 3, #a-c 6.75 6.75

Souvenir Sheet

2186 A454 $6 multi 4.50 4.50

No. 2185 contains three 42x28mm stamps.

Berlin Film Festival Type of 2000

No. 2187: a, James Stewart. b, Sachiko Hidari. c, Juliette Mayniel. d, Le Bonheur. e, La Notte. f, Lee Marvin.

$6, The Thin Red Line.

2000, May 15

2187 A455 $1.50 Sheet of 6, #a-f 6.75 6.75

Souvenir Sheet

2188 A455 $6 multi 4.50 4.50

Souvenir Sheets

Olympics Type of 2000

No. 2189: a, Frantz Reichel. b, Discus throw. c, Seoul Sports Complex and Korean flag. d, Ancient Greek wrestlers.

2000, May 15

2189 A457 $2 Sheet of 4, #a-d 6.00 6.00

Public Railways Type of 2000

No. 2190: a, Locomotion No. 1 and George Stephenson. b, Rocket.

2000, May 15

2190 A458 $3 Sheet of 2, #a-b 4.50 4.50

Bach Type of 2000

2000, May 15

2191 A459 $6 Statue of Bach 4.50 4.50

G168

Butterflies and Moths — G169

No. 2192: a, Clara satin moth. b, Spanish festoon. c, Giant silkmoth. d, Oak eggar. e, Common wall. f, Large oak blue.

No. 2193: a, Jersey tiger. b, Boisduval's autumnal moth. c, Orange swallow-tailed moth. d, Regent skipper. e, Hoop pine moth. f, Coppery oysphania.

No. 2194: a, Grecian shoemaker. b, 88. c, Cramer's mesene. d, Salt marsh moth. e, Ruddy dagger wing. f, Blue night.

No. 2195: a, Heliconius charitonius. b, Tiger pierid. c, Hewiton's blue hairstreak. d, Esmeralda. e, California dogface. f, Orange theope.

No. 2196: a, Hummingbird glearing. b, Gold-drop helicopis. c, Great tiger moth. d, Staudinger's longtail.

No. 2197: a, Common map. b, Papilio machaon. c, Purple emperor. d, Red-lined geometrid.

No. 2198, Peacock royal. No. 2199, Queen Alexandra's birdwing. No. 2200, Giant leopard moth. No. 2201, Robin moth, vert.

Illustrations reduced.

2000, May 29 *Perf. 14*

Sheets of 6, #a-f

2192-2193 G168 $1.50 each 6.75 6.75
2194-2195 G169 $1.50 each 6.75 6.75

Sheets of 4, #a-d

2196-2197 G168 $2 each 6.00 6.00

Souvenir Sheets

2198-2199 G168 $6 each 4.50 4.50
2200-2201 G169 $6 each 4.50 4.50

Apollo-Soyuz Type

No. 2202, vert.: a, Thomas P. Stafford. b, Mission badge. c, Donald K. Slayton.

$6, Alexei Leonov, vert.

2000, May 15 Litho. *Perf. 14*

2202 A456 $3 Sheet of 3, #a-c 6.75 6.75

Souvenir Sheet

2203 A456 $6 Alexei Leonov 4.50 4.50

Einstein Type

Souvenir Sheet

2000, May 15 *Perf. 14¼*

2204 A460 $6 multi 4.50 4.50

Space Type

Nos. 2205: a, Foton (green and orange background). b, Sub-satellite and comet tail. c, NEAR Eros (green background). d, Explorer 16 and sun. e, Astro Challenger (green and orange background). f, Giotto (green background).

No. 2206: a, Foton and asteroid. b, Sub-satellite and asteroid. c, NEAR Eros and asteroid. d, Explorer 16 and planet surface. e, Space Shuttle. f, Giotto (blue background).

No. 2207, Lunar Prospector. No. 2208, Pegasus Saturn.

2000, May 15 ***Perf. 14***

Sheets of 6, #a-f

2205-2206 A461 $1.50 Set of 2 13.50 13.50

Souvenir Sheets

2207-2208 A461 $6 Set of 2 9.00 9.00

Nos. 2205-2206 depict different satellites, but have the same inscriptions. World Stamp Expo 2000, Anaheim.

Trains G170

Designs: 90c, Golsdorf 2-6-2, Vienna Metropolitan Railways. $1, Forrester 2-2-0, Dublin & Kingstown Railway. $2, Metro-Cammell Co-Co, Nigerian Railways. $3, TGV 001, French Natl. Railways.

No. 2213, $1.50: a, Braithwait 0-4-0, Eastern Counties Railway. b, The Philadelphia, Austria. c, Stephenson 2-2-2, Russia. d, L'aigle, Western Railway of France. e, Borsig Standard 2-2-2, Germany. f, The Ajax, Great Western Railway.

No. 2214, $1.50: a, Co-Co locomotive, Norwegian State Railways. b, Diesel-electric locomotive, Jamaica Railway. c, Diesel-electric locomotive, Railway of the People's Republic of China. d, Electric locomotive, Portuguese Railways. e, Re 6/6, Swiss Federal Railways. f, Dual-purpose Electric locomotive, Turkish State Railways.

No. 2215, $1.50: a, 4-4-0 engine, Perak Government Railway. b, 2-4-2 tank engine, Rhondda & Swansea Railway. c, 2-4-2 tank engine, Lancashire & Yorkshire Railway. d, 2-8-2 tank engine, Northwestern Railway of India. e, 4-2-2 Imperial Yellow Mail engine, Shanghai-Nanking Railway. f, 2-4-2 tank engine, Danish State Railway.

No. 2216, $1.50: a, Electric railcar, South Jersey Transit. b, Metroliner, US. c, HSST Mag-lev train. d, E60C, Amtrak. e, TEE Express "Parsifal." f, 2-Co-Co-2 electric, Amtrak.

No. 2217, $6, The Experiment, US. No. 2218, 2-8-2 locomotive, Central South African Railway. No. 2219, $6, The Prospector, Western Australian Government Railways. No. 2220, Diesel-electric locomotive, South African Railways.

2000, June 13

2209-2212 G170 Set of 4 5.25 5.25

Sheets of 6, #a-f

2213-2216 G170 $1.50 Set of 4 26.00 26.00

Souvenir Sheets

2217-2220 G170 $6 Set of 4 18.00 18.00

European Soccer Championships Type

No. 2221, horiz. - Denmark: a, Tofting. b, Team photo. c, Michael Laudrup. d, Jorgensen. e, Philips Stadium, Eindhoven. f, Moller.

No. 2222, horiz. - France: a, Thuram. b, Team photo. c, Barthez. d, Zidane. e, Jan Breydel Stadium, Brugge. f, Michel Platini.

No. 2223, horiz. - Netherlands: a, Giovanni Van Bronckhorst. b, Team photo. c, Patrick Kluivert. d, Johan Cruyff. e, Amsterdam Arena Stadium. f, Zenden.

No. 2224, Denmark coach Bo Johansson. No. 2225, France coach Roger Lemerre. No. 2226, Netherlands coach Frank Rijkaard.

2000, Aug. 8 ***Perf. 13¾***

Sheets of 6, #a-f

2221-2223 A464 $1.50 Set of 3 20.00 20.00

Souvenir Sheets

2224-2226 A464 $6 Set of 3 13.50 13.50

Popes Type

No. 2227: a, Adrian VI, 1522-23. b, Paul II, 1464-71. c, Calixtus III, 1455-58. d, Eugenius IV, 1431-47.

2000, Aug. 22

2227 A467 $1.50 Sheet of 4, #a-d 4.50 4.50

Souvenir Sheet

2228 A467 $6 Gregory IX, 1370-78 4.50 4.50

Monarchs Type

No. 2229: a, Louis XVI of France, 1774-92. b, Louis XVIII of France, 1814-24. c, Queen of Kublai Khan, China. d, Mary Tudor of England, 1553-58. e, Mohammed Ali of Iran, 1907-09. f, Ch'ien-lung (Qian-long, Hung-li) of China, 1735-96.

$6, Vladimir I, Grand Prince of Kiev, 980-1015.

2000, Aug. 22

2229 A468 $1.50 Sheet of 6, #a-f 6.75 6.75

Souvenir Sheet

2230 A468 $6 Vladimir I 4.50 4.50

Fauna G171

Designs: 75c, St. Lucia Amazon. 90c, Three-toed sloth. $1, Hispaniolan solenodon. $2,Thick-billed parrot.

No. 2235: a, Jaguarundi. b, Andean condor. c, Darwin's rhea. d, Central American tapir. e, Jaguar. f, Jamaican hutia.

No. 2236: a, Red vakari. b, San Andreas vireo. c, Golden lion tamarin. d, American crocodile. e, Spectacled caiman. f, Rhinoceros iguana.

No. 2237, Pronghorn. No. 2238, Kemp Ridley sea turtle.

2000, Sept. 5 ***Perf. 14***

2231-2234 G171 Set of 4 3.50 3.50

Sheets of 6, #a-f

2235-2236 G171 $1.50 Set of 2 13.50 13.50

Souvenir Sheets

2237-2238 G171 $6 Set of 2 9.00 9.00

The Stamp Show 2000, London (Nos. 2235-2238).

Souvenir Sheet

David Copperfield, Magician — G172

No. 2239: a, Copperfield's face at L, legs at R. b, Upper torso at L, face at R. c, Legs at L, face at R. d, Face at L, upper torso at R.

Illustration reduced.

2000, Sept. 14

2239 G172 $1.50 Sheet of 4, #a-d 4.50 4.50

Prado Paintings Type

#2240: a, St. John the Baptist and the Franciscan Maestro Henricus Werl, by Robert Campin. b, Justice and Peace, by Corrado Giaquinto. c, St. Barbara, by Campin. d, John Fane, 10th Count of Westmoreland, by Thomas Lawrence. e, The Marchioness of Manzanedo, by Jean-Louis-Ernest Meissonier. f, Mr. Storer, by Martin Archer Shee.

#2241: a, Isabella Carla Eugenia, by Alonso Sánchez Coello. b, Portrait of a Nobleman with His Hand on His Chest, by El Greco. c, Philip III, by Juan Pantoja de la Cruz. d, Madonna & child from The Holy Family with Saints Ildefons & John the Evangelist, & the Master Alonso de Villegas, by Blas del Prado. e, The Last Supper, by Bartolomé Carducci. f, Man with goblet from The Holy Family with Saints Ildefons & John the Evangelist, & the Master Alonso de Villegas.

#2242: a, Dominic of Silos, by Bartolomé Bermejo. b, Head of a Prophet, by Jaime Huguet. c, Christ Giving His Blessing, by Fernando Gallego. d, The Mystic Marriage of St. Catherine, by Alonso Sánchez Coello. e, St. Catherine of Alexandria, by Fernando Yáñez de la Almedina. f, Virgin and Child, by Luis de Morales.

#2243, The Holy Family with Saints Ildefons & John the Evangelist, & the Master Alonso de Villegas. #2244, The Last Supper, horiz. #2245, The Coronation of the Virgin, by El Greco, horiz.

2000, Oct. 19 ***Perf. 12x12¼, 12¼x12***

Sheets of 6, #a-f

2240-2242 A470 $1.50 Set of 3 20.00 20.00

Souvenir Sheets

2243-2245 A470 Set of 3 13.50 13.50

Espana 2000, Intl. Philatelic Exhibition.

Mushroom Type of 2000

No. 2246, $2: a, Cinnabar chanterelle. b, Blackening wax cap. c, Edible cort. d, Orange scaber-stalk bolete.

No. 2247, $2: a, Crab russula. b, Steel blue entoloma. c, Tiger lentinus. d, Yellow-white mycena.

No. 2248, $2, horiz.: a, Le Gal's bolete. b, Emetic russula. c, Silvery violet cort. d, Tree volvariella.

No. 2249, $6, Scaly vase chanterelle, horiz. No. 2250, $6, Common collybia, horiz.

2000, Mar. 3 **Litho.** ***Perf. 14***

Sheets of 4, #a-d

2246-2248 A448 Set of 3 18.00 18.00

Souvenir Sheets

2249-2250 A448 Set of 2 9.00 9.00

Dog Type of 2000

Designs: 45c, Irish setter. 90c, Dalmatian. $2, German shepherd.

No. 2254, $1.50: a, Alaskan malamute. b, Golden retriever. c, Afghan hound. d, Long-haired dachshund. e, Irish terrier. f, Miniature poodle.

No. 2255, $1.50: a, Great Dane. b, Newfoundland. c, Rottweiler. d, Bulldog. e, Japanese spitz. f, Bull terrier.

No. 2256, $6, Labrador retriever. No. 2257, $6, Basset hound, horiz.

2000, June 23

2251-2253 A473 Set of 3 2.50 2.50

Sheets of 6, #a-f

2254-2255 A473 Set of 2 13.50 13.50

Souvenir Sheets

2256-2257 A473 Set of 2 9.00 9.00

Cat Type of 2000

Designs: 75c, Blue point snowshoe. $3, Black and white Maine coon cat. $4, Brown tabby British shorthair.

No. 2261, $1.50: a, California spangled cat. b, Russian blue. c, Seal point Siamese. d, Black Devon rex. e, Silver tabby British shorthair. f, Tricolor Japanese bobtail.

No. 2262, $1.50: a, British white shorthair. b, Blue cream American shorthair. c, Bombay. d, Red Burmese. e, Sorrel Abyssinian. f, Ocicat.

$5, Silver classic tabby Persian, horiz.

No. 2263A, $5, Red-white bicolored British shorthair.

2000, June 23

2258-2260 A478 Set of 3 5.75 5.75

Sheets of 6, #a-f

2261-2262 A478 Set of 2 13.50 13.50

Souvenir Sheet

2263 A478 $5 multi 3.75 3.75

*2263A*A478 $5 multi 3.75 3.75

Battle of Britain Type of 2000

No. 2264: a, Women fire fighters, London. b, Family leaving after the Blitz. c, Searchlights, London. d, Winston Churchill in Coventry after German raid. e, Rescue after German bombing. f, Rescue after London bombing. g, Terror hits Buckingham Gate. h, After a German raid on Coventry.

No. 2265: a, Pilots scramble to their planes. b, Balloons to catch low-flying planes. c, Spitfire B. d, Speech by Princess Elizabeth. e, Fire Watchers, auxiliary fire service. f, Painting stripes to see at night. g, Bombed buildings in Britain. h, Air raid wardens, auxiliary police force.

No. 2266, Hawker Hurricane. No. 2267, British family survives German bombing, vert.

2000, Oct. 30

Sheets of 8, #a-h

2264-2265 A471 $1 Set of 2 12.00 12.00

Souvenir Sheets

2266-2267 A471 $6 Set of 2 9.00 9.00

Queen Mother Type of 2000

2000, Oct. 30

2268 A479 $1.50 multi 1.10 1.10

Printed in sheets of 6.

Photomosaic Type of 1999

No. 2269, $1: Various flowers making up a photomosaic of the Queen Mother.

No. 2270, $1: Various photographs with religious theme making up a photomosaic of Pope John Paul II.

2000, Oct. 30 ***Perf. 13¾***

2269-2270 A445 Set of 2 12.00 12.00

Harry Houdini, Magician — G173

2000 **Litho.** ***Perf. 14***

2271 G173 $1.50 multi 1.10 1.10

Issued in sheets of 4.

Souvenir Sheet

Barbara Taylor Bradford, Author — G174

Illustration reduced.

2000 **Litho.** ***Perf. 12¼***

2272 G174 $6 multi 4.50 4.50

Souvenir Sheet

Hong Kong Comic Strip "The Storm Riders" — G175

No. 2273: a, Character with arms folded. b, Character with sword. c, Character in brown cape. d, Character in green.

Illustration reduced.

2000 ***Perf. 13½***

2273 G175 $4 Sheet of 4, #a-d 9.00 9.00

New Year 2001 (Year of the Snake) — G176

No. 2274: a, Rat snake. b, Mangrove snake. c, Boomslang. d, Emerald tree boa. e, African egg-eating snake. f, Chinese green tree viper.

Illustration reduced.

2001, Jan. 2 ***Perf. 14***

2274 G176 90c Sheet of 6, #a-f 4.00 4.00

Souvenir Sheet

2275 G176 $4 King cobra 3.00 3.00

Rijksmuseum Type of 2001

No. 2276, $1.50: a, Person with red shirt from Dune Landcape, by Jan van Goyen. b, The Raampoortje, by Wouter Johannes van Troostwijk. c, House and horse from The Cattle Ferry, by Esaias van de Velde. d, The Departure of a Senior Functionary from Middleburg, by Adriaen van de Venne. e, Steeple and ferry from The Cattle Ferry. f, Four people near rock from Dune Landscape.

No. 2277, $1.50: a, Building, statue and dog from Garden Party, by Dirck Hals. b, Still Life with Gilt Cup, by Willem Claesz Heda. c, Cloud of smoke from Orestes and Pylades Disputing at the Altar, by Pieter Lastman. d, Buildings from Orestes and Pylades Disputing at the Altar. e, Self-portrait in a Yellow Robe, by Jan Lievens. f, Birds in sky from Garden Party.

No. 2278, $1.50: a, Beatrix from Marriage Portrait of Isaac Massa and Beatrix van der Laen, by Frans Hals. b, Winter Landscape With Ice Skaters, by Hendrick Avercamp. c, Man and woman from The Spendthrift, by Cornelis Troost. d, Men in brown from The Spendthrift. e, Men and woman from The Art Gallery of Jan Gildermeester Jansz, by Adriaan de Lelie. f, Three men from The Art Gallery of Jan Gildermeester Jansz.

No. 2279, $1.50: a, Man from A Music Party, by Rembrandt. b, Woman from A Music Party. c, Girl and boy from Rutger Jan Schimmelpennick With His Wife and Children, by Pierre-Paul Prud'hon. d, Girl from Rutger Jan Schimmelpennick With His Wife and Children. e, Two men from The Syndics, by Thomas de Keyser. f, Isaac and Beatrix from Marriage Portrait of Isaac Massa and Beatrix van der Laen.

No. 2280, $6, A Music Party. No. 2281, $6, Anna Accused by Tobit of Stealing a Kid, by Rembrandt. No. 2282, $6, Cleopatra's Banquet, by Gerard Lairesse, horiz. No. 2283, $6, View of Tivoli, by Isaac de Moucheron.

2001, Jan. 15 ***Perf. 13¾***

Sheets of 6, *#a-f*

2276-2279 A483 Set of 4 27.50 27.50

Souvenir Sheets

2280-2283 A483 Set of 4 18.00 18.00

Pokémon Type of 2001

No. 2284: a, Bellsprout. b, Vulpix. c, Dewgong. d, Oddish. e, Dratini. f, Jigglypuff.

2001, Feb. 1

2284 A484 $1.50 Sheet of 6, #a-f 6.75 6.75

Souvenir Sheet

2285 A484 $6 Pikachu 4.50 4.50

Animals of the Tropics G177

Designs: 75c, Greater flamingo, vert. 90c, Cuban crocodile. $1, Jaguarundi, vert. $2, Wedge-capped capuchin monkey.

No. 2290, $1.50, vert.: a, Cuban pygmy owl. b, Woody spider monkey. c, Bee hummingbirds. d, Dragonfly, poison dart frog. e, Red brocket deer. f, Cuban stream anole.

No. 2291, $1.50, vert.: a, Red-breasted toucan. b, Mexican black howler monkey. c, Fleck's pygmy boa. d, Red-eyed tree frog. e, Caiman. f, Jaguar.

No. 2292, $6, Ocelot, vert. No. 2293, $6, Western knight anole, vert.

2001, Feb. 1 ***Perf. 14***

2286-2289 G177 Set of 4 3.50 3.50

Sheets of 6, *#a-f*

2290-2291 G177 Set of 2 13.50 13.50

Souvenir Sheets

2292-2293 G177 Set of 2 9.00 9.00

Hong Kong 2001 Stamp Exhibition.

Fish Type of 2000 with Added WWF Emblem

No. 2294: a, Sparisoma rubripinne. b, Scarus vetula. c, Scarus taeniopterus. d, Sparisoma viride.

2001, Mar. 28 Litho. ***Perf. 14***

2294 G167 75c Strip of 4, #a-d 2.25 2.25

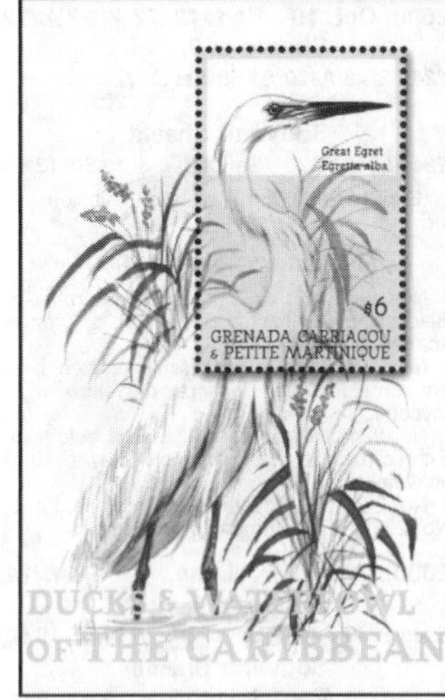

Waterfowl — G178

No. 2295, horiz.: a, Falklands streamer duck. b, Black-crowned night heron. c, Muscovy duck. d, Ruddy duck. e, Black-necked screamer. f, White-faced whistling duck.

2001, Mar. 28

2295 G178 $1.50 Sheet of 6, #a-f 6.75 6.75

Souvenir Sheet

2296 G178 $6 Great egret 4.50 4.50

Scenes From "The Littlest Rebel," Starring Shirley Temple — G179

Temple with - No. 2297, horiz.: a, Pointing soldier. b, Black woman. c, Soldier in carriage. d, Pres. Lincoln.

No. 2298: a, Spoon. b, Woman near tree. c, Soldier with hat. d, Woman. e, Black man and soldier. f, Man.

$6, Black man.

2001, Apr. 25 ***Perf. 13¾***

2297 G179 $2 Sheet of 4, #a-d 6.00 6.00

2298 G179 $2 Sheet of 6, #a-f 9.00 9.00

Souvenir Sheet

2299 G179 $6 multi 4.50 4.50

Clark Gable (1901-60) — G180

No. 2300, $1.50 - Color of photo: a, Purple. b, Sepia (wearing suit and tie). c, Yellow. d, Sepia (wearing sweater). e, Blue. f, Sepia (wearing bow tie).

No. 2301, $1.50 - Signature of Gable and Gable with: a, Cigar. b, Vest. c, Chair. d, Pen. e, Suit and tie. f, Pinstriped suit.

No. 2302, $6, Blue background. No. 2303, $6, Gable in uniform.

2001, Apr. 25 ***Perf. 14***

Sheets of 6, *#a-f*

2300-2301 G180 Set of 2 13.50 13.50

Souvenir Sheets

2302-2303 G180 Set of 2 9.00 9.00

Betty Boop Type of 2000

No. 2304 - Boop: a, With crown. b, With veil. c, With lei. d, At carnival. e, With flower in hair. f, With cowboy hat. g, With beret. h, In automobile. i, As Statue of Liberty.

No. 2305, $6, In sari. No. 2306, $6, In gondola.

2001, Apr. 25 ***Perf. 13¾***

2304 A481 $1 Sheet of 9, #a-i 6.75 6.75

Souvenir Sheets

2305-2306 A481 Set of 2 9.00 9.00

Phila Nippon Type of 2001

Designs: 75c, Scenes of Daily Life in Edo, by Choshun Miyagawa. 90c, Twelve Famous Places in Japan, by Eisenin Naganobu Kano. $1, Scenery Along the Length of the Sumida River, by Kyuei Kano. $1.25, Cranes, by Eisenin Michinobu Kano. No. 2311, $2, A Courtesan of Yoshiwara, by Shunei Katsukawa. $3, Rite of Bear Killing: Praying to the Bear's Spirit, by unknown artist.

No. 2313, $2, vert. - Bodhisattva Samantabhadra from the Lotus Sutra with: a, Surrounding rings, yellow elephant. b, White elephant. c, Temple at left. d, Surrounding rings with rays.

No. 2314, $2 (85x28mm) - Chapter illustrations from Genji Monogatari Emaki, by Ryusetsu Hidenobu Kano: a, Kiritsubo. b, Akashi. c, Hatsune. d, E-Awase.

No. 2315, $6, A Sage Pointing at the Moon, by Ranseki Takagiri. No. 2316, $6, Frontispiece for Devadatta, Lotus Sutra, vert.

2001, May 1 ***Perf. 14***

2307-2312 A487 Set of 6 6.75 6.75

Sheets of 4, *#a-d*

2313-2314 A488 Set of 2 12.00 12.00

Souvenir Sheets

2315-2316 A488 Set of 2 9.00 9.00

Marlene Dietrich Type of 2001

Dietrich with: a, Microphone. b, Robe. c, Flowered dress. d, Hat.

2001, May 15 ***Perf. 13¾***

2317 A489 $2 Sheet of 4, #a-d 6.00 6.00

Queen Victoria Type of 2001

No. 2318 - Queen Victoria with: a, Scepter. b, Flower. c, Sash.

$6, Sash, diff.

2001, May 15 ***Perf. 14***

2318 A490 $3 Sheet of 3, #a-c 6.75 6.75

Souvenir Sheet

2319 A490 $6 multi 4.50 4.50

Queen Elizabeth II Type of 2001

No. 2320 - Predominant background colors: a, Brown and yellow. b, Green. c, Blue. d, Black. e, Red and violet. f, Red and light blue.

No. 2320G: a, Green background. b, Purple background. c, Brown background.

$6, Tan.

2001, May 15 ***Perf. 14***

2320 A491 $1.25 Sheet of 6, #a-f 5.75 5.75

2320G A491 $2 Sheet of 3, #h-j 4.50 4.50

Souvenir Sheet

Perf. 13¾

2321 A491 $5 multi 3.75 3.75

No. 2321 contains one 38x51mm stamp.

Ship Type of 2001

Designs: 90c, Creole. $1, Britannia. $2, Ariel. $3, Sindia.

No. 2326, $1.25: a, William Fawcett. b, Sirius. c, S.S. Great Britain. d, Oriental. e, Lightning. f, Great Eastern.

No. 2327, $1.25: a, Santa Maria and Christopher Columbus. b, Sao Gabriel and Vasco da Gama. c, Victoria and Ferdinand Magellan. d, Golden Hind and Sir Francis Drake. e, Endeavour and Capt. James Cook. f, HMS Erebus and John Franklin.

No. 2328, $1.25, vert.: a, Mayflower. b, Gabriel. c, Beagle. d, Challenger. e, Vega. f, Fram.

No. 2329, $6, Challenge. No. 2330, $6, Cutty Sark.

2001, June 18 ***Perf. 14***

2322-2325 A497 Set of 4 5.25 5.25

Sheets of 6, *#a-f*

2326-2328 A497 Set of 3 17.00 17.00

Miniature Sheets

2329-2330 A497 Set of 2 9.00 9.00

Magician Type of Grenada Grenadines of 2000

Designs: No. 2331, $1.50, Howard Thurston. No. 2332, $1.50, Harry Kellar.

2001

2331-2332 G173 Set of 2 2.25 2.25

Issued in sheets of 4.

Mao Zedong Type of 2001

No. 2333, horiz.: a, Mao on stairs. b, Mao at right, with soldiers. c, Mao at left, with peasants. d, Mao seated, with officers.

$3, Portrait.

2001, May 15 Litho. ***Perf. 14***

2333 A493 $1.50 Sheet of 4, #a-d 4.50 4.50

Souvenir Sheet

2334 A493 $3 multi 2.25 2.25

Verdi Type of 2001

No. 2335 - Verdi and score: a, 25c. b, 75c. c, $2. d, $3.

$6, Portrait.

2001, May 15 ***Perf. 14***

2335 A494 Sheet of 4, #a-d 4.50 4.50

Souvenir Sheet

2336 A494 $6 multi 4.50 4.50

Toulouse-Lautrec Type of 2001

No. 2337, horiz.: a, Helene V. b, The Clownesse. c, Madame Berthe Bady. d, The Woman With The Black Boa.

$6, Loie Fuller at the Folies Bergére.

2001, May 15 ***Perf. 13¾***

2337 A495 $1 Sheet of 4, #a-d 3.00 3.00

Souvenir Sheet

2338 A495 $6 multi 4.50 4.50

Monet Type of 2001

No. 2339, horiz.: a, The Magpie. b, La Pointe de la Hève at Low Tide. c, Boats: Regatta at Argenteuil. d, La Grenouillère.

$6, Portrait of J. F. Jaquemart with Parasol.

2001, May 15

2339 A504 $1 Sheet of 4, #a-d 3.00 3.00

Souvenir Sheet

2340 A504 $6 multi 4.50 4.50

Orchids G181

Designs: 25c, Vanda Singapore. 50c, Vanda Joan Warne. 75c, Vanda lamellata. $2, Vanda merrillii.

No. 2345, $1.50: a, Papilionanthe teres. b, Vanda flabellata. c, Vanda tessellata (name at LL). d, Vanda pumila. e, Rhynchostylis gigantea. f, Vandopsis gigantea.

No. 2346, $1.50: a, Vanda tessellata (name at center left). b, Vanda helvola. c, Vanda brunnea. d, Vanda stangeana. e, Vanda limbata. f, Vandopsis tricolor.

No. 2347, $6, Vanda insignis. No. 2348, $6, Vandopsis lissochiloides.

2001, Oct. 15 ***Perf. 14***

2341-2344 G181 Set of 4 2.60 2.60

Sheets of 6, *#a-f*

2345-2346 G181 Set of 2 13.50 13.50

Souvenir Sheets

2347-2348 G181 Set of 2 9.00 9.00

Souvenir Sheets

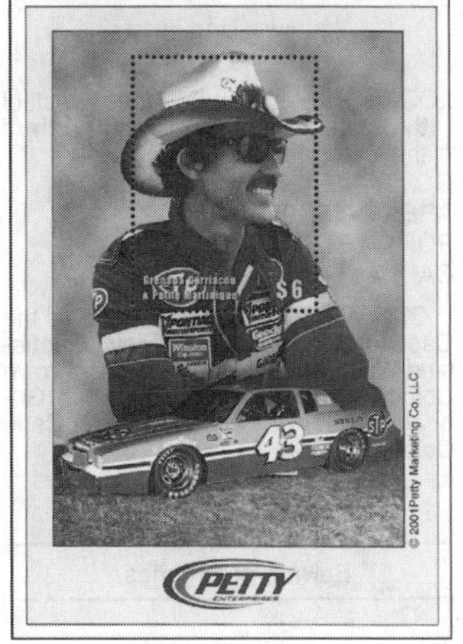

Richard Petty, Stock Car Racer — G182

Designs: No. 2349, $6, shown. No. 2350, $6, Petty speaking into microphone.

2001, Oct. 15 ***Perf. 13¾***
2349-2350 G182 Set of 2 9.00 9.00

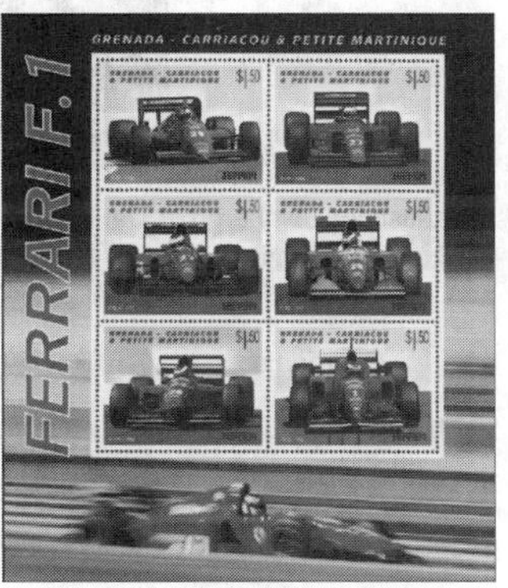

Ferrari Formula 1 Racing Cars — G183

No. 2351: a, 1986 F1 86. b, 1989 F1 89. c, 1992 F92A. d, 1993 F1 93. e, 1994 412T1. f, 1996 F310.

2001, Nov. 19 ***Perf. 13¾***
2351 G183 $1.50 Sheet of 6, #a-f 6.75 6.75

World Cup Soccer Championships Type of 2001

No. 2352, $1.50 - World Cup posters and badges from: a, 1950. b, 1954. c, 1958. d, 1962. e, 1966. f, 1970.
No. 2353, $1.50 - World Cup posters and badges from: a, 1978. b, 1982. c, 1986. d, 1990. e, 1994. f, 1998.
No. 2354, $6, World Cup poster and badge, 1930. No. 2355, $6, Head and globe from World Cup trophy.

2001, Nov. 29 ***Perf. 13¾x14¼***
Sheets of 6, #a-f
2352-2353 A505 Set of 2 13.50 13.50
Souvenir Sheets
2354-2355 A505 Set of 2 9.00 9.00

Christmas — G184

Designs: 25c, Coronation of the Virgin, by Filippo Lippi. 75c, Virgin and Child, by Mantegna. $1.50, Madonna and Child, by Masaccio. $3, Madonna and Child, by Raphael.
$6, Virgin and child Enthroned with Angels, by Mantegna.

2001, Dec. 3 ***Perf. 14***
2356-2359 G184 Set of 4 4.25 4.25
Souvenir Sheet
2360 G184 $6 multi 4.50 4.50

Royal Navy Ships — G185

Designs: 75c, HMS Renown in Portsmouth Harbor, 1922. 90c, Battle of the Saintes, 1782. $2, Battle of Trafalgar, 1805. $3, Embarkation at Dover, 1520.
No. 2365, $1.50, horiz.: a, Battle of Solebay, 1672. b, HMS Royal Prince, 1679. c, Battle of Texel, 1673. d, Battle of Scheveningen, 1653. e, Barbary Pirates, 1600s. f, Royal Charles, 1667.
No. 2366, $1.50, horiz.: a, Skirmishing preceding the Battle of the First of June. b, Moonlight Battle, 1780. c, Great ships of the Jacobean Navy, 1623. d, Battle of the Gulf of Genoa, 1795. e, Battle of the Nile, 1798. f, St. Lucia, 1778.
No. 2367, $6, Battle of Navarino, 1827, horiz. No. 2368, $6, HMS Repulse, 1924, horiz.

2001, Dec. 10 **Litho.**
2361-2364 G185 Set of 4 5.00 5.00
Sheets of 6, #a-f
2365-2366 G185 Set of 2 13.50 13.50
Souvenir Sheets
2367-2368 G185 Set of 2 9.00 9.00

Queen Mother Type of 1999 Redrawn

No. 2369: a, Lady Elizabeth Bowles-Lyon. b, In Rhodesia, 1957. c, With Princesses Elizabeth and Anne, 1950. d, In 1988.
$6, In Berlin.

2001, Dec. 13 ***Perf. 14***
Yellow Orange Frames
2369 A440 $2 Sheet of 4, #a-d, + label 6.00 6.00
Souvenir Sheet
Perf. 13¾
2370 A440 $6 multi 4.50 4.50

Queen Mother's 101st birthday. No. 2370 contains one 38x50mm stamp with a slightly darker appearance than that found on No. 2122. Sheet margins of Nos. 2369-2370 lack embossing and gold arms and frames found on Nos. 2121-2122.

Princess Diana Type of 2001
Souvenir Sheet

Diana in: a, Yellow dress. b, Red jacket. c, White pinstriped suit.

2001, Feb. 15 ***Perf. 14***
2371 A509 $1.50 Sheet of 2 each #a-c 6.75 6.75

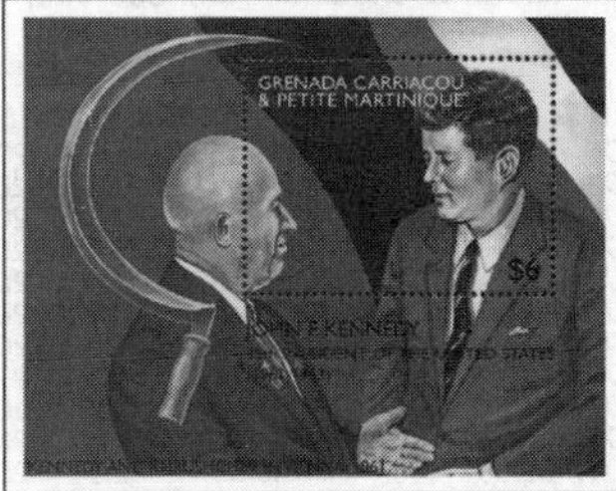

Pres. John F. Kennedy — G187

No. 2372, vert. - Pres. Kennedy: a, In boat. b, In chair. c, Profile. d, Close-up, smiling. e, Close-up. f, Looking down.
$6, With Nikita Khrushchev.

2001, Dec. 15 ***Perf. 13¾***
2372 G187 $1.50 Sheet of 6, #a-f 6.75 6.75
Souvenir Sheet
2373 G187 $6 multi 4.50 4.50

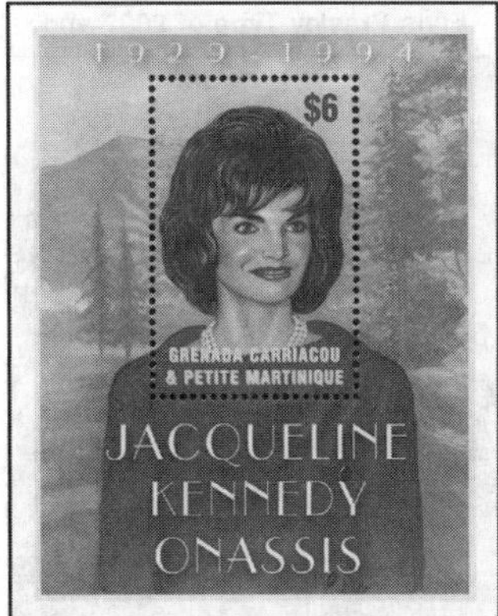

Jacqueline Kennedy Onassis (1929-94) — G188

No. 2374: a, Blue jacket, blue blouse. b, Red jacket, blue blouse. c, Green dress. d, Blue cape. e Pink and blue jacket. f, Blue jacket, yellow blouse.
No. 2375, $6, Mountain in background. No. 2376, $6, Beige background.

2001, Dec. 15 ***Perf. 14***
2374 G188 $1.50 Sheet of 6, #a-f 6.75 6.75
Souvenir Sheets
2375-2376 G188 Set of 2 9.00 9.00

G189

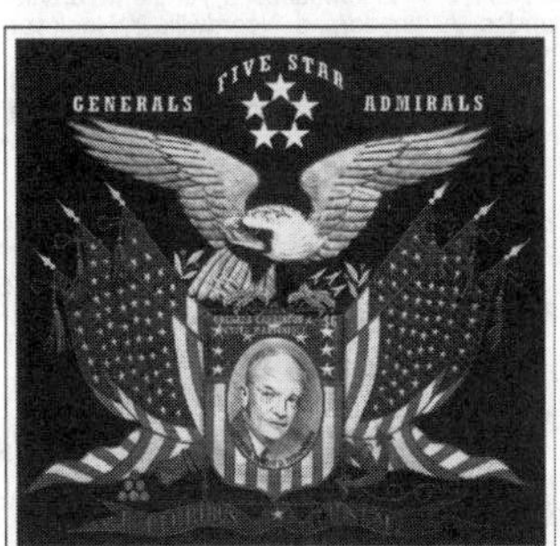

US Generals and Admirals — G190

No. 2377: a, Gen. Omar N. Bradley. b, Gen. George C. Marshall. c, Gen. Douglas MacArthur. d, Adm. William F. Halsey. e, Gen. Dwight D. Eisenhower. f, Adm. Chester Nimitz. g, Adm. William D. Leahy. h, Gen. Henry H. Arnold. i, Adm. Ernest J. King. j, Gen. George Washington. k, Gen. John J. Pershing.
No. 2378: a, Gen. George S. Patton, Jr. b, Gen. Joseph W. Stilwell. c, Adm. Thomas C. Kinkaid. d, Gen. Jonathan Wainwright. e, Lt. Gen. James H. Doolittle. f, Gen. Matthew B. Ridgway. g, Gen. Maxwell D. Taylor. h, Adm. Richmond Kelly Turner. i, Gen. Curtis E. LeMay. j, Gen. Hoyt S. Vandenberg. k, Gen. Carl Spaatz. l, Adm. Raymond Spruance.
No. 2379, $6, Eisenhower. No. 2380, $6, Douglas MacArthur.

2001, Dec. 15 ***Perf. 14***
2377 G189 75c Sheet of 11, #a-k, + label 6.25 6.25
2378 G189 75c Sheet of 12, #a-l 6.75 6.75
Souvenir Sheets
Perf. 13¾
2379-2380 G190 Set of 2 9.00 9.00

Moths G191

Designs: 75c, Pine emperor. 90c, Inquisitive monkey. $2, Oak eggar. $3, Madagascan sunset moth.
No. 2385, $1.50: a, Spanish moon moth. b, Coppery dysphania. c, Io moth. d, Large agarista. e, Millar's tiger. f, Tropical fruit-piercer.
No. 2386, $1.50: a, Indian moon moth. b, Beautiful tiger. c, Regal moth. d, Great tiger moth. e, Venus moth. f, Zodiac moth.
No. 2387, $6, Diva moth, vert. No. 2388, $6, African moon moth, vert.

2001, Dec. 17 ***Perf. 14***
2381-2384 G191 Set of 4 5.00 5.00
Sheets of 6, #a-f
2385-2386 G191 Set of 2 13.50 13.50
Souvenir Sheets
2387-2388 G191 Set of 2 9.00 9.00

Vegaspex (#2386).

Reign of Queen Elizabeth II, 50th Anniv. Type of 2002

No. 2389: a, White hat. b, Red hat. c, Tiara. d, Hatless.
$6, With Princes Philip, Charles, Princess Anne.

2002, Feb. 6 ***Perf. 14¼***
2389 A516 $2 Sheet of 4, #a-d 6.00 6.00
Souvenir Sheet
2390 A516 $6 multi 4.50 4.50

New Year 2002 (Year of the Horse) — G192

Various horses with background colors of-No. 2391: a, 75c, Light brown and light orange. b, $1.25, Light blue and olive green. c, $2, Tan and bister.
$6, Light orange and orange.

2002, Mar. 4 **Litho.** ***Perf. 13¾***
2391 G192 Sheet of 3, #a-c 3.00 3.00
Souvenir Sheet
2392 G192 $6 multi 4.50 4.50

United We Stand — G193

2002, May 21 ***Perf. 14***
2393 G193 80c multi .60 .60

Printed in sheets of 4.

Chiune Sugihara Type of 2002
Souvenir Sheets

Sugihara and: No. 2394, $6, Map of Asia. No. 2395, $6, Pink background.

2002, July 1 ***Perf. 13½x13¼***
2394-2395 A521 Set of 2 9.00 9.00

Winter Olympics Type of 2002

Montages of: No. 2396, $3, Skier in air, course flag, vert. No. 2397, $3, Skier, no flag, vert.

2002, July 1 ***Perf. 13½x13¼***
2396-2397 A522 Set of 2 4.50 4.50
2397a Souvenir sheet, #2396-2397 4.50 4.50

Intl. Year of Mountains Type of 2002

No. 2398: a, Mt. Kilimanjaro, Tanzania. b, Mt. Kenya, Kenya. c, Mauna Kea, Hawaii. d, Mt. Fuji, Japan.
$6, Koolau Mountains, Hawaii.

2002, July 1 ***Perf. 13¼x13½***
2398 A523 $2 Sheet of 4, #a-d 6.00 6.00

Souvenir Sheet

2399 A523 $6 multi 4.50 4.50

Intl. Year of Ecotourism Type of 2002

No. 2400, horiz.: a, Tourists at waterfall. b, Bird. c, Butterfly. d, Fish. e, Cactus. f, Orchid.
$6, Birds, horiz.

2002, July 1 ***Perf. 13¼x13½***
2400 A524 $1.50 Sheet of 6, #a-f 6.75 6.75

Souvenir Sheet

2401 A524 $6 multi 4.50 4.50

Scout Jamboree Type of 2002

No. 2402, horiz.: a, Campfire, Scout emblem. b, Scout with walking stick and backpack. c, Scout feeding calf. d, Girl giving Scout sign.
No. 2403, $6, Scout with hat.

2002, July 1 ***Perf. 13¼x13½***
2402 A525 $2 Sheet of 4, #a-d 6.00 6.00

Souvenir Sheet
Perf. 13½x13¼

2403 A525 $2 multi 1.50 1.50

Amerigo Vespucci (1454-1512), Explorer — G194

Various portraits with background colors of: $1, Purple. $2, Orange brown. $3, Green.
$6, Vespucci and map.

2002, July 1 ***Perf. 13½x13¼***
2404-2406 G194 Set of 3 4.50 4.50

Souvenir Sheet

2407 G194 $6 multi 4.50 4.50

Butterflies, Insects, Mushrooms and Whales Type of 2002

No. 2408, $1 - Whales: a, Sperm. b, Bottlenose. c, Sei. d, Killer. e, Humpback. f, Pygmy sperm.

No. 2409, $1 - Insects: a, Bumblebee. b, Dragonfly. c, Hercules beetle. d, Ladybug. e, Figure-of-eight butterfly. f, Praying mantis.

No. 2410, $2 - Butterflies: a, White peacock. b, Orange-barred sulphur. c, Blue night. d, Banded king shoemaker. e, Cramer's mesene. f, Common morpho.

No. 2411, $2 - Mushrooms: a, Shaggy mane. b, Shaggy parasol. c, Purple coincap. d, Sharp-scaled parasol. e, Thick-footed morel. f, Rosy-gill fairy helmet.

No. 2412, $6, Blue whale, horiz. No. 2413, $6, Dragonfly, horiz. No. 2414, $6, Blue night butterfly, horiz. No. 2415, $6, Death cap mushroom.

2002, Aug. 12 ***Perf. 14***

Sheets of 6, #a-f

2408-2411 A538 Set of 4 27.50 27.50

Souvenir Sheets

2412-2415 A538 Set of 4 18.00 18.00

Elvis Presley Type of 2002 and

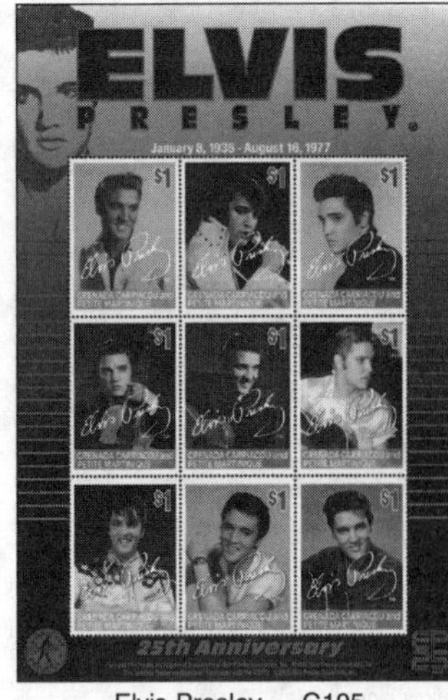

Elvis Presley — G195

No. 2416, Color portrait.

No. 2417: a, Wearing light plaid shirt. b, Holding microphone. c, Wearing dark shirt. d, Holding guitar with neck up. e, Wearing suit, holding guitar. f, Wearing short-sleeve shirt, holding guitar. g, Wearing shirt with flowers on shoulders. h, Wearing wrist watch and short-sleeve shirt. i, Wearing dark plaid shirt, holding guitar.

2002, Aug. 26 ***Perf. 13¾***
2416 A527 $1 multi .75 .75
2417 G195 $1 Sheet of 9, #a-i 6.75 6.75

No. 2416 printed in sheets of 9.

Dutch Nobel Prize Winners, Lighthouses and Women's Costumes Types of 2002

No. 2418 - Nobel Prize winners: a, Paul Crutzen, Chemistry, 1995. b, Nobel Medal for Physics, Chemistry, Physiology or Medicine, and Literature. c, Martinus J. G. Veltman, Physics, 1999. d, Hendrik A. Lorentz, Physics, 1902. e, Christiaan Eijkman, Physiology or Medicine, 1929. f, Gerardus 't Hooft, Physics, 1999.

No. 2419 - Lighthouses: a, Ameland. b, Vlieland. c, Julianadorp. d, Noordwijk. e, Hoek van Holland. f, Goeree.

No. 2420 - Women's costumes: a, Noord-Holland (woman with child). b, Overijssel (woman with blue dress and plaid neckerchief). c, Zeeland (woman with necklace).

2002, Aug. 29 ***Perf. 13½x13¼***
2418 A532 $1.50 Sheet of 6, #a-f 6.75 6.75
2419 A533 $1.50 Sheet of 6, #a-f 6.75 6.75

Perf. 13¼

2420 A534 $3 Sheet of 3, #a-c 6.75 6.75

Amphilex 2002 Intl. Stamp Exhibition, Amsterdam.

Teddy Bear Centenary Types of 2002

No. 2421 - Bear with: a, 15c, Tasseled helmet. b, $2, Black hat with red bullseye. c, $3, Hat and neck ruffle. d, $4, Gray hat.

No. 2422 - Bear with: a, 50c, Happy birthday heart. b, $1, Flower, vest, hat, and violin case. c, $2, Hat and trench coat. d, $5, Shorts.

2002, Sept. 23 ***Perf. 14***
2421 A529 Sheet of 4, #a-d 7.00 7.00
2422 A530 Sheet of 4, #a-d 6.50 6.50

Christmas Type of 2002

Carpaccio paintings: 15c, The Redeemer and the Four Apostles. 25c, The Miracle of the Relic of the Cross, vert. 50c, The Presentation in the Temple. $2, The Visitation. $3, The Birth of the Virgin.
$6, Madonna and Child and Two Angels, by Cimabue, vert.

2002, Nov. 4 ***Perf. 14***
2423-2427 A541 Set of 5 4.50 4.50

Souvenir Sheet

2428 A541 $6 multi 4.50 4.50

World Cup Soccer Matches Type of 2002

No. 2429, $1.50: a, Oliver Neuville, Eddie Pope. b, Claudio Reyna, Miroslav Klose. c, Christian Ziege, Frankie Hejduk. d, Nadal, Jung Hwan Ahn. e, Luis Enrique, Chong Gug Song. f, Park Ji Sung, Mendieta Gaizka.

No. 2430, $1.50: a, Danny Mills, Ronaldo. b, Roque Junior, Emile Heskey. c, Sol Campbell, Rivaldo. d, Lamine Diatta, Hakan Sukur. e, Umit Davala, Khalilou Fadiga. f, El Hadji Diouf, Tugay Kerimoglu.

No. 2431, $3: a, Oliver Kahn. b, Brad Friedel.

No. 2432, $3: a, Chun Soo Lee. b, Juan Carlos Valeron.

No. 2433, $3: a, David Beckham, Roberto Carlos. b, Ronaldinho, Nicky Butt.

No. 2434, $3: a, Alpay Ozalan. b, Fadiga.

2002, Nov. 18 ***Perf. 13¼***

Sheets of 6, #a-f

2429-2430 A542 Set of 2 13.50 13.50

Souvenir Sheets of 2, #a-b

2431-2434 A542 Set of 4 18.00 18.00

Dale Earnhardt Type of 2002

No. 2435: a, $2, 1980 photo. b, $2, 1986 photo. c, $2, 1987 photo. d, $2, 1990 photo. e, $2, 1991 photo. f, $2, 1993 photo. g, $2, 1994 photo. h, $4, Two cars (75x50mm).

2002 ***Perf. 13½x13¾***
2435 A518 Sheet of 8, #a-h 13.50 13.50

New Year 2003 (Year of the Ram) — G196

2003, Jan. 27 ***Perf. 14***
2436 G196 $1.25 multi .95 .95

Printed in sheets of 4.

SEMI-POSTAL STAMPS

1988 Seoul Olympics Type

1986, Dec. 1 ***Perf. 15***
B1 SP2 10c +5c Cycling .20 .20
B2 SP2 50c +20c Sailing .55 .55
B3 SP2 70c +30c Uneven Parallel Bars .75 .75
B4 SP2 $2 +$1 Dressage 2.25 2.25
Nos. B1-B4 (4) 3.75 3.75

Souvenir Sheet

B5 SP2 $3 +$1 Marathon 3.50 3.50

OFFICIAL STAMPS

Grenada Grenadines Nos. 396-408, 410, 440-442, 465-468 Overprinted "P.R.G."

1982, June ***Perf. 14, 15***

O1	G45	5c	multicolored	.20	.20
O2	G45	6c	multicolored	.20	.20
O3	G45	10c	multicolored	.20	.20
O4	G45	12c	multicolored	.20	.20
O5	G45	15c	multicolored	.20	.20
O6	G45	20c	multicolored	.20	.20
O7	G54	20c	multicolored	.20	.20
O8	G45	25c	multicolored	.20	.20
O9	G45	30c	multicolored	.20	.20
O10	G45	40c	multicolored	.25	.25
O11	CD331	40c	multicolored	.25	.25
O12	G54	40c	multicolored	.25	.25
O13	G45	50c	multicolored	.30	.30
O14	G45	90c	multicolored	.60	.60
O15	G45	$1	multicolored	.70	.70
O16	G54	$1	multicolored	.70	.70
O17	CD331	$2	multicolored	1.40	1.40
O18	G54	$2	multicolored	1.40	1.40
O19	G45	$3	multicolored	2.10	2.10
O20	CD331	$4	multicolored	2.75	2.75
O21	G45	$10	multicolored	7.00	7.00
			Nos. O1-O21 (21)	19.50	19.50

Royal Wedding stamps in changed colors, perf 15x14½ were also overprinted.

GRIQUALAND WEST

'gri-kwə-,land 'west

LOCATION — In South Africa west of the Orange Free State and north of the Orange River
GOVT. — British Crown Colony
AREA — 15,197 sq. mi.
POP. — 83,375 (1891)
CAPITAL — Kimberley

Originally a territorial division of the Cape of Good Hope Colony, Griqualand West was declared a British Crown Colony in 1873 and together with Griqualand East was annexed to the Cape Colony in 1880.

12 Pence = 1 Shilling

Beware of forgeries.

Stamps of Cape of Good Hope 1864-65 (Type I, 4p, 6p, 1sh) and 1871-76 (Type II, ½p, 1p, 4p, 5sh) Surcharged or Overprinted

Type I - With frame line around stamp.
Type II - Without frame line.

"Hope" — A1

Manuscript Surcharge in Dark Red

1874 **Wmk. 1** ***Perf. 14***
1 A1 1p on 4p blue (type I) 1,000. *1,400.*

Overprinted **G. W.**

1877 **Black Overprint**
2 1p rose 450.00 80.00
a. Double overprint *1,500.*

Red Overprint

3 4p blue (type II) 325.00 65.00

Overprinted

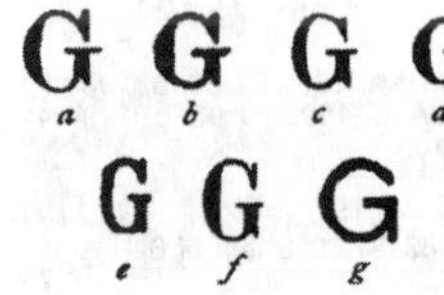

In Black on the One Penny, in Red on the Other Values

4	(a)	½p	gray black	17.00	20.00
5	(a)	1p	rose	18.00	12.00
6	(a)	4p	blue (type I)	150.00	24.00
7	(a)	4p	blue (type II)	110.00	19.00
8	(a)	6p	dull violet	85.00	21.00
9	(a)	1sh	green	110.00	18.00
a.			Inverted overprint		325.00
10	(a)	5sh	orange	400.00	22.50
11	(b)	½p	gray black	30.00	20.00
12	(b)	1p	rose	35.00	22.50
13	(b)	4p	blue (type I)	325.00	65.00
14	(b)	4p	blue (type II)		
15	(b)	6p	dull violet	160.00	37.50
16	(b)	1sh	green	200.00	30.00
a.			Inverted overprint	—	—
17	(b)	5sh	orange	—	35.00
18	(c)	½p	gray black	325.00	350.00
19	(c)	1p	rose	30.00	25.00
20	(c)	4p	blue (type I)	*1,350.*	450.00
21	(c)	4p	blue (type II)	*1,250.*	325.00
22	(c)	6p	dull violet	*1,000.*	400.00
23	(c)	1sh	green	*2,250.*	450.00
24	(c)	5sh	orange	*1,800.*	—
25	(d)	½p	gray black	22.50	*25.00*
26	(d)	1p	rose	22.50	18.00
27	(d)	4p	blue (type I)	250.00	37.50
28	(d)	4p	blue (type II)	160.00	25.00
29	(d)	6p	dull violet	125.00	27.50
30	(d)	1sh	green	175.00	22.50
31	(d)	5sh	orange	550.00	22.50
32	(e)	½p	gray black	37.50	*45.00*
33	(e)	1p	rose	37.50	29.00
34	(e)	4p	blue (type I)	350.00	70.00
35	(e)	4p	blue (type II)	250.00	42.50
36	(e)	6p	dull violet	190.00	45.00
37	(e)	1sh	green	200.00	37.50
a.			Inverted overprint		
38	(e)	5sh	orange		40.00
39	(f)	½p	gray black	40.00	*45.00*
40	(f)	1p	rose	45.00	32.50

41 (f) 4p blue (type I) 450.00 80.00
42 (f) 4p blue (type II) 300.00 57.50
43 (f) 6p dull violet 225.00 65.00
44 (f) 1sh green 250.00 45.00
45 (f) 5sh orange 925.00 50.00
46 (g) ½p gray black 25.00 21.00
47 (g) 1p rose 17.00 12.50
48 (g) 4p blue (type I) 200.00 35.00
49 (g) 4p blue (type II) 175.00 25.00
50 (g) 6p dull violet 110.00 27.50
51 (g) 1sh green 150.00 21.00
a. Inverted overprint
52 (g) 5sh orange 500.00 24.00

There are minor varieties of types e and f.

Overprinted in Black

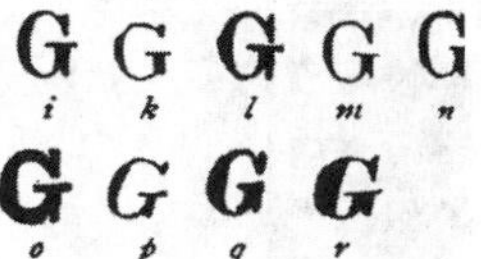

1878

54 (g) 4p blue (type II) 240.00 45.00
55 (g) 6p dull violet 375.00 85.00
56 (i) 1p rose 24.00 15.00
57 (i) 4p blue (type II) 110.00 20.00
58 (i) 6p dull violet 200.00 47.50
a. Double overprint *600.00*
59 (k) 1p rose 40.00 24.00
60 (k) 4p blue (type II) 240.00 45.00
61 (k) 6p dull violet 325.00 70.00
62 (l) 1p rose 20.00 15.00
63 (l) 4p blue (type II) 90.00 17.50
64 (l) 6p dull violet 175.00 40.00
65 (m) 1p rose
66 (m) 4p blue (type II)
67 (m) 6p dull violet
68 (n) 1p rose 60.00 *50.00*
69 (n) 4p blue (type II) 275.00 100.00
70 (n) 6p dull violet 400.00 100.00
a. Double overprint *700.00*
71 (o) 1p rose 40.00 32.50
72 (o) 4p blue (type II) 225.00 45.00
73 (o) 6p dull violet 350.00 100.00
74 (p) 1p rose 90.00 70.00
75 (p) 4p blue (type II) 425.00 100.00
76 (p) 6p dull violet 550.00 175.00
77 (q) 1p rose 55.00 50.00
78 (q) 4p blue (type II) 250.00 60.00
79 (q) 6p dull violet 350.00 125.00
80 (r) 1p rose 275.00 225.00
81 (r) 4p blue (type II) *1,350.* 375.00
82 (r) 6p dull violet *1,400.* 450.00

There are two minor varieties of type i and one of type p.

Overprinted in Red

G G
s t

1878

83 (s) ½p gray black 5.00 6.00
a. Double overprint 35.00
b. Inverted overprint 6.00 6.00
c. Double overprint, inverted 55.00
84 (s) 4p blue (type II) 225.00 100.00
a. Inverted overprint 700.00 100.00
85 (t) ½p gray black 6.00 6.00
a. Double overprint 55.00
b. Inverted overprint 6.00 *7.50*
86 (t) 4p blue (type II) 275.00 60.00
a. Inverted overprint 275.00 60.00

Black Overprint

87 (s) ½p gray black 200.00 150.00
a. Inverted overprint 200.00 *300.00*
b. With 2nd ovpt. (s) in red, invtd. 300.00
c. With 2nd ovpt. (t) in red, invtd. 110.00
88 (s) 1p rose 6.00 4.00
a. Double overprint 125.00 30.00
b. Inverted overprint 6.00 6.00
c. Double overprint, inverted 125.00 45.00
d. With second overprint (s) in red, inverted 22.50 *25.00*
89 (s) 4p blue (type I) 140.00
90 (s) 4p blue (type II) 62.50 14.00
a. Double overprint 150.00
b. Inverted overprint 110.00 60.00
c. Double overprint, inverted
91 (s) 6p dull violet 75.00 *22.50*
92 (t) ½p gray black 25.00 *30.00*
a. Inverted overprint 25.00 *35.00*
b. With 2nd ovpt. inverted 125.00
93 (t) 1p rose 6.00 5.50
a. Double overprint 60.00
b. Inverted overprint 55.00 20.00
c. Double overprint, inverted 75.00
d. With 2nd ovpt. (t) in red, invtd. 55.00 50.00
94 (t) 4p blue (type I) 125.00
95 (t) 4p blue (type II) 150.00 7.50
a. Double overprint 150.00
b. Inverted overprint 200.00 20.00
c. Double overprint, inverted
96 (t) 6p dull violet 27.50

G
Overprinted in Black

97 ½p gray black 7.00 5.50
a. Double overprint 250.00 225.00
98 1p rose 7.00 3.25
a. Double overprint 125.00
b. Triple overprint
c. Inverted overprint 75.00
99 4p blue (type II) 15.00 3.25
a. Double overprint 100.00
100 6p brt violet 75.00 6.00
a. Double overprint 425.00 140.00
b. Inverted overprint 32.50
101 1sh green 55.00 3.50
a. Double overprint 200.00 100.00
102 5sh orange 250.00 6.00
a. Double overprint 350.00 60.00
b. Triple overprint 275.00

These stamps were declared obsolete in 1880 and the remainders were used in Cape of Good Hope offices as ordinary stamps.

GUADELOUPE

ˈgwä-dəl-ˌüp

LOCATION — In the West Indies lying between Montserrat and Dominica
GOVT. — French colony
AREA — 688 sq. mi.
POP. — 271,262 (1946)
CAPITAL — Basse-Terre

Guadeloupe consists of two large islands, Guadeloupe proper and Grande-Terre, together with five smaller dependencies. Guadeloupe became an integral part of the Republic, acquiring the same status as the departments in metropolitan France, under a law effective Jan. 1, 1947.

100 Centimes = 1 Franc

Catalogue values for unused stamps in this country are for Never Hinged items, beginning with Scott 168 in the regular postage section, Scott B12 in the semi-postal section, Scott C1 in the airpost section, and Scott J38 in the postage due section.

See France Nos. 850, 909, 1280, 1913 for French stamps inscribed "Guadeloupe."

Stamps of French Colonies Surcharged

1884 Unwmk. *Imperf.*

1 A8 20c on 30c brn, *bis* 32.50 30.00
a. Large "2" 160.00 140.00
2 A8 25c on 35c blk, *org* 32.50 30.00
a. Large "2" 160.00 140.00
b. Large "5" 80.00 60.00

The 5c on 4c (French Colonies No. 40) was not regularly issued. Value $150.

c

d

1889 *Perf. 14x13½*

Surcharged Type c

3 A9 3c on 20c red, *grn* 2.00 2.00
4 A9 15c on 20c red, *grn* 17.50 17.50
5 A9 25c on 20c red, *grn* 17.00 15.00
Nos. 3-5 (3) 36.50 34.50

Surcharged Type d

6 A9 5c on 1c blk, *lil bl* 7.00 6.75
a. Inverted surcharge *700.00*
b. Double surcharge *250.00 250.00*
7 A9 10c on 40c red, *straw* 15.00 14.50
a. Double surcharge 225.00 200.00
8 A9 15c on 20c red, *grn* 15.00 13.50
a. Double surcharge 225.00 200.00
9 A9 25c on 30c brn, *bis* 22.50 18.00
a. Double surcharge 225.00 200.00
Nos. 6-9 (4) 59.50 52.75

The word "centimes" in surcharges "b" and "c" varies from 10 to 12½mm.

Issue dates: No. 6, June 25, others, Mar. 22.

1891

10 A9 5c on 10c blk, *lav* 7.50 6.25
11 A9 5c on 1fr brnz grn, *straw* 7.50 6.25

Stamps of French Colonies Overprinted in Black **GUADELOUPE**

1891 *Imperf.*

12 A7 30c brn, *yelsh* 275.00 275.00
13 A7 80c car, *pnksh* 700.00 700.00

Perf. 14x13½

14 A9 1c blk, *lil bl* 1.00 1.00
a. Double overprint 20.00 15.00
b. Inverted overprint 70.00 70.00
15 A9 2c brn, *buff* 1.50 1.00
a. Double overprint 20.00 15.00
16 A9 4c claret, *lav* 3.50 2.50
17 A9 5c grn, *grnsh* 5.00 4.00
a. Double overprint 20.00 15.00
b. Inverted overprint 80.00 80.00
18 A9 10c blk, *lavender* 8.50 7.00
19 A9 15c blue 29.00 2.50
a. Double overprint 55.00 55.00
20 A9 20c red, *grn* 25.00 16.00
a. Double overprint 140.00 140.00
21 A9 25c blk, *rose* 26.00 2.50
a. Double overprint 140.00 140.00
b. Inverted overprint 100.00 100.00
22 A9 30c brn, *bister* 24.00 18.00
a. Double overprint 140.00 140.00
23 A9 35c dp vio, *org* 52.50 40.00
24 A9 40c red, *straw* 35.00 25.00
a. Double overprint 450.00 275.00
25 A9 75c car, *rose* 87.50 75.00
26 A9 1fr brnz grn, *straw* 52.50 47.50
Nos. 14-26 (13) 351.00 242.00

The following errors may be found in all values: "GNADELOUPE," "GUADELOUEP," "GUADELONPE" and "GUADBLOUPE."

Navigation and Commerce — A7

Perf. 14x13½

1892-1901 Typo. Unwmk.

Colony Name in Blue or Carmine

27 A7 1c blk, *lil bl* .70 .55
28 A7 2c brn, *buff* .60 .55
29 A7 4c claret, *lav* .60 .60
30 A7 5c grn, *grnsh* 1.60 .55
31 A7 5c yel grn ('01) 2.00 .85
32 A7 10c blk, *lavender* 6.50 1.40
33 A7 10c red ('00) 3.50 1.25
a. Imperf. 65.00
34 A7 15c blue, quadrille paper 5.50 .55
35 A7 15c gray, *lt gray* ('00) 5.50 .75
36 A7 20c red, *grn* 4.50 2.00
37 A7 25c blk, *rose* 4.50 .75
38 A7 25c blue ('00) 65.00 65.00
39 A7 30c brn, *bister* 11.00 7.00
40 A7 40c red, *straw* 12.50 6.50
41 A7 50c car, *rose* 20.00 10.00
42 A7 50c brn, *az* ('00) 24.00 17.00
43 A7 75c dp vio, *org* 20.00 11.00
44 A7 1fr brnz grn, *straw* 20.00 18.00
Nos. 27-44 (18) 208.00 144.30

Perf. 13½x14 stamps are counterfeits.

For surcharges see Nos. 45-53, 83-85.

Nos. 39-41, 43-44 Surcharged in Black:

f

g

G & D
h 1 fr.

1903

45 A7 (f) 5c on 30c 2.00 2.00
a. "C" instead of "G" 13.00 13.00
b. Inverted surcharge 20.00 20.00
c. Double surcharge 75.00 75.00
d. Double surch., inverted 85.00
46 A7 (g) 10c on 40c 3.50 3.50
a. "C" instead of "G" 15.00 15.00
b. "1" inverted 30.00 30.00
c. Inverted surcharge 22.50 22.50
47 A7 (f) 15c on 50c 5.50 5.50
a. "C" instead of "G" 18.00 18.00
b. Inverted surcharge 57.50 57.50
c. "15" inverted 200.00 200.00
48 A7 (g) 40c on 1fr 6.50 6.50
a. "C" instead of "G" 20.00 20.00
b. "4" inverted 70.00 70.00
c. Inverted surcharge 60.00 60.00
d. Double surcharge 100.00 100.00
49 A7 (h) 1fr on 75c 22.50 22.50
a. "C" instead of "G" 75.00 75.00
b. "1" inverted 90.00 90.00
c. Value above "G & D" 175.00 175.00
d. Inverted surcharge 65.00 65.00
Nos. 45-49 (5) 40.00 40.00

Letters and figures from several fonts were used for these surcharges, resulting in numerous minor varieties.

Nos. 48-49 With Additional Overprint "1903" in a Frame

1904, Mar.

Red Overprint

50 A7 (g) 40c on 1fr 27.50 27.50
51 A7 (h) 1fr on 75c 42.50 42.50

Blue Overprint

52 A7 (g) 40c on 1fr 22.50 22.50
53 A7 (h) 1fr on 75c 45.00 45.00
Nos. 50-53 (4) 137.50 137.50

The date "1903" may be found in 19 different positions and type faces within the frame. These stamps may also be found with the minor varieties of Nos. 48-49.

The 40c exists with black overprint. Value, $200.

Harbor at Basse-Terre — A8

View of La Soufrière A9

Pointe-à-Pitre, Grand-Terre — A10

1905-27 Typo. *Perf. 14x13½*

54 A8 1c blk, *bluish* .20 .20
55 A8 2c vio brn, *straw* .20 .20
56 A8 4c bis brn, *az* .20 .20
57 A8 5c green .90 .30
58 A8 5c dp blue ('22) .20 .20
59 A8 10c rose .60 .20
60 A8 10c green ('22) .35 .35
61 A8 10c red, *bluish* ('25) .20 .20
62 A8 15c violet .25 .20
63 A9 20c red, *grn* .20 .20
64 A9 20c bl grn ('25) .20 .20
65 A9 25c blue .25 .20
66 A9 25c ol grn ('22) .20 .20
67 A9 30c black 2.50 1.50
68 A9 30c rose ('22) .20 .20
69 A9 30c brn ol, *lav* ('25) .20 .20
70 A9 35c blk, *yel* ('06) .30 .25
71 A9 40c red, *straw* .40 .40
72 A9 45c ol gray, *lil* ('07) .30 .30
73 A9 45c rose ('25) .40 .40
74 A9 50c gray grn, *straw* 3.50 1.50
75 A9 50c dp bl ('22) .50 .50
76 A9 50c violet ('25) .25 .25
77 A9 65c blue ('27) .40 .40
78 A9 75c car, *bl* .50 .50
79 A10 1fr blk, *green* 1.10 .85
80 A10 1fr lt bl ('25) .65 .60
81 A10 2fr car, *org* 1.10 .85
82 A10 5fr dp bl, *org* 3.75 3.75
Nos. 54-82 (29) 20.00 15.20

Nos. 57 and 59 exist imperf.

For surcharges see #86-95, 167, B1-B2.

Nos. 29, 39 and 40 Surcharged in Carmine or Black

a

b

1912, Nov.

83 A7 5c on 4c claret, *lav* (C) .50 .50
84 A7 5c on 30c brn, *bis* (C) .70 .70
85 A7 10c on 40c red, *straw* 1.00 1.00
Nos. 83-85 (3) 2.20 2.20

Two spacings between the surcharged numerals are found on Nos. 83 to 85.

Stamps and Types of 1905-27 Surcharged with New Value and Bars

1924-27

86 A10 25c on 5fr dp bl, *org* .35 .35
87 A10 65c on 1fr gray grn .60 .60
88 A10 85c on 1fr gray grn .60 .60
89 A9 90c on 75c dl red .60 .60
90 A10 1.05fr on 2fr ver (Bl) .35 .35
91 A10 1.25fr on 1fr lt bl (R) .20 .20
92 A10 1.50fr on 1fr dk bl .60 .60
93 A10 3fr on 5fr org brn .50 .50
94 A10 10fr on 5fr vio rose, *org* 6.00 6.00
95 A10 20fr on 5fr rose lil, *pnksh* 6.75 6.75
Nos. 86-95 (10) 16.55 16.55

Years issued: Nos. 87-88, 1925. Nos. 90-91, 1926. Nos. 89, 92-95, 1927.

Sugar Mill — A11

Saints Roadstead A12

Harbor Scene A13

Perf. 14x13½

1928-40 Unwmk. Typo.

96 A11 1c yel & vio .20 .20
97 A11 2c blk & lt red .20 .20
98 A11 3c yel & red vio ('40) .20 .20
99 A11 4c yel grn & org brn .20 .20
100 A11 5c ver & grn .20 .20
101 A11 10c bis brn & dp bl .20 .20
102 A11 15c brn red & blk .20 .20
103 A11 20c lil & ol brn .25 .20
104 A12 25c grnsh bl & olvn .25 .20
105 A12 30c gray grn & yel grn .20 .20
106 A12 35c bl grn ('38) .20 .20
107 A12 40c yel & vio .20 .20
108 A12 45c vio brn & slate .40 .40
109 A12 45c bl grn & dl grn ('40) .55 .55
110 A12 50c dl grn & org .20 .20
111 A12 55c ultra & car ('38) .40 .35
112 A12 60c ultra & car ('40) .20 .20
113 A12 65c gray blk & ver .25 .25
114 A12 70c gray blk & ver ('40) .20 .20
115 A12 75c dl red & bl grn .40 .35
116 A12 80c car & brn ('38) .25 .25
117 A12 90c dl red & dl rose 1.25 1.10
118 A12 90c rose red & bl ('39) .60 .60
119 A13 1fr lt rose & lt bl 3.00 1.50
120 A13 1fr rose red & org ('38) .55 .55
121 A13 1fr bl gray & blk brn ('40) .25 .25
122 A13 1.05fr lt bl & rose .65 .65
123 A13 1.10fr lt red & grn 1.75 1.60
124 A13 1.25fr bl gray & blk brn ('33) .20 .20
125 A13 1.25fr brt rose & red org ('39) .50 .50
126 A13 1.40fr lt bl & lil rose ('40) .30 .30
127 A13 1.50fr dl bl & bl .20 .20
128 A13 1.60fr lil rose & yel brn ('40) .30 .30
129 A13 1.75fr lil rose & yel brn ('33) 2.50 1.75
130 A13 1.75fr vio bl ('38) 3.25 2.50
131 A13 2fr bl grn & dk brn .20 .20
132 A13 2.25fr vio bl ('39) .45 .45
133 A13 2.50fr pale org & grn ('40) .55 .55
134 A13 3fr org brn & sl .25 .20
135 A13 5fr dl bl & org .40 .30
136 A13 10fr vio & ol brn .50 .40
137 A13 20fr green & mag .60 .60
Nos. 96-137 (42) 23.60 19.85

Nos. 96-97 exist imperf.
For surcharges see Nos. 161-166.
For 10c, type A11, without "RF," see No. 163A.

Common Design Types pictured following the introduction.

Colonial Exposition Issue
Common Design Types

1931, Apr. 13 Engr. *Perf. 12½*
Name of Country in Black

138 CD70 40c deep green 1.50 1.50
139 CD71 50c violet 1.50 1.50
140 CD72 90c red orange 3.00 3.00
141 CD73 1.50fr dull blue 2.50 2.50
Nos. 138-141 (4) 8.50 8.50

Cardinal Richelieu Establishing French Antilles Co., 1635 — A14

Victor Hugues and his Corsairs — A15

1935 ***Perf. 13***

142 A14 40c gray brown 5.00 5.00
143 A14 50c dull red 5.00 5.00
144 A14 1.50fr dull blue 5.00 5.00
145 A15 1.75fr lilac rose 5.00 5.00
146 A15 5fr dark brown 5.00 5.00
147 A15 10fr blue green 5.00 5.00
Nos. 142-147 (6) 30.00 30.00

Tercentenary of the establishment of the French colonies in the West Indies.

Paris International Exposition Issue
Common Design Types

1937 ***Perf. 13***

148 CD74 20c deep violet .70 .70
149 CD75 30c dark green .70 .70
150 CD76 40c car rose .90 .90
151 CD77 50c dk brn & blk .90 .90
152 CD78 90c red .90 .90
153 CD79 1.50fr ultra .90 .90
Nos. 148-153 (6) 5.00 5.00

Colonial Arts Exhibition Issue
Souvenir Sheet
Common Design Type

1937 ***Imperf.***

154 CD75 3fr dark blue 5.00 5.00

New York World's Fair Issue
Common Design Type

1939 Engr. *Perf. 12½x12*

155 CD82 1.25fr car lake .55 .55
156 CD82 2.25fr ultra .55 .55

For surcharges see Nos. 159-160.

La Soufrière View and Marshal Pétain A16

1941 Engr. *Perf. 12½x12*

157 A16 1fr lilac .40
158 A16 2.50fr blue .40

Nos. 157-158 were issued by the Vichy government in France, but were not placed on sale in Guadeloupe.

For surcharges, see Nos. B11A-B11B.

Nos. 155, 156, 113, 117 and 118 Surcharged with New Values in Black

1943 *Perf. 14x13½, 12½x12*

159 CD82 40c on 1.25fr .40 .40
160 CD82 40c on 2.25fr .75 .75
161 A12 50c on 65c .55 .55
162 A12 1fr on 90c (#117) .75 .75
163 A12 1fr on 90c (#118) .55 .55
Nos. 159-163 (5) 3.00 3.00

Type of 1928 Without "RF "

1943 ***Perf. 14x13½***

163A A11 10c bis brn & dp blue .35

No. 163A was issued by the Vichy government in France, and was not placed on sale in Guadeloupe.

Nos. 104, 106, 113 and 90 Surcharged with New Values in Black

1944 ***Perf. 14x13½***

164 A12 40c on 35c .40 .40
165 A12 50c on 25c .20 .20
166 A12 1fr on 65c .50 .50
a. Double surcharge 82.50
167 A10 4fr on 1.05fr on 2fr .90 .90
Nos. 164-167 (4) 2.00 2.00

The surcharge on No. 166 is spelled out.

Catalogue values for unused stamps in this section, from this point to the end of the section, are for Never Hinged items.

Dolphins A17

1945 Unwmk. Photo. *Perf. 11½*

168 A17 10c chlky bl & red org .20 .20
169 A17 30c lt yel grn & red .20 .20
170 A17 40c lt bl & car .60 .50
171 A17 50c red org & yel grn .20 .20
172 A17 60c ol bis & lt bl .20 .20
173 A17 70c lt gray & yel grn .60 .50
174 A17 80c lt bl grn & yel .60 .50
175 A17 1fr brn vio & grn .20 .20
176 A17 1.20fr brt red vio & yel grn .20 .20
177 A17 1.50fr dl brn & car .60 .40
178 A17 2fr cer & bl .60 .40
179 A17 2.40fr sal & yel grn 1.25 .75
180 A17 3fr gray brn & bl vio .60 .30
181 A17 4fr ultra & buff .30 .20
182 A17 4.50fr brn org & grn .60 .20
183 A17 5fr dk vio & grn .75 .35
184 A17 10fr gray grn & red vio .75 .35
185 A17 15fr sl gray & org .90 .75
186 A17 20fr pale gray & dl org 1.50 1.00
Nos. 168-186 (19) 10.85 7.40

Eboue Issue
Common Design Type

1945 Engr. *Perf. 13*

187 CD91 2fr black .30 .30
188 CD91 25fr Prussian green .70 .70

Basse-Terre Harbor and Woman A18

Cutting Sugar Cane — A19

Pineapple Bearer — A20

Guadeloupe Woman — A21

Gathering Coffee — A22

Guadeloupe Woman — A23

1947 Unwmk. Engr. *Perf. 13*

189 A18 10c red brown .20 .20
190 A18 30c sepia .20 .20
191 A18 50c blue grn .20 .20
192 A19 60c black brn .30 .20
193 A19 1fr dp carmine .60 .40
194 A19 1.50fr dk gray bl 1.10 .75
195 A20 2fr blue grn 1.25 .90
196 A20 2.50fr dp car 1.00 .75
197 A20 3fr deep blue 1.25 .90
198 A21 4fr violet 1.00 .80
199 A21 5fr blue grn 1.00 .80
200 A21 6fr red 1.00 .75
201 A22 10fr deep blue 1.00 .75
202 A22 15fr dk vio brn 1.50 1.25
203 A22 20fr rose red 1.75 1.50
204 A23 25fr blue green 3.50 2.25
205 A23 40fr red 3.75 3.50
Nos. 189-205 (17) 20.60 16.10

SEMI-POSTAL STAMPS

Nos. 59 and 62 Surcharged in Red

1915-17 Unwmk. *Perf. 14 x 13½*

B1 A8 10c + 5c rose 2.75 1.40
B2 A8 15c + 5c violet 1.90 1.50
a. Double surcharge 85.00 85.00

Curie Issue
Common Design Type

1938, Oct. 24 ***Perf. 13***

B3 CD80 1.75fr + 50c brt ultra 6.50 6.50

French Revolution Issue
Common Design Type
Name and Value Typo. in Black

1939, July 5 Photo. *Perf. 13*

B4 CD83 45c + 25c green 5.00 5.00
B5 CD83 70c + 30c brown 5.00 5.00
B6 CD83 90c + 35c red org 5.00 5.00
B7 CD83 1.25fr + 1fr rose pink 5.00 5.00
B8 CD83 2.25fr + 2fr blue 5.00 5.00
Nos. B4-B8 (5) 25.00 25.00

Common Design Type and

Colonial Artillery SP1

Colonial Infantry — SP2

1941 Photo. Perf. 13½

B9	SP1	1fr + 1fr red	.60
B10	CD86	1.50fr + 3fr maroon	.60
B11	SP2	2.50fr + 1fr blue	.60
		Nos. B9-B11 (3)	1.80

Nos. B9-B11 were issued by the Vichy government in France, but were not placed on sale in Guadeloupe.

Petain Type of 1941
Surcharged in Black or Red

1944 Engr. Perf. 12½x12

B11A	50c + 1.50fr on 2.50fr blue (R)	.40
B11B	+ 2.50fr on 1fr lilac	.40

Colonial Development Fund.
Nos. B11A-B11B were issued by the Vichy government in France, but were not placed on sale in Guadeloupe.

Catalogue values for unused stamps in this section, from this point to the end of the section, are for Never Hinged items.

Red Cross Issue
Common Design Type

1944 Perf. 14½x14

B12	CD90	5fr + 20fr ultra	.60	.60

The surtax was for the French Red Cross and national relief.

AIR POST STAMPS

Catalogue values for unused stamps in this section are for Never Hinged items.

Common Design Type

1945 Unwmk. Photo. Perf. 14½x14

C1	CD87	50fr green	1.25	.60
C2	CD87	100fr deep plum	1.75	.90

Victory Issue
Common Design Type

1946, May 8 Engr. Perf. 12½

C3	CD92	8fr redsh brn	.65	.65

Chad to Rhine Issue
Common Design Types

1946, June 6

C4	CD93	5fr dk slate grn	1.25	1.00
C5	CD94	10fr deep blue	1.25	1.00
C6	CD95	15fr brt violet	1.25	1.00
C7	CD96	20fr brown car	1.25	1.00
C8	CD97	25fr black	1.25	1.00
C9	CD98	50fr red brown	1.25	1.00
		Nos. C4-C9 (6)	7.50	6.00

Gathering Bananas — AP1

Seaplane at Roadstead — AP2

Pointe-a-Pitre Harbor and Guadeloupe Woman — AP3

1947 Unwmk. Perf. 13

C10	AP1	50fr dk brown violet	5.25	2.00
C11	AP2	100fr deep blue	6.00	2.50
C12	AP3	200fr red	7.50	3.00
		Nos. C10-C12 (3)	18.75	7.50

AIR POST SEMI-POSTAL STAMPS

Mother & Nurse with Children — SPAP1

1942, June 22 Engr. Perf. 13

CB1	SPAP1	1.50fr + 3.50fr green	.50
CB2	SPAP1	2fr + 6fr brown & red	.50

Native children's welfare fund.
Nos. CB1-CB2 were issued by the Vichy government in France, but were not placed on sale in Guadeloupe.

Colonial Education Fund
Common Design Type

1942, June 22

CB3	CD86a	1.20fr + 1.80fr blue & red	.50

No. CB3 was issued by the Vichy government in France, but was not placed on sale in Guadeloupe.

POSTAGE DUE STAMPS

D1 D2 D3

1876 Unwmk. Typeset Imperf.

J1	D1	25c black	625.	450.
J2	D2	40c black, *blue*		*20,000.*
J3	D3	40c black	750.	650.

Twenty varieties of each.
Nos. J1 and J3 have been reprinted on thinner and whiter paper than the originals.

D4

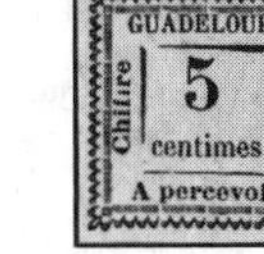

D5

1879

J4	D4	15c black, *blue*	25.00	18.00
a.		Period after "c" omitted	100.00	100.00
J5	D4	30c black	60.00	40.00
a.		Period after "c" omitted	140.00	125.00

Twenty varieties of each.

1884

J6	D5	5c black	12.50	12.50
J7	D5	10c black, *blue*	32.50	22.50
J8	D5	15c black, *violet*	57.50	40.00
J9	D5	20c black, *rose*	90.00	60.00
a.		Italic "2" in "20"	575.00	475.00
J10	D5	30c black, *yellow*	85.00	82.50
J11	D5	35c black, *gray*	27.50	20.00
J12	D5	50c black, *green*	12.50	11.00
		Nos. J6-J12 (7)	317.50	248.50

There are ten varieties of the 35c, and fifteen of each of the other values, also numerous wrong font and missing letters.

Postage Due Stamps of French Colonies Surcharged in Black

G & D
30

1903

J13	D1	30c on 60c brn, *cr*	200.	200.
a.		"3" with flat top	400.	400.
b.		Inverted surcharge	550.	550.
c.		As "a," inverted	900.	900.
J14	D1	30c on 1fr rose, *cr*	250.	250.
a.		Inverted surcharge	550.	550.
b.		"3" with flat top	500.	500.
c.		As "b," inverted	1,000.	1,000.

Gustavia Bay — D6

Avenue of Royal Palms — D7

1905-06 Typo. Perf. 14x13½

J15	D6	5c blue	.20	.20
J16	D6	10c brown	.20	.20
J17	D6	15c green	.50	.50
J18	D6	20c black, *yel* ('06)	.50	.50
J19	D6	30c rose	.60	.60
J20	D6	50c black	2.00	2.00
J21	D6	60c brown orange	1.00	1.00
J22	D6	1fr violet	2.00	2.00
		Nos. J15-J22 (8)	7.00	7.00

Type of 1905-06 Issue Surcharged

1926-27

J23	D6	2fr on 1fr gray	1.10	1.10
J24	D6	3fr on 1fr ultra ('27)	1.40	1.40

1928, June 18

J25	D7	2c olive brn & lil	.20	.20
J26	D7	4c bl & org brn	.20	.20
J27	D7	5c gray grn & dk brn	.20	.20
J28	D7	10c dl vio & yel	.20	.20
J29	D7	15c rose & olive grn	.20	.20
J30	D7	20c brn org & ol grn	.20	.20
J31	D7	25c brn red & bl grn	.30	.30
J32	D7	30c slate & olivine	.30	.30
J33	D7	50c ol brn & lt red	.40	.40
J34	D7	60c dp bl & blk	.50	.50
J35	D7	1fr green & orange	1.75	1.75
J36	D7	2fr bis brn & lt red	1.25	1.25
J37	D7	3fr vio & bl blk	.60	.60
		Nos. J25-J37 (13)	6.30	6.30

Type of 1928 Without "RF"

1944

J37A	D7	60c dp bl & blk	.20
J37B	D7	1fr green & orange	.35
J37C	D7	2fr bis brn & lt red	.35
		Nos. J37A-J37C (3)	.90

Nos. J37A-J37C were issued by the Vichy government in France, but were not placed on sale in Guadeloupe.

Catalogue values for unused stamps in this section, from this point to the end of the section, are for Never Hinged items.

D8

Perf. 14x13

1947, June 2 Unwmk. Engr.

J38	D8	10c black	.20	.20
J39	D8	30c dull blue green	.20	.20
J40	D8	50c bright ultra	.20	.20
J41	D8	1fr dark green	.35	.25
J42	D8	2fr dark blue	.70	.50
J43	D8	3fr black brown	.75	.55
J44	D8	4fr lilac rose	.80	.65
J45	D8	5fr purple	1.10	.85
J46	D8	10fr red	1.40	1.10
J47	D8	20fr dark violet	1.75	1.25
		Nos. J38-J47 (10)	7.45	5.75

GUATEMALA

ˌgwä-lə-ˈmä-lə

LOCATION — Central America, bordering on Atlantic and Pacific Oceans
GOVT. — Republic
AREA — 42,042 sq. mi.
POP. — 12,335,580 (1999 est.)
CAPITAL — Guatemala City

100 Centavos = 8 Reales = 1 Peso
100 Centavos de Quetzal = 1 Quetzal (1927)

Catalogue values for unused stamps in this country are for Never Hinged items, beginning with Scott 316 in the regular postage section, Scott B5 in the semi-postal section, Scott C137 in the air post section, Scott CB5 in the air post semi-postal section and Scott E2 in the special delivery section.

Coat of Arms
A1 A2

Two types of 10c:
Type I - Both zeros in "10" are wide.
Type II - Left zero narrow.

Perf. 14x13½

1871, Mar. 1 Typo. Unwmk.

1	A1	1c ocher	.75	*10.00*
a.		Imperf., pair	5.00	
b.		Printed on both sides, imperf.	75.00	
2	A1	5c lt bister brn	4.00	*7.50*
a.		Imperf. pair	35.00	
b.		Tête bêche pair	150.00	
c.		Tête bêche pair, imperf.	2,600.	
3	A1	10c blue (I)	5.00	*8.00*
a.		Imperf., pair (I)	45.00	
b.		Type II	8.00	*10.00*
c.		Imperf. pair (II)	60.00	
4	A1	20c rose	4.00	*7.50*
a.		Imperf., pair	45.00	
b.		20c blue (error)	125.00	125.00
c.		As "b," imperf.	*800.00*	
		Nos. 1-4 (4)	13.75	*33.00*

Forgeries exist. Forged cancellations abound. See No. C458.

1873 Litho. Perf. 12

5	A2	4r dull red vio	300.00	75.00
6	A2	1p dull yellow	150.00	100.00

Forgeries exist.

Liberty
A3 A4

A5

A6

1875, Apr. 15 **Engr.**

7 A3 ¼r black 1.00 *3.50*
8 A4 ½r blue green 1.00 *3.00*
9 A5 1r blue 1.00 *3.00*
a. Half used as ½r on cover *1,700.*
10 A6 2r dull red 1.00 *3.00*
Nos. 7-10 (4) 4.00 *12.50*

Nos. 7-10 normally lack gum.

Forgeries and forged cancellations exist.

Indian Woman — A7

Quetzal — A8

Typographed on Tinted Paper

1878, Jan. 10 ***Perf. 13***

11 A7 ½r yellow grn .75 *3.00*
12 A7 2r carmine rose 1.25 *4.00*
13 A7 4r violet 1.25 *4.50*
14 A7 1p yellow 2.00 *9.00*
c. Half used as 4r on cover *2,200.*
Nos. 11-14 (4) 5.25 *20.50*

Some sheets of Nos. 11-14 have papermaker's watermark, "LACROIX FRERES," in double-lined capitals appearing on six stamps.

Part perforate pairs of Nos. 11, 12 and 14 exist. Value for each, about $100.

Forgeries of Nos. 11-14 are plentiful. Forged cancellations exist.

For surcharges see Nos. 18, 20.

Imperf., Pairs

11a A7 ½r yellow green 50.00
12a A7 2r carmine rose 50.00
13a A7 4r violet 50.00
14a A7 1p yellow 50.00

1879 **Engr.** ***Perf. 12***

15 A8 ¼r brown & green 2.50 *2.75*
16 A8 1r black & green 2.50 *3.75*
a. Half used as ½r on cover *1,800.*

For similar types see A11, A72, A103, A121, A146. For surcharges see Nos. 17, 19.

Nos. 11, 12, 15, 16 Surcharged in Black

1881 ***Perf. 12 and 13***

17 A8 1c on ¼r brn & grn 5.00 *6.00*
a. "ecntavo," 30.00 20.00
b. Pair, one without surcharge 200.00
18 A7 5c on ½r yel grn 5.00 *7.50*
a. "ecntavos," 35.00 35.00
b. "5" omitted 100.00
c. Double surcharge 75.00 *85.00*
19 A8 10c on 1r blk & grn 7.50 7.50
a. "s" of "centavos" missing 75.00 75.00
b. "ecntavos" 40.00 *45.00*
20 A7 20c on 2r car rose 35.00 *40.00*
a. Horiz. pair, imperf. between 425.00
Nos. 17-20 (4) 52.50 *61.00*

The 5c had three settings.

Surcharge varieties found on Nos. 17-20 include: Period omitted; comma instead of period; "ecntavo." or "ecntavos."; "s" omitted; spaced "centavos."; wider "0" in "20."

Counterfeits of Nos. 17-20 are plentiful.

Quetzal — A11

1881, Nov. 7 **Engr.** ***Perf. 12***

21 A11 1c black & grn .75 .50
22 A11 2c brown & grn .50 .50
a. Center inverted 400.00 300.00
23 A11 5c red & grn 2.25 .75
a. Center inverted *3,000.* 1,300.
24 A11 10c gray vio & grn .75 .50
25 A11 20c yellow & grn .75 1.00
a. Center inverted 500.00 350.00
Nos. 21-25 (5) 5.00 3.25

Gen. Justo Rufino Barrios — A12

Black Surcharge

Correos Nacionales
25 c. 25 c.
Guatemala.
25 c. 25 c.
25 centavos.

1886, Mar. 6

26 A12 25c on 1p ver .50 .50
a. "centovos" 1.00
b. "centanos" 1.00
c. "255" instead of "25" 150.00
d. Inverted "S" in "Nacionales" 20.00
f. "cen avos" 20.00
h. "Corre cionales" 20.00
i. Inverted surcharge 75.00
27 A12 50c on 1p ver .50 .50
a. "centovos" 1.00
b. "centanos" 1.00
c. "Carreos" 1.00
d. Inverted surcharge 50.00
e. Double surcharge 75.00
f. Inverted "S" in "Nacionales" 10.00
g. "centavo" 20.00
h. "cen avos" 20.00
28 A12 75c on 1p ver .50 .50
a. "centovos" 1.00
b. "centanos" 1.00
c. "Carreos" 1.00
d. "50" for "75" at upper right 1.50
e. Inverted "S" in "Nacionales" 10.00
f. Double surcharge 75.00
g. "ales" inverted 100.00
29 A12 100c on 1p ver .75 .60
a. "110" at upper left and "á" at lower left, instead of "100" 4.00
b. Inverted surcharge 75.00
c. "Guatemala" bolder; 23mm instead of 18½mm wide 1.50
d. Double surcharge, one diagonal 100.00
30 A12 150c on 1p ver .50 .50
a. Inverted "G" 5.00
b. "Guetemala" and italic "5" in upper 4 numerals 5.00
d. Inverted surcharge 90.00
e. Pair, one without surcharge 100.00
f. Double surcharge 100.00
Nos. 26-30 (5) 2.75 2.60

There are many other minor varieties, such as wrong font letters, etc. The surcharge on Nos. 29 and 30 has different letters and ornaments. On No. 29, "Guatemala" normally is 18½mm wide.

Used values of Nos. 26-30 are for canceled to order stamps. Postally used sell for much more.

National Emblem — A13

1886, July 1 **Litho.** ***Perf. 12***

31 A13 1c dull blue 5.00 2.00
32 A13 2c brown 5.00 3.00
33 A13 5c purple 37.50 .75
34 A13 10c red 10.00 .75
35 A13 20c emerald 15.00 1.25
36 A13 25c orange 15.00 1.50
37 A13 50c olive green 10.00 2.00
38 A13 75c carmine rose 10.00 3.00
39 A13 100c red brown 10.00 3.00
40 A13 150c dark blue 15.00 3.75
41 A13 200c orange yellow 17.50 4.75
Nos. 31-41 (11) 150.00 25.75

Used values of Nos. 38-41 are for canceled to order stamps. Postally used sell for more.

See Nos. 43-50, 99-107. For surcharges see Nos. 42, 51-59, 75-85, 97-98, 108-110, 124-130.

No. 32 Surcharged in Black

Two settings:
I - "1886" (no period).
II - "1886." (period).

1886, Nov. 12

42 A13 1c on 2c brown, I 2.00 *2.50*
a. Date inverted, I 75.00
b. Date double, I 75.00
c. Date omitted, I 60.00
d. Date double, one invtd., I 100.00
e. Date triple, one inverted, I 100.00
f. Setting II 1.50 1.00
g. Inverted surcharge, II 4.00
h. Double surcharge, II 100.00

Forgeries exist.

Type I

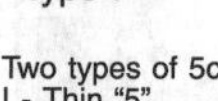
Type II

Two types of 5c:
I - Thin "5"
II - Larger, thick "5"

1886-95 **Engr.** ***Perf. 12***

43 A13 1c blue .75 .20
44 A13 2c yellow brn 2.25 .20
a. Half used as 1c on cover 100.00
45 A13 5c purple (I) 50.00 1.00
46 A13 5c vio (II) ('88) 1.50 .20
47 A13 6c lilac ('95) .60 .20
48 A13 10c red ('90) 1.50 .20
49 A13 20c green ('93) 3.00 .75
50 A13 25c red org ('93) 7.50 1.25
Nos. 43-44,46-50 (7) 17.10 3.00

The impression of the engraved stamps is sharper than that of the lithographed. On the engraved stamps the top four lines at left are heavier than those below them. (This is also true of the 1c litho., which is distinguished from the engraved only by a slight color difference and the impression.)

The "2" and "5" (I) are more open than the litho. numerals. The "10" of the engraved is wider. The 20c and 25c of the engraved have a vertical line at right end of the "centavos" ribbon.

No. 38 Surcharged in Blue Black

"1894" 14½mm wide

1894, Apr. 25

51 A13 10c on 75c car rose 4.50 4.50
a. Double surcharge 75.00
b. Inverted surcharge 100.00

Same on Nos. 38-41 in Blue or Red
"1894" 14mm wide

1894, June 13

52 A13 2c on 100c 7.50 4.25
53 A13 6c on 150c (R) 7.50 3.50
54 A13 10c on 75c 550.00 500.00
55 A13 10c on 200c 7.50 4.25
c. Inverted surcharge 75.00

Nos. 54-55 exist with thick or thin "1" in new value.

Same on Nos. 39-41 in Black or Red
"1894" 12mm wide

1894, July 14

52a A13 2c on 100c red brn (Bk) 4.00 3.50
b. Vert. pair, one without surcharge 150.00
53a A13 6c on 150c dk bl (R) 4.50 3.50
55a A13 10c on 200c org yel (Bk) 5.00 3.50
d. Inverted surcharge 100.00
e. Vert. pair, one without surcharge 150.00

Nos. 44 and 46 Surcharged in Black, Blue Black, or Red:

1894
1
CENTAVO
b

c

d

e

1894-96

56 A13 (b) 1c on 2c (Bk) .75 .30
a. "Centav" 5.00 5.00
b. Double surcharge 75.00
c. As "a," dbl. surcharge 150.00
d. Blue black surcharge 20.00 20.00
e. Dbl. surch., one inverted 150.00
57 A13 (c) 1c on 5c (R) ('95) .50 .20
a. Inverted surcharge 3.00 3.00
b. "1894" instead of "1895" 3.50 3.00
c. Double surcharge 50.00
58 A13 (d) 1c on 5c (R) ('95) .75 .20
a. Inverted surcharge 50.00 50.00
b. Double surcharge 50.00
59 A13 (e) 1c on 5c (R) ('96) 1.25 .40
a. Inverted surcharge 50.00 50.00
b. Double surcharge 50.00
Nos. 56-59 (4) 3.25 1.10

Nos. 56-58 may be found with thick or thin "1" in the new value.

National Arms and President J. M. Reyna Barrios A21

1897, Jan. 1 **Engr.** **Unwmk.**

60 A21 1c blk, *lil gray* .50 .50
61 A21 2c blk, *grnsh gray* .50 .50
62 A21 6c blk, *brn org* .50 .50
63 A21 10c blk, *dl bl* .50 .50
64 A21 12c blk, *rose red* .50 .50
65 A21 18c blk, *grysh white* 8.00 7.50
66 A21 20c blk, *scarlet* 1.00 1.00
67 A21 25c blk, *bis brn* 1.50 1.00
68 A21 50c blk, *redsh brn* 1.00 1.00
69 A21 75c blk, *gray* 50.00 50.00
70 A21 100c blk, *bl grn* 1.00 1.00
71 A21 150c blk, *dl rose* 100.00 *125.00*
72 A21 200c blk, *magenta* 1.00 1.00
73 A21 500c blk, *yel grn* 1.00 1.00
Nos. 60-73 (14) 167.00 *191.00*

Issued for Central American Exposition.

Stamps often sold as Nos. 65, 69 and 71 are copies with telegraph overprint removed.

Used values for Nos. 60-73 are for canceled-to-order copies. Postally used examples are worth more.

The paper of Nos. 64 and 66 was originally colored on one side only, but has "bled through" on some copies.

No. 64 Surcharged in Violet

1897, Nov.

74 A21 1c on 12c *rose red* 1.00 1.00
a. Inverted surcharge 30.00 30.00
b. Pair, one without surcharge 75.00
c. Dbl. surch., one invtd. 100.00

Stamps of 1886-93 Surcharged in Red

f

g

1898

75 (f) 1c on 5c violet 1.00 1.00
a. Inverted surcharge 75.00
76 (f) 1c on 50c ol grn 1.50 1.25
a. Inverted surcharge 100.00 100.00
77 (f) 6c on 5c violet 4.50 1.50
78 (f) 6c on 150c dk bl 4.50 3.25
79 (g) 10c on 20c emerald 5.00 4.00
a. Double surch., one inverted 125.00 125.00
Nos. 75-79 (5) 16.50 11.00

Black Surcharge

80 (f) 1c on 25c red org 2.00 2.00
81 (f) 1c on 75c car rose 1.50 1.50
a. Double surcharge 100.00
82 (f) 6c on 10c red 10.00 9.00
83 (f) 6c on 20c emer 5.00 4.00
84 (f) 6c on 100c red brn 5.00 4.00
85 (f) 6c on 200c org yel 5.00 4.00
a. Inverted surcharge 50.00 50.00
Nos. 80-85 (6) 28.50 24.50

Information that we have see indicates that No. 77 inverted and double surcharges are counterfeits.

National Emblem
A24 A25

Revenue Stamp Overprinted or Surcharged in Carmine

Perf. 12, 12x14, 14x12

1898, Oct. 8 **Litho.**

86 A24 1c dark blue .75 .50
a. Inverted overprint 12.50 12.50
87 A24 2c on 1c dk bl 1.00 .50
a. Inverted surcharge 12.50 12.50

Counterfeits exist.

See type A26.

Revenue Stamps Surcharged in Carmine

1898 Engr. *Perf. 12½ to 16*

88 A25 1c on 10c bl gray .75 .75
a. "ENTAVO" 5.00 5.00
89 A25 2c on 5c pur 1.25 1.00
90 A25 2c on 10c bl gray 6.50 *7.00*
a. Double surch., car & blk 100.00 75.00
91 A25 2c on 50c dp bl 8.00 *9.00*
a. Double surch., car & blk 100.00 100.00
Nos. 88-91 (4) 16.50 *17.75*

Black Surcharge

92 A25 2c on 1c lil rose 3.50 2.00
93 A25 2c on 25c red 7.50 8.00
94 A25 6c on 1p purple 4.00 4.50
95 A25 6c on 5p gray vio 7.50 7.50
96 A25 6c on 10p emer 7.50 7.50
Nos. 92-96 (5) 30.00 29.50

Nos. 88 and 90 are found in shades ranging from Prussian blue to slate blue.

Varieties other than those listed are bogus. Counterfeits exist of No. 92.

Soaking in water causes marked fading.

See type A27.

No. 46 Surcharged in Red

1899, Sept. *Perf. 12*

97 A13 1c on 5c violet .40 .25
a. Inverted surcharge 7.50 7.50
b. Double surcharge 15.00 15.00
c. Double surcharge, one inverted 15.00 15.00

No. 48 Surcharged in Black

1900, Jan.

98 A13 1c on 10c red .50 .50
a. Inverted surcharge 10.00 10.00
b. Double surcharge 75.00 75.00

Quetzal Type of 1886

1900-02 Engr.

99 A13 1c dark green .60 .25
100 A13 2c carmine .60 .25
101 A13 5c blue (II) 2.25 1.25
102 A13 6c lt green .75 .25
103 A13 10c bister brown 7.50 1.00
104 A13 20c purple 7.50 7.50
105 A13 20c bister brn ('02) 7.50 7.50
106 A13 25c yellow 7.50 7.50
107 A13 25c blue green ('02) 7.50 7.50
Nos. 99-107 (9) 41.70 33.00

No. 49 Surcharged in Black

1901, May

108 A13 1c on 20c green .50 .50
a. Inverted surcharge 20.00 20.00
b. Double surch., one diagonal 50.00
109 A13 2c on 20c green 1.50 1.50

No. 50 Surcharged in Black

1901, Apr.

110 A13 1c on 25c red org .60 .60
a. Inverted surcharge 25.00 25.00
b. Double surcharge 50.00 50.00

A26

A27

Revenue Stamps Surcharged in Carmine or Black

1902, July *Perf. 12, 14x12, 12x14*

111 A26 1c on 1c dk blue 1.00 1.00
a. Double surcharge 20.00
b. Inverted surcharge 20.00
112 A26 2c on 1c dk blue 1.00 1.00
a. Double surcharge 75.00
b. Inverted surcharge 25.00

Perf. 14, 15

113 A27 6c on 25c red (Bk) 2.00 2.50
a. Double surch., one invtd. 75.00 75.00
Nos. 111-113 (3) 4.00 4.50

National Emblem — A28

Statue of Justo Rufino Barrios — A29

"La Reforma" Palace — A30

Temple of Minerva — A31

Lake Amatitlán — A32

Cathedral in Guatemala — A33

Columbus Theater — A34

Artillery Barracks — A35

Monument to Columbus — A36

School for Indians — A37

1902 Engr. *Perf. 12 to 16*

114 A28 1c grn & claret .20 .20
a. Horiz. pair, imperf. vert. 100.00
115 A29 2c lake & blk .20 .20
a. Horiz. or vert. pair, imperf. btwn. 150.00
116 A30 5c blue & blk .20 .20
a. 5c ultra & blk .60 .20
b. Imperf., pair 100.00 100.00
c. Horiz. pair, imperf. vert. 100.00
117 A31 6c bister & grn .20 .20
a. Horiz. pair, imperf. btwn. 150.00
118 A32 10c orange & bl .25 .20
a. Horiz. pair, imperf. vert. 100.00
119 A33 20c rose lil & blk .40 .20
a. Horiz. pair, imperf. vert. 100.00
120 A34 50c red brn & bl .30 .20
a. Vert. pair, imperf. btwn. 350.00
121 A35 75c gray lil & blk .30 .20
a. Horiz. pair, imperf. btwn. 150.00
b. Horiz. pair, imperf. vert. 100.00
122 A36 1p brown & blk .55 .20
a. Horiz. pair, imperf. btwn. 150.00
123 A37 2p ver & blk .65 .40
Nos. 114-123 (10) 3.25 2.20

See Nos. 210, 212-214, 219, 223, 239-241, 243. For overprints and surcharges see Nos. 133, 135-139, 144-157, 168, 170-171, 178, 192-194, 298-299, 301, C19, C27, C123.

Issues of 1886-1900 Surcharged in Black or Carmine

1903, Apr. 18 *Perf. 12*

124 A13 25c on 1c dk grn 1.25 .50
a. Inverted surcharge 40.00 40.00
125 A13 25c on 2c carmine 1.50 .50
126 A13 25c on 6c lt grn 2.50 1.75
a. Inverted surcharge 40.00 40.00
127 A13 25c on 10c bis brn 7.50 7.00
128 A13 25c on 75c rose 10.00 10.00
129 A13 25c on 150c dk bl (C) 9.00 9.00
130 A13 25c on 200c yellow 10.00 10.00
Nos. 124-130 (7) 41.75 38.75

Forgeries and bogus varieties exist.

Declaration of Independence A38

1907, Jan. 1 *Perf. 13½ to 15*

132 A38 12½c ultra & blk .25 .20
a. Horiz. pair, imperf. btwn. 150.00

For surcharge see No. 134.

Nos. 118, 119 and 132 Surcharged in Black or Red

1908, May

133 A32 1c on 10c org & bl .30 .25
a. Double surcharge 25.00
b. Inverted surcharge 15.00 15.00
c. Pair, one without surcharge 50.00
134 A38 2c on 12½c ultra & blk (R) .25 .25
a. Horiz. or vert. pair, imperf. btwn. 100.00
b. Inverted surcharge 15.00 10.00
c. Double surcharge 30.00
135 A33 6c on 20c rose lil & blk .45 .25
a. Inverted surcharge 20.00 20.00
Nos. 133-135 (3) 1.00 .75

Similar Surcharge, Dated 1909, in Red or Black on Nos. 121 and 120

1909, Apr.

136 A35 2c on 75c (R) .50 .50
137 A34 6c on 50c (R) 50.00 50.00
a. Double surcharge 100.00 100.00
138 A34 6c on 50c (Bk) .30 .30
Nos. 136-138 (3) 50.80 50.80

Counterfeits exist of Nos. 137, 137a.

No. 123 Surcharged in Black

139 A37 12½c on 2p ver & blk .30 .30
a. Inverted surcharge 25.00 25.00
b. Period omitted after "1909" 12.50 12.50

Counterfeits exist.

Gen. Miguel García Granados, Birth Cent. (in 1909) — A39

1910, Feb. 11 *Perf. 14*

140 A39 6c bis & indigo .50 .40
a. Imperf., pair 50.00

Some sheets used for this issue contained a two-line watermark, "SPECIAL POSTAGE PAPER / LONDON." For surcharge see No. 143.

General Post Office — A40

Pres. Manuel Estrada Cabrera — A41

1911, June *Perf. 12*

141 A40 25c bl & blk .50 .20
a. Center inverted *1,750.* 900.00
142 A41 5p red & blk .65 .65
a. Center inverted 30.00 27.50

Nos. 116, 118 and 140 Surcharged in Black or Red:

h

i

j

1911 ***Perf. 14***

143 A39 (h) 1c on 6c 20.00 7.50
a. Double surcharge 75.00 75.00
144 A30 (i) 2c on 5c (R) 1.50 .75
145 A32 (j) 6c on 10c 1.25 1.25
a. Double surcharge 50.00
Nos. 143-145 (3) 22.75 9.50

See watermark note after No. 140. Forgeries exist.

Nos. 119-121 Surcharged in Black:

k

l

m

1912, Sept.

147 A33 (k) 1c on 20c .30 .30
a. Inverted surcharge 12.50 12.50
b. Double surcharge 15.00 15.00
148 A34 (l) 2c on 50c .30 .30
a. Inverted surcharge 12.50 12.50
b. Double surcharge 12.50
c. Double inverted surcharge 25.00
149 A35 (m) 5c on 75c .75 .75
a. "191" for "1912" 7.50 7.50
b. Double surcharge 15.00 15.00
c. Inverted surcharge 10.00
Nos. 147-149 (3) 1.35 1.35

Forgeries exist.

Nos. 120, 122 and 123 Surcharged in Blue, Green or Black:

n

o

p

1913, July

151 A34 (n) 1c on 50c (Bl) .25 .25
a. Inverted surcharge 10.00
b. Double surcharge 17.50
c. Horiz. pair, imperf. btwn. 100.00

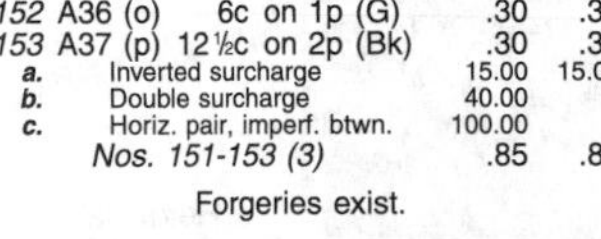

152 A36 (o) 6c on 1p (G) .30 .30
153 A37 (p) 12½c on 2p (Bk) .30 .30
a. Inverted surcharge 15.00 15.00
b. Double surcharge 40.00
c. Horiz. pair, imperf. btwn. 100.00
Nos. 151-153 (3) .85 .85

Forgeries exist.

Nos. 114 and 115 Surcharged in Black:

q

r

s

t

1916-17

154 A28 (q) 2c on 1c ('17) .20 .20
155 A28 (r) 6c on 1c .20 .20
156 A28 (s) 12½c on 1c .20 .20
157 A29 (t) 25c on 2c .20 .20
Nos. 154-157 (4) .80 .80

Numerous errors of value and color, inverted and double surcharges and similar varieties are in the market. They were not regularly issued, but were surreptitiously made and sold.

Counterfeit surcharges abound.

"Liberty" and President Estrada Cabrera — A51

Estrada Cabrera and Quetzal — A52

1917, Mar. 15 ***Perf. 14, 15***

158 A51 25c dp blue & brown .25 .20

Re-election of President Estrada Cabrera.

1918 ***Perf. 12***

161 A52 1.50p dark blue .25 .20

Radio Station — A54

"Joaquina" Maternity Hospital — A55

"Estrada Cabrera" Vocational School — A56

National Emblem — A57

1919, May 3 ***Perf. 14, 15***

162 A54 30c red & blk 2.00 .75
163 A55 60c ol grn & blk .75 .50
164 A56 90c red brn & blk .75 .75
165 A57 3p dp grn & blk 1.75 .50
Nos. 162-165 (4) 5.25 2.50

See Nos. 215, 227. For surcharges see Nos. 166-167, 179-185, 188, 195-198, 245-246, C8-C11, C21-C22.

No. 162 Surcharged

Blue Overprint and Black Surcharge

1920, Jan. **Unwmk.**

166 A54 2c on 30c red & blk .25 .25
a. Inverted surcharge 12.50 12.50
b. "1920" double 10.00 10.00
c. "1920" omitted 15.00 15.00
d. "2 centavos" omitted 20.00
e. Imperf, pair 100.00
f. Pair, imperf. btwn. 100.00

Nos. 123 and 163 Surcharged:

u

v

1920

167 A55 2c on 60c (Bk & R) .25 .25
a. Inverted surcharge 10.00 10.00
b. "1920" inverted 7.50 7.50
c. "1920" omitted 10.00 10.00
d. "1920" only 10.00
e. Double surcharge 25.00
168 A37 25c on 2p (Bk) .30 .25
a. "35" for "25" 10.00 10.00
b. Large "5" in "25" 10.00 10.00
c. Inverted surcharge 15.00 15.00
d. Double surcharge 25.00

A61

1920

169 A61 25c green .25 .20
a. Double overprint 50.00
b. Double overprint, inverted 75.00

See types A65-A66.

No. 119 Surcharged

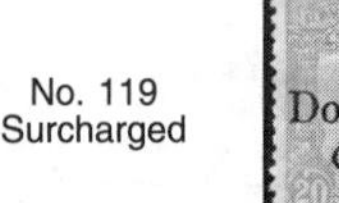

1921, Apr.

170 A33 12½c on 20c .25 .20
a. Double surcharge 15.00
b. Inverted surcharge 15.00

No. 121 Surcharged

1921, Apr.

171 A35 50c on 75c lil & blk .40 .30
a. Double surcharge 22.50
b. Inverted surcharge 25.00 25.00

Mayan Stele at Quiriguá — A62

Monument to President Granados — A63

"La Penitenciaria" Bridge — A64

1921, Sept. 1 ***Perf. 13½, 14, 15***

172 A62 1.50p blue & org .75 .25
173 A63 5p brown & grn 2.50 1.25
174 A64 15p black & ver 9.00 5.00
Nos. 172-174 (3) 12.25 6.50

See Nos. 216, 228, 229. For surcharges see Nos. 186-187, 189-191, 199-201, 207, 231, 247-251, C1-C5, C12, C23-C24.

A65

A66

Telegraph Stamps Overprinted or Surcharged in Black or Red

1921 ***Perf. 14***

175 A65 25c green .25 .20
176 A66 12½c on 25c grn (R) .20 .20
177 A66 12½c on 25c grn 15.00 15.00
Nos. 175-177 (3) 15.45 15.40

Nos. 119, 163 and 164 Surcharged in Black or Red:

w

x

1922, Mar.

178 A33(w) 12½c on 20c .20 .20
a. Inverted surcharge 10.00
179 A55(w) 12½c on 60c (R) .50 .50
a. Inverted surcharge 25.00
180 A56(w) 12½c on 90c .50 .50
a. Inverted surcharge 25.00
181 A55(x) 25c on 60c 1.00 1.00
a. Inverted surcharge 20.00
182 A55(x) 25c on 60c (R) 125.00 125.00
183 A56(x) 25c on 90c 1.00 1.00
a. Inverted surcharge 25.00
184 A56(x) 25c on 90c (R) 4.00 4.00
Nos. 178-181,183-184 (6) 7.20 7.20

Counterfeits exist.

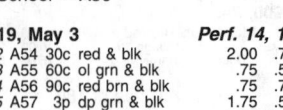

Nos. 165, 173-174 Surcharged in Red or Dark Blue

1922, May

185 A57 12½c on 3p grn & blk (R) .20 .20
186 A63 12½c on 5p brn & grn .50 .45
187 A64 12½c on 15p blk & ver .50 .45
Nos. 185-187 (3) 1.20 1.10

Nos. 165, 173-174 Surcharged in Red or Black

25 25 25 25
I II III IV

1922

188 A57 25c on 3p (I) (R) .20 .20
a. Type II .60 .60
b. Type III .60 .60
c. Type IV .30 .30
d. Inverted surcharge 40.00
e. Horiz. or vert. pair, imperf. btwn. (I) 125.00
189 A63 25c on 5p (I) 1.00 *2.00*
a. Type II 2.00 *3.00*
b. Type III 2.00 *3.00*
c. Type IV 1.00 *2.00*
190 A64 25c on 15p (I) 1.00 *1.50*
a. Type II 2.00 *3.00*
b. Type III 2.00 *3.00*
c. Type IV 1.00 *1.50*
191 A64 25c on 15p (I) (R) 22.50 *30.00*
a. Type II 40.00 *45.00*
b. Type III 45.00 45.00
c. Type IV 30.00 *35.00*
Nos. 188-191 (4) 24.70 *33.70*

Stamps of 1902-21 Surcharged in Dark Blue or Red

25 25 25
V VI VII

25 25
VIII IX

1922, Aug. **On Nos. 121-123**

192 A35 25c on 75c (V) .35 .35
a. Type VI .35 .35
b. Type VII 1.75 1.75
c. Type VIII 5.50 4.00
d. Type IX 6.50 6.00
193 A36 25c on 1p (V) .30 .30
a. Type VI .30 .30
b. Type VII 1.25 1.25
c. Type VIII 2.50 2.50
d. Type IX 4.00 3.50
e. Inverted surcharge 40.00
194 A37 25c on 2p (V) .45 .45
a. Type VI .45 .45
b. Type VII 1.25 1.25
c. Type VIII 4.00 4.00
d. Type IX 6.50 6.50

On Nos. 162-165

195 A54 25c on 30c (V) .45 .45
a. Type VI .45 .45
b. Type VII 1.25 1.25
c. Type VIII 5.50 5.50
d. Type IX 6.50 6.50
196 A55 25c on 60c (V) 1.00 *1.50*
a. Type VI 1.00 *1.50*
b. Type VII 5.50 *7.50*
c. Type VIII 8.00 *9.00*
d. Type IX 10.00 *11.00*
197 A56 25c on 90c (V) 1.00 *1.50*
a. Type VI 1.50 *2.00*
b. Type VII 5.50 *6.50*
c. Type VIII 8.00 *9.00*
d. Type IX 10.00 *11.00*
198 A57 25c on 3p (R) (V) .35 .35
a. Type VI .35 .35
b. Type VII 1.25 1.00
c. Type VIII 6.00 4.50
d. Type IX 6.50 6.00
e. Inverted surcharge 50.00

On Nos. 172-174

199 A62 25c on 1.50p (V) .30 .30
a. Type VI .30 .25
b. Type VII 1.25 1.00
c. Type VIII 3.00 3.00
d. Type IX 4.50 4.00
e. Inverted surcharge 40.00
200 A63 25c on 5p (V) .75 *.90*
a. Type VI .80 *1.00*
b. Type VII 3.00 *3.50*
c. Type VIII 5.50 *6.00*
d. Type IX 8.00 *8.50*
201 A64 25c on 15p (V) .85 *.90*
a. Type VI 1.50 1.50
b. Type VII 5.00 *5.50*
c. Type VIII 6.50 6.50
d. Type IX 12.00 12.00
Nos. 192-201 (10) 5.80 7.00

Centenary Palace — A69

National Palace at Antigua — A70

1922 ***Perf. 14, 14½***

Printed by Waterlow & Sons

202 A69 12½c green .20 .20
a. Horiz. or vert. pair, imperf. btwn. 100.00
203 A70 25c brown .20 .20

See Nos. 211, 221, 234.

Columbus Theater A71

Quetzal A72

Granados Monument — A73

Litho. by Castillo Bros.

1924, Feb. ***Perf. 12***

204 A71 50c rose .50 .20
a. Imperf., pair 7.50
b. Horiz. or vert. pair, imperf. btwn. 25.00
205 A72 1p dark green .75 .20
a. Imperf. vertically 15.00
b. Vert. pair, imperf. btwn. 20.00
c. Imperf., pair 7.50
206 A73 5p orange 1.25 .50
a. Imperf., pair 8.50
b. Horiz. pair, imperf. btwn. 20.00
Nos. 204-206 (3) 2.50 .90

For surcharges see Nos. 208-209.

Nos. 172 and 206 Surcharged

1924, July

207 A62 1p on 1.50p bl & org .30 .20
208 A73 1.25p on 5p orange .50 .50
a. "UN PESO 25 Cents." omitted 40.00
b. Horiz. pair, imperf. btwn. 25.00

#208 with two bars over "25 Cents."

1924

209 A73 1p on 5p orange .50 .50

Types of 1902-22 Issues

Engr. by Perkins Bacon & Co.

1924, Aug. **Re-engraved** ***Perf. 14***

210 A31 6c bister .20 .20
211 A70 25c brown .20 .20
212 A34 50c red .25 .20
213 A36 1p orange brn .25 .20
214 A37 2p orange .35 .25
215 A57 3p deep green 2.00 .50
216 A64 15p black 2.25 .75
Nos. 210-216 (7) 5.50 2.30

The designs of the stamps of 1924 differ from those of the 1902-22 issues in many details which are too minute to illustrate. The re-engraved issue may be readily distinguished by the imprint "Perkins Bacon & Co. Ld. Londres."

Pres. Justo Rufino Barrios A74

Lorenzo Montúfar A75

1924, Aug.

217 A74 1.25p ultra .20 .20
218 A75 2.50p dk violet 1.00 .25

See Nos. 224, 226. For surcharges see Nos. 232, C6, C20.

Aurora Park — A76

National Post Office — A77

National Observatory A78

Types of 1921-24 Re-engraved and New Designs Dated 1926

Engraved by Waterlow & Sons, Ltd.

1926, July-Aug. ***Perf. 12½***

219 A31 6c ocher .20 .20
220 A76 12½c green .20 .20
221 A70 25c brown .20 .20
222 A77 50c red .20 .20
223 A36 1p orange brn .20 .20
224 A74 1.50p dk blue .20 .20
225 A78 2p orange 1.25 1.00
226 A75 2.50p dk violet 1.50 1.25
227 A57 3p dark green .45 .20
228 A63 5p brown vio 1.00 .40
229 A64 15p black 1.25 .60
Nos. 219-229 (11) 6.65 4.65

These stamps may be distinguished from those of the same designs in preceding issues by the imprint "Waterlow & Sons, Limited, Londres," the date, "1926," and the perforation.

See Nos. 233, 242. For surcharge see No. 230.

Nos. 225-226, 228 Surcharged in Various Colors

1928

230 A78 ½c on 2p (Bl) .60 .45
a. Inverted surcharge 12.50
231 A63 ½c on 5p (Bk) .30 .20
a. Inverted surcharge 10.00 10.00
b. Double surcharge 50.00
c. Blue surcharge 45.00 45.00
d. Blue and black surcharge 50.00 50.00
232 A75 1c on 2.50p (R) .30 .20
b. Double surcharge 50.00
Nos. 230-232 (3) 1.20 .85

Barrios — A79

Montúfar — A80

Granados A81

General Orellana A82

Coat of Arms of Guatemala City — A83

Engraved by T. De la Rue & Co.

1929, Jan. ***Perf. 14***

233 A78 ½c yellow grn .75 .20
234 A70 1c dark brown .25 .20
235 A79 2c deep blue .25 .20
236 A80 3c dark violet .20 .20
237 A81 4c orange .25 .20
238 A82 5c dk carmine .50 .20
239 A31 10c brown .40 .20
240 A36 15c ultra .50 .20
241 A29 25c brown org 1.00 .25
242 A76 30c green .90 .30
243 A32 50c pale rose 2.00 .60
244 A83 1q black 3.00 .40
Nos. 233-244 (12) 10.00 3.15

Nos. 233, 234 and 239 to 243 differ from the illustrations in many minor details, particularly in the borders.

See No. 300 for bisect of No. 235. For overprints and surcharges see Nos. 297, C13, C17-C18, C25-C26, C28, E1, RA17-RA18.

No. 227 Surcharged in Black or Red

1929, Dec. 28 ***Perf. 12½, 13***

245 A57 3c on 3p dk grn (Bk) 1.25 *1.75*
a. Inverted surcharge 15.00 15.00
246 A57 5c on 3p dk grn (R) 1.25 *1.75*
a. Inverted surcharge 15.00 15.00

Inauguration of the Eastern Railroad connecting Guatemala and El Salvador.

No. 229 Surcharged in Red

1930, Mar. 30 **Unwmk.**

247 A64 1c on 15p black 1.00 1.10
248 A64 2c on 15p black 1.00 *1.10*
249 A64 3c on 15p black 1.00 *1.10*
250 A64 5c on 15p black 1.00 *1.10*
251 A64 15c on 15p black 1.00 1.10
Nos. 247-251 (5) 5.00 *5.50*

Opening of Los Altos electric railway.

Hydroelectric Dam — A85

Los Altos Railway A86

Railroad Station A87

1930, Mar. 30 Typo. *Perf. 12*

252 A85 2c brn vio & blk	1.00	*1.40*
a. Horiz. pair, imperf. btwn.	125.00	
253 A86 3c dp red & blk	2.00	*2.00*
a. Vert. pair, imperf. btwn.	125.00	
254 A87 5c buff & dk bl	2.00	*2.00*
Nos. 252-254 (3)	5.00	*5.40*

Opening of Los Altos electric railway. Exist imperf.

Mayan Stele at Quiriguá — A91

1932, Apr. 8 Engr.

258 A91 3c carmine rose	1.00	.20

See Nos. 302-303.

Flag of the Race, Columbus and Tecum Uman A92

1933, Aug. 3 Litho. *Perf. 12½*

259 A92 ½c dark green	.50	*.75*
260 A92 1c dull brown	1.00	*1.10*
261 A92 2c deep blue	1.00	*1.10*
262 A92 3c dull violet	1.00	.75
263 A92 5c rose	1.00	1.00
Nos. 259-263 (5)	4.50	*4.70*

Day of the Race and 441st anniv. of the sailing of Columbus from Palos, Spain, Aug. 3, 1492, on his 1st voyage to the New World.
The 3c and 5c exist imperf.

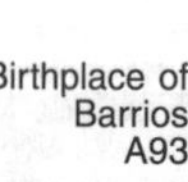

Birthplace of Barrios A93

View of San Lorenzo A94

Justo Rufino Barrios A95

National Emblem and Locomotive A96

General Post Office — A97

Telegraph Building and Barrios A98

Military Academy A99

National Police Headquarters — A100

Jorge Ubico and J. R. Barrios A101

1935, July 19 Photo.

264 A93 ½c yel grn & mag	.50	*.60*
265 A94 1c org red & pck bl	.50	*.60*
266 A95 2c orange & blk	.50	*.70*
267 A96 3c car rose & pck bl	2.00	1.00
268 A97 4c pck bl & org red	4.50	*7.50*
269 A98 5c bl grn & brn	3.00	*3.00*
270 A99 10c slate grn & rose lake	4.50	*4.75*
271 A100 15c ol grn & org brn	4.50	*4.75*
272 A101 25c scarlet & bl	4.50	*4.75*
Nos. 264-272 (9)	24.50	*27.65*

General Barrios. See Nos. C29-C31.

Lake Atitlán A102

Quetzal A103

Legislative Building — A104

1935, Oct. 10

273 A102 1c brown & crim	.25	.20
274 A103 3c rose car & pck grn	.70	.20
275 A103 3c red org & pck grn	.70	.20
276 A104 4c brt bl & dp rose	.35	.20
Nos. 273-276 (4)	2.00	.80

See No. 277. For surcharges see Nos. B1-B3.

No. 273 perforated diagonally through the center

1936, June *Perf. 12½x12*

277 A102 (½c) brown & crimson	.20	.20
a. Unsevered pair	.50	.60

Bureau of Printing — A105

Map of Guatemala A106

1936, Sept. 24 *Perf. 12½*

278 A105 ½c green & pur	.20	.20
279 A106 5c blue & dk brn	.75	.20

For surcharge see No. B4.

Quetzal A107

Union Park, Quezaltenango A108

Gen. Jorge Ubico on Horseback A109

1c, Tower of the Reformer. 3c, National Post Office. 4c, Government Building, Retalhuleu. 5c, Legislative Palace entrance. 10c, Custom House. 15c, Aurora Airport Custom House. 25c, National Fair. 50c, Residence of Presidential Guard. 1.50q, General Ubico, portrait standing, no cap.

1937, May 20

280 A107 ½c pck bl & car rose	.25	*.30*
281 A107 1c ol gray & red brn	.50	.30
282 A108 2c vio & car rose	.45	.35
283 A108 3c brn vio & brt bl	.40	.25
284 A108 4c yel & dl ol grn	1.75	*1.75*
285 A107 5c crim & brt vio	1.75	1.50
286 A107 10c mag & brn blk	3.00	*3.50*
287 A108 15c ultra & cop red	2.50	*3.50*
288 A108 25c red org & vio	3.00	*3.75*
289 A108 50c dk grn & org red	3.75	*4.50*
290 A109 1q magenta & blk	*20.00*	*22.50*
291 A109 1.50q red brn & blk	*20.00*	*22.50*
Nos. 280-291 (12)	*57.35*	*64.70*

Second term of President Ubico.

Mayan Calendar A119

Natl. Flower (White Nun Orchid) A120

Quetzal — A121

Map of Guatemala A122

1939, Sept. 7 *Perf. 13x12, 12½*

292 A119 ½c grn & red brn	.25	.20
293 A120 2c bl & gray blk	1.50	.25
294 A121 3c red org & turq grn	1.00	.40
295 A121 3c ol bis & turq grn	1.00	.40
296 A122 5c blue & red	1.75	1.25
Nos. 292-296 (5)	5.50	2.50

For overprints see Nos. 324, C157.

No. 235 Surcharged with New Value in Red

1939, Sept. *Perf. 14*

297 A79 1c on 2c deep blue	.20	.20

Stamps of 1929 Surcharged in Blue:

y

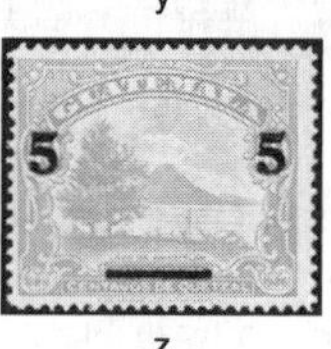

z

1940, June

298 A29 (y) 1c on 25c brn org	.25	.20
299 A32 (z) 5c on 50c pale rose (bar 10x¾mm)	.25	.20
a. Bar 12½x2mm	.30	.20
b. Bar 12½x1mm	50.00	5.00

No. 235 perforated diagonally through the center

1941, Aug. 16 *Perf. 14x11½*

300 A79 (1c) deep blue	.20	.20
a. Unsevered pair	.40	.40

No. 241 Surcharged in Black

1941, Dec. 24 *Perf. 14*

301 A29 ½c on 25c brn org	.20	.20

Type of 1932 Inscribed "1942"

1942 Engr. *Perf. 12*

302 A91 3c green	.75	.20
303 A91 3c deep blue	.75	.20

Issued to publicize the coffee of Guatemala.

Vase of Guastatoya A123

Home for the Aged A124

1942, July 13 Unwmk.

304 A123 ½c red brown	.35	.20
305 A124 1c carmine rose	.35	.20

National Printing Works A125 — Rafael Maria Landivar A126

1943, Jan. 25 Engr. *Perf. 11, 12*
307 A125 2c scarlet .25 .20
a. Vert. pair, imperf. horiz. 35.00

1943, Aug. *Perf. 11*
308 A126 5c brt ultra .25 .20

Death of Rafael Landivar, poet, 150th anniv.

National Palace A127

1944, June 30 *Perf. 11*
309 A127 3c dk blue green .20 .20

Inauguration of the Natl. Palace, Nov. 10, 1943.

See Nos. C137A-C139. For overprints see Nos. 311-311A, C133.

Ruins of Zakuleu A128

1945, Jan. 6
310 A128 ½c black brown .20 .20

Type of 1944 Overprinted in Blue

1945, Jan. 15
311 A127 3c deep blue .25 .20

Overprint Bar 1mm Thick
311A A127 3c deep blue .75 .40

Allegory of the Revolution A129 — Torch A130

1945, Feb. 20
312 A129 3c grayish blue .20 .20
Nos. 312,C128-C131 (5) 1.80 1.00

Revolution of 10/20/44.

1945, Oct. 20
313 A130 3c deep blue .20 .20

1st anniv. of the Revolution of Oct. 20, 1944. See No. C135-C136.

José Milla y Vidaurre A131 — Payo Enriquez de Rivera A132

1945 *Perf. 11, 12½*
314 A131 1c deep green .20 .20
315 A132 2c dull lilac .20 .20
Nos. 314-315,C134-C134A (4) 1.60 1.65

See Nos. 343-346, 379, C137, C269, C311-C315.

Catalogue values for unused stamps in this section, from this point to the end of the section, are for Never Hinged items.

José Batres y Montufar A133 — UPU Monument Bern, Switzerland A134

1946 Unwmk.
316 A133 ½c sepia .20 .20
317 A133 3c deep blue .20 .20

See Nos. 319, C142.

1946, Aug. 5 Photo. *Perf. 14x13*
318 A134 1c vio & gray brn .30 .20
Nos. 318,C140-C141 (3) 1.15 .60

Centenary of the first postage stamp.

Batres Type of 1946

1947, Nov. 11 Engr. *Perf. 11, 12½*
319 A133 3c dull green .20 .20

Symbolical of Labor — A135 — Bartolomé de las Casas and Indian — A136

1948, May 14 Unwmk. *Perf. 11*
320 A135 1c deep green .20 .20
a. Perf. 12½ 5.00
321 A135 2c sepia .20 .20
a. Perf. 12½ 5.00
322 A135 3c deep ultra .20 .20
a. Perf. 12½ 5.00
323 A135 5c rose carmine .20 .20
a. Perf. 12½ 5.00
Nos. 320-323 (4) .80 .80

Labor Day, May 1, 1948. Other perfs. and compound perfs. exist.

No. 296 Overprinted "1948" in Carmine at Lower Right

1948, May 14 *Perf. 12½*
324 A122 5c blue & red .20 .20

1949, Oct. 8 Engr. *Perf. 12½, 13½*
325 A136 ½c red .20 .20
326 A136 1c black brown .20 .20
327 A136 2c dk blue grn .20 .20
a. 2c green, perf. 11, 11½ ('60) .20 .20
328 A136 3c rose pink .20 .20
a. 3c car, perf. 11, 12½, 13½ ('64) .30 .20
329 A136 4c ultra .20 .20
Nos. 325-329 (5) 1.00 1.00

See Nos. 384-386.

Gathering Coffee — A137

1c, Poptun Agricultural Colony. 2c, Banana trees. 3c, Sugar cane field. 6c, Intl. Bridge.

1950, Feb. Photo. *Perf. 14*
330 A137 ½c vio bl, pink & ol gray .20 .20
331 A137 1c red brn, yel & grnsh gray .20 .20
332 A137 2c ol grn, pink & bl gray .20 .20
333 A137 3c pur, bl & org brn .20 .20
334 A137 6c dp org, aqua & vio .35 .20
Nos. 330-334 (5) 1.15 1.00

See Nos. 347-349.

Badge of Public and Social Assistance Ministry — A138 — Nurse — A139

Map Showing Hospitals — A140

1950-51 Litho. *Perf. 12, 12½x12*
335 A138 1c car rose & bl .20 .20
336 A139 3c dl grn & rose red .30 .20

Perf. 12
337 A140 5c dk bl & choc ('51) .40 .20
a. Souvenir sheet, #335-337 2.50 2.50
Nos. 335-337 (3) .90 .60

Issued to publicize the National Hospitals Fund.

No. 337a exists perf. and imperf., same values.

A perforated souvenir sheet is known which is similar to No. 337a, but with the 5c stamp like the basic stamp of No. C232 (with "BRITISH HONDURAS" inscription).

See #C177-C180a. For overprint see #C232.

Motorcycle Messenger A141

1951, May 22 *Perf. 14x12½*
337B A141 4c bl grn & gray blk .45 .20

Issued for regular postage, although inscribed "Expreso." See No. E2.

Souvenir Sheet

A142

Typographed and Engraved

1951, Oct. 22 *Imperf.*
338 A142 Sheet of 2 1.50 1.50
a. 1c rose carmine .50 .40
b. 10c deep ultramarine .50 .40

75th anniv. (in 1949) of the UPU. For overprint see No. 419.

A143

Modern Model Schools A144

1951, Oct. 22 Photo. *Perf. 13½x14*
339 A143 ½c purple & sepia .25 .20
340 A144 1c brn car & dl grn .25 .20
341 A143 2c grnsh bl & red brn .25 .20
342 A144 4c blk brn & rose vio .25 .20
Nos. 339-342 (4) 1.00 .80

Enriquez de Rivera Type of 1945 Re-engraved

1952, June 4 *Perf. 12½*
343 A132 ½c violet .20 .20
344 A132 1c rose carmine .20 .20
345 A132 2c green .20 .20
346 A132 4c orange .30 .20
Nos. 343-346 (4) .90 .80

A panel containing the dates "1660-1951" has been added below the portrait.

Produce Type of 1950

Designs: ½c, Sugar cane field. 1c, Banana trees. 2c, Poptun Agricultural Colony.

1953, Feb. 11 Photo. *Perf. 13½*
347 A137 ½c dk brn & dp bl .20 .20
348 A137 1c red org & ol grn .20 .20
349 A137 2c dk car & gray blk .20 .20
Nos. 347-349 (3) .60 .60

Issued to publicize farming.

Rafael Alvarez Ovalle and José Joaquin Palma A145

1953, May 13
350 A145 ½c purple & blk .25 .20
351 A145 1c dk grn & org brn .30 .20
352 A145 2c org brn & ol grn .30 .20
353 A145 3c dk bl & ol brn .30 .20
Nos. 350-353 (4) 1.15 .80

Authors of Guatemala's national anthem. For overprints see Nos. 374-378.

Quetzal — A146

1954, Sept. 27 Engr. *Perf. 12½, 11*
354 A146 1c dp violet blue .25 .20

See Nos. 367-373, 380-382A, 434-444. For overprint see No. 395.

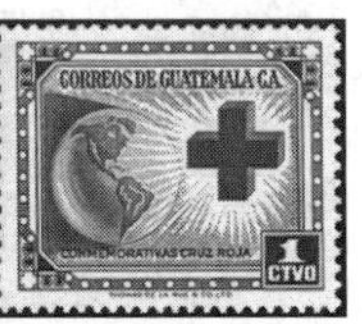

Mario Camposeco A147 — Globe and Red Cross A148

10c, Carlos Aguirre Matheu. 15c, Goalkeeper.

1955-56 Unwmk. *Perf. 12½*
355 A147 4c violet .90 .25
356 A147 4c carmine ('56) .90 .25
357 A147 4c blue grn ('56) .90 .25

358 A147 10c bluish grn 2.75 .75
359 A147 15c dark blue 2.75 2.00
Nos. 355-359 (5) 8.20 3.50

50 years of Soccer in Guatemala.

1956, May 23 ***Perf. 13x12½***

Designs: 3c, Red Cross, Telephone and "5110." 4c, Nurse, patient and Red Cross flag.

360 A148 1c brown & car .25 .20
361 A148 3c dk green & red .25 .20
362 A148 4c dk sl grn & red .25 .20
Nos. 360-362 (3) .75 .60

Red Cross. See Nos. B5-B7, CB5-CB7. For surcharges see Nos. CB8-CB10.

Dagger-Cross of the Liberation — A149

1c, Map showing 2,000 km. (1,243 miles) of new roads. 3c, Oil production.

1956 **Engr.** ***Perf. 12½***

363 A149 ½c violet .20 .20
364 A149 1c dk blue grn .20 .20

Perf. 11

365 A149 3c sepia .20 .20
Nos. 363-365 (3) .60 .60

Liberation of 1954-55. Issue dates: ½c, 1c, July 27; 3c, Oct. 31. See Nos. C210-C218.

Quetzal Type of 1954

1957-58 ***Perf. 11, 12½***

367 A146 2c violet .20 .20
368 A146 3c carmine rose .20 .20
369 A146 3c ultra .20 .20
a. 3c dark blue, perf. 11½ ('72) — —
370 A146 4c orange .30 .20
371 A146 5c brown .35 .20
372 A146 5c org ver ('58) .35 .20
373 A146 6c yellow grn .35 .20
Nos. 367-373 (7) 1.95 1.40

No. 368 is only perf. 12½. The 2c, 4c and No. 369 are found in perf. 11 and 12½. Other values are only perf. 11.

No. 350 Overprinted in Blue, Black, Carmine, Red Orange or Green:

1958, Nov.-Dec. **Photo.** ***Perf. 13½***

374 A145 ½c purple & blk (Bl) .20 .30
375 A145 ½c purple & blk (Bk) .20 .30
376 A145 ½c purple & blk (C) .20 .30
377 A145 ½c purple & blk (RO) .20 .30
378 A145 ½c purple & blk (G) .20 .30
Nos. 374-378 (5) 1.00 1.50

Cent. of the birth of Rafael Alvarez Ovalle, composer of Guatemala's national anthem.

Re-engraved Rivera Type of 1945

1959, Sept. 12 **Engr.** ***Perf. 11, 12½***

379 A132 4c gray blue .20 .20

See note after No. 346.

Quetzal Type of 1954

1960-63 **Unwmk.** ***Perf. 11***

380 A146 2c brown ('61) .20 .20
381 A146 4c lt violet .25 .20
382 A146 5c blue green .30 .20

Perf. 12½

382A A146 5c slate gray ('63) .60 .40
Nos. 380-382A (4) 1.35 1.00

Romulus and Remus Statue, Rome — A150

1871 Stamp — A151

1961 **Photo.** ***Perf. 14***

383 A150 3c blue .20 .20

Inauguration of the Plaza Italia.

Las Casas Type of 1949

Perf. 11, 11½, 12½, 13½

1962-64 **Engr.**

384 A136 ½c blue .20 .20
385 A136 1c brt violet ('64) .20 .20
386 A136 4c brown ('64) .20 .20
Nos. 384-386 (3) .60 .60

1963-66 **Unwmk.** ***Perf. 11***

387 A151 10c carmine .20 .20
388 A151 10c slate ('64) .25 .20

Perf. 11½

389 A151 10c olive brn ('66) .25 .20
390 A151 20c dp purple ('64) .40 .25
391 A151 20c dk blue ('65) .40 .25
Nos. 387-391 (5) 1.50 1.10

For souvenir sheet, see No. C310.

Pedro Bethancourt Comforting Sick Man — A152

1964, Jan. 6 **Engr.** ***Perf. 11***

394 A152 2½c olive bister .20 .20

Beatification (1962-63) of Pedro Bethancourt (1626-67). See Nos. C319-C322. For overprints see Nos. C381-C382.

Quetzal Type of 1957-58 Overprinted in Blue

1964, Dec. 29 **Engr.** ***Perf. 12½***

395 A146 4c orange .25 .20

15th anniv. (in 1963) of the Intl. Soc. of Guatemala Collectors.

Map of Guatemala and British Honduras A153

1967, Apr. 28 **Litho.** ***Perf. 14x13½***

396 A153 4c ol, vio bl & dp rose .25 .25
397 A153 5c ocher, vio bl & dp org .20 .20
398 A153 6c dp org, vio bl & gray .20 .20
Nos. 396-398 (3) .65 .65

Issued to state Guatemala's claim to British Honduras.
For overprints see Nos. C411-C413.

Quetzal, Mayan Ball Game Goal — A154

Lithographed and Engraved

1968, Oct. 15 ***Perf. 11½***

399 A154 1c blk, lt grn & red .20 .20
400 A154 5c yel, lt grn & red .20 .20
401 A154 8c org, lt grn & red .20 .20
402 A154 15c bl, lt grn & red .30 .20
403 A154 30c lt vio, lt grn & red .75 1.00
Nos. 399-403 (5) 1.65 1.80

19th Olympic Games, Mexico City, 10/12-27.
The 1c, 5c, 8c, 15c also exist perf 12½, 1c, 8c, perf 13½.
See Nos. 412-415. For overprints see Nos. 408-411, C431-C435.

Child and Poinsettia — A155

1968-70 **Typo.** ***Perf. 13½***

404 A155 2½c grn, dp bis & car .20 .20
405 A155 2½c grn, org & car ('70) .40 .50
406 A155 5c green, gray & car .40 .20
407 A155 21c green, lil & car .50 .50
Nos. 404-407 (4) 1.50 1.40

Issued to help abandoned children.

Type of 1968 Overprinted in Black or Red

1970, Mar. 19 **Litho.** ***Perf. 13½***

408 A154 8c org, lt grn & red .25 .50
409 A154 8c org, lt grn & red (R) .25 .50

Perf. 12½

410 A154 15c bl, lt grn & red .40 .75
411 A154 15c bl, lt grn & red (R) .40 .75
Nos. 408-411 (4) 1.30 2.50

50th anniv. of ILO. Gold overprint believed to be a trial color.

Type of 1968

1971 **Typo. & Engr.** ***Perf. 11½***

412 A154 1c gray, yel grn & red .20 .20

Typo.

413 A154 5c brt pink, yel grn & red .35 .20
414 A154 5c brown, grn & red .35 .20
415 A154 5c dk bl, grn & red .35 .20
Nos. 412-415 (4) 1.25 .80

Mayas and CARE Package — A156

1971-72 **Typo.** ***Perf. 13½***

416 A156 1c black & multi .20 .20

Perf. 11½

417 A156 1c violet & multi ('72) .20 .20
418 A156 1c brown & multi ('72) .20 .20
Nos. 416-418 (3) .60 .60

10th anniv. of CARE in Guatemala, a US-Canadian Cooperative for American Relief Everywhere. Exist imperf. See No. C459.

No. 338 (trimmed) Overprinted in Orange with Olympic Rings and: "JUEGOS OLIMPICOS / MUNICH 1972"

Souvenir Sheet

Typo. & Engr.

1972, Oct. 23 ***Imperf.***

419 A142 Sheet of 2 .50 .75
a. 1c rose carmine ("Munich") .20 .25
b. 10c deep ultra ("1972") .30 .50

20th Olympic Games, Munich, Aug. 26-Sept. 11. Commemorative inscriptions on No. 338 at left, top and right have been trimmed off. Size: 61x45mm (approximately). Many varieties exist. Gold overprints probably are proofs.

Pres. Carlos Arana Osorio A157

Designs: 3c, 5c, President Osorio seated, vert. 8c, Pres. Osorio standing, vert.

1973-74 **Typo.** ***Perf. 12½***

420 A157 2c blue & blk .20 .20
421 A157 3c orange & brn .20 .20
422 A157 5c rose car & blk .25 .20
423 A157 8c black & brt grn .35 .20
a. Lithographed ('74) .20 .20
Nos. 420-423 (4) 1.00 .80

8th population and 3rd dwellings census, Mar. 26-Apr. 7, 1973.

Francisco Ximenez — A158

Typographed, Lithographed (#426)

1973-77 ***Perf. 11½, 13½ (#426)***

424 A158 2c black & emer .20 .20
425 A158 3c dk brn & org .20 .20
426 A158 3c black & yellow .25 .20
427 A158 6c black & brt bl .25 .20
Nos. 424-427 (4) .90 .80

Brother Francisco Ximenez, discoverer and translator of National Book of Guatemala. No. 427 issued for Intl. Book Year 1972.

Issued: 6c, 8/2; 2c, 1/14/75; #425, 3/5/75; #426, 9/26/77.

Sculpture of Christ, by Pedro de Mendoza, 1643 — A159

8c, Sculpture by Lanuza Brothers, 18th century.

1977, Apr. 4 **Litho.** ***Perf. 11***

428 A159 6c purple & multi .20 .20
429 A159 8c purple & multi .25 .20
Nos. 428-429,C614-C619 (8) 2.45 2.40

Holy Week 1977.

INTERFER 77 Emblem — A160

1977, Oct. 31 Litho. *Perf. 11½*

430 A160 7c black & multi .20 .20

INTERFER 77, 4th International Fair, Guatemala, Oct. 31-Nov. 13.

Rotary Intl., 75th Anniv. A161

1980, July 31 Litho. *Perf. 11½*

431 A161	4c shown	.20	.20
432 A161	6c Diamond and Quetzal	.20	.20
433 A161	10c Paul P. Harris	.25	.20
	Nos. 431-433 (3)	.65	.60

Quetzal Type of 1954

1984-86 Engr. *Perf. 12½*

434 A146	1c deep green	.20	.20
435 A146	2c deep blue	.20	.20
436 A146	3c olive green	.20	.20
437 A146	3c sepia	.20	.20
438 A146	3c blue	.20	.20
439 A146	3c red	.20	.20
440 A146	3c orange	.20	.20
441 A146	3c vermilion	.20	.20
442 A146	4c lt red brn	.20	.20
443 A146	5c magenta	.20	.20
444 A146	6c deep blue	.20	.20
	Nos. 434-444 (11)	2.20	2.20

Issued: #436-439, 2/20; #441, 6c, 4/25/86; 1c, 4c, 5c, 2/16/87; 2c, 3/25/87.

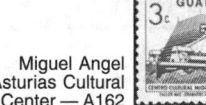

Miguel Angel Asturias Cultural Center — A162

Perf. 12½, 11½ (5c, 9c), 12½x11½ (4c), 13x12½ (6c)

1987-96 Litho.

445 A162	1c light blue		
446 A162	2c bister brown	.20	.20
447 A162	3c ultra	.20	.20
448 A162	4c bright pink	.20	.20
449 A162	5c orange	.20	.20
450 A162	6c pale green	.20	.20
451 A162	7c vermilion	.20	.20
452 A162	8c brt pink	.20	.20
453 A162	9c black	.20	.20
454 A162	10c pale green	.20	.20
	Nos. 446-454 (9)	1.80	1.80

Miguel Angel Asturias (1899-1974), 1967 Nobel laureate in literature.

Issued: 3c, 11/24; 7c, 11/17; 8c, 11/27; 10c, 12/8; 2c, 3/2/88; 5c, 3/23/90; 9c, 10/1/91; 4c, 6c, 3/16/93; 1c, 7/9/96.

Central American and Caribbean University Games A163

Toucan as a participant in various events.

1990 Litho. *Perf. 12½*

455 A163	15c shown	.30	.20
456 A163	20c Torch bearer, vert.	.40	.20
457 A163	25c Volleyball	.50	.20
458 A163	30c Soccer	.60	.20
459 A163	45c Karate	.90	.30
460 A163	1q Baseball	2.00	.65
461 A163	2q Basketball	4.00	1.25
462 A163	3q Hurdles	6.00	2.00
	Nos. 455-462 (8)	14.70	5.00

Issued: 20c, 8/22; 30c, 3q, 7/10; others, 4/25.

A164

A166

Oct. 20 Revolution, 50th Anniv. A165

Designs: 1q, Student holding book, rifle. 2q, Constitution, city buildings, San Carlos University, social security building.

1994, Nov. 8 Litho. *Perf. 11½*

463 A164	40c multicolored	.20	.20
464 A165	60c multicolored	.25	.20
465 A164	1q multicolored	.50	.20
466 A166	2q multicolored	1.00	.25
467 A166	3q multicolored	1.50	.35
	Nos. 463-467 (5)	3.45	1.20

UNICEF, 50th Anniv. — A167

Designs: 10c, Soldier hugging child, vert. 20c, Children flying on doves.

1997, May 21 Litho. *Perf. 12½*

468 A167 10c multicolored .20 .20

Perf. 11½x12½

469 A167 20c multicolored .20 .20

Landmark Buildings A168

Designs: 50c, Paraninfo University. 1q, Central American Services Building, vert.

1997, Mar. 6 *Perf. 12½*

470 A168	50c multicolored	.25	.20
471 A168	1q multicolored	.50	.20

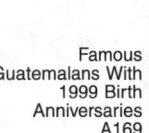

Famous Guatemalans With 1999 Birth Anniversaries A169

Designs: 3q, Francisco Marroquin (b. 1499), first Guatemalan bishop. 4q, Jacinto Rodriguez Diaz (b. 1899), aviator. 8.75q, Miguel Angel Asturias (1899-1974), 1967 Nobel Laureate for Literature. 10q, Cesar Brañas (b. 1899), writer.

2001, Oct. 9 Litho. *Perf. 12½x11½*

472-475 A169 Set of 4 7.00 3.50

Visit of Pope John Paul II and Canonization of St. Peter of San José Betancur (1626-67) — A170

Designs: Nos. 476, 483a, 20c, Saint and churches, vert. Nos. 477, 483b, 25c, Saint and bell, vert. Nos. 478, 483c, 50c, Pope, Saint and church. Nos. 479, 483d, 1q, Saint, painting of nativity, and bell, vert. Nos. 480, 483e, 2q, Pope and Guatemala Archbishop Quezada Toruño. Nos. 481, 483f, 5q, Pope, fountain and church decoration. Nos. 482, 483g, 8.75q, Pope and churches.

2002, July 16 Litho. *Perf. 12½*

476-482 A170 Set of 7 4.75 2.40

Souvenir Sheet

Rouletted 8½

483 A170 Sheet of 7, #a-g 4.75 2.40

SEMI-POSTAL STAMPS

Regular Issues of 1935-36 Surcharged in Blue or Red similar to illustration

1937, Mar. 15 Unwmk. *Perf. 12½*

B1	A102	1c + 1c brn & crim	.75	*1.00*
B2	A103	3c + 1c rose car & pck grn	.75	*1.00*
B3	A103	3c + 1c red org & pck grn	.75	*1.00*
B4	A106	5c + 1c bl & dk brn (R)	.75	*1.00*
		Nos. B1-B4 (4)	3.00	*4.00*

1st Phil. Exhib. held in Guatemala, Mar. 15-20.

Catalogue values for unused stamps in this section, from this point to the end of the section, are for Never Hinged items.

Type of Regular Issue, 1956

Designs: 5c+15c, Nurse, Patient and Red Cross Flag. 15c+50c, Red Cross, telephone and "5110." 25c+50c, Globe and Red Cross.

1956, June 19 Engr. *Perf. 13x12½*

B5	A148	5c + 15c ultra & red	.90	*1.25*
a.		Imperf., pair	75.00	
B6	A148	15c + 50c dk vio & red	2.00	*2.50*
B7	A148	25c + 50c bluish blk & car	2.00	*2.50*
		Nos. B5-B7 (3)	4.90	*6.25*

The surtax was for the Red Cross.

Jesus and Esquipulas Cathedral — SP1

1957, Oct. 29 *Perf. 13*

B8 SP1 1½c + ½c blk & brn .50 .20

The surtax was for the Esquipulas highway. See Nos. CB12-CB14.

Type of Air Post Semi-Postal Stamps and

Arms — SP2

3c+3c, Wounded man, Battle of Solferino.

1960, Apr. 9 Photo. *Perf. 13½x14*

Cross in Rose Red

B9	SP2	1c + 1c red brn & bl	.20	*.30*
B10	SPAP2	3c + 3c lil, bl & pink	.20	*.30*
B11	SP2	4c + 4c blk & bl	.20	*.30*
		Nos. B9-B11 (3)	.60	*.90*

Cent. (in 1959) of the Red Cross idea. The surtax went to the Red Cross. Exist imperf. See Nos. CB15-CB21.

AIR POST STAMPS

Surcharged in Red on No. 229

1929, May 20 Unwmk. *Perf. 12½*

C1	A64	3c on 15p blk	.50	.60
C2	A64	5c on 15p blk	.25	.20
C3	A64	15c on 15p blk	.75	.20
a.		Double surcharge (G & R)	100.00	
C4	A64	20c on 15p blk	1.00	1.00
a.		Inverted surcharge	100.00	
b.		Double surcharge	100.00	

Surcharged in Red on No. 216

1929, May 20 *Perf. 14*

C5	A64	5c on 15p black	1.50	1.00
		Nos. C1-C5 (5)	4.00	3.00

Surcharged in Black on No. 218

1929, Oct. 9

C6 A75 3c on 2.50p dk vio 1.00 1.00

Airplane and Mt. Agua AP3

1930, June 4 Litho. *Perf. 12½*

C7	AP3	6c rose red	.60	.40
a.		Double impression	25.00	25.00
b.		Imperf., pair	350.00	

For overprint see No. C14.

Nos. 227, 229 Surcharged in Black or Red

1930, Dec. 9 ***Perf. 12½***

C8 A57 1c on 3p grn (Bk) .40 .40
a. Double surcharge 100.00
C9 A57 2c on 3p grn (Bk) 1.10 *1.40*
C10 A57 3c on 3p grn (R) 1.10 *1.40*
C11 A57 4c on 3p grn (R) 1.10 *1.40*
C12 A64 10c on 15p blk (R) 1.40 *1.40*
a. Double surcharge 125.00
Nos. C8-C12 (5) 5.10 *6.00*

No. 237 Overprinted

1931, May 19 ***Perf. 14***

C13 A81 4c orange .35 .20
a. Double overprint 40.00 *50.00*

No. C7 Overprinted

Perf. 12½

C14 AP3 6c rose red 1.40 1.40
a. On No. C7a 30.00 30.00
b. Inverted overprint 6.00 *7.50*

Nos. 240, 242 Overprinted in Red

1931, Oct. 21 ***Perf. 14***

C15 A36 15c ultra 1.50 .20
a. Double overprint 100.00 100.00
C16 A76 30c green 2.50 .85
a. Double overprint 75.00 75.00

Nos. 235-236 Overprinted in Red or Green

1931, Dec. 5

C17 A79 2c dp bl (R) 2.50 *3.00*
C18 A80 3c dk vio (G) 2.50 *3.00*

No. 240 Overprinted in Red

C19 A36 15c ultra 2.50 *3.00*

Nos. C17-C19 were issued in connection with the 1st postal flight from Barrios to Miami.

No. 224 Surcharged in Red

1932-33 ***Perf. 12½***

C20 A74 2c on 1.50p dk bl .65 .50

Nos. 227, 229 Surcharged in Violet, Red or Blue

C21 A57 3c on 3p grn (V) .75 .20
a. Inverted surcharge 40.00 40.00
b. Vert. pair, imperf. horiz. 750.00
C22 A57 3c on 3p grn (R) .75 .20
C23 A64 10c on 15p blk (R) 7.50 6.00
b. First "I" of "Interior" missing 10.00 10.00
C24 A64 15c on 15p blk (Bl) 9.00 8.00
a. First "I" of "Interior" missing 15.00 15.00
Nos. C20-C24 (5) 18.65 14.90

Issued: #C22, 1/1/33; others, 2/11/32.

No. 237 Overprinted in Green

1933, Jan. 1 ***Perf. 14***

C25 A81 4c orange .25 .20
a. Double overprint 40.00 40.00

Nos. 235, 238 and 240 Overprinted in Red or Black

1934, Aug. 7

C26 A82 5c dk car (Bk) 1.50 .20
C27 A36 15c ultra (R) 1.50 .20

Overprinted in Red

C28 A79 2c deep blue .50 .20

View of Port Barrios — AP7

Designs: 15c, Tomb of Barrios. 30c, Equestrian Statue of Barrios.

1935, July 19 **Photo.** ***Perf. 12½***

C29 AP7 10c yel brn & pck grn 2.00 2.00
C30 AP7 15c gray & brn 2.00 2.00
C31 AP7 30c car rose & bl vio 2.00 1.50
Nos. C29-C31 (3) 6.00 5.50

Birth cent. of Gen. Justo Rufino Barrios.

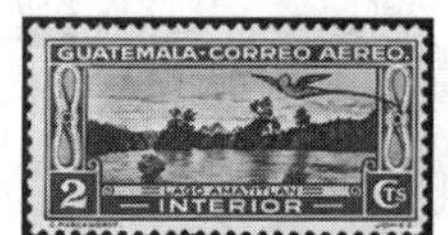

Lake Amatitlán AP10

#C36, C37, C45, C46. Different views of Lake Amatitlan. 3c, Port Barrios. #C34, C35, Ruins of Port San Felipe. 10c, Port Livingston. #C39, C40, Port San Jose. #C41, C42, View of Atitlan. #C43, C44, Aurora Airport.

Overprinted with Quetzal in Green

1935-37 **Size: 37x17mm**

C32 AP10 2c org brn .20 .20
C33 AP10 3c blue .20 .20
C34 AP10 4c black .25 .20
C35 AP10 4c ultra ('37) .20 .20
C36 AP10 6c yel grn .25 .20
C37 AP10 6c blk vio ('37) 4.00 .20
C38 AP10 10c claret .50 .25
C39 AP10 15c red org .65 .40
C40 AP10 15c yel grn ('37) .65 .65
C41 AP10 30c olive grn 6.00 6.50
C42 AP10 30c ol bis ('37) .75 .50
C43 AP10 50c rose vio 17.50 15.00
C44 AP10 50c Prus bl ('36) 4.00 3.00
C45 AP10 1q scarlet 17.50 20.00
C46 AP10 1q car ('36) 4.50 3.00
Nos. C32-C46 (15) 57.15 50.50

Issue dates follow No. C69.

For overprints and surcharges see Nos. C70-C79, CB1-CB2.

Central Park, Antigua AP11

Designs: 1c, Guatemala City. 2c, Central Park, Guatemala City. 3c, Monastery. Nos. C50-C51, Mouth of Dulce River. Nos. C52-C53, Plaza Barrios. Nos. C54-C55, Los Proceres Monument. No. C56, Central Park, Antigua. No. C57, Dulce River. Nos. C58-C59, Quezaltenango. Nos. C60-C61, Ruins at Antigua. Nos. C62-C63, Dock at Port Barrios. Nos. C64-C65, Port San Jose. Nos. C66-C67, Aurora Airport. 2.50q, Island off Atlantic Coast. 5q, Atlantic Coast view.

Overprinted with Quetzal in Green

Size: 34x15mm

C47 AP11 1c yel brn .20 .20
C48 AP11 2c vermilion .20 .20
C49 AP11 3c magenta .50 .25
C50 AP11 4c org yel ('36) 1.75 1.40
C51 AP11 4c car lake ('37) 1.00 .75
C52 AP11 5c dl bl .20 .20
C53 AP11 5c org ('37) .20 .20
C54 AP11 10c red brn .50 .40
C55 AP11 10c ol grn ('37) .50 .30
C56 AP11 15c rose red .25 .20
C57 AP11 15c ver ('37) .25 .20
C58 AP11 20c ultra 2.50 *3.00*
C59 AP11 20c dp cl ('37) .50 .25
C60 AP11 25c gray blk 3.00 *3.50*
C61 AP11 25c bl grn ('37) .45 .25
a. Quetzal omitted *1,100.*
C62 AP11 30c yel grn 1.50 1.50
C63 AP11 30c rose red ('37) 1.00 .20
C64 AP11 50c car rose 7.00 *8.00*
C65 AP11 50c pur ('36) 6.50 *7.50*
C66 AP11 1q dk bl 22.50 *25.00*
C67 AP11 1q dk grn ('36) 7.50 7.50

Size: 46x20mm

C68 AP11 2.50q rose red & ol grn ('36) 5.00 3.00
C69 AP11 5q org & ind ('36) 7.00 4.00
a. Quetzal omitted 1,500. 1,250.
Nos. C47-C69 (23) 70.00 *68.00*

Issued: #C32-C69, 11/1/35; 10/1/36; 1/1/37.

Value for No. C61a is for a sound copy.

For overprints and surcharges see Nos. C80-C91, CB3-CB4.

Types of Air Post Stamps, 1935 Overprinted with Airplane in Blue

2c, Quezaltenango. 3c, Lake Atitian. 4c, Progressive Colony, Lake Amatitlan. 6c, Carmen Hill. 10c, Relief map. 15c, National University. 30c, Espana Plaza. 50c, Police Station, Aurora Airport. 75c, Amphitheater, Aurora Airport. 1q, Aurora Airport.

1937, May 18

Center in Brown Black

C70 AP10 2c carmine .20 .20
C71 AP10 3c blue 1.00 *1.25*
C72 AP10 4c citron .20 .20
C73 AP10 6c yel grn .35 .25
C74 AP10 10c red vio 2.00 *2.25*
C75 AP10 15c orange 1.50 1.00
C76 AP10 30c ol grn 3.75 3.00
C77 AP10 50c pck bl 5.00 4.25
C78 AP10 75c dk vio 10.00 *11.00*
C79 AP10 1q dp rose 11.00 *12.00*
Nos. C70-C79 (10) 35.00 *35.40*

Overprinted with Airplane in Black

1c, 7th Ave., Guatemala City. 2c, Los Proceres Monument. 3c, Natl. Printing Office. 5c, Natl. Museum. 10c, Central Park. 15c, Escuintla. 20c, Motorcycle Police. 25c, Slaughterhouse, Escuintla. 30c, Exhibition Hall. 50c, Barrios Plaza. 1q, Polytechnic School. 1.50q, Aurora Airport.

Size: 33x15mm

C80 AP11 1c yel brn & brt bl .20 .20
C81 AP11 2c crim & dp vio .20 .20
C82 AP11 3c red vio & red brn .50 .50
C83 AP11 5c pck grn & cop red 4.00 3.00
C84 AP11 10c car & grn 1.25 1.00
C85 AP11 15c rose & dl ol grn .50 .25
C86 AP11 20c ultra & blk 3.00 1.75
C87 AP11 25c dk gray & scar 2.50 2.50
C88 AP11 30c grn & dp vio 1.25 1.25
C89 AP11 50c magenta & ultra 10.00 *12.00*

Size: 42x19mm

C90 AP11 1q ol grn & red vio 10.00 *12.00*
C91 AP11 1.50q scar & ol brn 10.00 *12.00*
Nos. C80-C91 (12) 43.40 *46.65*

Second term of President Ubico.

Souvenir Sheet

AP12

1938, Jan. 10 ***Perf. 12½***

C92 AP12 Sheet of 4 1.50 1.50
a. 15c George Washington .30 .30
b. 4c Franklin D. Roosevelt .30 .30
c. 4c Map of the Americas .30 .30
d. 15c Pan American Union Building, Washington, DC .30 .30

150th anniv. of US Constitution.

President Arosemena, Panama AP13

Flags of Central American Countries — AP19

Designs: 2c, Pres. Cortés Castro, Costa Rica. 3c, Pres. Somoza, Nicaragua. 4c, Pres. Carias Andino, Honduras. 5c, Pres. Martinez, El Salvador. 10c, Pres. Ubico, Guatemala.

1938, Nov. 20 **Unwmk.**

C93 AP13 1c org & ol brn .20 .20
C94 AP13 2c scar, pale pink & sl grn .20 .20
C95 AP13 3c grn, buff & ol brn .25 *.30*
C96 AP13 4c dk cl, pale lil & brn .30 *.35*
C97 AP13 5c bis, pale grn & ol brn .50 *.60*
C98 AP13 10c ultra, pale bl & brn 1.00 *1.25*
Nos. C93-C98 (6) 2.45 *2.90*

Souvenir Sheet

C99 AP19 Sheet of 6 1.00 1.00
a. 1c Guatemala .20 .20
b. 2c El Salvador .20 .20
c. 3c Honduras .20 .20
d. 4c Nicaragua .20 .20
e. 5c Costa Rica .20 .20
f. 10c Panama .20 .20

1st Central American Phil. Exhib., Guatemala City, Nov. 20-27.

For overprints see Nos. CO1-CO7.

La Merced Church, Antigua AP20

Designs: 2c, Ruins of Christ School, Antigua. 3c, Aurora Airport. 4c, Drill ground, Guatemala City. 5c, Cavalry barracks. 6c, Palace of Justice. 10c, Customhouse, San José. 15c, Communications Building, Retalhuleu. 30c, Municipal Theater, Quezaltenango. 50c, Customhouse, Retalhuleu. 1q, Departmental Building.

Inscribed "Aéreo Interior"
Overprinted with Quetzal in Green

1939, Feb. 14

C100 AP20 1c ol bis & chnt .20 .20
C101 AP20 2c rose red & sl grn .20 .20
C102 AP20 3c dl bl & bis .25 .20
C103 AP20 4c rose pink & yel grn .25 .20
C104 AP20 5c brn lake & brt ultra .30 .20
C105 AP20 6c org & gray brn .35 .20
C106 AP20 10c bis brn & gray blk .50 .20
C107 AP20 15c dl vio & blk .75 .20
C108 AP20 30c dp bl & dk car 1.10 .25
C109 AP20 50c org & brt vio 1.50 .40
a. Quetzal omitted *1,750.*
C110 AP20 1q yel grn & brt ultra 2.50 1.25
Nos. C100-C110 (11) 7.90 3.50

See Nos. C111-C122. For overprint and surcharge see No. C124, C132.

1939, Feb. 14

Designs: 1c, Mayan Altar, Aurora Park. 2c, Sanitation Building. 3c, Lake Amatitlan. 4c, Lake Atitlan. 5c, Tamazulapa River bridge. 10c, Los proceres Monument. 15c, Palace of Captains General. 20c, Church on Carmen Hill. 25c, Barrios Park. 30c, Mayan Altar. 50c, Charles III fountain. 1q, View of Antigua.

Inscribed "Aéreo International" or "Aérea Exterior"

Overprinted with Quetzal in Green

C111 AP20 1c ol grn & gldn brn .20 .20
C112 AP20 2c lt grn & blk .30 .20
C113 AP20 3c ultra & cob bl .20 .20
C114 AP20 4c org brn & yel grn .20 .20
C115 AP20 5c sage grn & red org .35 .20
C116 AP20 10c lake & sl blk 1.75 .20
C117 AP20 15c ultra & brt rose 1.75 .20
C118 AP20 20c yel grn & ap grn .60 .20
C119 AP20 25c dl vio & lt ol grn .60 .20
C120 AP20 30c dl rose & blk .80 .20
C121 AP20 50c scar & brt yel 1.50 .20
C122 AP20 1q org & yel grn 2.50 .35
Nos. C111-C122 (12) 10.75 2.55

No. 240 Overprinted in Carmine

1940, Apr. 14 ***Perf. 14***

C123 A36 15c ultra .55 .20

Pan American Union, 50th anniversary.

No. C112 Overprinted in Carmine

1941, Dec. 2 ***Perf. 12½***

C124 AP20 2c lt grn & blk .40 .20

Second Pan American Health Day.

San Carlos University, Antigua AP21

1943, June 25 **Engr.** ***Perf. 11***

C125 AP21 15c dk red brn .40 .20
a. Imperf., pair 100.00

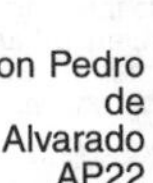

Don Pedro de Alvarado AP22

Type I- Diagonal shading lines at inner edges of commemorative tablet.
Type II- Overall shading added to tablet.

1943, Mar. 10 **Unwmk.** ***Perf. 11½***

C126 AP22 15c dp ultra (II) .40 .20
a. Type I 15.00 10.00

400th anniv. of the founding of Antigua.

National Police Building AP23

1943, Aug. 3 ***Perf. 11***

C127 AP23 10c dp rose vio .35 .20

Allegory of Revolution Type

1945, Apr. 27 **Engr.**

C128 A129 5c dp rose .40 .20
C129 A129 6c dk bl grn .40 .20
a. Imperf., pair 110.00
C130 A129 10c violet .40 .20
C131 A129 15c aqua .40 .20
Nos. C128-C131 (4) 1.60 .80

No. C113 Surcharged in Red

1945, July 25 ***Perf. 12½***

C132 AP20 2½c on 3c 1.10 *1.25*

The 1945 Book Fair.

Type of 1944 Overprinted "PALACIO NACIONAL" in Carmine

1945, Aug. **Engr.** ***Perf. 11***

C133 A127 5c rose car .20 .20
a. Triple ovpt., one inverted 50.00 25.00
b. Double ovpt., one inverted 65.00

See Nos. C137A-C139.

José Milla y Vidaurre Type

1945

C134 A131 7½c sepia .80 1.00
C134A A131 7½c dark blue .40 .25

Issued: #C134, Sept. 28; #C134A, Dec. 6.
For overprint see No. C230.

Torch Type

1945, Oct. 19

C135 A130 5c brt red vio .30 .20

Souvenir Sheet

Imperf

C136 A130 Sheet of 2 1.00 1.00
a. 5c bright red violet .40 .40

1st anniv. of the Revolution of Oct. 20, 1944.
See Nos. C147-C150.

Catalogue values for unused stamps in this section, from this point to the end of the section, are for Never Hinged items.

Payo Enriquez de Rivera Type

1946, Jan. 22 **Unwmk.** ***Perf. 11***

C137 A132 5c rose pink .30 .20

See Nos. C269, C311-C315.

Palace Type of 1944

1946-47

C137A A127 5c rose car ('47) .50 .20
C138 A127 10c deep lilac .25 .20
a. Imperf., pair 100.00
C139 A127 15c blue .50 .20
a. Imperf., pair 100.00
Nos. C137A-C139 (3) 1.25 .60

See No. C133 for #C137A without overprint.

Sir Rowland Hill — AP30 Globes, Quetzal — AP31

1946, Aug. 5 **Photo.** ***Perf. 14x13***

C140 AP30 5c slate & brn (blk ovpt.) .35 .20
a. Without "AEREO" ovpt. *400.00 400.00*
C141 AP31 15c car lake, ultra & emer .50 .20

Centenary of the first postage stamp.

José Batres y Montufar — AP32

Signing the Declaration of Independence AP33

1946, Sept. 16 **Engr.** ***Perf. 11***

C142 AP32 10c Prus grn .25 .20
a. Perf. 12½ 10.00 .20

1946, Dec. 19 ***Perf. 11***

C143 AP33 5c rose car .20 .20
C144 AP33 6c ol brn .20 .20
C145 AP33 10c violet .25 .20
C146 AP33 20c blue .35 .20
Nos. C143-C146 (4) 1.00 .80

125th anniv. of the signing of the Declaration of Independence.

Torch Type of 1945
Dated 1944-1946

1947, Feb. 3 **Engr.**

C147 A130 1c green .20 .20
C148 A130 2c carmine .20 .20
C149 A130 3c violet .20 .20
C150 A130 5c dp bl .30 .20
Nos. C147-C150 (4) .90 .80

Inscribed "II Aniversario de la Revolucion." "Aereo" in color on a white background.
2nd anniv. of the Revolution of 10/20/44.

Franklin D. Roosevelt — AP34

1947, June 6

C151 AP34 5c rose car .20 .20
C152 AP34 6c blue .20 .20
C153 AP34 10c dp ultra .30 .25
C154 AP34 30c gray blk 1.40 .90
C155 AP34 50c lt violet 2.25 2.25
a. Imperf., pair 125.00
C156 AP34 1q gray grn 3.75 3.75
a. Imperf., pair 125.00
Nos. C151-C156 (6) 8.10 7.55

No. 296 Overprinted in Carmine

1948, May 14 ***Perf. 12½***

C157 A122 5c blue & red .25 .20

Soccer Game AP35

1948, Aug. 31 **Engr.**

Center in Black

C158 AP35 3c brt carmine .75 .30
C159 AP35 5c blue green .90 .40
C160 AP35 10c dk violet 1.00 .95
C161 AP35 30c dp blue 2.00 *3.50*
C162 AP35 50c bister 4.50 4.50
Nos. C158-C162 (5) 9.15 9.65

4th Central American and Caribbean Soccer Championship, Mar. 1948.

Seal, University of Guatemala — AP36

1949, Nov. 29 ***Perf. 12½***

Center in Blue

C163 AP36 3c carmine .50 .40
C164 AP36 10c green 1.00 .75
C165 AP36 50c yellow 3.00 *3.25*
Nos. C163-C165 (3) 4.50 *4.40*

1st Latin American Cong. of Universities.

Lake Atitlan — AP37

Tecum Uman Monument — AP38

Designs: 8c, San Cristobal Church. 13c, Weaver. 35c, Momostenango Cliffs.

1950, Feb. 17 **Photo.** ***Perf. 14***

Multicolored Centers

C166 AP37 3c car rose .35 .20
C167 AP38 5c red brn .35 .20
C168 AP37 8c dk sl grn .40 .20
C169 AP38 13c brown .65 .25
C170 AP37 35c purple 2.25 2.75
Nos. C166-C170 (5) 4.00 3.60

See No. C181.

Soccer — AP39

Pole Vault — AP40

Designs: 3c, Foot race. 8c, Tennis. 35c, Diving. 65c, Stadium.

1950, Feb. 25 Engr. *Perf. 12½*

Center in Black

C171 AP39 1c purple .50 .20
C172 AP39 3c carmine .60 .20
C173 AP40 4c orange brn .75 .25
C174 AP39 8c red violet .90 .30
C175 AP40 35c lt blue 2.00 2.75

Center in Green

C176 AP40 65c dk slate grn 4.25 4.50
Nos. C171-C176 (6) 9.00 8.20

6th Central American and Caribbean Games.

Nurse and Patient AP41

Designs: 10c, School of Nurses. 50c, Zacapa Hospital. 1q, Roosevelt Hospital.

1950, Sept. 6 Litho. *Perf. 12*

Quetzal in Blue Green

C177 AP41 5c rose vio & car .25 .20
a. Double impression (frame) 25.00
C178 AP41 10c ol brn & emer .60 .35
C179 AP41 50c ver & red vio 2.00 *2.50*
C180 AP41 1q org yel & sage grn 2.75 *2.75*
a. Souv. sheet, #C177-C180 6.50 *7.50*
Nos. C177-C180 (4) 5.60 *5.80*

National Hospital Fund.
Nos. C177-C180 exist with colors reversed, perf. and imperf. These are proofs.

No. C168 perf. 12½ or 12 diagonally through center

1951, Apr. *Perf. 14*

C181 AP37 (4c) multi 10.00 7.50
a. Unsevered pair 25.00 15.00

Counterfeits of diagonal perforation exist.

Ceremonial Stone Ax — AP42

National Flag and Emblem — AP43

1953, Feb. 11 Photo. *Perf. 14x13½*

C182 AP42 3c dk bl & ol gray .20 .20
C183 AP42 5c dk gray & hn brn .30 .20
C184 AP42 10c dk pur & slate .40 .20
Nos. C182-C184 (3) .90 .60

1953, Mar. 14 *Perf. 13½*

Multicolored Center

C185 AP43 1c maroon .20 .20
C186 AP43 2c slate green .25 .20
C187 AP43 4c dark brown .30 .20
Nos. C185-C187 (3) .75 .60

Issued to mark the passing of the presidency from J. J. Arevalo to Col. Jacobo Arbenz Guzman.

Regional Dance — AP44

Horse Racing AP45

Designs: 4c, White nun - national flower. 5c, Allegory of the fair. 20c, Zakuleu ruins. 30c, Symbols of Agriculture. 50c, Champion bull. 65c, Bicycle racing. 1q, Quetzal.

1953, Dec. 18 Engr. *Perf. 12½*

C188 AP44 1c dp ultra & car .20 .20
C189 AP44 4c org & grn .50 .25
C190 AP44 5c emer & choc .30 .20
C191 AP45 15c choc & dk pur 1.25 1.00
C192 AP45 20c car & ultra .75 *1.00*
C193 AP44 30c dp ultra & choc 1.25 *1.50*
C194 AP45 50c pur & blk 1.50 1.50
C195 AP45 65c lt bl & dk grn 2.50 *2.75*
C196 AP44 1q dk bl grn & dk red 4.00 *4.75*
Nos. C188-C196 (9) 12.25 *13.15*

National Fair, Oct. 20, 1953.

Indian — AP46

1954, Apr. 21 Unwmk. *Perf. 12½*

C197 AP46 1c carmine .25 .20
C198 AP46 2c dp blue .25 .20
C199 AP46 4c yellow grn .25 .20
C200 AP46 5c aqua .50 .20
C201 AP46 6c orange .50 .20
C202 AP46 10c violet 1.00 .25
C203 AP46 20c black brn 3.00 3.00
Nos. C197-C203 (7) 5.75 4.25

Guatemala and ODECA Flags — AP47

1954, Oct. 13 Photo. *Perf. 14x13½*

C204 AP47 1c multicolored .20 .20
C205 AP47 2c multicolored .20 .20
C206 AP47 4c multicolored .20 .20
Nos. C204-C206 (3) .60 .60

3rd anniv. of the formation of the Organization of Central American States.

Rotary Emblem, Map of Guatemala AP48

1956, Sept. 8 Engr.

C207 AP48 4c bl & dl yel .25 .20
C208 AP48 6c lt bl grn & dl yel .25 .20
C209 AP48 35c pur & dl yel 1.25 *1.75*
Nos. C207-C209 (3) 1.75 *2.15*

50th anniv. of Rotary Intl. (in 1955).

Mayan Warrior Holding Dagger Cross of the Liberation AP49

4c, Family looking into the sun. 5c, The dagger of the Liberation destroying communist symbols. 6c, Hands holding cogwheel & map of Guatemala. 20c, Monument to the victims of communism & flag. 30c, Champerico harbor. 65c, Radio tower, Mercury & map of Guatemala. 1q, Flags of the American nations. 5q, Pres. Carlos Castillo Armas.

1956, Oct. 10 Photo. *Perf. 14x13½*

C210 AP49 2c dp grn, red, bl & brn .20 .20
C211 AP49 4c dp car & gray blk .20 .20
C212 AP49 5c bl & red brn .20 .20
C213 AP49 6c dk brn & dp ultra .25 .20
C214 AP49 20c vio, brn & bl 1.25 *1.50*
C215 AP49 30c dp bl & ol 1.40 *1.75*
C216 AP49 65c chnt brn & grn 2.25 *2.75*
C217 AP49 1q dk brn & multi 3.25 *3.50*
C218 AP49 5q multi 13.00 *14.00*
Nos. C210-C218 (9) 22.00 *24.30*

Liberation of 1954-55.
For overprints see Nos. C233, C243, C265-C266, C417.

Red Cross, Map and Quetzal AP50

Designs: 2c, José Ruiz Augulo and woman with child, vert 3c, Pedro de Bethancourt with sick man. 4c, Rafael Ayau.

Perf. 13½x14, 14x13½

1958, May 13 Unwmk.

C219 AP50 1c multicolored .25 .20
C220 AP50 2c multicolored .25 .20
C221 AP50 3c multicolored .25 .20
C222 AP50 4c multicolored .25 .20
Nos. C219-C222 (4) 1.00 .80

Issued in honor of the Red Cross.
For overprints and surcharges see Nos. C235-C242, C251-C254, C283-C298, C390-C394.

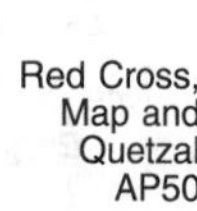

Col. Carlos Castillo Armas — AP51

Galleon of 1532 and Freighter "Quezaltenango" AP52

1959, Feb. 27 *Perf. 14x13½*

Center in Dark Blue and Yellow

C223 AP51 1c black .20 .20
C224 AP51 2c rose red .20 .20
C225 AP51 4c brown .20 .20
C226 AP51 6c dk bl grn .20 .20
C227 AP51 10c dk purple .25 .25
C228 AP51 20c blue grn .70 .70
C229 AP51 35c gray 1.25 1.25
Nos. C223-C229 (7) 3.00 3.00

Pres. Carlos Castillo Armas (1914-1957).

No. C134A Overprinted in Carmine: "HOMENAJE A LAS NACIONES UNIDAS"

1959, Mar. 4 Engr. *Perf. 11*

C230 A131 7½c dk blue .80 *1.00*

Issued to honor the United Nations.

1959, May 15 Litho. *Perf. 11*

C231 AP52 6c ultra & rose red .20 .20

Issued to honor the formation of the Guatemala-Honduras merchant fleet.
For overprint see No. C467.

Type of 1950 Overprinted in Dark Blue

1959, Oct. 9 *Perf. 12*

C232 A140 5c dk bl & lt brn .50 .20
a. Inverted overprint 200.00 35.00

Issued to state Guatemala's claim to British Honduras. Overprint reads: "Belize is ours." Map includes "BRITISH HONDURAS" and its borderline, and excludes bit extending above "A" of "GUATEMALA" on No. 337.
No. C232 is known without overprint in multiples.

No. C213 Overprinted in Red: "1859 Centenario Primera Exportacion de Cafe 1959"

1959, Oct. 26 Photo. *Perf. 14x13½*

C233 AP49 6c dk brn & dp ultra .50 .30

Centenary of coffee export.

Pres. and Mrs. Villeda of Honduras AP53

1959, Nov. 3 Litho. *Perf. 11*

C234 AP53 6c pale brown .25 .20

Visit of President Ramon Villeda Morales of Honduras, Oct. 12, 1958.
For overprint see No. C415.

Nos. C219-C222 Overprinted: "AÑO MUNDIAL DE REFUGIADOS" in Green, Violet, Blue or Brown

Perf. 13½x14, 14x13½

1960, Apr. 23 Photo. Unwmk.

C235 AP50 1c multi (G) 1.00 .75
C236 AP50 2c multi (V) .65 .60
C237 AP50 3c multi (Bl) .65 .60
C238 AP50 4c multi (Br) .65 .60

Nos. C219-C222 Overprinted as Above and Surcharged with New Value

C239 AP50 6c on 1c multi 2.50 2.25
C240 AP50 7c on 2c multi 2.50 2.25
C241 AP50 10c on 3c multi 4.00 4.25
C242 AP50 20c on 4c multi 4.50 4.50
Nos. C235-C242 (8) 16.45 15.80

Nos. C235-C242 issued to publicize World Refugee Year, July 1, 1959-June 30, 1960.

No. C213 Overprinted in Red: "Fundacion de la ciudad Melchor de Mencos, 30-IV-1960"

1960, Apr. 30 *Perf. 14x13½*

C243 AP49 6c dk brn & dp ultra 1.00 1.25

Founding of the city of Melchor de Mencos.

UNESCO and Eiffel Tower, Paris AP54

1960, Nov. 4 Photo. *Perf. 12½*
C244 AP54 5c dp mag & vio .20 .20
C245 AP54 6c ultra & vio brn .20 .20
C246 AP54 8c emer & magenta .35 .20
C247 AP54 20c red brn & dl bl 1.25 1.25
Nos. C244-C247 (4) 2.00 1.85

Issued to honor UNESCO.
For overprints see Nos. C258, C267-C268.

Abraham Lincoln — AP55

1960, Oct. 29 Engr. *Perf. 11*
C248 AP55 5c violet blue .20 .20
C249 AP55 30c violet 1.00 *1.25*
C250 AP55 50c gray 5.00 *6.00*
Nos. C248-C250 (3) 6.20 *7.45*

Sesquicentenary of the birth of Abraham Lincoln.
An 8c was also printed, but was not issued and all copies were destroyed.

Nos. C219-C222 Overprinted "Mayo de 1960" in Green, Blue or Brown
Perf. 13½x14, 14x13½
1961, Apr. 20 Photo. Unwmk.
C251 AP50 1c multi (G) .35 .25
C252 AP50 2c multi (Bl) .35 .25
C253 AP50 3c multi (Bl) .35 .25
C254 AP50 4c multi (Br) .35 .25
Nos. C251-C254 (4) 1.40 1.00

Issued to honor the Red Cross.

Proclamation of Independence — AP56

1962 Engr. *Perf. 11*
C255 AP56 4c sepia .20 .20
C256 AP56 5c violet blue .25 .20
C257 AP56 15c brt violet .75 .50
Nos. C255-C257 (3) 1.20 .90

140th anniv. of Independence (in 1961).
Issue dates: 4c, 5c, May 23; 15c, Aug. 10.

No. C245 Overprinted in Red: "1962 / EL MUNDO UNIDO / CONTRA LA MALARIA"
1962, Oct. 4 Photo. *Perf. 12½*
C258 AP54 6c ultra & vio brn .80 *1.25*

WHO drive to eradicate malaria.

Dr. José Luna — AP57

Guatemalan physicians: 4c, Rodolfo Robles. 5c, Narciso Esparragoza y Gallardo. 6c, Juan J. Ortega. 10c, Dario Gonzalez. 20c, José Felipe Flores.

1962, Dec. 12 Photo. *Perf. 14x13½*
C259 AP57 1c ol bis & dl pur .40 .20
C260 AP57 4c org yel & gray ol .40 .20
C261 AP57 5c pale bl & red brn .40 .20
C262 AP57 6c salmon & blk .40 .20
C263 AP57 10c pale grn & red brn .60 .20
C264 AP57 20c pale pink & bl .70 .60
Nos. C259-C264 (6) 2.90 1.60

No. C213 Overprinted in Red: "PRESIDENTE/ YDIGORAS/ FUENTES/ RECORRE POR TIERRA/ CENTRO AMERICA/ 14 A 20 DIC. 1962"
1962, Dec. Photo. *Perf. 14x13½*
C265 AP49 6c dk brn & dp ultra 1.00 .75

Pres. Ydigoras' tour of Central America, Dec. 14-20, 1962.

No. C213 Overprinted in Vermilion: "Reunion Presidents: Kennedy, EE. UU. - Ydigoras F., Guat. - Rivera. Salv. - Villeda M., Hond. - Somoza, Nic. - Orlich, C. R. - Chiari, Panama - San Jose, Costa Rica, 18 A 21 de Marzo de 1963"
Perf. 14x13½
1963, Mar. 18 Unwmk.
C266 AP49 6c dk brn & dp ultra 5.00 2.50

Meeting of Pres. John F. Kennedy with the Presidents of the Central American Republics, San Jose, Costa Rica, Mar. 18-21.

Nos. C245-C246 Overprinted "CONMEMORA / CION FIRMA / NUEVA CARTA / ODECA. - 1962" in Magenta or Black
1963, Mar. 14 *Perf. 12½*
C267 AP54 6c ultra & vio brn (M) .25 .20
C268 AP54 8c emerald & mag .35 .20

Signing of the new charter of the Organization of Central American States (ODECA).

Enriquez de Rivera Type of 1946
Perf. 11, 11½, 12½
1963, Mar. 26 Engr.
C269 A132 5c olive bister .20 .20

Woman Carrying Fruit Basket — AP58

1963, Mar. 14 Litho. *Perf. 11, 12½*
C270 AP58 1c multicolored .20 .20

Spring Fair, 1960.

Reaper — AP59

1963, July 25 Photo. *Perf. 14*
C271 AP59 5c Prus green .20 .20
C272 AP59 10c dark blue .35 .20

FAO "Freedom from Hunger" campaign.

Ceiba Tree — AP60

1963 Unwmk. *Perf. 12*
C273 AP60 4c brown & green .25 .20

Patzun Palace AP61

Buildings: 3c, Coban. 4c, Retalhuleu. 5c, San Marcos. 6c, Captains General of Antigua.

1964, Jan. 15 *Perf. 13½x14*
C274 AP61 1c rose red & brn .20 .20
C275 AP61 3c rose cl & Prus grn .20 .20
C276 AP61 4c vio bl & rose lake .20 .20
C277 AP61 5c brown & blue .25 .20
C278 AP61 6c green & slate .25 .20
Nos. C274-C278 (5) 1.10 1.00

City Hall, Guatemala City AP62

Design: 4c, Social Security Institute.

1964, Jan. 15 Photo. *Perf. 12x11½*
C279 AP62 3c brt bl & brn .20 .20
C280 AP62 4c brn & brt bl .20 .20

See Nos. C281-C282A. For overprints see Nos. C360-C361, C421.

1964-65 Engr. *Perf. 11½*

Designs: 3c, Social Security Institute. 4c, University administration building. No. C282, City Hall, Guatemala City. No. C282A, Engineering School.

Different Frames
C281 AP62 3c dull green .20 .20
C281A AP62 4c gray ('65) .20 .20
C282 AP62 7c blue .25 .20
C282A AP62 7c olive bis ('65) .20 .20
Nos. C281-C282A (4) .85 .80

Nos. C219-C222 Overprinted in Green, Blue or Black with Olympic Rings and: "OLIMPIADAS / TOKIO - 1964"
1964 Photo. *Perf. 13½x14, 14x13½*
C283 AP50 1c multi (G) .75 *1.00*
C284 AP50 2c multi (Bl) .75 *1.00*
C285 AP50 3c multi (G) .75 *1.00*
C286 AP50 4c multi (Bk) .75 *1.00*
Nos. C283-C286 (4) 3.00 *4.00*

18th Olympic Games, Tokyo, 10/10-25/64.

Nos. C219-C222 Surcharged in Green, Blue or Black with New Value and: "HABILITADA - 1964"
1964
C287 AP50 7c on 1c multi (G) .20 .20
C288 AP50 9c on 2c multi (Bl) .25 *.35*
C289 AP50 13c on 3c multi (Bl) .35 *.45*
C290 AP50 21c on 4c multi (Bk) .65 *.75*
Nos. C287-C290 (4) 1.45 *1.75*

Nos. C219-C222 Overprinted "FERIA MUNDIAL / DE NEW YORK" in Green, Blue or Black
1964, June 25
C291 AP50 1c multi (G) .50 *.75*
C292 AP50 2c multi (Bl) .50 *.75*
C293 AP50 3c multi (G) .50 *.75*
C294 AP50 4c multi (Bk) .50 *.75*
Nos. C291-C294 (4) 2.00 *3.00*

New York World's Fair.

Nos. C219-C222 Overprinted in Green, Blue or Black: "VIII VUELTA / CICLISTICA"
1964
C295 AP50 1c multi (G) .60 *.95*
C296 AP50 2c multi (Bl) .60 *.95*
C297 AP50 3c multi (G) .60 *.95*
C298 AP50 4c multi (Bk) 1.10 *1.50*
Nos. C295-C298 (4) 2.90 *4.35*

Eighth Bicycle Race.

Pres. John F. Kennedy — AP63

1964 Engr. *Perf. 11½*
C299 AP63 1c violet 1.00 .60
C300 AP63 2c yellow grn 1.00 .60
C301 AP63 3c brown 1.00 .60
C302 AP63 7c deep blue 1.00 .60
C303 AP63 50c dk gray 8.00 *6.50*
Nos. C299-C303 (5) 12.00 *8.90*

Minute letters "TEOK" are in lower right corner of 1c, 2c, 3c and 50c.
Issue dates: 7c, July 10; others, Aug. 21.

Centenary Emblem — AP64

Perf. 11x12
1964, Sept. 9 Unwmk. Photo.
C304 AP64 7c ultra, sil & red .50 .25
C305 AP64 9c org, sil & red .50 .40
C306 AP64 13c pur, sil & red .70 .55
C307 AP64 21c brt grn, sil & red .80 *1.00*
C308 AP64 35c brn, sil & red 1.25 *1.40*
C309 AP64 1q lem, sil & red 5.25 3.00
Nos. C304-C309 (6) 9.00 *6.60*

Centenary (in 1963) of the Intl. Red Cross.
For overprints see Nos. C323-C327, C395-C400.

Type of Regular Issue 1963
Souvenir Sheet
1964 Engr. *Imperf.*
C310 Sheet of 2 6.00 3.75
  a. A151 10c violet blue 2.50 1.50
  b. A151 20c carmine 2.50 1.50

15th UPU Congress, Vienna, May-June, 1964.

Enriquez de Rivera Type of 1946
1964, Dec. 18 Engr. *Perf. 11½*
C311 A132 5c gray .20 .20
C312 A132 5c orange .20 .20
C313 A132 5c lt green .20 .20
C314 A132 5c lt ultra .20 .20
C315 A132 5c dull violet .20 .20
Nos. C311-C315 (5) 1.00 1.00

Bishop Francisco Marroquin AP65

Guatemalan Boy Scout Emblem — AP66

1965, Jan. 21 Photo. Unwmk.
C316 AP65 4c lilac & brn .20 .20
C317 AP65 7c gray & sepia .20 .20
C318 AP65 9c vio bl & blk .25 .20
Nos. C316-C318 (3) .65 .60

Issued to honor Bishop Francisco Marroquin.

Bethancourt Type of Regular Issue, 1964
1965, Apr. 20 Engr. *Perf. 11½*
C319 A152 2½c violet blue .20 .20
C320 A152 3c orange .20 .20
C321 A152 4c purple .20 .20
C322 A152 5c yellow grn .20 .20
Nos. C319-C322 (4) .80 .80

For overprints see Nos. C381-C382.

Nos. C304-C308 Overprinted in Red: "AYUDENOS / MAYO 1965"

1965, June 18 Photo. *Perf. 11x12*

C323 AP64	7c ultra, sil & red	.35	.35
C324 AP64	9c org, sil & red	.40	.40
C325 AP64	13c pur, sil & red	.50	.50
C326 AP64	21c brt grn, sil & red	.65	.65
C327 AP64	35c brn, sil & red	1.00	1.10
	Nos. C323-C327 (5)	2.90	3.00

1966, Mar. 3 Photo. *Perf. 14x13½*

Designs: 9c, Campfire and Scouts. 10c, Scout emblem and Scout carrying torch and flag. 15c, Scout emblem, flags and Scout giving Scout sign. 20c, Lord Baden-Powell.

C328 AP66 5c multicolored	.50	.50
C329 AP66 9c multicolored	.50	.50
C330 AP66 10c multicolored	.70	.70
C331 AP66 15c multicolored	.80	.80
C332 AP66 20c multicolored	1.00	1.00
Nos. C328-C332 (5)	3.50	3.50

5th Interamerican Regional Training Conf., Guatemala City, Mar. 1-3.
For overprints see Nos. C376-C380.

Central American Independence Issue

Flags of Central American States — AP67

1966, Mar. 9 *Perf. 12½x13½*

C333 AP67 6c multicolored .20 .20

Queen Nefertari Temple, Abu Simbel AP68

1966, Oct. 3 Photo. *Perf. 12*

C334 AP68 21c violet & ocher .55 .30

UNESCO world campaign to save historic monuments in Nubia.

Coat of Arms — AP69

1966-70 Engr. *Perf. 13½*

C335 AP69 5c orange	.25	.20
C336 AP69 5c green	.25	.20
a. 5c yel grn, perf. 11½ ('69)	.25	.20

Perf. 11½

C337 AP69 5c blue ('67)	.25	.20
a. 5c dk bl, perf. 12½ ('69)	.25	.20

Perf. 12½

C338 AP69 5c gray ('67)	.25	.20
C339 AP69 5c purple ('67)	.25	.20
a. 5c bright violet ('69)	.25	.20

Perf. 11½

C339B AP69 5c dp mag ('70)	.25	.20
C339C AP69 5c grn, *yel* ('70)	.30	.20
Nos. C335-C339C (7)	1.80	1.40

Issued: #C335, 10/31; #C336, 12/15/66; #C337, 2/9/67; #C338-C339, 4/28/67; #C336a, 12/3/69; #C339a, 12/11/69; #C339B, 7/8/70; #C339C, 10/16/70.

Msgr. Mariano Rossell y Arellano AP70

1966, Nov. 3 Engr. *Perf. 13½*

C340 AP70 1c dp violet	.20	.20
C341 AP70 2c green	.20	.20
C342 AP70 3c brown	.20	.20
C343 AP70 7c blue	.35	.20
C344 AP70 50c gray	1.40	1.40
Nos. C340-C344 (5)	2.35	2.20

Issued to honor Msgr. Mariano Rossell y Arellano, apostolic delegate.

Mario Mendez Montenegro AP71

1966-67 *Perf. 13½*

C345 AP71 2c rose red ('67)	.20	.20
C346 AP71 3c orange ('67)	.20	.20
C347 AP71 4c rose claret ('67)	.20	.20
C348 AP71 5c gray	.35	.20
C349 AP71 5c lt ultra ('67)	.35	.20
C350 AP71 5c green ('67)	.35	.20
C351 AP71 5c bluish blk ('67)	.35	.20
Nos. C345-C351 (7)	2.00	1.40

Mario Mendez Montenegro (1910-65), founder of the Revolutionary Party.

Morning Glory and Map of Guatemala AP72

Flowers: 8c, Bird of paradise, horiz. 10c, White nun orchid, national flower, horiz. 20c, Nymphs of Amatitlan.

1967, Jan. 12 Photo. *Perf. 12*
Flowers in Natural Colors

C352 AP72 4c orange	.55	.25
C353 AP72 8c green	.55	.25
C354 AP72 10c dk blue	.65	.50
C355 AP72 20c dk red	1.25	1.00
Nos. C352-C355 (4)	3.00	2.00

Pan-American Institute Emblem — AP73

1967, Apr. 13 Photo. *Perf. 13½*

C356 AP73 4c lt brn, lil & blk	.20	.20
C357 AP73 5c ol, bl & blk	.35	.20
C358 AP73 7c org yel, bl & blk	.45	.20
Nos. C356-C358 (3)	1.00	.60

8th Gen. Assembly of the Pan-American Geographical and Historical Institute in 1965.

No. C281 Overprinted

1967, Apr. 28 Engr. *Perf. 11½*

C360 AP62 3c dull green .50 .40

Guatemala's victory in the 3rd Norceca Soccer Games (Caribbean, Central and North American).

No. C281A Overprinted in Red: "REUNION JEFES DE ESTADO / AMERICANO, PUNTA DEL ESTE, / MONTEVIDEO, URUGUAY 1967"

1967, June 28 Engr. *Perf. 11½*

C361 AP62 4c gray .65 .65

Meeting of American Presidents, Punta del Este, Apr. 10-12.

Handshake AP74

1967, June 28 Photo. *Perf. 12*

C362 AP74 7c pink, brn & grn	.30	.20
C363 AP74 21c lt bl, grn & brn	.50	.50

"Peace and Progress through Cooperation."
For overprint see No. C416.

Church of Santo Domingo AP75

1c, Yurrita Church, vert. 3c, Church of St. Francis. 4c, Antonio Joséde Irisarri, vert. 5c, Church of the Convent, vert. 7c, Mercy Church, Antigua. 10c, Metropolitan Cathedral.

1967, Aug. *Perf. 11½x12, 12x11½*

C364 AP75 1c grn, lt bl & dk brn	.20	.20
C365 AP75 2c plum, sal pink & brn	.25	.20
C366 AP75 3c brt rose, gray & blk	.25	.20
C367 AP75 4c mar, sl grn & org	.25	.20
C368 AP75 5c lil, pale grn & dk brn	.25	.20
C369 AP75 7c ultra, lil rose & blk	.30	.20
C370 AP75 10c pur, yel & blk	.50	.25
Nos. C364-C370 (7)	2.00	1.45

Abraham Lincoln (1809-1865) AP76

1967 Engr. *Perf. 13½, 11½ (9c)*

C371 AP76 7c gray & dp org	.35	.20
C372 AP76 9c dk grn & grysh	.40	.25
C373 AP76 11c brn org & slate	.40	.30
C374 AP76 15c ultra & vio brn	.65	.35
C375 AP76 30c magenta & grn	1.50	1.50
Nos. C371-C375 (5)	3.30	2.60

Issued: 7c, 9c, Oct. 9; others, Dec. 12.
For surcharge see No. C554.

Nos. C328-C332 Overprinted: "VIII Camporee Scout / Centroamericano / Diciembre 1-8/1967"

1967, Dec. 1 Photo. *Perf. 14x13½*

C376 AP66 5c multicolored	.35	.35
C377 AP66 9c multicolored	.50	.50
C378 AP66 10c multicolored	.65	.65
C379 AP66 15c multicolored	.70	.75
C380 AP66 20c multicolored	.80	.80
Nos. C376-C380 (5)	3.00	3.05

Issued to commemorate the 8th Central American Boy Scout Camporee, Dec. 1-8.

Nos. C320-C321 Overprinted in Four Lines: "Premio Nóbel de Literatura - 10 diciembre 1967 - Miguel Angel Asturias"

1967, Dec. 11 Engr. *Perf. 11½*

C381 A152 3c orange	.50	.50
C382 A152 4c purple	.50	.50

Awarding of the Nobel Prize for Literature to Miguel Angel Asturias, Guatemalan writer.

Institute Emblem — AP77

1967, Dec. 12 Engr. *Perf. 11½*

C383 AP77 9c black & grn	.65	.65
C384 AP77 25c car & brn	1.40	1.40
C385 AP77 1q ultra & bl	3.50	3.50
Nos. C383-C385 (3)	5.55	5.55

Inter-American Agriculture Institute, 25th anniv.

UNESCO Emblem and Children AP78

1967, Dec. 12

C386 AP78 4c blue green	.20	.20
C387 AP78 5c blue	.20	.20
C388 AP78 7c gray	.30	.30
C389 AP78 21c brt rose lil	.80	.80
Nos. C386-C389 (4)	1.50	1.50

20th anniv. (in 1966) of UNESCO.

Nos. C219-C221 and C304-C308 Overprinted in Black or Yellow Green: "III REUNION DE / PRESIDENTES / Nov. 15-18, 1967"

Perf. 13½x14, 14x13½, 11x12
1968, Jan. 23 Photo.

C390 AP50 1c multi	.65	.50
C391 AP50 1c multi (G)	.65	.75
C392 AP50 2c multi	.65	.75
C393 AP50 2c multi (G)	.65	.75
C394 AP50 3c multi	.65	.75
C395 AP64 3c multi (G)	.65	.75
C396 AP64 7c multi	.65	.75
C397 AP64 9c multi	1.00	1.00
C398 AP64 13c multi	1.40	1.00
C399 AP64 21c multi	2.00	1.00
C400 AP64 35c multi	1.60	1.75
Nos. C390-C400 (11)	10.55	9.75

3rd meeting of Central American Presidents, Nov. 15-18, 1967.

Our Lady of the Coro — AP79

Miguel Angel Asturias, Flags of Guatemala and Sweden — AP80

1968-74 Engr. *Perf. 13½, 11½*

C403 AP79 4c ultra	.40	.20
C404 AP79 7c slate	.35	.20
C405 AP79 9c green	.50	.20
C406 AP79 9c lilac ('74)	.20	.20
C407 AP79 10c brick red	.65	.20
C408 AP79 10c gray	.50	.20
C408A AP79 10c vio bl ('74)	.40	.20

C409 AP79 1q vio brn 3.50 3.00
C410 AP79 1q org yel 3.50 3.00
Nos. C403-C410 (9) 10.00 7.40

Perf. 13½ applies to 4c and Nos. C407, C409-C410; perf. 11½ to 4c, 7c, 9c and Nos. C408, C408A.

Nos. 396-398 Overprinted: "AEREO / XI VUELTA / CICLISTICA / 1967"

1968, Mar. 25 Litho. *Perf. 14x13½*
C411 A153 4c multicolored .50 .50
C412 A153 5c multicolored .50 .50
C413 A153 6c multicolored .40 .40
Nos. C411-C413 (3) 1.40 1.40

The 11th Bicycle Race.

1968, June 18 Engr. *Perf. 11½*
C414 AP80 20c ultra 1.00 .35

Awarding of the Nobel Prize for Literature to Miguel Angel Asturias.

No. C234 Overprinted in Carmine: "1968. - AÑO INTERNACIONAL / DERECHOS HUMANOS. - ONU"

1968, July 18 Litho. *Perf. 11*
C415 AP53 6c pale brown .50 .25

International Human Rights Year.

No. C362 Overprinted: "AYUDA A CONSERVAR / LOS BOSQUES. - 1968"

1968, July 18 Photo. *Perf. 12*
C416 AP74 7c pink, brn & grn .35 .20

Issued to publicize forest conservation.

No. C213 Overprinted in Brown: "Expedición / Científica / Nahakín / Guatemala-Peru / Ruta de los / Mayas"

1968, Aug. 23 Photo. *Perf. 14x13½*
C417 AP49 6c dk brn & dp ultra .25 .20

Nahakin scientific expedition along the route of the Mayas undertaken jointly with Peru.

Views, Quetzal and White Nun Orchid — AP81

1968, Aug. 23 Engr. *Perf. 13½*
C418 AP81 10c dp cl & grn .50 .20
C419 AP81 20c dp org & blk .75 .55
C420 AP81 50c ultra & car 1.25 1.25
Nos. C418-C420 (3) 2.50 2.00

Issued for tourist publicity.

No. C281A Overprinted in Carmine: "CONFEDERACION / DE UNIVERSIDADES / CENTROAMERICANAS / 1948 1968"

1968, Nov. 4 *Perf. 11½*
C421 AP62 4c gray .25 .25

20th anniv. of the Federation of Central American Universities.

Presidents Gustavo Diaz Ordaz and Julio Cesar Mendez Montenegro AP82

1968, Dec. 3 Litho. *Perf. 14x13½*
C422 AP82 5c multicolored .20 .20
C423 AP82 10c multicolored .35 .20
C424 AP82 25c multicolored .80 .75
Nos. C422-C424 (3) 1.35 1.15

Mutual visits of the Presidents of Mexico and Guatemala.

ITU Emblem, Old and New Communication Equipment — AP83

Engraved and Photogravure

1968-74 *Perf. 11½, 12½ (21c)*
C425 AP83 7c violet blue .25 .20
C426 AP83 15c gray & emer .35 .25
C426A AP83 15c vio brn & org ('74) .50 .25
C427 AP83 21c magenta .50 .35
C428 AP83 35c rose red & emer .90 .45
C429 AP83 75c green & red 2.00 2.00
C430 AP83 3q brown & red 6.50 6.50
Nos. C425-C430 (7) 11.00 10.00

Cent. (in 1965) of the ITU.
Nos. C425, C427 are engr. only; on others denominations are photo. No. C426A is on thin, toned paper.
Issued: #C426A, 2/18/74; others 12/13/68.
For surcharges see Nos. C454, C516.

Nos. 399-403 Overprinted in Red, Black or Gold

Lithographed and Engraved

1969 *Perf. 11½, 13½ (1c)*
C431 A154 1c blk, lt grn & red (R) .50 .50
C432 A154 5c yel, lt grn & red .65 .65
C433 A154 8c org, lt grn & red .80 .80
C434 A154 15c bl, lt grn & red 1.00 1.00
C435 A154 30c lt vio, lt grn & red (G) 1.40 1.40
Nos. C431-C435 (5) 4.35 4.35

Dante Alighieri — AP84

1969, July 17 Engr. *Perf. 12½*
C436 AP84 7c rose vio & ultra .20 .20
C437 AP84 10c dk blue .25 .20
C438 AP84 20c green .40 .20
C439 AP84 21c gray & brn .65 .70
C440 AP84 35c pur & brt grn 1.50 1.50
Nos. C436-C440 (5) 3.00 2.80

Dante Alighieri (1265-1321), Italian poet.

Map of Latin America — AP85

Design: 9c, Seal of University.

1969, Oct. 29 Typo. *Perf. 13*

Size: 44x27mm
C441 AP85 2c brt pink & blk .20 .20

Size: 35x27mm
C442 AP85 9c gray & blk .30 .20

Souvenir Sheet

Imperf
C443 AP85 Sheet of 2 .50 .50
a. 2c light blue & black .20 .20
b. 9c orange & black .20 .20

20th anniv. of the Union of Latin American Universities.

Moon Landing Issue

Moon Landing — AP86

1969-70 Engr. *Perf. 11½*
C444 AP86 50c maroon & blk 2.00 2.00
C445 AP86 1q ultra & blk 3.50 3.75

Souvenir Sheet

Imperf
C446 AP86 1q yel grn & ultra 3.75 4.00

See note after US No. C76. No. C446 contains one stamp with simulated perforations.
Issued: #C445-C446, 12/19/69; #C444, 1/6/70.

Giant Grebe Family on Lake Atitlan AP87

Designs: 4c, Lake Atitlan. 20c, Grebe chick, eggs atop floating nest, vert.

1970, Mar. 31 Litho. *Perf. 13½*
C447 AP87 4c red & multi .40 .20
C448 AP87 9c red & multi .60 .30
a. Souv. sheet of 2, #C447-C448 1.50 1.50
C449 AP87 20c red & multi 1.00 .75
Nos. C447-C449 (3) 2.00 1.25

Protection of zambullidor ducks.

Dr. Victor Manuel Calderon — AP88

Hand Holding Bible — AP89

1970 Litho. & Engr. *Perf. 13, 12½*
C450 AP88 1c lt bl & blk .20 .20
C451 AP88 2c pale grn & blk .20 .20

Perf. 13
C452 AP88 9c yellow & blk .30 .25
Nos. C450-C452 (3) .70 .65

Dr. Victor Manuel Calderon (1889-1969), who described microfilaria, a blood parasite.

1970 Litho. & Typo. *Perf. 13x13½*
C453 AP89 5c red & multi .25 .25

Fourth centenary of the Bible in Spanish.

No. C430 Surcharged

1971, Mar. 11 Engr. *Perf. 11½*
C454 AP83 50c on 3q brn & red 1.75 1.75

Arms of Guatemala, Newspapers — AP90

Official Decree of First Issue — AP91

1971 Litho. *Perf. 11½, 12½*
C455 AP90 2c dk bl & red .20 .20
C456 AP90 5c brn & red .20 .20
C457 AP90 25c brt bl & red .50 .25
Nos. C455-C457 (3) .90 .65

Souvenir Sheet

Lithographed and Engraved

Imperf
C458 AP91 Sheet of 5 1.50 1.50

Cent. of Guatemala's postage stamps.
Nos. C456-C457 have white value tablet.
No. C458 contains a litho. 4c black and engr. reproductions of Nos. 1-4 in colors similar to 1871 issue. Simulated perforations.
In 1974 No. C458 was overprinted "Conmemorativa / al Campeonato Mundial de Foot Ball / Munich 1974" and Munich Games emblem in black. Overprint in gold or other colors was not authorized.
See Nos. C569-C570.

Mayas with CARE Package — AP92

1971 Typo. *Perf. 11½*
C459 AP92 5c multi .30 .30
a. Souv. sheet of 2 1.50 1.50

25th anniversary of CARE, a US-Canadian Cooperative for American Relief Everywhere.
No. C459a contains imperf. stamps similar to Nos. 416 and C459.

J. Rufino Barrios, M. Garcia Granados, Map of Guatemala, Quetzal — AP93

1971, June 30 *Perf. 11½*
C460 AP93 2c multi, perf 13½ .25 .20
a. Value in pink ('72) .20 .20
C461 AP93 10c multi .40 .20
a. Value in pink, perf. 12½ ('72) .25 .20
C462 AP93 50c multi 1.50 1.50
C463 AP93 1q multi 3.00 3.00
Nos. C460-C463 (4) 5.15 4.90

Centenary of the liberal revolution of 1871.

Chavarry Arrué and León Bilak — AP94

Perf. 11½, 11x12½, 12½

1971-72 **Engr.**

C464	AP94	1c grn & blk ('72)	.20	.20
C465	AP94	2c lt brn & blk ('72)	.20	.20
C466	AP94	5c org & blk	.25	.20
		Nos. C464-C466 (3)	.65	.60

Honoring J. Arnoldo Chavarry Arrué, stamp engraver; León Bilak, philatelist.

No. C231 Overprinted

1971, Oct. 25 **Litho.** ***Perf. 11½***

C467	AP52	6c ultra & rose red	.25	.25

INTERFER 71, Intl. Fair, Guatemala, Oct. 30-Nov. 21.

Flag and Map of Guatemala AP95

UNICEF Emblem and Mayan Figure — AP96

Perf. 13½ (1c), 12½ (3c, 9c), 11 (5c)

1971-75 **Typo.**

C468	AP95	1c blk, bl & lil	.20	.20
a.		Lithographed ('75)	.20	.20
C469	AP95	3c brn, brt pink & bl	.20	.20
C470	AP95	5c brn, org & bl	.20	.20
a.		Lithographed, perf. 12½ ('74)	.20	.20
C471	AP95	9c blk, emer & bl	.20	.20
		Nos. C468-C471 (4)	.80	.80

Central American independence, sesqui. Date of issue: #C469-C471, July 10, 1972.

1971-75 **Engr.** ***Perf. 11½***

C472	AP96	1c yel grn	.20	.20
C472A	AP96	2c purple	.20	.20
C473	AP96	50c vio brn	1.75	1.75
C474	AP96	1q ultra	3.00	3.00
		Nos. C472-C474 (4)	5.15	5.15

25th anniv. UNICEF. Issued: 2c, 2/24/75; others, 11/71.

Early Boeing Planes — AP97

Design: 10c, Bleriot's plane.

1972 **Typo.** ***Perf. 11½***

C475	AP97	5c lt brn & brt bl	.25	.20
C476	AP97	10c dark blue	.50	.20

Military aviation in Guatemala, 50th anniv.

Arches, Antigua — AP98

1972-73 **Typo.** ***Perf. 11½***

Dark Blue and Light Blue

C480	AP98	1c shown	.20	.20
C481	AP98	1c Cathedral	.20	.20
C482	AP98	1c Fountain, Central Park	.20	.20
C483	AP98	1c Capuchin Monastery	.20	.20
C484	AP98	1c Fountain and Santa Clara	.20	.20
C485	AP98	1c Portal of San Francisco	.20	.20
a.		Block of 6, #C480-C485	1.00	.60

Black, Lilac Rose, and Silver

C486	AP98	2½c shown	.35	.20
C487	AP98	2½c Catherdral	.35	.20
C488	AP98	2½c Fountain and Santa Clara	.35	.20
C489	AP98	2½c Portal of San Francisco	.35	.20
C490	AP98	2½c Fountain	.35	.20
C491	AP98	2½c Capuchin Monastery	.35	.20
a.		Block of 6, #C3486-C491	2.10	1.00

Blue, Orange and Black

C492	AP98	5c shown	.65	.20
C493	AP98	5c Cathedral	.65	.20
C494	AP98	5c Santa Clara	.65	.20
C495	AP98	5c Portal of San Francisco	.65	.20
C496	AP98	5c Fountain	.65	.20
C497	AP98	5c Capuchin Monastery	.65	.20
a.		Block of 6, #C492-C497	4.00	1.00

Nos. C492-C497 exist perf. 12½, same value.

Perf. 12½

Red, Blue and Black

C498	AP98	1q Fountain	3.75	2.50
C499	AP98	1q Capuchin Monastery	3.75	2.50
C500	AP98	1q shown	3.75	2.50
C501	AP98	1q Cathedral	3.75	2.50
C502	AP98	1q Fountain and Santa Clara	3.75	2.50
C503	AP98	1q Portal of San Francisco	3.75	2.50
a.		Block of 6, #C498-C503	22.50	15.00
		Nos. C480-C503 (24)	29.70	18.60

Earthquake ruins of Antigua. 1c printed se-tenant in sheets of 90 (10x9); 2½c, 5c se-tenant in sheets of 30 (5x6); 1q se-tenant in sheets of 6 (3x2).

On Nos. C498-C503 the inks were applied by a thermographic process giving a shiny raised effect.

Issued: #C480-C485, 12/14; #C486-C491, 1/22/73; #C492-C497, 3/12/73; #C498-C503, 8/22/73.

Nos. C480-C485 were overprinted "II Feria Internacional / INTERFER/73 / 31 Octubre - Noviembre 18 / 1973 / GUATEMALA" in black or lilac rose and issued 11/3/73. Value $3.

The same overprint exists in black on Nos. C480-C485, but these stamps were not decreed or issued.

See Nos. C528-C545, C770-C775F. For overprints see Nos. C517-C523.

Simon Bolivar and Map of Americas AP99

1973-74 ***Perf. 11½***

C504	AP99	3c brt lil rose & blk	.20	.20
C505	AP99	3c org & dk bl ('74)	.20	.20
C506	AP99	5c yel & multi	.20	.20
C507	AP99	5c brt grn & blk	.20	.20
		Nos. C504-C507 (4)	.80	.80

Indian with CARE Package, World Map AP100

CARE Package AP101

1973, June 14 **Typo.** ***Perf. 12½***

C508	AP100	2c blk & multi	.20	.20
C509	AP101	10c blk & multi	.40	.40
a.		Souvenir sheet of 2	.80	.90

25th anniversary of CARE (in 1971), a US-sponsored relief organization and 10th anniversary of its work in Guatemala.

No. C509a contains 2 stamps similar to Nos. C508-C509 with simulated perforations.

Guatemala No. 1, Laurel AP102

1973-74 **Engr.** ***Perf. 12½, 11½ (1q)***

C510	AP102	1c yel brn ('74)	.20	.20
C511	AP102	1q rose claret	2.50	2.50

Centenary (in 1971) of Guatemala postage stamps. See Nos. C574-C576A.

Oak Wreath and Star AP103

1973, Aug. 22 **Typo.** ***Perf. 12½***

C512	AP103	5c brn, yel & bl	.20	.20

Centenary of Escuela Politecnica, Guatemala's military academy.

See Nos. C552-C553.

Eleanor Roosevelt AP104

1973, Sept. 11 **Engr.** ***Perf. 12½***

C513	AP104	7c blue	.20	.20

Eleanor Roosevelt (1884-1962), lecturer, writer, UN delegate.

Boys' School, Chiquimula AP105

1973-74 **Typo.** ***Perf. 12½***

C514	AP105	3c blk & bl	.20	.20
C515	AP105	5c blk & dp lil rose	.20	.20

Centenary of the Instituto Varones in Chiquimula.

Issued: 5c, 12/5/73; 3c, 6/13/74.

No. C430 Surcharged in Red: "Desvalorizadas a Q0.50" and Ornamental Obliteration of Old Denomination

1974 **Engr. & Photo.** ***Perf. 11½***

C516	AP83	50c on 3q brn & red	1.25	1.25

Nos. C480-C485 and C509a Overprinted with UPU Emblem, "UPU / HOMENAJE CENTENARIO / 1874 1974"

1974, June 13 **Typo.** ***Perf. 11½***

C517	AP98	1c dk bl & lt bl	.25	.30
C518	AP98	1c dk bl & lt bl	.25	.30
C519	AP98	1c dk bl & lt bl	.25	.30
C520	AP98	1c dk bl & lt bl	.25	.30
C521	AP98	1c dk bl & lt bl	.25	.30
C522	AP98	1c dk bl & lt bl	.25	.30
		Nos. C517-C522 (6)	1.50	1.80

Souvenir Sheet

C523		Sheet of 2	6.50	7.50

Centenary of Universal Postal Union.

No. C523 consists of an overprint on No. C509a, including "UNIVERSAL POSTAL UNION" instead of "UPU."

The overprint on No. C523 in red was not authorized by the Post Office.

Antigua Type of 1972-73

1974, Oct. 8 **Typo.** ***Perf. 11½***

Black and Light Brown

C528	AP98	2c Capuchin Monastery	.20	.20
C529	AP98	2c Arches	.20	.20
C530	AP98	2c Cathedral	.20	.20
C531	AP98	2c Fountain and Santa Clara	.20	.20
C532	AP98	2c Portal of San Francisco	.20	.20
C533	AP98	2c Fountain	.20	.20
		Nos. C528-C533 (6)	1.20	1.20

1974, Sept. 24

Black and Yellow

C540	AP98	20c Capuchin Monastery	.50	.50
C541	AP98	20c Arches	.50	.50
C542	AP98	20c Cathedral	.50	.50
C543	AP98	20c Fountain and Santa Clara	.50	.50
C544	AP98	20c Portal of San Francisco	.50	.50
C545	AP98	20c Fountain	.50	.50
		Nos. C540-C545 (6)	3.00	3.00

Earthquake ruins of Antigua. Each group of six printed se-tenant in sheets of 30 (5x6).

Nos. C528-C533 were printed in 1975 in black and bister se-tenant in sheets of 24 (4x6) on whiter paper.

Generals Justo Rufino Barrios and M. Garcia Granados — AP106

Polytechnic School AP107

1974-75 Typo. *Perf. 12½, 11½ (25c)*

C552 AP106 6c red, gray & bl .20 .20
C553 AP107 25c multi .35 .25

Centenary (in 1973) of Escuela Politecnica, Guatemala's military academy.
Issued: 6c, 9/17; 25c, 1/1/75.

No. C373 Surcharged in Black and Green

1974, Dec. 3 Engr. *Perf. 13½*

C554 AP76 10c on 11c multi .25 .20

Nature protection. The quetzal, Guatemala's national bird.

Costume San Martin Sacatepequez AP108

Costumes of Women: 2c, Solola. 9c, Coban. 20c, Chichicastenango.

1974-75 Typo. *Perf. 12½*

C556 AP108 2c car & multi .20 .20
C557 AP108 2½c bl, car & brn .20 .20
C559 AP108 9c bl & multi .30 .20
a. Perf. 12½x13½ .30 .20
C561 AP108 20c red & multi .50 .25
Nos. C556-C561 (4) 1.20 .85

Issue dates: 2½c, Dec. 16, 1974; 20c, Jan. 14, 1975; 2c, 9c, May 19, 1975.

Quetzals and Maya Quekchi Woman Wearing Huipil — AP109

1975, June 25 Litho. *Perf. 13½*

C565 AP109 8c bl & multi .35 .20
C566 AP109 20c red & multi .65 .20

International Women's Year 1975.

Rotary Emblem AP110

1975-76 Typo. *Perf. 13½*

C567 AP110 10c bl & multi .20 .20

Perf. 11½

C568 AP110 15c bl & multi .40 .20

Guatemala City Rotary Club, 50th anniv.
Issued: 10c, 10/1; 15c, 12/21/76.

Gaceta Type of 1971 Redrawn

1975-76 Typo. *Perf. 12½*

C569 AP90 5c brn & red .20 .20
C570 AP90 50c brt rose & brn 1.25 1.25

The white background around numeral and on right of arms has been filled in.
Issued: 5c, 12/12; 50c, 12/1/76.

IWY Emblem and White Nun Orchid — AP111

1975-76 *Perf. 12½x13½, 11½ (8c)*

C571 AP111 1c multi .20 .20
C572 AP111 8c yel & multi .25 .20
C573 AP111 26c rose & multi .65 .20
Nos. C571-C573 (3) 1.10 .60

International Women's Year 1975.
Issued: 1c, 12/19; 8c, 12/12; 26c, 5/10/76.

Stamp Centenary Type of 1973

1975-77 Engr. *Perf. 11½*

C574 AP102 6c orange .20 .20
C575 AP102 6c green ('76) .20 .20
C576 AP102 6c gray ('77) .20 .20
C576A AP102 6c vio bl ('77) .20 .20
Nos. C574-C576A (4) .80 .80

Issued: #C574, 12/31; #C575, 5/10; others, 8/10.

Destroyed Joyabaj Village — AP112

Designs (Guatemala Flag and): 3c, Emergency food distribution. 5c, Jaguar Temple, Tikal. 10c, Destroyed bridge. 15c, Outdoors emergency hospital. 20c, Sugar cane harvest. 25c, Destroyed house. 30c, New building, Tecpan. 50c, Destroyed Cerro del Carmen church. 75c, Cleaning up debris. 1q, Military help. 2q, Lake Atitlan.

1976, June 4 Litho. *Perf. 12½*

C577 AP112 1c red & multi .20 .20
C578 AP112 3c multi .20 .20
C579 AP112 5c pink & multi .20 .20
C580 AP112 10c red & multi .25 .20
C581 AP112 15c multi .35 .20
C582 AP112 20c pink & multi .45 .30
C583 AP112 25c red & multi .60 .35
C584 AP112 30c multi .75 .20
C585 AP112 50c red & multi 1.25 .75
C586 AP112 75c multi 2.00 1.00
C587 AP112 1q multi 2.50 1.25
C588 AP112 2q multi 5.00 3.00
Nos. C577-C588 (12) 13.75 7.85

Earthquake of Feb. 4, 1976, and gratitude for foreign help. Inscriptions in colored panels vary. 3 imperf. souvenir sheets exist (50c, 1q, 2q). Size: 112x83mm.

Allegory of Independence — AP113

Designs: 2c, Boston Tea Party. 3c, Thomas Jefferson, vert. 4c, 20c, 35c, Allegory of Independence (each different; 4c, 35c, vert.). 5c, Warren's Death at Bunker Hill. 10c, Washington at Valley Forge. 15c, Washington at Monmouth. 25c, The Generals at Yorktown. 30c, Washington Crossing the Delaware. 40c, Declaration of Independence. 45c, Patrick Henry, vert. 50c, Congress Voting Independence. 1q, Washington, vert. 2q, Lincoln, vert. 3q, Franklin, vert. 5q, John F. Kennedy, vert. The historical designs and portraits are after paintings.

1976, July 30 Litho. *Perf. 12½*
Size: 46x27mm, 27x46mm

C592 AP113 1c multicolored .20 .20
C593 AP113 2c multicolored .20 .20
C594 AP113 3c multicolored .20 .20
C595 AP113 4c multicolored .20 .20
C596 AP113 5c multicolored .20 .20
C597 AP113 10c multicolored .20 .20
C598 AP113 15c multicolored .30 .20
C599 AP113 20c multicolored .35 .20
C600 AP113 25c multicolored .45 .20
C601 AP113 30c multicolored .60 .20
C602 AP113 35c multicolored .65 .45
C603 AP113 40c multicolored .80 .55
C604 AP113 45c multicolored .90 .65
C605 AP113 50c multicolored 1.10 .45
C606 AP113 1q multicolored 2.00 2.00
a. Souvenir sheet 2.00 2.25
C607 AP113 2q multicolored 3.75 3.75
a. Souvenir sheet 4.50 4.75
C608 AP113 3q multicolored 5.50 5.50
a. Souvenir sheet 6.00 6.25

Size: 35x55mm

C609 AP113 5q multicolored 9.00 3.50
a. Souvenir sheet 11.00 11.50
Nos. C592-C609 (18) 26.60 18.85

American Bicentennial. Souvenir sheets contain one imperf. stamp each.

1974 Quetzal Coin AP114

Lithographed and Engraved

1976, Dec. 1 *Perf. 11½*

C610 AP114 8c org, blk & bl .20 .20

Perf. 13½

C611 AP114 20c brt rose, bl & blk .40 .20

50th anniv. of introduction of Quetzal currency.

Engineers at Work AP115

1976, Dec. 21 Engr. *Perf. 11½*

C612 AP115 9c ultra .20 .20
C613 AP115 10c green .20 .20

School of Engineering, Guatemala City, centenary.

Holy Week Type of 1977

Designs: Sculptures of Christ from various Guatemalan churches. 4c, 7c, 9c, 20c, vert.

1977, Apr. 4 Litho. *Perf. 11*

C614 A159 3c pur & multi .20 .20
C615 A159 4c pur & multi .20 .20
C616 A159 7c pur & multi .20 .20
C617 A159 9c pur & multi .25 .25
C618 A159 20c pur & multi .50 .50
C619 A159 26c pur & multi .65 .65
Nos. C614-C619 (6) 2.00 2.00

Souvenir Sheet

Roulette 7½

C620 A159 30c pur & multi .65 1.00

Holy Week 1977.

City Hall and Bank of Guatemala — AP116

Designs: 6c, Deed to original site, vert. 8c, Church and farm house, site of first legislative session. 9c, Coat of arms of Pedro Cortes, first archbishop. 22c, Arms of Guatemala City, vert.

Perf. 13½ (6c); 11½ (others)

1977, Aug. 10 Litho.

C621 AP116 6c multicolored .20 .20
C622 AP116 7c multicolored .20 .20
C623 AP116 8c multicolored .20 .20
C624 AP116 9c multicolored .25 .20
a. Souvenir sheet .25 .50
C625 AP116 22c multicolored .40 .20
a. Souvenir sheet .50 .75
Nos. C621-C625 (5) 1.25 1.00

Bicentenary of the founding of Nueva Guatemala de la Asuncion (Guatemala City). Nos. C624a-C625a contain one stamp each with simulated perforations.

Arms of Quetzaltenango AP117

City Hall and Torch AP118

1977, Sept. 11 Litho. *Perf. 11½*

C626 AP117 7c blk & sil .20 .20
C627 AP118 30c bl & yel .80 .20

Founding of Quetzaltenango, 150th anniv.

Mayan Bas-relief — AP119

1977, Nov. 7

C628 AP119 10c brt car & blk .20 .20

14th Intl. Cong. of Latin Notaries.

Children Bringing Gifts to Christ Child — AP120

Christmas: 1c, Mother and children, horiz. 4c, Guatemalan children's Nativity scene.

1977, Dec. 16 Litho. *Perf. 11½*

C629 AP120 1c multicolored .20 .20
C630 AP120 2c multicolored .20 .20
C631 AP120 4c multicolored .20 .20
Nos. C629-C631 (3) .60 .60

Almolonga Costume, Cancer League Emblem — AP121

Virgin of Sorrows, Antigua — AP122

Regional Costumes after Paintings by Carlos Mérida and Cancer League Emblem: 2c, Nebaj woman. 5c, San Juan Cotzal couple. 6c, Todos Santos couple. 20c, Regidores men. 30c, San Cristobal woman.

Perf. 14 (1c, 5c, No. C636); Perf. 12 (2c, 6c, No. C636a, 30c)

1978, Apr. 3 **Litho.**

C632 AP121 1c gold & multi .20 .20
C633 AP121 2c gold & multi .20 .20
C634 AP121 5c gold & multi .20 .20
C635 AP121 6c gold & multi .20 .20
C636 AP121 20c gold & multi .65 .50
a. Souv. sheet of 1 .65 .75
C637 AP121 30c gold & multi .65 .50
Nos. C632-C637 (6) 2.10 1.80

Part of proceeds from sale of stamps went to National League to Fight Cancer.

1978 **Litho.** ***Perf. 11½***

Statues from Various Churches: 4c, Virgin of Mercy, Antigua. 5c, Virgin of Anguish, Yurrita. 6c, Virgin of the Rosary, Santo Domingo. 8c, Virgin of Sorrows, Santo Domingo. 9c, Virgin of the Rosary, Quetzaltenango. 10c, Virgin of the Immaculate Conception, Church of St. Francis. 20c, Virgin of the Immaculate Conception, Cathedral Church.

C638 AP122 2c multicolored .20 .20
C639 AP122 4c multicolored .20 .20
C640 AP122 5c multicolored .20 .20
C641 AP122 6c multicolored .20 .20
C642 AP122 8c multicolored .20 .20
C643 AP122 9c multicolored .20 .20
C644 AP122 10c multicolored .20 .20
C645 AP122 20c multicolored .50 .20
Nos. C638-C645 (8) 1.90 1.60

Holy Week 1978. A 30c imperf. souvenir sheet shows the Pietà from Calvary Church, Antigua. Size: 71x101mm.

Issued: 6c, 10c, 20c, 9/28; others, 5/22.

Soccer Player, Argentina '78 Emblem AP123

1978, July 3 **Litho.** ***Perf. 12***

C646 AP123 10c multicolored .20 .20

11th World Cup Soccer Championship, Argentina, June 1-25.

Gymnastics AP124

1978, Sept. 4 ***Perf. 12***

C647 AP124 6c shown .20 .20
C648 AP124 6c Volleyball .20 .20
C649 AP124 6c Target shooting .20 .20
C650 AP124 6c Weight lifting .20 .20
a. Block of 4, #C647-C650 .40 .20
C651 AP124 8c Track & field .20 .20
Nos. C647-C651 (5) 1.00 1.00

13th Central American and Caribbean Games, Medellin, Colombia.

Cattleya Pachecoi AP125

Designs: Orchids.

1978, Dec. 7 **Litho.** ***Perf. 12***

C652 AP125 1c shown .20 .20
C653 AP125 1c Sobralia .20 .20
C654 AP125 1c Cypripedium .20 .20
C655 AP125 1c Oncidium .20 .20
a. Block of 4, #C652-C655 .30 .30
C656 AP125 3c Cattleya bowrigiana .20 .20
C657 AP125 3c Encyclia .20 .20
C658 AP125 3c Epidendrum .20 .20
C659 AP125 3c Barkeria .20 .20
a. Block of 4, #C656-C659 .30 .30
C660 AP125 8c Spiranthes .50 .50
C661 AP125 20c Lycaste 2.00 2.00
Nos. C652-C661 (10) 4.10 4.10

Seal of University AP126

Students of Different Departments AP127

Designs: 12c, Student in 17th cent. clothes. 14c, Students, 1978, and molecular model.

1978, Dec. 7

C662 AP126 6c multicolored .20 .20
C663 AP127 7c multicolored .20 .20
C664 AP126 12c multicolored .20 .20
C665 AP126 14c multicolored .25 .20
Nos. C662-C665 (4) .85 .80

San Carlos University of Guatemala, tercentenary.

Brown and White Children AP128

A Helping Hand — AP129

Designs: 7c, Child at play. 14c, Hands sheltering Indian girl.

1978, Dec. 7

C666 AP128 6c multicolored .20 .20
C667 AP128 7c multicolored .20 .20
C668 AP129 12c multicolored .20 .20
C669 AP129 14c multicolored .25 .20
Nos. C666-C669 (4) .85 .80

Year of the Children of Guatemala.

Tree Planting and FAO Emblem — AP130

Forest protection: 8c, Burnt forest. 9c, Watershed, river and trees. 10c, Sawmill. 26c, Forests, river and cultivated terraces.

1979, Apr. 16 **Litho.** ***Perf. 13½***

C670 AP130 6c multicolored .20 .20
C671 AP130 8c multicolored .20 .20
C672 AP130 9c multicolored .20 .20
C673 AP130 10c multicolored .20 .20
C674 AP130 26c multicolored .35 .20
a. Souv. sheet of 5, #C670-C674 .90 *1.25*
Nos. C670-C674 (5) 1.15 1.00

Peten Wild Turkey — AP131

Clay Jar, 50-100 A.D. — AP132

Wildlife conservation: 3c, White-tailed deer, horiz. 5c, King buzzard. 7c, Horned owl. 9c, Young wildcat. 30c, Quetzal.

1979, June 14 **Litho.** ***Perf. 13½***

C675 AP131 1c multicolored .20 .20
C676 AP131 3c multicolored .20 .20
C677 AP131 5c multicolored .20 .20
C678 AP131 7c multicolored .20 .20
C679 AP131 9c multicolored .20 .20
Nos. C675-C679 (5) 1.00 1.00

Souvenir Sheet

C680 AP131 30c multicolored 2.50 .75

1979, Sept. 19 **Litho.** ***Perf. 13***

Archaeological Treasures from Tikal: 3c, Mayan woman, ceramic head, 900 A.D. 4c, Earring, 50-100 A.D. 5c, vase, 700 A.D. 6c, Boy, 200-50 B.C. 7c, Bone carving, 700 A.D. 8c, Striped vase, 700 A.D. 10c, Covered vase on tripod, 450 B.C.

C681 AP132 2c multi .20 .20
C682 AP132 3c multi .20 .20
C683 AP132 4c multi .20 .20
C684 AP132 5c multi .20 .20
C685 AP132 6c multi .20 .20
C686 AP132 7c multi .20 .20
C687 AP132 8c multi .20 .20
C688 AP132 10c multi .20 .20
Nos. C681-C688 (8) 1.60 1.60

Presidential Guard Patches AP133

Presidential Guard, 30th anniv.: 10c, Guard Headquarters.

1979, Dec. 6 **Litho.** ***Perf. 11½***

C689 AP133 8c multi .20 .20
C690 AP133 10c multi .20 .20

National Coat of Arms — AP134

Arms of Guatemalan Municipalities.

1979, Dec. 27 **Litho.** ***Perf. 13½***

C691 AP134 8c shown .25 .20
C692 AP134 8c Alta Verapaz .25 .20
C693 AP134 8c Baja Verapaz .25 .20
C694 AP134 8c Chimal Tenango .25 .20
C695 AP134 8c Chiquimula .25 .20
C696 AP134 8c Escuintla .25 .20
C697 AP134 8c Flores .25 .20
C698 AP134 8c Guatemala .25 .20
C699 AP134 8c Huehuetenango .25 .20
C700 AP134 8c Izabal .25 .20
C701 AP134 8c Jalapa .25 .20
C702 AP134 8c Jutiapa .25 .20
C703 AP134 8c Mazatenango .25 .20
C704 AP134 8c Progreso .25 .20
C705 AP134 8c Quezaltenango .25 .20
C706 AP134 8c Quiche .25 .20
C707 AP134 8c Retalhuleu .25 .20
C708 AP134 8c Sacatepequez .25 .20
C709 AP134 8c San Marcos .25 .20
C710 AP134 8c Santa Rosa .25 .20
C711 AP134 8c Solola .25 .20
C712 AP134 8c Totonicapan .25 .20
C713 AP134 8c Zacapa .25 .20
Nos. C691-C713 (23) 5.75 4.60

Miniature Sheet

Imperf

C714 AP134 50c 1st & current natl. arms 1.50 .50

No. C714 is horizontal.

The Creation of the World — AP135

Designs: Scenes from The Creation, Popul Vuh (Sacred Book of the Ancient Quiches of Guatemala): No. C716, Origin of the Twin Semi-gods. No. C717, Populating the earth. No. C718, Balam Quitze. No. C719, Quiche monarch Cotuha. No. C720, Birth of the Stick Men. No. C721, Princess Xquic's punishment. No. C722, Caha Paluma. No. C723, Cotuha and Iztayul invincible. No. C724, Odyssey of Hun Ahpu and Xbalanque. No. C725, Balam Acab. No. C726, Chief of all Nations. No. C727, Destruction of the Stick Men. No. C728, The Test in Xibalba. No. C729, Chomiha. No. C730, Warrior with captive. No. C731, Creation of the Corn Men. No. C732, Multiplication of the Prodigies. No. C733, Mahucutah. No. C734, Undefeatable king. No. C735, Thanksgiving. No. C736, Deification of Hun Ahpu and Xbalanque. No. C737, Tzununiha. No. C738, Greatness of the Quiches (battle scene).

1981 Litho. *Perf. 12*

C715 AP135 1c multi .20 .20
C716 AP135 1c multi .20 .20
C717 AP135 2c multi .20 .20
C718 AP135 2c multi .20 .20
C719 AP135 3c multi .20 .20
C720 AP135 4c multi .20 .20
C721 AP135 4c multi .20 .20
C722 AP135 4c multi .20 .20
C723 AP135 4c multi .20 .20
C724 AP135 6c multi .20 .20
C725 AP135 6c multi .20 .20
C726 AP135 6c multi .20 .20
C727 AP135 8c multi .20 .20
C728 AP135 8c multi .20 .20
C729 AP135 8c multi .20 .20
C730 AP135 8c multi .20 .20
C731 AP135 10c multi .25 .20
C732 AP135 10c multi .25 .20
C733 AP135 10c multi .25 .20
C734 AP135 10c multi .25 .20
C735 AP135 22c multi .50 .20
C736 AP135 26c multi .60 .20
C737 AP135 30c multi .75 .25
C738 AP135 50c multi 1.25 .35
Nos. C715-C738 (24) 7.30 5.00

Issued: #C715, C717, 3c, C727, C731, 22c, 1/29; #C716, C718, C721-C722, C724-C725, C728-C729, C732-C733, 26c, 30c, 3/16; others, 1981.

Thomas Edison (Phonograph Centenary) AP136

Talking Movies, 50th Anniv. — AP137

Telephone Centenary (1976) — AP138

Lindbergh's Atlantic Flight, 50th Anniv. (1977) AP139

12c, Jose Cecilio del Valle, patriot. 25c, Jesus Castillo (1877-1949), composer.

Perf. 11½, 12½ (25c)

1981, June 1 Litho.

C739 AP136 3c multi .20 .20
C740 AP137 5c multi .20 .20
C741 AP138 6c multi .20 .20
C742 AP139 7c multi .20 .20
C743 AP139 12c multi .30 .20
C744 AP139 25c multi .60 .20
Nos. C739-C744 (6) 1.70 1.20

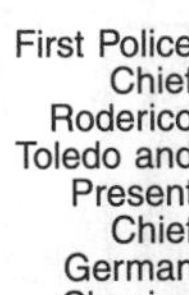

First Police Chief Roderico Toledo and Present Chief German Chupina AP140

1981, Sept. 12 Litho. *Perf. 11½*

C745 AP140 2c shown .20 .20
C746 AP140 4c Headquarters .20 .20

Mayan Rock of the Sun Calendar AP141

1981, Oct. 9

C747 AP141 1c multi .20 .20

Gen. Jose Gervasio Artigas of Uruguay AP142

Liberators of the Americas: 2c, Bernardo O'Higgins (Chile). 4c, Jose de San Martin (Argentina). 10c, Miguel Garcia Granados. 2c, 4c, 10c, 31x47mm.

1982, Apr. 2 Litho. *Perf. 11½*

C748 AP142 2c multi .20 .20
C749 AP142 3c multi .20 .20

Perf. 12½

C750 AP142 4c multi .20 .20
C751 AP142 10c tan & blk .20 .20
Nos. C748-C751 (4) .80 .80

Occidents Bank Centenary (1981) AP143

1c, Justo Rufino Barrios (1st pres.), Main Office, Quezaltenango. 2c, Main Office, 3c, Emblem, vert. 4c, Commemorative medals, vert.

1982, July 28 Litho. *Perf. 11½*

C752 AP143 1c multi .20 .20
C753 AP143 2c multi .20 .20
C754 AP143 3c multi .20 .20
C755 AP143 4c multi .20 .20
Nos. C752-C755 (4) .80 .80

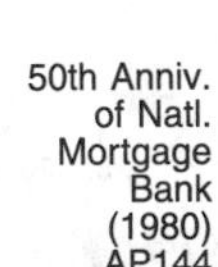

50th Anniv. of Natl. Mortgage Bank (1980) AP144

Various emblems. 5c vert.

1982, Oct. 18 Litho. *Perf. 11½*

C756 AP144 1c multi .20 .20
C757 AP144 2c multi .20 .20
C758 AP144 5c multi .20 .20
C759 AP144 10c multi .20 .20
Nos. C756-C759 (4) .80 .80

AP145

AP146

1983, May 16 Litho. *Perf. 11½*

C760 AP145 1c Portrait .20 .20
C761 AP145 20c Aparition, horiz. .25 .20

20th Anniv. of Beatification of Pedro Bethancourt (1626-1667).

1983, July 25 Litho. *Perf. 11½*

C762 AP146 10c multi .20 .20

World Telecommunications and Health Day, May 17, 1981

Evangelical Church Centenary (1982) — AP147

1983, Aug. 9

C763 AP147 3c Hands holding bible .20 .20
C764 AP147 5c Church .20 .20

Natl. Railroad Centenary — AP148

10c, 1st locomotive crossing Puenta de Las Vacas. 25c, General Justo Rufino Barrios, Railroad Yard. 30c, Spanish Diesel, Amatitlan crossing.

1983, Sept. 28 Litho. *Perf. 11½*

C765 AP148 10c multi .20 .20
C766 AP148 25c multi .25 .20
C767 AP148 30c multi .40 .20
Nos. C765-C767 (3) .85 .60

World Food Day AP149

1983, Oct. 16 Photo. *Perf. 11½*

C768 AP149 8c Globe, wheat, vert. .20 .20
C769 AP149 1q shown 1.40 1.00

Architecture Type of 1972

1984, Feb. 20 Typo. *Perf. 12½*

Black and Green

C770 AP98 1c like #C480 .20 .20
C771 AP98 1c like #C481 .20 .20
C772 AP98 1c like #C482 .20 .20
C773 AP98 1c like #C483 .20 .20
C774 AP98 1c like #C484 .20 .20
C775 AP98 1c like #C485 .20 .20
g. Strip of 6, #C770-C775 .30 .30

Black, Brown and Orange Brown

C775A AP98 5c like #C484 .20 .20
C775B AP98 5c like #C485 .20 .20
C775C AP98 5c like #C482 .20 .20
C775D AP98 5c like #C483 .20 .20
C775E AP98 5c like #C480 .20 .20
C775F AP98 5c like #C481 .20 .20
h. Strip of 6, #C775A-C775F .60 .60

Visit of Pope John Paul II, Mar. 8-9, 1983 AP150

1984, Mar. 26 Litho. *Perf. 11½*

C776 AP150 4c Pope, arms .20 .20
C777 AP150 8c Receiving Mayan indian .20 .20

Rafael Landivar (1731-93), Poet — AP151

Cardinal Mario Casariego y Acevedo AP152

1984, Aug. 6 Litho. *Perf. 11½*

C778 AP151 2c Portrait, vert. .20 .20
C779 AP151 4c Tomb .20 .20

1984, Aug. 6

C780 AP152 10c 16th archbishop of Guat. (1909-83) .20 .20

Central American Bank for Economic Integration, 20th Anniv. — AP153

1984, Sept. 10 Litho. *Perf. 11½*

C781 AP153 30c Bank emblem, map .40 .20

Coffee Production, 1870 AP154

Modern Coffee Production AP155

Designs: 1c, Planting coffee. 2c, Harvesting. 3c, Drying beans. 4c, Loading beans on steamer. 5c, Reyna plant grafting method. 10c, Picking beans, coffee cup. 12c, Drying unripened beans, Gardiola Freeze-drying machine. 25c, Cargo transports.

1984, Dec. 19 ***Perf. 11½***

C782 AP154 1c sep & pale brn .20 .20
C783 AP154 2c sep & pale org brn .20 .20
C784 AP154 3c sep & beige .20 .20
C785 AP154 4c sep & pale yel brn .20 .20
C786 AP155 5c multi .20 .20
C787 AP155 10c multi .20 .20
C788 AP155 12c multi .20 .20
C789 AP155 25c multi .35 .20
Nos. C782-C789 (8) 1.75 1.60

Natl. coffee production and export. An 86x112mm 25c stamp of Type AP154 and a 105x85mm 30c stamp of Type AP155 exist.

Natl. Scouting Assoc. — AP156

Scouting emblems and: 5c, Beaver scout, Pyramid of Tikal. 6c, Wolf scout, Palace of the Captains-General and Ahua Volcano. 8c, Scout, San Pedro Volcano and Marimba player. 10c, Rover scout and conquest mask dance. 20c, Lord Baden-Powell and Col. Carlos Cipriani, natl. founder.

1985, July 1

C792 AP156 5c multi .20 .20
C793 AP156 6c multi .20 .20
C794 AP156 8c multi .20 .20
C795 AP156 10c multi .20 .20
C796 AP156 20c multi .20 .20
Nos. C792-C796 (5) 1.00 1.00

Inter-American Family Unity Year — AP157

Central American Aeronautics Admin., 25th Anniv. — AP158

1985, Oct. 16

C797 AP157 10c multi .20 .20

1985, Nov. 11

C798 AP158 10c multi .20 .20

Natl. Telegraph, Cent. — AP159

Portraits: Samuel Morse, telegraph inventor, and Justo Rufino Barrios, communications pioneer.

1985, Nov. 20 ***Perf. 12***

C799 AP159 4c brn & blk .20 .20

Intl. Olympic Committee, 90th Anniv. — AP160

Designs: 8c, Mayan bust of ancient sportsman. 10c, Baron Pierre de Coubertin (1863-1937), father of modern Games, 1st committee president.

1986, Jan. 28 Litho. ***Perf. 11½***

C800 AP160 8c multi .20 .20
C801 AP160 10c multi .20 .20

Volunteer Fire Department AP161

1986, Feb. 6 Litho. ***Perf. 11½***

C802 AP161 6c multi .20 .20

Temple of Minerva — AP162

Quetzeltenango Coat of Arms, City Hall — AP163

1986, July 16 Litho. ***Perf. 12½, 11½***

C803 AP162 8c multi .20 .20
C804 AP163 10c multi .20 .20

Quetzeltenango Independence Fair, cent.

Volunteer Fire Department AP164

1986, Oct. 10 Litho. ***Perf. 11½***

C805 AP164 8c Rescue .20 .20
C806 AP164 10c Ruins .20 .20

Assoc. of Telegraphers and Radio-Telegraph Operators, 25th Anniv. — AP165

1986, Oct. 10 ***Perf. 12***

C807 AP165 6c multi .20 .20

San Carlos University School of Architecture, 25th Anniv. — AP166

1987, Feb. 16 Litho. ***Perf. 11½***

C808 AP166 10c multi .20 .20

ICAO, 40th Anniv. (in 1984) AP167

1987, Apr. 2 Litho. ***Perf. 11½***

C809 AP167 8c Aviateca Airlines jet .20 .20
C810 AP167 10c Jet, vert. .20 .20

Chixoy Hydroelectric Power Plant — AP168

1987, May 18 Litho. ***Perf. 11½***

C811 AP168 2c multi .20 .20

Nat'l. Electrification Institute inauguration (in 1985).

San Jose de los Infantes College, 200th Anniv. (in 1981) AP169

8c, Portrait of Archbishop Cayetano Francos y Monroy, founder. 10c, College crest.

1987, June 10

C812 AP169 8c multi, vert. .20 .20
C813 AP169 10c multi .20 .20

Promotion of Literacy in Latin America and Caribbean AP170

1987, Aug. 20 Litho. ***Perf. 11½***

C814 AP170 12c apple grn, blk & brt org .25 .20

19th Natl. Folklore Carnival of Coban, Alta Verapaz, July 25 — AP171

1987, Oct. 12

C815 AP171 1q Three girls from Tamahu 2.10 .70

1987, Dec. 8

C816 AP171 50c Girl weaving 1.50 .50

See No. C831.

9th Pan American Games, Caracas AP172

1987, Nov. 5 ***Perf. 12½***

C817 AP172 10c blk & sky blue .20 .20

Writers and Historians AP173

Esquipulas II — AP174

Designs: 1c, Flavio Herrera, poet, novelist. 2c, Rosendo Santa Cruz, novelist. 3c, Werner Ovalle Lopez, poet. 4c, Enrique A. Hidalgo, poet, humorist. 5c, Enrique Gomez Carrillo (1873-1927), novelist. 6c, Cesar Branas (1899-1976), journalist. 7c, Clemente Marroquin Rojas, historian. 8c, Rafael Arevalo Martinez (1884-1975), poet. 9c, Jose Milla y Vidaurre (1822-1882), historian. 10c, Miguel Angel Asturias, Nobel laureate for literature.

1987-90 ***Perf. 11½***

C818 AP173 1c blk & lil .20 .20
C819 AP173 2c blk & dl org .20 .20
C820 AP173 3c blk & brt bl .20 .20
C821 AP173 4c blk & ver .20 .20
C822 AP173 5c blk & org brn .20 .20
C823 AP173 6c blk & org .20 .20
C824 AP173 7c blk & grn .20 .20
C825 AP173 8c blk & brt red .20 .20
C826 AP173 9c blk & brt rose lil .20 .20
C827 AP173 10c blk & yel .20 .20
Nos. C818-C827 (10) 2.00 2.00

Issued: 6c, 8c, 9c, 11/5/87; 4c, 5c, 1/13/88; 7c, 3/23/90; 1c, 2c, 3c, 10c, 4/9/90.

1988, Jan. 15 ***Perf. 12½***

C828 AP174 10c dark olive grn .20 .20
C829 AP174 40c plum .85 .30
C830 AP174 60c deep blue vio 1.25 .40
Nos. C828-C830 (3) 2.30 .90

2nd Meeting of the Central American Peace Plan. Nos. C828-C829 horiz.

Folklore Festival Type of 1987

1988, Dec. 6 Litho. ***Imperf.***

Souvenir Sheet

C831 AP171 2q Music ensemble, horiz. 4.00 1.40

St. John Bosco (1815-1888), Educator AP175

1989, Feb. 1 Litho. ***Perf. 11½***

C832 AP175 40c gold & blk .80 .30

French Revolution, Bicent. AP176

1989, Oct. 18 Litho. *Perf. 11½*

C833 AP176 1q dark red, blk & deep blue 2.00 .70

America Issue — AP177

UPAE emblem and: 10c, Detail of the *Madrid Codex.* 20c, Temple of the Gran Jaguar of Tikal, Tikal Natl. Park.

1990, Jan. 25 Litho. *Perf. 11½*

C834 AP177 10c shown .25 .20
C835 AP177 20c brown & multi .50 .20
C836 AP177 20c black & multi .50 .20
Nos. C834-C836 (3) 1.25 .60

Institute of Nutrition of Central America and Panama, 40th Anniv. AP178

1990, May 18

C837 AP178 20c multicolored .40 .20

Red Cross, Red Crescent Societies, 125th Anniv. AP179

1990, June 8

C838 AP179 50c multicolored 1.00 .35

Defense Ministry General Staff, Cent. AP180

1991, May 8 Litho. *Perf. 11½*

C839 AP180 20c multicolored .40 .20

America AP181

UPAE: 10c, Pacaya Volcano Erupting at Night. 60c, Lake Atitlan.

1991, July 30 Litho. *Perf. 11½*

C840 AP181 10c multicolored .20 .20
C841 AP181 60c multicolored 1.25 .30

America Issue AP182

Designs: 40c, Pinzon brothers, Nina. 60c, Columbus, Santa Maria, vert.

1992, July 27 Litho. *Perf. 11½*

C842 AP182 40c green & black .90 .20
C843 AP182 60c green & black 1.25 .30

AP183

AP184

1992, Oct. 6 Litho. *Perf. 12½*

C844 AP183 10c multicolored .20 .20

Interamerican Institute for Agricultural Cooperation, 50th anniv.

1992, Dec. 1 Photo. *Perf. 11½*

C845 AP184 1q multicolored 2.00 .50

World campaign against AIDS.

Orchids — AP185

20c, Phragmipedium caudatum. 50c, Encyclia cochleata. 1q, Encyclia vitellina. 1.50q, Odontoglossum laeve 2q, Odontoglossum uroskinneri.

1994, Aug. 9 Litho. *Perf. 11½*

C845A AP185 20c multi
C846 AP185 50c multi .20 .20
C847 AP185 1q multi .35 .20
C847A AP185 1.50q multi
C848 AP185 2q multi .65 .25

#C845A, C847A put on sale 8/16/96.

Tourism — AP186

Designs: 20c, Rafting. 40c, Water sports. 60c, Boats on Lake Atitlan, volcanic mountain. 80c, Tourist boat on Lake Atitlan. 1q, Mt. Pacaya erupting. 2q, Guatemala City. 3q, Macaws, vert. 4q, Temple of the Gran Jaguar, vert. 5q, Holy Week procession from Antigua, carpet of colored saw dust, vert.

1995-96 Litho. *Perf. 12½*

C849 AP186 20c multicolored .20 .20
C850 AP186 40c multicolored .20 .20
C851 AP186 60c multicolored .30 .20
C852 AP186 80c multicolored .35 .20
C853 AP186 1q multicolored .35 .20
C854 AP186 2q multicolored .70 .20
C855 AP186 3q multicolored 1.00 .35
C856 AP186 4q multicolored 1.40 .45
C857 AP186 5q multicolored 1.75 .60
Nos. C849-C857 (9) 6.25 2.60

Issued: #C850, 7/5/96; #C852, 7/9/96.

Visit of Pope John Paul II — AP187

Papal arms, quotation, Pope John Paul II: 10c, With arms outstreached, dove, "That all the people join hands for peace." 1q, Kissing infant, "Let the children come unto me." 1.75q, Holding crucifix, "The house of the Lord is my house." 1.90q, Looking forward, "Blessed is he who comes in the name of the Lord." 2.90q, Waving hand, "Remember that all men are our brothers."

1996, Jan. 5 Litho. *Perf. 12½*

C858 AP187 10c multicolored .25 .20
C859 AP187 1q multicolored .40 .20
C860 AP187 1.75q multicolored .60 .20
C861 AP187 1.90q multicolored .75 .20
C862 AP187 2.90q multicolored 1.25 .30
Nos. C858-C862 (5) 3.25 1.10

Distinguished Guatemalans AP188

Designs: 40c, Carlos Merida (Self-portrait). 50c, José Eulalio Samayoa. 60c, Manuel Montufar y Coronado.

1996, Oct. 21 Litho. *Perf. 12½*

C863 AP188 40c multicolored .20 .20
C864 AP188 50c multicolored .20 .20
C865 AP188 60c multicolored .25 .20
Nos. C863-C865 (3) .65 .60

Mother Breastfeeding — AP190

1997, Mar. 6 *Perf. 11½*

C868 AP190 1q multicolored .40 .20

Public Finance Projects — AP191

Designs: 20c, Education. 60c, Health care. 80c, Road construction. 1q, Family security.

1997, Oct. 6 Litho. *Perf. 11½x12½*

C869 AP191 20c multicolored .20 .20
C870 AP191 60c multicolored .30 .20
C871 AP191 80c multicolored .40 .20
C872 AP191 1q multicolored .50 .20
Nos. C869-C872 (4) 1.40 .80

Jorge Rybar and Machine — AP192

1998 Litho. *Perf. 12½*

C873 AP192 10c multi .20 .20

Plastics industry in Guatemala, 50th anniv.

Intl. Society of Guatemala Collectors, 50th Anniv. — AP193

1999, May 14 Litho. *Perf. 11½x12½*

C874 AP193 1q Quetzel note .40 .25

AIR POST SEMI-POSTAL STAMPS

Air Post Stamps of 1937 Surcharged in Red or Blue

1937, Mar. 15 Unwmk. *Perf. 12½*

CB1 AP10 4c + 1c ultra (R) .75 *.85*
CB2 AP10 6c + 1c blk vio (R) .75 *.85*
CB3 AP11 10c + 1c ol grn (Bl) .75 *.85*
CB4 AP11 15c + 1c ver (Bl) .75 *.85*
Nos. CB1-CB4 (4) 3.00 *3.40*

1st Phil. Exhib. held in Guatemala, 3/15-20.

Catalogue values for unused stamps in this section, from this point to the end of the section, are for Never Hinged items.

Type of Regular Issue, 1956

Designs: 35c+1q, Red Cross, Ambulance and Volcano. 50c+1q, Red Cross, Hospital and Nurse. 1q+1q, Nurse and Red Cross.

Perf. 13x12½

1956, June 19 Engr. Unwmk.

CB5 A148 35c + 1q red & ol grn 5.00 *5.50*
CB6 A148 50c + 1q ultra & red 5.00 *5.50*
CB7 A148 1q + 1q dk grn & dk red 5.00 *5.50*
Nos. CB5-CB7 (3) 15.00 *16.50*

The surtax was for the Red Cross.

Nos. B5-B7 Overprinted

1957, May 11

CB8 A148 5c + 15c 6.50 *7.00*
  a. Imperf., pair 225.00
CB9 A148 15c + 50c 6.50 *7.00*
  a. Overprint inverted 275.00
CB10 A148 25c + 50c 6.50 *7.00*
Nos. CB8-CB10 (3) 19.50 *21.00*

The surtax was for the Red Cross.

Type of Semi-Postal Stamps, 1957 and

Esquipulas Cathedral SPAP1

15c+1q, Cathedral & crucifix. 20c+1q, Christ with crown of thorns and part of globe. 25c+1q, Archbishop Mariano Rossell y Arellano.

Perf. 13½x14½, 13

1957, Oct. 29 Engr. Unwmk.

CB11 SPAP1	10c + 1q choc & emer	6.25	*6.75*
CB12 SP1	15c + 1q dl grn & sep	6.25	*6.75*
CB13 SP1	20c + 1q bl gray & brn	6.25	*6.75*
CB14 SP1	25c + 1q lt vio & car	6.25	*6.75*
	Nos. CB11-CB14 (4)	25.00	*27.00*

The tax was for the Esquipulas highway.

Wounded Man, Battle of Solferino SPAP2

Designs: 6c+6c, 20c+20c, Flood disaster. 10c+10c, 25c+25c, Earth, moon and stars. 15c+15c, 30c+30c, Red Cross headquarters.

1960, Apr. 9 Photo. *Perf. 13½x14*

CB15 SPAP2	5c + 5c multi	2.25	*2.50*
CB16 SPAP2	6c + 6c multi	2.25	*2.50*
CB17 SPAP2	10c + 10c multi	2.25	*2.50*
CB18 SPAP2	15c + 15c multi	2.25	*2.50*
CB19 SPAP2	20c + 20c multi	2.25	*2.50*
CB20 SPAP2	25c + 25c multi	2.25	*2.50*
CB21 SPAP2	30c + 30c multi	2.25	*2.50*
	Nos. CB15-CB21 (7)	15.75	*17.50*

Cent. (in 1959) of the Red Cross idea. The surtax went to the Red Cross. Exist imperf.

AIR POST OFFICIAL STAMPS

Nos. C93-C98 Overprinted in Black

1939, Apr. 29 Unwmk. *Perf. 12½*

CO1 AP13	1c org & ol brn	1.00	1.10
CO2 AP13	2c multi	1.00	1.10
CO3 AP13	3c multi	1.00	1.10
CO4 AP13	4c multi	1.00	1.10
CO5 AP13	5c multi	1.00	1.10
CO6 AP13	10c multi	1.00	1.10
	Nos. CO1-CO6 (6)	6.00	6.60

No. C99 with Same Overprint on each Stamp

1939

CO7 AP19	Sheet of 6	2.25	2.25
a.	1c yel org, blue & blk	.30	.25
b.	2c lake, org, blue & blk	.30	.25
c.	3c olive, blue & orange	.30	.25
d.	4c dk claret, bl, org & blk	.30	.25
e.	5c grnsh bl, bl, red, org & blk	.30	.25
f.	10c olive bister, red & org	.30	.25

SPECIAL DELIVERY STAMPS

No. 237 Overprinted in Red

1940, June Unwmk. *Perf. 14*

E1 A81 4c orange 1.50 .35

No. E1 paid for express service by motorcycle messenger between Guatemala City and Coban.

Catalogue values for unused stamps in this section, from this point to the end of the section, are for Never Hinged items.

Motorcycle Messenger SD1

Black Surcharge

1948, Sept. 3 Photo. *Perf. 14x12½*

E2 SD1 10c on 4c bl grn & gray blk 3.00 .85

No. E2 without surcharge was issued for regular postage, not special delivery. See No. 337B.

OFFICIAL STAMPS

O1

National Emblem — O2

1902, Dec. 18 Typeset *Perf. 12*

O1 O1	1c green	3.75	1.75
O2 O1	2c carmine	3.75	1.75
O3 O1	5c ultra	4.50	1.50
O4 O1	10c brown violet	5.00	1.50
O5 O1	25c orange	5.25	1.50
a.	Horiz. pair, imperf. between	100.00	
	Nos. O1-O5 (5)	22.25	8.00

Nos. O1-O5 printed on thin paper with sheet watermark "AMERICAN LINEN BOND." Nos. O1-O3 also printed on thick paper with sheet watermark "ROYAL BANK BOND." Values are for copies that do not show the watermark. Counterfeits of Nos. O1-O5 exist.

During the years 1912 to 1926 the Post Office Department perforated the word "OFICIAL" on limited quantities of the following stamps: Nos. 114-123, 132, 141-149, 151-153, 158, 202, 210-229 and RA2. The perforating was done in blocks of four stamps at a time and was of two types.

A rubber handstamp "OFICIAL" was also used during the same period and was applied in violet, red, blue or black to stamps No. 117-118, 121-123, 163-165, 172 and 202-218.

Both perforating and handstamping were done in the post office at Guatemala City and use of the stamps was limited to that city.

1929, Jan. Engr. *Perf. 14*

O6 O2	1c pale grnsh bl	.25	.25
O7 O2	2c dark brown	.25	.25
O8 O2	3c green	.25	.25
O9 O2	4c deep violet	.35	.30
O10 O2	5c brown car	.35	.35
O11 O2	10c brown orange	.60	.60
O12 O2	25c dark blue	1.25	1.00
	Nos. O6-O12 (7)	3.30	3.00

POSTAL TAX STAMPS

National Emblem — PT1

Perf. 13½, 14, 15

1919, May 3 Engr. Unwmk.

RA1 PT1 12½c carmine .20 .20

Tax for rebuilding post offices.

G. P. O. and Telegraph Building — PT2

1927, Nov. 10 Typo. *Perf. 14*

RA2 PT2 1c olive green .20 .20

Tax to provide a fund for building a post office in Guatemala City.

No. RA2 Overprinted in Green

1936, June 30

RA3 PT2 1c olive green .50 .40

Liberal revolution, 65th anniversary.

No. RA2 Overprinted in Blue

1936, Sept. 15

RA4 PT2 1c olive green .40 .30

Independence of Guatemala, 2115th anniv.

No. RA2 Overprinted in Red Brown

1936, Nov. 15

RA5 PT2 1c olive green .50 .40

National Fair.

No. RA2 Overprinted in Red

1937, Mar. 15

RA6 PT2 1c olive green .40 .40

No. RA2 Overprinted in Blue

1938, Jan. 10 *Perf. 14x14½*

RA7 PT2	1c olive green	.25	.20
a.	"1937-1939" omitted	110.00	

150th anniv. of the US Constitution.

No. RA2 Overprinted in Blue or Red

1938 *Perf. 14*

RA8 PT2	1c olive green (Bl)	.30	.20
RA9 PT2	1c olive green (R)	.30	.20

No. RA2 Overprinted in Violet

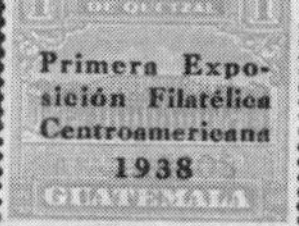

1938, Nov. 20

RA10 PT2 1c olive green .30 .20

1st Central American Philatelic Exposition.

No. RA2 Overprinted in Green or Black

1939

RA11 PT2	1c olive green (G)	.35	.20
RA12 PT2	1c olive green (Bk)	.35	.20

No. RA2 Overprinted in Violet or Brown

1940

RA13 PT2	1c olive green (V)	.35	.20
RA14 PT2	1c olive green (Br)	.35	.20

No. RA2 Overprinted in Red

1940, Apr. 14

RA15 PT2 1c olive green .25 .20

Pan American Union, 50th anniversary.

No. RA2 Overprinted in Red

1941

RA16 PT2 1c olive green .50 .20

No. 235 Surcharged in Red

RA17 A79 1c on 2c deep blue .25 .20

No. 235 Surcharged in Carmine

1942, Jan.
RA18 A79 1c on 2c deep blue .50 .20

Arch of Communications Building
PT3 PT4
With Imprint Below Design

1942, June 3 Engr. *Perf. 11, 12x11*
RA19 PT3 1c black brown 5.00 1.25

No imprint; Thin Paper

Perf. 11, 12x11, 11x12, 11x12x11x11

1942, July 18
RA20 PT3 1c black brown .35 .20

1943 *Perf. 11, 12x11, 12*
RA21 PT4 1c orange .25 .20

PT5

Perf. 11, 12½ and Compound

1945, Feb. Unwmk.
RA22 PT5 1c orange .20 .20

1949 *Perf. 12½*
RA23 PT5 1c deep ultra .30 .20

GUINEA

ˈgi-nē

LOCATION — Coast of West Africa, between Guinea-Bissau and Sierra Leone
GOVT. — Republic
AREA — 94,926 sq. mi.
POP. — 7,538,953 (1999 est.)
CAPITAL — Conakry

This former French Overseas Territory of French West Africa proclaimed itself an independent republic on October 2, 1958.

100 Centimes = 1 Franc
100 Caury = 1 Syli (1973)
100 Centimes = 1 CFA Franc (1986)

Catalogue values for all unused stamps in this country are for Never Hinged items.

Common Design Types pictured following the introduction.

French West Africa No. 79 Overprinted

1959 Unwmk. Photo. *Perf. 12x12½*
168 CD104 10fr multi 1.50 1.75

French West Africa No. 78 Surcharged in Red

Engr.
Perf. 13
169 A33 45fr on 20fr multi 1.60 1.75

Map, Dove and Pres. Sékou Touré A12

1959 Unwmk. Engr. *Perf. 13*
170 A12 5fr rose car .20 .20
171 A12 10fr ultramarine .25 .20
172 A12 20fr orange .45 .25
173 A12 65fr slate green 1.25 .65
174 A12 100fr violet 2.10 1.40
Nos. 170-174 (5) 4.25 2.70

Proclamation of independence, Oct. 2, 1958.

Bananas — A13

Flag Raising, Labé — A15

Fishing Boats and Tamara Lighthouse A14

1959 Litho. *Perf. 11½*
175 A13 10fr shown .20 .20
176 A13 15fr Grapefruit .20 .20
177 A13 20fr Lemons .35 .20
178 A13 25fr Avocados .45 .20
179 A13 50fr Pineapple .80 .20
Nos. 175-179 (5) 2.00 1.00

For overprints see Nos. 209-213.

1959 Engr. *Perf. 13½*

5fr, Coco palms & sailboat, vert. 10fr, Launching fishing pirogue. 15fr, Elephant's head. 20fr, Pres. Sékou Touré & torch, vert. 25fr, Elephant.

180 A14 1fr rose .20 .20
181 A14 2fr green .20 .20
182 A14 3fr brown .20 .20
183 A14 5fr blue .20 .20
184 A14 10fr claret .20 .20
185 A14 15fr light brn .25 .20
186 A14 20fr claret .35 .20
187 A14 25fr red brown .40 .20
Nos. 180-187 (8) 2.00 1.60

1959 Litho. *Perf. 12*
188 A15 50fr multicolored .40 .20
189 A15 100fr multicolored .90 .30

For overprints see Nos. 201-202.

UN Headquarters, New York, and People of Guinea — A16

1959 *Perf. 12*
190 A16 1fr vio blue & org .20 .20
191 A16 2fr red lil & emer .20 .20
192 A16 3fr brn & crimson .20 .20
193 A16 5fr brn & grnsh bl .20 .20
Nos. 190-193,C22-C23 (6) 1.75 1.70

Guinea's admission to the UN, first anniv.
For overprints see Nos. 205-208, C27-C28.

Uprooted Oak Emblem — A17

1960 Photo. *Perf. 11½*
Granite Paper
194 A17 25fr multicolored .40 .20
195 A17 50fr multicolored .60 .20

World Refugee Year, 7/1/59-6/30/60.
For surcharges see Nos. B17-B18.

UPU Monument, Bern — A18

1960 Granite Paper Unwmk.
196 A18 10fr gray brn & blk .20 .20
197 A18 15fr lil & purple .25 .20
198 A18 20fr ultra & dk blue .35 .20
199 A18 25fr yel grn & sl grn .45 .20
200 A18 50fr red org & brown .50 .20
Nos. 196-200 (5) 1.75 1.00

Nos. 199-200 are vertical.
Admission to the UPU, first anniv.

Nos. 188-189 Overprinted in Black, Orange or Carmine: "Jeux Olympiques Rome 1960" and Olympic Rings

1960 Litho. *Perf. 12*
201 A15 50fr multi (Bk) 3.25 3.25
202 A15 100fr multi (O or C) 5.00 5.00
Nos. 201-202,C24-C26 (5) 40.00 34.50

17th Olympic Games, Rome, 8/25-9/11.

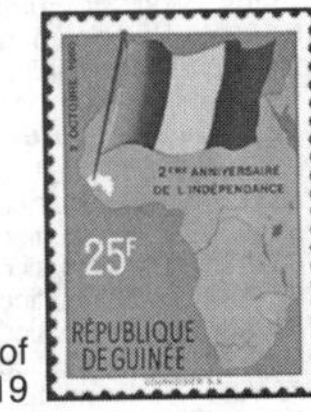

Map and Flag of Guinea — A19

1960 Photo. *Perf. 11½*
203 A19 25fr multicolored .25 .25
204 A19 30fr multicolored .35 .25

Second anniversary of independence.

Nos. 190-193 Overprinted

1961 Litho. *Perf. 12*
205 A16 1fr vio blue & org .20 .20
206 A16 2fr red lil & emer .20 .20
207 A16 3fr brn & crimson .20 .20
208 A16 5fr brn & grnsh bl .20 .20

Nos. 175-179 Overprinted in Black or Orange

Perf. 11½
Fruits in Natural Colors
209 A13 10fr red .20 .20
210 A13 15fr grn & pink .20 .20
211 A13 20fr red brn & bl .25 .20
212 A13 25fr bl & yel (O) .25 .25
213 A13 50fr dk vio blue .50 .40
Nos. 205-213,C27-C28 (11) 3.30 3.00

15th anniversary of United Nations.

Defassa Waterbuck A20

1961, Sept. 1 Photo. *Perf. 11½*
Multicolored Design; Granite Paper
214 A20 5fr bright grn .20 .20
215 A20 10fr emerald .20 .20
216 A20 25fr lilac .25 .20
217 A20 40fr orange .45 .20
218 A20 50fr red orange 1.00 .25
219 A20 75fr ultramarine 1.40 .25
Nos. 214-219 (6) 3.50 1.30

For surcharges see Nos. B19-B24.

Exhibition Hall — A21

1961, Oct. 2 *Perf. 11½*
Flag in Red, Yellow & Green
Granite Paper
220 A21 5fr ultra & red .20 .20
221 A21 10fr brown & red .20 .20
222 A21 25fr gray grn & red .20 .20
Nos. 220-222 (3) .60 .60

First Three-Year Plan.

Gray-breasted Helmet Guinea Fowl — A22

1961 Unwmk. *Perf. 13x14*
223 A22 5fr rose lil, sepia & bl .20 .20
224 A22 10fr dp org, sepia & bl .25 .20
225 A22 25fr cerise, sepia & bl .35 .20
226 A22 40fr ocher, sepia & bl .60 .20
227 A22 50fr lemon, sepia & bl .75 .20
228 A22 75fr apple grn, sep & bl 1.50 .30
Nos. 223-228 (6) 3.65 1.30

For surcharges see Nos. B30-B35.

Patrice Lumumba and Map of Africa — A23

1962, Feb. 13 Photo. *Perf. 11½*

229	A23	10fr multicolored	.40	.25
230	A23	25fr multicolored	.50	.25
231	A23	50fr multicolored	.30	.25
		Nos. 229-231 (3)	1.20	.75

Death anniv. (on Feb. 12, 1961) of Patrice Lumumba, Premier of the Congo Republic.

King Mohammed V of Morocco and Map of Africa — A24

1962, Mar. 15 Litho. *Perf. 13*

232	A24	25fr multicolored	.40	.20
233	A24	75fr multicolored	.90	.30

First anniv. of the conference of African heads of state at Casablanca.

For surcharges see Nos. B36-B37.

African Postal Union Issue

Map of Africa and Post Horn — A25

1962, Apr. 23 Photo. *Perf. 13½x13*

234	A25	25fr org, blk & grn	.50	.20
235	A25	100fr deep brn & org	1.25	.25

Establishment of African Postal Union.

Bolon Player A26

Musical Instruments: 30c, 25fr, 50fr, Bote, vert. 1fr, 10fr, Flute, vert. 1.50fr, 3fr, Koni. 2fr, 20fr, Kora. 40fr, 75fr, Bolon.

Perf. 13½x13, 13x13½

1962, June 15

236	A26	30c bl, dk grn & red	.20	.20
237	A26	50c sal, brn & brt grn	.20	.20
238	A26	1fr yel grn, grn & lil	.20	.20
239	A26	1.50fr yel, red & bl	.20	.20
240	A26	2fr rose lil, red lil & grn	.20	.20
241	A26	3fr brn grn, grn & lil	.20	.20
242	A26	10fr org, brn & bl	.20	.20
243	A26	20fr ol, dk ol & car	.20	.20
244	A26	25fr ol, dk ol & lil	.20	.20
245	A26	40fr bl, grn & red lil	.30	.20
246	A26	50fr rose, dp rose & Prus bl	.40	.25
247	A26	75fr dl yel, brn & Prus bl	.50	.35
		Nos. 236-247,C32-C34 (15)	7.75	5.60

Hippopotamus — A27

25fr, 75fr, Lion. 30fr, 100fr, Leopard.

1962, Aug. 25 Litho. *Perf. 13x13½*

248	A27	10fr org, grn & brn	.20	.20
249	A27	25fr emer, blk & brn	.25	.20
250	A27	30fr yel grn, dk brn & yel	.30	.20
251	A27	50fr vio bl, dk brn & grn	.40	.25
252	A27	75fr lil, lt lil & red brn	.55	.35
253	A27	100fr grnsh bl, dk brn & yel	.65	.50
		Nos. 248-253 (6)	2.35	1.70

See Nos. 340-345

Child at Blackboard — A28

Designs: 10fr, 20fr, Adult class.

1962, Sept. 19 Photo. *Perf. 13½x13*

254	A28	5fr yel, dk brn & org	.20	.20
255	A28	10fr org & dk brn	.20	.20
256	A28	15fr yel grn, dk brn & red	.20	.20
257	A28	20fr bl & dk brn	.20	.20
		Nos. 254-257 (4)	.80	.80

Campaign against illiteracy.

Imperforates
From late 1962 onward, most Guinea stamps exist imperforate.

Alfa Yaya — A29

1962, Oct. 2 *Perf. 13½*

30fr, King Behanzin. 50fr, King Ba Bemba. 75fr, Almamy Samory. 100fr, Tierno Aliou.

Gold Frame

258	A29	25fr brt bl & sepia	.25	.20
259	A29	30fr yel & sepia	.35	.20
260	A29	50fr brt pink & sepia	.40	.25
261	A29	75fr yel grn & sepia	1.00	.40
262	A29	100fr org, red & sepia	1.25	.60
		Nos. 258-262 (5)	3.25	1.65

Heroes and martyrs of Africa.

Gray Parrot A30

Birds: 30c, 3fr, 50fr, Crowned crane (vert). 1fr, 20fr, Abyssinian ground hornbill. 1.50fr, 25fr, White spoonbill. 2fr, 40fr, Bateleur eagle.

1962, Dec. *Perf. 13½x13, 13x13½*

263	A30	30c multicolored	.20	.20
264	A30	50c multicolored	.20	.20
265	A30	1fr multicolored	.20	.20
266	A30	1.50fr multicolored	.20	.20
267	A30	2fr multicolored	.20	.20
268	A30	3fr multicolored	.20	.20
269	A30	10fr multicolored	.20	.20
270	A30	20fr multicolored	.20	.20
271	A30	25fr multicolored	.20	.20
272	A30	40fr multicolored	.30	.20
273	A30	50fr multicolored	.40	.25
274	A30	75fr multicolored	.50	.35
		Nos. 263-274,C41-C43 (15)	8.90	5.70

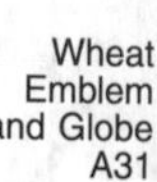

Wheat Emblem and Globe A31

1963, Mar. 21 Photo. *Perf. 13x14*

275	A31	5fr red & yellow	.20	.20
276	A31	10fr emerald & yel	.20	.20
277	A31	15fr brown & yel	.20	.20
278	A31	25fr dark ol & yel	.20	.20
		Nos. 275-278 (4)	.80	.80

FAO "Freedom from Hunger" campaign.

Basketball — A32

50c, 4fr, 30fr, Boxing. 1fr, 5fr, Running. 1.50fr, 10fr, Bicycling. 2fr, 20fr, Single sculls.

1963, Mar. 16 Unwmk. *Perf. 14*

279	A32	30c ver, dp claret & grn	.20	.20
280	A32	50c lilac & blue	.20	.20
281	A32	1fr dl org, sep & grn	.20	.20
282	A32	1.50fr org, ultra & mag	.20	.20
283	A32	2fr aqua, dk bl & mag	.20	.20
284	A32	3fr ol, dp cl & grn	.20	.20
285	A32	4fr car rose, pur & bl	.20	.20
286	A32	5fr brt grn, ol & mag	.20	.20
287	A32	10fr lil rose, ultra & mag	.20	.20
288	A32	20fr red org, dk bl & crim	.20	.20
289	A32	25fr emer, dp cl & dk grn	.25	.20
290	A32	30fr gray, pur & bl	.30	.20
		Nos. 279-290,C44-C46 (15)	7.70	5.40

For overprints and surcharges see Nos. 312-314, C58-C60.

A33

Various Butterflies.

1963, May 10 Photo. *Perf. 12*

291	A33	10c dp rose, blk & gray	.20	.20
292	A33	30c rose, blk & yel	.20	.20
293	A33	40c yel grn, brn & yel	.20	.20
294	A33	50c pale vio, blk & grn	.20	.20
295	A33	1fr yel, blk & emer	.20	.20
296	A33	1.50fr bluish grn, blk & sep	.20	.20
297	A33	2fr multi	.20	.20
298	A33	3fr multi	.20	.20
299	A33	10fr rose lil, blk & grn	.20	.20
300	A33	20fr gray, blk & grn	.20	.20
301	A33	25fr yel grn, blk & gray	.30	.20
302	A33	40fr multi	.40	.20
303	A33	50fr ultra, blk & yel	.50	.20
304	A33	75fr yel, blk & grn	.60	.35
		Nos. 291-304,C47-C49 (17)	9.95	5.55

Handshake, Map and Dove — A34

1963, May 22 *Perf. 13½x14*

305	A34	5fr bluish grn & dk brn	.20	.20
306	A34	10fr org yel & dk brn	.20	.20
307	A34	15fr ol & dk brn	.20	.20
308	A34	25fr bis brn & dk brn	.20	.20
		Nos. 305-308 (4)	.80	.80

Conference of African heads of state for African Unity, Addis Ababa.

Globe Encircled by Satellite — A35

1963, July 25 Engr. *Perf. 10½*

309	A35	5fr green & car	.20	.20
310	A35	10fr vio bl & car	.20	.20
311	A35	15fr yellow & car	.20	.20
		Nos. 309-311,C50 (4)	.85	.80

Centenary of the International Red Cross.

Nos. 279-281 Surcharged in Carmine, Yellow or Orange: "COMMISSION PRÉPARATOIRE AUX JEUX OLYMPIQUES À CONAKRY," New Value and Olympic Rings

1963, Nov. 20 Photo. *Perf. 14*

312	A32	40fr on 30c (C or Y)	1.10	1.00
313	A32	50fr on 50c (C or O)	1.50	1.40
314	A32	75fr on 1fr (C or O)	2.50	2.00
		Nos. 312-314,C58-C60 (6)	15.20	12.80

Meeting of the Olympic Games Preparatory Commission at Conakry. The overprint is in a circular line on #312, in 3 lines on each side on #313-314.

Jewelfish A36

Fish: 40c, 30fr, Golden pheasant. 50c, 40fr, Blue gularis. 1fr, 75fr, Banded Jewelfish. 1.50fr, African lyretail. 2fr, Six-barred epiplatys. 5fr, Jewelfish.

1964, Feb. 15 Litho. *Perf. 14x13½*

315	A36	30c car rose & multi	.20	.20
316	A36	40c pur & multi	.20	.20
317	A36	50c car rose & multi	.20	.20
318	A36	1fr blue & multi	.20	.20
319	A36	1.50fr blue & multi	.20	.20
320	A36	2fr pur & multi	.20	.20
321	A36	5fr blue & multi	.20	.20
322	A36	30fr grn & multi	.20	.20
323	A36	40fr pur & multi	.50	.25
324	A36	75fr multi	.65	.35
		Nos. 315-324,C54-C55 (12)	5.45	3.60

John F. Kennedy A37

1964, Mar. 5 Engr. *Perf. 10½*

Flag in Red and Blue

325	A37	5fr blk & pur	.20	.20
326	A37	25fr grn & pur	.20	.20
327	A37	50fr brn & pur	.40	.25
		Nos. 325-327,C56 (4)	1.60	1.45

Issued in sheets of 20 with marginal quotations in English and French. Two sheets for each denomination. See No. C56.

Workers Welding Pipe — A38

5fr, Pipe line over mountains, vert. 10fr, Waterworks. 30fr, Transporting pipe. 50fr, Laying pipe.

1964, May 1 Photo. *Perf. 11½*

328 A38 5fr deep mag .20 .20
329 A38 10fr bright pur .20 .20
330 A38 20fr org red .20 .20
331 A38 30fr ultra .20 .20
332 A38 50fr yel grn .20 .20
Nos. 328-332 (5) 1.00 1.00

Completion of the water-supply pipeline to Conakry, Mar. 1964.

Ice Hockey — A39

1964, May 15 *Perf. 13x12½*

333 A39 10fr shown .20 .20
334 A39 25fr Ski jump .30 .20
335 A39 50fr Slalom .60 .35
Nos. 333-335,C57 (4) 1.75 1.15

9th Winter Olympic Games, Innsbruck, Jan. 29-Feb. 9, 1964.

Eleanor Roosevelt Reading to Children — A40

1964, June 1 Engr. *Perf. 10½*

336 A40 5fr green .20 .20
337 A40 10fr red org .20 .20
338 A40 15fr bright bl .20 .20
339 A40 25fr car rose .20 .20
Nos. 336-339,C61 (5) 1.20 1.05

Eleanor Roosevelt, 15th anniv. of the Universal Declaration of Human Rights (in 1963).

Animal Type of 1962

Designs: 5fr, 30fr, Striped hyenas. 40fr, 300fr, Black buffaloes. 75fr, 100fr, Elephants.

1964, Oct. 8 Litho. *Perf. 13x13½*

340 A27 5fr yellow & blk .20 .20
341 A27 30fr light bl & blk .20 .20
342 A27 40fr lil rose & blk .25 .20
343 A27 75fr yel grn & blk .55 .25
344 A27 100fr bister & blk .65 .40
345 A27 300fr orange & blk 1.90 1.10
Nos. 340-345 (6) 3.75 2.35

Guinea Exhibit, World's Fair — A41

1964, Oct. 26 Engr. *Perf. 10½*

346 A41 30fr vio & emerald .20 .20
347 A41 40fr red lil & emer .30 .20
348 A41 50fr sepia & emer .40 .20
349 A41 75fr rose red & dk bl .60 .25
Nos. 346-349 (4) 1.50 .85

New York World's Fair, 1964-65.
See Nos. 372-375, C62-C63, C69-C70.

Queen Nefertari Crowned by Isis and Hathor — A42

Designs: 25fr, Ramses II in battle. 50fr, Submerged sphinxes, sailboat, Wadies-Sebua. 100fr, Ramses II holding crook and flail, Abu Simbel. 200fr, Feet and legs of Ramses statues, Abu Simbel.

1964, Nov. 19 Photo. *Perf. 12*

350 A42 10fr dk bl, red brn & cit .20 .20
351 A42 25fr blk, dl red & brn .20 .20
352 A42 50fr dk brn, bl & vio .25 .20
353 A42 100fr dk brn, yel & pur .40 .30
354 A42 200fr pur, dl grn & buff .90 .55
Nos. 350-354,C64 (6) 3.85 2.55

UNESCO campaign to preserve Nubian monuments.
For overprint see No. 415.

Weight Lifter and Caucasian, Japanese and Negro Children — A43

1965, Jan. 18 Photo. *Perf. 13x12½*

10fr, Runner carrying torch. 25fr, Pole vaulting and flags. 40fr, Runners. 50fr, Judo. 75fr, Japanese woman, flags and stadium.

355 A43 5fr gold, claret & blk .20 .20
356 A43 10fr gold, blk, ver & bl .20 .20
357 A43 25fr gold, blk, yel grn & red .20 .20
358 A43 40fr gold, blk, brn & yel .20 .20
359 A43 50fr gold, blk & grn .35 .25
360 A43 75fr gold & multi .60 .35
Nos. 355-360,C65 (7) 2.75 1.75

18th Olympic Games, Tokyo, 10/10-25/64.
For overprints see Nos. 410-414.

Doudou Mask, Boké — A44

Designs: 40c, 1fr, 15fr, Various Niamou masks, N'Zérékoré region. 60c, "Yoki," wood-carved statuette of a girl, Boke. 80c, Masked woman dancer from Guekedou. 2fr, Masked dancer from Macenta. 20fr, Beater from Tam-tam. 60fr, Bird dancer from Macenta. 80fr, Bassari dancer from Koundara. 100fr, Sword dancer from Karana.

1965, Feb. 15 Unwmk. *Perf. 14*

361 A44 20c multicolored .20 .20
362 A44 40c multicolored .20 .20
363 A44 60c multicolored .20 .20
364 A44 80c multicolored .20 .20
365 A44 1fr multicolored .20 .20
366 A44 2fr multicolored .20 .20
367 A44 15fr multicolored .20 .20
368 A44 20fr multicolored .20 .20
369 A44 60fr multicolored .50 .35
370 A44 80fr multicolored .50 .40
371 A44 100fr multicolored .70 .40
Nos. 361-371,C68 (12) 5.55 3.65

World's Fair Type of 1964 Inscribed "1965"

1965, Mar. 24 Engr. *Perf. 10½*

372 A41 30fr grn & orange .20 .20
373 A41 40fr car & brt grn .25 .20
374 A41 50fr brt grn & vio .35 .25
375 A41 75fr brown & vio .50 .35
Nos. 372-375 (4) 1.30 1.00

See Nos. C69-C70.

Blacksmith A45

Handicrafts: 20fr, Potter. 60fr, Cloth dyers. 80fr, Basketmaker.

1965, May 1 Photo. *Perf. 14*

376 A45 15fr multicolored .20 .20
377 A45 20fr multicolored .20 .20
378 A45 60fr multicolored .40 .25
379 A45 80fr multicolored .45 .35
Nos. 376-379,C71-C72 (6) 3.85 2.15

ITU Emblem, Old and New Communication Equipment — A46

1965, May 17 Unwmk.

380 A46 25fr yel, gray, gold & blk .20 .20
381 A46 50fr yel, grn, gold & blk .30 .25
Nos. 380-381,C73-C74 (4) 2.75 1.25

ITU centenary.

Maj. Virgil I. Grissom — A47

Moon from 258mi. — A48

Sputnik Over Earth A49

American Achievements in Space: 10fr, Lt. Com. John W. Young. 25fr, Moon from 115mi. 30fr, Moon from 58mi. 100fr, Grissom and Young in Gemini 2 spaceship.

1965, July 19 Photo. *Perf. 13*

Size: 21x29mm

382 A47 5fr dk red & multi .20 .20
383 A47 10fr dk red & multi .20 .20
384 A48 15fr gold, bl & dk bl .20 .20

Size: 39x28mm

385 A48 25fr gold, bl & dk bl .20 .20

Size: 21x29mm

386 A48 30fr gold, bl & dk bl .20 .20

Size: 39x28mm

387 A47 100fr multi & dk red .50 .40
a. Sheet of 15, #382-387 4.00

Russian Achievements in Space: 5fr, Col. Pavel Belyayev. 10fr, Lt. Col. Alexei Leonov. 15fr, Vostoks 3 & 4 in space. 30fr, Vostoks 5 & 6 over Earth. 100fr, Leonov floating in space.

Size: 21x29mm

388 A47 5fr bl & multi .20 .20
389 A47 10fr bl & multi .20 .20
390 A49 15fr bl & multi .20 .20

Size: 39x28mm

391 A49 25fr bl & multi .20 .20

Size: 21x29mm

392 A49 30fr bl & multi .20 .20

Size: 39x28mm

393 A47 100fr blk, dk red & gold .50 .40
a. Sheet of 15, #388-393 4.00
Nos. 382-393 (12) 3.00 2.80

American and Russian achievements in space. Nos. 387a and 393a contain five triptychs each: four rows with 5fr, 100fr and 10fr, and a center row with 15fr, 25fr and 30fr stamps each.

ICY Emblem, UN Headquarters and Skyline, New York — A50

1965, Sept. 8 *Perf. 10½*

394 A50 25fr yel grn & ver .20 .20
395 A50 45fr vio & orange .25 .20
396 A50 75fr red brn & org .40 .25
Nos. 394-396,C75 (4) 1.65 1.00

Intl. Cooperation Year, 1965.

Polytechnic Institute, Conakry — A51

New Projects, Conakry: 30fr, Hotel Camayenne. 40fr, Gbessia Airport. 75fr, Stadium "28 September."

1965, Oct. 2 Photo. *Perf. 13½*

397 A51 25fr multicolored .20 .20
398 A51 30fr multicolored .25 .20
399 A51 40fr multicolored .40 .25
400 A51 75fr multicolored .50 .35
Nos. 397-400,C76-C77 (6) 7.10 3.80

Seventh anniversary of independence.

Photographing Far Side of Moon — A52

10fr, Trajectories of Ranger VII on flight to moon. 25fr, Relay satellite. 45fr, Vostoks I & II & globe.

1965, Nov. 15 Litho. *Perf. 14x13½*

401 A52 5fr blk, pur & ocher .20 .20
402 A52 10fr red brn, lt grn & yel .20 .20
403 A52 25fr blk, bl & bis .20 .20
404 A52 45fr blk, lt ultra & bis .40 .20
Nos. 401-404,C78-C79 (6) 3.25 1.70

For overprints and surcharges see Nos. 529-530, C112-C112B.

Sword Dance, Karana — A53

Designs: 30c, Dancing girls, Lower Guinea. 50c, Behore musicians of Tiekere playing "Eyoro," horiz. 5fr, Doundouba dance of Kouroussa. 40fr, Bird man's dance of Macenta.

1966, Jan. 5 Photo. *Perf. 13½*

Size: 26x36mm

405 A53 10c multicolored .20 .20
406 A53 30c multicolored .20 .20

Size: 36x28½mm

407 A53 50c multicolored .20 .20

Size: 26x36mm

408 A53 5fr multicolored .20 .20
409 A53 40fr multicolored .35 .20
Nos. 405-409,C80 (6) 1.85 1.35

Festival of African Art and Culture. See Nos. 436-441.

Engraved Overprint in Red or Orange on Nos. 355-356 and Nos. 358-360

1966, Mar. 14 *Perf. 13x12½*

410 A43 5fr multi (R) .20 .20
411 A43 10fr multi (R) .20 .20
412 A43 40fr multi (O) .35 .25
413 A43 50fr multi (R) .45 .35
414 A43 75fr multi (R) .80 .60
Nos. 410-414,C81 (6) 2.80 2.00

4th Pan Arab Games, Cairo, Sept. 2-11, 1965. The same overprint was also applied to imperf. sheets of No. 357.

Engraved Red Orange Overprint on No. 352:
"CENTENAIRE DU TIMBRE CAIRE 1966"

1966, Mar. 14 *Perf. 12*

415 A42 50fr dk brn, bl & vio .35 .35

1st Egyptian postage stamps, cent. See #C82.

Vonkou Rock, Telimélé — A54

Views: 25fr, Artificial lake, Coyah. 40fr, Kalé waterfalls. 50fr, Forécariah bridge. 75fr, Liana bridge.

1966, Apr. 4 Photo. *Perf. 13½*

416 A54 20fr multicolored .20 .20
417 A54 25fr multicolored .20 .20
418 A54 40fr multicolored .20 .20
419 A54 50fr multicolored .30 .20
420 A54 75fr multicolored .40 .25
Nos. 416-420,C83 (6) 2.00 1.40

See Nos. 475-478, C90-C91. For overprints see Nos. 482-488, C93-C95.

UNESCO Emblem A55

1966, May 2 Photo. Unwmk.

421 A55 25fr multicolored .20 .20

20th anniv. of UNESCO. See Nos. C84-C85.

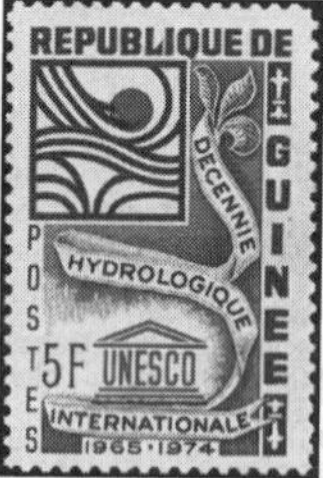

Woman of Guinea and Morning Glory — A56

Symbolic Water Cycle and UNESCO Emblem — A57

Designs: Women and Flowers of Guinea.

1966, May 30 Photo. *Perf. 13½*
Size: 23x34mm

422 A56 10c multicolored .20 .20
423 A56 20c multicolored .20 .20
424 A56 30c multicolored .20 .20
425 A56 40c multicolored .20 .20
426 A56 3fr multicolored .20 .20
427 A56 4fr multicolored .20 .20
428 A56 10fr multicolored .20 .20
429 A56 25fr multicolored .25 .20

Size: 28x43mm

430 A56 30fr multicolored .30 .20
431 A56 50fr multicolored .40 .25
432 A56 80fr multicolored .60 .30
Nos. 422-432,C86-C87 (13) 7.05 4.05

1966, Sept. 26 Engr. *Perf. 10½*

433 A57 5fr bl & dp org .20 .20
434 A57 25fr grn & dp org .20 .20
435 A57 100fr brt rose lil & dp org .60 .35
Nos. 433-435 (3) 1.00 .75

Hydrological Decade (UNESCO), 1965-74.

Dance Type of 1966

Various folk dances. 25fr, 75fr, horizontal.

1966, Oct. 24 Photo. *Perf. 13½*
Sizes: 26x36mm, 36x28½mm

436 A53 60c multicolored .20 .20
437 A53 1fr multicolored .20 .20
438 A53 1.50fr multicolored .20 .20
439 A53 25fr multicolored .20 .20
440 A53 50fr multicolored .35 .20
441 A53 75fr multicolored .45 .35
Nos. 436-441 (6) 1.60 1.35

Guinean National Dancers.

Child's Drawing and UNICEF Emblem — A58

Children's Drawings: 2fr, Elephant. 3fr, Girl. 20fr, Village, horiz. 25fr, Boy playing soccer. 40fr, Still life. 50fr, Bird in a tree.

1966, Dec. 12 Photo. *Perf. 13½*

442 A58 2fr multicolored .20 .20
443 A58 3fr multicolored .20 .20
444 A58 10fr multicolored .20 .20
445 A58 20fr multicolored .20 .20
446 A58 25fr multicolored .20 .20
447 A58 40fr multicolored .25 .20
448 A58 50fr multicolored .35 .20
Nos. 442-448 (7) 1.60 1.40

20th anniv. of UNICEF. Printed in sheets of 10 stamps and 2 labels with ornamental borders and inscriptions.

Laboratory Technician — A59

WHO Emblem and: 50fr, Physician examining infant. 75fr, Pre-natal care & instruction. 80fr, WHO Headquarters, Geneva.

1967, Jan. 20 Photo. *Perf. 13½*

449 A59 30fr multicolored .20 .20
450 A59 50fr multicolored .25 .20
451 A59 75fr multicolored .40 .25
452 A59 80fr multicolored .45 .35
Nos. 449-452 (4) 1.30 1.00

Inauguration (in 1966) of WHO Headquarters, Geneva.

Niamou Mask, N'Zerekore — A60

Designs: 10c, 1fr, 30fr, Small Banda mask, Kanfarade, Boké region. 1.50fr, 50fr, Like 30c. 50c, 5fr, 75fr, Bearded Niamou mask. 60c, 25fr, 100fr, Horned Yinadjinkele mask, Kankan region.

1967, Mar. 25 Photo. *Perf. 14x13*

453 A60 10c org & multi .20 .20
454 A60 30c cit & brn blk .20 .20
455 A60 50c dp lil rose, blk & red .20 .20
456 A60 60c dp org, blk & bis .20 .20
457 A60 1fr yel grn & multi .20 .20
458 A60 1.50fr sal pink & brn blk .20 .20
459 A60 5fr ap grn, blk & red .20 .20
460 A60 25fr red lil, blk & bis .20 .20
461 A60 30fr bis & multi .25 .20
462 A60 50fr grnsh bl & brn blk .40 .20
463 A60 75fr yel, blk & red .60 .25
464 A60 100fr lt ultra, blk & bis .90 .40
Nos. 453-464 (12) 3.75 2.65

Ball Python — A61

20c, Pastoria Research Institute. 50c, 75fr, Extraction of snake venom. 1fr, 50fr, Rock python. 2fr, Men holding rock python. 5fr, 30fr, Gaboon viper. 20fr, West African mamba.

1967, May 15 Litho. *Perf. 13½*
Size: 43½x20mm

465 A61 20c multicolored .20 .20
466 A61 30c multicolored .20 .20
467 A61 50c multicolored .20 .20
468 A61 1fr multicolored .20 .20
469 A61 2fr multicolored .20 .20
470 A61 5fr multicolored .20 .20

Size: 56x26mm

471 A61 20fr multicolored .20 .20
472 A61 30fr multicolored .35 .20
473 A61 50fr multicolored .40 .20
474 A61 75fr multicolored .65 .20
Nos. 465-474,C88-C89 (12) 6.45 3.80

Research Institute for Applied Biology of Guinea (Pastoria). For souvenir sheet see No. C88a.

Scenic Type of 1966

Views: 5fr, Loos Island. 30fr, Tinkisso Waterfalls. 70fr, "The Elephant's Trunk" Hotel, Mt. Kakoulima. 80fr, Evening at the shore, Ratoma.

1967, June 20 Photo. *Perf. 13½*

475 A54 5fr multicolored .20 .20
476 A54 30fr multicolored .20 .20
477 A54 70fr multicolored .40 .20
478 A54 80fr multicolored .60 .20
Nos. 475-478,C90-C91 (6) 3.40 1.90

People's Palace, Conakry — A62

Elephant A63

1967, Sept. 28 Photo. *Perf. 13½*

479 A62 5fr silver & multi .20 .20
480 A63 30fr silver & multi .25 .20
481 A62 55fr gold & multi .40 .20
Nos. 479-481 (3) .85 .60

20th anniv. of the Democratic Party of Guinea and the opening of the People's Palace, Conakry. See No. C92.

Nos. 418-420 and 475-478 Overprinted with Lions Emblem and: "AMITIE DES PEUPLES GRACE AU TOURISME 1917-1967"

1967, Nov. 6

482 A54 5fr multicolored .20 .20
483 A54 30fr multicolored .40 .20
484 A54 40fr multicolored .35 .20
485 A54 50fr multicolored .45 .20
486 A54 70fr multicolored .55 .25
487 A54 75fr multicolored .80 .40
488 A54 80fr multicolored 1.00 .40
Nos. 482-488,C93-C95 (10) 6.85 3.35

50th anniversary of Lions International.

WHO Office for Africa — A64

1967, Dec. 4 Photo. *Perf. 13½*

489 A64 30fr lt ol grn, bis & dk grn .25 .20
490 A64 75fr red org, bis & dk bl .55 .25

Inauguration of the WHO Regional Office for Africa in Brazzaville, Congo.

Human Rights Flame — A65

1968, Jan. 15 Photo. *Perf. 13½*

491 A65 30fr ocher, grn & dk car .25 .20
492 A65 40fr vio, grn & car .30 .20

International Human Rights Year, 1968.

Coyah, Dubréka Region A66

Homes and People: 30c, 30fr, Kankan Region. 40c, Kankan, East Guinea. 50c, 15fr, Woodlands Region. 60c, Fulahmori, Gaoual Region. 5fr, Cognagui, Kundara Region. 40fr, Fouta Djallon, West Guinea. 100fr, Labé, West Guinea.

1968, Apr. 1 Photo. *Perf. 13½x14*
Size: 36x27mm

493 A66 20c gold & multi .20 .20
494 A66 30c gold & multi .20 .20
495 A66 40c gold & multi .20 .20
496 A66 50c gold & multi .20 .20

Perf. 14x13½
Size: 57x36mm

497 A66 60c gold & multi .20 .20
498 A66 5fr gold & multi .20 .20
499 A66 15fr gold & multi .20 .20
500 A66 20fr gold & multi .20 .20
501 A66 30fr gold & multi .25 .20
502 A66 40fr gold & multi .40 .20
503 A66 100fr gold & multi .90 .25
Nos. 493-503,C100 (12) 5.15 3.05

The Storyteller — A67

African Legends: 15fr, The Little Genie of Mt. Nimba. No. 506, The Legend of the Moons and the Stars. No. 507, Lan, the Child Buffalo, vert. 40fr, Nianablas and the Crocodiles. 50fr, Leuk the Hare Playing the Drum, vert. 75fr, Leuk the Hare Selling his Sister, vert. 80fr, The Hunter and the Antelope-woman. The designs are from paintings by students of the Academy of Fine Arts in Bellevue.

1968 Photo. *Perf. 13½*

504 A67 15fr multicolored .20 .20
505 A67 25fr multicolored .20 .20
506 A67 30fr multicolored .20 .20
507 A67 30fr multicolored .20 .20
508 A67 40fr multicolored .30 .20
509 A67 50fr multicolored .40 .20
a. Souv. sheet of 4 3.75 3.75
510 A67 75fr multicolored .40 .25
511 A67 80fr multicolored .65 .25
Nos. 504-511,C101-C104 (12) 7.70 3.30

Issued in sheets of 10 plus 2 labels. No. 509a contains 4 imperf. stamps similar to Nos. 508-509, C101 and C104. "Poste Aerienne" omitted on the 70fr and 300fr of the souvenir sheet.

Issued: #505-506, 510-511, 5/16; #504, 507-509, 9/16.

Anubius Baboon — A68

African Animals: 10fr, Leopards. 15fr, Hippopotami. 20fr, Nile crocodile. 30fr, Ethiopian wart hog. 50fr, Defassa waterbuck. 75fr, Cape buffaloes.

1968, Nov. 25 Photo. *Perf. 13½*
Size: 44x31mm

512 A68 5fr gold & multi .20 .20
513 A68 10fr gold & multi .20 .20
514 A68 15fr gold & multi .20 .20
a. Souv. sheet of 3, #512-514 .30 .30
515 A68 20fr gold & multi .25 .20
516 A68 30fr gold & multi .30 .20
517 A68 50fr gold & multi .40 .20
a. Souv. sheet of 3, #515-517 .90 .90
518 A68 75fr gold & multi .60 .25
a. Souv. sheet of 3 3.25 3.25
Nos. 512-518,C105-C106 (9) 4.55 2.35

No. 518a contains one No. 518 and one each similar to Nos. C105-C106 without "POSTE AERIENNE" inscription. The three souvenir sheets contain 3 stamps and one green and gold label inscribed "FAUNE AFRICAINE."

Senator Robert F. Kennedy A69

Portraits: 75fr, Rev. Martin Luther King, Jr. 100fr, Pres. John F. Kennedy.

1968, Dec. 16

519 A69 30fr yel & multi .20 .20
520 A69 75fr multicolored .50 .20
521 A69 100fr multicolored .65 .25
Nos. 519-521,C107-C109 (6) 4.00 1.50

Robert F. Kennedy, John F. Kennedy and Martin Luther King, Jr., martyrs for freedom.

The stamps are printed in sheets of 15 (3x5) containing 10 stamps and five yellow-green and gold center labels. Sheets come either with English or French inscriptions on label.

Sculpture and Runner A70

Sculpture and Soccer — A71

Designs (Sculpture and): 10fr, Boxing. 15fr, Javelin. 30fr, Steeplechase. 50fr, Hammer throw. 75fr, Bicycling.

1969, Feb. 18 Photo. *Perf. 13½*

522 A70 5fr multicolored .20 .20
523 A70 10fr multicolored .20 .20
524 A70 15fr multicolored .25 .20
525 A71 25fr multicolored .25 .20
526 A70 30fr multicolored .25 .20
527 A70 50fr multicolored .40 .20
528 A70 75fr multicolored .55 .20
Nos. 522-528,C110-C111A (10) 6.40 2.65

19th Olympic Games, Mexico City, 10/12-27.

No. 404 Surcharged and Overprinted in Red

1969, Mar. 17 Litho. *Perf. 14x13½*

529 A52 30fr on 45fr multi .35 .35
530 A52 45fr multicolored .35 .35
Nos. 529-530,C112-C112B (5) 3.55 2.55

US Apollo 8 mission, the first men in orbit around the moon, Dec. 21-27, 1968.

Nos. 529-530 also exist with surcharge and overprint in black. These sell for about 10% more.

Tarzan — A72

Designs: 30fr, Tarzan sitting in front of Pastoria Research Institute gate. 75fr, Tarzan and his family. 100fr, Tarzan sitting in a tree.

1969, June 6 Photo. *Perf. 13½*

531 A72 25fr orange & multi .20 .20
532 A72 30fr bl grn & multi .25 .20
533 A72 75fr yel grn & multi .50 .20
534 A72 100fr yellow & multi .80 .30
Nos. 531-534 (4) 1.75 .90

Tarzan was a Guinean chimpanzee with superior intelligence and ability.

Campfire A73

25fr, Boy Scout & tents. 30fr, Marching Boy Scouts. 40fr, Basketball. 45fr, Senior Scouts, thatched huts & mountain. 50fr, Guinean Boy Scout badge.

1969, July 1

535 A73 5fr gold & multi .20 .20
536 A73 25fr gold & multi .20 .20
537 A73 30fr gold & multi .20 .20
538 A73 40fr gold & multi .30 .20
539 A73 45fr gold & multi .35 .20
540 A73 50fr gold & multi .40 .20
a. Min. sheet of 6, #535-540 2.00 2.00
Nos. 535-540 (6) 1.65 1.20

Issued to honor the Boy Scouts of Guinea.

Launching Apollo 11 — A74

Designs: 30fr, Earth showing Africa as seen from moon. 50fr, Separation of lunar landing module and spaceship. 60fr, Astronauts and module on moon. 75fr, Module on moon and earth. 100fr, Module leaving moon. 200fr, Splashdown. "a" stamps are inscribed in French. "b" stamps are inscribed in English.

1969, Aug. 20 Photo. *Perf. 13½*
Size: 34x55mm

541 A74 25fr Pair, #541a, 541b .35 .20
542 A74 30fr Pair, #542a, 542b .45 .20
543 A74 50fr Pair, #543a, 543b .65 .20
544 A74 60fr Pair, #544a, 544b 1.10 .30
545 A74 75fr Pair, #545a, 545b 1.25 .35

Size: 34x71mm

546 A74 100fr Pair, #546a, 546b 2.10 .50

Size: 34x55mm

547 A74 200fr Pair, #547a, 547b 4.25 1.25
Nos. 541-547 (7) 10.15 3.00

Man's 1st landing on the moon, 7/20/69.

Harvest and ILO Emblem A75

ILO, 50th Anniv.: 25fr, Power lines and blast furnaces. 30fr, Women in broadcasting studio. 200fr, Potters.

1969, Oct. 28 Photo. *Perf. 13½*

548 A75 25fr gold & multi .20 .20
549 A75 30fr gold & multi .20 .20
550 A75 75fr gold & multi .50 .20
551 A75 200fr gold & multi 1.50 .50
Nos. 548-551 (4) 2.40 1.10

Mother and Sick Child — A76

25fr, Sick child. 40fr, Girl receiving vaccination. 50fr, Boy receiving vaccination. 60fr, Mother receiving vaccination. 200fr, Edward Jenner, M.D.

1970, Jan. 15 Photo. *Perf. 13½*

552 A76 25fr multicolored .20 .20
553 A76 30fr multicolored .20 .20
554 A76 40fr multicolored .25 .20
555 A76 50fr multicolored .40 .20
556 A76 60fr multicolored .45 .20
557 A76 200fr multicolored 1.50 .75
Nos. 552-557 (6) 3.00 1.75

Campaign against smallpox and measles.

Map of Africa — A77

1970, Feb. 3 Litho. *Perf. 14½x14*

558 A77 30fr lt bl & multi .20 .20
559 A77 200fr lt vio & multi 1.40 .75

Meeting of statesmen of countries bordering on Senegal River: Mali, Guinea, Senegal and Mauritania.

Open Book and Radar A78

1970, July 6 Litho. *Perf. 14*

560 A78 5fr lt bl & blk .20 .20
561 A78 10fr rose & blk .20 .20
562 A78 50fr yellow & blk .40 .20
563 A78 200fr lilac & blk 1.40 .75
Nos. 560-563 (4) 2.20 1.35

International Telecommunications Day.

Lenin — A79

Designs: 20fr, Meeting with Lenin, by V. Serov. 30fr, Lenin Addressing Workers, by V. Serov. 40fr, Lenin with Red Guard Soldier and Sailor, by P. V. Vasiliev. 100fr, Lenin Speaking from Balcony, by P. V. Vasiliev. 200fr, Like 5fr.

1970, Nov. 16 Photo. *Perf. 13*

564 A79 5fr gold & multi .20 .20
565 A79 20fr gold & multi .20 .20
566 A79 30fr gold & multi .25 .20
567 A79 40fr gold & multi .40 .20
568 A79 100fr gold & multi .80 .25
569 A79 200fr gold & multi 1.60 .65
Nos. 564-569 (6) 3.45 1.70

Lenin (1870-1924), Russian communist leader.

Phenecogrammus Interruptus — A80

Designs: Various fish from Guinea.

1971, Apr. 1 Photo. *Perf. 13*

570 A80 5fr gold & multi .20 .20
571 A80 10fr gold & multi .20 .20
572 A80 15fr gold & multi .20 .20
573 A80 20fr gold & multi .20 .20
574 A80 25fr gold & multi .20 .20
575 A80 30fr gold & multi .25 .20
576 A80 40fr gold & multi .25 .20
577 A80 45fr gold & multi .30 .20
578 A80 50fr gold & multi .35 .20
579 A80 75fr gold & multi .60 .25
580 A80 100fr gold & multi .70 .35
581 A80 200fr gold & multi 1.40 .80
Nos. 570-581 (12) 4.85 3.20

Violet-crested Touraco — A81

Birds: 20fr, European golden oriole. 30fr, Blue-headed coucal. 40fr, Northern shrike. 75fr, Vulturine guinea fowl. 100fr, Southern ground hornbill.

1971, June 18 Photo. *Perf. 13*

Size: 34x34mm

582 A81	5fr gold & multi	.20	.20
583 A81	20fr gold & multi	.20	.20
584 A81	30fr gold & multi	.20	.20
585 A81	40fr gold & multi	.30	.20
586 A81	75fr gold & multi	.70	.22
587 A81	100fr gold & multi	.90	.35
	Nos. 582-587,C113-C113B (9)	5.50	2.37

UNICEF Emblem, Map of Africa — A82

1971, Dec. 24 *Perf. 12x12½*

Map in Olive

588 A82	25fr orange & blk	.20	.20
589 A82	30fr pink & black	.20	.20
590 A82	50fr gray grn & blk	.35	.20
591 A82	60fr gray bl & blk	.40	.20
592 A82	100fr lil rose & blk	.70	.20
	Nos. 588-592 (5)	1.85	1.00

UNICEF, 25th anniv.

For overprints see Nos. 625-629.

Imaginary Prehistoric Space Creature — A83

Various imaginary prehistoric space creatures.

1972, Apr. 1 *Perf. 13½x13*

593 A83	5fr multicolored	.20	.20
594 A83	20fr multicolored	.20	.20
595 A83	30fr multicolored	.20	.20
596 A83	40fr multicolored	.25	.20
597 A83	100fr multicolored	.60	.30
598 A83	200fr multicolored	1.10	.60
	Nos. 593-598 (6)	2.55	1.70

Black Boy, Men of 4 Races, Emblem — A84

Designs: 20fr, Oriental boy. 30fr, Indian youth. 50fr, Caucasian girl. 100fr, Men of 4 races and Racial Equality emblem.

1972, May 14 *Perf. 13x13½*

599 A84	15fr gold & multi	.20	.20
600 A84	20fr gold & multi	.20	.20
601 A84	30fr gold & multi	.20	.20
602 A84	50fr gold & multi	.25	.20
603 A84	100fr gold & multi	.50	.25
	Nos. 599-603,C119 (6)	1.95	1.40

Intl. Year Against Racial Discrimination, 1971.

Map of Africa, Syncom Satellite — A85

Designs (Map of Africa and Satellites): 30fr, Relay. 75fr, Early Bird. 80fr, Telstar.

1972, May 17 Litho. *Perf. 13*

604 A85	15fr multicolored	.20	.20
605 A85	30fr red org & multi	.20	.20
606 A85	75fr grn & multi	.40	.20
607 A85	80fr multicolored	.45	.30
	Nos. 604-607,C120-C121 (6)	2.75	1.65

4th World Telecommunications Day.

Carrier Pigeon, UPAF Emblem — A86

1972, July 10

608 A86	15fr brt bl & multi	.20	.20
609 A86	30fr multicolored	.20	.20
610 A86	75fr lil & multi	.40	.20
611 A86	80fr multicolored	.45	.30
	Nos. 608-611,C122-C123 (6)	3.10	1.80

Book Year Emblem, Reading Child — A87

Designs (Book Year Emblem and): 15fr, Book as sailing ship. 40fr, Young woman with flower and book. 50fr, Book as key. 75fr, Man reading and globe. 200fr, Book and laurel.

1972, Aug. 2 Photo. *Perf. 14x13½*

612 A87	5fr red & multi	.20	.20
613 A87	15fr multicolored	.20	.20
614 A87	40fr yel & multi	.20	.20
615 A87	50fr blue & multi	.30	.20
616 A87	75fr dk red & multi	.50	.30
617 A87	200fr org & multi	.90	.60
	Nos. 612-617 (6)	2.30	1.70

International Book Year 1972.

Javelin, Olympic Emblems, Arms of Guinea A88

1972, Aug. 26 Photo. *Perf. 13*

618 A88	5fr shown	.20	.20
619 A88	10fr Pole vault	.20	.20
620 A88	25fr Hurdles	.20	.20
621 A88	30fr Hammer throw	.20	.20
622 A88	40fr Boxing	.25	.20
623 A88	50fr Vaulting	.25	.20
624 A88	75fr Running	.40	.25
	Nos. 618-624,C124-C125 (9)	3.45	2.35

20th Olympic Games, Munich, 8/26-9/11.

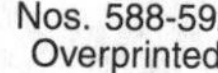

Nos. 588-592 Overprinted

1972, Sept. 28 Photo. *Perf. 12x12½*

Map in Olive

625 A82	25fr org & blk	.20	.20
626 A82	30fr pink & blk	.20	.20
627 A82	50fr gray grn & blk	.25	.20
628 A82	60fr gray bl & blk	.40	.20
629 A82	100fr lil rose & blk	.45	.20
	Nos. 625-629 (5)	1.50	1.00

UN Conference on Human Environment, Stockholm, June 5-16.

Dimitrov at Leipzig Trial — A89

1972, Sept. 28 *Perf. 13*

Gold, Dark Green & Black

630 A89	5fr shown	.20	.20
631 A89	25fr In Moabit Prison, 1933	.20	.20
632 A89	40fr Writing his memoirs	.20	.20
633 A89	100fr Portrait	.55	.25
	Nos. 630-633 (4)	1.15	.85

George Dimitrov (1882-1949), Bulgarian Communist party leader and Premier.

Emperor Haile Selassie — A90

Design: 200fr, Emperor facing right.

1972, Oct. 2

634 A90	40fr blk & multi	.25	.20
635 A90	200fr multicolored	1.10	.65

Syntomeida Epilais — A91

1973, Mar. 5 Photo. *Perf. 14x13½*

Designs: Various insects.

636 A91	5fr shown	.20	.20
637 A91	15fr Ladybugs	.20	.20
638 A91	30fr Green locust	.20	.20
639 A91	40fr Honey bee	.20	.20
640 A91	50fr Photinus pyralis	.25	.20
641 A91	200fr Ancyluris formosissima	1.10	.70
	Nos. 636-641 (6)	2.15	1.70

Kwame Nkrumah A92

Various portraits of Kwame Nkrumah.

1973, May 25 Photo. *Perf. 13½*

642 A92	1.50s lt grn, gold & brn	.20	.20
643 A92	2.50s lt grn, gold & brn	.20	.20
644 A92	5s lt grn, gold & brn	.25	.20
645 A92	10s gold & dark vio	.50	.40
	Nos. 642-645 (4)	1.15	1.00

OAU, 10th anniversary.

Institute for Applied Biology, Kindia A93

WHO Emblem and: 2.50s, Technicians inoculating egg. 3s, Filling vaccine into ampules. 4s, Sterilization of vaccine. 5s, Assembling of vaccine and vaccination gun. 10s, Inoculation of steer. 20s, Vaccination of woman.

1973, Nov. 16 Photo. *Perf. 13½*

Size: 40x36mm

646 A93	1s gold & multi	.20	.20
647 A93	2.50s gold & multi	.20	.20
648 A93	3s gold & multi	.20	.20
649 A93	4s gold & multi	.25	.20

Size: 47½x31mm

650 A93	5s gold & multi	.40	.20
651 A93	10s gold & multi	.50	.25
652 A93	20s gold & multi	1.25	.55
	Nos. 646-652 (7)	3.00	1.80

WHO, 25th anniversary.

Copernicus, Heliocentric System, Primeval Landscape — A94

Nicolaus Copernicus — A95

Designs (Copernicus and): 2s, Sun rising over volcanic desert, and spacecraft. 4s, Earth, moon and spacecraft. 5s, Moon scape and spacecraft. 10s, Jupiter and spacecraft. 20s, Saturn and heliocentric system.

1973, Dec. 17 Photo. *Perf. 13½*

653 A94	50c gold & multi	.20	.20
654 A94	2s gold & multi	.20	.20
655 A94	4s gold & multi	.20	.20
656 A94	5s gold & multi	.30	.20
657 A94	10s gold & multi	.60	.25
658 A94	20s gold & multi	1.25	.60
	Nos. 653-658 (6)	2.75	1.65

Souvenir Sheet

659		Sheet of 4	6.00	6.00
a.	A95	20s Single stamp	1.40	1.00

Nicolaus Copernicus (1473-1543), Polish astronomer. No. 659 contains center label showing rocket and heliocentric system in gold margin.

Loading Bauxite on Freighter — A96

1974, Mar. 1 Litho. *Perf. 13½*

660	A96	4s shown	.20	.20
661	A96	6s Freight train	.30	.20
662	A96	10s Mining	.50	.30
		Nos. 660-662 (3)	1.00	.70

Bauxite mining, Boke.

Clappertonia Ficifolia — A97

1974, May 20 Photo. *Perf. 13*

Size: 25x36mm

663	A97	50c shown	.20	.20
664	A97	1s Rothmannia longiflora	.20	.20
665	A97	2s Oncoba spinosa	.20	.20
666	A97	3s Venidium fastuosum	.20	.20

Size: 31x42mm

667	A97	4s Bombax costatum	.20	.20
668	A97	5s Clerodendrum splendens	.25	.20
669	A97	7.50s Combretuni grandiflorum	.40	.20
670	A97	10s Mussaendra erythrophylla	.55	.30

Size: 38x38mm (Diamond)

671	A97	12s Argemone mexicana	.65	.40
		Nos. 663-671,C127-C129 (12)	7.10	4.35

Drummers, Pigeon, UPAF and UPU Emblems — A98

Designs (Carrier Pigeon, African Postal Union and UPU Emblems): 6s, Runner with letter stick. 7.50s, Monorail and mail truck. No. 675, Jet and ocean liner. No. 676, Balloon and dugout canoe. 20s, Satellites over earth.

1974, Oct. 16 Photo. *Perf. 13½x14*

672	A98	5s mag & multi	.25	.20
673	A98	6s grn & multi	.35	.20
674	A98	7.50s ver & multi	.45	.25
675	A98	10s Prus bl & multi	.55	.45
		Nos. 672-675 (4)	1.60	1.10

Souvenir Sheets

Perf. 13½

676	A98	10s ocher & multi	3.50	
677		Sheet of 4, multi	4.00	
a.	A98	20s Single stamp	.90	.70

Centenary of Universal Postal Union. No. 676 contains one 70x60mm stamp.

Rope Bridge — A99

Designs (Pioneers): 2s, Field observation. 4s, Communication. 5s, Cooking in camp. 7.50s, Salute. 10s, Basketball.

1974, Nov. 22 Photo. *Perf. 14x13½*

678	A99	50c multicolored	.20	.20
679	A99	2s multicolored	.20	.20
680	A99	4s multicolored	.20	.20
681	A99	5s multicolored	.25	.20
682	A99	7.50s multicolored	.40	.20
683	A99	10s multicolored	.50	.30
a.		Souv. sheet of 2, #682-683	1.60	1.60

National Pioneer Movement.

Souvenir Sheet

Fruit — A100

1974, Nov. 22 Photo. *Perf. 13x14*

684	A100	Sheet of 5	3.50	
a.		4s Limes	.25	
b.		4s Oranges	.25	
c.		5s Bananas	.35	
d.		5s Mangos	.35	
e.		12s Pineapple	.80	

Chimpanzee — A101

1975, May 14 Photo. *Perf. 13½*

685	A101	1s shown	.20	.20
686	A101	2s Impala	.20	.20
687	A101	3s Wart hog	.20	.20
688	A101	4s Kobus defassa	.20	.20
a.		Souv. sheet of 4, #685-688	.65	.65
689	A101	5s Leopard	.20	.20
690	A101	6s Greater kudu	.25	.20
691	A101	6.50s Zebra	.30	.25
692	A101	7.50s Cape buffalo	.35	.25
a.		Souv. sheet of 4, #689-692	1.40	1.40
693	A101	8s Hippopotamus	.40	.25
694	A101	10s Lion	.45	.30
695	A101	12s Black rhinoceros	.50	.35
696	A101	15s Elephant	.65	.50
a.		Souv. sheet of 4, #693-696	2.25	2.25
		Nos. 685-696 (12)	3.90	3.10

Sheets exist perf. and imperf.

Stamps in Nos. 692a, 696a are inscribed "Poste Aerienne."

Lions, Pipe Line and ADB Emblem A102

Designs (African Development Bank Emblem, Pipe Line and): 7s, Elephants. 10s, Male lions. 20s, Elephant and calf.

1975, June 16 Photo. *Perf. 13½*

697	A102	5s gold & multi	.25	.20
698	A102	7s gold & multi	.30	.20
699	A102	10s gold & multi	.45	.25
700	A102	20s gold & multi	1.00	.60
		Nos. 697-700 (4)	2.00	1.25

African Development Bank, 10th anniv.

Women Musicians, IWY Emblem A103

IWY Emblem and: 7s, Women banjo & guitar players. 9s, Woman railroad shunter & train. 15s, Woman physician examining infant. 20s, Male & female symbols.

1976, Apr. 12 Photo. *Perf. 13½*

701	A103	5s multicolored	.25	.20
702	A103	7s multicolored	.40	.20
703	A103	9s blue & multi	.45	.30
704	A103	15s multicolored	.70	.50
a.		Souvenir sheet	.80	.80
705	A103	20s vio bl & multi	1.00	.70
a.		Souvenir sheet of 4	4.25	4.25
		Nos. 701-705 (5)	2.80	1.90

International Women's Year 1975. No. 704a contains one stamp similar to No. 704 with gold frame. No. 705a contains 4 stamps similar to No. 705 with gold frame.

Woman Gymnast A104

Montreal Olympic Games Emblem and: 4s, Long jump. 5s, Hammer throw. 6s, Discus. 6.50s, Hurdles. 7s, Javelin. 8s, Running. 8.50s, Bicycling. 10s, High jump. 15s, Shot put. 20s, Pole vault. #717, Soccer. #718, Swimming.

1976, May 17 Photo. *Perf. 13½*

Size: 38x38mm

706	A104	3s multicolored	.20	.20
707	A104	4s grn & multi	.20	.20
708	A104	5s yel & multi	.25	.20
709	A104	6s multicolored	.30	.20
710	A104	6.50s plum & multi	.35	.20
711	A104	7s blue & multi	.40	.25
712	A104	8s ultra & multi	.90	.25
713	A104	8.50s org & multi	.40	.25
714	A104	10s multicolored	.50	.30
715	A104	15s multicolored	.70	.50
716	A104	20s multicolored	1.00	.80
717	A104	25s grn & multi	1.40	.80
		Nos. 706-717 (12)	6.60	4.15

Souvenir Sheet

718	A104	25s multicolored	2.25	2.25

21st Olympic Games, Montreal, Canada, July 17-Aug. 1. No. 718 contains one 32x32mm stamp. See No. C130.

A. G. Bell, Telephone, 1900 — A105

7s, Wall telephone, 1910. 12s, Syncom telecommunications satellite. #722, Telstar satellite. #723, Telephone switchboard operator, 1914.

1976, Nov. 15 Photo. *Perf. 13*

719	A105	5s multicolored	.25	.20
720	A105	7s multicolored	.40	.20
721	A105	12s multicolored	.65	.40
722	A105	15s multicolored	.80	.55
a.		Souvenir sheet of 4, #719-722	2.25	2.25
		Nos. 719-722 (4)	2.10	1.35

Souvenir Sheet

723	A105	15s multicolored	1.00	1.00

Centenary of first telephone call by Alexander Graham Bell, Mar. 10, 1876.

Collybia Fusipes — A106

Mushrooms: 7s, Lycoperdon perlatum. 9s, Boletus edulis. 9.50s, Lactarius deliciosus. 11.50s, Agaricus campestris.

1977, Feb. 6 Photo. *Perf. 13*

Size: 48x26mm

724	A106	5s multicolored	.25	.20
725	A106	7s multicolored	.40	.20
726	A106	9s multicolored	.45	.25
a.		Souvenir sheet of 2, #724, 726	1.00	1.00
727	A106	9.50s multicolored	.55	.30

Size: 48x31mm

728	A106	11.50s multicolored	.65	.40
		Nos. 724-728,C131-C133 (8)	4.30	2.50

Hexaplex Hoplites — A107

Sea Shells: 2s, Perrona lineata. 4s, Marginella pseudofaba. 5s, Tympanotonos radula. 7s, Marginella strigata. 8s, Harpa doris. 10s, Demoulia pinguis. 20s, Bursa scrobiculator. 25s, Marginella adansoni.

1977, Apr. 25 Photo. *Perf. 13*

Size: 50x25mm

729	A107	1s gold & multi	.20	.20
730	A107	2s gold & multi	.20	.20
731	A107	4s gold & multi	.25	.20
732	A107	5s gold & multi	.35	.20
733	A107	7s gold & multi	.45	.30
734	A107	8s gold & multi	.55	.35

Size: 50x30mm

735	A107	10s gold & multi	.65	.40
736	A107	20s gold & multi	1.40	.80
737	A107	25s gold & multi	1.60	1.00
		Nos. 729-737 (9)	5.65	3.65

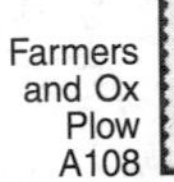

Farmers and Ox Plow A108

Designs: 5s, Pres. Touré addressing rally. 20s, Soldier driving farm tractor. 25s, Pres. Touré addressing UN General Assembly. 30s, 40s, Pres. Sékou Touré, vert.

1977, May 14 *Perf. 13½x13, 13x13½*

738	A108	5s gold & multi	.35	.20
739	A108	10s gold & multi	.65	.40
740	A108	20s gold & multi	1.40	.80
741	A108	25s gold & multi	1.60	1.00
a.		Souvenir sheet of 4, #738-741	4.25	3.50
742	A108	30s gold & dk brn	2.00	1.25
743	A108	40s gold & sl grn	2.50	1.60
a.		Souvenir sheet of 2, #742-743	5.00	4.00
		Nos. 738-743 (6)	8.50	5.25

Democratic Party of Guinea, 30th anniv.

Nile Monitor — A109

Reptiles and Snakes: 4s, Frogs. 5s, Lizard (uromastix). 6s, Sand skink. 6.50s, Agama. 7s, Black-lipped spitting cobra. 8.50s, Ball python. 20s, Toads.

1977, Oct. 10 Photo. *Perf. 13½*

Size: 46x20mm

744	A109	3s multi	.20	.20
745	A109	4s multi	.25	.20
746	A109	5s multi	.35	.20

Size: 46x30mm

747	A109	6s multi	.40	.25
748	A109	6.50s multi	.40	.25
749	A109	7s multi	.45	.30
750	A109	8.50s multi	.55	.35
751	A109	20s multi	1.40	.80
		Nos. 744-751,C134-C136 (11)	7.25	4.55

Eland — A110

Endangered Animals: 2s, Chimpanzee. 2.50s, Pygmy elephant. 3s, Lion. 4s, Palm squirrel. 5s, Hippopotamus. Each animal shown male, female and young.

1977, Dec. 12 Photo. *Perf. 14x13½*

752	A110	Strip of 3	.25	.20
a.-c.		1s any single	.20	
753	A110	Strip of 3	.40	.25
a.-c.		2s any single	.20	
754	A110	Strip of 3	.50	.30
a.-c.		2.50s any single	.20	
755	A110	Strip of 3	.60	.40
a.-c.		3s any single	.20	
756	A110	Strip of 3	.80	.50
a.-c.		4s any single	.20	
757	A110	Strip of 3	1.05	.60
a.-c.		5s any single	.35	
		Nos. 752-757,C137-C142 (12)	15.50	9.00

Russian October Revolution, 60th Anniv. — A111

Designs: 2.50s, First Lenin debate, Moscow. 5s, Lenin speaking, 1917. 7.50s, Lenin and people. 8s, Lenin in first parade on Red Square.

1978, Feb. 27 Photo. *Perf. 14*

758	A111	2.50s gold & multi	.20	.20
759	A111	5s gold & multi	.35	.20
760	A111	7.50s gold & multi	.50	.30
761	A111	8s gold & multi	.55	.35
		Nos. 758-761,C143-C144 (6)	4.25	2.70

Pres. Giscard d'Estaing at Microphones — A112

Pres. Valery Giscard d'Estaing of France and Pres. Sekou Toure of Guinea: 5s, 10s, In conference. 6.50s, Signing agreement. 7s, Attending official meeting. 8.50s, With their wives. 20s, Drinking a toast.

1979, Sept. 14 Photo. *Perf. 13*

762	A112	3s lt brn & brn	.20	.20
763	A112	5s green & brn	.35	.20
764	A112	6.50s red lil & brn	.40	.25
765	A112	7s ultra & brn	.45	.30
766	A112	8.50s dk red & brn	.55	.35
767	A112	10s vio & brown	.65	.40
768	A112	20s yel grn & brn	1.40	.80
		Nos. 762-768,C145 (8)	5.60	3.50

Visit of Pres. Valery Giscard d'Estaing to Guinea.

Twenty Thousand Leagues Under the Sea — A113

Jules Verne Stories: 3s, Children of Capt. Grant. 5s, Mysterious Island. 7s, A Captain at Fifteen. 10s, The Borsac Mission.

1979, Nov. 8 Litho. *Perf. 12x12½*

769	A113	1s multicolored	.20	.20
770	A113	3s multicolored	.20	.20
771	A113	5s multicolored	.35	.20
772	A113	7s multicolored	.45	.30
773	A113	10s multicolored	.65	.40
		Nos. 769-773,C146-C147 (7)	4.85	3.10

Jules Verne (1828-1905), French science fiction writer.

"Aerial Steam Carriage," 1842 — A114

Aviation Retrospect: 5s, Wright's Flyer 1 1903. 6.50s, Caudron, 1934. 7s, Spirit of St. Louis, 1927. 8.50s, Bristol Beaufighter, 1940. 10s, Bleriot XI, 1909. #780, Concorde. #781, Boeing 727, 1963.

1979, Nov. 22 Photo. *Perf. 14*

774	A114	3s multi	.25	.20
775	A114	5s multi	.40	.20
776	A114	6.50s multi	.50	.30
777	A114	7s multi	.55	.30
778	A114	8.50s multi	.65	.40
779	A114	10s multi	.80	.40
780	A114	20s multi	1.60	.80
781	A114	20s multi	1.60	.80
		Nos. 774-781 (8)	6.35	3.40

Hafia Soccer Team — A115

Designs: 2s, Players and Sekou Touré cup, vert. 5s, Pres. Touré presenting cup. 7s, Pres. Touré and player holding cup, vert. 8s, Sekou Touré cup, vert. 10s, Team captains and referees, vert. 20s, The winning goal.

Perf. 12½x12, 12x12½

1979, Dec. 18 Litho.

782	A115	1s multicolored	.20	.20
783	A115	2s multicolored	.20	.20
784	A115	5s multicolored	.40	.20
785	A115	7s multicolored	.55	.30
786	A115	8s multicolored	.65	.35
787	A115	10s multicolored	.80	.40
788	A115	20s multicolored	1.60	.65
		Nos. 782-788 (7)	4.40	2.30

Hafia Soccer Team, African triple champions, 1977.

Train, IYC Emblem A116

IYC Emblem and: 2s, Children dancing around tree, vert. 4s, "1979" and leaves, vert. 7s, Village. 10s, Boy climbing tree. 25s, Boys of different races, flowers, sun.

1980, Jan. 14 *Perf. 13x13½, 13½x13*

789	A116	2s multicolored	.20	.20
790	A116	4s multicolored	.40	.20
791	A116	5s multicolored	.50	.20
792	A116	7s multicolored	.65	.30
793	A116	10s multicolored	1.00	.40
794	A116	25s multicolored	2.50	1.00
		Nos. 789-794 (6)	5.25	2.30

International Year of the Child (1979).

Butterflyfish — A117

1980, Apr. 1 *Perf. 12½x12, 12x12½*

795	A117	1s shown	.20	.20
796	A117	2s Porgy	.20	.20
797	A117	3s Zeus conchifer, vert.	.20	.20
798	A117	4s Grouper	.25	.20
799	A117	5s Sea horse, vert.	.35	.20
800	A117	6s Hatchet fish	.40	.25
801	A117	7s Pisodonophis semicinctus	.45	.30
802	A117	8s Flying gurnard, vert.	.55	.35
803	A117	9s Squirrelfish	.60	.40
804	A117	10s Psettus sebae, vert.	.65	.40
805	A117	12s Abudefuf hoeffleri	.80	.50
806	A117	15s Triggerfish	1.00	.60
		Nos. 795-806 (12)	5.65	3.80

Apollo 11 Take-Off — A118

1980, July 20 Photo. *Perf. 14*

807	A118	1s shown	.20	.20
808	A118	2s Earth from moon	.20	.20
809	A118	4s Armstrong leaving module	.35	.20
810	A118	5s Armstrong on moon	.40	.20
811	A118	7s Collecting samples	.60	.30
812	A118	8s Re-entry	.65	.35
813	A118	12s Recovery	1.00	.50
814	A118	20s Crew	1.60	.80
		Nos. 807-814 (8)	5.00	2.75

Apollo 11 moon landing, 10th anniv. (1979).

Intl. Palestinian Solidarity Day — A119

1981, Nov. 21 Photo. *Perf. 13½*

815	A119	8s multicolored	.65	.35
816	A119	11s multicolored	1.00	.40

Soccer — A120

1982 Litho. *Perf. 12½x12*

817	A120	1s shown	.20	.20
818	A120	2s Basketball	.20	.20
819	A120	3s Diving	.20	.20
820	A120	4s Gymnast	.25	.20
821	A120	5s Boxing	.35	.20
822	A120	6s Pole vault	.40	.25
823	A120	7s Running	.45	.30
824	A120	8s Long jump	.55	.35
		Nos. 817-824,C148-C152 (13)	7.60	5.00

22nd Summer Olympic Games, Moscow, July 19-Aug. 3, 1980.

5th Anniv. of West African Economic Community — A121

1982, May 14 *Perf. 13½*

825	A121	6s multicolored	.50	.25
826	A121	7s multicolored	.65	.35
827	A121	9s multicolored	.85	.50
		Nos. 825-827 (3)	2.00	1.10

Kemal Ataturk Birth Centenary A122

1982, July 19 Photo. *Perf. 13½*

828	A122	7s multi	.45	.30
829	A122	10s multi, diff.	.65	.40
830	A122	25s multi, horiz.	1.60	1.00
		Nos. 828-830,C153 (4)	4.30	2.70

1982 World Cup A123

Designs: Various soccer players.

1982, Aug. 23

831	A123	6s multicolored	.40	.25
832	A123	8s multicolored	.55	.35
833	A123	9s multicolored	.60	.40
834	A123	10s multicolored	.65	.40
		Nos. 831-834,C154-C156 (7)	5.85	3.60

Soccer Type of 1982
#831-834 Overprinted in Red and Green:
"CHAMPION ITALIE-11 JUILLET 1982" and Italian Flag

1982, Aug. 23 Photo. *Perf. 13½*

835	A123	6s multicolored	.40	.25
836	A123	8s multicolored	.55	.35
837	A123	9s multicolored	.60	.40
838	A123	10s multicolored	.65	.40
		Nos. 835-838,C157-C159 (7)	5.85	3.60

Italy's victory in 1982 World Cup.

23rd Olympic Games, Los Angeles, July 28-Aug. 12, 1984
A124

1983, July 1 Litho. *Perf. 13½*

839	A124	5s Wrestling	.35	.20
840	A124	7s Weightlifting	.45	.30
841	A124	10s Gymnastics	.65	.40
842	A124	15s Discus	1.00	.60
843	A124	20s Kayak	1.40	.80
844	A124	25s Equestrian	1.60	1.00
		Nos. 839-844 (6)	5.45	3.30

Litho. & Embossed
Size: 39x58mm

844A A124 100s Running

Souvenir Sheets
Litho.

845 A124 30s Running 2.00 1.40

Litho. & Embossed

845A A124 100s Show jumping

Nos. 844A, 845A are airmail. No. 845A contains one 58x39mm stamp.

First Manned Balloon Flight, 200th Anniv. — A125

Designs: 5s, Marquis D'Arlandes, Pilatre de Rozier. 7s, Marie Antoinette Balloon, Rozier. 10s, Dirigible, Dupuy De Lome, horiz. 15s, Dirigible, Major A. Perseval, horiz.

1983, Aug. 1 Litho. *Perf. 13½*

846	A125	5s multicolored	.35	.20
847	A125	7s multicolored	.45	.30
848	A125	10s multicolored	.65	.50
849	A125	15s multicolored	1.00	.60
		Nos. 846-849,C160-C161 (6)	5.45	3.40

Intl. Year of the Handicapped — A126

1983, Aug. 24 Litho.

850	A126	10s multicolored	.80	.40
851	A126	20s multicolored	1.60	.80

Dr. Robert Koch (1843-1910), TB Bacillus
A127

Various phases of research.

1983, Aug. 24 Litho.

852	A127	6s multicolored	.40	.25
853	A127	10s multicolored	.65	.40
854	A127	11s multicolored	.70	.40
855	A127	12s multicolored	.80	.45
856	A127	15s multicolored	1.10	.60
857	A127	20s multicolored	1.40	.80
858	A127	25s multicolored	1.60	1.00
		Nos. 852-858 (7)	6.65	3.90

Mosque, Conakry
A128

1983, Oct. 2 Litho. *Perf. 13½*

859	A128	1s multicolored	.20	.20
860	A128	2s multicolored	.20	.20
861	A128	5s multicolored	.30	.20
862	A128	10s multicolored	.60	.30
		Nos. 859-862 (4)	1.30	.90

Souvenir Sheet

863 A128 25s multicolored 1.50 .70

Natl. independence, 25th anniv. No. 863 airmail.

Mano River Union, 10th Anniv.
A129

2s, Development program graduates. 7s, Emblem. 8s, Pres. Toure of Guinea, Stevens of Sierra Leone, Doe of Liberia. 10s, 20s, Signing treaty.

1983, Oct. 3

864	A129	2s multicolored	.20	.20
865	A129	7s multicolored	.40	.20
866	A129	8s multicolored	.50	.25
867	A129	10s multicolored	.60	.30
		Nos. 864-867 (4)	1.70	.95

Souvenir Sheet

868 A129 20s multicolored 1.10 .55

No. 868 airmail.

14th Winter Olympics, Sarajevo, Feb. 8-19, 1984 — A130

1983, Dec. 5 Litho. *Perf. 13½*

869	A130	5s Biathlon	.35	.20
870	A130	7s Bobsledding	.45	.30
871	A130	10s Downhill skiing	.65	.40
872	A130	15s Speed skating	1.00	.60
873	A130	20s Ski jumping	1.40	.80
874	A130	25s Figure skating	1.60	1.00
		Nos. 869-874 (6)	5.45	3.30

Litho. & Embossed
Size: 58x39mm

874A A130 100s Downhill skiing

Souvenir Sheets
Litho.

875 A130 30s Hockey 2.00 1.40

Litho. & Embossed

875A A130 100s 4-man bobsled

Nos. 873-875A airmail. No. 875A contains one 58x39mm stamp.

Self-portrait and Virgin with Blue Diadem, by Raphael
A131

Designs: 7s, Self-portrait and Holy Family, by Rubens. 10s, Self-portrait and Portrait of Saskia, by Rembrandt. 15s, Portrait of Goethe and scene from Young Werther. 20s, Scouting Year. 25s, Paul Harris, Rotary emblem. 30s, J.F. Kennedy, Apollo XI. 100s, Paul Harris, 3 other men in Rotary meeting.

1984, Jan 2 Litho. *Perf. 13*

876	A131	5s multicolored	.35	.20
877	A131	7s multicolored	.45	.30
878	A131	10s multicolored	.65	.40
879	A131	15s multicolored	1.00	.60
880	A131	20s multicolored	1.40	.80
881	A131	25s multicolored	1.60	1.20
		Nos. 876-881 (6)	5.45	3.50

Souvenir Sheets

882 A131 30s multicolored 2.00 1.40

Litho. & Embossed
Perf. 13½

882A A131 100s gold & multi

Nos. 880-882A airmail. No. 882A contains one 51x42mm stamp.
For overprints see Nos. C164-C165.

Transportation — A132

1984, May 7 Litho. *Perf. 13½*

883	A132	5s Congo River steamer	.25	.20
884	A132	7s Graf Zeppelin LZ 127	.40	.20
885	A132	10s Daimler automobile, 1886	.55	.30
886	A132	15s E. African RR Beyer-Garrat	.70	.45
887	A132	20s Latecoere 28, 1929	1.10	.60
888	A132	25s Sial Marchetti S.M. 73, 1934	1.40	.80
		Nos. 883-888 (6)	4.40	2.55

Souvenir Sheet

889 A132 30s Series B locomotive 1.60 .90

Nos. 887-889 airmail.

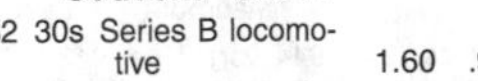

Anniversaries and Events — A133

Famous men: 5s, Abraham Lincoln, log cabin, the White House. 7s, Jean-Henri Dunant, Red Cross at Battle of Solferino. 10s, Gottlieb Daimler, 1892 Motor Carriage. 15s, Louis Bleriot, monoplane. 20s, Paul Harris, Rotary Intl. 25s, Auguste Piccard, bathyscaphe Trieste. 30s, Anatoly Karpov, world chess champion, chessboard and knight. 100s, Paul Harris, Rotary Intl. emblem.

1984, Aug. 20 Litho. *Perf. 13½*

890	A133	5s multicolored	.30	.20
891	A133	7s multicolored	.40	.20
892	A133	10s multicolored	.60	.30
893	A133	15s multicolored	.90	.45
894	A133	20s multicolored	1.10	.55
895	A133	25s multicolored	1.50	.70
		Nos. 890-895 (6)	4.80	2.40

Litho. & Embossed
Size: 60x30mm

895A A133 100s gold & multi
b. Min. sheet of 1, 91x70mm
c. Min. sheet of 1, 121x70mm

Souvenir Sheet

896 A133 30s multicolored 1.90 .90

Nos. 894-896 are airmail.
For overprints see Nos. C163, C166.

The Holy Family, by Durer — A134

Painting details: 5s, The Mystic Marriage of St. Catherine and St. Sebastian, by Correggio. 10s, The Veiled Woman, by Raphael. 15s, Portrait of a Young Man, by Durer. 20s, Portrait of Soutine, by Modigliani. 25s, Esterhazy Madonna, by Raphael. 30s, Impannata Madonna, by Raphael.

1984, Aug. 23

897	A134	5s multicolored	.25	.20
898	A134	7s multicolored	.40	.25
899	A134	10s multicolored	.55	.30
900	A134	15s multicolored	.70	.45
901	A134	20s multicolored	1.10	.60
902	A134	25s multicolored	1.40	.80
		Nos. 897-902 (6)	4.40	2.60

Souvenir Sheet

903 A134 30s multicolored 1.60 .90

Nos. 901-903 airmail.

1984 Winter Olympics, Sarajevo
A135

Gold medalists: 5s, East German two-man bobsled. 7s, Thomas Wassberg, Sweden, 50-kilometer cross-country. 10s, Gaetan Boucher, Canada, 1000 and 1500-meter speed skating. 15s, Katarina Witt, DDR, singles figure skating. 20s, Bill Johnson, US, men's downhill. 25s, Soviet Union, ice hockey. 30s, Jens Weissflog, DDR, 70-meter ski jump. No. 909A, Phil Mahre, US, slalom skiing. No. 910A, Jayne Torvill & Christopher Dean, Great Britain, ice dancing.

1985, Sept. 23 Litho. *Perf. 13½*

904	A135	5s multicolored	.30	.20
905	A135	7s multicolored	.40	.20
906	A135	10s multicolored	.60	.30
907	A135	15s multicolored	.90	.45
908	A135	20s multicolored	1.10	.55
909	A135	25s multicolored	1.50	.70
		Nos. 904-909 (6)	4.80	2.40

Litho. & Embossed
Size: 51x36mm

909A A135 100s gold & multi

Souvenir Sheets
Litho.

910 A135 30s multicolored 1.90 .90

Litho. & Embossed

910A A135 100s gold & multi

Nos. 908A-910A are airmail. No. 910A contains one 51x36mm stamp.

1984 Los Angeles Summer Olympics — A136

Medalists and various satellites: 5s, T. Ruiz and C. Costie, US, synchronized swimming. 7s, West Germany, team dressage. 10s, US, yachting, flying Dutchman class. 15s, Mark Todd, New Zealand, individual 3-day equestrian event. 20s, Daley Thompson, G.B., decathlon. 25s, US, team jumping. 30s, Carl Lewis, US, long jump, 100 and 200-meter run, 4x100 relay.

1985, Mar. 18 Litho. Perf. 13½

911 A136 5s multicolored .20 .20
912 A136 7s multicolored .30 .20
913 A136 10s multicolored .40 .25
914 A136 15s multicolored .60 .40
915 A136 20s multicolored .70 .45
916 A136 25s multicolored 1.00 .60
Nos. 911-917 (7) 4.60 2.90

Souvenir Sheet

917 A136 30s multicolored 1.40 .80

Nos. 915-917 airmail.

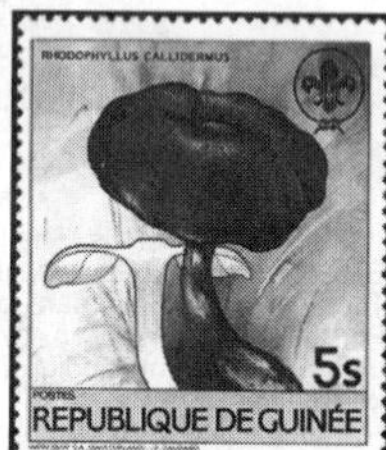

Fungi — A137

1985, Mar. 21 Litho. Perf. 13½

918 A137 5s Rhodophyllus callidermus .25 .20
919 A137 7s Agaricus niger .40 .20
920 A137 10s Thermitomyces globulus .55 .25
921 A137 15s Amanita robusta .80 .40
922 A137 20s Lepiota subradicans 1.10 .55
923 A137 25s Cantharellus rhodophyllus 1.40 .65
Nos. 918-923 (6) 4.50 2.25

Souvenir Sheet

924 A137 30s Phlebopus sylvaticus 1.60 .80

Nos. 922-924 airmail.
For surcharges see Nos. 962-968.

Scientist Herman J. Oberth, and Two-Stage Rocket A138

Space achievements: 10s, Lunik 1, USSR, 1959. 15s, Lunik 2 on the Moon, 1959. 20s, Lunik 3 photographing the Moon, 1959. 30s, US astronauts Armstrong, Aldrin, Collins and Apollo 11, 1969. 35s, Sally Ride, 1st American woman in space, 1983. 50s, Recovering a Palapa B satellite, 1984. No. 930A, Guion S. Bluford, 1st black American astronaut. No. 931A, Viking probe on Mars.

1985, May 26 Litho. Perf. 13½

925 A138 7s multicolored .30 .20
926 A138 10s multicolored .40 .25
927 A138 15s multicolored .60 .40
928 A138 20s multicolored .70 .45
929 A138 30s multicolored 1.40 .80
930 A138 35s multicolored 1.50 .85
Nos. 925-930 (6) 4.90 2.95

Litho. & Embossed

Size: 51x36mm

930A A138 200s gold & multi

Souvenir Sheet

Litho.

931 A138 50s multicolored 2.00 1.10

Litho. & Embossed

931A A138 200s gold & multi

Nos. 929-931A are airmail. No. 931A contains one 51x36mm stamp.

Maimonides (1135-1204), Jewish Scholar, Cordoba Jewish Quarter — A139

Anniversaries and events: 10s, Christopher Columbus departing from Palos for New World, 1492. 15s, Frederic Auguste Bartholdi (1834-1904), sculptor, architect, and Statue of Liberty, cent. 20s, Queen Mother, 85th birthday. 30s, Ulf Merbold, German physicist, US space shuttle Columbia. 35s, Wedding of Prince Charles and Lady Diana, 1981. 50s, Charles, Diana, Princes Henry and William. 100s, Queen Mother Elizabeth's 85th birthday.

1985, Sept. 23

932 A139 7s multicolored .40 .20
933 A139 10s multicolored .55 .25
934 A139 15s multicolored .80 .40
935 A139 20s multicolored 1.10 .55
936 A139 30s multicolored 1.60 .80
937 A139 35s multicolored 1.90 .90
Nos. 932-937 (6) 6.35 3.10

Litho. & Embossed

Size: 42x51mm

937A A139 100s gold & multi

Souvenir Sheet

Litho.

938 A139 50s multicolored 2.50 1.40

Nos. 936-938 airmail. No. 938 contains one 51x36mm stamp. Nos. 934 and 937A exist in souvenir sheets of one.

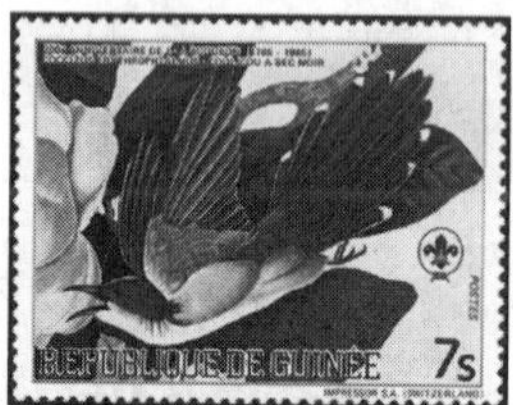

Audubon Birth Bicent. — A140

Illustrations of bird species from Birds of America.

1985, Sept. 23 Litho. Perf. 13½

939 A140 7s Coccizus erythrophtalmus .40 .20
940 A140 10s Conuropsis carolinensis .60 .30
941 A140 15s Anhinga anhinga .90 .45
942 A140 20s Buteo lineatus 1.10 .60
943 A140 30s Otus asio 1.90 .90
944 A140 35s Toxostoma rufum 2.00 1.10
Nos. 939-944 (6) 6.90 3.55

Souvenir Sheet

945 A140 50s Zenaidura macroura 3.00 2.25

Nos. 941, 944 vert. Nos. 943-945 are airmail. No. 945 contains one 51x36mm stamp. No. 944 exists in souvenir sheet of one.

1986 World Cup Soccer Championships, Mexico — A141

Famous soccer players: 7s, Bebeto, Brazil. 10s, Rinal Dassaev, USSR. 15s, Phil Neal, Great Britain. 20s, Jean Tigana, France. 30s, Fernando Chalana, Portugal. 35s, Michel Platini, France. 50s, Karl Heinz Rummenigge, West Germany.

1985, Oct. 26

946 A141 7s multicolored .40 .20
947 A141 10s multicolored .55 .25
948 A141 15s multicolored .80 .40
949 A141 20s multicolored 1.10 .55
950 A141 30s multicolored 1.60 .80
951 A141 35s multicolored 1.90 .90
Nos. 946-951 (6) 6.35 3.10

Souvenir Sheet

952 A141 50s multicolored 2.50 1.40

Nos. 950-952 airmail.

Cats and Dogs A142

1985, Oct. 26

953 A142 7s Blue-point Siamese .40 .20
954 A142 10s Cocker spaniel .55 .25
955 A142 15s Poodles .80 .40
956 A142 20s Blue Persian 1.10 .55
957 A142 25s European red-and-white tabby 1.40 .65
958 A142 30s German shepherd 1.60 .80
959 A142 35s Abyssinians 1.90 .90
960 A142 40s Boxer 2.25 1.10
Nos. 953-960 (8) 10.00 4.85

Souvenir Sheet

961 A142 50s Pyrenean mountain dog, chartreux cat 2.50 1.40

Nos. 958-961 airmail. No. 961 contains one 51x30mm stamp.

Nos. 918-924 Surcharged with 4 Bars

1985, Nov. 15

962 A137 1s on 5s multi .20 .20
963 A137 2s on 7s multi .20 .20
964 A137 8s on 10s multi .40 .25
965 A137 30s on 15s multi 1.60 .80
966 A137 35s on 20s multi 1.90 .90
967 A137 40s on 25s multi 2.25 1.10
Nos. 962-967 (6) 6.55 3.45

Souvenir Sheet

968 A137 50s on 30s multi 2.50 1.40

Nos. 966-968 airmail.

Locomotives — A143

Designs: 7s, 8F Class steam, Great Britain. 15s, Bobo 5500 Series III electric, German Fed. Railways. 25s, Pacific A Mazout No. 270, African Railways. 35s, Serie 420 electric train set, Suburban S-Bahn, Germany. 50s, ICE high-speed train, German Fed. Railways.

1985, Dec. 18 Litho. Perf. 13½

969 A143 7s multicolored .40 .20
970 A143 15s multicolored .80 .40
971 A143 25s multicolored 1.40 .65
972 A143 35s multicolored 1.90 .90
Nos. 969-972 (4) 4.50 2.15

Souvenir Sheet

973 A143 50s multicolored 2.50 1.40

Nos. 972-973 airmail.
For surcharges see Nos. 991-995.

Columbus Discovering America, 1492 — A144

1985, Dec. 18

974 A144 10s Pinta .55 .25
975 A144 20s Santa Maria 1.10 .55
976 A144 30s Nina 1.60 .80
977 A144 40s Santa Maria, sighting land 2.25 1.10
Nos. 974-977 (4) 5.50 2.70

Souvenir Sheet

978 A144 50s Columbus and Nina 2.50 1.40

Nos. 976-979 airmail.

Intl. Youth Year — A145

1986, Jan. 21

979 A145 10s Chopin .80 .40
980 A145 20s Botticelli 1.60 .80
981 A145 25s Picasso 2.00 1.00
982 A145 35s Rossini 2.75 1.40
Nos. 979-982 (4) 7.15 3.60

Souvenir Sheet

983 A145 50s Michelangelo 4.00 2.00

Nos. 981, 983 airmail.
For surcharges see Nos. 996-1000.

Halley's Comet — A146

Sightings: 5fr, Bayeux Tapestry (detail), c. 1092, France. 30fr, Arab, astrolabe, 1400. 40fr, Montezuma II, Aztec deity. 50fr, Edmond Halley, trajectory diagram. 300fr, Halley, Sir Isaac Newton. 500fr, Giotto, Soviet and NASA space probes, comet. 600fr, Hally commemorative medal, Giotto probe.

1986, July 1 Litho. Perf. 13½

5fr-500fr Surcharged with New Currency in Silver or Black

984 A146 5fr multi .20 .20
985 A146 30fr multi .20 .20
986 A146 40fr multi .25 .20
987 A146 50fr multi .30 .20
988 A146 300fr multi 1.60 .80
989 A146 500fr multi 2.75 1.40
Nos. 984-989 (6) 5.30 3.00

Souvenir Sheet

990 A146 600fr multi 3.25 1.60

Nos. 988-990 are airmail. Nos. 984-989 not issued without surcharge.

Nos. 969-973 Surcharged in Black or Black on Silver

1986, Aug. 25 Litho. Perf. 13½

991 A143 2fr on 7s multi (B on S) .20 .20
992 A143 25fr on 15s multi .20 .20
993 A143 50fr on 25s multi .30 .20
994 A143 90fr on 35s multi .50 .25
Nos. 991-994 (4) 1.20 .85

Souvenir Sheet

995 A143 500fr on 50s multi 2.75 1.40

Nos. 979-983 Surcharged

1986, Aug. 25

996 A145 5fr on 10s multi .20 .20
997 A145 35fr on 20s multi .20 .20
998 A145 50fr on 25s multi .30 .20
999 A145 90fr on 35s multi .50 .25
Nos. 996-999 (4) 1.20 .85

Souvenir Sheet

1000 A145 500fr on 50s multi 2.75 1.40

Locomotives — A147

Designs: 20fr, Dietrich 640 CV. 100fr, T.13 7906. 300fr, Vapeur 01220. 400fr, ABH Type 3 5020. 600fr, Renault ABH 3 (300 CV).

1986, Nov. 1

1001 A147	20fr multi		.20	.20
1002 A147	100fr multi		.55	.30
1003 A147	300fr multi		1.60	.80
1004 A147	400fr multi		2.25	1.10
	Nos. 1001-1004 (4)		4.60	2.40

Souvenir Sheet

1005 A147	600fr multi	3.25	1.60

Nos. 1004-1005 are airmail.

Discovery of America, 500th Anniv. (in 1992) — A148

Designs: 40fr, Columbus at Ft. Navidad construction, Santa Maria, 1492. 70fr, Landing at Hispaniola, 2nd voyage, 1494. 200fr, Aboard ship, 3rd voyage, 1498. 500fr, Trading with Indians. 600fr, At court of Ferdinand and Isabella, 1493.

1986, Nov. 1

1006 A148	40fr multi	.25	.20
1007 A148	70fr multi	.40	.20
1008 A148	200fr multi	1.10	.55
1009 A148	500fr multi	2.75	1.40
	Nos. 1006-1009 (4)	4.50	2.35

Souvenir Sheet

1010 A148	600fr multi	3.25	1.60

Nos. 1009-1010 are airmail.

Anniversaries & Events A149

30fr, Prince Charles and Diana, 5th wedding anniv. 40fr, Alain Prost, San Marino, 1985 Formula 1 Grand Prix world champion. 100fr, Wedding of Prince Andrew and Sarah Ferguson. 300fr, Elvis Presley. 500fr, Michael Jackson. 600fr, M. Dassault (1892-1986), aerospace engineer.

1986, Nov. 12

1011 A149	30fr multi	.20	.20
1012 A149	40fr multi	.25	.20
1013 A149	100fr multi	.55	.30
1014 A149	300fr multi	1.60	.80
1015 A149	500fr multi	2.75	1.40
	Nos. 1011-1015 (5)	5.35	2.90

Souvenir Sheet

1016 A149	600fr multi	3.30	1.60

Nos. 1015-1016 are airmail.

1986 World Cup Soccer Championships — A150

Various players and final scores.

1986, Nov. 12

1017 A150	100fr Pfaff	.55	.30
1018 A150	300fr Platini	1.60	.80
1019 A150	400fr Matthaus	2.25	1.10
1020 A150	500fr D. Maradona	2.75	1.40
	Nos. 1017-1020 (4)	7.15	3.60

Souvenir Sheet

1021 A150	600fr Maradona, trophy	3.25	1.60

Nos. 1020-1021 are airmail. No. 1021 contains one 51x42mm stamp.

For surcharge see No. 1182A.

1988 Summer Olympics, Seoul — A151

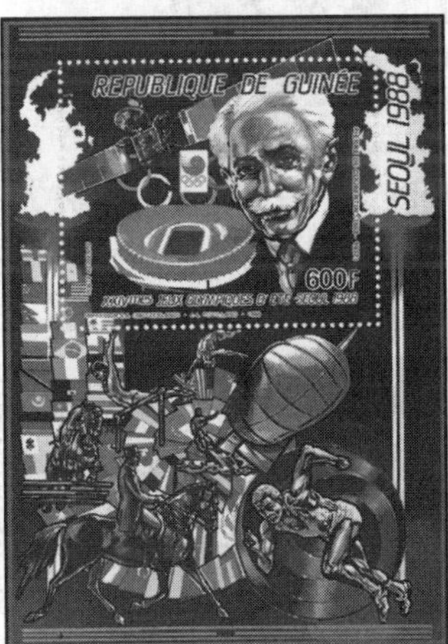

Pierre de Coubertin (1863-1937), Seoul Stadium, Telecommunications Satellite — A151a

1987, Jan. 17 Litho. *Perf. 13½*

1022 A151	20fr Judo	.20	.20
1023 A151	30fr High jump	.20	.20
1024 A151	40fr Team handball	.20	.20
1025 A151	100fr Women's gymnastics	.40	.20
1026 A151	300fr Javelin	1.25	.60
1027 A151	500fr Equestrian	2.00	1.00
	Nos. 1022-1027 (6)	4.25	2.40

Souvenir Sheet

1028 A151a	600fr multi	2.25	1.25

Dated 1986. Nos. 1026-1028 are airmail.

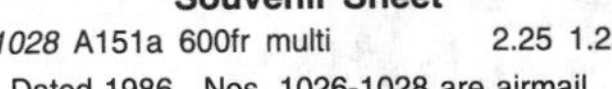

1988 Winter Olympics, Calgary — A152

1987, Mar. 23 Litho. *Perf. 13½*

1029 A152	50fr on 40fr Biathlon	.30	.20
1030 A152	100fr Cross-country skiing	.55	.30
1031 A152	400fr Ski jumping	2.25	2.25
1032 A152	500fr Two-man bobsled	2.75	1.40
	Nos. 1029-1032 (4)	5.85	4.15

Souvenir Sheet

1033 A152	600fr Woman skater, satellite	3.50	1.75

No. 1029 not issued without overprint. Nos. 1031-1033 are airmail.

1988 Winter Olympics, Calgary A153

Telecommunications satellite, athletes and emblem.

1987, May 1

1034 A153	25fr Women's slalom	.20	.20
1035 A153	50fr Hockey	.30	.20
1036 A153	100fr Men's figure skating	.55	.30
1037 A153	150fr Men's downhill skiing	.85	.40
1038 A153	300fr Speed skating	1.75	.90
1039 A153	500fr Four-man bobsled	2.75	1.40
	Nos. 1034-1039 (6)	6.40	3.40

Souvenir Sheet

1040 A153	600fr Ski jumping	3.50	1.75

Nos. 1038-1040 are airmail.

Famous Men — A154

Intl. Cardiology Congresses in Chicago, Washington and New York — A155

Designs: 50fr, Lafayette, military leader during American and French revolutions. 100fr, Ettore Bugatti (1881-1947), Italian automobile manufacturer, 200fr, Garri Kasparov, Russian chess champion. 300fr, George Washington. 400fr, Boris Becker, 1987 Wimbledon tennis champion. 500fr, Sir Winston Churchill.

1987, Nov. 1 Litho. *Perf. 13½*

1041 A154	50fr multi	.35	.20
1042 A154	100fr multi	.70	.35
1043 A154	200fr multi	1.40	.70
1044 A154	300fr multi	2.00	1.00
1045 A154	400fr multi	2.75	1.40
1046 A154	500fr multi	3.50	1.75
	Nos. 1041-1046 (6)	10.70	5.40

Souvenir Sheet

1047 A155	1500fr multi	10.00	5.00

Nos. 1045-1047 are airmail. Stamp in No. 1047 divided into three sections by simulated perforations.

For surcharge see No. 1182B.

Cave Bear — A156

Prehistoric Animals — A157

1987, Nov. 1

1048 A156	50fr Dimetrodon	.35	.20
1049 A156	100fr Iguanodon	.70	.35
1050 A156	200fr Tylosaurus	1.40	.70
1051 A156	300fr shown	2.00	1.00
1052 A156	400fr Saber-tooth tiger	2.75	1.40
1053 A156	500fr Stegosaurus	3.50	1.75
	Nos. 1048-1053 (6)	10.70	5.40

Souvenir Sheet

1054 A157	600fr Triceratops	4.25	2.10

Nos. 1052-1054 are airmail.

For surcharge see No. 1182C.

1988 Summer Olympics, Seoul — A158

Male and female tennis players in action.

1987, Nov. 28

1055 A158	50fr multi	.35	.20
1056 A158	100fr multi, diff.	.70	.35
1057 A158	150fr multi, diff.	1.10	.55
1058 A158	200fr multi, diff.	1.40	.70
1059 A158	300fr multi, diff.	2.10	1.10
1060 A158	500fr multi, diff.	3.50	1.75
	Nos. 1055-1060 (6)	9.15	4.65

Souvenir Sheet

1061 A158	600fr multi	4.50	2.25

Reintroduction of tennis as an Olympic event. Nos. 1059-1061 are airmail.

1992 Summer Olympics, Barcelona A159

Athletes participating in events, Barcelona highlights: 50fr, Discus, courtyard of St. Croix and St. Paul Hospital. 100fr, High jump, Pablo Casals playing cello. 150fr, Long jump, Labyrinth of Horta. 170fr, Javelin, lizard from Guell Park. 400fr, Gymnastics, Mercy Church. 500fr, Tennis, Picasso Museum. 600fr, Running, tapestry by Miro.

1987, Dec. 28 Litho. *Perf. 13½*

1062 A159	50fr multi	.35	.20
1063 A159	100fr multi	.70	.35
1064 A159	150fr multi	1.00	.55
1065 A159	170fr multi	1.25	.60

1066 A159 400fr multi 2.75 1.40
1067 A159 500fr multi 3.50 1.75
Nos. 1062-1067 (6) 9.55 4.85

Souvenir Sheet

1068 A159 600fr multi 4.25 2.10

Nos. 1066-1068 are airmail.
For surcharges see Nos. 1182D-1182E.

Wildlife
A160

1987, Dec. 28

1069 A160 50fr African wild dog pups 1.25 .20
1070 A160 70fr Adult 1.50 .20
1071 A160 100fr Adults circling gazelle 2.00 .35
1072 A160 170fr Chasing gazelle 3.25 .60
1073 A160 400fr Crown cranes 2.75 1.40
1074 A160 500fr Derby elands 3.50 1.75
Nos. 1069-1074 (6) 14.25 4.50

Souvenir Sheet

1075 A160 600fr Vervet monkeys 4.25 2.10

Nos. 1069-1072 picture World Wildlife Fund emblem; Nos. 1073, 1075, picture Scouting trefoil and No. 1074 pictures Rotary Intl. emblem. Nos. 1073-1075 are airmail.
For surcharges see Nos. 1182F-1182G.

Reconciliation Summit Conference, July 11-12, 1986 — A161

Heads of state and natl. flags: Dr. Samuel Kanyon Doe of Liberia, Colonel Lansana Conte of Guinea and Maj.-Gen. Joseph Saidu Momoh of Sierra Leone.

1987 Litho. *Perf. 13½*

1076 A161 40fr multi .35 .20
1077 A161 50fr multi .40 .20
1078 A161 75fr multi .65 .30
1079 A161 100fr multi .85 .40
1080 A161 150fr multi 1.25 .60
Nos. 1076-1080 (5) 3.50 1.70

Space Exploration — A162

1988, Apr. 16

1081 A162 50fr Galaxie-Grasp .35 .20
1082 A162 150fr Energia-Mir 1.00 .50
1083 A162 200fr NASA Space Station 1.40 .70
1084 A162 300fr Ariane 5-E.S.A. 2.10 1.00
1085 A162 400fr Mars-Rover 2.75 1.40
1086 A162 450fr Venus-Vega 3.25 1.60
Nos. 1081-1086 (6) 10.85 5.40

Souvenir Sheet

1087 A162 500fr Mars-Phobos 3.50 1.75

Nos. 1085-1087 are airmail.

A163

A163a

Boy Scouts watching birds and butterflies.

1988, July 5 Litho. *Perf. 13½*

1088 A163 50fr Spermophaga ruficapilla .30 .20
1089 A163 100fr Medon nymphalidae .65 .30
1090 A163 150fr Euplecte orix 1.00 .50
1091 A163 300fr Nectarinia pulchella 2.00 1.00
1092 A163 400fr Sophia nymphalidae 2.60 1.25
1093 A163 450fr Rumia nymphalidae 2.90 1.50
Nos. 1088-1093 (6) 9.45 4.75

Souvenir Sheet

1094 A163 750fr Opis nymphalidae, Psittacula krameri 4.75 2.50

1990, Aug. 3 Litho. & Embossed

1094A A163a 1500fr Druya antimachus

Nos. 1092-1094A are airmail. No. 1094 contains one 35x50mm stamp.
#1094A exists in souvenir sheet of 1.
For surcharge and overprints see Nos. 1182H, 1240-1246.

A164

Famous People: 200fr, Queen Elizabeth II, Prince Philip and crown jewels. 250fr, Fritz von Opel (1899-1971), German automotive industrialist, and 1928 RAK 2 Opel. 300fr, Wolfgang Amadeus Mozart, composer, and Masonic emblem. 400fr, Steffi Graf, tennis champion. 450fr, Buzz Aldrin and Masonic emblem. 500fr, Paul Harris, Rotary Intl. founder, and organization emblem. 750fr, Thomas Jefferson, horiz.

1988, July 5

1095 A164 200fr multi 1.25 .65
1096 A164 250fr multi 1.60 .80
1097 A164 300fr multi 2.00 1.00
1098 A164 400fr multi 2.60 1.25
1099 A164 450fr multi 2.90 1.40
1100 A164 500fr multi 3.25 1.60
Nos. 1095-1100 (6) 13.60 6.70

Souvenir Sheet

1101 A164 750fr multi 4.75 2.50

40th wedding anniv. of Queen Elizabeth II and Prince Philip (200fr).
Nos. 1099-1101 are airmail. No. 1101 contains one 42x36mm stamp.
For surcharges see Nos. 1182I, 1182Q.

1988 Winter Olympics Gold Medalists — A165

Designs: 50fr, Vreni Schneider, Switzerland, women's giant slalom and slalom. 100fr, Frank-Peter Roetsch, East Germany, 10 and 20-kilometer biathlon. 150fr, Matti Nykaenen, Finland, 70 and 90-meter ski jumping. 250fr, Marina Kiehl, West Germany, women's downhill. 400fr, Frank Piccard, France, super giant slalom. 450fr, Katarina Witt, East Germany, women's figure skating. 750fr, Pirmin Zurbriggen, Switzerland, men's downhill.

1988, Oct. 2 Litho. *Perf. 13½*

1102 A165 50fr multi, vert. .30 .20
1103 A165 100fr multi, vert. .60 .30
1104 A165 150fr multi, vert. 1.00 .50
1105 A165 250fr multi, vert. 1.60 .80
1106 A165 400fr multi, vert. 2.60 1.25
1107 A165 450fr multi, vert. 2.90 1.40
Nos. 1102-1107 (6) 9.00 4.45

Souvenir Sheet

1108 A165 750fr multi 5.00 2.50

Nos. 1103, 1107-1108 are airmail.
For surcharge see No. 1182J.

African Postal Union, 25th Anniv. A165a

1988 Litho. *Perf. 13½*

1108A A165a 50fr multicolored .35 .20
1108B A165a 75fr multicolored .55 .30
1108C A165a 100fr multicolored .70 .35
1108D A165a 150fr multicolored 1.10 .55
Nos. 1108A-1108D (4) 2.70 1.40

World Health Day — A165b

1988, Oct. 2 Litho. *Perf. 13½*

1108E A165b 50fr Medical research .40 .20
1108F A165b 150fr Immunization 1.10 .60
1108G A165b 500fr Dentistry 3.75 2.00
Nos. 1108E-1108G (3) 5.25 2.80

For surcharge see No. 1182K.

Opening of MT 20 Intl. Communications Center — A165c

1988, Dec. 8 Litho. *Perf. 13½*

1108H A165c 50fr multicolored
1108I A165c 100fr multicolored
1108J A165c 150fr multicolored

Pierre de Coubertin, Founder of Intl. Olympic Committee A165d

1988 Litho. *Perf. 13½x*

1108K A165d 50fr multi .75 .35
1108L A165d 100fr multi 1.50 .75
1108M A165d 150fr multi 2.50 1.25
1108N A165d 500fr multi 7.75 3.75
Nos. 1108K-1108N (4) 12.50 6.10

For surcharge see No. 1182L.

1992 Summer Olympics, Barcelona — A166

1989, May 3 Litho. *Perf. 13½*

1109 A166 50fr Diving .30 .20
1110 A166 100fr Running, vert. .65 .30
1111 A166 150fr Shooting 1.00 .50
1112 A166 250fr Tennis, vert. 1.60 .80
1113 A166 400fr Soccer 2.60 1.25
1114 A166 500fr Equestrian, vert. 3.25 1.60
Nos. 1109-1114 (6) 9.40 4.65

Souvenir Sheet

1115 A166 750fr Yachting, vert. 5.00 2.50

Nos. 1113-1115 are airmail.
For surcharge see No. 1182M.

French Revolution, Bicent. — A167

Personalities of and scenes from the revolution: 250fr, Jean-Sylvain Bailly (1736-1793) leading proceedings in Tennis Court, June 20, 1789. 300fr, Count Mirabeau (1749-1791) at royal session, June 23, 1789. 400fr, Lafayette (1757-1834), federation anniversary celebration, July 18, 1790. 450fr, Jerome Petion de Villeneuve (1756-1794), king's arrest at Varennes-en-Argonne, June 21, 1791. 750fr, Camille Desmoulins (1760-1794), destruction of the Bastille, July 1789.

1989, July 7 Litho. *Perf. 13½*

1116 A167 250fr multi 1.50 .75
1117 A167 300fr multi 1.75 .90
1118 A167 400fr multi 2.40 1.25
1119 A167 450fr multi 2.75 1.40
Nos. 1116-1119 (4) 8.40 4.30

Souvenir Sheet

1120 A167 750fr multi 4.50 2.25

Nos. 1119-1120 airmail.
Nos. 1116-1119 exist in souvenir sheets of 1. Sold for 100fr extra.
For surcharge and overprints see Nos. 1182N, 1216-1220.

Planting A168

1989 Litho. *Perf. 13½*

1121 A168 25fr shown .20 .20
1122 A168 50fr Irrigation .35 .20
1123 A168 75fr Milking .50 .25
1124 A168 100fr Fishing .70 .35
1125 A168 150fr Farmers in corn field 1.00 .50
1126 A168 300fr Public well 2.10 1.00
Nos. 1121-1126 (6) 4.85 2.50

Natl. Campaign for Self-sufficiency in Food Production and 10th anniv. of the Intl. Fund for Agricultural Development (in 1988). Dated 1988.

African Development Bank, 25th Anniv. — A169

1989, Nov. 4 Litho. *Perf. 13½*
1127 A169 300fr multicolored 2.10 1.10

Mano River Union, 15th Anniv. A170

Design: 300fr, Map of Guinea, Sierra Leone and Liberia, leaders' portraits.

1989, Nov. 4
1128 A170 150fr multicolored 1.10 .55
1129 A170 300fr multicolored 2.10 1.10

World Cup Soccer, Italy — A171

Various soccer plays and: 200fr, Spire of San Domenico, Naples. 250fr, Piazza San Carlo, Turin. 300fr, Church of San Cataldo. 450fr, Church of San Francesco, Utine. 750fr, Statue of Dante, Florence and World Cup Soccer Trophy.

1990, Aug. 3 Litho. *Perf. 13½*
1130 A171 200fr multicolored 1.50 .75
1131 A171 250fr multicolored 1.90 .95
1132 A171 300fr multicolored 2.25 1.10
1133 A171 450fr multicolored 3.50 1.75
Nos. 1130-1133 (4) 9.15 4.55

Souvenir Sheet

1134 A171 750fr multicolored 5.75 2.75

No. 1133-1134 airmail.
For overprints see Nos. 1221-1225.

Concorde, TGV Atlantic — A172

1990, Aug. 3
1135 A172 400fr multicolored 3.00 1.50

No. 1135 exists in a souvenir sheet of 1.
For surcharge see No. 1182O.

Pope John Paul II, Pres. Gorbachev — A173

1990, Aug. 3
1136 A173 300fr multicolored 2.25 1.10

Summit Meeting, Dec. 2, 1989. No. 1136 exists in a souvenir sheet of 1.

1992 Winter Olympics, Albertville — A174

1990, Aug. 3
1137 A174 150fr Downhill skiing 1.10 .60
1138 A174 250fr Cross country skiing 1.90 1.00
1139 A174 400fr Two-man bobsled 3.00 1.50
1140 A174 500fr Speedskating 3.75 1.90
Nos. 1137-1140 (4) 9.75 5.00

Souvenir Sheet

1141 A174 750fr Slalom skiing 5.75 2.75

Nos. 1140-1141 airmail. Nos. 1137-1140 exist in souvenir sheets of 1.
For overprints and surcharge see Nos. 1182P, 1225-1230.

Pres. Bush, Pres. Gorbachev — A175

1990, Aug. 3 Litho. *Perf. 13½*
1142 A175 200fr multicolored 1.50 .75

Summit Meeting Dec. 3, 1989. No. 1142 exists in a souvenir sheet of 1.

De Gaulle's Call for French Resistance, 50th Anniv. — A176

1990
1143 A176 250fr multicolored 1.90 .95

No. 1143 exists in a souvenir sheet of 1.

A177

World Cup Soccer Championships, Italy 1990 — A178

No. 1152, Player, Chateau Saint-Ange.

1991, Apr. 1 Litho. *Perf. 13½*
1144 A177 200fr Rudi Voller 1.50 .75
1145 A177 250fr Uwe Bein 1.90 .95
1146 A177 300fr Pierre Littbarski 2.25 1.10
1147 A177 400fr Jurgen Klinsmann 3.50 1.75
1148 A177 450fr Lothar Matthaus 3.40 1.70
1149 A177 500fr Andreas Brehme 3.75 1.90
Nos. 1144-1149 (6) 16.30 8.15

Litho. & Embossed

1150 A178 1500fr gold & multi

Souvenir Sheets

Litho.

1151 A177 750fr Brehme, diff. 5.75 2.75

Litho. & Embossed

1152 A178 1500fr gold & multi

Nos. 1148-1152 are airmail. Nos. 1144-1150 exist in souvenir sheets of 1.

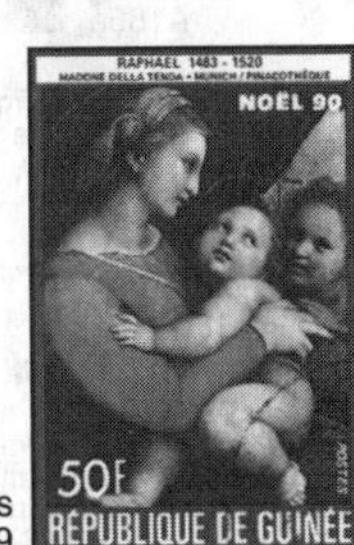

Christmas A179

Paintings by Raphael: 50fr, Della Tenda Madonna. 100fr, Cowper Madonna. 150fr, Tempi Madonna. 250fr, Niccolini Madonna. 300fr, Orleans Madonna. 500fr, Solly Madonna. 750fr, Madonna of the Fish.

1991, Apr. 1 Litho.
1153 A179 50fr multi .40 .20
1154 A179 100fr multi .75 .40
1155 A179 150fr multi 1.10 .60
1156 A179 250fr multi 1.90 .95
1157 A179 300fr multi 2.25 1.10
1158 A179 500fr multi 3.75 1.90
Nos. 1153-1158 (6) 10.15 5.15

Souvenir Sheet

1159 A179 750fr multi 5.75 2.75

Nos. 1157-1159 are airmail. Nos. 1153-1158 exist in souvenir sheets of 1.

A180

World War II Battles — A181

Designs: No. 1160, Sinking of the Bismarck, May 27, 1941, Adm. Raeder and Adm. Tovey. No. 1161, Battle of Midway, June 3, 1942, Adm. Yamamoto and Adm. Nimitz. 200fr, Guadalcanal, Oct. 7, 1942, Adm. Kondo and Adm. Halsey. 250fr, Battle of El Alamein, Oct. 23, 1942, Field Marshal Erwin Rommel, Field Marshal Montgomery. 300fr, Battle of the Bulge, Dec. 16, 1944, Gen. Guderian and Gen. Patton. 450fr, Sinking of the Yamato, Apr., 7, 1945, Adm. Kogo and Gen. MacArthur. No. 1166, Review of Free French Forces, July 14, 1940, Gen. Charles De Gaulle. 750fr, Boeing B-17G, Gen. Dwight Eisenhower. No. 1168, De Gaulle's Call for French Resistance, June 18, 1940.

1991, Apr. 8 Litho. *Perf. 13½*
1160 A180 100fr multicolored .75 .40
1161 A180 150fr multicolored 1.10 .60
1162 A180 200fr multicolored 1.50 .75
1163 A180 250fr multicolored 1.90 .95
1164 A180 300fr multicolored 2.25 1.10
1165 A180 450fr multicolored 5.00 2.50
a. Sheet of 6, #1160-1165 12.50 6.25

Litho. & Embossed

1166 A181 1500fr gold & multi

Souvenir Sheets

Litho.

1167 A180 750fr multicolored 5.75 2.75

Litho. & Embossed

1168 A181 1500fr gold & multi

Nos. 1164-1168 are airmail. No. 1160-1166 exist in souvenir sheets of 1.
For overprint see No. C177.

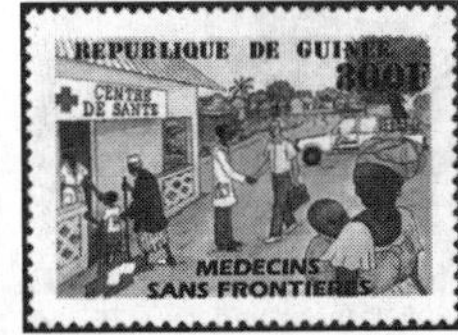

Doctors Without Borders A182

1991, Feb. 22 Litho. *Perf. 13½*
1169 A182 300fr multicolored 2.40 1.25

Telecom '91 A183

1991, Jan. 15
1170 A183 150fr multi, vert. 2.00 1.00
1171 A183 300fr shown 4.00 2.00

6th World Forum and Exposition on Telecommunications, Geneva, Switzerland.

American Entertainers and Films — A184

Designs: 100fr, Nat King Cole Trio. 150fr, Yul Brynner, The Magnificent Seven. 250fr, Judy Garland, The Wizard of Oz. 300fr, Steve McQueen, Papillon. 500fr, Gary Cooper, Sergeant York. 600fr, Bing Crosby, High Society. 750fr, John Wayne, How the West Was Won.

1991, Oct. 2 Litho. *Perf. 13½*
1172 A184 100fr multicolored .75 .45
1173 A184 150fr multicolored 1.10 .60
1174 A184 250fr multicolored 1.90 .95
1175 A184 300fr multicolored 2.25 1.10
1176 A184 500fr multicolored 3.75 1.90
1177 A184 600fr multicolored 8.00 4.00
Nos. 1172-1177 (6) 17.75 9.00

Souvenir Sheet

1178 A184 750fr multicolored 5.75 2.75

Nos. 1176-1178 are airmail. No. 1172-1177 exist in souvenir sheets of 1.

Care Bears Promoting Environmental Protection — A184a

Designs: 50fr, Care Bears circling earth, vert. 100fr, Save water, vert. 200fr, Recycle, vert. 300fr, Control noise, vert. 400fr, Elephant. 500fr, Care Bear emblem, end of rainbow. 600fr, Scout, tent, Lord Baden-Powell.

1991 Litho. *Perf. 13½*
1178A A184a 50fr multi .40 .25
1178B A184a 100fr multi .85 .40
1178C A184a 200fr multi 1.75 .85
1178D A184a 300fr multi 2.50 1.25
1178E A184a 400fr multi 3.50 1.75
Nos. 1178A-1178E (5) 9.00 4.50

Souvenir Sheets

1178F	A184a	500fr multi	4.25	2.25
1178G	A184a	600fr multi	5.00	2.50

Nos. 1178F-1178G each contain one 39x27mm stamp. No. 1178G is airmail.

African Tourism Year A185

1991, Aug. 16 Litho. *Perf. 13½*

1179	A185	100fr Dancer, vert.	.75	.40
1180	A185	150fr Baskets	1.10	.60
1181	A185	250fr Drum	1.90	.90
1182	A185	300fr Flute player, vert.	2.25	1.10
		Nos. 1179-1182 (4)	6.00	3.00

Stamps of 1986-92 Surcharged in Black or Silver (#1182A-1182B, 1182D, 1182H-1182I, 1182M-1182N, 1182P)

1991 Litho. *Perfs. as Before*

1182A	A150	100fr on 400fr #1019	.85	.40
1182B	A154	100fr on 400fr #1045	.85	.40
1182C	A156	100fr on 400fr #1052	.85	.40
1182D	A159	100fr on 170fr #1065	.85	.40
1182E	A159	100fr on 400fr #1066	.85	.40
1182F	A160	100fr on 170fr #1072	60.00	—
1182G	A160	100fr on 400fr #1073	.85	.40
1182H	A163	100fr on 400fr #1092	.85	.40
1182I	A164	100fr on 400fr #1098	.85	.40
1182J	A165	100fr on 400fr #1106	.85	.40
1182K	A165b	100fr on 500fr #1108G	.85	.40
1182L	A165d	100fr on 500fr #1108N	.85	.40
1182M	A166	100fr on 400fr #1113	.85	.40
1182N	A167	100fr on 250fr #1116	.85	.40
1182O	A172	100fr on 400fr #1135	.85	.40
1182P	A174	100fr on 400fr #1139	.85	.40
1182Q	A164	300fr on 450fr #1099	2.50	1.25
1182R	AP14	300fr on 450fr #C170	2.50	1.25
		Nos. 1182A-1182R (18)	77.75	8.50

Nos. 1182B-1182C, 1182E, 1182G, 1182M, 1182Q-1182R are airmail.

Visit by Pope John Paul II — A185a

1992, Feb. 24 Litho. *Perf. 13½*

1182S	A185a	150fr multicolored	1.25	.60

1994 World Cup Soccer, US — A186

A186a

Player, World Cup Trophy and scenes of Atlanta: 100fr, Little Five Points. 300fr, Fulton County Stadium. 400fr, Inman Park. 500fr, High Museum of Art. 1000fr, Intelsat VI, Capitol.

#1187A, Player in white shirt. #1187B, Player in red.

1992, Apr. 27 Litho. *Perf. 13½*

1183	A186	100fr multi	.75	.40
1184	A186	300fr multi	2.25	1.10
1185	A186	400fr multi	3.00	1.50
1186	A186	500fr multi	3.75	1.90
		Nos. 1183-1186 (4)	9.75	4.90

Souvenir Sheet

1187	A186	1000fr multi	7.50	3.75

Litho. & Embossed

1187A	A186a	1500fr gold & multi		

Souvenir Sheet

1187B	A186a	1500fr gold & multi		

Nos. 1186-1187B are airmail. Nos. 1183-1186A exist in souvenir sheets of 1.

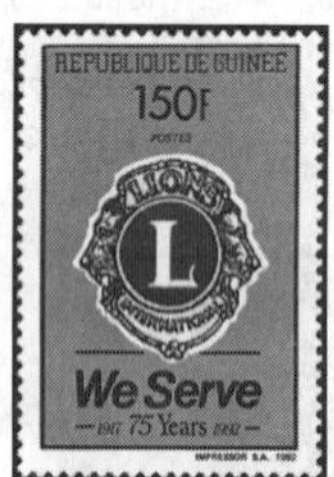

Lions Intl., 75th Anniv. — A187

1992, May 22 Litho. *Perf. 13½*

1188	A187	150fr blue & multi	1.25	.65
1188A	A187	400fr lilac rose & multi	3.50	1.75

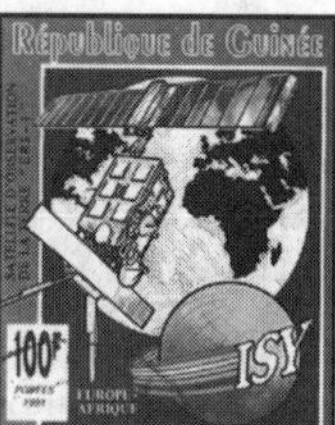

Anniversaries and Events — A188

Designs: 100fr, Satellite ERS-1 in orbit. 150fr, Vase with Fourteen Sunflowers, by Vincent van Gogh. 200fr, Napoleon Bonaparte. 250fr, Henri Dunant, Red Cross workers. 300fr, Brandenburg Gate. 400fr, Pope John Paul II. 450fr, Garry Kasparov, Anatoly Karpov, chess pieces. 500fr, African child, dove, emblems of Rotary and Lions Clubs.

1992, Nov. 10 Litho. *Perf. 13½*

1189	A188	100fr multicolored	.85	.40
1190	A188	150fr multicolored	1.25	.65
1191	A188	200fr multicolored	1.75	.85
1192	A188	250fr multicolored	2.10	1.10
1193	A188	300fr multicolored	2.50	1.25
1194	A188	400fr multicolored	3.25	1.75
1195	A188	450fr multicolored	3.75	1.90
1196	A188	500fr multicolored	4.25	2.10
		Nos. 1189-1196 (8)	19.70	10.00

Intl. Space Year (#1189). Vincent van Gogh, cent. of death (in 1990) (#1190). Napolean Bonaparte, 170th anniv. of death (in 1991) (#1191). Founding of Red Cross (in 1864) (#1192). Brandenburg Gate, bicent. (#1193). Pope John Paul II's visit to Africa in 1989 (#1194). World Chess Championships (#1195). Lions Intl., 75th anniv. (#1196).

Nos. 1195-1196 are airmail. Nos. 1189-1196 exist in souvenir sheets of one.

For overprint see No. C178.

Anniversaries and Events — A189

Designs: 200fr, The Devil and Kate, Antonin Dvorak. 300fr, Antonio Vivaldi. 350fr, Graf Zeppelin, flying boat, Count Ferdinand von Zeppelin. 400fr, English Channel Euro-Tunnel Train. 450fr, Konrad Adenauer, Brandenburg Gate. 500fr, Japanese naval ensign, Emperor Hirohito. 750fr, Tunnel Train, diff.

1992, Nov. 10

1197	A189	200fr multicolored	1.70	.85
1198	A189	300fr multicolored	2.50	1.25
1199	A189	350fr multicolored	2.90	1.40
1200	A189	400fr multicolored	3.25	1.75
1201	A189	450fr multicolored	3.75	1.90
a.		Souvenir sheet of 2, #1199, 1201	6.75	3.25
1202	A189	500fr multicolored	4.25	2.10
		Nos. 1197-1202 (6)	18.35	9.25

Souvenir Sheet

1203	A189	750fr multicolored	6.25	3.00

Antonin Dvorak, 90th anniv. of death (in 1994) (#1197). Antonio Vivaldi, 250th anniv. of death (in 1991) (#1198). Count Ferdinand von Zeppelin, 75th anniv. of death (#1199). Opening of English Channel Tunnel (in 1994) (#1200, 1203). Konrad Adenauer, 25th anniv. of death, Brandenburg Gate, bicent. (#1201). Death of Emperor Hirohito (in 1989) (#1202).

Nos. 1201-1203 are airmail. Nos. 1197-1202 exist imperf. and in souvenir sheets of one. No. 1203 exists imperf. and contains one 60x42mm stamp.

Anniversaries and Events A190

Designs: 50fr, Modern Times, film by Charlie Chaplin. 100fr, Expo '92 Seville, Columbus. 150fr, St. Peter's Square, Rome. 200fr, Marlene Dietrich, roses. 250fr, Michael Schumacher, Benetton Ford B192. 300fr, Mercury rocket, John Glenn. 400fr, Bill Koch, America 3. 450fr, Mark Rypien, quarterback of Washington Redskins. 500fr, Rescue of Intelsat VI by shuttle Endeavour.

1992, Dec. 3

1204	A190	50fr multicolored	.40	.20
1205	A190	100fr multicolored	.85	.40
1206	A190	150fr multicolored	1.25	.65
1207	A190	200fr multicolored	1.75	.85
1208	A190	250fr multicolored	2.10	1.10
1209	A190	300fr multicolored	2.50	1.25
1210	A190	400fr multicolored	3.25	1.75
1211	A190	450fr multicolored	3.75	1.90
1212	A190	500fr multicolored	4.25	2.10
		Nos. 1204-1212 (9)	20.10	10.20

Discovery of America, 500th anniv. (#1205). First US orbital space flight, 30th anniv. (#1209). Americas Cup yacht race (#1210). Super Bowl XXVI football game (#1211).

Nos. 1210-1212 are airmail. Nos. 1204-1212 exist in souvenir sheets of one.

Intl. Conference on Nutrition, Rome — A191

1992, Nov. 10 Litho. *Perf. 13½*

1213	A191	150fr multi	1.25	.65
1214	A191	400fr multi	3.25	1.75
1215	A191	500fr multi	4.25	2.10
		Nos. 1213-1215 (3)	8.75	4.50

Nos. 1116-1120 Ovptd. in Silver "BICENTENAIRE / DE L'AN I / DE LA REPUBLIQUE / FRANCAISE"

1992, Feb. 24 Litho. *Perf. 13½*

1216	A167	250fr multicolored	2.00	1.00
1217	A167	300fr multicolored	2.50	1.25
1218	A167	400fr multicolored	3.25	1.60
1219	A167	450fr multicolored	3.75	1.90
		Nos. 1216-1219 (4)	11.50	5.75

Souvenir Sheet

1220	A167	750fr multicolored	6.25	3.25

Nos. 1219-1220 are airmail. Nos. 1216-1219 exist in souvenir sheets of 1. Sold for 100fr extra.

Nos. 1130-1134 Ovptd. in Gold "1. ALLEMAGNE / 2. ARGENTINE / 3. ITALIE"

1992, Feb. 24 Litho. *Perf. 13½*

1221	A171	200fr multicolored	1.50	.75
1222	A171	250fr multicolored	1.90	.95
1223	A171	300fr multicolored	2.25	1.10
1224	A171	450fr multicolored	3.50	1.75
		Nos. 1221-1224 (4)	9.15	4.55

Souvenir Sheet

1225	A171	750fr multicolored	5.75	2.75

Nos. 1137-1141 Ovptd. in Gold

1992 Litho. *Perf. 13½*

1226	A174	150fr multicolored	1.25	.65
1227	A174	250fr multicolored	2.00	1.00
1228	A174	400fr multicolored	3.25	1.60
1229	A174	500fr multicolored	4.00	2.00
		Nos. 1226-1229 (4)	10.50	5.25

Souvenir Sheet

1230	A174	750fr multicolored	6.25	3.00

Overprints read: 150fr, 750fr, "SLALOM GEANT / Alberto Tomba, Italie." 250fr, "SKI NORDIQUE / Vegard Ulvang, Norvege." 400fr, "BOB A DEUX / G. Weder / D Acklin, Suisse." 500fr, "PATINAGE DE VITESSE / Olaf Zinke 1000m., Allemagne."

A192

1994 World Cup Soccer Championships, US — A192a

Soccer player, city skyline: 100fr, San Francisco. 300fr, Washington, DC. 400fr, Detroit. 500fr, Dallas. 1000fr, New York.

1993, Sept. 24 Litho. *Perf. 13½*

1233	A192	100fr multicolored	.80	.40
1234	A192	300fr multicolored	2.50	1.25
1235	A192	400fr multicolored	3.25	1.60
1236	A192	500fr multicolored	4.00	2.00
		Nos. 1233-1236 (4)	10.55	5.25

Souvenir Sheet

1237	A192	1000fr multicolored	8.25	4.25

Litho. & Embossed

1237A	A192a	1500fr gold & multi		

Nos. 1236-1237A are airmail. No. 1237A exists in a souvenir sheet of 1.

Miniature Sheet

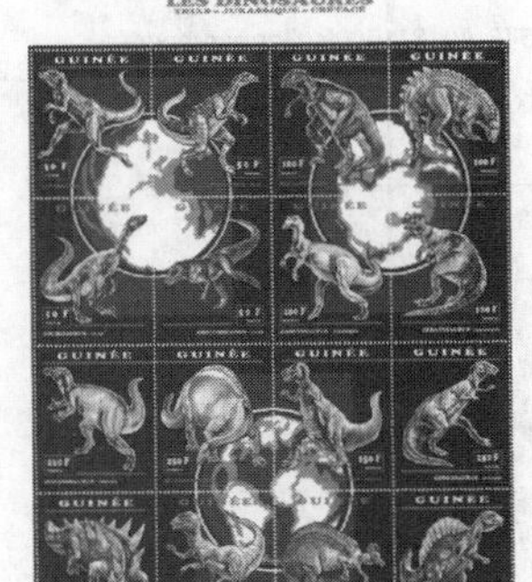

Dinosaurs — A193

No. 1238: a, 50fr, Euparkeria. b, 50fr, Plateosaurus. c, 50fr, Anchisaurus. d, 50fr, Ornithosuchus. e, 100fr, Megalosaurus. f, 100fr, Scelidosaurus. g, 100fr, Camptosaurus. h, 100fr, Ceratosaurus. i, 250fr, Ouranosaurus. j, 250fr, Dicraeosaurus. k, 250fr, Tarbosaurus. l, 250fr, Gorgosaurus. m, 250fr, Polacanthus. n, 250fr, Deinonychus. o, 250fr, Corythosaurus. p, 250fr, Spinosaurus.
1000fr, Tyrannosaurus rex.

1993, Oct. 27

1238 A193 Sheet of 16, #a.-p. 21.00 10.50

Souvenir Sheet

1239 A193 1000fr multicolored 8.25 4.00

No. 1239 is airmail and contains one 50x60mm stamp.

Nos. 1088-1094 Ovptd. in Silver "50eme ANNIVERSAIRE DE LA MORT DE BADEN POWEL"

1993, Feb. 24 Litho. *Perf. 13½*

1240 A163 50fr multicolored .40 .20
1241 A163 100fr multicolored .75 .40
1242 A163 150fr multicolored 1.10 .55
1243 A163 300fr multicolored 2.25 1.10
1244 A163 400fr multicolored 3.00 1.50
1245 A163 450fr multicolored 3.50 1.75
Nos. 1240-1245 (6) 11.00 5.50

Souvenir Sheet

1246 A163 750fr multicolored 5.75 3.00

Nos. 1244-1246 are airmail.

A194

1994 Winter Olympic Games, Lillehammer A195

Views of Lillehammer: 150fr, Ice hockey. 250fr, Bobsled. 400fr, Biathlon. 450fr, Ski jump.
1000fr, Slalom skiing. 1500fr, Ice skating.

1993, July 16 Litho. *Perf. 13½*

1247 A194 150fr multicolored 1.25 .65
1248 A194 250fr multicolored 2.25 1.10
1249 A194 400fr multicolored 3.50 1.75
1250 A194 450fr multicolored 4.00 1.90
Nos. 1247-1250 (4) 11.00 5.40

Souvenir Sheet

1251 A194 1000fr multicolored 8.50 4.25

Litho. & Embossed

1252 A195 1500fr gold & multi

Nos. 1249-1252 are airmail.
For overprints see #1267A-1267E.

A196

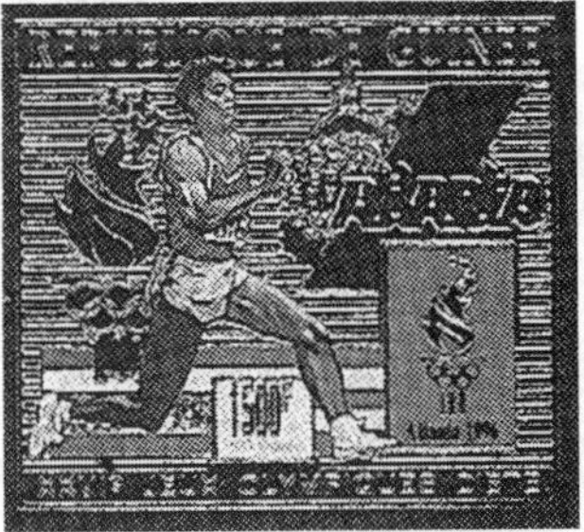

1996 Summer Olympic Games, Atlanta—A197 — 1257A

Event, scenes of Atlanta: 150fr, Soccer, "Little White House." 250fr, Cycling, Georgia World Congress Center. 400fr, Basketball, underground Atlanta. 500fr, Baseball, new Georgia Railroad.
1000fr, Tennis, Atlanta at night. 1500fr, Running, Georgia State Capitol, Olympic torch.

1993, July 16 Litho. *Perf. 13½*

1253 A196 150fr multi 1.25 .65
1254 A196 250fr multi 2.00 1.00
1255 A196 400fr multi 3.50 1.75
1256 A196 500fr multi 4.25 2.10
Nos. 1253-1256 (4) 11.00 5.50

Souvenir Sheet

1257 A196 1000fr multi 8.50 4.25

Litho. & Embossed

1257A A197 1500fr gold & multi

Nos. 1256-1257A are airmail.
#1253-1256 exist in souvenir sheets of 1.

First Manned Moon Landing, 25th Anniv. — A197a

d, Luna 3, 1959. e, Ranger 7, 1964. f, Luna 9, 1966. g, Surveyor 1, 1966. h, Lunar Orbiter 1, 1966. i, Launch of Apollo 11, Neil Armstrong, 1969. j, Michael Collins, Apollo 11 command module. k, Apollo 11 landing on Moon, "Buzz" Aldrin. l, Apollo 12, 1969. m, Apollo 13, 1969. n, Luna 16, 1970. o, Luna 17, 1970. p, Apollo 14, 1971. q, Apollo 15, 1971. r, Apollo 16, 1972. s, Apollo 17, 1972.

1993, July 27 Litho. *Perf. 13½*
Sheet of 16

1257B A197a 150fr #d.-s. 20.50 10.50

D-Day Landings, Normandy, 50th Anniv. — A198

Battle scenes and: No. 1258a, 150fr, Field Marshal Irwin Rommel (1891-1944), Germany. b, 600fr, Gen. Dwight D. Eisenhower (1890-1969), Allies. c, 150fr, Gen. George S. Patton, Jr. (1885-1945), Allies.
Battle of the Bulge, 1944: No. 1259a, 150fr, Lt. Gen. William H. Simpson. b, 600fr, Battle scene. c, 150fr, Gen. Heinz Guderian (1888-1954).
Austerlitz, Dec. 2, 1805: No. 1260a, 150fr, John I, Prince of Liechtenstein (1760-1836). b, 600fr, Napoleon I. c, 150fr, Marshal Joachim Murat (1767-1815).
Battle of Borodino, Sept. 7, 1812: No. 1261a, 150fr, Marshal Michael Ney (1769-1815). b, 600fr, Battle scene. c, 150fr, Prince Pytor Ivanovich Bagration (1765-1812).

1994, Jan. 26 Litho. *Perf. 13½*

1258 A198 Strip of 3, #a.-c. 7.25 3.75
1259 A198 Strip of 3, #a.-c. 7.25 3.75
1260 A198 Strip of 3, #a.-c. 7.25 3.75
1261 A198 Strip of 3, #a.-c. 7.25 3.75
Nos. 1258-1261 (4) 29.00 15.00

No. 1258b, 1259b, 1260b, 1261b are 60x46mm. Nos. 1258-1261 are each a continuous design.

Astronomers and Spacecraft A199

Designs: a, 300fr, Johannes Kepler, Pluto probe. b, 500fr, Copernicus, Galileo probe. b, 300fr, Sir Isaac Newton, Voyager.

1994, Jan. 26

1262 A199 Strip of 3, #a.-c. 8.75 4.50

No. 1262b is 60x46mm. No. 1262 has a continuous design.

Nos. 1233-1237 Ovptd. in Silver "1. BRESIL / 2. ITALIE / 3. SUEDE"

1994, Sept. 14 Litho. *Perf. 13½*

1263 A192 100fr multicolored .85 .40
1264 A192 300fr multicolored 2.50 1.25
1265 A192 400fr multicolored 3.50 1.75
1266 A192 500fr multicolored 4.25 2.00
Nos. 1263-1266 (4) 11.10 5.40

Souvenir Sheet

1267 A192 1000fr multicolored 8.50 4.25

Nos. 1266-1267 are airmail.

Nos. 1247-1251 Overprinted in Gold

1994, Sept. 14 Litho. *Perf. 13½*

1267A A194 150fr multi 1.25 .65
1267B A194 250fr multi 2.25 1.10
1267C A194 400fr multi 3.50 1.75
1267D A194 450fr multi 4.00 1.90
Nos. 1267A-1267D (4) 11.00 5.40

Souvenir Sheet

1267E A194 1000fr multi 8.50 4.25

Overprints read: 150fr, MEDAILLE D'OR / SUEDE. 250fr, G. WEDER / D. ACKLIN / SUISSE. 400fr, F.B. LUNDBERG / NORVEGE. 450fr, J. WEISSFLOG / ALLEMAGNE. 1000fr, T. MOE / U.S.A.
Nos. 1267C-1267E are airmail.

Birds — A200

150fr, Carduelis carduelis. 250fr, Luscinia megarhynchos. #1270, Serinus canaria. #1271, Fringilla coelebs. #1272, Carduelis chloris.
No. 1273, Erithacus rubecula.

1995, Aug. 31 Litho. *Perf. 13*

1268 A200 150fr multicolored .50 .25
1269 A200 250fr multicolored .80 .35
1270 A200 500fr multicolored 1.60 .80
1271 A200 500fr multicolored 1.60 .80
1272 A200 500fr multicolored 1.60 .80
Nos. 1268-1272 (5) 6.10 3.00

Souvenir Sheet

1273 A200 1000fr multicolored *4.75 2.50*

No. 1273 contains one 32x40mm stamp.

1996 Summer Olympics, Atlanta — A201

1995, Aug. 5

1274 A201 150fr Javelin .50 .25
1275 A201 250fr Boxing .80 .40
1276 A201 500fr Basketball 1.60 .80
1277 A201 500fr Weight lifting 1.60 .80
1278 A201 500fr Soccer 1.60 .80
Nos. 1274-1278 (5) 6.10 3.05

Souvenir Sheet

1279 A201 1000fr Archery *4.75 2.50*

No. 1279 contains one 32x40mm stamp.

African Animals A202

Designs: 150fr, Cercopithecus mona, vert. 250fr, Cercopithecus aethiops, vert. No. 1282, Galagoides demidovi, vert. No. 1283, Manis gigantea. No. 1284, Lepus crawshayi.
1000fr, Aonyx capensis, vert.

1995, Sept. 25

1280 A202 150fr multicolored .50 .25
1281 A202 250fr multicolored .80 .35
1282 A202 500fr multicolored 1.60 .80
1283 A202 500fr multicolored 1.60 .80
1284 A202 500fr multicolored 1.60 .80
Nos. 1280-1284 (5) 6.10 3.00

Souvenir Sheet

1285 A202 1000fr multicolored *4.75 2.50*

1998 World Cup Soccer Championships, France — A203

Opposing two players wearing: No. 1288, Yellow shirt & blue shorts, red shirt & white shorts. No. 1289, Red & white uniform, red shirt & white shorts. No. 1290, Striped shirt & blue shorts, red & yellow shirt & green shorts.
1000fr, Three players.

1995, Oct. 30 Litho. *Perf. 13*

1286 A203 150fr multicolored .50 .25
1287 A203 250fr multicolored .80 .35
1288 A203 500fr multicolored 1.60 .80
1289 A203 500fr multicolored 1.60 .80
1290 A203 500fr multicolored 1.60 .80
Nos. 1286-1290 (5) 6.10 3.00

Souvenir Sheet

1291 A203 1000fr multicolored *4.75 2.50*

No. 1291 contains one 32x40mm stamp.

Domestic Cats A204

150fr, Tortoiseshell. 250fr, Tabby and white. #1294, Tortoiseshell and white longhair. #1295, Red tabby. #1296, Smoke long-haired.
1000fr, Chinchilla.

1995, July 25

1292 A204 150fr multicolored .50 .25
1293 A204 250fr multicolored .80 .35
1294 A204 500fr multicolored 1.60 .80
1295 A204 500fr multicolored 1.60 .80
1296 A204 500fr multicolored 1.60 .80
Nos. 1292-1296 (5) 6.10 3.00

Souvenir Sheet

Perf. 12½

1297 A204 1000fr multicolored *4.75 2.50*

No. 1297 contains one 40x32mm stamp.

Production of Electrical Power — A205

Designs: 100fr, Banéa Dam. 150fr, Water Chamber, Donkea. 200fr, Tinkisso Spillway, vert. 250fr, Cascades of Grand Falls. 500fr, Building, Kinkon.

1995, July 18 *Perf. 12½*

1298 A205 100fr multicolored .50 .25
1299 A205 150fr multicolored .75 .35
1300 A205 200fr multicolored 1.00 .50
1301 A205 250fr multicolored 1.25 .65
1302 A205 500fr multicolored 2.50 1.25
Nos. 1298-1302 (5) 6.00 3.00

FAO, 50th Anniv. A206

Designs: 200fr, Man, oxen, boy. 750fr, Instructing women, children on nutrition.

1995, Oct. 16 *Perf. 13*

1303 A206 200fr multicolored .70 .35
1304 A206 750fr multicolored 2.50 1.25

Light Aircraft — A207

100fr, Pup-150, UK. 150fr, Gardan GY-80 Horizon, France. 250fr, Piper Cub J-3, US. No. 1308, Valmet L-90TP Redigo, Finland. No. 1309, Pilatus PC-6 Porter, Switzerland. No. 1310, Piper PA-28 Cherokee Arrow, US.
1000fr, Stol DO-27, Germany.

1995, Oct. 1 *Perf. 12½*

1305 A207 100fr multicolored .30 .20
1306 A207 150fr multicolored .50 .25
1307 A207 250fr multicolored .90 .45
1308 A207 500fr multicolored 1.60 .80
1309 A207 500fr multicolored 1.60 .80
1310 A207 500fr multicolored 1.60 .80
Nos. 1305-1310 (6) 6.50 3.30

Souvenir Sheet

1311 A207 1000fr multicolored *4.75 2.50*

No. 1311 contains one 40x32mm stamp.

Flowers — A208

100fr, Sprekelia formosissima. 150fr, Rudbeckia purpurea. 250fr, Meconopsis betonicifolia. #1314, Gail Borden rose. #1315, Lathyrus odoratus. #1316, Iris starshine.
1000fr, Cypripedium alma gaevert.

1995, Oct. 12

1312 A208 100fr multicolored .30 .20
1313 A208 150fr multicolored .50 .25
1314 A208 250fr multicolored .80 .40
1315 A208 500fr multicolored 1.60 .80
1316 A208 500fr multicolored 1.60 .80
1317 A208 500fr multicolored 1.60 .80
Nos. 1312-1317 (6) 6.40 3.25

Souvenir Sheet

1318 A208 1000fr multicolored *4.75 2.50*

No. 1318 contains one 32x40mm stamp.

Historic Buses — A209

250fr, 1832 Omnibus. 300fr, 1898 Daimler. 400fr, 1904 V.H. Bussing. 450fr, 1906 Autobus M.A.N. 500fr, 1904 Autocar M.A.N.

1995, Dec. 3 Litho. *Perf. 12½*

1319 A209 250fr multicolored .75 .35
1320 A209 300fr multicolored .90 .45
1321 A209 400fr multicolored 1.25 .60
1322 A209 450fr multicolored 1.40 .70
1323 A209 500fr multicolored 1.50 .75
Nos. 1319-1323 (5) 5.80 2.85

Arabian Horses A210

Various horses.

1995

Background Colors

1324 A210 100fr dk bl, vert. .30 .20
1325 A210 150fr tan, vert. .45 .20
1326 A210 250fr lt bl, vert. .75 .35
1327 A210 500fr pink, vert. 1.50 .75
1328 A210 500fr lilac, vert. 1.50 .75
1329 A210 500fr sage 1.50 .75
Nos. 1324-1329 (6) 6.00 3.00

Souvenir Sheet

1330 A210 1000fr white & gray *4.50 2.25*

No. 1330 contains one 32x40mm stamp.

Mushrooms A211

150fr, Leccinum nigrescens. 250fr, Boletus rhodoxanthus. #1333, Paxillus involutus. #1334, Cantharellus lutescens. #1335, Xerocomus rubellus.
1000fr, Gymnopilus junonius.

1995 Litho. *Perf. 12½*

1331 A211 150fr multicolored .45 .20
1332 A211 250fr multicolored .75 .40
1333 A211 500fr multicolored 1.50 .75
1334 A211 500fr multicolored 1.50 .75
1335 A211 500fr multicolored 1.50 .75
Nos. 1331-1335 (5) 5.70 2.85

Souvenir Sheet

1336 A211 1000fr multicolored *4.50 2.25*

No. 1336 contains one 32x40mm stamp.

Tourism — A212

1996, Sept. 5 Litho. *Perf. 12½*

1337 A212 200fr Mountain cliff .60 .30
1338 A212 750fr Young child 2.25 1.10
1339 A212 1000fr Women carrying wood 2.90 1.50
Nos. 1337-1339 (3) 5.75 2.90

Dogs — A213

1996, Oct. 20

1340 A213 200fr Bull terrier .60 .30
1341 A213 250fr Elkhound .75 .40
1342 A213 300fr Akita .90 .45
1343 A213 400fr Collie 1.10 .60
1344 A213 450fr Rottweiler 1.25 .65
1345 A213 500fr Boxer 1.50 .75
Nos. 1340-1345 (6) 6.10 3.15

Souvenir Sheet

Perf. 13

1346 A213 1000fr German pointer 4.50 2.25

No. 1346 contains one 32x40mm stamp.

Mushrooms A214

1996, Dec. 20 Litho. *Perf. 12½*

1347 A214 200fr Chestnut .60 .30
1348 A214 250fr Granular .75 .35
1349 A214 300fr Destroying angel .90 .45
1350 A214 400fr Milky blue 1.10 .60
1351 A214 450fr Violet cortinarius 1.25 .65
1352 A214 500fr Rough-stemmed 1.50 .75
Nos. 1347-1352 (6) 6.10 3.10

Souvenir Sheet

Perf. 13

1353 A214 1000fr Hygrophorus *4.50 2.25*

No. 1353 contains one 32x40mm stamp.

Locomotives — A215

Designs: 200fr, Tom Thumb, 1829. 250fr, Genf, 1858. 300fr, Dübs and Company, 1873. 400fr, W.G. Bagnall of Castle Engine Works, 1932. 450fr, Werner von Siemens, 1879. 500fr, North London Tramways Co., 1885-89.
1000fr, General, 1862.

1996, Aug. 30 *Perf. 12½*

1354 A215 200fr multicolored .60 .30
1355 A215 250fr multicolored .75 .40
1356 A215 300fr multicolored .90 .45
1357 A215 400fr multicolored 1.25 .60
1358 A215 450fr multicolored 1.40 .70
1359 A215 500fr multicolored 1.50 .75
Nos. 1354-1359 (6) 6.40 3.20

Souvenir Sheet

1360 A215 1000fr multicolored *4.50 2.25*

Nos. 1355, 1358 are each 68x27mm. No. 1360 contains one 40x32mm stamp.

Cats A216

200fr, Tortoiseshell short-hair. 250fr, Black and white short-hair. 300fr, Japanese. 400fr, Himalayan. 450fr, Brown long-hair. 500fr, Blue Persian.
1000fr, Tortoiseshell long-hair.

1996, Nov. 15 *Perf. 12½*

1361 A216 200fr multicolored .60 .30
1362 A216 250fr multicolored .75 .40
1363 A216 300fr multicolored .90 .45
1364 A216 400fr multicolored 1.25 .60
1365 A216 450fr multicolored 1.40 .70
1366 A216 500fr multicolored 1.50 .75
Nos. 1361-1366 (6) 6.40 3.20

Souvenir Sheet

1367 A216 1000fr multicolored *4.50 2.25*

No. 1367 contains one 32x40mm stamp.

Birds — A217

Designs: 200fr, Carduelis cucullata. 250fr, Uraeginthus bengalus. 300fr, Lonchura castaneothorax. 400fr, Amadina erythrocephala. 450fr, Chloebia gouldiae. 500fr, Euplectes orix.
1000fr, Poephila guttata.

1996, Sept. 28 ***Perf. 12½***

1368	A217	200fr multicolored	.60	.30
1369	A217	250fr multicolored	.75	.40
1370	A217	300fr multicolored	.90	.45
1371	A217	400fr multicolored	1.25	.60
1372	A217	450fr multicolored	1.40	.70
1373	A217	500fr multicolored	1.50	.75
		Nos. 1368-1373 (6)	6.40	3.20

Souvenir Sheet

1374	A217	1000fr multicolored	*4.50*	*2.25*

No. 1374 contains one 32x40mm stamp.

Orchids A218

Designs: 200fr, Paphiopedilum millmoore. 250fr, Paphiopedilum ernest read. 300fr, Paphiopedilum harrisianum. 400fr, Paphiopedilum gaudianum. 450fr, Paphiopedilum papa röhl. 500fr, Paphiopedilum sea cliffl.
1000fr, Paphiopedilum gowenanum.

1997, Mar. 3 **Litho.** ***Perf. 12½***

1375	A218	200fr multicolored	.55	.30
1376	A218	250fr multicolored	.70	.35
1377	A218	300fr multicolored	.80	.40
1378	A218	400fr multicolored	1.10	.55
1379	A218	450fr multicolored	1.25	.60
1380	A218	500fr multicolored	1.40	.70
		Nos. 1375-1380 (6)	5.80	2.90

Souvenir Sheet

1381	A218	1000fr multicolored	4.00	2.00

No. 1381 contains one 32x40mm stamp.

1998 World Cup Soccer Championships, France — A219

Various soccer plays.

1997, Jan. 15

1382	A219	200fr multi, vert.	.55	.30
1383	A219	250fr multi, vert.	.70	.35
1384	A219	300fr multi, vert.	.80	.40
1385	A219	400fr multicolored	1.10	.55
1386	A219	450fr multicolored	1.25	.60
1387	A219	500fr multicolored	1.40	.70
		Nos. 1382-1387 (6)	5.80	2.90

Souvenir Sheet

1388	A219	1000fr Goalie at net	4.00	2.00

No. 1388 contains one 32x40mm stamp.

Wild Animals A220

Designs: 200fr, Giraffa camelopardalis. 250fr, Cerothoterium simun, vert. 300fr, Phacochoerus aethiopicus. 400fr, Acinonyx jubatus. 450fr, Loxodonta africana, vert. 500fr, Choeropsis liberiensis.
1000fr, Okapia johnstoni.

1997, Apr. 15 **Litho.** ***Perf. 12½***

1389	A220	200fr multicolored	.50	.25
1390	A220	250fr multicolored	.65	.30
1391	A220	300fr multicolored	.75	.40
1392	A220	400fr multicolored	1.00	.50
1393	A220	450fr multicolored	1.10	.55
1394	A220	500fr multicolored	1.25	.65
		Nos. 1389-1394 (6)	5.25	2.65

Souvenir Sheet

1395	A220	1000fr multicolored	*3.75*	*1.90*

19th Century Warships — A221

Designs: 200fr, Captain, England, 1870. 250fr, Konig Wilhelm, Germany, 1869. 300fr, Téméraire, England, 1877. 400fr, Mouillage, Italy, 1866. 450fr, Inflexible, England, 1881. 500fr, Magenta, France, 1862.
1000fr, Redoutable, France, 1878.

1997, May 20 **Litho.** ***Perf. 12½***

1396	A221	200fr multicolored	.50	.25
1397	A221	250fr multicolored	.60	.30
1398	A221	300fr multicolored	.75	.40
1399	A221	400fr multicolored	1.00	.50
1400	A221	450fr multicolored	1.10	.55
1401	A221	500fr multicolored	1.25	.60
		Nos. 1396-1401 (6)	5.20	2.60

Souvenir Sheet

1402	A221	1000fr multicolored	3.50	1.75

No. 1402 contains one 32x40mm stamp.

Fish A222

Designs: 200fr, Siganus trispilos. 250fr, Scarus niger. 300fr, Choerodon fasciata. 400fr, Naso lituratus. 450fr, Hypoplectrus gemma. 500fr, Acanthurus achilles.
1000fr, Zebrasoma flavescens.

1997, June 15 **Litho.** ***Perf. 13***

1403	A222	200fr multicolored	.45	.25
1404	A222	250fr multicolored	.55	.30
1405	A222	300fr multicolored	.70	.35
1406	A222	400fr multicolored	.90	.45
1407	A222	450fr multicolored	1.00	.50
1408	A222	500fr multicolored	1.10	.55
		Nos. 1403-1408 (6)	4.70	2.40

Souvenir Sheet

Perf. 12½

1409	A222	1000fr multicolored	3.50	1.75

No. 1409 contains one 40x32mm stamp.

Chess Pieces A222a

200fr, Thailand, 14th cent. 250fr, China, 1930. 300fr, Portugal, 1920. 400fr, Germany. 450fr, Russia. 500fr, Pieces by Max Ernst.
1000fr, France, 18th cent.

1997, Oct. 20 **Litho.** ***Perf. 13***

1409A	A222a	200fr multi	.75	.35
1409B	A222a	250fr multi	.90	.45
1409C	A222a	300fr multi	1.10	.55
1409D	A222a	400fr multi	1.40	.70
1409E	A222a	450fr multi	1.60	.80
1409F	A222a	500fr multi	1.75	.90
		Nos. 1409A-1409F (6)	7.50	3.75

Souvenir Sheet

Perf. 12½

1409G	A222a	1000fr multi	3.75	1.90

No. 1409G contains one 32x40mm stamp.

Dogs A223

1997, Nov. 10 **Litho.** ***Perf. 12½***

Stamp plus Label

1410	A223	200fr Siberian husky	.70	.35
1411	A223	250fr Dachshund	.85	.45
1412	A223	300fr Boston terrier	1.00	.50
1413	A223	400fr Basset hound	1.40	.70
1414	A223	450fr Dalmatian	1.50	.75
1415	A223	500fr Rottweiler	1.70	.85
		Nos. 1410-1415 (6)	7.15	3.60

Souvenir Sheet

1416	A223	1000fr Golden retriever	3.50	1.75

Nos. 1410-1415 are each printed with se-tenant label.

Prehistoric Animals — A224

200fr, Dilophosaurus. 250fr, Psittacosaurus. 300fr, Dromiceiomimus. 400fr, Stenonychosaurus. 450fr, Opisthocoelicaudia. 500fr, Ornitholestes.
1000fr, Anchiceratops.

1997 **Litho.** ***Perf. 12½***

1417	A224	200fr multi	.70	.35
1418	A224	250fr multi, vert.	.85	.45
1419	A224	300fr multi	1.00	.50
1420	A224	400fr multi, vert.	1.40	.70
1421	A224	450fr multi	1.50	.75
1422	A224	500fr multi	1.75	.85
		Nos. 1417-1422 (6)	7.20	3.60

Souvenir Sheet

1423	A224	1000fr multicolored	3.50	1.75

No. 1423 contains one 40x32mm stamp.

UNICEF — A224a

Design: 750fr, Mother nursing child.

1997 **Litho.** ***Perf. 13¼***

1423C	A224a	750fr multi	—	—

Numbers have been reserved for three additional stamps in this set. The editors would like to examine any examples.

Butterflies — A225

200fr, Eueides cleobaea. 250fr, Danaus cleophile. 300fr, Dryas julia. 400fr, Dismorphia cubana. 450fr, Pyrrhocalles antiga. 500fr, Phoebis orbis.
1000fr, Morpho adonis.

1998

1424	A225	200fr multicolored	.70	.35
1425	A225	250fr multicolored	.85	.45
1426	A225	300fr multicolored	1.00	.50
1427	A225	400fr multicolored	1.40	.70
1428	A225	450fr multicolored	1.50	.75
1429	A225	500fr multicolored	1.75	.85
		Nos. 1424-1429 (6)	7.20	3.60

Souvenir Sheet

1430	A225	1000fr multicolored	3.50	1.75

No. 1430 contains one 40x32mm stamp.

Domestic Cats — A226

200fr, English shorthair bicolor. 250fr, Scottish fold. 300fr, Birman. 400fr, American coarse hair. 450fr, Snowshoe. 500fr, Maine coon.
1000fr, Malaysian.

1998 **Litho.** ***Perf. 12½***

1431	A226	200fr multicolored	.65	.30
1432	A226	250fr multicolored	.85	.40
1433	A226	300fr multicolored	1.00	.50
1434	A226	400fr multicolored	1.25	.65
1435	A226	450fr multicolored	1.50	.75
1436	A226	500fr multicolored	1.70	.85
		Nos. 1431-1436 (6)	6.95	3.45

Souvenir Sheet

Perf. 13

1437	A226	1000fr multicolored	3.50	1.75

No. 1437 contains one 32x40mm stamp.

Diana, Princess of Wales (1961-97) A227

Various portraits.

1998 Litho. *Perf. 13½*

Sheets of 9

1438 A227 200fr #a.-i. 6.75 3.50
1439 A227 300fr #a.-i 10.00 5.00
1440 A227 750fr #a.-i. 25.00 12.50

Souvenir Sheets

1441 A227 1500fr multicolored 5.50 2.75
1442 A227 2000fr multicolored 7.50 3.75

Dated 1997.

1998 World Cup Soccer Championships, France — A228

Various soccer plays.

1998 Litho. *Perf. 12½*

1443 A228 200fr multi, vert. .70 .35
1444 A228 250fr multi, vert. .85 .45
1445 A228 300fr multi, vert. 1.00 .50
1446 A228 400fr multi, vert. 1.40 .70
1447 A228 450fr multi 1.50 .75
1448 A228 500fr multi 1.75 .85
Nos. 1443-1448 (6) 7.20 3.60

Souvenir Sheet

Perf. 13

1449 A228 1000fr multi 3.50 1.75

No. 1449 contains one 32x40mm stamp.

Old Germanic Military Uniforms A228a

Designs: 200fr, Officer, Von Witerfeldt's Regiment. 250fr, Non-commissioned officer, Von Kanitz's Regiment. 300fr, Private, Prince Franz von Anhalt-Dessau's Regiment. 400fr, Private, Von Kalnein's Regiment. 450fr, Grenadier, Duke Ferdinand of Brunswick's Regiment. 500fr, Musician, Rekow's Guards Battalion.
1000fr, Pioneer.

1997, Aug. 17 Litho. *Perf. 12½*

1449A-1449F A228a Set of 6 7.50 3.75

Souvenir Sheet

1449G A228a 1000fr multi 3.75 1.75

No. 1449G contains one 32x40mm stamp.

Steam Locomotives — A229

200fr, Baldwin Locomotive Works, 0-4-2. 250fr, American Locomotive Co., 0-6-0. 300fr, Vulcan Iron Works, 0-6-0. 400fr, Baldwin Locomotive Works, 0-6-0. 450fr, H.K. Porter Co., 0-6-0. 500fr, Vulcan Iron Works, 0-6-0, diff.
1000fr, Baldwin Locomotive Works, 0-6-0, diff.

1997, Sept. 10 Litho. *Perf. 12½*

1450-1455 A229 Set of 6 7.25 3.50

Souvenir Sheet

1456 A229 1000fr multicolored 3.50 1.75

No. 1456 contains one 40x32mm stamp.

Nectophrynoides Occidentalis — A230

Color of border: 200fr, green. 300fr, blue. 750fr, pale rose.

1998 *Perf. 13½*

1457-1459 A230 Set of 3 4.25 2.25

Intl. Year of the Ocean A231

Marine life - #1460: a, Physeter macrocephalus, neophova cinerea. b, Melanogrammus aeglefinus. c, Delphinapterus leucas. d, Megaptera novaengliae. e, Notorhynchus cependianus. f, Manta birostris. g, Delphinaterusleucas, macrozoarces americanus. h, Physalia physalis, pollachius virens. i, Manta birostris. j, Odontapis taurus. k, Thalassoma ruppelli, octopus vulgaris. l, Sebestes marinus.
1500fr, Megaptera novaengliae, diff.

1998

1460 A231 200fr Sheet of 12, #a.-l. 8.00 4.00

Souvenir Sheet

1461 A231 1500fr multicolored 5.25 2.50

Antique Cars A232

200fr, 1932 Chrysler, 8 cylinders, US. 300fr, 1907 Napier, 60HP, England. 450fr, 1903 Mercedes, 60HP, Germany. 750fr, 1925 Fiat 509, Italy.
No. 1466: a, 1929 Alfa Romeo 6C 1750 Zagato, Italy. b, 1932 Hispano-Suiza Type 68, Spain. c, 1931 Horce V12, Germany. d, 1909 Rolland Pilain, 16hp, France. e, 1920 McLaughlin, Canada. f, 1930 Walter 6B, Czechoslovakia.
No. 1467: a, 1914 Fischer SS, Switzerland. b, 1922 Excelsior Adex C, Belgium. c, 1912 Pilain Torpedo, France. d, 1932 Franklin, 6 cylinders, US. e, 1912 Abadal 18/24hp, Spain. f, 1923 Alvis 12/50, England.
No. 1468, 1925 Rolls Royce Phantom 1, England. No. 1469, 1932 Ford V8, US.

1998, Aug. 21

1462-1465 A232 Set of 4 5.75 3.00

Sheets of 6

1466 A232 450fr #a.-f. 9.25 4.75
1467 A232 750fr #a.-f. 15.50 7.50

Souvenir Sheets

1468-1468A A232 1500fr each 5.25 2.50

Nos. 1468-1468A each contain one 56x42mm stamp.

Greenpeace — A233

Designs: a, Albatross looking left. b, Albatross in flight. c, Stern of Greenpeace ship, helicopter. d, Bow of Greenpeace ship. e, Albatross nesting. f, Albatross looking right.
2000fr, Albatross with chick.

1998 Litho. *Perf. 13½*

1469 A233 450fr Sheet of 6, #a.-f. 7.00 3.50

Souvenir Sheet

1470 A233 2000fr multicolored 9.50 4.75

No. 1470 contains one 40x46mm stamp.

Endangered Species — A234

Designs, vert: 200fr, Lynx pardellus. 300fr, Lepilemur mustelinus. 450fr, Canis rufus. 750fr, Bison bonasus.
No. 1475: a, Leopard. b, Civet (f). c, Bird (d). d, Hawk. e, Rhinoceros, impala. f, Okapi (e, h, i). g, Lion. h, Chimpanzee. i, Gorilla. j, Bird (long, curved beak). k, Hippopotamus (l). l, Antelope (h).
No. 1476: a, Falco peregrinus. b, Acinonyx jubatus. c, Antilocapre americana. d, Mustela nigripes. e, Ursus maritimus. f, Rhinoceros unicornis.
No. 1477: a, Gymnobelideus leadbeater. b, Felis concolor. c, Felis pardalis. d, Panthera pardus. e, Bufo hemiophyrs. f, Mustela rutorius.
No. 1478, Muscardinus avellanarius. No. 1479, Aepyceros melampus, vert. No. 1480, Panthera uncia.

1998, Sept. 8

1471-1474 A234 Set of 4 5.75 3.00

Sheets of 12 & 6

1475 A234 200fr #a.-l. 8.00 4.00
1476 A234 450fr #a.-f. 9.25 4.50
1477 A234 750fr #a.-f. 15.00 7.50

Souvenir Sheets

1478-1480 A234 1500fr each 5.00 2.50

Locomotives of the World — A235

No. 1481: a, Sir Nigel Gresley, England. b, Switzerland. c, Canada. d, EMU 102-6 Tobu Railway Spacia, Japan. e, Krauss Maffei V200, Germany. f, IC 580 Portugal. g, Amtrak No. 5, US. h, TGV, France.
No. 1482: a, Nippon Pacific No. 82, Middle East. b, Russia. c, Freight train, Albania. d, Dart No. 8319, Ireland. e, No. 141-F-177, France. f, EMU No. 69625, Norway. g, Bo-Bo, New Zealand. h, Azusa, Japan.
No. 1483: a, Syrian Railways 2-8-0, Iraq. b, The Irish Mail, England. c, Four car EMU, Italy. d, Sprinter, England. e, Van Golu Express, Turkey. f, No. 11.2110, Norway. g, Two-car EMU, New Zealand. h, Grey Mouse, France.
No. 1484: a, The Flying Scotman, United Kingdom. b, National Railways, Japan. c, North Africa. d, F-40M Winnebago, US. e, Federal Railways Class 10, three cylinder 4-6-2, Germany. f, DX5500, New Zealand. g, CIE, Ireland. h, Intercity class 43, England.
No. 1485, D2157, New Zealand. No. 1486, 140.7410, German Railways. No. 1487, JR Shinkansen 221-204, Japan. No. 1488, Egyptian Railways, Bo-Bo.

1998, Oct. 30

Sheets of 8

1481 A235 200fr #a.-h. 5.25 2.50
1482 A235 300fr #a.-h. 8.25 4.00
1483 A235 450fr #a.-h. 12.00 6.00
1484 A235 750fr #a.-h. 20.00 10.00

Souvenir Sheets

1485-1488 A235 1500fr each 5.00 2.50

Aircraft A236

Amphibians & flying boats - #1489: a, Boeing Model 1, 1916. b, Grumman G-21 Goose, 1937. c, Latecoere 631, 1942. d, Cessna Model 205. e, Sikorsky S-42, 1934. f, Boeing Model 314 Clipper. g, De Havilland Canada DHC-2 Beaver, 1947. h, Lake Buccaneer, 1979.
Balloons and Dirigibles - #1490: a, Henri Giffard, 1852. b, Santos-Dumont "Baladeuse," 1903. c, Zeppelin L37. d, R101, 1930. e, Santos-Dumont, 1898. f, Baldwin, 1908. g, Norge, 1926. h, Hindenburg, 1936.
Helicopters - #1491: a, Sikorsky VS-300, 1940. b, Sikorsky S-61, 1957. c, Bell Long Ranger, 1966. d, Dauphin SA 365, 1972. e, Bell 47, 1946. f, Boeing Vertol 243LR, 1958. g, Aerospatial SA 315 Blama. h, Bell Model 222, 1981.
Spacecraft - #1492: a, Mercury Capsule, 1961. b, Gemini 8, 1966. c, Apollo Lunar Module, 1968. d, Soviet Vostok, 1961. e, Apollo Command Module, 1968. f, Soviet Soyuz, 1975.
No. 1493, Cessna 208 Caravan, 1980. No. 1494, Goodyear Blimp. No. 1495, Miles Mi-26, 1983. No. 1496, Space Shuttle Columbia, 1981.

1998, Oct. 30

Sheets of 8 & 6

1489 A236 200fr #a.-h. 5.50 2.75
1490 A236 300fr #a.-h. 8.25 4.00
1491 A236 450fr #a.-h. 12.00 6.00
1492 A236 750fr #a.-f. 15.00 7.50

Souvenir Sheets

1493-1496 A236 1500fr each 5.00 2.50

No. 1489a incorrectly inscribed "1961."

Dinosaurs A237

No. 1497: a, Dicraeosaurus. b, Parasaurolophus. c, Sauronithoides. d, Dilophosaurus. e, Titanosaurus, bagaceratops. f, Iguanodon. g, Tenontosaurus. h, Dryosaurus. i, Ceratosaurus.
1500fr, Yangchuanosaurus, brachiosaurus.

1998 Litho. *Perf. 13½*

1497 A237 750fr Sheet of 9, #a.-i. 27.50 13.50

Souvenir Sheet

1498 A237 1500fr multicolored 6.00 3.00

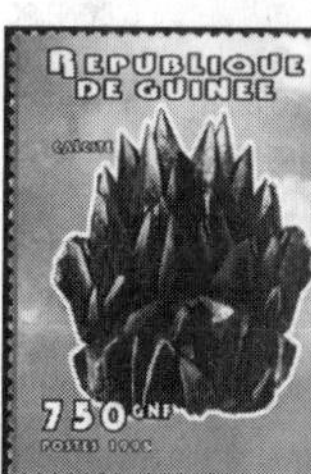

Minerals — A238

a, Calcite. b, Wolframite. c, Spodumene. #1500D: e, Psilomelane. f, Heterosite. g, Columbo-tantalite.

1998 Litho. *Perf. 13½*

Strip of 3

1499 A238 750fr Green back-ground, #a.-c. 8.75 4.50

Souvenir Sheets of 3

1500 A238 750fr Gray blue back-ground, #a.-c. 8.75 4.50
1500D A238 1500fr #e-g 12.00 12.00

Sailing Ships A239

No. 1501: a, "Theseus." b, "Euphrates." c, Phoenician War Galley. d, Chinese Junk.

No. 1502: a, "Juan Sebastian." b, "Santa Maria." c, Frigate. d, Madurese Jukung rig.

No. 1503, vert.: a, Windjammer, "Wavertree." b, British frigate, "Rose." c, Tromp's flagship, "Golden Leeuw." d, Danish Timber Barque.

No. 1504, vert.: a, Kraeck. b, Clipper ship, "Golden State." c, English ship, "Resolution." d, "Eagle."

No. 1505, British barque, "Garthpool." No. 1506, HMS Victory.

1998, Nov. 10 *Perf. 14*

Sheets of 4, #a.-d.

1501-1502 A239 450fr each 6.50 3.25
1503-1504 A239 750fr each 10.50 5.25

Souvenir Sheets

1505-1506 A239 1500fr each 5.50 5.50

Novotel Hotel, Conakry - A239a

1998 Litho. *Perf. 13x13½*

1506A A239a 200fr multi — —
1506B A239a 750fr multi — —

The editors suspect that additional stamps may have been issued in this set and would like to examine any examples. Numbers may change.

Horses A240

Designs: 150fr, Trotteur Russe. 200fr, Brabant. 300fr, Camargue. No. 1510, 450fr, Unidentified breed. No. 1511, 450fr, Dales pony. No. 1512, 750fr, Fjord.

No. 1513, vert.: a, Kabardin. b, Shire. c, Arabian. d, Mustang. e, Quarter horse. f, Appaloosa.

No. 1514, vert.: a, Thoroughbred. b, Lipizzaner. c, Belgian. d, Palomino. e, Haflinger. f, Fjord, diff.

No. 1515, Mustang, diff. No. 1516, Thorougbred colt.

1999, May 1 Litho. *Perf. 14*

1507-1512 A240 Set of 6 3.00 3.00

Sheets of 6

1513 A240 450fr #a.-f. 3.50 3.50
1514 A240 750fr #a.-f. 6.00 6.00

Souvenir Sheets

1515-1516 A240 1500fr each 2.00 2.00

Guinea - People's Republic of China Diplomatic Relations, 40th Anniv. — A240a

1999 Litho. *Perf. 13¼x13*

1516A A240a 200fr multi — —

The editors suspect additional stamps may have been issued in this set and would like to examine any examples. Number may change.

Dogs A241

Designs: 200fr, Newfoundland. No. 1518, 750fr, St. Bernard.

No. 1519, vert.: a, Bulldog. b, Miniature schnauzer. c, Dachshund. d, Beagle. e, Bloodhound. f, Miniature pinscher.

1500fr, Irish setter.

1999, May 1

1517-1518 A241 Set of 2 1.25 1.25

Sheet of 6

1519 A241 750fr #a.-f. 6.00 6.00

Souvenir Sheet

1520 A241 1500fr multi 2.00 2.00

A242

Dinosaurs & Prehistoric Animals — A243

Designs: 300fr, Ouranosaurus. No. 1522, 450fr, Centrosaurus. No. 1523, 450fr, Dilophosaurus, vert.

No. 1524: a, Cymbospondylus. b, Kronosaurus. c, Ichthyosaurus. d, Eurhinosaurus. e, Stenopterygius. f, Ophthalmosaurus. g, Shonisaurus. h, Temnodontosaurus. i, Mixosaurus.

No. 1525, vert.: a, Eudimorphodon. b, Sordes. c, Dimorphodon. d, Albertosaurus. e, Triceratops. f, Alioramus. g, Mesosaurus. h, Labidosaurus. i, Struthiomimus.

No. 1526: a, Saltosaurus. b, Corythosaurus. c, Protoceratops. d, Baryonyx. e, Pachycephalosaurus. f, Maiasaurus. g, Spinosaurus. h, Lambeosaurus.

2500fr, Elasmosaurus, vert. No. 1528, Tyrannosaurus Rex. No. 1529, Utahraptor. No. 1530, Parasaurolophus, vert.

1999, Aug. 12

1521-1523 A242 Set of 3 1.60 1.60

Sheets of 9

1524 A243 350fr #a.-i. 4.25 4.25
1525 A243 450fr #a.-i. 5.25 5.25

Sheet of 8

1526 A242 450fr #a.-h 4.75 4.75

Souvenir Sheets

1527 A243 2500fr multi 3.25 3.25
1528 A243 3000fr multi 4.00 4.00
1529-1530 A242 3000fr each 4.00 4.00

No. 1527 contains one 42x56mm stamp. No. 1528 contains one 56x42mm stamp.

Return of Macao to People's Republic of China, Dec. 20, 1999 A244

No. 1531: a, Current view of Nam Van (tall buildings). b, Nam Van in 1850s (hilltop and bay). c, Current view of Largo de Senado. d, Largo de Senado in 1900s.

No. 1532: a, Current view of Nam Van (highway). b, Nam Van in 1850s (buildings at water's edge). c, Current view of Nam Van (boat). d, Nam Van in 1850s (ships).

1999, Aug. 20 *Perf. 14¼x14½*

Sheets of 4, #a.-d.

1531-1532 A244 650fr each 3.50 3.50

China 1999 World Philatelic Exhibition.

Paintings of Zhang Daqian (1899-1983) — A245

No. 1533: a, Ink Lotus. b, Ink Peony. c, Red Cliff Excursion at Night. d, Poetic Landscape. e, Landscape in the Evening. f, Spring Landscape. g, Chatting at Leisure in Mountains. h, Pine Nesting. i, Pine in Thunder. j, Blue and Green Landscape.

No. 1534: a, Landscape. b, Versing in the Landscape.

1999, Aug. 20 Litho. *Perf. 13¼*

1533 A245 330fr Sheet of 10, #a.-j. 4.50 4.50

Souvenir Sheet of 2

Perf. 13

1534 A245 1150fr #a.-b. 3.00 3.00

No. 1534 contains two 51x39mm stamps. China 1999 World Philatelic Exhibition

Trains A246

100fr, Diesel TGV, East Germany. No. 1536, 200fr, 1900 horsepower Diesel-electric, Finland. No. 1537, 200fr, Type MLW 3000 horsepower Diesel-electric. No. 1538, 250fr, A-4, Britain. No. 1539, 250fr, Class R 4-6-4. No. 1540, 250fr, Class M, 4-6-2, Tasmania. No. 1541, 450fr, Class 68000 Diesel-electric, France. No. 1542, 450fr, 4-8-4 Daylight Express. No. 1543, 450fr, Electric TGV, Italy. No. 1544, 450fr, Western Class Hydraulic-Diesel.

No. 1545: a, Class 10 3-cylinder 4-6-2. b, SD18 Diesel-electric. c, Hikari Super Express Train, Japan. d, Diesel-electric No. 10000. e, PA-1 Diesel-electric. f, 2500 horsepower experimental gas turbine locomotive.

No. 1546: a, YP Class, India. b, Class 47, Standard Type 4 Diesel-electric. c, DSI Class 2-8-2, Japan. d, Class D-341 Diesel-electric. e, S1 Class 2-6-4. f, 3600 horsepower electric, India.

No. 1547: a, 2000 horsepower GP-20 Diesel-electric. b, Class C-53 3-cylinder, Japan. c, Multiple-unit Diesel, Japan. d, Royal Scot Class 4-6-0. e, Deltic electric prototype. f, W.P. Standard 4-6-2.

2500fr, Class 40 electric, England. No. 1549, GP-40 Diesel-electric. No. 1550, 9780 horsepower DM-3, Sweden. No. 1551, 1750 horsepower Diesel-electric, Denmark.

1999, Oct. 25 *Perf. 14*

1535-1544 A246 Set of 10 4.00 4.00

Sheets of 6

1545 A246 300fr #a.-f. 2.40 2.40
1546 A246 450fr #a.-f. 3.50 3.50
1547 A246 750fr #a.-f. 6.00 6.00

Souvenir Sheets

1548 A246 2500fr multi 3.25 3.25
1549-1551 A246 3000fr each 4.00 4.00

Mushrooms and Insects — A247

Mushrooms and unidentified insects: No. 1552, 100fr, Lentinellus cochleatus. No. 1553, 100fr, Lactarius blennius. No. 1554, Lactarius sanguifluus. No. 1555, 150fr, Leucocortinarius bulbiger. No. 1556, 300fr, Clitocybe phyllophila. No. 1557, 300fr, Calocybe ionides. No. 1558, 300fr, Lactarius porninsis. No. 1559, 300fr, Cystoderma amianthinum. No. 1560, 300fr, Limacella guttata. No. 1561, 450fr, Suillus placidus. No. 1562, 450fr, Suillus grevillei. No. 1563, 450fr, Suillus luteus. No. 1564, 450fr, Suillus granulatus. No. 1565, 450fr, Pleurotus cornuscopiae. No. 1566, 450fr, Calocybe carnea. No. 1567, 450fr, Panus tigrinus.

Mushrooms and insects - No. 1568: a, Hygrocybe nigreseens, Argynnis paphia. b, Hygrocybe subglobispora, Pterophoridae. c, Oudemansiella mucida, Tettigonia viridissima. d, Amanita rubescens, unidentified insect. e, Amanita muscaria, Oedipoda caerulescens. f, Suillus luteus, Happarchia fagi. g, Coprinus picaceus, Aphantopus hyperantus. h, Gymnopilus junonius, Ourapteryx sambucaria. i, Amanita muscaria, Catocala nupta.

No. 1569: a, Macrolepiota procera, Pieris brassicae. b, Lactarius britannicus, Pyrochroa cocci. c, Cortinarius sanguineus, Tabicina haematodes. d, Amanita muscaria, Sympetrum. e, Aerocomus badius, Issoria lathonia. f, Laccaria amethystea, Sympetrum. g, Paxillus atrotomentosus, Inachis io. h, Armillaria mellea, Chrystoxum cautum. i, Amanita echinocephala, Vanessa atalanta.

No. 1570, Lactarius brittanicus, Coccinella punctala. No. 1571, Amanita phalloides, Ochlodes venatus. No. 1572, Coprinus atramentarius, unidentified insect. No. 1573, Amanita citrina, unidentified insect. No. 1574, Amanita pantherina, Aperia syringaria.

1999, Nov. 11

1552-1567 A247 Set of 16 6.75 6.75

Sheets of 9

1568 A247 300fr #a.-i. 3.50 3.50
1569 A247 450fr #a.-i. 5.50 5.50

Souvenir Sheets

1570-1572 A247 2500fr each 3.25 3.25
1573-1574 A247 3000fr each 4.00 4.00

Birds

A248 A249

Designs: No. 1575, 200fr, Catamblyrhychus diadema. No. 1576, 200fr, Tichodrome. No. 1577, 300fr, Turtle dove. No. 1578, 300fr, Flamingo. No. 1579, 300fr, Duck. No. 1580, 300fr, Woodpecker. No. 1581, 450fr, Warbler. No. 1582, 450fr, Bullfinch.

No. 1583: a, Wild turkey. b, Ring-necked pheasant. c, Gray partridge. d, Woodcock. e, Capercaillie. f, Rock partridge.

No. 1584: a, Cuban hummingbird. b, Rufous-breated hermit. c, Green-throated hummingbird. d, Bee-eater. e, Puerto Rican hummingbird. f, Antillean hummingbird.

No. 1585: a, Gould's finch. b, Oriole. c, Psarismus dalhousiae. d, Red-headed woodpecker. e, Pitta guajana. f, Neodreponis coruscans.

No. 1586, horiz.: a, Purple-throated Carib. b, Bahamas hummingbird. c, Blue-bearded hummingbird. d, Green hummingbird. e, Jamaican hummingbird. f, Vervaine.

No. 1587, Spotted waxwing. No. 1588, Red-banded bee-eater. No. 1589, Bahamas hummingbird, horiz. No. 1590, Antillean crested hummingbird. No. 1591, Emerald hummingbird.

1999, Nov. 22

1575-1582 A248 Set of 8 3.25 3.25

Sheets of 6

1583 A248 450fr #a.-f. 3.50 3.50
1584 A249 500fr #a.-f. 4.00 4.00
1585 A248 600fr #a.-f. 4.75 4.75
1586 A249 750fr #a.-f. 6.00 6.00

Souvenir Sheets

1587-1588 A248 2500fr each 3.25 3.25
1589-1590 A249 2500fr each 3.25 3.25
1591 A249 3000fr multi 4.00 4.00

Butterflies A250

Designs: No. 1592, 300fr, Acraea acerata. No. 1593, 300fr, Charaxes protoclea. No. 1594, 300fr, Charaxes hadrianus. No. 1595, 300fr, Colotis halimede. No. 1596, 300fr, Colotis eucharis. No. 1597, Papilio dardanus.

No. 1598, vert.: a, Papilio charopus. b, Papilio dardanus. c, Acraea zetes. d, Hypolimnas salmacis. e, Cymothoe beckeri. f, Papilio nobilis.

No. 1599, vert.: a, Iolaus Ialos. b, Graphium gudenusi. c, Hewitsonia boisduvali. d, Graphium ucalegon. e, Danaus chrysippus. f, Acraea satis.

No. 1600, Euxanthe tiberius. No. 1601, Colotis danae.

1999, Nov. 22

1592-1597 A250 Set of 6 2.40 2.40

Sheets of 6

1598 A250 450fr #a.-f. 3.50 3.50
1599 A250 750fr #a.-f. 6.00 6.00

Souvenir Sheets

1600-1601 A250 2500fr each 3.25 3.25

Wedding of Prince Edward and Sophie Rhys-Jones A251

No. 1602: a, Edward in blue striped shirt. b, Sophie with scarf. c, Edward looking left. d, Sophie looking right. e, Edward with blue checked shirt. f, Sophie with black blouse.
3000fr, Couple.

1999, Dec. 6

1602 A251 750fr Sheet of 6, #a.-f. 6.00 6.00

Souvenir Sheet

1603 A251 3000fr multi 4.00 4.00

Hokusai Paintings A252

No. 1604: a, Actor Ichikawa Ebizo. b, Drawings (man with fan). c, Actor Sakata Hangoro. d, Geisha and Madam. e, Drawings (man with sword). f, Kabuki Actor Hanshiro IV.

No. 1605: a, Kintaro and Wild Animals. b, Drawings (man with clasped hands). c, Lady Walking in the Snow. d, Lady and Maiden on an Outing. e, Drawings (man with incense burner). f, Girls at Their Toilette.

No. 1606, Sumo Wrestlers. No. 1607, Geisha House and Madam at Leisure with Child.

1999, Dec. 6 ***Perf. 12¼***

Sheets of 6, #a.-f.

1604-1605 A252 750fr each 6.00 6.00

Souvenir Sheets

1606-1607 A252 3000fr each 4.00 4.00

Johann Wolfgang von Goethe (1749-1832), German Poet — A253

No. 1608: a, Mephistopheles tempts Faust with Margaret. b, Goethe and Friedrich von Schiller. c, The witches' kitchen, a potion brewed.
3000fr, Euphorion.

1999, Dec. 6 ***Perf. 14***

1608 A253 1000fr Sheet of 3, #a.-c. 4.00 4.00

Souvenir Sheet

1609 A253 3000fr multi 4.00 4.00

A254

A255

Space Exploration — A256

Designs: No. 1610, 300fr, Pioneer 10. No. 1611, 300fr, Viking 1.

No. 1612: a, Takao Doi. b, Frank Borman. c, Alan B. Shepard, Jr. d, M. Scott Carpenter. e, Ulf Merbold. f, David R. Scott. g, Mamoru Mohri. h, Gherman Titov. i, Sally K. Ride. j, Walter M. Schirra. k, John L. Swigert, Jr. l, Yuri A. Gagarin.

No. 1613: a, Venus. b, Neptune. c, Jupiter. d, Uranus. e, Saturn. f, Mercury.

No. 1614: a, Mariner 4. b, HL-20. c, Mariner 2. d, Voyager 1. e, Venture Star. f, Phobos.

No. 1615: a, 1961 drawing of lunar ferry. b, 1960 drawing of lunar lander. c, 1959 drawing of lunar lander. d, 1962 drawing of lunar lander. e, 1962 drawing of lunar lander trainer. f, 1961 drawing of lunar lander.

No. 1616, vert.: a, Apollo 5. b, Apollo 6, c, Apollo 7. d, Apollo escape test. e, Apollo "Little Joe." f, Apollo 4.

No. 1617, John Glenn. No. 1618, Apollo 11 command module, vert. No. 1619, Collecting moon rocks. No. 1620, Viking, diff. No. 1621, Mars Global Surveyor. No. 1622, Sojourner.

1999, Dec. 9

1610-1611 A254 Set of 2 .80 .80

Sheet of 12, #a.-l.

1612 A255 450fr multi 7.25 7.25

Sheets of 6, #a.-f.

1613-1614 A254 500fr each 4.00 4.00
1615-1616 A256 750fr each 6.00 6.00

Souvenir Sheets

1617 A255 1500fr multi 2.00 2.00
1618-1619 A256 1500fr each 2.00 2.00
1620-1622 A254 2000fr each 2.60 2.60

Nos. 1620-1622 each contain one 50x37mm stamp.

Queen Mother (b. 1900) — A257

No. 1623: a, In 1934. b, With tiara. c, Lady of the Garter. d, In 1997.
3000fr, With tiara, diff.

1999, Dec. 6 ***Perf. 14***

1623 A257 1000fr Sheet of 4, #a.-d., + label 5.25 5.25

Souvenir Sheet

Perf. 13¾

1624 A257 3000fr multi 4.00 4.00

No. 1624 contains one 38x50mm stamp.

Cats A257a

Designs: 300fr, Ragdoll. No. 1626, 400fr, Egyptian Mau.

No. 1627, vert.: a, Tonkinese. b, Korat. c, Siamese. d, British Shorthair. e, Bengal. f, Persian.
1500fr, Calico Shorthair, vert.

1999 ***Perf. 14***

1625-1626 A257a Set of 2 1.00 1.00

Sheet of 6

1627 A257a 450fr #a.-f. 3.50 3.50

Souvenir Sheet

1628 A257a 1500fr multi 2.00 2.00

Romance of the Three Kingdoms A258

No. 1629: a, Archer and four men. b, Two men and tea pot. c, Spear carrier, man, woman. d, Horsemen jousting. e, Four men.

No. 1630: a, Swordsman on white horse. b, Spear carrier on black horse. c, Bed chamber. d, Man being speared. e, At sea.
2000fr, Three men with tea cups.

1999 ***Perf. 13¼***

Sheets of 5, #a.-e.

1629-1630 A258 460fr each 3.00 3.00

Souvenir Sheet

1631 A258 2000fr multi 2.60 2.60

No. 1631 contains one 48x58mm stamp.

SEMI-POSTAL STAMPS

Eye Examination — SP1

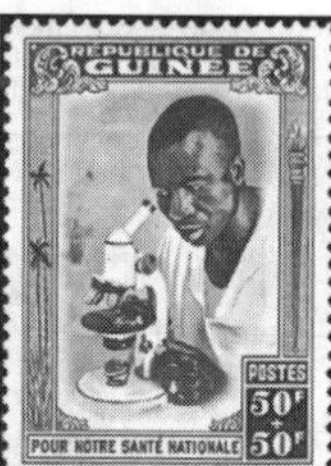

Microscopic Examination SP2

#B13, Medical laboratory. #B14, Insect control. #B16, Surgical operation.

Engraved and Lithographed

1960 Unwmk. ***Perf. 11½***

B12 SP1 20fr + 10fr ultra & car .45 .45
B13 SP1 30fr + 20fr brn org & violet .45 .45
B14 SP1 40fr + 20fr rose lil & blue .55 .55
B15 SP2 50fr + 50fr grn & brn .90 .90
B16 SP2 100fr + 100fr lil & grn 1.10 1.10
Nos. B12-B16 (5) 3.45 3.45

Issued for national health propaganda.
For overprints see Nos. B25-B29.

Nos. 194-195 Surcharged "1961" and New Value in Red or Orange

1961, June 6 **Photo.**

B17 A17 25fr + 10fr (R or O) 2.75 2.75
B18 A17 50fr + 20fr (R or O) 2.75 2.75

Nos. B17-B18 exist with orange surcharges transposed: "1961 + 10FRS." on 50fr and "1961 + 20FRS." on 25fr.

Nos. 214-219 Surcharged in Green, Lilac, Orange or Blue: "POUR LA PROTECTION DE NOS ANIMAUX +5 FRS"

Photo., Surcharge Engr.

1961, Dec. 8

Multicolored Design; Granite Paper

B19 A20 5fr + 5fr brt grn (G) .20 .20
B20 A20 10fr + 5fr emer (G) .20 .20
B21 A20 25fr + 5fr lilac (L) .30 .20
B22 A20 40fr + 5fr org (O) .40 .25
B23 A20 50fr + 5fr red org (O) .55 .35
B24 A20 75fr + 5fr ultra (B) .80 .45
Nos. B19-B24 (6) 2.45 1.65

The surtax was for animal protection.

Nos. B12-B16 Overprinted in Red or Orange

Engr. & Litho.

1962, Feb. ***Perf. 11½***

B25 SP1 20fr + 10fr (R or O) .25 .25
B26 SP1 30fr + 20fr (R or O) .35 .35
B27 SP1 40fr + 20fr (R or O) .40 .40
B28 SP2 50fr + 50fr (R or O) .80 .80
B29 SP2 100fr + 100fr (R or O) 1.60 1.60
Nos. B25-B29 (5) 3.40 3.40

WHO drive to eradicate malaria.
No. B25 also exists with black overprint.

Nos. 223-228 Surcharged in Red: "POUR LA PROTECTION DE NOS OISEAUX + 5 FRS"

Photo., Surcharge Engr.

1962, May 14 ***Perf. 13x14***

B30 A22 5fr + 5fr multi .20 .20
B31 A22 10fr + 5fr multi .20 .20
B32 A22 25fr + 5fr multi .25 .20
B33 A22 40fr + 5fr multi .35 .25
B34 A22 50fr + 5fr multi .60 .40
B35 A22 75fr + 5fr multi 1.40 .70
Nos. B30-B35 (6) 3.00 1.95

The surtax was for bird protection.

Nos. 232-233 Surcharged in Orange or Red and Overprinted: "Aide aux Réfugiés Algeriens"

1962, Nov. 1 Litho. ***Perf. 13***

B36 A24 25fr + 15fr multi .40 .40
B37 A24 75fr + 25fr multi .80 .80

Issued to help Algerian refugees.

Astronomers and Space Phenomena — SP3

1989, Mar. 7 Litho. ***Perf. 13½***

B38 SP3 100fr +25fr Helical nebula .80 .40
B39 SP3 150fr +25fr Orion nebula 1.10 .60
B40 SP3 200fr +25fr Eagle nebula 1.50 .75
B41 SP3 250fr +25fr Trifide nebula 1.75 .90
B42 SP3 300fr +25fr Eta-carinae nebula 2.10 1.10
B43 SP3 500fr +25fr NGC-2264 nebula 3.50 1.75
Nos. B38-B43 (6) 10.75 5.50

Souvenir Sheet

B44 SP3 750fr +50fr Horse's Head nebula 5.25 2.60

Nos. B42-B44 are airmail.

AIR POST STAMPS

Lockheed Constellation — AP1

Design: 500fr, Plane on ground.

Lithographed and Engraved

1959, July 13 Unwmk. *Perf. 11½*

Size: 52½x24mm

C14	AP1	100fr dp car, ultra & emer	1.00	.65
C15	AP1	200fr emer, brn & lil	1.40	1.00

Size: 56½x26mm

C16	AP1	500fr multicolored	3.50	2.00
		Nos. C14-C16 (3)	5.90	3.65

For overprints see Nos. C24-C26, C52-C53.

Doves with Letter and Olive Twig — AP2

1959, Oct. 16 Engr. *Perf. 13½*

C17	AP2	40fr blue	.20	.20
C18	AP2	50fr emerald	.40	.30
C19	AP2	100fr dk car rose	.70	.50
C20	AP2	200fr rose red	1.25	1.00
C21	AP2	500fr red orange	3.50	2.50
		Nos. C17-C21 (5)	6.05	4.50

For overprints see Nos. C35-C38.

Admission to UN Type of 1959

Engr. & Litho.

1959, Dec. 12 *Perf. 12*

Size: 44x26mm

C22	A16	50fr multicolored	.40	.40
C23	A16	100fr multicolored	.55	.50

For overprints see Nos. C27-C28.

Nos. C14-C16 Overprinted in Carmine, Orange or Blue: "Jeux Olympiques Rome 1960" and Olympic Rings

1960 Litho. & Engr. *Perf. 11½*

Size: 52½x24mm

C24	AP1	100fr multi (C or O)	4.25	3.00
C25	AP1	200fr multi (Bl)	7.50	4.25

Size: 56½x26mm

C26	AP1	500fr multi (C or O)	20.00	19.00
		Nos. C24-C26 (3)	31.75	26.25

17th Olympic Games, Rome, 8/25-9/11.

Nos. C22-C23 Overprinted

Engr. & Litho.

1961, Oct. 24 *Perf. 12*

C27	A16	50fr multicolored	.45	.40
C28	A16	100fr multicolored	.65	.55

United Nations, 15th anniversary.

Mosquito and Malaria Eradication Emblem AP3

1962, Apr. 7 Engr. *Perf. 10½*

C29	AP3	25fr orange & blk	.25	.20
C30	AP3	50fr car rose & blk	.40	.25
C31	AP3	100fr green & blk	.70	.45
		Nos. C29-C31 (3)	1.35	.90

WHO drive to eradicate malaria.

A souvenir sheet exists containing a 100fr green & sepia stamp, imperf. Sepia coat of arms in margin. Size: 102x76mm.

Musician Type of Regular Issue

Musical Instruments: 100fr, 200fr, Kora. 500fr, Balafon.

1962, June 15 Photo. *Perf. 13x13½*

C32	A26	100fr brt pink, dk car & Prus bl	.50	.40
C33	A26	200fr lt & dk ultra & car rose	1.00	.60
C34	A26	500fr dl org, pur & Prus bl	3.25	2.00
		Nos. C32-C34 (3)	4.75	3.00

Nos. C17-C20 Overprinted in Carmine, Orange or Black: "La Conquête De L'Espace"

Perf. 13½

1962, Nov. 15 Unwmk. Engr.

C35	AP2	40fr blue (C or O)	.40	.25
C36	AP2	50fr emer (C or O)	.40	.25
C37	AP2	100fr dk car rose (B)	.65	.45
C38	AP2	200fr rose red (B)	1.25	.90
		Nos. C35-C38 (4)	2.70	1.85

The conquest of space. Two types of overprint: Straight lines on 40fr and 50fr in carmine, 100fr (black). Curved lines on 40fr and 50fr in orange, 200fr (black).

Bird Type of Regular Issue

Birds: 100fr, Hornbill. 200fr, White spoonbill. 500fr, Bateleur eagle.

1962, Dec. Photo. *Perf. 13x13½*

C41	A30	100fr multicolored	.90	.40
C42	A30	200fr multicolored	1.50	.70
C43	A30	500fr multicolored	3.50	2.00
		Nos. C41-C43 (3)	5.90	3.10

Sports Type of Regular Issue, 1963

Designs: 100fr, Running. 200fr, Bicycling. 500fr, Single sculls.

1963, Mar. 16 *Perf. 14*

C44	A32	100fr dp rose, sep & grn	.65	.30
C45	A32	200fr ol bis, ultra & mag	1.50	.70
C46	A32	500fr ocher, dk bl & red	3.00	2.00
		Nos. C44-C46 (3)	5.15	3.00

Butterfly Type of Regular Issue

Various Butterflies.

1963, May 10 Unwmk. *Perf. 12*

C47	A33	100fr cit, dk brn & gray	.65	.30
C48	A33	200fr sal pink, blk & green	2.00	.70
C49	A33	500fr multicolored	3.50	1.60
		Nos. C47-C49 (3)	6.15	2.60

Red Cross Type of Regular Issue

1963, July 25 Engr. *Perf. 10½*

C50	A35	25fr black & car	.25	.20

Souvenir Sheet

Imperf

C51	A35	100fr green & car	1.50	1.50

Nos. C14-C15 Overprinted:

Lithographed and Engraved

1963, Oct. 28 *Perf. 11½*

C52	AP1	100fr dp car, ultra & emer	1.10	.70
C53	AP1	200fr emer, brn & lil	2.50	1.25

1st Pan American air service from Conakry to New York, July 30, 1963.

Fish Type of Regular Issue, 1964

100fr, African lyretail. 300fr, Six-barred epiplatys.

1964, Feb. 15 Litho. *Perf. 14x13½*

C54	A36	100fr grn & multi	.70	.40
C55	A36	300fr brn & multi	2.00	1.00

Kennedy Type of Regular Issue, 1964

1964, Mar. 5 Engr. *Perf. 10½*

C56	A37	100fr multicolored	.80	.80

See note after No. 327.

Olympic Type of Regular Issue

Design: 100fr, Women's ice skating.

1964, May 15 Photo. *Perf. 13x12½*

C57	A39	100fr gold, brn org & ind	.65	.40

Nos. C44-C46 Overprinted in Carmine or Orange: "Jeux Olympiques Tokyo 1964" and Olympic Rings

1964, May 15 Unwmk. *Perf. 14*

C58	A32	100fr (C or O)	1.60	1.40
C59	A32	200fr (C or O)	2.50	2.00
C60	A32	500fr (C or O)	6.00	5.00
		Nos. C58-C60 (3)	10.10	8.40

18th Olympic Games, Tokyo, Oct. 10-25.

Mrs. Roosevelt Type of Regular Issue

1964, June 1 Engr. *Perf. 10½*

C61	A40	50fr violet	.40	.25

Souvenir Sheets

Unisphere, "Rocket Thrower" and Guinea Pavilion — AP4

1964, Oct. 26 Engr. *Imperf.*

C62	AP4	100fr dk bl & org	.80	.80
C63	AP4	200fr rose red & emer	1.90	1.90

NY World's Fair, 1964-65. See Nos. C69-C70.

Nubian Monuments Type of Regular Issue

300fr, Queen Nefertari, Abu Simbel.

1964, Nov. 19 Photo. *Perf. 12*

C64	A42	300fr gold, dl red brn & sal	1.90	1.10

For overprint see No. C82.

Japanese Hostess, Plane and Map of Africa AP5

1965, Jan. 18 *Perf. 12½x13*

C65	AP5	100fr gold, blk & red lil	1.00	.35

18th Olympic Games, Tokyo, Oct. 10-25, 1964. Two multicolored souvenir sheets (200fr vert. and 300fr horiz.) exist, showing different views of Mt. Fuji. Sizes: 86x119mm, 119x86mm.

For overprint see No. C81.

Mask Type of Regular Issue

300fr, Niamou mask from N'Zérékoré.

1965, Feb. 15 Photo. *Perf. 14*

C68	A44	300fr multicolored	2.25	.90

World's Fair Type of 1964 Souvenir Sheets

1965, Mar. 24 Engr. *Imperf.*

C69	AP4	100fr green & brn	1.00	1.00
C70	AP4	200fr grn & car rose	2.00	2.00

Handicraft Type of Regular Issue

100fr, Cabinetmaker. 300fr, Ivory carver.

1965, May 1 Photo. *Perf. 14*

C71	A45	100fr multicolored	.60	.35
C72	A45	300fr multicolored	2.00	.80

ITU Type of Regular Issue, 1965

1965, May 17 Unwmk.

C73	A46	100fr multicolored	.65	.30
C74	A46	200fr multicolored	1.60	.50

Exist imperf.

ICY Type of Regular Issue, 1965

1965, Sept. 8 Engr. *Perf. 10½*

C75	A50	100fr bl & yel org	.80	.35

West Facade, Polytechnic Institute — AP6

Design: 200fr, North facade.

1965, Oct. 2 Photo. *Perf. 13½*

C76	AP6	200fr gold & multi	1.50	.80
C77	AP6	500fr gold & multi	4.25	2.00

Seventh anniversary of independence.

For overprints see Nos. C84-C85.

Moon Type of 1965

100fr, Ranger VII approaching moon, vert. 200fr, Launching of Ranger VII, Cape Kennedy, vert.

1965, Nov. 15 Litho. *Perf. 13½x14*

C78	A52	100fr rose red, yel & dk brown	.65	.30
C79	A52	200fr multicolored	1.60	.60

For overprints & surcharge see #C112-C112B.

Dancer Type of Regular Issue, 1966

100fr, Kouyate Kandia, national singer.

1966, Jan. 5 Photo. *Perf. 13½*

Size: 36x28½mm

C80	A53	100fr multi, horiz.	.70	.35

Engraved Overprint on No. C65

1966, Mar. 14 Photo. *Perf. 12½x13*

C81	AP5	100fr gold, blk & red lil	.80	.40

Fourth Pan Arab Games, Cairo, Sept. 2-11, 1965. The same overprint was applied to two souvenir sheets noted after No. C65 (red ovpt. on 200fr, black ovpt. on 300fr).

Engraved Dark Blue Overprint on No. C64: "CENTENAIRE DU TIMBRE / CAIRE 1966"

1966, Mar. 14 *Perf. 12*

C82	A42	300fr gold, dl red brn & sal	2.00	1.25

Centenary of first Egyptian postage stamp.

Scenic Type of Regular Issue

View: Boulbinet Lighthouse.

1966, Apr. 4 *Perf. 13½*

C83	A54	100fr multicolored	.70	.35

See #C90-C91. For overprints see #C93-C95.

Nos. C76-C77 Overprinted in Blue or Yellow

1966, May 2 Photo. *Perf. 13½*

C84	AP6	200fr multi (Bl)	1.40	.90
C85	AP6	500fr multi (Y)	3.25	2.00

UNESCO, 20th anniv.

Woman-Flower Type of Regular Issue

Designs: Women and flowers of Guinea.

1966, May 30 Photo. ***Perf. 13½***
Size: 28x34mm

C86 A56 200fr multicolored 1.60 .60
C87 A56 300fr multicolored 2.50 1.10

Snake Type of Regular Issue

Designs: 200fr, Pastoria Research Institute. 300fr, Men holding rock python.

1967, May 15 Litho. ***Perf. 13½***
Size: 56x20mm

C88 A61 200fr multicolored 1.40 .70
a. Souv. sheet of 3, #471, 474, C88 4.00 3.50
C89 A61 300fr multicolored 2.25 1.10

Scenic Type of Regular Issue

Views: 100fr, House of explorer Olivier de Sanderval. 200fr, Conakry.

1967, June 20 Photo. ***Perf. 13½***

C90 A54 100fr multicolored .60 .40
C91 A54 200fr multicolored 1.40 .70

For overprints see Nos. C94-C95.

Elephant Type of Regular Issue, 1967

1967, Sept. 28 Photo. ***Perf. 13½***

C92 A63 200fr gold & multi 1.40 .65

Nos. C83 and C90-C91 Overprinted with Lions Emblem and: "AMITIE DES PEUPLES GRACE AU TOURISME 1917-1967"

1967, Nov. 6

C93 A54 100fr multi (#C83) .80 .40
C94 A54 100fr multi (#C90) .80 .40
C95 A54 200fr multi (#C91) 1.50 .70
Nos. C93-C95 (3) 3.10 1.50

50th anniversary of Lions International.

Detail from Mural by José Vela Zanetti — AP7

Family, Mural by Per Krohg — AP8

The designs of the 30fr, 50fr and 200fr show mankind's struggle for a lasting peace after the mural in the lobby of the UN Conference Building, NY. The designs of the 100fr and of Nos. C98a-C98b show mankind's hope for the future after a mural in the UN Security Council Chamber.

1967, Nov. 11

C96 AP7 30fr multicolored .25 .20
C97 AP7 50fr multicolored .30 .20
C98 AP8 100fr multicolored .65 .30
a. Souv. sheet of 3, English inscription 1.50 1.50
b. As "a," French inscription 1.50 1.50
C99 AP7 200fr multi 1.40 .45
Nos. C96-C99 (4) 2.60 1.15

Nos. C98a and C98b each contain a 100fr stamp similar to No. C98 and two 50fr stamps showing festival scenes. The 50fr stamps have not been issued individually.

People and Dwellings Type of Regular Issue

Design: 300fr, People and village of Les Bassari, Kundara Region.

1968, Apr. 1 Photo. ***Perf. 14x13½***
Size: 57x36mm

C100 A66 300fr gold & multi 2.00 .80

Legends Type of Regular Issue

70fr, The Girl and the Hippopotamus. 100fr, Old Faya's Inheritance, vert. 200fr, Soumangourou Kante Killed by Djegue (woman on horseback). 300fr, Little Gouné, Son of the Lion, vert.

1968 Photo. ***Perf. 13½***

C101 A67 70fr multicolored .50 .20
C102 A67 100fr multicolored .80 .20
C103 A67 200fr multicolored 1.60 .40
a. Souv. sheet of 4 4.00 4.00
C104 A67 300fr multicolored 2.25 .80
Nos. C101-C104 (4) 5.15 1.60

Issued in sheets of 10 plus 2 labels. No. C103a contains 4 imperf. stamps similar to Nos. 510-511 and C102-C103.;
For souvenir sheet see No. 509a.
Issued: #C102-C103, 5/16; #C101, C104, 9/16.

African Animal Type of Regular Issue

1968, Nov. 25 Photo. ***Perf. 13½***
Size: 49x35mm

C105 A68 100fr Lions .90 .30
C106 A68 200fr Elephant 1.50 .60

For souvenir sheet see No. 518a.

Robert F. Kennedy Type of Regular Issue, 1968

Portraits: 50fr, Senator Robert F. Kennedy. 100fr, Rev. Martin Luther King, Jr. 200fr, Pres. John F. Kennedy.

1968, Dec. 16

C107 A69 50fr yel & multi .35 .20
C108 A69 100fr multicolored .70 .20
C109 A69 200fr multicolored 1.60 .45
Nos. C107-C109 (3) 2.65 .85

The stamps are printed in sheets of 15 (3x5) containing 10 stamps and five green and gold center labels. Sheets come either with English or French inscriptions on label.

Olympic Type of Regular Issue

Sculpture &: 100fr, Gymnast on vaulting horse. 200fr, Gymnast on rings. 300fr, High jump.

1969, Feb. 1 Photo. ***Perf. 13½***

C110 A71 100fr multicolored .65 .25
C111 A71 200fr multicolored 1.40 .40
C111A A71 300fr multicolored 2.25 .60
Nos. C110-C111A (3) 4.30 1.25

Nos. C78-C79 Surcharged and Overprinted in Red

1969, Mar. 17 Litho. ***Perf. 13½x14***

C112 A52 25fr on 200fr multi .35 .20
C112A A52 100fr multicolored .90 .65
C112B A52 200fr multicolored 1.60 1.00
Nos. C112-C112B (3) 2.85 1.85

See note after No. 530.
Nos. C112-C112B also exist with surcharge and overprint in orange (25fr, 200fr) or black (100fr). These sell for a small premium.

Bird Type of Regular Issue

Birds: 50fr, Violet-crested touraco. 100fr, European golden oriole. 200fr, Vulturine guinea fowl.

1971, June 18 Photo. ***Perf. 13***
Size: 41x41mm

C113 A81 50fr gold & multi .55 .20
C113A A81 100fr gold & multi .85 .30
C113B A81 200fr gold & multi 1.60 .50
Nos. C113-C113B (3) 3.00 1.00

John and Robert Kennedy, Martin Luther King, Jr. — AP9

Embossed on Metallic Foil

1972 ***Die Cut Perf. 10½***

C114 AP9 300fr silver

Embossed & Typo.

C114A AP9 1500fr gold, cream & green

Jules Verne, Moon Rocket — AP10

Embossed on Metallic Foil

1972 ***Die Cut Perf. 10½***

C115 AP10 300fr silver
C115A AP10 1200fr gold

Richard Nixon — AP11

Nixon and Mao — AP12

Nixon's Trip to People's Republic of China: a, Nixon. b, Chinese table tennis player. c, American table tennis player, Capitol dome. d, Mao Tse-tung.

Embossed on Metallic Foil

1972 ***Die Cut Perf. 10½***

C116 AP11 90fr Block of 4, #a.-d., silver
C117 AP11 290fr Block of 4, #a.-d., gold

Embossed & Typo.

C118 AP12 1200fr gold & red

Perforations within blocks of 4 are perf. 11.

Racial Equality Year Type of Regular Issue

Design: 100fr, Men of 4 races and racial equality emblem (like No. 603).

1972, May 14 Photo. ***Perf. 13x13½***

C119 A84 100fr gold & multi .60 .35

Satellite Type of Regular Issue

Designs: 100fr, Map of Africa and Relay. 200fr, Map of Africa and Early Bird.

1972, May 17 Litho. ***Perf. 13***

C120 A85 100fr yel & multi .50 .25
C121 A85 200fr multicolored 1.00 .50

African Postal Union Type of Regular Issue

Air mail envelope and UPAF emblem.

1972, July 10

C122 A86 100fr multicolored .60 .30
C123 A86 200fr multicolored 1.25 .60

Olympic Type of Regular Issue

1972, Aug. 26 Photo. ***Perf. 13***

C124 A88 100fr Gymnast on rings .65 .30
C125 A88 200fr Bicycling 1.10 .60

Souvenir Sheet

C126 A88 300fr Soccer 1.90 1.90

Flower Type of 1974

1974, May 20 Photo. ***Perf. 13***
Size: 38x38mm (Diamond)

C127 A97 20s Thunbergia alata .90 .45
C128 A97 25s Diascia barberae 1.10 .60
C129 A97 50s Kigelia africana 2.25 1.20
Nos. C127-C129 (3) 4.25 2.25

Olympic Games Type of 1976

Souvenir Sheet

1976, May 17 Photo. ***Perf. 13½***

C130 Sheet of 4 6.50 6.50
a. A104 25s Soccer 1.40 .80

No. C130 contains 32x32mm stamps.

Mushroom Type of 1977

Mushrooms: 10s, Morchella esculenta. 12s, Lepiota procera. 15s, Cantharellus cibarius.

1977, Feb. 6 Photo. ***Perf. 13***
Size: 48x31mm

C131 A106 10s multicolored .55 .30
C132 A106 12s multicolored .65 .40
C133 A106 15s multicolored .80 .45
Nos. C131-C133 (3) 2.00 1.15

Reptile Type of 1977

Reptiles: 10s, Flap-necked chameleon. 15s, Nile crocodiles. 25s, Painted tortoise.

1977, Oct. 10 Photo. ***Perf. 13½***
Size: 46x30mm

C134 A109 10s multicolored .65 .40
C135 A109 15s multicolored 1.00 .60
C136 A109 25s multicolored 1.60 1.00
Nos. C134-C136 (3) 3.25 2.00

Animal Type of 1977

Endangered Animals: 5s, Eland. 8s, Pygmy elephant. 9s, Hippopotamus. 10s, Chimpanzee. 12s, Palm squirrel. 13s, Lion. Male, female and young of each animal shown.

1977, Dec. 12 Photo. ***Perf. 14x13½***

C137 A110 Strip of 3 1.10 .60
a.-c. 5s any single .35
C138 A110 Strip of 3 1.75 .90
a.-c. 8s any single .55
C139 A110 Strip of 3 1.90 1.10
a.-c. 9s any single .60
C140 A110 Strip of 3 2.00 1.25
a.-c. 10s any single .65
C141 A110 Strip of 3 2.40 1.40
a.-c. 12s any single .80
C142 A110 Strip of 3 2.75 1.50
a.-c. 13s any single .90
Nos. C137-C142 (6) 11.90 6.75

Russian Revolution Type, 1978

10s, Russian ballet. 30s, Pushkin Monument.

1978, Feb. 27 Photo. ***Perf. 14***

C143 A111 10s gold & multi .65 .40
C144 A111 30s gold & multi 2.00 1.25

Giscard d'Estaing Type of 1979

Pres. Valery Giscard d'Estaing of France, vert.

1979, Sept. 14 Photo. ***Perf. 13***

C145 A112 25s multicolored 1.60 1.00

Jules Verne Type of 1979

Designs: 20s, Five Weeks in a Balloon. 25s, Robur the Conqueror.

1979, Nov. 8 Litho. ***Perf. 12x12½***

C146 A113 20s multicolored 1.40 .80
C147 A113 25s multicolored 1.60 1.00

Olympic Type of 1982

1982 Litho. ***Perf. 12½x12, 12x12½***

C148 A120 9s Fencing .60 .40
C149 A120 10s Soccer, vert. .65 .40
C150 A120 11s Basketball, vert. .75 .40

C151 A120 20s Diving, vert. 1.40 .80
C152 A120 25s Boxing, vert. 1.60 1.10
Nos. C148-C152 (5) 5.00 3.10

Ataturk Type of 1982

1982, July 19 Photo. *Perf. 13½*
C153 A122 25s like #830 1.60 1.00

World Cup Type of 1982

Designs: Various soccer players.

1982, Aug. 23
C154 A123 10s multicolored .65 .40
C155 A123 20s multicolored 1.40 .80
C156 A123 25s multicolored 1.60 1.00
Nos. C154-C156 (3) 3.65 2.20

Nos. C154-C156 Overprinted like #835-838

1982, Aug. 23 Photo. *Perf. 13½*
C157 A123 10s multicolored .65 .40
C158 A123 20s multicolored 1.40 .80
C159 A123 25s multicolored 1.60 1.00
Nos. C157-C159 (3) 3.65 2.20

Location of flag in overprint varies.

Balloon Type

Designs: 20s, Graf Zeppelin, Airship, horiz. 25s, Double Eagle II, L. Newman, B. Abruzzo, M. Anderson. 30s, Le Geant Hot Air Balloon, Nadar; Dirigible, Dumont.

1983, Aug. 1 Litho. *Perf. 13½*
C160 A125 20s multicolored 1.40 .80
C161 A125 25s multicolored 1.60 1.00

Souvenir Sheet

C162 A125 30s multicolored 2.00 1.25

Nos. 894, 880-881 and 896 Overprinted

1985, Nov. 5 Litho. *Perf. 13½*
C163 A133 20s "80c Anniversaire / 1905-1985" 1.10 .60
C164 A131 20s "Rassemblement / Jambville-1985" 1.10 .60
C165 A131 25s "80e Anniversaire / 1905-1985" 1.50 .70
Nos. C163-C165 (3) 3.70 1.90

Souvenir Sheet

C166 A133 30s "Kasparov / champion / du Monde" 1.90 .90

US Space Shuttle Challenger Explosion, Jan. 28, 1986 — AP13

Designs: 100fr, Lift-off, crew names. 170fr, Shuttle design, Christa McAuliffe holding shuttle model. 600fr, Lift-off, vert.

1986, July 1

100fr, 170fr Surcharged in Silver and Black

C167 AP13 100fr multicolored .55 .30
C168 AP13 170fr multicolored .95 .50

Souvenir Sheet

C169 AP13 600fr multicolored 3.25 1.60

#C167-C168 not issued without surcharge.
Souvenir sheets of one exist containing Nos. C167 and C168.

Robin Yount, Milwaukee Brewers Baseball Player — AP14

1990, Aug. 3 Litho. *Perf. 13½*
C170 AP14 450fr multicolored 3.50 1.75

No. C170 exists in a souvenir sheet of 1.
For surcharge see No. 1182R.

Souvenir Sheet

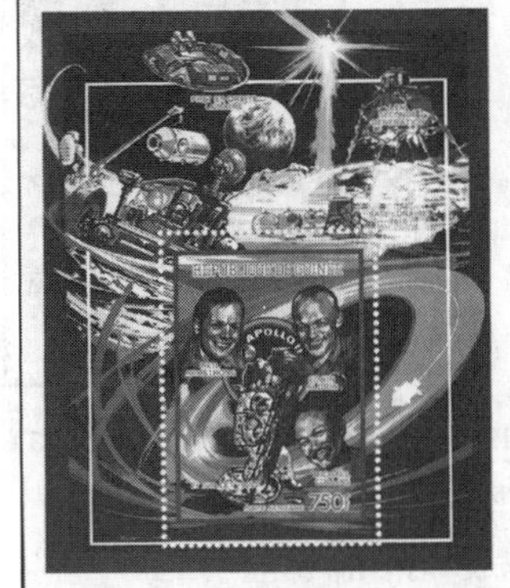

Armstrong, Aldrin, Collins and Apollo 11 Emblem — AP15

1990, Aug. 3 Litho. *Perf. 13½*
C171 AP15 750fr multicolored 5.75 2.75

Galileo Spacecraft — AP16

1990, Aug. 3
C172 AP16 500fr multicolored 3.75 1.90

No. C172 exists as a souvenir sheet of 1.

Pope John Paul II, Visit to Africa AP18

Portrait and: No. C174, Raising hand in benediction. No. C175, Child.

Litho. & Embossed

1992, Oct. 26 *Perf. 13½*
C174 AP18 1500fr gold & multi

Souvenir Sheet

C175 AP18 1500fr gold & multi

No. C175 exists imperf.

Elvis Presley, 15th Anniv. of Death — AP19

1992, Nov. 10
C176 AP19 1500fr gold & multi

No. C176 exists in miniature sheet of one.

De Gaulle Type of 1991 Overprinted "6 JUNE 1944 / DEBARQUEMENT"

1994 Litho. & Embossed *Perf. 13½*
C177 A181 1500fr like #1168

No. 1195 Ovptd. in Silver "RENCONTHE / FISCHER-SPASSKY / 4 SEPT au 5 NOV 1992 / AU MONTENEGRO"

1993, Feb. 24 Litho. *Perf. 13½*
C178 A188 450fr multicolored 4.50 2.25

No. C178 exists in souvenir sheet of 1.

POSTAGE DUE STAMPS

D5 D6

1959 Unwmk. Litho. *Perf. 11½*
J36 D5 1fr emerald .20 .20
J37 D5 2fr lilac rose .20 .20
J38 D5 3fr brown .20 .20
J39 D5 5fr blue .20 .20
J40 D5 10fr orange .50 .45
J41 D5 20fr rose lilac 1.00 .75
Nos. J36-J41 (6) 2.30 2.00

1960 Engr. *Perf. 13½*
J42 D6 1fr dark carmine .20 .20
J43 D6 2fr brown orange .20 .20
J44 D6 3fr dark car rose .20 .20
J45 D6 5fr bright green .45 .30
J46 D6 10fr dark brown .85 .45
J47 D6 20fr dull blue 1.75 1.00
Nos. J42-J47 (6) 3.65 2.35

GUINEA-BISSAU

'gi-nē-bi-'sau̧ⁿ

LOCATION — West coast of Africa between Senegal and Guinea
GOVT. — Republic
AREA — 13,948 sq. mi.
POP. — 1,234,555 (1999 est.)
CAPITAL — Bissau

Guinea-Bissau, the former Portuguese Guinea, attained independence September 10, 1974. The state includes the Bissagos Islands.

100 Centavos = 1 Escudo
100 Centavos = 1 Peso

Catalogue values for all unused stamps in this country are for Never Hinged items.

Amilcar Cabral, Map of Africa and Flag — A27

Design: Flag of the PAIGC (African Party of Independence of Guinea-Bissau and Cape Verde) shows location of Guinea-Bissau on map of Africa.

Perf. 11x10½

1974, Sept. 10 Litho. Unwmk.
345 A27 1p brown & multi .50 .40
346 A27 2.50p brown & multi .70 .60
347 A27 5p brown & multi *16.00 8.00*
348 A27 10p brown & multi 1.90 1.50
Nos. 345-348 (4) *19.10 10.50*

First anniv. of Proclamation of Independence, Sept. 24, 1973.

WMO Emblem — A28

Portuguese Guinea No. 344 Overprinted in Black

1975 Litho. *Perf. 13*
349 A28 2c brown & multi .50 .50

No. 349 exists with overprint in brown. Value, $5.

Amilcar Cabral, Map of Africa, Flag — A29

1975, Sept. Litho. *Perf. 11*
350 A29 1p brown & multi
351 A29 2.50p brown & multi
352 A29 5p brown & multi
353 A29 10p brown & multi
Nos. 350-353 (4) 9.00 6.75

Flag and Arms of Guinea-Bissau and Amilcar Cabral — A30

Flag, Arms and: 2e, #358, Family. 3e, 5e, Pres. Luiz Cabral. #359, like 1e.

1975, Sept. *Perf. 14*
354 A30 1e yel & multi .30 .20
355 A30 2e multicolored .30 .20
356 A30 3e red & multi .30 .20
357 A30 5e yel & multi .30 .20
358 A30 10e red & multi .40 .25
359 A30 10e brt grn & multi .50 .25
Nos. 354-359 (6) 2.10 1.30

Amilcar Cabral's 51st birth anniv. (1e, No. 359); African Party of Independence of Guinea-Bissau and Cape Verde, 19th anniv. (2e, No. 358); Proclamation of Independence, 2nd anniv. (3e, 5e).
For surcharges see Nos. 367-367E.

Henry Knox, Cannons of Ticonderoga — A30a

Designs: 10e, Israel Putnam, Battle of Bunker Hill. 15e, Washington crossing the Delaware. 20e, Tadeusz Kosciuszko, Battle of Saratoga. 30e, Von Steuben, winter at Valley Forge. 40e, Lafayette, Washington rallying troops at Monmouth. 50e, Signing the Declaration of Independence.

1976, May 5 Litho. *Perf. 13½*
360 A30a 5e multicolored
360A A30a 10e multicolored
360B A30a 15e multicolored
360C A30a 20e multicolored
360D A30a 30e multicolored
360E A30a 40e multicolored

Nos. 360-360E (6) 4.00

Souvenir Sheet

360F A30a 50e multicolored 4.00

American Revolution, bicentennial. Nos. 360D-360F are airmail. Nos. 360-360E exist in miniature sheets of 1, perf. and imperf. No. 360F contains one 75x45mm stamp and exists imperf.

See Nos. 371-371A.

Masked Dancer A30b

1976, May 10 ***Perf. 11***

Denomination in Black on Silver Block

361 A30b 2p shown
361A A30b 3p Dancer, drummer
361B A30b 5p Dancers on stilts
361C A30b 10p Dancer with spear, bow
361D A30b 15p Masked dancer, diff.
361E A30b 20p Dancer with striped cloak
Nos. 361-3601 (6) 4.00

Souvenir Sheet

361F A30b 50p Like No. 361E 4.00

Nos. 361C-361F are airmail. Silver block obliterates original denomination. Not issued without surcharge.

Nos. 361-361F Ovptd. in Black

1976, June 8 ***Perf. 11***

362 A30b 2p on No. 361
362A A30b 3p on No. 361A
362B A30b 5p on No. 361B
362C A30b 10p on No. 361C
362D A30b 15p on No. 361D
362E A30b 20p on No. 361E
Nos. 362-362E (6) 4.00

Souvenir Sheet

362F A30b 50p on No. 361F 4.00

Nos. 362C-362F are airmail. UPU cent. (in 1974). Nos. 362-362F exist imperf, and Nos. 362-362E in imperf miniature sheets of 1, all with black or red overprints.

Cabral, Guinean Mother and Children — A31

1976, Aug. **Litho.** ***Perf. 13½***

363 A31 3p multicolored .20 .20
364 A31 5p multicolored .20 .20
365 A31 6p multicolored .25 .20
366 A31 10p multicolored .35 .20
Nos. 363-366 (4) 1.00 .80

3rd anniv. of assassination of Amilcar Cabral (1924-1973), revolutionary leader.

Nos. 354-359 Surcharged in Black on Silver

1976, Sept. 12 **Litho.** ***Perf. 14***

367 A30 1p on 1e No. 354
367A A30 2p on 2e No. 355
367B A30 3p on 3e No. 356
367C A30 5p on 5e No. 357
367D A30 10p on 10e No. 358
367E A30 10p on 10e No. 359
Nos. 367-367E (6) 3.00

1876 Bell Telephone and Laying First Trans-Atlantic Cable — A31a

Telephones of: 3p, France, 1890, and first telephone booth, 1893. 5p, Germany, 1903, and automatic telephone, 1898. 10p, England, 1910, and relay station, 1963. 15p, France, 1924, and communications satellite. 20p, Modern telephone, 1970, and Molniya satellite. 50p, Picture phone.

1976, Oct. 18 ***Perf. 13½***

368 A31a 2p multicolored
368A A31a 3p multicolored
368B A31a 5p multicolored
368C A31a 10p multicolored
368D A31a 15p multicolored
368E A31a 20p multicolored
Nos. 368-368E (6) 6.00

Souvenir Sheet

368F A31a 50p multicolored 6.00

Nos. 368C-368F are airmail. No. 368F contains one 68x42mm stamp. No. 368F exists imperf. Nos. 368-368E exist in souvenir sheets of one, perf. and imperf.

1976 Winter Olympics, Innsbruck — A31b

1976, Nov. 3 ***Perf. 14x13½***

369 A31b 1p Women's figure skating
369A A31b 3p Ice hockey
369B A31b 5p Two-man bobsled
369C A31b 10p Pairs figure skating
369D A31b 20p Cross country skiing
369E A31b 30p Speed skating
Nos. 369-369E (6) 4.00

Souvenir Sheet

369F A31b 50p Downhill skiing 4.00

Nos. 369C-369F are airmail. No. 369F exists imperf. Nos. 369-369E exist in souvenir sheets of one, perf. and imperf.

1976 Summer Olympics, Montreal A31c

1976, Nov. 24 ***Perf. 13½***

370 A31c 1p Soccer
370A A31c 3p Pole vault
370B A31c 5p Women's hurdles
370C A31c 10p Discus
370D A31c 20p Sprinting
370E A31c 30p Wrestling
Nos. 370-370E (6) 6.00

Souvenir Sheet

370F A31c 50p Cycling, horiz. 4.00

Nos. 370E-370F are airmail. No. 370F contains one 47x38mm stamp. No. 370F exists imperf. Nos. 370-370E exist in souvenir sheets of one, perf. and imperf.

American Revolution Type of 1976

Designs: 3.50p, Crispus Attucks, Boston Massacre. 5p, Martin Luther King, US Capitol.

1977, Jan. 27 ***Perf. 13½***

Denomination in Black on Gold Block

371 A30a 3.50p multicolored
371A A30a 5p multicolored
Nos. 371-371A (2) 1.50

Gold block obliterates original denomination. Not issued without surcharge. Exist in souvenir sheets of one, perf. and imperf.

Cabral Addressing UN General Assembly — A32

Design: 50c, Cabral and guerrilla fighters.

1977, July **Litho.** ***Perf. 13½***

372 A32 50c multicolored .20 .20
373 A32 3.50p multicolored .30 .20

For surcharges see Nos. C12-C13.

Henri Dunant, Nobel Peace Prize, 1901 A32a

Nobel Prize Winners: 5p, Einstein, Physics, 1921. 6p, Irene and Frederic Joliot-Curie, Chemistry, 1935. 30p, Fleming, Medicine, 1945. 35p, Hemingway, Literature, 1954. 40p, J. Tinbergen, Economics, 1969. 50p, Nobel Prize Medal.

1977, July 27

374 A32a 3.50p multicolored
374A A32a 5p multicolored
374B A32a 6p multicolored
374C A32a 30p multicolored
374D A32a 35p multicolored
374E A32a 40p multicolored
Nos. 374-374E (6) 5.00

Souvenir Sheet

374F A32a 50p multicolored 5.00

Nos. 374D-374F are airmail. No. 374F contains one 57x39mm stamp. No. 374F exists imperf. Nos. 374-374E exist in souvenir sheets of one, perf. and imperf.

Postal Runner, Telstar Satellite — A32b

UPU Centenary (in 1974): 5p, Biplane, satellites encircle globe. 6p, Mail truck, satellite control room. 30p, Stagecoach, astronaut canceling letters on Moon. 35p, Steam locomotive, communications satellite. 40p, Space shuttle, Apollo-Soyuz link-up. 50p, Semaphore signalling system, satellite dish.

1977, Sept. 30

375 A32b 3.50p multicolored
375A A32b 5p multicolored
375B A32b 6p multicolored
375C A32b 30p multicolored
375D A32b 35p multicolored
375E A32b 40p multicolored
Nos. 375-375E (6) 6.00

Souvenir Sheet

375F A32b 50p multicolored 6.00

Nos. 375D-375F are airmail. No. 375F exists imperf. Nos. 375-375E exist in souvenir sheets of one, perf. and imperf.

Torch and Party Emblem — A33

1977, Sept. **Litho.** ***Perf. 14***

376 A33 3p yel & multi .20 .20
377 A33 15p sal & multi .60 .40
378 A33 50p lt grn & multi 1.50 1.00
Nos. 376-378 (3) 2.30 1.60

African Party of Independence of Guinea-Bissau and Cape Verde, 20th anniversary.

Queen Elizabeth II, Silver Jubilee — A33a

Designs: 5p, Coronation ceremony. 10p, Yeoman of the Guard, Crown Jewels. 20p, Trumpeter. 25p, Royal Horse Guard. 30p, Royal Family. 50p, Queen Elizabeth II.

1977, Oct. 15

379 A33a 3.50p multicolored
379A A33a 5p multicolored
379B A33a 10p multicolored
379C A33a 20p multicolored
379D A33a 25p multicolored
379E A33a 30p multicolored
Nos. 379-379E (6) 5.00

Souvenir Sheet

379F A33a 50p multicolored 4.00

Nos. 379D-379F are airmail. No. 379F contains one 42x39mm stamp. No. 379F exists imperf. Nos. 379-379E exist in souvenir sheets of one, perf. and imperf.

Massacre of the Innocents by Rubens A33b

Paintings by Peter Paul Rubens: 5p, Rape of the Daughters of Leukippos. 6p, Lamentation of Christ, horiz. 30p, Francisco IV Gonzaga, Prince of Mantua. 35p, The Four Continents. 40p, Marquise Brigida Spinola Doria. 50p, The Wounding of Christ.

1977, Nov. 15

380 A33b 3.50p multicolored
380A A33b 5p multicolored
380B A33b 6p multicolored
380C A33b 30p multicolored
380D A33b 35p multicolored
380E A33b 40p multicolored
Nos. 380-380E (6) 3.00

Souvenir Sheet

380F A33b 50p multicolored 3.00

Nos. 380D-380F are airmail. Nos. 380-380F exist imperf. Nos. 380-380E exist in souvenir sheets of one, perf. and imperf.

Congress Emblem — A34

1977, Nov. 15 Litho. *Perf. 14*

381 A34 3.50p multicolored .20 .20

3rd PAIGC Congress, Bissau, Nov. 15-20.

Santos-Dumont's Airship, 1901 — A34a

Airships: 5p, R-34 crossing the Atlantic, 1919. 10p, Norge over North Pole, 1926. 20p, Graf Zeppelin over Abu Simbel, 1931. 25p, Hindenburg over New York, 1937. 30p, Graf Zeppelin, Concorde, space shuttle. 50p, Ferdinand von Zeppelin, horiz.

1978, Feb. 27

382 A34a 3.50p multicolored
382A A34a 5p multicolored
382B A34a 10p multicolored
382C A34a 20p multicolored
382D A34a 25p multicolored
382E A34a 30p multicolored
Nos. 382-382E (6) 4.00

Souvenir Sheet

382F A34a 50p multicolored 4.00

Nos. 382D-382F are airmail. No. 382F exists imperf. Nos. 382-382E exist in souvenir sheets of one, perf. and imperf.

World Cup Soccer Championships, Argentina — A34b

Soccer players and posters from previous World Cup Championships: 3.50p, 1930. 5p, 1938. 10p, 1950. 20p, 1962. 25p, 1970. 30p, 1974. 50p, Argentina '78 emblem.

1978, Mar. 15

383 A34b 3.50p multicolored
383A A34b 5p multicolored
383B A34b 10p multicolored
383C A34b 20p multicolored
383D A34b 25p multicolored
383E A34b 30p multicolored
Nos. 383-383E (6) 3.00

Souvenir Sheet

383F A34b 50p multicolored 3.00

Nos. 383D-383F are airmail. Nos. 383-383F exist imperf. Nos. 383-383E exist in miniature sheets of one, perf. and imperf.
For surcharges see Nos. 393-393F.

Endangered Species — A34c

1978, Apr. 17

384 A34c 3.50p Black antelope
384A A34c 5p Fennec
384B A34c 6p Secretary bird
384C A34c 30p Hippopotami
384D A34c 35p Cheetahs
384E A34c 40p Gorillas
Nos. 384-384E (6) 2.00

Souvenir Sheet

384F A34c 50p Cercopithecus erythotis 2.50

Nos. 384D-384F are airmail. No. 384F contains one 39x42mm stamp. No. 384F exists imperf. Nos. 384-384E exist in souvenir sheets of one, perf. and imperf.

Antenna, ITU Emblem A35

1978, May 17 Litho. *Perf. 13½*

385 A35 3.50p silver & multi .20 .20
386 A35 10p gold & multi .40 .25

10th World Telecommunications Day.

Boy — A36

3p, Infant and grandfather. 5p, Boys. 30p, Girls.

1978 *Perf. 14*

387 A36 50c yel grn & dk bl .20 .20
388 A36 3p claret & car rose .20 .20
389 A36 5p ocher & brown .20 .20
390 A36 30p car & ocher 1.10 .65
Nos. 387-390 (4) 1.70 1.25

Children's Day.

Queen Elizabeth II, Silver Jubilee A36a

Elizabeth, Imperial State Crown — A36b

Designs: 5p, Queen, Prince Philip in Coronation Coach. 10p, Queen, Prince Philip. 20p, Mounted drummer. 25p, Imperial State Crown, St. Edward's Crown. 30p, Queen holding orb and scepter. 50p, Queen on Throne flanked by Archbishops. No. 391H, Coronation Coach.

1978, June 15

391 A36a 3.50p multicolored
391A A36a 5p multicolored
391B A36a 10p multicolored
391C A36a 20p multicolored
391D A36a 25p multicolored
391E A36a 30p multicolored
Nos. 391-391E (6) 3.50

Litho. & Embossed

391F A36b 100p gold & multi 4.00

Souvenir Sheets

391G A36a 50p multicolored 3.50

Litho. & Embossed

391H A36b 100p gold & multi 4.00

Nos. 391D-391H are airmail. Nos. 391-391E exist in souvenir sheets of one, perf. and imperf. Nos. 391F-391H exist imperf.

History of Aviation — A36c

1978, June 15 Litho. *Perf. 13½*

392 A36c 3.50p Wright Brothers
392A A36c 10p Santos-Dumont
392B A36c 15p Bleriot
392C A36c 20p Lindbergh, Spirit of St. Louis
392D A36c 25p Lunar module
392E A36c 30p Space shuttle
Nos. 392-392E (6) 5.00

Souvenir Sheet

392F A36c 50p Concorde 5.00

Nos. 392D-392F are airmail. Nos. 392-392E exist in souvenir sheets of one, perf. and imperf. No. 392F exists imperf.

Nos. 383-383F Ovptd. in Gold

1978, Oct. 2

393 A34b 3.50p on No. 383
393A A34b 5p on No. 383A
393B A34b 10p on No. 383B
393C A34b 20p on No. 383C
393D A34b 25p on No. 383D
393E A34b 30p on No. 383E
Nos. 393-393E (6) 3.00

Souvenir Sheet

393F A34b 50p on No. 383F 3.00

Nos. 393D-393F are airmail. Nos. 393-393F exist imperf. Nos. 393-393E exist in miniature sheets of 1 perf. and imperf. No. 393F exists overprinted in silver.

Virgin and Child by Albrecht Durer — A36d

Different Paintings of the Virgin and Child (Virgin only on 30p) by Durer.

1978, Nov. 14

394 A36d 3.50p multicolored
394A A36d 5p multicolored
394B A36d 6p multicolored
394C A36d 30p multicolored
394D A36d 35p multicolored
394E A36d 40p multicolored
Nos. 394-394E (6) 3.00

Souvenir Sheet

394F A36d 50p multicolored 3.00

Nos. 394D-394F are airmail. No. 394F contains one 51x56mm stamp. Nos. 394-394E exist in souvenir sheets of one, perf. and imperf. No. 394F exists imperf.

Sir Rowland Hill (1795-1879), Wurttemberg No. 53 — A36e

Hill and: 5p, Belgium #1. 6p, Monaco #10. 30p, Spain 2r stamp of 1851 in blue. 35p, Switzerland #5. 40p, Naples #8. 50p, Portuguese Guinea #13 in brown.

1978, Dec. 15

395 A36e 3.50p multicolored
395A A36e 5p multicolored
395B A36e 6p multicolored
395C A36e 30p multicolored
395D A36e 35p multicolored
395E A36e 40p multicolored
Nos. 395-395E (6) 3.00

Souvenir Sheet

395F A36e 50p multicolored 3.00

Nos. 395D-395F are airmail. No. 395F contains one 51x42mm stamp. Nos. 395-395E exist in souvenir sheets of one, perf. and imperf. No. 395F exists imperf.

Intl. Day of the Child — A36f

1979, Jan. 15 *Perf. 14*

396 A36f 3.50p shown
396A A36f 10p Children drinking
396B A36f 15p Child with book
396C A36f 20p Space plane
396D A36f 25p Skylab
396E A36f 30p Children playing chess
Nos. 396-396E (6) 3.00

Souvenir Sheet

396F A36f 50p Children watching spaceship 3.00

Nos. 396C-396F are airmail. Nos. 396-396E exist in souvenir sheets of one, perf. and imperf. No. 396F exists imperf.

A36g

A36h

1979 **Litho.** *Perf. 13*

397 A36g 4.50p multicolored 1.00

Massacre of Pindjiguiti, 20th anniv.

1979 **Litho.** *Perf. 14*

397A A36h 50c shown .20
397B A36h 4p People, rainbow, diff. 1.40

World Telecommunications Day.

Family A37

1979, May **Litho.** *Perf. 12x11½*

398 A37 50c multicolored .20 .20
399 A37 2p multicolored .20 .20
400 A37 4p multicolored .20 .20
Nos. 398-400 (3) .60 .60

General population census, Apr. 16-30.

Ernst Udet and Fokker D.VII — A38

1980 **Litho.** *Perf. 13½*

401 A38 3.50p shown .20 .20
401A A38 5p Charles Nungesser, Nieuport 17 .20 .20
401B A38 6p von Richthofen, Fokker DR.1 .25 .20
401C A38 30p Francesco Baracca, Spad XIII 1.00 .55
Nos. 401-401C,C14-C14A (6) 4.40 2.45

Lake Placid Emblem, Speed Skating — A39

1980

402 A39 3.50p shown .20 .20
402A A39 5p Downhill skiing .20 .20
402B A39 6p Luge .25 .20
402C A39 30p Cross-country skiing 1.00 .55
Nos. 402-402C,C15-C16 (6) 4.40 2.45

13th Winter Olympic Games, Lake Placid, NY, Feb. 12-24.

Shot-put A40

1980, Aug. **Litho.** *Perf. 13½*

403 A40 3.50p shown .20 .20
403A A40 5p Athlete on rings .20 .20
403B A40 6p Running .25 .20
403C A40 30p Fencing 1.00 .55
Nos. 403-403C,C18-C19 (6) 4.40 2.45

22nd Summer Olympic Games, Moscow, 7/19-8/3.

Pres. Luis Caral, Children and Workers A41

5p, Pres. Caral holding books.

1980, Aug. **Litho.** *Perf. 13½*

404 A41 3.50p multicolored .20 .20
405 A41 5p multicolored .25 .20

Literacy campaign. See Nos. C21-C22.

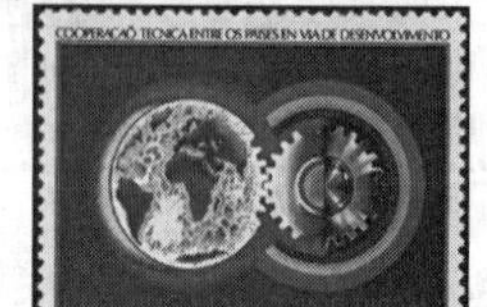

Cooperation Among Developing Countries — A42

1980, Aug.

406 A42 3.50p multicolored .20 .20
407 A42 6p multicolored .20 .20
408 A42 10p multicolored .40 .20
Nos. 406-408 (3) .80 .60

Baskets — A43

1980, Aug. **Litho.** *Perf. 13½*

409 A43 3p Bird, family wood statues, vert. .20 .20
410 A43 6p shown .20 .20
411 A43 20p Head, doll carvings .70 .40
Nos. 409-411 (3) 1.10 .80

Infant and Toy Train, Locomotive, IYC Emblem A44

1980

412 A44 6p Classroom, horiz. .25 .20
412A A44 10p Boy reading Jules Verne story .45 .30
412B A44 25p shown .90 .50
412C A44 35p Archer, boy with bow 1.40 .70
Nos. 412-412C (4) 3.00 1.70

Souvenir Sheet

412D A44 50p Students in lab 3.00 1.00

International Year of the Child (1979).

Columbia Space Shuttle and Crew — A45

Space Exploration: 3.50p, Galileo, satellites. 5p, Wernher von Braun. 6p, Jules Verne, rocket.

1981, May **Litho.** *Perf. 13½*

413 A45 3.50p multicolored .20 .20
413A A45 5p multicolored .25 .20
413B A45 6p multicolored .30 .20
413C A45 30p multicolored 1.50 .80
Nos. 413-413C,C23-C24 (6) 5.00 2.70

Soccer Players, World Cup, Argentina '78 and Espana '82 Emblems — A46

Soccer scenes and famous players: 3.50p, Platini, France. 5p, Bettega, Italy. 6p, Rensenbrink, Netherlands. 30p, Rivelino, Brazil.

1981, May

414 A46 3.50p multicolored .20 .20
414A A46 5p multicolored .25 .20
414B A46 6p multicolored .30 .20
414C A46 30p multicolored 1.50 .60
Nos. 414-414C,C26-C27 (6) 5.00 2.50

Prince Charles and Lady Diana, St. Paul's Cathedral A47

Royal Wedding (Couple and): 3.50p, Diana leading horse. 5p, Charles crowned Prince of Wales. 6p, Diana with kindergarten children.

1981 **Litho.** *Perf. 13½*

415 A47 3.50p multicolored .20 .20
415A A47 5p multicolored .25 .20
415B A47 6p multicolored .30 .20
415C A47 30p multicolored 1.00 .80
Nos. 415-415C,C29-C30 (6) 4.65 3.65

Woman Before a Mirror, by Picasso (1881-1973) A48

Picasso Birth Cent.: Various paintings.

1981, Dec. **Litho.** *Perf. 13½*

416 A48 3.50p multi .20 .20
417 A48 5p multi .25 .20
418 A48 6p multi .30 .20
419 A48 30p multi 1.50 .80
Nos. 416-419,C32-C33 (6) 6.15 3.65

Henrique Vermelho and his Ship, Drakkar A49

Navigators and their ships: 5p, Vasco de Gama, St. Gabriel. 6p, Ferdinand Magellan, Victoria. 30p, Jacques Cartier, Emerillon.

1981 **Litho.** *Perf. 13½*

420 A49 3.50p multicolored .20 .20
421 A49 5p multicolored .25 .20
422 A49 6p multicolored .30 .20
423 A49 30p multicolored 1.50 .80
Nos. 420-423,C35-C36 (6) 6.15 3.65

Christmas — A50

Designs: Virgin and Child paintings.

1981

424 A50 3.50p Mantegna .20 .20
425 A50 5p Bellini .25 .20
426 A50 6p Mantegna, diff. .30 .20
427 A50 25p Correggio 1.50 .80
Nos. 424-427,C38-C39 (6) 6.15 3.65

Scouting Year — A51

1982, June 9 Litho. *Perf. 13½*

428 A51	3.50p	Archery	.20	.20
429 A51	5p	First aid training	.20	.20
430 A51	6p	Bugler	.25	.20
431 A51	30p	Cub scouts	1.40	.60
		Nos. 428-431,C41-C42 (6)	5.45	2.90

1982 World Cup — A52

Various soccer players and cup.

1982, June 13 Litho. *Perf. 13½*

432 A52	3.50p	Keegan	.20	.20
433 A52	5p	Rossi	.20	.20
434 A52	6p	Zico	.25	.20
435 A52	30p	Arconada	1.40	.60
		Nos. 432-435,C44-C45 (6)	5.45	2.90

21st Birthday of Princess Diana — A53

Portraits and scenes of Diana.

1982

436 A53	3.50p	multicolored	.20	.20
437 A53	5p	multicolored	.20	.20
438 A53	6p	multicolored	.25	.20
439 A53	30p	multicolored	1.40	.60
		Nos. 436-439,C47-C48 (6)	5.45	2.90

For overprints see Nos. 450-456.

Visit by Portuguese President Eanes — A54

4.50p, Portugal and Guinea-Bissau flags.

1982 Litho. *Perf. 13½*

440 A54	4.50p	multicolored
441 A54	20p	multicolored

Manned Flight Bicentenary — A55

Various hot air balloons.

1983, Jan. 15 Litho. *Perf. 11*

442 A55	50c	multicolored	.20	.20
443 A55	2.50p	multicolored	.20	.20
444 A55	3.50p	multicolored	.20	.20
445 A55	5p	multicolored	.20	.20
446 A55	10p	multicolored	.30	.20
447 A55	20p	multicolored	.70	.30
448 A55	30p	multicolored	1.00	.40
		Nos. 442-448 (7)	2.80	1.70

Souvenir Sheet

Perf. 12½

449 A55	50p	multicolored	1.75	.85

No. 449 contains one 47x47mm stamp.

Nos. 436-439, C47-C48, C49A-C49B Overprinted: "21 DE JULHO . GUILHERMO ARTUR FILIPE LUIS PRINCIPE DE GALES"

1982 Litho. *Perf. 13½*

450 A53	3.50p	multicolored	.20	.20
451 A53	5p	multicolored	.20	.20
452 A53	6p	multicolored	.25	.20
453 A53	30p	multicolored	1.10	.65
454 A53	35p	multicolored	1.40	.75
455 A53	40p	multicolored	1.60	1.00
		Nos. 450-455 (6)	4.75	3.00

Souvenir Sheet

456 A53	50p	multicolored	2.25	1.10

Litho. & Embossed

456A A53a	200p	gold & multi	4.00

Souvenir Sheet

456B A53a	200p	gold & multi, vert.	4.00

Nos. 454-456A are airmail.

African Apes and Monkeys A56

1983, Mar. 15 Litho. *Perf. 13½*

457 A56	1p	Comopithecus hamadryas	.20	.20
458 A56	1.50p	Gorilla gorilla	.20	.20
459 A56	3.50p	Theropithecus gelada	.20	.20
460 A56	5p	Mandrillus sphinx	.20	.20
461 A56	8p	Pan trogladytes	.20	.20
462 A56	20p	Colobus abyssinicus	.55	.25
463 A56	30p	Cercopithecus diana	.80	.35
		Nos. 457-463 (7)	2.35	1.60

Souvenir Sheet

TEMBAL '83, Stamp Exhibition, Basel — A57

1983, May 21

464 A57	50p	Space shuttle	3.00	1.00

A58

Designs: Various telecommunications satellites and space shuttles.

1983, May 25 Litho. *Perf. 13½*

465 A58	1p	multicolored	.20	.20
466 A58	1.50p	multicolored	.20	.20
467 A58	3.50p	multicolored	.20	.20
468 A58	5p	multicolored	.20	.20
469 A58	8p	multicolored	.35	.20
470 A58	20p	multicolored	.85	.35
471 A58	30p	multicolored	1.25	.55
		Nos. 465-471 (7)	3.25	1.90

Souvenir Sheet

472 A58	50p	multicolored	2.00	.85

History of Chess — A59

Early Chess Game — A60

Various chess pieces.

1983, June 13 Litho. *Perf. 12*

473 A59	1p	multicolored	.20	.20
474 A59	1.50p	multicolored	.20	.20
475 A59	3.50p	multicolored	.20	.20
476 A59	5p	multicolored	.20	.20
477 A59	10p	multicolored	.25	.20
478 A59	20p	multicolored	.45	.20
479 A59	40p	multicolored	1.00	.45
		Nos. 473-479 (7)	2.50	1.65

Souvenir Sheet

480 A60	50p	brown & blk	1.90	.80

Raphael, 500th Birth Anniv. A61

Various paintings.

1983, June 30 Litho. *Perf. 12½*

481 A61	1p	gold & multi	.20	.20
482 A61	1.50p	gold & multi	.20	.20
483 A61	3.50p	gold & multi	.20	.20
484 A61	5p	gold & multi	.20	.20
485 A61	8p	gold & multi	.25	.20
486 A61	15p	gold & multi	.50	.20
487 A61	30p	gold & multi	.95	.35
		Nos. 481-487 (7)	2.50	1.55

Souvenir Sheet

488 A61	50p	gold & multi	1.75	.85

1984 Summer Olympics, Los Angeles — A62

1983, July 20 Litho. *Perf. 12½*

489 A62	1p	Swimming	.20	.20
490 A62	1.50p	Jumping	.20	.20
491 A62	3.50p	Fencing	.20	.20
492 A62	5p	Weightlifting	.20	.20
493 A62	10p	Running	.25	.20
494 A62	20p	Equestrian	.55	.25
495 A62	40p	Bicycling	1.10	.55
		Nos. 489-495 (7)	2.70	1.80

Souvenir Sheet

496 A62	50p	Stadium	1.75	.85

Souvenir Sheet

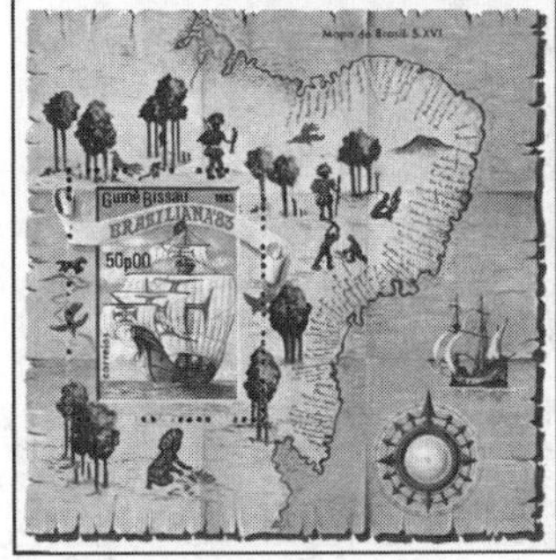

BRASILIANA '83, Philatelic Exhibition — A63

1983, July 29 Litho. *Perf. 13*

497 A63	50p	multicolored	*10.00*	*7.50*

Local Fish — A64

Perf. 12x11½, 11½x12

1983, Dec. 8 Litho.

498 A64	1p	Monodactylus sebae, vert.	.20	.20
499 A64	1.50p	Botia macracanthus	.20	.20
500 A64	3.50p	Ctenopoma acutirostre	.20	.20
501 A64	5p	Roloffia bertholdi	.20	.20
502 A64	8p	Aphyosemion bualanum	.30	.20
503 A64	10p	Aphyosemion bivittatum	.45	.20
504 A64	30p	Aphyosemion australe	1.25	.60
		Nos. 498-504 (7)	2.80	1.80

1984 Winter Olympics, Sarajevo — A65

1983, Oct. 10 Litho. *Perf. 13*

505 A65	1p	Speed skating	.20	.20
506 A65	1.50p	Ski jumping	.20	.20
507 A65	3p	Biathlon	.20	.20
508 A65	5p	Bobsledding	.20	.20
509 A65	10p	Hockey	.20	.20
510 A65	15p	Figure skating	.40	.20
511 A65	20p	Luge	.50	.25
		Nos. 505-511 (7)	1.90	1.45

Souvenir Sheet

512 A65	50p	Downhill skiing	1.75	.85

No. 512 contains one 31x40mm stamp.

A66

A67

1983, Nov. 7 *Perf. 12½*

513 A66 4.50p Emblem .20 .20
514 A66 7.50p Woman, flag .20 .20
515 A66 9p Sewing .25 .20
516 A66 12p Farm workers .35 .20
Nos. 513-516 (4) 1.00 .80

First anniv. of Women's Federation.

1983, Nov. 12 **Litho.** *Perf. 13*

Designs: Local flowers.

517 A67 1p Canna coccinea .20 .20
518 A67 1.50p Bouganville litoralis .20 .20
519 A67 3.50p Euphorbia milii .20 .20
520 A67 5p Delonix regia .25 .20
521 A67 8p Bauhinia variegata .40 .20
522 A67 10p Spathodea campanulata .55 .20
523 A67 30p Hibiscus rosa sinensis 1.50 .70
Nos. 517-523 (7) 3.30 1.90

JAAC Congress, Sept. 8-12 — A68

1983, Sept. 1 **Litho.** *Perf. 13*

524 A68 4p shown .20 .20
524A A68 5p Emblem .20 .20

World Food Day A69

1983, Oct. 16 **Litho.** *Perf. 12½x12*

525 A69 1.50p multicolored .20 .20
526 A69 2p multicolored .20 .20
527 A69 4p multicolored .20 .20

Imperf

Size: 61x62mm

528 A69 10p Hoeing .50 .50
Nos. 525-528 (4) 1.10 1.10

1984 Winter Olympics, Sarajevo A70

1984, Feb. 8 *Perf. 12*

529 A70 50c Ski jumping .20 .20
530 A70 2.50p Speed skating .20 .20
531 A70 3.50p Hockey .20 .20
532 A70 5p Biathlon .20 .20
533 A70 6p Downhill skiing .20 .20
534 A70 20p Figure skating .55 .30
535 A70 30p Bobsledding .95 .35
Nos. 529-535 (7) 2.50 1.65

Souvenir Sheet

Perf. 11½

536 A70 50p Skiing 1.75 .85

No. 536 contains one 32x43mm stamp.

World Communications Year — A71

1983, Aug. 30 **Litho.** *Perf. 12½*

537 A71 50c Rowland Hill .20 .20
538 A71 2.50p Samuel Morse .20 .20
539 A71 3.50p H.R. Hertz .20 .20
540 A71 5p Lord Kelvin .25 .20
541 A71 10p Alex. Graham Bell .50 .20
542 A71 20p G. Marconi 1.00 .50
543 A71 30p V. Zworykin 1.40 .65
Nos. 537-543 (7) 3.75 2.15

Souvenir Sheet

544 A71 50p Satellites 2.50 1.25

No. 544 contains one stamp 31x39mm.

Vintage Cars A72

1984, Mar. 20 *Perf. 12*

545 A72 5p Duesenberg, 1928 .20 .20
546 A72 8p MG Midget, 1932 .40 .20
547 A72 15p Mercedes, 1928 .50 .20
548 A72 20p Bentley, 1928 .60 .30
549 A72 24p Alfa Romeo, 1929 .75 .35
550 A72 30p Datsun, 1932 1.00 .45
551 A72 35p Lincoln, 1932 1.25 .50
Nos. 545-551 (7) 4.70 2.20

Souvenir Sheet

552 A72 100p Gottlieb Daimler 3.00 1.50

No. 552 contains one stamp 50x42mm.

Madonna and Child, by Morales — A73

Paintings by Spanish Artists (Espana '84): 6p, Dona Tadea Arias de Enriquez, by Goya. 10p, Santa Cassilda, by Zurbaran. 12p, Saints Andrew and Francis, by El Greco. 15p, Infanta Isabel Clara Eugenia, by Coello. 35p, Queen Maria of Austria, by Velazquez. 40p, Holy Trinity, by El Greco. 100p, Clothed Maja, by Goya.

1984, Apr. 20

553 A73 3p multicolored .20 .20
554 A73 6p multicolored .20 .20
555 A73 10p multicolored .30 .20
556 A73 12p multicolored .35 .20
557 A73 15p multicolored .40 .25
558 A73 35p multicolored 1.10 .60
559 A73 40p multicolored 1.25 .65
Nos. 553-559 (7) 3.80 2.30

Souvenir Sheet

560 A73 100p multicolored 3.00 1.50

No. 560 contains one stamp 29x50mm.

Carnivorous Animals — A74

1984, June 28

561 A74 3p Panthera tigris .20 .20
562 A74 6p Panthera leo .20 .20
563 A74 10p Neofelis nebulosa .20 .20
564 A74 12p Acinonyx jubatus .20 .20
565 A74 15p Lynx lynx .25 .20
566 A74 35p Panthera pardus .65 .35
567 A74 40p Uncia uncia .70 .35
Nos. 561-567 (7) 2.40 1.70

Intl. Civil Aviation Org., 40th Anniv. — A75

1984, Apr. 4 **Litho.** *Perf. 12½*

568 A75 8p Caravelle .20
569 A75 22p DC-6B .40
570 A75 80p IL-76 1.50
Nos. 568-570 (3) 2.10

1984 Summer Olympics, Los Angeles — A76

1984, May 24 *Perf. 12*

571 A76 6p Soccer .20
572 A76 8p Dressage .20
573 A76 15p Yachting .35
574 A76 20p Field hockey .45
575 A76 22p Women's team handball .50
576 A76 30p Canoeing .70
577 A76 40p Boxing .90
Nos. 571-577 (7) 3.30

Souvenir Sheet

Perf. 11½

578 A76 100p Windsurfing 2.25

World Heritage — A77

Wood sculptures: 3p, Pearl throne, Cameroun and Central Africa. 6p, Antelope, South Sudan. 10p, Kneeling woman, East Africa. 12p, Mask, West African coast. 15p, Leopard, Guinea coast. 35p, Standing woman, Zaire. 40p, Funerary statues, Southeast Africa and Madagascar.

1984, Aug. 15 *Perf. 12½*

579 A77 3p multicolored .20
580 A77 6p multicolored .20
581 A77 10p multicolored .20
582 A77 12p multicolored .30
583 A77 15p multicolored .40
584 A77 35p multicolored .80
585 A77 40p multicolored .90
Nos. 579-585 (7) 3.00

Amilcar Cabral, 60th Birth Anniv. — A78

1984, Sept. 12 *Perf. 13*

586 A78 5p Public speaking .20
587 A78 12p In combat fatigues .20
588 A78 20p Memorial building, Bafata .35
589 A78 50p Mausoleum, Bissau .90
Nos. 586-589 (4) 1.65

Independence, 11th Anniv. — A79

1984, Sept. 24

590 A79 3p Mechanic .20
591 A79 6p Student .20
592 A79 10p Mason .20
593 A79 12p Health care, vert. .30
594 A79 15p Seamstress, vert. .40
595 A79 35p Telecommunications .80
596 A79 40p PAIGC building .90
Nos. 590-596 (7) 3.00

Whales A80

1984, Sept. 30 *Perf. 12*

597 A80 5p Eschrichtius gibbosus .20
598 A80 8p Balaenoptera musculus .20
599 A80 15p Tursiops truncatus .25
600 A80 20p Physeter macrocephalus .35
601 A80 24p Orcinus orca .45
602 A80 30p Balaena mysticetus .55
603 A80 35p Balaenoptera borealis .60
Nos. 597-603 (7) 2.60

Butterflies A81

1984, Oct. 6 *Perf. 12½x13*

604 A81 3p Hypolimnas dexithea .20
605 A81 6p Papilio arcturus .25
606 A81 10p Morpho menelaus terrestris .30
607 A81 12p Apaturina erminea papuana .40
608 A81 15p Prepona praeneste .50
609 A81 35p Ornithoptera paradisea .75
610 A81 40p Morpho hecuba obidona 1.00
Nos. 604-610 (7) 3.40

1984 Olympic Winners — A82

National flag, medal and: 6p, Carl Lewis, 4x100 relay, US. 8p, Koji Gushiken, gymnastics, Japan. 15p, Reiner Klimke, equestrian, Federal Republic of Germany. 20p, Tracie Ruiz, synchronized swimming, US. 22p, Mary Lou Retton, gymnastics, US. 30p, Michael Gross, swimming, Federal Republic of Germany. 40p, Edwin Moses, hurdler, US. 100p, Daley Thompson, decathlon, Great Britain.

1984, Nov. 27 *Perf. 13*

611 A82 6p multicolored .20
612 A82 8p multicolored .20
613 A82 15p multicolored .35

614	A82	20p	multicolored	.45
615	A82	22p	multicolored	.50
616	A82	30p	multicolored	.70
617	A82	40p	multicolored	.90
			Nos. 611-617 (7)	3.30

Souvenir Sheet

Perf. 12½

618 A82 100p multicolored 2.25

No. 618 contains one stamp 32x40mm.

Locomotives — A83

1984, Dec. 15 ***Perf. 13***

619	A83	5p	White Mountain Central No. 4	.20
620	A83	8p	Kessler 2-6-OT, 1886	.20
621	A83	15p	Langen tram, 1901	.25
622	A83	20p	Gurjao No. 6	.30
623	A83	24p	Achenseebahn	.35
624	A83	30p	Vitznau-Rigi steam locomotive	.45
625	A83	35p	Riggenbach rackrail, 1873	.50
			Nos. 619-625 (7)	2.25

Souvenir Sheet

Perf. 12½

625A A83 100p like #621 1.50

No. 625A contains one stamp 40x32mm.

Native Crafts — A83a

LUBRAPEX '84: a, Numbe mask. b, Sono statue. c, Erande statue. d, Kokumba arms. e, Oma mask. f, Koni mask.

1984 **Litho.** ***Perf. 13½***

626 A83a 7.50p Strip of 6, #a.-f. *3.00*

Motorcycle Cent. — A84

1985, Feb. 20 ***Perf. 13x12½***

627	A84	5p	Harley-Davidson	*.25*
628	A84	8p	Kawasaki	*.35*
629	A84	15p	Honda	*.40*
630	A84	20p	Yamaha	*.75*
631	A84	25p	Suzuki	*1.00*
632	A84	30p	BMW	*1.25*
633	A84	35p	Moto Guzzi	*2.00*
			Nos. 627-633 (7)	*6.00*

Souvenir Sheet

Perf. 12½

634 A84 100p Daimler Motorized Bicycle, 1885, vert. *5.00*

No. 634 contains one 32x40mm stamp.

Miniature Sheet

Mushrooms A85

1985, May 15 ***Perf. 13***

635	Sheet of 6	3.00
a.	A85 7p Clitocybe gibba	.20
b.	A85 9p Morchella elata	.20
c.	A85 12p Lepista nuda	.30
d.	A85 20p Lactarius deliciosus	.45
e.	A85 30p Russula virescens	.70
f.	A85 35p Chroogomphus rutilus	.80

Henri Dunant (1828-1910), Red Cross Founder, Plane — A87

1985, June 12 ***Perf. 12½***

643	A87	20p	shown	.45
644	A87	25p	Ambulance	.50
645	A87	40p	Helicopter	.90
646	A87	80p	Speed boat	2.00
			Nos. 643-646 (4)	3.85

Cats — A88

1985, July 5 ***Perf. 13***

647	A88	7p	multicolored	*.20*
648	A88	10p	multicolored	*.30*
649	A88	12p	multicolored	*.50*
650	A88	15p	multicolored	*.75*
651	A88	20p	multicolored	*1.00*
652	A88	40p	multicolored	*1.50*
653	A88	45p	multicolored	*2.25*
			Nos. 647-653 (7)	*6.50*

Souvenir Sheet

654 A88 100p multicolored *5.00*

ARGENTINA '85. No. 654 contains one 40x32mm stamp.

Composers and Musical Instruments A89

Designs: 4p, Vincenzo Bellini (1801-1835), harp, 1820, and descant viol, 16th cent. 5p, Schumann (1810-1856) and Viennese pyramid piano, 1829. 7p, Chopin (1810-1849) and piano-forte, 1817. 12p, Luigi Cherubini (1760-1842) and 18th cent. Baryton violin and Quinton viol. 20p, G. B. Pergolesi (1710-1736) and double-manual harpsichord, 1734. 30p, Handel (1685-1759), valve trumpet, 1825, and timpani drum, 18th cent. 50p, Heinrich Schutz (1585-1672), bass viol and two-stop oboe, 17th cent. 100s, Bach (1685-1750) and St. Thomas Church organ, Leipzig.

1985, Aug. 5 ***Perf. 12***

655	A89	4p	multicolored	.20
656	A89	5p	multicolored	.20
657	A89	7p	multicolored	.20
658	A89	12p	multicolored	.30
659	A89	20p	multicolored	.45
660	A89	30p	multicolored	.70
661	A89	50p	multicolored	1.10
			Nos. 655-661 (7)	3.15

Souvenir Sheet

Perf. 11½

662 A89 100p multicolored 2.25

No. 662 contains one 30x50mm stamp.

Santa Maria, 15th Cent., Spain — A90

Ships: 15p, Carack, 16th cent., Netherlands. 20p, Mayflower, 17th cent., Great Britain. 30p, St. Louis, 17th cent., France. 35p, Royal Sovereign, 1635, Great Britain. 45p, Soleil Royal, 17th cent., France. 80p, English brig, 18th-19th cent.

1985, Sept. 12 ***Perf. 13***

663	A90	8p	multicolored	.20
664	A90	15p	multicolored	.20
665	A90	20p	multicolored	.25
666	A90	30p	multicolored	.40
667	A90	35p	multicolored	.45
668	A90	45p	multicolored	.60
669	A90	80p	multicolored	1.10
			Nos. 663-669 (7)	3.20

UN, 40th Anniv. A91

1985, Oct. 17

670	A91	10p	Emblem, doves, vert.	.20
671	A91	20p	Emblem, 40	.45

Venus and Mars, by Sandro Botticelli (1445-1510) A92

Botticelli paintings (details): 7p, Virgin with Child and St. John. 12p, St. Augustine in the Work Hall. 15p, Awakening of Spring. 20p, Virgin and Child. 40p, Virgin with Child and St. John, diff. 45p, Birth of Venus. 100p, Virgin and Child with Two Angels.

1985, Oct. 25 ***Perf. 12½x13***

672	A92	7p	multicolored	.20
673	A92	10p	multicolored	.20
674	A92	12p	multicolored	.25
675	A92	15p	multicolored	.30
676	A92	20p	multicolored	.40
677	A92	40p	multicolored	.75
678	A92	45p	multicolored	.95

Size: 73x106mm

Imperf

679 A92 100p multicolored 2.00
Nos. 672-679 (8) 5.05

ITALIA '85.

Intl. Youth Year A93

1985, Nov. 29 **Litho.** ***Perf. 12½***

680	A93	7p	Dance	.20
681	A93	13p	Wind surfing	.20
682	A93	15p	Rollerskating	.20
683	A93	25p	Hang gliding	.35
684	A93	40p	Surfing	.60
685	A93	50p	Skateboarding	.75
686	A93	80p	Parachuting	1.25
			Nos. 680-686 (7)	3.55

Souvenir Sheet

Perf. 13

687 A93 100p Self-defense 1.50

No. 687 contains one 40x32mm stamp.

Miniature Sheet

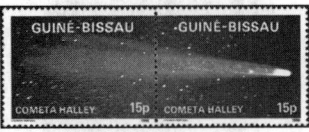

Halley's Comet — A94

1986 World Cup Soccer Championships, Mexico — A95

24th Summer Olympics, Seoul, 1988 A96

Italian Automobile Industry, Cent. A97

German Railways, 150th Anniv. A98

Discovery of America, 500th Anniv. (in 1992) A99

First American Manned Space Flight, 25th Anniv. — A100

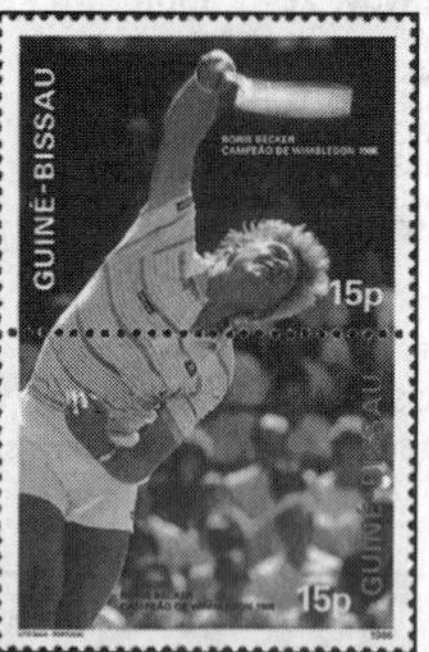

1986 Wimbledon Tennis Championships — A101

1986 Masters Tennis Championships — A102

Giotto Space Probe — A103

Designs: a, Comet tail. b, Comet. c, Trophy. d, Trophy base. e, Five-ring Olympic emblem. f, Alfa Tourer, Italy, c. 1905. g, Railway station, Frankfurt-on Main, c. 1914. h, Barcelona, site of Discovery of America exhibition and 1992 Olympics. i, Space station solar panels and tanks. j, Space station. k, Removing cargo from space shuttle. l, Docking facility, station panels. m, Boris Becker swinging tennis racket. n, Becker, diff. o, Ivan Lendl holding racket. p, Lendl, diff.

1986, Dec. 30 Litho. Perf. 13½

688 Sheet of 16 *60.00*
a.-p. A94-A102 15p any single

Souvenir Sheet

689 A103 100p multicolored 6.50

Nos. 688a-688b, 688c-688d, 688i-688l, 688m-688n, 688o-688p are se-tenant in continuous designs. Inscription on Nos. 688i-688l incorrect; should read "TRIPULADO MERCURY / 5-5-1961."

Discovery of America, 500th Anniv. (in 1992) — A104

Designs: No. 690, Christopher Columbus aboard caravelle. No. 691, Guadalquivir Port, Seville, c. 1490. No. 692, Pedro Alvars Cabral landing at Bahia, Brazil. No. 693, Bridge over the Guadalquivir River, Seville. No. 694, Port, Lisbon, 15th cent.

1987, Feb. 27

690 A104 50p multicolored 1.50
691 A104 50p multicolored 1.50
692 A104 50p multicolored 1.50
693 A104 50p multicolored 1.50
Nos. 690-693 (4) 6.00

Souvenir Sheet

694 A104 150p multicolored 10.00

No. 694 exists with pink or yellow anniv. emblem pictured in vignette.

Portuguese Guinea Nos. 306-309, 313, 316-317, Ovptd., Guinea-Bissau No. 349 Surcharged

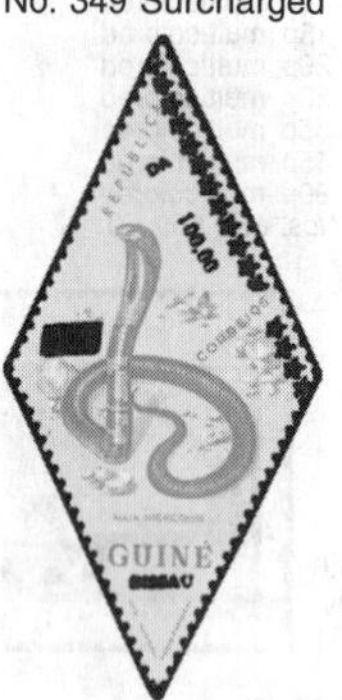

1987, July Litho. Perf. 13½

696 A21 100p on 20c #306 *4.00*
697 A21 200p on 35c #307 *9.00*
698 A21 300p on 70c #308 *12.00*
699 A21 400p on 80c #309 *20.00*
700 A21 500p on 3.50e #313 *25.00*
701 A21 1000p on 15e #316 *40.00*
702 A21 2000p on 20e #317 *65.00*

Perf. 13

703 CD61 2500p on 2e #349 *100.00*
Nos. 696-703 (8) *275.00*

Placement of "Bissau," new denomination and obliterating bar varies.

1988 Winter Olympics, Calgary — A106

1988, Jan. 15 Litho. Perf. 13

704 A106 5p Pairs figure skating .20
705 A106 10p Luge .20
706 A106 50p Skiing .20
707 A106 200p Slalom skiing .25
708 A106 300p Skibobbing .40
709 A106 500p Ski jumping, vert. .60
710 A106 800p Speed skating, vert. 1.00
Nos. 704-710 (7) 2.85

Souvenir Sheet

710A A106 900p Two-man luge 1.00

No. 710A contains one 40x32mm stamp.

Soccer — A107

Various soccer plays.

1988, Apr. 14 Litho. Perf. 13

711 A107 5p multi .20
712 A107 10p multi, diff. .20
713 A107 50p multi, diff. .20
714 A107 200p multi, diff. .40
715 A107 300p multi, diff. .60
716 A107 500p multi, diff. .90
717 A107 800p multi, diff. 1.50
Nos. 711-717 (7) 4.00

Souvenir Sheet

718 A107 900p multi, diff. 2.00

ESSEN '88 stamp exhibition. No. 718 contains one 32x40mm stamp.

1988 Summer Olympics, Seoul — A108

Perf. 12½x12, 12x12½

1988, Feb. 26 Litho.

719 A108 5p Yachting, vert. .20
720 A108 10p Equestrian .20
721 A108 50p High jump .20
722 A108 200p Shooting .55
723 A108 300p Long jump, vert. .80
724 A108 500p Tennis, vert. 1.25
725 A108 800p Women's archery, vert. 2.00
Nos. 719-725 (7) 5.20

Souvenir Sheet

Perf. 12½

726 A108 900p Soccer 2.00

No. 726 contains one 40x32mm stamp.

Ancient Ships — A109

Designs: 5p, Egyptian, c. 3300 B.C. 10p, Pharaoh Sahure's ship, c. 2700 B.C. 50p, Queen Hatsepsowe's ship, c. 1500 B.C. 200p, Ramses III's ship, c. 1200 B.C. 300p, Greek trireme, 480 B.C. 500p, Etruscan bireme, 600 B.C. 800p, Venetian galley, 12th cent.

1988 Litho. Perf. 13x12½

727 A109 5p multi .20
728 A109 10p multi .20
729 A109 50p multi .20
730 A109 200p multi .45
731 A109 300p multi .65
732 A109 500p multi 1.10
733 A109 800p multi 1.75
Nos. 727-733 (7) 4.55

FINLANDIA '88 — A110

Chess champions, board and chessmen.

1988 Litho. Perf. 12x12½

734 A110 5p Philidor .20
735 A110 10p Staunton .20
736 A110 50p Anderssen .20
737 A110 200p Morphy .45
738 A110 300p Steinitz .65
739 A110 500p Lasker 1.10
740 A110 800p Capablanca 1.75
Nos. 734-740 (7) 4.55

Souvenir Sheet

Perf. 13

741 A110 900p Ruy Lopez 1.90

No. 741 contains one 40x32mm stamp.

Dogs A111

1988 Perf. 13x12½

742 A111 5p Basset hound .20 .20
743 A111 10p Great blue of Gascony .20 .20
744 A111 50p Sabujo of Italy .20 .20
745 A111 200p Yorkshire terrier .50 .50
746 A111 300p Small musterlander .75 .75
747 A111 500p Pointer 1.25 1.25
748 A111 800p German setter 2.00 2.00
Nos. 742-748 (7) 5.10 5.10

Souvenir Sheet

Perf. 12½

749 A111 900 German shepherd 2.25 2.25

No. 749 contains one 40x32mm stamp.

Intl. Red Cross and Red Crescent Organizations, 125th Annivs. — A112

1988 Perf. 13

750 A112 10p Jean-Henri Dunant .45
751 A112 50p Dr. T. Maunoir .20
752 A112 200p Dr. Louis Appia .70
753 A112 800p Gustave Moynier 3.00
Nos. 750-753 (4) 4.35

Maps and Fauna — A113

1988 Perf. 12½x13, 13x12½

754 A113 5p *Panthera leo* .20
755 A113 10p *Glaucidium brasilianum* .20
756 A113 50p *Upupa epops* .20

757 A113 200p *Equus burchelli antiquorum* .45
758 A113 300p *Loxodonta africana* .65
759 A113 500p *Acryllium vulturinum* 1.10
760 A113 800p *Diceros bicornis* 1.75
Nos. 754-760 (7) 4.55

Nos. 754-755, 758-760 vert. The genus *"Upupa"* is misspelled on the 50p and *"Loxodonta"* is misspelled on the 300p.

Samora Machel (1933-1986), Pres. of Mozambique
A114

1988 *Perf. 13*

761 A114 10p shown .20
762 A114 50p Raising fist .20
763 A114 200p With sentry .75
764 A114 300p Wearing earphones at UN 1.10
Nos. 761-764 (4) 2.25

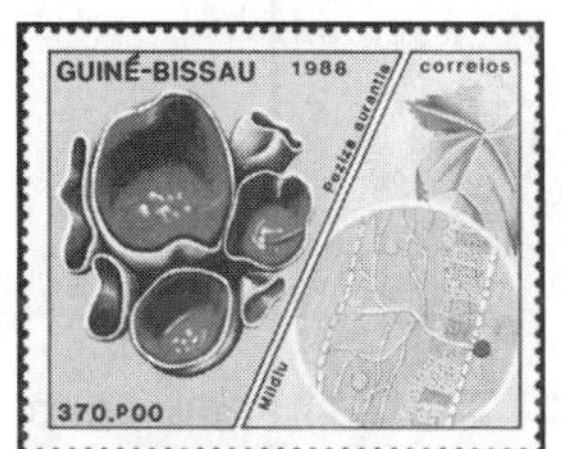

Mushrooms — A115

1988 Litho. *Perf. 13x12½*

765 A115 370p *Peziza aurantia* .75
766 A115 470p *Morchella* .90
767 A115 600p *Amanita caesarea* 1.25
768 A115 780p *Amanita muscaria* 1.60
769 A115 800p *Amanita phalloides* 1.60
770 A115 900p *Agaricus bisporus* 1.90
771 A115 945p *Cantharellus cibarius* 2.00
Nos. 765-771 (7) 10.00

1992 Winter Olympics, Albertville — A116

1989, Oct. 12 Litho. *Perf. 12½x12*

772 A116 50p Speed skating .20
773 A116 100p Women's figure skating .20
774 A116 200p Ski jumping .35
775 A116 350p Skiing .55
776 A116 500p Skiing, diff. .90
777 A116 800p Bobsled 1.40
778 A116 1000p Ice hockey 1.75
Nos. 772-778 (7) 5.35

Souvenir Sheet

Perf. 12½

779 A116 1500p Ice hockey, diff. 2.50

No. 779 contains one 32x40mm stamp.

World Cup Soccer Championships, Italy — A117

Various soccer players.

1989 Litho. *Perf. 12½*

780 A117 50p multicolored .20 .20
781 A117 100p multicolored .20 .20
782 A117 200p multicolored .30 .30
783 A117 350p multicolored .50 .50
784 A117 500p multicolored .55 .55
785 A117 800p multicolored 1.10 1.10
786 A117 1000p multicolored 1.40 1.40
Nos. 780-786 (7) 4.25 4.25

Souvenir Sheet

Perf. 13

786A A117 1500p multicolored 3.00 3.00

No. 786A contains one 40x32mm stamp.

Lilies (Lilium) — A118

1989 *Perf. 12½*

787 A118 50p Limelight .20 .20
788 A118 100p Candidum .20 .20
789 A118 200p Pardalinum .35 .35
790 A118 350p Auratum .60 .60
791 A118 500p Canadense .65 .65
792 A118 800p Enchantment 1.40 1.40
793 A118 1000p Black Dragon 1.75 1.75
Nos. 787-793 (7) 5.15 5.15

Souvenir Sheet

794 A118 1500p Lilium pyrenaicum 3.75 3.75

No. 794 contains one 32x40mm stamp.

Trains A119

Various railroad engines.

1989, May 24 Litho. *Perf. 13*

795 A119 50p multicolored .20 .20
796 A119 100p multicolored .20 .20
797 A119 200p multicolored .35 .35
798 A119 350p multicolored .65 .65
799 A119 500p multicolored .90 .90
800 A119 800p multicolored 1.40 1.40

Perf. 12½

Size: 68x27mm

801 A119 1000p multicolored 1.75 1.75
Nos. 795-801 (7) 5.45 5.45

Souvenir Sheet

Perf. 12½

802 A119 1500p multicolored 2.75 2.75

No. 802 contains one 32x40mm stamp.

La Marseillaise by Francois Rude — A120

Paintings: 100p, Armed mob. 200p, Storming the Bastille. 350p, Lafayette, Liberty, vert. 500p, Dancing around the Liberty tree. 800p, Rouget de Lisle singing La Marseillaise by Pils. 1000p, Storming the Bastille, diff. 1500p, Arms of the Republic of France.

Perf. 12½, 12x12½ (350p)

1989, July 5

803 A120 50p shown .20 .20
804 A120 100p multicolored .20 .20
805 A120 200p multicolored .35 .35
806 A120 350p multicolored, 27x44mm .65 .65
807 A120 500p multicolored .90 .90
808 A120 800p multicolored 1.40 1.40
809 A120 1000p multicolored 1.75 1.75
Nos. 803-809 (7) 5.45 5.45

Souvenir Sheet

Perf. 13

810 A120 1500p multicolored 2.50 2.50

Birds A121

Designs: 50p, Alectroenas pulcherrima. 100p, Streptopelia senegalensis. 200p, Oena capensis. 350p, Claravis mondetoura. 500p, Streptopelia roseogrisea. 800p, Otidiphaps nobilis. 1000p, Chalophapa indica. 1500p, Reinwardtoena Reinwardtsi.

1989 Litho. *Perf. 12½*

811 A121 50p multicolored .20
812 A121 100p multicolored .20
813 A121 200p multicolored .35
814 A121 350p multicolored .60
815 A121 500p multicolored .85
816 A121 800p multicolored 1.40
817 A121 1000p multicolored 1.60
Nos. 811-817 (7) 5.20

Souvenir Sheet

818 A121 1500p multicolored 3.25 3.25

Pioneers Organization — A122

1989 *Perf. 13*

819 A122 10p Children presenting flag, vert. .20 .20
820 A122 50p Children saluting, vert. .20 .20
821 A122 200p shown .85 .85
822 A122 300p Children playing ball 1.25 1.25
Nos. 819-822 (4) 2.50 2.50

Town of Cacheu, 400th Anniv. A123

1989, Nov. 30

823 A123 10p Monument, vert. .20 .20
824 A123 50p shown .20 .20
825 A123 200p Old building .85 .85
826 A123 300p Church 1.25 1.25
Nos. 823-826 (4) 2.50 2.50

Dated 1988.

A124

Designs: Prehistoric creatures.

Perf. 13, 12½x12 (100p)

1989, Sept. 15

827 A124 50p Trachodon .20 .20
828 A124 100p Edaphosaurus, 68x27mm .20 .20
829 A124 200p Mesosaurus .35 .35
830 A124 350p Elephas primigenius .60 .60
831 A124 500p Tyrannosaurus .85 .85
832 A124 800p Stegosaurus 1.40 1.40
833 A124 1000p Cervus megaceros 1.60 1.60
Nos. 827-833 (7) 5.20 5.20

Nos. 828, 831-833 horiz.

A125

1989, Apr. 10 Litho. *Perf. 13*

Designs: Musical instruments.

834 A125 50p Bombalon .20 .20
835 A125 100p Flauta .30 .20
836 A125 200p Tambor .60 .25
837 A125 350p Dondon 1.00 .35
838 A125 500p Balafon 1.25 .40
839 A125 800p Kora 1.50 .50
840 A125 1000p Nhanhero 1.75 .60
Nos. 834-840 (7) 6.60 2.50

A126

1989, July 13 *Perf. 12x12½*

Designs: Indian artifacts.

841 A126 50p Teotihuacan .20 .20
842 A126 100p Mochica .20 .20
843 A126 200p Jaina .35 .35
844 A126 350p Nayarit .60 .60
845 A126 500p Inca .85 .85
846 A126 800p Hopewell 1.40 1.40
847 A126 1000p Taina 1.60 1.60
Nos. 841-847 (7) 5.20 5.20

Souvenir Sheet

Perf. 12½

848 A126 1500p Indian statuette 2.25 2.25

Brasiliana '89 Philatelic Exhibition. Nos. 841-847 printed se-tenant with multicolored label showing scenes of colonization. No. 848 contains one 32x40mm stamp.

1992 Summer Olympics, Barcelona A127

1989, June 3 *Perf. 12½x13*

849 A127 50p Hurdles .20 .20
850 A127 100p Boxing .20 .20
851 A127 200p High jump .20 .20
852 A127 350p Sprinters in the blocks .30 .30
853 A127 500p Woman sprinter .50 .50

854 A127 800p Gymnastics .80 .80
855 A127 1000p Pole vault 1.00 1.00
Nos. 849-855 (7) 3.20 3.20

Souvenir Sheet

856 A127 1500p Soccer 1.50 1.50

No. 856 contains one 32x40mm stamp.

Wild Animals — A128

1989, Nov. 24 ***Perf. 12½***

857 A128 50p Syncerus caffer .20 .20
858 A128 100p Equus quagga .20 .20
859 A128 200p Diceros bicornis .25 .25
860 A128 350p Okapia johnstoni .40 .40
861 A128 500p Macaca mulatta .55 .55
862 A128 800p Hippopotamus amphibius .90 .90
863 A128 1000p Acinonyx jubatus 1.10 1.10
864 A128 1500p Panthera leo 1.60 1.60
Nos. 857-864 (8) 5.20 5.20

Christmas A129

Paintings of the Madonna and Child (50p) and the Adoration of the Magi.

1989, Dec. 10 ***Perf. 13***

865 A129 50p Fra Filippo Lippi .20 .20
866 A129 100p Pieter Brueghel .20 .20
867 A129 200p Mostaert .20 .20
868 A129 350p Durer .35 .35
869 A129 500p Rubens .50 .50
870 A129 800p Van der Weyden .80 .80
871 A129 1000p Francia, horiz. 1.00 1.00
Nos. 865-871 (7) 3.25 3.25

Womens' Hairstyles A130

Various hairstyles.

1989, Mar. 8 ***Perf. 12½x13***

872 A130 50p multicolored .20 .20
873 A130 100p multicolored .20 .20
874 A130 200p multicolored .30 .30
875 A130 350p multicolored .55 .55
875A A130 500p multicolored .75 .75
876 A130 800p multicolored 1.25 1.25
877 A130 1000p multicolored 1.50 1.50
Nos. 872-877 (7) 4.75 4.75

Vegetables — A131

1989, May 20 ***Perf. 12½***

878 A131 50p Capisium annum .20 .20
879 A131 100p Solanium .20 .20
880 A131 200p Curcumis peco .20 .20
881 A131 350p Solanium licopersicum .35 .35
882 A131 500p Solanium itiopium .50 .50
883 A131 800p Hibiscus esculentus .80 .80
884 A131 1000p Oseille de guine 1.00 1.00
Nos. 878-884 (7) 3.25 3.25

Visit of Pope John Paul II — A132

1990, Jan. 27 **Litho.** ***Perf. 13½***

885 A132 500p shown 1.50 1.50
886 A132 1000p multi, diff. 3.00 3.00

Souvenir Sheet

887 A132 1500p multi, diff., vert. 4.00 4.00

Souvenir Sheet

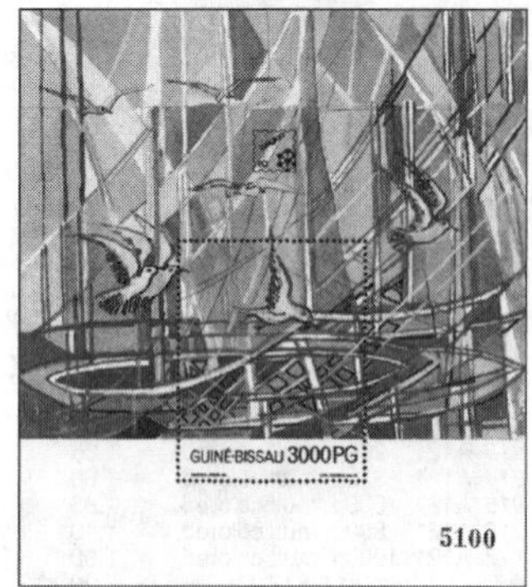

Belgica '90 — A133

1990, June 1 ***Perf. 14½***

888 A133 3000p multicolored 3.25 3.25

World Meteorology Day — A134

1990, Oct. 1 **Litho.** ***Perf. 13***

889 A134 1000p Radar weather map 1.25
890 A134 3000p Heliograph 4.00

LUBRAPEX '90 — A135

1990, Sept. 21 ***Perf. 14***

891 A135 500p Rooster, hen .65
892 A135 800p Turkey 1.00
893 A135 1000p Duck, ducklings 1.25
Nos. 891-893 (3) 2.90

Souvenir Sheet

Perf. 13½

894 A135 1500p Rooster, turkey, ducks 2.00

UN Development Program, 40th Anniv. — A136

1990 **Litho.** ***Perf. 14***

895 A136 1000p multicolored 1.40

Fight against AIDS.

Textile Manufacturing A137

No. 896: a, Gossypium hirsutum. b, Processing cotton. c, Spinning thread. d, Picking cotton. e, Moth, silkworms. f, Dyeing thread. g, Weaving. h, Animal design. i, Multicolored stripes design. j, Stripes, dots design.

1990

896 Sheet of 10 1.50
a.-j. A137 150p any single .20
897 A137 400p like #896a .35
898 A137 500p like #896g .45
899 A137 600p like #896h .55
Nos. 896-899 (4) 2.85

Carnival Masks A138

1990 **Litho.** ***Perf. 14***

900 A138 200p Mickey Mouse .20
901 A138 300p Hippopotamus .30
902 A138 600p Bull .55
903 A138 1200p Bull, diff. 1.10
Nos. 900-903 (4) 2.15

Fish A139

Designs: 300p, Pentanemus quinquarius. 400p, Psettias sabae. 500p, Chaetodipterus goreensis. 600p, Trachinotus goreensis.

1991, Mar. 10 **Litho.** ***Perf. 14***

904 A139 300p multicolored .25 .25
905 A139 400p multicolored .35 .35
906 A139 500p multicolored .40 .40
907 A139 600p multicolored .50 .50
Nos. 904-907 (4) 1.50 1.50

Fire Trucks A140

1991, Aug. 19 **Litho.** ***Perf. 14***

908 A140 200p shown .20 .20
909 A140 500p Ladder truck .40 .40
910 A140 800p Rescue vehicle .60 .60
911 A140 1500p Ambulance 1.10 1.10
Nos. 908-911 (4) 2.30 2.30

Birds — A141

Designs: 100p, Kaupifalco monogrammicus. 250p, Balearica pavonina. 350p, Bucorvus abyssinicus. 500p, Ephippiorhynchus senegalensis. 1500p, Kaupifalco monogrammicus, diff.

1991, Sept. 10

912 A141 100p multicolored .20 .20
913 A141 250p multicolored .20 .20
914 A141 350p multicolored .30 .30
915 A141 500p multicolored .40 .40
Nos. 912-915 (4) 1.10 1.10

Souvenir Sheet

Perf. 14½

916 A141 1500p multicolored 1.10 1.10

No. 916 contains one 40x50mm stamp.

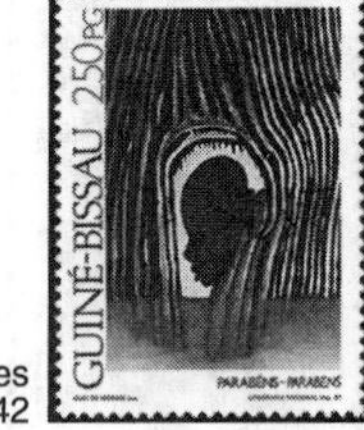

Messages A142

1991, Oct. 28 **Litho.** ***Perf. 14***

917 A142 250p Congratulations .20 .20
918 A142 400p With love .35 .35
919 A142 800p Happiness .65 .65
920 A142 1000p Seasons Greetings .80 .80
Nos. 917-920 (4) 2.00 2.00

Fruits — A143

Designs: 500p, Landolfia owariensis. 1500p, Dialium guineensis. 2000p, Adansonia digitata. 3000p, Parkia biglobosa.

1992, Mar. 25 **Litho.** ***Perf. 14***

921 A143 500p multicolored .30 .30
922 A143 1500p multicolored .75 .75
923 A143 2000p multicolored 1.10 1.10
924 A143 3000p multicolored 1.75 1.75
Nos. 921-924 (4) 3.90 3.90

Healthy Hearts — A144

1992, Apr. 7

Designs: 1500p, Cigarette butts, healthy heart. 4000p, Heart running over junk food.

925 A144 1500p multicolored .75 .75
926 A144 4000p multicolored 2.00 2.00

Traditional Costumes A145

Designs: a, 400p, Fula. b, 600p, Balanta. c, 1000p, Fula, diff. d, 1500p, Manjaco.

1992, Feb. 28 **Litho.** ***Perf. 14***

927 A145 Strip of 4, #a.-d. 1.75 1.75

Canoes A146

Designs: Nos. 928-931, Various types of canoes. No. 932, Alcedo cristata galerita.

1992, May 10

928 A146 750p multicolored .40 .40
929 A146 800p multicolored .45 .45
930 A146 1000p multicolored .60 .60
931 A146 1300p multicolored .75 .75
Nos. 928-931 (4) 2.20 2.20

Souvenir Sheet

Perf. 13½

932 A146 1500p multicolored .90 .90

Trees — A147

a, 100p, Cassia alata. b, 400p, Perlebia purpurea. c, 1000p, Caesalpina pulcherrima. d, 1500p, Adenanthera pavonina. 3000p, Caesalpina pulcherrima, diff.

1992, May 8 ***Perf. 14***

933 A147 Block of 4, #a.-d. 1.75 1.75

Souvenir Sheet

Perf. 13½

934 A147 3000p multicolored 1.75 1.75

1992 Summer Olympics, Barcelona A148

1992, July 28 Litho. *Perf. 14*

935 A148 600p Basketball .35 .35
936 A148 1000p Volleyball .60 .60
937 A148 1500p Team handball .90 .90
938 A148 2000p Soccer 1.25 1.25
Nos. 935-938 (4) 3.10 3.10

Trees A149

Designs: 1000p, Afzelia africana Smith. 1500p, Kaya senegalenses. 2000p, Militia regia. 3000p, Pterocarpus erinaceus.

1992, Sept. 11 ***Perf. 12***

939 A149 1000p multicolored .40 .40
940 A149 1500p multicolored .55 .55
941 A149 2000p multicolored .75 .75
942 A149 3000p multicolored 1.10 1.10
Nos. 939-942 (4) 2.80 2.80

Souvenir Sheet

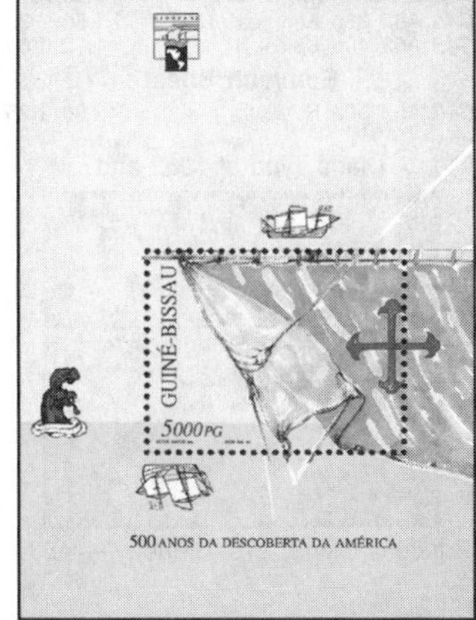

Discovery of America, 500th Anniv. — A150

1992, Sept. 18

943 A150 5000p multicolored 2.00 2.00

Genoa '92.

Procolobus Badius Temminckii A151

Designs: a, Pair in tree. b, Adult seated in vegetation c, Adult seated in tree fork. d, Female with young.

1992 Litho. *Perf. 12x11½*

944 A151 2000p Strip of 4, #a.-d. 1.75 1.75

World Wildlife Fund.

Reptiles A152

1993, May 18 Litho. *Perf. 14*

945 A152 1500p Bitis sp. .25 .25
946 A152 3000p Osteolaemus tetraspis .50 .50
947 A152 4000p Varanus nitolicus .65 .65
948 A152 5000p Agama agama .80 .80
a. Souvenir sheet of 4, #945-948 2.25 2.25
Nos. 945-948 (4) 2.20 2.20

Souvenir Sheet

Union of Portuguese Speaking Capitals — A153

1993, July 30 Litho. *Perf. 13½*

949 A153 6000p Fort 1.00 1.00

Brasiliana '93.

Tourism — A154

Designs: a, 1000p. b, 2000p. c, 4000p. d, 5000p. Illustration reduced.

1993, Nov. 15 Litho. *Perf. 14*

950 A154 Block of 4, #a.-d. 2.00 2.00

Traditional Jewelry A155

1993, Nov. 30 ***Perf. 14½***

951 A155 1500p Bracelet .20 .20
952 A155 3000p Mask pendant .45 .45
953 A155 4000p Circle pendant .60 .60
954 A155 5000p Filigree pendant .75 .75
Nos. 951-954 (4) 2.00 2.00

1994, Nov. 30

Souvenir Sheet

955 A155 18,000p like #952 3.75 3.75

Hong Kong '94 (No. 955). No. 955 has continuous design.

1994 World Cup Soccer Championships, US — A156

Various stylized designs of player, ball, net.

1994, June 17 Litho. *Perf. 14*

956 A156 4000p multicolored .85 .85
957 A156 5000p multicolored 1.00 1.00
958 A156 5500p multicolored 1.10 1.10
959 A156 6500p multicolored 1.40 1.40
Nos. 956-959 (4) 4.35 4.35

Flowering Plants — A157

Designs: 2000p, Erythrina senegalensis. 3000p, Cassia occidentalis. 4000p, Gardenia ternifolia. 6000p, Cochlospermum tinctorium.

1994, May 30 Litho. *Perf. 14*

960 A157 2000p multicolored .40 .40
961 A157 3000p multicolored .60 .60
962 A157 4000p multicolored .75 .75
963 A157 6000p multicolored 1.25 1.25
Nos. 960-963 (4) 3.00 3.00

Snakes — A158

#964: a, Dasypeltis scabra. b, Philothamnus. c, Naja melanoleuca. d, Python sebae.
15,000p, Thelotornis kirtlandii.

1994, Aug. 16 Litho. *Perf. 14*

964 A158 5000p Block of 4, #a.-d. 4.50 4.50

Souvenir Sheet

Perf. 13½

965 A158 15,000p multicolored 3.25 3.25

PHILAKOREA '94, SINGPEX '94. No. 965 contains one 60x50mm stamp.

Palmeira Dendem — A159

3000p, Climbing tree to pick fruit. 6500p, Hand processing palm fruit into baskets. 7500p, Mechanical processing. 8000p, Palm oil, uses.

1995, Feb. 27 Litho. *Perf. 14*

966 A159 3000p multicolored .30 .30
967 A159 6500p multicolored .60 .60
968 A159 7500p multicolored .70 .70
969 A159 8000p multicolored .75 .75
Nos. 966-969 (4) 2.35 2.35

FAO, 50th Anniv. A160

1995 Litho. *Perf. 13½*

970 A160 3000p Net fishing .40 .40
971 A160 6500p Disking field .80 .80
972 A160 7500p Hands holding fruit .95 .95
973 A160 8000p Vendors along road 1.00 1.00
a. Souvenir sheet of 2, #973-973 2.00 2.00
Nos. 970-973 (4) 3.15 3.15

UN, 50th Anniv. — A161

1995, Oct. 24 Litho. *Perf. 13½*

974 A161 4000p shown .50 .50
975 A161 5500p UN flag .70 .70
976 A161 7500p Natl. flag .95 .95
977 A161 8000p Hand on dove 1.00 1.00
Nos. 974-977 (4) 3.15 3.15

Souvenir Sheet

978 A161 15,000p UN emblem 2.00 2.00

AIR POST STAMPS

Liftoff of Soyuz Spacecraft AP1

Apollo-Soyuz mission: 10p, Launch of Apollo spacecraft. 15p, Leonov, Stafford and meeting in space. 20p, Eclipse of the sun. 30p, Infra-red photo of Earth. 40p, Return to Earth. 50p, Apollo and Soyuz docked, horiz.

1976, Oct. 4 *Perf. 13½*

C10 AP1 5p multicolored
C10A AP1 10p multicolored
C10B AP1 15p multicolored
C10C AP1 20p multicolored
C10D AP1 30p multicolored
C10E AP1 40p multicolored
Nos. C10-C10E (6) 6.50

Souvenir Sheet

C10F AP1 50p multicolored 3.50

No. C10F contains one 60x42mm stamp. Nos. C10-C10E exist in souvenir sheets of one, perf. and imperf.

Viking Spacecraft Orbiting Mars AP2

35p, Viking gathering Martian soil samples.

1977, Jan. 27

C11 AP2 25p multicolored 2.00 1.00
C11A AP2 35p multicolored 2.00 1.00

Nos. 372-373 Surcharged with New Value and "CORREIO AEREO" in Black on Silver Panels

1978 Litho. *Perf. 13½*

C12 A32 15p on 3.50p multi .80 .40
C13 A32 30p on 50c multi 1.00 .60

History of Aviation Type of 1980

1980 Litho. *Perf. 13½*

C14 A38 35p Willy de Houthulst, Hanriot HD.1 1.25 .60
C14A A38 40p Charles Guynemer, Spad S. VII 1.50 .70

Souvenir Sheet

C14B A38 50p Comdr. de Rose, Nieuport 3.00 1.00

No. C14B contains one stamp 37x55mm.

Winter Olympics Type of 1980

1980

C15 A39 35p Slalom 1.25 .60
C16 A39 40p Figure skating 1.50 .70

Souvenir Sheet

C17 A39 50p Ice hockey, horiz. 2.25 1.00

Summer Olympics Type of 1980

1980, Aug. Litho. *Perf. 13½*

C18 A40 35p Somersault 1.25 .60
C19 A40 40p Running 1.50 .70

Souvenir Sheet

C20 A40 50p Emblem 3.50 1.00

Literacy Type of 1980

1980, Aug. Litho. *Perf. 13½*

C21 A41 15p like #391 .75 .30
C22 A41 25p like #392 1.25 .50

Space Type of 1981

35p, Viking 1 & 2. 40p, Apollo-Soyuz craft & crew. 50p, Apollo 11 crew, craft & emblem.

1981, May Litho. *Perf. 13½*

C23 A45 35p multicolored 1.25 .60
C24 A45 40p multicolored 1.50 .70

Souvenir Sheet

C25 A45 50p multicolored 2.25 1.25

No. C25 contains one stamp 60x42mm.

Soccer Type of 1981

Designs: 35p, Rummenigge, Germany. 40p, Kempes, Argentina. 50p, Juanito, Spain.

1981, May

C26 A46 35p multicolored 1.25 .60
C27 A46 40p multicolored 1.50 .70

Souvenir Sheet

C28 A46 50p multicolored 2.25 1.25

No. C28 contains one stamp 56x40mm.

Royal Wedding Type of 1981

1981 Litho. *Perf. 13½*

C29 A47 35p Palace 1.40 1.00
C30 A47 40p Prince of Wales arms 1.50 1.25

Souvenir Sheet

C31 A47 50p Couple 2.25 1.25

Picasso Type of 1981

1981, Dec. Litho. *Perf. 13½*

C32 A48 35p multicolored 1.90 1.00
C33 A48 40p multicolored 2.00 1.25

Souvenir Sheet

C34 A48 50p multicolored 2.25 1.25

No. C34 contains one stamp 41x50mm.

Navigator Type of 1981

35p, Francis Drake, Golden Hinde. 40p, James Cook, Endeavor. 50p, Columbus, Santa Maria.

1981 Litho. *Perf. 13½*

C35 A49 35p multicolored 1.90 1.00
C36 A49 40p multicolored 2.00 1.25

Souvenir Sheet

C37 A49 50p multicolored 2.25 1.25

Christmas Type of 1981

1981

C38 A50 30p Memling 1.90 1.00
C39 A50 35p Bellini, diff. 2.00 1.25

Souvenir Sheet

C40 A50 50p Fra Angelico 3.50 1.25

No. C40 contains one 35x59mm stamp.

Scout Type of 1982

1982, June 9 Litho. *Perf. 13½*

C41 A51 35p Canoeing 1.50 .70
C42 A51 40p Flying model planes 1.90 1.00

Souvenir Sheet

C43 A51 50p Playing chess 2.25 1.25

No. C43 contains one 48x38mm stamp.

Soccer Type of 1982

1982, June 13 Litho. *Perf. 13½*

C44 A52 35p Kempes 1.50 .70
C45 A52 40p Kaltz 1.90 1.00

Souvenir Sheet

C46 A52 50p Stadium 3.00 1.25

Diana Type of 1982 and

Princess Diana, 21st Birthday — A53a

1982

C47 A53 35p multicolored 1.50 .70
C48 A53 40p multicolored 1.90 1.00

Souvenir Sheet

C49 A53 50p multi, vert. 2.00 1.00

1982, Oct. 1 Litho. & Embossed

C49A A53a 200p gold & multi 5.00

Souvenir Sheet

C49B A53a 200p gold & multi, vert. 5.00

For overprints see Nos. 456A-456B.

Audubon Birth Bicent. — AP3

1985, Apr. 16 Litho. *Perf. 12*

C50 AP3 5p Brown pelican .40
C51 AP3 10p American white pelican .60
C52 AP3 20p Great blue heron .75
C53 AP3 40p American flamingo 1.50
Nos. C50-C53 (4) 3.25

GUYANA

gī-ˈa-nə

LOCATION — Northeast coast of South America
GOVT. — Republic
AREA — 83,000 sq. mi.
POP. — 705,156 (1999 est.)
CAPITAL — Georgetown

The former Crown Colony of British Guiana became an independent member of the British Commonwealth May 26, 1966, taking the name Guyana. On February 23, 1970, Guyana became a republic, remaining a Commonwealth nation.

100 Cents = 1 Dollar

Catalogue values for all unused stamps in this country are for Never Hinged items.

Watermark

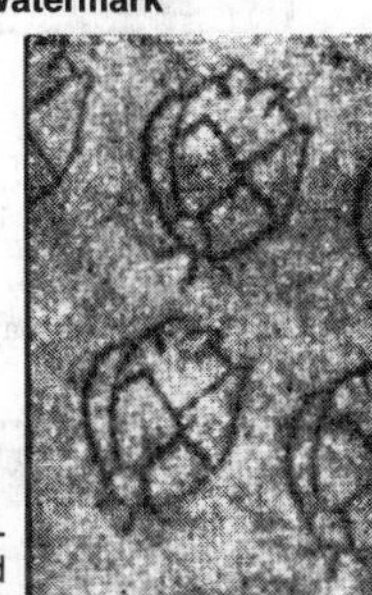

Wmk. 364- Lotus Bud Multiple

British Guiana #254-256, 258-260, 267 Overprinted

Perf. 12½x13, 13

1966, May 26 Wmk. 4 Engr.

1	A60	2c	dark green	.30	.20
1A	A60	3c	red brn & ol	2.50	2.50
2	A61	4c	violet	1.00	.20
3	A60	6c	yellow green	.30	.20
4	A60	8c	ultra	1.00	.20
5	A61	12c	brn & blk	1.25	.20
6	A61	$5	blk & ultra	24.00	*42.50*
			Nos. 1-6 (7)	30.35	46.00

Same Overprint on British Guiana Stamps and Types of 1954

Engr.; Center Litho. on $1

1966-67 Wmk. 314 Upright

7	A60	1c	black ('67)	.20	.20
8	A60	3c	red brn & ol (#279)	.20	.20
9	A61	4c	violet ('67)	.20	.20
10	A60	5c	blk & red (#280)	.20	.20
10A	A60	6c	yel green ('67)	.20	.20
11	A60	8c	ultra ('67)	.20	.20
12	A61	12c	brn & blk (#281)	.20	.20
13	A60	24c	org & blk (#282)	.50	.25
14	A60	36c	blk & rose (#283)	.30	.25
15	A61	48c	red brn & ultra (#284)	4.00	4.00
16	A61	72c	emer & rose (#285)	.50	.40
17	A60	$1	blk & multi (#286)	.65	.55
18	A60	$2	mag (#287)	1.40	.95
19	A61	$5	black & ultra	4.50	4.00
			Nos. 7-19 (14)	13.25	11.80

For surcharges see Nos. 543, 544A, 625-626, 1446.

1966-67 Wmk. 314 Sideways

7a	A60	1c	black	.20	.20
9a	A61	4c	violet	.20	.20
11a	A60	8c	ultramarine	.20	.20
12a	A61	12c	brown & black ('67)	.20	.20
13a	A60	24c	orange & black	1.75	.45
14a	A60	36c	black & rose ('67)	.25	*1.10*
15a	A61	48c	red brown & ultra	.25	.25
16a	A61	72c	emerald & rose ('67)	1.50	2.75
17a	A60	$1	black & multi ('67)	2.10	2.75
18a	A60	$2	magenta ('67)	2.50	2.75
19a	A61	$5	black & ultra ('67)	1.25	2.50
			Nos. 7a-19a (11)	10.40	13.35

See Nos. 32-32T and note. For surcharges see Nos. 544, 627-628, 1447.

Flag and Map of Guyana — A1

Designs: 25c, $1, Arms of Guyana.

Unwmk.

1966, May 26 Photo. *Perf. 14*

20	A1	5c	violet & multi	.20	.20
21	A1	15c	dk red brown & multi	.20	.20
22	A1	25c	brt blue & multi	.25	.25
23	A1	$1	sepia & multi	.80	.80
			Nos. 20-23 (4)	1.45	1.45

Guyana's independence, May 26, 1966.

Bank of Guyana A2

1966, Oct. 11 *Perf. 13½x14*

24	A2	5c	yel grn, blue, blk & gold	.20	.20
25	A2	25c	blue, black & gold	.20	.20

Establishment of the Bank of Guyana.

British Guiana No. 13 — A3

1967, Feb. 23 Litho. *Perf. 12½*

26	A3	5c	multicolored	.20	.20
	a.		Imperf., pair		
27	A3	25c	multicolored	.20	.20

Issued to honor the unique British Guiana 1c black on magenta stamp of 1856.

Canceled to Order

Remainders of Nos. 26-30, 33-38 and 54-67 were canceled and sold by the Post Office in 1969. Values are for these canceled to order stamps. Postally used copies do not command a significant premium.

Chateau Margot — A4

Designs: 15c, Independence Arch. 25c, Guyana Fort, Fort Island, horiz. $1, Parliament, National Assembly Hall, horiz.

Perf. 14, 14½x14, 14x14½

1967, May 26 Photo. Unwmk.

28	A4	6c	multicolored	.20	.20
29	A4	15c	multicolored	.20	.20
30	A4	25c	multicolored	.20	.20
31	A4	$1	multicolored	.30	.20
			Nos. 28-31 (4)	.90	.80

First anniversary of independence.

British Guiana Stamps and Types of 1954 Locally Overprinted

1967 Wmk. 4

32	A60	1c	black	.20	.20
32A	A60	2c	dark green	.20	.20
32B	A60	3c	red brown & ol	.55	.20
32C	A61	4c	violet	.20	.20
32D	A60	6c	yellow green	.20	.20
32E	A60	8c	ultramarine	.20	.20
32F	A61	12c	brown & black	.20	.20
32G	A60	$2	magenta	2.25	2.25
32H	A61	$5	black & ultra	2.50	2.50
			Nos. 32-32H (9)	6.50	6.15

The 24c with Wmk. 4 also exists with this overprint. Value $225.

1967-68 Wmk. 314 Upright

32I	A60	1c	black ('68)	.20	.20
32J	A60	2c	dk green ('68)	.20	.20
32K	A60	3c	red brown & ol	.20	.20
32L	A61	4c	violet ('68)	.20	.20
32M	A60	5c	black & red	1.10	1.10
32N	A60	6c	yel green ('68)	.20	.20
32O	A60	24c	orange & blk	2.00	.25
32P	A60	36c	black & rose	.85	.20
32Q	A61	48c	red brn & ultra	.85	.50
32R	A61	72c	emer & rose	1.25	.75
32S	A60	$1	black & multi	1.60	1.00
32T	A60	$2	magenta	1.60	1.60
			Nos. 32I-32T (12)	10.25	6.40

The 1c, 4c, 6c, 8c and $5 with Wmk. 314 were not issued without overprint.

For surcharges see Nos. 540, 542, 543A.

"Millie," the Bilingual Macaw — A5

Wicketkeeper, Emblem of West Indies Cricket Team — A6

Christmas Issues

1967, Nov. 6 *Perf. 14½x14*

33	A5	5c	olive green & multi	.20	.20
33A	A5	25c	purple & multi	.20	.20

1968, Jan. 22

34	A5	5c	red & multi	.20	.20
35	A5	25c	yel green & multi	.20	.20

1968, Jan. 8 Photo. *Perf. 14*

Designs: 6c, Batsman and emblem of Marylebone Cricket Club. 25c, Bowler and emblem of West Indies Cricket Team.

36	A6	5c	multicolored	.20	.20
37	A6	6c	multicolored	.20	.20
38	A6	25c	multicolored	.35	.20
	a.		Strip of 3, #36-38	.75	.30

Visit of the Marylebone Cricket Club to the West Indies, Jan.-Feb. 1968. Printed in sheets of 9.

Pike Cichlid — A7

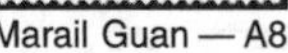

Marail Guan — A8

Christ of St. John of the Cross, by Salvador Dali — A9

Designs: 2c, Piranha. 3c, Cichla ocellaris (fish). 5c, Armored catfish. 6c, Two-spotted cichlid. 15c, Harpy eagle. 20c, Hoatzin. 25c, Andean cock-of-the-rock. 40c, Great kiskadee. 50c, Agouti. 60c, Peccary. $1, Paca. $2, Armadillo. $5, Ocelot.

Perf. 14x14½, 14½x14

1968, Mar. 4 Photo. Unwmk.

39	A7	1c	chalky blue & multi	.20	.20
40	A7	2c	gray & multi	.20	.20
41	A7	3c	grnsh bl & multi	.20	.20
42	A7	5c	ultra & multi	.20	.20
43	A7	6c	brt olive & multi	.45	.20
44	A8	10c	yel green & multi	.50	.20
45	A8	15c	green & multi	1.50	.20
46	A8	20c	ap grn & multi	.55	.20
47	A8	25c	brt green & multi	.55	.20
48	A8	40c	pale brn & multi	1.40	.65
49	A7	50c	rose brn & multi	.75	.50
50	A7	60c	lilac rose & multi	.75	.20
51	A7	$1	dp orange & multi	.75	.20
52	A7	$2	ocher & multi	.95	*1.90*
53	A7	$5	red & multi	.95	*2.75*
			Nos. 39-53 (15)	9.90	8.00

See Nos. 68-82.

For overprints & surcharges see #357, 410-413, 603, 752, 756, 761a, 1463, 1501, 1839, 2045.

1968, Mar. 25 ***Perf. 14x14½***

54 A9 5c car rose & multi .20 .20
55 A9 25c brt violet & multi .25 .20

Easter.

"Efficiency Year" — A10

Designs: 30c, 40c, "Savings bonds."

1968, July 22 Litho. ***Perf. 14***

56 A10 6c green & multi .20 .20
57 A10 25c fawn & multi .20 .20
58 A10 30c multicolored .20 .20
59 A10 40c multicolored .20 .20
Nos. 56-59 (4) .80 .80

Issued to promote the sale of savings bonds and to publicize Efficiency Year.

Open Koran A11

Perf. 14x13½

1968, Oct. 9 Photo. Unwmk.

60 A11 6c sal pink, gold & blk .20 .20
61 A11 25c pale vio, gold & blk .20 .20
62 A11 30c pale yel grn, gold & blk .20 .20
63 A11 40c pale blue, gold & blk .20 .20
Nos. 60-63 (4) .80 .80

Koran's 1400th anniversary.

For overprints & surcharges see #354, 355, 441, 445, 487-488, 575, 630, 1464-1465.

Dish Aerials, Thomas Lands, Guyana — A12

Designs: 30c, 40c, Map showing connection between Guyana and Trinidad. All stamps are inscribed: "Guyana Sends Christmas Greetings to the World."

Wmk. 364

1968, Nov. 11 Litho. ***Perf. 14***

64 A12 6c blue, gray, ocher & emer .20 .20
65 A12 25c brt rose lil, brn & emer .20 .20
66 A12 30c blue grn & dk blue grn .20 .20
67 A12 40c blue grn & red .20 .20
Nos. 64-67 (4) .80 .80

Christmas; communications link with Trinidad by the tropospheric scatter system.

Types of 1968

Designs as before.

Perf. 14x14½, 14½x14

1968 Photo. Wmk. 364

68 A7 1c chalky bl & multi .20 .20
69 A7 2c gray & multi .20 *.25*
70 A7 3c grnsh bl & multi .20 *.55*
71 A7 5c ultra & multi .20 .20
72 A7 6c brt olive & multi .20 *.55*
73 A8 10c yel grn & multi .65 .55
74 A8 15c green & multi .65 .20
75 A8 20c apple grn & multi .65 .65
76 A8 25c brt green & multi .65 .20
77 A8 40c pale brn & multi 1.25 .65
78 A7 50c rose brn & multi .70 .20
79 A7 60c lilac rose & multi .75 *.90*
80 A7 $1 dp org & multi 1.50 1.10
81 A7 $2 ocher & multi 2.10 *3.00*
82 A7 $5 red & multi 2.10 *4.50*
Nos. 68-82 (15) 12.00 13.70

For overprints & surcharges see #373, 376-377, 413D, 565-566, 633, 635, 704-705, 744, 749, 752a, 757-758, 761-762, 1862-1863, 1981, O2.

Celebrants Spraying Perfumed Powder — A13

Phagwah (Holi) Hindu Festival: 25c, 40c, Two celebrants spraying colored water.

1969, Feb. 26 Litho. ***Perf. 13½***

83 A13 6c multicolored .20 .20
84 A13 25c multicolored .20 .20
85 A13 30c multicolored .20 .20
86 A13 40c multicolored .20 .20
Nos. 83-86 (4) .80 .80

The Last Supper, by Salvador Dali A14

1969, Mar. 10 Photo. ***Perf. 13***

87 A14 6c dp carmine & multi .20 .20
88 A14 25c green & multi .20 .20
89 A14 30c org brown & multi .20 .20
90 A14 40c dp violet & multi .20 .20
Nos. 87-90 (4) .80 .80

Easter. For overprints and surcharges see Nos. 393-394, 482-485, 572, 576, 634, 765, 772, 1407-1410, 1813, 1815-1817, 2050.

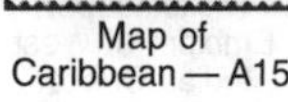

Map of Caribbean — A15

Prow of Aluminum Ship — A16

Design: 25c, "Strength in Unity," horiz.

Wmk. 364

1969, Apr. 30 Litho. ***Perf. 13½***

91 A15 6c violet blue & multi .20 .20
92 A15 25c brt rose, yel & brown .20 .20

1st anniv. of CARIFTA (Caribbean Free Trade Area).

1969, Apr. 30 ***Perf. 12x11, 11x12***

50th Anniv. of the ILO: 40c, Bauxite processing plant, horiz.

93 A16 30c black, blue & silver .40 .20
94 A16 40c multicolored .50 .25

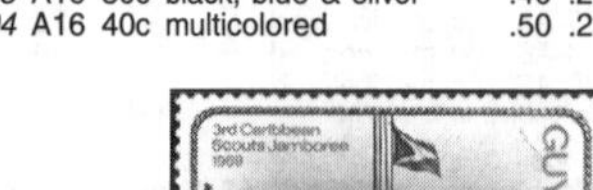

Flag Raising A17

Designs: 8c, 30c, Campfire.

1969, Aug. 13 Litho. ***Perf. 13½x13***

95 A17 6c pale green & multi .20 .20
96 A17 8c orange & multi .20 .20
97 A17 25c pale brown & multi .20 .20
98 A17 30c multicolored .20 .20
99 A17 50c rose & multi .20 .20
Nos. 95-99 (5) 1.00 1.00

60th anniv. of Scouting in Guyana; 3rd Caribbean Scout Jamboree, Georgetown, Aug. 13-22. For overprints and surcharges see Nos. 392, 395, 397, 402, 404-405, 453.

Gandhi and Spinning Wheel A18

1969, Oct. 1 ***Perf. 14½x14***

100 A18 6c olive, blk & lt brn .20 *.50*
101 A18 15c rose lilac, blk & lt brn .60 .50

Mohandas K. Gandhi (1868-1948), leader in India's fight for independence.

Mother Sally Troupe — A19

City Hall, Georgetown — A20

1969, Nov. 17 ***Perf. 14x13½***

102 A19 5c multicolored .20 .20
103 A20 6c blue & multi .20 .20
104 A19 25c multicolored .20 .20
105 A20 60c orange & multi .20 .20
Nos. 102-105 (4) .80 .80

Christmas. The 5c, 6c, and 25c exist without the "Christmas 1969" overprint.

Prime Minister Forbes Burnham and Map — A21

Descent from the Cross, by Rubens — A22

6c, "Rural Self Help Project" (man & woman building house). 15c, University of Guyana, horiz. 25c, President's Residence, horiz.

1970, Feb. 23 Litho. ***Perf. 14***

106 A21 5c blue, brn & ocher .20 .20
107 A21 6c blue, blk ocher & brn .20 .20
108 A21 15c apple grn & multi .20 .20
109 A21 25c multicolored .20 .20
Nos. 106-109 (4) .80 .80

Issued for Republic Day, Feb. 23, 1970.

1970, Mar. 24 ***Perf. 14x14½***

Easter: 6c, 25c, Christ on the Cross, by Rubens.

110 A22 5c blue & multi .20 .20
111 A22 6c rose lilac & multi .20 .20
112 A22 15c dark red & multi .20 .20
113 A22 25c yellow & multi .20 .20
Nos. 110-113 (4) .80 .80

"Peace" and UN Emblem A23

UN 25th Anniv.: 6c, 25c, UN emblem, panning for gold and drilling for minerals.

1970, Oct. 26 ***Perf. 14½x14***

114 A23 5c red & multi .20 .20
115 A23 6c blue & multi .20 .20
116 A23 15c multicolored .20 .20
117 A23 25c brown & multi .20 .20
Nos. 114-117 (4) .80 .80

Mother and Child, by Philip Moore — A24

1970, Dec. 8 Litho. ***Perf. 13½***

118 A24 5c violet & multi .20 .20
119 A24 6c brown & multi .20 .20
120 A24 15c dk green & multi .20 .20
121 A24 25c maroon & multi .20 .20
Nos. 118-121 (4) .80 .80

Christmas.

National Cooperative Bank — A25

1971, Feb. 23 Wmk. 364 ***Perf. 14***

122 A25 6c red & multi .20 .20
123 A25 15c yellow & multi .20 .20
124 A25 25c ultra & multi .20 .20
Nos. 122-124 (3) .60 .60

Republic Day.

"Togetherness, Vision, Understanding" A26

Volunteer Felling Tree, by John Criswick — A27

1971, Mar. 22 ***Perf. 14½x14***

125 A26 5c yel grn & multi .20 .20
126 A26 6c lil rose & multi .20 .20
127 A26 15c multicolored .20 .20
128 A26 25c yellow & multi .20 .20
Nos. 125-128 (4) .80 .80

Intl. year against racial discrimination.

1971, July 19 ***Perf. 14***

129 A27 5c blue & multi .20 .20
130 A27 20c green & multi .20 .20
131 A27 25c yellow & multi .20 .20
132 A27 50c brown & multi .40 *1.25*
Nos. 129-132 (4) 1.00 1.85

1st anniv. of the Natl. Self-help Road Project.

Yellow Allamanda — A28

Flora: 1c, Pitcher plant of Mt. Roraima. 3c, Hanging heliconia. 5c, Annatto tree. 6c, Cannonball tree. 10c, Cattleya violacea. 15c, Christmas orchid. 20c, Paphinia cristata. 25c, Gongora quinquinervis. 40c, Tiger beard. 50c, Guzmania lingulata. 60c, Soldier's cap. $1,

Chelonanthus uliginoides. $2, Norantea guianensis. $5, Odontadenia grandiflora.

1971-76 Litho. *Perf. 13x13½*

133 A28 1c multi ('72) .20 .20
134 A28 2c lilac & multi .20 .20
135 A28 3c multicolored .20 .20
136 A28 5c lt blue & multi .20 .20
137 A28 6c dull rose & multi .20 .20

Perf. 13½

138 A28 10c multi ('72) 2.50 .20
a. Perf. 13
139 A28 15c multi ('72) .50 .20
a. Perf. 13 ('76) .20 .20
140 A28 20c multi ('72) 2.25 .25
a. Perf. 13
141 A28 25c multi, 25c at center ('72) 3.75 *5.75*
141A A28 25c multi, 25c right of center ('73) .25 .25
b. Perf. 13 ('76) .25 .25
142 A28 40c multi ('72) 2.75 .20
143 A28 50c multi ('73) .30 .30
144 A28 60c multi ('73) .25 .25
145 A28 $1 multi ('73) .25 .25
146 A28 $2 multi ('73) .30 .30
147 A28 $5 multi ('73) .40 .40
Nos. 133-147 (16) 14.50 9.35

No. 141 has 2 blossoms at left, 3 at right; this is reversed on No. 141A.

The overprint "REVENUE / ONLY" between rules was applied to Nos. 134-136, 141A, 142-147 in 1975. Postal use was permitted in Nov.-Dec., 1975.

See Nos. 433-434, 731-732.

For overprints and surcharges see Nos. 192, 209, 234, 331-335, 351, 358-359, 367, 370, 372, 374-375A, 379-383, 385-390A, 401, 407, 422-425, 433-434, 438-440, 447, 450, 451, 457-458, 460-461, 464-466, 497-500, 545-546, 550, 563-564, 597, 602, 618, 631-632, 641-642, 666-667, 727, 747-748, 750-751, 753-754, 759-760, 803, 805, 807-808, 810-812, 847-848, 910-911, 995, 1361, 1382-1383, 1385-1386, 1391-1392, 1452, 1454, 1456-1460, 1466, 1499, 1778-1779, 1781-1784, 1837-1838, 1870-1872, 1898-1900, 2046-2049, 2225-2227, C2-C4, O1, O3-O5, O7, O13-O14, Q1-Q4, QO1.

The Lord's Prayer, by School Girl Veronica Bassoo — A29

Guyana Masker, by School Boy Michael Austin — A30

Perf. 13½x14, 14x13½

1971, Nov. 15 Litho. Wmk. 364

148 A29 5c brt green & multi .20 .20
149 A29 20c brt green & multi .20 .20
150 A30 25c multicolored .20 .20
151 A30 50c multicolored .30 .30
Nos. 148-151 (4) .90 .90

Christmas.

Guyana Dollar — A31

Handclasp and Mosque — A32

1972, Feb. 23 Litho. *Perf. 14½x14*

152 A31 5c blk, dp org & silver .20 .20
153 A31 20c blk, dp lil rose & sil .20 .20
154 A31 25c black, ultra & silver .20 .20
155 A31 50c black, emerald & silver .35 .35
Nos. 152-155 (4) .95 .95

Republic Day.

1972, Apr. 3 *Perf. 14*

156 A32 5c brown & multi .20 .20
157 A32 25c blue & multi .20 .20
158 A32 30c green & multi .20 .20
159 A32 60c yellow brn & multi .30 .30
Nos. 156-159 (4) .90 .90

Youman Nabi (Peaceful Prophet), Mohammedan festival.

Map of South America, Emblem of Non-aligned Countries — A33

CARIFESTA '72 Emblem — A34

1972, July 20

160 A33 8c violet & multi .20 .20
161 A33 25c yellow grn & multi .20 .20
162 A33 40c orange & multi .20 .20
163 A33 50c red brown & multi .25 .25
Nos. 160-163 (4) .85 .85

Conf. of Foreign Ministers of Nonaligned Countries, Georgetown, Aug. 7-12.

For overprints & surcharges see #573, 611, O17.

1972, Aug. 25

164 A34 8c orange & multi .20 .20
165 A34 25c orange & multi .20 .20
166 A34 40c orange & multi .20 .25
167 A34 50c orange & multi .25 .35
Nos. 164-167 (4) .85 1.00

Caribbean Festival of Arts (CARIFESTA), Georgetown, Aug. 25-Sept. 15.

Holy Family — A35

1972, Oct. 18 Litho. *Perf. 13x13½*

168 A35 8c blue & multi .20 .20
169 A35 25c blue & multi .20 .20
170 A35 40c blue & multi .20 .25
171 A35 50c blue & multi .20 .30
Nos. 168-171 (4) .80 .95

Christmas.

Umana Yana (Meeting Place of Wai Wai Chiefs) — A36

1973, Feb. 23 Litho. *Perf. 14x14½*

Designs: 25c, 40c, Bethel Chapel.

172 A36 8c brt blue & multi .20 .20
173 A36 25c rose red & multi .20 .20
174 A36 40c emerald & multi .20 .20
175 A36 50c black & multi .25 .25
Nos. 172-175 (4) .85 .85

Republic Day.

Pomegranate, Fertility and Church Symbol — A37

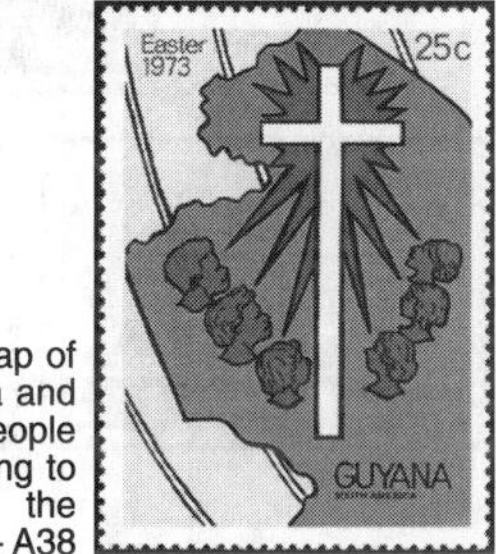

Map of Guyana and People Looking to the Cross — A38

1973, Apr. 19 *Perf. 14x14½, 13½*

176 A37 8c pink & multi .20 .20
177 A38 25c yellow & multi .20 .20
178 A38 40c ultra & multi .20 .20
179 A37 50c yellow & multi .20 .20
Nos. 176-179 (4) .80 .80

Easter.

Symbolic of Blood Donation — A39

Perf. 14x14½

1973, Oct. 1 Wmk. 364

180 A39 8c red & black .20 .20
181 A39 25c red & lilac .20 .20
182 A39 40c red & vio blue .30 *.35*
183 A39 50c red & brown .40 *.75*
Nos. 180-183 (4) 1.10 1.50

Guyana Red Cross, 25th anniversary.

Steel Band, Star, Pegasus Hotel — A40

Madonna and Child, St. Philip's Anglican Church, Georgetown — A41

1973, Nov. 20 Litho. *Perf. 14x14½*

184 A40 8c lilac & multi .20 .20
185 A40 25c lilac & multi .20 .20

Perf. 13½x14

186 A41 40c violet blue & multi .25 *.50*
187 A41 50c violet blue & multi .35 *.50*
Nos. 184-187 (4) 1.00 1.40

Christmas.

"One People, One Nation, One Destiny" — A42

Designs: 25c, 50c, Wai Wai Indian.

1974, Feb. 23 Litho. *Perf. 13½*

188 A42 8c multicolored .20 .20
189 A42 25c multicolored .20 .20
190 A42 40c multicolored .20 *.30*
191 A42 50c multicolored .20 *.40*
Nos. 188-191 (4) .80 1.10

Republic Day.

No. 137 Surcharged with New Value and 2 Bars

Perf. 13x13½

1974, Mar. 18 Wmk. 364

192 A28 8c on 6c multi .20 .20

For overprints and surcharges see Nos. 424, 459, 474-478, 1453, 1500, 1780.

Crucifix Super-imposed on Eddy Bow Kite — A43

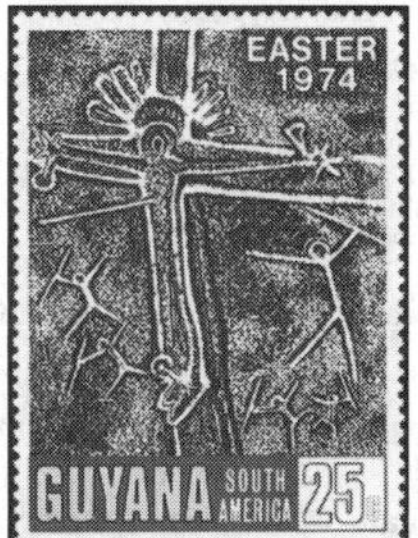

Crucifix in Pre-Columbian Timehri Style — A44

1974, Apr. 8 *Perf. 13½x14*

193 A43 8c green & multi .20 .20
194 A44 25c black, green & gray .20 .20
195 A44 40c black, gray & car .20 .20
196 A43 50c gold & multi .20 .20
Nos. 193-196 (4) .80 .80

Easter.

UPU Emblem and British Guiana Type of 1863 — A45

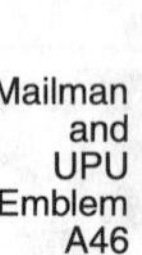

Mailman and UPU Emblem A46

1974, June 18 Litho. *Perf. 14, 14½*

197 A45 8c rose & multi .25 .20
198 A46 25c yellow green & multi .35 .20
199 A45 40c blue & multi .35 .25
200 A46 50c yellow green & multi .45 .35
Nos. 197-200 (4) 1.40 1.00

Centenary of Universal Postal Union.

Girl Guides Holding Banner A47

Designs: 25c, 40c, Guides in camp cooking and carrying water. 50c, Like 8c.

1974, Aug. 1 *Perf. 14½*

201 A47 8c multicolored .20 .20
202 A47 25c multicolored .30 .20
203 A47 40c multicolored .45 .30
204 A47 50c multicolored .45 .40
a. Souvenir sheet of 4, #201-204 1.50 1.50
Nos. 201-204 (4) 1.40 1.10

Girl Guides of Guyana, 50th anniv. For overprints see Nos. 574, 1352.

Buck Toyeau — A48

Christmas (Fruit): 35c, Carambola (starfruit) and awaras. 50c, Pawpaw and tangerine. $1, Pineapple and sapodillas.

1974, Nov. 18 Litho. *Perf. 14x13½*

205 A48 8c multicolored .20 .20
206 A48 35c multicolored .20 .20
207 A48 50c multicolored .20 .20
208 A48 $1 multicolored .30 .50
a. Souvenir sheet of 4, #205-208 1.00 *2.50*
Nos. 205-208 (4) .90 1.10

For overprints & surcharges see #551, 612, 716.

No. 135 Surcharged with New Value and Two Bars

1975, Jan. 20 Litho. *Perf. 13x13½*

209 A28 8c on 3c multi .20 .20

For surcharge see No. 423.

Golden Arrow of Courage — A49

Republic Day: 35c, Cacique's Crown of Honour. 50c, Cacique's Crown of Valour. $1, Order of Excellence.

1975, Feb. 23 *Perf. 13x13½*

210 A49 10c brown & multi .20 .20
211 A49 35c brown red & multi .20 .20
212 A49 50c green & multi .20 .25
213 A49 $1 violet bl & multi .35 .50
Nos. 210-213 (4) .95 1.15

For overprints and surcharges see Nos. 360, 368, 398, 637, 1359.

Old Sluice Gate — A50

Modern Sluice Gate A51

1975, May 2 *Perf. 14*

214 A50 10c bister & multi .20 .20
215 A51 35c brown & multi .20 .20
216 A50 50c bister & multi .20 .25
217 A51 $1 green & multi .35 .50
a. Souvenir sheet of 4, #214-217 1.25 *2.50*
Nos. 214-217 (4) .95 1.15

Intl. Commission on Irrigation and Drainage, 25th anniv.

For overprints see Nos. 361, 592, 794-795, 1374-1375.

IWY Emblem, Symbolic Man and Woman A52

Designs: IWY emblem and petroglyph designs of men and women.

1975, July 1 Litho. Wmk. 364

218 A52 10c yellow & dull grn .20 .20
219 A52 35c Prus blue & pur .20 .20
220 A52 50c orange & dk blue .25 .25
221 A52 $1 ultra & brown .40 .40
a. Souvenir sheet of 4, #218-221, perf. 14½ 1.25 *2.75*
Nos. 218-221 (4) 1.05 1.05

Intl. Women's Year. For overprints and surcharges see Nos. 362, 399, 555.

Freedom Monument, Georgetown A53

"GNS," Flower and Clasped Hands A54

Designs: Various views of Freedom Monument, Georgetown.

1975, Aug. 26 Litho. *Perf. 14*

222 A53 10c gray & multi .20 .20
223 A53 35c yellow & multi .20 .20
224 A53 50c lilac & multi .25 .25
225 A53 $1 olive & multi .35 .35
Nos. 222-225 (4) 1.00 1.00

Namibia Day (independence for South-West Africa).

For overprints and surcharges see Nos. 330, 582, 593, 619, 1360.

1975, Oct. 2 Wmk. 364 *Perf. 14*

"GNS" and Clasped hands: 35c, Wheel. 50c, Soccer ball. $1, Uniform cap.

226 A54 10c violet, yel & grn .20 .20
227 A54 35c brt bl, org & grn .20 .20
228 A54 50c lt brn, brt bl & grn .25 .25
229 A54 $1 grn, vio & brt grn .35 .35
a. Souvenir sheet of 4, #226-229 1.25 *2.00*
Nos. 226-229 (4) 1.00 1.00

Guyana National Service, 1st anniv. For overprint & surcharges see #448, 636, 638.

Foresters' Building and Badge A55

35c, Rock painting of hunter. 50c, Crossed axes and hunting horn. $1, Bow and arrow.

1975, Nov. 14 Litho. Wmk. 364

230 A55 10c red, black & gold .20 .20
231 A55 35c red, black & gold .20 .20
232 A55 50c gold & multi .25 .25
233 A55 $1 gold & multi .35 .35
a. Souvenir sheet of 4, #230-233 1.00 *2.00*
Nos. 230-233 (4) 1.00 1.00

Ancient Order of Foresters, centenary.

For overprints and surcharges see Nos. 356, 363, 400, 422, 583.

No. 144 Surcharged

1976, Feb. 10 *Perf. 13½*

234 A28 35c on 60c multi .20 .20

For overprints see Nos. 703-703b, 852.

St. John Ambulance Emblem — A56

Independence Arch, 1966 — A57

1976, Mar. 29 Litho. *Perf. 14*

235 A56 8c black, lil rose & sil .20 .20
236 A56 15c black, orange & sil .20 .20
237 A56 35c black, emer & silver .25 .25
238 A56 40c black, blue & sil .30 .30
Nos. 235-238 (4) .95 .95

Guyana St. John Ambulance, 50th anniv. For surcharges see Nos. 715, 717, 1411.

1976, May 25 *Perf. 13½*

Stylized Designs: 15c, Victoria regia. 35c, Letter "S" for socialism. 40c, Worker with pitchfork.

239 A57 8c silver & multi .20 .20
240 A57 15c silver & multi .20 .20
241 A57 35c silver & multi .20 .20
242 A57 40c silver & multi .20 .20
a. Souvenir sheet of 4, #239-242, perf. 14 .50 *1.25*
Nos. 239-242 (4) .80 .80

10th anniv. of independence. For surcharges see Nos. 567, 639, 1444.

Map of West Indies, Bats, Wicket and Ball A57a

Prudential Cup — A57b

Unwmk.

1976, Aug. 3 Litho. *Perf. 14*

243 A57a 15c light blue & multi 1.00 *1.50*
244 A57b 15c lilac rose & black 1.00 *1.50*

World Cricket Cup, won by West Indies Team, 1975.

For overprints & surcharges see #352-353, 653-654.

Lamp — A58

Guitar-Sitar, Benin Head — A59

Designs: 15c, Hand and flame. 35c, Flame. 40c, Lakshmi, Hindu goddess of wealth.

1976, Oct. 21 *Perf. 14*

245 A58 8c multicolored .20 .20
246 A58 15c orange & multi .20 .20
247 A58 35c purple & multi .20 .25
248 A58 40c ultra & multi .20 .30
a. Souvenir sheet of 4, #245-248 .75 *1.25*
Nos. 245-248 (4) .80 .95

Deepavali, Hindu Festival of Lights.

For surcharges see Nos. 719-721.

1977, Feb. 1 Litho. *Perf. 14½*

249 A59 10c gold & multi .20 .20
250 A59 35c gold & multi .20 .20
251 A59 50c gold & multi .35 .35
252 A59 $1 gold & multi .50 .50
a. Souvenir sheet of 4, #249-252 1.25 *3.00*
Nos. 249-252 (4) 1.25 1.25

2nd World Black and African Festival, Lagos, Nigeria, Jan. 15-Feb. 12. Nos. 249-252a were not issued without black bar.

For overprints see Nos. 364, 369, 584.

1c and 5c Coins A60

Coins (Obverse): 15c, 10c and 25c. 35c, 50c and $1. 40c, $5 and $10. $1, $50 and $100. $2, Reverse, Coat of arms.

1977, May 26 *Perf. 14*

253 A60 8c multicolored .25 .25
254 A60 15c multicolored .30 .30
255 A60 35c multicolored .55 .55
256 A60 40c multicolored .65 .65

257 A60 $1 multicolored 1.00 1.00
258 A60 $2 multicolored 1.50 1.50
Nos. 253-258 (6) 4.25 4.25

New coinage. For overprints and surcharges see Nos. 539-541, 568, 594, O18, O20, Q5.

Hand Pump, c. 1850 A61

National Fire Prevention Week: 15c, Steam engine, c. 1860. 35c, Fire engine, c. 1930. 40c, Fire engine, 1977.

Perf. 14x14½

1977, Nov. 15 Litho. Wmk. 364

259 A61 8c multicolored .85 .20
260 A61 15c multicolored 1.25 .20
261 A61 35c multicolored 1.40 .50
262 A61 40c multicolored 1.50 .85
Nos. 259-262 (4) 5.00 1.75

For surcharges see Nos. 1370-1371.

Cuffy Monument — A62

8c, 35c, Cuffy statue from monument.

1977, Dec. 7 Litho. *Perf. 14*

263 A62 8c multicolored .20 .20
264 A62 15c multicolored .20 .20
265 A62 35c multicolored .20 .20
266 A62 40c multicolored .20 .20
Nos. 263-266 (4) .80 .80

Cuffy, Guyana's national hero, led a slave revolution in 1763. The monument was unveiled in 1976. For overprints see Nos. 446, 569, 613.

Wildlife Protection — A63

1978, Feb. 15 *Perf. 14*

267 A63 8c Manatee .75 .20
268 A63 15c Giant sea turtle 1.00 .20
269 A63 35c Harpy eagle 3.75 1.75
270 A63 40c Iguana 3.75 1.75
Nos. 267-270 (4) 9.25 3.90

8c, 15c are horiz. For overprints and surcharges see Nos. 443, 722-723, 1416.

Parliament and Prime Minister Burnham — A64

Prime Minister and: 15c, Student and school children. 35c, Bauxite mine. 40c, Cooperative village.

1978, Apr. 27 Litho. *Perf. 13½x14*

271 A64 8c violet & black .20 .20
272 A64 15c gray, blk & bl .20 .20
273 A64 35c multicolored .20 .20
274 A64 40c gray, blk & org .20 .20
a. Souvenir sheet of 4, #271-274 .75 1.50
Nos. 271-274 (4) .80 .80

Prime Minister Linden Forbes Burnham, 25th anniv. of his entry into parliament. For surcharges see Nos. 648-649.

Dr. George Giglioli, Anopheles Mosquito — A65

Agrias Claudina — A66

30c, Institute of Applied Science & Technology, proposed for University of Guyana. 50c, Map of Guyana & National Science Research Council emblem. 60c, Commonwealth Science Council emblem.

Perf. 13½x14, 14x13½

1978, Sept. 4 Litho. Wmk. 364

275 A65 10c multi .20 .20
276 A65 30c multi, horiz. .20 .20
277 A65 50c multi .25 .25
278 A65 60c multi, horiz. .35 .35
Nos. 275-278 (4) 1.00 1.00

For overprints see Nos. 577, 585, 590.

1978-80 *Perf. 14x13½*

Size: 22x16mm

279 A66 5c Prepona pheridamas 1.75 .20
280 A66 10c Archonias bellona 1.75 .20
281 A66 15c Eryphanis polyxena 1.75 .20
282 A66 20c Helicopis cupido 1.75 .20
283 A66 25c Nessaea batesii 1.75 .20
283A A66 30c Nymphidium mantus ('80) 1.40 *2.00*
284 A66 35c Siderone galanthis 1.75 .20
285 A66 40c Morpho rhetenor, male 1.75 .20
286 A66 50c Hamadryas amphinone 1.75 .25
286A A66 60c Papilio androgeus ('80) 1.40 1.25

Perf. 13½x13

287 A66 $1 Agrias claudina 4.25 .25
288 A66 $2 Morpho rhetenor, female 6.25 .50
289 A66 $5 Morpho deidamia 7.00 1.00
289A A66 $10 Elbella patrobas, perf. 14 ('80) 5.25 4.50
Nos. 279-289A (14) 39.55 11.15

Issued: #279-283, 284-286, 287-289, 10/1/78. For overprints and surcharges see Nos. 391, 406, 436-436A, 481, 486, 554, 668-670, 733-743, 871, 936-939, 944, 969, 1373, 1418, 1455, 1786, 1812, 1814, 1832-1833, 1873, 1901, 1912-1913, 1984-1988, 2051, 2053, 2054C, 2055, 2057, 2057B-2057C, 2058-2059, 2082-2111, C5-C6, O15-O16, O23-O29.

Indian Making Stone Chip Grater — A67

UNESCO Emblem and: 30c, Arawak Cassiri jar and decorated Amerindian jar. 50c, Gate to old Dutch fort, Kykover-al. 60c, Fort Island, Dutch ruins.

1978, Dec. 27 Wmk. 364 *Perf. 14*

290 A67 10c green & multi .20 .20
291 A67 30c green & multi .20 .20
292 A67 50c green & multi .25 .25
293 A67 60c green & multi .25 .25
Nos. 290-293 (4) .90 .90

National and International Heritage Year. For surcharges see Nos. 604-606.

Earth Station at Dawn, Georgetown A68

Designs: 30c, Earth Station in daylight, Georgetown. 50c, Intelsat V. $3, Intelsat IVa.

1979, Feb. 7 Litho. *Perf. 14x14½*

294 A68 10c multicolored .20 .20
295 A68 30c multicolored .25 .20
296 A68 50c multicolored .40 .20
297 A68 $3 multicolored 1.40 1.40
Nos. 294-297 (4) 2.25 2.00

For surcharges see Nos. 384, 655, 714, 1376-1377, 1380, O9.

British Guyana No. 5 — A69

Designs: 30c, British Guiana No. 13, vert. 50c, British Guiana No. 152. $3, Printing press used for 1c Magenta, vert.

1979, May 30 Wmk. 364 *Perf. 14*

298 A69 10c multicolored .20 .20
299 A69 30c multicolored .25 .20
300 A69 50c multicolored .30 .20
301 A69 $3 multicolored .50 .50
Nos. 298-301 (4) 1.25 1.10

Sir Rowland Hill (1795-1879), originator of penny postage.

For overprints & surcharges see #409, 426, 428, 449, 479, 480, 578, 586, 598, 614, O6.

"Fun with the Fowls" and IYC Emblem — A70

Children's Drawings and IYC Emblem: 10c, "Me and my sister," vert. 50c, "Two boys catching ducks." $3, "Mango season."

1979, Aug. 20 Litho. *Perf. 13½*

302 A70 10c multicolored .20 .20
303 A70 30c multicolored .20 .20
304 A70 50c multicolored .35 .35
305 A70 $3 multicolored 1.50 1.50
Nos. 302-305 (4) 2.25 2.25

Intl. Year of the Child. For overprints and surcharges see Nos. 435, 579, 587, 599, 615, 943.

H. N. Critchlow, Worker Hauling Sack — A71

Critchlow and: 30c, Baker, horiz. 50c, Flag and crowd. $3, Portrait only.

1979, Sept. 27 Litho. *Perf. 14*

306 A71 10c multicolored .20 .20
307 A71 30c multicolored .20 .20
308 A71 50c multicolored .25 .25
309 A71 $3 multicolored .90 .90
Nos. 306-309 (4) 1.55 1.55

Guyana Labor Union, 60th anniversary. For surcharges see Nos. 403, 429, 718.

Cooperative Republic, 10th Anniv. — A72

Wmk. 364

1980, Feb. 23 Litho. *Perf. 14*

313 A72 10c shown .20 .20
314 A72 35c Demerara River Bridge .30 .20
315 A72 60c Kaieteur Falls .50 .20
316 A72 $3 Makanaima, American Indian .75 .75
Nos. 313-316 (4) 1.75 1.35

For overprints and surcharges see Nos. 365, 371, 450A, 442, 591, 656.

Miniature Sheet

Snoek, London 1980 Emblem A73

London 80 Emblem and Fish; a, Snoek. b, Haimara. c, Electric eel. d, Golden rivulus. e, Pencil fish. f, Four-eyed fish. g, Pirai. h, Smoking hassar. i, Devil ray. j, Flying patwa. k, Arapaima. l, Lukanani.

1980, May 6 Wmk. 373 *Perf. 14*

317 Sheet of 12 3.50 3.50
a.-l. A73 35c any single .30 .30

London 1980 Intl. Stamp Exhib., May 6-14. For overprints & surcharges see #444, 725-726, 1414.

Children's Convalescent Home, Rotary Emblem — A74

Rotary International, 75th anniversary (Emblem and): 30c, Georgetown club emblem. 50c, District 404 emblem (hibiscus), vert. $3, Anniversary emblem, vert.

Perf. 14x14½, 14½x14

1980, June 23 Litho. Wmk. 364

318 A74 10c multicolored .20 .20
319 A74 30c multicolored .20 .20
320 A74 50c multicolored .60 .50
321 A74 $3 multicolored 1.50 1.25
Nos. 318-321 (4) 2.50 2.15

For overprints and surcharges see Nos. 552, 580, 601, C1.

Emblem and Caduceus A75

Wmk. 364

1980, Sept. 23 Litho. *Perf. 13½*

322 A75 10c shown .20 .20
323 A75 60c Scientist, beach scene .55 .30

324 A75 $3 Emblems over island 1.25 1.10
Nos. 322-324 (3) 2.00 1.60

Commonwealth Caribbean Medical Research Council, 25th anniversary. For overprints and surcharges see Nos. 366, 427, 430, 494, 553.

Virola Surinamensis (Christmas 1980) — A76

1980, Nov. 1 Wmk. 373 *Perf. 14*
325 A76 10c shown .20 .20
326 A76 30c Hymenaea courbaril .20 .20
327 A76 50c Mora excelsa .35 .35
328 A76 $3 Peltogyne venosa 1.50 1.25
Nos. 325-328 (4) 2.25 2.00

For overprints and surcharges see Nos. 431, 773, 790, 792-793.

Miniature Sheet

A77

Designs: a, Tree porcupine. b, Howler monkeys. c, Squirrel monkeys. d, Two-toed sloth. e, Tapir. f, Collared peccary. g, Six-banded armadillo. h, Anteater. i, Great anteaters. j, Mouse opossums. k, Four-eyed opossum. l, Orange-rumped agouti.

1981, Mar. 2 Wmk. 364 *Perf. 14*
329 Sheet of 12 7.00 7.00
a.-l. A77 30c any single .60 .60
m. As #329g, perf. 12 3.00 .20

For overprints see #581, 819, 1399, 1503, 1844.

From this point on there seem to be numerous sources creating stamps for Guyana. According to our information as many as 5-7 parties are active at any one time.

No. 222 Surcharged

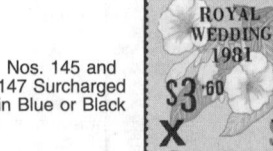

1981, May 4
330 A53 $1.05 on 10c multi .75

For surcharges see Nos. 396, 620.

Nos. 135, 146-147 Surcharged

Nos. 145 and 147 Surcharged in Blue or Black

1981 Litho. Wmk. 364 *Perf. 13½*
331 A28 60c on 3c #135 2.50
332 A28 75c on $5 #147 2.50
333 A28 $1.10 on $2 #146 2.50
334 A28 $3.60 on $5 #147 (Blk) 3.50
a. Blue overprint 3.50
335 A28 $7.20 on $1 #145 (Bl) 3.50
a. Black overprint 5.00

No. 333 is airmail. Issue dates: $3.60, $7.20, May 6. Others July 22. Diagonal overprint on No. 332. Vertical overprint on No. 333. Location of surcharge varies.

See Nos. 621, 666-667, Q4, QO5. For overprints and surcharges see Nos. 378, 489-496, 547, 549, 646, 818, 867-868, O11, Q3, QO3.

Map of Guyana — A78

1981, May 11 Photo. *Perf. 13½*
336 A78 10c on 3c multi 1.00
337 A78 30c on 2c multi 1.00
338 A78 50c on 2c multi 1.00
339 A78 60c on 2c multi 1.00
340 A78 75c on 3c multi 1.00
Nos. 336-340 (5) 5.00

Revenue stamps surcharged for postal use. For similar stamp, see #934a. For surcharge see #503.

Nos. J5-J8 Surcharged in Red, Black, or Brown

a

b

1981, June 8 Typo. *Perf. 13½x14*

Type "a"

341 D1 10c on 2c #J6
342 D1 15c on 12c #J8 (Blk)
343 D1 20c on 1c #J5
344 D1 45c on 2c #J6
345 D1 55c on 4c #J7
346 D1 60c on 4c #J7 (Brn)
347 D1 65c on 2c #J6
348 D1 70c on 4c #J7
349 D1 80c on 4c #J7
Nos. 341-349 (9) 10.50

Type "b"

341a D1 10c on 2c #J6
342a D1 15c on 12c #J8 (Blk)
343a D1 20c on 1c #J5
344a D1 45c on 2c #J6
345a D1 55c on 4c #J7
347a D1 65c on 2c #J6
348a D1 70c on 4c #J7
349a D1 80c on 4c #J7
Nos. 341a-349a (8) 9.00

Pairs with types a and b exist for all values except the 60c.

Nos. 48, 61-62, 74, 139, 142-143, 145-147, 212-213, 216, 220, 231-232, 243-244, 251-252, 315-316, and 323 Overprinted in Black or Red

1981 *Perfs. as Before*

Watermarks & Printing Methods as Before

350 A8 15c on #74 (R) 10.00
351 A28 15c on #139
a. Red overprint 7.00
b. On #139a, red overprint 8.00
352 A57a 15c on #243 6.00
353 A57b 15c on #244 4.00
354 A11 25c on #61 (R) .50
355 A11 30c on #62 (R) .50
356 A55 35c on #231 (R) 3.00
357 A8 40c on #48 8.50
358 A28 40c on #142
359 A28 50c on #143 3.00
360 A49 50c on #212 2.50
361 A50 50c on #216 1.00
362 A52 50c on #220 22.50
363 A55 50c on #232 2.75
364 A59 50c on #251 13.00
365 A72 60c on #315 .60
366 A75 60c on #323 .60
367 A28 $1 on #145 3.50
a. Red overprint 2.00
368 A49 $1 on #213 6.00
369 A59 $1 on #252 5.00
370 A28 $2 on #146 8.00
a. Red overprint 2.00
b. Black ovpt. with serifs 25.00
371 A72 $3 on #316 2.00
372 A28 $5 on #147 3.25
Nos. 350-372 (23) 50.00

Issued: #354-356, 367, 6/8; #350, 357, 370, 7/1; #351-353, 359-366, 368-369, 371-372, 7/7.

Location and size of overprint varies. Refer to second paragraph in footnote following No. 147 for Nos. 358-359.

For surcharges and overprints see Nos. 556, 607, 659, 745, 849-850, 1362.

Nos. 68, 135-136, 139, 145-147, 297, 333 Surcharged or Overprinted

1981 Litho. *Perfs. as Before*

Watermarks & Printing Methods as Before

373 A8 15c on 1c #68 1.00
374 A28 50c on 5c #136 2.50
375 A28 75c on 5c #136 30.00
375A A28 80c on 15c #139
376 A8 100c on 1c #68 .70
377 A8 110c on 1c #68 .70
a. Strip of 3, #373, 376-377 5.00
378 A28 $1.10 on #333 15.00
379 A28 120c on $1 #145 2.50
380 A28 140c on $1 #145 2.50
381 A28 150c on $2 #146 2.50
382 A28 210c on $5 #147 30.00
383 A28 220c on 5c #136 30.00
384 A68 220c on $3 #297 4.50
385 A28 250c on $5 #147 2.75
386 A28 280c on $5 #147 2.75
387 A28 360c on $2 #146 2.50
388 A28 375c on $5 #147 2.75
389 A28 $7.20 on 3c #135 90.00
390 A28 720c on 60c #144 2.50
390A A28 $20 on 5c #136

Location and size of surcharge and obliterator varies. Obliterator is an "X" on Nos. 381-388, 390, two solid boxes on Nos. 379-380, and five bars on No. 389. Numeral "7" is placed before 5 make surcharge on No. 375. "Royal Wedding 1981" obliterated by three bars on No. 378. New denomination on No. 375A does not have cent sign. Obliterator on No. 390A is three horizontal bars.

Refer to second paragraph in footnote following No. 147 for Nos. 381, 387 and 390. Nos. 376-378 are airmail.

Issued: #375, 382, 6/8; #373-374, 376-388, 390, 7/1.

For overprint and surcharges see Nos. 408, 788, 859-860, 863-864, 1379, 1417.

No. 281 Overprinted "ESSEQUIBO / IS OURS"

1981, July Litho. *Perf. 14x13½*
391 A66 15c on #281 4.50
a. Ovpt. without serifs

Nos. 87, 95-96, 142, 146, 210, 218, 230, 309, 330, O15 Surcharged

1981 *Perfs. as Before*

Watermarks & Printing Methods as Before

392 A17 55c on 6c #95 4.50
393 A14 70c on 6c #87 1.25
394 A14 100c on 6c #87 1.25
395 A17 100c on 8c #96 4.50
396 A53 100c on #330 (surcharge reading down 35.00
a. Surcharge reading up 40.00
397 A17 110c on 6c #95 3.00
398 A49 110c on 10c #210 3.00
399 A52 110c on 10c #218 6.00
400 A55 110c on 10c #230 6.00
401 A28 125c on $2 #146 14.00
402 A17 180c on 6c #95 4.50
403 A71 240c on $3 #309 10.50
404 A17 400c on 6c #95 4.00
405 A17 $4.40 on 6c #95 2.25
a. Fours same size 11.00
406 A66 550c on $10 #O15 9.00
407 A28 625c on 40c #142 15.00

Issued: #392, 394-395, 397-399, 405, 405a, 407, July 7; #393, 402-404, 406, Sept. 15. Refer to 2nd paragraph in footnote following #147 for #407. For overprints and surcharges see #651-652, 996, 1858-1859, 1861, O8, O10, O12.

No. 383 Ovptd. "Espana 82"

No. 301 Surcharged "1831-1981 / Von Stephan"

Perfs. as Before

1981, July 22 Litho. Wmk. 364
408 A28 220c on #383 2.00
409 A69 330c on $3 #301 10.00

For surcharges see Nos. 616, 622.

Nos. 43, 72 Surcharged

1981 Photo. Unwmk. *Perf. 14x14½*
410 A7 12c on 12c on 6c #43
411 A7 Pair, #a.-b.
a. 15c on 10c on 6c #43
b. 15c on 30c on 6c #43
412 A7 Pair, #a.-b.
a. 15c on 50c on 6c #43
b. 15c on 60c on 6c #43
413 A7 Strip of 3, #a.-c.
a. 12c On 6c #43
b. 50c On 6c #43
c. $1 On 6c #43

Wmk. 364

413D A7 Strip of 3, #e.-g.
e. 12c On 6c #72
f. 50c On 6c #72
g. $1 On 6c #72

Issue dates: Nos. 410-412, Aug. 24. No. 413-413D, Nov. 10.

Nos. 410-412 were not issued without large numeral surcharges. Obliterator is black box on Nos. 410-412, "X" on Nos. 413a & 413De. Nos. 413b-413c, 413Df-g are airmail.

For overprints and surcharges see Nos. 728-728a, 914, 994, 994a, 1400-1401.

16th Anniv. of the Guyana Defense Force — A79

1981, Oct. 1 Wmk. 364 *Perf. 13½*
414 A79 15c on 10c Armed Ranger, 1772 .20 .20
415 A79 50c Private, Foot Regiment, 1825 .60 .40
416 A79 $1 on 30c Marine Private, 1775 1.10 .75
417 A79 $1.10 on $3 Defense Force officers, 1966 1.25 .80
Nos. 414-417 (4) 3.15 2.15

Nos. 414, 416-417 not issued without surcharge. For overprints see Nos. 570, 588, 595, 1368-1369.

Louis Braille and Boy Reading Braille — A80

Intl. Year of the Disabled: 50c, Helen Keller and Rajkumari Singh. $1, Beethoven and Sonny Thomas. $1.10, Renoir and painting.

1981, Nov. 2 *Perf. 13½x14*
418 A80 15c on 10c multi .20 .20
419 A80 50c multi .45 .40
420 A80 $1 on 60c multi .85 .75
421 A80 $1.10 on $3 multi .95 .80
Nos. 418-421 (4) 2.45 2.15

Nos. 418, 420-421 not issued without surcharge. For overprints and surcharge see #571, 589, 596, 1913A.

Nos. 192, 209, 230, 298, 301, 309, 322, 324, 328, O1 Surcharged in Blue or Red

1981, Nov. 14 ***Perfs. as Before***
Watermarks & Printing Methods as Before

422 A55 110c on 10c #230 3.00
423 A28 110c on #209 5.00
424 A28 110c on #192 5.00
425 A28 110c on #O1 3.75
426 A69 110c on 10c #298 (R) 2.75
427 A75 110c on 10c #322 15.00
428 A69 110c on $3 #301 (R) 2.50
429 A71 110c on $3 #309 7.00
430 A75 110c on $3 #324 3.00
a. Red surcharge 8.00
431 A76 110c on $3 #328 6.00
a. Red surcharge 55.00
Nos. 422-431 (10) 53.00

Nos. 423-424 were issued with two 110c surcharges of different sizes. Refer to second paragraph in footnote below No. 147 for No. 425. For overprints and surcharges see Nos. 791, 820, 855, 1000, 1364-1366.

Flower Type of 1971-76 Surcharged

1981, Nov. 24 Photo. ***Perf. 15x14***
Size: 20x23mm
Coil Stamps

433 A28 15c on 2c like #134 .20
434 A28 15c on 8c Mazaruni Pride .20
a. Pair, #433-434 .50

Nos. 433-434 were not issued without surcharge. See Nos. 731-732.

No. 305 Surcharged "U.N.I.C.E.F. / 1946-1981"

Wmk. 364
1981, Nov. 14 Litho. ***Perf. 13½***

435 A70 125c on $3 #305 3.25

For surcharge see No. 942.

No. 279 Surcharged "Nov. 81" (#436) or "Cancun 81" (#436A)

1981, Nov. 14 ***Perf. 14x13½***

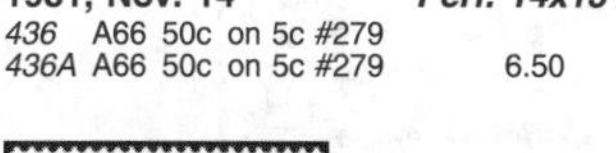

436 A66 50c on 5c #279
436A A66 50c on 5c #279 6.50

Conversion to Metric System, Jan. 2 — A81

a, Tape measure. b, Juggler. c, Man, envelope. d, Baby on scale. e, Canje Bridge. f, Liter bucket.

Perf. 14½x14
1982, Jan. 18 **Wmk. 364**

437 A81 15c Sheet of 6, #a.-f. 1.40 1.40

For surcharge see No. 557.

Nos. 61, 63, 139, 140, 141A, 143-144, 146-147, 228, 266, 269, 300, 314 and 316-317 Ovptd. "1982" Vertically or Horizontally in Blue or Violet

1982-83 ***Perfs. as Before***
Watermarks & Printing Methods as Before

438 A28 15c on #139 8.00
a. On #139a 65.00
439 A28 20c on #140 4.00
440 A28 25c on #141A 6.50
441 A11 25c on #61 (V) 2.00
442 A72 35c on #314 1.00
443 A63 35c on #269 6.00
444 A73 35c on block of 6, #317a-317f 20.00
445 A11 40c on #63 (V) 1.00
446 A62 40c on #266 1.00
447 A28 50c on #143 3.00
448 A54 50c on #228 2.00
449 A69 50c on #300 1.00
449A A28 60c on #144 6.00
450 A28 $2 on #146 1.50
450A A72 $3 on #316 1.75
451 A28 $5 on #147 1.50
Nos. 438-451 (16) 66.25

Issued: #439-441, 2/8; #450-451, 4/23; #445-446, 4/27; #438, 6/17; #443-444, 8/16; #447-449, 10/11; #449A, 7/1/83; #450A, 11/3/83.

For other stamps overprinted "1982" only, see Nos 482-483, 555.

For overprints and surcharges see Nos. 600, 806, 809, 813-814, 851, 999, 1354, 1415.

Nos. 97, O3, O4, O9-O10 Ovptd. "POSTAGE" in Blue

1982 ***Perfs. as Before***
Watermarks and Printing Methods as Before

452 A28 15c on #O3 10.00
453 A17 25c on #97 *6.00*
454 A28 50c on #O4 1.50
455 A68 100c on #O9 2.50
456 A17 110c on #O10 *3.00*

For surcharge see No. 853. For similar overprints see Nos. 729-730. Refer to second paragraph in footnote following No. 147 for No. 454.

Nos. 133, 137, 142, and 192 Surcharged in Blue or Green

Perfs. as Before
1982 Litho. Wmk. 364

457 A28 20c on 6c #137 .90
458 A28 20c on 6c #137 (G) .90
459 A28 125c on #192 .90
460 A28 180c on #142 ovpt. "1982" 5.75
461 A28 220c on 1c #133 2.00
Nos. 457-461 (5) 10.45

No. 458 has no obliterator, "20c" is 23mm long.

Issued: #457-459, 2/8; #460, 4/8; #461, 4/23.

Refer to 2nd paragraph in footnote following #147 for #460.

For overprints see #755, 856, 862.

Savings Campaign A81a

1982 Litho. ***Perf. 14½***

462 A81a $1 Soldier & flag .60
463 A81a $1.10 on $5, two soldiers, flag 7.00
a. Inverted comma before "OURS"

Size of obliterator differs on Nos. 463 and 463a. Nos. 462-463a are revenue stamps ovptd. for postal use.

Issued: #462, 2/8; #463, 3/3; #463a, 7/13.

Nos. 134, 136, & 192 Surcharged in Black or Green
"BADEN-POWELL / 1857-1982" (#464a, 465a, 466a)
"Scout Movement / 1907-1982" (#464b, 465b, 466b)
"1907-1982" (#464c, 465c, 466c)
"1857-1982" (#464d, 465d, 466d)
"1982" (#464e, 465e, 466e)

Perf. 13x13½
1982, Feb. 22 Litho. Wmk. 364
Sheets of 25

464 8 #a.-b., 4 #c.-d., 1 #e. 9.00
a.-e. A28 15c on 2c #134, any single .40
465 8 #a.-b., 4 #c.-d., 1 #e. 20.00
a.-e. A28 110c on 5c #136, any single .80
466 8 #a.-b., 4 #c.-d., 1 #e. 20.00
a.-e. A28 125c on #192, any single (G) .80

Lord Robert Baden-Powell, 125th anniv. of birth. Boy Scout Movement, 75th anniv.

For overprints and surcharges see Nos. 558, 778-784, 836-837, 1347.

Nos. 289, 299, 301 Surcharged or Overprinted in Black or Blue

Perfs. as Before
1982, Feb. 15 Litho. Wmk. 364

479 A69 100c on $3 #301 1.40
480 A69 400c on 30c #299 2.00
481 A66 $5 #289 (Bl) 10.00
Nos. 479-481 (3) 13.40

For surcharges see Nos. 617, 904-906, 937-939, O22-O29.

Nos. 88-89 Ovptd. "1982" in Blue and Nos. 87, 90 Surcharged in Blue or Red

1982, Mar. 15 Photo. ***Perf. 13***

482 A14 25c on #88
483 A14 30c on #89
484 A14 45c on 6c #87
485 A14 75c on 40c #90 (R)
Nos. 482-485 (4) 2.25

For overprints see Nos. 766-767.

Nos. 60, 284, 324, and 331-333 Surcharged in Black or Blue

1982 ***Perfs. as Before***
Watermarks & Printing Methods as Before

486 A66 20c on 35c #284 5.00
487 A11 80c on 6c #60 (Bl) 3.00
488 A11 85c on 6c #60 (Bl) 3.00
489 A28 85c on #331 5.00
490 A28 130c on #331 3.00
491 A28 160c on #333 (Bl) 3.00
a. Black surcharge 5.00
492 A28 170c on #333 15.00
493 A28 210c on #332 (Bl) 3.00
494 A75 210c on $3 #324 (Bl) 4.00
495 A28 235c on #332 4.00
a. Blue surcharge 4.00
496 A28 330c on #333 3.50
Nos. 486-496 (11) 51.50

Nos. 491-491a, 492, & 496 are airmail. Obliterators differ.

Issue dates: #486, Mar. 15. Others, Apr. 27.

For surcharges see Nos. 647, 1367.

Nos. 135, 137, 144 & 145 Overprinted or Surcharged in Blue or Black "ESPANA / 1982" or "ESPANA / 1982" and "ITALY" (#499)

Wmk. 364
1982, May 15 Litho. ***Perf. 13½***

497 A28 $1 on #145 (Blk) 1.50
498 A28 110c on 3c #135 1.50
499 A28 $2.35 on 180c on 60c #144 *14.00*
500 A28 250c on 6c #137 2.00

Refer to second paragraph in footnote below No. 147 for No. 499.

#499 not issued without $2.35 surcharge.

See No. 597 for stamp with one-line Espana 1982 overprint. For surcharges see #774-777.

Map Revenue Type A78 Surcharged in Black, Blue, or Red

1982-83 Photo. Wmk. 364 ***Perf. 13***

501 A78 15c on 2c (Bl)
502 A78 20c on 2c (Bl)
503 A78 20c on 10c #336 (Bl)
504 A78 25c on 2c
a. Blue surcharge
b. Red surcharge 1.00
505 A78 30c on 2c (Bl)
506 A78 40c on 2c
a. Blue surcharge
507 A78 45c on 2c (Bl)
508 A78 50c on 2c (Bl)
509 A78 60c on 2c (Bl)
510 A78 75c on 2c (Bl)
511 A78 80c on 2c (Bl)
512 A78 85c on 2c (Bl)
513 A78 $1.00 on 3c
514 A78 $1.10 on 3c
515 A78 $1.20 on 3c
516 A78 $1.25 on 3c
517 A78 $1.30 on 3c
518 A78 $1.50 on 3c
519 A78 $1.60 on 3c
520 A78 $1.70 on 3c
521 A78 $1.75 on 3c
522 A78 $1.80 on 3c
523 A78 $2.00 on 3c
524 A78 $2.10 on 3c
525 A78 $2.20 on 3c
526 A78 $2.35 on 3c
527 A78 $2.40 on 3c
528 A78 $2.50 on 3c
529 A78 $3.00 on 3c
530 A78 $3.30 on 3c
531 A78 $3.75 on 3c
532 A78 $4.00 on 3c
533 A78 $4.40 on 3c
534 A78 $5.00 on 3c
535 A78 $5.50 on 3c
536 A78 $6.25 on 3c
537 A78 $15 on 2c (R)
538 A78 $20 on 2c (R)
Nos. 501-538 (38) 175.00

Revenue stamps surcharged for postal use. Issue dates: Nos. 501-502, 504-538, May 17, 1982; No. 503, Mar. 14, 1983.

For surcharge see No. 935.

British Guiana Nos. 254, 255, 279, Guyana 10A, 13, 13a, 32J, 32K, 32N Surcharged "H.R.H. / Prince William / 21st June 1982" in Blue

British Guiana stamps also have "GUYANA."

1982, July 12 ***Perfs. as Before***
Watermarks & Printing Methods as Before

539 A60 50c on 2c #254
540 A60 50c on 2c #32J 10.00
541 A60 $1.10 on 3c #279 3.00
541A A60 $1.10 on 3c #255
542 A60 $1.10 on 3c #32K
543 A60 $1.25 on 6c #10A
543A A60 $1.25 on 6c #32N
544 A60 $2.20 on 24c #13a 3.00
544A A60 $2.20 on 24c #13

For surcharges see Nos. 797-800.

Nos. 133-134 Surcharged "C.A. & CARIB / Games / 1982"

Perf. 13x13½
1982, Aug. 16 Litho. Wmk. 364

545 A28 50c on 2c #134
546 A28 60c on 1c #133
Nos. 545-546 (2) 3.00

Central American and Caribbean Games, Havana. For overprint see No. 816.

Nos. 331, C2 Surcharged

1982, Sept. 15

547 A28 130c on #331 2.00
548 A28 170c on #C2 2.50
549 A28 440c on #331 ovptd. "1982" 3.00
a. Without "1982" 75.00
Nos. 547-549 (3) 7.50

For surcharge see No. 802.

No. 137 Surcharged "Commonwealth / GAMES / AUSTRALIA / 1982" in Blue

1982, Sept. 27

550 A28 $1.25 on 6c #137 1.50

For surcharge see No. 789.

No. 207 Ovptd. "INT. / FOOD DAY / 1982" in Dark Blue
No. 320 Ovptd. "INT. YEAR / OF THE / ELDERLY" in Dark Blue
No. 323 Ovptd. "Dr. R. KOCH / CENTENARY / TBC BACILLUS / DISCOVERY" in Dark Blue
No. 287 Ovptd. "F.D. ROOSEVELT / 1882-1982 " in Green
No. 221 Ovptd. "1982" in Blue
No. 332 Surcharged "GAC Inaug. Flight / Georgetown- / Boa Vista, Brasil" in Blue and "1982" in Blue Green

1982, Oct. 15 ***Perfs. as Before***
Watermarks & Printing Methods as Before

551 A48 50c on #207 20.00
552 A74 50c on #320 8.00
553 A75 60c on #323 5.00
554 A66 $1 on #287 5.00
555 A52 $1 on #221 5.00
556 A28 200c on #332 20.00
Nos. 551-556 (6) 63.00

For surcharges see Nos. 895, 902, 936, 1363.

No. 437 Surcharged "CARICOM / Heads of Gov't / Conference / July 1982"

Perf. 14½x14

1982, Jan. 18 Litho. Wmk. 364
557 Sheet of 6 4.50
a.-f. A81 50c on 15c, any single

Nos. 464 Ovptd. "CHRISTMAS / 1982" in Red

1982, Dec. 1 ***Perf. 13x13½***
558 Sheet of 25, 8 #a.-b., 4 #c.-d., 1 #e. 3.00
a.-e. A28 15c on #464a-464e, any single

Nos. 134, 137 Surcharged

Perf. 13x13½

1982-83 Litho. Wmk. 364
563 A28 15c on 2c #134 (Bl) .50
a. Red surcharge 2.00
b. Black surcharge .75
564 A28 20c on 6c #137 (Bk) .50
a. Green surcharge .75

Issued: #563, Dec. 15; #564, Jan. 5, 1983.
Compare No. 564 with Nos. 631-632. For surcharges see Nos. 846, 846a, 846b.

No. 72 Surcharged

1982, Dec. 15 Photo. ***Perf. 14x14½***
565 A7 50c on 6c #72
566 A7 $1.00 on 6c #72
Nos. 565-566 (2) 2.00

Nos. 62, 88-89, 144, 161, 202, 217, 224-225, 232, 240, 251, 254, 257, 264, 276-278, 299-301, 303-305, 315, 319, 321, 329m, 414-416, and 418-420 Ovptd. "1983" Vertically or Horizontally

1983 ***Perfs. as Before***
Watermarks & Printing Methods as Before

567 A57 15c on #240 6.00
568 A60 15c on #254 1.50
569 A62 15c on #264 1.00
570 A79 15c on 10c #414 1.00
571 A80 15c on 10c #418 .25
572 A14 25c on #88 .50
573 A33 25c on #161 14.00
574 A47 25c on #202
575 A11 30c on #62 1.50
576 A14 30c on #89 .50
577 A65 30c on #276 12.50
578 A69 30c on #299 5.00
579 A70 30c on #303 10.00
580 A74 30c on #319 6.00
581 A77 30c on #329m 3.00
582 A53 50c on #224 2.00
583 A55 50c on #232 5.00
584 A59 50c on #251 7.00
585 A65 50c on #277 5.00
586 A69 50c on #300 2.00
587 A70 50c on #304 30.00
588 A79 50c on #415 1.00
589 A80 50c on #419 2.00
590 A65 60c on #278 5.50
591 A72 60c on #315 7.00
592 A51 $1 on #217 10.00
593 A53 $1 on #225 10.00
594 A60 $1 on #257 6.00
595 A79 $1 on 30c #416 2.75
596 A80 $1 on 60c #420 7.50
597 A28 180c on 60c #144 2.00
598 A69 $3 on #301 12.00
599 A70 $3 on #305 15.00
601 A74 $3 on #321 75.00
602 A28 360c on $2 #146 2.25

Issued: #565-571, 583, 585-586, 2/1; #596, 3/7; #573, 3/11; #572, 576, 3/17; #582, 584, 587, 589, 592-595, 588, 598-599, 601, 4/1; #574, 5/23; #575, 577-580, 590-591, 7/1; #602, 11/3; #581, 11/15; #597, 12/14.

Refer to the second paragraph in footnote under No. 147 for Nos. 597 & 602. No. 597 contains unissued overprint, "ESPANA 1982."

For overprints and surcharges see Nos. 724, 901, 940, 943A.

No. O2 Ovptd. "POSTAGE" in Red

Perf. 14½x14

1983, Feb. 1 Photo. Wmk. 364
603 A7 15c on #O2 10.00

For surcharge see Nos. 746-746a.

Nos. 291-293, 356 Surcharged in Blue or Black

Wmk. 364

1983, Feb. 8 Litho. ***Perf. 14***
604 A67 90c on 30c #291 (Blk)
605 A67 90c on 50c #292
606 A67 90c on 60c #293
607 A55 90c on #356
Nos. 604-607 (4) 6.50

For overprints and surcharges see Nos. 763-764, 768-769, 770-771.

Flag A82

Cooperative Youth Palace — A83

1983, Feb. 19 ***Perf. 14½x14***
608 A82 Pair .60 .60
a. 25c Flag flying right .30 .30
b. 25c Flag flying left .30 .30

Perf. 13½

609 A83 $1.30 shown 1.00 1.00

Size: 43x25mm

Perf. 14½

610 A83 $6 Map 3.25 3.25

60th birthday of Pres. Linden Forbes Burnham. No. 608a inscribed for birthday; No. 608b for Burnham's 30th anniv. of election to parliament.

See #660, 913. For overprints & surcharges see #826-835, 924-926, 1404-1406.

Nos. 160, 205, 222, 263, 298, 302, 330, 333, 408-409, 480, C4, O1 and Q3 Ovptd. in Blue or Red

1983 Litho. ***Perfs. as Before***
Watermarks & Printing Methods as Before

611 A33 50c on 8c #160 (R) 14.00
612 A48 50c on 8c #205 2.25
613 A62 50c on 8c #263 8.00
614 A69 50c on 10c #298 (R) 1.50
615 A70 50c on 10c #302 4.00
616 A69 50c on #409 4.50
617 A69 50c on #480 2.00
618 A28 50c on #O1 5.00
619 A53 $1 on #222 8.50
620 A53 $1 on #330 5.00
621 A28 $1 on #333
622 A28 $1 on #408 10.00
623 A28 $1 on #C4 1.50
624 A28 $1 on #Q3 25.00

#621 has Royal Wedding ovpt. similar to #331. #624 also ovptd. "1982." See #648-649 for similar surcharges. For overprint see #815, 941. Issued: #614, 617, 619-624, 3/7; #611, 3/11; thers, 4/1.

Nos. 10A, 13a Surcharged "Commonwealth / Day / 14 March 1983" and Emblem in Blue or Black

Wmk. 314 Upright

1983, Mar. 14 Engr. ***Perf. 12½x13***
625 A60 25c on 6c #10A
626 A60 $1.20 on 6c #10A (Bl)

Wmk. 314 Sideways

627 A60 $1.30 on 24c #13a
628 A60 $2.40 on 24c #13a (Bl)
Nos. 625-628 (4) 4.25

For overprints see Nos. 1823-1825.

Intl. Maritime Organization, 25th Anniv. — A84

Perf. 14

1983, Mar. 17 Typo. Wmk. 3
Red Overprint on British Guiana Revenue Stamp

629 A84 $4.80 grn & blue 6.75

Nos. 60, 72, 87 & 137 Surcharged in Black or Blue

1983 ***Perfs. as Before***
Watermarks & Printing Methods as Before

630 A11 15c on 6c #60 .75
a. Blue surcharge 1.00
631 A28 20c on 6c #137, two obliterators 1.00
632 A28 20c on 6c #137 1.00
633 A7 50c on 6c #72 .75
634 A14 50c on 6c #87 1.00
Nos. 630-634 (5) 4.50

Issued: #630, 632-633, 5/23; #630a, 631, 634, 5/2.

Surcharge on No. 632 has "c" after value. No. 564 does not.

For surcharge see No. 916.

No. 72 Surcharged in Black or Red

Perf. 14x14½

1983 Photo. Wmk. 364
635 A7 $1 on 6c #72 1.50
a. Red overprint, 4mm high 1.50

Issue dates: #635, May 2. #635a, May 23.

For surcharge see No. 916A.

Nos. 142, 147, 211, 226-227, 239 & 249 Surcharged in Blue

1983 ***Perfs. as Before***
Watermarks & Printing Methods as Before

636 A54 110c on 10c #226 2.50
637 A49 120c on 35c #211 4.00
638 A54 120c on 35c #227 4.00
639 A57 120c on 8c #239 4.00
640 A59 120c on 10c #249 4.00
641 A28 250c on 40c #142 10.00
642 A28 400c on $5 #147 8.00
Nos. 636-642 (7) 36.50

Issue dates: Nos. 636, 641-642, May 2. Others, July 1. For surcharge see No. 865.

Nos. 332, 495a, C3 Surcharged in Red or Blue
"ITU / 1983" or (#643)
"WHO / 1983" or (#644)
"17 MAY '83 / ITU/WHO /" (#645)
"ITU/WHO / 17 MAY / 1983" (#646-647)

1983, May 17 ***Perfs. as Before***
Watermarks & Printing Methods as Before

643 A28 25c on #C3 2.50
644 A28 25c on #C3 2.50
645 A28 25c on #C3 2.50
a. Strip of 3, #643-645 7.50
646 A28 $4.50 on #332 (Bl) 15.00
647 A28 $4.50 on #495a (Bl)

Nos. 643-645 issued in sheets of 25 with 8 each Nos. 643-644 and 9 No. 645.

Nos. 272, 274 Surcharged in Dark Blue

Perf. 13½x14

1983, May 18 Litho. Wmk. 364
648 A64 $1 on 15c #272
649 A64 $1 on 40c #274
Nos. 648-649 (2) 7.00

Surcharge on No. 648 also contains overprint "1983."

Nos. 402, 404, O8 Surcharged or Overprinted "CANADA 1983"

1983, June 15 ***Perf. 13½x13***
650 A17 $1.30 on #O8
651 A17 180c on #402
652 A17 $3.90 on #404
Nos. 650-652 (3) 4.75

For surcharge see No. 1860.

Nos. 243-244 Surcharged

1983, June 22 Unwmk. ***Perf. 14***
653 A57a 60c on 15c #243
654 A57b $1.50 on 15c #244
Nos. 653-654 (2) 20.00

Nos. 297, 313 Surcharged

Perfs. as Before

1983, July 1 Wmk. 364
655 A68 120c on #297 4.00
656 A72 120c on 10c #313 (R) 4.00

No. 655 has unissued surcharge, "INTERNATIONAL / SCIENCE YEAR / 375."

British Guiana No. J1 and Guyana No. J5 Surcharged "120 / GUYANA" in Dark Blue

1983, July 1 Wmk. 4 ***Perf. 13½x14***
657 D1 120c on 1c #J1 5.00

Wmk. 364

658 D1 120c on 1c #J5 5.00

No. 371 Surcharged in Red "CARICOM DAY 1983"

1983, July 1 Wmk. 364 ***Perf. 14***
659 A72 60c on $3 #371 3.00

Type A82 Without Inscription

1983, July 1 Litho. ***Perf. 14½x14***
660 A82 Pair .30 .30
a. 25c, Flag flying right .20 .20
b. 25c, Flag flying left .20 .20

River Steamers A85

1983, July 11 Litho. ***Perf. 14***
661 A85 30c Kurupukari .20 .20
662 A85 60c Makouria .40 .40
a. Tete-beche pair
663 A85 120c Powis .85 .85
664 A85 130c Pomeroon .95 .95
665 A85 150c Lukanani 1.10 1.10
Nos. 661-665 (5) 3.50 3.50

No. 146 Surcharged in Dark Blue

1983, July 22 ***Perf. 13½***
666 A28 $2.30 on $1.10 on $2
667 A28 $3.20 on $1.10 on $2
Nos. 666-667 (2) 6.00

Nos. 666-667 have unissued surcharge of "$1.10 / Royal Wedding / 1981" similar to No. 331.

Nos. 282-283 & 283A Overprinted as Shown or with Various Initials in Red or Blue

Overprints: No. 668a, BW. b, LM. c, GY 1963 / 1983. d, JW. e, CU. f. Mont Golfier / 1783-1983.

No. 669a, BGI. b, GEO. c, MIA. d, BVB. e, PBM. f, Mont Golfier / 1783-1983. g, POS. h, JFK.

No. 670a, AHL. b, BCG. c, BMJ. d, EKE. e, GEO. f, GFO. g, IBM. h, Mont Golfier / 1783-1983. i, KAI. j, KAR. k, KPG. l, KRG. m, KTO. n, LTM. o, MHA. p, MWI. q, MYM. r, NAI. s, ORJ. t, USI. u, VEG.

1983, Sept. 5 ***Perf. 14x13½***

Sheets of 25

668 A66 20c 4 each #a.-e., 5 #f
669 A66 25c 2 each #a., c.-e., g.-h., 8 #b., 5 #f.
670 A66 30c #a.-e., g.-u., 5 #f., (Bl)

Manned flight, bicentennial and Guyana Airways, 20th anniv. For ovpts. see #871, 969.

No. 234 Surcharged in Dark Blue

1983, Sept. 14 ***Perf. 13½***

703 A28 240c on #234
a. "4" with serif

Nos. 703, 703a appear in same sheet.

Nos. 68, 70 Surcharged "FAO 1983" in Red

Perf. 14x14½

1983, Sept. 15 Photo. Wmk. 364

704 A7 30c on 1c #68
705 A7 $2.60 on 3c #70
Nos. 704-705 (2) 2.75

For overprints see Nos. 1497-1498.

Great Britain, Postal Use In British Guiana, 150th Anniv. — A86

Stamps: a, #20. b, #26. c, #27. d, #28.

1983, Oct. 1 Litho. ***Perf. 14***

Inscribed in Black

706 A86 25c #20 .20 .20
707 A86 30c #26 .20 .20
708 A86 60c #27 .35 .35
709 A86 120c #28 .70 .70

Inscribed in Blue

710 Block of 4 .60 .60
a.-d. A86 25c any single .20 .20
711 Block of 4 .70 .70
a.-d. A86 30c any single .20 .20
712 Block of 4 1.10 1.10
a.-d. A86 45c any single .25 .25
713 Block of 4 3.75 3.75
a. A86 120c #20 .70 .70
b. A86 130c #26, Demerara .75 .75
c. A86 150c #27, Berbice .90 .90
d. A86 200c #28, Essequibo 1.25 1.25
Nos. 706-713 (8) 7.60 7.60

Nos. 706-709 printed in sheets with bottom two rows inverted. Nos. 710-712 printed in sheets of 60. No. 713 printed in sheets with blue marginal text.

For overprints and surcharges see Nos. 796, 903, 912, 1448, 1982.

#235 & 238 Surcharged

#297 Surcharged "INT. / COMMUNICATIONS / YEAR"

#206 Surcharged "Int. Food Day / 1983"

#309 Surcharged "1918-1983 / I.L.O."

1983, Oct. 15 ***Perfs. as Before***

Watermarks & Printing Methods as Before

714 A68 50c on 375c on $3 #297 6.00
715 A56 75c on 8c #235 7.00
716 A48 $1.20 on 35c #206 1.75
717 A56 $1.20 on 40c #238 7.00
718 A71 240c on $3 #309 2.00
Nos. 714-718 (5) 23.75

No. 714 was not issued without 375c surcharge. For overprint see No. 821.

Nos. 245, 247-248 Surcharged

Unwmk.

1983, Nov. 1 Litho. ***Perf. 14***

719 A58 25c on 8c #245
720 A58 $1.50 on 35c #247
721 A58 $1.50 on 40c #248
Nos. 719-721 (3) 3.00

Nos. 268 & 270 Surcharged

1983, Nov. 15 Wmk. 364

722 A63 60c on 15c #268 1.90
723 A63 $1.20 on 40c #270 1.90

No. 601 Ovptd. "Human Rights / Day"

1983, Dec. 1 ***Perf. 14½x14***

724 A74 $3 on #601 2.75

For surcharge see footnote following No. 998.

Nos. 317 and 726 Surcharged "LOS ANGELES / 1984"

1983, Dec. 6 Wmk. 373

725 Sheet of 12
a.-l. A73 55c on 125c on 35c #726a-726l, any single
726 Sheet of 12
a.-l. A73 125c on 35c #317a-317l, any single

For surcharge see No. 1897.

No. 133 Surcharged "COMMONWEALTH / HEADS OF GOV'T / MEETING--INDIA / 1983"

Perf. 13x13½

1983, Dec. 14 Litho. Wmk. 364

727 A28 150c on 1c #133 1.50

Nos. 413a, 413e Surcharged "CHRISTMAS / 1983"

1983, Dec. 14 Photo. ***Perf. 14x14½***

Watermarks as before

728 A7 20c on #413a .50
a. 20c on #413De .50

Nos. 146, O15 Ovptd. "POSTAGE" in Blue

1984, Jan. 8 ***Perfs. as before***

729 A28 $2 on #146 3.50
730 A66 550c on $10 #O15 12.00

Refer to second paragraph in footnote following No. 147 for No. 729.

Flower Type of 1971-76 Surcharged in Blue

Perf. 15x14

1984, Jan. Photo. Unwmk.

Size: 20x23mm

Coil Stamps

731 A28 17c on 2c, like #134 .75
732 A28 17c on 8c, Mazaruni Pride .75
a. Pair, #731-732 1.50

Nos. 731-732 were intended for use on 8c envelopes to increase postage rate to 25c and were not issued without surcharge.

Nos. 284, 286A Surcharged in Black or Overprinted in Dark Blue
(1) "ALL / OUR HERITAGE"
(2) "1984" 7mm long
(3) "REPUBLIC / DAY"
(4) "BERBICE"
(5) "DEMERARA"
(6) "ESSEQUIBO"
(7) "1984" 18mm long

Perf. 14x13½

1984, Feb. 24 Litho. Wmk. 364

733 A66 25c on 35c (1)
734 A66 25c on 35c (2)
735 A66 25c on 35c (3)
736 A66 25c on 35c #284
737 A66 25c on 35c (4)
738 A66 25c on 35c (5)
739 A66 25c on 35c (6)
740 A66 25c on 35c (7)
741 A66 60c on #286A (1) (DBl)
742 A66 60c on #286A (3) (DBl)
743 A66 60c on #286A (2) (DBl)

Nos. 733-740 were issued in sheets of 25, 6 #733, 4 each #734-736, 2 each #737-739, 1 #740. Nos. 741-743 were issued in sheets of 25, 8 each #741-742, 9 #743.

Nos. 49-50, 52, 73-74, 77-80, 82, 139, 141A-143, 350, 603 Surcharged or Overprinted in Black and/or Blue "Protecting Our Heritage"

1984, Mar. 5 ***Perfs. as Before***

Watermarks & Printing Methods as Before

744 A8 20c on 15c #74 6.00
a. Blue surcharge (value and words) 15.00
745 A8 20c on 15c #350 6.00
746 A8 20c on 15c #603 (Bl) 12.50
a. "Protecting our Heritage" in black
747 A28 25c on #141A 10.00
a. 25c on #141b 50.00
748 A28 30c on 15c #139 15.00
749 A8 40c on #77 7.50
750 A28 50c on #143 1.00
751 A28 50c on #143 (Revenue Ovpt.) 1.00
752 A7 60c on #50 10.00
a. 60c on #79 75.00
753 A28 90c on 40c #142 12.00
754 A28 90c on 40c #142 (Revenue ovpt.) 100.00
755 A28 180c on #460 10.00
756 A7 $2 on #52 50.00
757 A8 225c on 10c on #73 17.00
758 A7 260c on $1 #80 10.00
759 A28 320c on 40c #142 10.00
760 A28 350c on 40c #142 15.00
761 A7 390c on 50c #78 6.00
a. 390c on #49 100.00
762 A7 450c on $5 #82 8.00
Nos. 744-762 (19) 307.00

Nos. 748, 753-754, 759-760 use row of "X", 6mm high, as obliterator. Nos. 744-746, 757 have new value printed vertically over old value. Nos. 758, 761-762 have new value printed horizontally over old value. Refer to second paragraph in footnote under No. 147 for Nos. 751, 754-755.

Nos. 89, 484-485, 606 Overprinted or Surcharged in Dark Blue "1984"

No. 87 Surcharged

No. 606 Surcharged "INT. / CHESS / FED. / 1924-1984" in Dark Blue (#764a, 769a, 771a)

1984 ***Perfs. as Before***

Watermarks & Printing Methods as Before

763 A67 25c on #606 2.00
764 A67 25c on #606 4.00
a. Pair, #763-764 10.00
765 A14 30c on #89 .50
766 A14 45c on 6c #484 .50
767 A14 75c on 40c #485 .50
768 A67 75c on #606 1.00
769 A67 75c on #606 3.00
a. Pair, #768-769 8.00
770 A67 90c on #606 1.00
771 A67 90c on #606 3.00
a. Pair, #770-771 9.00
772 A14 130c on 6c #87 .50
773 A76 $3 on #328 1.50
Nos. 763-773 (11) 17.50

Issued: #765-767, 772, Mar. 17; #773, June 15; #763-764, 768-769, 770-771, July 20.

No. 767 exists with surcharge either above old value or in center of stamp.

Nos. 497-500 Surcharged

1984, Apr. 2 Litho. ***Perf. 13½***

774 A28 75c on #497 10.00
775 A28 75c on #498 12.00
776 A28 225c on #500 3.00
777 A28 230c on #499 3.50
Nos. 774-777 (4) 28.50

Nos. 464e, 465a, 465b, 465e, 466a, 466b, 466e Surcharged Like No. 748

1984, May 2

778 A28 20c on #464e 2.00
779 A28 75c on #465e 10.00
780 A28 90c on #465a
781 A28 90c on #465b 8.50
782 A28 120c on #466a 10.00
783 A28 120c on #466e 10.00
784 A28 120c on #466b 3.00

No. C3 Surcharged "ITU DAY / 1984" (#785)

No. C3 Surcharged "WHO DAY / 1984" (#786)

Nos. C3, 386 Surcharged "ITU/WHO / DAY / 1984" (#787-788)

1984, May 17

785 A28 25c on #C3 1.60
786 A28 25c on #C3 1.60
787 A28 25c on #C3 1.60
788 A28 $4.50 on #386 2.50
Nos. 785-788 (4) 7.30

The surcharge is vertical on Nos. 785-787, horizontal on No. 788.

No. 550 Surcharged

1984, June 11

789 A28 120c on #550 8.00

Nos. 325-327, 431 Surcharged in Blue or Black

Wmk. 373

1984, June 15 Litho. ***Perf. 14***

790 A76 55c on 30c #326 (Blk) 1.10
791 A76 75c on #431 1.10
792 A76 160c on 50c #327 1.10
793 A76 260c on 10c #325 1.10
Nos. 790-793 (4) 4.40

No. 214 Surcharged

1984, June 18 Litho. Wmk. 364

794 A50 55c on 110c on 10c 1.00
795 A50 90c on 110c on 10c 1.00

No. 214 surcharged 110c only was never issued.

No. 713 Ovptd. "UPU / Congress 1984 / Hamburg"

1984, June 19

796 Block of 4 3.50
a. A86 120c on #713a
b. A86 130c on #713b
c. A86 150c on #713c
d. A86 200c on #713d

Nos. 539, 541, 543-544 Surcharged in Black, Blue or Dark Green

1984, June 21 ***Perfs. as Before***

Watermarks & Printing Methods as Before

797 A60 45c on #539
798 A60 60c on #541 (DkG)
a. 60c on British Guiana #255 (DkG)
799 A60 120c on #543
800 A60 200c on #544 (Bl)
Nos. 797-800 (4) 10.00

Nos. 135, 548, C2-C3 Surcharged in Blue or Black

No. C4 Overprinted "1984"

Perf. 13x13½

1984, June 30 Litho. Wmk. 364

801 A28 75c on #C2 (Blk) 3.75
802 A28 120c on #548 (Blk) 3.75
803 A28 150c on #135 1.00
804 A28 200c on #C3 3.75
804A A28 330c on #C4 3.75
Nos. 801-804A (5) 16.00

Surcharge on Nos. 801-802, 804 is like No. 748. Surcharge on No. 803 is like No. 457.

No. 135 Surcharged "CARICOM / HEADS OF GOV'T / CONFERENCE / JULY 1984"

No. 450A Surcharged "CARICOM DAY 1984"

1984, June 30 ***Perfs. as Before***

Watermarks & Printing Methods as Before

805 A28 60c on 3c #135 .50
806 A72 60c on #450A 1.00

Nos. 140-141, 141A, 329, 334, 427, 439a-440, 546, 611, 718, O13 Ovptd. "1984" in Black or Blue

1984 ***Perfs. as Before***

Watermarks & Printing Methods as Before

807 A28 20c on #140 12.50
a. On #140a 150.00
808 A28 20c on #140 55.00
a. On #140a 150.00
809 A28 20c on #439, 1984 omitted 60.00
810 A28 25c on #141 100.00
a. 1984 omitted 100.00
811 A28 25c on #141 (Revenue Only) 6.00
812 A28 25c on #141A
813 A28 25c on #141, 1982 ovpt., 1984 omitted 40.00
814 A28 25c on #440, 1984 omitted
815 A33 50c on #611 (Bl) 10.00
816 A28 60c on #546 (Bl) 1.00
817 A28 $2 on #O13 (Bl) 2.50
818 A28 $3.60 on #334 4.00
c. As #818, fleur-de-lis omitted 10.00
d. On #334a (Bl) 10.00
e. As "d," fleur-de-lis omitted 5.00
819 Sheet of 12 4.00
a.-l. A77 30c on #329a-329l, any single
820 A71 240c on #429 4.75
821 A71 240c on #718 4.75

Overprint on Nos. 808-814, 818 contains fleur-de-lis. Refer to second paragraph in footnote below No. 147 for Nos. 811-812, 817.

Issued: #819, Sept. 15; #820-821, Oct. 15.

Teachers' Assoc. Centenary — A87

1984, July 16 Wmk. 364 ***Perf. 14***

822 A87 25c Children dancing .20 .20
823 A87 25c Torch, graduate .20 .20
824 A87 25c Torch concentric circles .20 .20
825 A87 25c Teachers, school .20 .20
a. Block of 4 .80 .80

No. 609 Surcharged in Blue:
"CYCLING" (#826, 831)
"TRACK / AND / FIELD" (#827, 832)
"OLYMPIC / GAMES / 1984" (#828, 833)
"BOXING" (#829, 834)

"OLYMPIC / GAMES / 1984 / LOS ANGELES" (#830, 835)

Perf. 14½x14

1984, July 28 Litho. Wmk. 364

826 A83 25c on $1.30
827 A83 25c on $1.30
828 A83 25c on $1.30
829 A83 25c on $1.30
830 A83 25c on $1.30
831 A83 $1.20 on $1.30
832 A83 $1.20 on $1.30
833 A83 $1.20 on $1.30
834 A83 $1.20 on $1.30
835 A83 $1.20 on $1.30

Nos. 826-828 and 831-833 exist in strips of 3. Nos. 827, 829-830 and 832, 834-835 exists in booklets.

Nos. 465-466 Surcharged "GIRL / GUIDES / 1924-1984" in Blue

1984, Aug. 15 *Perf. 13x13½*

Sheets of 25

836 8 #a.-b., 4 #c.-d., 1 #e.
a.-e. A28 25c on #465a-465e, any single
837 8 #a.-b., 4 #c.-d., 1 #e.
a.-e. A28 25c on #466a-466e, any single
Nos. 836-837 (2) 7.50

Nos. 138-139, 234, 335, 351, 378, 380, 388, 401, 423, 438, 452, 459, 461, 563, 642, O3, O11-O12, O14 Surcharged

1984 *Perfs. as Before*

Watermarks & Printing Methods as Before

846 A28 20c on #563 1.00
a. 20c on #563a (Blk over R) 1.00
b. 20c on #563b (Blk over Bl) 1.00
847 A28 25c on #138 27.50
a. 25c on #138a 55.00
848 A28 25c on #139 150.00
849 A28 25c on #351a 20.00
a. 25c on #351 70.00
850 A28 25c on #351b 8.50
851 A28 25c on #438 8.00
a. 25c on #438a 150.00
852 A28 25c on #234 100.00
853 A28 25c on #452 8.00
854 A28 25c on #O3 8.00
855 A28 60c on #423, two obliterators, small 110 only 45.00
a. Single obliterator, small 110 only
856 A28 120c on #459 5.00
857 A28 120c on #401 35.00
858 A28 120c on #O12 2.00
859 A28 120c on #380 6.00
860 A28 130c on #378 100.00
861 A28 130c on #O11 12.50
862 A28 200c on #461 5.00
863 A28 320c on #378 5.50
864 A28 350c on #388 5.00
865 A28 390c on #642 6.00
866 A28 450c on #O14 5.75
867 A28 600c on #335 15.00
a. 600c on #335a 17.50
868 A28 600c on #335a 3.00
a. 600c on #335 4.00
Nos. 846-868 (23) 581.75

Nos. 860-861 are airmail. Obliterator on Nos. 846, 856-859, 862-866 is row of "X", on Nos. 847, 850, 852 is single line, on Nos. 848-849, 851, 853-854 is fleur-de-lis, on No. 855 is a block of 6 lines, on No. 867 is 3 lines, on No. 868 is 3 lines and fleur-de-lis.

Nos. 556, 670, C4 Overprinted in Blue or Surcharged in Blue and Black

Overprints: #a-f, ICAO on #670a-670f. g, IMB/ICAO on #g. h, KCV/ICAO on #h. i, KAI/ICAO on #i. j-k, ICAO on #670j-670k. l, 1984 on #h. m, KPM/ICAO on #h. n-p, ICAO on #670 l-670n. q, PMT/ICAO on #h. r-x, ICAO on #670o-670u.

Perf. 14x13½

1984, Sept. 6 Litho. Wmk. 364

871 A66 30c Sheet of 25, #a.-k., m.-x., 2 #l
895 A28 200c ICAO on #556 4.00
896 A28 200c ICAO on #C4 (Bl & Blk) 2.00

No. 896 is airmail with unissued "GAC" overprint. For surcharge see No. 1470.

Nos. J3-J4, J7-J8 Surcharged "120 / GUYANA" in Blue

Perf. 13½x14

1984, Oct. 1 Typo. Wmk. 314

897 D1 120c on 4c #J3
898 D1 120c on 12c #J4

Wmk. 364

899 D1 120c on 4c #J7
900 D1 120c on 12c #J8
Nos. 897-900 (4) 40.00

Nos. 551, 571 Surcharged in Black or Blue

Perfs. as Before

1984, Oct. 15 Wmk. 364

901 A80 $1.50 on #571 (Bl) 7.50
902 A48 150c on 50c #551 1.00

Obliterator is "X" on No. 901. Surcharge on No. 902 places "1" before existing 50c value, obliterates "1982" and adds "1984."

Nos. 712, 479-481 Surcharged

1984, Oct. 22 *Perf. 14*

903 Block of 4 .60
a.-d. A86 25c on 45c on #712a-712d, any single
904 A69 120c on #479 4.00
905 A69 120c on #480 .60
906 A66 320c on #481 6.00
Nos. 903-906 (4) 11.20

Nos. 135-136 Surcharged "MAHA SABHA / 1934-1984" in Blue

1984, Nov. 1 *Perf. 13x13½*

910 A28 25c on 5c #136
911 A28 $1.50 on 3c #135
Nos. 910-911 (2) 1.00

No. 713 Ovptd. "Philatelic Exhibition / New York 1984" in Red

1984, Nov. 15 *Perf. 14*

912 Block of 4 2.75
a. A86 120c on No. 713a
b. A86 130c on No. 713b
c. A86 150c on No. 713c
d. A86 200c on No. 713d

Type A83 Inscribed with Olympic Rings and "OLYMPIC GAMES 1984 / LOS ANGELES"

1984, Nov. 16 *Perf. 13½*

913 A83 $1.20 multicolored 2.00 2.00

Copies with numbers stamped on back are coils.

For similar stamp overprinted see No. 923.
For surcharges see Nos. 1953-1957.

Nos. 410, 413e, 633, 635a Surcharged

1984, Nov. 24 Photo. *Perf. 14x14½*

Watermarks as Before

914 A7 20c on #410 1.00
915 A7 20c on #413De
916 A7 25c on #633 .50
916A A7 60c on #635a .50

No. 914 has an "X" obliterating a "1" and no obliterating lines. No. 1400 has obliterating lines and small "20" in UR.

Elanoides Forficatus
A88

Designs: a, Pair in tree. b, Landing on branch. c, In flight, wings up. d, In flight, wings down. e, In flight, wings outstretched.

1984, Dec. 3 Wmk. 364 *Perf. 14½*

917 A88 60c Strip of 5, #a.-e. 6.00 6.00

Inscribed "Christmas 1982."
For surcharges see Nos. 1502, 1840.

High Street Architecture — A89

Designs: 25c, St. George's Cathedral, 1892, Colonial Life Insurance Co. 60c, No. 920a, Demerara Mutual Life Assurance Soc., Ltd. No. 920b, 200c, Town Hall, 1888, City Engineers Office. No. 920c, 300c, Victoria Law Courts, 1887.

1985, Feb. 8 *Perf. 14*

918 A89 25c multi .20 .20
919 A89 60c multi .40 .40
920 Triptych 1.40 1.40
a.-c. A89 120c, any single .45 .45
d. Triptych, unwmkd. 1.75 1.75
e.-g. As "d," any single .60 .60
921 A89 200c multi 1.25 1.25
922 A89 300c multi 1.75 1.75
Nos. 918-922 (5) 5.00 5.00

For surcharge see No. 1850.

Type A83 Ovptd. "INTERNATIONAL / YOUTH YEAR 1985"

Wmk. 364

1985, Feb. 15 Litho. *Perf. 14½*

923 A83 $1.20 multi 2.50

Bars obliterate Olympic Games inscription with second line spelled "LOS ANGELLES." No. 913 spells "Los Angeles" correctly.

Nos. 608, 610 Ovptd. in Red "Republic / Day / 1970-1985" or "1970 / 1985 / Republic / Day"

1985, Feb. 22 *Perfs. as Before*

924 A82 25c on #608
925 A83 120c on $6 #610
926 A83 130c on $6 #610
Nos. 924-926 (3) 1.75

Ocelot Cub Xica — A90

Macaw Nena — A90a

Perf. 12½x13

1985, Mar. 11 Wmk. 364

927 A90 25c multi .30 .30
928 A90 60c multi .60 .60
929 Triptych 3.50 3.50
a.-c. A90 120c, like #927-928, 930 1.10 1.10
930 A90 130c multi 1.25 1.25

Perf. 14½

931 A90a 320c shown 3.25 3.25
932 A90a 330c Cub on hind legs 3.25 3.25
Nos. 927-932 (6) 12.15 12.15

No. 929, perf. 14, inscribed "1986," were from the liquidation of stock held by the printer, value 75c.

For overprints see #1903-1905, 1983, 2032.

Map Revenue Type A78 and Nos. 481, 501, 554, O6 Surcharged in Black or Blue

1985 *Perfs as Before*

Watermarks & Printing Methods as Before

933 A69 30c on 50c on #O6 (Bl) 1.00
934 A78 55c on 2c multi 1.00
a. "ESSEQUIBO IS OURS" omitted 15.00
935 A78 55c on #501 .50
936 A66 90c on #554 (Bl) 5.00
937 A66 225c on #481 5.00
938 A66 230c on #481 (Bl) 5.00
939 A66 260c on #481 (Bl) 5.00
Nos. 933-939 (7) 22.50

Issued: #933-936, 938-939, 3/11; #937, 4/11.
Obliterator on Nos. 934-935 is fleur-de-lis.

Nos. 305, 435, 587, 599, & 615 Ovptd. "INTERNATIONAL / YOUTH YEAR / 1985" in Blue

Wmk. 364

1985, Apr. 15 Litho. *Perf. 13½*

940 A70 50c on #587 1.10
941 A70 50c on #615 3.00
942 A70 120c on #435 1.10
943 A70 $3 on #305 8.75
943A A70 $3 on #599 1.10
Nos. 940-943A (5) 15.05

No. 280 Surcharged with Names of 1860 Post Offices or Postal Agencies in Blue

Overprints: a, Airy Hall. b, Belfield / Arab. Coast. c, Belfield / E.C. Dem. d, Belladrum. e, Beterver- / wagting. f, Blairmont / Ferry. g, Boeraserie. h, Brahn. i, Bushlot. j, De / Kinderen. k, Fort / Wellington. l, Georgetown. m, Hague. n, Leguan. o, Mahaica. p, Mahaicony. q, New / Amsterdam. r, Plaisance. s, No. 6 Police / Station. t, Queenstown. u, Vertenoegen. v, Vigilance. w, Vreed-en- / Hoop. x, Wakenaam. y, Windsor / Castle.

Perf. 14x13½

1985, May 2 Litho. Wmk. 364

Sheet of 25

944 A66 25c on 10c, #a.-y.

Colonial Post Office, 125th anniv.

Nos. 670 Ovptd. "1985" or with Letters in Red

Overprints: a-f, 1985 on #670a-670f. g, I on #670g. h, T on #670h. i, U on #670i. j-k, 1985 on #670j-670k. l, W on #670h. m, H on #670h. n, O on #670h. o-p, 1985 on #670 l-670m. q, D on #670n. r, A on #670h. s, Y on #670o. t-y, 1985 on #670p-#670u.

1985, May 17

Sheet of 25

969 A66 30c #a.-y.

Nos. 413a & 413e Surcharged

1985, May 21 Photo. *Perf. 14x14½*

Watermarks as Before

994 A7 20c on #413a 8.75
a. 20c on #413De 11.00

#994a has "20" at left and 11 obliterating lines. #1401 has "20" at right and 12 lines.

No. 135 Surcharged "CARDI / 1975-1985"

Perf. 13x13½

1985, May 29 Litho. Wmk. 364

995 A28 60c on 3c #135 .50

Caribbean Agricultural Research Development Institute, 10th anniv.

No. 407 Surcharged

1985, June 3

996 A28 600c on #407 7.50

Nos. 288, 724, C1 Surcharged "ROTARY / INTERNATIONAL / 1905-1985" in Red

1985, June 21 *Perfs. as Before*

Watermarks & Printing Methods as Before

997 A74 120c on #C1 5.75
998 A66 300c on #288 3.50

No. 724 with a similar surcharge is usually found on first day covers.

No. 450A Surcharged "CARICOM DAY / 1985" and No. 426 Surcharged "135th Anniversary / Cotton Reel / 1850-1985" in Red

1985, June 28 *Perfs. as Before*

Watermarks & Printing Methods as Before

999 A72 60c on #450A .75
1000 A69 120c on #426 .75

Orchids from Reichenbachia, by Sanders — A91

1985-87 *Perf. 14*

Wmk. 364 (#1027, 1031, 1036, 1046, 1049, 1052, 1054, 1071, 1074, 1076, 1079, 1084, 1091, 1108), Unwmkd.

Series 1

1021 A91 120c Plate No. 1 .60 .60
1022 A91 60c Plate No. 2 .30 .30
1023 A91 130c Plate No. 3 .65 .65
1024 A91 200c Plate No. 4 1.00 1.00
1025 A91 60c Plate No. 5 .45 .45
1026 A91 75c like #1025 .40 .40
a. Wmk. 364 ('87) 7.50 7.50
1027 A91 100c Plate No. 6 .75 .75
1028 A91 130c like #1027 .65 .65
a. Wmk. 364 ('86) .65 .65
1029 A91 60c Plate No. 7 .30 .30
1030 A91 25c Plate No. 8 .20 .20
1031 A91 50c Plate No. 9 .40 .40
1032 A91 55c like #1031 .30 .30
a. Wmk. 364 ('86) .30 .30
1033 A91 60c Plate No. 10 .30 .30
1034 A91 120c Plate No. 11 .60 .60
1035 A91 25c Plate No. 12 .20 .20
1036 A91 100c Plate No. 13 .75 .75
1037 A91 130c like #1036 .65 .65
a. Wmk. 364 ('86) .65 .65
1038 A91 200c Plate No. 14 1.00 1.00
1039 A91 55c Plate No. 15 .45 .45
1040 A91 180c like #1039 .90 .90
a. Wmk. 364 ('87) 8.00 8.00
Nos. 1021-1040 (20) 10.85 10.85

Issued: #1022-1024, 1028-1029, 1033, 1035, 1037, 7/9; #1032, 8/12; #1021, 1030, 1034, 1038, 9/16; #1026, 2/26/86; #1040, 7/24/86; #1025, 1027, 1031, 1036, 1039, 8/21/86.

Nos. 1021, 1034 horiz.

1041 A91 130c Plate No. 16 .65 .65
1042 A91 55c Plate No. 17 .30 .30
a. Wmk. 364 ('87) 4.25 4.25
1043 A91 80c like #1042 .40 .40
1044 A91 130c Plate No. 18 .65 .65
1045 A91 60c Plate No. 19 .30 .30
1046 A91 100c Plate No. 20 .75 .75
1047 A91 130c like #1046 .65 .65
a. Wmk. 364 ('86) .65 .65
1048 A91 200c Plate No. 21 1.00 1.00
1049 A91 50c Plate No. 22 .40 .40
1050 A91 55c like #1049 .30 .30
a. Wmk. 364 ('86) .30 .30
1051 A91 25c Plate No. 23 .20 .20
1052 A91 50c Plate No. 24 .40 .40
1053 A91 225c like #1052 1.10 1.10
a. Wmk. 364 ('86) 1.10 1.10
1054 A91 100c Plate No. 25 .75 .75
1055 A91 130c like #1054 .65 .65
a. Wmk. 364 ('86) .65 .65
1056 A91 150c Plate No. 26 .75 .75
1057 A91 120c Plate No. 27 .60 .60
1058 A91 120c Plate No. 28 .60 .60
1059 A91 130c Plate No. 29 .65 .65
1060 A91 130c Plate No. 30 .65 .65
Nos. 1041-1060 (20) 11.75 11.75

Issued: #1044-1045, 1047, 1055, 1057, 1059-1060, 7/9; #1041, 1050, 8/12; #1048, 1051, 1058, 9/16; #1042, 1053, 1056, 7/10/86; #1046, 1049, 1052, 1054, 8/21/86; #1043, 11/25/86.

Nos. 1048, 1058 horiz.

1061 A91 60c Plate No. 31 .30 .30
1062 A91 150c Plate No. 32 .75 .75
1063 A91 200c Plate No. 33 1.00 1.00
1064 A91 150c Plate No. 34 .75 .75
1065 A91 150c Plate No. 35 .75 .75
1066 A91 120c Plate No. 36 .60 .60
1067 A91 120c Plate No. 37 .60 .60
1068 A91 130c Plate No. 38 .65 .65
1069 A91 80c Plate No. 39 .60 .60
1070 A91 260c like #1069 1.25 1.25
a. Wmk. 364 ('87) 4.25 4.25
1071 A91 100c Plate No. 40 .75 .75
1072 A91 150c like #1071 .75 .75
a. Wmk. 364 ('86) .75 .75
1073 A91 150c Plate No. 41 .75 .75
1074 A91 100c Plate No. 42 .75 .75
1075 A91 150c like #1075 .75 .75
a. Wmk. 364 ('86) .75 .75
1076 A91 100c Plate No. 43 .75 .75
1077 A91 200c like #1076 1.00 1.00
a. Wmk. 364 ('86) 1.00 1.00
1078 A91 60c Plate No. 44 .30 .30
1079 A91 100c Plate No. 45 .75 .75
1080 A91 150c like #1079 .75 .75
a. Wmk. 364 ('86) .75 .75
Nos. 1061-1080 (20) 14.55 14.55

Issued: #1061, 7/9; #1062, 1064-1066, 1068, 1073, 1078, 8/12; #1072, 1075, 1077, 1080, 9/16; #1063, 1067, 1070, 7/10/86; #1069, 1071, 1074, 1076, 1079, 8/21/86.

Nos. 1063, 1071-1072, 1074-1077, 1079-1080 horiz.

1081 A91 120c Plate No. 46 .60 .60
1082 A91 60c Plate No. 47 .30 .30
1083 A91 150c Plate No. 48 .75 .75
1084 A91 50c Plate No. 49 1.00 1.00
1085 A91 55c like #1084 .30 .30
a. Wmk. 364 ('86) .30 .30
1086 A91 60c Plate No. 50 .40 .40
1087 A91 320c like #1086 1.60 1.60
a. Wmk. 364 ('87) 7.50 7.50
1088 A91 25c Plate No. 51 .20 .20
1089 A91 25c Plate No. 52 .20 .20
1090 A91 30c Plate No. 53 .20 .20
a. Wmk. 364 ('86) .20 .20
1091 A91 50c like #1090 .40 .40
1092 A91 45c Plate No. 54 .25 .25
a. Wmk. 364 ('87) 7.50 7.50
1093 A91 60c like #1092 .45 .45
1094 A91 50c Plate No. 55 1.00 1.00
1095 A91 60c like #1094 1.25 1.25
1096 A91 75c like #1094 .40 .40
a. Wmk. 364 .40 .40
1097 A91 120c Plate No. 56 .60 .60
1098 A91 60c Plate No. 57 .30 .30
1099 A91 120c Plate No. 58 .60 .60
1100 A91 25c Plate No. 59 .20 .20
a. Dark red flowers ('86) .20 .20
Nos. 1081-1100 (20) 11.00 11.00

Issued: #1082-1083, 1085, 1089, 8/12; #1088, 9/16; #1095, 10/7; #1087, 1092, 2/26/86; #1081, 1090, 1096-1100, 7/10/86; #1086, 1091, 1093, 8/21/86; #1084, 12/22/86; #1094, 1/16/87.

No. 1098 horiz.

1101 A91 75c Plate No. 60 .55 .55
1102 A91 225c like #1101 1.10 1.10
a. Wmk. 364 ('87) 8.50 8.50
1103 A91 25c Plate No. 61 .20 .20
1104 A91 150c Plate No. 62 .75 .75
1105 A91 25c Plate No. 63 .20 .20
1106 A91 50c Plate No. 64 1.00 1.00
1107 A91 55c like #1106 .30 .30
a. Wmk. 364 ('86) .30 .30
1108 A91 50c Plate No. 65 .40 .40
1109 A91 100c like #1108 .50 .50
a. Wmk. 364 .50 .50
1110 A91 130c Plate No. 66 .65 .65
1111 A91 120c Plate No. 67 .60 .60
1112 A91 40c Plate No. 68 1.00 1.00
1113 A91 100c like #1112 .50 .50
a. Wmk. 364 ('87) 4.25 4.25
1114 A91 60c Plate No. 69 .45 .45
1115 A91 120c like #1114 .60 .60
a. Wmk. 364 ('87) 8.25 8.25
1116 A91 25c Plate No. 70 .20 .20
1117 A91 25c Plate No. 71 .20 .20
a. Wmk. 364 ('87) 8.25 8.25
1118 A91 60c like #1117 .45 .45
1119 A91 25c Plate No. 72 .20 .20
1120 A91 60c Plate No. 73 .30 .30
Nos. 1101-1120 (20) 10.15 10.15

Issued: #1104, 1107, 8/12; #1103, 1105, 1116, 1119, 9/16; #1102, 1115, 1117, 4/4/86; #1109-1111, 1113, 1120, 7/10/86; #1101, 1108, 1114, 1118, 8/21/86; #1112, 11/25/86.

No. 1114-1115, 1117-1118, 1120 horiz.

1121 A91 80c Plate No. 74 .60 .60
1122 A91 250c like #1121 1.25 1.25
a. Wmk. 364 ('87) 4.25 4.25
1123 A91 60c Plate No. 75 .30 .30
1124 A91 65c Plate No. 76 .50 .50
1125 A91 150c like #1124 .75 .75
a. Wmk. 364 ('87) 8.00 8.00
1126 A91 40c Plate No. 77 .20 .20
a. Wmk. 364 ('87) 7.50 7.50
1127 A91 45c like #1126 .35 .35
1128 A91 45c Plate No. 78 .35 .35
1129 A91 150c like #1128 .75 .75
a. Wmk. 364 ('87) 7.50 7.50
1130 A91 60c Plate No. 79 .45 .45
1131 A91 200c like #1130 1.00 1.00
a. Wmk. 364 ('87) 7.50 7.50
1132 A91 65c Plate No. 80 .50 .50
1133 A91 330c like #1132 1.60 1.60
a. Wmk. 364 ('87) 8.00 8.00
1134 A91 45c Plate No. 81 .25 .25
a. Wmk. 364 ('87) 8.00 8.00
1135 A91 55c like #1134 .45 .45
1136 A91 55c Plate No. 82 .45 .45
1137 A91 320c like #1136 1.60 1.60
a. Wmk. 364 ('87) 8.00 8.00
1138 A91 75c Plate No. 83 .55 .55
1139 A91 300c like #1138 1.50 1.50
a. Wmk. 364 ('87) 8.25 8.25
1140 A91 45c Plate No. 84 .35 .35
1141 A91 90c like #1140 .45 .45
a. Wmk. 364 ('87) 7.50 7.50
Nos. 1121-1141 (21) 14.20 14.20

Issued: #1126, 1129, 1131, 1139, 1141, 2/26/86; #1122-1123, 7/10/86; #1125, 1133-1134, 1137, 7/24/86; #1121, 1124, 1127-1128, 1130, 1132, 1135-1136, 1138, 1140, 8/21/86.

No. 1123 horiz.

1142 A91 45c Plate No. 85 .35 .35
1143 A91 360c like #1142 1.75 1.75
a. Wmk. 364 ('87) 7.50 7.50
1144 A91 30c Plate No. 86 .20 .20
a. Wmk. 364 ('87) 4.25 4.25
1145 A91 40c like #1144 1.00 1.00
1146 A91 60c Plate No. 87 .45 .45
1147 A91 150c like #1146 .75 .75
a. Wmk. 364 ('87) 8.25 8.25
1148 A91 65c Plate No. 88 .45 .45
1149 A91 100c like #1148 .50 .50
a. Wmk. 364 ('87) 8.00 8.00
1150 A91 55c Plate No. 89 .40 .40
1151 A91 90c like #1150 .45 .45
a. Wmk. 364 ('87) 8.00 8.00
1152 A91 40c Plate No. 90 .30 .30
1153 A91 375c like #1152 1.90 1.90
a. Wmk. 364 ('87) 4.25 4.25
1154 A91 40c Plate No. 91 1.75 1.75
1155 A91 130c like #1154 .65 .65
a. Wmk. 364 ('87) 4.25 4.25
1156 A91 50c Plate No. 92 .25 .25
a. Wmk. 364 ('87) 8.25 8.25
1157 A91 75c like #1156 .55 .55
1158 A91 60c Plate No. 93 .30 .30
a. Wmk. 364 ('87) 4.25 4.25
1159 A91 80c like #1158 .60 .60
1160 A91 60c Plate No. 94 .45 .45
1161 A91 350c like #1160 1.75 1.75
a. Wmk. 364 ('87) 8.25 8.25
1162 A91 60c Plate No. 95 .30 .30
a. Wmk. 364 ('87) 8.25 8.25
1163 A91 75c like #1162 .55 .55
1164 A91 40c Plate No. 96 .20 .20
a. Wmk. 364 ('87) 8.00 8.00
1165 A91 65c like #1164 .50 .50
Nos. 1142-1165 (24) 16.35 16.35

See note below #1341. Issued: #1143, 1156, 1162, 2/26/86; #1147, 1161, 4/4/86; #1144, 1153, 1155, 1158, 7/10/86; #1149, 1151, 1164, 7/24/86; #1142, 1146, 1148, 1150, 1152, 1157, 1159-1160, 1163, 1165, 8/21/86; #1154, 9/26/86; #1145, 10/23/86.

Some stamps printed in sheets of 25, blocks of 4 each of different stamps separated by gutter containing 2 #1337 and strip of 5 #1339. Margin contains separation marks for #1337, 1339.

Nos. 1146-1147, 1160-1161 horiz.

Nos. 1025, 1027, 1031, 1036, 1039, 1046, 1049, 1052, 1054, 1069, 1071, 1074, 1076, 1079, 1086, 1091, 1093, 1101, 1108, 1114, 1118, 1121, 1124, 1127-1128, 1130, 1132, 1135-1136, 1138, 1140, 1142, 1146, 1148, 1150, 1152, 1157, 1159-1160, 1163, 1165 sold as singles in booklets only. Two booklets of 48 stamps each contain these numbers and previous values issued in the series.

See #1372. For overprints and surcharges see #1342-1346, 1393, 1402-1403, 1412-1413, 1494, 1511-1670F, 1731-1740, 1742-1750, 1755-1759, 1761, 1764-1773, 1785, 1845-1849, 1906-1909, 1914-1933, 1939-1941, 1943-1947, 1958-1959, 1960-1979, 2000, C7, C9-C12, E2, E4.

1986-89 **Litho.** **Unwmk.** *Perf. 14*

Series 2

1166 A91 175c Plate No. 1 .65 .65
1167 A91 560c like #1166 1.60 1.60
1168 A91 90c Plate No. 2 1.00 1.00
1169 A91 200c like #1168 1.00 1.00
1170 A91 50c Plate No. 3 .20 .20
1171 A91 90c like #1170 .45 .45
1172 A91 90c Plate No. 4 .45 .45
1173 A91 140c like #1172 .50 .50
1174 A91 130c Plate No. 5 .50 .50
1175 A91 160c like #1174 .80 .80
1176 A91 50c Plate No. 6 .20 .20
1177 A91 390c like #1176 2.00 2.00
1178 A91 30c Plate No. 7 .20 .20
1179 A91 40c like #1178 .20 .20
1180 A91 70c Plate No. 8 .25 .25
1181 A91 75c like #1180 .40 .40
1182 A91 70c Plate No. 9 .25 .25
1183 A91 200c like #1182 1.00 1.00
1184 A91 90c Plate No. 10 1.25 1.25
1185 A91 320c like #1184 1.60 1.60
Nos. 1166-1185 (20) 14.50 14.50

Issued: #1172, 1175, 1181, 1183, 9/23; #1184, 10/23; #1177, 1185, 10/31; #1169, 11/25; #1171, 1179, 12/27; #1168, 1/5/87; #1167, 4/24/87; #1166, 1170, 1173-1174, 1176, 1178, 1180, 1182, 8/23/88.

Nos. 1174-1175 horiz.

1186 A91 200c Plate No. 11 .75 .75
1187 A91 70c Plate No. 12 .25 .25
1188 A91 320c like #1187 1.60 1.60
1189 A91 50c Plate No. 13 1.25 1.25
1190 A91 90c like #1189 .45 .45
1191 A91 30c Plate No. 14 .20 .20
1192 A91 120c like #1191 .60 .60
1193 A91 50c Plate No. 15 3.75 3.75
1194 A91 85c like #1193 .45 .45
1195 A91 260c Plate No. 16 .55 .55
1196 A91 320c like #1195 1.25 1.25
1197 A91 45c Plate No. 17 .20 .20
1198 A91 70c like #1197 .25 .25
1199 A91 85c Plate No. 18 .45 .45
1200 A91 320c like #1199 1.60 1.60
1201 A91 175c Plate No. 19 .65 .65
1202 A91 450c like #1201 1.25 1.25
1203 A91 25c Plate No. 20 .20 .20
1204 A91 50c like #1203 .20 .20
1205 A91 45c Plate No. 21 1.50 1.50
Nos. 1186-1205 (20) 17.40 17.40

Issued: #1188, 1205, 9/23; #1190, 1197, 10/31; #1189, 12/3; #1192, 1194, 1200, 1203, 12/27; #1193, 1199, 1/5/87; #1202, 4/24/87; #1196, 6/1/88; #1186-1187, 1191, 1198, 1201, 1204, 8/23/88; #1195, 7/7/89.

Nos. 1201-1202, 1205, horiz.

1206 A91 30c Plate No. 22 .20 .20
1207 A91 150c like #1206 .75 .75
1208 A91 200c Plate No. 23 .75 .75
1209 A91 85c Plate No. 24 1.00 1.00
1210 A91 225c like #1209 3.25 3.25
1211 A91 140c Plate No. 25 .50 .50
1212 A91 230c like #1211 .60 .60
1213 A91 200c Plate No. 26 .75 .75
1214 A91 60c Plate No. 27 .30 .30
1215 A91 90c like #1214 1.00 1.00
1216 A91 30c Plate No. 28 .20 .20
1217 A91 330c like #1216 1.60 1.60
1218 A91 130c Plate No. 29 .50 .50
1219 A91 350c like #1218 1.75 1.75
1220 A91 30c Plate No. 30 2.50 2.50
1221 A91 875c Plate No. 31 3.50 3.50
1222 A91 50c Plate No. 32 .20 .20
1223 A91 130c like #1222 .65 .65
1224 A91 50c Plate No. 33 .25 .25
1225 A91 100c like #1224 .75 .75
Nos. 1206-1225 (20) 21.00 21.00

Issued: #1219, 1220, 9/23; #1214, 1224, 10/31; #1210, 11/25; #1209, 1215, 12/15; #1207, 1217, 1223, 12/27; #1212, 2/14/87; #1221, 6/15/88; #1206, 1208, 1211, 1213, 1216, 1218, 1222, 1225, 8/23/88.

Nos. 1218-1219 horiz.

1226 A91 140c Plate No. 34 .50 .50
1227 A91 360c like #1226 1.75 1.75
1228 A91 380c Plate No. 35 1.40 1.40
1229 A91 525c Plate No. 36 2.25 2.25
1230 A91 175c Plate No. 37 .65 .65
1231 A91 390c like #1230 1.25 1.25
1232 A91 130c Plate No. 38 .65 .65
1233 A91 140c like #1232 .50 .50
1234 A91 175c Plate No. 39 .65 .65
1235 A91 260c like #1234 .75 .75
1236 A91 250c Plate No. 40 .90 .90
1237 A91 $10 like #1236 4.25 4.25
1238 A91 140c Plate No. 41 .50 .50
1239 A91 180c like #1238 .45 .45
1240 A91 80c Plate No. 42 .40 .40
1241 A91 130c like #1240 .50 .50
1242 A91 200c Plate No. 43 .55 .55
1243 A91 100c Plate No. 44 .75 .75
1244 A91 200c like #1243 1.00 1.00
1245 A91 35c Plate No. 45 .20 .20
1246 A91 85c like #1245 .40 .40
Nos. 1226-1246 (21) 20.25 20.25

Issued: #1227, 1232, 1240, 9/23; #1244, 1246, 10/31; #1245, 1/5/87; #1239, 2/14/87; #1231, 1235, 4/24/87; #1242, 9/29/87; #1237, 3/24/88; #1229, 6/1/88; #1226, 1228, 1230, 1233-1234, 1236, 1238, 1241, 1243, 8/23/88.

Nos. 1230-1231, 1240-1241 horiz.

1247 A91 225c Plate No. 46 .80 .80
1248 A91 175c Plate No. 47 .65 .65
1249 A91 240c like #1248 .70 .70
1250 A91 200c Plate No. 48 .55 .55
1251 A91 200c Plate No. 49 .55 .55
1252 A91 720c like #1251 3.00 3.00
1253 A91 160c Plate No. 50 .55 .55
1254 A91 300c like #1253 1.50 1.50
1255 A91 175c Plate No. 51 .60 .60
1256 A91 500c like #1255 1.50 1.50
1257 A91 140c Plate No. 52 .40 .40
1258 A91 590c like #1257 1.50 1.50
1259 A91 200c Plate No. 53 .55 .55
1260 A91 290c like #1259 1.25 1.25
1261 A91 175c Plate No. 54 .60 .60
1261A A91 460c like #1261 1.40 1.40
1262 A91 120c Plate No. 55 .35 .35
1263 A91 75c Plate No. 56 .40 .40
1264 A91 100c like #1263 .30 .30
1265 A91 225c Plate No. 57 .60 .60
Nos. 1247-1265 (20) 17.75 17.75

Issued: #1254, 1263, 10/31; #1258, 2/14/87; #1249, 1256, 1261A, 4/24/87; #1250, 9/29/87; #1252, 1260, 11/23/87; #1247-1248, 8/23/88; #1253, 1255, 11/3/88; #1251, 1257, 1259, 1261-1262, 1264-1265, 1/3/89.

Nos 1261, 1261A horiz.

1266 A91 175c Plate No. 58 .50 .50
1267 A91 275c like #1266 .85 .85
1268 A91 775c Plate No. 59 3.25 3.25
1269 A91 200c Plate No. 60 .55 .55
1270 A91 575c like #1269 1.50 1.50
1271 A91 255c Plate No. 61 1.00 1.00
1272 A91 280c Plate No. 62 .95 .95
1273 A91 700c like #1272 3.00 3.00
1274 A91 285c Plate No. 63 1.00 1.00
1275 A91 200c Plate No. 64 .55 .55
1276 A91 680c like #1275 2.75 2.75
1277 A91 140c Plate No. 65 .40 .40
1278 A91 650c like #1277 1.60 1.60
1279 A91 280c Plate No. 66 .75 .75
1280 A91 750c like #1279 3.00 3.00
1281 A91 280c Plate No. 67 .75 .75
1282 A91 $15 like #1281 6.25 6.25
1283 A91 325c Plate No. 68 .85 .85
1284 A91 530c Plate No. 69 2.25 2.25
1285 A91 550c Plate No. 70 2.75 2.75
Nos. 1266-1285 (20) 34.50 34.50

Issued: #1278, 2/14/87; #1267, 4/24/87; #1270, 1283, 10/26/87; #1271, 1276, 1280, 11/23/87; #1282, 1284, 6/1/88; #1268, 1273, 6/15/88; #1285, 8/15/88; #1272, 1274, 11/3/88; #1266, 1269, 1275, 1277, 1279, 1281, 1/3/89.

No. 1266-1267, 1283, 1285 horiz.

1286 A91 670c Plate No. 71 3.25 3.25
1287 A91 300c Plate No. 72 .80 .80
1288 A91 $25 like #1287 6.50 6.50
1289 A91 130c Plate No. 73 .25 .25
1290 A91 475c like #1289 2.00 2.00
1291 A91 350c Plate No. 74 1.50 1.50
1291A A91 900c like #1291 4.00 4.00
1291B A91 600c on 900c #1291A
1292 A91 200c Plate No. 75 .70 .70
1293 A91 250c Plate No. 76 .65 .65
1294 A91 850c like #1293 3.50 3.50
1295 A91 300c Plate No. 77 .80 .80
1296 A91 480c like #1295 1.25 1.25
1297 A91 280c Plate No. 78 .75 .75
1298 A91 950c like #1298 4.00 4.00
1299 A91 250c Plate No. 79 .90 .90
1300 A91 800c like #1299 3.25 3.25
1301 A91 300c Plate No. 80 .80 .80
1302 A91 400c like #1301 1.10 1.10
1303 A91 305c Plate No. 81 .80 .80
1304 A91 250c Plate No. 82 .65 .65
1305 A91 330c like #1304 .85 .85
Nos. 1286-1291A,1292-1305 (21) 38.30 38.30

Issued: #1305, 2/14/87; #1288, 1296, 1302, 7/22/87; #1291A-1291B, 10/9/87; #1294, 1300, 11/23/87; #1290, 6/1/88; #1298, 6/15/88; #1291, 6/22/88; #1286, 8/15/88;

#1292, 1299, 11/3/88; #1287, 1293, 1295, 1297, 1301, 1303-1304, 1/3/89; #1289, 7/7/89.
No. 1286 horiz.

1306 A91 350c Plate No. 83 .95 .95
1307 A91 $20 like #1306 5.25 5.25
1308 A91 360c Plate No. 84 1.75 1.75
1309 A91 250c Plate No. 85 .65 .65
1310 A91 300c like #1309 .75 .75
1311 A91 350c Plate No. 86 .95 .95
1312 A91 500c like #1311 1.25 1.25
1313 A91 250c Plate No. 87 .65 .65
1314 A91 425c like #1313 1.00 1.00
1315 A91 250c Plate No. 88 .65 .65
1316 A91 440c like #1315 1.10 1.10
1317 A91 350c Plate No. 89 .95 .95
1318 A91 520c like #1317 1.40 1.40
1319 A91 270c Plate No. 90 1.25 1.25
1320 A91 250c Plate No. 91 .65 .65
1321 A91 $12 like #1320 5.00 5.00
1322 A91 200c Plate No. 92 .55 .55
1323 A91 200c Plate No. 93 .70 .70
1324 A91 300c Plate No. 94 .80 .80
1325 A91 600c like #1324 1.60 1.60
1326 A91 420c Plate No. 95 1.25 1.25
1327 A91 200c Plate No. 96 .40 .40
1328 A91 375c like #1327 1.50 1.50
Nos. 1306-1328 (23) 31.00 31.00

Issued: #1310, 1314, 1316, 2/14/87; #1307, 1312, 1318, 6/2/87; #1325, 7/22/87/ #1322, 9/29/87; #1326, 10/26/87; #1328, 11/23/87; #1321, 3/24/88; #1308, 1319, 8/15/88; #1323, 11/3/88; #1306, 1309, 1311, 1313, 1315, 1317, 1320, 1324, 1/3/89; #1327, 7/7/89.

No. 1326, horiz.

Nos. 1166, 1170, 1174, 1176, 1178, 1180, 1182, 1187, 1191, 1193, 1198, 1201, 1204, 1206, 1211, 1216, 1218, 1222, 1225-1226, 1230, 1233-1234, 1236, 1238, 1248, 1257, 1261, 1264, 1266, 1277, 1279, 1281, 1287, 1293, 1295, 1297, 1301, 1304, 1306, 1308-1309, 1311, 1313, 1315, 1317, 1320, 1324 sold as singles in booklets only. Two booklets of 48 stamps each contain these numbers and previous values issued in the series.

Miniature Sheets of 4

Designs: Nos. 1329a, 1330b, 1331b, like #1303. Nos. 1329b, 1330a, 1332a, like #1265. Nos. 1329c, 1330c, 1332b, like #1247. Nos. 1330d, 1331a, 1332c, like #1262.

1329 #1262, 1329a-1329c 1.10 1.10
a.-c. A91 120c any single .25 .25
1330 #a.-d. 1.25 1.25
a.-d. A91 150c any single .30 .30
1331 #1247, 1265, 1331a-1331b 2.50 2.50
a.-b. A91 225c any single .45 .45
1332 #1303, 1332a-1332c 2.75 2.75
a.-c. A91 305c any single .60 .60
1333 4.50 4.50
a. A91 320c like #1262 .95 .95
b. A91 330c like #1247 .95 .95
c. A91 350c like #1303 1.00 1.00
d. A91 500c like #1265 1.50 1.50
1334 4.50 4.50
a. A91 320c like #1247 .95 .95
b. A91 330c like #1262 .95 .95
c. A91 350c like #1265 1.00 1.00
d. A91 500c like #1303 1.50 1.50
1335 4.50 4.50
a. A91 320c like #1303 .95 .95
b. A91 330c like #1265 .95 .95
c. A91 350c like #1262 1.00 1.00
d. A91 500c like #1247 1.50 1.50
1336 4.50 4.50
a. A91 320c like #1265 .95 .95
b. A91 330c like #1303 .95 .95
c. A91 350c like #1247 1.00 1.00
d. A91 500c like #1262 1.50 1.50

Issued: #1329-1332, 7/7/89; others, 2/26/88.

For surcharges & overprints see #1671-1727, 1776-1777, 1834-1835, 1942, 1948-1952, 1998-1999, 2031, 2033-2044, 2064, 2907A-2907G, 2928A-2928D, E3, E5, O40-O56.

Natl. Arms — A92

1985-87 ***Perf. 14 Vert.***
1337 A92 25c multi .50 .50
1338 A92 25c multi ('87) .50 .50

Perf. 14 Horiz.
1339 A92 25c multi .20 .20
1340 A92 25c multi ('87) .20 .20
Nos. 1337-1340 (4) 1.40 1.40

Perf. 14
1341 A92 25c multi

Nos. 1337-1340 were cut from orchid sheet gutters. Stamps vary considerably in size.

Nos. 1338, 1340 are Nos. 1337 and 1339 redrawn to include black border.

Issue dates: Nos. 1337, 1339, 1341, July 1985. No. 1338, 1340 June 2, 1987.

See Nos. 1467-1468. For surcharges see Nos. 1777A-1777C.

Nos. 1024, 1044, 1047, 1059, 1060 Surcharged or Overprinted in Blue or Black "QUEEN MOTHER 1900-1985" on 1 or 2 Lines

1985 ***Perfs. as Before***
1342 A91 130c on #1044
1343 A91 130c on #1059
1344 A91 130c on #1060
Nos. 1342-1344 (3) 6.25

Miniature sheets
1345 Sheet of 4 7.50
a.-d. A91 200c on #1024, any single
1346 Sheet of 4 8.25
a.-d. A91 200c on 130c #1047, any single (Bk)

Issued: #1342-1345, July 9; #1346, Sept. 12.

Nos. 1345a, 1346a overprinted "LADY BOWES-LYON 1900-1923". Nos. 1345b, 1346b overprinted "DUCHESS OF YORK 1923-1937". Nos. 1345c, 1346c overprinted "QUEEN ELIZABETH 1937-1952". Surcharge on No. 1346 sans serif.

For overprints see #1741, 1751-1754, 1774-1775.

Nos. 465 Surcharged in Red "INTERNATIONAL / YOUTH YEAR / 1985"

Perf. 13x13½
1985, July 18 Litho. Wmk. 364
1347 Sheet of 25, 8 #a.-b., 4 #c.-d., 1 #e. 3.00
a.-e. A28 25c on #465a-465e, any single

No. 203 Surcharged "1910-1985" and

No. 443 Surcharged

1985, July 26 ***Perfs. as Before***
Watermarks & Printing Methods as Before
1352 A47 225c on #203
1354 A63 240c on #443 12.00

Girl Guides, 75th anniv. (#1352), John J. Audubon, bicentennial of birth. No. 203 surcharged only with 350c, $2.25 or surcharged with both was not issued.

Abolition of Slavery, Sesquicent. — A93

Designs: 25c, Revolution leaders, 1763. 60c, Damon's execution, 1834. 130c, Demerara Uprising, 1823. 150c Den Arendt slave ship.

Unwmk.
1985, July 29 Litho. ***Perf. 14***
1355 A93 25c gray & black .25 .25
1356 A93 60c pink & black .65 .65
1357 A93 130c blue grn & blk 1.40 1.40
1358 A93 150c lilac & blk 1.60 1.60
Nos. 1355-1358 (4) 3.90 3.90

See Nos. 1994-1997 for changed colors.

No. 210 Surcharged "Guyana/Libya / Friendship 1985" No. 223 Surcharged in Brown No. 135 Surcharged "Mexico / 1986"

1985, Aug. 16 ***Perfs. as Before***
Watermarks and Printing Methods as Before
1359 A49 150c on #210 6.00
1360 A53 150c on #223 1.75
1361 A28 275c on 3c #135 1.75
Nos. 1359-1361 (3) 9.50

Refer to 2nd paragraph under No. 147 for No. 1361. See No. 1452 for 225c Mexico 1986 surcharge.

Nos. 366, 427, 430, 430a, 494, & 553 Ovptd. or Surcharged "1955-1985" Vertically or Horizontally

Wmk. 364
1985, Sept. 23 Litho. ***Perf. 13½***
1362 A75 60c on #366
1363 A75 60c on #553
1364 A75 120c on #427
1365 A75 120c on #430
1366 A75 120c on #430a
1367 A75 120c on #494
Nos. 1362-1367 (6) 4.00

No. 417 Surcharged "1965-1985" Vertically

1985, Sept. 30
1368 A79 25c on #417
1369 A79 225c on #417
Nos. 1368-1369 (2) 2.25

Nos. 260 & 262 Surcharged "1985"

1985, Oct. 5 Litho. ***Perf. 14x14½***
1370 A61 25c on 40c #262 10.00
1371 A61 320c on 15c #260 17.50

Orchid Type of 1985 Surcharged in Red "CRISTOBAL COLON / 1492-1992"

1985, Oct. 12 ***Perf. 14***
1372 A91 350c on 120c like #1108 5.00

No. 1372 not issued without surcharge. For overprint see No. E1. For surcharge see No. 1591A.

No. 288 Overprinted "SIR WINSTON CHURCHILL / 1965-1985"

1985, Oct. 15 ***Perf. 13½x13***
1373 A66 $2 on #288 7.00

No. 214 Surcharged "1950-1985"

1985, Oct. 15 ***Perf. 14***
1374 A50 25c on 110c on 10c
1375 A50 200c on 110c on 10c
Nos. 1374-1375 (2) 1.50

#214 with 110c surcharge only was not issued.

Nos. 295-297, 384, and O9 Overprinted or Surcharged "United / Nations / 1945-1985"

1985, Oct. 28 ***Perf. 14x14½***
1376 A68 30c on #295
1377 A68 50c on #296
1378 A68 100c on #O9
1379 A68 225c on #384
1380 A68 $3 on #297
Nos. 1376-1380 (5) 7.75

Nos. 142-144, 289A, O4-O5, O7, O15, and QO1-QO2 Ovptd. "POSTAGE"

1985, Oct. 29 ***Perfs. as Before***
Watermarks and Printing Methods as Before
1381 A28 30c on #O4 1.00
1382 A28 40c on #142 30.00
1383 A28 50c on #143 1.00
1384 A28 50c on #O5 1.00
1385 A28 60c on #144 3.00
1386 A28 60c on #144 (Revenue Only) 1.00
1387 A28 60c on #O7 2.50
1388 A66 $10 on #O15 15.00
1389 A28 $15 on #QO1 15.00
1390 A28 $20 on #QO2 17.50
Nos. 1381-1390 (10) 87.00

Refer to 2nd paragraph in footnote following #147 for #1381, 1384, 1386-1387.

Nos. 133-134 Surcharged "Deepavali / 1985"

1985, Nov. 1
1391 A28 25c on 2c #134
1392 A28 150c on 1c #133
Nos. 1391-1392 (2) 1.00

Miniature Sheet No. 1050 Ovptd. in Red

Overprinted: a, "Christmas 1985." b, "Happy New Year." c, "Merry Christmas." d, "Happy Holidays."

1985, Nov. 3 Unwmk. ***Perf. 14***
1393 A91 55c Sheet of 4, #a.-d. 12.00

For surcharge see No. 1670F.

Clive Lloyd, Cricketer — A94

Lloyd Holding Intl. Cup — A95

Designs: #a, $2.25, Lloyd playing cricket. #b, $1.30, Lloyd, bat and wicket. #c, 60c, Gloves, wicket, bat, natl. flag.

1985, Nov. 7 ***Perf. 14½x14***
1394 Triptych .55 .55
a.-c. A94 25c any single .20 .20

Size: 30x38mm
Perf. 14x14½
1395 A94 60c multi .40 .40
1396 A94 $1.30 multi .85 .85
1397 A94 $2.25 multi 1.50 1.50
1398 A95 $3.50 multi 2.50 2.50
Nos. 1394-1398 (5) 5.80 5.80

For surcharge see No. 1504.

Miniature Sheet No. 329 Ovptd. "1985" in Red

Wmk. 364
1985, Nov. 15 Litho. ***Perf. 14***
1399 A77 30c Sheet of 12, #a.-l.

Nos. 410 and 413e Surcharged

1985, Dec. 23 Photo. ***Perf. 14x14½***
Watermarks as Before
1400 A7 20c on #410
1401 A7 20c on #413De
Nos. 1400-1401 (2) 1.50

Compare No. 1400 with No. 914 and 1401 with No. 994a.

Nos. 1075, 1077 Ovptd. "REICHENBACHIA 1886-1986" in Purple

1986, Jan. 13 Litho. ***Perf. 14]***
1402 A91 150c on #1075 1.00
1403 A91 200c on #1077 1.25

For surcharge and overprints see Nos. 1553, 1760, 1762-1763.

Nos. 608, 610 Surcharged "Republic Day / 1986"

Perfs. as Before
1986, Feb. 22 Wmk. 364
1404 A82 25c on #608
1405 A83 120c on $6 #610
1406 A83 225c on $6 #610
Nos. 1404-1406 (3) 2.00

No. 87 Surcharged "1986"

1986, Mar. 24 Photo. *Perf. 13*

1407 A14 25c on 6c #87
1408 A14 50c on 6c #87
1409 A14 100c on 6c #87
1410 A14 200c on 6c #87
Nos. 1407-1410 (4) 2.75

No. 237 Surcharged "1926 / 1986"

1986, Mar. 27 Litho. *Perf. 14*

1411 A56 150c on 35c #237 5.00

St. John Ambulance, 60th anniv.

Nos. 1028, 1037 Surcharged "Queen Elizabeth / 1926 1986"

1986, Apr. 21 Unwmk.

1412 A91 Sheet of 4 6.25
a. 130c on 130c #1028
b. 200c on 130c #1028
c. 260c on 130c #1028
d. 330c on 130c #1028
1413 A91 130c on #1037 1.00

Location of overprint on No. 1413 differs from No. 1412.
For overprints & surcharges see #1670A, 1738B.

Nos. 267, 317g-317 l, 444a-444f Surcharged "Protect the"

Wmk. 373

1986, May 3 Litho. *Perf. 14*

1414 A73 60c on 35c #317g-317l, block of 6, #a.-f. 3.00
1415 A73 60c on 35c #444, block of 6, #a.-f. 2.50

Wmk. 364

1416 A63 $6 on 8c #267 5.00

No. 390 Surcharged

1986, May 5 Litho. *Perf. 13*

1417 A28 600c on #390 4.75

No. 283A Surcharged

Overprints: a, Abary. b, Anna Regina. c, Aurora. d, Bartica Grove. e, Bel Air. f, Belle Plaine. g, Clonbrook. h, T.P.O. Dem. / Railway. i, Enmore. j, Fredericks / burg. k, Good Success. l, 1986. m, Mariabba. n, Massaruni. o, Nigg. p, No. 50. q, No. 63 / Benab. r, Philadelphia. s, Sisters. t, Skeldon. u, Suddie. v, Taymouth / Manor. w, Wales. x, Whim.

Perf. 14x13½

1986, May 15 Litho. Wmk. 364

1418 Sheet of 25, #a.-k., m.-x., 2 #l.
a.-x. A66 25c on 30c, any single

British Guiana No. 254 Surcharged "GUYANA / INDEPENDENCE 1966-1986"

Nos. 10A and 13a Surcharged "1986"

No. 237 Surcharged

No. 713a-713d Surcharged "INDEPENDENCE / 1966-1986"

1986, May 26 *Perfs. as Before*

Watermarks and Printing Methods as Before

1443 A60 25c on 2c British Guiana #254
1444 A57 25c on 35c #241
1445 A60 60c on 2c British Guiana #254
1446 A60 120c on 6c #10A
1447 A60 130c on 24c #13a
1448 Block of 4
a. A86 25c on 120c #713a
b. A86 25c on 130c #713b
c. A86 25c on 150c #713c
d. A86 225c on 200c #713d
Nos. 1443-1448 (6) 6.00

No. 135 Surcharged "MEXICO / 1986" in Blue

Perf. 13x13½

1986, May 31 Litho. Wmk. 364

1452 A28 225c on 3c #135 2.50

World Cup Soccer Championships, Mexico City.

Nos. 135 and 192 Surcharged "CARICOM HEADS OF GOV'T / CONFERENCE / JULY 1986" in Blue

No. 286A Ovptd. "CARICOM / DAY 1986" in Blue

1986 *Perfs. as Before*

Watermarks and Printing Methods as Before

1453 A28 25c on #192 .75
1454 A28 60c on 3c #135 .75
1455 A66 60c on #286A 2.00
Nos. 1453-1455 (3) 3.50

Issued: #1455, June 28; #1453-1454, July 1.

Nos. 133 and 137 Surcharged "INT. YEAR / OF PEACE" in Black or Blue

1986, July 14 Litho. *Perf. 13x13½*

1456 A28 25c on 1c #133 (Bl)
1457 A28 60c on 6c #137
1458 A28 120c on 6c #137
1459 A28 130c on 6c #137
1460 A28 150c on 6c #137
Nos. 1456-1460 (5) 3.00

Halley's Comet — A96

Designs: a, Br. Guiana #172. b, Guyana #931.

1986, July 19 *Perf. 14*

1461 A96 320c Pair, #a.-b. 3.00 3.00
c. Imperf. 5.00

No. 1461 has continuous design. No. 1461 exists imperf. between. Most were overprinted.
For overprints and surcharges see Nos. 1822, 1836, 2029, E5-E6, E11, E14.

No. 43 Surcharged

1986, July 28 Photo. *Perf. 14x14½*

1463 A7 20c on 6c #43 3.00

Nos. 60-61 Surcharged "GUSIA / 1936-1986"

Perf. 14x13½

1986, Aug. 15 Photo. Unwmk.

1464 A11 25c on #61
1465 A11 $1.50 on 6c #60
Nos. 1464-1465 (2) 2.00

No. 136 Surcharged "REGIONAL / PHARMACY / CONFERENCE / 1986" in Blue

Perf. 13x13½

1986, Aug. 15 Litho. Wmk. 364

1466 A28 130c on 5c #136

Nos. 1337, 1339, 1341 Inscribed "1966-1986"

Perfs. as Before

1986, Sept. 23 Unwmk.

1467 A92 25c on #1337
1468 A92 25c on #1339
1469 A92 25c on #1341

No. 871 Surcharged

Perf. 14x13½

1986, Oct. 1 Litho. Wmk. 364

Sheet of 25

1470 #a.-k., m.-x., 2 #l
a.-x. A66 120c any single

No. 1145 Surcharged "12th World Orchid Conference" / "TOKYO JAPAN MARCH 1987"

Unwmk.

1986, Oct. 6 Litho. *Perf. 14*

1494 A91 650c on 40c #1145 5.00

For overprint see No. 1851.

Orchid Type like No. 1052 Surchd. "1492-1992" and "CHRISTOPHER COLUMBUS" in Black and Red or Red

1986, Oct.

1495 A91 320c on 150c
1496 A91 320c on 150c (R)
Nos. 1495-1496 (2) 4.00

Issued: #1495, 10/10; #1496, 10/30. #1495-1496 not issued without surcharge.

Nos. 704 and 705 Surcharged "1986"

Perf. 14x14½

1986, Oct. 15 Photo. Wmk. 364

1497 A7 50c on #704
1498 A7 225c on #705
Nos. 1497-1498 (2) 2.00

Nos. 134, 192 Surcharged "Deepavali /1986"

1986, Nov. 3 Litho. *Perf. 13x13½*

1499 A28 25c on 2c #134
1500 A28 200c on #192
Nos. 1499-1500 (2) 1.00

No. 43 Surcharged "CHRISTMAS / 1986" in Red

No. 917 Surcharged in Red

1986, Nov. 26 *Perfs. as Before*

Watermarks and Printing Methods as Before

1501 A7 20c on 6c #43 1.00

Miniature Sheet

1502 A88 120c on 60c on #a.-e.

No. 1502 is surcharged on an unissued miniature sheet containing No. 917.

No. 329 Ovptd. "1986" in Blue

Wmk. 364

1986, Nov. 26 Litho. *Perf. 14*

1503 A77 30c Sheet of 12, #a.-l.

No. 1398 Surcharged in Red

1986, Dec. 1 Litho. *Perf. 14x14½*

1504 A95 $15 on $3.50 #1398 15.00

L.F.S. Burnham, President 1980-85 A97

1986, Dec. 13 Litho. *Perf. 12½x13*

1505 A97 25c Tomb .20 .20
1506 A97 120c Flags, map .35 .35
1507 A97 130c Government building .40 .40
1508 A97 $6 Portrait, necklace, vert. 1.90 1.90
Nos. 1505-1508 (4) 2.85 2.85

Orchid Type of 1985-87 Surcharged "GPOC / 1977 - 1987"

1987, Jan. 19 *Perf. 14*

1509 A91 225c on 25c like #1090 1.25
1510 A91 $10 on 50c like #1052 4.00

Nos. 1509-1510 not issued without surcharge. No. 1509 adds "2" to 25c value, No. 1510 uses flower as obliterator.

Stamps of Type A91 Surcharged in Black or Red

a

b

c

d

e

f

g

h

i

j

k

l

1987-89 ***Perfs. as Before***

Design A91
Series 1
(Plate Number in Parentheses)
On Nos. 1022-1039

1511 (a) 120c on 60c (2) 2.50
1512 (b) 120c on 60c (2) 1.00
1513 (a) 120c on 60c (5) 2.00
1514 (c) 200c on 60c (5) 1.00
1515 (c) 200c on 75c (5) 1.00

Obliterator invtd. in surch. on #1514-1515.

1516 (d) 200c on 60c (7) 1.00
1517 (d) 200c on 25c (8) 1.50
1518 (e) 200c on 25c (8) 1.00
1519 (a) 120c on 50c (9) 1.00
1520 (b) 120c on 50c (9)
1521 (f) 120c on 50c (9) 1.00
1522 (g) 120c on 50c (9)
1523 (a) 120c on 55c (9) 2.00
1524 (f) 120c on 55c (9) 1.50
a. 120c on 55c #1032a 1.50
1525 (g) 120c on 55c (9) 1.00
1526 (a) 120c on 60c (10) 2.00
1527 (d) 200c on 60c (10) 1.00
1528 (h) $2 on 25c (12) 1.00

Surcharge on No. 1528 lacks obliterator.

1529 (f) 120c on 55c (15) 1.25
1530 (a) 200c on 55c (15) 5.00

Issued: #1518, 1528, 3/6; #1514-1515, 3/17; #1516-1517, 1522, 1525, 1527, 3/87; #1521, 1524, 1529, 7/87; #1511, 1513, 1519, 1523, 1526, 1530, 9/87; #1512, 1520, 7/88.

On Nos. 1042-1061

1531 (b) 120c on 55c (17)
1532 (d) 200c on 55c (17) 1.50
1533 (a) 600c on 80c (17) 3.00
1534 (a) 120c on 60c (19) 2.00
1535 (d) 200c on 60c (19) 1.00
1536 (a) 120c on 50c (22)
1537 (b) 120c on 50c (22)
1538 (f) 120c on 50c (22) 1.00
1539 (c) 200c on 50c (22) 1.00
1540 (i) 225c on 50c (22) 1.50
1541 (a) 120c on 55c #1050a (22) 2.00
1542 (f) 120c on 55c #1050a (22) 1.50
1543 (c) 200c on 55c #1050a (22) 1.00
1544 (h) $2 on 25c (23) 1.25
1545 (a) 120c on 50c (24) 2.00
1546 (a) 200c on 50c (24)
1547 (d) 200c on 50c (24) 1.00
1548 (a) 120c on 60c (31) 2.00
1549 (d) 200c on 60c (31) 1.00

Issued: #1544, 3/6; #1539, 1543, 3/17; #1532, 1535, 1547, 1549, 3/87; #1540, 6/87; #1538, 1542, 7/87; #1533-1534, 1536, 1541, 1545-1546, 1548, 9/87; #1531, 1537, 7/88.

On Nos. 1069-1091

1550 (b) 120c on 80c (39)
1551 (a) 600c on 80c (39) 3.00
1552 (g) $15 on 80c (39) 4.00
1553 (i) 225c on #1402 (42) 1.50
1554 (d) 200c on 60c (44) 1.00
1555 (d) 200c on 60c (47) 1.00
1556 (a) 120c on 50c (49)
1557 (f) 120c on 50c (49) 1.50
1558 (a) 120c on 55c #1085a (49) 2.00
1559 (f) 120c on 55c (49) 1.25
a. 120c on 55c on #1085a 1.50
1560 (d) 200c on 55c (49) 1.00
a. 200c on 55c on #1085a 2.50
1561 (a) 120c on 60c (50) 2.00
1562 (b) 120c on 60c (50)
1563 (e) 200c on 25c (51) 1.25
1564 (d) 200c on 25c (52) 1.00
1565 (b) 120c on 30c (53)
a. 120c on 30c on #1090a
1566 (a) 120c on 50c (53) 2.00
1567 (d) 200c on 30c #1090a (53) 1.00
1568 (a) 200c on 50c (53)
1569 (d) 200c on 50c (53) 1.00
1570 (g) $10 on 25c (53) 3.25
1571 (g) $25 on 25c (53) 6.00

Surcharge on #1571 lacks obliterator and places a "$" in front of original denomination. #1570-1571 not issued without surcharge.

Issued: #1563, 3/6; #1552, 1554-1555, 1560, 1564, 1567, 1569-1571, 3/87; #1553, 6/87; #1557, 1559, 7/87; #1551, 1556, 1558, 1561, 1566, 1568, 9/87; #1550, 1562, 1565, 7/88.

On Nos. 1092-1108, 1372

1572 (b) 120c on 45c (54)
1573 (a) 120c on 60c (54) 2.00
1574 (b) 120c on 60c (54) 1.00
1575 (a) 200c on 50c (55)
1576 (i) 225c on 60c (55) 1.50
1577 (b) 120c on 60c (57) 1.00
a. New value at bottom
1578 (d) 200c on 60c (57) 1.00
1579 (b) 120c on 25c (59) 1.00
1580 (a) 120c on 75c (60) 2.00
1581 (c) 200c on 75c (60) 2.50
1582 (b) 120c on 25c (61)
1583 (b) 120c on 25c (63) 1.00
1584 (a) 120c on 50c (64)
1585 (f) 120c on 50c (64) 1.50
1586 (a) 120c on 55c, wmkd. (64) 2.00
1587 (f) 120c on 55c (64) 1.00
a. 120c on 55c on #1107a 1.25
1588 (g) 120c on 55c (64) 1.00
a. 120c on 55c on #1107a 1.00

Surcharge on Nos. 1522, 1525, 1588-1588a does not contain date.

1589 (a) 120c on 50c (65) 2.00
1590 (a) 200c on 50c (65)
1591 (d) 200c on 50c (65) 1.00
1591A (i) 225c on #1372 (65)

Issued: #1581, 3/17; #1578, 1588, 1591, 3/87; #1576, 6/87; #1585, 1587, 7/87; #1573, 1575, 1580, 1584, 1586, 1589-1590, 9/87; #1591A, 10/9/87; #1572, 1574, 1577, 1579, 1582-1583, 7/88.

On Nos. 1112-1124

1592 (b) 120c on 40c (68) 1.00
a. New value at LL
1593 (c) 200c on 40c (68) 1.00
a. Obliterator inverted 1.00
1594 (a) 225c on 40c (68) 2.50
1595 (a) 120c on 60c (69)
1596 (b) 120c on 60c (69) 1.00
1597 (b) 120c on 25c (70)
1598 (b) 120c on 25c (71)
1599 (a) 120c on 60c (71) 2.00
1600 (d) 200c on 25c (71) 1.00
1601 (d) 200c on 60c (71) 1.00
1602 (j) 120c on 25c (72)
1603 (d) 200c on 25c (72) 1.00
1604 (b) 120c on 60c (73)
1605 (d) 200c on 60c (73) .75
1606 (b) 120c on 80c (74)
1607 (a) 600c on 80c (74) 3.00
1608 (g) $12 on 80c (74) 3.50
1609 (b) 120c on 60c (75)
a. New value at bottom
1610 (d) 200c on 60c (75) 1.00
1611 (a) 225c on 65c (76) 2.50

Issued: #1593, 3/17; #1600-1601, 1603, 1605, 1608, 1610, 3/87; #1594-1595, 1599, 1611, 9/87; #1592, 1596-1598, 1604, 1606-1607, 1609, 7/88; #1602, 9/88.

On Nos. 1126-1142

1612 (b) 120c on 40c (77)
a. New value at UL
1613 (d) 200c on 40c (77) 1.00
1614 (a) 200c on 45c (77) 3.00
1615 (d) 200c on 45c (77) 1.00
1616 (a) 200c on 45c (78) 3.00
1617 (d) 200c on 45c (78) 1.00
1618 (a) 120c on 60c (79) 3.00
1619 (b) 120c on 60c (79)
1620 (a) 225c on 65c (80) 3.00
1621 (b) 120c on 45c (81)
1622 (f) 120c on 55c (81) 1.25
1623 (d) 200c on 45c (81) 1.00
1624 (a) 200c on 55c (81) 4.00
1625 (f) 120c on 55c (82) 1.50
1626 (a) 200c on 55c (82) 10.00
1627 (a) 120c on 75c (83) 3.00
1628 (b) 120c on 90c (84)
1629 (a) 200c on 45c (84) 3.00
1630 (a) 200c on 45c (85) 3.00
1631 (d) 200c on 45c (85) 1.00

Issued: #1613, 1615, 1617, 1623, 1631, 3/87; #1622, 1625, 7/87; #1614, 1616, 1618, 1620, 1624, 1626-1627, 1629-1630, 9/87; #1612, 1619, 1621, 1628, 7/88.

On Nos. 1144-1153

1632 (b) 120c on 30c (86)
1633 (b) 120c on 40c (86) 1.00
1634 (d) 200c on 30c (86) 1.00
1635 (d) 200c on 40c (86)
1636 (a) 225c on 40c (86) 3.00
a. Inscribed "ONTOGLOSSUM" 2.50
1637 (a) 120c on 60c (87) 2.00
a. Surcharge reading up
1638 (d) 200c on 60c (87) 1.00
1639 (a) 225c on 65c (88) 2.50
1640 (f) 120c on 55c (89) 1.25
1641 (b) 120c on 90c (89)
1642 (a) 200c on 55c (89) 5.00
1643 (d) 225c on 90c (89) 1.00
1644 (a) 120c on 40c (90) 2.00
1645 (b) 120c on 40c (90) 1.00
1646 (c) 200c on 40c (90) 1.00
1647 (d) 200c on 40c (R) (90) 1.25
1648 (c) 200c on 375c (90) 1.00
a. 200c on 375c #1153a 3.00
1649 (a) 225c on 40c (90) 2.50
1650 (i) 225c on 40c (90) 1.50
1651 (k) 260c on 375c (90) 1.00

Issued: #1647, 2/9/87; #1646, 1648, 3/17/87; #1634-1635, 1638, 1643, 3/87; #1650, 6/87; #1640, 7/87; #1636-1637, 1639, 1642, 1644, 1649, 9/87; #1632-1633, 1641, 1645, 7/88; #1651, 10/88.

Surcharge on #1651 is placed over original value and has no obliterator.

On Nos. 1154-1165

1652 (a) 120c on 40c (91) 2.00
1653 (b) 120c on 40c (91) 1.00
a. New value at LR
1654 (a) 225c on 40c (91) 3.00
1655 (i) 225c on 40c (91) 1.50
1656 (b) 120c on 50c (92)
1657 (a) 120c on 75c (92) 2.50
1658 (c) 200c on 50c (92)
1659 (c) 200c on 75c (92) 1.00
1660 (b) 120c on 60c (93)
1661 (b) 120c on 80c (93)
1662 (i) 225c on 60c (93) 1.50
1663 (i) 225c on 80c (93) 1.50
1664 (a) 600c on 80c (93)
1665 (a) 120c on 60c (94)
1666 (b) 120c on 60c (94)
1667 (b) 120c on 60c (95) 1.00
1668 (a) 120c on 75c (95) 3.00
1669 (b) 120c on 40c (96)
1670 (a) 225c on 65c (96) 2.50

Miniature Sheets

1670A Sheet of 4 20.00
b. (a) 600c on 130c #1412a (6)
c. (a) 600c on 200c #1412b (6)
d. (a) 600c on 260c #1412c (6)
e. (a) 600c on 330c #1412d (6)
1670F Sheet of 4
g. (i) 225c on #1393a (22)
h. (i) 225c on #1393b (22)
i. (i) 225c on #1393c (22)
j. (i) 225c on #1393d (22)

Issued: #1658-1659, 3/17/87; #1655, 1662-1663, 6/87; #1652, 1654, 1657, 1664-1665, 1668, 1670, 9/87; #1670F, 11/9/87; #1670A, 11/20/87; #1653, 1656, 1660-1661, 1666-1667, 1669, 7/88.

For overprints see Nos. 1975, 1979.

Series 2
On Nos. 1168-1204

1671 (b) 120c on 90c (2) 1.00
1672 (b) 120c on 50c (3) 1.00
1673 (f) 120c on 50c (3) 1.00
1674 (b) 200c on 90c (4)
1675 (b) 120c on 50c (6) 1.00
1676 (f) 120c on 50c (6) 1.00
1677 (b) 120c on 30c (7) 1.00
1678 (b) 120c on 70c (8) 1.00
1679 (b) 120c on 70c (9) 1.00
a. New value at LR
1680 (b) 120c on 90c (10) 1.00
1681 (b) 120c on 70c (12) 1.00
a. New value at LL
1682 (b) 120c on 50c (13) 1.00
1683 (b) 120c on 90c (13)
1684 (b) 120c on 30c (14) 1.00
a. New value at UR
1685 (b) 120c on 50c (15) 1.00
1686 (b) 120c on 85c (15)
1687 (b) 120c on 70c (17) 11.00
1688 (b) 120c on 85c (18) 1.00
1689 (c) 200c on 85c (18)
1690 (b) 120c on 50c (20) 1.00
1691 (f) 120c on 50c (20) 1.50

Issued: #1689, 3/17/87; #1673, 1676, 1691, 7/87; #1671-1672, 1674-1675, 1677-1688, 1690, 7/88.

On Nos. 1205-1240

1692 (b) 120c on 45c (21) 1.00
1693 (b) 120c on 30c (22) 1.00
1694 (l) 350c on 330c #O52 (23) 1.00
1695 (b) 120c on 85c (24) 1.00
1696 (j) 120c on 140c (R) (25) 1.00
1697 (l) 250c on 225c #O46 (26) 1.00
a. New value at UL
1698 (b) 120c on 60c (27) 1.50
1699 (b) 120c on 90c (27)
1700 (b) 120c on 30c (28) 1.00
a. New value at UL 1.00
1701 (b) 120c on 30c (30) 1.00
1702 (k) 240c on 140c (30) 1.00

No. 1702 not issued without surcharge.

1703 (l) 150c on 175c #O44 (31) 1.00
1704 (b) 120c on 50c (32) 1.00
1705 (f) 120c on 50c (32) 1.00
1706 (k) 240c on 140c (34) 1.00
1707 (l) 125c on 140c #O42 (36) 1.00
1708 (k) 120c on 140c (38) 1.00
1709 (k) 120c on 140c (41) 1.00
1710 (b) 200c on 80c (42)
1711 (l) 150c on #O43 (43) 1.00

Issued: #1705, 7/87; #1692-1693, 1695, 1698-1701, 1704, 1710, 7/88; #1702, 1706, 10/88; #1696, 1708-1709, 2/22/89; #1694, 1697, 1703, 1707, 1711, 3/89.

On Nos. 1245-1314

1712 (b) 120c on 35c (45) 1.00
1713 (b) 120c on 85c (45)
1714 (j) 120c on 140c (R) (52) 1.00
1715 (k) 300c on 290c (53) 1.00
1716 (j) 120c on 175c (R) (54) 1.00
1717 (k) 170c on 175c (58) 1.00
1718 (l) 250c on #O48 (59) 1.00
1719 (j) 120c on 140c (R) (65) 1.00
1720 (k) 250c on 280c (66) 1.00
1721 (k) 250c on 280c (67) 1.00
1722 (l) 250c on 230c #O47 (68) 1.00
1723 (l) 250c on 260c #O49 (69) 1.00
a. New value at UR 1.00
1724 (l) 600c on #O54 (70) 1.00
1725 (l) $12 on #O55 (71) 1.00
1726 (l) $15 on #O56 (84) 1.00
1727 (k) 240c on 425c (87) 1.00
1728 (l) 300c on 275c #O50 (90) 1.00
1729 (l) 125c on 130c #O41 (92) 1.00
1730 (l) 350c on #O53 (95) 1.00

On No. 1730 "Postage" reads up or down.

Issued: #1712-1713, 7/88; #1727, 10/88; #1714, 1716, 1719, 2/22/89; #1715, 1717-1718, 1720-1726, 1728-1730, 3/89.

Obliterator on Nos. 1708-1709, 1715, 1717, 1720-1721 has two thick bars.

Stamps of Type A91 Overprinted

m

n

o

p

1987 ***Perfs. as Before***

Series 1

1731 (m) 120c on #1021 (1) 5.00
1732 (n) 130c on #1023 (3) 1.00
1733 (m) 130c on #1028a (6) 3.00
1734 (n) 130c on #1028 (6) 1.25
a. 130c on #1028a 1.25
1735 (m) 120c on #1034 (11) 3.00
1736 (m) 130c on #1037a (13) 3.00
1737 (n) 130c on #1413 (13) 2.50
1738 (o) 130c on #1037 (13) 1.00
a. 130c on #1037a 1.00
1738B (p) 130c on #1413 (13)
1739 (n) 200c on #1038 (14) 1.50
1740 (n) 130c on #1041 (16) 1.00
1741 (n) 130c on #1342 (18) 1.00
1742 (p) 130c on #1342 (18) 1.00
1743 (m) 130c on #1047a (20) 2.00
1744 (n) 130c on #1047a (20) 1.00
a. 130c on #1047 1.25
1745 (m) 200c on #1048 (21) 2.00
1746 (n) 200c on #1048 (21)
1747 (m) 130c on #1055a (25) 2.50
1748 (o) 130c on #1055 (25) 1.00
a. 130c on #1055a 1.00
1749 (p) 150c on #1056 (26) 1.00
1750 (m) 120c on #1058 (28) 4.00
1751 (n) 130c on #1343 (29) 1.00
1752 (p) 130c on #1343 (29) 1.00

Issued: #1732, 1734, 1737-1741, 1744, 1746, 1748, 1751, Mar; #1731, 1733, 1735-1736, 1743, 1745, 1747, 1750, July; #1738B, Nov. 20; #1742, 1749, 1752, Dec.

1753 (n) 130c on #1344 (30) 1.00
1754 (p) 130c on #1344 (30) 1.00
1755 (n) 200c on #1063 (33) 1.00
1756 (m) 120c on #1067 (37) 1.50
1757 (n) 260c on #1070 (39) 2.00
1758 (m) 150c on #1072a, ovpt. reading up (40) 1.50
a. 150c on #1072 2.50
1759 (m) 150c on #1075a (42) 3.00
1760 (m) 150c on #1402 (42) 5.00
1761 (m) 200c on #1077a (43) 5.00
1762 (m) 200c on #1403 (43) 5.00
1763 (n) 200c on #1403 (43) 3.00
1764 (m) 150c on #1080 reading down (45) 2.00
a. 150c on #1080a reading up 2.50
1765 (m) 120c on #1081 (46) 8.00
1766 (m) 120c on #1097 (56) 3.00
1767 (m) 120c on #1099 (58) 3.00
1768 (n) 130c on #1110 (66) 3.00
1769 (p) 130c on #1110 (66) 1.00
1770 (p) 120c on #1111 (67) 1.00
1771 (n) 250c on #1122 (74) 1.25
1772 (n) 200c on #1131 (79) 1.00
1773 (o) 130c on #1155 (91) 1.50

Miniature Sheets of 4

1774 (n) 200c on #1345 (4) 3.00
1775 (n) 200c on 130c #1346 (20) 4.00

Series 2

1776 (n) 200c on #1169 (2) 5.00
1777 (n) 200c on #1183 (9) 1.00

Issued: #1753, 1755, 1757, 1763, 1768, 1771-1777, Mar.; #1756, 1758, 1759-1762, 1764-1767, July. #1754, 1769-1770, Dec.

Overprint reads up on #1759, 1761. Overprint reads down on #1731, 1735, 1745, 1750, 1755, 1758a, 1760, 1762, 1763.

See Nos. 1813-1814, 1844 for other stamps overprinted "1987" only.

Nos. 1337, 1339, 1341 Surcharged

1987, Mar. 6 ***Perfs. as Before***

1777A A92 200c on #1337
1777B A92 200c on #1339
1777C A92 200c on #1341

See note following No. 1341.

Nos. 134, 136, 139a, and 192 Surcharged "Post Office / Corp. / 1977-1987" in Blue

Perfs. as Before

1987, Feb. 17 Litho. Wmk. 364

1778 A28 25c on 2c #134
1779 A28 25c on 5c #136
1780 A28 25c on #192
1781 A28 25c on 15c #139a
1782 A28 60c on 15c #139a
1783 A28 $1.20 on 2c #134
1784 A28 $1.30 on 15c #139a
Nos. 1778-1784 (7) 8.00

Nos. 1032, 1032a Surcharged "12th World Orchid Conference" and "TOKYO JAPAN"

1987, Mar. 12 Unwmk. ***Perf. 14***

1785 A91 650c on 55c #1032 5.00
a. 650c on 55c #1032a 5.00

No. 280 Surcharged with Names of Post Offices Operating in 1885

Overprints: a, AGRICOLA. b, BAGOTVILLE. c, BOURDA. d, BUXTON. e, CABACABURI. f, CAR- / MICHAEL STREET. g, COTTON / TREE. h, DUNOON. i, FELLOW- / SHIP. j, GROVE. k, HACKNEY. l, LEONORA. m, 1987. n, MALLALI. o, PROVI- / DENCE. p, RELI-ANCE. q, SPARTA. r, STEWART- / VILLE. s, TARLOGY. t, T.P.O. / BERBICE RIV. u, T.P.O. / DEM. RIV. v, T.P.O. / ESSEQ. RIV. w, T.P.O. / MASSARUNI / RIV. x, TUSCHEN / (De / VRIENDEN). y, ZORG.

Perf. 14x13½

1987, Mar. 17 Wmk. 364

1786 Sheet of 25, #a.-y.
a.-y. A66 25c on 10c, any single

British Guiana Post Office, 125th Anniv.

Columbus' Discovery of America, 500th Anniv. (in 1992) — A98

Paintings: 120c, Discovery of America, by Dali. 225c, Preparations Before the Journey, by unknown artist. 360c, Catholic Kings from Prado Museum.

$6, Columbus' Fleet, by R. Monleon.

1987, Mar. 30 Litho. ***Perf. 13½***

1787 A98 120c multicolored
1788 A98 225c multicolored
1789 A98 360c multicolored
a. Strip of 3, #1787-1789

Souvenir Sheet

1790 A98 $6 gold & multi

No. 1790 exists with silver border.

No. 289A Ovptd. "28 MARCH 1927 / PAA / GEO-POS"

1987, Mar. 28 ***Perf. 13½x13***

1811 A66 $10 on #289A 6.00

First Georgetown to Port-of-Spain Flight, 50th Anniv.

No. 285 Surcharged

1987, Apr. 6 ***Perf. 14x13½***

1812 A66 25c on 40c #285 3.00

Nos. 87-88, 90, 287 Surcharged or Overprinted "1987"

1987, Apr. ***Perfs. as Before***

Watermarks and Printing Methods as Before

1813 A14 25c on #88 .75
1814 A66 $1 on #287 5.00
1815 A14 120c on 6c #87 .75
1816 A14 320c on 6c #87 .75
1817 A14 500c on 40c #90 .75
Nos. 1813-1817 (5) 8.00

Issued: #1813, 1815-1817, Apr. 21; #1814, Apr.

No. 1461 Ovptd. "CAPEX '87"

1987, June 10 Litho. ***Perf. 14***

1822 A96 320c Pair, #a.-b. 2.00
c. on #1461, imperf. between 5.00

For surcharges see Nos. 2030, E15.

Nos. 626-628 Ovptd. "1987"

Wmk. 314 Upright

1987, July 15 Engr. ***Perf. 12½x13***

1823 A60 $1.20 on #626

Wmk. 314 Sideways

1824 A60 $1.30 on #627
1825 A60 $2.40 on #628
Nos. 1823-1825 (3) 3.00

A99

A100

Locomotives — A101

#1826a, 1827a, Alexandra 4. #1826b, 1827b, Diesel locomotive facing right. #1826c, 1827c, Steam locomotive facing right. #1826d, 1827d, Diesel locomotive No. 21 facing left.

#1829a, 1830b, Alexandra 4. #1829b, 1830a, Diesel locomotive. #1829c, 1830d, Steam locomotive facing right. #1829d, 1830c, Diesel locomotive No. 21. #1830e, Photograph of trains in Georgetown Station. #1831, Steam locomotive pulling cattle cars, map of routes from Parika to Vreedenhoop and from Georgetown to Rosignol.

1987, Aug. 3 ***Perf. 15***

1826 Block of 4 1.00 1.00
a.-d. A99 $1.20 green, any single .25 .25
1827 Block of 5 3.25 3.25
a.-d. A99 $3.20 blue, any single .65 .65
e. A100 $3.20 blue .65 .65
1828 A101 $12 shown 2.50 2.50
Nos. 1826-1828 (3) 6.75 6.75

1987, Dec. 4

1829 Block of 4 1.25 1.25
a.-d. A99 $1.20 rose lake, any single .30 .30
1830 Block of 5 3.75 3.75
a.-d. A99 $3.30 blk, any single .75 .75
e. A100 $3.30 black .75 .75
1831 A101 $10 multi 2.25 2.25
Nos. 1829-1831 (3) 7.25 7.25

Sizes: #1827e, 1830e, 84x57mm. #1828, 1831, 90x40mm.

For surcharges see #E12-E13. For overprints see #1910-1911, 1935-1938, 2024-2028F, 2054, 2056.

No. 287 Ovptd. "FAIREY NICHOLL / 15 AUG 1927 / GEO-MAB" or "FAIREY NICHOLL / 8 AUG 1927 / GEO-MAZ"

1987, Aug. 7 Litho. ***Perf. 13½x13***

1832 A66 $1 "MAB" on #287
1833 A66 $1 "MAZ" on #287
a. Pair, #1832-1833

No. 1291A Surcharged "CRISTOVAO COLOMBO / 1492 - 1992" (#1834) or "CHRISTOPHE COLOMB / 1492 - 1992" (#1835)

No. 1461c Surcharged "THE PASSING OF HALLEY'S COMET: / PROPHESY OF THE ARRIVAL OF / HERNAN CORTES 1519. / V CENTENARY OF THE LANDING OF / CHRISTOPHER COLUMBUS / IN THE AMERICAS"

Unwmk.

1987, Oct. 9 Litho. ***Perf. 14***

1834 A91 950c on 900c #1291A
1835 A91 950c on 900c #1291A
a. Pair, #1834-1835 15.00

Imperf

1836 A96 $20 on 320c #1461c

Nos. 135-136 Surcharged "DEEPAVALI / 1987"

1987, Nov. 2 Litho. ***Perf. 13x13½***

1837 A28 25c on 3c #135
1838 A28 $3 on 5c #136

No. 43 Surcharged "CHRISTMAS / 1987" in Red

No. 1502 Surcharged "1987" in Blue

1987, Nov. 9 ***Perfs. as Before***

Watermarks and Printing Methods as Before

1839 A7 20c on 6c #43

Miniature Sheet

1840 A88 120c on 60c #1502

No. 329 Overprinted "1987"

No. 920 Surcharged "Protect Our Heritage '87" in Red

Nos. 1037, 1040, 1056, 1110-1111, 1494 Surcharged "PROTECT OUR HERITAGE '87"

1987, Dec. 9 ***Perfs. as Before***

Watermarks and Printing Methods as Before

1844 A77 30c Sheet of 12, #a.-l, on #329
1845 A91 120c on #1111 2.50
1846 A91 130c on #1110 2.50
1847 A91 150c on #1056 2.50
1848 A91 180c on #1040 2.50
1849 A91 320c on #1137 5.00
1850 A89 320c Triptych, #a.-c, on 120c #920
1851 A91 650c on #1494 8.00

1988 Summer Olympics, Seoul — A102

1987, Dec. 30 Litho. *Perf. 13½x14*

1852 A102 $2 Jumping
1853 A102 $3 Discus
1854 A102 $5 Vase
a. Strip of 3, #1852-1854 8.00

Souvenir Sheet

Perf. 14

1855 A102 $3.50 Olympic Rings, horiz.

Christmas 1987 — A103

Paintings: #a, The Virgin of the Rocks, by Da Vinci. #b, Virgin with Grapes, by Mignard. #c, Sacred Family, by Raphael. #d, Virgin Mary, by Lucas Cranach. No. 1857, Adoration of Three Kings, by Rubens.

1988, Jan. 7 Litho. *Perf. 14*

1856 A103 $2 Strip of 4, #a.-d. 5.00

Souvenir Sheet

1857 A103 $10 Sheet of 1 7.00

Dated 1987.

Nos. 397, 405 and 651 Ovptd. or Surcharged "*AUSTRALIA* / 1987 JAMBOREE 1988" in Red

1988, Jan. 7 Litho. *Perf. 13½x13*

1858 A17 $4.40 on #405
1859 A17 $10 on #397
1860 A17 $10 on #651
1861 A17 $10 on #405
a. $10 on #405a

Obliterator on Nos. 1859-1861 is red fleur-de-lis. Size and location of overprint varies.

Nos. 68 and 70 Surcharged "IFAD / For a World / Without Hunger"

Perf. 14x14½

1988, Jan. 26 Photo. Wmk. 364

1862 A68 25c on 1c #68
1863 A68 $5 on 3c #70
Nos. 1862-1863 (2) 1.50

No. 1862 uses new denomination as obliterator and No. 1863 uses "X."

Flora and Fauna — A104

Mushrooms - #1864: a, Corprinus comatus. b, Amanita muscaria. c, Pholiota aurivella. d, Laccaria amethstina.

Birds - #1865: a, Starling. b, Reed warbler. c, Kingfisher. d, Goldcrest.

Cats - #1866: a, Himalayan. b, American shorthaired. c, Maine coon. d, Abyssinian.

Cactus flowers - #1866: e, Sulcorebutia densiseta. f, Subutia hyalacantha. g, Echinopsis. h, Lobivia polycephala.

Nos. 1866a-1866h horiz.

1988, Jan. 28 *Perf. 14*

1864 A104 $2 Strip of 4, #a.-d. 4.00
1865 A104 $2 Strip of 4, #a.-d. 4.00

Miniature Sheet

Perf. 14x13½

1866 A104 $2 Sheet of 8, #a.-h. 4.00

Dated 1987.

Santa Maria — A105

Ships: a, Santa Maria. b, Grande Francoise. #1869, San Martin, horiz.

1988, Feb. 10 Litho. *Perf. 13½x14*

1867 A105 $7 Pair, #a.-b., pale yel & multi
1868 A105 $7 Pair, #a.-b., bl & multi

Souvenir Sheet

Perf. 14

1869 A105 $7 silver & multi

Discovery of America, 500th anniv. (in 1992). Nos. 1867-1868 printed checkerwise with se-tenant labels describing ship dimensions. No. 1869 exists with gold border.

Nos. 136, 139a, and 146 Surcharged "Republic / Day / 1988" in Blue

Perfs. as Before

1988, Feb. 23 Litho. Wmk. 364

1870 A28 25c on 5c #136
1871 A28 120c on 15c #139a
1872 A28 $10 on $2 #146
Nos. 1870-1872 (3) 5.00

No. 283A Surcharged with Names of Post Offices Operating in 1900

Overprints: a, Albouystown. b, Anns Grove. c, Amacura. d, Arakaka. e, Baramanni. f, Cuyuni. g, Hope Placer. h, HMPS. i, Kitty. j, M'M'Zorg. k, Maccaseema. l, 1988. m, Morawhanna. n, Naamryck. o, Purini. p, Potaro / Landing. q, Rockstone. r, Rosignol. s, Stanleytown. t, Santa Rosa. u, Tumatumari. v, Weldaad. w, Wismar. x, TPO Berbice / Railway.

1988, Apr. 5 *Perf. 14x13½*

1873 A66 25c Sheet of 25, #a.-k., m.-x., 2 #l.

British Guiana Post Office, 125th Anniv.

No. 725 Surcharged "Olympic / Games / 1988"

Perf. 14½x14

1988, May 3 Litho. Wmk. 373

1897 A73 120c Sheet of 12, #a.-l.

Nos. 136-137 and 146 Surcharged "Caricom Day / 1988"

Perf. 13x13½

1988, June 15 Litho. Wmk. 364

1898 A28 25c on 5c #136
1899 A28 $1.20 on 6c #137
1900 A28 $10 on $2 #146
Nos. 1898-1900 (3) 2.00

No. 286A Overprinted

Overprints: a, 1988. b, WHO / 1948-1988.

1988, June 17 Litho. *Perf. 14x13½*

1901 Sheet of 25, 24 #a., 1 #b.
a.-b. A28 60c any single

World Health Day, 40th anniv.

Nos. 929d Overprinted as Indicated Nos. 1053a, 1063, 1131, and 1161 Overprinted "CONSERVE / WATER"

Overprints: No. 1903, "CONSERVE TREES" on ocher stamp, "CONSERVE ELECTRICITY on green stamp, "CONSERVE WATER on brown stamp. No. 1904, "CONSERVE ELECTRICITY" on ocher stamp, "CONSERVE WATER on green stamp, "CONSERVE TREES on brown stamp. No. 1905, "CONSERVE WATER" on ocher stamp, "CONSERVE TREES on green stamp, "CONSERVE ELECTRICITY on brown stamp.

Perfs. as Before

1988, July 15 Litho.

Watermarks as Before

1903 Triptych
a.-c. A90 120c any single
1904 Triptych
a.-c. A90 120c any single
1905 Triptych
a.-c. A90 120c any single
1906 A91 200c on #1063
1907 A91 200c on #1131
1908 A91 225c on #1053a
1909 A91 350c on #1161

Location and size of overprint varies.

Nos. 1826a and 1829a Ovptd. "BEWARE / OF ANIMALS" (a.)
Nos. 1826b and 1829b Ovptd. "BEWARE / OF CHILDREN" (b.)
Nos. 1826c and 1829c Ovptd. "DRIVE SAFELY" (c.)
Nos. 1826d and 1829d Ovptd. "DO NOT / DRINK AND DRIVE" (d.)

Unwmk.

1988, July 15 Litho. *Perf. 15*

Block of 4, #a.-d.

1910 A99 $1.20 on #1826
1911 A99 $1.20 on #1829
Nos. 1910-1911 (2) 10.00

No. 287 Ovptd. or Surcharged

Perf. 13½x13

1988, July Litho. Wmk. 364

1912 A66 $1 "1988" on #287
1913 A66 120c on $1 #287

No. 421 Surcharged with New Value and "1988"

1988? Litho. *Perf. 13½x14*

1913A A80 $1.20 on $1.10 on $3 #421

Nos. 1037a, 1047a, 1056-1057, 1066-1068, 1097, 1099, 1109-1109a, 1110-1111, 1113, 1115, 1122, 1125, 1129, 1147, 1149, and 1155 Ovptd. "CONSERVE / OUR RESOURCES"

1988, July *Perf. 14*

Watermarks as Before

Series 1

Plate Numbers in Parentheses

1914 130c on #1037a (13)
a. Overprint inverted 1.50

#1914a probably is as common as #1914.

1915 A91 130c on #1047a (20)
1916 A91 150c on #1056 (26)
1917 A91 120c on #1057 (27)
1918 A91 120c on #1066 (36)
1919 A91 120c on #1067 (37)
1920 A91 130c on #1068 (38)
1921 A91 120c on #1097 (56)
1922 A91 120c on #1099 (58)
1923 A91 100c on #1109 (65)
a. 100c on #1109a
1924 A91 130c on #1110 (66)
1925 A91 120c on #1111 (67)
1926 A91 100c on #1113 (68)
1927 A91 120c on #1115 (69)
1928 A91 250c on #1122 (74)
1929 A91 150c on #1125 (76)
1930 A91 150c on #1129 (78)
1931 A91 150c on #1147 (87)
1932 A91 100c on #1149 (88)
1933 A91 130c on #1155 (91)

Nos. 1827a-1827d and 1830a-1830d Ovptd. with Red Cross

1988, Aug. 3 Litho. *Perf. 15*

1935 A99 $3.20 Pair, #a.-b., on #1827a, 1827c
1936 A99 $3.20 Pair, #a.-b., on #1827b, 1827d
1937 A99 $3.30 Pair, #a.-b., on #1830a, 1830c
1938 A99 $3.30 Pair, #a.-b., on #1830b, 1830d

Intl. Red Cross, 125th anniv.

Nos. 1038, 1131 Ovptd. and Nos. 1147, 1175 Surcharged "1928-1988 / CRICKET / JUBILEE"

1988, Sept. 5 Litho. *Perf. 14*

Watermarks as Before

Plate Numbers in Parentheses

1939 A91 200c on #1038 (14)
1940 A91 200c on #1131 (79)
1941 A91 800c on 150c #1147 (87)
1942 A91 800c on 160c #1175 (5)

Nos. 1063, 1081, 1139, 1147, 1161, 1185, 1219, 1232, and 1305 Ovptd. and No. 1227 Surcharged "OLYMPIC GAMES / 1988"

1943 A91 200c on #1063 (33)
1944 A91 120c on #1081 (46)
1945 A91 300c on #1139 (83)
1946 A91 150c on #1147 (87)
1947 A91 350c on #1161 (94)
1948 A91 320c on #1185 (10)
1949 A91 350c on #1219 (29)
1950 A91 300c on 360c #1227 (34)
1951 A91 130c on #1232 (38)
1952 A91 330c on #1305 (82)

Overprint reads up on No. 1947.

Type A83 Ovptd. or Surcharged "OLYMPICS 1988" (a.) or "KOREA 1988" (b.)

1988 Litho. Wmk. 364 *Perf. 13½*

1953 A83 $1.20 Pair, #a.-b.
1954 A83 130c on $1.20, pair, #a.-b.
1955 A83 150c on $1.20, pair, #a.-b.
1956 A83 200c on $1.20, pair, #a.-b.
1957 A83 350c on $1.20, pair, #a.-b.
c. Strip of 5, #1953a-1957a 2.50
d. Strip of 5, #1953b-1957b 2.50

Overprint obliterates inscription spelled "LOS ANGELLES."

No. 1087 Ovptd. and No. 1143 Surcharged "V CENTENARY OF / THE LANDING OF / CHRISTOPHER COLUMBUS / IN THE AMERICAS"

Unwmk.

1988, Oct. 12 Litho. *Perf. 14*

1958 A91 320c on #1087
1959 A91 $15 on 360c #1143
Nos. 1958-1959 (2) 2.00

Nos. 1027, 1036, 1040, 1046, 1054, 1062, 1070, 1071, 1074, 1076, 1079, 1102, 1104, 1133, 1137 and 1143 Surcharged "SEASON'S / GREETINGS" in Blue or Black
Nos. 1053, 1053a, 1102, 1591A and 1670F Ovptd. or Surcharged "SEASON'S / GREETINGS / 1988" in Blue

1988, Nov. 10 *Perfs. as Before*

Watermarks and Printing Methods as Before

Plate Numbers in Parentheses

1960 A91 120c on 100c #1027 (6) 2.00
1961 A91 120c on 100c #1036 (13) 2.00
1962 A91 240c on 180c #1040 (15) (Bk) 1.00
1963 A91 120c on 100c #1046 (20) 2.00
1964 A91 225c on #1053 (24) 1.00
a. 225c on #1053a
1965 A91 120c on 100c #1054 (25) 2.00
1966 A91 150c on #1062 (32) (Bk) 1.00
1967 A91 260c on #1070 (39) (Bk) 1.00
1968 A91 120c on 100c #1071 (40) 2.00
1969 A91 120c on 100c #1074 (42) 2.00
1970 A91 120c on 100c #1076 (43) 2.00
1971 A91 120c on 100c #1079 (45) 2.00
1972 A91 225c on #1102 (60) (Bk) 1.00
1973 A91 225c on #1102 (60) 1.00
1974 A91 150c on #1104 (62) (Bk) 1.00
1975 A91 225c on #1591A (65) 1.50
1976 A91 330c on #1133 (80) (Bk) 1.00
1977 A91 320c on #1137 (82) (Bk) 1.00
1978 A91 360c on #1143 (85) (Bk) 1.00
Nos. 1960-1978 (19) 27.50

Miniature Sheet

1979 A91 225c on #1670F (22) 4.00

Size and location of overprint varies.

Nos. 72, 713 and 932 Surcharged or Ovptd. "CHRISTMAS / 1988" in Red or Black

1988, Nov. 16 *Perfs. as Before*

Watermarks and Printing Methods as Before

1981 A7 20c on 6c #72
1982 A86 Block of 4 (Bk)
a. 120c on #713a
b. 120c on 130c #713b
c. 120c on 150c #713c
d. 120c on 200c #713d

1983 A90a 500c on 330c #932
Nos. 1981-1983 (6) 3.00

Overprint reads up on No. 1983.

Nos. 288, 289, and 289A Surcharged or Ovptd. for Prevention of AIDS

Beginnning of overprint reads: Nos. 1984a, 1985e, "Get information..." Nos. 1984b, 1985a, "Get the facts..." Nos. 1984c, 1985b, "Say no to drugs..." Nos. 1984d, 1985c, $2, $5, $10, "Protect yourself..." Nos. 1984e, 1985d, "Be compassionate..."

Perf. 13½x13

1988, Dec. 1 Litho. Wmk. 364

1984 A66 120c Strip of 5, #a.-e., on #289
1985 A66 120c Strip of 5, #a.-e., on #289A
1986 A66 $2 on #288
1987 A66 $5 on #289
1988 A66 $10 on #289A
Nos. 1984-1988 (13) 50.00

1988 Winter Olympics, Calgary A106

Design: $3.50, Olympic rings.

1988, Dec. 1 ***Perf. 14***

1989 A106 $7 Downhill skiing 8.25

Souvenir Sheet

1990 A106 $3.50 Sheet of 1 5.00

No. 1989 exists in souvenir sheet of 1.

Christmas — A107

Paintings: No. 1991a, Virgin and Child Between St. George and St. Catherine, by Titian. b, Adoration of the Magi, by Titian.
No. 1992a, Holy Family, by Rubens. b, Adoration of the Shepherds, by Rubens.
$8, The Madonna, by Titian.

Perf. 14x13½, 13½x14

1988, Dec. 15 Litho.

1991 A107 $2 Pair, #a.-b. 3.50
1992 A107 $2 Pair, #a.-b. 3.50

Souvenir Sheet

Perf. 13½x14

1993 A107 $8 multicolored 8.00

Nos. 1991a-1991b, 1992a-1992b exist in souvenir sheets of 1.

Abolition of Slavery Type of 1985

1988, Dec. 16 Litho. ***Perf. 14***

Designs as Before

1994 A93 25c brown & black .25 .25
1995 A93 60c magenta & black .50 .50
1996 A93 130c green & black 1.00 1.00
1997 A93 150c blue & black 1.25 1.25
Nos. 1994-1997 (4) 3.00 3.00

Nos. 1087, 1167, and 1200 Surcharged "SALUTING WINNERS / OLYMPIC GAMES / 1988"

Unwmk.

1989, Jan. 3 Litho. ***Perf. 14***

1998 A91 $5.50 on 560c #1167
1999 A91 $9 on 320c #1200
2000 A91 $10.50 on 320c #1087
Nos. 1998-2000 (3) 6.00

Miniature Sheets

Red Cross, 125th Anniv. — A108

Designs: No. 2001, Henri Dunant, vert. No. 2002, First maritime ambulance. No. 2003, Red Cross hospital ship in African War. No. 2004, Red Cross air ambulance. No. 2005, Red Cross train.
Nos. 2001-2004 printed with red cross in center of sheet. Each stamp contains part of the red cross at the: a, LR. b, LL. c, UR. d, UL.

Perf. 13½x14, 14x13½

1989, Jan. 5 Litho.

2001 A108 $2 Sheet of 4, #a.-d.
2002 A108 $2 Sheet of 4, #a.-d.
2003 A108 $2 Sheet of 4, #a.-d.
2004 A108 $2 Sheet of 4, #a.-d.
Nos. 2001-2004 (4) 30.00

Souvenir Sheet

Perf. 14x13½

2005 A108 $7 Sheet of 1 8.00

Dated 1988.

Trains — A109

Designs: a, Hernalser sleeping carriage. b, 5 Forney locomotive. c, Austrian sleeping carriage. d, Pacific 231 locomotive.
$10, First Japanese imperial train.

1989, Jan. 5 Litho. ***Perf. 14***

2006 A109 $2 Sheet of 4, #a.-d.

Souvenir Sheet

2007 A109 $10 multicolored

Nos. 2006a-2006d exist in souvenir sheets of 1.
Dated 1988.

Naval Airship LZ 92, 1916 — A110

#2008: a, Astronaut on moon. b, Graf Zeppelin over San Francisco Bay, 1929. c, Testu-Brissy on horseback ascending in balloon, 1798.
#2009, Naval Airship LZ 92, 1916, diff.

1989, Jan. 26 ***Perf. 14***

2007A A110 $2 black
2008 A110 $2 Strip of 3, #a.-c.

Souvenir Sheet

2009 A110 $2 Sheet of 1

Nos. 2007A, 2008b, 2009, Ferdinand von Zeppelin, 150th birth anniv. in 1988. No. 2008a, 1st moon landing, 20th anniv. in 1989. The inscriptions on Nos. 2007A and 2009 are in error. Dated 1988.

Mushrooms — A111

#2010: a, Cortinarius bolaris. b, Cortinarius laniger. c, Tricholoma sulphureum. d, Lepiota cristata.
#2011, Sarcoscypha coccinea, vert.

1989, Feb. 1 ***Perf. 14x13½***

2010 A111 $2 Block of 4, #a.-d. 9.00

Souvenir Sheet

Perf. 13½x14

2011 A111 $5 Sheet of 1 8.00

Dated 1988.

Boy Scout Jamboree, Australia — A112

Design: $8, Scouts of different races.

1989, Feb. 10

2012 A112 $10 grn, black & yel 15.00

Souvenir Sheet

2013 A112 $8 Sheet of 1 15.00

Dated 1988. #2012 exists in souvenir sheet of 1.

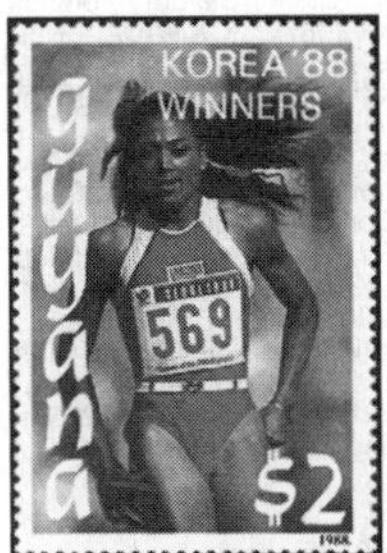

1988 Summer Olympics, Seoul — A113

Designs: No. 2014, Florence Griffith-Joyner. No. 2015, Carl Lewis. No. 2016, Equestrian. No. 2017, Runners, horiz. No. 2018, City skyline, Olympic Rings, horiz. No. 2019, 1988 & 1992 Olympic mascots, horiz. No. 2022, Griffith-Joyner, Lewis, horiz. No. 2023, Cosmic Athlete by Dali, horiz.

1989, Feb. 15 Litho. ***Perf. 14***

2014 A113 $2 multicolored
2015 A113 $2 multicolored
2016 A113 $2 multicolored
2017 A113 $2 multicolored
2018 A113 $2 multicolored
2019 A113 $2 multicolored

Souvenir Sheets

2022 A113 $3.50 multicolored
2023 A113 $3.50 multicolored
Nos. 2022-2023 (2) 24.00

No. 2023 exists with gold border and inscriptions. Nos. 2014-2019 inscribed 1988.

Nos. 1826, 1829 and 1831 Ovptd. "REPUBLIC DAY 1989" in Red

1989, Feb. 22 Litho. ***Perf. 15***

2024 A99 $1.20 Block of 4, #a.-d., on #1826 1.00
2025 A99 $1.20 Block of 4, #a.-d., on #1829 1.00
2026 A101 $10 on #1831

Nos. 1827a-1827d and 1830a-1830d Surcharged in Red

1989, Feb. 22

2027 A99 $5 Pair, #a.-b., on $3.20 #a., c.
2028 A99 $5 Pair, #a.-b., on $3.20 #b., d.
2028C A99 $5 Pair, #d.-e., on $3.30 #a., c.
2028F A99 $5 Pair, #g-h., on $3.30 #b., d.

Nos. 1461, 1822 Surcharged in Red

1989, Feb. 22 Litho. ***Perf. 14***

2029 A96 $10 #a.-b. on #1461
2030 A96 $10 #a.-b. on #1822
Nos. 2029-2030 (2) 7.50

No. 1188 Surcharged "EASTER"

1989, Mar. 22 ***Perf. 14***

2031 A91 Sheet of 4 on #1188 3.00
- *a.* 125c on 320c #1188
- *b.* 250c on 320c #1188
- *c.* 300c on 320c #1188
- *d.* 350c on 320c #1188

No. 927 Surcharged

1989, Mar. Wmk. 364 ***Perf. 14***

2032 A90 250c on 25c #927 2.00

Inscribed "1986."

No. 1197 Surcharged "RED CROSS / 1948 / 1988"

1989, Apr. Unwmk. ***Perf. 14***

2033 A91 375c on 45c #1197
2034 A91 425c on 45c #1197
Nos. 2033-2034 (2) 3.00

Guyana Red Cross, 40th anniv.

#1263 & 1252 Surcharged in Pairs "ALL FOR / HEALTH" (a.) or "HEALTH / FOR ALL" (b.)

1989, Apr. 3

2035 A91 250c on 75c #1263 (56), pair
2036 A91 675c on 720c #1252 (49), pair
Nos. 2035-2036 (2) 5.00

For surcharge see No. 2052.

Nos. 1224-1225, and 1254 Overprinted or Surcharged "BOY SCOUTS / 1909 1989" (a.) or "GIRL GUIDES / 1924 1989" (b.) Nos. 1272-1273 Surcharged "LADY BADEN POWELL / 1889-1989"

1989, Apr. 11

2037 A91 250c on 100c, pair, #a.-b. 5.00
2038 A91 $2.50 on 50c, pair, #a.-b.
2039 A91 300c Pair, #a.-b.
- *c.* Pair, #d.-e., Prussian bl ovpt.

2040 A91 $25 on 280c #1272
- *a.* Prussian blue overprint

2041 A91 $25 on 700c #1273
- *a.* Prussian blue overprint

Nos. 2037-2039, Boy Scouts in Guyana, 80th anniversary and Girl Guides, 65th anniversary. Nos. 2040-2041, Lady Baden Powell, birth centenary.

No. 1177 Surcharged "PHOTOGRAPHY / 1839-1989"

1989, Apr. 15

2042 A91 550c on 390c
2043 A91 650c on 390c, 2 bar obliterator
- *a.* 6 bar obliterator

Nos. 2042-2043, 2043a (3) 4.00

Nos. 2042-2043 printed in sheets of 4 with alternating overprints.

No. 1263 Surcharged "I.L.O. / 1919-1989"

1989, May 2

2044 A91 300c on 75c #1263 1.00

Intl. Labor Organization, 70th anniversary.

Nos. 43, 87, 134-137, 279-280, 284-285, and 286A 288, 1827, 1830, and 2035-2036 Surcharged in Black or Blue

q

s

r

t

1989 ***Perfs. as Before***

Watermarks and Printing Methods as Before

2045 A7(q) 80c on 6c #43
 a. A7 80c on 6c #43
2046 A28(q) $1 on 2c #134
 a. A28(r) $1 on 2c #134
2047 A28(q) $2.05 on 3c #135
2048 A28(q) $2.55 on 5c #136
 a. A28(r) $2.55 on 5c #136
2049 A28(q) $3.25 on 6c #137
 a. A28(r) $3.25 on 6c #137
2050 A14(q) $5 on 6c #87
 a. A14(s) $5 on 6c #87
2051 A66(q) $6 on 5c #279
2052 A91 640c Pair, #2036 5.00
2053 A66(q) $6.40 on 10c #280
 a. A66 $6.40 on 10c #280
 b. A66(r) $6.40 on 10c #280
2054 Block of 5, #a.-e. on #1830
 a.-d. A99(t) $6.40 on $3.30 #a.-d.
 e. A100(t) $190 on $3.30 #e.
2054F A66(r) $7.65 on 35c #284
2055 A66 $7.65 on 40c #285
2056 Block of 5, #a.-e. on #1827 15.00
 a.-d. A99(t) $7.65 on $3.20 #a.-d.
 e. A100(t) $225 on $3.20 #e.
2057 A66(q) $8.90 on 60c #286A
 a. A66 $8.90 on 60c #286A
2057B A66(q) $30 on 10c #280
2057C A66(q) $35 on 35c #284
2058 A66(r) $50 on $2 #288 (Bl)
2059 A66(r) $100 on $2 #288

Issued: #2045a, 2053-2053a, 2054F, 2055, May 18; #2057, May 26; #2058-2059, June 5; #2045, 2049, 2046a, 2048a, 2049a, June 15; #2050-2050a, 2051, 2052, 2054, 2056, Aug. 16.

Nos. 2045a, 2053a, 2055, 2057a have no obliterator. New denominations are larger on Nos. 2045a, 2053a and 2057a. No. 2045a has no cent sign.

Nos. 2054e, 2056b additionally overprinted "SPECIAL DELIVERY."

No. 1244 Surcharged "CARICOM / DAY"

Unwmk.

1989, June 26 **Litho.** ***Perf. 14***

2064 A91 125c on 200c #1244, 2 bar obliterator 1.00
 a. 6 bar obliterator 2.00

No. 280 Ovptd. in Gold or Silver for Gold Medalists at 1988 Summer Olympics

Overprints read: Nos. 2082a, 2083a, "SEOUL / OLYMPICS." Nos. 2082b, 2083b, "Men's 800M / Ereng / Kenya." Nos. 2082c, 2083c, "KOREA." Nos. 2082d, 2083d, "Men's / Gymnastics / Artemov / USSR." Nos. 2082e, 2083e, "Men's / Swimming / Louganis / USA." Nos. 2082f, 2083f, "Woman's / Swimming / Otto / DDR." Nos. 2082g, 2083g, "Men's Fencing / Lamour / France." Nos. 2082h, 2083h, "Men's / Gymnastics / Lou / China." Nos. 2082i, 2083i, "Women's / Cycling / Knol / Holland." Nos. 2082j, 2083j, "Men's / Swimming / Szabo / Hungary." Nos. 2082k, 2083k, "1988." Nos. 2082l, 2083l, "Men's / Swimming / Nesty / Suriname." Nos. 2082m, 2083m, "Men's Boxing / Lewis / Canada." Nos. 2082n, 2083n, "Men's Javelin / Korjus / Finland." Nos. 2082o, 2083o, "Basketball / USA." Nos. 2082p, 2083p, "Men's / Equestrian / Klimke / W. Germany." Nos. 2082q, 2083q, "Men's Boxing / Park / Korea." Nos. 2082r, 2083r, "Women's / Marathon / Mota / Portugal." Nos. 2082s, 2083s, "Men's / Swimming / Suzuki / Japan."

Nos. 2084a, 2085a, "Men's 100M / Lewis / USA." Nos. 2084b, 2085b, "Men's / Pole Vault / Bubka / USSR." Nos. 2084c, 2085c, "Women's / 100-200m / Joyner / USA." Nos. 2084d, 2085d, "Men's Pentathlon / Martinek / Hungary." Nos. 2084e, 2085e, "Men's Wrestling / Sako / Japan." Nos. 2084f, 2085f, "Men's Judo / Saito / Japan." Nos. 2084g, 2085g, "Women's 800M / Wodars / DDR." Nos. 2084h, 2085h, "Men's Boxing / Gross / W. Germany." Nos. 2084i, 2085i, "Men's Boxing / Maske / DDR." Nos. 2084j, 2085j, "Men's Boxing / Kim / Korea." Nos. 2084k, 2085k, "Woman's / Swimming / Evans / USA." Nos. 2084l, 2085l, "Soccer / USSR." Nos. 2084m, 2085m, "Woman's / Gymnastics / Silivas / Romania." Nos. 2084n, 2085n, "Men's Boxing / Mercer / USA." Nos. 2084o, 2085o, "Men's Marathon / Bordin / Italy." Nos. 2084p, 2085p, "Women's Tennis / Graf / W. Germany."

Perf. 14x13½

1989, Apr. **Litho.** **Wmk. 364**

Sheets of 25

2082 5 #a., 3 #c., #b., d.-s.
 a.-s. A66 10c on #280, any single
2083 5 #a., 3 #c., #b., d.-s. (S)
 a.-s. A66 10c on #280, any single
2084 #a.-p., 5 #2082a, 3 #2082c, #2082k
 a.-p. A66 10c on #280, any single
2085 #a.-p., 5 #2083a, 3 #2083c, #2083k (S)
 a.-p. A66 10c on #280, any single

Nos. 280 Ovptd. in Gold or Silver for Gold Medalists at 1988 Winter Olympics

Overprints read: Nos. 2086a, 2087a, "Gold Medal / Winners." Nos. 2086b, 2087b, "Ice Hockey / USSR." Nos. 2086c, 2087c, "CALGARY / OLYMPICS." Nos. 2086d, 2087d, "Bobsled / Kipours-Kozlov / USSR." Nos. 2086e, 2087e, "Women's Skating / 1500-3000-5000M / Gennip / Netherlands." Nos. 2086f, 2087f, "Men's / Speed / Skating / 5000-10000M / Gustafson / Sweden." Nos. 2086g, 2087g, "Men's Figure / Skating / Boitano / USA." Nos. 2086h, 2087h, "Women's / 500M Skating / Blair / USA." Nos. 2086i, 2087i, "Women's / Figure Skating / Witt / DDR." Nos. 2086j, 2087j, "Men's Giant / Slalom / Tomba / Italy." Nos. 2086k, 2087k, "CANADA." Nos. 2086l, 2087l, "Men's Super / Giant Slalom / Picard / France." Nos. 2086m, 2087m, "Women's / Downhill Skiing / Kiehl / W. Germany." Nos. 2086n, 2087n, "Men's 50km Skiing Svan / Sweden." Nos. 2086o, 2087o, "Men's Nordic / Combined Skiing / Mueller-Pohl / Schwarz / W. Germany." Nos. 2086p, 2087p, "Women's / Giant Slalom / Schneider / Switzerland." Nos. 2086q, 2087q, "Women's / 5-km Skiing / Matikainen / Finland." Nos. 2086r, 2087r, "Men's Downhill / Alpine Skiing / Zurbriggen / Switzerland." Nos. 2086s, 2087s, "Men's Ski / Jumping / Nykanen / Finland."

1989, Apr.

2086 4 #a., 3 #c., #b., d.-s., #2082k
 a.-s. A66 10c on #280, any single
2087 4 #a., 3 #c., #b., d.-s., #2083k (S)
 a.-s. A66 10c on #280, any single

No. 281 Ovptd. in Gold or Silver in Memory of Hirohito, Emperor of Japan

Overprints read: Nos. 2088a, 2089a, "Emperor / Hirohito." Nos. 2088b, 2089b, "Showa / Era." Nos. 2088c, 2089c, "Chrysanthemum / Dynasty." Nos. 2088d, 2089d, "Emperor / of Japan." Nos. 2088e, 2089e, "1901." Nos. 2088f, 2089f, "1989." Nos. 2088g, 2089g, "Emperor / Hirohito / 1901-1989."

1989, Apr.

2088 5 #a., 4 #c.-d., 9 #b., #e.-g.
 a.-g. A66 15c on #281, any single
2089 5 #a., 4 #c.-d., 9 #b., #e.-g. (S)
 a.-g. A66 15c on #281, any single

No. 280 Ovptd. in Gold or Silver for Enthronement of Akihito, Emperor of Japan

Overprints reads: Nos. 2090a, 2091a, "Honoring / His / Majesty." Nos. 2090b, 2091b, "Emperor / of / Japan." Nos. 2090c, 2091c, "1989." Nos. 2090d, 2091d, "HEISI / ERA."

1989, Apr.

2090 12 #a, 8 #b., 4 #c., #d.
 a.-d. A66 10c on #280, any single
2091 12 #a., 8 #b., 4 #c., #d. (S)
 a.-d. A66 10c on #280, any single

Overprint is 10mm long on #2090c, 2091c.

Nos. 280-281 and 283 Ovptd. with Emblems of Scouts, Rotary Intl., and Lions Intl. in Gold, Silver, Metallic Red, Metallic Green and Black

Overprints: Nos. 2092a, 2093a, 2094a, 2095a, 2096b, 2097b, 2098b, 2099b, 2100c, 2101c, 2102c, 2103c, Scouting emblem. Nos. 2092b, 2093b, 2094b, 2095b, 2096a, 2097a, 2098a, 2099a, 2100b, 2101b, 2102b, 2103b, Rotary emblem. Nos. 2092c, 2093c, 2094c, 2095c, 2096c, 2097c, 2098c, 2099c, 2100a, 2101a, 2102a, 2103a, Lions emblem. Nos. 2092d, 2093d, 2094d, 2095d, 2096d, 2097d, 2098d, 2099d, 2100d, 2101d, 2102d, 2103d, "1989." Nos. 2092e, 2093e, 2094e, 2095e, Large scouting emblem. Nos. 2096e, 2097e, 2098e, 2099e, Large Rotary emblem. Nos. 2100e, 2101e, 2102e, 2103e, Large Lions emblem.

1989, Apr.

2092 8 #a.-b., 6 #c., 2 #d., #e.
 a.-e. A66 10c on #280, any single
2093 8 #a.-b., 6 #c., 2 #d., #e. (S)
 a.-e. A66 10c on #280, any single
2094 8 #a.-b., 6 #c., 2 #d., #e. (R)
 a.-e. A66 10c on #280, any single
2095 8 #a.-b., 6 #c., 2 #d., #e. (Bk)
 a.-e. A66 10c on #280, any single
2096 8 #a.-b., 6 #c., 2 #d., #e.
 a.-e. A66 15c on #281, any single
2097 8 #a.-b., 6 #c., 2 #d., #e. (S)
 a.-e. A66 15c on #281, any single
2098 8 #a.-b., 6 #c., 2 #d., #e. (R)
 a.-e. A66 15c on #281, any single
2099 8 #a.-b., 6 #c., 2 #d., #e. (Gr)
 a.-e. A66 15c on #281, any single
2100 8 #a.-b., 6 #c., 2 #d., #e.
 a.-e. A66 25c on #283, any single
2101 8 #a.-b., 6 #c., 2 #d., #e. (S)
 a.-e. A66 25c on #283, any single
2102 8 #a.-b., 6 #c., 2 #d., #e. (R)
 a.-e. A66 25c on #283, any single
2103 8 #a.-b., 6 #c., 2 #d., #e. (Gr)
 a.-e. A66 25c on #283, any single

"1989" overprints are 7½mm long.

No. 280 Ovptd. in Gold or Silver for Halley's Comet

Overprints read: Nos. 2104a, 2105a, "Halley's / Comet." Nos. 2104b, 2105b, "Famous / Space Event." Nos. 2104c, 2105c, "Edmund / Halley / 1656-1742." Nos. 2104d, 2105d, "1910." Nos. 2104e, 2105e, "1986."

1989, Apr.

2104 11 #a., 6 #b., 4 #c., 2 #d.-e.
 a.-e. A66 10c on #280, any single
2105 11 #a., 6 #b., 4 #c., 2 #d.-e. (S)
 a.-e. A66 10c on #280, any single

No. 280 Ovptd. in Gold or Silver for Space Achievements

Overprints read: Nos. 2106a, 2107a, "Sputnik I / Oct. 4, 1957." Nos. 2106b, 2107b, "Explorer I / Jan. 31, 1958." Nos. 2106c, 2107c, "Sputnik II / Laika / Spacedog / Nov. 3, 1957." Nos. 2106d, 2107d, "Alan Shepard, Jr. / Mercury III / May 5, 1961." Nos. 2106e, 2107e, "Yuri Gagarin / Vostok I / April 12, 1961." Nos. 2106f, 2107f, "John Glenn / Mercury VI / Feb. 20, 1962." Nos. 2106g, 2107g, "Vostok III / Vostok IV / Aug. 12, 1962." Nos. 2106h, 2107h, "Grissom-Young / Gemini III / March 23, 1965." Nos. 2106i, 2107i, "Luna III / Oct. 4, 1959." Nos. 2106j, 2107j, "Edward H. White II / Gemini IV / June 3, 1965." Nos. 2106k, 2107k, "V. Tereshkova / First Woman / in Space / June 16-19, 1963." Nos. 2106 l, 2107 l, "Surveyor I / June 2, 1966." Nos. 2106m, 2107m, "Space / Achievements." Nos. 2106n, 2107n, "Voskod I / First 3 Man Crew / Oct. 12-13, 1964." Nos. 2106o, 2107o, "Apollo I / Jan. 27, 1967." Nos. 2106p, 2107p, "Alexei A. Leonov / First Walk in Space / March 18-19, 1965." Nos. 2106q, 2107q, "Apollo VIII / Dec. 21-27, 1968." Nos. 2106r, 2107r, "V. Komarov / Soyuz I / April 24, 1967." Nos. 2106s, 2107s, "Apollo XI / First Man on Moon / July 20, 1969." Nos. 2106t, 2107t, "Lunokhod I / Dec. 10, 1970." Nos. 2106u, 2107u, "Apollo XIII / April 11-17, / 1970." Nos. 2106v, 2107v, "Soyuz XI / June 30, 1971." Nos. 2106w, 2107w, "Viking I / July 20, 1976." Nos. 2106x, 2107x, "Vega I / March 6, 1986." Nos. 2106y, 2107y, "Columbia Sts-1 / April 12-14, / 1981."

1989, Apr.

2106 #a.-y.
 a.-y. A66 10c on #280, any single
2107 #a.-y. (S)
 a.-y. A66 10c on #280, any single

No. 280 Ovptd. in Gold or Silver

Overprints read: Nos. 2108a, 2109a, "1969- / 1989." Nos. 2108b, 2109b, "Apollo XI." Nos. 2108c, 2109c, "First Man / on Moon." Nos. 2108d, 2109d, "USA." Nos. 2108e, 2109e, "Neil A. / Armstrong." Nos. 2108f, 2109f, "Col. Edwin E. / Aldrin, Jr." Nos. 2108g, 2109g, "Lt. Col. / Michael / Collins."

1989, Apr.

2108 5 #a, 7 b, 4 c, 6 d, e-g
 a.-g. A66 10c on #280, any single
2109 5 #a, 7 b, 4 c, 6 d, e-g (S)
 a.-g. A66 10c on #280, any single

Moon Landing, 20th anniv.

No. 281 Ovptd. in Gold or Silver for Space Shuttle Program

Overprints read: Nos. 2110a, 2111a, "Enterprise / Aug. 12, 1977." Nos. 2110b, 2111b, "Columbia / April 12, 1981." Nos. 2110c, 2111c, "Space / Shuttles." Nos. 2110d, 2111d, "Discovery / Aug. 30, 1984." Nos. 2110e, 2111e, "Atlantis / Oct. 3, 1985." Nos. 2110f, 2111f, "Challenger / Heroes." Nos. 2110g, 2111g, "Resnik / McAuliffe / Jarvis." Nos. 2110h, 2111h, "In Memoriam / Challenger / Jan. 28, 1986." Nos. 2110i, 2111i, "Onizuka / Smith / McNair / Scobee."

1989, Apr.

2110 4 #a.-e., 2 #f., #g.-i.
 a.-i. A66 15c on #281, any single
2111 4 #a.-e., 2 #f., #g.-i. (S)
 a.-i. A66 15c on #281, any single

Butterflies — A115

A116

1989, Sept. 7 **Litho.** ***Perf. 14***

2208	A115	80c	Stalachtis calliope	.20	.20
2209	A115	$2.25	Morpho rhetenor	.20	.20
2210	A115	$5	Agrias claudia	.30	.30
2211	A115	$6.40	Marpesia marcella	.40	.40
2212	A115	$7.65	Papilio zagreus	.45	.45
2213	A115	$8.90	Chorinea faunus	.55	.55
2214	A115	$25	Cepheuptychia cephus	1.50	1.50
2215	A115	$100	Nessaea regina	6.00	6.00
			Nos. 2208-2215 (8)	9.60	9.60

See Nos. E16-E17. For overprints see Nos. 2251-2254, 2256-2257, 2260-2261, 2283-2290, E19-E22, E24, E26-E27, E31.

1989, Nov. 8

Women in Space, 25th Anniv. (in 1988): $6.40, Kathryn Sullivan, 1st US woman to walk in space. $12.80, Svetlana Savitskaya, 1st Soviet woman to walk in space. $15.30, Judy Resnik & Christa McAuliffe, astronauts killed in Challenger explosion. $100, Sally Ride, 1st US woman astronaut.

2216	A116	$6.40	multicolored	.40	.40
2217	A116	$12.80	multicolored	.75	.75
2218	A116	$15.30	multicolored	.90	.90
2219	A116	$100	multicolored	6.40	6.40
			Nos. 2216-2219 (4)	8.45	8.45

See No. E18. For overprints see Nos. 2255, 2258-2259, 2262, E23, E25, E28, E32.

1990 World Cup Soccer Championships, Italy — A117

Various soccer players.

Perf. 14x13½, 13½x14

1989, Nov. 20

2220 A117 $2.55 shown
2221 A117 $2.55 Yellow shirt, vert.
2222 A117 $2.55 Goalie

2223 A117 $2.55 Green shirt, vert.

Souvenir Sheet

2224 A117 $20 Championships emblem, vert.

#2220-2223 exist in souvenir sheets of 1.
For surcharges see Nos. 2263-2267.

No. 134-136 Surcharged "AHMADIYYA / CENTENARY / 1889-1989"

Perf. 13x13½

1989, Nov. 22 Litho. Wmk. 364

2225 A28 80c on 2c #134
2226 A28 $6.40 on 3c #135
2227 A28 $8.90 on 5c #136

1992 Summer Olympics, Barcelona
A118

1989, Dec. 5 *Perf. 13½x14, 14x13½*

2228 A118 $2.55 shown
2229 A118 $2.55 Boxing, horiz.
2230 A118 $2.55 Chariot racing, horiz.
2231 A118 $2.55 Javelin, horiz.
2232 A118 $2.55 Running, horiz.
2233 A118 $2.55 Wrestling
Nos. 2228-2233 (6) 14.00

Souvenir Sheets

2234 A118 $10 Running, horiz., diff.
2235 A118 $10 Columbus Walk by Picasso
Nos. 2234-2235 (2) 20.00

#2228-2233 exist in souvenir sheets of 1.

Christmas — A119

Paintings: No. 2236, Child Declaring in Favor of His Mother, by Titian. No. 2237, The Sacred Family, by Rubens. No. 2238, Saint Anne, the Virgin and Child, by Durer. No. 2239, Madonna Enthroned, Surrounded by Saints, by Rubens. $20, Saint Ildefonso, by Rubens.

1989, Dec. 26 *Perf. 14x13½, 13½x14*

2236 A119 $2.55 multi
2237 A119 $2.55 multi, vert.
2238 A119 $2.55 multi, vert.
2239 A119 $2.55 multi, vert.
Nos. 2236-2239 (4) 6.00

Souvenir Sheet

2240 A119 $20 multi, vert.

#2236-2239 exist in souvenir sheets of 1.

Harpy Eagle — A120

Channel-billed Toucan — A121

1990, Jan. 23 Litho. *Perf. 14*

2241 A120 $2.25 Eagle's head .75 .25
2242 A120 $5 Eagle with prey 1.00 .30
2243 A120 $8.90 Eagle facing right 1.50 .50
2244 A121 $15 shown 1.00 .40
2245 A121 $25 Blue & yellow macaw 1.50 .70
2246 A120 $30 Eagle facing left 3.50 3.25
2247 A121 $50 Wattled jacana, horiz. 2.75 2.25
2248 A121 $60 Hoatzin, horiz. 3.00 2.50
Nos. 2241-2248 (8) 15.00 10.15

Souvenir Sheets

2249 A121 $100 Great kiskadee, horiz. 6.25 6.25
2250 A121 $100 Amazon kingfisher, horiz. 6.25 6.25

Nos. 2241-2243, 2246, World Wildlife Fund.

Nos. 2208-2184 Ovptd. in Silver with Rotary Emblem and "ROTARY INTERNATIONAL 1905-1990" on 2 or 3 Lines

1990, Mar. 15

2251 A115 80c on #2208
2252 A115 $2.25 on #2209
2253 A115 $5 on #2210
2254 A115 $6.40 on #2211
2255 A116 $6.40 on #2216
2256 A115 $7.65 on #2212
2257 A115 $8.90 on #2213
2258 A116 $12.80 on #2217
2259 A116 $15.30 on #2218
2260 A115 $25 on #2214
2261 A115 $100 on #2215
2262 A116 $100 on #2219

Nos. 2220-2222, 2224 Surcharged "GERMANY / CHAMPION"

No. 2223 Surcharged "GERMANY / CHAMPION / ARGENTINA / SUB-CHAMPION"

1990 *Perfs. as Before*

2263 A117 $75 on #2220
2264 A117 $75 on #2221
2265 A117 $75 on #2222
2266 A117 $75 on #2223
Nos. 2263-2266 (4) 10.00

Souvenir Sheet

2267 A117 $225 on #2224 8.00

#2263-2266 exist in souvenir sheets of 1.

Miniature Sheets

Penny Black, 150th Anniv., 500th Anniv. of Thurn & Taxis Postal Service
A122

No. 2268: a, Banghy Post runner, 1832. b, Penny Black, Sir Rowland Hill. c, Dutch mail ship. d, Paddle steamer Monarch, 1830. e, Paddle steamer Hindostan, 1842. f, Mail steamer Chusan. g, Sailing ship Madagascar, 1853. h, Paddle steamer Orinoco, 1855. i, Packet Orpheus, 1835.

No. 2269: a, Imperial postal messenger. b, Swiss messenger, 1499. c, River messenger, 15th century. d, Russian courier, Middle Ages. e, Oldenburg postilions, 1820. f, Indian mail coach, 1829. g, Baden mail coach postilions, 1820. h, Pony Express, 1860. i, Camel rider.

No. 2270: a, Mail coach, 1840. b, Danish Ball Post, 1815. c, Australian Bush mailman, 1838. d, Japanese postmen, 1870. e, Mail cart, 1857. f, Russian mail troika. g, Wells, Fargo Overland Express. h, Phantoms of the Night, 1853. i, Cobb & Co. coach, Australia.

No. 2271: a, Postilions, 1850. b, Mounted postilion, Holland. c, Paddle steamer Arctic, 1850. d, Peruvian swimming couriers. e, First London post box, 1855. f, Indian mail cart, 1870. g, Balloon post, 1870. h, Bath Mail Coach. i, Postrider, 1837.

No. 2272: a, Northeastern Railway post office. b, Traveling post office, 1838. c, American Express. d, Graf Zeppelin. e, Columbia Post airplane, 1925. f, Calcutta flying boat. g, Junkers JU-52/3M mail plane. h, Douglas M2 mail plane. i, US air mail service, DH-4.

No. 2273: a, First Atlantic Airways. b, Morris post office van, 1931. c, Swiss post-passenger bus. d, Westland-Sikorsky S51 helicopter mail flight. e, Union Pacific Railway. f, Boeing Model 314 flying boat, Yankee Clipper. g, Boeing 747. h, Concorde. i, Apollo 11, US #C76.

No. 2274, Mounted postilion. No. 2275, Thurn & Taxis #7. No. 2276, Thurn & Taxis #45.

1990, May 3

Sheets of 9

2268 A122 $15.30 #a.-i. 7.00 7.00
2269 A122 $15.30 #a.-i. 7.00 7.00
2270 A122 $15.30 #a.-i. 7.00 7.00
2271 A122 $17.80 #a.-i. 8.00 8.00
2272 A122 $20 #a.-i. 9.00 9.00
2273 A122 $20 #a.-i. 9.00 9.00
Nos. 2268-2273 (6) 47.00 47.00

Souvenir Sheets

2274 A122 $150 multi 7.50 7.50
2275 A122 $150 multi 7.50 7.50
2276 A122 $150 multi 7.50 7.50

For overprint see No. 2551.

Nos. 1028, 1032, 1055, 1085, 1107 Surcharged "ROTARY / DISTRICT 405 / 9th CONFERENCE / MAY 1990 / GEORGETOWN"

Unwmk.

1990, May 8 Litho. *Perf. 14*

Design A91

Plate Numbers in Parentheses

2277 80c on 55c #1032 (9)
2278 80c on 55c #1085 (49)
2279 80c on 55c #1107 (64)
2280 $6.40 on 130c #1028 (6)
2281 $6.40 on 130c #1055 (25)
2282 $7.65 on 130c #1055 (25)

Nos. 2208-2215 Overprinted

90th Birthday
H.M. The Queen Mother

1990, June 8 Litho. *Perf. 14*

2283 A115 80c on #2208 .20 .20
2284 A115 $2.25 on #2209 .20 .20
2285 A115 $5 on #2210 .30 .30
2286 A115 $6.40 on #2211 .40 .40
2287 A115 $7.65 on #2212 .45 .45
2288 A115 $8.90 on #2213 .55 .55
2289 A115 $25 on #2214 1.50 1.50
2290 A115 $100 on #2215 6.00 6.00
Nos. 2283-2290 (8) 9.60 9.60

See Nos. E26-E27.

Locomotives — A123

1990, July 15 *Perf. 14x13½*

2291 A123 $2.55 Class 3F
2292 A123 $2.55 Class A4
2293 A123 $2.55 Liner Class A34
2294 A123 $2.55 Pacific Class
2295 A123 $2.55 Grange Class
Nos. 2291-2295 (5) 10.00

Souvenir Sheets

Perf. 13½x14, 14x13½

2296 A123 $20 Castle Class, vert.
2297 A123 $20 Southern Railway
Nos. 2296-2297 (2) 20.00

Still Life with Guitar, by Picasso — A124

Paintings: No. 2299, Horseman, by Velazquez. No. 2300, Sunflowers, by Van Gogh, vert. No. 2301, Man Wearing Striped Shirt, by Miro, vert. No. 2302, Franz von Taxis, by Durer, vert. No. 2303, Virgin and Child, by Titian, vert. No. 2304, Presentation of Marie de Medici, by Rubens, vert.

Perf. 14x13½, 13½x14

1990, Aug. 1 Litho.

2298 A124 $2.55 multicolored
2299 A124 $2.55 multicolored
2300 A124 $2.55 multicolored
2301 A124 $2.55 multicolored
2302 A124 $2.55 multicolored
Nos. 2298-2302 (5) 10.00

Souvenir Sheets

2303 A124 $20 multicolored
2304 A124 $20 multicolored
Nos. 2303-2304 (2) 20.00

Postal System of Thurn and Taxis, 500th anniv. (#2302). Titian, 500th birth anniv. (#2303). Rubens, 350th death anniv. (#2304).

Birds — A125

Designs: 80c, Guiana partridge, horiz. $2.55, Collared trogon. $3.25, Derby aracari. $5, Black-necked aracari. $5.10, Green aracari. $5.80, Ivory-billed aracari. $6.40, Guiana toucanet. $6.50, Sulphur-breasted toucan. $7.55, Red-billed toucan. $7.65, Toco toucan. $8.25, Natterers toucanet. $8.90, Welcome trogon. $9.75, Doubtful trogon. $11.40, Banded aracari. $12.65, Golden-headed train bearer. $12.80, Rufus-breasted hermit. $13.90, Band-tail barbthroat. $15.30, White-tipped sickle bill. $17.80, Black jacobin. $19.20, Fiery topaz. $22.95, Tufted coquette. $26.70, Ecuadorian pied-tail. $30, Quetzal. $50, Green-crowned brilliant. $100, Emerald-chinned hummingbird. $190, Lazuline sabrewing. $225, Berylline hummingbird.

1990, Sept. 12 Litho. *Perf. 14*

2305 A125 80c multi .20 .20
2306 A125 $2.55 multi .20 .20
2307 A125 $3.25 multi .20 .20
2308 A125 $5 multi .20 .20
2309 A125 $5.10 multi .20 .20
2310 A125 $5.80 multi .20 .20
2311 A125 $6.40 multi .20 .20
2312 A125 $6.50 multi .20 .20
2313 A125 $7.55 multi .20 .20
2314 A125 $7.65 multi .20 .20
2315 A125 $8.25 multi .20 .20
2316 A125 $8.90 multi .25 .25
2317 A125 $9.75 multi .25 .25
2318 A125 $11.40 multi .30 .30
2319 A125 $12.65 multi .30 .30
2320 A125 $12.80 multi .30 .30
2321 A125 $13.90 multi .35 .35
2322 A125 $15.30 multi .40 .40
2323 A125 $17.80 multi .45 .45
2324 A125 $19.20 multi .50 .50
2325 A125 $22.95 multi .60 .60
2326 A125 $26.70 multi .70 .70
2327 A125 $30 multi .75 .75
2328 A125 $50 multi 1.25 1.25
2329 A125 $100 multi 2.50 2.50
2330 A125 $190 multi 4.75 4.75
2331 A125 $225 multi 5.75 5.75
Nos. 2305-2331 (27) 21.60 21.60

Butterflies — A126

No. 2340: a, Thecla falerina. b, Pheles heliconides. c, Echenais leucocyana. d, Heliconius xanthocles. e, Mesopthalma idotea. f, Parides aeneas. g, Heliconius numata. h, Thecla critola. i, Themone pais. j, Nymula agle. k, Adelpha cocala. l, Anaea eribotes. m, Prepona demophon. n, Selenophanes cassiope. o, Consul hippona. p, Antirrhaea avernus.

No. 2341: a, Thecla telemus. b, Thyridia confusa. c, Heliconius burneyi. d, Parides lysander. e, Eunica orphise. f, Adelpha melona. g, Morpho menelaus. h, Nymula phylleus. i, Stalachtis phlegia. j, Theope barea. k, Morpho perseus. l, Lycorea ceres. m, Archonias bellona. n, Caerois chorinaeus. o, Vila azeca. p, Nessaea batesii.

No. 2342: a, Heliconius silvana. b, Eunica alcmena. c, Mechanitis polymnia. d, Mesosemia ephyne. e, Thecla erema. f, Callizona acesta. g, Stalachtis phaedusa. h, Battus belus. i, Nymula phliasus. j, Parides childrenae. k, Stalachtis euterpe. l, Dysmathia portia. m, Tithorea hermias. n, Prepona pheridamas. o, Dismorphia fortunata. p, Hamadryas amphinome.

No. 2343: a, Heliconius vetustus. b, Mesosemia eumene. c, Parides phosphorus. d, Polystichtis emylius. e, Xanthocleis aedesia. f, Doxocopa agathina. g, Adelpha plesaure. h, Heliconius wallacei. i, Notheme eumeus. j, Melinaea mediatrix. k, Theritas coronata. l, Dismorphia orise. m, Phyciodes ianthe. n, Morpho aega. o, Zaretis isidora. p, Pierella lena.

Nos. 2340-2341 are horiz.

1990, Sept. 26 Litho. *Perf. 14*

2332	A126	80c	Melinaea idae	.20	.20
2333	A126	$2.55	Rhetus dysonii	.20	.20
2334	A126	$5	Actinote anteas	.20	.20
2335	A126	$6.40	Heliconius tales	.20	.20
2336	A126	$7.65	Thecla telemus	.20	.20
2337	A126	$8.90	Theope eudocia	.25	.25
2338	A126	$50	Heliconius vicini	1.25	1.25
2339	A126	$100	Amarynthis meneria	2.50	2.50
			Nos. 2332-2339 (8)	5.00	5.00

Miniature Sheets

Sheets of 16

2340	A126	$10	#a.-p.	4.00	4.00
2341	A126	$10	#a.-p.	4.00	4.00
2342	A126	$10	#a.-p.	4.00	4.00
2343	A126	$10	#a.-p.	4.00	4.00

Souvenir Sheets

2344	A126	$150	Heliconius aoede	3.75	3.75
2345	A126	$150	Phyciodes clio, horiz.	3.75	3.75
2346	A126	$190	Nymphidium caricae	4.75	4.75
2347	A126	$190	Thecla hemon	4.75	4.75

For surcharges see #2415-2425, 2596-2606.

Mushrooms A127

1990, Oct. 12

2348	A127	$2.55	Oudemanseilla mucida	
2349	A127	$2.55	Pholiota squarosa	
2350	A127	$2.55	Coprinus comatus	
2351	A127	$2.55	Anellaria semiovaja	
			Nos. 2348-2351 (4)	8.00

Souvenir Sheet

2352	A127	$20	Phallus impudicus	8.00

Sailing Ships — A128

1990, Oct. 12

2353	A128	$2.55	Brig century	
2354	A128	$2.55	Dutch marine ship	
2355	A128	$2.55	Galleon, 1588	
2356	A128	$2.55	Warship, 16th cent.	
2357	A128	$2.55	Hulk, 17th cent.	
			Nos. 2353-2357 (5)	8.00

Souvenir Sheet

2358	A128	$20	Dutch ships, 16th-17th cent.	8.00

No. 2358 printed in continuous design. Discovery of America, 500th anniv. (in 1992).

Flora — A129

Orchids: $7.65, Vanilla inodora. $8.90, Epidendrum ibaguense. No. 858, Maxillaria parkeri. $15.30, Epidendrum nocturnum. $17.80, Catasetum discolor. $20, Scuticaria hadwenii. $25, Epidendrum fragrans. $100, Epistephium parviflorum.

No. 2367: a, Dichea muricata. b, Octomeria erosilabia. c, Spiranthes orchiodes. d, Brassavola nodosa. e, Epidendrum rigidum. f, Brassia caudata. g, Pleurothallis diffusa. h, Aspasia variegata. i, Stenia pallida. j, Cyrtopodium punctatum. k, Cattleya deckeri. l, Cryptarrhena lunata. m, Cattleya violacea. n, Caularthron bicornutum. o, Oncidium carthagenense. p, Galeandra devoniana.

No. 2368: a, Bifrenaria aurantiaca. b, Epidendrum ciliare. c, Dichaea picta. d, Scaphyglottis violacea. e, Cattleya percivaliana. f, Map of Guyana (no flower). g, Epidendrum difforme. h, Eulophia maculata. i, Spiranthes tenuis. j, Peristeria guttata. k, Pleurothallis pruinosa. l, Cleistes rosea. m, Maxillaria variabilis. n, Brassavola cucullata. o, Epidendrum moyobambae. p, Oncidium orthostates.

No. 2369: a, Brassavola martiana. b, Paphinia cristata. c, Aganisia pulchella. d, Oncidium lanceanum. e, Lockhartia imbricata. f, Caularthron bilamellatum. g, Oncidium nanum. h, Pleurothallis ovalifolia. i, Galeandra dives. j, Cycnoches loddigesii. k, Ada aurantiaca. l, Catasetum barbatum. m, Palmorchis pubescens. n, Epidendrum anceps. o, Huntleya meleagris. p, Sobralia sessilis.

No. 2370: a, Maxillaria camaridii. b, Vanilla pompona. c, Stanhopea grandiflora. d, Oncidium pusillum. e, Polycycnis vittata. f, Cattleya lawrenceana. g, Menadenium labiosum. h, Rodriguezia secunda. i, Mormodes buccinator. j, Otostylis brachystalix. k, Maxillaria discolor. l, Liparis elata. m, Gongora maculata. n, Koellensteinia graminea. o, Rudolfiella aurantiaca. p, Scuticaria steelei.

Flowering Trees: No. 2371: a, Cochlospermum vitifolium. b, Eugenia malaccensis. c, Plumiera rubra. d, Erythrina glauca. e, Spathodea campanulata. f, Jacaranda filicifolia. g, Samanea saman. h, Cassia fistula. i, Abutilon integerrimum. j, Lagerstroemia speciosa. k, Tabebuia serratifolia. l, Guaiacum officinale. m, Solanum macranthum. n, Peltophorum roxburghii. o, Bauhinia variegata. p, Plumiera alba.

Flowering Vines: No. 2372: a, Gloriosa rothschildiana. b, Pseudocalymma alliaceum. c, Callichlamys latifolia. d, Distictis riversii. e, Maurandya barclaiana. f, Beaumontia fragrans. g, Phaseolus caracalla. h, Mandevilla splendens. i, Solandra longiflora. j, Passiflora coccinea. k, Allamanda cathartica. l, Bauhinia galpini. m, Verbena maritima. n, Mandevilla suaveolens. o, Phryganocydia corymbosa. p, Jasminum sambac.

1990, Oct. 16 Litho. *Perf. 14*

2359	A129	$7.65	multicolored	.30	.30
2360	A129	$8.90	multicolored	.40	.40
2361	A129	$12.80	multicolored	.55	.55
2362	A129	$15.30	multicolored	.65	.65
2363	A129	$17.80	multicolored	.75	.75
2364	A129	$20	multicolored	.85	.85
2365	A129	$25	multicolored	1.10	1.10
2366	A129	$100	multicolored	4.25	4.25
			Nos. 2359-2366 (8)	8.85	8.85

Miniature Sheets

Sheets of 16

2367	A129	$10	#a.-p.	7.00	7.00
2368	A129	$10	#a.-p.	7.00	7.00
2369	A129	$12.80	#a.-p.	8.50	8.50
2370	A129	$12.80	#a.-p.	8.50	8.50
2371	A129	$12.80	#a.-p.	8.50	8.50
2372	A129	$12.80	#a.-p.	8.50	8.50
			Nos. 2367-2372 (6)	48.00	48.00

Souvenir Sheets

2373	A129	$150	Coleandra devoniana	6.75	6.75
2374	A129	$150	Delonix regia	6.75	6.75
2375	A129	$150	Hexisea bidentata	6.75	6.75
2376	A129	$150	Lecythis ollaria	6.75	6.75
2377	A129	$190	Ionopsis utricularioides	8.50	8.50
			Nos. 2373-2377 (5)	35.50	35.50

Nos. 2370-2375 are horiz. For surcharges see Nos. 2593-2595.

Souvenir Sheet

Cenozoic Era Wildlife — A130

Designs: a, Palaelodus. b, Archaeotrogon. c, Vulture. d, Bradyrus tridactylus. e, Natalus stramineus bat. f, Cebidae. g, Cuvieronius. h, Phororhacos. i, Smilodectes. j, Megatherium. k, Titanotylopus. l, Teleoceras. m, Macrauchenia. n, Mylodon. o, Smilodon. p, Glyptodon. q, Protohydrocherus. r, Archaeohyrax. s, Pyrotherium. t, Platypittamys.

1990, Nov. 6

2378	A130	$12.80	Sheet of 20, #a.-t.	12.00	12.00

Miniature Sheets

Endangered Wildlife — A131

#2379: a, Ivory-billed woodpecker. b, Cauca guan. c, Sun conure. d, Quetzal. e, Long-wattled umbrellabird. f, Banded cotinga. g, Blue-chested parakeet. h, Rufous-bellied chachalaca. i, Yellow-faced amazon. j, Toucan barbet. k, Red siskin. l, Cock-of-the-rock. m, Hyacinth macaw. n, Yellow cardinal. o, Bare-necked umbrellabird. p, Saffron toucanette. q, Red-billed curassow. r, Spectacled parrotlet. s, Lovely cotinga. t, Black-breasted gnateater.

#2380: a, Swallow-tailed kite. b, Hoatzin. c, Ruby topaz hummingbird. d, Black vulture. e, Rufous-tailed jacamar. f, Scarlet macaw. g, Rose-breasted thrush tanager. h, Toco toucan. i, Bearded bellbird. j, Blue-crowned motmot. k, Green oropendola. l, Pompadour cotinga. m, Vermilion flycatcher. n, Blue and yellow macaw. o, White-barred piculet. p, Great razor-billed curassow. q, Ruddy quail-dove. r, Paradise tanager. s, Anhinga. t, Greater flamingo.

#2381: a, Harpy eagle. b, Andean condor. c, Amazonian umbrellabird. d, Spider monkeys. e, Hyacinth macaw, diff. f, Red siskin, diff. g, Toucan barbet, diff. h, Three-toed sloth. i, Guanaco. j, Spectacled bear. k, White-lipped peccary. l, Maned wolf. m, Jaguar. n, Spectacled caiman. o, Giant armadillo. p, Giant anteater. q, South American river otter. r, Yapok. s, Central American river turtle. t, Cauca guan, diff.

Perf. 14x13½, 13½x14

1990, Nov. 6 Litho.

Sheets of 20

2379	A131	$12.80	#a.-t.	12.50	12.50
2380	A131	$12.80	#a.-t.	12.50	12.50
2381	A131	$12.80	#a.-t.	12.50	12.50

#2381a-2381t are horiz. #2380s incorrectly inscribed Anhigna. See #E29-E30.

Numbers have been reserved for additional values in this set.

Independence, 25th Anniv. — A132

Illustration reduced.

1991, June 25 Litho. *Imperf.*

2389	A132	$225	multicolored	10.00	10.00

Miniature Sheets

Olympic Gold Medal Winners A133

No. 2390: a, Ramon Fonst. b, Lucien Gaudin. c, Ole A. Lilloe-Olsen. d, Morris Fisher. e, Ray C. Ewry. f, Hubert Van Innes. g, Alvin Kraenzlein. h, Johnny Weissmuller. i, Hans Winkler.

No. 2391: a, Viktor Chukarin. b, Agnes Keleti. c, Barbel Wochel. d, Eric Heiden. e, Alvodar Gerevich. f, Guiseppe Delfino. g, Alexander Tikhonov. h, C.F. Pahud de Mortanges. i, Patricia McCormick.

No. 2392: a, Nelli Kim. b, Viktor Krovopuskov. c, Viktor Sidiak. d, Nikolai Andrianov. e, Nadia Comaneci. f, Mitsuo Tsukahara. g, Yelena Novikova-Belova. h, John Naber. i, Kornelia Ender.

No. 2393: a, Olga Korbut. b, Lyudmila Turischeva. c, Lasse Viren. d, George Miez. e, Roland Matthes. f, Pal Kovaks. g, Jesse Owens. h, Mark Spitz. i, Eduardo Mangiarotti.

No. 2394: a, Sawao Kato. b, Rudolf Karpati. c, Jeno Fuchs. d, Emil Zatopek. e, Fanny Blankers-Koen. f, Melvin Sheppard. g, Gert Fredriksson. h, Paul Elvstrom. i, Harrison W. Dillard.

No. 2395: a, Lydia Skoblikova. b, Ivar Ballangrud. c, Clas Thunberg. d, Anton Heida. e, Akinori Nakayama. f, Sixten Jernberg. g, Yevgeniy Grischin. h, Paul Radmilovic. i, Charles Daniels.

No. 2396: a, Betty Cuthbert. b, Vera Caslavska. c, Galina Kulakova. d, Yukio Endo. e, Vladimir Morozov. f, Boris Shaklin. g, Don Schollander. h, Gyozo Kulscar. i, Christian D'Oriola.

No. 2397: a, Al Oerter. b, Polina Astakhova. c, Takashi Ono. d, Valentin Muratov. e, Henri St. Cyr. f, Iain Murray Rose. g, Larissa Latynina. h, Carlo Pavesi. i, Dawn Fraser.

No. 2398, Paavo Nurmi, vert. No. 2399, Johannes Kolehmainen, vert. $190. Nedo Nadi, vert.

1991, Aug. 12 Litho. *Perf. 14x13½*

Sheets of 9

2390	A133	$15.30	#a.-i.	2.75	2.75
2391	A133	$17.80	#a.-i.	3.25	3.25
2392	A133	$20	#a.-i.	3.50	3.50
2393	A133	$20	#a.-i.	3.50	3.50
2394	A133	$25	#a.-i.	4.50	4.50
2395	A133	$25	#a.-i.	4.50	4.50
2396	A133	$30	#a.-i.	5.50	5.50
2397	A133	$30	#a.-i.	5.50	5.50
			Nos. 2390-2397 (8)	33.00	33.00

Souvenir Sheets

Perf. 13x13½

2398	A133	$150	multicolored	3.00	3.00
2399	A133	$150	multicolored	3.00	3.00
2400	A133	$190	multicolored	3.75	3.75

For overprints see Nos. 2552-2557.

Discovery of America, 500th Anniv. (in 1992) — A134

Birds: $6.40, Phoenicopterus ruber. $7.65, Ostinops decumanus. $50, Falco peregrinus. $100, Nymphicus hollandicus. $190, Vultur feriphus. $260, Merganetta armata, horiz.

1991, Sept. 15 Litho. *Perf. 13½x14*

2401 A134 $6.40 multicolored
2402 A134 $7.65 multicolored
2403 A134 $50 multicolored
2404 A134 $100 multicolored
2405 A134 $190 multicolored
Nos. 2401-2405 (5) 12.00

Souvenir Sheet

Perf. 14x13½

2406 A134 $260 multicolored 13.00

A135

Various orchids.

Perf. 13½x14, 14x13½

1991, Sept. 30

2407 A135 $6.40 multicolored
2408 A135 $7.65 multi, horiz.
2409 A135 $50 multicolored
2410 A135 $100 multicolored
2411 A135 $190 Odontoglossum

Souvenir Sheets

2412 A135 $360 multicolored
2413 A135 $360 Cycnoches ventricosum
2414 A135 $360 Miltonia hibrida, horiz.

Nos. 2332-2339, 2343-2345 Ovptd. or Surcharged

Overprints: 80c, $2.55, Nos. 2421-2422, 2423a, 2423p, Rotary emblem and "1905-1990." $5.00, $6.40, $7.65, Nos. 2420, 2423d, 2423m, Rotary emblem and "Paul Percy Harris Founder 1868-1947" on 2 or 3 lines. Nos. 2423b, 2423l, 2423n, Boy Scout emblem and "1907-1992." Nos. 2423c, 2423i, 2423o, Lions Intl. emblem and "1917-1992." Nos. 2423e, 2423h, Red Cross emblem and "125 Years / Red Cross." Nos. 2423f-2423g, 2423j-2423k have parts of larger Rotary emblem. Nos. 2424-2425 ovptd. with service emblems in sheet margins.

1991, Oct. 29 *Perfs. as Before*

2415 A126 80c on #2332 .20 .20
2416 A126 $2.55 on #2333 .20 .20
2417 A126 $5 on #2334 .20 .20
2418 A126 $6.40 on #2335 .20 .20
2419 A126 $7.65 on #2336 .20 .20
2420 A126 $100 on $8.90 #2337 2.50 2.50
2421 A126 $190 on $50 #2338 4.75 4.75
2422 A126 $225 on $100 #2339 5.50 5.50
Nos. 2415-2422 (8) 13.75 13.75

Miniature Sheet

2423 A126 Sheet of 16 11.50 11.50
a.-l. $10 any single .20 .20
m. $50 on $10 #2343m 1.00 1.00
n. $75 on $10 #2343n 1.60 1.60
o. $100 on $10 #2343o 2.00 2.00
p. $190 on $10 #2343p 4.00 4.00

Souvenir Sheets

2424 A126 $400 on $150 #2344 10.00 10.00
2425 A126 $500 on $150 #2345 12.50 12.50

Swiss Confederation, 700th Anniv. — A136

$6.40, Painting by Diego Giacometti. $7.65, Swiss puppets. $50, Man in top hat by Goya. $100, Stained glass window of Mary & Joseph. $190, Stained glass window of Jesus healing the sick.

No. 2431, Ship's cross-section, by Le Corbusier. No. 2432, Portrait of Giovanna Tornabuoni.

1991, Oct. 30 *Perf. 13½x14*

2426 A136 $6.40 multicolored
2427 A136 $7.65 multicolored
2428 A136 $50 multicolored
2429 A136 $100 multicolored
2430 A136 $190 multicolored
a. Sheet of 5 + label, #2426-2430

Souvenir Sheets

2431 A136 $360 multicolored
2432 A136 $360 multicolored

Phila Nippon '91 — A137

Trains: $6.40, Class 581 12-car. $7.65, Class EF-81. $50, Class 381 9-car. $100, Kodama 8-car. $190, Shin-Kansen 16-car. No. 2438, Shin-Kansen 16-car, diff. No. 2439, Japanese locomotives in Calcutta.

1991, Nov. 16 *Perf. 14x13½*

2433 A137 $6.40 multicolored
2434 A137 $7.65 multicolored
2435 A137 $50 multicolored
2436 A137 $100 multicolored
2437 A137 $190 multicolored
Nos. 2433-2437 (5) 12.00

Souvenir Sheets

2438 A137 $360 multicolored
2439 A137 $360 multicolored
Nos. 2438-2439 (2) 25.00

Swiss Confederation, 700th anniv., #2439.

Common Design Types pictured following the introduction.

Royal Family Birthday, Anniversary

Common Design Type

1991, Nov. Litho. *Perf. 14*

2440 CD347 $8.90 multi .20 .20
2441 CD347 $12.80 multi .30 .30
2442 CD347 $15.30 multi .30 .30
2443 CD347 $50 multi 1.10 1.10
2444 CD347 $75 multi 1.60 1.60
2445 CD347 $100 multi 2.25 2.25
2446 CD347 $130 multi 2.75 2.75
2447 CD347 $150 multi 3.25 3.25
2448 CD347 $190 multi 4.00 4.00
2449 CD347 $200 multi 4.50 4.50
Nos. 2440-2449 (10) 20.25 20.25

Souvenir Sheets

2450 CD347 $225 Elizabeth 5.00 5.00
2451 CD347 $225 Charles, Diana, sons 5.00 5.00

$8.90, $50, $75, $190, No. 2451, Charles and Diana, 10th wedding anniversary. $130, $150, Prince Philip, 70th birthday. Others, Queen Elizabeth II, 65th birthday.

Miniature Sheet

Japanese Attack on Pearl Harbor, 50th Anniv. A138

Designs: a, Akagi launches attack planes. b, Sakamaki's midget submarine beached. c, Mistubishi ASM Zero fighter. d, USS Arizona under attack. e, Aichi D3A1 Val dive bomber. f, USS California. g, P40 defends Pearl Harbor. h, USS Cassin and Downes hit at dry dock. i, B17 crash lands at Bellows Field. j, USS Nevada burns at Hospital Point.

1991, Dec. 7 *Perf. 14½x15*

2452 A138 $50 Sheet of 10, #a.-j. 11.00 11.00

1992 Winter Olympics, Albertville — A139

Walt Disney characters at the Olympics: $6.40, Gus Gander playing ice hockey. $7.65, Mickey, Minnie in bobsled. $8.90, Huey, Dewey, Louie pretending to luge. $12.80, Goofy freestyle skiing. $50, Goofy ski jumping. $100, Donald, Daisy Duck speed skating. $130, Pluto cross-country skiing. $190, Mickey, Minnie ice dancing. No. 2461, Scrooge McDuck slalom skiing. No. 2462, Huey curling.

1991, Dec. 12 *Perf. 13½x13*

2453 A139 $6.40 multi .20 .20
2454 A143 $7.65 multi .20 .20
2455 A139 $8.90 multi .20 .20
2456 A143 $12.80 multi .30 .30
2457 A143 $50 multi 1.10 1.10
2458 A139 $100 multi 2.25 2.25
2459 A139 $130 multi 2.75 2.75
2460 A143 $190 multi 4.25 4.25
Nos. 2453-2460 (8) 11.25 11.25

Souvenir Sheets

2461 A139 $225 multi 5.00 5.00
2462 A143 $225 multi 5.00 5.00

Mushrooms — A140

Designs: $6.40, Boletus satanoides. $7.65, Russula nigricans. $50, Cortinarius glaucopus. $100, Lactarius camphoratus. $190, Cortinarius callisteus. No. 2468, Russula integra. No. 2469, Coprinus micaceus, vert.

1991, Dec. 16 Litho. *Perf. 14x13½*

2463 A140 $6.40 multicolored
2464 A140 $7.65 multicolored
2465 A140 $50 multicolored
2466 A140 $100 multicolored
2467 A140 $190 multicolored
Nos. 2463-2467 (5) 12.00

Souvenir Sheets

Perf. 14x13½, 13½x14

2468 A140 $360 multicolored
2469 A140 $360 multicolored
Nos. 2468-2469 (2) 25.00

Walt Disney Christmas Cards — A141

Designs and year of issue: 80c, Mickey, friends singing carols, 1989. $2.55, Mickey, friends riding trolley car, 1962. $5, Donald, Pluto wrapping package, 1971. $6.40, Mickey holding candle, 1948. $7.65, Mickey with Santa mask, 1947. $8.90, Pinocchio's shadow, 1939. $50, Three Little Pigs, dancing on wolf's back, 1933. $200, Mickey, mice singing carols, 1949.

No. 2478: a, Conductor, Donald. b, Elephant with book. c, Goofy, centaurs. d, Snow White, dwarfs. e, Pluto, dinosaur.

No. 2479: a, Mickey in sleigh. b, Three little pigs, Winnie-the-Pooh, Bambi. c, Dalmatian, bear, monkey, Lady and the Tramp. d, Alice, Goofy, Mad Hatter. e, Pinocchio, Tinker Bell, Peter Pan, Seven Dwarfs, Donald Duck. f, Pluto, 1974.

No. 2480, Mickey and friends riding in coach, 1932. No. 2481, Mickey, Pluto greeting friends, 1935. No. 2482, Donald, Jose Carioca, 1944. No. 2483, Couple dancing, baseball batter, 1945. No. 2484, Mickey, Donald, Goofy, 1946. No. 2485, Santa in chimney, 1969. No. 2486, Portrait of Winnie-the-Pooh hanging on wall, 1969. No. 2487, Mickey, 1978.

1991, Dec. 17 *Perf. 14x13½*

2470 A141 80c multi .20 .20
2471 A141 $2.55 multi .20 .20
2472 A141 $5 multi .20 .20
2473 A141 $6.40 multi .20 .20
2474 A141 $7.65 multi .20 .20
2475 A141 $8.90 multi .20 .20
2476 A141 $50 multi 1.10 1.10
2477 A141 $200 multi 4.25 4.25
2478 A141 $50 Strip of 5, #a.-e. 5.50 5.50
2479 A141 $50 Strip of 5, #a.-e. 5.50 5.50
Nos. 2470-2479 (10) 17.55 17.55

Souvenir Sheets

2480 A141 $260 multi 5.75 5.75
2481 A141 $260 multi 5.75 5.75
2482 A141 $260 multi 5.75 5.75
2483 A141 $260 multi 5.75 5.75
2484 A141 $260 multi 5.75 5.75
2485 A141 $260 multi 5.75 5.75
2486 A141 $260 multi 5.75 5.75
2487 A141 $260 multi 5.75 5.75
Nos. 2480-2487 (8) 46.00 46.00

Nos. 2478a-2478e, 2479a-2479f, 2480-2481, 2485 and 2487 are vert.

Christmas A142

Paintings: $6.40, Madonna and Child with Angels, by Titian, horiz. $7.65, Madonna and Child with Angels, by Rubens. $50, Madonna and Child, by Raphael. $100, Madonna and Child, by Durer. $190, Madonna, by Durer. No. 2493, Madonna and Child, by Rubens, horiz. No. 2494, Madonna, by Durer, diff.

1991, Dec. 30 *Perf. 14x13½, 13½x14*

2488 A142 $6.40 multicolored
2489 A142 $7.65 multicolored
2490 A142 $50 multicolored
2491 A142 $100 multicolored
2492 A142 $190 multicolored
Nos. 2488-2 92(5) 12.00

Souvenir Sheets

2493 A142 $360 multicolored
2494 A142 $360 multicolored
Nos. 2493-2494 (2) 25.00

Brandenburg Gate, Bicent. — A143

Designs: $10, Map of Berlin. $25, US Pres. George Bush, Polish Pres. Lech Walesa. $100, German Chancellor Helmut Kohl, Foreign Minister Hans-Dietrich Genscher. $190, Armored helmet.

1991, Dec. *Perf. 14*

2495 A143 $10 multicolored .25 .25
2496 A143 $25 multicolored .55 .55
2497 A143 $100 multicolored 2.20 2.20
Nos. 2495-2497 (3) 3.00 3.00

Souvenir Sheet

2498 A143 $190 multicolored 4.25 4.25

Wolfgang Amadeus Mozart, Death Bicent. A144

Portrait of Mozart and: $75, Laxenburg. $80, Death of Leopold II. $100, Mozart's birthplace, Salzburg.

1991, Dec.

2499 A144 $75 multicolored 1.60 1.60
2500 A144 $80 multicolored 1.75 1.75
2501 A144 $100 multicolored 2.10 2.10
Nos. 2499-2501 (3) 5.45 5.45

Souvenir Sheet

2502 A144 $190 Bust of Mozart, vert. 4.25 4.25

17th World Scout Jamboree, Korea — A145

Designs: $30, Scouts hiking. $40, Emblems, flag. $100, Lord Baden-Powell, vert. $190, Rocket cover with US No. 1145.

1991, Dec.

2503 A145 $25 multicolored .55 .55
2504 A145 $30 multicolored .65 .65
2505 A145 $40 multicolored .90 .90
2506 A145 $100 multicolored 2.25 2.25
Nos. 2503-2506 (4) 4.35 4.35

Souvenir Sheet

2507 A145 $190 multicolored 4.25 4.25

Charles de Gaulle A146

De Gaulle: $60, In Venice, 1944. $75, With Khrushchev, 1960. $80, In Algiers, 1958. $100, With Pope Paul VI, 1967.

1991, Dec.

2508 A146 $60 multicolored 1.25 1.25
2509 A146 $75 multicolored 1.60 1.60
2510 A146 $80 multicolored 1.75 1.75
2511 A146 $100 multicolored 2.25 2.25
Nos. 2508-2511 (4) 6.85 6.85

Souvenir Sheets

2512 A146 $150 Portrait, vert. 3.25 3.25
2513 A146 $190 Portrait, diff, vert. 4.25 4.25

Anniversaries and Events — A147

Designs: No. 2515, Caroline Herschel, astronomer, Old Town Hall, Hanover. No. 2516, Map of Switzerland, woman in traditional dress. $80, Otto Lilienthal's glider No. 3. $100, Locomotive. $190, Arms of Bern and Solothurn.

1991, Dec.

2515 A147 $75 multicolored 1.60 1.60
2516 A147 $75 multicolored 1.60 1.60
2517 A147 $80 multicolored 1.75 1.75
2518 A147 $100 multicolored 2.25 2.25
Nos. 2515-2518 (4) 7.20 7.20

Souvenir Sheet

2519 A147 $190 multicolored 4.25 4.25

Hanover, 750th anniv. (#2515), Swiss Confederation, 700th anniv. (#2516, 2519), first glider flight, cent. (#2517), Trans-Siberian Railway, cent. (#2518).

Discovery of America, 500th Anniv. A148

: $6.40, Columbus lands on Trinidad. $7.65, Columbus, globe. $8.90, Ships blown off course by hurricane. $12.80, Map, hands in chains. $15.30, Land sighted. $50, Nina, Pinta. $75, Santa Maria. $100, Columbus trading with natives. $125, Superstitions & sea monsters. $130, Map, Columbus ashore. $140, Priest & natives. $150, Columbus kneeling before King Ferdinand and Queen Isabella. #2532, Map of New World. #2533, One of Columbus' ships, vert. #2534, Columbus.

1992, Jan. 2 ***Perf. 14***

2520 A148 $6.40 multi .20 .20
2521 A148 $7.65 multi .20 .20
2522 A148 $8.90 multi .20 .20
2523 A148 $12.80 multi .30 .30
2524 A148 $15.30 multi .35 .35
2525 A148 $50 multi 1.10 1.10
2526 A148 $75 multi 1.60 1.60
2527 A148 $100 multi 2.25 2.25
2528 A148 $125 multi 2.75 2.75
2529 A148 $130 multi 2.75 2.75
2530 A148 $140 multi 3.00 3.00
2531 A148 $150 multi 3.25 3.25
Nos. 2520-2531 (12) 17.95 17.95

Souvenir Sheets

2532 A148 $280 multi 6.25 6.25
2533 A148 $280 multi 6.25 6.25
2534 A148 $280 multi 6.25 6.25

Movie Posters — A149

Designs: $8.90, The Great K & A Train Robbery. $12.80, Cimarron. $15.30, Buzzin' Around. $25, Adventures of Captain Marvel. $30, The Mummy. $50, A Sainted Devil. $75, A Tale of Two Cities. $100, A Tugboat Romeo. $130, Thief of Bagdad. $150, Bacon Grabbers. $190, A Night at the Opera. $200, Citizen Kane. No. 2547, She Done Him Wrong. No. 2548, The Circus. No. 2549, Babe Comes Home. No. 2550, Zeppelin, horiz.

1992, Mar. 11 Litho. ***Perf. 14***

2535 A149 $8.90 multi .20 .20
2536 A149 $12.80 multi .30 .30
2537 A149 $15.30 multi .35 .35
2538 A149 $25 multi .55 .55
2539 A149 $30 multi .65 .65
2540 A149 $50 multi 1.10 1.10
2541 A149 $75 multi 1.60 1.60
2542 A149 $100 multi 2.25 2.25
2543 A149 $130 multi 2.75 2.75
2544 A149 $150 multi 3.25 3.25
2545 A149 $190 multi 4.25 4.25
2546 A149 $200 multi 4.50 4.50
Nos. 2535-2546 (12) 21.75 21.75

Size: 70x100mm, 100x70mm

Imperf

2547 A149 $225 multi 5.00 5.00
2548 A149 $225 multi 5.00 5.00
2549 A149 $225 multi 5.00 5.00
2550 A149 $225 multi 5.00 5.00

No. 2273 Overprinted or Surcharged with Olympic Rings and "ALBERTVILLE '92" or "XVIth Olympic Winter / Games in Albertville" (No. 2551e)

1992 ***Perfs. as Before***

2551 A122 Sheet of 9
a.-f. $20 on #2273a-2273f
g. $70 on $20 #2273g
h. $100 on $20 #2273h
i. $190 on $20 #2273i

Nos. 2391g, 2395c, 2396c, 2398, 2400 Ovptd. "ALBERTVILLE '92"
No. 2399 Ovptd. "Barcelona '92" and emblems in Sheet Margin

1992 ***Perfs. as Before***

2552 A133 $17.80 on #2391g
2553 A133 $25 on #2395c
2554 A133 $30 on #2396c

Souvenir Sheets

2555 A133 $150 on #2398
2556 A133 $150 on #2399 3.00 3.00
2557 A133 $190 on #2400

Nos. 2552-2554 printed in sheets of 9, overprint applied to only one stamp per sheet. Overprint on Nos. 2555, 2557 applied to sheet margin.

Easter A150

Various details from paintings by Durer: $6.40, $12.80, $50, $130, No. 2567, The Martyrdom of Ten Thousand. $7.65, $15.30, $100, $190, No. 2566, Adoration of the Trinity.

1992 Litho. ***Perf. 13½x14***

2558 A150 $6.40 multi .20 .20
2559 A150 $7.65 multi .20 .20
2560 A150 $12.80 multi .30 .30
2561 A150 $15.30 multi .35 .35
2562 A150 $50 multi 1.10 1.10
2563 A150 $100 multi 2.25 2.25
2564 A150 $130 multi 2.75 2.75
2565 A150 $190 multi 4.25 4.25
Nos. 2558-2565 (8) 11.40 11.40

Souvenir Sheets

2566 A150 $225 multi 5.00 5.00
2567 A150 $225 multi 5.00 5.00

Queen Elizabeth II's Accession to the Throne, 40th Anniv. A151

Queen Elizabeth II: $8.90, With Prince Philip. $12.80, In uniform. $100, At coronation. $130, Wearing black cape and hat. No. 2572, Coronation portrait. No. 2573, Fortieth anniv. portrait.

1992 Litho. ***Perf. 14***

2568 A151 $8.90 multicolored .20 .20
2569 A151 $12.80 multicolored .30 .30
2570 A151 $100 multicolored 2.25 2.25
2571 A151 $130 multicolored 2.75 2.75
Nos. 2568-2571 (4) 5.50 5.50

Souvenir Sheets

2572 A151 $225 multicolored 5.00 5.00
2573 A151 $225 multicolored 5.00 5.00

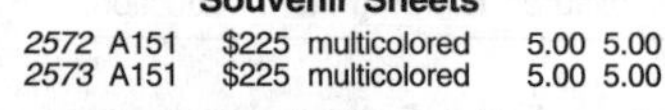

Diocese of Guyana, 150th Anniv. A152

Designs: $6.40, Holy Cross Church, Annai Bupununi. $50, St. Peter's Church. $100, St. George's Cathedral, interior, vert. $190, Map, vert. $225, Religious symbols.

1992 Litho. ***Perf. 14***

2574 A152 $6.40 multicolored .25 .25
2575 A152 $50 multicolored 1.00 1.00
2576 A152 $100 multicolored 2.00 2.00
2577 A152 $190 multicolored 3.75 3.75
Nos. 2574-2577 (4) 7.00 7.00

Souvenir Sheet

2578 A152 $225 multicolored 4.50 4.50

Miniature Sheet

Horses — A153

Designs: No. 2579a, Palomino. b, Appaloosa. c, Clydesdale. d, Arab. e, Morgan. f, Friesian. g, Pinto. h, Thoroughbred. No. 2580, Lipizzaner.

1992, Aug. 10

2579 A153 $190 Sheet of 8, #a.-h. 30.00 30.00

Souvenir Sheet

2580 A153 $190 multicolored 3.75 3.75

No. 2580 contains one 58x29mm stamp.

Cats — A154

Designs: No. 2588b, Russian blue. c, Havana brown. d, Himalayan. e, Manx. f, Cornish rex. g, Black Persian. h, Scottish fold. i, Siamese.

1992, Aug. 10 ***Perf. 14½x14***

2581 A154 $5 Burmese .20 .20
2582 A154 $6.40 Turkish van .20 .20
2583 A154 $12.80 American shorthair .25 .25
2584 A154 $15.30 Egyptian .35 .35
2585 A154 $50 Egyptian mau 1.00 1.00
2586 A154 $100 Japanese bobtail 2.00 2.00
2587 A154 $130 Abyssinian 2.50 2.50
2588 A154 $225 Oriental shorthair 4.50 4.50
Nos. 2581-2588 (8) 11.00 11.00

Miniature Sheet

Perf. 14x13½

2588A A154 $50 Sheet of 8, #b.-i. 8.00 8.00

Souvenir Sheets

Perf. 14x14½

2589 A152 $250 Chartreuse, vert. 4.50 4.50
2590 A154 $250 Turkish angora 5.00 5.00
2591 A154 $250 Maine coon 5.00 5.00
2592 A154 $250 Chinchilla 5.00 5.00

No. 2589 has continuous design. Nos. 2590-2592 are vert. and have continous design.

Nos. 2368-2369 Surcharged on 4 stamps and Overprinted in Red "PHILA NIPPON '91 / WORLD STAMP EXHIBITION NIPPON '91" and Show Emblem in Sheet Margin
No. 2376 Surcharged in Red

1992 ***Perfs. as Before***

Sheets of 12

2593 A129 #a.-d., #2368a-2368l
a. $25 on $10 #2368m
b. $50 on $10 #2368n
c. $75 on $10 #2368o
d. $130 on $10 #2368p

2594 A129 #a.-d., 2369a-2369l
- *a.* $25 on $12.80 #2369m
- *b.* $50 on $12.80 #2369n
- *c.* $75 on $12.80 #2369o
- *d.* $100 on $12.80 #2369p

Souvenir Sheet

2595 A129 $250 on $150 #2376

Nos. 2332-2340, 2346-2347 Overprinted or Surcharged

Overprints: 80c, $2.55, Nos. 2602-2603, Lions emblem and "Lions International / 1917-1992." $5, $6.40, $7.65, Nos. 2601, 2604d, 2604m, Lions emblem and "Melvin Jones Founder 1880-1961" on 2 or 3 lines. Nos. 2604a, 2604p, Lions emblem and "1917-1992." Nos. 2604b, 2604i, 2604o, Rotary emblem and "1905-1990." Nos. 2604c, 2604l, 2604n, Boy Scout emblem and "1907-1992." Nos. 2604e, 2604h, Red Cross emblem and "125 Years Red Cross." Nos. 2604f-2604g, 2604j-2604k have parts of larger Lions emblem. Nos. 2605-2606 have service organization emblems in sheet margins.

1992 ***Perfs. as Before***

2596 A126 80c on #2332
2597 A126 $2.55 on #2333
2598 A126 $5 on #2334
2599 A126 $6.40 on #2335
2600 A126 $7.65 on #2336
2601 A126 $100 on $8.90 #2337
2602 A126 $190 on $50 #2338
2603 A126 $225 on $100 #2339

Miniature Sheet

2604 Sheet of 16
- *a.-l.* A126 $10 any single
- *m.* A126 $50 on $10 #2340m
- *n.* A126 $75 on $10 #2340n
- *o.* A126 $100 on $10 #2340o
- *p.* A126 $190 on $10 #2340p

Souvenir Sheets

2605 A126 $400 on $190 #2346
2606 A126 $500 on $190 #2347

Elephants — A155

Designs: No. 2607a, Mammoth, Oligocene Epoch. b, Stegodon, mid- Miocene Epoch. c, Mammoth, Pliocene Epoch. d, Hannibal's army crossing Alps. e, Royal elephant of the Maharaja of Mysore, India. f, Elephant pulling tree trunks, Burma. g, Tiger hunt, India. h, Elephant towing raft on River Kwai, Thailand.
$225, African elephants, Kenya.

1992, Aug. 10 **Litho.** ***Perf. 14***

2607 A155 $50 Sheet of 8, #a.-h. 8.00 8.00

Souvenir Sheet

2608 A155 $225 multicolored 4.50 4.50

No. 2607 has continuous design.

Animals of Guyana A156

1992, Aug. 10

2609 A156 $8.90 Red howler monkey .20 .20
2610 A156 $12.80 Ring-tailed coati .25 .25
2611 A156 $15.30 Jaguar .30 .30
2612 A156 $25 Two-toed sloth .50 .50
2613 A156 $50 Giant armadillo 1.00 1.00
2614 A156 $75 Giant anteater 1.50 1.50
2615 A156 $100 Capybara 2.00 2.00
2616 A156 $130 Ocelot 2.60 2.60
Nos. 2609-2616 (8) 8.35 8.35

Souvenir Sheets

2617 A156 $225 Wooly opossum, vert. 4.50 4.50
2618 A156 $225 Night monkey, vert. 4.50 4.50

Souvenir Sheet

Statue of Liberty, New York — A157

1992, Oct. 28

2619 A157 $325 multicolored 6.50 6.50

Postage Stamp Mega Event '92, New York City.

Miniature Sheets

Model Trains A158

Marklin toy locomotives: No. 2620a, 2-4-4-2 Crocodile locomotive, 1 gauge, 1933. b, French prototype streetcar, 1 gauge, 1933. c, British prototype Flatiron 2-4-4 tank engine, O gauge, 1913. d, German National Railways 0-6-0 switching engine, Z gauge, 1970. e, Smoking/non-smoking third class car, 1 gauge, 1909. f, American style 0-4-0 locomotive, O gauge, 1904. g, Zurich, Switzerland prototype streetcar, O gauge, 1928. h, Central London Railway Bo-Bo, 1 gauge, 1904. i, "The Great Bear" Pacific, 1 gauge, 1909.

No. 2621: a, 0-4-4 American style locomotive, 2 gauge, 1907. b, German first and second class passenger car, 1 gauge, 1908. c, British Great Eastern Railway 4-4-0, 1 gauge, 1908. d, English prototype steeplecab, O gauge, 1904. e, Santa Fe Railroad diesel, 1962. f, British Great Northern 4-4-0, 3 gauge, live steam model, 1903. g, Caledonian Railway "Cardean" of Scotland, 1 gauge, 1904. h, British LNWR passenger car, 1 gauge, 1903. i, Swiss Gotthard Rwy. 0-4-0 locomotive, O gauge, 1920.

No. 2622: a, British LB & SCR tank engine, O gauge, 1920. b, Central London Railway, tunnel locomotive, 1 gauge, 1904. c, "Borsig" 4-6-4 streamliner, O gauge, 1935. d, French PLM first class car, 1 gauge, 1929. e, American style 0-4-0 locomotive #1021, 1 gauge, 1904. f, "Paris-Orsay" long-nose steeplecab, 1 gauge, 1920. g, British "Cock O' The North," 1 gauge, 1936. h, Prussian State Railways P8 4-6-0 live steam model, 1 gauge, 1975. i, 1937 German "Schnell Treibwagen," O gauge, 1937.

No. 2623: a, Marklin North British Railway "Atlantic," 1 gauge, 1913. b, Bing British London & Western Railway 4-4-2 "Precursor," O gauge, clockwork model, 1916. c, Marklin British Great Western "King George V," O gauge, 1937. d, Marklin passenger car, "Kaiser Train," 1 gauge, 1901. e, Bing 4-4-0 side tank engine, 1 gauge, live steam model, 1904. f, Marklin short-nose steeplecab, 1 gauge, 1912. g, Marklin "Der Adler", 1 gauge, 1935. h, Bing British Great Western Railway "County of Northampton," 1 gauge, live steam model, 1909. i, Bing British Midland Railway "Black Prince," 3 gauge, live steam model, 1908.

Bing toy locomotives: No. 2624: a, Midland Railway "Deeley Type" 4-4-0, 1 gauge clockwork model, 1909. b, No. 2631, British Midland Railway 0-4-0, 3 gauge clockwork model, 1903. c, German 4-6-2 Pacific, O gauge clockwork model, 1927. d, British Great Western Railway, third class coach, O gauge, 1926. e, British London & Southwestern "M7" 0-4-4, 1 gauge clockwork model, 1909. f, "Pilot" 4-4-0 side tank engine, 3 gauge live steam model, 1901. g, British London & Northwestern Railway Webb "Cauliflower," O gauge clockwork model, 1912. h, No. 112, 4-4-0 side tank locomotive, 1 gauge live steam model, 1910. i, British Great Northern Railway, "Stirling Single," 2 gauge live steam model, 1904.

Carette toy locomotives: No. 2625: a, Lithographed tin "Penny Bazaar" train, 1904. b, Winteringham 0-4-0 locomotive, O gauge, 1917. c, British Northeastern Railway, Smith Compound, 3 gauge, 1905. d, SE & CR 2-2-4 steam railcar, 1 gauge, live steam model, 1908. e, No. 776 British Great Northern Railway Stirling "Single," 3 gauge, live steam model, 1903. f, British Midland Railway 4-4-0, O gauge, clockwork model, 1911. g, London Metropolitan Railway "Westinghouse," 1 gauge, 1908. h, Clestory coach, 1 gauge, 1907. i, Steam railcar No. 1, O gauge, live steam model, 1906.

Marklin toy locomotives: No. 2626: a, LMS "Precursor" 4-4-2 tank engine, O gauge clockwork model, 1923. b, American "Congressional Limited" passenger car, 1 gauge, 1908. c, Swiss prototype "Ae 3/6" locomotive, O gauge, 1934. d, German National Railways class 80, 0-6-0, 1 gauge, 1975. e, British Southern Railway third class coach, O gauge, 1926. f, "Bowen-Cooke" 4-6-2 tank engine, O gauge, 1913. g, First electric prototype model, "Two Penny Tube," London, 1 gauge clockwork model, 1901. h, "Paris-Orsay" steeplecab, 1 gauge, 1920. i, 0-2-2 Passenger engine, O gauge clockwork model, 1895.

Bing toy locomotives: No. 2627: a, 2-2-0 engine and tender, 2 gauge live steam model, 1895. b, British Midland Railway "single," O gauge clockwork model, 1913. c, #524/510 reversible express passenger locomotive, 1 gauge, 1916. d, "Kaiser Train" passenger car with Gothic windows, 1 gauge, 1902. e, Tinplate model, British rural station, 1 gauge, 1915. f, British LSMR "M7" side tank locomotive, O gauge clockwork model, 1909. g, 4-4-4 "Windcutter," 1 gauge live steam model, 1912. h, British Great Central Railway "Sir Sam Fay," 1 gauge clockwork model, 1914. i, "Dunalastair" locomotive Caledonian Railway, 1 gauge clockwork model, 1910.

No. 2628, German National Railroad class 0-1 Pacific, O gauge, 1937. No. 2629, Bing 0-4-0 Contractor's locomotive, 4 gauge, 1904. No. 2630, Rack Railway "Steeplecab" locomotive, 2 gauge, 1908. No. 2631, Bing Pabst Blue Ribbon Beer refrigerator car, O gauge, 1925. No. 2632, Marklin "Commodore Vanderbilt," O gauge, 1937. No. 2633, Bing British Great Western Railway "County of Northampton," 1 gauge, live steam model, 1909. No. 2634, Marklin French Prototype PLM Pacific, 1 gauge, live steam model, 1912. No. 2635, Marklin "Mountain Etat" second series, O gauge, 1933.

1992, Nov. 19 ***Perf. 14***

Sheets of 9

2620 A158 $45 #a.-i. 8.25 8.25
2621 A158 $45 #a.-i. 8.25 8.25
2622 A158 $45 #a.-i. 6.50 6.50
2623 A158 $45 #a.-i. 6.50 6.50
2624 A158 $45 #a.-i. 6.50 6.50
2625 A158 $45 #a.-i. 6.50 6.50
2626 A158 $45 #a.-i. 6.50 6.50
2627 A158 $45 #a.-i. 6.50 6.50

Souvenir Sheets

2628 A158 $350 multicolored 7.00 7.00
2629 A158 $350 multicolored 7.00 7.00

Perf. 14x13½

2630 A158 $350 multicolored 7.00 7.00

Perf. 13x13½, 13½x13

2631 A158 $350 multicolored 5.50 5.50
2632 A158 $350 multicolored 5.50 5.50
2633 A158 $350 multicolored 5.75 5.75
2634 A158 $350 multicolored 5.75 5.75
2635 A158 $350 multicolored 5.75 5.75

Genoa '92. Nos. 2628-2635 each contain one 50x39mm stamp.

While Nos. 2622-2623 & 2631 have the issue date as Nos. 2620-2621 & 2628-2630, the face value of of Nos. 2622-2623 & 2631 was lower when they were released.

Anniversaries and Events — A159

Designs: $12.80, Zeppelin over Lake Constance, 1909. No. 2638, Voyager 1, Jupiter. No. 2639, Konrad Adenauer, John F. Kennedy. No. 2640, Aeromedical airlift. No. 2641, Amazon dolphins. No. 2642, Lift-off of Voyager 1, 1977. No. 2643, Baby gorilla. No. 2644, America's Cup yacht Stars and Stripes. No. 2644A, Eye screening van, doctor with patient. $190, Adenauer, Charles de Gaulle. $225, Zeppelin preparing for takeoff. No. 2647, Count Zeppelin, vert. No. 2648 View of Earth from space, vert. No. 2649, Konrad Adenauer, vert. No. 2650, Tree frog, vert.

1993, Jan. **Litho.** ***Perf. 14***

2637 A159 $12.80 multi .35 .35
2638 A159 $50 multi 1.00 1.00
2639 A159 $50 multi 1.00 1.00
2640 A159 $100 multi 2.00 2.00
2641 A159 $100 multi 2.00 2.00
2642 A159 $130 multi 2.60 2.60
2643 A159 $130 multi 2.60 2.60
2644 A159 $130 multi 2.60 2.60
2644A A159 $130 multi 2.60 2.60
2645 A159 $190 multi 3.75 3.75
2646 A159 $225 multi 4.50 4.50
Nos. 2637-2646 (11) 25.00 25.00

Souvenir Sheets

2647 A159 $225 multi 4.50 4.50
2648 A159 $225 multi 4.50 4.50
2649 A159 $225 multi 4.50 4.50
2650 A159 $225 multi 4.50 4.50

Count Zeppelin, 75th anniv. of death (#2637, 2646-2647). Intl. Space Year (#2638, 2642, 2648). Konrad Adenaurer, 25th anniv. of death (#2639, 2645, 2649). World Health Organization (#2640). Earth Summit, Rio (#2641, 2643, 2650). America's Cup Yacht Race (#2644). Lions Intl., 75th anniv. (#2644A).

Miniature Sheet

Biblical Story of David and Goliath — A160

Designs: No. 2651a, City of Jerusalem, two birds in flight. b, City, bird in flight at right. c, City, sun above. d, City, bird in flight at left. e, City with clouds above. f, Philistine army (i-k, q-r). g, Goliath. h, Goliath's arm, spear shaft (b, i, n). l, Goliath's leg (m, q-s), shield. n, David (r-t, w) with slingshot. o, Jewish soldiers with spears or swords (p-y).

1992, Dec. 29 **Litho.** ***Perf. 14***

2651 A160 $25 Sheet of 25, #a.-y. 12.50 12.50

No. 2651 has a continuous design.

Parrots A161

1993, Mar. 10

2652 A161 80c Hyacinth macaw .20 .20
2653 A161 $6.40 Scarlet macaw .20 .20
2654 A161 $7.65 Green macaw, vert. .20 .20
2655 A161 $15.30 Tovi parakeet .25 .25
2656 A161 $50 Blue & yellow macaw .80 .80
2657 A161 $100 Military macaw, vert. 2.00 2.00
2658 A161 $130 Red & green macaw, vert. 2.60 2.60
2659 A161 $190 Severa macaw 3.00 3.00
Nos. 2652-2659 (8) 9.25 9.25

Souvenir Sheet

2660 A161 $225 Scarlet macaw, diff. 4.50 4.50
2661 A161 $225 Green parakeet, vert. 3.75 3.75

While Nos. 2654-2656, 2659, 2661 have the same issue date as Nos. 2652-2653, 2657-2658, 2660, the value of Nos. 2654-2656, 2659, 2661 was lower when released.

Miniature Sheets

Dinosaurs — A162

#2662: a, Archaeopteryx. b, Pteranodon. c, Quetzalcoatlus. d, Protoavis. e, Dicraeosaurus. f, Moschops. g, Lystrosaurus. h, Dimetrondon. i, Staurikosaurus. j, Cacops. k, Diarthrognathus. l, Estemmenosuchus.

#2663: a, Pteranodon. b, Cearadactylus. c, Eudimorphodon. d, Pterodactylus. e, Stauirkosaurus. f, Euoplocephalus. g, Tuojiangosaurus. h, Oviraptor. i, Protoceratops. j,

Panaoplosaurus. k, Psittacosaurus. l, Corythosaurus.

#2664: a, Sordes. b, Quetzalcoatlus. c, Archaeopteryx. d, Rhamphorynchus. e, Spinosaurus. f, Anchisaurus. g, Stegosaurus. h, Leaellynosaurus. i, Minmi. j, Heterdontosaurus. k, Lesothosaurus. l, Deninonychus.

1993, Mar. 10 Litho. *Perf. 14*

Sheets of 12

2662 A162 $30 #a.-l. 6.00 6.00
2663 A162 $30 #a.-l. 6.00 6.00
2664 A162 $30 #a.-l. 6.00 6.00

Miniature Sheet

Signs of the Zodiac A163

Designs: a, Aquarius. b, Pisces. c, Aries. d, Taurus. e, Gemini. f, Cancer. g, Leo. h, Virgo. i, Libra. j, Scorpio. k, Sagittarius. l, Capricorn.

1993, Dec. 29 Litho. *Perf. 14x13½*

Sheet of 12

2665 A163 $30 #a.-l. 5.75 5.75

Caribbean Manatee A164

$6.40, Adult sticking head out of water. $7.65, Adult, eating, with young. $8.90, Adult swimming underwater. $50, Adult swimming with young.

1993, Mar. 10 Litho. *Perf. 15x14½*

2666 A164 $6.40 multicolored .65 .20
2667 A164 $7.65 multicolored .65 .20
2668 A164 $8.90 multicolored .65 .20
2669 A164 $50 multicolored 2.50 2.50
Nos. 2666-2669 (4) 4.45 3.10

World Wildlife Federation.

Miniature Sheets

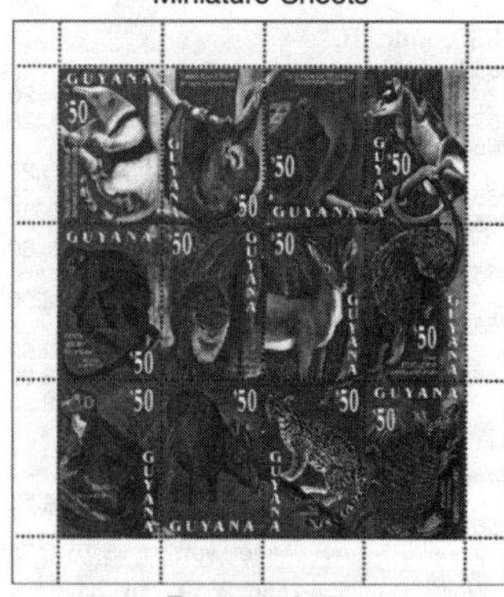

Fauna — A165

No. 2670: a, Southern tamandua. b, Three-toed sloth. c, Red howler monkey. d, Four-eyed opossum. e, Black spider monkey. f, Giant otter. g, Red brocket. h, Tree porcupine. i, Tayra. j, Tapir. k, Ocelot. l, Giant armadillo.

No. 2671: a, Crimson topaz hummingbird. b, Bearded bellbird (f). c, Amazonian umbrellabird. d, Paradise jacamar (h). e, Paradise tanager. f, White-tailed trogon (i-j). g, Scarlet macaw (k). h, Red fan parrot. i, Red-billed toucan. j, White plumed antbird. k, Crimson-hooded manakin. l, Guyanan cock-of-the-rock.

No. 2672, Paca. No. 2673, Tufted coquettes, horiz.

1993, Mar. 10 *Perf. 14*

Sheets of 12

2670 A165 $50 #a.-l. 10.00 10.00
2671 A165 $50 #a.-l. 10.00 10.00

Souvenir Sheets

2672 A165 $325 multicolored 5.25 5.25
2673 A165 $325 multicolored 5.25 5.25

Miniature Sheet

Coronation of Queen Elizabeth II, 40th Anniv. A166

a, $25, Official coronation photograph. b, $50, Gems from royal collection. c, $75, Queen, Duke of Edinburgh. d, $130, Queen opening Parliament.

$325, State Portrait, by Sir James Gunn, 1954-56.

1993, June 2 Litho. *Perf. 13½x14*

2674 A166 Sheet, 2 each #a.-d. 9.00 9.00

Souvenir Sheet

Perf. 14

2675 A166 $325 multicolored 5.25 5.25

No. 2675 contains one 28x42mm stamp. For overprints see Nos. 2793-2795.

Miniature Sheets

A167

Famous People A168

Athletes: No. 2676: a, O. J. Simpson, football. b, Rohan B. Kanhai, cricket. c, Gabriela Sabatini, tennis. d, Severiano Ballesteros, golf. e, Peace dove. f, Franz Beckenbauer, soccer. g, Pele, soccer. h, Wilt Chamberlain, basketball, i, Nadia Comaneci, gymnastics.

Scientists: No. 2677: a, Louis Leakey, archaeology. b, Jonas Salk, polio vaccine. c, Hideyo Noguchi, yellow fever. d, Karl Landsteiner, blood transfusions. e, Peace dove. f, Sigmund Freud, psychoanalysis. g, Louis Pasteur. h, Madame Curie, radium tubes. i, Jean Baptiste Perrin, physics.

Artists, entertainers: No. 2678: a, Gabriel Marquez, writer. b, Pablo Picasso, artist. c, Cecil DeMille, film director. d, Martha Graham, dance. e, Peace dove. f, Charles Chaplin, actor. g, Paul Robeson, singer. h, Rudolph Dunbar, musician. i, Louis Armstrong, musician.

Politicians: No. 2679: a, Jawaharlal Nehru. b, Dr. Eric Williams, first prime minister of Trinidad and Tobago. c, John F. Kennedy. d, Hugh Desmond Hoyte, president of Guyana. e, Peace dove over map. f, Friedrich Ebert. g, Franklin D. Roosevelt. h, Mikhail Gorbachev. i, Winston Churchill.

Humanitarians: No. 2680: a, Gandhi. b, Dalai Lama. c, Michael Manley, prime minister of Jamaica. d, Javier Perez de Cuellar, former UN Secretary General. e, Peace dove, globe. f, Mother Teresa. g, Martin Luther King, Jr. h, Nelson Mandela. i, Raoul Wallenberg.

Transportation, communication: No. 2681: a, DC-3 cargo plane. b, Space shuttle. c, Concorde. d, Ferdinand von Zeppelin. e, Peace dove. f, Guglielmo Marconi. g, Adrian Thompson, mountaineer. h, Bullet train, Japan. i, John von Neuman, mathematician.

#2682, UN Flag, natl. flags. #2683, Jackie Robinson. #2684, Einstein's formula. #2685, Elvis Presley. #2686, Nobel Peace Prize certificate. #2687, Apollo Moon Landing.

1993, July 26 Litho. *Perf. 14*

Sheets of 9

2676 A167 $50 #a.-i. 7.25 7.25
2677 A167 $50 #a.-i. 7.25 7.25
2678 A167 $50 #a.-i. 7.25 7.25
2679 A168 $100 #a.-i. 14.50 14.50
2680 A168 $100 #a.-i. 14.50 14.50
2681 A168 $100 #a.-i. 14.50 14.50

Souvenir Sheets

2682 A168 $250 multi, vert. 4.00 4.00
2683 A167 $250 multi, vert. 4.00 4.00
2684 A167 $250 multi, vert. 4.00 4.00
2685 A167 $250 multi, vert. 4.00 4.00
2686 A168 $250 multi, vert. 4.00 4.00
2687 A168 $250 multi 4.00 4.00

Willy Brandt (1913-1992), German Chancellor — A169

Designs: $25, Brandt, Golda Meir, 1969. $190, Brandt at steel mill, 1969. $325, Brandt.

1993, Aug. 16 Litho. *Perf. 14*

2688 A169 $25 multicolored .40 .40
2689 A169 $190 multicolored 3.00 3.00

Souvenir Sheet

2690 A169 $325 multicolored 5.25 5.25

Armillary Sphere — A170

Copernicus (1473-1543): $190, Satellite antenna. $300, Copernicus.

1993, Aug. 16

2691 A170 $50 multicolored .80 .80
2692 A170 $190 multicolored 3.00 3.00

Souvenir Sheet

2693 A170 $300 multicolored 4.75 4.75

Georg Hackl, Luge Gold Medalist, 1992 — A171

1993, Aug. 16

1994 Winter Olympics, Lillehammer, Norway: $130, Karen Magnussen, figure skater, 1972. $325, German bobsled team, 1992.

2694 A171 $50 multicolored .80 .80
2695 A171 $130 multicolored 2.00 2.00

Souvenir Sheet

2696 A171 $325 multicolored 5.25 5.25

A172

World War II — A173

Designs: $6.40, Audie Murphy. $7.65, British, US forces link up in France, June 8, 1944. $8.90, Monte Cassino falls to Allies, May 18, 1944. $12.80, Battleship Yamato attacked by US in Battle of East China Sea, Apr. 7, 1945. $15.30, St. Basil's Cathedral, Moscow, Foreign Ministers Conf., Oct. 19, 1943. $50, US forces cross Rhine River, Mar. 7, 1945. $130, Gen. George S. Patton, Jr., Battle of Sicily ends, Aug. 17, 1943. $190, Battleship Tirpitz sunk, Nov. 12, 1944. $200, US Sherman tank, US forces enter Brittany after taking Normandy, Aug. 1, 1944. $100, B-29s begin bombing raids on Japan from China, June 15, 1944. $225, End of fighting in Italy, May 2, 1945.

War at Sea, 1943: No. 2708: a, Adm. Yamamoto launches air offensive, Apr. 7. b, PT-109 in Blackett Strait, Aug. 1. c, USS Enterprise. d, Allied ships attack Rabaul, Oct. 12. e, US troops land at Cape Gloucester, Dec. 26. f, USS Bogue enters service, Feb. g, Wildcat fighters sink U-118. h, Battle of Atlantic reaches peak, U-boats sink 108 ships. i, Italian fleet surrenders at Malta, Sept. 10. j, Battleship Duke of York sinks Scharnhorst, Dec. 26.

War in the Air, 1943: No. 2709: a, Royal Australian Air Force Beaufighter, Battle of Bismark Sea, Mar. 2-4. b, P-38 Lightening shoots down Adm. Yamamoto's plane over Bougainville, Apr. 7. c, B-24 Liberators bomb Tarawa prior to landings, Sept. 17-19. d, B-25 Mitchell of Fifth Air Force bombs Rabaul, Oct. 12. e, US Navy aircraft attack Makin, Nov. 19. f, US Army Air Force's first daylight raid over Germany, Jan. 27. g, Royal Air Force Mosquito bombers make first daylight raid on Berlin, Jan. 30. h, Allies devastate Hamburg with first firestorm, July 24-30. i, B-24 bombers raid Ploesti oil refineries in Romania, Aug. 1. j, Battle of Berlin begins, Nov. 18.

No. 2710, $325, US, Russian infantry meeting at Elbe River, Apr. 25, 1945.

1993, Oct. 18 Litho. *Perf. 14*

2697 A172 $6.40 multicolored .20 .20
2698 A172 $7.65 multicolored .20 .20
2699 A172 $8.90 multicolored .20 .20
2700 A172 $12.80 multicolored .20 .20
2701 A172 $15.30 multicolored .25 .25
2702 A172 $50 multicolored .75 .75
2703 A172 $100 multicolored 1.50 1.50
2704 A172 $130 multicolored 2.00 2.00
2705 A172 $190 multicolored 3.00 3.00
2706 A172 $200 multicolored 3.00 3.00
2707 A172 $225 multicolored 3.50 3.50
Nos. 2697-2707 (11) 14.80 14.80

Miniature Sheets

Perf. 15

2708 A173 $50 Sheet of 10, #a.-j. 8.00 8.00
2709 A172 $50 Sheet of 10, #a.-j. 8.00 8.00

Nos. 2709a-2709j are 35½x22mm.

Souvenir Sheet

Perf. 14

2710 A172 $325 multicolored 5.00 5.00

1994 World Cup Soccer Championships, U.S. — A174

Player, country: $5, Stuart Pearce, England. $6.40, Ronald Koeman, Holland. $7.65, Gianluca Vialli, Italy. $12.80, McStay, Scotland, Alemao, Brazil. $15.30, Ceulemans, Belgium, Butcher, England. $50, Dragan Stojkovic, Yugoslovia. $100, Ruud Gullit, Holland. $130, Miloslav Kadlec, Czechoslovakia. $150, Ramos, Uruguay, Berthold, Germany. $190, Baggio, Italy; Wright, England. $200, Yarentchuck, Russia, Renquin, Belgium. $225, Timofte, Romania; Aleinikov, Russia. No. 2724, Rene Higuita, Colombia. No. 2723, Salvatore Schillaci, Italy, horiz.

1993, Oct. 18 Litho. *Perf. 14*

2711 A174 $5 multicolored .20 .20
2712 A174 $6.40 multicolored .20 .20
2713 A174 $7.65 multicolored .20 .20
2714 A174 $12.80 multicolored .20 .20
2715 A174 $15.30 multicolored .25 .25
2716 A174 $50 multicolored .70 .70
2717 A174 $100 multicolored 1.50 1.50
2718 A174 $130 multicolored 2.00 2.00
2719 A174 $150 multicolored 2.25 2.25
2720 A174 $190 multicolored 2.75 2.75
2721 A174 $200 multicolored 3.25 3.25
2722 A174 $225 multicolored 3.50 3.50
Nos. 2711-2722 (12) 17.00 17.00

Souvenir Sheets

2723 A174 $325 multicolored 5.25 5.25
2724 A174 $325 multicolored 5.25 5.25

Order of the Caribbean Community
A175

1993, Sept. 27 Litho. *Perf. 14*

2725 A175 $7.65 William Demas .20 .20
2726 A175 $7.65 Derek Walcott .20 .20
2727 A175 $7.65 Sir Shridath Ramphal .20 .20
Nos. 2725-2727 (3) .60 .60

Christmas
A176

Details from Holy Family Under the Apple Tree, by Rubens: $6.40, $12.80, $130, $190.
Details from The Virgin in Glory, by Durer: $7.65, $15.30, $50, $250.
No. 2736, Holy Family Under the Apple Tree (entire). No. 2737, The Virgin in Glory (entire).

1993, Dec. 1 *Perf. 13½x14*

2728-2735 A176 Set of 8 10.50 10.50

Souvenir Sheets

2736 A174 $325 multicolored 5.25 5.25
2737 A174 $325 multicolored 5.25 5.25

Miniature Sheets

Louvre Museum, Bicent.
A177

Details or entire paintings: No. 2738, Mona Lisa, by Da Vinci.
No. 2739: a, La Femme A La Puce, by Crespi. b, La Femme Hydropique, by Dou. c, Portrait of a Couple, by Ittenbach. d, Cleopatra Enthroned, by Moreau. e, La Richesse, by Vouet. f, Vieillard Et Jeune Garcon, by Ghirlandaio. g, Louis XIV, by Rigaud. h, La Buveuse, by Pieter De Hooch.
No. 2740: a, Self-portrait Wearing Spectacles, by Chardin. b, L'Infante Marie-Therese, by Velasquez. c, Spring, by Arcimboldo. d, The Virgin of Sorrows, by Bouts. e, The Study, by Fragonard. f. Francis I, by Clouet. g, Le Condottiere, by Antonello Da Messina. h, La Bohemienne, by Hals.
No. 2741: a, Le Femme A La Puce, entire, by Crespi. b, Self-portrait, by Rembrandt. c, Femmes D'Alger Dans Leur Appartement, by Delacroix. d, Tete De Jeune Homme, by Raphael. e, Venus and the Graces, by Botticelli. f, Nature Morte A L'Echiquier, by Lubin Baugin. g, Lady MacBeth Sleepwalking, by Fussli. h, La Tabagie, by Chardin.
Nos. 2742: a-c, L'Accordee de Village (left, center, right), by Greuze. d, Self-portrait, by Melendez. e, Knight and Young Girl on Horseback, by Baldung-Grien. f, The Young Begger, by Murillo. g-h, The Pilgrims of Emmaus (left, right), by Mathieu Le Nain.
No. 2743: a-b, The Virgin and the Rabbit (diff. details), by Titian. c, La Belle Jardiniere, by Raphael. d, The Lacemaker, by Vermeer. e, Jeanne D'Aragon, by Raphael. f, The Astronomer, by Vermeer. g, The Bridge at Rialto, by Canaletto. h, Sigismond Malatesta, by Piero Della Francesca.
No. 2744, Cour De Ferme, by Jan Brueghel, the Younger. No. 2745, The Bridge at Rialto, by Canaletto. No. 2746, The Coronation of Napoleon I, by David. No. 2747, Details and painting of Mona Lisa. No. 2748, The Fortune Teller, by Caravaggio. No. 2749, The Marriage at Cana, by Veronese.

1993, Dec. 6 Litho. *Perf. 13½x14*

2738 A177 $50 multicolored .80 .80
a. Sheet of 8 + label 6.50 6.50

Sheets of 8 + label

2739 A177 $50 #a.-h. 6.50 6.50
2740 A177 $50 #a.-h. 6.50 6.50
2741 A177 $50 #a.-h. 6.50 6.50
2742 A177 $50 #a.-h. 6.50 6.50
2743 A177 $50 #a.-h. 6.50 6.50

Souvenir Sheets

Perf. 12

2744-2749 A177 $325 each 5.25 5.25

Nos. 2744-2746 each contain one 80x47mm stamp. Nos. 2747-2749 one 80x53mm stamp.

Christmas
A177a

Entire paintings or details: $7.65, St. Anne with Mary and the Child Jesus, by Dürer. $8.90, Mary Being Crowned by Two Angels, by Dürer. $50, Pentecost, by Titian. $100, Samson and Delilah, by Rubens. $250, Origin of the Milky Way, by Rubens.
No. 2749F, The Descent from the Cross, by Rubens, horiz. No. 2749G, The Descent from the Cross, by Dürer, horiz.

1993 Litho. *Perf. 13½x14, 14x13½*

2749A-2749E A177a Set of 5 6.50 6.50

Souvenir Sheets

2749F-2749G A177a $500 ea 8.00 8.00

Polska '93 (Paintings) — A178

$50, $130, Pantaloons, by Tadeusz Brzozowski, 1966. $75, Fortress, by Miedzyrecz. $325, Children in the Garden, by Wladyslaw Podkowinski, 1892, horiz.

1993 *Perf. 14*

2750 A178 $50 multicolored .80 .80
2751 A178 $75 multicolored 1.10 1.10
2752 A178 $130 multicolored 2.00 2.00
a. A178 Pair, #2750, #2752 2.80 2.80
Nos. 2750-2752 (3) 3.90 3.90

Souvenir Sheet

2753 A178 $325 multicolored 5.25 5.25

Picasso (Paintings) — A179

1993, Nov. Litho. *Perf. 14*

$15.30, Bather, Paris, 1909. $100, Two Nudes, 1906. $190, Nude Seated on a Rock, 1921. $325, The Rescue, 1922.

2754 A179 $15.30 multicolored .20 .20
2755 A179 $100 multicolored 1.60 1.60
2756 A179 $190 multicolored 3.00 3.00
Nos. 2754-2756 (3) 4.80 4.80

Souvenir Sheet

2756A A179 $325 multicolored 5.25 5.25

Rebirth of Democracy, 1st Anniv. — A180

$6.40, Dr. Cheddie B. Jagan, Guyana Pres. $325, Sunburst, "REBIRTH OF DEMOCRACY," horiz.

1993, Dec. 17 Litho. *Perf. 13½x14*

2757 A180 $6.40 multicolored .20 .20

Souvenir Sheet

Perf. 13

2757A A180 $325 multicolored 5.00 5.00

Miniature Sheet

Aladdin — A181

Nos. 2758a-2758h, Various characters from Disney animated film, vert. Nos. 2759a-2759i, Various film scenes. Nos. 2760a-2760i, Various scenes from Disney animated film.
No. 2761, Genie, Jasmine, and Aladdin. No. 2762, Aladdin, the Genie, Abu, Magic Carpet. No. 2763, Aladdin as Prince Ali Ababwa. No. 2764, Aladdin, Abu, Jasmine.

1993, Dec. 20 Litho. *Perf. 14x13½*

Sheets of 8 & 9

2758 A181 $7.65 #a.-h. 1.10 1.10
2759 A181 $50 #a.-i. 7.25 7.25
2760 A181 $65 #a.-i. 9.00 9.00
Nos. 2758-2760 (3) 17.35 17.35

Souvenir Sheets

2761 A181 $325 multicolored 5.00 5.00
2762 A181 $325 multicolored 5.00 5.00
2763 A181 $325 multicolored 5.00 5.00
2764 A181 $325 multicolored 5.00 5.00

A182

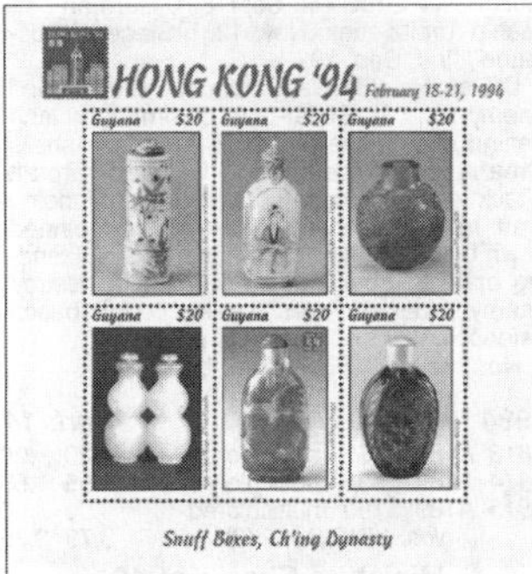

Hong Kong '94 — A183

Stamps, photograph of Happy Valley Horse Race Course: No. 2765, Hong Kong #437, scoreboard. No. 2766, Track, horses, #2545.
Snuff boxes, Qing Dynasty: No. 2767: a, Painted enamel in shape of bamboo. b, Painted enamel with human figure. c, Amber with lions playing ball. d, Agate in shape of two gourds. e, Glass overlay with dog. f, Glass, foliage design.
Porcelain, Ch'ing Dynasty: No. 2768: a, Covered jar with dragon. b, Rotating brush holder. c, Covered jar with horses. d, Amphora vase with bats & peaches. e, Tea caddy with Fo dogs. f, Vase with wild camellia & peaches.

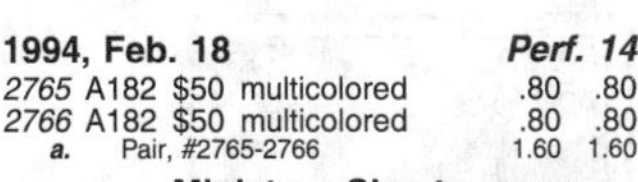

1994, Feb. 18 *Perf. 14*

2765 A182 $50 multicolored .80 .80
2766 A182 $50 multicolored .80 .80
a. Pair, #2765-2766 1.60 1.60

Miniature Sheets

2767 A183 $20 Sheet of 6, #a.-f. 2.00 2.00
2768 A183 $20 Sheet of 6, #a.-f. 2.00 2.00

Nos. 2765-2766 issued in sheets of 5 pairs. No. 2766a is continuous design.
New Year 1994 (Year of the Dog) (#2767e, #2768e).

Miniature Sheets of 6 and 8

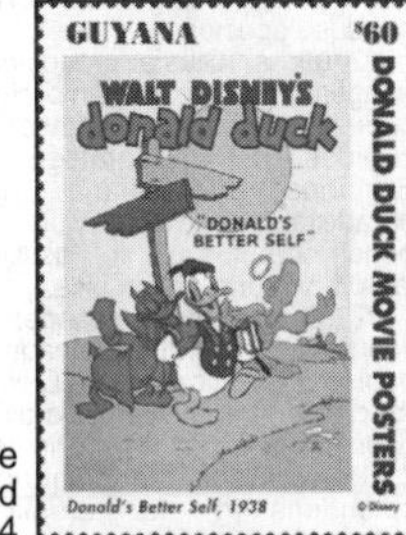

Vintage Donald Duck — A184

Movie posters: No. 2769: a, Donald's Better Self, 1938. b, Donald's Golf Game, 1938. c, Sea Scouts, 1939. d, Donald's Penguin, 1939. e, A Good Time for a Dime, 1941. f, Truant Officer Donald. g, Orphan's Benefit, 1941. h, Chef Donald, 1941.
No. 2770: a, The Village Smithy, 1942. b, Donald's Snow Fight, 1942. c, Donald's Garden, 1942. d, Donald's Gold Mine, 1942. e, The Vanishing Private, 1942. f, Sky Trooper, 1942. g, Bellboy Donald, 1942. h, The New Spirit, 1942.
No. 2771: a, Saludos Amigos, 1943. b, The Eyes Have It, 1945. c, Donald's Crime, 1945. d, Straight Shooters, 1947. e, Donald's Dilemma, 1947. f, Bootle Beetle, 1947. g, Daddy Duck, 1948. h, Soup's On, 1948.
Story boards from Pirate Gold, horiz.: No. 2772: a, Pirate ship. b, Carrying treasure chest. c, Donald Duck with map. d, Donald, souvenir shop. e, Donald following Aracuan bird. f, Angry Donald.
Movie posters: No. 2773: a, Donald's Happy Birthday, 1949. b, Sea Salts, 1949. c, Honey Harvester, 1949. d, All in a Nutshell, 1949. e, The Greener Yard, 1949. f, Slide, Donald, Slide, 1949. g, Lion Around, 1950. h, Trailer Horn, 1950.
No. 2774: a, Bee at the Beach, 1950. b, Out on a Limb, 1950. c, Corn Chips, 1951. d, Test Pilot Donald, 1951. e, Lucky Number, 1951. f, Out of Scale, 1951. g, Bee on Guard, 1951. h, Let's Stick Together, 1952.
No. 2775: a, Trick or Treat, 1952. b, Don's Fountain of Youth, 1953. c, Rugged Bear, 1953. d, Canvas Back Duck, 1953. e, Dragon Around, 1954. f, Grin and Bear It, 1954. g, The Flying Squirrel, 1954. h, Up a Tree, 1955.
No. 2776, Studio Fan Card, Melody Time, 1948.
No. 2777, Scene from picture book of first movie, The Wise Little Hen, 1944, horiz. No. 2778, Sketch for closing scene of Timber, 1941. No. 2779, Donald Duck, horiz. No. 2780, Studio fan card, The Three Caballeros, 1945, horiz.
Movie posters contained in No. 2780A are listed as designs for Nos. 2769-2771, 2774-2775, 2777, 2780.

Perf. 14x13½, 13½x14

1993, Dec. 6 Litho.

2769-2771 A184 $60 #a.-h., each 7.75 7.75
2772 A184 $80 #a.-f. 7.50 7.50
2773-2775 A184 $80 #a.-h, each 10.00 10.00

Size: 130x104mm

Imperf

2776 A184 $500 multi 7.75 7.75

Souvenir Sheets

Perf. 14x13½, 13½x14

2777-2780 A184 $500 each 8.00 8.00

Imperf

Self-Adhesive

Size: 64x89mm

2780A A184 $60 Set of 50 50.00

No. 2780A exists with backing labels printed in English or French. Value is for either set. No. 2780A was printed on thin card and sold in sealed cellophane packages containiong 10 stamps. To affix stamps, backing containing film information must be removed.
#2769-2771, 2773-2775 exist in sheets of 7 $5 stamps + label. The label replaces #2769f, 2770b, 2771h, 2773a, 2774d, 2775e. These sheets became available Nov. 20, 1996.

Tropical Flowers
A185

#2781, $6.40, Cestrum parqui. #2782, $7.65, Brunfelsia calycina. #2783, $12.80, Datura rosei. #2784, $15.30, Ruellia macrantha. #2785, $50, Portlandia albiflora. #2786, $130, Pachystachys coccinea. #2787, $190, Beloperone guttata. #2788, $250, Ferdinandusa speciosa.

#2789: a, Clusia grandiflora. b, Begonia haageana. c, Fuchsia simplicicaulis. d, Guaiacum officinale (a). e, Pithecoctenium cynanchoides. f, Sphaeralcea umbellata. g, Erythrina poeppigiana. h, Steriphoma paradoxa. i, Allemanda violacea (f). j, Centropogon cornutus (g). k, Passiflora quadrangularis. l, Victoria amazonica.

#2790: a, Cobaea scandens. b, Pyrostegia venusta (c). c, Petrea kohautiana (b). d, Hippobroma longiflora (a). e, Cleome hassleriana (b, d, f, h, i). f, Verbena peruviana (c). g, Tropaeolum peregrinum. h, Plumeria rubra (g, i). i, Selenicereus grandiflorus. j, Mandevilla splendens (g). k, Pereskia aculeata. l, Ipomoea learii.

#2791, Columnea fendleri. #2792, Lophospermum erubescens.

1994, Feb. 10 Litho. *Perf. 13½*

2781-2788 A185 Set of 8 10.00 10.00

Miniature Sheets of 12

Perf. 14

2789-2790 A185 $50 each 10.00 10.00

Souvenir Sheets

Perf. 13

2791-2792 A185 $325 each 5.25 5.25

Nos. 2674-2675 Ovptd. "ROYAL VISIT FEB 19-22, 1994" in One or Two Lines

1994 Litho. *Perf. 13½x14*

2793 A166 Sheet, 2 each #a.-d. 9.00 9.00

Souvenir Sheet

Perf. 14

2794 A166 $325 multicolored 5.25 5.25

Hummel Figurines — A186

Designs: $20, #2803a ($30), Girl holding basket and heart. $25, Boy holding heart. $35, #2804a ($20), Chef holding dessert. $50, #2804b ($130), Girl holding planter of mushrooms. $60, Girl holding plant, horn. No. 2800 ($130), #2803b ($6), Four girls. $190, Two girls, boy and puppy. $250, #2804c ($35), Boy holding covered dish, puppy.

1994, May 5 Litho. *Perf. 14*

2795-2802 A186 Set of 8 11.50 11.50

Souvenir Sheets

2803 A186 #a.-b, #2796, 2801 4.00 4.00
2804 A186 #a.-c, #2799 4.00 4.00

Miniature Sheets

Sierra Club, Cent.
A187

Various animals or scenic places: No. 2805a-2805b, American alligator. c.-d, Italian Alps. e.-f, Mono Lake.

No. 2806: a, Red kangaroo. b.-d, Whooping crane. e.-f, Alaskan brown bear. g, Bald eagle. h, Giant panda.

No. 2807, vert.: a.-b, Red kangaroo. c, American alligator. d, Alaskan brown bear. e.-f, Bald eagle. g.-h, Giant panda.

No. 2808, vert.: a.-c, Sea lion. d, Mono Lake. e, Sierra Club centennial emblem. f, Italian Alps. g.-i, Matterhorn.

1994, May 20 Litho. *Perf. 14*

Sheets of 6, 8 & 9

2805 A187 $70 #a.-f. 6.50 6.50
2806 A187 $70 #a.-h. 8.75 8.75
2807 A187 $70 #a.-h. 8.75 8.75
2808 A187 $70 #a.-i. 10.00 10.00
Nos. 2805-2808 (4) 34.00 34.00

Miniature Sheets of 6

First Manned Moon Landing, 25th Anniv.
A188

Famous men, aviation & space scenes: No. 2809a, Robert R. Gilruth, Apollo 16. b, Ernst Stuhlinger, Apollo 17. c, Christopher C. Kraft, X-30 National Aero-Space Plane. d, Rudolf Opitz, Me-163, July 24, 1943. e, Clyde W. Tombaugh, "Face on Mars." f, Hermann Oberth, Scene from "The Girl in the Moon."

No. 2810: a, Werner von Braun, Apollo 11. b, Rocco A. Petrone, Apollo 11. c, Eberhard Rees, Apollo 12. d, Charles A. Berry, Apollo 13. e, Thomas O. Paine, Apollo 14. f, A.F. Staats, Apollo 15.

No. 2811: a, Walter Dornberger, 1st A-4 launch. b, Rudolph Nebel, Surveyor 1. c, Robert H. Goddard, Apollo 7. d, Kurt Debus, Apollo 8. e, James T. Webb, Apollo 9. f, George E. Mueller, Apollo 10.

No. 2812, Frank J. Everest, Jr.

1994, July 20 Litho. *Perf. 14*

2809-2811 A188 $60 #a.-f, each 5.75 5.75

Souvenir Sheet

2812 A188 $325 multicolored 5.00 5.00

A189

World War II — A190

Designs: $6, Photo reconnaissance Spitfire. $35, 226 Squadron B-25. $190, 76 Squadron P-47 Thunderbolts.

Europe and North Africa, 1944: No. 2816: a, Allied landings, Anzio, Jan. 22. b, RAF bombs Amiens prison, Feb. 18. c, Sevastopol falls to Red Army, May 9. d, Allies breach Gustav Line, May 19. e, D-Day, June 6. f, V-1 attacks on London begin, June 13. g, Cease fire declared for Paris, Aug. 19. h, Germany launches V-2 rockets, Sept. 8. i, German battleship Tirpitz sunk, Nov. 12. j, Siege of Bastogne lifted, Dec. 29.

D-Day: No. 2817: a, Paratroops drop behind enemy lines. b, Glider-born commandos land behind enemy lines. c, USS Arkansas shells Omaha beach defenses. d, Allied aircraft attack enemy movements. e, Allied landing craft hit the beach. f, Allied troops pinned down by enemy fire. g, Commandos exit landing craft. h, Specialized Allied tanks destroy enemy mines. i, Allies break through beach defenses. j, Consolidation of position.

No. 2818, RAF Lancaster bomber.

1994, June 20 *Perf. 14*

2813 A189 $6 multicolored .20 .20
2814 A189 $35 multicolored .55 .55
2815 A189 $190 multicolored 3.00 3.00
Nos. 2813-2815 (3) 3.75 3.75

Miniature Sheets of 10

Perf. 13

2816 A190 $60 #a.-j. 9.50 9.50
2817 A190 $60 #a.-j. 9.50 9.50

Souvenir Sheet

Perf. 14

2818 A189 $325 multicolored 5.00 5.00

A191

Butterflies
A192

Designs: $6, Heliconius melpomene. $20, Helicopius cupido. $25, Agrias claudina. $30, Parides coelus. $50, Heliconius hecale. $60, Morpho diana. $190, Dismorphia orise. $250, Morpho deidamia.

No. 2827: a, Anaea marthesia. b, Brassolis astyra. c, Heliconius melpomene. d, Haetera piera. e, Morpho diana dixey. f, Parides coelus. g, Catagramma pitheas. h, Nessaea obrinus. i, Automeris janus. j, Papilio torquatus. k, Eunica sophonisba. l, Ceratinia nise. m, Panacea procilla. n, Pyrrhogyra neaerea. o, Morpho deidamia. p, Dismorphia orise.

No. 2829, Eunica sophonisba. No. 2830, Anaea eribotes. No. 2831, Hamadryas velutina. No. 2832, Agrias claudina.

1994, July 5 Litho. *Perf. 14*

2819-2826 A191 Set of 8 10.00 10.00

Miniature Sheet of 16

2827 A192 $50 #a.-p. 12.50 12.50

Souvenir Sheets

2829-2830 A191 $325 each 5.00 5.00
2831-2832 A192 $325 each 5.00 5.00

Nos. 2829-2830 each contain one 43x28mm stamp.

Miniature Sheets of 24

Bible Stories — A193

Story of Ruth and Naomi: Nos. 2833a-2833f: Ruth & Naomi preparing to leave Moab & return to Israel. g.-l: Ruth harvesting grain in fields of Boaz. m-r: Boaz receives a man's sandal, finalizing sale of Naomi's field. s-x: Naomi, Boaz, Ruth and Obed, who was David's grandfather.

Story of Joseph: Nos. 2834a-2834d, Jacob made Joseph a coat of many colors. e-h, Joseph's brothers take his coat and cast him into pit. i-l, Joseph is sold to the Ishmaelites. m-p, Joseph is accused by Potiphar's wife and thrown into prison. q-t, Joseph interprets Pharoah's dreams. u-x, Joseph is reunited with his brothers.

Parting of the Red Sea: Nos. 2835a-2835x, Moses leading Israelites through sea, Pharoah's army drowning.

Daniel and the Lions: No. 2836a-2836x, Daniel in lion's den surrounded by various animals, angel.

1994, Aug. 4 Litho. *Perf. 14*

2833-2836 A193 $20 #a.-x, each 7.75 7.75

Nos. 2835-2836 have continuous design.

A194

PHILAKOREA '94 — A195

Designs: $6, Statues of socialist ideals, Pyongyang. $25, Statue of Adm. Yi Sun-sin. $120, Sokkat'ap Pagoda, Pulguksa. $130, Village guardian, Chejudo Island.

Ten-fold screens: Nos. 2841b-2841e, Cranes. h-i, Deer. j, Deer, mushrooms, waterfall.

Nos. 2842b-2842d, Cranes. f-h, Deer. c, h, Waterfalls. i-j, Mushrooms.

No. 2843, Falled Rock, horiz. No. 2844, Westerners at Korean Court, horiz.

1994, June 20 Litho. *Perf. 14*

2837-2840 A194 Set of 4 5.00 5.00

Miniature Sheets of 10

Perf. 13

2841-2842 A195 $60 each, #a.-j. 11.00 11.00

Souvenir Sheets

Perf. 14

2843-2844 A194 $325 each 5.75 5.75

Nos. 2841-2842 have continuous design.

Miniature Sheet of 8

Entertainers of Takarazuka Revue, Japan
A196

Designs: a, $60, Mira Anju. b, $60, Yuki Amami. c, $60, Maki Ichiro. d, $60, Yu Shion. e, $20, Miki Maya. f, $20, Fubuki Takane. g, $20, Seika Juze. h, $20, Saki Asaji.

1994 *Perf. 14½*

2845 A196 #a.-h. + 4 labels 5.75 5.75

Nos. 2845a-2845d are 34x47mm.

A197

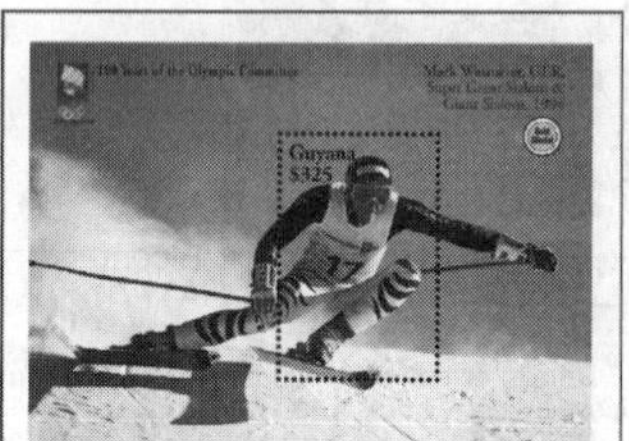
Intl. Olympic Committee, Cent. — A198

Designs: $20, Nancy Kerrigan, US, figure skating, 1994. $35, Sawao Kato, Japan, gymnastics, 1976. $130, Florence Griffith-Joyner, US, 100-, 200-meters, 1988.

$325, Mark Wasmeier, Germany, super giant & giant slalom, 1994.

1994, June 20

2846-2848 A197 Set of 3 3.00 3.00

Souvenir Sheet

2849 A198 $325 multicolored 5.25 5.25

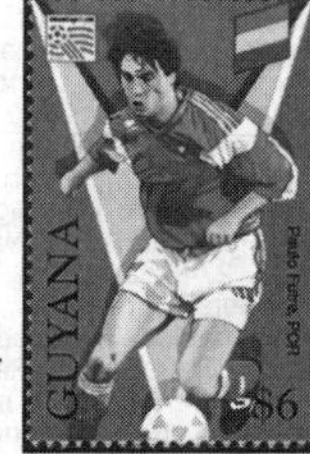
1994 World Cup Soccer Championships, U.S. — A199

Player, country: $6, Paulo Futre, Portugal. $35, Lyndon Hooper, Canada. $60, Enzo Francescoli, Uruguay. $190, Freddy Rincon, Colombia.

No. 2854: a, Paolo Maldini, Italy. b, Guyana player. c, Bwalya Kalusha, Zambia. d, Diego Maradona, Argentina. e, Andreas Brehme, Germany. f, Eric Wynalda, US.
No. 2855: a, John Doyle, US. b, Eric Wynalda, US, diff. c, Thomas Dooley, US. d, Ernie Stewart, US. f, Marcelo Balboa, US. g, Coach Bora Milutinovic, US.
No. 2856, 1994 World Cup program cover. No. 2857, Oiler Watson.

1994, Aug. 8

2850-2853 A199 Set of 4 4.00 4.00

Miniature Sheets of 6

2854-2855 A199 $60 #a.-f., each 4.75 4.75

Souvenir Sheets

2856-2857 A199 $325 each 5.25 5.25

Birds — A200

No. 2858: a, Goshawk. b, Lapwing. c, Ornate umbrellabird. d, Slatey-headed parakeet. e, Regent bowerbird. f, Egytian goose. g, White-winged crossbill. h, Waxwing. i, Ruff. j, Hoopoe. k, Superb starling. l, Great jacamar.
No. 2859: a, Peregrine falcon. b, Great spotted woodpecker. c, White-throated kingfisher. d, Peruvian cock-of-the-rock. e, Yellow-headed Amazon. f, Victoria crowned pigeon. g, Little owl. h, Pheasant. i, Goldfinch. j, Jay. k, Sulphur-brasted toucan. l, Japanese blue flycatcher.
#2860, Gould's violet-ear. #2861, Bald eagle.

1994, Sept. 15

Sheets of 12, #a.-i.

2858-2859 A200 $35 each 6.75 6.75

Souvenir Sheets

2860-2861 A200 $325 each 5.25 5.25

PHILAKOREA '94.

1996 Summer Olympics, Atlanta — A201

1994, Sept. 28

German athletes: $6, Anja Fichtel, fencing, 1988, horiz. $25, Annegret Richter, 100-meter dash, 1976. $30, Heike Henkel, high jump, 1982. $35, Armin Hary, 100-meter dash, 1960. $50, Heide Rosendahl, long jump, 1972. $60, Josef Neckermann, equestrian grand prix, 1968. $130, Heike Drechsler, long jump, 1988. $190, Ulrike Mayfarth, high jump, 1984. $250, Michael Gross, swimming, 1984, horiz.
No. 2871, Franziska van Almsick, swimming, 1992. No. 2872, Steffi Graf, tennis, 1992.
No. 2870b, $135, Markus Wasmeier, skiing, 1994. c, $190, Katja Seizinger, skiing, 1994.

2862-2870 A201 Set of 9 12.50 12.50

Souvenir Sheets

2870A A201 Sheet of 2, #b.-c. 5.25 5.25
2871-2872 A201 $325 each 5.25 5.25

Miniature Sheets of 9

Space Missions, First Manned Moon Landing, 25th Anniv. A202

Designs: No. 2873a, Laika, first dog in space. b, Yuri Gagarin, first man in space. c, John Glenn, first American to orbit earth. d, Edward White, first American to walk in space. e, Neil Armstrong, first to step foot onto moon. f, Luna 16. g, Luna 17. h, Skylab 1. i, 1975 Apollo-Soyuz.
Unmanned probes: No. 2874a, Mars 3, Mars. b, Mariner 10, Mercury. c, Voyager, planetary grand tour. d, Pioneer, Venus. e, Giotto, Halley's Comet. f, Megellan, Venus. g, Galileo, Jupiter. h, Ulysses, Sun. i, Cassini, Titan.
No. 2875, "Buzz" Aldrin, Neil Armstrong, Michael Collins. No. 2876, Pioneer 1, 2.

1994, Nov. 10 Litho. *Perf. 13½*

2873-2874 A202 $60 #a.-i, each 8.75 8.75

Souvenir Sheets

2875-2876 A202 $325 each 5.25 5.25

Steam Locomotives — A203

No. 2877, $25, South Eastern Railway #285, 1882. No. 2878, $25, West Point Foundry, 1830. No. 2879, $300, Mt. Washington Cog Railway, 1886. No. 2880, $300, Stroudley-Brighton, 1872.
No. 2881: a, "John Bull," 1831. b, Stephenson, 1837. c, "Atlantic," 1832. d, Stourbridge Lion, 1829. e, Polonceau, 1854. f, Rogers, 1856. g, "Vulcan," 1858. h, "Namur," 1846.
No. 2882: a, West Point Foundry, 1832. b, Sequin, 1830. c, Stephenson's Planet, 1830. d, Norris 4-2-0, 1840. e, Union Iron Works os San Francisco, 1867. f, Andrew Jackson, 1832. g, Herald, 1831. h, Cumberland, 1845.
No. 2883: a, Pennsylvania's Class K, 1880. b, Cooke, 1885. c, John B. Turner, 1867. d, Baldwin, 1871. e, Richard Trevithick, 1804. f, John Stephens, 1825. g, John Blenkinsop, 1814. h, Pennsylvania, 1803.
$250, Est Railway, 1878. $300, "Claud Hamilton," 1840.

1994, Nov. 15 *Perf. 14*

2877-2880 A203 Set of 4 4.50 4.50

Miniature Sheets of 8 + Label

2881-2883 A203 $30 #a.-h, each 3.75 3.75

Souvenir Sheets

2884 A203 $250 multicolored 4.00 4.00
2885 A203 $300 multicolored 4.75 4.75

English Touring Cricket, Cent. A204

$20, C.H. Lloyd, Guyana/West Indies, vert. $35, C.W. Hooper, Guyana/West Indies, Wisden Trophy. $60, G.A. Hick, England, Wisden Trophy.
$200, First English Team, 1895.

1994, June 20 Litho. *Perf. 14*

2886-2888 A204 Set of 3 1.75 1.75

Souvenir Sheet

2889 A204 $200 multicolored 3.00 3.00

Christmas A205

Paintings: $6, Joseph with the Christ Child, by Guido Reni. $20, Adoration of the Christ Child, by Girolamo Romanino. $25, Adoration of the Christ Child with St. Barbara and St. Martin, by Raffaello Botticini. $30, Holy Family, by Pompeo Girolam Batoni. $35, Flight into Egypt, by Bartolommeo Carducci. $60, Holy Family and the Baptist, by Andrea del Sarto. $120, Sacred Conversation, by Cesare de Sesto. $190, Madonna and Child with Sts. Joseph & John the Baptist, by Pontormo.
No. 2898, Holy Family and St. Elizabeth and St. John the Baptist, by Francisco Primaticcio. No. 2899, Presentation of Christ in the Temple, by Fra Bartolommeo.

1994, Dec. 5 *Perf. 13½x14*

2890-2897 A205 Set of 8 7.50 7.50

Souvenir Sheets

2898-2899 A205 $325 each 5.00 5.00

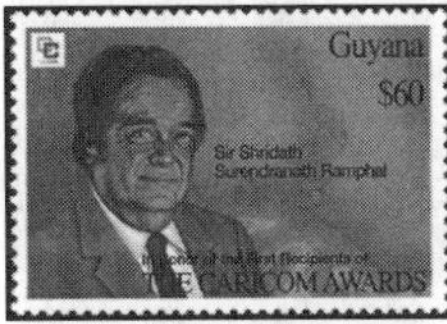

Order of the Caribbean Community — A206

First award recipients: No. 2900, Sir Shridath Ramphal, statesman, Guyana. No. 2901, William Demas, economist, Trinidad & Tobago. No. 2902, Derek Walcott, writer, St. Lucia.

1994 *Perf. 14*

2900-2902 A206 $60 Set of 3 2.75 2.75

Motion Picture, Star Trek Generations A207

A207a

No. 2903, "Boldly Go," Starship Enterprise.
No. 2904: a, Capt. Picard. b, Cmdr. Riker. c, Capt. Kirk. d, Villain with phaser. e, Kirk, Picard on horseback. f, Klingons L'rsa and B'tor. g, Kirk, Picard, diff. h, Counselor Troi. i, Picard, Lcdr. Data.
No. 2905: a, Troi, Riker. b, Worf. c, Picard. d, Worf, Lcdr. LaForge. e, Sailing ship, Enterprise. f, Picard, Riker. g. Data. h, Worf. i, Dr. Crusher.
$500, Like No. 2903, horiz.
$1000, Capt. Kirk, Capt. Picard.
#2906e, Capt. Picard. 2906f, Capt. Kirk.
Illustration A207a reduced.

1994, Dec. 7 *Perf. 13½x14*

2903 A207 $100 multicolored 1.50 1.50

Miniature Sheets of 9

2904-2905 A207 $100 #a.-i., each 14.00 14.00

Souvenir Sheet

Perf. 14x13½

2906 A207 $500 multicolored 7.75 7.75

No. 2903 was issued in sheets of 9.

Litho. & Embossed

1994, Nov. 18 *Perf. 9*

2906C A207a $1000 gold & multi

1994, Dec. 7

Miniature Sheet of 2

2906D A207a $500 #e.-f.

No. 2906D is perf. 9 around the outside. Nos. 2906e-2906f are imperf.

Sisters of Mercy of Guyana, Cent. — A208

1994, Dec. 12 *Perf. 14*

2907 A208 $60 multicolored .95 .95

Nos. 1037a, 1097, 1099 Surcharged "ILO / 75th Anniversary / 1919-1994"

Perfs & Printing Methods as Before

1994

2907A A91 $6 on 130c #1037a
2907B A91 $30 on 120c #1099
2907C A91 $35 on 120c #1097

Nos. 1063, 1098, 1120, 1123 Surcharged in Blue "CENTENARY / Sign For The / MAHDI / 1894-1994"

Perfs. & Printing Methods as Before

1994

2907D A91 $6 on 60c #1120
2907E A91 $20 on 200c #1063
2907F A91 $30 on 60c #1098
2907G A91 $35 on 60c #1123

Cricket A209

Designs: $20, Sobers congratulates Lara. $30, Brian Lara setting world record, vert. $375, Lara, Chanderpaul.
$300, Brian Lara walking under "avenue of bats," vert.

1995, Feb. 3 Litho. *Perf. 14*

2908-2910 A209 Set of 3 6.00 6.00

Souvenir Sheet

2911 A209 $300 multicolored 4.25 4.25

A210

A211

Babe Ruth (1895-1948) — A212

Type A211 various portraits like #2914. $2000, Portrait, Ruth holding bat, vert. Type A212 illustration reduced.

1995, Feb. 6 Litho. *Perf. 14*
2912 A210 $65 multi .90 .90

Self-Adhesive
Size: 64x89mm
2913 A211 $350 Set of 12 60.00 60.00

No. 2912 issued in sheets of 9. Portraits of Babe Ruth in No. 2913 are same as in No. 2915, but surrounded by gold frame, gold autograph, baseballs, and simulated perfs. No. 2913 was sold in sealed celophane package. To affix stamps, backing containing biographical information must be removed.

Litho. & Embossed
Perf. 12
2914 A212 $1000 gold & sep

Embossed
2914A A212 $2000 gold

Litho.
Perf. 14
Miniature Sheet of 12
2915 A211 $65 #a.-l. 11.00 11.00

Souvenir Sheet
2916 A211 $500 like #2912a, horiz. 7.00 7.00

Miniature Sheets of 8 or 9

Disney Characters at Work — A213

Animal workers: No. 2917: a, Veterinarian. b, Animal trainer. c, Animal psychiatrist. d, Ornithologist. e, Dog groomer. f, Herpetologist. g, Pet shop keeper. h, Park ranger. i, Aquarist.

Arts & crafts: No. 2918: a, Mickey the animator, Pluto. b, Goofy the tailor, Mickey. c, Pete the glass blower, Morty. d, Clarabelle modeling for Minnie the artist. e, Daisy sculpts Donald. f, Donald, nephews working with clay. g, Watchmakers, Chip & Dale. h, Locksmith Donald, nephews. i, Grandma Duck makes a quilt.

Medical group: No. 2919: a, Family doctor. b, Optometrist. c, Nurse. d, Psychiatrist. e, Physical therapist. f, Dentist. g, Radiologist. h, Pharmacist. i, Chiropractor.

Hard hat & company, vert.: No. 2920: a, Mickey, Pluto in truck. b, Mickey at work. c, Goofy jackhammer. d, Minnie at work. e, Forklifters. f, Construction contractor. g, Carpenter. h, Bulldozer.

Home services, vert.: No. 2921: a, Mickey, plumber. b, Mickey, paperboy. c, Huey, Dewey, Louie, moving service. d, Pete, handyman. e, Donald, newphews' house painting service. f, Goofy, washer repairman. g, Minnie, babysitter. h, Daisy cares for Grandma Duck.

Public service workers, vert.: No. 2922a, Policeman. b, Fireman. c, Ambulance driver. d, Crossing guard. e, Museum docent. f, Census taker. g, Street maintenance workers. h, Sanitation worker.

No. 2923, Goofy, zoo keeper. No. 2924, Camera, Pluto, vert. No. 2925, Goofy, surgeon. No. 2926, Minnie, pups, tool chest. No. 2927, Minnie, maid. No. 2928, Horace, politician.

1995, Feb. 23 Litho. *Perf. 13½x14*
2917-2919 A213 $30 #a.-i., ea 4.00 4.00

Perf. 14x13½
2920-2922 A213 $35 #a.-h., ea 4.25 4.25

Souvenir Sheets
2923-2928 A213 $200 each 3.00 3.00

#2917-2922 exist in sheets of 7 or 8 $5 stamps + label. The label replaces #2917e, 2918e, 2919g, 2920h, 2921h, 2922e. These sheets became available Nov. 20, 1996.

Nos. 1022, 1033, 1045, 1061
Surcharged in Red
"SALVATION / ARMY / 1895-1995"

1995, Apr. 24 Litho. *Perf. 14*
2928A A91 $6 on 60c #1033
2928B A91 $20 on 60c #1045
2928C A91 $30 on 60c #1022
2928D A91 $35 on 60c #1061

A214

New Year 1995 (Year of the Boar) Stylized boars: a, $20, f, "Abundant Year of the Pig." b, $30, g, "Fortunate Year of the Pig." c, $50, Facing forward, denomination LR. d, $100, h, Facing forward, denomination LL.

$150, Face, Chinese inscriptions.

1995, May 4 Litho. *Perf. 14½*
2929 A214 Block of 4, #a.-d. 2.75 2.75
e. $50 Souvenir sheet of 4, #c, f.-h. 2.75 2.75

Souvenir Sheet
2930 A214 $150 multicolored 2.00 2.00

#2929 was issued in miniature sheets of 4.

Birds: $5, Goshawk. $6, Lapwing. $8, Ornate umbrellabird. $15, Slatey-headed parakeet. $19, Regent bowerbird. $20, Egyptian goose. $25, White-winged crossbill. $30, Waxwing. $35, Ruff. $60, Hoopoe. $100, Superb starling. $500, Great jacamar.

A215

1995, May 8 Litho. *Perf. 14½x13½*

2931	A215	$5 multicolored	.20	.20
2932	A215	$6 multicolored	.20	.20
2933	A215	$8 multicolored	.20	.20
2934	A215	$15 multicolored	.25	.25
2935	A215	$19 multicolored	.25	.25
2936	A215	$20 multicolored	.30	.30
2937	A215	$25 multicolored	.35	.35
2938	A215	$30 multicolored	.40	.40
2939	A215	$35 multicolored	.50	.50
2940	A215	$60 multicolored	.85	.85
2941	A215	$100 multicolored	1.40	1.40
2942	A215	$500 multicolored	7.00	7.00
		Nos. 2931-2942 (12)	11.90	11.90

Nolan Ryan, Baseball Player — A216

Designs, team: No. 2943a, Looking left, Mets. b, With bat, Mets. c, Pitching, Mets. d, Looking toward home plate, Angels. e, Pitching, Angels. f, Without hat, Angels. g, In red cap, Astros. h, Pitching, Astros. i, In black cap, Astros. j, Pitching, Rangers. k, Getting ready to pitch, Rangers. l, Up close, Rangers.

1995 Litho. *Imperf.*
Self-Adhesive
Size: 64x89mm
2943 A216 $350 Set of 12, #a.-l. 60.00 60.00

Nos. 2943a-2943l are printed on thin cards, distributed in boxed sets containing certificate of authenticity and sealed in celophane packages. To affix stamps, backing containing biographical information must be removed.

Miniature Sheets of 12

Singapore '95 — A217

Dogs: No. 2944: a, Gordon setter. b, Long-haired chihuahua. c, Dalmation. d, Afghan. e, English bulldog. f, Miniature schnauzer. g, Clumber spaniel. h, Pekingese. i, St. Bernard. j, English cocker spaniel. k, Alaskan malamute. l, Rottweiler.

Cats: No. 2945: a, Norwegian forest cat. b, Scottish fold. c, Red burmese. d, British bluehair. e, Abyssinian. f, Siamese. g, Exotic shorthair. h, Turkish van cat. i, Black Persian. j, Black-tipped burmilla. k, Singapura. l, Calico shorthair.

Horses: No. 2946: a, Chestnut thoroughbred colt. b, Liver chestnut quarter horse. c, Black Freisian. d, Chestnut Belgian. e, Appaloosa. f, Lipizzanas. g, Chestnut hunter. h, British shire. i, Palomino. j, Seal brown point. k, Arab. l, Afghanistan Kabardin.

No. 2947, Golden retriever. No. 2948, Maine coon. No. 2949, American Anglo-Arab.

1995, June 1 *Perf. 14*
2944-2946 A217 $35 #a.-l., ea 6.00 6.00

Souvenir Sheets
2947-2949 A217 $300 each 4.25 4.25

Miniature Sheet of 8

Pocahontas A218

Characters from Disney animated film - #2950: a, Pocahontas, Meeko. b, John Smith. c, Chief Powhatan. d, Kocoum. e, Ratcliffe. f, Wiggins. g, Nakoma. h, Thomas.

No. 2951, Meeko, horiz.

1995, June 23 Litho. *Perf. 13½x14*
2950 A218 $50 #a.-h. 5.50 5.50

Souvenir Sheet
Perf. 14x13½
2951 A218 $300 multicolored 4.25 4.25

See Nos. 2985-2990.

UN, 50th Anniv. — A219

Map: No. 2952a, $35, North, South America. b, $60, Europe, Africa. c, $200, Asia, Australia.

$300, Secretary General Boutros Boutros-Ghali.

1995, July 6 *Perf. 14*
2952 A219 Strip of 3, #a.-c. 4.25 4.25

Souvenir Sheet
2953 A219 $300 multicolored 4.25 4.25

Miniature Sheets of 6 or 8

End of World War II, 50th Anniv. A220

No. 2954: a, P61 Black Widow. b, PT boat. c, B26 Marauder. d, Cruiser USS San Juan. e, US Gato class submarine. f, US destroyer.

No. 2955: a, Jan. 1945, Battle of Bulge is over. b, Sigfried Line is breached. c, Liberation of concentration camps. d, Operation "Manna," Allies drop food to starving Dutch. e, GIs looking for snipers at end of Italian campaign. f, Newspaper headline announces Hitler's suicide. g, Soviet tanks pour into Berlin. h, U-858, first German warship to surrender in US waters.

No. 2956, Battleship, aircraft carrier. No. 2957, Top of Brandenburg Gate.

1995, July 6
2954 A220 $60 #a.-f. + label 5.00 5.00
2955 A220 $60 #a.-h. + label 6.75 6.75

Souvenir Sheets
2956-2957 A220 $300 each 4.25 4.25

No. 2957 contains one 57x42mm stamp.

FAO, 50th Anniv. — A221

No. 2958: a, $35, Girl carrying sack on head. b, $60, Man carrying sack, woman sorting sacks. c, $200, Woman lifting sack.

$300, Pouring from ladle into bowl.

1995, July 6 Litho. *Perf. 14*
2958 A221 Strip of 3, #a.-c. 4.25 4.25

Souvenir Sheet
2959 A221 $300 multicolored 4.25 4.25

No. 2958 is a continuous design.

Rotary Intl., 90th Anniv. A222

Designs: $200, Paul Harris, Rotary emblem. $300, Old, new Rotary emblems.

1995, July 6
2960 A222 $200 multicolored 3.00 3.00

Souvenir Sheet
2961 A222 $300 multicolored 4.25 4.25

1995 Boy Scout Jamboree, Holland — A223

Slogan, emblem, and: $20, Campfire. $25, Scout, beach. $30, Hiking. $35, Snorkeling. $60, Natl. flag, scout salute. $200, Fishing from boat.
No. 2968, Canoeing. No. 2969, Camping.

1995, July 6
2962-2967 A223 Set of 6 5.25 5.25

Souvenir Sheets
2968-2969 A223 $300 each 4.25 4.25

Queen Mother, 95th Birthday A224

No. 2970: a, Drawing. b, Violet hat. c, Formal portrait. d, Green blue hat.
$325, As younger woman.

1995, July 6 ***Perf. 13½x14***
2970 A224 $100 Strip or block of 4, #a.-d. 4.75 4.75

Souvenir Sheet
2971 A224 $325 multicolored 4.50 4.50

No. 2970 issued in sheets of 2.
Sheets of #2970 and 2971 exist with black border in margin with text "In Memoriam/1900-2002."

Miniature Sheet of 8

Holidays of the World A225

No. 2972: a, Thanksgiving, US. b, Christmas, Germany. c, Hanukkah, Israel. d, Easter, Spain. e, Carnivale, brazil. f, Bastill Day, France. g, Independence Day, India. h, St. Patrick's Day, Ireland.
$300, Chinese New Year, China.

1995, Aug. 8 **Litho.** ***Perf. 14***
2972 A225 $60 #a.-h. 6.75 6.75

Souvenir Sheet
2973 A225 $300 multicolored 4.25 4.25

Marine Life A226

No. 2974, vert: a, Cocoa damselfish. b, Sergeant major. c, Beau gregory. d, Yellowtail damselfish.
No. 2975: a, $30, Butterflyfish. b, $35, Bluehead. c, $60, Yellow damselfish. d, $200, Clown wrasse.
No. 2976: a, $30, Lemon shark. b, $35, Green turtle. c, $60 Sawfish. d, $200, Stingray.
No. 2977: a, Tiger shark. b, Needlefish. c, Horse-eye jack. d, Princess parrotfish. e, Yellowtail snapper. f, Spotted snake eel. g, Trunkfish. h, Cherubfish. i, French angelfish.
No. 2978: a, Sei whale. b, Barracuda. c, Mutton snapper. d, Hawksbill turtle. e, Spanish hogfish. f, Queen angelfish. g, Porkfish. h, Trumpetfish. i, Electric ray.
No. 2979, Carcharodon carcharias. No. 2980, Dermochelys coriacea.

1995, Sept. 5 **Litho.** ***Perf. 14***
2974 A226 $80 Strip of 4, #a.-d. 4.50 4.50

Miniature Sheets of 4
2975-2976 A226 #a.-d., each 4.50 4.50

Miniature Sheets of 9
2977-2978 A226 $60 #a.-i., ea 7.50 7.50

Souvenir Sheets
2979-2980 A226 $300 each 4.25 4.25

No. 2974 was issued in sheets of 4.

Miniature Sheets of 8

1996 Summer Olympics, Atlanta — A227

No. 2981: a, Shot put. b, Relay. c, Balance beam. d, Cycling. e, Synchronized swimming. f, Hurdles. g, Pommel horse. h, Discus thrower, head down.
No. 2982: a, Pole vault. b, Long jump. c, Track. d, Wrestling. e, Discus thrower, head up. f, Basketball. g, Boxing. h, Weight lifting.
No. 2983, Long jump. No. 2984, Runners.

1995, Oct. 2 **Litho.** ***Perf. 14***
2981-2982 A227 $60 #a.-h., ea 6.75 6.75

Souvenir Sheets
2983-2984 A227 $300 each 4.50 4.50

Pocahontas Type of 1995
Miniature Sheets

Nos. 2985-2987: Various scenes from Disney animated film, horiz.
No. 2988, Pocahontas behind tree branch, horiz. No. 2989, Pocahontas, Powhatan, horiz. No. 2990, Pocahontas kneeling.

Perf. 14x13½, 13½x14 (#2990)
1995, Oct. 9 **Litho.**
2985 A218 $8 Sheet of 9, #a.-i. 1.00 1.00
2986 A218 $30 Sheet of 9, #a.-i. 3.75 3.75
2987 A218 $35 Sheet of 9, #a.-i. 5.00 5.00

Souvenir Sheets
2988-2990 A218 $325 each 4.50 4.50

Fauna — A228

No. 2991: a, $35, House martin. b, $60. Hobby. c, $20, Sand martin (a). d, $200, Long-tailed skua (b).
No. 2992: a, Olive colobus. b, Violet-backed starling. c, Diana monkey. d, African palm civet. e, Giraffe, zebras. f, African linsang. g, Royal antelope (fawn). h, Royal antelope (adult, fawn) (g, i). i, Palm squirrel.
No. 2993, Brush pig. No. 2994, Chimpanzee.

1995, Oct. 18 **Litho.** ***Perf. 14***
2991 A228 Block of 4, #a.-d. 4.50 4.50

Miniature Sheet of 9
2992 A228 $60 #a.-i. 7.50 7.50

Souvenir Sheets
2993-2994 A228 $300 each 4.25 4.25

No. 2991 was issued in sheets of 16 stamps.

Queenstown Holy Mosque, Georgetown, Cent. — A229

1995, Dec. 1 **Litho.** ***Perf. 14***
2995 A229 $60 multicolored .85 .85

Christmas A230

Details or entire paintings, by Carracci: $25, The Angel of Annunciation. $30, Annunciation of the Virgin. $35, Assumption of the Virgin. $60, Baptism of Christ. $100, Madonna and Child. $300, Birth by the Virgin.
No. 3002, Madonna and Ten Saints, by Fiorentino. No. 3003, Mystical Marriage of St. Catherine, by Carracci.

1995, Dec. 4 ***Perf. 13½x14***
2996-3001 A230 Set of 6 7.75 7.75

Souvenir Sheets
3002-3003 A230 $325 each 4.50 4.50

Guyana Defense Force, 30th Anniv. — A231

1995, Dec. 7 ***Perf. 14***
3004 A231 $6 Woman with gun .20 .20
3005 A231 $60 Man with gun .85 .85

John Lennon (1940-80) — A232

1995
3006 A232 $35 multicolored .50 .50

No. 3006 was issued in sheets of 16.

Miniature Sheets of 9

Nobel Prize Fund Established, Cent. — A233

Recipients: #3007: a, Henri Becquerel, physics, 1903. b, Igor Tamm, physics, 1958. c, Georges Köhler, medicine, 1984. d, Gerhard Domagk, medicine, 1939. e, Yasunari Kawabata, literature, 1968. f, Maurice Allais, economics, 1988. g, Aristide Briand, peace, 1926. h, Pavel Cherenkov, physics, 1958. i, Feodor Lynen, medicine, 1964.
#3008: a, Adolf von Baeyer, chemistry, 1905. b, Hideki Yukawa, physics, 1949. c, George W. Beadle, medicine, 1958. d, Edwin M. McMillian, chemistry, 1951. e, Samuel C.C. Ting, physics, 1976. f, Saint-John Perse, literature, 1960. g, John F. Enders, medicine, 1954. h, Felix Bloch, physics, 1952. i, P.B. Medawar, medicine, 1960.
#3009: a, Albrecht Kossel, medicine, 1910. b, Arthur H. Compton, physics, 1927. c, N.M. Butler, peace, 1931. d, Charles Laveran, medicine, 1907. e, George R. Minot, medicine, 1934. f, Henry H. Dale, medicine, 1936. g, Jacques Monod, medicine, 1965. h, Alfred Hershey, medicine, 1969. i, Pär Lagerkvist, literature, 1951.
#3010: a, Francis Crick, medicine, 1962. b, Manne Siegbahn, physics, 1924. c, Eisaku Sato, peace, 1974. d, Robert Koch, medicine, 1905. e, Edgar D. Adrian, medicine, 1932. f, Erwin Neher, medicine, 1991. g, Henry Taube, chemistry, 1983. h, Norman Angell, peace, 1933. i, Robert Robinson, chemistry, 1947.
#3011: a, Nikolai Basov, physics, 1964. b, Klas Arnoldson, peace, 1908. c, René Sully-Prudhomme, literature, 1901. d, Robert W. Wilson, physics, 1978. e, Hugo Theorell, medicine, 1955. f, Nelly Sachs, literature, 1966. g, Hans von Euler-Chelpin, chemistry, 1929. h, Mairead Corrigan, peace, 1976. i, Willis E. Lamb, Jr, physics, 1955.
#3012: a, Norman F. Ramsey, physics, 1989. b, Chen Ning Yang, physics, 1957. c, Earl W. Sutherland, Jr., medicine, 1971. d, Paul Karrer, chemistry, 1937. e, Harmut Michel, chemistry, 1988. f, Richard Kuhn, chemistry, 1938. g, P.A.M. Dirac, physics, 1933. h, Victor Grignard, chemistry, 1912. i, Richard Willstätter, chemistry, 1915.
#3013, Le Duc Tho, peace, 1973. #3014, Yasunari Kawabata, literature, 1968. #3015, Heinrich Böll, literature, 1972. #3016, Henry Kissinger, peace, 1973. #3017, Kenichi Fukui, chemistry, 1981. #3018, Lech Walesa, peace, 1983.

1995, Dec. 20 **Litho.** ***Perf. 14***
3007-3012 A233 $35 #a.-i., ea 4.50 4.50

Souvenir Sheets
3013-3018 A233 $300 each 4.25 4.25

Caribbean Development Bank, 25th Anniv. — A234

1995, Dec. 29 **Litho.** ***Perf. 14***
3019 A234 $60 multicolored .85 .85

Miniature Sheet of 9

Marilyn Monroe (1926-62) A235

#3020, Various portraits. #3021, Portrait, horiz.

1995, Dec. 29 ***Perf. 13½x14***
3020 A235 $60 #a.-i. 7.50 7.50

Souvenir Sheet
Perf. 14x13½
3021 A235 $300 multicolored 4.25 4.25

Miniature Sheet of 9

David Copperfield, Magician A236

Nos. 3022-3023, Various portraits, magic acts.

1995, Dec. 29 ***Perf. 13½x14***
3022 A236 $60 #a.-i. 7.50 7.50

Souvenir Sheet

3023 A236 $300 multicolored 4.25 4.25

New Year 1996 (Year of the Rat) — A237

Stylized rats: No. 3024: a, $20. b, $30. c, $50, light brown & multi. d, $100.
No. 3025: a, like #3024a, b, like #3024b. c, like #3024c, darker brown & multi. d, like #3024d.
No. 3026, Rat facing forward.

1996, Jan. 2 ***Perf. 14½***
3024 A237 Block of 4, #a.-d. 2.75 2.75

Miniature Sheet

3025 A237 $50 Sheet of 4, #a.-d. 2.75 2.75

Souvenir Sheet

3026 A237 $150 multicolored 2.25 2.25

No. 3024 was issued in sheets of 16 stamps.

Miniature Sheet of 4

UNICEF, 50th Anniv. A238

Designs: a, Children, building in background. b, Man, boy, tree in background. c, Children behind tree. d, Man, children.

1996, Jan. 2 ***Perf. 14***
3027 A238 $1100 #a.-d. 62.00 62.00

No. 3027 is a continuous design.

Paintings by Peter Paul Rubens A239

Details or entire paintings: $6, The Garden of Love. $10, Two Sleeping Children. $20, All Saints Day. $25, Sacrifice of Abraham. $30, The Last Supper. $35, The Birth of Henry of Navarre. $40, Standing Female Saint Study. $50, $60, The Garden of Love, each diff. No. 3037, $200, The Martyrdom of St. Livinus. No. 3038, $200, Der Heilige Franz Von Paula. $300, The Union of Maria de Medici and Henry IV.
No. 3039, The Three Crosses. No. 3040, Decius Mus Addressing the Legions, horiz. No. 3041, Triumph of Henry IV, horiz.

1996, Jan. 29 **Litho.** ***Perf. 14***
3028-3038A A239 Set of 11 14.00 14.00

Souvenir Sheets

3039-3041 A239 $325 each 4.50 4.50

Nos. 3039-3041 each contain one 57x85mm or 85x57mm stamp.

Miniature Sheets

A240

Prehistoric Animals — A241

#3042: a, Tarbosaurus. b, Hadrosaurus. c, Polacanthus. d, Psittacosaurus. e, Ornitholestes. f, Yangchuanosaurus. g, Scelidosaurus. h, Kentrosaurus. i, Coelophysis. j, Lesothosaurus. k, Plateosaurus. l, Staurikosaurus.
#3043: a, Eudimorphodon. b, Criorynchus. c, Elasmosaurus. d, Rhomaleosaurus. e, Ceresiosaurus. f, Mesosaurus. g, Grendelius. h, Nothosaurus. i, Mixosaurus. j, Placodus. k, Coelacanth. l, Mosasaurus.
#3044: a, Ornithomimus. b, Pteranodon. c, Rhamphorynchus. d, Ornitholestes. e, Brachiosaurus. f, Parasaurolophus. g, Ceratosaurus. h, Camarasaurus. i, Euoplocephalus. j, Scutellosaurus. k, Compsognathus. l, Stegoceras.
#3045: a, Apatosaurus. b, Archaeopteryx. c, Dimorphodon. d, Deinonychus. e, Coelophysis. f, Tyrannosaurus. g, Triceratops. h, Anatosaurus. i, Saltasaurus. j, Allosaurus. k, Oviraptor. l, Stegosaurus.
#3046: a, Heterodontosaurus (b). b, Compsognathus (c). c, Ornithomimus (b).
#3047: a, Saurolophus. b, Muttaburrasaurus (a). c, Dicraeosaurus (b).
#3048, Apatosaurus, allosaurus, horiz. #3049, Tyrannosaurus rex. #3050, Quetzalcoatlus. #3051, Lagosuchus. #3052, Struthiomimus.

1996, Feb. 12

Sheets of 12 & 3

3042 A240 $35 #a.-l. 6.00 6.00
3043-3045 A241 $35 #a.-l., ea 6.00 6.00
3046-3047 A240 $60 #a.-c., ea 2.50 2.50

Souvenir Sheets

3048-3049 A240 $300 each 4.25 4.25
3050-3052 A241 $300 each 4.25 4.25

A242

A243

Giant pandas, in tree: No. 3053: a, Lying on back, looking right. b, Arms, legs around branch. c, Paws holding onto tree. d, Sitting, looking left.
On rocks by stream: No. 3054: a, Standing. b, Sitting, holding bamboo stick. c, Holding bamboo to mouth. d, Lying on stomach.

1996, Apr. 12 **Litho.** ***Perf. 14***

Miniature Sheets

3053 A242 $60 Sheet of 4, #a.-d. 3.50 3.50
3054 A242 $60 Sheet of 4, #a.-d. 3.50 3.50

China '96, 9th Asian Intl. Philatelic Exhibtion.

1996, May 3 **Litho.** ***Perf. 14***

Mushrooms, Insects, Coral: $20, Yellow morce, leaf beetle. $25, Green spored mushroom. $30, Leaf beetle, common mushroom. $35, Monarch caterpillars, pine cone mushroom.
No. 3059: a, Green-beaded jelly club. b, Aspic puffball. c, Stalkless paxillus. d, Stout-stalked amanita.
No. 3060: a, Fly agaric. b, Graying yellow russula, click beetle. c, Netted stinkhorn, housefly. d, Butterfly hunter, stropharia.
No. 3061: a, Cockle-shell lentinus. b, Parasitic volvariella. c, Deadly lepiota. d, Shaggy-stalked boleta.
No. 3062: a, Armillauella mellea. b, Sealy vase chanterelle. c, Bitter pholiota. d, Flute white helvella. e, Fading scarlet waxy cap. f, Jask's lantern. g, Hygzocybe acutoconica. h, Mycena viscosa.
No. 3063, Orange mycena. No. 3064, Violet-branched coral, Red raspberry slime, yellow-tipped coral, horiz.

3055-3058 A243 Set of 4 1.50 1.50
3059-3061 A243 $60 Strips of 4, #a.-d., ea 3.50 3.50
3062 A243 $60 Sheet of 8, #a.-h. 6.75 6.75

Souvenir Sheets

3063-3064 A243 $300 each 4.25 4.25

Nos. 3059-3061 were issued in sheets of 8 stamps.

Deng Xiaoping, Chinese Communist Leader — A244

a, Painting inscription. b, With dignitaries, waving. c, Signing autograph. d, Waving.
$300, Wearing white shirt, vert.

1996 ***Perf. 13***
3065 A244 $30 Strip or block of 4, #a.-d. 1.75 1.75

Souvenir Sheet

3066 A244 $300 multicolored 4.25 4.25

No. 3065 issued in sheets of 16 stamps.

Queen Elizabeth II, 70th Birthday A245

Designs: a, Portrait wearing blue dress. b, Wearing blue green dress, hat. c, On throne, opening Parliament.
$325, In ceremonial attire.

1996, May 3 **Litho.** ***Perf. 13½x14***
3067 A245 $100 Strip of 3, #a.-c. 4.25 4.25

Souvenir Sheet

3068 A245 $325 multicolored 4.50 4.50

No. 3067 was issued in sheets of 9 stamps, with each strip having a different order.

A246

A247

Jerusalem, 3000th Anniv.: a, $30. The Hulda Gates. b, $35, Old City, View from Mt. of Olives. c, $200, Absalom's Memorial, Kidron Valley.
$300, Children's Memorial.

1996 **Litho.** ***Perf. 14***
3069 A246 Sheet of 3, #a.-d. 3.75 3.75

Souvenir Sheet

3070 A246 $300 multicolored 4.25 4.25

1996, July 10

#3071: a, Blue & yellow macaw. b, Andean condor. c, Crested eagle. d, White-tailed trogon. e, Toco toucan. f, Great horned owl. g, Andean cock-of-the-rock. h, Great curassow.
Hummingbirds: j, Long-billed starthroat. k, Velvet-purple coronet. l, Racket-tailed coquette. m, Violet-tailed sylph. n, Broad-tailed hummingbird. o, Blue-tufted starthroat. p, White-necked jacobin. q, Ruby-throated hummingbird.
#3072, Ornate hawk eagle, horiz. No. 3073, Gould's violet-ear.

Sheets of 8

3071 A247 $60 #a.-h. 6.75 6.75
3071I A247 $60 #j.-q. 6.75 6.75

Souvenir Sheets

3072 A247 $300 multicolored 4.25 4.25
3073 A247 $300 multicolored 4.25 4.25

Radio, Cent. A248

Entertainers: $20, Frank Sinatra. $35, Gene Autry. $60, Groucho Marx. $200, Red Skelton. $300, Burl Ives.

1996, July 25
3074-3077 A248 Set of 4 4.50 4.50

Souvenir Sheet

3078 A248 $300 multicolored 4.25 4.25

1996 Summer Olympic Games, Atlanta A249

$20, Pancratium. $30, Olympic Stadium, 1956. $60, Leonid Spirin, 20k walk, 1956, vert. $200, Lars Hall, modern pentathlon, 1952, 1956, vert.
Female gold medalists: No. 3083, vert.: a, Florence Griffith-Joyner. b, Ines Geissler. c, Nadia Comaneci. d, Tatiana Gutsu. e, Olga Korbut. f, Barbara Krause. g, Olga Bryzgina. h, Fanny Blankers-Koen. i, Irena Szewinska.
Male gold medalists: No. 3084, vert.: a, Gerd Wessig. b, Jim Thorpe. c, Norman Read. d, Lasse Viren. e, Milt Campbell. f, Abebe Bikila. g, Jesse Owens. h, Viktor Saneev. i, Waldemer Cierpinski.
Gold medalists: No. 3085, vert.: a, Ditmar Schmidt. b, Pam Shriver. c, Zina Garrison. d, Hyun Jung-Hua. e, Steffi Graf. f, Michael Jordan. g, Karch Kiraly. h, "Magic" Johnson. i, Ingolf Weigert.
Sporting events: No. 3086: a, Volleyball. b, Basketball. c, Tennis. d, Table tennis. e, Baseball. f, Handball. g, Field hockey. h, Water polo. i, Soccer.
Sporting events: No. 3087, vert.: a, Cycling. b, Hurdles. c, High jump. d, Diving. e, Weight lifting. f, Canoeing. g, Wrestling. h, Gymnastics. i, Running.
No. 3088, Carl Lewis, track and field gold medalist. No. 3089, US defeats Korea for gold medal in baseball, 1988.

1996, July 25
3079-3082 A249 Set of 4 4.25 4.25

Sheets of 9

3083-3087 A249 $50 #a.-i., ea 6.25 6.25

Souvenir Sheets

3088-3089 A249 $300 each 4.25 4.25

Olymphilex '96 (#3088).

Disney Cartoons — A250

Mickey outdoors: No. 3090: a, Mickey's Bait Shop. b, Ol' Mickey, The Lumbercamp Legend and Pluto the Yellow Dog. c, For All Men Are Equal Before Fish.
Super sports: No. 3091, vert.: a, BMX Championships. b, Goofy, Hockey Superstar. c, Malibu Surf City.
Nautical Mickey: No. 3092, vert.: a, The Path to Adventure is Shown in the Stars. b, Captain Mickey's Steamship School. c, Ahoy, Follow the Wind on Waves of Fortune.
No. 3093, M. Mouse, ESQ, Lawman, vert.: No. 3094, All Aboard, Ride the Great American Transcontinental Railroad. No. 3095, Mouse and Pinkerton, Wild West Detective Agency, vert. $300, Donald's Rock & Ice Mountaineers. $325, Guided by The Great Spirit, vert.

1996, July 26 ***Perf. 14x13½, 13½x14***

3090 A250 $60 Strip of 3, #a.-c. 2.50 2.50
3091 A250 $80 Strip of 3, #a.-c. 3.50 3.50
3092 A250 $100 Strip of 3, #a.-c. 4.25 4.25

Souvenir Sheets

3093-3095 A250 $250 each 3.50 3.50
3096 A250 $300 multi 4.25 4.25
3097 A250 $325 multi 4.50 4.50

Nos. 3090-3092 were issued in sheets of 9 stamps.

Disney Antique Toys — A251

No. 3098: a, Two-Gun Mickey. b, Wood-jointed Mickey doll. c, Donald Jack-in-the Box. d, Rocking Minnie. e, Fireman Donald Duck. f, Long-billed Donald Duck. g, Painted wood Mickey doll. h, Wind-up Jiminy Cricket.
#3099, Mickey doll. #3100, Carousel train.

1996, July 26 ***Perf. 13½x14***

3098 A251 $6 Sheet of 8, #a.-h. .70 .70

Souvenir Sheets

3099-3100 A251 $300 each 4.25 4.25

Elvis Presley's First "Hit" Year, 40th Anniv. A252

Various portraits.

1996, Sept. 8 **Litho.** ***Perf. 13½x14***

3101 A252 $100 Sheet of 6, #a.-f. 8.50 8.50

Domestic Cats A253

No. 3102: a, Birman. b, American curl. c, Turkish Angora. d, European shorthair. e, Persian. f, Scottish fold. g, Sphynx. h, Malayan. i, Cornish rex.
No. 3103, vert: a, Norwegian forest. b, Russian shorthair. c, European shorthair. d, Birman. e, Ragdoll. f, Egyptian mau. g, Persian. h, Angora. i, Siamese.
#3104, Maine coon, vert. #3105, Himalayan.

1996, Sept. 18 ***Perf. 14***

Sheets of 9

3102-3103 A253 $60 #a.-i., ea 7.50 7.50

Souvenir Sheets

3104-3105 A253 $300 each 4.25 4,25

Deep Ocean Exploration — A254

No. 3106: a, Goblin shark, coelacanth. b, Remote operated vehicle, JASON. c, Deep water invertebrates. d, Submarine NR1 (e). e, Giant squid (b, c, f, g, h, j, m). f, Sperm whale (b, c). g, Volcanic vents, submersible ALVIN. h, Air-recycling pressure suit, shipwreck. i, Bacteria survey, submersible SHINKAI 6500. j, Giant tube worms. k, Anglerfish. l, Six-gill shark (k). m. Autonomous underwater vehicle ABE. n, Viperfish. o, Swallower, hatchetfish.
$300, Sea anemone.

1996, Dec. 2 **Litho.** ***Perf. 14***

3106 A254 $30 Sheet of 15, #a.-o. 6.50 6.50

Souvenir Sheet

3107 A254 $300 multicolored 4.25 4.25

Characters from Disney's Snow White in Christmas Scenes A255

Designs: $6, Snow White. $20, Doc. $25, Dopey, Sneezy. $30, Sleepy, Happy, Bashful. $35, Dopey, Santa. $60, Dopey, fireplace. $100, Dopey, Grumpy. $200, Dopey as Santa.
No. 3116, Snow White looking at squirrel in box. No. 3117, Dopey placing star on tree.

1996, Dec. 16 ***Perf. 13½x14***

3108-3115 A255 Set of 8 6.75 6.75

Souvenir Sheets

3116-3117 A255 $300 each 4.25 4.25

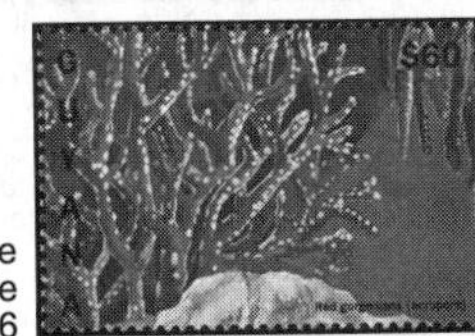

Marine Life A256

a, Red gorgonians. b, Plexaura homomalla, butterflyfish (a, c). c, Dendronephtbya. d, Common clownfish, anemone, mushroom coral (a). e, Anemone, horse-eyed jack (d, g-h). f, Slender snappers (c), splendid coral trout. g, Anemones. h, Brain coral, Indo-Pacific hard coral. i, Cup coral (f, h).

1996, Dec. 2 **Litho.** ***Perf. 14***

3118 A256 $60 Sheet of 9, #a.-i. 7.50 7.50

New Year 1997 (Year of the Ox) — A257

Denomination at: No. 3119: a, $20, LR. b, $30, LL. c, $35, UR. d, $50, UL.
No. 3120: a, like #3119a. b, like #3119b. c, like #3119c.
$150, Ox, facing.

1997, Jan. 2 **Litho.** ***Perf. 14½***

3119 A257 Block of 4, #a.-d. 1.90 1.90
3120 A257 $50 Sheet of 4, #a.-c. + #3119d 2.75 2.75

Souvenir Sheet

3121 A257 $150 multicolored 2.10 2.10

No. 3119 was issued in sheets of 16 stamps.

Mickey and Friends Celebrate Chinese Lunar New Year — A258

#3122: a, $6, Mickey. b, $20, Home visit. c, $25, Fortune lantern. d, $30, Silhouette. e, $35, Flower market. f, $60, Harmonious man, woman.
#3123: a, Red-pocket money. b, Lion dance. c, Calligraphy. d, Surplus every year. e, Fireworks. f, Ox.
$150, Mickey marching, vert. $200, Mickey, ox.

1997, Jan. 2 ***Perf. 14x13½***

Sheets of 6

3122 A258 #a.-f. 2.50 2.50
3123 A258 $30 #a.-f. 2.60 2.60

Souvenir Sheets

Perf. 13½x14, 14x13½

3124 A258 $150 multicolored 2.25 2.25
3125 A258 $200 multicolored 2.75 2.75

Marine Life A259

No. 3126, $6, Angelfish. No. 3127, $6, Hyed snapper. $20, Box fish. $25, Golden damselfish. $35, Clown triggerfish. $200, Harlequin tuskfish.
$300, Caribbean flower coral.

1996 **Litho.** ***Perf. 14***

3126-3131 A259 Set of 6 4.50 4.50

Souvenir Sheet

3132 A259 $300 multicolored 4.75 4.75

Hotel Tower, 50th Anniv. — A260

1996, Dec. 28

3133 A260 $30 multicolored .45 .45

Souvenir Sheet

The Summer Palace, Beijing — A261

Illustration reduced.

1996, Apr. 12 **Litho.** ***Perf. 13***

3134 A261 $60 multicolored .85 .85

China '96. No. 3134 was not available until March 1997.

Transfer of Hong Kong — A262

No. 3135: a, Tortoise. b, Dragon. c, Unicorn. d, Phoenix.
No. 3136, vert.: a, Swallow & willow. b, Kingfisher & chrysanthemum. c, Crane & pine. d, Peacock & peony.
No. 3137a-3137d, vert.: Various kites.
No. 3138a-3138b, vert.: Paintings of mountains and lakes.

1997, Feb. 12 ***Perf. 14***

Sheets of 4 & 2

3135-3137 A262 $80 #a.-d., each 4.50 4.50
3138 A262 $200 #a.-b. 5.50 5.50

Hong Kong '97. No. 3138 contains two 70x44mm stamps.

Motion Pictures, Cent. A263

Movie star, World War II films: No. 3139: a, Burgess Meredith, "The Story of GI Joe." b, M.E. Clifton-James, "I Was Monty's Double." c, Audie Murphy, "To Hell and Back." d, Gary Cooper, "The Story of Dr. Wassell." e, James Mason, "The Desert Fox." f, Manart Kippen, "Mission to Moscow." g, Robert Taylor, "Above and Beyond." h, James Cagney, "The Gallant Hours." i, John Garfield, "Pride of the Marines."
$300, George C. Scott, "Patton," horiz.

1997, Feb. 21 ***Perf. 13½x14***

3139 A263 $50 Sheet of 9, #a.-i. 6.25 6.25

Souvenir Sheet

Perf. 14x13½

3140 A263 $300 multicolored 4.25 4.25

Pres. John F. Kennedy (1917-63) — A264

1997, Mar. 14 **Litho.** ***Perf. 14***

3141 A264 $50 blue .70 .70

George Washington A265

Designs from works of art: No. 3142: a, Washington in battle. b, Washington taking oath. c, Washington Seated in Armchair, from engraving after Chappel. d, Col. Washington of Virginia Militia, by Charles W. Peale. e, George Washington, by Rembrandt Peale. f, Washington Addressing Constitutional Convention, by Junius Brutus Stearns. g, Washington on His Way to the Continental Congress. h, Washington on a White Charger, by John Faed. i, Washington as a Surveyor, from an engraving by G.R. Hall after Darley's drawing. j, Bas-relief of Washington Praying at Valley Forge. k, Death of Gen. Mercer at Battle of Princeton, by John Trumbull. l, Washington Taking Command of the Continental Army at Cambridge. m, George Washington, by Gilbert Stuart.

No. 3143: a, Washington Before the Battle of Trenton, by John Trumbull. b, Washington, His Family at Mt. Vernon, by Alonzo Chappel. c, Inauguration of Washington in New York City, by Chappel. d, Washington, by Adolph Ulrich Wertmuller. e, Washington Accepts His Commission as Commander-in-Chief, June 1775, Currier & Ives lithograph. f, Washington from a mezzotint by Sartain. g, On the Lawn at Mt. Vernon after the War. h, Washington Conversing with a Farmhand During the Baling Season with Nelly and Washington Custus Playing Nearby, from anonymous print after Junius Brutus Stearns. i, Nellie Custis' Wedding on Washington's Last Birthday, by Ogden. j, Washington Crossing the Delaware, by Leutze. k, Washington Receives Orders from Mortally Wounded Gen. Braddock at 1755 Battle of Monongahela. l, Washington Birthplace (supposed) on the Potomac, Currier & Ives lithograph. m, Washington at Yorktown, by James Peale.

1997, Mar. 14 Litho. *Perf. 14*

3142 Sheet of 13 16.00 16.00
a.-l. A265 $60 each .95 .95
m. A265 $300 imperf. 4.75 4.75
3143 Sheet of 13 16.00 16.00
a.-l. A265 $60 each .95 .95
m. A265 $300 imperf. 4.75 4.75

Nos. 3142m, 3143m are each 66x91mm and have simulated perforations.

No. 3142m exists perf. 14½.

A266

Mushrooms: $6, Morchella hortensis. $20, Boletus chrysenteron. $25, Hygrophorus agathosmus. $30, Cortinarius violaceus. $35, Acanthocystis geogenius. $60, Mycena polygramma. $200, Hebeloma radicosum. $300, Coprinus comatus.

No. 3152: a, Coprinus picaceus. b, Stropharia umbonatescens. c, Paxillus involutus. d, Amanita inaurata. e, Lepiota rhacodes. f, Russula amoena.

No. 3153: a, Volvaria volvacea. b, Psalliota augusta. c, Tricholoma aurantium. d, Pholiota spectabilis. e, Cortinarius armillatus. f, Agrocybe dura.

No. 3154, Pholiota mutabilis. No. 3155, Amanita muscaria.

1997, Apr. 2 Litho. *Perf. 14*

3144-3151 A266 Set of 8 9.50 9.50

Sheets of 6

3152-3153 A266 $80 #a.-f., ea 7.50 7.50

Souvenir Sheets

3154-3155 A266 $300 each 4.75 4.75

A267

Flowers: No. 3156, $6, Pineapple lily. No. 3157, $6, Blue columbine. $20, Petunia. $25, Lily of the Nile. $30, Bird of Paradise. $35, African daisy. $60, Cape daisy. $80, Gazania. $100, Cape water lily. $200, Insigne lady's slipper.

No. 3166: a, Monarch supperwart. b, Passion flower. c, Butterfly iris. d, Red-hot poker. e, Dir. G.T. Moore water lily. f, Superbissima painted tongue. g, Orchid. h, Annual chrysanthemum.

No. 3167: a, Tulips. b, Liatris. c, Roses. d, Gerber daisies. e, Sunflowers. f, Chrysanthemums.

No. 3168, Petunia.

1997, Apr. 2

3156-3165 A267 Set of 10 8.00 8.00
3166 A267 $60 Sheet of 8, #a.-h. 7.50 7.50
3167 A267 $80 Sheet of 6, #a.-f, 7.50 7.50

Souvenir Sheet

3168 A267 $300 multicolored 4.50 4.50

Deng Xiaoping (1904-97) — A268

Illustration reduced.

1997, May 1

3169 A268 $100 shown 1.75 1.75

Souvenir Sheet

3170 A268 $150 Portrait, diff. 2.50 2.50

No. 3169 was issued in sheets of 3.

UNESCO, 50th Anniv. — A269

Designs: $20, Horyu-Ji, Japan. $25, Scandola Nature Reserve, France. $30, Great Wall Defenses, China. $35, Wurzburg, Germany. $60, Monastery of Batalha, Portugal. $200, Dubrovnik, Croatia.

Sites in Germany, vert: No. 3177: a, Cathedral of Aquisgran, Aachen. b, Cathedral at Trier. c, Column of Augusta Treveror, Trier. d, f, Residences, Wurzburg. e, Church interior, Wurzburg. g, House of the River at Inselstadt, Bamberg. h, Cathedral interior, Speyer.

Sites in Greece, vert: No. 3178: a, Monastery of Thessaloniki. b, d, e, Monastery at Mystras. c, Church of Santa Sofia, Thessaloniki. f, City, Thessaloniki. g, Painting, Mystras. h, Museum of Byzantine Art, Thessaloniki.

No. 3179, vert.: a, Monastery of Poblet Catalonia, Spain. b, Old City of Salamanca, Spain. c, Toledo, Spain. d, Cathedral of Florence, Italy. e, Tower of Pisa, Italy. f, g, h, Convent of Christ, Tomar, Portugal.

Sites in Japan: No. 3180: a, d, e, Horyu-Ji. b, c, Kyoto.

Sites in the Americas: No. 3181: a, Cuzco, Peru. b, Potosi, Bolivia. c, Fortress, San Lorenzo, Panama. d, Sangay Natl. Park, Ecuador. e, Los Glaciares Natl. Park, Argentina.

Sites in US: No. 3182: a, Monticello. b, Yosemite Natl. Park. c, Yellowstone Natl. Park. d, Olympic Natl. Park. e, Everglades.

No. 3183, Mount Taishan Shrine, China. No. 3184, Monastery of Batalha, Portugal. No. 3185, Bamberg Cathedral (detail), Germany. No. 3186, Monastery, Mount Athos, Greece.

1997, May 20

3171-3176 A269 Set of 6 5.25 5.25

Sheets of 8 or 5 + Label

3177-3179 A269 $60 #a.-h., ea 6.75 6.75

Sheets of 5

3180-3182 A269 $80 #a.-e., ea 5.50 5.50

Souvenir Sheets

3183-3186 A269 $300 each 4.25 4.25

Queen Elizabeth II, Prince Philip, 50th Wedding Anniv. A270

No. 3187: a, Queen. b, Royal Arms. c, Wedding portrait. d, Queen, Prince. e, Broadlands House. f, Prince Philip.

$300, Queen Elizabeth II.

1997, May 20 Litho. *Perf. 14*

3187 A270 $60 Sheet of 6, #a.-f. 5.00 5.00

Souvenir Sheet

3188 A270 $300 multicolored 4.25 4.25

Paintings, by Hiroshige (1797-1858) A271

No. 3189: a, Oumayagashi. b, Ryogoku Ekoin & Moto-Yanagibashi Bridge. c, Pine of Success and Oumayagashi Asakusa River. d, Fireworks at Ryogoku. e, Dyers' Quarter, Kanda. f, Cotton-goods Lane, Odenma-cho.

No. 3190, Suruga-cho. No. 3191, Yatsukoji, inside Sujikai Gate.

1997, May 20 *Perf. 13½x14*

3189 A271 $80 Sheet of 6, #a.-f. 6.75 6.75

Souvenir Sheets

3190-3191 A271 $300 each 5.00 5.00

Heinrich von Stephan (1831-97), Founder of UPU A272

No. 3192: a, Frieze of Roman post service. b, UPU emblem. c, Cable car, Boston, 1907.

$300, Von Stephan, Egyptian messenger.

1997, May 20 Litho. *Perf. 14*

3192 A272 $100 Sheet of 3, #a.-c. 4.25 4.25

Souvenir Sheet

3193 A272 $300 multicolored 4.25 4.25

PACIFIC 97.

Paul P. Harris (1868-1947), Founder of Rotary, Intl. — A273

Designs: $200, Health, hunger and humanity, portrait of Harris. $300, Mutual respect among all faiths, races and cultures.

1997, May 20

3194 A273 $200 multicolored 2.75 2.75

Souvenir Sheet

3195 A273 $300 multicolored 4.25 4.25

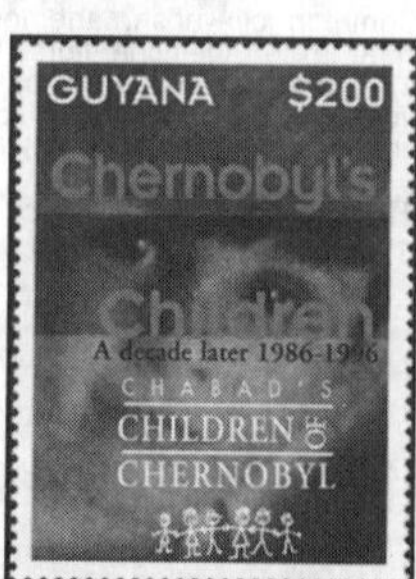

Chernobyl Disaster, 10th Anniv. A274

Designs: No. 3196, Chabad's Children of Chernobyl. No. 3197, UNESCO.

1997, May 20 *Perf. 13½x14*

3196 A274 $200 multicolored 2.75 2.75
3197 A274 $200 multicolored 2.75 2.75

Grimm's Fairy Tales — A275

Mother Goose — A276

Scenes from "Hansel & Gretel:" No. 3198: a, Hansel & Gretel in forest. b, Gingerbread house. c, Wicked witch. $500, Witch trying to capture Gretel, horiz.

$300, Rooster from "Cock-A-Doodle-Do."

1997, May 20 *Perf. 13½x14*

3198 A275 $100 Sheet of 3, #a.-c. 4.25 4.25

Souvenir Sheets

Perf. 14, 14x13½

3199 A276 $300 multicolored 4.25 4.25
3200 A275 $500 multicolored 7.00 7.00

US Pres. Bill Clinton's Visit to Caribbean, May 1997 — A277

Designs: $30, Guyana Pres. Cheddi Jagan, Pres. Clinton, map of Caribbean, vert. $100, Clinton, Jagan, flags of US, Guyana, palm trees, beach.

Perf. 13½x14, 14x13½

1997, June 23

3201 A277 $30 multicolored .45 .45
3202 A277 $100 multicolored 1.40 1.40

#3201-3202 each issued in sheets of 9.

See Nos. 3201-3202.

1998 Winter Olympic Games, Nagano

A278 A279

Medalists: $30, Georg Thoma. $35, Katja Seizinger. $60, Georg Hackl. $200, Katarina Witt.

No. 3207: a, Gunda Niemann, 3000- & 5000-m speed skating, 1992. b, Tony Nash, Robin Dixon, 2-man bobsled, 1964. c, Switzerland 4-man bobsled, 1988. d, Piet Kleine, speed skating, 1976.

No. 3208: a, Oksana Baiul, figure skating, 1994. b, Cathy Turner, 500-m short track speed skating, 1994. c, Brian Boitano, figure skating, 1988. d, Nancy Kerrigan, figure skating, 1994.

No. 3209: a, Markus Wasmeier. b, Jens Weissflog. c, Erhard Keller. d, Rosi Mittermaier. e, Gunda Niemann. f, Peter Angerer.

No. 3210, Swiss 4-Man bobsled team. No. 3211, Jean-Claude Killy, slalom, 1968. No. 3212, Chen Lu, figure skating, 1992.

1997, July 1 ***Perf. 14***

3203-3206 A278 Set of 4 4.50 4.50

Strips or Blocks of 4

3207-3208 A279 $60 #a.-d., each 3.50 3.50

Sheet of 6

3209 A278 $30 #a.-f. 2.50 2.50

Souvenir Sheets

3210 A278 $300 multicolored 4.25 4.25
3211-3212 A279 $300 each 4.25 4.25

Nos. 3207-3208 issued in sheets of 8 stamps.

Souvenir Sheet

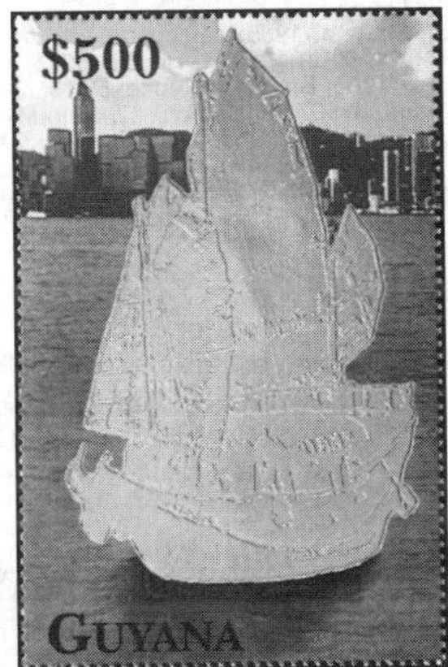

Return of Hong Kong to China — A280

Litho. & Embossed

1997, July 1 ***Perf. 14***

3213 A280 $500 gold & multi

Domestic Cats A281

Designs, vert.: $30, Norwegian forest cat. $35, Oriental spotted tabby. $200, Asian smoke.

No. 3217: a, Abyssinian. b, Chocolate colorpoint shorthair. c, Silver tabby. d, Persian. e, Maine coon cat & kitten. f, Brown shaded Burmese. g, Persian kitten. h, Siamese. i, British shorthair.

$300, Manx, vert.

1997, July 29

3214-3216 A281 Set of 3 3.75 3.75
3217 A281 $60 Sheet of 9, #a.-i. 7.50 7.50

Souvenir Sheet

3218 A281 $300 multicolored 4.25 4.25

Birds A282

$25, Verdin. $30, Wood thrush, vert. $60, Rofous-sided towhee. $200, Pygmy nuthatch, vert.

No. 3223: a, Groove-billed ani. b, Green honeycreeper. c, Toucanet. d, Wire-tailed manakin. e, Hoatzin. f, Tiger heron.

Hummingbirds: No. 3224: a, Magenta-throated woodstar. b, Long-tailed hermit. c, Red-footed plumeleteer. d, Anna's. e, White-tipped sicklebill. f, Fiery-throated.

No. 3225, Pinnated bittern. No. 3226, Keel-billed toucan.

1997, Aug. 12 **Litho.** ***Perf. 14***

3219-3222 A282 Set of 4 4.50 4.50

Sheets of 6

3223-3224 A282 $80 #a.-f., each 6.75 6.75

Souvenir Sheets

3225-3226 A282 $300 each 4.25 4.25

Dogs — A283

Designs: $20, Chihuahua. $25, Norfolk terrier. $60, Welsh terrier.

No. 3230: a, Shar-pei. b, Chihuahua. c, Chow chow. d, Sealyham terrier. e, Collie. f, German shorthair pointer. g, Bulldog. h, German shepherd. i, Old English sheepdog.

$300, Tibetan spaniel.

1997, July 29 **Litho.** ***Perf. 14***

3227-3229 A283 Set of 3 1.50 1.50
3230 A283 $60 Sheet of 9, #a.-i. 7.50 7.50

Souvenir Sheet

3231 A283 $300 multicolored 4.25 4.25

Pres. Cheddi Jagan's 1st Election to Parliament, 50th Anniv. — A284

1997, Oct. 6 **Litho.** ***Perf. 14***

3232 A284 $6 green & multi .20 .20
3233 A284 $30 pale yellow & multi 4.25 4.25

#3232-3233 each issued in sheets of 9.

Diana, Princess of Wales (1961-97) — A285

No. 3234a-3234f, Various portraits.

No. 3235, Wearing red dress. No. 3236, With longer hair.

1997, Oct. 15

3234 A285 $80 Sheet of 6, #a.-f. 8.00 8.00

Souvenir Sheets

Perf. 14½

3235-3236 A285 $300 each 4.25 4.25

Nos. 3235-3236 each contain one 34x52mm stamp.

US Pres. Bill Clinton's Visit Type of 1997

#3238, Clinton, Jagan, flags, sun on horizon.

Perf. 13½x14, 14x13½

1997, Nov. 10

3237 A277 $6 like #3201 .20 .20
3238 A277 $30 multicolored .45 .45

#3237-3238 each issued in sheets of 9.

Souvenir Sheets

Chinese Pres. Jiang Zemin's Visit to New York — A286

Pres. Zemin, New York skyline, and: $200, Flags of China, UN, US. $300, Flags of China, US.

Illustration reduced.

1997, Nov. 10 ***Perf. 14***

3239 A286 $200 multicolored 2.75 2.75
3240 A286 $300 multicolored 4.25 4.25

Buildings in Guyana — A287

1997, Dec. 8 **Litho.** ***Perf. 14***

3241 A287 $6 W. Fogarty #1 .20 .20
3242 A287 $30 Public building .40 .40

Christmas A288

Entire paintings, details, or sculptures: $24, $30, Diff. angels from The Triumph of Galatea, by Raphael. $35, Primavera, by Botticelli. $60, Angel Muscicians, by Agostino di Duccio, (bas relief). $100, From cover of Life Magazine, #1212, 1906. $200, Madonna and Saints, by Rosso Fiorentino.

No. 3249, The Gardens of Love, by Rubens. No. 3250, Cherubs, by Philippe de Champaigne.

1997, Dec. 8

3243-3248 A288 Set of 6 6.25 6.25

Souvenir Sheets

3249-3250 A288 $300 each 4.25 4.25

Historical Events A289

Events of 1922: No. 3251, Explorers discover tomb of Tutankhamun. No. 3252, Lincoln Memorial dedicated, Washington, DC. No. 3253, Alexander Graham Bell dies.

Events of 1923: No. 3254, Calvin Coolidge becomes President. No. 3255, John L. Baird develops 1st experimental television. No. 3256, Warren G. Harding dies.

Event of 1924: No. 3257, First Winter Olympic Games, Chamonix, France.

Events of 1925: No. 3258, Tennessee bans teaching of evolution in schools. No. 3259, Chinese leader Sun Yat-Sen dies.

Events of 1926: No. 3260, Robert Goddard launches 1st liquid fuel rocket. No. 3261, Richard E. Byrd is 1st to fly over North Pole. No. 3262, Sesquicentennial Exposition, Philadelphia.

1997, Dec. 8

3251-3262 A289 $60 Set of 12 10.00 10.00

New Year 1998 (Year of the Tiger) — A290

Various stylized tigers with denomination in: a, LR. b, LL. c, UR. d, UL.

$150, Tiger, red background.

1998, Jan. 5 **Litho.** ***Perf. 14½***

3263 A290 $50 Sheet of 4, #a.-d. 2.75 2.75

Souvenir Sheet

3264 A290 $150 multicolored 2.10 2.10

Prehistoric Wildlife — A291

Designs: $25, Kentrosaurus. $30, Lesothosaurus. $35, Stegoceras. $60, Lagosuchus. $100, Herrerasaurus. $200, Iguanodon.

No. 3271: a, Quetzalcoatlus (d). b, Pteranodon (a, c). c, Peteinosaurus. d, Criorhychus (g). e, Pterodaustro. f, Eudimorphodon. g, Archeopteryx. h, Dimorphodon. i, Sharovipteryx.

No. 3272: a, Ceresiosaurus. b, Nothosaurus. c, Rhomaleosaurus. d, Grendelius. e, Mixosaurus. f, Mesosaurus. g, Placodus. h, Stethacanthus. i, Coelacanth.

No. 3273, Styracosaurus, vert. No. 3274, Yangchuanosaurus, vert.

1998, Feb. 23 **Litho.** ***Perf. 14***

3265-3270 A291 Set of 6 6.25 6.25

Sheets of 9

3271-3272 A291 $55 #a.-i., each 7.00 7.00

Souvenir Sheets

3273-3274 A291 $300 each 4.25 4.25

1998 World Cup Soccer Championships, France — A292

Team pictures: Group A: #3275, Brazil. #3276, Morocco. #3277, Norway. #3278, Scotland.

Group B: #3279, Austria. #3280, Cameroun. #3281, Chile. #3282, Italy.

Group C: #3283, Denmark. #3284, France. #3285, Saudi Arabia. #3286, South Africa.

Group D: #3287, Bulgaria. #3288, Nigeria. #3289, Paraguay. #3290, Spain.

Group E: #3291, Belgium. #3292, Holland. #3293, S. Korea. #3294, Mexico.

Group F: #3295, Germany. #3296, Iran. #3297, US. #3298, Yugoslavia.

Group G: #3299, Colombia. #3300, England. #3301, Romania. #3302, Tunisia.

Group H: #3303, Argentina. #3304, Croatia. #3305, Jamaica. #3306, Japan.

Japanese players, vert.: #3306A, Okada. #3306B, Nakata.

1998, Apr. 8 **Litho.** ***Perf. 14x13½***

3275-3306 A292 $30 Set of 32 13.50 13.50

Perf. 13½x14
Souvenir Sheets

3306A-3306B A292 $300 each 4.25 4.25

Nos. 3275-3306 were each issued in sheets of 8 + 1 label.
For overprints see Nos. 3317-3324.

The Titanic A293

No. 3307: a, J. Bruce Ismay, managing director, White Star Line. b, Jack Phillips, radio operator. c, Margaret "Unsinkable Molly" Brown, passenger. d, Capt. Edward J. Smith. e, Frederick Fleet, lookout. f, Thomas Andrews, managing director of Harland and Wolff.
$300, Titanic sinking.

1998, June 17 Litho. *Perf. 14*

3307 A293 $80 Sheet of 6, #a.-f. 6.75 6.75

Souvenir Sheet

3308 A293 $300 multicolored 4.25 4.25

Sailing Ships A294

No. 3309: a, Viking double-ended ship, 14th cent. b, Portuguese caravel. c, "Nina." d, Fannie, 1896. e, "Victoria," 1519. f, Arab sambook.
No. 3310: a, "Dutch Fluyt." b, "Alastor." c, "Falcon." d, "Red Rover." e, "British Anglesey." f, "Archibald Russel."
No. 3311, Oseberg ship. No. 3312, "Half Moon," 1609.

1998, June 17 Litho. *Perf. 14*
Sheets of 6

3309-3310 A294 $80 #a.-f., ea 6.75 6.75

Souvenir Sheets

3311-3312 A294 $300 each 4.25 4.25

Diana, Princess of Wales (1961-97) — A295

#3313, Diana in black and brown fur trimmed hat and coat. #3314, Diana wearing suit and hat.

Litho. & Embossed
1998, Aug. 3 *Die Cut 7½*

3313-3314 A295 $1500 gold & multi

Queen Mother A296

1998, Aug. 4 *Perf. 13½*

3315 A296 $90 multicolored 1.25 1.25

CARICOM, 25th Anniv. — A297

1998, July 4 Litho. *Perf. 13½*

3316 A297 $20 multicolored .30 .30

Nos. 3275, 3282-3286, 3289, 3304 Ovptd. "FRANCE WINNERS" in Gold

1998, Aug. 20 Litho. *Perf. 14x13½*

3317-3324 A292 $30 Set of 8 3.50 3.50

Nos. 3317-3324 were each issued in sheets of 8+label. Each sheet contains additional overprints in sheet margins.

National Hockey League Players — A298

Designs: a, Bryan Berard. b, Ray Bourque. c, Martin Brodeur. d, Pavel Bure. e, Chris Chelios. f, Sergei Fedorov. g, Peter Forsberg. h, Wayne Gretzky. i, Dominik Hasek. j, Brett Hull. k, Jarome Iginla. l, Jaromir Jagr. m, Paul Kariya. n, Saku Koivu. o, John LeClair. p, Brian Leetch. q, Eric Lindros. r, Patrick Marleau. s, Mark Messier. t, Mike Modano. u, Chris Osgood. v, Zigmund Palffy. w, Felix Potvin. x, Jeremy Roenick. y, Patrick Roy. z, Joe Sakic. aa, Sergei Samsonov. ab, Teemu Selanne. ac, Brendan Shanahan. ad, Ryan Smyth. ae, Jocelyn Thibault. af, Joe Thornton. ag, Keith Tkachuk. ah, John Vanbiesbrouck. ai, Steve Yzerman. aj, Dainius Zubrus.

1998, Apr. 1 Litho. *Perf. 13½*

3325 A298 $35 Sheet of 36, #a.-aj. 17.50 17.50

Aircraft A299

Military aircraft - #3326: a, A7K Corsair II. b, A6E Intruder. c, U2 Spy plane. d, Blackhawk. e, F-16. f, Phantom II.
Pioneers of aviation - #3327: a, Wright Brothers, 1903. b, Bleriot, 1911. c, Curtiss Jenny, 1919. d, Airship Schwaben, 1911. e, W-8B, 1923. f, DH-66, 1926.
#3328, A-10 Warthog. #3329, HH-65A Dolphin.

1998, Sept. 28 *Perf. 14*
Sheets of 6

3326-3327 A299 $80 #a.-f, each 6.75 6.75

Souvenir Sheets

3328-3329 A299 $300 each 4.25 4.25

Endangered Species — A300

Nos. 3330, 3332, Various pictures of the giant panda.
Nos. 3331, 3333, Various pictures of the mountain gorilla.

1998, Oct. 8
Sheets of 6

3330-3331 A300 $80 #a.-f., ea 6.75 6.75

Souvenir Sheets

3332-3333 A300 $300 each 4.25 4.25

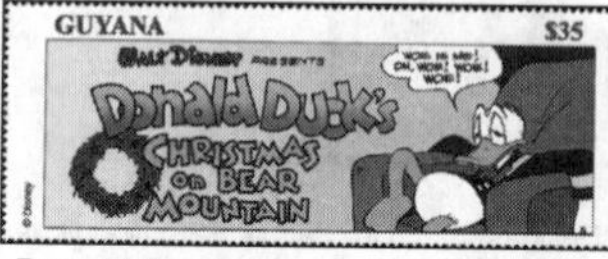

Donald Duck Adventures, Christmas on Bear Mountain — A301

Cartoon panels: a, 1-8. b, 9-16. c, 17-24. d, 25-32. e, 33-40. f, 41-48. g, 49-56. h, 57-64. i, 65-72. j, 73-80. k, Pane of 2, Carl Barks, vert., bears and duck.
Illustration reduced.

1998, Oct. 15 *Perf. 14x13½, 13½x14*

3334 Complete booklet 27.50 27.50
a.-j. A301 $35 Panes of 4, each 1.90
k. A301 $300 Pane of 2 8.25

Disney's Uncle Scrooge, by Carl Barks, 50th anniv.

Organization of American States, 50th Anniv. A302

1998, Oct. 29 *Perf. 14*

3335 A302 $40 multicolored .55 .55

Ferrari Automobiles — A302a

No. 3335A: c, 212 Export. d, 410 Superamerica chassis. e, 125 S.
$300, 512 S Racer.
Illustration reduced.

1998, Oct. 29 Litho. *Perf. 14*

3335A A302a $100 Sheet of 3, #c-e 4.00 4.00

Souvenir Sheet

3335B A302a $300 multi 4.00 4.00

No. 3335A contains three 39x25mm stamps.

Diana, Princess of Wales (1961-97) A303

1998, Oct. 29

3336 A303 $60 multicolored .85 .85

Self-Adhesive
Serpentine Die Cut Perf. 11½
Sheet of 1
Size: 53x65mm

3336A A303 $300 Diana, buildings, bridge

No. 3336 was issued in sheets of 6.
Soaking in water may affect the multi-layer image of No. 3336A.
Issued: $60, 10/29; $300, 11/5/98.

Grand Prix Champion Racing Cars and Drivers—A304 — 3337

No. 3337: a, 1914 Grand Prix Mercedes, Christian Lautenschlager. b, 1930 Bugati Type 35B, P. Etancelin. c, 1934 Alfa Romeo P3, Louis Chiron. d, 1938 Mercedes Benz W154, Richard Seaman. e, 1938 Auto Union D Type, Tazio Nuvolari. f, 1951 Alfa Romeo 158, Juan Manuel Fangio.
No. 3338: a, 1955 Mercedes Benz W196, Stirling Moss. b, 1960 Ferrari Dino 246, Phil Hill. c, 1966 Brabham-Repco BT19, Jack Brabham. d, 1970 Lotus Ford 72, John Miles. e, 1983 Renault RE40, Alain Prost. f, 1998 McLaren Mercedes MP4/13, David Coulthard.
No. 3339, 1906 Grand Prix Renault, Ferenc Szisz. No. 3340, 1956 Maserati 250F, Stirling Moss.

1998, Oct. 29
Sheets of 6

3337-3338 A304 $80 #a.-f., ea 6.75 6.75

Souvenir Sheets

3339-3340 A304 $300 each 4.25 4.25

Nos. 3339-3340 contain one 57x42mm stamp.

Tigger's Happy New Year — A304a

No. 3340A, vert. - Tigger: d, Giving gift to Winnie the Pooh. e, With fireworks. f, Giving flowers to Kanga. g, With Piglet. h, At door. i, With Eeyore.
No. 3340B, $300,Tigger beating drum. No. 3340C, $300, Tigger carrying staff for dragon.

1998, Oct. 29 Litho. *Perf. 13¼*

3340A A304a $60 Sheet of 6, #a-f 5.00 5.00

Souvenir Sheets

3340B-3340C A304a Set of 2 8.00 8.00

Gandhi — A305

No. 3341: a, Age 37, 1906. b, Age 77, 1946. c, Age 78, 1948. d, Age 77, 1947.
$300, Age 76, 1946, horiz.

1998, Oct. 29

3341 A305 $100 Sheet of 4, #a.-d. 5.50 5.50

Souvenir Sheet

3342 A305 $300 multicolored 4.25 4.25

No. 3341b-3341c are each 53x38mm.

Pablo Picasso A306

Paintings, details: $25, Sleeping Peasants, 1919. $60, Large Nude in Red Armchair, 1929, vert. $200, Sculpture, "Female Head," 1931, vert.
$300, Man and Woman, 1971, vert.

1998, Oct. 29 ***Perf. 14½***

3343-3345 A306 Set of 3 4.00 4.00

Souvenir Sheet

3346 A306 $300 multicolored 4.25 4.25

Royal Air Force, 80th Anniv. A307

No. 3347: a, Avro Lancaster B2. b, PBY-5A Catalina Amphibian. c, BAe Hawk TIA trainers (Red Arrows). d, Avro Lancaster, DeHavilland Mosquito.
No. 3348: a, BAe Hawk TIA. b, C130 Hercules. c, Panavia Tornado GRI. d, BAe Hawk 200.
No. 3349: a, BAe Nimrod RIP. b, Panavia Tornado F3 ADV. c, CH-47 Chinook helicopter. d, Panavia Tornado GRIA.
No. 3350, Biplane, hawks in flight. No. 3351, Eurofighter, Spitfire. No. 3352, Eurofighters. No. 3353, Head of hawk, hawk spreading wings, biplane. No. 3354, Tiger Moth, Eurofighter. No. 3355, Hawk spreading wings, biplane.

1998, Oct. 29 ***Perf. 14***

Sheets of 4, #a.-d.

3347-3348 A307 $100 each 5.50 5.50
3349 A307 $150 #a.-d. 8.25 8.25

Souvenir Sheets

3350-3351 A307 $200 each 2.75 2.75
3352-3355 A307 $300 each 4.25 4.25

1998 World Scout Jamboree, Chile — A308

a, James E. West, 1st scout executive with early Eagle Scouts. b, Pres. . Kennedy greets Explorers, 51st Scouts anniv., 1961. c, Astronaut Walter Schirra receives a special merit badge, 1962.

1998, Oct. 29 **Litho.** ***Perf. 14***

3356 A308 $160 Sheet of 3, #a.-c. 6.75 6.75

A309

Paintings by Eugène Delacroix (1798-1863) - #3357: a, The Sultan of Morocco Receives the Count de Mornay. b, Armed Indian with a Gurkha Scimitar. c, Portrait presumed to be of the Singer Baroihet in Turkish Dress. d, Moroccan Notebook: Studies of Jewish Women. e, Arab Horseman Giving a Signal. f, Arab Cavalry Practicing a Charge. g, A Seated Moor. h, Jewish Woman in Traditional Dress.
#3358: a, Corner of the Studio; the Stove. b, Room in the Apartment the Count de Mornay. c, Hamlet and Horatio in the Graveyard. d, George Sand. e, The Bride of Abydos. f, Elysian Fields. g, A Lioness Standing by a Tree. h, Monsieur Alfred Bruyas.
Details, horiz: No. 3359, Moroccan Jewish Wedding. No. 3360, Death of Sardanapulus.

1998, Oct. 29

Sheets of 8, #a.-h.

3357-3358 A309 $60 each 6.75 6.75

Souvenir Sheets

3359-3360 A309 $300 each 4.25 4.25

A310

St. Andrew's Church, Georgetown, 180th anniv. - Various views of front of church: $6, $30, $60.

1998 **Litho.** ***Perf. 14***

3361-3363 A310 Set of 3 1.25 1.25

New Year 1999 (Year of the Rabbit) — A311

Various stylized rabbits, location of denomination - #3364: a, LR. b, LL. c, UR. d, UL.
$150, Red background, Chinese inscription.

1999, Jan. 4 **Litho.** ***Perf. 14½***

3364 A311 $50 Sheet of 4, #a.-d. 2.75 2.75

Souvenir Sheet

3365 A311 $150 multicolored 2.10 2.10

Disney Characters in Sporting Activities A312

Skate boarding - #3366: a, Huey. b, Mickey. c, Dewey. d, Louie. e, Goofy. f, Donald.
Roller blading - #3367: a, Minnie. b, Goofy. c, Daisy. d, Baby Duck. e, Donald. f, Mickey.
Skate boarding, roller blading, red, white & blue background - #3368: a, Baby Duck. b, Daisy. c, Mickey. d, Goofy. e, Dewey. f, Donald.
No. 3369, Dewey. No. 3370, Daisy. No. 3371, Goofy, horiz.

Perf. 13½x14, 14X13½

1999, Mar. 1 **Litho.**

Sheets of 6

3366-3368 A312 $80 #a.-f., ea 7.00 7.00

Souvenir Sheets

3369-3371 A312 $300 each 4.50 4.50

Mickey Mouse, 70th anniv.

Disney Characters in Trains — A313

101 Dalmatians Express - #3372: a, Locomotive. b, Flatcar. c, Car with pillars. d, "Basket" car. e, Caboose.
Robin Hood Train - #3373: a, Engine. b, Marian, Robin Hood. c, Royal coach. d, Flatcar. e, Caboose.
Snow White, Diamond Mine Railroad - #3374: a, Engine. b, Flatcar. c, Snow White, Prince Charming. d, Passenger car. e, Pump car.
Little Mermaid Railroad - #3375: a, Engine. b, Fish holding pearls. c, Little Mermaid. d, Various marine life in car. e, "Bah Hum Bug!"
No. 3376: a, Dwarf from Diamond Mine Railroad driving locomotive. b, Dwarf on pump car.
No. 3377, Bandits, Cruela De Vil. No. 3378, Robin Hood, Bear. No. 3379, Little Mermaid kissing Prince under mistletoe. No. 3380, Little Mermaid holding starfish.

1999, Mar. 1 ***Perf. 13½x14***

Sheets of 5 & 2

3372-3375 A313 $100 #a.-e., ea 7.00 7.00
3376 A313 $200 #a.-b. 5.50 5.50

Souvenir Sheets

3377-3380 A313 $300 each 4.25 4.25

Caribbean Butterflies — A314

No. 3381: a, Scarce Bamboo Page. b, Spicebush swallowtail. c, Isabella. d, The mosaic. e, Gulf fritillary. f, Figure-of-eight.
No. 3382: a, Hewitson's blue hairstreak. b, Polydamas swallowtail. c, Common morpho. d, Blue-green reflector. e, Malachite. f, Grecian shoemaker.
No. 3383, Giant swallowtail, vert. No. 3384, Pipevine swallowtail, vert.

1999, Mar. 15 ***Perf. 14***

Sheets of 6

3381-3382 A314 $80 #a.-f., ea 6.75 6.75

Souvenir Sheets

3383-3384 A314 $300 each 4.25 4.25

Flowers A315

No. 3385: a, Geranium. b, Oncidium macranthum. c, Bepi orchidglades. d, Sunflowers (2). e, Cattleya walkeriana. f, Cattleya frasquita. g, Helianthus maximilani (one). h, Paphiopedilum insigne sanderae, lily. i, Lily (2).
No. 3386: a, Dendrobium nobile. b, Phalaenopsis schilleriana. c, Cymbidium alexette. d, Rhododendron. e, Phragmipedium besseae, laelia cinnabarina. f, Masdevallia veitchiana. g, Calochortus nuttallii. h, Brassolaeliocattleya pure gold. i, Laelia cinnabarina.
No. 3387: a, Leptotes bicolor, masdevallia ignea. b, Sophrolaeliocattleya, anguloa clowesii. c, Laelia pumila. d, Masdevallia ignea. e, Dendrodium phalaenopsis. f, Anguloa clowesii.
No. 3388, Asocentrum miniatum, vert. No. 3389, Iris pseudacorus.

1999, Mar. 15 **Litho.** ***Perf. 14***

Sheets of 9

3385-3386 A315 $60 #a.-i., each 7.50 7.50
3387 A315 $90 Sheet of 6, #a.-f. 7.50 7.50

Souvenir Sheet

3388-3389 A315 $300 each 4.25 4.25

Akira Kurosawa (1910-98), Film Director — A316

Films by Kurosawa, vert. - #3390: a, "The Dream." b, "Rashomon." c, "Kagemusha." d, "Red Beard." e, "Seven Samurai." f, "Yojimbo."
Portraits - #3391: a, Pointing. b, Hand on face. c, Standing. d, With camerman.
$300, Scene from "Dreams."

1999, Mar. 22

Sheets of 6 & 4

3390 A316 $80 #a.-f. 6.75 6.75
3391 A316 $130 #a.-d. 7.25 7.25

Souvenir Sheet

3392 A316 $300 multicolored 4.25 4.25

Mushrooms A317

Designs: $25, Coprinus atramentarius. $35, Hebeloma crustuliniforme. $100, Russula nigricans. $200, Tricholoma aurantium.
No. 3397: a, Boletus aereus. b, Coprinus comatus. c, Inocybe godeyi. d, Morchella crassipes. e, Lepiota acutesquamosa. f, Amanita phalloides. g, Boletus spadiceus. h, Cortinarius collinitus. i, Lepiota procera.
No. 3398: a, Russula ochroleuca. b, Hygrophorus hypotheius. c, Amanita rubescens. d, Boletus satanas. e, Amanita echinocephala. f, Amanita muscaria. g, Boletus badius. h, Hebeloma radicosum. i, Mycena polygramma.
No. 3399, Lepiota acutequamoso. No. 3400, Pluteus cervinus.

1999, May 6 **Litho.** ***Perf. 14***

3393-3396 A317 Set of 4 .50 .50

Sheets of 9 32x41mm Stamps

Perf. 14½

3397-3398 A317 $60 #a.-i., ea 7.50 7.50

Souvenir Sheet

3399-3400 A317 $300 each 4.25 4.25

Nos. 3399-3400 each contain one 32x41mm stamp.

Australia '99, World Stamp Expo — A318

Trains - #3401: a, Burlington Northern GP 39-2, 1974. b, CSX GP40-2, 1967. c, Erie Lackawana Railroad GP 9, 1956. d, Amtrak P 42 Genesis, 1993. e, Erie Railroad S-2, 1948. f, Pennsylvania Railroad S-1, 1947.
No. 3402: a, Northern and Western #610, c. 1933. b, Pennsylvania Railroad M1B Mountain, 1930. c, Reading Railroad FP7A, 1951. d, New York Central 2-8-4, c. 1940. e, Union Pacific Challenger Big Boy, 1963. f, GP 15-15-1, 1956.
No. 3403: a, Shinkansen Bullet 100 series, 1984, Japan. b, Ukranian Diesel ZMGR, 1983, Russia. c, Rhatische Bahn GE 6/6 II, Germany. d, Eurostar TGV, 1986, France. e, Atlantique TGV, 1989, France. f, Class 86-6, UK.
No. 3404: a, Joseph Clark 0-4-0, 1868. b, Diamond Stack Bethel 4-4-0, 1863. c, New

York Central #999, 1890. d, Boston & Maine Ballardville 0-4-0, 1876. e, Atlantic 4-4-0 Portland Rochester Railroad, 1863. f, America 4-4-0 Baltimore & Ohio Railroad, 1881.

Railroad pioneers: No. 3405, George Stephen, vert. No. 3406, Alfred de Glehn, vert. No. 3407, George Nagelmackers, vert. No. 3408, R.F. Trevithick, vert.

1999, May 10 *Perf. 14*

Sheets of 6, #a.-f.

3401-3404 A318 $80 each 6.75 6.75

Souvenir Sheets

3405-3408 A318 $300 each 4.25 4.25

Wedding of Prince Edward and Sophie Rhys-Jones — A319

Various portraits: Nos. 3409, 3411, rose lilac sheet margin. Nos. 3410a, 3412, yellow brown sheet margin.

1999, June 19 Litho. *Perf. 14¼*

Sheets of 4, #a.-d.

3409-3410 A319 $150 each 8.00 8.00

Souvenir Sheets

3411-3412 A319 $300 each 4.00 4.00

Nos. 3411-3412 are horiz.

Johann Wolfgang von Goethe (1749-1832), Poet — A320

No. 3413: a, Lynceus sings from the watchtower. b, Portaits of Von Goethe and Friedrich von Schiller (1759-1805), poet. c, The fallen Icarus.

$300, Mephistopheles appears as salamander, vert.

1999, June 22 Litho. *Perf. 14*

3413 A320 $150 Sheet of 3, #a.-c. 6.25 6.25

Souvenir Sheet

3414 A320 $300 multicolored 4.25 4.25

IBRA '99, World Philatelic Exhibition, Nuremberg — A321

$60, Class E10 Bo-bo electric locomotive, BMW offices, Munich, 1952, vert. $200, Class 01, 4-6-2 steam express train, 1926.

Illustration reduced.

1999, June 22

3415 A321 $60 multicolored .85 .85
3416 A321 $200 multicolored 2.75 2.75

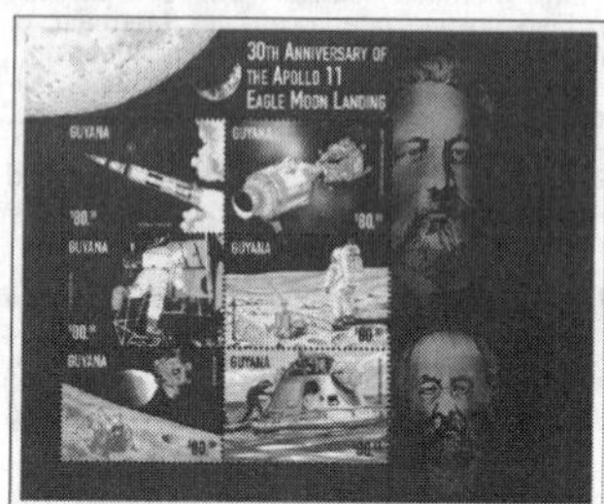

Apollo 11 Moon Landing, 30th Anniv. — A322

No. 3417: a, Blast off. b, Command Module docked with Lunar Lander. c, First man on moon. d, Seismic experiments package. e, Back to the orbiter. f, Astronauts being picked up.

No. 3418, vert: a, Sputnik, 1959, Konstantin Tsiolkovsky. b, Apollo 11 liftoff. c, On the moon. d, Collecting samples of lunar rocks. e, Apollo 11 Lunar Module. f, Splashdown.

No. 3419, Salute to the flag. No. 3420, Michael Collins.

1999, June 22

Sheets of 6

3417-3418 A322 $80 #a.-f., ea 6.25 6.25

Souvenir Sheet

3419-3420 A322 $300 each 4.00 4.00

Souvenir Sheets

PhilexFrance '99, World Philatelic Exhibition — A323

#3421, Co-co 7000 Class High Speed 1949-55. #3422, 241-P Class 4-8-2 Express 1947-49.

Illustration reduced.

1999, June 22

3421-3422 A323 $300 each 4.25 4.25

Paintings by Hokusai (1760-1849) — A324

Details or entire paintings - #3423: a, Travelers Climbing a Mountain Path. b, Washing in a River. c, The Blind (eyes & mouth open). d, The Blind (eyes & mouth shut). e, Convolvulus and Tree-Frog. f, Fishermen Hauling a Net.

No. 3424: a, Hibiscus and Sparrow. b, Hydrangea and Swallow. c, The Blind (eyes shut, mouth open). d, The Blind (eyes open, mouth shut). e, Irises. f, Lilies.

No. 3425, Flowering Cherries at Mount Yoshino, vert. No. 3426, A View of a Stone Causeway, vert.

1999, June 22 Litho. *Perf. 14x13¾*

Sheets of 6

3423-3424 A324 $80 #a.-f., ea 6.75 6.75

Souvenir Sheets

Perf. 13¾x14

3425-3426 A324 $300 each 4.25 4.25

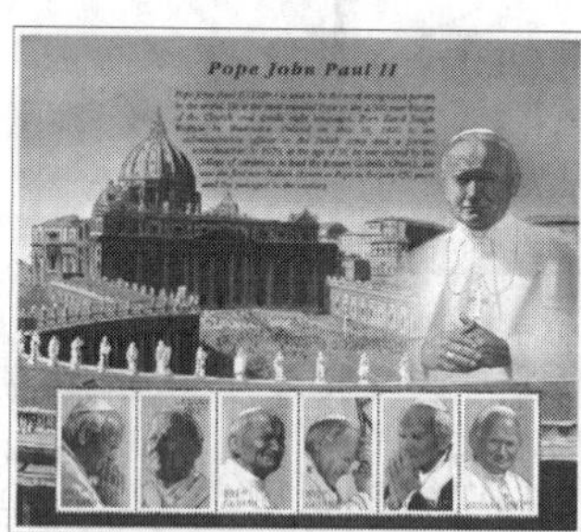

Pope John Paul II — A325

1999, June 22 *Perf. 14*

3427 A325 $80 Sheet of 6, #a.-f. 6.25 6.25

John Glenn's return to space — A326

1999, June 22 *Perf. 14½x14¼*

#3428: a, In space suit, 1962. b, After landing, 1962. c, As Senator. d, With helmet, 1998. e, Without helmet, 1998.

3428 A326 $100 Sheet of 5, #a.-e. 6.50 6.50

Parrots and Parakeets — A327

No. 3429: a, Hyacinth macaw. b, Blue and gold macaw. c, Blue-fronted Amazon parrot. d, Amazon parrot. e, Sun Conure. f, Tivi parakeet. g, Bavaria's conure. h, Fairy lorikeet.

No. 3430: a, Marron macaw. b, Thick-billed parrot. c, Golden-crowned canure. d, Yellow-naped macaw. e, Double yellow-headed parrot. f, Golden-fronted parakeet. g, Maroon-billed conure. h, Nandaya conure.

No. 3431, Jendaya conure, horiz. No. 3432, Gray-cheeked parakeet.

1999, Aug. 3 *Perf. 14*

Sheets of 8, #a.-h.

3429-3430 A327 $60 each 6.25 6.25

Souvenir Sheets

3431-3432 A327 $300 each 4.00 4.00

Queen Mother, 100th Birthday (in 2000) — A328

Gold frames

No. 3433: a, Duchess of York, Princess Elizabeth, 1928. b, Lady Elizabeth Bowles-Lyon, 1914. c, Queen Elizabeth, Princess Elizabeth, 1940. d, Queen Mother, Venice, 1984.

$400, Queen Mother, Canada, 1988.

1999, Aug. 4

Sheet of 4

3433 A328 $130 #a.-d. + label 7.00 7.00

Souvenir Sheet

3434 A328 $400 multicolored 5.25 5.25

No. 3434 contains one 38x50mm stamp. Margins of sheets are embossed.

See Nos. 3689-3690.

China Soccer League Superstars A329

Nos. 3435a-3435g, 3436a-3436g, Various players. Nos. 3435h, 3436h, League emblem.

1999, Aug. 16 *Perf. 14½x14¼*

3435 A329 $50 Sheet of 8, #a.-h. 5.00 5.00
3436 A329 $60 Sheet of 8, #a.-h. 6.00 6.00

A330

Rights of the Child - #3437: a, Denomination at LL, flag at UR. b, Denomination at UL, flag at LL. c, Denomination at UL, flag at UR.
$300, Prince Talal.

1999, June 22 Litho. *Perf. 14*

3437 A330 $150 Sheet of 3, #a.-c. 5.00 5.00

Souvenir Sheet

3438 A330 $300 multicolored 3.50 3.50

A331

1999, June 22 Litho. *Perf. 14*

Intl. Year of the Elderly - #3439: a, Kurt Masur. b, Rupert Murdoch. c, Margaret Thatcher. d, Pope John Paul II. e, Mikhail Gorbachev. f, Ted Turner. g, Sophia Loren. h, Nelson Mandela. i, John Glenn. j, Luciano Pavarotti. k, Queen Mother. l, Jimmy Carter.
#3440 - Ronald Reagan: a, As young man. b, In uniform. c, Feeding chimp. d, With campaign poster. e, With cowboy hat. f, With wine glass.
$300, Reagan in star.

3439 A331 $50 Sheet of 12, #a.-l. 6.75 6.75
3440 A331 $100 Sheet of 6, #a.-f. 3.50 3.50

Souvenir Sheet

3441 A331 $300 multicolored 3.50 3.50

Souvenir Sheet

Mei Lan Fang, Chinese Actor — A332

1999, Aug. 16 Litho. *Perf. 13¾*

3442 A332 $400 multicolored 4.50 4.50

First Balloon Flight Around the World — A333

No. 3443: a, Orbiter 3. b, Emblem. c, Bertrand Piccard. d, Brian Jones.
$300, Orbiter 3, flight path.

1999, Aug. 16 Litho. *Perf. 14*

3443 A333 $150 Sheet of 4, #a.-d. 6.75 6.75

Souvenir Sheet

3444 A333 $300 multicolored 3.50 3.50

The Kennedy Family A334

No. 3445: a, Jacqueline and John, Jr. b, John and John, Jr. c, John and Jacqueline. d, Jacqueline. e, John, Jr. and Caroline. f, John.
No. 3445G: h, John, Jr. as adult and child. i, John, Jr. and Jacqueline. j, John Jr.

1999, Oct. 4 Litho. *Perf. 13¾*

3445 A334 $80 Sheet of 6, #a.-f. 5.50 5.50
3445G A334 $160 Sheet of 3, #h.-j. 5.50 5.50

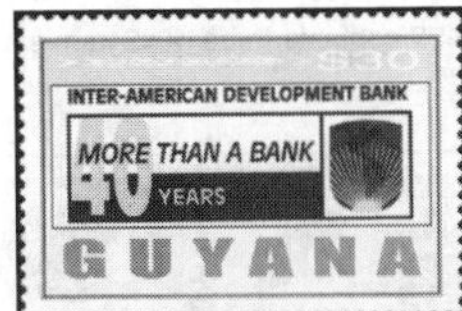

Inter-American Development Bank, 40th Anniv. — A335

1999, Nov. 15 Litho. *Perf. 14*

3446 A335 $30 multicolored .30 .30

Ferrari Automobiles — A336

$30, 312 T2. $35, 553 F.1. $60, D 50. $200, 246 F.1. $300, 126/C2. $400, 312/B2.

1999 Litho. *Perf. 14*

3447-3452 A336 Set of 6 11.50 11.50

Sidney Sheldon, Novelist — A337

1999 Litho. *Perf. 14*

3453 A337 $80 multicolored .90 .90

Issued in sheets of 4.

A338

No. 3454: a, During World War II. b, Wedding photo. c, As child. d, At coronation of George VI. e, In 1971. f, In 1991. g, in 1914. h, In 1988. i, At Royal Agricultural show. j, On 60th birthday.
$1,000, Portrait.

1999 Litho. *Perf. 12*

3454 A338 $60 Sheet of 10, #a.-j. 6.75 6.75

Imperf

Size: 51x76mm

3455 A338 $1000 multicolored 11.00 11.00

Sheets of #3454 exist with black border in margin with text "In Memoriam/1900-2002."

Queen Mother (b. 1900) — A339

Litho. & Embossed

1999, Aug. 4 *Die Cut Perf. 8¾*

3456 A339 $1500 gold & multi

Millennium A340

Highlights of the 11th Century: No. 3457, Founding of first university.
No. 3458: a, Anasazi trade center. b, "Black Virgin." c, Seljuk warrior. d, Appearance of Halley's Comet. e, Battle of Hastings. f, William of Normandy crowned King of England. g, Power of the Fujiwara is checked. h, Holy Roman Emperor Henry IV. i, Muslims build Timbuktu. j, Like No. 3457. k, Gondolas come into use in Venice. l, El Cid. m, First crusade. n, Crusaders capture Jerusalem. o, Chinese statue of Guanyin. p, Rubiayat of Omar Khayyam (60x40mm). q, Syrian storage jar.
Highlights of the 1910s - No. 3459: a, Manet and Post-impressionists show, Grafton Gallery, London. b, Standard Oil loses Supreme Court antitrust suit. c, Harriet Quimby, 1st female pilot in US d, US enters World War I. e, Titanic sinks. f, Pu Yi resigns as Chinese Emperor. g, Grand Central Station built in NYC. h, Assassination of Archduke Francis Ferdinand. i, Panama Canal opens. j, Lawrence of Arabia. k, Easter Uprising, Ireland. l, 1917 Russian Revolution. m, Execution of the Romanovs. n, Treaty of Versailles ends World War I. o, Influenza epidemic. p, Leo Tolstoy & Mark Twain die (60x40mm). q, Bauhaus opens, Weimar, Germany.

1999, Dec. 20 Litho. *Perf. 13¼x13*

3457 A340 $35 multi .40 .40

Perf. 12¾x12½

3458 A340 $35 Sheet of 17, #a.-q. 6.50 6.50
3459 A340 $35 Sheet of 17, #a.-q., + label 6.50 6.50

Flowers — A341

#3460: Various flowers making up a photomosaic of Princess Diana.
#3461: Various details of paper money of the world making up a photomosaic of George Washington's portrait on $1 bill.

1999-2000 Litho. *Perf. 13¾*

3460 A341 $80 Sheet of 8, #a.-h. 7.00 7.00
3461 A341 $80 Sheet of 8, #a.-h. 7.00 7.00

Issued: #3460, 12/31; #3461, 3/27/00.
See Nos. 3568-3569.

New Year 2000 (Year of the Dragon) — A342

No. 3462 - Dragons with denomination in: a, LR. b, LL. c, UR, d, UL.
$300, LR.

2000, Feb. 5 *Perf. 14¾*

3462 A342 $100 Sheet of 4, #a.-d. 4.50 4.50

Souvenir Sheet

3463 A342 $300 multi 3.25 3.25

A343

Automobiles — A344

No. 3464: a, Nicholas Cugnot's steam-powered Fardier, 1769. b, Siegfried Marcus's motor carriage, 1875. c, Karl Benz's Velo, 1894. d, Virgilio Bordino's steam carriage, 1854. e, 1886 Benz. f, 1908 Ford Model T.

No. 3465: a,1926 Duesenberg Model A Phaeton. b, 1927 Mercedes-Benz Model K. c, 1928, Rolls-Royce Phantom I limousine. d, 1935 Auburn 851 Speedster. e, 1936 Mercedes-Benz 540K Cabriolet B. f, 1949, Volkswagen Cabriolet Beetle.

No. 3466: a, 1957 Ford Thunderbird. b, 1957 Jaguar XK150. c, 1968 Chevrolet Corvette Stingray. d, 1973 BMW 2002 Turbo. e, 1975 Porsche 911 Turbo. f, 1999 Volkswagen Beetle.

No. 3467: a, 1886 Daimler motor car. b, 1898 Opel Luzman. c, 1899 Benz Landaulet coupe. d, 1892 Peugeot Vis-a-vis. e, 1886 Benz. f, 1894 Benz Velo, diff.

No. 3468: a, 1896 Ford. b, 1903 De Dion-Bouton Populare. c, 1900 Adler. d, 1904 Vauxhall. e, 1908 Rolls-Royce Silver Ghost. f, 1908 Ford Model T, diff.

No. 3469, 1904 Mercedes-Benz 60/70. No. 3470, 1939 Mercedes-Benz Type 320 Cabriolet. No. 3471, 1954 Mercedes-Benz 300SL Gullwing. No. 3472, 1904 Turner-Miesse. No. 3473, 1910 Runabout.

Illustrations reduced.

2000, Mar. 13 Litho. *Perf. 13½*

Sheets of 6, #a.-f.

3464-3466 A343 $100 each 6.75 6.75

Perf. 14

3467-3468 A344 $100 each 6.75 6.75

Souvenir Sheets

Perf. 14½

3469-3471 A343 $400 each 4.50 4.50

Perf. 14¼

3472-3473 A344 $400 each 4.50 4.50

Size of stamps from Nos. 3463-3466, 41x25mm; from Nos. 3467-3468, 42x28mm.

Marine Life A345

Designs: $30, Lachnolaimus maximus. $35, Cyphoma gibbosum. $60, Trachinotus falcatus. $100, Bodianus pulchellus. $200, Anisotremus virginicus. $300, Etheostoma spectabile.

No. 3480: a, Hypoplectrus indigo. b, Chlamys hastata. c, Sebastes rubrivinctus. d, Selene vomer. e, Marginella carnea. f, Phoca vitulina. g, Coryphaena hippurus. h, Epinephelus fulvus.

No. 3481: a, Sphyraena barracuda. b, Saccopharynx sp. c, Chromodoris amoena. d, Makaira nigricans. e, Orcinus orca. f, Hippocampus reidi. g, Chelonia mydas. h, Emblemaria pandionis.

No. 3482, vert.: a, Pterois volitans. b, Tursiops truncatus. c, Diplulmaris antarctica. d, Pomacanthus arcuatus. e, Aetobatus narinari. f, Carcharhinus amblyrhynchos. g, Sacura margaritacea. h, Octopus dolfeini.

No. 3483, Asteroschema tenue, vert. No. 3484, Apodichthys flavidus, vert. No. 3485, Periclimenes pedersoni.

2000, May 15 *Perf. 14*

3474-3479 A345 Set of 6 8.00 8.00

Sheets of 8, #a.-h.

3480-3482 A345 $80 each 7.00 7.00

Souvenir Sheets

3483-3485 A345 $400 each 4.50 4.50

No. 3485 contains one 57x42mm stamp.

Souvenir Sheet of 2

1999 Return of Macao to People's Republic of China — A346

No. 3486: a, Flag. b, Skyline.
Illustration reduced.

2000, May 15

3486 A346 $150 #a.-b. 3.50 3.50

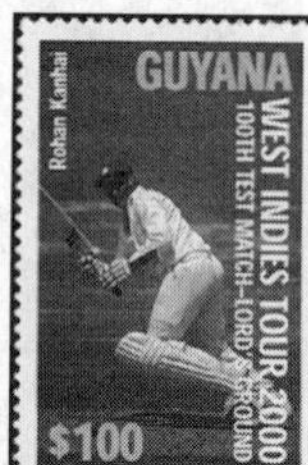

100th Test Match at Lord's Ground — A347

$100, Rohan Kanhai. $300, Clive Lloyd. $400, Lord's Ground, horiz.

2000, May 15 Litho. *Perf. 14*

3487-3488 A347 Set of 2 4.50 4.50

Souvenir Sheet

3489 A347 $400 multi 4.50 4.50

Prince William, 18th Birthday — A348

No. 3490: a, With Prince Harry. b, Wearing sweater. c, In profile. d, In suit.
$400, In ski wear.
Illustration reduced.

2000, May 15 *Perf. 14*

3490 A348 $100 Sheet of 4, #a-d 4.50 4.50

Souvenir Sheet

Perf. 13¾

3491 A348 $400 multi 4.50 4.50

No. 3490 contains four 28x42mm stamps. It exists imperf.

First Zeppelin Flight, Cent. — A349

No. 3492 - Ferdinand von Zeppelin and: a, LZ-1. b, LZ-2. c, LZ-9.
$400, LZ-127.

2000, May 15 *Perf. 14*

3492 A349 $200 Sheet of 3, #a-c 6.75 6.75

Souvenir Sheet

3493 A349 $400 multi 4.50 4.50

No. 3492 contains three 40x24mm stamps.

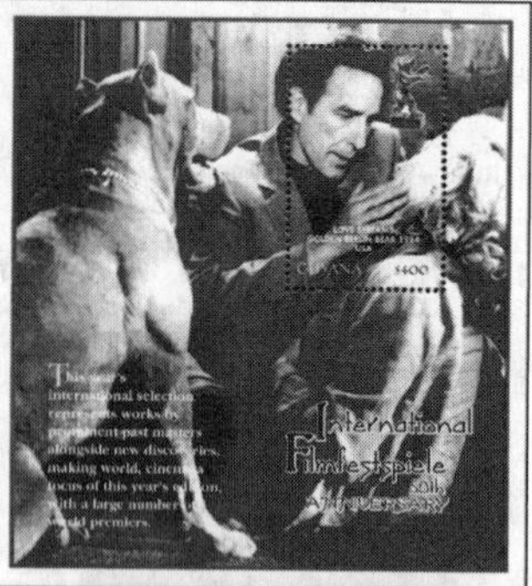

Berlin Film Festival, 50th Anniv. — A350

No. 3494: a, Das Boot Ist Voll. b, David. c, Hong Gao Liang (Red Sorghum). d, Die Ehe der Maria Braun. e, Edith Evans. f, Michel Simon.
$400, Love Streams.
Illustration reduced.

2000, May 15

3494 A350 $100 Sheet of 6, #a-f 6.75 6.75

Souvenir Sheet

3495 A350 $400 multi 4.50 4.50

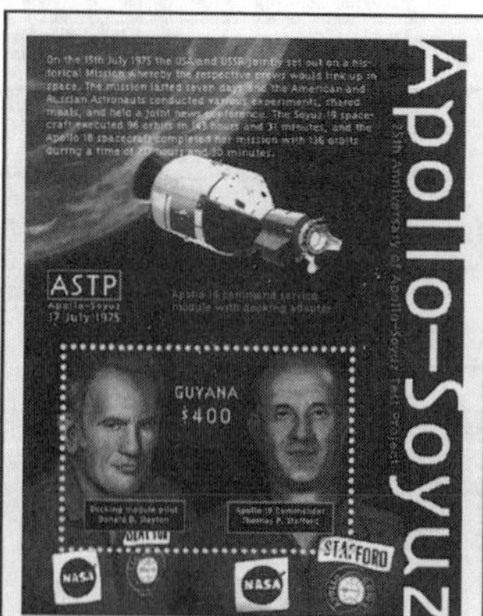

Apollo-Soyuz Mission, 25th Anniv. — A351

No. 3496: a, Vance D. Brand, Thomas P. Stafford. b, Apollo 18, docking adapter. c, Stafford, Valeri Kubasov.
$400, Stafford, Donald K. Slayton.
Illustration reduced.

2000, May 15

3496 A351 $200 Sheet of 3, #a-c 6.75 6.75

Souvenir Sheet

3497 A351 $400 multi 4.50 4.50

Souvenir Sheets

2000 Summer Olympics, Sydney — A352

No. 3498: a, Henry Robert Pearce. b, Volleyball. c, Olympic Park, Montreal, and Canadian flag. d, Ancient Greek runners.
Illustration reduced.

2000, May 15

3498 A352 $160 Sheet of 4, #a-d 7.25 7.25

Public Railways, 175th Anniv. — A353

No. 3499: a, Timothy Hackworth. b, Sans Pareil. c, Branhope Tunnel.
Illustration reduced.

2000, May 15

3499 A353 $200 Sheet of 3, #a-c 6.75 6.75

Johann Sebastian Bach (1685-1750) — A354

Illustration reduced.

2000, May 15

3500 A354 $400 multi 4.50 4.50

Souvenir Sheet

Albert Einstein (1879-1955) — A355

Illustration reduced.

2000, May 15 Litho. *Perf. 14¼*
3501 A355 $400 multi 4.50 4.50

Space — A356

No. 3502, $100: a, Amsat IIIc. b, SRET. c, Inspector. d, Stardust. e, Temisat. f, Arsene.
No. 3503, $100, horiz.: a, Sun and Echo satellite (inscribed Apollo 11). b, Saturn, and-Pioneer. c, Moon and Apollo 11 (inscribed Echo satellite). d, Mars and Mars Explorer. e, Space Shuttle, Intl. Space Station. f, Halley's Comet and Giotto.
No. 3504, $100, horiz.: a, Cesar, Argentine, Spanish flags. b, Sirio 2, Italian flag. c, Taos S.80, French flag. d, Viking, Swedish flag. e, SCD 1, Brazilian flag. f, Offeq 1, Israeli flag.
No. 3505, $400, Clementine. No. 3506, $400, Solar Max, horiz.
Illustration reduced.

2000, May 15 Litho. *Perf. 14*
Sheets of 6, #a-f
3502-3504 A356 Set of 3 20.00 20.00
Souvenir Sheets
3505-3506 A356 Set of 2 9.00 9.00

World Stamp Expo 2000, Anaheim.

The Three Stooges — A357

No. 3507: a, Shemp, Moe, Larry, man with glasses. b, Skeleton, Larry, Moe. c, Shemp. d, Stooges with fingers in mouths. e, Stooges reading book. f, Stooges attacking man. g, Stooges with candle. h, Stooges, man, fire bucket. i, Moe, Shemp, man in window.
No. 3508, $400, Moe in doorway. No. 3509, $400, Larry, skeleton.
Illustration reduced.

2000, July 27 *Perf. 13¾*
3507 A357 $80 Sheet of 9, #a-i 8.00 8.00
Souvenir Sheets
3508-3509 A357 Set of 2 9.00 9.00

See Nos. 3542-3544.

Betty Boop — A358

No. 3510: a, In striped blouse. b, With shopping bags. c, On cushion. d, As belly dancer. e, In red lingerie. f, In cutoff shorts. g, With musical notes. h, In flowered pants. i, In black dress.
No. 3511, $400, In fur coat. No. 3512, $400, In polka dot bathing suit, with flamingos.
Illustration reduced.

2000, July 27 *Perf. 13¾*
3510 A358 $80 Sheet of 9, #a-i 8.00 8.00
Souvenir Sheets
3511-3512 A358 Set of 2 9.00 9.00

See Nos. 3545-3552.

Third Annual Caribbean Media Conference A359

2000, Aug. 14 *Perf. 14*
3513 A359 $100 multi 1.10 1.10

European Soccer Championships — A360

No. 3514, $80, horiz.: a, Denmark. b, Germany. c, Italy. d, Netherlands. e, Portugal. f, Romania. g, Czech Republic. h, Norway.
No. 3515, $80, horiz.: a, Turkey. b, Slovenia. c, Yugoslavia. d, Sweden. e, Belgium. f, Spain. g, France. h, England.
No. 3516, $400, Jurgen Klinsmann. No. 3517, $400, Stefan Kuntz.
Illustration reduced.

2000, Aug. 21 *Perf. 13¾*
Sheets of 8, #a-h, + label
3514-3515 A360 Set of 2 14.00 14.00
Souvenir Sheets
3516-3517 A360 Set of 2 9.00 9.00

Mushrooms — A361

No. 3518, $100, horiz.: a, Sealy vase chanterelle. b, Caesar's mushroom. c, Green-headed jelly club. d, Salmon unicorn entoloma. e, White oysterette. f, Variable cort.
No. 3519, $100, horiz.: a, Coccora. b, Winter polypore. c, Turpentine waxy cap. d, Aerdyginosa. e, Fly agaric. f, Honey mushroom.
No. 3520, $100, horiz: a, Salmon waxy cap. b, Shellfish-scented russula. c, Scarlet waxy cap. d, Stuntz's blue legs. e, Netted rhodotus. f, Indigo milky.
No. 3521, $400, Tiny volvariella. No. 3522, $400, Turkey tail, horiz. No. 3523, $400, Pinwheel marasmius, horiz.
Illustration reduced.

2000, Oct. 4 *Perf. 14*
Sheets of 6, #a-f
3518-3520 A361 Set of 3 20.00 20.00
Souvenir Sheets
3521-3523 A361 Set of 3 13.50 13.50

The Stamp Show 2000, London.

A362

Flowers — A363

Designs: No. 3524, $35, Bougainvillea spectabilis. No. 3525, $60, Euphorbia milii. No. 3526, $200, Catharanthus roseus. No. 3527, $300, Ipomoea carnea.
No. 3528, $35, Russelia equisetiformis. No. 3529, $60, Sprekelia formosissima. No. 3530, $200, Passiflora quadrangularis. No. 3531, $300, Mirabilis jalapa.
No. 3532, $100: a, Lantana camara. b, Jatropha integerrima. c, Plumeria alba. d, Strelitzia reginae. e, Clerodendrum splendens. f, Thunbergia grandiflora.
No. 3533, $100, vert.: a, Cordia sebestena. b, Heliconia wagneriana. c, Dendrobium phalaenopsis. d, Passiflora caerulea. e, Oncidium nubigenum. f, Hibiscus rosa-sinensis.
No. 3534, $100: a, Ipomoea tricolor. b, Lantana camara (inscribed canara). c, Cantua buxifolia. d, Fuchsia. e, Eichornia crassipes. f, Cosmos sulphureus.
No. 3535, $100: a, Bignonia capreolata. b, Calceolaria herbeo-hybrida. c, Canna generalis. d, Bauhinia grandiflora. e, Amaranthus caudatus. f, Abutilon megapotamicum.
No. 3536, $400, Guzmania lingulata. No. 3537, $400, Cattleya granulosa, vert.
No. 3538, $400, Tacsonia van-volxemii. No. 3539, $400, Oeceoclades maculata.

2000, Oct. 30 *Perf. 14*
3524-3527 A362 Set of 4 6.75 6.75
3528-3531 A363 Set of 4 6.75 6.75
Sheets of 6, #a-f
3532-3533 A362 Set of 2 13.50 13.50
3534-3535 A363 Set of 2 13.50 13.50
Souvenir Sheets
3536-3537 A362 Set of 2 9.00 9.00
3538-3539 A363 Set of 2 9.00 9.00

Munich Olympics Massacre — A364

No. 3540: a, Yaakov Springer. b, Andrei Schpitzer. c, Amitsur Shapira. d, David Berger. e, Ze'ev Friedman. f, Joseph Gottfreund. g, Moshe Weinberg. h, Kahat Shor. i, Mark Slavin. j, Eliezer Halefin. k, Joseph Romano. l, Poster of Munich Olympics.
Illustration reduced.

2000, Oct. 30
3540 A364 $40 Sheet of 12, #a-l 5.25 5.25
Souvenir Sheet
3541 A364 $400 Torch bearer 4.50 4.50

Three Stooges Type of 2000

No. 3542: a, Moe with seltzer bottle, Shemp, Larry. b, As cave men trying to break rock. c, Moe with cow. d, Two women, Shemp, Moe. e, As cave men, seated. f, As cave men, Shemp holding large rock. g, Stooges wearing pith helmets. h, Stooges, picture frames. i, Stooges with fake beards.
No. 3543, $400, Larry, woman, vert. No. 3544, $400, Moe in plaid shirt, vert.

2000, July 27 Litho. *Perf. 13¾*
3542 A357 $80 Sheet of 9, #a-i 8.00 8.00
Souvenir Sheets
3543-3544 A357 Set of 2 9.00 9.00

Betty Boop Type of 2000
Souvenir Sheets

#3545, At football field. #3546, With tennis racquet. #3547, With ankh earrings, winking. #3548, With red swimsuit. #3549, As portrait of queen. #3550, As Can-can girl. #3551, Standing on shell. #3552, As Mona Lisa, horiz.

2000, July 27
3545-3552 A358 $400 Set of 8 36.00 36.00

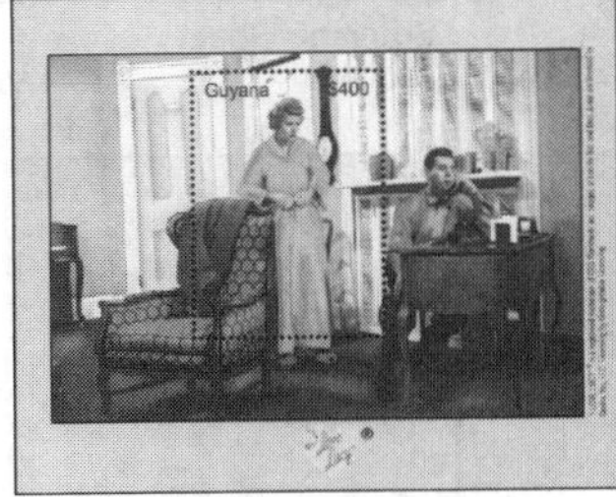

I Love Lucy — A365

No. 3553: a, Lucy reading book. b, Ricky, Lucy with book. c, Ricky kissing Lucy. d, Lucy near window. e, Lucy grabbing Ethel. f, Ricky holding scarf, Lucy in bed. g, Ethel, Lucy, frying pan. h, Ricky with frying pan. i, Lucy, Ethel, coffee table.
No. 3554, $400, Lucy in pink robe. No. 3555, $400, Lucy with garbage can lid.
Illustration reduced.

2000, July 27

3553 A365 $60 Sheet of 9, #a-i 6.00 6.00

Souvenir Sheets

3554-3555 A365 Set of 2 9.00 9.00

FIN. K. L — A366

No. 3556: a, Lee Hyo-Ri. b, Ok Ju-Hyun. c, Lee Jin. d, Lee Jin. e, Group. f, Sung Yu-Ri. g, Lee Hyo-Ri. h, Sung Yu-Ri. i, Ok Ju-Hyun. #d, f, i, full color, others, sepia tone.

2000, Sept. 7 ***Perf. 13½***

3556 A366 $80 Sheet of 9, #a-i 8.00 8.00

Queen Mother, 100th Birthday — A367

2000, Dec. 1 ***Perf. 14***

3557 A367 $100 multi 1.10 1.10

Printed in sheets of 6.

Christmas — A368

$60, #3562b, Heads of 2 angels, org background. $90, #3562a, 2 full angels, bl background. $120, #3562c, Heads of 2 angels, bl background. #3561, $400, #3562d, 2 full angels, org background.

No. 3563, Baby Jesus, horiz.

2000, Dec. 18

3558-3561 A368 Set of 4 7.50 7.50

3562 A368 $180 Sheet of 4, #a-d 8.00 8.00

Souvenir Sheet

3563 A368 $400 multi 4.50 4.50

New Year 2001 (Year of the Snake) — A369

No. 3564: a, Green snake head. b, Red snake head. c, Blue snake head. d, Yellow snake head.

$250, Purple snake head, vert.

Illustration reduced.

2001, Jan. 2 Litho. ***Perf. 13½x13***

3564 A369 $80 Sheet of 4, #a-d 3.50 3.50

Souvenir Sheet

Perf. 13x13½

3565 A369 $250 multi 2.75 2.75

Tourist Attractions — A370

Designs: No. 3566, $90, Prime Minister's residence. No. 3567, $90, Kaiteur Falls, vert.

2001, Jan. 30 ***Perf. 13¼***

3566-3567 A370 Set of 2 2.00 2.00

Flower Photomosaic Type of 1999

No. 3568, $80: Various photographs of flowers making up a photomosaic of the Queen Mother.

No. 3569, $100: Various photographs of religious sites making up a photomosaic of Pope John Paul II.

2001, Feb. 13 ***Perf. 13¾***

Sheets of 8, #a-h

3568-3569 A341 Set of 2 16.00 16.00

Souvenir Sheet

Chow Yun-Fat, Actor — A371

Background color: a, Blue green. b, Dark red. c, Olive brown. d, Red violet. e, Dark blue. f, Purple.

2001, Feb. 13 ***Perf. 13¾x13¼***

3570 A371 $60 Sheet of 6, #a-f 4.00 4.00

Pokémon — A372

No. 3571: a, Staryu. b, Seaking. c, Tentacool. d, Magikarp. e, Seadra. f, Goldeen.

Illustration reduced.

2001, Feb. 13 ***Perf. 13¾***

3571 A372 $100 Sheet of 6, #a-f 6.75 6.75

Souvenir Sheet

3572 A372 $400 Horsea 4.50 4.50

Betty Boop Type of 2000

Designs: No. 3573, $400, In pink hat. No. 3574, $400, As singer on stage. No. 3575, $400, With red top and necklace, on beach. No. 3576, $400, In orange and black hat, horiz.

2001 ? Litho. ***Perf. 13¾***

3573-3576 A358 Set of 4 18.00 18.00

I Love Lucy Type of 2000

Designs: No. 3577, $400, Dressed like Carmen Miranda. No. 3578, $400, With blue hat and gloves. No. 3579, $400, As knife thrower's target. No. 3580, $400, At table, wearing blue hat. No. 3581, $400, Wearing glasses with thick black frames.

2001 ?

3577-3581 A365 Set of 5 22.50 22.50

A373

A374

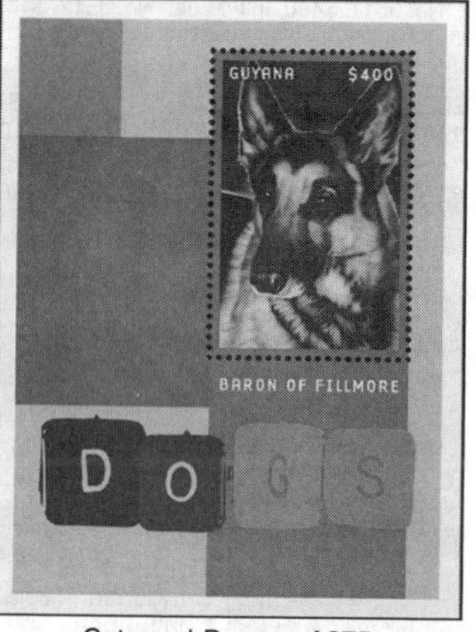

Cats and Dogs — A375

Designs: No. 3582, $35, Boxer. No. 3583, $60, Cinnamon ocicat. No. 3584, $100, Smooth dachshund. $300, White Manx.

No. 3586, $35, Chihuahua. No. 3587, $60, Persian tabby. No. 3588, $100, Colorpoint shorthair. $200, Cocker spaniel.

No. 3590 - Names of dogs (border color and location of denomination), $100: a, Pup (pink, bottom). b, Yogi (orange, bottom). c, Hooch (yellow, bottom) d, Huxley Blu (orange, top) e, Snowflake (yellow, top). f, Red (pink, top).

No. 3591 - Names of cats (border color and location of denomination), $100: a, Tom (orange, bottom). b, Puff (yellow, bottom). c, Jag (pink, bottom). d, Fritz (yellow, top). e, Smokey (pink, top). f, Thor, (orange, top).

No. 3592, $60: a, Devon rex. b, Egyptian mau. c, Turkish angora. d, Sphynx. e, Persian. f, American wirehair. g, Exotic shorthair. h, American curl.

No. 3593, $80: a, Airedale terrier. b, Greyhound. c, Afghan hound. d, Samoyed. e, Field spaniel. f, Scottish terrier. g, Brittany spaniel. h, Boston terrier.

No. 3594, $80: a, American shorthair. b, Somali. c, Singapura. d, Balinese. e, Egyptian mau. f, Scottish fold. g, Sphynx. h, Korat.

No. 3595, $80: a, Rottweiler. b, German shepherd. c, Bernese mountain dog. d, Sharpei. e, Dachshund. f, Jack Russell terrier. g, Boston terrier. h, Welsh corgi.

No. 3596, $400, Dalmatian. No. 3597, $400, Birman. No. 3598, $400, Abyssinian. No. 3599, $400, Beagle. No. 3600, $400, German shepeherd named Baron of Fillmore. No. 3601, $400, Cat named Spike.

2001, Mar. 1 ***Perf. 14***

3582-3585 A373 Set of 4 5.50 5.50

3586-3589 A374 Set of 4 4.50 4.50

Sheets of 6, #a-f

3590-3591 A375 Set of 2 13.50 13.50

Sheets of 8, #a-h

3592-3593 A373 Set of 2 12.50 12.50

3594-3595 A374 Set of 2 14.00 14.00

Souvenir Sheets

3596-3597 A373 Set of 2 9.00 9.00

3598-3599 A374 Set of 2 9.00 9.00

3600-3601 A375 Set of 2 9.00 9.00

Hong Kong 2001 Stamp Exhibition (Nos. 3592-3593, 3596-3597).

Souvenir Sheets

Hello Kitty — A376

Western children's stories with Hello Kitty characters: No. 3602, $400, Cinderella. No. 3603, $400, The Wizard of Oz. No. 3604, $400, Little Red Riding Hood. No. 3605, $400, Peter Pan. No. 3606, $400, Heidi. No. 3607, $400, Alice in Wonderland.

Oriental children's stories with Hello Kitty characters: No. 3608, $400, The Fishermen. No. 3609, $400, In the Snow. No. 3610, $400, Bamboo Princess. No. 3611, $400, Three in a Boat. No. 3612, $400, Up a Tree. No. 3613, $400, On a Bear.

2001, Mar. 28 Litho. ***Perf. 13¾***

3602-3613 A376 Set of 12 52.50 52.50

Phila Nippon '01, Japan — A377

Designs: No. 3614, $25, Hanaogi with Maidservant, by Choki Eishosai. No. 3615, $25, Girl at a Hot Spring Resort, by Goyo Hashiguchi. No. 3616, $30, Morokoshi of the Echizenya, by Eiri Rekisentei. No. 3617, $30, Courtesan Receiving Letter of Invitation, by Harunobu Suzuki. No. 3618, $35, Two Girls on Their Way to or from the Bathhouse, by Suzuki. No. 3619, $35, Mother and Daughter on an Outing, by Hokusai. No. 3620, $60, Matron in Love, by Utamaro. No. 3621, $60, Girl and Frog, by Suzuki. No. 3622, $100, The Courtesan Midorigi, by Eisho Chokosai. No. 3623, $100, Three Beauties of High Fame, by Utamaro. No. 3624, $200, Maiko, by Bakusen Tsuchida. No. 3625, $200, Girl Breaking Off the Branch of a Flowering Tree, by Suzuki.

No. 3626 - Paintings by Jakuchu Ito (28x84mm): a, Insects, Reptiles and Amphibians at a Pond. b, Rose Mallows and Fowl. c, Rooster, Sunflower and Morning Glories. d, A Group of Roosters. e, Black Rooster and Nandina. f, Birds and Autumn Maples. g, Wagtail and Roses. h, Cockatoos in a Pine.

No. 3627 - Predominate features of sections of Procession to the Shugakuin Imperial Villa, by Sesshin Kakimoto (28x84mm): a, Bridge. b, High mountain, road and bridge. c, Large tree in foreground. d, Small island in foreground. e, Building at bottom. f, Building and large tree at bottom.

No. 3628 - Paintings of Women (28x84mm): a, Girls After the Bath, by Utamaro. b, Summer Evening on the Riverbank at Hama-cho, by Kiyonaga Torii. c, A Beauty in the Wind, by Ando Kaigetsudo. d, Sisters by Kako Tsuji. e, Kasamori Osen, by Suzuki.

No. 3629 - Details from Ichikawa Ebizo, by Sharaku Toshusai (30x38mm): a, Top of screen. b, Man with red kimono. c, Man with stringed instrument. e, Man on chair.

No. 3630, $400, Portrait of Senseki Takami, by Kazan Watanabe. No. 3631, $400, Fish and Octopus From the Colorful Realm of Living Beings, by Ito. No. 3632, $400, Woman Holding a Flower, by Hisako Kajiwara, horiz. No. 3633, $400, Palace of Immortals in an Autumn Valley, by Yako Okochi, horiz. No. 3634, $400, Wintry Sky, by Hosen Higashibara, horiz.

2001, June 18 ***Perf. 14***

3614-3625 A377 Set of 12 10.00 10.00
3626 A377 $80 Sheet of 8, #a-h 7.00 7.00
3627 A377 $100 Sheet of 6, #a-f 6.75 6.75
3628 A377 $120 Sheet of 5, #a-e 6.75 6.75
3629 A377 $160 Sheet of 4, #a-d 7.00 7.00

Sizes: 90x120mm, 120x90mm

Imperf

3630-3634 A377 Set of 5 22.50 22.50

Giuseppe Verdi (1813-1901), Opera Composer — A378

No. 3635: a, Verdi, score at LR. b, Actor, score from Rigoletto. c, Actor, score from Ernani. d, Verdi, scores at left.
$400, Verdi and scores.

2001, June 18 ***Perf. 14***

3635 A378 $160 Sheet of 4, #a-d 7.00 7.00

Souvenir Sheet

3636 A378 $400 multi 4.50 4.50

Toulouse-Lautrec Paintings — A379

No. 3637, horiz.: a, Maurice Joyant in the Baie de Somme. b, Monsieur Boileau. c, Monsieur, Madame and the Dog.
$300, Man from Monsieur, Madame and the Dog.

2001, June 18 ***Perf. 13¾***

3637 A379 $160 Sheet of 3, #a-c 5.25 5.25

Souvenir Sheet

3638 A379 $300 multi 3.25 3.25

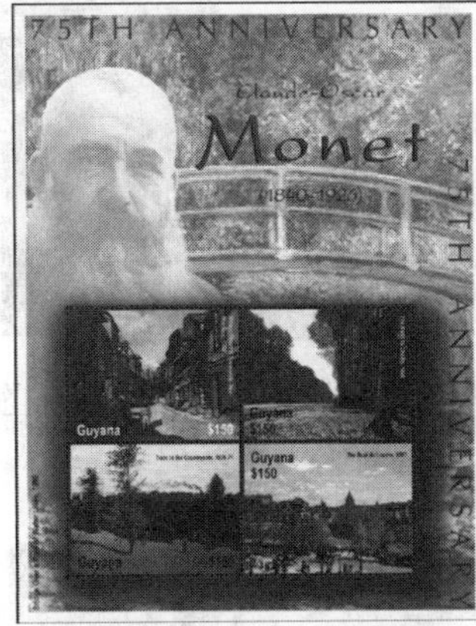

Monet Paintings — A380

No. 3639, horiz.: a, Village Street in Normandy, Near Honfleur. b, The Road to Chailly. c, Train in the Countryside. d, The Quai du Louvre.
$400, Flowering Garden.

2001, June 18

3639 A380 $150 Sheet of 4, #a-d 6.75 6.75

Souvenir Sheet

3640 A380 $400 multi 4.50 4.50

Queen Victoria (1819-1901) — A381

Pictures of Victoria from - No. 3641, $200: a, 1829. b, 1837. c, 1840. d, 1897 (with crown).
No. 3642, $200: a, 1850. b, 1843. c, 1859. d, 1897 (with hat).
No. 3643, $400, 1885 (with crown). No. 3644, $400, Undated.

2001, June 18 ***Perf. 14***

Sheets of 4, #a-d

3641-3642 A381 Set of 2 18.00 18.00

Souvenir Sheets

3643-3644 A381 Set of 2 9.00 9.00

Queen Elizabeth II, 75th Birthday — A382

No. 3645: a, Pink hat. b, Red hat. c, White hat. d, Tiara.

2001, June 18 ***Perf. 14***

3645 A382 $150 Sheet of 4, #a-d 6.75 6.75

Souvenir Sheet

Perf. 13¾

3646 A382 $400 shown 4.50 4.50

No. 3645 contains four 28x42mm stamps.

Photomosaic of Queen Elizbeth II — A383

2001, June 18 ***Perf. 14***

3647 A383 $80 multi .90 .90

Printed in sheets of 8, with and without inscription reading "In Celebration of the 50th Anniversary of H.M. Queen Elizabeth II's Accession to the Throne."

Flower Photomosaic Type of 1999-2000

No. 3648: Various pictures of American scenes making up a photomosaic of Pres. John F. Kennedy.

2001, June 18

3648 A341 $80 Sheet of 8, #a-h 7.00 7.00

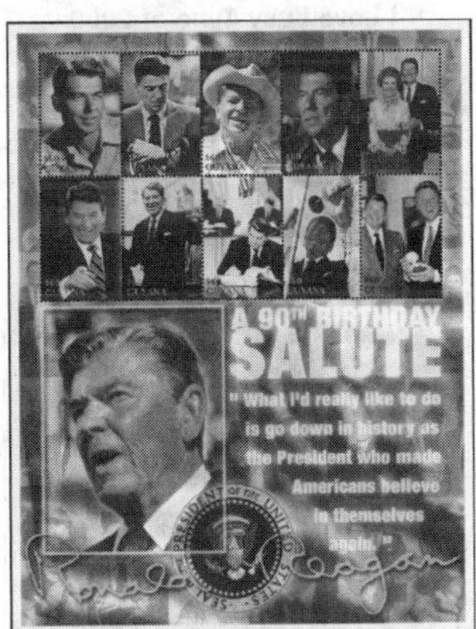

Pres. Ronald Reagan — A384

Reagan: a, In checked shirt. b, With Bonzo. c, With cowboy hat. d, With dark tie. e, With wife, Nancy. f, With striped tie. g, Waving. h, Signing treaty with Mikhail Gorbachev. i, With hammer and chisel. j, With Pres. Clinton.

2001, June 18

3649 A384 $60 Sheet of 10, #a-j 6.75 6.75

Betty Boop Type of 2000

Designs: No. 3650, $400, With swimsuit and sunglasses. No. 3651, $400, With lilac headdress. No. 3652, $400, With purple top and pirate's hat. No. 3653, $400, Dancing on radio, horiz.

2001 ***Perf. 13¾***

3650-3653 A358 Set of 4 18.00 18.00

Betty Boop Type of 2000

Designs: No. 3654, $400, In orange and yellow polka dot swimsuit, holding gift. No. 3655, $400, Holding on to anchor. No. 3556, $400, In red bikini, surfing. No. 3557, $400, Wearing birthday hat, horiz.

2001 **Litho.** ***Perf. 13¾***

3654-3657 A358 Set of 4 18.00 18.00

Historical Events Type of 1997

No. 3658: a, Securities and Exchange Commission formed, 1934. b, Herbert Hoover is elected president, 1928. c, The Jazz Singer is first talking movie, 1927. d, J. Edgar Hoover becomes director of FBI, 1924. e, Alexander Fleming discovers penicillin, 1928. f, FCC established to regulate broadcasting, 1934. g, Lindbergh becomes first to fly solo across Atlantic, 1927. h, Albert Einstein is awarded Nobel Prize for Physics, 1921. i, Hindenburg dies and Hitler becomes German Führer, 1934. j, Social Security Act provides safety for Americans, 1935. k, Earhart is first to fly solo from Hawaii to California, 1935. l, Marcus Garvey's prison sentence is commuted, 1927.

2001, Mar. 28 ***Perf. 14¼x14¾***

3658 A289 $60 Sheet of 12, #a-l 8.00 8.00

Prehistoric Animals — A385

Designs: $20, Allosaurus. $30, Spinosaurus. $35, Pteranodon. $60, Cetiosaurus. $200, Archaeopteryx. $300, Parasaurolophus.
No. 3665, $100, horiz.: a, Alamosaurus. b, Archaeopteryx, diff. c, Pachycephalosaurus. d, Parasaurolophus, diff. e, Edmontosaurus. f, Triceratops.
No. 3666, $100, horiz.: a, Brachiosaurus and two palm trees. b, Dimorphodon. c, Coelophysis. d, Velociraptor. e, Antrodemus. f, Euparkeria.
No. 3667, $100, horiz.: a, Ichthyostega. b, Eryops. c, Ichthyosaur. d, Pliosaur. e, Dunklosteus. f, Eogyrinus.
No. 3668, $100, horiz.: a, Brachiosaurus and palm tree. b, Pteranodon, diff. c, Compsognathus. d, Corythosaurus. e, Allosaurus, diff. f, Torosaurus.
No. 3669, $400, Brachiosaurus, diff. No. 3670, $400, Torosaurus, diff., horiz. No. 3671, $400, Ichthyosaur, diff., horiz. No. 3672, $400, Pteranodon, diff., horiz.

2001, Oct. 15 ***Perf. 14***

3659-3664 A385 Set of 6 7.25 7.25

Sheets of 6, #a-f

3665-3668 A385 Set of 4 27.50 27.50

Souvenir Sheets

3669-3672 A385 Set of 4 18.00 18.00

Vegaspex (#3665-3672).

Animals of Tropical Rainforests A386

Designs: $35, Mandrill, vert. $100, Leaf cutting ants.
No. 3675, $80: a, Elephant. b, Impala. c, Leopard. d, Gray parrot. e, Hippopotamus. f, Pygmy chimp. g, African green python. h, Mountain gorilla.
No. 3676, $80: a, Three-toed sloth. b, Lion tamarin. c, Ringtail lemur. d, Sugar glider. e, Toucan. f, Trogons. g, Pygmy marmoset. h, Poison arrow frog.
No. 3677, $400, Tapir, vert. No. 3678, $400, Sable antelope, vert.

2001, Oct. 15

3673-3674 A386 Set of 2 1.50 1.50

Sheets of 8, #a-h

3675-3676 A386 Set of 2 14.50 14.50

Souvenir Sheets

3677-3678 A386 Set of 2 9.00 9.00

Tropical Birds — A387

No. 3679, $100, horiz.: a, Rainbow lorikeet. b, King bird of paradise. c, Yellow-chevroned parakeet. d, Masked lovebird. e, Scarlet ibis. f, Toco toucan.

No. 3680, $100, horiz.: a, Hyacinth macaw. b, Wire-tailed manakin. c, Scarlet macaw. d, Sun parakeet. e, Roseate spoonbill. f, Red-billed toucan.

No. 3681, $400, Eclectus parrot. No. 3682, $400, Sulfur-crested cockatoo.

2001, Oct. 15 Litho.

Sheets of 6, #a-f

3679-3680 A387 Set of 2 13.50 13.50

Souvenir Sheets

3681-3682 A387 Set of 2 9.00 9.00

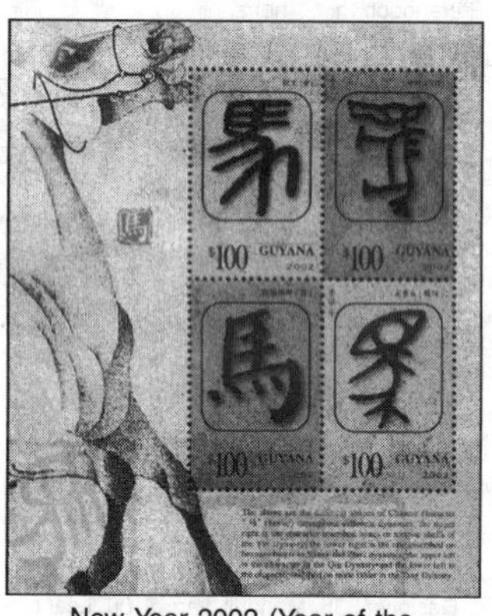

New Year 2002 (Year of the Horse) — A388

No. 3683 - Evolution of Chinese character for "horse": a, Two characters outside, one character inside parentheses at UR. b, Three characters outside, one character inside parentheses at UR. c, Four characters outside, one character inside parentheses at UR. d, Three characters outside, two characters inside parentheses at UR.

No. 3684 - Figure on horse: a, Denomination at UL. b, Denomination at UR.

2001, Oct. 15 *Perf. 13*

3683 A388 $100 Sheet of 4, #a-d 4.50 4.50

Perf. 13¼

3684 A388 $150 Sheet of 2, #a-b 3.50 3.50

No. 3684 contains two 38x50mm stamps.

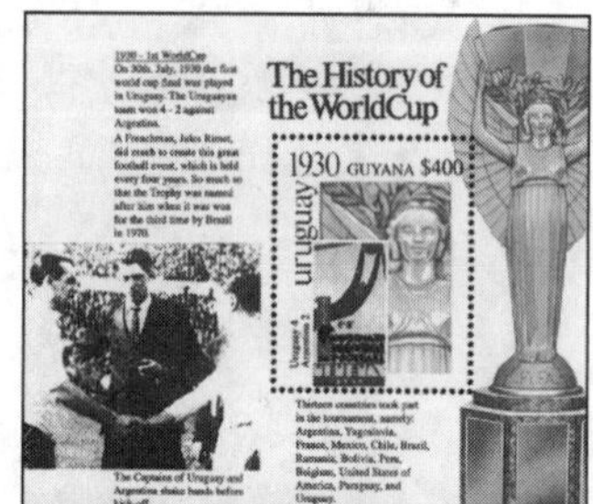

2002 World Cup Soccer Championships, Japan and Korea — A389

No. 3685, $100 - Posters from: a, 1950, and player. b, 1954, and Jules Rimet. c, 1958, Pelé and teammates. d, 1962, and Zito scoring goal. e, 1966, and English players celebrating. f, 1970, and Jairzinho.

No. 3686, $100 - Posters from: a, 1978, and Daniel Passarella. b, 1982, and Paolo Rossi. c, 1986, and Diego Maradona. d, 1990, and German players celebrating. e, 1994, and Brazilian players celebrating. f, 1998, and Zinedine Zidane.

No. 3687, $400, 1930 poster, head from Jules Rimet Trophy. No. 3688, $400, Head and globe from World Cup trophy.

2001, Dec. 26 *Perf. 13¾x14¼*

Sheets of 6, #a-f

3685-3686 A389 Set of 2 13.50 13.50

Souvenir Sheets

Perf. 14¼

3687-3688 A389 Set of 2 9.00 9.00

Queen Mother Type of 1999 Redrawn

No. 3689: a, With Princess Elizabeth, 1928. b, Lady Elizabeth-Bowles Lyon, 1914. c, With Princess Elizabeth, 1950. d, In Venice, 1984. $400, In Canada, 1988.

2001, Dec. *Perf. 14*

Yellow Orange Frames

3689 A328 $130 Sheet of 4, #a-d, + label 5.75 5.75

Souvenir Sheet

Perf. 13¾

3690 A328 $400 multi 4.50 4.50

Queen Mother's 101st birthday. No. 3690 contains one 38x50mm stamp with a bluer cast than that found on No. 3434. Sheet margins of Nos. 3689-3690 lack embossing and gold arms and frames found on Nos. 3433-3434.

I Love Lucy Type of 2000

Souvenir Sheets

Designs: No. 3691, $400, Lucy wearing leis, with hands up. No. 3692, $400, Lucy with checked shirt and apron, with mouth open.

2001 ? *Perf. 13¾*

3691-3692 A365 Set of 2 9.00 9.00

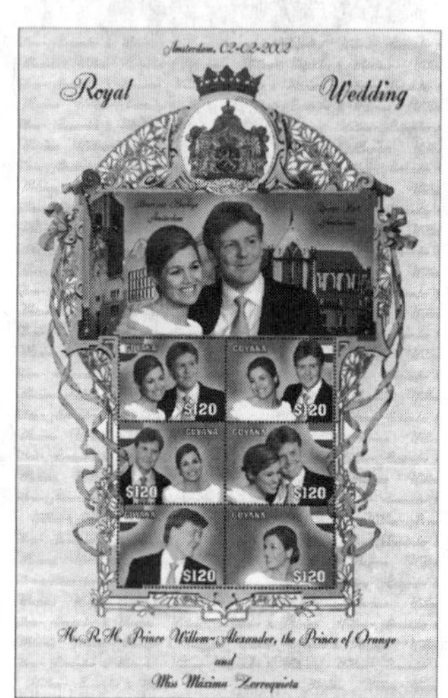

Wedding of Netherlands Prince Willem-Alexander and Máxima Zorreguieta — A390

No. 3693: a, Couple (Máxima at left), flag colors at left. b, Couple (heads apart), flag colors at right. c, Couple (Máxima at right), flag colors at left. d, Couple (heads together), flag colors at right. e, Willem-Alexander. f, Máxima.

2002, Jan. 7 Litho. *Perf. 14¾x14¼*

3693 A390 $120 Sheet of 6, #a-f 8.00 8.00

United We Stand — A391

2002, Feb. 6 *Perf. 13½x13¼*

3694 A391 $200 multi 2.25 2.25

Printed in sheets of four.

Reign of Queen Elizabeth II, 50th Anniv. — A392

No. 3695: a, Blue hat. b, Feathered hat. c, Waving. d, With horse at right. $400, With horse at left.

2002, Feb. 6 *Perf. 14½*

3695 A392 $150 Sheet of 4, #a-d 6.75 6.75

Souvenir Sheet

3696 A392 $400 multi 4.50 4.50

Flower Photomosaic Type of 1999-2000

No. 3697: Various science photographs making up a photomosaic of Albert Einstein.

2002, Feb. 25 *Perf. 13¾*

3697 A341 $80 Sheet of 8, #a-h 7.25 7.25

Nobel Prizes, Cent. (in 2001) — A393

No. 3698, $100 - Chemistry laureates: a, Harold C. Urey, 1934. b, Willard F. Libby, 1960. c, Frederick Sanger, 1958 and 1980. d, Theodor Svedberg, 1926. e, Cyril N. Hinshelwood, 1956. f, Nikolai Semenov, 1956.

No. 3699, $100: a, Alexander Todd, Chemistry, 1957. b, John Steinbeck, Literature, 1962. c, Edward C. Kendall, Physiology or Medicine, 1950. d, Frederick G. Banting, Physiology or Medicine, 1923. e, Charles Nicolle, Physiology or Medicine, 1928. f, Charles Richet, Physiology or Medicine, 1913.

No. 3700, $400, International Red Cross, Peace, 1917. No. 3701, $400, John J. R. MacLeod, Physiology or Medicine, 1923. No. 3702, $400, Derek H. R. Barton, Chemistry, 1969.

2002, Feb. 25 *Perf. 14*

Sheets of 6, #a-f

3698-3699 A393 Set of 2 13.50 13.50

Souvenir Sheets

3700-3702 A393 Set of 3 13.50 13.50

2002 Winter Olympics, Salt Lake City A394

Designs: No. 3703, $200, Skier. No. 3704, $200, Figure skater.

2002, July 1 Litho. *Perf. 13¼x13½*

3703-3704 A394 Set of 2 4.50 4.50

a. Souvenir sheet, #3703-3704 4.50 4.50

Guyana - People's Republic of China Diplomatic Relations, 30th Anniv. — A395

Designs: No. 3705, $100, Chinese flag, Kaieteur Falls, Guyana. No. 3706, $100, Guyanese flag, Great Wall of China.

2002, July 1 *Perf. 14*

3705-3706 A395 Set of 2 2.25 2.25

Intl. Volunteers Year (in 2001) A396

Emblem, Guyanese flag and: $35, Person on ladder touching Guyana on map. $60, Map of Guyana and IVY emblem. $300, People.

2002, July 1

3707-3709 A396 Set of 3 4.50 4.50

Intl. Year of Ecotourism — A397

No. 3710: a, Owl. b, Waterfall and tourists. c, Baboon. d, Butterfly. e, Flower. f, Otter. $400, Leopard.

2002, July 1 *Perf. 13¼x13*

3710 A397 $100 Sheet of 6, #a-f 6.75 6.75

Souvenir Sheet

3711 A397 $400 multi 4.50 4.50

Intl. Year of Mountains — A398

No. 3712: a, Devil's Tower, US. b, Schreckhorn, Switzerland. c, Mt. Rainier, US. d, Mt. Everest, Nepal and Tibet.

2002, July 1 *Perf. 13½x13¼*

3712 A398 $200 Sheet of 4, #a-d 9.00 9.00

Souvenir Sheet

3713 A398 $400 multi 4.50 4.50

20th World Scout Jamboree, Thailand — A399

No. 3714: a, Environmental Science merit badge. b, Citizenship in the World merit badge. c, Life Saving merit badge.
$400, Mascot, Scout emblem.

2002, July 1
3714 A399 $200 Sheet of 3, #a-c 6.75 6.75

Souvenir Sheet

3715 A399 $400 multi 4.50 4.50

Flora and Fauna — A400

No. 3716, $100 - Butterflies: a, Sweet oil. b, Swallowtail. c, Southern white admiral. d, Prepona pheridamas. e, Plain tiger. f, Common eggfly.
No. 3717, $100 - Moths: a, Burgena varia. b, Lime hawkmoth. c, Spurge hawkmoth. d, Eligma laetipicta. e, Io moth. f, Pine hawkmoth.
No. 3718, $100 - Birds: a, Flycatcher. b, Barbary shrike. c, Red-faced mousebird. d, Red-footed booby. e, White-fronted goose. f, Great crested grebe.
No. 3719, $100 - Whales: a, Sperm. b, Pygmy sperm. c, Blue. d, Bottlenose. e, Killer. f, True's beaked.
No. 3720, $100, vert. - Orchids: a, Masdevallia tovarensis. b, Encyclia vitellina. c, Dendrobium nobile. d, Masdevallia falcata. e, Calanthe vestita. f, Brassolaeliacattleya Rising Sun.
No. 3721, $400, Zebra butterfly. No. 3722, $400, Callimorpha quadripuntaria. No. 3723, $400, Whiskered tern. No. 3724, $400, Beluga whale. No. 3725, $400, Brassavola nodosa.

2002, Aug. 7 ***Perf. 14***

Sheets of 6, #a-f

3716-3720 A400 Set of 5 35.00 35.00

Souvenir Sheets

3721-3725 A400 Set of 5 22.50 22.50

Elvis Presley (1935-77) A401

Designs: No. 3726, $60, In army uniform. No. 3727, $60, Singing.

2002, Aug. 16 ***Perf. 13¾***
3726-3727 A401 Set of 2 1.40 1.40

Each stamp was printed in a sheet of nine.

Popeye — A402

No. 3728: a, Popeye. b, Olive Oyl. c, Wimpy. d, Jeep. e, Swee'Pea and Olive Oyl. f, Swee'Pea.
$400, Popeye, diff.

2002, Oct. 7 ***Perf. 14***
3728 A402 $100 Sheet of 6, #a-f 6.75 6.75

Souvenir Sheet

3729 A402 $400 multi 4.50 4.50

New Year 2003 (Year of the Ram) — A403

Rams and background color of: a, Red. b, Orange. c, Bright pink. d, Yellow green.

2003, Jan. 27 Litho. ***Perf. 14¼x14½***
3730 A403 $100 Sheet of 4, #a-d 4.50 4.50

Pres. John F. Kennedy (1917-63) — A404

No. 3731, vert.: a, Pres. Kennedy, Presidential seal. b, Pres. Kennedy, Dr. Martin Luther King, Jr. c, Pres. Kennedy, space capsule. d, Pres. Kennedy, US flag, White House. e, Pres. Kennedy, map of Cuba, missile. f, Jacqueline and John F. Kennedy, Jr., US flag.
$400, Pres. Kennedy and wife, Jacqueline.

2003, Jan. 27 ***Perf. 14***
3731 A404 $100 Sheet of 6, #a-f 6.75 6.75

Souvenir Sheet

3732 A404 $400 multi 4.50 4.50

Pres. Ronald Reagan — A405

No. 3733, vert. - Pres. Reagan: a, And eagle. b, As actor. c, And Mt. Rushmore. d, And wife Nancy. e, And White House. f, Riding horse.
$400, With Mikhail Gorbachev.

2003, Jan. 27
3733 A405 $100 Sheet of 6, #a-f 6.75 6.75

Souvenir Sheet

3734 A405 $400 multi 4.50 4.50

Princess Diana (1961-97) — A406

No. 3735: a-f, Various depictions of Princess wearing tiaras or bridal veils.
$400, Wearing pink and yellow dress.

2003, Jan. 27
3735 A406 $100 Sheet of 6, #a-f 6.75 6.75

Souvenir Sheet

3736 A406 $400 multi 4.50 4.50

AIR POST STAMPS

No. 321 Surcharged in Blue "HUMAN RIGHTS / DAY / 1981 / 110 AIR"

1981, Nov. 14 ***Perfs. as Before***
C1 A74 110c on $3 No. 321 3.50

For surcharge see No. 997.

Nos. 133, 136 and 146 Surcharged in Red, Black or Blue "AIR / Princess / of Wales / 1961-1982"

1982, June 25 ***Perfs. as Before***

Printing Methods as Before

C2 A28 110c on 5c No. 136 (R)
C3 A28 220c on 1c No. 133
C4 A28 330c on $2 No. 146 (Bl)
Nos. C2-C4 (3) 7.25

For surcharges see Nos. 623, 785-787, 801, 804-804A, O19, O21, O30-O39.

No. 287 Surcharged in Dark Blue "UNICEF / 1946-1986 / AIR" or "UNESCO / 1946-1986 / AIR"

Perfs. as Before

1986, Oct. 24 **Litho.**
C5 A66 120c on $1 UNICEF
C6 A66 120c on $1 UNESCO
a. Pair, #C5-C6 2.10

Nos. 1026, 1095, 1096, 1096a, 1100, 1138, 1163 Surcharged "AIR"

1987-88 Litho. ***Perf. 14***

Design A91

Plate Numbers in Parentheses

C7 75c on 25c No. 1100 (59) 5.00
C8 60c on No. 1095 (55) — —
C9 75c on No. 1026 (5)
C10 75c on No. 1096 (55)
a. 75c on No. 1096a
C11 75c on No. 1138 (83)
C12 75c on No. 1163 (95)

Issued: #C7, 11/87; #C8, 12/87; #C9-C12, 8/88.

SPECIAL DELIVERY STAMPS

Orchid Type of 1985 Overprinted or Surcharged "EXPRESS"

1986-87 Litho. ***Perf. 14***

Plate Numbers in Parentheses

E1 A91 $12 on #1372 (65) 6.25
E2 A91 $15 on 40c #1145 (86) 6.25
E3 A91(p) $15 on #E2 (86) 6.00
E4 A91 $25 on 25c like #1090 (53) 8.50
Nos. E1-E4 (4) 27.00

Issue dates: $12, $25, #E2, Nov. 10. #E3, Dec. 1987. #E4 not issued without surcharge.

No. 1461c Surcharged "EXPRESS"

1986-87 Litho. ***Imperf.***
E5 A96 $20 on 320c #1461c 10.00

No. E5 Ovptd. with Maltese Cross

1987, Mar. 3
E6 A96 $20 on No. E5 8.00

Orchid Type of 1985 Inscribed "Express"

1987-88 Litho. ***Perf. 14***

Series 2

Plate Numbers in Parentheses

E7 A91 $15 like #1186 (11) 4.00 4.00
E8 A91 $20 like #1323 (93) 7.50 7.50
E9 A91 $25 like #1274 (63) 6.50 6.50
E10 A91 $45 like #1228 (35) 12.00 12.00
Nos. E7-E10 (4) 30.00 30.00

Issued: $45, 9/1; $15, 9/29; $25, 10/26; $20, 5/17/88.

No. "1461" Surcharged "EXPRESS / FORTY DOLLARS"

1987, Nov. ***Perf. 14***
E11 A96 $40 on 320c No. 1461, imperf. btwn. 10.00

A five-pointed star appears between the lines of the surcharge on #E11. See #E14.

Nos. 1827e, 1830e Surcharged in Red "SPECIAL DELIVERY"

1988, Aug. 10 ***Perf. 15***
E12 A100 $40 on $3.20 #1827e 3.50
E13 A100 $45 on $3.30 #1830e 3.50

See Nos. 2054b, 2056b.

Nos. "1461," 1822c Surcharged in Red "EXPRESS / FORTY DOLLARS"

1989, Mar. ***Perf. 14***
E14 A96 $40 on 320c #1461, imperf. btwn.
E15 A96 $40 on 320c #1822c, imperf. btwn.

Butterflies Type of 1989 Inscribed "EXPRESS"

Souvenir Sheets

1989, Sept. 7 Litho. ***Perf. 14***
E16 A115 $130 Phareas coeleste 7.75 7.75
E17 A115 $190 Papilio torquatus 12.50 12.50

For overprints see #E19-E22, E24, E26-E27, E31.

Women in Space Type of 1989 Inscribed "EXPRESS"

Souvenir Sheets

1989, Nov. 8
E18 A116 $190 Valentina Tereshkova 12.50 12.50

For overprints see No. E23, E25, E28, E32.

Nos. E16-E17 Ovptd. with World Stamp Expo '89 Emblem

1989, Nov. 17
E19 A115 $130 on No. E16 8.00
E20 A115 $190 on No. E17

Nos. E16-E18 Ovptd. in Sheet Margin "Stamp World London 90" and Show Emblem

1990, May 3
E21 A115 $130 on No. E16
E22 A115 $190 on No. E17
E23 A116 $190 on No. E18
Nos. E21-E23 (3) 30.00

Nos. E17-E18 Ovptd. in Sheet Margin with Rotary Emblem and "ROTARY / INTERNATIONAL / 1905-1990"

1990, Mar.
E24 A115 $190 on No. E17
E25 A116 $190 on No. E18
Nos. E24-E25 (2) 22.50

Nos. E16-E18 Ovptd. in Sheet Margin "90th BIRTHDAY / H.M. THE / QUEEN MOTHER"

1990, June 8 Litho. ***Perf. 14***
E26 A115 $130 on No. E16 7.75 7.75
E27 A115 $190 on No. E17 12.50 12.50
E28 A116 $190 on No. E18 12.50 12.50
Nos. E26-E28 (3) 32.75 32.75

Endangered Wildlife Type

Souvenir Sheets

1990, Nov. 6 Litho. ***Perf. 14***
E29 A131 $130 Harpy eagle 6.25 6.25
E30 A131 $150 Ocelot 7.25 7.25

Nos. E29-E30 each contain one 43x57mm stamp.

Nos. E16, E18 Ovptd. in Sheet Margin with "BELGICA PHILATELIC / EXPOSITION 1990" and Scout, Lions, Rotary and Show Emblems

1990, June 2

E31 A115 $130 on No. E16
E32 A116 $190 on No. E18

No. E31 has Scout and Lions emblems. No. E32 has Scout and Rotary emblems.

POSTAGE DUE STAMPS

Type of British Guiana Inscribed "Guyana"

Perf. 13½x14

1967-68 Wmk. 314 Typo.

J2 D1 2c black ('68) .60 .60
J3 D1 4c ultramarine .20 .20
J4 D1 12c carmine .40 .40
Nos. J2-J4 (3) 1.20 1.20

For surcharges see Nos. 897-898.

1973 Wmk. 364

J5 D1 1c green .20 .20
J6 D1 2c black .20 .20
J7 D1 4c ultramarine .20 .20
J8 D1 12c carmine .25 .25
Nos. J5-J8 (4) .85 .85

For surcharges see #341-349, 658, 899-900.

OFFICIAL STAMPS

Nos. 74, 139, 141, 143-144, 146-147, 289A, 297, 300, 333, 395, 397, 401 Surcharged in Black, Red, or Black and Red

1981-82 *Perfs. as Before*

Printing Methods as Before

O1 A28 10c on 25c #141 (Bk & R) 3.00
O2 A8 15c on #74 7.00
O3 A28 15c on #139 10.00
O4 A28 30c on $2 #146 (Bk & R) 2.00
O5 A28 50c on #143 (R) 3.00
O6 A69 50c on #300 2.00
O7 A28 60c on #144 (R) 3.00
O8 A17 100c on #395
O9 A68 100c on $3 #297 (Bk & R) 5.00
O10 A17 110c on #397 3.50
O11 A28 $1.10 on #333 (R)
O12 A28 125c on #401 (R) 4.50
O13 A28 $2 on #146 (R) 12.50
O14 A28 $5 on #147 (R) 6.00
O15 A66 $10 on #289A 20.00

Issued: #O1, O5, O7, O15, 6/8; #O2, O4, O9, O11-O12, 7/1; #O13, 7/12/82; others, 7/7.
Surcharge on Nos. O3, O6, O8, O10, O13-O14 have no obliterator. No. O11 is airmail.
Refer to 2nd paragraph in footnote following #147 for #O1, O4-O5, O7 and O13.
For overprints and surcharges see No. 406, 425, 452, 454-456, 603, 618, 650, 817, 854, 861, 866, 933, 1378, 1381, 1384, 1387-1388.

Nos. 162, 256, 258, 282, 480, C2-C3 Surcharged in Blue or Black

1982 *Perfs. as Before*

Printing Methods as Before

O16 A66 20c on #282 10.00
O17 A33 40c on #162 3.00
O18 A60 40c on #256 2.00
O19 A28 110c on #C2 (Bk) 4.00
O20 A60 $2 on #258 8.00
O21 A28 220c on #C3 4.00
O22 A69 250c on #480 2.00
Nos. O16-O22 (7) 33.00

Issue dates: 110c, Sept. 15; others, May 17. Nos. O19, O21 are airmail.

No. 481 Surcharged "OPS" Reading Up in Blue Violet or Blue Violet and Black

1984, Apr. 2 *Perfs. as Before*

O23 A66 150c on $5
O24 A66 200c on $5
O25 A66 225c on $5 (BV & Bk)
O25A A66 230c on $5
O26 A66 260c on $5
O27 A66 320c on $5
O28 A66 350c on $5
O29 A66 600c on $5
Nos. O23-O29 (8) 32.50

Nos. C2-C3 Surcharged "OPS" in Black and Blue, Black or Blue

1984, June 25 *Perfs. as Before*

O30 A28 25c on No. C2 (Bk)
O31 A28 30c on No. C2
O32 A28 45c on No. C3
O33 A28 55c on No. C2 (Bk)
O34 A28 60c on No. C3
O35 A28 75c on No. C3
O36 A28 90c on No. C3 (Bl)
O37 A28 120c on No. C3
O38 A28 130c on No. C3 (Bl)
O39 A28 330c on No. C3 (Bl)
Nos. O30-O39 (10) 8.00

Overprint reads up on No. O39.

Orchid Type of 1985

1987-88 Litho. Unwmk. *Perf. 14*

Series 2

Plate Numbers in Parentheses

O40 A91 120c like #1250 (48) .25 .25
O41 A91 130c like #1322 (92) .25 .25
O42 A91 140c like #1229 (36) .30 .30
O43 A91 150c like #1242 (43) .30 .30
O44 A91 175c like #1221 (31) .40 .40
O45 A91 200c like #1271 (61) .40 .40
O46 A91 225c like #1213 (26) .45 .45
O47 A91 230c like #1283 (68) .45 .45
O48 A91 250c like #1268 (59) .50 .50
O49 A91 260c like #1284 (69) .55 .55
O50 A91 275c like #1319 (90) .55 .55
O51 A91 320c like #1292 (75) .60 .60
O52 A91 330c like #1208 (23) .65 .65
O53 A91 350c like #1326 (95) .70 .70
O54 A91 600c like #1285 (70) 1.25 1.25
O55 A91 $12 like #1286 (71) 2.50 2.50
O56 A91 $15 like #1308 (84) 3.00 3.00
Nos. O40-O56 (17) 13.10 13.10

Nos. O47, O53-O56 horiz.
Issued: #O42, O44, O48, O49, 10/5/88; others, 10/5/87.
For overprints & surcharges see #1694, 1697, 1703, 1707, 1722-1726, 1728-1730.

PARCEL POST STAMPS

No. 145 Surcharged "PARCEL POST"

1981, June 8 Litho. *Perf. 13½*

Q1 A28 $15 on $1 No. 145
Q2 A28 $20 on $1 No. 145
Nos. Q1-Q2 (2) 27.50

For overprints see Nos. QO1-QO2.

No. 333 Surcharged "PARCEL POST" in Blue

1983, Jan. 15

Q3 A28 $12 on No. 333 12.50

For surcharge see No. 624.

No. 146 Surcharged "Parcel Post"

1983, Sept. 14

Q4 A28 $12 on $1.10 on $2 5.00

No. Q4 has a horizontal Royal Wedding / 1981 surcharge similar to No. 331. For overprint see No. QO5.

No. 255 Surcharged in Red "TWENTY FIVE DOLLARS / PARCEL POST 25.00"

1985, Apr. 25 *Perf. 14*

Q5 A60 $25 on 35c No. 255 16.00

PARCEL POST OFFICIAL STAMPS

Nos. Q1-Q2 Overprinted "OPS" in Red

1981, June 8

QO1 A28 $15 on No. Q1 12.00
QO2 A28 $20 on No. Q2 12.50

For surcharges see Nos. 1389-1390.

No. 333 Surcharged in Blue "OPS / 1982 / Parcel Post / $12.00"

1983, Jan. 15

QO3 A28 $12 on No. 333 75.00

No. QO3 Overprinted "OPS" in Black

1983, Aug. 22

QO4 A28 $12 on No. QO3 30.00

No. Q4 Overprinted "OPS" in Blue

1983, Nov. 3

QO5 A28 $12 on No. Q4 15.00

HAITI

'hā-tē

LOCATION — Western part of Hispaniola
GOVT. — Republic
AREA — 10,714 sq. mi.
POP. — 6,884,264 (1999 est.)
CAPITAL — Port-au-Prince

100 Centimes = 1 Piaster (1906)
100 Centimes = 1 Gourde

Catalogue values for unused stamps in this country are for Never Hinged items, beginning with Scott 370 in the regular postage section, Scott B2 in the semi-postal section, Scott C33 in the air post section, Scott CB10 in the air post semi-postal section, Scott CO6 in the air post official section, Scott CQ1 in the air post parcel post seciton, Scott E1 in the special delivery section, Scott J21 in the postage due section, Scott Q1 in the parcel post section, Scott RA1 in the postal tax section, and Scott RAC1 in the air post postal tax section.

Watermark

Wmk. 131- RH

Liberty Head — A1

A3

A4

On A3 (#18, 19) there are crossed lines of dots on face. On A4 the "5" is 3mm wide, on A1 2½mm wide.

1881 Unwmk. Typo. *Imperf.*

1 A1 1c vermilion, *yelsh* 7.00 4.50
2 A1 2c dk violet, *pale lil* 9.00 4.50
3 A1 3c bister, *pale bis* 16.00 5.00
4 A1 5c green, *grnsh* 27.50 8.00
5 A1 7c blue, *grysh* 18.00 3.00
6 A1 20c red brown, *yelsh* 67.50 20.00
Nos. 1-6 (6) 145.00 45.00

Nos. 1-6 were printed from plate I, Nos. 7-13 from plates II and III.

1882 *Perf. 13½*

7 A1 1c ver, *yelsh* 4.50 1.50
c. Horiz. pair, imperf. btwn. 160.00
d. Vert. pair imperf. btwn. 150.00 125.00
8 A1 2c dk vio, *pale lil* 7.50 2.25
a. 2c dark violet 9.00 5.50
b. 2c red violet, *pale lilac* 6.75 2.60
c. Horiz. pair, imperf. vert. 125.00
d. Vert. pair, imperf. horiz. 125.00
e. Horiz. pair, imperf. between 150.00 150.00
9 A1 3c bister, *pale bis* 9.00 2.50
10 A1 5c grn, *grnsh* 6.50 1.00
a. 5c yellow green, *greenish* 5.50 1.00
b. 5c deep green, *greenish* 5.50 1.00
c. Horiz. pair, imperf. vert. 225.00
d. Horiz. or vert. pair, imperf. btwn. 150.00
11 A1 7c blue, *grysh* 8.25 1.50
a. Horiz. pair, imperf. between
12 A1 7c ultra, *grysh* 13.00 2.50
a. Vert. pair, imperf. between
b. Horiz. pair, imperf. vert.
13 A1 20c pale brn, *yelsh* 6.50 1.40
a. 20c red brown, *yellowish* 13.50 2.25
b. Horiz. pair, imperf. vert 110.00
c. Vert. pair, imperf. horiz. 140.00
d. Horiz. or vert. pair, imperf. btwn. 150.00 140.00
Nos. 7-13 (7) 55.25 12.65

Stamps perf. 14, 16 are postal forgeries.

1886-87 *Perf. 13½*

18 A3 1c vermilion, *yelsh* 4.50 1.40
a. Horiz. pair, imperf. vert. 150.00
b. Horiz. pair, imperf. between 150.00 150.00
19 A3 2c dk violet, *lilac* 35.00 3.50
20 A4 5c green ('87) 13.50 1.75
Nos. 18-20 (3) 53.00 6.65

General Louis Etienne Félicité Salomon — A5

1887 Engr. *Perf. 14*

21 A5 1c lake .30 .30
22 A5 2c violet .80 .60
23 A5 3c blue .60 .40
24 A5 5c green 3.75 .40
a. Double impression —
Nos. 21-24 (4) 5.45 1.70

Some experts believe the imperfs. of Nos. 21-24 are plate proofs. Value per pair, $20.

No. 23 Handstamp Surcharged in Red

1890

25 A5 2c on 3c blue .50 .40

This surcharge being handstamped is to be found double, inverted, etc. This applies to succeeding surcharged issues.

Coat of Arms A7

Coat of Arms (Leaves Drooping) A9

1891 *Perf. 13*

26 A7 1c violet .40 .30
27 A7 2c blue .60 .30
28 A7 3c gray lilac .80 .40
a. 3c slate .80 .50
29 A7 5c orange 2.75 .30
30 A7 7c red 6.00 2.25
Nos. 26-30 (5) 10.55 3.55

Nos. 26-30 exist imperf. Value of unused pairs, each $20.
The 2c, 3c and 7c exist imperf. vertically.

No. 28 Surcharged Like No. 25 in Red

1892

31 A7 2c on 3c gray lilac 1.00 .80
a. 2c on 3c slate 1.00 .80

1892-95 Engr., Litho. (20c) *Perf. 14*

32 A9 1c lilac .30 .20
a. Imperf., pair
33 A9 2c deep blue .40 .20
34 A9 3c gray .60 .40
35 A9 5c orange 2.00 .30
36 A9 7c red .30 .20
a. Imperf., pair 5.00
37 A9 20c brown 1.40 .85
Nos. 32-37 (6) 5.00 2.15

Nos. 32, 33, 35 exist in horiz. pairs, imperf. vert., Nos. 33, 35, in vert. pairs, imperf. horiz.

1896 Engr. *Perf. 13½*

38 A9 1c light blue .20 .20
39 A9 2c red brown .20 .20
40 A9 3c lilac brown .20 .20
41 A9 5c slate green .20 .20
42 A9 7c dark gray .20 .20
43 A9 20c orange .20 .20
Nos. 38-43 (6) 1.20 1.20

Nos. 32-37 are 23¾mm high, Nos. 38-43 23¼mm to 23½mm. The "C" is closed on Nos. 32-37, open on Nos. 38-43. Other differences exist. The stamps of the two issues may be readily distinguished by their colors and perfs.

Nos. 38-43 exist imperf. and in horiz. pairs, imperf. vert. The 1c, 3c, 5c, 7c exist in vert. pairs, imperf. horiz. or imperf. between. The 5c, 7c exist in horiz. pairs, imperf. between. Value of unused pairs, $5 and up.

#37, 43 Surcharged Like #25 in Red

1898

44 A9 2c on 20c brown 1.00 .75
45 A9 2c on 20c orange .60 .50

No. 45 exists in various part perf. varieties.

Coat of Arms — A11

1898 Wmk. 131 *Perf. 11*

46 A11 1c ultra 1.10 .75
47 A11 2c brown carmine .40 .20
48 A11 3c dull violet .95 .60
49 A11 5c dark green .40 .25
50 A11 7c gray 2.25 1.60
51 A11 20c orange 2.25 1.60
Nos. 46-51 (6) 7.35 5.00

All values exist imperforate. They are plate proofs.

Pres. T. Augustin Simon Sam — A12

Coat of Arms — A13

1898-99 Unwmk. *Perf. 12*

52 A12 1c ultra .20 .20
53 A13 1c yel green ('99) .20 .20
54 A12 2c deep orange .20 .20
55 A13 2c car lake ('99) .20 .20
56 A12 3c green .20 .20
57 A13 4c red .20 .20
58 A12 5c red brown .20 .20
59 A13 5c pale blue ('99) .20 .20
60 A12 7c gray .20 .20
61 A13 8c carmine .20 .20
62 A13 10c orange red .20 .20
63 A13 15c olive green .50 .35
64 A12 20c black .50 .35
65 A12 50c rose brown .55 .35
66 A12 1g red violet 1.50 1.40
Nos. 52-66 (15) 5.25 4.65

For overprints see Nos. 67-81, 110-124, 169, 247-248.

Stamps of 1898-99 Handstamped in Black

1902

67 A12 1c ultra .45 .40
68 A13 1c yellow green .35 .20
69 A12 2c deep orange .70 .70
70 A13 2c carmine lake .35 .20
71 A12 3c green .35 .35
72 A13 4c red .45 .45
73 A12 5c red brown 1.00 1.00
74 A13 5c pale blue .35 .35
75 A12 7c gray .70 .70
76 A13 8c carmine .70 .70
77 A13 10c orange red .70 .70
78 A13 15c olive green 3.50 2.50
79 A12 20c black 3.50 2.75
80 A12 50c rose brown 8.75 4.25
81 A12 1g red violet 10.50 8.75
Nos. 67-81 (15) 32.35 24.00

Many forgeries exist of this overprint.

Centenary of Independence Issues

Coat of Arms A14

Pierre D. Toussaint L'Ouverture A15

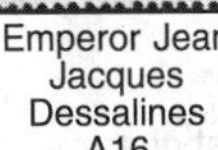

Emperor Jean Jacques Dessalines A16

Pres. Alexandre Sabes Pétion A17

1904 Engr. *Perf. 13½, 14*

82 A14 1c green .20 .20

Center Engr., Frame Litho.

83 A15 2c rose & blk .20 .20
84 A15 5c dull blue & blk .20 .20
85 A16 7c plum & blk .20 .20
86 A16 10c yellow & blk .20 .20
87 A17 20c slate & blk .20 .20
88 A17 50c olive & blk .20 .20
Nos. 82-88 (7) 1.40 1.40

Nos. 82 to 88 exist imperforate.

Nos. 83-88 exist with centers inverted. Some are known with head omitted.

Forgeries exist.

Same Handstamped in Blue

1904

89 A14 1c green .30 .30
90 A15 2c rose & blk .30 .30
91 A15 5c dull blue & blk .30 .30
92 A16 7c plum & blk .40 .40
93 A16 10c yellow & blk .40 .40
94 A17 20c slate & blk .40 .40
95 A17 50c olive & blk .40 .40
Nos. 89-95 (7) 2.50 2.50

Two dies were used for the handstamped overprint on Nos. 89-95. Letters and figures are larger on one than on the other. All values exist imperforate.

Pres. Pierre Nord-Alexis — A18

1904 Engr. *Perf. 13½, 14*

96 A18 1c green .20 .20
97 A18 2c carmine .20 .20
98 A18 5c dark blue .20 .20
99 A18 10c orange brown .20 .20
100 A18 20c orange .20 .20
101 A18 50c claret .20 .20
a. Tête bêche pair *110.00*
Nos. 96-101 (6) 1.20 1.20

Used values are for c-t-o's. Postally used examples are worth more.

Nos. 96-101 exist imperforate.

This issue, and the overprints and surcharges, exist in horiz. pairs, imperf. vert., and in vert. pairs, imperf. horiz.

For overprints and surcharges see Nos. 102-109, 150-161, 170-176, 217-218, 235-238, 240-242, 302-303.

Forgeries of Nos. 96, 101, 101a exist.

Reprints or very accurate imitations of this issue exist, including No. 101a.

Some are printed in very bright colors on very white paper and are found both perforated and imperforate. Generally the original stamps are perf. 13¼, the reprints perf 13½.

Same Handstamped in Blue like #89-95

1904

102 A18 1c green .50 .50
103 A18 2c carmine .50 .50
104 A18 5c dark blue .50 .50
105 A18 10c orange brown .50 .50
106 A18 20c orange .50 .50
107 A18 50c claret .50 .50
Nos. 102-107 (6) 3.00 3.00

The note after No. 95 applies also to Nos. 102-107. All values exist imperf.

Forgeries exist.

Regular Issue of 1904 Handstamp Surcharged in Black:

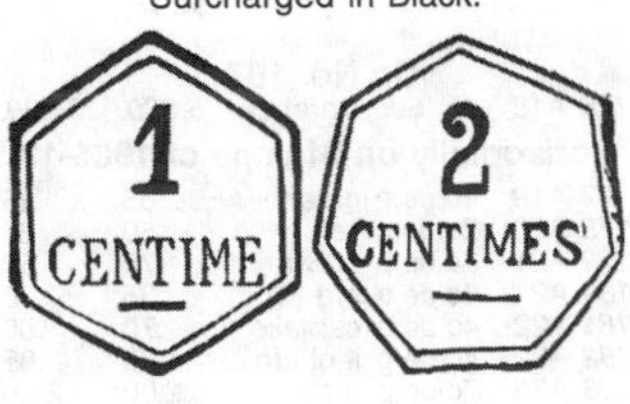

1906, Feb. 20

108 A18 1c on 20c orange .20 .20
a. 1c on 50c claret *500.00*
109 A18 2c on 50c claret .20 .20

No. 108a is known only with inverted surcharge.

Forgeries exist.

Nos. 52-66 Handstamped in Red

1906

110 A12 1c ultra .90 .70
111 A13 1c yellow green .50 .50
112 A12 2c deep orange 1.75 1.75
113 A13 2c carmine lake 1.00 1.00
114 A12 3c green 1.00 1.00
115 A13 4c red 4.25 3.50
116 A12 5c red brown 5.25 4.25
117 A13 5c pale blue .70 .45
118 A12 7c gray 3.50 3.50
119 A13 8c carmine .70 .70
120 A13 10c orange red 1.40 .90
121 A13 15c olive green 1.75 1.00
122 A12 20c black 4.25 3.50
123 A12 50c rose brown 4.25 2.75
124 A12 1g red violet 7.00 5.50
Nos. 110-124 (15) 38.20 31.00

Forgeries of this overprint are plentiful.

Coat of Arms — A19

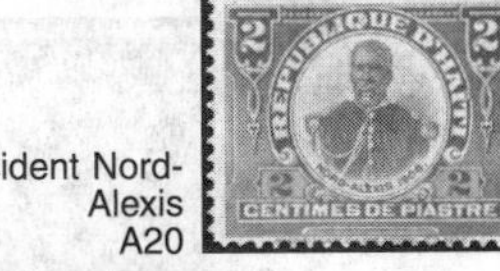

President Nord-Alexis A20

Market at Port-au-Prince A21

Sans Souci Palace — A22

Independence Palace at Gonaives — A23

Entrance to Catholic College at Port-au-Prince A24

Monastery and Church at Port-au-Prince A25

Seat of Government at Port-au-Prince A26

Presidential Palace at Port-au-Prince A27

For Foreign Postage (centimes de piastre)

1906-13 *Perf. 12*

125 A19 1c de p green .20 .20
126 A20 2c de p ver .35 .20
127 A21 3c de p brown .50 .20
128 A21 3c de p org yel ('11) 5.00 2.75
129 A22 4c de p car lake .50 .30
130 A22 4c de p lt ol grn ('13) 7.00 4.25
131 A20 5c de p dk blue 1.75 .20
132 A23 7c de p gray 1.40 .70
133 A23 7c de p org red ('13) 21.00 14.00
134 A24 8c de p car rose 1.40 .60
135 A24 8c de p ol grn ('13) 12.00 8.50
136 A25 10c de p org red .90 .20
137 A25 10c de p red brn ('13) 12.00 8.50
138 A26 15c de p sl grn 1.75 .70
139 A26 15c dp p yel ('13) 5.25 2.75
140 A20 20c de p blue grn 1.75 .70
141 A19 50c de p red 2.75 2.00
142 A19 50c de p org yel ('13) 6.00 4.25

143 A27 1p claret 5.50 3.50
144 A27 1p red ('13) 6.00 5.00
Nos. 125-144 (20) 93.00 59.50

All 1906 values exist imperf. These are plate proofs.

For overprints and surcharges see Nos. 177-195, 213-216, 239, 245, 249-260, 263, 265-277, 279-284, 286-301, 304.

Nord-Alexis
A28

Coat of Arms — A29

For Domestic Postage (centimes de gourde)

1906-10

145 A28 1c de g blue .20 .20
146 A29 2c de g org yel .35 .20
147 A29 2c de g lemon ('10) .50 .20
148 A28 3c de g slate .30 .20
149 A29 7c de g green .90 .35
Nos. 145-149 (5) 2.25 1.15

For overprints see Nos. 196-197.

Regular Issue of 1904 Handstamp Surcharged in Red like #108-109

1907

150 A18 1c on 5c dk bl .30 .20
151 A18 1c on 20c org .20 .20
152 A18 2c on 10c org brn .25 .20
153 A18 2c on 50c claret .35 .20

Black Surcharge

154 A18 1c on 5c dk bl .35 .20
155 A18 1c on 10c org brn .25 .20
156 A18 2c on 20c org .20 .20

Brown Surcharge

157 A18 1c on 5c dk bl .35 .35
158 A18 1c on 10c org brn .55 .35
159 A18 2c on 20c org 1.75 1.40
160 A18 2c on 50c claret 17.50 16.00

Violet Surcharge

161 A18 1c on 20c org 70.00

The handstamps are found sideways, diagonal, inverted and double.

Forgeries exist.

A30

President Antoine T. Simon — A31

For Foreign Postage

1910

162 A30 2c de p rose red & blk .50 .35
163 A30 5c de p bl & blk 10.00 .50
164 A30 20c de p yel grn & blk 7.00 5.50

For Domestic Postage

165 A31 1c de g lake & blk .20 .20
Nos. 162-165 (4) 17.70 6.55

For overprint and surcharges see Nos. 198, 262, 278, 285.

A32

A33

Pres. Cincinnatus Leconte — A34

1912

166 A32 1c de g car lake .20 .20
167 A33 2c de g dp org .25 .20

For Foreign Postage

168 A34 5c de p dp blue .55 .20
Nos. 166-168 (3) 1.00 .60

For overprints see Nos. 199-201.

Stamps of Preceding Issues Handstamped Vertically

1914

On No. 61

169 A13 8c carmine 8.75 7.00

On Nos. 96-101

170 A18 1c green 25.00 21.00
171 A18 2c carmine 25.00 21.00
172 A18 5c dk blue .45 .25
173 A18 10c orange brn .45 .25
174 A18 20c orange .70 .35
175 A18 50c claret 2.00 .90
Nos. 170-175 (6) 53.60 43.75

Perforation varieties of Nos. 172-175 exist.

No. 175 overprinted "T. M." is a revenue stamp. The letters are the initials of "Timbre Mobile."

On No. 107

176 A18 50c claret *5,000. 5,000.*

Horizontally on Stamps of 1906-13

177 A19 1c de p green .35 .25
178 A20 2c de p ver .50 .25
179 A21 3c de p brown .75 .50
180 A21 3c de p org yel .35 .25
181 A22 4c de p car lake .70 .60
182 A22 4c de p lt ol grn 1.25 .65
183 A23 7c de p gray 2.00 2.00
184 A23 7c de p org red 2.75 2.75
185 A24 8c de p car rose 3.50 3.50
186 A24 8c de p ol grn 3.50 3.50
187 A25 10c de p org red 1.00 .50
188 A25 10c de p red brn 1.40 .90
189 A26 15c de p sl grn 2.75 2.75
190 A26 15c de p yellow 1.25 .70
191 A20 20c de p bl grn 2.50 .90
192 A19 50c de p red 4.25 4.25
193 A19 50c de p org yel 4.25 4.25
194 A27 1p claret 4.25 4.25
195 A27 1p red 4.25 4.25
196 A29 2c de g lemon .35 .20
197 A28 3c de g slate .35 .20
Nos. 177-197 (21) 42.25 37.40

On No. 164

198 A30 20c de p yel grn & blk 2.75 2.75

Vertically on Nos. 166-168

199 A32 1c de g car lake .25 .20
200 A33 2c de g dp org .45 .35
201 A34 5c de p dp blue .70 .20
Nos. 199-201 (3) 1.40 .75

Two handstamps were used for the overprints on Nos. 169-201. They may be distinguished by the short and long foot of the "L" of "GL" and the position of the first "1" in "1914" with regard to the period above it. Both handstamps are found on all but #176, 294, 295, 306, 308.

Handstamp Surcharged

On Nos. 141 and 143

213 A19 1c de p on 50c de p red .30 .20
214 A27 1c de p on 1p claret .45 .40

On Nos. 142 and 144

215 A19 1c de p on 50c de p org yel .45 .35
216 A27 1c de p on 1p red .50 .40

Handstamp Surcharged

On Nos. 100 and 101

217 A18 7c on 20c orange .40 .20
218 A18 7c on 50c claret .35 .20

The initials on the preceding handstamps are those of Gen. Oreste Zamor; the date is that of his triumphal entry into Port-au-Prince.

Pres. Oreste Zamor

Coat of Arms

Pres. Tancrède Auguste

Owing to the theft of a large quantity of this 1914 issue, while in transit from the printers, the stamps were never placed on sale at post offices. A few copies have been canceled through carelessness or favor. Value, set of 10, $4.75.

Preceding Issues Handstamp Surcharged in Carmine or Blue

On Nos. 98-101

1915-16

235 A18 1c on 5c dk bl (C) 1.10 1.10
236 A18 1c on 10c org brn .50 .50
237 A18 1c on 20c orange .40 .35
238 A18 1c on 50c claret .40 .40

On No. 132

239 A23 1c on 7c de p gray (C) .40 .40

On Nos. 106-107

240 A18 1c on 20c orange .50 .70
241 A18 1c on 50c claret 1.75 .50
242 A18 1c on 50c cl (C) 27.50 21.00
Nos. 235-242 (8) 32.55 24.95

Nos. 240-242 are known with two types of the "Post Paye" overprint. No. 237 with red surcharge and any stamps with violet surcharge are unofficial.

No. 143 Handstamp Surcharged in Red

1917-19

245 A27 2c on 1p claret .40 .40

Stamps of 1906-14 Handstamp Surcharged in Various Colors

1c, 5c

On Nos. 123-124

247 A12 1c on 50c (R) 17.50 12.50
248 A12 1c on 1g (R) 21.00 16.00

On #127, 129, 134, 136, 138, 140-141

249 A22 1c on 4c de p (Br) .40 .50
250 A25 1c on 10c de p (Bl) .40 .50
252 A20 1c on 20c de p (R) .40 .50
253 A20 1c on 20c de p (Bk) .40 .50
254 A19 1c on 50c de p (R) .40 .50
255 A19 1c on 50c de p (Bk) .40 .50
256 A21 2c on 3c de p (R) .40 .50
257 A24 2c on 8c de p (R) .40 .50
258 A24 2c on 8c de p (Bk) .40 .50
259 A26 2c on 15c de p (R) .40 .50
260 A20 2c on 20c de p (R) .40 .50
Nos. 249-260 (11) 4.40 5.50

The 1c on 10c de p stamp in black is actually a blue ink which bled into the stamps.

On Nos. 164, 128

262 A30 1c on 20c de p (Bk) 3.50 3.50
263 A21 2c on 3c de p (R) .40 .30

On #130, 133, 135, 137, 139, 142, 144

265 A22 1c on 4c de p (R) .40 .30
266 A23 1c on 7c de p (Br) .40 .30
267 A26 1c on 15c de p (R) .40 .30
268 A19 1c on 50c de p (Bk) .90 .90
269 A27 1c on 1p (Bk) .90 .90
270 A24 2c on 8c de p (R) .40 .35
271 A25 2c on 10c de p (Br) .40 .20
272 A26 2c on 15c de p (R) .45 .45
273 A25 5c on 10c de p (Bl) .70 .70
274 A25 5c on 10c de p (VBk) .45 .45
275 A26 5c on 15c de p (R) 3.50 3.50
Nos. 265-275 (11) 8.90 8.35

"O. Z." Stamps of 1914 Handstamp Surcharged in Red or Brown

276 A26 1c on 15c de p sl grn .40 .40
277 A20 1c on 20c de p bl grn .40 .40
278 A30 1c on 20c de p yel grn & blk .40 .40
279 A27 1c on 1p claret (Br) .40 .40
280 A27 1c on 1p claret 1.25 1.25
281 A27 5c on 1p red (Br) .40 .40
Nos. 276-281 (6) 3.25 3.25

"O. Z." Stamps of 1914 Handstamp Surcharged in Violet, Green, Red, Magenta or Black
1 ct and 2 cts as in 1917-19 and

1919-20

282 A22 2c on 4c de p car lake (V) .35 .35
283 A24 2c on 8c de p car rose (G) .30 .20
284 A24 2c on 8c de p ol grn (R) .20 .20
285 A30 2c on 20c de p yel grn & blk (R) .30 .20
286 A19 2c on 50c de p red (G) .20 .20
288 A19 2c on 50c de p red (R) .45 .35
289 A19 2c on 50c de p org yel (R) .25 .20
290 A27 2c on 1pi claret (R) 2.00 1.75
291 A27 2c on 1pi red (R) 1.50 1.50
292 A21 3c on 3c de p brn (R) .35 .35
293 A23 3c on 7c de p org red (R) .35 .20
294 A21 5c on 3c de p brn (R) .40 .20
295 A21 5c on 3c de p org yel (R) 1.40 1.40
296 A22 5c on 4c de p car lake (R) .45 .45
297 A22 5c on 4c de p ol grn (R) .25 .25
298 A23 5c on 7c de p gray (V) .30 .25
299 A23 5c on 7c de p org red (V) .35 .35
300 A25 5c on 10c de p org red (V) .25 .25
301 A26 5c on 15c de p yel (M) .35 .35
Nos. 282-301 (19) 10.00 9.00

Nos. 217 and 218 Handstamp Surcharged with New Value in Magenta

302 A18 5c on 7c on 20c orange .35 .35
303 A18 5c on 7c on 50c claret 2.75 2.75

No. 187 Handstamp Surcharged in Magenta

304 A25 5c de p on 10c de p .45 .45

Postage Due Stamps of 1906-14 Handstamp Surcharged in Black or Magenta (#308)

On Stamp of 1906

305 D2 5c on 50c ol gray 8.50 6.75

On Stamp of 1914

306 D2 5c on 10c violet .30 .30
307 D2 5c on 50c olive gray .40 .40
308 D2 5c on 50c ol gray (M) 1.40 1.40
Nos. 305-308 (4) 10.60 8.85

Nos. 299 with red surcharge and 306-307 with violet are trial colors or essays.

Allegory of Agriculture A40

Allegory of Commerce A41

1920, Apr. **Engr.** ***Perf. 12***

310 A40 3c deep orange .20 .20
311 A40 5c green .20 .20
312 A41 10c vermilion .40 .30
313 A41 15c violet .35 .25
314 A41 25c deep blue .40 .20
Nos. 310-314 (5) 1.55 1.15

Nos. 311-313 overprinted "T. M." are revenue stamps. The letters are the initials of "Timbre Mobile."

President Louis J. Borno — A42

Christophe's Citadel — A43

Old Map of West Indies — A44

Borno — A45

National Capitol — A46

1924, Sept. 3

315 A42 5c deep green .20 .20
316 A43 10c carmine .25 .20
317 A44 20c violet blue .65 .20
318 A45 50c orange & blk .65 .20
319 A46 1g olive green 1.25 .20
Nos. 315-319 (5) 3.00 1.00

For surcharges see Nos. 359, C4A.

Coffee Beans and Flowers — A47

1928, Feb. 6

320 A47 35c deep green 2.75 .35

For surcharge see No. 337.

Pres. Louis Borno — A48

1929, Nov. 4

321 A48 10c carmine rose .25 .20

Signing of the "Frontier" treaty between Haiti and the Dominican Republic.

Presidents Salomon and Vincent — A49

Pres. Sténio Vincent — A50

1931, Oct. 16

322 A49 5c deep green .90 .35
323 A50 10c carmine rose .90 .35

50th anniv. of Haiti's joining the UPU.

President Vincent — A52

Aqueduct at Port-au-Prince A53

Fort National — A54

Palace of Sans Souci — A55

Christophe's Chapel at Milot — A56

King's Gallery Citadel — A57

Vallières Battery — A58

1933-40

325 A52 3c orange .20 .20
326 A52 3c dp ol grn ('39) .20 .20
327 A53 5c green .20 .20
328 A53 5c olive grn ('40) .40 .20
329 A54 10c rose car .35 .20
a. 10c vermilion .50 .20
330 A54 10c red brn ('40) .35 .20
331 A55 25c blue .65 .20
332 A56 50c brown 1.75 .35
333 A57 1g dark green 1.75 .35
334 A58 2.50g olive bister 2.75 .50
Nos. 325-334 (10) 8.60 2.60

For surcharges see Nos. 357-358, 360.

Alexandre Dumas, His Father and Son — A59

1935, Dec. 29 **Litho.** ***Perf. 11½***

335 A59 10c rose pink & choc .65 .25
336 A59 25c blue & chocolate 1.25 .30
Nos. 335-336,C10 (3) 5.15 2.45

Visit of a delegation from France to Haiti.
No. 335 exists imperf and in horiz. pair, imperf. between. #336 exists as pair, imperf horiz.

No. 320 Surcharged in Red

1939, Jan. 24 ***Perf. 12***

337 A47 25c on 35c dp grn .70 .30

Statue of Liberty, Map of Haiti and Flags of American Republics A60

1941, June 30 **Engr.** ***Perf. 12***

338 A60 10c rose carmine .75 .30
339 A60 25c dark blue .65 .35
Nos. 338-339,C12-C13 (4) 6.15 1.70

3rd Inter-American Caribbean Conf., held at Port-au-Prince.

Patroness of Haiti, Map and Coat of Arms — A61

1942, Dec. 8

Size: 26x36¼mm

340 A61 3c dull violet .25 .20
341 A61 5c brt green .35 .20
342 A61 10c rose car .35 .20
343 A61 15c orange .45 .35
344 A61 20c brown .45 .40
345 A61 25c deep blue .95 .40
346 A61 50c red orange 1.25 .55
347 A61 2.50g olive black 4.50 1.10

Size: 32x45mm

348 A61 5g purple 9.00 2.25
Nos. 340-348,C14-C18 (14) 21.95 7.25

Issued in honor of Our Lady of Perpetual Help, patroness of Haiti.
For surcharges see Nos. 355-356.

Adm. Hammerton Killick and Destruction of "La Crête-à-Pierrot" — A62

1943, Sept. 6

349 A62 3c orange .30 .20
350 A62 5c turq green .35 .20
351 A62 10c carmine rose .35 .20
352 A62 25c deep blue .40 .20
353 A62 50c olive .90 .30
354 A62 5g brown black 4.50 2.50
Nos. 349-354,C22-C23 (8) 8.80 5.10

Nos. 343 and 345 Surcharged with New Value and Bars in Red

1944, July 19

355 A61 10c on 15c orange .30 .20
356 A61 10c on 25c dp blue .30 .20

Nos. 319, 326 and 334 Surcharged with New Values and Bars in Red

1944-45

357 A52 2c on 3c dp ol grn .20 .20
358 A52 5c on 3c dp ol grn .20 .20
359 A46 10c on 1g ol grn .40 .20
a. Surcharged "01.0"
360 A58 20c on 2.50g ol bis .40 .30
Nos. 357-360 (4) 1.20 .90

Nurse and Wounded Soldier on Battlefield — A63

1945, Feb. 20

Cross in Rose

361 A63 3c gray black .20 .20
362 A63 5c dk blue grn .20 .20
363 A63 10c red orange .20 .20
364 A63 20c black brn .20 .20
365 A63 25c deep blue .25 .20
366 A63 35c orange .25 .20
367 A63 50c car rose .40 .20
368 A63 1g olive green .65 .30
369 A63 2.50g pale violet 2.00 .35
Nos. 361-369,C25-C32 (17) 12.60 5.60

Issued to honor the Intl. Red Cross.
20c, 1g, 2.50g, Aug. 14. Others, Feb. 20.
For overprints and surcharges see Nos. 456-457, C153-C160.

Catalogue values for unused stamps in this section, from this point to the end of the section, are for Never Hinged items.

Col. François Capois
A64

Jean Jacques Dessalines
A65

Unwmk.

1946, July 18 Engr. *Perf. 12*

370 A64 3c red orange .20 .20
371 A64 5c Prus green .20 .20
372 A64 10c red .20 .20
373 A64 20c olive black .20 .20
374 A64 25c deep blue .20 .20
375 A64 35c orange .20 .20
376 A64 50c red brown .25 .20
377 A64 1g olive brown .35 .20
378 A64 2.50g gray 1.00 .35
Nos. 370-378,C35-C42 (17) 6.30 4.55

For surcharges see Nos. 383, 392, C43-C45, C49-C51, C61-C62.

1947-54

379 A65 3c orange yel .20 .20
380 A65 5c green .20 .20
380A A65 5c dp vio ('54) .40 .20
381 A65 10c carmine rose .20 .20
382 A65 25c deep blue .20 .20
Nos. 379-382,C46 (6) 1.40 1.20

No. 375 Surcharged with New Value and Rectangular Block in Black

1948

383 A64 10c on 35c orange .20 .20

Arms of Port-au-Prince
A66

Engraved and Lithographed

1950, Feb. 12 *Perf. 12½*

384 A66 10c multicolored .20 .20
Nos. 384,C47-C48 (3) 1.60 .85

200th anniv. (in 1949) of the founding of Port-au-Prince.

Nos. RA10-RA12 and RA16 Surcharged or Overprinted in Black

1950, Oct. 4 Unwmk. *Perf. 12*

385 PT2 3c on 5c ol gray .20 .20
386 PT2 5c green .25 .20
387 PT2 10c on 5c car rose .25 .20
388 PT2 20c on 5c blue .35 .35
Nos. 385-388,C49-C51 (7) 2.30 2.15

75th anniv. (in 1949) of the UPU.
Exist with inverted or double surcharge and 10c on 5c green.

Cacao — A67

Pres. Paul E. Magloire and Day Nursery, Saline — A68

1951, Sept. 3 Photo. *Perf. 12½*

389 A67 5c dark green .25 .20
Nos. 389,C52-C54 (4) 4.75 3.55

1953, May 4 Engr. *Perf. 12*

Design: 10c, Applying asphalt.

390 A68 5c green .20 .20
391 A68 10c rose carmine .20 .20
Nos. 390-391,C57-C60 (6) 2.40 1.85

No. 375 Surcharged in Black

1953, Apr. 7

392 A64 50c on 35c orange .35 .20

Gen. Pierre Dominique Toussaint L'Ouverture, 1743-1803, liberator.

J. J. Dessalines and Paul E. Magloire — A69

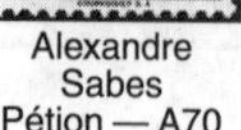

Alexandre Sabes Pétion — A70

Battle of Vertieres — A71

Design: No. 395, Larmartiniere. No. 396, Boisrond-Tonnerre. No. 397, Toussaint L'Ouverture. No. 399, Capois. No. 401, Marie Jeanne and Lamartiniere leading attack.

1954, Jan. 1 Photo. *Perf. 11½*

Portraits in Black

393 A69 3c blue gray .20 .20
394 A70 5c yellow green .20 .20
395 A70 5c yellow green .20 .20
396 A70 5c yellow green .20 .20
397 A70 5c yellow green .20 .20
398 A69 10c crimson .20 .20
399 A70 15c rose lilac .20 .20

Perf. 12½

400 A71 25c dark gray .20 .20
401 A71 25c deep orange .20 .20
Nos. 393-401 (9) 1.80 1.80
Nos. 393-401,C63-C74 (21) 8.60 7.70

150th anniv. of Haitian independence.
See Nos. C95-C96.

Mme. Yolette Magloire — A72

1954, Jan. 1 *Perf. 11½*

402 A72 10c orange .20 .20
403 A72 10c blue .20 .20
Nos. 402-403,C75-C80 (8) 4.15 3.60

Henri Christophe, Paul Magloire and Citadel
A73

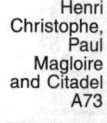

Tomb and Arms of Henri Christophe — A74

Perf. 13½x13

1954, Dec. 6 Litho. Unwmk.

404 A73 10c carmine .20 .20

Perf. 13

405 A74 10c red, blk & car .20 .20
Nos. 404-405,C81-C90 (12) 9.55 6.80

Restoration of Christophe's Citadel.

J. J. Dessalines
A75

Pres. Magloire and Dessalines Memorial, Gonaives
A76

1955-57 Photo. *Perf. 11½*

406 A75 3c ocher & blk .20 .20
407 A75 5c pale vio & blk ('56) .20 .20
408 A75 10c rose & blk .20 .20
a. 10c salmon pink & black ('57) .20 .20
409 A75 25c chalky bl & blk ('56) .20 .20
a. 25c blue & black ('57) .20 .20
Nos. 406-409,C93-C94 (6) 1.20 1.20

1955, Aug. 1

410 A76 10c deep blue & blk .25 .20
411 A76 10c crimson & blk .25 .20
Nos. 410-411,C97-C98 (4) 1.40 .80

21st anniv. of the new Haitian army.
Nos. 410-411 were printed in a single sheet of 20 (5x4). The two upper rows are of No. 410, the two lower No. 411, providing five se-tenant pairs.

Flamingo
A77

Mallard
A78

1956, Apr. 14 Photo. *Perf. 11½*

Granite Paper

412 A77 10c blue & ultra .20 .20
413 A78 25c dk grn & bluish grn .40 .20
Nos. 412-413,C99-C104 (8) 7.25 3.75

Immanuel Kant — A79

1956, July 19 *Perf. 12*

Granite Paper

414 A79 10c brt ultra .20 .20
Nos. 414,C105-C107 (4) 1.55 .95

10th anniv. of the 1st Inter-American Philosophical Congress.

Zim Waterfall
A80

J. J. Dessalines and Dessalines Memorial, Gonaives
A81

1957, Dec. 16 Unwmk. *Perf. 11½*

Granite Paper

415 A80 10c orange & blue .20 .20
Nos. 415,C108-C111 (5) 2.90 2.45

For surcharge & overprint see #CB49, CQ2.

1958, July 1 Photo.

416 A81 5c yel grn & blk .20 .20

Bicentenary of birth of J. J. Dessalines.
See Nos. 470-471, C112, C170. For overprints see Nos. 480-482, C183-C184, CQ1, Q1-Q3.

"Atomium" — A82

View of Brussels Exposition A83

Perf. 13x13½, 13½x13

1958, July 22 Litho. Unwmk.

417 A82 50c brown .20 .20
418 A83 75c brt green .20 .20
419 A82 1g purple .50 .20
420 A83 1.50g red orange .40 .20
Nos. 417-420,C113-C114 (6) 2.85 1.85

Issued for the Universal and International Exposition at Brussels.

For surcharges see Nos. B2-B3, CB9.

Sylvio Cator — A84

U. S. Satellite — A85

1958, Aug. 16 Photo. *Perf. 11½*

Granite Paper

421 A84 5c green .20 .20
422 A84 10c brown .20 .20
423 A84 20c lilac .20 .20
Nos. 421-423,C115-C118 (7) 2.80 1.90

30th anniversary of the world championship record broad jump of Sylvio Cator.

1958, Oct. 8 *Perf. 14x13½*

Designs: 20c, Emperor penguins. 50c, Modern observatory. 1g, Ocean exploration.

424 A85 10c brt bl & brn red .20 .20
425 A85 20c black & dp org .30 .20
426 A85 50c grn & rose brn .40 .20
427 A85 1g black & blue .60 .20
Nos. 424-427,C119-C121 (7) 4.05 1.70

Issued for the International Geophysical Year 1957-58.

President François Duvalier — A86

Engraved and Lithographed

1958, Oct. 22 Unwmk. *Perf. 11½*

Commemorative Inscription in Ultramarine

428 A86 10c blk & dp pink .20 .20
429 A86 50c blk & lt grn .30 .20
430 A86 1g blk & brick red .40 .25
431 A86 5g blk & sal 1.75 1.25
Nos. 428-431,C122-C125 (8) 7.20 4.90

1st anniv. of the inauguration of Pres. Dr. François Duvalier. See note on souvenir sheets after No. C125.

1958 Nov. 20

Without Commemorative Inscription

432 A86 5c blk & lt vio bl .20 .20
433 A86 10c blk & dp pink .20 .20
434 A86 20c blk & yel .20 .20
435 A86 50c blk & lt grn .20 .20
436 A86 1g blk & brick red .30 .20
437 A86 1.50g blk & rose pink .40 .30
438 A86 2.50g blk & gray vio .65 .40
439 A86 5g blk & sal 1.25 .90
Nos. 432-439,C126-C132 (15) 8.90 6.10

For surcharges see Nos. B13, B22-B24.

Map of Haiti — A87

1958, Dec. 5 Photo. *Perf. 11½*

Granite Paper

440 A87 10c rose pink .20 .20
441 A87 25c green .20 .20
Nos. 440-441,C133-C135 (5) 1.15 1.00

Tribute to the UN. See No. C135a. For overprints and surcharges see Nos. 442-443, B4-B5, CB11-CB12.

Nos. 440-441 Overprinted "10th ANNIVERSARY OF THE / UNIVERSAL DECLARATION / OF HUMAN RIGHTS" in English (a), French (b), Spanish (c) or Portuguese (d)

1959, Jan. 28

442 Block of 4 .35 .35
a.-d. A87 10c any single .20 .20
443 Block of 4 .90 .70
a.-d. A87 25c any single .20 .20
Nos. 442-443,C136-C138 (5) 10.65 10.45

10th anniv. of the signing of the Universal Declaration of Human Rights.

Pope Pius XII and Children — A88

50c, Pope praying. 2g, Pope on throne.

1959, Feb. 28 Photo. *Perf. 14x13½*

444 A88 10c vio bl & ol .20 .20
445 A88 50c green & dp brn .20 .20
446 A88 2g dp claret & dk brn .65 .35
Nos. 444-446,C139-C141 (6) 2.25 1.45

Issued in memory of Pope Pius XII.

For surcharges see Nos. B6-B8.

Abraham Lincoln — A89

1959, May 12 Photo. *Perf. 12*

447 A89 50c lt bl & deep claret .30 .20
Nos. 447,C142-C144 (4) 1.45 .90

Sesquicentennial of the birth of Abraham Lincoln. Imperf. pairs exist.

For surcharges see #B9, CB16-CB18.

Chicago's Skyline and Dessables House — A90

Jean Baptiste Dessables and Map of American Midwest, c. 1791 — A91

Design: 50c, Discus thrower and flag of Haiti.

1959, Aug. 27 Unwmk. *Perf. 14*

448 A90 25c blk brn & lt bl .20 .20
449 A90 50c multicolored .40 .30
450 A91 75c brown & blue .50 .40
Nos. 448-450,C145-C147 (6) 2.85 1.75

3rd Pan American Games, Chicago, 8/27-9/7.

For surcharges see #B10-B12, CB19-CB21.

No. 449 Overprinted

1960, Feb. 29

451 A90 50c multicolored 1.25 1.00
Nos. 451,C148-C150 (4) 4.60 4.35

8th Olympic Winter Games, Squaw Valley, Calif., Feb. 18-29, 1960.

Uprooted Oak Emblem and Hands — A92

1960, Apr. 7 Litho. *Perf. 12½x13*

452 A92 10c salmon & grn .20 .20
453 A92 50c violet & mag .20 .20
Nos. 452-453,C151-C152 (4) .90 .80

World Refugee Year, July 1, 1959-June 30, 1960. See Nos. 489-490, C191-C192. For surcharges see Nos. B14-B17, B28-B29, CB24-CB27, CB45-CB46.

No. 406 Surcharged with New Values

1960, Apr. 27 Photo. *Perf. 11½*

454 A75 5c on 3c ocher & blk .20 .20
455 A75 10c on 3c ocher & blk .20 .20

No. 369 Surcharged or Overprinted in Red: "28eme ANNIVERSAIRE"

1960, May 8 Engr. *Perf. 12*

Cross in Rose

456 A63 1g on 2.50g pale vio .65 .30
457 A63 2.50g pale violet .90 .70
Nos. 456-457,C153-C160 (10) 4.30 3.40

28th anniversary of the Haitian Red Cross.

Claudinette Fouchard, Miss Haiti, Sugar Queen — A93

Sugar Queen and: 20c, Sugar harvest. 50c, Beach. 1g, Sugar plantation.

Perf. 11½

1960, May 30 Photo. Unwmk.

Granite Paper

458 A93 10c ol bis & vio .20 .20
459 A93 20c red brn & blk .20 .20
460 A93 50c brt bl & brn .35 .20
461 A93 1g green & brn .70 .20
Nos. 458-461,C161-C162 (6) 2.70 1.35

Haitian sugar industry.

Olympic Victors, Athens, 1896, Melbourne Stadium and Olympic Torch A94

Designs: 20c, Discus thrower and Rome stadium. 50c, Pierre de Coubertin and victors, Melbourne, 1956. 1g, Athens stadium, 1896.

1960, Aug. 18 Photo. *Perf. 12*

462 A94 10c black & org .20 .20
463 A94 20c dk blue & crim .20 .20
464 A94 50c green & ocher .20 .20
465 A94 1g dk brn & grnsh bl .30 .20
Nos. 462-465,C163-C165 (7) 2.15 1.50

17th Olympic Games, Rome, Aug. 25-Sept. 11. For surcharges see Nos. B18-B19, CB28-CB29.

Occide Jeanty and Score from "1804" A95

20c, Occide Jeanty and National Capitol.

1960, Oct. 19 *Perf. 14x14½*

466 A95 10c orange & red lilac .20 .20
467 A95 20c blue & red lilac .20 .20
468 A95 50c green & sepia .40 .20
Nos. 466-468,C166-C167 (5) 1.60 1.00

Cent. of the birth of Occide Jeanty, composer. Printed in sheets of 12 (3x4) with commemorative inscription and opening bars of "1804," Jeanty's military march, in top margin.

UN Headquarters, NYC — A96

1960, Nov. 25 Engr. *Perf. 10½*

469 A96 1g green & blk .25 .20
Nos. 469,C168-C169 (3) .80 .65

15th anniv. of the UN. For surcharges see Nos. B20-B21, CB30-CB31, CB35-CB36.

Exists with center inverted.

Dessalines Type of 1958

Perf. 11½

1960, Nov. 5 Unwmk. Photo.

Granite Paper

470 A81 10c red org & blk .20 .20
471 A81 25c ultra & blk .20 .20
Nos. 470-471,C170 (3) .60 .60

Alexandre Dumas Père and Musketeer — A97

5c, Map of Haiti & birthplace of General Alexandre Dumas, horiz. 50c, Alexandre Dumas, father & son, French & Haitian flags, horiz.

1961, Feb. 10 ***Perf. 11½***

Granite Paper

472 A97 5c lt blue & choc .20 .20
473 A97 10c rose, blk & sep .20 .20
474 A97 50c dk blue & crim .20 .20
Nos. 472-474,C177-C179 (6) 1.40 1.25

Gen. Dumas (Alexandre Davy de la Pailleterie), born in Jeremie, Haiti, and his son and grandson, French authors.

Three Pirates — A98

Tourist publicity: 5c, Map of Tortuga. 15c, Pirates. 20c, Privateer in battle. 50c, Pirate with cutlass in rigging.

1961, Apr. 4 **Litho.** ***Perf. 12***

475 A98 5c blue & yel .20 .20
476 A98 10c lake & yel .20 .20
477 A98 15c ol grn & org .20 .20
478 A98 20c choc & org .20 .20
479 A98 50c vio bl & org .20 .20
Nos. 475-479,C180-C182 (8) 1.65 1.60

For surcharges and overprints see Nos. 484-485, C186-C187.

Nos. 416, 470-471 and 378 Overprinted: "Dr. F. Duvalier / Président / 22 Mai 1961"

1961, May 22 **Photo.** ***Perf. 11½***

480 A81 5c yel grn & blk .20 .20
481 A81 10c red org & blk .20 .20
482 A81 25c ultra & blk .20 .20

Engr.

Perf. 12

483 A64 2.50g gray .70 .50
Nos. 480-483,C183-C185 (7) 2.00 1.75

Re-election of Pres. Francois Duvalier.

No. 475 Surcharged: "EXPLORATION SPATIALE JOHN GLENN," Capsule and New Value

1962, May 10 **Litho.**

484 A98 50c on 5c bl & yel .30 .20
485 A98 1.50g on 5c bl & yel 1.00 .70
Nos. 484-485,C186-C187 (4) 2.55 1.95

US achievement in space exploration and for the 1st orbital flight of a US astronaut, Lt. Col. John H. Glenn, Jr., Feb. 20, 1962.

Malaria Eradication Emblem — A99

Design: 10c, Triangle pointing down.

Unwmk.

1962, May 30 **Litho.** ***Perf. 12***

486 A99 5c crimson & dp bl .20 .20
487 A99 10c red brn & emer .20 .20
488 A99 50c blue & crimson .20 .20
Nos. 486-488,C188-C190 (6) 1.30 1.20

WHO drive to eradicate malaria.
Sheets of 12 with marginal inscription.
For surcharges see Nos. B25-B27, CB42-CB44.

WRY Type of 1960 Dated "1962"

1962, June 22 ***Perf. 12½x13***

489 A92 10c lt blue & org .20 .20
490 A92 50c rose lil & ol grn .20 .20
Nos. 489-490,C191-C192 (4) .80 .80

Issued to publicize the plight of refugees. For souvenir sheet see note after #C191-C192.

Haitian Scout Emblem — A100

5c, 50c, Scout giving Scout sign. 10c, Lord and Lady Baden-Powell, horiz.

Perf. 14x14½, 14½x14

1962, Aug. 6 **Photo.**

491 A100 3c blk, ocher & pur .20 .20
492 A100 5c cit, red brn & blk .20 .20
493 A100 10c ocher, blk & grn .20 .20
494 A100 25c maroon, ol & bl .20 .20
495 A100 50c violet, grn & red .25 .20
Nos. 491-495,C193-C195 (8) 1.80 1.70

22nd anniv. of the Haitian Boy Scouts.
For surcharges and overprints see Nos. B31-B34, C196-C199.

TIMBRE MOBILE, etc.
From 1970 through 1979 postage and airmail stamps were overprinted for use as revenue stamps. The overprints used were: "TIMBRE MOBILE," "TIMBRE DE SOLIDARITE," "SOLIDARITE," "TIMBRE SOLIDARITE," "OBLIGATION PELIGRE."

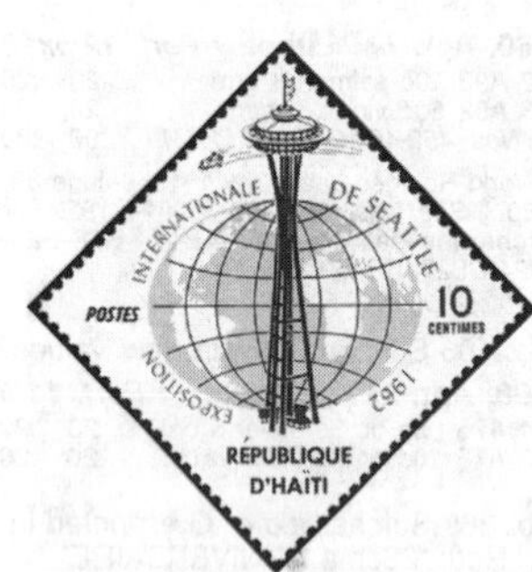

Space Needle, Space Capsule and Globe — A101

1962, Nov. 19 **Litho.** ***Perf. 12½***

496 A101 10c red brn & lt bl .20 .20
497 A101 20c vio bl & pink .20 .20
498 A101 50c emerald & yel .20 .20
499 A101 1g car & lt grn .35 .20
Nos. 496-499,C200-C202 (7) 1.95 1.40

"Century 21" International Exposition, Seattle, Wash., Apr. 21-Oct. 21.
For overprints see #503-504, C206-C207.

Plan of Duvalier Ville and Stamp of 1904 — A102

1962, Dec. 10 **Photo.** ***Perf. 14x14½***

500 A102 5c vio, yel & blk .20 .20
501 A102 10c car rose, yel & blk .20 .20
502 A102 25c bl gray, yel & blk .20 .20
Nos. 500-502,C203-C205 (6) 1.70 1.50

Issued to publicize Duvalier Ville.
For surcharge see No. B30.

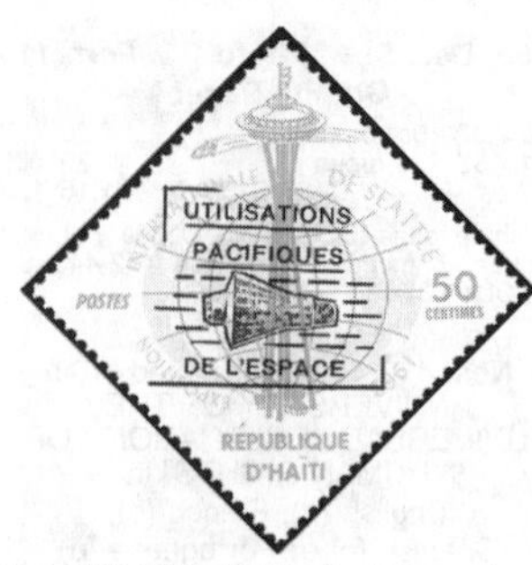

Nos. 498-499 with Vertical Overprint in Black Similar to

1963, Jan. 23 **Litho.** ***Perf. 12½***

503 A101 50c emerald & yel .50 .30
a. Claret overprint, horiz. .45 .30
504 A101 1g car & lt grn .90 .35
a. Claret overprint, horiz. .75 .40
Nos. 503-504,C206-C207 (4) 3.55 1.80
Nos. 503a-504a,C206a-C207a (4) 3.70 2.40

"Peaceful Uses of Outer Space." The black vertical overprint has no outside frame lines and no broken shading lines around capsule. Nos. 503a and 504a were issued Feb. 20.

Symbolic Harvest A103

1963, July 12 **Photo.** ***Perf. 13x14***

505 A103 10c orange & blk .20 .20
506 A103 20c bluish grn & blk .20 .20
Nos. 505-506,C208-C209 (4) .90 .80

FAO "Freedom from Hunger" campaign.

J. J. Dessalines A104

Weight Lifter A105

1963, Oct. 17 ***Perf. 14x14½***

507 A104 5c tan & ver .20 .20
508 A104 10c yellow & blue .20 .20
Nos. 507-508,C214-C215 (4) .80 .80

For overprints see Nos. 509, C216-C217.

No. 508 Overprinted: "FETE DES MERES / 1964"

1964, July 22

509 A104 10c yellow & blue .20 .20
Nos. 509,C216-C218 (4) .95 .80

Issued for Mother's Day, 1964.

1964, Nov. 12 **Photo.** ***Perf. 11½***

Granite Paper

Design: 50c, Hurdler.

510 A105 10c lt bl & dk brn .20 .20
511 A105 25c salmon & dk brn .20 .20
512 A105 50c pale rose lil & dk brn .20 .20
Nos. 510-512,C223-C226 (7) 1.60 1.40

18th Olympic Games, Tokyo, Oct. 10-25. Printed in sheets of 50 (10x5), with map of Japan in background extending over 27 stamps.
For surcharges see #B35-B37, CB51-CB54.

Madonna of Haiti and International Airport, Port-au-Prince A106

1964, Dec. 15 ***Perf. 14½x14***

513 A106 10c org yel & blk .20 .20
514 A106 25c bl grn & blk .20 .20
515 A106 50c brt yel grn & blk .25 .20
516 A106 1g vermilion & blk .35 .25
Nos. 513-516,C227-C229 (7) 2.50 1.75

Same Overprinted "1965"

1965, Feb. 11

517 A106 10c org, yel & blk .20 .20
518 A106 25c blue grn & blk .20 .20
519 A106 50c brt yel grn & blk .25 .20
520 A106 1g vermilion & blk .35 .25
Nos. 517-520,C230-C232 (7) 2.40 1.85

Unisphere, NY World's Fair — A107

1965, Mar. 22 **Photo.** ***Perf. 13½***

20c, "Rocket Thrower" by Donald De Lue.

521 A107 10c grn, yel ol & dk red .20 .20
522 A107 20c plum & orange .20 .20
523 A107 50c dk brn, dk red, yel & grn .25 .20
Nos. 521-523,C233-C235 (6) 2.95 2.60

New York World's Fair, 1964-65.

Merchantmen — A108

1965, May 13 **Unwmk.** ***Perf. 11½***

524 A108 10c blk, lt grn & red .20 .20
525 A108 50c blk, lt bl & red .20 .20
Nos. 524-525,C236-C237 (4) 1.00 .90

The merchant marine.

ITU Emblem, Old and New Communication Equipment — A109

1965, Aug. 16 **Litho.** ***Perf. 13½***

526 A109 10c gray & multi .20 .20
527 A109 25c multicolored .20 .20
528 A109 50c multicolored .20 .20
Nos. 526-528,C242-C245 (7) 2.15 1.90

Cent. of the ITU.
For overprints see #537-539, C255-C256.

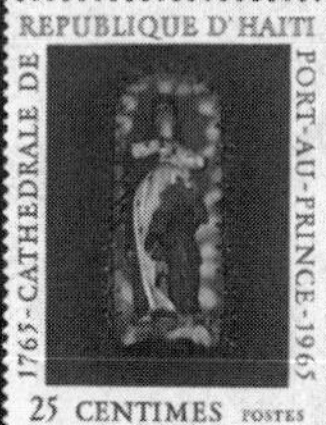

Statue of Our Lady of the Assumption A110

Designs: 5c, Cathedral of Port-au-Prince, horiz. 10c, High altar.

Perf. 14x13, 13x14

1965, Nov. 19 **Photo.**

Size: 39x29mm, 29x39mm

529 A110	5c	multicolored	.20	.20
530 A110	10c	multicolored	.20	.20
531 A110	25c	multicolored	.20	.20
		Nos. 529-531,C246-C248 (6)	3.10	2.75

200th anniv. of the Metropolitan Cathedral of Port-au-Prince.

Passionflower A111

Flowers: 5c, 15c, American elder. 10c, Okra.

1965, Dec. 20 **Photo.** *Perf. 11½*

Granite Paper

532 A111	3c	dk vio, lt vio bl & grn	.20	.20
533 A111	5c	grn, lt bl & yel	.20	.20
534 A111	10c	multicolored	.20	.20
a.		"0.10" omitted		
535 A111	15c	grn, pink & yel	.20	.20
536 A111	50c	dk vio, yel & grn	.20	.20
		Nos. 532-536,C249-C254 (11)	3.80	3.55

For surcharges see Nos. 566, B38-B40, CB55-CB56.

Nos. 526-528 Overprinted in Red: "20e. Anniversaire / UNESCO"

1965, Aug. 27 **Litho.** *Perf. 13½*

537 A109	10c	gray & multi	.20	.20
538 A109	25c	yel brn & multi	.35	.35
539 A109	50c	pale grn & multi	.70	.70
		Nos. 537-539,C255-C256 (5)	4.25	2.30

20th anniversary of UNESCO.

Amulet — A112

Ceremonial Stool — A113

Perf. 14x½x14, 14x14½

1966, Mar. 14 **Photo.** **Unwmk.**

540 A112	5c	grnsh bl, blk & yel	.20	.20
541 A113	10c	multi	.20	.20
542 A112	50c	scar, yel & blk	.20	.20
		Nos. 540-542,C257-C259 (6)	2.20	1.75

For overprints and surcharges see Nos. 543, 567-570, C260-C261, C280-C281.

No. 541 Overprinted in Red: "Hommage / a Hailé Sélassiéler / 24-25 Avril 1966"

1966, Apr. 24

543 A113	10c	multi	.20	.20
		Nos. 543,C260-C262 (4)	1.80	1.50

Visit of Emperor Haile Selassie of Ethiopia, Apr. 24-25.

Space Rendezvous of Gemini VI and VII, Dec. 15, 1965 A114

1966, May 3 *Perf. 13½*

544 A114	5c	vio bl, brn & lt bl	.20	.20
545 A114	10c	pur, brn & lt bl	.20	.20
546 A114	25c	grn, brn & lt bl	.20	.20
547 A114	50c	dk red, brn & lt bl	.20	.20
		Nos. 544-547,C263-C265 (7)	1.90	1.70

Walter M. Shirra, Thomas P. Stafford, Frank A. Borman, James A. Lovell and Gemini VI.

For overprint see No. 584.

Soccer Ball within Wreath and Pres. Duvalier A115

Design: 10c, 50c, Soccer player within wreath and Duvalier.

Lithographed and Photogravure

1966, June 16 *Perf. 13x13½*

Portrait in Black; Gold Inscription; Green Commemorative Inscription in Two Lines

548 A115	5c	pale sal & grn	.20	.20
549 A115	10c	lt ultra & grn	.20	.20
550 A115	15c	lt grn & grn	.20	.20
551 A115	50c	pale lil rose & grn	.20	.20

Green Commemorative Inscription in 3 Lines; Gold Inscription Omitted

552 A115	5c	pale sal & grn	.20	.20
553 A115	10c	lt ultra & grn	.20	.20
554 A115	15c	lt grn & grn	.20	.20
555 A115	50c	pale lil rose & grn	.20	.20
		Nos. 548-555,C266-C269 (12)	3.00	2.80

Caribbean Soccer Festival, June 10-22. Nos. 548-551 also for the Natl. Soccer Championships, May 8-22.

For surcharges and overprint see Nos. 578-579, C288, CB57.

"ABC," Boy and Girl — A116

10c, Scout symbols. 25c, Television set, book and communications satellite, horiz.

Perf. 14x13½, 13½x14

1966, Oct. 18 **Litho. & Engr.**

556 A116	5c	grn, sal pink & brn	.20	.20
557 A116	10c	red brn, lt brn & blk	.20	.20
558 A116	25c	grn, bl & dk vio	.20	.20
		Nos. 556-558,C270-C272 (6)	1.50	1.50

Issued to publicize education through literacy, Scouting and by audio-visual means.

Dr. Albert Schweitzer, Maps of Alsace and Gabon — A117

Designs: 10c, Dr. Schweitzer and pipe organ. 20c, Dr. Schweitzer and Albert Schweitzer Hospital, Deschapelles, Haiti.

Perf. 12½x13

1967, Apr. 20 **Photo.** **Unwmk.**

559 A117	5c	pale lil & multi	.20	.20
560 A117	10c	buff & multi	.20	.20
561 A117	20c	gray & multi	.20	.20
		Nos. 559-561,C273-C276 (7)	2.30	2.25

Issued in memory of Dr. Albert Schweitzer (1875-1965), medical missionary to Gabon, theologian and musician.

Watermelon and J. J. Dessalines — A118

1967, July 4 **Photo.** *Perf. 12½*

562 A118	5c	shown	.20	.20
563 A118	10c	Cabbage	.20	.20
564 A118	20c	Tangerine	.20	.20
565 A118	50c	Chayote	.20	.20
		Nos. 562-565,C277-C279 (7)	1.70	1.55

No. 532 Surcharged

1967, Aug. 21 **Photo.** *Perf. 11½*

566 A111	50c	on 3c multi	.20	.20
		Nos. 566,B38-B40,CB55-CB56 (6)	1.30	1.30

12th Boy Scout World Jamboree, Farragut State Park, Idaho, Aug. 1-9.

Nos. 540-542 Overprinted and Surcharged

Perf. 14½x14, 14x14½

1967, Aug. 30 **Photo.**

567 A112	5c	grnsh bl, blk & yel	.20	.20
568 A113	10c	multi	.20	.20
569 A112	50c	scar, yel & blk	.20	.20
570 A112	1g	on 5c multi	.28	.25
		Nos. 567-570,C280-C281 (6)	2.08	1.80

EXPO '67 Intl. Exhibition, Montreal, 4/28-10/27.

Pres. Duvalier and Brush Turkey A119

1967, Sept. 22 **Photo.** *Perf. 14x13*

571 A119	5c	car rose & gold	.20	.20
572 A119	10c	ultra & gold	.20	.20
573 A119	25c	dk red brn & gold	.20	.20
574 A119	50c	dp red lil & gold	.20	.20
		Nos. 571-574,C282-C284 (7)	2.35	2.05

10th anniversary of Duvalier revolution.

Writing Hands A120

Designs: 10c, Scout emblem and Scouts, vert. 25c, Audio-visual teaching of algebra.

1967, Dec. 11 **Litho.** *Perf. 11½*

575 A120	5c	multicolored	.20	.20
576 A120	10c	multicolored	.20	.20
577 A120	25c	dk grn, lt bl & yel	.20	.20
		Nos. 575-577,C285-C287 (6)	1.50	1.40

Issued to publicize the importance of education.

For surcharges see Nos. CB58-CB60.

Nos. 552 and 554 Surcharged

Lithographed and Photogravure

1968, Jan. 18 *Perf. 13x13½*

578 A115	50c	on 15c	.20	.20
579 A115	1g	on 5c	.25	.20
		Nos. 578-579,C288,CB57 (4)	1.95	1.70

19th Olympic Games, Mexico City, Oct. 12-27.

The 1968 date is missing on 2 stamps in every sheet of 50.

Caiman Woods, by Raoul Dupoux A121

1968, Apr. 22 **Photo.** *Perf. 12*

Size: 36x26mm

580 A121	5c	multi	.20	.20
581 A121	10c	rose red & multi	.20	.20
582 A121	25c	multi	.20	.20
583 A121	50c	dl lil & multi	.20	.20
		Nos. 580-583,C289-C295 (11)	4.30	3.70

Caiman Woods ceremony during the Slaves' Rebellion, Aug. 14, 1791.

No. 547 Overprinted

1968, Apr. 19 **Photo.** *Perf. 13½*

584 A114	50c	dk red, brn & lt bl	.70	.70
		Nos. 584,C296-C298 (4)	3.95	2.35

10th Winter Olympic Games, Grenoble, France, Feb. 6-18, 1968.

Monument to the Unknown Maroon — A122

Palm Tree and Provincial Coats of Arms — A123

Madonna, Papal Arms and Arms of Haiti — A124

1968, May 22 *Perf. 11½*

Granite Paper

585 A122 5c bl & blk .20 .20
586 A122 10c rose brn & blk .20 .20
587 A122 20c vio & blk .20 .20
588 A122 25c lt ultra & blk .20 .20
589 A122 50c brt bl grn & blk .25 .20
Nos. 585-589,C299-C301 (8) 2.15 1.80

Unveiling of the monument to the Unknown Maroon, Port-au-Prince.
For surcharges see Nos. C324-C325.

Perf. 13x14, 12½x13½

1968, Aug. 16 **Photo.**

Design: 25c, Cathedral, arms of Pope Paul VI and arms of Haiti.

590 A123 5c grn & multi .20 .20
591 A124 10c brn & multi .20 .20
592 A124 25c multi .20 .20
Nos. 590-592,C302-C305 (7) 2.20 2.05

Consecration of the Bishopric of Haiti, 10/28/66.

Air Terminal, Port-au-Prince — A125

1968, Sept. 22 **Photo.** *Perf. 11½*

Portrait in Black

593 A125 5c brn & lt ultra .20 .20
594 A125 10c brn & lt bl .20 .20
595 A125 25c brn & pale lil .20 .20
Nos. 593-595,C306-C308 (6) 1.90 1.80

Inauguration of the Francois Duvalier Airport in Port-au-Prince.

Slave Breaking Chains, Map of Haiti, Torch, Conch — A126

1968, Oct. 28 **Litho.** *Perf. 14½x14*

596 A126 5c brn, lt bl & brt pink .20 .20
597 A126 10c brn, lt ol & brt pink .20 .20
598 A126 25c brn, bis & brt pink .20 .20
Nos. 596-598,C310-C313 (7) 2.05 1.85

Slaves' Rebellion, of 1791.

Children Learning to Read A127

10c, Children watching television. 50c, Hands setting volleyball and sports medal.

1968, Nov. 14 *Perf. 11½*

599 A127 5c multi .20 .20
600 A127 10c multi .20 .20
601 A127 50c multi .20 .20
Nos. 599-601,C314-C316 (6) 1.60 1.40

Issued to publicize education through literacy, audio-visual means and sport.
For surcharges see #B41-B42, CB61-CB62.

Winston Churchill — A128

Churchill: 5c, as painter. 10c, as Knight of the Garter. 15c, and soldiers at Normandy. 20c, and early seaplane. 25c, and Queen Elizabeth II. 50c, and Big Ben, London.

1968, Dec. 23 **Photo.** *Perf. 13*

602 A128 3c gold & multi .20 .20
603 A128 5c gold & multi .20 .20
604 A128 10c gold & multi .20 .20
605 A128 15c gold & multi .20 .20
606 A128 20c gold & multi .20 .20
607 A128 25c gold & multi .20 .20
608 A128 50c gold & multi .20 .20
Nos. 602-608,C319-C322 (11) 2.50 2.40

Exist imperf. For surcharge see No. 828.

1968 Winter Olympics, Grenoble A128a

Designs: 5c, 1.50g, Peggy Fleming, US, figure skating. 10c, Harold Groenningen, Norway, cross-country skiing. 20c, Belousova & Protopopov, USSR, pairs figure skating. 25c, Toini Gustafsson, Sweden, cross country skiing. 50c, Eugenio Monti, Italy, 4-man bobsled. 2g, Erhard Keller, Germany, speed skating. 4g, Jean-Claude Killy, France, downhill skiing.

1968 **Litho.** *Perf. 14x13½*

609 A128a 5c brt bl & multi
609A A128a 10c bl grn & multi
609B A128a 20c brt rose & multi
609C A128a 25c sky bl & multi
609D A128a 50c ol bis & multi
609E A128a 1.50g vio & multi

Size: 36x65mm

Perf. 12x12½

609F A128a 2g emer grn & multi

Souvenir Sheet

609G A128a 4g brn & multi

No. 609G contains one 36x65mm stamp. Nos. 609F-609G are airmail. No. 609G exists imperf. with green, brown and blue margin.

No. 589 Surcharged with New Value and Rectangle

1969, Feb. 21 **Photo.** *Perf. 11½*

610 A122 70c on 50c .30 .20
Nos. 610,C324-C325 (3) 1.00 .80

Blue-headed Euphonia — A129

Birds of Haiti: 10c, Hispaniolan trogon. 20c, Palm chat. 25c, Stripe-headed tanager. 50c, Like 5c.

1969, Feb. 26 *Perf. 13½*

611 A129 5c lt grn & multi .20 .20
612 A129 10c yel & multi .20 .20
613 A129 20c cream & multi .20 .20
614 A129 25c lt lil & multi .20 .20
615 A129 50c lt gray & multi .25 .20
Nos. 611-615,C326-C329 (9) 2.50 2.30

For overprints see Nos. C344A-C344D.

Olympic Marathon Winners, 1896-1968 — A130

Designs: Games location, date, winner, country and time over various stamp designs.
Souvenir sheets do not show location, date, country or time.

1969, May 16 *Perf. 12½x12*

Size: 66x35mm (Nos. 616, 616C, 616F, 616O)

616 A130 5c like Greece #124
616A A130 10c like France #124
616B A130 15c US #327
616C A130 20c like Great Britain #142
616D A130 20c Sweden #68
616E A130 25c Belgium #B49
616F A130 25c like France #198
616G A130 25c Netherlands #B30
616H A130 30c US #718
616I A130 50c Germany #B86
616J A130 60c Great Britain #274
616K A130 75c like Finland #B110
616L A130 75c like Australia #277
616M A130 90c Italy #799
616N A130 1g like Japan #822
616O A130 1.25g like Mexico #C328

Souvenir Sheets

616P A130 1.50g US #718, diff.

Imperf

616Q A130 1.50g Germany #B86, diff.

Nos. 616H-616O are airmail. Nos. 616P-616Q contain one 66x35mm stamp. A 2g souvenir sheet exists, perf. & imperf.

Power Lines and Light Bulb — A131

1969, May 22 **Litho.** *Perf. 13x13½*

617 A131 20c lilac & blue .20 .20

Issued to publicize the Duvalier Hydroelectric Station. See Nos. C338-C340.

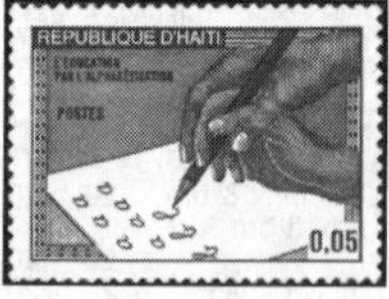

Learning to Write — A132

Designs: 10c, children playing, vert. 50c, Peace poster on educational television, vert.

1969, Aug. 12 **Litho.** *Perf. 13½*

618 A132 5c multi .20 .20
619 A132 10c multi .20 .20
620 A132 50c multi .20 .20
Nos. 618-620,C342-C344 (6) 1.70 1.35

Issued to publicize national education.

ILO Emblem A133

1969, Sept. 22 *Perf. 14*

621 A133 5c bl grn & blk .20 .20
622 A133 10c brn & blk .20 .20
623 A133 20c vio bl & blk .20 .20
Nos. 621-623,C345-C347 (6) 1.70 1.40

50th anniv. of the ILO.

Apollo Space Missions — A133a

Designs: 10c, Apollo 7 rendezvous of command module, third stage. 15c, Apollo 7, preparation for re-entry. 20c, Apollo 8, separation of third stage. 25c, Apollo 8, mid-course correction. 70c, Apollo 8, approaching moon. 1g, Apollo 8, orbiting moon, Christmas 1968, vert. 1.25, Apollo 8, leaving moon. 1.50g, Apollo 8, crew, vert. 1.75g, 2g, Apollo 11, first lunar landing.

1969, Oct. 6 *Perf. 12x12½*

624 A133a 10c brt rose & multi
624A A133a 15c vio & multi
624B A133a 20c ver & multi
624C A133a 25c emer grn & multi
624D A133a 70c brt bl & multi
624E A133a 1g bl grn & multi
624F A133a 1.25g dk bl & multi
624G A133a 1.50g dp rose lil & multi

Souvenir Sheets

624H A133a 1.75g grn & multi
624I A133a 2g sky bl & multi

Nos. 624D-624I are airmail. Nos. 624-624I exist imperf. in different colors.

Papilio Zonaria — A134

Butterflies: 20c, Zerene cesonia cynops. 25c, Papilio machaonides.

1969, Nov. 14 **Photo.** *Perf. 13½*

625 A134 10c pink & multi .20 .20
626 A134 20c gray & multi .20 .20
627 A134 25c lt bl & multi .20 .20
Nos. 625-627,C348-C350 (6) 1.75 1.70

Martin Luther King, Jr. A135

1970, Jan. 12 **Litho.** *Perf. 12½x13½*

628 A135 10c bis, red & blk .20 .20
629 A135 20c grnsh bl, red & blk .20 .20
630 A135 25c brt rose, red & blk .20 .20
Nos. 628-630,C351-C353 (6) 1.70 1.40

Martin Luther King, Jr. (1929-1968), American civil rights leader.

Laeliopsis Dominguensis A136

UPU Monument and Map of Haiti A137

Haitian Orchids: 20c, Oncidium Haitiense. 25c, Oncidium calochilum.

1970, Apr. 3 Litho. *Perf. 13x12½*

631 A136 10c yel, lil & blk .20 .20
632 A136 20c lt bl grn, yel & brn .20 .20
633 A136 25c bl & multi .30 .20
Nos. 631-633,C354-C356 (6) 1.95 1.70

1970, June 23 Photo. *Perf. 11½*

Designs: 25c, Propeller and UPU emblem, vert. 50c, Globe and doves.

634 A137 10c blk, brt grn & ol bis .20 .20
635 A137 25c blk, brt rose & ol bis .20 .20
636 A137 50c blk & bl .35 .25
Nos. 634-636,C357-C359 (6) 2.15 1.75

16th Cong. of the UPU, Tokyo, Oct. 1-Nov. 16, 1970.

For overprints see Nos. 640, C360-C362.

Map of Haiti, Dam and Generator A138

Design: 25c, Map of Haiti, dam and pylon.

1970 Litho. *Perf. 14x13½*

637 A138 20c lt grn & multi .20 .20
638 A138 25c lt bl & multi .20 .20

François Duvalier Central Hydroelectric Plant.

For surcharges see #B43-B44, RA40-RA41.

Apollo 12 A138a

1970, Sept. 7 *Perf. 13½x14*

639 A138a 5c Lift-off
639A A138a 10c 2nd stage ignition
639B A138a 15c Docking preparations
639C A138a 20c Heading for moon
639D A138a 25c like 639B
639E A138a 25c Lunar exploration
639F A138a 30c Landing on Moon
639G A138a 30c Lift-off from Moon
639H A138a 40c 3rd stage separation
639I A138a 40c Lunar module, crew
639J A138a 50c Lunar orbital activities
639K A138a 50c Leaving Moon orbit
639L A138a 75c In Earth orbit
639M A138a 1g Re-entry
639N A138a 1.25g Landing at sea
639O A138a 1.50g Docking with lunar module
Nos. 639-639O (16) 7.50 3.75

Nos. 639E, 639G, 639I, 639K-639O are airmail. Nos. 639-639O exist imperf. with brighter colors.

For overprints see Nos. 656-656O.

No. 636 Overprinted in Red with UN Emblem and: "XXVe ANNIVERSAIRE / O.N.U."

1970, Dec. 14 Photo. *Perf. 11½*

640 A137 50c blk & bl .20 .20
Nos. 640,C360-C362 (4) 1.60 1.30

UN, 25th anniv.

Fort Nativity, Drawing by Columbus — A139

Ascension, by Castera Bazile — A140

1970, Dec. 22

641 A139 3c dk brn & buff .20 .20
642 A139 5c dk grn & pale grn .20 .20

Christmas 1970.

1971, Apr. 29 Litho. *Perf. 12x12½*

Paintings: 5c, Man with Turban, by Rembrandt. 20c, Iris in a Vase, by Van Gogh. 50c, Baptism of Christ, by Castera Bazile. No. 647, Young Mother Sewing, by Mary Cassatt. No. 648, The Card Players, by Cezanne.

Size: 20x40mm

643 A140 5c multi .20 .20
644 A140 10c multi .20 .20

Perf. 13x12½

Size: 25x37mm

645 A140 20c multi .20 .20

Perf. 12x12½

Size: 20x40mm

646 A140 50c multi .30 .20
Nos. 643-646,C366-C368 (7) 2.00 1.70

Souvenir Sheets

Imperf

647 A140 3g multi 1.00 1.00
648 A140 3g multi 1.00 1.00

No. 647 contains one stamp, size: 20x40mm, No. 648 size: 25x37mm.

Nos. 643-646, C366-C368 exist imperf in changed colors.

Soccer Ball — A141

Design: No. 651, 1g, 5g, Jules Rimet cup.

1971, June 14 Photo. *Perf. 11½*

649 A141 5c salmon & blk .20 .20
650 A141 50c tan & blk .20 .20
651 A141 50c rose pink, blk & gold .20 .20
652 A141 1g lil, blk & gold .40 .30
653 A141 1.50g gray & blk .50 .40
654 A141 5g gray, blk & gold 1.75 1.50
Nos. 649-654 (6) 3.25 2.80

Souvenir Sheet

Imperf

655 Sheet of 2 8.50 7.00
a. A141 70c light violet & black 2.50
b. A141 1g light green, blue & gold 2.50

9th World Soccer Championships for the Jules Rimet Cup, Mexico City, May 30-June 21, 1970. The surface tint of the sheets of 50 (10x5) of Nos. 649-654 includes a map of Brazil covering 26 stamps. Positions 27, 37 and 38 inscribed "Brasilia," "Santos," "Rio de Janeiro" respectively. On soccer ball design the 4 corner stamps are inscribed "Pele."

Nos. 655a and 655b have portions of map of Brazil in background; No. 655a inscribed "Pele" and "Santos," No. 655b "Brasilia."

Nos. 639-639O Ovptd. in Gold

1971, Mar. 15

656 A138a 5c multicolored
656A A138a 10c multicolored
656B A138a 15c multicolored
656C A138a 20c multicolored
656D A138a 25c multicolored
656E A138a 25c multicolored
656F A138a 30c multicolored
656G A138a 30c multicolored
656H A138a 40c multicolored
656I A138a 40c multicolored
656J A138a 50c multicolored
656K A138a 50c multicolored
656L A138a 75c multicolored
656M A138a 1g multicolored
656N A138a 1.25g multicolored
656O A138a 1.50g multicolored
Nos. 656-656O (16) 7.50

Nos. 656E, 656G, 656I, 656K-656O are airmail.

Exist overprinted in silver.

J. J. Dessalines — A142

1972, Apr. 28 Photo. *Perf. 11½*

657 A142 5c grn & blk .20 .20
658 A142 10c brt bl & blk .20 .20
659 A142 25c org & blk .20 .20
Nos. 657-659,C378-C379 (5) 1.30 1.20

See Nos. 697-700, C448-C458, 727, C490-C493, C513-C514. For surcharges see Nos. 692, 705-709, 724-726, C438, C512.

"Sun" and EXPO '70 Emblem — A143

1972, Oct. 27 Photo. *Perf. 11½*

660 A143 10c ocher, brn & grn .20 .20
661 A143 25c ocher, brn & mar .20 .20
Nos. 660-661,C387-C390 (6) 2.25 1.60

EXPO '70 International Exposition, Osaka, Japan, Mar. 15-Sept. 13, 1970.

Gold Medalists, 1972 Summer Olympics, Munich — A143a

Designs: 5c, L. Linsenhoff, dressage, W. Ruska, judo. 10c, S. Kato, gymnastics, S.Gould, women's swimming. 20c, M. Peters, women's pentathlon, K. Keino, steeplechase. 25c, L. Viren, 5,000, 10,000m races, R. Milburn, 110m hurdles. No. 662D, D. Morelon, cycling, J. Akii-Bua, 400m hurdles. No. 662E, R. Williams, long jump. 75c, G. Mancinelli, equestrian. 1.50g, W. Nordwig, pole vault. 2.50g, K. Wolferman, javelin. 5g, M. Spitz, swimming.

1972, Dec. 29 *Perf. 13½*

662 A143a 5c multicolored
662A A143a 10c multicolored
662B A143a 20c multicolored
662C A143a 25c multicolored
662D A143a 50c multicolored
662E A143a 50c multicolored
662F A143a 75c multicolored
662G A143a 1.50g multicolored
662H A143a 2.50g multicolored
662I A143a 5g multicolored

Nos. 662E-662I are airmail.

Basket Vendors A144

Designs: 80c, 2.50g, Postal bus.

1973, Jan. Photo. *Perf. 11½*

665 A144 50c blk & multi .20 .20
666 A144 80c blk & multi .30 .20
667 A144 1.50g blk & multi .50 .30
668 A144 2.50g blk & multi 1.25 .50
Nos. 665-668 (4) 2.25 1.20

20th anniv. of Caribbean Travel Assoc.

Space Exploration

A set of 12 stamps for US-USSR space exploration, the same overprinted for the centenary of the UPU and 3 overprinted in silver for Apollo 17 exist but we have no evidence that they were printed with the approval of the Haitian postal authorities.

Micromelo Undata A145

Designs: Marine life; 50c horizontal.

1973, Sept. 4 Litho. *Perf. 14*

669 A145 5c *shown* .20 .20
670 A145 10c *Nemaster rubiginosa* .20 .20
671 A145 25c *Cyerce cristallina* .20 .20
672 A145 50c *Desmophyllum riisei* .20 .20
Nos. 669-672,C395-C398 (8) 2.20 1.90

For surcharge see No. C439.

Gramma Loreto — A146

1973 *Perf. 13½*

673 A146 10c *shown* .20 .20
674 A146 50c *Acanthurus coeruleus* .20 .20
Nos. 673-674,C399-C402 (6) 2.65 2.10

For surcharges see Nos. 693, C440.

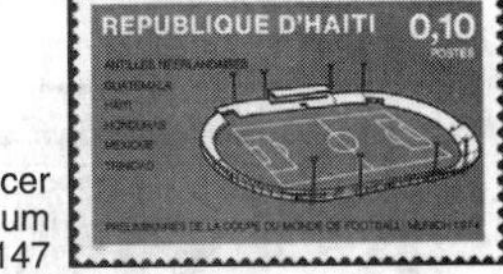

Soccer Stadium A147

Design: 20c, Haiti No. 654.

1973, Nov. 29 ***Perf. 14x13***

675 A147 10c bis, blk & emer	.20	.20
676 A147 20c rose lil, blk & tan	.20	.20
Nos. 675-676,C407-C410 (6)	4.10	3.15

Caribbean countries preliminary games of the World Soccer Championships, Munich, 1974.

Jean Jacques Dessalines A148

Nicolaus Copernicus A149

1974, Apr. 22 **Photo.** ***Perf. 14***

677 A148 10c lt bl & emer	.20	.20
678 A148 20c rose & blk	.20	.20
679 A148 25c yel & vio	.20	.20
Nos. 677-679,C411-C414 (7)	1.85	1.60

For surcharges see Nos. 694, C443.

1974, May 24 **Litho.** ***Perf. 14x13½***

Design: 10c, Symbol of heliocentric system.

680 A149 10c multi	.20	.20
681 A149 25c brt grn & multi	.20	.20
Nos. 680-681,C415-C419 (7)	1.85	1.55

For overprint and surcharges see Nos. 695, C444, C460-C463.

Pres. Jean-Claude Duvalier — A151

1974 **Photo.** ***Perf. 14x13½***

689 A151 10c grn & gold	.20	.20
690 A151 20c car rose & gold	.20	.20
691 A151 50c bl & gold	.20	.20
Nos. 689-691,C421-C426 (9)	3.60	2.85

For surcharge and overprints see Nos. C445, C487-C489.

Audubon Birds

In 1975 or later various sets of bird paintings by Audubon were produced by government employees without official authorization. They were not sold by the Haiti post office and were not valid for postage. The first set consisted of 23 values and was sold in 1975. A second set containing some of the original stamps and some new stamps appeared unannounced several years later. More sets may have been printed as there are 75 different stamps. These consist of 5 denominations each for the 15 designs.

Perf and imperf souvenir sheets picturing Audubon were also produced.

Nos. 659, 673 and 679-680 Surcharged with New Value and Bar

Perf. 11½, 13½, 14, 14x13½

1976 **Photo.; Litho.**

692 A142 80c on 25c	.35	.20
693 A146 80c on 10c	.35	.20
694 A148 80c on 25c	.35	.20
695 A149 80c on 10c	.35	.20
Nos. 692-695 (4)	1.40	.80

Haiti No. C11 and Bicentennial Emblem — A152

1976, Apr. 22 **Photo.** ***Perf. 11½***

Granite Paper

696 A152 10c multi	.20	.20
Nos. 696,C434-C437 (5)	3.05	2.40

American Bicentennial.

Dessalines Type of 1972

1977 **Photo.** ***Perf. 11½***

697 A142 10c rose & blk	.20	.20
698 A142 20c lemon & blk	.20	.20
699 A142 50c vio & blk	.20	.20
700 A142 50c tan & blk	.20	.20
Nos. 697-700 (4)	.80	.80

Dessalines Type of 1972 Surcharged in Black or Red

1978 **Photo.** ***Perf. 11½***

705 A142 1g on 20c (#698)	.35	.20
706 A142 1g on 1.75g (#C454)	.35	.20
707 A142 1.25g on 75c (#C448)	.60	.25
708 A142 1.25g on 1.50g (#C453)	.60	.25
709 A142 1.25g on 1.50g (#C453; R)	.60	.25
Nos. 705-709 (5)	2.50	1.15

Rectangular bar obliterates old denomination on Nos. 705-709 and "Par Avion" on Nos. 706-709.

J. C. Duvalier Earth Telecommunications Station — A153

Designs: 20c, Video telephone. 50c, Alexander Graham Bell, vert.

1978, June 19 **Litho.** ***Perf. 13½***

710 A153 10c multi	.20	.20
711 A153 20c multi	.20	.20
712 A153 50c multi	.20	.20
Nos. 710-712,C466-C468 (6)	1.80	1.45

Centenary of first telephone call by Alexander Graham Bell, Mar. 10, 1876.

Athletes' Inaugural Parade — A154

1978, Sept. 4 **Litho.** ***Perf. 13½x13***

713 A154 5c shown	.20	.20
714 A154 25c Bicyclists	.20	.20
715 A154 50c High jump	.20	.20
Nos. 713-715,C469-C471 (6)	3.85	2.10

21st Olympic Games, Montreal, 7/17-8/1/76.

Mother Nursing Child — A155

Mother Feeding Child — A156

1979, Jan. 15 **Photo.** ***Perf. 14x14½***

716 A155 25c multi	.20	.20
Nos. 716,C472-C473 (3)	1.10	.85

Inter-American Children's Inst., 50th anniv.

1979, May 11 **Photo.** ***Perf. 11½***

717 A156 25c multi	.20	.20
718 A156 50c multi	.20	.20
Nos. 717-718,C474-C476 (5)	1.60	1.25

30th anniversary of CARE (Cooperative for American Relief Everywhere).

Human Rights Emblem — A157

1979, July 20 **Litho.** ***Perf. 14***

719 A157 25c multi	.20	.20
Nos. 719,C477-C479 (4)	1.85	1.05

30th anniversary of declaration of human rights.

Anti-Apartheid Year Emblem, Antenor Firmin, "On the Equality of Human Races" A158

1979, Nov. 22 **Photo.** ***Perf. 12x11½***

720 A158 50c tan & black	.20	.20
Nos. 720,C480-C482 (4)	1.85	1.05

Anti-Apartheid Year (1978).

Children Playing, IYC Emblem A159

1979, Dec. 19 **Photo.** ***Perf. 12***

721 A159 10c multi	.20	.20
722 A159 25c multi	.20	.20
723 A159 50c multi	.30	.20
Nos. 721-723,C483-C486 (7)	4.60	2.60

International Year of the Child.

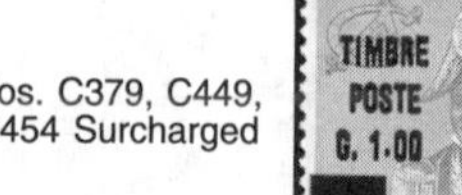

Nos. C379, C449, C454 Surcharged

1980 **Photo.** ***Perf. 11½***

Granite Paper

724 A142 1g on 2.50g lil & blk	.30	.20
725 A142 1.25g on 80c emer & blk	.35	.30
726 A142 1.25g on 1.75g rose & blk	.35	.30
Nos. 724-726 (3)	1.00	.80

Dessalines Type of 1972

1980, Aug. 27 **Photo.** ***Perf. 11½***

Granite Paper

727 A142 25c org yel & blk	.20	.20
Nos. 727,C490-C493 (5)	2.80	2.05

Henry Christophe Citadel — A160

1980, Dec. 2 **Litho.** ***Perf. 12½x12***

728 A160 5c shown	.20	.20
729 A160 25c Sans Souci Palace	.20	.20
730 A160 50c Vallieres market	.20	.20
Nos. 728-730,C494-C498 (8)	2.90	2.25

World Tourism Conf., Manila, Sept. 27.
For surcharges see Nos. 738, C511.

Soccer Players, World Cup, Flag of Uruguay (1930 Champion) — A161

1980, Dec. 30 **Litho.** ***Perf. 14***

731 A161 10c shown	.20	.20
732 A161 20c Italy, 1934	.20	.20
733 A161 25c Italy, 1938	.20	.20
Nos. 731-733,C499-C506 (11)	4.50	3.60

World Cup Soccer Championship, 50th anniv.
For surcharges see Nos. 741, 829.

Going to Church, by Gregoire Etienne A162

Paintings: 5c, Woman with Birds and Flowers, by Hector Hyppolite, vert. 20c, Street Market, by Petion Savain. 25c, Market Vendors, by Michele Manuel.

1981, May 12 **Photo.** ***Perf. 11½***

734 A162 5c multi	.20	.20
735 A162 10c multi	.20	.20
736 A162 20c multi	.20	.20
737 A162 25c multi	.20	.20
Nos. 734-737,C507-C510 (8)	3.30	2.65

For surcharges see Nos. 739-740.

Nos. 728, 734-735, 732 Surcharged

Perf. 12½x12, 14, 11½

1981, Dec. 30 **Litho., Photo.**

738 A160 1.25g on 5c multi	.35	.30
739 A162 1.25g on 5c multi	.35	.30
740 A162 1.25g on 10c multi	.35	.30
741 A161 1.25g on 20c multi	.35	.30
Nos. 738-741,C511-C512 (6)	2.30	1.95

10th Anniv. of Pres. Duvalier Reforms — A163

1982, June 21 **Photo.** ***Perf. 11½x12***

Granite Paper

742 A163 25c yel grn & blk	.20	.20
743 A163 50c olive & blk	.20	.20
744 A163 1g rose & blk	.30	.20
745 A163 1.25g bl & blk	.35	.30
746 A163 2g org red & blk	.55	.40
747 A163 5g org & blk	1.40	1.00
Nos. 742-747 (6)	3.00	2.30

Nos. 742, 744-746 Overprinted in Blue: "1957-1982 / 25 ANS DE REVOLUTION"

1982, Nov. 29 **Photo.** ***Perf. 11½x12***

Granite Paper

748 A163 25c yel grn & blk	.20	.20
749 A163 1g rose & blk	.30	.20
750 A163 1.25g blue & blk	.35	.30
751 A163 2g org red & blk	.55	.40
Nos. 748-751 (4)	1.40	1.10

25th anniv. of revolution.

Scouting Year A164

Perf. 13½x14, 14x13½

1983, Feb. 26 **Litho.**

752 A164 5c Building campfire .20 .20
753 A164 10c Baden-Powell, vert. .20 .20
754 A164 25c Boat building .20 .20
755 A164 50c like 10c .30 .20
756 A164 75c like 25c .50 .20
757 A164 1g like 5c .75 .20
758 A164 1.25g like 25c .85 .30
759 A164 2g like 10c 1.00 .40
Nos. 752-759 (8) 4.00 1.90

Nos. 756-759 airmail.
For surcharge see No. 827.

Patroness of Haiti — A165

1983, Mar. 9 **Litho.** *Perf. 14*

760 A165 10c multi .20 .20
761 A165 20c multi .20 .20
762 A165 25c multi .20 .20
763 A165 50c multi .20 .20
764 A165 75c multi .20 .20
765 A165 1g multi .30 .20
766 A165 1.25g multi .35 .30
767 A165 1.50g multi .40 .35
768 A165 1.75g multi .50 .40
769 A165 2g multi .55 .40
770 A165 5g multi 1.40 1.00
a. Souvenir sheet, 116x90mm 1.40 1.00
j. Souvenir sheet, 90x116mm 1.40 1.00
Nos. 760-770 (11) 4.50 3.65

Centenary of the Miracle of Our Lady of Perpetual Help. Nos. 764-770 airmail.
For surcharge see No. 875.

UPU Admission, 100th Anniv. A165a

1983, June 10 **Litho.** *Perf. 15x14*

770B A165a 5c shown .20 .20
770C A165a 10c L.F. Salomon, J.C. Duvalier .20 .20
770D A165a 25c No. 1, UPU emblem .20 .20
770E A165a 50c like 5c .20 .20
770F A165a 75c like 10c .20 .20
770G A165a 1g like 5c .30 .20
770H A165a 1.25g like 25c .35 .30
770I A165a 2g like 25c .55 .40
Nos. 770B-770I (8) 2.20 1.90

Nos. 770F-770I airmail.
For surcharge see No. 825.

1982 World Cup — A166

Games and scores. Nos. 776-780 airmail, horiz.

1983, Nov. 22 **Litho.** *Perf. 14*

771 A166 5c Argentina, Belgium .20 .20
772 A166 10c Northern Ireland, Yugoslavia .20 .20
773 A166 20c England, France .20 .20
774 A166 25c Spain, Northern Ireland .20 .20
775 A166 50c Italy (champion) .20 .20
776 A166 1g Brazil, Scotland .30 .20
777 A166 1.25g Northern Ireland, France .35 .30
778 A166 1.50g Poland, Cameroun .40 .30
779 A166 2g Italy, Germany .55 .40
780 A166 2.50g Argentina, Brazil .70 .70
Nos. 771-780 (10) 3.30 2.90

For surcharge see No. 826.

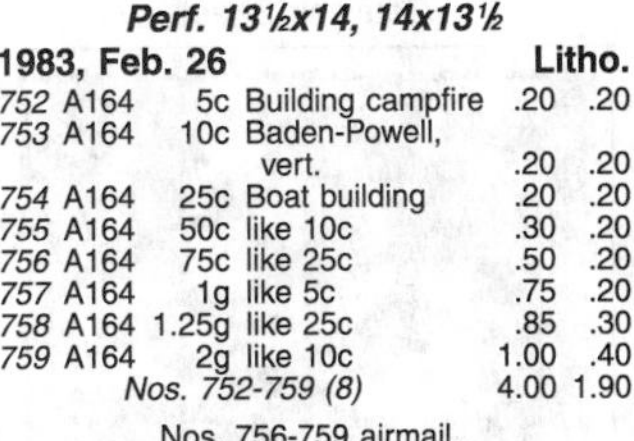

Haiti Postage Stamp Centenary — A167

1984, Feb. 28 **Litho.** *Perf. 14½*

781 A167 5c #1 .20 .20
782 A167 10c #2 .20 .20
783 A167 25c #3 .20 .20
784 A167 50c #5 .20 .20
785 A167 75c Liberty, Salomon .20 .20
786 A167 1g Liberty, Salomon .30 .20
787 A167 1.25g Liberty, Duvalier .35 .30
788 A167 2g Liberty, Duvalier .55 .40
Nos. 781-788 (8) 2.20 1.90

Nos. 785-788 airmail.
For surcharge see No. 826A.

A168

A169

1984, May 30 **Photo.** *Perf. 11½*

Granite Paper

789 A168 25c Broadcasting equipment, horiz. .20 .20
790 A168 50c like 25c .25 .20
791 A168 1g Drum .40 .20
792 A168 1.25g like 1g .50 .30
793 A168 2g Globe .75 .40
794 A168 2.50g like 2g 1.00 .55
Nos. 789-794 (6) 3.10 1.85

World Communications Year.

1984, July 27

Granite Paper

795 A169 5c Javelin, running, pole vault, horiz. .20 .20
796 A169 10c like 5c .20 .20
797 A169 25c Hurdles, horiz. .20 .20
798 A169 50c like 25c .25 .20
799 A169 1g Long jump .35 .20
800 A169 1.25g like 1g .45 .30
801 A169 2g like 1g .75 .40
Nos. 795-801 (7) 2.40 1.70

Souvenir Sheet

802 A169 2.50g like 1g .70 .50

1984 Summer Olympics. No. 802 exists imperf.
For surcharge see No. 874.

Arrival of Europeans in America, 500th Anniv. — A170

The Unknown Indian, detail or full perspective of statue. Nos. 807-809 are vert. and airmail.

1984, Dec. 5 **Litho.** *Perf. 14*

803 A170 5c multi .20 .20
804 A170 10c multi .20 .20
805 A170 25c multi .20 .20
806 A170 50c multi .20 .20
807 A170 1g multi .25 .20
808 A170 1.25g multi .30 .25
809 A170 2g multi .50 .40
a. Souvenir sheet of #806, 809
Nos. 803-809 (7) 1.85 1.65

For surcharge see No. 881.

Simon Bolivar and Alexander Petion — A171

Designs: 25c, 1.25g, 7.50g, Portraits reversed. 50c, 4.50g, Bolivar, flags of Grand Colombian Confederation member nations.

1985, Aug. 30 *Perf. 13½x14*

810 A171 5c multi .20 .20
811 A171 25c multi .20 .20
812 A171 50c multi .20 .20
813 A171 1g multi .25 .20
814 A171 1.25g multi .30 .25
815 A171 2g multi .50 .40
816 A171 7.50g multi 1.75 1.40
Nos. 810-816 (7) 3.40 2.85

Souvenir Sheet

Imperf

817 A171 4.50g multi 1.10 .80

Nos. 813-817 airmail.
For surcharge see No. 876.

Arrival of Europeans in America, 500th Anniv. — A172

Designs: 10c, 25c, 50c, Henri, cacique of Bahoruco, hero of the Spanish period, 1492-1625. 1g, 1.25g, 2g, Henri in tropical forest.

1986, Apr. 11 **Litho.** *Perf. 14*

818 A172 10c multi .20 .20
819 A172 25c multi .20 .20
820 A172 50c multi .20 .20
821 A172 1g multi .30 .20
822 A172 1.25g multi .35 .25
823 A172 2g multi .55 .40
Nos. 818-823 (6) 1.80 1.45

Nos. 821-823 are airmail. A 3g souvenir sheet exists picturing Henri in tropical forest.
For surcharge see No. 883.

Nos. 770B, 771, 781, 756, C322, C500 Surcharged

1986, Apr. 18

825 A165a 25c on 5c No. 770B .20 .20
826 A166 25c on 5c No. 771 .20 .20
826A A167 25c on 5c No. 781 .20 .20
827 A164 25c on 75c No. 756 .20 .20
828 A128 25c on 1.50g No. C322 .20 .20
829 A161 25c on 75c No. C500 .20 .20
Nos. 825-829 (6) 1.20 1.20

Intl. Youth Year — A173

UNESCO, 40th Anniv. (in 1986) — A174

1986, May 20 **Litho.** *Perf. 14x15*

830 A173 10c Afforestation .20 .20
831 A173 25c IYY emblem .20 .20
832 A173 50c Girl Guides .20 .20
833 A173 1g like 10c .30 .20
834 A173 1.25g like 25c .35 .25
835 A173 2g like 50c .55 .40
Nos. 830-835 (6) 1.80 1.45

Souvenir Sheet

836 A173 3g multi *3.50 3.50*

Nos. 833-836 are airmail.
For surcharge see No. 873.

1987, May 29 **Photo.** *Perf. 11½*

Granite Paper

837 A174 10c multi .20 .20
838 A174 25c multi .20 .20
839 A174 50c multi .20 .20
840 A174 1g multi .40 .30
841 A174 1.25g multi .50 .35
842 A174 2.50g multi 1.00 .75
Nos. 837-842 (6) 2.50 2.00

Souvenir Sheet

Granite Paper

843 A174 2g multi *1.10 1.10*

Nos. 840-842 are airmail.
For surcharge see No. 882.

Charlemagne Peralte, Resistance Leader — A175

1988, Oct. 18 **Litho.** *Perf. 14*

844 A175 25c multi .20 .20
845 A175 50c multi .25 .20
846 A175 1g multi .45 .35
847 A175 2g multi .90 .70
a. Souvenir sheet of 1 .90 .90
848 A175 3g multi 1.35 1.00
Nos. 844-848 (5) 3.15 2.45

Nos. 846-848, 847a are airmail.

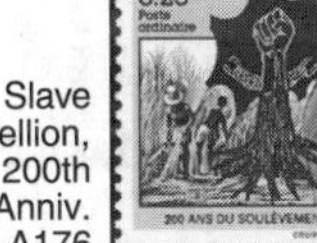

Slave Rebellion, 200th Anniv. A176

Design: 1g, 2g, 3g, Slaves around fire, vert.

1991, Aug. 22 **Litho.** *Perf. 12x11½*

849 A176 25c brt green & multi .25 .20
850 A176 50c pink & multi .50 .40

Perf. 11½x12

851 A176 1g blue & multi 1.00 .75
852 A176 2g yellow & multi 2.00 1.50
a. Souv. sheet of 2, #850 & 852 2.50 1.90
853 A176 3g buff & multi 3.00 2.25
Nos. 849-853 (5) 6.75 5.10

Nos. 851-853 are airmail.

Discovery of America, 500th Anniv. A177

Designs: 25c, 50c, Ships at anchor, men coming ashore, native. 1g, 2g, 3g, Ships, beached long boats, vert.

1993, July 30 **Litho.** *Perf. 11½*

854 A177 25c green & multi .20 .20
855 A177 50c yellow & multi .20 .20
856 A177 1g blue & multi .20 .20
857 A177 2g pink & multi .30 .25
a. Souvenir sheet of 2, #856-857 *6.50*
858 A177 3g orange yellow & multi .50 .40
Nos. 854-858 (5) 1.40 1.25

Nos. 856-858, 857a are airmail.

25th Genl. Assembly of the Organization of American States A178

Designs: 50c, 75c, 7.50g, Emblem, map of Haiti. 1g, 2g, 3g, 5g, Emblems, map of North, South America, vert.

Perf. 14x12½, 12½x14

1995, June 25 Litho.

859 A178 50c violet & multi .25 .20
860 A178 75c green & multi .40 .30
861 A178 1g gray blue & multi .50 .40
862 A178 2g lilac rose & multi 1.00 .75
863 A178 3g green & multi 1.50 1.10
864 A178 5g violet & multi 2.50 1.90
Nos. 859-864 (6) 6.15 4.65

Souvenir Sheet

Imperf

865 A178 7.50g green blue & multi 3.75 2.75

UN, 50th Anniv. A179

Designs: 50c, 75c, Dove holding UN, Haitian flags. 1g, 2g, 3g, 5g, Haitian, UN flags, dove carrying olive branch.

1995, Nov. 24 Litho. *Perf. 12x11½*

866 A179 50c blue & multi *.20 .20*
867 A179 75c lilac & multi *.20 .20*
868 A179 1g apple green & multi *.20 .20*
869 A179 2g yellow & multi *.20 .20*
870 A179 3g orange brown & multi *.30 .25*
871 A179 5g blue green & multi *.55 .40*
Nos. 866-871 (6) *1.65 1.45*

Souvenir Sheet

872 A179 5g multicolored *4.50 3.50*

Nos. 868-872 are airmail.

Nos. 766, 800, 814, 834 Surcharged

1996 *Perfs., Etc., as Before*

873 A173 1g on 1.25g #834 .55 .40
874 A169 2g on 1.25g #800 1.10 .80
875 A165 3g on 1.25g #766 1.60 1.25
876 A171 3g on 1.25g #814 1.60 1.25
Nos. 873-876 (4) 4.85 3.70

Size and location of surcharge varies. Nos. 873, 875-876 are airmail.

1996 Summer Olympic Games, Atlanta — A180

1996, Aug. 2 Litho. *Perf. 14*

877 A180 3g Hurdler .40 .30
878 A180 10g Athlete up close 1.25 1.00

Volleyball Federation, 1996 Summer Olympics, Atlanta — A181

#879: a, 50c, Three players in yellow shirts. b, 75c, Three players in red shirts. c, 1g, Two players in white shirts, torch. d, 2g, Players in yellow, in red.
15g, Player in red.

1996, Aug. 2

879 A181 Sheet of 4, #a.-d. .55 .40

Souvenir Sheet

880 A181 15g multicolored 1.90 1.40

Volleyball, cent. (#880).

Nos. 803, 818, 837 Surcharged

1996, Nov. Litho. *Perfs. as Before*

881 A170 1g on 5c #803 *.40 .30*
882 A174 4g on 10c #837 *1.50 1.10*
883 A172 6g on 10c #818 *2.25 1.60*
Nos. 881-883 (3) *4.15 3.00*

Size and location of surcharge varies.

Christmas A182

Paintings: 2g, The Virgin and Infant, by Jacopo Bellini. 3g, Adoration of the Shepherds, by Strozzi. 6g, Virgin and the Infant, by Giovanni Bellini. 10g, Virgin and the Infant, by Francesco Mazzola. #888, Adoration of the Magi, by Gentile da Fabriano.
#889 The Nativity, by Jan de Beer, horiz.

1996, Dec. 16 Litho. *Perf. 13½x14*

884 A182 2g multicolored .20 .20
885 A182 3g multicolored .30 .25
886 A182 6g multicolored .60 .45
887 A182 10g multicolored 1.00 .75
888 A182 25g multicolored 2.50 2.00
Nos. 884-888 (5) 4.60 3.65

Souvenir Sheet

Perf. 14x13½

889 A182 25g multicolored 2.50 2.00

UNICEF, 50th Anniv. — A183

1997, Jan. 28 *Perf. 14*

890 A183 4g green & multi .40 .30
891 A183 5g pink & multi .50 .40
892 A183 6g blue & multi .60 .45
893 A183 10g brown & multi 1.00 .75
894 A183 20g bister & multi 2.00 1.50
Nos. 890-894 (5) 4.50 3.40

Souvenir Sheet

895 A183 25g like #890-894, vert. 2.50 2.50

#890-894 were each issued in sheets of 6.

Grimm's Fairy Tales — A184

2g, #902a, Sleeping Beauty. 3g, #902b, Snow White. 4g, #902c, Prince awakening Sleeping Beauty. 6g, #902d, Old man sleeping from "The Drink of Life." 10g, #902e, Cinderella. 20g, #902f, Old man awakened after taking drink.
No. 903, Cottage of the Seven Dwarfs, horiz.

1998, Jan. 5 Litho. *Perf. 13½*

896-901 A184 Set of 6 4.75 3.50

Size: 38x50mm

Perf. 14

902 A184 Sheet of 6, #a.-f. 4.75 3.50

Souvenir Sheet

903 A184 25g multicolored *6.00* 2.00

Abstract paintings A185

1998, Oct. 30 Litho. *Perf. 12½*

2g, "Coconut on Pastel Stairs," by Luce Turnier. 3g, "Ogou," by Rose Marie Desruisseau. 5g, "Lantern," by Hilda Williams. 6g, Woman using artist's brush and palette.
15g, Fish, flower and geometric design with faces, snakes by Philippe Dodar.

904 A185 2g multicolored .35 .35
905 A185 3g multicolored .50 .50
906 A185 5g multicolored .85 .85
907 A185 6g multicolored 1.00 1.00
Nos. 904-907 (4) 2.70 2.70

Souvenir Sheet

Perf. 13

908 A185 15g multicolored *4.50 4.50*

Tourism. Nos. 904-907 exist in imperf. souvenir sheet of 4. No. 908 contains one 28x36mm stamp.

Birds A186

Designs: 2g, Priotelus roseigaster. 4g, Xenoligeo mantana. 10g, Phoenicophilus poliocephalus. 20g, Phoenicopterus ruber.

1999, Aug. 27 Litho. *Perf. 14*

909 A186 2g multicolored .25 .25
910 A186 4g multicolored .50 .50
911 A186 10g multicolored 1.25 1.25
912 A186 20g multicolored 2.50 2.50
a. Souvenir sheet, #909-912 4.50 4.50
Nos. 909-912 (4) 4.50 4.50

Nos. 911-912 are airmail.

Worldwide Fund for Nature — A187

No. 913: a, 2g, Hyla vasta. b, 4g, Head of Hyla vasta. c, 2g, Cyclura ricordii. d, 4g, Head of Cyclura ricordii.

1999, Aug. 27 Litho. *Perf. 14*

913 A187 Block of 4, #a.-d. 1.50 1.50

Issued in sheets of 16 (4x4) and 8 (2x4).

Souvenir Sheet

Protection of Natural Resources — A188

1999 Litho. *Perf. 13¾*

914 A188 20g multicolored 2.50 2.50

Chinese Inventions — A189

No. 915, 2g, Movable type. No. 916, 3g, Paper. No. 917, 6g, Gunpowder, cannon. No. 918, 10g, Compass.

1999, Dec. 20 Litho. *Perf. 13¾*

915-918 A189 Set of 4 2.25 2.25
a. Souv. sheet, #915-918 2.25 2.25

UPU, 125th anniv.

Tourism A190

Designs: 2g, Pirogue. 3g, Smiling girl. 4g, Zim Pond, vert. 5g, Ardadins Island, vert. 6g, Gingerbread House. 10g, National Palace.20g, Peligre Reservoir, vert.

Perf. 14¼x14½, 14½x14¼

2000, June 5 Litho.

919-925 A190 Set of 7 5.50 5.50
a. Souv. sheet, #919-925 + label 5.50 5.50

Souvenir Sheet

926 A190 25g Boat "Pays," vert. 3.75 3.75

1801 Constitution, Bicent. A191

Designs: 1g, 2g, 5g, 10g, 25g, 50g, Toussaint L'Ouverture and 1801 Constitution.
No. 933: a, Toussaint L'Ouverture. b, 1801 Constitution.

2001 Litho. *Perf. 13¾x13¼*

927 A191 1g multi — —
928 A191 2g multi — —
929 A191 5g multi — —
930 A191 10g multi — —
931 A191 25g multi — —
932 A191 50g multi — —
Nos. 927-932 (0) .00 .00

Souvenir Sheet

Perf. 12¾

933 A191 25g Sheet of 2, #a-b — —

Nos. 929-932 are airmail. No. 933 contains two 25x29mm stamps.

SEMI-POSTAL STAMPS

Pierre de Coubertin
SP1

Unwmk.
1939, Oct. 3 Engr. *Perf. 12*
B1 SP1 10c + 10c multi 15.00 15.00
Nos. B1,CB1-CB2 (3) 45.00 45.00

Pierre de Coubertin, organizer of the modern Olympic Games. The surtax was used to build a Sports Stadium at Port-au-Prince.

Catalogue values for unused stamps in this section, from this point to the end of the section, are for Never Hinged items.

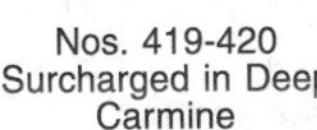

Nos. 419-420 Surcharged in Deep Carmine

Perf. 13x13½, 13½x13
1958, Aug. 30 Litho. Unwmk.
B2 A82 1g + 50c purple 1.75 1.75
B3 A83 1.50g + 50c red org 1.75 1.75
Nos. B2-B3,CB9 (3) 5.50 5.50

The surtax was for the Red Cross. Overprint arranged horizontally on No. B3.

Similar Surcharge in Red on One Line on Nos. 440-441

1959, Apr. 7 Photo. *Perf. 11½*
Granite Paper
B4 A87 10c + 25c rose pink .20 .20
B5 A87 25c + 25c green .25 .20

Nos. 444-446 Surcharged Like Nos. B2-B3 in Red
Perf. 14x13½
B6 A88 10c + 50c vio bl & ol .50 .35
B7 A88 50c + 50c grn & dp brn .50 .40
B8 A88 2g + 50c dp cl & dk brn .70 .70
Nos. B6-B8,CB10-CB15 (9) 4.70 4.25

The surtax was for the Red Cross.

No. 447 Surcharged Diagonally

Unwmk.
1959, July 23 Photo. *Perf. 12*
B9 A89 50c + 20c lt bl & dp cl .50 .50
Nos. B9,CB16-CB18 (4) 2.50 2.35

Issued for the World Refugee Year, July 1, 1959-June 30, 1960.

Nos. 448-450 Surcharged in Dark Carmine

1959, Oct. 30 *Perf. 14*
B10 A90 25c + 75c blk brn & lt bl .50 .50
B11 A90 50c + 75c multi .65 .50
B12 A91 75c + 75c brn & bl .65 .50
Nos. B10-B12,CB19-CB21 (6) 3.75 3.15

The surtax was for Haitian athletes.
On No. B12, surcharge lines are spaced to total depth of 16mm.

No. 436 Surcharged in Red: "Hommage a l'UNICEF +G. 0,50"
Engraved and Lithographed
1960, Feb. 2 *Perf. 11½*
B13 A86 1g + 50c blk & brick red .65 .65
Nos. B13,CB22-CB23 (3) 2.60 2.60

UNICEF.

Nos. 452-453 Surcharged with Additional Value and Overprinted "ALPHABETISATION" in Red or Black
Perf. 12½x13
1960, July 12 Litho. Unwmk.
B14 A92 10c + 20c sal & grn (R) .20 .20
B15 A92 10c + 30c sal & grn .20 .20
B16 A92 50c + 20c vio & mag (R) .30 .20
B17 A92 50c + 30c vio & mag .40 .35
Nos. B14-B17,CB24-CB27 (8) 3.10 2.55

Olympic Games Issue
Nos. 464-465 Surcharged with Additional Value
1960, Sept. 9 Photo. *Perf. 12*
B18 A94 50c + 25c grn & ocher .25 .20
B19 A94 1g + 25c dk brn & grnsh bl .30 .20
Nos. B18-B19,CB28-CB29 (4) 1.10 .90

No. 469 Surcharged: "UNICEF +25 centimes"
1961, Jan. 14 Engr. *Perf. 10½*
B20 A96 1g + 25c grn & blk .30 .20
Nos. B20,CB30-CB31 (3) .85 .65

UNICEF.

No. 469 Surcharged: "OMS SNEM +20 CENTIMES"
1961, Dec. 11
B21 A96 1g + 20c grn & blk .55 .50
Nos. B21,CB35-CB36 (3) 2.70 2.65

Haiti's participation in the UN malaria eradication drive.

Nos. 434, 436 and 438 Surcharged in Black or Red:

(Surcharge arranged to fit shape of stamp.)

1961-62 Engr. & Litho. *Perf. 11½*
B22 A86 20c + 25c blk & yel .20 .20
B23 A86 1g + 50c blk & brick red (R) ('62) .40 .35
B24 A86 2.50g + 50c blk & gray vio (R) ('62) .65 .50
Nos. B22-B24,CB37-CB41 (8) 3.75 3.40

The surtax was for the benefit of the urban rehabilitation program in Duvalier Ville.

Nos. 486-488 Surcharged: "+25 centimes"
1962, Sept. 13 Litho. *Perf. 12*
B25 A99 5c + 25c crim & dp bl .20 .20
B26 A99 10c + 25c red brn & emer .20 .20
B27 A99 50c + 25c bl & crim .20 .20
Nos. B25-B27,CB42-CB44 (6) 1.40 1.20

Nos. 489-490 Surcharged in Red: "+0.20"
1962 Unwmk. *Perf. 12½x13*
B28 A92 10c + 20c bl & org .20 .20
B29 A92 50c + 20c rose lil & ol grn .20 .20
Nos. B28-B29,CB45-CB46 (4) .90 .80

No. 502 Surcharged: "ALPHABETISATION" and "+0,10"
1963, Mar. 15 Photo. *Perf. 14x14½*
B30 A102 25c + 10c bl gray, yel & blk .25 .20
Nos. B30,CB47-CB48 (3) .80 .70

Nos. 491-494 Surcharged and Overprinted in Black or Red With Olympic Emblem and: "JEUX OLYMPIQUES / D'HIVER / INNSBRUCK 1964"
Perf. 14x14½, 14½x14
1964, July 27 Unwmk.
B31 A100 50c + 10c on 3c (R) .30 .20
B32 A100 50c + 10c on 5c .30 .20
B33 A100 50c + 10c on 10c (R) .30 .20
B34 A100 50c + 10c on 25c .30 .20
Nos. B31-B34,CB49 (5) 1.80 1.20

9th Winter Olympic Games, Innsbruck, Austria, Jan. 20-Feb. 9, 1964. The 10c surtax went for charitable purposes.

Nos. 510-512 Surcharged: "+ 5c." in Black
1965, Mar. 15 Photo. *Perf. 11½*
Granite Paper
B35 A105 10c + 5c lt bl & dk brn .20 .20
B36 A105 25c + 5c sal & dk brn .30 .20
B37 A105 50c + 5c pale rose lil & dk brn .40 .20
Nos. B35-B37,CB51-CB54 (7) 2.20 1.75

Nos. B35-B37 and CB51-CB54 also exist with this surcharge (without period after "c") in red. They also exist with a similar black surcharge which lacks the period and is in a thinner, lighter type face.

Nos. 533 and 535-536 Surcharged and Overprinted with Haitian Scout Emblem and "12e Jamboree / Mondial 1967" Like Regular Issue
1967, Aug. 21 Photo. *Perf. 11½*
B38 A111 10c + 10c on 5c multi .20 .20
B39 A111 15c + 10c multi .20 .20
B40 A111 50c + 10c multi .20 .20
Nos. B38-B40,CB55-CB56 (5) 1.20 1.15

12th Boy Scout World Jamboree, Farragut State Park, Idaho, Aug. 1-9. The surcharge on No. B38 includes 2 bars through old denomination.

Nos. 600-601 Surcharged in Red with New Value, Red Cross and: "50ème. Anniversaire / de la Ligue des / Sociétés de la / Croix Rouge"
1969, June 25 Litho. *Perf. 11½*
B41 A127 10c + 10c multi .20 .20
B42 A127 50c + 20c multi .20 .20
Nos. B41-B42,CB61-CB62 (4) 1.30 1.05

50th anniv. of the League of Red Cross Societies.

Nos. 637-638 Surcharged with New Value and: "INAUGURATION / 22-7-71"
1971, Aug. 3 Litho. *Perf. 14x13½*
B43 A138 20c + 50c multi .25 .20
B44 A138 25c + 1.50g multi .65 .40

Inauguration of the François Duvalier Central Hydroelectric Plant, July 22, 1971.

AIR POST STAMPS

Plane over Port-au-Prince — AP1

1929-30 Unwmk. Engr. *Perf. 12*
C1 AP1 25c dp grn ('30) .30 .25
C2 AP1 50c dp vio .40 .20
C3 AP1 75c red brn ('30) 1.25 1.00
C4 AP1 1g dp ultra 1.40 1.25
Nos. C1-C4 (4) 3.35 2.70

AP1a

Red Surcharge

1933, July 6
C4A AP1a 60c on 20c blue 40.00 50.00

Non-stop flight of Capt. J. Errol Boyd and Robert G. Lyon from New York to Port-au-Prince.

Plane over Christophe's Citadel — AP2

1933-40
C5 AP2 50c org brn 3.50 .65
C6 AP2 50c ol grn ('35) 3.25 .65
C7 AP2 50c car rose ('37) 2.00 1.25
C8 AP2 50c blk ('38) 1.50 .65
C8A AP2 60c choc ('40) .65 .20
C9 AP2 1g ultra 1.25 .35
Nos. C5-C9 (6) 12.15 3.75

For surcharge see No. C24.

Dumas Type of Regular Issue
1935, Dec. 29 Litho. *Perf. 11½*
C10 A59 60c brt vio & choc 3.25 1.90

Visit of delegation from France to Haiti.

Arms of Haiti and Portrait of George Washington — AP4

1938, Aug. 29 Engr. *Perf. 12*
C11 AP4 60c deep blue .40 .20

150th anniv. of the US Constitution.

Caribbean Conference Type of Regular Issue
1941, June 30
C12 A60 60c olive 2.50 .65
C13 A60 1.25g purple 2.25 .40

Madonna Type of Regular Issue
1942, Dec. 8 *Perf. 12*
C14 A61 10c dk olive .30 .20
C15 A61 25c brt ultra .40 .30
C16 A61 50c turq grn .70 .30
C17 A61 60c rose car 1.00 .40
C18 A61 1.25g black 2.00 .40
Nos. C14-C18 (5) 4.40 1.60

Souvenir Sheets
Perf. 12, Imperf.

C19 A61 Sheet of 2, #C14, C16 3.50 3.50
C20 A61 Sheet of 2, #C15, C17 3.50 3.50
C21 A61 Sheet of 1, #C18 3.50 3.50

Our Lady of Perpetual Help, patroness of Haiti.

Killick Type of Regular Issue

1943, Sept. 6
C22 A62 60c purple .50 .25
C23 A62 1.25g black 1.50 1.25

No. C8A Surcharged with New Value and Bars in Red

1944, Nov. 25
C24 AP2 10c on 60c choc .35 .25
a. Bars at right vertical 1.75
b. Double surcharge 52.50

Red Cross Type of Regular Issue

1945 **Cross in Rose**
C25 A63 20c yel org .20 .20
C26 A63 25c brt ultra .20 .20
C27 A63 50c ol blk .20 .20
C28 A63 60c dl vio .25 .20
C29 A63 1g yellow 1.00 .20
C30 A63 1.25g carmine .70 .20
C31 A63 1.35g green .70 .35
C32 A63 5g black 5.00 2.00
Nos. C25-C32 (8) 8.25 3.55

Issue dates: 1g, Aug. 14; others, Feb. 20.
For surcharges see Nos. C153-C160.

Catalogue values for unused stamps in this section, from this point to the end of the section, are for Never Hinged items.

Franklin D. Roosevelt — AP11

1946, Feb. 5 **Unwmk.** ***Perf. 12***
C33 AP11 20c black .20 .20
C34 AP11 60c black .20 .20

Capois Type of Regular Issue

1946, July 18 **Engr.**
C35 A64 20c car rose .20 .20
C36 A64 25c dk grn .20 .20
C37 A64 50c orange .20 .20
C38 A64 60c purple .20 .20
C39 A64 1g gray blk .30 .20
C40 A64 1.25g red vio .40 .25
C41 A64 1.35g black .50 .35
C42 A64 5g rose car 1.50 1.00
Nos. C35-C42 (8) 3.50 2.60

For surcharges see Nos. C43-C45, C49-C51, C61-C62.

Nos. C37 and C41 Surcharged with New Value and Bar or Block in Red or Black

1947-48
C43 A64 5c on 1.35g (R) ('48) .40 .20
C44 A64 30c on 50c .30 .20
C45 A64 30c on 1.35g (R) .30 .25
Nos. C43-C45 (3) 1.00 .65

Dessalines Type of 1947-54 Regular Issue

1947, Oct. 17 **Engr.**
C46 A65 20c chocolate .20 .20

Christopher Columbus and Fleet — AP14

Pres. Dumarsais Estiméand Exposition Buildings — AP15

1950, Feb. 12 ***Perf. 12½***
C47 AP14 30c ultra & gray .70 .35
C48 AP15 1g black .70 .30

200th anniversary (in 1949) of the founding of Port-au-Prince.

Nos. C36, C39 and C41 Surcharged or Overprinted in Carmine

1950, Oct. 4 ***Perf. 12***
C49 A64 30c on 25c dk grn .20 .20
a. 30c on 1g gray black 70.00
C50 A64 1g gray blk .40 .35
a. "P" of overprint omitted 42.50 42.50
C51 A64 1.50g on 1.35g blk .65 .65
Nos. C49-C51 (3) 1.25 1.20

75th anniv. (in 1949) of the UPU.

Bananas AP16

Coffee AP17

Sisal AP18

Isabella I AP19

1951, Sept. 3 **Photo.** ***Perf. 12½***
C52 AP16 30c dp org .35 .20
C53 AP17 80c dk grn & sal pink .90 .40
C54 AP18 5g gray 3.25 2.75
Nos. C52-C54 (3) 4.50 3.35

For surcharge see No. C218.

1951, Oct. 12 ***Perf. 13***
C55 AP19 15c brown .20 .20
C56 AP19 30c dull blue .30 .30

Queen Isabella I of Spain, 500th birth anniv.

Type of Regular Issue

1953, May 4 **Engr.** ***Perf. 12***

20c, Cap Haitien Roadstead. 30c, Workers' housing, St. Martin. 1.50g, Restored cathedral. 2.50g, School lunchroom.

C57 A68 20c dp bl .20 .20
C58 A68 30c red brn .25 .20
C59 A68 1.50g gray blk .55 .35
C60 A68 2.50g violet 1.00 .70
Nos. C57-C60 (4) 2.00 1.45

Nos. C38 and C41 Surcharged in Black

1953, May 18
C61 A64 50c on 60c pur .30 .20
a. Double surcharge 50.00 50.00
C62 A64 50c on 1.35g blk .30 .20
a. Double surcharge 50.00

150th anniv. of the adoption of the natl. flag.

Dessalines and Magloire Type and:

Henri Christophe — AP21

1954, Jan. 1 **Photo.** ***Perf. 11½***
C63 AP21 50c shown .25 .20
C64 AP21 50c Toussaint L'Ouverture .25 .20
C65 AP21 50c Dessalines .25 .20
C66 AP21 50c Petion .25 .20
C67 AP21 50c Boisrond-Tonerre .25 .20
C68 AP21 1g Petion .50 .20
C69 AP21 1.50g Lamartiniere 1.00 .65
C70 A69 7.50g shown 3.25 3.25
Nos. C63-C70 (8) 6.00 5.10

See Nos. C95-C96.

Marie Jeanne and Lamartinière Leading Attack — AP23

Design: Nos. C73, C74, Battle of Vertieres.

1954, Jan. 1 ***Perf. 12½***
C71 AP23 50c black .20 .20
C72 AP23 50c carmine .20 .20
C73 AP23 50c ultra .20 .20
C74 AP23 50c sal pink .20 .20
Nos. C71-C74 (4) .80 .80

150th anniv. of Haitian independence.

Mme. Magloire Type of Regular Issue

1954, Jan. 1 ***Perf. 11½***
C75 A72 20c red org .20 .20
C76 A72 50c brown .20 .20
C77 A72 1g gray grn .35 .30
C78 A72 1.50g crimson .40 .35
C79 A72 2.50g bl grn .70 .65
C80 A72 5g gray 1.90 1.50
Nos. C75-C80 (6) 3.75 3.20

Christophe Types of Regular Issue

1954, Dec. 6 **Litho.** ***Perf. 13½x13***
Portraits in Black
C81 A73 50c orange .25 .20
C82 A73 1g blue .40 .35
C83 A73 1.50g green .65 .50
C84 A73 2.50g gray 1.25 .70
C85 A73 5g rose car 2.00 1.40

Perf. 13
Flag in Black and Carmine
C86 A74 50c orange .30 .20
C87 A74 1g dp bl .40 .35
C88 A74 1.50g bl grn .65 .50
C89 A74 2.50g gray 1.25 .70
C90 A74 5g red org 2.00 1.50
Nos. C81-C90 (10) 9.15 6.40

Fort Nativity, Drawing by Christopher Columbus — AP27

1954, Dec. 14 **Engr.** ***Perf. 12***
C91 AP27 50c dk rose car .40 .20
C92 AP27 50c dk gray .40 .20

Dessalines Type of 1955-57 Issue
Perf. 11½

1955, July 14 **Unwmk.** **Photo.**
C93 A75 20c org & blk .20 .20
C94 A75 20c yel grn & blk .20 .20

For overprint see No. C183a.

Portrait Type of 1954
Dates omitted

Design: J. J. Dessalines.

1955, July 19
Portrait in Black
C95 AP21 50c gray .20 .20
C96 AP21 50c blue .20 .20

Dessalines Memorial Type of Regular Issue

1955, Aug. 1
C97 A76 1.50g gray & blk .40 .20
C98 A76 1.50g grn & blk .50 .20

Types of 1956 Regular Issue and

Car and Coastal View — AP30

Designs: No. C100, 75c, Plane, steamship and Haiti map. 1g, Car and coastal view. 2.50g, Flamingo. 5g, Mallard.

1956, Apr. 14 **Unwmk.** ***Perf. 11½***
Granite Paper
C99 AP30 50c hn brn & lt bl .25 .20
C100 AP30 50c blk & gray .20 .20
C101 AP30 75c dp grn & bl grn .35 .30
C102 AP30 1g ol grn & lt bl .35 .20
C103 A77 2.50g dp org & org 2.00 .70
C104 A78 5g red & buff 3.50 1.75
Nos. C99-C104 (6) 6.65 3.35

For overprint see No. C185.

Kant Type of Regular Issue

1956, July 19 **Photo.** ***Perf. 12***
Granite Paper
C105 A79 50c chestnut .20 .20
C106 A79 75c dp yel grn .25 .20
C107 A79 1.50g dp magenta .90 .35
a. Miniature sheet of 3 2.50 1.90
Nos. C105-C107 (3) 1.35 .75

No. C107a exists both perf. and imperf. Each sheet contains Nos. C105, C106 and a 1.25g gray black of same design.

Waterfall Type of Regular Issue

1957, Dec. 16 ***Perf. 11½***
Granite Paper
C108 A80 50c grn & grnsh bl .20 .20
C109 A80 1.50g ol grn & grnsh bl .35 .30
C110 A80 2.50g dk bl & brt bl .65 .50
C111 A80 5g bluish blk & saph 1.50 1.25
Nos. C108-C111 (4) 2.70 2.25

For surcharge and overprint see Nos. CB49, CQ2.

Dessalines Type of Regular Issue

1958, July 2
C112 A81 50c org & blk .20 .20

For overprints see Nos. C184, CQ1.

Brussels Fair Types of Regular Issue, 1958

Perf. 13x13½, 13½x13

1958, July 22 **Litho.** **Unwmk.**
C113 A82 2.50g pale car rose .65 .40
C114 A83 5g bright blue .90 .65
a. Souv. sheet of 2, #C113-C114, imperf. 2.50 2.50

For surcharge see No. CB9.

Sylvio Cator — AP33

1958, Aug. 16 **Photo.** ***Perf. 11½***
Granite Paper
C115 AP33 50c green .20 .20
C116 AP33 50c blk brn .20 .20
C117 AP33 1g org brn .30 .20
C118 AP33 5g gray 1.50 .70
Nos. C115-C118 (4) 2.20 1.30

30th anniversary of the world championship record broad jump of Sylvio Cator.

IGY Type of Regular Issue, 1958

Designs: 50c, US Satellite. 1.50g, Emperor penguins. 2g, Modern observatory.

1958, Oct. 8 *Perf. 14x13½*

C119 A85 50c dp ultra & brn red .30 .20
C120 A85 1.50g brn & crim 1.00 .35
C121 A85 2g dk bl & crim 1.25 .35
a. Souv. sheet of 4, #427, C119-C121, imperf. 3.00 2.50
Nos. C119-C121 (3) 2.55 .90

President Francois Duvalier AP34

Engraved and Lithographed
1958, Oct. 22 Unwmk. *Perf. 11½*
Commemorative Inscription in Ultramarine

C122 AP34 50c blk & rose .65 .20
C123 AP34 2.50g blk & ocher .90 .40
C124 AP34 5g blk & rose lil 1.25 1.00
C125 AP34 7.50g blk & lt bl grn 1.75 1.40
Nos. C122-C125 (4) 4.55 3.00

See note after No. 431.
Souvenir sheets of 3 exist, perf. and imperf., containing one each of Nos. C124-C125 and No. 431. Sheets measure 132x77mm. with marginal inscription in ultramarine. Value, $6.25 each.
For surcharges see Nos. CB37-CB39.

Same Without Commemorative Inscription

1958, Nov. 20

C126 AP34 50c blk & rose .20 .20
C127 AP34 1g blk & vio .35 .20
C128 AP34 1.50g blk & pale brn .50 .30
C129 AP34 2g blk & rose pink .65 .30
C130 AP34 2.50g blk & ocher .65 .35
C131 AP34 5g blk & rose lil 1.25 .90
C132 AP34 7.50g blk & lt bl grn 1.90 1.25
Nos. C126-C132 (7) 5.50 3.50

For surcharges see #CB22-CB23, CB40-CB41.

Type of Regular Issue and

Flags of Haiti and UN — AP35

Perf. 11½
1958, Dec. 5 Unwmk. Photo.
Granite Paper

C133 AP35 50c pink, car & ultra .20 .20
C134 A87 75c brt bl .20 .20
C135 A87 1g brown .35 .20
a. Souv. sheet of 2, #C133, C135, imperf. 2.25 2.25
Nos. C133-C135 (3) .75 .60

For surcharges see Nos. CB10-CB12.

Nos. C133-C135 Overprinted: "10th ANNIVERSARY OF THE UNIVERSAL DECLARATION OF HUMAN RIGHTS," in English (a), French (b), Spanish (c) or Portuguese (d)

1959, Jan. 28

C136 Block of 4 1.90 1.90
a.-d. AP35 50c any single .35 .35
C137 Block of 4 2.50 2.50
a.-d. A87 75c any single .45 .45
C138 Block of 4 5.00 5.00
a.-d. A87 1g any single 1.00 1.00
Nos. C136-C138 (3) 9.40 9.40

Pope Pius XII — AP36

1.50g, Pope praying. 2.50g, Pope on throne.

1959, Feb. 28 Photo. *Perf. 14x13½*

C139 AP36 50c grn & lil .20 .20
C140 AP36 1.50g ol & red brn .35 .20
C141 AP36 2.50g pur & dk bl .65 .30
Nos. C139-C141 (3) 1.20 .70

Issued in memory of Pope Pius XII.
For surcharges see Nos. CB13-CB15.

Lincoln Type of Regular Issue, 1959

Designs: Various Portraits of Lincoln.

1959, May 12 *Perf. 12*

C142 A89 1g lt grn & chnt .25 .20
C143 A89 2g pale lem & sl grn .40 .20
C144 A89 2.50g buff & vio bl .50 .30
a. Min. sheet of 4, #447, C142-C144, imperf. 2.00 2.00
Nos. C142-C144 (3) 1.15 .70

Imperf. pairs exist.
For surcharges see Nos. CB16-CB18.

Pan American Games Types of Regular Issue

Designs: 50c, Jean Baptiste Dessables and map of American Midwest, c. 1791. 1g, Chicago's skyline and Dessables house. 1.50g, Discus thrower and flag of Haiti.

Unwmk.
1959, Aug. 27 Photo. *Perf. 14*

C145 A91 50c hn brn & aqua .40 .20
C146 A90 1g lil & aqua .65 .30
C147 A90 1.50g multi .70 .35
Nos. C145-C147 (3) 1.75 .85

For surcharges see Nos. CB19-CB21.

Nos. C145-C147 Overprinted like No. 451

1960, Feb. 29

C148 A91 50c hn brn & aqua .70 .70
C149 A90 1g lil & aqua 1.25 1.25
C150 A90 1.50g multi 1.40 1.40
Nos. C148-C150 (3) 3.35 3.35

WRY Type of Regular Issue, 1960

1960, Apr. 7 Litho. *Perf. 12½x13*

C151 A92 50c bl & blk .20 .20
C152 A92 1g lt grn & mar .30 .20
a. Souv. sheet of 4, #452-453, C151-C152, imperf. 3.00 3.00

See Nos. C191-C192. For surcharges see Nos. CB24-CB27, CB45-CB46.

Nos. C31, C28 and 369 Surcharged or Overprinted in Red: "28ème ANNIVERSAIRE"

1960, May 8 Engr. *Perf. 12*
Cross in Rose

C153 A63 20c on 1.35g grn .20 .20
C154 A63 50c on 60c dl vio .20 .20
C155 A63 50c on 1.35g grn .20 .20
C156 A63 50c on 2.50g pale vio .20 .20
C157 A63 60c dl vio .25 .20
C158 A63 1g on 1.35g grn .30 .30
C159 A63 1.35g green .50 .40
C160 A63 2g on 1.35g grn .90 .70
Nos. C153-C160 (8) 2.75 2.40

28th anniv. of the Haitian Red Cross. Additional overprint "Avion" on No. C156.

Sugar Type of Regular Issue

Miss Fouchard &: 50c, Harvest. 2.50g, Beach.

Perf. 11½
1960, May 30 Unwmk. Photo.
Granite Paper

C161 A93 50c lil rose & brn .35 .20
C162 A93 2.50g ultra & brn .90 .35

Olympic Type of Regular Issue

Designs: 50c, Pierre de Coubertin, Melbourne stadium and torch. 1.50g, Discus thrower and Rome stadium. 2.50g, Victors' parade, Athens, 1896, and Melbourne, 1956.

1960, Aug. 18 *Perf. 12*

C163 A94 50c mar & bis .20 .20
C164 A94 1.50g rose car & yel grn .40 .20
C165 A94 2.50g sl grn & mag .65 .30
a. Souv. sheet of 2, #465, C165, imperf. 2.00 2.00
Nos. C163-C165 (3) 1.25 .70

For surcharges see Nos. CB28-CB29.

Jeanty Type of Regular Issue

50c, Occide Jeanty and score from "1804." 1.50g, Occide Jeanty and National Capitol.

1960, Oct. 19 *Perf. 14x14½*

C166 A95 50c yel & bl .30 .20
C167 A95 1.50g lil rose & sl grn .50 .20

Printed in sheets of 12 (3x4) with inscription and opening bars of "1804," Jeanty's military march, in top margin.

UN Type of Regular Issue, 1960

1960, Nov. 25 Engr. *Perf. 10½*

C168 A96 50c red org & blk .20 .20
C169 A96 1.50g dk bl & blk .35 .25
a. Souv. sheet of 3, #469, C168-C169, imperf. 1.75 1.75

For surcharges see #CB30-CB31, CB35-CB36.
Nos. C168-C169 exist with centers inverted.

Dessalines Type of Regular Issue

1960, Nov. 5 Photo. *Perf. 11½*
Granite Paper

C170 A81 20c gray & blk .20 .20

For overprint see No. C183.

Sud-Caravelle Jet Airliner and Orchid — AP37

Designs: 50c, Boeing 707 jet airliner, facing left, and Kittyhawk. 1g, Sud-Caravelle jet airliner and Orchid. 1.50g, Boeing 707 jet airliner and air post stamp of 1933.

1960, Dec. 17 Photo. Unwmk.
Granite Paper

C171 AP37 20c dp ultra & car .20 .20
C172 AP37 50c rose brn & grn .20 .20
C173 AP37 50c brt grnsh bl & ol grn .20 .20
C174 AP37 50c gray & grn .20 .20
C175 AP37 1g gray ol & ver .30 .20
C176 AP37 1.50g brt pink & dk bl .50 .30
a. Souv. sheet of 3, #C174-C176, imperf. 1.00 .70
Nos. C171-C176 (6) 1.60 1.30

Issued for Aviation Week, Dec. 17-23.
#C172-C174 are dated 17 Decembre 1903.
For overprints and surcharges see Nos. CB32-CB34, CO1-CO5.

Dumas Type of Regular Issue.

Designs: 50c, The Three Musketeers and Dumas père, horiz 1g, The Lady of the Camellias and Dumas fils. 1.50g, The Count of Monte Cristo and Dumas père.

1961, Feb. 10 Photo. *Perf. 11½*
Granite Paper

C177 A97 50c brt bl & blk .20 .20
C178 A97 1g blk & red .25 .20
C179 A97 1.50g brt grn & bl blk .35 .25
Nos. C177-C179 (3) .80 .65

Type of Regular Issue, 1961

Tourist publicity: 20c, Privateer in Battle. 50c, Pirate with cutlass in rigging. 1g, Map of Tortuga.

1961, Apr. 4 Litho. *Perf. 12*

C180 A98 20c dk bl & yel .20 .20
C181 A98 50c brt pur & org .20 .20
C182 A98 1g Prus grn & yel .25 .20
Nos. C180-C182 (3) .65 .60

For overprint and surcharge see #C186-C187.

Nos. C170, C112 and C101 Overprinted: "Dr. F. Duvalier Président 22 Mai 1961"

1961, May 22 Photo. *Perf. 11½*

C183 A81 20c gray & blk .20 .20
a. On No. C93
C184 A81 50c org & blk .20 .20
C185 AP30 75c dp grn & bl grn .30 .25
Nos. C183-C185 (3) .70 .65

Re-election of Pres. Francois Duvalier.

No. C182 Overprinted or Surcharged: "EXPLORATION SPATIALE JOHN GLENN" and Capsule

1962, May 10 Litho. *Perf. 12*

C186 A98 1g Prus grn & yel .35 .30
C187 A98 2g on 1g Prus grn & yel .90 .75

See note after No. 485.

Malaria Type of Regular Issue

Designs: 20c, 1g, Triangle pointing down. 50c, Triangle pointing up.

1962, May 30 Unwmk.

C188 A99 20c lilac & red .20 .20
C189 A99 50c emer & rose car .20 .20
C190 A99 1g org & dk vio .30 .20
a. Souv. sheet of 3 1.40 1.40
Nos. C188-C190 (3) .70 .60

Sheets of 12 with marginal inscription.
No. C190a contains stamps similar to Nos. 488 and C189-C190 in changed colors and imperf. Issued July 16.
A similar sheet without the "Contribution . . ." inscription was issued May 30.
For surcharges see Nos. CB42-CB44.

WRY Type of 1960 Dated "1962"

1962, June 22 *Perf. 12½x13*

C191 A92 50c lt bl & red brn .20 .20
C192 A92 1g bister & blk .20 .20

A souvenir sheet exists containing one each of #489-490, C191-C192, imperf. Value, $2.
For surcharges see Nos. CB45-CB46.

Boy Scout Type of 1962

Designs: 20c, Scout giving Scout sign. 50c, Haitian Scout emblem. 1.50g, Lord and Lady Baden-Powell, horiz.

Perf. 14x14½, 14½x14
1962, Aug. 6 Photo. Unwmk.

C193 A100 20c multi .20 .20
C194 A100 50c multi .20 .20
C195 A100 1.50g multi .35 .30
Nos. C193-C195 (3) .75 .70

A souvenir sheet contains one each of Nos. C194-C195 imperf. Value, 90 cents.
A similar sheet inscribed in gold, "Epreuves De Luxe," was issued Dec. 10. Value $2.

Nos. 495 and C193-C195 Overprinted: "AÉROPORT INTERNATIONAL 1962"

1962, Oct. 26 *Perf. 14x14½, 14½x14*

C196 A100 20c multi, #C193 .20 .20
C197 A100 50c multi, #495 .20 .20
C198 A100 50c multi, #C194 .20 .20
C199 A100 1.50g multi, #C195 .20 .20
Nos. C196-C199 (4) .80 .80

Proceeds from the sale of Nos. C196-C199 were for the construction of new airport at Port-au-Prince. The overprint on No. C197 has "Poste Aérienne" added.

Seattle Fair Type of 1962

Design: Denomination at left, "Avion" at right.

1962, Nov. 19 Litho. *Perf. 12½*

C200 A101 50c blk & pale lil .20 .20
C201 A101 1g org brn & gray .35 .20
C202 A101 1.50g red lil & org .45 .20
Nos. C200-C202 (3) 1.00 .60

An imperf. sheet of two exists containing one each of Nos. C201-C202 with simulated gray perforations. Size: 133x82mm. Value, $2.50.

Street in Duvalier Ville and Stamp of 1881 — AP38

1962, Dec. 10 Photo. *Perf. 14x14½*
Stamp in Dark Brown

C203 AP38 50c orange .20 .20
C204 AP38 1g blue .35 .30
C205 AP38 1.50g green .55 .40
Nos. C203-C205 (3) 1.10 .90

Issued to publicize Duvalier Ville.
For surcharges see Nos. CB47-CB48.

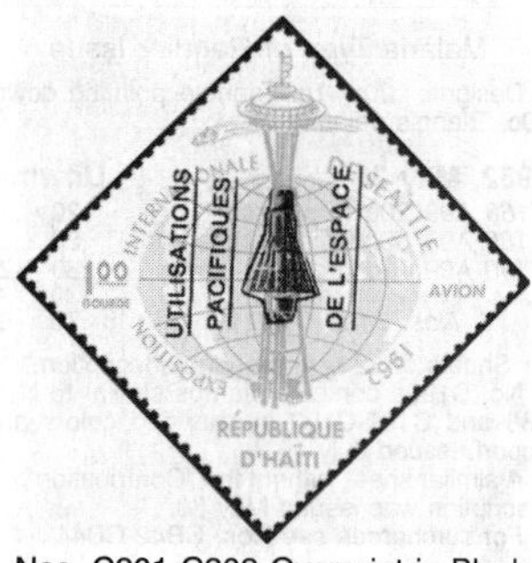

Nos. C201-C202 Overprint in Black

1963, Jan. 23 Litho. *Perf. 12½*

C206 A101 1g org brn & gray .90 .45
a. Claret overprint, horiz. 1.10 .60
C207 A101 1.50g red lil & org 1.25 .70
a. Claret overprint, horiz. 1.40 1.10

"Peaceful Uses of Outer Space." The black vertical overprint has no outside frame lines and no broken shading lines around capsule. Nos. C206a and C207a were issued Feb. 20.

Hunger Type of Regular Issue

Perf. 13x14

1963, July 12 Unwmk. Photo.

C208 A103 50c lil rose & blk .20 .20
C209 A103 1g lt ol grn & blk .30 .20

Dag Hammarskjold and UN Emblem — AP39

Lithographed and Photogravure

1963, Sept. 28 *Perf. 13½x14*

Portrait in Slate

C210 AP39 20c buff & brn .20 .20
C211 AP39 50c lt bl & car .20 .20
a. Souvenir sheet of 2 1.25 1.25
C212 AP39 1g pink & bl .30 .20
C213 AP39 1.50g gray & grn .45 .40
Nos. C210-C213 (4) 1.15 1.00

Dag Hammarskjold, Sec. Gen. of the UN, 1953-61. Printed in sheets of 25 (5x5) with map of Sweden extending over 9 stamps in second and third vertical rows. No. C211a contains 2 imperf. stamps: 50c blue and carmine and 1.50g ocher and brown with map of southern Sweden in background.

For overprints see Nos. C219-C222, C238-C241, CB50.

Dessalines Type of Regular Issue, 1963

1963, Oct. 17 Photo. *Perf. 14x14½*

C214 A104 50c bl & lil rose .20 .20
C215 A104 50c org & grn .20 .20

Nos. C214-C215 and C53 Overprinted in Black or Red: "FETE DES MERES / 1964"

1964, July 22 *Perf. 14x14½, 12½*

C216 A104 50c bl & lil rose .20 .20
C217 A104 50c org & grn .20 .20
C218 AP17 1.50g on 80c dk grn & sal pink (R) .35 .20
Nos. C216-C218 (3) .75 .60

Issued for Mother's Day, 1964.

Nos. C210-C213 Overprinted in Red

Lithographed and Engraved

1964, Oct. 2 *Perf. 13½x14*

Portrait in Slate

C219 AP39 20c buff & brn .20 .20
C220 AP39 50c lt bl & car .20 .20
C221 AP39 1g pink & bl .35 .30
C222 AP39 1.50g gray & grn .40 .35
Nos. C219-C222,CB50 (5) 2.05 1.75

Cent. (in 1963) of the Intl. Red Cross.

Olympic Type of Regular Issue

#C223, Weight lifter. #C224-C226, Hurdler.

1964, Nov. 12 Photo. *Perf. 11½*

Granite Paper

C223 A105 50c pale lil & dk brn .20 .20
C224 A105 50c pale grn & dk brn .20 .20
C225 A105 75c buff & dk brn .20 .20
C226 A105 1.50g gray & dk brn .40 .20
a. Souv. sheet of 4 .90 .90
Nos. C223-C226 (4) 1.00 .80

Printed in sheets of 50 (10x5), with map of Japan in background extending over 27 stamps.

No. C226a contains four imperf. stamps similar to Nos. C223-C226 in changed colors and with map of Tokyo area in background.

For surcharges see Nos. CB51-CB54.

Airport Type of Regular Issue, 1964

1964, Dec. 15 *Perf. 14½x14*

C227 A106 50c org & blk .20 .20
C228 A106 1.50g brt lil rose & blk .40 .20
C229 A106 2.50g lt vio & blk .90 .50
Nos. C227-C229 (3) 1.50 .90

Same Overprinted "1965"

1965, Feb. 11 Photo.

C230 A106 50c org & blk .20 .20
C231 A106 1.50g brt lil rose & blk .50 .25
C232 A106 2.50g lt vio & blk .70 .55
Nos. C230-C232 (3) 1.40 1.00

World's Fair Type of Regular Issue, 1965

Designs: 50c, 1.50g, "Rocket Thrower" by Donald De Lue. 5g, Unisphere, NY World's Fair.

1965, Mar. 22 Unwmk. *Perf. 13½*

C233 A107 50c dp bl & org .20 .20
C234 A107 1.50g gray & org .35 .30
C235 A107 5g multi 1.75 1.50
Nos. C233-C235 (3) 2.30 2.00

Merchant Marine Type of Regular Issue, 1965

1965, May 13 Photo. *Perf. 11½*

C236 A108 50c blk, lt grnsh bl & red .20 .20
C237 A108 1.50g blk, lt vio & red .40 .30

Nos. C210-C213 Overprinted

Lithographed and Photogravure

1965, June 26 *Perf. 13½x14*

Portrait in Slate

C238 AP39 20c buff & brn .20 .20
C239 AP39 50c lt bl & car .20 .20
C240 AP39 1g pink & bl .25 .20
C241 AP39 1.50g gray & grn .20 .30
Nos. C238-C241 (4) .85 .90

20th anniversary of the United Nations.

ITU Type of Regular Issue

Perf. 13½

1965, Aug. 16 Unwmk. Litho.

C242 A109 50c multi .20 .20
C243 A109 1g multi .30 .25
C244 A109 1.50g bl & multi .40 .35
C245 A109 2g pink & multi .65 .50
Nos. C242-C245 (4) 1.55 1.30

A souvenir sheet, released in 1966, contains 50c and 2g stamps resembling Nos. C242 and C245, with simulated perforations.

For overprints see Nos. C255-C256.

Cathedral Type of Regular Issue, 1965

Designs: 50c, Cathedral, Port-au-Prince, horiz. 1g, High Altar. 7.50g, Statue of Our Lady of the Assumption.

Perf. 14x13, 13x14

1965, Nov. 19 Photo.

Size: 39x29mm, 29x39mm

C246 A110 50c multi .20 .20
C247 A110 1g multi .30 .20

Size: 38x52mm

C248 A110 7.50g multi 2.00 1.75
Nos. C246-C248 (3) 2.50 2.15

Flower Type of Regular Issue

#C249, 5g, Passionflower. #C250, C252, Okra. #C251, C253, American elder.

1965, Dec. 20 Photo. *Perf. 11½*

Granite Paper

C249 A111 50c dk vio, yel & grn .20 .20
C250 A111 50c multi .20 .20
C251 A111 50c grn, gray & yel .20 .20
C252 A111 1.50g multi .40 .35
C253 A111 1.50g grn, tan & yel .40 .35
C254 A111 5g dk vio, yel grn & grn 1.40 1.25
Nos. C249-C254 (6) 2.80 2.55

For surcharges see Nos. CB55-CB56.

Nos. C242-C243 Overprinted in Red: "20e. Anniversaire / UNESCO"

1965, Aug. 27 Litho. *Perf. 13½*

C255 A109 50c lt vio & multi 1.00 .35
C256 A109 1g citron & multi 2.00 .70

20th anniversary of UNESCO.

The souvenir sheet noted below No. C245 was also overprinted "20e. Anniversaire / UNESCO" in red. Value, $20.00.

Culture Types of Regular Issue and

Modern Painting — AP40

Designs: 50c, Ceremonial stool. 1.50g, Amulet.

Perf. 14x14½, 14½x14, 14

1966, Mar. 14 Photo. Unwmk.

C257 A113 50c lil, brn & brnz .20 .20
C258 A112 1.50g brt rose lil, yel & blk .50 .35
C259 AP40 2.50g multi .90 .60
Nos. C257-C259 (3) 1.60 1.15

For overprints and surcharge see Nos. C260-C262, C280-C281.

Nos. C257-C259 Overprinted in Black or Red: "Hommage / a Hailé Sélassiéler / 24-25 Avril 1966"

1966, Apr. 24

C260 A112 50c (R) .20 .20
C261 A113 1.50g (vert. ovpt.) .50 .40
C262 AP40 2.50g (R) .90 .70
Nos. C260-C262 (3) 1.60 1.30

See note after No. 543.

Walter M. Schirra, Thomas P. Stafford, Frank A. Borman, James A. Lovell and Gemini VI and VII — AP41

1966, May 3 *Perf. 13½*

C263 AP41 50c vio bl, brn & lt bl .20 .20
C264 AP41 1g grn, brn & lt bl .35 .30
C265 AP41 1.50g car, brn & bl .55 .40
Nos. C263-C265 (3) 1.10 .90

See No. 547.

For overprints see Nos. C296-C298.

Soccer Type of Regular Issue

Designs: 50c, Pres. Duvalier and soccer ball within wreath. 1.50g, President Duvalier and soccer player within wreath.

Lithographed and Photogravure

1966, June 16 *Perf. 13x13½*

Portrait in Black; Gold Inscription; Green Commemorative Inscription in Two Lines

C266 A115 50c lt ol grn & plum .20 .20
C267 A115 1.50g rose & plum .50 .40

Green Commemorative Inscription in 3 Lines; Gold Inscription Omitted

C268 A115 50c lt ol grn & plum .20 .20
C269 A115 1.50g rose & plum .50 .40
Nos. C266-C269 (4) 1.40 1.20

Caribbean Soccer Festival, June 10-22. Nos. C266-C267 also for the National Soccer Championships, May 8-22.

For overprint and surcharge see Nos. C288, CB57.

Education Type of Regular Issue

Designs: 50c, "ABC", boy and girl. 1g, Scout symbols. 1.50g, Television set, book and communications satellite, horiz.

Perf. 14x13½, 13½x14

Litho. and Engraved

1966, Oct. 18

C270 A116 50c grn, yel & brn .20 .20
C271 A116 1g dk brn, org & blk .30 .30
C272 A116 1.50g grn, bl grn & dk bl .40 .40
Nos. C270-C272 (3) .90 .90

Schweitzer Type of Regular Issue

Designs (Schweitzer and): 50c, 1g, Albert Schweitzer Hospital, Deschapelles, Haiti. 1.50g, Maps of Alsace and Gabon. 2g, Pipe organ.

Perf. 12½x13

1967, Apr. 20 Photo. Unwmk.

C273 A117 50c multi .20 .40
C274 A117 1g multi .35 .30
C275 A117 1.50g lt bl & multi .50 .40
C276 A117 2g multi .65 .55
Nos. C273-C276 (4) 1.70 1.65

Fruit-Vegetable Type of Regular Issue, 1967

1967, July 4 Photo. *Perf. 12½*

C277 A118 50c Watermelon .20 .20
C278 A118 1g Cabbage .30 .20
C279 A118 1.50g Tangerine .40 .35
Nos. C277-C279 (3) .90 .75

No. C258 Overprinted or Surcharged Like EXPO '67 Regular Issue

1967, Aug. 30 Photo. *Perf. 14½x14*

C280 A112 1.50g multi .50 .40
C281 A112 2g on 1.50g multi .70 .55

Issued to commemorate EXPO '67 International Exhibition, Montreal, Apr. 28-Oct. 27.

Duvalier Type of Regular Issue, 1967

1967, Sept. 22 Photo. *Perf. 14x13*

C282 A119 1g brt grn & gold .35 .30
C283 A119 1.50g vio & gold .50 .40
C284 A119 2g org & gold .70 .55
Nos. C282-C284 (3) 1.55 1.25

Education Type of Regular Issue, 1967

50c, Writing hands. 1g, Scout emblem and Scouts, vert. 1.50g, Audio-visual teaching of algebra.

1967, Dec. 11 Litho. *Perf. 11½*

C285 A120 50c multi .20 .20
C286 A120 1g multi .30 .25
C287 A120 1.50g multi .40 .35
Nos. C285-C287 (3) .90 .80

For surcharges see Nos. CB58-CB60.

No. C269 Overprinted

Lithographed and Photogravure

1968, Jan. 18 *Perf. 13x13½*

C288 A115 1.50g rose & plum .50 .40

See note after No. 579.

Caiman Woods Type of Regular Issue

1968, Apr. 22 Photo. *Perf. 12*

Size: 36x26mm

C289 A121 50c multi .20 .20
C290 A121 1g multi .30 .30

Perf. 12½x13½

Size: 49x36mm

C291 A121 50c multi .20 .20
C292 A121 1g multi .30 .25
C293 A121 1.50g multi .40 .40
C294 A121 2g gray & multi .70 .55
C295 A121 5g multi 1.40 1.00
Nos. C289-C295 (7) 3.50 2.90

Nos. C263-C265 Overprinted

1968, Apr. 19 *Perf. 13½*

C296 AP41 50c multi .50 .25
C297 AP41 1g multi 1.00 .50
C298 AP41 1.50g multi 1.75 .90
Nos. C296-C298 (3) 3.25 1.65

See note after No. 584.

Monument Type of Regular Issue

1968, May 22 *Perf. 11½*

Granite Paper

C299 A122 50c ol bis & blk .20 .20
C300 A122 1g brt rose & blk .35 .25
C301 A122 1.50g org & blk .55 .35
Nos. C299-C301 (3) 1.10 .80

For surcharges see Nos. C324-C325.

Types of Regular Bishopric Issue

50c, Palm tree & provincial coats of arms. 1g, 2.50g, Madonna, papal arms & arms of Haiti. 1.50g, Cathedral, arms of Pope Paul VI & arms of Haiti.

Perf. 13x14, 12½x13½

1968, Aug. 16 Photo.

C302 A123 50c lil & multi .20 .20
C303 A124 1g multi .30 .25
C304 A124 1.50g multi .40 .35
C305 A124 2.50g multi .70 .65
Nos. C302-C305 (4) 1.60 1.45

Airport Type of Regular Issue

50c, 1.50g, 2.50g, Front view of air terminal.

1968, Sept. 22 Photo. *Perf. 11½*

Portrait in Black

C306 A125 50c rose lake & pale vio .20 .20
C307 A125 1.50g rose lake & bl .40 .35
C308 A125 2.50g rose lake & lt grnsh bl .70 .65
Nos. C306-C308 (3) 1.30 1.20

Pres. Francois Duvalier — AP42

Embossed & Typo. on Gold Foil

1968, Sept. 22 ***Die Cut Perf. 14***

C309 AP42 30g black & red *25.00 25.00*

Freed Slaves' Type of Regular Issue

1968, Oct. 28 Litho. *Perf. 14½x14*

C310 A126 50c brn, lil & brt pink .20 .20
C311 A126 1g brn, yel grn & brt pink .30 .25
C312 A126 1.50g brn, lt vio bl & brt pink .40 .35
C313 A126 2g brn, lt grn & brt pink .55 .45
Nos. C310-C313 (4) 1.45 1.25

Education Type of Regular Issue, 1968

50c, 1.50g, Children watching television. 1g, Hands throwing ball, and sports medal.

1968, Nov. 14 *Perf. 11½*

C314 A127 50c multi .20 .20
C315 A127 1g multi .30 .25
C316 A127 1.50g multi .50 .35
Nos. C314-C316 (3) 1.00 .80

For surcharges see Nos. CB61-CB62.

Jan Boesman and his Balloon — AP43

1968, Nov. 28 Litho. *Perf. 13½*

C317 AP43 70c lt yel grn & sepia .35 .30
C318 AP43 1.75g grnsh bl & sepia .90 .70

Dr. Jan Boesman's balloon flight, Mexico City, Nov. 1968.

Miniature Sheet

Cachet of May 2, 1925 Flight — AP44

1968, Nov. 28 Litho. *Perf. 13½x14*

Black Cachets, Magenta Inscriptions and Rose Lilac Background

C318A Sheet of 12 5.50 *7.50*
b. AP44 70c 2 Mai 1925 .35 *.45*
c. AP44 70c 2 Septembre 1925 .35 *.45*
d. AP44 70c 28 Mars 1927 .35 *.45*
e. AP44 70c 12 Juillet 1927 .35 *.45*
f. AP44 70c 13 Septembre 1927 .35 *.45*
g. AP44 70c 6 Fevrier 1928 .35 *.45*

Galiffet's 1784 balloon flight and pioneer flights of the 1920's. No. C318A contains 2 each of Nos. C318b-C318g. The background of the sheet shows in white outlines a balloon and the inscription "BALLON GALIFFET 1784." The design of each stamp shows a different airmail cachet, date of a special flight and part of the white background design.

Churchill Type of Regular Issue

Churchill: 50c, and early seaplane. 75c, and soldiers at Normandy. 1g, and Queen Elizabeth II. 1.50g, and Big Ben, London. 3g, and coat of arms, horiz.

1968, Dec. 23 Photo. *Perf. 13*

C319 A128 50c gold & multi .20 .20
C320 A128 75c gold & multi .20 .20
C321 A128 1g gold & multi .30 .25
C322 A128 1.50g gold & multi .40 .35
Nos. C319-C322 (4) 1.10 1.00

Souvenir Sheet

Perf. 12½x13, Imperf.

C323 A128 3g sil, blk & red 1.00 1.00

Nos. C319-C322 exist imperf. Value, $4.00.

No. C323 contains one horizontal stamp, size: 38x25½mm.

Nos. C299-C300 Surcharged with New Value and Rectangle

1969, Feb. 21 Photo. *Perf. 11½*

C324 A122 70c on 50c .20 .20
C325 A122 1.75g on 1g .50 .40

Bird Type of Regular Issue

Birds of Haiti: 50c, Hispaniolan trogon. 1g, Black-cowled oriole. 1.50g, Stripe-headed tanager. 2g, Striated woodpecker.

1969, Feb. 26 *Perf. 13½*

C326 A129 50c multi .20 .20
C327 A129 1g lt bl & multi .30 .25
C328 A129 1.50g multi .40 .35
C329 A129 2g gray & multi .55 .50
Nos. C326-C329 (4) 1.45 1.30

For overprints see Nos. C344A-C344D.

Electric Power Type of 1969

1969, May 22 Litho. *Perf. 13x13½*

C338 A131 20c dk bl & lil .20 .20
C339 A131 25c grn & rose red .20 .20
C340 A131 25c rose red & grn .20 .20
Nos. C338-C340 (3) .60 .60

Education Type of 1969

Designs: 50c, Peace poster on educational television, vert. 1g, Learning to write. 1.50g, Playing children, vert.

1969, Aug. 12 Litho. *Perf. 13½*

C342 A132 50c multi .20 .20
C343 A132 1g multi .35 .20
C344 A132 1.50g multi .55 .35
Nos. C342-C344 (3) 1.10 .75

Nos. C326-C329 Overprinted

1969, Aug. 29 Photo. *Perf. 13½*

C344A A129 50c multi
C344B A129 1g lt bl & multi
C344C A129 1.50g multi
C344D A129 2g gray & multi

ILO Type of Regular Issue

1969, Sept. 22 *Perf. 14*

C345 A133 25c red & blk .20 .20
C346 A133 70c org & blk .25 .20
C347 A133 1.75g brt pur & blk .65 .40
Nos. C345-C347 (3) 1.10 .80

Butterfly Type of Regular Issue

50c, Danaus eresimus kaempfferi. 1.50g, Anaea marthesia nemesis. 2g, Prepona antimache.

1969, Nov. 14 Photo. *Perf. 13½*

C348 A134 50c multi .20 .20
C349 A134 1.50g multi .40 .35
C350 A134 2g yel & multi .55 .55
Nos. C348-C350 (3) 1.15 1.10

King Type of Regular Issue

1970, Jan. 12 Litho. *Perf. 12½x13½*

C351 A135 50c emer, red & blk .20 .20
C352 A135 1g brick red, red & blk .35 .25
C353 A135 1.50g brt bl, red & blk .55 .35
Nos. C351-C353 (3) 1.10 .80

Orchid Type of Regular Issue

Haitian Orchids: 50c, Tetramicra elegans. 1.50g, Epidendrum truncatum. 2g, Oncidium desertorum.

1970, Apr. 3 Litho. *Perf. 13x12½*

C354 A136 50c buff, brn & mag .20 .20
C355 A136 1.50g multi .40 .35
C356 A136 2g lilac & multi .65 .55
Nos. C354-C356 (3) 1.25 1.10

UPU Type of Regular Issue

Designs: 50c, Globe and doves. 1.50g, Propeller and UPU emblem, vert. 2g, UPU Monument and map of Haiti.

1970, June 23 Photo. *Perf. 11½*

C357 A137 50c blk & vio .20 .20
C358 A137 1.50g multi .50 .35
C359 A137 2g multi .70 .55
a. Souvenir sheet of 3, #C357-C359, imperf. 1.50
Nos. C357-C359 (3) 1.40 1.10

Nos. C357-C359a Overprinted in Red with UN Emblem and: "XXVe ANNIVERSAIRE / O.N.U."

1970, Dec. 14 Photo. *Perf. 11½*

C360 A137 50c blk & vio .20 .20
C361 A137 1.50g multi .50 .35
C362 A137 2g multi .70 .55
a. Souvenir sheet of 3 1.90
Nos. C360-C362 (3) 1.40 1.10

United Nations, 25th anniversary.

Haitian Nativity AP45

1970, Dec. 22

C363 AP45 1.50g sepia & multi .50 .35
C364 AP45 1.50g ultra & multi .50 .35
C365 AP45 2g multi .90 .50
Nos. C363-C365 (3) 1.90 1.20

Christmas 1970.

Painting Type of Regular Issue

Paintings: 50c, Nativity, by Rigaud Benoit. 1g, Head of a Negro, by Rubens. 1.50g, Ascension, by Castera Bazile (like No. 648).

1971, Apr. 29 Litho. *Perf. 12x12½*

Size: 20x40mm

C366 A140 50c multi .20 .20
C367 A140 1g multi .35 .30
C368 A140 1.50g multi .55 .40
Nos. C366-C368 (3) 1.10 .90

Nos. C366-C368 exist imperf in changed colors.

Balloon and Haiti No. C2 — AP46

No. C370, as #C369. No. C373, Haiti #C2. 1g, 1.50g, Supersonic transport & Haiti #C2.

1971, Dec. 22 Photo. *Perf. 11½*

C369 AP46 20c bl, red org & blk .20 .20
C370 AP46 50c ultra, red org & blk .20 .20
C371 AP46 1g org & blk .40 .20
C372 AP46 1.50g lil rose & blk .70 .30
Nos. C369-C372 (4) 1.50 .90

Souvenir Sheet

Imperf

C373 AP46 50c brt grn & blk 3.50

40th anniv. (in 1969) of air post service in Haiti.

For overprints see #C374-C377, C380-C386.

Nos. C369-C372 Overprinted

1972, Mar. 17 *Perf. 11½*

C374 AP46 20c multi .20
C375 AP46 50c multi .20
C376 AP46 1g org & blk .35
C377 AP46 1.50g lil rose & blk .50
Nos. C374-C377 (4) 1.25

14th INTERPEX, NYC, Mar. 17-19.

Dessalines Type of Regular Issue

1972, Apr. 28 Photo. *Perf. 11½*

C378 A142 50c yel grn & blk .20 .20
C379 A142 2.50g lil & blk .50 .40

For surcharge see No. C438.

Nos. C369-C372 Overprinted

1972, May 4

C380 AP46 20c multi .20 .20
C381 AP46 50c multi .20 .20
C382 AP46 1g org & blk .35 .20
C383 AP46 1.50g lil rose & blk .50 .30
Nos. C380-C383 (4) 1.25 .90

HAIPEX, 5th Congress.

Nos. C370-C372 Overprinted

1972, July

C384 AP46 50c multi .20 .20
C385 AP46 1g org & blk .35 .20
C386 AP46 1.50g lil rose & blk .55 .30
Nos. C384-C386 (3) 1.10 .70

Belgica '72, International Philatelic Exhibition, Brussels, June 24-July 9.

Tower of the Sun, EXPO '70 Emblem AP47

1972, Oct. 27

C387 AP47 50c bl, plum & dk bl .20 .20
C388 AP47 1g bl, plum & red .35 .20
C389 AP47 1.50g bl, plum & blk .40 .30
C390 AP47 2.50g bl, plum & grn .90 .50
Nos. C387-C390 (4) 1.85 1.20

EXPO '70 International Exposition, Osaka, Japan, Mar. 15-Sept. 13, 1970.
For surcharges see Nos. C447-C447A.

Souvenir Sheets

1972 Summer Olympics, Munich — AP47a

Designs: 2.50g, Israeli delegation, opening ceremony in Munich Stadium. 5g, Assassinated Israeli athlete David Berger.

1973 ***Perf. 13½***

C390A AP47a 2.50g multi 1.10 .75
C390B AP47a 5g multi 2.25 1.50

No. C390B contains one 22½x34mm stamp.

Headquarters and Map of Americas — AP48

1973, May 11 Litho. ***Perf. 14½***

C391 AP48 50c dk bl & multi .20 .20
C392 AP48 80c multi .25 .20
C393 AP48 1.50g vio & multi .40 .30
C394 AP48 2g brn & multi .55 .40
Nos. C391-C394 (4) 1.40 1.10

70th anniversary (in 1972) of the Panamerican Health Organization.

Marine Life Type of Regular Issue

50c, 1.50g horizontal.

1973, Sept. 4 ***Perf. 14***

C395 A145 50c *Platypodia spectabilis* .20 .20
C396 A145 85c *Goniaster tessellatus* .25 .20
C397 A145 1.50g *Stephanocyathus diadema* .40 .30
C398 A145 2g *Phyllangia americana* .55 .40
Nos. C395-C398 (4) 1.40 1.10

For surcharge see No. C439.

Fish Type of Regular Issue

Designs: Tropical fish.

1973 ***Perf. 13½***

C399 A146 50c *Gramma melacara* .20 .20
C400 A146 85c *Holacanthus tricolor* .25 .20
C401 A146 1.50g *Liopropoma rubre* .40 .30
C402 A146 5g *Clepticus parrai* 1.40 1.00
Nos. C399-C402 (4) 2.25 1.70

For surcharge see No. C440.

Haitian Flag AP49

Nos. C404, C405, Haitian flag and coat of arms. No. C406, Flag and Pres. Jean-Claude Duvalier.

1973, Nov. 18 ***Perf. 14½x14***

Size: 35x22½mm

C403 AP49 80c blk & red .25 .20
C404 AP49 80c red & blk .25 .20

Perf. 14x13½

Size: 42x27mm

C405 AP49 1.85g blk & red .50 .30
C406 AP49 1.85g red & blk .50 .30
Nos. C403-C406 (4) 1.50 1.00

For overprints and surcharges see Nos. C427-C428, C432-C433, C441-C442.

Soccer Type of Regular Issue

50c, 80c, Soccer Stadium. 1.75g, 10g, Haiti #654.

1973, Nov. 29 ***Perf. 14x13***

C407 A147 50c multi .20 .20
C408 A147 80c multi .25 .20
C409 A147 1.75g multi .50 .35
C410 A147 10g multi 2.75 2.00
Nos. C407-C410 (4) 3.70 2.75

Dessalines Type of 1974

1974, Apr. 22 Photo. ***Perf. 14***

C411 A148 50c brn & grnsh bl .20 .20
C412 A148 80c gray & brn .25 .20
C413 A148 1g lt grn & mar .30 .20
C414 A148 1.75g lil & ol brn .50 .40
Nos. C411-C414 (4) 1.25 1.00

For surcharge see No. C443.

Copernicus Type of 1974

Designs: No. C415, 80c, 1.50g, 1.75g, Symbol of heliocentric system. No. C416, 1g, 2.50g, Nicolaus Copernicus.

1974, May 24 Litho. ***Perf. 14x13½***

C415 A149 50c org & multi .20 .20
C416 A149 50c yel & multi .20 .20
C417 A149 80c multi .25 .20
C418 A149 1g multi .30 .20
C419 A149 1.75g brn & multi .50 .35
Nos. C415-C419 (5) 1.45 1.15

Souvenir Sheet

Imperf

C420 Sheet of 2 1.25
a. A149 1.50g light green & multi .42
b. A149 2.50g deep orange & multi .70

For overprint and surcharges see Nos. C444, C460-C463.

Pres. Duvalier Type of 1974

1974 Photo. ***Perf. 14x13½***

C421 A151 50c vio brn & gold .20 .20
C422 A151 80c rose red & gold .20 .20
C423 A151 1g red lil & gold .30 .20
C424 A151 1.50g Prus bl & gold .40 .30
C425 A151 1.75g brt vio & gold .50 .35
C426 A151 5g ol grn & gold 1.40 1.00
Nos. C421-C426 (6) 3.00 2.25

For surcharge and overprints see Nos. C445, C487-C489.

Nos. C405-C406 Surcharged in Violet Blue

1975, July 15 Litho. ***Perf. 14x13½***

C427 AP49 80c on 1.85g, #C405
C428 AP49 80c on 1.85g, #C406

Nos. C405-C406 Overprinted in Blue

1975, July 15 Litho. ***Perf. 14x13½***

C432 AP49 1.85g blk & red .50 .30
C433 AP49 1.85g red & blk .50 .30

Centenary of Universal Postal Union. "100 ANS" in 2 lines on No. C433.

Names of Haitian Participants at Siege of Savannah — AP50

1976, Apr. 22 Photo. ***Perf. 11½***

Granite Paper

C434 AP50 50c multi .20 .20
C435 AP50 80c multi .25 .20
C436 AP50 1.50g multi .40 .30
C437 AP50 7.50g multi 2.00 1.50
Nos. C434-C437 (4) 2.85 2.20

American Bicentennial.

Stamps of 1972-74 Surcharged with New Value and Bar in Black or Violet Blue

Photogravure; Lithographed

1976 ***Perf. 11½, 13½, 14x13½, 14***

C438 A142 80c on 2.50g, #C379 .25 .20
C439 A145 80c on 85c, #C396 .25 .20
C440 A146 80c on 85c, #C400 .25 .20
C441 AP49 80c on 1.85g, #C405 .25 .20
C442 AP49 80c on 1.85g, #C406 .25 .20
C443 A148 80c on 1.75g, #C414 (VB) .25 .20
C444 A149 80c on 1.75g, #C419 (VB) .25 .20
C445 A151 80c on 1.75g, #C425 .25 .20
C446 AP50 80c on 1.50g, #C436 .25 .20
C447 AP47 80c on 1.50g, #C389
C447A AP47 80c on 2.50g #C390
Nos. C438-C446 (9) 2.25 1.80

Black surcharge of Nos. C441-C442 differs from the violet blue surcharge of Nos. C427-C428 in type face, arrangement of denomination and bar, and size of bar (10x6mm).

Dessalines Type of 1972

1976-77 Photo. ***Perf. 11½***

Granite Paper

C448 A142 75c yel & blk .20 .20
C449 A142 80c emer & blk .25 .20
C450 A142 1g bl & blk .30 .20
C451 A142 1g red brn & blk .30 .20
C452 A142 1.25g yel grn & blk .35 .25
C453 A142 1.50g bl gray & blk .40 .30
C454 A142 1.75g rose & blk .50 .40
C455 A142 2g yel & blk .55 .40
C457 A142 5g bl grn & blk 1.40 1.00
C458 A142 10g ocher & blk 2.75 2.00
Nos. C448-C458 (10) 7.00 5.15

Issued: 75c, 80c, #C451, 1,75g, 5g, 10g, 1977.

Nos. C415-C416, C418-C419 Overprinted or Surcharged in Black, Dark Blue or Green

1977, July 6 Litho. ***Perf. 14x13½***

C460 A149 1g (Bk) .30 .20
C461 A149 1.25g on 50c (DB) .35 .25
C462 A149 1.25g on 50c (G) .35 .25
C463 A149 1.25g on 1.75g (Bk) .35 .25
Nos. C460-C463 (4) 1.35 .95

Charles A. Lindbergh's solo transatlantic flight from NY to Paris, 50th anniv.

Telephone Type of 1978

Designs: 1g, Telstar over globe. 1.25g, Duvalier Earth Telecommunications Station. 2g, Wall telephone, 1890, vert.

1978, June 19 Litho. ***Perf. 13½***

C466 A153 1g multi .30 .20
C467 A153 1.25g multi .35 .25
C468 A153 2g multi .55 .40
Nos. C466-C468 (3) 1.20 .85

Olympic Games Type of 1978

Montreal Olympic Games' Emblem and: 1.25g, Equestrian. 2.50g,Basketball. 5g, Yachting.

1978, Sept. 4 Litho. ***Perf. 13½x13***

C469 A154 1.25g multi .50 .25
C470 A154 2.50g multi 1.00 .50
C471 A154 5g multi 1.75 .75
Nos. C469-C471 (3) 3.25 1.50

Children's Institute Type, 1979

Designs: 1.25g, Mother nursing child. 2g, Nurse giving injection.

1979, Jan. 15 Photo. ***Perf. 14x14½***

C472 A155 1.25g multi .35 .25
C473 A155 2g multi .55 .40

Haitians Spinning Cotton, CARE Workshop AP51

1979, May 11 Photo. ***Perf. 11½***

C474 AP51 1g multi .30 .20
C475 AP51 1.25g multi .35 .25
C476 AP51 2g multi .55 .40
Nos. C474-C476 (3) 1.20 .85

30th anniversary of CARE.

Human Rights Type of 1979

1979, July 20 Litho. ***Perf. 14***

C477 A157 1g multi .40 .20
C478 A157 1.25g multi .50 .25
C479 A157 2g multi .75 .40
Nos. C477-C479 (3) 1.65 .85

Anti-Apartheid Year Type of 1979

1979, Nov. 22 Photo. ***Perf. 12x11½***

C480 A158 1g yel grn & blk .40 .20
C481 A158 1.25g bl & blk .50 .25
C482 A158 2g gray olive .75 .40
Nos. C480-C482 (3) 1.65 .85

IYC Type of 1979

1979, Dec. 19 Photo. ***Perf. 12***

C483 A159 1g multi .40 .20
C484 A159 1.25g multi .50 .25
C485 A159 2.50g multi 1.00 .55
C486 A159 5g multi 2.00 1.00
Nos. C483-C486 (4) 3.90 2.00

Nos. C421, C424-C425 Overprinted:

1980, May 17 Photo. *Perf. 14x13½*

C487 A151 50c multi .20 .20
C488 A151 1.50g multi .40 .30
C489 A151 1.75g multi .50 .40
Nos. C487-C489 (3) 1.10 .90

Wedding of Pres. Duvalier, May 27.

Dessalines Type of 1972

1980, Aug. 27 Photo. *Perf. 11½*

Granite Paper

C490 A142 1g gray vio & blk .30 .20
C491 A142 1.25g sal pink & blk .35 .25
C492 A142 2g pale grn & blk .55 .40
C493 A142 5g lt bl & blk 1.40 1.00
Nos. C490-C493 (4) 2.60 1.85

For surcharge see No. C512.

Tourism Type

1980, Dec. 2 Litho. *Perf. 12½x12*

C494 A160 1g like #728 .30 .20
C495 A160 1.25g like #729 .35 .25
C496 A160 1.50g Carnival dancers .40 .30
C497 A160 2g Vendors .55 .40
C498 A160 2.50g like #C497 .70 .50
Nos. C494-C498 (5) 2.30 1.65

For surcharge see No. C511.

Soccer Type of 1980

1980, Dec. 30 Litho. *Perf. 14*

C499 A161 50c Uruguay, 1950 .20 .20
C500 A161 75c Germany, 1954 .20 .20
C501 A161 1g Brazil, 1958 .30 .20
C502 A161 1.25g Brazil, 1962 .35 .25
C503 A161 1.50g Gt. Britain, 1966 .40 .35
C504 A161 1.75g Brazil, 1970 .50 .40
C505 A161 2g Germany, 1974 .55 .40
C506 A161 5g Argentina, 1978 1.40 1.00
Nos. C499-C506 (8) 3.90 3.00

Painting Type of 1981

1981, May 12 Photo. *Perf. 11½*

C507 A162 50c like #734 .20 .20
C508 A162 1.25g like #735 .35 .25
C509 A162 2g like #736 .55 .40
C510 A162 5g like #737 1.40 1.00
Nos. C507-C510 (4) 2.50 1.85

Nos. C496, C493 Surcharged

Perf. 12½x12, 11½

1981, Dec. 30 Litho., Photo.

C511 A160 1.25g on 1.50g multi .35 .30
C512 A142 2g on 5g multi .55 .45

Dessalines Type of 1972

1982, Jan. 25 Photo. *Perf. 11½*

Granite Paper

C513 A142 1.25g lt brn & blk .35 .30
C514 A142 2g lilac & blk .55 .45

AIR POST SEMI-POSTAL STAMPS

Coubertin Semipostal Type of 1939

Unwmk.

1939, Oct. 3 Engr. *Perf. 12*

CB1 SP1 60c + 40c multi 15.00 15.00
CB2 SP1 1.25g + 60c multi 15.00 15.00

Mosquito and National Sanatorium — SPAP2

1949, July 22 Cross in Carmine

CB3 SPAP2 20c + 20c sep 7.00 5.00
CB4 SPAP2 30c + 30c dp grn 7.00 5.00
CB5 SPAP2 45c + 45c lt red brn 7.00 5.00
CB6 SPAP2 80c + 80c pur 7.00 5.00
CB7 SPAP2 1.25g + 1.25g car rose 7.00 5.00
 a. Souvenir sheet 24.00 18.00
CB8 SPAP2 1.75g + 1.75g bl 7.00 5.00
 a. Souvenir sheet 24.00 18.00
Nos. CB3-CB8 (6) 42.00 30.00

The surtax was used for fighting tuberculosis and malaria.

No. C113 Surcharged in Deep Carmine

1958, Aug. 30 Litho. *Perf. 13x13½*

CB9 A82 2.50g + 50c 2.00 2.00

The surtax was for the Red Cross.

Catalogue values for unused stamps in this section, from this point to the end of the section, are for Never Hinged items.

Similar Surcharge in Red on One Line on Nos. C133-C135

1959, Apr. 7 Photo. *Perf. 11½*

Granite Paper

CB10 AP35 50c + 25c pink, car & ultra .25 .20
CB11 A87 75c + 25c brt bl .30 .25
CB12 A87 1g + 25c brn .40 .35

Nos. C139-C141 Surcharged Like No. CB9 in Red

CB13 AP36 50c + 50c grn & lil .65 .65
CB14 AP36 1.50g + 50c ol & red brn .65 .65
CB15 AP36 2.50g + 50c pur & dk bl .75 .70
Nos. CB10-CB15 (6) 3.00 2.80

Surtax for the Red Cross.

Nos. C142-C144 Surcharged Diagonally

1959, July 23 Unwmk. *Perf. 12*

CB16 A89 1g + 20c .65 .50
CB17 A89 2g + 20c .65 .65
CB18 A89 2.50g + 20c .70 .70
Nos. CB16-CB18 (3) 2.00 1.85

World Refugee Year, July 1, 1959-June 30, 1960. A similar surcharge of 50c was applied horizontally to stamps in No. C144a. Value $17.50.

C145-C147 Surcharged in Dark Carmine

1959, Oct. 30 Photo. *Perf. 14*

CB19 A91 50c + 75c hn brn & aqua .65 .50
CB20 A90 1g + 75c lil & aqua .65 .50
CB21 A90 1.50g + 75c multi .65 .65
Nos. CB19-CB21 (3) 1.95 1.65

The surtax was for Haitian athletes.

On No. CB19, surcharge lines are spaced to total depth of 16mm.

Nos. C129-C130 Surcharged in Red: "Hommage a l'UNICEF +G. 0,50"

Engraved and Lithographed

1960, Feb. 2 *Perf. 11½*

CB22 AP34 2g + 50c .70 .70
CB23 AP34 2.50g + 50c 1.25 1.25

Issued to honor UNICEF.

Nos. C151-C152 Surcharged and Overprinted: "ALPHABETISATION" in Red or Black.

1960, July 12 Litho. *Perf. 12½x13*

CB24 A92 50c + 20c (R) .30 .20
CB25 A92 50c + 30c .40 .30
CB26 A92 1g + 20c (R) .65 .55
CB27 A92 1g + 30c .65 .55
Nos. CB24-CB27 (4) 2.00 1.60

Olympic Games Issue

Nos. C163-C164 Surcharged

1960, Sept. 9 Photo. *Perf. 12*

CB28 A94 50c + 25c .20 .20
CB29 A94 1.50g + 25c .35 .30

Nos. C168-C169 Surcharged: "UNICEF +25 centimes"

1961, Jan. 14 Engr. *Perf. 10½*

CB30 A96 50c + 25c red org & blk .20 .20
CB31 A96 1.50g + 25c dk bl & blk .35 .25

Nos. C171, C175-C176 Surcharged with Additional Value, Scout Emblem and: "18e Conference Internationale du Scoutisme Mondial Lisbonne Septembre 1961"

1961, Sept. 30 Photo. *Perf. 11½*

CB32 AP37 20c + 25c .20 .20
CB33 AP37 1g + 25c .20 .20
CB34 AP37 1.50g + 25c .30 .30
Nos. CB32-CB34 (3) .70 .70

Issued to commemorate the 18th Boy Scout World Conference, Lisbon, Sept. 19-24, 1961.

The surtax was for the Red Cross. Additional proceeds from the sale of Nos. CB32-CB34 benefited the Port-au-Prince airport project.

The same surcharge was also applied to No. C176a.

Nos. C168-C169 Surcharged: "OMS SNEM +20 CENTIMES"

1961, Dec. 11 Engr. *Perf. 10½*

CB35 A96 50c + 20c .90 .90
CB36 A96 1.50g + 20c 1.25 1.25

Issued to publicize Haiti's participation in the UN malaria eradication drive.

Nos. C123, C126-C127 and C131-C132 Surcharged in Black or Red:

Engraved and Lithographed

1961-62 *Perf. 11½*

CB37 AP34 50c + 25c .20 .20
CB38 AP34 1g + 50c .20 .20
CB39 AP34 2.50g + 50c (R) ('62) .40 .35
CB40 AP34 5g + 50c .70 .70
CB41 AP34 7.50g + 50c (R) ('62) 1.00 .90
Nos. CB37-CB41 (5) 2.50 2.35

The surtax was for the benefit of the urban rehabilitation program in Duvalier Ville.

Nos. C188-C190 Surcharged: "+25 centimes"

1962, Sept. 13 Litho. *Perf. 12*

CB42 A99 20c + 25c .20 .20
CB43 A99 50c + 25c .25 .20
CB44 A99 1g + 25c .35 .20
Nos. CB42-CB44 (3) .80 .60

#C191-C192 Surcharged in Red: "+0.20"

1962 *Perf. 12½x13*

CB45 A92 50c + 20c .20 .20
CB46 A92 1g + 20c .30 .20

Nos. C203 and C205 Surcharged: "ALPHABETISATION" and "+0, 10"

1963, Mar. 15 Photo. *Perf. 14x14½*

CB47 AP38 50c + 10c .20 .20
CB48 AP38 1.50g + 10c .35 .30

No. C110 Surcharged in Red with Olympic Emblem and: "JEUX OLYMPIQUES / D'HIVER / INNSBRUCK 1964"

1964, July 27 Photo. *Perf. 11½*

CB49 A80 2.50g + 50c + 10c .60 .40

See note after No. B34. The 50c+10c surtax went for charity.

No. C213 Surcharged in Red

Engraved and Photogravure

1964, Oct. 2 *Perf. 13½x14*

CB50 AP39 2.50g + 1.25g on 1.50g .90 .70

Issued to commemorate the centenary (in 1963) of the International Red Cross.

Nos. C223-C226 Surcharged: "+ 5c."

1965, Mar. 15 Photo. *Perf. 11½*

CB51 A105 50c + 5c pale lil & dk brn .20 .20
CB52 A105 50c + 5c pale grn & dk brn .20 .20
CB53 A105 75c + 5c buff & dk brn .30 .25
CB54 A105 1.50g + 5c gray & dk brn .60 .50
Nos. CB51-CB54 (4) 1.30 1.15

The souvenir sheet No. C226a was surcharged "+25c." Value, $7.50.

See note following No. B37.

Nos. C251 and C253 Surcharged and Overprinted with Haitian Scout Emblem and "12e Jamboree / Mondial 1967" Like Regular Issue

1967, Aug. 21 Photo. *Perf. 11½*

CB55 A111 50c + 10c multi .20 .20
CB56 A111 1.50g + 50c multi .40 .35

See note after No. B40.

No. C269 Surcharged Like Regular Issue

Lithographed and Photogravure

1968, Jan. 18 *Perf. 13x13½*

CB57 A115 2.50g + 1.25g on 1.50g 1.00 .90

See note after No. 579.

#C285-C287 Surcharged "CULTURE + 10"

1968, July 4 Litho. *Perf. 11½*

CB58 A120 50c + 10c multi .20 .20
CB59 A120 1g + 10c multi .30 .30
CB60 A120 1.50g + 10c multi .35 .35
Nos. CB58-CB60 (3) .85 .85

Nos. C314 and C316 Surcharged in Red with New Value, Red Cross and: "50ème. Anniversaire / de la Ligue des / Sociétés de la / Croix Rouge"

1969, June 25 Litho. *Perf. 11½*

CB61 A127 50c + 20c multi .25 .25
CB62 A127 1.50g + 25c multi .65 .40

League of Red Cross Societies, 50th anniv.

AIR POST OFFICIAL STAMPS

Nos. C172-C176 and C176a Overprinted: "OFFICIEL"

Perf. 11½

1961, Mar. Unwmk. Photo.

CO1 AP37 50c rose brn & grn .25
CO2 AP37 50c brt grnsh bl & ol grn .25
CO3 AP37 50c gray & grn .25
CO4 AP37 1g gray ol & ver .35
CO5 AP37 1.50g brt pink & dk bl .50
a. Sheet of 3 1.50
Nos. CO1-CO5 (5) 1.60

Nos. CO1-CO5a only available canceled.

Catalogue values for unused stamps in this section, from this point to the end of the section, are for Never Hinged items.

Jean Jacques Dessalines — OA1

1962, Mar. 7 Photo. *Perf. 14x14½*
Size: 20½x38mm

CO6 OA1 50c dk bl & sepia .25 .20
CO7 OA1 1g lt bl & maroon .35 .25
CO8 OA1 1.50g bister & bl .50 .35

Size: 30x40mm

CO9 OA1 5g rose & ol grn 1.40 1.10
Nos. CO6-CO9 (4) 2.50 1.90

Inscription at bottom of #CO9 is in 2 lines.

AIR POST PARCEL POST STAMPS

Catalogue values for unused stamps in this section are for Never Hinged items.

Nos. C112 and C111 Overprinted in Red

Perf. 11½

1960, Nov. 21 Unwmk. Photo.

CQ1 A81 50c orange & black .30 .25
CQ2 A80 5g bluish blk & saph 2.00 1.75

Type of Parcel Post Stamps, 1961 Inscribed "Poste Aerienne"

1961, Mar. 24 *Perf. 14*

CQ3 PP1 2.50g yel grn & mar .90 .70
CQ4 PP1 5g org & green 1.75 1.40

SPECIAL DELIVERY STAMP

The catalogue value for the unused stamp in this section is for Never Hinged.

Postal Administration Building — SD1

Unwmk.

1953, May 4 Engr. *Perf. 12*

E1 SD1 25c vermilion .70 .60

POSTAGE DUE STAMPS

D1

D2

1898, May Unwmk. Engr. *Perf. 12*

J1 D1 2c black .25 .25
J2 D1 5c red brown .35 .35
J3 D1 10c brown orange .60 .20
J4 D1 50c slate 1.25 .70
Nos. J1-J4 (4) 2.45 1.50

For overprints see Nos. J5-J9, J14-J16.

Stamps of 1898 Handstamped like #67-81

1902 Black Overprint

J5 D1 2c black .70 .50
J6 D1 5c red brown .70 .50
J7 D1 10c brown orange .85 .50
J8 D1 50c slate 6.00 3.50

Red Overprint

J9 D1 2c black .85 .85
Nos. J5-J9 (5) 9.10 5.85

1906

J10 D2 2c dull red .60 .45
J11 D2 5c ultra 1.75 1.75
J12 D2 10c violet 1.75 1.75
J13 D2 50c olive gray 7.50 4.25
Nos. J10-J13 (4) 11.60 8.20

For surcharges and overprints see Nos. 305-308, J17-J20.

Preceding Issues Handstamped like #169-201

1914 On Stamps of 1898

J14 D1 5c red brown .60 .45
J15 D1 10c brown orange .55 .55
J16 D1 50c slate 3.75 2.50
Nos. J14-J16 (3) 4.90 3.50

On Stamps of 1906

J17 D2 2c dull red .45 .30
J18 D2 5c ultra .75 .45
J19 D2 10c violet 3.00 2.50
J20 D2 50c olive gray 5.50 3.50
Nos. J17-J20 (4) 9.70 6.75

The note after No. 201 applies to Nos. J14-J20 also.

Catalogue values for unused stamps in this section, from this point to the end of the section, are for Never Hinged items.

Unpaid Letter — D3

1951, July Litho. *Perf. 11½*

J21 D3 10c carmine .20 .20
J22 D3 20c red brown .20 .20
J23 D3 40c green .25 .25
J24 D3 50c orange yellow .35 .35
Nos. J21-J24 (4) 1.00 1.00

PARCEL POST STAMPS

Catalogue values for unused stamps in this section are for Never Hinged items.

Nos. 416, 470-471 and 378 Overprinted in Red

Photogravure, Engraved
Perf. 11½, 12

1960, Nov. 21 Unwmk.

Q1 A81 5c yel grn & blk .20 .20
Q2 A81 10c red org & blk .20 .20
Q3 A81 25c ultra & black .20 .20
Q4 A64 2.50g gray 1.00 1.00
Nos. Q1-Q4 (4) 1.60 1.60

Coat of Arms — PP1

Unwmk.

1961, Mar. 24 Photo. *Perf. 14*

Q5 PP1 50c bister & purple .35 .20
Q6 PP1 1g pink & dark blue .50 .30

See Nos. CQ3-CQ4.

POSTAL TAX STAMPS

Catalogue values for unused stamps in this section, are for Never Hinged items.

Haitian Woman, War Invalids and Ruined Buildings PT1

Unwmk.

1944, Aug. 16 Engr. *Perf. 12*

RA1 PT1 5c dull purple .70 .30
RA2 PT1 5c dark blue .70 .30
RA3 PT1 5c olive green .70 .30
RA4 PT1 5c black .70 .30

1945, Dec. 17

RA5 PT1 5c dark green .70 .30
RA6 PT1 5c sepia .70 .30
RA7 PT1 5c red brown .70 .30
RA8 PT1 5c rose carmine .70 .30
Nos. RA1-RA8 (8) 5.60 2.40

The proceeds from the sale of Nos. RA1 to RA8 were for United Nations Relief.

George Washington, J.J. Dessalines and Simón Bolivar — PT2

1949, Sept. 20

RA9 PT2 5c red brown .20 .20
RA10 PT2 5c olive gray .20 .20
RA11 PT2 5c blue .20 .20
RA12 PT2 5c green .20 .20
RA13 PT2 5c violet .20 .20
RA14 PT2 5c black .20 .20
RA15 PT2 5c orange .20 .20
RA16 PT2 5c carmine rose .20 .20
Nos. RA9-RA16 (8) 1.60 1.60

Bicentenary of Port-au-Prince.
For overprint and surcharges see #385-388.

Helicopter Inspection of Hurricane Damage PT3

Helicopter PT4

1955, Jan. 3 Photo. *Perf. 11½*

RA17 PT3 10c bright green .20 .20
RA18 PT3 10c bright blue .20 .20
RA19 PT3 10c gray black .20 .20
RA20 PT3 10c orange .20 .20
RA21 PT3 20c rose carmine .20 .20
RA22 PT3 20c deep green .20 .20
Nos. RA17-RA22 (6) 1.20 1.20

1955, May 3

RA23 PT4 10c black, *gray* .20 .20
RA24 PT4 20c violet blue, *blue* .20 .20

The surface tint of the sheets of 50, (10x5) of #RA23-RA24, RAC1-RAC2 includes a map of Haiti's southern peninsula which extends over the three center rows of stamps.
The tax was for reconstruction.
See Nos. RAC1-RAC2.

PT5

1959-60 Unwmk. Photo. *Perf. 11½*
Size: 38x22½mm

RA25 PT5 5c green .20 .20
RA26 PT5 5c black ('60) .20 .20
RA27 PT5 10c red .20 .20
Nos. RA25-RA27 (3) .60 .60

1960-61
Size: 28x17mm

RA28 PT5 5c green .20 .20
RA29 PT5 10c red .20 .20
RA30 PT5 10c blue ('61) .20 .20
Nos. RA28-RA30 (3) .60 .60

PT6

1963, Sept. *Perf. 14½x14*
Size: 13½x21mm

RA31 PT6 10c red orange .20 .20
RA32 PT6 10c bright blue .20 .20
RA33 PT6 10c olive .20 .20
Nos. RA31-RA33,RAC6-RAC8 (6) 1.20 1.20

1966-69 Photo. *Perf. 14x14½*
Size: 17x25mm

RA34 PT6 10c bright green .20 .20
RA35 PT6 10c violet .20 .20
RA36 PT6 10c violet blue .20 .20
RA37 PT6 10c brown ('69) .20 .20
Nos. RA34-RA37,RAC9-RAC15 (11) 2.20 2.20

Nos. RA25-RA37 represent a tax for a literacy campaign.
See Nos. RA42-RA45, RAC20-RAC22.

Duvalier de Peligre Hydroelectric Works — PT7

1970-72

RA38 PT7 20c violet & olive .20 .20
RA39 PT7 20c ultra & blk ('72) .20 .20

See Nos. RA46, RAC16-RAC19, RAC23.

Nos. 637-638 Surcharged: "ALPHABETISATION +10"

1971, Dec. 23 Litho. ***Perf. 14x13½***

RA40 A138 20c + 10c multi .20 .20
a. Inverted surcharge 2.00
RA41 A138 25c + 10c multi .20 .20

Tax was for the literacy campaign.

"CA" Type of 1963

1972-74 Photo. ***Perf. 14x14½***
Size: 17x25mm

RA42 PT6 5c violet blue .20 .20
RA43 PT6 5c deep carmine .20 .20
RA44 PT6 5c ultra ('74) .20 .20
RA45 PT6 5c carmine rose ('74) .20 .20
Nos. RA42-RA45 (4) .80 .80

Tax was for literacy campaign.

Hydroelectric Type of 1970

1980 Photo. ***Perf. 14x14½***

RA46 PT7 25c choc & green .25 .20

AIR POST POSTAL TAX STAMPS

Catalogue values for unused stamps in this section, are for Never Hinged items.

Helicopter Type of 1955

1955 Unwmk. Photo. ***Perf. 11½***

RAC1 PT4 10c red brn, *pale sal* .20 .20
RAC2 PT4 20c rose pink, *pink* .20 .20

See note after No. RA24.

Type of Postal Tax Stamps, 1960-61

1959
Size: 28x17mm

RAC3 PT5 5c yellow .20 .20
RAC4 PT5 10c dull salmon .20 .20
RAC5 PT5 10c blue .20 .20
Nos. RAC3-RAC5 (3) .60 .60

Type of Postal Tax Stamps, 1963

1963, Sept. ***Perf. 14½x14***
Size: 13½x21mm

RAC6 PT6 10c dark gray .20 .20
RAC7 PT6 10c violet .20 .20
RAC8 PT6 10c brown .20 .20
Nos. RAC6-RAC8 (3) .60 .60

1966-69 ***Perf. 14x14½***
Size: 17x25mm

RAC9 PT6 10c orange .20 .20
RAC10 PT6 10c sky blue .20 .20
RAC11 PT6 10c yellow ('69) .20 .20
RAC12 PT6 10c carmine ('69) .20 .20
RAC13 PT6 10c gray grn ('69) .20 .20
RAC14 PT6 10c lilac ('69) .20 .20
RAC15 PT6 10c dp claret ('69) .20 .20
Nos. RAC9-RAC15 (7) 1.40 1.40

Nos. RAC3-RAC15, RAC20-RAC21 represent a tax for a literacy campaign.

Hydroelectric Type of 1970

1970-74

RAC16 PT7 20c tan & slate .20 .20
RAC17 PT7 20c brt bl & dl vio .20 .20
RAC18 PT7 25c sal & bluish blk ('74) .20 .20
RAC19 PT7 25c yel ol & bluish blk ('74) .20 .20
Nos. RAC16-RAC19 (4) .80 .80

"CA" Type of 1963

1973 Photo. ***Perf. 14x14½***
Size: 17x26mm

RAC20 PT6 10c brn & blue .20 .20
RAC21 PT6 10c brn & green .20 .20
RAC22 PT6 10c brn & orange .20 .20
Nos. RAC20-RAC22 (3) .60 .60

Hydroelectric Power Type of 1970

1979(?) Photo. ***Perf. 14x14½***

RAC23 PT7 25c blue & vio brn .20 .20

HATAY

hä-'tī

LOCATION — Northwest of Syria, bordering on Mediterranean Sea
GOVT. — Semi-independent republic
AREA — 10,000 sq. mi. (approx.)
POP. — 273,350 (1939)
CAPITAL — Antioch

Alexandretta, a semi-autonomous district of Syria under French mandate, was renamed Hatay in 1938 and transferred to Turkey in 1939.

100 Santims = 1 Kurush
40 Paras = 1 Kurush (1939)

Stamps of Turkey, 1931-38, Surcharged in Black:

On A77

On A78

1939 Unwmk. ***Perf. 11½x12***

1 A77 10s on 20pa dp org .20 .20
a. "Sent" instead of "Sant" 20.00 20.00
2 A78 25s on 1ku dk sl grn .20 .20
a. Small "25" 2.25 1.50
3 A78 50s on 2ku dk vio .60 .60
a. Small "50" 2.25 2.00
4 A77 75s on 2½ku green .40 .35
5 A78 1ku on 4ku slate 4.50 4.25
6 A78 1ku on 5ku rose red 1.50 1.40
7 A78 1½ku on 3ku brn org .60 .60
8 A78 2½ku on 4ku slate .60 .60
9 A78 5ku on 8ku brt blue .60 .60
10 A77 12½ku on 20ku ol grn 1.50 1.40
11 A77 20ku on 25ku Prus bl 5.25 4.75
Nos. 1-11 (11) 15.95 14.95

Map of Hatay — A1

Lions of Antioch A2

Flag of Hatay A3

Post Office A4

1939 Unwmk. Typo. ***Perf. 12***

12 A1 10p orange & aqua .75 .75
13 A1 30p lt vio & aqua .75 .75
14 A1 1½ku olive & aqua .75 .75
15 A2 2½ku turq grn 1.00 1.00
16 A2 3ku light blue 1.00 1.00
17 A2 5ku chocolate 1.00 1.00
18 A3 6ku brt blue & car 1.25 1.25
19 A3 7½ku dp green & car 1.25 1.25
20 A3 12ku violet & car 1.25 1.25
21 A3 12½ku dk blue & car 1.50 1.50
22 A4 17½ku brown car 3.00 3.00
23 A4 25ku olive brn 3.50 3.50
24 A4 50ku slate blue 8.50 8.50
Nos. 12-24 (13) 25.50 25.50

Stamps of 1939 Overprinted in Black

1939

25 A1 10p orange & aqua .50 .50
a. Overprint reading up 20.00
26 A1 30p lt vio & aqua .50 .50
27 A1 1½ku ol & aqua .50 .50
28 A2 2½ku turq grn .45 .45
29 A2 3ku light blue .55 .55
30 A2 5ku chocolate 1.00 1.00
a. Overprint inverted 20.00
31 A3 6ku brt bl & car 1.00 1.00
32 A3 7½ku dp grn & car 1.00 1.00
33 A3 12ku vio & car .75 .75
34 A3 12½ku dk bl & car 1.00 1.00
35 A4 17½ku brn car 1.75 1.75
a. Overprint inverted 20.00
36 A4 25ku olive brn 3.75 3.75
37 A4 50ku slate blue 8.00 8.00
Nos. 25-37 (13) 20.75 20.75

The overprint reads "Date of annexation to the Turkish Republic, June 30, 1939."

On Nos. 25-27, the overprint reads down. On Nos. 28-37, it is horizontal.

POSTAGE DUE STAMPS

Postage Due Stamps of Turkey, 1936, Surcharged or Overprinted in Black

1939 Unwmk. ***Perf. 11½***

J1 D6 1ku on 2ku lt bl .45 .30
J2 D6 3ku bright violet .85 .75
J3 D6 4ku on 5ku Prus bl .85 .75
J4 D6 5ku on 12ku brt rose .85 .75
J5 D6 12ku bright rose 22.00 20.00
Nos. J1-J5 (5) 25.00 22.55

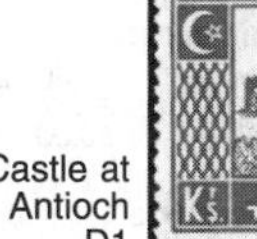

Castle at Antioch D1

1939 Typo. ***Perf. 12***

J6 D1 1ku red orange 1.00 1.00
J7 D1 3ku dk olive brown 1.00 1.00
J8 D1 4ku turqoise green 1.50 1.50
J9 D1 5ku slate black 2.00 2.00
Nos. J6-J9 (4) 5.50 5.50

Nos. J6-J9 Overprinted in Black like Nos. 25-37

1939

J10 D1 1ku red orange 1.00 1.00
J11 D1 3ku dk olive brown 1.25 1.25
J12 D1 4ku turqoise green 1.50 1.50
J13 D1 5ku slate black 1.75 1.75
a. Overprint inverted 20.00
Nos. J10-J13 (4) 5.50 5.50

HELIGOLAND

'he-lə-gō-,land

LOCATION — An island in the North Sea near the northern coast of Germany
GOVT. — Former British Possession
AREA — ¼ sq. mi.
POP. — 2,307 (1900)

Great Britain ceded Heligoland to Germany in 1890. It became part of Schleswig-Holstein province. Stamps of Heligoland were superseded by those of the German Empire.

16 Schillings = 1 Mark
100 Pfennig = 1 Mark = 1 Schilling (1875)

Queen Victoria
A1 A2

A3

A4

HALF SCHILLING
A1: Curl below chignon is rounded.
A2: Curl resembles hook or comma.

Typo., Head Embossed

1867-68 Unwmk. ***Rouletted***

1 A1 ½sch bl grn & rose 350.00 *775.00*
1A A2 ½sch bl grn & rose 700.00 *1,000.*
2 A1 1sch rose & dp grn 175.00 *175.00*
3 A3 2sch rose & pale green 10.00 *50.00*
4 A3 6sch gray green & rose 12.50 *240.00*

Reprints of No. 2 lack the large curl, those of No. 1A are not in blue green, and those of Nos. 3 and 4 are on slightly porous paper and the colors are either too deep or too bright. The 2sch and 6sch perforated exist only as reprints.

1869-71 ***Perf. 13½x14½***
Thick Soft Paper

5 A2 ½sch ol grn & car 100.00 *150.00*
a. ½sch blue green & rose 175.00 *200.00*
b. ½sch yellow green & rose 300.00 *275.00*
6 A2 1sch rose & yel grn 140.00 *175.00*

Reprints are on thinner paper and in too dark colors.

1873 Thick Quadrille Paper

7 A4 ¼sch pale rose & pale grn 25.00 *1,500.*
a. ¼sch deep rose & pale grn *85.00* *1,750.*
8 A4 ¼sch yel grn & rose 150.00 *3,000.*
9 A2 ½sch brt grn & rose 100.00 *175.00*
10 A4 ¾sch gray grn & pale rose 27.50 *1,100.*
a. ¾sch gray green & dp rose 27.50 *1,100.*
11 A2 1sch rose & pale grn 110.00 *175.00*
12 A4 1½sch yel grn & rose 65.00 *240.00*

Reprints are never on quadrille paper.

1874 Thin Wove Paper

13 A4 ¼sch rose & yel grn 15.00

Originals have the large curl. The early reprints have the small curl. The later reprints are on thin hard paper with smooth white gum and the colors are too bright.

A5

A6

A7

Coat of Arms — A8

1875 Wove Paper

14 A5 1pf dk rose & dk grn 10.00 *475.00*
15 A5 2pf yel grn & dk rose 10.00 *575.00*

16 A6 5pf dk rose & dk grn 15.00 *35.00*
17 A6 10pf blue grn & red 10.00 *22.50*
a. 10pf yel green & dark rose 75.00 *20.00*
b. 10pf lt green & pale red 125.00 *27.50*
18 A7 25pf rose & dk grn 11.50 *25.00*
a. 25pf dk rose & dk green 11.50 *25.00*
19 A7 50pf grn & brick red 17.50 *50.00*
a. 50pf dl grn & dk rose 55.00 *30.00*

The 1pf and 2pf have been reprinted on very white paper with white gum. The colors are too bright and too light.

1876-88 **Typo.**
20 A8 3pf grn & bright red ('77) 150.00 *900.00*
a. 3pf dp grn & dl red 225.00 *1,100.*
21 A8 20pf ver & brt grn ('88) 12.00 *27.50*
a. 20pf brn org & grn ('87) 375.00 *37.50*
b. 20pf vio car & yel grn ('80) 140.00 *47.50*
c. 20pf anil rose & dk grn ('85) 375.00 *30.00*
d. 20pf lilac rose & dk green 250.00 *125.00*
e. 20pf rose red & dk grn ('80) 150.00 *75.00*

The coat-of-arms on Nos. 20, 21 and sub-varieties is printed in three colors: varying shades of yellow, red and green.

The 3pf has been reprinted. The colors are usually too pale, especially the red, which is either orange or orange red.

A9

A10

1879 **Typo.**
22 A9 1m dp green & car 150.00 *190.00*
a. 1m blue green & salmon 150.00 *190.00*
b. 1m dark green & vermilion 65.00
23 A10 5m blue grn & sal 175.00 *900.00*

Perf. 11½

24 A9 1m dp grn & car 1,000.
25 A10 5m bl grn & rose red 1,000.
a. Horiz. pair, imperf. vert. *3,250.*

Nos. 13, 22b, 24 and 25 were never placed in use. Forged cancellations of Nos. 1-23 are plentiful.

Heligoland stamps were replaced by those of the German Empire in 1890.

HONDURAS

hän-ˈdur-əs

LOCATION — Central America, between Guatemala on the north and Nicaragua on the south
GOVT. — Republic
AREA — 43,277 sq. mi.
POP. — 5,997,327 (1999 est.)
CAPITAL — Tegucigalpa

8 Reales = 1 Peso
100 Centavos = 1 Peso (1878)
100 Centavos = 1 Lempira (1933)

Catalogue values for unused stamps in this country are for Never Hinged items, beginning with Scott 344 in the regular postage section, Scott B1 in the semi-postal section, Scott C144 in the airpost section, Scott CB5 in the airpost semi-postal section, Scott CE3 in the airpost special delivery section, Scott CO110 in the airpost official section, and Scott RA6 in the postal tax section.

Values for unused stamps are for examples with original gum as defined in the catalogue introduction. Very fine examples of the locally printed Nos. 95-110, 127, 140, 151-210C, and 218-279 will have margins clear of the perforations but will be noticeably off center.

Watermark

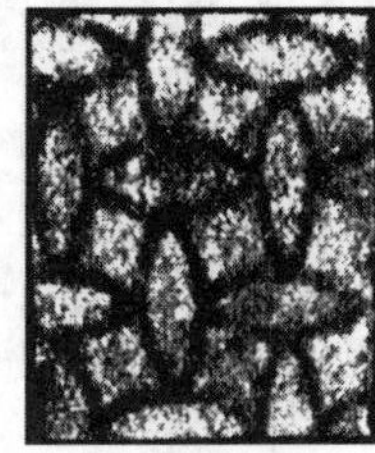
Wmk. 209- Multiple Ovals

Coat of Arms — A1

1865, Dec. Unwmk. Litho. *Imperf.*
1 A1 2r black, *green* .50 —
2 A1 2r black, *pink* .50 —

Comayagua

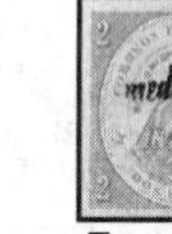

Tegucigalpa

The actual surcharges are very blurry, distorted and generally unreadable. The above illustrations are from proof impressions.
Medio real = ½ real
Un real = 1 real
Dos reales = 2 reales

Comayagua Issue

1877, May

Red Surcharge

3 A1 ½r on 2r blk, *grn* 60.00

Blue Surcharge

5 A1 2r on 2r blk, *grn* —
6 A1 2r on 2r blk, *pink* 200.00 —

Black Surcharge

7 A1 1r on 2r blk, *grn* 100.00
8 A1 2r on 2r blk, *grn* *500.00*
9 A1 2r on 2r blk, *pink* 350.00

Tegucigalpa Issue

1877, July

Black Surcharge

13 A1 1r on 2r blk, *grn* 15.00 *35.00*
a. Surcharged on #5 *500.00*
14 A1 1r on 2r blk, *pink* *50.00*
16 A1 2r on 2r blk, *pink* —

Blue Surcharge

18 A1 ½r on 2r blk, *grn* *50.00*
19 A1 ½r on 2r blk, *pink* *25.00*
20 A1 1r on 2r blk, *pink* *35.00*
23 A1 2r on 2r blk, *pink* 15.00 *25.00*

Red Surcharge

24 A1 ½r on 2r blk, *grn* 15.00 *35.00*
25 A1 ½r on 2r blk, *pink* 50.00

Only the stamps valued used were postally used. The others were sold as remainders.

The blue surcharges range from light blue to violet black. The black surcharge has no tinge of blue. The red surcharges range from light to dark carmine. Some exist double or inverted, but genuine errors are rare. Normal cancel is a blue or black 7-bar killer. Target cancels on Nos. 1-24 are forgeries and surcharges with target cancels also are forgeries. Surcharges and cancels have been extensively forged.

Regular Issue

President Francisco Morazán — A4

Thin, hard paper, colorless gum
Various Frames

1878, July Engr. *Perf. 12*
Printed by National Bank Note Co. of N.Y.

30 A4 1c violet .50 .50
31 A4 2c brown .50 .50
32 A4 ½r black 5.00 .50
33 A4 1r green 25.00 .50
34 A4 2r deep blue 3.00 *5.00*
35 A4 4r vermilion 5.00 *10.00*
36 A4 1p orange 6.00 *25.00*
Nos. 30-36 (7) 45.00 *42.00*

Various counterfeit cancellations exist on Nos. 30-36. Most used copies of Nos. 35-36 offered are actually 35a-36a with fake or favor cancels.

Re-Issue
Soft paper, yellowish gum
Various Frames

1889
Printed by American Bank Note Co. of N.Y.

30a A4 1c deep violet *10.00*
31a A4 2c red brown .25
32a A4 ½r black .25
33a A4 1r blue green .25
34a A4 2r ultramarine *5.00*
35a A4 4r scarlet vermilion .25
36a A4 1p orange yellow .25
Nos. 30a-36a (7) 16.25

Although Nos. 30a-36a were not intended for postal use, they were valid, and genuine cancels are known on Nos. 31a-34a.

Arms of Honduras — A5

1890, Jan. 6
40 A5 1c yellow green .30 .30
41 A5 2c red .30 .30
42 A5 5c blue .30 .30
43 A5 10c orange .35 *.40*
44 A5 20c ocher .35 *.40*
45 A5 25c rose red .35 *.40*
46 A5 30c purple .50 *.60*
47 A5 40c dark blue .50 *.80*
48 A5 50c brown .55 *.80*
49 A5 75c blue green .55 *2.00*
50 A5 1p carmine .70 *2.25*
Nos. 40-50 (11) 4.75 *8.55*

The tablets and numerals of Nos. 40 to 50 differ for each denomination.

For overprints see Nos. O1-O11.

Used values of Nos. 1-110 are for stamps with genuine cancellations applied while the stamps were valid. Various counterfeit cancellations exist.

A6

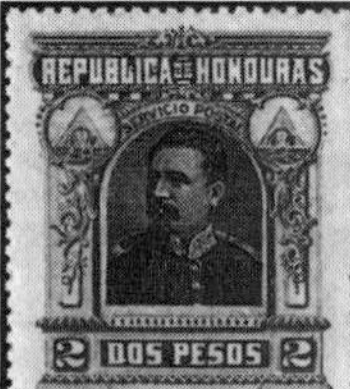
President Luis Bográn — A7

1891, July 31
51 A6 1c dark blue .30 .30
52 A6 2c yellow brown .30 .30
53 A6 5c blue green .30 .30
54 A6 10c vermilion .30 .30
55 A6 20c brown red .30 .30
56 A6 25c magenta .40 *.55*
57 A6 30c slate .40 *.55*
58 A6 40c blue green .40 *.55*
59 A6 50c black brown .50 *.80*
60 A6 75c purple .50 *1.25*
61 A6 1p brown .50 *1.60*
62 A7 2p brn & black 1.50 *5.00*
a. Head inverted 225.00
63 A7 5p pur & black 1.50 *5.75*
a. Head inverted 60.00
64 A7 10p green & blk 1.50 *5.75*
a. Head inverted 75.00
Nos. 51-64 (14) 8.70 *23.30*

#62, 64 exist with papermakers watermark.

For overprints see Nos. O12-O22.

Columbus Sighting Honduran Coast — A8

General Trinidad Cabanas — A9

1892, July 31
65 A8 1c slate .40 *.45*
66 A8 2c deep blue .40 *.45*
67 A8 5c yellow green .40 *.45*
68 A8 10c blue green .40 *.45*
69 A8 20c red .40 *.45*
70 A8 25c orange brown .50 *.55*
71 A8 30c ultramarine .50 *.60*
72 A8 40c orange .50 *.90*
73 A8 50c brown .60 *.85*
74 A8 75c lake .60 *1.25*
75 A8 1p purple .60 *1.40*
Nos. 65-75 (11) 5.30 *7.80*

Discovery of America by Christopher Columbus, 400th anniv.

1893, Aug.
76 A9 1c green .25 *1.50*
77 A9 2c scarlet .25 *1.50*
78 A9 5c dark blue .25 *1.50*
79 A9 10c orange brn .25 *1.50*
80 A9 20c brown red .25 *1.50*
81 A9 25c dark blue .30 *1.50*
82 A9 30c red orange .45 *1.50*
83 A9 40c black .45 *1.50*
84 A9 50c olive brn .45 *1.50*
85 A9 75c purple .60 *1.50*
86 A9 1p deep magenta .60 *1.75*
Nos. 76-86 (11) 4.10 *16.75*

"Justice" A10

President Celio Arias A11

1895, Feb. 15
87 A10 1c vermilion .30 .30
88 A10 2c deep blue .30 .30
89 A10 5c slate .30 *.50*
90 A10 10c brown rose .40 *.50*
91 A10 20c violet .40 *.50*
92 A10 30c deep violet .40 *.85*
93 A10 50c olive brown .50 *1.25*
94 A10 1p dark green .55 *1.60*
Nos. 87-94 (8) 3.15 *5.80*

The tablets and numerals of Nos. 76-94 differ for each denomination.

1896, Jan. 1 Litho. *Perf. 11½*
95 A11 1c dark blue .30 *.35*
96 A11 2c yellow brn .30 *.35*
97 A11 5c purple 1.10 .30
a. 5c red violet .55 *1.10*
98 A11 10c vermilion .40 .40
a. 10c red 4.50 *4.50*
99 A11 20c emerald .75 .50
a. 20c deep green
100 A11 30c ultramarine .65 *.70*
101 A11 50c rose .90 *1.00*
102 A11 1p black brown 1.25 *1.50*
Nos. 95-102 (8) 5.65 *5.10*

Counterfeits are plentiful. Nos. 95-102 exist imperf. between horiz. or vertically.

Originals of Nos. 95 to 102 are on both thin, semi-transparent paper and opaque paper; reprints are on thicker, opaque paper and usually have a black cancellation "HONDURAS" between horizontal bars.

Railroad Train — A12

1898, Aug. 1
103 A12 1c brown .50 .20
104 A12 2c rose .50 .20
105 A12 5c dull ultra 1.00 .25
b. 5c red violet (error) 1.50 .70

106 A12 6c red violet .90 .25
b. 6c dull rose (error)
107 A12 10c dark blue 1.00 .30
108 A12 20c dull orange 1.25 .75
109 A12 50c orange red 2.00 1.25
110 A12 1p blue green 4.00 3.00
Nos. 103-110 (8) 11.15 6.20

Excellent counterfeits of Nos. 103-110 exist.
For overprints see Nos. O23-O27.

Laid Paper

103a A12 1c 1.00 .50
104a A12 2c 1.25 .50
105a A12 5c 1.50 .50
106a A12 6c 1.50 .75
107a A12 10c 1.50 1.00
Nos. 103a-107a (5) 6.75 3.25

General Santos Guardiola
A13

President José Medina
A14

1903, Jan. 1 Engr. *Perf. 12*

111 A13 1c yellow grn .35 .20
112 A13 2c carmine rose .35 .30
113 A13 5c blue .35 .30
114 A13 6c dk violet .35 .30
115 A13 10c brown .40 .30
116 A13 20c dull ultra .45 .40
117 A13 50c vermilion 1.25 1.10
118 A13 1p orange 1.25 1.10
Nos. 111-118 (8) 4.75 4.00

"PERMITASE" handstamped on stamps of 1896-1903 was applied as a control mark by the isolated Pacific Coast post office of Amapala to prevent use of stolen stamps.

1907, Jan. 1 *Perf. 14*

119 A14 1c dark green .20 .20
120 A14 2c scarlet .25 .25
120A A14 2c carmine 9.00 5.50
121 A14 5c blue .30 .30
122 A14 6c purple .35 .30
a. 6c dark violet .80 .60
123 A14 10c gray brown .40 .35
124 A14 20c ultra .90 .85
a. 20c blue violet 110.00 110.00
125 A14 50c deep lake 1.10 1.10
126 A14 1p orange 1.50 1.50
a. 1p orange yellow —
Nos. 119-126 (9) 14.00 10.35

All values of the above set exist imperforate, imperforate horizontally and in horizontal pairs, imperforate between. No. 124a imperf is worth only 10% of the listed perforated variety.
For surcharges see Nos. 128-130.

1909 Typo. *Perf. 11½*

127 A14 1c green 1.25 1.00
a. Imperf., pair 3.50 3.50
b. Printed on both sides 7.50

The 1909 issue is roughly typographed in imitation of the 1907 design. It exists pin perf. 8, 13, etc.

No. 124 Handstamp Surcharged in Black, Green or Red:

1910, Nov. *Perf. 14*

128 A14 1c on 20c ultra 7.00 5.75
129 A14 5c on 20c ultra (G) 7.00 5.75
130 A14 10c on 20c ultra (R) 7.00 5.75
Nos. 128-130 (3) 21.00 17.25

As is usual with handstamped surcharges inverts and double exist.

Honduran Scene — A15

1911, Jan. Litho. *Perf. 14, 12 (1p)*

131 A15 1c violet .35 .20
132 A15 2c green .35 .20
a. Perf. 12 5.00 1.25
133 A15 5c carmine .40 .20
a. Perf. 12 8.00 3.50
134 A15 6c ultramarine .45 .30
135 A15 10c blue .60 .40
136 A15 20c yellow .60 .50
137 A15 50c brown 2.00 1.75
138 A15 1p olive green 2.25 2.00
Nos. 131-138 (8) 7.00 5.55

For overprints and surcharges see Nos. 139, 141-147, O28-O47.

No. 132a Overprinted in Red

1911, Sept. 19 *Perf. 12*

139 A15 2c green 18.00 18.00
a. Inverted overprint 22.50 22.50

90th anniversary of Independence.
Counterfeit overprints on perf. 14 stamps exist.

President Manuel Bonilla — A16

1912, Feb. 1 Typo. *Perf. 11½*

140 A16 1c orange red 12.00 12.00

Election of Pres. Manuel Bonilla.

Stamps of 1911 Surcharged in Black, Red or Blue:

a

b

1913 Litho. *Perf. 14*

141 A15(a) 2c on 1c violet 1.25 .75
a. Double surcharge 3.25
b. Inverted surcharge 4.50
c. Double surch., one invtd. 6.75
d. Red surcharge 40.00 40.00
142 A15(b) 2c on 1c violet 7.00 5.75
a. Inverted surcharge 14.00
143 A15(b) 2c on 10c blue 2.75 2.25
a. Double surcharge 5.75 5.75
b. Inverted surcharge
144 A15(b) 2c on 20c yellow 7.00 6.75
145 A15(b) 5c on 1c violet 2.50 .75
146 A15(b) 5c on 10c bl (Bl) 2.75 1.50
147 A15(b) 6c on 1c violet 2.75 2.25
Nos. 141-147 (7) 26.00 20.00

Counterfeit surcharges exist.

Terencio Sierra — A17

Bonilla — A18

ONE CENTAVO:
Type I - Solid border at sides below numerals.
Type II - Border of light and dark stripes.

1913-14 Typo. *Perf. 11½*

151 A17 1c dark brn, I .20 .20
a. 1c brown, type II .75 .45
152 A17 2c carmine .25 .20
153 A18 5c blue .40 .20
154 A18 5c ultra ('14) .40 .20
155 A18 6c gray vio .50 .25
156 A18 6c purple ('14) .40 .25
a. 6c red lilac .60 .35
157 A17 10c blue .75 .75
158 A17 10c brown ('14) 1.25 .50
159 A17 20c brown 1.00 .75
160 A18 50c rose 2.00 2.00
161 A18 1p gray green 2.25 2.25
Nos. 151-161 (11) 9.40 7.55

For overprints and surcharges see Nos. 162-173, O48-O57.

Surcharged in Black or Carmine

1914

162 A17 1c on 2c carmine .75 .75
163 A17 5c on 2c carmine 1.25 .90
164 A18 5c on 6c gray vio 2.00 2.00
165 A17 10c on 2c carmine 2.00 2.00
166 A18 10c on 6c gray vio 2.00 2.00
a. Double surcharge 10.00
167 A18 10c on 6c gray vio (C) 2.00 2.00
168 A18 10c on 50c rose 6.50 5.00
Nos. 162-168 (7) 16.50 14.65

No. 158 Surcharged with New Value

1915

173 A17 5c on 10c brown 2.50 1.75

Ulua Bridge — A19

Bonilla Theater — A20

1915-16 Typo.

174 A19 1c chocolate .20 .20
175 A19 2c carmine .20 .20
a. Tête bêche pair 1.00 1.00
176 A20 5c bright blue .25 .20
177 A20 6c deep purple .35 .20
178 A19 10c dull blue .75 .20
179 A19 20c red brown 1.25 1.00
a. Tête bêche pair 4.00 4.00
180 A20 50c red 1.50 1.50
181 A20 1p yellow grn 2.50 2.50
Nos. 174-181 (8) 7.00 6.00

For overprints & surcharges see #183, 231-232, 237, 239-240, 285, 292, C1-C13, C25, C28, C31, C36, C57, CO21, CO30-CO32, CO42, O58-O65.

Imperf., Pairs

174a A19 1c 2.00 2.00
175b A19 2c 2.00 2.00
176a A20 5c 3.50
178a A19 10c 3.50
179b A19 20c 5.25
180b A20 50c 7.00
181a A20 1p 8.75 8.75

Francisco Bertrand
A21

Statue to Francisco Morazán
A22

1916, Feb. 1

182 A21 1c orange 2.00 2.00

Election of Pres. Francisco Bertrand.
Unauthorized reprints exist.

Official Stamp No. O60 Overprinted

1918

183 A20 5c bright blue 2.00 1.50
a. Inverted overprint 5.00 5.00

1919 Typo.

184 A22 1c brown .20 .20
a. Printed on both sides 2.00
b. Imperf., pair .70
185 A22 2c carmine .25 .20
186 A22 5c lilac rose .25 .20
187 A22 6c brt violet .25 .20
188 A22 10c dull blue .25 .25
189 A22 15c light blue .75 .20
190 A22 15c dark violet .60 .20
191 A22 20c orange brn 1.00 .30
a. 20c gray brown 10.00 .30
b. Imperf., pair 2.75
192 A22 50c light brown 4.00 2.50
a. Imperf. pair 15.00
193 A22 1p yellow green 7.50 *20.00*
a. Imperf., pair 20.00
b. Printed on both sides 9.00
c. Tête bêche pair 15.00
Nos. 184-193 (10) 15.05 24.25

See note on handstamp following No. 217.
Unauthorized reprints exist.
For overprints and surcharges see Nos. 201-210C, 230, 233, 235-236, 238, 241-243, 287, 289, C58, C61, CO23, CO25, CO33, CO36-CO38, CO39, CO40, O66-O74.

"Dawn of Peace" — A23

1920, Feb. 1

Size: 27x21mm

194 A23 2c rose 2.50 2.50
a. Tête bêche pair 12.50 12.50
b. Imperf., pair 12.50 12.50

Size: 51x40mm

195 A23 2c gold 10.00 10.00
196 A23 2c silver 10.00 10.00
197 A23 2c bronze 10.00 10.00
198 A23 2c red 12.00 12.00
Nos. 194-198 (5) 44.50 44.50

Assumption of power by Gen. Rafael Lopez Gutierrez.
Nos. 195-198 exist imperf.
Unauthorized reprints of #195-198 exist.

Type of 1919, Dated "1920"

1921

201 A22 6c dark violet 10.00 *5.00*
a. Tête bêche pair 15.00
b. Imperf., pair 15.00

Unauthorized reprints exist.

No. 185 Surcharged in Antique Letters

1922

202 A22 6c on 2c carmine .40 .40
a. "ALE" for "VALE" 2.00 2.00
b. Comma after "CTS" 2.00 2.00
c. Without period after "CTS" 2.00 2.00
d. "CT" for "CTS" 2.00 2.00
e. Double surcharge 4.25
f. Inverted surcharge 4.25

Stamps of 1919 Surcharged in Roman Figures and Antique Letters in Green

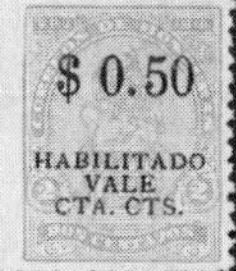

1923

203 A22 10c on 1c brown 1.50 1.50
204 A22 50c on 2c carmine 2.00 2.00
a. Inverted surcharge 10.00 10.00
b. "HABILTADO" 6.00 6.00

Surcharged in Black or Violet Blue

205 A22 1p on 5c lil rose (Bk) 3.50 3.50
a. "PSEO" 20.00 20.00
b. Inverted surcharge 20.00 20.00
206 A22 1p on 5c lil rose (VB) 20.00 20.00
a. "PSEO" 70.00

On Nos. 205-206, "Habilitado Vale" is in Antique letters, "Un Peso" in Roman.

No. 185 Surcharged in Roman Letters in Green

207 A22 6c on 2c carmine 3.50 2.75

Nos. 184-185 Surcharged in Roman Letters in Green

208 A22 10c on 1c brown 1.75 1.25
a. "DIES" 4.00
b. "DEIZ" 4.00
c. "DEIZ CAS" 4.00
d. "TTS" for "CTS" 4.00
e. "HABILTADO" 4.00
f. "HABILITAD" 4.00
g. "HABILITA" 4.00
h. Inverted surcharge 20.00
209 A22 50c on 2c carmine 3.75 2.75
a. "CAT" for "CTA" 7.50
b. "TCA" for "CTA" 7.50
c. "TTS" for "CTS" 7.50
d. "CAS" for "CTS" 7.50
e. "HABILTADO" 7.50

Surcharge on No. 209 is found in two spacings between value and HABILITADO: 5mm (illustrated) and 1½mm.

No. 186 Surcharged in Antique Letters in Black

$ 1.00
HABILITADO
VALE
UN PESO

210 A22 1p on 5c lil rose 25.00 *25.00*
a. "PFSO" 75.00

In the surcharges on Nos. 202 to 210 there are various wrong font, inverted and omitted letters.

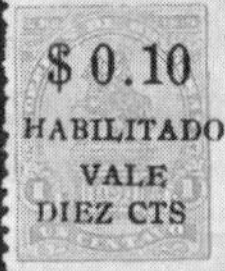

No. 184 Surcharged in Large Antique Letters in Green

210C A22 10c on 1c brown 15.00 15.00
d. "DIFZ" 55.00 55.00

Dionisio de Herrera A24

Pres. Miguel Paz Baraona A25

1924, June Litho. *Perf. 11, 11½*

211 A24 1c olive green .30 .20
212 A24 2c deep rose .35 .20
213 A24 6c red violet .40 .20
214 A24 10c blue .40 .20
215 A24 20c yellow brn .80 .35
216 A24 50c vermilion 1.75 1.10
217 A24 1p emerald 4.00 2.75
Nos. 211-217 (7) 8.00 5.00

In 1924 a facsimile of the signatures of Santiago Herrera and Francisco Caceres, covering four stamps, was handstamped in violet to prevent the use of stamps that had been stolen during a revolution.

Imperfs exist.

For overprints and surcharges see Nos. 280-281, 290-291, C14-C24, C26-C27, C29-C30, C32-C35, C56, C60, C73-C76, CO1-CO5, CO22, CO24, CO28-CO29, CO34-CO35, CO38A, CO39A, CO41, CO43, O75-O81.

1925, Feb. 1 Typo. *Perf. 11½*

218 A25 1c dull blue 2.00 2.00
a. 1c dark blue 2.00 2.00
219 A25 1c car rose 5.00 5.00
a. 1c brown carmine 5.00 5.00
220 A25 1c olive brn 14.00 14.00
a. 1c orange brown 14.00 14.00
b. 1c dark brown 14.00 14.00
c. 1c black brown 14.00 14.00
221 A25 1c buff 12.00 12.00
222 A25 1c red 60.00 60.00
223 A25 1c green 40.00 40.00
Nos. 218-223 (6) 133.00 133.00

Imperf

225 A25 1c dull blue 5.50 5.50
a. 1c dark blue 5.50 5.50
226 A25 1c car rose 8.75 8.75
a. 1c brown carmine 8.75 8.75
227 A25 1c olive brn 8.75 8.75
a. 1c orange brown 8.75 8.75
b. 1c deep brown 8.75 8.75
c. 1c black brown 8.75 8.75
228 A25 1c buff 8.75 8.75
229 A25 1c red 60.00 60.00
229A A25 1c green 27.50 27.50
Nos. 225-229A (6) 119.25 119.25

Inauguration of President Baraona.
Counterfeits and unauthorized reprints exist.

No. 187 Overprinted in Black and Red

1926, June *Perf. 11½*

230 A22 6c bright violet 1.25 1.00

Many varieties of this two-part overprint exist: one or both inverted or double, and various combinations. Value, each $10.

Nos. 177 and 187 Overprinted in Black or Red

1926

231 A20 6c deep pur (Bk) 2.00 2.00
a. Inverted overprint 5.50 5.50
b. Double overprint 5.50 5.50
232 A20 6c deep pur (R) 2.50 2.50
a. Double overprint 5.00 5.00
233 A22 6c lilac (Bk) .60 .60
a. 6c violet .75 .75
b. Inverted overprint 5.00 5.00
c. Double overprint 5.00 5.00
d. Double ovpt., one inverted 5.00 5.00
e. "192" 7.50 7.50
f. Double ovpt., both inverted 7.50 7.50

Same Overprint on No. 230

235 A22 6c violet 20.00 20.00
a. "1926" inverted 20.00 20.00
b. "Habilitado" triple, one invtd. 20.00 20.00

No. 188 Surcharged in Red or Black

236 A22 6c on 10c blue (R) .50 .20
c. Double surcharge 3.50 3.50
d. Without bar
e. Inverted surcharge 2.50 2.50
f. "Vale" omitted
g. "6cts" omitted
h. "cts" omitted
k. Black surcharge *55.00 55.00*

Nos. 175 and 185 Overprinted in Green

237 A19 2c carmine .20 .20
a. Tête bêche pair 4.00 4.00
b. Double overprint 2.00 1.40
c. "HARILITADO" 2.00 1.40
d. "1926" only 2.75 2.75
e. Double overprint, one inverted 2.75 2.75
f. "1926" omitted 3.50 3.50
g. Triple overprint, two inverted 5.25 5.25
h. Double on face, one on back 5.25 5.25
238 A22 2c carmine .20 .20
a. "HARILITADO" .90 .90
b. Double overprint 1.40 1.40
c. Inverted overprint 2.00 2.00

No. 177 Overprinted in Red **1926**

Large Numerals, 12x5mm

1927

239 A20 6c deep purple 25.00 25.00
a. "1926" over "1927" 35.00 35.00
b. Invtd. ovpt. on face of stamp, normal ovpt. on back 30.00

No. 179 Surcharged

1927

240 A19 6c on 20c brown .75 .75
a. Tête bêche pair 2.75 2.75
c. Interted surcharge 2.00 2.00
d. Double surcharge 8.50 8.50

Nos. 8 and 10 in the setting have no period after "cts" and No. 50 has the "t" of "cts" inverted.

Same Surcharge on Nos. 189-191

241 A22 6c on 15c blue 27.50 27.50
a. "c" of "cts" omitted
242 A22 6c on 15c vio .70 .70
a. Double surcharge 1.75 1.75
b. Double surch., one invtd. 2.00 2.00
c. "L" of "Vale" omitted
243 A22 6c on 20c yel brn .60 .60
a. 6c on 20c deep brown
b. "6" omitted 1.75 1.75
c. "Vale" and "cts" omitted 3.50 3.50
Nos. 240-243 (4) 29.55 29.55

On Nos. 242 and 243 stamps Nos. 12, 16 and 43 in the setting have no period after "cts" and No. 34 often lacks the "s." On No. 243 the "c" of "cts" is missing on stamp No. 38. On No. 241 occur the varieties "ct" or "ts" for "cts." and no period.

Southern Highway — A26

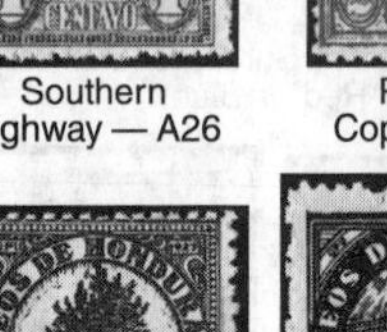

Ruins of Copán — A27

Pine Tree — A28

Presidential Palace — A29

Ponciano Leiva — A30

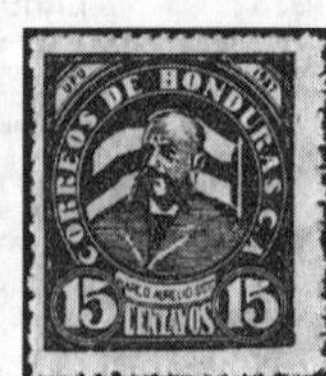

Pres. M.A. Soto — A31

Lempira — A32

Map of Honduras — A33

President Juan Lindo — A34

Statue of Columbus — A35

1927-29 Typo. Wmk. 209

244 A26 1c ultramarine .30 .20
a. 1c blue .30 .20
245 A27 2c carmine .30 .20
246 A28 5c dull violet .30 .20
247 A28 5c bl gray ('29) 12.00 7.00
248 A29 6c blue black .75 .50
a. 6c gray black .75 .50
249 A29 6c dark bl ('29) .40 .20
a. 6c light blue .40 .20
250 A30 10c blue .70 .20
251 A31 15c deep blue 1.00 .50
252 A32 20c dark blue 1.25 .60
253 A33 30c dark brown 1.50 1.00
254 A34 50c light blue 2.50 1.50
255 A35 1p red 5.00 2.50
Nos. 244-255 (12) 26.00 14.60

In 1929 a quantity of imperforate sheets of No. 249 were stolen from the Litografia Nacional. Some of them were perforated by sewing machine and a few copies were passed through the post. To prevent the use of stolen stamps of the 1927-29 issues they were declared invalid and the stock on hand was overprinted "1929 a 1930."

For overprints and surcharges see Nos. 259-278, CO19-CO20B.

Pres. Vicente Mejia Colindres and Vice-Pres. Rafael Diaz Chávez — A36

President Mejia Colindres — A37

1929, Feb. 25

256 A36 1c dk carmine 2.75 2.75
257 A37 2c emerald 2.75 2.75

Installation of Pres. Vicente Mejia Colindres. Printed in sheets of ten.

Nos. 256 and 257 were surreptitiously printed in transposed colors. They were not regularly issued.

Stamps of 1927-29 Overprinted in Various Colors

1929, Oct.

259 A26 1c blue (R) .20 .20
a. 1c ultramarine (R) .50 .20
b. Double overprint 2.50 1.75
c. As "a", double overprint 2.50 1.75
260 A26 1c blue (Bk) 6.50 6.50
a. 1c ultramarine (Bk)
261 A27 2c car (R Br) 3.50 3.50
a. Double overprint
262 A27 2c car (Bl Gr) 1.00 1.00
a. Double overprint

263 A27 2c car (Bk) 1.00 .50
264 A27 2c car (V) .50 .25
a. Double overprint
b. Double ovpt., one inverted
265 A27 2c org red (V) 1.50
266 A28 5c dl vio (R) .40 .30
a. Double overprint (R+V)
267 A28 5c bl gray (R) 1.00 .75
a. Double overprint (R+Bk)
269 A29 6c gray blk (R) 2.50 2.00
a. Double overprint 6.00 6.00
272 A29 6c dk blue (R) .40 .20
a. 6c light blue (R) .40 .20
b. Double overprint 2.00 2.00
c. Double overprint (R+V)
273 A30 10c blue (R) .40 .20
a. Double overprint 2.50 1.75
274 A31 15c dp blue (R) .50 .25
a. Double overprint 3.50 2.50
275 A32 20c dark bl (R) .50 .35
276 A33 30c dark brn (R) .75 .60
a. Double overprint 3.50 2.50
277 A34 50c light bl (R) 2.00 1.00
278 A35 1p red (V) 5.00 2.50
Nos. 259-278 (17) 27.65

Nos. 259-278 exist in numerous shades. There are also various shades of the red and violet overprints. The overprint may be found reading upwards, downwards, inverted, double, triple, tête bêche or combinations.

Status of both 6c stamps with overprint in black is questioned.

A38

1929, Dec. 10

279 A38 1c on 6c lilac rose .70 .70
a. "1992" for "1929"
b. "9192" for "1929"
c. Surcharge reading down 8.00
d. Dbl. surch., one reading down

Varieties include "1992" reading down and pairs with one surcharge reading down, double or with "1992."

No. 214 Surcharged in Red

Perf. 11, 11½

1930, Mar. 26 **Unwmk.**

280 A24 1c on 10c blue .35 .30
a. "1093" for "1930" 1.40
b. "tsc" for "cts" 1.40
281 A24 2c on 10c blue .35 .30
a. "tsc" for "cts" 2.00
b. "Vale 2" omitted

Official Stamps of 1929 Overprinted in Red or Violet

1930, Mar. Wmk. 209 ***Perf. 11½***

282 O1 1c blue (R) .50 .50
a. Double overprint 2.00 2.00
284 O1 2c carmine (V) .90 .90

Stamps of 1915-26 Overprinted in Blue

On No. 174

1930, July 19 **Unwmk.**

285 A19 1c chocolate .30 .25
a. Double overprint 1.00 1.00
b. Inverted overprint 1.40 1.40
c. Dbl. ovpt., one inverted 1.40 1.40

On No. 184

287 A22 1c brown 15.00 15.00
a. Double overprint
c. Inverted overprint

On No. 204

289 A22 50c on 2c carmine 90.00 90.00
b. Inverted surcharge

On Nos. 211 and 212

290 A24 1c olive green .20 .20
a. Double overprint 1.75 1.75
b. Inverted overprint 1.75 1.75
d. On No. O75 12.00
291 A24 2c carmine rose .25 .25
a. Double overprint 1.75 1.75
b. Inverted overprint 1.75 1.75

On No. 237

292 A19 2c car (G & Bl) 100.00 100.00

From Title Page of Government Gazette, First Issue — A39

1930, Aug. 11 Typo. Wmk. 209

295 A39 2c orange .90 .90
296 A39 2c ultramarine .90 .90
297 A39 2c red .90 .90
Nos. 295-297 (3) 2.70 2.70

Publication of the 1st newspaper in Honduras, cent. The stamps were on sale and available for postage on Aug. 11th, 1930, only. Not more than 5 copies of each color could be purchased by an applicant.

Nos. 295-297 exist imperf. and part-perforate. Unauthorized reprints exist.

For surcharges see Nos. CO15-CO18A.

Paz Baraona — A40

Manuel Bonilla — A41

Lake Yojoa — A42

View of Palace at Tegucigalpa A43

City of Amapala A44

Mayan Stele at Copán A45

Christopher Columbus A46

Discovery of America A47

Loarque Bridge A48

Unwmk.

1931, Jan. 2 Engr. *Perf. 12*

298 A40 1c black brown .50 .20
299 A41 2c carmine rose .50 .20
300 A42 5c dull violet .60 .20
301 A43 6c deep green .60 .20
302 A44 10c brown 1.00 .25
303 A45 15c dark blue 1.00 .30
304 A46 20c black 2.50 .40
305 A47 50c olive green 3.50 1.50
306 A48 1p slate black 7.00 2.50
Nos. 298-306 (9) 17.20 5.75

Regular Issue of 1931 Overprinted in Black or Various Colors

1931

307 A40 1c black brown .40 .30
308 A41 2c carmine rose .60 .30
309 A45 15c dark blue .90 .30
310 A46 20c black 2.00 .40

Overprinted

311 A42 5c dull violet .50 .30
312 A43 6c deep green .50 .30
315 A44 10c brown 1.00 .35
316 A47 50c olive green 6.00 4.00
317 A48 1p slate black 7.50 6.00
Nos. 307-317 (9) 19.40 12.25
Nos. 307-317,C51-C55 (14) 44.40 33.25

The overprint is a control mark. It stands for "Tribunal Superior de Cuentas" (Superior Tribunal of Accounts).

Overprint varieties include: inverted; double; double, one or both inverted; on back; pair, one without overprint; differing colors (6c exists with overprint in orange, yellow and red).

President Carías and Vice-President Williams — A49

1933, Apr. 29

318 A49 2c carmine rose .50 .35
319 A49 6c deep green .75 .40
320 A49 10c deep blue 1.00 .50
321 A49 15c red orange 1.25 .75
Nos. 318-321 (4) 3.50 2.00

Inauguration of Pres. Tiburico Carias Andino and Vice-Pres. Abraham Williams, Feb. 1, 1933.

Columbus' Fleet and Flag of the Race — A50

Wmk. 209

1933, Aug. 3 Typo. *Perf. 11½*

322 A50 2c ultramarine 1.00 .65
323 A50 6c yellow 1.00 .65
324 A50 10c lemon 1.40 .85

Perf. 12

325 A50 15c violet 2.00 1.50
326 A50 50c red 4.00 3.50
327 A50 1 l emerald 7.00 7.00
Nos. 322-327 (6) 16.40 14.15

"Day of the Race," an annual holiday throughout Spanish-American countries. Also for the 441st anniv. of the sailing of Columbus to the New World, Aug. 3, 1492.

Masonic Temple, Tegucigalpa — A51

Designs: 2c, President Carias. 5c, Flag. 6c, Tomás Estrada Palma.

Unwmk.

1935, Jan. 12 Engr. *Perf. 12*

328 A51 1c green .40 .20
329 A51 2c carmine .40 .20
330 A51 5c dark blue .40 .25
331 A51 6c black brown .40 .25
a. Vert. pair, imperf. btwn. 20.00 20.00
Nos. 328-331 (4) 1.60 .90
Nos. 328-331,C77-C83 (11) 10.15 5.40

Gen. Carías Bridge — A55

1937, June 4

332 A55 6c car & ol green .75 .35
333 A55 21c grn & violet 1.25 .65
334 A55 46c orange & brn 1.75 1.25
335 A55 55c ultra & black 2.50 2.00
Nos. 332-335 (4) 6.25 4.25

Prolongation of the Presidential term to Jan. 19, 1943.

Seal of Honduras A56

Central District Palace — A57

Designs: 3c, Map of Honduras. 5c, Bridge of Choluteca. 8c, Flag.

1939, Mar. 1 *Perf. 12½*

336 A56 1c orange yellow .20 .20
337 A57 2c red orange .20 .20
338 A57 3c carmine .30 .20
339 A57 5c orange .30 .20
340 A56 8c dark blue .50 .20
Nos. 336-340 (5) 1.50 1.00
Nos. 336-340,C89-C98 (15) 14.00 7.30

Nos. 336-340 exist imperf.

For overprints see #342-343.

Nos. 336 and 337 Overprinted in Green

1944 *Perf. 12½*

342 A56 1c orange yellow .30 .30
 a. Inverted overprint 5.00 5.00
343 A57 2c red orange 1.25 .75
 a. Inverted overprint 5.00 5.00

Catalogue values for unused stamps in this section, from this point to the end of the section, are for Never Hinged items.

International Peace Movement — A58

1984, Feb. 15 **Litho.** *Perf. 12*

344 A58 78c multi .70 .65
345 A58 85c multi .80 .30
346 A58 95c multi .85 .35
347 A58 1.50 l multi 1.40 .55
348 A58 2 l multi 1.75 .70
349 A58 5 l multi 4.50 1.75
 Nos. 344-349 (6) 10.00 4.30

Central American Aeronautics Corp., 25th Anniv. — A59

Designs: 2c, Edward Warner Award issued by the Intl. Civil Aviation Organization, vert. 5c, Corp. emblem, flags of Guatemala, Honduras, El Salvador, Costa Rica and Panama. 60c, Transmission tower, plane. 75c, Corp. emblem, vert. 1 l, 1.50 l, Emblem, flags, diff.

1987, Feb. 26 **Litho.** *Perf. 12*

350 A59 2c multi .20 .20
351 A59 5c multi .20 .20
352 A59 60c multi .50 .25
353 A59 75c multi .65 .30
354 A59 1 l multi .90 .40
 Nos. 350-354 (5) 2.45 1.35

Souvenir Sheet

355 A59 1.50 l multi 1.75

Housing Institute (INVA), 30th Anniv. A60

1987, Oct. 9 **Litho.** *Perf. 13½*

356 A60 5c shown .20 .20
357 A60 95c Map, emblem, text .85 .40

EXFILHON '88 — A61

1988, Sept. 11 **Litho.** *Imperf.*

358 A61 3 l dull red brn & brt ultra 3.25 3.00

1988 Summer Olympics, Seoul — A62

1988, Sept. 30 **Litho.** *Imperf.*

359 A62 4 l multi 4.75 4.75
 Nos. 359,C772-C773 (3) 7.05 5.65

Luis Bogran Technical Institute, Cent. A63

85c, Cogwheel, map, flag of Honduras.

1990, Sept. 28 **Litho.** *Perf. 10½*

360 A63 20c multicolored .20
361 A63 85c multicolored .55

Size: 114x82mm

Imperf

362 A63 2 l like #360 1.25
 Nos. 360-362 (3) 2.00

Nos. 360-361 are airmail.

America Issue A64

UPAE emblem, land and seascapes showing produce and fish.

1990, Oct. 31 **Litho.** *Perf. 13½*

363 A64 20c multi, vert. .20 .20
364 A64 1 l multicolored .60 .30

A65

1992, Feb. 17

365 A65 50c shown .30
366 A65 3 l Cross-country skiing 1.80

1992 Winter Olympics, Albertville.

A66

1992, May 21 **Litho.** *Perf. 13½*

Mother's Day (Paintings): 20c, Saleswoman, by Manuel Rodriguez. 50c, The Grandmother and Baby, by Rodriguez. 5 l, Saleswomen, by Maury Flores.

367 A66 20c shown .20
368 A66 50c multicolored .30
369 A66 5 l multicolored 3.00
 Nos. 367-369 (3) 3.50

Butterflies A67

Designs: 25c, Melitaeinae chlosyne janais. 85c, Heliconiinae agrilus vanillae. 3 l, Morphinae morpho granadensis. 5 l, Heliconiinae dryadula phalusa.

1992, June 22

370 A67 25c multicolored .20
371 A67 85c multicolored .50
372 A67 3 l multicolored 1.75

Size: 108x76mm

Imperf

373 A67 5 l multicolored 3.25
 Nos. 370-373 (4) 5.70

1992 Summer Olympics, Barcelona — A68

1992, Mar. 16 **Litho.** *Perf. 13½*

374 A68 20c Running .20
375 A68 50c Tennis .30
376 A68 85c Soccer .50
 Nos. 374-376 (3) 1.00

Japanese Overseas Cooperation Volunteers in Honduras, 20th Anniv. — A69

Designs: 1.40 l, Volunteers working on Japanese letter, vert. 4.30 l, Folding screen showing Mayan Gods. 5.40 l, Men, women of Honduras in traditional costumes, volunteer.

1995, Sept. 20 **Litho.** *Perf. 13½*

377 A69 1.40 l multicolored .40 .40
378 A69 4.30 l multicolored 1.25 1.25
379 A69 5.40 l multicolored 1.50 1.50
 Nos. 377-379 (3) 3.15

Nos. 378-379 are airmail.

Birds — A70

Designs: 1.40 l, Buteo jamaicensis. 1.50 l, Ramphastos sulfuratus. 2 l, Dendrocygna autumnalis. 2.15 l, Micrastur semitorguatus. 3 l, Polyporus plancus. 5.40 l, 10 l, Sacroamphus papa.

1997, Apr. 29 **Litho.** *Perf. 13½*

380 A70 1.40 l multicolored .20
381 A70 1.50 l multicolored .25
382 A70 2 l multicolored .30
383 A70 2.15 l multicolored .35
 a. Pair, #382, 383 .65
384 A70 3 l multicolored .45
 a. Pair, #380, 384 .65
385 A70 5.40 l multicolored .85
 a. Pair, #381, 385 1.10
 Nos. 380-385 (6) 2.40

Size: 50x73mm

Imperf

386 A70 20 l multicolored 3.00

No. 386 is airmail.

No. RA8 Surcharged in Gold

1999, June 25 **Litho.** *Perf. 13½*

387 PT6 2.60 l on 1c .65 .35
388 PT6 7.85 l on 1c 1.90 .95
389 PT6 10.65 l on 1c 2.60 1.25
390 PT6 11.55 l on 1c 2.75 1.40
391 PT6 12.45 l on 1c 3.00 1.50
392 PT6 13.85 l on 1c 3.50 1.75
 Nos. 387-392 (6) 14.40 7.20

SEMI-POSTAL STAMPS

Catalogue values for unused stamps in this section are for Never Hinged items.

Indiginous Musical Instruments — SP1

No. B1: a, Garífuna drum. b, Flutes. c, Toltec drum. d, Hornpipe. e, Maya drum. f, Conch shell.

2000, Apr. 7 **Litho.** *Perf. 13¼*

B1 Sheet of 6, "Pro filatelia" in black 12.00 12.00
 a.-f. SP1 10 l + 1 l Any single 2.00 2.00
 g. As #B1, "Pro filatelia" in gold 12.00 12.00

See No. C1073.

AIR POST STAMPS

Regular Issue of 1915-16 Overprinted in Black, Blue or Red

1925 **Unwmk.** *Perf. 11½*

C1 A20 5c lt blue (Bk) 87.50 87.50
C2 A20 5c lt blue (Bl) 300.00 300.00
 a. Inverted overprint *400.00*
 b. Vertical overprint *600.00*
 c. Double overprint *800.00*
C3 A20 5c lt blue (R) *7,250.*

Value for No. C3 is for copy without gum.

C4 A19 10c dk blue (R) 175.00
 a. Inverted overprint 325.00
 b. Overprint tête bêche, pair *800.00*
C5 A19 10c dk blue (Bk) *1,100.*
C6 A19 20c red brn (Bk) 175.00 175.00
 a. Inverted overprint 250.00
 b. Tête bêche pair 400.00
 c. Overprint tête bêche, pair *725.00*
 d. "AFRO" *1,400.*
 e. Double overprint *600.00*
C7 A19 20c red brn (Bl) 175.00 175.00
 a. Inverted overprint *700.00*
 b. Tête bêche pair *1,000*
 c. Vertical overprint 900.00
C8 A20 50c red (Bk) 450.00 300.00
 a. Inverted overprint *550.00*
 b. Overprint tête bêche, pair *900.00*
C9 A20 1p yel grn (Bk) 600.00 600.00

Surcharged in Black or Blue

AERO
CORREO
25

C10 A19 25c on 1c choc 125.00 125.00
 a. Inverted surcharge 700.00
C11 A20 25c on 5c lt bl (Bl) 225.00 225.00
 a. Inverted surcharge 700.00
 b. Double inverted surcharge *675.00*
C12 A19 25c on 10c dk bl *75,000.*
C13 A19 25c on 20c brn (Bl) 200.00 200.00
 a. Inverted surcharge 325.00
 b. Tête bêche pair 450.00

Counterfeits of Nos. C1-C13 are plentiful.

Monoplane and Lisandro Garay AP1

1929, June 5 Engr. *Perf. 12*

C13C AP1 50c carmine 2.00 1.75

No. 216 Surcharged in Blue

1929 *Perf. 11, 11½*

C14 A24 25c on 50c ver 5.00 3.50

In the surcharges on Nos. C14 to C40 there are various wrong font and defective letters and numerals, also periods omitted.

Nos. 215-217 Surcharged in Green, Black or Red

1929, Oct.

C15 A24 5c on 20c yel brn (G) 1.40 1.40
- *a.* Double surcharge (R+G) 45.00

C16 A24 10c on 50c ver (Bk) 2.25 1.90
C17 A24 15c on 1p emer (R) 3.50 3.50
Nos. C15-C17 (3) 7.15 6.80

a b

Nos. 214 and 216 SurchargedVertically in Red or Black

1929, Dec. 10

C18 A24(a) 5c on 10c bl (R) .50 .50
C19 A24(b) 20c on 50c ver .95 .95
- *a.* "1299" for "1929" 190.00
- *b.* "cts. cts." for "cts. oro." 190.00
- *c.* "r" of "Aereo" omitted 2.00
- *d.* Horiz. pair, imperf. btwn. 20.00

Nos. 214, 215 and 180 Surcharged in Various Colors

1930, Feb.

C20 A24 5c on 10c (R) .50 .50
- *a.* "1930" reading down 3.50
- *b.* "1903" for "1930" 3.50
- *c.* Surcharge reading down 10.00
- *d.* Double surcharge 14.00
- *e.* Dbl. surch., one downward 14.00

C21 A24 5c on 10c (Y) *450.00 450.00*
C22 A24 5c on 20c (Bl) 125.00 125.00
C23 A24 10c on 20c (Bk) .70 .70
- *a.* "0" for "10" 3.50
- *b.* Double surcharge 8.75
- *c.* Dbl. surch., one downward 12.00
- *d.* Horiz. pair, imperf. btwn. 70.00

C24 A24 10c on 20c (V) *750.00 750.00*
- *a.* "0" for "10" *1,600.*

C25 A20 25c on 50c (Bk) .95 .95
- *a.* "Internaoicnal" 3.50
- *b.* "o" for "oro" 3.50
- *c.* Inverted surcharge 17.50
- *d.* As "a," invtd. surch. *175.00*
- *e.* As "b," invtd. surch. *175.00*

Surcharge on Nos. C20-C24 are vertical.

Nos. 214, 215 and 180 Surcharged

1930, Apr. 1

C26 A24 5c on 10c blue .50 .50
- *a.* Double surcharge 9.50
- *b.* "Servicioa" 3.50

C27 A24 15c on 20c yel brn .55 .55
- *a.* Double surcharge 7.00

C28 A20 20c on 50c red, surch. reading down .95 .95
- *a.* Surcharge reading up 7.00

Nos. C26-C28 (3) 2.00 2.00

Nos. C22 and C23 Surcharged Vertically in Red

1930

C29 A24 10c on 5c on 20c (Bl+R) .90 .90
- *a.* "1930" reading down 9.00 9.00
- *b.* "1903" for "1930" 9.00 9.00
- *c.* Red surcharge, reading down 14.00

C30 A24 10c on 10c on 20c (Bk+R) 87.50 87.50
- *a.* "0" for "10" 190.00

No. 181 Surcharged as No. C25 and Re-surcharged

C31 A20 50c on 25c on 1p grn 4.25 4.25
- *a.* "Internaoicnal" 7.00
- *b.* "o" for "oro" 7.00
- *c.* 25c surcharge inverted 17.50 17.50
- *d.* 50c surcharge inverted 17.50 17.50
- *e.* As "a" and "c"
- *f.* As "a" and "d"
- *g.* As "b" and "c"
- *h.* As "b" and "d"

Nos. C29-C31 (3) 92.65 92.65

No. 215 Surcharged in Dark Blue

1930, May 22

C32 A24 5c on 20c yel brn 1.00 1.00
- *a.* Double surcharge 5.25 5.25
- *b.* Horiz. pair, imperf. btwn. 60.00 60.00
- *c.* Vertical pair, imperf. between 20.00 20.00

Nos. O78-O80 Surcharged like Nos. C20 to C25 in Various Colors

1930

C33 A24 5c on 10c (R) 450.00 350.00
- *a.* "1930" reading down *875.00*
- *b.* "1903" for "1930" *875.00*

C34 A24 5c on 20c (Bl) 400.00 400.00
C35 A24 25c on 50c (Bk) 225.00 225.00
- *a.* 55c on 50c vermilion 325.00 325.00

No. C35 exists with inverted surcharge.

No. O64 Surcharged like No. C28

C36 A20 20c on 50c red (dbl. surch., reading up) *350.00 350.00*
- *a.* Dbl. surch., reading down *350.00 350.00*

No. O87 Overprinted

1930, Feb. 21 Wmk. 209 *Perf. 11½*

C37 O1 50c yel, grn & blue 1.25 1.25
- *a.* "Internacional" 5.25
- *b.* "Iuternacional" 5.25
- *c.* Double overprint 5.25

Nos. O86-O88 Overprinted in Various Colors

1930, May 23

C38 O1 20c dark blue (R) 1.00 .85
- *a.* Double overprint 8.75
- *b.* Triple overprint 12.00

C39 O1 50c org, grn & bl (Bk) 1.00 .90
C40 O1 1p buff (Bl) 1.25 1.25
- *a.* Double overprint 10.50

Nos. C38-C40 (3) 3.25 3.00

National Palace AP3

Unwmk.

1930, Oct. 1 Engr. *Perf. 12*

C41 AP3 5c yel orange .50 .30
C42 AP3 10c carmine .75 .60
C43 AP3 15c green 1.00 .75
C44 AP3 20c dull violet 1.25 .60
C45 AP3 1p light brown 4.00 4.00
Nos. C41-C45 (5) 7.50 6.25

Same Overprinted in Various Colors

1931 *Perf. 12*

C51 AP3 5c yel orange (R) *2.00 1.50*
C52 AP3 10c carmine (Bk) *3.00 2.50*
C53 AP3 15c green (Br) *5.00 4.00*
C54 AP3 20c dull vio (O) *5.00 4.25*
C55 AP3 1p lt brown (G) *10.00 8.75*
Nos. C51-C55 (5) *25.00 21.00*

See note after No. 317.

Stamps of Various Issues Surcharged in Blue or Black (#C59)

Servicio aéreo
interior.
Vale 15 cts.
Octubre 1931.

1931, Oct. *Perf. 11½*

On No. 215

C56 A24 15c on 20c yel brn 3.50 2.75
- *a.* Horiz. pair, imperf. btwn. 42.50
- *b.* Green surcharge 20.00 20.00

On No. O64

C57 A20 15c on 50c red 4.25 3.50
- *a.* Inverted surcharge 10.50 10.50

On No. O72

C58 A22 15c on 20c brn 4.25 4.25
- *a.* Vert. pair, imperf. between 12.00

On Nos. C57 and C58 the word "OFICIAL" is canceled by two bars.

On No. O88

Wmk. 209

C59 O1 15c on 1p buff 4.25 4.25
- *a.* Vert. pair, imperf. horiz. 25.00
- *b.* "Sevricio" 14.00 14.00

The varieties "Vaie" for "Vale," "aereo" with circumflex accent on the first "e" and "Interior" with initial capital "I" are found on #C56, C58-C59. #C57 is known with initial capital in "Interior."

A similar surcharge, in slightly larger letters and with many minor varieties, exists on Nos. 215, O63, O64 and O73. The authenticity of this surcharge is questioned.

Nos. 215, O73, O87-O88 Surcharged in Green, Red or Black

S.—Aéreo
VI. 15 cts.
XI 1931.

1931, Nov. Unwmk.

C60 A24 15c on 20c (G) 3.50 2.75
- *a.* Inverted surcharge 6.25
- *b.* "XI" omitted 6.25
- *c.* "X" for "XI" 6.25
- *d.* "PI" for "XI" 6.25

C61 A22 15c on 50c (R) 3.50 2.75
- *a.* "XI" omitted 6.75
- *b.* "PI" for "XI" 6.75
- *c.* Double surcharge 20.00 20.00

On No. C61 the word "OFICIAL" is not barred out.

Wmk. 209

C62 O1 15c on 50c (Bk) 2.75 2.50
- *a.* "1391" for "1931" 10.50 10.50
- *b.* Double surcharge 8.75 8.75

C63 O1 15c on 1p (Bk) 2.50 2.25
- *a.* "1391" for "1931" 12.50
- *b.* Surcharged on both sides 7.00

Nos. O76-O78 Surcharged in Black or Red

Aéreo
interior
VALE
15 Cts.
1932

1932 Unwmk. *Perf. 11, 11½*

C73 A24 15c on 2c .75 .75
- *a.* Double surcharge 5.50
- *b.* Inverted surcharge 4.25
- *c.* "Ae" of "Aero" omitted 1.00
- *d.* On No. 212 (no "Official")

C74 A24 15c on 6c .75 .75
- *a.* Double surcharge 3.50
- *b.* Horiz. pair, imperf. btwn. 17.50
- *c.* "Aer" omitted
- *d.* "A" omitted 1.00
- *e.* Inverted surcharge 3.50

C75 A24 15c on 10c (R) .75 .75
- *a.* Double surcharge 5.50
- *b.* Inverted surcharge 3.50
- *c.* "r" of "Aereo" omitted 1.00

Same Surcharge on No. 214 in Red

C76 A24 15c on 10c dp bl *150.00 100.00*

There are various broken and missing letters in the setting.

A similar surcharge with slightly larger letters exists.

Post Office and National Palace AP4

View of Tegucigalpa — AP5

Designs: 15c, Map of Honduras. 20c, Mayol Bridge. 40c, View of Tegucigalpa. 50c, Owl. 1 l, Coat of Arms.

1935, Jan. 10 *Perf. 12*

C77 AP4 8c blue .20 .20
C78 AP5 10c gray .25 .20
C79 AP5 15c olive gray .40 .20
C80 AP5 20c dull green .50 .20
C81 AP5 40c brown .70 .20
C82 AP4 50c yellow 4.00 1.25
C83 AP4 1 l green 2.50 2.25
Nos. C77-C83 (7) 8.55 4.50

Flags of US and Honduras — AP11

Engr. & Litho.

1937, Sept. 17 Unwmk.

C84 AP11 46c multicolored 1.00 1.00

US Constitution, 150th anniv..

Comayagua Cathedral AP12

Founding of Comayagua AP13

Alonzo Cáceres and Pres. Carías AP14

Lintel of Royal Palace AP15

1937, Dec. 7 **Engr.**

No.	Type	Description	Unused	Used
C85	AP12	2c copper red	.20	.20
C86	AP13	8c dark blue	.30	.20
C87	AP14	15c slate black	.50	.50
C88	AP15	50c dark brown	3.00	2.00
		Nos. C85-C88 (4)	4.00	2.90

City of Comayagua founding, 400th anniv.
For surcharges see Nos. C144-C146.

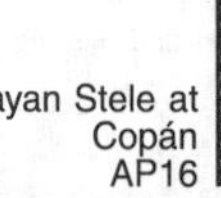

Mayan Stele at Copán AP16

Mayan Temple, Copán AP17

Designs: 15c, President Carias. 30c, José C. de Valle. 40c, Presidential House. 46c, Lempira. 55c, Church of Our Lady of Suyapa. 66c, J. T. Reyes. 1 l, Hospital at Choluteca. 2 l, Ramón Rosa.

1939, Mar. 1 ***Perf. 12½***

No.	Type	Description	Unused	Used
C89	AP16	10c orange brn	.20	.20
C90	AP16	15c grnsh blue	.25	.20
C91	AP17	21c gray	.45	.20
C92	AP16	30c dk blue grn	.45	.20
C93	AP17	40c dull violet	.90	.20
C94	AP16	46c dk gray brn	.90	.45
C95	AP16	55c green	1.10	.60
a.		Imperf., pair	22.50	
C96	AP16	66c black	1.50	1.10
C97	AP16	1 l olive grn	2.75	.90
C98	AP16	2 l henna red	4.00	2.25
		Nos. C89-C98 (10)	12.50	6.30

For surcharges see #C118-C119, C147-C152.

Souvenir Sheets

AP26

14c, Francisco Morazan. 16c, George Washington. 30c, J. C. de Valle. 40c, Simon Bolivar.

1940, Apr. 13 **Engr.** ***Perf. 12***

Centers of Stamps Lithographed

No.	Type	Description	Unused	Used
C99	AP26	Sheet of 4	2.25	2.25
a.		14c black, yellow, ultra & rose	.35	.30
b.		16c black, yellow, ultra & rose	.40	.35
c.		30c black, yellow, ultra & rose	.65	.55
d.		40c black, yellow, ultra & rose	.75	.70

Imperf

No.	Type	Description	Unused	Used
C100	AP26	Sheet of 4	2.25	2.25
a.		14c black, yellow, ultra & rose	.35	.30
b.		16c black, yellow, ultra & rose	.40	.35
c.		30c black, yellow, ultra & rose	.65	.55
d.		40c black, yellow, ultra & rose	.75	.70

Pan American Union, 50th anniv.
For overprints see Nos. C153-C154, C187.

Air Post Official Stamps of 1939 Overprinted in Red

1940, Oct. 12 ***Perf. 12½***

No.	Type	Description	Unused	Used
C101	OA2	2c dp bl & green	.20	.20
C102	OA2	5c dp blue & org	.20	.20
C103	OA2	8c deep bl & brn	.20	.20
C104	OA2	15c dp blue & car	.40	.40
C105	OA2	46c dp bl & ol grn	.70	.70
C106	OA2	50c dp bl & vio	.80	.80
C107	OA2	1 l dp bl & red brn	3.50	3.50
C108	OA2	2 l dp bl & red org	7.00	7.50
		Nos. C101-C108 (8)	13.00	13.50

Erection and dedication of the Columbus Memorial Lighthouse.

Air Post Official Stamps of 1939 Overprinted in Black

1941, Aug. 2

No.	Type	Description	Unused	Used
C109	OA2	5c deep bl & org	3.00	.25
C110	OA2	8c dp blue & brn	5.00	.25
a.		Overprint inverted		*225.00*

Nos. CO44, CO47-CO51 Surcharged in Black

1941, Oct. 28

No.	Type	Description	Unused	Used
C111	OA2	3c on 2c	.40	.20
C112	OA2	8c on 2c	.50	.50
C113	OA2	8c on 15c	.50	.20
C114	OA2	8c on 46c	.60	.60
C115	OA2	8c on 50c	.75	.50
C116	OA2	8c on 1 l	1.25	.70
C117	OA2	8c on 2 l	2.00	1.50
		Nos. C111-C117 (7)	6.00	4.20

Once in each sheet a large "h" occurs in "ocho."

Nos. C90, C94 Surcharged in Red

1942, July 14

No.	Type	Description	Unused	Used
C118	AP16	8c on 15c	.70	.25
a.		"Cerreo"	2.00	2.00
b.		Double surcharge	25.00	25.00
c.		As "a," double surcharge	*175.00*	
C119	AP16	16c on 46c	.70	.25
a.		"Cerreo"	2.00	2.00

Plaque AP27

Morazán's Tomb, San Salvador — AP28

Designs: 5c, Battle of La Trinidad. 8c, Morazán's birthplace. 16c, Statue of Morazán. 21c, Church where Morazán was baptized. 1 l, Arms of Central American Federation. 2 l, Gen. Francisco Morazán.

1942, Sept. 15 ***Perf. 12***

No.	Type	Description	Unused	Used
C120	AP27	2c red orange	.20	.20
C121	AP27	5c turq green	.20	.20
C122	AP27	8c sepia	.20	.20
C123	AP28	14c black	.30	.30
C124	AP27	16c olive gray	.20	.20
C125	AP27	21c light blue	.90	.65
C126	AP27	1 l brt ultra	2.75	2.25
C127	AP28	2 l dl ol brn	7.25	7.25
		Nos. C120-C127 (8)	12.00	11.25

Gen. Francisco Morazan (1799-1842).
For surcharges see Nos. C349-C350.

Coat of Arms AP35

Cattle AP36

Bananas — AP37

Pine Tree — AP38

Tobacco Plant AP39

Orchid AP40

Coco Palm — AP41

Map of Honduras AP42

Designs: 2c, Flag. 8c, Rosario. 16c, Sugar cane. 30c, Oranges. 40c, Wheat. 1 l, Corn. 2 l, Map of Americas.

1943, Sept. 14 ***Perf. 12½***

No.	Type	Description	Unused	Used
C128	AP35	1c light grn	.20	.20
C129	AP35	2c blue	.20	.20
C130	AP36	5c green	.30	.20
C131	AP37	6c dark bl grn	.25	.20
C132	AP36	8c lilac	.30	.20
C133	AP38	10c lilac brn	.30	.20
C134	AP39	15c dp claret	.35	.20
C135	AP38	16c dark red	.35	.20
C136	AP40	21c deep blue	.75	.20
C137	AP39	30c org brown	.60	.20
C138	AP40	40c red orange	.60	.20
C139	AP41	55c black	1.00	.50
C140	AP41	1 l dark olive	1.50	1.25
C141	AP37	2 l brown red	5.00	3.75
C142	AP42	5 l orange	12.50	12.50
a.		Vert. pair, imperf. btwn.	150.00	
		Nos. C128-C142 (15)	24.20	20.20

Pan-American School of Agriculture AP50

1944, Oct. 12 ***Perf. 12***

No.	Type	Description	Unused	Used
C143	AP50	21c dk blue grn	.30	.20

Inauguration of the Pan-American School of Agriculture, Tegucigalpa.

Catalogue values for unused stamps in this section, from this point to the end of the section, are for Never Hinged items.

Air Post Stamps of 1937-39 Surcharged in Red or Green

1945, Mar. 13 ***Perf. 11, 12½***

No.	Type	Description	Unused	Used
C144	AP15	1c on 50c dk brn	.20	.20
C145	AP12	2c on 2c cop red	.20	.20
C146	AP14	8c on 15c sl blk	.25	.20
C147	AP16	10c on 10c org brown (G)	.40	.25
C148	AP16	15c on 15c grnsh blue (G)	.25	.20
C149	AP17	30c on 21c gray (G)	4.00	2.75
C150	AP17	40c on 40c dull violet (G)	2.00	1.10
C151	AP16	1 l on 46c dk gray brown (G)	2.00	1.10
C152	AP16	2 l on 66c blk (G)	4.00	2.75
		Nos. C144-C152 (9)	13.30	8.75

Souvenir Sheets

Nos. C99 and C100 Overprinted in Red "VICTORIA DE LAS NACIONES UNIDAS, ALEMANIA SE RINDE INCONDICIONALMENTE 8 DE MAYO DE 1945. ACDO. No. 1231 QUE AUTORIZA LA CONTRAMARCA"

1945, Oct. 1 ***Perf. 12***

No.	Type	Description	Unused	Used
C153	AP26	Sheet of 4	2.50	1.90

Imperf

No.	Type	Description	Unused	Used
C154	AP26	Sheet of 4	4.50	3.00

Allied Nations' victory and Germany's unconditional surrender, May 8, 1945.

Seal of Honduras AP51

Arms of Gracias and Trujillo AP52

Franklin D. Roosevelt ("F.D.R." under Column)
AP53

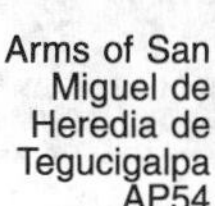

Arms of San Miguel de Heredia de Tegucigalpa
AP54

Designs (Coats of Arms): 5c, Comayagua and San Jorge de Olancho. 15c, Province of Honduras and San Juan de Puerto Caballas. 21c, Comayagua and Tencoa. 1 l, Jerez de la Frontera de Choluteca and San Pedro de Zula.

Perf. 12½

1946, Oct. 15 Unwmk. Engr.

C155 AP51	1c red	.20	.20
a.	Vert. pair, imperf. between	17.50	
b.	Imperf., pair	70.00	
C156 AP52	2c red orange	.20	.20
a.	Imperf., pair	70.00	
C157 AP52	5c violet	.30	.20
C158 AP53	8c brown	1.00	.50
a.	Horiz. pair, imperf. btwn.	70.00	
C159 AP52	15c sepia	.50	.20
C160 AP52	21c deep blue	.50	.30
a.	Horiz. pair, imperf. btwn.	15.00	
b.	Imperf., pair	70.00	
C161 AP52	1 l green	2.10	1.00
C162 AP54	2 l dark grn	3.00	1.75
	Nos. C155-C162 (8)	7.80	4.35

No. C158 commemorates the death of Franklin D. Roosevelt and the Allied victory over Japan in World War II.

Type AP53 Redrawn ("Franklin D. Roosevelt" under Column)
AP59

1947, Oct. *Perf. 12½*

C163 AP59	8c brown	.45	.30
a.	Vert. pair, imperf. between	87.50	
b.	Horiz. pair, imperf. btwn.		
c.	Perf. 12x6	*175.00*	

Map, Ancient Monuments and Conference Badge
AP60

1947, Oct. 20 *Perf. 11x12½*

Various Frames

C164 AP60	16c green	.40	.20
C165 AP60	22c orange yel	.30	.20
C166 AP60	40c orange	.65	.35
C167 AP60	1 l deep blue	1.10	.90
C168 AP60	2 l lilac	4.00	3.50
C169 AP60	5 l brown	10.50	8.00
	Nos. C164-C169 (6)	16.95	13.15

1st Intl. Archeological Conf. of the Caribbean.

For overprints and surcharges see Nos. C181-C186, C351, C353-C354, C379, C544.

Flag and Arms of Honduras
AP61

Juan Manuel Galvez
AP62

J. M. Galvez, Gen. Tiburcio Carias A. and Julio Lozano
AP63

National Stadium
AP64

Designs: 5c, 15c, Julio Lozano. 9c, Juan Manuel Galvez. 40c, Custom House. 1 l, Recinto Hall. 2 l, Gen. Tiburcio Carias A. 5 l, Galvez and Lozano.

Various frames inscribed: "Conmemorativa de la Sucesion Presidencial para el Periodo de 1949-1955."

1949, Sept. 17 Engr. *Perf. 12*

C170 AP61	1c deep blue	.20	.20
C171 AP62	2c rose car	.20	.20
C172 AP62	5c deep blue	.20	.20
C173 AP62	9c sepia	.20	.20
C174 AP62	15c red brown	.25	.20
C175 AP63	21c gray black	.45	.20
C176 AP64	30c olive gray	.60	.20
C177 AP64	40c slate gray	.90	.20
C178 AP61	1 l red brown	1.40	.40
C179 AP62	2 l violet	3.25	1.50
C180 AP64	5 l rose car	9.25	5.50
	Nos. C170-C180 (11)	16.90	9.00

Presidential succession for the 1949-1955 term.

For overprints and surcharges see Nos. C188-C197, C206-C208, C346, C355, C419-C420, C478, C545.

Nos. C164-C169 Overprinted in Carmine

1951, Feb. 26 *Perf. 11x12½*

C181 AP60	16c green	.50	.40
a.	Inverted overprint	45.00	45.00
C182 AP60	22c orange yel	.65	.55
a.	Inverted overprint	45.00	
C183 AP60	40c orange	.65	.55
C184 AP60	1 l deep blue	2.00	1.75
C185 AP60	2 l lilac	3.25	2.75
a.	Inverted overprint	60.00	
C186 AP60	5 l brown	27.50	24.00
	Nos. C181-C186 (6)	34.55	30.00

Souvenir Sheets

Same Overprint in Carmine on Nos. C99 and C100

Perf. 12

C187 AP26	Sheet of 4	3.00	2.25
a.	Imperf.	*250.00*	*250.00*

UPU, 75th anniv. (in 1949).

Nos. C170 to C179 Overprinted in Carmine

1951, Feb. 27 *Perf. 12*

C188 AP61	1c deep blue	.20	.20
C189 AP62	2c rose car	.20	.20
C190 AP62	5c deep blue	.20	.20
C191 AP62	9c sepia	.20	.20
C192 AP62	15c red brown	.20	.20
C193 AP63	21c gray black	.25	.20
C194 AP64	30c olive gray	.60	.30
C195 AP64	40c slate gray	.75	.50
C196 AP61	1 l red brown	1.75	1.25
C197 AP62	2 l violet	6.00	4.50
	Nos. C188-C197 (10)	10.35	7.75

Founding of Central Bank, July 1, 1950.

Discovery of America
AP65

Queen Isabella I — AP66

2c, 1 l, Columbus at court. 8c, Surrender of Granada. 30c, Queen Isabella offering her jewels.

Perf. 13½x14, 14x13½

1952, Oct. 11 Engr. Unwmk.

C198 AP65	1c red org & blk	.20	.20
C199 AP65	2c bl & red brn	.20	.20
C200 AP65	8c dk grn & dk brown	.20	.20
C201 AP66	16c dk bl & blk	.40	.25
C202 AP65	30c pur & dk grn	.70	.70
C203 AP65	1 l dp car & blk	1.75	1.40
C204 AP65	2 l brn & vio	3.75	3.50
C205 AP66	5 l rose lil & ol	9.25	8.75
	Nos. C198-C205 (8)	16.45	15.20

500th birth anniv. of Isabella I of Spain.

For overprints and surcharges see Nos. C209-C221, C377-C378, C404-C406, C489, CO52-CO59.

No. C175 Surcharged in Carmine

1953, May 13 *Perf. 12*

C206 AP63	5c on 21c gray blk	.20	.20
C207 AP63	8c on 21c gray blk	.30	.20
C208 AP63	16c on 21c gray blk	.50	.20
	Nos. C206-C208 (3)	1.00	.60

Nos. CO52-CO54 Surcharged "HABILITADO 1953" and New Value in Red

1953, Dec. 8 *Perf. 13½x14, 14x13½*

C209 AP65	10c on 1c	.20	.20
a.	Inverted surcharge	50.00	50.00
C210 AP65	12c on 1c	.20	.20
C211 AP65	15c on 2c	.20	.20
C212 AP65	20c on 2c	.30	.20
C213 AP65	24c on 2c	.30	.20
a.	Inverted surcharge	50.00	50.00
C214 AP65	25c on 2c	.30	.25
C215 AP65	30c on 8c	.35	.25
C216 AP65	35c on 8c	.45	.45
C217 AP65	50c on 8c	.60	.45
C218 AP65	60c on 8c	.80	.60

Same Overprint on Nos. CO57-CO59

C219 AP65	1 l dk grn & dk brown	3.00	2.00
C220 AP65	2 l bl & red brn	6.00	5.00
C221 AP66	5 l red org & blk	12.00	12.00
a.	Date inverted	150.00	
	Nos. C209-C221 (13)	24.70	22.00

Flags of UN and Honduras
AP67

2c, UN emblem. 3c, UN building. 5c, Shield. 15c, Juan Manuel Galvez. 30c, UNICEF. 1 l, UNRRA. 2 l, UNESCO. 5 l, FAO.

Engraved; Center of 1c Litho.

1953, Dec. 18 *Perf. 12½*

Frames in Black

C222 AP67	1c ultra & vio bl	.20	.20
C223 AP67	2c blue	.20	.20
C224 AP67	3c rose lilac	.20	.20
C225 AP67	5c green	.20	.20
C226 AP67	15c red brown	.30	.25
C227 AP67	30c brown	.80	.45
C228 AP67	1 l dp carmine	6.25	4.50
C229 AP67	2 l orange	8.00	5.00
C230 AP67	5 l blue green	19.00	15.00
	Nos. C222-C230 (9)	35.15	26.00

Issued to honor the United Nations.

For overprints and surcharges see Nos. C231-C249, C331-C335, C472, C490, CO60-CO68.

Nos. CO60-CO66 Overprinted in Red

1955, Feb. 23 Unwmk. *Perf. 12½*

Frames in Black

C231 AP67	1c ultra & vio bl	.20	.20
C232 AP67	2c dp blue grn	.20	.20
C233 AP67	3c orange	.20	.20
C234 AP67	5c dp carmine	.25	.25
C235 AP67	15c dk brown	.35	.35
C236 AP67	30c purple	1.00	.90
C237 AP67	1 l olive gray	20.00	15.00

Overprint exists inverted on 1c, 3c.

Nos. C231 to C233 Surcharged with New Value in Black

C238 AP67	8c on 1c	.20	.20
C239 AP67	10c on 2c	.20	.20
C240 AP67	12c on 3c	.20	.20
	Nos. C231-C240 (10)	22.80	17.70

50th anniv. of the founding of Rotary International (Nos. C231-C240).

Nos. CO60-CO63, C226-C230 Overprinted

1956, July 14 Unwmk. *Perf. 12½*

Frames in Black

C241 AP67	1c ultra & vio bl	.20	.20
C242 AP67	2c dp bl grn	.20	.20
C243 AP67	3c orange	.20	.20
C244 AP67	5c dp car	.25	.25
C245 AP67	15c red brn	.30	.30
C246 AP67	30c brown	.50	.40
C247 AP67	1 l dp car	3.75	2.75
C248 AP67	2 l orange	5.75	4.00
C249 AP67	5 l bl grn	14.00	11.50
	Nos. C241-C249 (9)	25.15	19.80

10th anniv. of UN (in 1955). The red "OFICIAL" overprint was not obliterated.

The "ONU" overprint exists inverted on 1c, 3c, 5c and 1-lempira.

Basilica of Suyapa
AP68

Pres. Julio Lozano Diaz — AP69

3c, Southern Highway. 4c, Genoveva Guardiola de Estrada Palma. 5c, Maria Josefa Lastiri de Morazan. 8c, Landscape and cornucopia (5-Year Plan). 10c, National Stadium. 12c, US School. 15c, Central Bank. 20c, Legislative Palace. 25c, Development Bank (projected). 30c, Toncontin Airport. 40c, Juan Ramon Molina Bridge. 50c, Peace Monument. 60c, Treasury Palace. 1 l, Blood bank. 2 l, Communications Building. 5 l, Presidential Palace.

Engraved; #C255 Litho.

1956, Oct. 3 ***Perf. 13x12½, 12½x13***

C250 AP68 1c black & vio bl .20 .20
C251 AP69 2c black & dk bl .20 .20
C252 AP68 3c black & brown .20 .20
C253 AP69 4c black & lilac .20 .20
C254 AP69 5c black & dk red .20 .20
C255 AP68 8c brown & multi .20 .20
C256 AP68 10c black & emer .20 .20
C257 AP68 12c black & green .20 .20
C258 AP68 15c dk red & blk .30 .20
C259 AP68 20c black & ultra .30 .20
C260 AP69 24c black & lil .35 .20
C261 AP68 25c black & green .40 .25
C262 AP68 30c black & car rose .40 .25
C263 AP68 40c black & red brn .50 .25
C264 AP69 50c black & bl grn .60 .35
C265 AP68 60c black & orange .80 .45
C266 AP68 1 l black & rose vio 2.00 1.00
C267 AP69 2 l black & mag 3.75 2.25
C268 AP69 5 l black & brn car 9.00 5.00
Nos. C250-C268 (19) 20.00 12.00

Issued to publicize the Five-Year Plan.

For overprints and surcharges see Nos. C414-C418, C491-C493, C537-C538, C542, C550.

Types AP68 and AP69 in different colors, overprinted "OFICIAL," see Nos. CO69-CO87.

Flag of Honduras AP70

Designs: 2c, 8c, Monument and mountains. 10c, 15c, 1 l, Lempira. 30c, 2 l, Coat of arms.

1957, Oct. 21 Litho. ***Perf. 13***

Frames in Black

C269 AP70 1c buff & ultra .20 .20
C270 AP70 2c org, pur & emerald .20 .20
C271 AP70 5c pink & ultra .20 .20
C272 AP70 8c org, vio & ol .20 .20
C273 AP70 10c violet & brown .20 .20
C274 AP70 12c lt grn & ultra .25 .20
C275 AP70 15c green & brown .30 .20
C276 AP70 30c pink & slate .45 .25
C277 AP70 1 l blue & brown 1.75 1.50
C278 AP70 2 l lt grn & slate 3.25 3.00
Nos. C269-C278 (10) 7.00 6.15

First anniv. of the October revolution.

For overprints and surcharge, see Nos. C551, CO88-CO97.

Control marks were handstamped in violet on many current stamps in July and August, 1958, following fire and theft of stamps at Tegucigalpa in April.

All post offices were ordered to honor only stamps overprinted with the facsimile signature of their departmental revenue administrator. Honduras has 18 departments.

Flags of Honduras and US — AP71

1958, Oct. 2 Engr. ***Perf. 12***

Flags in National Colors

C279 AP71 1c light blue .20 .20
C280 AP71 2c red .20 .20
C281 AP71 5c green .20 .20
C282 AP71 10c brown .20 .20
C283 AP71 20c orange .35 .20
C284 AP71 30c deep rose .35 .25
C285 AP71 50c gray .45 .40
C286 AP71 1 l orange yel 1.00 1.00
C287 AP71 2 l gray olive 2.40 2.00
C288 AP71 5 l vio blue 5.25 4.00
Nos. C279-C288 (10) 10.60 8.65

Honduras Institute of Inter-American Culture. The proceeds were intended for the Binational Center, Tegucigalpa.

For overprints see Nos. C320-C324.

Abraham Lincoln — AP72

Lincoln's Birthplace AP73

Designs: 3c, 50c, Gettysburg Address. 5c, 1 l, Freeing the slaves. 10c, 2 l, Assassination. 12c, 5 l, Memorial, Washington.

1959, Feb. 12 Unwmk. ***Perf. 13½***

Flags in National Colors

C289 AP72 1c green .20 .20
C290 AP73 2c dark blue .20 .20
C291 AP73 3c purple .25 .20
C292 AP73 5c dk carmine .25 .20
C293 AP73 10c black .30 .20
C294 AP73 12c dark brown .30 .20
C295 AP72 15c red orange .40 .25
C296 AP73 25c dull pur .60 .40
C297 AP73 50c ultra .75 .65
C298 AP73 1 l red brown 1.50 1.40
C299 AP73 2 l gray olive 2.40 1.75
C300 AP73 5 l ocher 5.50 5.00
a. Miniature sheet 8.00 8.00
Nos. C289-C300 (12) 12.65 10.65

Birth sesquicentennial of Abraham Lincoln.

No. C300a contains one each of the 1c, 3c, 10c, 25c, 1 l and 5 l, imperf.

For overprints and surcharges see Nos. C316-C319, C325-C330, C345, C347-C348, C352, C356-C364, C494-C495, C539-C541, C552-C553.

Types AP72 and AP73 in different colors, overprinted "OFICIAL," see Nos. CO98-CO109.

Constitution AP74

Designs: 2c, 12c, Inauguration of Pres. Villeda Morales, horiz. 3c, 25c, Pres. Ramon Villeda Morales. 5c, 50c, Allegory of Second Republic (Torch and olive branches).

Engr.; Seal Litho. on 1c, 10c

1959, Dec. 21 ***Perf. 13½***

C301 AP74 1c red brn, car & ultra .20 .20
C302 AP74 2c bister brn .20 .20
C303 AP74 3c ultra .20 .20
C304 AP74 5c orange .20 .20
C305 AP74 10c dull green, car & ultra .25 .20
C306 AP74 12c rose red .35 .20
C307 AP74 25c dull lilac .85 .20
C308 AP74 50c dark blue 1.10 .50
Nos. C301-C308 (8) 3.35 1.90

Second Republic of Honduras, 2nd anniv.

For surcharge see No. C543.

King Alfonso XIII and Map AP75

Designs: 2c, 1906 award of King Alfonso XIII of Spain. 5c, Arbitration commission delivering its award, 1907. 10c, Intl. Court of Justice. 20c, Verdict of the Court, 1960. 50c, Pres. Morales, Foreign Minister Puerto and map. 1 l, Pres. Davila and Pres. Morales.

1961, Nov. 18 Engr. ***Perf. 14½x14***

C309 AP75 1c dark blue .20 .20
C310 AP75 2c magenta .20 .20
C311 AP75 5c deep green .20 .20
C312 AP75 10c brn orange .20 .20
C313 AP75 20c vermilion .30 .20
C314 AP75 50c brown .95 .40
C315 AP75 1 l vio black 1.25 .60
Nos. C309-C315 (7) 3.30 2.00

Judgment of the Intl. Court of Justice at The Hague, Nov. 18, 1960, returning a disputed territory to Honduras from Nicaragua.

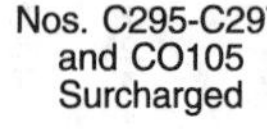

Nos. C295-C297 and CO105 Surcharged

1964, Apr. 7 ***Perf. 13½***

Flags in National Colors

C316 AP72 6c on 15c red org .25 .20
C317 AP73 8c on 25c dull pur .25 .20
C318 AP73 10c on 50c ultra .30 .20
C319 AP73 20c on 25c black .50 .30
Nos. C316-C319 (4) 1.30 .90

The red "OFICIAL" overprint on No. C319 was not obliterated.

See Nos. C345-C355, C419-C421.

Nos. C279-C281, C284 and C287 Overprinted: "FAO / Lucha Contra / el Hambre"

1964, Mar. 23 Unwmk. ***Perf. 12***

Flags in National Colors

C320 AP71 1c light blue .20 .20
C321 AP71 2c red .20 .20
C322 AP71 5c green .20 .20
C323 AP71 30c deep rose .75 .75
C324 AP71 2 l gray olive 5.50 5.50
Nos. C320-C324 (5) 6.85 6.85

FAO "Freedom from Hunger Campaign" (1963).

Nos. CO98-CO101, CO104 and CO106 Overprinted in Blue or Black: "IN MEMORIAM / JOHN F. KENNEDY / 22 NOVEMBRE 1963"

1964, May 29 ***Perf. 13½***

Flags in National Colors

C325 AP72 1c ocher (Bl) .20 .20
C326 AP73 2c gray ol (Bl) .20 .20
C327 AP73 3c red brn (Bl) .20 .20
C328 AP73 5c ultra (Bk) .30 .30
C329 AP72 15c dk brn (Bl) 1.25 1.25
C330 AP73 50c dk car (Bl) 6.25 6.25
Nos. C325-C330 (6) 8.40 8.40

Pres. John F. Kennedy (1917-63). The red "OFICIAL" overprint was not obliterated. The same overprint was applied to the stamps in miniature sheet No. C300a and seal of Honduras and Alliance for Progress emblem added in margin.

Nos. C222-C224, C226 and CO67 Overprinted with Olympic Rings and "1964"

Engr.; Center of 1c Litho.

1964, July 23 ***Perf. 12½***

Frames in Black

C331 AP67 1c ultra & vio bl .20 .20
C332 AP67 2c blue .20 .20
C333 AP67 3c rose lilac .25 .25
C334 AP67 15c red brown .50 .50
C335 AP67 2 l lilac rose 6.25 6.25
Nos. C331-C335 (5) 7.40 7.40

18th Olympic Games, Tokyo, Oct. 10-25. The red "OFICIAL" overprint on No. C335 was not obliterated.

The same overprint was applied in black to the 6 stamps in #CO108a, with additional rings and "1964" in margins of souvenir sheet. Value $50.

View of Copan AP76

Designs: 2c, 12c, Stone marker from Copan. 5c, 1 l, Mayan ball player (stone). 8c, 2 l, Olympic Stadium, Tokyo.

Unwmk.

1964, Nov. 27 Photo. ***Perf. 14***

Black Design and Inscription

C336 AP76 1c yellow grn .20 .20
C337 AP76 2c pale rose lil .20 .20
C338 AP76 5c light ultra .25 .20
C339 AP76 8c bluish green .30 .25
C340 AP76 10c buff .40 .30
C341 AP76 12c lemon .60 .35
C342 AP76 1 l light ocher 1.60 1.25
C343 AP76 2 l pale ol grn 4.25 3.50
C344 AP76 3 l rose 4.75 4.00
Nos. C336-C344 (9) 12.55 10.25

18th Olympic Games, Tokyo, Oct. 10-25. Perf. and imperf. souvenir sheets of four exist containing one each of Nos. C338-C339, C341 and C344. Size: 129x110mm.

For overprints, see Nos. CO111-CO119.

Nos. C292, C174, CO106, CO104, C124-C125, C165, CO105, C167-C168 and C178 Surcharged

1964-65

C345 AP73 4c on 5c dk car, bl & red .20 .20
C346 AP62 10c on 15c red brn .20 .20
C347 AP73 10c on 50c dk car, bl & red .20 .20
C348 AP72 12c on 15c dk brn, bl & red .30 .20
C349 AP27 12c on 16c ol gray .30 .20
C350 AP27 12c on 21c lt blue .30 .20
C351 AP60 12c on 22c org yel .30 .20
C352 AP73 12c on 25c blk, bl & red .30 .20
C353 AP60 30c on 1 l dp blue .50 .25
C354 AP60 40c on 2 l lilac ('65) .70 .50
C355 AP61 40c on 1 l red brown ('65) .70 .30
Nos. C345-C355 (11) 4.00 2.65

The red "OFICIAL" overprint on Nos. C347-C348 and C352 was not obliterated.

Nos. C289, CO99, C291-C292, C295-C296, CO106 and C299-C300 Overprinted in Black or Green: "Toma de Posesión / General / Oswaldo López A. / Junio 6, 1965"

1965, June 6 Engr. ***Perf. 13½***

Flags in National Colors

C356 AP72 1c green .20 .20
C357 AP73 2c gray ol (G) .20 .20
C358 AP73 3c purple (G) .20 .20
C359 AP73 5c dk car (G) .20 .20
C360 AP72 15c red orange .25 .25
C361 AP73 25c dull pur (G) .40 .40
C362 AP73 50c dk carmine (G) .85 .85
C363 AP73 2 l gray olive (G) 3.00 3.00
C364 AP73 5 l ocher (G) 7.50 7.50
Nos. C356-C364 (9) 12.80 12.80

Inauguration of Gen. Oswaldo López Arellano as president. The red "OFICIAL" overprint on Nos. C358 and C362 was not obliterated.

Ambulance and Maltese Cross AP77

Designs (Maltese Cross and): 5c, Hospital of Knights of Malta. 12c, Patients treated in village. 1 l, Map of Honduras.

1965, Aug. 30 Litho. *Perf. 12x11*

C365 AP77 1c ultra .20 .20
C366 AP77 5c dark green .30 .30
C367 AP77 12c dark brown .50 .50
C368 AP77 1 l brown 1.90 1.90
Nos. C365-C368 (4) 2.90 2.90

Knights of Malta; campaign against leprosy.

Father Manuel de Jesus Subirana — AP78

Designs: 1c, Jicaque Indian. 2c, Preaching to the Indians. 10c, Msgr. Juan de Jesus Zepeda. 12c, Pope Pius IX. 20c, Tomb of Father Subirana, Yore. 1 l, Mission church. 2 l, Jicaque mother and child.

Perf. 13½x14

1965, July 27 Litho. Unwmk.

C369 AP78 1c multicolored .20 .20
C370 AP78 2c multicolored .20 .20
C371 AP78 8c multicolored .20 .20
C372 AP78 10c multicolored .20 .20
C373 AP78 12c multicolored .20 .20
C374 AP78 20c multicolored .35 .30
C375 AP78 1 l multicolored 1.75 1.50
C376 AP78 2 l multicolored 3.50 3.00
a. Souv. sheet of 4, #C371, C373, C375-C376 17.50 17.50
Nos. C369-C376 (8) 6.60 5.80

Centenary (in 1964) of the death of Father Manuel de Jesus Subirana (1807-64), Spanish missionary to the Central American Indians.

For overprints and surcharges see Nos. C380-C386, C407-C413, C487-C488, C554.

Nos. C198-C199 and C168 Overprinted: "IN MEMORIAM / Sir Winston Churchill / 1874-1965."

1965, Dec. 20 Engr. *Perf. 13½x14*

C377 AP65 1c red org & blk .30 .30
C378 AP65 2c blue & red brn .70 .70
C379 AP60 2 l lilac 6.00 6.00
Nos. C377-C379 (3) 7.00 7.00

Sir Winston Spencer Churchill (1874-1965), statesman and World War II leader.

Nos. C369-C375 Overprinted

1966, Mar. 10 Litho. *Perf. 13½x14*

C380 AP78 1c multicolored .20 .20
C381 AP78 2c multicolored .20 .20
C382 AP78 8c multicolored .25 .20
C383 AP78 10c multicolored .25 .20
C384 AP78 12c multicolored .30 .20
C385 AP78 20c multicolored .35 .35
C386 AP78 1 l multicolored 3.25 3.25
Nos. C380-C386 (7) 4.80 4.60

Visit of Pope Paul VI to the UN, New York City, Oct. 4, 1965.

Stamp of 1866, #1 — AP79

Tomas Estrada Palma — AP80

Post Office, Tegucigalpa AP81

Designs: 2c, Air post stamp of 1925, #C1. 5c, Locomotive. 6c, 19th cent. mail transport with mules. 7c, 19th cent. mail room. 8c, Sir Rowland Hill. 9c, Modern mail truck. 10c, Gen. Oswaldo Lopez Arellano. 12c, Postal emblem. 15c, Heinrich von Stephan. 20c, Mail plane. 30c, Flag of Honduras. 40c, Coat of Arms. 1 l, UPU monument, Bern. 2 l, José Maria Medina.

Perf. 14½x14, 14x14½

1966, May 31 Litho. Unwmk.

C387 AP79 1c gold, blk & grnsh gray .20 .20
C388 AP79 2c org, blk & lt bl .20 .20
C389 AP80 3c brt rose, gold & dp plum .20 .20
C390 AP81 4c bl, gold & blk .20 .20
C391 AP81 5c pink, gold & blk .50 .20
C392 AP81 6c lil, gold & blk .20 .20
C393 AP81 7c lt bl grn, gold & black .20 .20
C394 AP80 8c lt bl, gold & blk .20 .20
C395 AP81 9c lt ultra, gold & black .20 .20
C396 AP80 10c cit, gold & blk .20 .20
C397 AP79 12c gold, blk, yel & emerald .20 .20
C398 AP80 15c brt pink, gold & dp claret .25 .25
C399 AP81 20c org, gold & blk .30 .30
C400 AP79 30c gold & bl .35 .35
C401 AP79 40c multi .60 .55
C402 AP79 1 l emer, gold & dk green 1.25 1.00
C403 AP80 2 l gray, gold & black 2.75 2.75
a. Souv. sheet of 6, #C387-C388, C396-C397, C402-C403 3.50 3.50
Nos. C387-C403 (17) 8.00 7.40

Centenary of the first Honduran postage stamp. #C403a exists perf. and imperf. See #CE3. For surcharges see #C473-C474, C479, C486, C496.

Nos. CO53, C201 and C204 Overprinted: "CAMPEONATO DE FOOTBALL Copa Mundial 1966 Inglaterra-Alemania Wembley, Julio 30"

Perf. 13½x14, 14x13½

1966, Nov. 25 Engr.

C404 AP65 2c brown & vio .20 .20
C405 AP66 16c dk bl & blk .30 .30
C406 AP65 2 l brn & vio 8.50 8.50
Nos. C404-C406 (3) 9.00 9.00

Final game between England and Germany in the World Soccer Cup Championship, Wembley, July 30, 1966. The overprint on the 2c and 2 l is in 5 lines, it is in 8 lines on the 16c. There is no hyphen between "Inglaterra" and "Alemania" on the 16c.

Nos. C369-C371 and C373-C376 Overprinted in Red: "CONMEMORATIVA / del XX Aniversario / ONU 1966"

1967, Jan. 31 Litho. *Perf. 13½x14*

C407 AP78 1c multicolored .20 .20
C408 AP78 2c multicolored .20 .20
C409 AP78 8c multicolored .30 .30
C410 AP78 12c multicolored .50 .40
C411 AP78 20c multicolored .65 .55
C412 AP78 1 l multicolored 1.50 1.50
C413 AP78 2 l multicolored 3.25 3.25
Nos. C407-C413 (7) 6.60 6.40

UN, 20th anniversary.

Nos. C250, C252, C258, C261 and C267 Overprinted in Red: "Siméon Cañas y Villacorta / Libertador de los esclavos / en Centro America / 1767-1967"

1967, Feb. 27 Engr.

C414 AP68 1c blk & vio bl .20 .20
C415 AP68 3c blk & brown .25 .25
C416 AP68 15c dk red & blk .35 .35
C417 AP68 25c blk & grn .70 .70
C418 AP69 2 l blk & mag 2.50 2.50
Nos. C414-C418 (5) 4.00 4.00

Birth bicentenary of Father José Siméon Canas y Villacorta, D.D. (1767-1838), emancipator of the Central American slaves. The overprint is in 6 lines on the 2 l, in 4 lines on all others.

Nos. C178-C179 and CE2 Surcharged

1967

C419 AP61 10c on 1 l .35 .20
C420 AP62 10c on 2 l .35 .20
C421 APSD1 10c on 20c .35 .20
Nos. C419-C421 (3) 1.05 .60

José Cecilio del Valle, Honduras AP82

Designs: 12c, Ruben Dario, Nicaragua. 14c, Batres Montufar, Guatemala. 20c, Francisco Antonio Gavidia, El Salvador. 30c, Juan Mora Fernandez, Costa Rica. 40c, Federation Emblem with map of Americas. 50c, Map of Central America.

1967, Aug. 4 Litho. *Perf. 13*

C422 AP82 11c gold, ultra & blk .20 .20
C423 AP82 12c lt bl, yel & blk .20 .20
C424 AP82 14c sil, grn & blk .20 .20
C425 AP82 20c pink, grn & blk .25 .25
C426 AP82 30c bluish lil, yel & black .40 .35
C427 AP82 40c pur, lt bl & gold .70 .70
C428 AP82 50c lem, grn & car rose .70 .70
Nos. C422-C428 (7) 2.65 2.60

Founding of the Federation of Central American Journalists.

For surcharges see Nos. C475-C476.

Olympic Rings, Flags of Mexico and Honduras AP83

Olympic Rings and Winners of 1964 Olympics: 2c, Like 1c. 5c, Italian flag and boxers. 10c, French flag and women skiers. 12c, German flag and equestrian team. 50c, British flag and women runners. 1 l, US flag and runners (Bob Hayes).

1968, Mar. 4 Litho. *Perf. 14x13½*

C429 AP83 1c gold & multi .20 .20
C430 AP83 2c gold & multi .20 .20
C431 AP83 5c gold & multi .25 .25
C432 AP83 10c gold & multi .30 .25
C433 AP83 12c gold & multi .50 .25
C434 AP83 50c gold & multi 1.90 1.10
C435 AP83 1 l gold & multi 6.25 6.25
Nos. C429-C435 (7) 9.60 8.50

19th Olympic Games, Mexico City, Oct. 12-27.

Exist imperf. Perf. and imperf. souvenir sheets of 2 exist containing 20c and 40c stamps in design of 1c. Value $7 each.

For surcharge see No. C499.

John F. Kennedy, Rocket at Cape Kennedy AP84

ITU Emblem and: 2c, Radar and telephone. 3c, Radar and television set. 5c, Radar and globe showing Central America. 8c, Communications satellite. 10c, 20c, like 1c.

1968, Nov. 28 *Perf. 14x13½*

C436 AP84 1c vio & multi .20 .20
C437 AP84 2c sil & multi .20 .20
C438 AP84 3c multicolored .25 .25
C439 AP84 5c org & multi .30 .30
C440 AP84 8c multicolored .35 .35
C441 AP84 10c olive & multi .40 .40
C442 AP84 20c multicolored .50 .50
Nos. C436-C442 (7) 2.20 2.20

ITU, cent. A 30c in design of 2c, a 1 l in design of 5c and a 1.50 l in design of 1c exist; also two souvenir sheets, one containing 10c, 50c and 75c, the other one 1.50 l.

For overprints see Nos. C446-C453.

Nos. C436, C441-C442 Overprinted: "In Memoriam / Robert F. Kennedy / 1925-1968"

1968, Dec. 23

C446 AP84 1c vio & multi .20 .20
C447 AP84 10c olive & multi .30 .30
C448 AP84 20c multicolored .50 .50
Nos. C446-C448 (3) 1.00 1.00

In memory of Robert F. Kennedy. Same overprint was also applied to a 1.50 l and to a souvenir sheet containing one 1.50 l.

Nos. C437-C440 Overprinted in Blue or Red with Olympic Rings and: "Medalias de Oro / Mexico 1968"

1969, Mar. 3

C450 AP84 2c multi (Bl) .50 .50
C451 AP84 3c multi (Bl) 1.00 1.00
C452 AP84 5c multi (Bl) 1.50 1.50
C453 AP84 8c multi (R) 2.00 2.00
Nos. C450-C453 (4) 5.00 5.00

Gold medal winners in 19th Olympic Games, Mexico City. The same red overprint was also applied to a 30c and a 1 l. The souvenir sheet of 3 noted after No. C442 exists with this overprint in black.

Rocket Blast-off AP85

Designs: 10c, Close-up view of moon. 12c, Spacecraft, horiz. 20c, Astronaut and module on moon, horiz. 24c, Lunar landing module.

Perf. 14½x13½, 13½x14

1969, Oct. 29

C454 AP85 5c multicolored .20 .20
C455 AP85 10c multicolored .30 .30
C456 AP85 12c multicolored .40 .40
C457 AP85 20c multicolored .50 .50
C458 AP85 24c multicolored 1.00 1.00
Nos. C454-C458 (5) 2.40 2.40

Man's first landing on the moon, July 20, 1969. A 30c showing re-entry of capsule, a 1 l in design of 20c and a 1.50 l in design of 24c exist. Two souvenir sheets exist, one containing #C454-C455 and 1.50 l, and the other #C456, 30c and 1 l.

For the safe return of Apollo 13, overprints were applied in 1970 to #C454-C458, the 3 unlisted denominations and the 2 souvenir sheets.

For overprints and surcharges see Nos. C500-C504, C555.

Nos. C224, C393, C395, C422, C424, CE2 and C178 Surcharged with New Value

1970, Feb. 20 Engr.; Litho.

C472 AP67 4c on 3c blk & rose lil .20 .20
C473 AP81 5c on 7c multi .25 .20
C474 AP81 10c on 9c multi .30 .20

C475 AP82 10c on 11c multi .30 .20
C476 AP82 12c on 14c multi .35 .20
C477 APSD1 12c on 20c blk & red .35 .20
C478 AP61 12c on 1 l red brn .35 .20
Nos. C472-C478 (7) 2.10 1.40

No. CE3 Overprinted "HABILITADO"

1970 Litho. *Perf. 14x14½*
C479 AP81 20c bis brn, brn & gold .75 .35

Julio Adolfo Sanhueza AP86

Emblems, Map and Flag of Honduras — AP87

Designs: 8c, Rigoberto Ordoñez Rodriguez. 12c, Forest Fire Brigade emblem (with map of Honduras) and emblems of fire fighters, FAO and Alliance for Progress, horiz. 1 l, Flags of Honduras, UN and US, Arms of Honduras and emblems as on 12c.

Perf. 14½x14, 14x14½

1970, Aug. 15 Litho.
C480 AP86 5c gold, emer & ind .30 .20
C481 AP86 8c gold, org brn & indigo .40 .20
C482 AP87 12c bl & multi .50 .20
C483 AP87 20c yel & multi .70 .25
C484 AP87 1 l gray & multi 3.50 1.75
a. Souvenir sheet of 5 3.00 2.00
Nos. C480-C484 (5) 5.40 2.60

Campaign against forest fires and in memory of the men who lost their lives fighting forest fires. No. C484a contains 5 imperf. stamps with simulated perforations and without gum similar to Nos. C480-C484. Sold for 1.45 l.
For surcharges see Nos. C497-C498.

Hotel Honduras Maya AP88

1970, Oct. 24 Litho. *Perf. 14*
C485 AP88 12c sky blue & blk .30 .25

Hotel Honduras Maya, Tegucigalpa, opening.

Stamps of 1952-1968 Surcharged

1971 Litho.; Engr.
C486 AP79 4c on 1c (#C387) .20
C487 AP78 5c on 1c (#C369) .20
C488 AP78 8c on 2c (#C370) .25
C489 AP65 10c on 2c (#C199) .35
C490 AP67 10c on 3c (#C224) .35
a. Inverted surcharge
C491 AP68 10c on 3c (#C252) .35
C492 AP68 10c on 3c (#CO71) .35
C493 AP69 10c on 2c (#C251) .35
C494 AP73 10c on 2c (#CO99) .35
C495 AP73 10c on 3c (#CO100) .35
C496 AP80 10c on 3c (#C389) .35
C497 AP87 15c on 12c (#C482) .50
C498 AP87 30c on 12c (#C482) 1.00
C499 AP83 40c on 50c (#C434) 1.25
C500 AP85 40c on 24c (#C458) 1.25
Nos. C486-C500 (15) 7.45

Red "OFICIAL" overprint was not obliterated on Nos. C492, C494-C495.
No. C491 exists with inverted surcharge.

Nos. C454, C456-C458 Overprinted and Surcharged

Perf. 14½x13½, 13½x14½

1972, May 15 Litho.
C501 AP85 5c multi .70 .40
C502 AP85 12c multi 1.50 .75
C503 AP85 1 l on 20c multi 3.50 3.00
C504 AP85 2 l on 24c multi 6.00 5.00
Nos. C501-C504 (4) 11.70 9.15

Masonic Grand Lodge of Honduras, 50th anniv. Overprint varies to fit stamp shape.

Soldier's Bay, Guanaja AP89

Designs: 5c, 7c, 9c, 10c, 2 l, vertical.

1972, May 19 *Perf. 13*
C505 AP89 4c shown .20 .20
C506 AP89 5c Taps .20 .20
C507 AP89 6c Yojoa Lake .20 .20
C508 AP89 7c Banana Carrier, by Roberto Aguilar .20 .20
C509 AP89 8c Military parade .20 .20
C510 AP89 9c Orchid, national flower .25 .20
C511 AP89 10c like 9c .25 .20
C512 AP89 12c Soldier with machine gun .20 .20
C513 AP89 15c Sunset over beach .30 .20
C514 AP89 20c Litter bearers .30 .20
C515 AP89 30c Landscape, by Antonio Velasquez .50 .25
C516 AP89 40c Ruins of Copan .75 .40
a. Souv. sheet of 4, #C508, C513, C515-C516 1.40 1.40
C517 AP89 50c Girl from Huacal, by Pablo Zelaya Sierra .60 .35
a. Souv. sheet of 4, #C506-C507, C514, C517 1.40 1.40
C518 AP89 1 l Trujillo Bay 1.50 1.00
a. Souv. sheet of 4, #C505, C509, C512, C518 2.00 1.75
C519 AP89 2 l Orchid, national flower 4.00 3.00
a. Souv. sheet of 3, #C510-C511, C519 4.50 3.25
Nos. C505-C519,CE4 (16) 9.95 7.30

Sesquicentennial of independence (stamps inscribed 1970).
For surcharge see No. CE5.

Sister Maria Rosa and Child — AP90

Designs: 15c, SOS Children's Village emblem, horiz. 30c, Father José Trinidad Reyes. 40c, Kennedy Center, first SOS village in Central America, horiz. 1 l, Boy.

Perf. 13½x13, 13x13½

1972, Nov. 10 Photo.
C520 AP90 10c grn, gold & brn .20 .20
C521 AP90 15c grn, gold & brn .25 .20
C522 AP90 30c grn, gold & brn .40 .20
C523 AP90 40c grn, gold & brn .50 .20
C524 AP90 1 l grn, gold & brn 2.00 1.50
Nos. C520-C524 (5) 3.35 2.30

Children's Villages in Honduras (Intl. SOS movement to save homeless children).
For overprints and surcharges see #C531, C534-C536, C546-C549, C556, C560-C561.

Map of Honduras and Society Emblem AP91

Design: 12c, Map of Honduras, emblems of National Geographic Institute and Interamerican Geodesic Service.

1973, Mar. 27 Litho. *Perf. 13*
C525 AP91 10c multicolored .55 .30
C526 AP91 12c multicolored .65 .30

25th annivs. of Natl. Cartographic Service (10c) and of joint cartographic work (12c).
For overprints and surcharges see Nos. C532-C533, C557-C558.

Juan Ramón Molina AP92

Designs: 8c, Illustration from Molina's book "Habitante de la Osa." 1 l, Illustration from "Tierras Mares y Cielos." 2 l, "UNESCO."

1973, Apr. 17 Litho. *Perf. 13½*
C527 AP92 8c brn org, blk & red brn .20 .20
C528 AP92 20c brt bl & multi .65 .25
C529 AP92 1 l green & multi 1.40 1.00
C530 AP92 2 l org & multi 2.75 2.75
a. Sheet of 4 5.25 5.25
Nos. C527-C530 (4) 5.00 4.20

Molina (1875-1908), poet, and 25th anniv. (in 1971) of UNESCO. #C530a contains 4 stamps similar to #C527-C530. Exists perf. & imperf.
For surcharge see No. C559.

Nos. C520-C523, C525-C526 Overprinted in Red or Black: "Censos de Población y Vivienda, marzo 1974. 1974, Año Mundial de Población"

Perf. 13½x13, 13x13½, 13

1973, Dec. 28 Photo; Litho.
C531 AP90 10c multi (R) .20 .20
C532 AP91 10c multi (B) .20 .20
C533 AP91 12c multi (B) .20 .20
C534 AP90 15c multi (R) .20 .20
C535 AP90 30c multi (R) .30 .25
C536 AP90 40c multi (R) .35 .35
Nos. C531-C536 (6) 1.45 1.40

1974 population and housing census; World Population Year. The overprint is in 7 lines on vertical stamps, in 5 lines on horizontal.

Issues of 1947-59 Surcharged in Red or Black

Perf. 13x12½, 13½, 11x12½, 12

1974, June 28 Engr.
C537 AP68 2c on 1c (#C250) (R) .20 .20
C538 AP68 2c on 1c (#CO69) .20 .20
C539 AP72 2c on 1c (#C289) .20 .20
C540 AP72 2c on 1c (#CO98) .20 .20
C541 AP72 3c on 1c (#C289) .20 .20
C542 AP68 3c on 1c (#C250) (R) .20 .20
C543 AP74 1 l on 50c (#C308) 1.40 1.40
C544 AP60 1 l on 2 l (#C168) 1.40 1.40
C545 AP62 1 l on 2 l (#C179) (R) 1.40 1.40
Nos. C537-C545 (9) 5.40 5.40

Red "OFICIAL" overprint was not obliterated on Nos. C538 and C540.

Nos. C520-C523 Overprinted in Bright Green: "1949-1974 SOS Kinderdorfer International Honduras-Austria"

1974, July 25 Photo.
C546 AP90 10c grn, gold & brn .20 .20
C547 AP90 15c grn, gold & brn .20 .20
C548 AP90 30c grn, gold & brn .25 .25
C549 AP90 40c grn, gold & brn .35 .35
Nos. C546-C549 (4) 1.00 1.00

25th anniversary of Children's Villages in Honduras. Overprint in 6 lines on 10c and 30c, in 4 lines on 15c and 40c.

Stamps of 1956-73 Surcharged

1975, Feb. 24 Litho.; Engr.
C550 AP68 16c on 1c (#C250) .20 .20
C551 AP70 16c on 1c (#C269) .20 .20
C552 AP72 16c on 1c (#C289) .20 .20
C553 AP72 16c on 1c (#CO98) .20 .20
C554 AP78 16c on 1c (#C369) .30 .30
C555 AP85 18c on 12c (#C456) .40 .25
C556 AP90 18c on 10c (#C520) .25 .20
C557 AP91 18c on 10c (#C525) .25 .20
C558 AP91 18c on 12c (#C526) .25 .20
C559 AP92 18c on 8c (#C527) .25 .20
C560 AP90 50c on 30c (#C522) .75 .50
C561 AP90 1 l on 30c (#C522) 1.25 .90
Nos. C550-C561,CE5 (13) 5.35 4.15

Denominations not obliterated on Nos. C551, C553-C558, C560-C561; "OFICIAL" overprint not obliterated on No. C553.

Flags of Germany and Austria AP93

Designs (Flags): 2c, Belgium & Denmark. 3c, Spain & France. 4c, Hungary & Russia. 5c, Great Britain & Italy. 10c, Norway & Sweden. 12c, Honduras. 15c, US & Switzerland. 20c, Greece & Portugal. 30c, Romania & Serbia. 1 l, Egypt & Netherlands. 2 l, Luxembourg & Turkey.

1975, June 18 Litho. *Perf. 13*

Gold & Multicolored; Colors Listed are for Shields
C562 AP93 1c lilac .20 .20
C563 AP93 2c gold .20 .20
C564 AP93 3c rose gray .20 .20
C565 AP93 4c light blue .20 .20
C566 AP93 5c yellow .20 .20
C567 AP93 10c gray .20 .20
C568 AP93 12c lilac rose .25 .25
C569 AP93 15c bluish green .30 .30
C570 AP93 20c bright blue .30 .30
C571 AP93 30c pink .50 .50
C572 AP93 1 l salmon 1.50 1.50
C573 AP93 2 l yellow green 3.25 3.25
Nos. C562-C573 (12) 7.30 7.30

Souvenir Sheet
C574 AP93 Sheet of 12 *9.50 9.50*

UPU, cent. (in 1974). No. C574 contains 12 stamps similar to Nos. C562-C573 with shields in different colors.

Humuya Youth Center and Mrs. Arellano AP94

Designs (Portrait of First Lady, Gloria de Lopez Arellano, IWY Emblem and): 16c, Jalteva Youth Center. 18c, Mrs. Arellano (diff. portrait) and IWY emblem. 30c, El Carmen de San Pedro Sula Youth Center. 55c, Flag of National Social Welfare Organization, vert. 1 l, La Isla sports and recreational facilities. 2 l, Women's Social Center.

1976, Mar. 5 Litho. *Perf. 13½*
C575 AP94 8c sal & multi .20 .20
C576 AP94 16c yel & multi .20 .20
C577 AP94 18c pink & multi .20 .20
C578 AP94 30c org & multi .35 .35
C579 AP94 55c multicolored .50 .50
C580 AP94 1 l multicolored 1.10 1.10
C581 AP94 2 l multicolored 2.00 2.00
Nos. C575-C581 (7) 4.55 4.55

International Women's Year (1975).
For surcharges see #C736-C737, C781, C798, C885, C887, C919.

"CARE" and Globe AP95

Designs: 1c, 16c, 30c, 55c, 1 l, Care package and globe, vert. Others like 5c.

1976, May 24 Litho. *Perf. 13½*

C582	AP95	1c blk & lt blue	.20	.20
C583	AP95	5c rose brn & blk	.20	.20
C584	AP95	16c black & org	.20	.20
C585	AP95	18c lemon & blk	.25	.25
C586	AP95	30c blk & blue	.35	.35
C587	AP95	50c yel grn & blk	.50	.50
C588	AP95	55c blk & buff	.50	.50
C589	AP95	70c brt rose & blk	.70	.70
C590	AP95	1 l blk & lt grn	1.10	1.10
C591	AP95	2 l ocher & blk	2.00	2.00
		Nos. C582-C591 (10)	6.00	6.00

20th anniversary of CARE in Honduras.
For surcharges see Nos. C735, C738, C788, C888, C922.

Fawn in Burnt-out Forest — AP96

"Sons of Liberty" — AP97

Forest Protection: 16c, COHDEFOR emblem (Corporacion Hondureña de Desarollo Forestal). 18c, Forest, horiz. 30c, 2 l, Live and burning trees. 50c, like 10c. 70c, Emblem. 1 l, Young forest, horiz.

1976, May 28 Litho. *Perf. 13½*

C592	AP96	10c multicolored	.20	.20
C593	AP96	16c multicolored	.25	.20
C594	AP96	18c multicolored	.25	.20
C595	AP96	30c grn & multi	.50	.20
C596	AP96	50c multicolored	.75	.30
C597	AP96	70c brn & multi	1.00	.40
C598	AP96	1 l yel & multi	2.00	.75
C599	AP96	2 l vio & multi	3.50	3.50
		Nos. C592-C599,CE6 (9)	9.05	6.20

For surcharges see Nos. C784, C787, C917.

1976, Aug. 29 Litho. *Perf. 12*

American Bicentennial: 2c, Raising flag of "Liberty and Union." 3c, Bunker Hill flag. 4c, Washington's Cruisers' flag. 5c, 1st Navy Jack. 6c, Flag of Honduras over Presidential Palace, Tegucigalpa. 18c, US flag over Capitol. 55c, Grand Union flag. 2 l, Bennington flag. 3 l, Betsy Ross and her flag.

C601	AP97	1c multicolored	.20	.20
C602	AP97	2c multicolored	.20	.20
C603	AP97	3c multicolored	.20	.20
C604	AP97	4c multicolored	.20	.20
C605	AP97	5c multicolored	.20	.20
C606	AP97	6c multicolored	.20	.20
C607	AP97	18c multicolored	.30	.35
C608	AP97	55c multicolored	.75	.70
a.		Souv. sheet of 4, #C603, C606-C608	*1.50*	*1.50*
C609	AP97	2 l multicolored	2.00	1.75
a.		Souv. sheet of 3, #C601, C604, C609	*3.25*	*3.25*
C610	AP97	3 l multicolored	4.50	4.50
a.		Souv. sheet of 3, #C602, C605, C610	*4.75*	*4.75*
		Nos. C601-C610 (10)	8.75	8.50

For surcharges see Nos. C883-C884, C885, C889.

King Juan Carlos of Spain — AP98

Designs: 16c, Queen Sophia. 30c, Queen Sophia and King Juan Carlos. 2 l, Arms of Honduras and Spain, horiz.

1977, Sept. 13 Litho. *Perf. 14*

C611	AP98	16c multicolored	.20	.20
C612	AP98	18c multicolored	.20	.20
C613	AP98	30c multicolored	.30	.25
C614	AP98	2 l multicolored	1.90	1.90
		Nos. C611-C614 (4)	2.60	2.55

Visit of King and Queen of Spain.
For surcharges see Nos. C890, C918.

Mayan Steles, Exhibition Emblems AP99

Designs: 18c, Giant head. 30c, Statue. 55c, Sun god. 1.50 l, Mayan pelota court.

1978, Apr. 28 Litho. *Perf. 12*

C615	AP99	15c multi	.20	.20
C616	AP99	18c multi	.25	.25
C617	AP99	30c multi	.35	.35
C618	AP99	55c multi	.70	.70

Imperf

C619	AP99	1.50 l multi	1.75	1.75
		Nos. C615-C619 (5)	3.25	3.25

Honduras '78 Philatelic Exhibition.
For overprints and surcharges see Nos. C642-C645, C786, C920, C924, CB5.

Del Valle's Birthplace AP100

Designs: 14c, La Merced Church, Choluteca, where del Valle was baptized. 15c, Baptismal font, vert. 20c, Del Valle reading independence acts. 25c, Portrait, documents, map of Central America. 40c, Portrait, vert. 1 l, Monument, Central Park, Choluteca, vert. 3 l, Bust, vert.

1978, Apr. 11 Litho. *Perf. 14*

C620	AP100	8c multicolored	.20	.20
C621	AP100	14c multicolored	.20	.20
C622	AP100	15c multicolored	.20	.20
C623	AP100	20c multicolored	.20	.20
C624	AP100	25c multicolored	.30	.30
C625	AP100	40c multicolored	.40	.40
C626	AP100	1 l multicolored	1.00	1.00
C627	AP100	3 l multicolored	3.50	3.50
		Nos. C620-C627 (8)	6.00	6.00

Bicentenary of the birth of José Cecilio del Valle (1780-1834), Central American patriot and statesman.
For surcharges see Nos. C739, C793, C795, C886A.

Rural Health Center AP101

Designs: 6c, Child at water pump. 10c, Los Laureles Dam, Tegucigalpa. 20c, Rural aqueduct. 40c, Teaching hospital, Tegucigalpa. 2 l, Parents and child. 3 l, National vaccination campaign. 5 l, Panamerican Health Organization Building, Washington, DC.

1978, May 10 Litho. *Perf. 14*

C628	AP101	5c multicolored	.20	.20
C629	AP101	6c multicolored	.20	.20
C630	AP101	10c multicolored	.20	.20
C631	AP101	20c multicolored	.25	.25
C632	AP101	40c multicolored	.45	.45
C633	AP101	2 l multicolored	1.90	1.90
C634	AP101	3 l multicolored	3.00	3.00
C635	AP101	5 l multicolored	4.50	4.50
		Nos. C628-C635 (8)	10.70	10.70

75th anniv. of Panamerican Health Organization (in 1977).
For surcharge see No. C783.

Luis Landa and his "Botanica" AP102

Designs (Luis Landa and): 16c, Map of Honduras showing St. Ignacio. 18c, Medals received by Landa. 30c, Landa's birthplace in St. Ignacio. 2 l, Brassavola (orchid), national flower. 3 l, Women's Normal School.

1978, Aug. 29 Photo. *Perf. 13x13½*

C636	AP102	14c multicolored	.20	.20
C637	AP102	16c multicolored	.20	.20
C638	AP102	18c multicolored	.20	.20
C639	AP102	30c multicolored	.40	.20
C640	AP102	2 l multicolored	3.00	1.00
C641	AP102	3 l multicolored	3.50	3.50
		Nos. C636-C641 (6)	7.50	5.30

Prof. Luis Landa (1875-1975), botanist.
For surcharges see Nos. C740, C794, C888A, C923.

Nos. C615-C618 Overprinted in Red with Argentina '78 Soccer Cup Emblem and: "Argentina Campeon / Holanda Sub-Campeon / XI Campeonato Mundial / de Football"

1978, Sept. 6 Litho. *Perf. 12*

C642	AP99	15c multicolored	.20	.20
C643	AP99	18c multicolored	.25	.20
C644	AP99	30c multicolored	.35	.30
C645	AP99	55c multicolored	.75	.50
		Nos. C642-C645 (4)	1.55	1.20

Argentina's victory in World Cup Soccer Championship. Same overprint was applied to No. C619.
For surcharge see No. C924.

Central University and Coat of Arms — AP103

Designs show for each denomination a 19th century print and a contemporary photograph of same area (except 1.50 l, 5 l): No. C647, University City. 8c, Manuel Bonilla Theater. No. C650, Court House, vert. No. C651, North Boulevard highway intersection, vert. No. C652, Natl. Palace. No. C653, Presidential Palace. 20c, Hospital. 40c, Cathedral. 50c, View of Tegucigalpa. 1.50 l, Aerial view of Tegucigalpa. No. C660, Arms of San Miguel de Tegucigalpa, 18th cent., vert. No. C661, Pres. Marco Aurelio Soto (1846-1908) (painting), vert.

1978, Sept. 29

C646	AP103	6c black & brn	.20	.20
C647	AP103	6c multicolored	.20	.20
a.		Pair, #C646-C647	.20	.20
C648	AP103	8c black & brn	.20	.20
C649	AP103	8c multicolored	.20	.20
a.		Pair, #C648-C649	.25	.20
C650	AP103	10c black & brn	.20	.20
C651	AP103	10c multicolored	.20	.20
a.		Pair, #C650-C651	.30	.20
C652	AP103	16c black & brn	.25	.20
C653	AP103	16c multicolored	.25	.20
a.		Pair, #C652-C653	.50	.30
C654	AP103	20c black & brn	.30	.20
C655	AP103	20c multicolored	.30	.20
a.		Pair, #C654-C655	.60	.30
C656	AP103	40c black & brn	.60	.45
C657	AP103	40c multicolored	.60	.45
a.		Pair, #C656-C657	1.25	.90
C658	AP103	50c black & brn	.75	.50
C659	AP103	50c multicolored	.75	.50
a.		Pair, #C658-C659	1.50	1.00
C660	AP103	5 l black & brn	6.00	6.00
C661	AP103	5 l multicolored	6.00	6.00
a.		Pair, #C660-C661	12.00	12.00
		Nos. C646-C661 (16)	17.00	15.90

Souvenir Sheet

C662	AP103	1.50 l multi	2.00	2.00

400th anniv. of the founding of Tegucigalpa.
In the listing the first number is for the 19th cent. design, the second for the 20th cent. design.
For overprints and surcharges see #C724-C725, C740A-C746, C766-C769, C779-C780.

Goalkeeper — AP104

Designs: Various soccer scenes.

1978, Nov. 26 Litho. *Perf. 12*

C663	AP104	15c multi, vert.	.20	.20
C664	AP104	30c multi	.30	.30
C665	AP104	55c multi, vert.	.50	.50
C666	AP104	1 l multi	1.00	1.00
C667	AP104	2 l multi	2.00	2.00
		Nos. C663-C667 (5)	4.00	4.00

7th Youth Soccer Championship, Nov. 26.
For surcharge see No. C797.

UPU Emblem — AP105

2c, Postal emblem of Honduras. 25c, Dr. Ramon Rosa, vert. 50c, Pres. Marco Aurelio Soto, vert.

1979, Apr. 1 Litho. *Perf. 12*

C668	AP105	2c multicolored	.20	.20
C669	AP105	15c multicolored	.20	.20
C670	AP105	25c multicolored	.20	.20
C671	AP105	50c multicolored	.40	.40
		Nos. C668-C671 (4)	1.00	1.00

Centenary of Honduras joining UPU.

Rotary Emblem and "50" AP106

1979, Apr. 26 Litho. *Perf. 14*

C672	AP106	3c multi	.20	.20
C673	AP106	5c multi	.20	.20
C674	AP106	50c multi	.40	.40
C675	AP106	2 l multi	1.60	1.60
		Nos. C672-C675 (4)	2.40	2.40

Rotary Intl. of Honduras, 50th anniv.
For surcharge see No. C884A.

Map of Caratasca Lagoon AP107

Designs: 10c, Fort San Fernando de Omoa. 24c, Institute anniversary emblem, vert. 5 l, Map of Santanilla islands.

1979, Sept. 15 Litho. *Perf. 13½*

C676	AP107	5c multi	.20	.20
C677	AP107	10c multi	.20	.20
C678	AP107	24c multi	.20	.20
C679	AP107	5 l multi	3.75	3.75
		Nos. C676-C679 (4)	4.35	4.35

Panamerican Institute of History and Geography, 50th anniversary.
For surcharge see No. C891.

General Post Office, 1979 — AP108

UPU Membership Cent.: 3 l, Post Office, 19th cent.

1980, Feb. 20 Litho. *Perf. 12*

C680 AP108 24c multi .20 .20
C681 AP108 3 l multi 2.50 2.50

For surcharge see No. C925.

Workers in the Field, IYC Emblem AP109

1980, Dec. 9 Litho. *Perf. 14½*

C682 AP109 1c shown .20 .20
C683 AP109 5c Landscape, vert. .20 .20
C684 AP109 15c Sitting boy, vert. .20 .20
C685 AP109 20c IYC emblem, vert. .20 .20
C686 AP109 30c Beach scene .30 .30
Nos. C682-C686 (5) 1.10 1.10

Souvenir Sheet

C687 AP109 1 l UNICEF and IYC emblems, vert. 1.00 1.00

International Year of the Child (1979).

Intibucana Mother and Child — AP111

Inter-American Women's Commission, 50th Anniv.: 2c, Visitacion Padilla, Honduras Section founder. 10c, Maria Trinidad del Cid, Section member. 1 l, Emblem, horiz.

1981, June 15 Litho. *Perf. 14½*

C695 AP111 2c multicolored .20 .20
C696 AP111 10c multicolored .20 .20
C697 AP111 40c multicolored .30 .30
C698 AP111 1 l multicolored .80 .80
Nos. C695-C698 (4) 1.50 1.50

Bernardo O'Higgins, by Jose Gil de Castro — AP112

1981, June 29

Paintings of O'Higgins: 16c, Liberation of Chile, by Cosme San Martin, horiz. 20c, Portrait of Ambrosio O'Higgins (father). 1 l, Abdication of Office, by Antonio Caro, horiz.

C699 AP112 16c multicolored .20 .20
C700 AP112 20c multicolored .20 .20
C701 AP112 30c multicolored .25 .25
C702 AP112 1 l multicolored .85 .50
Nos. C699-C702 (4) 1.50 1.15

For surcharges see Nos. C785, C888B.

CONCACAF 81 Soccer Cup — AP113

1981, Dec. 30 Litho. *Perf. 14*

C703 AP113 20c Emblem .20 .20
C704 AP113 50c Player .35 .25
C705 AP113 70c Flags .60 .40
C706 AP113 1 l Stadium .85 .85
Nos. C703-C706 (4) 2.00 1.70

Souvenir Sheet

C707 AP113 1.50 l like #C703 1.25 1.25

For overprint see No. C797.

50th Anniv. of Air Force (1981) AP114

Designs: 3c, Curtiss CT-32 Condor. 15c, North American NA-16. 25c, Chance Vought F4U-5. 65c, Douglas C47. 1 l Cessna A37-B. 2 l, Super Mister SMB-11.

1983, Jan. 14 Litho. *Perf. 12*

C708 AP114 3c multi .20 .20
C709 AP114 15c multi .20 .20
C710 AP114 25c multi .25 .20
C711 AP114 65c multi .55 .35
C712 AP114 1 l multi .85 .50
C713 AP114 2 l multi 1.75 1.75
Nos. C708-C713 (6) 3.80 3.20

Souvenir Sheet

C714 AP114 1.55 l Helicopter 1.50 1.50

For surcharge see No. C884B.

UPU Executive Council Membership, 3rd Anniv. — AP115

1983, Jan. 14

C715 AP115 16c UPU monument .20 .20
C716 AP115 18c 18th UPU Congress emblem .20 .20
C717 AP115 30c Natl. Postal Service emblem .30 .30
C718 AP115 55c Rio de Janeiro .45 .45
C719 AP115 2 l Dove on globe 1.75 1.75
Nos. C715-C719 (5) 2.90 2.90

Souvenir Sheet

C720 AP115 1 l like 2 l .90 .90

For surcharge see No. C921.

Natl. Library and Archives Centenary (1980) AP116

1983, Feb. 11 Litho. *Perf. 12*

C721 AP116 9c Library .25 .20
C722 AP116 1 l Books 1.00 .40

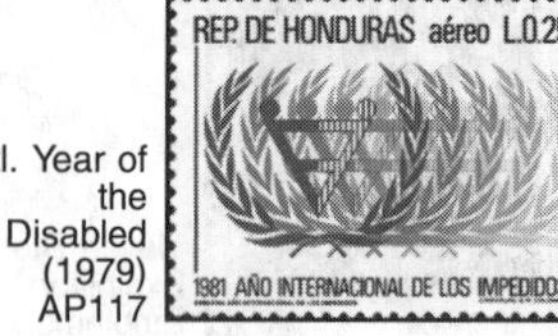

Intl. Year of the Disabled (1979) AP117

1983, Feb. 11

C723 AP117 25c Emblem .25 .25

No. C657a Overprinted in Red: "CONMEMORATIVA DE LA VISITA / DE SS. JUAN PABLO II / 8 de marzo de 1983"

1983, Mar. 8

C724 AP103 40c multicolored 3.00 2.50
C725 AP103 40c multicolored 3.00 2.50
a. Pair, #C724-C725 6.00 5.00

Visit of Pope John Paul II.

Literacy Campaign (1980) — AP118

World Food Day, Oct. 16, 1981 — AP119

1983, May 18 Litho. *Perf. 12*

C726 AP118 40c Hands, open book .35 .35
C727 AP118 1.50 l People holding books 1.40 1.40

1983, May 18

C728 AP119 65c Produce, emblem .60 .60

20th Anniv. of Inter-American Development Bank (1980) — AP120

1983, June 17 Litho. *Perf. 12*

C729 AP120 1 l Comayagua River Bridge .85 .50
C730 AP120 2 l Luis Bogran Technical Institute of Physics 1.60 1.00

2nd Anniv. of Return to Constitutional Government — AP121

1984, Jan. 27 Litho. *Perf. 12*

C731 20c Arms, text .20 .20
C732 20c Pres. Suazo Cordova .20 .20
a. AP121 Pair, #C731-C732 .35 .30

La Gaceta Newspaper Sesquicentenary (1980) — AP122

1984, May 25 Litho. *Perf. 12*

C733 AP122 10c multicolored .20 .20
C734 AP122 20c multicolored .20 .20

Nos. C582 and C575-C576 Surcharged

1985, June 26 Litho. *Perf. 13½*

C735 AP95 5c on 1c #C582 .20 .20
C736 AP94 10c on 8c #C575 .20 .20
C737 AP94 20c on 16c #C576 .20 .20
C738 AP95 1 l on 1c #C582 .90 .40
Nos. C735-C738 (4) 1.50 1.00

Nos. C621, C636, C647a Surcharged

Litho., Photo. (No. C740)

1986, Aug. 21 *Perfs. as before*

C739 AP100 50c on 14c #C621 .45 .25
C740 AP102 60c on 14c #C636 .55 .30
C740A AP103 85c on 6c #C646 .75 .40
C740B AP103 85c on 6c #C647 .75 .40
c. Pair, #C740A-C740B 1.50 .80
C741 AP103 95c on 6c #C646 .85 .45
C742 AP103 95c on 6c #C647 .85 .45
a. Pair, #C741-C742 1.70 .90
Nos. C739-C742 (6) 4.20 2.25

Black bar obliterating old values on #C739-C740 also cover "aereo."

Nos. C656-C657 Ovptd. in Red "EXFILHON '86," "MEXICO '86" and: No. C743 "ARGENTINA CAMPEON" No. C744 "ALEMANIA FEDERAL Sub Campeon" No. C745 "FRANCIA TERCER LUGAR" No. C746 "BELGICA CUARTO LUGAR"

1986, Sept. 12 Litho. *Perf. 12*

C743 AP103 40c No. C656 .40 .20
C744 AP103 40c No. C657 .40 .20
C745 AP103 40c No. C657 .40 .20
C746 AP103 40c No. C656 .40 .20
a. Block of 4, #C743-C746 1.60

AP123

San Fernando de Omoa Castle — AP124

Maltese Cross, Hill AP110

1980, Dec. 17

C688 AP110 1c shown .20 .20
C689 AP110 2c Penny Black .20 .20
C690 AP110 5c Honduras type A1 .20 .20
C691 AP110 10c Honduras type A1 .20 .20

Size: 47x34mm

C692 AP110 15c Postal emblem .20 .20
C693 AP110 20c Flags of Honduras, Gt. Britain .20 .20
Nos. C688-C693 (6) 1.20 1.20

Souvenir Sheet

C694 AP110 1 l Honduras #C402 .85 .85

Sir Rowland Hill (1795-1879), originator of penny postage. No. C694 contains one stamp 47x34mm.

20c, Phulapanzak Falls. 78c, Bahia Isls. beach. 85c, Bahia Isls. cove. 95c, Yojoa Lake. 1 l, Woman painting pottery.

Perf. 13½x14, 14x13½

1986, Nov. 10 Litho.

C747 AP123 20c multi, vert. .20 .20
C748 AP123 78c multi .70 .35
C749 AP123 85c multi .75 .35
C750 AP123 95c multi, vert. .85 .40
C751 AP123 1 l multi, vert. .90 .45

Size: 84x59mm

Imperf

C752 AP124 1.50 l multi 1.40 1.40
Nos. C747-C752 (6) 4.80 3.15

For overprint see No. C782.

AP125

Flora — AP126

1987, Feb. 2 Litho. *Perf. 13½*

National flag, Pres. Jose Azcona Hoyo.

C753 AP125 20c multicolored .20 .20
C754 AP125 85c multicolored .75 .30

Democratic government, 1st anniv.

1987, July 8 Litho. *Perf. 13½x14*

C755 AP126 10c Eupatorium cyril-linelsonii .20 .20
C756 AP126 20c Salvia ernesti-vargasii .20 .20
C757 AP126 95c Robinsonella er-asmi-sosae .85 .40
Nos. C755-C757 (3) 1.25 .80

Birds — AP127

AP128

1987, Sept. 10 Litho. *Perf. 13½x14*

C758 AP127 50c Eumomota superciliosa .45 .25
C759 AP127 60c Ramphastos sulfuratus .60 .30
C760 AP127 85c Amazona autumnalis .75 .45
Nos. C758-C760 (3) 1.80 1.00

1987, Dec. 10 Litho. *Perf. 13½*

C761 AP128 1 l blk, brt yel & dark red .90 .45

Natl. Autonomous University of Honduras, 30th anniv.

AP129

AP130

1987, Dec. 23 Litho. *Perf. 13½*

C762 AP129 20c red & dk ultra .20 .20

Natl. Red Cross, 50th anniv.

1988, Jan. 27 Litho. *Perf. 13½*

C763 AP130 95c brt blue & org yel .85 .40

17th regional meeting of Lions Intl.

Atlantida Bank, 75th Anniv. AP131

Main offices: 10c, La Ceiba, Atlantida, 1913. 85c, Tegucigalpa, 1988.

1988, Feb. 10

C764 AP131 10c multi .20 .20
C765 AP131 85c mutli .75 .40
a. Souv. sheet of 2, #358-359, imperf. .90 .90

No. C765a sold for 1 l.

No. C649a Surcharged

1988, June 9 Litho. *Perf. 12*

C766 AP103 20c on 8c #C648 .20 .20
C767 AP103 20c on 8c #C649 .20 .20
a. Pair, #C766-C767 .30 .20

No. C647a Surcharged

1988, July 8 Litho. *Perf. 12*

C768 AP103 5c on 6c #C646 .20 .20
C769 AP103 5c on 6c #C647 .20 .20
a. Pair, #C768-C769 .20 .20

Postman AP132

Tegucigalpa Postmark on Stampless Cover, 1789 — AP133

1988, Sept. 11 Litho. *Perf. 13½*

C770 AP132 85c dull red brn 1.10 .40
C771 AP133 2 l dull red brn & ver 2.50 1.00

EXFILHON '88.

Summer Olympics Type of 1988

1988, Sept. 30 Litho. *Perf. 13½*

Size: 28x33mm

C772 A62 85c Running, vert. 1.10 .40

Size: 36x27mm

C773 A62 1 l Baseball, soccer, basketball 1.20 .50

Discovery of America, 500th Anniv. (in 1992) AP134

Pre-Colombian pottery artifacts: 10c, Footed vase, vert. 25c, Bowl. 30c, Footed bowl. 50c, Pitcher, vert. 1 l, Rectangular footed bowl.

1988 Litho. *Perf. 13½*

C774 AP134 10c multicolored .30 .20
C775 AP134 25c multicolored .75 .25
C776 AP134 30c multicolored .90 .30
C777 AP134 50c multicolored 1.50 .50
Nos. C774-C777 (4) 3.45 1.25

Size: 115x83mm

Imperf

C778 AP134 1 l multicolored 3.00

Nos. C653a and C576 Surcharged

1988 Litho. *Perf. 12, 13½*

C779 AP103 10c on 16c #C652 .20 .20
C780 AP103 10c on 16c #C653 .20 .20
a. Pair, #C779-C780 .30 .30
C781 AP94 50c on 16c #C576 .60 .40
Nos. C779-C781 (3) 1.00 .80

Nos. C779-C780 exist with double surcharge. Issued: 10c, Apr. 7, 50c, May 25.

No. C752 Overprinted

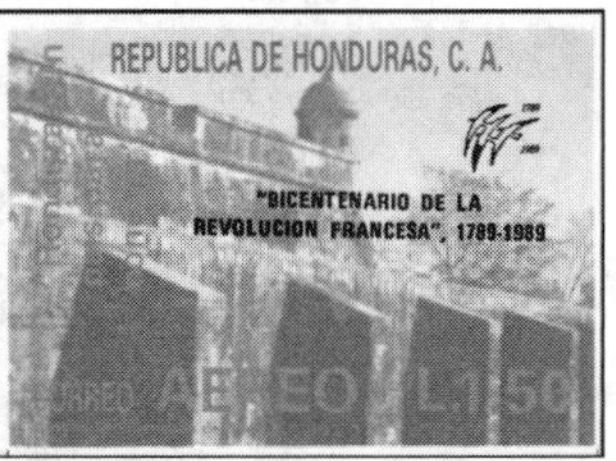

1989, July 14 Litho. *Imperf.*

C782 AP124 1.50 l multi 1.75

French revolution, bicent.

Nos. C629 and C593 Surcharged

I

II

1989 Litho. *Perf. 14, 13½*

C783 AP101 15c on 6c, I .20
C783A AP101 15c on 6c, II 1.00
C784 AP96 1 l on 16c 1.25
Nos. C783-C784 (3) 2.45

Issue date: 1 l, June 15.

Nos. C699 and C616 Surcharged

1989, Dec. 15 Litho. *Perf. 14½, 12*

C785 AP112 20c on 16c #C699 .20
C786 AP99 95c on 18c #C616 .75

No. C786 exists with inverted surcharge. Issued: #C785, Dec. 15; #C786, Dec. 28.

Nos. C594 and C585 Surcharged with New Denomination and "IV Juegos / Olimpicos / Centroamericanos"

1990, Jan. 12 *Perf. 13½*

C787 AP96 75c on 18c #C594 (S) 1.00
C788 AP95 85c on 18c #C585 1.10

No. C787 exists with double and inverted surcharge.

World Wildlife Fund — AP135

Various *Mono ateles.*

1990, Apr. 18 Litho. *Perf. 13½*

C789 AP135 10c shown 1.50
C790 AP135 10c Adult, young 1.50
C791 AP135 20c Adult hanging, diff. 2.50
C792 AP135 20c Adult, young, diff. 2.50
Nos. C789-C792 (4) 8.00

No. C621 Surcharged

1990, Feb. 8 Litho. *Perf. 14*

C793 AP100 20c on 14c multi .20

Nos. C621 and C636 Surcharged "50 Aniversario / IHCI" / 1939-1989

1990, Mar. 29

C794 AP102 20c on 14c No. 636 .20
C795 AP100 1 l on 14c No. 621 .45

No. C665 Surcharged

1990, June 14 Litho. *Perf. 12*

C796 AP104 1 l on 55c multi .45

World Cup Soccer Championships, Italy.

No. C707 Ovptd. in Margin "CAMPEONATO MUNDIAL DE FUTBOL Italia '90," and Character Trademark Souvenir Sheet

1990, June 14 *Perf. 14*

C797 AP113 1.50 l multi .70

No. C577 Surcharged in Black

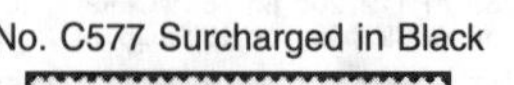

1990, Feb. 22 Litho. *Perf. 13½*

C798 AP94 20c on 18c multi .20

FAO, 45th Anniv. — AP136

1990, Oct. 16 Litho. *Perf. 13½*

C799 AP136 95c yel, blk, bl, grn .55

17th Interamerican Congress of Industry and Construction — AP137

1990, Nov. 21 Litho. *Perf. 13½*

C800 AP137 20c Map, vert. .20

C801 AP137 1 l Jose Cecilio Del Valle Palace .60

AP138

Christmas — AP139

1990, Nov. 30 Litho. *Perf. 13½*

C802 AP138 20c shown .20

C803 AP138 95c Madonna and Child, vert. .55

Size: 112x82mm

Imperf

C804 AP139 3 l Poinsettia 1.75

Nos. C802-C804 (3) 2.50

Salesian Order in Honduras, 80th Anniv. AP140

1990, Dec. 28 Litho. *Perf. 13½*

C805 AP140 75c St. John Bosco .45

C806 AP140 1 l Natl. Youth Sanctuary .60

Pres. Rafael Leonardo Callejas — AP141

1991, Jan. 31

C807 AP141 30c Taking oath .20

C808 AP141 2 l Portrait 1.20

Moths and Butterflies AP142

1991, Feb. 28 Litho. *Perf. 13½*

C809 AP142 85c Strymon melinus .50

C810 AP142 90c Diorina sp. .60

C811 AP142 1.50 l Hyalophora cecropia .90

Size: 114x82mm

Imperf

C812 AP142 5 l Papilio polixenes 3.00

Nos. C809-C812 (4) 5.00

Notary Day — AP143

1991, May 22 Litho. *Perf. 13½*

C813 AP143 50c multicolored .35

Rafael Heliodoro Valle, Birth Cent. — AP144

1991, July 26 Litho. *Perf. 13½*

C815 AP144 2 l pale pink & blk 1.25

Churches AP145

Discovery of America, 500th Anniv. emblem and: 30c, Church of St. Manuel of Colohete, Gracias. 95c, Church of Our Lady of Mercy, Gracias. 1 l, Comayagua Cathedral.

1991, Aug. 30 Litho. *Perf. 13½*

C816 AP145 30c multicolored .20

C817 AP145 95c multicolored .55

C818 AP145 1 l multicolored .60

Nos. C816-C818 (3) 1.35

Latin American Institute, 25th Anniv. AP146

1991, June 20

C819 AP146 1 l multicolored .60

Flowers AP147

1991, Apr. 30

C820 AP147 30c Rhyncholaelia glauca .20

C821 AP147 50c Oncidium splendidum, vert. .30

C822 AP147 95c Laelia anceps, vert. .60

C823 AP147 1.50 l Cattleya skinneri .90

Nos. C820-C823 (4) 2.00

Espamer '91, Buenos Aires AP148

1991, July 1

C824 AP148 2 l multicolored 1.25

Size: 101x82mm

Imperf

C825 AP148 5 l like #C824 3.25

Discovery of America, 500th anniv. (in 1992).

11th Pan American Games, Havana AP149

1991, Aug. 8

C826 AP149 30c Equestrian .20

C827 AP149 85c Judo .50

C828 AP149 95c Men's swimming .55

Size: 114x83mm

Imperf

C829 AP149 5 l Women's swimming 3.25

Nos. C826-C829 (4) 4.50

Pre-Columbian Culture — AP150

UPAEP emblem, artifacts and: 25c, ears of corn. 40c, ear of corn, map. 1.50 l, map.

1991, Sept. 30 Litho. *Perf. 13½*

C830 AP150 25c multicolored .20

C831 AP150 40c multicolored .25

C832 AP150 1.50 l multicolored .90

Nos. C830-C832 (3) 1.35

4th Intl. Congress on Control of Insect Pests AP151

Designs: 30c, Tactics to control pests. 75c, Integration of science. 1 l, Cooperation between farmers and scientists. 5 l, Pests and biological controls.

1991, Nov. 22

C833 AP151 30c multicolored .20

C834 AP151 75c multicolored .45

C835 AP151 1 l multicolored .60

Size: 115x83mm

Imperf

C836 AP151 5 l multicolored 3.00

Nos. C833-C836 (4) 4.25

America Issue AP152

1992, Jan. 27 Litho. *Perf. 13½*

C837 AP152 90c Sighting land .55

C838 AP152 1 l Columbus' ships .60

C839 AP152 2 l Ship, map, birds 1.20

Nos. C837-C839 (3) 2.35

Christmas AP153

1991, Dec. 19

C840 AP153 1 l shown .60

C841 AP153 2 l Poinsettias in rooster vase 1.25

Honduran Savings Insurance Company, 75th Anniv. AP154

1992, Jan. 17

C842 AP154 85c multicolored .50
C843 AP154 1 l Priest saying mass .60

Size: 115x83mm

Imperf

C844 AP154 5 l like #C842 3.00
Nos. C842-C844 (3) 4.10

First mass in New World, 490th anniv. (No. C843). Taking possession of new continent, 490th anniv. (Nos. C842, C844).

Pres. Rafael Leonardo Callejas, 2nd Year in Office AP155

Callejas with: 20c, Italian president Francesco Cossiga. 2 l, Pope John Paul II.

1992, Jan. 27 Litho. *Perf. 13½*

C845 AP155 20c black & purple .20
C846 AP155 2 l black & multi 1.25

Flowers AP156

1992, July 25 Litho. *Perf. 13½*

C847 AP156 20c Bougainvillea glabra .20
C848 AP156 30c Canna indica .20
C849 AP156 75c Epiphyllum .45
C850 AP156 95c Sobralia macrantha .60
Nos. C847-C850 (4) 1.45

Gen. Francisco Morazan Hydroelectric Complex — AP157

1992, Aug. 17

C851 AP157 85c Dam face, vert. .50
C852 AP157 4 l Rear of dam 2.40

AP158

AP159

1992, Aug. 24

C853 AP158 95c black & multi .60
C854 AP158 95c multicolored .60

Intl. Conference on Agriculture, 50th anniv.

1992, Sept. 18 Litho. *Perf. 13½*

Gen. Francisco Morazan (1792-1842): 5c, Morazan mounted on horseback. 10c, Statue of Morazan. 50c, Watch and sword, horiz. 95c, Portrait of Josefa Lastiri de Morazan. 5 l, Portrait of Morazan in uniform.

C855 AP159 5c multicolored .20
C856 AP159 10c multicolored .20
C857 AP159 50c multicolored .30
C858 AP159 95c multicolored .55

Size: 76x108mm

Imperf

C859 AP159 5 l multicolored 2.75
Nos. C855-C859 (5) 4.00

Children's Day — AP160

Paintings of children: 25c, Musicians. 95c, Boy, dog standing in doorway. 2 l, Flower girl.

1992, Sept. 7

C860 AP160 25c multicolored .20
C861 AP160 95c multicolored .50
C862 AP160 2 l multicolored 1.10
Nos. C860-C862 (3) 1.80

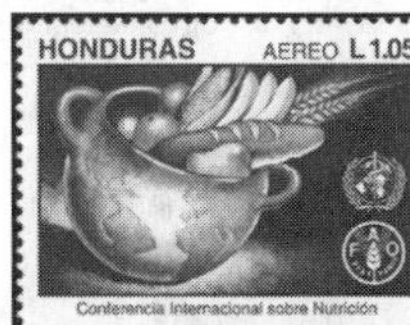

Intl. Conference on Nutrition AP161

1992, Sept. 30 Litho. *Perf. 13½*

C863 AP161 1.05 l multicolored .60

Pan-American Agricultural School, 50th Anniv. — AP162

1992, Oct. 9

C864 AP162 20c Bee keepers .20
C865 AP162 85c Woman, goats .45
C866 AP162 1 l Plowing .55
C867 AP162 2 l Man with tool, vert. 1.10
Nos. C864-C867 (4) 2.30

Exfilhon '92 — AP163

Birds: 1.50 l, F. triquilidos. 2.45 l, Ara macao. 5 l, Quetzal pharomachrus mocinno.

1992, Oct. 2

C868 AP163 1.50 l multicolored .85
C869 AP163 2.45 l multicolored 1.40

Size: 76x108mm

Imperf

C870 AP163 5 l multicolored 2.75
Nos. C868-C870 (3) 5.00

Discovery of America, 500th anniv.

America Issue — AP164

Discovery of America, 500th Anniv. — AP165

UPAEP emblem and: 35c, Native settlement. 5 l, Explorers meeting natives in boats.

1992, Oct. 30 Litho. *Perf. 13½*

C871 AP164 35c multicolored .20
C872 AP164 5 l multicolored 2.75

Printed on both thick and thin paper.

1992, Oct. 30

Details from First Mass, by Roque Zelaya: 95c, Ships off-shore. 1 l, Holding services with natives, horiz. 2 l, Natives, countryside, temples, horiz.

C873 AP165 95c multicolored .50
C874 AP165 1 l multicolored .55
C875 AP165 2 l multicolored 1.10
Nos. C873-C875 (3) 2.15

City of El Progreso, Cent. AP166

1992, Oct. 17

C876 AP166 1.55 l multicolored .85

First Road Conservation Congress of Panama and Central America — AP167

1992, Nov. 16 *Perf. 13½*

C878 AP167 20c shown .20
C879 AP167 85c Bulldozer on highway .45

Pan-American Health Organization, 90th Anniv. — AP168

1992, Nov. 27

C880 AP168 3.95 l multicolored 2.10

Christmas AP169

Paintings by Roque Zelaya: 20c, Crowd watching people climb pole in front of church, vert. 85c, Nativity scene.

1992, Nov. 24

C881 AP169 20c multicolored .20
C882 AP169 85c multicolored .45

Surcharges on:

No. C601

Nos. C606-C607

Nos. C584, C612, C637

Nos. C672, C678, C708

Nos. C575-C576, C603, C620, C699

1992-93

Perfs. and Printing Methods as Before

C883	AP97	20c on 1c #C601	.20
C884	AP97	20c on 3c #C603	.20
C884A	AP106	20c on 3c #C672	.20
C884B	AP114	20c on 3c #C708	.20
C885	AP97	20c on 6c #C606	.20
C886	AP94	20c on 8c #C575	.20
C886A	AP100	20c on 8c #C620	.20
C887	AP94	50c on 16c #C576	.40
C888	AP95	50c on 16c #C584	.25
C888A	AP102	50c on 16c #C637	.25
C888B	AP112	50c on 16c #C699	.40
C889	AP97	85c on 18c #C607	.45
C890	AP98	85c on 18c #C612	.45
C891	AP107	85c on 24c #C678	.40
		Nos. C883-C891 (14)	4.00

Size and location of surcharge varies.

Issued: #C883, 12/18/92; #C889, 1/22/93; #C885, 3/8/93; #C888A, 9/7/93; #C888, 9/13/93; #C890, 9/24/93; #C891, 10/1/93; #C884A, 10/5/93; #C884B, 10/8/93; #C884, C886A, 10/21/93; #C886, 10/29/93; #C887, C888B, 11/3/93.

Intl. Court of Justice Decision on Border Dispute Between Honduras & El Salvador
AP170

Designs: 90c, Pres. of El Salvador and Pres. Callejas of Honduras, vert. 1.05 l, Country flags, map of Honduras and El Salvador.

1993, Feb. 24 Litho. *Perf. 13½*

C893 AP170 90c multicolored .45
C894 AP170 1.05 l multicolored .55

Third year of Pres. Callejas' term.

Mother's Day — AP171

Endangered Animals — AP172

Paintings of a mother and child, by Sandra Pendrey.

1993, May 5 Litho. *Perf. 13½*

C895 AP171 50c Red blanket .25
C896 AP171 95c Green blanket .50

1993, May 14 *Perf. 13½*

C897 AP172 85c Manatee, horiz .50
C898 AP172 2.45 l Puma, horiz. 1.50
C899 AP172 10 l Jaguar 6.00
Nos. C897-C899 (3) 8.00

Natl. Symbols AP173

1993, June 25 Litho. *Perf. 13½*

C900 AP173 25c Ara macao .20
C901 AP173 95c Odocoileus virginianus .45

First Brazilian Postage Stamps, 150th Anniv. AP174

1993, Sept. 10 Litho. *Perf. 13½*

C902 AP174 20c Brazil No. 1 .20
C903 AP174 50c Brazil No. 2 .25
C904 AP174 95c Brazil No. 3 .45
Nos. C902-C904 (3) .90

Departments in Honduras — AP175

Various scenes, department name: No. C905a, Atlantida. b, Colon. c, Cortes. d, Choluteca. e, El Paraiso. f, Francisco Morazan.
No. C906a, Comayagua. b, Copan. c, Intibuca. d, Islas de la Bahia. e, Lempira. f, Ocotepeque.
No. C907a, La Paz. b, Olancho. c, Santa Barbara. d, Valle. e, Yoro. f, Gracias a Dios.

1993, Sept. 20 Litho. *Perf. 13½*

C905 AP175 20c Strip of 6, #a.-f. .60
C906 AP175 50c Strip of 6, #a.-f. 1.40
C907 AP175 1.50 l Strip of 6, #a.-f. 4.00
Nos. C905-C907 (3) 6.00

No. C906 is vert.

Endangered Birds — AP176

UN Development Program AP177

1993, Oct. 11 Litho. *Perf. 13½*

C908 AP176 20c Spizaetus ornatus .20
C909 AP176 80c Cairina moschata, horiz. .40
C910 AP176 2 l Harpia harpija, horiz. .95
Nos. C908-C910 (3) 1.55

1993, Oct. 19

C911 AP177 95c multicolored .45

Christmas AP178

1993, Nov. 5

C912 AP178 20c Church .20
C913 AP178 85c Woman, flowers .40

Nos. C577, C585, C593, C611, C616, C638, C643, C680, C716 Surcharged

1993
Perfs. and Printing Methods as Before

C917 AP96 50c on 16c #C593 .25
C918 AP98 50c on 16c #C611 .25
C919 AP94 50c on 18c #C577 .25
C920 AP99 50c on 18c #C616 .25
C921 AP115 50c on 18c #C716 .40
C922 AP95 85c on 18c #C585 .40
C923 AP102 85c on 18c #C638 .40
C924 AP99 85c on 18c #C643 .40
C925 AP108 85c on 24c #C680 .40
Nos. C917-C925 (9) 3.00

Size and location of surcharge varies. This is an expanding set. Numbers may change.
Issued: #C917-C918, 11/12; #C920, C924, 11/23; #C921, C925, 11/30; #C922-C923, 12/3; #C919, 12/10.

Fish AP179

1993, Dec. 7 Litho. *Perf. 13½*

C931 AP179 20c Pomacanthus arcuatus .20
C932 AP179 85c Holacanthus ciliaris .40
C933 AP179 3 l Chaetodon striatus 1.50
Nos. C931-C933 (3) 2.10

Famous Men — AP180

1993, Nov. 17

C934 AP180 25c Ramon Rosa .20
C935 AP180 65c Jesus Aguilar Paz .30
C936 AP180 85c Augusto C. Coello .40
Nos. C934-C936 (3) .90

Pres. Rafael Leonardo Callejas, 4th Year in Office AP181

95c, Wife, Norma, planting tree, vert.

1994, Jan. 21 Litho. *Perf. 13½*

C937 AP181 95c multicolored .40
C938 AP181 1 l multicolored .45

AP182

AP183

1994, Mar. 8 Litho. *Perf. 13 ½*

C939 AP182 1 l multicolored .45

Intl. Year of the Family.

1994, Oct. 24 Litho. *Perf. 13½*

C940 AP183 1 l multicolored .40

Intl. Conference on Peace and Development in Central America, Tegucigalpa.

Christmas AP184

UN, 50th Anniv. — AP185

Paintings by Gelasio Gimenez: 95c, Madonna and Child. 1 l, Holy Family.

1994, Dec. 15 Litho. *Perf. 13½*

C941 AP184 95c multicolored .35
C942 AP184 1 l multicolored .40

1995, Jan. 17

Designs: 1 l, The Sowing: Ecological Family, by Elisa Dulcey. 2 l, Family Scene, by Delmer Mejia. 3 l, UN emblem, "50."

C943 AP185 1 l multicolored .40
C944 AP185 2 l multicolored .75
C945 AP185 3 l multicolored 1.10
Nos. C943-C945 (3) 2.25

Pres. Carlos Roberto Reina, 1st Anniv. of Taking Office AP186

Designs: 80c, Beside flag, vert. 1 l, Summit meeting of area presidents & vice presidents.

1995, Jan. 27

C946 AP186 80c multicolored .30
C947 AP186 95c multicolored .35
C948 AP186 1 l multicolored .40
Nos. C946-C948 (3) 1.05

America Issue AP187

Postal vehicles.

1995, Feb. 28 Litho. *Perf. 13½*

C949 AP187 1.50 l Van .55
C950 AP187 2 l Motorcycle .75

Miniature Sheet of 30

Mushrooms AP188

1 l: a, Marasmius cohaerens. b, Lepista nuda. c, Polyporus pargamenus. d, Fomes. e, Paneolus sphinctrinus. f, Hygrophorus aurantiaca.

1.50 l, vert: g, Psathyrella. h, Amanita rubescens. i, Boletellus russelli. j, Boletus frostii. k, Marasmius spegazzinii. l, Fomes annosus.

2 l, vert: m, Craterellus cornucopioides. n, Amanita. o, Auricularia delicata. p, Psllocybe cubensis. q, Clavariadelphus pistilaris. r, Boletus regius.

2.50 l: s, Scleroderma aurantium. t, Amanita praegraveolens. u, Cantharellus cibarius. v, Geastrum triplex. w, Russula emetica. x, Boletus pinicola.

3 l: y, Fomes versicolor. z, Cantharellus pupurascens. aa, Lyophyllum decastes. ab, Pleurotus ostreatus. ac, Boletus ananas. ad, Amanita caesarea.

1995, Apr. 7

C951	AP188	#a.-ad.	27.50

FAO, 50th Anniv. AP189

1995, May 25 Litho. *Perf. 13½*

C952	AP189	3 l multicolored	.65

CARE, 50th Anniv. AP190

Designs: 1.40 l, Family, farm. No. C954, Orchid, wildlife, couple working in soil. No. C955, Couple in vegetable garden.

1995, Aug. 4 Litho. *Perf. 13½*

C953	AP190	1.40 l multicolored	.50	
C954	AP190	5.40 l multicolored	2.00	
C955	AP190	5.40 l multicolored	2.00	
		Nos. C953-C955 (3)	4.50	

El Puente Archaeological Park — AP191

Illustration reduced.

1995, Aug. 8 *Imperf.*

C956	AP191	20 l multicolored	6.25

America Issue AP192

1.40 l, Kinosternon scorpioides. 4.54 l, Alpinia purpurata, vert. 10 l, Polyborus plancus, vert.

1995, Oct. 10 Litho. *Perf. 13½*

C957	AP192	1.40 l multicolored	.50
C958	AP192	4.54 l multicolored	1.60
C959	AP192	10 l multicolored	3.50
		Nos. C957-C959 (3)	5.60

Reptiles AP193

1995, Nov. 10 Litho. *Perf. 13*

C960	AP193	5.40 l Iguana iguana	2.00
C961	AP193	5.40 l Agalychnis	2.00

Christmas AP194

1995, Dec. 4 Litho. *Perf. 13½*

C962	AP194	1.40 l Bell, vert.	.50
C963	AP194	5.40 l Nativity figurines	2.00
C964	AP194	6.90 l Carved deer, vert.	2.50
		Nos. C962-C964 (3)	5.00

Integration System of Central America AP195

1.40 l, Map of Central America, Tegucigalpa Protocol, 1991. 4.30 l, Functions listed, 1993. 5.40 l, 17th Summit of Presidents of Central America.

1996, Feb. 19 Litho. *Perf. 13½*

C965	AP195	1.40 l multicolored	.50
C966	AP195	4.30 l multicolored	1.60
C967	AP195	5.40 l multicolored	2.00
		Nos. C965-C967 (3)	4.10

UN Fight Against Drug Trafficking and Abuse, 10th Anniv. AP196

Designs: 1.40 l, Stylized picture of minds on drugs. 5.40 l, Person with butterfly for brain, vert. 10 l, Musical score, "Viva la Vida."

1996, May 3

C968	AP196	1.40 l multicolored	.40
C969	AP196	5.40 l multicolored	1.50
C970	AP196	10 l multicolored	2.75
		Nos. C968-C970 (3)	4.65

Arrival of the Garifunas in Honduras, Bicent. AP197

Designs: 1.40 l, Headdress, vert. 5.40 l, Dancers, men playing drums. 10 l, Drums.

1996, June 13 Litho. *Perf. 13½*

C971	AP197	1.40 l multicolored	.40
C972	AP197	5.40 l multicolored	1.50
C973	AP197	10 l multicolored	2.75
		Nos. C971-C973 (3)	4.65

EXFILHON '96, 7th Philatelic Exhibition AP198

1996, July 12 Litho. *Perf. 13½*

C974	AP198	5.40 l Steam locomotive	1.50
C975	AP198	5.40 l Passenger railcar	1.50

73x52mm

Imperf

C976	AP198	20 l +2 l like #C974	6.00
		Nos. C974-C976 (3)	9.00

6th Central American Games AP199

1996, Aug. 30 Litho. *Perf. 13½*

C977	AP199	4.30 l Soccer	1.25	.60
C978	AP199	4.54 l Volleyball	1.25	.65
C979	AP199	5.40 l Mascot, vert.	1.50	.75
		Nos. C977-C979 (3)	4.00	2.00

Scouting in Honduras, 75th Anniv. AP200

1996, Oct. 25 Litho. *Perf. 13½*

C980	AP200	2.15 l Emblems	.40	.20
C981	AP200	5.40 l Emblem, vert.	1.00	.45
C982	AP200	6.90 l Scout feeding deer, vert.	1.50	.60
		Nos. C980-C982 (3)	2.90	1.25

Christmas AP201

Poinsettia and: 1.40 l, Candles. 5.40 l, Candles, vert.

1996, Dec. 23 Litho. *Perf. 13½*

C983	AP201	1.40 l multicolored	.30	.20
C984	AP201	3 l shown	.60	.25
C985	AP201	5.40 l multicolored	1.00	.45
		Nos. C983-C985 (3)	1.90	.90

Traditional Costumes AP202

America issue: 4.55 l, Man in costume. 5.40 l, Woman in costume. 10 l, Couple in costumes.

1997, Jan. 17 Litho. *Perf. 13½*

C986	AP202	4.55 l multicolored	.80	.35
C987	AP202	5.40 l multicolored	1.00	.45
C988	AP202	10 l multicolored	2.50	.80
		Nos. C986-C988 (3)	4.30	1.60

Honduras Plan, 20th Anniv., Intl. Plan, 60th Anniv. AP203

Children's paintings: 1.40 l, Outdoor scene, children swimming, vert. 5.40 l, Girl standing beside lake, fish. 9.70 l, People working between buildings.

1997, Feb. 7 Litho. *Perf. 13½*

C989	AP203	1.40 l multicolored	.35	.20
C990	AP203	5.40 l multicolored	1.25	.65
C991	AP203	9.70 l multicolored	2.40	2.40
		Nos. C989-C991 (3)	4.00	3.25

Heinrich von Stephan (1831-97) AP205

1997, May 9 Litho. *Perf. 13½*

C995	AP205	5.40 l multicolored	.85	.40

World Population Day AP206

Designs: 6.90 l, Child's drawing of people outside, trees, houses.

1997, July 11 Litho. *Perf. 13½*

C996	AP206	1.40 l shown	.20	.20
C997	AP206	6.90 l multicolored	1.00	.50

Butterflies AP207

Designs: 1 l, Rothchildia forbesi. 1.40 l, Parides photinus. 2.15 l, Morpho peleides. 3 l, Eurytides marcellus. 4.30 l, Parides iphidamas. 5.40 l, Danaus plexippus. 20 l+2 l, Hamadryas arinome.

1997, July 31

C998	AP207	1 l multicolored	.20	.20
C999	AP207	1.40 l multicolored	.20	.20
C1000	AP207	2.15 l multicolored	.30	.20
C1001	AP207	3 l multicolored	.45	.20
C1002	AP207	4.30 l multicolored	.65	.30
C1003	AP207	5.40 l multicolored	.80	.40

Imperf

Size: 80x53mm

C1004	AP207	20 l +2 l multi	5.00	2.50
		Nos. C998-C1004 (7)	7.60	4.00

St. Teresa of Jesus, Death Cent. — AP208

1997, Aug. 20 Litho. *Perf. 13½*

C1005	AP208	1.40 l shown	.30	.20
C1006	AP208	5.40 l Portrait, diff.	1.25	.60

Astronomical Observatory AP209

Designs: 5.40 l, Statue of Father Jose Trinidad Reyes. 10 l, Woman with book leading child up steps.

1997, Sept. 19 Litho. *Perf. 13½*

C1007 AP209 1.40 l multicolored .30 .20
C1008 AP209 5.40 l multicolored 1.25 .60
C1009 AP209 10 l multicolored 2.25 1.10
Nos. C1007-C1009 (3) 3.80 1.90

Alma Mater Foundation, 150th anniv., Autonomous University, 40th anniv.

Alcoholics Anonymous in Honduras, 37th anniv. — AP210

1997, Oct. 27

C1010 AP210 5.40 l multicolored 1.25 .60

Diana, Princess of Wales (1961-97) AP211

1.40 l, Portrait, vert. 5.40 l, Diana dressed to walk through mine field, warning sign.
20 l, Mother Teresa, Princess Diana.

1997, Oct. 15

C1011 AP211 1.40 l multicolored .30 .20
C1012 AP211 5.40 l multicolored 1.25 .55

Size: 51x78mm

Imperf

C1013 AP211 20 l multicolored 4.50 2.25
Nos. C1011-C1013 (3) 6.05 3.00

Christmas AP212

1997, Dec. 2 Litho. *Perf. 13½*

C1014 AP212 1.40 l Christ of Picacho .20 .20
C1015 AP212 5.40 l Virgin of Suyapa .85 .45

Mascot — AP213

C1016: a, Basketball. b, At bat, baseball. c, Soccer. d, Racquetball. e, Spiking volleyball. f, Setting volleyball. g, Bowling. h, Table tennis. i, Rings over map of Central America. j, Pitching, baseball.

No. C1017: a, Kicking, karate. b, Chopping, karate. c, Bowing, karate. d, Wrestling. e, Weight lifting. f, Boxing. g, Body building. h, Fencing. i, Program cover. j, Shooting.

No. C1018: a, Riding bicycle. b, Riding bicycle by shoreline. c, Swimming. d, Water polo. e, Hurdles. f, Gymnastics. g, Riding horse. h, Tennis. i, Program cover with mascot. j, Chess.

1997

Sheets of 10

C1016 AP213 1.40 l #a.-j. 3.25 1.60
C1017 AP213 1.50 l #a.-j. 3.50 1.75
C1018 AP213 2.15 l #a.-j. 4.75 2.40

6th Central American Games, San Pedro Sula.

Fish AP214

1.40 l, Cichlasoma dovii. 2 l, Cichlasoma spilurum. 3 l, Cichlasoma spilurum facing right. 5.40 l, Astyanay fasciatus.

1997 Litho. *Perf. 13½*

C1019 AP214 1.40 l multicolored .20 .20
C1020 AP214 2 l multicolored .30 .20
C1021 AP214 3 l multicolored .45 .25
C1022 AP214 5.40 l multicolored .80 .35
Nos. C1019-C1022 (4) 1.75 1.00

Marine Life, Islas de la Bahía (Bay Islands) — AP215

Designs: a, Balistes vetula. b, Haemudon plumieri. c, Pomacanthus paru. d, Juvenile halichoeres garnoti. e, Pomacanthus arcuatus. f, Holacanthus ciliaris. g, Diver's face, pseud opterogorgia. h, Diver's oxygen tanks, pseud opterogorgia. i, Dendrogya cylindrus. j, Holocentrus adscensionis. k, Dendrogya cylindrus, diff. l, Stegastes fuscus. m, Gorgonia mariae. n, Pillar coral. o, Pomacanthus arcuatus, diff. p, Holocentrus adscensionis, diff. q, Eusmilia fastigiata. r, Scarus coelestinus. s, Pillar coral, diff. t, Lachnolaimus masimus.

1998, Mar. 13 Litho. *Perf. 13½*

Sheet of 20

C1023 AP215 2.50 l #a.-t. 11.50 5.50

Bancahsa, 50th anniv.

America Issue AP216

1998, May 29 Litho. *Perf. 13½*

C1024 AP216 5.40 l Post Office headquarters .80 .40
C1025 AP216 5.40 l Postman on motorcycle .80 .40

Maya Artifacts — AP217

Designs: 1 l, Large carving on temple. 1.40 l, Stele of Mayan king. 2.15 l, Large stelae. 5.40 l, Small ornamental carving.
20 l, Maya Ruins, Copán.

1998, June 19 Litho. *Perf. 13½*

C1026 AP217 1 l multicolored .20 .20
C1027 AP217 1.40 l multicolored .30 .20
C1028 AP217 2.15 l multicolored .45 .20
C1029 AP217 5.40 l multicolored 1.10 .55

Size: 78x52mm

Imperf

C1030 AP217 20 l multicolored 4.25 2.00
Nos. C1026-C1030 (5) 6.30 3.15

1998 World Cup Soccer Championships, France — AP218

No. C1033: a, Stadium, Tegucigalpa. b, St. Denis Stadium, France.

1998, July 3 Litho. *Perf. 13½*

C1031 AP218 5.40 l shown 1.10 .55
C1032 AP218 10 l Players, vert. 2.25 1.10

Imperf

C1033 AP218 10 l Pair, #a.-b. 4.25 2.00

No. C1033 contains two 53x42mm stamps.

Reptiles AP219

Designs: 1.40 l, Green iguana. 2 l, Rattlesnake. 3 l, Two iguanas. 5.40 l, Coral snake.
20 l + 2 l, Marine turtle.

1998, July 31 Litho. *Perf. 13½*

C1034 AP219 1.40 l multicolored .20 .20
C1035 AP219 2 l multicolored .30 .20
C1036 AP219 3 l multicolored .45 .25
C1037 AP219 5.40 l multicolored .80 .40

Size: 77x52mm

Imperf

C1038 AP219 20 l +2 l multi 3.25 1.60
Nos. C1034-C1038 (5) 5.00 2.65

Christmas AP220

Designs: 3 l, Girl taking ornament from bird, vert. 5.40 l, Christ Child asleep on bed of holly, dove, stars. 10 l, Boy with lantern leading donkey, cabin in the snow, vert.

1998, Dec. 8 Litho. *Perf. 13½*

C1039 AP220 3 l multicolored .65 .30
C1040 AP220 5.40 l multicolored 1.10 .55
C1041 AP220 10 l multicolored 2.00 1.00
Nos. C1039-C1041 (3) 3.75 1.85

Pres. Carlos Roberto Flores, 1st Anniv. of Taking Office AP221

Designs: 5.40 l, Pres. and Mrs. Flores, Pope John Paul II. 10 l, Portrait of Pres., Mrs. Flores, vert.

1999, Jan. 27 Litho. *Perf. 13½*

C1042 AP221 5.40 l multicolored 1.10 .55
C1043 AP221 10 l multicolored 2.00 1.00

Hurricane Mitch — AP222

No. C1044: a, Men working to clean up. b, Helicopter distributing aid. c, Vehicles under water, North Zone. d, Tipper Gore, Mary de Flores cleaning. e, Working to save banana crop. f, Destruction of Tegucigalpa. g, Cars, buses, trucks blocked by rock slide. h, Destruction of Comayagüela. i, Streets of Comayagüela. j, Oriental Zone. k, Loading debris, help from Mexico. l, Streets of Limpieza. m, Pres. Flores with Pres. Chirac of Fance. n, Business district of Comayagüela. o, Flooding, Tegucigalpa. p, Car in street, Comayagüela.

No. C1045: a, Central Zone. b, South Zone. c, Prince Felipe de Borbon, Mary de Flores. d, Small child crying. e, Cleaning up debris, Comayagüela. f, Families, man carrying baby, North Zone. g, Two men looking at destruction of building, Tegucigalpa. h, Man, child, woman wading in water, North Zone. i, Destruction in rural area. j, Cars piled up, concrete abutment along roadway. k, Cars, buildings along roadway. l, Mexican troops, airplane. m, Boys swimming. n, Pres. & Mrs. Flores, Hillary Clinton. o, People walking over rubble and debris, South Zone. p, Pres. Flores, former US Pres. George Bush.

Illustration reduced.

1999, Feb. 19 *Rouletted*

Sheets of 16

C1044 AP222 5.40 l #a.-p. 17.50 9.00
C1045 AP222 5.40 l #a.-p. 17.50 9.00

Famous Honduran Women — AP223

America Issue: 2.60 l, Maria del Pilar Salinas (b. 1914), scholar. 7.30 l, Clementina Suarez (1902-91), poet, writer. 10.65 l, Mary Flake de Flores, first lady of Honduras.

1999, Apr. 20 Litho. *Perf. 13½*

C1046 AP223 2.60 l multi .55 .25
C1047 AP223 7.30 l multi 1.50 .75
C1048 AP223 10.65 l multi 2.25 1.10
Nos. C1046-C1048 (3) 4.30 2.10

Dated 1998.

Mother's Day AP224

Designs: 20 l, Police officer Orellana breastfeeding baby, vert. 30 l, Paphiopedilum urbanianum. 50 l, Miltoniopsis vexillaria.

1999, May 14 Litho. *Perf. 13½*

C1049 AP224 20 l multicolored 4.00 2.00
C1050 AP224 30 l multicolored 6.00 3.00
C1051 AP224 50 l multicolored 10.00 5.00
Nos. C1049-C1051 (3) 20.00 10.00

Endangered Birds — AP225

No. C1052, 5 l: a, Sarcorampohus papa. b, Leucopternis albicollis. c, Harpia harpyja. d, Pulsatrix perspicallata. e, Spizaetus ornatus. f, Pharomarchrus mocinno. g, Aulacorhynchus prasinus. h, Amazilia luciae. i, Ara macao. j, Centurus pygmaeus.

3 l: k, Aratinga canicularis. l, Amazona albifrons. m, Amazona auropalliata. n, Amazona autumnalis. o, Eurypyga helias. p, Crax rubra. q, Brotogeris jugularis. r, Pionus senilis. s, Aratinga rubritorques. t, Tinamus major.

No. C1053: a, Jaberu mycteria. b, Chondrohierax uncinatus. c, Pharomachrus mocinno. d, Ramphastos sulfuratus.

1999, July 8

C1052 AP225 Sheeet of 20, #a.-t. 16.00 8.00
C1053 AP225 10 l Sheet of 4, #a.-d. 8.00 4.00

Banco Sogerin, 30th anniv.

Inter-American Development Bank, 40th Anniv. — AP226

1999, Nov. 22 Litho. *Perf. 13½*

C1054 AP226 18.30 l multi 3.50 1.75

Blessed Josemaría Escrivá de Balaguer (1902-75), Founder of Opus Dei — AP227

1999, Nov. 29

C1055 AP227 2.60 l multi .50 .25
C1056 AP227 16.40 l multi 3.00 1.50

Millennium AP228

Designs: 2 l, Salvador Moncada, discoverer of nitric oxide in blood, vert. 8.65 l, Albert Einstein, vert. 10 l, Wilhelm Röntgen, vert. 14.95 l, George Stephenson and locomotive "Rocket."

1999, Oct. 18

C1057 AP228 2 l multi .40 .20
C1058 AP228 8.65 l multi 1.60 .80
C1059 AP228 10 l multi 1.90 .95
C1060 AP228 14.95 l multi 2.75 1.40
Nos. C1057-C1060 (4) 6.65 3.35

National Congress, 175th Anniv. AP229

Designs: 4.30, Statue of Francisco Morazán. 10 l, Congress President Rafael Pineda Ponce, Congress Building.

1999, Dec. 17 Litho. *Perf. 13¼*

C1061 AP229 4.30 l multi .80 .40
C1062 AP229 10 l multi 1.90 .95

AP230

Holy Year 2000 — AP231

Holy Year Emblem and: 4 l, Pope John Paul II, people. 4.30 l, St. Peter. 6.90 l, Jesus, Jerusalem, horiz. 7.30 l, John Paul II, crowd, horiz. 10 l, John Paul II giving blessing. 14 l, Pres. Carlos Roberto Flores, John Paul II.

2000, Jan. 1 Litho. *Perf. 13¼*

C1063 AP230 4 l multi .75 .35
C1064 AP230 4.30 l shown .80 .40
C1065 AP230 6.90 l multi 1.25 .65
C1066 AP230 7.30 l multi 1.40 .70
C1067 AP230 10 l multi 1.90 .95
C1068 AP231 14 l shown 2.60 1.25

Nos. C1064, C1068 Redrawn

C1069 AP230 4.30 l multi .80 .40
C1070 AP231 14 l multi 2.60 1.25
Nos. C1063-C1070 (8) 12.10 5.95

#C1066 issued in panes of 6. #C1069 has "HONDURAS" in yellow; #C1064 in white. #C1070 has "HONDURAS" at right, reading up; #C1068 at top.

2nd Anniv. of Inauguration of Pres. Flores — AP232

Pres. Flores and: 10 l, Conference delegates. 10.65 l, Mario Hung Pacheco.

2000, Jan. 27

C1071 AP232 10 l multi 1.90 .95
C1072 AP232 10.65 l multi 2.00 1.00

Musical Instruments Type of Semi-postals of 2000

No. 1073, vert.: a, 1.40 l, Marimba, denomination at L. b, 1.40 l, Marimba, denomination at L. c, 1.40 l, Ayotl. d, 10 l, Maya drum. e, 10 l, Teponaxtle. f, 2.60 l, Maracas. g, 2.60 l, Güiro. h, 2.60 l, Chinchín. i, 2.60 l, Raspador. j, 2.60 l, Horse's jawbone. k, 3 l, Green zoomorphic whistle. l, 3 l, Aztec drum. m, 3 l, One-tone zoomorphic whistle. n, 3 l, Two-tone zoomorphic whistle. o, 3 l, Tun. p, 4 l, Gourd. q, 4 l, Deer hide drum. r, 4 l, Guacalitos. s, 4 l, Five musicians, marimba. t, 4 l, Four musicians, marimba.

2000, Apr. 7 Litho. *Perf. 13¼*

C1073 SP1 Sheet of 20, #a-t 13.50 6.75

Paintings of Pablo Zelaya Sierra — AP233

No. C1074: a, 2 l, Green City (building and tree). b, 2 l, Old Woman With Rosary. c, 2 l, Rural Women (women with jars). d, 2 l, Woman With Green Robe. e, 2 l, City. f, 1.40 l, Shoulders of a Man. g, 1.40 l, Goat. h, 1.40 l, Spanish City. i, 1.40 l, Woman With Chignon. j, 1.40 l, Woman With Calabash. k, 2.60 l, Goat and Birds. l, 2.60 l, Tree Trunks. m, 2.60 l, Nuns. n, 2.60 l, Archers. o, 2.60 l, Moon and Boats. p, 2.60 l, Bust. q, 10 l, Still-life. r, 10 l, Composition With Books. s, 2.60 l, Landscape. t, 2.60 l, Head, Fan and Book.

2000, July 1

C1074 AP233 Sheet of 20, #a-t 10.50 5.25

Airmail Anniv. Type of Semi-postals

Designs: 7.30 l, #C12. 10 l, Thomas Canfield Pounds, owner of Central American Airline, vert. 10.65 l, Pres. Rafael López Gutiérrez, signer of first airmail contract, vert.

2000, July 7

Size: 35x25mm

C1075 SP2 7.30 l multi 1.40 .70

Size: 25x35mm

C1076 SP2 10 l multi 1.75 .90
C1077 SP2 10.65 l multi 1.90 .95
Nos. C1075-C1077 (3) 5.05 2.55

America Issue, A New Millennium Without Arms — AP234

Designs: 10 l, Sobralia macrantha, "No guns," vert. 10.65 l, Dove, "No soldiers," vert. 14 l, Train, "No bombs."

2000, July 28 Litho. *Perf. 13¼*

C1078-C1080 AP234 Set of 3 6.25 3.25

2000 Summer Olympics, Sydney AP235

Designs: 2.60 l, Soccer players Ivan Guerrero, Mario Chirinos. 10.65 l, Swimmer Ramon Valle, vert. 12.45 l, Runner Gina Coello.

No. C1084: a, 4.30 l, Swimmer. b, 4.30 l, Soccer player Danilo Turcios. c, 10.65 l, Runner Pedro Ventura. d, 12.45 l, Soccer player David Suazo.

2000, Sept. 13

C1081-C1083 AP235 Set of 3 3.50 1.75

Souvenir Sheet

C1084 AP235 Sheet of 4, #a-d 4.25 2.10

No. C1084 exists imperf.

Intl. Voluntarism Year — AP236

Emblem, people and: 2.60 l, White-crowned parrot. 10.65 l, Telipogon ampliflorus.

2000, Dec. 5

C1085-C1086 AP236 Set of 2 2.40 1.25

Christmas AP237

Designs: 2.60 l, Madonna and child. 7.30 l, Nativity, vert. 14 l, Carpet painter.

2000, Dec. 18

C1087-C1089 AP237 Set of 3 4.25 2.10

America Issue, Birds — AP238

Designs: 2.60 l, Amazona auropalliata caribea. 4.30 l, Columbina passerina, horiz. 10.65 l, Ara macao. 20 l, Aguila harpia.

2001, Feb. 16 Litho. *Perf. 13¼*

C1090-C1093 AP238 Set of 4 6.75 3.50

Nos. C584, C593, C606, C611, C646-C647, C652-C653, C699 Surcharged - c

Nos. C620, C672, C708, C721 Surcharged - d

No. C637 Surcharged - e

Methods and Perfs. as Before

2001

C1094 AP103(c) 2 l on 16c #C652 .35 .20
C1095 AP103(c) 2 l on 16c #C653 .35 .20
a. Pair, #C1094-C1095 .70 .35
C1096 AP106(d) 2.60 l on 3c #C672 .45 .20
C1097 AP114(d) 2.60 l on 3c #C708 .45 .20
C1098 AP100(d) 2.60 l on 8c #C620 .45 .20
C1099 AP102(e) 2.60 l on 16c #C637 .45 .20
C1100 AP96(c) 3 l on 16c #C593 .55 .25
C1101 AP116(d) 4 l on 9c #C721 .70 .35
C1102 AP97(c) 4.30 l on 6c #C606 .75 .35
C1103 AP103(c) 7.30 l on 6c #C646 1.25 .60
C1104 AP103(c) 7.30 l on 6c #C647 1.25 .60
a. Pair, #C1103-C1104 2.50 1.20
C1105 AP95(c) 10 l on 16c #C584 1.75 .90
C1106 AP112(c) 10.65 l on 16c #C699 1.90 .95
C1107 AP98(c) 14 l on 16c #C611 2.50 1.25
Nos. C1094-C1107 (14) 13.15 6.45

Size and location of surcharge varies. Issued: Nos. C1096-C1099, 3/26; others, 4/3.

Oscar Cardinal Rodriguez — AP239

No. C1108: a, 2.60 l, With father, 1946. b, 2.60 l, In Sanctuary of Our Lady of Suyapa. c, 2.60 l, As seminarian, 1964. d, 2.60 l, Installation as archbishop. e, 2.60 l, Ordination, 1960. f, 2.60 l, At Vatican, Feb. 21, 2001. g, 2.60 l, At mass in Guatemala, 1970. h, 2.60 l, Standing behind Honduran flag. i, 2.60 l, With Pope John Paul II, 1993. j, 2.60 l, Returning to Honduras as Cardinal. k, 2.60 l, Giving address as Cardinal, Mar. 10, 2001. l, 10.65 l, With Pope and woman, 1993. m, 10.65 l, Papal audience, Feb. 23, 2001. n, 10.65 l, Celebration of the Eucharist. o, 10.65 l, Kneeling before Pope, 1993. p, 10.65 l, Installation as Cardinal, Feb. 21, 2001. q, 15 l, Installation as Cardinal, St. Peter's Square.

2001, May 9 Litho. *Perf. 13¼*
C1108 AP239 Sheet of 17, #a-q 16.00 16.00

Stamp sizes: Nos. C1108a-C1108j, 29x40mm; C1108k-C1108p, 49x40mm; C1108q, 163x131mm. No. C1108 exists imperf.

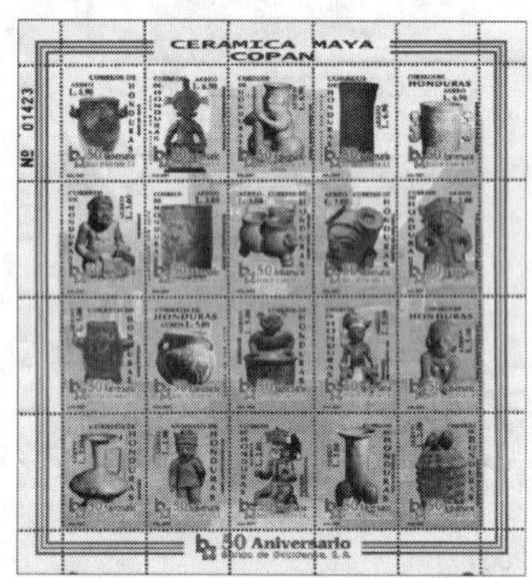

Banco de Occidente, S.A., 50th Anniv. — AP240

Mayan ceramics: a, 2 l, Flower pot. b, 2 l, Anthropomorphic jar. c, 2 l, Anthropomorphic cover. d, 2 l, Cylindrical vase. e, 2 l, Censer tripod. f, 3 l, Scribe. g, 3 l, Cylindrical jar with anthropomorphic figures. h, 3 l, Three-part container. i, 3 l, Ceramic face. j, 3 l, Anthropomorphic jar, diff. k, 5 l, Three-legged vessel. l, 5 l, Pot with handles. m, 5 l, Censer. n, 5 l, Anthropomorphic cover. o, 5 l, Anthropomorphic jar, diff. p, 6.90 l, Pot with handles, diff. q, 6.90 l, Anthropomorphic cover, diff. r, 6.90 l, Anthropomorphic jar, diff. s, 6.90 l, Red cylindrical container. t, 6.90 l, Decorated container.

2001, Sept. 1 Litho. *Perf. 13¼*
C1109 AP240 Sheet of 20, #a-t 15.00 7.50

UN High Commissioner for Refugees, 50th Anniv. — AP241

Designs: 2.60 l, Refugee and child, vert. 10.65 l, Refugees running.

2001
C1110-C1111 AP241 Set of 2 2.25 1.10

Souvenir Sheet

Juan Ramon Molina Bridge — AP242

No. C1112: a, 2.60 l, Aerial view from end. b, 10 l, Close-up view from side. c, 10.65 l, Aerial view from side. d, 13.65 l, Side view showing river.

2001, Dec. 20 Litho. *Rouletted 6½*
C1112 AP242 Sheet of 4, #a-d 6.50 6.50

Stamp sizes: No. C1112b, 152x93mm; others, 40x30mm.

America Issue - Wildlife AP243

Designs: 10 l, Bird, Yojoa Lake. 10.65 l, Iguana, Cisne Islands. 20 l, Chrysina quetzalcoatli, Morpho sp., Pulaphanzhak Cataracts.

2002, Jan. 31 *Perf. 13¼*
C1113-C1115 AP243 Set of 3 7.00 7.00

Pan-American Health Organization, Cent. — AP244

2002, Apr. 7
C1116 AP244 10 l multi 1.25 1.25

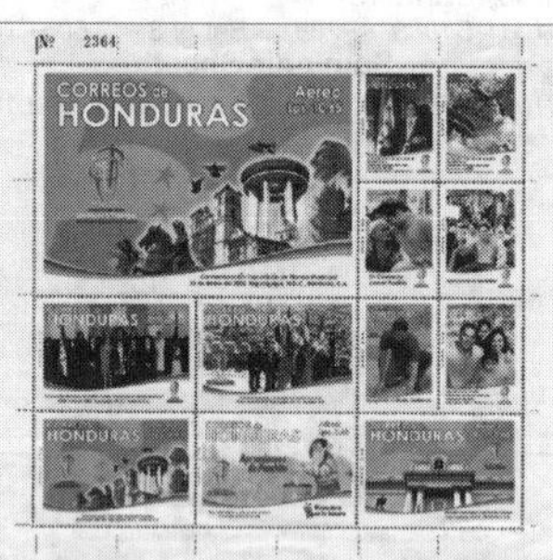

Miguel R. Pastor, Central District Mayor — AP245

Central District emblem and: a, 1.40 l, Cathedral of San Miguel, statues, birds (57x35mm). b, 1.40 l, Chimpanzee throwing banana peel in trash can (57x35mm). c, 1.40 l, Municipal building (57x35mm). d, 2.60 l, Mayor Pastor, flags (27x35mm). e, 2.60 l, Mayor Pastor under tree (27x35mm). f, 2.60 l, Mayor Pastor with old woman (27x35mm). g, 2.60 l, Mayor Pastor with crowd (27x35mm). h, 2.60 l, Mayor Pastor planting seedling (27x35mm). i, 2.60 l, Mayor Pastor and family (27x35mm). j, 10 l, Municipal council (57x35mm). k, 10 l, Mayor with guests (57x35mm). l, 10.65 l, Cathedral of San Miguel, statues, birds (114x75mm).

2002, June 13 Litho. *Perf. 13¼*
C1117 AP245 Sheet of 12, #a-l 6.25 6.25

Souvenir Sheet

Discovery of Honduras, 500th Anniv. — AP246

No. C1118: a, 10.65 l, Boat on shore, jungle. b, 12.45 l, Natives on shore. c, 13.65 l, Spaniards coming ashore. d, 20 l, Spanish ship.

2002, Aug. 14
C1118 AP246 Sheet of 4, #a-d 7.00 7.00

Exfilhon 2002.

Souvenir Sheet

Christianity in Honduras, 500th Anniv. — AP247

No. C1119: a, 2.60 l, Natives and cross. b, 3 l, Santa Barbara Trujillo Fort. c, 10 l, 400 Years of History, by Mario Castillo. d, 10 l, Spaniards on shore, ships at sea.

2002, Aug. 14
C1119 AP247 Sheet of 4, #a-d 3.25 3.25

America issue.

AIR POST SEMI-POSTAL STAMPS

No. C13C Surcharged with Plus Sign and Surtax in Black

Unwmk.

1929, June 5 Engr. *Perf. 12*
CB1 AP1 50c + 5c carmine .40 .30
CB2 AP1 50c + 10c carmine .50 .35
CB3 AP1 50c + 15c carmine .70 .50
CB4 AP1 50c + 20c carmine .90 .70
Nos. CB1-CB4 (4) 2.50 1.85

Catalogue values for unused stamps in this section, from this point to the end of the section, are for Never Hinged items.

Souvenir Sheet

Airmail Pilot Sumner B. Morgan and Airplane — SP2

2000, July 7
CB5 SP2 50 l + 5 l multi 10.00 10.00

First airmail flight in Honduras, 75th anniv., EXFILHON 2000. See Nos. C1075-C1077.

No. C619 Surcharged With New Value in Black and 2000 Sydney Olympics Emblem in Red

2000, Sept. 13 Litho. *Imperf.*
CB6 AP99 48.50 l +1.50 l multi 9.00 9.00

AIR POST SPECIAL DELIVERY STAMPS

No. CO52 Surcharged in Red

Perf. 13½x14
1953, Dec. 8 Engr. Unwmk.
CE1 AP65 20c on 1c 2.50 1.00

Transport Plane APSD1

1956, Oct. 3 *Perf. 13x12½*
CE2 APSD1 20c black & red .75 .40

Surcharges on No. CE2 (see Nos. C421, C477) eliminate its special delivery character.

Catalogue values for unused stamps in this section, from this point to the end of the section, are for Never Hinged items.

Stamp Centenary Type of Air Post Issue

Design: 20c, Mailman on motorcycle.

1966, May 31 Litho. *Perf. 14x14½*
CE3 AP81 20c bis brn, brn & gold .60 .40

Centenary (in 1965) of the first Honduran postage stamp.

The "HABILITADO" overprint on No. CE3 (see No. C479) eliminates its special delivery character.

Independence Type of Air Post Issue

1972, May 19 Litho. *Perf. 13*
CE4 AP89 20c Corsair plane .30 .30

Same Surcharged

1975
CE5 AP89 60c on 20c .85 .60

Forest Protection Type of Air Post

1976, May 28 Litho. *Perf. 13½*
CE6 AP96 60c Stag in forest .60 .45

AIR POST OFFICIAL STAMPS

Official Stamps Nos. O78 to O81 Overprinted in Red, Green or Black

1930 *Perf. 11, 11½*
CO1 A24 10c deep blue (R) 1.25 1.25
CO2 A24 20c yellow brown 1.25 1.25
 a. Vert. pair, imperf. btwn. 14.00
CO3 A24 50c vermilion (Bk) 1.40 1.40
CO4 A24 1p emerald (R) 1.25 1.25
Nos. CO1-CO4 (4) 5.15 5.15

OA1

Green Surcharge

CO5 OA1 5c on 6c red vio 1.00 1.00
 a. "1910" for "1930" 2.75 2.75
 b. "1920" for "1930" 2.75 2.75

The overprint exists in other colors and on other denominations but the status of these is questioned.

Official Stamps of 1931 Overprinted

1931 Unwmk. Perf. 12

CO6 O2 1c ultra .35 .35
CO7 O2 2c black brown .85 .85
CO8 O2 5c olive gray 1.00 1.00
CO9 O2 6c orange red 1.00 1.00
 a. Inverted overprint 24.00 24.00
CO10 O2 10c dark green 1.25 1.25
CO11 O2 15c olive brown 2.00 1.75
 a. Inverted overprint 20.00 20.00
CO12 O2 20c red brown 2.00 1.75
CO13 O2 50c gray violet 1.40 1.40
CO14 O2 1p deep orange 2.00 1.75
 Nos. CO6-CO14 (9) 11.85 11.10

In the setting of the overprint there are numerous errors in the spelling and punctuation, letters omitted and similar varieties.
This set is known with blue overprint. A similar overprint is known in larger type, but its status has not been fully determined.

Postage Stamps of 1918-30 Surcharged Type "a" or Type "b" (#CO22-CO23) in Green, Black, Red and Blue

a

b

1933 Wmk. 209, Unwmk.

CO15 A39 20c on 2c #295 (G) 3.25 3.25
CO16 A39 20c on 2c #296 (G) 3.25 3.25
CO17 A39 20c on 2c #297 (G) 3.25 3.25
CO17A A39 40c on 2c #295 2.00 2.00
CO18 A39 40c on 2c #297 (G) 7.00 7.00
CO18A A39 40c on 2c #297 4.25 4.25
CO19 A28 40c on 5c #246 4.25 4.25
CO19A A28 40c on 5c #247 7.00 7.00
CO20 A28 40c on 5c #266 15.00 15.00
CO20A A28 40c on 5c #267 9.00 9.00
CO20B A28 40c on 5c #267 (R) 14.00 14.00
CO21 A20 70c on 5c #183 3.00 3.00
CO22 A24 70c on 10c #214 (R) 3.25 3.25
CO23 A22 1 l on 20c #191 (Bl) 3.25 3.25
CO24 A24 1 l on 50c #216 (Bl) 14.00 14.00
CO25 A22 1.20 l on 1p #193 (Bl) 1.00 1.00
 Nos. CO15-CO25 (16) 96.75 96.75

Official Stamps of 1915-29 Surcharged Type "a" or Type "b" (#CO28-CO29, CO33-CO41, CO43) in Black, Red, Green, Orange, Carmine or Blue

CO26 O1 40c on 5c #O84 (Bk) 1.00 1.00
CO27 O1 40c on 5c #O84 (R) 25.00 25.00
CO28 A24 60c on 6c #O77 (Bk) .70 .70
CO29 A24 60c on 6c #O77 (G) 25.00 25.00
CO30 A20 70c on 5c #O60 (Bk) 5.25 5.25
CO31 A19 70c on 10c #O62 (R) 9.00 9.00
CO32 A19 70c on 10c #O62 (Bk) 7.75 7.75
CO33 A22 70c on 10c #O70 (R) 4.50 4.00
CO34 A24 70c on 10c #O78 (O) 3.50 3.50
CO35 A24 70c on 10c #O78 (C) 4.50 4.50
CO36 A22 70c on 15c #O71 (R) 87.50 87.50
CO37 A22 90c on 10c #O70 (R) 5.25 5.25
CO38 A22 90c on 15c #O71 (R) 8.00 8.00
CO38A A24 1 l on 2c #O76 1.40 1.40
CO39 A22 1 l on 20c #O72 2.50 2.50
CO39A A24 1 l on 20c #O79 3.75 3.75
CO40 A22 1 l on 50c #O73 1.90 1.90
CO41 A24 1 l on 50c #O80 4.25 4.25
CO42 A20 1.20 l on 1p #O65 9.00 7.00
CO43 A24 1.20 l on 1p #O81 3.00 3.00
 Nos. CO26-CO43 (20) 212.75 210.25

Varieties of foregoing surcharges exist.

Merchant Flag and Seal of Honduras
OA2

1939, Feb. 27 Unwmk. Perf. 12½

CO44 OA2 2c dp blue & grn .20 .20
CO45 OA2 5c dp blue & org .20 .20
CO46 OA2 8c dp blue & brn .20 .20
CO47 OA2 15c dp blue & car .30 .20
CO48 OA2 46c dp blue & ol grn .40 .30
CO49 OA2 50c dp blue & vio .50 .30
CO50 OA2 1 l dp blue & red brn 1.75 1.25
CO51 OA2 2 l dp blue & red org 3.75 2.25
 Nos. CO44-CO51 (8) 7.30 4.90

For overprints and surcharges see #C101-C117.

Types of Air Post Stamps of 1952 Overprinted in Red

Perf. 13½x14, 14x13½

1952 Engr. Unwmk.

CO52 AP65 1c rose lil & ol .20 .20
CO53 AP65 2c brown & vio .20 .20
CO54 AP65 8c dp car & blk .20 .20
CO55 AP66 16c pur & dk grn .25 .25
CO56 AP65 30c dk bl & blk .50 .50
CO57 AP65 1 l dk grn & dk brown 1.75 1.75
CO58 AP65 2 l bl & red brn 3.50 3.50
CO59 AP66 5 l red org & blk 8.50 8.50
 Nos. CO52-CO59 (8) 15.10 15.10

Queen Isabella I of Spain, 500th birth anniv.
For overprints and surcharge, see Nos. CE1, CO110.

No. C222 and Types of Air Post Stamps of 1953 Overprinted in Red

Engraved; Center of 1c Litho.

1953, Dec. 18 Perf. 12½

Frames in Black

CO60 AP67 1c ultra & vio bl .20 .20
CO61 AP97 2c dp blue grn .20 .20
CO62 AP67 3c orange .20 .20
CO63 AP67 5c dp carmine .20 .20
CO64 AP67 15c dk brown .20 .20
CO65 AP67 30c purple .35 .35
CO66 AP67 1 l olive gray 3.25 2.25
CO67 AP67 2 l lilac rose 4.00 3.00
CO68 AP67 5 l ultra 9.25 7.00
 Nos. CO60-CO68 (9) 17.85 13.60

Issued to honor the United Nations.

Types of Air Post Stamps Overprinted in Red

Engraved; 8c Lithographed

1956, Oct. 3 Perf. 13x12½

CO69 AP68 1c blk & brn car .20 .20
CO70 AP69 2c black & mag .20 .20
CO71 AP68 3c blk & rose vio .20 .20
CO72 AP69 4c black & org .20 .20
CO73 AP69 5c black & bl grn .20 .20
CO74 AP68 8c violet & multi .20 .20
CO75 AP68 10c blk & red brn .20 .20
CO76 AP68 12c blk & car rose .20 .20
CO77 AP68 15c carmine & blk .20 .20
CO78 AP68 20c black & ol brn .20 .20
CO79 AP69 24c black & blue .20 .20
CO80 AP68 25c blk & rose vio .20 .20
CO81 AP68 30c black & grn .20 .20
CO82 AP69 40c blk & red org .25 .25
CO83 AP69 50c blk & brn red .30 .30
CO84 AP68 60c blk & rose vio .40 .40
CO85 AP68 1 l black & brn 1.40 1.10
CO86 AP69 2 l black & dk bl 2.75 2.25
CO87 AP69 5 l black & vio bl 5.75 5.25
 Nos. CO69-CO87 (19) 13.45 12.15

OFICIAL

Nos. C269-C278 Overprinted Vertically in Red (Horizontally on Nos. CO89 and CO91)

1957, Oct. 21 Litho. Perf. 13

Frames in Black

CO88 AP70 1c buff & aqua .20 .20
CO89 AP70 2c org, pur & emer .20 .20
CO90 AP70 5c pink & ultra .20 .20
 a. Inverted overprint
CO91 AP70 8c orange, vio & ol .20 .20
CO92 AP70 10c violet & brn .20 .20
CO93 AP70 12c lt grn & ultra .20 .20
CO94 AP70 15c green & brn .20 .20
CO95 AP70 30c pink & sl .55 .25
CO96 AP70 1 l blue & brn 1.40 1.00
CO97 AP70 2 l lt grn & sl 2.75 2.25
 Nos. CO88-CO97 (10) 6.10 4.90

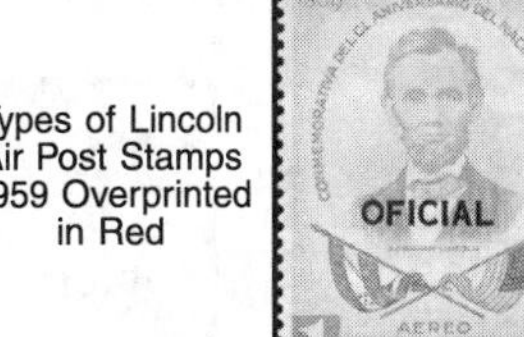

Types of Lincoln Air Post Stamps 1959 Overprinted in Red

1959 Engr. Perf. 13½

Flags in National Colors

CO98 AP72 1c ocher .20 .20
CO99 AP73 2c gray olive .20 .20
 a. Inverted overprint
CO100 AP73 3c red brown .20 .20
CO101 AP73 5c ultra .20 .20
CO102 AP73 10c dull purple .20 .20
 a. Overprint omitted
CO103 AP73 12c red orange .20 .20
CO104 AP72 15c dark brown .20 .20
CO105 AP73 25c black .20 .20
CO106 AP73 50c dark car .30 .25
CO107 AP73 1 l purple .75 .65
CO108 AP73 2 l dark blue 1.40 1.10
 a. Min. sheet of 6, 2c, 5c, 12c, 15c, 50c, 2 l, imperf. 2.50 2.00
CO109 AP73 5 l green 4.50 3.75
 Nos. CO98-CO109 (12) 8.55 7.35

Catalogue values for unused stamps in this section, from this point to the end of the section, are for Never Hinged items.

No. CO55 Overprinted: "IN MEMORIAM / Sir Winston / Churchill / 1874-1965"

1965, Dec. 20 Perf. 14x13½

CO110 AP66 16c purple & dk grn 1.00 1.00

See note after No. C379.

Nos. C336-C344 Overprinted in Red:

1965 Photo. Perf. 14

Black Design and Inscription

CO111 AP76 1c yellow green .20 .20
CO112 AP76 2c pale rose lil .20 .20
CO113 AP76 5c light ultra .20 .20
CO114 AP76 8c bluish grn .20 .20
CO115 AP76 10c buff .25 .25
CO116 AP76 12c lemon .30 .30
CO117 AP76 1 l light ocher 3.50 3.25
CO118 AP76 2 l pale olive grn 7.75 7.00
CO119 AP76 3 l rose 9.50 8.50
 Nos. CO111-CO119 (9) 22.10 20.10

OFFICIAL STAMPS

Type of Regular Issue of 1890 Overprinted in Red

1890 Unwmk. Perf. 12

O1 A5 1c pale yellow .20
O2 A5 2c pale yellow .20
O3 A5 5c pale yellow .20
O4 A5 10c pale yellow .20
O5 A5 20c pale yellow .20
O6 A5 25c pale yellow .20
O7 A5 30c pale yellow .20
O8 A5 40c pale yellow .20
O9 A5 50c pale yellow .20
O10 A5 75c pale yellow .20
O11 A5 1p pale yellow .20
 Nos. O1-O11 (11) 2.20

Type of Regular Issue of 1891 Overprinted in Red

1891

O12 A6 1c yellow .20
O13 A6 2c yellow .20
O14 A6 5c yellow .20
O15 A6 10c yellow .20
O16 A6 20c yellow .20
O17 A6 25c yellow .20
O18 A6 30c yellow .20
O19 A6 40c yellow .20
O20 A6 50c yellow .20
O21 A6 75c yellow .20
O22 A6 1p yellow .20
 Nos. O12-O22 (11) 2.20

Nos. O1 to O22 were never placed in use. Cancellations were applied to remainders. They exist with overprint inverted, double, triple and omitted; also, imperf. and part perf.

Regular Issue of 1898 Overprinted

1898-99 Perf. 11½

O23 A12 5c dl ultra .20
O24 A12 10c dark bl .20
O25 A12 20c dull org .30
O26 A12 50c org red .35
O27 A12 1p blue grn .60
 Nos. O23-O27 (5) 1.65

Counterfeits of basic stamps and of overprint exist.

Regular Issue of 1911 Overprinted

1911-15 *Perf. 12, 14*

Carmine Overprint

O28 A15 1c violet 1.50 .65
a. Inverted overprint 2.00
b. Double overprint 2.00
O29 A15 6c ultra 2.50 2.00
a. Inverted overprint 2.50
O30 A15 10c blue 1.50 1.25
a. "OFICAIL" 2.50
b. Double overprint 3.50
O31 A15 20c yellow 15.00 12.00
O32 A15 50c brown 8.00 7.00
O33 A15 1p ol grn 12.00 10.00
Nos. O28-O33 (6) 40.50 32.90

Black Overprint

O34 A15 2c green 1.00 .70
a. "CFICIAL" 5.00
O35 A15 5c carmine 1.50 1.00
a. Perf. 12 7.50 5.00
O36 A15 6c ultra 4.50 4.50
O37 A15 10c blue 4.00 4.00
O38 A15 20c yellow 5.00 5.00
O39 A15 50c brown 5.50 4.00
Nos. O34-O39 (6) 21.50 19.20

Counterfeits of overprint of Nos. O28-O39 exist.

With Additional Surcharge

1913-14

O40 A15 1c on 5c car 1.75 1.50
O41 A15 2c on 5c car 2.00 1.50
O42 A15 10c on 1c vio 4.00 3.50
a. "OFICIAL" inverted 7.50
O43 A15 20c on 1c vio 3.00 2.50
Nos. O40-O43 (4) 10.75 9.00

On No. O40 the surcharge reads "1 cent."
Nos. O40-O43 exist with double surcharge.

No. O43 Surcharged Vertically in Black, Yellow or Maroon

1914

O44 A15 10c on 20c on 1c 20.00 20.00
a. Maroon surcharge 20.00 20.00
O45 A15 10c on 20c on 1c (Y) 40.00 40.00

No. O35 Surcharged

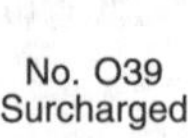

1915

O46 A15 10c on 5c car *20.00 20.00*

No. O39 Surcharged

O47 A15 20c on 50c brn 5.00 5.00

Regular Issues of 1913-14 Overprinted in Red or Black

1915 *Perf. 11½*

O48 A17 1c brn (R) .40 .40
a. "OFICAIL" 5.00
O49 A17 2c car (Bk) .40 .40
a. "OFICAIL" 5.00
b. Double overprint 4.00
O50 A18 5c ultra (Bk) .45 .45
a. "OFIC" 4.00
O51 A18 5c ultra (R) 1.00 1.00
a. "OFIC"
b. "OFICAIL" 5.00
O52 A18 6c pur (Bk) 1.50 1.50
a. 6c red lil (Bk)
O53 A17 10c brn (Bk) 1.25 1.25
O54 A17 20c brn (Bk) 3.00 3.00
O55 A17 20c brn (R) 3.00 3.00
a. Double overprint (R+Bk) 10.00
b. "OFICAIL" 5.00
O56 A18 50c rose (Bk) 6.00 6.00
Nos. O48-O56 (9) 17.00 17.00

The 10c blue has the overprint "OFICIAL" in different type from the other stamps of the series. It is stated that forty copies were overprinted for the Postmaster General but the stamp was never put in use or on sale at the post office.

No. 152 Surcharged

O57 A17 1c on 2c car 2.00 2.00
a. "0.10" for "0.01" 4.25 4.25
b. "0.20" for "0.01" 4.25 4.25
c. Double surcharge 8.50 8.50
d. As "a," double surcharge 77.50
e. As "b," double surcharge 77.50

Regular Issue of 1915-16 Overprinted in Black or Red.

1915-16

O58 A19 1c choc (Bk) .20 .20
O59 A19 2c car (Bk) .20 .20
a. Tête bêche pair 1.25 1.25
b. Double overprint 2.00
c. Double overprint, one inverted 2.00
d. "b" and "c" in tête bêche pair
O60 A20 5c brt blue (R) .30 .30
a. Inverted overprint 3.00
O61 A20 6c deep pur (R) .40 .40
a. Black overprint 3.00
b. Inverted overprint 2.00 2.00
O62 A19 10c dl bl (R) .40 .40
O63 A19 20c red brn (Bk) .60 .60
a. Tête bêche pair 2.50
O64 A20 50c red (Bk) 1.75 1.75
O65 A20 1p yel grn (C) 3.75 3.75
Nos. O58-O65 (8) 7.60 7.60

The 6c, 10c and 1p exist imperf.

Regular Issue of 1919 Overprinted

1921

O66 A22 1c brown *2.25 2.25*
a. Inverted overprint 3.00 3.00
O67 A22 2c carmine *6.50 6.50*
a. Inverted overprint 3.00 3.00
O68 A22 5c lilac rose *6.50 6.50*
a. Inverted overprint 3.00
O69 A22 6c brt vio .50 .50
a. Inverted overprint
O70 A22 10c dull blue .60 .60
a. Double overprint
O71 A22 15c light blue .70 .70
a. Inverted overprint 2.00
b. Double ovpt., one inverted 4.00
O72 A22 20c brown 1.00 1.00
O73 A22 50c light brown 1.50 1.50
O74 A22 1p yellow green 3.00 3.00
Nos. O66-O74 (9) 22.55 22.55

Regular Issue of 1924 Overprinted

1924 *Perf. 11, 11½*

O75 A24 1c olive brn .20 .20
O76 A24 2c deep rose .20 .20
O77 A24 6c red vio .30 .30
O78 A24 10c deep bl .45 .45
O79 A24 20c yel brn .60 .60
O80 A24 50c vermilion 1.25 1.25
O81 A24 1p emerald 2.00 2.00
Nos. O75-O81 (7) 5.00 5.00

J. C. del Valle — O1

Designs: 2c, J. R. Molina. 5c, Coffee tree. 10c, J. T. Reyes. 20c, Tegucigalpa Cathedral. 50c, San Lorenzo Creek. 1p, Radio station.

1929 **Litho.** **Wmk. 209** *Perf. 11½*

O82 O1 1c blue .20 .20
O83 O1 2c carmine .20 .20
a. 2c rose .20 .20
O84 O1 5c purple .35 .35
O85 O1 10c emerald .50 .35
O86 O1 20c dk bl .60 .60
O87 O1 50c org, grn & bl 1.00 1.00
O88 O1 1p buff 1.75 1.75
Nos. O82-O88 (7) 4.60 4.45

Nos. O82-O88 exist imperf.
For overprints and surcharges see Nos. 282, 284, C37-C40, C59, C62-C63, CO26-CO27.

View of Tegucigalpa O2

1931 **Unwmk.** **Engr.** *Perf. 12*

O89 O2 1c ultra .30 .20
O90 O2 2c black brn .30 .20
O91 O2 5c olive gray .35 .25
O92 O2 6c orange red .40 .30
O93 O2 10c dark green .50 .35
O94 O2 15c olive brn .65 .40
O95 O2 20c red brown .75 .50
O96 O2 50c gray vio 1.00 .65
O97 O2 1p dp orange 1.75 1.75
Nos. O89-O97 (9) 6.00 4.60

For overprints see #CO6-CO14, O98-O105.

Official Stamps of 1931 Overprinted in Black

1936-37

O98 O2 1c ultra .25 .25
O99 O2 2c black brn .25 .25
a. Inverted overprint 10.00
O100 O2 5c olive gray .30 .30
O101 O2 6c red orange .40 .40
O102 O2 10c dark green .40 .40
O103 O2 15c olive brown .50 .50
a. Inverted overprint 5.00
O104 O2 20c red brown 1.00 1.00
a. "1938-1935"
O105 O2 50c gray violet 4.00 3.00
Nos. O98-O105 (8) 7.10 6.10

Double overprints exist on 1c and 2c. No. O97 with this overprint is fraudulent.

POSTAL TAX STAMPS

Red Cross PT1

Francisco Morazán PT2

Engr.; Cross Litho.

1941, Aug. 1 **Unwmk.** *Perf. 12*

RA1 PT1 1c blue & carmine .25 .20

Obligatory on all domestic or foreign mail, the tax to be used by the Honduran Red Cross.

1941, Aug. 1 **Engr.**

RA2 PT2 1c copper brown .40 .20

Francisco Morazan, 100th anniv. of death.

Mother and Child — PT3

Henri Dunant — PT4

1945 **Engr.; Cross Litho.**

RA3 PT3 1c ol brn, car & bl .25 .20

The tax was for the Honduran Red Cross.

Similar to Type of 1945
Large Red Cross

1950

RA4 PT3 1c olive brn & red .25 .20

The tax was for the Honduran Red Cross.

1959 *Perf. 13x13½*

RA5 PT4 1c blue & red .25 .20

The tax was for the Red Cross.

Catalogue values for unused stamps in this section, from this point to the end of the section, are for Never Hinged items.

Henri Dunant — PT5

No. RA7, as PT5, but redrawn; country name panel at bottom, value at right, "El poder . . ." at top.

1964, Dec. 15 **Litho.** *Perf. 11*

RA6 PT5 1c brt grn & red .25 .20
RA7 PT5 1c brown & red .25 .20

The tax was for the Red Cross.

Nurse and Patient — PT6

1969, June **Litho.** *Perf. 13½*

RA8 PT6 1c light blue & red .25 .20

The tax was for the Red Cross.
For surcharges see Nos. 387-391.

HONG KONG

'häŋ,käŋ

LOCATION — A peninsula and island in southeast China at the mouth of the Canton River
GOVT. — Special Administrative Area of China (PRC) (as of 7/1/97)
AREA — 426 sq. mi.
POP. — 6,847,125 (1999 est.)
CAPITAL — Victoria

100 Cents = 1 Dollar

Catalogue values for unused stamps in this country are for Never Hinged items, beginning with Scott 174 in the regular postage section, Scott B1 in the semi-postal section and Scott J13 in the postage due section.

Watermark

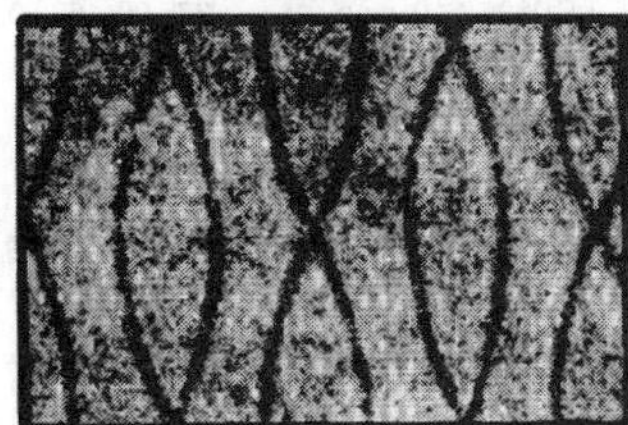

Wmk. 340

Values for unused stamps are for examples with original gum as defined in the catalogue introduction. Very fine examples of Nos. 1-25, 29-48, 61-66d and 69-70a will have perforations touching the design on at least one side due to the narrow spacing of the stamps on the plates. Stamps with perfs clear of the design on all four sides are scarce and will command higher prices.

Queen Victoria — A1

Unwmk.

1862, Dec. 8 Typo. Perf. 14

1 A1 2c pale brown 300.00 75.00
a. 2c deep brown 450.00 85.00
2 A1 8c buff 475.00 40.00
3 A1 12c blue 400.00 40.00
4 A1 18c lilac 400.00 35.00
5 A1 24c green 1,000. 80.00
6 A1 48c rose 2,750. 175.00
7 A1 96c gray 3,500. 300.00

1863-80 Wmk. 1

8 A1 2c brown ('65) 100.00 6.00
a. 2c deep brown ('64) 225.00 24.00
9 A1 2c dull rose ('80) 110.00 15.00
10 A1 4c slate 90.00 7.50
a. 4c greenish grey 275.00 37.50
b. 4c bluish slate 450.00 20.00
11 A1 5c ultra ('80) 400.00 27.50
12 A1 6c lilac 325.00 7.50
a. 6c violet 375.00 9.00
13 A1 8c org buff ('65) 375.00 10.00
a. 8c bright orange 325.00 9.00
b. 8c brownish orange 350.00 10.00
14 A1 10c violet ('80) 425.00 13.50
15 A1 12c light blue 27.50 5.00
a. 12c light greenish blue 850.00 27.50
b. 12c deep blue 175.00 10.00
16 A1 16c yellow ('77) 1,400. 60.00
17 A1 18c lilac ('66) 5,500. 250.00
18 A1 24c green ('65) 450.00 9.00
a. 24c deep green 800.00 24.00
19 A1 30c vermilion 800.00 12.00
20 A1 30c violet ('71) 190.00 5.50
21 A1 48c rose carmine 800.00 22.50
22 A1 48c brown ('80) 1,200. 50.00
23 A1 96c bister ('65) *30,000.* 575.00
24 A1 96c gray ('66) 1,000. 42.50

Imperfs. are plate proofs.

1874 Perf. 12½

25 A1 4c slate 8,500. 250.

See #36-49. For surcharges or overprints on stamps of type A1 see #29-35B, 51-56, 61-66, 69-70.

A2

A3

A4

1874 Engr. Wmk. 1 Perf. 15½x15

26 A2 $2 sage green 400.00 50.00
27 A3 $3 violet 275.00 32.50
28 A4 $10 rose 9,000. 625.00

Nos. 26-28 are revenues which were used postally. Used values are for postally canceled copies. Black "Paid All" cancels are fiscal usage.

See Nos. 57-59. For surcharges see Nos. 50, 60, 67.

Nos. 17 and 20 Surcharged in Black:

16 cents. *28 cents.*

1876 Perf. 14

29 A1 16c on 18c lilac 2,250. 140.00
30 A1 28c on 30c violet 1,250. 45.00

Stamps of 1863-80 Surcharged in Black — 5 cents.

1879-80

31 A1 5c on 8c org ('80) 900.00 80.00
a. Inverted surcharge *10,000.*
b. Double surcharge *17,500.*
32 A1 5c on 18c lilac 700.00 55.00
33 A1 10c on 12c blue 800.00 55.00
34 A1 10c on 16c yellow 7,500. 125.00
a. Inverted surcharge *30,000.*
35 A1 10c on 24c green ('80) 1,400. 75.00

Most copies of No. 31a are damaged.

Nos. 16-17, 35B Surcharged in Black

A5

A6

1879

35A A5 3c on 16c on card 325.00 1,550.
Stamp off card 325.00
35B A5 5c on 18c on card 325. 1,825.
Stamp off card 350.00
35C A6 3c on 5c on 18c on card 6,500. *7,000.*
Stamp off card *6,500.*

Nos. 35A-35C were sold affixed to postal cards. Most used copies are found off card so values are given for these.

Type of 1862

1882-1902 Wmk. 2 Perf. 14

36 A1 2c rose 18.00 1.00
a. 2c dull rose 18.00 1.00
37 A1 2c green ('00) 14.00 1.00
38 A1 4c slate ('96) 10.00 1.00
39 A1 4c car rose ('00) 15.00 1.00
40 A1 5c ultramarine 22.50 1.00
41 A1 5c yellow ('00) 24.00 6.00
42 A1 10c lilac 525.00 9.00
43 A1 10c green 100.00 1.50
a. 10c blue green 1,800. 27.50
44 A1 10c vio, *red* ('91) 20.00 1.00
45 A1 10c ultra ('00) 50.00 1.75
46 A1 12c blue ('02) 40.00 *50.00*
47 A1 30c gray grn ('91) 80.00 15.00
a. 30c yellow green 125.00 19.00
48 A1 30c brown ('01) 35.00 19.00
Nos. 36-48 (13) 953.50 108.25

No. 47 has fugitive ink. Both colors will turn dull green upon soaking.

The 2c rose, perf 12, is most likely a proof.

No. 28 Surcharged in Black — 12 CENTS.

1880 Wmk. 1 Perf. 15½x15

50 A4 12c on $10 rose 800.00 300.00

Surcharged in Black

1885-91 Wmk. 2 Perf. 14

51 A1 20c on 30c ver 87.50 5.00
a. Double surcharge —
52 A1 20c on 30c gray grn ('91) 110.00 *125.00*
53 A1 50c on 48c brown 425.00 22.50
54 A1 50c on 48c lil ('91) 225.00 *240.00*
55 A1 $1 on 96c ol gray 575.00 50.00
56 A1 $1 on 96c vio, *red* ('91) 750.00 300.00

For overprints see Nos. 61-63.

Types of 1874 and

A7

1890-1902 Wmk. 2 Perf. 14

56A A7 2c dull purple 70.00 17.00

Wmk. 1

57 A2 $2 gray green 375.00 200.00
58 A3 $3 lilac ('02) 475.00 325.00
59 A4 $10 gray grn ('92) *11,500. 11,500.*

Due to a shortage of 2c postage stamps, No. 56A was authorized for postal use December 24-30, 1890.

Fake postmarks are known on No. 59. Beware also of fiscal cancels altered to resemble postal cancels.

For surcharge see No. 68.

Type of 1874 Surcharged in Black — 5 DOLLARS

1891, Jan. 1 Wmk. 2

60 A4 $5 on $10 vio, *red* 325.00 92.50

Nos. 52, 54 and 56 Handstamped with Chinese characters

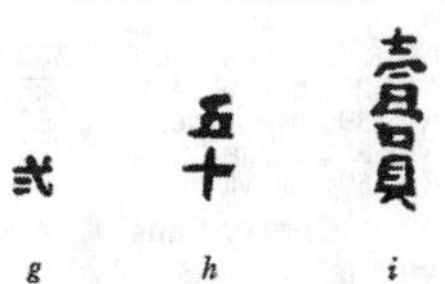

g h i

61 A1 (g) 20c on 30c gray green 30.00 4.50
a. 20c on 30c dull green 55.00 5.75
b. "20 CENTS" double
62 A1 (h) 50c on 48c lilac 67.50 5.00
63 A1 (i) $1 on 96c vio, *red* 375.00 22.50

No. 61 may be found with Chinese character 2, 2½ or 3mm high.

The handstamped Chinese surcharges on Nos. 61-63 exist in several varieties including inverted, double, triple, misplaced, omitted and (on #63) on both front and back.

Nos. 43 and 20 Surcharged

1891

64 A1 7c on 10c green 60.00 7.50
a. Double surcharge *6,000. 1,500.*

Wmk. 1

65 A1 14c on 30c violet 140.00 47.50

Beware of faked varieties.

No. 36 Overprinted in Black

1891, Jan. 22 Wmk. 2

66 A1 2c rose *550.00* 110.00
a. Double overprint *17,500. 11,000.*
b. "U" of "JUBILEE" shorter *800.00* 140.00
c. "J" of "JUBILEE" shorter *800.00* 140.00
d. Tall "K" in "KONG" *1,100.* 400.00

50th anniversary of the colony.
Beware of faked varieties.

No. 26 Surcharged (Chinese Handstamped)

1897, Sept. Wmk. 1 Perf. 15½x15

67 A2 $1 on $2 sage green 225.00 95.00
a. Without Chinese surcharge 5,000. 4,000.

On No. 57

Perf. 14

68 A2 $1 on $2 gray green 250.00 100.00
a. Without Chinese surcharge 1,600. 1,300.

Handstamp Surcharged in Black

1898 Wmk. 2

69 A1 10c on 30c gray grn 50.00 *65.00*
a. Large Chinese surcharge 1,250. 900.00
b. Without Chinese surcharge 600.00 *1,000.*
70 A1 $1 on 96c black 160.00 25.00
a. Without Chinese surcharge 2,800. *3,500.*

The Chinese surcharge is added separately.
See notes below Nos. 61-63. The small Chinese surcharge is illustrated.

King Edward VII — A10

1903 Wmk. 2

71 A10 1c brown & lilac 2.00 .40
72 A10 2c gray green 7.00 1.25
73 A10 4c violet, *red* 9.00 .35
74 A10 5c org & gray grn 10.00 7.75
75 A10 8c violet & black 8.00 1.10
76 A10 10c ultra & lil, *bl* 30.00 1.25
77 A10 12c red vio & gray grn, *yel* 8.00 3.75
78 A10 20c org brn & brnsh gray 38.00 2.75
79 A10 30c blk & gray grn 38.00 17.50
80 A10 50c red vio & gray green 30.00 26.00
81 A10 $1 olive grn & lil 65.00 19.00
82 A10 $2 scar & black 190.00 *200.00*

83 A10 $3 dp blue & blk 240.00 *275.00*
84 A10 $5 blue grn & lil 375.00 375.00
85 A10 $10 org & blk, *bl* 850.00 350.00
Nos. 71-85 (15) 1,900. 1,281.

1904-11 Wmk. 3

Ordinary or Chalky Paper

86 A10 1c brown ('10) 1.00 .20
a. Booklet pane of 4
87 A10 2c gray green 2.75 1.10
88 A10 2c deep green 17.00 1.50
a. Booklet pane of 4
b. Booklet pane of 12
89 A10 4c violet, *red* 3.00 .20
90 A10 4c carmine 3.75 .35
a. Booklet pane of 4
b. Booklet pane of 12
91 A10 5c org & gray grn 6.50 4.50
92 A10 6c red vio & org ('07) 12.00 2.75
93 A10 8c vio & blk ('07) 5.00 1.25
94 A10 10c ultra & lil, *bl* 15.00 .35
95 A10 10c ultramarine 9.00 .40
96 A10 12c red vio & gray grn, *yel* ('07) 7.50 5.75
97 A10 20c org brn & brnsh gray 16.00 1.50
98 A10 20c ol grn & vio ('11) 40.00 37.50
99 A10 30c blk & gray grn 17.50 7.00
100 A10 30c org & vio ('11) 60.00 16.50
101 A10 50c red vio & gray green 37.50 7.50
102 A10 50c blk, *grn* ('11) 32.50 12.50
103 A10 $1 ol grn & lil 90.00 12.50
104 A10 $2 scar & black 125.00 82.50
105 A10 $2 blk & car ('10) 250.00 175.00
106 A10 $3 dp bl & blk 150.00 150.00
107 A10 $5 bl grn & lil 325.00 275.00
108 A10 $10 org & blk, *bl* 1,300. 700.00
Nos. 86-108 (23) 2,526. 1,495.

Nos. 86, 88, 90, 94 and 95 are on ordinary paper only. Nos. 92, 93, 96, 98, 100, 102, 105, 106 and 107 are on chalky paper and the others of the issue are on both papers.

The 4c, 5c, 8c, 12c 20c, 50c, $2 and $5 denominations of type A10 are expressed in colored letters or numerals and letters on a colorless background.

King George V
A11 A12

A13

A14

A15

1912-14 Ordinary Paper

109 A11 1c brown 1.75 .35
a. Booklet pane of 12
110 A11 2c deep green 5.00 .35
a. Booklet pane of 12
111 A12 4c carmine 4.00 .35
a. Booklet pane of 12
b. Booklet pane of 4
112 A13 6c orange 4.00 .65
113 A12 8c gray 22.50 3.75
114 A11 10c ultramarine 35.00 .35

Chalky Paper

115 A14 12c vio, *yel* 3.00 *4.00*
116 A14 20c ol grn & vio 4.00 .65
117 A15 25c red vio & dl violet 13.00 *16.00*
118 A13 30c org & violet 27.50 4.00
119 A14 50c black, *green* 8.50 .40
a. 50c black, *emerald* 20.00 15.00
b. 50c black, *bl grn*, ol back 1,000. 25.00
c. 50c black, *emer*, ol back 21.00 4.00
120 A11 $1 blue & vio, *bl* 25.00 1.40
121 A14 $2 black & red 110.00 30.00
122 A13 $3 vio & green 160.00 55.00
123 A14 $5 red & grn, *grn* 400.00 225.00
a. $5 red & grn, *bl grn*, ol back 900.00 200.00
124 A13 $10 blk & vio, *red* 600.00 67.50
Nos. 109-124 (16) 1,423. 409.75

For overprints see British Offices in China #1-27.

1914, May Surface-colored Paper

125 A14 12c violet, *yel* 7.00 *10.50*
126 A14 50c black, *green* 13.00 4.00
127 A14 $5 red & grn, *grn* 475.00 240.00
Nos. 125-127 (3) 495.00 254.50

Stamp of 1912-14 Redrawn

二 instead of 弍 at upper left.

1919, Sept. Chalky Paper

128 A15 25c red vio & dl vio 125.00 47.50

Types of 1912-14 Issue

1921-37 Wmk. 4

Ordinary Paper

129 A11 1c brown 1.00 .40
130 A11 2c deep green 2.25 .35
131 A11 2c gray ('37) 15.00 5.50
132 A12 3c gray ('31) 4.00 1.00
133 A12 4c rose red 3.50 .75
134 A12 5c violet ('31) 4.50 .20
135 A12 8c gray 12.00 *42.50*
136 A12 8c orange 2.50 1.10
137 A11 10c ultramarine 2.25 .20

Chalky Paper

138 A14 12c vio, *yel* ('33) 11.00 .65
139 A14 20c ol grn & dl vio 3.50 .25
140 A15 25c red vio & dl vio, redrawn 2.75 .45
141 A13 30c yel & violet 12.00 2.00
142 A14 50c blk, *emerald* 12.00 .20
143 A11 $1 ultra & vio, *bl* 25.00 .80
144 A14 $2 black & red 100.00 6.00
145 A13 $3 dl vio & grn ('26) 175.00 47.50
146 A14 $5 red & grn, *emer* ('25) 350.00 60.00
Nos. 129-146 (18) 738.25 169.85

Common Design Types pictured following the introduction.

Silver Jubilee Issue

Common Design Type

1935, May 6 Engr. *Perf. 11x12*

147 CD301 3c black & ultra 3.00 1.25
148 CD301 5c indigo & grn 10.00 1.25
149 CD301 10c ultra & brn 25.00 4.00
150 CD301 20c brn vio & ind 30.00 7.50
Nos. 147-150 (4) 68.00 14.00
Set, never hinged 175.00

Coronation Issue

Common Design Type

1937, May 12 *Perf. 11x11½*

151 CD302 4c deep green 4.00 1.00
152 CD302 15c dark carmine 8.75 1.75
153 CD302 25c deep ultra 11.25 3.50
Nos. 151-153 (3) 24.00 6.25
Set, never hinged 40.00

King George VI — A16

1938-48 Typo. *Perf. 14*

Ordinary Paper

154 A16 1c brown .40 .40
155 A16 2c gray .55 .20
156 A16 4c orange .70 .70
157 A16 5c green .35 .20
157B A16 8c brown red ('41) .75 *1.40*
c. Imperf., pair — —
158 A16 10c violet 1.75 .50
159 A16 15c carmine .35 .20
159A A16 20c gray ('46) .35 .20
159B A16 20c rose red ('48) 1.75 .25
160 A16 25c ultramarine 12.00 .80
160A A16 25c gray ol ('46) 1.25 .80
161 A16 30c olive bister 77.50 .85
161B A16 30c lt ultra ('46) 1.50 .20
162 A16 50c red violet 1.75 .50

Chalky Paper

162B A16 80c lilac rose ('48) 1.40 .60
163 A16 $1 lilac & ultra 3.75 1.75
163B A16 $1 dp org & grn ('46) 2.50 .20
164 A16 $2 dp org & grn 37.50 9.50
164A A16 $2 vio & red ('46) 4.50 1.50
165 A16 $5 lilac & red 27.50 *30.00*
165A A16 $5 grn & vio ('46) 25.00 3.25
166 A16 $10 grn & vio 200.00 55.00
166A A16 $10 vio & ultra ('46) 47.50 16.00
Nos. 154-166A (23) 450.60 125.00
Set, never hinged 900.00

Coarse Impressions

Ordinary Paper

1941-46 *Perf. 14½x14*

155a A16 2c gray 1.50 *4.50*
156a A16 4c orange ('46) 3.50 3.00
157a A16 5c green 2.00 4.50
158a A16 10c violet 7.00 .20
161a A16 30c dull olive bister 18.00 7.00
162a A16 50c red lilac 22.50 1.00
Nos. 155a-162a (6) 54.50 20.20
Set, never hinged 85.00

A17

1938, Jan. 11 Wmk. 4

167 A17 5c green 30.00 20.00
Never hinged 45.00

No. 167 is a revenue stamp officially authorized to be sold and used for postal purposes. Used Jan. 11-20, 1938. The used price is for the stamp on cover. CTO covers exist.

Street Scene — A18

Hong Kong Bank — A22

Liner and Junk — A19

University of Hong Kong — A20

Harbor — A21

China Clipper and Seaplane A23

Perf. 13½x13, 13x13½

1941, Feb. 26 Engr. Wmk. 4

168 A18 2c sepia & org 1.25 .55
169 A19 4c rose car & vio 3.00 1.40
170 A20 5c yel grn & blk 1.50 .35
171 A21 15c red & black 5.50 1.40
172 A22 25c dp blue & dk brn 9.50 2.75
173 A23 $1 brn org & brt bl 30.00 8.25
Nos. 168-173 (6) 50.75 14.70
Set, never hinged 95.00

Centenary of British rule.

Catalogue values for unused stamps in this section, from this point to the end of the section, are for Never Hinged items.

Peace Issue

Phoenix Rising from Flames A24

1946, Aug. 29 *Perf. 13x12½*

174 A24 30c car & dp blue 3.50 1.90
175 A24 $1 car & brown 5.75 1.10

Return to peace after WWII.

Silver Wedding Issue

Common Design Types

Perf. 14x14½

1948, Dec. 22 Photo. Wmk. 4

178 CD304 10c purple 2.00 .50

Engr.; Name Typo.

Perf. 11½x11

179 CD305 $10 rose car 375.00 62.50
Set, hinged 175.00

UPU Issue

Common Design Types

Engr.; Name Typo. on 20c & 30c

1949, Oct. 10 *Perf. 13½, 11x11½*

180 CD306 10c violet 3.75 .35
181 CD307 20c deep car 15.00 2.25
182 CD308 30c indigo 12.50 1.25
183 CD309 80c red violet 35.00 7.00
Nos. 180-183 (4) 66.25 10.85
Set, hinged 30.00

Coronation Issue

Common Design Type

1953, June 2 Engr. *Perf. 13½x13*

184 CD312 10c purple & black 8.00 .50
Hinged 3.00

Elizabeth II A25

Arms of University A26

1954-60 Typo. *Perf. 13½x14*

185 A25 5c orange 1.75 .20
a. Imperf., pair *1,100.*
186 A25 10c violet 3.00 .20
187 A25 15c green 4.75 .40
188 A25 20c brown 6.00 .25
189 A25 25c rose red 3.75 .80
190 A25 30c gray 5.50 .20
191 A25 40c blue 4.75 .35
192 A25 50c red violet 5.75 .20
193 A25 65c lt gray ('60) 22.50 7.25
194 A25 $1 org & green 9.00 .20
195 A25 $1.30 bl & ver ('60) 27.50 .85
196 A25 $2 violet & red 15.00 .35
197 A25 $5 green & vio 92.50 1.50
198 A25 $10 violet & ultra 72.50 7.25
Nos. 185-198 (14) 274.25 20.00
Set, hinged 125.00

Nos. 185-187 are on ordinary paper; Nos. 188-198 on chalky paper.

Perf. 11½x12

1961, Sept. 11 Photo. Wmk. 314

199 A26 $1 bl, blk, red, grn & gold 12.00 2.00
a. Gold omitted 1,400.

University of Hong Kong, 50th anniv.

Queen Victoria Statue, Victoria Park, Hong Kong — A27

Queen Elizabeth II — A28

1962, May 4 ***Perf. 14***
200 A27 10c car rose & black .65 .20
201 A27 20c blue & black 2.50 .35
202 A27 50c bister & black 5.50 .75
Nos. 200-202 (3) 8.65 1.30

1st postage stamps of Hong Kong, cent.

Wmk. 314 Upright
1962, Oct. 4 Photo. ***Perf. 14½x14***
Size: 17x21mm
203 A28 5c red orange .60 .20
a. Booklet pane of 4 2.50
204 A28 10c purple 1.40 .20
a. Booklet pane of 4 5.00
205 A28 15c green 3.00 .20
206 A28 20c red brown 1.75 .20
a. Booklet pane of 4 11.00
207 A28 25c lilac rose 2.50 .20
208 A28 30c dark blue 2.50 .20
209 A28 40c Prus green 2.00 .20
210 A28 50c crimson 1.75 .20
a. Booklet pane of 4 25.00
211 A28 65c ultramarine 17.50 1.50
212 A28 $1 dark brown 17.50 .20

Perf. 14x14½
Size: 25½x30½mm
Portrait in Natural Colors
213 A28 $1.30 sky blue 5.00 .20
a. Ocher (sash) omitted 40.00
b. Yellow omitted 40.00
214 A28 $2 fawn 7.00 .20
a. Yellow and ocher (sash) omitted 75.00
b. Yellow omitted 40.00
215 A28 $5 orange 17.50 .95
a. Ocher (sash) omitted 50.00
216 A28 $10 green 30.00 1.90
217 A28 $20 violet blue 140.00 24.00
Nos. 203-217 (15) 250.00 30.55

1966-72 **Wmk. 314 Sideways**
203b A28 5c ('67) .20 .20
204b A28 10c ('67) .40 .20
205a A28 15c ('67) .55 .20
206b A28 20c .75 .20
207a A28 25c ('67) 1.00 .20
208a A28 30c ('70) 1.10 .20
209a A28 40c ('67) 1.25 .20
210b A28 50c ('67) 2.00 .20
211a A28 65c ('67) 8.00 2.75
212a A28 $1 ('67) 8.00 .30
213c A28 $1.30 ('72) 5.75 .90
214c A28 $2 ('71) 16.00 2.50
215b A28 $5 ('71) 65.00 5.50
217a A28 $20 ('72) 190.00 55.00
Nos. 203b-217a (14) 300.00 68.55

Freedom from Hunger Issue
Common Design Type
Perf. 14x14½
1963, June 4 Photo. Wmk. 314
218 CD314 $1.30 green 65.00 9.50

Red Cross Centenary Issue
Common Design Type
1963, Sept. 2 Litho. ***Perf. 13***
219 CD315 10c black & red 1.75 .45
220 CD315 $1.30 ultra & red 45.00 5.50

ITU Issue
Common Design Type
1965, May 17 ***Perf. 11x11½***
221 CD317 10c red lil & yel 4.00 .25
222 CD317 $1.30 apple grn & turq blue 26.00 4.00

Intl. Cooperation Year Issue
Common Design Type
1965, Oct. 25 ***Perf. 14½***
223 CD318 10c blue grn & cl 4.00 .35
224 CD318 $1.30 lt violet & grn 25.00 3.25

Churchill Memorial Issue
Common Design Type
1966, Jan. 24 Photo. ***Perf. 14***
Design in Black, Gold and Carmine Rose
225 CD319 10c bright blue 3.00 .40
226 CD319 50c green 3.50 .85
227 CD319 $1.30 brown 24.00 4.25
228 CD319 $2 violet 37.50 5.75
Nos. 225-228 (4) 68.00 11.25

WHO Headquarters Issue
Common Design Type
1966, Sept. 20 Litho. ***Perf. 14***
229 CD322 10c multicolored 3.00 .25
230 CD322 50c multicolored 10.00 1.75

UNESCO Anniversary Issue
Common Design Type
1966, Dec. 1 Litho. ***Perf. 14***
231 CD323 10c "Education" 4.00 .45
232 CD323 50c "Science" 16.00 2.25
233 CD323 $2 "Culture" 67.50 16.00
Nos. 231-233 (3) 87.50 18.70

Three Rams' Heads A29

Lunar New Year: $1.30, Three rams.

1967, Jan. 17 Photo. ***Perf. 14***
234 A29 10c red, citron & grn 2.25 .50
235 A29 $1.30 red, cit & brt grn 37.50 9.50

Outline of Telephone with Map of South East Asia and Australia A30

1967, Mar. 30 Photo. ***Perf. 12½***
236 A30 $1.30 dk red & blue 22.50 4.50

Completion of the Hong Kong-Malaysia link of the South East Asia Commonwealth Cable, SEACOM.

Monkeys A31

Lunar New Year: $1.30, Two monkey families.

1968, Jan. 23 Wmk. 314 ***Perf. 14***
237 A31 10c crim, blk & gold 2.00 .45
238 A31 $1.30 crim, blk & gold 37.50 8.00

Liner and New Sea Terminal A32

Seacraft: 20c, Pleasure launch and sailing cruiser. 40c, Vehicle ferry. 50c, Passenger ferry. $1, Sampan. $1.30, Junk.

Perf. 13x12½
1968, Apr. 24 Litho. Unwmk.
239 A32 10c multicolored 1.25 .20
240 A32 20c sky blue, bis & black 3.50 .75
241 A32 40c org, rose lil & black 8.75 8.00
242 A32 50c brt red, emer & black 10.00 .55
243 A32 $1 yel, cop red & black 24.00 4.50
244 A32 $1.30 dk bl, brt pink & black 47.50 3.50
Nos. 239-244 (6) 95.00 17.50

Bauhinia Blakeana — A33

Perf. 14x14½
1968, Sept. 25 Photo. Wmk. 314
245 A33 65c shown 9.00 .50
a. Wmkd. sideways ('72) 50.00 16.00
246 A33 $1 Coat of Arms 9.00 .50
a. Wmkd. sideways ('71) 10.00 2.25

Human Rights Flame and "Lamp of Life" A34

1968, Nov. 20 Litho. ***Perf. 13½***
247 A34 10c green, org & blk 3.25 .75
248 A34 50c magenta, yel & blk 9.75 2.00

International Human Rights Year.

Cock A35

Design: $1.30, Cock, vert.

Perf. 13x13½, 13½x13
1969, Feb. 11 Photo. Unwmk.
249 A35 10c brown, blk, org & red 5.75 .50
a. Red omitted 175.00
250 A35 $1.30 ocher, blk, org & red *75.00* 9.50

Lunar New Year, Feb. 17, 1969.

Chinese University Seal — A36

1969, Aug. 26 Unwmk. ***Perf. 13***
251 A36 40c multicolored 10.50 2.00

Chinese University of Hong Kong, founded 1963.

Radar, Globe and Satellite A37

Perf. 14x14½
1969, Sept. 24 Photo. Wmk. 314
252 A37 $1 scar, blk, sil & bl 25.00 5.00

Opening of the satellite earth station (connected through the Indian Ocean satellite Intelsat III) on Stanley Peninsula, Hong Kong.

Chow — A38

Emblem — A39

Lunar New Year (Year of the Dog): $1.30, Chow, horiz.

1970, Jan. 28 ***Perf. 14***
253 A38 10c black & multi 5.00 .50
254 A38 $1.30 green & multi 95.00 12.00

Perf. 13½x13, 13x13½
1970, Mar. 14 Litho. Wmk. 314

25c, Emblem and Chinese junks, horiz.

255 A39 15c multicolored 1.10 .50
256 A39 25c multicolored 2.25 1.00

EXPO '70 Intl. Exposition, Osaka, Japan, Mar. 15-Sept. 13.

"A Compassionate Ship on the Bitter Sea" — A40

1970, Apr. 9 Photo. ***Perf. 14***
257 A40 10c yel green & multi 1.25 .25
258 A40 50c scarlet & multi 5.25 1.00

Centenary of the Tung Wah Group of Hospitals (including schools and various charitable organizations).

A.P.Y. Emblem — A41

1970, Aug. 5 Litho. Wmk. 314
259 A41 10c yellow & multi 1.60 .35

Issued for Asian Productivity Year.

Boar A42

Perf. 13x13½
1971, Jan. 20 Photo. Unwmk.
260 A42 10c yel grn, gold & black 2.75 .50
261 A42 $1.30 vio, gold & blk 40.00 7.00

Lunar New Year.

Scout Emblem and "60" — A43

Perf. 14x14½
1971, July 23 Litho. Wmk. 314
262 A43 10c red, yellow & black .75 .35
263 A43 50c blue, emer & black 4.25 .80
264 A43 $2 vio, lil rose & blk 22.50 4.00
Nos. 262-264 (3) 27.50 5.15

60th anniversary of Hong Kong Boy Scouts.

Festival Emblem A44

Symbolic Flower A45

Festival of Hong Kong: 50c, Dancers, horiz.

1971, Nov. 2 ***Perf. 14***
265 A44 10c lilac & orange 1.50 .20

Perf. 14½
266 A45 50c lilac & multi 3.50 .80
267 A45 $1 lilac & multi 11.00 6.50
Nos. 265-267 (3) 16.00 7.50

Rats A46

Perf. 13½x13

1972, Feb. 8 Photo. Unwmk.

268 A46 10c black, red & gold 5.00 .50
269 A46 $1.30 black, gold & red 45.00 9.50

Lunar New Year.

Cross Harbor Tunnel Entrance — A47

Perf. 14x14½

1972, Oct. 20 Litho. Wmk. 314

270 A47 $1 multicolored 6.50 1.00

Inauguration of Cross Harbor Tunnel linking Victoria and Kowloon.

Silver Wedding Issue, 1972
Common Design Type

Design: Queen Elizabeth II, Prince Philip, phoenix and dragon.

1972, Nov. 20 Photo. Perf. 14x14½

271 CD324 10c citron & multi .65 .25
272 CD324 50c gray & multi 2.50 .65

Ox A48

Lunar New Year: 10c, Ox, vert.

1973, Feb. 3 Perf. 14

273 A48 10c dk brown & red 3.25 .50
274 A48 $1.30 dk brn, yel & org *9.25* 4.50

Elizabeth II — A49

Wmk. 314 Upright; Sideways (15c, 30c, 40c)

1973, June 12 Photo. Perf. 14½x14

Size: 20x24mm

275 A49 10c orange .90 .20
 b. Booklet pane of 4 ('75) 1.40
 d. Watermark sideways (coil) 1.75 1.25
276 A49 15c olive green 7.75 .20
 b. Booklet pane of 4 ('75) 2.10
277 A49 20c bright purple .55 .20
 b. Booklet pane of 4 ('75) 3.75
278 A49 25c deep brown 11.00 .20
279 A49 30c ultramarine 1.10 .20
280 A49 40c blue green 2.75 .20
281 A49 50c red 1.40 .20
 b. Booklet pane of 4 ('75) 9.25
282 A49 65c dp bister 13.00 5.00
283 A49 $1 dk slate green 2.50 .55

Perf. 14x14½

Wmk. 314 Sideways

Size: 28x32mm

284 A49 $1.30 dk pur & yel 7.75 .75
285 A49 $2 dp brn & lt grn 8.75 .90
286 A49 $5 dk vio bl & rose 12.00 3.00

Photo. & Embossed

287 A49 $10 dk sl green & pink 16.50 7.50
288 A49 $20 black & rose 27.50 20.00
 Nos. 275-288 (14) 113.45 39.10

1975-78 Wmk. 373 Perf. 14½x14

Size: 20x24mm

275a A49 10c orange .20 .20
 c. Booklet pane of 4 ('76) .80
276a A49 15c olive green .25 .20
 c. Booklet pane of 4 1.00
277a A49 20c bright purple .25 .20
 c. Booklet pane of 4 ('76) 1.10
278a A49 25c deep brown .45 .20
279a A49 30c ultramarine .60 .25
280a A49 40c blue green .75 .30
281a A49 50c red 1.00 .45
 c. Booklet pane of 4 4.25
282a A49 65c deep bister 1.50 .55
283a A49 $1 dark slate green 2.00 .70

Perf. 14x14½

Size: 28x32mm

284a A49 $1.30 dark purple & yel 2.75 .90
285a A49 $2 dp brn & lt grn 4.75 1.60
286a A49 $5 dk vio bl & rose ('78) 11.00 4.00
287a A49 $10 dk sl grn & pink ('78) 21.00 8.25
288a A49 $20 black & rose ('78) 42.50 19.00
 Nos. 275a-288a (14) 89.00 36.80

See Nos. 316-327.

Princess Anne's Wedding Issue
Common Design Type
Wmk. 314

1973, Nov. 14 Litho. Perf. 14

289 CD325 50c ocher & multi 1.00 .25
290 CD325 $2 lilac & multi 3.50 1.50

Chinese Character "Hong" — A50

Designs: 50c, "Kong." $1, "Festival."

1973, Nov. 23 Litho. Perf. 14½x14

291 A50 10c red & green .40 .20
292 A50 50c plum & red 2.10 .60
293 A50 $1 emerald & plum 5.50 1.60
 Nos. 291-293 (3) 8.00 2.40

Festival of Hong Kong 1973.

Tiger A51

Lunar New Year: $1.30, Tiger, vert.

Perf. 14½x14, 14x14½

1974, Jan. 8 Wmk. 314

294 A51 10c green & multi 2.00 .30
295 A51 $1.30 lilac & multi 10.50 3.00

Chinese Opera Mask — A52

Designs: Chinese opera masks.

1974, Feb. 1 Photo. Perf. 12x12½

296 A52 10c black, red & org .40 .25
297 A52 $1 multicolored 4.50 1.00
298 A52 $2 black, org & gold 11.50 2.75
 a. Souvenir sheet of 3, #296-298, perf. 14x13 *50.00* *35.00*
 Nos. 296-298 (3) 16.40 4.00

Hong Kong Arts Festival.

Carrier Pigeons A53

Cent. of UPU: 50c, Symbolic globe in envelope. $2, Hands holding letters.

1974, Oct. 9 Litho. Perf. 14

299 A53 10c blue, grn & blk .50 .20
 a. Unwatermarked 30.00
300 A53 50c magenta & multi 1.25 .20
301 A53 $2 violet & multi 5.75 1.75
 Nos. 299-301 (3) 7.50 2.15

Rabbit A54

Lunar New Year: $1.30, Two rabbits.

1975, Feb. 5 Wmk. 314 Perf. 14

302 A54 10c silver & red .75 .35
 a. Unwatermarked 1.00 1.00
303 A54 $1.30 gold & green 6.50 3.00
 a. Unwatermarked 8.50 8.50

Queen Elizabeth II, Prince Philip, Hong Kong Arms — A55

Wmk. 373

1975, Apr. 30 Litho. Perf. 13½

304 A55 $1.30 blue & multi 3.00 1.00
305 A55 $2 yellow & multi 4.00 2.00

Royal Visit 1975.

Mid-Autumn Festival — A56 Brown Laughing Thrush — A57

Abstract Designs: $1, Dragon Boat Festival (boats). $2, Tin Hau Festival (ships with flags).

1975, July 31 Unwmk. Perf. 14

306 A56 50c rose lil & multi 2.25 .25
307 A56 $1 brt grn & multi 9.00 1.50
308 A56 $2 orange & multi 32.50 5.75
 a. Souv. sheet of 3, #306-308 *100.00* *45.00*
 Nos. 306-308 (3) 43.75 7.50

Hong Kong Festivals, 1975.

1975, Oct. 29 Litho. Wmk. 373

Birds: $1.30, Chinese bulbul. $2, Black-capped kingfisher.

309 A57 50c lt blue & multi 3.00 .75
310 A57 $1.30 pink & multi 10.50 3.50
311 A57 $2 yellow & multi 19.00 6.00
 Nos. 309-311 (3) 32.50 10.25

Dragon A58

Lunar New Year: $1.30, like 20c, pattern reversed.

1976, Jan. 21 Litho. Perf. 14½

312 A58 20c gold, pur & lilac .75 .50
313 A58 $1.30 gold, red & grn 7.75 2.50

Queen Elizabeth Type of 1973

Wmk. 373 (#320-323), Unwmkd.

1976-81 Photo. Perf. 14½x14

Size: 20x24mm

316 A49 20c bright purple 3.75 1.00
318 A49 30c ultramarine 7.50 1.75
320 A49 60c lt violet ('77) 1.75 1.75
321 A49 70c yellow ('77) 1.75 .35
322 A49 80c brt magenta ('77) 2.50 2.40
323 A49 90c sepia ('81) 8.25 1.50

Size: 28x32mm

Perf. 14x14½

324 A49 $2 dp brn & lt grn 9.75 3.00
325 A49 $5 dk vio bl & rose 9.75 5.75

Photo. & Embossed

326 A49 $10 dk sl grn & pink 80.00 35.00
327 A49 $20 black & rose 175.00 47.50
 Nos. 316-327 (10) 300.00 100.00

"60" and Girl Guides Emblem A59

$1.30, "60," tents and Girl Guides emblem.

1976, Apr. 23 Wmk. 314 Perf. 14½

328 A59 20c silver & multi .75 .25
329 A59 $1.30 silver & multi 7.25 2.25

60th anniv. of Hong Kong Girl Guides.

"Postal Services" (in Chinese) — A60

Designs: $1.30, General Post Office, 1911-1976. $2, New G.P.O., 1976.

1976, Aug. 11 Litho. Wmk. 373

330 A60 20c gray, green & black .75 .20
331 A60 $1.30 gray, red & black 3.50 1.50
332 A60 $2 gray, yel & black 6.25 2.50
 Nos. 330-332 (3) 10.50 4.20

Opening of new GPO building.

Snake A61

Lunar New Year: $1.30, Snake & branch face left.

1977, Jan. 6 Perf. 13½

333 A61 20c multicolored .75 .25
334 A61 $1.30 multicolored 5.25 3.25

Queen Dotting Eye of Dragon, 1975 Visit — A62

20c, Presentation of the orb. $2, Orb, vert.

1977, Feb. 7 Litho.

335 A62 20c multicolored .60 .25
336 A62 $1.30 multicolored 1.90 .75
337 A62 $2 multicolored 2.25 1.00
 Nos. 335-337 (3) 4.75 2.00

25th anniv. of the reign of Elizabeth II.

Streetcars — A63

Designs: 60c, Star ferryboat. $1.30, Funicular railway. $2, Junk and sampan.

1977, June 30 Wmk. 373 *Perf. 13½*

338	A63	20c	multicolored	.60	.20
339	A63	60c	multicolored	1.40	1.10
340	A63	$1.30	multicolored	2.75	1.10
341	A63	$2	multicolored	3.25	1.60
			Nos. 338-341 (4)	8.00	4.00

Tourist publicity.

Buttercup Orchid — A64

1977, Oct. 12 Litho. *Perf. 14*

$1.30, Lady's-slipper. $2, Susan orchid.

342	A64	20c	blue & multi	1.25	.25
343	A64	$1.30	yellow & multi	4.00	1.50
344	A64	$2	green & multi	6.00	3.25
			Nos. 342-344 (3)	11.25	5.00

Horse and Chinese Character "Ma" — A65

1978, Jan. 26 Litho. *Perf. 14½*

345	A65	20c	multicolored	.75	.20
346	A65	$1.30	multicolored	4.75	.70

Lunar New Year.

Elizabeth II — A66

1978, June 2 Litho. *Perf. 14x14½*

347	A66	20c	carmine & dk blue	.50	.20
348	A66	$1.30	dk blue & carmine	1.50	1.25

25th anniv. of coronation of Elizabeth II.

Boy and Girl A67

Design: $1.30, Ring-around-a-rosy.

1978, Nov. 8 Wmk. 373 *Perf. 14½*

349	A67	20c	multicolored	.25	.20
350	A67	$1.30	multicolored	1.50	.80

Centenary of Po Leung Kuk, society for help and education of orphans and poor children.

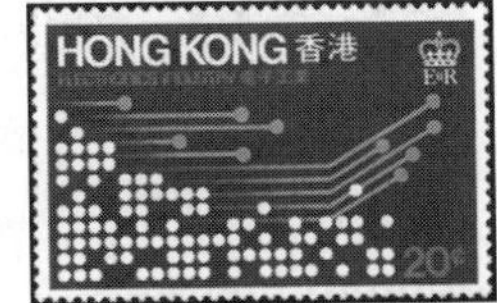

Electronics — A68

Industries: $1.30, Toy (bear and drum). $2, Garment (mannequins).

1979, Jan. 9 Litho. *Perf. 14½*

351	A68	20c	multicolored	.20	.20
352	A68	$1.30	multicolored	1.10	.75
353	A68	$2	multicolored	1.10	1.00
			Nos. 351-353 (3)	2.40	1.95

Precis Orithya — A69

Butterflies: $1, Graphium sarpedon. $1.30, Heliophorus epicles phoenicoparyphus. $2, Danaus genutia.

1979, June 20 Photo. Unwmk.

354	A69	20c	multicolored	.30	.20
355	A69	$1	multicolored	.60	.30
356	A69	$1.30	multicolored	.80	.30
357	A69	$2	multicolored	.90	.55
			Nos. 354-357 (4)	2.60	1.35

Cross Section of Station A70

Mass Transit Railroad: $1.30, Front, rear and side views of train. $2, Map of routes.

1979, Oct. 1 Litho. *Perf. 13½*

358	A70	20c	multicolored	.35	.20
359	A70	$1.30	multicolored	1.00	.30
360	A70	$2	multicolored	1.10	.50
			Nos. 358-360 (3)	2.45	1.00

Ching Chung Koon Temple, Tuen Mun — A71

Rural Architecture: 20c, Tsui Shing Lau Pagoda, Sheung Cheung Wai, vert. $1.30, Village house, Sai O.

Perf. 13x13½, 13½x13

1980, May 14 Litho. Wmk. 373

361	A71	20c	multicolored	.30	.20
362	A71	$1.30	multicolored	.90	.30
363	A71	$2	multicolored	1.25	.50
			Nos. 361-363 (3)	2.45	1.00

Queen Mother Elizabeth Birthday Issue

Common Design Type

1980, Aug. 4 Litho. *Perf. 14*

364	CD330	$1.30	multicolored	1.00	.75

Botanical Gardens — A72

1980, Nov. 12 Litho. *Perf. 13½*

365	A72	20c	shown	.30	.20
366	A72	$1	Ocean Park	.55	.20
367	A72	$1.30	Kowloon Park	.60	.25
368	A72	$2	Country Park	1.25	.75
			Nos. 365-368 (4)	2.70	1.40

Epinephelus Akaara — A73

1981, Jan. 28 Litho. *Perf. 13½*

369	A73	20c	shown	.20	.20
370	A73	$1	Nemipterus virgatus	.55	.25
371	A73	$1.30	Choerodon azurio	.75	.30
372	A73	$2	Scarus ghobban	1.10	.75
			Nos. 369-372 (4)	2.60	1.50

Royal Wedding Issue

Common Design Type

1981, July 29 Photo. *Perf. 14*

373	CD331	20c	Bouquet	.40	.20
374	CD331	$1.30	Charles	1.10	.30
375	CD331	$5	Couple	3.50	1.25
			Nos. 373-375 (3)	5.00	1.75

Public Housing Development A74

Various public housing developments.

1981, Oct. 14 Litho. *Perf. 13½*

376	A74	20c	multicolored	.20	.20
377	A74	$1	multicolored	.65	.35
378	A74	$1.30	multicolored	.95	.35
379	A74	$2	multicolored	1.10	.50
	a.		Souvenir sheet of 4, #376-379	5.00	5.00
			Nos. 376-379 (4)	2.90	1.40

Port of Hong Kong A75

Various views of Port of Hong Kong.

1982, Jan. 12 Litho. *Perf. 14½*

380	A75	20c	multicolored	.40	.20
381	A75	$1	multicolored	1.25	.90
382	A75	$1.30	multicolored	1.60	1.25
383	A75	$2	multicolored	2.25	1.50
			Nos. 380-383 (4)	5.50	3.85

Five-banded Civet — A76

1982, May 4 Litho. *Perf. 14½*

384	A76	20c	shown	.25	.20
385	A76	$1	Pangolin	.55	.40
386	A76	$1.30	Chinese porcupine	1.10	.80
387	A76	$5	Barking deer	3.25	2.25
			Nos. 384-387 (4)	5.15	3.65

Queen Elizabeth II
A77 A78

Perf. 14½x14

1982, Aug. 30 Photo. Wmk. 373

388	A77	10c	yellow & dk red	.60	.60
389	A77	20c	blue vio & vio	.80	.70
390	A77	30c	orange & pur	1.10	.30
391	A77	40c	lt blue & red	1.10	.30
392	A77	50c	pale grn & brn	1.10	.30
393	A77	60c	gray & brt mag	2.40	1.50
394	A77	70c	brt org & dk grn	2.50	.40
395	A77	80c	gray ol & brn ol	2.50	1.50
396	A77	90c	grnsh bl & grn	4.00	.30
397	A77	$1	brt pink & brn org	2.25	.30
398	A77	$1.30	rose vio & dk bl	3.50	.30
399	A77	$2	buff & blue	5.75	1.00

Photo. & Embossed

Perf. 14x14½

400	A78	$5	lemon & lake	6.25	2.50
401	A78	$10	brn & blk brn	7.25	5.00
402	A78	$20	lt blue & lake	12.50	15.00
403	A78	$50	gray & lake	32.50	30.00
			Nos. 388-403 (16)	86.10	60.00

Nos. 388 and 397 also issued in coils.

1985-87 Unwmk.

388a	A77	10c		.75	.20
389a	A77	20c		18.50	5.00
391a	A77	40c		1.00	.40
392a	A77	50c		1.00	.30
393a	A77	60c		1.60	.60
394a	A77	70c		1.90	.50
395a	A77	80c		2.25	1.00
396a	A77	90c		2.25	.50
397a	A77	$1		1.90	.40
398b	A77	$1.30		2.50	.35
398A	A77	$1.70	brt yel grn & dp bl	3.75	.75
399a	A77	$2		4.00	.75
400a	A78	$5		7.00	2.00
401a	A78	$10		8.25	3.00
402a	A78	$20		11.00	6.00
403a	A78	$50		32.50	20.00
			Nos. 388a-403a (16)	100.15	41.75

Issued: $1.30, 6/13/86; $1.70, 9/2/86; 20c, 6/87; others, 10/10/85.

3rd Far East and South Pacific Games for the Disabled A79

Perf. 14x14½

1982, Oct. 31 Litho. Wmk. 373

404	A79	30c	Table tennis	.30	.20
405	A79	$1	Racing	.45	.40
406	A79	$1.30	Basketball	1.75	.75
407	A79	$5	Archery	3.00	2.00
			Nos. 404-407 (4)	5.50	3.35

Performing Arts — A80

1983, Jan. 26 Litho. *Perf. 14½x14*

408	A80	30c	Dancing	.35	.20
409	A80	$1.30	Theater	1.40	.60
410	A80	$5	Music	4.25	2.00
			Nos. 408-410 (3)	6.00	2.80

A81

1983, Mar. 14 *Perf. 14½x13½*

411 A81	30c	Aerial view	.75	.20
412 A81	$1	Liverpool Bay	1.90	.80
413 A81	$1.30	Flag	1.90	.85
414 A81	$5	Queen Elizabeth II	3.75	2.00
		Nos. 411-414 (4)	8.30	3.85

Commonwealth Day.

Views by Night A82

1983, Aug. 17 **Litho.** *Perf. 14½*

415 A82	30c	Victoria Harbor	1.25	.65
416 A82	$1	Space Museum	3.75	2.10
417 A82	$1.30	Chinese New Year Fireworks	5.00	2.25
418 A82	$5	Jumbo Restaurant	15.00	6.00
		Nos. 415-418 (4)	25.00	11.00

Royal Observatory Centenary — A83

1983, Nov. 23 **Litho.** *Perf. 14½*

419 A83	40c	Technical facilities	.60	.25
420 A83	$1	Wind measurement	1.75	.70
421 A83	$1.30	Temperature measurement	1.90	.90
422 A83	$5	Earthquake measurement	6.75	3.00
		Nos. 419-422 (4)	11.00	4.85

Training Plane, Dorado A84

1984, Mar. 7 **Wmk. 373** *Perf. 13½*

423 A84	40c	shown	.65	.25
424 A84	$1	Hong Kong Clipper seaplane	1.75	.75
425 A84	$1.30	Jumbo jet, Kai Tak Airport	2.50	1.00
426 A84	$5	Baldwin Brothers balloon, vert.	6.00	2.25
		Nos. 423-426 (4)	10.90	4.25

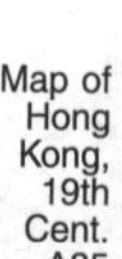

Map of Hong Kong, 19th Cent. A85

Various maps.

1984, June 21 **Litho.** *Perf. 14*

427 A85	40c	multicolored	.90	.35
428 A85	$1	multicolored	1.60	.90
429 A85	$1.30	multicolored	2.50	1.00
430 A85	$5	multicolored	10.00	2.75
		Nos. 427-430 (4)	15.00	5.00

Chinese Lanterns A86

1984, Sept. 6 **Litho.** *Perf. 13½x13*

431 A86	40c	Rooster	.75	.35
432 A86	$1	Bull	1.60	.90
433 A86	$1.30	Butterfly	2.75	1.00
434 A86	$5	Fish	8.50	2.75
		Nos. 431-434 (4)	13.60	5.00

Jockey Club Centenary — A87

1984, Nov. 21 **Litho.** *Perf. 14½*

435 A87	40c	Supporting health care	.65	.40
436 A87	$1	Supporting disabled	1.60	1.10
437 A87	$1.30	Supporting the arts	2.00	1.40
438 A87	$5	Supporting Ocean Park	5.00	3.50
a.		Souvenir sheet of 4, #435-438	20.00	14.00
		Nos. 435-438 (4)	9.25	6.40

Historic Buildings A88

Perf. 13½

1985, Mar. 14 **Unwmk.** **Litho.**

439 A88	40c	Hung Sing Temple	.60	.30
440 A88	$1	St. John's Cathedral	1.75	.65
441 A88	$1.30	Old Supreme Court Building	2.25	.85
442 A88	$5	Wan Chai Post Office	7.00	2.50
		Nos. 439-442 (4)	11.60	4.30

Intl. Dragon Boat Festival A89

Perf. 13½x13

1985, June 19 **Wmk. 373** **Litho.**

443 A89	40c	multicolored	.40	.30
444 A89	$1	multicolored	1.40	.60
445 A89	$1.30	multicolored	2.40	.75
446 A89	$5	multicolored	8.00	3.25
a.		Strip of 4, #443-446	12.20	4.90
b.		Souvenir sheet of 4, #443-446, perf. 13x12½	22.50	15.00
		Nos. 443-446 (4)	12.20	4.90

Nos. 443-446 when placed together form a continuous design.

Queen Mother 85th Birthday Issue
Common Design Type

1985, Aug. 7 **Litho.** *Perf. 14½x14*

447 CD336	40c	At Glamis Castle, age 9	.50	.25
448 CD336	$1	On balcony with Princes William and Charles	1.25	.45
449 CD336	$1.30	Photograph by Cecil Beaton,1980	1.50	.50
450 CD336	$5	Holding Prince Henry	4.00	1.60
		Nos. 447-450 (4)	7.25	2.80

Indigenous Flowers — A90

1985, Sept. 25 **Litho.** *Perf. 13½*

451 A90	40c	Melastoma	1.75	.60
452 A90	50c	Chinese lily	2.00	.65
453 A90	60c	Grantham's camellia	2.25	.75
454 A90	$1.30	Narcissus	3.50	1.10
455 A90	$1.70	Bauhinia	4.00	1.40
456 A90	$5	Chinese New Year flower	7.25	4.50
		Nos. 451-456 (6)	20.75	9.00

See No. 898.

Modern Architecture — A91

1985, Nov. 27 *Perf. 15*

457 A91	50c	Hong Kong Academy for Performing Arts	.60	.30
458 A91	$1.30	Exchange Square, vert.	1.25	.60
459 A91	$1.70	Hong Kong Bank Hdqtrs., vert.	2.00	.90
460 A91	$5	Hong Kong Coliseum	7.25	2.60
		Nos. 457-460 (4)	11.10	4.40

Halley's Comet A92

1986, Feb. 26 **Litho.** *Perf. 13½x13*

461 A92	50c	Comet, solar system	.85	.20
462 A92	$1.30	Edmond Halley	1.40	.60
463 A92	$1.70	Hong Kong, trajectory	2.00	.95
464 A92	$5	Comet, Earth	7.50	2.60
a.		Souvenir sheet of 4, #461-464	21.00	16.00
		Nos. 461-464 (4)	11.75	4.35

Queen Elizabeth II 60th Birthday
Common Design Type

Designs: 50c, At the wedding of Cecillia Bowes-Lyon, Brompton Parish Church, 1939. $1, Most Noble Order of the Garter, service at St. George's Chapel, Windsor Castle, 1977. $1.30, State visit, 1975. $1.70, Queen Mother's 80th birthday celebration, Royal Lodge, Windsor, 1980. $5, Visiting Crown Agents' offices, 1983.

1986, Apr. 21 *Perf. 14½*

465 CD337	50c	scar, blk & sil	.50	.20
466 CD337	$1	ultra & multi	1.00	.35
467 CD337	$1.30	green & multi	1.25	.45
468 CD337	$1.70	violet & multi	1.40	.55
469 CD337	$5	rose vio & multi	4.25	1.90
		Nos. 465-469 (5)	8.40	3.45

EXPO '86, Vancouver — A93

1986, July 18 **Litho.** *Perf. 13½*

470 A93	50c	Transportation	.60	.20
471 A93	$1.30	Finance	1.25	.50
472 A93	$1.70	Trade	1.90	.70
473 A93	$5	Communications	6.00	2.25
		Nos. 470-473 (4)	9.75	3.65

Fishing Vessels A94

1986, Sept. 24 **Litho.**

474 A94	50c	Hand-liner sampan	.50	.20
475 A94	$1.30	Stern trawler	1.25	.65
476 A94	$1.70	Long liner junk	1.60	.90
477 A94	$5	Junk trawler	3.50	2.10
		Nos. 474-477 (4)	6.85	3.85

19th Cent. Paintings — A95

50c, Possibly, Second puan khequa, by Spoilum. $1.30, Chinese woman, artist unknown. $1.70, Self-portrait at age 52, by Kwan Kiu Chin. $5, Possibly, Wife of a merchant, by George Chinnery.

1986, Dec. 9 **Litho.** *Perf. 14*

478 A95	50c	multicolored	.40	.20
479 A95	$1.30	multicolored	1.10	.70
480 A95	$1.70	multicolored	1.25	.95
481 A95	$5	multicolored	4.00	2.25
		Nos. 478-481 (4)	6.75	4.10

New Year (Year of the Hare) A96

Embroideries of various rabbits.

1987, Jan. 21 **Litho.** *Perf. 13½x14*

482 A96	50c	multicolored	.50	.30
483 A96	$1.30	multicolored	1.40	.75
484 A96	$1.70	multicolored	1.50	.95
485 A96	$5	multicolored	6.00	2.75
a.		Souvenir sheet of 4, #482-485	37.50	25.00
		Nos. 482-485 (4)	9.40	4.75

19th Century Paintings in the Hong Kong Museum of Art and Shanghai Banking Corp. A97

Scenes: 50c, A Village Square, Hong Kong Island, 1838, by Auguste Borget (1809-1877). $1.30, Boat Dwellers in Kowloon Bay, 1838, by Borget. $1.70, Flagstaff House, Lt. Governor D'Aguilar's Residence, 1846, by Murdoch Bruce. $5, A View of Wellington Street, late 19th century, by C. Andrasi.

1987, Apr. 23 **Litho.** *Perf. 14*

486 A97	50c	multicolored	.65	.25
487 A97	$1.30	multicolored	1.75	.85
488 A97	$1.70	multicolored	2.25	1.00
489 A97	$5	multicolored	7.00	3.00
		Nos. 486-489 (4)	11.65	5.10

Elizabeth II, Hong Kong Waterfront A98

Queen, Natl. Landmarks A99

Type I-Darker Shading Under Chin

Type II-Lighter Shading Under Chin

Designs: $5, Tsim Shah Tsui, Kowloon. $10, Victoria Harbor. $20, Legislative Council Building. $50, Government House.

1987, July 13 Litho. *Perf. 14½x14*

490 A98 10c yel grn, gray & blk .20 .20
491 A98 40c bluish grn, lt yel & blk .20 .20
492 A98 50c brn org, buff & blk .20 .20
493 A98 60c lt blue, pale rose & blk .20 .20
494 A98 70c vio, pale rose & blk .45 .25
495 A98 80c brt rose lil, lt blue & blk .50 .35
496 A98 90c pink, pale beige & blk .60 .40
497 A98 $1 brt lem & blk .70 .40
498 A98 $1.30 rose claret, brt yel grn & blk 1.00 .50
499 A98 $1.70 lt blue & blk 1.00 .60
500 A98 $2 yel grn, cream & blk 1.25 .70

Perf. 14

501 A99 $5 grn, lt grn & blk 3.50 2.00
502 A99 $10 brn, yel brn & blk 6.75 3.50
503 A99 $20 rose vio, lil & blk 15.00 7.50
504 A99 $50 sep, gray & blk 37.50 20.00
Nos. 490-504 (15) 69.05 37.00

1988, Sept. 1 Type II

490a A98 10c .25 .20
491a A98 40c .60 .20
492a A98 50c .40 .20
493a A98 60c .55 .25
494a A98 70c .60 .30
495a A98 80c .65 .35
496a A98 90c .75 .40
497a A98 $1 .80 .45
498a A98 $1.30 1.90 .60
499a A98 $1.70 1.40 .70
500a A98 $2 1.50 .75
501a A99 $5 4.75 2.25
502a A99 $10 8.50 4.50
b. Souv. sheet of 1, inscribed "1990" *110.00*
c. As "b," inscribed "1991" *50.00*
d. As "b," inscribed "1991" *20.00*
503a A99 $20 16.00 9.00
504a A99 $50 40.00 22.50
Nos. 490a-504a (15) 78.65 42.65

No. 502b for the New Zealand 1990 World Stamp Exhibition. No. 502c for Phila Nippon '91 Intl. Philatelic Exhibition. No. 502d for Hong Kong Post Office sponsorship of 1992 Olympic Games.

Issued: #502b, 8/24; #502c, 11/16/91; #502d, 12/4/91.

Nos. 490a-498a, 500a-504a reissued inscribed "1989," "1990." Nos. 490a, 492a-497a, 499a-504a, "1991."

See Nos. 532-533, 592-593, 629.

Nethersole Hospital, Cent. — A100

1987, Sept. 8 *Perf. 14½*

505 A100 50c Hospital, 1887 .70 .20
506 A100 $1.30 Patients, staff 1.60 .70
507 A100 $1.70 Technology, 1987 1.90 .85
508 A100 $5 Treatment 4.75 2.50
Nos. 505-508 (4) 8.95 4.25

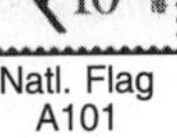

Natl. Flag A101

Map of Hong Kong A101a

Coil Stamps

1987, July 13 *Perf. 15x14*

509 A101 10c shown *1.00 1.00*
510 A101a 50c olive green *1.00 1.00*

Nos. 509-510 reissued inscribed "1989," No. 509, "1990." See Nos. 611-614.

Folk Costumes — A102

1987, Nov. 18 *Perf. 13½*

511 A102 50c multicolored .35 .20
512 A102 $1.30 multi, diff. 1.00 .50
513 A102 $1.70 multi, diff. 1.40 .65
514 A102 $5 multi, diff. 4.25 2.10
Nos. 511-514 (4) 7.00 3.45

New Year (Year of the Dragon) A103

1988, Jan. 27 Litho. *Perf. 13½*

515 A103 50c multicolored .75 .30
516 A103 $1.30 multi, diff. 1.75 .90
517 A103 $1.70 multi, diff. 2.00 1.25
518 A103 $5 multi, diff. 4.25 3.50
a. Souv. sheet of 4, #515-518 *14.00 6.75*
Nos. 515-518 (4) 8.75 5.95

See No. 838e.

Indigenous Birds — A104

Indigenous Trees — A105

1988, Apr. 20 *Perf. 13½x14*

519 A104 50c White-breasted kingfisher .30 .20
520 A104 $1.30 Fukien niltava .95 .55
521 A104 $1.70 Black kite 1.25 .65
522 A104 $5 Pied kingfisher 3.50 1.90
Nos. 519-522 (4) 6.00 3.30

1988, June 16 Litho. *Perf. 13½*

523 A105 50c Chinese banyan .35 .20
524 A105 $1.30 Bauhinia blakeana 1.10 .50
525 A105 $1.70 Cotton tree 1.40 .65
526 A105 $5 Schima 4.00 1.90
a. Souv. sheet of 4, #523-526 *11.00 8.75*
Nos. 523-526 (4) 6.85 3.25

See note after No. 940.

Peak Tramway, Victoria, Cent. — A106

Catholic Cathedral, Caine Road, Cent. — A107

Various views of Hong Kong and the tram line.

1988, Aug. 4 Litho. *Perf. 15*

527 A106 50c multicolored .50 .20
528 A106 $1.30 multi, diff. 1.00 .85
529 A106 $1.70 multi, diff. 1.10 1.10
530 A106 $5 multi, diff. 3.50 3.50
a. Souvenir sheet of 4, #527-530 *9.00 6.00*
Nos. 527-530 (4) 6.10 5.65

1988, Sept. 30 Litho. *Perf. 14*

531 A107 60c multicolored 1.25 .50

Queen and Waterfront Type of 1987

Type II

1988, Sept. 1 Litho. *Perf. 14½x14*

532 A98 $1.40 multicolored 2.25 .60
533 A98 $1.80 multicolored 3.75 .75

Nos. 532-533 reissued inscribed "1989," "1990," No. 533, "1991."

New Year (Year of the Snake) A108

1989, Jan. 18 Litho. *Perf. 13½x14*

534 A108 60c multicolored .45 .20
535 A108 $1.40 multi, diff. 1.10 .40
536 A108 $1.80 multi, diff. 1.25 .50
a. Bklt. pane, 5 each #534, 536 11.00
537 A108 $5 multi, diff. 4.00 1.40
a. Souv. sheet of 4, #534-537 *12.00 10.00*
Nos. 534-537 (4) 6.80 2.50

See No. 838g.

Cheung Chau Bun Festival — A109

1989, May 4 Unwmk. *Perf. 13½*

538 A109 60c Girl, doll .40 .20
539 A109 $1.40 Girl .90 .45
540 A109 $1.80 Festival paper god 1.10 .55
541 A109 $5 Bun tower gate 2.75 1.60
Nos. 538-541 (4) 5.15 2.80

Modern Art — A110

Hong Kong People — A111

60c, Twin, sculpture by Cheung Yee (b. 1936). $1.40, Figures, painted by Luis Chan (b. 1905). $1.80, Lotus, sculpture by Van Lau (b. 1933). $5, Zen, painted by Lui Shou-kwan (1919-1975).

1989, July 19 *Perf. 12x13*

542 A110 60c multicolored .45 .25
543 A110 $1.40 multicolored .95 .45
544 A110 $1.80 multicolored 1.25 .65
545 A110 $5 multicolored 3.00 1.75
Nos. 542-545 (4) 5.65 3.10

1989, Sept. 6 *Perf. 13x14½*

Designs: 60c, Youth holding autumn festival decoration, lunar year festival dragon. $1.40, Shadow boxer, horse racing. $1.80, Office and construction workers. $5, Two women, two men (ethnic multiplicity).

546 A111 60c multicolored .55 .25
547 A111 $1.40 multicolored 1.00 .50
548 A111 $1.80 multicolored 1.25 .60
549 A111 $5 multicolored 3.75 2.00
Nos. 546-549 (4) 6.55 3.35

See No. 762.

Construction Projects A112

1989, Oct. 5 Unwmk. *Perf. 13*

550 A112 60c University of Science and Technology .45 .20
551 A112 70c Cultural center .50 .20
552 A112 $1.30 Eastern Harbor Crossing 1.00 .35
553 A112 $1.40 Bank of China 1.00 .35
554 A112 $1.80 Convention center 1.10 .50
555 A112 $5 Light rail transit 4.00 1.40
Nos. 550-555 (6) 8.05 3.00

Visit of the Prince and Princess of Wales — A113

Portraits and view of Hong Kong: 60c, Charles and Diana. $1.40, Diana. $1.80, Charles. $5, Couple wearing formal attire.

1989, Nov. 8 Wmk. 340 *Perf. 14½*

556 A113 60c multicolored .65 .30
557 A113 $1.40 multicolored 1.25 .60
558 A113 $1.80 multicolored 1.75 .90
559 A113 $5 multicolored 5.25 2.40
a. Souvenir sheet of 1 *14.00 11.00*
Nos. 556-559 (4) 8.90 4.20

New Year 1990 (Year of the Horse) A114

Perf. 13½x12½

1990, Jan. 23 Unwmk.

560 A114 60c multicolored .70 .35
561 A114 $1.40 multi, diff. 1.40 .70
562 A114 $1.80 multi, diff. 1.75 1.00
a. Bklt. pane, 3 each 60c, $1.80 *15.00*
563 A114 $5 multi, diff. 5.00 2.75
a. Souvenir sheet of 4, #560-563 *16.00*
Nos. 560-563 (4) 8.85 4.80

Copies of No. 562a ovptd. with marginal inscription were released on May 3 to publicize Stamp World London '90.

See No. 838k.

Intl. Cuisine — A115

Pollutants — A116

1990, Apr. 26 Litho. ***Perf. 12½x13***

564 A115 60c Chinese .50 .25
565 A115 70c Indian .50 .30
566 A115 $1.30 Chinese, diff. .80 .45
567 A115 $1.40 Thai .80 .65
568 A115 $1.80 Japanese 1.25 .70
569 A115 $5 French 4.00 1.90
Nos. 564-569 (6) 7.85 4.25

Wmk. 340

1990, June 5 Litho. ***Perf. 14½***

570 A116 60c Air .40 .20
571 A116 $1.40 Noise .75 .35
572 A116 $1.80 Water 1.10 .50
573 A116 $5 Land 2.75 1.40
Nos. 570-573 (4) 5.00 2.45

World Environment Day.

Electrification of Hong Kong, Cent. — A117

Views of Hong Kong and streetlights.

1990, Oct. 2 Litho. ***Perf. 14½***

574 A117 60c 1890 .30 .20
575 A117 $1.40 1940 .70 .30
576 A117 $1.80 1960 1.00 .45
577 A117 $5 1980 2.50 1.25
a. Souvenir sheet of 2, #575, 577 *4.75 4.75*
Nos. 574-577 (4) 4.50 2.20

Christmas — A118

1990, Nov. 8

578 A118 50c shown .25 .20
579 A118 60c Dove, holly .35 .20
580 A118 $1.40 Skyline, snowman .80 .40
581 A118 $1.80 Santa Claus' hat, skyscraper 1.00 .45
582 A118 $2 Children, Santa Claus 1.10 .50
583 A118 $5 Candy cane, skyline 2.75 1.40
Nos. 578-583 (6) 6.25 3.15

New Year 1991 (Year of the Sheep) A119

Different embroidered rams.

1991, Jan. 24 Litho. ***Perf. 13½x12½***

584 A119 60c multicolored .35 .20
585 A119 $1.40 multicolored .90 .40
586 A119 $1.80 multicolored 1.00 .50
a. Bklt. pane, 3 each #584, 586 4.25
587 A119 $5 multicolored 2.75 1.40
a. Souv. sheet of 4, #584-587 *9.00 8.50*
Nos. 584-587 (4) 5.00 2.50

See No. 838j.

Education — A120

Perf. 13½x13

1991, Apr. 18 Litho. Unwmk.

588 A120 80c Kindergarten .35 .25
589 A120 $1.80 Primary & secondary .80 .55
590 A120 $2.30 Vocational 1.10 .70
591 A120 $5 Tertiary 2.25 1.60
Nos. 588-591 (4) 4.50 3.10

Queen and Waterfront Type of 1987 Type II

1991, Apr. 2 Litho. ***Perf. 14½x14***

592 A98 $1.20 multicolored *.45* .30
593 A98 $2.30 multicolored *.90* .60

Transportation A121

1991, June 6 Unwmk. ***Perf. 14***

594 A121 80c Rickshaw .55 .30
595 A121 90c Bus .60 .35
596 A121 $1.70 Ferry 1.10 .75
597 A121 $1.80 Tram 1.25 .80
598 A121 $2.30 Mass transit railway 1.60 1.00
599 A121 $5 Hydrofoil 3.75 2.40
Nos. 594-599 (6) 8.85 5.60

A122

Historic Landmarks A123

Royal postboxes with contemporary envelopes: 80c, Stamp of Type A1, Queen Victoria. $1.70, Stamps of Type A10, King Edward VII. $1.80, #149, King George V. $2.30, Stamps of Type A16, King George VI. $5, $10, Stamp of Type A98, Queen Elizabeth II.

1991, Aug. 25 Litho. ***Perf. 14***

600 A122 80c multicolored .75 .30
601 A122 $1.70 multicolored 1.50 .70
602 A122 $1.80 multicolored 1.75 .80
603 A122 $2.30 multicolored 2.25 .95
604 A122 $5 multicolored 5.00 2.25
Nos. 600-604 (5) 11.25 5.00

Souvenir Sheet

605 A122 $10 multicolored *16.00 5.25*

Hong Kong Post Office, 150th anniv.

See No. 792.

1991, Oct. 24

606 A123 80c Bronze Buddha .65 .25
607 A123 $1.70 Peak Pavilion 1.10 .55
608 A123 $1.80 Clock Tower 1.25 .60
609 A123 $2.30 Catholic Cathedral 1.75 .75
610 A123 $5 Wong Tai Sin Temple 4.25 1.75
Nos. 606-610 (5) 9.00 3.90

Map of Hong Kong Type

1992, Mar. 26 Photo. ***Perf. 14½x14***

Coil Stamps

Color of Map

611 A101a 80c red lilac *.30* .25
612 A101a 90c blue *.45* .35
613 A101a $1.80 brt yel grn *.85* .60
614 A101a $2.30 red brown *1.00* .80
Nos. 611-614 (4) 2.60 2.00

Inscribed 1991.

New Year 1992 (Year of the Monkey) A125

Various embroidery designs of monkeys.

1992, Jan. 22 Litho. ***Perf. 14½***

615 A125 80c multicolored .40 .25
616 A125 $1.80 multicolored 1.00 .50
617 A125 $2.30 multicolored 1.75 .75
a. Bklt. pane, 3 ea #615, 617 7.00
618 A125 $5 multicolored 3.75 1.60
a. Sheet of 4, #615-618 11.00 5.50
Nos. 615-618 (4) 6.90 3.10

See No. 838i.

Queen Elizabeth II's Accession to the Throne, 40th Anniv.

Common Design Type

Unwmk.

1992, Feb. 11 Litho. ***Perf. 14***

619 CD349 80c multicolored .35 .20
620 CD349 $1.70 multicolored .70 .35
621 CD349 $1.80 multicolored .75 .40
622 CD349 $2.30 multicolored 1.10 .55
623 CD349 $5 multicolored 2.75 1.10
Nos. 619-623 (5) 5.65 2.60

1992 Summer Olympics, Barcelona — A126

1992, Apr. 2 Litho. ***Perf. 14½***

Black Inscription

624 A126 80c Running .25 .20
625 A126 $1.80 Swimming and javelin .55 .40
626 A126 $2.30 Cycling .70 .55
627 A126 $5 High jump 1.50 1.10
Nos. 624-627 (4) 3.00 2.25

Souvenir Sheet

628 Sheet of 4 4.50 2.50
a. A126 80c red inscription .20 .20
b. A126 $1.80 green inscription .45 .45
c. A126 $2.30 blue inscription .60 .60
d. A126 $5 orange yellow inscription 1.25 1.25
e. Sheet of 4 with inscription in margin 3.75 2.50

Issue date: No. 628e, July 25. New inscription on No. 628e sheet margin reads "To Commemorate the Opening of the 1992 Summer Olympic Games 25 July 1992" in English and Chinese.

Queen and Landmarks Type of 1987 Souvenir Sheet

Perf. 14

1992, May 22 Litho. Type II

629 A99 $10 lt violet & black 6.00 4.75

World Columbian Stamp Expo '92.

A127

Perf. 15x14

1992-97 Photo. Unwmk.

Color of Chinese Inscription

630 A127 10c pink .30 .30
630A A127 20c black 1.00 1.00
631 A127 50c red orange .30 .25
632 A127 60c blue 1.00 .40
633 A127 70c red lilac .65 .55
634 A127 80c rose .30 .20
635 A127 90c gray green .30 .20
636 A127 $1 orange brown .35 .20
637 A127 $1.10 carmine .55 .45
638 A127 $1.20 violet .35 .20
639 A127 $1.30 dark blue 1.50 .65
640 A127 $1.40 apple green .35 .25
641 A127 $1.50 brown .80 .80
642 A127 $1.60 green .45 .45
643 A127 $1.70 ultramarine .80 .80
644 A127 $1.80 rose lilac 1.25 .55
645 A127 $1.90 green .80 .80
646 A127 $2 blue green 1.50 .50
647 A127 $2.10 claret 1.25 1.10
648 A127 $2.30 gray 1.25 .65
649 A127 $2.40 dark blue 2.00 1.25
650 A127 $2.50 olive green .55 .55
a. Sheet of 6, 2 #647, 4 #650 *9.00*
d. Booklet pane, 2 #647, 4 #650 *6.50*
651 A127 $2.60 dark brown 1.25 1.25
651A A127 $3.10 salmon .65 .65
l. Sheet of 6, 2 #642, 4 #651A *8.00*
o. Booklet pane, 2 #642, 4 #651A *6.00*
651B A127 $5 bright green 2.50 1.75
k. Souvenir sheet of 1 *7.00* 1.75
m. Sheet of 6, 4 #639, 2 #651B *12.00*
n. Booklet pane, 4 #639, 2 #651B *18.00*
p. Souvenir booklet, #650d, 651Ao, 651Bn *35.00*

Size: 25x30mm

Perf. 14½x14

651C A127 $10 brown 3.25 2.50
h. Souvenir sheet of 1 *5.00* 2.50
651D A127 $20 orange red 4.50 4.00
651E A127 $50 gray 10.50 9.75
Nos. 630-651E (28) 40.25 32.00

Issued: 20c, $1.30, $1.90, $2.40, 11/1/93; #651i, 2/18/94; #651h, 8/16/94; $1.10, $1.50, $2.10, $2.60, 6/1/95; $1.40, $1.60, $2.50, $3.10, 9/2/96; #651Bp, 2/14/97; others, 6/16/92.

10c, 50c, 80c, 90c, $1, $1.20, $1.30, $1.50, $1.60, $1.80, $1.90, $2.10, 2.30, $2.40, $2.50, $2.60, $3.10 also issued in coils. These have numbers on the back of every fifth stamp.

No. 651i issued for Hong Kong '94; No. 651h, for Conference of Commonwealth Postal Administrations.

Nos. 650a, 651Al, 651Bm are 130x85mm.

Nos. 650d, 651Ao, 651Bn are 180x130mm and are rouletted at left.

See Nos. 656, 677-678, 683, 688, 724, 729, 738, 743, 756-757.

1993-96 Litho. ***Perf. 15x14***

636a A127 $1 Litho. .35 .35
b. As "a," bklt. pane of 10 3.50
638a A127 $1.20 Litho. .30 .30
b. As "a," bklt. pane of 10 3.00
Complete booklet, #638b 3.00
639a A127 $1.30 Litho. .35 .35
b. As "a," booklet pane of 10 3.50
645a A127 $1.90 Litho. .65 .65
b. As "a," bklt. pane of 10 6.50
647a A127 $2.10 Litho. .55 .55
b. As "a," bklt. pane of 10 5.50
Complete booklet, #647b 5.50
649a A127 $2.40 Litho. .85 .85
b. As "a," bklt. pane of 10 8.50
650b A127 $2.50 Litho. .65 .65
c. As "b," booklet pane of 10 6.50
651f A127 $2.60 Litho. .70 .70
g. As "f," bklt. pane of 10 7.00
Complete booklet, #651g 7.00
651Ai A127 $3.10 Litho. .80 .80
j. As "i," booklet pane of 10 8.00
Nos. 636a-651Ai (9) 5.20 5.20

Chinese characters on Nos. 636a, 638a, 645a, 647a, 649a, 651f are lighter in shade and contrast less with the background color than characters on Nos. 636, 638, 645, 647, 649, 651.

Issued: #636a, 12/14/93; #645a, 649a, 12/28/93; #638a, 647a, 651f, 6/1/95; #639a, 650a, 651Ai, 9/2/96.

Stamp Collecting — A128

Stamps and: 80c, Perforation gauge, #559, 586a. $1.80, Canceler, #66, stamp tongs. $2.30, Magnifying glass, #174, 180, 181. $5, Watermark detector, Type A1.

1992, July 15 Litho. *Perf. 14½*

652	A128	80c	multicolored	.30	.20
653	A128	$1.80	multicolored	.70	.40
654	A128	$2.30	multicolored	1.00	.60
655	A128	$5	multicolored	2.00	1.40
			Nos. 652-655 (4)	4.00	2.60

Queen Type of 1992

Souvenir Sheet

Perf. 14½x14

1992, Sept. 1 Photo. Unwmk.

Background Color

656	A127	$10	blue	5.75	3.75

Kuala Lumpur Philatelic Exhibition '92. Size of stamp: 25x30mm.

Chinese Opera — A129

1992, Sept. 24 Litho. *Perf. 13½*

657	A129	80c	Principal male role	.45	.25
658	A129	$1.80	Martial role	1.00	.60
659	A129	$2.30	Principal female role	1.40	.75
660	A129	$5	Comic role	2.25	1.50
			Nos. 657-660 (4)	5.10	3.10

Greetings Stamps — A130

1992, Nov. 19 Litho. *Perf. 14½*

661	A130	80c	Hearts	.25	.20
662	A130	$1.80	Stars	.60	.30
663	A130	$2.30	Presents	.70	.50
664	A130	$5	Balloons	1.60	1.00
a.			Bklt. pane of 5, #662-664, 3 #661	4.00	2.50
			Nos. 661-664 (4)	3.15	2.00

New Year 1993 (Year of the Rooster) A131

Various embroidery designs of a rooster.

1993, Jan. 7 Litho. *Perf. 13½*

665	A131	80c	multicolored	.25	.20
666	A131	$1.80	multicolored	.60	.30
667	A131	$2.30	multicolored	.75	.50
a.			Bklt. pane, 3 ea #665, 667	4.75	
668	A131	$5	multicolored	1.60	1.00
a.			Souvenir sheet of 4, #665-668	5.00	3.75
			Nos. 665-668 (4)	3.20	2.00

See No. 838h.

Chinese String Instruments A132

1993, Apr. 14 Litho. *Perf. 14½*

669	A132	80c	Pipa	.25	.20
670	A132	$1.80	Erhu	.60	.30
671	A132	$2.30	Ruan	.75	.50
672	A132	$5	Gehu	1.60	1.00
			Nos. 669-672 (4)	3.20	2.00

Coronation of Queen Elizabeth II, 40th Anniv. A133

Different views of Hong Kong with portraits of Queen that appear on Types A25, A28, A49 and A127.

1993, June 3 Litho. *Perf. 14*

673	A133	80c	multicolored	.25	.20
674	A133	$1.80	multicolored	.65	.40
675	A133	$2.30	multicolored	.85	.50
676	A133	$5	multicolored	1.75	1.10
			Nos. 673-676 (4)	3.50	2.20

Queen Type of 1992

Souvenir Sheets

1993, July 6 Litho. *Perf. 14½x14*

Background Color

677	A127	$10	brown	4.50	4.25

1993, Aug. 12 Background Color

678	A127	$10	bright blue	4.50	4.25

Hong Kong '94 Stamp Exhibition. Nos. 677-678 contain a 25x30mm stamp.

No. 678 exists with gold, silver or red overprints with the Hong Kong Philatelic Society emblem and Chinese characters. These sheets were sold only at various philatelic exhibitions.

Science and Technology — A134

Designs: 80c, Education, Hong Kong University of Science and Technology. $1.80, Public presentation, Hong Kong Science Museum. $2.30, Achievement regognition, Governor's Award. $5, World class telecommunications, telecommunications industry.

1993, Sept. 8 *Perf. 14½*

679	A134	80c	multicolored	.25	.20
680	A134	$1.80	multicolored	.60	.45
681	A134	$2.30	multicolored	.80	.55
682	A134	$5	multicolored	1.75	1.10
			Nos. 679-682 (4)	3.40	2.30

Queen Type of 1992

Souvenir Sheet

1993, Oct. 5 Litho. *Perf. 14½x14*

Background Color

683	A127	$10	bright green	4.50	3.75

Bangkok '93 Stamp Exhibition. No. 683 contains one 25x30mm stamp.

Goldfish A135

1993, Nov. 17 Litho. *Perf. 14½*

684	A135	$1	Red calico egg-fish	.35	.35
685	A135	$1.90	Red cap oranda	.65	.45
686	A135	$2.40	Red & white fringetail	1.00	.70
687	A135	$5	Black & gold dragon-eye	2.00	1.60
a.			Souvenir sheet of 4, #684-687	7.00	6.50
			Nos. 684-687 (4)	4.00	3.10

Queen Type of 1992

Perf. 15x14

1994, Jan. 27 Photo. Wmk. 373

688		Souvenir booklet	10.50	12.00
a.	A127	Sheet of #630, 5 #646	3.50	3.50
b.	A127	Sheet of #643, 5 #644	3.50	3.50
c.	A127	Sheet of 5 #636, #651B	3.50	3.50

First Hong Kong stamps, 130th anniv. No. 688 sold for $38.

Year of the Dog A136

Various embroidery designs of dogs.

1994, Jan. 27 Litho. *Perf. 14½*

689	A136	$1	multicolored	.35	.20
690	A136	$1.90	multicolored	.65	.45
691	A136	$2.40	multicolored	.80	.55
a.			Bklt. pane, 3 ea #689, 691	5.50	
692	A136	$5	multicolored	1.75	1.10
a.			Souvenir sheet of 4, #689-692	*6.00*	*6.00*
			Nos. 689-692 (4)	3.55	2.30

See No. 838f.

Royal Hong Kong Police Force, 150th Anniv. — A137

Designs: $1, Traffic policeman, woman. $1.20, Marine policeman. $1.90, Male, female officers of 1950. $2, Policeman holding M-16. $2.40, Policemen, 1906, pre-1920. $5, Policemen, 1900.

1994, May 4 Litho. *Perf. 13½*

693	A137	$1	multicolored	.35	.30
694	A137	$1.20	multicolored	.40	.35
695	A137	$1.90	multicolored	.65	.55
696	A137	$2	multicolored	.70	.60
697	A137	$2.40	multicolored	.80	.70
698	A137	$5	multicolored	2.00	1.50
			Nos. 693-698 (6)	4.90	4.00

Traditional Chinese Festivals — A138

Designs: $1, Dragon Boat Festival. $1.90, Lunar New Year. $2.40, Seven Sisters Festival. $5, Mid-Autumn Festival.

1994, June 8 Litho. *Perf. 14*

699	A138	$1	multicolored	.25	.25
700	A138	$1.90	multicolored	.50	.50
701	A138	$2.40	multicolored	.60	.60
702	A138	$5	multicolored	1.25	1.25
			Nos. 699-702 (4)	2.60	2.60

XV Commonwealth Games, Victoria, BC, Canada — A139

Unwmk.

1994, Aug. 25 Litho. *Perf. 14*

703	A139	$1	Swimming	.25	.25
704	A139	$1.90	Lawn bowling	.50	.50
705	A139	$2.40	Gymnastics	.60	.60
706	A139	$5	Weight lifting	1.25	1.25
			Nos. 703-706 (4)	2.60	2.60

Dr. James Legge (1815-97), Religious Leader, Translator — A140

1994, Oct. 5 Litho. *Perf. 14*

707	A140	$1	multicolored	.25	.25

Corals — A141

1994, Nov. 17 Litho. *Perf. 14*

708	A141	$1	Alcyonium	.35	.20
709	A141	$1.90	Zoanthus	.65	.45
710	A141	$2.40	Tubastrea	.80	.55
711	A141	$5	Platygyra	1.75	1.10
a.			Souv. sheet of 4, #708-711	*5.00*	2.50
			Nos. 708-711 (4)	3.55	2.30

New Year 1995 (Year of the Boar) A142

Various embroidery designs of pigs.

1995, Jan. 17 Litho. *Perf. 14½*

712	A142	$1	multicolored	.40	.35
713	A142	$1.90	multicolored	.85	.65
714	A142	$2.40	multicolored	1.10	.75
a.			Bklt. pane, 3 each #712, 714	4.50	
			Complete booklet, 2 #714a	9.00	
715	A142	$5	multicolored	2.10	1.50
a.			Souvenir sheet of 4, #712-715	*8.50*	6.75
			Nos. 712-715 (4)	4.45	3.25

See No. 838d.

Intl. Sporting Events A143

Designs: $1, Hong Kong Rugby Sevens. $1.90, China Sea Race. $2.40, Intl. Dragon Boat Races. $5, Hong Kong Intl. Horse Races.

1995, Mar. 22 Litho. *Perf. 14½*

716	A143	$1	multicolored	.20	.20
717	A143	$1.90	multicolored	.45	.40
718	A143	$2.40	multicolored	.60	.50
719	A143	$5	multicolored	1.25	1.00
			Nos. 716-719 (4)	2.50	2.10

Traditional Buildings — A144

Litho. & Engr.

1995, May 24 *Perf. 13½*

720 A144 $1 Tsui Shing Lau .40 .20
721 A144 $1.90 Sam Tung UK .75 .45
722 A144 $2.40 Lo Wai .85 .50
723 A144 $5 Man Shek Tong 2.00 1.10
Nos. 720-723 (4) 4.00 2.25

Queen Type of 1992
Souvenir Sheet

1995, Aug. 25 Litho. *Perf. 14*
Background Color

724 A127 $10 carmine *6.00* 2.50

Singapore '95 World Stamp Exhibition. No. 724 contains one 25x30mm stamp.

Royal Hong Kong Regiment (1854-1995) — A145

$1.20, Modern Regimental Badge, vert. $2.10, Current flag. $2,60, Former flag. $5, Royal Hong Kong Defense Force, 1951 soldier's badge, vert.

1995, Aug. 16 Litho. *Perf. 14½*

725 A145 $1.20 multicolored .30 .30
726 A145 $2.10 multicolored .50 .50
727 A145 $2.60 multicolored .60 .60
728 A145 $5 multicolored 1.10 1.10
Nos. 725-728 (4) 2.50 2.50

Queen Type of 1992
Souvenir Sheet

1995, Oct. 9 Litho. *Perf. 14*
Background Color

729 A127 $10 brown 6.00 5.25

End of World War II, 50th anniv. No. 729 contains one 25x30mm stamp.

Hong Kong Movie Stars A146

1995, Nov. 15 Litho. *Perf. 13½*

730 A146 $1.20 Bruce Lee 1.25 .60
731 A146 $2.10 Leung Sing-Por 2.25 1.10
732 A146 $2.60 Yam Kim-Fai 3.00 1.40
733 A146 $5 Lin Dai 5.50 2.50
Nos. 730-733 (4) 12.00 5.60

New Year 1996 (Year of the Rat) A147

Various embroidery designs of rats.

1996, Jan. 31 Litho. *Perf. 13½*

734 A147 $1.20 multicolored .30 .30
735 A147 $2.10 multicolored .55 .55
736 A147 $2.60 multicolored .70 .70
a. Bklt. pane, 3 ea #734, 736 3.00
Complete booklet, 2 #736a 6.00
737 A147 $5 multicolored 1.25 1.25
a. Souvenir sheet of 4, #734-737 3.00
Nos. 734-737 (4) 2.80 2.80

See No. 838a.

Queen Type of 1992
Souvenir Sheet
Unwmk.

1996, Feb. 23 Litho. *Perf. 14*
Background Color

738 A127 $10 orange 3.00 3.00

Hong Kong '97 Stamp Exhibition. No. 738 contains one 25x30mm stamp.

1996 Summer Olympics, Atlanta — A148

1996, Mar. 20 Litho. *Perf. 13½*

739 A148 $1.20 Gymnastics .30 .30
740 A148 $2.10 Diving .55 .55
741 A148 $2.60 Running .70 .70
742 A148 $5 Basketball 1.25 1.25
Nos. 739-742 (4) 2.80 2.80

Souvenir Sheet

742A Sheet of 4, #742b-742e 3.00 3.00
f. As #742A, different sheet margin 3.75 3.75

No. 742Af shows Olympic gold medal at top of sheet margin.

Nos. 748-751 have denominations in color and Olympic rings in gold. Nos. 739-742 have denominations in black, Olympic rings in different colors. No. 742Ab-742Ae have gold Olympic rings.

No. 742f issued 7/19/96.

Queen Type of 1992
Souvenir Sheet
Unwmk.

1996, May 18 Litho. *Perf. 14*
Background Color

743 A127 $10 brt grn & bl vio 2.60 2.60

Hong Kong '97 Stamp Exhibition. No. 743 contains one 25x30mm stamp.

Archaeological Finds — A149

1996, June 26 Litho. *Perf. 13½*

744 A149 $1.20 Painted pottery basin .30 .30
745 A149 $2.10 Stone "Yue" .55 .55
746 A149 $2.60 Stone "GE" .70 .70
747 A149 $5 Pottery tripod 1.25 1.25
Nos. 744-747 (4) 2.80 2.80

1996 Summer Olympic Games Type

1996, July 19 Litho. *Perf. 14x14½*
Color of Denomination

748 A148 $1.20 like #739, red .20 .20
749 A148 $2.10 like #740, blue .40 .40
750 A148 $2.60 like #741, green .50 .50
751 A148 $5 like #742, org .90 .90
Nos. 748-751 (4) 2.00 2.00

Nos. 748-751 have denominations in color and Olympic rings in gold. Nos. 739-742 have denonminations in black, Olympic rings in different colors.

Mountains in Hong Kong — A150

Unwmk.

1996, Sept. 24 Litho. *13½x14*

752 A150 $1.30 Pat Sing Leng .45 .45

Perf. 14x14½, 14½x14

753 A150 $2.50 Ma On Shan .90 .90
754 A150 $3.10 Lion Rock, vert. 1.10 1.10

Perf. 14x13½

755 A150 $5 Lantau Peak, vert. 1.75 1.75
Nos. 752-755 (4) 4.20 4.20

No. 753 is 40x36mm, No. 754 36x40mm. See #899, 905.

Queen Type of 1992
Souvenir Sheets

1996 Photo. Unwmk. *Perf. 14*
Background Color

756 A127 $10 red 2.60 2.60
757 A127 $10 brown 2.60 2.60

Issued: No. 756, 10/16; No. 757, 10/29.

Visit Hong Kong '97 Stamp Exhibition (#756). 1996 Summer Olympic Games, Atlanta (#757). Nos. 756-757 each contain one 25x30mm stamp.

Urban Heritage A151

Designs: $1.30, Main building, University of Hong Kong, 1912. $2.50, Western Market, 1906. $3.10, Old Pathological Institute, 1905. $5, Flagstaff House, 1846.

Litho. & Engr.

1996, Nov. 20 *Perf. 13½*

758 A151 $1.30 multicolored .45 .45
759 A151 $2.50 multicolored .75 .75
760 A151 $3.10 multicolored .90 .90
761 A151 $5 multicolored 1.50 1.50
Nos. 758-761 (4) 3.60 3.60

Hong Kong People Type of 1989
Souvenir Sheet
Perf. 13x13½

1997, Jan. Photo. Unwmk.

762 A111 $5 like No. 549 1.50 1.50

No. 762 contains one 23x33mm stamp that has darker colors and a different perf. than No. 549.

Panoramic Views of Hong Kong Skyline — A152

#763-775: Various daytime views from harbor.

#776-778, Various nighttime views from harbor.

Perf. 13½x13

1997, Jan. 26 Litho. Unwmk.
Background Color

763 A152 10c pink .20 .20
764 A152 20c vermilion .20 .20
765 A152 50c orange .20 .20
766 A152 $1 orange yellow .25 .25
767 A152 $1.20 olive .30 .30
768 A152 $1.30 apple green .35 .35
a. Booklet pane of 10 3.50
Complete booklet, #768a 3.50
769 A152 $1.40 green .35 .35
770 A152 $1.60 blue green .40 .40
771 A152 $2 green blue .55 .55
772 A152 $2.10 blue .55 .55
773 A152 $2.50 purple .65 .65
a. Booklet pane of 10 6.50
Complete booklet, #773a 6.50
774 A152 $3.10 rose .80 .80
a. Booklet pane of 10 8.00
Complete booklet, #774a 8.00
c. Sheet of 4, #771-774 2.50 2.50
775 A152 $5 orange 1.25 1.25
a. Sheet of 13, #763-775 5.75 5.75

Size: 28x33mm
Perf. 14x13½

776 A152 $10 blue 2.50 2.50
a. Souv. sheet of 1 (Series #4) *8.00*
b. Souv. sheet of 1 (Series #5) *8.00*
c. Souv. Sheet of 1 (Sheet #12) 2.50 2.50
d. Souv. sheet of 1, perf14x13¼ (Sheet #14) 2.60 2.60
777 A152 $20 bl, pur & rose 5.25 5.25
778 A152 $50 purple & rose 13.00 13.00
a. Sheet of 3, #776-778 *21.00*
Nos. 763-778 (16) 26.80 26.80

Hong Kong '97 (#776a-776b). 1996 Atlanta Paralympic Games (#776c). 13th Asian Games, Bangkok, Thailand (#774c). China 1999 World Philatelic Exhibition (#776d).

Perforations are alternating small and large holes.

#775a and 778a are continuous designs.

Issued: #776a, 2/12; #776b, 2/16; #774c, 3/27/99; #776d, 8/21/99.

See note after No. 940.

Coil Stamps

Photo. *Perf. 14½x14*

763a A152 10c .20 .20
765a A152 50c .20 .20
768b A152 $1.30 .35 .35
770a A152 $1.60 .40 .40
773b A152 $2.50 .65 .65
774b A152 $3.10 .80 .80
Nos. 763a-774b (6) 2.60 2.60

These have numbers on back of every fifth stamp.

Perforations are the same size.

New Year 1997 (Year of the Ox) A153

Various designs of oxen.

Perf. 14½

1997, Feb. 27 Litho. Unwmk.
Background Color

780 A153 $1.30 pink .30 .30
781 A153 $2.50 orange yellow .65 .65
782 A153 $3.10 green .80 .80
a. Booklet pane, 3 each #780, 782, perf. 13½ 3.50
Complete booklet, 2 #782a 7.00
783 A153 $5 blue 1.25 1.25
a. Souvenir sheet of 4, #780-783 4.50 4.50
Nos. 780-783 (4) 3.00 3.00

See Nos. 838b, 838c.

Perf. 13½

780a A153 $1.30 .40 .40
781a A153 $2.50 .75 .75
782b A153 $3.10 .90 .90
783b A153 $5 1.50 1.50
c. Souvenir sheet of 4, #780a-781a, 782b-783b 3.50 3.50

Migratory Birds — A154

$1.30, Yellow-breasted bunting. $2.50, Great knot. $3.10, Falcated teal. $5, Black-faced spoonbill.

Perf. 13½

1997, Apr. 27 Unwmk. Photo.

784 A154 $1.30 multicolored .30 .30
785 A154 $2.50 multicolored .65 .65
786 A154 $3.10 multicolored .80 .80
787 A154 $5 multicolored 1.25 1.25
Nos. 784-787 (4) 3.00 3.00

Landmarks — A155

$1.30, Hong Kong Stadium. $2.50, The Peak Tower. $3.10, Hong Kong Convention & Exhibition Center. $5, The Lantau Link (bridge).

1997, May 18 *Perf. 13½*

788 A155 $1.30 multicolored .30 .30
789 A155 $2.50 multicolored .65 .65
790 A155 $3.10 multicolored .80 .80
791 A155 $5 multicolored 1.25 1.25
a. Souvenir sheet of 1 1.25 1.25
Nos. 788-791 (4) 3.00 3.00

Opening of the Lantau Link (bridge) (#791a).

Nos. 788-791 and 791a also exist perf 14x14½. Values are the same.

Royal Postbox Type of 1991
Souvenir Sheet

1997, June 30 Litho. *Perf. 11½*
792 A122 $5 like No. 604 1.25 1.25

No. 792 contains one 19x29mm stamp.

Special Administrative Region of People's Republic of China

First Issue Under Chinese Administration A156

Sights and symbols of Hong Kong: $1.30, Chinese architecture. $1.60, Modern buildings, methods of transportation. $2.50, Skyscrapers, Hong Kong Convention & Exhibition Center. $2.60, Cargo ship entering port. $3.10, Chinese junks, dolphins jumping in water. $5, Hibiscus flower.

1997, July 1 Litho. *Perf. 12x12½*
793 A156 $1.30 multicolored .35 .35
794 A156 $1.60 multicolored .40 .40
795 A156 $2.50 multicolored .65 .65
796 A156 $2.60 multicolored .70 .70
797 A156 $3.10 multicolored .80 .80
798 A156 $5 multicolored 1.25 1.25
a. Souvenir sheet of 1 1.25 1.25
Nos. 793-798 (6) 4.15 4.15

1997 World Bank Group/Intl. Monetary Fund Annual Meetings — A157

Designs: $1.30, Finance, banking. $2.50, Investment, stock exchange. $3.10, Trade, telecommunications. $5, Infrastructure, transport.

Perf. 14½
1997, Sept. 21 Litho. Unwmk.
799 A157 $1.30 multicolored .30 .30
800 A157 $2.50 multicolored .65 .65
801 A157 $3.10 multicolored .80 .80
802 A157 $5 multicolored 1.25 1.25
Nos. 799-802 (4) 3.00 3.00

Shells — A158

1997, Nov. 9 Photo. *Perf. 13½*
803 A158 $1.30 Clam .35 .35
804 A158 $2.50 Cowrie .65 .65
805 A158 $3.10 Cone .80 .80
806 A158 $5 Murex 1.25 1.25
Nos. 803-806 (4) 3.05 3.05

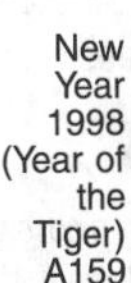

New Year 1998 (Year of the Tiger) A159

Various embroidery designs of tigers.

1998, Jan. 4 Litho. *Perf. 13½*
807 A159 $1.30 multicolored .30 .30
808 A159 $2.50 multicolored .65 .65
809 A159 $3.10 multicolored .80 .80
a. Bklt. pane, 6 ea #807, 809 7.00
Complete booklet, #809a 7.00
810 A159 $5 multicolored 1.25 1.25
a. Souvenir sheet, #807-810 3.00 3.00
Nos. 807-810 (4) 3.00 3.00

See No. 838.

Star Ferry, Cent. A160

Star Ferry during: $1.30, 1900's. $2.50, 1910's-1920's. $3.10, 1920's-1950's. $5, Mid-1950's on.

1998, Apr. 26 Photo. *Perf. 13½*
811 A160 $1.30 multicolored .30 .30
812 A160 $2.50 multicolored .65 .65
813 A160 $3.10 multicolored .80 .80
814 A160 $5 multicolored 1.25 1.25
Nos. 811-814 (4) 3.00 3.00

Souvenir Sheet

The Closing of Kai Tak Airport — A161

Illustration reduced.

1998, July 5 Photo. *Perf. 13½*
815 A161 $5 multicolored 1.25 1.25

New Hong Kong Airport A162

$1.30, Passengers on terminal's moving sidewalks. $1.60, Couple entering Automated People Mover. $2.50, Airport Railway, Tsing Ma Bridge. $2.60, Terminal building, Airmail Center. $3.10, Aircraft gates. $5, Terminal departure level.

1998, July 5 *Perf. 14*
816 A162 $1.30 multicolored .35 .35
817 A162 $1.60 multicolored .40 .40
818 A162 $2.50 multicolored .65 .65
819 A162 $2.60 multicolored .70 .70
820 A162 $3.10 multicolored .80 .80
821 A162 $5 multicolored 1.25 1.25
a. Souvenir sheet of 1 1.25 1.25
b. Block of 6, #816-821 4.25 4.25

See note after No. 940.

A163

A164

Scouting in Hong Kong: Rope tied in various knots, different scouting divisions: $1.30, Grasshopper Scouts, Cub Scouts. $2.50, Tower, tents, Boy Scouts, Girl Scouts. $3.10, Helicopter, sailboats, Venture Scouts. $5, City buildings, Rover Scouts, adult leaders.

Unwmk.
1998, July 26 Litho. *Perf. 14*
822 A163 $1.30 multicolored .30 .30
823 A163 $2.50 multicolored .65 .65
824 A163 $3.10 multicolored .80 .80
825 A163 $5 multicolored 1.25 1.25
Nos. 822-825 (4) 3.00 3.00

1998, Sept. 20 Litho. *Perf. 13½*
Hong Kong designs.
826 A164 $1.30 Graphic .35 .35
827 A164 $2.50 Product .65 .65
828 A164 $3.10 Interior .85 .85
829 A164 $5 Fashion 1.25 1.25
Nos. 826-829 (4) 3.10 3.10

Kites — A165

1998, Nov. 15 Litho. *Perf. 13½*
830 A165 $1.30 Dragonfly .30 .30
831 A165 $2.50 Dragon .65 .65
832 A165 $3.10 Butterfly .80 .80
833 A165 $5 Goldfish 1.25 1.25
a. Souvenir sheet, #830-833 3.00 3.00
Nos. 830-833 (4) 3.00 3.00

A166

1999, Jan. 31 Photo. *Perf. 14x13½*
New Year 1999 (Year of the Rabbit): White rabbit with flower designs in various positions.
834 A166 $1.30 yel org & multi .35 .35
Scratched panel .35
a. Sheet of 10 3.50
835 A166 $2.50 green & multi .65 .65
Scratched panel .35
a. Sheet of 10 6.50
836 A166 $3.10 orange & multi .80 .80
Scratched panel .35
a. Sheet of 10 8.00
837 A166 $5 red lilac & multi 1.25 1.25
Scratched panel .35
a. Sheet of 10 12.50
Nos. 834-837 (4) 3.05 3.05

Nos. 834-837 are printed with a layering of gold "scratch off" ink, which, when removed, reveals a Chinese greeting.

New Year Types of 1987-98

Designs: a, Like #734. b, Like #780. c, Like #783. d, Like #712. e Like 515. f, Like #691. g, Like #534. h, Like #668. i, Like #615. j, Like #584. k, Like #560. #a.-k. have 4 Chinese characters at UL instead of crown and ER.

1999, Feb. 21 Litho. *Perf. 13½*
Sheet of 12
838 $1.30 #a.-k, #807 + label 4.00 4.00

Design in label and sheet selvage is engraved.

Intl. Year of Older Persons — A167

Perf. 14½
1999, Mar. 14 Litho. Unwmk.
839 A167 $1.30 Calligraphy .35 .35
840 A167 $2.50 Bird raising .65 .65
841 A167 $3.10 Playing Go .80 .80
842 A167 $5 Voluntary services 1.25 1.25
Nos. 839-842 (4) 3.05 3.05

Souvenir Sheet

Giant Pandas in Hong Kong — A168

Illustration reduced.

1999, Apr. 25 Litho. *Perf. 14¼*
843 A168 $10 multicolored 2.50 2.50

No. 843 contains one circular stamp 38mm in diameter.

Public Transport — A169

1999, May 23
844 A169 $1.30 Bus .35 .35
845 A169 $2.40 Minibus .60 .60
846 A169 $2.50 Tram .65 .65
847 A169 $2.60 Taxi .70 .70
848 A169 $3.10 Airport express .80 .80
Nos. 844-848 (5) 3.10 3.10

Hong Kong and Singapore Tourism — A170

Designs: $1.20, Hong Kong Harbor. $1.30, Singapore Skyline. $2.50, Giant Buddha, Hong Kong. $2.60, Merlion, Sentosa Island, Singapore. $3.10, Hong Kong street scene. $5, Bugis Junction, Singapore.

Perf. 13¼
1999, July 1 Litho. Unwmk.
849 A170 $1.20 multicolored .30 .30
850 A170 $1.30 multicolored .35 .35
851 A170 $2.50 multicolored .65 .65
852 A170 $2.60 multicolored .65 .65
853 A170 $3.10 multicolored .80 .80
854 A170 $5 multicolored 1.25 1.25
a. Souvenir sheet, #849-854 4.00 4.00
Nos. 849-854 (6) 4.00 4.00

See Singapore Nos. 896-902.

People's Republic of China, 50th Anniv. — A171

Designs: $1.30, Flags of People's Republic and Hong Kong Special Administrative District. $2.50 Bauhinia blakeana flower, Hong Kong skyline. $3.10, Dragon dance. $5, Fireworks.

Perf. 14¼ Syncopated
1999, Oct. 1 Photo.
Granite Paper
855 A171 $1.30 multicolored .35 .35
856 A171 $2.50 multicolored .65 .65
857 A171 $3.10 multicolored .75 .75
858 A171 $5 multicolored 1.25 1.25
a. Block or strip of 4, #855-858 3.00 3.00

Issued in sheets of 4 blocks or strips and individually in sheets of 20..

Landmarks — A172

10c, Museum of Tea Ware. 20c, St. John's Cathedral. 50c, Legislative Council building. $1, Tai Fu Tai. $1.20, Wong Tai Sin Temple. $1.30, Victoria Harbor. $1.40, Hong Kong Railway Museum. $1.60, Tsim Sha Tsui Clock Tower. $2, Happy Valley Racecourse. $2.10, Kowloon-Canton Railway. $2.50, Chi Lin Nunnery. $3.10, Buddha at Po Lin Monastery. $5, Aw Boon Haw Gardens. $10, Tsing Ma Bridge. $20, Hong Kong Convention & Exhibition Center. $50, Hong Kong Intl. Airport.

Perf. 13x13¾ Syncopated

1999, Oct. 18 **Photo.**

Granite Paper

859 A172 10c multi .20 .20
a. Booklet pane of 1 *.20*
860 A172 20c multi .20 .20
a. Booklet pane of 1 *.20*
861 A172 50c multi .20 .20
a. Booklet pane of 1 *.25*
862 A172 $1 multi .25 .25
a. Booklet pane of 1 *.50*
863 A172 $1.20 multi .30 .30
a. Booklet pane of 1 *.60*
864 A172 $1.30 multi .35 .35
a. Booklet pane of 1 *.70*
865 A172 $1.40 multi .35 .35
a. Booklet pane of 1 *.70*
b. Booklet pane of 10 3.50 —
Booklet, #865b 3.50
866 A172 $1.60 multi .40 .40
a. Booklet pane of 1 *.80*
867 A172 $2 multi .50 .50
a. Booklet pane of 1 *1.00*
868 A172 $2.10 multi .55 .55
a. Booklet pane of 1 *1.10*
869 A172 $2.50 multi .60 .60
a. Booklet pane of 1 *1.25*
870 A172 $3.10 multi .75 .75
a. Booklet pane of 1 *1.50*
871 A172 $5 multi 1.25 1.25
a. Booklet pane of 1 *2.50*
Souv. booklet, #859a-871a *12.00*
b. Sheet of 13, #859-871 5.50 5.50
c. Souvenir sheet of 1 (Definitive #4) 1.25 1.25
d. Souv. sheet of 1 (Definitive #6) 1.25 1.25

Size: 26x32mm

Perf. 13¼

872 A172 $10 blue & multi 2.50 2.50
a. Souv. sheet of 1 (Definitive #1) 2.50 2.50
b. Souv. sheet of 1 (Exhibition #1) 2.50 2.50
c. Souv. sheet of 1 (Exhibition #2) 2.50 2.50
d. Souv. sheet of 1 (Definitive #2) 2.50 2.50
e. Souv. sheet of 1 (Definitive #5) 2.50 2.50
873 A172 $20 multi 5.00 5.00
874 A172 $50 multi 12.50 12.50
a. Sheet of 3, #872-874 20.00 20.00
Nos. 859-874 (16) 25.90 25.90

Coil Stamps

13¾x13¼ Syncopated

Size: 18x22mm

874B A172 10c multi .20 .20
874C A172 50c multi .20 .20
874D A172 $1.30 multi .35 .35
874E A172 $1.60 multi .40 .40
874F A172 $2.50 multi .60 .60
874G A172 $3.10 multi .75 .75
Nos. 874B-874G (6) 2.50 2.50

#872a-872b are Syncopated perf 14x14¼. #872c is Syncopated perf 13¼x13. #872d is Syncopated perf 14x14½. No. 872e is Syncopated perf. 13¼x13.

Issued: #872a, 1/31/00; #872b, 2/10/00; #872c, 4/15/00; #872d, 12/2/00; #871c, 4/21/01; #872e, 8/1/01; #874B-874E, 874G, 10/18/99; #874F, 10/18/99; #871d, 1/19/02. #865b, 4/1/02.

See note after No. 940.

Chinese White Dolphin — A173

Various views of dolphin.

1999, Nov. 14 **Litho.** ***Perf. 14½***

Granite Paper

875 A173 $1.30 green & multi .35 .35
876 A173 $2.50 bl grn & multi .65 .65
877 A173 $3.10 blue & multi .75 .75
878 A173 $5 pur & multi 1.25 1.25

Souvenir Sheet

879 Sheet of 4, #a.-d. 3.00 3.00

Nos. 875-878 have Worldwide Fund for Nature (WWF) emblem; Nos. 879a-879d do not.

See No. 900.

Souvenir Sheet

Millennium — A174

No. 880: a, Dragon boat races, skyline. b, Bridge, birds.

Illustration reduced.

Perf. 14¼ Syncopated

1999, Dec. 31 **Photo.**

Granite Paper

880 A174 $5 Sheet of 2, #a.-b. 2.50 2.50

New Millennium Children's Stamp Design Contest Winners — A175

Designs: $1.30, Scales. $2.50, Children planting tree on planet. $3.10, Planets. $5, Inhabited planets, space shuttle, rocket.

2000, Jan. 1 **Granite Paper**

881 A175 $1.30 multi .35 .35
882 A175 $2.50 multi .65 .65
883 A175 $3.10 multi .75 .75
884 A175 $5 multi 1.25 1.25
Nos. 881-884 (4) 3.00 3.00

Victoria Harbor A176

Litho. & Embossed with Foil Application

2000, Jan. 1 ***Perf. 13¼***

885 A176 $50 gold & multi 12.50 12.50

New Year 2000 (Year of the Dragon) — A177

Various dragons.

Perf. 14¼ Syncopated

2000, Jan. 23 **Litho.**

Granite Paper

886 A177 $1.30 multi .35 .35
887 A177 $2.50 multi .65 .65
888 A177 $3.10 multi .75 .75
889 A177 $5 multi 1.25 1.25
a. Souvenir sheet of 1, imperf. 1.25 1.25
b. Souvenir sheet, #886-889 3.00 3.00
Nos. 886-889 (4) 3.00 3.00

Museums and Libraries — A178

Designs: $1.30, Heritage Museum. $2.50, Central Library. $3.10, Museum of Coastal Defense. $5 Museum of History.

Illustration reduced.

Perf. 14½x14¼

2000, Mar. 26 **Photo.**

Granite Paper

890 A178 $1.30 multi .35 .35
891 A178 $2.50 multi .65 .65
892 A178 $3.10 multi .75 .75
893 A178 $5 multi 1.25 1.25
a. Block, #890-893 3.00 3.00
Nos. 890-893 (4) 3.00 3.00

Nos. 890-893 issued in sheets of 24. No. 893a issued only in sheet containing 4 blocks.

Red Cross — A179

Designs: $1.30, Blood transfusion. $2.50, Special education. $3.10, Disaster relief. $5, Voluntary service.

Perf. 14¼ Syncopated

2000, May 7 **Photo.**

Granite Paper

894 A179 $1.30 multi .35 .35
895 A179 $2.50 multi .65 .65
896 A179 $3.10 multi .75 .75
897 A179 $5 multi 1.25 1.25
a. Souvenir sheet, #894-897 3.00 3.00
Nos. 894-897 (4) 3.00 3.00

Flower Type of 1989, Mountain Type of 1996 Inscribed "Hong Kong, China," and Dolphin Type of 1999

Perf. 14¼ Syncopated

2000, June 17 **Photo.**

Granite Paper

898 A90 $5 Booklet pane of 1, like #455 3.00 3.00
899 A150 $5 Booklet pane of 1, like #755 3.00 3.00
900 A173 $5 Booklet pane of 1, like #879d 3.00 3.00
Booklet, #898-900 9.00

Hong Kong 2001 Stamp Exhibition. Booklet sold for $35.

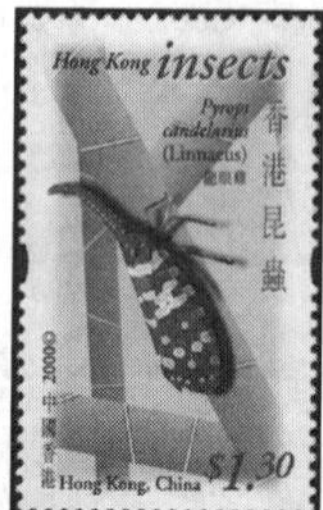

Insects — A180

Designs: $1.30, Pyrops candelarius. $2.50, Macromidia ellenae. $3.10, Troides helena spilotia. $5, Chiridopsis bowringi.

Perf. 13½x13¼ Syncopated

2000, July 16 **Litho.**

Granite Paper

901-904 A180 Set of 4 3.00 3.00
904a Souvenir sheet, #901-904 3.00 3.00

Mountain Type of 1996 Inscribed "Hong Kong, China"

Souvenir Sheet

Perf. 13¼ Syncopated

2000, Aug. 12 **Photo.**

Granite Paper

905 A150 $10 Like #754 2.50 2.50

Hong Kong 2001 Stamp Exhibition.

2000 Summer Olympics, Sydney — A181

Designs: $1.30, Cycling, badminton. $2.50, Table tennis, running. $3.10, Judo, rowing. $5, Swimming, sailboarding.

Perf. 14¼ Syncopated

2000, Aug. 27 **Litho.**

Granite Paper

906-909 A181 Set of 4 3.00 3.00

Birds A182

2000, Sept. 30 **Photo.**

Granite Paper

910 Booklet pane of 2 2.00
a. A182 $1.30 Yellow-breasted bunting .70 .70
b. A182 $2.50 Great knot 1.25 1.25
911 Booklet pane of 2 4.25
a. A182 $3.10 Falcated teal 1.60 1.60
b. A182 $5 Black-faced spoonbill 2.60 2.60
Booklet, #910-911 6.25

Booklet containing Nos. 910-911 sold for $25.

Chinese General Chamber of Commerce, Cent. — A183

Designs: $1.30, Hong Kong in 1900. $2.50, Headquarters buildings. $3.10, People reading notice for distribution of relief funds. $5, Hand with computer mouse, currency symbols.

Perf. 13¾ Syncopated

2000, Oct. 22 **Litho.**

Granite Paper

912-915 A183 Set of 4 3.00 3.00

Coral Type of 1994 Inscribed "Hong Kong, China"

Souvenir Sheet

Perf. 13¼ Syncopated

2000, Nov. 25 **Photo.**

Granite Paper

916 A141 $10 Like #709 2.50 2.50

Landmarks Type of 1999

Souvenir Sheet

Litho. & Holography

2000, Dec. 31

917 A172 $20 Like #873 5.00 5.00

Soaking in water may affect hologram.

New Year 2001 (Year of the Snake) — A184

Various snakes. Denominations: $1.30, $2.50, $3.10, $5.

918-921	A184	Set of 4	3.00	3.00
921a		Souvenir sheet of 1, imperf.	1.25	1.25
921b		Souvenir sheet, #918-921	3.00	3.00

Souvenir Sheet

Opening of Hong Kong 2001 Stamp Exhibition — A185

No. 922: a, Year of the Dragon. b, Year of the Snake.

Litho. & Embossed with Foil Application

2001, Feb. 1 ***Perf. 13¼***

922 A185 $50 Sheet of 2, #a-b 25.00 25.00

Indiginous Trees Type of 1988 Inscribed "Hong Kong, China"

2001 Photo. ***Perf. 14¼ Syncopated***

Granite Paper

923	A105	$5 multi, sheetlet #5	1.25	1.25
a.		Sheetlet #6	1.25	1.25
b.		Sheetlet #7	1.25	1.25
c.		Sheetlet #8	1.25	1.25

Issued: No. 923, 2/2; No. 923a, 2/3; No. 923b, 2/4; No. 923c, 2/5. No. 923b with gold overprint in margin reading "To commemorate the FIAP Day of HONG KONG 2001 Stamp Exhibition on 4th February, 2001" is a private emission.

See note after No. 940 for unsyncopated stamp.

Greetings — A186

Designs: $1.30, Maple leaves. $1.60, Swans. $2.50, Chicks. $2.60, Cherry blossoms. $3.10, Bamboo. $5, Snow-covered plant.

2001, Feb. 1 **Photo.**

Granite Paper

Stamps + Labels

924-929 A186 Set of 6 4.00 4.00

A sheet of 18 $1.30 stamps with labels with Chinese inscriptions only to the right of the stamp, and labels depicting various celebrities was sold for $120 in limited quantities.

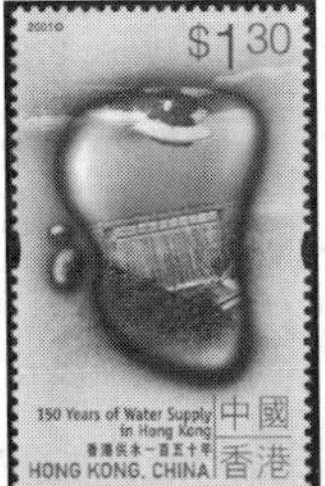

Hong Kong Water Supply, 150th Anniv. — A187

Designs: $1.30, Tai Tam Tuk Reservoir. $2.50, Plover Cove Reservoir. $3.10, Pipelines. $5, Beakers, chemical symbols.

2001, Mar. 18 **Litho. & Embossed**

Granite Paper

930-933	A187	Set of 4	3.00	3.00
a.		Block of 4, #930-933	3.00	3.00

Movie Stars A188

Designs: $1.30, Ng Cho-fan (1911-93) and Pak Yin (1920-87). $2.50, Sun Ma Si-tsang (1916-97) and Tang Bik-wan (1926-91). $3.10, Cheung Wood-yau (1910-85) and Wong Manlei (1913-98). $5, Mak Bing-wing (1915-84) and Fung Wong-nui (1925-92).

2001, Apr. 8 **Litho.**

Granite Paper

934-937	A188	Set of 4	3.00	3.00
a.		Block of 4, #934-937	3.00	3.00

Values are for stamps with surrounding selvage.

On June 12, 2001 Hong Kong sold for $120 limited numbers of a sheet containing 18 examples of the $1.30 stamp, No. 924. The 18 labels to the right of the stamps on this sheet differ from those found on examples of No. 924 sold on the stamp's original date of issue, and the 18 labels to the left of the stamps depict Chinese celebrities.

Dragon Boat Races A189

Dragon boats and: No. 938, $5, Sydney Opera House. No. 939, Hong Kong Convention and Exhibition Center.

2001, June 25 **Litho.** ***Perf. 14x14½***

Granite Paper

938-939	A189	Set of 2	2.50	2.50
a.		Souvenir sheet, #938-939	2.50	2.50

See Australia Nos. 1977-1978.

Emblem of 2008 Summer Olympics, Beijing — A190

2001, July 14 **Photo.** ***Perf. 13x13¼***

940 A190 $1.30 multi + label .35 .35

No. 940 printed in sheets of 12 stamp + label pairs with one large central label. See People's Republic of China No. 3119, Macao No. 1067. No. 940 with different label is from People's Republic of China No. 3119a.

On July 21, 2001 Hong Kong sold a booklet containing stamps with a face value of $12.40 for $30. The stamps are the Indigenous Trees type of 1988 with the inscription "Hong Kong, China." The first pane in the booklet contained $1.30 and $2.50 stamps, and those on the second pane contained $3.10 and $5 stamps.

On Aug. 25, 2001 Hong Kong sold a booklet containing stamps with a face value of $30 for $65. The first pane in the booklet contained four stamps with a face value of $1.80 of the Stamp Collecting type of 1992 with the inscription "Hong Kong, China." The second pane contained two $3.10 perf. 13½x13 stamps on granite paper of type A152, and two $3.10 perf. 13¾ syncopated stamps on granite paper of type A172. The third pane contained four $2.60 perf. 14¼ stamps on granite paper of type A162.

Tea Culture — A191

Various tea services and background colors of: $1.30, Lilac. $2.50, Orange brown. $3.10, Bright orange. $5, Green.

Perf. 14¼x14½ Syncopated

2001, Sept. 9 **Litho.**

944-947 A191 Set of 4 3.00 3.00

Herbs — A192

Designs: $1.30, Centella asiatica. $2.50, Lobelia chinensis. $3.10, Gardenia jasminoides. $5, Scutellaria indica.

Perf. 14½ Syncopated

2001, Oct. 7 **Litho.**

Granite Paper

948-951 A192 Set of 4 3.00 3.00

Children's Stamp Coloring Contest — A193

Designs: $1.30, Bear. $2.50, Penguin. $3.10, Flower. $5, Bee.

Die Cut Perf. 13¾x13¼ Sync.

2001, Nov. 18

Granite Paper

Self-Adhesive

952-955	A193	Set of 4	3.00	3.00
a.		Souvenir sheet, #952-955	3.00	3.00

New Year 2002 (Year of the Horse) — A194

Various horses. Denominations: $1.30, $2.50, $3.10, $5.

2002, Jan. 13 ***Perf. 14½ Syncopated***

Granite Paper

956-959	A194	Set of 4	3.00	3.00
a.		Souvenir sheet of 1, imperf.	1.25	1.25
b.		Souvenir sheet, #956-959	3.00	3.00

Souvenir Sheet

New Year 2002 (Year of the Horse) — A195

No. 960: a, Snake. b, Horse.

Litho. & Embossed with Foil Application

2002, Feb. 9 ***Perf. 13¼***

960 A195 $50 Sheet of 2, #a-b 25.00 25.00

Works of Art — A196

Details from: $1.30, Lines in Motion, by Chui Tze-hung. $2.50, Volume and Time, by Hon Chi-fun. $3.10, Bright Sun, by Aries Lee. $5, Midsummer, by Irene Chou.

Perf. 14½ Syncopated

2002, Feb. 24 **Litho.**

Granite Paper

961-964 A196 Set of 4 3.00 3.00

Landmarks Type of 1999

Designs: $1.40, Hong Kong Railway Museum. $1.80, Hong Kong Stadium. $1.90, Western Market. $2.40, Kwun Yam statue, Repulse Bay. $3, Peak Tower. $13, Hong Kong Cultural Center.

Perf. 13x13¾ Syncopated

2002, Apr. 1 **Photo.**

Granite Paper

965	A172	$1.80 multi	.45	.45
966	A172	$1.90 multi	.50	.50
967	A172	$2.40 multi	.60	.60
a.		Booklet pane of 10	6.00	—
		Booklet, #967a	6.00	
968	A172	$3 multi	.75	.75
a.		Booklet pane of 10	7.50	—
		Booklet, #968a	7.50	

Size: 26x32mm

Perf. 13¼ Syncopated

969	A172	$13 multi	3.50	3.50
		Nos. 965-969 (5)	5.80	5.80

Coil Stamps

Size: 18x22mm

Perf. 14¾x13¼ Syncopated

970	A172	$1.40 multi	.35	.35
971	A172	$1.80 multi	.45	.45
972	A172	$2.40 multi	.60	.60
973	A172	$3 multi	.75	.75
		Nos. 970-973 (4)	2.15	2.15

Cyberindustry in Hong Kong — A197

Designs: $1.40, Innovation. $2.40, Connectivity. $3, Trend. $5, Strength.

Perf. 13¾ Syncopated

2002, Apr. 14 Litho.

Granite Paper

974-977 A197 Set of 4 3.00 3.00
a. Block of 4, #974-977 3.00 3.00

A booklet of two panes, one containing one each of Nos. 974 and 976, and another containing one each of Nos. 975 and 977, sold for $30.

2002 World Cup Soccer Championships, Japan and Korea — A198

No. 978: a, Goalie. b, Crowd and players.

Perf. 12 Syncopated

2002, May 16 Photo.

978 Horiz. pair, with central label .70 .70
a.-b. A198 $1.40 Either single .35 .35

No. 978 was printed in sheets of 5 pairs and five different labels.

Corals A199

Designs: $1.40, North Atlantic pink tree, Pacific orange cup, and North Pacific horn corals. $2.40, North Atlantic giant orange tree, and Black corals. $3, Dendronepthea gigantea and Dendronepthea corals. $5, Tubastrea and Echinogorgia corals.

Perf. 13¾x14 Syncopated

2002, May 19 Litho.

Granite Paper

979-982 A199 Set of 4 3.00 3.00
a. Souvenir sheet, #979-982 3.00 3.00

See Canada Nos. 1948-1951.

Beijing - Kowloon Through Trains A200

Train and: $1.40, Hong Kong commercial buildings. $2.40, Wuhan-Changjiang Bridge, Wuchang. $3, Shaolin Monastery Pagodas, Zhengzhou. $5, Temple of Heaven, Beijing.

2002, June 9 *Perf. 14¼ Syncopated*

Granite Paper

983-986 A200 Set of 4 3.00 3.00
a. Horiz. strip of 4, #983-986 3.00 3.00

Hong Kong Special Administrative Region, 5th Anniv. — A201

Designs: $1.40, White dolphins, corals. $2.40, Students, bauhinia flowers. $3, Flying cranes, Hong Kong International Airport. $5, Flags of Hong Kong and People's Republic of China, fireworks over skyline.

2002, July 1 Granite Paper

987-990 A201 Set of 4 3.00 3.00
a. Souvenir sheet, #987-990 3.00 3.00

Landmarks Type of 1999 with Pink Denomination and Country Name

Souvenir Sheet

Design: Tsing Ma Bridge.

Perf. 13¼ Syncopated

2002, July 27 Photo.

Granite Paper

991 A172 $10 pink & multi 2.60 2.60

Philakorea 2002.

Landmarks Type of 1999 With Olive Green Denomination and Country Name

Souvenir Sheet

Design: Tsing Ma Bridge.

Perf. 13¼ Syncopated

2002, Aug. 24 Photo.

Granite Paper

992 A172 $10 ol green & multi 2.60 2.60

Amphilex 2002 Intl. Stamp Exhibition, Amsterdam.

Landmarks Type of 1999 With Buff Background

Souvenir Sheet

Design: Tsing Ma Bridge.

2002, Sept. 7

993 A172 $10 blue, buff & multi 2.60 2.60

Rocks A202

Designs: $1.40, Ping Chau (siltstone). $2.40, Port Island (conglomerate). $3, Po Pin Chau (tuff). $5, Lamma Island (granite).

Perf. 13¼x12¾

2002, Sept. 15 Litho.

994-997 A202 Set of 4 3.00 3.00
a. Souvenir sheet, #994-997 3.00 3.00

Portions of the designs were applied by a thermographic process, producing a shiny, raised effect.

Eastern and Western Cultures A203

Designs: 10c, Radar screen, luopan. 20c, Calculator, abacus. 50c, Incense coil, stained glass window. $1, Chair, Chinese bed. $1.40, Dim sum, loaves of bread. $1.80, Silverware, chopsticks and spoon. $1.90, Canned drinks, tea caddies. $2, Western and Eastern wedding cakes. $2.40, Erhu, violin. $2.50, Letter boxes, internet. $3, Sailboats, dragon boat. $5, Tiled roof, glass wall. $10, Ballet, Chinese opera. $13, Chess, Xiangqi. $20, Christmas decorations, lanterns. $50, Eastern and Western sculptures.

Perf. 13¼x13 Syncopated

2002, Oct. 14 Photo.

Granite Paper

998 A203 10c multi .20 .20
999 A203 20c multi .20 .20
1000 A203 50c multi .20 .20
1001 A203 $1 multi .25 .25
1002 A203 $1.40 multi .35 .35
a. Booklet pane of 10 3.50
Booklet, #1002a 3.50
1003 A203 $1.80 multi .45 .45
1004 A203 $1.90 multi .50 .50
1005 A203 $2 multi .50 .50
1006 A203 $2.40 multi .60 .60
a. Booklet pane of 10 6.00
Booklet, #1006a 6.00
1007 A203 $2.50 multi .65 .65
1008 A203 $3 multi .75 .75
a. Booklet pane of 10 7.50
Booklet, #1008a 7.50
1009 A203 $5 multi 1.25 1.25
a. Souvenir sheet, #998-1009 5.75 5.75
b. Booklet pane, #998-1009 5.75
Booklet, #1009b 5.75

Size: 40x24mm

Perf. 14¾ Syncopated

1010 A203 $10 multi 2.60 2.60
1011 A203 $13 multi 3.25 3.25
1012 A203 $20 multi 5.25 5.25
1013 A203 $50 multi 13.00 13.00
Nos. 998-1013 (16) 30.00 30.00

Coil Stamps

Size: 22x19mm

Perf. 13¼x14¾ Syncopated

1014 A203 $1.40 multi .35 .35
1015 A203 $1.80 multi .45 .45
1016 A203 $2.40 multi .60 .60
1017 A203 $3 multi .75 .75
Nos. 1014-1017 (4) 2.15 2.15

Christmas — A204

Designs: $1.40, Christmas tree. $2.40, Ornament. $3, Snowman. $5, Bell.

Photo. with Hologram Applied

Perf. 13½ Syncopated

2002, Nov. 24

Granite Paper

1018-1021 A204 Set of 4 3.00 3.00

Perforations within the stamp outline the designs.

Hong Kong Disneyland A205

Designs: $1.40, Main Street. $2.40, Fantasyland. $3, Adventureland. $5, Tomorrowland.

Perf. 13¾ Syncopated

2003, Jan. 12 Litho. & Embossed

Granite Paper

1022-1025 A205 Set of 4 3.00 3.00
a. Souvenir sheet, #1022-1025 3.00 3.00

New Year 2003 (Year of the Ram) — A206

Various rams: $1.40, $2.40, $3, $5.

Perf. 14¼ Syncopated

2003, Jan. 19 Litho.

Granite Paper

1026-1029 A206 Set of 3 3.00 3.00
a. Souvenir sheet of 1, imperf. 1.25 1.25
b. Souvenir sheet, #1026-1029 3.00 3.00

SEMI-POSTAL STAMPS

Catalogue values for unused stamps in this section are for Never Hinged items.

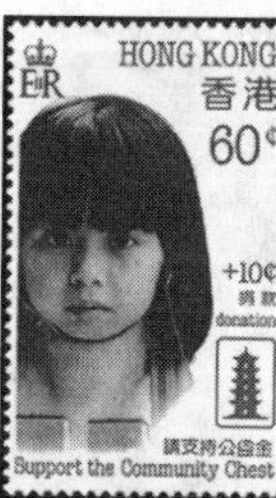

Community Chest of Hong Kong — SP1

1988, Nov. 30 Litho. *Perf. 14½*

B1 SP1 60c +10c Girl .60 .35
B2 SP1 $1.40 +20c Elderly woman .75 .70
B3 SP1 $1.80 +30c Blind youth 1.40 1.00
B4 SP1 $5 +$1 Mother and child 3.75 2.75
Nos. B1-B4 (4) 6.50 4.80

Surtax for the social welfare organization.

POSTAGE DUE STAMPS

Scales Showing Letter Overweight — D1

1923, Dec. Typo. Wmk. 4 *Perf. 14*

J1 D1 1c brown 1.60 .50
a. Chalky paper, wmkd. sideways .70 .75
J2 D1 2c green 7.00 1.00
J3 D1 4c red 19.00 1.50
J4 D1 6c orange 18.00 5.00
J5 D1 10c ultramarine 16.00 2.00
Nos. J1-J5 (5) 61.60 10.00
Set, never hinged 160.00

No. J1a issued Mar. 21, 1956.

1938-47 *Perf. 14*

J6 D1 2c gray .60 .35
J7 D1 4c orange yellow 1.40 .45
J8 D1 6c carmine 4.75 1.40
J9 D1 8c fawn ('46) 2.75 1.40
J10 D1 10c violet 7.50 .65
J11 D1 20c black ('46) 5.00 2.00
J12 D1 50c blue ('47) 19.00 11.50
Nos. J6-J12 (7) 41.00 17.75
Set, never hinged 110.00

Nos. J6-J7 and J10 exist on both ordinary and chalky paper.

Catalogue values for unused stamps in this section, from this point to the end of the section, are for Never Hinged items.

Wmk. 314 Sideways

1965-69 *Perf. 14*

J13 D1 4c orange yellow 6.50 1.75
J14 D1 5c orange ver ('69) 3.25 .40
a. 5c carmine, wmk. upright ('67) 5.00 .40
J15 D1 10c purple ('67) 5.50 .85
J16 D1 20c black 12.00 2.00
J17 D1 50c dark blue 22.00 3.00
a. Wmk. upright ('70) 50.00 10.00
Nos. J13-J17 (5) 49.25 8.00

Size of 5c, 21x18mm.; others, 22x18mm.

Wmk. 314 Upright

1972-74 *Perf. 13½x14*

J18 D1 5c red brown ('74) 2.50 1.00

Perf. 14x14½

J19 D1 10c lilac 7.00 .60
J20 D1 20c black 8.25 1.25
J21 D1 50c dull blue 5.00 3.50
Nos. J18-J21 (4) 22.75 6.35

Nos. J18-J22 are on glazed paper.

1976, Mar. 19 Wmk. 373

J19a D1 10c lilac .50 .20
J20a D1 20c black .50 .20
J21a D1 50c dull blue 1.25 .30
b. Unwatermarked 1.25 .30
J22 D1 $1 yellow 3.00 .60
a. Unwatermarked 2.00 .60
Nos. J19a-J22 (4) 5.25 1.30

Size of $1, 20½x17mm; others, 22x18mm. Issue date: No. J21b, J22, Jan. 11, 1986.

D2

Perf. 14x15

1986, Mar. 25 Litho. Unwmk.

J23	D2	10c light green	.20	.20
J24	D2	20c dark red brown	.20	.20
J25	D2	50c lilac	.20	.20
J26	D2	$1 light orange	.30	.20
J27	D2	$5 grayish blue	1.10	.90
J28	D2	$10 rose red	2.00	1.75
		Nos. J23-J28 (6)	4.00	3.45

OCCUPATION STAMPS

Issued under Japanese Occupation

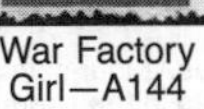
War Factory Girl—A144

Gen. Maresuke Nogi — A84

Admiral Heihachiro Togo — A86

Stamps of Japan, 1942-43 Surcharged in Black

Wmk. 257

1945, Apr. Typo. *Perf. 13*

N1	A144	1½y on 1s org brn	17.50	15.00
N2	A84	3y on 2s ver	12.00	*17.50*
N3	A86	5y on 5s brn lake	700.00	125.00
		Nos. N1-N3 (3)	729.50	157.50

No. N1 has eleven characters.

HORTA

hȯr-tə

LOCATION — An administrative district of the Azores, consisting of the islands of Pico, Fayal, Flores and Corvo

GOVT. — A district of the Republic of Portugal

AREA — 305 sq. mi.

POP. — 49,000 (approx.)

CAPITAL — Horta

1000 Reis = 1 Milreis

King Carlos
A1 A2

Chalk-surfaced Paper

Perf. 11½, 12½, 13½

1892-93 Typo. Unwmk.

1	A1	5r yellow	1.75	1.00
2	A1	10r reddish violet	1.75	1.25
3	A1	15r chocolate	3.00	2.00
4	A1	20r lavender	4.00	2.25
5	A1	25r dp grn, perf. 11½	4.25	.50
a.		Perf. 13½	2.50	2.50
6	A1	50r blue	4.75	2.25
a.		Perf. 13½	10.00	5.25
7	A1	75r carmine	6.00	7.00
8	A1	80r yellow green	9.50	7.50
9	A1	100r brn, *yel* ('93)	7.50	3.75
a.		Perf. 12½	110.00	52.50
10	A1	150r car, *rose* ('93)	30.00	27.50
11	A1	200r dk bl, *bl* ('93)	40.00	27.50
12	A1	300r dark blue ('93)	40.00	30.00
		Nos. 1-12 (12)	152.50	112.50

Bisects of No. 1 were used in Aug. 1894.

The reprints have shiny white gum and clean-cut perforation 13½. The white paper is thinner than that of the originals. Value unused, $12 each.

1897-1905 *Perf. 11½*

Name and Value in Black Except 500r

13	A2	2½r gray	.50	.30
14	A2	5r orange	.50	.30
15	A2	10r lt green	.50	.30
16	A2	15r brown	5.25	3.00
17	A2	15r gray grn ('99)	1.25	.80
18	A2	20r gray violet	1.75	.85
19	A2	25r sea green	2.25	.45
20	A2	25r car rose ('99)	.90	.50
21	A2	50r blue	3.00	.70
22	A2	50r ultra ('05)	13.00	9.00
23	A2	65r slate blue ('98)	.70	.55
24	A2	75r rose	1.90	.95
25	A2	75r brn, *yel* ('05)	17.00	12.50
26	A2	80r violet	1.25	1.10
27	A2	100r dk blue, *bl*	1.75	.95
28	A2	115r org brn, *pink* ('98)	2.00	1.50
29	A2	130r gray brn, *buff* ('98)	2.00	1.50
30	A2	150r lt brn, *buff*	2.00	1.50
31	A2	180r sl, *pnksh* ('98)	2.00	1.75
32	A2	200r red vio, *pale lil*	5.50	4.00
33	A2	300r dk blue, *rose*	7.50	6.75
34	A2	500r blk & red, *bl*	10.50	8.50
		Nos. 13-34 (22)	83.00	57.75

Stamps of Portugal replaced those of Horta.

HUNGARY

'həŋ-gə-ˌrē

LOCATION — Central Europe
GOVT. — Republic
AREA — 35,911 sq. mi.
POP. — 10,186,372 (1999 est.)
CAPITAL — Budapest

Prior to World War I, Hungary together with Austria comprised the Austro-Hungarian Empire. The Hungarian post became independent on May 1, 1867. During 1850-1871 stamps listed under Austria were also used in Hungary. Copies showing clear Hungarian cancels sell for substantially more.

100 Krajczár (Kreuzer) = 1 Forint 100 Fillér = 1 Korona (1900) 100 Fillér = 1 Pengő (1926) 100 Fillér = 1 Forint (1946)

Catalogue values for unused stamps in this country are for Never Hinged items, beginning with Scott 503 in the regular postage section, Scott B92 in the semi-postal section, Scott C35 in the airpost section, Scott CB1 in the airpost semi-postal section, Scott F1 in the registrtation section, Scott J130 in the postage due section, and Scott Q9 in the parcel post section.

Watermarks

Wmk. 91- "ZEITUNGS-MARKEN" in Double-lined Capitals across the Sheet

Wmk. 106- Multiple Star

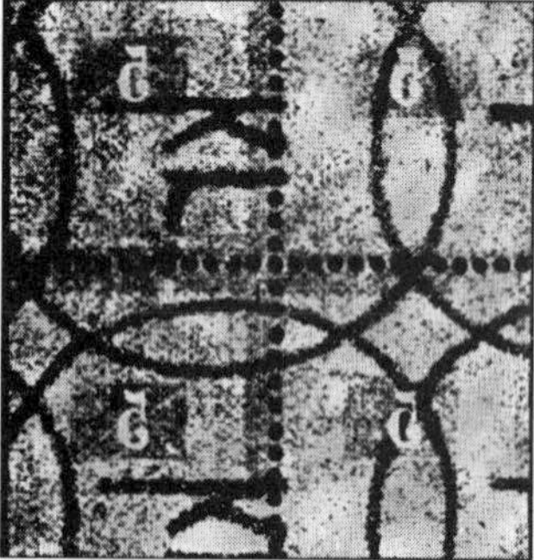

Wmk. 132- kr in Oval

Wmk. 133- Four Double Crosses

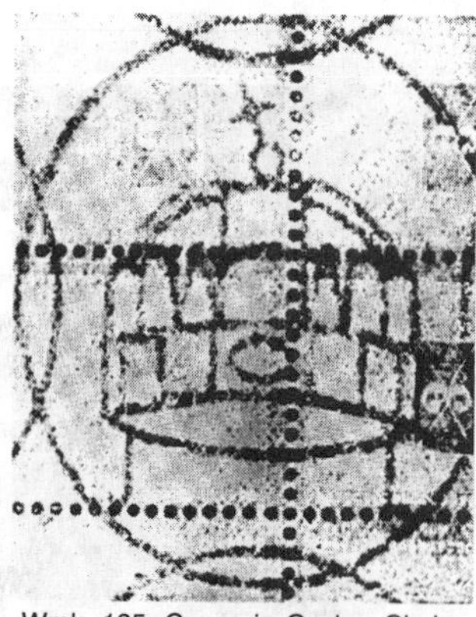

Wmk. 135- Crown in Oval or Circle, Sideways

Wmk. 136

Wmk. 136a

Wmk. 137- Double Cross

Wmk. 210- Double Cross on Pyramid

Wmk. 266- Double Barred Cross, Wreath and Crown

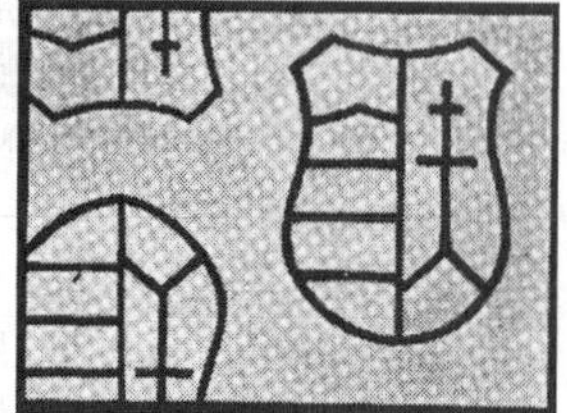

Wmk. 283- Double Barred Cross on Shield, Multiple

Watermarks 132, 135, 136 and 136a can be found normal, reversed, inverted, or reversed and inverted.

Values for unused stamps are for examples with original gum as defined in the catalogue introduction. Very fine examples of Nos. 1-12 will have perforations touching the framelines on one or two sides due to imperfect perforating methods. Stamps with perfs clear on all four sides are very scarce and will command substantial premiums.

Issues of the Monarchy

Franz Josef I — A1

1871 Unwmk. Litho. ***Perf. 9½***

1	A1	2k orange	225.00	75.00
a.		2k yellow	1,300.	225.00
2	A1	3k lt green	725.00	475.00
3	A1	5k rose	300.00	17.50
a.		5k brick red	600.00	45.00
4	A1	10k blue	700.00	90.00
a.		10k pale blue	950.00	150.00
5	A1	15k yellow brn	750.00	100.00
6	A1	25k violet	750.00	150.00
a.		25k bright violet	850.00	275.00

The first printing of No. 1, in dark yellow, was not issued because of spots on the King's face. A few copies were used at Pest in 1873. Value, $3,500.

1871-72 **Engr.**

7	A1	2k orange	37.50	7.50
a.		2k yellow	150.00	14.00
b.		Bisect on cover		—
8	A1	3k green	85.00	20.00
a.		3k blue green	110.00	30.00
9	A1	5k rose	50.00	1.75
a.		5k brick red	125.00	8.00
10	A1	10k deep blue	200.00	10.00
11	A1	15k brown	225.00	15.00
a.		15k copper brown	—	900.00
b.		15k black brown	875.00	85.00
12	A1	25k lilac	140.00	40.00
		Nos. 7-12 (6)	737.50	94.25

Reprints are perf. 11½ and watermarked "kr" in oval. Value, set $225.

Crown of St. Stephen
A2 A3

Design A3 has an overall burelage of dots. Compare with design N3.

1874-76 ***Perf. 12½ to 13½***

13	A2	2k rose lilac	25.00	1.50
14	A2	3k yellow green	25.00	1.50
a.		3k blue green	32.50	1.50
15	A2	5k rose	12.50	.25
a.		5k dull red	27.50	.95
16	A2	10k blue	50.00	1.00
17	A2	20k slate	350.00	8.00
		Nos. 13-17 (5)	462.50	12.25

Perf. 11½ and Compound

13a	A2	2k rose lilac	57.50	5.00
14b	A2	3k yellow green	40.00	6.00
c.		3k blue green	40.00	6.00
d.		Perf. 9½	*1,000.*	*700.00*
15b	A2	5k rose	35.00	.70
c.		5k dull red	35.00	.70
d.		Perf. 9½	*500.00*	*300.00*
16a	A2	10k blue	70.00	3.00
17a	A2	20k slate	775.00	40.00

1881 Wmk. 132 ***Perf. 11½, 12x11½***

18	A2	2k violet	1.75	.25
a.		2k rose lilac	1.75	.25
b.		2k slate	8.50	.45
19	A2	3k blue green	1.60	.20
20	A2	5k rose	10.00	.20
21	A2	10k blue	5.00	.35
22	A2	20k slate	8.50	.65
		Nos. 18-22 (5)	26.85	1.65

Perf. 12½ to 13½ and Compound

18c	A2	2k violet	85.00	4.00
19a	A2	3k blue green	62.50	1.25
20a	A2	5k rose	60.00	1.25
21a	A2	10k blue	42.50	2.00
22b	A2	20k slate	600.00	8.50
		Nos. 18c-22b (5)	850.00	17.00

1888-98 Typo. ***Perf. 11½, 12x11½***

Numerals in Black

22A	A3	1k black, one plate	.55	.20
c.		"1" printed separately	10.50	.90
23	A3	2k red violet	.80	.20
a.		Perf. 11½	725.00	45.00
24	A3	3k green	1.00	.30
a.		Perf. 11½	50.00	15.00
25	A3	5k rose	1.10	.20
a.		Perf. 11½	50.00	1.10
26	A3	8k orange	4.00	.40
a.		"8" double	*150.00*	
27	A3	10k blue	3.50	.80
a.		Perf. 11½	450.00	325.00
28	A3	12k brown & green	8.00	.45
29	A3	15k claret & blue	6.75	.20
30	A3	20k gray	6.75	1.25
a.		Perf. 11½	*1,400.*	*600.00*
31	A3	24k brn vio & red	17.50	.60
32	A3	30k ol grn & brn	20.00	.30
33	A3	50k red & org	32.50	.80

Numerals in Red

34	A3	1fo gray bl & sil	125.00	1.25
a.		Perf. 11½	150.00	1.50
35	A3	3fo lilac brn & gold	11.00	4.00
		Nos. 22A-35 (14)	238.45	10.95

Most of Nos. 22A to 103 exist imperforate, but were never so issued.

1898-99 Wmk. 135 ***Perf. 12x11½***

Numerals in Black

35A	A3	1k black	.80	.30
36	A3	2k violet	3.25	.30
37	A3	3k green	2.75	.30
38	A3	5k rose	2.75	.20
39	A3	8k orange	10.00	2.00
40	A3	10k blue	2.75	.40
41	A3	12k red brn & grn	47.50	5.50
42	A3	15k rose & blue	2.75	.30
43	A3	20k gray	4.00	1.25
44	A3	24k vio brn & red	4.75	2.50
45	A3	30k ol grn & brn	4.00	2.00
46	A3	50k dull red & org	12.00	10.00
		Nos. 35A-46 (12)	97.30	25.05

In the watermark with circles, a four-pointed star and "VI" appear four times in the sheet in the large spaces between the intersecting circles. The paper with the circular watermark is often yellowish and thinner than that with the oval watermark and sell for much higher prices.

See note after No. 35.

Perf. 11½

35Ab	A3	1k black	*30.00*	*2.00*
36a	A3	2k violet	*90.00*	*9.00*
37a	A3	3k green	*75.00*	*6.75*
38a	A3	5k rose	*75.00*	*2.25*
39a	A3	8k orange	*10.00*	*6.00*
40a	A3	10k blue	*190.00*	*25.00*
41a	A3	12k red brn & grn	—	*30.00*
42a	A3	15k rose & blue	—	*15.00*
43a	A3	20k gray	*750.00*	*25.00*
44a	A3	24k vio brn & red	*200.00*	*75.00*
45a	A3	30k ol grn & brn	*450.00*	*15.00*
46a	A3	50k dull red & org	*275.00*	*75.00*

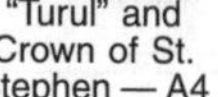

"Turul" and Crown of St. Stephen — A4

Franz Josef I Wearing Hungarian Crown—A5

1900-04 Wmk. 135 ***Perf. 12x11½***

Numerals in Black

47	A4	1f gray	.45	.40
a.		1f dull lilac	.55	.40
48	A4	2f olive yel	.45	.20
49	A4	3f orange	.35	.25
50	A4	4f violet	.40	.20
a.		Booklet pane of 6	60.00	
51	A4	5f emerald	2.25	.20
a.		Booklet pane of 6	35.00	
52	A4	6f claret	.65	.25
a.		6f violet brown	1.00	.25
53	A4	6f bister ('01)	8.00	.40
54	A4	6f olive grn ('02)	3.00	.25
55	A4	10f carmine	2.25	.20
a.		Booklet pane of 6	35.00	
56	A4	12f violet ('04)	1.50	.50
57	A4	20f brown ('01)	1.90	.35
58	A4	25f blue	2.25	.35
a.		Booklet pane of 6	60.00	
59	A4	30f orange brn	18.00	.25
60	A4	35f red vio ('01)	12.50	.25
a.		Booklet pane of 6	100.00	
61	A4	50f lake	10.00	1.10
62	A4	60f green	40.00	.55
63	A5	1k brown red	45.00	.70
64	A5	2k gray blue ('01)	275.00	10.00
65	A5	3k sea green	85.00	3.00
66	A5	5k vio brown ('01)	85.00	15.00
		Nos. 47-66 (20)	593.95	34.40

The watermark on Nos. 47 to 66 is always the circular form of Wmk. 135 described in the note following No. 46.

Pairs imperf between of Nos. 47-49, 51 were favor prints made for an influential Budapest collector. Value, $90 each.

For overprints & surcharges see #B35-B52, 2N1-2N3, 6N1-6N6, 6NB127N1-7N6, 7NB1, 10N1.

See note after No. 35.

Perf. 11½

No.	Type	Denom.	Color	Unused	Used
47b	A4	1f	gray	90.00	17.50
48a	A4	2f	olive yel	90.00	12.50
49a	A4	3f	orange	22.50	2.25
50b	A4	4f	violet	70.00	1.50
51b	A4	5f	emerald	5.50	1.40
52b	A4	6f	claret	110.00	12.50
53a	A4	6f	bister ('01)	80.00	22.50
54a	A4	6f	olive grn ('02)	160.00	90.00
55b	A4	10f	carmine	90.00	3.00
56a	A4	12f	violet ('04)	70.00	27.50
57a	A4	20f	brown ('01)	140.00	45.00
58b	A4	25f	blue	140.00	15.00
59a	A4	30f	orange brn	150.00	35.00
60b	A4	35f	red vio ('01)	190.00	80.00
61a	A4	50f	lake	190.00	80.00
62a	A4	60f	green	250.00	20.00
63a	A5	1k	brown red	45.00	3.25
64a	A5	2k	gray blue ('01)	550.00	120.00
65a	A5	3k	sea green	—	*1,500.*
66a	A5	5k	vio brown ('01)	550.00	225.00

1908-13 Wmk. 136 *Perf. 15*

No.	Type	Denom.	Color	Unused	Used
67	A4	1f	slate	.25	.20
68	A4	2f	olive yellow	.20	.20
69	A4	3f	orange	.25	.20
70	A4	5f	emerald	.20	.20
c.			Booklet pane of 6	100.00	
71	A4	6f	olive green	.30	.20
72	A4	10f	carmine	.20	.20
c.			Booklet pane of 6	100.00	
73	A4	12f	violet	.40	.20
74	A4	16f	gray green ('13)	.20	.40
75	A4	20f	dark brown	2.50	.20
76	A4	25f	blue	2.25	.20
77	A4	30f	orange brown	2.50	.20
78	A4	35f	red violet	3.75	.20
79	A4	50f	lake	.75	.30
80	A4	60f	green	4.00	.20
81	A5	1k	brown red	7.25	.25
82	A5	2k	gray blue	50.00	.55
83	A5	5k	violet brown	75.00	7.50
			Nos. 67-83 (17)	150.00	11.40

See note after No. 35.

1904-05 Wmk. 136a *Perf. 12x11½*

No.	Type	Denom.	Color	Unused	Used
67a	A4	1f	slate	.90	.60
68a	A4	2f	olive yellow	2.75	.20
69a	A4	3f	orange	.90	.25
70a	A4	5f	emerald	2.00	.20
71a	A4	6f	olive green	1.25	.20
72a	A4	10f	carmine	3.75	.20
73a	A4	12f	violet	1.50	.65
75a	A4	20f	dark brown	8.75	.60
76a	A4	25f	blue	18.00	.80
77a	A4	30f	orange brown	4.50	.40
78a	A4	35f	red violet	14.00	.80
79a	A4	50f	lake	10.50	2.50
c.			50f magenta	.40	2.25
80a	A4	60f	green	200.00	.75
81a	A5	1k	brown red	150.00	2.00
82a	A5	2k	gray blue	*550.00*	60.00
c.			Perf. 11½	*575.00*	87.50
83a	A5	5k	violet brown	175.00	80.00
			Nos. 67a-83a (16)	*1,143.*	150.15

1906 *Perf. 15*

No.	Type	Denom.	Color	Unused	Used
67b	A4	1f	slate	.75	.45
68b	A4	2f	olive yellow	.40	.20
69b	A4	3f	orange	.70	.20
70b	A4	5f	emerald	.35	.20
71b	A4	6f	olive green	.90	.20
72b	A4	10f	carmine	.75	.20
73b	A4	12f	violet	1.10	.20
75b	A4	20f	dark brown	2.25	.30
76b	A4	25f	blue	2.75	.20
77b	A4	30f	orange brown	3.00	.20
78b	A4	35f	red violet	13.00	.20
79b	A4	50f	lake	2.25	.50
80b	A4	60f	green	30.00	.45
81b	A5	1k	brown red	30.00	.65
82b	A5	2k	gray blue	100.00	8.00
			Nos. 67b-82b (15)	188.20	12.15

1913-16 Wmk. 137 Vert. *Perf. 15*

No.	Type	Denom.	Color	Unused	Used
84	A4	1f	slate	.30	.20
85	A4	2f	olive yellow	.20	.20
86	A4	3f	orange	.20	.20
87	A4	5f	emerald	.50	.20
88	A4	6f	olive green	.20	.20
89	A4	10f	carmine	.20	.20
90	A4	12f	violet, *yel*	.20	.20
91	A4	16f	gray green	.35	.50
92	A4	20f	dark brown	.75	.20
93	A4	25f	ultra	.85	.20
94	A4	30f	orange brown	.75	.20
95	A4	35f	red violet	.75	.20
96	A4	50f	lake, *blue*	.35	.20
a.			Cliché of 35f in plate of 50f	250.00	—
97	A4	60f	green	4.25	1.75
98	A4	60f	green, *salmon*	.60	.20
99	A4	70f	red brn, *grn* ('16)	.30	.20
100	A4	80f	dull violet ('16)	.30	.20
101	A5	1k	dull red	1.25	.20
102	A5	2k	dull blue	2.75	.30
103	A5	5k	violet brown	9.00	2.00
			Nos. 84-103 (20)	24.05	7.75

See note after No. 35.

For overprints and surcharges see Nos. 2N1-2N3, 6N1-6N6, 6NB12, 7N1-7N6, 7NB1, 10N1.

Wmk. 137 Horiz.

No.	Type	Denom.	Color	Unused	Used
84a	A4	1f	slate	.80	1.25
85a	A4	2f	olive yellow	2.10	.60
87a	A4	5f	emerald	.50	.60
88a	A4	6f	olive green	1.00	.60
89b	A4	10f	carmine	1.10	.35
90a	A4	12f	violet, *yellow*	2.10	.45
92a	A4	20f	dark brown	6.25	.50
94a	A4	30f	orange brown	42.50	.35
95a	A4	35f	red violet	150.00	.50
96b	A4	50f	lake, *blue*	10.50	9.50
97a	A4	60f	green	3.75	2.50
98a	A4	60f	green, *salmon*	1.60	.30
101a	A5	1k	dull red	16.00	.50
102a	A5	2k	dull blue	75.00	2.50
			Nos. 84a-102a (14)	313.20	20.50

A5a

1916, July 1 *Perf. 15*

No.	Type	Denom.	Color	Unused	Used
103A	A5a	10f	violet brown	.80	.50

Although issued as a postal savings stamp, No. 103A was also valid for postage. Used value is for postal usage.

For overprints and surcharges see Nos. 2N59, 5N23, 6N50, 8N13, 10N42.

Queen Zita — A6

Charles IV — A7

1916, Dec. 30

No.	Type	Denom.	Color	Unused	Used
104	A6	10f	violet	.35	.25
105	A7	15f	red	.35	.25

Coronation of King Charles IV and Queen Zita on Dec. 30, 1916.

Harvesting (White Numerals) — A8

1916

No.	Type	Denom.	Color	Unused	Used
106	A8	10f	rose	.50	.20
107	A8	15f	violet	.50	.20

For overprints and surcharges see Nos. B56-B57, 2N4-2N5, 5N1.

Harvesting Wheat — A9

Parliament Building at Budapest — A10

1916-18 *Perf. 15*

No.	Type	Denom.	Color	Unused	Used
108	A9	2f	brown orange	.20	.20
109	A9	3f	red lilac	.20	.20
110	A9	4f	slate gray ('18)	.20	.20
111	A9	5f	green	.20	.20
112	A9	6f	grnsh blue	.20	.20
113	A9	10f	rose red	.35	.20
114	A9	15f	violet	.20	.20
115	A9	20f	gray brown	.20	.20
116	A9	25f	dull blue	.20	.20
117	A9	35f	brown	.20	.20
118	A9	40f	olive green	.20	.20

Perf. 14

No.	Type	Denom.	Color	Unused	Used
119	A10	50f	red vio & lil	.20	.20
120	A10	75f	brt bl & pale bl	.20	.20
121	A10	80f	grn & pale grn	.20	.20
122	A10	1k	red brn & claret	.20	.20
123	A10	2k	ol brn & bister	.20	.20
124	A10	3k	dk vio & indigo	.35	.20
125	A10	5k	dk brn & lt brn	.35	.20
126	A10	10k	vio brn & vio	.65	.20
			Nos. 108-126 (19)	4.70	3.80

See Nos. 335-377, 388-396. For overprints and surcharges see Nos. 153, 167, C1-C5, J76-J99, 1N1-1N21, 1N26-1N30, 1N33, 1N36-1N39, 2N6-2N27, 2N33-2N38, 2N41, 2N43-2N48, 4N1-4N4, 5N2-5N17, 6N7-6N24, 6N29-6N39, 7N7-7N30, 7N38, 7N41-7N42, 8N1-8N4, 9N1-9N2, 9N4, 10N2-10N16, 10N25-10N29, 10N31, 10N33-10N41, Szeged 1-15, 20-24, 27, 30, 32-33.

During 1921-24 the two center rows of panes of various stamps then current were punched with three holes forming a triangle. These were sold at post offices. Collectors and dealers who wanted the stamps unpunched would have to purchase them through the philatelic agency at a 10% advance over face value.

Charles IV — A11

Queen Zita — A12

1918 *Perf. 15*

No.	Type	Denom.	Color	Unused	Used
127	A11	10f	scarlet	.20	.20
128	A11	15f	deep violet	.20	.20
129	A11	20f	dark brown	.20	.20
130	A11	25f	brt blue	.20	.20
131	A12	40f	olive green	.20	.20
132	A12	50f	lilac	.20	.20
			Nos. 127-132 (6)	1.20	1.20

For overprints see Nos. 168-173, 1N32, 1N34-1N35, 2N28-2N32, 2N39-2N40, 2N42, 2N49-2N51, 5N18-5N22, 6N25-6N28, 6N40-6N43, 7N31-7N37, 7N39-7N40, 8N5, 9N3, 10N17-10N21, 10N30, 10N32, Szeged 16-19, 25-26, 28-29, 31.

Issues of the Republic

Hungarian Stamps of 1916-18 Overprinted in Black

1918-19 Wmk. 137 *Perf. 15, 14*

On Stamps of 1916-18

No.	Type	Denom.	Color	Unused	Used
153	A9	2f	brown orange	.20	.20
154	A9	3f	red lilac	.20	.20
155	A9	4f	slate gray	.20	.20
156	A9	5f	green	.20	.20
157	A9	6f	grnsh blue	.20	.20
158	A9	10f	rose red	.20	.20
159	A9	20f	gray brown	.25	.20
162	A9	40f	olive green	.20	.20
163	A10	1k	red brn & claret	.20	.20
164	A10	2k	ol brn & bis	.20	.20
165	A10	3k	dk violet & ind	.45	.40
166	A10	5k	dk brn & lt brn	1.25	1.50
167	A10	10k	vio brn & vio	.75	.90

On Stamps of 1918

No.	Type	Denom.	Color	Unused	Used
168	A11	10f	scarlet	.20	.20
169	A11	15f	deep violet	.20	.20
170	A11	20f	dark brown	.20	.20
171	A11	25f	brt blue	.25	.20
172	A12	40f	olive green	.25	.20
173	A12	50f	lilac	.25	.20
			Nos. 153-173 (19)	5.85	6.00

Nos. 153-162, 168-173 exist with overprint inverted. Vaue, each $1.

A13

A14

1919-20 *Perf. 15*

No.	Type	Denom.	Color	Unused	Used
174	A13	2f	brown orange	.20	.20
176	A13	4f	slate gray	.20	.20
177	A13	5f	yellow grn	.20	.20
178	A13	6f	grnsh blue	.20	.20
179	A13	10f	red	.20	.20
180	A13	15f	violet	.20	.20
181	A13	20f	dark brown	.20	.20
182	A13	20f	green ('20)	.20	.20

183 A13 25f dull blue .20 .20
184 A13 40f olive green .20 .20
185 A13 40f rose red ('20) .20 .20
186 A13 45f orange .20 .20

Perf. 14

187 A14 50f brn vio & pale vio .20 .20
188 A14 60f brown & bl ('20) .20 .20
189 A14 95f dk bl & bl .20 .20
190 A14 1k red brn .20 .20
191 A14 1k dk bl & dull bl ('20) .20 .20
192 A14 1.20k dk grn & grn .20 .20
193 A14 1.40k yellow green .20 .20
194 A14 2k ol brn & bis .20 .20
195 A14 3k dk vio & ind .20 .20
196 A14 5k dk brn & brn .20 .20
197 A14 10k vio brn & red vio .60 .60
Nos. 174-197 (23) 5.00 5.00

The 3f red lilac, type A13, was never regularly issued without overprint (Nos. 204 and 312). In 1923 a small quantity was sold by the Government at public auction. Value $2.50.

For overprints see Nos. 203-222, 306-330, 1N40, 2N52-2N58, 6N44-6N49, 8N6-8N12, 10N22-10N24, Szeged 34-35.

Issues of the Soviet Republic

Karl Marx — A15

Sándor Petőfi — A16

Ignác Martinovics — A17

György Dózsa — A18

Friedrich Engels — A19

Wmk. 137 Horiz.

1919, June 14 Litho. *Perf. 12½x12*

198 A15 20f rose & brown .25 *.40*
199 A16 45f brn org & dk grn .25 *.40*
200 A17 60f blue gray & brn .80 *1.25*
201 A18 75f claret & vio brn .80 *1.25*
202 A19 80f olive db & blk brn .80 *1.25*
Nos. 198-202 (5) 2.90 *4.55*

Values are for favor cancels.

Wmk. Vertical

198a A15 20f 5.00
199a A16 45f 5.00
200a A17 60f 5.00
201a A18 75f 5.00
202a A19 80f 15.00
Nos. 198a-202a (5) 35.00

Nos. 198a-202a were not used postally. "Canceled" examples exist.

Stamps of 1919 Overprinted in Red

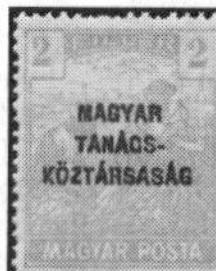

1919, July 21 Typo. *Perf. 15*

203 A13 2f brown orange .20 .20
204 A13 3f red lilac .20 .20
205 A13 4f slate gray .20 .20
206 A13 5f yellow green .20 .20
207 A13 6f grnsh blue .20 .20
208 A13 10f red .20 .20
209 A13 15f violet .20 .20
210 A13 20f dark brown .20 .20
211 A13 25f dull blue .20 .20
212 A13 40f olive green .20 .20
213 A13 45f orange .20 .20

Overprinted in Red

Perf. 14

214 A14 50f brn vio & pale vio .20 .20
215 A14 95f dk blue & blue .20 .20
216 A14 1k red brown .20 .20
217 A14 1.20k dk grn & grn .20 .20
218 A14 1.40k yellow green .20 .20
219 A14 2k ol brn & bister .35 .35
220 A14 3k dk vio & ind .35 .35
221 A14 5k dk brn & brn .35 .35
222 A14 10k vio brn & red vio .60 .60
Nos. 203-222 (20) 4.85 4.85

"Magyar Tanacsköztarsasag" on Nos. 198 to 222 means "Hungarian Soviet Republic."

Issues of the Kingdom

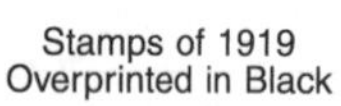

Stamps of 1919 Overprinted in Black

1919, Nov. 16

306 A13 5f green .50 .50
307 A13 10f rose red .50 .50
308 A13 15f violet .50 .50
309 A13 20f gray brown .50 .50
310 A13 25f dull blue .50 .50
Nos. 306-310 (5) 2.50 2.50

Issued to commemorate the Romanian evacuation. The overprint reads: "Entry of the National Army-November 16, 1919."

Forged overprints exist.

Nos. 203 to 213 Overprinted in Black

1920, Jan. 26 *Perf. 15*

311 A13 2f brown orange .45 *.80*
312 A13 3f red lilac .20 .20
313 A13 4f slate gray .45 *.80*
314 A13 5f yellow green .20 .20
315 A13 6f blue green .20 .20
316 A13 10f red .20 .20
317 A13 15f violet .20 .20
318 A13 20f dark brown .20 .20
319 A13 25f dull blue .20 .20
320 A13 40f olive green .45 *.80*
321 A13 45f orange .45 *.80*

Nos. 214 to 222 Overprinted in Black

Perf. 14

322 A14 50f brn vio & pale vio .45 *.80*
323 A14 95f dk bl & bl .45 *.80*
324 A14 1k red brown .45 *.80*
325 A14 1.20k dk grn & grn 1.10 1.25
326 A14 1.40k yellow green 1.10 1.25
327 A14 2k ol brn & bis 1.60 2.50
328 A14 3k dk vio & ind 1.60 2.50
329 A14 5k dk brn & brn .35 .35
330 A14 10k vio brn & red vio 2.50 2.75
Nos. 311-330 (20) 12.80 17.60

Counterfeit overprints exist.

Types of 1916-18 Issue Denomination Tablets Without Inner Frame on Nos. 350 to 363

1920-24 Wmk. 137 *Perf. 15*

335 A9 5f brown orange .20 .20
336 A9 10f red violet .20 .20
337 A9 40f rose red .20 .20
338 A9 50f yellow green .20 .20
339 A9 50f blue vio ('22) .20 .20
340 A9 60f black .20 .20
341 A9 1k green ('22) .20 .20
342 A9 1½k brown vio ('22) .20 .20
343 A9 2k grnsh blue ('22) .20 .20
344 A9 2½k dp green ('22) .20 .20
345 A9 3k brown org ('22) .20 .20
346 A9 4k lt red ('22) .20 .20
347 A9 4½k dull violet ('22) .40 .20
348 A9 5k deep brown ('22) .20 .20
349 A9 6k dark blue ('22) .20 .20
350 A9 10k brown ('23) .20 .20
351 A9 15k slate ('23) .20 .20
352 A9 20k red vio ('23) .20 .20
353 A9 25k orange ('23) .20 .20
354 A9 40k gray grn ('23) .20 .20
355 A9 50k dark blue ('23) .20 .20
356 A9 100k claret ('23) .20 .20
357 A9 150k dark green ('23) .20 .20
358 A9 200k green ('23) .20 .20
359 A9 300k rose red ('24) .20 .20
360 A9 350k violet ('23) .40 .20
361 A9 500k dark gray ('24) .45 .20
362 A9 600k olive bis ('24) .45 .20
363 A9 800k org yel ('24) .75 .20

Perf. 14

364 A10 2.50k bl & gray bl .20 .20
365 A10 3.50k gray .20 .20
366 A10 10k brown ('22) .20 .20
367 A10 15k dk gray ('22) .20 .20
368 A10 20k red vio ('22) .20 .20
369 A10 25k orange ('22) .20 .20
370 A10 30k claret ('22) .20 .20
371 A10 40k gray grn ('22) .20 .20
372 A10 50k dp blue ('22) .20 .20
373 A10 100k yel brn ('22) .20 .20
374 A10 400k turq bl ('23) .65 .30
375 A10 500k brt vio ('23) .50 .20
376 A10 1000k lilac ('24) .50 .20
377 A10 2000k car ('24) 1.75 .20
Nos. 335-377 (43) 12.65 8.70

Nos. 372 to 377 have colored numerals.

Madonna and Child — A23

1921-25 Typo. *Perf. 12*

378 A23 50k dk brn & bl .55 .20
379 A23 100k ol bis & yel brn .80 .40

Wmk. 133

380 A23 200k dk bl & ultra .40 .20
381 A23 500k vio brn & vio .40 .25
382 A23 1000k vio & red vio .40 .30
383 A23 2000k grnsh bl & vio .50 .45
384 A23 2500k ol brn & buff .55 .35
385 A23 3000k brn red & vio .65 .35
386 A23 5000k dk grn & yel grn .65 .35
a. Center inverted *11,000. 6,000.*
387 A23 10000k gray vio & pale bl 1.60 1.25
Nos. 378-387 (10) 6.50 4.10

Issue dates: 50k, 100k, Feb. 27, 1921; 2500k, 10,000k, 1925; others, 1923.

Types of 1916-18 Denomination Tablets Without Inner Frame on Nos. 388-394

1924 Wmk. 133 *Perf. 15*

388 A9 100k claret .45 .30
389 A9 200k yellow grn .25 .20
390 A9 300k rose red .25 .20
391 A9 400k deep blue .25 .20
392 A9 500k dark gray .25 .20
393 A9 600k olive bister .25 .25
a. "800" in upper right corner 140.00 140.00
394 A9 800k org yel .50 .35

Perf. 14½x14

395 A10 1000k lilac .75 .20
396 A10 2000k carmine .95 .30
Nos. 388-396 (9) 3.90 2.20

Nos. 395 and 396 have colored numerals.

Maurus Jókai (1825-1904), Novelist — A24

1925, Feb. 1 Unwmk. *Perf. 12*

400 A24 1000k dp grn & blk brn .90 1.60
401 A24 2000k lt brn & blk brn .60 .50
402 A24 2500k dk bl & blk brn .90 1.90
Nos. 400-402 (3) 2.40 4.00

Crown of St. Stephen — A25

Matthias Cathedral — A26

Palace at Budapest — A27

Perf. 14, 15

1926-27 Wmk. 133 Litho.

403 A25 1f dk gray .25 .20
404 A25 2f lt blue .25 .20
405 A25 3f orange .25 .20
406 A25 4f violet .25 .20
407 A25 6f lt green .35 .20
408 A25 8f lilac rose .50 .20

Typo.

409 A26 10f deep blue .40 .20
410 A26 16f dark violet .40 .20
411 A26 20f carmine .40 .20
412 A26 25f lt brown .40 .20

Perf. 14½x14

413 A27 32f dp vio & brt vio 1.25 .20
414 A27 40f dk blue & blue 1.50 .20
Nos. 403-414 (12) 6.20 2.40

See Nos. 428-436. For surcharges see Nos. 450-456, 466-467.

Madonna and Child — A28

1926-27 Engr. *Perf. 14*

415 A28 1p violet 14.00 .50
416 A28 2p red 7.75 .75
417 A28 5p blue ('27) 14.00 2.75
Nos. 415-417 (3) 35.75 4.00

Palace at Budapest A29

St. Stephen A30

1926-27 Typo.

418 A29 30f blue grn ('27) 1.25 .20
419 A29 46f ultra ('27) 1.75 .30
420 A29 50f brown blk ('27) 1.25 .20
421 A29 70f scarlet 1.75 .20
Nos. 418-421 (4) 6.00 .90

For surcharge see No. 480.

1928-29 Engr. *Perf. 15*

422 A30 8f yellow grn .40 .30
423 A30 8f rose lake ('29) .40 .30
424 A30 16f orange red .55 .30
425 A30 16f violet ('29) .45 .30
426 A30 32f ultra 1.25 1.10
427 A30 32f bister ('29) 1.25 1.10
Nos. 422-427 (6) 4.30 3.40

890th death anniversary of St. Stephen, the first king of Hungary.

Types of 1926-27 Issue

Perf. 14, 15

1928-30 Typo. Wmk. 210

428	A25	1f black	.25	.20
429	A25	2f blue	.20	.20
430	A25	3f orange	.20	.20
431	A25	4f violet	.20	.20
432	A25	6f blue grn	.20	.20
433	A25	8f lilac rose	.25	.20
434	A26	10f dp blue ('30)	2.50	.20
435	A26	16f violet	.50	.20
436	A26	20f dull red	.40	.20
		Nos. 428-436 (9)	4.70	1.80

On #428-433 the numerals have thicker strokes than on the same values of the 1926-27 issue.

Palace at Budapest — A31

Type A31 resembles A27 but the steamer is nearer the right of the design.

1928-31 *Perf. 14*

437	A31	30f emerald ('31)	.70	.20
438	A31	32f red violet	.90	.30
439	A31	40f deep blue	.80	.20
440	A31	46f apple green	.80	.20
441	A31	50f ocher ('31)	.80	.20
		Nos. 437-441 (5)	4.00	1.10

Admiral Nicholas Horthy — A32

1930, Mar. 1 Litho. *Perf. 15*

445	A32	8f myrtle green	1.40	.30
446	A32	16f purple	1.40	.35
447	A32	20f carmine	3.75	1.10
448	A32	32f olive brown	3.75	3.75
449	A32	40f dull blue	7.00	1.65
		Nos. 445-449 (5)	17.30	7.15

10th anniv. of the election of Adm. Nicholas Horthy as Regent, Mar. 1, 1920.

Stamps of 1926-28 Surcharged

1931, Jan. 1 *Perf. 14, 15*

450	A25	2f on 3f orange	1.00	.40
451	A25	6f on 8f magenta	1.00	.20
	a.	Perf. 14	25.00	25.00
452	A26	10f on 16f violet	.90	.20

Wmk. 133

453	A25	2f on 3f orange	3.50	3.00
454	A25	6f on 8f magenta	2.75	3.00
	a.	Perf. 14	65.00	65.00
455	A26	10f on 16f dk vio	2.25	1.50
456	A26	20f on 25f lt brn	2.25	1.25
	a.	Perf. 14	1.60	1.50
		Nos. 450-456 (7)	13.65	9.55

For surcharges see Nos. 466-467.

St. Elizabeth A33

Ministering to Children A34

Wmk. 210

1932, Apr. 21 Photo. *Perf. 15*

458	A33	10f ultra	.65	.30
459	A33	20f scarlet	.65	.35

Perf. 14

460	A34	32f deep violet	1.90	2.10
461	A34	40f deep blue	1.50	1.25
		Nos. 458-461 (4)	4.70	4.00

700th anniv. of the death of St. Elizabeth of Hungary.

Madonna, Patroness of Hungary — A35

1932, June 1 *Perf. 12*

462	A35	1p yellow grn	13.50	.65
463	A35	2p carmine	14.00	.95
464	A35	5p deep blue	52.50	3.75
465	A35	10p olive bister	70.00	25.00
		Nos. 462-465 (4)	150.00	30.35

Nos. 451 and 454 Surcharged

1932, June 14 Wmk. 210 *Perf. 15*

466	A25	2f on 6f on 8f mag	1.50	.40

Wmk. 133

467	A25	2f on 6f on 8f mag	30.00	30.00

Imre Madách — A36

Designs: 2f, Janos Arany. 4f, Dr. Ignaz Semmelweis. 6f, Baron Roland Eotvos. 10f, Count Stephen Szechenyi. 16f, Ferenc Deak. 20f, Franz Liszt. 30f, Louis Kossuth. 32f, Stephen Tisza. 40f, Mihaly Munkacsy. 50f, Alexander Csoma. 70f, Farkas Bolyai.

1932 Wmk. 210 *Perf. 15*

468	A36	1f slate violet	.20	.20
469	A36	2f orange	.20	.20
470	A36	4f ultra	.20	.20
471	A36	6f yellow grn	.20	.20
472	A36	10f Prus green	.20	.20
473	A36	16f dull violet	.25	.20
474	A36	20f deep rose	.20	.20
475	A36	30f brown	.45	.20
476	A36	32f brown vio	.70	.45
477	A36	40f dull blue	.70	.20
478	A36	50f deep green	1.10	.20
479	A36	70f cerise	1.50	.20
		Nos. 468-479 (12)	5.90	2.65
		Set, never hinged	7.50	

Issued in honor of famous Hungarians. See Nos. 509-510.

No. 421 Surcharged

1933, Apr. 15 Wmk. 133 *Perf. 14*

480	A29	10f on 70f scarlet	.40	.20
		Never hinged	1.00	

Leaping Stag and Double Cross — A47

Wmk. 210

1933, July 10 Photo. *Perf. 15*

481	A47	10f dk green	.90	1.00
482	A47	16f violet brn	2.50	2.25
483	A47	20f car lake	1.60	1.25
484	A47	32f yellow	3.75	4.00
485	A47	40f deep blue	3.75	4.00
		Nos. 481-485 (5)	12.50	12.50
		Set, never hinged	16.50	

Boy Scout Jamboree at Gödöllö, Hungary, July 20 - Aug. 20, 1933.

Souvenir Sheet

Franz Liszt — A48

1934, May 6 *Perf. 15*

486	A48	20f lake	45.00	45.00
		Never hinged	75.00	

2nd Hungarian Phil. Exhib., Budapest, and Jubilee of the 1st Hungarian Phil. Soc. Sold for 90f, including entrance fee. Size: 64x76mm.

Francis II Rákóczy (1676-1735), Prince of Transylvania A49

1935, Apr. 8 *Perf. 12*

487	A49	10f yellow green	.50	.50
488	A49	16f brt violet	2.00	*2.50*
489	A49	20f dark carmine	.50	.50
490	A49	32f brown lake	4.00	*4.50*
491	A49	40f blue	4.00	4.00
		Nos. 487-491 (5)	11.00	12.00
		Set, never hinged	20.00	

Cardinal Pázmány — A50

Signing the Charter — A51

1935, Sept. 25

492	A50	6f dull green	1.00	1.00
493	A51	10f dark green	.35	.35
494	A50	16f slate violet	1.25	1.25
495	A50	20f magenta	.40	.40
496	A51	32f deep claret	2.75	1.60
497	A51	40f dark blue	2.25	1.60
		Nos. 492-497 (6)	8.00	6.20
		Set, never hinged	11.00	

Tercentenary of the founding of the University of Budapest by Peter Cardinal Pázmány.

Ancient City and Fortress of Buda — A52

Guardian Angel over Buda — A53

Shield of Buda, Cannon and Massed Flags — A54

First Hungarian Soldier to Enter Buda — A55

1936, Sept. 2 *Perf. 11½x12½*

498	A52	10f dark green	.50	.25
499	A53	16f deep violet	1.75	1.75
500	A54	20f car lake	.50	.25
501	A55	32f dark brown	1.75	2.25
502	A52	40f deep blue	1.75	2.50
		Nos. 498-502 (5)	6.25	7.00
		Set, never hinged	12.00	

250th anniv. of the recapture of Budapest from the Turks.

Catalogue values for unused stamps in this section, from this point to the end of the section, are for Never Hinged items.

Budapest International Fair — A56

1937, Feb. 22			*Perf. 12*	
503 A56	2f	deep orange	.20	.20
504 A56	6f	yellow green	.25	.20
505 A56	10f	myrtle green	.30	.20
506 A56	20f	deep cerise	.50	.25
507 A56	32f	dark violet	1.00	.70
508 A56	40f	ultra	1.25	.70
		Nos. 503-508 (6)	3.50	2.25

Portrait Type of 1932

5f, Ferenc Kolcsey. 25f, Mihaly Vorosmarty.

1937, May 5			*Perf. 15*	
509 A36	5f	brown orange	.20	.20
510 A36	25f	olive green	.45	.20

Pope Sylvester II, Archbishop Astrik — A59

Designs: 2f, 16f, Stephen the Church builder. 4f, 20f, St. Stephen enthroned. 5f, 25f, Sts. Gerhardt, Emerich, Stephen. 6f, 30f, St. Stephen offering holy crown to Virgin Mary. 10f, same as 1f. 32f, 50f, Portrait of St. Stephen. 40f, Madonna and Child. 70f, Crown of St. Stephen.

See designs A75-A77 for smaller stamps of designs similar Nos. 521-524, but with slanted "MAGYAR KIR POSTA."

1938, Jan. 1			*Perf. 12*	
511 A59	1f	deep violet	.20	.25
512 A59	2f	olive brown	.20	.20
513 A59	4f	brt blue	.40	.20
514 A59	5f	magenta	.40	.25
515 A59	6f	dp yel grn	.40	.20
516 A59	10f	red orange	.40	.20
517 A59	16f	gray violet	.75	.50
518 A59	20f	car lake	.55	.20
519 A59	25f	dark green	1.10	.50
520 A59	30f	olive bister	1.60	.20
521 A59	32f	dp claret, *buff*	2.25	1.00
522 A59	40f	Prus green	1.60	.20
523 A59	50f	rose vio, *grnsh*	2.25	.30
524 A59	70f	ol grn, *bluish*	2.50	.40
		Nos. 511-524 (14)	14.60	4.60

900th anniv. of the death of St. Stephen.

For overprints see Nos. 535-536.

Admiral Horthy — A67

1938, Jan. 1			*Perf. 12½x12*	
525 A67	1p	peacock green	1.10	.20
526 A67	2p	brown	1.90	.25
527 A67	5p	sapphire blue	6.75	1.75
		Nos. 525-527 (3)	9.75	2.20

Souvenir Sheet

St. Stephen — A68

1938, May 22	Wmk. 210	*Perf. 12*	
528 A68	20f carmine lake	13.00	8.50

3rd Hungarian Phil. Exhib., Budapest. Sheet sold only at exhibition with 1p ticket.

College of Debrecen A69

Three Students — A71

George Marothy — A73

10f, 18th cent. view of College. 20f, 19th cent. view of College. 40f, Stephen Hatvani.

Perf. 12x12½, 12½x12

1938, Sept. 24			Wmk. 210	
529 A69	6f	deep green	.20	.20
530 A69	10f	brown	.20	.20
531 A71	16f	brown car	.30	.20
532 A69	20f	crimson	.25	.20
533 A73	32f	slate green	.80	.45
534 A73	40f	brt blue	.90	.30
		Nos. 529-534 (6)	2.65	1.55

Founding of Debrecen College, 400th anniv.

Types of 1938 Overprinted in Blue (#535) or Carmine (#536):

a

HAZATÉRÉS 1938

b

1938			*Perf. 12*	
535 A59(a)	20f	salmon pink	.70	.25
536 A59(b)	70f	brn, *grnsh*	.80	.25
a.		Overprint omitted	*9,000.*	*7,500.*

Restoration of the territory ceded by Czechoslovakia.

Forgeries exist of No. 536a.

Crown of St. Stephen A75

St. Stephen A76

Madonna, Patroness of Hungary A77

Coronation Church, Budapest A78

Reformed Church, Debrecen A79

Cathedral, Esztergom A80

Deak Square Evangelical Church, Budapest — A81

Cathedral of Kassa — A82

Wmk. 210

1939, June 1		Photo.	*Perf. 15*	
537 A75	1f	brown car	.20	.20
538 A75	2f	Prus green	.20	.20
539 A75	4f	ocher	.20	.20
540 A75	5f	brown violet	.20	.20
541 A75	6f	yellow green	.20	.20
542 A75	10f	bister brn	.20	.20
543 A75	16f	rose violet	.20	.20
544 A76	20f	rose red	.20	.20
545 A77	25f	blue gray	.20	.20
		Perf. 12		
546 A78	30f	red violet	.50	.20
547 A79	32f	brown	.40	.20
548 A80	40f	greenish blue	.50	.20
549 A81	50f	olive	.50	.20
550 A82	70f	henna brown	.55	.20
		Nos. 537-550 (14)	4.25	2.80

See #578-596. For overprints see #559-560.

Girl Scout Sign and Olive Branch — A83

6f, Scout lily, Hungary's shield, Crown of St. Stephen. 10f, Girls in Scout hat & national headdress. 20f, Dove & Scout emblems.

1939, July 20		Photo.	*Perf. 12*	
551 A83	2f	brown orange	.40	.35
552 A83	6f	green	.45	.35
553 A83	10f	brown	.75	.35
554 A83	20f	lilac rose	.90	.70
		Nos. 551-554 (4)	2.50	1.75

Girl Scout Jamboree at Gödöllö.

Admiral Horthy at Szeged, 1919 — A87

Admiral Nicholas Horthy A88

Cathedral of Kassa and Angel Ringing "Bell of Liberty" A89

1940, Mar. 1				
555 A87	6f	green	.30	.20
556 A88	10f	ol blk & ol bis	.30	.20
557 A89	20f	brt rose brown	.60	.35
		Nos. 555-557 (3)	1.20	.75

20th anniversary of the election of Admiral Horthy as Regent of Hungary.

Crown of St. Stephen A90

1940, Sept. 5				
558 A90	10f	dk green & yellow	.20	.20

Issued in commemoration of the recovery of northeastern Transylvania from Romania.

Nos. 542, 544 Overprinted in Red or Black

1941, Apr. 21			*Perf. 15*	
559 A75	10f	bister brn (R)	.25	.20
560 A76	20f	rose red (Bk)	.25	.20

Return of the Bacska territory from Yugoslavia.

Admiral Nicholas Horthy — A92

Wmk. 210

1941, June 18		Photo.	*Perf. 12*	
570 A92	1p	dk green & buff	.25	.20
571 A92	2p	dk brown & buff	.25	.20
572 A92	5p	dk rose vio & buff	2.00	*2.50*
		Nos. 570-572 (3)	2.50	2.90

See Nos. 597-599.

KIR·POSTA MAGYAR 10f

Count Stephen Széchenyi A93

Count Széchenyi and Royal Academy of Science A94

Representation of the Narrows of Kazán — A95

Chain Bridge, Budapest A96

Mercury, Train and Boat — A97

1941, Sept. 21

573	A93	10f dk olive grn	.20	.20
574	A94	16f olive brown	.20	.20
575	A95	20f carmine lake	.20	.20
576	A96	32f red orange	.30	.20
577	A97	40f royal blue	.30	.20
		Nos. 573-577 (5)	1.20	1.00

Count Stephen Szechenyi (1791-1860).

Types of 1939

Perf. 12x12½, 12½x12, 15

1941-43 **Wmk. 266**

578	A75	1f rose lake ('42)	.20	.20
579	A75	3f dark brown	.20	.20
580	A75	5f violet gray ('42)	.20	.20
581	A75	6f lt green ('42)	.20	.20
582	A75	8f slate grn	.20	.20
583	A75	10f olive brn ('42)	.20	.20
584	A75	12f red orange	.20	.20
585	A76	20f rose red ('42)	.20	.20
586	A76	24f brown violet	.20	.20
587	A78	30f lilac ('42)	.20	.20
588	A82	30f rose red ('43)	.20	.20
589	A80	40f blue green ('42)	.20	.20
590	A79	40f gray black ('43)	.20	.20
591	A81	50f olive grn ('42)	.20	.20
592	A80	50f brt blue ('43)	.20	.20
593	A82	70f copper red ('42)	.20	.20
594	A81	70f gray green ('43)	.20	.20
595	A77	80f brown bister	.20	.20
596	A78	80f bister brn ('43)	.20	.20
		Nos. 578-596 (19)	3.80	3.80

Horthy Type of 1941

Perf. 12x12½

1941, Dec. 18 **Wmk. 266**

597	A92	1p dk green & buff	.40	.20
598	A92	2p dk brown & buff	.40	.20
599	A92	5p dk rose vio & buff	.40	.20
		Nos. 597-599 (3)	1.00	.60

Stephen Horthy — A98

1942, Oct. 15 ***Perf. 12***

600	A98	20f black	.20	.20

Death of Stephen Horthy (1904-42), son of Regent Nicholas Horthy, who died in a plane crash.

Arpád — A99 A109

Portraits: 2f, King Ladislaus I. 3f, Miklós Toldi. 4f, János Hunyadi. 5f, Paul Kinizsi. 6f, Count Miklós Zrinyi. 8f, Francis II Rákóczy. 10f, Count Andrew Hadik. 12f, Arthur Görgei. 18f, 24f, Virgin Mary, Patroness of Hungary.

1943-45 ***Perf. 15***

601	A99	1f grnsh black	.20	.20
602	A99	2f red orange	.20	.20
603	A99	3f ultra	.20	.20
604	A99	4f brown	.20	.20
605	A99	5f vermilion	.20	.20
606	A99	6f slate blue	.20	.20
607	A99	8f dk ol grn	.20	.20
608	A99	10f brown	.20	.20
609	A99	12f dp blue grn	.20	.20
610	A99	18f dk gray	.20	.20
611	A109	20f chestnut brn	.20	.20
612	A99	24f rose violet	.20	.20
613	A109	30f brt carmine	.20	.20
614	A109	50f blue	.20	.20
615	A109	80f yellow brn	.20	.20
616	A109	1p green	.20	.20
616A	A109	2p brown ('45)	.20	.20
616B	A109	5p dk red violet ('45)	.30	.30
		Nos. 601-616B (18)	3.70	3.70

For overprints and surcharges see Nos. 631-658, 660-661, 664, 666-669, 671-672, 674-677, 679, 680, 682, 685-689, 691-698, 801-803, 805-806, 810-815, F2, Q2-Q3, Q7.

Message to the Shepherds A110

St. Margaret — A113

20f, Nativity. 30f, Adoration of the Magi.

1943, Dec. 1 ***Perf. 12x12½***

617	A110	4f dark green	.20	.20
618	A110	20f dull blue	.20	.20
619	A110	30f brown orange	.20	.20
		Nos. 617-619 (3)	.60	.60

1944, Jan. 19 ***Perf. 15***

620	A113	30f deep carmine	.20	.20

Canonization of St. Margaret of Hungary. For surcharges see Nos. 662, 673A.

Kossuth with Family — A114 Lajos Kossuth — A117

Honvéd Drummer A115

Design: 30f, Kossuth orating.

1944, Mar. 20 ***Perf. 12½x12, 12x12½***

621	A114	4f yellow brown	.20	.20
622	A115	20f dk olive grn	.20	.20
623	A115	30f henna brown	.20	.20
624	A117	50f slate blue	.20	.20
		Nos. 621-624 (4)	.80	.80

Louis (Lajos) Kossuth (1802-94). For surcharges see Nos. B175-B178.

St. Elizabeth — A118

Portraits: 24f, St. Margaret. 30f, Elizabeth Szilágyi. 50f, Dorothy Kanuizsai. 70f, Susanna Lórántffy. 80f, Ilona Zrinyi.

1944, Aug. 1 ***Perf. 15***

625	A118	20f olive	.20	.20
626	A118	24f rose violet	.20	.20
627	A118	30f copper red	.20	.20
628	A118	50f dark blue	.20	.20
629	A118	70f orange red	.20	.20
630	A118	80f brown car	.20	.20
		Nos. 625-630 (6)	1.20	1.20

For overprints and surcharges see Nos. 659, 663, 665, 670, 673, 678, 681, 683-684, 690, 804, 807-809, F1, F3, Q1, Q4-Q6, Q8.

Issues of the Republic

Types of Hungary, 1943 Surcharged in Carmine

1945, May 1 **Wmk. 266**

Blue Surface-tinted Paper

631	A99	10f on 1f grnsh blk	1.50	1.50
632	A99	20f on 3f ultra	1.50	1.50
633	A99	30f on 4f brown	1.50	1.50
634	A99	40f on 6f slate bl	1.50	1.50
635	A99	50f on 8f dk ol grn	1.50	1.50
636	A99	1p on 10f brown	1.50	1.50
637	A99	150f on 12f dp bl grn	1.50	1.50
638	A99	2p on 18f dk gray	1.50	1.50
639	A109	3p on 20f chnt brn	1.50	1.50
640	A99	5p on 24f rose vio	1.50	1.50
641	A109	6p on 50f blue	1.50	1.50
642	A109	10p on 80f yel brn	1.50	1.50
643	A109	20p on 1p green	1.50	1.50

Yellow Surface-tinted Paper

644	A99	10f on 1f grnsh blk	1.50	1.50
645	A99	20f on 3f ultra	1.50	1.50
646	A99	30f on 4f brown	1.50	1.50
647	A99	40f on 6f slate bl	1.50	1.50
648	A99	50f on 8f dk ol grn	1.50	1.50
649	A99	1p on 10f brown	1.50	1.50
650	A99	150f on 12f dp bl grn	1.50	1.50
651	A99	2p on 18f dk gray	1.50	1.50
652	A109	3p on 20f chnt brn	1.50	1.50
653	A99	5p on 24f rose vio	1.50	1.50
654	A109	6p on 50f blue	1.50	1.50
655	A109	10p on 80f yel brn	1.50	1.50
656	A109	20p on 1p green	1.50	1.50
		Nos. 631-656 (26)	39.00	39.00

Hungary's liberation.

Types of Hungary, 1943-45, Surcharged in Carmine or Black

1945

Blue Surface-tinted Paper

657	A99	10f on 4f brn (C)	.20	.20
658	A99	10f on 10f brn (C)	.45	.45
659	A118	20f on 20f ol (C)	.20	.20
660	A99	28f on 5f ver	.20	.20
661	A109	30f on 30f brt car	.20	.20
662	A113	30f on 30f dp car	.20	.20
663	A118	30f on 30f cop red	.20	.20
664	A99	40f on 10f brown	.20	.20
665	A118	1p on 70f org red	.25	.25
666	A109	1p on 80f yel brn (C)	.20	.20
667	A99	2p on 4f brown	.20	.20
668	A109	2p on 2p brn (C)	.20	.20
669	A109	4p on 30f brt car	.20	.20
670	A118	8p on 20f olive	.20	.20
671	A99	10p on 2f red org	7.25	7.25
672	A109	10p on 80f yel brn	.20	.20
673	A118	20p on 30f cop red	.20	.20

Same Surcharge with Thinner Unshaded Numerals of Value

673A	A113	300p on 30f dp car	.20	.20

Surcharged as Nos. 657-673 Yellow Surface-tinted Paper

674	A99	10f on 12f dp bl grn (C)	.20	.20
675	A99	20f on 1f grnsh blk (C)	.20	.20
676	A99	20f on 18f dk gray (C)	.20	.20
a.		Double surcharge		
677	A99	40f on 24f rose vio (C)	.20	.20
678	A118	40f on 24f rose vio (C)	.20	.20
679	A109	42f on 20f chnt brn (C)	.20	.20
680	A109	50f on 50f bl (C)	.20	.20
681	A118	50f on 50f dk bl (C)	.20	.20
682	A99	60f on 8f dk ol grn (C)	.20	.20
683	A118	80f on 24f rose vio	.20	.20
684	A118	80f on 80f brn car (C)	.20	.20
685	A109	1p on 20f chnt brn	.20	.20
686	A109	1p on 1p grn (C)	.20	.20
687	A99	150f on 6f sl bl (C)	.90	.90
688	A99	1.60p on 12f dp bl grn	.20	.20
689	A99	3p on 3f ultra (C)	.30	.30
690	A118	3p on 50f dk bl	.20	.20
691	A99	5p on 8f dk ol grn	.20	.20
692	A109	5p on 5p dk red vio (C)	.25	.25
693	A109	6p on 50f blue	.20	.20
694	A109	7p on 1p grn	.20	.20
695	A99	9p on 1f grnsh blk	.20	.20

Same Surcharge with Thinner, Unshaded Numerals of Value

696	A99	40p on 8f dk ol grn	.20	.20
697	A99	60p on 18f dk gray	.20	.20
698	A99	100p on 12f dp bl grn	.20	.20
		Nos. 657-698 (43)	16.80	16.80

Various shades and errors of overprint exist on Nos. 657-698.

These surface-tinted stamps exist without surcharge, but were not so issued.

Construction A124

Designs: 1.60p, Manufacturing. 2p, Railroading. 3p, Building. 5p, Agriculture. 8p, Communications. 10p, Architecture. 20p, Writing.

Wmk. 266

1945, Sept. 11 **Photo.** ***Perf. 12***

700	A124	40f gray black	5.00	5.00
701	A124	1.60p olive bis	5.00	5.00
702	A124	2p slate green	5.00	5.00
703	A124	3p dark purple	5.00	5.00
704	A124	5p dark red	5.00	5.00
705	A124	8p brown	5.00	5.00
706	A124	10p deep claret	5.00	5.00
707	A124	20p slate blue	5.00	5.00
		Nos. 700-707 (8)	40.00	40.00

World Trade Union Conf., Paris, Sept. 25 to Oct. 10, 1945.

"Reconstruction" — A132

1945-46

708	A132	12p brown olive	.25	.25
709	A132	20p brt green	.20	.20
710	A132	24p orange brn	.25	.25
711	A132	30p gray black	.20	.20
712	A132	40p olive green	.20	.20
713	A132	60p red orange	.20	.20
714	A132	100p orange yel	.20	.20
715	A132	120p brt ultra	.20	.20
716	A132	140p brt red	.40	.40
717	A132	200p olive brn	.20	.20
718	A132	240p brt blue	.20	.20
719	A132	300p dk carmine	.20	.20
720	A132	500p dull green	.20	.20
721	A132	1000p red violet	.20	.20
722	A132	3000p brt red ('46)	.20	.20
		Nos. 708-722 (15)	3.30	3.30

#708-721 exist tête bêche. Value: $12.50.

"Liberation" A133

1946, Feb. 12

723	A133	3ez p dark red	.20	.20
724	A133	15ez p ultra	.20	.20

Postrider — A134

Photo.; Values Typo.

1946 ***Perf. 15***

725	A134	4ez p brown org	.20	.20
726	A134	10ez p brt red	.20	.20
727	A134	15ez p ultra	.20	.20
728	A134	20ez p dk brown	.20	.20
729	A134	30ez p red violet	.20	.20
730	A134	50ez p gray black	.20	.20
731	A134	80ez p brt ultra	.20	.20

732	A134	100ez p rose car	.20	.20
733	A134	160ez p gray green	.20	.20
734	A134	200ez p yellow grn	.20	.20
735	A134	500ez p red	.20	.20
736	A134	640ez p olive bis	.20	.20
737	A134	800ez p rose violet	.20	.20
		Nos. 725-737 (13)	2.60	2.60

Abbreviations:
Ez (Ezer) = Thousand
Mil (Milpengo) = Million
Mlrd (Milliard) = Billion
Bil (Billio-pengo) = Trillion

Arms of Hungary — A135

1946 **Wmk. 210**

738	A135	1mil p vermilion	.20	.20
a.		"1" in center omitted	400.00	
739	A135	2mil p ultra	.20	.20
740	A135	3mil p brown	.20	.20
741	A135	4mil p slate gray	.20	.20
742	A135	5mil p rose violet	.20	.20
743	A135	10mil p green	.20	.20
744	A135	20mil p carmine	.20	.20
745	A135	50mil p olive	.20	.20

Arms and Post Horn
A136 A137

746	A136	100mil p henna brn	.20	.20
747	A136	200mil p henna brn	.20	.20
748	A136	500mil p henna brn	.20	.20
749	A136	1000mil p henna brn	.20	.20
750	A136	2000mil p henna brn	.20	.20
751	A136	3000mil p henna brn	.20	.20
752	A136	5000mil p henna brn	.20	.20
753	A136	10,000mil p henna brn	.20	.20
754	A136	20,000mil p henna brn	.20	.20
755	A136	30,000mil p henna brn	.25	.20
756	A136	50,000mil p henna brn	.25	.25

Denomination in Carmine

757	A137	100mlrd p olive	.20	.20
758	A137	200mlrd p olive	.20	.20
759	A137	500mlrd p olive	.20	.20

Dove and Letter — A138

Denomination in Carmine

760	A138	1bil p grnsh blk	.20	.20
761	A138	2bil p grnsh blk	.20	.20
763	A138	5bil p grnsh blk	.20	.20
764	A138	10bil p grnsh blk	.20	.20
765	A138	20bil p grnsh blk	.20	.20
766	A138	50bil p grnsh blk	.20	.20
767	A138	100bil p grnsh blk	.20	.20
768	A138	200bil p grnsh blk	.20	.20
769	A138	500bil p grnsh blk	.20	.20
770	A138	1000bil p grnsh blk	.20	.20
771	A138	10,000bil p grnsh blk	.20	.20
772	A138	50,000bil p grnsh blk	.25	.25
773	A138	100,000bil p grnsh blk	.25	.25
774	A138	500,000bil p grnsh blk	.25	.25

Denomination in Black

775	A137	5ez ap green	.20	.20
776	A137	10ez ap green	.20	.20
777	A137	20ez ap green	.20	.20
778	A137	50ez ap green	.20	.20
779	A137	80ez ap green	.20	.20
780	A137	100ez ap green	.20	.20
781	A137	200ez ap green	.20	.20
782	A137	500ez ap green	.20	.20
783	A137	1mil ap vermilion	.20	.20
784	A137	5mil ap vermilion	.20	.20
		Nos. 738-784 (46)	9.40	9.40

Denominations are expressed in "ado" or "tax" pengos.

Early Steam Locomotive A139

Designs: 20,000ap, Recent steam locomotive. 30,000ap, Electric locomotive. 40,000ap, Diesel locomotive.

1946, July 15 **Wmk. 266** ***Perf. 12***

785	A139	10,000ap vio brn	3.00	3.50
786	A139	20,000ap dk blue	3.00	3.50
787	A139	30,000ap dp yel grn	3.00	3.50
788	A139	40,000ap rose car	3.00	3.50
b.		"40,000 ap" omitted	*1,750.*	
		Nos. 785-788 (4)	12.00	14.00

Centenary of Hungarian railways.

Industry A143

Agriculture A144

1946 **Wmk. 210** **Photo.** ***Perf. 15***

788A	A143	8f henna brn	.20	.20
789	A143	10f henna brn	.20	.20
790	A143	12f henna brn	.20	.20
791	A143	20f henna brn	.20	.20
792	A143	30f henna brn	.20	.20
793	A143	40f henna brn	.20	.20
794	A143	60f henna brn	.20	.20
795	A144	1fo dp yel grn	.30	.20
796	A144	1.40fo dp yel grn	.45	.20
797	A144	2fo dp yel grn	.55	.20
798	A144	3fo dp yel grn	4.00	.20
799	A144	5fo dp yel grn	1.50	.20
800	A144	10fo dp yel grn	3.50	.35
		Nos. 788A-800 (13)	11.70	2.75

For surcharges see Nos. Q9-Q11.

Stamps and Types of 1943-45 Overprinted in Carmine or Black to Show Class of Postage for which Valid

"Any." or "Nyomtatv."=Printed Matter.
"Hl" or "Helyi levél"=Local Letter.
"Hlp." or "Helyi lev.-lap"=Local Postcard.
"Tl." or "Távolsági levél"=Domestic Letter.
"Tlp." or "Távolsági lev.-lap"=Domestic Postcard.

a

b

1946 **Wmk. 266**

801	A99(a)	"Any 1." on 1f (#601;C)	.20	.20
802	A99(a)	"Any 2," on 1f (#601;C)	.20	.20
803	A99(b)	"Nyomtatv. 20gr" on 60f on 8f (#682;Bk + C)	.20	.20
804	A118(a)	"Hl. 1" on 50f (#628;C)	.20	.20
805	A99(a)	"Hl. 2" on 40f on 10f (#664;C + Bk)	.20	.20
806	A99(b)	"Helyi levél" on 10f brn, *bl* (Bk)	.20	.20
807	A118(a)	"Hlp.1" on 8p on 20f (#670;C + Bk)	.20	.20
808	A118(a)	"Hlp.2." on 8p on 20f (#670;C + Bk)	.20	.20
809	A118(b)	"Helyi lev.-lap" on 20f ol, *bl* (C)	.20	.20
810	A99(a)	"Tl.1" on 10f (#608;Bk)	.20	.20
811	A99(a)	"Tl.2." on 10f on 4f (#657;Bk + C)	.20	.20
812	A99(b)	"Tavolsagi level" on 18f (#610;C)	.20	.20
813	A99(a)	"Tlp.1." on 4f (#604;Bk)	.20	.20
814	A99(a)	"Tlp.2." on 4f (#604;Bk)	.20	.20
815	A99(b)	"Tavolsagi lev.-lap" on 4f (#604;Bk)	.20	.20
		Nos. 801-815 (15)	3.00	3.00

Nos. 806, 809 not issued without overprint.

György Dózsa — A145

Designs: 10f, Antal Budai-Nagy. 12f, Tamas Esze. 20f, Ignac Martinovics. 30f, Janos Batsanyi. 40f, Lajos Kossuth. 60f, Mihaly Tancsics. 1fo, Alexander Petőfi. 2fo, Andreas Ady. 4fo, Jozsef Attila.

1947, Mar. 15 **Photo.** **Wmk. 210**

816	A145	8f rose brown	.25	.20
817	A145	10f deep ultra	.25	.20
818	A145	12f deep brown	.25	.20
819	A145	20f dk yel grn	.25	.20
820	A145	30f dk ol bis	.20	.20
821	A145	40f brown car	.20	.20
822	A145	60f cerise	.35	.20
823	A145	1fo dp grnsh bl	.45	.20
824	A145	2fo dk violet	1.10	.35
825	A145	4fo grnsh black	1.50	.70
		Nos. 816-825 (10)	4.80	2.65

Peace and Agriculture A155

Postal Savings Emblem A156

1947, Sept. 22 ***Perf. 12***

826	A155	60f bright red	.30	.20
a.		"60f." omitted	*1,250.*	

Peace treaty.

1947, Oct. 31

60f, Postal Savings Bank, Budapest.

827	A156	40f rose brown	.20	.20
828	A156	60f brt rose car	.40	.20

Savings Day, Oct. 31, 1947.

Hungarian Flag — A157

1848 Printing Press A158

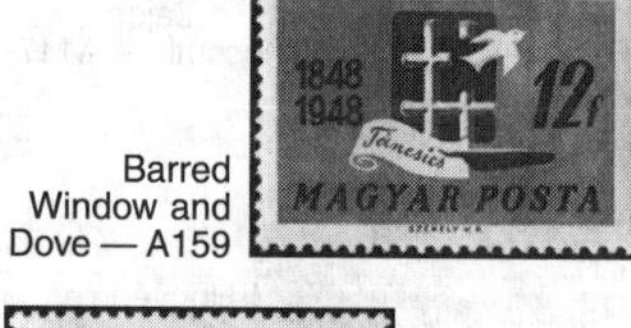

Barred Window and Dove — A159

1848 Shako, Sword and Trumpet A160

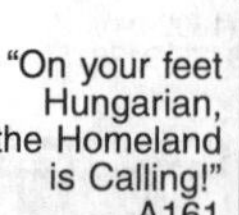

"On your feet Hungarian, the Homeland is Calling!" A161

Arms of Hungary — A162

Perf. 12½x12, 12x12½

1948 **Wmk. 283** **Photo.**

829	A157	8f dk rose red	.25	.20
830	A158	10f ultra	.25	.20
831	A159	12f copper brn	.40	.25
832	A160	20f deep green	.80	.20
833	A161	30f olive brown	.40	.20
834	A157	40f dk vio brn	.65	.20
835	A161	60f carmine lake	1.00	.20
a.		Printed on both sides	550.00	
836	A162	1fo brt ultra	1.00	.20
837	A162	2fo red brown	1.40	.25
838	A162	3fo green	1.60	.60
839	A162	4fo scarlet	4.25	.80
		Nos. 829-839 (11)	12.00	3.30

Cent. of the beginning of Hungary's war for independence.
#834 is inscribed "Kossuth," #835 "Petofi."

Baron Roland Eötvös A163

1948, July 27

840	A163	60f deep red	.60	.25

Roland Eötvös, physicist, birth cent.

Hungarian Workers — A164

1948, Oct. 17 **Wmk. 283** ***Perf. 12***

841	A164	30f dk carmine rose	.40	.30
a.		Sheet of 4	20.00	20.00

The 17th Trade Union Congress, Budapest, October 1948. No. 841a was sold for 2 forint.

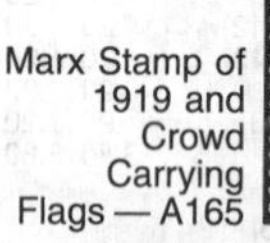

Marx Stamp of 1919 and Crowd Carrying Flags — A165

Petőfi Stamp of 1919 and Flags — A166

1949, Mar. 19

Flags in Carmine

842	A165	40f brown	.35	.25
843	A166	60f olive gray	.35	.25

1st Hungarian Soviet Republic, 30th anniv.

Workers of the Five Continents and Flag — A167

1949, June 29 ***Perf. 12x12½***

Flag in Red

844	A167	30f yellow brown	3.00	3.00
845	A167	40f brown violet	3.00	3.00
846	A167	60f lilac rose	3.00	3.00
847	A167	1fo violet blue	3.00	3.00
		Nos. 844-847 (4)	12.00	12.00

2nd Congress of the World Federation of Trade Unions, Milan, 1949.

Sándor Petőfi — A168

Youth of Three Races — A169

Perf. 12½x12

1949, July 31 Engr. Unwmk.

848 A168 40f claret .40 .20
849 A168 60f dark red .30 .20
850 A168 1fo deep blue .40 .20
Nos. 848-850 (3) 1.10 .60

Cent. of the death of Sándor Petőfi, poet.
See Nos. 867-869.

Perf. 12½x12

1949, Aug. 14 Photo. Wmk. 283

Designs: 30f, Three fists. 40f, Soldier breaking chain. 60f, Soviet youths carrying flags. 1fo, Young workers displaying books.

851 A169 20f dk violet brn .70 .70
a. 20f blue green 3.00 3.00
852 A169 30f blue green .80 .80
a. 30f violet brown 3.00 3.00
853 A169 40f olive bister 1.00 1.00
a. 40f ultramarine 3.00 3.00
854 A169 60f rose pink 1.00 1.00
855 A169 1fo ultra 1.50 1.50
a. 1fo olive bister 3.50 3.50
b. Souv. sheet of 5, #851a-853a, 854, 855a 25.00 25.00
Nos. 851-855 (5) 5.00 5.00

World Festival of Youth and Students, Budapest, Aug. 14-28, 1949.

Arms of Hungarian People's Republic A170

1949 Wmk. 283

Arms in Bister, Carmine, Blue and Green

856 A170 20f green .90 .50
a. Unwatermarked 1.00 .50
857 A170 60f carmine .35 .20
a. Unwatermarked .50 .20
858 A170 1fo blue .90 .55
a. Unwatermarked 1.00 .55
Nos. 856-858 (3) 2.15 1.25

Adoption of the Hungarian People's Republic constitution.
Nos. 856-858 exist with papermaker's watermark. These sell for more.

Imperforates

Nearly all Hungarian stamps from No. 859 on were issued imperforate as well as with perforations. In most cases the imperforate quantities were smaller than the perforated ones. The imperforates were sold at five times face value, and all issued before Feb. 22, 1958, were invalid. Late in 1958, Philatelica Hungarica started selling the imperforates at four to six times face value.

Philatelica Hungarica announced in 1991 that, beginning with the 1992 issues, imperforates would no longer be produced.

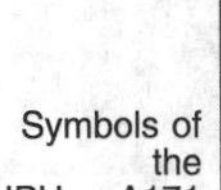

Symbols of the UPU — A171

1949, Nov. 1 ***Perf. 12x12½***

859 A171 60f rose red .20 .20
a. Booklet pane of 6 7.50
860 A171 1fo blue .30 .30
a. Booklet pane of 6 10.00
Nos. 859-860,C63 (3) 1.00 1.00

75th anniv. of the UPU.
Nos. 859 and 860 exist imperf. and stamps from 859a and 860a in horiz. pairs, imperf. between.
See No. C81.

Chain Bridge A172

1949, Nov. 20 Wmk. 283

861 A172 40f blue green .20 .20
862 A172 60f red brown .20 .20
863 A172 1fo blue .25 .25
Nos. 861-863,C64-C65 (5) 2.25 1.90

Cent. of the opening of the Chain Bridge at Budapest to traffic. For souvenir sheet see No. C66.

Joseph V. Stalin — A173

Perf. 12½x12

1949, Dec. 21 Engr. Unwmk.

864 A173 60f dark red .40 .20
865 A173 1fo deep blue .40 .30
866 A173 2fo brown .95 .50
Nos. 864-866 (3) 1.75 1.00

70th anniv. of the birth of Joseph V. Stalin.
See Nos. 1034-1035.

Petőfi Type of 1949

1950, Feb. 5 ***Perf. 12½x12***

867 A168 40f brown .20 .20
868 A168 60f dark carmine .30 .20
869 A168 1fo dark green .75 .20
Nos. 867-869 (3) 1.25 .60

Philatelic Museum, Budapest A174

Perf. 12x12½

1950, Mar. 12 Photo. Wmk. 283

870 A174 60f gray & brown 3.50 3.00

20th anniv. of the establishment of the Hungarian PO Phil. Museum. See No. C68.

Coal Mining A175

Designs: 10f, Heavy industry. 12f, Power production. 20f, Textile industry. 30f, "Cultured workers." 40f, Mechanized agriculture. 60f, Village cooperative. 1fo, Train. 1.70fo, "Holiday." 2fo, Defense. 3fo, Shipping. 4fo, Livestock. 5fo, Engineering. 10fo, Sports.

1950 Wmk. 283

871 A175 8f gray .45 .20
872 A175 10f claret .45 .20
873 A175 12f orange ver .70 .35
874 A175 20f blue green .25 .20
875 A175 30f rose violet .35 .20
876 A175 40f sepia .45 .20
877 A175 60f red .40 .20
878 A175 1fo gray brn, yel & lil 1.90 .25
879 A175 1.70fo dk grn & yel 5.50 .40
880 A175 2fo vio brn & cr 2.75 .20
881 A175 3fo slate & cream 4.50 .20
882 A175 4fo blk brn & sal 19.00 4.00
883 A175 5fo rose vio & yel 9.75 1.90
884 A175 10fo dk brn & yel 45.00 11.00
Nos. 871-884 (14) 91.45 19.50
Hinged set 70.00

Issued to publicize Hungary's Five Year Plan. See Nos. 945-958.

Citizens Welcoming Liberators — A176

1950, Apr. 4 Unwmk. ***Perf. 12***

885 A176 40f gray black .85 .50
886 A176 60f rose brown .40 .20
887 A176 1fo deep blue .75 .20
888 A176 2fo brown 1.00 .60
Nos. 885-888 (4) 3.00 1.50

Fifth anniversary of Hungary's liberation.

Chess Players A177

Design: 1fo, Iron Workers Union building and chess emblem.

1950, Apr. 9 Wmk. 106

889 A177 60f deep magenta .70 .40
890 A177 1fo deep blue 1.25 .85
Nos. 889-890,C69 (3) 3.70 2.25

World Chess Championship Matches, Budapest.

Workers Symbolizing International Proletariat — A178

Design: 60f, Blast furnace, tractor, workers holding Maypole.

1950, May 1

891 A178 40f orange brown .50 .35
892 A178 60f rose carmine .30 .20
893 A178 1fo deep blue .80 .45
Nos. 891-893 (3) 1.60 1.00

Issued to publicize Labor Day, May 1, 1950.

Liberty, Cogwheel, Dove and Globes — A179

Inscribed: "1950. V. 10.-24."

Design: 60f, Three workers and flag.

1950, May 10 Photo. ***Perf. 12x12½***

894 A179 40f olive green .20 .20
895 A179 60f dark carmine .30 .20
Nos. 894-895,C70 (3) 1.00 .60

Meeting of the World Federation of Trade Unions, Budapest, May 1950.

Doctor Inspecting Baby's Bath — A180

Children's Day: 30f, Physical Culture. 40f, Education. 60f, Boys' Camp. 1.70fo, Model plane building.

1950, June 4 Wmk. 106

896 A180 20f gray & brn .80 .55
897 A180 30f brn & rose lake .40 .20
898 A180 40f indigo & dk grn .40 .20
899 A180 60f SZABAD .40 .20
a. UTANPOTLASUNK . . 600.00 600.00
900 A180 1.70fo dp grn & gray 1.50 .55
Nos. 896-900 (5) 3.50 1.70

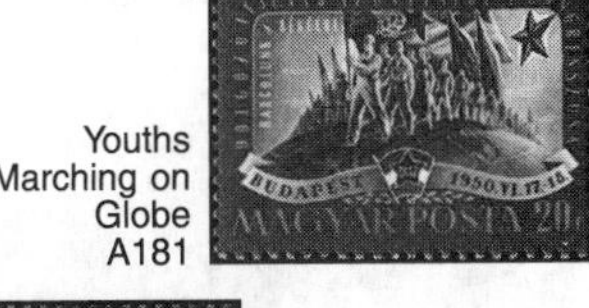

Youths Marching on Globe A181

Working Man and Woman — A182

30f, Foundry worker. 60f, Workers on Mt. Gellert. 1.70fo, Worker, peasant & student; flags.

Inscribed: Budapest 1950. VI. 17-18.

Perf. 12x12½, 12½x12

1950, June 17

901 A181 20f dark green .60 .40
902 A181 30f deep red org .20 .20
903 A182 40f dark brown .20 .20
904 A182 60f deep claret .35 .20
905 A182 1.70fo dark olive grn .90 .30
Nos. 901-905 (5) 2.25 1.30

Issued to publicize the First Congress of the Working Youth, Budapest, June 17-18, 1950.

Peonies — A183

Designs: 40f, Anemones. 60f, Pheasant's-eye. 1fo, Geraniums. 1.70fo, Bluebells.

Engraved and Lithographed

Perf. 12½x12

1950, Aug. 20 Unwmk.

906 A183 30f rose brn, rose pink & grn .40 .20
907 A183 40f dk green, lil & yel .55 .20
908 A183 60f red brn, yel & grn .80 .35
909 A183 1fo purple, red & grn 1.75 1.25
910 A183 1.70fo dk violet & grn 2.50 1.00
Nos. 906-910 (5) 6.00 3.00

Miner — A184

Designs: 60f, High speed lathe. 1fo, Prefabricated building construction.

Perf. 12x12½

1950, Oct. 7 Photo. Wmk. 106

911 A184 40f brown	.20	.20
912 A184 60f carmine rose	.20	.20
913 A184 1fo brt blue	.60	.45
Nos. 911-913 (3)	1.00	.85

2nd National Exhibition of Inventions.

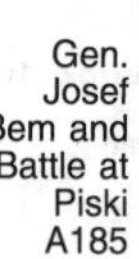

Gen. Josef Bem and Battle at Piski A185

Perf. 12½x12

1950, Dec. 10 Engr. Unwmk.

914 A185 40f dark brown	.90	.60
915 A185 60f deep carmine	.80	.30
916 A185 1fo deep blue	1.10	.65
Nos. 914-916 (3)	2.80	1.55

Gen. Josef Bem, death centenary.
See No. C80.

Signing Petition A186

Peace Demonstrator Holding Dove — A187

1fo, Mother and Children with soldier.

Wmk. 106

1950, Nov. 23 Photo. *Perf. 12*

917 A186 40f ultra & red brn	8.75	6.50
918 A187 60f red org & dk grn	2.00	1.50
919 A186 1fo ol grn & dk brn	8.75	5.50
Nos. 917-919 (3)	19.50	13.50

Women Swimmers A188

Designs: 20f, Vaulting. 1fo, Mountain climbing. 1.70fo, Basketball. 2fo, Motorcycling.

1950, Dec. 2 *Perf. 12x12½*

920 A188 10f blue & gray	.20	.20
921 A188 20f salmon & dk brn	.20	.20
922 A188 1fo olive & grn	.50	.45
923 A188 1.70fo ver & brn car	.80	.55
924 A188 2fo salmon & pur	1.60	1.00
Nos. 920-924,C82-C86 (10)	8.65	5.70

Canceled to Order

The government stamp agency started about 1950 to sell canceled sets of new issues. Values in the second ("used") column are for these canceled-to-order stamps. Postally used copies are worth more.

The practice was to end Apr. 1, 1991.

A189

Worker, Peasant, Soldier and Party Flag — A190

60f, Matthias Rakosi & allegory. 1fo, House of Parliament, columns of workers & banner.

Inscribed: "Budapest * 1951 * Februar 24."

1951, Feb. 24 *Perf. 12½x12, 12x12½*

925 A189 10f yellow green	.20	.20
926 A190 30f brown	.25	.20
927 A190 60f carmine rose	.30	.25
928 A189 1fo blue	.75	.35
Nos. 925-928 (4)	1.50	1.00

2nd Congress of the Hungarian Workers' Party.

Mare and Foal — A191

Designs: 30f, Sow and shoats. 40f, Ram and ewe. 60f, Cow and calf.

1951, Apr. 5 *Perf. 12x12½*

929 A191 10f ol bis & rose brn	.30	.20
930 A191 30f rose brn & ol bis	.45	.30
931 A191 40f dk green & brn	.45	.25
932 A191 60f brown org & brn	.60	.30
Nos. 929-932,C87-C90 (8)	5.90	3.95

Issued to encourage increased livestock production.

Flags of Russia and Hungary — A192

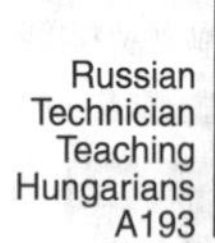

Russian Technician Teaching Hungarians A193

1951, Apr. 4 *Perf. 12½x12, 12x12½*

933 A192 60f brnsh carmine	.20	.20
934 A193 1fo dull violet	.30	.20

Issued to publicize the "Month of Friendship" between Hungary and Russia, 1951.

Worker Holding Olive Branch and Mallet A194

Workers Carrying Flags — A195

1fo, Workers approaching Place of Heroes.

Perf. 12x12½, 12½x12

1951, May 1 Photo. Wmk. 106

935 A194 40f brown	.20	.20
936 A195 60f scarlet	.25	.20
937 A194 1fo blue	.40	.20
Nos. 935-937 (3)	.85	.60

Issued to publicize Labor Day, May 1, 1951.

Leo Frankel — A196

Paris Street Fighting, 1871 — A197

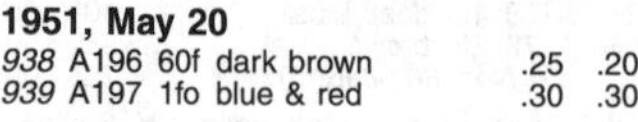

1951, May 20

938 A196 60f dark brown	.25	.20
939 A197 1fo blue & red	.30	.30

80th anniv. of the Commune of Paris.

Children of Various Races — A198

1951, June 3 *Perf. 12½x12*

Designs: 40f, Boy and girl at play. 50f, Street car and Girl Pioneer. 60f, Chemistry students. 1.70fo, Pioneer bugler.

Inscribed: "Nemzetkozi Gyermeknap 1951"

940 A198 30f dark brown	.25	.20
941 A198 40f green	.25	.20
942 A198 50f brown red	.35	.25
943 A198 60f plum	.50	.35
944 A198 1.70fo blue	1.00	1.00
Nos. 940-944 (5)	2.35	2.00

International Day of Children, 6/3/51.

5-Year-Plan Type of 1950

Designs as before.

1951-52 Wmk. 106 *Perf. 12x12½*

945 A175 8f gray	.60	.20
946 A175 10f claret	.35	.20
947 A175 12f orange ver	.35	.20
948 A175 20f blue green	.35	.20
949 A175 30f rose violet	.35	.20
950 A175 40f sepia	.65	.20
951 A175 60f red	.75	.20
952 A175 1fo gray brn, yel & lil	.85	.20
953 A175 1.70fo dk grn & yel	1.75	.20
954 A175 2fo vio brn & cr	2.25	.20
955 A175 3fo slate & cream	3.25	.25
956 A175 4fo blk brn & sal	4.00	.35
957 A175 5fo rose vio & yel ('52)	4.50	.75
958 A175 10fo dk brn & yel ('52)	10.00	2.00
Nos. 945-958 (14)	30.00	5.35

Maxim Gorky — A199

Perf. 12½x12

1951, June 17 Engr. Unwmk.

959 A199 60f copper red	.20	.20
960 A199 1fo deep blue	.35	.25
961 A199 2fo rose violet	1.00	.75
Nos. 959-961 (3)	1.55	1.20

15th anniversary of the death of Gorky.

Budapest Buildings

Railroad Workshop A200

Building in Lehel Street A201

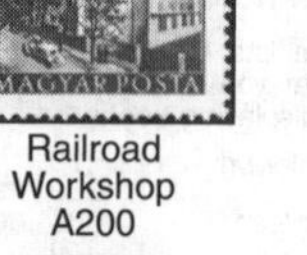

Suburban Bus Terminal A202

Rakosi House of Culture A203

George Kilian Street School A204

Central Construction Headquarters A205

1951 Wmk. 106 Photo. *Perf. 15*

962 A200 20f green	.20	.20
963 A201 30f red orange	.20	.20
964 A202 40f brown	.25	.20
965 A203 60f red	.35	.20
966 A204 1fo blue	.75	.20
967 A205 3fo deep plum	2.25	.20
Nos. 962-967 (6)	4.00	1.20

The original size of Nos. 962-967, 22x18mm, was changed to 21x17mm starting in 1958. Values are the same.

See Nos. 1004-1011, 1048-1056C.

Tractor Manufacture A206

30f, Fluoroscope examination. 40f, Checking lathework. 60f, Woman tractor operator.

1951, Aug. 20 *Perf. 12x12½*

968 A206 20f black brown	.20	.20
969 A206 30f deep blue	.20	.20
970 A206 40f crimson rose	.40	.20
971 A206 60f brown	.45	.20
Nos. 968-971,C91-C93 (7)	3.25	1.80

The successful conclusion of the first year under Hungary's 5-year plan.

Soldiers of the People's Army — A207

1951, Sept. 29

972 A207 1fo brown	1.00	.30

Issued to publicize Army Day, Sept. 29, 1951. See No. C94.

Stamp of 1871, Portrait Replaced by Postmark A208

Cornflower A209

Perf. 12½x12

1951, Sept. 12 Engr. Unwmk.

973 A208 60f olive green		2.00	1.50
Nos. 973,B207-B208 (3)		22.00	20.00

80th anniv. of Hungary's 1st postage stamp. See Nos. C95, CB13-CB14.

1951, Nov. 4 Engr. & Litho.

974	A209	30f shown	.25	.20
975	A209	40f Lily of the Valley	1.25	.45
976	A209	60f Tulip	.35	.20
977	A209	1fo Poppy	.75	.40
978	A209	1.70fo Cowslip	.90	1.00
		Nos. 974-978 (5)	3.50	2.25

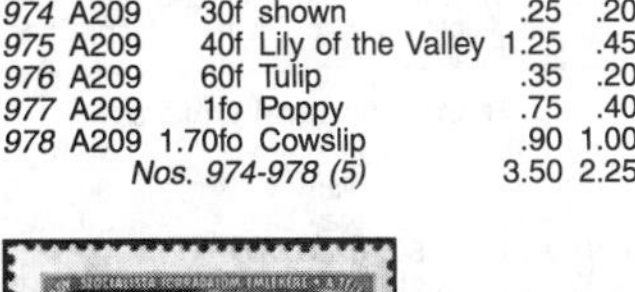

Storming of the Winter Palace A210

Designs: 60f, Lenin speaking to soldiers. 1fo, Lenin and Stalin.

Perf. 12x12½

1951, Nov. 7 Photo. Wmk. 106

979 A210 40f gray green	.65	.25
980 A210 60f deep blue	.50	.20
981 A210 1fo rose lake	.85	.40
Nos. 979-981 (3)	2.00	.85

34th anniversary of the Russian Revolution.

Marchers Passing Stalin Monument — A211

1951, Dec. 16 Wmk. 106

982 A211 60f henna brown	.45	.20
983 A211 1fo deep blue	.85	.30

Joseph V. Stalin, 72nd birthday.

Grand Theater, Moscow A212

Views of Moscow: 1fo, Lenin Mausoleum. 1.60fo, Kremlin.

1952, Feb. 20 ***Perf. 12***

984	A212	60f ol grn & rose brn	.30	.20
985	A212	1fo lil rose & ol brn	.55	.30
986	A212	1.60fo red brn & ol	.90	.50
		Nos. 984-986 (3)	1.75	1.00

Hungarian-Soviet Friendship Month.

Rakosi and Farmers A213

Matyas Rakosi — A214

Design: 2fo, Rakosi and Workers.

Perf. 12x12½, 12½x12

1952, Mar. 9 Engr. Unwmk.

987 A213 60f deep plum	.25	.20
988 A214 1fo dk red brown	.35	.20
989 A213 2fo dp violet blue	1.10	.50
Nos. 987-989 (3)	1.70	.90

60th anniv. of the birth of Matyas Rakosi, communist leader.

Lajos Kossuth and Speech at Debrecen A215

Designs: 30f, Sándor Petőfi. 50f, Gen. Josef Bem. 60f, Mihaly Tancsics. 1fo, Gen. János Damjanich. 1.50fo, Gen. Alexander Nagy.

1952, Mar. 15 ***Perf. 12***

990	A215	20f green	.20	.20
991	A215	30f rose violet	.20	.20
992	A215	50f grnsh blk	.25	.25
993	A215	60f brown car	.35	.20
994	A215	1fo blue	.45	.30
995	A215	1.50fo redsh brown	.55	.50
		Nos. 990-995 (6)	2.00	1.65

Heroes of the 1848 revolution.

No. B204 Surcharged in Black with Bars Obliterating Inscription and Surtax

Perf. 12½x12

1952, Apr. 27 Photo. Wmk. 283

996 SP121 60f magenta	35.00	30.00

Budapest Philatelic Exhibition. Counterfeits exist.

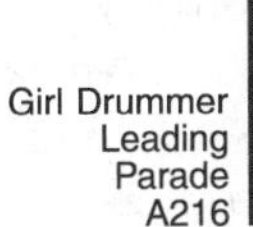

Girl Drummer Leading Parade A216

Designs: 60f, Workers and soldier. 1fo, Worker, flag-encircled globe and dove.

Perf. 12x12½

1952, May 1 Photo. Wmk. 106

997 A216 40f dk grn & dull red	.40	.25
998 A216 60f dk red brn & dull red	.40	.25
999 A216 1fo sepia & dull red	.70	.40
Nos. 997-999 (3)	1.50	.90

Issued to publicize Labor Day, May 1, 1952.

Runner — A217

Designs: 40f, Swimmer. 60f, Fencer. 1fo, Woman gymnast.

1952, May 26 ***Perf. 11***

1000 A217 30f dark red brown	.30	.20
1001 A217 40f deep green	.35	.20
1002 A217 60f deep lilac rose	.45	.25
1003 A217 1fo deep blue	.70	.50
Nos. 1000-1003,C107-C108 (6)	3.50	2.05

Issued to publicize Hungary's participation in the Olympic Games, Helsinki, 1952

Building Types of 1951

Buildings: 8f, School, Stalinvarost. 10f, Szekesfehervar Station. 12f, Building, Ujpest. 50f, Metal works, Inotai. 70f, Grain elevator, Hajdunanas. 80f, Tiszalok dam. 4fo, Miners' union headquarters. 5fo, Workers' apartments, Ujpest.

1952 Wmk. 106 ***Perf. 15***

1004	A202	8f green	.35	.20
1005	A200	10f purple	.40	.20
1006	A202	12f carmine	.35	.20
1007	A202	50f gray blue	.50	.20
1008	A202	70f yellow brn	.65	.20
1009	A200	80f maroon	1.00	.20
1010	A202	4fo olive grn	1.75	.20
1011	A202	5fo gray black	3.00	.20
		Nos. 1004-1011 (8)	8.00	1.60

The original size of Nos. 1004-1011 was 22x18mm. Starting in 1958, this was changed to 21x17mm. Values are the same.

Approaching Train — A218

Railroad Day: 1fo, Railroad Construction.

1952, Aug. 10 ***Perf. 12x12½***

1012 A218 60f red brown	.40	.20
1013 A218 1fo deep olive grn	.45	.35

Coal Excavator A219

Miners' Day: 1fo, Coal breaker.

1952, Sept. 7

1014 A219 60f brown	.60	.20
1015 A219 1fo dark green	.85	.25

Lajos Kossuth — A220

Janos Hunyadi — A221

Design: 60f, Kossuth statue.

1952, Sept. 19 ***Perf. 12½x12***

1016 A220 40f ol brn, *pink*	.40	.25
1017 A220 60f black brn, *bl*	.20	.20
1018 A220 1fo purple, *citron*	.40	.20
Nos. 1016-1018 (3)	1.00	.65

150th anniv. of the birth of Lajos Kossuth.

1952, Sept. 28 Engr. Unwmk.

Portraits: 30f, Gyorgy Dozsa. 40f, Miklos Zrinyi. 60f, Ilona Zriuyi. 1fo, Bottyan Vak. 1.50fo, Aurel Stromfeld.

1019	A221	20f purple	.20	.20
1020	A221	30f dark green	.20	.20
1021	A221	40f indigo	.20	.20
1022	A221	60f dk violet brn	.20	.20
1023	A221	1fo dk blue grn	.50	.35
1024	A221	1.50fo dark brown	1.25	.85
		Nos. 1019-1024 (6)	2.55	2.00

Army Day, Sept. 28, 1952.

Lenin and Conference at Smolny Palace A222

Designs: 60f, Stalin and Cavalry Attack. 1fo, Marx, Engels, Lenin and Stalin.

1952, Nov. 7 Wmk. 106

Portraits in Olive Gray

1025 A222 40f deep claret	.75	.40
1026 A222 60f gray	.50	.20
1027 A222 1fo rose red	1.00	.30
Nos. 1025-1027 (3)	2.25	.90

Russian Revolution, 35th anniversary.

Peasant Woman Holding Wheat — A223

Peace Meeting A224

Perf. 12½x12, 12x12½

1952, Nov. 22

1028 A223 60f brn red, *citron*	.50	.20
1029 A224 1fo brown, *blue*	.70	.40

Third Hungarian Peace Congress, 1952.

Subway Construction A225

Design: 1fo, Station and map.

1953, Jan. 19 Photo. ***Perf. 12x12½***

1030 A225 60f dk slate green	.55	.25
1031 A225 1fo brown red	.75	.45

Completion of the Budapest subway extension.

Tank and Flag — A226

Stalin — A227

60f, Map of Central Europe and Soldier.

1953, Feb. 18

1032 A226 40f dark car rose	.60	.25
1033 A226 60f chocolate	.60	.20

Battle of Stalingrad, 10th anniversary.

Perf. 12x11½

1953 Engr. Wmk. 106

1034	A227	60f pur blk	.40	.20

Souvenir Sheet

1035	A227	2fo purple black	13.50	11.00

Death of Joseph Stalin (1879-1953).
Issue dates: #1034, Mar. 27; #1035, Mar. 9.

Workers' Rest Home, Galyateto A228

Designs: 40f, Home at Mecsek. 50f, Parad Mineral Baths. 60f, Home at Kekes. 70f, Balatonfured Mineral Baths.

1953, Apr. Photo. *Perf. 12x12½*

1036	A228	30f fawn	.25	.20
1037	A228	40f deep blue	.25	.20
1038	A228	50f dk olive bis	.30	.20
1039	A228	60f dp yellow grn	.35	.20
1040	A228	70f scarlet	.75	.25
		Nos. 1036-1040,C121-C122 (7)	2.75	1.70

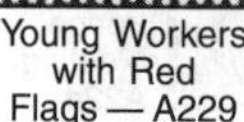

Young Workers with Red Flags — A229

Karl Marx — A230

1953, May 1 *Perf. 12½x12*

1041	A229	60f brn & red, *yel*	.35	.20

Issued to publicize Labor Day, May 1, 1953.

1953, May 1 Engr. *Perf. 11½x12*

1042	A230	1fo black, *pink*	.35	.20

70th anniv. of the death of Karl Marx. See No. 1898.

Insurgents in the Forest — A231

30f, Drummer & fighters. 40f, Battle scene. 60f, Cavalry attack. 1fo, Francis Rákóczy II.

1953, June 14 Photo. *Perf. 11*

1043	A231	20f dk ol grn & org red, *grnsh*	.40	.30
1044	A231	30f vio brn & red org	.60	.40
1045	A231	40f gray bl & red org, *pink*	.75	.40
1046	A231	60f dk ol brn & org, *yel*	1.00	.75
1047	A231	1fo dk red brn & org red, *yel*	1.25	1.00
		Nos. 1043-1047 (5)	4.00	2.85

250th anniv. of the insurrection of 1703.

Building Types of 1951

Buildings: 8f, Day Nursery, Ozd. 10f, Medical research institute, Szombathely. 12f, Apartments, Komlo. 20f, Department store, Ujpest. 30f, Brick factory, Maly. 40f, Metropolitan hospital. 50f, Sports building, Stalinvaros. 60f, Post office, Csepel. 70f, Blast furnace, Diosgyor. 1.20fo, Agricultural school, Ajkacsinger Valley. 1.70fo, Iron Works School, Csepel. 2fo, Optical works house of culture.

1953 Wmk. 106 *Perf. 15*

1048	A204	8f olive green	.30	.20
1049	A204	10f purple	.40	.20
1050	A205	12f rose carmine	.40	.20
1051	A204	20f dark green	.45	.20
1052	A204	30f orange	.45	.20
1053	A204	40f dark brown	.45	.20
1054	A205	50f blue violet	.70	.20
1055	A205	60f rose red	.70	.20
1056	A204	70f yellow brown	1.00	.20
1056A	A205	1.20fo red	1.50	.20
1056B	A204	1.70fo blue	1.40	.20
1056C	A204	2fo green	1.75	.20
		Nos. 1048-1056C (12)	9.50	2.40

The original size of Nos. 1048-1056C was 22x18mm. Starting in 1958, this was changed to 21x17mm. Values are the same.

Cycling — A232

1953, Aug. 20 *Perf. 11*

1057	A232	20f shown	.35	.25
1058	A232	30f Swimming	.20	.20
1059	A232	40f Calisthenics	.25	.20
1060	A232	50f Discus	.30	.20
1061	A232	60f Wrestling	.35	.20
		Nos. 1057-1061,C123-C127 (10)	6.25	3.75

Opening of the People's Stadium, Budapest.

Kazar Costume A233

Lenin — A234

Provincial Costumes: 30f, Ersekcsanad. 40f, Kalocsa. 60f, Sioagard. 1fo, Sarkoz. 1.70fo, Boldog. 2fo, Orhalom. 2.50fo, Hosszuheteny.

1953, Sept. 12 Engr. *Perf. 12*

1062	A233	20f blue green	.60	.30
1063	A233	30f chocolate	.60	.20
1064	A233	40f ultra	1.40	.30
1065	A233	60f red	1.40	.45
1066	A233	1fo grnsh blue	1.75	.85
1067	A233	1.70fo brt green	2.75	1.25
1068	A233	2fo carmine rose	4.00	2.00
1069	A233	2.50fo purple	8.00	4.25
		Nos. 1062-1069 (8)	20.50	9.60

See No. 1189.

1954, Jan. 21 Wmk. 106 *Perf. 12*

Designs: 60f, Lenin and Stalin at meeting. 1fo, Lenin, facing left.

1073	A234	40f dk blue grn	.55	.55
1074	A234	60f black brown	.70	.25
1075	A234	1fo dk car rose	1.00	.65
		Nos. 1073-1075 (3)	2.25	1.45

30th anniversary, death of Lenin.

Worker Reading A235

Revolutionary and Red Flag — A236

Design: 1fo, Soldier.

Perf. 12x12½, 12½x12

1954, Mar. 21 Photo.

1076	A235	40f gray blue & red	1.25	.65
1077	A236	60f brown & red	1.75	1.50
1078	A235	1fo gray & red	2.50	2.25
		Nos. 1076-1078 (3)	5.50	4.40

35th anniversary of the "First Hungarian Communist Republic."

Blood Test — A237

Maypole — A238

Designs: 40f, Mother receiving newborn baby. 60f, Medical examination of baby.

1954, Mar. 8 *Perf. 12*

1079	A237	30f brt blue	.20	.20
1080	A237	40f brown bister	.25	.20
1081	A237	60f purple	.35	.20
		Nos. 1079-1081,C146-C148 (6)	2.35	1.80

1954, May 1 *Perf. 12½x12*

Design: 60f, Flag bearer.

1082	A238	40f olive	.20	.20
1083	A238	60f orange red	.25	.20

Issued to publicize Labor Day, May 1, 1954.

Farm Woman with Fruit A239

1954, May 24 *Perf. 12*

1084	A239	60f red orange	.25	.20

3rd Congress of the Hungarian Workers Party, Budapest, May 24, 1954.

Natl. Museum, Budapest — A240

Peppers A241

Designs: 60f, Arms of People's Republic. 1fo, Dome of Parliament Building.

1954, Aug. 20 *Perf. 12½x12*

1085	A240	40f brt blue	.25	.20
1086	A240	60f redsh brown	.20	.20
1087	A240	1fo dark brown	.40	.25
		Nos. 1085-1087 (3)	.85	.65

People's Republic Constitution, 5th anniv.

1954, Sept. 11 Engr., Fruit Litho.

Fruit: 50f, Tomatoes. 60f, Grapes. 80f, Apricots. 1fo, Apples. 1.20fo, Plums. 1.50fo, Cherries. 2fo, Peaches.

Fruit in Natural Colors

1088	A241	40f gray blue	.30	.20
1089	A241	50f plum	.30	.20
1090	A241	60f gray blue	.30	.20
1091	A241	80f chocolate	.40	.20
1092	A241	1fo rose violet	.40	.25
1093	A241	1.20fo dull blue	.70	.35
1094	A241	1.50fo plum	1.00	.65
1095	A241	2fo gray blue	.90	.45
		Nos. 1088-1095 (8)	4.30	2.50

National agricultural fair.

Maurus Jokai — A242

1954, Oct. 17 Engr.

1096	A242	60f dk brown olive	.45	.25
1097	A242	1fo deep claret	.85	.70

50th anniv. of the death of Maurus Jokai, writer.

No. 1097 in violet blue is from the souvenir sheet, No. C157.

Janos Apacai Csere A243

1954, Dec. 5 Photo. *Perf. 12x12½*

Scientists: 10f, Csoma Sandor Korosi. 12f, Anyos Jedlik. 20f, Ignaz Semmelweis. 30f, Janos Irinyi. 40f, Frigyes Koranyi. 50f, Armin Vambery. 60f, Karoly Than. 1fo, Otto Herman. 1.70fo, Tivadar Puskas. 2fo, Endre Hogyes.

1098	A243	8f dk vio brn, *yel*	.20	.20
1099	A243	10f brn, car, *pink*	.20	.20
1100	A243	12f gray, *bl*	.20	.20
1101	A243	20f brn, *yel*	.20	.20
1102	A243	30f vio bl, *pink*	.20	.20
1103	A243	40f dk grn, *yel*	.20	.20
1104	A243	50f red brn, *pale grn*	.20	.20
1105	A243	60f blue, *pink*	.20	.20
1106	A243	1fo olive	.40	.20
1107	A243	1.70fo rose brn, *yel*	.60	.25
1108	A243	2fo blue green	.80	.40
		Nos. 1098-1108 (11)	3.40	2.45

Readers in Industrial Library — A244

Industry A245

1fo, Agriculture. 2fo, Liberation monument.

1955, Apr. 4 ***Perf. 12½x12, 12x12½***

1109 A244	40f dk car & ol brn	.20	.20
1110 A245	60f dk green & red	.20	.20
1111 A245	1fo choc & grn	.50	.20
1112 A244	2fo blue grn & brn	.85	.50
Nos. 1109-1112 (4)		1.75	1.10

10th anniversary of Hungary's liberation.

Date, Flags, Grain Elevator and Tractor A246

1955, May 1 ***Perf. 12x12½***

1113 A246 1fo rose carmine .45 .20

Labor Day, May 1, 1955.

Government Printing Plant — A247

1955, May 28 **Wmk. 106**

1114 A247 60f gray grn & hn brn .25 .20

Centenary of the establishment of the government printing plant.

Young Citizens and Hungarian Flag — A248

1955, June 15 ***Perf. 12***

1115 A248 1fo red brown .40 .20

Issued to publicize the second national congress of the Hungarian Youth Organization.

Truck Farmer A249

10f, Fisherman. 12f, Bricklayer. 20f, Radio assembler. 30f, Woman potter. 40f, Railwayman & train. 50f, Clerk & scales. 60f, Postman emptying mail box. 70f, Cattle & herdsman. 80f, Textile worker. 1fo, Riveter. 1.20fo, Carpenter. 1.40fo, Streetcar conductor. 1.70fo, Herdsman & pigs. 2fo, Welder. 2.60fo, Woman tractor driver. 3fo, Herdsman in national costume & horse. 4fo, Bus driver. 5fo, Lineman. 10fo, Coal miner.

1955 **Wmk. 106** ***Perf. 12x12½***

1116 A249	8f	chestnut	.20	.20
1117 A249	10f	Prus green	.20	.20
1118 A249	12f	red orange	.20	.20
1119 A249	20f	olive green	.20	.20
1120 A249	30f	dark red	.45	.20
1121 A249	40f	brown	.20	.20
1122 A249	50f	violet bl	.20	.20
1123 A249	60f	brown red	.35	.20
1124 A249	70f	olive	.35	.20
1125 A249	80f	purple	.45	.20
1126 A249	1fo	blue	.25	.20
1127 A249	1.20fo	olive bis	.25	.20
1128 A249	1.40fo	deep green	.45	.20
1129 A249	1.70fo	purple	.45	.20
1130 A249	2fo	rose brown	.45	.20
1131 A249	2.60fo	vermilion	.60	.20
1132 A249	3fo	green	1.00	.20
1133 A249	4fo	peacock blue	1.25	.20
1134 A249	5fo	orange brown	1.75	.25
1135 A249	10fo	violet	2.75	.55
Nos. 1116-1135 (20)			12.00	4.40

For surcharges see Nos. B211-B216.

Postrider Blowing Horn — A250

1955, June 25 ***Perf. 12½x12***

1136 A250 1fo rose violet .35 .20

Hungarian Postal Museum, 25th anniv.

Exists tete-beche. Value: 2½ times the value of a single.

Mihaly Csokonai Vitez A251

1fo, Mihaly Vorosmarty. 2fo, Attila József.

1955, July 28 ***Perf. 12***

1137 A251 60f olive black	.40	.30
1138 A251 1fo dark blue	.70	.25
1139 A251 2fo rose brown	.90	.65
Nos. 1137-1139 (3)	2.00	1.20

Issued to honor three Hungarian poets.

Bela Bartok — A252

1955, Oct. 9

1140 A252 60f light brown	1.00	.50
Nos. 1140,C168-C169 (3)	4.75	3.10

10th anniversary of the death of Bela Bartok, composer.

Diesel Train A253

Designs: 60f, Bus. 80f, Motorcycle. 1fo, Truck. 1.20fo, Steam locomotive. 1.50fo, Dump truck. 2fo, Freighter.

1955, Dec. 20 ***Perf. 14½***

1141 A253	40f	grn & vio brn	.20	.20
1142 A253	60f	dp grn & ol	.20	.20
1143 A253	80f	ol grn & brn	.25	.20
1144 A253	1fo	ocher & grn	.45	.30
1145 A253	1.20fo	salmon & blk	.65	.35
1146 A253	1.50fo	grnsh blk & red brn	.80	.50
1147 A253	2fo	aqua & brown	1.10	.75
Nos. 1141-1147 (7)			3.65	2.50

Puli (Sheepdog) — A254

Puli and Steer A255

Hungarian Pointer — A256

Hungarian Dogs: 60f, Pumi (sheepdog). 1fo, Retriever with fowl. 1.20fo, Kuvasz (sheepdog). 1.50fo, Komondor (sheepdog) and cottage. 2fo, Komondor (head).

Perf. 11x13 (A254), 12

1956, Mar. 17 **Engr. & Litho.**

1148 A254	40f	yel, blk & red	.20	.20
1149 A255	50f	blue, bis & blk	.20	.20
1150 A254	60f	yel grn, blk & red	.20	.20
1151 A256	80f	bluish grn, ocher & blk	.25	.20
1152 A256	1fo	turq, ocher & blk	.30	.20
1153 A254	1.20fo	salmon, blk & chnt	.50	.20
1154 A255	1.50fo	ultra, blk & buff	.90	.40
1155 A254	2fo	cerise, blk & chnt	1.25	.70
Nos. 1148-1155 (8)			3.80	2.30

Pioneer Emblem A257

Perf. 12x12½

1956, June 2 **Photo.** **Wmk. 106**

1156 A257 1fo red	.25	.20
1157 A257 1fo gray	.25	.20

Pioneer movement, 10th anniversary.

Janos Hunyadi Statue — A258

Miner — A259

1956, Aug. 12 ***Perf. 12***

1158 A258 1fo brown, *yelsh* .50 .35

500th anniv. of the defeat of the Turks at the battle of Pecs under Janos Hunyadi.

Printed in sheets of 50 with alternate vertical rows inverted and center row of perforation omitted, providing 25 tête bêche pairs, of which 5 are imperf. between.

1956, Sept. 2

1159 A259 1fo dark blue .30 .20

Issued in honor of Miners' Day 1956.

Kayak Racer A260

Sports: 30f, Horse jumping hurdle. 40f, Fencing. 60f, Women hurdlers. 1fo, Soccer. 1.50fo, Weight lifting. 2fo, Gymnastics. 3fo, Basketball.

1956, Sept. 25 **Wmk. 106** ***Perf. 11***

Figures in Brown Olive

1160 A260	20f	lt blue	.20	.20
1161 A260	30f	lt olive grn	.20	.20
1162 A260	40f	deep orange	.20	.20
1163 A260	60f	bluish grn	.20	.20
1164 A260	1fo	vermilion	.20	.20
1165 A260	1.50fo	blue violet	.25	.25
1166 A260	2fo	emerald	.30	.30
1167 A260	3fo	rose lilac	.45	.40
Nos. 1160-1167 (8)			2.00	1.95

16th Olympic Games at Melbourne, Nov. 22-Dec. 8, 1956.

Franz Liszt A261

Portrait: 1fo, Frederic Chopin facing left.

1956, Oct. 7 **Photo.** ***Perf. 12x12½***

1168 A261 1fo violet blue	.90	.90
1169 A261 1fo magenta	.90	.90
a. Pair, #1168-1169	2.25	1.90

29th Day of the Stamp. Sold only at the Philatelic Exhibition together with entrance ticket for 4fo.

Janos Arany — A262

1957, Sept. 15 **Wmk. 106** ***Perf. 12***

1170 A262 2fo bright blue .50 .20

75th anniv. of the death of Janos Arany, poet.

Arms of Hungary A263

1957, Oct. 1

1171 A263 60f brt red	.20	.20
1172 A263 1fo dp yellow grn	.30	.20

Trade Union Congress Emblem A264

1957, Oct. 4
1173 A264 1fo dk carmine .25 .20

4th Intl. Trade Union Cong., Leipzig, 10/4-15.

Dove and Colors of Communist Countries — A265

Design: 1fo, Lenin.

1957, Nov. 7 Litho. *Perf. 12*
1174 A265 60f gray, blk & multi .25 .20
1175 A265 1fo ol bis & indigo .25 .20

Russian Revolution, 40th anniversary.

Komarom Tumbler Pigeons A266

Pigeons: 40f, Two short-beaked Budapest pigeons. 60f, Giant domestic pigeon. 1fo, Three Szeged pigeons. 2fo, Two Hungarian fantails.

Perf. 12x12½
1957-58 Photo. Wmk. 106
1176 A266 30f yel grn, cl & ocher .25 .20
1177 A266 40f ocher & blk .25 .20
1178 A266 60f blue & gray .25 .20
1179 A266 1fo gray & red brn .25 .20
1180 A266 2fo brt pink & gray .60 .40
Nos. 1176-1180,C175 (6) 2.35 1.70

Intl. Pigeon Exhibition, Budapest, 12/14-16. Issued: 30f, 1/12/58; others, 12/14/57.

Television Station — A267

1958, Feb. 22 Engr. *Perf. 11*
1181 A267 2fo rose violet .80 .65
a. Perf. 12 2.00 2.00

Souvenir Sheet

1182 A267 2fo green 22.50 22.50

Issued to publicize the television industry. No. 1182 sold for 25fo.

Mother and Child A268

Designs: 30f, Old man feeding pigeons. 40f, School boys. 60f, "Working ants and fiddling grasshopper." 1fo, Honeycomb and bee. 2fo, Handing over money.

1958, Mar. 9 Photo. *Perf. 12*
1183 A268 20f yel grn & ol gray .20 .20
1184 A268 30f lt olive & mar .20 .20
1185 A268 40f yel bis & brn .20 .20
1186 A268 60f rose car & grnsh blk .30 .20
1187 A268 1fo ol gray & dk brn .55 .35
1188 A268 2fo org & ol gray 1.40 .50
Nos. 1183-1188 (6) 2.85 1.65

Issued to publicize the value of savings and insurance.

Kazar Costume Type of 1953
Souvenir Sheet

1958, Apr. 17 Engr. *Perf. 12*
1189 A233 10fo magenta 15.00 15.00

Issued for the Universal and International Exposition at Brussels.

Arms of Hungary A269

1958, May 23 Litho. Wmk. 106
Arms in Original Colors
1190 A269 60f lt red brn & red .20 .20
1191 A269 1fo gray grn & grn .20 .20
1192 A269 2fo gray & dk brn .45 .20
Nos. 1190-1192 (3) .85 .60

1st anniv. of the law amending the constitution.

Youth Holding Book — A270

1958, June 14 Photo. *Perf. 12½x12*
1193 A270 1fo brown carmine .45 .20

5th Hungarian Youth Festival at Keszthely. Printed with alternating label, inscribed: V. IFJUSAGI TALALKOZO KESZTHELY 1958.

Post Horn and Town Hall, Prague — A271

1958, June 30
1194 A271 60f green .20 .20
a. Pair, #1194, C184 .55 .40

Conference of Postal Ministers of Communist Countries at Prague, June 30-July 8.

Dolomite Flax — A272

Hungarian Thistles — A273

30f, Kitaibelia vitifolia. 60f, Crocuses. 1fo, Hellebore. 2fo, Lilies. 2.50fo, Pinks. 3fo, Dog roses.

Perf. 11x13, 12½x12 (A273)
1958, Aug. 12 Photo. Wmk. 106
1195 A272 20f red vio & yel 1.00 .20
1196 A272 30f blue, yel & grn .20 .20
1197 A273 40f brown & bis .25 .20
1198 A273 60f bl grn & pink .30 .20
1199 A273 1fo rose car & yel grn .55 .25
1200 A273 2fo grn & yel .95 .20
1201 A272 2.50fo vio bl & pink 1.10 .45
1202 A272 3fo green & pink 1.90 .70
a. Souv. sheet of 4, perf. 12 14.00 14.00
Nos. 1195-1202 (8) 6.25 2.40

No. 1202a and a similar imperf. sheet were issued for the International Philatelic Congress at Brussels, Sept. 15-17, 1958. They contain the triangular 20f, 30f, 2.50fo and 3fo stamps printed in different colors. Sheets measure 111x111mm. and are printed on unwatermarked, linen-finish paper. Background of stamps, marginal inscriptions and ornaments in green. No. 1202a also exists perf. 11; same value.

Paddle, Ball and Olive Branch A274

Designs: 30f, Table tennis player, vert. 40f, Wrestlers, vert. 60f, Wrestlers, horiz. 1fo, Water polo player, vert. 2.50fo, High dive, vert. 3fo, Swimmer.

1958, Aug. 30 Wmk. 106 *Perf. 12*
1203 A274 20f rose red, *pnksh* .20 .20
1204 A274 30f olive, *grnsh* .20 .20
1205 A274 40f mag, *yel* .25 .20
1206 A274 60f brown, *bluish* .30 .20
1207 A274 1fo ultra, *bluish* .35 .20
1208 A274 2.50fo dk red, *yel* .50 .30
1209 A274 3fo grnsh bl, *grnsh* .75 .50
Nos. 1203-1209 (7) 2.55 1.80

Intl. Wrestling and European Swimming and Table Tennis Championships, held at Budapest.

Red Flag — A275

Design: 2fo, Hand holding newspaper.

1958, Nov. 21 *Perf. 12½x12*
1210 A275 1fo brown & red .20 .20
1211 A275 2fo dk gray bl & red .30 .20

40th anniversary of the founding of the Hungarian Communist Party and newspaper.

Satellite, Sputnik and American Rocket A276

Designs: 10f, Eötvös Torsion Balance and Globe. 20f, Deep sea exploration. 30f, Icebergs, penguins and polar light. 40f, Soviet Antarctic camp and map of Pole. 60f, "Rocket" approaching moon. 1fo, Sun and observatory.

1959, Mar. 14 *Perf. 12x12½*
Size: 32x21mm
1212 A276 10f car rose & sepia .30 .20
1213 A276 20f brt blue & gray .25 .20
1214 A276 30f dk slate grn & bis .35 .20

Perf. 12
Size: 35x26mm
1215 A276 40f slate bl & lt bl .25 .20

Perf. 15
Size: 58x21mm
1216 A276 60f Prus bl & lemon .40 .20

Perf. 12
Size: 35x26mm
1217 A276 1fo scarlet & yel .65 .30
1218 A276 5fo brn & red brn 1.50 .80
Nos. 1212-1218 (7) 3.70 2.10

Intl. Geophysical Year. See No. 1262.

"Revolution" — A277

1959, Mar. 21 *Perf. 12½x12*
1219 A277 20f vio brn & red .20 .20
1220 A277 60f blue & red .20 .20
1221 A277 1fo brown & red .45 .20
Nos. 1219-1221 (3) .85 .60

40th anniv. of the proclamation of the Hungarian Soviet Republic.

Rose — A278

1959, May 1 Photo. *Perf. 11*
1222 A278 60f lilac, dp car & grn .30 .20
1223 A278 1fo lt brn, dl red & grn .45 .20

Issued for Labor Day, May 1, 1959.

Early Locomotive — A279

Designs: 30f, Diesel coach. 40f, Early semaphore, vert. 60f, Csonka automobile. 1fo, Icarus bus. 2fo, First Lake Balaton steamboat. 2.50fo, Stagecoach.

1959, May 26 Litho. *Perf. 14½x15*
1224 A279 20f multi .20 .20
1225 A279 30f multi .20 .20
1226 A279 40f multi .20 .20
1227 A279 60f multi .20 .20
1228 A279 1fo multi .35 .20
1229 A279 2fo multi .45 .20
1230 A279 2.50fo multi .65 .30
Nos. 1224-1230,C201 (8) 3.50 1.90

Transport Museum, Budapest.

Perf. 10½x11½
1959, May 29 Wmk. 106
1231 A279 2.50fo multi 2.00 2.00

Designer's name on No. 1231. Printed in sheets of four with four labels to commemorate the congress of the International Federation for Philately in Hamburg.

Post Horn and World Map — A280

1959, June 1 Photo. *Perf. 12*

1232 A280 1fo cerise .40 .30

Postal Ministers Conference, Berlin.
Printed in sheets of 25 stamps with 25 alternating gray labels showing East Berlin Opera House.

Great Cormorant A281

Warrior, 10th Century — A282

Birds: 20f, Little egret and nest. 30f, Purple heron and nest. 40f, Great egret. 60f, White spoonbill. 1fo, Gray heron. 2fo, Squacco heron and nest. 3fo, Glossy ibis.

1959, June 14

1233 A281 10f green & indigo .20 .20
1234 A281 20f gray bl & ol grn .20 .20
1235 A281 30f org, grnsh blk & vio .20 .20
1236 A281 40f dark grn & gray .20 .20
1237 A281 60f dp cl & pale rose .35 .20
1238 A281 1fo dp bl grn & blk .50 .20
1239 A281 2fo dp orange & gray .85 .30
1240 A281 3fo bister & brn lake 1.50 .70
Nos. 1233-1240 (8) 4.00 2.20

1959, July 11

Designs: 20f, Warrior, 15th century. 30f, Soldier, 18th century. 40f, Soldier, 19th century. 60f, Cavalry man, 19th century. 1fo, Fencer, assault. 1.40fo, Fencer on guard. 3fo, Swordsman saluting.

1241 A282 10f gray & blue .20 .20
1242 A282 20f gray & dull yel .20 .20
1243 A282 30f gray & gray vio .20 .20
1244 A282 40f gray & ver .20 .20
1245 A282 60f gray & rose lil .20 .20
1246 A282 1fo ind & lt bl grn .30 .20
1247 A282 1.40fo orange & blk .60 .25
1248 A282 3fo blk & ol grn .90 .70
Nos. 1241-1248 (8) 2.80 2.15

24th World Fencing Championships, Budapest.

Sailboat, Lake Balaton — A283

40f, Vintager & lake, horiz. 60f, Bathers. 1.20fo, Fishermen. 2fo, Summer guests & ship.

1959, July 11 Photo. Wmk. 106

1249 A283 30f blue, *yel* .20 .20
1250 A283 40f carmine rose .20 .20
1251 A283 60f dp red brown .20 .20
1252 A283 1.20fo violet .30 .20
1253 A283 2fo red org, *yel* .60 .35
Nos. 1249-1253,C202-C205 (9) 2.60 2.05

Issued to publicize Lake Balaton and the opening of the Summer University.

Haydn's Monogram A284

Esterhazy Palace A285

Haydn and Schiller Monograms — A286

Design: 1fo, Joseph Haydn and score.

1959, Sept. 20 Wmk. 106 *Perf. 12*

1254 A284 40f dp claret & yel .20 .20
1255 A285 60f Prus bl, gray & yel .75 .75
1256 A284 1fo dk vio, lt brn & org .65 .20

Designs: 40f, Schiller's monogram. 60f, Pegasus rearing from flames. 1fo, Friedrich von Schiller.

1257 A284 40f olive grn & org .20 .20
1258 A285 60f violet bl & lil .40 .20
1259 A284 1fo dp cl & org brn .80 .20
Nos. 1254-1259 (6) 3.00 1.75

Souvenir Sheet

Imperf

1260 A286 Sheet of 2 8.75 8.75
a. 3fo magenta 2.25 2.25
b. 3fo green 2.25 2.25

150th anniv. of the death of Joseph Haydn, Austrian composer, Nos. 1254-1256; 200th anniv. of the birth of Friedrich von Schiller, German poet and dramatist, Nos. 1257-1259; No. 1260 honors both Haydn and Schiller.

Shepherd — A287

1959, Sept. 25 Engr. *Perf. 12*

1261 A287 2fo deep claret 1.50 1.50
a. With ticket 1.75 1.75

Day of the Stamp and Natl. Stamp Exhib. Issued in sheets of 8 with alternating ticket. The 4fo sale price marked on the ticket was the admission fee to the Natl. Stamp Exhib.

Type of 1959 Overprinted in Red

1959, Sept. 24 Photo. *Perf. 15*

1262 A276 60f dull bl & lemon .40 .25
a. Overprint omitted 1,400.

Landing of Lunik 2 on moon, Sept. 14.

Handing over Letter A288

1959, Oct. 4 Litho. *Perf. 12*

1263 A288 60f multicolored .25 .20

Intl. Letter Writing Week, Oct. 4-10.

Szamuely and Lenin — A289

Designs: 40pf, Aleksander Pushkin. 60pf, Vladimir V. Mayakovsky. 1fo, Hands holding peace flag.

1959, Nov. 14 Photo. Wmk. 106

1264 A289 20f dk red & bister .20 .20
1265 A289 40f brn & rose lil, *bluish* .20 .20
1266 A289 60f dk blue & bis .20 .20
1267 A289 1fo bl, car, buff, red & grn .40 .30
Nos. 1264-1267 (4) 1.00 .90

Soviet Stamp Exhibition, Budapest.

European Swallowtail A290

Butterflies: 30f, Arctia hebe, horiz. 40f, Lysandra hylas, horiz. 60f, Apatura ilia.

Perf. 11½x12, 12x11½

1959, Nov. 20

Butterflies in Natural Colors

1268 A290 20f blk & yel grn .20 .20
1269 A290 30f lt blue & blk .25 .20
1270 A290 40f dk gray & org brn .25 .20
1271 A290 60f dk gray & dl yel .35 .20
Nos. 1268-1271,C206-C208 (7) 4.90 2.10

Worker with Banner — A291

Design: 1fo, Congress flag.

1959, Nov. 30 *Perf. 14½*

1272 A291 60f brown, grn & red .20 .20
1273 A291 1fo brn, red, red & grn .20 .20

Issued to commemorate the 7th Congress of the Hungarian Socialist Workers' Party.

Teacher Reading Fairy Tales — A292

Fairy Tales: 30f, Sleeping Beauty. 40f, Matt, the Goose Boy. 60f, The Cricket and the Ant. 1fo, Mashenka and the Three Bears. 2fo, Hansel and Gretel. 2.50fo, Pied Piper. 3fo, Little Red Riding Hood.

1959, Dec. 15 Litho. *Perf. 11½*

Designs in Black

1274 A292 20f gray & multi .20 .20
1275 A292 30f brt pink .20 .20
1276 A292 40f lt blue grn .20 .20
1277 A292 60f lt blue .20 .20
1278 A292 1fo yellow .25 .25
1279 A292 2fo brt yellow grn .40 .25
1280 A292 2.50fo orange .50 .40
1281 A292 3fo crimson .80 .60
Nos. 1274-1281 (8) 2.75 2.30

Sumeg Castle — A293

Castles: 20fr, Tata. 30f, Diosgyor. 60f, Saros-Patak. 70f, Nagyvazsony. 1.40fo, Siklos. 1.70fo, Somlo. 3fo, Csesznek, vert. 5fo, Koszeg, vert. 10fo, Sarvar, vert.

Wmk. 106

1960, Feb. 1 Photo. *Perf. 14½*

Size: 21x17½mm

1282 A293 8f purple .20 .20
1283 A293 20f dk yel grn .20 .20
1284 A293 30f orange brn .20 .20
1285 A293 60f rose red .20 .20
1286 A293 70f emerald .20 .20

Perf. 12x11½, 11½x12

Size: 28x21mm, 21x28mm

1287 A293 1.40fo ultra .20 .20
1288 A293 1.70fo dl vio, "Somlo" .25 .20
b. "Somlyo" .45 .20
1289 A293 3fo red brown .35 .20
a. Unwatermarked .70 .25
1290 A293 5fo yellow green .70 .20
a. Unwatermarked 1.50 .40
1291 A293 10fo carmine rose 1.50 .35
Nos. 1282-1291 (10) 4.00 2.15

Tinted Paper

Perf. 14½

Size: 21x17½mm

1282a A293 8f pur, *bluish* .20 .20
1283a A293 20f dk yel grn, *grnsh* .20 .20
1284a A293 30f org brn, *yel* .25 .20
1285a A293 60f rose red, *pnksh* .20 .20
1286a A293 70f emer, *bluish* .50 .20

Perf. 12x11½

Size: 28x21mm

1287a A293 1.40fo ultra, *bluish* .55 .25
1288a A293 1.70fo dull vio, *bluish* .70 .25
Nos. 1282a-1288a (7) 2.60 1.50

See Nos. 1356-1365, 1644-1646.

Halas Lace — A294

Cross-country Skier — A295

Designs: Various Halas lace patterns.

Wmk. 106

1960, Feb. 15 Litho. *Perf. 11½*

Sizes: 20f, 60f, 1fo, 3fo: 27x37mm
30f, 40f, 1.50fo, 2fo: 37½x43½mm

Inscriptions in Orange

1292	A294	20f	brown black	.20	.20
1293	A294	30f	violet	.20	.20
1294	A294	40f	Prus blue	.40	.20
1295	A294	60f	dark brown	.20	.20
1296	A294	1fo	dark green	.25	.20
1297	A294	1.50fo	green	.40	.20
1298	A294	2fo	dark blue	.85	.25
1299	A294	3fo	dk carmine	1.50	.40
			Nos. 1292-1299 (8)	4.00	1.85

See Nos. 1570-1577.

Souvenir Sheet

Design as on No. 1299.

1960, Sept. 3

Inscriptions in Orange

1300	Sheet of 4 + 4 labels	6.75	5.75
a.	3fo brown olive	1.25	1.25
b.	3fo bright violet	1.25	1.25
c.	3fo emerald	1.25	1.25
d.	3fo bright blue	1.25	1.25

Fédération Internationale de Philatélie Congress, Warsaw, Sept. 3-11. No. 1300 contains 4 stamps and 4 alternating labels, printed in colors of adjoining stamps.

1960, Feb. 29 Photo. *Perf. 11½x12*

Sports: 40f, Ice hockey player. 60f, Ski jumper. 80f, Woman speed skater. 1fo, Downhill skier. 1.20fo, Woman figure skater.

Inscriptions and Figures in Bister

1301	A295	30f	deep blue	.20	.20
1302	A295	40f	brt green	.20	.20
1303	A295	60f	scarlet	.20	.20
1304	A295	80f	purple	.20	.20
1305	A295	1fo	brt grnsh blue	.45	.20
1306	A295	1.20fo	brown red	.55	.45
			Nos. 1301-1306,B217 (7)	2.50	1.80

8th Olympic Winter Games, Squaw Valley, Calif., Feb. 18-29, 1960.

Clara Zetkin — A296

Portraits: No. 1308, Kato Haman. No. 1309, Lajos Tüköry. No. 1310, Giuseppe Garibaldi. No. 1311, István Türr. No. 1312, Ottó Herman. No. 1313, Ludwig van Beethoven. No. 1314, Ferenc Mora. No. 1315, Istvan Toth Bucsoki. No. 1316, Donat Banki. No. 1317, Abraham G. Pattantyus. No. 1318, Ignaz Semmelweis. No. 1319, Frédéric Joliot-Curie. No. 1320, Ferenc Erkel. No. 1321, Janos Bolyai. No. 1322, Lenin.

1960 Photo. *Perf. 10½*

1307	A296	60f	lt red brn	.20	.20

Engr.

1308	A296	60f	pale purple	.20	.20
1309	A296	60f	rose red	.20	.20
1310	A296	60f	violet	.20	.20
1311	A296	60f	blue green	.20	.20
1312	A296	60f	blue	.20	.20
1313	A296	60f	gray brown	.20	.20
1314	A296	60f	salmon pink	.20	.20
1315	A296	60f	gray	.20	.20
1316	A296	60f	rose lilac	.20	.20
1317	A296	60f	green	.20	.20
1318	A296	60f	violet blue	.20	.20
1319	A296	60f	brown	.20	.20
1320	A296	60f	rose brown	.20	.20
1321	A296	60f	grnsh blue	.20	.20
1322	A296	60f	dull red	.20	.20
			Nos. 1307-1322 (16)	3.20	3.20

Nos. 1307-1308 commemorate International Women's Day, Mar. 8.

Flower and Quill — A297

Wmk. 106

1960, Apr. 2 Photo. *Perf. 12*

1323	2fo brn, yel & grn	1.25	1.25
a.	A297 With ticket	1.50	1.50

Issued for the stamp show of the National Federation of Hungarian Philatelists. The olive green 4fo ticket pictures the Federation's headquarters and served as entrance ticket to the show. Printed in sheets of 35 stamps and 35 tickets.

Soviet Capt. Ostapenko Statue — A298

Perf. 12½x11½, 11½x12½

1960, Apr. 4

Designs: 60f, Youth holding flag, horiz.

1324	A298	40f	dp carmine & brn	.20	.20
1325	A298	60f	red brn, red & grn	.20	.20

Hungary's liberation from the Nazis, 15th anniv.

Boxers — A299

Sports: 10f, Rowers. 30f, Archer. 40f, Discus thrower. 50f, Girls playing ball. 60f, Javelin thrower. 1fo, Rider. 1.40fo, Wrestlers. 1.70fo, Swordsmen. 3fo, Hungarian Olympic emblem.

1960, Aug. 21 *Perf. 11½x12*

Designs in Ocher and Black

1326	A299	10f	blue	.20	.20
1327	A299	20f	salmon	.20	.20
1328	A299	30f	lt violet	.20	.20
1329	A299	40f	yellow	.20	.20
1330	A299	50f	deep pink	.20	.20
1331	A299	60f	gray	.20	.20
1332	A299	1fo	pale brn vio	.25	.20
1333	A299	1.40fo	lt violet bl	.25	.20
1334	A299	1.70fo	ocher	.45	.20
1335	A299	3fo	multi	1.00	.50
			Nos. 1326-1335,B218 (11)	3.90	2.60

17th Olympic Games, Rome, 8/25-9/11.

Souvenir Sheet

Romulus and Remus Statue and Olympic Flame — A300

1960, Aug. 21

1336	A300	10fo	multicolored	8.00	*9.00*

Winter and Summer Olympic Games, 1960.

Woman of Mezokovesd Writing Letter — A301

Perf. 11½x12

1960, Oct. 15 Photo. Wmk. 106

1337	A301 2fo multicolored	1.40	1.40
a.	With ticket	1.75	1.75

Day of the Stamp and Natl. Stamp Exhib. Issued in sheets of 8 with alternating ticket. The 4fo sale price marked on the ticket was the admission fee to the Natl. Stamp Exhib.

The Turnip, Russian Fairy Tale — A302

Brown Bear — A303

Fairy Tales: 30f, Snow White and the Seven Dwarfs. 40f, The Miller, His Son and the Donkey. 60f, Puss in Boots. 80f, The Fox and the Raven. 1fo, The Maple-Wood Pipe. 1.70fo, The Fox and the Stork. 2fo, Momotaro (Japanese).

1960, Dec. 1 *Perf. 11½x12*

1338	A302	20f	multi	.20	.20
1339	A302	30f	multi	.20	.20
1340	A302	40f	multi	.20	.20
1341	A302	60f	multi	.20	.20
1342	A302	80f	multi	.20	.20
1343	A302	1fo	multi	.35	.20
1344	A302	1.70fo	multi	.65	.35
1345	A302	2fo	multi	1.00	.50
			Nos. 1338-1345 (8)	3.00	2.05

1961, Feb. 24 *Perf. 11½x12*

Animals: 20f, Kangaroo. 30f, Bison. 60f, Elephants. 80fr, Tiger with cubs. 1fo, Ibex. 1.40fo, Polar bear. 2fo, Zebra and young. 2.60fo, Bison cow with calf. 3fo, Main entrance to Budapest Zoological Gardens. 30f, 60f, 80f, 1.40fo, 2fo, 2.60fo are horizontal.

1346	A303	20f	orange & blk	.20	.20
1347	A303	30f	yel grn & blk brn	.20	.20
1348	A303	40f	org brn & brn	.20	.20
1349	A303	60f	lil rose & gray	.20	.20
1350	A303	80f	gray & yel	.20	.20
1351	A303	1fo	blue grn & brn	.20	.20
1352	A303	1.40fo	grnsh bl, gray & blk	.30	.20
1353	A303	2fo	pink & black	.40	.25
1354	A303	2.60fo	brt vio & brn	.60	.40
1355	A303	3fo	multicolored	1.10	.75
			Nos. 1346-1355 (10)	3.60	2.80

Issued for the Budapest Zoo.

Castle Type of 1960

10f, Kisvárda. 12f, Szigliget. 40f, Simon Tornya. 50f, Füzér. 80f, Egervár. 1fo, Vitány. 1.20fo, Sirok. 2fo, Boldogkő. 2.60fo, Hollókő. 4fo, Eger.

1961, Mar. 3 Photo. *Perf. 14½*

Size: 21x17½mm

1356	A293	10f	orange brn	.20	.20
1357	A293	12f	violet blue	.20	.20
1358	A293	40f	brt green	.20	.20
1359	A293	50f	brown	.20	.20
1360	A293	80f	dull claret	.20	.20

Perf. 12x11½

Size: 28x21mm

1361	A293	1fo	brt blue	.20	.20
1362	A293	1.20fo	rose violet	.25	.20
1363	A293	2fo	olive bister	.40	.20
1364	A293	2.60fo	dull blue	.60	.20
1365	A293	4fo	brt violet	.75	.20
			Nos. 1356-1365 (10)	3.20	2.00

Child Chasing Butterfly A304

Ferenc Rozsa, Journalist A305

40f, Man on operating table. 60f, Ambulance & stretcher. 1fo, Traffic light & scooter. 1.70fo, Syringe. 4fo, Emblem of Health Information Service (torch & serpent).

1961, Mar. 17 Litho. *Perf. 10½*

Cross in Red

Size: 18x18mm

1366	A304	30f	org brn & blk	.20	.20
1367	A304	40f	bl grn, bl & sepia	.20	.20

Size: 25x30mm

1368	A304	60f	multi	.20	.20
1369	A304	1fo	multi	.20	.20
1370	A304	1.70fo	multi	.45	.20
1371	A304	4fo	gray & yel grn	1.25	.50
			Nos. 1366-1371 (6)	2.50	1.50

Health Information Service.

Wmk. 106, Unwmk.

1961 Photo. *Perf. 12*

Portraits: No. 1373, Gyorgy Kilian. No. 1374, Jozsef Rippl-Ronai. No. 1375, Sandor Latinka. No. 1376, Maté Zalka. No. 1377, Jozsef Katona.

1372	A305	1fo	red brown	.20	.20
1373	A305	1fo	greenish blue	.20	.20
1374	A305	1fo	rose brown	.20	.20
1375	A305	1fo	olive bister	.20	.20
1376	A305	1fo	olive green	.20	.20
1377	A305	1fo	maroon	.20	.20
			Nos. 1372-1377 (6)	1.20	1.20

Press Day (#1372); the inauguration of the Gyorgy Kilian Sports Movement (#1373); birth cent. of Jozsef Rippl-Ronai, painter (#1374); Sandor Latinka, revolutionary leader, 75th death anniv. (#1375); Mate Zalka, author and revolutionist (#1376); Jozsef Katona, dramatist (#1377).

Nos. 1374, 1375, 1377 are unwmkd. Others in this set have wmk. 106.

Yuri A. Gagarin and Vostok 1 A306

Roses — A307

Design: 1fo, Launching Vostok 1.

Perf. 11½x12

1961, Apr. 25 **Wmk. 106**

1381	A306	1fo dk bl & bis brn	.55	.25
1382	A306	2fo dp ultra & bis brn	2.50	2.00

1st man in space, Yuri A. Gagarin, 4/12/61.

1961, Apr. 29 *Perf. 12½x11½*

Design: 2fo, as 1fo, design reversed.

1383	A307	1fo grn & dp car	.20	.20
1384	A307	2fo grn & dp car	.30	.20
a.		Pair, #1383-1384	.50	.30

Issued for May Day, 1961.

"Venus" and Moon A308

Designs: Various Stages of Rocket.

1961, May 24 **Wmk. 106** *Perf. 14½*

1385	A308	40f grnsh bl, bis & blk	.35	.20
1386	A308	60f brt bl, bis & blk	.50	.20
1387	A308	80f ultra & blk	.75	.60
1388	A308	2fo violet & yel	2.40	1.50
		Nos. 1385-1388 (4)	4.00	2.50

Soviet launching of the Venus space probe, Feb. 12, 1961. No. 1388 was also printed in sheets of four, perf. and imperf. Size: 130x76mm.

Warsaw Mermaid, Letter and Sea, Air and Land Transport — A309

Mermaid and: 60f, Television screen and antenna. 1fo, Radio.

1961, June 19 **Photo.** *Perf. 13½*

1389	A309	40f red org & blk	.20	.20
1390	A309	60f lilac & blk	.25	.20
1391	A309	1fo brt blue & blk	.40	.20
		Nos. 1389-1391 (3)	.85	.60

Conference of Postal Ministers of Communist Countries held at Warsaw.

Flag and Parliament — A310

Designs: 1.70fo, Orchid. 2.60fo, Small tortoise-shell butterfly. 3fo, Goldfinch.

1961, June 23 *Perf. 11*

Background in Silver

1392	A310	1fo green, red & blk	.40	.35
1393	A310	1.70fo red & multi	.50	.45
1394	A310	2.60fo purple & multi	.75	.75
1395	A310	3fo blue & multi	1.00	1.00

1961, Aug. 19

Background in Gold

1396	A310	1fo green & blk	.35	.30
1397	A310	1.70fo red & multi	.50	.40
1398	A310	2.60fo purple & multi	.75	.75
1399	A310	3fo blue & multi	1.00	1.00
		Nos. 1392-1399 (8)	5.25	5.00

Issued to publicize the International Stamp Exhibition, Budapest, Sept. 23-Oct. 3, 1961.

#1392-1399 eachprinted in sheets of 4.

In gold background issue the top left inscription is changed on 1fo and 3fo.

George Stephenson A311

Winged Wheel, Steering Wheel and Road A312

Design: 2fo, Jenö Landler.

Perf. 12½x11½

1961, July 4 **Photo.** **Wmk. 106**

1400	A311	60f yellow olive	.20	.20
1401	A312	1fo blue & bister	.25	.20
1402	A311	2fo yellow brown	.40	.25
		Nos. 1400-1402 (3)	.85	.65

Conference of Transport Ministers of Communist Countries held at Budapest.

Soccer A313

1961, July 8 **Unwmk.** *Perf. 14½*

1403	A313	40f shown	.20	.20
1404	A313	60f Wrestlers	.20	.20
1405	A313	1fo Gymnast	.30	.20
		Nos. 1403-1405 (3)	.70	.60

50th anniv. of the Steel Workers Sport Club (VASAS). See No. B219.

Galloping Horses — A314

40f, Hurdle Jump. 60f, Two trotters. 1fo, Three trotters. 1.70fo, Mares & foals. 2fo, Race horse "Baka." 3fo, Race horse "Kincsem."

1961, July 22

1406	A314	30f multi	.20	.20
1407	A314	40f multi	.20	.20
1408	A314	60f multi	.20	.20
1409	A314	1fo multi	.35	.20
1410	A314	1.70fo multi	.50	.20
1411	A314	2fo multi	.80	.30
1412	A314	3fo multi	1.25	.50
		Nos. 1406-1412 (7)	3.50	1.80

Keyboard, Music and Liszt Silhouette A315

Liszt Monument, Budapest A316

Designs: 2fo, Academy of Music, Budapest, and bar of music. 10fo, Franz Liszt.

1961, Oct. 2 **Unwmk.** *Perf. 12*

1413	A315	60f gold & blk	.20	.20
1414	A316	1fo dark gray	.35	.20
1415	A315	2fo dk bl & gray grn	.50	.40
		Nos. 1413-1415 (3)	1.05	.80

Souvenir Sheet

1416	A316	10fo multi	6.00	6.00

150th anniv. of the birth, and the 75th anniv. of the death of Franz Liszt, composer.

Lenin — A317

Monk's Hood — A318

1961, Oct. 22 *Perf. 11½*

1417	A317	1fo deep brown	.25	.20

22nd Congress of the Communist Party of the USSR, Oct. 17-31.

Wmk. 106

1961, Nov. 4 **Photo.** *Perf. 12*

1418	A318	20f shown	.20	.20
1419	A318	30f Centaury	.20	.20
1420	A318	40f Blue iris	.20	.20
1421	A318	60f Thorn apple	.20	.20
1422	A318	1fo Purple holly-hock	.25	.20
1423	A318	1.70fo Hop	.35	.20
1424	A318	2fo Poppy	.70	.30
1425	A318	3fo Mullein	1.10	.50
		Nos. 1418-1425 (8)	3.20	2.00

Nightingale A319

Mihaly Karolyi A320

Birds: 40f, Great titmouse. 60f, Chaffinch, horiz. 1fo, Eurasian jay. 1.20fo, Golden oriole, horiz. 1.50fo, European blackbird, horiz. 2fo, Yellowhammer, 3fo, Lapwing, horiz.

1961, Dec. 18 **Unwmk.** *Perf. 12*

1426	A319	30f multi	.20	.20
1427	A319	40f multi	.20	.20
1428	A319	60f multi	.20	.20
1429	A319	1fo multi	.20	.20
1430	A319	1.20fo multi	.20	.20
1431	A319	1.50fo multi	.45	.20
1432	A319	2fo multi	.55	.25
1433	A319	3fo multi	.75	.35
		Nos. 1426-1433 (8)	2.75	1.80

1962, Mar. 18

1434	A320	1fo black	.20	.20

Mihaly Karolyi, (1875-1955), Prime Minister of Hungarian Republic (1918-19).

1962, Mar. 29

Portrait: No. 1435, Ferenc Berkes.

1435	A320	1fo red brown	.20	.20

Fifth Congress of the Hungarian Cooperative Movement, and to honor Ferenc Berkes, revolutionary. See Nos. 1457, 1459.

Map of Europe, Train Signals and Emblem — A321

1962, May 2 **Photo.**

1436	A321	1fo blue green	.20	.20

14th Intl. Esperanto Cong. of Railway Men.

Xiphophorus Helleri A322

Tropical Fish: 30f, Macropodus opercularis. 40f, Lebistes reticulatus. 60f, Betta splendens. 80c, Puntius tetrazona. 1fo, Pterophyllum scalare. 1.20fo, Mesogonistius chaetodon. 1.50fo, Aphyosemion australe. 2fo, Hyphessobrycon innesi. 3fo, Symphysodon aequifasciata haraldi.

1962, May 5 *Perf. 11½x12*

Fish in Natural Colors, Black Inscriptions

1437	A322	20f blue	.20	.20
1438	A322	30f citron	.20	.20
1439	A322	40f lt blue	.20	.20
1440	A322	60f lt yellow grn	.20	.20
1441	A322	80f blue green	.30	.20
1442	A322	1fo brt bl grn	.20	.20
1443	A322	1.20fo blue green	.20	.20
1444	A322	1.50fo grnsh blue	.25	.20
1445	A322	2fo green	.50	.25
1446	A322	3fo gray grn & yel	.75	.50
		Nos. 1437-1446 (10)	3.00	2.35

Globe, Soccer Ball and Flags of Colombia and Uruguay — A323

Goalkeeper — A324

Flags of: 40f, USSR and Yugoslavia. 60f, Switzerland and Chile. 1fo, Germany and Italy. 1.70fo, Argentina and Bulgaria. 3fo, Brazil and Mexico.

Unwmk.

1962, May 21 Photo. *Perf. 11*

Flags in National Colors

1447	A323	30f	rose & bis	.20	.20
1448	A323	40f	pale grn & bis	.20	.20
1449	A323	60f	pale lil & bis	.20	.20
1450	A323	1fo	blue & bis	.35	.20
1451	A323	1.70fo	ocher & bis	.25	.25
1452	A323	3fo	pink & blue bis	.70	.40
			Nos. 1447-1452,B224,C209A (8)	3.50	2.05

Souvenir Sheet

Perf. 12

1453	A324	10fo	multicolored	6.50	6.50

World Cup Soccer Championship, Chile, May 30-June 17.

Type of 1961 and

Johann Gutenberg A325

#1456, Miklós Misztófalusi Kis, Hungarian printer (1650-1702). #1457, Jozsef Pach. #1458, András Cházár. #1459, Dr. Ferenc Hutyra. #1460, Gábor Egressy & National Theater.

1962 Unwmk. Photo. *Perf. 12*

1455	A325	1fo	blue black	.20	.20
1456	A325	1fo	red brown	.20	.20
1457	A320	1fo	blue	.20	.20
1458	A325	1fo	violet	.20	.20
1459	A320	1fo	deep blue	.30	.20
1460	A325	1fo	rose red	.40	.20
			Nos. 1455-1460 (6)	1.50	1.20

Cent. of Printers' and Papermakers' Union (Nos. 1455-1456). 75th anniv. of founding, by Joszef Pech, of Hungarian Hydroelectric Service (No. 1457). András Cházár, founder of Hungarian deaf-mute education (No. 1458). Dr. Ferenc Hutyra, founder of Hungarian veterinary medicine (No. 1459). 125th anniv. of National Theater (No. 1460).

Malaria Eradication Emblem — A327

1962, June 25 *Perf. 15*

1461	A327	2.50fo	lemon & blk	.50	.40
a.			2.50fo grn & blk, sheet of 4, perf. 11	4.00	3.75

WHO drive to eradicate malaria. Imperf. sheets with control numbers exist.

Sword-into-Plowshare Statue, United Nations, NY — A328

1962, July 7 *Perf. 12*

1462	A328	1fo	brown	.20	.20

World Congress for Peace and Disarmament, Moscow, July 9-14.

Floribunda Rose — A329

Festival Emblem — A330

1962 *Perf. 12½x11½*

Various Roses in Natural Colors

1465	A329	20f	orange brn	.20	.20
1466	A329	40f	slate grn	.20	.20
1467	A329	60f	violet	.20	.20
1468	A329	80f	rose red	.20	.20
1469	A329	1fo	dark green	.25	.20
1470	A329	1.20fo	orange	.30	.20
1471	A329	2fo	dk blue grn	.50	.45
1472	A330	3fo	multi	.75	.35
			Nos. 1465-1472 (8)	2.60	2.00

No. 1472 was issued for the 8th World Youth Festival, Helsinki, July 28-Aug. 6.

Weight Lifter — A331

Oil Derrick and Primitive Oil Well — A332

1962, Sept. 16 *Perf. 12*

1473	A331	1fo	copper red	.30	.20

European Weight Lifting Championships.

Perf. 12x11½

1962, Oct. 8 Photo. Unwmk.

1474	A332	1fo	green	.20	.20

25th anniv. of the Hungarian oil industry.

Racing Motorcyclist — A333

Designs: 30f, Stunt racing. 40f, Uphill race. 60f, Cyclist in curve. 1fo, Start. 1.20fo, Speed racing. 1.70fo, Motorcyclist with sidecar. 2fo, Motor scooter. 3fo, Racing car.

1962, Dec. 28 *Perf. 11*

1475	A333	20f	multi	.20	.20
1476	A333	30f	multi	.20	.20
1477	A333	40f	multi	.20	.20
1478	A333	60f	multi	.20	.20
1479	A333	1fo	multi	.20	.20
1480	A333	1.20fo	multi	.20	.20
1481	A333	1.70fo	multi	.35	.20
1482	A333	2fo	multi	.50	.25
1483	A333	3fo	multi	.75	.40
			Nos. 1475-1483 (9)	2.80	2.05

Ice Skater — A334

Designs: 20f-3fo, Various figure skating and ice dancing positions. 20f, 3fo horiz. 10fo, Figure skater and flags of participating nations.

Perf. 12x11½, 11½x12

1963, Feb. 5 Photo. Unwmk.

1484	A334	20f	multi	.20	.20
1485	A334	40f	multi	.20	.20
1486	A334	60f	multi	.20	.20
1487	A334	1fo	multi	.30	.20
1488	A334	1.40fo	multi	.30	.20
1489	A334	2fo	multi	.35	.25
1490	A334	3fo	multi	.75	.50
			Nos. 1484-1490 (7)	2.30	1.75

Souvenir Sheet

Perf. 11½x12

1491	A334	10fo	multi	4.75	4.25

European Figure Skating and Ice Dancing Championships, Budapest, Feb. 5-10.

János Batsányi (1763-1845) — A335

#1493, Helicon Monument. #1494, Actors before Szeged Cathedral. #1495, Leo Weiner, composer. #1496, Ferenc Entz,horticulturist. #1497, Ivan Markovits, inventor of Hungarian shorthand,1863. #1498, Dr. Frigyes Koranyi. #1499, Ferenc Erkel (1810-93), composer. #1500, Geza Gardonyi (1863-1922), writer of Hungarian historical novels for youth. #1501, Pierre de Coubertin, Frenchman, reviver of Olympic Games. #1502, Jozsef Eötvös, author, philosopher, educator. #1503, Budapest Industrial Fair emblem. #1504, Stagecoach and Arc de Triomphe, Paris. #1505, Hungary map and power lines. #1506, Roses.

1963 Unwmk. *Perf. 11*

1492	A335	40f	dk car rose	.20	.20
1493	A335	40f	blue	.20	.20
1494	A335	40f	violet blue	.20	.20
1495	A335	40f	olive	.20	.20
1496	A335	40f	emerald	.20	.20
1497	A335	40f	dark blue	.20	.20
1498	A335	60f	dull violet	.20	.20
1499	A335	60f	bister brn	.20	.20
1500	A335	60f	gray green	.20	.20
1501	A335	60f	red brown	.40	.20
1502	A335	60f	lilac	.20	.20
1503	A335	1fo	purple	.20	.20
1504	A335	1fo	rose red	.25	.20
1505	A335	1fo	gray	.25	.20
1506	A335	2fo	multi	.50	.20
			Nos. 1492-1506 (15)	3.60	3.00

#1493, 10th Youth Festival, Keszthely. #1494, Outdoor plays, Szeged. #1495, Budapest Music Competition. #1496, Cent. of professional horticultural training. #1498, 50th anniv. of the death of Prof. Koranyi, pioneer in fight against tuberculosis. #1499, Erkel Memorial Festival, Gyula. #1501, 10th anniv. of the People's Stadium, Budapest. #1502, 150th anniv. of birth of Jozsef Eötvös, organizer of modern public education in Hungary. #1504, Paris Postal Conf., 1863. #1505, Rural electrification. #1506, 5th Natl. Rose Show.

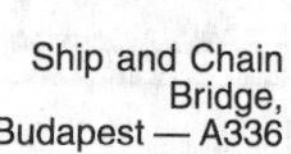

Ship and Chain Bridge, Budapest — A336

Bus and Parliament A337

20f, Trolley. 30f, Sightseeing bus & Natl. Museum. 40f, Bus & trailer. 50f, Railroad tank car. 60f, Trolley bus. 70f, Railroad mail car. 80f, Motorcycle messenger. #1516, Mail plane, vert. #1517, Television transmitter, Miskolc, vert. 1.40fo, Mobile post office. 1.70fo, Diesel locomotive. 2fo, Mobile radio transmitter & stadium. 2.50fo, Tourist bus. 2.60fo, Passenger train. 3fo, P.O. parcel conveyor. 4fo, Television transmitters, Pecs, vert. 5fo, Hydraulic lift truck & mail car. 6fo, Woman teletypist. 8fo, Map of Budapest & automatic dial phone. 10fo, Girl pioneer &woman letter carrier.

1963-64 Photo. *Perf. 11*

1507	A336	10f	brt blue	.20	.20
1508	A336	20f	dp yellow grn	.20	.20
1509	A336	30f	violet	.20	.20
1510	A336	40f	orange	.20	.20
1511	A336	50f	brown	.20	.20
1512	A336	60f	crimson	.20	.20
1513	A336	70f	olive gray	.20	.20
1514	A336	80f	red brn ('64)	.25	.20

Perf. 12x11½, 11½x12

1515	A337	1fo	rose claret	.20	.20
1516	A337	1.20fo	orange brn	.80	.60
1517	A337	1.20fo	dp vio ('64)	.20	.20
1518	A337	1.40fo	dp yel grn	.20	.20
1519	A337	1.70fo	maroon	.25	.20
1520	A337	2fo	grnsh blue	.30	.20
1521	A337	2.50fo	lilac	.35	.20
1522	A337	2.60fo	olive	.35	.20
1523	A337	3fo	dk blue ('64)	.25	.20
1524	A337	4fo	blue ('64)	.35	.20
1525	A337	5fo	ol brn ('64)	.45	.20
1526	A337	6fo	dk ol bis ('64)	.55	.20
1527	A337	8fo	red lilac ('64)	.80	.20
1528	A337	10fo	emerald ('64)	.80	.40
			Nos. 1507-1528 (22)	7.50	5.00

Size of 20f, 60f: 20½-21x16¾-17mm.

Minute inscription in lower margin includes year date, number of stamp in set and designer's name (Bokros F. or Legrady S.).

See Nos. 1983-1983B, 2196-2204.

Coil Stamps

1965-67 *Perf. 14*

Size: 21½x16½mm

1508a	A336	20f	deep yellow green	.30	.20
1512a	A336	60f	crimson ('67)	.50	.20

Black control number on back of every 3rd stamp.

Motorboat — A338

Girl, Steamer and Castle — A339

Design: 60f, Sailboat.

1963, July 13 *Perf. 11*

1529	A338	20f	sl grn, red & blk	.20	.20
1530	A339	40f	multicolored	.20	.20
1531	A338	60f	bl, blk, brn & org	.40	.25
			Nos. 1529-1531 (3)	.80	.65

Centenary of the summer resort Siofok.

Child with Towel and Toothbrush A340

Karancsság Woman A341

Designs: 40f, Child with medicines. 60f, Girls of 3 races. 1fo, Girl and heart. 1.40fo, Boys of 3 races. 2fo, Medical examination of child. 3fo, Hands shielding plants.

1963, July 27 ***Perf. 12x11½***

1532 A340 30f multi .20 .20
1533 A340 40f multi .20 .20
1534 A340 60f multi .20 .20
1535 A340 1fo multi .20 .20
1536 A340 1.40fo multi .20 .20
1537 A340 2fo multi .25 .25
1538 A340 3fo multi .50 .40
Nos. 1532-1538 (7) 1.75 1.65

Centenary of the International Red Cross.

1963, Aug. 18 Engr. ***Perf. 11½***

Provincial Costumes: 30f, Kapuvár man. 40f, Debrecen woman. 60f, Hortobágy man. 1fo, Csököly woman. 1.70fo, Dunántul man. 2fo, Buják woman. 2.50fo, Alföld man. 3fo, Mezökövesd bride.

1539 A341 20f claret .20 .20
1540 A341 30f green .20 .20
1541 A341 40f brown .25 .20
1542 A341 60f brt blue .25 .20
1543 A341 1fo brown red .30 .20
1544 A341 1.70fo purple .40 .20
1545 A341 2fo dk blue grn .25 .20
1546 A341 2.50fo dk carmine .55 .25
1547 A341 3fo violet blue .85 .45
Nos. 1539-1547 (9) 3.25 2.10

Popular Art Exhibition in Budapest.

Slalom and 1964 Olympic Emblem — A342

Sports: 60f, Downhill skiing. 70f, Ski jump. 80f, Rifle shooting on skis. 1fo, Figure skating pair. 2fo, Ice hockey. 2.60fo, Speed ice skating. 10fo, Skier and mountains, vert.

1963-64 Photo. ***Perf. 12***

1964 Olympic Emblem in Black and Red

1548 A342 40f yel grn & bis .20 .20
1549 A342 60f violet & bis .20 .20
1550 A342 70f ultra & bis .20 .20
1551 A342 80f emerald & bis .20 .20
1552 A342 1fo brn org & bis .20 .20
1553 A342 2fo brt blue & bis .40 .20
1554 A342 2.60fo rose lake & bis .60 .40
Nos. 1548-1554,B234 (8) 2.70 1.90

Souvenir Sheet

Perf. 11½x12

1555 A342 10fo grnsh bl, red & brn ('64) 4.25 4.00

9th Winter Olympic Games, Innsbruck, Austria, Jan. 29-Feb. 9, 1964.

Four-Leaf Clover — A343

Good Luck Symbols: 20f, Calendar and mistletoe, horiz. 30f, Chimneysweep and clover. 60f, Top hat, pig and clover. 1fo, Clown with balloon and clover, horiz. 2fo, Lanterns, mask and clover.

Perf. 12x11½, 11½x12

1963, Dec. 12 Photo. Unwmk.

Sizes: 28x22mm (20f, 1fo); 22x28mm (40f); 28x39mm (30f, 60f, 2fo)

1556 A343 20f multi .20 .20
1557 A343 30f multi .20 .20
1558 A343 40f multi .20 .20
1559 A343 60f multi .20 .20
1560 A343 1fo multi .20 .20
1561 A343 2fo multi .45 .20
Nos. 1556-1561,B235-B236 (8) 2.65 1.80

New Year 1964. The 20f and 40f issued in booklet panes of 10, perf. and imperf.; sold for 2 times and 1½ times face respectively.

Moon Rocket — A344

U.S. & USSR Spacecraft: 40f, Venus space probe. 60f, Vostok I, horiz. 1fo, Friendship 7. 1.70fo, Vostok III & IV. 2fo, Telstar 1 & 2, horiz. 2.60fo, Mars I. 3fo, Radar, rockets and satellites, horiz.

1964, Jan. 8 ***Perf. 11½x12, 12x11½***

1562 A344 30f grn, yel & brnz .20 .20
1563 A344 40f pur, bl & sil .20 .20
1564 A344 60f bl, blk, yel, sil & red .20 .20
1565 A344 1fo dk brn, red & sil .20 .20
1566 A344 1.70fo vio bl, blk, tan & red .30 .20
1567 A344 2fo sl grn, yel & sil .40 .20
1568 A344 2.60fo dp bl, yel & brnz .60 .30
1569 A344 3fo dp vio, lt bl & sil .75 .50
Nos. 1562-1569 (8) 2.85 2.00

Achievements in space research.

Lace Type of 1960

Various Halas Lace Designs.
Sizes: 20f, 2.60fo: 38x28mm. 30f, 40f, 60f, 1fo, 1.40fo, 2fo: 38x45mm.

Engr. & Litho.

1964, Feb. 28 ***Perf. 11½***

1570 A294 20f emerald & blk .20 .20
1571 A294 30f dull yel & blk .20 .20
1572 A294 40f deep rose & blk .20 .20
1573 A294 60f olive & blk .20 .20
1574 A294 1fo red org & blk .30 .20
1575 A294 1.40fo blue & blk .40 .20
1576 A294 2fo bluish grn & blk .50 .25
1577 A294 2.60fo lt vio & blk .75 .45
Nos. 1570-1577 (8) 2.75 1.90

Special Anniversaries-Events Issue

Imre Madach (1823-64) — A345

Shakespeare A346

Karl Marx and Membership Card of International Working Men's Association — A347

Michelangelo — A348

Lajos Kossuth and György Dózsa — A349

Budapest Fair Buildings — A350

#1579, Ervin Szabo. #1580, Writer Andras Fay (1786-1864). #1581, Aggtelek Cave scene. #1582, Excavating bauxite. #1584, Equestrian statue, Szekesfehervar. #1585, Bowler. #1586, Waterfall and forest. #1587, Architect Miklos Ybl (1814-91) and Budapest Opera. #1590, Armor, saber, sword & foil. #1592, Galileo Galilei. #1593, Women basketball players. #1595, Two runners breaking tape.

Perf. 11½x12, 12x11½, 11

1964 Photo. Unwmk.

Inscribed: "ÉVFORDULÓK-ESEMÉNYEK"

1578 A345 60f brt purple .20 .20
1579 A345 60f olive .20 .20
1580 A345 60f olive grn .20 .20
1581 A346 60f bluish grn .20 .20
1582 A346 60f Prus blue .20 .20
1583 A347 60f rose red .20 .20
1584 A348 60f slate blue .20 .20
1585 A345 1fo car rose .20 .20
1586 A346 1fo dull blue grn .20 .20
1587 A348 1fo orange brn .20 .20
1588 A349 1fo ultra .20 .20
1589 A350 1fo brt green .20 .20
1590 A345 2fo yellow brn .20 .20
1591 A346 2fo magenta .35 .20
1592 A346 2fo red brown .25 .20
1593 A346 2fo brt blue .25 .20
1594 A348 2fo gray brown .30 .20
1595 A348 2fo brown red .25 .20
Nos. 1578-1595 (18) 4.00 3.60

No. 1579, Municipal libraries, 60th anniv., and librarian Szabo (1877-1918). No. 1582, Bauxite mining in Hungary, 30th year. No. 1583, Cent. of 1st Socialist Intl. No. 1584, King Alba Day in Székesfehérvár. No. 1585, 1st European Bowling Championship, Budapest.

No. 1586, Cong. of Natl. Forestry Federation. No. 1588, City of Cegléd, 600th anniv. No. 1589, Opening of 1964 Budapest Intl. Fair. No. 1590, Hungarian Youth Fencing Association, 50th anniv. Nos. 1591-1592, Shakespeare and Galileo, 400th birth anniversaries. No. 1593, 9th European Women's Basketball Championship. No. 1594, Michelangelo's 400th death anniv. No. 1595, 50th anniv. of 1st Hungarian-Swedish athletic meet.

Eleanor Roosevelt — A351

Design, horiz.: a, d, Portrait at right. b, c, Portrait at left.

1964, Apr. 27 ***Perf. 12½***

1596 A351 2fo gray, black & buff .30 .20

Miniature Sheet

Perf. 11

1597 Sheet of 4 3.00 2.75
a. A351 2fo dp claret, brn & blk .65 .65
b. A351 2fo dk bl, brn & blk .65 .65
c. A351 2fo grn, brn & blk .65 .65
d. A351 2fo olive, brn & blk .65 .65

Fencing — A352

Sport: 40f, Women's gymnastics. 60f, Soccer. 80f, Equestrian. 1fo, Running. 1.40fo, Weight lifting. 1.70fo, Gymnast on rings. 2fo, Hammer throw and javelin. 2.50fo, Boxing.

1964, June 12 Photo. ***Perf. 11***

Multicolored Design and Inscription

1598 A352 30f lt ver .20 .20
1599 A352 40f blue .20 .20
1600 A352 60f emerald .20 .20
1601 A352 80f tan .20 .20
1602 A352 1fo yellow .20 .20
1603 A352 1.40fo bis brn .20 .20
1604 A352 1.70fo bluish gray .30 .20
1605 A352 2fo gray grn .35 .20
1606 A352 2.50fo vio gray .55 .40
Nos. 1598-1606,B237 (10) 3.00 2.75

18th Olympic Games, Tokyo, Oct. 10-25.

Elberta Peaches A353

Peaches: 40h, Blossoms (J. H. Hale). 60h, Magyar Kajszi. 1fo, Mandula Kajszi. 1.50fo, Borsi Rozsa. 1.70fo, Blossoms (Alexander). 2fo, Champion. 3fo, Mayflower.

1964, July 24 ***Perf. 11½***

1607 A353 40f multi .20 .20
1608 A353 60f multi .20 .20
1609 A353 1fo multi .20 .20
1610 A353 1.50fo multi .20 .20
1611 A353 1.70fo multi .25 .20
1612 A353 2fo multi .35 .20
1613 A353 2.60fo multi .45 .30
1614 A353 3fo multi .65 .50
Nos. 1607-1614 (8) 2.50 2.00

National Peach Exhibition, Szeged.

Crossing Street in Safety Zone — A354

60f, "Watch out for Children" (child & ball). 1fo, "Look before Crossing" (mother & child).

1964, Sept. 27 *Perf. 11*

1615	A354	20f	multicolored	.20	.20
1616	A354	60f	multicolored	.20	.20
1617	A354	1fo	lilac & multi	.25	.20
			Nos. 1615-1617 (3)	.65	.60

Issued to publicize traffic safety.

Souvenir Sheet

Voskhod 1 and Globe — A355

1964, Nov. 6 *Perf. 12x11½*

1618	A355	10fo	multicolored	3.75	3.50

Russian space flight of Vladimir M. Komarov, Boris B. Yegorov and Konstantine Feoktistov.

Arpad Bridge — A356

Danube Bridges, Budapest: 30f, Margaret Bridge. 60f, Chain Bridge. 1fo, Elizabeth Bridge. 1.50fo, Freedom Bridge. 2fo, Petőfi Bridge. 2.50fo, Railroad Bridge.

1964, Nov. 21 **Photo.** *Perf. 11x11½*

1619	A356	20f	multi	.20	.20
1620	A356	30f	multi	.20	.20
1621	A356	60f	multi	.20	.20
1622	A356	1fo	multi	.25	.20
1623	A356	1.50fo	multi	.30	.20
1624	A356	2fo	multi	.50	.20
1625	A356	2.50fo	multi	.85	.40
			Nos. 1619-1625 (7)	2.50	1.60

Opening of the reconstructed Elizabeth Bridge. See No. C250.

Ring-necked Pheasant and Hunting Rifle — A357

Designs: 30f, Wild boar. 40f, Gray partridges. 60f, Varying hare. 80f, Fallow deer. 1fo, Mouflon. 1.70fo, Red deer. 2fo, Great bustard. 2.50fo, Roebuck and roe deer. 3fo, Emblem of National Federation of Hungarian Hunters (antlers).

1964, Dec. 30 **Photo.** *Perf. 12x11½*

1626	A357	20f	multi	.20	.20
1627	A357	30f	multi	.20	.20
1628	A357	40f	multi	.20	.20
1629	A357	60f	multi	.20	.20
1630	A357	80f	multi	.20	.20
1631	A357	1fo	multi	.20	.20
1632	A357	1.70fo	multi	.25	.20
1633	A357	2fo	multi	.30	.20
1634	A357	2.50fo	multi	.50	.30
1635	A357	3fo	multi	.75	.50
			Nos. 1626-1635 (10)	3.00	2.40

Castle Type of 1960

3fo, Czesznek, vert. 4fo, Eger. 5fo, Koszeg, vert.

1964 *Perf. 11½x12, 12x11½*

Size: 21x28mm, 28x21mm

1644	A293	3fo	red brown	.50	.20
1645	A293	4fo	brt violet	1.00	.20
1646	A293	5fo	yellow grn	1.25	.20
			Nos. 1644-1646 (3)	2.75	.60

Equestrian, Gold and Bronze Medals — A358

Medals: 30f, Women's gymnastics, silver & bronze. 50f, Small-bore rifle, gold & bronze. 60f, Water polo, gold. 70f, Shot put, bronze. 80f, Soccer, gold. 1fo, Weight lifting, 1 bronze, 2 silver. 1.20fo, Canoeing, silver. 1.40fo, Hammer throw, silver. 1.50fo, Wrestling, 2 gold. 1.70fo, Javelin, 2 silver. 3fo, Fencing, 4 gold.

1965, Feb. 20 *Perf. 12*

Medals in Gold, Silver or Bronze

1647	A358	20f	lt ol grn & dk brn	.20	.20
1648	A358	30f	violet & dk brn	.20	.20
1649	A358	50f	olive & dk brn	.20	.20
1650	A358	60f	lt bl & red brn	.20	.20
1651	A358	70f	lt gray & red brn	.20	.20
1652	A358	80f	yel grn & dk brn	.20	.20
1653	A358	1fo	lil, vio & red brn	.20	.20
1654	A358	1.20fo	lt bl, ultra & red brn	.20	.20
1655	A358	1.40fo	gray & red brn	.20	.20
1656	A358	1.50fo	tan, lt brn & red brn	.25	.20
1657	A358	1.70fo	pink & red brn	.50	.25
1658	A358	3fo	grnsh blue & brn	.70	.55
			Nos. 1647-1658 (12)	3.25	2.80

Victories by the Hungarian team in the 1964 Olympic Games, Tokyo, Oct. 10-25.

Arctic Exploration A359

Chrysanthemums A360

Designs: 30f, Radar tracking rocket, ionosphere research. 60f, Rocket and earth with reflecting layer diagrams, atmospheric research. 80f, Telescope and map of Milky Way, radio astronomy. 1.50fo, Earth, compass rose and needle, earth magnetism. 1.70fo, Weather balloon and lightning, meteorology. 2fo, Aurora borealis and penguins, arctic research. 2.50fo, Satellite, earth and planets, space research. 3fo, IQSY emblem and world map. 10fo, Sun with flares and corona, snow crystals and rain.

Perf. 11½x12

1965, Mar. 25 **Photo.** **Unwmk.**

1659	A359	20f	blue, org & blk	.20	.20
1660	A359	30f	gray, blk & emer	.20	.20
1661	A359	60f	lilac, blk & yel	.20	.20
1662	A359	80f	lt grn, yel & blk	.20	.20
1663	A359	1.50fo	lemon, bl & blk	.20	.20
1664	A359	1.70fo	blue, pink & blk	.20	.20
1665	A359	2fo	ultra, sal & blk	.25	.20
1666	A359	2.50fo	org brn, yel & blk	.40	.20
1667	A359	3fo	lt bl, cit & blk	.70	.40
			Nos. 1659-1667 (9)	2.55	2.00

Souvenir Sheet

1668	A359	10fo	ultra, org & blk	2.50	2.50

Intl. Quiet Sun Year, 1964-65.

1965, Apr. 4

30f, Peonies. 50f, Carnations. 60f, Roses. 1.40fo, Lilies. 1.70fo, Anemones. 2fo, Gladioli. 2.50fo, Tulips. 3fo, Mixed flower bouquet.

Flowers in Natural Colors

1669	A360	20f	gold & gray	.20	.20
1670	A360	30f	gold & gray	.20	.20
1671	A360	50f	gold & gray	.20	.20
1672	A360	60f	gold & gray	.20	.20
1673	A360	1.40fo	gold & gray	.20	.20
1674	A360	1.70fo	gold & gray	.20	.20
1675	A360	2fo	gold & gray	.20	.20
1676	A360	2.50fo	gold & gray	.30	.20
1677	A360	3fo	gold & gray	.60	.50
			Nos. 1669-1677 (9)	2.30	2.10

20th anniversary of liberation from the Nazis.

"Head of a Combatant" by Leonardo da Vinci — A361

Perf. 11½x12

1965, May 4 **Photo.** **Unwmk.**

1678	A361	60f	bister & org brn	.30	.20

Issued to publicize the First International Renaissance Conference, Budapest.

Nikolayev, Tereshkova and View of Budapest — A362

1965, May 10 *Perf. 11*

1679	A362	1fo	dull blue & brn	.25	.20

Visit of the Russian astronauts Andrian G. Nikolayev and Valentina Tereshkova (Mr. & Mrs. Nikolayev) to Budapest.

ITU Emblem, Old and New Communication Equipment A363

1965, May 17

1680	A363	60f	violet blue	.20	.20

Cent. of the ITU.

Souvenir Sheet

Austrian WIPA Stamp of 1933 — A363a

1965, June 4 **Photo.** *Perf. 11*

1681	A363a		Sheet of 2 + 2 labels	3.50	3.50
	a.		2fo gray & deep ultra	1.50	1.50

1965 Vienna Intl. Phil. Exhib. WIPA, 6/4-13.

Marx and Lenin, Crowds with Flags — A364

ICY Emblem and Pulley — A365

1965, June 15 *Perf. 11½x12*

1682	A364	60f	red, blk & yel	.20	.20

6th Conference of Ministers of Post of Socialist Countries, Peking, June 21-July 15.

1965, June 25

1683	A365	2fo	dark red	.20	.20
	a.		Min. sheet of 4, perf. 11	2.25	2.25

Intl. Cooperation Year, 1965. No. 1683a contains rose red, olive, Prussian green and violet stamps.

Musical Clown — A366

Dr. Semmelweis A367

Circus Acts: 20f, Equestrians. 40f, Elephant. 50f, Seal balancing ball. 60f, Lions. 1fo, Wildcat jumping through burning hoops. 1.50fo, Black leopards. 2.50fo, Juggler. 3fo, Leopard and dogs. 4fo, Bear on bicycle.

1965, July 26 **Photo.** *Perf. 11½x12*

1684	A366	20f	multi	.20	.20
1685	A366	30f	multi	.20	.20
1686	A366	40f	multi	.20	.20
1687	A366	50f	multi	.20	.20
1688	A366	60f	multi	.20	.20
1689	A366	1fo	multi	.20	.20
1690	A366	1.50fo	multi	.25	.20
1691	A366	2.50fo	multi	.35	.20
1692	A366	3fo	multi	.40	.20
1693	A366	4fo	multi	.50	.40
			Nos. 1684-1693 (10)	2.70	2.20

1965, Aug. 20 **Photo.** **Unwmk.**

1694	A367	60f	red brown	.20	.20

Dr. Ignaz Philipp Semmelweis (1818-1865), discoverer of the cause of puerperal fever and introduced antisepsis into obstetrics.

Runner — A368

Sport: 30f, Swimmer at start. 50f, Woman diver. 60f, Modern dancing. 80f, Tennis. 1.70fo, Fencing. 2fo, Volleyball. 2.50fo, Basketball. 4fo, Water polo. 10fo, People's Stadium, Budapest, horiz.

1965, Aug. 20 *Perf. 11*

Size: 38x38mm

1695 A368	20f	multi	.20	.20
1696 A368	30f	blue & red brn	.20	.20
1697 A368	50f	bl grn, blk & red brn	.20	.20
1698 A368	60f	vio, blk & red brn	.20	.20
1699 A368	80f	tan, ol & red brn	.20	.20
1700 A368	1.70fo	multi	.25	.20
1701 A368	2fo	multi	.30	.20
1702 A368	2.50fo	gray, blk & red brn	.45	.25
1703 A368	4fo	bl, red brn & blk	.75	.45
		Nos. 1695-1703 (9)	2.75	2.10

Souvenir Sheet

Perf. 12x11½

1704 A368	10fo	bis, red brn & gray	3.00	2.75

Intl. College Championships, "Universiade," Budapest. No. 1704 contains one 38x28mm stamp.

Hemispheres and Warsaw Mermaid — A369

1965, Oct. 8 Photo. *Perf. 12x11½*

1705 A369	60f	brt blue	.20	.20

Sixth Congress of the World Federation of Trade Unions, Warsaw.

Phyllocactus Hybridus A370

Flowers from Botanical Gardens: 30f, Cattleya Warszewiczii (orchid). 60f, Rebutia calliantha. 70f, Paphiopedilum hybridium. 80f, Opuntia cactus. 1fo, Laelia elegans (orchid). 1.50fo, Christmas cactus. 2fo, Bird-of-paradise flower. 2.50fo, Lithops Weberi. 3fo, Victoria water lily.

1965, Oct. 11 *Perf. 11½x12*

1706 A370	20f	gray & multi	.20	.20
1707 A370	30f	gray & multi	.20	.20
1708 A370	60f	gray & multi	.20	.20
1709 A370	70f	gray & multi	.20	.20
1710 A370	80f	gray & multi	.20	.20
1711 A370	1fo	gray & multi	.20	.20
1712 A370	1.50fo	gray & multi	.25	.20
1713 A370	2fo	gray & multi	.25	.20
1714 A370	2.50fo	gray & multi	.40	.25
1715 A370	3fo	gray & multi	.60	.35
		Nos. 1706-1715 (10)	2.70	2.20

"The Black Stallion" A371

Tales from the Arabian Nights: 30f, Shahriar and Scheherazade. 50f, Sinbad's Fifth Voyage (ship). 60f, Aladdin, or The Wonderful Lamp. 80f, Harun al-Rashid. 1fo, The Flying Carpet. 1.70fo, The Fisherman and the Genie. 2fo, Ali Baba and the Forty Thieves. 3fo, Sinbad's Second Voyage (flying bird).

1965, Dec. 15 Litho. *Perf. 11½*

1716 A371	20f	multi	.20	.20
1717 A371	30f	multi	.20	.20
1718 A371	50f	multi	.20	.20
1719 A371	60f	multi	.20	.20
1720 A371	80f	multi	.20	.20
1721 A371	1fo	multi	.20	.20
1722 A371	1.70fo	multi	.35	.20
1723 A371	2fo	multi	.45	.25
1724 A371	3fo	multi	.75	.45
		Nos. 1716-1724 (9)	2.75	2.10

Congress Emblem A372

Callimorpha Dominula A373

1965, Dec. 9 Photo. *Perf. 11½x12*

1725 A372	2fo	dark blue	.30	.20

Fifth Congress of the International Federation of Resistance Fighters (FIR), Budapest.

1966, Feb. 1 Photo. *Perf. 11½x12*

Various Butterflies in Natural Colors; Black Inscription

1726 A373	20f	lt aqua	.20	.20
1727 A373	60f	pale violet	.20	.20
1728 A373	70f	tan	.20	.20
1729 A373	80f	lt ultra	.20	.20
1730 A373	1fo	gray	.20	.20
1731 A373	1.50fo	emerald	.40	.20
1732 A373	2fo	dull rose	.30	.20
1733 A373	2.50fo	bister	.45	.30
1734 A373	3fo	blue	.70	.50
		Nos. 1726-1734 (9)	2.85	2.20

Lal Bahadur Shastri A374

Designs: 60f, Bela Kun. 2fo, Istvan Széchenyi and Chain Bridge.

Lithographed; Photogravure (#1736)

1966 *Perf. 11½x12, 12x11½*

1735 A374	60f	red & black	.20	.20
1736 A374	1fo	brt violet	.20	.20
1737 A374	2fo	dull yel, buff & sepia	.25	.20
		Nos. 1735-1737 (3)	.65	.60

Kun (1886-1939), communist labor leader; Shastri (1904-66), Indian Prime Minister; Count Istvan Széchenyi (1791-1860), statesman.

See Nos. 1764-1765, 1769-1770.

Luna 9 — A375

Design: 3fo, Luna 9 sending signals from moon to earth, horiz.

1966, Mar. 12 Photo. *Perf. 12*

1738 A375	2fo	violet, blk & yel	.45	.20
1739 A375	3fo	lt ultra, blk & yel	.85	.60

1st soft landing on the moon by the Russian satellite Luna 9, Feb. 3, 1966.

Crocus — A376

1966, Mar. 12 *Perf. 11*

Flowers: 30f, Cyclamen. 60f, Ligularia sibirica. 1.40fo, Lilium bulbiferum. 1.50fo, Snake's head. 3fo, Snapdragon and emblem of Hungarian Nature Preservation Society.

Flowers in Natural Colors

1740 A376	20f	brown	.20	.20
1741 A376	30f	aqua	.20	.20
1742 A376	60f	rose claret	.20	.20
1743 A376	1.40fo	gray	.30	.20
1744 A376	1.50fo	ultra	.45	.25
1745 A376	3fo	mag & sepia	.65	.40
		Nos. 1740-1745 (6)	2.00	1.45

1966, Apr. 16

Designs: 20f, Barn swallows. 30f, Long-tailed tits. 60f, Red crossbill and pine cone. 1.40fo, Middle spotted woodpecker. 1.50fo, Hoopoe feeding young. 3fo, Forest preserve, lapwing and emblem of National Forest Preservation Society.

Birds in Natural Colors

1746 A376	20f	brt green	.20	.20
1747 A376	30f	vermilion	.20	.20
1748 A376	60f	brt green	.20	.20
1749 A376	1.40fo	vio blue	.25	.20
1750 A376	1.50fo	blue	.65	.35
1751 A376	3fo	brn, mag & grn	.75	.50
		Nos. 1746-1751 (6)	2.25	1.65

Nos. 1740-1751 issued to promote protection of wild flowers and birds.

Locomotive, 1947; Monoplane, 1912; Autobus, 1911; Steamer, 1853, and Budapest Railroad Station, 1846 — A377

Designs: 2fo, Transportation, 1966: electric locomotive V.43; turboprop airliner IL-18; Ikarusz autobus; Diesel passenger ship, and Budapest South Railroad Station.

1966, Apr. 2 Photo. *Perf. 12*

1752 A377	1fo	yel, brn & grn	.20	.20
1753 A377	2fo	pale grn, bl & brn	.35	.20

Re-opening of the Transport Museum, Budapest.

Bronze Order of Labor — A378

Decorations: 30f, Silver Order of Labor. 50f, Banner Order, third class. 60f, Gold Order of Labor. 70f, Banner Order, second class. 1fo, Red Banner Order of Labor. 1.20fo, Banner Order, first class. 2fo, Order of Merit. 2.50fo, Hero of Socialist Labor. Sizes: 20f, 30f, 60f, 1fo, 2fo, 2.50fo: 19½x38mm. 50f: 21x29mm. 70f, 25x31mm. 1.20fo: 28x38mm.

1966, Apr. 2 Unwmk. *Perf. 11*

Decorations in Original Colors

1754 A378	20f	dp ultra	.20	.20
1755 A378	30f	lt brown	.20	.20
1756 A378	50f	blue green	.20	.20
1757 A378	60f	violet	.20	.20
1758 A378	70f	carmine	.20	.20
1759 A378	1fo	violet bl	.20	.20
1760 A378	1.20fo	brt blue	.20	.20
1761 A378	2fo	olive	.25	.20
1762 A378	2.50fo	dull blue	.35	.20
		Nos. 1754-1762 (9)	2.00	1.80

Portrait Type of 1966 and

Dubna Nuclear Research Institute — A379

WHO Headquarters, Geneva — A380

Designs: No. 1764, Pioneer girl. No. 1765, Tamás Esze (1666-1708), military hero. No. 1767, Old view of Buda and UNESCO emblem. No. 1768, Horse-drawn fire pump and emblem of Sopron Fire Brigade. No. 1769, Miklos Zrinyi (1508-66), hero of Turkish Wars. No. 1770, Sandor Koranyi (1866-1944), physician and scientist.

1966 Litho. *Perf. 11½x12*

1763 A379	60f	blue grn & blk	.20	.20
1764 A374	60f	multicolored	.20	.20
1765 A374	60f	brt bl & blk	.20	.20
1766 A380	2fo	lt ultra & blk	.20	.20
1767 A380	2fo	lt blue & pur	.25	.20
1768 A380	2fo	orange & blk	.25	.20

1769 A374 2fo ol bis & brn .20 .20
1770 A374 2fo multicolored .20 .20
Nos. 1763-1770 (8) 1.70 1.60

No. 1763, 10th anniv. of the United Institute for Nuclear Research, Dubna, USSR; No. 1764, 20th anniv. of Pioneer Movement; No. 1766, Inauguration of the WHO Headquarters, Geneva; No. 1767, 20th anniv. of UNESCO and 72nd session of Executive Council, Budapest, May 30-31; No. 1768, Cent. of Volunteer Fire Brigade.

Hungarian Soccer Player and Soccer Field — A381

Jules Rimet, Cup and Soccer Ball — A382

Designs (Views of Soccer play): 30f, Montevideo 1930 (Uruguay 4, Argentina 2). 60f, Rome 1934 (Italy 2, Czechoslovakia 1). 1fo, Paris 1938 (Italy 4, Hungary 2). 1.40fo, Rio de Janeiro 1950 (Uruguay 2, Brazil 1). 1.70fo, Bern 1954 (Germany 3, Hungary 2). 2fo, Stockholm 1958 (Brazil 5, Sweden 2). 2.50fo, Santiago 1962 (Brazil 3, Czechoslovakia 1).

Souvenir Sheet

1966, May 16 Photo. *Perf. 11½x12*

1771 A381 10fo multi 3.25 3.00

1966, June 6 *Perf. 12x11½*

1772 A382 20f blue & multi .25 .20
1773 A382 30f orange & multi .25 .20
1774 A382 60f multi .20 .20
1775 A382 1fo multi .20 .20
1776 A382 1.40fo multi .20 .20
1777 A382 1.70fo multi .20 .20
1778 A382 2fo multi .25 .20
1779 A382 2.50fo multi .60 .40
Nos. 1772-1779,B258 (9) 2.75 2.30

World Cup Soccer Championship, Wembley, England, July 11-30.

European Red Fox — A383

Hunting Trophies: 60f, Wild boar. 70f, Wildcat. 80f, Roebuck. 1.50fo, Red deer. 2.50fo, Fallow deer. 3fo, Mouflon.

1966, July 4 Photo. *Perf. 11½x12*
Animals in Natural Colors

1780 A383 20f gray & lt brn .20 .20
1781 A383 60f buff & gray .20 .20
1782 A383 70f lt bl & gray .20 .20
1783 A383 80f pale grn & yel bis .25 .20
1784 A383 1.50fo pale lem & brn .35 .20
1785 A383 2.50fo gray & brn .60 .35
1786 A383 3fo pale pink & gray .95 .50
Nos. 1780-1786 (7) 2.75 1.85

The 80f and 1.50fo were issued with and without alternating labels, which show date and place when trophy was taken; the 2.50fo was issued only with labels, 20f, 60f, 70f and 3fo without labels only.

Discus Thrower and Matthias Cathedral A384

30f, High jump & Agriculture Museum. 40f, Javelin (women's) & Parliament. 50f, Hammer throw, Mt. Gellert & Liberty Bridge. 60f, Broad jump & view of Buda. 1fo, Shot put & Chain Bridge. 2fo, Pole vault & Stadium. 3fo, Long distance runners & Millenium Monument.

1966, Aug. 30 Photo. *Perf. 12x11½*

1787 A384 20f grn, brn & org .20 .20
1788 A384 30f multi .30 .20
1789 A384 40f multi .20 .20
1790 A384 50f multi .20 .20
1791 A384 60f multi .20 .20
1792 A384 1fo multi .25 .20
1793 A384 2fo multi .50 .20
1794 A384 3fo multi .75 .50
Nos. 1787-1794 (8) 2.60 1.90

8th European Athletic Championships, Budapest, Aug. 30-Sept. 4. See No. C261.

Girl in the Forest by Miklos Barabas A385

Paintings: 1fo, Mrs. Istvan Bitto by Miklos Barabas (1810-98). 1.50fo, Hunyadi's Farewell by Gyula Benczur (1844-1920). 1.70fo, Reading Woman by Gyula Benczur, horiz. 2fo, Woman with Fagots by Mihaly Munkacsi (1844-1900). 2.50fo, Yawning Boy by Mihaly Munkacsi. 3fo, Lady in Violet by Pal Szinyei Merse (1845-1920). 10fo, Picnic in May by Pal Szinyei Merse, horiz.

1966, Dec. 9 *Perf. 12½*
Gold Frame

1795 A385 60f multi .20 .20
1796 A385 1fo multi .25 .20
1797 A385 1.50fo multi .40 .20
1798 A385 1.70fo multi .40 .20
1799 A385 2fo multi .40 .20
1800 A385 2.50fo multi .45 .20
1801 A385 3fo multi .90 .80
Nos. 1795-1801 (7) 3.00 2.00

Souvenir Sheet

1802 A385 10fo multi 6.00 6.00

Issued to honor Hungarian painters. Size of stamp in No. 1802: 56x51mm.

Vostoks 3 and 4 — A386

Space Craft: 60f, Gemini 6 and 7. 80f, Vostoks 5 and 6. 1fo, Gemini 9 and target rocket. 1.50fo, Alexei Leonov walking in space. 2fo, Edward White walking in space. 2.50fo, Voskhod. 3fo, Gemini 11 docking Agena target.

1966, Dec. 29 *Perf. 11*

1803 A386 20f multi .20 .20
1804 A386 60f multi .20 .20
1805 A386 80f multi .20 .20
1806 A386 1fo multi .20 .20
1807 A386 1.50fo multi .30 .20
1808 A386 2fo multi .30 .20
1809 A386 2.50fo multi .50 .30
1810 A386 3fo multi .75 .50
Nos. 1803-1810 (8) 2.65 2.00

American and Russian twin space flights.

Pal Kitaibel and Kitaibelia Vitifolia — A387

Flowers of the Carpathian Basin: 60f, Dentaria glandulosa. 1fo, Edraianthus tenuifolius. 1.50fo, Althaea pallida. 2fo, Centaurea mollis. 2.50fo, Sternbergia colchiciflora. 3fo, Iris Hungarica.

1967, Feb. 7 Photo. *Perf. 11½x12*
Flowers in Natural Colors

1811 A387 20f rose, blk & gold .20 .20
1812 A387 60f green .20 .20
1813 A387 1fo violet gray .20 .20
1814 A387 1.50fo blue .20 .20
1815 A387 2fo light olive .25 .20
1816 A387 2.50fo gray grn .45 .30
1817 A387 3fo yellow grn .75 .50
Nos. 1811-1817 (7) 2.25 1.80

Pal Kitaibel (1757-1817), botanist, chemist and physician.

Militiaman A388

1967, Feb. 18 Photo. *Perf. 11½x12*

1818 A388 2fo blue gray .40 .20

Workers' Militia, 10th anniversary.

Mme. Du Barry and Louis XV, by Gyula Benczur (1844-1920) — A390

Souvenir Sheet

Painting: 10fo, Milton dictating "Paradise Lost" to his daughters, by Soma Orlai Petrics.

1967, May 6 Photo. *Perf. 12½*

1819 A390 10fo multi 4.75 4.50

1967, June 22

Paintings: 60f, Franz Liszt by Mihaly Munkacsi (1844-1900). 1fo, Samuel Lanyi, self-portrait, 1840. 1.50fo, Lady in Fur-lined Jacket by Jozsef Borsos (1821-83). 1.70fo, The Lovers, by Pal Szinyei Merse (1845-1920). 2fo, Portrait of Szidonia Deak, 1861, by Alajos Gyorgyi (1821-63). 2.50fo, National Guardsman, 1848, by Jozsef Borsos.

Gold Frame

1820 A390 60f multi .20 .20
1821 A390 1fo multi .20 .20
1822 A390 1.50fo multi .20 .20
1823 A390 1.70fo multi, horiz. .30 .20
1824 A390 2fo multi .35 .20
1825 A390 2.50fo multi .45 .20
1826 A390 3fo multi .75 .70
Nos. 1820-1826 (7) 2.45 1.90

Issued to honor Hungarian painters. No. 1819 commemorates AMPHILEX 67 and the F.I.P. Congress, Amsterdam, May 11-21. No. 1819 contains one 56x50mm stamp.

See #1863-1870, 1900-1907, 1940-1947.

Map of Hungary, Tourist Year Emblem, Plane, Train, Car and Ship A391

1967, May 6 *Perf. 12x11½*

1827 A391 1fo brt blue & blk .20 .20

International Tourist Year, 1967.

S.S. Ferencz Deak, Schönbüchel Castle, Austrian Flag — A392

Designs: 60f, Diesel hydrobus, Bratislava Castle and Czechoslovak flag. 1fo, Diesel ship Hunyadi, Buda Castle and Hungarian flag. 1.50fo, Diesel tug Szekszard, Golubac Fortress and Yugoslav flag. 1.70fo, Towboat Miskolc, Vidin Fortress and Bulgarian flag. 2fo, Cargo ship Tihany, Galati shipyard and Romanian flag. 2.50fo, Hydrofoil Siraly I, Izmail Harbor and Russian flag.

1967, June 1 *Perf. 11½x12*
Flags in National Colors

1828 A392 30f lt blue grn .20 .20
1829 A392 60f orange brn .20 .20
1830 A392 1fo grnsh blue .50 .25
1831 A392 1.50fo lt green .75 .30
1832 A392 1.70fo blue 1.10 .45
1833 A392 2fo rose lilac 1.75 .75
1834 A392 2.50fo lt olive grn 4.50 1.10
Nos. 1828-1834 (7) 9.00 3.25

25th session of the Danube Commission.

Poodle A393

Collie — A394

1fo, Hungarian pointer. 1.40fo, Fox terriers. 2fo, Pumi, Hungarian sheep dog. 3fo, German shepherd. 4fo, Puli, Hungarian sheep dog.

1967, July 7 Litho. *Perf. 12*

1835 A393 30f multi .25 .20
1836 A394 60f multi .25 .20
1837 A393 1fo multi .20 .20
1838 A394 1.40fo multi .25 .25
1839 A393 2fo multi .35 .20
1840 A394 3fo multi .60 .35
1841 A393 4fo multi .95 .60
Nos. 1835-1841 (7) 2.85 2.00

Sterlets A395

Fish: 60f, Pike perch. 1fo, Carp. 1.70fo, European catfish. 2fo, Pike. 2.50fo, Rapfin.

1967, Aug. 22 Photo. *Perf. 12x11½*

No.	Type	Value	Description	Unused	Used
1842	A395	20f	multi	.20	.20
1843	A395	60f	bister & multi	.20	.20
1844	A395	1fo	multi	.20	.20
1845	A395	1.70fo	multi	.20	.20
1846	A395	2fo	green & multi	.30	.20
1847	A395	2.50fo	gray & multi	.75	.55
			Nos. 1842-1847,B263 (7)	2.75	2.00

14th Cong. of the Intl. Federation of Anglers (C.I.P.S.), Dunaujvaros, Aug. 20-28.

Prince Igor, by Aleksandr Borodin — A396

Opera Scenes: 30f, Freischütz, by Karl Maria von Weber. 40f, The Magic Flute, by Mozart. 60f, Prince Bluebeard's Castle, by Bela Bartok. 80f, Carmen, by Bizet, vert. 1fo, Don Carlos, by Verdi, vert. 1.70fo, Tannhäuser, by Wagner, vert. 3fo. Laszlo Hunyadi, by Ferenc Erkel, vert.

1967, Sept. 26 Photo. *Perf. 12*

No.	Type	Value	Description	Unused	Used
1848	A396	20f	multi	.20	.20
1849	A396	30f	multi	.20	.20
1850	A396	40f	multi	.20	.20
1851	A396	60f	multi	.20	.20
1852	A396	80f	multi	.20	.20
1853	A396	1fo	multi	.20	.20
1854	A396	1.70fo	multi	.45	.30
1855	A396	3fo	multi	1.00	.70
			Nos. 1848-1855 (8)	2.65	2.20

Teacher, Students and Stone from Pecs University, 14th Century A397

1967, Oct. 9 Photo. *Perf. 11½x12*

No.	Type	Value	Description	Unused	Used
1856	A397	2fo	gold & dp grn	.40	.20

600th anniv. of higher education in Hungary; University of Pecs was founded in 1367.

Eötvös University, and Symbols of Law and Justice — A398

1967, Oct. 12 *Perf. 12x11½*

No.	Type	Value	Description	Unused	Used
1857	A398	2fo	slate	.40	.20

300th anniv. of the School of Political Science and Law at the Lorand Eötvös University, Budapest.

Lenin as Teacher, by Sandor Legrady A399

Paintings by Sandor Legrady: 1fo, Lenin. 3fo, Lenin on board the cruiser Aurora.

1967, Oct. 31 *Perf. 12½*

No.	Type	Value	Description	Unused	Used
1858	A399	60f	gold & multi	.20	.20
1859	A399	1fo	gold & multi	.20	.20
1860	A399	3fo	gold & multi	.60	.25
			Nos. 1858-1860 (3)	1.00	.65

50th anniv. of the Russian October Revolution.

Venus 4 Landing on Venus — A400

1967, Nov. 6 *Perf. 12*

No.	Type	Value	Description	Unused	Used
1861	A400	5fo	gold & multi	1.25	1.10

Landing of the Russian automatic space station Venus 4 on the planet Venus.

Souvenir Sheet

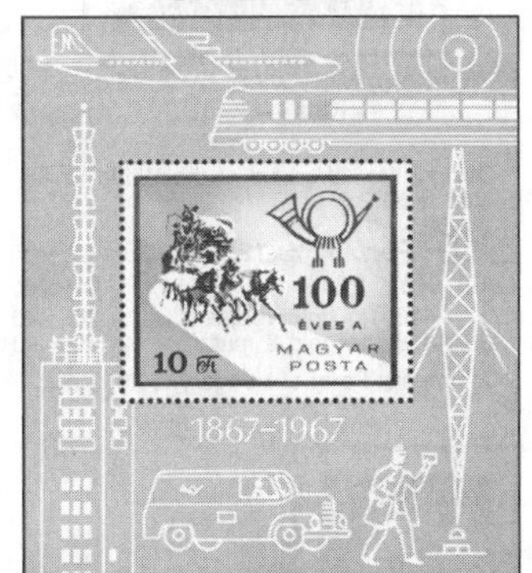

19th Century Mail Coach and Post Horn — A401

Photogravure; Gold Impressed

1967, Nov. 21 *Perf. 12½*

No.	Type	Value	Description	Unused	Used
1862	A401	10fo	multicolored	3.25	3.00

Hungarian Postal Administration, cent.

Painting Type of 1967

Paintings: 60f, Brother and Sister by Adolf Fenyes (1867-1945). 1fo, Wrestling Boys by Oszkar Glatz (1872-1958). 1.50fo, "October" by Karoly Ferenczy (1862-1917). 1.70fo, Women at the River Bank by Istvan Szönyi (1894-1960), horiz. 2fo, Godfather's Breakfast by Istvan Csok (1865-1961). 2.50fo, "Eviction Notice" by Gyula Derkovits (1894-1934). 3fo, Self-portrait by M. T. Czontvary Kosztka (1853-1919). 10fo, The Apple Pickers by Bela Uitz (1887-).

1967, Dec. 21 Photo. *Perf. 12½*

No.	Type	Value	Description	Unused	Used
1863	A390	60f	multi	.20	.20
1864	A390	1fo	multi	.20	.20
1865	A390	1.50fo	multi	.20	.20
1866	A390	1.70fo	multi	.20	.20
1867	A390	2fo	multi	.30	.20
1868	A390	2.50fo	multi	.40	.25
1869	A390	3fo	multi	.70	.45
			Nos. 1863-1869 (7)	2.20	1.70

Miniature Sheet

No.	Type	Value	Description	Unused	Used
1870	A390	10fo	multi	2.75	2.50

Issued to honor Hungarian painters.

Biathlon — A402

Sport (Olympic Rings and): 60f, Figure skating, pair. 1fo, Bobsledding. 1.40fo, Slalom. 1.70fo, Women's figure skating. 2fo, Speed skating. 3fo, Ski jump. 10fo, Ice hockey.

1967, Dec. 30 Photo. *Perf. 12½*

Souvenir Sheet

No.	Type	Value	Description	Unused	Used
1871	A402	10fo	lilac & multi	2.50	2.00

1968, Jan. 29 *Perf. 11*

No.	Type	Value	Description	Unused	Used
1872	A402	30f	multi	.20	.20
1873	A402	60f	multi	.20	.20
1874	A402	1fo	multi	.20	.20
1875	A402	1.40fo	rose & multi	.20	.20
1876	A402	1.70fo	multi	.20	.20
1877	A402	2fo	multi	.30	.20
1878	A402	3fo	ol & multi	.80	.30
			Nos. 1872-1878,B264 (8)	2.80	1.80

10th Winter Olympic Games, Grenoble, France, Feb. 6-18. No. 1871 contains one 43x43mm stamp.

Kando Statue, Miskolc, Kando Locomotive and Map of Hungary A403

1968, Mar. 30 Photo. *Perf. 11½x12*

No.	Type	Value	Description	Unused	Used
1879	A403	2fo	dark blue	.40	.20

Kalman Kando (1869-1931), engineer, inventor of Kando locomotive.

Domestic Cat A404

1968, Mar. 30 *Perf. 11*

No.	Type	Value	Description	Unused	Used
1880	A404	20f	shown	.20	.20
1881	A404	60f	Cream Persian	.20	.20
1882	A404	1fo	Smoky Persian	.20	.20
1883	A404	1.20fo	Domestic kitten	.20	.20
1884	A404	1.50fo	White Persian	.30	.20
1885	A404	2fo	Brown-striped Persian	.30	.20
1886	A404	2.50fo	Siamese	.60	.25
1887	A404	5fo	Blue Persian	1.25	.55
			Nos. 1880-1887 (8)	3.25	2.00

Zoltan Kodaly, by Sandor Légrády A405

1968, Apr. 17 Photo. *Perf. 12½*

No.	Type	Value	Description	Unused	Used
1888	A405	5fo	gold & multi	1.00	.75

Kodaly (1882-1967), composer & musicologist.

White Storks A406

Birds: 50f, Golden orioles. 60f, Imperial eagle. 1fo, Red-footed falcons. 1.20fo, Scops owl. 1.50fo, Great bustard. 2fo, European bee-eaters. 2.50fo, Graylag goose.

1968, Apr. 25

Birds in Natural Colors

No.	Type	Value	Description	Unused	Used
1889	A406	20f	ver & lt ultra	.20	.20
1890	A406	50f	ver & gray	.20	.20
1891	A406	60f	ver & lt bl	.20	.20
1892	A406	1fo	ver & yel grn	.25	.20
1893	A406	1.20fo	ver & brt grn	.25	.20
1894	A406	1.50fo	ver & lt vio	.25	.20
1895	A406	2fo	ver & pale lil	.55	.30
1896	A406	2.50fo	ver & bl grn	1.10	.50
			Nos. 1889-1896 (8)	3.00	2.00

International Bird Preservation Congress.

City Hall, Kecskemét A407

Student and Agricultural College A408

1968, Apr. 25 *Perf. 12x11½*

No.	Type	Value	Description	Unused	Used
1897	A407	2fo	brown orange	.30	.20

600th anniversary of Kecskemét.

Marx Type of 1953

1968, May 5 Engr. *Perf. 12*

No.	Type	Value	Description	Unused	Used
1898	A230	1fo	claret	.20	.20

Karl Marx (1818-1883).

1968, May 24 Photo. *Perf. 12x11½*

No.	Type	Value	Description	Unused	Used
1899	A408	2fo	dk olive green	.30	.20

150th anniv. of the founding of the Agricultural College at Mosonmagyaróvár.

Painting Type of 1967

Paintings: 40f, Girl with Pitcher, by Goya (1746-1828). 60f, Head of an Apostle, by El Greco (c. 1541-1614). 1fo, Boy with Apple Basket and Dogs, by Pedro Nunez (1639-1700), horiz. 1.50fo, Mary Magdalene, by El Greco. 2.50fo, The Breakfast, by Velazquez (1599-1660), horiz. 4fo, The Virgin from The Holy Family, by El Greco. 5fo, The Knife Grinder, by Goya. 10fo, Portrait of a Girl, by Palma Vecchio (1480-1528).

1968, May 30 *Perf. 12½*

1900	A390	40f multi	.20	.20
1901	A390	60f multi	.20	.20
1902	A390	1fo multi	.20	.20
1903	A390	1.50fo multi	.20	.20
1904	A390	2.50fo multi	.50	.20
1905	A390	4fo multi	.70	.20
1906	A390	5fo multi	1.00	.35
		Nos. 1900-1906 (7)	3.00	1.55

Souvenir Sheet

1907	A390	10fo multi	3.25	3.00

Issued to publicize art treasures in the Budapest Museum of Fine Arts and to publicize an art exhibition.

Lake Balaton at Badacsony A409

Views on Lake Balaton: 40f like 20f. 60f, Tihanyi Peninsula. 1fo, Sailboats at Almadi. 2fo, Szigliget Bay.

1968-69 Litho. *Perf. 12*

1908	A409	20f multi	.20	.20
1908A	A409	40f multi ('69)	.20	.20
b.		Bklt. pane, #1909, 1911, 2 each #1908A, 1910	.75	
c.		Bklt. pane, #1909-1911, 3 #1908A	.75	
d.		Bklt. pane, #1911, 3 #1908A, 2 #1909	.75	
1909	A409	60f multi	.20	.20
1910	A409	1fo multi	.20	.20
1911	A409	2fo multi	.45	.20
		Nos. 1908-1911 (5)	1.25	1.00

Locomotive, Type 424 — A410

1968, July 14 Photo. *Perf. 12x11½*

1912	A410	2fo gold, lt bl & slate	.60	.20

Centenary of the Hungarian State Railroad.

Horses Grazing — A411

Designs: 40f, Horses in storm. 60f, Horse race on the steppe. 80f, Horsedrawn sleigh. 1fo, Four-in-hand and rainbow. 1.40fo, Farm wagon drawn by 7 horses. 2fo, One rider driving five horses. 2.50fo, Campfire on the range. 4fo, Coach with 5 horses.

1968, July 25 *Perf. 11*

1913	A411	30f multi	.20	.20
1914	A411	40f multi	.20	.20
1915	A411	60f multi	.20	.20
1916	A411	80f multi	.20	.20
1917	A411	1fo multi	.20	.20
1918	A411	1.40fo multi	.30	.20
1919	A411	2fo multi	.30	.20
1920	A411	2.50fo multi	.40	.25
1921	A411	4fo multi	.75	.45
		Nos. 1913-1921 (9)	2.75	2.10

Horse breeding on the Hungarian steppe (Puszta).

Mihály Tompa (1817-68), Poet — A412

1968, July 30 Photo. *Perf. 12x11½*

1922	A412	60f blue black	.20	.20

Festival Emblem, Bulgarian and Hungarian National Costumes — A413

1968, Aug. 3 Litho. *Perf. 12*

1923	A413	60f multicolored	.30	.20

Issued to publicize the 9th Youth Festival for Peace and Friendship, Sofia, Bulgaria.

Souvenir Sheet

Runners and Aztec Calendar Stone — A414

1968, Aug. 21 Photo. *Perf. 12½*

1924	A414	10fo multicolored	2.50	2.25

19th Olympic Games, Mexico City, 10/12-27.

Scientific Society Emblem — A415

Perf. 12½x11½

1968, Dec. 10 **Photo.**

1925	A415	2fo brt blue & blk	.35	.20

Society for the Popularization of Scientific Knowledge.

Hesperis A416

Garden Flowers: 60f, Pansy. 80f, Zinnias. 1fo, Morning-glory. 1.40fo, Petunia. 1.50fo, Portulaca. 2fo, Michaelmas daisies. 2.50fo, Dahlia.

1968, Oct. 29 *Perf. 11½x12*

Flowers in Natural Colors

1926	A416	20f gray	.20	.20
1927	A416	60f lt green	.20	.20
1928	A416	80f bluish lilac	.25	.20
1929	A416	1fo buff	.25	.20
1930	A416	1.40fo lt grnsh bl	.20	.20
1931	A416	1.50fo lt blue	.25	.20
1932	A416	2fo pale pink	.30	.25
1933	A416	2.50fo lt blue	.60	.40
		Nos. 1926-1933 (8)	2.25	1.85

Pioneers Saluting Communist Party — A417

Children's Paintings: 60f, Four pioneers holding banner saluting Communist Party. 1fo, Pioneer camp.

1968, Nov. 16 Photo. *Perf. 12x11½*

1934	A417	40f buff & multi	.20	.20
1935	A417	60f buff & multi	.20	.20
1936	A417	1fo buff & multi	.30	.20
		Nos. 1934-1936 (3)	.70	.60

50th anniv. of the Communist Party of Hungary. The designs are from a competition among elementary school children.

Workers, Monument by Z. Olcsai-Kiss — A418

Design: 1fo, "Workers of the World Unite!" poster by N. Por, vert.

Perf. 11½x12, 12x11½

1968, Nov. 24 **Photo.**

1937	A418	1fo gold, red, & blk	.20	.20
1938	A418	2fo gold & multi	.20	.20

Communist Party of Hungary, 50th anniv.

Human Rights Flame — A419

1968, Dec. 10 *Perf. 12½x11½*

1939	A419	1fo dark red brown	.25	.20

International Human Rights Year.

Painting Type of 1967

Italian Paintings: 40f, Esterhazy Madonna, by Raphael. 60f, The Annunciation, by Bernardo Strozzi. 1fo, Portrait of a Young Man, by Raphael. 1.50fo, The Three Graces, by Battista Naldini. 2.50fo, Portrait of a Man, by Sebastiano del Piombo. 4fo, The Doge Marcantonio Trevisani, by Titian. 5fo, Venus, Cupid and Jealousy, by Angelo Bronzino. 10fo, Bathsheba Bathing, by Sebastiano Ricci, horiz.

1968, Dec. 10 Photo. *Perf. 12½*

1940	A390	40f multi	.20	.20
1941	A390	60f multi	.20	.20
1942	A390	1fo multi	.20	.20
1943	A390	1.50fo multi	.20	.20
1944	A390	2.50fo multi	.30	.20
1945	A390	4fo multi	.60	.25
1946	A390	5fo multi	.80	.35
		Nos. 1940-1946 (7)	2.50	1.60

Miniature Sheet

Perf. 11

1947	A390	10fo multi	2.75	2.50

Issued to publicize art treasures in the Budapest Museum of Fine Arts. No. 1947 contains one stamp size of stamp: 62x45mm.

1869 and 1969 Emblems of Athenaeum Press — A420

1969, Jan. 27 *Perf. 12½x11½*

1948	A420	2fo gold, gray, lt bl & blk	.30	.20

Centenary of Athenaeum Press, Budapest.

Endre Ady (1877-1919), Lyric Poet — A421

1969, Jan. 27 *Perf. 11½x12*

1949	A421	1fo multicolored	.20	.20

Olympic Medal and Women's Javelin — A422

Olympic Medal and: 60f, Canadian singles (canoeing). 1fo, Soccer. 1.20fo, Hammer throw. 2fo, Fencing. 3fo, Greco-Roman Wrestling. 4fo, Kayak single. 5fo, Equestrian. 10fo, Head of Mercury by Praxiteles and Olympic torch.

1969, Mar. 7 Photo. *Perf. 12*

1950	A422	40f multi	.20	.20
1951	A422	60f multi	.20	.20
1952	A422	1fo multi	.20	.20
1953	A422	1.20fo multi	.20	.20
1954	A422	2fo multi	.20	.20
1955	A422	3fo multi	.30	.20
1956	A422	4fo multi	.70	.20
1957	A422	5fo multi	.75	.45
		Nos. 1950-1957 (8)	2.75	1.85

Souvenir Sheet

Litho. *Perf. 11½*

1958	A422	10fo multi	2.75	2.75

Victories won by the Hungarian team in the 1968 Olympic Games, Mexico City, Oct. 12-27, 1968. No. 1958 contains one 45x33mm stamp.

1919 Revolutionary Poster — A423

Revolutionary Posters: 60f, Lenin. 1fo, Man breaking chains. 2fo, Industrial worker looking at family and farm. 3fo, Militia recruiter. 10fo, Shouting revolutionist with red banner, horiz.

1969, Mar. 21 Photo. *Perf. 11½x12*

Gold Frame

1960	A423	40f red & black	.20	.20
1961	A423	60f red & black	.20	.20
1962	A423	1fo red & black	.20	.20
1963	A423	2fo black, gray & red	.25	.20
1964	A423	3fo multicolored	.35	.20
		Nos. 1960-1964 (5)	1.20	1.00

Souvenir Sheet

Perf. 12½

1965	A423	10fo red, gray & blk	1.50	1.50

50th anniv. of the proclamation of the Hungarian Soviet Republic.

The 60f red lilac with 4-line black printing on back was given away by the Hungarian PO.

No. 1965 contains one 51x38½mm stamp.

Jersey Tiger A424

Designs: Various Butterflies and Moths.

1969, Apr. 15 Litho. *Perf. 12*

1966	A424	40f shown	.20	.20
1967	A424	60f Eyed hawk moth	.20	.20
1968	A424	80f Painted lady	.20	.20
1969	A424	1fo Tiger moth	.20	.20
1970	A424	1.20fo Small fire moth	.25	.20
1971	A424	2fo Large blue	.35	.20
1972	A424	3fo Belted oak egger	.65	.45
1973	A424	4fo Peacock	.90	.50
		Nos. 1966-1973 (8)	2.95	2.15

ILO Emblem A426

1969, May 22 Photo. *Perf. 12x11½*

1974	A426	1fo car lake & lake	.20	.20

50th anniv. of the ILO.

Black Pigs, by Paul Gauguin A427

French Paintings: 60f, These Women, by Toulouse-Lautrec, horiz. 1fo, Venus in the Clouds, by Simon Vouet. 2fo, Lady with Fan, by Edouard Manet, horiz. 3fo, La Petra Camara (dancer), by Théodore Chassériau. 4fo, The Cowherd, by Constant Troyon, horiz. 5fo, The Wrestlers, by Gustave Courbet. 10fo, Pomona, by Nicolas Fouché.

1969, May 28 Photo. *Perf. 12½*

1975	A427	40f multicolored	.20	.20
1976	A427	60f multicolored	.20	.20
1977	A427	1fo multicolored	.20	.20
1978	A427	2fo multicolored	.30	.20
1979	A427	3fo multicolored	.50	.20
1980	A427	4fo multicolored	.70	.25
1981	A427	5fo multicolored	1.00	.50
		Nos. 1975-1981 (7)	3.10	1.75

Miniature Sheet

1982	A427	10fo multicolored	3.25	3.00

Art treasures in the Budapest Museum of Fine Arts. No. 1982 contains one 40x62mm stamp.

Hotel Budapest A428

Budapest Post Office 100 A429

1969, May Photo. *Perf. 11*

1983	A428	1fo brown	.20	.20

Coil Stamps

1970, Aug. 3 *Perf. 14*

1983B	A429	40f gray	.30	.20
1983a	A428	1fo brown	.40	.20

Yellow control number on back of every 5th stamp.

Arms and Buildings of Vac A430

Towns of the Danube Bend: 1fo, Szentendre. 1.20fo, Visegrad. 3fo, Esztergom.

1969, June 9 Litho. *Perf. 12*

1984	A430	40f multi	.20	.20
a.		Bklt. pane, #1985, 1987, 4 #1984	2.75	
b.		Bklt. pane, #1986, 3 #1984, 2 #1985	2.75	
1985	A430	1fo multi	.20	.20
1986	A430	1.20fo multi	.20	.20
1987	A430	3fo multi	.30	.25
		Nos. 1984-1987 (4)	.90	.85

Stamps in booklet panes Nos. 1984a-1984b come in two arrangements.

"PAX" and Men Holding Hands — A431

1969, June 17 Photo. *Perf. 11½x12*

1988	A431	1fo lt bl, dk bl & gold	.20	.20

20th anniversary of Peace Movement.

The Scholar, by Rembrandt A432

1969, Sept. 15 *Perf. 11½x12*

1989	A432	1fo sepia	.20	.20

Issued to publicize the 22nd International Congress of Art Historians, Budapest.

Fossilized Zelkova Leaves — A433

1969, Sept. 21 Photo.

Designs: 60f, Greenockit calcite sphalerite crystals. 1fo, Fossilized fish, clupea hungarica. 1.20fo, Quartz crystals. 2fo, Ammonite. 3fo, Copper. 4fo, Fossilized turtle, placochelys placodonta. 5fo, Cuprite crystals.

1990	A433	40f red, gray & sep	.20	.20
1991	A433	60f violet, yel & blk	.20	.20
1992	A433	1fo blue, tan & brn	.20	.20
1993	A433	1.20fo emer, gray & lil	.20	.20
1994	A433	2fo olive, tan & brn	.20	.20
1995	A433	3fo orange, brt & dk grn	.30	.20
1996	A433	4fo dull blk grn, brn & blk	.55	.30
1997	A433	5fo multicolored	.90	.40
		Nos. 1990-1997 (8)	2.75	1.90

Centenary of the Hungarian State Institute of Geology.

Steeplechase — A434

Designs: 60f, Fencing. 1fo, Pistol shooting. 2fo, Swimmers at start. 3fo, Relay race. 5fo, Pentathlon.

1969, Sept. 15 Photo. *Perf. 12x11½*

1998	A434	40f blue & multi	.20	.20
1999	A434	60f multi	.20	.20
2000	A434	1fo multi	.20	.20
2001	A434	2fo violet & multi	.30	.20
2002	A434	3fo lemon & multi	.50	.30
2003	A434	5fo bluish grn, gold & dk red	.75	.50
		Nos. 1998-2003 (6)	2.15	1.60

Hungarian Pentathion Championships.

First Hungarian Postal Card — A435

1969, Oct. 1

2004	A435	60f ver & ocher	.20	.20

Centenary of the postal card. Hungary and Austria both issued cards in 1869.

Mahatma Gandhi — A436

1969, Oct. 1 *Perf. 11½x12*

2005	A436	5fo green & multi	1.25	.70

Mohandas K. Gandhi (1869-1948), leader in India's fight for independence.

World Trade Union Emblem A437

1969, Oct. 17 Photo. *Perf. 12x11½*

2006	A437	2fo fawn & dk blue	.30	.20

Issued to publicize the 7th Congress of the World Federation of Trade Unions.

Janos Balogh Nagy, Self-portrait A438

1969, Oct. 17 *Perf. 11½x12*

2007	A438	5fo gold & multi	1.50	.80

Janos Balogh Nagy (1874-1919), painter.

St. John the Evangelist, by Anthony Van Dyck — A439

Dutch Paintings: 60f, Three Fruit Pickers (by Pieter de Molyn?). 1fo, Boy Lighting Pipe, by Hendrick Terbrugghen. 2fo, The Feast, by Jan Steen. 3fo, Woman Reading Letter, by Pieter de Hooch. 4fo, The Fiddler, by Dirk Hals. 5fo, Portrait of Jan Asselyn, by Frans Hals. 10fo, Mucius Scaevola before Porsena, by Rubens and Van Dyck.

1969-70 Photo. *Perf. 12½*

2008	A439	40f multi	.20	.20
2009	A439	60f multi	.20	.20
2010	A439	1fo multi	.20	.20
2011	A439	2fo multi	.25	.20
2012	A439	3fo multi	.40	.20
2013	A439	4fo multi	.50	.30
2014	A439	5fo multi	1.00	.50
		Nos. 2008-2014 (7)	2.75	1.80

Miniature Sheet

2015	A439	10fo multi	3.25	3.25

Treasures in the Museum of Fine Arts, Budapest and the Museum in Eger.

Issued: 40f-5fo, 12/2/69; 10fo, 1/70.

Kiskunfelegyhaza Circling Pigeon — A440

1969, Dec. 12 Photo. *Perf. 11½x12*

2016	A440	1fo multicolored	.20	.20

Issued to publicize the International Pigeon Show, Budapest, Dec. 1969.

Subway A441

1970, Apr. 3 Photo. *Perf. 12*

2017	A441	1fo blk, lt grn & ultra	.20	.20

Opening of new Budapest subway.

Souvenir Sheet

Panoramic View of Budapest 1945 and 1970, and Soviet Cenotaph — A442

Illustration reduced.

1970, Apr. 3 ***Perf. 12x11½***

2018	A442	Sheet of 2	2.75	2.50
a.		5fo "1945"	1.00	1.00
b.		5fo "1970"	1.00	1.00

25th anniv. of the liberation of Budapest.

Cloud Formation, Satellite, Earth and Receiving Station — A443

1970, Apr. 8 **Litho.** ***Perf. 12***

2019 A443 1fo dk bl, yel & blk .20 .20

Centenary of the Hungarian Meteorological Service.

Lenin Statue, Budapest — A444

Design: 2fo, Lenin portrait.

1970, Apr. 22 **Photo.** ***Perf. 11***

2020	A444	1fo gold & multi	.20	.20
2021	A444	2fo gold & multi	.20	.20

Lenin (1870-1924), Russian communist leader.

Franz Lehar and "Giuditta" Music — A445

1970, Apr. 30 **Photo.** ***Perf. 12***

2022 A445 2fo multicolored .50 .20

Franz Lehar (1870-1948), composer.

Samson and Delilah, by Michele Rocca A446

Paintings: 60f, Joseph Telling Dream, by Giovanni Battista Langetti. 1fo, Clio, by Pierre Mignard. 1.50fo, Venus and Satyr, by Sebastiano Ricci, horiz. 2.50fo, Andromeda, by Francesco Furini. 4fo, Venus, Adonis and Cupid, by Luca Giordano. 5fo, Allegorical Feast, by Corrado Giaquinto. 10fo, Diana and Callisto, by Abraham Janssens, horiz.

1970, June 2 **Photo.** ***Perf. 12½***

2023	A446	40f	gold & multi	.20	.20
2024	A446	60f	gold & multi	.20	.20
2025	A446	1fo	gold & multi	.20	.20
2026	A446	1.50fo	gold & multi	.25	.20
2027	A446	2.50fo	gold & multi	.30	.20
2028	A446	4fo	gold & multi	.60	.30
2029	A446	5fo	gold & multi	.75	.50
	Nos. 2023-2029 (7)			2.50	1.80

Miniature Sheet

Perf. 11

2030 A446 10fo gold & multi 3.50 3.00

No. 2030 contains one 63x46mm horizontal stamp.

Beethoven Statue, by Janos Pasztor, at Martonvasar A447

1970, June 27 **Litho.** ***Perf. 12***

2031 A447 1fo plum, gray grn & org yel .75 .20

Ludwig van Beethoven, composer. The music in the design is from his Sonatina No. 1.

Foundryman A448

King Stephen I — A449

1970, July 28 **Litho.** ***Perf. 12***

2032 A448 1fo multicolored .25 .20

200th anniversary of the first Hungarian steel foundry at Diosgyor, now the Lenin Metallurgical Works.

1970, Aug. 19 **Photo.** ***Perf. 11½x12***

2033 A449 3fo multicolored 1.00 .50

Millenary of the birth of Saint Stephen, first King of Hungary.

Women's Four on Lake Tata and Tata Castle — A450

1970, Aug. 19 **Litho.** ***Perf. 12***

2034 A450 1fo multicolored .35 .20

17th European Women's Rowing Championships, Lake Tata.

Mother Giving Bread to her Children, FAO Emblem — A451

1970, Sept. 21 **Litho.** ***Perf. 12***

2035 A451 1fo lt blue & multi .20 .20

7th European Regional Cong. of the UNFAO, Budapest, Sept. 21-25.

Boxing and Olympic Rings A452

Designs (Olympic Rings and): 60f, Canoeing. 1fo, Fencing. 1.50fo, Water polo. 2fo, Woman gymnast. 2.50fo, Hammer throwing. 3fo, Wrestling. 5fo, Swimming, butterfly stroke.

1970, Sept. 26 **Photo.** ***Perf. 11***

2036	A452	40f	lt violet & multi	.20	.20
2037	A452	60f	sky blue & multi	.20	.20
2038	A452	1fo	orange & multi	.20	.20
2039	A452	1.50fo	multi	.20	.20
2040	A452	2fo	multi	.25	.20
2041	A452	2.50fo	multi	.30	.20
2042	A452	3fo	multi	.40	.25
2043	A452	5fo	multi	.60	.40
	Nos. 2036-2043 (8)			2.35	1.85

75th anniv. of the Hungarian Olympic Committee. The 5fo also publicizes the 1972 Olympic Games in Munich.

Flame and Family A453

1970, Sept. 28 **Litho.** ***Perf. 12***

2044 A453 1fo ultra, org & emer .20 .20

5th Education Congress, Budapest.

Chalice, by Benedek Suky, 1440 — A454

Hungarian Goldsmiths' Art: 60f, Altar burette, 1500. 1fo, Nadasdy goblet, 16th century. 1.50fo, Coconut goblet, 1600. 2fo, Silver tankard, by Mihaly Toldalaghy, 1623. 2.50fo, Communion cup of Gyorgy Rakoczy I, 1670. 3fo, Tankard, 1690. 4fo, Bell-flower cup, 1710.

1970, Oct. **Photo.** ***Perf. 12***

2045	A454	40f	gold & multi	.20	.20
2046	A454	60f	gold & multi	.20	.20
2047	A454	1fo	gold & multi	.20	.20
2048	A454	1.50fo	gold & multi	.20	.20
2049	A454	2fo	gold & multi	.20	.20
2050	A454	2.50fo	gold & multi	.25	.20
2051	A454	3fo	gold & multi	.40	.30
2052	A454	4fo	gold & multi	.60	.40
	Nos. 2045-2052 (8)			2.25	1.90

Virgin and Child, by Giampietrino — A455

Paintings from Christian Museum, Esztergom: 60f, "Love" (woman with 3 children), by Gregorio Lazzarini. 1fo, Legend of St. Catherine, by Master of Bat. 1.50fo, Adoration of the Shepherds, by Francesco Fontebasso, horiz. 2.50fo, Adoration of the Kings, by Master of Aranyosmarot. 4fo, Temptation of St. Anthony the Hermit, by Jan de Cock. 5fo, St. Sebastian, by Marco Palmezzano. 10fo, Lady with the Unicorn, by Painter of Lombardy.

1970, Dec. 7 **Photo.** ***Perf. 12½***

2053	A455	40f	silver & multi	.20	.20
2054	A455	60f	silver & multi	.20	.20
2055	A455	1fo	silver & multi	.20	.20
2056	A455	1.50fo	silver & multi	.20	.20
2057	A455	2.50fo	silver & multi	.40	.20
2058	A455	4fo	silver & multi	.65	.30
2059	A455	5fo	silver & multi	.90	.40
	Nos. 2053-2059 (7)			2.75	1.70

Souvenir Sheet

2060 A455 10fo silver & multi 3.00 2.75

No. 2060 contains one 50½x56mm stamp.

Monument to Hungarian Martyrs, by A. Makrisz — A456

1970, Dec. 30 **Photo.** ***Perf. 12x11½***

2061 A456 1fo ultra & sepia .20 .20

The 25th anniversary of the liberation of the concentration camps at Auschwitz, Mauthausen and Dachau.

"Souvenir Sheets"

Beginning in 1971, the government stamp agency, as well as a number of other state sanctioned organizations, have created souvenir sheets that do not have postal validity. These are not listed in this catalogue.

Marseillaise, by Francois Rude — A457

1971, Mar. 18 **Litho.** ***Perf. 12***

2062 A457 3fo bister & green .40 .20

Centenary of the Paris Commune.

Béla Bartók (1881-1945), Composer
A458

1971

Design: No. 2064, András L. Achim (1871-1911), peasant leader.

2063 A458 1fo gray & dk car .55 .20
2064 A458 1fo gray & green .20 .20

Issued: #2063, Mar. 25; #2064, Apr. 17.

Györ Castle, 1594
A459

1971, Mar. 27
2065 A459 2fo lt blue & multi .40 .20

700th anniversary of Györ.

Bison Hunt — A460

Designs: 60f, Wild boar hunt. 80f, Deer hunt. 1fo, Falconry. 1.20fo, Felled stag and dogs. 2fo, Bustards. 3fo, Net fishing. 4fo, Angling.

1971, May Photo. *Perf. 12*
2066 A460 40f ver & multi .20 .20
2067 A460 60f plum & multi .20 .20
2068 A460 80f multi .20 .20
2069 A460 1fo lilac & multi .20 .20
2070 A460 1.20fo multi .25 .20
2071 A460 2fo multi .25 .20
2072 A460 3fo multi .40 .30
2073 A460 4fo green & multi .55 .40
Nos. 2066-2073 (8) 2.25 1.90

World Hunting Exhibition, Budapest, Aug. 27-30. See No. C313.

Souvenir Sheet

Portrait of a Man, by Dürer — A461

1971, May 21 *Perf. 12½*
2074 A461 10fo gold & multi 2.75 2.50

Albrecht Dürer (1471-1528), German painter and etcher.

Carnation and Pioneers' Emblem — A462

1971, June 2 Photo. *Perf. 12*
2075 A462 1fo dark red & multi .20 .20

Hungarian Pioneers' Organization, 25th anniv.

FIR Emblem, Resistance Fighters — A463

1971, July 3
2076 A463 1fo brown & multi .20 .20

International Federation of Resistance Fighters (FIR), 20th anniversary.

Walking in Garden, Tokyo School
A464

Japanese Prints from Museum of East Asian Art, Budapest: 60f, Geisha in Boat, by Yeishi (1756-1829). 1fo, Woman with Scroll, by Yeishi. 1.50fo, Courtesans, by Kiyonaga (1752-1815). 2fo, Awabi Fisher Women, by Utamaro (1753-1806). 2.50fo, Seated Courtesan, by Harunobu (1725-1770). 3fo, Peasant Woman Carrying Fagots, by Hokusai (1760-1849). 4fo, Women and Girls Walking, by Yeishi.

1971, July 9 *Perf. 12½*
2077 A464 40f gold & multi .20 .20
2078 A464 60f gold & multi .20 .20
2079 A464 1fo gold & multi .20 .20
2080 A464 1.50fo gold & multi .20 .20
2081 A464 2fo gold & multi .25 .20
2082 A464 2.50fo gold & multi .30 .20
2083 A464 3fo gold & multi .50 .25
2084 A464 4fo gold & multi .75 .45
Nos. 2077-2084 (8) 2.60 1.90

Locomotive, Map of Rail System and Danube — A465

1971, July 15 Litho. *Perf. 12*
2086 A465 1fo multi .30 .20

125th anniversary of first Hungarian railroad between Pest and Vac.

Griffin Holding Ink Balls
A466

1971, Sept. 11 Photo. *Perf. 12x11½*
2087 A466 1fo multicolored 1.00 .75

Centenary of stamp printing in Hungary. Printed se-tenant with 2 labels showing printing presses of 1871 and 1971 and Hungary Nos. P1 and 1171. Value unused, $1.

OIJ Emblem and Printed Page — A467

1971, Sept. 21 *Perf. 11½x12*
2088 A467 1fo dk bl, bl & gold .25 .20

25th anniversary of the International Organization of Journalists (OIJ).

Josef Jacob Winterl and Barren Strawberry — A468

Plants: 60f, Bromeliaceae. 80f, Titanopsis calcarea. 1fo, Periwinkle. 1.20fo, Gymnocalycium. 2fo, White water lily. 3fo, Iris arenaria. 5fo, Peony.

1971, Oct. 29 Litho. *Perf. 12*
2089 A468 40f lt vio & multi .20 .20
2090 A468 60f gray & multi .20 .20
2091 A468 80f multi .20 .20
2092 A468 1fo multi .20 .20
2093 A468 1.20fo lilac & multi .20 .20
2094 A468 2fo gray & multi .30 .20
2095 A468 3fo multi .50 .25
2096 A468 5fo multi .75 .40
Nos. 2089-2096 (8) 2.55 1.85

Bicentenary of Budapest Botanical Gardens.

Galloping — A469

Equestrian Sports: 60f, Trotting. 80f, Horses fording river. 1fo, Jumping. 1.20fo, Start. 2fo, Polo. 3fo, Steeplechase. 5fo, Dressage.

1971, Nov. 22 Photo. *Perf. 12*
2097 A469 40f blue & multi .20 .20
2098 A469 60f ocher & multi .20 .20
2099 A469 80f olive & multi .20 .20
2100 A469 1fo red & multi .20 .20
2101 A469 1.20fo multi .25 .20
2102 A469 2fo multi .30 .20
2103 A469 3fo violet & multi .50 .30
2104 A469 5fo blue & multi .75 .50
Nos. 2097-2104 (8) 2.60 2.00

Beheading of Heathen Chief Koppany
A470

Designs: 60f, Samuel Aba pursuing King Peter. 1fo, Basarad's victory over King Charles Robert. 1.50fo, Strife between King Salomon and Prince Geza. 2.50fo, Founding of Obuda Church by King Stephen I and Queen Gisela. 4fo, Reconciliation of King Koloman and his brother Almos. 5fo, Oradea Church built by King Ladislas I. 10fo, Funeral of Prince Emeric and blinding of Vazul.

1971, Dec. 10 Litho.
2105 A470 40f buff & multi .20 .20
2106 A470 60f buff & multi .20 .20
2107 A470 1fo buff & multi .20 .20
2108 A470 1.50fo buff & multi .20 .20
2109 A470 2.50fo buff & multi .25 .20
2110 A470 4fo buff & multi .50 .30
2111 A470 5fo buff & multi .75 .50
Nos. 2105-2111 (7) 2.30 1.80

Miniature Sheet

Perf. 11½
2112 A470 10fo buff & multi 3.00 2.75

History of Hungary, from miniatures from Illuminated Chronicle of King Louis the Great, c. 1370. No. 2112 contains one stamp (size 44½x52mm).

Equality Year Emblem
A471

1971, Dec. 30 Litho. *Perf. 12*
2113 A471 1fo bister & multi .20 .20

Intl. Year Against Racial Discrimination.

Ice Hockey and Sapporo '72 Emblem — A472

Sport and Sapporo '72 Emblem: 60f, Men's slalom. 80f, Women's figure skating. 1fo, Ski jump. 1.20fo, Long-distance skiing. 2fo, Men's figure skating. 3fo, Bobsledding. 4fo, Biathlon. 10fo, Buddha.

1971, Dec. 30 *Perf. 12*
2114 A472 40f black & multi .20 .20
2115 A472 60f black & multi .20 .20
2116 A472 80f black & multi .20 .20
2117 A472 1fo black & multi .20 .20
2118 A472 1.20fo black & multi .25 .20
2119 A472 2fo black & multi .35 .20
2120 A472 3fo black & multi .50 .30
2121 A472 4fo black & multi .75 .50
Nos. 2114-2121 (8) 2.65 2.00

Souvenir Sheet

Perf. 11½
2122 A472 10fo gold & multi 2.75 2.50

11th Winter Olympic Games, Sapporo, Japan, Feb. 3-13, 1972. No. 2122 contains one 86x48mm stamp.

Hungarian Locomotive — A473

Locomotives: 60f, Germany. 80f, Italy. 1fo, Soviet Union. 1.20fo, Japan. 2fo, Great Britain. 4fo, Austria. 5fo, France.

1972, Feb. 23 Photo. *Perf. 12x11½*

2123	A473	40f multi	.20	.20
2124	A473	60f ocher & multi	.20	.20
2125	A473	80f multi	.20	.20
2126	A473	1fo olive & multi	.20	.20
2127	A473	1.20fo ultra & multi	.35	.30
2128	A473	2fo ver & multi	.20	.20
2129	A473	4fo multi	.50	.25
2130	A473	5fo multi	.90	.45
		Nos. 2123-2130 (8)	2.75	2.00

Janus Pannonius, by Andrea Mantegna A474

1972, Mar. 27 Litho. *Perf. 12*

2131	A474	1fo gold & multi	.25	.20

Janus Pannonius (Johannes Czezmiczei, 1434-1472), humanist and poet.

Mariner 9 — A475

Design: No. 2133, Mars 2 and 3 spacecraft.

1972, Mar. 30 Photo. *Perf. 11½x12*

2132	A475	2fo dk blue & multi	.45	.45
2133	A475	2fo multi	.45	.45
a.		Strip #2132-2133 + label	1.25	1.25

Exploration of Mars by Mariner 9 (US), and Mars 2 and 3 (USSR). Issued in sheets containing 4 each of Nos. 2132-2133 and 4 labels inscribed in Hungarian, Russian and English.

13th Century Church Portal — A476

1972, Apr. 11

2134	A476	3fo greenish black	.40	.20

Centenary of the Society for the Protection of Historic Monuments.

Hungarian Greyhound — A477

Hounds: 60f, Afghan hound (head). 80f, Irish wolfhound. 1.20fo, Borzoi. 2fo, Running greyhound. 4fo, Whippet. 6fo, Afghan hound.

1972, Apr. 14 Litho. *Perf. 12*

2135	A477	40f multi	.20	.20
2136	A477	60f brown & multi	.20	.20
2137	A477	80f multi	.20	.20
2138	A477	1.20fo multi	.20	.20
2139	A477	2fo multi	.30	.20
2140	A477	4fo multi	.70	.20
2141	A477	6fo multi	1.10	.60
		Nos. 2135-2141 (7)	2.90	1.80

József Imre, Emil Grósz, László Blaskovics (Ophthalmologists) — A478

Design: 2fo, Allvar Gullstrand, V. P. Filatov, Jules Gonin, ophthalmologists.

1972, Apr. 17

2142	A478	1fo red, brn & blk	.40	.20
2143	A478	2fo blue, brn & blk	.95	.45

First European Ophthalmologists' Congress, Budapest.

Girl Reading and UNESCO Emblem A479

Roses — A480

1972, May 27 Photo. *Perf. 11½x12*

2144	A479	1fo multicolored	.40	.20

International Book Year 1971.

1972, June 1

2145	A480	1fo multicolored	.40	.20

15th Rose Exhibition, Budapest.

George Dimitrov A481

1972, June 18 Litho. *Perf. 12*

2146	A481	3fo black & multi	.40	.20

90th anniversary, birth of George Dimitrov (1882-1949), communist leader.

Souvenir Sheet

St. Martin and the Beggar, Stained-glass Window — A482

1972, June 20 *Perf. 10½*

2147	A482	10fo multi	2.75	2.50

Belgica 72, International Philatelic Exhibition, Brussels, June 24-July 9.

Gyorgy Dozsa (1474-1514), Peasant Leader — A483

1972, June 25 Photo. *Perf. 11½x12*

2148	A483	1fo red & multi	.20	.20

Olympic Rings, Soccer — A484

Designs (Olympic Rings and): 60f, Water polo. 80f, Javelin, women's. 1fo, Kayak, women's. 1.20fo, Boxing. 2fo, Gymnastics, women's. 5fo, Fencing.

1972, July 15 *Perf. 11*

2149	A484	40f multi	.20	.20
2150	A484	60f multi	.20	.20
2151	A484	80f multi	.20	.20
2152	A484	1fo lilac & multi	.20	.20
2153	A484	1.20fo blue & multi	.20	.20
2154	A484	2fo multi	.40	.25
2155	A484	5fo green & multi	.75	.50
		Nos. 2149-2155,B299 (8)	2.65	2.05

20th Olympic Games, Munich, Aug. 26-Sept. 11. See No. C325.

Prince Geza Selecting Site of Székesfehérvár — A485

Designs: 60f, St. Stephen, first King of Hungary. 80f, Knights (country's defense). 1.20fo, King Stephen dictating to scribe (legal organization). 2fo, Sculptor at work (education). 4fo, Merchants before king (foreign relations). 6fo, View of castle and town of Székesfehérvár, 10th century. 10fo, King Andreas II presenting Golden Bull to noblemen.

1972, Aug. 20 Photo. *Perf. 12*

2156	A485	40f slate & multi	.20	.20
2157	A485	60f multi	.20	.20
2158	A485	80f lilac & multi	.20	.20
2159	A485	1.20fo multi	.20	.20
2160	A485	2fo bister & multi	.40	.20
2161	A485	4fo blue & multi	.55	.25
2162	A485	6fo purple & multi	.75	.50
		Nos. 2156-2162 (7)	2.50	1.75

Souvenir Sheet

Perf. 12½

2163	A485	10fo black & multi	3.00	3.00

Millennium of the town of Székesfehérvár; 750th anniv. of the Golden Bull granting rights to lesser nobility. #2163 contains one 94x45mm stamp.

Parliament, Budapest A486

Design: 6fo, Session room of Parliament.

1972, Aug. 20 Litho.

2164	A486	5fo dk blue & multi	.60	.20
2165	A486	6fo multicolored	.75	.30

Constitution of 1949.

Eger, 17th Century View, and Bottle of Bull's Blood — A487

Design: 2fo, Contemporary view of Tokay and bottle of Tokay Aszu.

1972, Aug. 21 Litho. *Perf. 12*

2166	A487	1fo buff & multi	.30	.20
2167	A487	2fo green & multi	.65	.20

1st World Wine Exhibition, Budapest, Aug. 1972.

Georgikon Emblems, Grain, Potato Flower — A488

1972, Sept. 3

2168	A488	1fo multi	.20	.20

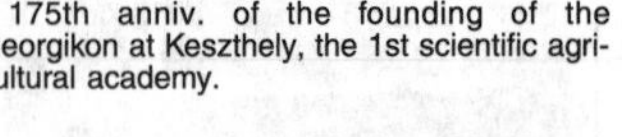

175th anniv. of the founding of the Georgikon at Keszthely, the 1st scientific agricultural academy.

Covered Candy Dish A489

Herend Porcelain: 40f, Vase with bird. 80f, Vase with flowers and butterflies. 1fo, Plate with Mexican landscape. 1.20fo, Covered dish. 2fo, Teapot, cup and saucer. 4fo, Plate with flowers. 5fo, Baroque vase showing Herend factory.

1972, Sept. 15
Sizes: 23x46mm (40f, 80f, 2fo, 5fo); 33x36mm, others

2169	A489	40f gray & multi	.20	.20
2170	A489	60f ocher & multi	.20	.20
2171	A489	80f multi	.20	.20
2172	A489	1fo multi	.20	.20
2173	A489	1.20fo green & multi	.20	.20
2174	A489	2fo multi	.30	.20
2175	A489	4fo red & multi	.50	.30
2176	A489	5fo multi	.70	.50
		Nos. 2169-2176 (8)	2.50	2.00

Herend china factory, founded 1839.

UIC Emblem and M-62 Diesel Locomotive — A490

1972, Sept. 19 Photo. *Perf. 11½x12*

2177	A490	1fo dark red	.35	.20

50th anniversary of International Railroad Union Congress, Budapest, Sept. 19.

"25" and Graph — A491

1972, Sept. *Perf. 11½x12*

2178	A491	1fo yellow & brown	.35	.20

Planned national economy, 25th anniv.

Budapest, 1972 — A492

#2179, View of Obuda, 1872. #2181, Buda, 1872. #2183, Pest, 1872. #2182, 2184, Budapest, 1972.

1972, Sept. 26 *Perf. 12x11½*

2179	A492	1fo Prus bl & rose car	.20	.20
2180	A492	1fo rose car & Prus bl	.20	.20
a.		Pair, #2179-2180	.30	.20
2181	A492	2fo ocher & olive	.30	.20
2182	A492	2fo olive & ocher	.30	.20
a.		Pair, #2181-2182	.60	.35
2183	A492	3fo green & lt brn	.40	.20
2184	A492	3fo lt brown & grn	.40	.20
a.		Pair, #2183-2184	.80	.50
		Nos. 2179-2184 (6)	1.80	1.20

Centenary of unification of Obuda, Buda and Pest into Budapest.

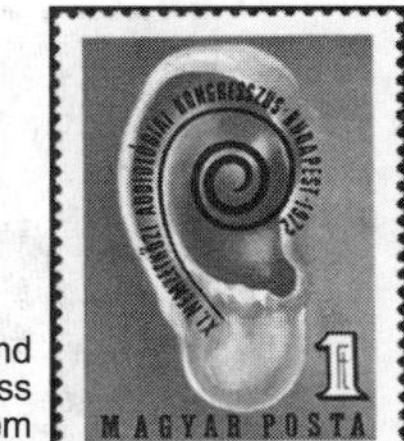

Ear and Congress Emblem A493

1972, Oct. 3 *Perf. 11½x12*

2185	A493	1fo brown, yel & blk	.20	.20

11th Intl. Audiology Cong., Budapest.

Flora Martos — A494

1972 Photo. *Perf. 11½x12*

Portrait: No. 2187, Miklós Radnóti.

2186	A494	1fo green & multi	.20	.20
2187	A494	1fo brown & multi	.20	.20

Flora Martos (1897-1938), Hungarian Labor Party leader, & Miklós Radnóti (1909-44), poet.

Issued: #2186, Nov. 5; #2187, Nov. 11.

Muses, by Jozsef Rippl-Ronai A495

Stained-glass Windows, 19th-20th Centuries: 60f, 16th century scribe, by Ferenc Sebesteny. 1fo, Flight into Egypt, by Karoly Lotz and Bertalan Székely. 1.50fo, Prince Arpad's Messenger, by Jenö Percz. 2.50fo, Nativity, by Lili Sztehlo. 4fo, Prince Arpad and Leaders, by Karoly Kernstock. 5fo, King Matthias and Jester, by Jenö Haranghy.

1972, Nov. 15 *Perf. 12*

2188	A495	40f multi	.20	.20
2189	A495	60f multi	.20	.20
2190	A495	1fo multi	.20	.20
2191	A495	1.50fo multi	.20	.20
2192	A495	2.50fo multi	.35	.20
2193	A495	4fo multi	.65	.30
2194	A495	5fo multi	1.10	.50
		Nos. 2188-2194 (7)	2.90	1.80

Weaver, Cloth and Cogwheel — A496

1972, Nov. 27 Litho. *Perf. 12*

2195	A496	1fo silver & multi	.25	.20

Opening of Museum of Textile Techniques, Budapest.

Main Square, Szarvas — A497

Designs: 1fo, Modern buildings, Salgotarjan. 3fo, Tokay and vineyard. 4fo, Esztergom Cathedral. 7fo, Town Hall, Kaposvar. 20fo, Veszprem.

1972 Litho. *Perf. 11*

2196	A497	40f brown & orange	.20	.20
2197	A497	1fo dk & lt blue	.20	.20

Church and City Hall, Vac — A498

1973 *Perf. 12x11½*

2198	A498	3fo dk & lt green	.40	.20
2199	A498	4fo red brn & org	.50	.20
2200	A498	7fo blue vio & lil	1.00	.20
2200A	A498	20fo multicolored	2.50	.40
		Nos. 2196-2200A (6)	4.80	1.40

See Nos. 2330-2335.

Coil Stamps
Type of 1963-64

Designs as before.

1972, Nov. Photo. *Perf. 14*
Size: 21½x17½mm, 17½x21½mm

2201	A336	2fo blue green	.40	.20
2202	A336	3fo dark blue	.55	.20
2203	A336	4fo blue, vert.	.75	.25
2204	A336	6fo bister	1.10	.35
		Nos. 2201-2204 (4)	2.80	1.00

Black control number on back of every 5th stamp.

Minute inscription centered in lower margin: "Legrady Sandor."

Arms of Soviet Union — A498a

1972, Dec. 30 Photo. *Perf. 11½x12*

2205	A498a	1fo multicolored	.20	.20

50th anniversary of Soviet Union.

Petöfi Speaking at Pilvax Cafe A499

2fo, Portrait. 3fo, Petöfi on horseback, 1848-49.

1972, Dec. 30 Engr. *Perf. 12*

2206	A499	1fo rose carmine	.20	.20
2207	A499	2fo violet	.35	.20
2208	A499	3fo Prus green	.45	.25
		Nos. 2206-2208 (3)	1.00	.65

Sesquicentennial of the birth of Sandor Petöfi (1823-49), poet and revolutionary.

Postal Zone Map of Hungary and Letter-carrying Crow — A500

1973, Jan. 1 Litho. *Perf. 12*

2209	A500	1fo red & black	.20	.20

Introduction of postal code system.

Imre Madách (1823-64), Poet and Dramatist A501

1973, Jan. 20 Photo. *Perf. 11½x12*

2210	A501	1fo multicolored	.20	.20

Busho Mask — A502

Designs: Various Busho masks.

1973, Feb. 17 Litho. *Perf. 12*

2211	A502	40f tan & multi	.20	.20
2212	A502	60f dull grn & multi	.20	.20
2213	A502	80f lilac & multi	.20	.20
2214	A502	1.20fo multi	.20	.20
2215	A502	2fo tan & multi	.30	.20
2216	A502	4fo multi	.50	.30
2217	A502	6fo lilac & multi	.75	.40
		Nos. 2211-2217 (7)	2.35	1.70

Busho Walk at Mohacs, ancient ceremony to drive out winter.

Nicolaus Copernicus A503

1973, Feb. 19 Engr. *Perf. 12*

2218	A503	3fo bright ultra	.75	.50

Printed with alternating label showing heliocentric system and view of Torun.

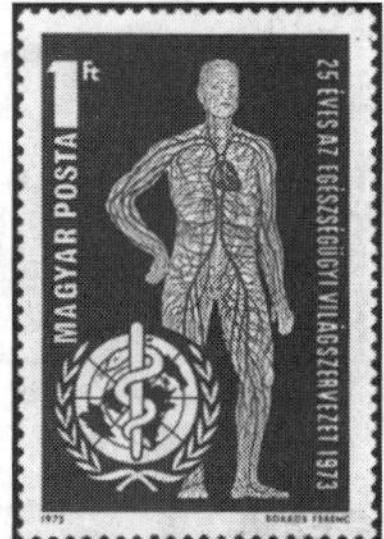

Vascular System and WHO Emblem
A504

1973, Apr. 16 Photo. *Perf. 12*

2219 A504 1fo sl grn & brn red .25 .20

25th anniv. of WHO.

Tank, Rocket, Radar, Plane, Ship and Soldier
A505

1973, May 9 Litho. *Perf. 12*

2220 A505 3fo blue & multi .40 .20

Philatelic Exhibition of Military Stamp Collectors of Warsaw Treaty Member States. No. 2220 was printed with alternating label showing flags of Warsaw Treaty members.

Hungary No. 1396 and IBRA '73 Emblem — A506

1973, May 11 Litho. *Perf. 12*

2221 A506 40f shown .20 .20
2222 A506 60f No. 1397, POLSKA '73 .20 .20
2223 A506 80f No. 1398, IBRA '73 .20 .20
2224 A506 1fo No. 1399, POLSKA .20 .20
2225 A506 1.20fo No. B293a, IBRA .20 .20
2226 A506 2fo No. B293b, POLSKA .25 .20
2227 A506 4fo No. B293c, IBRA .50 .30
2228 A506 5fo No. B293d, POLSKA .75 .40
Nos. 2221-2228 (8) 2.50 1.90

Publicity for IBRA '73 International Philatelic Exhibition, Munich, May 11-20; and POLSKA '73, Poznan, Aug. 15-Sept. 2. See No. C345.

Typesetting, from "Orbis Pictus," by Comenius
A507

3fo, Printer & wooden screw press, woodcut from Hungarian translation of Gospels.

1973, June 5 Photo. *Perf. 11½x12*

2229 A507 1fo black & gold .20 .20
2230 A507 3fo black & gold .40 .20

500th anniv. of book printing in Hungary.

Storm over Hortobagy Puszta, by Csontvary — A508

Paintings: 60f, Mary's Well, Nazareth. 1fo, Carriage Ride by Moonlight in Athens, vert. 1.50fo, Pilgrimage to Cedars of Lebanon, vert. 2.50fo, The Lonely Cedar. 4fo, Waterfall at Jajce. 5fo, Ruins of Greek Theater at Taormina. 10fo, Horseback Riders on Shore.

1973, June 18 *Perf. 12½*

2231 A508 40f gold & multi .20 .20
2232 A508 60f gold & multi .20 .20
2233 A508 1fo gold & multi .20 .20
2234 A508 1.50fo gold & multi .20 .20
2235 A508 2.50fo gold & multi .40 .20
2236 A508 4fo gold & multi .65 .35
2237 A508 5fo gold & multi .80 .50
Nos. 2231-2237 (7) 2.65 1.85

Souvenir Sheet

2238 A508 10fo gold & multi 3.50 3.00

Paintings by Tividar Kosztka Csontvary (1853-1919). No. 2238 contains one stamp (size: 90x43mm).

Hands Holding Map of Europe — A509

Flowers — A510

1973, July 3 Photo. *Perf. 11½x12*

2239 A509 2.50fo blk & gldn brn 3.00 3.00
a. Souv. sheet of 4 + 2 labels 10.00 9.00

Conference for European Security and Cooperation. Helsinki, July 1973. No. 2239 was printed in souvenir sheet of 4 stamps and 2 blue labels showing conference sites.

1973, Aug. 4

2240 A510 40f Provence roses .20 .20
2241 A510 60f Cyclamen .20 .20
2242 A510 80f Lungwort .20 .20
2243 A510 1.20fo English daisies .20 .20
2244 A510 2fo Buttercups .30 .20
2245 A510 4fo Violets .70 .30
2246 A510 6fo Poppies 1.00 .50
Nos. 2240-2246 (7) 2.80 1.80

"Let's be Friends in Traffic" — A511

Designs: 60f, "Not even one drink." 1fo, "Light your bicycle."

1973, Aug. 18 Photo. *Perf. 12x11½*

2247 A511 40f green & orange .20 .20
2248 A511 60f purple & orange .20 .20
2249 A511 1fo indigo & orange .20 .20
Nos. 2247-2249 (3) .60 .60

To publicize traffic rules.

Adoration of the Kings
A512

Paintings: 60f, Angels playing violin and lute. 1fo, Adoration of the Kings. 1.50fo, Annunciation. 2.50fo, Angels playing organ and harp. 4fo, Visitation of Mary. 5fo, Legend of St. Catherine of Alexandria. 10fo, Nativity.

1973, Nov. 3 Photo. *Perf. 12½*

2250 A512 40f gold & multi .20 .20
2251 A512 60f gold & multi .20 .20
2252 A512 1fo gold & multi .20 .20
2253 A512 1.50fo gold & multi .25 .20
2254 A512 2.50fo gold & multi .40 .25
2255 A512 4fo gold & multi .60 .30
2256 A512 5fo gold & multi .80 .50
Nos. 2250-2256 (7) 2.65 1.85

Souvenir Sheet

Perf. 11

2257 A512 10fo gold & multi 3.00 2.75

Paintings by Hungarian anonymous early masters from the Christian Museum at Esztergom. No. 2257 contains one 49x74mm stamp.

Mihaly Csokonai Vitez — A513

1973, Nov. 17 Photo. *Perf. 11½x12*

2258 A513 2fo bister & multi .35 .20

Mihaly Csokonai Vitez (1773-1805), poet.

José Marti and Cuban Flag — A514

1973, Nov. 30

2259 A514 1fo dk brn, red & bl .20 .20

Marti (1853-95), Cuban natl. hero and poet.

Barnabas Pesti (1920-44), Member of Hungarian Underground Communist Party — A515

1973, Nov. 30

2260 A515 1fo blue, brn & buff .20 .20

Women's Double Kayak — A516

Designs: 60f, Water polo. 80f, Men's single kayak. 1.20fo, Butterfly stroke. 2fo, Men's fours kayak. 4fo, Men's single canoe. 6fo, Men's double canoe.

1973, Dec. 29 Litho. *Perf. 12x11*

2261 A516 40f red & multi .20 .20
2262 A516 60f blue & multi .20 .20
2263 A516 80f multicolored .20 .20
2264 A516 1.20fo green & multi .25 .20
2265 A516 2fo car & multi .35 .20
2266 A516 4fo violet & multi .45 .30
2267 A516 6fo multicolored .50 .50
Nos. 2261-2267 (7) 2.15 1.80

Hungarian victories in water sports at Tampere and Belgrade.

Souvenir Sheet

Map of Europe — A517

1974, Jan. 15 Photo. *Perf. 12x11½*

2268 Sheet of 2 + label 8.50 8.00
a. A517 5fo multicolored 2.25 2.25

European Peace Conference (Arab-Israeli War), Geneva, Jan. 1974.

Lenin — A518

1974, Jan. 21 Photo. *Perf. 11½x12*

2269 A518 2fo gold, dull bl & brn .25 .20

50th anniv. of the death of Lenin (1870-1924).

Jozsef Boczor, Imre Békés, Tamás Elek — A519

1974, Feb. 21 *Perf. 12½*

2270 A519 3fo brown & multi .25 .20

30th anniversary of the death in France of Hungarian resistance fighters.

Comecon Building, Moscow and Flags
A520

1974, Feb. 26 Photo. *Perf. 12x11½*

2271 A520 1fo multicolored .25 .20

25th anniversary of the Council of Mutual Economic Assistance.

Bank Emblem, Coins and Banknote A521

1974, Mar. 1 *Perf. 11½x12*
2272 A521 1fo lt green & multi .25 .20

25th anniversary of the State Savings Bank.

Spacecraft on Way to Mars — A522

Designs: 60f, Mars 2 over Mars. 80f, Mariner 4. 1fo, Mars and Mt. Palomar Observatory. 1.20fo, Soft landing of Mars 3. 5fo, Mariner 9 with Mars satellites Phobos and Deimos.

1974, Mar. 11 **Photo.** *Perf. 12½*

2273	A522	40f	gold & multi	.20	.20
2274	A522	60f	silver & multi	.20	.20
2275	A522	80f	gold & multi	.20	.20
2276	A522	1fo	silver & multi	.20	.20
2277	A522	1.20fo	gold & multi	.25	.20
2278	A522	5fo	silver & multi	.75	.40
	Nos. 2273-2278,C347 (7)			2.55	1.90

Exploration of Mars. See No. C348.

Salvador Allende (1908-73), Pres. of Chile — A523

1974, Mar. 27 **Photo.** *Perf. 11½x12*
2279 A523 1fo black & multi .20 .20

Mona Lisa, by Leonardo da Vinci A524

1974, Apr. 19 *Perf. 12½*
2280 A524 4fo gold & multi 6.25 6.00

Exhibition of the Mona Lisa in Asia.
Printed in sheets of 6 stamps and 6 labels with commemorative inscription. Value, $45.

Souvenir Sheet

Issue of 1874 and Flowers — A525

a, Mallow. b, Aster. c, Daisy. d, Columbine.

1974, May 11 **Litho.** *Perf. 11½*
2281 A525 Sheet of 4 2.75 2.75
a.-d. 2.50fo any single .50 .50

Centenary of the first issue inscribed "Magyar Posta" (Hungarian Post).

Carrier Pigeon, World Map, UPU Emblem — A526

1974, May 22 **Litho.** *Perf. 12*

2282	A526	40f	shown	.20	.20
2283	A526	60f	Mail coach	.20	.20
2284	A526	80f	Old mail auto-mobile	.20	.20
2285	A526	1.20fo	Balloon post	.20	.20
2286	A526	2fo	Mail train	.35	.20
2287	A526	4fo	Mail bus	.75	.40
	Nos. 2282-2287,C349 (7)			2.65	2.00

Centenary of the Universal Postal Union.

Dove of Basel, Switzerland No. 3L1, 1845 — A527

1974, June 7 **Photo.** *Perf. 11½x12*
2288 A527 3fo gold & multi 1.25 1.25

INTERNABA 1974 Philatelic Exhibition, Basel, June 7-16. No. 2288 issued in sheets of 3 stamps and 3 labels showing Internaba 1974 emblem. Size: 104x125mm.

Chess Players, from 13th Century Manuscript A528

Designs: 60f, Chess players, 15th century English woodcut. 80f, Royal chess party, 15th century Italian chess book. 1.20fo, Chess players, 17th century copper engraving by Selenus. 2fo, Farkas Kempelen's chess playing machine, 1769. 4fo, Hungarian Grand Master Geza Maroczy (1870-1951). 6fo, View of Nice and emblem of 1974 Chess Olympiad.

1974, June 6 **Litho.** *Perf. 12*

2289	A528	40f	multi	.20	.20
2290	A528	60f	multi	.20	.20
2291	A528	80f	multi	.20	.20
2292	A528	1.20fo	multi	.25	.20
2293	A528	2fo	multi	.25	.20
2294	A528	4fo	multi	.70	.30
2295	A528	6fo	multi	1.10	.50
	Nos. 2289-2295 (7)			2.90	1.80

50th anniv. of Intl. Chess Federation and 21st Chess Olympiad, Nice, June 6-30.

Souvenir Sheet

Cogwheel Railroad — A529

Designs: a, Passenger train, 1874. b, Freight train, 1874. c, Electric train, 1929-73. d, Twin motor train, 1973.

1974, June 25 **Litho.** *Perf. 12*
2296 A529 Sheet of 4 3.50 3.25
a.-d. 2.50fo, any single .50 .50

Cent. of Budapest's cogwheel railroad.

Congress Emblem (Globe and Parliament) — A530

1974, Aug. 18 **Photo.** *Perf. 12*
2297 A530 2fo silver, dk & lt bl .35 .20

4th World Congress of Economists, Budapest, Aug. 19-24.

Bathing Woman, by Károly Lotz A531

Paintings of Nudes: 60f, Awakening, by Károly Brocky. 1fo, Venus and Cupid, by Brocky, horiz. 1.50fo, After the Bath, by Lotz. 2.50fo, Resting Woman, by Istvan Csok, horiz. 4fo, After the Bath, by Bertalan Szekely. 5fo, "Devotion," by Erzsebet Korb. 10fo, Lark, by Pál Szinyei Merse.

1974, Aug. *Perf. 12½*

2298	A531	40f	gold & multi	.20	.20
2299	A531	60f	gold & multi	.20	.20
2300	A531	1fo	gold & multi	.20	.20
2301	A531	1.50fo	gold & multi	.30	.20
2302	A531	2.50fo	gold & multi	.35	.20
2303	A531	4fo	gold & multi	.70	.25
2304	A531	5fo	gold & multi	.90	.40
	Nos. 2298-2304 (7)			2.85	1.65

Souvenir Sheet

Perf. 11

2305 A531 10fo gold & multi 3.25 3.00

No. 2305 contains one stamp (45x70mm).

Mimi, by Béla Czóbel A532

1974, Sept. 4
2306 A532 1fo multicolored .40 .20

91st birthday of Béla Czóbel, Hungarian painter.

Intersputnik Tracking Station — A533

High Voltage Line "Peace" and Pipe Line "Friendship" A534

Perf. 11½x12, 12x11½

1974, Sept. 5 **Litho.**
2307 A533 1fo blue & violet .20 .20
2308 A534 3fo multicolored .60 .20

Technical assistance and cooperation between Hungary and USSR, 25th anniv.

Pablo Neruda — A535

1974, Sept. 11 **Photo.** *Perf. 11½x12*
2309 A535 1fo multicolored .20 .20

Pablo Neruda (Neftali Ricar do Reyes, 1904-1973), Chilean poet.

Sweden No. 1 and Lion from Royal Palace, Stockholm A536

1974, Sept. 21 *Perf. 12x11½*
2310 A536 3fo ultra, yel grn & gold 1.25 1.25

Stockholmia 74 Intl. Philatelic Exhibition, Stockholm, Sept. 21-29. No. 2310 issued in sheets of 3 stamps and 3 labels showing Stockholmia emblem. White margin inscribed "UPU" multiple in white. Size: 126x104mm.

Tank Battle and Soldier with Anti-tank Grenade — A537

1974, Sept. 28 Litho. *Perf. 12*
2311 A537 1fo gold, orange & blk .20 .20
Nos. 2311,C351-C352 (3) .90 .60

Army Day.

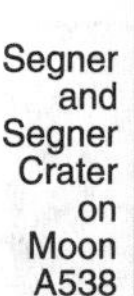

Segner and Segner Crater on Moon A538

1974, Oct. 5
2312 A538 3fo multicolored .60 .25

270th anniversary of the birth of Janos Andras Segner, naturalist. No. 2312 printed se-tenant with label arranged checkerwise in sheet. Label shows Segner wheel.

Rhyparia Purpurata — A539

Lepidoptera: 60f, Melanargia galathea. 80f, Parnassius Apollo. 1fo, Celerio euphorbia. 1.20fo, Catocala fraxini. 5fo, Apatura iris. 6fo, Palaeochrysophanus hyppothoe.

1974, Nov. 11 Photo. *Perf. 12½*
2313 A539 40f multicolored .20 .20
2314 A539 60f violet & multi .20 .20
2315 A539 80f multicolored .20 .20
2316 A539 1fo brown & multi .20 .20
2317 A539 1.20fo blue & multi .25 .25
2318 A539 5fo purple & multi .75 .30
2319 A539 6fo multicolored 1.00 .40
Nos. 2313-2319 (7) 2.80 1.75

Motherhood A540

1974, Dec. 24 Litho. *Perf. 12*
2320 A540 1fo lt blue, blk & yel .25 .20

Robert Kreutz — A541

1974, Dec. 24
2321 A541 1fo shown .20 .20
2322 A541 1fo István Pataki .20 .20

30th death anniv. of anti-fascist martyrs Kreutz (1923-44) and Pataki (1914-44).

Puppy A542

Young Animals: 60f, Siamese kittens, horiz. 80f, Rabbit. 1.20fo, Foal, horiz. 2fo, Lamb. 4fo, Calf, horiz. 6fo, Piglet.

1974, Dec. 30
2323 A542 40f lt blue & multi .20 .20
2324 A542 60f multicolored .20 .20
2325 A542 80f olive & multi .20 .20
2326 A542 1.20fo green & multi .20 .20
2327 A542 2fo brown & multi .30 .20
2328 A542 4fo orange & multi .70 .30
2329 A542 6fo violet & multi 1.10 .50
Nos. 2323-2329 (7) 2.90 1.80

See Nos. 2403-2409.

Building Type of 1972

4fo, Szentendre. 5fo, View of Szolnok across Tisza River. 6fo, Skyscraper, Dunáujváros. 8fo, Chrch and city hall, Vac. 10fo, City Hall, Kiskunfélegyháza. 50fo, Church (Turkish Mosque), Hunyadi Statue & TV tower, Pecs.

1974-80 Litho. *Perf. 12x11½*
2330 A498 4fo red brn & pink .60 .20
2331 A498 5fo dk blue & ultra .75 .20
2332 A498 6fo dk brn & org .90 .20
2333 A498 8fo dk & brt grn 1.25 .20
2334 A498 10fo brown & yel 1.75 .20
2335 A498 50fo multi 6.00 1.25
Nos. 2330-2335 (6) 11.25 2.25

Issued: 8fo, 12/7; 10fo, 50fo, 12/30; 5fo, 3/8/75; 6fo, 6/10/75; 4fo, 6/20/80.

Hospital, Lambarene — A544

60f, Dr. Schweitzer, patient & microscope. 80f, Patient arriving by boat. 1.20fo, Hospital supplies arriving by ship. 2fo, Globe, Red Cross, carrier pigeons. 4fo, Nobel Peace Prize medal. 6fo, Portrait & signature of Dr. Schweitzer, organ pipes & "J. S. Bach."

1975, Jan. 14 Photo. *Perf. 12*
2340 A544 40f gold & multi .20 .20
2341 A544 60f gold & multi .20 .20
2342 A544 80f gold & multi .20 .20
2343 A544 1.20fo gold & multi .20 .20
2344 A544 2fo gold & multi .25 .20
2345 A544 4fo gold & multi .60 .30
2346 A544 6fo lil & multi .80 .45
Nos. 2340-2346 (7) 2.45 1.75

Dr. Albert Schweitzer (1875-1965), medical missionary and musician, birth centenary.

Farkas Bolyai — A545

1975, Feb. 7 Litho. *Perf. 11½x12*
2347 A545 1fo gray & red brown .20 .20

Bolyai (1775-1856), mathematician.

Mihály Károlyi A546

1975, Mar. 4 Litho. *Perf. 12*
2348 A546 1fo lt blue & brown .20 .20

Birth centenary of Count Mihály Károlyi (1875-1955), prime minister, 1918-1919.

Woman, IWY Emblem A547

1975, Mar. 8 *Perf. 12x11½*
2349 A547 1fo aqua & black .20 .20

International Women's Year 1975.

"Let us Build up the Railroads" — A548

Posters: 60f, "Bread starts here." 2fo, "Hungarian Communist Party-a Party of Action." 4fo, "Heavy Industry-secure base of Three-year Plan." 5fo, "Our common interest-a developed socialist society."

1975, Mar. 17 Photo. *Perf. 11*
2350 A548 40f red & multi .20 .20
2351 A548 60f red & multi .20 .20
2352 A548 2fo red & multi .20 .20
2353 A548 4fo red & multi .40 .20
2354 A548 5fo red & multi .50 .30
Nos. 2350-2354 (5) 1.50 1.10

Hungary's liberation from Fascism, 30th anniv.

Arrow, 1915, Pagoda and Mt. Fuji — A549

Antique Cars: 60f, Swift, 1911, Big Ben and Tower of London. 80f, Model T Ford, 1908, Capitol and Statue of Liberty. 1fo, Mercedes, 1901, Towers of Stuttgart. 1.20fo, Panhard Levassor, 1912, Arc de Triomphe and Eiffel Tower. 5fo, Csonka, 1906, Fishermen's Bastion and Chain Bridge. 6fo, Emblems of Hungarian Automobile Club, Alliance Internationale de Tourisme and Federation Internationale de l'Automobile.

1975, Mar. 27 Litho. *Perf. 12*
2355 A549 40f lt blue & multi .20 .20
2356 A549 60f lt green & multi .20 .20
2357 A549 80f pink & multi .20 .20
2358 A549 1fo lilac & multi .20 .20
2359 A549 1.20fo orange & multi .20 .20
2360 A549 5fo ultra & multi .65 .30
2361 A549 6fo lilac rose & multi 1.00 .50
Nos. 2355-2361 (7) 2.65 1.80

Hungarian Automobile Club, 75th anniv.

The Creation of Adam, by Michelangelo — A550

1975, Apr. 23 Photo. *Perf. 12½*
2362 A550 10fo gold & multi 3.50 3.25

Michelangelo Buonarroti (1475-1564), Italian painter, sculptor and architect.

Academy of Science A551

Designs: 2fo, Dates "1975 1825." 3fo, Count Istvan Szechenyi.

1975, May 5 Litho. *Perf. 12*
2363 A551 1fo green & multi .20 .20
2364 A551 2fo green & multi .30 .20
2365 A551 3fo green & multi .50 .30
Nos. 2363-2365 (3) 1.00 .70

Sesquicentennial of Academy of Science, Budapest, founded by Count Istvan Szechenyi.

Emblem of 1980 Olympics and Proposed Moscow Stadium — A553

1975, May 8 Photo. *Perf. 11½x12*
2366 A553 5fo lt blue & multi 1.50 1.25

Socfilex 75 Intl. Philatelic Exhibition, Moscow, 5/8-18. #2366 issued in sheets of 3 stamps and 3 labels showing Socfilex 75 emblem (War Memorial, Berlin-Treptow).

France No. 1100 and Venus of Milo — A554

1975, June 3 Photo. *Perf. 11½x12*
2367 A554 5fo lilac & multi 1.50 1.25

ARPHILA 75 International Philatelic Exhibition, Paris, June 6-16. No. 2367 issued in sheets of 3 stamps and 3 labels showing ARPHILA 75 emblem.

Early Transformer, Kando Locomotive, 1902, Pylon — A555

1975, June 10 Litho. *Perf. 12*
2368 A555 1fo multicolored .30 .20

Hungarian Electrotechnical Association, 75th anniversary.

Epée, Saber, Foil and Globe — A556

1975, July 11
2369 A556 1fo multicolored .25 .20

32nd World Fencing Championships, Budapest, July 11-20.

Souvenir Sheet

Whale Pavilion, Oceanexpo 75 — A557

1975, July 21 Photo. *Perf. 12½*
2370 A557 10fo gold & multi 3.00 2.75

Oceanexpo 75, International Exhibition, Okinawa, July 20, 1975-Jan. 1976.

Dr. Agoston Zimmermann (1875-1963), Veterinarian A558

1975, Sept. 4 Litho. *Perf. 12*
2371 A558 1fo brown & blue .20 .20

Symbolic of 14 Cognate Languages A559

1975, Sept. 9
2372 A559 1fo gold & multi .20 .20

International Finno-Ugrian Congress.

Voters — A560

Design: No. 2374, Map of Hungary with electoral districts.

1975, Oct. 1
2373 A560 1fo multicolored .20 .20
2374 A560 1fo multicolored .20 .20

Hungarian Council System, 25th anniv.

Fish and Waves (Ocean Pollution) A561

Designs: 60f, Skeleton hand reaching for rose in water glass. 80f, Fish gasping for raindrop. 1fo, Carnation wilting in polluted soil. 1.20fo, Bird dying in polluted air. 5fo, Sick human lung and smokestack. 6fo, "Stop Pollution" (raised hand protecting globe from skeleton hand).

1975, Oct. 16 Litho. *Perf. 11½*
2375 A561 40f multi .20 .20
2376 A561 60f multi .20 .20
2377 A561 80f multi .20 .20
2378 A561 1fo multi .20 .20
2379 A561 1.20fo multi .25 .20
2380 A561 5fo multi .60 .30
2381 A561 6fo multi .85 .40
Nos. 2375-2381 (7) 2.50 1.70

Environmental Protection.

Mariska Gárdos (1885-1973) A562

Portraits: No. 2383, Imre Mezö (1905-56). No. 2384, Imre Tarr (1900-37).

1975, Nov. 4 Litho. *Perf. 12*
2382 A562 1fo black & red org .20 .20
2383 A562 1fo black & red org .20 .20
2384 A562 1fo black & red org .20 .20
Nos. 2382-2384 (3) .60 .60

Famous Hungarians, birth anniversaries.

Treble Clef, Organ and Orchestra — A563

1975, Nov. 14
2385 A563 1fo multicolored .40 .20

Franz Liszt Musical Academy, centenary.

Szigetcsep Icon — A564

Virgin and Child, 18th Century Icons: 60f, Graboc. 1fo, Esztergom. 1.50fo, Vatoped. 2.50fo, Tottos. 4fo, Gyor. 5fo, Kazan.

1975, Nov. 25 Photo. *Perf. 12½*
2386 A564 40f gold & multi .20 .20
2387 A564 60f gold & multi .20 .20
2388 A564 1fo gold & multi .20 .20
2389 A564 1.50fo gold & multi .20 .20
2390 A564 2.50fo gold & multi .35 .20
2391 A564 4fo gold & multi .70 .30
2392 A564 5fo gold & multi .90 .60
Nos. 2386-2392 (7) 2.75 1.90

Members' Flags, Radar, Mother and Child — A565

1975, Dec. 15 Litho. *Perf. 12*
2393 A565 1fo multicolored .20 .20

20th anniversary of the signing of the Warsaw Treaty (Bulgaria, Czechoslovakia, German Democratic Rep., Hungary, Poland, Romania, USSR).

Ice Hockey, Winter Olympics' Emblem — A566

Designs (Emblem and): 60f, Slalom. 80f, Ski race. 1.20fo, Ski jump. 2fo, Speed skating. 4fo, Cross-country skiing. 6fo, Bobsled. 10fo, Figure skating, pair.

1975, Dec. 29 Photo. *Perf. 12x11½*
2394 A566 40f silver & multi .20 .20
2395 A566 60f silver & multi .20 .20
2396 A566 80f silver & multi .20 .20
2397 A566 1.20fo silver & multi .20 .20
2398 A566 2fo silver & multi .35 .20
2399 A566 4fo silver & multi .70 .30
2400 A566 6fo silver & multi .90 .50
Nos. 2394-2400 (7) 2.75 1.80

Souvenir Sheet

Perf. 12½

2401 A566 10fo silver & multi 3.25 3.00

12th Winter Olympic Games, Innsbruck, Austria, Feb. 4-15, 1976. No. 2401 contains one stamp (59x36mm).

"P," 5-pengö and 500-pengö Notes — A567

1976, Jan. 16 Litho. *Perf. 12*
2402 A567 1fo multicolored .25 .20

Hungarian Bank Note Co., 50th anniversary.

Animal Type of 1974

Young Animals: 40f, Wild boars, horiz. 60f, Squirrels. 80f, Lynx, horiz. 1.20fo, Wolves. 2fo, Foxes, horiz. 4fo, Bears. 6fo, Lions, horiz.

1976, Jan. 26
2403 A542 40f multi .20 .20
2404 A542 60f blue & multi .20 .20
2405 A542 80f multi .20 .20
2406 A542 1.20fo multi .20 .20
2407 A542 2fo violet & multi .30 .20
2408 A542 4fo yellow & multi .65 .30
2409 A542 6fo multi .75 .40
Nos. 2403-2409 (7) 2.50 1.70

A.G. Bell, Telephone, Molniya I and Radar — A568

1976, Mar. 10 Litho. *Perf. 11½x12*
2410 A568 3fo multicolored .75 .75

Centenary of first telephone call by Alexander Graham Bell, Mar. 10, 1876. Issued in sheets of 4.

Battle of Kuruc-Labantz — A569

Paintings: 60f, Meeting of Rakoczi and Tamas Esze, by Endre Veszprem. 1fo, Diet of Onod, by Mor Than. 2fo, Camp of the Kurucs. 3fo, Ilona Zrinyi (Rakoczi's mother), vert. 4fo, Kuruc officers, vert. 5fo, Prince Francis II Rakoczy, by Adam Manyoki, vert. Painters of 40f, 2fo, 3fo, 4fo, are unknown.

1976, Mar. 27 Photo. *Perf. 12½*
2411 A569 40f gold & multi .20 .20
2412 A569 60f gold & multi .20 .20
2413 A569 1fo gold & multi .30 .20
2414 A569 2fo gold & multi .60 .20
2415 A569 3fo gold & multi .85 .25
2416 A569 4fo gold & multi 1.25 .30
2417 A569 5fo gold & multi 1.60 .50
Nos. 2411-2417 (7) 5.00 1.85

Francis II Rakoczy (1676-1735), leader of Hungarian Protestant insurrection, 300th birth anniversary.

Standard Meter, Hungarian Meter Act — A570

2fo, Istvan Krusper, his vacuum balance, standard kilogram. 3fo, Interferometer & rocket.

1976, Apr. 5 ***Perf. 11½x12***

2418 A570 1fo multicolored .20 .20
2419 A570 2fo multicolored .30 .20
2420 A570 3fo multicolored .50 .30
Nos. 2418-2420 (3) 1.00 .70

Introduction of metric system in Hungary, cent.

US No. 1353 and Independence Hall, Philadelphia — A571

Photogravure and Foil Embossed

1976, May 29 ***Perf. 11½x12***

2421 A571 5fo blue & multi 1.40 1.25

Interphil 76 International Philatelic Exhibition, Philadelphia, Pa., May 29-June 6. No. 2421 issued in sheets of 3 stamps and 3 labels showing bells. Size: 115x125mm.

"30" and Various Pioneer Activities — A572

1976, June 5 Litho. ***Perf. 12***

2422 A572 1fo multicolored .25 .20

Hungarian Pioneers, 30th anniversary.

Trucks, Safety Devices, Trade Union Emblem — A573

1976, June ***Perf. 12½***

2423 A573 1fo multicolored .20 .20

Labor safety.

Intelstat 4, Montreal Olympic Emblem, Canadian Flag — A574

Designs: 60f, Equestrian. 1fo, Butterfly stroke. 2fo, One-man kayak. 3fo, Fencing. 4fo, Javelin. 5fo, Athlete on vaulting horse.

1976, June 29 Photo. ***Perf. 11½x12***

2424 A574 40f dk blue & multi .20 .20
2425 A574 60f slate grn & multi .20 .20
2426 A574 1fo blue & multi .20 .20
2427 A574 2fo green & multi .35 .20
2428 A574 3fo brown & multi .45 .20
2429 A574 4fo bister & multi .60 .30
2430 A574 5fo maroon & multi .75 .40
Nos. 2424-2430 (7) 2.75 1.70

21st Olympic Games, Montreal, Canada, July 17-Aug. 1. See No. C365.

Denmark No. 2 and Mermaid, Copenhagen — A575

1976, Aug. 19 Photo. ***Perf. 11½x12***

2431 A575 3fo multicolored 1.25 1.25

HAFNIA 76 Intl. Phil. Exhib., Copenhagen, Aug. 20-29. No. 2431 issued in sheets of 3 stamps and 3 labels showing HAFNIA emblem.

Souvenir Sheet

Discovery of Body of Lajos II, by Bertalan Székely — A576

1976, Aug. 27 Photo. ***Perf. 12½***

2432 A576 20fo multicolored 3.00 2.75

450th anniversary of the Battle of Mohacs against the Turks.

Flora, by Titian A577

1976, Aug. 27

2433 A577 4fo gold & multi .75 .25

Titian (1477-1576), Venetian painter.

Hussar, Herend China — A578

1976, Sept. 28 Litho. ***Perf. 12***

2434 A578 4fo multicolored .75 .25

Herend China manufacture, sesqui.

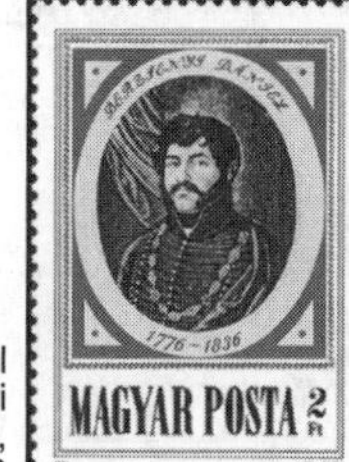

Daniel Berzsenyi (1776-1836), Poet — A579

1976, Sept. 28

2435 A579 2fo black, gold & yel .25 .20

Pal Gyulai (1826-1909), Poet and Historian A580

1976, Sept. 28

2436 A580 2fo orange & black .25 .20

Tuscany No. 1 and Emblem — A581

1976, Oct. 13 Photo. ***Perf. 11½x12***

2437 A581 5fo orange & multi 1.75 1.75

ITALIA 76 International Philatelic Exhibition, Milan, Oct. 14-24. No. 2437 issued in sheets of 3 stamps and 3 labels showing Italia 76 emblem. Size: 106x127mm.

Jozsef Madzsar, M.D. — A582

Labor leaders: No. 2439, Ignac Bogar (1876-1933), secretary of printers' union. No. 2440, Rudolf Golub (1901-44), miner.

1976, Nov. 4 Litho. ***Perf. 12***

2438 A582 1fo deep brown & red .20 .20
2439 A582 1fo deep brown & red .20 .20
2440 A582 1fo deep brown & red .20 .20
Nos. 2438-2440 (3) .60 .60

Science and Culture House, Georgian Dancer, Hungarian and USSR Flags A583

1976, Nov. 4 ***Perf. 12½x12***

2441 A583 1fo multicolored .40 .20

House of Soviet Science and Culture, Budapest, 2nd anniversary.

Koranyi Sanitarium and Statue — A584

1976, Nov. 11 ***Perf. 12***

2442 A584 2fo multicolored .35 .20

Koranyi TB Sanitarium, founded by Dr. Frigyes Koranyi, 75th anniversary.

Locomotive, 1875, Enese Station — A585

Designs: 60f, Steam engine No. 17, 1885, Rabatamasi Station. 1fo, Railbus, 1925, Fertoszentmiklos Station. 2fo, Express steam engine, Kapuvar Station. 3fo, Engine and trailer, 1926, Gyor Station. 4fo, Eight-wheel express engine, 1934, and Fertoboz Station. 5fo, Raba-Balaton engine, Sopron Station.

1976, Nov. 26 Litho. ***Perf. 12***

2443 A585 40f multicolored .20 .20
2444 A585 60f multicolored .20 .20
2445 A585 1fo multicolored .20 .20
2446 A585 2fo multicolored .30 .20
2447 A585 3fo multicolored .50 .20
2448 A585 4fo multicolored .70 .35
2449 A585 5fo multicolored .90 .50
Nos. 2443-2449 (7) 3.00 1.85

Gyor-Sopron Railroad, centenary.

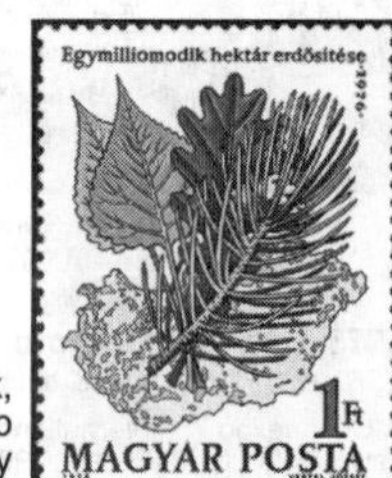

Poplar, Oak, Pine and Map of Hungary A586

1976, Dec. 14

2450 A586 1fo multicolored .25 .20

Millionth hectare of reforestation.

Weight Lifting and Wrestling, Silver Medals — A587

60f, Kayak, men's single & women's double. 1fo, Horse vaulting. 4fo, Women's fencing. 6fo, Javelin. 20fo, Water polo.

1976, Dec. 14 Photo. ***Perf. 11½x12***

2451 A587 40f multicolored .20 .20
2452 A587 60f multicolored .20 .20
2453 A587 1fo multicolored .20 .20
2454 A587 4fo multicolored .75 .30
2455 A587 6fo multicolored .90 .50
Nos. 2451-2455 (5) 2.25 1.40

Souvenir Sheet

Perf. 12½x11½

2456 A587 20fo multicolored 3.25 3.25

Hungarian medalists in 21st Olympic Games.

Spoonbills — A588

Birds: 60f, White storks. 1fo, Purple herons. 2fo, Great bustard. 3fo, Common cranes. 4fo, White wagtails. 5fo, Garganey teals.

1977, Jan. 3 Litho. *Perf. 12*

2457 A588 40f multicolored .20 .20
2458 A588 60f multicolored .20 .20
2459 A588 1fo multicolored .25 .20
2460 A588 2fo multicolored .40 .20
2461 A588 3fo multicolored .45 .30
2462 A588 4fo multicolored .90 .40
2463 A588 5fo multicolored 1.10 .50
Nos. 2457-2463 (7) 3.50 2.00

Birds from Hortobagy National Park.

1976 World Champion Imre Abonyi Driving Four-in-hand — A589

Designs: 60f, Omnibus on Boulevard, 1870. 1fo, One-horse cab at Budapest Railroad Station, 1890. 2fo, Mail coach, Buda to Vienna route. 3fo, Covered wagon of Hajduszoboszlo. 4fo, Hungarian coach, by Jeremias Schemel, 1563. 5fo, Post chaise, from a Lübeck wood panel, 1430.

1977, Jan. 31 Litho. *Perf. 12x11½*

2464 A589 40f multicolored .20 .20
2465 A589 60f multicolored .20 .20
2466 A589 1fo multicolored .20 .20
2467 A589 2fo multicolored .30 .20
2468 A589 3fo multicolored .30 .20
2469 A589 4fo multicolored .50 .35
2470 A589 5fo multicolored .70 .45
Nos. 2464-2470 (7) 2.40 1.80

History of the coach.

Peacock A590

Birds: 60f, Green peacock. 1fo, Congo peacock. 3fo, Argus pheasant. 4fo, Impeyan pheasant. 6fo, Peacock pheasant.

1977, Feb. 22 Litho. *Perf. 12*

2471 A590 40f multicolored .20 .20
2472 A590 60f multicolored .20 .20
2473 A590 1fo multicolored .20 .20
2474 A590 3fo multicolored .40 .20
2475 A590 4fo multicolored .60 .30
2476 A590 6fo multicolored .90 .50
Nos. 2471-2476 (6) 2.50 1.60

Newspaper Front Page, Factories A591

1977, Mar. 3 Litho. *Perf. 12*

2477 A591 1fo gold, black & ver .20 .20

Nepszava newspaper, centenary.

Flowers, by Mihaly Munkacsy A592

Flowers, by Hungarian Painters: 60f, Jakab Bogdany. 1fo, Istvan Csok, horiz. 2fo, Janos Halapy. 3fo, Jozsef Rippl-Ronai, horiz. 4fo, Janos Tornyai. 5fo, Jozsef Koszta.

1977, Mar. 18 Photo. *Perf. 12½*

2478 A592 40f gold & multi .20 .20
2479 A592 60f gold & multi .20 .20
2480 A592 1fo gold & multi .20 .20
2481 A592 2fo gold & multi .30 .20
2482 A592 3fo gold & multi .40 .20
2483 A592 4fo gold & multi .55 .30
2484 A592 5fo gold & multi .75 .50
Nos. 2478-2484 (7) 2.60 1.80

Newton and Double Convex Lens A593

1977, Mar. 31 Litho. *Perf. 12*

2485 A593 3fo tan & multi 1.00 .80

Isaac Newton (1643-1727), natural philosopher and mathematician, 250th death anniversary. No. 2485 issued in sheets of 4 stamps and 4 blue and black labels showing illustration from Newton's "Principia Mathematica," and Soviet space rocket.

Janos Vajda (1827-97), Poet — A594

1977, May 2 Litho. *Perf. 12*

2486 A594 1fo green, cream & blk .20 .20

Netherlands No. 1 and Tulips — A595

1977, May 23 Photo. *Perf. 11½x12*

2487 A595 3fo multicolored 1.25 1.25

AMPHILEX '77, Intl. Stamp Exhib., Amsterdam, May 26-June 5. Issued in sheets of 3 stamps + 3 labels showing Amphilex poster.

Scene from "Wedding at Nagyrede" A596

1977, June 14 Litho. *Perf. 12*

2488 A596 3fo multicolored .50 .20

State Folk Ensemble, 25th anniversary.

Souvenir Sheet

Bath of Bathsheba, by Rubens — A597

1977, June 14 Photo. *Perf. 11*

2489 A597 20fo multicolored 3.75 3.50

Peter Paul Rubens (1577-1640), Flemish painter.

Medieval View of Sopron, Fidelity Tower, Arms A598

1977, June 25 Litho. *Perf. 12x11½*

2490 A598 1fo multicolored 1.40 1.40

700th anniv. of Sopron. Printed se-tenant with label showing European Architectural Heritage medal awarded Sopron in 1975.

Race Horse Kincsem A599

1977, July 16 Litho. *Perf. 12*

2491 A599 1fo multicolored 1.00 .90

Sesquicentennial of horse racing in Hungary. Printed se-tenant with label showing portrait of Count Istvan Szechenyi and vignette from his 1827 book "Rules of Horse Racing in Hungary."

German Democratic Republic No. 370 — A600

1977, Aug. 18 Photo. *Perf. 12x11½*

2492 A600 3fo multicolored 1.25 1.10

SOZPHILEX 77 Philatelic Exhibition, Berlin, Aug. 19-28. No. 2492 issued in sheets of 3 stamps and 3 labels showing SOZPHILEX emblem.

Scythian Iron Bell, 6th Century B.C. — A601

Panel, Crown of Emperor Constantin Monomakhos — A602

Designs: No. 2494, Bronze candlestick in shape of winged woman, 12th-13th centuries. No. 2495, Centaur carrying child, copper aquamanile, 12th century. No. 2496, Gold figure of Christ, from 11th century Crucifix. Designs show art treasures from Hungarian National Museum, founded 1802.

1977, Sept. 3 Litho. *Perf. 12*

2493 A601 2fo multicolored .75 .75
2494 A601 2fo multicolored .75 .75
2495 A601 2fo multicolored .75 .75
2496 A601 2fo multicolored .75 .75
a. Horiz. strip of 4, #2493-2496 3.00 3.00

Souvenir Sheet

2497 A602 10fo multicolored 3.50 3.00

50th Stamp Day.

Sputnik A603

Spacecraft: 60f, Skylab. 1fo, Soyuz-Salyut 5. 3fo, Luna 24. 4fo, Mars 3. 6fo, Viking.

1977, Sept. 20

2498 A603 40f multicolored .20 .20
2499 A603 60f multicolored .20 .20
2500 A603 1fo multicolored .20 .20
2501 A603 3fo multicolored .40 .20

2502 A603 4fo multicolored .65 .35
2503 A603 6fo multicolored .90 .45
Nos. 2498-2503 (6) 2.55 1.60

Space explorations, from Sputnik to Viking. See No. C375.

Janos Szanto Kovacs (1852-1908), Agrarian Movement Pioneer A604

Ervin Szabo (1877-1918), Revolutionary Workers' Movement Pioneer A605

1977, Nov. 4 Litho. *Perf. 12*
2504 A604 1fo red & black .20 .20
2505 A605 1fo red & black .20 .20

Monument to Hungarian October Revolutionists, Omsk — A606

1977, Nov. 4
2506 A606 1fo black & red .20 .20

60th anniv. of Russian October Revolution.

Hands and Feet Bathed in Thermal Spring — A607

1977, Nov. 1
2507 A607 1fo multicolored .25 .20

World Rheumatism Year.

Endre Ady — A608

1977, Nov. 22 Engr. *Perf. 12*
2508 A608 1fo violet blue .35 .35

Endre Ady (1877-1919), lyric poet. Issued in sheets of 4.

Lesser Panda — A609

Designs: 60f, Giant panda. 1fo, Asiatic black bear. 4fo, Polar bear. 6fo, Brown bear.

1977, Dec. 16 Litho. *Perf. 11½x12*
2509 A609 40f yellow & multi .20 .20
2510 A609 60f yellow & multi .20 .20
2511 A609 1fo yellow & multi .35 .20
2512 A609 4fo yellow & multi .75 .30
2513 A609 6fo yellow & multi 1.00 .50
Nos. 2509-2513 (5) 2.50 1.40

Souvenir Sheet

Flags and Ships along Intercontinental Waterway — A610

Flags: a, Austria. b, Bulgaria. c, Czechoslovakia. d, France. e, Luxembourg. f, Yugoslavia. g, Hungary. h, Fed. Rep. of Germany. i, Romania. j, Switzerland. k, USSR.

1977, Dec. 28 Litho. *Perf. 12*
2514 A610 Sheet of 11 8.00 7.75
a.-k. 2fo, any single 1.00 1.00

European Intercontinental Waterway: Danube, Main and Rhine.

Lancer, 17th Century A611

Hussars: 60f, Kuruts, 1710. 1fo, Baranya, 1762. 2fo, Palatine officer, 1809. 4fo, Sandor, 1848. 6fo, Trumpeter, 5th Honved Regiment, 1900.

1978, Jan. Litho. *Perf. 11½x12*
2515 A611 40f lilac & multi .20 .20
2516 A611 60f yel grn & multi .20 .20
2517 A611 1fo red & multi .20 .20
2518 A611 2fo dull bl & multi .35 .20
2519 A611 4fo olive bis & multi .70 .30
2520 A611 6fo gray & multi 1.10 .50
Nos. 2515-2520 (6) 2.75 1.60

School of Arts and Crafts A612

1978, Mar. 31 Litho. *Perf. 12*
2521 A612 1fo multicolored .20 .20

School of Arts and Crafts, 200th anniv.

Soccer Players, Flags of West Germany and Poland — A613

Designs (Various Soccer Scenes and Flags): No. 2523, Hungary and Argentina. No. 2524, France and Italy. No. 2525, Tunisia and Mexico. No. 2526, Sweden and Brazil. No. 2527, Spain and Austria. No. 2528, Peru and Scotland. No. 2529, Iran and Netherlands. Flags represent first round of contestants. 20fo, Argentina '78 emblem.

1978, May 25 Litho. *Perf. 12*
2522 A613 2fo multicolored .20 .20
2523 A613 2fo multicolored .20 .20
2524 A613 2fo multicolored .20 .20
2525 A613 2fo multicolored .20 .20
2526 A613 2fo multicolored .25 .20
2527 A613 2fo multicolored .25 .20
2528 A613 2fo multicolored .55 .30
2529 A613 2fo multicolored .90 .40
Nos. 2522-2529 (8) 2.75 1.90

Souvenir Sheet

Perf. 11½
2530 A613 20fo multicolored 3.75 3.75

Argentina '78 11th World Cup Soccer Championships, Argentina, June 2-25.

Vase, Star and Glass Blower's Tube A614

1978, May 20 Litho. *Perf. 12*
2531 A614 1fo multicolored .20 .20

Ajka Glass Works, centenary.

Canada No. 1 and Trillium — A615

1978, June 2
2532 A615 3fo multicolored 1.00 .90

CAPEX '78, Canadian International Philatelic Exhibition, Toronto, Ont., June 9-18. Issued in sheets of 3 stamps and 3 labels showing CAPEX '78 emblem.

Souvenir Sheets

Leif Ericson and his Ship — A616

Explorers and their ships: #2533b, Columbus. c, Vasco da Gama. d, Magellan. #2534a, Drake. b, Hudson. c, Cook. d, Peary.

1978, June 10 Litho. *Perf. 12x11½*
2533 Sheet of 4 3.25 3.00
a.-d. A616 2fo, any single .70 .70
2534 Sheet of 4 3.25 3.00
a.-d. A616 2fo, any single .70 .70

Diesel Train, Pioneer's Kerchief — A617

Congress Emblem as Flower — A618

1978, June 10 *Perf. 12*
2535 A617 1fo multicolored .20 .20

30th anniversary of Pioneer Railroad.

1978, June

Design: No. 2537, Congress emblem, "Cuba" and map of Cuba.

2536 A618 1fo multi .25 .20
2537 A618 1fo multi .25 .20
a. Pair, #2536-2537 .50 .30

11th World Youth Festival, Havana.

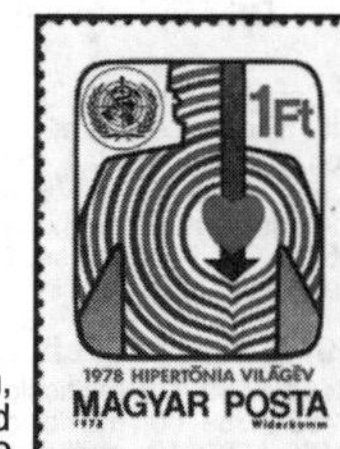
WHO Emblem, Stylized Body and Heart — A619

Clenched Fist, Dove and Olive Branch — A620

1978, Aug. 21 Litho. *Perf. 12*
2538 A619 1fo multicolored .20 .20

Drive against hypertension.

1978, Sept. 1 Litho. *Perf. 12*
2539 A620 1fo gray, red & black .20 .20

Publication of review "Peace and Socialism," 20th anniversary.

Train, Telephone, Space Communication — A621

1978, Sept. 8 Litho. *Perf. 12*
2540 A621 1fo multicolored .25 .20

20th anniv. of Organization for Communication Cooperation of Socialist Countries.

"Toshiba" Automatic Letter Sorting Machine — A622

1978, Sept. 15 Litho. *Perf. 11½x12*

2541	A622	1fo multicolored	.25	.20

Introduction of automatic letter sorting. No. 2541 printed with se-tenant label showing bird holding letter.

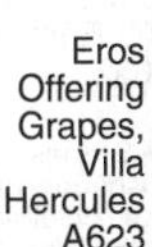

Eros Offering Grapes, Villa Hercules A623

Roman Mosaics Found in Hungary: No. 2543, Tiger (Villa Hercules, Budapest). No. 2544, Bird eating berries (Balacapuszta). No. 2545, Dolphin (Aquincum). 10fo, Hercules aiming at Centaur fleeing with Deianeira (Villa Hercules).

Photogravure and Engraved

1978, Sept. 16 *Perf. 11½*

2542	A623	2fo multicolored	1.50	1.25
2543	A623	2fo multicolored	1.50	1.25
2544	A623	2fo multicolored	1.50	1.25
2545	A623	2fo multicolored	1.50	1.25
		Nos. 2542-2545 (4)	6.00	5.00

Souvenir Sheet

2546	A623	10fo multicolored	9.00	8.50

Stamp Day. No. 2546 contains one stamp (52x35mm).

Count Imre Thököly — A624

1978, Oct. 1 Photo. *Perf. 12½*

2547	A624	1fo black & yellow	.25	.20

300th anniv. of Hungary's independence movement, led by Imre Thököly (1657-1705).

Souvenir Sheet

Hungarian Crown Jewels — A625

1978, Oct. 10

2548	A625	20fo gold & multi	5.50	5.25

Return of Crown Jewels from US, 1/6/78.

"The Red Coach" A626

1978, Oct. 21 Litho. *Perf. 12*

2549	A626	3fo red & black	.50	.20

Gyula Krudy, 1878-1933, novelist.

St. Ladislas I Reliquary, Györ Cathedral A627

1978, Nov. 15 *Perf. 11½x12½*

2550	A627	1fo multicolored	.20	.20

Ladislas I (1040-1095), 900th anniversary of accession to throne of Hungary.

Miklos Jurisics Statue, Köszeg — A628

1978, Nov. 15 *Perf. 12*

2551	A628	1fo multicolored	.20	.20

650th anniversary of founding of Köszeg.

Samu Czaban and Gizella Berzeviczy — A629

Photogravure and Engraved

1978, Nov. 24 *Perf. 11½x12*

2552	A629	1fo brown, buff & red	.20	.20

Samu Czaban (1878-1942) and Gizella Berzeviczy (1878-1954), Communist teachers during Soviet Republic (1918-1919).

Communist Party Emblem A630

1978, Nov. 24 Litho. *Perf. 12*

2553	A630	1fo gray, red & blk	.20	.20

Hungarian Communist Party, 60th anniv.

Woman Cutting Bread A631

Ceramics by Margit Kovacs (1902-1976): 2fo, Woman with pitcher. 3fo, Potter.

1978, Nov. 30 Litho. *Perf. 11½x12*

2554	A631	1fo multicolored	.20	.20
2555	A631	2fo multicolored	.30	.20
2556	A631	3fo multicolored	.70	.60
		Nos. 2554-2556 (3)	1.20	1.00

Virgin and Child, by Dürer A632

Dürer Paintings: 60f, Adoration of the Kings, horiz. 1fo, Self-portrait, 1500. 2fo, St. George. 3fo, Nativity, horiz. 4fo, St. Eustatius. 5fo, The Four Apostles. 20fo, Dancing Peasant Couple, 1514 (etching).

1979, Jan. 8 Photo. *Perf. 12½*

2557	A632	40f gold & multi	.20	.20
2558	A632	60f gold & multi	.20	.20
2559	A632	1fo gold & multi	.20	.20
2560	A632	2fo gold & multi	.30	.20
2561	A632	3fo gold & multi	.35	.20
2562	A632	4fo gold & multi	.70	.30
2563	A632	5fo gold & multi	.80	.60
		Nos. 2557-2563 (7)	2.75	1.90

Souvenir Sheet

Litho.

2564	A632	20fo buff & brown	3.50	3.25

Albrecht Dürer (1471-1528), German painter and engraver.

Human Rights Flame — A633

1979, Feb. 8 Litho. *Perf. 11½x12*

2565	A633	1fo dk & lt blue	1.25	1.25

Universal Declaration of Human Rights, 30th anniversary. No. 2565 issued in sheets of 12 stamps (3x4) and 4 labels. Alternating horizontal rows inverted.

Child at Play — A634

IYC Emblem and: No. 2567, Family. No. 2568, 3 children (international friendship).

1979, Feb. 26 *Perf. 12*

2566	A634	1fo multicolored	.75	.75
2567	A634	1fo multicolored	.75	.75
2568	A634	1fo multicolored	6.50	5.50
		Nos. 2566-2568 (3)	8.00	7.00

Soldiers of the Red Army, by Bela Uitz A635

1979, Mar. 21 Litho. *Perf. 12*

2569	A635	1fo silver, blk & red	.20	.20

60th anniv. of Hungarian Soviet Republic.

Calvinist Church, Nyirbator — A636

1979, Mar. 28 *Perf. 11*

2570	A636	1fo brown & yellow	.20	.20

700th anniv. of Nyirbator. See No. 2601.

Chessmen, Gold Cup, Flag — A637

1979, Apr. 12 Litho. *Perf. 12*

2571	A637	3fo multicolored	.50	.50

Hungarian victories in 23rd Chess Olympiad, Buenos Aires, 1978.

Alexander Nevski Cathedral, Sofia, Bulgaria No. 1 — A638

1979, May 18 Litho. *Perf. 11½x12*

2572	A638	3fo multicolored	.75	.75

Philaserdica '79 Philatelic Exhibition, Sofia, Bulgaria, May 18-27. No. 2572 issued in sheets of 3 stamps and 3 labels showing Philaserdica emblem and arms of Sofia.

Stephenson's Rocket, 1829, IVA '79 Emblem — A639

Railroad Development: 60f, Siemens' first electric locomotive, 1879. 1fo, "Pioneer," Chicago & Northwestern Railroad, 1836. 2fo, Orient Express, 1883. 3fo, Trans-Siberian train, 1898. 4fo, Express train on Tokaido line, 1964. 5fo, Transrapid-O5 train, exhibited 1979. 20fo, Map of European railroad network.

1979, June 8 Litho. *Perf. 12x11½*

2573	A639	40f multi	.20	.20
2574	A639	60f multi	.20	.20
2575	A639	1fo multi	.20	.20
2576	A639	2fo multi	.30	.20
2577	A639	3fo multi	.45	.25

2578 A639 4fo multi .60 .45
2579 A639 5fo multi .90 .50
Nos. 2573-2579 (7) 2.85 2.00

Souvenir Sheet

Perf. 12½x11½

2580 A639 20fo multi 4.00 3.75

Intl. Transportation Exhibition (IVA '79), Hamburg. #2580 contains one 47x32mm stamp.

Natural Gas Pipeline and Compressor A640

2fo, Lenin power station & dam, Dnieprope-trovsk & pylon. 3fo, Comecon Building, Moscow, & star symbolizing 10 member states.

1979, June 26 ***Perf. 11½x12***

2581 A640 1fo multi .20 .20
2582 A640 2fo multi .25 .20
2583 A640 3fo multi .40 .20
Nos. 2581-2583 (3) .85 .60

30th anniversary of the Council of Mutual Economic Assistance, Comecon.

Zsigmond Moricz (1879-1942), Writer, by Jozsef Ripple-Ronai A641

1979, June 29 ***Perf. 12***

2584 A641 1fo multi .20 .20

Town Hall, Helsinki, Finnish Flag, Moscow '80 Emblem A642

Designs (Moscow '80 Emblem and): 60f, Colosseum, Rome, Italian flag. 1fo, Asakusa Temple, Tokyo, Japanese flag. 2fo, Mexico City Cathedral, Mexican flag. 3fo, Our Lady's Church, Munich, German flag. 4fo, Skyscrapers, Montreal, Canadian flag. 5fo, Lomonosov University, Misha the bear and Soviet flag.

1979, July 31 ***Perf. 12x11½***

2585 A642 40f multi .20 .20
2586 A642 60f multi .20 .20
2587 A642 1fo multi .20 .20
2588 A642 2fo multi .20 .20
2589 A642 3fo multi .30 .25
2590 A642 4fo multi .40 .30
2591 A642 5fo multi .70 .45
Nos. 2585-2591 (7) 2.20 1.80

Pre-Olympic Year.

Boy with Horse and Greyhounds, by Janos Vaszary — A643

Paintings of Horses: 60f, Coach and Five, by Karoly Lotz. 1fo, Boys on Horseback, by Celesztin Pallya. 2fo, Farewell, by Lotz. 3fo, Horse Market, by Pallya. 4fo, Wanderer, by Bela Ivanyi-Grunwald. 5fo, Ready for the Hunt, by Karoly Sterio.

1979, Aug. 11 **Photo.** ***Perf. 12½***

2592 A643 40f multi .20 .20
2593 A643 60f multi .20 .20
2594 A643 1fo multi .20 .20
2595 A643 2fo multi .25 .20
2596 A643 3fo multi .40 .20
2597 A643 4fo multi .50 .30
2598 A643 5fo multi .75 .40
Nos. 2592-2598 (7) 2.50 1.70

Sturgeons, Map of Danube, "Calypso" — A644

1979, Aug. 11

2599 A644 3fo multi .50 .20

Environmental protection of rivers and seas.

Pentathlon A645

1979, Aug. 12 **Litho.** ***Perf. 12***

2600 A645 2fo multi .50 .20

Pentathlon World Championship, Budapest, Aug. 12-18.

Architecture Type of 1979

Design: Vasvar Public Health Center.

1979, Aug. 15 **Litho.** ***Perf. 11***

2601 A636 40f multi .20 .20

700th anniversary of Vasvar.

Denarius of Stephen I, 1000-1038, Reverse A646

Hungarian Coins: 2fo, Copper coin of Bela III, 1172-1196. 3fo, Golden groat of King Louis the Great, 1342-1382. 4fo, Golden forint of Matthias I, 1458-1490. 5fo, Silver gulden of Wladislaw II, 1490-1516.

Engraved and Photogravure

1979, Sept. 3 ***Perf. 12x11½***

2602 A646 1fo multi .20 .20
2603 A646 2fo multi .25 .20
2604 A646 3fo multi .35 .25
2605 A646 4fo multi .50 .40
2606 A646 5fo multi 1.00 .70
Nos. 2602-2606 (5) 2.30 1.75

9th International Numismatic Congress, Berne, Switzerland.

Souvenir Sheet

Unofficial Stamp, 1848 — A647

1979, Sept. 15 **Litho.** ***Perf. 12***

2607 A647 10fo dk brown, blk & red 2.75 2.50

Stamp Day.

Souvenir Sheet

Gyor-Sopron-Ebenfurt rail service, cent. — A648

Designs: a, Elbel Locomotive. b, Type 424 steam engine. c, "War Locomotive." d, Hydraulic diesel locomotive.

1979, Oct. 19 **Litho.** ***Perf. 12***

2608 A648 Sheet of 4 3.25 3.00
a.-d. A648 5fo any single .65 .65

Vega-Chess, by Victor Vasarely A649

1979, Oct. 29

2609 A649 1fo multi .20 .20

International Savings Day — A650

1979, Oct. 29 **Litho.** ***Perf. 12***

2610 A650 1fo multi .20 .20

Otter — A651

Wildlife Protection: 60f, Wild cat. 1fo, Pine marten. 2fo, Eurasian badger. 4fo, Polecat. 6fo, Beech marten.

1979, Nov. 20

2611 A651 40f multi .20 .20
2612 A651 60f multi .20 .20
2613 A651 1fo multi .20 .20
2614 A651 2fo multi .30 .20
2615 A651 4fo multi .60 .25
2616 A651 6fo multi .90 .60
Nos. 2611-2616 (6) 2.40 1.65

Tom Thumb, IYC Emblem A652

IYC Emblem and Fairy Tale Scenes: 60f, The Ugly Duckling. 1fo, The Fisherman and the Goldfish. 2fo, Cinderella. 3fo, Gulliver's Travels. 4fo, The Little Pigs and the Wolf. 5fo, Janos the Knight. 20fo, The Fairy Ilona.

1979, Dec. 29 **Litho.** ***Perf. 12x11½***

2617 A652 40f multi .20 .20
2618 A652 60f multi .20 .20
2619 A652 1fo multi .20 .20
2620 A652 2fo multi .35 .20
2621 A652 3fo multi .50 .30
2622 A652 4fo multi .70 .30
2623 A652 5fo multi 1.00 .60
Nos. 2617-2623 (7) 3.15 2.00

Souvenir Sheet

2624 A652 20fo multi 3.75 3.50

Trichodes Apairius and Yarrow — A653

Insects Pollinating Flowers: 60f, Bumblebee and blanketflower. 1fo, Red admiral butterfly and daisy. 2fo, Cetonia aurata and rose. 4fo, Graphosoma lineatum and petroselinum hortense. 6fo, Chlorophorus varius and thistle.

1980, Jan. 25 **Litho.** ***Perf. 12***

2625 A653 40f multi .20 .20
2626 A653 60f multi .20 .20
2627 A653 1fo multi .25 .20
2628 A653 2fo multi .35 .20
2629 A653 4fo multi .50 .25
2630 A653 6fo multi .75 .30
Nos. 2625-2630 (6) 2.25 1.35

Hanging Gardens of Semiramis, 6th Century B.C., Map showing Babylon — A654

Seven Wonders of the Ancient World (and Map): 60f, Temple of Artemis, Ephesus, 6th century B.C. 1fo, Zeus, by Phidias, Olympia. 2fo, Tomb of Maussolos, Halikarnassos, 3rd century B.C. 3fo, Colossos of Rhodes. 4fo, Pharos Lighthouse, Alexandria, 3rd century B.C. 5fo, Pyramids, 26th-24th centuries B.C.

1980, Feb. 29 **Litho.** ***Perf. 12x11½***

2631 A654 40f multi .20 .20
2632 A654 60f multi .20 .20
2633 A654 1fo multi .20 .20
2634 A654 2fo multi .25 .20
2635 A654 3fo multi .35 .25
2636 A654 4fo multi .55 .35
2637 A654 5fo multi .70 .60
Nos. 2631-2637 (7) 2.45 2.00

Tihany Benedictine Abbey and Deed — A655

1980, Mar. 19 **Litho.** ***Perf. 12***
2638 A655 1fo multi .20 .20

Benedictine Abbey, Tihany, 925th anniversary of deed (oldest document in Hungarian).

Gabor Bethlen, Copperplate Print — A656

1980, Mar. 19
2639 A656 1fo multi .20 .20

Gabor Bethlen (1580-1629), Prince of Transylvania (1613-29) and King of Hungary (1620-29).

Easter Casket of Garamszentbenedek, 15th Century (Restoration) — A657

1980, Mar. 19

2640	A657	1fo shown	.20	.20
2641	A657	2fo Three Marys	.25	.25
2642	A657	3fo Apostle James	.35	.35
2643	A657	4fo Thaddeus	.55	.55
2644	A657	5fo Andrew	.75	.55
		Nos. 2640-2644 (5)	2.10	1.90

Liberation from Fascism, 35th Anniversary A658

1980, Apr. 3 **Litho.** ***Perf. 12***
2645 A658 1fr multi .20 .20

Jozsef Attila, Poet and Lyricist — A659

1980, Apr. 11
2646 A659 1fo rose car & olive .20 .20

See No. 2675.

Hungarian Postal Museum, 50th anniv. — A660

1980, Apr. 28 ***Perf. 11½x12***
2647 A660 1fo multi 1.90 1.50

Features Hungary No. 386a.

Two Pence Blue, Mounted Guardsman, London 1980 Emblem — A661

1980, Apr. 30 ***Perf. 11½x12***
2648 A661 3fo multi 1.00 1.00

London 1980 International Stamp Exhibition, May 6-14. No. 2648 issued in sheets of 3 stamps and 3 labels showing London 1980 emblem and arms of city. Size: 104x125mm.

Norway No. B51, Mother with Child, by Gustav Vigeland — A662

1980, June 9 **Litho.** ***Perf. 11½x12***
2649 A662 3fo multi 1.00 1.00

NORWEX '80 Stamp Exhibition, Oslo, June 13-22. No. 2649 issued in sheets of 3 stamps and 3 labels showing NORWEX emblem. Size: 108x125mm.

Margit Kaffka (1880-1918), Writer — A663

1980, June 9 ***Perf. 12***
2650 A663 1fo blk & pur, *cr* .25 .20

Zoltan Schönherz (1905-42), Anti-fascist Martyr — A664

1980, July 25 **Litho.**
2652 A664 1fo multi .20 .20

Dr. Endre Hogyes and Congress Emblem A665

1980, July 25
2653 A665 1fo multi .20 .20

28th International Congress of Physiological Sciences, Budapest, Dr. Hogyes (1847-1906) first described equilibrium reflex-curve and modified Pasteur's rabies vaccine.

Decanter, c. 1850 — A666

1980, Sept. **Litho.** ***Perf. 12***

2654	A666	1fo shown	.25	.25
2655	A666	2fo Decorated glass	.35	.35
2656	A666	3fo Stem glass	.65	.65
		Nos. 2654-2656 (3)	1.25	1.25

Souvenir Sheet

2657 A666 10fo Pecs glass 2.50 2.25

53rd Stamp Day.

Bertalan Por, Self-portrait A667

1980, Nov. 4 **Litho.** ***Perf. 12***
2658 A667 1fo Artist (1880-1964) .35 .20

Graylag Goose — A668

1980, Nov. 11 ***Perf. 11½x12***

2659	A668	40f shown	.20	.20
2660	A668	60f Black-crowned night heron	.20	.20
2661	A668	1fo Shoveler	.20	.20
2662	A668	2fo Chlidonias leucopterus	.30	.20
2663	A668	4fo Great crested grebe	.60	.30
2664	A668	6fo Black-necked stilt	1.00	.50
		Nos. 2659-2664 (6)	2.50	1.60

Souvenir Sheet

2665 A668 20fo Great white heron 4.25 4.00

European Nature Protection Year. No. 2665 contains one stamp (37x59mm).

Souvenir Sheet

Dove on Map of Europe — A669

1980, Nov. 11 ***Perf. 12½x11½***
2666 A669 20fo multi 4.50 4.00

European Security and Cooperation Conference, Madrid.

Johannes Kepler and Model of his Theory — A670

1980, Nov. 21 **Litho.** ***Perf. 12***
2667 A670 1fo multi .35 .20

Johannes Kepler (1571-1630), German astronomer, 350th anniversary of death. No. 2667 printed se-tenant with label showing rocket and satellites orbiting earth.

Karoly Kisfaludy (1788-1830), Poet and Dramatist A671

1980, Nov. 21
2668 A671 1fo brn red & dull brn .20 .20

UN Headquarters, New York — A672

UN membership, 25th anniversary.

Photogravure and Engraved

1980, Dec. 12 ***Perf. 11½x12***

2669	A672	40f shown	.20	.20
2670	A672	60f Geneva headquarters	.20	.20
2671	A672	1fo Vienna headquarters	.20	.20
2672	A672	2fo UN & Hungary flags	.25	.20
2673	A672	4fo UN, Hungary arms	.50	.30
2674	A672	6fo World map	.85	.50
		Nos. 2669-2674 (6)	2.20	1.60

Attila Type of 1980

Ferenc Erdei (1910-71), economist & statesman.

1980, Dec. 23 **Litho.** ***Perf. 12***
2675 A659 1fo dk green & brown .20 .20

Bela Szanto — A674

Count Lajos Batthyany A675

1981, Jan. 31 Litho. *Perf. 12*

2676 A674 1fo multi .20 .20

Bela Szanto (1881-1951), labor movement leader.

See Nos. 2698, 2724, 2767.

1981, Feb. 14

2677 A675 1fo multi .20 .20

Count Lajos Batthyany (1806-1849), prime minister, later executed.

Bela Bartok (1881-1945), Composer A677

Design: b, Cantata Profana illustration.

1981, Mar. 25 Litho. *Perf. 12½*

2685 Sheet of 2 2.50 2.50
a.-b. A677 10fo any single 1.25 1.25

Telephone Exchange System Cent. — A678

1981, Apr. 29 Litho. *Perf. 12*

2686 A678 2fo multi .25 .20

Belling Stag — A679

1981, Apr. 29

2687 A679 2fo multi .25 .20

Flag of the House of Arpad, 11th Cent. A680

1981, Apr. 29

2688 A680 40f shown .20 .20
2689 A680 60f Hunyadi family, 15th cent. .20 .20
2690 A680 1fo Gabor Bethlen, 1600 .20 .20
2691 A680 2fo Ferenc Rakoczi II, 1716 .25 .20
2692 A680 4fo Honved, 1848 .60 .25
2693 A680 6fo Troop flag, 1919 .80 .35
Nos. 2688-2693 (6) 2.25 1.40

Red Cross and Ambulance Vehicles A681

Map of Europe and J. Henry Dunant (Red Cross Founder) — A682

1981, May 4

2694 A681 2fo multi .25 .20

Souvenir Sheet

Perf. 12½x11½

2695 A682 20fo multi 2.50 2.50

Hungarian Red Cross cent. (2fo); 3rd European Red Cross Conf., Budapest, May 4-7 (20fo).

Souvenir Sheet

1933 WIPA Exhibition Seals — A683

1981, May 15 *Perf. 12x12½*

2696 Sheet of 4 2.75 2.75
a.-d. A683 5fo any single .65 .65

WIPA 1981 Phil. Exhib., Vienna, May 22-31.

Stephenson and his Nonpareil — A684

1981, June 12 Litho. *Perf. 12*

2697 A684 2fo multi .25 .20

George Stephenson (1781-1848), British railroad engineer, birth bicentenary.

Famous Hungarians Type

Bela Vago (1881-1939), anti-fascist martyr.

1981, Aug. 7 Litho. *Perf. 12*

2698 A674 2fo ocher & brn ol .25 .20

Alexander Fleming (1881-1955), Discoverer of Penicillin — A686

1981, Aug. 7

2699 A686 2fo multi .25 .20

Bridal Chest A687

Designs: Bridal chests.

1981, Sept. 12 Litho. *Perf. 12*

2700 A687 1fo Szentgal, 18th cent. .20 .20
2701 A687 2fo Hodmezovasarhely, 19th cent. .30 .20

Souvenir Sheet

2702 A687 10fo Bacs County, 17th cent. 1.75 1.75

54th Stamp Day. No. 2702 contains one stamp (44x25mm).

Calvinist College, Papa, 450th Anniv. A688

1981, Oct. 3 Litho. *Perf. 12*

2703 A688 2fo multi .25 .20

World Food Day — A689

1981, Oct. 16

2704 A689 2fo multi .25 .20

Passenger Ship Rakoczi, 1964, No. 1834 — A690

Sidewheelers and Hungarian stamps.

1981, Nov. 25 *Perf. 12x11½*

2705 A690 1fo Franz I, #1828 .20 .20
2706 A690 1fo Arpad, #1829 .20 .20
2707 A690 2fo Szechenyi, #1830 .30 .20
2708 A690 2fo Grof Szechenyi Istvan, #1831 .30 .20
2709 A690 4fo Sofia, #1832 .65 .30
2710 A690 6fo Felszabadulas, #1833 .95 .50
2711 A690 8fo shown 1.25 .65
Nos. 2705-2711 (7) 3.85 2.25

Souvenir Sheet

Perf. 13

2712 A690 20fo Hydrofoil Solyom, #1830 3.00 3.00

European Danube Commission, 125th anniv.

Souvenir Sheet

Slovakian Natl. Costumes — A691

Perf. 12½x11½

1981, Nov. 18 Litho.

2713 Sheet of 4 2.00 1.90
a. A691 1fo shown .20 .20
b. A691 2fo German .40 .35
c. A691 3fo Croatian .60 .60
d. A691 4fo Romanian .80 .75

Christmas 1981 — A692

Sculptures: 1fo, Mary Nursing the Infant Jesus, by Margit Kovacs. 2fo, Madonna of Csurgo.

1981, Dec. 4 *Perf. 12½x11½*

2714 A692 1fo multi .20 .20
2715 A692 2fo multi .25 .20

Pen Pals, by Norman Rockwell A693

1981, Dec. 29 *Perf. 11½x12*

Norman Rockwell Illustrations.

2716 A693 1fo shown .20 .20
2717 A693 2fo Courting Under the Clock at Midnight .20 .20
2718 A693 2fo Maiden Voyage .20 .20
2719 A693 4fo Threading the Needle .45 .25
Nos. 2716-2719,C435-C437 (7) 3.10 2.50

Souvenir Sheet

La Toilette, by Pablo Picasso (1881-1973) — A694

1981, Dec. 29 Litho. *Perf. 11½*

2720 A694 20fo multicolored 2.75 2.75

25th Anniv. of Worker's Militia A695

1982, Jan. 26 Litho. *Perf. 12*

2721 A695 1fo Shooting practice .20 .20
2722 A695 4fo Members, 3 generations .50 .35

10th World Trade Union Congress — A696

1982, Feb. 12 Litho. ***Perf. 12x11½***

2723 A696 2fo multicolored .25 .20

Famous Hungarians Type

Gyula Alpri (1882-1944), anti-fascist martyr.

1982, Mar. 24 ***Perf. 12***

2724 A674 2fo multicolored .25 .20

Robert Koch — A698

1982, Mar. 24 Litho. ***Perf. 12***

2725 A698 2fo multicolored .25 .20

TB Bacillus centenary.

1982 World Cup — A699

Designs: Hungary in competition with other World Cup teams.

#2733: a, Barcelona Stadium. b, Madrid Stadium.

1982, Apr. 16 ***Perf. 11***

2726	A699 1fo Egypt, 1934	.20	.20
2727	A699 1fo Italy, 1938	.20	.20
2728	A699 2fo Germany, 1954	.20	.20
2729	A699 2fo Mexico, 1958	.20	.20
2730	A699 4fo England, 1962	.45	.25
2731	A699 6fo Brazil, 1966	.70	.40
2732	A699 8fo Argentina, 1978	.90	.55
	Nos. 2726-2732 (7)	2.85	2.00

Souvenir Sheet

2733	Sheet of 2	3.00	3.00
a.-b.	A699 10fo any single	1.40	1.40

No. 2733 contains 44x44mm stamps.

European Table Tennis Championship, Budapest, Apr. 17-25 — A700

1982, Apr. 16 Litho. ***Perf. 11½x12***

2734 A700 2fo multi .25 .20

Roses A701

25 Years of Space Travel — A702

1982, Apr. 30 ***Perf. 12***

2735	A701 1fo Pascali	.20	.20
2736	A701 1fo Michele Meilland	.20	.20
2737	A701 2fo Diorama	.30	.20
2738	A701 2fo Wendy Cussons	.30	.20
2739	A701 3fo Blue Moon	.40	.25
2740	A701 3fo Invitation	.40	.25
2741	A701 4fo Tropicana	.60	.30
	Nos. 2735-2741 (7)	2.40	1.60

Souvenir Sheet

2742 A701 10fo Bouquet 2.50 2.50

No. 2742 contains one stamp (34x59mm, perf. 11).

1982, May 18 Photo. ***Perf. 11½***

2743	A702 1fo Columbia shuttle, 1981	.20	.20
2744	A702 1fo Armstrong, Apollo 11, 1969	.20	.20
2745	A702 2fo A. Leonov, Voskhod 2, 1965	.30	.20
2746	A702 2fo Yuri Gagarin, Vostok	.30	.20
2747	A702 4fo Laika, Sputnik 2, 1957	.55	.35
2748	A702 4fo Sputnik I, 1957	.55	.35
2749	A702 6fo Space researcher K.E. Tsiolkovsky	.90	.50
	Nos. 2743-2749 (7)	3.00	2.00

A703

1982, May 7 Litho. ***Perf. 12***

2750 A703 2fo multi .25 .20

George Dimitrov (1882-1947), 1st prime minister of Bulgaria. SOZPHILEX '82 Stamp Exhib., Sofia, Bulgaria, May. No. 2750 se-tenant with label showing Bulgarian 1300th anniv. emblems.

Diosgyor paper mill, bicent. — A704

1982, May 27 Litho. ***Perf. 12x11½***

2751 A704 2fo multi .25 .20

First Rubik's Cube World Championship, Budapest, June 5 — A705

1982, June 4 ***Perf. 11½x12***

2752 A705 2fo multi .25 .20

Souvenir Sheet

George Washington, by F. Kemmelmeyer — A706

Washington's 250th Birth Anniv.: a, Michael Kovats de Fabricy (1724-1779), Cavalry Commandant, by Sandor Finta.

1982, July 2 Litho. ***Perf. 11***

2753	A706 Sheet of 2	2.50	2.50
a.-b.	5fo any single	.75	.75

World Hematology Congress, Budapest — A707

Zirc Abbey, 800th Anniv. — A708

1982, July 30 ***Perf. 12½x11½***

2754 A707 2fo multi .25 .20

1982, Aug. 19 ***Perf. 11½x12***

2755 A708 2fo multi .25 .20

KNER Printing Office, Gyoma, Centenary — A709

1982, Sept. 23 Litho. ***Perf. 12x11½***

2756 A709 2fo Emblem .25 .20

AGROFILA '82 Intl. Agricultural Stamp Exhibition, Godollo — A710

1982, Sept. 24 ***Perf. 11½x12***

2757 A710 5fo Map 1.00 .95

Issued in sheets of 3 stamps and 3 labels showing Godollo Agricultural University, emblem. Size: 109x127mm.

Public Transportation Sesquicentennial — A711

1982, Oct. 5 Litho. ***Perf. 12x11½***

2758 A711 2fo multi .25 .20

Vuk and a Bird — A712

Scenes from Vuk the Fox Cub, Cartoon by Attila Dargay.

1982, Nov. 11 ***Perf. 12½***

2759	A712 1fo shown	.20	.20
2760	A712 1fo Dogs	.20	.20
2761	A712 2fo Rooster	.25	.20
2762	A712 2fo Owl	.25	.20
2763	A712 4fo Geese	.50	.30
2764	A712 6fo Frog	.70	.55
2765	A712 8fo Master fox	1.00	.70
	Nos. 2759-2765 (7)	3.10	2.35

Engineering Education Bicentenary A713

1982, Oct. 13 ***Perf. 12***

2766 A713 2fo Budapest Polytechnical Univ. .25 .20

Famous Hungarians Type

Gyorgy Boloni (1882-1959), writer and journalist.

1982, Oct. 29

2767 A674 2fo multi .25 .20

October Revolution, 65th Anniv. — A715

Works of Art in Hungarian Chapel, Vatican — A716

1982, Nov. 5 Litho. *Perf. 11½x12*

2768 A715 5fo Lenin .75 .40

1982, Nov. 30 *Perf. 12x11½*

Designs: No. 2769, St. Stephen, first King of Hungary (1001-1038). No. 2770, Pope Sylvester II making donation to St. Stephen. No. 2771, Pope Callixtus III ordering noon victory bell ringing by St. John of Capistrano, 1456. No. 2772, Pope Paul VI showing Cardinal Lekai location of Hungarian Chapel. No. 2773, Pope John Paul II consecrating chapel, 1980. No. 2774, Madonna and Child. Nos. 2769, 2774 sculptures by Imre Varga; others by Amerigo Tot. Nos. 2770-2773, size 37x18mm, in continuous design in block of 4 between Nos. 2769 and 2774.

2769 A716 2fo multi .40 .40
2770 A716 2fo multi .40 .40
2771 A716 2fo multi .40 .40
2772 A716 2fo multi .40 .40
2773 A716 2fo multi .40 .40
2774 A716 2fo multi .40 .40
a. Block of 6, #2769-2774 2.60 2.60

Souvenir Sheet

Zoltan Kodaly (1882-1967), Composer — A717

1982, Dec. 16 *Perf. 11½*

2775 A717 20fo multi 2.75 2.75

A718

Perf. 12½x11½

1982, Dec. 16 Litho.

2776 A718 2fo multi .25 .20

New Year 1983.

A719

1982, Dec. 29 *Perf. 11½x12½*

Design: Johann Wolfgang Goethe (1749-1832), German poet, by Heinrich Kolbe.

Souvenir Sheet

2777 A719 20fo multi 2.75 2.75

10th Anniv. of Postal Code — A720

1983, Jan. 24 *Perf. 11½x12*

2778 A720 2fo multi .25 .20

3rd Budapest Spring Festival, Mar. 18-27 A721

1983, Mar. 18 Litho. *Perf. 12x11½*

2779 A721 2fo Ship of Peace, by Engre Szasz .25 .20

Gyula Juhasz (1883-1937), Poet — A722

1983, Apr. 15 *Perf. 12*

2780 A722 2fo multi .25 .20

City of Szentgotthard, 800th Anniv. — A723

1983, May 4 Litho. *Perf. 11½*

2781 A723 2fo Monastery, seal, 1489 .25 .20

Malomto Lake, Tapolca — A724

1983, May 17 *Perf. 11½x12*

2782 A724 5fo multi .80 .80

TEMBAL '83 Intl. Topical Stamp Exhibition, Basel, May 21-29. Issued in sheets of 3 stamps and 3 labels.

Souvenir Sheet

5th Interparliamentary Union Conference on European Cooperation, Budapest, May 30-June 5 — A725

1983, May 30 Litho. *Perf. 12½*

2783 A725 20fo Budapest Parliament 3.50 3.25

Jeno Hamburger (1883-1936) A726

1983, May 31 *Perf. 12*

2784 A726 2fo multi .25 .20

Lady with Unicorn, by Raphael (1483-1517) A727

Paintings: No. 2786, Joan of Aragon. No. 2787, Granduca Madonna. No. 2788, Madonna and Child with St. John. 4fo, La Muta. 6fo, La Valeta. 8fo, La Fornarina. 20fo, Esterhazy Madonna.

Perf. 11½x12½

1983, June 29 Litho.

2785 A727 1fo multi .20 .20
2786 A727 1fo multi .20 .20
2787 A727 2fo multi .25 .20
2788 A727 2fo multi .25 .20
2789 A727 4fo multi .45 .30
2790 A727 6fo multi .65 .30
2791 A727 8fo multi .75 .45
Nos. 2785-2791 (7) 2.75 1.85

Souvenir Sheet

2792 A727 20fo multi 3.00 3.00

No. 2792 contains one stamp (24x37mm).

Simon Bolivar (1783-1830) A728

1983, July 22 Litho. *Perf. 12*

2793 A728 2fo multi .25 .20

Istvan Vagi (1883-1940), Anti-fascist Martyr A729

1983, July 22 *Perf. 11½x12½*

2794 A729 2fo multi .25 .20

68th World Esperanto Congress, Budapest, July 30-Aug. 6 — A730

1983, July 29 *Perf. 12*

2795 A730 2fo multi .25 .20

Souvenir Sheet

Martin Luther (1483-1546) — A731

1983, Aug. 12 *Perf. 12½*

2796 A731 20fo multi 2.75 2.50

Birds — A732

Designs: Protected birds of prey and World Wildlife Fund emblem

1983, Aug. 18 *Perf. 11½x12*

2797 A732 1fo Aquila heliaca .20 .20
2798 A732 1fo Aquila pomarina .20 .20
2799 A732 2fo Haliaetus albicilla .25 .20
2800 A732 2fo Falco vespertinus .25 .20
2801 A732 4fo Falco cherrug .45 .30
2802 A732 6fo Buteo lagopus .75 .35
2803 A732 8fo Buteo buteo .90 .75
Nos. 2797-2803 (7) 3.00 2.20

29th Intl. Apicultural Congress, Budapest, Aug. 25-31 — A733

1983, Aug. 25 *Perf. 12*
2804 A733 1fo Bee collecting pollen .20 .20

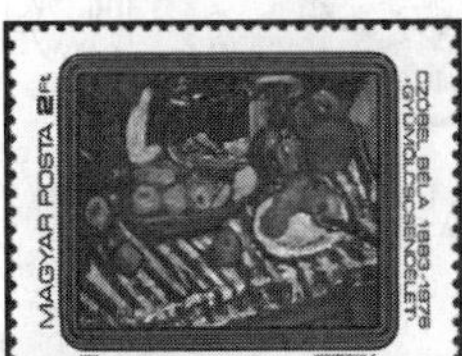

Fruit, by Bela Czobel (1883-1976) — A734

1983, Sept. 15 Litho. *Perf. 12x11½*
2805 A734 2fo multi .25 .20

World Communications Year — A735

No. 2806, Telecommunications, Earth Satellite. No. 2807, Intersputnik Earth Station. 2fo, TMM-81 Telephone Service. 3fo, Intelligent Terminal System. 5fo, OCR Optical Reading Instrument. 8fo, Teletext. 20fo, Molina Communications Satellite.

1983, Oct. 7 Litho. *Perf. 11½x12*
2806 A735 1fo multi .20 .20
2807 A735 1fo multi .20 .20
2808 A735 2fo multi .25 .20
2809 A735 3fo multi .40 .25
2810 A735 5fo multi .70 .40
2811 A735 8fo multi 1.10 .65
Nos. 2806-2811 (6) 2.85 1.90

Souvenir Sheet
Perf. 12x12½
2812 A735 20fo multi 3.00 3.00

34th Intl. Astronautical Federation Congress — A736

1983, Oct. 10 Photo. *Perf. 12*
2813 A736 2fo multi .25 .20

SOZPHILEX 83, Moscow — A737

1983, Oct. 14 Litho. *Perf. 12*
2814 A737 2fo Kremlin .50 .50

Issued in sheets of 3 stamps and 3 labels showing emblem. Size: 101x133mm.

Mihaly Babits (1883-1941), Poet and Translator — A738

1983, Nov. 25
2815 A738 2fo multi .25 .20

Souvenir Sheet

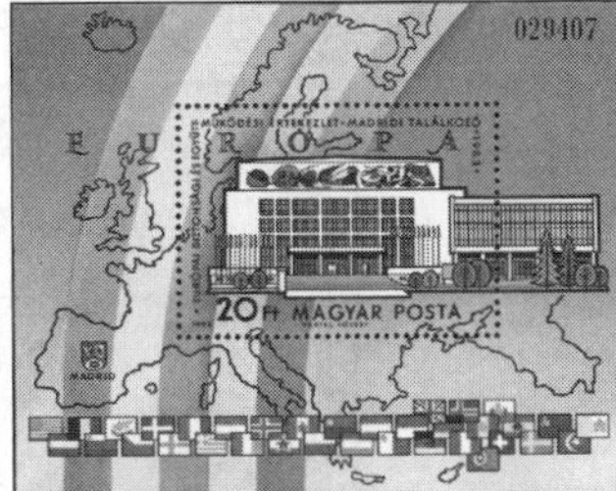

European Security and Cooperation Conference, Madrid — A739

Perf. 12½x11½
1983, Nov. 10 **Litho.**
2816 A739 20fo multi 3.75 3.75

1984 Winter Olympics, Sarajevo — A740

Designs: Ice dancers representing the seven phases of a figure cut.

1983, Dec. 22 Litho. *Perf. 12x12½*
2817 A740 1fo Emblem upper right .20 .20
2818 A740 1fo Emblem upper left .20 .20
2819 A740 2fo Arms extended .25 .20
2820 A740 2fo Arms bent .25 .20
2821 A740 4fo Man looking down .55 .30
2822 A740 4fo Girl looking up .55 .30
2823 A740 6fo multi .85 .45
a. Strip of 7, #2817-2823 3.00 2.00

Souvenir Sheet
Perf. 12½
2824 A740 20fo multi 3.00 3.00

No. 2824 contains one 49x39mm stamp.

Christmas A741

Resorts and Spas — A742

Designs: 1fo, Madonna with Rose, Kassa, 1500. 2fo, Altar piece, Csikmenasag, 1543.

1983, Dec. 13 Litho. *Perf. 11½x12*
2825 A741 1fo multi .20 .20
2826 A741 2fo multi .30 .20

1983, Dec. 18
2827 A742 1fo Zanka, Lake Balaton .20 .20
2828 A742 2fo Hajduszoboszlo .30 .20
2829 A742 5fo Heviz .70 .35
Nos. 2827-2829 (3) 1.20 .75

Virgin with Six Saints, by Giovanni Battista Tiepolo — A743

Rest During Flight into Egypt, by Giovanni Domenico Tiepolo — A744

Paintings Stolen and Later Recovered, Museum of Fine Arts, Budapest: b, Esterhazy Madonna, by Raphael. c, Portrait of Giorgione, 16th cent. d, Portrait of a Woman, by Tintoretto. e, Pietro Bempo, by Raphael. f, Portrait of a Man, by Tintoretto.

1984, Feb. 16 *Perf. 12½x12*
2839 Sheet of 7 3.75 3.75
a.-f. A743 2fo multi .35
g. A744 8fo multi 1.50

Energy Conservation A745

1984, Mar. 30 Litho. *Perf. 11½x12*
2840 A745 1fo multi .25 .20

Sandor Korosi Csoma (1784-1842), Master of Tibetan Philology A746

1984, Mar. 30 *Perf. 11½x12½*
2841 A746 2fo multi .25 .20

Stamps with silver inscription and with back inscription "Gift of the Hungarian Post" issued to members of Natl. Fed. of Hungarian Philatelists.

Miniature Sheet

No. 1900 — A747

Designs: b, No. 1346. c, No. 1259.

1984, Apr. 20 Litho. *Perf. 12x11½*
2842 Sheet of 3 + 3 labels 2.75 2.75
a.-c. A747 4fo multi .70

Espana '84; Ausipex '84; Philatelia '84.

Post-Roman Archaeological Discoveries — A748

#2843, Round gold disc hair ornaments, Rakamaz. #2844, Saber belt plates, Szolnok-Strazsahalom and Galgocz. #2845, Silver disc hair ornaments, Sarospatak. #2846, Swords. 4fo, Silver and gold bowl, Ketpo. 6fo, Bone walking stick handles, Hajdudorog and Szabadbattyan. 8fo, Ivory saddle bow, Izsak; bit, stirrups, Muszka.

1984, May 15 *Perf. 12*
2843 A748 1fo dk brn & tan .20 .20
2844 A748 1fo dk brn & tan .20 .20
2845 A748 2fo dk brn & tan .25 .20
2846 A748 2fo dk brn & tan .25 .20
2847 A748 4fo dk brn & tan .50 .20
2848 A748 6fo dk brn & tan .75 .30
2849 A748 8fo dk brn & tan 1.00 .40
Nos. 2843-2849 (7) 3.15 1.70

View of Cracow — A749

1984, May 21 Litho. *Perf. 12½x11½*
2850 A749 2fo multi .25 .20

Permanent Committee of Posts and Telecommunications, 25th Session, Cracow.

Butterflies A750

1984, June 7 *Perf. 11½x12*
2851 A750 1fo Epiphille dilecta .20 .20
2852 A750 1fo Agra sara .20 .20
2853 A750 2fo Morpho cypris .25 .20
2854 A750 2fo Ancylusis formossissima .25 .20
2855 A750 4fo Danaus chrysippus .50 .20
2856 A750 6fo Catagramma cynosura .75 .30
2857 A750 8fo Ornithoptera paradisea 1.00 .45
Nos. 2851-2857 (7) 3.15 1.75

A751

A752

Archer, by Kisfaludy Strobl (1884-1975).

1984, July 26 Litho. *Perf. 12½x11½*
2858 A751 2fo multicolored .25 .20

1984, July 26
2859 A752 2fo multicolored .25 .20

Akos Hevesi (1884-1937), revolutionary. See Nos. 2884-2885, 2910, 2915, 2962.

Kepes Ujsag Peace Festival A753

Aerobatic Championship A754

1984, Aug. 3 Litho. ***Perf. 12½x11½***
2860 A753 2fo Map, building .25 .20

1984, Aug. 14
2861 A754 2fo Plane, map .25 .20

Horse Team World Championship, Szilvasvarad, Aug. 17-20 — A755

1984, Aug. 17 ***Perf. 12***
2862 A755 2fo Horse-drawn wagon .25 .20

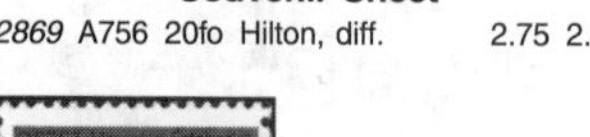

Budapest Riverside Hotels — A756

1984, Sept.
2863 A756 1fo Atrium Hyatt .20 .20
2864 A756 2fo Duna Intercontinental .25 .20
2865 A756 4fo Forum .50 .25
2866 A756 4fo Thermal Hotel, Margaret Isld. .50 .25
2867 A756 5fo Hilton .70 .35
2868 A756 8fo Gellert 1.00 .50
Nos. 2863-2868 (6) 3.15 1.75

Souvenir Sheet
2869 A756 20fo Hilton, diff. 2.75 2.75

14th Conference of Postal Ministers, Budapest — A757

1984, Sept. 10 ***Perf. 12½x11½***
2870 A757 2fo Building, post horn .25 .20

57th Stamp Day A758

1984, Sept. 21 ***Perf. 12***
2871 A758 1fo Four-handled vase, Zsolnay .20 .20
2872 A758 2fo Platter, vert. .25 .20

Souvenir Sheet
2872A A758 10fo #19 on cover 1.75 1.75

No. 2872A contains one stamp (44x27mm, perf. 11).

Edible Mushrooms A759

Photogravure and Engraved
1984, Oct. ***Perf. 12x11½***
2873 A759 1fo Boletus edulis .20 .20
2874 A759 1fo Marasmius oreades .20 .20
2875 A759 2fo Morchella esculenta .30 .20
2876 A759 2fo Agaricus campester .30 .20
2877 A759 3fo Macrolepiota procera .45 .25
2878 A759 3fo Cantharellus cibarius .45 .25
2879 A759 4fo Armillariella mellea .65 .30
Nos. 2873-2879 (7) 2.55 1.60

Budapest Opera House Centenary — A760

1984, Sept. 27 ***Perf. 12x11½***
2880 A760 1fo Fresco by Mor Than .20 .20
2881 A760 2fo Hallway .25 .20
2882 A760 5fo Auditorium .65 .30
Nos. 2880-2882 (3) 1.10 .70

Souvenir Sheet
2883 A760 20fo Building 2.75 2.75

No. 2883 contains one stamp (49x40mm, perf. 12½).

Famous Hungarians Type of 1984

#2884, Bela Balazs, writer (1884-1949); #2885, Kato Haman, labor leader (1884-1936).

1984, Dec. 3 Litho. ***Perf. 12½x11½***
2884 A752 2fo multi .25 .20
2885 A752 2fo multi .25 .20

Madonna and Child, Trensceny A763

1984, Dec. 17 Litho. ***Perf. 11½x12***
2886 A763 1fo multi .20 .20

Owls — A764

Photogravure and Engraved
1984, Dec. 28 ***Perf. 12½x11½***
2887 A764 1fo Athene Noctua .20 .20
2888 A764 1fo Tyto alba .20 .20
2889 A764 2fo Strix aluco .25 .20
2890 A764 2fo Asio otus .25 .20
2891 A764 4fo Nyctea scadiaca .45 .30
2892 A764 6fo Strix uralensis .75 .40
2893 A764 8fo Bubo bubo .90 .50
Nos. 2887-2893 (7) 3.00 2.00

Torah Crown, Buda — A765

19th Cent. Art from Jewish Museum, Budapest.

1984, Dec. Litho. ***Perf. 12***
2894 A765 1fo shown .20 .20
2895 A765 1fo Chalice, Moscow .20 .20
2896 A765 2fo Torah shield, Vienna .25 .20
2897 A765 2fo Chalice, Warsaw .25 .20
2898 A765 4fo Container, Augsburg .55 .20
2899 A765 6fo Candlestick holder, Warsaw .80 .35
2900 A765 8fo Money box, Pest 1.10 .45
Nos. 2894-2900 (7) 3.35 1.80

Souvenir Sheet

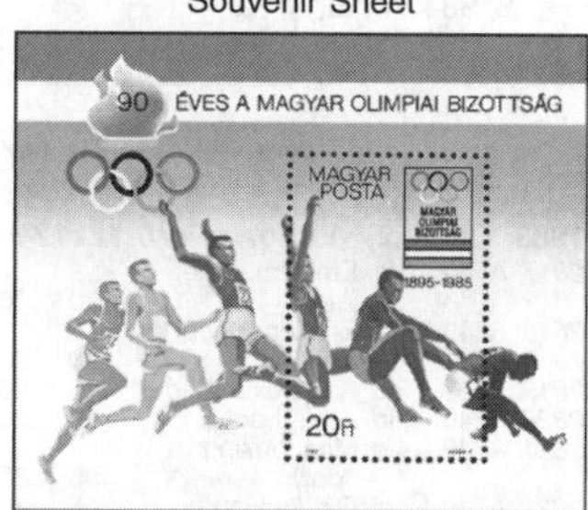

Hungarian Olympic Committee, 90th Anniv. — A766

1985, Jan. 2 Photo. ***Perf. 12x12½***
2901 A766 20fo Long jump 2.75 2.75

Novi Sad, Yugoslavia — A767

Danube Bridges: No. 2903, Baja. No. 2904, Arpad Bridge, Budapest. No. 2905, Bratislava, Czechoslovakia. 4fo, Reichsbrucke, Vienna. 6fo, Linz, Austria. 8fo, Regensburg, Federal Rep. of Germany. 20fo, Elizabeth Bridge, Budapest, and map.

1985, Feb. 12 Litho. ***Perf. 12x11½***
2902 A767 1fo multi .20 .20
2903 A767 1fo multi .20 .20
2904 A767 2fo multi .25 .20
2905 A767 2fo multi .25 .20
2906 A767 4fo multi .50 .25
2907 A767 6fo multi .75 .40
2908 A767 8fo multi 1.00 .45
Nos. 2902-2908 (7) 3.15 1.90

Souvenir Sheet
Perf. 12½
2909 A767 20fo multi 3.00 3.00

Famous Hungarians Type of 1984

Design: Laszlo Rudas (1885-1950), communist philosopher.

1985, Feb. 21 ***Perf. 12½x11½***
2910 A752 2fo gold & brn .25 .20

Intl. Women's Day, 75th Anniv. A769

1985, Mar. 5 Photo. ***Perf. 11½x12½***
2911 A769 2fo gold & multi .25 .20

OLYMPHILEX '85, Lausanne A770

1985, Mar. 14 Litho. ***Perf. 11½x12***
2912 A770 4fo No. B81 .50 .25
2913 A770 5fo No. B82 .65 .30

Souvenir Sheet

Liberation of Hungary From German Occupation Forces, 40th Anniv. — A771

Design: Liberty Bridge, Budapest and silhouette of the Liberation Monument on Gellert Hill illuminated by fireworks.

1985, Mar. 28 ***Perf. 12½***
2914 A771 20fo multi 2.75 2.75

Famous Hungarians Type of 1984

Design: Gyorgy Lukacs (1885-1971) communist philosopher, educator.

1985, Apr. 12 ***Perf. 12½x11½***
2915 A752 2fo gold & brn .25 .20

Totfalusi Bible, 300th Anniv. — A773

1985, Apr. 25 ***Perf. 12***
2916 A773 2fo gold & black .25 .20

1st Bible printed in Hungarian by Nicolas Totfalusi Kis (1650-1702), publisher, in 1685.

Lorand Eotvos Univ., 350th Anniv. — A774

Design: Archbishop Peter Pazmany (1570-1637), founder.

1985, May 14

2917 A774 2fo magenta & gray .25 .20

No. 2917 printed se-tenant with label picturing obverse and reverse of university commemorative medal.

26th European Boxing Championships, Budapest — A775

1985, May 25

2918 A775 2fo multi .25 .20

Intl. Youth Year — A776

1985, May 29 ***Perf. 11½x12***

2919 A776 1fo Girl's soccer	.20	.20
2920 A776 2fo Windsurfing	.20	.20
2921 A776 2fo Aerobic exercise	.20	.20
2922 A776 4fo Karate	.45	.20
2923 A776 4fo Go-kart racing	.45	.20
2924 A776 5fo Hang gliding	.65	.25
2925 A776 6fo Skateboarding	.70	.35
Nos. 2919-2925 (7)	2.85	1.60

Electro-magnetic High-speed Railway — A777

EXPO '85, Tsukuba, Japan: futuristic technology.

1985, May 29 ***Perf. 12x11½***

2926 A777 2fo shown	.25	.20
2927 A777 4fo Fuyo (robot) Theater	.50	.20

Audubon Birth Bicentenary A778

Audubon illustrations

1985, June 19 ***Perf. 12***

2928 A778 2fo Colaptes cafer	.30	.20
2929 A778 2fo Bombycilla garrulus	.30	.20
2930 A778 2fo Dryocopus pileatus	.30	.20
2931 A778 4fo Icterus galbula	.55	.30
Nos. 2928-2931,C446-C447 (6)	2.90	1.75

Mezohegyes Stud Farm, Bicent. — A779

Horses: No. 2932, Nonius-36, 1883, a dark chestnut. No. 2933, Furioso-23, 1889, a light chestnut. No. 2934, Gidrian-1, 1935, a blond breed. No. 2935, Ramses-3, 1960, gray sporting horse. No. 2936, Krozus-1, 1970, chestnut sporting horse.

1985, June 28

2932 A779 1fo multi	.20	.20
2933 A779 2fo multi	.25	.20
2934 A779 4fo multi	.55	.20
2935 A779 4fo multi	.55	.20
2936 A779 6fo multi	.85	.35
Nos. 2932-2936 (5)	2.40	1.15

Prevention of Nuclear War — A780

Design: Illustration of a damaged globe and hands, by Imre Varga (b. 1923), 1973 Kossuth prize-winner.

1985, June 28 ***Perf. 11½x12***

2937 A780 2fo multi .25 .20

Intl. Physician's Movement for the Prevention of Nuclear War, 5th Congress.

European Music Year — A781

1985, July 10 ***Perf. 11***

Composers and instruments: 1fo, George Frideric Handel (1685-1759), kettle drum, horn. 2fo, Johann Sebastian Bach (1685-1750), Thomas Church organ. No. 2940, Luigi Cherubini (1760-1842), harp, bass viol, baryton. No. 2941, Frederic Chopin (1810-1849), piano, 1817. 5fo, Gustav Mahler (1860-1911), pardessus de viole, kettle drum, double horn. 6fo, Erkel Ferenc (1810-1893), bass tuba, violin.

2938 A781 1fo multi	.20	.20
2939 A781 2fo multi	.25	.20
2940 A781 4fo multi	.50	.20
2941 A781 4fo multi	.50	.20
2942 A781 5fo multi	.65	.25
2943 A781 6fo multi	.75	.30
Nos. 2938-2943 (6)	2.85	1.35

Souvenir Sheet

12th World Youth Festival, Moscow — A782

1985, July 22 ***Perf. 12½***

2944 A782 20fo Emblem, Red Square 2.75 2.50

Souvenir Sheet

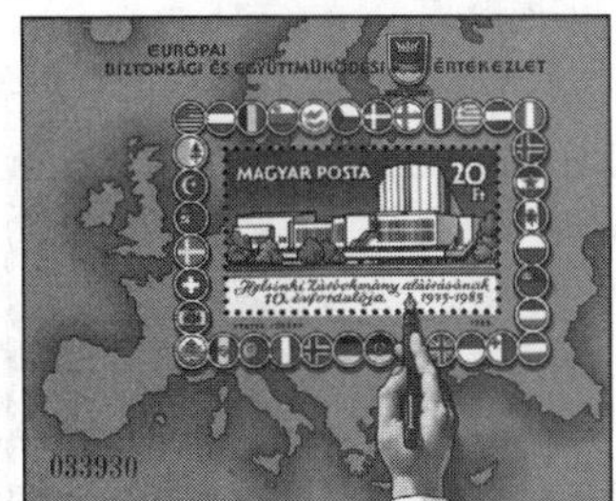
Helsinki Agreement, 10th Anniv. — A783

1985, Aug. 1 ***Perf. 11***

2945 A783 20fo Finlandia Hall, Helsinki 3.00 3.00

World Tourism Day — A784

Perf. 12½x11½

1985, Sept. 27 **Litho.**

2946 A784 2fo Key, globe, heart .25 .20

COMNET '85 — A785

1985, Oct. 1 ***Perf. 11½***

2947 A785 4fo Computer terminal .60 .30

3rd Computer Sciences Conference, Budapest, Oct. 1-4.

Souvenir Sheet

Danube River, Budapest Bridges — A786

1985, Oct. 15 ***Perf. 12***

2948 A786 20fo multi 3.25 3.25

European Security and Cooperation Conference and Cultural Forum, Budapest, Oct. 15-Nov. 25. Exists inscribed "Kuturalis Forum Resztvevoi Tiszteletere" in gold on front and "Gift of the Hungarian Post" on back. Not valid for postage.

16-17th Century Ceramics — A787

1fo, Faience water jar and dispenser, 1609. 2fo, Tankard, 1670. 10fo, Hexagonal medicine jar, 1774.

1985, Oct. 18 ***Perf. 12½x11½***

2949 A787 1fo multi	.20	.20
2950 A787 2fo multi	.35	.20

Souvenir Sheet

2951 A787 10fo multi 1.75 1.75

EUROPHILEX '85, Oct. 14-31.

Italy No. 799, view of Rome — A788

1985, Oct. 21 ***Perf. 12x11½***

2952 A788 5fo multi .90 .90

Italia '85, Rome, Oct. 25-Nov. 3.

Issued in sheets of 3 stamps and 3 labels showing emblem.

UN, 40th Anniv. — A789

1985, Oct. 24 ***Perf. 11½x12***

2953 A789 4fo Dove, globe, emblem .50 .30

Indigenous Lilies — A790

Photogravure and Engraved

1985, Oct. 28 *Perf. 12x11½*

2954 A790 1fo Lilium bulbiferum .20 .20
2955 A790 2fo Lilium martagon .25 .20
2956 A790 2fo Erythronium dens-canis .25 .20
2957 A790 4fo Fritillaria meleagris .55 .20
2958 A790 4fo Lilium tigrinum .55 .20
2959 A790 5fo Hemerocallis lilio-asphodelus .70 .30
2960 A790 6fo Bulbocodium vernum .85 .35
Nos. 2954-2960 (7) 3.35 1.65

Christmas 1985 — A791

1985, Nov. 6 Litho. *Perf. 13½x13*

2961 A791 2fo Youths caroling .25 .20

Famous Hungarians Type of 1984

Design: Istvan Ries (1885-1950), Minister of Justice (1949), labor movement.

1985, Nov. 11 *Perf. 12½x11½*

2962 A752 2fo gold & ol brn .25 .20

Motorcycle Centenary — A793

Photogravure & Engraved

1985, Dec. 28 *Perf. 11½x12*

2963 A793 1fo Fantic Sprinter, 1984 .20 .20
2964 A793 2fo Suzuki Katana GSX, 1983 .20 .20
2965 A793 2fo Harley-Davidson Duo-Glide, 1960 .20 .20
2966 A793 4fo Rudge-Whitworth, 1935 .45 .20
2967 A793 4fo BMW R47, 1927 .45 .20
2968 A793 5fo NSU, 1910 .60 .20
2969 A793 6fo Daimler, 1885 .70 .25
Nos. 2963-2969 (7) 2.80 1.45

Bela Kun (1886-1939), Communist Party Founder — A794

Perf. 12½x11½

1986, Feb. 20 **Litho.**

2970 A794 4fo multi .50 .30

Souvenir Sheet

US Shuttle Challenger — A795

1986, Feb. 21 *Perf. 11½*

2971 A795 20fo multi 3.25 3.25

Memorial to the US astronauts who died when the Challenger exploded during takeoff, Jan. 28.

Halley's Comet — A796

#2972, US Ice satellite, dinosaurs. #2973, USSR Vega and Bayeaux tapestry detail, 1066, France. #2974, Japanese Suisei and German engraving, 1507. #2975, European Space Agency Giotto and The Three Magi, tapestry by Giotto. #2976, USSR Astron and Apianis constellation, 1531. #2977, US space shuttle and Edmond Halley.

Perf. 11½x13½

1986, Feb. 14 **Litho.**

2972 A796 2fo multi .25 .20
2973 A796 2fo multi .25 .20
2974 A796 2fo multi .25 .20
2975 A796 4fo multi .45 .20
2976 A796 4fo multi .45 .20
2977 A796 6fo multi .80 .35
Nos. 2972-2977 (6) 2.45 1.35

Seeing-eye Dog, Red Cross A797

Soccer Players in Blue and Red Uniforms A798

Perf. 12½x11½

1986, Mar. 20 **Litho.**

2978 A797 4fo multi .50 .20

Assistance for the blind.

1986, Apr. 2 *Perf. 11*

Color of Uniforms

2979 A798 2fo shown .25 .20
2980 A798 2fo blue & green .25 .20
2981 A798 4fo red & black .55 .20
2982 A798 4fo yellow & red .55 .20
2983 A798 4fo yellow & green .55 .20
2984 A798 6fo orange & white .75 .30
Nos. 2979-2984 (6) 2.90 1.30

Souvenir Sheet

Perf. 12½

2985 A798 20fo Victors 3.50 3.50

1986 World Cup Soccer Championships, Mexico. No. 2979 contains one stamp (size: 41x32mm). Also exists with added inscription "In honor of the winner . . ." and red control number.

Buda Castle Cable Railway Station Reopening — A799

1986, Apr. 30 *Perf. 11½x12*

2986 A799 2fo org, brn & pale yel .40 .20

A800

A801

AMERIPEX '86, Chicago, May 22-June 1: a, Yankee doodle rose. b, America rose. c, George Washington, statue by Gyula Bezeredy (1858-1935), Budapest.

1986, Apr. 30 *Perf. 12½x11½*

Souvenir Sheet

2987 Sheet of 3 3.25 3.00
a.-b. A800 5fo any single .75 .75
c. A800 10fo multi 1.50 1.50

Size of No. 2987c: 27x74mm.

1986, May 6 *Perf. 11½x12*

2988 A801 4fo Folk dolls .50 .30

Hungary Days in Tokyo.

Andras Fay (1786-1864), Author, Politician — A802

Lithographed and Engraved

1986, May 29 *Perf. 12*

2989 A802 4fo beige & fawn .50 .30

Printed se-tenant with label picturing First Hungarian Savings Bank Union, founded by Fay.

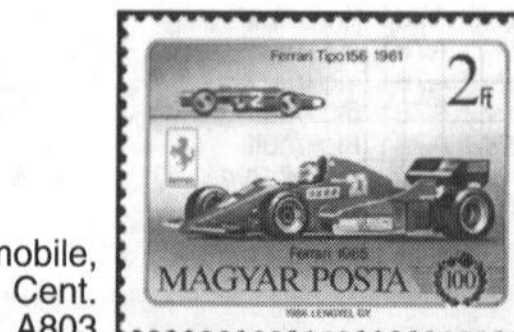

Automobile, Cent. A803

#2990, 1961 Ferrari Tipo 156, 1985 race car. #2991, 1932 Alfa Romeo Tipo B, 1984 race car. #2992, 1936 Volkswagen, 1986 Porsche 959. #2993, 1902 Renault 14CV, 1985 Renault 5 GT Turbo. #2994, 1899 Fiat 3½, 1985 Fiat Ritmo. 6fo, 1886 Daimler, 1986 Mercedes-Benz 230SE.

1986, July 24 Litho. *Perf. 12*

2990 A803 2fo multi .25 .20
2991 A803 2fo multi .25 .20
2992 A803 2fo multi .25 .20
2993 A803 4fo multi .55 .20
2994 A803 4fo multi .55 .20
2995 A803 6fo multi .85 .35
Nos. 2990-2995 (6) 2.70 1.35

Wasa, 1628, Warship — A804

1986, Aug. 15 Litho. *Perf. 11½x12*

2996 A804 2fo multi .50 .50

STOCKHOLMIA '86, 8/28-9/7. Printed se-tenant with label (size: 27x34mm) picturing exhibition emblem. Printed in sheets of 3.

14th Intl. Cancer Congress, Budapest — A805

Design: Moritz Kaposi (1837-1902), Austrian cancer researcher.

1986, Aug. 21 *Perf. 12½x11½*

2997 A805 4fo multicolored .50 .30

Recapture of Buda Castle, by Gyula Benzcur (1844-1920) — A806

1986, Sept. 2 *Perf. 12*

2998 A806 4fo multicolored .50 .30

Recapture of Buda from the Turks, 300th anniv.

Tranquility — A807

Hope — A808

Stamp Day: Paintings by Endre Szasz.

1986, Sept. 5

2999 A807 2fo shown .30 .20
3000 A807 2fo Confidence .30 .20

Souvenir Sheet

Perf. 11½

3001 A808 10fo shown 1.75 1.75

5th Intl. Conference on Oriental Carpets, Vienna and Budapest A809

1986, Sept. 17 Litho. *Perf. 11*

3002 A809 4fo Anatolia crivelli, 15th cent. .60 .30

Franz Liszt, Composer A810

1986, Oct. 21 Engr. *Perf. 12*

3003 A810 4fo grayish green .50 .30

Intl. Peace Year — A811

1986, Oct. 24 Litho.

3004 A811 4fo multicolored .50 .30

No. 3004 printed se-tenant with label.

Souvenir Sheet

Hofburg Palace, Vienna, and Map — A812

1986, Nov. 4 *Perf. 11*

3005 A812 20fo multicolored 3.00 2.75

European Security and Cooperation Conference, Vienna.

Fruits A813

Photogravure & Engraved

1986, Nov. 25 *Perf. 12x11½*

3006 A813 2fo Sour cherries .25 .20
3007 A813 2fo Apricots .25 .20
3008 A813 4fo Peaches .50 .25
3009 A813 4fo Raspberries .50 .25
3010 A813 4fo Apples .50 .25
3011 A813 6fo Grapes .80 .35
Nos. 3006-3011 (6) 2.80 1.50

Natl. Heroes — A814

Designs: No. 3012, Jozseph Pogany (1886-1939), journalist, martyr. No. 3013, Ferenc Munnich (1886-1967), prime minister, 1958-61.

1986 Litho. *Perf. 12½x11½*

3012 A814 4fo multi .65 .30
3013 A814 4fo multi .65 .30

Issued: #3012, Nov. 6; #3013, Nov. 14.

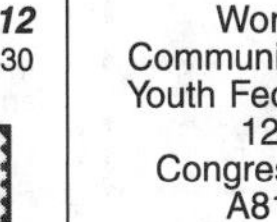

World Communist Youth Fed., 12th Congress A815

1986, Nov. 21 *Perf. 12*

3014 A815 4fo multi .50 .30

Castles — A816

Festetics Castle, Keszthely A816a

2fo, Forgach, Szecseny. 3fo, Savoya, Rackeve. 4fo, Batthyany, Kormend. 5fo, Szechenyi, Nagycenk. 6fo, Rudnyanszky, Nagyteteny. 7fo, Esterhazy, Papa. 8fo, Szapary, Buk. 10fo, Festetics, Keszthely. 12fo, Dory Castle, Mihalyi. 20fo, Brunswick, Martonvasar. 30fo, De la Motte, Nosvaj. 40fo, L'Huillier-Coborg, Edeleny. 50fo, Teleki-Degenfeld, Szirak. 70fo, Magochy, Pacin. 100fo, Eszterhazy, Fertod.

Perf. 12x11½, 11½x12½ (7fo)

1986-91 Litho.

3015 A816 2fo multi .20 .20
3016 A816 3fo multi .20 .20
3017 A816 4fo multi .20 .20
3018 A816 5fo multi .30 .20
3019 A816 6fo multi .35 .20
3020 A816 7fo multi .50 .30
3021 A816 8fo multi .50 .30
3022 A816 10fo multi .85 .40
3023 A816 12fo multi .90 .50
3024 A816 20fo multi 1.75 .75
3025 A816 30fo multi 2.25 1.10
3026 A816 40fo multi 3.00 1.60
3027 A816 50fo multi 4.00 1.90
3028 A816 70fo multi 5.00 2.75
3029 A816 100fo multi 8.00 4.00
Nos. 3015-3029 (15) 28.00 14.60

The 7fo, 12fo are inscribed "Magyarorszag."
Issued: 2-6, 8fo, 11/28; 10, 20-30, 100fo, 5/28/87; 40-60fo, 7/30/87; 7fo, 6/27/91; 12fo, 9/6/91.
For overprint see No. 3320.

1989-92 Litho. & Engr. *Perf. 12*

3030 A816a 10fo multi 1.50 .85

Litho.

3031 A816a 15fo multi 1.10 .65

The 15fo is inscribed "Magyarorszag."
Issued: 10fo, Feb. 28; 15fo, Mar. 27, 1992.

Wildlife Conservation A817

1986, Dec. 15 *Perf. 12*

3035 A817 2fo Felis silvestris .30 .20
3036 A817 2fo Lutra lutra .30 .20
3037 A817 2fo Mustela erminea .30 .20
3038 A817 4fo Sciurus vulgaris .55 .30
3039 A817 4fo Erinaceus concolor .55 .30
3040 A817 6fo Emys orbicularis .80 .40
Nos. 3035-3040 (6) 2.80 1.60

Portraits of Hungarian Kings in the Historical Portrait Gallery — A818

King and reign: No. 3041, St. Steven, 997-1038. No. 3042, Geza I, 1074-1077. No. 3043, St. Ladislas, 1077-1095. No. 3044, Bela III, 1172-1196. No. 3045, Bela IV, 1235-1270.

1986, Dec. 10 *Perf. 11½x12*

3041 A818 2fo multi .30 .20
3042 A818 2fo multi .30 .20
3043 A818 4fo multi .60 .30
3044 A818 4fo multi .60 .30
3045 A818 6fo multi .90 .45
Nos. 3041-3045 (5) 2.70 1.45

See Nos. 3120-3122.

Fungi — A819

Lithographed and Engraved

1986, Dec. 30 *Perf. 11½*

3046 A819 2fo Amanita phalloides .30 .20
3047 A819 2fo Inocybe patouillardi .30 .20
3048 A819 2fo Amanita muscaria .30 .20
3049 A819 4fo Omphalotus olearius .55 .30
3050 A819 4fo Amanita pantherina .55 .30
3051 A819 6fo Gyromitra esculenta .80 .40
Nos. 3046-3051 (6) 2.80 1.60

Saltwater Fish — A820

1987, Jan. 15 Photo. *Perf. 11½*

3052 A820 2fo Colisa fasciata .30 .20
3053 A820 2fo Pseudotropheus zebra .30 .20
3054 A820 2fo Iriatherina werneri .30 .20
3055 A820 4fo Aphyosemion multicolor .55 .30
3056 A820 4fo Papiliochromis ramirezi .55 .30
3057 A820 6fo Hyphessobrycon erythrostigma .80 .40
Nos. 3052-3057 (6) 2.80 1.60

Seated Woman, 1918, by Bela Uitz (1887-1972), Painter A821

Abstract, 1960, by Lajos Kassak (1887-1967) A822

1987, Mar. 6 Litho. *Perf. 12*

3058 A821 4fo multicolored .50 .30

1987, Mar. 20

3059 A822 4fo black & red .50 .30

Medical Pioneers — A823

Designs: 2fo, Hippocrates (460-377 B.C.), Greek physician. No. 3061, Avicenna or Ibn Sina (A.D. 980-1037), Islamic pharmacist, diagnostician. No. 3062, Ambroise Pare (1510-1590), French surgeon. No. 3063, William Harvey (1578-1657), English physician, anatomist. 6fo, Ignaz Semmelweis (1818-1865), Hungarian obstetrician.

1987, Mar. 31

3060 A823 2fo black & dk red brn .30 .20
3061 A823 4fo black & dk grn .55 .30
3062 A823 4fo black & steel bl .55 .30
3063 A823 4fo black & olive blk .55 .30
3064 A823 6fo black & grn blk .80 .40
Nos. 3060-3064 (5) 2.75 1.50

Neolithic and Copper Age Artifacts — A824

1987, Apr. 15 Litho. *Perf. 12*

Designs: 2fo, Urn, Hodmezovasarhely. No. 3066, Altar, Szeged. No. 3067, Deity, Szegvar-Tuzkoves. 5fo, Vase, Center.

3065 A824 2fo pale bl grn & sep .25 .20
3066 A824 4fo buff & sepia .55 .30
3067 A824 4fo pale org & sepia .55 .30
3068 A824 5fo pale yel grn & sep .80 .40
Nos. 3065-3068 (4) 2.15 1.20

Souvenir Sheet

Esztergom Cathedral Treasury Reopening — A825

1987, Apr. 28 ***Perf. 11***
3069 A825 20fo Calvary of King Matthias 3.50 3.50

No. 3069 margin pictures the Horn Chalice of King Sigismund, Rhineland, 1408 (UL), Crozier of Archbishop Miklos Olah, Hungary, c. 1490 (UR), Monstrance of Imre Eszterhazy, by Gaspar Meichl, Vienna, 1728 (LL), and the Chalice of Matthias, Hungary, c. 1480.

Hungarian First Aid Assoc., Cent. — A826

1987, May 5 ***Perf. 11½x12***
3070 A826 4fo Ambulances, 1887-1987 .50 .30

Souvenir Sheet

CAPEX '87, Toronto A827

Stamp exhibitions: b, OLYMPHILEX '87, Rome. c, HAFNIA '87, Copenhagen.

1987, May 20 **Litho.** ***Perf. 11***
3071 Sheet of 3 + 3 labels 3.50 2.75
a.-c. A827 5fo any single 1.25 .90

Jozsef Marek (1886-1952), Veterinarian — A828

1987, May 25 ***Perf. 12x11½***
3072 A828 4fo multicolored .50 .30

Veterinary education, bicent.

Teleki's African Expedition, Cent. — A829

1987, June 10
3073 A829 4fo multicolored .50 .30

Samuel Teleki (1845-1916), explorer.

Woodcut by Abraham von Werdt, 18th Cent. — A830

Litho. & Engr.

1987, June 25 ***Perf. 12***
3074 A830 4fo beige & sepia .50 .30

Hungarian Printing, Paper and Press Workers' Union, 125th anniv.

Antarctic Research, 75th Anniv. — A831

Helicopter Landing, Mirnij Research Station — A832

1987, June 30 **Litho.**

Map, explorer and scene: No. 3075, James Cook (1728-1779) and ship. No. 3076, Fabian von Bellingshausen (1778-1852) and seals. No. 3077, Ernest H. Shackleton (1874-1922) and penguins. No. 3078, Roald Amundsen (1872-1928) discovering South Pole, dog team. No. 3079, Robert F. Scott (1868-1912) and ship. No. 3080, Richard E. Byrd (1888-1957) and Floyd Bennett monoplane.

3075 A831 2fo multi .30 .20
3076 A831 2fo multi .30 .20
3077 A831 2fo multi .30 .20
3078 A831 4fo multi .55 .30
3079 A831 4fo multi .55 .30
3080 A831 6fo multi .80 .40
Nos. 3075-3080 (6) 2.80 1.60

Souvenir Sheet

Perf. 11½

3081 A832 20fo multi 3.00 3.00

Railway Officers Training Institute, Cent. — A833

1987, Sept. 4 **Litho.** ***Perf. 11½x12***
3082 A833 4fo blue & black .75 .50

Stamp Day, 60th Anniv. — A834

Litho. & Engr.

1987, Sept. 18 ***Perf. 12***

Masonry of the medieval Buda Castle: 2fo, Flowers, dolphin. 4fo, Arms of King Matthias. 10fo, "ONDIDIT/GENEROSVM" inscribed on capital.

3083 A834 2fo multi .35 .20
3084 A834 4fo multi .70 .45

Souvenir Sheet

Perf. 11

3085 A834 10fo multi 1.75 1.75

A835

1987, Sept. 30 **Litho.** ***Perf. 12***
3086 A835 4fo multi .80 .50
a. Se-tenant with label .80 .50

No 3086 printed in sheet of 50 and in sheet of 25 plus 25 labels picturing 13th cent. church at Gyongyospata which houses the altar.

A836

Orchids A837

1987, Oct. 29 **Litho.** ***Perf. 11***
3087 A836 2fo Cypripedium calceolus .35 .25
3088 A836 2fo Orchis purpurea .35 .25
3089 A836 4fo Himantoglossum hircinum .60 .50
3090 A836 4fo Ophrys scolopax cornuta .65 .50
3091 A836 5fo Cephalanthera rubra .75 .60
3092 A836 6fo Epipactis atrorubens .80 .75
Nos. 3087-3092 (6) 3.50 2.85

Miniature Sheet

3093 A837 20fo shown 3.50 3.25

1988 Winter Olympics, Calgary — A838

1987, Nov. 24
3094 A838 2fo Speed skating .35 .25
3095 A838 2fo Cross-country skiing .35 .25
3096 A838 4fo Biathlon .65 .40
3097 A838 4fo Ice hockey .65 .40
3098 A838 4fo 4-Man bobsled .65 .40
3099 A838 6fo Ski-jumping 1.00 .65
Nos. 3094-3099 (6) 3.65 2.35

Souvenir Sheet

3100 A838 20fo Slalom 3.50 3.25

Souvenir Sheet

U.S.-Soviet Summit, Dec. 7-10 — A839

1987, Dec. 7 ***Perf. 12***
3101 A839 20fo Shaking hands 3.50 3.25

Meeting of Gen. Secretary Gorbachev and Pres. Reagan to discuss and sign nuclear arms reduction treaty.

Fairy Tales — A840

Designs: No. 3102, The White Crane, from Japan. No. 3103, The Fox and the Crow, Aesop's Fables. No. 3104, The Tortoise and the Hare, Aesop's Fables. No. 3105, The Ugly Duckling, by Hans Christian Andersen. No. 3106, The Steadfast Tin Soldier, by Andersen.

1987, Dec. 11
3102 A840 2fo multi .40 .25
3103 A840 2fo multi .40 .25
3104 A840 4fo multi .75 .50
3105 A840 4fo multi .75 .50
3106 A840 6fo multi 1.00 .75
Nos. 3102-3106 (5) 3.30 2.25

Count Ferdinand von Zeppelin (1838-1917), Designer of Dirigibles — A841

1988, Jan. 29 **Litho.** ***Perf. 12***
3107 A841 2fo LZ-2, 1905 .35 .25
3108 A841 4fo LZ-4, 1908 .75 .40
3109 A841 4fo LZ-10, Schwaben, 1911 .75 .40
3110 A841 8fo LZ-127, Graf Zeppelin, 1928 1.40 .80
Nos. 3107-3110 (4) 3.25 1.85

1988 World Figure Skating Championships, Budapest — A842

Various athletes wearing period costumes.

1988, Feb. 29 **Photo.** ***Perf. 11½***
3111 A842 2fo Male, 20th cent. .35 .25
3112 A842 2fo Male, (cap), 19th cent. .35 .25
3113 A842 4fo Male (hat), 18th cent. .60 .40
3114 A842 4fo Woman, c. 1930 .60 .40

3115 A842	5fo Woman (contemporary)	.75	.50
3116 A842	6fo Pair	1.00	.65
	Nos. 3111-3116 (6)	3.65	2.45

Souvenir Sheet

Perf. 12x11½

3117 A842	20fo Death spiral	3.50	3.25

No. 3117 contains one 37x52mm stamp.

Illes Monus (1888-1944), Party Leader — A843

1988, Mar. 11 Litho. *Perf. 11½x12*

3118 A843	4fo multi	.75	.50

See Nos. 3152, 3160.

Miniature Sheet

Postmaster's Coat, Hat and Post Horn, 18th Cent. — A844

1988, Mar. 18 Litho. *Perf. 13*

3119 A844	4fo + 4 labels	1.25	1.25

Intl. stamp exhibitions, 1988. No. 3119 contains 4 labels picturing exhibition emblems: JUVALUX '88, Luxembourg, Mar. 29-Apr. 4 (UL), SYDPEX '88, Sydney, Australia, July 30-Aug.7 (UR), FINLANDIA '88, Helsinki, Finland, June 1-12 (LR), and PRAGA '88, Prague, Czechoslovakia, Aug. 26-Sept. 4 (LL).

King Type of 1986

Portraits of Hungarian kings in the Historical Portrait Gallery. King and reign: 2fo, Charles Robert (1308-1342). 4fo, Louis I (1342-1382). 6fo, Sigismund (1387-1437).

1988, Mar. 31 *Perf. 11½x12*

3120 A818	2fo pale grn, sep & red	.30	.20
3121 A818	4fo pale ultra, sep & red	.60	.45
3122 A818	6fo pale vio, sep & red	.90	.65
	Nos. 3120-3122 (3)	1.80	1.30

1988 Summer Olympics, Seoul — A845

1988, Apr. 20 Litho. *Perf. 13½x13*

3123 A845	2fo Rowing	.30	.20
3124 A845	4fo Hurdling	.60	.45
3125 A845	4fo Fencing	.60	.45
3126 A845	6fo Boxing	.90	.65
	Nos. 3123-3126 (4)	2.40	1.75

Souvenir Sheet

Perf. 12½

3127 A845	20fo Tennis	3.75	3.25

Computer Animation A846

1988, May 12 *Perf. 12*

Design: Graphic from the computer-animated film *Dilemma*, 1972, by graphic artist Janos Kass (b. 1927) and cartoon film director John Halas (b. 1912).

3128 A846	4fo black, pur & ver	.75	.50

Eurocheck Congress, June 10, Budapest — A847

1988, June 10 Litho. *Perf. 12*

3129 A847	4fo multicolored	.75	.50

Eurocheck as legal tender, 20th anniv.

Sovereign of the Seas — A848

1988, June 30

3130 A848	2fo shown	.35	.20
3131 A848	2fo *Santa Maria*	.35	.25
3132 A848	2fo *Mayflower*	.35	.25
3133 A848	4fo *Jylland*	.75	.50
3134 A848	6fo *St. Jupat*	1.10	.80
	Nos. 3130-3134 (5)	2.90	2.00

Fight Drug Abuse — A849

1988, July 7 Litho. *Perf. 12*

3135 A849	4fo multicolored	.75	.50

Ducks A850

1988, July 29 Litho. *Perf. 13x13½*

3136 A850	2fo Anas crecca	.30	.20
3137 A850	2fo Bucephala clangula	.30	.20
3138 A850	4fo Anas penelope	.65	.45
a.	Pane of 10 #3136 + 10 #3138 with gutter btwn.	12.00	
	Complete booklet, #3138a, with text and cover in either English or German	12.00	
3139 A850	4fo Netta rufina	.65	.50
3140 A850	6fo Anas strepera	1.10	.65
	Nos. 3136-3140 (5)	3.00	2.00

Souvenir Sheet

Perf. 12½x11½

3141 A850	20fo Anas platyrhynchos	4.00	3.50

No. 3141 contains one 52x37mm stamp.
For surcharges see Nos. 3199-3200.

Antique Toys — A851

1988, Aug. 12 *Perf. 12*

3142 A851	2fo Train	.30	.25
3143 A851	2fo See-saw	.30	.25
3144 A851	4fo +2fo Pecking chickens	1.00	.65
3145 A851	5fo String-manipulated soldier	.85	.55
	Nos. 3142-3145 (4)	2.45	1.70

Surtax for youth philately programs.

Calvinist College, Debrecen, 450th Anniv. — A852

1988, Aug. 16 Litho. *Perf. 13½x13*

3146 A852	4fo multi	.75	.50

58th American Society of Travel Agents World Congress, Oct. 23-29, Budapest A853

1988, Aug. 30 *Perf. 12*

3147 A853	4fo multi	.75	.50

P.O. Officials Training School, Cent. — A854

1988, Sept. 9 Litho. *Perf. 12*

3148 A854	4fo Badge on collar	.75	.50

Gabor Baross (1848-1892), Minister of Commerce and Communication — A855

Portrait and: 2fo, Postal Savings Bank, Budapest, emblem and postal savings stamp. 4fo, Telephone and telegraph apparatus, registration label and cancellations. 10fo, East Railway Station, Budapest.

1988, Sept. 16

3149 A855	2fo multi	.30	.25
3150 A855	4fo multi	.65	.50

Souvenir Sheet

Perf. 11½

3151 A855	10fo multi	2.25	2.00

No. 3151 contains one 50x29mm stamp.

Famous Hungarians Type of 1988

Gyula Lengyel (1888-1941), political writer.

1988, Oct. 7 *Perf. 11½x12*

3152 A843	4fo multi	.75	.50

Christmas — A857

Perf. 12½x11½

1988, Nov. 10 Litho.

3153 A857	2fo multi	.40	.25

Nobel Prize Winners — A858

Designs: No. 3154, Richard Adolf Zsigmondy (1865-1929), Germany, chemistry (1925). No. 3155, Robert Barany (1876-1936), Austria, medicine (1914). No. 3156, Georg von Hevesy (1885-1966), Hungary, chemistry (1943). No. 3157, Albert Szent-Gyorgyi (1893-1986), Hungary-US, medicine (1937). No. 3158, Georg von Bekesy (1899-1972), US, medicine (1961). 6fo, Denis Gabor (1900-1979), Great Britain, physics (1971).

Litho. & Engr.

1988, Nov. 30 *Perf. 12*

3154 A858	2fo red brown	.35	.25
3155 A858	2fo green	.35	.25
3156 A858	2fo deep claret	.35	.25
3157 A858	4fo rose lake	.60	.40
3158 A858	4fo steel blue	.60	.40
3159 A858	6fo sepia	.75	.65
	Nos. 3154-3159 (6)	3.00	2.20

Famous Hungarians Type of 1988

Arpad Szakasits (1888-1965), party leader.

1988, Dec. 6 *Perf. 11½x12*

3160 A843	4fo multicolored	.75	.50

Souvenir Sheet

Medals Won by Hungarian Athletes at the 1988 Seoul Olympic Games — A860

1988, Dec. 19 Litho. *Perf. 12*

3161 A860	20fo multicolored	3.75	3.50

Silver and Cast Iron — A861

1988, Dec. 28 Litho. & Engr.

3162 A861 2fo Teapot, Pest, 1846	.35	.25
3163 A861 2fo Coffee pot, Buda, 18th cent.	.35	.25
3164 A861 4fo Sugar bowl, Pest, 1822	.65	.45
3165 A861 5fo Cast iron plate, Romania, 1850	.85	.55
Nos. 3162-3165 (4)	2.20	1.50

Postal Savings Bank Inauguration — A862

1989, Jan. 20 Litho. *Perf. 12x11½*

3166 A862 5fo royal blue, blk & silver .90 .55

Kalman Wallisch (1889-1934), Labor Leader — A863

1989, Feb. 28 Litho. *Perf. 12*

3167 A863 3fo dk red & brt bl .55 .35

See No. 3170.

World Indoor Sports Championships, Budapest, Mar. 3-5 — A864

1989, Mar. 3 *Perf. 13x13½*

3168 A864 3fo multicolored .55 .35

Souvenir Sheet

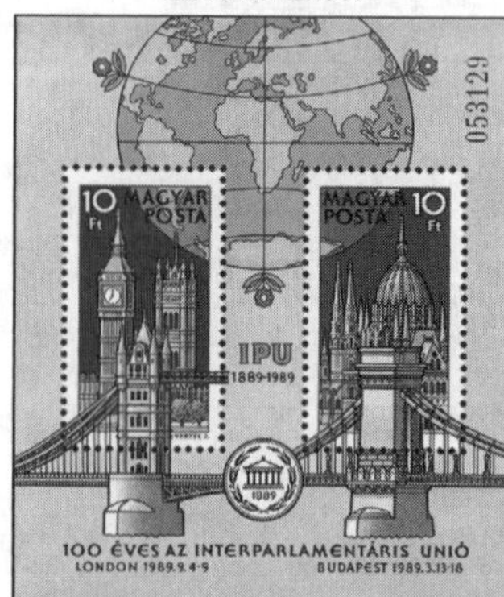

Interparliamentary Union Cent. and 81st Session, Budapest, Mar. 13-18 — A865

a, Parliament, Big Ben & Tower Bridge, London. b, Parliament & Chain Bridge, Budapest.

1989, Mar. 13 Litho. *Perf. 11*

3169 A865 Sheet of 2 3.75 3.50
a.-b. 10fo any single 1.75 1.60

Exists with red inscriptions and control number.

Famous Hungarians Type of 1989

Janos Gyetvai (1889-1967), journalist, diplomat.

1989, Apr. 7 Litho. *Perf. 12*

3170 A863 3fo dark red & brt grn .55 .35

Stud Farm at Babolna, 200th Anniv. A867

Horses: a, O Bajan. b, Meneskari Csikos. c, Gazal II.

1989, May 18 Litho. *Perf. 12*

3171 Strip of 3 1.75 1.10
a.-c. A867 3fo any single .55 .35

ART '89, May 23-27, Budapest A868

1989, May 23 *Perf. 12x11½*

3172 A868 5fo multi .90 .55

Exhibition for disabled artists.

Flower Arrangements — A869

1989, May 31 *Perf. 12*

3173 A869 2fo multi, vert.	.35	.25
3174 A869 3fo multi, vert.	.40	.30
3175 A869 3fo shown	.40	.30
3176 A869 5fo multi, diff.	.85	.50
3177 A869 10fo multi, vert.	1.50	1.00
Nos. 3173-3177 (5)	3.50	2.35

French Revolution, Bicent. A870

1989, June 1 *Perf. 12*

3178 A870 5fo brt blue, blk & red .75 .50

Souvenir Sheet

Perf. 11½

3179 A870 20fo like 5fo 3.50 3.25

No. 3179 contains one 50x30mm stamp.

Medieval Church of the Csolts Near Veszto — A871

Photography, 150th Anniv. — A872

1989, June 15 Litho. *Perf. 12*

3180 A871 3fo multi .50 .30

1989, June 15

3181 A872 5fo multi .80 .50

Old Mills — A873

Designs: 2fo, Water mill, Turistvandi, 18th cent. 3fo, Horse-driven mill, Szarvas, 1836. 5fo, Windmill, Kiskunhalas, 18th cent. 10fo, Water wheel on the Drava River.

1989, June 20

3182 A873 2fo multi	.30	.20
3183 A873 3fo multi	.45	.30
3184 A873 5fo multi	.75	.50
3185 A873 10fo multi	1.50	1.00
Nos. 3182-3185 (4)	3.00	2.00

Souvenir Sheet

1st Moon Landing, 20th Anniv. — A874

1989, July 12 Litho. *Perf. 12½*

3186 A874 20fo multi 3.75 3.50

Gliders — A875

1989, July 20 *Perf. 12*

3187 A875 3fo Futar .45 .30
3188 A875 5fo Cimbora .80 .60

17th Intl. Old Timers Rally, Budakeszi Airport, and 60th anniv. of glider flying in Hungary.

Reptiles A876

1989, July 26 *Perf. 11*

3189 A876 2fo *Lacerta agilis*	.25	.20
3190 A876 3fo *Lacerta viridis*	.45	.25
3191 A876 5fo *Vipera rakosiensis*	.70	.40
3192 A876 5fo *Natrix natrix*	.70	.40
3193 A876 10fo *Emys orbicularis*	1.25	.75
Nos. 3189-3193 (5)	3.35	2.00

31st Modern Pentathlon World Championships, Aug. 30-Sept. 4, Budapest — A877

1989, July 31 *Perf. 13½x13*

3194 A877 5fo multi .80 .50

Caves — A878

10th World Speleology Congress, Aug. 13-20, Sofia.

1989, Aug. 14 Litho. *Perf. 11*

3195 A878 3fo Baradla	.30	.20
3196 A878 5fo Szemlohegy	.55	.40
3197 A878 10fo Anna	.90	.70
3198 A878 12fo Lake Cave of Tapolca	1.25	.80
Nos. 3195-3198 (4)	3.00	2.10

Nos. 3136 and 3138 Surcharged

1989, Aug. 14 *Perf. 13x13½*

3199 A850 3fo on 2fo #3136 .45 .25
3200 A850 5fo on 4fo #3138 .80 .40
a. Pane of 10 #3199 + pane of 10 #3200 with gutter between 15.00
Complete booklet, #3200a, with text and cover in either English or German 15.00

A879

1989, Aug. 24 *Perf. 12*

3201 A879 5fo multi .80 .45

Third World Two-in-Hand Carriage-driving Championships, Balatonfenyves, Aug. 24-27.

A880

1989, Sept. 8 Litho. *Perf. 12*

Nurses: 5fo, Zsuzsanna Kossuth (1820-1854) and emblem. 10fo, Florence Nightingale (1820-1910) and medal awarded in her name by the Red Cross.

3202 A880 5fo multi .65 .40
3203 A880 10fo multi 1.10 .75

Stamp Day. See No. B341.

Pro-Philatelia 1989 — A881

1989, Oct. 10 Litho. *Imperf.*

3204 A881 50fo #2665, C426, 2742, 3005, B233 6.25 5.75

Dismantling of the Electronic Surveillance System (Iron Curtain) on the Hungary-Austria Border — A882

1989, Oct. 30 *Perf. 11*

3205 A882 5fo multi .75 .45

Conquest of Hungary, by Mor Than — A883

1989, Oct. 31

3206 A883 5fo multi .75 .45

Arpad, chief who founded the 1st Magyar dynasty of Hungary in 889.

Christmas — A884

1989, Nov. 10 Litho. *Perf. 11½x12*

3207 A884 3fo Flight to Egypt .45 .25

Jawaharlal Nehru — A885

Litho. & Engr.

1989, Nov. 14 *Perf. 12*

3208 A885 3fo buff & rose brn .45 .25

Jawaharlal Nehru, 1st prime minister of independent India.

Modern Art (Paintings) A886

3fo, *Mike,* by Dezso Korniss. 5fo, *Sunrise,* by Lajos Kassak. 10fo, *Grotesque Burial,* by Endre Balint. 12fo, *Memory of Toys,* by Tihamer Gyarmathy.

1989, Dec. 18 Litho. *Perf. 12*

3209 A886 3fo multicolored .35 .25
3210 A886 5fo multicolored .65 .50
3211 A886 10fo multicolored 1.40 .95
3212 A886 12fo multicolored 1.60 1.10
Nos. 3209-3212 (4) 4.00 2.80

Medical Pioneers — A887

1989, Dec. 29 Engr. *Perf. 12*

#3213, Galen (129-c.199), Greek physician. #3214, Paracelsus (1493-1541), German alchemist. 4fo, Andreas Vesalius (1514-64), Belgian anatomist. 6fo, Rudolf Virchow (1821-1902), German pathologist. 10fo, Ivan Petrovich Pavlov (1849-1936), Russian physiologist.

3213 A887 3fo olive gray .40 .25
3214 A887 3fo brown .40 .25
3215 A887 4fo black .70 .45
3216 A887 6fo intense black .85 .55
3217 A887 10fo brown violet 1.40 .80
Nos. 3213-3217 (5) 3.75 2.30

Hungarian Savings Bank, 150th Anniv. — A888

1990, Jan. 11 Litho.

3218 A888 5fo multicolored .75 .45

A889

A890

1990, Jan. 15 *Perf. 12*

3219 A889 5fo brown & sepia .75 .45

Singer Sewing Machine, 25th anniv.

1990, Jan. 29

3fo, Telephone, Budapest Exchange. 5fo, Mailbox and main p.o., Budapest, c. 1900.

3220 A890 3fo multicolored .40 .20
3221 A890 5fo multicolored .60 .30

Coil Stamps
Size: 17x22mm
Perf. 14
Photo.

3222 A890 3fo shown .40 .20
3223 A890 5fo multi .60 .30
Nos. 3220-3223 (4) 2.00 1.00

Nos. 3220-3221 inscribed "Pj 1989." Nos. 3222-3223 inscribed "1989."
Nos. 3222-3223 do not exist imperf.

A891

A892

Designs: Protected bird species.

1990, Feb. 20 Litho. *Perf. 11½x12*

3224 A891 3fo *Alcedo atthis* .45 .30
3225 A891 3fo *Pyrrhula pyrrhula* .45 .30
3226 A891 3fo *Dendrocopos syriacus* .45 .30
3227 A891 5fo *Upupa epops* .75 .50
3228 A891 5fo *Merops apiaster* .75 .50
3229 A891 10fo *Coracias garrulus* 1.50 1.00
Nos. 3224-3229 (6) 4.35 2.90

1990, Mar. 14 Litho. *Perf. 12*

Flowers of the continents (Africa).

3230 A892 3fo *Leucadendron* .40 .25
3231 A892 3fo *Protea compacta* .40 .25
3232 A892 3fo *Leucadendron spissifolium* .40 .25
3233 A892 5fo *Protea barbigera* .70 .40
3234 A892 5fo *Protea lepidocarpodendron* .70 .40
3235 A892 10fo *Protea cynaroides* 1.25 .85
Nos. 3230-3235 (6) 3.85 2.40

Souvenir Sheet
Perf. 12½x12

3236 A892 20fo Montage of African flowers 3.75 3.75

No. 3236 contains one 27x38mm stamp.
See Nos. 3278-3283, 3371-3375, 3377-3381, 3451-3455.

A893

Portraits of Hungarian kings in the Historical Portrait Gallery. King and reign: No. 3237, Janos Hunyadi (c. 1407-1409). No. 3238, Matthias Hunyadi (1443-1490).

1990, Apr. 6 Litho. *Perf. 11½x12*

3237 A893 5fo multicolored .70 .40
3238 A893 5fo multicolored .70 .40
a. Pair, #3237-3238 1.40 1.00

Souvenir Sheet

A894

Litho. & Engr.

1990, Apr. 17 *Perf. 12½x12*

3239 A894 20fo black & buff 3.75 3.25

Penny Black 150th anniv., Stamp World London '90.

Karoli Bible, 400th Anniv. — A895

1990, Apr. 24 Litho.

3240 A895 8fo Gaspar Karoli 1.00 .70

No. 3240 printed se-tenant with label picturing Bible frontispiece.

1990 World Cup Soccer Championships, Italy — A896

Various athletes.

1990, Apr. 27 *Perf. 11½x12*

3241 A896 3fo Dribble .30 .20
3242 A896 5fo Heading the ball .55 .35
3243 A896 5fo Kick .55 .35
3244 A896 8fo Goal attempt .80 .55
3245 A896 8fo Dribble, diff. .80 .55
3246 A896 10fo Dribble, diff. 1.00 .75
Nos. 3241-3246 (6) 4.00 2.75

Souvenir Sheet
Perf. 12½

3247 A896 20fo Dribble, diff. 3.50 3.50

No. 3247 contains one 32x42mm stamp.

Kelemen Mikes (1690-1761), Writer — A897

1990, May 31 Litho. *Perf. 13½x13*

3248 A897 8fo black & gold 1.10 .75

Noemi and Beni Ferenczy, Birth Cent. — A898

Designs: 3fo, Painting by Noemi Ferenczy. 5fo, Sculpture by Beni Ferenczy.

1990, June 18 Litho. *Perf. 12*
3249 A898 3fo multicolored .30 .20
3250 A898 5fo multicolored .50 .30

Ferenc Kazinczy (1759-1831), Hungarian Language Reformer A899

1990, July 18 Litho. *Perf. 12*
3251 A899 8fo multicolored .60 .40

Ferenc Kolcsey (1790-1838), Poet — A900

1990, Aug. 3
3252 A900 8fo multicolored .60 .40

New Coat of Arms A901

1990, Aug. 17 Litho. *Perf. 13½x13*
3253 A901 8fo multicolored .60 .40

Souvenir Sheet

Perf. 11

3254 A901 20fo multicolored 2.50 1.25

No. 3254 contains one 34x50mm stamp.

A souvenir sheet like No. 3254 was released with a hologram as the stamp. The sheet exists with black or red control numbers on the reverse.

Grapes and Wine Producing Areas — A902

Grapes and Growing Area: 3fo, Cabernet franc, Hajos-Vaskut. 5fo, Cabernet sauvignon, Villany-Siklos. No. 3257, Italian Riesling, Badacsony. No. 3258, Kadarka, Szekszard. No. 3259, Leanyka, Eger. 10fo, Furmint, Tokaj-Hegyalja.

1990, Aug. 31 *Perf. 13x13½*
3255 A902 3fo multicolored .25 .20
3256 A902 5fo multicolored .45 .30
3257 A902 8fo multicolored .65 .45
3258 A902 8fo multicolored .65 .45
3259 A902 8fo multicolored .65 .45
3260 A902 10fo multicolored .85 .60
Nos. 3255-3260 (6) 3.50 2.45

See Nos. 3580-3582, 3656-3657, 3704-3705.

Paintings by Endre Szasz A903

1990, Oct. 12 Litho. *Perf. 12*
3261 A903 8fo Feast .70 .45
3262 A903 12fo Message 1.10 .65

Stamp Day. See No. B344.

Prehistoric Animals A904

1990, Nov. 16 Litho. *Perf. 12*
3263 A904 3fo Tarbosaurus .25 .20
3264 A904 5fo Brontosaurus .40 .25
3265 A904 5fo Stegosaurus .40 .25
3266 A904 5fo Dimorphodon .40 .25
3267 A904 8fo Platybelodon .70 .35
3268 A904 10fo Mammoth .85 .40
Nos. 3263-3268 (6) 3.00 1.70

Intl. Literacy Year — A905

1990, Nov. 21 *Perf. 13x13½*
3269 A905 10fo multicolored 1.00 .65

Budapest Stamp Museum, 60th Anniv. — A906

1990, Nov. 23 *Perf. 12½*
3270 A906 5fo brn red & grn .50 .30

Souvenir Sheet

Thurn & Taxis Postal System, 500th Anniv. — A907

Illustration reduced.

1990, Nov. 30 Litho. *Perf. 12½x12*
3271 A907 50fo multicolored *6.75 5.00*

Antique Clocks — A908

1990, Dec. 14 *Perf. 12*
3272 A908 3fo Travelling clock, 1576 .25 .20
3273 A908 5fo Table clock, 1643 .45 .30
3274 A908 5fo Mantel clock, 1790 .45 .30
3275 A908 10fo Table clock, 1814 .85 .60
Nos. 3272-3275 (4) 2.00 1.40

Madonna with Child by Botticelli — A909

1990, Dec. 14 *Perf. 12½x11½*
3276 A909 5fo multicolored .45 .25

Lorand Eotvos (1848-1919) and Torsion Pendulum A910

1991, Jan. 31 Litho. *Perf. 11*
3277 A910 12fo multicolored 1.10 .65

Flowers of the Continents Type

Flowers of the Americas.

1991, Feb. 28 Litho. *Perf. 12*
3278 A892 5fo Mandevilla splendens .35 .20
3279 A892 7fo Lobelia cardinalis .45 .30
3280 A892 7fo Cobaea scandens .45 .30
3281 A892 12fo Steriphoma paradoxa .75 .50
3282 A892 15fo Beloperone guttata 1.00 .70
Nos. 3278-3282 (5) 3.00 2.00

Souvenir Sheet

Perf. 11

3283 A892 20fo Flowers of the Americas 2.50 1.75

No. 3283 contains one 27x44mm stamp.

Post Office, Budapest A911

Designs: 7fo, Post Office, Pecs.

Perf. 11½x12½

1991, Mar. 22 Litho.
3284 A911 5fo multicolored 1.25 .60
3285 A911 7fo multicolored 1.75 .90
a. Pair, #3284-3285 3.00 1.50

Admission to CEPT.

Europa — A912

1991, Apr. Litho. *Perf. 12½*
3286 A912 12fo Ulysses probe .90 .65
3287 A912 30fo Cassini-Huygens probe 2.50 1.75

Budapest Zoological and Botanical Gardens, 125th Anniv. — A913

1991, May 15 *Perf. 13½x13*
3288 A913 7fo Gorilla .60 .35
3289 A913 12fo Rhinoceros .85 .60
3290 A913 12fo Toucan .85 .60
3291 A913 12fo Polar bear .85 .60
3292 A913 20fo Orchid 1.40 1.00
Nos. 3288-3292 (5) 4.55 3.15

A914

A915

1991, May 24 Litho. *Perf. 12*
3293 A914 12fo multi 1.00 .60

Count Pal Teleki (1879-1941), politician.

1991, June 13 *Perf. 13x13½*
3294 A915 12fo multicolored 1.00 .60

44th World Fencing Championships, Budapest.

Images of the Virgin and Child in Hungarian Shrines
A916

Designs: 7fo, Mariapocs. No. 3296, Mariagyud. No. 3297, Celldomolk. No. 3298, Mariaremete. 20fo, Esztergom.

1991, June 17 *Perf. 12½*

3295 A916 7fo multicolored .55 .35
3296 A916 12fo multicolored .85 .60
3297 A916 12fo multicolored .85 .60
3298 A916 12fo multicolored .85 .60
3299 A916 20fo multicolored 1.40 1.00
Nos. 3295-3299 (5) 4.50 3.15

Compare with design A927.

Souvenir Sheet

Visit of Pope John Paul II, Aug. 16-20, 1991 — A917

Litho. & Engr.

1991, July 15 *Perf. 12*

3300 A917 50fo multicolored 4.50 3.50

Karoly Marko (1791-1860), Painter — A918

1991, June 17 *Perf. 12*

3301 A918 12fo multicolored 1.00 .65

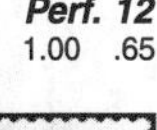

Basketball, Cent. — A919

1991, June 27 Litho. *Perf. 12*

3302 A919 10fo multicolored .90 .55

Otto Lilienthal's First Glider Flight, Cent. — A920

Aircraft of aviation pioneers.

1991, June 27

3303 A920 7fo Otto Lilienthal .50 .35
3304 A920 12fo Wright Brothers .80 .65
3305 A920 20fo Alberto Santos-Dumont 1.40 1.00
3306 A920 30fo Aladar Zselyi 2.00 1.50
Nos. 3303-3306 (4) 4.70 3.50

3rd Intl. Hungarian Philological Congress
A921

1991, Aug. 12 Litho. *Perf. 13½x13*

3307 A921 12fo multicolored 1.10 .65

A922

A923

1991, Sept. 6 Engr. *Perf. 12*

3308 A922 12fo dark red .65 .45

Count Istvan Szechenyi (1791-1860), founder of Academy of Sciences.

1991, Sept. 6 **Litho.**

Wolfgang Amadeus Mozart (1756-91).

3309 A923 12fo As child .95 .50
3310 A923 20fo As adult 1.50 .80

Souvenir Sheet

3311 A923 30fo +15fo, in red coat 3.25 2.50

Stamp Day. No. 3311 contains one 30x40mm stamp.

Telecom '91 — A924

1991, Sept. 30 Litho. *Perf. 12*

3312 A924 12fo multicolored .90 .50

6th World Forum and Exposition on Telecommunications, Geneva, Switzerland.

A925

A926

1991, Oct. 30 Litho. *Perf. 13½x13*

3313 A925 12fo multicolored .90 .50

Sovereign Order of the Knights of Malta.

1991, Oct. 30 *Perf. 12*

Early explorers and Discovery of America, 500th anniv. (in 1992): 7fo, Sebastian Cabot, Labrador Peninsula, Nova Scotia. No. 3315, Amerigo Vespucci, South American region. No. 3316, Hernando Cortez, Mexico. 15fo, Ferdinand Magellan, Straits of Magellan. 20fo, Francisco Pizarro, Peru, Andes Mountain region. 30fo, Christopher Columbus and coat of arms.

3314 A926 7fo multicolored .50 .25
3315 A926 12fo multicolored .80 .45
3316 A926 12fo multicolored .80 .45
3317 A926 15fo multicolored 1.00 .60
3318 A926 20fo multicolored 1.40 .75
Nos. 3314-3318 (5) 4.50 2.50

Souvenir Sheet

3319 A926 30fo multicolored 2.50 2.00

No. 3319 contains one 26x37mm stamp.

No. 3023 Overprinted in Brown

1991, Oct. 22 Litho. *Perf. 12x11½*

3320 A816 12fo on #3021A .90 .45

Anniversary of Hungarian revolution, 1956.

Christmas — A927

Images of the Virgin and Child from: 7fo, Mariapocs. 12fo, Mariaremete.

1991, Nov. 20 *Perf. 13½x13*

3322 A927 7fo multicolored .50 .25
3323 A927 12fo multicolored .90 .45

Nos. 3322-3323 issued in sheets of 20 plus 20 labels.

A928

1991, Nov. 20 *Perf. 12*

3324 A928 12fo multicolored .90 .45

Fight for human rights.

A929

1991, Dec. 6 *Perf. 13½x13*

3325 A929 7fo Cross-country skiing .35 .20
3326 A929 12fo Slalom skiing .70 .30
3327 A929 15fo Four-man bob-sled .80 .45
3328 A929 20fo Ski jump 1.10 .60
3329 A929 30fo Hockey 1.60 .85
Nos. 3325-3329 (5) 4.55 2.40

Souvenir Sheet

Perf. 12½x11½

3330 A929 30fo Pairs figure skating 2.50 2.00

1992 Winter Olympics, Albertville.

Souvenir Sheet

First Hungarian Postage Stamp, 120th Anniv. — A930

1991, Dec. 20 Litho. *Perf. 12x12½*

3331 A930 50fo No. 6 4.00 3.00

Piarist Order in Hungary, 350th Anniv. — A931

1992, Jan. 22 *Perf. 13½x13*

3332 A931 10fo multicolored .85 .40

World Heritage Village of Holloko
A932

1992, Jan. 22 *Perf. 12*

3333 A932 15fo multicolored 1.10 .60

1992 Summer Olympics, Barcelona — A933

1992, Feb. 26 Litho. *Perf. 13½x13*

3334 A933 7fo Swimming .50 .25
3335 A933 9fo Cycling .65 .40
3336 A933 10fo Gymnastics .85 .45
3337 A933 15fo Running 1.25 .65
Nos. 3334-3337 (4) 3.25 1.75

Discovery of America, 500th Anniv. — A934

Expo '92, Seville: No. 3338, Map shaped as Indian, Columbus' fleet. No. 3339, Face-shaped map of ocean, sailing ship. No. 3340, Map shaped as European face, ship. No. 3341, Map, square, protractor, compass.

1992, Mar. 27 Litho. *Perf. 12*

3338 A934 10fo multicolored .60 .35
3339 A934 10fo multicolored .60 .35
3340 A934 15fo multicolored 1.00 .55
3341 A934 15fo multicolored 1.00 .55
Nos. 3338-3341 (4) 3.20 1.80

Jozsef Cardinal Mindszenty (1892-1975), Leader of Hungarian Catholic Church — A935

1992, Mar. 27 *Perf. 12½x11½*

3342 A935 15fo red, brn & buff 1.10 .60

A936

1992, Mar. 27 *Perf. 13½x13*

3343 A936 15fo multicolored 1.10 .60

Jan Amos Komensky (Comenius), writer, 400th birth anniv.

A937

1992, Apr. 14 Litho. *Perf. 13½x13*

3344 A937 15fo Maya Indian sculpture 1.00 .50
3345 A937 40fo Indian sculpture, diff. 2.75 .90

Europa. Discovery of America, 500th anniv..

European Gymnastics Championships, Budapest — A938

1992, May 15 Litho. *Perf. 12*

3346 A938 15fo multicolored 1.10 .60

A939

1992, June 26 Litho. *Perf. 13½x13*

3347 A939 15fo multicolored 1.00 .50

St. Margaret, 750th Anniv. (in 1991). No. 3347 printed with se-tenant label.

A940

1992, June 26 *Perf. 13x13½*

Protected birds.

3348 A940 9fo Falco cherrug .40 .20
3349 A940 10fo Hieraaetus pennatus .60 .20
3350 A940 15fo Circaetus gallicus .85 .50
3351 A940 40fo Milvus milvus 1.60 1.00
Nos. 3348-3351 (4) 3.45 1.90

Raoul Wallenberg, Swedish Diplomat, 80th Anniv. of Birth — A941

1992, July 30 Litho. *Perf. 12*

3352 A941 15fo gray & red .90 .45

Theodore von Karman (1881-1963), Physicist and Aeronautical Engineer — A942

Design: 40fo, John von Neumann (1903-1957), mathematician.

1992, Aug. 3 Litho. *Perf. 12x11½*

3353 A942 15fo multicolored .45 .25
3354 A942 40fo multicolored 1.90 .70

3rd World Congress of Hungarians A943

1992, Aug. 3 *Perf. 13½x13*

3355 A943 15fo multicolored .80 .35

Telecom '92 — A945

1992, Oct. 6 Litho. *Perf. 12½x11½*

3360 A945 15fo multicolored .80 .35

Stamp Day — A946

1992, Sept.4 *Perf. 12*

3361 A946 10fo +5fo Coat of arms, vert. .80 .35
3362 A946 15fo shown .80 .35
3363 A946 15fo +5fo like #3362, inscribed "65. Belyegnap" 1.00 .45
Nos. 3361-3363 (3) 2.60 1.15

Souvenir Sheet

3364 A946 50fo +20fo Postilion 3.50 3.25

Eurofilex '92 (#3361, 3363-3364). Nos. 3361, 3363 printed with se-tenant label. No. 3364 contains one 40x30mm stamp.

Famous Men — A947

Postal Uniforms — A948

Designs: 10fo, Stephen Bathory (1533-1586), Prince of Transylvania and King of Poland. 15fo, Stephen Bocskay (1557-1606), Prince of Transylvania. 40fo, Gabriel Bethlen (1580-1629), Prince of Transylvania and King of Hungary.

1992, Oct. 28 Litho. *Perf. 12*

3365 A947 10fo multicolored .40 .20
3366 A947 15fo multicolored .70 .30
3367 A947 40fo multicolored 1.25 .85
Nos. 3365-3367 (3) 2.35 1.35

1992, Nov. 20 *Perf. 13½x13*

Designs: 10fo, Postrider, 1703-1711. 15fo, Letter carrier, 1874.

3368 A948 10fo multicolored .65 .30
3369 A948 15fo multicolored 1.00 .50

Christmas A949

Litho. & Engr.

1992, Nov. 20 *Perf. 12*

3370 A949 15fo blue & black 1.00 .50

Flowers of the Continents Type of 1990

Flowers of Australia: 9fo, Clianthus formosus. 10fo, Leschenaultia biloba. 15fo, Anigosanthos manglesii. 40fo, Comesperma ericinum. 50fo, Bouquet of flowers.

1992, Nov. 20 Litho.

3371 A892 9fo multicolored .50 .25
3372 A892 10fo multicolored .55 .40
3373 A892 15fo multicolored .75 .50
3374 A892 40fo multicolored 1.75 1.25
Nos. 3371-3374 (4) 3.55 2.40

Souvenir Sheet

Perf. 12½

3375 A892 50fo multicolored 2.75 2.00

No. 3375 contains one 32x41mm stamp.

1992 European Chess Championships A950

1992, Oct. 28 *Perf. 11*

3376 A950 15fo multicolored .70 .35

Flowers of the Continents Type of 1990

Flowers of Asia: No. 3377, Dendrobium densiflorum. No. 3378, Arachnis flos-aeris. No. 3379, Lilium speciosum. No. 3380, Meconopsis aculeata. 50fo, Bouquet of flowers.

1993, Jan. 27 Litho. *Perf. 13½x13*

3377 A892 10fo multicolored .40 .25
3378 A892 10fo multicolored .40 .25
3379 A892 15fo multicolored .85 .50
3380 A892 15fo multicolored .85 .50
Nos. 3377-3380 (4) 2.50 1.50

Souvenir Sheet

Perf. 12½

3381 A892 50fo multicolored 3.75 3.25

No. 3381 contains one 32x41mm stamp.

Scythian Archaeological Artifacts — A951

1993, Feb. 25 Litho. *Perf. 13x13½*

3382 A951 10fo Horse standing .30 .20
3383 A951 17fo Horse lying down .75 .25

Hungarian Rowing Association, Cent. — A952

1993, Feb. 25 Litho. *Perf. 12*

3384 A952 17fo multicolored .60 .20

Missale Romanum of Matthias Corvinus (Matyas Hunyadi, King of Hungary) — A953

Design: 40fo, Illuminated page.

1993, Mar. 12 Litho. *Perf. 12*

3385 A953 15fo multicolored .50 .25

Souvenir Sheet

3386 A953 40fo multicolored 2.00 1.50

Illustration reduced. No. 3386 contains one 60x38mm stamp.

See Belgium Nos. 1474, 1476.

Motocross World Championships A954

1993, May 5 Litho. *Perf. 11½x12*

3387 A954 17fo multicolored .60 .25

Europa — A955

Buildings designed by Imre Makovecz: 17fo, Roman Catholic Church, Paks. 45fo, Hungarian Pavilion, Expo '92, Seville.

1993, May 5 *Perf. 13x13½*

3388 A955 17fo multicolored .55 .25

3389 A955 45fo multicolored 1.75 .65

Heliocentric Solar System, Copernicus — A956

1993, May 5 *Perf. 12*

3390 A956 17fo multicolored .65 .25

Polska '93. No. 3390 issued in sheets of 8 + 4 labels.

Edible Mushrooms A957

1993, June 18 Litho. *Perf. 13½x13*

3391 A957 10fo Ramaria botrytis .40 .20

3392 A957 17fo Craterellus cornucopioides .70 .25

3393 A957 45fo Amanita caesarea 2.25 .80

Nos. 3391-3393 (3) 3.35 1.25

St. Christopher, by Albrecht Durer — A958

1993, June 18 *Perf. 12*

3394 A958 17fo sil, blk & buff .65 .20

Year of the Elderly.

City of Mohacs, 900th Anniv. — A959

1993, June 18 *Perf. 13½x13*

3395 A959 17fo buff, mar & red brn .65 .20

Hungarian State Railways, 125th Anniv. A960

1993, June 18 *Perf. 13x13½*

3396 A960 17fo lt blue & blue .65 .20

Comedians A961

1993, July 28 Litho. *Perf. 12*

3397 A961 17fo Kalman Latabar .70 .25

3398 A961 30fo Charlie Chaplin 1.10 .65

Butterflies A962

1993, July 28 *Perf. 13½x13*

3399 A962 10fo Limenitis populi .30 .20

3400 A962 17fo Aricia artaxerxes .70 .25

3401 A962 30fo Plebejides pylaon 1.25 .65

Nos. 3399-3401 (3) 2.25 1.10

Souvenir Sheet

Helsinki Conference on European Security and Cooperation, 20th Anniv. — A963

1993, July 28 *Perf. 12*

3402 A963 50fo multicolored 2.75 2.50

Intl. Solar Energy Society Congress, Budapest — A964

Perf. 12½x11½

1993, Aug. 23 Litho.

3403 A964 17fo multicolored .35 .20

No. 3403 printed se-tenant with label.

Writers — A965

1993, Aug. 23 *Perf. 12*

Designs: No. 3404, Laszlo Nemeth (1901-75). No. 3405, Dezso Szabo (1879-1945). No. 3406, Antal Szerb (1901-45).

3404 A965 17fo blue .45 .20

3405 A965 17fo blue .45 .20

3406 A965 17fo blue .45 .20

Nos. 3404-3406 (3) 1.35 .60

School of Agronomy, Pannon Agricultural Univ., 175th Anniv. — A966

1993, Oct. 22 Litho. *Perf. 12*

3407 A966 17fo multicolored .60 .30

Ships A967

1993, Oct. 27 *Perf. 13x13½*

3408 A967 10fo Steamer with sails .35 .20

3409 A967 30fo Battleship 1.00 .50

a. Pair, #3408-3409 1.40 .70

Prehistoric Man — A968

1993, Oct. 27 *Perf. 13½x13*

3410 A968 17fo Skull fragment .60 .30

3411 A968 30fo Stone tool 1.00 .50

Souvenir Sheet

Roman Roads — A969

1993, Oct. 27 *Perf. 11*

3412 A969 50fo multicolored 2.25 1.50

Christmas A970

Altarpiece: 10fo, Virgin and Christ Child, Cathedral of Szekesfehervar, by F. A. Hillebrant.

1993, Nov. 24 *Perf. 13½x13*

3413 A970 10fo multicolored .35 .20

Sights of Budapest — A971

Designs: 17fo, Szechenyi Chain Bridge. 30fo, Opera House. 45fo, Matthias Church, vert. Illustration reduced.

Photo. & Engr.

1993, Dec. 16 *Perf. 12*

3414 A971 17fo lt grn & dk grn .50 .30

3415 A971 30fo lt mag & dk mag 1.00 .50

3416 A971 45fo lt brn & dk brn 1.50 .75

Nos. 3414-3416 (3) 3.00 1.55

Expo '96.

Josef Antall (1932-93) — A972

1993 Litho. *Perf. 11*

3417 A972 19fo multicolored .65 .30

a. Souvenir sheet .65 .30

ICAO, 50th Anniv. A973

1994, Jan. 13 *Perf. 13x13½*
3418 A973 56fo multicolored 1.90 .95

1994 Winter Olympics, Lillehammer — A974

1994, Jan. 13 *Perf. 12*
3419 A974 12fo Downhill skiing .40 .20
3420 A974 19fo Ice hockey .65 .30

A975

Easter: 12fo, Golgotha, by Mihaly Munkacsy.

1994, Feb. 17 Litho. *Perf. 11½x12*
3421 A975 12fo multicolored .40 .20

A976

1994, Feb. 17

Artists: 12fo, Gyula Benczur (1844-1920). 19fo, Mihaly Munkacsy (1844-1900).

3422 A976 12fo multicolored .40 .20
3423 A976 19fo multicolored .65 .30

Lajos Kossuth (1802-94) A977

1994, Feb. 17
3424 A977 19fo multicolored .65 .30

Gen. Joseph Bem (1794-1850) A978

1994, Mar. 10 *Perf. 12*
3425 A978 19fo multicolored .65 .30

Otis Tarda — A979

World Wildlife Fund: No. 3426, Female, male with feathers ruffled in mating dance. No. 3427, Nestlings, female on nest. No. 3428, Nestlings, female standing. No. 3429, Three flying.

1994, Mar. 14
3426 A979 10fo multicolored .30 .20
3427 A979 10fo multicolored .30 .20
3428 A979 10fo multicolored .30 .20
3429 A979 10fo multicolored .30 .20
a. Block of 4, #3426-3429 1.40 .70

A980

Europa: 19fo, Sailing steamer Tegetthoff, Franz-Joseph Land, Julius Payer (1842-1915), Austrian explorer. 50fo, Mark Aurel Stein (1862-1943), explorer, archeologist, geographer, Asian scenes.

1994, Apr. 1 Litho. *Perf. 13x13½*
3430 A980 19fo multicolored .65 .30
3431 A980 50fo multicolored 1.60 .85

Austro-Hungarian Arctic Expedition, 120th anniv. (#3430).

A981

#3432, Baron Miklos Josika (1794-1865), Novelist. #3433, Balint Balassi (1551-94), poet.

1994, May 19 Litho. *Perf. 12*
3432 A981 19fo gray .65 .30
3433 A981 19fo rose lake .65 .30

Creation of Magyar Hungary, 1100th Anniv. (in 1996) — A982

Designs: No. 3434, Two soldiers on horseback. No. 3435, Soldier on white horse, others in background with flags. No. 3436, Soldier on black horse, others in background. No. 3437, Man with staff, oxen pulling carts. No. 3438, Oxen pulling royal cart. No. 3439, Man with staff on shoulder, oxen with packs. No. 3440, Minstrels, bard celebrating. No. 3441, Soldiers preparing to sacrifice white horse. No. 3442, Shaman before fire, headsman.

1994-96
3434 A982 19fo multicolored .65 .30
3435 A982 19fo multicolored .65 .30
3436 A982 19fo multicolored .65 .30
a. Strip of 3, #3434-3436 2.00 2.00
3437 A982 22fo multicolored .65 .30
3438 A982 22fo multicolored .65 .30
3439 A982 22fo multicolored .65 .30
a. Strip of 3, #3437-3439 2.00 2.00
3440 A982 24fo multicolored .55 .30
3441 A982 24fo multicolored .55 .30
3442 A982 24fo multicolored .55 .30
a. Strip of 3, #3440-3442 1.65 .90
Nos. 3434-3442 (9) 5.55 2.70

Nos. 3436a, 3439a, 3442a are continuous design. #3436a sold for 59fo.
Nos. 3435, 3438, 3441 are 60x40mm.
Issued: #3434-3436, 5/19/94; #3437-3439, 2/23/95; #3440-3442, 2/29/96.

Souvenir Sheet

1996, Apr. 18
3442B A982 195fo multicolored 6.00 6.00

Nos. 3436a, 3439a, 3442a are continuous design. #3436a sold for 59fo. No. 3442B contains one each of Nos. 3436a, 3439a, 3442a.

Intl. Olympic Committee, Cent. — A985

Designs: 12fo, 1896, 1992 medals. No. 3444, Flag, runners, Olympic flame. No. 3445, Athens Stadium, 1896. 35fo, Pierre de Coubertin (1863-1937), first president.

1994, June 16 Litho. *Perf. 12½*
3443 A985 12fo multicolored .45 .20
3444 A985 19fo multicolored .65 .30
3445 A985 19fo multicolored .65 .30
3446 A985 35fo multicolored 1.25 .60
Nos. 3443-3446 (4) 3.00 1.40

1994 World Cup Soccer Championships, US — A986

US flag, soccer players and: No. 3447, Elvis Presley. No. 3448, Marilyn Monroe. No. 3449, John Wayne.

1994, June 16 *Perf. 12*
3447 A986 19fo multicolored .65 .30
3448 A986 19fo multicolored .65 .30
3449 A986 35fo multicolored 1.25 .60
Nos. 3447-3449 (3) 2.55 1.20

Intl. Year of the Family A987

1994, July 21 Litho. *Perf. 11*
3450 A987 19fo multicolored .65 .30

Flowers of the Continents Type of 1990

Flowers of Europe: 12fo, Leucojum aestivum. 19fo, Helianthemum nummularium. 35fo, Eryngium alpinum. 50fo, Thlaspi rotundifolium. 100fo, Bouquet of European flowers.

1994, Aug. 18 Litho. *Perf. 11½x12*
3451 A892 12fo multicolored .40 .20
3452 A892 19fo multicolored .65 .35
3453 A892 35fo multicolored 1.25 .60
3454 A892 50fo multicolored 1.60 .85
Nos. 3451-3454 (4) 3.90 2.00

Souvenir Sheet
Perf. 12½
3455 A892 100fo multicolored 3.25 2.50

No. 3455 contains one 32x41mm stamp.

UPU, 120th Anniv. A988

UPU emblem and: 19fo, Heinrich Von Stephan (1831-97). 35fo, Mihaly Gervay (1819-96).
#3458: a, Von Stephan, vert. b, Gervay, vert.

1994, Sept. 9 Litho. *Perf. 12*
3456 A988 19fo multicolored .55 .30
3457 A988 35fo multicolored 1.00 .50

Souvenir Sheet of 2
3458 A988 50fo +25fo, #a.-b. 4.50 2.25

Stamp Day, 67th anniv.

Folk Designs — A989

Various ornate designs.

1994-96 Litho. *Perf. 11½x12*

3459	A989	1fo	bl vio & blk	.20	.20
3460	A989	2fo	multi	.20	.20
3461	A989	3fo	multi	.20	.20
3461A	A989	9fo	multi	.20	.20
3462	A989	11fo	multi	.35	.20
3463	A989	12fo	multi	.35	.20
3463A	A989	13fo	grn, red & blk	.20	.20
3464	A989	14fo	multi	.25	.20
3465	A989	16fo	bl, red & blk	.30	.20
3466	A989	17fo	red & blk	.30	.20
3467	A989	19fo	multi	.50	.25
3468	A989	22fo	multi	.35	.20
3469	A989	24fo	multi	.40	.20
3470	A989	32fo	multi	.95	.50
3471	A989	35fo	multi	1.00	.50
3472	A989	38fo	multi	.65	.30
3473	A989	40fo	multi	1.10	.55
3474	A989	50fo	multi	1.40	.70
3475	A989	75fo	multi	1.25	.65
3476	A989	80fo	multi	1.40	.70
3477	A989	300fo	multi	5.25	2.60
3478	A989	500fo	multi	8.75	4.50
	Nos. 3459-3478 (22)			25.55	13.65

Issued: 11fo, 12fo, 19fo, 32fo, 35fo, 40fo, 50fo, 10/10/94; 1fo, 1/10/95; 2fo, 3fo, 9fo, 14fo, 22fo, 38fo, 4/3/95; 13fo, 16fo, 17fo, 24fo, 75fo, 80fo, 7/1/96.
See #3561, 3615, 3630, 3644-3646, 3649-3650. For surcharge see #3583.

Souvenir Sheet

Summit Meeting of the Conference for European Security & Cooperation — A990

1994, Sept. 10 Litho. *Perf. 12*
3479 A990 100fo Budapest 3.00 2.50

Holocaust, 50th Anniv. — A991

1994, Oct. 20
3480 A991 19fo multicolored .55 .30

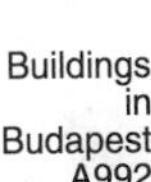

Buildings in Budapest A992

#3481, Vajdahunyadvar Castle. #3482, Nemzeti Museum. #3483, Muszaki Palace.

1994, Nov. 17 **Engr.**
3481 A992 19fo violet .55 .30
3482 A992 19fo green .55 .30
3483 A992 19fo brown .55 .30
Nos. 3481-3483 (3) 1.65 .90

Christmas — A993

1994, Nov. 17 **Litho.**
3484 A993 12fo shown .40 .20
3485 A993 35fo Flight into Egypt 1.25 .60

Hungarian Shipping Co., Cent. — A994

Design: 22fo, Early steamer Francis Joseph I, cargo ship Baross.

1995, Jan. 24 **Litho.** ***Perf. 13***
3486 A994 22fo multicolored .65 .30

Easter — A995

1995, Mar. 7 ***Perf. 12***
3487 A995 14fo black & lilac .45 .25

Hungarian Shipping — A996

Designs: 14fo, Tug-wheeled steamship, map of first navigable section of the Tisza, view of Szeged. 60fo, Pal Vasarhelyi, Tisza survey ship, surveyor.

1995, Mar. 7 ***Perf. 13***
3488 A996 14fo multicolored .45 .25
3489 A996 60fo multicolored 2.00 1.00

Natl. Meteorological Service, 125th Anniv. — A997

1995, Apr. 7 ***Perf. 12***
3490 A997 22fo multicolored .65 .30

FAO, 50th Anniv. — A998

1995, Apr. 7
3491 A998 22fo multicolored .65 .30

European Nature Conservation Year — A999

#3492, Crane, frog, flowers. #3493, Squirrel, insect. #3494, Bird, berries, flowers. #3495, Butterfly, hedgehog, flowers.

1995, May 9 **Litho.** ***Perf. 13½x13***
3492 A999 14fo multicolored .40 .20
3493 A999 14fo multicolored .40 .20
3494 A999 14fo multicolored .40 .20
3495 A999 14fo multicolored .40 .20
a. Strip of 4, #3492-3495 1.60 .75

Peace & Liberty — A1000

1995, May 9
3496 A1000 22fo multicolored .60 .30

Europa.

Hungarian Olympic Committee, Cent. — A1001

22fo, Diver, Pierre de Coubertin. 60fo, Javelin. 100fo, Fencing.

1995, June 12 **Litho.** ***Perf. 12***
3497 A1001 22fo multicolored .60 .30
3498 A1001 60fo multicolored 1.60 .80
3499 A1001 100fo multicolored 2.75 1.40
Nos. 3497-3499 (3) 4.95 2.50

St. Ladislas I (1040?-1095) A1002

1995, June 12
3500 A1002 22fo multicolored .60 .30

Laszlo Almasy, Sahara Researcher, Birth Cent. — A1003

1995, Aug. 22 **Litho.** ***Perf. 13x13½***
3501 A1003 22fo multicolored .60 .30

Odon Lechner, Architect, 150th Birth Anniv. — A1004

Design: 22fo, Museum of Applied Arts, Lechner. Illustration reduced.

Litho. & Engr.

1995, Aug. 22 ***Perf. 12***
3502 A1004 22fo multicolored .60 .30

Contemporary Paintings A1005

No. 3503, Abstract, by Laszlo Moholy-Nagy (1895-1946). No. 3504, Woman with a violin, by Aurel Bernath (1895-1982).

1995, Sept. 18 **Litho.**
3503 A1005 22fo multicolored .60 .30
3504 A1005 22fo multicolored .60 .30

Eotvos College, Cent. — A1006

60fo, Eotvos College, Josef Eotvos (1813-71), statesman, writer, educational leader.

1995, Sept. 18
3505 A1006 60fo red brn, blk 1.60 .80

Stamp Day A1007

Designs: 22fo, Horse-drawn mail chaise. 40fo, Jet, map. 100fo + 30fo, Man, boys looking at stamp album, vert.

1995, Sept. 29 **Litho.** ***Perf. 13½x13***
3506 A1007 22fo multicolored .60 .30
3507 A1007 40fo multicolored 1.10 .55

Souvenir Sheet

Perf. 12x12½
3508 A1007 100fo +30fo multi 3.50 2.50

Buildings of Budapest A1008

#3509, Nyugati Palyaudvar. #3510, Vigado.

1995 **Engr.** ***Perf. 12***
3509 A1008 22fo dark olive brn .60 .30
3510 A1008 22fo deep claret .60 .30

UN, 50th Anniv. A1009

1995, Oct. 24 **Litho.** ***Perf. 11***
3511 A1009 60fo multicolored 1.60 .80

Christmas — A1010

1995, Nov. 16 ***Perf. 12***

Children's designs: 14fo, Spark thrower. 60fo, The Three Magi.

3512 A1010 14fo multicolored .40 .20
3513 A1010 60fo multicolored 1.60 .80

Nobel Prize Fund Established, Cent. — A1011

1995, Nov. 16
3514 A1011 100fo Medals 2.75 1.40

No. 3514 is printed se-tenant with label.

St. Elizabeth of Hungary Bathing Lepers — A1012

1995, Nov. 16 ***Perf. 13***
3515 A1012 22fo multicolored .60 .30

No. 3515 is printed se-tenant with label.

A1013

Archaeological Finds from Karos: a, Gold and silver saber. b, Badge.

1996, Mar. 14 Litho. *Perf. 13½x13*

3516 A1013 24fo #a.-b. + 2 labels 1.10 .55

Souvenir Sheet

Pannonhalma, Benedictine Monastery, 1000th Anniv. — A1014

1996, Mar. 21 Engr. *Perf. 12*

3517 A1014 100fo deep violet 2.25 1.75

Sheet margin is litho. and multicolored.

1996 Summer Olympics, Atlanta A1015

1996, Apr. 18 Litho. *Perf. 11½x12*

3518 A1015 24fo Swimming .55 .30
3519 A1015 50fo Tennis 1.10 .60
3520 A1015 75fo Kayak 1.75 .85
Nos. 3518-3520 (3) 3.40 1.75

National Productivity A1016

1996, Apr. 18 Litho. *Perf. 12*

3521 A1016 24fo multicolored .55 .30

Natl. Writers Assoc., Cent. — A1017

1996, Apr. 18 *Perf. 12x11½*

3522 A1017 50fo multicolored 1.10 .60

Budapest Subway, Cent. — A1018

1996, May 2 *Perf. 12*

3523 A1018 24fo multicolored .55 .30

Famous Women A1019

Europa: 24fo, Queen Gizella. 75fo, Bavarian Princess Elisabeth Wittelsbach.

1996, May 2 Litho. *Perf. 12*

3524 A1019 24fo multicolored .55 .30
3525 A1019 75fo multicolored 2.75 .85

Pannonhalma, Benedictine Monastery, 1000th Anniv. A1020

Designs: 17fo, Entrance to cathedral. 24fo, Monks in northern wing.

1996, June 21 Engr. *Perf. 12*

3526 A1020 17fo red brown .40 .20
3527 A1020 24fo dark blue .55 .30

See Nos. 3536-3537.

Intl. Anti-Drug Day — A1021

1996, June 21 Litho. *Perf. 14*

3528 A1021 24fo multicolored .55 .30

Hungarian Developers of Technolgy — A1022

Inventor, invention: 24fo, Denes Mihaly (1894-1953), Telehor. 50fo, Jozsef Biro Laszlo (1899-1985), mass-produced ball-point pen. 75fo, Zoltan Bay (1900-92), lunar radar set.

1996, June 21 *Perf. 12x11½*

3529 A1022 24fo multicolored .55 .30
3530 A1022 50fo multicolored 1.10 .60
3531 A1022 75fo multicolored 1.75 .85
Nos. 3529-3531 (3) 3.40 1.75

Hungarian Railways, 150th Anniv. — A1023

Designs: 17fo, 303-Series steam tender locomotive. No. 3533, 325-Series locomotive . No. 3534, "Pest," steam locomotive made by Cokerill and Co.

1996, July 12 *Perf. 13½x13*

3532 A1023 17fo multicolored .40 .20
3533 A1023 24fo multicolored .55 .30
3534 A1023 24fo multicolored .55 .30
Nos. 3532-3534 (3) 1.50 .80

Second European Congress of Mathematicians A1024

1996, July 12 *Perf. 12*

3535 A1024 24fo multicolored .55 .30

Pannonhalma, Benedictine Monastery, Type of 1996

Designs: 17fo, Refectory. 24fo, Main library.

1996, Aug. 12 Engr. *Perf. 12*

3536 A1020 17fo dark brown .30 .20
3537 A1020 24fo dark green .45 .20

Nature Expo '96 A1025

1996, Aug. 12 Litho. *Perf. 12x11½*

3538 A1025 13fo Egretta alba .20 .20
3539 A1025 13fo Iris sibirica .20 .20
3540 A1025 13fo Lynx lynx .20 .20
3541 A1025 13fo Ropalopus ungaricus .20 .20
a. Block of 4, #3538-3541 .80 .40

A1026 A1027

1996, Aug. 12 *Perf. 12*

3542 A1026 24fo No. 4 .45 .20

Hungarian postage stamps, 125th anniv.

1996, Aug. 21 Litho. *Perf. 11½x12*

Stamp Day, Budapest '96: 17fo, Prince Arpad, people from 14th cent. "Vienna Picture Chronicle," man stirring liquid in pot. 24fo, Prince on horseback, archer.

150fo+50fo, #601, first page from "The Deeds of Hungarians."

3543 A1027 17fo multicolored .30 .20
3544 A1027 24fo multicolored .45 .20

Souvenir Sheet

Perf. 12x12½

3545 A1027 150fo +50fo multi 4.00 3.00

Steamships on Lake Balaton, 150th Anniv. — A1028

Steamer Kisfaludy.

1996, Sept. 17 Litho. *Perf. 12*

3548 A1028 17fo multicolored .30 .20

Hungarian Revolution, 40th Anniv. — A1029

Newspaper clippings and: 13fo, People marching. 16fo, Troops on back of truck. 17fo, Two men with guns. 24fo, Imre Nagy addressing people.

40fo, Nagy Cabinet.

1996, Oct. 23 Litho. *Perf. 12*

3549 A1029 13fo multicolored .25 .20
3550 A1029 16fo multicolored .30 .20
3551 A1029 17fo multicolored .30 .20
3552 A1029 24fo multicolored .45 .20
Nos. 3549-3552 (4) 1.30 .80

Souvenir Sheet

3553 A1029 40fo multicolored .75 .40

Souvenir Sheet

1996 Summer Olympic Games, Atlanta — A1030

Illustration reduced.

1996, Oct. 22

3554 A1030 150fo multicolored 3.00 2.25

A1036

1996, Nov. 14 Litho. *Perf. 11½x12*

3555 A1036 24fo multicolored .30 .20

Miklos Wesselenyi (1796-1850), writer.

A1037

1996, Nov. 14 *Perf. 13½x13*

3556 A1037 24fo multicolored .30 .20

UNICEF, 50th anniv.

Christmas A1038

Paintings: 17fo, Mary with Infant Jesus and Two Angels, by Matteo di Giovanni. 24fo, Adoration of the Kings, by unknown painter of Salsburg.

1996, Nov. 14 *Perf. 12*

3557 A1038 17fo multicolored .20 .20
3558 A1038 24fo multicolored .30 .20

Hungarian Literature — A1039

Designs: No. 3559, Scenes from "The Umbrella of St. Peter," Kalman Mikszath (1847-1910). No. 3560, Scenes of men and dogs from "Abel in the Vast Trackless Forest" and "Matthias the Ice-breaker," Aron Tamasi (1897-1966).

1997, Jan. 16 Litho. *Perf. 12x11½*

3559 A1039 27fo multicolored .50 .25
3560 A1039 27fo multicolored .50 .25

Folk Art Type of 1994

1997, Mar. 26 *Perf. 11½x12*

3561 A989 27fo multicolored .50 .25

Coat of Arms of Budapest and Counties — A1040

No. 3562: a, Hajdú-Bihar. b, Baranya. c, Bács-Kiskun. d, Békés. e, Borsod-Abaúj-Zemplén.

No. 3563: a, Fejér. b, Györ-Moson-Sopron. c, Heves. d, Jász-Nagykun-Szolnok. e, Komárom-Esztergom. f, Nógrád.

No. 3564: a, Pest. b, Somogy. c, Toina. d, Vas. e, Veszprém. f, Zala.

No. 3565: a, Budapest. b, Csongrád. c, Szaboics-Szatmár-Bereg.

1997, Mar. 26 *Perf. 11½x12*

3562 A1040 27fo Sheet of 5, #a.-e. + label 2.40 1.25
3563 A1040 27fo Sheet of 6, #a.-f. 2.75 1.40
3564 A1040 27fo Sheet of 6, #a.-f. 2.75 1.40
3564G A1040 27fo Hajdu-Bihar .45 .25

Size: 51x33mm

3565 A1040 27fo Sheet of 3, #a.-c. 1.40 .70

No. 3564G is 51x33mm and has the same design as No. 3562a which has a se-tenant label, but lacks the perforations separating these items. Nos. 3256b-3256e, 3563a-3563f, 3564a-3564f, 3565a-3565c were also printed in individual sheets.

A1041

Youth Stamps — A1042

Designs: 20fo, Scouting emblem, tents, sailboat, waterfall. 27fo+10fo, Knights on horseback from "Toldi," by Janos Arany.

1997, Apr. 23 *Perf. 12*

3566 A1041 20fo multicolored .35 .20
3567 A1042 27fo +10fo multi .65 .35

A1043

1997, Apr. 23 *Perf. 13½x13*

3568 A1043 90fo multicolored 1.60 .80

World Meeting of Custom Directors.

A1044

1997, Apr. 23 Engr. *Perf. 12*

3569 A1044 80fo deep violet 1.40 .70

St. Adalbert (956-997). See Germany No. 1964, Poland No. 3307, Czech Republic No. 3012, Vatican City No. 1040..

Stories and Legends A1045

Europa: 27fo, Hunters on horseback shooting bow and arrow at deer. 90fo, Preparing body in sarcophagus of Prince Geza.

1997, May 5 Litho. *Perf. 13x13½*

3570 A1045 27fo multicolored .35 .20
3571 A1045 90fo multicolored 1.25 .60

African Animals A1046

16fo, Oryx gazella. #3573, Equus burchelli. #3574, Diceros bicornis. 27fo, Panthera leo. 90fo, Loxodonta africana.

1997, May 5 *Perf. 12*

3572 A1046 16fo multicolored .25 .20
3573 A1046 20fo multicolored .30 .20
3574 A1046 20fo multicolored .30 .20
3575 A1046 27fo multicolored .40 .20
Nos. 3572-3575 (4) 1.25 .80

Souvenir Sheet

3576 A1046 90fo multicolored 1.50 1.25

A1047

1997, June 8 Litho. *Perf. 12*

3577 A1047 90fo multicolored 1.40 .70

Polish Queen Jadwiga (1373-99).

A1048

World Congress on Stress, Budapest: Janos (Hans) Selye (1907-82), founder of theory of stress, face of person under stress.

1997, July 1

3578 A1048 90fo multicolored 1.40 .70

Indigenous Fish A1049

Designs: a, Gymnocephalus schraetzer. b, Cottus gobio. c, Alburnoides bipunctatus. d, Cobitis taenia.

1997, June 6 Litho. *Perf. 13x13½*

3579 A1049 20fo Strip of 4, #a.-d. 1.25 .60

Grapes and Wine Producing Areas Type of 1990

Grapes and growing area: No. 3580, Nemes kadarka, Great Kiskoros. No. 3581, Teitfürtü ezerjo, Mor. No. 3582, Harslevelu, Gyongyos.

1997, Aug. 12 Litho. *Perf. 13x13½*

3580 A902 27fo multicolored .40 .20
3581 A902 27fo multicolored .40 .20
3582 A902 27fo multicolored .40 .20
Nos. 3580-3582 (3) 1.20 .60

No. 3469 Surcharged in Red

1997, July 10 Litho. *Perf. 11½x12*

3583 A989 60fo on 24fo multi .90 .45

Christmas A1050

20fo, Holy family. 27fo, Adoration of the Magi.

1997, Oct. 31 Litho. *Perf. 13x13½*

3584 A1050 20fo multicolored .30 .20
3585 A1050 27fo multicolored .40 .20

World Weight Lifting Championships, Thailand A1051

1997, Nov. 12 *Perf. 12*

3586 A1051 90fo multicolored 1.25 .65

Zsigmond Szechenyi, African Explorer A1052

1998, Jan. 22 Litho. *Perf. 12*

3587 A1052 60fo multicolored .90 .45

Natl. Anthem by Ferenc Kolcsey, 175th Anniv. A1053

1998, Jan. 22

3588 A1053 75fo multicolored 1.10 .55

1998 Winter Olympic Games, Nagano — A1054

1998, Jan. 22 *Perf. 13½x13*

3589 A1054 30fo Downhill skiing .45 .25
3590 A1054 100fo Snowboarding 1.50 .75

Valentine's Day — A1055

1998, Feb. 11 *Perf. 11½x12*

3591 A1055 24fo multi .40 .20

A1056

A1057

1998, Feb. 11 ***Perf. 12***

3592 A1056 50fo multicolored .75 .40

Leo Szilard (1898-1964), physicist.

1998, Feb. 11 ***Perf. 11½x12***

Balint Postas (Post Office Mascot) in front of printed material: 23fo, Holding letter. 24fo, Bowing. 30fo, Standing straight with arms outstretched. 65fo, Flying.

3593 A1057 23fo multicolored .35 .20
3594 A1057 24fo multicolored .35 .20
3595 A1057 30fo multicolored .45 .25
3596 A1057 65fo multicolored .95 .50
Nos. 3593-3596 (4) 2.10 1.15

Easter
A1058 A1059

1998, Mar. 13 **Litho.** ***Perf. 13½x13***

3597 A1058 24fo Stylized egg .40 .20

Perf. 11

3598 A1059 30fo Christ's resurrection .45 .20

1848-49 Revolution, War of Independence, 150th Anniv. — A1060

23fo, Sandor Petofi (1823-49), poet, handwriting, tricolor. 24fo, Mihaly Tancsics, writer & politician, ink well. 30fo, Lajos Kossuth (1802-94), seal.

1998, Mar. 13 ***Perf. 12***

3599 A1060 23fo multicolored .35 .20
3600 A1060 24fo multicolored .40 .20
3601 A1060 30fo multicolored .45 .20
Nos. 3599-3601 (3) 1.20 .60

See Nos. 3640-3643.

Art Nouveau — A1061

Ceramics: 20fo, Vase with relief design of young girl picking flowers, 1899. 24fo, Flower holder with peacock-eyed butterflies, 1901. 30fo, Vase with tulip stems, 1899. 95fo, Round container with legs, 1912.

1998, Mar. 31 **Litho.** ***Perf. 12***

3602 A1061 20fo multi, vert. .30 .20
Complete booklet, 10 #3602 3.00
3603 A1061 24fo multi .35 .20
Complete booklet, 10 #3603 3.50
3604 A1061 30fo multi, vert. .45 .25
Complete booklet, 10 #3604 4.50
3605 A1061 95fo multi 1.40 .70
Nos. 3602-3605 (4) 2.50 1.35

Postal Regulation, 250th Anniv. — A1062

Designs: 24fo+10fo, Courier of 1748, detail of postal route connecting counties of Zala and Gyor. 30fo+10fo, Mounted courier, blowing post horn, script of regulation.
150fo, Horse-drawn postal coach, detail of postal route.

1998, Apr. 10

3606 A1062 24fo +10fo multi .50 .25
3607 A1062 30fo +10fo multi .60 .30

Souvenir Sheet

3608 A1062 150fo multicolored 2.25 1.75

Stamp Day.

Animals of the Americas A1063

23fo, Bison bison. #3610, Ursus horribilis. #3611, Alligator mississippiensis. 30fo, Leopardus pardalis.
150fo, Loddigesia mirabilis.

1998, Apr. 30

3609 A1063 23fo multicolored .70 .35
3610 A1063 24fo multicolored .70 .35
3611 A1063 24fo multicolored .70 .35
3612 A1063 30fo multicolored .90 .45
Nos. 3609-3612 (4) 3.00 1.50

Souvenir Sheet

3613 A1063 150fo multicolored 2.25 1.75

Gyorgy Jendrassik, Engineer, Birth Cent. A1064

1998, May 4 **Engr.**

3614 A1064 100fo dark blue 1.50 .75

Folk Designs Type of 1994

1998, June 5 **Litho.** ***Perf. 11½x12***

3615 A989 5fo multicolored .20 .20

1998 Canoe-Kayak World Championships, Szeged — A1065

1998, June 5 ***Perf. 12***

3616 A1065 30fo multicolored .45 .20

1998 World Cup Soccer Championships, France — A1066

Different soccer players.

1998, June 5

3617 A1066 30fo multicolored .45 .20
3618 A1066 110fo multicolored 1.60 .80
a. Pair, 3617-3618 2.10 1.00

1998 European Track & Field Championships, Budapest — A1067

1998, June 5 ***Perf. 12x11***

3619 A1067 24fo Hurdles .35 .20
3620 A1067 65fo Pole vault .95 .50
3621 A1067 80fo Hammer throw 1.25 .60
Nos. 3619-3621 (3) 2.55 1.30

Gabor Baross (1848-92), Postal Administrator A1068

1998, June 5 ***Perf. 12***

3622 A1068 60fo multicolored .90 .45

A1069

1998, July 31 **Litho.** ***Perf. 12***

3623 A1069 24fo multicolored .35 .20
Complete booklet, 10 #3623 3.50

Széchenyi Hill Children's Railway, 50th anniv.

A1070

1998, July 31 ***Perf. 12x11½***

3624 A1070 65fo multicolored .95 .50

World Congress of Computer Technology, Budapest.

Natl. Holidays — A1071

Europa: 50fo, Sculptures, Festival of the 1956 Revolution, Proclamation of the Republic, 1989, October 23. 60fo, Sheaf of grain, Natl. arms, National Day, August 20.

1998, Aug. 19 **Litho.** ***Perf. 12***

3625 A1071 50fo multicolored .65 .35
3626 A1071 60fo multicolored .80 .40

A1072

1998, Aug. 19

3627 A1072 100fo multicolored 1.40 .70

World Federation of Hungarians, 60th Anniv.

National Parks A1073

Various flora, fauna, explorer of given region: 24fo, Dr. Miklós Udvardy, Hortobágy Natl. Park. 70fo, Adám Boros, Kiskunság Natl. Park.

1998, Oct. 6 **Litho.** ***Perf. 12***

3628 A1073 24fo multicolored .35 .20
3629 A1073 70fo multicolored 1.00 .50

See Nos. 3689-3690.

Folk Designs Type of 1994

1998 **Litho.** ***Perf. 11½x12***

3630 A989 200fo multicolored 1.40 .70

Christmas A1074

Designs: 20fo, Painting, "Visit of the Shepherds," by Agnolo Bronzino (1503-72). 24fo, Artwork, "Mary Upon the Throne with the Infant," by Carlo Crivelli (1430?-94?), vert.

1998, Oct. 30 ***Perf. 12x11½, 11½x12***

3631 A1074 20fo multicolored .30 .20
Complete booklet, 10 #3631 3.00
3632 A1074 24fo multicolored .35 .20
Complete booklet, 10 #3632 3.50

See No. 3676.

Easter A1075

1999, Feb. 11 **Litho.** ***Perf. 12***

3633 A1075 27fo Decorated eggs .35 .20
3634 A1075 32fo Shroud of Turin .40 .20

No. 3634 is 38x53mm.

Intl. Year of the Elderly A1076

1999, Feb. 11 ***Perf. 12½x13½***

3635 A1076 32fo multicolored .40 .20

Sailing Ships A1077

1999, Feb. 11 *Perf. 12*

3636 A1077	32fo	Novara	.40	.20
3637 A1077	79fo	Phoenix	1.00	.50
3638 A1077	110fo	Galley, 15th cent.	1.40	.70
		Nos. 3636-3638 (3)	2.80	1.40

Souvenir Sheet

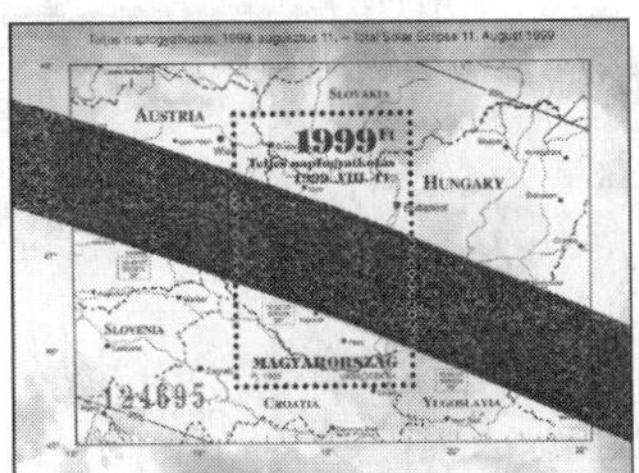
Total Solar Eclipse, Aug. 11 — A1078

Illustration reduced.

1999, Feb. 11

3639 A1078 1999fo multi 18.00 12.00

No. 3639 contains a holographic image. Soaking in water may affect the hologram.

Revolution of 1848-49 Type of 1998

24fo, Sword, Artúr Görgey (1818-1916), general. 27fo, Military decoration, Lajos Batthyány (1806-49), premier of 1st Hungarian ministry. 32fo, Military decoration, József Bem (1794-1850), Polish General who joined Hungarian army.
100fo, Battle scene.

1999, Mar. 12

3640 A1060	24fo	multicolored	.30	.20
3641 A1060	27fo	multicolored	.35	.20
3642 A1060	32fo	multicolored	.40	.20
		Nos. 3640-3642 (3)	1.05	.60

Souvenir Sheet

3643 A1060 100fo multicolored 1.25 .85

No. 3643 contains one 45x28mm stamp.

Folk Designs Type of 1994

1999 **Litho.** *Perf. 12½*

3644 A989	24fo	multicolored	.30	.20
3645 A989	65fo	red & black	.60	.30
3646 A989	90fo	multicolored	1.10	.55
		Nos. 3644-3646 (3)	2.00	1.05

Nos. 3644-3646 are inscribed "1999."

Entrance into NATO — A1079

1999, Mar. 12 **Litho.** *Perf. 12x11½*

3647 A1079 110fo multicolored 1.10 .55

Souvenir Sheet

1999 Modern Pentathlon World Championships, Budapest — A1080

Illustration reduced.

1999, Mar. 24 *Perf. 12½*

3648 A1080 100fo multicolored 1.25 .60

Folk Designs Type of 1994

Various ornate designs.

1999, Apr. 19 **Litho.** *Perf. 11½x12*

3649 A989	79fo	multicolored	.85	.45
3650 A989	100fo	multicolored	1.25	.60

A1081

A1082

1999, May 3 *Perf. 12*

3651 A1081 50fo slate & bister .65 .30

Ferenc Pápai Páriz (1649-1716).

1999, May 3

3652 A1082 100fo multicolored 1.25 .65

Ferencvárosi Torna Sport Club, cent.

World Science Conference A1082a

1999, May 3 **Litho.** *Perf. 11½x12½*

3652A A1082a 65fo multicolored .65 .30

Council of Europe, 50th Anniv. A1083

1999, May 4 *Perf. 13x13¼*

3653 A1083 50fo multicolored .50 .25

National Parks Type of 1998

Europa: 27fo, Aggteleki National Park. 32fo, Bükki National Park.

1999, May 6 *Perf. 12*

3654 A1073	27fo	multicolored	.25	.20
3655 A1073	32fo	multicolored	.30	.20

Grapes and Wine Producing Areas Type of 1990

Grapes, growing area and: 24fo, Castle ruins, Somló region. 27fo, 17th cent. view of Sopron.

1999, May 6 **Litho.** *Perf. 12¼x12½*

3656 A902	24fo	multi, horiz.	.25	.20
3657 A902	27fo	multi, horiz.	.30	.20

Animals of Asia A1085

Designs: 27fo, Tigris regalis. 32fo, Ailuropodus melanoleucus. 52fo, Panthera pardus. 79fo, Pongo pygmaeus.
100fo, Aix galericulata.

1999, May 6 *Perf. 12*

3658 A1085	27fo	multicolored	.25	.20
3659 A1085	32fo	multicolored	.30	.20
3660 A1085	52fo	multicolored	.50	.25
3661 A1085	79fo	multicolored	.75	.35
		Nos. 3658-3661 (4)	1.80	1.00

Souvenir Sheet

3662 A1085 100fo multicolored .95 .60

No. 3662 contains one 50x30mm stamp.

Queen Maria Theresa's Introduction of Mail Coach Service, 250th Anniv. A1086

Stamp Day: 32fo+15fo, Decree by Maria Theresa, coach, street. 52fo+20fo, People entering coach, woman with letters, portion of decree.
150fo, Horse-drawn coach arriving a station.

1999, May 21 **Litho.** *Perf. 12½x12¼*

3663 A1086	32fo	+15fo multi	.45	.20
3664 A1086	52fo	+20fo multi	.65	.30

Souvenir Sheet

3665 A1086 150fo multicolored 1.40 1.00

#3665 contains one 32x42mm stamp.

Red Poppy — A1087

1999, July 7 **Litho.** *Perf. 12x11½*

3666 A1087	27fo	shown	.25	.20
3667 A1087	32fo	Stalkless gentian	.25	.20

George Cukor (1899-1983), Film Director — A1088

1999, July 7 **Litho.** *Perf. 12*

3668 A1088 50fo multicolored .45 .20

UPU, 125th Anniv. A1089

1999, Aug. 13 **Litho.** *Perf. 12*

3669 A1089 32fo multicolored .25 .20

Issued in sheets of 3.

Frankfurt Book Fair — A1090

1999, Sept. 9 **Litho.** *Perf. 12*

3670 A1090 40fo multicolored .40 .20

Antique Furniture A1091

Designs: 10fo, Chair, 17th cent, vert. 20fo, Chair by Károly Lingel, 1915, vert. 50fo, Chair by Pál Esterházy, vert. 70fo, Upholstered chair, vert. 100fo, Couch by Lajos Kozma.

Perf. 11½x12, 12x11½

1999, Oct. 7 **Litho.**

3671 A1091	10fo	bister & dk brn	.20	.20
3672 A1091	20fo	green & dk grn	.20	.20
3673 A1091	50fo	blue & dk bl	.45	.25
3674 A1091	70fo	red & dk red	.60	.30
3675 A1091	100fo	brown & dk brn	.90	.45
		Nos. 3671-3675 (5)	2.35	1.40

See Nos. 3711-3721.

Bronzino Christmas Painting Type of 1998 and

Magi — A1092

Madonna and Child, Stained Glass by Miksa Róth — A1093

1999, Oct. 15 *Perf. 12x11½, 11½x12*

3676 A1074	24fo	multi	.20	.20
		Complete booklet, 10 #3676	2.00	
3677 A1092	27fo	multi	.25	.20
		Complete booklet, 10 #3677	2.50	
3678 A1093	32fo	multi	.30	.20
		Complete booklet, 10 #3678	3.00	
		Nos. 3676-3678 (3)	.75	.60

Jenő Wigner (1902-95), Winner of 1963 Nobel Physics Prize — A1094

1999, Nov. 3 *Perf. 12*

3679 A1094 32fo blue .30 .20

Souvenir Sheet

Chain Bridge, 150th Anniv. — A1095

Illustration reduced.

1999, Nov. 3

3680 A1095 150fo multi 1.40 1.00

Hungarian Millennium A1096

Designs: 28fo, 30fo, Coronation scepter. 34fo, 40fo, Millennium flag.

2000 Litho. *Perf. 12x11½*

3681 A1096 28fo multi	.20	.20
3682 A1096 30fo multi	.25	.20
3683 A1096 34fo multi	.30	.20
3684 A1096 40fo multi	.35	.20
Nos. 3681-3684 (4)	1.10	.80

Coronation of Stephen I, Hungarian conversion to Christianity, 1000th anniv.

Issued: 30fo, 40fo, 1/1; 28fo, 24fo, 2/24.

No. 3681 exists dated 2001.

Souvenir Sheet

Famous Hungarians A1097

No. 3685: a, 30fo, Miklós Misztófalusi Kis (1650-1702), scientist. b, 40fo, Anyos Jedlik (1800-95), physicist. c, 50fo, Jeno Kvassay (1850-1919), engineer. d, 80fo, Jeno Barcsay (1900-88), painter.

2000, Jan. 11 *Perf. 11½x12*

3685 A1097 Sheet of 4, #a.-d. 1.75 1.00

Souvenir Sheet of 5

Literary and Theatrical Personalities A1098

No. 3686: a, Mihály Vörösmarty (1800-55), dramatist. b, Mari Jászai (1850-1926), actress. c, Sándor Márai (1900-89), writer. d, Lujza Blaha (1850-1926), actress. e, Lorinc Szabó (1900-57), writer.

2000, Feb. 24 *Perf. 12*

3686 A1098 50fo #a.-e. 2.00 1.50

A1099

Easter — A1100

2000, Mar. 20

3687 A1099 26fo multi	.20	.20
3688 A1100 28fo multi	.20	.20

National Parks Type of 1998

Designs: 29fo, Bluethroat, Siberian iris, ornithologist György Breuer (1887-1955), Ferto-Hanság Park. 34fo, Black stork, fritillary, scientist Pál Kitaibel (1757-1817), Duna-Dráva Park.

2000, Mar. 20 Litho. *Perf. 12*

3689 A1073 29fo multi	.20	.20
Complete booklet, 10 #36892	2.00	
3690 A1073 34fo multi	.25	.20
Complete booklet, 10 #3690	2.50	

Ferihegy Airport, 50th Anniv. — A1101

2000, May 3 *Perf. 12x11½*

3691 A1101 136fo multi 1.00 .50

István Türr (1825-1908) and Canal Boat — A1102

2000, May 9 *Perf. 12*

3692 A1102 80fo multi .60 .30

Expo 2000, Hanover.

Australian Wildlife — A1103

2000, May 9

3693 A1103 26fo shown	.20	.20
3694 A1103 28fo Opossum	.20	.20
3695 A1103 83fo Koala	.60	.30
3696 A1103 90fo Red kangaroo	.65	.35
Nos. 3693-3696 (4)	1.65	1.05

Souvenir Sheet

3697 A1103 110fo Platypus .80 .60

Souvenir Sheet

Millennium — A1104

Litho., Hologram in Margin

2000, May 9

3698 A1104 2000fo multi 15.00 10.00

Soaking in water may affect the hologram.

Europa, 2000

Common Design Type and

A1105

2000, May 9 Litho.

3699 A1105 34fo multi	.25	.20
3700 CD17 54fo multi	.40	.20

Stamp Day — A1106

26fo, Queen Gisela in coronation gown. 28fo, King Stephen I in coronation gown.

2000, May 18

3701 A1106 26fo multi	.20	.20
3702 A1106 28fo multi	.20	.20

Austria No. 4 and Bisect A1107

2000, May 18

3703 A1107 110fo multi .80 .40

WIPA 2000 Philatelic Exhibition, Vienna.

Grapes and Wine Producing Areas Type of 1990

Grapes and: 29fo, Winery building, Balatonfüred-Csopak region, horiz. 34fo, Storage containers, Aszár-Neszmély region, horiz.

2000, May 25 *Perf. 13¼x13*

3704 A902 29fo multi	.20	.20
3705 A902 34fo multi	.25	.20

Houses of Worship A1108

Designs: No. 3706, 30fo, Abbey Church, Ják. No. 3707, 30fo, Reformed Church, Tákos. No. 3708, 30fo, St. Antal's Church, Eger. No. 3709, 30fo, Deák Evangelical Church, Budapest. 120fo, Dohany Synagogue, Budapest.

2000 Litho. *Perf. 12*

3706-3710 A1108 Set of 5 1.75 .85

Issued: 120fo, 9/19; others 6/30. See Israel No. 1416.

Furniture Type of 1999

Designs: 2fo, Wooden chair, 1838, vert. 3fo, 19th cent. chair, vert. 4fo, Chair by Géza Maróti, 1900, vert. 5fo, Chair by Odon Farago, 1900, vert. 6fo, Chair by Márton Kovács, 1893, vert. 9fo, 18th cent. chair from Dunapataj, vert. 26fo, 1850 chair, vert. 29fo, 19th cent. chair with animal designs, vert. 30fo, Chair by Károly Nagy, 1935, vert. 80fo, 1840-50 chair, vert. 90fo, Chair by Lajos Kozma, 1928, vert.

2000 *Perf. 11½x12*

3711-3721 A1091 Set of 11 2.00 1.00

Issued: 2fo, 3fo, 9fo, 26fo, 29fo, 30fo, 6/30; others, 10/9.

Hungarian Aviation, 90th Anniv. A1109

2000, Aug. 18 *Perf. 12¾x12¼*

3722 A1109 120fo multi .85 .45

Souvenir Sheets

Hungarian History A1110

No. 3723: a, King with orb, knights. b, St. Laszlo with sword. c, St. Elizabeth, Mongol invasion. d, King Sigismund, knight on horseback. e, Janos Hunuyadi and Janos Kapisztran.

No. 3724: a, King Matthias. b, Crucifixion scene, Miklos Zrinyi. c, Trumpeter on horseback, battle scenes. d, Gabor Bethlen (in black hat). e, Peer Parmany, university.

2000, Aug. 18 *Perf. 12*

3723 Sheet of 5	1.75	1.75
a.-e. A1110 50fo Any single	.35	.35
3724 Sheet of 5	1.75	1.75
a.-e. A1110 50fo Any single	.35	.35

A1111

A1112

Christmas A1113

2000, Oct. 16 *Perf. 12¼x11½*

3725 A1111 26fo shown .20 .20

Perf. 13¼x13

3726 A1112 28fo shown	.20	.20
Booklet, 10 #3726	2.00	
3727 A1112 29fo Christmas tree	.20	.20

Perf. 12

3728 A1113 34fo shown	.25	.20
Booklet, 10 #3728	2.50	
Nos. 3725-3728 (4)	.85	.80

European Convention on Human Rights, 50th Anniv. — A1114

2000, Nov. 3 *Perf. 12½*

3729 A1114 50fo multicolored .35 .20

2000 Summer Olympics, Sydney A1115

Sports and total of medals won: 30fo, Shooting, three bronzes. 40fo, Weight lifting, six silvers. 80fo, Men's rings, eight golds. 120fo, Rowing, total count.

2000, Nov. 22 *Perf. 12*

3730-3732 A1115 Set of 3 1.10 .55

Souvenir Sheet

3733 A1115 120fo multi .85 .45

European Language Year A1116

2001, Jan. 15 Litho. *Perf. 13x13¼*

3734 A1116 100fo multi .75 .35

Souvenir Sheet

Greetings — A1117

No. 3735: a, Bugler on pig. b, Man, woman, flower. c, Baby in cradle. d, Clown. e, Mother and child.

2001, Feb. 9 ***Perf. 11½x12***
3735 A1117 36fo Sheet of 5, #a-f 1.40 .70

World Speed Skating Championships, Budapest — A1118

2001, Feb. 9 Litho. ***Perf. 13***
3736 A1118 140fo multi 1.00 .50

Furniture Type of 1999

Designs: 1fo, Three-legged stool, by János Vincze, 1910, vert. 7fo, 1853 chair, vert. 8fo, 19th cent. chair, vert. 31fo, Like No. 3717, vert. 40fo, Armchair by Ignác Alpár, 1896, vert. 60fo, Armchair by Ferenc Steindl, 1840, vert. 200fo, Settee by Sebestyén Vogel, 1810.

2001 ***Perf. 11½x12, 12x11½***
3737-3743 A1091 Set of 7 2.50 1.25

Issued: 31fo, 3/5; others, 2/9.

Hungarian Millennium Type of 2000

2001, Mar. 5 ***Perf. 12x11½***
3744 A1096 36fo Millennium flag .25 .20

National Parks Type of 1998

Designs: 28fo, Balaton. 36fo, Körös-maros. 70fo, Duna-Ipoly.

2001, Mar. 5 ***Perf. 12***
3745-3747 A1073 Set of 3 1.00 .50

Easter A1119

2001, Mar. 5 ***Perf. 13***
3748 A1119 28fo multi .25 .20

Locomotives — A1120

Designs: 31fo, Mk. 48. 36fo, 490. 100fo, 394. 150fo, C50.

2001, Apr. 13 ***Perf. 13¼x13***
3749-3752 A1120 Set of 4 2.25 1.10

Esztergom Archbishopric, 1000th Anniv. — A1121

2001, Apr. 18 ***Perf. 12***
3753 A1121 124fo multi .90 .45

Organizations — A1122

No. 3754: a, 70fo, Emblems of European and Mediterranean Plant Protection Organization and Intl. Plant Protection Convention. b, 80fo, UN High Commissioner for Refugees, 50th anniv.

Illustration reduced.

2001, Apr. 18 ***Perf. 13¼x13***
3754 A1122 Horiz. pair, #a-b 1.10 .55

Europa A1123

Designs: 36fo, Open chest with water. 90fo, Split globe with water.

2001, May 9 ***Perf. 12***
3755-3756 A1123 Set of 2 .95 .45

Animals A1124

Designs: 28fo, Phoca hispida. 36fo, Canis lupus. 70fo, Testudo hermanni. 90fo, Alcedo atthis ispida.
200fo, Cervus elaphus.

2001, May 9 ***Perf. 12***
3757-3760 A1124 Set of 4 1.75 .85

Souvenir Sheet

3761 A1124 200fo multi 1.50 .75

A1125

Stamp Day — A1126

Designs: 36fo, #N2. 90fo, #2.
200fo+40fo, Pigeon Post, by Miklos Barabás.

2001, May 25 ***Perf. 12¼x11½***
3762-3763 A1125 Set of 2 .95 .45
3763a Sheet, 6 each # 3762-3763 5.75 3.00

Souvenir Sheet

Perf. 12½

3764 A1126 200fo +40fo multi 1.75 .90

European Water Polo Championships A1127

2001, June 14 ***Perf. 13½x13***
3765 A1127 150fo multi 1.10 .55

Intl. Scouting Conference — A1128

2001, June 21 ***Perf. 12***
3766 A1128 150fo multi 1.10 .55

World Youth Track and Field Championships, Debrecen — A1129

2001, July 12 Litho. ***Perf. 13x13¼***
3767 A1129 140fo multi .95 .50

Artist's Colony, Gödöllö, Cent. — A1130

Fészek Arts Club, Cent. — A1131

2001, July 12 ***Perf. 12***
3768 A1130 100fo multi .70 .35
3769 A1131 150fo blue & blk 1.00 .50

Hungarian History Type of 2000

Souvenir Sheets

No. 3770: a, Prince Francis II Rákóczy, swordsman on horseback, Ilona Zrinyi. b, Rider from Royal Horse Guard, Castle at Munkács, Queen Maria Theresa. c, Count Stephen Széchenyi, Chain Bridge. d, Lajos Kossuth, Artúr Görgey with sword on horseback, battle scene. e, Poet János Arany, Parliament building.

No. 3771: a, World War I soldier on horseback, outline map of Hungary and lost parts of empire, Hungarian people. b, Albert Szent-Gyorgi and chemistry equipment. c, Chain Bridge, World War II soldiers, Bishop Vilmos Apor. d, Pictures of 1956 revolution, Polish-Hungarian Solidarity banner. e, Barbed wire, children representing Hungary's future, Hungarian millennium flag.

2001, Aug. 15
3770 Sheet of 5 1.75 1.75
a.-e. A1110 50fo Any single .35 .35
3771 Sheet of 5 1.75 1.75
a.-e. A1110 50fo Any single .35 .35

Souvenir Sheet

Crown of St. Stephen — A1132

Litho. & Embossed

2001, Aug. 15 ***Perf. 13x12¾***
3772 A1132 2001fo multi 14.50 7.25

Grapes and Wine Producing Areas Type of 1990

Grapes and: 60fo, Pannonhalma Abbey, Pannonhalma-Sokoróalja region, horiz. 70fo, Spherical observatory and Red Chapel, Balatonboglár, horiz.

2001, Aug. 17 Litho. ***Perf. 13¼x13***
3773-3774 A902 Set of 2 .95 .50

Attempt To Create World's Largest Stamp Mosaic — A1133

2001, Oct. 9 ***Perf. 12***
3775 A1133 10fo multi .20 .20

Maria Valeria Bridge Reconstruction — A1134

2001, Oct. 11 ***Perf. 13¼x13***
3776 A1134 36fo multi .25 .20

See Slovakia No. 388.

Christmas A1135

2001, Oct. 16 ***Perf. 12***
3777 A1135 36fo multi .25 .20

State Printers, 150th Anniv. — A1136

2001, Nov. 23 Litho. ***Perf. 13¼x13***
3778 A1136 150fo multi 1.10 .55

2002 Winter Olympics, Salt Lake City — A1137

2002, Feb. 8 Litho. ***Perf. 12***
3779 A1137 160fo multi 1.25 .60

Souvenir Sheet

History of the Bicycle — A1138

No. 3780: a, Large-wheeled bicycle and rider, c. 1880. b, Tricycle, early 1900s. c, Károly Iszer (1860-1929), Budapest Sport Club chairman and bicycle. d, Tandem bicycle.

2002, Feb. 20 ***Perf. 11½x12¼***
3780 A1138 40fo Sheet of 4, #a-d 1.25 .60

Souvenir Sheet

Hungarian - Ottoman Battles of 1552 — A1139

No. 3781: a, 50fo, Siege of Eger Castle (25x30mm). b, 50fo, Battle of Temesvár (25x30mm). c, 100fo+50fo, Battle of Drégely Castle (40x30mm).

2002, Feb. 20 ***Perf. 12***
3781 A1139 Sheet of 3, #a-c 1.90 .95

Easter — A1140

2002, Mar. 14 ***Perf. 11½x12¼***
3782 A1140 30fo multi .25 .20

Airplanes Designed by Hungarians — A1141

Designs: 180fo, Libelle, by János adorján, 1910. 190fo, Magyar Lloyd, by Tibor Melczer, 1914.

2002, Mar. 14 ***Perf. 12½***
3783-3784 A1141 Set of 2 2.75 1.40

Famous Hungarians A1142

Designs: 33fo, Lajos Kossuth (1802-94), leader of Hungarian independence movement. 134fo, János Bolyai (1802-60), mathematician. 150fo, Gyula Illyés (1902-83), writer.

2002, Mar. 14 ***Perf. 13x13½***
3785-3787 A1142 Set of 3 2.40 1.25

Souvenir Sheet

Parliament Building, Cent. — A1143

2002, Mar. 14 ***Perf. 11½x12¼***
3788 A1143 500fo multi 3.75 1.90

Souvenir Sheet

Opening of National Theater — A1144

2002, Mar. 14
3789 A1144 500fo multi 3.75 1.90

Furniture Type of 1999

Designs: 33fo, Chair, 1809, vert. 134fo, Theater armchair, 1900.

2002, Mar. 28 ***Perf. 11½x12, 12x11½***
3790-3791 A1091 Set of 2 1.25 .60

Environmental Protection — A1145

2002, Mar. 28 ***Perf. 12***
3792 A1145 158fo multi 1.25 .60

Souvenir Sheet

Founding of Hungarian National Museum and National Széchényi Library, Bicent. — A1146

No. 3793: a, Mihály Apafi psalter, 1686. b, Illuminated letter from Graduale Pars II. c, Standard of the Civil Guard of Pest, 1848. d, Basin for holy water, 12th cent.

2002, Apr. 29
3793 A1146 150fo Sheet of 4, #a-d 4.75 2.40

Halas Lace, Cent. — A1147

Designs: 100fo, Tablecloth with Two Deer, by Mrs. Béla Bazala, 1916. 110fo, Swan Tablecloth, by Erno Stepanek, 1930. 140fo, Jancsi and Iluska, by Antal Tar, 1935.

Litho. & Embossed

2002, May 3 ***Perf. 12***
3794-3796 A1147 Set of 3 2.75 1.40

Europa A1148

2002, May 9 Litho. ***Perf. 11***
3797 A1148 62fo multi .50 .25

2002 World Cup Soccer Championships, Japan and Korea — A1149

2002, May 9 ***Perf. 13x13½***
3798 A1149 160fo multi + label 1.25 .60

Fauna A1150

Designs: 30fo, Felis sylvestris. 38fo, Podarcis taurica. 110fo, Garrulus glandarius. 160fo, Rosalia alpina.
500fo, Acipenser ruthenus.

2002, May 9 ***Perf. 12***
3799-3802 A1150 Set of 4 2.60 1.25

Souvenir Sheet

3803 A1150 500fo multi 3.75 1.90

Greetings — A1151

No. 3804: a, Etesd meg! b, Megszülettem! c, Sok boldogságot! d, Ontözd meg! e, Ennyire szeretlek!

Serpentine Die Cut 12¼x12¾

2002, May 29

Self-Adhesive

3804 Booklet pane of 5 1.50
a.-e. A1151 38fo Any single .30 .20

Flower Type of 1999

Designs: 30fo, Red poppy. 38fo, Stalkless gentian.

2002, June 24 ***Perf. 12¼x11½***
3805-3806 A1087 Set of 2 .55 .30

Art — A1152

Designs: 62fo, Kodobálók, by Károly Ferenczy. 188fo, Táncosno, sculpture by Ferenc Megyessy, vert.

Perf. 12¾x12¼, 12¼x12¾

2002, June 24
3807-3808 A1152 Set of 2 2.10 1.10

UNESCO World Heritage Sites — A1153

Designs: 100fo, Budapest. 150fo, Hollóko. 180fo, Caves of Aggtelek Karst, horiz.

2002, June 24 ***Perf. 12***
3809-3811 A1153 Set of 3 3.50 1.75

Kalocsa Archbishopric, 1000th Anniv. — A1154

2002, Aug. 1 Litho. ***Perf. 13¼x12½***
3812 A1154 150fo multi 1.25 .65

Medical Congresses A1155

No. 3813: a, 100fo, 38th European Diabetes Association Congress. b, 150fo, 16th European Arm and Shoulder Surgeons Congress.

2002, Aug. 23 ***Perf. 13x13¼***
3813 A1155 Vert. pair, #a-b 2.10 1.10

Printed in sheets of two pairs.

Ceramics by Margit Kovács — A1156

No. 3814: a, 33fo, Madonna and Child, 1938. b, 38fo, Mother and Children, 1953.
400fo+200fo, St. George, 1936.

2002, Oct. 3 ***Perf. 13¼x13***
3814 A1156 Pair, #a-b .60 .30

Souvenir Sheet
Perf. 12¼x11½

3815 A1156 400fo +200fo multi 5.00 2.50

Stamp Day. No. 3814 printed in sheets of two pairs. No. 3815 contains one 25x36mm stamp.

Christmas A1157

Designs: 30fo, Adoration of the Magi. 38fo, Bethlehem.

Litho. with Foil Application

2002, Oct. 30 ***Perf. 12***
3816-3817 A1157 Set of 2 .60 .30

World Gymnastics Championships, Debrecen — A1158

2002, Nov. 20 Litho. ***Perf. 13x13¼***
3818 A1158 160fo multi 1.40 .70

SEMI-POSTAL STAMPS

Issues of the Monarchy

"Turul" and St. Stephen's Crown — SP1

Franz Josef I Wearing Hungarian Crown — SP2

Wmk. Double Cross (137)

1913, Nov. 20 Typo. ***Perf. 14***

B1	SP1	1f slate	.20	.20
B2	SP1	2f olive yellow	.20	.20
B3	SP1	3f orange	.20	.20
B4	SP1	5f emerald	.20	.20
B5	SP1	6f olive green	.20	.20
B6	SP1	10f carmine	.20	.20
B7	SP1	12f violet, *yellow*	.35	.20
B8	SP1	16f gray green	.40	.20
B9	SP1	20f dark brown	.80	.30
B10	SP1	25f ultra	.40	.20
B11	SP1	30f orange brown	.55	.20
B12	SP1	35f red violet	.55	.20
B13	SP1	50f lake, *blue*	1.25	.40
B14	SP1	60f green, *salmon*	1.25	.35
B15	SP2	1k dull red	12.50	1.40
B16	SP2	2k dull blue	32.50	21.00
B17	SP2	5k violet brown	15.00	10.50
		Nos. B1-B17 (17)	66.75	36.15

Nos. B1-B17 were sold at an advance of 2f over face value, as indicated by the label at bottom. The surtax was to aid flood victims.

For overprints see Nos. 5NB1-5NB10, 6NB1-6NB11.

Semi-Postal Stamps of 1913 Surcharged in Red, Green or Brown:

a

b

1914

B18	SP1(a)	1f slate	.20	.20
B19	SP1(a)	2f olive yel	.20	.20
B20	SP1(a)	3f orange	.20	.20
B21	SP1(a)	5f emerald	.20	.20
B22	SP1(a)	6f olive green	.20	.20
B23	SP1(a)	10f carmine (G)	.20	.20
B24	SP1(a)	12f violet, *yel*	.20	.20
B25	SP1(a)	16f gray green	.20	.20
B26	SP1(a)	20f dark brown	.50	.20
B27	SP1(a)	25f ultra	.50	.20
B28	SP1(a)	30f orange brn	.75	.20
B29	SP1(a)	35f red violet	1.25	.20
B30	SP1(a)	50f lake, *bl*	.90	.25
B31	SP1(a)	60f green, *salmon*	1.50	.35
B32	SP2(b)	1k dull red (Br)	32.50	12.50
B33	SP2(b)	2k dull blue	17.00	13.00
B34	SP2(b)	5k violet brn	13.50	9.50
		Nos. B18-B34 (17)	70.00	38.00

Regular Issue of 1913 Surcharged in Red or Green:

c

d

1915, Jan. 1

B35	A4(c)	1f slate	.20	.20
B36	A4(c)	2f olive yel	.20	.20
B37	A4(c)	3f orange	.20	.20
B38	A4(c)	5f emerald	.20	.20
B39	A4(c)	6f olive grn	.20	.20
B40	A4(c)	10f carmine (G)	.20	.20
B41	A4(c)	12f violet, *yel*	.20	.20
B42	A4(c)	16f gray green	.25	.25
B43	A4(c)	20f dark brown	.30	.30
B44	A4(c)	25f ultra	.20	.20
B45	A4(c)	30f orange brn	.20	.20
B46	A4(c)	35f red violet	.20	.20
B47	A4(c)	50f lake, *bl*	.20	.20
a.		On No. 96a	5,500.	
B48	A4(c)	60f green, *salmon*	.35	.30
B49	A5(d)	1k dull red	.40	.45
B50	A5(d)	2k dull blue	1.25	1.25
B51	A5(d)	5k violet brown	5.25	5.25

Surcharged as Type "c" but in Smaller Letters

B52	A4	60f green, *salmon*	1.00	1.00
		Nos. B35-B52 (18)	11.00	11.00

Nos. B18-B52 were sold at an advance of 2f over face value. The surtax to aid war widows and orphans.

Soldiers Fighting SP3 SP4

Eagle with Sword SP5

Harvesting SP6

1916-17 ***Perf. 15***

B53	SP3	10f + 2f rose red	.20	.20
B54	SP4	15f + 2f dull violet	.20	.20
B55	SP5	40f + 2f brn car ('17)	.20	.20
		Nos. B53-B55 (3)	.60	.60

For overprints and surcharge see Nos. B58-B60. 1NB1-1NB3, 2NB1-2NB6, 4NJ1, 5NB11-5NB13, 6NB13-6NB15, 7NB2-7NB3, 9NB1, 10NB1-10NB4, Szeged B1-B4.

1917, Sept. 15

Surcharge in Red

B56	SP6	10f + 1k rose	.25	.25
B57	SP6	15f + 1k violet	.25	.25

Nos. B56 and B57 were issued in connection with the War Exhibition of Archduke Josef.

Issues of the Republic

Semi-Postal Stamps of 1916-17 Overprinted in Black

1918

B58	SP3	10f + 2f rose red	.20	.20
B59	SP4	15f + 2f dull violet	.20	.20
B60	SP5	40f + 2f brown car	.20	.20
		Nos. B58-B60 (3)	.60	.60

Nos. B58-B60 exist with inverted overprint.

Postally used copies of Nos. B69-B174 sell for more.

Issues of the Kingdom

Released Prisoner Walking Home — SP7

Prisoners of War — SP8

Homecoming of Soldier — SP9

Wmk. 137 Vert. or Horiz.

1920, Mar. 11 ***Perf. 12***

B69	SP7	40f + 1k dull red	.25	.40
B70	SP8	60f + 2k gray brown	.25	.30
B71	SP9	1k + 5k dk blue	.25	.30
		Nos. B69-B71 (3)	.75	1.00
		Set, never hinged	1.75	

The surtax was used to help prisoners of war return home from Siberia.

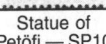

Statue of Petőfi — SP10

Griffin — SP11

Sándor Petőfi — SP12

Petőfi Dying — SP13

Petőfi Addressing People — SP14

1923, Jan. 23 ***Perf. 14 (10k, 40k), 12***

B72	SP10	10k slate green	.20	.30
B73	SP11	15k dull blue	.85	1.25
B74	SP12	25k gray brown	.25	.30
B75	SP13	40k brown violet	.85	1.25
B76	SP14	50k violet brown	.85	1.25
		Nos. B72-B76 (5)	3.00	4.35
		Set, never hinged	5.50	

Birth centenary of the Hungarian poet Sándor Petőfi. The stamps were on sale at double face value, for a limited time and in restricted quantities, after which the remainders were given to a charitable organization.

Child with Symbols of Peace — SP15

Mother and Infant — SP16

Instruction in Archery — SP17

Wmk. 133

1924, Apr. 8 Engr. ***Perf. 12***

B77	SP15	300k dark blue	1.25	1.25
a.		Perf. 11½	25.00	25.00
B78	SP16	500k black brown	1.25	1.25
B79	SP17	1000k black green	1.25	1.25
		Nos. B77-B79 (3)	3.75	3.75
		Set, never hinged	5.75	

Each stamp has on the back an inscription stating that it was sold at a premium of 100 per cent over the face value.

Parade of Athletes SP18

Skiing — SP19

Skating — SP20

Diving — SP21

Fencing SP22

Scouts Camping — SP23

Soccer SP24

Hurdling — SP25

Perf. 12, 12½ and Compound

1925		**Typo.**		**Unwmk.**
B80 SP18	100k	bl grn & brn	1.00	*1.50*
B81 SP19	200k	lt brn & myr grn	1.60	*2.50*
B82 SP20	300k	dark blue	2.00	*3.00*
B83 SP21	400k	dp bl & dp grn	2.40	*3.50*
B84 SP22	500k	purple brown	3.00	*5.00*
B85 SP23	1000k	red brown	4.00	*6.00*
B86 SP24	2000k	brown violet	4.75	*7.00*
B87 SP25	2500k	olive brown	5.75	*8.00*
		Nos. B80-B87 (8)	24.50	*36.50*
		Set, never hinged	45.00	

These stamps were sold at double face value, plus a premium of 10 per cent on orders sent by mail. They did not serve any postal need and were issued solely to raise funds to aid athletic associations. An inscription regarding the 100 per cent premium is printed on the back of each stamp. Exist imperf.

St. Emerich SP26

Sts. Stephen and Gisela SP27

St. Ladislaus SP28

Sts. Gerhardt and Emerich SP29

1930, May 15	**Wmk. 210**		***Perf. 14***
B88 SP26	8f + 2f deep green	.45	.40
B89 SP27	16f + 4f brt violet	.50	*.70*
B90 SP28	20f + 4f deep rose	1.75	*2.25*
B91 SP29	32f + 8f ultra	2.50	*3.25*
	Nos. B88-B91 (4)	5.20	*6.60*
	Set, never hinged	9.00	

900th anniv. of the death of St. Emerich, son of Stephen I, king, saint and martyr.

Catalogue values for unused stamps in this section, from this point to the end of the section, are for Never Hinged items.

St. Ladislaus — SP30

Holy Sacrament SP31

SP32

1938 May 16	**Photo.**		***Perf. 12***
B92 SP30	16f + 16f dull slate bl	2.50	2.50
B93 SP31	20f + 20f dk car	2.50	2.50

Souvenir Sheet

B94 SP32	Sheet of 7	25.00	15.00
a.	6f + 6f St. Stephen	1.90	1.10
b.	10f + 10f St. Emerich	1.90	1.10
c.	16f + 16f slate blue (B92)	1.90	1.10
d.	20f + 20f dark carmine (B93)	1.90	1.10
e.	32f + 32f St. Elizabeth	1.90	1.10
f.	40f + 40f St. Maurice	1.90	1.10
g.	50f + 50f St. Margaret	1.90	1.10

Printed in sheets measuring 136½x155mm. Nos. B94c and B94d are slightly smaller than B92 and B93.

Eucharistic Cong. in Budapest, May, 1938.

St. Stephen, Victorious Warrior SP33

St. Stephen, Offering Crown SP34

SP35

1938, Aug. 12			***Perf. 12***
B95 SP33	10f + 10f violet brn	3.00	3.00
B96 SP34	20f + 20f red org	3.00	3.00

Souvenir Sheet

B97 SP35	Sheet of 7	20.00	15.00
a.	6f + 6f St. Stephen the Missionary	1.40	1.25
b.	10f + 10f violet brown (B95)	1.40	1.25
c.	16f + 16f Seated Upon Throne	1.40	1.25
d.	20f + 20f red orange (B96)	1.40	1.25
e.	32f + 32f Receives Bishops and Monks	1.40	1.25
f.	40f + 40f St. Gisela, St. Stephen and St. Emerich	1.40	1.25
g.	50f + 50f St. Stephen on Bier	1.40	1.40

Death of St. Stephen, 900th anniversary.

No. B97 is on brownish paper, Nos. B95-B96 on white.

Statue Symbolizing Recovered Territories SP36

Castle of Munkács SP37

Admiral Horthy Entering Komárom SP38

Cathedral of Kassa SP39

Girl Offering Flowers to Soldier — SP40

1939, Jan. 16			
B98 SP36	6f + 3f myrtle grn	.60	.35
B99 SP37	10f + 5f olive grn	.25	.20
B100 SP38	20f + 10f dark red	.25	.20
B101 SP39	30f + 15f grnsh blue	1.10	.60
B102 SP40	40f + 20f dk bl gray	1.10	.65
	Nos. B98-B102 (5)	3.30	2.00

The surtax was for the aid of "Hungary for Hungarians" patriotic movement.

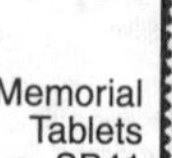

Memorial Tablets SP41

Gáspár Károlyi, Translator of the Bible into Hungarian SP42

Albert Molnár de Szenci, Translator of the Psalms SP43

Prince Gabriel Bethlen — SP44

Susanna Lórántffy — SP45

Perf. 12x12½, 12½x12

1939	**Photo.**		**Wmk. 210**
B103 SP41	6f + 3f green	.70	.55
B104 SP42	10f + 5f claret	.70	.55
B105 SP43	20f + 10f copper red	.80	.75
B106 SP44	32f + 16f bister	1.25	1.00
B107 SP45	40f + 20f chalky blue	1.40	1.00
	Nos. B103-B107 (5)	4.85	3.85

Souvenir Sheets

Perf. 12

B108 SP44	32f olive & vio brn	14.00	10.00

Imperf

B109 SP44	32f bl grn, cop red & gold	14.00	10.00

National Protestant Day. The surtax was used to erect an Intl. Protestant Institute.

The souvenir sheets sold for 1.32p each.

Issue dates: Nos. B103-B107, Oct. 2. Nos. B108-B109, Oct. 27.

Boy Scout Flying Kite — SP47

Allegory of Flight — SP48

Archangel Gabriel from Millennium Monument, Budapest, and Planes — SP49

1940, Jan. 1			***Perf. 12½x12***
B110 SP47	6f + 6f yellow grn	.25	.25
B111 SP48	10f + 10f chocolate	.40	.35
B112 SP49	20f + 20f copper red	.90	.80
	Nos. B110-B112 (3)	1.55	1.40

The surtax was used for the Horthy National Aviation Fund.

SP50

Soldier Protecting Family from Floods — SP51

Souvenir Sheet

Wmk. 210

1940, May 6 Photo. *Perf. 12*

B113 SP50 20f + 1p dk blue grn 5.00 5.00

1940, May

B114 SP51 10f + 2f gray brown .25 .25
B115 SP51 20f + 4f orange red .25 .25
B116 SP51 20f + 50f red brown .70 .70
Nos. B114-B116 (3) 1.20 1.20

The surtax on Nos. B113-B116 was used to aid flood victims.

Hunyadi Coat of Arms SP52

King Matthias SP54

Hunyadi Castle SP53

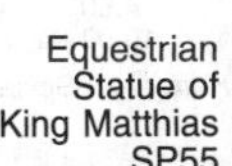

Equestrian Statue of King Matthias SP55

Corvin Codex — SP56

Equestrian Statue of King Matthias — SP57

1940 *Perf. 12½x12, 12x12½*

B117 SP52 6f + 3f blue grn .30 .30
B118 SP53 10f + 5f gldn brn .25 .25
B119 SP54 16f + 8f dk ol bis .30 .30
B120 SP55 20f + 10f brick red .50 .40
B121 SP56 32f + 16f dk gray 1.00 .70
Nos. B117-B121 (5) 2.35 1.95

Souvenir Sheet

B122 SP57 20f + 1p dk bl grn & pale grn 4.50 4.50

King Matthias (1440-1490) at Kolozsvar, Transylvania. The surtax was used for war relief.

Issued: #B117-B121, July 1. #B122. Nov. 7.

Hungarian Soldier — SP58

20f+50f, Virgin Mary and Szekley, symbolizing the return of transylvania. 32f+50f, Szekley Mother Offering Infant Son to the Fatherland.

1940, Dec. 2 Photo. *Perf. 12½x12*

B123 SP58 10f + 50f dk blue grn .65 .50
B124 SP58 20f + 50f brown car .65 .50
B125 SP58 32f + 50f yellow brn .95 .75
Nos. B123-B125 (3) 2.25 1.75

Occupation of Transylvania. The surtax was for the Pro-Transylvania movement.

Symbol for Drama SP61

Symbol for Sculpture — SP62

Symbols: 16f+16f, Art. 20f+20f, Literature.

1940, Dec. 15 *Perf. 12x12½, 12½x12*

B126 SP61 6f + 6f dark green .90 .75
B127 SP62 10f + 10f olive bis .90 .75
B128 SP62 16f + 16f dk violet .90 .75
B129 SP61 20f + 20f fawn .90 .75
Nos. B126-B129 (4) 3.60 3.00

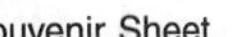

Souvenir Sheet

1941, Jan. 5 *Imperf.*

B130 Sheet of 4 2.75 2.00
a. SP61 6f + 6f olive brown .55 .40
b. SP62 10f + 10f henna brown .55 .40
c. SP62 16f + 16f dk blue green .55 .40
d. SP61 20f + 20f rose violet .55 .40

Surtax on #B126-B130 was used for the Pension and Assistance Institution for Artists.

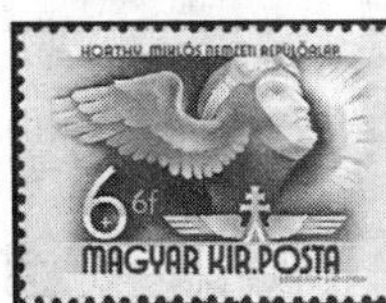

Winged Head of Pilot — SP66

Designs: 10f+10f, Boy Scout with model plane. 20f+20f, Glider in flight. 32f+32f, Our Lady of Loreto, patroness of Hungarian pilots.

1941, Mar. 24 *Perf. 12x12½*

B131 SP66 6f + 6f grn olive .45 .35
B132 SP66 10f + 10f dp claret .45 .35
B133 SP66 20f + 20f org ver .45 .35
B134 SP66 32f + 32f turq blue .90 .80
Nos. B131-B134 (4) 2.25 1.85

The surtax was used to finance civilian and army pilot training through the Horthy National Aviation Fund.

Infantry SP70

12f+18f, Heavy artillery. 20f+30f, Plane and tanks. 40f+60f, Cavalryman and cyclist.

1941, Dec. 1 Photo. Wmk. 266

Inscribed: "Honvedeink Karacsonyara 1941"

B135 SP70 8f + 12f dk green .25 .20
B136 SP70 12f + 8f olive grn .25 .20
B137 SP70 20f + 30f slate .30 .25
B138 SP70 40f + 60f red brown .50 .45
Nos. B135-B138 (4) 1.30 1.10

The surtax was for the benefit of the Army.

Soldier and Emblem SP74

1941, Dec. 1

B139 SP74 20f + 40f dark red 1.50 1.25

The surtax was for the soldiers' Christmas.

Aviator and Plane — SP75

Planes and Ghostly Band of Old Chiefs SP76

Plane and Archer SP77

Aviators and Plane — SP78

1942, Mar. 15 *Perf. 12½x12, 12x12½*

B140 SP75 8f + 8f dark green .45 .35
B141 SP76 12f + 12f sapphire .45 .35
B142 SP77 20f + 20f brown .45 .35
B143 SP78 30f + 30f dark red .45 .35
Nos. B140-B143 (4) 1.80 1.40

The surtax aided the Horthy National Aviation Fund.

Blood Transfusion — SP79

Designs: 8f+32f, Bandaging wounded soldier. 12f+50f, Radio and carrier pigeons. 20f+1p, Widows and orphans.

1942, Sept. 1 *Perf. 12½x12*

B144 SP79 3f + 18f dk ol & red .80 .85
B145 SP79 8f + 32f dp brn & red .80 .85
B146 SP79 12f + 50f dp cl & red .80 .85
B147 SP79 20f + 1p slate bl & red .80 .85
Nos. B144-B147 (4) 3.20 3.40

The surtax aided the Hungarian Red Cross. Sheets of 10.

Widow of Stephen Horthy — SP83

Red Cross Nurse Aiding Soldier SP84

Magdalene Horthy Mother of Stephen Horthy — SP85

1942, Dec. 1 *Perf. 13, Imperf.*

B148 SP83 6f + 1p vio bl & red 2.00 1.50
a. Sheet of 4 13.00 13.00
B149 SP84 8f + 1p dk ol grn & red 2.00 1.50
a. Sheet of 4 13.00 13.00
B150 SP85 20f + 1p dk red brn & red 2.00 1.50
a. Sheet of 4 13.00 13.00
Nos. B148-B150 (3) 6.00 4.50

The surtax aided the Hungarian Red Cross.

King Ladislaus I
SP86 SP87

1942, Dec. 21 Wmk. 266 *Perf. 12*

B151	SP86	6f + 6f olive gray	.35	.40
B152	SP87	8f + 8f green	.35	.40
B153	SP86	12f + 12f dull violet	.35	.40
B154	SP87	20f + 20f Prus green	.35	.40
B155	SP86	24f + 24f brown	.35	.40
B156	SP87	30f + 30f rose car	.35	.40
		Nos. B151-B156 (6)	2.10	2.40

900th anniv. of the birth of St. Ladislaus (1040-95), the 700th anniv. of the beginning of the country's reconstruction by King Béla IV (1206-70) and the 600th anniv. of the accession of King Lajos the Great (1326-82).

The surtax aided war invalids and their families.

Archer on Horseback
SP92

Knight with Sword and Shield — SP93

Old Magyar Arms — SP94

Designs: 3f+1f, 4f+1f, Warrior with shield and battle ax. 12f+2f, Knight with lance, 20f+2f, Musketeer. 40f+4f, Hussar. 50f+6f, Artilleryman.

1943

B157	SP92	1f + 1f dk gray	.20	.25
B158	SP93	3f + 1f dull violet	.30	.30
B159	SP93	4f + 1f lake	.20	.25
B160	SP93	8f + 2f green	.20	.25
B161	SP92	12f + 2f bister brn	.20	.25
B162	SP93	20f + 2f dp claret	.20	.25
B163	SP92	40f + 4f gray vio	.20	.25
B164	SP93	50f + 6f org brn	.25	.25
B165	SP94	70f + 8f slate blue	.25	.25
		Nos. B157-B165 (9)	2.00	2.30

The surtax aided war invalids.

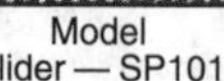

Model Glider — SP101

Gliders — SP102

White-tailed Sea Eagle and Planes — SP103

ME-109E Fighter and Gliders — SP104

1943, July 17

B166	SP101	8f + 8f green	.40	.50
B167	SP102	12f + 12f royal blue	.40	.50
B168	SP103	20f + 20f chestnut	.40	.50
B169	SP104	30f + 30f rose car	.40	.50
		Nos. B166-B169 (4)	1.60	2.00

The surtax aided the Horthy National Aviation Fund.

Stephen Horthy
SP105

1943, Aug. 16

B170	SP105	30f + 20f dp rose vio	.30	.25

The surtax aided the Horthy National Aviation Fund.

Nurse and Soldier
SP106

Designs: 30f+30f, Soldier, nurse, mother and child. 50f+50f, Nurse keeping lamp alight. 70f+70f, Wounded soldier and tree shoot.

1944, Mar. 1

Cross in Red

B171	SP106	20f + 20f brown	.20	.25
B172	SP106	30f + 30f henna	.20	.25
B173	SP106	50f + 50f brown vio	.20	.25
B174	SP106	70f + 70f Prus blue	.20	.25
		Nos. B171-B174 (4)	.80	1.00

The surtax aided the Hungarian Red Cross.

Issues of the Republic

Types of 1944 Surcharged in Red or Black:

a

b

1945, July 23 Wmk. 266 *Perf. 12*

B175	A115(a)	3p + 9p on 20f dk ol grn, *yel*	.20	.20
B176	A114(b)	4p + 12p on 4f yel brn, *bl* (Bk)	.20	.20
B177	A117(b)	8p + 24p on 50f sl bl, *yel*	.20	.20
B178	A115(a)	10p + 30p on 30f hn brn, *bl* (Bk)	.20	.20
		Nos. B175-B178 (4)	.80	.80

The surtax was for the Peoples Universities. "Béke" means "peace".

Imre Sallai and Sandor Fürst
SP110

Designs: 3p+3p, L. Kabok and Illes Monus. 4p+4p, Ferenc Rozsa and Zoltan Schonerz. 6p+6p, Anna Koltai and Mrs. Paul Knurr. 10p+10p, George Sarkozi and Imre Nagy. 15p+15p, Vilmos Tartsay and Jeno Nagy. 20p+20p, Janos Kiss and Andreas Bajcsy-Zsilinszky. 40p+40p, Endre Sagvari and Otto Hoffmann.

1945, Oct. 6 Photo.

B179	SP110	2p + 2p yel brn	1.10	1.25
B180	SP110	3p + 3p deep red	1.10	1.25
B181	SP110	4p + 4p dk pur	1.10	1.25
B182	SP110	6p + 6p dk yel grn	1.10	1.25
B183	SP110	10p + 10p dp car	1.10	1.25
B184	SP110	15p + 15p dk sl grn	1.10	1.25
B185	SP110	20p + 20p dk brn	1.10	1.25
B186	SP110	40p + 40p dp bl	1.10	1.25
		Nos. B179-B186 (8)	8.80	10.00

The surtax was for child welfare.

Andreas Bajcsy-Zsilinszky and Eagle — SP111

1945, May 27

B187	SP111	1p + 1p dk brn vio	.25	.25

1st anniv. of the death of Andreas Bajcsy-Zsilinszky, hanged by the Nazis for anti-fascist activities.

Lion with Broken Shackles
SP112

1946, May 1

B188	SP112	500ez + 500ez p	.95	.95
B189	SP112	1mil p + 1mil p	.95	.95
B190	SP112	1.5mil p + 1.5mil p	.95	.95
B191	SP112	2mil p + 2mil p	.95	.95
		Nos. B188-B191 (4)	3.80	3.80

75th anniv. of Hungary's 1st postage stamp. The surtax was for the benefit of postal employees.

"Agriculture" Holding Wheat — SP113

Physician with Syringe — SP114

1946, Sept. 7 Photo.

B192	SP113	30f + 60f dp yel grn	3.75	3.75
B193	SP113	60f + 1.20fo rose brn	3.75	3.75
B194	SP113	1fo + 2fo dp blue	3.75	3.75
		Nos. B192-B194 (3)	11.25	11.25

1st Agricultural Congress and Exhibition.

Perf. 12½x12

1947, May 16 Wmk. 210

Designs: 12f+50f, Physician examining X-ray picture. 20f+50f, Nurse and child. 60f+50f, Prisoner of war starting home.

B195	SP114	8f + 50f ultra	3.00	3.25
B196	SP114	12f + 50f choc	3.00	3.25
B197	SP114	20f + 50f dk grn	3.00	3.25
B198	SP114	60f + 50f dk red	1.00	1.25
		Nos. B195-B198 (4)	10.00	11.00

The surtax was for charitable purposes.

Franklin D. Roosevelt and Freedom of Speech Allegory
SP115

Pres. F. D. Roosevelt and Allegory: 12f+12f, Freedom of Religion. 20f+20f, Freedom from Want. 30f+30f, Freedom from Fear.

1947, June 11 Photo. *Perf. 12x12½*

Portrait in Sepia

B198A	SP115	8f + 8f dark red	2.00	2.25
B198B	SP115	12f + 12f deep green	2.00	2.25
B198C	SP115	20f + 20f brown	2.00	2.25
B198D	SP115	30f + 30f blue	2.00	2.25
		Nos. B198A-B198D,CB1-CB1C (8)	18.00	20.00

Nos. B198A-B198D and CB1-CB1C were also printed in sheets of 4 of each denomination (size: 117x96mm). Value, set of 8, $250.

A souvenir sheet contains one each of Nos. B198A-B198D with border inscriptions and decorations in brown. Size: 161x122mm. Value $60.

Lenin — SP118

XVI Century Mail Coach
SP119

Designs: 60f+60f, Soviet Cenotaph, Budapest. 1fo+1fo, Joseph V. Stalin.

1947, Oct. 29 Photo. Wmk. 283

B199	SP118	40f + 40f ol grn & org brn	4.50	5.50
B200	SP118	60f + 60f red & sl bl	1.00	1.00
B201	SP118	1fo + 1fo vio & brn blk	4.50	5.50
		Nos. B199-B201 (3)	10.00	12.00

The surtax was for the Hungarian-Soviet Cultural Association.

1947, Dec. 21 *Perf. 12x12½*

B202	SP119	30f (+ 50f) hn brn	9.50	10.00
		Sheet of 4	42.50	42.50

Stamp Day. The surtax paid admission to a philatelic exhibition in any of eight Hungarian towns, where the stamps were sold.

Globe and Carrier Pigeon — SP120

Woman Worker — SP121

1948, Oct. 17 ***Perf. 12½x12***
B203 SP120 30f (+ 1fo) grnsh bl 4.00 4.00
Sheet of 4 24.00 24.00

5th Natl. Hungarian Stamp Exhib., Budapest. Each stamp sold for 1.30 forint, which included admission to the exhibition.

1949, Mar. 8
B204 SP121 60f + 60f magenta .75 .75

Intl. Woman's Day, Mar. 8, 1949. The surtax was for the Democratic Alliance of Hungarian Women.

Aleksander S. Pushkin — SP122

SP123

1949, June 6 **Photo.**
B205 SP122 1fo + 1fo car lake 7.50 7.50

Souvenir Sheet
Perf. 12½x12, Imperf
B206 SP123 1fo + 1fo red vio & car lake 14.00 14.00

150th anniversary of the birth of Aleksander S. Pushkin. The surtax was for the Hungarian-Russian Culture Society.

1st Stamp Type
Perf. 12½x12
1951, Oct. 6 **Engr.** **Unwmk.**
B207 A208 1fo + 1fo red 7.50 7.00
B208 A208 2fo + 2fo blue 12.50 11.50

Postwoman Delivering Mail — SP124

1953, Nov. 1 **Wmk. 106** ***Perf. 12***
B209 SP124 1fo + 1fo blue grn 1.75 1.75
B210 SP124 2fo + 2fo rose vio 1.75 1.75

Stamp Day, Nov. 1, 1953.

Stamps of 1955 Surcharged in Red or Lake

1957, Jan. 31 **Photo.** ***Perf. 12x12½***
B211 A249 20f + 20f olive grn .20 .20
B212 A249 30f + 30f dk red (L) .25 .25
B213 A249 40f + 40f brown .30 .25
B214 A249 60f + 60f brn red (L) .50 .30
B215 A249 1fo + 1fo blue .75 .50
B216 A249 2fo + 2fo rose brn 1.00 .75
Nos. B211-B216 (6) 3.00 2.25

The surtax was for the Hungarian Red Cross.

Winter Olympic Type of 1960
Design: Olympic Games emblem.

Perf. 11½x12
1960, Feb. 29 **Wmk. 106**
B217 A295 2fo + 1fo multi .70 .35

Olympic Type of 1960
Design: 2fo+1fo, Romulus and Remus.

Perf. 11½x12
1960, Aug. 21 **Photo.** **Wmk. 106**
B218 A299 2fo + 1fo multi .75 .30

Sport Club Type of 1961
Sport: 2fo+1fo, Sailboats.

1961, July 8 **Unwmk.** ***Perf. 14½***
B219 A313 2fo + 1fo multi .75 .50

St. Margaret's Island and Danube — SP125

Views of Budapest: No. B221, Fishermen's Bastion. No. B222, Coronation Church and Chain Bridge. No. B223, Mount Gellert.

Unwmk.
1961, Sept. 24 **Photo.** ***Perf. 12***
B220 SP125 2fo + 1fo multi .70 .70
B221 SP125 2fo + 1fo multi .70 .70
B222 SP125 2fo + 1fo multi .70 .70
B223 SP125 2fo + 1fo multi .70 .70
a. Horiz. strip of 4, #B220-B223 3.00 3.00

Stamp Day, 1961, and Budapest Intl. Stamp Exhibition.
No. B223a has a continuous design.
Miniature presentation sheets, perf. and imperf., contain one each of Nos. B220-B223; size: 204x66½mm. Value for both sheets, $600.

Soccer Type of Regular Issue, 1962
Design: Flags of Spain and Czechoslovakia.

1962, May 21 ***Perf. 11***
Flags in Original Colors
B224 A323 4fo + 1fo lt grn & bister 1.10 .30

Austrian Stamp of 1850 with Pesth Postmark SP126

Stamps: No. B226, #201. No. B227, #C164. No. B228, #C208.

Lithographed and Engraved
1962, Sept. 22 **Unwmk.** ***Perf. 11***
Design and Inscription in Dark Brown
B225 SP126 2fo + 1fo yellow .55 .55
B226 SP126 2fo + 1fo pale pink .55 .55
B227 SP126 2fo + 1fo pale blue .55 .55
B228 SP126 2fo + 1fo pale yel grn .55 .55
a. Horiz. strip of 4, #B225-B228 2.50 2.25
b. Souv. sheet of 4, #B225-B228 5.25 5.25

35th Stamp Day and 10th anniv. of Mabeosz, the Hungarian Phil. Fed.

Emblem, Cup and Soccer Ball — SP127

1962, Nov. 18 **Photo.** ***Perf. 11½x12***
B229 SP127 2fo + 1fo multi .60 .50

Winning of the "Coupe de l'Europe Centrale" by the Steel Workers Sport Club (VASAS) in the Central European Soccer Championships.

Stamp Day — SP128

1963, Oct. 24 ***Perf. 11½x12***
Size: 32x43mm
B230 SP128 2fo + 1fo Hyacinth .50 .50
B231 SP128 2fo + 1fo Narcissus .50 .50
B232 SP128 2fo + 1fo Chrysanthemum .50 .50
B233 SP128 2fo + 1fo Tiger lily .50 .50
a. Horiz. strip of 4, #B230-B233 3.00 3.00
b. Min. sheet of 4, #B230-B233 3.50 3.50

#B233b contains 25x32mm stamps, perf. 11.

Winter Olympic Type of 1963
Design: 4fo+1fo, Bobsledding.

1963, Nov. 11 ***Perf. 12***
B234 A342 4fo + 1fo grnsh bl & bis .70 .30

New Year Type of Regular Issue
Good Luck Symbols: 2.50fo+1.20fo, Horseshoe, mistletoe and clover. 3fo+1.50fo, Pigs, clover and balloon, horiz.

Perf. 12x11½, 11½x12
1963, Dec. 12 **Photo.** **Unwmk.**
Sizes: 28x39mm (#B235); 28x22mm (#B206)
B235 A343 2.50fo + 1.20fo multi .50 .25
B236 A343 3fo + 1.50fo multi .70 .35

The surtax was for the modernization of the Hungarian Postal and Philatelic Museum.

Olympic Type of Regular Issue
Design: 3fo+1fo, Water polo.

1964, June 12 ***Perf. 11***
B237 A352 3fo + 1fo multi .60 .75

Exhibition Hall — SP129

1964, July 23 **Photo.**
B238 SP129 3fo + 1.50fo blk, red org & gray .60 .35

Tennis Exhibition, Budapest Sports Museum.

Twirling Woman Gymnast SP130

1964, Sept. 4 ***Perf. 11½x12***
Size: 27x38mm
B239 SP130 2fo + 1fo Lilac .45 .45
B240 SP130 2fo + 1fo Mallards .45 .45
B241 SP130 2fo + 1fo Gymnast .45 .45
B242 SP130 2fo + 1fo Rocket & globe .45 .45
a. Horiz. strip of 4, #B239-B242 2.25 2.25
b. Souv. sheet of 4, #B239-B242 3.25 3.25

37th Stamp Day and Intl. Topical Stamp Exhib., IMEX. No. B242b contains 4 20x28mm stamps, perf. 11.

13th Century Tennis SP131

History of Tennis: 40f+10f, Indoor tennis, 16th century. 60f+10f, Tennis, 18th century. 70f+30f, Tennis court and castle. 80f+40f, Tennis court, Fontainebleau (buildings). 1fo+50f, Tennis, 17th century. 1.50fo+50f, W. C. Wingfield, Wimbledon champion 1877, and Wimbledon Cup. 1.70fo+50f, Davis Cup, 1900. 2fo+1fo, Bela Kehrling (1891-1937), Hungarian champion.

Lithographed and Engraved
1965, June 15 **Unwmk.** ***Perf. 12***
B243 SP131 30f + 10f mar, *dl org* .20 .20
B244 SP131 40f + 10f blk, *pale lil* .20 .20
B245 SP131 60f + 10f grn, *ol* .20 .20
B246 SP131 70f + 30f lil, *brt grn* .25 .20
B247 SP131 80f + 40f dk bl, *lt vio* .25 .20
B248 SP131 1fo + 50f grn, *yel* .25 .20
B249 SP131 1.50fo + 50f sep, *lt ol grn* .30 .25
B250 SP131 1.70fo + 50f ind, *lt bl* .35 .25
B251 SP131 2fo + 1fo dk red, *lt grn* .50 .30
Nos. B243-B251 (9) 2.50 2.00

Flood Scene SP132

10fo+5fo, Relief commemorating 1838 flood.

1965, Aug. 14 **Photo.** ***Perf. 12x11½***
B252 SP132 1fo + 50f org brn & bl .30 .30

Souvenir Sheet
B253 SP132 10fo + 5fo gldn brn & buff 2.75 2.75

Surtax for aid to 1965 flood victims.

Geranium Stamp of 1950 (No. 909) SP133

Stamp Day: No. B255, #120. No. B256, #1489. No. B257, #1382.

Perf. 12x11½
1965, Oct. 30 **Photo.** **Unwmk.**
Stamps in Original Colors
B254 SP133 2fo + 1fo gray & dk bl .65 .60
B255 SP133 2fo + 1fo gray & red .65 .60
B256 SP133 2fo + 1fo gray & ocher .65 .60
B257 SP133 2fo + 1fo gray & vio .65 .60
a. Horiz. strip of 4, #B254-B257 3.00 3.00
b. Souv. sheet of 4, #B254-B257 3.50 3.25

#B254b contains 32x23mm stamps, perf. 11.

Soccer Type of Regular Issue

Design: 3fo+1fo, Championship emblem and map of Great Britain showing cities where matches were held.

1966, June 6 Photo. ***Perf. 12x11½***
B258 A382 3fo + 1fo multi .60 .50

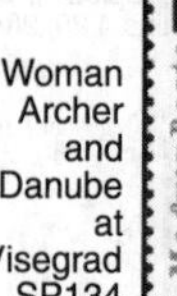

Woman Archer and Danube at Visegrad
SP134

Stamp Day: No. B260, Gloria Hungariae grapes and Lake Balaton. No. B261, Red poppies and ruins of Diosgyor Castle. No. B262, Russian space dogs Ugolek and Veterok.

1966, Sept. 16 Photo. ***Perf. 12x11½***
B259 SP134 2fo + 50f multi .60 .60
B260 SP134 2fo + 50f multi .60 .60
B261 SP134 2fo + 50f multi .60 .60
B262 SP134 2fo + 50f multi .60 .60
a. Horiz. strip of 4, #B259-B262 2.75 2.75
b. Souv. sheet of 4, #B259-B262 2.75 2.75

#B262b contains 4 29x21mm stamps, perf. 11.

Anglers, C.I.P.S. Emblem and View of Danube
SP135

1967, Aug. 22 Photo. ***Perf. 12x11½***
B263 SP135 3fo + 1fo multi .90 .45

See note after No. 1847

Olympic Type of Regular Issue

Indoor stadium & Winter Olympics emblem.

1968, Jan. 29 Photo. ***Perf. 11***
B264 A402 4fo + 1fo multi .70 .30

Jug, Western Hungary, 1618
SP136

Hungarian Earthenware: No. B266, Tiszafüred vase, 1847. No. B267, Toby jug, 1848. No. B268, Decorative Baja plate, 1870. No. B269a, Jug, Northern Hungary, 1672. No. B269b, Decorative Mezőcsat plate, 1843. No. B269c, Decorative Moragy plate, 1860. No. B269d, Pitcher, Debrecen, 1793.

1968, Oct. 5 Litho. ***Perf. 12***
B265 SP136 1fo + 50f ultra & multi .50 .50
B266 SP136 1fo + 50f sky bl & multi .50 .50
B267 SP136 1fo + 50f sepia & multi .50 .50
B268 SP136 1fo + 50f yel brn & multi .50 .50
Nos. B265-B268 (4) 2.00 2.00

Miniature Sheet

B269 Sheet of 4 2.75 2.50
a. SP136 2fo + 50f ultra & multi .45 .40
b. SP136 2fo + 50f yel brn & multi .45 .40
c. SP136 2fo + 50f olive & multi .45 .40
d. SP136 2fo + 50f brt rose & multi .45 .40

Issued for 41st Stamp Day. No. B269 contains 4 25x36mm stamps. See Nos. B271-B275.

Suspension Bridge, Buda Castle and Arms of Budapest — SP137

Lithographed and Engraved

1969, May 22 ***Perf. 12***
B270 SP137 5fo + 2fo sep, pale yel & gray 1.00 1.00

Budapest 71 Philatelic Exposition.

Folk Art Type of 1968

Hungarian Wood Carvings: No. B271, Stirrup cup from Okorag, 1880. No. B272, Jar with flower decorations from Felsötiszavidek, 1898. No. B273, Round jug, Somogyharsagy, 1935. No. B274, Two-legged jug, Alföld, 1740. No. B275a, Carved panel (farm couple), Csorna, 1879. No. B275b, Tankard, Okany, 1914. No. B275c, Round jar with soldiers, Sellye, 1899. No. B275d, Square box with 2 women, Lengyeltoti, 1880.

1969, Sept. 13 Litho. ***Perf. 12***
B271 SP136 1fo + 50f rose cl & multi .60 .60
B272 SP136 1fo + 50f dp bis & multi .60 .60
B273 SP136 1fo + 50f bl & multi .60 .60
B274 SP136 1fo + 50f lt bl grn & multi .60 .60
Nos. B271-B274 (4) 2.40 2.40

Miniature Sheet

B275 Sheet of 4 2.75 2.50
a. SP136 2fo + 50f ultra & multi .50 .45
b. SP136 2fo + 50f brn org & multi .50 .45
c. SP136 2fo + 50f lt brn & multi .50 .45
d. SP136 2fo + 50f bl grn & multi .50 .45

Issued for the 42nd Stamp Day. No. B275 contains 4 stamps (size: 25x36mm).

Fishermen's Bastion, Coronation Church and Chain Bridge — SP138

Designs: No. B277, Parliament and Elizabeth Bridge. No. B278, Castle and Margaret Bridge.

1970, Mar. 7 Litho. ***Perf. 12***
B276 SP138 2fo + 1fo gldn brn & multi .50 .50
B277 SP138 2fo + 1fo bl & multi .50 .50
B278 SP138 2fo + 1fo lt vio & multi .50 .50
Nos. B276-B278 (3) 1.50 1.50

Budapest 71 Philatelic Exhibition, commemorating the centenary of Hungarian postage stamps.

King Matthias I Corvinus
SP139

Initials and Paintings from Bibliotheca Corvina: No. B280, Letter "A." No. B281, Letter "N." No. B282, Letter "O." No. B283a, Ransanus Speaking before King Matthias. No. B283b, Scholar and letter "Q." No. B283c, Portrait of Appianus and letter "C." No. B283d, King David and letter "A."

1970, Aug. 22 Photo. ***Perf. 11½x12***
B279 SP139 1fo + 50f multi .40 .40
B280 SP139 1fo + 50f multi .40 .40
B281 SP139 1fo + 50f multi .40 .40
B282 SP139 1fo + 50f multi .40 .40
Nos. B279-B282 (4) 1.60 1.60

Miniature Sheet

B283 Sheet of 4 2.75 2.50
a.-d. SP139 2fo + 50f, any single .50 .45

Issued for the 43rd Stamp Day. No. B283 contains 4 stamps (size: 22½x32mm).

View of Buda, 1470 — SP140

#B285, Buda, 1600. #B286, Buda and Pest, about 1638. #B287, Buda and Pest, 1770. #B288a, Buda, 1777. #B288b, Buda, 1850. #B288c, Buda, 1895. #B288d, Budapest, 1970.

1971, Feb. 26 Litho. ***Perf. 12***
B284 SP140 2fo + 1fo blk & yel .60 .60
B285 SP140 2fo + 1fo blk & pink .60 .60
B286 SP140 2fo + 1fo blk & pale grn .60 .60
B287 SP140 2fo + 1fo blk & pale sal .60 .60
Nos. B284-B287 (4) 2.40 2.40

Souvenir Sheet

Perf. 10½

B288 Sheet of 4 2.50 2.25
a. SP140 2fo + 1fo blk & pale sal .50 .45
b. SP140 2fo + 1fo blk & pale grn .50 .45
c. SP140 2fo + 1fo blk & lilac .50 .45
d. SP140 2fo + 1fo blk & pink .50 .45

Budapest 71 Intl. Stamp Exhib. for the cent. of Hungarian postage stamps, Budapest, Sept. 4-12. No. B288 contains 4 stamps, size: 39½x18mm.

Iris and #P1
SP141

Designs: No. B290, Daisy and #199. No. B291, Poppy and #391. No. B292, Rose and #B128. No. B293a, Carnations and #200. No. B293b, Dahlia and #1069. No. B293c, Tulips and #C196. No. B293d, Anenomes and #C251.

1971, Sept. 4 Photo. ***Perf. 12x11½***
B289 SP141 2fo + 1fo sil & multi .70 .70
B290 SP141 2fo + 1fo sil & multi .70 .70
B291 SP141 2fo + 1fo sil & multi .70 .70
B292 SP141 2fo + 1fo sil & multi .70 .70
Nos. B289-B292 (4) 2.80 2.80

Souvenir Sheet

Perf. 11½

B293 Sheet of 4 2.75 2.50
a.-d. SP141 2fo + 1fo, any single .50 .45

Cent. of 1st Hungarian postage stamps and in connection with Budapest 71 Intl. Stamp Exhib., Sept. 4-12.

Miskólcz Postmark, 1818-43 — SP142

Postmarks: No. B295, Szegedin, 1827-48. No. B296, Esztergom, 1848-51. No. B297, Budapest 1971 Exhibition. No. B298a, Paar family signet, 1593. No. B298b, Courier letter, 1708. No. B298c, First well-known Hungarian postmark "V. TOKAI," 1752. No. B298d, Letter, 1705.

1972, May ***Perf. 12x11½***
B294 SP142 2fo + 1fo blue & blk .70 .70
B295 SP142 2fo + 1fo yel & blk .70 .70
B296 SP142 2fo + 1fo yel grn & blk .70 .70
B297 SP142 2fo + 1fo ver & multi .70 .70
Nos. B294-B297 (4) 2.80 2.80

Souvenir Sheet

B298 Sheet of 4 2.50 2.25
a. SP142 2fo + 1fo yel grn & multi .50 .45
b. SP142 2fo + 1fo brn & multi .50 .45
c. SP142 2fo + 1fo ultra & multi .50 .45
d. SP142 2fo + 1fo red & multi .50 .45

9th Congress of National Federation of Hungarian Philatelists (Mabeosz). No. B298 contains 4 stamps (size: 32x23mm).

Olympic Type of Regular Issue

Design: Wrestling and Olympic rings.

1972, July 15 Photo. ***Perf. 11***
B299 A484 3fo + 1fo multi .50 .30

Historic Mail Box, Telephone and Molnya Satellite — SP143

Design: No. B301, Post horn, Tokai postmark, and Nos. 183, 1802, 1809.

1972, Oct. 27 Litho. ***Perf. 12***
B300 SP143 4fo + 2fo grn & multi .80 .70
B301 SP143 4fo + 2fo bl & multi .80 .70

Reopening of the Post and Philatelic Museums, Budapest.

Bird on Silver Disk, 10th Century
SP144

Treasures from Hungarian Natl. Museum. No. B303, Ring with serpent's head, 11th cent. No. B304, Lovers, belt buckle, 12th cent. No. B305, Flower, belt buckle, 15th cent. No. B306a, Opal pendant, 16th cent. No. B306b, Jeweled belt buckle, 18th cent. No. B306c, Flower pin, 17th cent. No. B306d, Rosette pendant, 17th cent.

1973, Sept. 22 Litho. ***Perf. 12***
B302 SP144 2fo + 50f brn & multi .65 .65
B303 SP144 2fo + 50f brt rose lil & multi .65 .65
B304 SP144 2fo + 50f dk bl & multi .65 .65
B305 SP144 2fo + 50f grn & multi .65 .65
Nos. B302-B305 (4) 2.60 2.60

Souvenir Sheet

B306 Sheet of 4 2.50 2.50
a. SP144 2fo + 50f brown & multi .35 .35
b. SP144 2fo + 50f car & multi .35 .35
c. SP144 2fo + 50f ol grn & multi .35 .35
d. SP144 2fo + 50f brt bl & multi .35 .35

46th Stamp Day. No. B306 contains 4 stamps (size: 25x35mm).

Gothic Wall Fountain
SP145

Visegrad Castle and Bas-reliefs — SP146

Designs: No. B308, Wellhead, Anjou period. No. B309, Twin lion-head wall fountain. B310, Fountain with Hercules riding dolphin. No. B311a, Raven panel. No. B311b, Visegrad Madonna. B311c, Lion panel. No. B311d, Visegrad Castle. Designs show artworks from Visegrad Palace of King Matthias Corvinus I, 15th century. Illustration SP146 is reduced.

1975, Sept. 13 Litho. *Perf. 12*

Multicolored and:

B307 SP145 2fo + 1fo green 2.00 2.00
B308 SP145 2fo + 1fo ver 2.00 2.00
B309 SP145 2fo + 1fo blue 2.00 2.00
B310 SP145 2fo + 1fo lilac 2.00 2.00
a. Horizontal strip of 4 9.00 8.50

Souvenir Sheet

B311 SP146 Sheet of 4 10.00 10.00
a. 2fo + 1fo 21x32mm 1.40 1.40
b. 2fo + 1fo 47x32mm 1.40 1.40
c. 2fo + 1fo 21x32mm 1.40 1.40
d. 2fo + 1fo 99x32mm 1.40 1.40

European Architectural Heritage Year 1975 and 48th Stamp Day.

Knight SP147

Gothic Sculptures, Buda Castle — SP148

Gothic sculptures from Buda Castle.

1976 Photo. *Perf. 12*

B312 SP147 2.50 + 1fo shown .60 .60
B313 SP147 2.50 + 1fo Armor-bearer .60 .60
B314 SP147 2.50 + 1fo Apostle .60 .60
B315 SP147 2.50 + 1fo Bishop .60 .60
a. Horizontal strip of 4, #B312-B315 2.75 2.75

Souvenir Sheet

Designs: a, Man with hat. b, Woman with wimple. c, Man with cloth cap. d, Man with fur hat.

B316 Sheet of 4 3.00 3.00
a.-d. SP148 2.50 + 1fo any single .55 .55

49th Stamp Day.

No. B316 issued in connection with 10th Congress of National Federation of Hungarian Philatelists (Mabeosz).

Issued: #B316, May 22; #B312-B315, Sept. 4.

Young Runners SP149

1977, Apr. 2 Litho. *Perf. 12*

B317 SP149 3fo + 1.50fo multi .85 .85

Sports promotion among young people.

Young Man and Woman, Profiles SP150

1978, Apr. 1 Litho. *Perf. 12*

B318 SP150 3fo + 1.50fo multi .90 .90

Hungarian Communist Youth Movement, 60th anniversary.

"Generations," by Gyula Derkovits SP151

1978, May 6 Litho. *Perf. 12*

B319 SP151 3fo + 1.50fo multi .90 .90

Szocfilex '78, Szombathely. No. B319 printed in sheets of 3 stamps and 3 labels showing Szocfilex emblem.

Girl Reading Book, by Ferenc Kovacs SP152

1979, Mar. 31 Litho. *Perf. 12*

B320 SP152 3fo + 1.50fo blk & ultra .45 .45

Surtax was for Junior Stamp Exhibition, Bekescsaba.

Watch Symbolizing Environmental Protection SP153

1980, Apr. 3 Litho. *Perf. 12*

B321 SP153 3fo + 1.50fo multi .70 .70

Surtax was for Junior Stamp Exhibition, Dunaujvaros.

International Year of the Disabled SP154

Youths and Factory SP155

1981, May 15 Litho. *Perf. 12*

B322 SP154 2fo + 1fo multi .45 .45

1981, May 29 *Perf. 12x11½*

B323 SP155 4fo + 2fo multi .80 .80

Young Communist League, 10th Congress, Budapest, May 29-31.

European Junior Tennis Cup, July 25-Aug. 1 — SP156

1982, Apr. 2 Litho. *Perf. 12x11½*

B324 SP156 4fo + 2fo multi .80 .80

Souvenir Sheet

SP157

Perf. 12½x11½

1982, June 11 Litho.

B325 SP157 20fo + 10fo multi 4.00 4.00

PHILEXFRANCE '82 Stamp Exhibition, Paris, June 11-21.

55th Stamp Day — SP158

Budapest Architecture and Statues: No. B326, Fishermen's Bastion, Janos Hunyadi (1403-1456). No. B327, Parliament, Ferenc Rakoczi the Second (1676-1735).

1982, Sept. 10 Litho. *Perf. 12*

B326 SP158 4fo + 2fo multi .90 .90
B327 SP158 4fo + 2fo shown .90 .90

Souvenir Sheet

Parliament, Chain Bridge, Buda Castle, Budapest — SP159

Illustration reduced.

1982, Sept. 10 *Perf. 11½*

B328 SP159 20fo + 10fo multi 3.75 3.75

European Security and Cooperation Conference, 10th anniv.

21st Junior Stamp Exhibition, Baja, Mar. 31-Apr. 9 — SP160

1983, Mar. 31 Litho. *Perf. 12x11½*

B329 SP160 4fo + 2fo multi .90 .90

Surtax was for show.

56th Natl. Stamp Day SP161

Budapest Architecture (19th Cent. Engravings by): Rudolph Alt, H. Luders (No. B331).

1983, Sept. 9 Litho. *Perf. 12*

B330 SP161 4fo + 2fo Old Natl. Theater .90 .90
B331 SP161 4fo + 2fo Municipal Concert Hall .90 .90

Souvenir Sheet

Lithographed and Engraved

Perf. 11

B332 SP161 20fo + 10fo Holy Trinity Square 3.75 3.75

No. B332 contains one stamp (28x45mm).

SP162

1984, Apr. 2 Litho. *Perf. 12½x11½*

B333 SP162 4fo + 2fo Mother & Child .75 .75

Surtax was for children's foundation.

SP163

Little Red Riding Hood, by the Brothers Grimm.

1985, Apr. 2 Litho. *Perf. 11½x12*

B334 SP163 4fo + 2fo multi .75 .75

Jacob (1785-1863) and Wilhelm (1786-1859) Grimm, fabulists and philologists.

Natl. SOS Children's Village Assoc., 3rd Anniv. SP164

1985, Dec. 10 Litho. *Perf. 11*

B335 SP164 4fo + 2fo multi .75 .75

Surtax for natl. SOS Children's Village.

Natl. Young Pioneers Org., 40th Anniv. SP165

1986, May 30 ***Perf. 11½x12½***
B336 SP165 4fo + 2fo multi .75 .60

Souvenir Sheet

Budapest Natl. Theater — SP166

Lithographed and Engraved
1986, Oct. 10 ***Perf. 11***
B337 SP166 20fo + 10fo tan, brn & buff 4.00 4.00

Surtax benefited natl. theater construction.

Natl. Communist Youth League, 30th Anniv. — SP167

1987, Mar. 20 ***Perf. 13½x13***
B338 SP167 4fo + 2fo multi .60 .60

Souvenir Sheet

SOCFILEX '88, Aug. 12-21, Kecskemet — SP168

1988, Mar. 10 Litho. ***Perf. 11½***
B339 SP168 20fo +10fo multi 4.00 4.00

Surtax for SOCFILEX '88.

Sky High Tree, a Tapestry by Erzsebet Szekeres SP169

1989, Apr. 12 Litho. ***Perf. 12***
B340 SP169 5fo +2fo multi 1.50 1.50

Surtax to promote youth philately.

Souvenir Sheet

Battle of Solferino, by Carlo Bossoli — SP170

1989, Sept. 8 Litho. ***Perf. 10½***
B341 SP170 20fo +10fo multi 3.75 3.75

Stamp Day.

Souvenir Sheet

Martyrs of Arad, Arad, Romania, 1849 — SP171

1989, Oct. 6 ***Perf. 11½x12½***
B342 SP171 20fo +10fo multi 3.75 3.75

Surtax to fund production of another statue.

Teacher's Training High School, Sarospatak Municipal Arms — SP172

1990, Mar. 30 Litho. ***Perf. 12x11½***
B343 SP172 8fo +4fo multi 1.75 1.75

28th Youth Stamp Exhib., Sarospatak, Apr. 6-22.

Souvenir Sheet

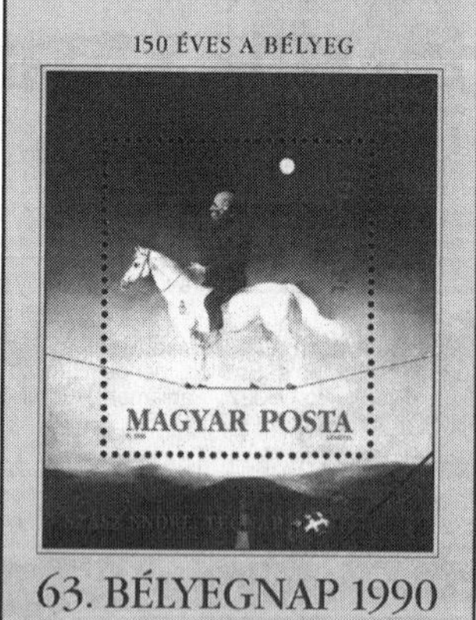
Yesterday, by Endre Szasz — SP173

1990, Oct. 12 Litho. ***Perf. 12***
B344 SP173 20fo +10fo multi 3.75 3.75

Stamp Day. Surtax for National Federation of Hungarian Philatelists.

Tapestry, Peter and the Wolf, by Gabriella Hajnal — SP174

1991, Apr. 30 Litho. ***Perf. 12***
B345 SP174 12fo +6fo multi 1.50 .80

Surtax to promote youth philately.

Children's Drawings SP175

Designs: 9fo + 4fo, Girl holding flower, vert. 10fo + 4fo, Child standing beneath sun. 15fo + 4fo, Boy wearing crown, vert.

1992, May 15 Litho. ***Perf. 12***
B346 SP175 9fo +4fo multi 1.10 1.10
B347 SP175 10fo +4fo multi 1.25 1.25
B348 SP175 15fo +4fo multi 1.65 1.65
Nos. B346-B348 (3) 4.00 4.00

Surtax for children's welfare.

Souvenir Sheet

1992 Summer Olympics, Barcelona — SP176

1992, Sept. 4 Litho. ***Perf. 12***
B349 SP176 50fo +20fo multi 3.00 3.00

Textile Art, by Erzsebet Szekeres SP177

1993, Apr. 14 Litho. ***Perf. 12***
B350 SP177 10fo +5fo Outdoor scene .40 .40
B351 SP177 17fo +8fo Tree of life 1.00 1.00

Stamp Day SP178

Stamp designers, stamps: 10fo + 5fo, Zoltan Nagy (1916-1987), #1062. 17fo + 5fo, Sandor Legrady (1906-1987), #523. 50fo + 20fo, Ferenc Helbing (1870-1959), #465.

1993, Sept. 10 Litho. ***Perf. 12***
B352 SP178 10fo +5fo multi .30 .20
B353 SP178 17fo +5fo multi .45 .25

Souvenir Sheet

B354 SP178 50fo +20fo multi 2.00 1.75

No. B354 contains one 35x27mm stamp.

The Little Prince, by Antoine de Saint-Exupery SP179

1994, Apr. 1 Litho. ***Perf. 13½x13***
B355 SP179 19fo +5fo multi .80 .40

Surtax for children's welfare.

Poem, "John the Hero," 150th Anniv. SP180

1995, Apr. 7 Litho. ***Perf. 12***
B356 SP180 22fo +10fo multi .90 .45

Surtax to promote youth philately.

Olympiafila '95, Budapest — SP181

1995, June 12 Litho. ***Perf. 11***
B357 SP181 22fo +11fo yellow rings .90 .45
B358 SP181 22fo +11fo purple rings .90 .45
a. Pair, #B357-B358 1.90 .90

No. B358a also sold in a strip of 3 pairs in a booklet.

World Festival of Puppet Players, Budapest SP182

Laszlo Vitez puppet and ghost puppet.

1996, June 21 Litho. ***Perf. 12***
B359 SP182 24fo +10fo multi .75 .40

Oder River Flood of 1997 SP183

1997, Sept. 12 Litho. *Perf. 12*

B360 SP183 27fo +100fo flower in water 1.90 .95

Surtax is for aid to flood victims.

Stamp Day SP184

Early postman using: 27fo + 5fo, Motorized tricycle. 55fo + 5fo, Experimental registered letter-receiving machine, vert. 90fo + 30fo, Postal van.

1997, Sept. 19

B361 SP184 27fo +5fo multi .45 .25
B362 SP184 55fo +5fo multi .90 .45

Souvenir Sheet

B363 SP184 90fo +30fo multi 1.75 .90

Souvenir Sheet

Revolution of 1848 — SP185

Design: Seven members of movement, newspaper *Nemzeti dal.*
Illustration reduced.

1998, Mar. 13 Litho. *Perf. 12*

B364 SP185 150fo +50fo multi 2.90 1.50

Surtax to promote youth philately.

Youth Stamp SP186

1999, Mar. 12 Litho. *Perf. 12*

B365 SP186 52fo +25fo multi .95 .50

István Fekete (1900-70), Writer — SP187

2000, Jan. 11 Litho. *Perf. 12*

B366 SP187 60fo +30fo multi .80 .40

Surtax for youth philately.

Hunphilex 2000 Stamp Exhibition, Budapest SP188

2000, Jan. 11

B367 SP188 200fo +100fo multi 2.60 1.25

Surtax to support stamp exhibition.

Souvenir Sheet

Hunphilex 2000 Stamp Exhibition, Budapest — SP189

2000, Aug. 18 Litho. *Perf. 12*

B368 SP189 200fo +100fo Coronation robe 2.10 1.10
a. Sheet of 2 4.25 2.25

Star Over Eger, by Geza Gardonyi SP190

2001, Jan. 15 Litho. *Perf. 13¼x13*

B369 SP190 60fo +30fo multi .65 .30

Surtax for youth philately.

AIR POST STAMPS

Issues of the Monarchy

Nos. 120, 123 Surcharged in Red or Blue

REPÜLŐ POSTA
4 K 50 f

Wmk. 137

1918, July 4 Typo. *Perf. 14*

C1 A10 1k 50f on 75f (R) 8.25 10.00
C2 A10 4k 50f on 2k (Bl) 6.75 8.00

Counterfeits exist.

LEGI POSTA

No. 126 Surcharged

12 korona

1920, Nov. 7

C3 A10 3k on 10k (G) .85 1.50
C4 A10 8k on 10k (R) .85 1.50
C5 A10 12k on 10k (Bl) .85 1.50
Nos. C3-C5 (3) 2.55 4.50
Set, never hinged 4.75

Icarus — AP3

1924-25 *Perf. 14*

C6 AP3 100k red brn & red .50 .40
C7 AP3 500k bl grn & yel grn .50 .40
C8 AP3 1000k bis brn & brn .50 .40
C9 AP3 2000k dk bl & lt bl .50 .40

Wmk. 133

C10 AP3 5000k dl vio & brt vio .75 .75
C11 AP3 10000k red & dl vio 1.00 1.00
Nos. C6-C11 (6) 3.75 3.35
Set, never hinged 4.75

Issued: 100k-2000k, 4/11; others, 4/20/25.
Forgeries exist.
For surcharges see Nos. J112-J116.

Mythical "Turul" — AP4

"Turul" Carrying Messenger
AP5 AP6

1927-30 Engr. *Perf. 14*

C12 AP4 4f orange ('30) .25 .20
C13 AP4 12f deep green .25 .20
C14 AP4 16f red brown .25 .20
C15 AP4 20f carmine .25 .20
C16 AP4 32f brown vio 1.50 1.00
C17 AP4 40f dp ultra 1.50 .20
C18 AP5 50f claret 1.50 .75
C19 AP5 72f olive grn 1.50 .50
C20 AP5 80f dp violet 1.50 .60
C21 AP5 1p emerald ('30) 2.50 .60
C22 AP5 2p red ('30) 3.75 2.00
C23 AP5 5p dk blue ('30) 7.50 8.75
Nos. C12-C23 (12) 22.25 15.20
Set, never hinged 29.00

1931, Mar. 27

Overprinted

C24 AP6 1p orange (Bk) 24.00 20.00
C25 AP6 2p dull vio (G) 24.00 20.00
Set, never hinged 75.00

Monoplane over Danube Valley — AP7

Worker Welcoming Plane, Double Cross and Sun Rays — AP8

Spirit of Flight on Plane Wing AP9

"Flight" Holding Propeller AP10

Wmk. 210

1933, June 20 Photo. *Perf. 15*

C26 AP7 10f blue green 1.00 .20
C27 AP7 16f purple .85 .20

Perf. 12½x12

C28 AP8 20f carmine 2.00 .20
C29 AP8 40f blue 1.90 .20
C30 AP9 48f gray black 3.25 .60
C31 AP9 72f bister brn 9.00 1.50
C32 AP10 1p yellow grn 14.50 1.10
C33 AP10 2p violet brn 35.00 6.00
C34 AP10 5p dk gray 52.50 *55.00*
Nos. C26-C34 (9) 120.00 65.00
Set, never hinged 225.00

Catalogue values for unused stamps in this section, from this point to the end of the section, are for Never Hinged items.

Fokker F VII over Mail Coach AP11

Plane over Parliament AP12

Airplane AP13

1936, May 8 *Perf. 12x12½*

C35 AP11 10f brt green .35 .20
C36 AP11 20f crimson .35 .20
C37 AP11 36f brown .55 .25
C38 AP12 40f brt blue .55 .25
C39 AP12 52f red org 1.40 .90
C40 AP12 60f brt violet 9.50 .90
C41 AP12 80f dk sl grn 1.90 1.00
C42 AP13 1p dk yel grn 2.00 .50
C43 AP13 2p brown car 4.25 1.25
C44 AP13 5p dark blue 14.00 7.00
Nos. C35-C44 (10) 34.85 12.45

Issues of the Republic

Loyalty Tower, Sopron — AP14

Designs: 20f, Cathedral of Esztergom. 50f, Liberty Bridge, Budapest. 70f, Palace Hotel, Lillafüred. 1fo, Vajdahunyad Castle, Budapest. 1.40fo, Visegrád Fortress on the Danube. 3fo, Lake Balaton. 5fo, Parliament Building, Budapest.

Perf. 12½x12

1947, Mar. 5 Photo. Wmk. 210

C45 AP14 10f rose lake 1.00 .25
C46 AP14 20f gray green .35 .20
C47 AP14 50f copper brn .40 .20
C48 AP14 70f olive grn .40 .20
C49 AP14 1fo gray blue .75 .25
C50 AP14 1.40fo brown .90 .40
C51 AP14 3fo green 1.90 .25
C52 AP14 5fo rose violet 4.00 1.00
Nos. C45-C52 (8) 9.70 2.75

Johannes Gutenberg and Printing Press AP22

Designs: 2f, Columbus. 4f, Robert Fulton. 5f, George Stephenson. 6f, David Schwarz and Ferdinand von Zeppelin. 8f, Thomas A. Edison. 10f, Louis Bleriot. 12f, Roald Amundsen. 30f, Kalman Kando. 40f, Alexander S. Popov.

Perf. 12x12½

1948, May 15 Wmk. 283

C53 AP22 1f orange red .20 .20
C54 AP22 2f dp magenta .20 .20
C55 AP22 4f blue .20 .20
C56 AP22 5f orange brn .20 .20
C57 AP22 6f green .20 .20
C58 AP22 8f dp red vio .20 .20
C59 AP22 10f brown .25 .25
C60 AP22 12f blue grn .30 .30
C61 AP22 30f brown rose .55 .85
C62 AP22 40f blue violet .70 1.00
Nos. C53-C62 (10) 3.00 3.60

Explorers and inventors.
See Nos. CB3-CB12.

UPU Type

1949, Nov. 1

C63 A171 2fo orange brn .50 .50
a. Booklet pane of 6 27.50

75th anniv. of the UPU. See No. C81.

Chain Bridge Type and

Symbols of Labor — AP25

1949, Nov. 20

C64 A172 1.60fo scarlet .70 .50
C65 A172 2fo olive .90 .75

Souvenir Sheet

Perf. 12½x12

C66 AP25 50fo car lake 160.00 110.00

Opening of the Chain Bridge, Budapest, cent.

Postman and Mail Carrying Vehicles AP26

1949, Dec. 11 ***Perf. 12***

C67 AP26 50f lilac gray 4.00 4.00
Sheet of 4 17.50 17.50

Stamp Day, 1949.

Plane, Globe, Stamps and Stagecoach — AP27

1950, Mar. 12 ***Perf. 12x12½***

C68 AP27 2fo red brn & yel 3.50 3.00

20th anniv. of the establishment of the Hungarian Post Office Philatelic Museum.

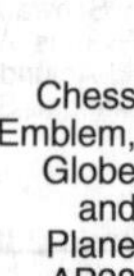

Chess Emblem, Globe and Plane AP28

1950, Apr. 9 **Wmk. 106** ***Perf. 12***

C69 AP28 1.60fo brown 1.75 1.00

World Chess Championship Matches, Budapest.

Globes, Parliament Building and Chain Bridge — AP29

1950, May 16 ***Perf. 12x12½***

C70 AP29 1fo red brown .50 .20

Meeting of the World Federation of Trade Unions, Budapest, May 1950.

Statue of Liberty and View of Budapest — AP30

Designs: 30f, Crane and apartment house. 70f, Steel mill. 1fo, Stalinyec tractor. 1.60fo, Steamship. 2fo, Reaping-threshing machine. 3fo, Passenger train. 5fo, Matyas Rakosi Steel Mill, Csepel. 10fo, Budaörs Airport.

Perf. 12½x12

1950, Oct. 29 **Engr.** **Unwmk.**

C71 AP30 20f claret .50 .25
C72 AP30 30f blue vio .50 .20
C73 AP30 70f violet brn .25 .20
C74 AP30 1fo yellow brn .25 .20
C75 AP30 1.60fo ultra .50 .40
C76 AP30 2fo red org .55 .25
C77 AP30 3fo olive blk .75 .40
C78 AP30 5fo gray blue 1.50 1.25
C79 AP30 10fo chestnut 4.75 1.75
Nos. C71-C79 (9) 9.55 4.90

See Nos. C167 and C172.

Bem Type
Souvenir Sheet

1950, Dec. 10 **Engr.** ***Imperf.***

C80 A185 2fo deep plum 20.00 18.00

Stamp Day and Budapest Stamp Exhibition.

UPU Type of 1949

Perf. 12x12½, Imperf.

1950, July 2 **Photo.** **Wmk. 106**

C81 A171 3fo dk car & dk brn 17.50 17.00
Sheet of 4 225.00 175.00

Sports Type

Designs: 30f, Volleyball. 40f, Javelin-throwing. 60f, Sports badge. 70f, Soccer. 3fo, Glider meet.

1950, Dec. 2

C82 A188 30f lilac & magenta .25 .20
C83 A188 40f olive & indigo .45 .20
C84 A188 60f ol, dk brn & org red .80 .40
C85 A188 70f gray & dk brn 1.10 .50
C86 A188 3fo buff & dk brn 2.75 2.00
Nos. C82-C86 (5) 5.35 3.30

Livestock Type

1951, Apr. 5 **Photo.** ***Perf. 12x12½***

C87 A191 20f Mare & foal .25 .25
C88 A191 70f Sow & shoats .60 .35
C89 A191 1fo Ram & ewe 1.25 .90
C90 A191 1.60fo Cow & calf 2.00 1.40
Nos. C87-C90 (4) 4.10 2.90

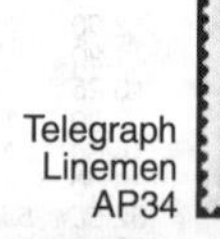

Telegraph Linemen AP34

Tank Column — AP35

Designs: 1fo, Workers on vacation. 2fo, Air view of Stalin Bridge.

1951, Aug. 20

C91 AP34 70f henna brown .35 .25
C92 AP34 1fo blue green .55 .30
C93 AP34 2fo deep plum 1.10 .45
Nos. C91-C93 (3) 2.00 1.00

Successful conclusion of the 1st year under Hungary's 5-year plan.

1951, Sept. 29 ***Perf. 12½x12***

C94 AP35 60f deep blue .30 .20

Army Day, Sept. 29, 1951.

1st Stamp Type
Souvenir Sheet

1951, Oct. 6 **Engr.** **Unwmk.**

C95 A208 60f olive green 37.50 37.50

Stamp exhibition to commemorate the 80th anniv. of Hungary's 1st postage stamp.

Twelve hundred copies in rose lilac, perf. and imperf., were presented to exhibitors and members of the arranging committee of the exhibition. Value, each $500.

Avocet — AP37

Hungarian Birds: 30f, White stork. 40f, Golden oriole. 50f, Kentish plover. 60f, Black-winged stilt. 70f, Lesser gray shrike. 80f, Great bustard. 1fo, Redfooted falcon. 1.40fo, European bee-eater. 1.60fo, Glossy ibis. 2.50fo, Great white egret.

Perf. 13x11

1952, Mar. 16 **Photo.** **Wmk. 106**

Birds in Natural Colors

C96 AP37 20f emer, *grnsh* .20 .20
C97 AP37 30f sage grn, *grysh* .20 .20
C98 AP37 40f brown, *cr* .20 .20
C99 AP37 50f orange, *cr* .20 .20
C100 AP37 60f deep carmine .30 .20
C101 AP37 70f red org, *cr* .30 .20
C102 AP37 80f olive, *cr* .45 .20
C103 AP37 1fo dp blue, *bluish* .55 .25
C104 AP37 1.40fo gray, *grysh* 1.00 .50
C105 AP37 1.60fo org brn, *cr* 1.00 .55
C106 AP37 2.50fo rose vio, *cr* 1.50 .75
Nos. C96-C106 (11) 5.90 3.45

Olympic Games Type

Design: 2fo, Stadium, Budapest.

1952, May 26 ***Perf. 11***

C107 A217 1.70fo dp red orange .80 .40
C108 A217 2fo olive brown .90 .50

Issued to publicize Hungary's participation in the Olympic Games, Helsinki, 1952.

Leonardo da Vinci — AP39

1952, June 15 ***Perf. 12½x12***

C109 AP39 1.60fo shown .60 .55
C110 AP39 2fo Victor Hugo .70 .60

AP40

AP41

1953, Mar. 4 ***Perf. 12x12½***

C111 AP40 20f Red squirrel .40 .20
C112 AP41 30f Hedgehog .40 .20
C113 AP41 40f Hare .85 .20
C114 AP40 50f Beech marten .55 .20
C115 AP41 60f Otter .55 .20
C116 AP41 70f Red fox .55 .25
C117 AP40 80f Fallow deer .75 .40
C118 AP41 1fo Roe deer .90 .25
C119 AP41 1.50fo Boar 1.25 .85
C120 AP40 2fo Red deer 1.90 1.00
Nos. C111-C120 (10) 8.10 3.75

Type of Regular Issue

Designs: 1fo, Children at Balaton Lake. 1.50fo, Workers' Home at Lillafured.

1953, Apr. 19 ***Perf. 12***

C121 A228 1fo brt grnsh blue .25 .25
C122 A228 1.50fo dp red lilac .60 .40

People's Stadium Type

1953, Aug. 20 ***Perf. 11***

C123 A232 80f Water polo .35 .20
C124 A232 1fo Boxing .35 .20
C125 A232 2fo Soccer .80 .40
C126 A232 3fo Track 1.40 .90
C127 A232 5fo Stadium 1.90 1.00
Nos. C123-C127 (5) 4.80 2.70

No. C125 Overprinted in Black

1953, Dec. 3

C128 A232 2fo green & brown 12.00 12.00

Hungary's success in the soccer matches at Wembley, England, Nov. 25, 1953. Counterfeits exist.

Janos Bihari and Scene from Verbunkos AP44

Portraits: 40f, Ferenc Erkel. 60f, Franz Liszt. 70f, Mihaly Mosonyi. 80f, Karl Goldmark. 1fo, Bela Bartok. 2fo, Zoltan Kodaly.

1953, Dec. 5 **Photo.** ***Perf. 12***

Frames and Portraits in Brown

C129 AP44 30f blue gray .20 .20
C130 AP44 40f orange .20 .20
C131 AP44 60f green .20 .20
C132 AP44 70f red .20 .20
C133 AP44 80f gray blue .20 .25
C134 AP44 1fo olive bis .50 .30
C135 AP44 2fo violet 1.00 .65
Nos. C129-C135 (7) 2.50 2.00

Hungarian composers.

Carrot Beetle — AP45

May (or June) Beetle AP46

Designs: Various beetles. 60f, Bee.

Perf. 12½x12, 12x12½

1954, Feb. 6 **Wmk. 106**

C136 AP45 30f dp org & dk brn .30 .20
C137 AP46 40f grn & dk brn .30 .20
C138 AP46 50f rose brn & blk .50 .30
C139 AP46 60f vio, dk brn & yel .30 .30
C140 AP45 80f grnsh gray, pur & rose .30 .30
C141 AP45 1fo ocher & blk 1.00 .25

C142 AP46 1.20fo dl grn & dk brn .90 .35
C143 AP46 1.50fo ol brn & dk brn .90 .40
C144 AP46 2fo hn brn & dk brn 1.25 .60
C145 AP45 3fo bl grn & dk brn 2.00 1.00
Nos. C136-C145 (10) 7.75 3.90

Lunchtime at the Nursery AP47

Designs: 1.50fo, Mother taking child from doctor. 2fo, Nurse and children.

1954, Mar. 8 ***Perf. 12***
C146 AP47 1fo olive green .20 .20
C147 AP47 1.50fo red brown .45 .35
C148 AP47 2fo blue green .90 .65
Nos. C146-C148 (3) 1.55 1.20

Model Glider Construction — AP48

Boy Flying Model Glider AP49

Designs: 60f, Gliders. 80f, Pilot leaving plane. 1fo, Parachutists. 1.20fo, Biplane. 1.50fo, Plane over Danube. 2fo, Jet planes.

1954, June 25 ***Perf. 11***
C149 AP48 40f brn, ol & dk bl gray .20 .20
C150 AP49 50f gray & red brn .20 .20
C151 AP48 60f red brn & dk bl gray .20 .20
C152 AP49 80f violet & sep .20 .20
C153 AP48 1fo brn & dk bl gray .20 .20
C154 AP49 1.20fo olive & sep .55 .25
C155 AP48 1.50fo cl & dk bl gray .90 .50
C156 AP49 2fo blue & dk brn 1.10 .50
Nos. C149-C156 (8) 3.55 2.25

Jokai Type
Souvenir Sheet

1954, Oct. 17 Engr. ***Perf. 12½x12***
C157 A242 1fo violet blue 13.00 12.00

Stamp Day. Exists imperforate.

Children on Sled — AP51

Skaters AP52

50f, Ski racer. 60f, Ice yacht. 80f, Ice hockey. 1fo, Ski jumper. 1.50fo, Downhill ski racer. 2fo, Man and woman exhibition-skating.

1955 Photo. ***Perf. 12***
C158 AP51 40f multi .60 .20
C159 AP52 50f multi .25 .20
C160 AP51 60f multi .35 .20
C161 AP52 80f multi .40 .20
C162 AP51 1fo multi .60 .30
C163 AP52 1.20fo multi .80 .30
C164 AP51 1.50fo multi 1.25 .60
C165 AP52 2fo multi 1.25 .50
Nos. C158-C165 (8) 5.50 2.50

Issued: 1.20fo, 2fo, Jan. 27; others Feb. 26.

Government Printing Plant Type
Souvenir Sheet

1955, May 28 ***Perf. 12x12½***
C166 A247 5fo hn brn & gray grn 12.50 11.00

Cent. of the establishment of the government printing plant.

No. C78 Printed on Aluminum Foil

Perf. 12½x12
1955, Oct. 5 Engr. Unwmk.
C167 AP30 5fo gray blue 7.50 7.50

Intl. Cong. of the Light Metal Industry and for 20 years of aluminum production in Hungary. Imperfs. exist.

Bartok Type
Wmk. 106

1955, Oct. 9 Photo. ***Perf. 12***
C168 A252 1fo gray green 1.25 .85
C169 A252 1fo violet brn 2.50 1.75
a. With ticket 12.50 12.50

10th anniv. of the death of Bela Bartok, composer. No. C169a was issued for the Day of the Stamp, Oct. 16, 1955. The 5fo sales price, marked on the attached ticket, was the admission fee to any one of 14 simultaneous stamp shows.

"Esperanto" — AP55

Lazarus Ludwig Zamenhof AP56

1957, June 8
C170 AP55 60f red brown .30 .25
C171 AP56 1fo dark green .35 .30

10th anniversary of the death of L. L. Zamenhof, inventor of Esperanto.

Type of 1950

Design: 20fo, Budaörs Airport.

Perf. 12½x12
1957, July 18 Engr. Unwmk.
C172 AP30 20fo dk slate grn 6.00 4.00
Punched 3 holes 7.00 4.50

A few days after issuance, stocks of No. C172 were punched with three holes and used on domestic surface mail.

Courier and Fort Buda AP57

Design: No. C174, Plane over Budapest.

Wmk. 106

1957, Oct. 13 Photo. ***Perf. 12***
C173 AP57 1fo ol bis & brn, *buff* .75 .75
C174 AP57 1fo ol bis & dp cl, *buff* .75 .75
a. Strip of #C173-C174 + label 2.25 2.25

Stamp Day, Oct. 20th. The triptych sold for 6fo.

Type of Regular Pigeon Issue

Design: 3fo, Two carrier pigeons.

1957, Dec. 14 ***Perf. 12x12½***
C175 A266 3fo red, grn, gray & blk .75 .50

Hungarian Pavilion, Brussels — AP58

Designs: 40f, Map, lake and local products. 60f, Parliament. 1fo, Chain Bridge, Budapest. 1.40fo, Arms of Hungary and Belgium. 2fo, Fountain, Brussels, vert. 3fo, City Hall, Brussels vert. 5fo, Exposition emblem.

Perf. 14½x15
1958, Apr. 17 Litho. Wmk. 106
C176 AP58 20f red org & red brn .20 .20
C177 AP58 40f lt blue & brn .20 .20
C178 AP58 60f crimson & sep .20 .20
C179 AP58 1fo bis & red brn .20 .20
C180 AP58 1.40fo dull vio & multi .20 .20
C181 AP58 2fo gldn brn & dk brn .25 .20
C182 AP58 3fo bl grn & sep .55 .40
C183 AP58 5fo gray ol, blk, red, bl & yel 1.00 .60
Nos. C176-C183 (8) 2.80 2.20

Universal and Intl. Exposition at Brussels.

View of Prague and Morse Code AP59

1958, June 30 Photo. ***Perf. 12x12½***
C184 AP59 1fo rose brown .35 .20

See No. 1194a for se-tenant pair.
Conference of Postal Ministers of Communist Countries at Prague, June 30-July 8.

Post Horn, Pigeon and Pen AP60

No. C185, Stamp under magnifying glass.

1958, Oct. 25 Wmk. 106 ***Perf. 12***
C185 AP60 1fo dp car & bis .55 .55
C186 AP60 1fo yel grn & bis .55 .55
a. Strip, #C185-C186 + label 1.50 1.50

Natl. Stamp Exhib., Budapest, 10/25-11/2. #C185 inscribed: "XXXI Belyegnap 1958."

1958, Oct. 26

Designs: 60f, as No. C186. 1fo, Ship, plane, locomotive and pen surrounding letter.

C187 AP60 60f dp plum & grysh buff .30 .20
C188 AP60 1fo bl & grysh buff .45 .20

Issued for Letter Writing Week.

Plane over Heroes' Square Budapest — AP61

Design: 5fo, Plane over Tower of Sopron.

Perf. 12½x12
1958, Nov. 3 Engr. Wmk. 106
C189 AP61 3fo gray, rose vio & red 1.25 .60
C190 AP61 5fo gray, dk bl & red 1.50 .90

40th anniv. of Hungarian air post stamps.

Same Without Commemorative Inscription

Plane over: 20f, Szeged. 30f, Sarospatak. 70f, Gyor. 1fo, Budapest, Opera House. 1.60fo, Veszprém. 2fo, Budapest, Chain Bridge. 3fo, Sopron. 5fo, Heroes' Square, Budapest. 10fo, Budapest, Academy of Science and Parliament. 20fo, Budapest.

1958, Dec. 31 Engr. Wmk. 106
Yellow Paper
and Vermilion Inscriptions
C191 AP61 20f green .20 .20
C192 AP61 30f violet .20 .20
C193 AP61 70f brown vio .20 .20
C194 AP61 1fo blue .20 .20
C195 AP61 1.60fo purple .20 .20
C196 AP61 2fo Prus green .25 .20
C197 AP61 3fo brown .30 .20
C198 AP61 5fo olive green .45 .20
C199 AP61 10fo dark blue 1.25 .30
C200 AP61 20fo brown 2.50 .60
Nos. C191-C200 (10) 5.75 2.50

Transport Type of Regular Issue

Design: 3fo, Early plane.

1959, May Litho. ***Perf. 14½x15***
C201 A279 3fo dl lil, blk, yel & brn 1.25 .40

Tihany — AP62

Designs: 70f, Ship. 1fo, Heviz and water lily. 1.70fo, Sailboat and fisherman statue.

1959, July 15 Photo. ***Perf. 11½x12***
C202 AP62 20f brt green .20 .20
C203 AP62 70f brt blue .20 .20
C204 AP62 1fo ultra & car rose .20 .20
C205 AP62 1.70fo red brn, *yel* .50 .30
Nos. C202-C205 (4) 1.10 .90

Issued to publicize Lake Balaton and the opening of the Summer University.

Moth-Butterfly Type of 1959

Butterflies: 1fo, Lycaena virgaureae. 2fo, Acherontia atropos, horiz. 3fo, Red admiral.

Perf. 11½x12, 12x11½
1959, Nov. 20 Wmk. 106
Butterflies in Natural Colors
C206 A290 1fo black & lt bl grn .70 .20
C207 A290 2fo black & lilac 1.25 .35
C208 A290 3fo dk gray & emer 1.90 .75
Nos. C206-C208 (3) 3.85 1.30

Souvenir Sheet

Rockets in Orbit, Gagarin, Titov & Glenn — AP63

Perf. 11, Imperf.

1962, Mar. 29 **Unwmk.**

C209	AP63	10fo multi	8.00	7.00

Cosmonants Yuri A. Gagarin and Gherman Titov, USSR and astronaut John H. Glenn, Jr., US.

Soccer Type of 1962

Flags of Hungary and Great Britain.

1962, May 21 **Photo.** ***Perf. 11***

Flags in National Colors

C209A	A323	2fo greenish bister	.50	.30

Glider and Lilienthal's 1898 Design — AP64

Designs: 30f, Icarus and Aero Club emblem. 60f, Light monoplane and 1912 aerobatic plane. 80f, Airship GZ-1 and Montgolfier balloon. 1fo, IL-18 Malev and Wright 1903 plane. 1.40fo, Stunt plane and Nyesterov's 1913 plane. 2fo, Helicopter and Asboth's 1929 helicopter. 3fo, Supersonic bomber and Zhukovski's turbomotor. 4fo, Space rocket and Tsiolkovsky's rocket.

1962, July 19 **Unwmk.** ***Perf. 15***

C210	AP64	30f blue & dull yel	.20	.20
C211	AP64	40f yel grn & ultra	.20	.20
C212	AP64	60f ultra & ver	.20	.20
C213	AP64	80f grnsh bl & sil	.20	.20
C214	AP64	1fo lilac, sil & bl	.20	.20
C215	AP64	1.40fo blue & org	.20	.20
C216	AP64	2fo bluish grn & brn	.25	.20
C217	AP64	3fo vio, sil & bl	.50	.25
C218	AP64	4fo grn, sil & blk	.80	.35
		Nos. C210-C218 (9)	2.75	2.00

Issued to show flight development: "From Icarus to the Space Rocket."

Earth, TV Screens and Rockets — AP65

Design: 2fo, Andrian G. Nikolayev, Pavel R. Popovich and rockets.

1962, Sept. 4 ***Perf. 12***

C219	AP65	1fo dk bl & org brn	.60	.35
C220	AP65	2fo dk bl & org brn	.70	.55
a		Pair, #C219-C220	1.30	.90

First group space flight of Vostoks 3 and 4, Aug. 11-15, 1962. Printed in alternating horizontal rows.

John H. Glenn, Jr. AP66

Astronauts: 40f, Yuri A. Gagarin. 60f, Gherman Titov. 1.40fo, Scott Carpenter. 1.70fo, Andrian G. Nikolayev. 2.60fo, Pavel R. Popovich. 3fo, Walter Schirra.

1962, Oct. 27 ***Perf. 12x11½***

Portraits in Bister

C221	AP66	40f purple	.20	.20
C222	AP66	60f dark green	.20	.20
C223	AP66	1fo dark bl grn	.20	.20
C224	AP66	1.40fo dark brown	.20	.20
C225	AP66	1.70fo deep blue	.30	.25
C226	AP66	2.60fo violet	.65	.30
C227	AP66	3fo red brown	1.10	.45
		Nos. C221-C227 (7)	2.85	1.80

Issued to honor the first seven astronauts and in connection with the Astronautical Congress in Paris.

Eagle Owl — AP67

Birds: 40f, Osprey. 60f, Marsh harrier. 80f, Booted eagle. 1fo, African fish eagle. 2fo, Lammergeier. 3fo, Golden eagle. 4fo, Kestrel.

1962, Nov. 18 **Litho.** ***Perf. 11½***

Birds in Natural Colors

C228	AP67	30f yel grn & blk	.20	.20
C229	AP67	40f org yel & blk	.20	.20
C230	AP67	60f bister & blk	.20	.20
C231	AP67	80f lt grn & blk	.20	.20
C232	AP67	1fo ol bis & blk	.20	.20
C233	AP67	2fo bluish grn & blk	.25	.20
C234	AP67	3fo lt vio & blk	.50	.30
C235	AP67	4fo dp org & blk	1.00	.50
		Nos. C228-C235 (8)	2.75	2.00

Radio Mast and Albania No. 623 AP68

Designs (Communication symbols and rocket stamps of various countries): 30f, Bulgaria #C77, vert. 40f, Czechoslovakia #1108. 50f, Communist China #380. 60f, North Korea. 80f, Poland #875. 1fo, Hungary #1386. 1.20fo, Mongolia #189, vert. 1.40fo, DDR #580. 1.70fo, Romania #1200. 2fo, Russia #2456, vert. 2.60fo, North Viet Nam.

Perf. 12x11½, 11½x12

1963, May 9 **Photo.** **Unwmk.**

Stamp Reproductions in Original Colors

C236	AP68	20f olive green	.20	.20
C237	AP68	30f rose lake	.20	.20
C238	AP68	40f violet	.20	.20
C239	AP68	50f brt blue	.20	.20
C240	AP68	60f orange brn	.20	.20
C241	AP68	80f ultra	.20	.20
C242	AP68	1fo dull red brn	.20	.20
C243	AP68	1.20fo aqua	.20	.20
C244	AP68	1.40fo olive	.25	.20
C245	AP68	1.70fo brown olive	.25	.20
C246	AP68	2fo rose lilac	.30	.20
C247	AP68	2.60fo bluish green	.60	.40
		Nos. C236-C247 (12)	3.00	2.60

5th Conference of Postal Ministers of Communist Countries, Budapest.

Souvenir Sheet

Globe and Spaceships — AP69

Perf. 11½x12, Imperf.

1963, July 13 **Unwmk.**

C248	AP69	10fo dk & lt blue	8.00	7.00

Space flights of Valeri Bykovski, June 14-19, and Valentina Tereshkova, 1st woman cosmonaut, June 16-19, 1963.

Souvenir Sheet

Mt. Fuji and Stadium — AP70

1964, Sept. 22 **Photo.** ***Perf. 11½x12***

C249	AP70	10fo multi	4.00	3.50

18th Olympic Games, Tokyo, Oct. 10-24. Exists imperf.

Bridge Type of 1964

Souvenir Sheet

Design: Elizabeth Bridge.

1964, Nov. 21 **Photo.** ***Perf. 11***

C250	A356	10fo silver & dp grn	3.75	3.50

No. C250 contains one 59x20mm stamp.

Lt. Col. Alexei Leonov in Space — AP71

Design: 2fo, Col. Pavel Belyayev, Lt. Col. Alexei Leonov and Voskhod 2.

1965, Apr. 17 **Photo.** ***Perf. 11½x12***

C251	AP71	1fo violet & gray	.45	.20
C252	AP71	2fo rose claret & ocher	1.10	.65

Space flight of Voskhod 2 and of Lt. Col. Alexei Leonov, the first man floating in space.

Mariner IV (USA) — AP72

New achievements in space research: 30f, San Marco satellite, Italy. 40f, Molniya satellite, USSR. 60f, Moon rocket, 1965, USSR. 1fo, Shapir rocket, France. 2.50fo, Zond III satellite, USSR. 3fo, Syncom III satellite, US. 10fo, Rocket sending off satellites, horiz.

1965, Dec. 31 **Photo.** ***Perf. 11***

C253	AP72	20f ultra, blk & org yel	.20	.20
C254	AP72	30f brn, vio & yel	.20	.20
C255	AP72	40f vio, brn & pink	.20	.20
C256	AP72	60f lt pur, blk & org yel	.20	.20
C257	AP72	1fo red lil, blk & buff	.30	.25
C258	AP72	2.50fo rose cl, blk & gray	.60	.35
C259	AP72	3fo bl grn, blk & bis	.75	.60
		Nos. C253-C259 (7)	2.45	2.00

Souvenir Sheet

1965, Dec. 20

C260	AP72	10fo brt bl, yel & dk ol	3.50	3.00

Sport Type of Regular Issue

Souvenir Sheet

10fo, Women hurdlers and Ferihegy airport.

1966, Sept. 4 **Photo.** ***Perf. 12x11½***

C261	A384	10fo brt bl, brn & red	4.00	3.75

Plane over Helsinki — AP73

Plane over Cities Served by Hungarian Airlines: 50f, Athens. 1fo, Beirut. 1.10fo, Frankfort on the Main. 1.20fo, Cairo. 1.50fo, Copenhagen. 2fo, London. 2.50fo, Moscow. 3fo, Paris. 4fo, Prague. 5fo, Rome. 10fo, Damascus. 20fo, Budapest.

1966-67 **Photo.** ***Perf. 12x11½***

C262	AP73	20f brown org	.20	.20
C263	AP73	50f brown	.20	.20
C264	AP73	1fo blue	.20	.20
C265	AP73	1.10fo black	.20	.20
C266	AP73	1.20fo orange	.20	.20
C267	AP73	1.50fo blue grn	.25	.20
C268	AP73	2fo brt blue	.30	.20
C269	AP73	2.50fo brt red	.30	.20
C270	AP73	3fo yel grn	.40	.20
C271	AP73	4fo brown red	1.10	1.00
C272	AP73	5fo brt pur	.55	.20
C273	AP73	10fo violet bl ('67)	.75	.20
C274	AP73	20fo gray ol ('67)	1.10	.35
		Nos. C262-C274 (13)	5.75	3.55

See No. C276.

Souvenir Sheet

Icarus Falling — AP73a

1968, May 11 Photo. *Perf. 11*
C275 AP73a 10fo multicolored 2.75 2.50

In memory of the astronauts Edward H. White, US, Vladimir M. Komarov and Yuri A. Gagarin, USSR.

Type of 1966-67 without "Legiposta" Inscription

Design: 2.60fo, Malev Airlines jet over St. Stephen's Cathedral, Vienna.

1968, July 4 Photo. *Perf. 12x11½*
C276 AP73 2.60fo violet .50 .20

50th anniv. of regular airmail service between Budapest and Vienna.

Women Swimmers and Aztec Calendar Stone — AP74

Aztec Calendar Stone, Olympic Rings and: 60f, Soccer. 80f, Wrestling. 1fo, Canoeing. 1.40fo, Gymnast on rings. 3fo, Fencing. 4fo, Javelin.

1968, Aug. 21 Photo. *Perf. 12*

C277 AP74	20f	brt bl & multi	.20	.20
C278 AP74	60f	green & multi	.20	.20
C279 AP74	80f	car rose & multi	.20	.20
C280 AP74	1fo	grnsh bl & multi	.20	.20
C281 AP74	1.40fo	violet & multi	.20	.20
C282 AP74	3fo	brt lilac & multi	.65	.35
C283 AP74	4fo	green & multi	1.00	.55
		Nos. C277-C283,CB31 (8)	3.00	2.25

Issued to publicize the 19th Olympic Games, Mexico City, Oct. 12-27.

Souvenir Sheet

Apollo 8 Trip Around the Moon — AP75

1969, Feb. Photo. *Perf. 12½*
C284 AP75 10fo multi 3.50 3.50

Man's 1st flight around the moon, Dec. 21-27, 1968.

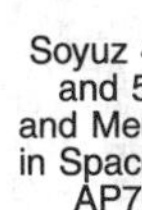

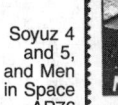

Soyuz 4 and 5, and Men in Space AP76

Design: No. C286, Soyuz 4 and 5.

1969, Mar. 21 Photo. *Perf. 12x11½*
C285 AP76 2fo multi .35 .35
C286 AP76 2fo dk bl, lt bl & red .35 .35
a. Strip, # C285-C286 + label .85

First team flights of Russian spacecraft Soyuz 4 and 5, Jan. 16, 1969.

Journey to the Moon, by Jules Verne — AP77

Designs: 60f, Tsiolkovski's space station. 1fo, Luna 1. 1.50fo, Ranger 7. 2fo, Luna 9 landing on moon. 2.50fo, Apollo 8 in orbit around moon. 3fo, Soyuz 4 and 5 docking in space. 4fo, Lunar landing module landing on moon. 10fo, Apollo 11 astronauts on moon and lunar landing module.

1969 Photo. *Perf. 12x11½*

C287 AP77	40f	multi	.20	.20
C288 AP77	60f	multi	.20	.20
C289 AP77	1fo	multi	.20	.20
C290 AP77	1.50fo	multi	.20	.20
C291 AP77	2fo	multi	.20	.20
C292 AP77	2.50fo	multi	.25	.20
C293 AP77	3fo	multi	.50	.20
C294 AP77	4fo	multi	.75	.40
		Nos. C287-C294 (8)	2.50	1.80

Souvenir Sheet

Perf. 11

C295 AP77 10fo multi 5.00 5.00

Moon landing issue. See note after Algeria No. 427.

No. C295 contains one 74x49mm stamp. Issued: #C287-C294, Nov. 1; #C295, Aug. 15.

Daimler, 1886 — AP78

Automobiles: 60f, Peugeot, 1894. 1fo, Benz, 1901. 1.50fo, Cudell mail truck, 1902. 2fo, Rolls Royce, 1908. 2.50fo, Model T Ford, 1908. 3fo, Vermorel, 1912. 4fo, Csonka mail car, 1912.

1970, Mar. Photo. *Perf. 12*

C296 AP78	40f	ocher & multi	.20	.20
C297 AP78	60f	multi	.20	.20
C298 AP78	1fo	red & multi	.20	.20
C299 AP78	1.50fo	bl & multi	.20	.20
C300 AP78	2fo	multi	.25	.20
C301 AP78	2.50fo	vio & multi	.30	.20
C302 AP78	3fo	multi	.40	.30
C303 AP78	4fo	multi	.70	.50
		Nos. C296-C303 (8)	2.45	2.00

American Astronauts on Moon — AP79

No. C305, Soyuz 6, 7 and 8 in space.

1970, Mar. 20 Photo. *Perf. 11*
C304 AP79 3fo blue & multi .75 .75
C305 AP79 3fo car rose & multi .75 .75

Landing of Apollo 12 on the moon, Nov. 14, 1969, and group flight of Russian spacecraft Soyuz 6, 7 & 8, Oct. 11-13, 1969.

Nos. C304-C305 issued in sheets of 4. Size: 112½x78mm.

"Rain at Foot of Fujiyama," by Hokusai, and Pavilion — AP80

3fo, Sun Tower, Peace Bell and globe.

1970, Apr. 30 Photo. *Perf. 12½*
C306 AP80 2fo multi .75 .75
C307 AP80 3fo multi .75 .75

Issued to publicize EXPO '70 International Exhibition, Osaka, Japan, Mar. 15-Sept. 13.

Miniature Sheets

Phases of Apollo 13 Moon Flight — AP81

Vignettes of No. C308: Apollo 13 over moon; return to earth; capsule with parachutes; capsule floating, aircraft carrier and helicopter.

Vignettes of No. C309: Soyuz 9 on way to launching pad; launching of Soyuz 9 capsule in orbit; cosmonauts Andrian Nikolayev and Vitaly Sevastyanov.

Vignettes of No. C310: Luna 16 approaching moon; module on moon; landing; nose cone on ground.

Vignettes of No. C311: Lunokhod 1 on moon; trajectories of Luna 17 around earth and moon.

1970-71 Litho. *Perf. 11½*
C308 AP81 Sheet of 4 2.25 2.25

Photo.

C309 AP81 Sheet of 4 2.25 2.25
C310 AP81 Sheet of 4 ('71) 2.25 2.25
C311 AP81 Sheet of 4 ('71) 2.25 2.25

Nos. C308-C311 were valid for postage only as full sheets. Each contains four 2.50fo vignettes.

No. C308 for the aborted moon flight and safe return of Apollo 13, 4/11-17/70.

No. C309 for the 424-hour flight of Soyuz 9, 6/1-9.

No. C310 for Luna 16, the unmanned, automated moon mission, 9/12-24/70.

No. C311 for Luna 17, unmanned, automated moon mission, 11/10-17/70.

Issued: #C308, 6/10; #C309, 9/4; #C310, 1/15; #C311 3/8.

Souvenir Sheet

American Astronauts on Moon — AP82

1971, Mar. 31 *Perf. 12½*
C312 AP82 10fo multi 2.25 2.25

Apollo 14 moon landing, 1/31-2/9/71. See Nos. C315, C326-C328.

Hunting Type of Regular Issue Souvenir Sheet

Design: 10fo, Red deer group.

1971, Aug. 27 Photo. *Perf. 11*
C313 A460 10fo multi 3.00 2.50

No. C313 contains one 70x45mm stamp.

Astronauts Volkov, Dobrovolsky and Patsayev — AP83

Souvenir Sheet

1971, Oct. 4 Photo. *Perf. 12½*
C314 AP83 10fo multi 2.25 2.25

In memory of the Russian astronauts Vladislav N. Volkov, Lt. Col. Georgi T. Dobrovolsky and Victor I. Patsayev, who died during the Soyuz 11 space mission, June 6-30, 1971.

Apollo 14 Type of 1971 Souvenir Sheet

10fo, American Lunar Rover on moon.

1972, Jan. 20 Photo. *Perf. 12½*
C315 AP82 10fo multi 2.75 2.50

Apollo 15 moon mission, 7/26-8/7/71.

Soccer and Hungarian Flag — AP84

Various Scenes from Soccer and Natl. Flags of: 60f, Romania. 80f, DDR. 1fo, Great Britain. 1.20fo, Yugoslavia. 2fo, USSR. 4fo, Italy. 5fo, Belgium.

1972, Apr. 29

C316 AP84	40f	gold & multi	.20	.20
C317 AP84	60f	gold & multi	.20	.20
C318 AP84	80f	gold & multi	.20	.20
C319 AP84	1fo	gold & multi	.20	.20
C320 AP84	1.20fo	gold & multi	.20	.20
C321 AP84	2fo	gold & multi	.30	.20
C322 AP84	4fo	gold & multi	.75	.40
C323 AP84	5fo	gold & multi	1.10	.70
a.		Sheet of 8, #C316-C323	3.00	2.50
		Nos. C316-C323 (8)	3.15	2.30

European Soccer Championships for the Henri Delaunay Cup.

Nos. C316-C321 were later issued individually in sheets of 20 and in partly changed colors.

Souvenir Sheet

Olympic Rings and Globe — AP85

1972, June 10 Photo. *Perf. 12½*
C324 AP85 10fo multi 6.00 5.75

20th Olympic Games, Munich, 8/26-9/11.

Olympic Type of Regular Issue Souvenir Sheet

Design: Equestrian and Olympic Rings.

1972, July 15 Photo. *Perf. 12½*
C325 A484 10fo multi 2.50 2.50

20th Olympic Games, Munich, Aug. 26-Sept. 11. #C325 contains one 43x43mm stamp.

Apollo 14 Type of 1971
Souvenir Sheets

Design: 10fo, Astronaut in space, Apollo 16 capsule and badge.

1972, Oct. 10 Photo. *Perf. 12½*

C326 AP82 10fo blue & multi 2.75 2.75

Apollo 16 US moon mission, 4/15-27/72.

1973, Jan. 15

Design: Astronaut exploring moon, vert.

C327 AP82 10fo blue & multi 2.75 2.75

Apollo 17 US moon mission, Dec. 7-19, 1972. No. C327 contains one vertical stamp.

1973, Mar. 12 Photo. *Perf. 12½*

C328 AP82 10fo Venus 8 2.75 2.75

Venus 8 USSR space mission, Mar. 27-July 22, 1972.

Equestrian (Pentathlon), Olympic Rings and Medal — AP86

Designs (Olympic Rings and Medals): 60f, Weight lifting. 1fo, Canoeing. 1.20fo, Swimming, women's. 1.80fo, Boxing. 4fo, Wrestling. 6fo, Fencing. 10fo, Allegorical figure lighting flame, vert.

1973, Mar. 31

C329	AP86	40f multi	.20	.20
C330	AP86	60f multi	.20	.20
C331	AP86	1fo blue & multi	.20	.20
C332	AP86	1.20fo multi	.20	.20
C333	AP86	1.80fo multi	.30	.20
C334	AP86	4fo multi	.65	.30
C335	AP86	6fo multi	1.00	.50
		Nos. C329-C335 (7)	2.75	1.80

Souvenir Sheet

Perf. 11

C336 AP86 10fo blue & multi 3.75 3.75

Hungarian medalists at 20th Olympic Games. #C336 contains one 44x71mm stamp.

Wrens — AP87

1973, Apr. 16 Litho. *Perf. 12*

C337	AP87	40f shown	.20	.20
C338	AP87	60f Rock thrush	.20	.20
C339	AP87	80f Robins	.20	.20
C340	AP87	1fo Firecrests	.20	.20
C341	AP87	1.20fo Linnets	.20	.20
C342	AP87	2fo Blue titmice	.25	.20
C343	AP87	4fo White-spotted blue throat	.50	.25
C344	AP87	5fo Gray wagtails	1.00	.55
		Nos. C337-C344 (8)	2.75	2.00

Exhibition Type of Regular Issue
Souvenir Sheet

10fo, Bavaria #1 with mill wheel cancellation; Munich City Hall, TV Tower and Olympic tent.

1973, May 11 Litho. *Perf. 11*

C345 A506 10fo multi 2.75 2.75

No. C345 contains one 83x45mm stamp.

Souvenir Sheet

Skylab over Earth — AP88

1973, Oct. 16 Photo. *Perf. 12½*

C346 AP88 10fo dk bl, lt bl & yel 2.75 2.75

First US manned space station.

Space Type of Regular Issue

Designs: 6fo, Mars "canals" and Giovanni V. Schiaparelli. 10fo, Mars 7 spacecraft.

1974, Mar. 11 Photo. *Perf. 12½*

C347 A522 6fo gold & multi .75 .50

Souvenir Sheet

C348 A522 10fo gold & multi 2.75 2.50

UPU Type of 1974

Designs: a, Mail coach. b, Old mail automobile. c, Jet. d, Apollo 15.

1974, May 22 Litho. *Perf. 12*

C349 A526 6fo UPU emblem and TU-154 jet .75 .60

Souvenir Sheet

C350 Sheet of 4 2.75 2.75
a.-d. A526 2.50fo, any single .40 .40

No. C350 has bister UPU emblem in center where 4 stamps meet.

Army Day Type of 1974

Designs: 2fo, Ground-to-air missiles, vert. 3fo, Parachutist, helicopter, supersonic jets.

1974, Sept. 28 Litho. *Perf. 12*

C351 A537 2fo gold, emer & blk .25 .20
C352 A537 3fo gold, blue & blk .45 .20

Carrier Pigeon, Elizabeth Bridge, Mt. Gellert AP89

1975, Feb. 7 Litho. *Perf. 12*

C353 AP89 3fo multi 1.25 1.25

Carrier Pigeons' Olympics, Budapest, Feb. 7-9. No. C353 printed checkerwise with black and violet coupon showing Pigeon Olympics emblem.

Sputnik 2, Apollo-Soyuz Emblem AP90

Spacecraft and Apollo-Soyuz Emblem: 60f, Mercury-Atlas 5. 80f, Lunokhod I on moon. 1.20fo, Lunar rover, Apollo 15 mission. 2fo, Soyuz take-off, Baikonur. 4fo, Apollo take-off, Cape Kennedy. 6fo, Apollo-Soyuz link-up. 10fo, Apollo, Soyuz, American and Russian flags over earth, horiz.

1975, July 7 Photo. *Perf. 12x11½*

C354	AP90	40f silver & multi	.20	.20
C355	AP90	60f silver & multi	.20	.20
C356	AP90	80f silver & multi	.20	.20
C357	AP90	1.20fo silver & multi	.20	.20
C358	AP90	2fo silver & multi	.25	.20
C359	AP90	4fo silver & multi	.45	.30
C360	AP90	6fo silver & multi	.75	.45
		Nos. C354-C360 (7)	2.25	1.75

Souvenir Sheet

Perf. 12½

C361 AP90 10fo blue & multi 3.25 3.00

Apollo Soyuz space test project (Russo-American cooperation), launching July 15; link-up July 17. No. C361 contains one 59x38mm stamp.

Souvenir Sheet

Map of Europe and Cogwheels — AP91

1975, July 30 Litho. *Perf. 12½*

C362 AP91 10fo multi 4.50 3.75

European Security and Cooperation Conference, Helsinki, July 30-Aug. 1.

Souvenir Sheet

Hungary Nos. 1585, 1382, 2239, 2280, C81 — AP92

1975, Sept. 9 Photo. *Perf. 12½*

C363 AP92 10fo multi 2.75 2.50

30 years of stamps.

A similar souvenir sheet with blue margin, no denomination and no postal validity was released for the 25th anniversary of Filatelica Hungarica.

Souvenir Sheet

Paintings by Károly Lotz and János Halápi — AP93

1976, Mar. 19 Photo. *Perf. 12½*

C364 AP93 Sheet of 2 3.25 2.50
a. 5fo Horses in Storm 1.00 1.00
b. 5fo Morning at Tihany 1.00 1.00

Tourist publicity. #C364a and C364b are imperf. between.

Souvenir Sheet

Montreal Olympic Stadium — AP94

1976, June 29 Litho. *Perf. 12½*

C365 AP94 20fo red, gray & blk 3.75 3.75

21st Olympic Games, Montreal, Canada, July 17-Aug. 1.

US Mars Mission AP95

60f, Viking in space. 1fo, Viking on Mars. 2fo, Venus, rocket take-off. 3fo, Venyera 9 in space. 4fo, Venyera 10, separation in space. 5fo, Venyera on moon. 20fo, Viking 1 landing on Mars, vert.

1976, Nov. 11 Photo. *Perf. 11*

C366	AP95	40f silver & multi	.20	.20
C367	AP95	60f silver & multi	.20	.20
C368	AP95	1fo silver & multi	.20	.20
C369	AP95	2fo silver & multi	.25	.20
C370	AP95	3fo silver & multi	.35	.20
C371	AP95	4fo silver & multi	.55	.30
C372	AP95	5fo silver & multi	.75	.40
		Nos. C366-C372 (7)	2.50	1.70

Souvenir Sheet

Perf. 12½

C373 AP95 20fo black & multi 3.00 2.75

US-USSR space missions. No. C373 contains one stamp (size: 41x64mm).

Hungary No. CB33 — AP96

1977, Apr. Litho. *Perf. 11½x12*

C374 AP96 3fo multi 1.50 1.50

European stamp exhibitions. Issued in sheets of 3 stamps and 3 labels. Labels show exhibition emblems respectively: 125th anniversary of Brunswick stamps, Brunswick, May 5-8; Regiofil XII, Lugano, June 17-19; centenary of San Marino Stamps, Riccione, Aug. 27-29.

Space Type 1977
Souvenir Sheet

Design: 20fo, Viking on Mars.

1977, Sept. 20 Litho. *Perf. 11½*

C375 A603 20fo multi 3.75 3.75

Souvenir Sheet

"EUROPA," Map and Dove — AP97

1977, Oct. 3 *Perf. 12½*

C376 AP97 20fo multi 5.25 4.75

European Security Conference, Belgrade, Oct.-Nov.

TU-154, Malev over Europe AP98

Planes, Airlines, Maps: 1.20fo, DC-8, Swissair, Southeast Asia. 2fo, IL-62, CSA, North Africa. 2.40fo, A 300B Airbus, Lufthansa, Northwest Europe. 4fo, Boeing 747, Pan Am, North America. 5fo, TU-144, Aeroflot, Northern Europe. 10fo, Concorde, Air France, South America. 20fo, IL-86, Aeroflot, Northeast Asia.

1977, Oct. 26 Litho. *Perf. 11½x12*

Size: 32x21mm

C377 AP98 60f orange & blk .20 .20
C378 AP98 1.20fo violet & blk .35 .20
C379 AP98 2fo yellow & blk .35 .20
C380 AP98 2.40fo bl grn & blk .50 .20
C381 AP98 4fo ultra & blk .50 .20
C382 AP98 5fo dp rose & blk .70 .25
C383 AP98 10fo blue & blk 1.25 .40

Perf. 12x11½

Size: 37½x29mm

C384 AP98 20fo green & blk 1.40 .90
Nos. C377-C384 (8) 5.25 2.55

Montgolfier Brothers and Balloon, 1783 — AP99

Designs: 60f, David Schwarz and airship, 1850. 1fo, Alberto Santos-Dumont and airship flying around Eiffel Tower, 1901. 2fo, Konstantin E. Tsiolkovsky, airship and Kremlin, 1857. 3fo, Roald Amundsen, airship Norge, Polar bears and map, 1872. 4fo, Hugo Eckener, Graf Zeppelin over Mt. Fuji, 1930. 5fo, Count Ferdinand von Zeppelin, Graf Zeppelin over Chicago, 1932. 20fo, Graf Zeppelin over Budapest, 1931.

1977, Nov. 1 Photo. *Perf. 12x11½*

C385 AP99 40f gold & multi .20 .20
C386 AP99 60f gold & multi .20 .20
C387 AP99 1fo gold & multi .20 .20
C388 AP99 2fo gold & multi .25 .20
C389 AP99 3fo gold & multi .40 .25
C390 AP99 4fo gold & multi .50 .30
C391 AP99 5fo gold & multi .75 .50
Nos. C385-C391 (7) 2.50 1.85

Souvenir Sheet

Perf. 12½

C392 AP99 20fo silver & multi 3.25 3.00

History of airships. No. C392 contains one 60x36mm stamp.

Moon Station — AP100

Science Fiction Paintings by Pal Varga: 60f, Moon settlement. 1fo, Spaceship near Phobos. 2fo, Exploration of asteroids. 3fo, Spaceship in gravitational field of Mars. 4fo, Spaceship and rings of Saturn. 5fo, Spaceship landing on 3rd Jupiter moon.

1978, Mar. 10 Litho. *Perf. 11*

C393 AP100 40f multi .20 .20
C394 AP100 60f multi .20 .20
C395 AP100 1fo multi .20 .20
C396 AP100 2fo multi .25 .20
C397 AP100 3fo multi .40 .25
C398 AP100 4fo multi .50 .30
C399 AP100 5fo multi .75 .40
Nos. C393-C399 (7) 2.50 1.75

Louis Bleriot and La Manche AP101

60f, J. Alcock & R. W. Brown, Vickers Vimy, 1919. 1fo, A. C. Read, Navy Curtiss NC-4, 1919. 2fo, H. Köhl, G. Hünefeld, J. Fitzmaurice, Junkers W33, 1928. 3fo, A. Johnson, J. Mollison, Gipsy Moth, 1930. 4fo, G. Endresz, S. Magyar, Lockheed Sirius, 1931. 5fo, W. Gronau, Dornier WAL, 1932. 20fo, Wilbur & Orville Wright & their plane.

1978, May 10 Litho. *Perf. 12*

C400 AP101 40f multi .20 .20
C401 AP101 60f multi .20 .20
C402 AP101 1fo multi .20 .20
C403 AP101 2fo multi .25 .20
C404 AP101 3fo multi .40 .25
C405 AP101 4fo multi .55 .30
C406 AP101 5fo multi .85 .40
Nos. C400-C406 (7) 2.65 1.75

Souvenir Sheet

C407 AP101 20fo multi 3.00 2.75

75th anniv. of 1st powered flight by Wright brothers. #C407 contains one 75x25mm stamp.

Souvenir Sheet

Jules Verne and "Voyage from Earth to Moon" — AP102

1978, Aug. 21 *Perf. 12½x11½*

C408 AP102 20fo multi 3.00 2.75

Jules Verne (1828-1905), French science fiction writer.

Vladimir Remek Postmarking Mail on Board Salyut 6 — AP103

1978, Sept. 1 Photo. *Perf. 11½x12*

C409 AP103 3fo multi .75 .75

PRAGA '78 International Philatelic Exhibition, Prague, Sept. 8-17. Issued in sheets of 3 stamps and 3 labels, showing PRAGA '78 emblem and Golden Tower, Prague. FISA emblems in margin.

Ski Jump — AP104

Lake Placid '80 Emblem and: 60f, 20fo, Figure skating, diff. 1fo, Downhill skiing. 2fo, Ice hockey. 4fo, Bobsledding. 6fo, Cross-country skiing.

1979, Dec. 15 Litho. *Perf. 12*

C410 AP104 40f multi .20 .20
C411 AP104 60f multi .20 .20
C412 AP104 1fo multi .20 .20
C413 AP104 2fo multi .30 .20
C414 AP104 4fo multi .60 .30
C415 AP104 6fo multi 1.00 .55
Nos. C410-C415 (6) 2.50 1.65

Souvenir Sheet

C416 AP104 20fo multi 2.75 2.75

13th Winter Olympic Games, Lake Placid, NY, Feb. 12-24, 1980.

Soviet and Hungarian Cosmonauts AP105

1980, May 27 Litho. *Perf. 11½x12*

C417 AP105 5fo multi .60 .25

Intercosmos cooperative space program.

Women's Handball, Moscow '80 Emblem, Olympic Rings — AP106

1980, June 16 Photo. *Perf. 11½x12*

C418 AP106 40f shown .20 .20
C419 AP106 60f Double kayak .20 .20
C420 AP106 1fo Running .20 .20
C421 AP106 2fo Gymnast .25 .20
C422 AP106 3fo Equestrian .40 .25
C423 AP106 4fo Wrestling .55 .35
C424 AP106 5fo Water polo .65 .50
Nos. C418-C424 (7) 2.45 1.90

Souvenir Sheet

C425 AP106 20fo Torch bearers 3.00 3.00

22nd Summer Olympic Games, Moscow, July 19-Aug. 3.
See No. C427.

Souvenir Sheet

Cosmonauts Bertalan Farkes and Valery Kubasov, Salyut 6-Soyuz 35 and 36 — AP107

1980, July 12 Litho. *Perf. 12½*

C426 AP107 20fo multi 3.25 3.00

Intercosmos cooperative space program (USSR-Hungary).

Olympic Type of 1980

Souvenir Sheet

1980, Sept. 26 Litho. *Perf. 12½*

C427 AP106 20fo Greek Frieze and gold medal 3.25 3.00

Olympic Champions.

Kalman Kittenberger (1881-1958), Zoologist and Explorer — AP108

1981, Mar. 6 Photo. *Perf. 11½*

C427A AP108 40f Cheetah .20 .20
C427B AP108 60f Lion .20 .20
C427C AP108 1fo Leopard .20 .20
C427D AP108 2fo Rhinoceros .35 .20
C427E AP108 3fo Antelope .55 .25
C427F AP108 4fo African elephant .65 .30
C427G AP108 5fo shown .85 .40
Nos. C427A-C427G (7) 3.00 1.75

Graf Zeppelin over Tokyo, First Worldwide Flight, Aug. 7-Sept. 4, 1929 — AP109

Graf Zeppelin Flights (Zeppelin and): 2fo, Icebreaker Malygin, Polar flight, July 24-31, 1931. 3fo, Nine Arch Bridge, Hortobagy, Hungary, Mar. 28-30, 1931. 4fo, Holsten Tor, Lubeck, Baltic Sea, May 12-15, 1931. 5fo, Tower Bridge, England, Aug. 18-20, 1931. 6fo, Federal Palace, Chicago World's Fair, 50th crossing of Atlantic, Oct. 14-Nov. 2, 1933. 7fo, Lucerne, first flight across Switzerland, Sept. 26, 1929.

Perf. 12½x11½

1981, Mar. 16 Litho.

C428 AP109 1fo multi .20 .20
C429 AP109 2fo multi .25 .20
C430 AP109 3fo multi .40 .25
C431 AP109 4fo multi .55 .35
C432 AP109 5fo multi .65 .40
C433 AP109 6fo multi .75 .55
C434 AP109 7fo multi .85 .60
Nos. C428-C434 (7) 3.65 2.55

LURABA '81, First Aviation and Space Philatelic Exhibition, Lucerne, Switzerland, Mar. 20-29. No. C434 se-tenant with label showing exhibition emblem.

Illustrator Type of 1981

Designs: Illustrations by A. Lesznai.

1981, Dec. 29 Litho. *Perf. 11½x12*

C435 A693 4fo At the End of the Village .55 .50
C436 A693 5fo Dance .70 .55
C437 A693 6fo Sunday .80 .60
Nos. C435-C437 (3) 2.05 1.65

Manned Flight Bicentenary AP110

Various hot air balloons.

1983, Apr. 5 Litho. *Perf. 12x11½*

C438 AP110 1fo 1811 .20 .20
C439 AP110 1fo 1896 .20 .20
C440 AP110 2fo 1904 .25 .20
C441 AP110 2fo 1977 .25 .20
C442 AP110 4fo 1981 .50 .25

C443	AP110	4fo 1982	.50	.25
C444	AP110	5fo 1981	.70	.35
		Nos. C438-C444 (7)	2.60	1.65

Souvenir Sheet

Perf. 12½

C445	AP110	20fo 1983	2.75	2.75

No. C445 contains one 39x49mm stamp.

Audubon Type of 1985

1985, June 19 Litho. *Perf. 12*

C446	A778	4fo Colaptes auratus	.60	.35
C447	A778	6fo Richmondena cardinalis	.85	.50

Aircraft — AP111

1988, Aug. 31 Litho. *Perf. 11*

C448	AP111	1fo Lloyd CII	.20	.20
C449	AP111	2fo Brandenburg CI	.30	.20
C450	AP111	4fo UFAG CI	.50	.35
C451	AP111	10fo Gerle 13	1.40	.90
C452	AP111	12fo WM 13	1.60	1.10
		Nos. C448-C452 (5)	4.00	2.75

AIR POST SEMI-POSTAL STAMPS

Catalogue values for unused stamps in this section are for Never Hinged items.

Roosevelt Type of Semipostal Stamps, 1947

F. D. Roosevelt, Plane and Place: 10f+10f, Casablanca. 20f+20f, Tehran. 50f+50f, Yalta (map). 70f+70f, Hyde Park.

Perf. 12x12½

1947, June 11 Photo. Wmk. 210

Portrait in Sepia

CB1	SP115	10f + 10f red vio	2.50	2.75
CB1A	SP115	20f + 20f brn ol	2.50	2.75
CB1B	SP115	50f + 50f vio	2.50	2.75
CB1C	SP115	70f + 70f blk	2.50	2.75
		Nos. CB1-CB1C (4)	10.00	11.00

A souvenir sheet contains one each of Nos. CB1-CB1C with border inscriptions and decorations in gray. Size: 161x122mm. Value $60.

See note below Nos. B198A-B198D.

Souvenir Sheet

Chain Bridge, Budapest — SPAP1

Perf. 12x12½

1948, May 15 Photo. Wmk. 283

CB1D	SPAP1	2fo + 18fo brn car	45.00	50.00

Souvenir Sheet

Chain Bridge — SPAP2

1948, Oct. 16

CB2	SPAP2	3fo + 18fo dp grnsh bl	45.00	45.00

Type of Air Post Stamps of 1948 Portraits at Right

Writers: 1f, William Shakespeare. 2f, Francois Voltaire. 4f, Johann Wolfgang von Goethe. 5f, Lord Byron. 6f, Victor Hugo. 8f, Edgar Allen Poe. 10f, Sandor Petőfi. 12f, Mark Twain. 30f, Count Leo Tolstoy. 40f, Maxim Gorky.

1948, Oct. 16 Photo.

CB3	AP22	1f dp ultra	.20	.20
CB4	AP22	2f rose carmine	.20	.20
CB5	AP22	4f dp yellow grn	.20	.20
CB6	AP22	5f dp rose lilac	.20	.20
CB7	AP22	6f deep blue	.20	.20
CB8	AP22	8f olive brn	.20	.20
CB9	AP22	10f red	.20	.20
CB10	AP22	12f deep violet	.20	.20
CB11	AP22	30f orange brn	.50	.60
CB12	AP22	40f sepia	.75	.90
		Nos. CB3-CB12 (10)	2.85	3.10

Sold at a 50 per cent increase over face, half of which aided reconstruction of the Chain Bridge and the other half the hospital for postal employees.

1st Stamp Type Souvenir Sheets

Perf. 12½x12

1951, Sept. 12 Engr. Unwmk.

CB13	A208	1fo + 1fo red	45.00	45.00
CB14	A208	2fo + 2fo blue	45.00	45.00

Children Inspecting Stamp Album — SPAP3

2fo+2fo, Children at stamp exhibition.

Perf. 12x12½

1952, Oct. 12 Photo. Wmk. 106

CB15	SPAP3	1fo + 1fo blue	2.25	2.25
CB16	SPAP3	2fo + 2fo brn red	2.25	2.25

Stamp week, Oct. 11-19, 1952.

Globe and Mailbox SPAP4

Designs: 1fo+50f, Mobile post office. 2fo+1fo, Telegraph pole. 3fo+1.50fo, Radio. 5fo+2.50fo, Telephone. 10fo+5fo, Post horn.

1957, June 20 *Perf. 12x12½, 12*

Cross in Red

Size: 32x21mm

CB17	SPAP4	60f + 30f bister brn	.50	.20
CB18	SPAP4	1fo + 50f lilac	.70	.35
CB19	SPAP4	2fo + 1fo org ver	.95	.45
CB20	SPAP4	3fo + 1.50fo blue	1.25	.70
CB21	SPAP4	5fo + 2.50fo gray	1.90	1.75

Size: 46x31mm

CB22	SPAP4	10fo + 5fo pale grn	4.00	4.00
		Nos. CB17-CB22 (6)	9.30	7.45

The surtax was for the benefit of hospitals for postal and telegraph employees.

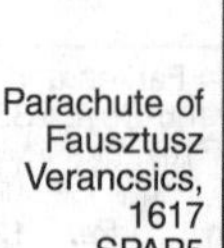

Parachute of Fausztusz Verancsics, 1617 SPAP5

History of Hungarian Aviation: No. CB24, Balloon of David Schwarz, 1897. No. CB25, Monoplane of Ernő Horvath, 1911. No. CB26, PKZ-2 helicopter, 1918.

Engraved and Lithographed

1967, May 6 *Perf. 10½*

CB23	SPAP5	2fo + 1fo sep & yel	.50	.50
CB24	SPAP5	2fo + 1fo sep & lt bl	.50	.50
CB25	SPAP5	2fo + 1fo sep & lt grn	.50	.50
CB26	SPAP5	2fo + 1fo sep & pink	.50	.50
a.		Horiz. strip of 4, #CB23-CB26	2.75	2.75
b.		Souv. sheet of 4, #CB23-CB26	3.00	2.75

"AEROFILA 67" International Airmail Exhibition, Budapest, Sept. 3-10.

1967, Sept. 3

Aviation, 1967: No. CB27, Parachutist. No. CB28, Helicopter Mi-1. No. CB29, TU-154 jet. No. CB30, Space station Luna 12.

CB27	SPAP5	2fo + 1fo slate & lt grn	.50	.50
CB28	SPAP5	2fo + 1fo slate & buff	.50	.50
CB29	SPAP5	2fo + 1fo slate & yel	.50	.50
CB30	SPAP5	2fo + 1fo slate & pink	.50	.50
a.		Horiz. strip of 4, #CB27-CB30	2.75	2.75
b.		Souv. sheet of 4, #CB27-CB30	3.75	3.75

Issued to commemorate (in connection with AEROFILA 67) the 7th Congress of FISA (Fédération Internationale des Sociétés Aérophilatéliques) and the 40th Stamp Day.

Olympic Games Airmail Type

Design: 2fo+1fo, Equestrian.

1968, Aug. 21 Photo. *Perf. 12*

CB31	AP74	2fo + 1fo multi	.35	.35

1st Hungarian Airmail Letter, 1918, Plane — SPAP6

Designs: No. CB33, Letter, 1931, and Zeppelin. No. CB34, Balloon post letter, 1967, and balloon. No. CB35, Letter, 1969, and helicopter.

#CB36a, #C1. b, #C7. c, #C305. d, #C312.

1974, Oct. 19 Litho. *Perf. 12*

CB32	SPAP6	2fo + 1fo multi	.95	.95
CB33	SPAP6	2fo + 1fo multi	.95	.95
a.		Pair, #CB32-CB33	2.00	2.00
CB34	SPAP6	2fo + 1fo multi	.95	.95
CB35	SPAP6	2fo + 1fo multi	.95	.95
a.		Pair, #CB34-CB35	2.00	2.00
		Nos. CB32-CB35 (4)	3.80	3.80

Souvenir Sheet

CB36		Sheet of 4	3.50	3.50
a.		SPAP6 2fo+1fo any single	.50	.50

AEROPHILA, International Airmail Exhibition, Budapest, Oct. 19-27.

No. CB36 contains 4 35x25mm stamps.

SPECIAL DELIVERY STAMPS

Issue of the Monarchy

SD1

SD2

1916 Typo. Wmk. 137 *Perf. 15*

E1	SD1	2f gray green & red	.20	.20

For overprints and surcharges see Nos. 1NE1, 2NE1, 4N5, 5NE1, 6NE1, 7NE1, 8NE1, 10NE1, Szeged E1, J7-J8.

Issue of the Republic

Special Delivery Stamp of 1916 Overprinted

1919

E2	SD1	2f gray green & red	.20	.20

General Issue

1919

E3	SD2	2f gray green & red	.20	.20

REGISTRATION STAMPS

Catalogue values for unused stamps in this section are for Never Hinged items.

Nos. 625, 609 and 626 Overprinted in Carmine

a

b

"Ajl." or "Ajánlás" = Registered Letter.

1946 Wmk. 266 *Perf. 15*

F1	A118(a)	"Ajl.1." on 20f	.20	.20
a.		"Ajj.1."	12.00	
F2	A99(a)	"Ajl.2." on 12f	.20	.20
F3	A118(b)	"Ajánlás" on 24f	.20	.20
		Nos. F1-F3 (3)	.60	.60

POSTAGE DUE STAMPS

Issues of the Monarchy

D1

Perf. 11½, 11½x12

1903 Typo. Wmk. 135

J1	D1	1f green & blk	.50	.20
J2	D1	2f green & blk	3.00	1.00
J3	D1	5f green & blk	9.50	4.00
J4	D1	6f green & blk	7.00	3.50
J5	D1	10f green & blk	45.00	2.25
J6	D1	12f green & blk	2.50	1.50
a.		Perf. 11½	80.00	50.00
J7	D1	20f green & blk	11.00	1.50
a.		Perf. 11½	100.00	24.00
J8	D1	50f green & blk	10.50	9.50
a.		Perf. 11½	125.00	110.00
J9	D1	100f green & blk	1.00	.70
		Nos. J1-J9 (9)	90.00	24.15

See Nos. J10-J26, J28-J43. For overprints and surcharges see Nos. J27, J44-J50, 1NJ1-1NJ5, 2NJ1-2NJ16, 4NJ2-4NJ3, 5NJ1-5NJ8, 6NJ1-6NJ9, 7NJ1-7NJ4, 9NJ1-9NJ3, 10NJ1-10NJ6, Szeged J1-J6.

1908-09 Wmk. 136 *Perf. 15*

J10	D1	1f green & black	.45	.45
J11	D1	2f green & black	.30	.30
J12	D1	5f green & black	2.50	1.10
J13	D1	6f green & black	.50	.40
J14	D1	10f green & black	1.50	.40
J15	D1	12f green & black	.50	.40
J16	D1	20f green & black	10.00	.45
c.		Center inverted		*4,000.*
J17	D1	50f green & black	.95	.95
		Nos. J10-J17 (8)	16.70	4.45

1905 Wmk. 136a *Perf. 11½x12*

J12a	D1	5f green & black	75.00	50.00
J13a	D1	6f green & black	7.50	7.50
J14a	D1	10f green & black	75.00	5.00
J15a	D1	12f green & black	12.50	10.00
J17a	D1	50f green & black	7.50	5.00
J18	D1	100f green & black	2.00	

1906 *Perf. 15*

J11b	D1	2f green & black	2.50	1.90
J12b	D1	5f green & black	2.00	1.75
J13b	D1	6f green & black	2.00	1.25
J14b	D1	10f green & black	10.00	.60

J15b D1 12f green & black .60 .60
J16b D1 20f green & black 15.00 .60
d. Center inverted 3,000.
J17b D1 50f green & black 1.00 .70
Nos. J11b-J17b (7) 33.10 7.40

1914 Wmk. 137 Horiz. *Perf. 15*

J19 D1 1f green & black .20 .20
J20 D1 2f green & black .20 .20
J21 D1 5f green & black .40 .40
J22 D1 6f green & black .60 .60
J23 D1 10f green & black .70 .70
J24 D1 12f green & black .35 .35
J25 D1 20f green & black .35 .35
J26 D1 50f green & black .40 .40
Nos. J19-J26 (8) 3.20 3.20

1914 Wmk. 137 Vert.

J20a D1 2f green & black 57.50 57.50
J21a D1 5f green & black 7.50 6.25
J22a D1 6f green & black 16.00 16.00
J25a D1 20f green & black 2,750. 900.00
J26a D1 50f green & black 7.50 7.50

No. J9 Surcharged in Red

1915 Wmk. 135

J27 D1 20f on 100f grn & blk 1.25 .90
a. On No. J18, Wmk. 136a 25.00 20.00

1915-22 Wmk. 137

J28 D1 1f green & red .20 .20
J29 D1 2f green & red .20 .20
J30 D1 5f green & red .20 .20
J31 D1 6f green & red .20 .20
J32 D1 10f green & red .20 .20
J33 D1 12f green & red .20 .20
J34 D1 15f green & red .20 .20
J35 D1 20f green & red .20 .20
J36 D1 30f green & red .20 .20
J37 D1 40f green & red ('20) .20 .20
J38 D1 50f green & red ('20) .20 .20
a. Center inverted 60.00
J39 D1 120f green & red ('20) .20 .20
J40 D1 200f green & red ('20) .20 .20
J41 D1 2k green & red ('22) .40 .40
J42 D1 5k green & red ('22) .20 .20
J43 D1 50k green & red ('22) .20 .20
Nos. J28-J43 (16) 3.40 3.40

Issues of the Republic

Postage Due Stamps of 1914-18 Overprinted in Black

1918-19

On Issue of 1914

J44 D1 50f green & black .60 .60

On Stamps and Type of 1915-18

J45 D1 2f green & red .20 .20
J46 D1 3f green & red .20 .20
a. "KOZTARSASAG" omitted 650.00
J47 D1 10f green & red .20 .20
J48 D1 20f green & red .20 .20
J49 D1 40f green & red .20 .20
a. Inverted overprint 20.00 20.00
J50 D1 50f green & red .20 .20
a. Center and overprint inverted 25.00 25.00
Nos. J44-J50 (7) 1.80 1.80

Issues of the Kingdom

D3

1919-20 Typo.

J65 D3 2f green & black .20 .20
a. Inverted center 1,000.
J66 D3 3f green & black .20 .20
J67 D3 20f green & black .20 .20
J68 D3 40f green & black .20 .20
J69 D3 50f green & black .20 .20
Nos. J65-J69 (5) 1.00 1.00

Postage Due Stamps of this type have been overprinted "Magyar Tancskztarsasag" but have not been reported as having been issued without the additional overprint "heads of wheat."

For overprints see Nos. J70-J75.

New Overprint in Black over "Magyar Tanacskoztarsasag"

1920

J70 D3 2f green & black .45 .45
J71 D3 3f green & black .45 .45
J72 D3 10f green & black 1.60 1.75
J73 D3 20f green & black .45 .45
J74 D3 40f green & black .45 .45
J75 D3 50f green & black .45 .45
Nos. J70-J75 (6) 3.85 4.00

Counterfeit overprints exist.

Postage Issues Surcharged

1921-25

Red Surcharge

J76 A9 100f on 15f violet .20 .20
J77 A9 500f on 15f violet .20 .20
J78 A9 2½k on 10f red vio .20 .20
J79 A9 3k on 15f violet .20 .20
J80 A9 6k on 1½k violet .20 .20
J81 A9 9k on 40f ol grn .20 .20
J82 A9 10k on 2½k green .20 .20
J83 A9 12k on 60f blk brn .20 .20
J84 A9 15k on 1½k vio .20 .20
J85 A9 20k on 2½k grn .20 .20
J86 A9 25k on 1½k vio .20 .20
J87 A9 30k on 1½k vio .20 .20
J88 A9 40k on 2½k grn .20 .20
J89 A9 50k on 1½k vio .20 .20
J90 A9 100k on 4½k dl vio .20 .20
J91 A9 200k on 4½k dl vio .20 .20
J92 A9 300k on 4½k dl vio .20 .20
J93 A9 500k on 2k grnsh bl .30 .20
J94 A9 500k on 3k org brn .30 .30
J95 A9 1000k on 2k grnsh bl .30 .20
J96 A9 1000k on 3k org brn .45 .20
J97 A9 2000k on 2k grnsh bl .35 .20
J98 A9 2000k on 3k org brn .70 .35
J99 A9 5000k on 5k brown .90 .50
Nos. J76-J99 (24) 6.70 5.35

Year of issue: 6k, 15k, 25k, 30k, 50k, 1922. 10k, 20k, 40k, 100k - No. J93, Nos. J95, J97, 1923. 5,000k, 1924. Nos. J94, J96, J98, 1925. Others, 1921.

D6

1926 Wmk. 133 Litho. *Perf. 14, 15*

J100 D6 1f rose red .20 .20
J101 D6 2f rose red .20 .20
J102 D6 3f rose red .20 .20
J103 D6 4f rose red .20 .20
J104 D6 5f rose red .50 .25
a. Perf. 15 1.10 .45
J105 D6 8f rose red .20 .20
J106 D6 10f rose red .20 .20
J107 D6 16f rose red .35 .20
J108 D6 32f rose red .50 .20
J109 D6 40f rose red .50 .20
J110 D6 50f rose red .50 .20
J111 D6 80f rose red 1.75 .35
Nos. J100-J111 (12) 5.30 2.60

See Nos. J117-J123. For surcharges see Nos. J124-J129.

Nos. C7-C11 Surcharged in Red or Green

1926 Wmk. 137 *Perf. 14*

J112 AP3 1f on 500k (R) .30 .25
J113 AP3 2f on 1000k (G) .30 .30
J114 AP3 3f on 2000k (R) .30 .20

Wmk. 133

J115 AP3 5f on 5000k (G) .65 .55
J116 AP3 10f on 10000k (G) .45 .35
Nos. J112-J116 (5) 2.00 1.65

Type of 1926 Issue

1928-32 Wmk. 210 *Perf. 14, 15*

J117 D6 2f rose red .20 .20
J118 D6 4f rose red ('32) .20 .20
J119 D6 8f rose red .20 .20
J120 D6 10f rose red .20 .20
J121 D6 16f rose red .20 .20
J122 D6 20f rose red .30 .20
J123 D6 40f rose red .70 .20
Nos. J117-J123 (7) 2.00 1.40

Postage Due Stamps of 1926 Surcharged in Black

1931-33 Wmk. 133

J124 D6 4f on 5f rose red .35 .20
J125 D6 10f on 16f rose red 1.00 .80
J126 D6 10f on 80f rose red ('33) .45 .20
J127 D6 12f on 50f rose red ('33) .45 .20
J128 D6 20f on 32f rose red .45 .30
Nos. J124-J128 (5) 2.70 1.70

Surcharged on No. J121

1931 Wmk. 210 *Perf. 15*

J129 D6 10f on 16f rose red .85 .70

Catalogue values for unused stamps in this section, from this point to the end of the section, are for Never Hinged items.

Figure of Value — D7

1934 Photo. Wmk. 210

J130 D7 2f ultra .20 .20
J131 D7 4f ultra .20 .20
J132 D7 6f ultra .20 .20
J133 D7 8f ultra .20 .20
J134 D7 10f ultra .20 .20
J135 D7 12f ultra .20 .20
J136 D7 16f ultra .20 .20
J137 D7 20f ultra .20 .20
J138 D7 40f ultra .55 .20
J139 D7 80f ultra .70 .30
Nos. J130-J139 (10) 2.85 2.10

Coat of Arms and Post Horn — D8

1941

J140 D8 2f brown red .20 .20
J142 D8 4f brown red .20 .20
J143 D8 6f brown red .20 .20
J144 D8 8f brown red .20 .20
J145 D8 10f brown red .25 .20
J146 D8 12f brown red .30 .20
J147 D8 16f brown red .40 .20
J148 D8 20f brown red .50 .20
J150 D8 40f brown red .75 .25
Nos. J140-J150 (9) 3.00 1.85

1941-44 Wmk. 266

J151 D8 2f brown red .20 .20
J152 D8 3f brown red .20 .20
J153 D8 4f brown red .20 .20
J154 D8 6f brown red .20 .20
J155 D8 8f brown red .20 .20
J156 D8 10f brown red .20 .20
J157 D8 12f brown red .20 .20
J158 D8 16f brown red .20 .20
J159 D8 18f brown red ('44) .25 .20
J160 D8 20f brown red .20 .20
J161 D8 24f brown red .25 .20
J162 D8 30f brown red ('44) .20 .20
J163 D8 36f brown red ('44) .20 .20
J164 D8 40f brown red .20 .20
J165 D8 50f brown red .20 .20
J166 D8 60f brown red ('44) .30 .20
Nos. J151-J166 (16) 3.40 3.20

For surcharges see Nos. J167-J185.

Issues of the Republic

Types of Hungary Postage Due Stamps, 1941-44, Surcharged in Carmine

1945 Wmk. 266 Photo. *Perf. 15*

Blue Surface-tinted Paper

J167 D8 10f on 2f brn red .20 .20
J168 D8 10f on 3f brn red .20 .20
J169 D8 20f on 4f brn red .20 .20
J170 D8 20f on 6f brn red 5.50 5.50
J171 D8 20f on 8f brn red .20 .20
J172 D8 40f on 12f brn red .20 .20
J173 D8 40f on 16f brn red .20 .20
J174 D8 40f on 18f brn red .20 .20
J175 D8 60f on 24f brn red .20 .20
J176 D8 80f on 30f brn red .20 .20
J177 D8 90f on 36f brn red .20 .20
J178 D8 1p on 10f brn red .20 .20
J179 D8 1p on 40f brn red .20 .20
J180 D8 2p on 20f brn red .20 .20
J181 D8 2p on 50f brn red .20 .20
J182 D8 2p on 60f brn red .20 .20

Surcharged in Black, Thicker Type

J183 D8 10p on 3f brn red .20 .20
J184 D8 12p on 8f brn red .20 .20
J185 D8 20p on 24f brn red .20 .20
Nos. J167-J185 (19) 9.10 9.10

D9

1946-50 Wmk. 210 *Perf. 15*

Numerals in Deep Magenta

J186 D9 4f magenta .50 .20
J187 D9 10f magenta 1.25 .20
J188 D9 20f magenta .50 .20
J189 D9 30f magenta .50 .20
J190 D9 40f magenta .75 .20
J191 D9 50f mag ('50) 2.25 .50
J192 D9 60f magenta 1.50 .20
J193 D9 1.20fo magenta 2.25 .25
J194 D9 2fo magenta 3.75 .30
Nos. J186-J194 (9) 13.25 2.25

1951 Wmk. 106

Numerals in Deep Magenta

J194A D9 4f magenta .20 .20
J194B D9 10f magenta .20 .20
J194C D9 20f magenta .20 .20
j. "fiellr" 3.75
J194D D9 30f magenta .25 .20
J194E D9 40f magenta .30 .20
J194F D9 50f magenta 1.25 .20
J194G D9 60f magenta .45 .20
J194H D9 1.20fo magenta .75 .20
J194I D9 2fo magenta 1.50 .20
Nos. J194A-J194I (9) 5.10 1.80

Nos. J194A-J194I are found in both large format (about 18x22mm) and small (about 17x21mm).

D10

D11

1951 Unwmk. Typo. *Perf. 14½x15*

Paper with Vertical Lines in Green

Revenue Stamps with Blue Surcharge

J195 D10 8f dark brown .20 .20
J196 D10 10f dark brown .20 .20
J197 D10 12f dark brown .40 .40
Nos. J195-J197 (3) .80 .80

1951 Wmk. 106 Photo. *Perf. 14½*

J198 D11 4f brown .20 .20
J199 D11 6f brown .20 .20
J200 D11 8f brown .20 .20
J201 D11 10f brown .20 .20
J202 D11 14f brown .35 .25
J203 D11 20f brown .20 .20
J204 D11 30f brown .20 .20
J205 D11 40f brown .20 .20
J206 D11 50f brown .25 .20
J207 D11 60f brown .30 .20
J208 D11 1.20fo brown .30 .20
J209 D11 2fo brown .50 .30
Nos. J198-J209 (12) 3.10 2.55

D12

D13

Photo., Numeral Typo. in Black

1953

Numerals 3mm High

J210 D12 4f dull green .20 .20
J211 D12 6f dull green .20 .20
J212 D12 8f dull green .20 .20
J213 D12 10f dull green .20 .20
J214 D12 12f dull green .20 .20
J215 D12 14f dull green .20 .20
J216 D12 16f dull green .20 .20
J217 D12 20f dull green .20 .20
J218 D12 24f dull green .20 .20
J219 D12 30f dull green .20 .20
J220 D12 36f dull green .20 .20
J221 D12 40f dull green .20 .20
J222 D12 50f dull green .20 .20
J223 D12 60f dull green .20 .20
J224 D12 70f dull green .25 .20
J225 D12 80f dull green .30 .20

Numerals 4½mm High

J226 D12 1.20fo dull green .40 .20
J227 D12 2fo dull green .75 .20
a. Small "2" (3mm high) .90 .60
Nos. J210-J227 (18) 4.50 3.60

1st Hungarian postage due stamp, 50th anniv.

Photo., Numeral Typo. in Black on Nos. J228-J243

1958 Wmk. 106 *Perf. 14½*

Size: 21x16½mm

J228 D13 4f red .20 .20
J229 D13 6f red .20 .20
J230 D13 8f red .20 .20
J231 D13 10f red .20 .20
J232 D13 12f red .20 .20
J233 D13 14f red .20 .20
J234 D13 16f red .20 .20
J235 D13 20f red .20 .20
J236 D13 24f red .20 .20
J237 D13 30f red .20 .20
J238 D13 36f red .20 .20
J239 D13 40f red .20 .20
J240 D13 50f red .20 .20
J241 D13 60f red .20 .20
J242 D13 70f red .20 .20
J243 D13 80f red .25 .20

Perf. 12

Size: 31x21mm

J244 D13 1.20fo dk red brn .35 .20
J245 D13 2fo dk red brn .50 .25
Nos. J228-J245 (18) 4.10 3.65

Photo., Numeral Typo. in Black on Nos. J246-J261

1965-69 Unwmk. *Perf. 11½*

Size: 21x16½mm

J246 D13 4f red .20 .20
J247 D13 6f red .20 .20
J248 D13 8f red .20 .20
J249 D13 10f red .20 .20
J250 D13 12f red .20 .20
J251 D13 14f red .20 .20
J252 D13 16f red .20 .20
J253 D13 20f red .20 .20
J254 D13 24f red .20 .20
J255 D13 30f red .20 .20
J256 D13 36f red .20 .20
J257 D13 40f red .20 .20
J258 D13 50f red .20 .20
J259 D13 60f red .20 .20
J260 D13 70f red .20 .20
J261 D13 80f red .20 .20

Perf. 11½x12

Size: 31x21mm

J262 D13 1fo dk red brn ('69) .20 .20
J263 D13 1.20fo dk red brn .25 .20
J264 D13 2fo dk red brn .30 .20
J265 D13 4fo dk red brn ('69) .50 .20
Nos. J246-J265 (20) 4.45 4.00

Mail Plane and Truck — D14

Postal History — D15

Designs: 20f, Money order canceling machine. 40f, Scales in self-service P.O. 80f, Automat for registering parcels. 1fo, Keypunch operator. 1.20fo, Mail plane and truck. 2fo, Diesel mail train. 3fo, Mailman on motorcycle with sidecar. 4fo, Rural mail delivery. 8fo, Automatic letter sorting machine. 10fo, Postman riding motorcycle.

1973-85 Photo. *Perf. 11*

Size: 21x18mm

J266 D14 20f brown & ver .20 .20
J267 D14 40f dl bl & ver .20 .20
J268 D14 80f violet & ver .20 .20
J269 D14 1fo ol grn & ver .20 .20

Perf. 12x11½

Size: 28x22mm

J270 D14 1.20fo green & ver .20 .20
J271 D14 2fo lilac & ver .20 .20
J272 D14 3fo brt blue & ver .25 .20
J273 D14 4fo org brn & ver .35 .20
J274 D14 8fo deep mag & dark red 1.10 .30
J275 D14 10fo green & dark red 1.25 .35
Nos. J266-J275 (10) 4.15 2.25

Issued: 20f-4fo, 12/1973; 8fo, 10fo, 12/16/85.

1987, Dec. 10 Litho. *Perf. 12*

Designs: Excerpt from 18th cent. letter, innovations in letter carrying.

J276 D15 1fo Foot messenger, 16th cent. .20 .20
J277 D15 4fo Post rider, 17th cent. .55 .30
J278 D15 6fo Horse-drawn mail coach, 18th cent. .75 .45
J279 D15 8fo Railroad mail car, 19th cent. 1.00 .60
J280 D15 10fo Mail truck, 20th cent. 1.25 .65
J281 D15 20fo Airplane, 20th cent. 2.25 1.25
Nos. J276-J281 (6) 6.00 3.45

OFFICIAL STAMPS

O1

1921-23 Wmk. 137 Typo. *Perf. 15*

O1 O1 10f brn vio & blk .20 .20
O2 O1 20f ol brn & blk .20 .20
a. Inverted center 500.00 500.00
O3 O1 60f blk brn & blk .20 .20
O4 O1 100f dl rose & blk .20 .20
O5 O1 250f bl & blk .20 .20
O6 O1 350f gray & blk .25 .20
O7 O1 500f lt brn & blk .25 .20
O8 O1 1000f lil brn & blk .25 .20
O9 O1 5k brn ('23) .20 .20
O10 O1 10k choc ('23) .20 .20
O11 O1 15k gray blk ('23) .20 .20
O12 O1 25k org ('23) .20 .20
O13 O1 50k brn & red ('22) .20 .20
O14 O1 100k bis & red ('22) .20 .20
O15 O1 150k grn & red ('23) .20 .20
O16 O1 300k dl red & red ('23) .25 .20
O17 O1 350k vio & red ('23) .30 .20
O18 O1 500k org & red ('22) .30 .20
O19 O1 600k ol bis & red ('23) .80 .50
O20 O1 1000k bl & red ('22) .50 .20
Nos. O1-O20 (20) 5.30 4.30

Counterfeits of No. O2a exist.

Stamps of 1921 Surcharged in Red

1922

O21 O1 15k on 20f ol brn & blk .20 .20
O22 O1 25k on 60f blk brn & blk .20 .20

Stamps of 1921 Overprinted in Red

1923

O23 O1 350k gray & blk .25 .20

With Additional Surcharge of New Value in Red

O24 O1 150k on 100f dl rose & blk .25 .20
O25 O1 2000k on 250f bl & blk .60 .40
Nos. O23-O25 (3) 1.10 .80

1923-24

Paper with Gray Moiré on Face

O26 O1 500k org & red ('23) .25 .20
O27 O1 1000k bl & red ('23) .30 .20
O28 O1 3000k vio & red ('24) .60 .30
O29 O1 5000k bl & red ('24) .70 .50
Nos. O26-O29 (4) 1.85 1.20

1924 Wmk. 133

O30 O1 500k orange & red 1.10 .55
O31 O1 1000k blue & red 1.10 .55

NEWSPAPER STAMPS

Issues of the Monarchy

St. Stephen's Crown and Post Horn
N1 N2

Litho. (#P1), Typo. (#P2)

1871-72 Unwmk. *Imperf.*

P1 N1 (1k) ver red 40.00 15.00
P2 N2 (1k) rose red ('72) 10.00 2.00
a. (1k) vermilion 10.00 2.00
b. Printed on both sides

Reprints of No. P2 are watermarked. Value, $450.

Letter with Crown and Post Horn — N3

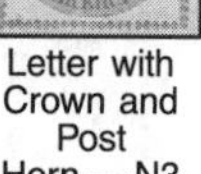
N5

1874

P3 N3 1k orange 3.75 .35

1881 Wmk. "kr" in Oval (132)

P4 N3 1k orange 1.25 .20
a. 1k lemon yellow 16.00 3.50
b. Printed on both sides

1898 Wmk. 135

P5 N3 1k orange 1.25 .20

See watermark note after No. 46.

1900 Wmk. Crown in Circle (135)

P6 N5 (2f) red orange .75 .20

1905 Wmk. Crown (136a)

P7 N5 (2f) red orange 1.00 .20
a. Wmk. 136 ('08) 1.00 .20

1914-22 Wmk. Double Cross (137)

P8 N5 (2f) orange .20 .20
a. Wmk. horiz. 4.50 3.75
P9 N5 (10f) deep blue ('20) .20 .20
P10 N5 (20f) lilac ('22) .20 .20
Nos. P8-P10 (3) .60 .60

For overprints and surcharges see Nos. 1NJ6-1NJ10, 1NP1, 2NP1, 5NP1, 6NP1, 8NP1, 10NP1, Szeged P1.

NEWSPAPER TAX STAMPS

Issues of the Monarchy

NT1

NT2

NT3

Wmk. 91; Unwmk. from 1871

1868 Typo. *Imperf.*

PR1 NT1 1k blue 5.50 1.50
a. Pair, one sideways
PR2 NT2 2k brown 17.50 15.00
a. 2k red brown 275.00 47.50

1868

PR2B NT3 1k blue *9,500. 6,000.*

No. PR2B was issued for the Military Border District only. All used copies are precanceled (newspaper text printed on the stamp). A similar 2k was not issued.

1889-90 Wmk. "kr" in Oval (132)

PR3 NT1 1k blue 2.00 .80
PR4 NT2 2k brown 5.50 4.00

1898 Wmk. Crown in Oval (135)

PR5 NT1 1k blue 7.50 5.50

These stamps did not pay postage, but represented a fiscal tax collected by the postal authorities on newspapers.

Nos. PR3 and PR5 have a tall "k" in "kr."

PARCEL POST STAMPS

Nos. 629, 613, 612, 615, 630, 667 and Type of 1943-45 Overprinted in Black or Carmine

a

b

"Cs." or "Csomag"=Parcel

1946 Wmk. 266 *Perf. 15*

Q1 A118 "Cs. 5-1." on 70f .20 .20
Q2 A109 "Cs. 5-1." on 30f 5.50 5.00
Q3 A99 "Cs. 5-2." on 24f .20 .20
Q4 A118 "Cs. 10-1." on 70f .20 .20
Q5 A118 "Cs. 10-1." on 80f 5.50 5.00
Q6 A118 "Cs. 10-2." on 80f .20 .20
Q7 A99 "Csomag 5kg." on 2p on 4f (C+Bk) .20 .20
Q8 A118 "Csomag 10kg." on 30f copper red, *bl* .20 .20
Nos. Q1-Q8 (8) 12.20 11.20

No. Q8 was not issued without overprint.

Catalogue values for unused stamps in this section, from this point to the end of the section, are for Never Hinged items.

No. 796 Surcharged with New Value in Red or Black

1954 Wmk. 210

Q9 A144 1.70fo on 1.40fo 1.00 .20
Q10 A144 2fo on 1.40fo (Bk) 1.25 .30
Q11 A144 3fo on 1.40fo 1.50 .50
Nos. Q9-Q11 (3) 3.75 1.00

OCCUPATION STAMPS

Issued under French Occupation

ARAD ISSUE

The overprints on this issue have been extensively forged. Even the inexpensive values are difficult to find with genuine overprints. Values are for genuine overprints. Collectors should be aware that stamps sold "as is" are likely to be forgeries, and unexpertized collections should be assumed to consist of mostly forged stamps. Education plus working with knowledgeable dealers is mandatory in this collecting area. More valuable stamps should be expertized.

Stamps of Hungary Overprinted in Red or Blue

On Issue of 1916-18

1919 Wmk. 137 *Perf. 15, 14*

1N1	A9	2f brn org (R)	1.60	1.60
1N2	A9	3f red lil (R)	.75	.75
1N3	A9	5f green (R)	20.00	20.00
1N4	A9	6f grnsh bl (R)	1.90	1.90
a.		Inverted overprint	30.00	30.00
1N5	A9	10f rose red	4.00	4.00
1N6	A9	15f violet (R)	1.75	1.75
a.		Double overprint	50.00	50.00
1N7	A9	20f gray brn (R)	50.00	50.00
1N8	A9	35f brown (R)	65.00	65.00
1N9	A9	40f ol grn (R)	37.50	37.50
1N10	A10	50f red vio & lil	6.00	6.00
1N11	A10	75f brt bl & pale bl	2.00	2.00
1N12	A10	80f grn & pale grn	2.75	2.75
1N13	A10	1k red brn & cl	15.00	15.00
1N14	A10	2k ol brn & bis	3.00	3.00
a.		Inverted overprint	50.00	50.00
1N15	A10	3k dk vio & ind	17.50	17.50
1N16	A10	5k dk brn & lt brn	13.50	13.50
1N17	A10	10k vio brn & vio	70.00	70.00
		Nos. 1N1-1N17 (17)	312.25	312.25

With Additional Surcharge:

a

b

c

d

1N18	A9 (a)	45f on 2f brn org	8.00	8.00
1N19	A9 (b)	45f on 2f brn org	8.00	8.00
1N20	A9 (c)	50f on 3f red lil	8.00	8.00
1N21	A9 (d)	50f on 3f red lil	8.00	8.00
		Nos. 1N18-1N21 (4)	32.00	32.00

Overprinted On Issue of 1918

1N22	A11	10f scarlet (Bl)	60.00	60.00
1N23	A11	20f dk brn	.90	.90
1N24	A11	25f brt bl	2.40	2.40
a.		Inverted overprint	30.00	30.00
1N25	A12	40f ol grn	3.25	3.25
		Nos. 1N22-1N25 (4)	66.55	66.55

Ovptd. On Issue of 1918-19, Overprinted "Koztarsasag"

1N26	A9	2f brn org	2.00	2.00
a.		Inverted overprint	50.00	50.00
1N27	A9	4f slate gray	2.00	2.00
1N28	A9	5f green	.60	.60
1N29	A9	6f grnsh bl	12.00	12.00
a.		Inverted overprint	30.00	30.00
1N30	A9	10f rose red (Bl)	60.00	60.00
1N31	A9	20f gray brn	15.00	15.00
1N32	A11	25f brt bl	2.75	2.75
a.		Inverted overprint	30.00	30.00
1N33	A9	40f ol grn	2.00	2.00
1N34	A12	40f ol grn	60.00	60.00
a.		Inverted overprint	125.00	125.00
1N35	A12	50f lilac	8.00	8.00
1N36	A10	1k red brn & cl (Bl)	3.25	3.25
1N37	A10	3k dk vio & ind (Bl)	15.00	15.00
		Nos. 1N26-1N37 (12)	182.60	182.60

No. 1N36 With Additional Surcharge:

e

f

1N38	A10 (e)	10k on 1k	13.50	13.50
1N39	A10 (f)	10k on 1k	13.50	13.50

On Issue of 1919
Inscribed "MAGYAR POSTA"

1N40	A13	10f red (Bl)	6.50	6.50

SEMI-POSTAL STAMPS

Hungarian Semi-Postal Stamps of 1916-17 Overprinted "Occupation francaise" in Blue or Red

1919 Wmk. 137 *Perf. 15*

1NB1	SP3	10f + 2f rose red	65.00	65.00
1NB2	SP4	15f + 2f dl vio (R)	9.50	9.50
1NB3	SP5	40f + 2f brn car	12.50	12.50
		Nos. 1NB1-1NB3 (3)	87.00	87.00

SPECIAL DELIVERY STAMP

Hungarian Special Delivery Stamp of 1916 Overprinted "Occupation francaise"

1919 Wmk. 137 *Perf. 15*

1NE1	SD1	2f gray green & red	.60	.60

POSTAGE DUE STAMPS

Hungarian Postage Due Stamps of 1915 Overprinted "Occupation francaise"

1919 Wmk. 137 *Perf. 15*

1NJ1	D1	2f green & red	7.50	7.50
1NJ2	D1	10f green & red	4.00	4.00
1NJ3	D1	12f green & red	32.50	32.50
1NJ4	D1	15f green & red	42.50	42.50
1NJ5	D1	20f green & red	3.00	3.00

Hungarian Newspaper Stamp of 1914 Surcharged

1NJ6	N5	12f on 2f orange	8.00	8.00
1NJ7	N5	15f on 2f orange	8.00	8.00
1NJ8	N5	30f on 2f orange	8.00	8.00
a.		Double surcharge	50.00	50.00
1NJ9	N5	50f on 2f orange	8.00	8.00
1NJ10	N5	100f on 2f orange	8.00	8.00
		Nos. 1NJ1-1NJ10 (10)	129.50	129.50

NEWSPAPER STAMP

Hungarian Newspaper Stamp of 1914 Overprinted "Occupation francaise"

1919 Wmk. 137 *Imperf.*

1NP1	N5	(2f) orange	1.25	1.25

ISSUED UNDER ROMANIAN OCCUPATION

FIRST DEBRECEN ISSUE

The first Debrecen overprint was applied to numerous other stamps, also in other colors than are listed. These varieties were not sold to the public but to a favored few.

The overprints on this issue have been extensively forged. Even the inexpensive values are difficult to find with genuine overprints. The more extensive note before No. 1N1 also applies to Nos. 2N1-2NP16.

Hungarian Stamps of 1913-19 Overprinted in Blue, Red or Black

1919 Wmk. 137 *Perf. 15, 14½x14*

On Stamps of 1913

2N1	A4	2f olive yellow	*90.00*	*90.00*
2N2	A4	3f orange	*125.00*	*125.00*
2N3	A4	6f olive grn (R)	50.00	50.00

On Stamps of 1916

2N4	A8	10f rose	75.00	75.00
2N5	A8	15f violet (Bk)	65.00	65.00

On Stamps of 1916-18

2N6	A9	2f brown org	1.50	1.50
2N7	A9	3f red lilac	.70	.70
2N8	A9	5f green	4.75	4.75
2N9	A9	6f grnsh bl (R)	1.60	1.60
2N10	A9	15f violet (Bk)	.80	.80
2N11	A9	20f gray brn	*125.00*	*125.00*
2N12	A9	25f dull bl (Bk)	4.50	4.50
2N13	A9	35f brown	60.00	60.00
2N14	A9	40f olive grn	3.75	3.75
2N15	A10	50f red vio & lil	8.25	8.25
2N16	A10	75f brt bl & pale bl (Bk)	2.00	2.00
2N17	A10	80f grn & pale grn (R)	3.50	3.50
2N18	A10	1k red brn & cl	4.75	4.75
2N19	A10	2k ol brn & bis (Bk)	1.75	1.75
2N20	A10	3k dk vio & ind (R)	30.00	30.00
a.		Blue overprint	*65.00*	*65.00*
b.		Black overprint	*250.00*	*250.00*
2N21	A10	5k dk brn & lt brn (Bk)	27.50	27.50
2N22	A10	10k vio brn & vio	*160.00*	*160.00*

With New Value Added

2N23	A9	35f on 3f red lil	2.00	2.00
2N24	A9	45f on 2f brn org	2.00	2.00
2N25	A10	3k on 75f brt bl & pale bl (Bk)	4.00	4.00
2N26	A10	5k on 75f brt bl & pale bl (Bk)	3.75	3.75
2N27	A10	10k on 80f grn & pale grn (R)	3.50	3.50

On Stamps of 1918

2N28	A11	10f scarlet	60.00	60.00
2N29	A11	20f dk brown (R)	6.25	6.25
a.		Black overprint	30.00	30.00
b.		Blue overprint	75.00	75.00
2N30	A11	25f brt blue (R)	7.00	7.00
a.		Black overprint	75.00	75.00
2N31	A12	40f olive green	3.00	3.00
2N32	A12	50f lilac	50.00	50.00

On Stamps of 1918-19, Overprinted "Koztarsasag"

2N33	A9	2f brn org	3.00	3.00
2N34	A9	3f red lilac	65.00	65.00
2N35	A9	4f sl gray (R)	1.75	1.75
2N36	A9	5f green	.65	.65
2N37	A9	6f grnsh bl (R)	30.00	30.00
2N38	A9	10f rose red	37.50	37.50
2N39	A11	10f scarlet	25.00	25.00
2N40	A11	15f dp vio (Bk)	45.00	45.00
2N41	A9	20f gray brn	3.25	3.25
2N42	A11	20f dk brn (Bk)	37.50	37.50
b.		Red overprint	50.00	50.00
2N43	A9	40f olive grn	1.75	1.75
2N44	A10	1k red brn & cl	2.75	2.75
2N45	A10	2k ol brn & bis (Bk)	60.00	60.00
2N46	A10	3k dk vio & ind (R)	9.75	9.75
a.		Blue overprint	60.00	60.00
b.		Black overprint	*200.00*	*200.00*
2N47	A10	5k dk & lt brn (Bk)	*225.00*	*225.00*
2N48	A10	10k vio brn & vio	*500.00*	*500.00*
2N49	A11	25f brt bl (R)	3.25	3.25
a.		Black overprint	25.00	25.00
2N50	A12	40f olive grn	*125.00*	*125.00*
2N51	A12	50f lilac	2.25	2.25

On Stamps of 1919

2N52	A13	5f green	.50	.50
2N53	A13	6f grnsh bl (Bk)	22.50	22.50
2N54	A13	10f red	.20	.20
2N55	A13	20f dk brown	.20	.20
2N56	A13	25f dl bl (Bk)	1.25	1.25
2N57	A13	45f orange	15.00	15.00
2N58	A14	5k dk brn & brn	3,000.	3,000.

#2N58 is handstamped. Counterfeits exist.

On No. 103A

2N59	A5a	10f violet brn (R)	50.00	50.00
		Nos. 2N1-2N57,2N59 (58)	*2,254.*	*2,254.*

SEMI-POSTAL STAMPS

Overprinted like Regular Issues in Blue or Black

1919 Wmk. 137 *Perf. 15*

2NB1	SP3	10f + 2f rose red	4.00	4.00
2NB2	SP4	15f + 2f dl vio (Bk)	17.00	17.00
2NB3	SP5	40f + 2f brown car	11.00	11.00
		Nos. 2NB1-2NB3 (3)	32.00	32.00

Same Overprint on Hungary Nos. B58-B60 (with "Köztarsasag")

1919

2NB4	SP3	10f + 2f rose red	42.50	42.50
2NB5	SP4	15f + 2f dl vio (Bk)	75.00	75.00
2NB6	SP5	40f + 2f brown car	32.50	32.50
		Nos. 2NB4-2NB6 (3)	150.00	150.00

SPECIAL DELIVERY STAMP

Hungarian Special Delivery Stamp of 1916 Overprinted like Regular Issues

1919 Wmk. 137 *Perf. 15*

2NE1	SD1	2f gray grn & red (Bl)	3.00	3.00

POSTAGE DUE STAMPS

Hungarian Postage Due Stamps of 1914-19 Overprinted in Black like Regular Issues

1919 Wmk. 137 *Perf. 15*

On Stamp of 1914

2NJ1	D1	50f grn & blk	*125.00*	*125.00*

On Stamps of 1915

2NJ2	D1	1f green & red	62.50	62.50
2NJ3	D1	2f green & red	2.00	2.00
2NJ4	D1	5f green & red	*225.00*	*225.00*
2NJ5	D1	6f green & red	*125.00*	*125.00*
2NJ6	D1	10f green & red	.80	.80
2NJ7	D1	12f green & red	*125.00*	*125.00*
2NJ8	D1	15f green & red	20.00	20.00
2NJ9	D1	20f green & red	4.50	4.50
2NJ10	D1	30f green & red	13.50	13.50

On Stamps of 1918-19, Overprinted "Koztarsasag"

2NJ11	D1	2f green & red	25.00	25.00
2NJ12	D1	3f green & red	30.00	30.00
2NJ13	D1	10f green & red	30.00	30.00
2NJ14	D1	20f green & red	30.00	30.00
2NJ15	D1	40f green & red	30.00	30.00
2NJ16	D1	50f green & red	30.00	30.00
		Nos. 2NJ1-2NJ16 (16)	*878.30*	
		Nos. 2NJ1-2NJ13,2NJ15-2NJ16 (15)		*848.30*

NEWSPAPER STAMP

Hungarian Newspaper Stamp of 1914 Overprinted like Regular Issues

1919 Wmk. 137 *Imperf.*

2NP1	N5	(2f) orange (Bl)	.55	.55
a.		Inverted overprint	50.00	50.00
b.		Double overprint	125.00	125.00

SECOND DEBRECEN ISSUE

Complete forgeries exist of this issue and are often found in large multiples or even complete sheets. Values are for genuine stamps.

Mythical "Turul" — OS5

Throwing Lariat — OS6

Hungarian Peasant OS7

1920 Unwmk. Typo. *Perf. 11½*

3N1	OS5	2f lt brown	2.25	2.25
3N2	OS5	3f red brown	2.25	2.25
3N3	OS5	4f gray	2.25	2.25
3N4	OS5	5f lt green	.50	.50
3N5	OS5	6f slate	2.25	2.25
3N6	OS5	10f scarlet	.50	.50
3N7	OS5	15f dk violet	3.00	3.00
3N8	OS5	20f dk brown	.60	.60
3N9	OS6	25f ultra	1.25	1.25
3N10	OS6	30f buff	.65	.65
3N11	OS6	35f claret	1.25	1.25
3N12	OS6	40f olive grn	.75	.75
3N13	OS6	45f salmon	1.00	1.00
3N14	OS6	50f pale vio	.75	.75
3N15	OS6	60f yellow grn	.90	.90
3N16	OS6	75f Prus blue	.75	.75
3N17	OS7	80f gray grn	.85	.85
3N18	OS7	1k brown red	3.00	3.00
3N19	OS7	2k chocolate	3.00	3.00
3N20	OS7	3k brown vio	2.25	2.25
3N21	OS7	5k bister brn	2.25	2.25
3N22	OS7	10k dull vio	2.25	2.25
		Nos. 3N1-3N22 (22)	34.50	34.50

Thick, Glazed Paper

3N23	OS5	2f lt brown	3.00	3.00
3N24	OS5	3f red brown	3.00	3.00
3N25	OS5	4f gray	3.00	3.00
3N26	OS5	5f lt green	3.00	3.00
3N27	OS5	6f slate	3.00	3.00
3N28	OS5	10f scarlet	.75	.75
3N29	OS5	15f dk vio	3.00	3.00
3N30	OS5	20f dk brown	1.00	1.00
3N31	OS7	80f gray grn	1.50	1.50
3N32	OS7	1k brown red	4.00	4.00
3N33	OS7	1.20k orange	8.00	8.00
3N34	OS7	2k chocolate	4.50	4.50
		Nos. 3N23-3N34 (12)	37.75	37.75

SEMI-POSTAL STAMPS

Carrying Wounded

1920 Unwmk. Typo. *Perf. 11½*

3NB1	SP1	20f green	1.25	1.25
3NB2	SP1	50f gray brn	2.25	2.25
3NB3	SP1	1k blue green	2.25	2.25
3NB4	SP1	2k dk green	2.25	2.25

Colored Paper

3NB5	SP1	20f green, *bl*	3.00	3.00
3NB6	SP1	50f brn, *rose*	3.00	3.00
3NB7	SP1	1k dk grn, *grn*	3.00	3.00
		Nos. 3NB1-3NB7 (7)	17.00	17.00

POSTAGE DUE STAMPS

D1

1920 Typo. *Perf. 15*

3NJ1	D1	5f blue green	1.50	1.50
3NJ2	D1	10f blue green	1.50	1.50
3NJ3	D1	20f blue green	.75	.75
3NJ4	D1	30f blue green	.75	.75
3NJ5	D1	40f blue green	1.25	1.25
		Nos. 3NJ1-3NJ5 (5)	5.75	5.75

TEMESVAR ISSUE

Issued under Romanian Occupation

Forgeries exist of the inverted and color error surcharges.

Hungary Nos. 108, 155, 109, 111, E1 Surcharged

1919 Wmk. 137 *Perf. 15*

4N1	A9	30f on 2f brn org (Bl)	.40	.40
a.		Red surcharge	2.00	2.00
b.		Inverted surcharge (R)	25.00	25.00
4N2	A9	1k on 4f sl gray (R)	.30	.30
4N3	A9	150f on 3f red lil (Bk)	.20	.20
4N4	A9	150f on 5f grn (Bk)	.40	.40
4N5	SD1	3k on 2f gray grn & red (Bk)	.50	.50
a.		Blue surcharge	2.00	2.00
		Nos. 4N1-4N5 (5)	1.80	1.80

POSTAGE DUE STAMPS

D1

D2

1919 Wmk. 137 *Perf. 15*

4NJ1	D1	40f on 15f + 2f vio (Bk)	.50	.50
a.		Red surcharge	2.00	2.00
4NJ2	D2	60f on 2f grn & red (Bk)	2.50	2.50
a.		Red surcharge	8.00	8.00
4NJ3	D2	60f on 10f grn & red (Bk)	1.25	1.25
a.		Red surcharge	4.00	4.00
		Nos. 4NJ1-4NJ3 (3)	4.25	4.25

FIRST TRANSYLVANIA ISSUE

Issued under Romanian Occupation

Both the first and second Transylvania overprints were applied to numerous other stamps and in colors other than listed. These varieties were not sold to the public but to a favored few.

The scarcer values of this issue have been extensively forged. Genuine common values are more easily found.

Issued in Kolozsvar (Cluj)

Hungarian Stamps of 1916-18 Overprinted

1919 Wmk. 137 *Perf. 15, 14*

On Stamp of 1916, White Numerals

5N1	A8	15b violet	4.75	4.75

On Stamps of 1916-18

5N2	A9	2b brown org	.20	.25
5N3	A9	3b red lilac	.20	.25
5N4	A9	5b green	.20	.25
5N5	A9	6b grnsh blue	.40	.40
5N6	A9	15b violet	.20	.25
5N7	A9	25b dull blue	.20	.25
5N8	A9	35b brown	.20	.25
5N9	A9	40b olive grn	.50	.50
5N10	A10	50b red vio & lil	1.00	1.00
5N11	A10	75b brt bl & pale bl	.30	.30
5N12	A10	80b grn & pale grn	.20	.25
5N13	A10	1 l red brn & cl	.20	.25
5N14	A10	2 l ol brn & bis	.60	.60
5N15	A10	3 l dk vio & ind	3.50	3.50
5N16	A10	5 l dk brn & lt brn	2.50	2.50
5N17	A10	10 l vio brn & vio	3.00	3.00

On Stamps of 1918

5N18	A11	10b scarlet	40.00	40.00
5N19	A11	15b dp violet	20.00	20.00
5N20	A11	20b dk brown	.25	.25
a.		Gold overprint	75.00	75.00
b.		Silver overprint	75.00	75.00
5N21	A11	25b brt blue	.65	.65
5N22	A12	40b olive grn	.30	.30

On No. 103A

5N23	A5a	10b violet brn	.35	.35
		Nos. 5N1-5N23 (23)	79.70	80.10

SEMI-POSTAL STAMPS

Hungarian Semi-Postal Stamps of 1913-17 Overprinted like Regular Issues

On Issue of 1913

1919 Wmk. 137 *Perf. 14*

5NB1	SP1	1 l on 1f slate	27.50	27.50
5NB2	SP1	1 l on 2f ol yel	70.00	70.00
5NB3	SP1	1 l on 3f org	37.50	37.50
5NB4	SP1	1 l on 5f emer	3.25	3.25
5NB5	SP1	1 l on 10f car	4.50	4.50
5NB6	SP1	1 l on 12f vio,*yel*	16.00	16.00
5NB7	SP1	1 l on 16f gray grn	6.25	6.25
5NB8	SP1	1 l on 25f ultra	60.00	60.00
5NB9	SP1	1 l on 35f red vio	10.00	10.00
5NB10	SP2	1 l on 1k dl red	60.00	60.00

On Issue of 1916-17

Perf. 15

5NB11	SP3	10b + 2b rose red	.20	.25
5NB12	SP4	15b + 2b dull vio	.20	.25
5NB13	SP5	40b + 2b brn car	.20	.25
		Nos. 5NB1-5NB13 (13)	295.60	295.75

SPECIAL DELIVERY STAMP

Hungarian Special Delivery Stamp of 1916 Overprinted like Regular Issues

1919 Wmk. 137 *Perf. 15*

5NE1	SD1	2b gray grn & red	.30	.30

POSTAGE DUE STAMPS

Hungarian Postage Due Stamps of 1914-18 Overprinted like Regular Issues

On Stamp of 1914

1919 Wmk. 137 *Perf. 15*

5NJ1	D1	50b green & blk	13.00	13.00

On Stamps of 1915

5NJ2	D1	1b green & red	*350.00*	*350.00*
5NJ3	D1	2b green & red	.70	.70
5NJ4	D1	5b green & red	60.00	60.00
5NJ5	D1	10b green & red	.45	.45
5NJ6	D1	15b green & red	20.00	20.00
5NJ7	D1	20b green & red	.40	.40
5NJ8	D1	30b green & red	30.00	30.00
		Nos. 5NJ1-5NJ8 (8)	*474.55*	*474.55*

NEWSPAPER STAMP

Hungarian Newspaper Stamp of 1914 Overprinted like Regular Issues

1919 Wmk. 137 *Imperf.*

5NP1	N5	2b orange	3.75	3.75

SECOND TRANSYLVANIA ISSUE

The scarcer values of this issue have been extensively forged. Genuine common values are more easily found.

Issued in Nagyvarad (Oradea)

Hungarian Stamps of 1916-19 Overprinted

1919 Wmk. 137 *Perf. 15, 14*

On Stamps of 1913-16

6N1	A4	2b olive yel	7.00	7.00
6N2	A4	3b orange	13.00	13.00
6N3	A4	6b olive grn	1.75	1.75
6N4	A4	16b gray grn	37.50	37.50
6N5	A4	50b lake, *bl*	1.75	1.75
6N6	A4	70b red brn & grn	26.00	26.00

On Stamps of 1916-18

6N7	A9	2b brown org	.20	.25
6N8	A9	3b red lilac	.20	.25
6N9	A9	5b green	.30	.30
6N10	A9	6b grnsh blue	1.60	1.60
6N11	A9	10b rose red	2.10	2.10
6N12	A9	15b violet	.20	.25
6N13	A9	20b gray brn	20.00	20.00
6N14	A9	25b dull blue	.30	.30
6N15	A9	35b brown	.45	.45
6N16	A9	40b olive grn	.30	.30
6N17	A10	50b red vio & lil	.60	.60
6N18	A10	75b brt bl & pale bl	.20	.25
6N19	A10	80b grn & pale grn	.30	.30
6N20	A10	1 l red brn & cl	.75	.75
6N21	A10	2 l ol brn & bis	.20	.25
6N22	A10	3 l dk vio & ind	6.50	6.50
6N23	A10	5 l dk brn & lt brn	3.25	3.25
6N24	A10	10 l vio brn & vio	1.50	1.50

On Stamps of 1918

6N25	A11	10b scarlet	3.25	3.25
6N26	A11	20b dk brown	.20	.25
6N27	A11	25b brt blue	.75	.75
6N28	A12	40b olive grn	1.10	1.10

On Stamps of 1918-19, Overprinted "Koztarsasag"

6N29	A9	2b brown org	4.00	4.00
6N30	A9	3b red lilac	.20	.25
6N31	A9	4b slate gray	.20	.25
6N32	A9	5b green	.50	.50
6N33	A9	6b grnsh bl	3.00	3.00
6N34	A9	10b rose red	17.50	17.50
6N35	A9	20b gray brn	2.50	2.50
6N36	A9	40b olive grn	.50	.50
6N37	A10	1 l red brn & cl	.20	.25
6N38	A10	3 l dk vio & ind	.75	.75
6N39	A10	5 l dk brn & lt brn	4.50	4.50
6N40	A11	10b scarlet	*75.00*	*75.00*
6N41	A11	20b dk brown	4.50	4.50
6N42	A11	25b brt blue	1.25	1.25
6N43	A12	50b lilac	.20	.25

On Stamps of 1919
Inscribed "MAGYAR POSTA"

6N44 A13 5b yellow grn .20 .25
6N45 A13 10b red .20 .25
6N46 A13 20b dk brown .40 .40
6N47 A13 25b dull blue 2.00 2.00
6N48 A13 40b olive grn .65 .65
6N49 A14 5 l dk brn & brn 6.50 6.50

On No. 103A

6N50 A5a 10b violet brn .85 .85
Nos. 6N1-6N50 (50) *256.85 257.45*

SEMI-POSTAL STAMPS

Hungarian Semi-Postal Stamps of 1913-17 Overprinted like Regular Issues

On Stamps of 1913

1919 Wmk. 137 *Perf. 14*

6NB1 SP1 1 l on 1f slate 2.25 2.25
6NB2 SP1 1 l on 2f olive yel 8.50 8.50
6NB3 SP1 1 l on 3f orange 2.75 2.75
6NB4 SP1 1 l on 5f emerald .25 .25
6NB5 SP1 1 l on 6f olive grn 2.25 2.25
6NB6 SP1 1 l on 10f carmine .30 .30
6NB7 SP1 1 l on 12f vio, *yel* 60.00 60.00
6NB8 SP1 1 l on 16f gray grn 2.50 2.50
6NB9 SP1 1 l on 20f dk brn 11.00 11.00
6NB10 SP1 1 l on 25f ultra 7.50 7.50
6NB11 SP1 1 l on 35f red vio 7.75 7.75

On Stamp of 1915

Wmk. 135 *Perf. 11½*

6NB12 A4 5b emerald 20.00 20.00

On Stamps of 1916-17

Wmk. 137 *Perf. 15*

6NB13 SP3 10b + 2b rose red 1.25 1.25
6NB14 SP4 15b + 2b dull vio .45 .45
6NB15 SP5 40b + 2b brown car .20 .25
Nos. 6NB1-6NB15 (15) 126.95 127.00

SPECIAL DELIVERY STAMP

Hungarian Special Delivery Stamp of 1916 Overprinted like Regular Issues

1919 Wmk. 137 *Perf. 15*

6NE1 SD1 2b gray grn & red .40 .40

POSTAGE DUE STAMPS

Hungarian Postage Due Stamps of 1915 Overprinted like Regular Issues

1919 Wmk. 137 *Perf. 15*

6NJ1 D1 1b green & red 30.00 30.00
6NJ2 D1 2b green & red .20 .25
6NJ3 D1 5b green & red 9.75 9.75
6NJ4 D1 6b green & red 6.75 6.75
6NJ5 D1 10b green & red .20 .25
6NJ6 D1 12b green & red 1.50 1.50
6NJ7 D1 15b green & red 1.50 1.50
6NJ8 D1 20b green & red .20 .25
6NJ9 D1 30b green & red 1.60 1.60
Nos. 6NJ1-6NJ9 (9) 51.70 51.85

NEWSPAPER STAMP

Hungarian Newspaper Stamp of 1914 Overprinted like Regular Issues

1919 Wmk. 137 *Imperf.*

6NP1 N5 2b orange .45 .45

FIRST BARANYA ISSUE

Issued under Serbian Occupation

The scarcer values of this issue have been extensively forged. Genuine common values are more easily found.

Hungarian Stamps of 1913-18 Overprinted in Black or Red:

On A4, A9, A11, A12

On A10

1919 Wmk. 137 *Perf. 15*

On Issue of 1913-16

7N1 A4 6f olive grn (R) .90 .90
7N2 A4 50f lake, *bl* .20 .20
7N3 A4 60f grn, *salmon* .75 .75
7N4 A4 70f red brn & grn (R) 2.00 2.00
7N5 A4 70f red brn & grn (Bk) .25 .25
7N6 A4 80f dl vio (R) 3.25 3.25

On Issue of 1916-18

7N7 A9 2f brown org (Bk) 4.25 4.25
7N8 A9 2f brown org (R) .20 .20
7N9 A9 3f red lilac (Bk) .20 .20
7N10 A9 3f red lilac (R) .80 .80
7N11 A9 5f green (Bk) .80 .80
7N12 A9 5f green (R) .20 .20
7N13 A9 6f grnsh bl (Bk) 1.75 1.75
7N14 A9 6f grnsh bl (R) 2.00 2.00
7N15 A9 15f violet .35 .35
7N16 A9 20f gray brn 20.00 20.00
7N17 A9 25f dull blue 3.50 3.50
7N18 A9 35f brown 5.75 5.75
7N19 A9 40f olive grn 20.00 20.00
7N20 A10 50f red vio & lil 2.00 2.00
7N21 A10 75f brt bl & pale bl .40 .40
7N22 A10 80f grn & pale grn .65 .65
7N23 A10 1k red brn & cl .55 .55
7N24 A10 2k ol brn & bis .65 .65
7N25 A10 3k dk vio & ind .65 .65
7N26 A10 5k dk brn & lt brn 1.25 1.25
7N27 A10 10k vio brn & vio 4.00 *4.00*

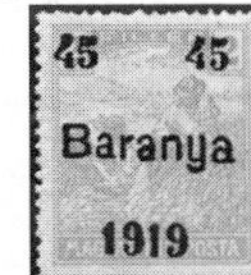

7N28 A9 45f on 2f brn org .35 .35
7N29 A9 45f on 5f green .20 .20
7N30 A9 45f on 15f violet .20 .20

On Issue of 1918

7N31 A11 10f scarlet (Bk) .20 .20
7N32 A11 20f dk brn (Bk) .20 .20
7N33 A11 20f dk brn (R) *65.00* 65.00
7N34 A11 25f dp blue (Bk) 1.90 1.90
7N35 A11 25f dp blue (R) 1.10 1.10
7N36 A12 40f olive grn (Bk) 4.50 4.50
7N37 A12 40f olive grn (R) 30.00 30.00

On Issue of 1918-19 (Koztarsasag)

7N38 A9 2f brown org (Bk) 3.50 3.50
7N39 A12 40f ol grn (Bk) *125.00 125.00*
7N40 A12 40f olive grn (R) 20.00 20.00

With New Value Added

7N41 A9 45f on 2f brn org (Bk) 2.00 2.00
7N42 A9 45f on 2f brn org (R) .45 .45

The overprints were set in groups of 25. In each group two stamps have the figures "1" of "1919" with serifs.

No. 7N33 is considered a proof by some specialists.

SEMI-POSTAL STAMPS

Hungarian Semi-Postal Stamps Overprinted Regular Issue First Type

On Stamp of 1915

1919 Wmk. 137 *Perf. 15*

7NB1 A4 50f + 2f lake, *bl* 16.00 16.00

On Stamps of 1916

7NB2 SP3 10f + 2f rose red .30 .30
7NB3 SP4 15f + 2f dull vio .40 .40
Nos. 7NB1-7NB3 (3) 16.70 16.70

SPECIAL DELIVERY STAMP

SD1

1919 Wmk. 137 *Perf. 15*

7NE1 SD1 105f on 2f gray grn & red 1.25 1.25

POSTAGE DUE STAMPS

Overprinted or Surcharged on Hungary Nos. J29, J32, J35

1919 Wmk. 137 *Perf. 15*

7NJ1 D1 2f green & red 3.75 3.75
7NJ2 D1 10f green & red 1.25 1.25
7NJ3 D1 20f green & red 1.60 1.60

With New Value Added

7NJ4 D1 40f on 2f grn & red 1.50 1.50
Nos. 7NJ1-7NJ4 (4) 8.10 8.10

SECOND BARANYA ISSUE

The scarcer values of this issue have been extensively forged. Genuine common values are more easily found.

Hungarian Stamps of 1916-19 Surcharged in Black and Red

1919 On Stamps of 1916-18

8N1 A9 20f on 2f brn org 4.25 4.25
8N2 A9 50f on 5f green 2.00 2.00
8N3 A9 150f on 15f violet 2.00 2.00
8N4 A10 200f on 75f brt bl & pale bl .75 .75

On Stamp of 1918-19, Overprinted "Koztarsasag"

8N5 A11 150f on 15f dp vio .50 .50

On Stamps of 1919

8N6 A13 20f on 2f brn org .35 .35
8N7 A13 30f on 6f grnsh bl .70 .70
8N8 A13 50f on 5f yel grn .20 .20
8N9 A13 100f on 25f dull bl .25 .25
8N10 A13 100f on 40f ol grn .25 .25
8N11 A13 100f on 45f orange 1.10 1.10
8N12 A13 150f on 20f dk brn 1.40 1.40

On No. 103A

8N13 A5a 10f on 10f vio brn .75 .75
Nos. 8N1-8N13 (13) 14.50 14.50

SPECIAL DELIVERY STAMP

Hungarian Special Delivery Stamp of 1916 Surcharged like Regular Issues

1919 Wmk. 137 *Perf. 15*

8NE1 SD1 10f on 2f gray grn & red .65 .65

NEWSPAPER STAMP

Hungarian Newspaper Stamp of 1914 Surcharged like Regular Issues

1919 Wmk. 137 *Imperf.*

8NP1 N5 10f on 2f orange .80 .80

TEMESVAR ISSUE

Issued under Serbian Occupation

Forgeries exist of the inverted and color error surcharges.

Hungarian Stamps of 1916-18 Surcharged in Black, Blue or Brown:

a

b

1919

9N1 A9(a) 10f on 2f brn org (Bl) .20 .25
a. Black surcharge 15.00 15.00
9N2 A9(b) 30f on 2f brn org .20 .25
a. Inverted surcharge 75.00 75.00
9N3 A11(b) 50f on 20f dk brn (Bl) .20 .25
a. Inverted surcharge
9N4 A9(b) 1k 50f on 15f vio .30 .30
a. Brown surcharge .75 .75
b. Double surcharge (Bk) 50.00 50.00
Nos. 9N1-9N4 (4) .90 1.05

SEMI-POSTAL STAMP

Hungarian Semi-Postal Stamp of 1916 Surcharged in Blue

1919 Wmk. 137 *Perf. 15*

9NB1 SP3 45f on 10f + 2f rose red .20 .25

POSTAGE DUE STAMPS

Hungarian Postage Due Stamps of 1915 Surcharged

1919 Wmk. 137 *Perf. 15*

9NJ1 D1 40f on 2f grn & red .80 .80
9NJ2 D1 60f on 2f grn & red .80 .80
9NJ3 D1 100f on 2f grn & red .80 .80
Nos. 9NJ1-9NJ3 (3) 4.25 4.25

BANAT, BACSKA ISSUE

Issued under Serbian Occupation

Postal authorities at Temesvar applied these overprints. The stamps were available for postage, but were chiefly used to pay postal employees' salaries.

The overprints on this issue have been extensively forged. Even the inexpensive values are difficult to find with genuine overprints. The more extensive note before 1N1 also applies to Nos. 10N1-10NP1.

Hungarian Stamps of 1913-19 Overprinted in Black or Red:

a

b

1919

Type "a" on Stamp of 1913

10N1 A4 50f lake, *blue* 4.00 4.00

Type "a" on Stamps of 1916-18

10N2 A9 2f brown org 4.00 4.00
10N3 A9 3f red lilac 4.00 4.00
10N4 A9 5f green 4.00 4.00
10N5 A9 6f grnsh blue 4.00 4.00
10N6 A9 15f violet 4.00 4.00
10N7 A9 35f brown 35.00 35.00

Type "b"

10N8 A10 50f red vio & lil (R) 30.00 30.00
10N9 A10 75f brt bl & pale bl 4.00 4.00
10N10 A10 80f grn & pale grn 4.00 4.00
10N11 A10 1k red brn & cl 4.00 4.00
10N12 A10 2k ol brn & bis 4.00 4.00
a. Red overprint 37.50 37.50
10N14 A10 3k dk vio & ind 65.00 65.00
10N15 A10 5k dk brn & lt brn 4.00 4.00
10N16 A10 10k vio brn & vio 4.00 4.00

Type "a" on Stamps of 1918

10N17 A11 10f scarlet 4.00 4.00
10N18 A11 20f dk brown 4.00 4.00
10N19 A11 25f brt blue 4.00 4.00
10N20 A12 40f olive grn 4.00 4.00
10N21 A12 50f lilac 4.00 4.00

Type "a" on Stamps of 1919 Inscribed "Magyar Posta"

10N22 A13 10f red *30.00 30.00*
10N23 A13 20f dk brown *30.00 30.00*
10N24 A13 25f dull blue *37.50 37.50*

Type "a" on Stamps of 1918-19 Overprinted "Koztarsasag"

10N25 A9 4f slate gray 3.50 3.50
10N26 A9 4f sl gray (R) 42.50 42.50
10N27 A9 5f green 4.00 4.00
10N28 A9 6f grnsh blue 4.00 4.00
10N29 A9 10f rose red 30.00 30.00
10N30 A11 15f dp violet 30.00 30.00
10N31 A9 20f gray brn 30.00 30.00
10N32 A11 25f brt blue 30.00 30.00
10N33 A9 40f olive grn 3.50 3.50
10N34 A9 40f ol grn (R) 32.50 32.50

Type "b"

10N35 A10 1k red brn & cl 4.00 4.00
10N36 A10 2k ol brn & bis 30.00 30.00
10N37 A10 3k dk vio & ind 30.00 30.00
10N38 A10 5k dk brn & lt brn 30.00 30.00
10N39 A10 10k vio brn & vio 30.00 30.00

Type "a" on Temesvár Issue

10N40 A9 10f on 2f brn org (Bl & Bk) 4.00 4.00
10N41 A9 1k50f on 15f vio 4.00 4.00

10N42 A5a 50f on 10f vio brn 4.00 4.00
Nos. 10N1-10N42 (41) *641.50 641.50*

SEMI-POSTAL STAMPS

Semi-Postal Stamps of 1916-17 Overprinted Type "a" in Black

1919

10NB1 SP3 10f + 2f rose red 4.00 4.00
10NB2 SP4 15f + 2f dull vio 4.00 4.00
10NB3 SP5 40f + 2f brn car 4.00 4.00

Same Overprint on Temesvar Issue

10NB4 SP3 45f on 10f + 2f rose red (Bl & Bk) 4.00 4.00
Nos. 10NB1-10NB4 (4) 16.00 16.00

SPECIAL DELIVERY STAMP

Hungary No. E1 Surcharged in Black

1919

10NE1 SD1 30f on 2f gray grn & red 4.00 4.00

POSTAGE DUE STAMPS

Postage Due Stamps of 1914-15 Overprinted Type "a" in Black

1919

10NJ1 D1 2f green & red 4.00 4.00
10NJ2 D1 10f green & red 4.00 4.00
10NJ3 D1 15f green & red 32.50 32.50
10NJ4 D1 20f green & red 4.00 4.00
10NJ5 D1 30f green & red 30.00 30.00
10NJ6 D1 50f green & blk 30.00 30.00
Nos. 10NJ1-10NJ6 (6) 104.50 104.50

NEWSPAPER STAMP

Stamp of 1914 Overprinted Type "a" in Black

1919

10NP1 N5 (2f) orange 4.00 4.00

SZEGED ISSUE

The "Hungarian National Government, Szeged, 1919," as the overprint reads, was an anti-Bolshevist government which opposed the Soviet Republic then in control at Budapest.

The overprints on this issue have been extensively forged. Even the inexpensive stamps are difficult to find with genuine overprints. The more extensive note before No. 1N1 also applies to Szeged Nos. 1-P1.

Hungary Stamps of 1916-19 Overprinted in Green, Red and Blue

On Stamps of 1916-18

1919 ***Perf. 15, 14***

1 A9 2f brn org (G) 2.25 2.25
2 A9 3f red lilac (G) .75 .75
3 A9 5f green 2.75 2.75
4 A9 6f grnsh blue 32.50 32.50
5 A9 15f violet 3.50 3.50
6 A10 50f red vio & lil 19.00 19.00
7 A10 75f brt bl & pale bl 4.25 4.25
8 A10 80f grn & pale grn 18.00 18.00
9 A10 1k red brn & cl (G) 2.25 2.25
10 A10 2k ol brn & bis 4.75 4.75
11 A10 3k dk vio & ind 7.25 7.25
12 A10 5k dk brn & lt brn 60.00 60.00
13 A10 10k vio brn & vio 60.00 60.00

With New Value Added

14 A9 45f on 3f red lil (R & G) .80 .80
15 A10 10k on 1k red brn & cl (Bl & G) 8.00 8.00

On Stamps of 1918

16 A11 10f scarlet (G) 2.50 2.50
17 A11 20f dk brown .60 .60
18 A11 25f brt blue 22.50 22.50
19 A12 40f olive grn 11.00 11.00

On Stamps of 1918-19 Overprinted "Koztarsasag"

20 A9 3f red lil (G) 42.50 42.50
21 A9 4f slate gray 11.00 11.00
22 A9 5f green 25.00 25.00
23 A9 6f grnsh blue 15.00 15.00
24 A9 10f rose red (G) 32.50 32.50
25 A11 10f scarlet) 30.00 30.00
26 A11 15f dp violet 10.00 10.00
27 A9 20f gray brown 50.00 50.00
28 A11 20f dk brown 65.00 65.00
29 A11 25f brt blue 20.00 20.00
30 A9 40f olive 2.25 2.25
31 A12 50f lilac 1.75 1.75
32 A10 3k dk vio & ind 37.50 37.50

With New Value Added

33 A9 20f on 2f brn org (R & G) .80 .80

On Stamps of 1919 Inscribed "Magyar Posta"

34 A13 20f dk brown 60.00 60.00
35 A13 25f dull blue 1.75 1.75
Nos. 1-35 (35) 667.70 667.70

SEMI-POSTAL STAMPS

Szeged Overprint on Semi-Postal Stamps of 1916-17 in Green or Red

1919

B1 SP3 10f + 2f rose red (G) .85 .85
B2 SP4 15f + 2f dl vio (R) 3.75 3.75
B3 SP5 40f + 2f brn car (G) 10.00 10.00

With Additional Overprint "Koztarsasag"

B4 SP5 40f + 2f brn car (Bk & G) 15.00 15.00
Nos. B1-B4 (4) 29.60 29.60

SPECIAL DELIVERY STAMP

Szeged Overprint on Special Delivery Stamp of 1916 in Red

1919

E1 SD1 2f gray grn & red 11.00 11.00

POSTAGE DUE STAMPS

Szeged Overprint on Stamps of 1915-18 in Red

1919

J1 D1 2f green & red 3.00 3.00
J2 D1 6f green & red 9.75 9.75
J3 D1 10f green & red 3.75 3.75
J4 D1 12f green & red 4.75 4.75
J5 D1 20f green & red 6.00 6.00
J6 D1 30f green & red 9.00 9.00

Red Surcharge

J7 SD1 50f on 2f gray grn & red 2.75 2.75
J8 SD1 100f on 2f gray grn & red 2.75 2.75
Nos. J1-J8 (8) 41.75 41.75

NEWSPAPER STAMP

Szeged Overprint on Stamp of 1914 in Green

1919 **Wmk. 137** ***Imperf.***

P1 N5 (2f) orange .85 .85

ICELAND

'is-lənd

LOCATION — Island in the North Atlantic Ocean, east of Greenland
GOVT. — Republic
AREA — 39,758 sq. mi.
POP. — 272,069 (1997)
CAPITAL — Reykjavik

Iceland became a republic on June 17, 1944. Formerly this country was united with Denmark under the government of King Christian X who, as a ruling sovereign of both countries, was assigned the dual title of king of each. Although the two countries were temporarily united in certain affairs beyond the king's person, both were acknowledged as sovereign states.

96 Skillings = 1 Rigsdaler
100 Aurar (singular "Eyrir") = 1 Krona (1876)

Catalogue values for unused stamps in this country are for Never Hinged items, beginning with Scott 246 in the regular postage section, Scott B7 in the semi-postal section and Scott C21 in the air post section.

Watermarks

Wmk. 112- Crown

Wmk. 113- Crown

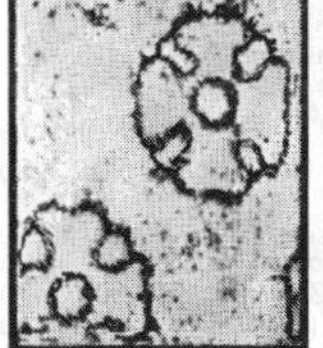

Wmk. 47- Multiple Rosette

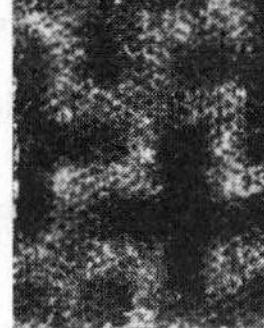

Wmk. 114- Multiple Crosses

Values for unused stamps are for examples with original gum as defined in the catalogue introduction. Very fine examples of Nos. 1-33A and O1-O12 will have centering with perforations clear of the framelines but with design noticeably off center, and Nos. 1-7 and O1-O3 additionally will have some irregular or shorter perforations. Well centered stamps are quite scarce and will command higher prices.

A1

Perf. 14x13½

1873 Typo. Wmk. 112

No.	Type	Description	Unused	Used
1	A1	2s ultra	825.	*1,750.*
a.		Imperf.	525.	
2	A1	4s dark carmine	140.	*825.*
a.		Imperf.	500.	—
3	A1	8s brown	240.	*925.*
a.		Imperf.	250.	
4	A1	16s yellow	1,250.	*2,000.*
a.		Imperf.	300.	

Perf. 12½

No.	Type	Description	Unused	Used
5	A1	3s gray	400.	*1,250.*
a.		Imperf.	600.	
6	A1	4s carmine	1,100.	*1,750.*
7	A1	16s yellow	90.	*500.*

Fake and favor cancellations are often found on Nos. 1-7. Values are considerably less than those shown. The imperforate varieties lack gum.

A2

1876

No.	Type	Description	Unused	Used
8	A2	5a blue	275.00	*600.00*

Perf. 14x13½

No.	Type	Description	Unused	Used
9	A2	5a blue	325.00	*675.00*
a.		Imperf.	1,600.	
10	A2	6a gray	100.00	24.00
11	A2	10a carmine	175.00	6.25
a.		Imperf.	450.00	*575.00*
12	A2	16a brown	87.50	40.00
13	A2	20a dark violet	26.00	*400.00*
14	A2	40a green	82.50	*200.00*

Fake and favor cancellations are often found on No. 13 and value is considerably less than that shown.

A3
Small "3"

A3a
Large "3"

1882-98

No.	Type	Description	Unused	Used
15	A3	3a orange	50.00	15.00
16	A2	5a green	40.00	10.00
17	A2	20a blue	250.00	40.00
a.		20a ultramarine	575.00	250.00
18	A2	40a red violet	35.00	35.00
a.		Perf. 13 ('98)	*4,000.*	
19	A2	50a bl & car ('92)	72.50	*82.50*
20	A2	100a brn & vio ('92)	67.50	*110.00*
		Nos. 15-20 (6)	515.00	*292.50*

See note after No. 68.

1896-1901 ***Perf. 13***

No.	Type	Description	Unused	Used
21	A3	3a orange ('97)	77.50	9.25
22	A3a	3a yellow ('01)	4.00	*18.00*
23	A2	4a rose & gray ('99)	16.00	*18.00*
24	A2	5a green	3.00	2.50
25	A2	6a gray ('97)	14.00	*15.00*
26	A2	10a carmine ('97)	7.25	2.50
27	A2	16a brown	62.50	*92.50*
28	A2	20a dull blue ('98)	40.00	30.00
a.		20a dull ultramarine	350.00	35.00
29	A2	25a yel brown & blue ('00)	16.00	*27.50*
30	A2	50a bl & car ('98)	350.00	*550.00*

See note after No. 68.
For surcharges see Nos. 31-33A, 45-68.

Black and Red Surcharge

Surcharged þrir 3

1897 ***Perf. 13***

No.	Type	Description	Unused	Used
31	A2	3a on 5a green	400.	350.
a.		Perf. 14x13½		*3,100.*
b.		Inverted surcharge	925.	775.

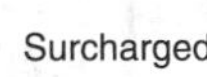

Surcharged

No.	Type	Description	Unused	Used
32	A2	3a on 5a green	575.	500.
a.		Inverted surcharge	1,000.	800.
b.		Perf. 14x13½	*9,000.*	*1,750.*

Unused value for #32b is for stamp without gum.

Black Surcharge

Surcharged þrir

No.	Type	Description	Unused	Used
33	A2	3a on 5a green	750.	650.
b.		Inverted surcharge	1,200.	1,000.

þrir

Surcharged

No.	Type	Description	Unused	Used
33A	A2	3a on 5a green	550.	450.
c.		Inverted surcharge	950.	800.

Excellent counterfeits are known.

King Christian IX — A4

1902-04 Wmk. 113 ***Perf. 13***

No.	Type	Description	Unused	Used
34	A4	3a orange	5.00	3.25
35	A4	4a gray & rose	3.25	1.10
36	A4	5a yel green	25.00	1.00
37	A4	6a gray brown	17.00	9.00
38	A4	10a car rose	5.00	1.00
39	A4	16a chocolate	7.00	*9.00*
40	A4	20a deep blue	2.50	*4.00*
a.		Inscribed "PJONUSTA"	50.00	*75.00*
41	A4	25a brn & grn	3.50	*6.00*
42	A4	40a violet	4.00	*5.50*
43	A4	50a gray & bl blk	5.00	*21.00*
44	A4	1k sl bl & yel brn	6.00	*9.00*
44A	A4	2k olive brn & brt blue ('04)	25.00	*65.00*
44B	A4	5k org brn & slate blue ('04)	110.00	*200.00*
		Nos. 34-44B (13)	218.25	*334.85*

For surcharge see No. 142.

Stamps of 1882-1901 Overprinted

1902-03 Wmk. 112 ***Perf. 13***

Red Overprint

No.	Type	Description	Unused	Used
45	A2	5a green	.50	*6.50*
a.		Inverted overprint	37.50	55.00
b.		"I" before Gildi omitted	90.00	
c.		'03-'03	190.00	
d.		02'-'03	190.00	
e.		Pair, one without overprint	75.00	
46	A2	6a gray	.50	*6.50*
a.		Double overprint	47.50	
b.		Inverted overprint	37.50	
c.		'03-'03	275.00	
d.		02'-'03	275.00	
e.		Pair, one with invtd. ovpt.	190.00	
f.		Pair, one without overprint	110.00	
g.		As "f", inverted	150.00	
47	A2	20a dull blue	.70	*8.50*
a.		Inverted overprint	29.00	*42.50*
b.		"I" before Gildi omitted	75.00	
c.		02'-'03	240.00	
48	A2	25a yel brn & bl	.70	*13.50*
a.		Inverted overprint	37.50	*47.50*
b.		'03-'03	175.00	
c.		02'-'03	175.00	
d.		Double overprint	92.50	

Black Overprint

No.	Type	Description	Unused	Used
49	A3	3a orange	140.00	*400.00*
b.		Inverted overprint	500.00	
c.		"I" before Gildi omitted	225.00	
d.		'03-'03	275.00	
e.		02'-'03	275.00	
50	A3a	3a yellow	1.00	*1.75*
a.		Double overprint	240.00	
b.		Inverted overprint	37.50	47.50
c.		"I" before Gildi omitted	175.00	
d.		02'-'03	225.00	
51	A2	4a rose & gray	30.00	*45.00*
a.		Double overprint	140.00	
b.		Inverted overprint	85.00	
c.		Dbl. ovpt., one invtd.	190.00	
d.		"I" before Gildi omitted	140.00	
e.		'03-'03	240.00	
f.		02'-'03	240.00	
g.		Pair, one with invtd. ovpt.	190.00	
52	A2	5a green	275.00	*400.00*
a.		Inverted overprint	350.00	
b.		Pair, one without overprint	425.00	
c.		As "b", inverted	475.00	
53	A2	6a gray	475.00	*650.00*
a.		Inverted overprint	575.00	
b.		Pair, one without overprint	550.00	
54	A2	10a carmine	1.00	*8.00*
a.		Inverted overprint	37.50	55.00
b.		Pair, one without overprint	65.00	
55	A2	16a brown	19.00	*30.00*
a.		Inverted overprint	92.50	
b.		"I" before Gildi omitted	140.00	
c.		'03-'03	240.00	
d.		02'-'03	240.00	
56	A2	20a dull blue	*6,500.*	
a.		Inverted overprint	*7,000.*	
57	A2	25a yel brn & bl	*6,000.*	
a.		Inverted overprint	*6,500.*	
58	A2	40a red vio	.70	*30.00*
a.		Inverted overprint	37.50	
59	A2	50a bl & car	3.00	*55.00*
a.		Double overprint	190.00	
b.		02'-'03	190.00	
c.		'03-'03	190.00	

Perf. 14x13½

Red Overprint

No.	Type	Description	Unused	Used
60	A2	5a green	1,200.	—
a.		'03-'03	—	
b.		02'-'03	—	
61	A2	6a gray	1,200.	—
a.		02'-'03	—	
62	A2	20a blue	*3,500.*	—

Black Overprint

No.	Type	Description	Unused	Used
63	A3	3a orange	750.00	*1,200.*
a.		Inverted overprint	1,000.	
b.		02'-'03	1,100.	
c.		'03-'03	1,100.	
64	A2	10a carmine	*4,500.*	—
65	A2	16a brown	800.00	*1,200.*
a.		Inverted overprint	1,100.	
b.		02'-'03	1,100.	
d.		'03-'03	1,100.	
65C	A2	20a dull blue	*4,500.*	—
66	A2	40a red vio	15.00	*75.00*
a.		Inverted overprint	—	—
b.		'03-'03	190.00	
c.		02'-'03	190.00	
67	A2	50a bl & car	30.00	*100.00*
a.		Inverted overprint	140.00	
b.		'03-'03	225.00	
c.		02'-'03	225.00	
d.		As "c," inverted	—	
68	A2	100a brn & vio	40.00	*65.00*
a.		Inverted overprint	100.00	
b.		02'-'03	190.00	
c.		'03-'03	190.00	

"I GILDI" means "valid."

In 1904 Nos. 20, 22-30, 45-59 (except 49, 52, 53, 56 and 57) and No. 68 were reprinted for the Postal Union. The reprints are perforated 13 and have watermark type 113. Value $50 each. Without overprint, $100 each.

Kings Christian IX and Frederik VIII — A5

Typo., Center Engr.

1907-08 Wmk. 113 *Perf. 13*

No.	Type	Description	Unused	Used
71	A5	1e yel grn & red	1.40	.90
72	A5	3a yel brn & ocher	3.00	1.00
73	A5	4a gray & red	1.50	1.40
74	A5	5a green	60.00	1.00
75	A5	6a gray & gray brn	30.00	2.50
76	A5	10a scarlet	100.00	1.10
77	A5	15a red & green	6.00	1.00
78	A5	16a brown	7.00	*32.50*
79	A5	20a blue	7.00	5.00
80	A5	25a bis brn & grn	4.75	*10.00*
81	A5	40a claret & vio	5.00	*12.00*
82	A5	50a gray & vio	6.00	*12.00*
83	A5	1k blue & brn	20.00	*55.00*
84	A5	2k dk brn & dk grn	27.50	*60.00*
85	A5	5k brn & slate	150.00	*300.00*
		Nos. 71-85 (15)	429.15	*495.40*

See Nos. 99-107.

For surcharges and overprints see Nos. 130-138, 143, C2, O69.

Jon Sigurdsson A6

Frederik VIII A7

1911 Typo. and Embossed

No.	Type	Description	Unused	Used
86	A6	1e olive green	2.00	2.00
87	A6	3a light brown	3.75	*11.00*
88	A6	4a ultramarine	1.00	*1.50*
89	A6	6a gray	10.00	*20.00*
90	A6	15a violet	12.00	1.50
91	A6	25a orange	21.00	*40.00*
		Nos. 86-91 (6)	49.75	*76.00*

Sigurdsson (1811-79), statesman and author.

For surcharge see No. 149.

1912, Feb. 17

No.	Type	Description	Unused	Used
92	A7	5a green	25.00	10.00
93	A7	10a red	25.00	10.00
94	A7	20a pale blue	37.50	15.00
95	A7	50a claret	8.00	*30.00*
96	A7	1k yellow	25.00	*62.50*
97	A7	2k rose	20.00	*50.00*
98	A7	5k brown	125.00	*175.00*
		Nos. 92-98 (7)	265.50	*352.50*

For surcharges and overprints see Nos. 140-141, O50-O51.

Type of 1907-08 and

Christian X — A8

Typo., Center Engr.

1915-18 Wmk. 114 *Perf. 14x14½*

No.	Type	Description	Unused	Used
99	A5	1e yel grn & red	7.00	*15.00*
100	A5	3a bister brn	3.50	2.40
101	A5	4a gray & red	3.50	*8.00*
102	A5	5a green	75.00	1.10
103	A5	6a gray & gray brn	15.00	*110.00*
104	A5	10a scarlet	3.00	1.00
107	A5	20a blue	175.00	19.00
		Nos. 99-107 (7)	282.00	*156.50*

Revenue cancellations consisting of "TOLLUR" boxed in frame are found on stamps used to pay the tax on parcel post packages entering Iceland.

1920-22 Typo.

No.	Type	Description	Unused	Used
108	A8	1e yel grn & red	.70	*1.00*
109	A8	3a bister brn	4.50	*12.50*
110	A8	4a gray & red	3.50	2.10
111	A8	5a green	1.50	*1.60*
112	A8	5a ol green ('22)	3.25	1.25
113	A8	6a dark gray	10.00	6.75
114	A8	8a dark brown	6.00	2.00
115	A8	10a red	1.50	*9.00*
116	A8	10a green ('21)	2.50	1.40
117	A8	15a violet	32.50	1.10
118	A8	20a deep blue	2.00	*14.00*
119	A8	20a choc ('22)	45.00	1.25
120	A8	25a brown & grn	13.50	1.40
121	A8	25a red ('21)	11.00	*40.00*
		Revenue cancellation		3.25
122	A8	30a red & green	45.00	3.00
		Revenue cancellation		7.50
123	A8	40a claret	40.00	2.50
124	A8	40a dk bl ('21)	65.00	12.00
		Revenue cancellation		8.25
125	A8	50a dk gray & cl	150.00	10.00
		Revenue cancellation		11.00
126	A8	1k dp bl & dk brn	75.00	1.50
		Revenue cancellation		1.40
127	A8	2k ol brn & myr green	175.00	25.00
		Revenue cancellation		2.50
128	A8	5k brn & ind	45.00	13.00
		Revenue cancellation		2.50
		Nos. 108-128 (21)	732.45	*162.35*

See Nos. 176-187, 202.

For surcharges and overprints see Nos. 139, 150, C1, C9-C14, O52, O70-O71.

1921-25 Wmk. 113 *Perf. 13*

No.	Type	Description	Unused	Used
130	A4	5a on 16a brown	3.00	*25.00*
131	A5	5a on 16a brown	2.00	*7.00*
132	A4	20a on 25a brn & green	6.00	7.00
133	A5	20a on 25a bis brn & green	4.00	*7.00*
134	A4	20a on 40a violet	7.00	*17.00*
135	A5	20a on 40a cl & vio	8.00	*17.50*
137	A4	30a on 50a gray & bl blk ('25)	25.00	*30.00*
		Revenue cancellation		13.00
138	A9	50a on 5k org brn & sl bl ('25)	50.00	42.50
		Revenue cancellation		13.00
		Nos. 130-138 (8)	105.00	*153.00*

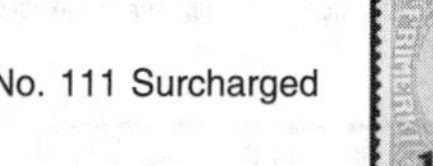

No. 111 Surcharged

1922 Wmk. 114 *Perf. 14x14½*

No.	Type	Description	Unused	Used
139	A8	10a on 5a green	5.00	2.50

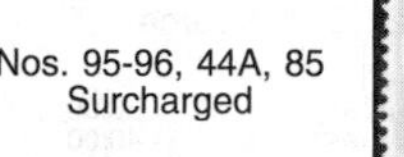

Nos. 95-96, 44A, 85 Surcharged

1924-30 Wmk. 113 *Perf. 13*

No.	Type	Description	Unused	Used
140	A7	10k on 50a ('25)	210.00	*375.00*
		Revenue cancellation		27.50
141	A7	10k on 1k	275.00	*500.00*
		Revenue cancellation		52.50
142	A4	10k on 2k ('29)	55.00	25.00
		Revenue cancellation		7.50
143	A5	10k on 5k ('30)	350.00	500.00
		Revenue cancellation		18.00

"Tollur" is a revenue cancellation.

Landing the Mail — A12

Designs: 7a, 50a, Landing the mail. 10a, 35a, View of Reykjavik. 20a, Museum building.

Perf. 14x15

1925, Sept. 12 Typo. Wmk. 114

No.	Type	Description	Unused	Used
144	A12	7a yel green	35.00	6.50
145	A12	10a dp bl & brn	35.00	.60
146	A12	20a vermilion	35.00	.60
147	A12	35a deep blue	57.50	8.00
148	A12	50a yel grn & brn	57.50	1.25
		Nos. 144-148 (5)	220.00	16.95

No. 91 Surcharged

1925 Wmk. 113 *Perf. 13*

No.	Type	Description	Unused	Used
149	A6	2k on 25a orange	90.00	*110.00*
		Revenue cancellation		12.50

No. 124 Surcharged in Red

1926

No.	Type	Description	Unused	Used
150	A8	1k on 40a dark blue	110.00	30.00
		Revenue cancellation		19.00

Parliament Building A15

Designs: 5a, Viking ship in storm. 7a, Parliament meeting place, 1690. 10a, Viking funeral. 15a, Vikings naming land. 20a, The dash for Thing. 25a, Gathering wood. 30a, Thingvalla Lake. 35a, Iceland woman in national costume. 40a, Iceland flag. 50a, First Althing, 930 A.D. 1k, Map of Iceland. 2k, Winter-bound home. 5k, Woman spinning. 10k, Viking Sacrifice to Thor.

Perf. 12½x12

1930, Jan. 1 Litho. Unwmk.

No.	Type	Description	Unused	Used
152	A15	3a dull vio & gray vio	3.00	*8.00*
153	A15	5a dk bl & sl grn	3.00	*8.00*
154	A15	7a grn & gray grn	2.50	*8.00*
155	A15	10a dk vio & lilac	8.00	*15.00*
156	A15	15a dp ultra & bl gray	2.00	*8.50*
157	A15	20a rose red & sal	35.00	*70.00*
a.		Double impression	275.00	
158	A15	25a dk brn & lt brown	6.00	*12.00*
159	A15	30a dk grn & sl grn	5.00	*11.50*
160	A15	35a ultra & bl gray	5.50	*11.00*
161	A15	40a dk ultra, red & slate grn	5.00	*11.50*
162	A15	50a red brn & cinnamon	50.00	*125.00*
163	A15	1k ol grn & gray green	50.00	*125.00*
164	A15	2k turq bl & gray green	70.00	*140.00*
165	A15	5k org & yellow	40.00	*110.00*
166	A15	10k mag & dl rose	40.00	*110.00*
		Nos. 152-166 (15)	325.00	*773.50*

Millenary of the "Althing," the Icelandic Parliament, oldest in the world.

Imperfs were privately printed.

For overprints see Nos. O53-O67.

Gullfoss (Golden Falls) — A30

1931-32 Unwmk. Engr. *Perf. 14*

No.	Type	Description	Unused	Used
170	A30	5a gray	11.50	.80
171	A30	20a red	10.00	.25
172	A30	35a ultramarine	20.00	11.50
		Revenue cancellation		1.25
173	A30	60a red lil ('32)	10.00	1.00
174	A30	65a red brn ('32)	1.75	1.00
175	A30	75a grnsh bl ('32)	80.00	26.00
		Revenue cancellation		3.75
		Nos. 170-175 (6)	133.25	40.55

Issued: 5a-35a, Dec. 15; 60a-75a, May 30.

Type of 1920 Christian X Issue Redrawn

Perf. 14x14½

1931-33 Typo. Wmk. 114

No.	Type	Description	Unused	Used
176	A8	1e yel grn & red	.70	*1.00*
177	A8	3a bister brown	8.50	*12.00*
		Revenue cancellation		6.25
178	A8	4a gray & red	1.50	1.10
179	A8	6a dark gray	1.50	*3.25*
180	A8	7a yel grn ('33)	.50	1.50
181	A8	10a chocolate	100.00	.95
182	A8	25a brn & green	15.00	3.00
		Revenue cancellation		2.50
183	A8	30a red & green	25.00	5.00
184	A8	40a claret	200.00	18.00
		Revenue cancellation		9.00
185	A8	1k dk bl & lt brn	35.00	6.50
		Revenue cancellation		2.50
186	A8	2k choc & dk grn	200.00	62.50
		Revenue cancellation		6.25
187	A8	10k yel grn & blk	240.00	160.00
		Revenue cancellation		9.00
		Nos. 176-187 (12)	827.70	274.80

On the redrawn stamps the horizontal lines of the portrait and the oval are closer together than on the 1920 stamps and are crossed by many fine vertical lines.

See No. 202.

Dynjandi Falls — A31

Mount Hekla — A32

Perf. 12½

1935, June 28 Engr. Unwmk.

193 A31 10a blue 19.00 .20

Never hinged 55.00

194 A32 1k greenish gray 35.00 .20

Never hinged 90.00

Matthias Jochumsson — A33

1935, Nov. 11

195 A33 3a gray green .60 *3.50*

196 A33 5a gray 12.00 1.10

197 A33 7a yel green 16.00 1.50

198 A33 35a blue .50 *1.10*

Nos. 195-198 (4) 29.10 *7.20*

Set, never hinged 80.00

Birth cent. of Matthias Jochumsson, poet.

For surcharges see Nos. 212, 236.

King Christian X — A34

1937, May 14 *Perf. 13x12½*

199 A34 10a green 1.75 *20.00*

200 A34 30a brown 1.75 *8.50*

201 A34 40a claret 1.75 *8.50*

Nos. 199-201 (3) 5.25 *37.00*

Set, never hinged 9.50

Reign of Christian X, 25th anniv.

Christian X Type of 1931-33

1937 Unwmk. Typo. *Perf. 11½*

202 A8 1e yel grn & red .70 *1.60*

Never hinged 1.50

Geyser

A35 A36

1938-47 Engr. *Perf. 14*

203 A35 15a dp rose vio 5.00 *10.00*

a. Imperf., pair *550.00*

Never hinged 600.00

204 A35 20a rose red 20.00 .20

205 A35 35a ultra .60 .90

206 A36 40a dk brn ('39) 10.00 *25.00*

207 A36 45a brt ultra ('40) .70 .90

208 A36 50a dk slate grn 18.00 .90

208A A36 60a brt ultra ('43) 5.00 1.00

c. Perf. 11½ ('47) 2.50 *9.00*

Never hinged (#208Ac) 5.00

208B A36 1k indigo ('45) 1.60 .25

d. Perf. 11½ ('47) 2.50 *9.00*

Never hinged (#208Bd) 5.00

Nos. 203-208B (8) 60.90 *39.15*

Set, never hinged 125.00

University of Iceland A37

1938, Dec. 1 *Perf. 13½*

209 A37 25a dark grn 6.50 *14.00*

210 A37 30a brown 6.50 *14.00*

211 A37 40a brt red vio 6.50 *14.00*

Nos. 209-211 (3) 19.50 *42.00*

Set, never hinged 26.00

20th anniversary of independence.

No. 198 Surcharged with New Value

1939, Mar. 17 *Perf. 12½*

212 A33 5a on 35a blue .70 *1.40*

Never hinged 1.10

a. Double surcharge *150.00*

Never hinged 175.00

Trylon and Perisphere A38

Leif Ericsson's Ship and Route to America A39

Statue of Thorfinn Karlsefni — A40

1939 Engr. *Perf. 14*

213 A38 20a crimson 3.00 *6.00*

214 A39 35a bright ultra 3.50 *7.50*

215 A40 45a bright green 3.75 *9.00*

216 A40 2k dark gray 45.00 *125.00*

Nos. 213-216 (4) 55.25 *147.50*

Set, never hinged 85.00

New York World's Fair.

For overprints see Nos. 232-235.

Codfish — A41

Herring — A42

Flag of Iceland — A43

1939-45 Engr. *Perf. 14, 14x13½*

217 A41 1e Prussian blue .30 *4.00*

a. Perf. 14x13½ 1.25 *4.50*

218 A42 3a dark violet .30 *.70*

a. Perf. 14x13½ 2.00 *7.00*

219 A41 5a dark brown .30 .25

c. Perf. 14x13½ 1.50 1.00

220 A42 7a dark green 5.00 *8.00*

221 A42 10a green ('40) 27.50 .65

b. Perf. 14x13½ 45.00 1.40

Never hinged 125.00

222 A42 10a slate gray ('45) .30 .20

223 A42 12a dk grn ('43) .30 .45

224 A41 25a brt red ('40) 18.00 .20

b. Perf. 14x13½ 40.00 1.75

Never hinged (#224b) 110.00

225 A41 25a hn brn ('45) .25 .20

226 A42 35a carmine ('43) .50 .25

227 A41 50a dk bl grn ('43) .50 .20

Typo.

228 A43 10a car & ultra 2.00 1.10

Nos. 217-228 (12) 55.25 *16.20*

Set, never hinged 110.00

Statue of Thorfinn Karlsefni — A44

1939-45 Engr. *Perf. 14*

229 A44 2k dark gray 2.50 .20

230 A44 5k dk brn ('43) 20.00 .40

231 A44 10k brn yel ('45) 10.00 1.50

Nos. 229-231 (3) 32.50 2.10

Set, never hinged 75.00

1947

Perf. 11½

229a A44 2k 6.75 1.40

230a A44 5k 25.00 1.75

231a A44 10k 10.00 *40.00*

Nos. 229a-231a (3) 41.75 *43.15*

Set, never hinged 125.00

New York World's Fair Issue of 1939 Overprinted "1940" in Black

1940, May 11 *Perf. 14*

232 A38 20a crimson 7.00 *25.00*

233 A39 35a bright ultra 7.00 *25.00*

234 A40 45a bright green 7.00 *25.00*

235 A40 2k dark gray 80.00 *350.00*

Nos. 232-235 (4) 101.00 *425.00*

Set, never hinged 200.00

No. 195 Surcharged in Red

1941, Mar. 6 *Perf. 12½*

236 A33 25a on 3a gray green .75 *1.40*

Never hinged 1.40

Statue of Snorri Sturluson A45

Jon Sigurdsson A46

1941, Nov. 17 Engr. *Perf. 14*

237 A45 25a rose red .80 1.75

238 A45 50a deep ultra 1.00 3.50

239 A45 1k dk olive grn 1.00 3.50

Nos. 237-239 (3) 2.80 8.75

Set, never hinged 5.00

Snorri Sturluson, writer and historian, 700th death anniv.

Republic

1944, June 17 *Perf. 14x13½*

240 A46 10a gray black .30 *.75*

241 A46 25a dk red brn .40 *.75*

242 A46 50a slate grn .40 *.75*

243 A46 1k blue black .70 *.75*

244 A46 5k henna 2.00 *10.00*

245 A46 10k golden brn 30.00 *85.00*

Nos. 240-245 (6) 33.80 *98.00*

Set, never hinged 80.00

Founding of Republic of Iceland, June 17, 1944.

Catalogue values for unused stamps in this section, from this point to the end of the section, are for Never Hinged items.

A47

A48

Eruption of Hekla Volcano: 35a, 60a, Close view of Hekla.

Unwmk.

1948, Dec. 3 Engr. *Perf. 14*

246 A47 12a dark vio brn .20 .40

247 A48 25a green 1.25 .20

248 A47 35a carmine rose .35 .25

249 A47 50a brown 1.60 .20

250 A47 60a bright ultra 5.75 3.25

251 A48 1k orange brown 8.00 .20

252 A48 10k violet black 40.00 .35

Nos. 246-252 (7) 57.15 4.85

Set, hinged 25.00

For surcharge see No. 283.

Pack Train and UPU Monument, Bern — A49

UPU, 75th Anniv.: 35a, Reykjavik. 60a, Map. 2k, Thingvellir Road.

1949, Oct. 9

253 A49 25a dark green .25 *.40*

254 A49 35a deep carmine .25 *.40*

255 A49 60a blue .40 *.90*

256 A49 2k orange red 1.10 1.00

Nos. 253-256 (4) 2.00 *2.70*

Trawler — A50

Jon Arason — A51

Designs: 20a, 75a, 1k, Tractor plowing. 60a, 5k, Flock of sheep. 5a, 90a, 2k, Vestmannaeyjar harbor.

1950-54 *Perf. 13*

257 A50 5a dk brn ('54) .20 .20

258 A50 10a gray .20 .20

259 A50 20a brown .20 .20

260 A50 25a car ('54) .20 .20

261 A50 60a green 9.75 *17.00*

262 A50 75a red org ('52) .35 .20

263 A50 90a carmine .40 .25

264 A50 1k chocolate 4.25 .20

265 A50 1.25k red vio ('52) 14.50 .20

266 A50 1.50k deep ultra 10.00 .40

267 A50 2k purple 18.00 .25

268 A50 5k dark grn 25.00 .80

Nos. 257-268 (12) 83.05 20.10

Set, hinged 35.00

For surcharges see Nos. B12-B13.

1950, Nov. 7 *Perf. 14*

269 A51 1.80k carmine 2.50 *2.75*

270 A51 3.30k green 1.10 *1.75*

Bishop Jon Arason, 400th anniv. of death.

Mail Delivery, 1776 — A52

Design: 3k, Airmail, 1951.

1951, May 13

271 A52 2k deep ultra 2.10 2.00

272 A52 3k dark purple 2.75 2.50

175th anniv. of Iceland's postal service.

Parliament Building — A53

1952, Apr. 1 *Perf. 13x12½*

273 A53 25k gray black 140.00 12.50

Hinged 52.50

Sveinn Björnsson A54

Reykjabok A55

1952, Sept. 1 *Perf. 13½*

274 A54 1.25k deep blue	2.10	.20
275 A54 2.20k deep green	.50	*3.25*
276 A54 5k indigo	7.00	1.10
277 A54 10k brown red	30.00	20.00
Nos. 274-277 (4)	39.60	24.55

Sveinn Björnsson, 1st President of Iceland.

1953, Oct. 1 *Perf. 13½x13*

Designs: 70a, Lettering manuscript. 1k, Corner of 15th century manuscript, "Stjorn." 1.75k, Reykjabok. 10k, Corner from law manuscript.

278 A55 10a black	.20	.20
279 A55 70a green	.25	.25
280 A55 1k carmine	.30	.20
281 A55 1.75k blue	20.00	1.00
282 A55 10k orange brn	8.75	.75
Nos. 278-282 (5)	29.50	2.40

No. 248 Surcharged With New Value and Bars in Black

1954, Mar. 31 *Perf. 14*

283 A47 5a on 35a car rose	.25	.25
a. Bars omitted	75.00	
b. Inverted surcharge	—	

Hannes Hafstein A56

Icelandic Wrestling A57

Portraits: 2.45k, in oval. 5k, fullface.

1954, June 1 **Engr.** *Perf. 13*

284 A56 1.25k deep blue	4.00	.55
285 A56 2.45k dark green	21.00	*32.50*
286 A56 5k carmine	22.50	5.00
Nos. 284-286 (3)	47.50	*38.05*

Appointment of the first native minister to Denmark, 50th anniv.

1955, Aug. 9 **Unwmk.** *Perf. 14*

287 A57 75a shown	.20	.20
288 A57 1.25k Diving	.50	.25

See Nos. 300-301.

Skoga Falls — A58

Ellidaar Power Plant — A59

Waterfalls: 60a, Goda. 2kr, Detti. 5kr, Gull. Electric Power Plants: 1.50kr, Sogs. 2.45kr, Andakilsar. 3kr, Laxar.

Perf. 11½, 13½x14 (A59)

1956, Apr. 4 **Unwmk.**

289 A58 15a vio blue	.20	.20
290 A59 50a dull green	.30	.20
291 A59 60a brown	2.50	*3.25*
292 A59 1.50k violet	27.50	.20
293 A59 2k sepia	1.50	.35
294 A59 2.45k gray black	6.00	*7.00*
295 A59 3k dark blue	5.00	.75
296 A58 5k dark green	12.00	1.25
Nos. 289-296 (8)	55.00	13.20

Telegraph-Telephone Emblem and Map — A60

1956, Sept. 29 **Engr.** *Perf. 13*

297 A60 2.30k ultramarine	.45	*.55*

Telegraph and Telephone service in Iceland, 50th anniv.

Northern Countries Issue

Whooper Swans — A60a

1956, Oct. 30 *Perf. 12½*

298 A60a 1.50k rose red	.50	*1.00*
299 A60a 1.75k ultra	9.50	*10.00*

To emphasize the bonds among Denmark, Finland, Iceland, Norway and Sweden.

Sports Type of 1955

1.50k, Icelandic wrestling. 1.75k, Diving.

1957, Apr. 1 **Engr.** *Perf. 14*

300 A57 1.50k carmine	.90	.25
301 A57 1.75k ultramarine	.35	.25

Type of 1952 Air Post Stamps Plane Omitted

Glaciers: 2k, Snaefellsjokull. 3k, Eiriksjokull. 10k, Oraefajokull.

1957, May 8 *Perf. 13½x14*

302 AP16 2k green	2.50	.30
303 AP16 3k dark blue	3.25	.20
304 AP16 10k reddish brn	5.00	.30
Nos. 302-304 (3)	10.75	.80

Bessastadir, President's Residence A61

1957, Aug. 1 **Engr.** **Unwmk.**

305 A61 25k gray blk	20.00	4.25

Evergreen and Volcanoes A62

Jonas Hallgrimsson A63

1957, Sept. 4 *Perf. 13½x13*

306 A62 35a shown	.20	.20
307 A62 70a Birch	.20	.20

Issued to publicize a reforestation program.

1957, Nov 16

308 A63 5k grn & blk	1.50	.55

150th birth anniv. of Jonas Hallgrimsson, poet.

Willow Herb — A64

Icelandic Pony — A65

1958, July 8 **Litho.** **Unwmk.**

309 A64 1k shown	.20	.20
310 A64 2.50k Wild pansy	.35	.35

1958, Sept. 27 **Engr.**

311 A65 10a gray black	.20	.20
312 A65 2.25k brown	.65	.25

See No. 324.

Flag — A66

Old Icelandic Government Building — A67

Perf. 13½x14

1958, Dec. 1 **Litho.** **Unwmk.**

Size: 17½x21mm

313 A66 3.50k brt ultra & red	1.75	.65

Size: 23x26½mm

314 A66 50k brt ultra & red	6.75	4.50

40th anniversary of Icelandic flag.

1958, Dec. 9 **Photo.** *Perf. 11½*

315 A67 2k deep green	.45	.20
316 A67 4k deep brown	.55	.35

See Nos. 333-334.

Jon Thorkelsson Teaching — A68

1959, May 5 **Engr.** *Perf. 13½*

317 A68 2k green	.40	*.40*
318 A68 3k dull purple	.60	*.60*

Death bicentenary of Jon Thorkelsson, headmaster of Skaholt.

Sockeye Salmon A69

Eider Ducks — A70

Design: 25k, Gyrfalcon.

1959-60 **Engr.** *Perf. 14*

319 A69 25a dark blue	.20	.20
320 A70 90a chestnut & blk	.20	.20
321 A70 2k olive grn & blk	.35	.20
322 A69 5k gray green	7.25	.90

Litho. *Perf. 11½*

323 A70 25k dl pur, gray & yel	12.00	*14.00*
Nos. 319-323 (5)	20.00	*15.50*

Issued: 25k, Mar. 1, 1960; others, Nov. 25.

Pony Type of 1958

1960, Apr. 7 **Engr.** *Perf. 13½x13*

324 A65 1k dark carmine	.30	.20

"The Outlaw" by Einar Jonsson A71

Wild Geranium A72

1960, Apr. 7 *Perf. 14*

325 A71 2.50k reddish brn	.20	.20
326 A71 4.50k ultramarine	.65	.75

World Refugee Year, 7/1/59-6/30/60.

Common Design Types pictured following the introduction.

Europa Issue, 1960

Common Design Type

1960, Sept. 18 **Photo.** *Perf. 11½*

Size: 32½x22mm

327 CD3 3k grn & lt grn	.50	.35
328 CD3 5.50k dk bl & lt bl	.50	*1.10*

1960-62 **Photo.** *Perf. 11½*

Flowers: 50a, Bellflower. 2.50k, Dandelion. 3.50k, Buttercup.

329 A72 50a gray grn, grn & violet ('62)	.20	.20
330 A72 1.20k sep, vio & grn	.20	.20
331 A72 2.50k brn, yel & grn	.20	.20
332 A72 3.50k dl bl, yel & green ('62)	.55	.20
Nos. 329-332 (4)	1.15	.80

See Nos. 363-366, 393-394.

Building Type of 1958

1961, Apr. 11 **Unwmk.** *Perf. 11½*

333 A67 1.50k deep blue	.25	.20
334 A67 3k dark carmine	.25	.20

Jon Sigurdsson A73

Reykjavik A74

Typographed and Embossed

1961, June 17 *Perf. 12½x14*

335 A73 50a crimson	.20	.20
336 A73 3k dark blue	1.10	.90
337 A73 5k deep plum	.60	.55
Nos. 335-337 (3)	1.90	1.65

Jon Sigurdsson (1811-1879), statesman and scholar.

1961, Aug. 18 **Photo.** *Perf. 11½*

338 A74 2.50k blue & grn	.45	.25
339 A74 4.50k lilac & vio bl	.70	.40

Municipal charter of Reykjavik, 175th anniv.

Europa Issue, 1961

Common Design Type

1961, Sept. 18

Size: 32x22½mm

340 CD4 5.50k multicolored	.35	*.55*
341 CD4 6k multicolored	.35	*.55*

Benedikt Sveinsson — A75

University of Iceland — A76

Design: 1.40k, Björn M. Olsen.

1961, Oct. 6 Photo. *Perf. 11½*
342 A75 1k red brown .20 .20
343 A75 1.40k ultramarine .20 .20
344 A76 10k green 1.40 .75
a. Souv. sheet of 3, #342-344, imperf. .45 *1.00*
Nos. 342-344 (3) 1.80 1.15

50th anniv. of the University of Iceland; Benedikt Sveinsson (1827-1899), statesman; and Björn M. Olsen (1850-1919), first rector.

Production Institute — A77

New Buildings: 4k, Fishing Research Institute. 6k, Farm Bureau.

1962, July 6 Unwmk. *Perf. 11½*
345 A77 2.50k ultramarine .35 .25
346 A77 4k dull green .45 .25
347 A77 6k brown .55 .30
Nos. 345-347 (3) 1.35 .80

Europa Issue, 1962
Common Design Type

1962, Sept. 17 *Perf. 11½*
Size: 32½x22½mm
348 CD5 5.50k yel, lt grn & brn .20 *.25*
349 CD5 6.50k lt grn, grn & brn .35 *.50*

Map Showing Submarine Telephone Cable — A78

1962, Nov. 20
Granite Paper
350 A78 5k multicolored 1.10 .55
351 A78 7k grn, lt bl & red .65 .45

Inauguration of the submarine telephone cable from Newfoundland, via Greenland and Iceland to Scotland.

Sigurdur Gudmundsson, Self-portrait A79

Herring Boat A80

5.50k, Knight slaying dragon, Romanesque door from Valthjofsstad Church, ca. 1200 A.D.

1963, Feb. 20 Photo. *Perf. 11½*
352 A79 4k bis brn & choc .50 .30
353 A79 5.50k gray ol & brn .50 .30

National Museum of Iceland, cent., and its first curator, Sigurdur Gudmundsson.

1963, Mar. 21
354 A80 5k multicolored .90 .30
355 A80 7.50k multicolored .25 .20

FAO "Freedom from Hunger" campaign.

View of Akureyri A81

1963, July 2 Unwmk. *Perf. 11½*
356 A81 3k gray green .25 .20

Europa Issue, 1963
Common Design Type

1963, Sept. 16
Size: 32½x23mm
357 CD6 6k org brn & yel .35 .40
358 CD6 7k blue & yellow .35 .40

M.S. Gullfoss A82

1964, Jan. 17 Photo. *Perf. 11½*
359 A82 10k ultra, blk & gray 1.60 1.25
a. Accent on 2nd "E" omitted 17.00 12.50

Iceland Steamship Company, 50th anniv.

Scout Emblem and "Be Prepared" A83

Icelandic Coat of Arms A84

1964, Apr. 24
360 A83 3.50k multicolored .55 .20
361 A83 4.50k multicolored .55 .30

Issued to honor the Boy Scouts.

1964, June 17 *Perf. 11½*
362 A84 25k multicolored 2.00 1.75

20th anniversary, Republic of Iceland.

Flower Type of 1960-62

Flowers: 50a, Eight-petal dryas. 1k, Crowfoot (Ranunculus glacialis). 1.50k, Buck bean. 2k, Clover (trifolium repens).

1964, July 15
Flowers in Natural Colors
363 A72 50a vio bl & lt vio bl .20 .20
364 A72 1k gray & dk gray .20 .20
365 A72 1.50k brn & pale brn .20 .20
366 A72 2k ol & pale olive .40 .20
Nos. 363-366 (4) 1.00 .80

Europa Issue, 1964
Common Design Type

1964, Sept. 14 Photo. *Perf. 11½*
Granite Paper
Size: 22½x33mm
367 CD7 4.50k golden brn, yel & Prus grn .55 .35
368 CD7 9k bl, yel & dk brn .55 .50

Runner — A85

1964, Oct. 20 Unwmk. *Perf. 11½*
369 A85 10k lt grn & blk .85 .65

18th Olympic Games, Tokyo, Oct. 10-25.

ITU Emblem A86

1965, May 17 Photo. *Perf. 11½*
370 A86 4.50k green .75 .60
371 A86 7.50k bright ultra .20 .20

ITU, centenary.

Surtsey Island, April 1964 — A87

1.50k, Underwater volcanic eruption, Nov. 1963, vert. 3.50k, Surtsey, Sept. 1964.

1965, June 23 Unwmk. *Perf. 11½*
372 A87 1.50k bl, bis & blk .50 .50
373 A87 2k multicolored .50 .50
374 A87 3.50k bl, blk & red .75 .65
Nos. 372-374 (3) 1.75 1.65

Emergence of a new volcanic island off the southern coast of Iceland.

Europa Issue, 1965
Common Design Type

1965, Sept. 27 Photo. *Perf. 11½*
Size: 33x22½mm
375 CD8 5k tan, brn & brt grn *1.25* .90
376 CD8 8k brt grn, brn & yel green *.75* .75

Einar Benediktsson A88

Engr. & Litho.
1965, Nov. 16 *Perf. 14*
377 A88 10k brt blue & brn 2.50 *3.25*

Einar Benediktsson, poet (1864-1940).

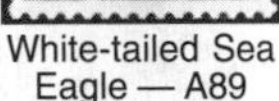
White-tailed Sea Eagle — A89

National Costume — A90

1965-66 Photo. *Perf. 11½*
378 A89 50k multicolored 8.25 8.25
379 A90 100k multicolored 6.50 6.25

Issued: #378, 4/26/66; #379, 12/3/65.

West Iceland — A91

1966, Aug. 4 Photo. *Perf. 11½*
380 A91 2.50k shown .40 .20
381 A91 4k North Iceland .35 .20
382 A91 5k East Iceland .45 .25
383 A91 6.50k South Iceland .60 .25
Nos. 380-383 (4) 1.80 .90

Europa Issue, 1966
Common Design Type

1966, Sept. 26 Photo. *Perf. 11½*
Size: 22½x33mm
384 CD9 7k grnsh bl, lt bl & red *1.50* 1.25
385 CD9 8k brn, buff & red *1.50* 1.25

Literary Society Emblem A92

1966, Nov. 18 Engr. *Perf. 11½*
386 A92 4k ultramarine .35 .30
387 A92 10k vermilion .90 .60

Icelandic Literary Society, 150th anniv.

Common Loon — A93

1967, Mar. 16 Photo. *Perf. 11½*
388 A93 20k multicolored 4.25 3.50

Europa Issue, 1967
Common Design Type

1967, May 2 Photo. *Perf. 11½*
Size: 22½x33mm
389 CD10 7k yel, brn & dk bl *1.50* 1.00
390 CD10 8k emer, gray & dk bl *1.50* 1.00

Old and New Maps of Iceland and North America A94

1967, June 8 Photo. *Perf. 11½*
391 A94 10k blk, tan & lt bl .35 .30

EXPO '67 Intl. Exhibition, Montreal, Apr. 28-Oct. 27, 1967. The old map, drawn about 1590 by Sigurdur Stefansson, is at the Royal Library, Copenhagen.

Symbols of Trade, Fishing, Husbandry and Industry A95

1967, Sept. 14 Photo. *Perf. 11½*
392 A95 5k dk bl, yel & emerald .30 .25

Icelandic Chamber of Commerce, 50th anniv.

Flower Type of 1960-62

Flowers: 50a, Saxifraga oppositifolia. 2.50k, Orchis maculata.

1968, Jan. 17 Photo. *Perf. 11½*
Flowers in Natural Colors
393 A72 50a green & dk brn .25 .20
394 A72 2.50k dk brn, yel & grn .25 .20

Europa Issue, 1968
Common Design Type

1968, Apr. 29 Photo. *Perf. 11½*
Size: 33½x23mm
395 CD11 9.50k dl yel, car rose & blk *1.25* .85
396 CD11 10k brt yel grn, blk & org *1.10* .85

Right-hand Driving — A96

1968, May 21 Photo. *Perf. 11½*
397 A96 4k yellow & brn .20 .20
398 A96 5k lt reddish brn .20 .20

Introduction of right-hand driving in Iceland, May 26, 1968.

Fridrik Fridriksson, by Sigurjón Olafsson — A97

1968, Sept. 5 Photo. *Perf. 11½*

399 A97 10k sky bl & dk gray .45 .45

Rev. Fridrik Fridriksson (1868-1961), founder of the YMCA in Reykjavik and writer.

Reading Room, National Library A98

Prime Minister Jon Magnusson (1859-1926) A99

1968, Oct. 30 Photo. *Perf. 11½*

Granite Paper

400 A98 5k yellow & brn .25 .20
401 A98 20k lt bl & dp ultra .85 .70

Natl. Library, Reykjavik, sesquicentennial.

1968, Dec. 12

Granite Paper

402 A99 4k carmine lake .50 .50
403 A99 50k dark brown 3.75 3.75

50th anniversary of independence.

Nordic Cooperation Issue

Five Ancient Ships — A99a

1969, Feb. 28 Engr. *Perf. 12½*

404 A99a 6.50k vermilion .50 .50
405 A99a 10k bright blue .50 .50

See footnote after Norway No. 524.

Europa Issue, 1969

Common Design Type

1969, Apr. 28 Photo. *Perf. 11½*

Size: 32½x23mm

406 CD12 13k pink & multi *3.50* 2.10
407 CD12 14.50k yel & multi *.50* .50

Flag of Iceland and Rising Sun — A100

1969, June 17 Photo. *Perf. 11½*

408 A100 25k gray, gold, vio bl & red 1.10 .70
409 A100 100k lt bl, gold, vio bl & red 5.75 5.25

25th anniversary, Republic of Iceland.

Boeing 727 A101

Design: 12k, Rolls Royce 400.

1969, Sept. 3 Photo. *Perf. 11½*

410 A101 9.50k dk bl & sky bl .50 .50
411 A101 12k dk bl & ultra .50 .50

50th anniversary of Icelandic aviation.

Snaefellsjökull Mountain A102

1970, Jan. 6 Photo. *Perf. 11½*

412 A102 1k shown .20 .20
413 A102 4k Laxfoss .35 .20
414 A102 5k Hattver, vert. .35 .20
415 A102 20k Fjardargill, vert. .90 .40
Nos. 412-415 (4) 1.80 1.00

First Meeting of Icelandic Supreme Court A103

1970, Feb. 16 Photo. *Perf. 11½*

416 A103 6.50k multicolored .25 .20

Icelandic Supreme Court, 50th anniv.

Column from "Skarosbók," 1363 (Law Book) — A104

Icelandic Manuscripts: 15k, Preface to "Flateyjarbók" (History of Norwegian Kings), 1387-1394. 30k, Initial from "Flateyjarbók" showing Harald Fairhair cutting fetters of Dofri.

1970, Mar. 20 Photo. *Perf. 11½*

417 A104 5k multicolored .25 .25
418 A104 15k multicolored .65 .65
419 A104 30k multicolored 1.25 1.25
Nos. 417-419 (3) 2.15 2.15

Europa Issue, 1970

Common Design Type

1970, May 4 Photo. *Perf. 11½*

Size: 32x22mm

420 CD13 9k brn & yellow *1.75* .75
421 CD13 25k brt grn & bister *3.25* 2.50

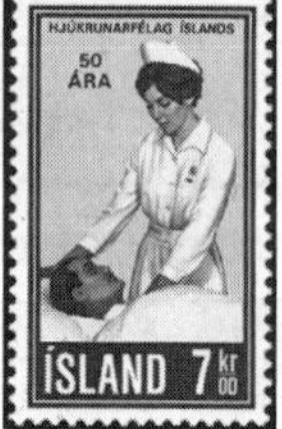

Nurse — A105

Grimur Thomsen — A106

The Rest, by Thorarinn B. Thorlaksson A107

1970, June 19 Photo. *Perf. 11½*

422 A105 7k ultra & lt bl .35 .20
423 A106 10k ind & lt grnsh bl .45 .30
424 A107 50k gold & multi 2.00 1.25
Nos. 422-424 (3) 2.80 1.75

50th anniv. (in 1969) of the Icelandic Nursing Association (No. 422); 150th birth anniv. of Grimur Thomsen (1820-1896), poet (No. 423); Intl. Arts Festival, Reykjavik, June 1970 (No. 424).

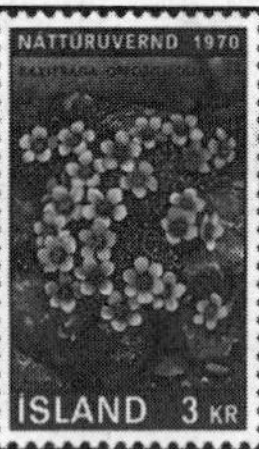

Saxifraga Oppositifolia A108

Lakagigar A109

1970, Aug. 25 Photo. *Perf. 11½*

425 A108 3k multicolored .30 .30
426 A109 15k multicolored .80 .80

European Nature Conservation Year.

UN Emblem and Map of Iceland A110

1970, Oct. 23 Photo. *Perf. 11½*

427 A110 12k multicolored .50 .50

25th anniversary of United Nations.

"Flight," by Asgrimur Jonsson A111

1971, Mar. 26 Photo. *Perf. 11½*

428 A111 10k multicolored .70 .50

Joint northern campaign for the benefit of refugees.

Europa Issue, 1971

Common Design Type

1971, May 3 Photo. *Perf. 11½*

Size: 33x22mm

429 CD14 7k rose cl, yel & blk *2.40* 1.75
430 CD14 15k ultra, yel & blk *2.25* 1.50

Postal Checking Service Emblem A112

1971, June 22 Photo. *Perf. 11½*

431 A112 5k vio bl & lt blue .20 .25
432 A112 7k dk grn & yel grn .30 .35

Introduction of Postal Checking Service, Apr. 30, 1971.

Tryggvi Gunnarsson A113

Haddock Freezing Plant A114

Design: 30k, Patriotic Society emblem.

1971, Aug. 19 Photo. *Perf. 11½*

433 A113 30k lt bl & vio blk 1.25 .90
434 A113 100k gray & vio blk 5.50 6.00

Icelandic Patriotic Society, cent.; Tryggvi Gunnarsson (1835-1917), founder and president.

1971, Nov. 18

Fish Industry: 7k, Cod fishing. 20k, Lobster canning plant.

435 A114 5k multicolored .20 .20
436 A114 7k multicolored .20 .20
437 A114 20k green & multi .60 .50
Nos. 435-437 (3) 1.00 .90

Herdubreid Mountain — A115

Engr. & Litho.

1972, Mar. 9 *Perf. 14*

438 A115 250k blue & multi .90 .35

Europa Issue 1972

Common Design Type

1972, May 2 Photo. *Perf. 11½*

Size: 22x32mm

439 CD15 9k lt vio & multi *1.10* .40
440 CD15 13k yel grn & multi *2.50* 1.40

"United Municipalities" — A116

1972, June 14 Photo. *Perf. 11½*

441 A116 16k multicolored .25 .20

Legislation for local government, cent.

Chessboard, World Map, Rook — A117

1972, July 2 Litho. *Perf. 13*

442 A117 15k lt ol & multi .45 .35

World Chess Championship, Reykjavik, July-Sept. 1972.

Hothouse Tomatoes A118

Designs: 12k, Steam valve and natural steam. 40k, Hothouse roses.

1972, Aug. 23 Photo. *Perf. 11½*

443 A118 8k Prus bl & multi .20 .20
444 A118 12k green & multi .20 .20
445 A118 40k dk pur & multi 1.25 .90
Nos. 443-445 (3) 1.65 1.30

Hothouse gardening in Iceland, using natural steam and hot springs.

Iceland and the Continental Shelf — A119

1972, Sept. 27 Litho. *Perf. 13*

446 A119 9k blue & multi .20 .20

To publicize Iceland's offshore fishing rights.

Europa Issue 1973
Common Design Type

1973, Apr. 30 Photo. *Perf. 11½*
Size: 32½x22mm

447 CD16 13k vio & multi *4.00* 1.75
448 CD16 25k olive & multi *.60* .40

Iceland No. 1 and Messenger — A120

Designs (First Issue of Iceland and): 15k, No. 5 and pony train. 20k, No. 2 and mailboat "Esja." 40k, No. 3 and mail truck. 80k, No. 4 and Beech-18 mail plane.

Litho. & Engr.

1973, May 23 *Perf. 13x13½*

449 A120 10k dl bl, blk & ultra .25 .25
450 A120 15k grn, blk & gray .20 .20
451 A120 20k maroon, blk & car .20 .20
452 A120 40k vio, blk & brn .20 .20
453 A120 80k olive, blk & yel 1.00 .65
Nos. 449-453 (5) 1.85 1.50

Centenary of Iceland's first postage stamps.

Nordic Cooperation Issue

Nordic House, Reykjavik A120a

1973, June 26 Engr. *Perf. 12½*

454 A120a 9k multicolored .35 .20
455 A120a 10k multicolored 1.00 .85

A century of postal cooperation among Denmark, Finland, Iceland, Norway and Sweden, and in connection with the Nordic Postal Conference, Reykjavik.

Ásgeir Ásgeirsson, (1894-1972),President of Iceland 1952-1968 — A121

1973, Aug. 1 Engr. *Perf. 13x13½*

456 A121 13k carmine .35 .25
457 A121 15k blue .20 .25

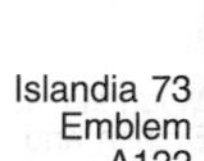

Islandia 73 Emblem A122

20k, Islandia 73 emblem; diff. arrangement.

1973, Aug. 31 Photo. *Perf. 11½*

458 A122 17k gray & multi .35 .35
459 A122 20k brn, ocher & yel .25 .25

Islandia 73 Philatelic Exhibition, Reykjavik, Aug. 31-Sept. 9.

Man and WMO Emblem A123

The Settlement, Tapestry by Vigdis Kristjansdottir A124

1973, Nov. 14 Photo. *Perf. 12½*

460 A123 50k silver & multi .50 .45

Intl. meteorological cooperation, cent.

1974 Photo. *Perf. 11½*

Designs: 13k, Establishment of Althing, painting by Johannes Johannesson, horiz. 15k, Gudbrandur Thorlakkson, Bishop ofHolar 1571-1627. 17k, Age of Sturlungar (Fighting Vikings), drawing by Thorvaldur Skulason. 20k, Stained glass window honoring Hallgrimur Petursson (1614-74), hymn writer. 25k, Illumination from Book of Flatey, 14th century. 30k, Conversion to Christianity (altarpiece, Skalholt), mosaic by Nina Tryggvadottir. 40k, Wood carving (family and plants), 18th century. 60k, Curing the Catch, cement bas-relief. 70k, Age of Writing (Saemundur Riding Seal), sculpture by Asmundur Sveinsson. 100k, Virgin and Child with Angels, embroidered antependium, Stafafell Church, 14th century.

461 A124 10k multicolored .20 .20
462 A124 13k multicolored .20 .20
463 A124 15k multicolored .20 .20
464 A124 17k multicolored .25 .20
465 A124 20k multicolored .25 .20
466 A124 25k multicolored .20 .20
467 A124 30k multicolored .65 .50
468 A124 40k multicolored .85 .60
469 A124 60k multicolored .85 .85
470 A124 70k multicolored .85 .75
471 A124 100k multicolored 1.10 .50
Nos. 461-471 (11) 5.60 4.40

1100th anniv. of settlement of Iceland.
Issued: 10k, 13k, 30k, 70k, 3/12; 17k, 25k, 100k, 6/11; 15k, 20k, 40k, 60k, 7/16.

Horseback Rider, Wood, 17th Century — A125

Europa: 20k, "Through the Sound Barrier," contemporary bronze by Asmundur Sveinsson.

1974, Apr. 29 Photo. *Perf. 11½*

472 A125 13k brn red & multi *.25* .20
473 A125 20k gray & multi *1.00* .50

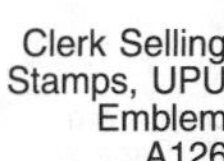

Clerk Selling Stamps, UPU Emblem A126

Design: 20k, Mailman delivering mail.

1974, Oct. 9 Photo. *Perf. 11½*

474 A126 17k ocher & multi .25 .25
475 A126 20k olive & multi .25 .25

Centenary of Universal Postal Union.

Volcanic Eruption, Heimaey, Jan. 23, 1973 — A127

Design: 25k, Volcanic eruption, night view.

1975, Jan. 23 Photo. *Perf. 11½*

476 A127 20k multicolored .50 .35
477 A127 25k multicolored .25 .25

Europa Issue 1975

Bird, by Thorvaldur Skulason A128

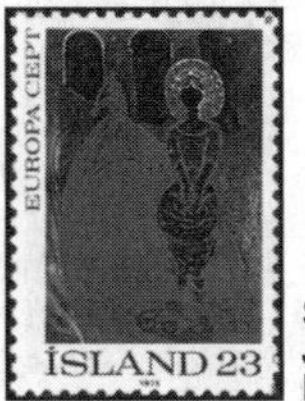

Sun Queen, by Johannes S. Kjarval — A129

1975, May 12 Photo. *Perf. 11½*

478 A128 18k multicolored .20 .20
479 A129 23k gold & multi .75 .35

Stephan G. Stephansson A130

1975, Aug. 1 Engr. *Perf. 13*

480 A130 27k green & brn .40 .25

Stephan G. Stephansson (1853-1927), Icelandic poet and settler in North America; centenary of Icelandic emigration to North America.

Petursson, by Hjalti Thorsteinsson A131

Einar Jonsson, Self-portrait A132

23k, Arni Magnusson, by Hjalti Thorsteinsson. 30k, Jon Eiriksson, sculpture by Olafur Olafsson.

1975, Sept. 18 Engr. *Perf. 13*

481 A131 18k slate green & indigo .20 .20
482 A131 23k Prussian blue .20 .20
483 A131 30k deep magenta .20 .20
484 A132 50k indigo .25 .20
Nos. 481-484 (4) .85 .80

Famous Icelanders: Hallgrimur Petursson (1614-1674), minister and religious poet; Arni Magnusson (1663-1730), historian, registrar and manuscript collector; Jon Eiriksson (1728-1787), professor of law and cabinet member; Einar Jonsson (1874-1954), sculptor, painter and writer.

Red Cross A133

1975, Oct. 15 Photo. *Perf. 11½x12*

485 A133 23k multicolored .30 .20

Icelandic Red Cross, 50th anniversary.

Abstract Painting, by Nina Tryggvadottir A134

1975, Oct. 15 *Perf. 12x12½*

486 A134 100k multicolored .85 .45

International Women's Year 1975.

Thorvaldsen Statue, by Thorvaldsen A135

Saplings Growing in Bare Landscape A136

1975, Nov. 19 Photo. *Perf. 11½*

487 A135 27k lt vio & multi .60 .30

Centenary of Thorvaldsen Society, a charity honoring Bertel Thorvaldsen (1768-1844), sculptor.

1975, Nov. 19 *Perf. 12x11½*

488 A136 35k multicolored .40 .30

Reforestation.

Lang Glacier, by Asgrimur Jonsson A137

1976, Mar. 18 Photo. *Perf. 11½*

489 A137 150k gold & multi 1.25 1.00

Asgrimur Jonsson (1876-1958), painter.

Wooden Bowl — A138

Europa: 45k, Spinning wheel, vert.

1976, May 3 Photo. *Perf. 11½*

490 A138 35k ver & multi *.80* .65
491 A138 45k blue & multi *.80* .80

No. 9 with First Day Cancel — A139

Decree Establishing Postal Service — A140

1976, Sept. 22 Photo. *Perf. 11½*
Granite Paper

492 A139 30k bis, blk & gray bl .25 .20

Centenary of aurar stamps.

1976, Sept. 22 Engr. *Perf. 13*

45k, Conclusion of Decree with signatures.

493 A140 35k dark brown .30 .25
494 A140 45k dark blue .30 .25

Iceland's Postal Service, bicentenary.

Federation Emblem, People — A141

1976, Dec. 2 Photo. *Perf. 12½*
Granite Paper

495 A141 100k multicolored .65 .50

Icelandic Federation of Labor, 60th anniv.

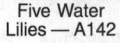

Five Water Lilies — A142 Ofaerufoss, Eldgja — A143

Photo. & Engr.

1977, Feb. 2 *Perf. 12½*

496 A142 35k brt grn & multi .60 .40
497 A142 45k ultra & multi .60 .40

Nordic countries cooperation for protection of the environment and 25th Session of Nordic Council, Helsinki, Feb. 19.

1977, May 2 Photo. *Perf. 12*

Europa: 85k, Kirkjufell Mountain, seen from Grundarfjord.

498 A143 45k multicolored *2.40* .50
499 A143 85k multicolored *.80* .25

Harlequin Duck — A144

1977, June 14 Photo. *Perf. 11½*

500 A144 40k multicolored .40 .25

Wetlands conservation, European campaign.

Society Emblem — A145

1977, June 14

501 A145 60k vio bl & ultra .60 .45

Federation of Icelandic Cooperative Societies, 75th anniversary.

Hot Springs, Therapeutic Bath, Emblem A146

1977, Nov. 16 Photo. *Perf. 11½*

502 A146 90k multicolored .50 .40

World Rheumatism Year.

Stone Marker — A147

1977, Dec. 12 Engr. *Perf. 11½*

503 A147 45k dark blue .70 .55

Touring Club of Iceland, 50th anniversary.

Thorvaldur Thoroddsen, (1855-1921), Geologist, Scientist and Writer — A148

Design: 60k, Briet Bjarnhedinsdottir (1856-1940), Founder of Icelandic Women's Association and Reykjavik city councillor.

1977, Dec. 12 Engr. *Perf. 11½*

504 A148 50k brn & slate grn .20 .20
505 A148 60k grn & vio brn .45 .35

Bailiff's Residence, Videy Island, 1752 — A149

Europa: 120k, Husavik Church, 1906.

1978, May 2 Photo. *Perf. 11½*

506 A149 80k multicolored *.75* .45
507 A149 120k multi, vert. *2.25* .40

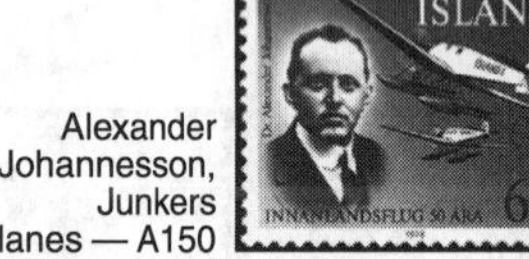

Alexander Johannesson, Junkers Planes — A150

100k, Fokker Friendship plane over mountains.

1978, June 21 Photo. *Perf. 12½*

508 A150 60k multicolored .40 .25
509 A150 100k multicolored .40 .35

50th anniv. of domestic flights in Iceland.

Skeioara River Bridge A151

1978, Aug. 17 Photo. *Perf. 11½*

510 A151 70k multicolored .20 .20

Lava Near Mt. Hekla, by Jon Stefansson — A152

1978, Nov. 16 Photo. *Perf. 12*

511 A152 1000k multicolored 3.00 2.50

Jon Stefansson (1881-1962), Icelandic painter.

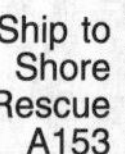

Ship to Shore Rescue A153

1978, Dec. 1 Engr. *Perf. 13*

512 A153 60k black .20 .20

National Life Saving Assoc., 50th anniv.

Halldor Hermannsson (1878-1958), Historian, Librarian — A154

1978, Dec. 1

513 A154 150k indigo .45 .35

Lighthouse A155 Telephone, c. 1900 A156

1978, Dec. 1 Photo. *Perf. 11½*

514 A155 90k multicolored .45 .35

Centenary of Icelandic lighthouses.

1979, Apr. 30 Photo. *Perf. 11½*

Europa: 190k, Post horn and satchel.

515 A156 110k multicolored *1.60* .35
516 A156 190k multicolored *3.00* .50

Jon Sigurdsson and Ingibjorg Einarsdottir A157

1979, Nov. 1 Engr. *Perf. 13x12½*

517 A157 150k black .45 .45

Jon Sigurdsson (1811-1879), Icelandic statesman and leader in independence movement.

Excerpt from Olafs Saga Helga — A158

1979, Nov. 1 Photo. *Perf. 11½*

518 A158 200k multicolored .60 .45

Snorri Sturluson (1178-1241), Icelandic historian and writer.

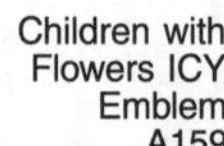

Children with Flowers ICY Emblem A159

1979, Nov. 12

519 A159 140k multicolored .60 .45

International Year of the Child.

A160 A161

Icelandic Arms, before 1904 and 1904-1919.

1979, Nov. 12

520 A160 500k multicolored 1.00 .65

Home rule, 75th anniversary.

1979 Engr. *Perf. 13*

Designs: 80k, Ingibjorg H. Bjarnason (1867-1941). 100k, Bjarni Thorsteinsson (1861-1938), composer. 120k, Petur Gudjohnsen (1812-77), organist. 130k, Sveinbjorn Sveinbjornson (1847-1927), composer. 170k, Torfhildur Holm (1845-1918), poet.

521 A161 80k rose violet .20 .20
522 A161 100k black .20 .20
523 A161 120k rose carmine .20 .20
524 A161 130k sepia .25 .25
525 A161 170k carmine rose .40 .30
Nos. 521-525 (5) 1.25 1.15

Issued: 80k, 170k, Aug. 3; others, Dec. 12.

Canis Familiaris — A162

Design: 90k, Alopex lagopus.

1980, Jan. 24

526 A162 10k black .20 .20
527 A162 90k sepia .20 .20

See Nos. 534-536, 543-545, 552, 553, 556-558, 610-612.

Jon Sveinsson Nonni (1857-1944), Writer — A163

Europa: 250k, Gunnar Gunnarsson (1889-1975), writer.

1980, Apr. 28 Photo. *Perf. 11½*
Granite Paper

528 A163 140k dl rose & blk .60 .35
529 A163 250k tan & blk .70 .50

Mountain Ash Branch and Berries — A164

1980, July 8 Photo. *Perf. 12½*

530 A164 120k multicolored .25 .25

Year of the Tree.

Laugardalur Sports Complex, Reykjavik A165

1980, July 8 Engr. *Perf. 13x12½*

531 A165 300k slate green .50 .40

1980 Olympic Games.

Carved and Painted Cabinet Door, 18th Cent. — A166

Radio Receiver, 1930 — A168

Nordic Cooperation: 180k, Embroidered cushion, 19th cent.

1980, Sept. 9 Photo. *Perf. 11½*
Granite Paper

532 A166 150k multicolored .45 .50
533 A166 180k multicolored .50 .60

Animal Type of 1980

1980, Oct. 16 Engr. *Perf. 13*

Designs: 160k, Sebastes marinus. 170k, Fratercula arctica. 190k, Phoca vitulina.

534 A162 160k rose violet .60 .20
535 A162 170k black .65 .40
536 A162 190k dark brown .20 .25
Nos. 534-536 (3) 1.45 .85

1980, Nov. 20 Photo. *Perf. 12½*
Granite Paper

537 A168 400k multicolored .75 .35

State Broadcasting Service, 50th anniv.

University Hospital, 50th Anniversary A169

1980, Nov. 20 *Perf. 11½*

538 A169 200k multicolored .35 .35

A170

Design: 170a, Magnus Stephensen (1762-1833), Chief Justice. 190a, Finnur Magnusson (1781-1847), Privy Archives keeper.

1981, Feb. 24 Engr. *Perf. 13*

539 A170 170a bright ultra .40 .25
540 A170 190a olive green .40 .25

Europa Issue 1981

Europa — A171

1981, May 4 Photo. *Perf. 11½*
Granite Paper

541 A171 180a Luftur the Sorcerer *1.10* .60
542 A171 220a Sea witch *1.10* .60

Animal Type of 1980

1981, Aug. 20 Engr. *Perf. 13*

Designs: 50a, Troglodytes troglodytes. 100a, Pluvialis apricaria. 200a, Corvus corax.

543 A162 50a brown .20 .20
544 A162 100a blue .20 .20
545 A162 200a black .20 .20
Nos. 543-545 (3) .60 .60

Intl. Year of the Disabled — A173

1981, Sept. 29 Photo. *Perf. 11½*

546 A173 200a multicolored .20 .20

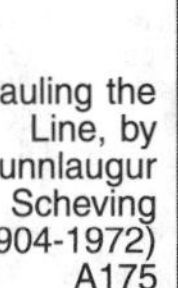

Skyggnir Earth Satellite Station, First Anniv. — A174

1981, Sept. 29 Photo. *Perf. 11½*

547 A174 500a multicolored .85 .40

Hauling the Line, by Gunnlaugur Scheving (1904-1972) A175

1981, Oct. 21 Photo. *Perf. 11½*

548 A175 5000a multi 5.25 2.75

Christian Missionary Work in Iceland Millennium A176

1981, Nov. 24 Engr. *Perf. 13*

549 A176 200a dark violet .20 .20

Christmas A177

1981, Nov. 24 Photo. *Perf. 12½*
Granite Paper

550 A177 200a Leaf bread .50 .50
551 A177 250a Leaf bread, diff. .50 .40

Animal Type of 1980

1982, Mar. 23 Engr. *Perf. 13*

Designs: 20a, Buccinum undatum, vert. 600a, Chlamys islandica.

552 A162 20a copper brn .20 .20
553 A162 600a vio brown .70 .35

Europa Issue 1982

First Norse Settlement, 874 — A179

1982, May 3 Photo. *Perf. 11½*
Granite Paper

554 A179 350a shown *2.75* .65
555 A179 450a Discovery of North America, 1000 *2.75* .65

Animal Type of 1980

1982, June 3 Engr. *Perf. 13*

Designs: 300a, Ovis aries, vert. 400a, Bos taurus, vert. 500a, Felis catus, vert.

556 A162 300a brown .60 .35
557 A162 400a lake .40 .25
558 A162 500a gray .20 .20
Nos. 556-558 (3) 1.20 .80

Kaupfelag Thingeyinga Cooperative Society Centenary — A181

1982, June 3

559 A181 1000a black & red .65 .35

Man Riding Iceland Pony — A182

1982, July 1 Photo. *Perf. 11½*
Granite Paper

560 A182 700a multicolored .60 .25

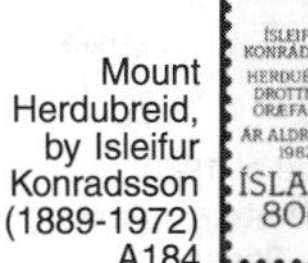

Centenary of School of Agriculture, Holar A183

1982, July 1
Granite Paper

561 A183 1500a multi .85 .50

Mount Herdubreid, by Isleifur Konradsson (1889-1972) A184

1982, Sept. 8 Photo. *Perf. 11½*
Granite Paper

562 A184 800a multicolored .50 .40

UN World Assembly on Aging, 7/26-8/6.

Borbjorg Sveinsdottir (1828-1903) — A185

1982, Sept. 8 Engr. *Perf. 13*

563 A185 900a red brown .40 .35

Borbjorg Sveinsdottir (1828-1903), midwife and Univ. founder.

Souvenir Sheet

NORDIA '84 — A186

Photo. & Engr.

1982, Oct. 7 *Perf. 13½*

564 Sheet of 2 4.50 4.50
a. A186 400a Reynistaour Monastery seal 2.25 2.25
b. A186 800a Bingeyrar 2.25 2.25

NORDIA '84 Intl. Stamp Exhibition, Reykjavik, July 3-8, 1984. Sold for 18k.

See No. 581.

Christmas A187

Score from The Night was Such a Splendid One.

1982, Nov. 16 Photo. *Perf. 11½*
Granite Paper

565 A187 3k Birds .65 .45
566 A187 3.50k Bells .75 .45

Caltha Palustris — A188

1983, Feb. 10 Photo.
Granite Paper

567 A188 7.50k shown .45 .45
568 A188 8k Lychnis alpina .65 .45
569 A188 10k Potentilla palustris 1.00 .45
570 A188 20k Myosotis scorpioides 1.75 .65
Nos. 567-570 (4) 3.85 2.00

See #586-587, 593-594, 602-605, 663-664.

Nordic Cooperation A189

1983, Mar. 24
Granite Paper

571 A189 4.50k Mt. Sulur .85 .60
572 A189 5k Urrida Falls .85 .60

Europa Issue, 1983

Thermal Energy Projects — A190

1983, May 5
Granite Paper

573 A190 5k shown *2.25* 1.10
574 A190 5.50k multi, diff. *16.00* 1.40

Fishing Industry A191

1983, June 8 Engr. *Perf. 13x12½*

575 A191 11k Fishing boats .25 .25
576 A191 13k Fishermen 1.00 .60

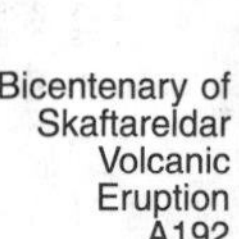

Bicentenary of Skaftareldar Volcanic Eruption
A192

1983, June 8 Photo. *Perf. 11½*
Granite Paper

577 A192 15k Volcano, by Finnur Jonsson .50 .40

Skiing — A193

1983, Sept. 8 Photo. *Perf. 11½*

578 A193 12k shown .60 .40
579 A193 14k Running .65 .50

World Communications Year — A194

1983, Sept. 8 *Perf. 12½*

580 A194 30k multi 1.75 .85

NORDIA '84 Type of 1982
Souvenir Sheet

Bishops' Seals: 8k, Magnus Eyjolfsson of Skalholt, 1477-90. 12k, Ogmundur Palsson of Skalhot, 1521-40.

Photo. & Engr.

1983, Oct. 6 *Perf. 13½*

581 Sheet of 2 6.25 6.25
a. A186 8k violet blue & black 2.75 2.75
b. A186 12k pale green & black 2.75 2.75

Sold for 30k.

Christmas
A195

Pres. Kristjan Eldjarn (1916-82)
A196

1983, Nov. 10 Photo. *Perf. 11½*
Granite Paper

582 A195 6k Virgin and Child .65 .40
583 A195 6.50k Angel .65 .40

1983, Dec. 6

584 A196 6.50k brn carmine .65 .50
585 A196 7k dark blue .25 .20

Flower Type of 1983

1984, Mar. 1 Photo. *Perf. 11½*
Granite Paper

586 A188 6k Rosa pimpinellifolia .65 .35
587 A188 25k Potentilla anserium .85 .35

Europa 1959-84
A197

1984, May 3

588 A197 6.50k grnsh bl & blk *1.60* .55
589 A197 7.50k rose & black *.75* .55

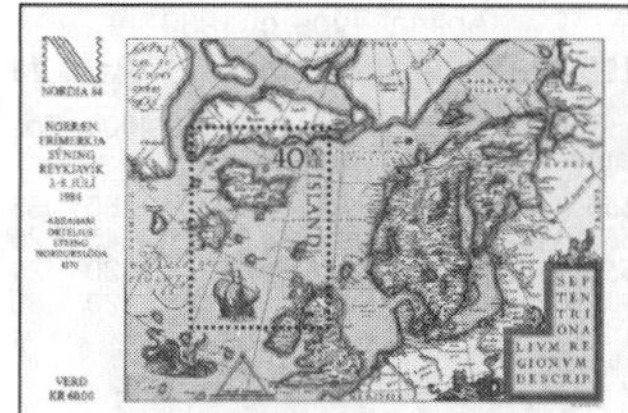

A198

Souvenir Sheet

Design: Abraham Ortelius' map of Northern Europe, 1570.

Photo. & Engr.

1984, June 6 *Perf. 14x13½*

590 A198 40k multi 9.00 9.00

NORDIA '84 Intl. Stamp Exhibition, Reykjavik, July 3-8. Sold for 60k.

A199

1984, June 17 Photo. *Perf. 11½*
Granite Paper

591 A199 50k Flags 4.00 2.10

40th Anniv. of Republic.

Good Templars Headquarters, Akureyri — A200

1984, July 18 Engr. *Perf. 13*

592 A200 10k green .50 .35

Order of the Good Templars, centenary in Iceland, temperance org.

Flower Type of 1983

1984, Sept. 11 Photo. *Perf. 11½*
Granite Paper

593 A188 6.50k Loiseleuria procumbens .40 .25
594 A188 7.50k Arctostaphylos uva-ursi .40 .25

Christmas
A201

Gudbrand's Bible, 400th Anniv.
A202

1984, Nov. 29 Photo.

595 A201 600a Madonna and Child .50 .25
596 A201 650a Angel, Christmas rose .50 .35

1984, Nov. 29 Engr. *Perf. 12½x13*

597 A202 6.50k Text .40 .25
598 A202 7.50k Illustration .25 .35

First Icelandic Bible.

Confederation of Employers, 50th Anniv.
A203

Bjorn Bjarnarson (1853-1918)
A204

1984, Nov. 9 Photo. *Perf. 12x12½*
Granite Paper

599 A203 30k Building blocks 1.00 .85

1984, Nov. 9 Photo. *Perf. 11½*
Granite Paper

600 A204 12k shown .40 .40
601 A204 40k New gallery building, horiz. 1.50 .85

Natl. Gallery centenary.

Flower Type of 1983

1985, Mar. 20 Photo. *Perf. 11½*
Granite Paper

602 A188 8k Rubus saxatilis .65 .25
603 A188 9k Veronica fruticans .65 .25
604 A188 16k Lathyrus japonicus 1.60 .40
605 A188 17k Draba alpina .50 .40
Nos. 602-605 (4) 3.40 1.30

Music Year Emblem, Woman Playing the Langspil — A205

Europa: 7.50k, Man playing the Icelandic violin.

1985, May 3 Photo. *Perf. 11½*
Granite Paper

606 A205 6.50k multicolored *1.60* .40
607 A205 7.50k multicolored *1.60* .40

Natl. Horticulture Soc., Cent. — A206

Intl. Youth Year — A207

1985, June 20 Photo. *Perf. 12*

608 A206 20k Sorbus intermedia .65 .40

1985, June 20 Photo. *Perf. 11½*

609 A207 25k Icelandic girl .85 .65

Animal Type of 1980

1985, Sept. 10 Engr. *Perf. 13*

Designs: 700a, Todarodes sagittatus. 800a, Hyas araneus. 900a, Tealia felina.

610 A162 700a brn carmine .20 .25
611 A162 800a dk brown .25 .20
612 A162 900a carmine .85 .35
Nos. 610-612 (3) 1.30 .80

Hannes Stephensen (1799-1856), Cleric, Politician, Translator — A209

Famous men: 30k, Jon Gudmudsson (1807-1875), editor, politician.

1985, Sept. 10 Engr.

613 A209 13k dp magenta .40 .35
614 A209 30k deep violet 1.00 .50

Yearning to Fly, by Johannes S. Kjarval (1885-1972), Reykjavik Natl. Museum
A210

1985, Oct. 15 Photo. *Perf. 12x11½*

615 A210 100k multi 4.00 3.25

A211

Birds — A212

Abstract ice crystal paintings, by Snorri Sveinn Fridriksson (b. 1934).

1985, Nov. 14 Photo. *Perf. 11½*

616 A211 8k Crucifix .60 .25
617 A211 9k Pine Trees .60 .25

Christmas.

1986, Mar. 19 Photo. *Perf. 11½*
Granite Paper

618 A212 6k Motacilla alba .20 .20
619 A212 10k Anas acuta 1.25 .40
620 A212 12k Falco columbarius .85 .40
621 A212 15k Alca torda .50 .35
Nos. 618-621 (4) 2.80 1.35

See Nos. 642-645, 665-666, 671-672, 686-687, 721, 725.

Europa Issue 1986

Natl. Parks — A213

1986, May 5

622 A213 10k Skaftafell *7.50* .85
623 A213 12k Jokulsargljufur *3.00* 1.00

Nordic Cooperation Issue
A214

Sister towns.

1986, May 27 *Perf. 11½*

624 A214 10k Stykkisholmur .85 .60
625 A214 12k Seydisfjordur .85 .60

Natl. Bank, Cent.
A215

1986, July 1 Engr. *Perf. 14*

626 A215 13k Headquarters, Reykjavik .65 .50
627 A215 250k Banknote reverse, 1928 7.00 6.25

Reykjavik Bicent. A216

1986, Aug. 18 Engr. *Perf. 13½x14*

628 A216 10k City seal, 1815 .50 .25
629 A216 12k View from bank, illustration, 1856 .50 .25
630 A216 13k Laugardalur hot water brook .50 .40
631 A216 40k City Theater 1.25 1.00
Nos. 628-631 (4) 2.75 1.90

Introduction of the Telephone in Iceland, 80th Anniv. — A217

1986, Sept. 29 Photo. *Perf. 11½*
Granite Paper

632 A217 10k Morse receiver, 1906 .35 .25
633 A217 20k Handset, microchip, 1986 .75 .40

Souvenir Sheet

Hvita River Crossing, Loa, 1836, by Auguste Mayer — A218

Photo. & Engr.
1986, Oct. 9 *Perf. 14*

634 A218 20k bluish black 3.75 3.75

Stamp Day. Sold for 30k to benefit philatelic organizations. See Nos. 646, 667.

Christmas — A219

Paintings by Bjoerg Thorsteinsdottir: 10k, Christmas at Peace. 12k, Christmas Night.

1986, Nov. 13 Photo. *Perf. 12*

635 A219 10k multicolored .75 .25
636 A219 12k multicolored .35 .25

Olafsvik Trading Station, 300th Anniv. A220

1987, Mar. 26 Engr. *Perf. 14x13½*

637 A220 50k Merchantman Svanur, 1777 2.10 .85

Keflavik Intl. Airport Terminal Inauguration — A221

1987, Apr. 14 Photo. *Perf. 12x11½*

638 A221 100k multi 3.75 1.25

Europa Issue 1987

Stained Glass Windows by Leifur Breidfjoerd, Fossvogur Cemetery Chapel A222

1987, May 4 Photo. *Perf. 12x11½*

639 A222 12k Christ carrying the cross *1.10* .55
640 A222 15k Soldiers, peace dove *1.10* .55

Rasmus Christian Rask (1787-1832), Danish Linguist — A223

1987, June 10 Engr. *Perf. 13½*

641 A223 20k black .65 .50

Preservation of the Icelandic language.

Bird Type of 1986

1987, Sept. 16 Photo. *Perf. 11½*
Granite Paper

642 A212 13k Asio flammeus .80 .25
643 A212 40k Turdus iliacus 1.50 .40
644 A212 70k Haematopus ostralegus 2.10 .65
645 A212 90k Anas platyrhynchos 3.25 1.00
Nos. 642-645 (4) 7.65 2.30

Stamp Day Type of 1986
Souvenir Sheet

1987, Oct. 9 Engr. *Perf. 13½x14*

Trading Station of Djupivogur in 1836, by Auguste Mayer.

646 A218 30k black 3.75 3.75

Stamp Day. Sold for 45k to benefit the Stamp and Postal History Fund.

Dental Protection — A226

1987, Oct. 9 Photo. *Perf. 11½x12*
Granite Paper

647 A226 12k multi .40 .25

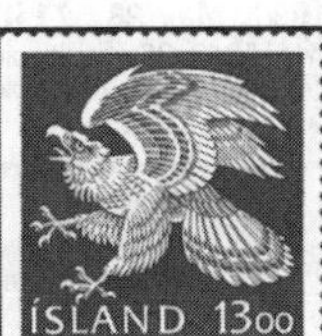

Vulture — A227

Perf. 13 on 3 sides
1987, Oct. 9 Engr.

Guardian Spirits of the North, East, South and West.

Booklet Stamps

648 A227 13k shown .35 .25
649 A227 13k Dragon .35 .25
650 A227 13k Bull .35 .25
651 A227 13k Giant .35 .25
a. Block of 4, #648-651 1.50 1.75
b. Bklt. pane of 12, 3 #651a 4.50 5.00

Legend of Heimskringla, the story of the Norse kings. Haraldur Gormsson, king of Denmark, deterred from invading Iceland after hearing of the guardian spirits.
See Nos. 656-659, 677, 688-695.

Christmas — A228

1987, Oct. 21 Photo. *Perf. 11½x12*

652 A228 13k Fir branch .50 .20
653 A228 17k Candle flame .50 .35

Steinn Steinarr (1908-1958) A229

Poets: 21k, David Stefansson (1895-1964).

1988, Feb. 25 Photo. *Perf. 12*

654 A229 16k multi .50 .25
655 A229 21k multi .60 .40

Guardian Spirit Type of 1987
Perf. 13 on 3 sides
1988, May 2 Engr.
Booklet Stamps

656 A227 16k Vulture .35 .40
657 A227 16k Dragon .35 .40
658 A227 16k Bull .35 .40
659 A227 16k Giant .35 .40
a. Block of 4, #656-659 1.50 1.75
b. Bklt. pane of 12, 3 #659a 4.75 5.25

Europa Issue, 1988

Modern Communication — A230

1988, May 2 Photo. *Perf. 12x11½*

660 A230 16k Data transmission system *.70* .35
661 A230 21k Facsimile machine *2.75* 1.00

1988 Summer Olympics, Seoul A231

1988, June 9 Photo. *Perf. 12*
Granite Paper

662 A231 18k Handball .50 .40

Flower Type of 1983

1988, June 9 *Perf. 11½*
Granite Paper

663 A188 10k Vicia cracca .40 .25
664 A188 50k Thymus praecox 2.00 .50

Bird Type of 1986

1988, Sept. 21 Photo. *Perf. 11½*
Granite Paper

665 A212 5k Limosa limosa .30 .20
666 A212 30k Clangula hyemalis 1.25 .50

Stamp Day Type of 1986
Souvenir Sheet

1988, Oct. 9 Engr. *Perf. 14*

Nupsstadur Farm, Fljotshverfi, 1836, by Auguste Mayer.

667 A218 40k black 3.25 3.25

Stamp Day. Sold for 60k to benefit the Stamp and Postal History Fund.

WHO, 40th Anniv. — A234

1988, Nov. 3 Photo. *Perf. 11½x12*
Granite Paper

668 A234 19k multicolored .60 .35

Christmas A235

1988, Nov. 3 *Perf. 11½*
Granite Paper

669 A235 19k Fisherman at sea .65 .25
670 A235 24k Ship, buoy .85 .50

Bird Type of 1986

1989, Feb. 2 Photo.

671 A212 19k Phalaropus lobatus .65 .25
672 A212 100k Plectrophenax nivalis 3.25 1.25

Women's Folk Costumes — A236

1989, Apr. 20 Photo. *Perf. 11½x12*
Granite Paper

673 A236 21k Peysufot 1.00 .35
674 A236 26k Upphlutur 1.00 .50

Nordic cooperation.

Europa 1989 A237

Children's games.

1989, May 30 Photo. *Perf. 11½*
Granite Paper

675 A237 21k Sailing toy boats *3.00* .60
676 A237 26k Hoop, stick pony *3.00* .60

Guardian Spirit Type of 1987

1989, June 27 Engr. *Perf. 13*

677 A227 500k Dragon 10.50 4.75

Landscapes A238

1989, Sept. 20 Photo. *Perf. 11½*

Granite Paper

678 A238 35k Mt. Skeggi, Arnarfjord 1.00 .50
679 A238 45k Thermal spring, Namaskard 1.25 .50

See Nos. 713-714, 728, 737.

Agricultural College at Hvanneyri, Cent. A239

1989, Sept. 20 Engr. *Perf. 14*

680 A239 50k multi 1.25 .65

Souvenir Sheet

NORDIA '91 — A240

Detail of *A Chart and Description of Northern Routes and Wonders to Be Found in the Nordic Countries,* 1539, by Olaus Magnus (1490-1557).

Litho. & Engr.

1989, Oct. 9 *Perf. 12½*

681 A240 Sheet of 3 6.00 6.00
a.-c. 30k any single 2.00 2.00

Stamp Day. Sold for 130k to benefit the exhibition.

See No. 715.

Natural History Soc., Cent. A241

Flowers or fish and: 21k, Stefan Stefansson (1863-1921), botanist and founder. 26k, Bjarni Saemundsson (1867-1940), chairman.

1989, Nov. 9 Photo. *Perf. 11½*

Granite Paper

682 A241 21k multi .50 .40
683 A241 26k multi .60 .40

Christmas — A242

Paintings like stained-glass windows by Johannes Johannesson (b. 1921): 21k, Madonna and Child. 26k, Three Wise Men.

1989, Nov. 9

Granite Paper

684 A242 21k multi .80 .30
685 A242 26k multi .80 .60

Bird Type of 1986

1990, Feb. 15

Granite Paper

686 A212 21k *Anas penelope* 1.00 .45
687 A212 80k *Anser brachyrhynchus* 1.75 .90

Guardian Spirit Type of 1987

Perf. 13 on 3 Sides

1990, Feb. 15 Engr.

688 A227 5k Vulture .20 .20
689 A227 5k Dragon .20 .20
690 A227 5k Bull .20 .20
691 A227 5k Giant .20 .20
a. Block of 4, #688-691 .50 .60
692 A227 21k Vulture .65 .65
693 A227 21k Dragon .65 .65
694 A227 21k Bull .65 .65
695 A227 21k Giant .65 .65
a. Block of 4, #692-695 1.75 2.00
b. Block of 8, #688-695 3.50 3.50
c. Bklt. pane, 2 each #691a, 695a 5.50 5.50

Famous Women — A243

No. 696, Gudrun Larusdottir (1880-1938), author and politician, by Halldor Petursson. No. 697, Ragnhildur Petursdottir (1880-1961), educator, by Asgrimur Jonsson.

1990, Mar. 22 Litho. *Perf. 13½x14*

696 A243 21k multicolored .50 .40
697 A243 21k multicolored .50 .40

Europa 1990 A244

Old and new post offices in Reykjavik and letter scales.

1990, May 7 Photo. *Perf. 12x11½*

Granite Paper

698 A244 21k 1915 *2.10* .45
699 A244 40k 1989 *2.10* .85

Sports — A245

1990-93 Litho. *Perf. 13x14½*

700 A245 21k Archery .50 .35
701 A245 21k Soccer .50 .35
706 A245 26k Golf .60 .35
707 A245 26k Icelandic wrestling .60 .35

Perf. 13½x14½

Photo.

708 A245 30k Volleyball .70 .45
709 A245 30k Skiing .70 .45
710 A245 30k Running .70 .45
711 A245 30k Team handball .70 .45

Litho.

Perf. 14x14½

711A A245 30k Swimming .70 .35
711B A245 30k Weight lifting .70 .35
Nos. 700-711B (10) 6.40 3.90

Issued: 21k, 6/28; 26k, 8/14/91; 30k, 2/20/92; #710-711, 3/10/93; #711A, 711B, 2/25/94.

This is an expanding set. Numbers will change if necessary.

European Tourism Year — A246

1990, Sept. 6 Litho. *Perf. 13½*

712 A246 30k multicolored .65 .45

Landscape Type of 1989

1990, Sept. 6 Photo. *Perf.*

713 A238 25k Hvitserkur .80 .45
714 A238 200k Lomagnupur 5.00 1.75

NORDIA '91 Map Type of 1989

Souvenir Sheet

Detail of 1539 Map by Olaus Magnus: a, Dania. b, Gothia. c, Gotlandia.

Litho. & Engr.**Litho. & Engr.**

1990, Oct. 9 *Perf. 12½*

715 A240 Sheet of 3 6.50 6.50
a.-c. 40k any single 2.00 2.00

Stamp Day. Sold for 170k to benefit the exhibition.

Christmas A247

1990, Nov. 8 *Perf. 13½x13*

716 A247 25k shown .85 .40
717 A247 30k Carolers .85 .50

Bird Type of 1986

1991, Feb. 7 Photo. *Perf. 11½*

Granite Paper

721 A212 25k Podiceps auritus .85 .40
725 A212 100k Sula bassana 3.00 .85

This is an expanding set. Numbers will change if necessary.

Landscape Type of 1989

1991, Mar. 7 Photo. *Perf. 11½*

Granite Paper

728 A238 10k Vestrahorn .40 .25
737 A238 300k Kverkfjoll 7.00 2.50

This is an expanding set. Numbers will change if necessary.

Europa A248

1991, Apr. 29 Litho. *Perf. 14*

738 A248 26k Weather map 4.00 .65
739 A248 47k Solar panels 2.10 1.10

NORDIA '91 Map Type of 1989

Souvenir Sheet

Detail of 1539 Map by Olaus Magnus: a, Iceland's west coast. b, Islandia. c, Mare Glacial.

Litho. & Engr.

1991, May 23 *Perf. 12½*

740 A240 Sheet of 3 7.25 7.25
a.-c. 50k any single 2.40 2.40

Sold for 215k to benefit the exhibition.

Jokulsarlon Lagoon A249

Design: 31k, Strokkur hot spring.

1991, May 23 Litho. *Perf. 15x14*

741 A249 26k multicolored .85 .40
742 A249 31k multicolored 1.00 .50

Ragnar Jonsson (1904-1984), Patron of the Arts — A250

70k, Pall Isolfsson (1893-1974), musician, vert.

1991, Aug. 14 Litho. *Perf. 14*

743 A250 60k multicolored 2.00 .90
744 A250 70k multicolored 2.25 .90

Ships A251

Designs: a, Soloven, schooner, 1840. b, Arcturus, steamer with sails, 1858. c, Gullfoss, steamer, 1915. d, Esja II, diesel ship, 1939.

1991, Oct. 9 Litho. *Perf. 14*

745 Block or strip of 4 8.00 8.00
a.-d. A251 30k any single 2.00 1.00
e. A251 Bklt. pane, 2 #745 16.00

Issued in sheet of 8. No. 745e is distinguished from sheet of 8 by rouletted selvage at left.

See Nos. 803-806.

College of Navigation, Reykjavik, Cent. A252

1991, Oct. 9 *Perf. 13½*

746 A252 50k multicolored 1.75 .90

Christmas — A253

Paintings by Eirikur Smith (b. 1925): 30k, Christmas star. 35k, Star over winter landscape.

1991, Nov. 7 Litho. *Perf. 13½*

747 A253 30k multicolored 1.00 .30
748 A253 35k multicolored 1.25 .80

Europa A254

Map and: No. 749, Viking longboat of Leif Eriksson. No. 750, Sailing ship of Columbus.

1992, Apr. 6 Litho. *Perf. 13½x14*

749 A254 55k multicolored *2.50* 1.10
750 A254 55k multicolored *2.50* 1.10

Souvenir Sheet

751 A254 Sheet of 2, #749-750 *6.50* 6.00

First landing in the Americas by Leif Erikson (#749). Discovery of America by Christopher Columbus, 500th anniv. (#750).

Stamps on #751 printed in continuous design. #749-751 have borders.

Export Trade and Commerce A255

Designs: 35k, Fishing boat, fish.

1992, June 16 Litho. *Perf. 13½*

752 A255 30k multicolored 1.10 .50
753 A255 35k multicolored 1.25 .60

Bridges A256

1992, Oct. 9 Litho. *Perf. 13½*

754 A256 5k Fnjoska, 1908 .20 .20
755 A256 250k Olfusa, 1891 6.25 3.50

See Nos. 766-767.

Mail Trucks A257

#756, Mail transport car RE 231, 1933. #757, Ford bus, 1946. #758, Ford TT, 1920-26. #759, Citroen snowmobile, 1929.

1992, Oct. 9 *Perf. 14*

756 A257 30k multicolored 1.10 .75
757 A257 30k multicolored 1.10 .75
758 A257 30k multicolored 1.10 .75
759 A257 30k multicolored 1.10 .75
a. Block or strip of 4, #756-759 4.50 4.50
b. Bklt. pane, 2 ea #756-759 9.00

Issued in sheets of 8. No. 759b has rouletted selvage at left.

See Nos. 820-823.

Christmas — A258

Paintings by Bragi Asgeirsson.

1992, Nov. 9 Litho. *Perf. 13½x13*

760 A258 30k shown 1.10 .30
761 A258 35k Sun over mountains 1.25 .60

Falco Rusticolus — A259

1992, Dec. 3 Photo. *Perf. 11½*

Granite Paper

762 A259 5k Adult, two young .25 .40
763 A259 10k Adult feeding .45 .40
764 A259 20k Adult, head up .80 .40
765 A259 35k Adult 1.50 1.25
Nos. 762-765 (4) 3.00 2.45

Bridges Type of 1992

1993, Mar. 10 Litho. *Perf. 13½x13*

766 A256 90k Hvita, 1928 3.00 1.25
767 A256 150k Jokulsa a Fjollum, 1947 4.75 1.75

Nordica '93 — A260

Designs: 30k, The Blue Lagoon therapeutic bathing area, hot water plant, Svartsengi. 35k, Perlan hot water storage tanks, restaurant.

1993, Apr. 26 Litho. *Perf. 13½x13*

768 A260 30k multicolored 1.00 .40
769 A260 35k multicolored 1.10 .70

Sculptures — A261

Europa: 35k, Sailing, by Jon Gunnar Arnason. 55k, Hatching of the Jet, by Magnus Tomasson.

1993, Apr. 26 *Perf. 13x13½*

770 A261 35k multicolored *1.25* .80
771 A261 55k multicolored *2.10* 1.25

Souvenir Sheet

Italian Group Flight, 60th Anniv. — A262

1993, Oct. 9 Litho. *Perf. 13½*

772 A262 Sheet of 3, #a.-c. 6.00 6.00
a. 10k #C12 .35 .35
b. 50k #C13 1.90 1.90
c. 100k #C14 3.75 3.75

No. 772 sold for 200k.

Seaplanes — A263

1993, Oct. 9 *Perf. 14*

773 A263 30k Junkers F-13 (D463) 1.25 .75
774 A263 30k Waco YKS-7 (TF-ORN) 1.25 .75
775 A263 30k Grumman G-21A/JRF-5 (RVK) 1.25 .75
776 A263 30k PBY-5 Catalina (TF-ISP) 1.25 .75
a. Block or strip of 4, #773-776 5.00 5.00
b. Bklt. pane, 2 ea #773-776 10.00

No. 776b is distinguished from sheet of 8 by rouletted selvage at left.

Issued in sheet of 8.

See Nos. 838-841.

Christmas A264

1993, Nov. 8 Litho. *Perf. 12½*

777 A264 30k Adoration of the Magi .90 .40
778 A264 35k Virgin and Child 1.00 .90

Intl. Year of the Family A265

1994, Feb. 25 Litho. *Perf. 13½x13*

779 A265 40k multicolored 1.10 .55

Voyages of St. Brendan (484-577) A266

Europa: 35k, St. Brendan, Irish monks sailing past volcano. 55k, St. Brendan on island with sheep, monks in boat.

1994, Apr. 18 Litho. *Perf. 14½x14*

780 A266 35k multicolored *1.60* .75
781 A266 55k multicolored *1.60* 1.00
a. Miniature sheet of 2, #780-781 *3.25* 3.25

See Ireland Nos. 923-924; Faroe Islands Nos. 264-265.

Icelandic Art and Culture A267

1994, May 25 Litho. *Perf. 13½x13*

782 A267 30k Music .90 .30
783 A267 30k Crafts .90 .60
784 A267 30k Film making .90 .60
785 A267 30k Ballet, modern dance .90 .60
786 A267 30k Theatre .90 .60
Nos. 782-786 (5) 4.50 2.70

Independence, 50th anniv.

Gisli Sveinsson (1880-1959), Politician — A268

1994, June 14 *Perf. 14*

787 A268 30k multicolored .90 .45

Proclamation of new constitution, 50th anniv.

Souvenir Sheet

Republic of Iceland, 50th Anniv. — A269

Presidents of Iceland: a, Sveinn Bjornsson (1881-1952). b, Asgeir Asgeirsson (1894-1972). c, Kristjan Eldjarn (1916-82). d, Vigdis Finnbogadottir (b. 1930).

1994, June 17 Photo. *Perf. 11½*

Granite Paper

788 A269 Sheet of 4, #a.-d. 4.25 4.25
a.-d. 50k any single 1.10 1.10

Souvenir Sheet

Stamp Day — A270

Designs: a, Boy, girl with stamp album. b, Nos. 672, 713, portions of other Icelandic stamps. c, Girl, elderly man looking at globe.

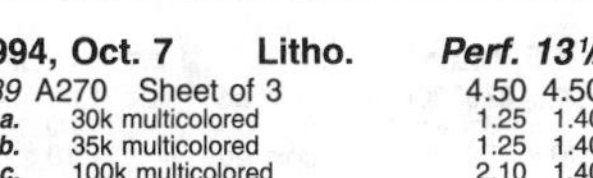

1994, Oct. 7 Litho. *Perf. 13½*

789 A270 Sheet of 3 4.50 4.50
a. 30k multicolored 1.25 1.40
b. 35k multicolored 1.25 1.40
c. 100k multicolored 2.10 1.40

No. 789 sold for 200k for the benefit of the Stamp and Postal History Fund.

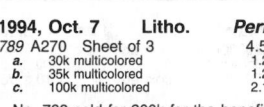

Christmas A271

1994, Nov. 9 Litho. *Perf. 14½*

790 A271 30k Woman, stars .95 .30
791 A271 35k Man, stars 1.10 .70

ICAO, 50th Anniv. A272

1994, Nov. 9 *Perf. 13½x14*

792 A272 100k multicolored 3.25 1.40

A273 A274

1995, Mar. 14 Litho. *Perf. 13*

793 A273 35k multicolored 1.10 .60

Salvation Army in Iceland, cent.

1995, Mar. 14

794 A274 90k multicolored 3.00 1.10

Town of Seydisfjordur, cent.

1995 Men's Team Handball World Championships, Iceland — A275

Federation emblem, handball and: No. 795, Geyser, landscape. No. 796, Silhouette of building, landscape. No. 797, Volcano, lake. No. 798, Inlet, sunlight on water.

1995, Mar. 14 Litho. *Perf. 14*

795 A275 35k multicolored 1.10 .90
796 A275 35k multicolored 1.10 .90
797 A275 35k multicolored 1.10 .90
798 A275 35k multicolored 1.10 .90
a. Block or strip of 4, #795-798 4.50 4.50
b. Booklet pane, 2 #798a 16.00
Complete booklet, #798b 16.00

Nos. 795-798 issued in sheets of 8 containing 2 each. No. 798b is separated from booklet by rouletted selvage at left, and sold for 480k in the complete booklet.

Norden 1995 — A276

Designs: 30k, Turf farmhouses, church. 35k, Volcano, Fjallsjokull glacier.

1995, May 5 Litho. ***Perf. 13½x13***
799 A276 30k multicolored 1.00 .40
Booklet, 10 #799 10.00
800 A276 35k multicolored 1.10 .75

Spell-Broken, by Einar Jonsson (1874-1954) — A277

1995, May 5 ***Perf. 13x13½***
801 A277 35k brown & multi 1.10 1.00
Booklet, 10 #801 12.00
802 A277 55k blue & multi 1.50 1.25
Booklet, 10 #802 16.00

Europa.

Ship Type of 1991

1995, June 30 Litho. ***Perf. 14***
803 A251 30k SS Laura 1.00 .75
804 A251 30k MS Dronning Alexandrine 1.00 .75
805 A251 30k MS Laxfoss 1.00 .75
806 A251 30k MS Godafoss III 1.00 .75
a. Block or strip of 4, #803-806 4.00 4.00
b. Bklt. pane, 2 ea #803-806 8.00
Prestige booklet, #806b 13.50

No. 806b is distinguished from sheet of 8 by rouletted selvage at left.
Issued in sheets of 8.
Prestige booklet sold for 400k.

Luxembourg-Reykjavik, Iceland Air Route, 40th Anniv. — A278

1995, Sept. 18 Litho. ***Perf. 13½***
807 A278 35k multicolored 1.10 .75

See Luxembourg No. 936.

Birds A279

1995, Sept. 18 ***Perf. 13½***
808 A279 25k Acanthis flammea .60 .50
809 A279 250k Gallinago gallinago 6.00 5.00

Souvenir Sheet

Nordia '96, Reykjavik — A280

Design: Hraunfossar Waterfalls, Hvita River. Illustration reduced.

1995, Oct. 9 ***Perf. 13½x14***
810 A280 Sheet of 2, #a.-b. 6.75 6.75
a. 10k multicolored .40 .40
b. 150k multicolored 6.25 6.25

See No. 830.

Christmas A281

1995, Nov. 8 Litho. ***Perf. 13½***
811 A281 30k Snowman, woman 1.00 .60
812 A281 35k Three trees 1.10 .75

UN, 50th Anniv. — A282

1995, Nov. 8 ***Perf. 13x13½***
813 A282 100k multicolored 2.50 1.75

Water Birds A283

Designs: 20k, Phalacrocorax carbo. 40k, Bucephala islandica.

1996, Feb. 7 Litho. ***Perf. 13½***
814 A283 20k multicolored .50 .40
815 A283 40k multicolored .90 .75

See Nos. 834-835.

Paintings A284

100k, Seamen in a Boat, by Gunnlaugur Scheving (1904-72). 200k, At the Washing Springs, by Kristín Jónsdóttir (1888-1959).

1996, Feb. 7
816 A284 100k multicolored 2.10 1.60
817 A284 200k multicolored 4.00 3.25

Famous Women A285

Europa: 35k, Halldóra Bjarnadóttir (1873-1981), educator. 55k, Olafía Jóhannsdóttir (1863-1924), representative of women's rights, temperance affairs.

1996, Apr. 18 Litho. ***Perf. 14½***
818 A285 35k multicolored .80 .60
819 A285 55k multicolored 1.25 1.10

Postal Vehicle Type of 1992

Designs: No. 820, 1931 Buick. No. 821, 1933 Studebaker, Reykjavík Municipal Bus Service. No. 822, 1937 Ford, Iceland Motor Coach Service. No. 823, 1946 REO, Post and Telecommunications.

1996, May 13 Litho. ***Perf. 14***
820 A257 35k multicolored 1.00 .75
821 A257 35k multicolored 1.00 .75
822 A257 35k multicolored 1.00 .75
823 A257 35k multicolored 1.00 .75
a. Block or strip of 4, #820-823 3.75 3.75
b. Bklt. pane, 2 ea #820-823 7.50 7.50
Souvenir booklet, #823b 11.00

No. 823a issued in sheets of 8 stamps. No. 823b has rouletted selvage at left.

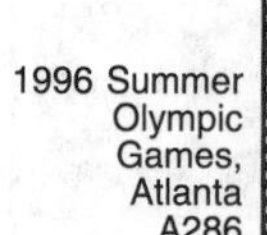
1996 Summer Olympic Games, Atlanta A286

1996, June 25 Litho. ***Perf. 12½***
824 A286 5k Running .20 .20
825 A286 25k Javelin .60 .35
826 A286 45k Long jump 1.10 1.00
827 A286 65k Shot put 1.60 1.25
Nos. 824-827 (4) 3.50 2.80

Order of the Sisters of St. Joseph in Iceland, Cent. — A287

1996, Sept. 17 Litho. ***Perf. 14½x13***
828 A287 65k multicolored 1.50 1.40

Reykjavik School, 150th Anniv. A288

1996, Sept. 17 ***Perf. 12½x13***
829 A288 150k multicolored 3.50 2.75

Nordia '96 Type of 1995

Design: Godafoss Waterfalls, Skjalfandafljot River. Illustration reduced.

1996, Oct. 9 Litho. ***Perf. 13½x14***
830 A280 Sheet of 3, #a.-c. 7.50 7.50
a. 45k multicolored 2.00 2.00
b. 65k multicolored 2.50 2.50
c. 90k multicolored 3.00 3.00

Reykjavik Cathedral, Bicent. — A289

1996, Nov. 5 ***Perf. 14***
831 A289 45k multicolored 1.40 .90

Christmas — A290

Artifacts from Natl. Museum of Iceland: 35k, Figurine of Madonna and Child carved from walrus tusk. 45k, Pax showing Nativity.

1996, Nov. 5 ***Perf. 13½***
832 A290 35k multicolored 1.10 .50
a. Booklet pane of 10 11.00
Booklet, #832a 11.00
833 A290 45k multicolored 1.40 .75

Bird Type of 1996

10k, Mergus serrator. 500k, Anas crecca.

1997, Apr. 2 Litho. ***Perf. 13½***
834 A283 10k multicolored .25 .20
835 A283 500k multicolored 12.50 12.50

Paintings A291

150k, Song of Iceland, by Svavar Guthnason. 200k, The Harbor, by Thorvaldur Skúlason.

1997, Mar. 6 Litho. ***Perf. 14***
836 A291 150k multicolored 3.50 2.50
837 A291 200k multicolored 4.50 3.50

Airplane Type of 1993

#838, De Havilland DH-89A (TF-ISM). #839, Stinson SR 8B Reliant (TF-RVB). #840, Douglas DC-3 (TF-ISH). #841, De Havilland DHC-6 Twin Otter (TF-REG).

1997, Apr. 15 Litho. ***Perf. 14***
838 A263 35k multicolored 1.10 .75
839 A263 35k multicolored 1.10 .75
840 A263 35k multicolored 1.10 .75
841 A263 35k multicolored 1.10 .75
a. Block or strip of 4, #838-841 4.50 4.50
b. Booklet pane, 2 each #838-841 9.00
Booklet, #841b 9.00

Issued in sheet of 8.
No. 841b has rouletted selvage at left.

European Games A292

1997, May 13 Litho. ***Perf. 14½***
842 A292 35k Hurdles 1.00 .70
843 A292 45k Sailing 1.25 .90

Europa A293

Stories and legends by Asgrimur Jonsson: 45k, Couple on galloping horse. 65k, Old woman reaching for children.

1997, May 13 ***Perf. 13½***
844 A293 45k multicolored 1.10 1.00
Complete booklet of 10 12.50
845 A293 65k multicolored 1.60 1.10
Complete booklet of 105 20.00

Union of Graphic Workers, Cent. — A294

1997, Sept. 3 Litho. ***Perf. 13½***
846 A294 90k multicolored 2.00 1.75

Reykjavik Theater, Cent. — A295

1997, Sept. 3 ***Perf. 13½x14***
847 A295 100k multicolored 1.75 1.75

Stamp Day — A296

Icelandic row boats: a, Gideon, eight-oared lugger, 1836. b, Breidafjördur double-ended transport, 1904. c, Engey, six-oared craft, 1912.

1997, Oct. 9 Litho. *Perf. 15*

848 A296 Sheet of 3	7.50	7.50
a. 35k multicolored	1.60	1.60
b. 100k multicolored	3.25	3.25
c. 65k multicolored	2.40	2.40

Christmas A297

1997, Nov. 5 Litho. *Perf. 13½x13*

849 A297 35k Magi	1.00	.70
a. Booklet pane of 10	10.00	
Booklet, #849a	10.00	
850 A297 45k Nativity	1.40	.90

Rural Postman A298

Litho. & Engr.

1997, Nov. 5 *Perf. 13½*

851 A298 50k multicolored	1.25	1.00

1998 Winter Olympic Games, Nagano A299

1998, Jan. 22 Litho. *Perf. 13½*

852 A299 35k Downhill skier	1.00	1.00
853 A299 45k Cross country skier	1.25	1.25

Nordic Stamps A300

1998, Mar. 5 Litho. *Perf. 13½x13*

854 A300 35k Sailboats	1.00	1.00
855 A300 45k Power boats	1.25	1.25

Fish — A301

1998, Apr. 16

856 A301 5k Cyclopterus lumpus	.20	.20
857 A301 10k Gadus morhua	.30	.30
858 A301 60k Raja batis	1.75	1.75
859 A301 300k Anarhicus lupus	8.75	8.75
a. Min. sheet of 4, #856-859	11.00	11.00
Nos. 856-859 (4)	11.00	11.00

Intl. Year of the Ocean (#859a).
See Nos. 915-916.

National Holidays and Festivals A302

Independence Day, June 17th: 45k, Children standing at attention, flag. 65k, Monument, parade.

1998, May 12 Litho. *Perf. 14½*

860 A302 45k multicolored	1.25	1.25
Complete booklet, 10 #860	12.50	
861 A302 65k multicolored	1.90	1.90
Complete booklet, 10 #861	19.00	

Europa.

Minerals — A303

1998, Sept. 3 Litho. *Perf. 13½*

862 A303 35k Stilbite	1.00	1.00
863 A303 45k Scolecite	1.25	1.25

See Nos. 885-886.

Leprosy Hospital, Laugarnes A304

1998, Sept. 3 *Perf. 13½x14*

864 A304 70k multicolored	2.00	2.00

First Icelandic Postage Stamp, 125th Anniv. — A305

1998, Oct. 9 Litho. *Perf. 13½*

865 A305 35k multicolored	1.00	1.00

Agricultural Tools — A306

1998, Oct. 9 *Perf. 15*

866 A306 Sheet of 3	7.50	7.50
a. 35k Turf scythe	1.25	1.25
b. 65k Hay mower	2.40	2.40
c. 100k Manure mincer	3.75	3.75

Stamp Day.

Christmas, Children's Drawings — A307

35k, Black cat, homes, mountains. 45k, Angels, Christmas tree, moon and stars.

1998, Nov. 5 Litho. *Perf. 13x13½*

867 A307 35k multicolored	1.10	1.10
a. Booklet pane of 10	11.00	
Complete booklet, #867a	11.00	
868 A307 45k multicolored	1.40	1.40

Universal Declaration of Human Rights, 50th Anniv. — A308

1998, Nov. 5 *Perf. 14½*

869 A308 50k multicolored	1.50	1.50

Jón Leifs (1899-1968), Composer — A309

1999, Jan. 22 Litho. *Perf. 14½*

870 A309 35k multicolored	1.00	1.00

Fish Type of 1998

35k, Pleuronectez platessa. 55k, Clupea harengus.

1999, Jan. 22 *Perf. 14½x15*

871 A301 35k multicolored	1.00	1.00
872 A301 55k multicolored	1.60	1.60

Marine Mammals — A311

Designs: 35k, Orcinus orca. 45k, Physeter macrocephalus. 65k, Balaenoptera musculus. 85k, Phocoena phocoena.

1999, Mar. 4 Litho. *Perf. 14½*

873 A311 35k multicolored	.95	.95
874 A311 45k multicolored	1.25	1.25
875 A311 65k multicolored	1.90	1.90
876 A311 85k multicolored	2.40	2.40
a. Sheet of 4, #873-876	6.50	6.50
Nos. 873-876 (4)	6.50	6.50

See Nos. 911-914.

Locomotive A312

Perf. 13 on 2 or 3 Sides

1999, Apr. 15

Booklet Stamps

877 A312 25k green & multi	.70	.70
878 A312 50k brown & multi	1.40	1.40
a. Booklet pane, 1 #877, 3 #878	5.00	
Complete booklet, #878a	5.00	
879 A312 75k Ship	2.10	2.10
a. Booklet pane of 4	8.50	
Complete booklet, #879a	8.50	
Nos. 877-879 (3)	4.20	4.20

See Nos. 908-909.

Council of Europe, 50th Anniv. A313

1999, Apr.15 *Perf. 13x13½*

880 A313 35k multicolored	1.00	1.00

Mushrooms A314

35k, Suillus grevillei. 75k, Agaricus campestris.

1999, May 20 Litho. *Perf. 14½*

881 A314 35k multicolored	1.00	1.00
882 A314 75k multicolored	2.10	2.10

See Nos. 898-899.

National Parks — A315

1999, May 20 *Perf. 13¼*

883 A315 50k Skutustadagigar	1.40	1.40
a. Booklet pane of 10	14.00	
Complete booklet, #883a	14.00	
884 A315 75k Vid Arnarstapa	2.10	2.10
a. Booklet pane of 10	21.00	
Complete booklet, #884a	21.00	

Europa.

Minerals Type of 1998

1999, Sept. 9 Litho. *Perf. 14¾*

885 A303 40k Calcite	1.10	1.10
886 A303 50k Heulandite	1.40	1.40

Nature Conservation A316

1999, Sept. 9 Litho. *Perf. 14¼*

887 A316 35k "Hreinar"	1.00	1.00
888 A316 35k "Markviss"	1.00	1.00
889 A316 35k "Hreint"	1.00	1.00
890 A316 35k "Endurheimt"	1.00	1.00
891 A316 35k "Eflum"	1.00	1.00
a. Strip of 5, #887-891	5.00	5.00

Reykjavik, European Cultural City for 2000 A317

35k, Facescape, by Erro. 50k, Book, violin, palette, masks, camera, computer.

1999, Oct. 7 Litho. *Perf. 13¼*

892 A317 35k multi	1.00	1.00
893 A317 50k multi	1.40	1.40

Souvenir Sheet

View of Skagafhordur, by Carl Emil Baagoe — A318

Illustration reduced.

1999, Oct. 7 *Perf. 13¼x13*

894 A318 200k olive & black	7.00	7.00

Stamp Day. #894 sold for 250k.

Children's Art — A319

1999, Nov. 4 Litho. *Perf. 13*

895 A319 35k multi 1.00 1.00

Christmas — A320

No. 896, Elf: a, With walking stick. b, Jumping over rock. c, Waving. d, Licking spoon. e, With hand in cauldron. f, With cup. g, At door. h, With ladle and barrel. i, With sausages. j, At window.

No. 897, Elf: a, Looking up. b, With ham. c, With candles.

1999, Nov. 4

896 Strip of 10 10.00 10.00
a.-j. A320 35k any single 1.00 1.00
k. Booklet pane, #896a-896j 10.00
Complete booklet, #896k 10.00
897 Strip of 3 4.25 4.25
a.-c. A320 50k any single 1.40 1.40

See Nos. 924-926.

Mushroom Type of 1999

Designs: 40k, Cantharellus cibarius. 50k, Coprinus comatus.

2000, Feb. 4 Litho. *Perf. 13*

898 A314 40k multi 1.10 1.10
a. Booklet pane of 10 11.00
Complete booklet, #898a 11.00
899 A314 50k multi 1.40 1.40

A321

Christianity in Iceland, 1000th Anniv. — A322

Illustration A322 reduced.

2000, Feb. 4 *Perf. 13¼x13¾*

900 A321 40k multi 1.10 1.10

Souvenir Sheet

Perf. 13¼x13

901 A322 40k multi 1.10 1.10

See Vatican City #1151.

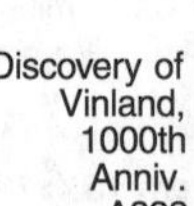

Discovery of Vinland, 1000th Anniv. A323

Designs: 40k, Viking with shield, globe. 50k, Viking ship sailing. 75k, Viking ship at shore. 90k, Viking without shield, globe.

Litho. & Engr.

2000, Mar. 16 *Perf. 12½x13*

902 A323 40k multi 1.10 1.10
903 A323 50k multi 1.40 1.40
904 A323 75k multi 2.00 2.00
905 A323 90k multi 2.50 2.50
a. Souvenir sheet, #902-905 7.00 7.00
Nos. 902-905 (4) 7.00 7.00

Millennium A324

Designs: 40k, Head, quill pen. 50k, Man, genealogical chart, circuit board.

2000, Apr. 27 Litho. *Perf. 13x13¼*

906 A324 40k multi 1.10 1.10
907 A324 50k multi 1.40 1.40

Locomotive Type of 1999

Perf. 13 on 2 or 3 sides

2000, Apr. 27 Litho.

Booklet Stamps

908 A312 50k Steam roller 1.40 1.40
a. Booklet pane of 4 5.75
Booklet, #908a 5.75
909 A312 75k Fire pumper 2.00 2.00
a. Booklet pane of 4 8.00
Booklet, #909a 8.00

Europa, 2000

Common Design Type

2000, May 18 Litho. *Perf. 13¼x13*

910 CD17 50k multi 1.40 1.40
a. Booklet pane of 10 14.00
Booklet, #910a 14.00

Marine Mammals Type of 1999

Designs: 5k, Hyperoodon ampullatus. 40k, Lagenorhynchus acutus. 50k, Megaptera novaeangliae. 75k, Balaenoptera acutorostrata.

2000, May 18 *Perf. 14½*

911 A311 5k multi .20 .20
912 A311 40k multi 1.10 1.10
913 A311 50k multi 1.40 1.40
914 A311 75k multi 2.00 2.00
Nos. 911-914 (4) 4.70 4.70

Fish Type of 1998

Designs: 10k, Melanogrammus aeglefinus. 250k, Mallotus villosus.

2000, Sept. 14 Litho. *Perf. 13*

915-916 A301 Set of 2 6.75 6.75

Flowers — A325

Designs: 40k, Viola x wittrockiana. 50k, Petunia x hybrida.

2000, Sept. 14 *Perf. 13*

917-918 A325 Set of 2 2.40 2.40

Butterflies A326

Designs: 40k, Chloroclysta citrata. 50k, Cerapteryx graminis.

2000, Oct. 9 *Perf. 14x14½*

919-920 A326 Set of 2 2.25 2.25

Souvenir Sheet

Stamp Day — A327

Illustration reduced.

Litho. & Engr.

2000, Oct. 9 *Perf. 13¼*

921 A327 200k multi 6.00 6.00

No. 921 sold for 250k.

Ancient Architecture — A328

Various buildings. Denominations: 45k, 75k.

2000, Nov. 9 Litho. *Perf. 14*

922-923 A328 Set of 2 3.00 3.00

Christmas Type of 1999

Designs: 40k, Elf grasping walking stick. 50k, Female elf carrying bag.

2000, Nov. 9 *Perf. 13*

924 A320 40k multi .95 .95
a. Perf. 12¾x13¼ .95 .95
b. Booklet pane, 4 #924a 4.00
c. Booklet pane, 6 #924a 5.75
Booklet, #924b, 924c 9.75
925 A320 50k multi 1.25 1.25

Souvenir Sheet

926 Sheet of 2 2.25 2.25
a. A320 40k As #924, 25x38mm .95 .95
b. A320 50k As #925, 25x38mm 1.25 1.25

Coast Guard, 75th Anniv. A329

2001, Jan. 18 Litho. *Perf. 13*

927 A329 (40k) multi .95 .95
a. Booklet pane of 10 9.50
Booklet, #927a 9.50

Fish Type of 1998

Designs: 55k, Reinhardtius hippoglossoides. 80k, Pollachius virens.

2001, Jan. 18

928-929 A301 Set of 2 3.25 3.25

UN High Commissioner for Refugees, 50th Anniv. — A330

2001, Mar. 8 *Perf. 13¼x13*

930 A330 50k multi 1.10 1.10

Flower Type of 2000

Designs: 55k, Calendula officinalis. 65k, Dorotheanthus bellidiformis.

2001, Mar. 8 *Perf. 13*

931-932 A325 Set of 2 2.75 2.75

Icelandic Sheepdog A331

Dog's coat: 40k, Brown. 80k, Black.

2001, Apr. 18 *Perf. 14¼*

933-934 A331 Set of 2 2.50 2.50

Airplanes A332

Designs: 55k: TF-OGN (biplane). 80k, Klemm TF-SUX (monoplane).

Perf. 13½x12¾ on 2 or 3 Sides

2001, Apr. 18

Booklet Stamps

935 A332 55k multi 1.10 1.10
a. Booklet pane of 4 4.50
Booklet, #935a 4.50
936 A332 80k multi 1.75 1.75
a. Booklet pane of 4 7.00
Booklet, #936a 7.00

Europa A333

Designs: 55k, Head, waterfall. 80k, Hand, wave.

2001, May 17 *Perf. 13*

937 A333 55k multi 1.10 1.10
a. Booklet pane of 10 11.00
Booklet, #937a 11.00
938 A333 80k multi 1.75 1.75
a. Booklet pane of 10 17.50
Booklet, #938a 17.50

Horses A334

Designs: 40k, Fet. 50k, Tölt. 55k, Brokk. 60k, Skeidh. 80k, Stökk.

2001, May 17 *Perf. 13x13¼*

939-943 A334 Set of 5 6.00 6.00

No. 873 Surcharged in Red

2001, July 10 Litho. *Perf. 14½*

944 A311 (53k) on 35k multi 1.10 1.10

Marine Mammals Type of 1999

Designs: 5k, Lagenorhynchus albirostris. 40k, Balaenoptera physalus. 80k, Balaenoptera borealis. 100k, Globicephala melas.

2001, Sept. 6 Litho. *Perf. 14½*

945 A311 5k multi .20 .20
946 A311 40k multi .85 .85
947 A311 80k multi 1.60 1.60
948 A311 100k multi 2.10 2.10
Nos. 945-948 (4) 4.75 4.75

Islands
A335

Designs: 40k, Grimsey. 55k, Papey.

2001, Oct. 9 Litho. *Perf. 13¼x13*
949-950 A335 Set of 2 1.90 1.90

Souvenir Sheet

Esja Mountain — A336

2001, Oct. 9 *Perf. 13¼*
951 A336 250k multi 5.00 5.00

Stamp Day.

Birds — A337

Designs: 42k, Oenanthe oenanthe. 250k, Charadrius hiaticula.

2001, Nov. 8 *Perf. 13¼x13*
952-953 A337 Set of 2 5.75 5.75

Christmas
A338

Churches: (42k), Brautarholt. 55k, Vidhmyri.

2001, Nov. 8

954 A338 (42k) multi		.80	.80
a.	Booklet pane of 6	4.80	—
	Booklet, #954a, 4 #954	8.00	
955 A338 55k multi		1.10	1.10

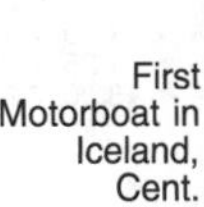

First
Motorboat in
Iceland,
Cent.
A339

2002, Jan. 17 Litho. *Perf. 13x13½*
956 A339 60k multi 1.25 1.25

Mushroom Type of 1999

Designs: (40k), Leccinum scabrum. 85k, Hydnum repandum.

2002, Jan. 17 *Perf. 13¼x12¾*
957-958 A314 Set of 2 2.50 2.50
Booklet, 10 #957 8.00

No. 957 is inscribed "Bref 20g."

Intl. Year of
Mountains
A340

2002, Mar. 7 Litho. *Perf. 13*
959 A340 (42k) multi .85 .85

Halldór
Laxness
(1902-98),
1955 Nobel
Literature
Laureate
A341

2002, Mar. 7 Litho. *Perf. 13x13¼*
960 A341 100k multi 2.00 2.00
a. Souvenir sheet of 1 2.00 2.00

Examples of No. 960a with Nobel Prize medal in margin printed in gold foil and embossed sold for 1700k.

Lighthouses — A342

Perf. 12¾x13¼ on 2 or 3 Sides
2002, Apr. 18
Booklet Stamps

961 A342 60k Grótta		1.25	1.25
a.	Booklet pane of 4	5.00	—
	Booklet, #961a	5.00	
962 A342 85k Kögur		1.75	1.75
a.	Booklet pane of 4	7.00	—
	Booklet, #962a	7.00	

Fyssa, by
Rúrí — A343

Spenna, by
Hafsteinn
Austmann
A344

2002, Apr. 18 Litho. *Perf. 14½x14¾*
963 A343 (42k) multi .90 .90
964 A344 60k multi 1.25 1.25

Nordic Council, 50th anniv. (No. 963).

Sesselja
Sigmundsdóttir
(1902-74),
Advocate for
Mentally
Handicapped
A345

2002, May 9
965 A345 45k multi 1.00 1.00

Europa
A346

Designs: 60k, Acrobats, juggling clown. 85k, Head on stick, lion jumping through ring of fire.

2002, May 9 *Perf. 13*

966 A346 60k multi		1.25	1.25
a.	Booklet pane of 10	12.50	
	Booklet, #966a	12.50	
967 A346 85k multi		1.90	1.90
a.	Booklet pane of 10	19.00	
	Booklet, #967a	19.00	

Flowers Type of 2000

Designs: 10k, Lobelia erinus. 200k, Centaurea cyanus.

2002, Sept. 5 Litho. *Perf. 14¾x14½*
968-969 A325 Set of 2 5.00 5.00

Fish of Lake Thingvallavatn — A347

Designs: (45k), Salvelinus alpinus (Murta). (55k), Salmo trutta, vert. 60k, Salvelinus alpinus (Sílableikja). 90k, Salvelinus alpinus (Kuthungableikja). 200k, Salvelinus alpinus (Dvergbleikja).

2002, Sept. 5 *Perf. 13¼x13, 13x13¼*

970 A347 (45k) multi		1.00	1.00
971 A347 (55k) multi		1.25	1.25
a.	Perf. 13¼x13	1.25	1.25
972 A347 60k multi		1.40	1.40
973 A347 90k multi		2.10	2.10
974 A347 200k multi		4.75	4.75
a.	Booklet pane, #970, 971a, 972-974	10.50	
	Booklet, #974a	10.50	

Islands Type of 2001

Designs: 45k, Vigur. 55k, Flatey.

2002, Oct. 9 *Perf. 14*
975-976 A335 Set of 2 2.40 2.40

Souvenir Sheet

Sudurgata, Reykjavik — A348

2002, Oct. 9 *Perf. 14½x14¾*
977 A348 250k multi 5.75 5.75

Stamp Day.

Birds
A349

Christmas
A350

Designs: 50k, Tringa totanus. 85k, Phalaropus fulicarius.

2002, Nov. 7 *Perf. 13¼x13*
978-979 A349 Set of 2 3.25 3.25

2002, Nov. 7 *Perf. 13*

Designs: 45k, Gifts and ornaments. 60k, Gifts.

980 A350 45k multi		1.10	1.10
a.	Booklet pane of 10	11.00	
	Booklet, #980a	11.00	
981 A350 60k multi		1.40	1.40

Flower Type of 2000

Designs: 45k, Phlox drummondii. 60k, Gazania x hybrida.

2003, Jan. 16 *Perf. 13*

982 A325 45k multi		1.10	1.10
a.	Booklet pane of 10	11.00	
	Booklet, #982a	11.00	
983 A325 60k multi		1.50	1.50

Icelandic Police
Force,
Bicent. — A351

Designs: 45k, Police officers, 2003. 55k, Policeman, 1803.

2003, Jan. 16
984-985 A351 Set of 2 2.50 2.50

SEMI-POSTAL STAMPS

Shipwreck
and Rescue
by
Breeches
Buoy
SP1

Children
Gathering
Rock
Plants
SP2

Old
Fisherman
at Shore
SP3

Unwmk.

1933, Apr. 28 Engr. *Perf. 14*

B1 SP1 10a + 10a red brown		1.50	*4.50*
B2 SP2 20a + 20a org red		1.50	*4.50*
B3 SP1 35a + 25a ultra		1.50	*4.50*
B4 SP3 50a + 25a blue grn		1.50	*4.50*
	Nos. B1-B4 (4)	6.00	*18.00*
	Set, never hinged	11.00	

Receipts from the surtax were devoted to a special fund for use in various charitable works especially those indicated on the stamps: "Slysavarnir" (Rescue work), "Barnahaeli" (Asylum for scrofulous children), "Ellhaeli" (Asylum for the Aged).

Souvenir Sheets

King Christian X — SP4

1937, May 15 Typo.

B5 SP4 Sheet of 3		35.00	*250.00*
	Never hinged	65.00	
a.	15a violet	7.50	*45.00*
b.	25a red	7.50	*45.00*
c.	50a blue	7.50	*45.00*

Reign of Christian X, 25th anniv. Sheet sold for 2kr.

SP5

Designs: 30a, 40a, Ericsson statue, Reykjavik. 60a, Iceland's position on globe.

1938, Oct. 9 Photo. *Perf. 12*

B6 SP5 Sheet of 3	3.50	*25.00*
Never hinged	7.50	
a. 30a scarlet	.90	*9.00*
b. 40a purple	.90	*9.00*
c. 60a deep green	.90	*9.00*

Leif Ericsson Day, Oct. 9, 1938.

Catalogue values for unused stamps in this section, from this point to the end of the section, are for Never Hinged items.

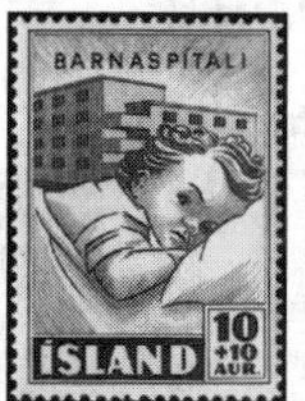
Ill Child — SP6

Red Cross Nurse and Patient — SP7

Nurse Covering Patient — SP8

Elderly Couple — SP9

Rescue at Sea — SP10

Unwmk.

1949, June 8 Engr. *Perf. 14*

B7 SP6 10a + 10a olive grn	.55	*.75*
B8 SP7 35a + 15a carmine	.55	*.75*
B9 SP8 50a + 25a choc	.60	*.75*
B10 SP9 60a + 25a brt ultra	.65	*.75*
B11 SP10 75a + 25a slate gray	.65	*.75*
Nos. B7-B11 (5)	3.00	*3.75*

The surtax was for charitable purposes.

Nos. 262 and 265 Surcharged in Black

1953, Feb. 12 Unwmk. *Perf. 13*

B12 A50 75a + 25a red org	1.25	*3.25*
B13 A50 1.25k + 25a red vio	1.75	*3.25*

The surtax was for flood relief in the Netherlands.

St. Thorlacus — SP11

Cathedral at Skalholt SP12

1.75k+1.25k, Bishop Jon Thorkelsson Vidalin.

1956, Jan. 23 *Perf. 11½*

B14 SP11 75a + 25a car	.35	*.45*
B15 SP12 1.25k + 75a dk brn	.35	*.45*
B16 SP11 1.75k + 1.25k black	.65	*1.25*
Nos. B14-B16 (3)	1.35	*2.15*

Bishopric of Skalholt, 900th anniv.

The surtax was for the rebuilding of Skalholt, former cultural center of Iceland.

Ambulance SP13

1963, Nov. 15 Photo. Unwmk.

B17 SP13 3k + 50a multi	.25	*.50*
B18 SP13 3.50k + 50a multi	.25	*.50*

Centenary of International Red Cross.

Rock Ptarmigan in Summer SP14

Design: #B20, Rock ptarmigan in winter.

1965, Jan. 27 Photo. *Perf. 12½*
Granite Paper

B19 SP14 3.50k + 50a multi	.55	*1.25*
B20 SP14 4.50k + 50a multi	.55	*1.25*

Ringed Plover's Nest — SP15

Design: 5k+50a, Rock ptarmigan's nest.

1967, Nov. 22 Photo. *Perf. 11½*

B21 SP15 4k + 50a multi	.55	*1.10*
B22 SP15 5k + 50a multi	.55	*1.10*

Arctic Terns — SP16

1972, Nov. 22 Litho. *Perf. 13*

B23 SP16 7k + 1k multi	.30	*.55*
B24 SP16 9k + 1k multi	.45	*.55*

AIR POST STAMPS

No. 115 Overprinted

Perf. 14x14½

1928, May 31 Wmk. 114

C1 A8 10a red	.70	*10.00*
Never hinged	1.10	

Same Overprint on No. 82

1929, June 29 Wmk. 113 *Perf. 13*

C2 A5 50a gray & violet	45.00	*95.00*
Never hinged	100.00	

Gyrfalcon AP1

Perf. 12½x12

1930, Jan. 1 Litho. Unwmk.

C3 AP1 10a dp ultra & gray blue	20.00	*55.00*
Never hinged	40.00	

Imperfs were privately printed.
For overprint see No. CO1.

Snaefellsjokull, Extinct Volcano — AP2

Parliament Millenary: 20a, Fishing boat. 35a, Iceland pony. 50a, Gullfoss (Golden Falls). 1k, Ingolfour Arnarson Statue.

Wmk. 47

1930, June 1 Typo. *Perf. 14*

C4 AP2 15a org brn & dl bl	25.00	*45.00*
C5 AP2 20a bis brn & sl bl	25.00	*45.00*
C6 AP2 35a olive grn & brn	47.50	*95.00*
C7 AP2 50a dp grn & dp bl	47.50	*95.00*
C8 AP2 1k olive grn & dk red	47.50	*95.00*
Nos. C4-C8 (5)	192.50	*375.00*
Set, never hinged	350.00	

Regular Issue of 1920 Overprinted

Perf. 14x14½

1931, May 25 Wmk. 114

C9 A8 30a red & green	30.00	*125.00*
C10 A8 1k dp bl & dk brn	11.00	*125.00*
C11 A8 2k ol brn & myr grn	50.00	*125.00*
Nos. C9-C11 (3)	91.00	*375.00*
Set, never hinged	160.00	

Nos. 185, 128 and 187 Overprinted in Red

1933, June 16

C12 A8 1k dk bl & lt brn	85.	*350.*
Never hinged	210.	
C13 A8 5k brn & indigo	325.	*900.*
Never hinged	800.	
C14 A8 10k yel grn & blk	750.	*2,250.*
Never hinged	1,900.	

Excellent counterfeit overprints exist.

Visit of the Italian Flying Armada en route from Rome to Chicago; also for the payment of the charges on postal matter sent from Iceland to the US via the Italian seaplanes.

Plane over Thingvalla Lake — AP7

10a-20a, Plane over Thingvalla Lake. 25a-50a, Plane and Aurora Borealis. 1k-2k, Map of Iceland.

Perf. 12½x14

1934, Sept. 1 Engr. Unwmk.

C15 AP7 10a blue	1.90	*2.50*
C16 AP7 20a emerald	3.50	*6.00*
a. Perf. 14	17.50	*17.50*
C17 AP7 25a dark violet, perf. 14	10.00	*16.00*
Revenue cancellation		18.00
a. Perf. 12½x14	17.50	*27.50*
C18 AP7 50a red vio, perf. 14	3.25	*7.00*
C19 AP7 1k dark brown	19.00	*30.00*
Revenue cancellation		20.00
C20 AP7 2k red orange	9.00	*12.00*
Nos. C15-C20 (6)	46.65	*73.50*
Set, never hinged	95.00	

Catalogue values for unused stamps in this section, from this point to the end of the section, are for Never Hinged items.

Thingvellir, Old Site of the Parliament AP10

Isafjörthur AP11

Eyjafjörthur AP12

Mt. Strandatindur AP13

Mt. Thyrill AP14

Aerial View of Reykjavik AP15

1947, Aug. 18 *Perf. 14*

C21 AP10 15a red orange	.65	*1.10*
C22 AP11 30a gray black	.65	*1.10*
C23 AP12 75a brown red	.60	*.95*
C24 AP13 1k indigo	.60	*.95*
C25 AP14 2k chocolate	1.25	*1.90*
C26 AP15 3k dark green	1.25	*1.90*
Nos. C21-C26 (6)	5.00	*7.90*

Snaefellsjokull AP16

Views: 2.50k, Eiriksjokull. 3.30k, Oraefajokull.

1952, May 2 Unwmk. *Perf. 13½x14*

C27 AP16 1.80k slate blue	16.00	*14.00*
C28 AP16 2.50k green	27.50	1.00
C29 AP16 3.30k deep ultra	6.50	5.00
Nos. C27-C29 (3)	50.00	*20.00*

See Nos. 302-304.

Vickers Viscount and Plane of 1919 AP17

4.05k, Skymaster and plane of 1919.

1959, Sept. 3 Engr. *Perf. 13½*
C30 AP17 3.50k steel blue .75 .55
C31 AP17 4.05k green .50 .45

40th anniv. of air transportation in Iceland.

AIR POST OFFICIAL STAMP

No. C3 Overprinted In Red

1930, Jan. 1 Unwmk. *Perf. 12½x12*
CO1 AP1 10a dp ultra & gray blue 20.00 *110.00*
Never hinged 40.00

Imperfs were privately printed.

OFFICIAL STAMPS

O1

O2

O3

Perf. 14x13½
1873 Typo. Wmk. 112
O1 O1 4s green 6,000. *7,500.*
a. Imperf. —
O2 O1 8s red lilac 500. *650.*
a. Imperf. 600.

Perf. 12½
O3 O1 4s green 75. *400.*

The imperforate varieties lack gum.
No. O1 values are for copies with perfs just touching the design on at least one side.
Fake and favor cancellations are often found on Nos. O1-O3. Values are considerably less than those shown.

1876-95 *Perf. 14x13½*
O4 O2 3a yellow 30.00 *55.00*
O5 O2 5a brown 8.00 *15.00*
a. Imperf. 300.00
O6 O2 10a blue 60.00 15.00
a. 10a ultramarine 375.00 55.00
O7 O2 16a carmine 17.50 *42.50*
O8 O2 20a yellow green 16.00 *30.00*
O9 O2 50a rose lilac ('95) 57.50 *75.00*
Nos. O4-O9 (6) 189.00 *232.50*

1898-1902 *Perf. 13*
O10 O2 3a yellow 12.00 *24.00*
O11 O2 4a gray ('01) 32.50 *35.00*
O12 O2 10a ultra ('02) 57.50 *110.00*
Nos. O10-O12 (3) 102.00 *169.00*

A 5a brown, perf. 13, Wmk. 112, exists. It was not regularly issued.
See note after No. O30.
For overprints see Nos. O20-O30.

1902 Wmk. 113 *Perf. 13*
O13 O3 3a buff & black 3.50 2.25
O14 O3 4a dp grn & blk 4.00 2.00
O15 O3 5a org brn & blk 3.00 3.00
O16 O3 10a ultra & black 3.50 3.00
O17 O3 16a carmine & blk 3.00 *13.00*
O18 O3 20a green & blk 15.00 7.00
O19 O3 50a violet & blk 7.00 *10.00*
Nos. O13-O19 (7) 39.00 *40.25*

Stamps of 1876-1901 Overprinted in Black

1902-03 Wmk. 112 *Perf. 13*
O20 O2 3a yellow .90 *2.40*
a. "I" before Gildi omitted 20.00
b. Inverted overprint 13.00 18.00
c. As "a," invtd. 100.00
d. Pair, one with invtd. ovpt. 50.00
e. '03-'03 100.00
f. 02'-'03 100.00
O21 O2 4a gray .75 *2.25*
a. "I" before Gildi omitted 40.00
b. Inverted overprint 25.00 14.00
e. '03-'03 125.00 *150.00*
f. 02'-'03 125.00
g. Pair, one without ovpt. 40.00
h. Pair, one with invtd. ovpt. 67.50 35.00
i. "L" only of "I GILDI" inverted 160.00
O22 O2 5a brown .75 *2.25*
O23 O2 10a ultramarine .75 *2.25*
a. "I" before Gildi omitted 25.00
b. Inverted overprint 20.00 8.75
c. '03-'03 150.00
d. 02'-'03 90.00
e. "L" only of "I GILDI" 25.00
f. As "e," inverted 35.00
g. "IL" only of "I GILDI" 26.00
O24 O2 20a yel green .75 *25.00*
Nos. O20-O24 (5) 3.90 *34.15*

Perf. 14x13½
O25 O2 3a yellow 300.00 *1,100.*
a. "02'-'03" 575.00
O26 O2 5a brown 8.00 *100.00*
a. Inverted overprint 20.00 *140.00*
b. '03-'03 125.00
c. 02'-'03 125.00
d. "L" only of "I GILDI" inverted 175.00
O27 O2 10a blue 425.00 *850.00*
a. "I" before Gildi omitted 600.00
b. Inverted overprint 600.00 *1,000.*
c. '03-'03 800.00
d. 02'-'03 700.00
O28 O2 16a carmine 13.00 *80.00*
a. "I" before Gildi omitted 140.00
b. Double overprint 75.00 *110.00*
c. Dbl. ovpt., one inverted 87.50
d. Inverted overprint 50.00 *100.00*
e. '03-'03 170.00
O29 O2 20a yel green 12.00 *75.00*
a. Inverted overprint 70.00 *110.00*
b. '03-'03 125.00
c. 02'-'03 125.00
d. "I" before Gildi omitted 90.00
O30 O2 50a red lilac 6.50 *60.00*
a. "I" before Gildi omitted 30.00
b. Inverted overprint 80.00
Nos. O25-O30 (6) 764.50 *2,265.*

Nos. O10-O12, O20-O24, O28 and O30 were reprinted in 1904. They have the watermark of 1902 (type 113) and are perf. 13. Value $50 each. Without overprint $100 each.

Christian IX, Frederick VIII — O4

Christian X — O5

Engraved Center

1907-08 Wmk. 113 *Perf. 13*
O31 O4 3a yellow & gray 5.75 *6.00*
O32 O4 4a green & gray 3.25 *6.00*
O33 O4 5a brn org & gray 9.50 3.50
O34 O4 10a deep bl & gray 2.00 *3.00*
O35 O4 15a lt blue & gray 4.00 *7.00*
O36 O4 16a carmine & gray 4.75 *20.00*
O37 O4 20a yel grn & gray 12.00 4.25
O38 O4 50a violet & gray 7.25 *10.00*
Nos. O31-O38 (8) 48.50 *59.75*

1918 Wmk. 114 *Perf. 14x14½*
O39 O4 15a lt bl & gray 12.00 *32.50*

1920-30 Typo.
O40 O5 3a yellow & gray 3.25 *2.50*
O41 O5 4a dp grn & gray .95 *2.50*
O42 O5 5a orange & gray .95 *1.10*
O43 O5 10a dk bl & gray 2.60 .90
O44 O5 15a lt blue & gray .70 *1.00*
O45 O5 20a yel grn & gray 45.00 4.00
O46 O5 50a violet & gray 40.00 1.50
O47 O5 1k car & gray 37.50 2.50
O48 O5 2k bl & blk ('30) 8.00 *16.00*
O49 O5 5k brn & blk ('30) 37.50 32.50
Nos. O40-O49 (10) 176.45 64.50

See No. O68.

Nos. 97 and 98 Overprinted

1922, May Wmk. 113 *Perf. 13*
O50 A7 2k rose, larger letters, no period 27.50 *55.00*
a. As shown 80.00 60.00
O51 A7 5k brown 225.00 *240.00*

No. 115 Surcharged

1923 Wmk. 114 *Perf. 14x14½*
O52 A8 20a on 10a red 17.50 2.50

Parliament Millenary Issue

#152-166 Overprinted in Red or Blue

1930, Jan. 1 Unwmk. *Perf. 12½x12*
O53 A15 3a (R) 12.50 *40.00*
O54 A15 5a (R) 12.50 *40.00*
O55 A15 7a (R) 12.50 *40.00*
O56 A15 10a (Bl) 12.50 *40.00*
O57 A15 15a (R) 12.50 *40.00*
O58 A15 20a (Bl) 12.50 *40.00*
O59 A15 25a (Bl) 12.50 *40.00*
O60 A15 30a (R) 12.50 *40.00*
O61 A15 35a (R) 12.50 *40.00*
O62 A15 40a (Bl) 12.50 *40.00*
O63 A15 50a (Bl) 140.00 *260.00*
O64 A15 1k (R) 140.00 *260.00*
O65 A15 2k (R) 175.00 *260.00*
O66 A15 5k (Bl) 140.00 *260.00*
O67 A15 10k (Bl) 140.00 *260.00*
Nos. O53-O67 (15) 860.00 *1,700.*

Type of 1920 Issue Redrawn

1931 Wmk. 114 Typo.
O68 O5 20a yel grn & gray 30.00 2.00

For differences in redrawing see note after No. 187.

No. 82 Overprinted in Black

Overprint 15mm long

1936, Dec. 7 Wmk. 113 *Perf. 13*
O69 A5 50a gray & vio 22.50 *25.00*

Same Overprint on Nos. 180 and 115

Perf. 14x14½
Wmk. 114
O70 A8 7a yellow green 3.50 *37.50*
O71 A8 10a red 4.50 2.00
Nos. O69-O71 (3) 30.50 *64.50*

IFNI

'if-nē

LOCATION — An enclave in southern Morocco on the Atlantic coast
GOVT. — Spanish possession
AREA — 580 sq. mi.
POP. — 51,517 (est. 1964)
CAPITAL — Sidi Ifni

Ifni was ceded to Spain by Morocco in 1860, but the Spanish did not occupy it until 1934. Sidi Ifni was also the administrative capital for Spanish West Africa. Spain turned Ifni back to Morocco June 30, 1969.

100 Centimos = 1 Peseta

Catalogue values for unused stamps in this country are for Never Hinged items, beginning with Scott 28 in the regular postage section, Scott B1 in the semi-postal section, and Scott C38 in the airpost section.

Stamps of Spain, 1936-40, Overprinted in Red or Blue

1941-42 Unwmk. *Imperf.*
1 A159 1c green 5.25 4.75

Perf. 10 to 11
2 A160 2c org brn (Bl) 5.25 4.75
3 A161 5c gray brown 1.10 1.00
5 A161 10c dk car (Bl) 3.00 1.60
a. Red overprint 15.00 7.50
6 A161 15c lt green 1.10 1.00
7 A166 20c brt violet 1.10 1.00
8 A166 25c deep claret 1.10 1.00
9 A166 30c blue 1.10 1.00
10 A166 40c Prus green 1.10 1.00
11 A166 50c indigo 6.00 1.25
12 A166 70c blue 6.00 3.25
13 A166 1p gray black 6.00 1.00
14 A166 2p dull brown 65.00 16.50
15 A166 4p dl rose (Bl) 275.00 92.50
16 A166 10p light brn 550.00 200.00
Nos. 1-16 (15) 928.10 331.60
Set, never hinged 1,400.

Counterfeit overprints exist.

Nomads — A1

Alcazaba Fortress — A3

Designs: 2c, 20c, 45c, 3p, Marksman.

1943 Litho. *Perf. 12½*
17 A1 1c brn & lil rose .20 .20
18 A1 2c yel grn & sl lil .20 .20
19 A3 5c magenta & vio .20 .20
20 A1 15c sl grn & grn .20 .20
21 A1 20c vio & red brn .20 .20
22 A1 40c rose vio & vio .20 .20
23 A1 45c brn vio & red .25 .25
24 A3 75c indigo & bl .25 .25
25 A1 1p red & brown 1.40 1.10
26 A1 3p bl vio & sl grn 1.75 1.60
27 A3 10p blk brn & blk 16.00 14.00
Nos. 17-27,E1 (12) 21.95 19.30
Set, never hinged 32.50

Nos. 17-27 exist imperforate. Value, set $85.

Catalogue values for unused stamps in this section, from this point to the end of the section, are for Never Hinged items.

1947, Feb. *Perf. 10*
28 A1 50c Nomad family 10.00 .55

Stamps of Spain, 1939-48, Overprinted in Carmine

1948, Aug. 2 *Perf. 9½x10½, 11, 13*
29 A161 5c gray brown 2.10 .35
30 A194 15c gray green 4.00 .45
31 A167 90c dark green 12.50 2.50
32 A166 1p gray black .40 .20
Nos. 29-32 (4) 19.00 3.50

Spain Nos. 769 and 770 Overprinted in Violet Blue or Carmine

1949, Oct. 9 *Perf. 12½x13*
33 A202 50c red brown (VB) 2.25 .70
34 A202 75c violet blue (C) 2.25 .70
Nos. 33-34,C40 (3) 7.00 2.35

75th anniv. of the UPU.

Stamps of Spain, 1938-48, Overprinted in Blue or Carmine like Nos. 29-32

Perf. 13, 13½, 12½x13, 9½x10½

1949 **Unwmk.**

35	A160	2c orange brn (Bl)	.20	.20
37	A161	10c dk carmine (Bl)	.20	.20
38	A161	15c dk green (II)	.20	.20
39	A166	25c brown violet	.20	.20
40	A166	30c blue	.20	.20
41	A195	40c red brown	.25	.20
42	A195	45c car rose (Bl)	.40	.30
43	A166	50c indigo	.30	.20
44	A195	75c dk vio bl	.50	.25
47	A167	1.35p purple	4.50	3.25
48	A166	2p dl brn	3.00	1.75
49	A166	4p dl rose (Bl)	12.00	4.50
50	A166	10p lt brn	22.50	16.00
		Nos. 35-50 (13)	44.45	27.45

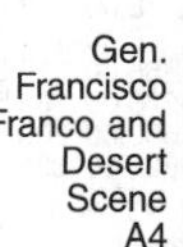

Gen. Francisco Franco and Desert Scene A4

Perf. 12½x13

1951, July 18 Photo. Unwmk.

51	A4	50c dp org	.50	.20
52	A4	1p chocolate	4.00	1.25
53	A4	5p bl grn	30.00	11.00
		Nos. 51-53 (3)	34.50	12.45

Visit of Gen. Francisco Franco, 1950.

View of Granada and Globe — A5

1952, Dec. 10 ***Perf. 13x12½***

54	A5	5c red org	.20	.20
55	A5	35c dk ol grn	.20	.20
56	A5	60c brown	.20	.20
		Nos. 54-56 (3)	.60	.60

400th anniversary of the death of Leo Africanus (c. 1485-c. 1554), Arab traveler and scholar, author of "Descrittione dell' Africa."

Musician A6

Design: 60c, Two musicians.

1953, June 1 ***Perf. 12½x13***

57	A6	15c olive gray	.20	.20
58	A6	60c brown	.20	.20
		Nos. 57-58,B13-B14 (4)	.80	.80

Issued to promote child welfare.

Fish and Branched Sponges A7

15c, Fish and jellyfish.

1953, Nov. 23

59	A7	15c dark green	.20	.20
60	A7	60c brown	.30	.20
		Nos. 59-60,B15-B16 (4)	.90	.80

Colonial Stamp Day, Nov. 23, 1953.

Sea Gull — A8

Cactus — A9

25c, 60c, 2p, 5p, Salsola vermiculata.

1954, Apr. 22 ***Perf. 12½x13, 13x12½***

61	A8	5c red org	.20	.20
62	A9	10c olive	.20	.20
63	A9	25c brn car	.20	.20
64	A8	35c olive gray	.20	.20
65	A9	40c rose lilac	.20	.20
66	A9	60c dk brn	.20	.20
67	A8	1p brown	7.50	.60
68	A9	1.25p car rose	.20	.20
69	A9	2p darp blue	.20	.20
70	A9	4.50p olive grn	.40	.35
71	A9	5p olive blk	35.00	9.50
		Nos. 61-71 (11)	44.50	12.05

Mother and Child
A10 A11

1954, June 1 ***Perf. 13x12½***

72	A10	15c dk gray grn	.20	.20
73	A11	60c dk brn	.20	.20
		Nos. 72-73,B17-B18 (4)	.80	.80

Lobster A12

Design: 60c, Hammerhead shark.

1954, Nov. 23 ***Perf. 12½x13***

74	A12	15c olive green	.20	.20
75	A12	60c rose brown	.20	.20
		Nos. 74-75,B19-B20 (4)	.80	.80

Issued to publicize Colonial Stamp Day.

Farmer Plowing and Statue of "Justice" A13

1955, June 1 Photo. Unwmk.

76	A13	50c gray olive	.20	.20
		Nos. 76,B21-B22 (3)	.60	.60

Squirrel A14

1955, Nov. 23

77	A14	70c yellow green	.20	.20
		Nos. 77,B23-B24 (3)	.60	.60

Issued to publicize Colonial Stamp Day.

Senecio Antheuphorbium A15

Design: 50c, Limoniastrum Ifniensis.

1956, June 1 ***Perf. 13x12½***

78	A15	20c bluish green	.20	.20
79	A15	50c brown	.20	.20
		Nos. 78-79,B25-B26 (4)	.80	.80

Arms of Sidi Ifni and Shepherd A16

1956, Nov. 23 ***Perf. 12½x13***

80	A16	70c light green	.20	.20

Issued for Colonial Stamp Day.

Rock Doves — A17

1957, June 1 Photo. ***Perf. 13x12½***

81	A17	70c yel grn & brn	.20	.20
		Nos. 81,B29-B30 (3)	.60	.60

See No. 86.

Jackal A18

Design: 70c, Jackal's head, vert.

Perf. 12½x13, 13x12½

1957, Nov. 23

82	A18	20c emerald & lt grn	.20	.20
83	A18	70c green & brown	.30	.20
		Nos. 82-83,B31-B32 (4)	.90	.80

Issued for the Day of the Stamp, 1957. See Nos. 87, B41.

Basketball Players A19

Red-legged Partridges A20

Design: 70c, Cyclists.

1958, June 1 ***Perf. 13x12½***

84	A19	20c bluish green	.20	.20
85	A19	70c olive green	.30	.20
		Nos. 84-85,B36-B37 (4)	.90	.80

Types of 1957 inscribed "Pro-Infancia 1959"

Designs: 20c, Goat. 70c, Ewe and lamb.

1959, June 1 ***Perf. 13x12½, 12½x13***

86	A17	20c dull green	.20	.20
87	A18	70c yellow green	.20	.20
		Nos. 86-87,B41-B42 (4)	.80	.80

Issued to promote child welfare.

1960, June 10 ***Perf. 13x12½***

88	A20	35c shown	.20	.20
89	A20	80c Camels	.20	.20
		Nos. 88-89,B46-B47 (4)	.80	.80

White Stork A21

Birds: 50c, 1.50p, 5p, European goldfinches. 75c, 2p, 10p, Skylarks, vert.

1960 Unwmk. ***Perf. 12½x13***

90	A21	25c violet	.20	.20
91	A21	50c olive black	.20	.20
92	A21	75c dull purple	.20	.20
93	A21	1p orange ver	.20	.20
94	A21	1.50p brt grnsh bl	.20	.20
95	A21	2p red lilac	.20	.20
96	A21	3p dark blue	.50	.20
97	A21	5p red brown	1.10	.35
98	A21	10p olive	4.50	1.25
		Nos. 90-98 (9)	7.30	3.00

Map of Ifni — A22

General Franco A23

Design: 70c, Government palace.

Perf. 13x12½, 12½x13

1961, Oct. 1 Photo.

99	A22	25c gray violet	.20	.20
100	A23	50c olive brown	.20	.20
101	A23	70c brt green	.20	.20
102	A23	1p red orange	.20	.20
		Nos. 99-102 (4)	.80	.80

25th anniv. of the nomination of Gen. Francisco Franco as Head of State.

Admiral Jofre Tenoria — A24

Mailman — A25

Design: 50c, Cesareo Fernandez-Duro (1830-1908), writer.

1962, July 10 ***Perf. 13x12½***

103	A24	25c dull violet	.20	.20
104	A24	50c deep blue grn	.20	.20
105	A24	1p orange brown	.20	.20
		Nos. 103-105 (3)	.60	.60

1962, Nov. 23 Unwmk.

Stamp Day: 35c, Hands, letter and winged wheel.

106	A25	15c dark blue	.20	.20
107	A25	35c lilac rose	.20	.20
108	A25	1p rose brown	.20	.20
		Nos. 106-108 (3)	.60	.60

Golden Tower, Seville
A26

Butterflies
A27

1963, Jan. 29 **Photo.**

109 A26 50c green .20 .20
110 A26 1p brown orange .20 .20

Issued for flood relief in Seville.

1963, July 6 ***Perf. 13x12½***

Design: 50c, Butterfly and flower.

111 A27 25c deep blue .20 .20
112 A27 50c light green .20 .20
113 A27 1p carmine rose .20 .20
Nos. 111-113 (3) .60 .60

Issued for child welfare.

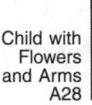

Child with Flowers and Arms
A28

1963, July 12 ***Perf. 12½x13***

114 A28 50c gray olive .20 .20
115 A28 1p reddish brown .20 .20

Issued for Barcelona flood relief.

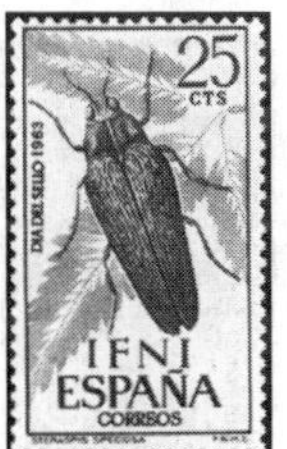

Beetle (Steraspis Speciosa)
A29

Mountain Gazelle
A30

Stamp Day: 50c, Grasshopper.

1964, Mar. 6 ***Perf. 13x12½***

116 A29 25c violet blue .20 .20
117 A29 50c olive green .20 .20
118 A29 1p red brown .20 .20
Nos. 116-118 (3) .60 .60

1964, June 1 **Photo.**

Design: 50c, Head of roebuck.

119 A30 25c brt violet .20 .20
120 A30 50c slate blk .20 .20
121 A30 1p orange red .20 .20
Nos. 119-121 (3) .60 .60

Issued for child welfare.

Bicycle Race
A31

Stamp Day: 1p, Motorcycle race.

1964, Nov. 23 ***Perf. 12½x13***

122 A31 50c brown .20 .20
123 A31 1p orange ver .20 .20
124 A31 1.50p Prus green .20 .20
Nos. 122-124 (3) .60 .60

Man — A32

Two Boys in School — A33

Cable Cars, Sidi Ifni — A34

Perf. 13x12½, 12½x13

1965, Mar. 1 **Photo.** **Unwmk.**

125 A32 50c dark green .20 .20
126 A33 1p orange ver .20 .20
127 A34 1.50p dark blue .20 .20
Nos. 125-127 (3) .60 .60

25 years of peace after the Spanish Civil War.

Eugaster Fernandezi
A35

Insect: 1p, Halter halteratus.

1965, June 1 **Photo.** **Unwmk.**

128 A35 50c purple .20 .20
129 A35 1p rose red .20 .20
130 A35 1.50p violet blue .20 .20
Nos. 128-130 (3) .60 .60

Issued for child welfare.

Eagle — A36

Arms of Sidi Ifni — A37

Perf. 13x12½, 12½x13

1965, Nov. 23 **Photo.**

131 A36 50c dk red brown .20 .20
132 A37 1p orange ver .20 .20
133 A36 1.50p grnsh blue .20 .20
Nos. 131-133 (3) .60 .60

Issued for Stamp Day 1965.

Jetliner over Sidi Ifni — A38

Design: 2.50p, Two 1934 biplanes, horiz.

Perf. 13x12½, 12½x13

1966, June 1 **Photo.** **Unwmk.**

134 A38 1p orange brn .20 .20
135 A38 1.50p brt blue .20 .20
136 A38 2.50p dull violet 2.00 1.60
Nos. 134-136 (3) 2.40 2.00

Issued for child welfare.

Syntomis Alicia — A39

1966, Nov. 23 **Photo.** ***Perf. 13***

40c, 4p, Danais chrysippus (butterfly).

137 A39 10c green & red .20 .20
138 A39 40c dk brn & gldn brn .20 .20
139 A39 1.50p violet & yel .20 .20
140 A39 4p dk pur & brt bl .25 .20
Nos. 137-140 (4) .85 .80

Issued for Stamp Day, 1966.

Coconut Palms — A40

Designs: 40c, 4p, Cactus.

1967, June 1 **Photo.** ***Perf. 13***

141 A40 10c dp grn & brn .20 .20
142 A40 40c Prus grn & ocher .20 .20
143 A40 1.50p bl grn & sepia .20 .20
144 A40 4p sepia & ocher .25 .20
Nos. 141-144 (4) .85 .80

Issued for child welfare.

Sidi Ifni Harbor
A41

1967, Sept. 28 **Photo.** ***Perf. 12½x13***

145 A41 1.50p grn & red brn .20 .20

Modernization of harbor installations.

Needlefish (Skipper) — A42

Fish: 1.50p, John Dory, vert. 3.50p, Gurnard (Trigla lucerna).

1967, Nov. 23 **Photo.** ***Perf. 13***

146 A42 1p blue & green .20 .20
147 A42 1.50p vio blk & yel .20 .20
148 A42 3.50p brt bl & scar .30 .20
Nos. 146-148 (3) .70 .60

Issued for Stamp Day 1967.

Zodiac Issue

Pisces — A43

Signs of the Zodiac: 1.50p, Capricorn. 2.50p, Sagittarius.

1968, Apr. 25 **Photo.** ***Perf. 13***

149 A43 1p brt mag, *lt yel* .20 .20
150 A43 1.50p brown, *pink* .20 .20
151 A43 2.50p dk vio, *yel* .30 .20
Nos. 149-151 (3) .70 .60

Issued for child welfare.

Mailing a Letter
A44

Designs: 1.50p, Carrier pigeon carrying letter. 2.50p, Stamp under magnifying glass.

1968, Nov. 23 **Photo.** ***Perf. 12½x13***

152 A44 1p org yel & sl grn .20 .20
153 A44 1.50p brt bl & vio blk .20 .20
154 A44 2.50p emer & vio blk .20 .20
Nos. 152-154 (3) .60 .60

Issued for Stamp Day.

SEMI-POSTAL STAMPS

Catalogue values for unused stamps in this section are for Never Hinged items.

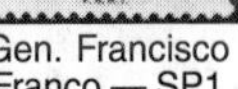

Gen. Francisco Franco — SP1

Fennec — SP2

Perf. 13x12½

1950, Oct. 19 **Unwmk.**

B1 SP1 50c + 10c sepia .55 .45
B2 SP1 1p + 25c blue 15.00 5.75
B3 SP1 6.50p + 1.65p dl grn 6.00 2.75
Nos. B1-B3 (3) 21.55 8.95

The surtax was for child welfare.

1951, Nov. 30

B4 SP2 5c + 5c brown .20 .20
B5 SP2 10c + 5c red org .20 .20
B6 SP2 60c + 15c olive brn .40 .20
Nos. B4-B6 (3) .80 .60

Colonial Stamp Day, Nov. 23, 1951.

Mother and Child — SP3

Common Shag — SP4

1952, June 1

B7 SP3 5c + 5c brn .20 .20
B8 SP3 50c + 10c brn blk .20 .20
B9 SP3 2p + 30c dp bl 1.60 .60
Nos. B7-B9 (3) 2.00 1.00

The surtax was for child welfare.

1952, Nov. 23

B10 SP4 5c + 5c brn .20 .20
B11 SP4 10c + 5c brn car .20 .20
B12 SP4 60c + 15c dk grn .35 .20
Nos. B10-B12 (3) .75 .60

Colonial Stamp Day, Nov. 23, 1952.

Musician Type of Regular Issue

1953, June 1 ***Perf. 12½x13***

B13 A6 5c + 5c as No. 57 .20 .20
B14 A6 10c + 5c as No. 58 .20 .20

The surtax was for child welfare.

Fish Type of Regular Issue

1953, Nov. 23

B15 A7 5c + 5c as No. 59 .20 .20
B16 A7 10c + 5c as No. 60 .20 .20

Colonial Stamp Day, Nov. 23, 1953.

Type of Regular Issue

1954, June 1 ***Perf. 13x12½***

B17 A10 5c + 5c org .20 .20
B18 A11 10c + 5c rose vio .20 .20

The surtax was for child welfare.

Type of Regular Issue

1954, Nov. 23 ***Perf. 12½x13***

B19 A12 5c + 5c as No. 74 .20 .20
B20 A12 10c + 5c as No. 75 .20 .20

"Dama de Elche" Protecting Caravan SP5

1955, June 1 **Photo.** **Unwmk.**

B21 A13 10c + 5c rose lilac .20 .20
B22 SP5 25c + 10c violet .20 .20

The surtax was to help Ifni people.

Squirrel Type of Regular Issue

Design: 15c+5c, Squirrel holding nut.

1955, Nov. 23

B23 A14 5c + 5c red brown .20 .20
B24 A14 15c + 5c olive bister .20 .20

Type of Regular Issue

1956, June 1 ***Perf. 13x12½***

B25 A15 5c + 5c as No. 78 .20 .20
B26 A15 15c + 5c as No. 79 .20 .20

The tax was for child welfare.

Dorcas Gazelles and Arms of Spain — SP6

Design: 15c+5c, Arms of Sidi Ifni, boat and woman with drum.

1956, Nov. 23

B27 SP6 5c + 5c dark brown .20 .20
B28 SP6 15c + 5c golden brn .20 .20

Issued for Colonial Stamp Day.

Dove Type of Regular Issue

1957, June 1 **Photo.** ***Perf. 13x12½***

B29 A17 5c + 5c as No. 81 .20 .20
B30 A17 15c + 5c Stock doves .20 .20

The surtax was for child welfare.

Type of Regular Issue

Perf. 12½x13, 13x12½

1957, Nov. 23 **Photo.** **Unwmk.**

B31 A18 10c + 5c as No. 82 .20 .20
B32 A18 15c + 5c as No. 83 .20 .20

Swallows and Arms of Valencia and Sidi Ifni — SP7

1958, Mar. 6 ***Perf. 12½x13***

B33 SP7 10c + 5c org brn .20 .20
B34 SP7 15c + 10c bister .20 .20
B35 SP7 50c + 10c brn olive .20 .20
Nos. B33-B35 (3) .60 .60

The surtax was to aid the victims of the Valencia flood, Oct. 1957.

Sport Type of Regular Issue, 1958

1958, June 1 **Photo.** ***Perf. 13x12½***

B36 A19 10c + 5c as No. 84 .20 .20
B37 A19 15c + 5c as No. 85 .20 .20

The surtax was for child welfare.

Guitarfish — SP8

Sailboats SP9

Stamp Day: 10c+5c, Spotted dogfish.

Perf. 13x12½, 12½x13

1958, Nov. 23

B38 SP9 10c + 5c brn red .20 .20
B39 SP8 25c + 10c dull vio .20 .20
B40 SP9 50c + 10c olive .25 .20
Nos. B38-B40 (3) .65 .60

Donkey and Man — SP10

Soccer — SP11

Type of 1957 and SP10

Design: 10c+5c, Ewe and lamb.

Perf. 12½x13, 13x12½

1959, June 1 **Photo.** **Unwmk.**

B41 A18 10c + 5c lt red brn .20 .20
B42 SP10 15c + 5c golden brn .20 .20

The surtax was for child welfare.

1959, Nov. 23 ***Perf. 13x12½***

Designs: 20c+5c, Soccer players. 50c+20c, Javelin thrower.

B43 SP11 10c + 5c fawn .20 .20
B44 SP11 20c + 5c slate green .20 .20
B45 SP11 50c + 20c olive gray .25 .20
Nos. B43-B45 (3) .65 .60

Issued for the day of the Stamp, 1959. See Nos. B52-B54.

Type of Regular Issue, 1960

1960, June 10 ***Perf. 13x12½***

B46 A20 10c + 5c as No. 89 .20 .20
B47 A20 15c + 5c Wild boars .20 .20

The surtax was for child welfare.

Santa Maria del Mar — SP12

Stamp Day: 20c+5c, 50c+20c, New school building, horiz.

Perf. 13x12½, 12½x13

1960, Dec. 29 **Photo.**

B48 SP12 10c + 5c org brn .20 .20
B49 SP12 20c + 5c dk sl grn .20 .20
B50 SP12 30c + 10c red brn .20 .20
B51 SP12 50c + 20c sepia .20 .20
Nos. B48-B51 (4) .80 .80

Type of 1959 inscribed: "Pro-Infancia 1961"

Designs: 10c+5c, 80c+20c, Pole vaulting, horiz. 25c+10c, Soccer player.

Perf. 12½x13, 13x12½

1961, June 21 **Unwmk.**

B52 SP11 10c + 5c rose brn .20 .20
B53 SP11 25c + 10c gray vio .20 .20
B54 SP11 80c + 20c dk green .20 .20
Nos. B52-B54 (3) .60 .60

The surtax was for child welfare.

Camel Rider and Truck SP13

Stamp Day: 25c+10c, 1p+10c, Ship in Sidi Ifni harbor.

1961, Nov. 23 ***Perf. 12½x13***

B55 SP13 10c + 5c rose brn .20 .20
B56 SP13 25c + 10c dk pur .20 .20
B57 SP13 30c + 10c dk red brn .20 .20
B58 SP13 1p + 10c red org .20 .20
Nos. B55-B58 (4) .80 .80

AIR POST STAMPS

Stamps formerly listed as Nos. C1-C29 were privately overprinted. These include 1936 stamps of Spain overprinted "VIA AEREA" and plane, and 1939 stamps of Spain, type AP30, overprinted "IFNI" or "Territorio de Ifni."

Oasis AP1

The Sanctuary AP2

1943 **Unwmk.** **Litho.** ***Perf. 12½***

C30 AP2 5c cer & vio brn .20 .20
C31 AP1 25c yel grn & ol grn .20 .20
C32 AP2 50c ind & turq grn .30 .30
C33 AP1 1p pur & grnsh bl .30 .30
C34 AP2 1.40p gray grn & bl .30 .30
C35 AP1 2p mag & org brn 1.00 1.00
C36 AP2 5p brn & pur 1.60 1.50
C37 AP1 6p brt bl & gray grn 19.00 17.50
Nos. C30-C37 (8) 22.90 21.30
Set, never hinged 32.50

Nos. C30-C37 exist imperforate. Value, set $85.

Catalogue values for unused stamps in this section, from this point to the end of the section, are for Never Hinged items.

Type of Spain, 1939-47, Overprinted in Carmine

1947, Nov. 29

C38 AP30 5c dull yellow 1.75 .75
C39 AP30 10c dk bl green 1.75 .75

Spain No. C126 Overprinted in Carmine like Nos. 33-34

1949, Oct. 9 ***Perf. 12½x13***

C40 A202 4p dk olive grn 2.50 .95

75th anniv. of the UPU.

Spain, Nos. C110 and C112 to C116, Overprinted in Blue or Carmine like Nos. 29-32

1949 ***Perf. 10***

C41 AP30 25c redsh brn (Bl) .35 .20
C42 AP30 50c brown .40 .20
C43 AP30 1p chalky blue .40 .20
C44 AP30 2p lt gray grn 2.00 .40
C45 AP30 4p gray blue 7.00 3.00
C46 AP30 10p brt purple 9.00 6.00
Nos. C41-C46 (6) 19.15 10.00

Lope Sancho de Valenzuela and Sheik — AP3

Woman Holding Dove — AP4

1950, Nov. 23 **Photo.** ***Perf. 13x12½***

C47 AP3 5p brown black 2.75 .70

Stamp Day, Nov. 23, 1950.

1951, Apr. 22 **Engr.** ***Perf. 10***

C48 AP4 5p red 18.00 5.75

500th anniversary of the birth of Queen Isabella I of Spain.

Ferdinand the Catholic — AP5

Perf. 13x12½

1952, July 18 **Photo.** **Unwmk.**

C49 AP5 5p brown 24.00 6.00

500th anniv. of the birth of Ferdinand the Catholic of Spain.

Plane and Mountain Gazelle — AP6

1953, Apr. 1

C50 AP6 60c light grn .20 .20
C51 AP6 1.20p brn car .25 .20
C52 AP6 1.60p lt brown .30 .20
C53 AP6 2p deep blue 2.25 .20
C54 AP6 4p grnsh blk 1.25 .20
C55 AP6 10p brt red vio 6.50 1.40
Nos. C50-C55 (6) 10.75 2.40

SPECIAL DELIVERY STAMPS

Type A3 inscribed "URGENTE"

1943 ***Perf. 12½***

E1 A3 25c slate green & car 1.10 .90

Spain, No. E20, Overprinted in Blue like Nos. 29-32

1949 **Unwmk.** ***Perf. 10***

E2 SD10 25c carmine .30 .20

INDIA

ˈin-dē-ə

LOCATION — Southern, central Asia
GOVT. — Republic
AREA — 1,266,732 sq. mi.
POP. — 1,000,848,550 (1999 est.)
CAPITAL — New Delhi

On August 15, 1947, India was divided into two self-governing dominions: Pakistan and India. India became a republic in 1950.

The stamps of pre-partition India fall into three groups:

1) Issues inscribed simply "East India" (to 1881) and "India" (from 1882), for use mainly in British India proper, but available and valid throughout the country;

2) Issues as above and overprinted with one of the names of the six "Convention" states (Chamba, Faridkot, Gwalior, Jind, Nabha and Patiala) which had a postal convention with British India, for use in these states.

3) Issues of the feudatory states, over which the British India government exercised little internal control, valid for use only within the states issuing them.

12 Pies = 1 Anna
16 Annas = 1 Rupee
100 Naye Paise = 1 Rupee (1957)
100 Paise = 1 Rupee (1964)

Catalogue values for unused stamps in this country are for Never Hinged items, beginning with Scott 168 in the regular postage section, Scott C7 in the air post section, Scott M44 in the military section, Scott O113 in the official section, Scott RA1 in the postal tax section, Scott 51 in Hyderabad regular issues, Scott O54 in Hyderabad officials, Scott 49 in Jaipur regular issues, Scott O30 in Jaipur officials, Scott 39 in Soruth regular issues and Scott O19 in Soruth official

All of the values are for Never Hinged for all of the items in the sections for the International Commission in Indo-China, Jasdan, Rajasthan, and Travancore-Cochin.

Watermarks

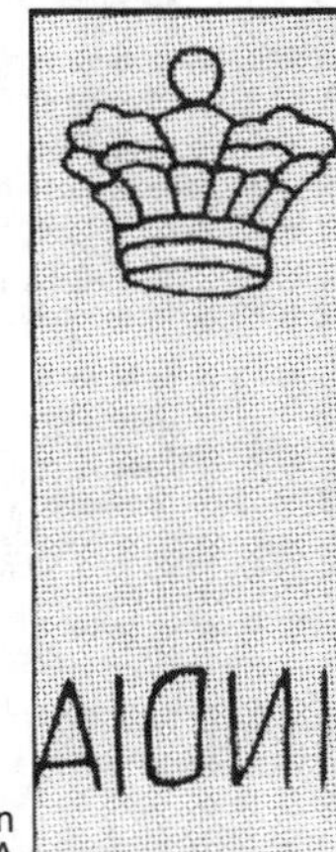

Wmk. 36- Crown and INDIA

Wmk. 37- Coat of Arms in Sheet. (Reduced illustration. Watermark covers a large section of the sheet.)

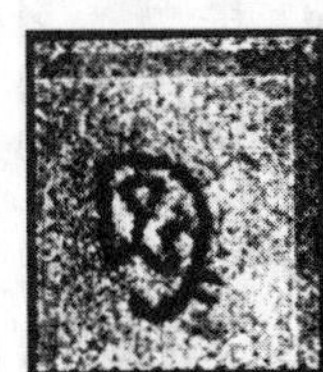
Wmk. 38- Elephant's Head

Wmk. 39- Star

Wmk. 40

Wmk. 41- Small Umbrella

Wmk. 42- Urdu Characters

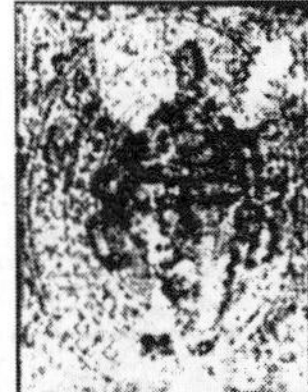
Wmk. 43- Shell

Wmk. 196- Multiple Stars

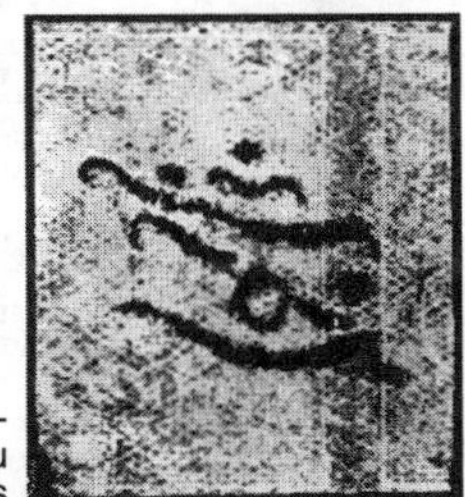
Wmk. 211- Urdu Characters

Wmk. 294- Letters and Ornaments in Sheet (size reduced)

Wmk. 324- Asoka Pillar, Multiple

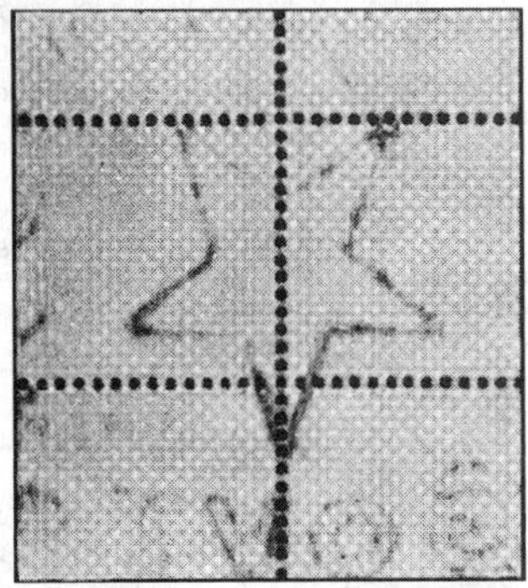
Wmk. 360- Star and GOVT INDIA

SCINDE DISTRICT POST

A1

1852, July 1	**Embossed**		***Imperf.***
A1 A1 ½a *white*		4,000.	500.
A2 A1 ½a blue		10,000.	1,750.
A3 A1 ½a *red*		—	6,750.

Obsolete October, 1854.

Nos. A1-A3 were issued without gum. No. A3 is embossed on red wafer. It is usually found with cracks and these examples are worth somewhat less than the values given, depending on the degree of cracking.

GENERAL ISSUES

Unused stamps of India are valued with original gum as defined in the catalogue introduction except for Nos. 1-7 which are valued without gum.

East India Company

Queen Victoria
A1 A2

A3

A4

A5

Litho.; Typo. (#5)

1854	**Wmk. 37**		***Imperf.***
1 A1 ½a red		700.00	
2 A2 ½a blue		40.00	15.00
a. ½a deep blue		65.00	17.50
b. Printed on both sides			*7,000.*
4 A3 1a red		65.00	30.00
a. 1a scarlet		110.00	32.50
5 A4 2a green		75.00	21.00
6 A5 4a red & blue		3,250.	350.00
a. 4a deep red & blue		3,250.	350.00
Cut to shape			14.00
c. Head inverted			*65,000.*
As "c," cut to shape			*35,000.*
e. Double impression of head			

No. 1 was not placed in use.

Nos. 2, 4, 5 and 6 are known with unofficial perforation.

There are 3 dies of No. 2, and 2 dies of No. 4, showing slight differences.

There are 4 dies of the head and 2 dies of the frame of No. 6.

Beware of forgeries.

A6

1855		
7 A6 1a red	700.00	140.00

No. 7 was printed from a lithographic transfer made from the original die retouched. The lines of the bust at the lower left are nearly straight and meet in a point.

Beware of forgeries.

Nos. 9-35 are normally found with very heavy cancelations, and values are for stamps so canceled. Lightly canceled copies are seldom seen. The same holds true for Nos. O1-O26.

Diadem includes Maltese Crosses — A7

1855-64 Unwmk. Typo. *Perf. 14*
Blue Glazed Paper

9 A7 4a black	325.00	12.00
a. Imperf., pair	2,000.	—
b. Half used as 2a on cover		*5,000.*
10 A7 8a rose	375.00	12.50
a. Imperf., pair	1,500.	—
b. Half used as 4a on cover		—

See #11-18, 20, 22-25, 31. For overprints see #O1-O5, O7-O9, O16-O19, O22-O24.

1855-64	**White Paper**	
11 A7 ½a blue	32.50	1.25
a. Imperf., pair	365.00	*600.00*
12 A7 1a brown	22.50	1.60
a. Imperf., pair	650.00	—
b. Vert. pair, imperf between		
c. Half used as ½a on cover		*6,500.*
13 A7 2a dull rose	250.00	20.00
a. Imperf., pair	2,000.	2,000.
14 A7 2a yellow green	575.00	
a. Imperf., pair	2,000.	
15 A7 2a buff	125.00	20.00
a. 2a orange	125.00	20.00
b. Imperf., pair	1,500.	—
16 A7 4a black	100.00	6.50
a. Imperf., pair	2,000.	—
b. Diagonal half used as 2a on cover		*4,000.*
17 A7 4a green ('64)	500.00	27.50
18 A7 8a rose	110.00	14.00
a. Half used as 4a on cover		*6,500.*

No. 14 was not regularly issued. See note after No. 25.

Crown Colony

Queen Victoria — A8

1860-64	**Unwmk.**		***Perf. 14***
19 A8 8p lilac		30.00	6.00
a. Diagonal half used as 4p on cover			*8,250.*
b. Imperf., pair		2,100.	—
19C A8 8p lilac, *bluish*		190.00	40.00

See #21. For overprint See #O6 and footnote after #O4.

1865-67 **Wmk. 38**

20 A7 ½a blue 5.50 .30
a. Imperf., pair 1,400.
21 A8 8p lilac 8.00 3.00
22 A7 1a brown 2.00 .20
23 A7 2a orange 27.50 1.00
a. 2a yellow 47.50 2.00
b. Imperf., pair 1,500.
24 A7 4a green 325.00 18.00
25 A7 8a rose 1,100. 72.50

No. 21 was variously surcharged locally, "NINE" or "NINE PIE," to indicate that it was being sold for 9 pies (the soldier's letter rate had been raised from 8 to 9 pies). These surcharges were made without government authorization.

Stamps of types A7 and A9 overprinted with crown and surcharged with new values were for use in Straits Settlements.

A9

A10

Diadem: Rows of pearls & diamonds — A11

FOUR ANNAS

Type I - Slanting line at corner of mouth extends downward only. Shading about mouth and chin. Pointed chin.

Type II - Line at corner of mouth extends both up and down. Upper lip and chin are defined by a colored line. Rounded chin.

1866-68

26 A9 4a grn, type I 50.00 .65
26B A9 4a bl grn, type II 14.50 .35
27 A10 6a8p slate 50.00 17.00
a. Imperf., pair 2,000.
28 A11 8a rose ('68) 21.00 3.50
Nos. 26-28 (4) 135.50 21.50

Type A11 is a redrawing of type A7. Type A7 has Maltese crosses in the diadem, while type A11 has shaded lozenges.

For overprints see #O10, O20-O21, O25-O26.

For designs A9-A85 overprinted CHAMBA, FARIDKOT, GWALIOR, JIND (JHIND, JEEND), NABHA, PATIALA (PUTTIALLA), see the various Convention States

A12

SIX ANNAS

Type I - "POSTAGE" 3½mm high
Type II - "POSTAGE" 2½mm high

Blue Glazed Paper
Green Overprint
Perf. 14 Vert.

1866, June 28 **Wmk. 36**

29 A12 6a violet, type I 625. 75.00
a. Inverted overprint *7,500.*
30 A12 6a violet, type II 900.00 125.00

Nos. 29 and 30 were made from revenue stamps with the labels at top and bottom cut off. Most and sometimes all of the watermark was removed with the labels.

These stamps are often found with cracked surface or scuffs. Such examples sell for somewhat less.

A13

A14

A15 A16

1873-76 **Wmk. 38** ***Perf. 14***

31 A7 ½a blue, redrawn 2.25 .25
32 A13 9p lilac ('74) 9.50 7.00
33 A14 6a bister ('76) 4.50 1.25
34 A15 12a red brown ('76) 6.00 *7.50*
35 A16 1r slate ('74) 27.50 19.00
Nos. 31-35 (5) 49.75 35.00

In the redrawn ½ anna the lines of the mouth are more deeply cut, making the lips appear fuller and more open, and the nostril is defined by a curved line.

Victorian and Edwardian stamps overprinted "Postal Service" and new denominations were customs fee due stamps, not postage stamps.

Empire

A17

A18

A19

A20

A21

A22

A23

A24

A25

A26

A27

1882-87 **Wmk. 39**

36 A17 ½a green 2.00 .20
a. Double impression 350.00
37 A18 9p rose 1.00 *1.75*
38 A19 1a maroon 2.50 .20
a. 1a violet brown 2.50 .20
39 A20 1a6p bister brown .50 *.60*
40 A21 2a ultra 2.50 .20
a. Double impression 650.00 *1,000.*
41 A22 3a brown org 4.25 .20
a. 3a orange 10.00 4.00
42 A23 4a olive green 9.50 .20
43 A24 4a6p green 12.00 4.25
44 A25 8a rose violet 11.00 1.50
a. 8a red lilac 12.50 1.50
45 A26 12a violet, *red* 5.50 1.50
46 A27 1r gray 12.50 4.00
Nos. 36-46 (11) 63.25 14.60

A 6a bister and a 12a Venetian red were prepared but not issued.

No. 40a used value is for copy with postal cancellation.

See Nos. 56-58. For surcharges see Nos. 47, 53 and British East Africa No. 59. For overprints see Nos. M2-M4, M6-M9, O27-O31, O34-O36, Gwalior O1-O5.

Beginning with the 1882-87 issue, higher denomination stamps exist used for telegrams. The telegraph cancellation has concentric circles. These sell for 10-15% of the postally used values.

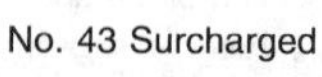
No. 43 Surcharged

1891, Jan. 1

47 A24 2½a on 4a6p green 1.90 .60

A28

A29

1892

48 A28 2a6p green 1.00 .35
49 A29 1r car rose & grn 8.00 1.90

See No. 59. For overprints see Nos. M5, M10, O32, Gwalior O6.

Queen Victoria
A30 A31

1895, Sept. 1

50 A30 2r brown & rose 30.00 10.00
51 A30 3r green & brown 22.50 9.00
52 A30 5r violet & ultra 27.50 20.00
Nos. 50-52 (3) 80.00 39.00

Used high values such as Nos. 50-52 and later issues are for postally used examples.

No. 36 Surcharged

1898

53 A17 ¼a on ½a green .20 .20
a. Double surcharge 100.00
b. Double impression of stamp 225.00

For #61, 81 with this overprint see #77, 105.

1899

54 A31 3p carmine rose .20 .20

See #55. For overprints see #M1, Gwalior O11.

1900

55 A31 3p gray .40 .20
56 A17 ½a light green .85 .20
57 A19 1a carmine rose .65 .20
58 A21 2a violet 2.75 2.00
59 A28 2a6p ultramarine 2.75 3.00
Nos. 55-59 (5) 7.40 5.60

For overprints see #M11, Gwalior O7-O10.

Edward VII — A32

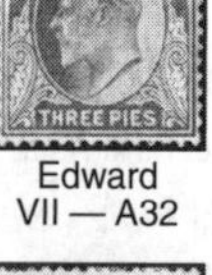
A33

A34

A35

A36

A37

A38

A39

A40

A41

A42

A43

1902-09

60 A32 3p gray .20 .20
61 A33 ½a green .20 .20
a. Booklet pane of 6 ('04) 32.50
62 A34 1a carmine rose .40 .20
a. Booklet pane of 6 ('04) 92.50
63 A35 2a violet 1.25 .20
64 A36 2a6p ultra 3.00 .20
65 A37 3a brown org 3.00 .20
66 A38 4a olive green 2.50 .20
67 A39 6a bister 8.50 1.75
68 A40 8a red violet 6.00 .60
69 A41 12a violet, *red* 6.50 2.00
70 A42 1r car rose & grn 5.75 .50
71 A43 2r brown & rose 26.00 3.25
72 A43 3r green & brn ('04) 22.50 11.50
73 A43 5r violet & ultra ('04) 45.00 32.50
74 A43 10r car rose & grn ('09) 80.00 22.50
75 A43 15r olive gray & ultra ('09) 140.00 45.00
76 A43 25r ultra & org brown 825.00 775.00
Telegraph cancel 300.00
Nos. 60-75 (16) 350.80 121.00

For overprints and surcharge see #M12-M20, O33, O37-O44, O47-O51, O67-O69, O73, Gwalior O12-O18.

No. 61 Surcharged Like No. 53

1905

77 A33 ¼a on ½a green .20 .20
a. Inverted surcharge 600.00

A44

A45

1906

78 A44 ½a green .20 .20
a. Booklet pane of 4 17.50
79 A45 1a carmine rose .20 .20
a. Booklet pane of 4 25.00

For overprints see #O45-O46, Gwalior O19-O20.

A46 A47

A48 A49

A50 A51

A52 A53

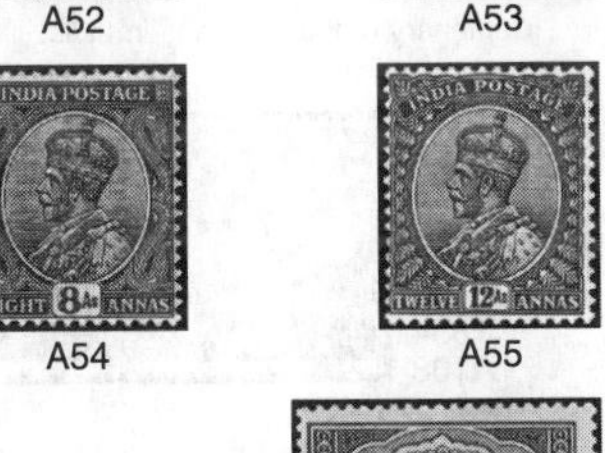

A54 A55

George V — A56

1911-23 **Wmk. 39**

80 A46 3p gray .20 .20
a. Booklet pane of 4 25.00
81 A47 ½a green .20 .20
a. Double impression 175.00
b. Booklet pane of 4 21.00
82 A48 1a carmine rose .20 .20
a. Printed on both sides
b. Booklet pane of 4 35.00
83 A48 1a dk brown ('22) .85 .20
a. Booklet pane of 4 42.50
84 A49 2a dull violet .80 .20
a. Booklet pane of 4 42.50
85 A50 2a6p ultramarine 1.00 .85
86 A51 3a brown org 1.50 .20
87 A51 3a ultra ('23) 5.25 .65
88 A52 4a olive green 2.50 .20
89 A53 6a yel bister 3.00 .70
90 A53 6a bister ('15) 3.00 .80
91 A54 8a red violet 4.00 .35
92 A55 12a claret 5.00 1.00
93 A56 1r grn & red brn 8.50 .60
94 A56 2r brn & car rose 13.00 1.00
95 A56 5r vio & ultra 35.00 4.00
96 A56 10r car rose & grn 55.00 5.50
97 A56 15r ol grn & ultra 92.50 16.00
98 A56 25r ultra & brn org 175.00 27.50
Nos. 80-98 (19) 406.50 60.35

See #106-108, 110-111, 113-125. For surcharges and overprints see #104-105, M23-M25, M27, M29-M37, M39-M43, O52-O66, O70-O71, O74, O78-O81, O85, O87-O92, Gwalior O28-O29.

A57

1913-26

99 A57 2a6p ultramarine 1.75 .25
100 A57 2a6p brown org ('26) 6.00 6.00

See #112. For overprints and surcharge see #M28, M38, O77, O84.

"One and Half" — A58

"One and a Half" — A59

1919

101 A58 1½a chocolate 1.50 .20
a. Booklet pane of 4 35.00

For overprint and surcharge see #M26, O75.

1921-26

102 A59 1½a chocolate .70 .30
103 A59 1½a rose ('26) .40 .20

See #109. For surcharge see #O76.

Type of 1911-26 Surcharged

1921

104 A48 9p on 1a rose .20 .20
a. Surcharged "NINE-NINE" 30.00 30.00
b. Surcharged "PIES-PIES" 30.00 30.00
c. Double surcharge 50.00 *55.00*
e. Booklet pane of 4 27.50

Forgeries exist of Nos. 104a-104c.

No. 81 Surcharged Like No. 53

1922

105 A47 ¼a on ½a green .20 .20
a. Inverted surcharge 8.00 8.00
b. Pair, one without surcharge 175.00

Types of 1911-26 Issues

1926-36 **Wmk. 196**

106 A46 3p slate .20 .20
107 A47 ½a green .20 .20
108 A48 1a dark brown .20 .20
a. Tete beche pair 1.50 *7.50*
b. Booklet pane of 4 16.00
109 A59 1½a car rose ('29) .45 .20
110 A49 2a dull violet .75 .20
a. Booklet pane of 4 32.50
111 A49 2a ver ('34) 7.50 .90
a. Small die ('36) 4.50 .60
112 A57 2a6p buff .40 .20
113 A51 3a ultramarine 5.00 1.25
114 A51 3a blue ('30) 5.00 .20
115 A51 3a car rose ('32) .50 .20
116 A52 4a olive green .75 .20
117 A53 6a bister ('35) 8.00 2.00
118 A54 8a red violet 1.90 .20
119 A55 12a claret 2.25 .20
120 A56 1r grn & brn 1.60 .20
121 A56 2r brn org & car rose 2.50 .25
122 A56 5r dk vio & ultra 13.00 1.10
123 A56 10r car & grn 37.50 2.00
124 A56 15r ol grn & ultra 16.00 16.00
125 A56 25r blue & ocher 100.00 25.00
Nos. 106-125 (20) 203.70 50.90

No. 111 measures 19x22½mm, while the small die, No. 111a, measures 18½x22mm.

For overprints see Gwalior #O30-O39, O44-O45.

A60

A61

1926-32 **Typo.**

126 A60 2a dull violet .45 .20
a. Tete beche pair 4.50 4.50
b. 2a rose violet .45 .20
c. Booklet pane of 4 19.00
127 A60 2a vermilion ('32) 7.50 4.00
128 A61 4a olive green 1.40 .20
Nos. 126-128 (3) 9.35 4.40

For overprints see #O82-O83, , O86, Gwalior O33-O34.

Fortress of Purana Qila — A62

George V Flanked by Dominion Columns A67

¼a, War Memorial Arch. 1a, Council Building. 2a, Viceroy's House. 3a, Parliament Building.

Wmk. 196 Sideways

1931, Feb. 9 **Litho.** ***Perf. 13½x14***

129 A62 ¼a brown & ol grn .85 1.00
130 A62 ½a green & violet .85 .25
131 A62 1a choc & red vio .85 .20
132 A62 2a blue & green 1.00 .80
133 A62 3a car & choc 2.25 1.75
134 A67 1r violet & green 7.50 14.00
Nos. 129-134 (6) 13.30 18.00

Change of the seat of Government from Calcutta to New Delhi.

A68 A69

A70

Wmk. 196

1932, Apr. 22 **Litho.** ***Perf. 14***

135 A68 9p dark green .30 .20
136 A69 1a3p violet .25 .20
137 A70 3a6p deep blue 1.25 .20
Nos. 135-137 (3) 1.80 .60

No. 135 exists both litho. and typo.

For overprints and surcharge see #O94, O96, O104, Gwalior O41, O43.

A71

A72

1934 **Typo.**

138 A71 ½a green .80 .20
139 A72 1a dark brown .80 .20

For overprints see #O93, O95, Gwalior O40, O42.

Silver Jubilee Issue

Gateway of India, Bombay A73

Designs: 9p, Victoria Memorial, Calcutta. 1a, Rameswaram Temple, Madras. 1¼a, Jain Temple, Calcutta. 2½a, Taj Mahal, Agra. 3½a, Golden Temple, Amritsar. 8a, Pagoda, Mandalay.

Wmk. 196 Sideways

1935 **Litho.** ***Perf. 13½x14***

142 A73 ½a lt green & black .20 .20
143 A73 9p dull green & blk .20 .20
144 A73 1a brown & black .20 .20
145 A73 1¼a violet & black .20 .20
146 A73 2½a brown org & blk .90 .40
147 A73 3½a blue & black 1.50 1.00
148 A73 8a rose lilac & blk 4.00 2.25
Nos. 142-148 (7) 7.20 4.45

25th anniv. of the reign of George V.

King George VI

A80 A82

Dak Runner A81

Mail transport: 2a6p, Dak bullock cart. 3a, Dak tonga. 3a6p, Dak camel. 4a, Mail train. 6a, Mail steamer. 8a, Mail truck. 12a, 14a, Mail plane.

Perf. 13½x14 or 14x13½

1937-40 **Typo.** **Wmk. 196**

150 A80 3p slate .30 .25
151 A80 ½a brown .80 .25
152 A80 9p green 2.40 .25
153 A80 1a carmine .25 .25
a. Tete beche pair .50 .50
b. Booklet pane of 4 4.25
154 A81 2a scarlet 1.60 .25
155 A81 2a6p purple .50 .25
156 A81 3a yel grn 3.00 .25
157 A81 3a6p ultramarine 2.00 .40
158 A81 4a dark brown 8.25 .25
159 A81 6a peacock blue 8.00 .25
160 A81 8a blue violet 4.75 .25
161 A81 12a car lake 10.00 .70
161A A81 14a rose vio ('40) 11.50 .25
162 A82 1r brn & slate .65 .25
163 A82 2r dk brn & dk vio 2.40 .25
164 A82 5r dp ultra & dk grn 9.50 .25
165 A82 10r rose car & dk vio 9.50 .90
166 A82 15r dk grn & dk brn 50.00 *65.00*
167 A82 25r dk vio & blue vio 65.00 12.50
Nos. 150-167 (19) 190.40 *83.00*

The King's portrait is larger on No. 161A than on other stamps of type A81.

For overprints see #O97-O103, Gwalior O48-O51.

Catalogue values for unused stamps in this section, from this point to the end of the section, are for Never Hinged items.

A83

A84

A85

Perf. 13½x14

1941-43 **Typo.** **Wmk. 196**

168 A83 3p slate ('42) .20 .20
169 A83 ½a rose vio ('42) .75 .20
170 A83 9p light green .75 .20
171 A83 1a car rose ('43) .75 .20
172 A84 1a3p bister .75 .20
172A A84 1½a dark pur ('42) .95 .20
173 A84 2a scarlet 1.10 .20
174 A84 3a violet 2.00 .20
175 A84 3½a ultramarine .75 .20
176 A85 4a chocolate .50 .20
177 A85 6a peacock blue 2.50 .20

178 A85 8a blue violet 1.25 .25
179 A85 12a carmine lake 2.25 .40
Nos. 168-179 (13) 14.50 2.85

Early printings of the 1½a and 3a were lithographed.
For surcharge see No. 199.

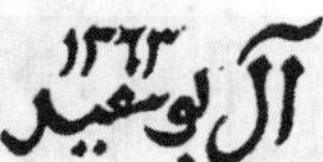

For stamps with this overprint, or a smaller type, see Oman (Muscat).

Symbols of Victory A86

1946, Jan. 2 Litho. *Perf. 13*
195 A86 9p green .20 .20
196 A86 1½a dull purple .20 .20
197 A86 3½a ultramarine .50 .40
198 A86 12a brown lake 1.25 .35
Nos. 195-198 (4) 2.15 1.15

Victory of the Allied Nations in WWII.

No. 172 Surcharged With New Value and Bars

1946, Aug. 8 *Perf. 13½x14*
199 A84 3p on 1a3p bister .20 .20

Dominion of India

Asoka Pillar — A87

National Flag A88

Four-Motor Plane A89

Perf. 14x13½, 13½x14
1947 Litho. Wmk. 196
200 A87 1½a greenish gray .20 .20
201 A88 3½a multicolored .25 .20
202 A89 12a ultramarine .90 .45
Nos. 200-202 (3) 1.35 .85

Elevation to dominion status, Aug. 15, 1947.

Mahatma Gandhi — A90

Design: 10r, Gandhi profile.

Perf. 11½
1948, Aug. 15 Unwmk. Photo.
Size: 22x32½mm
203 A90 1½a brown 1.75 .25
204 A90 3½a violet 4.50 1.50
205 A90 12a dark gray green 6.25 .85

Size: 22x37mm
206 A90 10r rose brn & brn 47.50 35.00
Nos. 203-206 (4) 60.00 37.60

Mohandas K. Gandhi, 1869-1948.
For overprints see #O112A-O112D.

Ajanta Panel — A91

Konarak Horse — A92

Bodhisattva A93

Tomb of Muhammad Adil Shah, Bijapur A95

Sanchi Stupa A94

Victory Tower, Chittorgarh A96

Red Fort, Delhi A97

Satrunjaya Temple, Palitana A98

9p, Trimurti. 2a, Nataraja. 3½a, Bodh Gaya Temple. 4a, Bhuvanesvara. 8a, Kandarya Mahadeva Temple. 12a, Golden Temple, Amritsar. 5r, Taj Mahal. 10r, Qutb Minar.

Perf. 13½x14, 14x13½
1949, Aug. 15 Typo. Wmk. 196
207 A91 3p gray violet .20 .20
208 A92 6p red brown .20 .20
209 A93 9p green .20 .20
210 A93 1a turquoise .20 .20
211 A93 2a carmine .20 .20
212 A94 3a red orange .40 .20
213 A94 3½a ultramarine 6.75 2.10
214 A94 4a brown lake 8.50 .20
215 A95 6a purple 3.00 .20
216 A95 8a blue green 3.00 .20
217 A95 12a blue 2.75 .20

Litho.
218 A96 1r dk green & pur 17.50 .20
219 A97 2r pur & rose red 7.50 .20
220 A97 5r brn car & dk grn 21.00 .70
221 A96 10r dp bl & brn car 30.00 4.00

Perf. 13½x13
222 A98 15r dp car & dk brn 21.00 12.00
Nos. 207-222 (16) 122.40 21.20

See #231, 235-236. For overprints see #M44-M46, M48-M55 and Intl. Commission in Indo-china issues for Cambodia, #1, 3-5, Laos #1, 3-5 and Vietnam #1, 3-5.

Symbols of UPU and Asoka Pillar — A99

1949, Oct. Litho. *Perf. 13½x13*
223 A99 9p dull green 1.25 .80
224 A99 2a carmine rose 1.25 .80
225 A99 3½a ultramarine 2.00 .90
226 A99 12a red brown 2.50 1.00
Nos. 223-226 (4) 7.00 3.50

75th anniv. of the formation of the UPU.

Republic of India

Rejoicing Crowds A100

Designs: 3½a, Quill pen, vert. 4a, Plow and wheat. 12a, Charkha and cloth.

Perf. 13½x13
1950, Jan. 26 Wmk. 196
227 A100 2a carmine 1.00 .40
228 A100 3½a ultramarine 1.60 *2.75*
229 A100 4a purple 1.60 .60
230 A100 12a claret 3.25 2.25
Nos. 227-230 (4) 7.45 6.00

Type of 1949 Redrawn

Bodhisattva — A101

1950, July 15 Typo. *Perf. 13½x14*
231 A101 1a turquoise 2.00 .20

For overprints see No. M47, Intl. Commission in Indo-china issues for Cambodia, No. 2, Laos, No. 2, and Vietnam, No. 2.

Extinct Stegodon Ganesa A102

1951, Jan. 13 *Perf. 13*
232 A102 2a deep carmine & black 2.25 .50

Geological Survey of India, cent.

Torch and Map — A103

Kabir — A104

1951, Mar. 4 Typo.
233 A103 2a red vio & red org 1.00 .25
234 A103 12a dark brown & ultra 4.00 1.00

First Asian Games, New Delhi.

Temple Type of 1949

2½a, Bodh Gaya Temple. 4a, Bhuvanesvara.

Perf. 13½x14
1951, Apr. 30 Wmk. 196
235 A94 2½a brown lake 2.50 2.50
236 A94 4a ultramarine 5.00 .20

1952, Oct. 1 Photo. *Perf. 14x13½*

1a, Tulsidas, poet & saint. 2a, Meera, Rajput princess. 4a, Surdas, blind poet and saint. 4½a, Ghalib, Urdu poet. 12a, Rabindranath Tagore.

237 A104 9p emerald .45 .40
238 A104 1a crimson .45 .20
239 A104 2a red orange 1.50 .20
240 A104 4a ultramarine 1.90 .60
241 A104 4½a red violet .45 .45
242 A104 12a brown 3.25 .90
Nos. 237-242 (6) 8.00 2.75

First Locomotive and Streamliner A105

1953, Apr. 16 *Perf. 14½x14*
243 A105 2a black .80 .20

Centenary of India's railroads.

Mt. Everest A106

1953, Oct. 2
244 A106 2a violet .25 .20
245 A106 14a brown 2.75 .30

Conquest of Mt. Everest, May 29, 1953.

Telegraph Poles of 1851 and 1951 A107

1953, Nov. 1
246 A107 2a blue green .25 .20
247 A107 12a blue 2.50 .30

Centenary of the telegraph in India.

Mail Transport, 1854 A108

Designs: 2a and 14a, Pigeon and plane. 4a, Mail transport, 1954.

1954, Oct. 1
248 A108 1a rose lilac .25 .20
249 A108 2a rose pink .25 .20
250 A108 4a yellow brown 2.50 .75
251 A108 14a blue 1.25 .30
Nos. 248-251 (4) 4.25 1.45

Centenary of India's postage stamps.

UN Emblem and Lotus Blossom A109

1954, Oct. 24
252 A109 2a Prussian green .40 .35

United Nations Day.

Forest Research Institute, Dehra Dun A110

1954, Dec. 11
253 A110 2a ultramarine .20 .20

4th World Forestry Cong., Dehra Dun.

Tractor
A111

Charkha
Operator
A112

Symbols of
Malaria
Control
A113

Designs: 6p, Power looms. 9p, Bullock irrigation pump. 1a, Damodar Valley dam. 3a, Naga woman at hand loom. 4a, Bullock team. 8a, Chittaranjan Locomotive Works. 10a, Plane over Marine Drive, Bombay. 12a, Hindustan aircraft factory. 14a, Plane over Kashmir valley. 1r, Telephone factory worker. 1r2a, Plane over Cape Comorin. 1r8a, Plane over Kanchenjunga Mountains. 2r, Rare earth factory. 5r, Sindri fertilizer factory. 10r, Steel mill.

Perf. 14x14½, 14½x14

1955, Jan. 26 **Photo.**

No.	Type	Value	Color	Unused	Used
254	A111	3p	rose lilac	.20	.20
255	A111	6p	deep violet	.20	.20
256	A111	9p	orange brown	.30	.20
257	A111	1a	dp blue green	.30	.20
258	A112	2a	blue	.20	.20
259	A112	3a	blue green	.35	.20
260	A111	4a	rose red	.35	.20
261	A113	6a	yellow brown	1.10	.20
262	A111	8a	deep blue	4.50	.20
263	A113	10a	aquamarine	2.25	1.40
264	A111	12a	violet blue	1.75	.20
265	A113	14a	emerald	3.00	.20
266	A111	1r	greenish black	3.00	.20
267	A113	1r2a	gray	1.50	*1.75*
268	A113	1r8a	claret	5.00	2.50
269	A111	2r	carmine rose	3.00	.20
270	A111	5r	brown	10.00	.25
271	A111	10r	orange	10.00	2.50
			Nos. 254-271 (18)	47.00	11.00

See Nos. 316-319.

Bodhi
Tree — A114

Ornament
and Bodhi
Tree
A115

1956, May 24 **Wmk. 196** ***Perf. 13***

No.	Type	Value	Color	Unused	Used
272	A114	2a	brown	.50	.20
273	A115	14a	brick red	4.00	3.00

2500th anniv. of the birth of Buddha.

Bal Gangadhar
Tilak — A116

Map of
India — A117

1956, July 23 **Photo.**

No.	Type	Value	Color	Unused	Used
274	A116	2a	orange brown	.20	.20

Birth cent. of Bal Gangadhar Tilak, independence leader.

1957-58 ***Perf. 14x14½***

No.	Type	Value	Color	Unused	Used
275	A117	1np	blue green	.20	.20
276	A117	2np	light brown	.20	.20
277	A117	3np	brown	.20	.20
278	A117	5np	emerald	3.50	.20
279	A117	6np	gray	.20	.20
280	A117	8np	brt green ('58)	4.50	.75
281	A117	10np	dark green	3.50	.20
282	A117	13np	brt carmine	.25	.20
283	A117	15np	violet ('58)	2.75	.20
284	A117	20np	bright blue	.25	.20
285	A117	25np	ultramarine	.25	.20
286	A117	50np	orange	1.75	.20
287	A117	75np	plum	1.00	.20
288	A117	90np	red lilac ('58)	2.75	1.00
			Nos. 275-288 (14)	21.30	4.15

Denominations of the 8np, 15np and 90np are inscribed nP.

See #302-315. For overprints see #M60 and Intl. Commission in Indo-China issues for Cambodia, #6-10, Laos, #6-10, and Vietnam, #6-10.

Laxmibai,
Rani of
Jhansi
A118

Banyan Sapling,
Arch and
Flames — A119

Perf. 14½x14, 13

1957, Aug. 15 **Wmk. 196**

No.	Type	Value	Color	Unused	Used
289	A118	15np	brown	.20	.20
290	A119	90np	bright red violet	1.50	.70

Centenary of the struggle for independence (Indian Mutiny).

Henri
Dunant
A120

1957, Oct. 28 ***Perf. 13½x13***

No.	Type	Value	Color	Unused	Used
291	A120	15np	car rose & black	.20	.20

19th Intl. Red Cross Conf., New Delhi.

Boy Eating
Banana
A121

Bankura
Horse — A122

Children's Day: 15np, Girl writing on tablet.

1957, Nov. 14 ***Perf. 13½***

No.	Type	Value	Color	Unused	Used
292	A121	8np	rose lilac	.20	.20
293	A121	15np	aquamarine	.20	.20
294	A122	90np	lt orange brown	.40	.20
			Nos. 292-294 (3)	.80	.60

Madras
University
A123

University Centenaries: No. 296, Calcutta. No. 297, Bombay, vert.

1957, Dec. 31 **Photo.**

Size: 29½x25mm

No.	Type	Value	Color	Unused	Used
295	A123	10np	light brown	.20	*.30*
296	A123	10np	gray	.20	*.30*

Size: 21½x38mm

No.	Type	Value	Color	Unused	Used
297	A123	10np	violet	.20	*.30*
			Nos. 295-297 (3)	.60	.90

J. N. Tata and Steel Works,
Jamshedpur — A124

1958, Mar. 1 ***Perf. 14½x14***

No.	Type	Value	Color	Unused	Used
298	A124	15np	red orange	.20	.20

50th anniv. of Indian steel industry.

Dr. Dhondo
Keshav
Karve — A125

1958, Apr. 18 ***Perf. 14x13½***

No.	Type	Value	Color	Unused	Used
299	A125	15np	orange brown	.20	.20

Cent. of the birth of Karve, educator and pioneer of women's education.

Wapiti and
Hunter
Planes
A126

1958, Apr. 30 ***Perf. 14½x14***

No.	Type	Value	Color	Unused	Used
300	A126	15np	bright blue	1.00	.20
301	A126	90np	ultramarine	1.25	1.25

25th anniv. of the Indian Air Force.

Map Type of 1957-58 and Industrial Type of 1955

1r, Telephone factory worker. 2r, Rare earth factory. 5r, Sindri fertilizer factory. 10r, Steel mill.

Perf. 14x14½

1958-63 **Photo.** **Wmk. 324**

No.	Type	Value	Color	Unused	Used
302	A117	1np	blue grn ('60)	.75	.20
a.			Imperf., pair	150.00	
303	A117	2np	light brown	.20	.20
304	A117	3np	brown	.20	.20
305	A117	5np	emerald	.20	.20
306	A117	6np	gray ('63)	.20	*2.50*
307	A117	8np	bright green	.20	.20
308	A117	10np	dark green	.20	.20
309	A117	13np	bright car ('63)	.75	*3.00*
310	A117	15np	violet ('59)	.45	.20
311	A117	20np	bright blue	.25	.20
312	A117	25np	ultramarine	.25	.20
313	A117	50np	orange ('59)	.25	.20
314	A117	75np	plum ('59)	.35	.20
315	A117	90np	red lilac ('60)	4.25	.20
316	A111	1r	dk grn ('59)	3.00	.20
317	A111	2r	lilac rose ('59)	4.25	.20
318	A111	5r	brown ('59)	7.25	.20
319	A111	10r	orange ('59)	17.00	3.50
			Nos. 302-319 (18)	40.00	12.00

For overprints see Nos. M56-M59, M61, Intl. Commission in Indo-china issues for Cambodia, No. 12, Laos, Nos. 12-16, and Vietnam Nos. 11-16.

Bipin Chandra
Pal — A128

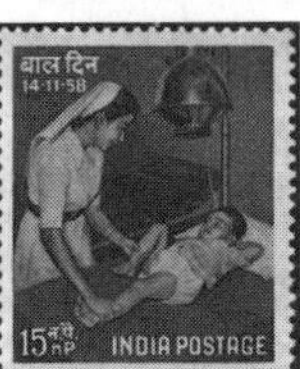

Nurse and
Child — A129

1958, Nov. 7 ***Perf. 13½***

No.	Type	Value	Color	Unused	Used
320	A128	15np	dull green	.20	.20

Birth cent. of Pal, early leader of India's freedom movement.

1958, Nov. 30

Portrait: Sir Jagadis Chandra Bose.

No.	Type	Value	Color	Unused	Used
321	A128	15np	brt greenish blue	.20	.20

Bose, physicist, plant physiologist, birth cent.

1958, Nov. 14 **Wmk. 324**

No.	Type	Value	Color	Unused	Used
322	A129	15np	violet	.20	.20

Children's Day, Nov. 14.

Exhibition
Gate
A130

1958, Dec. 30 ***Perf. 14½x14***

No.	Type	Value	Color	Unused	Used
323	A130	15np	claret	.20	.20

India 1958 Exhibition at Kampur.

Sir Jamsetjee
Jejeebhoy — A131

1959, Apr. 13 ***Perf. 13½***

No.	Type	Value	Color	Unused	Used
324	A131	15np	brown	.20	.20

Cent. of the death of Jejeebhoy, philosopher and philanthropist.

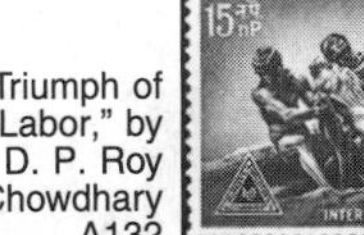

"Triumph of
Labor," by
D. P. Roy
Chowdhary
A132

1959, June 15 ***Perf. 14½x14***

No.	Type	Value	Color	Unused	Used
325	A132	15np	dull green	.20	.20

40th anniv. of the ILO.

Children Arriving at
Institution — A133

Perf. 14x14½

1959, Nov. 14 **Photo.** **Wmk. 324**

No.	Type	Value	Color	Unused	Used
326	A133	15np	dull green	.20	.20
a.			Imperf., pair	*500.00*	

Children's Day, Nov. 14.

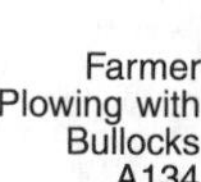

Farmer Plowing with Bullocks A134

1959, Dec. 30 ***Perf. 13***
327 A134 15np gray .20 .20

World Agriculture Fair, New Delhi.

Thiruvalluvar Holding Stylus and Palmyra Leaf — A135

1960, Feb. 15 ***Perf. 14***
328 A135 15np rose lilac .20 .20

Honoring the ancient and saintly Tamil poet, Thiruvalluvar.

Scene from Meghduta — A136

Scene from Sakuntala A137

1960, June 22 ***Perf. 13***
329 A136 15np gray .40 .20
330 A137 1.03r brown & bister 1.60 1.25

Honoring Kalidasa, 5th cent. poet and dramatist.

For surcharge see No. 371.

Subramania Bharati — A138

Dr. M. Visvesvaraya A139

1960, Sept. 11 Photo. ***Perf. 14x13½***
331 A138 15np bright blue .20 .20

Honoring the poet and statesman Subramania Bharati (1882-1921).

1960, Sept. 15 ***Perf. 13x13½***
332 A139 15np car rose & brown .20 .20

Birth cent. of Visvesvaraya, engineer and statesman.

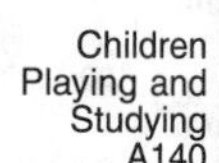

Children Playing and Studying A140

1960, Nov. 14 ***Perf. 13½x13***
333 A140 15np green .20 .20

Children's Day, Nov. 14.

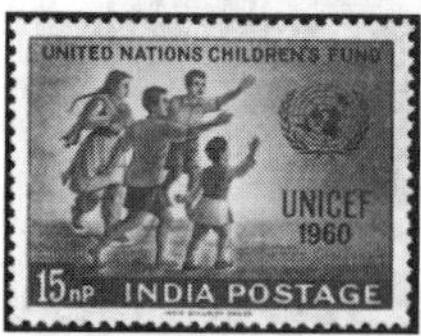

Children and UN Emblem A141

1960, Dec. 11 **Wmk. 324**
334 A141 15np olive gray & org brn .20 .20

UNICEF Day.

Tyagaraja, Indian Musician — A142

1961, Jan. 6 Photo. ***Perf. 14***
335 A142 15np bright blue .20 .20

114th anniv. of Tyagaraja's death.

First Airmail Postmark — A143

Boeing 707 Jetliner — A144

Design: 1r, Humber-Sommer biplane.

Perf. 14, 13x13½

1961, Feb. 18 **Wmk. 324**
336 A143 5np olive bister 1.00 .25
337 A144 15np gray & green 1.00 .25
338 A144 1r gray & claret 3.50 2.00
Nos. 336-338 (3) 5.50 2.50

50th anniv. of the world's 1st airmail. The flight was from Allahabad to Naini, Feb. 18, 1911.

Chatrapati Sivaji Maharaj (1627-1680) A145

1961, Apr. 17 ***Perf. 13x13½***
339 A145 15np gray green & brown .70 .30

Leader of the Maharattas in the fight against the Moguls.

Motilal Nehru — A146

Rabindranath Tagore — A147

1961, May 6 ***Perf. 14x13½***
340 A146 15np orange & ol gray .20 .20

Cent. of the birth of Motilal Nehru, leader in India's fight for freedom.

1961, May 7 ***Perf. 13***
341 A147 15np blue grn & org .70 .30

Cent. of the birth of Tagore, poet.

Radio Masts and All India Radio Emblem A148

1961, June 8 Photo. **Wmk. 324**
342 A148 15np ultramarine .20 .20

25th anniv. of All India Radio.

Prafulla Chandra Ray — A149

Vishnu Narayan Bhatkhande A150

1961, Aug. 2 ***Perf. 14x13½***
343 A149 15np gray .20 .20

Cent. of the birth of Ray, scientist.

1961, Sept. 1 ***Perf. 13***
344 A150 15np olive gray .20 .20

Bhatkhande (1860-1936), musician.

Boy Making Pottery — A151

Gate at Fair — A152

1961, Nov. 14 ***Perf. 13½***
345 A151 15np brown .20 .20

Children's Day, Nov. 14.

1961, Nov. 14 ***Perf. 14x14½***
346 A152 15np blue & carmine .20 .20

Indian Industries Fair at New Delhi.

Forest and Himalayas — A153

1961, Nov. 21 ***Perf. 13***
347 A153 15np brown & green .35 .20

Cent. of the introduction of scientific forestry in India.

Yaksha, God of Fertility — A154

Kalibangan Seal — A155

1961, Dec. 14 Photo. ***Perf. 14***
348 A154 15np orange brown .25 .20
349 A155 90np orange brn & olive .50 .20

Cent. of the Archaeological Survey of India.

Madan Mohan Malaviya — A156

Nunmati Refinery, Gauhati — A157

1961, Dec. 25 *Perf. 14x13½*

350 A156 15np slate .20 .20

Cent. of the birth of Malaviya, Pres. of the Indian Natl. Cong. and Vice Chancellor of Benares University.

1962, Jan. 1 **Photo.** *Perf. 13*

351 A157 15np blue .30 .20

1st Indian oil refinery at Gauhati.

Bhikaiji Cama — A158

Village Council, Banyan Tree, Parliament and Map — A159

1962, Jan. 26 *Perf. 14*

352 A158 15np rose lilac .20 .20

Cent. of the birth of Madame Cama, a leader in India's fight for independence.

1962, Jan. 26 *Perf. 13*

353 A159 15np red lilac .20 .20

Panchayati Raj, the system of government by village council.

Dayananda Sarasvati — A160

Ganesh Shankar Vidyarthi — A161

1962, Mar. 4 *Perf. 14*

354 A160 15np brown orange .20 .20

135th anniv. of the birth of Sarasvati, reformer of the Vedic religion and founder of the Arya Samaj educational institutions.

1962, Mar. 25

355 A161 15np reddish brown .20 .20

Vidyarthi (1890-1931), reformer of community life.

Malaria Eradication Emblem — A162

Dr. Rajendra Prasad — A163

1962, Apr. 7 *Perf. 13*

356 A162 15np dk car rose & yel .20 .20

WHO drive to eradicate malaria.

1962, May 13 *Perf. 13*

357 A163 15np bright red lilac .20 .20

Prasad, President of India (1950-62).

High Court, Calcutta A164

1962 **Photo.** *Perf. 13½x14*

358 A164 15np green .50 .20
359 A164 15np Madras .50 .20
360 A164 15np Bombay .50 .20
Nos. 358-360 (3) 1.50 .60

Indian High Courts, cent. Issued: No. 358, July 1; No. 359, Aug. 8; No. 360, Aug. 14.

Ramabai Ranade — A165

Indian Rhinoceros A166

1962, Aug. 15 *Perf. 14*

361 A165 15np brown orange .40 .20

Ramabai Ranade (1862-1924), woman social reformer.

1962-63 **Wmk. 324** *Perf. 14*

10np, Gaur. No. 363, Lesser panda, vert. 30np, Elephant, vert. 50np, Tiger. 1r, Lion.

Size: 30x26mm

361A	A166	10np yel org & blk ('63)	.70	*1.50*
362	A166	15np Prus blue & brn	.40	.20

Perf. 13x13½, 13½x13

Size: 25x36mm, 36x25mm

363	A166	15np green & red brown ('63)	1.40	.55
364	A166	30np bister & slate ('63)	3.50	1.50
365	A166	50np dp grn, ocher & brown ('63)	3.25	.75
366	A166	1r brt bl & pale brown ('63)	2.25	.50
		Nos. 361A-366 (6)	11.50	5.00

Child Reaching for Flag A167

1962, Nov. 14 *Perf. 13*

367 A167 15np lt bluish grn & ver .20 .20

Children's Day.

Eye within Lotus Blossom A168

1962, Dec. 3 **Photo.**

368 A168 15np olive gray .20 .20

16th Intl. Cong. of Ophthalmology, New Delhi, Dec. 1962.

Srinivasa Ramanujan A169

Swami Vivekananda — A170

1962, Dec. 22 *Perf. 13½x14*

369 A169 15np olive gray .60 .40

75th anniv. of the birth of Ramanujan (1887-1920), mathematician.

1963, Jan. 17 *Perf. 14x14½*

370 A170 15np olive & orange brn .20 .20

Cent. of the birth of Vivekananda (1863-1902), philosopher.

No. 330 Surcharged with New Value and Two Bars

1963, Feb. 2 *Perf. 13*

371 A137 1r on 1.03r brown & bis .30 .20

Hands Reaching for "FAO" Emblem — A171

Henri Dunant and Centenary Emblem — A172

1963, Mar. 21 **Photo.**

372 A171 15np chalky blue 1.00 .30

UNFAO Freedom from Hunger campaign.

1963, May 8 *Perf. 13*

373 A172 15np gray & red 2.25 .30

Centenary of the International Red Cross.

Field Artillery and Helicopter A173

Design: 1r, Soldier guarding frontier and plane dropping supplies.

1963, Aug. 15 *Perf. 13½x14*

374 A173 15np dull green .40 .20
375 A173 1r red brown .85 .80

Honoring the Armed Forces and the 16th anniv. of independence.

Dadabhoy Naoroji — A174

1963, Sept. 4 *Perf. 13*

376 A174 15np gray green .20 .20

Honoring Dadabhoy Naoroji (1825-1917), mathematician and statesman.

Annie Besant — A175

School Lunch — A176

1963, Oct. 1 **Photo.** *Perf. 14*

377 A175 15np blue green .20 .20

Besant (1847-1933), an English woman devoted to the cause of India's freedom, theosophist and writer. Stamp gives birth date as 1837.

1963, Nov. 14 **Wmk. 324** *Perf. 14*

378 A176 15np olive bister .20 .20

Children's Day.

Eleanor Roosevelt at Spinning Wheel
A177

1963, Dec. 10 ***Perf. 13***

379 A177 15np rose violet .20 .20

Honoring Eleanor Roosevelt on the 15th anniv. of the Universal Declaration of Human Rights.

Gopabandhu Das (1877-1928)
A178

Lakshmi, Goddess of Wealth — A179

1964, Jan. 4 ***Perf. 13***

380 A178 15np dull purple .20 .20

Gopabandhu Das, social reformer.

1964, Jan. 4 **Photo.**

381 A179 15np dull violet blue .20 .20

26th Intl. Cong. of Orientalists, New Delhi, Jan. 4-14.

Purandaradasa Holding Veena and Chipala — A180

1964, Jan. 14

382 A180 15np golden brown .20 .20

400th anniv. of the death of Purandaradasa (1484-1564), musician.

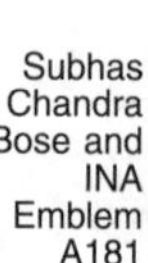

Subhas Chandra Bose and INA Emblem
A181

Design: 55np, Bose addressing troops.

1964, Jan. 23 ***Perf. 13***

383 A181 15np olive .40 .20

384 A181 55np red & black .40 .40

67th anniv. of the birth of Bose, organizer of the Indian Natl. Army.

Sarojini Haidu (1879-1949)
A182

Kasturba Gandhi
A183

1964, Feb. 13 ***Perf. 14x13½***

385 A182 15np dull lilac & slate grn .20 .20

Mrs. Sarojini Haidu, poet, politician, governor of United Provinces.

1964, Feb. 22 **Photo.** **Wmk. 324**

386 A183 15np brown orange .20 .20

20th anniv. of the death of Kasturba Gandhi (1869-1944), wife of Mahatma Gandhi.

Dr. Waldemar M. Haffkine (1860-1930)
A184

1964, Mar. 16 ***Perf. 13***

387 A184 15np violet brown, *buff* .20 .20

Haffkine, bacteriologist, who as director of Haffkine Institute introduced inoculations against cholera and plague.

Jawaharlal Nehru (1889-1964) and People
A185

1964, June 12 **Unwmk.** ***Perf. 13***

388 A185 15p grayish blue .20 .20

Prime Minister Jawaharlal Nehru.

Asutosh Mookerjee and High Court, Calcutta
A186

1964, June 29 **Wmk. 324**

389 A186 15p olive green & brn .20 .20

Cent. of the birth of Asutosh Mookerjee (1864-1924), educator, lawyer and judge.

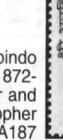

Sri Aurobindo Ghose (1872-1950), Writer and Philosopher
A187

1964, Aug. 15 **Photo.**

390 A187 15p violet brown .20 .20

Raja Rammohun Roy — A188

1964, Sept. 27 ***Perf. 13***

391 A188 15p reddish brown .20 .20

Roy (1772-1833), Hindu religious reformer.

Globe, Lotus, and Calipers — A189

Nehru Medal and Rose — A190

1964, Nov. 9 **Unwmk.** **Photo.**

392 A189 15p carmine rose .20 .20

6th gen. assembly of the Intl. Organization for Standardization.

1964, Nov. 14 ***Perf. 13½***

393 A190 15p blue gray .20 .20

Children's Day. For overprints, see Nos. M62, Intl. Commission in Indo-china issues for Laos and Vietnam, No. 1.

St. Thomas Statue, Ortona, Italy — A191

Globe and Pickax — A192

1964, Dec. 2 **Unwmk.** ***Perf. 13½***

394 A191 15p rose violet .20 .20

Visit of Pope Paul VI, Nov. 30-Dec. 2.

1964, Dec. 14 **Wmk. 324**

395 A192 15p bright green .30 .30

22nd Intl. Geological Cong., New Delhi.

Jamsetji N. Tata
A193

1965, Jan. 7 **Unwmk.** ***Perf. 13***

396 A193 15p dk brown & orange .30 .20

125th anniv. of the birth of Tata (1839-1904), founder of India's steel industry.

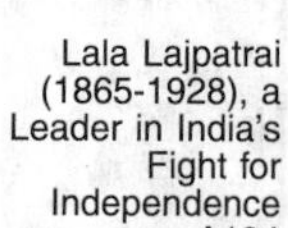

Lala Lajpatrai (1865-1928), a Leader in India's Fight for Independence
A194

1965, Jan. 28 **Photo.** ***Perf. 13***

397 A194 15p brown .20 .20

ICC Emblem and Globe
A195

1965, Feb. 8 **Litho.**

398 A195 15p dull green & car .20 .20

20th cong. of the Intl. Chamber of Commerce, New Delhi.

Freighter Jalausha at Visakhapatnam — A196

Perf. 14½x14

1965, Apr. 5 **Photo.** **Wmk. 324**

399 A196 15p ultramarine .30 .30

National Maritime Day.

Death Centenary of Abraham Lincoln — A197

1965, Apr. 15 ***Perf. 13***

400 A197 15p yellow & dk brown .20 .20

ITU Emblem, Old and New Communication Equipment — A198

1965, May 17 **Photo.** ***Perf. 14½x14***

401 A198 15p rose violet 1.00 .30

Cent. of the ITU.

Torch and Rose — A199

1965, May 27 **Wmk. 324** ***Perf. 13***

402 A199 15p carmine & blue .20 .20

1st anniv. of the death of Jawaharlal Nehru.

ICY Emblem
A200

1965, June 26 Photo. Unwmk.
403 A200 15p bister & dk green 1.00 .50

International Cooperation Year.

Indians Raising Flag on Everest — A201

1965, Aug. 15 Unwmk. *Perf. 13*
404 A201 15p plum .25 .20

Success of the Indian Mt. Everest Expedition, May 20, 1965.

Elephant from Konarak Temple, Orissa
A202

Tea Picking
A203

Woman Writing Letter, Chandella Carving, 11th Century — A204

Trombay Atomic Center
A205

Designs: 2p, Vase (bidri ware). 3p, Brass lamp. 4p, Coffee berries. 5p, Family (family planning). 8p, Axis deer (chital). 10p, Electric locomotive, 1961. 20p, Gnat plane. 30p, Male and female figurines. 40p, General Post Office, Calcutta, 1868. 50p, Mangoes. 60p, Somnath Temple. 70p, Stone chariot, Hampi, Mysore. 2r, Dal Lake, Kashmir. 5r, Bhakra Dam, Punjab.

Perf. 14½x14, 14x14½

1965-68 Photo. Wmk. 324

405	A202	2p	redsh brown ('67)	.20	*.35*
406	A202	3p	olive bis ('67)	.20	*1.75*
407	A203	4p	orange brn ('68)	.20	*1.50*
408	A202	5p	cerise ('67)	.20	.20
409	A202	6p	gray ('66)	.20	*1.90*
410	A202	8p	red brown ('67)	.30	*2.75*
411	A203	10p	brt blue ('66)	.35	.20
412	A203	15p	dk yel green	1.90	.20
413	A203	20p	plum ('67)	5.00	.20
414	A202	30p	brown ('67)	.20	.20
415	A203	40p	brown vio ('68)	.20	.20
416	A202	50p	green ('67)	.20	.20
417	A202	60p	dark gray ('67)	.30	.20
418	A203	70p	violet ('67)	.55	.20
419	A204	1r	deep claret & red brown ('66)	.55	.20
420	A205	2r	vio & brt bl ('67)	1.90	.20
421	A205	5r	brn & vio ('67)	2.25	.50
422	A205	10r	green & gray	13.50	.55
			Nos. 405-422 (18)	28.20	11.50

See Nos. 623, 666-670, 678, 680, 684-685. For overprints see Nos. RA1-RA2, Intl. Commission in Indo-china issues for Laos and Viet-nam, Nos. 2-9.

1975-76 Wmk. 360 *Perf. 14½x14*
423 A202 5p cerise .75 .20

Unwmk.
423A A202 5p cerise ('76) .50 .20

A206

A207

1965, Sept. 10 Unwmk. *Perf. 13*
424 A206 15p dark green & brown .20 .20

Govind Ballabh Pant (1887-1961), Home Minister of India.

1965, Oct. 31 *Perf. 14*
425 A207 15p gray .20 .20

Vallabhbhai Patel (1875-1950), Deputy Prime Minister of India.

Chittaranjan Das (1870-1925)
A208

Vidyapati, 15th Cent. Poet
A209

1965, Nov. 5 Photo. *Perf. 13*
426 A208 15p brown .20 .20

Das, freedom fighter, pres. of Indian Natl. Cong., mayor of Calcutta.

1965, Nov. 17 *Perf. 14x14½*
427 A209 15p brown .20 .20

Tomb of Akbar the Great, Sikandra
A210

1966, Jan. 24 *Perf. 14*
428 A210 15p dark gray .20 .20

Pacific Area Travel Assoc. Conf., New Delhi.

Soldier, Planes and Warships
A211

1966, Jan. 26
429 A211 15p bright violet .80 .30

Honoring the Indian armed forces.

Lal Bahadur Shastri
A212

Kambar
A213

1966, Jan. 26 *Perf. 13*
430 A212 15p gray .35 .20

Prime Minister Shastri (1904-66).

1966, Apr. 9 *Perf. 14x14½*
431 A213 15p green .20 .20

Kambar, 9th century Tamil poet.

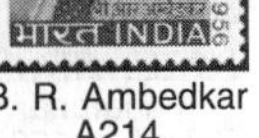

B. R. Ambedkar
A214

Kunwar Singh
A215

1966, Apr. 14 Unwmk. *Perf. 14*
432 A214 15p violet brown .20 .20

10th anniv. of the death of Dr. Bhimrao R. Ambedkar (1891-1956), lawyer and leader in social reform.

1966, Apr. 23 Photo.
433 A215 15p orange brown .20 .20

Kunwar Singh (1777-1858), hero of 1857 War of Independence (1857 Mutiny).

Gopal Krishna Gokhale
A216

1966, May 9 Unwmk. *Perf. 13*
434 A216 15p violet brown & yel .20 .20

Cent. of the birth of Gokhale (1866-1915), professor of history and political economy and leader of the opposition party.

A. M. P. Dvivedi (1864-1938)
A217

Ranjit Singh (1780-1839) — A218

1966, May 15 *Perf. 14*
435 A217 15p olive gray .20 .20

Acharya Mahavir Prasad Dvivedi, Hindi writer.

1966, June 28 Unwmk. *Perf. 14*
436 A218 15p plum .25 .20

Maharaja Ranjit Singh, ruler of Punjab.

Homi Bhabha and Atomic Reactor
A219

1966, Aug. 4 *Perf. 14½x14*
437 A219 15p brown violet .20 .20

Dr. Homi Bhabha (1909-1966), scientist.

Rama Tirtha
A220

1966, Nov. 11 Unwmk. *Perf. 13*
438 A220 15p greenish blue .20 .20

60th anniv. of the death of Swami Rama Tirtha (1873-1906).

A221

A222

1966, Nov. 11 Photo. *Perf. 13½*
439 A221 15p dark violet blue .20 .20

Abdul Kalam Azad (1888-1958), president of the All-India Congress.

1966, Nov. 14 *Perf. 13*
440 A222 15p Child and dove .35 .20

Children's Day.

Allahabad High Court, Cent.
A223

1966, Nov. 25 *Perf. 14½x14*
441 A223 15p violet brown .30 .30

Family
A224

1966, Dec. 12 *Perf. 13½x13*
442 A224 15p brown .20 .20

Intl. Conf. for Marriage Guidance, New Delhi, and Family Planning Week.

Hockey
A225

1966, Dec. 31 Unwmk. *Perf. 13*
443 A225 15p bright blue .20 .20

Victory of the Indian hockey team at the 5th Asian Games, Bangkok, Dec. 19.

Grain Harvest
A226

1967, Jan. 11 *Perf. 13½*
444 A226 15p yellow green .20 .20

1st anniv. of the death of Prime Minister Lal Bahadur Shastri, who advocated self-sufficiency in food production.

Voters — A227

Guru Dwara Shrine, Patna — A228

1967, Jan. 13 Photo.
445 A227 15p light red brown .20 .20

General elections, Feb. 1967.

1967, Jan. 17 *Perf. 14*
446 A228 15p violet .20 .20

300th anniv. of the birth of Gobind Singh (1666-1708), religious leader.

Taj Mahal
A229

1967, Mar. 19 *Perf. 14½x14*
447 A229 15p brown & orange .20 .20

International Tourist Year.

Nandalal Bose and Garuda — A230

1967, Apr. 16 *Perf. 13½*
448 A230 15p brown .20 .20

Nandalal Bose (1882-1966), painter.

Survey of India Emblem
A231

1967, May 1 Unwmk. *Perf. 13*
449 A231 15p lilac .40 .30

Bicentenary of Survey of India.

Basaveswara, 12th Cent. Statesman and Philosopher, at Work — A232

1967, May 11 *Perf. 13½x14*
450 A232 15p deep orange .20 .20

Narsinha Mehta — A233

Maharana Pratap — A234

1967, May 30 *Perf. 13½*
451 A233 15p gray brown .20 .20

Narsina Mehta, 15th cent. musician.

1967, June 11 *Perf. 14x14½*
452 A234 15p reddish brown .20 .20

Pratap (1540-1597), Mewar ruler.

Narayana Guru
A235

Dr. Sarvepalli Radhakrishnan
A236

1967, Aug. 21 Photo. *Perf. 14*
453 A235 15p brown .20 .20

Narayana Guru (1855-1928), religious reformer.

1967, Sept. 5 Unwmk. *Perf. 13*
454 A236 15p dull claret .45 .20

Radhakrishnan, Pres. of India 1962-67.

Martyrs' Memorial, Patna
A237

1967, Oct. 1 Photo. *Perf. 14½x14*
455 A237 15p dark carmine .20 .20

25th anniv. of the "Quit India" revolt led by Gandhi.

Map Showing Indo-European Telegraph
A238

1967, Nov. 9 Photo. *Perf. 13½*
456 A238 15p blue & black .30 .20

Cent. of the laying of the Indo-European telegraph line.

Wrestlers
A239

1967, Nov. 12
457 A239 15p ocher & plum .35 .20

World Wrestling Championships, New Delhi, Nov. 1967.

Nehru and Naga Tribesmen — A240

Rashbehari Basu — A241

1967, Dec. 4 Photo. *Perf. 13*
458 A240 15p ultramarine .20 .20

1967, Dec. 26 *Perf. 13½*
459 A241 15p dull purple .20 .20

Basu (1886-1945), Bengali leader.

Bugle, Scout Emblem and Scout Sign
A242

1967, Dec. 27 *Perf. 14½x14*
460 A242 15p orange brown .75 .20

Boy Scout Movement, 60th anniv.

People Encircling the Globe and Human Rights Flame
A243

1968, Jan. 1 *Perf. 13*
461 A243 15p dark green .35 .30

Intl. Human Rights Year.

Conference Emblem and Gopuram Temple — A244

1968, Jan. 3 Photo. Unwmk.
462 A244 15p purple .35 .20

2nd Intl. Conf. on Tamil Studies, Madras.

UN Emblem, Plane and Ship
A245

1968, Feb. 1 *Perf. 14½x14*
463 A245 15p greenish blue .40 .20

UN Conference on Trade and Development, New Delhi, Feb. 1968.

Symbolic Bow and Quill Pen — A246

1968, Feb. 20 *Perf. 13½x14*
464 A246 15p ocher & sepia .20 .20

Cent. of the newspaper Amrit Bazar Patrika, Calcutta.

Maxim Gorky (1868-1936), Russian Writer — A247

1968, Mar. 28 Photo. *Perf. 14*
465 A247 15p brown violet .20 .20

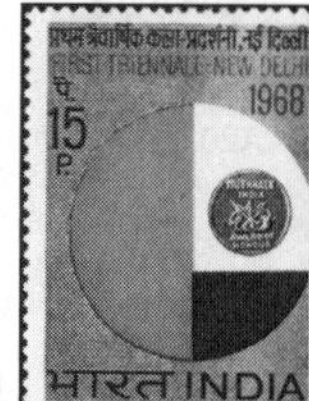

Exhibition Emblem — A248

Symbolic Mail Box — A249

1968, Mar. 31 *Perf. 13*
466 A248 15p dark blue & org .30 .20

First Triennial Exhibition, New Delhi.

1968, July 1 Unwmk. *Perf. 13*
467 A249 20p vermilion & blue .30 .20

Opening of 100,000th Indian post office.

Wheat and Indian Agricultural Research Institute
A250

1968, July 15 Photo. *Perf. 13*
468 A250 20p brt grn & brn org .30 .20

India's 1968 bumper wheat crop.

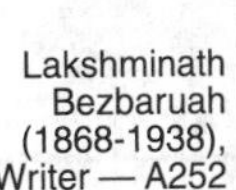

Gaganendranath Tagore (1867-1938), Self-portrait A251

1968, Sept. 17 Unwmk. *Perf. 13*
469 A251 20p ocher & deep clar .30 .20

Lakshminath Bezbaruah (1868-1938), Writer — A252

1968, Oct. 5 Photo. *Perf. 13½*
470 A252 20p sepia .20 .20

19th Olympic Games, Mexico City A253

1968, Oct. 12 *Perf. 14½x14*
471 A253 20p blue gray & red brn .20 .20
472 A253 1r olive gray & dk brn .40 .20

Bhagat Singh (1907-1931), Revolutionary — A254

1968, Oct. 19 Photo. *Perf. 13½x13*
473 A254 20p orange brown .20 .20

Bose Reading Proclamation A255

Sister Nivedita A256

1968, Oct. 21 *Perf. 14x14½*
474 A255 20p dark blue .20 .20

25th anniv. of the establishment of the Azad Hind (Free India) government by Subhas Chandra Bose (1897-1945), independence leader.

1968, Oct. 27
475 A256 20p blue green .30 .30

Sister Nivedita (Margaret Noble, 1867-1911), Irish-born friend of India.

Marie Curie and Patient Receiving Radiation A257

1968, Nov. 6 *Perf. 14½x14*
476 A257 20p purple 1.25 .50

Marie Sklodowska Curie (1867-1934), discoverer of radium and polonium.

World Map — A258

Interior of Cochin Synagogue A259

1968, Dec. 1 *Perf. 13*
477 A258 20p blue .20 .20

21st Intl. Geographical Congress.

Perf. 13x13½
1968, Dec. 15 Photo. Unwmk.
478 A259 20p vio bl & car rose .80 .40

400th anniv. of Cochin Synagogue.

Frigate Nilgiri A260

1968, Dec. 15 *Perf. 13½x13*
479 A260 20p dull violet blue 1.75 .40

Navy Day. The Nilgiri, launched Oct. 23, 1968, was the 1st Indian warship.

Redbilled Blue Magpie A261

Birds: 50p, Brown-fronted pied woodpecker. 1r, Slaty-headed scimitar babbler, vert. 2r, Yellow-backed sunbirds.

1968, Dec. 31 *Perf. 14½x14, 14x14½*
480 A261 20p pink & multi .65 .45
481 A261 50p multicolored 1.00 *1.40*
482 A261 1r multicolored 1.75 .90
483 A261 2r multicolored 1.60 1.25
Nos. 480-483 (4) 5.00 4.00

Chatterjee (1838-94) A262

Dr. Bhagavan Das A263

1969, Jan. 1 *Perf. 13½*
484 A262 20p ultramarine .20 .20

Bankim Chandra Chatterjee, writer.

1969, Jan. 12 Photo. *Perf. 13½*
485 A263 20p red brown .20 .20

Das (1869-1958), philosopher.

Martin Luther King, Jr. (1929-1968), American Civil Rights Leader — A264

1969, Jan. 25
486 A264 20p olive gray .20 .20

Mirza Ghalib A265

1969, Feb. 17 *Perf. 14½x14*
487 A265 20p dk gray & salmon .40 .20

Mirza Ghalib (Asad Ullah Beg Khan 1797-1869), poet who modernized the Urdu language.

Osmania University, Hyderabad, 50th Avviv. A266

1969, Mar. 15 Photo. *Perf. 14½x14*
488 A266 20p green .20 .20

Rafi Ahmed Kidwai A267

1969, Apr. 1 *Perf. 13*
489 A267 20p grayish blue .75 .30

Minister of communications and food, introduced around-the-clock airmail service.

ILO Emblems A268

1969, Apr. 11 *Perf. 14½x14*
490 A268 20p orange brown .20 .20

50th anniv. of the ILO.

Memorial Monument and Hands Strewing Flowers — A269

1969, Apr. 13 *Perf. 13½*
491 A269 20p rose carmine .20 .20

50th anniv. of Jallianwala Bagh, Amritsar, massacre.

Nageswara Rao (1867-1938), Journalist and Congressman A270

1969, May 1 Photo. *Perf. 13½x14*
492 A270 20p brown .20 .20

Ardaseer Cursetjee Wadia and Ships A271

1969, May 27 Photo. *Perf. 14½x14*
493 A271 20p blue green .40 .30

Wadia (1808-1877), shipbuilder.

Serampore College, 150th Anniv. — A272

1969, June 7 Photo. *Perf. 13½*
494 A272 20p violet brown .20 .20

Dr. Zakir Husain (1897-1969), President of India 1967-1969 A273

1969, June 11 *Perf. 13*
495 A273 20p olive gray .20 .20

Laxmanrao Kirloskar and Plow A274

1969, June 20
496 A274 20p gray .20 .20

Kirloskar (1869-1956), industrialist and social reformer, introduced the iron plow to India.

Mahatma Gandhi (1869-1948) A275

Gandhi on the Dandi March A276

20p, Gandhi and his wife Kasturba, horiz. 5r, Gandhi with spinning wheel, horiz.

1969, Oct. 2 Photo. Unwmk.
Size: 29x25mm
Perf. 13½
497 A275 20p sepia .50 .50
Size: 28x38mm
Perf. 13
498 A275 75p ol gray, sal & brn 1.25 .20
Size: 20x38mm
Perf. 14x14½
499 A276 1r bright blue 1.25 1.25
Size: 35½x25½mm
Perf. 13
500 A275 5r orange & sepia 4.50 4.50
Nos. 497-500 (4) 7.50 6.45

Freighter and IMCO Emblem
A277

1969, Oct. 14 ***Perf. 13***
501 A277 20p ultramarine 1.75 .40

10th anniv. of the Intergovernmental Maritime Consultative Organization.

Globe and Parliament, New Delhi
A278

1969, Oct. 30 Photo. ***Perf. 14½x14***
502 A278 20p bright blue .20 .20

57th Interparliamentary Conf., New Delhi.

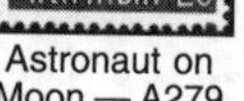

Astronaut on Moon — A279

Nanak Mausoleum, Talwandi, Punjab — A280

1969, Nov. 19 ***Perf. 14x14½***
503 A279 20p olive brown .45 .30

See note after US No. C76.

1969, Nov. 23 Photo. ***Perf. 13½***
504 A280 20p gray violet .20 .20

500th anniv. of the birth of the Guru Nanak, Sikh leader.

Tiger and Globe
A281

1969, Nov. 24 ***Perf. 14½x14***
505 A281 20p olive grn & red brn .60 .60

Intl. Union for the Conservation of Nature and Natural Resources.

T. L. Vaswani
A282

Thakkar Bapa
A283

1969, Nov. 25 ***Perf. 14x14½***
506 A282 20p dark gray .20 .20

T. L. Vaswani (1879-1966), writer and orator.

1969, Nov. 29 ***Perf. 13½***
507 A283 20p dark brown .20 .20

Thakkar Bapa (1869-1951), statesman who worked to help the untouchables.

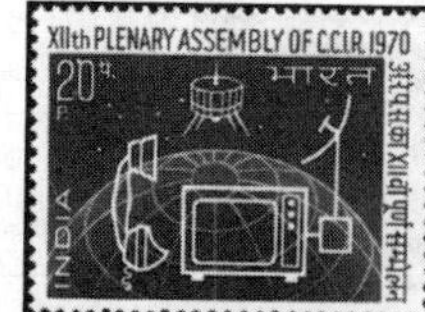

Globe and Telecommunications Symbols — A284

1970, Jan. 21 ***Perf. 13***
508 A284 20p Prussian blue .35 .20

12th Plenary Assembly of the Intl. Radio Consultative Committee.

C. N. Annadurai (1909-1969), Journalist — A285

Munshi Newal Kishore and Printing Plant — A286

1970, Feb. 2
509 A285 20p dk blue & magenta .20 .20

1970, Feb. 19 Photo. ***Perf. 13x13½***
510 A286 20p dark carmine .20 .20

Kishore (1836-1895), publisher.

Cent. of Nalanda College
A287

1970, Mar. 27 Photo. ***Perf. 14½x14***
511 A287 20p light red brown .60 .40

Swami Shraddhanand (1856-1926), Patriot — A288

1970, Mar. 30 ***Perf. 13½***
512 A288 20p orange brown .70 .40

Lenin
A289

1970, Apr. 22 Photo. ***Perf. 13***
513 A289 20p multicolored .60 .20

UPU Headquarters, Bern — A290

1970, May 20
514 A290 20p black & green .20 .20

New UPU Headquarters in Bern.

Sher Shah Suri — A291

1970, May 22 Photo. ***Perf. 13***
515 A291 20p blue green .20 .20

Suri, 15th cent. ruler of Delhi and postal service reformer.

Vir D. Savarkar and Prison at Port Blair, Andamans
A292

1970, May 28
516 A292 20p orange brown .20 .20

V. D. Savarkar (1883-1966), patriot.

"UN" and UN Emblem — A293

1970, June 26 Photo. ***Perf. 13***
517 A293 20p blue .35 .20

25th anniv. of the UN.

Harvest, Crane, Factory and Emblem
A294

1970, Aug. 18 ***Perf. 14½x14***
518 A294 20p violet .20 .20

Asian Productivity Year.

Dr. Maria Montessori and Education Symbol
A295

1970, Aug. 31 ***Perf. 13½x13***
519 A295 20p dull claret .30 .30

Intl. Education Year and Maria Montessori (1870-1952), Italian educator and physician.

Jatindra Nath Mukherjee
A296

1970, Sept. 9 ***Perf. 14½x14***
520 A296 20p dark red brown 1.00 .30

Mukherjee (1879-1915), revolutionary leader.

Srinivasa Sastri (1869-1946)
A297

Iswar Chandra Vidyasagar
A298

1970, Sept. 22 Photo. ***Perf. 13***
521 A297 20p dk brown & ocher .30 .30

V. S. Srinivasa Sastri, statesman.

1970, Sept. 26
522 A298 20p rose lilac & brown .30 .30

Vidyasagar (1820-91), educator and writer.

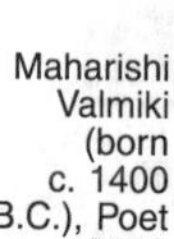

Maharishi Valmiki (born c. 1400 B.C.), Poet
A299

1970, Oct. 14 Photo. ***Perf. 13***
523 A299 20p plum .40 .30

Calcutta Harbor
A300

1970, Oct. 17
524 A300 20p blue 1.10 .50

Cent. of Calcutta Port Commissioners.

Jamia Millia Islamia University, 50th Anniv.
A301

1970, Oct. 29 ***Perf. 14½x14***
525 A301 20p yellow green .50 .40

Jamnalal Bajai (1889-1942), Patriot — A302

1970, Nov. 4 Wmk. 324 ***Perf. 13***
526 A302 20p sepia .25 .20

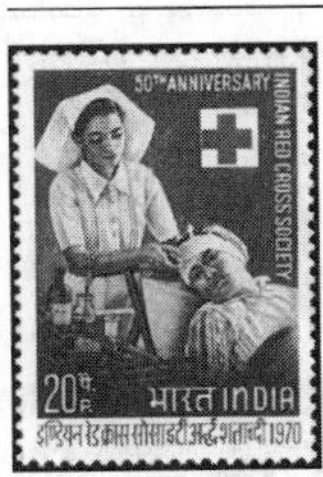
Nurse and Patient — A303

Ludwig van Beethoven A305

Sant Namdeo (1270-1350), Holy Man — A304

1970, Nov. 5
527 A303 20p Prus. blue & red .75 .40
50th anniv. of the Indian Red Cross Soc.

1970, Nov. 9 **Photo.**
528 A304 20p orange .20 .20

1970, Dec. 16 **Unwmk.** ***Perf. 13***
529 A305 20p dk brn & org 2.50 .60

Children with Stamp Album A306

Design: 1r, Hands holding magnifying glass over Gandhi stamp.

1970, Dec. 23 **Photo.** ***Perf. 13***
530 A306 20p dull green & lt brn .25 .20
531 A306 1r ocher & brown 2.50 .75
INPEX 1970, Indian Natl. Phil. Exhib., New Delhi, Dec. 23, 1970-Jan. 6, 1971.

Girl Guide and Sign — A307

Hands Shielding Flame — A308

1970, Dec. 27
532 A307 20p dark brown violet .75 .30
Girl Guides, 60th anniv.

1971, Jan. 11
533 A308 20p bis brn & dp clar .20 .20
Centenary of Indian Life Insurance.

Kashi Vidyapith, 50th Anniv. A309

1971, Feb. 10 ***Perf. 14½x14***
534 A309 20p black brown .20 .20
Kashi Vidyapith University, Benares.

Charles Freer Andrews (1871-1940), British Publicist, Friend of Gandhi — A310

1971, Feb. 12 ***Perf. 13x13½***
535 A310 20p orange brown .40 .30

Ravidas, 15th Cent. Poet and Holy Man A311

1971, Feb. ***Perf. 13***
536 A311 20p rose carmine .35 .30

Acharya Narendra Deo (1889-1956), Educator, Patriot, Statesman A312

1971, Feb. 18 **Photo.** ***Perf. 13***
537 A312 20p olive bister .20 .20

Cent. of Indian Census A313

1971, Mar. 10
538 A313 20p ultra & sepia .35 .30

Ramana Maharshi (1879-1950), Holy Man — A314

1971, Apr. 14 **Photo.** ***Perf. 13½x14***
539 A314 20p ol gray & orange .20 .20

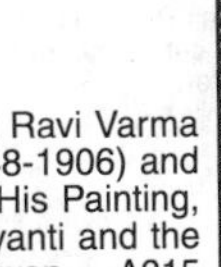

Raja Ravi Varma (1848-1906) and His Painting, Damayanti and the Swan — A315

1971, Apr. 29 ***Perf. 13x13½***
540 A315 20p deep yellow green .40 .40

Dadasaheb Phalke, Movie Camera A316

1971, Apr. 30 ***Perf. 13½x13***
541 A316 20p violet brown .75 .40
Dadasaheb Phalke (1870-1944), motion picture pioneer.

Abhisarika, by Abanindranath Tagore A317

Swami Virjanand A318

1971, Aug. 7 **Unwmk.** ***Perf. 14x14½***
542 A317 20p dark brn & ocher .35 .30
Tagore (1871-1951), painter.

1971, Sept. 14 ***Perf. 14x13½***
543 A318 20p orange brown .30 .30
Virjanand (1778-1868), scholar and sage.

Scuptures and Stairway, Persepolis Palace A319

1971, Oct. 12 ***Perf. 13***
544 A319 20p sepia .75 .50
2500th anniv. of the founding of the Persian empire by Cyrus the Great.

World Thrift Day A320

1971, Oct. 31 ***Perf. 14½x14***
545 A320 20p dark violet blue .20 .20

Bodhisatva Padampani, from Ajanta Cave — A321

Girls at Work, by Geeta Gupta — A322

1971, Nov. 4 ***Perf. 13***
546 A321 20p brown 1.60 .50
25th anniv. of UNESCO.

1971, Nov. 14 ***Perf. 14x14½***
547 A322 20p salmon pink .20 .20
Chidren's Day.

C. V. Raman A323

1971, Nov. 21 ***Perf. 13***
548 A323 20p brown & dp org .50 .30
Sir Chandrasekhara Venkata Raman (1888-1970), physicist, Nobel Prize winner.

Rabindranath Tagore, Visva-Bharati Building — A324

1971, Dec. 24 ***Perf. 14½x14***
549 A324 20p blk brn & org brn .20 .20
50th anniv. of Visva-Bharati, center for Eastern cultural studies.

Indian Cricket Victories A325

1971, Dec. 24
550 A325 20p green 2.50 .65

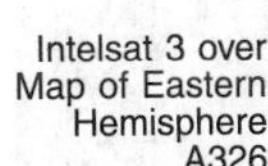

Intelsat 3 over Map of Eastern Hemisphere A326

1972, Feb. 26 **Photo.** ***Perf. 13½***
551 A326 20p dark purple .20 .20
Arvi Satellite Earth Station.

Plumb Line and Symbols — A327

Signal Panel and Route Diagram — A328

1972, May 29 **Photo.** ***Perf. 13***
552 A327 20p bluish gray & black .20 .20

India's Bureau of Standards, 25th anniv.

1972, June 30
553 A328 20p black & multi .75 .40

Intl. Railroad Union (UIC), 50th anniv.

Hockey, Olympic Rings A329

20th Olympic Games, Munich, Aug. 26-Sept. 11: 1.45r, "1972," Olympic rings, symbols for running, wrestling, shooting and hockey.

1972, Aug. 10 **Photo.** ***Perf. 13***
554 A329 20p dull violet 1.75 .25
555 A329 1.45r bl grn & dk red 2.25 2.00

Marchers with Flag, Parliament A330

1972, Aug. 15
556 A330 20p blue & multi .20 .20

25th anniv. of Independence.

Armed Forces' Emblems — A331

Symbol of Aurobindo and Sun — A332

1972, Aug. 15
557 A331 20p blue & multi .30 .30

Honoring India's defense forces.

1972, Aug. 15 ***Perf. 14x13½***
558 A332 20p yellow & blue .40 .40

Sri Aurobindo Ghose (1872-1950).

V.O. Chidambaram Pillai and Ship — A333

Perf. 13½x13

1972, Sept. 5 **Unwmk.**
559 A333 20p bl & dk red brn .75 .40

V.O. Chidambaram Pillai (1872-1936), founder of steamship company, trade union leader, resistance fighter.

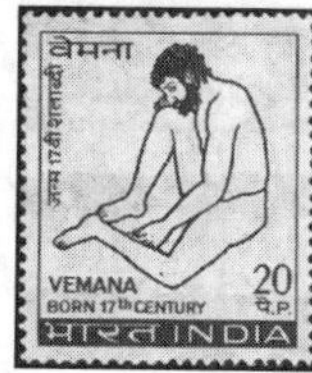

Vemana, 17th-18th Cent. Poet — A334

Bertrand Russell — A335

1972, Oct. 16 **Wmk. 324** ***Perf. 14***
560 A334 20p black .40 .40

1972, Oct. 16 **Unwmk.**
561 A335 1.45r black 3.50 2.50

British philosopher and pacifist (1872-1970).

Bhai Vir Singh — A336

T. Prakasam — A337

1972, Oct. 16 ***Perf. 13½***
562 A336 20p dull purple .20 .20

Bhai Vir Singh (1872-1957), poet and scholar.

1972, Oct. 16
563 A337 20p yellow brown .20 .20

T. Prakasam (1872-1957), national leader and lawyer.

Hand of Buddha, 9th Century Sculpture — A338

20p, Stylized Hand of Buddha as Fair emblem.

1972, Nov. 3 **Wmk. 324** ***Perf. 13***
564 A338 20p orange & black .20 .20
565 A338 1.45r orange, blk & ind .55 *1.75*

3rd Asian Intl. Trade Fair, ASIA 72, New Delhi.

Vikram Ambalal Sarabhai, Rohini Rocket and Dove A339

1972, Dec. 30 **Unwmk.**
566 A339 20p slate grn & brn .20 .20

1st anniv. of the death of Dr. Vikram Ambalal Sarabhai (1919-1971), chairman of Natl. Committee for Space Research.

Flag of USSR and Spasski Tower A340

1972, Dec. 30 ***Perf. 13***
567 A340 20p red & yellow .20 .20

50th anniv. of the Soviet Union.

INDIPEX 73 Emblem — A341

Wheel of Asoka, Naga (Serpent) — A342

India Gate, Gnat Planes, India's Colors A343

1973, Jan. 8 **Photo.** ***Perf. 13***
568 A341 1.45r black, pink & gold .45 *1.00*

Intl. Phil. Exhib., New Delhi, 11/14-23/73. See Nos. 597-599.

1973, Jan. 26 ***Perf. 13***
569 A342 20p orange & multi .20 .20

Perf. 14½x14
570 A343 1.45r violet & multi 1.25 1.50

Republic Day, 25th year of Independence.

Ramakrishna Paramahamsa (1836-86) — A344

Army Postal Service Corps Emblem — A345

1973, Feb. 18 **Photo.** ***Perf. 13***
571 A344 20p yellow brown .20 .20

Hindu spiritual leader; Ramakrishna Mission founded by his followers.

1973, Mar. 1
572 A345 20p violet blue & red .50 .50

1st anniv. of establishment of Army Postal Service Corps.

Flower, Flag, Map — A346

Kumaran Asan — A347

1973, Apr. 10 **Unwmk.** ***Perf. 13***
573 A346 20p blue & multi .20 .20

1st anniv. of Bangladesh independence.

1973, Apr. 12
574 A347 20p brown .20 .20

Kumaran Asan (1873-1924), Kerala social reformer and writer.

Flame and Flag of India — A348

1973, Apr. 13
575 A348 20p deep blue & multi .20 .20

In honor of the martyrs of the massacre of Jallianwala Bagh, Apr. 13, 1919.

B. R. Ambedkar and Parliament Building A349

1973, Apr. 14 ***Perf. 14½x14***
576 A349 20p olive & plum .20 .20

Bhimrao R. Ambedkar (1891-1956), lawyer, reformer of Hindu law and one of the writers of India's Constitution.

Radha-Kishangarh, by Nihal Chand, 1778 — A350

Indian Miniatures: 50p, Dancing Couple, late 17th century. 1r, Lovers on a Camel, by Nasir-ud-Din, c. 1605. 2r, Chained Elephant, by Zain-al-Abidin, 16th century.

1973, May 5 Photo. *Perf. 13½x13*

577 A350 20p gold & multi .30 *.35*
578 A350 50p lilac & multi .65 *1.25*
579 A350 1r ocher & multi .80 *1.40*
580 A350 2r gold & multi 1.25 *2.00*
Nos. 577-580 (4) 3.00 5.00

Himalayas A351

1973, May 15 *Perf. 13½x13*

581 A351 20p blue .60 .50

15th anniv. of Indian Mountaineering Foundation.

Air India Jet — A352

1973, June 8 Photo. *Perf. 13*

582 A352 1.45r multicolored 4.00 4.00

Air India, 25 years of intl. service.

Stone Cross on St. Thomas's Mount, Madras — A353

Michael Madhusudan Dutt — A354

1973, July 3

583 A353 20p gray ol & blue gray .20 .20

1900th anniv. of the death of St. Thomas.

1973, July 21 Photo. *Perf. 13*

584 A354 20p ocher & olive 1.00 1.00

Dutt (1824-1873), writer and poet.

Vishnu Dingambar Paluskar (1872-1931), Musician — A355

1973, July 21

585 A355 30p red brown 1.25 1.25

Dr. Armauer G. Hansen, Microscope, Petri Dish with Bacilli A356

1973, July 21

586 A356 50p deep brown 1.50 1.50

Cent. of the discovery by Hansen of the Hansen bacillus, the cause of leprosy.

Nicolaus Copernicus, Heliocentric System A357

1973, July 21

587 A357 1r vio blue & red brown 1.50 1.50

500th anniv. of the birth of Nicolaus Copernicus (1473-1543), Polish astronomer.

Allan Octavian Hume (1829-1912) A358

1973, July 31

588 A358 20p gray .20 .20

Hume, British civil servant and friend of India, on the 25th anniv. of independence.

Nehru and Gandhi A359

1973, Aug. 15 Photo. *Perf. 13*

589 A359 20p blue vio & red brown .20 .20

25th anniv. of India's independence.

Romesh Chunder Dutt — A360

Ranjit Sinhji — A361

Vithalbhai Patel (1873-1933), National Leader — A362

1973, Sept. 27 Photo. *Perf. 13*

590 A360 20p brown .20 .20
591 A361 30p dark green 3.50 3.50
592 A362 50p brown .20 .20
Nos. 590-592 (3) 3.90 3.90

Birth anniv.: Dutt (1848-1909), economist and pres. of Natl. Cong. in 1890; Sinhji, Maharaja of Nawanagar (1872-1933), cricketer.

President's Body Guard — A363

1973, Sept. 30

593 A363 20p multicolored .40 .40

Bicentenary of President's Body Guard.

INTERPOL Emblem — A364

1973, Oct. 9 Photo. *Perf. 13*

594 A364 20p brown .35 .35

50th anniv. of Intl. Criminal Police Org.

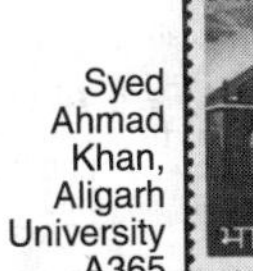

Syed Ahmad Khan, Aligarh University A365

1973, Oct. 17

595 A365 20p olive gray .20 .20

Khan (1817-1898), founder of Aligarh Muslim Univ.

Child's Drawing A366

1973, Nov. 14 Photo. *Perf. 13*

596 A366 20p multicolored .20 .20

Children's Day.

Elephant with Howdah, and No. 200 — A367

1973, Nov. 14

597 A367 20p Emblem .25 .25
598 A367 1r shown 1.00 1.00
599 A367 2r Peacock, vert. 1.25 1.25
a. Souvenir sheet of 4 5.00 5.00
Nos. 597-599 (3) 2.50 2.50

Intl. Phil. Exhib., INDIPEX 73, New Delhi, Nov. 14-23. No. 599a contains 4 imperf. stamps similar to Nos. 568, 597-599. The imperf. stamps from No. 599a were not valid individually.

NCC Emblem — A368

Rajagopalachari A369

1973, Nov. 25

600 A368 20p multicolored .20 .20

National Cadet Corps, 25th anniv.

1973, Dec. 25

601 A369 20p gray olive .20 .20

Chakravarti Rajagopalachari (1878-1972), statesman, governor general (1948-50).

Sun Mask — A370

Narasimha Mask — A371

Designs: Masks.

1974, Apr. 15 Photo. *Perf. 13*

602 A370 20p shown .20 .20
603 A370 50p Moon .30 .30
604 A371 1r shown .40 .40
605 A371 2r Ravana, horiz. .60 .60
a. Souvenir sheet of 4, #602-605 2.00 2.00
Nos. 602-605 (4) 1.50 1.50

300th Anniv. of the Coronation of Chatrapati Sivaji Maharaj (1627-1680), Military Leader of the Maharattas and Enlightened Ruler — A372

1974, June 2 Photo. *Perf. 13*
606 A372 25p gold & multi .40 .30

Maithili Sharan Gupta — A373

Utkal Gourab Madhusudan Das — A374

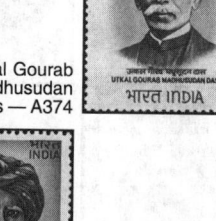

Kandukuri Veeresalingam A375

Tipu Sultan — A376

No. 608, Jainarain Vyas. 1r, Max Mueller.

1974 Photo. *Perf. 13*

607 A373 25p red brown	.20	.20
608 A373 25p brown	.20	.20
609 A374 25p olive gray	.20	.20
610 A375 25p red brown	.25	.25
611 A376 50p violet brown	.40	.40
612 A376 1r brown	.60	.60
Nos. 607-612 (6)	1.85	1.85

Gupta (1886-1964), poet and patriot; Vyas (1899-1963), writer and member of parliament; Das (1848-1934), writer and patriot. Veeresalingam (1848-1919), reformer; Sultan (1750-99), military leader and reformer; Mueller (1823-1900), German scholar of Sanskrit and Indian culture.

Issued: #607-609, 7/3; #610-612, 7/15.

Kamala Nehru — A377

1974, Aug 1 Photo. *Perf. 14½x14*
613 A377 25p multicolored .50 .50

Kamala Nehru (1899-1936), champion of India's freedom, mother of Indira Gandhi.

WPY Emblem — A378

V. V. Giri — A379

1974, Aug. 14 Unwmk. *Perf. 13½*
614 A378 25p buff & plum .20 .20

1974, Aug. 24 *Perf. 13x13½*
615 A379 25p green & multi .20 .20

Vaharagiri Venkata Giri, pres. of India, 1969-74.

Type of 1965-68 and

Tiger — A380

Veena A381

Design: 25p, Axis deer (chital).

1974 Wmk. 324 *Perf. 14½x14*

622 A380 15p dk brn (white "15")	3.25	.75
623 A202 25p brown	1.00	1.00
624 A381 1r black & brown	2.50	.25
Nos. 622-624 (3)	6.75	2.00

Issue dates: 25p, Aug. 20; 15p, 1r, Oct. 1.
See Nos. 671-682.

Madhubani Folk Design, UPU Emblem A384

Designs: 25p, UPU emblem. 2r, Arrows circling globe, UPU emblem, vert.

1974, Oct. 3 Unwmk. *Perf. 13*

634 A384 25p brt blue & gray	.20	.20
635 A384 1r olive & multi	.50	.20
636 A384 2r ocher & multi	.75	.25
a. Souvenir sheet of 3, #634-636	2.75	2.75
Nos. 634-636 (3)	1.45	.65

Cent. of UPU.

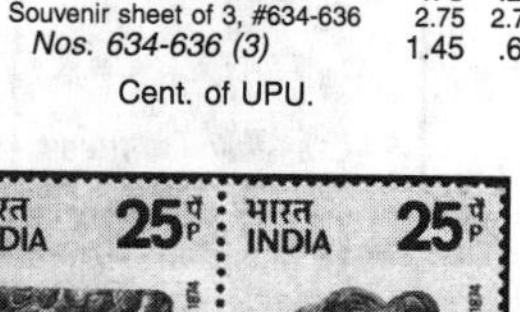

A385

1974, Oct. 9 Photo. *Perf. 13½*

637 25p Flute player	.50	.50
638 25p Vidyadhara with garland	.50	.50
a. A385 Pair, #637-638	1.00	1.00

Cent. of Mathura Museum.

Nicholas Konstantin Roerich, by Henry Dropsy A387

1974, Oct. 9 *Perf. 13*
639 A387 1r dark gray & yellow .50 .50

Roerich (1874-1947), Russian painter and sponsor of Roerich Peace Pact.

Pavapuri Temple, Bihar A388

1974, Nov. 13 Photo. *Perf. 13*
640 A388 25p slate .40 .20

2500th anniv. of attainment of Nirvana by Bhagwan Mahavira, leader and preacher of Jainism.

Dancers and Musician (Child's Drawing) A389

1974, Nov. 14 *Perf. 14½x14*
641 A389 25p multicolored .50 .50

UNICEF in India.

Cat (Child's Drawing) — A390

1974, Nov. 14 *Perf. 13*
642 A390 25p multicolored .65 .35

Children's Day.

Territorial Army Emblem — A391

1974, Nov. 16 *Perf. 13*
643 A391 25p green, yel & black .60 .40

Territorial Army, 25th anniv.

Cows, from Handpainted Rajasthan Cloth — A392

1974, Dec. 2 *Perf. 14*
644 A392 25p ocher & maroon .40 .30

19th Intl. Dairy Cong., New Delhi, Dec. 2-6.

Symbol of Retardates and Child A393

1974, Dec. 8 Photo. *Perf. 13½x13*
645 A393 25p black & vermilion .45 .45

Help the Retardates!

Guglielmo Marconi — A394

1974, Dec. 12 *Perf. 13x13½*
646 A394 2r slate 1.50 1.25

Marconi (1874-1937), Italian electrical engineer and inventor.

St. Francis Xavier's Tomb and Statue A395

1974, Dec. 24 *Perf. 13½x13*
647 A395 25p multicolored .20 .20

Showing of the body of St. Francis Xavier, Apostle to the Indies.

Saraswati, Goddess of Language and Learning, Inscription in Hindi — A396

1975, Jan. 10 Photo. *Perf. 14x14½*
648 A396 25p dark red & gray .30 .30

World Hindi Convention, Nagpur, Jan. 10-14. See No. 654.

Parliament House A397

1975, Jan. 26 ***Perf. 13***
649 A397 25p black, blue & silver .40 .30

Republic of India, 25th anniv.

Table Tennis Paddle and Ball — A398

1975, Feb. 6 ***Perf. 13½x13***
650 A398 25p black, red & olive .65 .30

33rd World Table Tennis Championship, Calcutta.

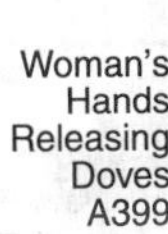

Woman's Hands Releasing Doves A399

1975, Feb. 16
651 A399 25p yellow & multi .85 .45

International Women's Year.

Bicentenary of Army Ordnance Corps — A400

1975, Apr. 8 Photo. ***Perf. 13x13½***
652 A400 25p black & vermilion .65 .40

Flame A401

1975, Apr. 11 ***Perf. 13½x13***
653 A401 25p orange & black .30 .30

Cent. of the founding of Arya Samaj, a movement dedicated to enlightenment and progress and to a revival of Vedic Law and Aryan culture.

Saraswati Type of 1975

25p, Saraswati and inscription in Telugu.

1975, Apr. 12 ***Perf. 14x14½***
654 A396 25p dp green & dk gray .40 .30

World Telugu Conf., Hyderabad, Apr. 12-18.

Aryabhata Satellite A402

1975, Apr. 20 ***Perf. 13½x13***
655 A402 25p multicolored .40 .40

Launching of 1st Indian satellite, Apr. 19, 1975.

Bluewinged Pitta A403

Birds: 50p, Black-headed oriole. 1r, Western tragopan, vert. 2r, Himalayan monal pheasant, vert.

1975, Apr. 28 ***Perf. 13½x13, 13x13½***
656 A403 25p multicolored .50 .20
657 A403 50p multicolored 1.00 1.00
658 A403 1r multicolored 1.50 1.50
659 A403 2r multicolored 2.00 2.00
Nos. 656-659 (4) 5.00 4.70

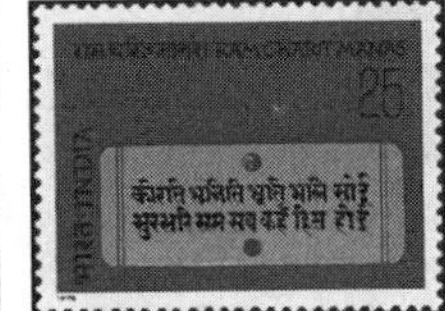

Quotation from Ram Charit Manas A404

1975, May 24 Photo. ***Perf. 13½x13***
660 A404 25p red, orange & black .50 .20

Ram Charit Manas, Hindi poem by Goswami Tulsidas (1532-1623).

Women and YWCA Emblem — A405

1975, June 20 Photo. ***Perf. 13x13½***
661 A405 25p gray & multi .30 .30

YWCA of India, cent.

Creation of Adam, by Michelangelo — A406

Design: Nos. 664-665, Creation of sun, moon and stars, by Michelangelo.

1975, June 28 ***Perf. 14x13½***
662 50p multicolored .50 .50
663 50p multicolored .50 .50
a. A406 Pair #662-663 1.00 1.00
664 50p multicolored .50 .50
665 50p multicolored .50 .50
a. Block of 4, #662-665 2.00 2.00
b. A406 Pair #664-665 1.00 1.00

Michelangelo Buonarroti (1475-1564), Italian sculptor, painter and architect.

Types of 1965-1974 Without Currency Designation and

Flying Crane — A408

Jawaharlal Nehru — A409

Mahatma Gandhi — A410

Himalayas A411

Designs: 2p, Bidri vase. 5p, Family. 10p, Electric locomotive. 15p, Tiger. 20p, Wooden toy horse. 30p, Male and female figurines. 60p, Somnath Temple. 1r, Veena. 5r, Bhakra Dam, Punjab. 10r, Trombay Atomic Center.

Perf. 14½x14, 14x14½, 14 (#674-676), 11½x12 (#681)
Wmk. 324; 360 (#667, 668, 670)
1975-88 **Photo.**

Three types of 25p Nehru:
Type I: Size at top, 25mm. Character before NEHRU has 2 lower points.
Type II: Smaller portrait. Size at top, 23mm. Character has 3 points.
Type III: Portrait as in type I. Size at top, 25½mm. Character has 3 points.

666 A202 2(p) redsh brn, wmk. 324 ('76) .80 *1.90*
667 A202 2(p) redsh brn, wmk. 360 ('79) .80 *1.90*
668 A202 5(p) cerise ('76) .40 .20
669 A203 10(p) brt blue ('76) .40 .20
670 A203 10(p) brt blue ('79) 2.75 .50
671 A380 15(p) dk brn (brown "15") 1.25 .20
672 A408 20(p) green .20 .20
673 A409 25(p) vio, I ('76) 6.25 .60
674 A409 25(p) vio, II ('76) 4.00 .60
675 A409 25(p) vio, III ('76) 3.00 .60
676 A410 25(p) red brn ('76) (23x29mm) .80 .20
677 A410 25(p) red brn ('78) (17x20mm) 5.00 1.90
678 A202 30(p) brown ('79) 2.75 .40
679 A408 50(p) violet blue 4.00 .20
680 A202 60(p) dk gray ('76) 1.25 .75
681 A410 60(p) black ('88) .60 .20
682 A381 1(r) brown & blk 2.75 .20
683 A411 2(r) violet & brn 9.50 .30
684 A205 5(r) brn & vio ('76) 1.50 .75
685 A205 10(r) dl grn & sl ('76) 1.00 .95
Nos. 666-685 (20) 49.00 12.75

See #841-842, 844-845, 846A-846B, 916.
Size of No. 681, 17x20mm.

Irrigation Commission Emblem — A412

"Educational Television" A413

Unwmk.

1975, July 28 **Photo.** ***Perf. 14***
686 A412 25p multicolored .20 .20

9th Intl. Cong. on Irrigation and Drainage, Moscow, and 25th anniv. of the Intl. Commission on Irrigation and Drainage.

1975, Aug. 1 ***Perf. 13x13½***
687 A413 25p multicolored .20 .20

Inauguration of the Satellite Instructional Television Experiment (SITE).

Arunagirinathar A414

1975, Aug. 14 **Photo.** ***Perf. 13½***
688 A414 50p rose lilac .25 .20

600th birth anniv. of Arunagirinathar, Advaita philosopher, saint and author of Tiruppugazh, a collection of songs.

A415

1975, Aug. 26 **Photo.** ***Perf. 13½***
689 A415 25p rose & black .20 .20

Namibia Day. See note after UN No. 241.

A416

1975, Sept. 4
690 A416 25p slate green .20 .20

Mir Anees (1803-1874), Urdu poet.

Chhatri at Maheshwar A417

1975, Sept. 4 ***Perf. 13x13½***
691 A417 25p red brown .20 .20

Queen Ahilyabai Holkar (1725-1795); building shown was place of last rites.

Bharata Natyam Dance — A418

1975, Oct. 20 Photo. ***Perf. 13x13½***

Designs: Indian traditional dances.

692 A418 25p shown .20 .20
693 A418 50p Orissi .20 .20
694 A418 75p Kathak .20 .20
695 A418 1r Kathakali .35 .20
696 A418 1.50r Kuchipudi .50 .20
697 A418 2r Manipuri .65 .25
Nos. 692-697 (6) 2.10 1.25

Krishna Menon — A419

Ameer Khusrau — A420

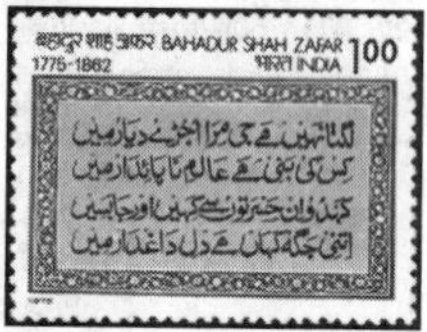

Poem by Bahadur Shah Zafar A421

Design: No. 699, Sardar Vallabhbhai Patel.

1975 ***Perf. 13x13½, 13½x13***

698 A419 25p olive .20 .20
699 A419 25p slate .20 .20
700 A420 50p yellow & brown .20 .20
701 A421 1r black, brn & buff .25 .20
Nos. 698-701 (4) .85 .80

Men of India: V. K. Krishna Menon (1896-1974), founder of India League and member of Parliament; Patel (1875-1950), statesman who unified India, birth cent.; Khusrau (1253-1325), poet; Zafar (1775-1862), last Mogul emperor and poet.

Issue dates: #699, Oct. 31; others Oct. 24.

Parliament Annex, New Delhi A422

1975, Oct. 28 ***Perf. 14½x14***

702 A422 2r gray olive .50 .25

21st Commonwealth Parliamentary Conf., New Delhi, Oct. 28-Nov. 4.

Karmavir Nabin Chandra Bardoloi (1875-1936), Writer and Gandhi Associate — A423

1975, Nov. 3 **Photo.** ***Perf. 13***

703 A423 25p reddish brown .20 .20

Cow, Child's Painting A424

1975, Nov. 14

704 A424 25p multicolored .20 .20

Children's Day.

Security Press Building A425

1975, Dec. 13 **Photo.** ***Perf. 13***

705 A425 25p multicolored .20 .20

India Security Press, 50th anniv.

Gurdwara Sisganj, Chandni Chawk — A426

Theosophical Society Emblem — A427

1975, Dec. 16

706 A426 25p multicolored .20 .20

300th anniv. of martyrdom of Tegh Bahadur (1621-75), 9th Sikh Guru; building shown was place of beheading.

1975, Dec. 20

707 A427 25p multicolored .20 .20

Centenary of Theosophical Society.

Meteorological Instruments A428

Indian Bishop Mark, 1775 — A430

Early Mail Cart A429

1975, Dec. 24 **Photo.** ***Perf. 13***

708 A428 25p blue vio, blk & grn .20 .20

Indian Meteorological Dept., cent.

1975, Dec. 25

709 A429 25p brown & black .20 .20
710 A430 2r reddish brn & blk .50 .25

INPEX 75, Indian Natl. Phil. Exhib., Calcutta, Dec. 25-31.

Lalit Narayan Mishra — A431

Tiger — A432

1976, Jan. 3

711 A431 25p sepia .20 .20

Mishra (1923-75), Minister of Railroads.

1976, Jan. 24

712 A432 25p multicolored .20 .20

Jim Corbett (1875-1955), conservationist.

Painted Storks A433

1976, Feb. 10 **Photo.** ***Perf. 13***

713 A433 25p sky blue & multi .20 .20

Keoladeo Ghana, Bharatpur Water Bird Sanctuary.

Tank A434

1976, Mar. 4 **Photo.** ***Perf. 13***

714 A434 25p multicolored .20 .20

16th Light Cavalry, senior regiment of Armoured Corps, bicentenary.

Alexander Graham Bell — A435

1976, Mar. 10 **Photo.** ***Perf. 13x13½***

715 A435 25p yellow & black .20 .20

Cent. of 1st telephone call by Bell, Mar. 10, 1876.

Muthuswami Dikshitar — A436

1976, Mar. 18 ***Perf. 14x13½***

716 A436 25p dull violet .20 .20

Dikshitar (1775-1835), musician, composer.

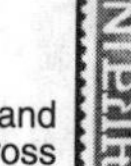

Eye and Red Cross A437

1976, Apr. 7 ***Perf. 13½x13***

717 A437 25p dark brown & red .20 .20

World Health Day: "Foresight prevents blindness."

"Industries" A438

Perf. 13x13½

1976, Apr. 30 **Unwmk.**

718 A438 25p multicolored .20 .20

Industrial development and progress.

1 F/I type, Ajmer, 1895 A439

Locomotives: 25p, WDM 2 Diesel Locomotive, 1963. 1r, 1 WP./1, 4-6-2 Pacific type, 1963. 2r, 1 GIP No. 1, 1853.

1976, May 15 ***Perf. 15x14***

719 A439 25p multicolored .20 .20
720 A439 50p multicolored .20 .20
721 A439 1r multicolored .40 .20
722 A439 2r multicolored .75 .25
Nos. 719-722 (4) 1.55 .85

Kumaraswamy Kamaraj (1903-1975), Independence Fighter — A440

1976, July 15 **Photo.** ***Perf. 13x13½***

723 A440 25p sepia .20 .20

Target, Olympic Rings — A441

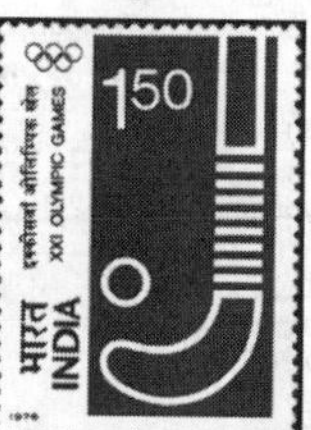

Hockey — A442

1976, July 17 ***Perf. 14***

724 A441 25p dk blue & carmine .20 .20
725 A441 1r "Team handball" .30 .20

726 A442 1.50r black & brt purple .40 .25
727 A441 2.80r "Running" .70 .35
Nos. 724-727 (4) 1.60 1.00

21st Olympic Games, Montreal, Canada, July 17-Aug. 1.

Subhadra Kumari Chauhan — A443

Param Vir Chakra Medal — A444

1976, Aug. 6 Photo. *Perf. 13x13½*
728 A443 25p grayish blue .20 .20

Chauhan (1904-1948), Hindi poetess and member of Legislative Assembly.

1976, Aug. 15
729 A444 25p yellow & multi .20 .20

Medal of Honor awarded for bravery to military men.

Women's University, Bombay A445

1976, Sept. 3 Photo. *Perf. 13½x14*
730 A445 25p violet .20 .20

Indian Women's Univ., 60th anniv.

Bharatendu Harishchandra A446

1976, Sept. 9 *Perf. 13*
731 A446 25p black brown .20 .20

Harishchandra (1850-1885), writer, "Father of Modern Hindi."

Sarat Chandra Chatterji — A447

1976, Sept. 15 Unwmk.
732 A447 25p dull purple .20 .20

Chatterji (1876-1938), writer.

Family Planning — A448

1976, Sept. 22 Photo. *Perf. 14x14½*
733 A448 25p multicolored .20 .20

Maharaja Agrasen, Coin and Brick Wall A449

1976, Sept. 24 *Perf. 13½x13*
734 A449 25p red brown .20 .20

Maharaja Agrasen, legendary ruler of Agra.

India Blood Donation Day — A450

Wildlife Protection A451

1976, Oct. 1 *Perf. 13x13½*
735 A450 25p bister, car & black .20 .20

1976, Oct. 1 *Perf. 14x14½, 14½x14*
736 A451 25p Swamp deer .20 .20
737 A451 50p Lion .20 .20
738 A451 1r Leopard, horiz. .30 .20
739 A451 2r Caracal, horiz. .70 .30
Nos. 736-739 (4) 1.40 .90

Suryakant Tripathi "Nirala" (1896-1961), Hindi poet — A452

1976, Oct. 15 *Perf. 13*
740 A452 25p dark violet .20 .20

Children's Day — A453

1976, Nov. 14 Unwmk. *Perf. 14*
741 A453 25p Mongoose and Woman .20 .20

Hiralal Shastri — A454

Hari Singh Gour — A455

1976, Nov. 24 *Perf. 13*
742 A454 25p red brown .20 .20

Hiralal Shastri (1899-1974), social worker and political leader.

1976, Nov. 26
743 A455 25p plum .20 .20

Hari Singh Gour (1870-1949), University administrator, member Indian Legislative and Constituent Assemblies.

Airbus A456

1976, Dec. 1 *Perf. 14½x14*
744 A456 2r multicolored .50 .25

Inauguration of Indian Airlines Airbus.

Hybrid Coconut Palm — A457

1976, Dec. 27 Photo. *Perf. 13x13½*
745 A457 25p multicolored .20 .20

75th anniv. of coconut research in India.

Vande Mataram, First Stanza A458

1976, Dec. 30 *Perf. 13*
746 A458 25p multicolored .20 .20

Vande Mataram, national song of India, music by Bankim Chandra Chatterjee, 1896, words by Rabindranath Tagore, 1911.

Film and Globe A459

1977, Jan. 3
747 A459 2r multicolored .50 .25

6th Intl. Film Festival, New Delhi, Jan. 3-16.

Earth's Crust with Fault, Seismograph A460

1977, Jan. 10
748 A460 2r dull purple .50 .25

6th World Conference on Earthquake Engineering, New Delhi, Jan. 10-14.

Tarun Ram Phookun — A461

1977, Jan. 22 Photo. *Perf. 13x13½*
749 A461 25p sepia .20 .20

Phookun (1877-1939), lawyer, Assam political leader.

Paramahansa Yogananda A462

1977, Mar. 7 Photo. *Perf. 13½*
750 A462 25p deep orange .20 .20

Yogananda (1893-1952), religious leader, founder of Self-realization Society in America.

Red Cross Conference Emblem — A463

Fakhruddin Ali Ahmed (1905-77) — A464

1977, Mar. 9
751 A463 2r multicolored .30 .20

1st Asian Regional Red Cross Conference, New Delhi, Mar. 9-16.

1977, Mar. 22 Photo. *Perf. 13½x13*
752 A464 25p multicolored .20 .20

Ahmed, Pres. of India, 1974-77.

Asian-Oceanic Postal Union Emblem — A465

1977, Apr, 1 ***Perf. 13***
753 A465 2r silver & multi .30 .20
Asian-Oceanic Postal Union, 15th anniv.

"Loyalty" and Morarjee A466

1977, Apr. 2 ***Perf. 13½x13***
754 A466 25p blue .20 .20
Narottam Morarjee (1877-1929), founder of Scindia Steam Ship Navigation Co.

Makhanlal Chaturvedi A467

1977, Apr. 4 ***Perf. 13***
755 A467 25p orange brown .20 .20
Chaturvedi (1889-1968), Hindi writer.

Mahaprabhu Vallabhacharya A468

1977, Apr. 14
756 A468 1r olive brown .20 .20
Vallabhacharya (1479-1531), philosopher.

Federation Emblem A469

1977, Apr. 23 ***Perf. 13½x13***
757 A469 25p ocher & purple .20 .20
Federation of Indian Chambers of Commerce, 50th anniv.

Protection of Environment A470

1977, June 5 **Photo.** ***Perf. 13***
758 A470 2r multicolored .30 .20

Council of States Chamber A471

1977, June 21
759 A471 25p multicolored .20 .20
Council of States, Rajya Sabha (Parliament), 25th anniv.

Lotus A472

50p and 1r are vert.

1977, July 1 ***Perf. 15x14, 14x15***
760 A472 25p shown .20 .20
761 A472 50p Rhododendron .20 .20
762 A472 1r Kadamba .20 .20
763 A472 2r Gloriosa lily .50 .20
Nos. 760-763 (4) 1.10 .80

Berliner Gramaphone — A473

1977, July 20 ***Perf. 13½x13***
764 A473 2r black & brown .40 .20
Centenary of the phonograph.

Ananda Kentish Coomaraswamy (1877-1947) and Dancing Shiva — A474

1977, Aug. 22 **Photo.** ***Perf. 13x13½***
765 A474 25p multicolored .20 .20
Coomaraswamy, art historian and critic.

Ganga Ram (1851-1927) and Hospital, New Delhi — A475

1977, Sept. 4 ***Perf. 14½x14***
766 A475 25p rose carmine .20 .20
Ram, social reformer and philanthropist.

Dr. Samuel Hahnemann and Cinchona — A476

19th Century Postman — A477

Lion and Palm Tree, East India Co. Essay — A478

1977, Oct. 6 **Photo.** ***Perf. 13***
767 A476 2r black & green .30 .20
32nd Intl. Homeopathic Cong., New Delhi.

1977, Oct. 12 ***Perf. 13***
768 A477 25p multicolored .20 .20
Perf. 13½
769 A478 2r mag & gray, *buff* .30 .20
INPEX '77 Phil. Exhib., Bangalore, 10/12-16.

Ram Manohar Lohia (1910-67), Founder of Congress Socialist Party, Sec. of Foreign Dept. — A479

1977, Oct. 12 ***Perf. 13x13½***
770 A479 25p red brown .20 .20

Red Scinde Dawks, 1852 A480

Design: 3r, Foreign mail arriving at Ballard Pier, Bombay, 1927.

1977, Oct. 19 ***Perf. 13½x13***
771 A480 1r orange & multi .20 .20
772 A480 3r orange & multi .45 .30
ASIANA 77, First Asian International Philatelic Exhibition, Bangalore, Oct. 19-23.

Statue of Rani Channamma — A481

1977, Oct. 23
773 A481 25p gray green .20 .20
Rani Channamma of Kittue (1778-1829), who fought against British rule.

Mother and Child, Khajuraho Sculpture — A482

1977, Oct. 23 ***Perf. 13x13½***
774 A482 2r gray & sepia .30 .20
15th Intl. Pediatrics Congress.

Sun and National Colors — A483

Stylized Grain — A484

1977, Nov. 8 **Photo.** ***Perf. 13***
775 A483 25p multicolored .20 .20
Union Public Service Commission, founded 1926.

1977, Nov. 13
776 A484 25p green .20 .20
AGRIEXPO '77, Intl. Agriculture Exhib.

Cats A485

1r, Friends. Designs are from children's drawings.

1977, Nov. 14
777 A485 25p multicolored .20 .20
778 A485 1r multicolored .20 .20
Children's Day.

Jotirao Phooley — A486

1977, Nov. 28 **Wmk. 324**
779 A486 25p gray olive .20 .20
Phooley (1827-1890), social reformer.

Senapati Bapat — A487

1977, Nov. 28
780 A487 25p brown orange .20 .20
Senapati Bapat (Pandurang Mahadev Bapat, 1880-1967), scholar and fighter for India's independence.

Diagram of Population Growth — A488

Perf. 13x13½

1977, Dec. 13 **Unwmk.**

781 A488 2r carmine & blue grn .30 .20

41st Session of Intl. Statistical Institute, New Delhi, Dec. 5-15.

Kamta Prasad (1875-1947) and Hindi Grammar A489

1977, Dec. 25 **Wmk. 324** ***Perf. 14***

782 A489 25p sepia .20 .20

Prasad, compiler of Hindi Grammar.

Spasski Tower, Russian Flag — A490

1977, Dec. 30 **Unwmk.** ***Perf. 13***

783 A490 1r multicolored .20 .20

60th anniv. of Russian October revolution.

Climber Crossing Crevasse — A491

Indian Flag near Summit A492

Perf. 13½x13, 13x13½

1978, Jan. 15 **Photo.**

784 A491 25p multicolored .20 .20

785 A492 1r multicolored .20 .20

Conquest of Kanchenjunga (Himalayas), by Indian team under Col. N. Kumar, May 31, 1977.

Tourists in Shikara on Dal Lake A493

1978, Jan. 23 ***Perf. 13x13½***

786 A493 1r multicolored .20 .20

27th Pacific Area Travel Assoc. Conf., New Delhi, Jan. 23-26.

Children in Library, Fair Emblem A494

1978, Feb. 11 **Photo.** ***Perf. 13***

787 A494 1r rose brown & indigo .20 .20

3rd World Book Fair, New Delhi, Feb. 1978.

Mother of Pondicherry A495

1978, Feb. 21

788 A495 25p dark & light brown .20 .20

Mother of the Sri Aurobindo Ashram, Pondicherry (Mira Richard, 1878-1973, born in Paris).

Wheat, Globe and Genetic Helix — A496

1978, Feb. 23

789 A496 25p yellow & blue green .20 .20

5th Intl. Wheat Genetics Symposium.

Nanalal Dalpatram Kavi — A497

Wmk. 324

1978, Mar. 16 **Photo.** ***Perf. 13***

790 A497 25p rose brown .20 .20

Kavi (1877-1946), Gujarati poet.

Surjya Sen (1894-1934), Patriot — A498

1978, Mar. 22

791 A498 25p ver, black & brown .20 .20

Two Vaishnavas (Vishnu Worshippers) by Jaminy Roy — A499

Modern Indian Paintings: 50p, The Mosque, by Sailoz Mookherjea. 1r, Woman's Head, by Rabindranath Tagore. 2r, Hill Women, by Amrita Sher Gil.

Perf. 13½x14

1978, Mar. 23 **Unwmk.**

792 A499 25p black & multi .20 .20

793 A499 50p black & multi .20 .20

794 A499 1r black & multi .20 .20

795 A499 2r black & multi .30 .20

Nos. 792-795 (4) .90 .80

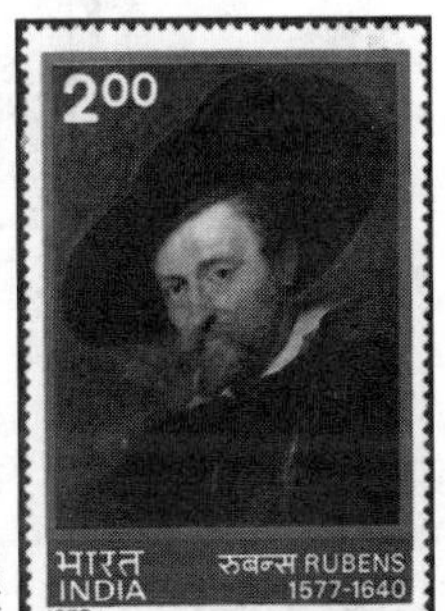

Rubens, Self-portrait A500

1978, Apr. 4 **Photo.** ***Perf. 13½x13***

796 A500 2r multicolored .30 .20

"The Little Tramp," Charlie Chaplin — A501

1978, Apr. 16 ***Perf. 13***

797 A501 25p gold & indigo .20 .20

Deendayal Upadhyaya (1916-68) — A502

1978, May 5 **Photo.** ***Perf. 13***

798 A502 25p multicolored .20 .20

Upadhyaya, social and political reformer.

Syama Prasad Mookerjee (1901-1953) A503

"Airavat," 19th Century Wood Carving — A504

Kushan Gold Coin, 1st Century A505

1978, July 6 **Photo.** ***Perf. 13***

799 A503 25p gray olive .20 .20

Dr. Mookerjee, educator, member of 1st natl. government.

1978, July 27

Designs: 50p, Wish-fulfilling tree, 2nd century B.C. 2r, Dagger and knife.

800 A504 25p multicolored .20 .20

801 A504 50p multicolored .20 .20

802 A505 1r multicolored .20 .20

803 A505 2r multicolored .30 .20

Nos. 800-803 (4) .90 .80

Treasures from Indian museums.

Krishna and Arjuna on Battlefield, Quotation A506

1978, Aug. 25 **Unwmk.** ***Perf. 13***

804 A506 25p orange red & gold .20 .20

Bhagavad Gita, part of Mahabharata Epic, the Divine Song of the Lord.

Bethune College for Women, Calcutta A507

1978, Sept. 4

805 A507 25p green & brown .20 .20

E. V. Ramasami A508

1978, Sept. 17

806 A508 25p black .20 .20

E. V. Ramasami (1879-1973), founder of Self-respect Movement, fighting caste system and social injustice.

Uday Shankar — A509

1978, Sept. 26
807 A509 25p buff & violet brown .20 .20

Uday Shankar (1900-77), dancer.

Leo Tolstoi — A510

Vallathol Narayana Menon — A511

1978, Oct. 2
808 A510 1r multicolored .20 .20

Tolstoi, novelist and philosopher.

1978, Oct. 15 Photo. *Perf. 13*
809 A511 25p multicolored .20 .20

Menon (1878-1958), poet.

"Two Friends" A512

1978, Nov. 14 Photo. *Perf. 13*
810 A512 25p multicolored .20 .20

Children's Day.

Worker at Lathe — A513

1978, Nov. 17 *Perf. 13½*
811 A513 25p green .20 .20

Small Industries Fair.

Skinner's Horse Soldiers — A514

Chakravarti Rajagopalachari A515

1978, Nov. 25 *Perf. 13*
812 A514 25p multicolored .20 .20

175th anniv. of Skinner's Horse Regiment.

1978, Dec. 10 Photo. *Perf. 13*
813 A515 25p maroon .20 .20

Chakravarti Rajagopalachari (1878-1972), first post-independence Governor General.

A516

A517

1978, Dec. 10
814 A516 25p olive green .20 .20

Mohammad Ali Jauhar (1878-1931), writer and patriot.

1978, Dec. 23 *Perf. 13x14*
815 A517 1r ocher & purple .20 .20

Wright Brothers, Flyer, 75th anniv. of 1st powered flight.

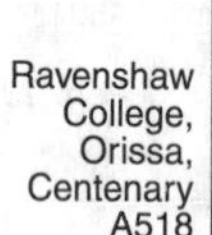

Ravenshaw College, Orissa, Centenary A518

1978, Dec. 24 *Perf. 14*
816 A518 25p green & maroon .20 .20

Franz Schubert (1797-1828), Austrian Composer — A519

1978, Dec. 25 *Perf. 13*
817 A519 1r multicolored .20 .20

Punjab Regiment, Uniforms and Crest A520

1979, Feb. 20 Photo. Unwmk.
818 A520 25p multicolored .20 .20

Oldest Indian infantry unit.

Bhai Parmanand (1876-1947) A521

Gandhi and Child — A522

1979, Feb. 24
819 A521 25p violet blue .20 .20

Parmanand, writer and educator.

1979, Mar. 5 Photo. *Perf. 13*
Design: 1r, IYC emblem.
820 A522 25p dk brown & red .20 .20
821 A522 1r dp org & dk brn .20 .20

Albert Einstein (1879-1955), Theoretical Physicist — A523

1979, Mar. 14
822 A523 1r black .20 .20

Rajarshi Shahu Chhatrapati (1874-1922), Ruler of Kolhapur — A524

1979, May 1 Photo. *Perf. 13x13½*
823 A524 25p dull purple .20 .20

Lotus, India '80 Emblem A525

1979, July 2 Photo. *Perf. 13*
824 A525 30p deep orange & green .20 .20

India '80 Phil. Exhib., New Delhi, Jan. 25-Feb. 3, 1980.

Postal Cards, 1879 and 1979 — A526

Raja Mahendra Pratap (1886-1979), Patriot — A527

1979, July 2
825 A526 50p multicolored .20 .20

1979, Aug. 15 Photo. *Perf. 13*
826 A527 30p olive gray .20 .20

Jatindra Nath Das (1904-1929) A528

1979, Sept. 13
827 A528 30p dark brown .20 .20

Das, political martyr.

Early and Modern Light Bulbs — A529

1979, Oct. 21 Photo. *Perf. 13*
828 A529 1r rose magenta .20 .20

Centenary of invention of electric light.

Buddhist Text A530

1979, Oct. 23 *Perf. 14½x14*
829 A530 30p brown & bister .20 .20

National Archives.

Hirakud Dam A531

Perf. 13½x13
1979, Oct. 29 Wmk. 324
830 A531 30p brown red & dull grn .20 .20

13th Congress (Golden Jubilee) of the Intl. Commission on Large Dams, New Delhi, 10/29-11/2.

Boy and Alphabet Book A532

1979, Nov. 10 Photo. *Perf. 14½x14*
831 A532 30p multicolored .20 .20

Intl. Children's Book Fair, New Delhi, 11/10-19.

Fair Emblem — A533

1979, Nov. 10 ***Perf. 13***
832 A533 1r black & orange .20 .20

India Intl. Trade Fair, New Delhi, 11/10-12/9.

Dove, Agency Emblem A534

1979, Dec. 4 ***Perf. 13½x13***
833 A534 1r multicolored .20 .20

23rd Intl. Atomic Energy Agency Conf., New Delhi, Dec. 4-10.

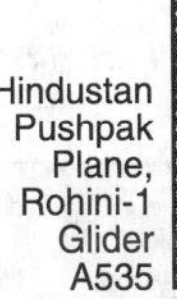

Hindustan Pushpak Plane, Rohini-1 Glider A535

1979, Dec. 10 ***Perf. 13½x13***
834 A535 30p multicolored .20 .20

Gurdwara Baoli Shrine, Goindwal — A536

1979, Dec. 21 ***Perf. 13x13½***
835 A536 30p multicolored .20 .20

Guru Amardas (1469-1574), Sikh spiritual leader.

Types of 1975-79 and

Women in Rice Field A537

Family Planning A537a

Designs: 2p, Adult education. 5p, Fish. 15p, Agricultural technology. 20p, Child nutrition. No. 840, Poultry. No. 840B, Farm, wheat, farmer plowing. 1r, Hybrid cotton. 2r, Weaving. 5r, Rubber tapping.

Perf. 14x14½, 14½x14, 13 (#840B)

1979-85 Photo. Wmk. 324

836	A537	2p	violet	.20	.20
837	A537	5p	blue	.20	.20
838	A537a	15p	blue grn ('80)	.20	.20
839	A537a	20p	henna brn ('81)	.20	.20
840	A537	25p	brown	.20	.20
840B	A537	25p	brt green ('85)	.20	.20
841	A409	30p	violet ('80)	.75	.25
842	A410	30p	red brown ('80)	.50	.25
843	A537	30p	yel green	.20	.20
844	A409	35p	violet ('80)	.50	.25
845	A410	35p	red brown ('80)	.35	.25
846	A537a	35p	cerise ('80)	.20	.20
846A	A409	50p	violet ('83)	.20	.20
846B	A410	50p	red brown ('83)	.50	.25

Size: 17x28mm

847	A537a	1r	brown ('80)	.20	.20
848	A537a	2r	rose violet ('80)	.30	.20

Size: 20x37mm

849	A537a	5r	multi ('80)	.45	.25
			Nos. 836-849 (17)	5.35	3.70

Size: #841-842, 844-845, 846A-846B, 17x20mm.

See Nos. 895-900A, 903-917.

1979-83 ***Perf. 13***

837a	A537	5p		.20	.20
837b	A537	5p	Litho. ('82)	.50	.30
838a	A537a	15p		.20	.20
839a	A537a	20p		.30	.20
840a	A537	25p	brown	.30	.20
843a	A537	30p		.50	.20
844a	A409	35p		.75	.30
845a	A410	35p		.25	.20
846c	A537a	35p		.50	.20
846d	A409	50p		.50	.20
846e	A410	50p		.20	.20

Perf. 12½x13

847a	A537a	1r		.20	.20

Perf. 13x13½, 13½x13

848a	A537a	2r ('83)		.20	.20
849a	A537a	5r ('83)		.40	.35
			Nos. 837a-849a (14)	5.00	3.15

People Holding Hands, UN Emblem — A538

1980, Jan. 21 Photo. ***Perf. 13***
851 A538 1r multicolored .20 .20

UN Industrial Development Org. (INIDO), 3rd Gen. Conf., New Delhi, Jan. 21-Feb. 8.

Field Post Office, Cancels — A539

Money Order Centenary — A540

2-Anna Copper Coins, 1774 — A541

Rowland Hill, Birthplace, Kidderminster A542

Wmk. 360, Unwmkd. (1r)

1980, Jan. 25

852	A539	30p	gray olive	.20	.20
853	A540	50p	brown & citron	.20	.20
854	A541	1r	bronze	.20	.20
855	A542	2r	dark gray	.25	.20
			Nos. 852-855 (4)	.85	.80

INDIA '80 Intl. Stamp Exhib., New Delhi, Jan. 25-Feb. 3.

India Institution of Engineers, 60th Anniversary A543

Uniforms, 1780 and 1980, Arms and Ribbon — A544

Perf. 13x13½

1980, Feb. 17 **Unwmk.**
856 A543 30p dark blue & gold .20 .20

1980, Feb. 26
857 A544 30p multicolored .20 .20

Madras Sappers bicentennial.

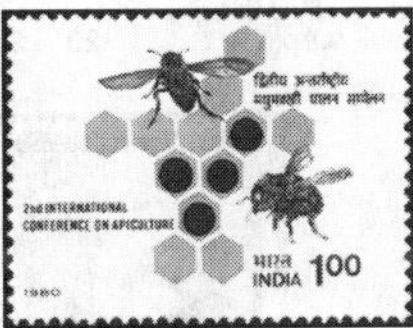
2nd Intl. Apiculture Conf., New Delhi A545

1980, Feb. 29 ***Perf. 13½***
858 A545 1r multicolored .20 .20

A546

A547

1980, Feb. 29 **Wmk. 360**
859 A546 30p bright blue .20 .20

4th World Book Fair, New Delhi.

1980, Mar. 18 ***Perf. 13x13½***
860 A547 30p blue gray .20 .20

Welthy Fisher (b. 1879), educator, Literacy House, Lucknow.

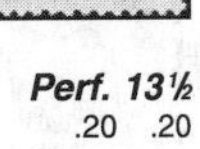
Darul Uloom Islamic School, Deoband A548

1980, Mar. 21 ***Perf. 13½***
861 A548 30p gray green .20 .20

Keshub Chunder Sen — A549

Sivaji, Raigad Fort — A550

Perf. 13x13½

1980, Apr. 15 Photo. Wmk. 360
862 A549 30p brown .20 .20

Sen (1838-84), scholar, writer, journalist.

1980, Apr. 21 **Unwmk.**
863 A550 30p multicolored .20 .20

Sivaji (1627-80), Indian patriot.

Narayan Malhar Joshi — A551

Ulloor S. Parameswara Iyer — A552

Perf. 13x13½

1980, June 5 **Wmk. 360**
864 A551 30p lilac rose .20 .20

Joshi (1879-1955), trade union pioneer.

1980, June 6
865 A552 30p dull purple .20 .20

Iyer (1877-1949), poet and scholar.

Syed Mohammad Zamin Ali — A553

1980, June 25
866 A553 30p dk yellow green .20 .20

Ali (1880-1955), linguist and educator.

Helen Keller (1880-1955) — A554

1980, June 27

867 A554 30p orange & black .20 .20

Keller, blind and deaf writer and lecturer.

High Jump, Olympic Rings A555

Prem Chand (1880-1936) A556

1980, July 19 Photo. *Perf. 13½x14*

868 A555 1r shown .20 .20
869 A555 2.80r Equestrian .35 .20

22nd Summer Olympic Games, Moscow, July 19-Aug. 3.

1980, July 31 *Perf. 13*

870 A556 30p red brown .20 .20

Pen name of Nawab Rai, writer.

Mother Teresa, Nobel Peace Prize Medallion A557

Perf. 13½x13

1980, Aug. 27 Photo. Wmk. 360

871 A557 30p violet, *grayish* .20 .20

Mother Teresa, founder of Missionaries of Charity, 70th birthday.

Earl Mountbatten of Burma — A558

Asian Table Tennis Championship A559

1980, Aug. 28 *Perf. 13x13½*

872 A558 2.80r multicolored .35 .20

Mountbatten (1900-79), 1st governor gen. of India.

1980, Sept. Photo. *Perf. 13x13½*

873 A559 30p magenta .20 .20

Scottish Church College, Calcutta, Sesquicentennial — A560

1980, Sept. 27 Photo. *Perf. 13½*

874 A560 35p dull purple .20 .20

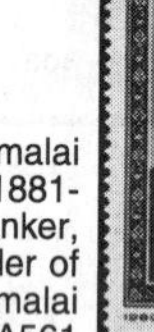

Rajah Annamalai Chettiar (1881-1948), Banker, Founder of Annamalai University — A561

1980, Sept. 30 Unwmk. *Perf. 14x15*

875 A561 35p dull purple .20 .20

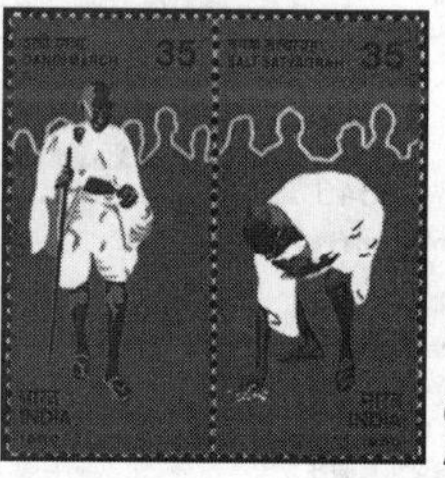

Gandhi A562

1980, Oct. 2 *Perf. 15x14*

876 35p Gandhi on Dandi March .20 .20
877 35p Gandhi Defying Salt Law .20 .20
a. A562 Pair, #876-877 .20 .20

Jayaprakash Narayan (1902-79), Writer — A564

1980, Oct. 8 Wmk. 360 *Perf. 14x15*

878 A564 35p red brown .20 .20

Intl. Symposium on Bustards, Jaipur — A565

1980, Nov. 1 Photo. *Perf. 13*

879 A565 2.30r Great Indian bustards .30 .20

Hegira (Pilgrimage Year) A566

1980, Nov. 3 *Perf. 13x13½*

880 A566 35p multicolored .20 .20

Children's Day — A567

Perf. 13½x13

1980, Nov. 14 Unwmk.

881 A567 35p multicolored .20 .20

Dhyan Chand — A568

Miner, Molten Gold — A569

1980, Dec. 3 Wmk. 360 *Perf. 14x15*

882 A568 35p dark rose brown .20 .20

Chand (1906-1979), field hockey player.

Perf. 13x13½

1980, Dec. 20 Unwmk.

883 A569 1r multicolored .20 .20

Kolar gold fields centenary.

Mukhtar Ahmad Ansari (1880-1936), Surgeon — A570

Perf. 14x15

1980, Dec. 25 Wmk. 360

884 A570 35p olive gray .20 .20

Government Mint, Bombay, Sesquicentennial — A571

Perf. 13½x13

1980, Dec. 27 Unwmk.

885 A571 35p multicolored .20 .20

Regional Bridal Outfits — A572

Mazharul Haque (1866-1930), Patriot — A573

1980, Dec. 30 *Perf. 13x13½*

886 A572 1r Kashmir .20 .20
887 A572 1r Bengal .20 .20
888 A572 1r Rajasthan .20 .20
889 A572 1r Tamilnada .20 .20
Nos. 886-889 (4) .80 .80

1981, Jan. 2 Wmk. 360 *Perf. 14x15*

890 A573 35p violet .20 .20

St. Stephen's College Centenary — A574

1981, Feb. 1 Photo. *Perf. 14x14½*

891 A574 35p dull red .20 .20

Gommateshwara Statue, Shravanabelgola A575

Ganesh V. Mavalankar (1888-1956) A576

1981, Feb. 9 Unwmk.

892 A575 1r multicolored .20 .20

1981, Feb. 27

893 A576 35p light red brown .20 .20

Mavalankar, 1st speaker of parliament.

Type of 1979

Perf. 14½x14

1981-86 Photo. Wmk. 324

Size: 19½x37½mm

895 A537 2.25r Cashew .75 .50
a. Perf. 14x14½ .30 .20
b. Perf. 13 .25 .20
896 A537 2.80r Apples 1.00 .60
a. Perf. 14x14½ .40 .20
897 A537 3.25r Oranges ('83) .60 .45
a. Perf. 13½x13 ('85) .30 .20
b. Perf. 13 .30 .20
900 A537 10r Trees on hillside ('84) .75 .40
b. Perf. 13x13½ 1.25 .60

Perf. 13½x13

Size: 37½x19½mm

900A A537 50r Windmill ('86) 2.00 1.25
Nos. 895-900A (5) 5.10 3.20

Homage to Martyrs — A577

1981, Mar. 23 Unwmk. *Perf. 14x15*

901 A577 35p multicolored .20 .20

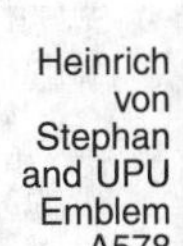

Heinrich von Stephan and UPU Emblem
A578

1981, Apr. 8 ***Perf. 15x14***

902 A578 1r red brown & brt blue .20 .20

Types of 1979 and

Telecommunications
A578a

Natural Gas
A578b

Perf. 14x14½, 14½x14, 13 (40p, 75p), 13x13½ (20r)

Wmk. 324, 360 (2p, 5p, 15p)

1981-90 **Photo.**

903 A537 2p violet .20 .20
904 A537 5p blue .20 .20
905 A537 10p Irrigation .20 .20
a. Perf. 13 .20 .20
906 A537a 15p blue green .20 .20
912 A578a 40p dull red .20 .20
914 A537 50p Dairy industry .20 .20
a. Perf. 13 .20 .20
915 A537a 75p vermilion .20 .20

Size: 17x20mm

916 A410 1r orange brown .20 .20
917 A578b 20r sepia & dark blue 1.00 .60
Nos. 903-917 (9) 2.60 2.20

Issued: 10p, 50p, 1/25/82; 40p, 10/15/88; 20r, 11/30/88; 75p, 1990; 1r, 1/30/91; others, 3/25/81.

Intl. Year of the Disabled
A579

Perf. 14½x14

1981, Apr. 20 **Photo.** **Unwmk.**

919 A579 1r blue & black .20 .20

Tribesman — A580

1981, May 30 ***Perf. 14x14½***

920 A580 1r Khiamngan Naga .20 .20
921 A580 1r Toda .20 .20
922 A580 1r Bhil .20 .20
923 A580 1r Dandami Maria .20 .20
Nos. 920-923 (4) .80 .80

World Environment Day — A581

1981, June 15

924 A581 1r multicolored .20 .20

Nilmoni Phukan (1880-1978), Writer — A582

1981, June 22

925 A582 35p red brown .20 .20

Sanjay Gandhi (1946-1980), Politician — A583

1981, June 23 ***Perf. 13x13½***

926 A583 35p multicolored .20 .20

SLV-3 Take-off — A584

1981, July 18 **Photo.** ***Perf. 14x15***

927 A584 1r multicolored .20 .20

Launching of India's 1st satellite, 1st anniv.

Mascot, Field Hockey
A585

1981, July 28 ***Perf. 13½x13***

928 A585 1r shown .20 .20
929 A585 1r Emblem .20 .20

9th Asian Games, New Delhi, 1982.

Flame of the Forest — A586

Designs: Flowering trees.

1981, Sept. 1 **Photo.** ***Perf. 13***

930 A586 35p shown .20 .20
931 A586 50p Crateva .20 .20
932 A586 1r Golden shower .20 .20
933 A586 2r Bauhinia .25 .20
Nos. 930-933 (4) .85 .80

World Food Day — A587

1981, Oct. 16 **Photo.** ***Perf. 14x14½***

934 A587 1r multicolored .20 .20

Cyrestis Achates — A588

1981, Oct. 20 ***Perf. 13***

935 A588 35p Stichophthalma camadeva, horiz. .20 .20
936 A588 50p Cethosia biblis, horiz. .20 .20
937 A588 1r shown .20 .20
938 A588 2r Treinopalpus imperialis .25 .20
Nos. 935-938 (4) .85 .80

Bellary Raghava (1880-1946), Actor — A589

1981, Oct. 31 ***Perf. 14½x14***

939 A589 35p olive gray .20 .20

40th Anniv. of Mahar Regiment — A590

Children's Day — A591

1981, Nov. 9 ***Perf. 13***

940 A590 35p multicolored .20 .20

1981, Nov. 14 ***Perf. 14x14½***

941 A591 35p multicolored .20 .20

Rajghat Stadium
A591a

1981 ***Perf. 13½x13***

942 A591a 1r shown .20 .20
943 A591a 1r Nehru Stadium .20 .20

Asian games. Issued: #942, 11/19; #943, 12/30.

Kashi Prasad Jayaswal (1881-1937), Historian — A592

1981, Nov. 27 ***Perf. 14x14½***

944 A592 35p chalky blue .20 .20

Intl. Palestinian Solidarity Day
A593

1981, Nov. 29 ***Perf. 14½x14***

945 A593 1r multicolored .20 .20

Naval Ship Taragiri
A594

1981, Dec. 4

946 A594 35p multicolored .20 .20

Henry Heras (1888-1955), Historian — A595

1981, Dec. 14 **Photo.** ***Perf. 14½x14***

947 A595 35p rose violet .20 .20

Indian Ocean Commonwealth Submarine Telephone Cable — A596

1981, Dec. 24 ***Perf. 13½***

948 A596 1r multicolored .20 .20

5th World Field Hockey Championship, Bombay — A597

1981, Dec. 29 ***Perf. 13½x13***

949 A597 1r multicolored .20 .20

Telephone Service Centenary — A598

Perf. 13x13½

1982, Jan. 28 **Unwmk.**
950 A598 2r multicolored .25 .20

12th Intl. Soil Science Congress, New Delhi, Feb. 8-16 — A599

1982, Feb. 8 ***Perf. 13½x13***
951 A599 1r multicolored .20 .20

Sir Jamsetjee Jejeebhoy School of Art, Bombay — A600

1981, Mar. 2 **Photo.** ***Perf. 14x14½***
952 A600 35p multicolored .20 .20

Three Musicians, by Pablo Picasso (1881-1973) — A601

1982, Mar. 15 **Photo.** ***Perf. 14***
953 A601 2.85r multicolored .35 .20

Deer, 5th Cent. Bas Relief — A602

Radio Telescope, Ooty — A603

Festival of India, England: No. 955, Krishna, 9th cent. bronze sculpture.

1982, Mar. 23 ***Perf. 14x15***
954 A602 2r multicolored .20 .20
955 A602 3.05r multicolored .40 .20

Perf. 13

956 A603 3.05r multicolored .40 .20
Nos. 954-956 (3) 1.00 .60

TB Bacillus Centenary — A604

1982, Mar. 24 ***Perf. 13***
957 A604 35p rose violet .20 .20

Durgabai Deshmukh (1909-1981), Social Worker — A605

1982, May 9 **Photo.** ***Perf. 14½x14***
958 A605 35p blue .20 .20

Himalayan Flowers — A606

1982, May 29 ***Perf. 14x14½***
959 A606 35p Blue poppies .20 .20
960 A606 1r Showy inula .20 .20
961 A606 2r Cobra lily .25 .20
962 A606 2.85r Brahma kamal .35 .20
Nos. 959-962 (4) 1.00 .80

Ariana Passenger Payload Experimental (APPLE) Satellite, First Anniv. — A607

1982, June 19 ***Perf. 13½x13***
963 A607 2r multicolored .25 .20

Bidhan Chandra Roy (1882-1962), Physician and Politician — A608

1982, July 1 ***Perf. 14½x14***
964 A608 50p orange brown .20 .20

Sagar Samrat Drilling Rig — A609

1982, Aug. 14 **Photo.** ***Perf. 13***
985 A609 1r multicolored .20 .20

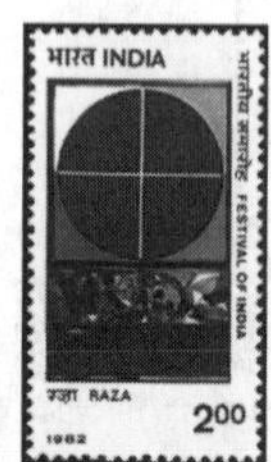

Bindu (Cosmic Spirit), by Raza — A610

Kashmir Stag — A611

Paintings; 3.05r, Between the Spider and the Lamp, 1956, by M.F. Husain.

1982, Sept. 17 ***Perf. 14x14½***
986 A610 2r multicolored .25 .20
987 A610 3.05r multicolored .40 .20

1982, Oct. 1 ***Perf. 13x13½***
988 A611 2.85r multicolored .35 .20

50th Anniv. of Indian Air Force — A612

1982, Oct. 8 ***Perf. 13½x13***
989 A612 1r Wapiti, MiG 25 .20 .20

50th Anniv. of Civil Aviation — A613

1982, Oct. 15
990 A613 3.25r J.R.D. Tata and his Puss Moth, 1932 .40 .20

Police Memorial Day — A614

1982, Oct. 21
991 A614 50p Beat patrol .20 .20

Post Office Savings Bank Centenary — A615

1982, Oct. 23
992 A615 50p brown .20 .20

9th Asian Games — A616

1982 ***Perf. 13½x14***
993 A616 1r Wrestling, by Janaki, 17th cent. .20 .20
993A A616 1r Archery .20 .20

Issued: #993, Oct. 30; #993A, Nov. 6.

India-USSR Troposcatter Communications Link — A617

1982, Nov. 2 ***Perf. 13½x13***
994 A617 3.05r multicolored .40 .20

Children's Day — A618

1982, Nov. 14 ***Perf. 14x15***
995 A618 50p multicolored .20 .20

9th Asian Games — A619

1982 ***Perf. 13***
996 A619 50p Cycling .20 .20
997 A619 2r Yachting .25 .20
998 A619 2r Javelin .25 .20
999 A619 2.85r Rowing .35 .20
1000 A619 2.85r Discus .35 .20
1001 A619 3.25r Soccer .40 .20
Nos. 996-1001 (6) 1.80 1.20

Issued: #997, 999, Nov. 25; others Nov. 19.

50th Anniv. of Indian Military Academy, Dehradun — A620

1982, Dec. 10 ***Perf. 13½x13***
1002 A620 50p multicolored .20 .20

Purushottamdas Tandon (1882-1962), Politician — A621

1982, Dec. 15 ***Perf. 13***
1003 A621 50p bister .20 .20

Darjeeling Himalayan Railway Centenary — A622

1982, Dec. 18 ***Perf. 13½x13***
1004 A622 2.85r multicolored .35 .20

Indian Railway Car — A623

Nos. 2 and 201 — A624

1982, Dec. 30 Photo. *Perf. 13, 14*

1005 A623 50p multicolored .20 .20
1006 A624 2r multicolored .25 .20

INPEX '82 Stamp Exhibition.

First Anniv. of Antarctic Expedition A625

1983, Jan. 9 Photo. *Perf. 13½x13*

1007 A625 1r multicolored .20 .20

Pres. Franklin D. Roosevelt (1882-1945) — A626

1983, Jan. 30 *Perf. 13*

1008 A626 3.25r brown .40 .20

Siberian Cranes — A627

1983, Feb. 7 *Perf. 13x13½*

1009 A627 2.85r multicolored .35 .20

180th Anniv. of Jat Regiment A628

1983, Feb. 16 *Perf. 13½x13*

1010 A628 50p Soldiers, emblem .20 .20

7th Non-aligned Summit Conference A629

1983, Mar. 7

1011 A629 1r Emblem .20 .20
1012 A629 2r Jawaharlal Nehru .25 .20

Commonwealth Day — A630

1983, Mar. 14 *Perf. 13*

1013 A630 1r Shore Temple, Mahabalipuram .20 .20
1014 A630 2r Mountains, Gomukh .25 .20

86th Session of Intl. Olympic Committee, New Delhi, Mar. 21-28 A631

1983, Mar. 25 Litho. *Perf. 13½x13*

1015 A631 1r Acropolis .20 .20

A632

A633

St. Francis of Assisi (1182-1226), by Giovanni Collina.

1983, Apr. 4 Photo. *Perf. 13*

1016 A632 1r brown .20 .20

1983, May 5 Photo. *Perf. 13x12½*

1017 A633 1r brown .20 .20

Karl Marx (1818-1883).

Charles Darwin (1809-1882) — A634

1983, May 18 *Perf. 12½x13*

1018 A634 2r multicolored .40 .20

50th Anniv. of Kanha Natl. Park A635

1983, May 30 *Perf. 13½x13*

1019 A635 1r Barasinga stag .20 .20

World Communications Year — A636

1983, July 18 Photo. *Perf. 13*

1020 A636 1r multicolored .20 .20

Simon Bolivar (1783-1830) — A637

1983, July 24

1021 A637 2r multicolored .40 .20

Quit India Resolution, Aug. 8, 1942 — A638

Meera Behn (Madeleine Slade). Disciple of Gandhi, d. 1982 — A639

Design: No. 1024, Mahadev Desai (1892-1942).

1983, Aug. 9 Photo. *Perf. 14*

1022 A638 50p shown .20 .20

Perf. 13½x13

1023 A639 50p shown .20 .20
1024 A639 50p org, green & brn .20 .20
 a. Pair, #1023-1024 .20 .20

See Nos. 1033, 1035, 1042, 1052-1057, 1077, 1093-1094, 1103, 1107, 1109, 1122, 1137-1139, 1144, 1147-1149, 1163, 1167, 1198, 1202-1205, 1229-1231, 1238, 1243, 1257, 1268-1271, 1277.

Ram Nath Chopra (1882-1973), Pharma- cologist — A640

1983, Aug. 17 *Perf. 13*

1025 A640 50p brown .20 .20

Indian Mountaineering Foundation, 25th Anniv. — A641

1983, Aug. 27 *Perf. 13½*

1026 A641 2r Nanda Devi, Himalayas .40 .20

Bombay Natural History Soc. — A642

1983, Sept. 15 *Perf. 13x13½*

1027 A642 1r multicolored .20 .20

Rock Garden, Chandigarh A643

1983, Sept. 23 *Perf. 13x13½*

1028 A643 1r multicolored .20 .20

Wildlife A644

1983, Oct. 1 *Perf. 13½x13*

1029 A644 1r Golden langur .20 .20
1030 A644 2r Lion-tailed macaque .40 .20

World Tourism, 5th General Assembly — A645

1983, Oct. 3 Photo. *Perf. 14*

1031 A645 2r Ghats of Varanasi .40 .20

Krishna Kanta Handique, Linguist, Sanskritist, Educator and Scholar — A646

1983, Oct. 7 Litho. *Perf. 13*

1032 A646 50p deep gray violet .20 .20

Famous Indians Type of 1983

Design: Hemu Kalani, revolutionary patriot.

1983, Oct. 18 Photo. *Perf. 13½x13*

1033 A639 50p org, grn & red brn .20 .20

Children's Day — A648

Painting: Festival, by Kashyap Premswala

1983, Nov. 14 Photo. *Perf. 13*

1034 A648 50p multicolored .20 .20

Famous Indians Type of 1983

Design: Acharya Vinoba Bhave (1895-1982), freedom fighter.

1983, Nov. 15 Photo. *Perf. 13½x13*

1035 A639 50p org, grn & dull brn .20 .20

Manned Flight Bicent. — A650

Project Tiger — A651

1983, Nov. 21 Photo. Perf. 13
1036 A650 1r 1st Indian Balloon .20 .20
1037 A650 2r Montgolfier Balloon .40 .20

1983, Nov. 22 Photo. Perf. 13
1038 A651 2r multicolored .40 .20

Commonwealth Heads of Government Meeting, New Delhi — A652

Design: 2r, Goanese Couple, 19th century.

1983, Nov. 23 Photo. Perf. 13
1039 A652 1r lt brnsh blue & multi .20 .20
1040 A652 2r pink & multi .40 .20

Pratiksha — A653

1983, Dec. 5 Photo. Perf. 13
1041 A653 1r multi .20 .20

Nanda Lal Bose (1882-1966), artist.

Famous Indians Type of 1983

Design: Surendranath Banerjee, journalist.

1983, Dec. 28 Photo. Perf. 13½x13
1042 A639 50p org, green & olive .20 .20

7th Light Cavalry Bicent. A655

Deccan Horse Regiment, 194th Anniv. A656

1984, Jan. 7
1043 A655 1r Soldier, banner .20 .20

1984, Jan. 9 Perf. 13x13½
1044 A656 1r multicolored .20 .20

Asiatic Society Bicentenary — A657

Design: Society building, Calcutta; founder William Jones.

1984, Jan. 15 Perf. 13
1045 A657 1r brt green & dp lilac .20 .20

Postal Life Insurance Centenary — A658

1984, Feb. 1 Photo. Perf. 13x13½
1046 A658 1r Emblem .20 .20

Presidential Review of Naval Fleet A659

1984, Feb. 3 Perf. 13½x13
1047 A659 1r Jet .20 .20
1048 A659 1r Aircraft carrier .20 .20
1049 A659 1r Submarine .20 .20
1050 A659 1r Missile destroyer .20 .20
a. Block of 4, #1047-1050 .80 .40

12th Intl. Leprosy Congress, New Delhi A660

1984, Feb. 10 Perf. 13x13½
1051 A660 1r Globe, emblem .20 .20

Famous Indians Type of 1983

#1052, Vasudeo Balvant Phadke (d. 1884), freedom fighter. #1053, Baba Kanshi Ram. #1054, Begum Hazrat Mahal. #1055, Mangal Pandey. #1056, Nana Sahib. #1057, Tatya Tope.

1984 Perf. 13½x13
1052 A639 50p org, grn & dk ol .20 .20
1053 A639 50p org, grn & brn .20 .20
1054 A639 50p org, grn, red org & gray .20 .20
1055 A639 50p org, grn, brn & gray .20 .20
1056 A639 50p org, grn, vio & gray .20 .20
1057 A639 50p org, grn, dk ol & gray .20 .20
Nos. 1052-1057 (6) 1.20 1.20

Issue dates: No. 1052, Feb. 23. No. 1053, Apr. 23. Nos. 1054-1057, May 10.

Indian-Russian Space Cooperation — A662

1984, Apr. 3 Photo. Perf. 14
1058 A662 3r Spacecraft .60 .30

G. D. Birla (1894-1983), Industrialist — A663

Birla, Birla Institute of Technology, Pilani.

1984, June 11
1060 A663 50p sepia .20 .20

1984 Summer Olympics — A664

Perf. 13x12½, 12½x13
1984, July 28 Photo.
1061 A664 50p Basketball .20 .20
1062 A664 1r High jump .20 .20
1063 A664 2r Gymnastics, horiz. .40 .20
1064 A664 2.50r Weight lifting, horiz. .50 .25
Nos. 1061-1064 (4) 1.30 .85

Vellore Fort — A665

1984, Aug. 3 Perf. 13½x13, 13x13½
1065 A665 50p Gwalior, horiz. .20 .20
1066 A665 1r shown .20 .20
1067 A665 1.50r Simhagad .30 .20
1068 A665 2r Jodhpur, horiz. .40 .20
Nos. 1065-1068 (4) 1.10 .80

B.V. Paradkar, Editor — A665a

1984, Sept. 14 Photo. Perf. 13x13½
1068A A665a 50p sepia .20 .20

Dr. D.N. Wadia (1883-1969), Geologist — A665b

1984, Oct. 23 Perf. 13
1068B A665b 1r multicolored .20 .20

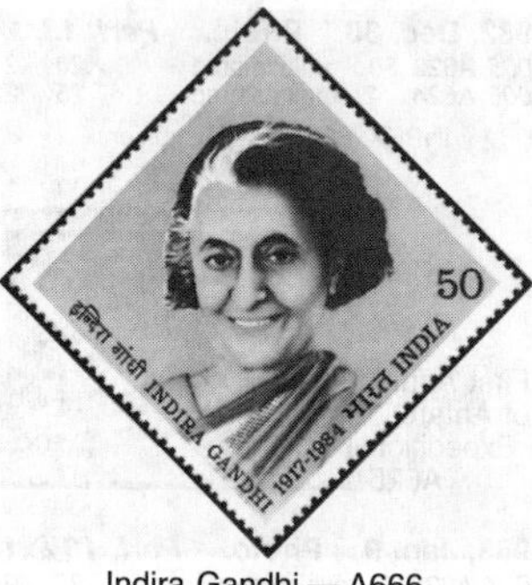
Indira Gandhi — A666

1984, Nov. 19 Photo. Perf. 15x14
1069 A666 50p multicolored .20 .20

Children's Day — A667

12th World Mining Congress — A668

1984, Nov. 14 Photo. Perf. 13
1070 A667 50p Birds in trees .20 .20

1984, Nov. 20 Photo. Perf. 13
1071 A668 1r Congress emblem .20 .20

Dr. Rajendra Prasad (1884-1963), 1st, Pres. — A669

1984, Dec. 3 Photo. Perf. 13
1072 A669 50p multicolored .20 .20

Roses — A670

1984, Dec. 23 Litho. Perf. 13
1073 A670 1.50r Mrinalini .20 .20
1074 A670 2r Sugandha .25 .20

Fergusson College Centenary A671

1985, Jan. 2 Photo. Perf. 13x13½
1076 A671 100p multicolored .20 .20

Famous Indians Type of 1983

Design: Narhar Vishnu Gadgil (1896-1966), freedom fighter.

1985, Jan. 10 Photo. Perf. 13½x13
1077 A639 50p org, grn & brn .20 .20

Artillery Regiment, 50th Anniv. A673

1985, Jan. 15 ***Perf. 13½x13***
1078 A673 1r Gunner, howitzer .20 .20

Indira Gandhi (1917-1984) — A674

1985, Jan. 31 ***Perf. 14***
1079 A674 2r Addressing UN General Assembly .25 .20

See Nos. 1098-1099.

Minicoy Lighthouse Cent. — A675

1985, Feb. 2 ***Perf. 13***
1080 A675 1r multicolored .20 .20

Bengal Medical College, 150th Anniv. A676

1985, Feb. 20 ***Perf. 13½x13***
1081 A676 1r multicolored .20 .20

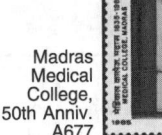

Madras Medical College, 150th Anniv. A677

1985, Mar. 8 ***Perf. 13½x13***
1082 A677 1r multicolored .20 .20

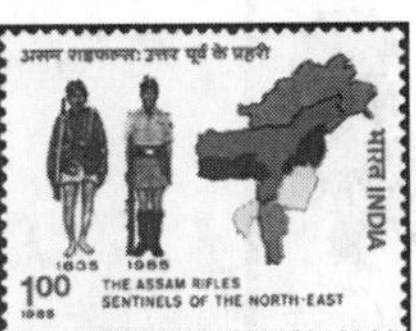

Assam Rifles, North-East Sentinels, 150th Anniv. A679

1985, Mar. 29
1084 A679 1r multicolored .20 .20

Potato Research, 50th Anniv. — A680

Baba Jassa Singh Ahluwalia, 1718-1783, Sikh Leader — A681

1985, Apr. 1 ***Perf. 13***
1085 A680 50p brown & pale brown .20 .20

1985, Apr. 4
1086 A681 50p rose violet .20 .20

St. Xavier's College, 125th Anniv. A682

1985, Apr. 12
1087 A682 1r multicolored .20 .20

White-winged Wood Duck — A683

Bougainvillea A684

1985, May 18 ***Perf. 14***
1088 A683 2r multicolored .30 .20

1985, June 5 ***Perf. 13***
1089 A684 50p multicolored .20 .20
1090 A684 1r multicolored .20 .20

Statue of Didarganj Yakshi, Indian Deity — A685

Yaudheya Tribal Republic Copper Coin, c. 200 B.C. — A686

1985
1091 A685 1r multicolored .20 .20
1092 A686 2r multicolored .30 .20

Festival of India, festival in France and the US for cultural exchange.

Issue dates: 1r, June 7. 2r, June 13.

Famous Indians Type of 1983

Designs: No. 1093, Jairamdas Doulatram (1891-1979), journalist and politician. No. 1094, Nellie (1909-1973) & Jatindra Mohan (d. 1933) Sengupta, political activists, horiz.

1985 ***Perf. 13½x13***
1093 A639 50p org, grn & dl red brn .20 .20

Perf. 13x13½
1094 A639 50p org, green & fawn .20 .20

Issued: #1093, July 21; #1094, July 22.

Swami Haridas (1478-1573), Philosopher A689

1985, Sept. 19 Photo. ***Perf. 13½x13***
1095 A689 1r multicolored .20 .20

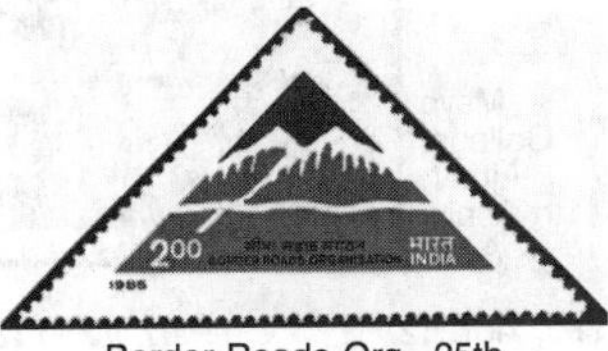

Border Roads Org., 25th Anniv. — A690

1985, Oct. 10 ***Perf. 13x14***
1096 A690 2r multicolored .20 .20

Prime Minister Nehru at Podium A691

1985, Oct. 24 ***Perf. 13x13½***
1097 A691 2r multicolored .30 .20

UN, 40th anniv.

Indira Gandhi Memorial Type of 1985

1985 ***Perf. 14***
1098 A674 2r Gandhi addressing crowd .30 .20
1099 A674 3r Portrait .50 .25

Issue dates: 2r, Oct. 31. 3r, Nov. 19.

Children's Day — A692

1985, Nov. 14 ***Perf. 13½x13***
1100 A692 50p multicolored .20 .20

Halley's Comet — A693

1985, Nov. 19 ***Perf. 13x13½***
1101 A693 1r multicolored .20 .20

Intl. Astronomical Union, 19th General Assembly, New Delhi, Nov. 19-28.

St. Stephen's Hospital, Delhi, Cent. A694

1985, Nov. 25 ***Perf. 13***
1102 A694 1r multicolored .20 .20

Famous Indians Type of 1983

Design: Kakasaheb Kalelkar (1885-1981), author.

1985, Dec. 2 ***Perf. 13½x13***
1103 A639 50p org, grn & ol brn .20 .20

Map of South Asia A696

Flags of India, Pakistan, Bangladesh, Nepal, Bhutan, Sri Lanka and the Maldive Islands — A697

1985, Dec. 8 ***Perf. 13½x13, 14***
1104 A696 1r multicolored .20 .20
1105 A697 3r multicolored .50 .25

South Asian Regional Cooperation, SARC.

Shyama Shastri (1762-1827), Composer — A698

1985, Dec. 21 ***Perf. 13½x13***
1106 A698 1r multicolored .20 .20

Famous Indians Type of 1983

Master Tara Singh (1885-1967), Sikh leader.

1985, Dec. 23 ***Perf. 13½x13***
1107 A639 50p org, green & blue .20 .20

Intl. Youth Year A700

1985, Dec. 24
1108 A700 2r multicolored .30 .20

Famous Indians Type of 1983

Design: Ravishankar Maharaj (1884-1984), freedom fighter, politician.

1985, Dec. 24 ***Perf. 13½x13***
1109 A639 50p org, green & slate .20 .20

Handel and Bach — A702

1985, Dec. 27 *Perf. 13x13½*
1110 A702 5r multicolored .80 .40

Congress Presidents, 1924-1985 A703

1985, Dec. 28 *Perf. 14*
1111 Block of 4 .65 .65
a.-d. A703 1r any single .20 .20

Indian Natl. Congress, cent. Withdrawn on day of issue for a period of two weeks.

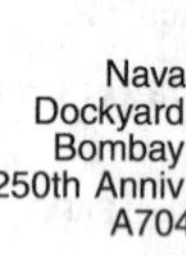

Naval Dockyard, Bombay, 250th Anniv. A704

1986, Jan. 11 Photo. *Perf. 13½*
1112 A704 2.50r multicolored .40 .20

INPEX '86, Jaipur, Feb. 14-19 A705

Designs: 50p, Hawa Mahal Palace, Jaipur No. 3. 2r, Khar Desert mobile post office.

1986, Feb. 14 *Perf. 13½x13*
1113 A705 50p multicolored .20 .20
1114 A705 2r multicolored .30 .20

Vikrant Aircraft Carrier, 25th Anniv. — A706

1986, Feb. 16 *Perf. 13x13½*
1115 A706 2r multicolored .30 .20

Inaugural Airmail Flight, 75th Anniv. A707

1986, Feb. 18 *Perf. 13½x13, 13x13½*
1116 A707 50p Biplane .20 .20

Size: 41x28mm

1117 A707 3r Jet .50 .25

Sixth Triennale of the Arts, Lalit Kala Academy A708

Sri Chaitanya Mahaprabhu A709

1986, Feb. 22 *Perf. 13x13½*
1118 A708 1r multicolored .20 .20

1986, Mar. 3 *Perf. 13*
1119 A709 2r multicolored .30 .20

Mayo College, Ajmer, 111th Anniv. A710

1986, Apr. 12 *Perf. 13½x13*
1120 A710 1r multicolored .20 .20

1986 World Cup Soccer Championships, Mexico — A711

1986, May 31 Photo. *Perf. 13*
1121 A711 5r multicolored .75 .40

Famous Indians Type of 1983

Bhim Sen Sachar (1894-1978), freedom fighter.

1986, Aug. 14 Photo. *Perf. 13½x13*
1122 A639 50p org, green & sepia .20 .20

Swami Sivananda (1887-1963), Religious Author — A713

1986, Sept. 8 Photo. *Perf. 13½x13*
1123 A713 2r multicolored .30 .20

10th Asian Games — A714

1986, Sept. 16 *Perf. 13x13½*
1124 A714 1.50r Women's volley-ball .25 .20
1125 A714 3r Hurdling .50 .25

Madras Post Office, Bicent. A715

1986, Oct. 9 Photo. *Perf. 13x13½*
1126 A715 5r black & brown orange .80 .40

1st Battalion of Parachutists Regiment, 225th Anniv. — A716

Indian Police Force, 125th Anniv. — A717

1986, Oct. 17
1127 A716 3r multicolored .50 .25

1986, Oct. 21 *Perf. 13½*

Uniforms, 1861-1986. No. 1129a has a continuous design.

1128 A717 1.50r multicolored .25 .20
1129 A717 2r multicolored .30 .20
a. Pair, #1129, 1128 .55 .35

Intl. Peace Year A718

1986, Oct. 24
1130 A718 5r sage grn, blue & rose .80 .40

Children's Day — A719

1986, Nov. 14 Photo. *Perf. 13x13½*
1131 A719 50p multicolored .20 .20

UN, 40th Anniv. A720

1986, Dec. 11 *Perf. 13½x13*
1132 A720 50p Growth monitoring .20 .20
1133 A720 5r Immunization .80 .40

Child Survival Campaign.

Miyan Tansen, 17th Cent. Dhrupad Singer, Playing the Surbahar — A721

1986, Dec. 12
1134 A721 1r multicolored .20 .20

Corbett Natl. Park, 50th Anniv. A722

1986, Dec. 15
1135 A722 1r Elephant .20 .20
1136 A722 2r Gavial .30 .20

Famous Indians Type of 1983

Designs: No. 1137, Alluri Seetarama Raju (b. 1897), freedom fighter. No. 1138, Sagarmal Gopa (b. 1900), freedom fighter. No. 1139, Veer Surendra Sai (b. 1809), freedom fighter.

1986, Dec. *Perf. 13½x13*
1137 A639 50p red, green & sepia .20 .20
1138 A639 50p red, green & sl blue .20 .20
1139 A639 50p red, green & dp red brn .20 .20
Nos. 1137-1139 (3) .60 .60

Issued: #1137, 26th; #1138, 29th; #1139, 30th.

St. Martha's Hospital, Bangalore, Cent. A724

1986, Dec. 30 *Perf. 13½*
1140 A724 1r multicolored .20 .20

Africa Fund — A726

Yacht Trishna A725

1987, Jan. 10
1141 A725 6.50r multicolored 1.10 .50

1st Indian Army circumnavigation of the world, Sept. 28, 1985 to 1987.

1987, Jan. 25 Photo. *Perf. 14x14½*
1142 A726 6.50r black 1.10 .50

ICC 29th Congress, New Delhi — A727

1987, Feb. 11 ***Perf. 13½***
1143 A727 5r multicolored .80 .40

Famous Indians Type of 1983

Design: Hakim Ajmal Khan (1864-1927), physician, politician.

1987, Feb. 13 ***Perf. 13½x13***
1144 A639 60p org, grn & brn .20 .20

A729

Family Planning A730

1987, Feb. 27 ***Perf. 13, 13x13½***
1145 A729 35p dark red .20 .20
1146 A730 60p green & dark red .20 .20

Famous Indians Type of 1983

Designs: No. 1147, Lala Har Dayal (1884-1939). No. 1148, Manabendra Nath Roy (1887-1954). No. 1149, T. Ramaswamy Chowdary (1887-1943).

1987 Photo. ***Perf. 13½x13***
1147 A639 60p org, green & purple .20 .20
1148 A639 60p org, green & red brn .20 .20
1149 A639 60p org, grn & brt blue .20 .20
Nos. 1147-1149 (3) .60 .60

Issued: #1147, 3/18; #1148, 3/21; #1149, 4/25.

SER Emblem, Blast Furnaces — A732

Electric Train Crossing Bridge — A734

Steam Locomotive No. 691 — A733

1987, Mar. 28 ***Perf. 13x13½, 13½x13***
1150 A732 1r shown .20 .20
1151 A733 1.50r shown .25 .20
1152 A734 2r shown .30 .20
1153 A733 4r Steam locomotive, c. 1890 .65 .30
Nos. 1150-1153 (4) 1.40 .90

Southeastern Railway, cent.

Kalia Bhomora Bridge, Assam A735

1987, Apr. 14 ***Perf. 13½***
1154 A735 2r multicolored .30 .20

Madras Christian College, 150th Anniv. A736

1987, Apr. 16 ***Perf. 13x13½***
1155 A736 1.50r black & rose lake .25 .20

A737

A738

1987, May 1 ***Perf. 13½***
1156 A737 1r dull brown .20 .20

Shree Shree Ma Anandamayee (1896-1982), spiritualist.

1987, May 8 ***Perf. 14***
1157 A738 2r multicolored .30 .20

Rabindranath Tagore (1861-1941), 1913 Nobel Laureate for literature.

A739

A740

1987, May 10 ***Perf. 13½***
1158 A739 1r multicolored .20 .20

Garhwal Rifles and Garhwal Scouts, cent.

1987, May 11
1159 A740 60p black brn & buff .20 .20

J. Krishnamurti (1895-1986), mystic.

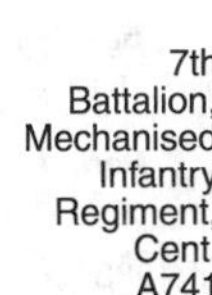

7th Battalion, Mechanised Infantry Regiment, Cent. A741

1987, June 3 ***Perf. 13½x13***
1160 A741 1r multicolored .20 .20

INDIA '89, New Delhi, Jan. 20-29, 1989 A742

1987, June 15
1161 A742 50p Swan emblem .20 .20
a. Bklt. pane of 4+inscribed margin ('89) .30
1162 A742 5r Hall of Nations, New Delhi .80 .40
a. Souv. sheet of 2, #1161-1162 1.25 1.25
b. Bklt. pane of 4+inscribed margin ('89) 3.25

Inscribed 1986. No. 1162a sold for 8r.

Famous Indians Type of 1983

Kailas Nath Katju (1887-1968), Chief Minister.

1987, June 17 ***Perf. 13½x13***
1163 A639 60p org, grn & yel brn .20 .20

Sadyah-Snata, Sanghol Sculpture, c. 2000 B.C. A744

1987, July 3
1164 A744 6.50r multicolored 1.10 .50

Festival of India in the USSR, July 3, 1987-88.

Natl. Independence, 40th Anniv. — A745

1987, Aug. 15 Photo. ***Perf. 13x13½***
1165 A745 60p orange, brt blue & dk green .20 .20

Sant Harchand Singh Longowal (1932-1985), Social Reformer — A746

1987, Aug. 20 ***Perf. 13½***
1166 A746 1r multicolored .20 .20

Famous Indians Type of 1983

Design: S. Satyamurti (1887-1943), political reformer, martyr.

1987, Aug. 22 ***Perf. 13½x13***
1167 A639 60p org, green & brn .20 .20

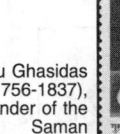

Guru Ghasidas (1756-1837), Founder of the Saman Sect — A748

1987, Sept. 1
1168 A748 60p henna brown .20 .20

Sri Sri Thakur Anukul Chandra (1888-1969), Physician, Guru — A749

1987, Sept. 2 ***Perf. 13½***
1169 A749 1r multicolored .20 .20

University of Allahabad, Cent. A750

1987, Sept. 23 ***Perf. 13½x13***
1170 A750 2r multicolored .30 .20

Phoolwalon Ki Sair — A751

Maharaja Chhatrasal A752

1987, Oct. 1 ***Perf. 13x13½***
1171 A751 2r Pankha (embroidered apron) .30 .20

Festival of thanksgiving for fulfilled prayers.

1987, Oct. 2 ***Perf. 14***
1172 A752 60p henna brown .20 .20

Chhatrasal (1649-1731), military commander during the war against the Moguls.

Intl. Year of Shelter for the Homeless A753

1987, Oct. 5 ***Perf. 13½x13***
1173 A753 5r multicolored .80 .40

Asia Regional Conference of Rotary Intl. — A754

1987, Oct. 14

1174 A754 60p shown .20 .20
1175 A754 6.50r Polio immunization 1.10 .50

Service to the Blind, Cent. A755

1987, Oct. 15

1176 A755 1r shown .20 .20
1177 A755 2r Eye donation .30 .20

World White Cane Day.

INDIA '89 — A756

Designs: 60p, The Iron Pillar, Quwwat-ul-Islam Mosque courtyard, 5th cent., Delhi. 1.50r, The India Gate, New Delhi, war memorial by Luytens, 1921. 5r, The Dewan-E-Khas, Hall of Private Audience, Red Fort, Delhi, c. 1648. 6.50r, Purana Qila, Old Fort, Delhi, c. 1540.

1987, Oct. 17

1178 A756 60p multicolored .20 .20
  a. Bklt. pane of 4 + inscribed margin ('89) .40
1179 A756 1.50r multicolored .25 .20
  a. Bklt. pane of 4 + inscribed margin ('89) 1.00
1180 A756 5r multicolored .80 .40
  a. Bklt. pane of 4 + inscribed margin ('89) 3.25
1181 A756 6.50r multicolored 1.10 .50
  a. Souv. sheet of 4, #1178-1811 2.50 1.25
  b. Bklt. pane of 4 + inscribed margin ('89) 4.25
  Nos. 1178-1181 (4) 2.35 1.30

No. 1181a sold for 15r.

Tyagmurti Goswami Ganeshdutt (1889-1959), Educator, Social Activist — A757

1987, Nov. 2 ***Perf. 13½***

1182 A757 60p terra cotta .20 .20

Children's Day — A758

1987, Nov. 14

1183 A758 60p multicolored .20 .20

Trees A759

1987, Nov. 19 **Photo.** ***Perf. 13½***

1184 A759 60p Chinar, vert. .20 .20
1185 A759 1.50r Pipal .25 .20
1186 A759 5r Sal, vert. .80 .40
1187 A759 6.50r Banyan 1.10 .50
  Nos. 1184-1187 (4) 2.35 1.30

Festival of the USSR in India — A760

Votive coin based on The Worker and the Peasant Woman, by Soviet sculptor Mukhina.

1987, Nov. 21 ***Perf. 14***

1188 A760 5r multicolored .80 .40

White Tiger — A761

Rameshwari Nehru (1886-1966), Human Rights and World Peace Activist — A762

1987, Nov. 29 **Photo.** ***Perf. 13½***

1189 A761 1r shown .20 .20
1190 A761 5r Snow leopard, horiz. .80 .40

1987, Dec. 10

1191 A762 60p red brown .20 .20

Execution of Veer Narayan Singh (1795-1857), Sikh Uprising Leader — A763

1987, Dec. 10

1192 A763 60p dark brown .20 .20

Father Kuriakose Elias Chavara (1806-1871), Theologian Beatified by Pope John Paul II Feb. 8, 1986 — A764

1987, Dec. 20

1193 A764 60p dark brown olive .20 .20

Dr. Rajah Sir M.A. Muthiah Chettiar (1905-1984), Politician, Pro-chancellor of Annamalai University — A765

1987, Dec. 21 ***Perf. 13***

1194 A765 60p chalky blue black .20 .20

Sri Harmandir Sahib (Gold Temple), Amritsar, 400th Anniv. — A766

1987, Dec. 26 ***Perf. 13½***

1195 A766 60p multicolored .20 .20

Rukmini Devi (1904-1986), Dancer, Choreographer — A767

1987, Dec. 27

1196 A767 60p dark red .20 .20

Dr. Hiralal (1867-1934), Historian — A768

1987, Dec. 31

1197 A768 60p dark blue .20 .20

Famous Indians Type of 1983

Design: Pandit Hriday Nath Kunzru (1887-1978), human rights activist, statesman.

1987, Dec. 31 ***Perf. 13½x13***

1198 A639 60p org, grn & red brn .20 .20

75th Session of the Indian Science Congress Assoc. A770

1988, Jan. 1

1199 A770 4r multicolored .65 .30

Solar Energy A771

13th Asia Pacific Dental Congress, New Delhi, Jan. 28-Feb.2 A772

Wmk. 324

1988, Jan. 1 **Photo.** ***Perf. 13***

1200 A771 5r dp orange & sepia .80 .40

1988, Jan. 28 **Unwmk.** ***Perf. 13***

1201 A772 4r multicolored .65 .30

Famous Indians Type of 1983

Designs: No. 1202, Mohan Lal Sukhadia (1916-1982). No. 1203, Dr. S.K. Sinha (1887-1961). No. 1204, Chandra Shekhar Azad (1906-1931). No. 1205, Govind Ballabh Pant (1887-1961).

1988 ***Perf. 13½x13***

1202 A639 60p org, grn & bluish blk .20 .20
1203 A639 60p org, grn & org brn .20 .20
1204 A639 60p org, grn & rose red .20 .20
1205 A639 60p org, grn & purple .20 .20
  Nos. 1202-1205 (4) .80 .80

Issue dates: Nos. 1202, Feb. 2; No. 1203, Feb. 4; No. 1204, Feb. 27; No. 1205, Mar. 7.

U. Tirot Sing (1800-1833), Patriot — A774

1988, Feb. 3

1206 A774 60p dull brown .20 .20

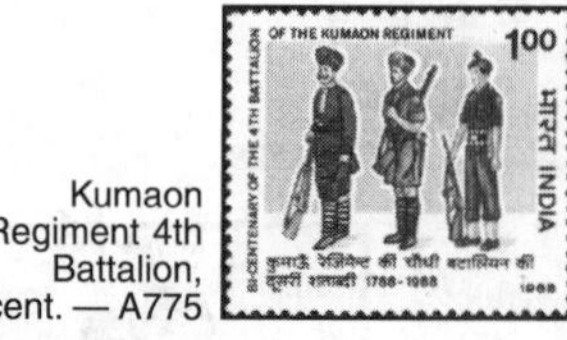

Kumaon Regiment 4th Battalion, Bicent. — A775

Balgandharva (1888-1967), Musician — A776

1988, Feb. 19 ***Perf. 14***

1207 A775 1r Uniforms of 1788, 1947, 1988 .20 .20

1988, Feb. 22 ***Perf. 13x13½***

1208 A776 60p brown .20 .20

Mechanised Infantry Regiment A777

1988, Feb. 24 ***Perf. 13½x13***

1209 A777 1r multicolored .20 .20

A778

1988, Feb. 26 ***Perf. 13***

1210 A778 60p bluish black .20 .20

Sir B.N. Rau (1887-1953), constitutional advisor.

A779

1988, Mar. 14 Photo. ***Perf. 13x13½***
1211 A779 1r bright rose .20 .20

Mohindra College, Patiala, founded in 1875 by Maharaja Mohinder Singh, is now part of Punjabi University.

Dr. D.V. Gundappa (1887-1975), Journalist, and Gikhala Institute of Public Affairs — A780

1988, Mar. 17 ***Perf. 13½x13***
1212 A780 60p slate blue .20 .20

Woman Warrior Riding into Battle — A781

1988, Mar. 20 ***Perf. 13x13½***
1213 A781 60p bright rose .20 .20

Rani Avantibai (d. 1858), heroine of the 1857 independence war.

Malayala Manorama Newspaper, Cent. — A782

1988, Mar. 23
1214 A782 1r blue & black .20 .20

Malayala Manorama, published in Kottayam, is the largest circulated daily newspaper in India.

Maharshi Dadhichi, Vedic Period Saint Purported to Have Introduced Fire to Man — A783

1988, Mar. 26
1215 A783 60p deep orange .20 .20

Mohammad Iqbal (1877-1938), Poet — A784

1988, Apr. 21
1216 A784 60p carmine & gold .20 .20

Samarth Ramdas (1608-1682), Philosopher A785

1988, May 1 ***Perf. 13***
1217 A785 60p dk yellow green .20 .20

Swati Tirunal Rama Varma (1813-1846), Carnatic Composer — A786

1988, May 2 ***Perf. 13x13½***
1218 A786 60p brt violet .20 .20

1st War of Independence, the "Indian Mutiny of 1857" — A787

Painting: Rani Laxmi Bai transformed from a queen into a warrior fighting for justice, by M.F. Husain.

1988, May 9 Photo. ***Perf. 13x13½***
1219 A787 60p multicolored .20 .20

Bhaurao Patil (b. 1887), Educator A788

1988, May 9 ***Perf. 13½x13***
1220 A788 60p red brown .20 .20

Himalayan Peaks A789

1988, May 19
1221 A789 1.50r Broad Peak .25 .20
1222 A789 4r Godwin Austin .65 .30
1223 A789 5r Kanchenjunga .75 .40
1224 A789 6.50r Nandadevi 1.00 .50
Nos. 1221-1224 (4) 2.65 1.40

Care for the Elderly — A790

1988, May 24 ***Perf. 13x13½***
1225 A790 60p multicolored .20 .20

Victoria Terminal, Bombay, Cent. A791

1988, May 30 ***Perf. 13½x13***
1226 A791 1r multicolored .20 .20

Lawrence School, Lovedale, 130th Anniv. A792

1988, May 31 ***Perf. 13***
1227 A792 1r dk green & red brown .20 .20

World Environment Day — A793

1988, June 5 ***Perf. 14***
1228 A793 60p Khejri tree .20 .20

Famous Indians Type of 1983

#1229, Dr. Anugrah Narain Singh (1887-1957), statesman. #1230, Kuladhor Chaliha (1886-1963), political and social reformer. #1231, Shivprasad Gupta (1883-1944), freedom fighter.

1988 ***Perf. 13½x13***
1229 A639 60p org, grn & rose vio .20 .20
1230 A639 60p org, grn & gray blk .20 .20
1231 A639 60p org, grn & dk vio .20 .20
Nos. 1229-1231 (3) .60 .60

Issued: #1229, 6/18; #1230, 6/19; #1231, 6/28.

Rani Durgawati (d. 1564), Ruler of Gondwana — A795

1988, June 24
1232 A795 60p red .20 .20

A796

A797

1988, July 28 Photo. ***Perf. 13x13½***
1233 A796 60p red brown .20 .20

Acharya Shanti Dev (687-765), Sanskrit and Pali scholar.

1988, Aug. 4
1234 A797 60p blue violet .20 .20

Yashwant Singh Parmar (1906-1981), administrator of Himachal Pradesh State.

Painting by M.F. Husain — A798

1988, Aug. 16 Photo. ***Perf. 13x13½***
1235 60p India at upper left .20 .20
1236 60p India at lower left .20 .20
a. A798 Pair, #1235-1236 .20 .20

Natl. Independence 40th anniv.

Durgadas Rathore (1638-1718), Guardian of King Ajit Singh — A799

1988, Aug. 26 **Litho.**
1237 A799 60p dark red brown .20 .20

Famous Indians Type of 1983

Design: Sarat Chandra Bose (1889-1950), politician, lawyer, publisher.

1988, Sept. 6 Photo. ***Perf. 13½x13***
1238 A639 60p org, grn & dk blue grn .20 .20

Gopinath Kaviraj (1887-1976), Scholar — A801

1988, Sept. 7 ***Perf. 13x13½***
1239 A801 60p brown olive .20 .20

Hindi Language Day, Sept. 14
A802

Indian Olympic Assoc. Emblem
A803

Glory of Sport, Independence 40th Anniv. — A804

1988, Sept. 14 Photo. ***Perf. 13x13½***
1240 A802 60p ver & dk olive green .20 .20

Perf. 13½x13, 13x13½

1988, Sept. 17
1241 A803 60p deep claret .20 .20
1242 A804 5r multicolored .80 .40

Famous Indians Type of 1983

Baba Kharak (1867-1963), nationalist.

1988, Oct. 6 ***Perf. 13½x13***
1243 A639 60p org, green & org brn .20 .20

Jerdon's Courser — A806

1988, Oct. 7 ***Perf. 13½***
1244 A806 1r multicolored .20 .20

The Times of India, Newspaper, 150th Anniv. — A807

1988, Nov. 3 ***Perf. 13½x14***
1245 A807 1.50r black & gold .25 .20

INDIA '89 — A808

Perf. 13½x13

1988, Oct. 9 Unwmk. Photo.
1246 A808 4r Bangalore P.O. .65 .30
a. Bklt. pane of 6+inscribed margin ('89) 4.00
1247 A808 5r Bombay P.O. .70 .35
a. Bklt. pane of 6+inscribed margin ('89) 4.25

Portrait of Azad by K.K. Hebbar — A809

1988, Nov. 11
1248 A809 60p multicolored .20 .20

Maulana Abul Kalam Azad (1888-1958), minister of education, natl. resources and scientific research.

Jawaharlal Nehru — A810

Perf. 13x13½, 13½x13 (1r)

1988, Nov. 14
1249 A810 60p dk gray, dk orange & dk grn .20 .20
1250 A810 1r Portrait, vert. .20 .20

Birsa, Munda Leader
A811

1988, Nov. 15 ***Perf. 13½x13***
1251 A811 60p brown .20 .20

Bhakra Dam, 25th Anniv. — A812

1988, Dec. 15 ***Perf. 14***
1252 A812 60p carmine rose .20 .20

INDIA '89 — A813

60p, Dead-letter cancellations, 1886. 6.50r, Traveling p.o. cancellation, 1864-69.

1988, Dec. 20 ***Perf. 13½x13***
1253 A813 60p multicolored .20 .20
a. Bklt. pane of 6+inscribed margin ('89) .50
1254 A813 6.50r multicolored 1.10 .50
a. Bklt. pane of 6+inscribed margin ('89) 6.25

K.M. Munshi (1887-1971), Environmentalist, Statesmen — A814

1988, Dec. 30
1255 A814 60p dark olive green .20 .20

Mannathu Padmanabhan (1878-1970), Social Reformer — A815

1989, Jan. 2 ***Perf. 13½x13***
1256 A815 60p dull brown .20 .20

Famous Indians Type of 1983

Hare Krushna Mahtab (1899-1987), author.

1989, Jan. 2 ***Perf. 13½x13***
1257 A639 60p orange, grn & black .20 .20

Lok Sabha Secretariat, 60th Anniv.
A817

1989, Jan. 10 ***Perf. 13½x13***
1258 A817 60p dark olive green .20 .20

State Museum, Lucknow, 125th Anniv. — A818

1989, Jan. 11 ***Perf. 14***
1259 A818 60p Goddess Durga, lion .20 .20

INDIA '89 — A819

1989, Jan. 20 ***Perf. 13½x13***
1260 A819 60p Youth collecting .20 .20
a. Bklt. pane of 6 + inscribed margin .60
1261 A819 1.50r Postal coach & p.o., 1842 .25 .20
a. Bklt. pane of 6 + inscribed margin 1.50
1262 A819 5r Travancore #2 .80 .40
a. Bklt. pane of 6 + inscribed margin 4.75
1263 A819 6.50r Philatelic journal mastheads 1.10 .50
a. Bklt. pane of 6 + inscribed margin 6.25
Nos. 1260-1263 (4) 2.35 1.30

St. John Bosco (1815-1888), Educator — A820

1989, Jan. 31 ***Perf. 13***
1264 A820 60p carmine rose .20 .20

3rd Cavalry, 148th Anniv.
A821

1989, Feb. 8 ***Perf. 13½x13***
1265 A821 60p multicolored .20 .20

Dargah Sharif Ajmer
A822

1989, Feb. 13 Litho. ***Perf. 13½x13***
1266 A822 1r multicolored .20 .20

President's Review of the Naval Fleet — A823

1989, Feb. 15 ***Perf. 14***
1267 A823 6.50r multicolored 1.10 .50

Famous Indians Type of 1983

#1268, Sheikh Mohammad Abdullah. #1269, Balasaheb Gangadhar Kher (1888-1957), politician. #1270, Saiffuddin Kitchlew (1888-1963), lawyer, diplomat. #1271, Rajkumari Amrit Kaur (d. 1964), minister of health and welfare.

1988-89 Photo. ***Perf. 13½x13***
1268 A639 60p org, grn & lil rose .20 .20
1269 A639 60p org, grn & dk vio .20 .20
1270 A639 60p org, grn & blk brn .20 .20
1271 A639 60p org, grn & grnsh blk .20 .20
Nos. 1268-1271 (4) .80 .80

Issue dates: No. 1268, Dec. 5; No. 1269, Mar. 8, 1989; Nos. 1270-1271, Apr. 13, 1989.

Freedom Fighters — A825

#1272, Baldev Ramji Mirdha (1889-1956). #1273, Rao Gopal Singh (1899-1939).

1989 ***Perf. 13x13½***
1272 A825 60p slate .20 .20
1273 A825 60p dark olive .20 .20

Issue dates: #1272, Jan. 17; #1273, Mar. 30.

Freedom Fighters A826

Designs: No. 1274, Shaheed Laxman Nayak (1899-1943), protest leader. No. 1275, Bishu Ram Medhi (1888-1981), politician.

1989 ***Perf. 13½x13***
1274 A826 60p org, sage grn & brn .20 .20

Size: 24x37mm

1275 A826 60p org, sage grn & dp yel grn .20 .20

Issued: #1274, Mar. 29; #1275, Apr. 24.
See #1292, 1299-1300, 1317, 1429, 1487.

Sydenham College, Bombay A827

1989, Apr. 19 ***Perf. 13½***
1276 A827 60p black .20 .20

Famous Indians Type of 1983

Design: Asaf Ali (1888-1953), patriot.

1989, May 11 Photo. ***Perf. 13½x13***
1277 A639 60p org, green & sepia .20 .20

N.S. Hardikar (1889-1975), Freedom Fighter — A829

1989, May 13 ***Perf. 13x13½***
1278 A829 60p chestnut brown .20 .20

Sankaracharya (b. 788), Philosopher — A830

1989, May 17 ***Perf. 14x13½***
1279 A830 60p multicolored .20 .20

Punjab University, Chandigarh A831

1989, May 19 ***Perf. 13½x13***
1280 A831 1r blue green & brn .20 .20

Film Industry, 75th Anniv. — A832

1989, May 30 Photo. ***Perf. 14***
1281 A832 60p dk olive bis & blk .20 .20

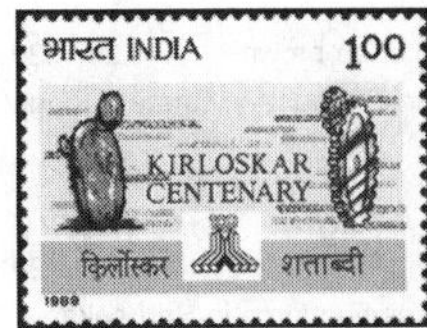

Kirloskar Corporation, Cent. A833

1989, June 20 Photo. ***Perf. 13½x13***
1282 A833 1r multicolored .20 .20

DAV Education Movement, Cent. A834

1989, June 27 Photo. ***Perf. 13½x13***
1283 A834 1r multicolored .20 .20

Dakshin Gangotri Post Office in the Antarctic, 1988 A835

1989, July 11 ***Perf. 14***
1284 A835 1r multicolored .20 .20

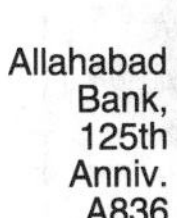
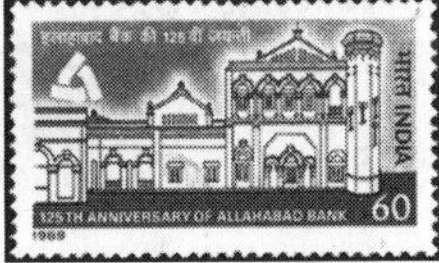

Allahabad Bank, 125th Anniv. A836

1989, July 19
1285 A836 60p multicolored .20 .20

Central Reserve Police Force, 50th Anniv. A837

1989, July 27 ***Perf. 13½x13***
1286 A837 60p golden brown .20 .20

Military Farms, Cent. A838

1989, Aug. 18
1287 A838 1r multicolored .20 .20

Kemal Ataturk (1881-1938), 1st President of Turkey — A839

1989, Aug. 30 ***Perf. 13x13½***
1288 A839 5r multicolored .80 .40

Sarvepalli Radhakrishnan, President of India, 1962-67 — A840

1989, Sept. 11 Photo. ***Perf. 13x13½***
1289 A840 60p black .20 .20

P. Subbarayan (1889-1962), Lawyer, Political Reformer — A841

1989, Sept. 30 ***Perf. 13x13½***
1290 A841 60p brown orange .20 .20

Mohun Bagan Soccer Team, Cent. A842

1989, Sept. 23 Photo. ***Perf. 13½x13***
1291 A842 1r multicolored .20 .20

Freedom Fighter Type of 1989

Shyamji Krishna Varma (1857-1930).

1989, Oct. 4 Photo. ***Perf. 13½x13***
1292 A826 60p org, sage grn & dk red brn .20 .20

Sayaji Rao Gaekwad III (1863-1939), Maharaja of the Former State of Baroda — A843

1989, Oct. 6 ***Perf. 13x13½***
1293 A843 60p black .20 .20

Use Pin Code A844

1989, Oct. 14 ***Perf. 14***
1294 A844 60p multicolored .20 .20

Namakkal Kavignar (1888-1972), Poet Laureate — A845

1989, Oct. 19 Photo. ***Perf. 13x13½***
1295 A845 60p black .20 .20

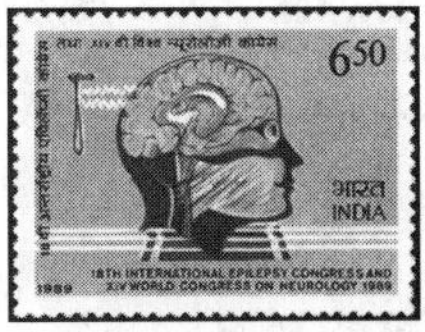

18th Intl. Epilepsy Congress and 14th World Neurology Congress, New Delhi A846

1989, Oct. 21 ***Perf. 13½x13***
1296 A846 6.50r multicolored .90 .45

Ramabai and Sharada Sadan School A847

1989, Oct. 26
1297 A847 60p brown .20 .20

Pandita Ramabai (1858-1920), women's rights activist, founder of mission to help destitute women and children.

Pigeon Post A848

1989, Nov. 3
1298 A848 1r brown orange .20 .20

Freedom Fighter Type of 1989

#1299, Acharya Narendra Deo (1889-1956), democratic socialist movement founder. #1300, Acharya Kripalani (1888-1982), politician.

1989 ***Perf. 13½x13***
1299 A826 60p org, sage grn & brn .20 .20
1300 A826 60p org, sage grn & dp gray .20 .20

Issue dates: #1299, Nov. 6; #1300, Nov. 11.

Jawaharlal Nehru, Birth Cent. — A849

1989, Nov. 14 ***Perf. 14x15***
1301 A849 1r buff, dk red brn & sepia .20 .20

8th Asian Track and Field Meet, Nov. 14-19, New Delhi — A850

1989, Nov. 19 ***Perf. 14x14½***
1302 A850 1r black, org & dp grn .20 .20

A851

1989, Nov. 20 ***Perf. 13x13½***
1303 A851 60p deep brown .20 .20

Gurunath Bewoor (b. 1888), 1st Indian appointed postmaster general.

A852

1989, Dec. 8 Photo. ***Perf. 13x13½***
1304 A852 60p black .20 .20

Balkrishna Sharma Navin (1897-1960), litterateur, politician.

Bombay Art Soc., Cent. A853

1989, Dec. 15 ***Perf. 13½x13***
1305 A853 1r multicolored .20 .20

Likh Florican — A854

Digboi Oil Field, 1889 — A855

1989, Dec. 20 ***Perf. 13x13½***
1306 A854 2r multicolored .30 .20

1989, Dec. 29 ***Perf. 14***
1307 A855 60p dark red brown .20 .20

Discovery of oil, Digboi, Assam, cent.

M.G. Ramachandran (1917-1987), Actor, Chief Minister — A856

1990, Jan. 17 ***Perf. 13x13½***
1308 A856 60p dark red brown .20 .20

Extracting Silt from Sukhna Lake, Chandigarh A857

1990, Jan. 29 ***Perf. 13½x13***
1309 A857 1r multicolored .20 .20

Sukhna Shramda, society for the preservation of Sukhna Lake.

Presentation of Colors by Pres. Venkataraman to the Bombay Sappers (Corps of Engineers), Feb. 21 — A858

Perf. 15x14x14

1990, Feb. 21 **Photo.**
1310 A858 60p multicolored .20 .20

Asian Development Bank — A859

1990, May 2 Photo. ***Perf. 14***
1311 A859 2r Seashell .20 .20

Great Britain No. 1, Simulated Cancel of India, Envelope A860

1990, May 6 ***Perf. 13x13½***
1312 A860 6r multicolored .40 .20

Penny Black, 150th anniv.

Residence and Portrait A861

1990, May 17 Photo. ***Perf. 13½x13***
1313 A861 2r red brown & green .20 .20

Ho Chi Minh (1890-1969), Vietnamese Communist Party leader.

A862

A863

1990, May 29
1314 A862 1r orange brown .20 .20

Prime Minister Chaudhary Charan Singh (1902-1987).

1990, July 30 Photo. ***Perf. 13x13½***
1315 A863 2r multicolored .25 .20

Indian peace keeping force in Sri Lanka.

Indian Council of Agricultural Research — A864

1990, July 31 ***Perf. 14***
1316 A864 2r multicolored .25 .20

Freedom Fighter Type of 1989

Design: Khudiram Bose (1889-1908), vert.

1990, Aug. 11 Photo. ***Perf. 13x13½***
Size: 26x35mm
1317 A826 1r orange, grn & red brn .20 .20

Russian Child's Drawing of India — A865

6.50r, Indian child's drawing of Red Square.

1990, Aug. 16 Photo. ***Perf. 14***
1318 A865 1r multicolored .20 .20
1319 A865 6.50r multicolored .80 .40
a. Pair, #1318-1319 .90 .50

See Russia Nos. 5925-5926.

A866

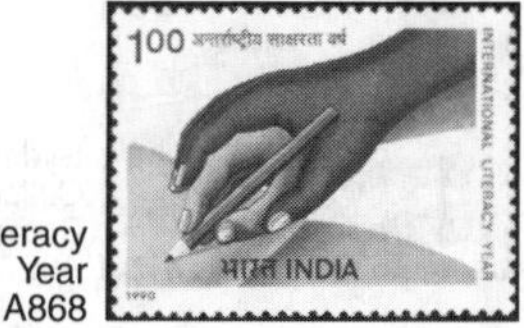

A867

1990, Aug. 24 ***Perf. 13***
1320 A866 1r lt red brown .20 .20

K. Kelappan (1889-1971), social revolutionary.

1990, Sept. 5 ***Perf. 13x13½***
1321 A867 1r multicolored .20 .20

Care for young girls.

Intl. Literacy Year A868

1990, Sept. 8 ***Perf. 13½x13***
1322 A868 1r blue, brn & tan .20 .20

A869

A870

1990, Sept. 10 ***Perf. 13x14***
1323 A869 4r blue grn & red .50 .25

Safe drinking water.

1990, Sept. 28 Photo. ***Perf. 13x13½***
1324 A870 60p rose lake .20 .20

Sunder Lal Sharma (1881-1940), social reformer.

11th Asian Games, Beijing — A871

1990, Sept. 29

1325	A871	1r Kabbadi	.20	.20
1326	A871	4r Sprinting	.50	.25
1327	A871	4r Cycling	.50	.25
1328	A871	6.50r Archery	.80	.40
		Nos. 1325-1328 (4)	2.00	1.10

A.K. Gopalan (1904-1977), Political and Social Reformer — A872

1990, Oct. 1
1329 A872 1r red brown .20 .20

5th Gurkha Rifles, 3rd and 5th Battalions — A873

1990, Oct. 1
1330 A873 2r yel brown & dk vio .25 .20

Suryamall Mishran (1815-1868), Poet — A874

1990, Oct. 19
1331 A874 2r brown & yel brown .25 .20

Children's Day — A875

Perf. 13½x13
1990, Nov. 14 Photo. Unwmk.
1332 A875 1r multicolored .20 .20

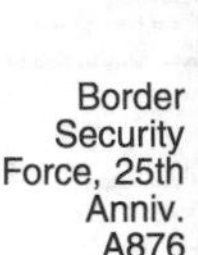

Border Security Force, 25th Anniv. A876

1990, Nov. 30
1333 A876 5r multicolored .60 .30

Greetings — A877

4r, Two elephants carrying riders, horiz.

Perf. 13x13½, 13½x13
1990, Dec. 17 Photo.
1334 A877 1r multicolored .20 .20
1335 A877 4r multicolored .50 .25

Cities of India A878

1990, Dec. 24 Photo. *Perf. 13½x13*
1336 A878 4r Bikaner .50 .25
1337 A878 5r Hyderabad .60 .30
1338 A878 6.50r Cuttack .70 .35
Nos. 1336-1338 (3) 1.80 .90

Bhakta Kanakadas (1488-1578), Mystic — A879

1990, Dec. 26 *Perf. 14*
1339 A879 1r red orange .20 .20

Dnyaneshwari, 700th Anniv. — A880

1990, Dec. 31 *Perf. 13½x13*
1340 A880 2r org red, red brown & blk .25 .20

Calcutta, 300th Anniv. — A881

Unwmk.
1990, Dec. 28 Photo. *Perf. 14*

Designs: 1r, Shaheed Minar. 6r, Sailing ships on Ganges River.

1341 A881 1r multicolored .20 .20

Size: 44x35mm

1342 A881 6r multicolored .85 .40

Pandit Mohan Malaviya, Banaras Hindu University A882

1991, Jan. 20 *Perf. 13½x13*
1343 A882 1r dk carmine rose .20 .20

Banaras Hindu University, 75th Anniv.

Intl. Conference on Traffic Safety A883

1991, Jan. 30 *Perf. 13½x13*
1344 A883 6.50r blue, red & blk .80 .40

7th Art Triennial — A884

1991, Feb. 12 Photo. *Perf. 13x13½*
1345 A884 6.50r multicolored .90 .45

Jagannath Sunkersett A885

1991, Feb. 15
1346 A885 2r ultra & henna brn .30 .20

Jagannath Sunkersett (1803-1865), educator, reformer.

Tata Memorial Center, 50th Anniv. A886

1991, Feb. 28 *Perf. 13½x13*
1347 A886 2r brown & buff .30 .20

River Dolphin A887

1991, Mar. 4
1348 A887 4r shown .55 .30
1349 A887 6.50r Sea cow .90 .45

Fight Against Drugs — A888

World Peace — A889

1991, Mar. 5 *Perf. 13x13½*
1350 A888 5r dp violet & red .70 .35

1991, Mar. 7 Photo. *Perf. 13x13½*
1351 A889 6.50r black & tan .90 .45

Indian Remote Sensing Satellite 1A — A890

1991, Mar. 18 *Perf. 14*
1352 A890 6.50r blue, red brn & blk .90 .45

Babu Jagjivan Ram (1908-1976), Politician — A891

1991, Apr. 5 Photo. *Perf. 13½*
1353 A891 1r yellow & brown .20 .20

Dr. B.R. Ambedkar (1891-1956), Social Reformer — A892

1991, Apr. 14 *Perf. 13½x13*
1354 A892 1r red brown & blue .20 .20

Tribal Dances A893

1991, Apr. 30 Photo. *Perf. 13½x13*
1355 A893 2.50r Valar .35 .20
1356 A893 4r Kayang .55 .30
1357 A893 5r Hozagiri .70 .35
1358 A893 6.50r Velakali .90 .45
Nos. 1355-1358 (4) 2.50 1.30

Ariyakudi Ramanuja Iyengar (1890-1967), Musician — A894

1991, May 18
1359 A894 2r green & red brown .30 .20

Karpoori Thakur (1924-1988), Politician — A895

1991, May 30 *Perf. 13x13½*
1360 A895 1r red brown .20 .20

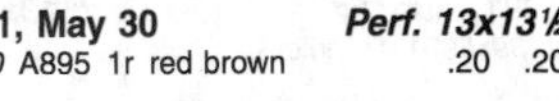

Antarctic Treaty, 30th Anniv. A896

1991, June 23 Photo. *Perf. 13½x13*
1361 A896 5r Penguins .70 .35
1362 A896 6.50r Map, penguins .90 .45
a. Pair, #1361-1362 1.60 .80

No. 1362a printed in continuous design.

New Delhi, 60th Anniv. A897

Views of New Delhi architecture.

1991, June 25
1363 A897 5r multicolored .70 .35
1364 A897 6.50r multicolored .90 .45
a. Pair, #1363-1364 1.60 .80

No. 1364a printed in continuous design.

Sri Ram Sharma Acharya (1911-1990), Social Reformer — A898

1991, June 27
1365 A898 1r red & blue green .20 .20

K. Shankar Pillai (1902-1989), Cartoonist — A899

1991, July 31 Photo. *Perf. 13½x13*
1366 A899 4r shown .55 .30

Perf. 13x13½
1367 A899 6.50r The Big Show, vert. .90 .45

Sriprakash (1890-1971), Politician — A900

1991, Aug. 3 *Perf. 13½x13*
1368 A900 2r yellow brown .30 .20

Gopinath Bardoloi (1890-1950), Politician — A901

1991, Aug. 5 *Perf. 13x13½*
1369 A901 1r violet .20 .20

Rajiv Gandhi (1944-1991), Prime Minister — A902

1991, Aug. 20 *Perf. 13*
1370 A902 1r multicolored .20 .20

Jain Muni Mishrimalji (1891-1984), Philospher — A903

1991, Aug. 24 Photo. *Perf. 13½*
1371 A903 1r brown .20 .20

Mahadevi Verma (1907-1987), Writer and Poet — A904

No. 1373: Jayshankar Prasad (1890-1937), poet and dramatist.

1991, Sept. 16
1372 A904 2r black & blue .30 .20
1373 A904 2r black & blue .30 .20
a. Pair, #1372-1373 .60 .30

37th Commonwealth Parliamentary Conference — A905

1991, Sept. 27 Photo. *Perf. 13½x13*
1374 A905 6.50r dk blue & brown .90 .45

Greetings — A906

Orchids — A907

1991, Sept. 30 *Perf. 13x13½*
1375 A906 1r Frog .20 .20
1376 A906 6.50r Bird .90 .45
a. Pair, #1375-1376 1.10 .50

1991, Oct. 12
1377 A907 1r Cymbidium aloifolium .20 .20
1378 A907 2.50r Paphiopedilum venustum .35 .20
1379 A907 3r Aerides crispum .40 .25
1380 A907 4r Cymbidium bicolour .60 .30
1381 A907 5r Vanda spathulata .70 .35
1382 A907 6.50r Cymbidium devonianum .90 .45
Nos. 1377-1382 (6) 3.15 1.75

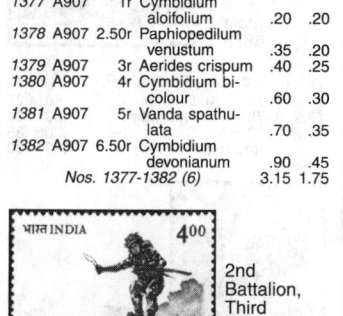

2nd Battalion, Third Gurkha Rifles A908

1991, Oct. 18 *Perf. 13½x13*
1383 A908 4r multicolored .60 .30

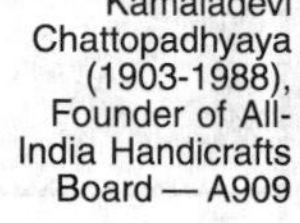

Kamaladevi Chattopadhyaya (1903-1988), Founder of All-India Handicrafts Board — A909

1991, Oct. 29 *Perf. 13x13½*
1384 A909 1r Horsemen .20 .20
1385 A909 6.50r Puppet .90 .45

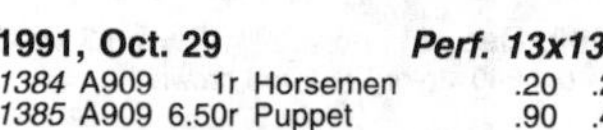

Chithira Tirunal Bala Rama Varma (1912-1991), Maharaja of Travancore — A910

1991, Nov. 7 Photo. *Perf. 13½x13*
1386 A910 2r violet .30 .20

Children's Day — A911

1991, Nov. 14 *Perf. 13x13½*
1387 A911 1r multicolored .20 .20

18th Cavalry, Sesquicentennial (in 1992) — A912

1991, Nov. 14 *Perf. 13½x13*
1388 A912 6.50r multicolored .90 .45

India Tourism Year A913

1991, Nov. 15
1389 A913 6.50r multicolored .90 .45

Intl. Conference on Youth Tourism — A914

Wolfgang Amadeus Mozart, Death Bicent. — A915

1991, Nov. 18 Photo. *Perf. 13x13½*
1390 A914 6.50r multicolored .90 .45

1991, Dec. 5
1391 A915 6.50r multicolored .90 .45

SAARC Year of Shelter A916

1991, Dec. 7 *Perf. 13½x13*
1392 A916 4r lake & bister .55 .30

Run for Your Heart A917

1991, Dec. 11
1393 A917 1r black, red & gray .20 .20

Siddhartha With An Injured Bird — A918

1991, Dec. 28 *Perf. 13x13½*
1394 A918 2r multicolored .30 .20

Asit Kumar Haldar (1890-1964), Painter

Yoga Exercises A919

1991, Dec. 30 Photo. *Perf. 13½x13*
1395 A919 2r Bhujangasana .20 .20
1396 A919 5r Dhanurasana .50 .25
1397 A919 6.50r Ustrasana .70 .35

1398 A919 10r Utthita trikonasana 1.10 .50
Nos. 1395-1398 (4) 2.50 1.30

Intl. Assoc. for Bridge and Structural Engineering A920

#1399, Hooghly River Bridge, Madurai Temple. #1400, Sanchi Stupa gates, Hall of Nations.

1992, Mar. 1 Photo. ***Perf. 13½x13***
1399 A920 2r sal, brn & blue .20 .20
1400 A920 2r sal, brn & blue .20 .20
a. Pair, #1399-1400 .40 .20

Fifth Intl. Conference on Goats — A921

Natl. Council of YMCAs, Cent. (in 1991) — A922

1992, Mar. 2 ***Perf. 13x13½***
1401 A921 6r dk blue & brown .60 .30

1992, Feb. 21
1402 A922 1r blue & vermilion .20 .20

National Archives A923

1992, Apr. 20 Photo. ***Perf. 13½x13***
1403 A923 6r multicolored .60 .30

Krushna Chandra Gajapathi — A924

Vijay Singh Pathik, Writer — A925

1992, Apr. 29 ***Perf. 13x13½***
1404 A924 1r violet .20 .20
1405 A925 1r red brown .20 .20

Adventure Sports A926

1992, Apr. 29 ***Perf. 13½x13***
1406 A926 2r Hang gliding .20 .20
1407 A926 4r Wind surfing .40 .20
1408 A926 5r River rafting .50 .25
1409 A926 11r Skiing 1.10 .55
Nos. 1406-1409 (4) 2.20 1.20

Henry Gidney (1873-1942), Physician and Politician — A927

1992, May 9 ***Perf. 13½x13***
1410 A927 1r blue & black .20 .20

Telecommunication Training Center, Jabalpur, 50th Anniv. — A928

1992, May 30
1411 A928 1r lemon .20 .20

A929

A930

1992, July 31 ***Perf. 13x13½***
1412 A929 1r black & brown .20 .20

Sardar Udham Singh (1899-1940), freedom fighter.

1992, Aug. 8
1413 A930 1r Discus .20 .20
1414 A930 6r Gymnastics .60 .30
1415 A930 8r Field hockey .80 .40
1416 A930 11r Boxing 1.10 .55
Nos. 1413-1416 (4) 2.70 1.45

1992 Summer Olympics, Barcelona.

Quit India Movement, 50th Anniv. A931

Designs: 1r, Spinning wheel, inscription. 2r, Mahatma Gandhi, inscription.

1992, Aug. 9 ***Perf. 13½x13***
1417 A931 1r pink, blk & pale pink .20 .20
1418 A931 2r gray, black & claret .20 .20

60th Parachute Field Ambulance, 50th Anniv. A932

1992, Aug. 10
1419 A932 1r multicolored .20 .20

Indian Air Force, 60th Anniv. A933

1992, Oct. 8 Photo. ***Perf. 13½x13***
1420 A933 1r shown .20 .20
1421 A933 10r Biplane, jet fighter 1.00 .50
a. Pair, #1420-1421 1.10 .55

Phad Painting of Dev Narayan A934

1992, Sept. 2 Photo. ***Perf. 13½x14***
1422 A934 5r multicolored .50 .25

Sisters of Jesus and Mary, 150th Anniv. — A935

1992, Nov. 13 Photo. ***Perf. 13x13½***
1423 A935 1r gray & blue .20 .20

Children's Day A936

1992, Nov. 14 ***Perf. 13½x13***
1424 A936 1r multicolored .20 .20

Shri Yogiji Maharaj, Religious Leader, Birth Cent. — A937

1992, Dec. 2 Photo. ***Perf. 13x13½***
1425 A937 1r blue .20 .20

Army Service Corps 1760-1992 A938

1992, Dec. 8 Photo. ***Perf. 13½x13***
1426 A938 1r multicolored .20 .20

Stephen Smith (1891-1951), Rocket Mail Pioneer — A939

1992, Dec. 19 Photo. ***Perf. 13½x13***
1427 A939 11r multicolored 1.10 .55

State of Haryana, 25th Anniv. A940

1992, Dec. 20
1428 A940 2r green & orange .20 .20

Freedom Fighter Type of 1989

Design: Madan Lal Dhingra, vert.

1992, Dec. 28 ***Perf. 13x13½***
1429 A826 1r org, grn & brn .20 .20

Dr. Shri Shiyali Ramamrita Ranganathan (1892-1972), Writer and Librarian — A941

1992, Aug. 30 Photo. ***Perf. 13½x13***
1430 A941 1r blue .20 .20

Hanuman Prasad Poddar — A942

Pandit Ravishankar Shukla — A943

1992, Sept. 19 Photo. ***Perf. 13x13½***
1431 A942 1r green .20 .20

1992, Dec. 31
1432 A943 1r rose lake .20 .20

Birds — A944

2r, Pandion haliaetus. 6r, Falco peregrinus. 8r, Gypaetus barbatus. 11r, Aquila chrysaetos.

1992, Dec. 30

1433 A944 2r multicolored .20 .20
1434 A944 6r multicolored .45 .25
1435 A944 8r multicolored .60 .30
1436 A944 11r multicolored .85 .40
Nos. 1433-1436 (4) 2.10 1.15

William Carey, Baptist Missionary to India, Bicent. of Appointment A945

1993, Jan. 9 Photo. ***Perf. 13½x13***

1437 A945 6r multicolored .50 .25

Fakir Mohan Senapati, Writer — A946

1993, Jan. 14 ***Perf. 13x13½***

1438 A946 1r orange brown .20 .20

Council of Scientific and Industrial Research, 50th Anniv. — A947

1993, Feb. 28 ***Perf. 13½x13***

1439 A947 1r violet brown .20 .20

Squadron No. 1, Indian Air Force, 60th Anniv. A948

1993, Apr. 1

1440 A948 1r shown .20 .20
1441 A948 1r Paratroopers, planes, artillery .20 .20

Parachute Field Regiment 9, 50th anniv. (#1441).

Rahul Sankrityayan (1893-1963), Politician — A949

1993, Apr. 9

1442 A949 1r multicolored .20 .20

Mountain Locomotives A950

1993, Apr. 16 ***Perf. 13½x13***

1443 A950 1r Neral Matheran .20 .20
1444 A950 6r DHR (Darjeeling) .50 .25
1445 A950 8r Nilgiri Mountain Railway .65 .30
1446 A950 11r Kalka-Simla .90 .45
Nos. 1443-1446 (4) 2.25 1.20

89th Inter-Parliamentary Union Conference, New Delhi — A951

1993, Apr. 11 Photo. ***Perf. 13x13½***

1447 A951 1r indigo .20 .20

Meerut College, Cent. (in 1992) — A952

1993, Apr. 25 ***Perf. 14***

1448 A952 1r indigo & red brown .20 .20

P.C. Mahalanobis (b. 1893), Statistician — A953

1993, June 29 ***Perf. 13x13½***

1449 A953 1r olive yellow .20 .20

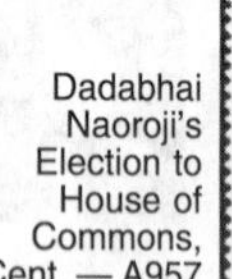

Dadabhai Naoroji's Election to House of Commons, Cent. — A957

1993, Aug. 26 Photo. ***Perf. 14***

1453 A957 6r blue & red brown .50 .25

A958

A959

1993, Sept. 11 ***Perf. 13x13½***

1454 A958 2r gray, red brn & org .20 .20

Swami Vivekananda, Chicago address, cent.

1993, Oct. 9 Photo. ***Perf. 13x13½***

Trees: 1r, Lagerstroemia speciosa. 6r, Cochlospermum religiosum. 8r, Erythrina variegata. 11r, Thespesia populnea.

1455 A959 1r multicolored .20 .20
1456 A959 6r multicolored .40 .20
1457 A959 8r multicolored .50 .25
1458 A959 11r multicolored .70 .35
Nos. 1455-1458 (4) 1.80 1.00

Dr. Dwarkanath Kotnis A960

1993, Dec. 9 Photo. ***Perf. 13½x13***

1459 A960 1r black & gray .20 .20

A961

A962

1993, Nov. 14 ***Perf. 14***

1460 A961 1r multicolored .20 .20

Children's Day.

1993, Nov. 8 ***Perf. 13x13½***

1461 A962 2r multicolored .30 .30

College of Military Engineering, Pune, 50th anniv.

A963

A964

Design: Dr. Dwarm Venkataswamy Naidu.

1993, Nov. 8

1462 A963 1r orange brown .20 .20

1993, July 31

1463 A964 2r multicolored .30 .20

Bombay Municipal Corporation Building, cent.

India Tea A965

1993, Dec. 11 ***Perf. 13***

1464 A965 6r green & red .40 .20

Papal Seminary, Pune, Cent. A966

1993, Dec. 16 ***Perf. 13½x13***

1465 A966 6r multicolored .40 .20

Natl. Integration A967

1993, Aug. 19

1466 A967 1r orange & green .20 .20

Khan Abdul Ghaffar Khan A968

1993, Aug. 9

1467 A968 1r multicolored .20 .20

Heart Care Festival A969

1993, Dec. 9

1468 A969 6.50r multicolored .40 .25

Inpex '93 — A970

1993

1469 A970 1r shown .20 .20
1470 A970 2r Boats, beach .30 .20

Issued: 1r, Dec. 25; 2r, Dec. 27.

Meghnad Saha (1893-1956), Astrophysicist A971

1993, Dec. 23 Photo. ***Perf. 13x13½***

1471 A971 1r dark blue .20 .20

Dinanath Mageshkar, Musician A972

1993, Dec. 29 ***Perf. 13½x13***

1472 A972 1r orange brown .20 .20

Nargis Dutt, Actress and Social Worker — A973

1993, Dec. 30 ***Perf. 13***

1473 A973 1r orange brown .20 .20

Indian Natl. Army, 50th Anniv. A974

1r, Netaji Subhash Bose inspecting soldiers.

1993, Dec. 31 ***Perf. 13½x13***

1474 A974 1r multicolored .20 .20

Satyendra Nath Bose (1894-1974), Mathematician and Physicist — A975

1994, Jan. 1

1475 A975 1r dark rose brown .20 .20

Satyajit Ray (1921-92) A976

6r, Scene from film, Pather Panchali.

1994, Jan. 11 ***Perf. 13***

1476 A976 6r multicolored .40 .20
1477 A976 11r multicolored .70 .35
a. Pair, #1476-1477 1.10 .55

No. 1476 is 68x30mm. No. 1477a is a continuous design.

Dr. Sampurnanand — A977

1994, Jan. 10 Photo. ***Perf. 13½x13***

1478 A977 1r multicolored .20 .20

Dr. Shanti Swarup Bhatnagar A978

1994, Feb. 21

1479 A978 1r dark blue .20 .20

Eighth Triennale A979

1994, Mar. 14

1480 A979 6r multicolored .40 .20

Prajapita Brahma (1876-1969), Religious Leader — A980

1994, Mar. 7 Photo. ***Perf. 13½x13***

1481 A980 1r multicolored .20 .20

Sanchi Stupa A981

Wmk. 324

1994, Apr. 4 Photo. ***Perf. 13***

1482 A981 5r blue green & brn .30 .20

ILO, 75th Anniv. A982

1994, May 1 Unwmk. ***Perf. 13½x13***

1483 A982 6r multicolored .40 .20

United Planters Assoc. of Southern India, Cent. — A983

1994, Mar. 26 Photo. ***Perf. 13x13½***

1484 A983 2r multicolored .20 .20

Rani Rashmoni (1793-1861), Philanthropist — A984

1994, Apr. 9 ***Perf. 13½x13***

1485 A984 1r brown .20 .20

Jallianwala Bagh Martyrdom, 75th Anniv. A985

1994, Apr. 13

1486 A985 1r red & black .20 .20

Freedom Fighters Type of 1988

1r, Chandra Singh Garhwali (1891-1979).

1994, Apr. 23

1487 A826 1r org, sage grn & grn .20 .20

IPTA A986

Small Families A987

1994, May 25 ***Perf. 13***

1488 A986 2r multi .20 .20

1994 ***Perf. 13x12½***

1r, Family of 3 in front of house.

1489 A987 75c red brn & brn .20 .20
1490 A987 1r green & rose .20 .20

4th Battalion Madras Regiment, Bicent. — A988

1994, Aug. 12

1491 A988 6.50r multicolored .45 .45

Institute of Mental Health, Madras, Bicent. A989

1994, Sept. 23 Photo. ***Perf. 13½x13***

1492 A989 2r multicolored .20 .20

Mahatma Gandhi (1869-1948) A990

Design: 11r, Flag colors, Gandhi walking and at spinning wheel.

1994, Oct. 2 ***Perf. 13***

1493 A990 6r multicolored .40 .40
1494 A990 11r multicolored .70 .70
a. Pair, #1493-1494 1.10 1.10

No. 1494 is 68x30mm.

16th Intl. Cancer Congress — A991

1994, Oct. 30 Photo. ***Perf. 13½***

1495 A991 6r multicolored .40 .40

World Conference on Human Resource Development — A992

1994, Nov. 8 ***Perf. 13½x13***

1496 A992 6r multicolored .40 .40

Intl. Year of the Family — A993

1994, Nov. 20 ***Perf. 13x12½***

1497 A993 2r multicolored .20 .20

Children's Day A994

1994, Nov. 14 ***Perf. 13½x13***

1498 A994 1r multicolored .20 .20

J.R.D. Tata (1904-93) — A995

1994, Nov. 29 ***Perf. 14***

1499 A995 2r multicolored .20 .20

Calcutta School for the Blind, Cent. A996

1994 Nov. 30 ***Perf. 13½x13***

1500 A996 2r brown & carmine .20 .20

Endangered Waterbirds - A996A

Designs: 1r, Andaman teal. 6r, Eastern white stork. 8r, Black-necked crane. 11r, Pink-headed duck.

1994, Nov. 23 ***Perf. 13***
1501 A996A 1r multicolored 2.00 2.00
1502 A996A 6r multicolored 3.00 3.00
1503 A996A 8r multicolored 3.50 3.50
1504 A996A 11r multicolored 4.50 4.50
a. Block of 4, #1501-1504 13.00 13.00

This set was withdrawn shortly after issue, when it was discovered that it was printed with water soluble ink.

Begum Akhtar - A996B

1994, Dec 2 ***Perf. 13x13½***
1504B A996B 2r multicolored 1.75 .75

No. 1504B was withdrawn shortly after issue, when it was discovered that it was printed with water soluble ink.

Remount Veterinary Corps, 215th Anniv. — A998

1994, Dec. 14 Photo. ***Perf. 13x13½***
1505 A998 6r multicolored .40 .40

College of Engineering, Guindy, Madras, Bicent. — A999

1994, Dec. 19 ***Perf. 14***
1506 A999 2r multicolored .20 .20

Baroda Museum, Vadodara — A1000

Designs: 6r, Ancient artifact. 11r, Ancient artifact, man standing on pedestal.

1994, Dec. 20 ***Perf. 14x13½***
1507 6r black & bister .40 .40
1508 11r black & bister .75 .75
a. A1000 Pair, #1507-1508 1.25 1.25

Khuda Bakhsh Oriental Public Library A1001

1994, Nov. 21 Photo. ***Perf. 14***
1509 A1001 6r multicolored .40 .40

A1002

A1003

1995, Jan. 9 Photo. ***Perf. 13x13½***
1510 A1002 1r Chhoturam .20 .20

1995, Jan. 7
1511 A1003 6r multicolored .20 .20

India Natl. Science Academy, 30th Anniv.

St. Xavier's College, Bombay, 125th Anniv. A1005

1994, Dec. 4 Photo. ***Perf. 13½***
1513 A1005 2r multicolored .20 .20

General Post Office, Bombay, Bicent. — A1006

Illustration reduced.

1994, Dec. 28 Litho. ***Perf. 13½***
1514 A1006 6r multicolored .40 .40

Motion Pictures, Cent. A1007

Designs: 6r, Colored film, world map. 11r, Early camera, black & white film.

1995, Jan. 11 Litho. ***Perf. 13***
1515 A1007 6r multicolored .40 .40
1516 A1007 11r multicolored .75 .75
a. Pair, #1515-1516 1.25 1.25

Oil Conservation A1008

Rafi Ahmed Kidwai A1009

1995, Feb. 18 Photo. ***Perf. 13***
1517 A1008 1r red brown & black .20 .20

1995, Feb. 18
1518 A1009 1r red brown .20 .20

K. L. Saigal A1010

1995, Apr. 4 Photo. ***Perf. 13½x13***
1519 A1010 5r black & brown .30 .30

A1011

A1012

1995, Jan. 5 Photo. ***Perf. 13***
1520 A1011 2r King Rajaraja Chola .20 .20

8th Intl. Conference of Tamil Studies.

1995, Jan. 12 Photo. ***Perf. 13½x13***
1521 A1012 2r multicolored .20 .20

SAARC Youth Year.

A1013

A1014

1995, Jan. 15
1522 A1013 2r multicolored .20 .20

Prithvi Theater, 50th anniv.

1995, Jan. 15

Field Marshall K.M. Cariappa (1900-93).

1523 A1014 2r multicolored .20 .20

A1015

A1017

1995, Jan. 18
1524 A1015 2r multicolored .20 .20

Tex-Styles India '95, National Textile Fair, Bombay.

1995, June 6 Photo. ***Perf. 13***

UN, 50th Anniv.: 6r, Planting seedling, mother and child, child reading.

1526 A1017 1r multicolored .20 .20
1527 A1017 6r multicolored .40 .40

R.S. Ruikar — A1018

Bharti Bhavan Library, Allahabad A1019

1995, May 1 Photo. ***Perf. 13½***
1528 A1018 1r brown violet .20 .20

1995, Aug. 30 ***Perf. 14***
1529 A1019 6r multicolored .35 .35

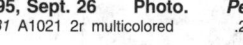

Asian Pacific Postal Training Center, Bangkok, 25th Anniv. A1020

1995, Sept. 4 Litho. ***Perf. 13½x13***
1530 A1020 10r multicolored .60 .60

Headquarters Delhi Area — A1021

1995, Sept. 26 Photo. ***Perf. 13***
1531 A1021 2r multicolored .20 .20

Louis Pasteur (1822-95) A1022

1995, Sept. 28
1532 A1022 5r pale yel & black .30 .30

La Martiniere College, Lucknow, 150th Anniv. A1023

1995, Oct. 1
1533 A1023 2r multicolored .20 .20

Mahatma Gandhi (1869-1948) — A1024

1995, Oct. 2
1534 1r As young man .20 .20
1535 2r As older man .20 .20
a. A1024 Pair, #1534-1535 .20 .20
b. Souvenir sheet, #1535a .20 .20

See South Africa Nos. 918-919.

FAO, 50th Anniv. A1025

1995, Oct. 16 ***Perf. 13½***
1536 A1025 5r multicolored .30 .30

A1026

1995, Oct. 30 ***Perf. 13***
1537 A1026 1r carmine .20 .20

P.M. Thevar (1908-63), politician.

A1027

1995, Nov. 8 Photo. ***Perf. 13x13½***
1538 A1027 6r multicolored .40 .40

Wilhelm Roentgen (1845-1923), discovery of the X-Ray, cent.

JAT Regiment, Bicent. A1028

1995, Nov. 20 ***Perf. 13***
1539 A1028 5r multicolored .35 .35

Radio Communication, Cent. — A1029

1995, May 17 Litho. ***Perf. 13½x13***
1540 A1029 5r multicolored .30 .30

Dehli Development Authority — A1030

1995, May 23
1541 A1030 2r multicolored .20 .20

Children's Day — A1031

1995, Nov. 14 Photo. ***Perf. 13x13½***
1542 A1031 1r multicolored .20 .20

Rajputana Rifles, 175th Anniv. A1032

1995, Nov. 28 ***Perf. 13½***
1543 A1032 5r multicolored .35 .35

Communal Harmony — A1033

1995, Nov. 19 Photo. ***Perf. 13***
1544 A1033 2r multicolored .35 .35

Sant Tukdoji Maharaj, Patriot, Social Worker A1034

1995, Dec. 10
1545 A1034 1r brown .20 .20

Dated 1993.

A1035

A1036

Design: Yellapragada Subbarow (1895-1948), biochemist.

1995, Dec. 19
1546 A1035 1r yellow brown .20 .20

1995, Dec. 25

Giani Zail Singh (1916-94), Pres. of India.

1547 A1036 1r multicolored .20 .20

Dome Barelvi's Mausoleum, Dargah — A1037

1995, Dec. 31 **Litho.**
1548 A1037 1r multicolored .20 .20

Ala Hazrat Barelvi (1856-1921), poet.

Cricket Players — A1038

1996, Mar. 13 Photo. ***Perf. 14***
1549 A1038 2r Deodhar .20 .20
1550 A1038 2r Vijay Merchant .20 .20
1551 A1038 2r Vinoo Mankad .20 .20
1552 A1038 2r C.K. Nayudu .20 .20
Nos. 1549-1552 (4) .80 .80

Dated 1995.

Homi Bhabha and Tata Institute of Fundamental Research — A1039

1996, Feb. 9 Photo. ***Perf. 13***
1553 A1039 2r multicolored .20 .20

Kasturba Trust — A1040

Cardiac Surgery, Cent. — A1041

1996, Feb. 22
1554 A1040 1r multicolored .20 .20

1996, Feb. 25 **Litho.**
1555 A1041 5r multicolored .30 .30

Miniature Paintings A1042

#1556, Two women picking berries from trees. #1557, Woman, man embracing. #1558, Women looking upward, men, animals. #1559, Ceremony, black clouds.

1996, Mar. 13 ***Perf. 13½***
1556 A1042 5r multicolored .30 .30
1557 A1042 5r multicolored .30 .30
1558 A1042 5r multicolored .30 .30
1559 A1042 5r multicolored .30 .30
Nos. 1556-1559 (4) 1.20 1.20

Pt. Kunjilal Dubey — A1043

1996, Mar. 18 Photo. ***Perf. 13***
1560 A1043 1r brown .20 .20

Himalayan Wildlife A1044

#1561, Saussurea simpsoniana. #1562, Capra falconeri. #1563, Ithaginis cruentus. #1564, Meconopsis horridula.

1996, May 10 **Litho.**
1561 A1044 5r multicolored .30 .30
1562 A1044 5r multicolored .30 .30
1563 A1044 5r multicolored .30 .30
1564 A1044 5r multicolored .30 .30
a. Souv. sheet of 4, #1561-1564 3.50 3.50
Nos. 1561-1564 (4) 1.20 1.20

No. 1564a sold for 30r. Stamps in No. 1564a do not have "1996."

Morarji Desai — A1045

1996, Apr. 10 Photo. ***Perf. 13x13½***
1565 A1045 1r carmine .20 .20

SKCG College A1047

1996, May 25 **Photo.**
1567 A1047 1r lt brn & dk brn .20 .20

Muhammad Ismail Sahib — A1048

1996 Summer Olympic Games, Atlanta — A1049

1996, June 5 ***Perf. 13x13½***

1568 A1048 1r claret .20 .20

1996, June 25

1569 A1049 5r Olympic stadium .30 .30
1570 A1049 5r Torch .30 .30

A1050

A1051

1996, July 19 ***Perf. 13x13½***

1571 A1050 1r blue & black .20 .20

Sister Alphonsa (1910-46).

1996, Aug. 2 **Litho.** ***Perf. 14***

1572 A1051 5r multicolored .30 .30

VSNL, 125th anniv.

A1052 A1053

1r, Chembai Vaidyanatha Bhagavathar. 2r, Ahilyabai Holkar.

1996 **Photo.** ***Perf. 13x13½***

1573 A1052 1r dk bl grn & brn .20 .20
1574 A1052 2r rose brn & lt brn .20 .20

Issued: 1r, 8/28; 2r, 8/25.

1996, Aug. 4 **Photo.** ***Perf. 13***

1575 A1053 1r Sir Pherozsha Mehta .20 .20

Poultry Production A1054

1996, Sept. 2

1576 A1054 5r Gallus gallus .30 .30

Rani Gaidinliu — A1055

1996, Sept. 12

1577 A1055 1r dark blue green .20 .20

Barrister Nath Pai — A1056

1996, Sept. 25

1578 A1056 1r blue .20 .20

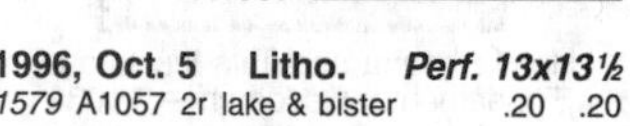

Indepex '97 World Philatelic Exhibition A1057

1996, Oct. 5 **Litho.** ***Perf. 13x13½***

1579 A1057 2r lake & bister .20 .20

Children's Day A1058

1996, Nov. 14 **Photo.** ***Perf. 13½x13***

1580 A1058 8r multicolored .50 .50

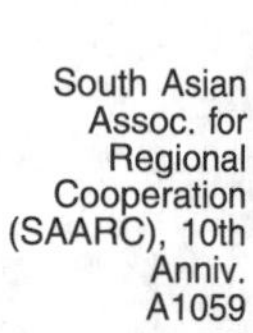

South Asian Assoc. for Regional Cooperation (SAARC), 10th Anniv. A1059

1996, Dec. 8 ***Perf. 13***

1581 A1059 11r multicolored .60 .60

Abai Konunbaev (1845-1904), Poet — A1060

2nd Intl. Crop Science Congress A1061

1996, Dec. 9 ***Perf. 13x13½***

1582 A1060 5r red brown & lake .40 .40

Dated 1995.

1996, Nov. 17 ***Perf. 13***

1583 A1061 2r multicolored .20 .20

Sikh Regiment, 150th Anniv. A1062

1996, Oct. 19

1584 A1062 5r multicolored .40 .40

Natl. Rail Museum, 25th Anniv. — A1063

1996, Oct. 7 **Litho.** ***Perf. 13½***

1585 A1063 5r multicolored .40 .40

Jananayak Debeswar Sarmah (1896-1993), Politician — A1064

1996, Oct. 10

1586 A1064 2r lt brn & red brn .20 .20

Dr. Salim Ali, Birth Cent. — A1065

1996, Nov. 12 **Photo.** ***Perf. 13***

1587 8r Dr. Salim Ali .50 .50
1588 11r Water fowl .60 .60
a. A1065 Pair, #1587-1588 1.10 1.10

Second Battalion, The Grenadiers, Bicent. A1066

1996, Dec. 4 ***Perf. 14***

1589 A1066 5r multicolored .40 .40

Vijay Divas A1067

1996, Dec. 16

1590 A1067 2r multicolored .20 .20

Vivekananda Rock Memorial, Kanyakumari — A1068

Illustration reduced.

1996, Dec. 26 **Litho.** ***Perf. 13***

1591 A1068 5r multicolored .30 .30

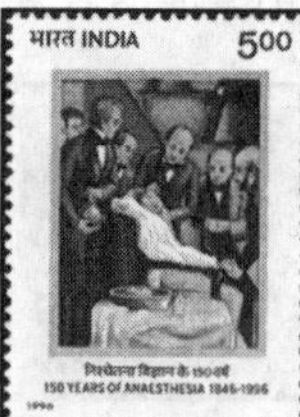

Use of Anesthesia, 150th Anniv. — A1069

1996, Dec. 27 ***Perf. 13***

1592 A1069 5r multicolored .40 .40

University of Roorkee, 150th Anniv. A1070

1997, Jan. 1 **Photo.** ***Perf. 13***

1593 A1070 8r multicolored .45 .45

Vrindavan Lal Verma, Writer — A1071

1997, Jan. 9 **Photo.** ***Perf. 13x13½***

1594 A1071 2r red .20 .20

Army Postal Service Corps. (APS), 25th Anniv. A1072

1997, Jan. 22 ***Perf. 13½x13***

1595 A1072 5r multicolored .40 .40

Jose Marti (1853-95), Cuban Revolutionary A1073

1997, Jan. 28 ***Perf. 13x13½***
1596 A1073 11r multicolored .60 .60

Inter-Parliamentary Specialized Conference, New Dehli — A1074

1997, Feb. 15 **Photo.** ***Perf. 13***
1597 A1074 5r multicolored .30 .30

A1075

1997, Mar. 4 **Photo.** ***Perf. 13***
1598 A1075 1r lt brn & dk brn .20 .20

Shyam Lal Gupt (b. 1896), composer of song on natl. flag.

A1076

1997, Mar. 8 ***Perf. 13x13½***
1599 5r Parijat Tree .30 .30
1600 6r Branch, flower .35 .35
a. A1076 Pair, #1599-1600 .65 .65

Rashtriya Indian Military College, Dehra Dun, 75th Anniv. A1077

1997, Mar. 13 ***Perf. 13½***
1601 A1077 2r multicolored .20 .20

Netaji Subhas Chandra Bose (1897-1945), Nationalist Leader — A1078

1997, Jan. 23 ***Perf. 13***
1602 A1078 1r dk brn & lt brn .20 .20

A1079

1997, Feb. 25 **Photo.** ***Perf. 13x13½***
1603 A1079 8r St. Andrews Church .45 .45

Morarji Desai, Prime Minister, 1977-79 — A1080

1997, Feb. 28 **Photo.** ***Perf. 13***
1604 A1080 1r brown & buff .20 .20

Saint Dnyaneshwar (1274-95), Poet — A1081

1997, Mar. 5 **Photo.** ***Perf. 13***
1605 A1081 5r multicolored .30 .30

Ram Manohar Lohia (1910-67), Politician — A1082

1997, Mar. 23 **Litho.** ***Perf. 13x13½***
1606 A1082 1r multicolored .20 .20

CENTIPEX '97 — A1083

1997, Mar. 27

Philatelic Society of India, Cent.: No. 1608, #1, Front cover of "The Philatelic Journal of India," 1897.

1607 2r multicolored .20 .20
1608 2r multicolored .20 .20
a. Pair, #1607-1608 .25 .25

Jnanpith Award Winners — A1084

K.V. Puttappa, D.R. Bendre, Prof. V.K. Gokak, Dr. Masti V. Iyengar, writers.

1997, Mar. 28 **Photo.** ***Perf. 13***
1609 A1084 2r multi .20 .20

Madhu Limaye (1922-95), Politician — A1085

1997, May 1
1610 A1085 2r green .20 .20

A1086

A1087

1997, June 24 **Photo.** ***Perf. 13x13½***
1611 A1086 2r Pandit Omkarnath Thakar .20 .20

1997, Aug. 6 **Photo.** ***Perf. 13***
1612 A1087 2r brown .20 .20

Thirumathi Rukmini Lakshmipathi (1892-1951), reformer.

Independence, 50th Anniv. — A1088

Officers from Indian Natl. Army, Shah Nawaz Khan, G.S. Dhillon, P.K. Sahgal.

1997, Aug. 15
1613 A1088 2r multicolored .20 .20

Newspaper Swantantra Bharat, 50th Anniv. A1089

1997, Aug. 15 ***Perf. 13½x13***
1614 A1089 2r multicolored .20 .20

A1090

A1091

1997, Aug. 20 ***Perf. 13***
1615 A1090 2r black & gray .20 .20

Sir Ronald Ross (1857-1932), physician, medical researcher.

1997, Sept. 6
1616 A1091 5r red brown .30 .30

Swami Bhaktivedanta (b. 1896), humanitarian.

A1092

A1093

1997, Sept. 14
1617 A1092 2r black & gray .20 .20

Swami Brahmanand (1894-1984), social reformer.

1997, Aug. 8
1618 A1093 2r Sri Basaveswara .20 .20

Maratha Parachute Regiment, Bicent. A1094

1997, Sept. 7 ***Perf. 13½x13***
1619 A1094 2r multicolored .20 .20

Hazari Prasad Dwivedi — A1095

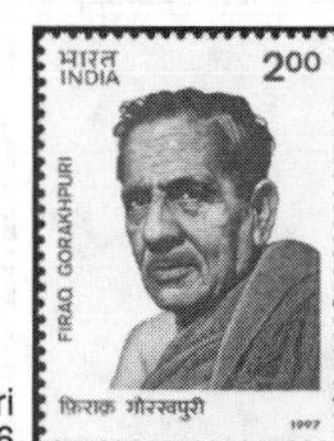

Firaq Gorakhpuri A1096

1997, Dec. 13 Photo. ***Perf. 13x13½***

1620	A1095	2r gray brown	.20	.20

1997, Aug. 28

1621	A1096	2r brown	.20	.20

Fossil Plants — A1097

Sir William Jones, 250th Birth Anniv. — A1098

No. 1622, Birbalsahnia divyadarshanii. No. 1623, Glossopteris. 6r, Pentoxylon. 10r, Williamsonia sewardiana.

1997, Sept. 11

1622	A1097	2r multicolored	.20	.20
1623	A1097	2r multicolored	.20	.20
1624	A1097	6r multicolored	.35	.35
1625	A1097	10r multicolored	.60	.60
		Nos. 1622-1625 (4)	1.35	1.35

1997, Sept. 28

1626	A1098	4r multicolored	.25	.25

Lawrence School, Sanawar, 150th Anniv. A1099

1997, Oct. 4 ***Perf. 13½x13***

1627	A1099	2r multicolored	.20	.20

Indepex '97 A1100

1997, June 6 Photo. ***Perf. 13½x13***

1628	A1100	2r Nalanda	.20	.20
1629	A1100	6r Bodhgaya	.30	.30
1630	A1100	10r Vaishali	.45	.45
1631	A1100	11r Kushinagar	.50	.50
a.		Block of 4, #1628-1631	1.40	1.40

66th General Assembly Session of Interpol, 1997 A1101

1997, Oct. 15 ***Perf. 13½***

1632	A1101	4r multicolored	.20	.20

V.K. Krishna Menon — A1102

1997, Oct. 6 ***Perf. 13***

1633	A1102	2r brown carmine	.20	.20

Indepex '97 World Philatelic Exhibition A1103

Rural Indian women.

1997, Oct. 15 Photo. ***Perf. 13x13½***

1634	A1103	2r Arunachal Pradesh	.20	.20
1635	A1103	6r Gujarat	.40	.40
1636	A1103	10r Ladakh	.60	.60
1637	A1103	11r Kerala	.65	.65
a.		Block of 4, #1634-1637	1.75	1.75

Scindia School, Cent. — A1104

Designs: No. 1638, Outdoor class. No. 1639, Founder, school building, aerial view.

1997, Oct. 20 ***Perf. 14***

1638		5r multicolored	.30	.30
1639		5r multicolored	.30	.30
a.	A1104	Pair, #1638-1639	.60	.60

Medicinal Plants A1105

2r, Ocimum sanctum. 5r, Curcuma longa. 10r, Rauvolfia serpentina. 11r, Aloe barbadensis.

1997, Oct. 28

1640	A1105	2r multicolored	.20	.20
1641	A1105	5r multicolored	.30	.30
1642	A1105	10r multicolored	.60	.60
1643	A1105	11r multicolored	.65	.65
a.		Block of 4, #1640-1643	1.75	1.75

A1106

A1107

1997, July 2 Litho. ***Perf. 13x13½***

1644	A1106	2r brown & sepia	.20	.20

Ram Sewak Yadav (1926-74), politician, social reformer.

1997, July 11

1645	A1107	2r multicolored	.20	.20

Sibnath Banerjee (1897-1982), politician, union leader.

Indepex '97 A1110

Indian beaches: 2r, Gopalpur on Sea, Orissa. 6r, Kovalam Beach, Thiruvananthapuram. 10r, Anjuna Beach, Goa. 11r, Bogmalo Beach, Goa.

1997, Aug. 11 Photo. ***Perf. 13½x13***

1648	A1110	2r multicolored	.20	.20
1649	A1110	6r multicolored	.40	.40
1650	A1110	10r multicolored	.60	.60
1651	A1110	11r multicolored	.65	.65
		Nos. 1648-1651 (4)	1.85	1.85

Sant Kavi Sunderdas (1596-1689) A1111

Kotamaraju Rama Rao — A1112

1997, Nov. 8 Photo. ***Perf. 13x13½***

1652	A1111	2r lt brn & dk brn	.20	.20

1997, Nov. 9

1653	A1112	2r dk brn & yel brn	.20	.20

Children's Day A1113

1997, Nov. 14 ***Perf. 13½x13***

1654	A1113	2r Nehru with child	.20	.20

A1114

A1115

1997, Nov. 23 Photo. ***Perf. 13***

1655	A1114	4r multicolored	.20	.20

World Convention on Reverence for All Life.

1997, Dec. 15 Photo. ***Perf. 13x13½***

1656	A1115	2r dk brn & lt brn	.20	.20

Sardar Vallabhbhai Patel (1875-1950), politician.

Indepex '97 A1116

Designs: 2r, Post Office Heritage Building. 6r, Indian River Mail. 10r, Cancellations, Jal Cooper. 11r, Mail ship, SS Hindosthan.

1997, Dec, 15 Photo. ***Perf. 13½x13***

1657	A1116	2r multicolored	.20	.20
1657A	A1116	6r multicolored	.30	.30
1657B	A1116	10r multicolored	.50	.50
1657C	A1116	11r multicolored	.55	.55
d.		Block of 4, #1657-1657C	1.50	1.50

Souvenir Sheet

Mother Teresa (1910-97) — A1117

Illustration reduced.

1997, Dec. 15 Litho. ***Perf. 13x13½***

1658	A1117	45r multicolored	2.75	2.75

Indian Armed Forces, 50th Anniv. A1118

1997, Dec. 16 Photo. ***Perf. 13½x13***

1659	A1118	2r multicolored	.20	.20

Dr. B. Pattabhi Sitaramayya (1880-1959), Author, Politician — A1119

1997, Dec. 17 ***Perf. 13x13½***

1660	A1119	2r dk brn & lt brn	.20	.20

Fr. Jerome D'Souza (1897-1977) A1120

1997, Dec. 18 ***Perf. 13½x13***
1661 A1120 2r red brown .20 .20

Ashfaquallah Khan and Ram Prasad Bismil, Revolutionaries A1121

1997, Dec. 19 ***Perf. 13***
1662 A1121 2r dk brn & brn .20 .20

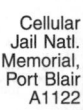

Cellular Jail Natl. Memorial, Port Blair A1122

1997, Dec. 30
1663 A1122 2r multicolored .20 .20

A1123

1998, Jan. 2
1664 A1123 2r red brown .20 .20

Nanak Singh (1897-1971), novelist.

A1124

1998, Jan. 9
1665 A1124 2r plum .20 .20

Nahar Singh, minor leader of Great Mutiny.

Rotary Intl., 1998 Council on Legislation, New Delhi A1125

1998, Jan. 12 ***Perf. 13½X13***
1666 A1125 8r multicolored .50 .50

A1126

A1127

#1667, Maharana Pratap (1540-97), ruler, warrior. #1668, Vishnu S. Khandekar (b. 1898), writer.

1998, Jan. 19 ***Perf. 13x13½***
1667 A1126 2r violet brown .20 .20
1668 A1127 2r rose red & dull red .20 .20

A1128 A1129

1998, Jan. 25
1669 A1128 10r multicolored .60 .60

Bharat Paryatan Diwas (India Tourism Day).

1998, Jan. 2 ***Perf. 13½x13***
1670 A1129 4r multicolored .25 .25

11th Gurkha Rifles, 50th anniv.

A1130

Mahatma Gandhi, 50th Anniv. of Death: 2r, Peasants' welfare. 6r, Social upliftment. 10r, Salt Satyagraha. 11r, Communal harmony.

1998, Jan. 30 **Photo.** ***Perf. 14***
1671 A1130 2r multicolored .20 .20
1672 A1130 6r multicolored .40 .40
1673 A1130 10r multicolored .60 .60
1674 A1130 11r multicolored .65 .65
a. Block of 4, #1671-1674 1.75 1.75

A1131

1998, Mar. 8 **Photo.** ***Perf. 13x13½***
1675 A1131 6r multicolored .40 .40

Universal Declaration of Human Rights, 50th anniv.

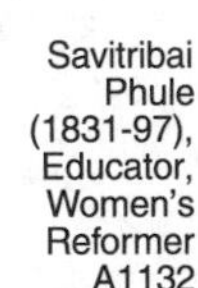

Savitribai Phule (1831-97), Educator, Women's Reformer A1132

1998, Mar. 10 ***Perf. 13½x13***
1676 A1132 2r dk brn & lt brn .20 .20

Jagdish Chandra Jain A1133

1998, Jan. 28 **Photo.** ***Perf. 13x13½***
1677 A1133 2r red brown .20 .20

Syed Ahmad Khan (1817-98), Writer — A1134

Sardar A. Vedaratnam A1135

1998, Mar. 27
1678 A1134 2r brn & olive brn .20 .20

1998, Feb. 25
1679 A1135 2r violet black .20 .20

Global Environment Facility First Assembly Meeting — A1136

1998, Apr. 1 ***Perf. 13***
1680 A1136 11r multicolored .55 .55

A1137

A1138

1998, Apr. 16 **Photo.** ***Perf. 14***
1681 A1137 6r carmine .35 .35

Defense Services Staff College.

1998, May 3 **Photo.** ***Perf. 13***

Design: Pres. Zakir Husain (1897-1969).

1682 A1138 2r sepia .20 .20

A1139 A1140

Jnanpith Literary Award winners, year: Shri Bishnu Dey (1909-82), 1971; Shri Tarashankar Bandopadhyay (1898-1971), 1966; Smt. Ashapurna Devi (1909-95), 1976.

1998, June 5
1683 A1139 2r olive brown .20 .20

1998, June 8 **Photo.** ***Perf. 13***

Designs: 5r, Parliament Clock Tower, London. 6r, Airplane, mascot, Gateway of India, Bombay.

1684 A1140 5r multicolored .30 .30

Size: 56x35mm

1685 A1140 6r multicolored .35 .35
a. Pair, #1684-1685 .55 .55

Air India's 1st intl. flight, 50th anniv.

A1141

A1142

Design: Salem C. Vijiaraghavachariar (1852-1944), freedom fighter.

1998, June 18
1686 A1141 2r red brown .20 .20

1998, May 1
1687 A1142 2r N.G. Goray .20 .20

Sri Ramana Maharshi A1143

1998, Apr. 14
1688 A1143 2r violet black .20 .20

Konkan Railway — A1143a

Illustration reduced.

1998, May 1 **Photo.** ***Perf. 13***
1689 A1143a 8r multicolored .50 .50

A1144

A1145

Mohammed Abdurahiman Shahib.

1998, May 15
1690 A1144 2r red brown .20 .20

1998, May 21 Photo. *Perf. 14*
1691 A1145 2r brown & sepia .20 .20

Lokanayak Omeo Kumar Das, freedom fighter.

Revolutionaries — A1146

Design: Satyendra Chandra Bardhan, Vakkom Abdul Khader, Fouja Singh.

1998, May 25 *Perf. 13*
1692 A1146 2r brn & red brn .20 .20

Natl. Savings Organization, 50th Anniv. — A1147

Design: 6r, Hand dropping coin into bank.

1998, June 30
1693 A1147 5r multicolored .25 .25
1694 A1147 6r multicolored .30 .30
a. Pair, #1693-1694 .55 .55

Bhagwan Gopinathji, Spiritual Leader, Birth Cent. — A1148

1998, July 3 *Perf. 13½*
1695 A1148 3r brown & sepia .20 .20

Ardeshir (1868-1926) & Pirojsha (1882-1972) Godrej, Environmentalists — A1149

1998, July 11 *Perf. 13*
1696 A1149 3r green .20 .20

Aruna Asaf Ali, Revolutionay A1150

1998, July 16
1697 A1150 3r brown .20 .20

Vidyasagar College, 125th Anniv. A1151

1998, July 29
1698 A1151 2r dark gray .20 .20

Shivpujan Sahai (1893-1963), Writer — A1152

1998, Aug. 9 Photo. *Perf. 13*
1699 A1152 2r brown .20 .20

Homage to Martyrs A1153

Designs: 3r, Minaret, silhouettes of soldiers standing in fort, flag of India. 8r, Symbols of industrial, scientific and technological developments.

1998, Aug. 15 *Perf. 14*
1700 A1153 3r multicolored .20 .20
1701 A1153 8r multicolored .40 .40
a. Pair, #1700-1701 .55 .55

Gostha Behari Paul (1896-1976), Soccer Player — A1154

1998, Aug. 20 *Perf. 13*
1702 A1154 3r sepia .20 .20

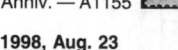

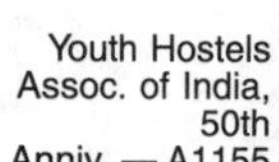
Youth Hostels Assoc. of India, 50th Anniv. — A1155

1998, Aug. 23 *Perf. 14*
1703 A1155 5r multicolored .25 .25

Brigade of the Guards, Fourth Battalion, Bicent. A1156

1998, Sept. 15 Photo. *Perf. 13½*
1704 A1156 6r multicolored .30 .30

Bhai Kanhaiyaji A1157

1998, Sept. 18 *Perf. 13*
1705 A1157 2r red .20 .20

20th Intl. Congress of Radiology A1158

1998, Sept. 18 *Perf. 13½x13*
1706 A1158 8r multicolored .40 .40

28th IBBY Congress A1159

1998, Sept. 20 *Perf. 13*
1707 A1159 11r multicolored .55 .55

Dr. Tristao Braganza Cunha — A1160

1998, Sept. 26
1708 A1160 3r dark brown .20 .20

Jananeta Hijam Irawat Singh — A1161

1998, Sept. 30
1709 A1161 3r brown .20 .20

Acharya Tulsi (1914-97) A1162

1998, Oct. 20 Photo. *Perf. 13½x13*
1710 A1162 3r brown & orange .20 .20

Indian Women in Aviation A1163

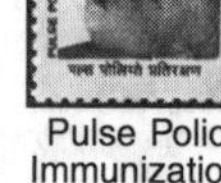
Pulse Polio Immunization A1164

1998, Oct. 15 *Perf. 13*
1711 A1163 8r blue .40 .40

1998, Sept. 21
1712 A1164 3r maroon .20 .20

2nd Battalion of the Rajput Regiment (Kalichindi), Bicent. — A1165

1998, Nov. 30
1713 A1165 3r multicolored .20 .20

David Sassoon Library & Reading Room, Mumbai — A1166

1998, Nov. 30
1714 A1166 3r lt blue & dk blue .20 .20

Army Postal Service Center, Kamptee, 50th Anniv. A1167

1998, Dec. 2
1715 A1167 3r multicolored .20 .20

Connemara Public Library, Chennai A1168

1998, Dec. 5 ***Perf. 13½x13***
1716 A1168 3r bister & brown .20 .20

A1169

A1170

1998, Dec. 10 **Litho.** ***Perf. 13½***
1717 A1169 3r multicolored .20 .20

Indian Pharmaceutical Cong. Assoc., 50th anniv.

1998, Dec. 12 **Photo.** ***Perf. 13***

Design: Baba Raghv Das (1896-1958), reformer, freedom fighter.

1718 A1170 2r deep gray violet .20 .20

Indra Lal Roy (1898-1918), World War I Pilot — A1171

1998, Dec. 19
1719 A1171 3r multicolored .20 .20

Sant Gadge Baba (1876-1956), Religious Philosopher — A1172

1998, Dec. 20
1720 A1172 3r multicolored .20 .20

Traditional Musical Instruments A1173

Designs: 2r, Rudra veena (stringed instrument). 6r, Flute (wind insrument). 8r, Pakhawaj (percussion instrument). 10r, Sarod (stringed instrument).

1998, Dec. 29
1721 A1173 2r multicolored .20 .20
1722 A1173 6r multicolored .30 .30
1723 A1173 8r multicolored .40 .40
1724 A1173 10r multicolored .50 .50
Nos. 1721-1724 (4) 1.40 1.40

Children's Day A1174

1998, Nov. 14 **Photo.** ***Perf. 13½***
1725 A1174 3r multicolored .20 .20

INS Delhi A1175

1998, Nov. 15
1726 A1175 3r multicolored .20 .20

President's Bodyguard A1176

1998, Nov. 16
1727 A1176 3r multicolored .20 .20

Shells A1177

Designs: No. 1728, Cypraea staphylaea. No. 1729, Cassis cornuta. No. 1730, Chicoreus brunneus. 11r, Lambis lambis.

1998, Dec. 30
1728 A1177 3r multicolored .20 .20
1729 A1177 3r multicolored .20 .20
1730 A1177 3r multicolored .20 .20
1731 A1177 11r multicolored .60 .60
Nos. 1728-1731 (4) 1.20 1.20

Indian Police Service, 50th Anniv. A1178

1999, Jan. 13 **Litho.** ***Perf. 13½x13¼***
1732 A1178 3r multicolored .20 .20

Defense Research & Development Organization — A1179

1999, Jan. 26 **Photo.** ***Perf. 13***
1733 A1179 10r multicolored .50 .50

Newpapers in Assam, 150th Anniv. — A1180

1999, Jan. 29 ***Perf. 13x13½***
1734 A1180 3r multicolored .20 .20

Sanskrit College, Calcutta, 175th Anniv. A1181

1999, Feb. 25 ***Perf. 13½x13***
1735 A1181 3r brown & yellow .20 .20

National Defense Academy, 50th Anniv. A1182

Perf. 13½x13¼
1999, Feb. 19 **Litho.**
1736 A1182 3r multicolored .20 .20

Hindu College, Delhi, Cent. A1183

1999, Feb. 17 **Photo.** ***Perf. 13½x13***
1737 A1183 3r blue .20 .20

Biju Patnaik (1916-97), Politician A1184

1999, Mar. 5
1738 A1184 3r multicolored .20 .20

A1185 A1186

1999, Mar. 12 ***Perf. 13***
1739 A1185 15r multicolored .75 .75

Press Trust of India, 50th anniv.

1999, Mar. 6
1740 A1186 15r multicolored .75 .75

Temple Complex of Khajuraho, 1000th anniv.

Dr. K.B. Hedgewar (1889-1940) A1187

1999, Mar. 18
1741 A1187 3r multicolored .20 .20

Bethune Collegiate School, 150th Anniv. A1188

1999 **Photo.** ***Perf. 13***
1742 A1188 3r green .20 .20

Creation of the Khalsa, 300th Anniv. A1189

1999, Apr. 14
1743 A1189 3r multicolored .20 .20

Maritime Heritage A1190

1999, Apr. 5 **Litho.** ***Perf. 13½x13¼***
1744 A1190 3r Boat from 2200 B.C. .20 .20
1745 A1190 3r Ship from 1700 .20 .20

Technology Day A1191

1999, May 11 **Litho.** ***Perf. 13½x13¼***
1746 A1191 3r multicolored .20 .20

Mumbai Port Trust, 125th Anniv. A1192

1999, June 26 **Photo.** ***Perf. 12¾x13***
1747 A1192 3r blue gray .20 .20

A1193

A1194

1999, June 30 Photo. ***Perf. 13x12¾***
1748 A1193 3r multicolored .20 .20

Mizoram Accord.

1999, July 4 Photo. ***Perf. 13¼***
1749 A1194 3r multicolored .20 .20

Gulzari Lal Nanda (b. 1899), interim Prime Minister.

Jijabai, Mother of Shivaji — A1195

1999, July 7 Photo. ***Perf. 14x13½***
1750 A1195 3r claret .20 .20

P. S. Kumaraswamy Raja — A1196

1999, July 8 Photo. ***Perf. 13¼***
1751 A1196 3r sky blue & brown .20 .20

Balai Chand Mukhopadhyay (1879-1979), Writer — A1197

1999, July 19 Photo. ***Perf. 13¼***
1752 A1197 3r slate blue .20 .20

Sindh River Festival A1198

Perf. 13½x13¼
1999, July 28 Photo.
1753 A1198 3r multicolored .20 .20

Geneva Conventions, 50th Anniv. — A1199

1999, Aug. 12 Photo. ***Perf. 13¾***
1754 A1199 15r black & red .70 .70

Freedom Fighters A1200

#1755, Swami Ramanand Teerth. #1756, Vishwambhar Dayalu Tripathi. #1757, Swami Keshawanand. #1758, Sardar Ajit Singh.

Perf. 13½x13¼
1999, Aug. 15 Photo.
1755 A1200 3r multicolored .20 .20
1756 A1200 3r multicolored .20 .20
1757 A1200 3r multicolored .20 .20
1758 A1200 3r multicolored .20 .20
Nos. 1755-1758 (4) .80 .80

Kalki Krishnamurthy (1899-1954), Novelist — A1201

1999, Sept. 9 Photo. ***Perf. 13¾***
1759 A1201 3r black .20 .20

Qazi Nazrul Islam (1899-1976), Poet — A1202

Rambriksh Benipuri, Writer A1203

Ramdhari Sinha "Dinkar," Poet A1204

Jhaverchand Kalidas Meghani (b. 1896), Poet — A1205

1999, Sept. 14 Photo. ***Perf. 13x13¼***
1760 A1202 3r multicolored .20 .20

Perf. 13¼
1761 A1203 3r multicolored .20 .20

Perf. 13¼x13
1762 A1204 3r multicolored .20 .20
1763 A1205 3r multicolored .20 .20
Nos. 1760-1763 (4) .80 .80

Arati Gupta, First Asian Woman to Swim Across English Channel A1206

1999, Sept. 29 Photo. ***Perf. 13x13¼***
1764 A1206 3r multi .20 .20

Worldwide Fund for Nature A1207

Asiatic lion: No. 1765, Male atop female. No. 1766, Two lions. No. 1767, Three lions. 15r, Two lions, diff.

1999, Oct. 4 ***Perf. 13¼x13***
1765 A1207 3r multi .20 .20
1766 A1207 3r multi .20 .20
1767 A1207 3r multi .20 .20
1768 A1207 15r multi .70 .70
Nos. 1765-1768 (4) 1.30 1.30

UPU, 125th Anniv. A1208

#1769, Muria ritual object. #1770, Mask for Chhau dance. #1771, Rathva wall painting. 15r, Angami ornament.

1999, Oct. 9 ***Perf. 13¼x13, 13x13¼***
1769 A1208 3r multi .20 .20
1770 A1208 3r multi .20 .20
1771 A1208 3r multi, vert. .20 .20
1772 A1208 15r multi, vert. .70 .70
Nos. 1769-1772 (4) 1.30 1.30

Dr. T. M. A. Pai (1898-1979) — A1209

Chhaganlal K. Parekh (1894-1968) — A1209a

A. B. Walawalkar, Draftsman for Konkar Railway — A1209b

A. D. Shroff — A1209c

1999, Oct. 9 ***Perf. 13x13¼***
1773 A1209 3r yel & brn .20 .20

Perf. 12¾x13¼
1774 A1209a 3r org brn & ind .20 .20

Perf. 13¼
1775 A1209b 3r lilac & maroon .20 .20
1776 A1209c 3r bister & olive .20 .20
Nos. 1773-1776 (4) .80 .80

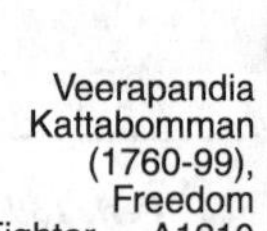
Veerapandia Kattabomman (1760-99), Freedom Fighter — A1210

1999, Oct. 16 Photo. ***Perf. 13x13¼***
1777 A1210 3r olive green .20 .20

Musicians A1211

#1778, Ustad Allauddin Khan Saheb (1870-1972), sarod player. #1779, Musiri Subramania Iyer (1899-1975), music teacher.

1999, Oct. 19 Photo. ***Perf. 13¾***
1778 A1211 3r multicolored .20 .20
1779 A1211 3r multicolored .20 .20

A1212

A1213

Perf. 13¼x13½
1999, Oct. 27 Photo.
1780 A1212 3r violet brown .20 .20

Brigadier Rajinder Singh (1899-1947).

1999, Nov. 14 Photo. ***Perf. 14***
1781 A1213 3r multi .20 .20

Children's Day.

Sri Sathya Sai Water Supply Project A1214

Perf. 12¾x13¼
1999, Nov. 23 Photo.
1782 A1214 3r multi .20 .20

Supreme Court, 50th Anniv. A1215

Perf. 12¾x13¼
1999, Nov. 26 Photo.
1783 A1215 3r multi .20 .20

Dr. Punjabrao Deshmukh, Agriculture Minister A1215a

A. Vaidyanatha Iyer (d. 1955), Advocate of Untouchables — A1216

P. Kakkan, Politician A1217

Indulal Kanaiyalal Yagnik, Politician A1218

1999, Dec. 9 *Perf. 13¼*

1784 A1215a 3r brown & grn .20 .20
1785 A1216 3r orange brown .20 .20
1786 A1217 3r green & brn .20 .20
1787 A1218 3r tan & black .20 .20
Nos. 1784-1787 (4) .80 .80

Thermal Power, Cent. A1219

1999, Dec. 14 Photo. *Perf. 13¼x13*

1788 A1219 3r bister & brn .20 .20

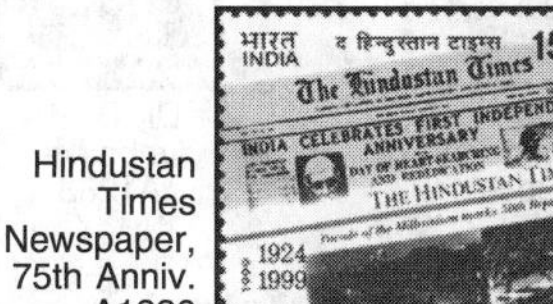

Hindustan Times Newspaper, 75th Anniv. A1220

1999, Dec. 16 Photo. *Perf. 13¼*

1789 A1220 15r multi .70 .70

Family Planning Assoc. of India, 50th Anniv. — A1221

1999, Dec. 18 *Perf. 14x13¾*

1790 A1221 3r multi .20 .20

Birth of Jesus Christ, 2000th Anniv. — A1222

1999, Dec. 25

1791 A1222 3r multi .20 .20

Tabo Monastery A1223

1999, Dec. 31 *Perf. 12¾x13¼*

1792 A1223 5r shown .25 .25
1793 A1223 10r People .45 .45
a. Pair, #1792-1793 .70 .70

First Sunrise of the Millennium A1224

2000, Jan. 1 *Perf. 13¼x13*

1794 A1224 3r multi .20 .20

Agni II Missile A1225

2000, Jan. 1 Litho. *Perf. 13x13¼*

1795 A1225 3r multi .20 .20

Mahatma Gandhi — A1226

2000, Jan. 27 *Perf. 14x13¾*

1796 A1226 3r red & black .20 .20

Republic of India, 50th anniv.

Gallantry Award Winners A1227

Designs: No. 1797, Karam Singh, regimental crest. No. 1798, Abdul Hamid, jeep-mounted artillery gun. No. 1799, Albert Ekka, grenades, knife. No. 1800, N. J. S. Sekhon, airplane. No. 1801, M. N. Mulla, ship.

2000, Jan. 27 *Perf. 13¼x13*

1797 A1227 3r multi .20 .20
1798 A1227 3r multi .20 .20
1799 A1227 3r multi .20 .20
1800 A1227 3r multi .20 .20
1801 A1227 3r multi .20 .20
a. Strip of 5, #1797-1801 .70 .70

Republic of India, 50th anniv.

Millepex 2000 A1228

Endangered reptiles: No. 1802, Batagur terrapin. No. 1803, Olive ridley turtle.

2000, Jan. 29 *Perf. 13¼*

1802 A1228 3r multi .20 .20
1803 A1228 3r multi .20 .20
a. Pair, #1802-1803 .30 .30

Famous Men — A1229

Designs: No. 1804, Balwantrai Mehta. No. 1805, Arun Kumar Chanda. No. 1806, Dr. Harekrushna Mahatab, politician.

2000, Feb. 17 Litho. *Perf. 13x13¼*

1804 A1229 3r multi .20 .20
1805 A1229 3r multi .20 .20
1806 A1229 3r multi .20 .20
Nos. 1804-1806 (3) .60 .60

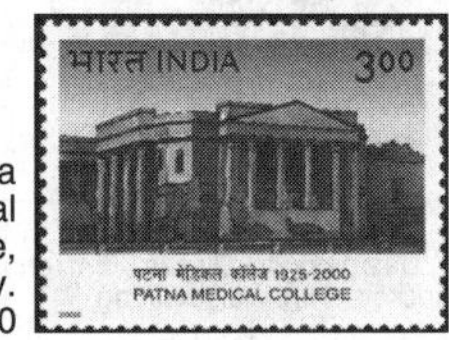

Patna Medical College, 75th Anniv. A1230

2000, Feb. 26 *Perf. 13¼x13*

1807 A1230 3r multi .20 .20

Dr. Burgula Ramakrishna Rao, Politician — A1231

2000, Mar. 13 *Perf. 13x13¾*

1808 A1231 3r brn & ocher .20 .20

Potti Sriramulu (1901-52), Advocate of Untouchables — A1232

2000, Mar. 16 *Perf. 13¼x13*

1809 A1232 3r red .20 .20

Basawon Sinha (1909-89), Socialist Party Leader — A1233

2000, Mar. 23 *Perf. 13x13¼*

1810 A1233 3r multi .20 .20

Indepex Asiana 2000 — A1234

2000, Mar. 31 *Perf. 13x13¼*

1811 A1234 3r Siroi lily .20 .20
1812 A1234 3r Wild guava .20 .20
1813 A1234 3r Sangai deer .20 .20
1814 A1234 15r Slow loris .70 .70
a. Souvenir sheet, #1811-1814 1.25 1.25
Nos. 1811-1814 (4) 1.30 1.30

See Nos. 1831-1834.

Arya Samaj, 125th Anniv. — A1235

Perf. 13x13¼

2000, Apr. 5 Litho. Unwmk.

1815 A1235 3r multi .20 .20

Indigenous Cattle Breeds A1236

Perf. 13¼x13

2000, Apr. 25 Litho. Unwmk.

1816 A1236 3r Gir .20 .20
1817 A1236 3r Kangayam .20 .20
1818 A1236 3r Kankrej .20 .20
1819 A1236 15r Hallikar .65 .65
Nos. 1816-1819 (4) 1.25 1.25

Blackbuck A1237

Patel A1237a

Smooth Indian Otter — A1238

Leopard Cat — A1239

Tiger A1240

Amaltaas — A1241

50p, Nilgiri tahr. 1r, Saras crane. 2r, Sardar Vallabhbhai Patel (1875-1950), Politician. 15r, Butterfly. 50r, Paradise flycatcher.

Perf. 12¾x13, 13x12¾

2000 Photo. Wmk. 324

1820 A1237 25p olive brn .20 .20
1821 A1237 50p yel brn .20 .20
1822 A1237 1r blue .20 .20
1823 A1237a 2r black .20 .20
1824 A1238 3r gray vio .20 .20
1825 A1239 5r multi .20 .20
1826 A1240 10r multi .45 .45
1827 A1240 15r multi .65 .65
1828 A1241 20r multi .85 .85
1829 A1241 50r multi 2.10 2.10
Nos. 1820-1829 (10) 5.25 5.25

Issued: 25p, 50p, 1r, 3r, 7/20; 2r, 10/31; 5r, 10r, 4/30; 15r, 20r, 11/20; 50r, 10/30.

Railways in Doon Valley, Cent. — A1244

Perf. 13¼

2000, May 6 Litho. Unwmk.

1830 A1244 15r multi .65 .65

Indepex Asiana Type of 2000

Birds: #1831, Rosy pastor. #1832, Garganey teal. #1833, Forest wagtail. #1834, White stork.

2000, May 24 ***Perf. 13¼x13***

1831 A1234 3r multi, horiz. .20 .20
1832 A1234 3r multi, horiz. .20 .20
1833 A1234 3r multi, horiz. .20 .20
1834 A1234 3r multi, horiz. .20 .20
a. Block of strip of 4, #1831-1834 .55 .55
b. Souvenir sheet, #1831-1834 .55 .55

Dr. Nandamuri Taraka Rama Rao (1923-96), Actor, Politician A1245

2000, May 28

1835 A1245 3r multi .20 .20

Swami Sahajanand Saraswati (1889-1950), Freedom Fighter — A1246

2000, June 26 ***Perf. 13x13¼***

1836 A1246 3r multi .20 .20

Christian Medical College and Hospital, Vellore, Cent. A1247

2000, Aug. 12 ***Perf. 13¼x13***

1837 A1247 3r multi .20 .20

Social and Political Leaders — A1248

Designs: No. 1838, Radha Gobinda Baruah (1900-75), newspaper publisher. No. 1839, Vijaya Lakshmi Pandit (1900-90), President of UN General Assembly. No. 1840, Jaglal Choudhary (1895-1975), politician. No. 1841, R. Srinivasan (1859-1945), advocate of untouchables, newspaper founder.

2000, Aug. 15 ***Perf. 13x13¼***

1838 A1248 3r multi .20 .20
1839 A1248 3r multi .20 .20
1840 A1248 3r multi .20 .20
1841 A1248 3r multi .20 .20
Nos. 1838-1841 (4) .80 .80

Kodaikanal Intl. School, Cent. A1249

Perf. 13¼x13

2000, Aug. 26 Litho. Unwmk.

1842 A1249 15r multi .65 .65

2000 Summer Olympics, Sydney A1250

Designs: 3r, Discus. 6r, Tennis. 10r, Field hockey. 15r, Weight lifting.

2000, Sept. 17 ***Perf. 13x13¼***

1843-1846 A1250 Set of 4 1.50 1.50

India in Space A1251

#1847, Oceansat 1. #1848, Insat 3B in orbit. No. 1849, vert.: a, Astronaut on planet, spacecraft. b, Earth, spacecraft.

Perf. 13¼x13, 13x13¼

2000, Sept. 29

1847-1848 A1251 3r Set of 2 .30 .30
1849 Pair .30 .30
a.-b. A1251 3r Any single .20 .20

Madhubani-Mithila Painting — A1252

#1850, 3 figures. #1851, 2 figures and bird. #1852, 2 figures and cow, vert.

No. 1853, vert.: a, Red fish, palanquin. b, Yellow fish, elephant.

2000, Oct. 15 ***Perf. 13¼***

1850-1852 A1252 3r Set of 3 .40 .40
1853 Pair .65 .65
a. A1252 5r multi .20 .20
b. A1252 10r multi .45 .45

Raj Kumar Shukla (b. 1875), Farmer — A1253

2000, Oct. 16 Litho. ***Perf. 13x13¼***

1854 A1253 3r multi .20 .20

Pres. Shanker Dayal Sharma (1918-99) A1254

2000, Oct. 29 Litho.

1855 A1254 3r multicolored .20 .20

Children's Day — A1255

2000, Nov. 14

1856 A1255 3r multicolored .20 .20

Maharaja Bijli Pasi A1256

2000, Nov. 16 ***Perf. 13¼x13***

1857 A1256 3r multicolored .20 .20

Gems and Jewelry — A1257

#1858, 3r, Ancient India. #1859, 3r, Sarpech. #1860, 3r. Taxila. #1861, 3r, Navratna. #1862, 3r, Temple. #1863, 3r, Bridal.

2000, Dec. 7 ***Perf. 13¼***

1858-1863 A1257 Set of 6 .80 .80
a. Block of 6, #1858-1863 .80 .80
b. Souvenir sheet, #1858, 1860-1861, 1863 .70 .70

Issued: No. 1863b, 12/11. No. 1863b sold fo 15r.

Warship of Adm. Mohammed Kunjali Marakkar — A1258

2000, Dec. 17 ***Perf. 13¼x13***

1864 A1258 3r multi .20 .20

Ustad Hafiz Ali Khan (1888-1972), Musician — A1259

2000, Dec. 28

1865 A1259 3r multi .20 .20

Famous Men A1260

#1866, Gen. Zorawar Singh (1786-1841). #1867, Rajarshi Bhagyachandra (1740-98), King of Manipur, vert. #1868, Samrat Prithviraj Chauhan (1162-92), ruler of Delhi, vert. #1869, Raja Bhamashah (c. 1542-98), military leader, vert.

2000, Dec. 31 ***Perf. 13¼x13, 13x13¼***

1866-1869 A1260 3r Set of 4 .55 .55

St. Aloysius College Chapel Paintings, Cent. A1261

Perf. 13¼

2001, Jan. 12 Litho. Unwmk.

1870 A1261 15r multi .65 .65

Subhas Chandra Bose A1262

Dr. B. R. Ambedkar A1263

Perf. 12¾x13

2001 Photo. Wmk. 324

1871 A1262 1r brown .20 .20
1872 A1263 3r blue green .20 .20

Issued: 1r, 1/23; 3r, 4/14.

Famous Men — A1264

Designs: No. 1873, 3r, Sane Guruji (1899-1950), social reformer. No. 1874, 3r, N. G. Ranga (1900-95), politician. No. 1875, 3r, E. M. S. Namboodiripad (1909-98), Marxist leader. No. 1876, 3r, Giani Gurmukh Singh Musafir (1899-1976), politician.

Perf. 13x13¼

2001, Jan. Litho. Unwmk.

1873-1876 A1264 Set of 4 .50 .50

Issued: No. 1873, 1/25; others, 1/27.

Famous Men — A1265

Designs: No. 1877, 3r, Sheel Bhadra Yajee (1906-96), freedom figher. No. 1878, 3r, Jubba Sahni (1906-44), revolt leader. No. 1879, 3r, Yogendra (1896-1966) and Baikunth (1907-34) Shukla, freedom fighters.

2001, Jan.
1877-1879 A1265 Set of 3 .40 .40

Issued: No. 1877, 1/28; others, 1/29.

Western Railways Building, Mumbai, Cent. (in 1999) A1266

2001, Feb. 6 ***Perf. 13¼x13***
1880 A1266 15r multi .65 .65

Dated 1999.

2001 Census — A1267

2001, Feb. 10 ***Perf. 13x13¼***
1881 A1267 3r multi .20 .20

President's International Fleet Review — A1268

Designs: No. 1882, 3r, Pal. No. 1883, 3r, Galbat. No. 1884, 3r, Tarangini. 15r, Emblem.

2001, Feb. 18 ***Perf. 13¼x13***
1882-1885 A1268 Set of 4 1.00 1.00

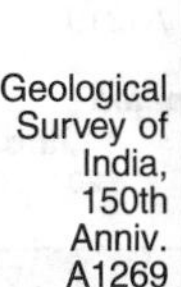

Geological Survey of India, 150th Anniv. A1269

2001, Mar. 4
1886 A1269 3r multi .20 .20

4th Battalion of Maratha Light Infantry, Bicent. — A1270

2001, Mar. 6 ***Perf. 13x13¼***
1887 A1270 3r multi .20 .20

Bhagwan Mahavira, 2600th Anniv. of Birth — A1271

2001, Apr. 6
1888 A1271 3r multi .20 .20

First Manned Space Flight, 40th Anniv. A1272

2001, Apr. 12 ***Perf. 13¼x13***
1889 A1272 15r multi .65 .65

Frederic Chopin (1810-49), Composer A1273

2001, May 4
1890 A1273 15r multi .65 .65

Suraj Narain Singh (1908-73), Politician A1274

2001, May 31 ***Perf. 13x13¼***
1891 A1274 3r multi .20 .20

B. P. Mandal (1918-82), Politician A1275

2001, June 1
1892 A1275 3r multi .20 .20

Samanta Chandra Sekhar (1835-1904), Astronomer A1276

2001, June 11
1893 A1276 3r multi .20 .20

Sant Ravidas, 15th Cent Religious Leader — A1277

2001, June 24
1894 A1277 3r multi .20 .20

Famous Men — A1278

Designs: No. 1895, 4r, Krishna Nath Sarmah (1887-1947), social reformer. No. 1896, 4r, C. Sankaran Nair (1857-1934), President of Indian National Congress. No. 1897, 4r, Syama Prasad Mookerjee (1901-53), politician. No. 1898, 4r, U Kiang Nongbah (d. 1862), soldier.

2001, July 6 **Litho.** ***Perf. 13x13¼***
1895-1898 A1278 Set of 4 .70 .70

Chandragupta Maurya, Emperor, 3rd Cent. B.C. — A1279

2001, July 21 **Litho.** ***Perf. 13¼***
1899 A1279 4r multi .20 .20

Jhalkari Bai — A1280

2001, July 22 **Litho.** ***Perf. 13x13¼***
1900 A1280 4r multi .20 .20

Corals A1281

Designs: No. 1901, 4r, Acropora digitifera. No. 1902, 4r, Fungia horrida. 15r, Montipora acquituberculata. 45r, Acropora formosa.

2001, Aug. 2 ***Perf. 13¼***
1901-1904 A1281 Set of 4 3.00 3.00

Dwarka Prasad Mishra (1901-88), Politician — A1282

2001, Aug. 5 ***Perf. 13x13¼***
1905 A1282 4r multi .20 .20

Chaudhary Brahm Parkash (1918-93), Government Minister — A1283

2001, Aug. 11
1906 A1283 4r multi .20 .20

Ballia Revolution of August 1942 — A1284

2001, Aug. 19
1907 A1284 4r multi .20 .20

Jagdev Prasad (1922-74), Socialist Politician — A1285

2001, Sept. 5
1908 A1285 4r multi .20 .20

Rani Avantibai (d. 1858), Queen of Ramgarh — A1286

2001, Sept. 19
1909 A1286 4r multi .20 .20

Painted Stork — A1287

Perf. 12¾x13

2001, Sept. 20 **Photo.** **Wmk. 324**
1910 A1287 4r bister brown .20 .20

Rao Tula Ram (1825-63), Chieftain — A1288

Perf. 13x13¼

2001, Sept. 23 Litho. Unwmk.

1911 A1288 4r multi .20 .20

Chaudhary Devi Lal (1914-2001), Deputy Prime Minister — A1289

2001, Sept. 25

1912 A1289 4r multi .20 .20

Satis Chandra Samanta (1900-83), Politician — A1290

2001, Sept. 29

1913 A1290 4r multi .20 .20

Sivaji Ganesan (1928-2001), Actor — A1291

2001, Oct. 1

1914 A1291 4r multi .20 .20

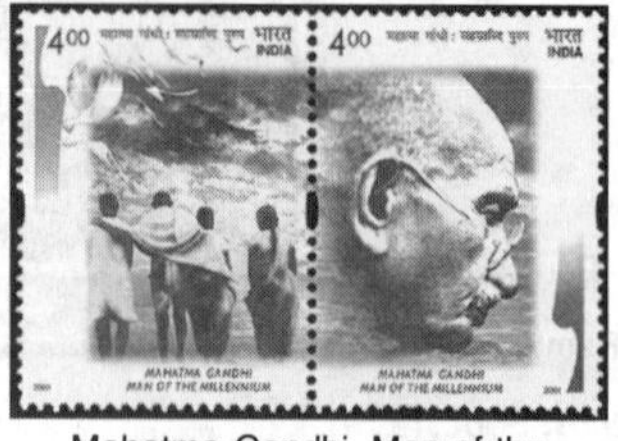

Mahatma Gandhi, Man of the Millennium — A1292

No. 1915: a, Gandhi and followers, birds. b, Gandhi.

Type A Syncopation (1st stamp #1915): On the two longer sides, an oval hole equal in width to 3 holes is located in the center, with an equal number of normal round holes to either side.

Perf. 13x13¼ Syncopated Type A

2001, Oct. 2

1915 A1292 4r Horiz. pair, #a-b .35 .35

Literary and Performing Arts Personalities A1293

Designs: No. 1916, 4r, Lachhu Maharaj (1901-78), choreographer. No. 1917, 4r, Master Mitrasen (1895-1946), playwright, theater founder. No. 1918, 4r, Bharathidasan (1891-1964), Tamil poet.

2001, Oct. 9 ***Perf. 13¼x13***

1916-1918 A1293 Set of 3 .50 .50

Jayaprakash Narayan (1902-79), Socialist Politician A1294

2001, Oct. 11

1919 A1294 4r multi .20 .20

Panchatantra Fables — A1295

No. 1920 - The Monkey and the Crocodile, 4r: a, Monkey in tree. b, Monkey on crocodile's back.

No. 1921 - The Lion and the Rabbit, 4r: a, Lion and rabbit. b, Lion and rabbit on bridge.

No. 1922 - The Crows and the Snake, 4r: a, Crows with necklace. b, Villagers pursuing snake.

No. 1923 - The Tortoise and the Geese, 4r: a, Tortoise in pond. b, Tortoise flying with geese.

Sizes: Nos. 1920a-1923a, 58x39mm; Nos. 1920b-1923b, 29x39mm. Illustration reduced.

2001, Oct. 17 ***Perf. 13x13¼***

Horiz. Pairs, #a-b

1920-1923 A1295 Set of 4 1.40 1.40

Global Iodine Deficiency Disorders Day — A1296

2001, Oct. 21

1924 A1296 4r multi .20 .20

Thangal Kunju Musaliar (1897-1966), Industrialist A1297

2001, Oct. 26

1925 A1297 4r multi .20 .20

Children's Day — A1298

2001, Nov. 14 Litho. ***Perf. 13x13¼***

1926 A1298 4r multi .20 .20

Dr. V. Shantaram (1901-90), Movie Producer A1299

Perf. 13¼x13 Syncopated

2001, Nov. 17

1927 A1299 4r multi .20 .20

Sobha Singh (1901-86), Artist — A1300

2001, Nov. 29 Litho. ***Perf. 13x13¼***

1928 A1300 4r multi .20 .20

Sun Temple, Konark — A1301

No. 1929: a, 4r, Carved wheel. b, 15r, Sun Temple.

Illustration reduced.

Perf. 13¼x13 Syncopated

2001, Dec. 1

1929 A1301 Horiz. pair, #a-b .80 .80

Intl. Volunteers Year A1302

2001, Dec. 5 Litho. ***Perf. 13¼x13***

1930 A1302 4r multi .20 .20

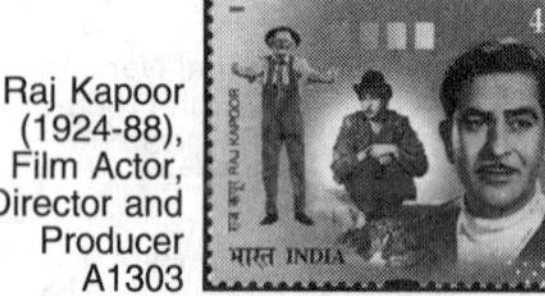

Raj Kapoor (1924-88), Film Actor, Director and Producer A1303

Perf. 13¼x13 Syncopated

2001, Dec. 14 Litho.

1931 A1303 4r multi .20 .20

Greetings — A1304

Flowers and: 3r, Fireworks. 4r, Butterflies.

Perf. 13x13¼ Syncopated

2001, Dec. 18 Litho.

1932-1933 A1304 Set of 2 .30 .30

Digboi Refinery, Cent. A1305

2001, Dec. 18 ***Perf. 13¼x13***

1934 A1305 4r multi .20 .20

Vijaye Raje Scindia (1919-2001), Politician — A1306

Perf. 13x13¼ Syncopated

2001, Dec. 20

1935 A1306 4r multi .20 .20

Temples A1307

Designs: No. 1936, 4r, Kedarnath. No. 1937, 4r, Tryambakeshwar. No. 1938, 4r, Aundha Nagnath. 15r, Rameswaram.

2001, Dec. 22 ***Perf. 13¼x13***

1936-1939 A1307 Set of 4 1.10 1.10

Cancer Awareness Day — A1308

2001, Nov. 7 ***Perf. 13x13¼***

1940 A1308 4r multi .20 .20

Maharaja Ranjit Singh (1780-1839), Founder of Sikh Kingdom of the Punjab — A1309

2001, Nov. 9

1941 A1309 4r multi .20 .20

Directorate General of Mine Safety, Cent. — A1310

Perf. 13x13¼ Syncopated

2002, Jan. 7 Litho.

1942 A1310 4r multi .20 .20

May 2001 Ascent of Mt. Everest by Indian Army Mountaineers A1311

2002, Jan. 15 ***Perf. 13x13¼***

1943 A1311 4r multi .20 .20

Bauddha Mahotsav Festival
A1312

Designs: No. 1944, 4r, Dhamek Stupa, Sarnath. No. 1945, 4r, Gridhakuta Hills, Rajgir. 8r, Mahaparinirvana Temple, Kushinagar. 15r, Mahabodhi Temple, Bodhgaya.

Perf. 13¼x13 Syncopated

2002, Jan. 21

1944-1947 A1312 Set of 4 1.40 1.40

Book Year
A1313

2002, Jan. 28 ***Perf. 13¼x13***

1948 A1313 4r multi .20 .20

Swami Ramanand
A1314

2002, Feb. 4 ***Perf. 13x13¼***

1949 A1314 4r multi .20 .20

Indian Munitions Factories, 50th Anniv.
A1315

Perf. 13¼ Syncopated

2002, Mar. 18 **Litho.**

1950 A1315 4r multi .20 .20

Sido and Kanhu Murmu, 1855-57 Revolt Leaders
A1316

2002, Apr. 6 ***Perf. 13¼***

1951 A1316 4r multi .20 .20

Indian Railways, 150th Anniv. — A1317

2002, Apr. 16 ***Perf. 13¼x13***

1952 A1317 15r multi .65 .65

India - Japan Diplomatic Relations, 50th Anniv. — A1318

No. 1953: a, Kathakali actor, India. b, Kabuki actor, Japan.

2002, Apr. 26 Litho. ***Perf. 13x13¼***

1953 A1318 15r Horiz. pair, #a-b 1.25 1.25

c. Souvenir sheet, #1953a-1953b 1.25 1.25

Parliament, 50th Anniv.
A1319

Litho. & Embossed

2002, May 13 ***Perf. 13¼***

1954 A1319 4r gold .20 .20

Prabodhankar Thackeray (1885-1973), Writer — A1320

Perf. 13x13¼ Syncopated

2002, May 19 **Litho.**

1955 A1320 4r black .20 .20

Cotton College, Guwahati
A1321

2002, May 26 Photo. ***Perf. 13¼x13***

1956 A1321 4r grn & claret .20 .20

P. L. Deshpande (1919-2000), Actor — A1322

2002, June 16 Litho. ***Perf. 13¼***

1957 A1322 4r multi .20 .20

Brajlal Biyani (1896-1968), Politician and Writer — A1323

Perf. 13x13¼ Syncopated

2002, June 22

1958 A1323 4r multi .20 .20

Writers — A1324

Designs: No. 1959, 5r, Babu Gulabrai (1888-1963). No. 1960, 5r, Pandit Suryanarayan Vyas (1902-76).

2002, June 22

1959-1960 A1324 Set of 2 .40 .40

Anna Bhau Sathe (1920-69), Writer — A1326

Perf. 13x13¼ Syncopated

2002, Aug. 1 **Litho.**

1962 A1326 4r gray & black .20 .20

Anand Rishiji Maharaj (1900-92), Humanitarian
A1327

2002, Aug. 9 ***Perf. 13¼***

1963 A1327 4r multi .20 .20

Vithalrao Vikhe Patil (1901-80), Initiator of Cooperatives
A1328

Perf. 13x13¼ Syncopated

2002, Aug. 10

1964 A1328 4r multi .20 .20

Sant Tukaram (1608-50), Poet — A1329

2002, Aug. 10

1965 A1329 4r multi .20 .20

Bhaurao Krishnaroao Gaikwad (1902-71), Politician — A1330

2002, Aug. 26

1966 A1330 4r multi .20 .20

Social Reformers
A1331

Designs: No. 1967, 5r, Ayyan Kali (1863-1941), advocate of rights for untouchables. No. 1968, 5r, Chandraprabha Saikiani (1901-72), women's rights advocate. No. 1969, 5r, Gora (1902-75), advocate of atheism.

Perf. 13¼x13 Syncopated

2002, Sept. 12

1967-1969 A1331 Set of 3 .60 .60

Ananda Nilayam Vimanam
A1332

2002, Oct. 11 ***Perf. 13¼x13***

1970 A1332 15r multi .65 .65

Kanika Bandopadhyay (1924-2000), Singer — A1333

2002, Oct. 12 Photo. ***Perf. 13x13¼***

1971 A1333 5r multi .20 .20

Arya Vaidya Sala Health Organization, Cent. — A1334

Perf. 13¼x13 Syncopated

2002, Oct. 12 **Litho.**

1972 A1334 5r multi .20 .20

Bhagwan Baba (1896-1965), Religious Leader — A1335

Perf. 13x13¼ Syncopated

2002, Oct. 15

1973 A1335 5r multi .20 .20

Bihar Chamber of Commerce, 75th Anniv. (in 2001) — A1336

2002, Oct. 28

1974 A1336 4r multi .20 .20

UN Climate Change Convention
A1337

Mangroves: No. 1975, 5r, Rhizophora mucronata. No. 1976, 5r, Nypa fruticans. No. 1977, 5r, Bruguiera gymnorrhiza. 15r, Sonneratia alba.

Perf. 13¼x13 Syncopated

2002, Oct. 30

1975-1978 A1337 Set of 4 1.25 1.25

AIR POST STAMPS

De Havilland Hercules over Lake AP1

Wmk. 196 Sideways

1929-30 Typo. *Perf. 14*
C1 AP1 2a dull green .55 .30
C2 AP1 3a deep blue .80 .55
C3 AP1 4a gray olive 2.25 1.10
a. 4a olive green ('30) 2.75 1.10
C4 AP1 6a bister 2.75 .70
C5 AP1 8a red violet 3.25 3.25
C6 AP1 12a brown red 9.75 9.75
Nos. C1-C6 (6) 19.35 15.65

Catalogue values for unused stamps in this section, from this point to the end of the section, are for Never Hinged items.

Dominion of India

Lockheed Constellation — AP2

Perf. 13½x14
1948, May 29 Litho. Wmk. 196
C7 AP2 12a ultra & slate blk .55 .30

Bombay-London flight of June 8, 1948.

Republic of India

The Spirit of '76, by Archibald M. Willard — AP3

1976, May 29 *Perf. 13x13½*
C8 AP3 2.80r multicolored .75 .55

American Bicentennial.

INDIA '80 Emblem, De Havilland Puss Moth AP4

1979, Oct. 15 Photo. *Perf. 14½x14*
C9 AP4 30p shown .20 .20
C10 AP4 50p Chetak helicopter .20 .20
C11 AP4 1r Boeing 737 .20 .20
C12 AP4 2r Boeing 747 .30 .20
Nos. C9-C12 (4) .90 .80

INDIA '80 Intl. Stamp Exhib., New Delhi, Jan. 25-Feb. 3, 1980.

MILITARY STAMPS

China Expeditionary Force

Regular Issues of India, 1882-99, Overprinted

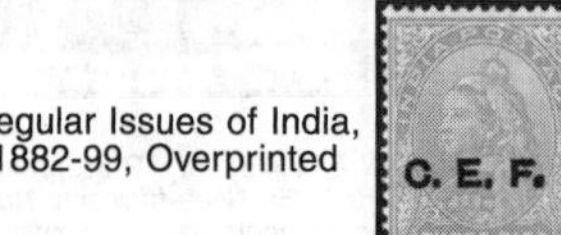

1900 Wmk. 39 *Perf. 14*
M1 A31 3p carmine rose .30 *.75*
M2 A17 ½a dark green .60 *.90*
M3 A19 1a maroon 3.25 1.00
M4 A21 2a ultra 2.50 *5.75*
M5 A28 2a6p green 10.00 *18.00*
M6 A22 3a orange 2.25 *15.00*
M7 A23 4a olive green 2.25 *6.50*
M8 A25 8a red violet 2.25 *10.00*
M9 A26 12a violet, *red* 12.00 *15.00*
M10 A29 1r car rose & grn 12.00 *12.50*
a. Double overprint
Nos. M1-M10 (10) 47.40 *85.40*

The 1a6p of this set was overprinted, but not issued. Value $165.

Overprinted on 1900 Issue of India

1904, Feb. 27
M11 A19 1a carmine rose 20.00 7.00

Overprinted on 1902-09 Issue of India

1904
M12 A32 3p gray 2.40 *3.25*
M13 A34 1a carmine rose 4.25 .60
M14 A35 2a violet 11.00 1.50
M15 A36 2a6p ultra 2.50 *3.50*
M16 A37 3a brown org 3.00 *3.25*
M17 A38 4a olive green 6.75 *9.00*
M18 A40 8a red violet 6.25 *6.75*
M19 A41 12a violet, *red* 8.50 *15.00*
M20 A42 1r car rose & grn 10.00 *21.00*
Nos. M12-M20 (9) 54.65 *63.85*

Overprinted on 1906 Issue of India

1909
M21 A44 ½a green 1.50 1.00
M22 A45 1a carmine rose 1.50 .40

Overprinted on 1911-19 Issues of India

1913-21
M23 A46 3p gray 2.60 *10.00*
M24 A47 ½a green 1.90 *2.00*
M25 A48 1a car rose 2.40 1.25
M26 A58 1½a chocolate 18.00 *42.50*
M27 A49 2a violet 8.25 *30.00*
M28 A57 2a6p ultra 6.75 *15.00*
M29 A51 3a brown org 19.00 *100.00*
M30 A52 4a olive green 15.00 *100.00*
M31 A54 8a red violet 15.00 *200.00*
M32 A55 12a claret 15.00 *82.50*
M33 A56 1r grn & red brn 47.50 *150.00*
Nos. M23-M33 (11) 151.40 *733.25*

Issue dates: No. M23, 1913; others, 1921.

Indian Expeditionary Force

Regular Issues of India, 1911-13, Overprinted

1914 Wmk. 39 *Perf. 14*
M34 A46 3p gray .20 .20
a. Double overprint 30.00 25.00
M35 A47 ½a green .20 .20
M36 A48 1a carmine rose .20 .20
M37 A49 2a violet .30 .25
M38 A57 2a6p ultra .30 .25
M39 A51 3a brown org .60 .60
M40 A52 4a olive green .65 .65
M41 A54 8a red violet 1.00 1.00
M42 A55 12a claret 1.75 1.75
a. Double overprint
M43 A56 1r grn & red brn 3.25 3.50
Nos. M34-M43 (10) 8.45 8.60

Catalogue values for unused stamps in this section, from this point to the end of the section, are for Never Hinged items.

Korea Custodial Unit

Regular Issues of India Overprinted in Black

Perf. 13½x14, 14x13½
1953 Wmk. 196
M44 A91 3p gray violet .30 *2.25*
M45 A92 6p red brown .30 *2.25*
M46 A91 9p green .30 *2.25*
M47 A101 1a turquoise .40 *2.50*
M48 A93 2a carmine .70 *2.50*
M49 A94 2½a brown lake 1.25 *3.00*
M50 A94 3a red orange 1.50 *3.00*
M51 A94 4a ultra 1.75 *3.00*
M52 A95 6a purple 6.75 *7.00*
M53 A95 8a blue green 4.75 *7.00*
M54 A95 12a blue 6.50 *14.00*
M55 A96 1r dk grn & pur 10.50 *14.00*
Nos. M44-M55 (12) 35.00 *62.75*

Hindi overprint reads "Indian Custodial Unit, Korea."

Indian UN Force in Congo

Nos. 302-303, 305, 307, 282 and 313 Overprinted: "U.N. FORCE (INDIA) CONGO"

Wmk. 324, 196 (13np)

1962, Jan. 15 Photo. *Perf. 14x14½*
M56 A117 1np blue green .20 .20
M57 A117 2np light brown .20 .20
M58 A117 5np emerald .20 .20
M59 A117 8np bright green .20 .20
M60 A117 13np brt carmine .40 .40
M61 A117 50np orange .80 .80
Nos. M56-M61 (6) 2.00 2.00

Indian UN Force in Gaza

No. 393 Overprinted in Carmine

1965, Jan. 15 Unwmk. *Perf. 13½*
M62 A190 15p blue gray .20 .20

Overprint letters stand for "United Nations Emergency Force."

INTERNATIONAL COMMISSION IN INDO-CHINA

Catalogue values for all unused stamps in this section are for Never Hinged items.

Cambodia

India Nos. 207, 231, 211, 216 and 217 Overprinted in Black

Perf. 13½x14
1954, Dec. 1 Wmk. 196
1 A91 3p gray violet .20 .20
2 A101 1a turquoise .25 .25
3 A93 2a carmine .40 *.40*
4 A95 8a blue green 1.40 *1.75*
5 A95 12a blue 2.25 *2.50*
Nos. 1-5 (5) 4.50 *5.10*

The overprint reads "International Commission Cambodia." Top line is 18mm on Nos. 4-5; 15½mm on Nos. 1-3, 6-12.

Same Overprint on India Nos. 276, 279, 282, 286 and 287

1957, Apr. 1 *Perf. 14x14½*
6 A117 2np light brown .20 .20
7 A117 6np gray .20 .20
8 A117 13np bright carmine .50 .35
9 A117 50np orange 1.25 1.00
10 A117 75np plum 2.50 2.25
Nos. 6-10 (5) 4.65 4.00

Same Overprint on India No. 303

1962 Wmk. 324
12 A117 2np light brown .65 .65

Laos

India Nos. 207, 231, 211, 216 and 217 Overprinted in Black

Perf. 13½x14
1954, Dec. 1 Wmk. 196
1 A91 3p gray violet .20 .20
2 A101 1a turquoise .25 .25
3 A93 2a carmine .40 .40
4 A95 8a blue green 1.40 *1.75*
5 A95 12a blue 2.25 *2.50*
Nos. 1-5 (5) 4.50 *5.10*

The overprint reads "International Commission Laos." Top line is 18mm on Nos. 4-5; 15½mm on Nos. 1-3, 6-16.

Same Overprint on India Nos. 276, 279, 282, 286 and 287

1957, Apr. 1 *Perf. 14x14½*
6 A117 2np light brown .20 .20
7 A117 6np gray .20 .20
8 A117 13np brt carmine .50 .35
9 A117 50np orange 1.25 1.00
10 A117 75np plum 2.50 2.25
Nos. 6-10 (5) 4.65 4.00

Same Overprint on India Nos. 303-305, 313-314

1962-65 Wmk. 324
12 A117 2np light brown .85 *1.00*
13 A117 3np brown ('63) .20 .20
14 A117 5np emerald ('63) .20 .20
15 A117 50np orange ('65) .65 *.75*
16 A117 75np plum ('65) 1.40 *1.60*
Nos. 12-16 (5) 3.30 *3.75*

Laos and Viet Nam

No. 393 Overprinted in Carmine

1965, Jan. 15 Unwmk. *Perf. 13½*
1 A190 15p blue gray .30 .30

Overprint letters stand for "International Control Commission."

Nos. 406-408, 411-412, 417 and 419-420 Overprinted in Carmine

Perf. 14½x14, 14x14½
1968, Oct. 2 Photo. Wmk. 324
2 A202 2p reddish brown .20 .20
3 A202 3p olive bister .20 .20
4 A202 5p cerise .20 .20
5 A203 10p bright blue .20 .20
6 A203 15p green .20 .20
7 A202 60p dark gray .45 .45
8 A204 1r dp cl & red brn .75 *.95*
9 A205 2r violet & brt blue 1.60 *2.25*
Nos. 2-9 (8) 3.80 *4.65*

The arrangement of the lines of the overprint varies on each denomination.

Viet Nam

India Nos. 207, 231, 211, 216 and 217 Overprinted in Black

Perf. 13½x14
1954, Dec. 1 Wmk. 196
1 A91 3p gray violet .20 .20
2 A101 1a turquoise .25 .25
3 A93 2a carmine .40 .40
4 A95 8a blue green 1.40 *1.75*
5 A95 12a blue 2.25 *2.50*
Nos. 1-5 (5) 4.50 *5.10*

The overprint reads "International Commission Viet Nam." Top line of overprint is 18mm on Nos. 4-5; 15½mm on Nos. 1-3, 6-16.

Same Overprint on India Nos. 276, 279, 282, 286 and 287

1957, Apr. 1 *Perf. 14x14½*
6 A117 2np light brown .20 .20
7 A117 6np gray .20 .20
8 A117 13np bright carmine .50 .35

9 A117 50np orange 1.25 1.00
10 A117 75np plum 2.50 2.25
Nos. 6-10 (5) 4.65 4.00

Same Overprint on India Nos. 302-305, 313-314

1961-65 Wmk. 324

11 A117 1np blue green .55 *.65*
12 A117 2np light brown ('62) 1.10 1.10
13 A117 3np brown ('63) .40 .40
14 A117 5np emerald ('63) .25 .30
15 A117 50np orange ('65) .85 *1.10*
16 A117 75np plum ('65) 1.60 *1.90*
Nos. 11-16 (6) 4.75 *5.45*

OFFICIAL STAMPS

Nos. O1-O26 are normally found with very heavy cancellations, and values are for stamps so canceled. Lightly canceled copies are seldom seen.

Nos. 11-12, 18, 20-22, 23a, 24, 26 Overprinted in Black **Service.**

1866, Aug. 1 Unwmk. *Perf. 14*

O1 A7 ½a blue 800.00 125.00
a. Inverted overprint
O3 A7 1a brown 130.00
O4 A7 8a rose 14.00 32.50

The 8p lilac unwatermarked (No. 19) with "Service" overprint was not officially issued.

Wmk. 38

O5 A7 ½a blue 200.00 12.50
a. Inverted overprint
b. Without period 160.00
O6 A8 8p lilac 17.00 *45.00*
O7 A7 1a brown 175.00 14.00
a. Inverted overprint
O8 A7 2a yellow 140.00 70.00
a. Imperf.
b. Inverted overprint
O9 A7 4a green 150.00 60.00
a. Inverted overprint
O10 A9 4a green (I) 850.00 200.00

Reprints were made of #O5, O7, O10 (type II).

Revenue Stamps Surcharged or Overprinted

Queen Victoria — O1

Blue Glazed Paper
Black Surcharge

1866 Wmk. 36 *Perf. 14 Vertically*

O11 O1 2a violet 350.00 250.00

The note after No. 30 will apply here also.

No. O10 is often found with cracked surface or scuffs. Such examples sell for somewhat less.

Reprints of No. O11 are surcharged in either black or green, and have the word "SERVICE" 16½x2½mm, instead of 16½x2¾mm and "TWO ANNAS" 18x3mm, instead of 20x3¼mm.

O2

O3

O4

1866

Green Overprint

O12 O2 2a violet 750. 325.
O13 O3 4a violet *2,750. 1,000.*
O14 O4 8a violet *3,500. 3,500.*

The note after No. 30 will apply here also.

These stamps are often found with cracked surface or scuffs. Such examples sell for somewhat less.

Reprints of No. O12 have the overprint in sans-serif letters 2¼mm high, instead of Roman letters 2½mm high. On the reprints of No. O13 "SERVICE" measures 16½x2¼mm, instead of 20¼x3mm and "POSTAGE" 18x2¼mm, instead of 22x3mm.

On No. O14 "SERVICE" is 20½mm long, instead of 20mm and "POSTAGE" is 23mm long, instead of 22mm. All three overprints are in a darker green than on the original stamps.

O5

Green Overprint

1866 Wmk. 40 *Perf. 15½x15*

Lilac Paper

O15 O5 ½a violet 350.00 75.00
a. Double overprint 2,500.

Nos. 20, 31, 22-23, 23a, 26, 28 Overprinted in Black

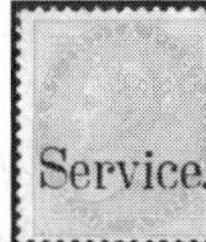

1866-73 Wmk. 38 *Perf. 14*

O16 A7 ½a blue 24.00 .20
O17 A7 ½a bl, re-engraved 125.00 60.00
a. Double overprint
O18 A7 1a brown 30.00 .40
O19 A7 2a orange 4.50 2.00
a. 2a yellow 15.00 2.25
O20 A9 4a green (I) 2.50 1.50
O21 A11 8a rose 3.00 1.25
Nos. O16-O21 (6) 189.00 65.35

The 6a8p with this overprint was not issued. Value $25.

Nos. 31, 22-23, 26, 28 Overprinted in Black

1874-82

O22 A7 ½a blue, re-engraved 7.00 .20
a. Blue overprint 300.00 37.50
O23 A7 1a brown 10.00 .20
a. Blue overprint 450.00 100.00
O24 A7 2a orange 32.50 12.50
O25 A9 4a green (I) 11.00 2.50
O26 A11 8a rose 4.25 3.50
Nos. O22-O26 (5) 64.75 18.90

Same Overprint on Nos. 36, 38, 40, 42, 44, 49

1883-97 Wmk. 39

O27 A17 ½a green .20 .20
a. Pair, one without overprint
b. Double overprint 900.00
O28 A19 1a maroon .20 .20
a. Inverted overprint 300.00 *400.00*
b. Double overprint 900.00
c. 1a violet brown 1.75 .35
O29 A21 2a ultramarine 4.50 .50
O30 A23 4a olive green 12.00 .40
O31 A25 8a red violet 7.00 .40
O32 A29 1r car rose & grn 8.50 .40
Nos. O27-O32 (6) 32.40 2.10

Same Overprint on No. 54

1899

O33 A31 3p carmine rose .20 .20

Same Overprint on Nos. 56-58

1900

O34 A17 ½a light green 1.25 .30
O35 A19 1a carmine rose 1.75 .20
a. Double overprint 1,250.
b. Inverted overprint 1,200.
O36 A21 2a violet 22.50 .50
Nos. O34-O36 (3) 25.50 1.00

Same Overprint on Nos. 60-63, 66-68, 70

1902-09

O37 A32 3p gray .75 .20
O38 A33 ½a green .90 .20
O39 A34 1a carmine rose .75 .20
O40 A35 2a violet *2.25* .20
O41 A38 4a olive green *4.00* .20
O42 A39 6a bister *2.10* .20
O43 A40 8a red lilac *5.00* .50
O44 A42 1r car rose & green ('05) *4.25* .20
Nos. O37-O44 (8) *20.00* 1.90

For surcharge see No. O73.

Same Overprint on Nos. 78-79

1906-07

O45 A44 ½a green 1.00 .20
O46 A45 1a carmine rose 1.75 .20
a. Pair, one without overprint
b. Overprint on back —

Same Overprint on Nos. 71, 73-76

1909

O47 A43 2r brown & rose *6.50* .90
O48 A43 5r violet & ultra *11.00* 1.00
O49 A43 10r car rose & grn *21.00* 8.50
a. 10r red & green 52.50 6.00
O50 A43 15r ol gray & ultra 47.50 27.50
O51 A43 25r ultra & org brn 110.00 42.50
Nos. O47-O51 (5) 196.00 80.40

For surcharges see Nos. O67-O69.

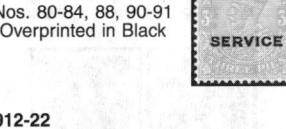

Nos. 80-84, 88, 90-91 Overprinted in Black **SERVICE**

1912-22

O52 A46 3p gray .25 .20
O53 A47 ½a green .25 .20
a. Double overprint 90.00
O54 A48 1a carmine rose .75 .20
a. Double overprint 750.00
O55 A48 1a dark brown ('22) 1.00 .20
a. Imperf., pair 75.00
O56 A49 2a violet .50 .20
O57 A52 4a olive green .75 .20
O58 A53 6a bister 1.25 *1.75*
O59 A54 8a red violet 1.75 .75

Nos. 93-98 Overprinted in Black **SERVICE**

O60 A56 1r grn & red brn 2.00 .80
O61 A56 2r yel brn & car rose 2.50 *3.50*
O62 A56 5r violet & ultra 10.50 *13.50*
O63 A56 10r car rose & grn 35.00 32.50
O64 A56 15r ol grn & ultra 67.50 *75.00*
O65 A56 25r ultra & brn org 150.00 125.00
Nos. O52-O65 (14) 274.00 254.00

For surcharges see Nos. O69b, O70-O71.

O6

O7

Black Surcharge on No. 82

1921 Black Surcharge

O66 O6 9p on 1a rose .75 .60

For overprint see Gwalior No. O28.

Nos. O49-O51 Surcharged

1925

O67 A43 1r on 15r 4.00 3.00
O68 A43 1r on 25r 20.00 *60.00*
O69 A43 2r on 10r red & grn 3.50 3.50
a. 2r on 10r carmine rose & green 175.00 47.50
b. Surcharge on #O63 (error) 700.00

Nos. O64-O65 Surcharged **ONE RUPEE**

O70 A56 1r on 15r 19.00 *65.00*
a. Inverted surcharge
O71 A56 1r on 25r 5.00 *9.00*
a. Inverted surcharge 475.00
Nos. O67-O71 (5) 51.50 *140.50*

Black Surcharge on No. O42

1926

O73 O7 1a on 6a bister .40 .40

Nos. 83, 101, 102, 99 Surcharged **SERVICE ONE ANNA**

O74 A48 1a on 1a dk brn (error) 175.00 175.00
O75 A58 1a on 1½a choc .20 .20
O76 A59 1a on 1½a choc 1.25 *3.50*
b. Double surcharge 30.00
O77 A57 1a on 2a6p ultra .50 .50
Nos. O73-O77 (5) 177.35 179.60

Nos. O74, O75 and O76 have short bars over the numerals in the upper corners.

Nos. 106-108, 111, 126-127, 112, 116, 128, 118-119 Overprinted

a

1926-35 Wmk. 196

O78 A46 3p slate ('29) .20 .20
O79 A47 ½a green ('31) 5.00 .40
O80 A48 1a dark brown .20 .20
a. Overprint as on No. O55 100.00 4.75
O81 A49 2a vermilion ('35) 1.00 1.00
a. Small die .85 .20
O82 A60 2a dull violet .20 .20
O83 A60 2a vermilion ('32) .90 2.00
O84 A57 2a6p buff ('32) .25 .20
O85 A52 4a olive green ('35) 1.00 .20
O86 A61 4a olive green .35 .20
O87 A53 6a bister('35) 18.00 9.00
O88 A54 8a red violet .50 .20
O89 A55 12a claret .50 *1.75*

Nos. 120-121, 123 Overprinted

b

O90 A56 1r green & brn ('30) 2.25 .90
O91 A56 2r brn org & car rose ('30) 6.00 6.00
O92 A56 10r car & green ('31) 70.00 50.00
Nos. O78-O92 (15) 106.35 72.45

#138, 135, 139, 136 Overprinted Type "a"

1932-35

O93 A71 ½a green ('35) .60 .20
O94 A68 9p dark green .25 .20
O95 A72 1a dark brown ('35) 1.90 .20
O96 A69 1a3p violet .25 .20
Nos. O93-O96 (4) 3.00 .80

Nos. 151-153, 162-165 Overprinted Type "a"

1937-39 ***Perf. 13½x14***

O97 A80 ½a brown ('38) 10.00 .25
O98 A80 9p green 11.50 .35
O99 A80 1a carmine 2.10 .20

Type "b" Overprint

O100 A82 1r brn & sl ('38) .30 .30
O101 A82 2r dk brown & dk vio ('38) .85 *1.90*
O102 A82 5r dp ultra & dk green ('38) 1.50 *4.25*
O103 A82 10r rose car & dark violet ('39) 8.50 3.75
Nos. O97-O103 (7) 34.75 11.00

No. 136 Surcharged in Black

1939, May **Wmk. 196** ***Perf. 14***

O104 A69 1a on 1a3p violet *10.00* 1.75

King George VI — O8

1939-43 **Typo.** ***Perf. 13½x14***

O105 O8 3p slate .20 .20
O106 O8 ½a brown 3.75 .20
O106A O8 ½a dk rose vio ('43) .20 .20
O107 O8 9p green .20 .20
O108 O8 1a car rose .20 .20
O108A O8 1a3p bister ('41) *3.25* .65
O108B O8 1½a dull pur ('43) .20 .20
O109 O8 2a scarlet .20 .20
O110 O8 2½a purple .20 .20
O111 O8 4a dark brown .20 .20
O112 O8 8a blue violet .30 .20
Nos. O105-O112 (11) *8.90* *2.65*

For overprints see Gwalior Nos. O52-O61. Stamps overprinted "Postal Service" or "I. P. N." were not used as postage stamps.

Catalogue values for unused stamps in this section, from this point to the end of the section, are for Never Hinged items.

Nos. 203-206 (Gandhi Issue) Overprinted Type "a"

Perf. 11½

1948, Aug. **Unwmk.** **Photo.**

O112A A90 1½a brown *37.50* *27.50*
O112B A90 3½a violet *750.00* *400.00*
O112C A90 12a dk gray green *1,750.* *1,500.*
O112D A90 10r rose brn & brown *10,000.*

Overprint forgeries exist.

Capital of Asoka Pillar
O9 O10

Perf. 13½x14

1950 **Wmk. 196** **Typo.**

O113 O9 3p violet blue .20 .20
O114 O9 6p chocolate .20 .20
O115 O9 9p green .35 .20
O116 O9 1a turquoise .50 .20
O117 O9 2a red .20 .20
O118 O9 3a vermilion 2.50 1.50
O119 O9 4a brown car 3.75 .20
O120 O9 6a purple 3.00 .20
O121 O9 8a orange brn 1.50 .20

Litho.

Perf. 14x13½

O122 O10 1r dark purple 2.00 .20
O123 O10 2r brown red .80 .20
O124 O10 5r dark green 1.50 1.25
O125 O10 10r red brown 4.50 *12.50*
Nos. O113-O125 (13) 21.00 *17.25*

Issue dates: 1r-10r, Jan. 2, others, July 1.

1951, Oct. 1 **Typo.**

O126 O9 4a violet blue .20 .20

Type of 1950 Redrawn; Denomination in Naye Paise

Typo. or Litho.

1957-58 ***Perf. 13½x14***

O127 O9 1np slate blue .20 .20
O128 O9 2np blue violet .20 .20
O129 O9 3np chocolate .20 .20
O130 O9 5np yellow green .20 .20
O131 O9 6np turquoise .20 .20
O132 O9 13np red .20 .20
O133 O9 15np dk purple ('58) .20 .20
O134 O9 20np vermilion .20 .20
O135 O9 25np violet blue .20 .20
O136 O9 50np reddish brown .35 .20
Nos. O127-O136 (10) 2.15 2.00

Issue dates: 15np, June; others, Apr. 1.

Redrawn Type of 1957-58

Typo. or Litho.

1958-71 **Wmk. 324** ***Perf. 13½x14***

O137 O9 1np slate blue ('59) .20 .20
O138 O9 2np blue violet ('59) .20 .20
O139 O9 3np chocolate .20 .20
O140 O9 5np yel green .20 .20
O141 O9 6np turquoise ('59) .20 .20
O142 O9 10np dk green ('63) .20 .20
O142A O9 13np red ('63) .20 .20
O143 O9 15np dk purple .20 .20
O144 O9 20np ver ('59) .20 .20
O145 O9 25np vio blue ('59) .20 .20
O146 O9 50np redsh brown ('59) .20 .20

Litho.

Perf. 14

O147 O10 1r rose vio ('59) .20 .20
O148 O10 2r rose red ('60) .35 .20
a. Watermark sideways ('69) .50 *.60*
O149 O10 5r green ('59) .90 .90
a. Watermark sideways ('69) .90 .30
O150 O10 10r rose lake ('59) 1.75 .75
a. Watermark sideways ('71) 2.50 2.50
Nos. O137-O150 (15) 5.40 4.25

Capital of Asoka Pillar
O11 O12

Perf. 14½x14

1967-76 **Photo.** **Wmk. 360**

Without Gum

O151 O11 2p violet black .20 .20
O152 O11 3p dk red brown .20 .20
O153 O11 5p bright green .20 .20
O154 O11 6p Prussian blue .75 .75
O155 O11 10p slate green .20 .20
O156 O11 15p purple .20 .20
O157 O11 20p orange ver .20 .20
O158 O11 25p deep car ('76) 6.50 2.50
O159 O11 30p violet blue .20 .20
O160 O11 50p red brown .20 .20
Nos. O151-O160 (10) 8.85 4.85

No. O153 Overprinted

1971, Nov. 15 **Wmk. 360**

Without Gum

O161 O11 5p green .40 .40

No. O153 Overprinted "Refugee / Relief"

O162 O11 5p green 1.00 1.00

No. O162 was used in Maharashtra state.

1971, Dec. 1(?)

Without Gum

O163 O12 5p green .20 .20

Nos. O161-O163 were obligatory on all official mail as a postal tax to benefit refugees from East Pakistan. The tax was paid out of the various governmental departments' budgets.

Type of 1968

1967-74 **Wmk. 324** ***Perf. 14½x14***

O164 O11 2p violet .80 *1.00*
O165 O11 5p brt green ('74) .80 .20
O166 O11 10p slate green ('74) 1.25 .20
O167 O11 15p purple ('73) 1.60 .40
O168 O11 20p dp orange ('74) 5.25 5.00
O169 O11 30p ultramarine 3.50 1.00
O170 O11 50p red brown ('73) 2.75 2.00
O171 O11 1r dull purple .55 .20
Nos. O164-O171 (8) 16.50 10.00

Without Currency Designation
O13 O14

Perf. 14½x14

1976-80 **Litho.** **Wmk. 360**

Without Gum

O172 O13 2p violet black .20 .20
O173 O13 5p bright green .20 .20
O174 O13 10p slate green .20 .20
O175 O13 15p purple .20 .20
O176 O13 20p brown orange .20 .20
O177 O13 25p carmine rose .45 .45
O178 O13 30p blue ('79) 1.50 1.50
O179 O13 35p violet ('80) .40 .20
O180 O13 50p red brown 2.00 1.00
O181 O13 1r dull purple ('80) 2.25 .50

Wmk. 324

O182 O13 1r dull purple .50 .50

Perf. 14x13½

O183 O14 2r salmon rose 1.90 1.90
O184 O14 5r deep green 2.00 2.00
O185 O14 10r red brown .75 .75
Nos. O172-O185 (14) 12.75 9.80

O15

Perf. 15x14

1981, Feb. **Litho.** **Wmk. 360**

Without Gum

O186 O15 2r orange vermilion .50 .25
O187 O15 5r dark green 1.25 .60
O188 O15 10r dark red brown 2.50 1.25
Nos. O186-O188 (3) 4.25 2.10

Unwmk.

1981, Dec. 10 **Litho.** ***Imperf.***

Cream Paper

O189 O13 5p bright green .50 *.75*
O190 O13 10p slate green .60 *.75*
O191 O13 15p purple .60 *.75*
O192 O13 20p brown orange .60 *.75*
O193 O13 25p carmine rose 1.25 *1.50*
O194 O13 35p violet .70 .50
O195 O13 50p brown 1.25 1.25
O196 O13 1r dull purple 1.40 1.25
O197 O15 2r salmon rose 1.40 *3.00*
O198 O15 5r deep green 1.60 *4.00*
O199 O15 10r red brown 2.10 *5.50*
Nos. O189-O199 (11) 12.00 20.00

Perf. 12½x13

1982, Nov. 22 **Photo.** **Wmk. 360**

Without Gum

O200 O13 5p bright green .40 *.55*
O201 O13 10p slate green .50 *.65*
O202 O13 15p purple .55 *.65*
O203 O13 20p fawn .65 .65
O204 O13 25p car rose .80 *1.25*
O205 O13 30p dark blue .80 *1.25*
O206 O13 35p violet .80 .35
O207 O13 50p light brown 1.25 1.25
O208 O13 1r dull purple 1.25 1.25
O209 O15 2r salmon rose 1.40 1.90
O210 O15 5r deep green 1.60 3.25
O211 O15 10r red brown 2.00 4.50
Nos. O200-O211 (12) 12.00 17.50

Perf. 12½x13

1984-99 **Photo.** **Wmk. 324**

Without Gum

O212 O13 5p green .20 .20
O213 O13 10p dark green .20 .20
O214 O13 15p rose lake .20 .20
O215 O13 20p fawn .20 .20
O216 O13 25p deep carmine .20 .20
O217 O13 30p blue .20 .20
O218 O13 35p purple .20 .20
O219 O13 40p violet .20 .20
O220 O13 50p brown .20 .20
O221 O13 60p brown .20 .20
O222 O15 1r violet brown .20 .20
O223 O15 2r orange ver .40 .20
O223A O15 3r orange .20 .20
O224 O15 5r gray green 1.00 .50
O225 O15 10r red brown 2.00 1.00
Nos. O213-O225 (14) 5.60 3.90

Issued: 25p, 1986. 60p, 4/15/88; 40p, 10/15/88; 3r, 3/22/99; others, 4/16/84.

This is an expanding set. Numbers may change again.

POSTAL TAX STAMPS

Catalogue values for unused stamps in this section are for Never Hinged items.

No. 408 Overprinted

Perf. 14½x14

1971, Nov. 15 **Photo.** **Wmk. 324**

RA1 A202 5p cerise .20 .20

No. 408 Overprinted "Refugee/Relief"

RA2 A202 5p cerise .20 .20

No. RA2 was used in Maharashtra. In order to make the obligatory tax stamps available immediately throughout India postmasters were authorized to overprint locally No. 408. This resulted in a great variety of mostly handstamped overprints of various types and sizes.

Refugees — PT1

Perf. 14x14½

1971, Dec. 1 **Photo.** **Wmk. 324**

RA3 PT1 5p cerise .20 .20

Nos. RA1-RA3 were obligatory on all mail. The tax was for refugees from East Pakistan.

See Nos. O161-O163.

CONVENTION STATES OF THE BRITISH EMPIRE IN INDIA

CONVENTION STATES OF THE BRITISH EMPIRE IN INDIA

Stamps of British India overprinted for use in the States of Chamba, Faridkot, Gwalior, Jhind, Nabha and Patiala.

These stamps had franking power throughout all British India.

Forgeries

Numerous forgeries exist of the high valued Convention States stamps, unused and used.

CHAMBA

'chəm-bə

LOCATION — A State of India located in the north Punjab, south of Kashmir.
AREA — 3,127 sq. mi.
POP. — 168,908 (1941)
CAPITAL — Chamba

The varieties with small letters in the overprint are not listed as the letters are merely broken and not from another font of type.

Indian Stamps Overprinted in Black

1886-95 Wmk. 39 *Perf. 14*
1 A17 ½a green .20 .35
a. "CHMABA" 300.00 350.00
c. Double overprint 500.00
2 A19 1a violet brown .75 .90
a. "CHMABA" 450.00 500.00
3 A20 1a6p bis brown ('95) .85 6.75
4 A21 2a ultramarine .95 1.00
a. "CHMABA" 1,750.
5 A28 2a6p green ('95) 24.00 52.50
6 A22 3a brn org 1.00 2.75
a. 3a orange 5.00 12.50
b. Inverted overprint
c. "CHMABA" 4,000.
7 A23 4a olive green 2.75 4.50
a. "CHMABA" 1,300.
8 A25 8a red violet 4.00 9.00
a. "CHMABA" 3,500. 3,500.
9 A26 12a vio, *red* ('90) 3.50 6.75
a. "CHMABA" 6,000.
b. 1st "T" of "STATE" invtd. 5,000.
10 A27 1r gray 25.00 72.50
a. "CHMABA" 8,000.
11 A29 1r car rose & grn ('95) 4.75 7.50
12 A30 2r brown & rose ('95) 62.50 175.00
13 A30 3r grn & brown ('95) 65.00 140.00
14 A30 5r vio & bl ('95) 72.50 260.00

Wmk. 38
15 A14 6a bister ('90) 2.25 9.00
Nos. 1-15 (15) 270.00 748.50

1900 Wmk. 39
15B A31 3p carmine rose .20 .20

1902-04
16 A31 3p gray ('04) .20 .20
a. Inverted overprint 67.50
17 A17 ½a light green .20 .20
18 A19 1a carmine rose .20 .20
19 A21 2a violet ('03) 6.25 15.00
Nos. 16-19 (4) 6.85 15.60

1903-05
20 A32 3p gray .20 .55
21 A33 ½a green .20 .20
22 A34 1a carmine rose .55 .20
23 A35 2a violet .65 1.40
24 A37 3a brown org ('05) 1.90 2.40
25 A38 4a olive green ('04) 2.50 8.75
26 A39 6a bister ('05) 2.25 11.00
27 A40 8a red violet ('04) 3.00 10.00
28 A41 12a violet, *red* 3.50 13.00
29 A42 1r car rose & grn ('05) 4.25 12.50
Nos. 20-29 (10) 19.00 60.00

1907
30 A44 ½a green .30 2.00
31 A45 1a carmine rose .50 2.50

1913-24
32 A46 3p gray .20 .40
33 A47 ½a green .20 .60
34 A48 1a carmine rose 2.50 2.75
35 A48 1a dark brown ('22) .80 1.50
36 A49 2a violet 1.10 3.25
37 A51 3a brown orange 1.25 2.25
38 A51 3a ultra ('24) 1.40 7.50
39 A52 4a olive green 1.00 1.50
40 A53 6a bister .95 1.50
41 A54 8a red violet 1.75 4.00
42 A55 12a claret 1.60 5.00
43 A56 1r green & red brown 7.25 9.75
Nos. 32-43 (12) 20.00 40.00

India No. 104 Overprinted

1921
44 A48 9p on 1a rose .90 14.00

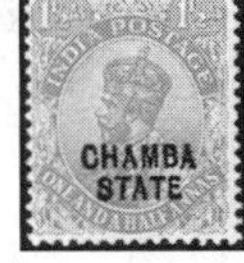

India Stamps of 1913-26 Overprinted

1922-27
45 A58 1½a chocolate 18.00 55.00
46 A59 1½a chocolate .90 2.50
47 A59 1½a rose .60 8.50
48 A57 2a6p ultramarine .50 1.75
49 A57 2a6p brown orange 1.00 7.25
Nos. 45-49 (5) 21.00 75.00

India Stamps of 1926 Overprinted

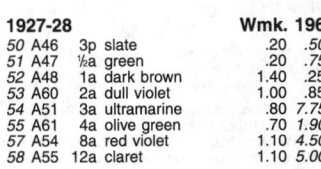

1927-28 Wmk. 196
50 A46 3p slate .20 .50
51 A47 ½a green .20 .75
52 A48 1a dark brown 1.40 .25
53 A60 2a dull violet 1.00 .85
54 A51 3a ultramarine .80 7.75
55 A61 4a olive green .70 1.90
57 A54 8a red violet 1.10 4.50
58 A55 12a claret 1.10 5.00

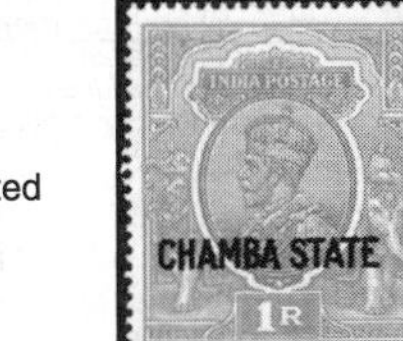

Overprinted

59 A56 1r green & brown 3.50 11.00
Nos. 50-55,57-59 (9) 10.00 32.50

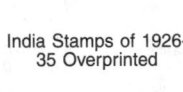

India Stamps of 1926-35 Overprinted

1932-37
60 A71 ½a green .60 3.25
61 A68 9p dark green .25 4.75
62 A72 1a dark brown .35 .25
63 A69 1a3p violet .20 2.00
64 A59 1½a carmine rose .20 4.00
65 A49 2a vermilion .40 9.00
a. Small die 100.00 100.00
66 A57 2a6p buff .20 6.00
67 A51 3a carmine rose .65 3.75
68 A52 4a olive green ('36) 3.25 5.00
69 A53 6a bister ('37) 45.00 65.00
Nos. 60-69 (10) 51.10 103.00

Same Overprint on India Stamps of 1937

1938 Wmk. 196 *Perf. 13½x14*
70 A80 3p slate .60 1.25
71 A80 ½a brown .30 .30
72 A80 9p green .70 1.90
73 A80 1a carmine .70 .60

Overprinted

74 A81 2a scarlet .40 2.50
75 A81 2a6p purple .30 5.00
76 A81 3a yellow green 3.00 8.00
77 A81 3a6p ultra 1.25 4.50
78 A81 4a dark brown 1.40 4.50
79 A81 6a peacock blue 6.25 15.00
80 A81 8a blue violet 1.25 4.50
81 A81 12a carmine lake 2.50 10.00

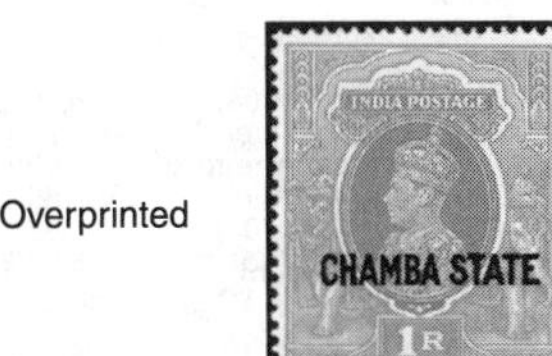

Overprinted

82 A82 1r brown & slate 20.00 25.00
83 A82 2r dk brn & dk vio 30.00 100.00
84 A82 5r dp ultra & dk green 55.00 200.00
85 A82 10r rose car & dk violet 95.00 300.00
86 A82 15r dk grn & dk brown 190.00 275.00
87 A82 25r dk vio & bl vio 225.00 450.00
Nos. 70-87 (18) 633.65 1,408.

India Nos. 151 and 153 Overprinted

1942
87B A80 ½a brown 22.50 12.50
88 A80 1a carmine 27.50 18.00

Same Ovpt. on India Stamps of 1941-42

1942-44
89 A83 3p slate .50 2.00
90 A83 ½a rose violet ('43) .50 1.10
91 A83 9p lt green ('43) .75 4.50
92 A83 1a carmine rose ('43) .75 1.25
93 A84 1½a dk purple ('44) .75 3.25
94 A84 2a scarlet ('43) 2.25 4.00
95 A84 3a violet ('43) 7.00 13.00
96 A84 3½a ultra ('43) 3.75 20.00
97 A85 4a chocolate ('43) 5.25 4.50
98 A85 6a pck blue ('43) 13.00 30.00
99 A85 8a blue violet ('43) 11.50 35.00
100 A85 12a car lake ('43) 22.50 45.00
Nos. 89-100 (12) 68.50 163.60

India Nos. 162-167 Overprinted

1943 Wmk. 196 *Perf. 13½x14*
101 A82 1r brown & slate 16.00 25.00
102 A82 2r dk brown & dk vio 21.00 95.00
103 A82 5r dp ultra & dk grn 45.00 110.00
104 A82 10r rose car & dk vio 70.00 225.00
105 A82 15r dk grn & dk brn 140.00 400.00
106 A82 25r dk vio & bl vio 250.00 450.00
Nos. 101-106 (6) 542.00 1,305.

India No. 161A Overprinted

1948
107 A81 14a rose violet 6.50 2.75

OFFICIAL STAMPS

Indian Stamps Overprinted in Black

1886-98 Wmk. 39 *Perf. 14*
O1 A17 ½a green .20 .20
a. "CHMABA" 175.00 175.00
c. "SERV CE"
O2 A19 1a violet brown .80 .30
a. "CHMABA" 325.00 300.00
c. "SERV CE" 1,800.
d. "SERVICE" double 1,000. 1,000.
O3 A21 2a ultra .80 .75
a. "CHMABA" 900.00 1,250.
O4 A22 3a brown orange 1.50 5.50
a. 3a orange — —
b. "CHMABA" 2,000. 2,100.
O5 A23 4a olive green 1.40 2.00
a. "CHMABA" 900.00 1,250.
c. "SERV CE" 2,250.
O6 A25 8a red violet .80 1.00
a. "CHMABA" 4,500. 4,500.
O7 A26 12a vio, *red* ('90) 5.75 17.50
a. "CHMABA" 5,000.
b. 1st "T" of "STATE" invtd.
O8 A27 1r gray ('90) 10.00 52.50
a. "CHMABA" 4,000.
O9 A29 1r car rose & grn ('98) 4.75 15.00

Wmk. 38
O10 A14 6a bister 3.00 5.25
Nos. O1-O10 (10) 29.00 100.00

1902-04 Wmk. 39
O11 A31 3p gray ('04) .20 .30
O12 A17 ½a light green .20 1.75
O13 A19 1a carmine rose .35 .25
O14 A21 2a violet 7.25 15.00
Nos. O11-O14 (4) 8.00 17.30

1903-05
O15 A32 3p gray .20 .35
O16 A33 ½a green .20 .20
O17 A34 1a carmine rose .45 .20
O18 A35 2a violet .65 .25
O19 A38 4a olive green ('05) 2.75 7.00
O20 A40 8a red violet ('05) 3.00 6.50
O21 A42 1r car rose & grn ('05) 1.40 3.50
Nos. O15-O21 (7) 8.65 18.00

1907
O22 A44 ½a green .25 .75
a. Inverted overprint 3,750. 3,750.
O23 A45 1a carmine rose 1.50 1.00

1913
O24 A49 2a violet 10.00
O25 A52 4a olive green 12.00

India No. 63 Overprinted

O26 A35 2a violet 60.00
No. O26 was never placed in use.

India Stamps of 1911-29 Overprinted:

a

b

1913-25
O27 A46 (a) 3p gray .20 .20
O28 A47 (a) ½a green .20 .20
O29 A48 (a) 1a carmine rose 2.40 .20
O30 A48 (a) 1a dk brown ('25) 1.10 .25
O31 A49 (a) 2a violet ('14) .65 5.00
O32 A52 (a) 4a olive green .65 6.00
O33 A54 (a) 8a red violet 1.10 6.50
O34 A56 (b) 1r grn & red brn 2.40 11.00
Nos. O27-O34 (8) 8.70 29.35

India No. O66 Overprinted

1921
O35 O6 9p on 1a rose .20 3.00

India Stamps of 1926-35 Overprinted

1927-39 Wmk. 196
O36 A46 3p slate .45 .20
O37 A47 ½a green .30 .20
O38 A68 9p dark green ('32) 1.50 4.75
O39 A48 1a dark brown .20 .20
O40 A69 1a3p violet ('32) 4.50 .40
O41 A60 2a dull violet .90 .40
O42 A61 4a olive green .90 .85
O43 A54 8a red violet 3.00 4.75
O44 A55 12a claret 2.00 11.50

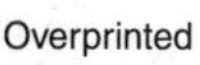
Overprinted

O45 A56 1r green & brown 9.75 *20.00*
O45A A56 2r brn org & car rose ('39) 19.00 *125.00*
O45B A56 5r dk vio & ultra ('39) 35.00 *175.00*
O45C A56 10r car & grn ('39) 47.50 *175.00*
Nos. O36-O45C (13) 125.00 518.25

India Stamps of 1926-35 Overprinted

1935-36
O46 A71 ½a green 1.75 .30
O47 A72 1a dark brown 2.00 .40
O48 A49 2a vermilion 2.75 .80
a. Small die 2.00 *10.00*
O49 A52 4a olive grn ('36) 3.50 2.50
Nos. O46-O49 (4) 10.00 *4.00*

Same Overprint on India Stamps of 1937

1938 ***Perf. 13½x14***
O50 A80 9p green 7.50 *25.00*
O51 A80 1a carmine 6.00 1.50

India Stamps of 1937 Overprinted **CHAMBA STATE SERVICE**

1940-41
O51A A82 1r brn & sl ('41) 600.00 *700.00*
O52 A82 2r dk brn & dk vio 40.00 *150.00*
O53 A82 5r dp ultra & dk grn 70.00 *250.00*
O54 A82 10r rose car & dk vio 125.00 *475.00*

India Official Stamps of 1939-43 Overprinted

1941-46 **Wmk. 196**
O55 O8 3p slate ('44) .20 *.65*
O56 O8 ½a brown 11.00 1.50
O57 O8 ½a dk rose vio ('44) .20 *1.60*
O58 O8 9p green .20 *5.50*
O59 O8 1a carmine rose .20 *1.25*
O60 O8 1a3p bister ('46) 50.00 12.50
O61 O8 1½a dull pur ('46) .85 *4.50*
O62 O8 2a scarlet ('44) 1.25 *3.75*
O63 O8 2½a purple ('44) 1.75 *14.50*
O64 O8 4a dark brown ('44) 3.00 *6.75*
O65 O8 8a blue vio ('41) 4.25 *37.50*
Nos. O55-O65 (11) 72.90 *90.00*

India Nos. 162-165 Overprinted

1944
O66 A82 1r brown & slate 22.50 *90.00*
O67 A82 2r dk brn & dk vio 30.00 *140.00*
O68 A82 5r dp ultra & dk grn 75.00 *190.00*
O69 A82 10r rose car & dk vio 110.00 *325.00*
Nos. O66-O69 (4) 237.50 *745.00*

FARIDKOT

fe-'rēd-,kōt

LOCATION — A State of India lying northeast of Nabha in the central Punjab.
AREA — 638 sq. mi.
POP. — 164,364
CAPITAL — Faridkot

Previous stamp issues are listed under Feudatory States. Stamps of Faridkot were superseded by those of India in 1901.

The varieties with small letters in the overprint are not listed as the letters are merely broken and not from another font.

India Stamps Overprinted in Black

1887-93 **Wmk. 39** ***Perf. 14***
4 A17 ½a green .95 .95
a. "ARIDKOT"
5 A19 1a violet brown .95 *1.90*
6 A21 2a ultramarine 2.50 *3.50*
7 A22 3a orange 4.75 *7.50*
8 A23 4a olive green 5.25 *12.50*
a. "ARIDKOT" 900.00
9 A25 8a red violet 9.00 *27.50*
a. "ARIDKOT" 2,000.
10 A27 1r gray 35.00 *275.00*
a. "ARIDKOT" *2,000.*
11 A29 1r car rose & grn ('93) 30.00 *75.00*

Wmk. 38
12 A14 6a bister 1.60 *11.00*
a. "ARIDKOT" 1,400.
Nos. 4-12 (9) 90.00 *414.85*

1900 **Wmk. Star. (39)**
13 A31 3p car rose .75 *35.00*
14 A26 12a violet, *red* 30.00 *300.00*

OFFICIAL STAMPS

India Stamps Overprinted in Black

1886 **Wmk. 39** ***Perf. 14***
O1 A17 ½a green .20 *.50*
a. "SERV CE" 1,400.
O2 A19 1a violet brown .50 *1.10*
a. "SERV CE" 1,800.
O3 A21 2a ultramarine 1.60 *7.00*
a. "SERV CE" 1,800.
O4 A22 3a orange 1.25 *3.50*
O5 A23 4a olive green 4.50 *6.00*
a. "SERV CE" 1,800.
O6 A25 8a red lilac 4.50 *20.00*
a. "SERV CE" 2,000.
O7 A27 1r gray 37.50 *150.00*

Wmk. 38
O8 A14 6a bister 22.50 *60.00*
a. "ARIDKOT" 1,000.
b. "SERVIC" 1,800.
Nos. O1-O8 (8) 72.55 *248.10*

1896 **Wmk. 39**
O9 A29 1r car rose & green 75.00 *350.00*

Obsolete March 31, 1901.

GWALIOR

'gwäl-ē-,o̦ə̦r

LOCATION — One of the Central Provinces of India
AREA — 26,008 sq. mi.
POP. — 4,006,159 (1941)
CAPITAL — Lashkar

The varieties with small letters in the overprint are not listed as the letters are merely broken and not from another font.

गवालियर
India Stamps Overprinted in Black
GWALIOR

Lines Spaced 16-17mm

1885 **Wmk. 39** ***Perf. 14***
1 A17 ½a green 35.00 20.00
2 A19 1a violet brown 40.00 *25.00*
3 A20 1a6p bister brown 55.00
4 A21 2a ultramarine 40.00 12.00
5 A25 8a red lilac 55.00
6 A27 1r gray 55.00

Wmk. 38
7 A9 4a green 60.00
8 A14 6a bister 60.00
Nos. 1-8 (8) 400.00 57.00

The Hindi overprint measures 13½-14x2mm and 15-15½x2½mm.

The two sizes are found in the same sheet in the proportion of one of the smaller to three of the larger.

The ½a, 1a, 2a, also exist with lines 13mm apart and the short Hindi overprint.

Reprints of the ½a and 1a have the 13mm spacing, the short Hindi overprint and usually carry the overprint "Specimen."

India Stamps Overprinted

Red Overprint

1885 **Wmk. 39**
9 A17 ½a green .50 .25
10 A21 2a ultramarine 8.50 *10.00*
11 A27 1r gray 6.00 *16.00*

Wmk. 38
12 A9 4a green 15.00 8.75
Nos. 9-12 (4) 30.00 35.00

Nos. 9-12 have been reprinted. They have the short Hindi overprint. Most copies bear the word "Reprint." Those without it cannot be distinguished from the originals.

Black Overprint

1885-91 **Wmk. 39**
13 A17 ½a green .20 .20
a. "GWALICR" 85.00 *100.00*
b. Double overprint —
14 A18 9p rose 30.00 *50.00*
15 A19 1a violet brown .70 .20
16 A20 1a6p bister brown .50 1.00
17 A21 2a ultramarine .60 .20
18 A22 3a orange 3.00 .20
19 A23 4a olive green 3.50 .75
20 A25 8a red violet 4.50 1.00
21 A26 12a violet, *red* 3.00 .75
22 A27 1r gray 2.50 1.10

Wmk. 38
23 A14 6a bister 1.50 6.00
Nos. 13-23 (11) 50.00 *61.40*

The Hindi overprint measures 13½-14x2mm and 15-15½x2½mm as in the preceding issue.

1896 **Wmk. 39**
24 A28 2a6p green 5.50 *16.00*
a. "GWALICR" 400.00
25 A29 1r car rose & grn 3.00 2.75
a. "GWALICR" 600.00 *750.00*
26 A30 2r bis brn & rose 5.50 3.00
27 A30 3r green & brown 7.00 3.50
28 A30 5r violet & blue 14.00 6.50
Nos. 24-28 (5) 35.00 31.75

The Hindi inscription varies from 13 to 15½mm long.

1899
29 A31 3p carmine rose .20 .20
a. Inverted overprint 750.00 400.00

1901-04
30 A31 3p gray ('04) 5.50 *50.00*
31 A17 ½a light green .20 *.95*
32 A19 1a carmine rose .60 .30
33 A21 2a violet .85 *3.25*
34 A28 2a6p ultra ('03) .85 *4.00*
Nos. 30-34 (5) 8.00 *58.50*

1903-08
35 A32 3p gray .50 .20
36 A33 ½a green .20 .20
37 A34 1a carmine rose .20 .20
38 A35 2a violet .50 .50
39 A36 2a6p ultra ('05) .75 *4.75*
40 A37 3a brown org ('04) 1.10 .25
41 A38 4a olive green 1.00 .35
42 A39 6a bister ('06) 1.90 1.90
43 A40 8a red violet 2.25 1.00
44 A41 12a vio, *red* ('05) 2.75 2.40
45 A42 1r car rose & grn ('05) 1.60 1.25
46 A43 2r brown & rose 6.75 *8.50*
47 A43 3r grn & brn ('08) 19.00 *32.50*
48 A43 5r vio & bl ('08) 14.00 *21.00*
Nos. 35-48 (14) 52.50 *75.00*

There are two settings of the overprint on Nos. 35, 37-46. In the first (1903), "GWALIOR" is 14mm long and lines are spaced 1¾mm. In the second (1908), "GWALIOR" is 13mm long and lines are 2¾mm apart. No. 36 exists only with first overprint, Nos. 47-48 only with second.

1907
49 A44 ½a green .20 *.70*
50 A45 1a carmine rose 1.25 .25

No. 49 exists with both settings of overprint. See note below No. 48.

1912-23
51 A46 3p gray .20 .20
52 A47 ½a green .20 .20
a. Inverted overprint *375.00*
53 A48 1a car rose .20 .20
a. Double overprint 37.50
54 A48 1a dk brown ('23) .40 .20
55 A49 2a violet .35 .20
56 A51 3a brown orange .40 .20
57 A52 4a olive grn ('13) .50 .50
58 A53 6a bister .80 .80
59 A54 8a red vio ('13) .95 .50
60 A55 12a claret ('14) 1.00 *2.10*
61 A56 1r green & red brn 4.25 .65
62 A56 2r brn & car rose 3.75 3.75
63 A56 5r violet & ultra 16.00 5.50
Nos. 51-63 (13) 29.00 15.00

India No. 104 Overprinted

1921
64 A48 9p on 1a rose .20 .20
a. Inverted overprint —

India Stamps of 1911-26 Overprinted

Hindi Overprint 15mm Long

1923-27
66 A59 1½a choc ('25) 1.25 .40
67 A59 1½a rose ('27) .20 .20
a. Inverted overprint — —
68 A57 2a6p ultra ('25) 1.25 *1.50*
69 A57 2a6p brown org ('27) .30 *.40*
70 A51 3a ultra ('24) 1.00 .50
Nos. 66-70 (5) 4.00 3.00

Similar Ovpt. on India Stamps of 1926-35

Hindi Overprint 13½mm Long

1928-32 **Wmk. 196**
71 A46 3p slate ('32) .65 .20
72 A47 ½a green ('30) 1.25 .20
73 A48 1a dark brown .65 .20
74 A60 2a dull violet .65 .30
75 A51 3a ultramarine .85 .40
76 A61 4a olive green .85 .85
77 A54 8a red violet 1.10 1.10
78 A55 12a claret 1.25 *2.50*

Overprinted

79 A56 1r green & brown 1.75 *2.75*
80 A56 2r brn org & car rose 5.00 4.00
81 A56 5r dk vio & ultra ('29) 13.50 *21.00*
82 A56 10r car & grn ('30) 37.50 29.00
83 A56 15r olive green & ultra ('30) 60.00 52.50
84 A56 25r bl & ocher ('30) 125.00 110.00
Nos. 71-84 (14) 250.00 225.00

India Stamps of 1932-35 Overprinted in Black

Hindi Overprint 13½mm Long

1933-36
85 A71 ½a green ('36) .40 .20
86 A68 9p dk green ('33) 1.75 .30
87 A72 1a dk brown ('36) .20 .20
88 A69 1a3p violet ('36) .40 .20
89 A49 2a vermilion ('36) 1.25 1.10
Nos. 85-89 (5) 4.00 2.00

Same Ovpt. on India Stamps of 1937

1938-40 ***Perf. 13½x14***
90 A80 3p slate ('40) 2.50 .25
91 A80 ½a brown 2.75 .20
92 A80 9p green ('40) 18.00 10.00
93 A80 1a carmine 2.50 .20
94 A81 3a yel green ('39) 7.00 2.00
95 A81 4a dark brown 21.00 5.00
96 A81 6a pck blue ('39) 1.25 *2.00*
Nos. 90-96 (7) 55.00 19.65

Same Overprinted on India Stamps of 1941-43

1942-49
100 A83 3p slate ('44) .20 .20
101 A83 ½a rose vio ('46) .20 .20
102 A83 9p light green .20 .20
103 A83 1a car rose ('44) .20 .20
104 A84 1½a dk purple ('44) .45 .20
105 A84 2a scarlet ('44) .20 .20
106 A84 3a violet ('44) .25 .20
108 A85 4a choc ('44) .25 .20
109 A85 6a pck blue ('48) 12.00 *18.00*
110 A85 8a blue violet 2.50 2.50
111 A85 12a carmine lake 5.50 *16.00*

India Nos. 162-167 Overprinted **GWALIOR गवालियर**

Perf. 13½x14
112 A82 1r brn & slate ('45) 3.75 1.40
113 A82 2r dk brn & dk vio ('49) 15.00 7.50
114 A82 5r dp ultra & dk grn ('49) 32.50 29.00
115 A82 10r rose car & dk vio ('49) 30.00 *35.00*
116 A82 15r dk grn & dk brn ('48) 87.50 *140.00*
117 A82 25r dk vio & blue vio ('48) 87.50 *100.00*
Nos. 100-106,108-117 (17) 278.20 351.00

India Stamps of 1941-43 Overprinted

1949
118 A83 3p slate .60 .45
119 A83 ½a rose violet .50 .45
120 A83 1a carmine rose .50 .50
121 A84 2a scarlet 11.00 1.60
122 A84 3a violet 27.50 20.00
123 A85 4a chocolate 2.40 2.00
124 A85 6a pck blue 25.00 *37.50*
125 A85 8a blue violet 57.50 37.50
126 A85 12a carmine lake 225.00 100.00
Nos. 118-126 (9) 350.00 200.00

OFFICIAL STAMPS

India Stamps Overprinted in Black

1895 **Wmk. 39** ***Perf. 14***
O1 A17 ½a green .20 .20
a. Double overprint 750.00
O2 A19 1a maroon .55 .20
O3 A21 2a ultramarine 1.00 .35
O4 A23 4a olive green 1.50 .75
O5 A25 8a red violet 1.00 .75
O6 A29 1r car rose & grn 3.75 2.50
Nos. O1-O6 (6) 8.00 4.75

Nos. O1 to O6 inclusive are known with the last two characters of the lower word transposed.

1901-04
O7 A31 3p gray ('04) 1.10 *1.90*
O8 A17 ½a light green .20 .20
O9 A19 1a carmine rose 3.25 .20
O10 A21 2a violet ('03) .45 *1.25*
Nos. O7-O10 (4) 5.00 *3.55*

1902
O11 A31 3p carmine rose .25 .25

1903-05
O12 A32 3p gray .30 .20
O13 A33 ½a green 1.75 .20
O14 A34 1a carmine rose .45 .20
O15 A35 2a violet 1.75 .20
O16 A38 4a olive grn ('05) 3.00 .60
O17 A40 8a red violet 3.50 .30
O18 A42 1r car rose & grn ('05) 2.75 .75
Nos. O12-O18 (7) 13.50 2.45

1907
O19 A44 ½a green .75 .20
O20 A45 1a carmine rose 4.00 .20

Two spacings of the overprint lines, 10mm and 8mm, are found on Nos. O12-O20.

1913
O21 A46 3p gray .25 .20
O22 A47 ½a green .25 .20
O23 A48 1a carmine rose .25 .20
a. Double overprint 57.50
O24 A49 2a violet .50 .25
O25 A52 4a olive green .50 *.75*
O26 A54 8a red violet .75 *1.00*
O27 A56 1r grn & red brn 17.50 15.00
Nos. O21-O27 (7) 20.00 17.60

India No. O66 Overprinted

1921
O28 O6 9p on 1a rose .20 .20

India No. 83 Overprinted

1923
O29 A48 1a dark brown 2.50 .20

Similar Ovpt. on India Stamps of 1926-35

1927-35 **Wmk. 196**
O30 A46 3p slate .25 .20
O31 A47 ½a green .20 .20
O32 A48 1a dark brown .20 .20
O33 A60 2a dull violet .20 .20
O34 A61 4a olive green .40 .30
O35 A54 8a red violet .40 *.65*

Overprinted

O36 A56 1r green & brown .85 *1.50*
O37 A56 2r brn org & car rose ('35) 7.00 *8.25*
O38 A56 5r dk vio & ultra ('32) 10.50 *125.00*
O39 A56 10r car & grn ('32) 80.00 *260.00*
Nos. O30-O39 (10) 100.00 *396.50*

India Stamps of 1926-35 Overprinted

1933-37 ***Perf. 13½x14, 14***
O40 A71 ½a green ('36) .35 .25
O41 A68 9p dk green ('35) .20 .25
O42 A72 1a dk brown ('36) .20 .20
O43 A69 1a3p violet ('33) .50 .20
O44 A49 2a ver ('36) .20 *.40*
a. Small die ('36) 1.75 1.00
O45 A52 4a olive green ('37) .40 *.50*
Nos. O40-O45 (6) 1.85 1.80

For surcharge see No. O62.

Same Overprint on India Stamps

1938 ***Perf. 13½x14***
O46 A80 ½a brown 2.00 .25
O47 A80 1a carmine 2.00 .20

India Nos. 162-165 Overprinted

1945-48 **Wmk. 196** ***Perf. 13½x14***
O48 A82 1r brown & slate 1.25 *10.00*
O49 A82 2r dk brn & dk vio 12.00 *50.00*
O50 A82 5r dp ultra & dk grn ('46) 37.50 *275.00*
O51 A82 10r rose car & dk vio ('48) 60.00 *550.00*
Nos. O48-O51 (4) 110.75 *885.00*

India Official Stamps of 1939-43 Overprinted

1940-44 **Wmk. 196** ***Perf. 13½x14***
O52 O8 3p slate .20 .20
O53 O8 ½a brown 1.50 .25
O54 O8 ½a dk rose vio ('43) .20 .20
O55 O8 9p green ('43) .30 .30
O56 O8 1a car rose ('41) 1.00 .20
O57 O8 1a3p bister ('42) 14.00 1.50
O58 O8 1½a dull purple ('43) .50 .30
O59 O8 2a scarlet ('41) .50 .30
O60 O8 4a dark brown ('44) .55 *1.50*
O61 O8 8a blue vio ('44) 1.25 *5.75*
Nos. O52-O61 (10) 20.00 10.50

Gwalior No. O43 with Additional Surcharge in Black

1942
O62 A69 1a on 1a3p violet 10.50 2.75

JIND

'jind

(Jhind)

LOCATION — A State of India in the north Punjab.
AREA — 1,299 sq. mi.
POP. — 361,812 (1941)
CAPITAL — Sangrur

Previous stamp issues are listed under Feudatory States.

The varieties with small letters are not listed as the letters are merely broken and not from another font.

India Stamps Overprinted in Black **JHIND STATE**

1885 **Wmk. 39** ***Perf. 14***
33 A17 ½a green .75 .75
a. Overprint reading down 52.50 52.50
34 A19 1a violet brown 15.00 *20.00*
a. Overprint reading down 500.00
35 A21 2a ultra 4.25 4.25
a. Overprint reading down 600.00
36 A25 8a red lilac 300.00
a. Overprint reading down *9,000.*
37 A27 1r gray 300.00
a. Overprint reading down *10,000.*

Wmk. 38
38 A9 4a green 19.00 *26.00*
Nos. 33-38 (6) 639.00 51.00

On the reprints of Nos. 33 to 38 "Jhind" measures 8mm instead of 9mm and "State" 9mm instead of 9½mm.

India Stamps Overprinted in Red or Black **JEEND STATE**

1885 **Wmk. 39**
39 A17 ½a green (R) 60.00
40 A19 1a violet brown 60.00
41 A21 2a ultra (R) 100.00
42 A25 8a red lilac 140.00
43 A27 1r gray (R) 150.00

Wmk. 38
44 A9 4a green (R) 125.00
Nos. 39-44 (6) 635.00

India Stamps Overprinted **JHIND STATE**

Red Overprint

1886 **Wmk. 39**
45 A17 ½a green 10.50
a. "JEIND" 1,200.
46 A21 2a ultramarine 12.50
a. "JEIND" 1,400.
47 A27 1r gray 27.50
a. "JEIND" 2,000.

Wmk. 38
48 A9 4a green 25.00
Nos. 45-48 (4) 75.50

Nos. 46, 47 and 48 were not placed in use.

Black Overprint

1886-98 **Wmk. 39**
49 A17 ½a green ('88) .20 .20
a. Inverted overprint 150.00
50 A19 1a violet brown .20 .20
a. "JEIND" 500.00
51 A20 1a6p bister brn ('97) .75 .75
52 A21 2a ultra .30 .25
53 A22 3a orange .25 .20
54 A23 4a olive green .35 .30
55 A25 8a red violet .60 *.75*
a. "JEIND" 2,000.
56 A26 12a vio, *red* ('97) .60 *.75*
57 A27 1r gray ('91) 6.00 *8.75*
58 A29 1r car rose & green ('98) 4.50 *7.50*
59 A30 2r brn & rose ('97) 150.00 *140.00*
60 A30 3r grn & brn ('97) 400.00 *140.00*
61 A30 5r vio & bl ('97) 450.00 *225.00*

Wmk. 38
62 A14 6a bister .90 *1.00*
Nos. 49-62 (14) 1,014. *525.65*

1900 **Wmk. 39**
63 A31 3p carmine rose .20 .20

1902-04
64 A31 3p gray ('04) .20 .20
65 A17 ½a light green .25 *.30*
66 A19 1a carmine rose .30 *.35*
Nos. 64-66 (3) .75 *.85*

1903-09
67 A32 3p gray .20 .20
a. Double overprint
68 A33 ½a green .20 .20
69 A34 1a car rose ('09) .20 .20
a. Double overprint
70 A35 2a violet ('06) .20 .20
70A A36 2a6p ultra ('09) .30 *.35*
71 A37 3a brown orange .25 .25
a. Double overprint 87.50
72 A38 4a olive green .30 *.35*
73 A39 6a bister ('05) .40 *.50*
74 A40 8a red violet .40 *.50*
75 A41 12a vio, *red* ('05) .60 *.75*
76 A42 1r car rose & grn ('05) .75 *.90*
Nos. 67-76 (11) 3.80 *4.40*

1907
77 A44 ½a green .20 .20
78 A45 1a carmine rose .25 .20

1913
80 A46 3p gray .20 .20
81 A47 ½a green .20 .20
82 A48 1a carmine rose .20 .20
83 A49 2a violet .25 .25
84 A51 3a brown orange .85 *1.00*
85 A53 6a bister 2.00 *2.25*
Nos. 80-85 (6) 3.70 *4.10*

India Stamps of 1911-26 Overprinted

1913-14

88 A46 3p gray .20 .20
89 A47 ½a green .20 .20
90 A48 1a carmine rose .20 .20
91 A49 2a violet .20 .20
92 A51 3a brown orange .20 .20
93 A52 4a olive green .20 .20
94 A53 6a bister .20 .20
95 A54 8a red violet .25 .25
96 A55 12a claret .30 *.35*
97 A56 1r grn & red brn .50 .50
Nos. 88-97 (10) 2.45 2.50

India No. 104 Overprinted

1921

98 A48 9p on 1a rose 2.00 *2.25*

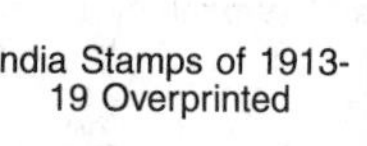

India Stamps of 1913-19 Overprinted

1922

99 A58 1½a chocolate .70 *.80*
100 A57 2a6p ultramarine .40 *.45*

Same Overprint on India Stamps of 1911-26

1924

101 A48 1a dark brown .20 .20
102 A59 1½a chocolate .40 *.45*

Same Overprint on India No. 87

1925

103 A51 3a ultramarine .20 *.25*

Same Overprint on India Stamps of 1911-26

1927

104 A59 1½a rose .20 .20
105 A57 2a6p brown orange .20 .20
106 A56 2r yel brn & car rose 5.25 *6.25*
107 A56 5r violet & ultra 24.00 *27.50*
Nos. 104-107 (4) 29.65 *34.15*

India Stamps of 1926-35 Overprinted

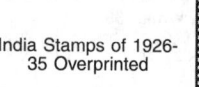

1927-32 **Wmk. 196**

108 A46 3p slate .20 .20
109 A47 ½a green .20 .20
110 A68 9p dark green ('32) .40 .55
111 A48 1a dark brown .20 .20
112 A69 1a3p violet ('32) .30 .40
113 A59 1½a carmine rose .25 .30
114 A60 2a dull violet .20 .20
115 A57 2a6p buff .20 .20
116 A51 3a ultramarine .40 .45
117 A61 4a olive green .25 .30
118 A54 8a red violet 1.25 *1.60*
119 A55 12a claret .75 *1.90*

Overprinted

120 A56 1r green & brown 1.00 *2.50*
121 A56 2r buff & car rose 13.00 *15.00*
122 A56 5r dk vio & ultra 14.00 *17.50*
123 A56 10r car rose & grn 25.00 *35.00*
124 A56 15r ol grn & blue 45.00 *110.00*
125 A56 25r blue & ocher 65.00 *140.00*
Nos. 108-125 (18) 167.60 *326.50*

India Stamps of 1926-35 Overprinted

1934-37

126 A71 ½a green .20 .20
127 A72 1a dark brown .20 .20
128 A49 2a vermilion .20 .20
129 A51 3a carmine rose .20 .20
130 A70 3a6p deep blue ('37) .20 .20
131 A52 4a olive green .25 .25
132 A53 6a bister ('37) .25 .25
Nos. 126-132 (7) 1.50 1.50

Same Overprint on India Stamps of 1937

1937-38 **Wmk. 196** ***Perf. 13½x14***

133 A80 3p slate ('38) .20 *.25*
134 A80 ½a brown ('38) .20 *.30*
135 A80 9p green .30 .30
136 A80 1a carmine .20 .20
137 A81 2a scarlet ('38) .20 .20
138 A81 2a6p purple ('38) .20 .20
139 A81 3a yel grn ('38) .20 .20
140 A81 3a6p ultra ('38) .30 *.35*
141 A81 4a dk brown ('38) .30 *.35*
142 A81 6a pck blue ('38) .35 *.60*
143 A81 8a blue vio ('38) .45 *1.75*
144 A81 12a car lake ('38) .65 *2.50*

Overprinted

1938

145 A82 1r brown & slate 8.00 *9.00*
146 A82 2r dk brn & dk violet 14.00 *15.00*
147 A82 5r dp ultra & dk green 37.50 *50.00*
148 A82 10r rose car & dk violet 75.00 *90.00*
149 A82 15r dk grn & dk brown 150.00 *300.00*
150 A82 25r dk vio & bl vio 190.00 *350.00*
Nos. 133-150 (18) 478.05 *821.20*

India Stamps of 1937 Overprinted

1942-43 **Wmk. 196** ***Perf. 13½x14***

155 A80 3p slate 2.75 2.75
156 A80 ½a brown 2.75 2.75
157 A80 9p green 2.75 2.75
158 A80 1a carmine 2.75 2.75
159 A82 1r brn & slate 3.00 *8.25*
160 A82 2r dk brn & dk violet 9.25 *15.00*
161 A82 5r dp ultra & dk green 35.00 *62.50*
162 A82 10r rose car & dk vio ('43) 47.50 *100.00*
163 A82 15r dk grn & dk brn ('43) 92.50 *140.00*
164 A82 25r dk vio & bl vio 100.00 *225.00*
Nos. 155-164 (10) 298.25 *561.75*

Same Overprint on India Stamps of 1941-43

165 A83 3p slate .30 .30
166 A83 ½a rose vio ('43) .20 .20
167 A83 9p light green .20 .20
168 A83 1a car rose ('43) .20 .20
169 A84 1a3p bister ('43) .45 .45
170 A84 1½a dark purple 1.90 1.90
171 A84 2a scarlet .20 .20
172 A84 3a violet ('43) 1.10 1.10
173 A84 3½a ultramarine .40 .40
174 A85 4a chocolate .40 .40
175 A85 6a peacock blue .45 .40
176 A85 8a blue violet 1.90 *2.25*
177 A85 12a carmine lake 4.50 *5.25*
Nos. 165-177 (13) 12.20 *13.25*

OFFICIAL STAMPS

India Stamps Overprinted in Black

1885 **Wmk. 39** ***Perf. 14***

O1 A17 ½a green .20 .20
a. "JHIND STATE" reading down 85.00 32.50
O2 A19 1a violet brown .25 .20
a. "JHIND STATE" reading down 7.00 7.00
O3 A21 2a ultra 17.50 17.50
a. "JHIND STATE" reading down *1,000.*
Nos. O1-O3 (3) 17.95 17.90

The reprints may be distinguished by the same measurements as the reprints of the corresponding regular issue.

SERVICE

India Stamps Overprinted in Red or Black

JEEND
STATE

1885

O4 A17 ½a green (R) 50.00
O5 A19 1a violet brown 50.00
O6 A21 2a ultra (R) 50.00
Nos. O4-O6 (3) 150.00

India Stamps Overprinted

1886

Red Overprint

O7 A17 ½a green 14.00
a. "JEIND" *600.00*
b. "ERVICE"
O8 A21 2a ultramarine 14.00
a. "JEIND" *750.00*
b. "ERVICE"

No. O8 was not placed in use.

1886-96

Black Overprint

O9 A17 ½a green ('88) .35 .25
O10 A19 1a violet brown 2.25 .25
a. "JEIND" *500.00*
b. "ERVICE"
O11 A21 2a ultramarine .25 .25
O12 A23 4a olive green .65 .40
O13 A25 8a red violet 1.90 1.90
O14 A29 1r car rose & grn ('96) 5.50 *10.50*
Nos. O9-O14 (6) 10.90 *13.55*

1902

O15 A17 ½a light green .25 .25

1903-06

O16 A32 3p gray .20 .20
O17 A33 ½a green 1.25 .20
a. "HIND" 175.00
O18 A34 1a carmine rose 1.75 .20
a. "HIND" 175.00
O19 A35 2a violet .30 .20
O20 A38 4a olive green .60 .35
O21 A40 8a red violet 2.50 2.00
O22 A42 1r car rose & grn ('06) 2.75 2.50
Nos. O16-O22 (7) 9.35 5.65

1907

O23 A44 ½a green .20 .20
O24 A45 1a carmine rose .30 .20

Indian Stamps of 1911-26 Overprinted

a

b

1914-27

O25 A46(a) 3p gray .20 .20
O26 A47(a) ½a green .40 .20
O27 A48(a) 1a car rose .40 .20
O28 A49(a) 2a violet .25 .20
O29 A52(a) 4a olive green .25 .20
a. Double overprint
O30 A54(a) 8a red violet .40 .40
O31 A56(b) 1r grn & red brn .65 .40
O32 A56(b) 2r yel brn & car rose ('27) 7.75 *10.50*
O33 A56(b) 5r vio & ultra ('27) 19.00 *21.00*
Nos. O25-O33 (9) 29.30 *33.30*

India Nos. 83 and 89 Overprinted Type "a"

1924-27

O34 A48 1a dark brown .20 .20
O35 A53 6a bister ('27) .30 .30

India Stamps of 1926-35 Overprinted

c

1927-32

O36 A46 3p slate .20 .20
O37 A47 ½a green .20 .20
O38 A68 9p dark green ('32) .20 .20
O39 A48 1a dark brown .20 .20
O40 A69 1a3p violet ('32) .20 .25
O41 A60 2a dull violet .20 .20
O42 A61 4a olive green .20 .20
O43 A54 8a red violet .25 .25
O44 A55 12a claret .30 .40

Overprinted

d

O45 A56 1r green & brown 1.75 *1.90*
O46 A56 2r buff & car rose 5.75 *6.50*
O47 A56 5r dk vio & ultra 12.00 *13.00*
O48 A56 10r car rose & grn 19.00 *26.00*
Nos. O36-O48 (13) 40.45 *49.50*

India Stamps of 1926-35 Overprinted Type "c"

1934-37

O49 A71 ½a green .25 .20
O50 A72 1a dark brown .20 .20
O51 A49 2a vermilion .20 .20
O52 A57 2a6p buff ('37) 1.10 1.10
O53 A52 4a olive green 1.25 1.25
O54 A53 6a bister ('37) 1.25 1.25
Nos. O49-O54 (6) 4.25 4.20

India Nos. 151-153 Overprinted Type "c"

1937-42 ***Perf. 13½x14***

O55 A80 ½a brown ('42) 32.50 .45
O56 A80 9p green .40 .20
O57 A80 1a carmine .40 .20

India Nos. 162-165 Overprinted Type "d"

O58 A82 1r brn & sl ('40) 16.00 11.00
O59 A82 2r dk brn & dk vio ('40) 25.00 *37.50*
O60 A82 5r dp ultra & dk grn ('40) 65.00 *67.50*
O61 A82 10r rose car & dk vio ('40) 110.00 *110.00*
Nos. O55-O61 (7) 249.30 *226.85*

India Official Stamps of 1939-43 Overprinted

1940-43

O62 O8 3p slate .20 .20
O63 O8 ½a brown 2.50 1.25
O64 O8 ½a dk rose vio ('43) .25 .20
O65 O8 9p green .20 .20
O66 O8 1a car rose .20 .20
O67 O8 1½a dull pur ('43) .90 .75
O68 O8 2a scarlet .20 .20

O69 O8 2½a purple .25 .25
O70 O8 4a dark brown .25 .20
O71 O8 8a blue violet .90 .90

India Nos. 162-165 Overprinted

1942 Wmk. 196 *Perf. 13½x14*
O72 A82 1r brown & slate 14.00 *22.50*
O73 A82 2r dk brn & dk vio 27.50 *40.00*
O74 A82 5r dp ultra & dk green 62.50 *110.00*
O75 A82 10r rose car & dk violet 110.00 *175.00*
Nos. O62-O75 (14) 219.85 *351.85*

NABHA

'näb-hə

LOCATION — A State of India in the eastern and southeastern Punjab
AREA — 966 sq. mi.
POP. — 340,044 (1941)
CAPITAL — Nabha

The varieties with small letters in the overprint are not listed as the letters are merely broken and not from another font.

Indian Stamps Overprinted in Black

1885 Wmk. 39 *Perf. 14*
1 A17 ½a green .45 *.55*
2 A19 1a violet brown 19.00 *30.00*
3 A21 2a ultramarine 9.50 *11.00*
4 A25 8a red lilac 300.00
5 A27 1r gray 200.00

Wmk. 38
6 A9 4a green 37.50 *45.00*

On the reprints "Nabha" and "State" each measure 9½mm. On the originals they measure 11 and 10mm respectively.

Indian Stamps Overprinted

Red Overprint

1885 Wmk. 39
7 A17 ½a green .50 .50
8 A21 2a ultramarine .80 .85
9 A27 1r gray 60.00 *80.00*

Wmk. 38
10 A9 4a green 17.50 *32.50*

Black Overprint

1885-97 Wmk. 39
11 A17 ½a green .25 .20
12 A18 9p rose ('92) .75 .85
13 A19 1a violet brown .20 .20
14 A20 1a6p bister brn .60 .60
a. "ABHA" 200.00
15 A21 2a ultramarine .60 .50
16 A22 3a orange 1.75 1.75
17 A23 4a olive green .75 .50
18 A25 8a red lilac 1.75 1.75
19 A26 12a vio, *red* ('89) 1.10 *1.50*
20 A27 1r gray 12.50 *25.00*
21 A29 1r car rose & grn ('93) 2.00 *2.50*
a. "N BHA"
22 A30 2r brn & rose ('97) 80.00 *125.00*
23 A30 3r grn & brn ('97) 80.00 *125.00*
24 A30 5r vio & blk ('97) 95.00 *140.00*

Wmk. 38
25 A14 6a bister ('89) 2.00 *2.50*
Nos. 11-25 (15) 279.25 *427.85*

Nos. 7, 8, 9, 10, 13, and 18 have been reprinted. They usually bear the overprint "Specimen."

1900 Wmk. 39
26 A31 3p carmine rose .20 .20

1903-09
27 A32 3p gray .20 .20
28 A33 ½a green .25 .25
a. "NABH"
29 A34 1a car rose .40 .35
30 A35 2a violet .40 .40
30A A36 2a6p ultra 27.50 *42.50*
31 A37 3a brown orange .70 .70
32 A38 4a olive green .70 .70
33 A39 6a bister .90 .90
34 A40 8a red violet .70 *.90*
35 A41 12a violet, *red* 1.75 *1.90*
36 A42 1r car rose & grn 1.75 *1.90*
Nos. 27-36 (11) 35.25 *50.70*

1907
37 A44 ½a green .20 .20
38 A45 1a carmine rose .25 .20

1913
40 A46 3p gray .20 .20
41 A47 ½a green .20 .20
42 A48 1a carmine rose .20 .20
43 A49 2a violet .20 .20
44 A51 3a brown orange .20 .20
45 A52 4a olive green .30 .30
46 A53 6a bister .20 *.25*
47 A54 8a red violet .30 .30
48 A55 12a claret .35 *.40*
49 A56 1r green & red brn 1.50 1.50
Nos. 40-49 (10) 3.65 3.75

1924
50 A48 1a dark brown .20 .20

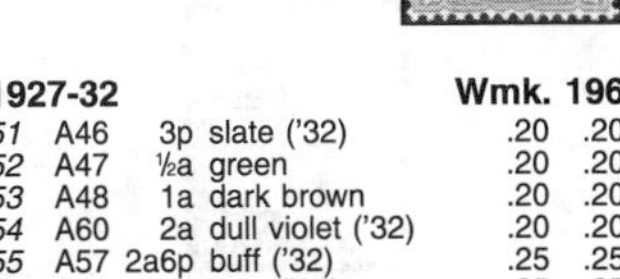

India Stamps of 1926-35 Overprinted

1927-32 Wmk. 196
51 A46 3p slate ('32) .20 .20
52 A47 ½a green .20 .20
53 A48 1a dark brown .20 .20
54 A60 2a dull violet ('32) .20 .20
55 A57 2a6p buff ('32) .25 .25
56 A51 3a blue ('30) .25 .25
57 A61 4a olive green ('32) .80 .80

Overprinted

58 A56 2r brown org & car rose ('32) 15.00 *7.75*
59 A56 5r dk violet & ultra ('32) 70.00 *27.50*
Nos. 51-59 (9) 87.10 *37.35*

India Stamps of 1926-35 Overprinted

1936-37
63 A71 ½a green .20 .20
64 A68 9p dark green ('37) .20 .20
65 A72 1a dark brown .20 .20
66 A69 1a3p violet ('37) .20 .20
67 A51 3a car rose ('37) .50 *.55*
68 A52 4a olive green ('37) .50 *.65*
Nos. 63-68 (6) 1.80 *2.00*

Same Overprint in Black on 1937 Stamps of India

1938-39 *Perf. 13½x14*
69 A80 3p slate 3.75 1.25
70 A80 ½a brown .50 .60
71 A80 9p green 15.00 11.00
72 A80 1a carmine .25 *.30*
73 A81 2a scarlet .20 *.25*
74 A81 2a6p purple .25 *.30*
75 A81 3a yel green .50 *.75*
76 A81 3a6p ultramarine .45 *.60*
77 A81 4a dark brown 1.40 *2.00*
78 A81 6a peacock blue 1.40 *3.00*
79 A81 8a blue violet 2.75 *3.75*
80 A81 12a car lake 3.50 *5.00*

Overprinted

81 A82 1r brown & slate 5.50 *9.00*
82 A82 2r dk brn & dk vio 12.50 *22.50*
83 A82 5r dp ultra & dk green 45.00 *65.00*
84 A82 10r rose car & dk vio ('39) 72.50 *110.00*
85 A82 15r dk grn & dk brn ('39) 125.00 *225.00*
86 A82 25r dk vio & blue vio ('39) 140.00 *250.00*
Nos. 69-86 (18) 430.45 *710.30*

India Stamps of 1937 Overprinted in Black

1942 *Perf. 13½x14*
87 A80 3p slate 22.50 4.00
88 A80 ½a brown 42.50 17.50
89 A80 9p green 17.50 4.50
90 A80 1a carmine 17.50 2.50
Nos. 87-90 (4) 100.00 28.50

Same on India Nos. 168-179

1942-46 Wmk. 196
100 A83 3p slate .35 .35
101 A83 ½a rose vio ('43) .45 .45
102 A83 9p lt green ('43) .45 .45
103 A83 1a car rose ('46) .45 .45
104 A84 1a3p bister ('44) .45 .45
105 A84 1½a dark pur ('43) .55 .55
106 A84 2a scarlet ('44) .80 .80
107 A84 3a violet ('44) 1.25 1.25
108 A84 3½a ultramarine 2.00 2.00
109 A85 4a choc ('43) 2.00 2.00
110 A85 6a pck blue ('44) 2.00 2.00
111 A85 8a blue vio ('44) 2.50 2.50
112 A85 12a car lake ('44) 5.00 5.00
Nos. 100-112 (13) 18.25 18.25

OFFICIAL STAMPS

Indian Stamps Overprinted in Black

1885 Wmk. 39 *Perf. 14*
O1 A17 ½a green .60 .60
O2 A19 1a violet brown .40 .40
O3 A21 2a ultra 37.50 *57.50*
Nos. O1-O3 (3) 38.50 *58.50*

The reprints have the same measurements as the reprints of the regular issue of the same date.

Indian Stamps Overprinted

1885

Red Overprint
O4 A17 ½a green .70 *.95*
O5 A21 2a ultramarine .50 *.55*

1885-97

Black Overprint
O6 A17 ½a green .20 .20
a. Period after "SERVICE" 85.00 1.75
O7 A19 1a violet brown .20 .20
a. "NABHA STATE" double *200.00*
b. Period after "SERVICE" 4.50 1.75
O8 A21 2a ultra .75 .20
O9 A22 3a orange 9.50 *27.50*
O10 A23 4a olive green .90 .30
O11 A25 8a red vio ('89) .65 .60
O12 A26 12a vio, *red* ('89) 3.25 *8.00*
O13 A27 1r gray ('89) 20.00 *110.00*
O14 A29 1r car rose & grn ('97) 16.00 *35.00*

Wmk. 38
O15 A14 6a bister ('89) 8.00 *9.50*
Nos. O6-O15 (10) 59.45 *191.50*

Nos. O4, O5, and O7 have been reprinted. They usually bear the overprint "Specimen."

1903-06 Wmk. 39
O16 A32 3p gray ('06) .20 .20
O17 A33 ½a green .20 .20
O18 A34 1a carmine rose .20 .20
O19 A35 2a violet .30 .30
O20 A38 4a olive green .30 .25
a. Double overprint
O21 A40 8a red violet .50 .40
O22 A42 1r car rose & grn .80 1.00
Nos. O16-O22 (7) 2.50 2.55

1907
O23 A44 ½a green .20 .20
O24 A45 1a carmine rose .20 .20

1913
O25 A52 4a olive green 17.50
O26 A56 1r grn & red brn 92.50

Indian Stamps of 1911-26 Overprinted:

a

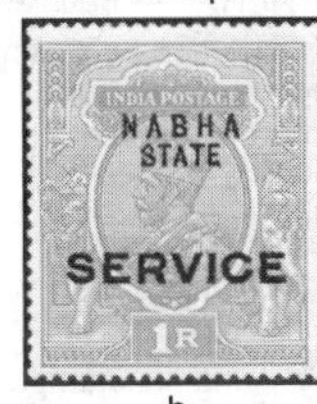

b

1913
O27 A46(a) 3p gray .20 .20
O28 A47(a) ½a green .20 .20
O29 A48(a) 1a carmine rose .20 .20
O30 A49(a) 2a violet .20 .20
O31 A52(a) 4a olive green .20 .20
O32 A54(a) 8a red violet .25 .25
O33 A56(b) 1r grn & red brn .50 .50
Nos. O27-O33 (7) 1.75 1.75

India Stamps of 1926-35 Overprinted

Perf. 13½x14, 14

1932-45 Wmk. 196
O34 A46 3p slate .20 .20
O35 A72 1a dark brown ('35) .20 .20
O36 A52 4a olive green ('45) 7.00 1.75
O37 A54 8a red violet ('37) .70 .85
Nos. O34-O37 (4) 8.10 3.00

Same Overprint in Black on India Stamps of 1937

1938
O38 A80 9p green 2.25 2.25
O39 A80 1a carmine .65 .65

Official Stamps of India 1939-43 Overprinted in Black

1942-44 *Perf. 13½x14*
O40 O8 3p slate .20 .20
O41 O8 ½a brown ('43) .20 .20
O42 O8 ½a dk rose vio ('44) 2.25 2.25
O43 O8 9p green ('43) .20 .20
O44 O8 1a car rose ('43) .20 .20
O45 O8 1½a dull purple ('43) .35 .35
O46 O8 2a scarlet ('43) .20 .20
O47 O8 4a dark brown ('43) 1.90 *2.75*
O48 O8 8a blue violet ('43) 1.90 *2.75*

India Nos. 162-164 Overprinted in Black

O49 A82 1r brown & slate 12.50 *25.00*
O50 A82 2r dk brn & dk vio 37.50 *90.00*
O51 A82 5r dp ultra & dk green 200.00 *200.00*
Nos. O40-O51 (12) 257.40 *324.10*

PATIALA

ˌpət-ē-ˈäl-ə

LOCATION — A State of India in the central Punjab
AREA — 5,942 sq. mi.
POP. — 1,936,259 (1941)
CAPITAL — Patiala

The varieties with small letters in the overprint are not listed as the letters are merely broken and not from another font.

Indian Stamps Overprinted in Red

1884 Wmk. 39 *Perf. 14*

1 A17 ½a green .85 *.90*
a. Double ovpt., one horiz. 1,500. 400.00
2 A19 1a violet brown 14.00 14.00
a. Double overprint
b. Double ovpt., one in black 500.00
c. Pair, one as "b," one without overprint
3 A21 2a ultra 5.25 5.75
4 A25 8a red lilac 200.00 *400.00*
a. Double ovpt., one in black 50.00
c. Overprint reversed
d. Pair like "a," one with overprint reversed
5 A27 1r gray 100.00 *100.00*

Wmk. 38

6 A9 4a green 14.00 16.00
Nos. 1-6 (6) 334.10 *536.65*

Indian Stamps Overprinted in Red

1885 Wmk. 39

7 A17 ½a green .40 .35
a. "AUTTIALLA" 8.50
c. "STATE" only
8 A21 2a ultra .85 .45
a. "AUTTIALLA" 15.00
9 A27 1r gray 5.00 *10.50*
a. "AUTTIALLA" 400.00

Wmk. 38

10 A9 4a green 1.10 1.10
a. Double overprint, one in black 200.00
b. Pair, one as "a," one with black overprint

Same, Overprinted in Black

Wmk. 39

11 A19 1a violet brown .25 .25
a. "AUTTIALLA" 35.00
c. Double overprint, one in red 4.00
d. Pair, one as "c," one without overprint
12 A25 8a red lilac 4.50 4.50
a. "AUTTIALLA" 200.00
Nos. 7-12 (6) 12.10 *17.15*

Nos. 7-12 have been reprinted. Most of them bear the word "Reprint." The few copies that escaped the overprint cannot be distinguished from the originals.

The error "AUTTIALLA" has been reprinted in entire sheets, in red on the ½, 2, 4a and 1r and in black on the ½, 1, 2, 4, 8a and 1r. "STATE" is 7¾mm long, instead of 8½mm. Most copies are overprinted "Reprint."

Same, Overprinted in Black

1891-96

13 A17 ½a green .20 .20
14 A18 9p rose .25 .30
15 A19 1a violet brown .20 .20
a. "STATE" only 150.00 *250.00*
16 A20 1a6p bister brown .35 .40
17 A21 2a ultra .55 .20
18 A22 3a orange .30 .30
19 A23 4a olive grn ('96) .25 .20
a. "STATE" only 325.00 175.00
20 A25 8a red violet ('96) .55 .55
21 A26 12a violet, *red* .45 .55
22 A29 1r car rose & grn ('96) 4.25 *7.00*
23 A30 2r brn & rose ('95) 70.00
24 A30 3r grn & brn ('95) 90.00
25 A30 5r vio & bl ('95) 110.00

Wmk. 38

26 A14 6a bister .35 .30
Nos. 13-26 (14) 277.70

1899 Wmk. 39

27 A31 3p carmine rose .20 .20

1902

28 A17 ½a light green .20 .20
29 A19 1a carmine rose .20 .20

1903-06

31 A32 3p gray .20 .20
32 A33 ½a green .20 .20
33 A34 1a carmine rose .20 .20
a. Pair, one without overprint *1,000.*
34 A35 2a violet .20 .20
35 A37 3a brown orange .25 .25
36 A38 4a olive green ('06) .75 .40
37 A39 6a bister ('05) .55 .50
38 A40 8a red violet ('06) .45 .40
39 A41 12a vio, *red* ('06) 1.25 1.25
40 A42 1r car rose & grn ('05) .70 .75
Nos. 31-40 (10) 4.75 4.35

1908

41 A44 ½a green .20 .20
42 A45 1a carmine rose .20 .20

1912-14

43 A46 3p gray .20 .20
44 A47 ½a green .20 .20
45 A48 1a carmine rose .20 .20
46 A49 2a violet .20 .20
47 A51 3a brown orange .25 .25
48 A52 4a olive green .25 .20
49 A53 6a bister .30 .30
50 A54 8a red violet .45 .25
51 A55 12a claret .65 .40
52 A56 1r green & red brn 2.50 2.50
Nos. 43-52 (10) 5.20 4.70

1922-26

53 A48 1a dk brown ('23) .25 .20
54 A58 1½a chocolate .30 .30
55 A51 3a ultra ('26) .25 .25
56 A56 2r yel brn & car rose ('26) 6.75 *7.25*
57 A56 5r vio & ultra ('26) 14.00 *15.00*
Nos. 53-57 (5) 21.55 *23.00*

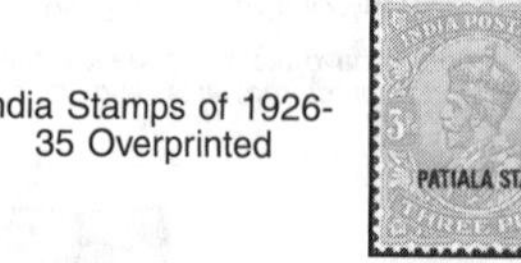

India Stamps of 1926-35 Overprinted

1928-34 Wmk. 196

60 A46 3p slate .20 .20
61 A47 ½a green .20 .20
62 A68 9p dark green .20 .20
63 A48 1a dark brown .20 .20
64 A69 1a3p violet .20 .20
65 A60 2a dull violet .20 .20
66 A57 2a6p buff 1.50 1.50
67 A51 3a blue .90 .90
68 A61 4a olive green .25 *.30*
69 A54 8a red violet .40 .40

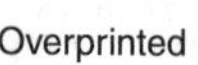

Overprinted

70 A56 1r green & brown 1.00 *1.25*
71 A56 2r buff & car rose 1.75 *2.00*
Nos. 60-71 (12) 7.00 *7.55*

India Stamps of 1926-35 Overprinted Like Nos. 60-69

1935-37 *Perf. 14*

75 A71 ½a green ('37) .20 .20
76 A72 1a dk brown ('36) .20 .20
77 A49 2a ver ('36) .20 .20
78 A51 3a car rose ('37) 1.50 1.50
79 A52 4a olive green .50 .50
Nos. 75-79 (5) 2.60 2.60

Same Overprint in Black on Stamps of India, 1937

1937-38 *Perf. 13½x14*

80 A80 3p slate ('38) 16.00 2.50
81 A80 ½a brown ('38) 3.50 .70
82 A80 9p green 1.25 .45
83 A80 1a carmine .80 .25
84 A81 2a scarlet ('38) 1.00 .25
85 A81 2a6p purple ('38) 1.25 .25
86 A81 3a yel green ('38) 1.25 .25
87 A81 3a6p ultra ('38) 1.60 .40
88 A81 4a dark brown ('38) 8.00 .35
89 A81 6a pck blue ('38) 9.50 .45
90 A81 8a blue violet ('38) 10.00 1.10
91 A81 12a car lake ('38) 10.00 1.10

Overprinted Like Nos. 70-71

1938

92 A82 1r brown & slate 11.00 8.50
93 A82 2r dk brn & dk vio 17.00 16.00
94 A82 5r dp ultra & dk green 27.50 *32.50*
95 A82 10r rose car & dk vit 42.50 *70.00*
96 A82 15r dk grn & dk brown 77.50 *125.00*
97 A82 25r dk vio & bl vio 100.00 *175.00*
Nos. 80-97 (18) 339.65 *435.05*

India Nos. 150-153 Overprinted in Black

1942-43 *Perf. 13½x14*

98 A80 3p slate 12.00 1.50
99 A80 ½a brown ('43) 5.50 1.10
100 A80 9p green ('43) 100.00 3.75
101 A80 1a carmine 15.00 1.50
Nos. 98-101 (4) 132.50 7.85

India Stamps of 1941-43 with same Overprint in Black

1942-47 *Perf. 13½x14*

102 A83 3p slate .35 .20
103 A83 ½a rose violet ('43) .35 .20
104 A83 9p lt green ('43) .35 .20
a. Pair, one without overprint *2,400.*
105 A83 1a car rose ('46) .35 .20
106 A84 1a3p bister ('43) 1.10 *1.60*
107 A84 1½a dk purple ('43) 2.25 .80
108 A84 2a scarlet ('46) 2.25 .20
109 A84 3a violet ('46) 1.25 .55
110 A84 3½a ultra ('46) 6.50 *15.00*
111 A85 4a choc ('46) 1.60 .55
112 A85 6a pck blue ('46) 1.25 *8.50*
113 A85 8a blue vio ('46) 1.60 *4.00*
114 A85 12a car lake ('45) 4.00 *27.50*

India No. 162 Overprinted in Black

115 A82 1r brown & slate ('47) 5.25 *40.00*
Nos. 102-115 (14) 28.45 *99.50*

OFFICIAL STAMPS

Indian Stamps Overprinted in Black and Red

1884 Wmk. 39 *Perf. 14*

O1 A17 ½a green 3.00 .25
O2 A19 1a vio brown .45 .20
a. "SERVICE" double 900.00 400.00
b. "SERVICE" inverted 900.00
c. "PUTTIALLA STATE" double 90.00
d. "PUTTIALLA STATE" inverted 900.00 90.00
O3 A21 2a ultra *2,250.* 200.00

Same, Overprinted in Red or Black:

a

b

1885-90

O4 A17(a) ½a grn (R & Bk) .55 .20
a. "AUTTIALLA" 45.00 15.00
d. "SERVICE" double 600.00
O5 A17(b) ½a green (Bk) .45 .20
O6 A19(a) 1a vio brn (Bk) .25 .20
a. "AUTTILLA" 500.00 37.50
c. "SERVICE" dble., one invtd. 500.00
d. "SERVICE" double 1,000. 190.00
O7 A21(b) 2a ultra (R) .20 .20
c. "SERVICE" dbl., one invtd. 40.00
Nos. O4-O7 (4) 1.45 .80

There are reprints of Nos. O4, O6 and O7. That of No. O4 has "SERVICE" overprinted in red in large letters and that of No. O6 has the same overprint in black. The originals have the word in small black letters. The reprints of No. O7, except those overprinted "Reprint," cannot be distinguished from the originals. These three reprints also exist with the error "AUTTIALLA."

Same, Overprinted in Black

1891-1900

O8 A17 ½a green ('95) .20 .20
b. "SERVICE" inverted 67.50
O9 A19 1a vio brown ('00) 2.25 .20
a. "SERVICE" inverted 72.50
O10 A21 2a ultramarine .95 .45
a. "SERVICE" inverted 72.50
O11 A22 3a orange .35 .25
O12 A23 4a olive green .20 .20
O13 A25 8a red violet .30 .25
O14 A26 12a violet, *red* .50 .30
O15 A27 1r gray .55 .30

Wmk. 38

O16 A14 6a bister .45 .40
Nos. O8-O16 (9) 5.75 2.55

1902 Wmk. 39

O17 A19 1a carmine rose .25 .20

1903

O18 A29 1r car rose & green 5.25 5.50

1903-09

O19 A32 3p gray .20 .20
O20 A33 ½a green .20 .20
O21 A34 1a carmine rose .20 .20
O22 A35 2a violet .20 .20
O23 A37 3a brown orange .75 .75
O24 A38 4a olive green ('05) .30 .20
O25 A40 8a red violet .30 .20
O26 A42 1r car rose & grn ('06) .85 .85
Nos. O19-O26 (8) 3.00 2.80

1907

O27 A44 ½a green .20 .20
O28 A45 1a carmine rose .20 .20

India Stamps of 1911-26 Overprinted:

a

b

1913-26

O29 A46(a) 3p gray .20 .20
O30 A47(a) ½a green 1.10 .20
O31 A48(a) 1a car rose .20 .20
O32 A49(a) 2a violet .20 .20
O33 A52(a) 4a olive green .20 .20
O34 A54(a) 8a red violet .25 .20
O35 A56(b) 1r grn & red brn .55 .45
O36 A56(b) 2r yel brn & car rose ('26) 5.50 *9.25*
O37 A56(b) 5r vio & ultra ('26) 11.00 *22.50*
Nos. O29-O37 (9) 19.20 *33.40*

Same Overprint on India Nos. 83 and 89

1925-26

O38 A48(a) 1a dark brown .20 .20
O39 A53(a) 6a bister ('26) .25 .20

India Stamps of 1926-35 Overprinted

1927-36 **Wmk. 196**

O40 A46 3p slate .20 .20
O41 A47 ½a green .20 .20
O42 A48 1a dark brown .20 .20
O43 A69 1a3p violet .20 .20
O44 A60 2a dull violet .20 .20
O45 A60 2a vermilion .20 .20
O46 A57 2a6p buff .20 .20
O47 A61 4a olive green .20 .20
O48 A54 8a red violet .25 .25

Overprinted

O49 A56 1r green & brown .75 .30
O50 A56 2r brn org & car rose ('36) 3.00 *3.25*
Nos. O40-O50 (11) 5.60 *5.40*

India Stamps of 1926-34 Overprinted

1935-36

O51 A71 ½a green ('36) .20 .20
O52 A72 1a dark brown ('36) .20 .20
O53 A49 2a vermilion .30 .20
a. Small die .25 .20
O54 A52 4a olive green ('36) .30 .20
Nos. O51-O54 (4) 1.00 *.80*

Same Overprint on India #151-153

1938-39 ***Perf. 13½x14***

O55 A80 ½a brown ('39) .60 .20
O56 A80 9p green ('39) 21.00 *27.50*
O57 A80 1a carmine .60 .20
Nos. O55-O57 (3) 22.20 *27.90*

India No. 136 Surcharged in Black

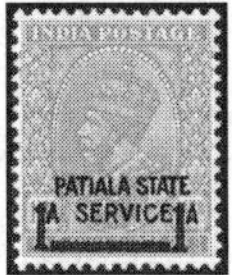

1939 ***Perf. 14***

O58 A69 1a on 1a3p violet 2.00 .70

"SERVICE" measures 9¼mm.

No. 64 Surcharged in Black

1940

O59 A69 1a on 1a3p violet 2.00 1.40

"SERVICE" measures 8½mm.

India Nos. 162-164 Overprinted

Perf. 13½x14

O60 A82 1r brown & slate 2.75 2.75
O61 A82 2r dk brn & dk vio 14.00 14.00
O62 A82 5r dp ultra & dk grn 27.50 27.50

India Official Stamps of 1939-43 Overprinted

1940-45

O63 O8 3p slate ('41) .20 .20
O64 O8 ½a brown .20 .20
O65 O8 ½a dk rose vio ('43) .20 .20
O66 O8 9p green .20 .20
O67 O8 1a carmine rose .25 .20
O68 O8 1a3p bister ('41) .20 .20
O69 O8 1½a dull purple ('45) .40 .20
O70 O8 2a scarlet ('41) .20 .20
O71 O8 2½a purple ('41) .20 .20
O72 O8 4a dk brown ('45) .30 .30
O73 O8 8a blue violet ('45) .90 *1.25*

India Nos. 162-164 Overprinted in Black

O74 A82 1r brn & slate ('43) 7.50 5.50
O75 A82 2r dk brn & dk vio ('45) 13.00 *32.50*
O76 A82 5r dp ultra & dk grn ('45) 20.00 *50.00*
Nos. O63-O76 (14) 43.75 *91.35*

NATIVE FEUDATORY STATES

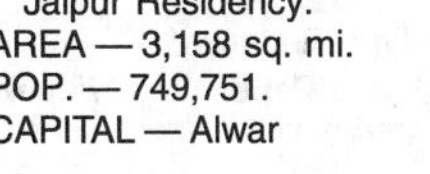

NATIVE FEUDATORY STATES
These stamps had franking power solely in the states in which they were issued, except for Cochin and Travancore which had a reciprocal postal agreement.

ALWAR

'əl-wər

LOCATION — A Feudatory State of India, lying southwest of Delhi in the Jaipur Residency.
AREA — 3,158 sq. mi.
POP. — 749,751.
CAPITAL — Alwar

Katar (Indian Dagger) — A1

1877 **Unwmk.** **Litho.** ***Rouletted***

1 A1 ¼a ultramarine 1.00 .75
a. ¼a blue 1.00 .75
b. Horiz. pair, imperf. vert. 32.50
2 A1 1a brown 1.00 1.00
a. 1a yellow brown 1.00 1.00
b. 1a red brown 1.00 1.00
c. Horiz. pair, imperf. vert. 55.00 55.00

Redrawn

1899-1901 ***Pin-perf. 12***

3 A1 ¼a sl blue, wide margins 6.00 3.50
4 A1 ¼a yel grn, narrow margins ('01) 5.25 3.50
a. Horiz. pair, imperf. btwn. 275.00
b. ¼a emer, wide margins ('99) 500.00
c. ¼a emer, narrow margins 5.25 4.75

Nos. 3 and 4b are printed farther apart in the sheet.

On Nos. 3 and 4, the shading of the left border line is missing.

Nos. 1 to 4 occasionally show portions of the papermaker's watermark, W. T. & Co.

Alwar stamps became obsolete in 1902.

BAMRA

'bäm-rə

LOCATION — A Feudatory State in the Eastern States, Orissa States Agency, Bengal.
AREA — 1,988 sq. mi.
POP. — 151,259
CAPITAL — Deogarh

Stamps of Bamra were issued without gum.

A1

A2

1888 **Unwmk.** **Typeset** ***Imperf.***

1 A1 ¼a black, *yellow* 80.00
a. "g" inverted *2,000.*
2 A1 ½a black, *rose* 52.50
a. "g" inverted *1,750.*
3 A1 1a black, *blue* 32.50
a. "g" inverted *1,350.*
b. "postge"
4 A1 2a black, *green* 45.00
a. "postge" *1,750.*
5 A1 4a black, *yellow* 32.50
a. "postge" *1,500.*
6 A1 8a black, *rose* 30.00
a. "postge" *1,350.*
Nos. 1-6 (6) 272.50

All values may be found with the scroll inverted, and with the long end of the scroll pointing to the right or left.

On No. 5 the last character on the 3rd line is a vertical line. On No. 1 it is not vertical.

On No. 2 the last character on the 3rd line looks like a backwards "R" with a bent leg. On No. 6 it looks like an apostrophe.

Nos. 1 and 2 have been reprinted in blocks of 8 and Nos. 1-6 in blocks of 20. In the reprints the 4th character of the native inscription often has the curved upper line broken at the left, but in many instances comparison with photographic reproductions of the original settings is the only certain test.

1890

7 A2 ¼a black, *rose lilac* 1.00 1.00
a. "Quatrer" 10.00 10.00
b. "e" of "Postage" inverted 10.00 10.00
c. "Eeudatory" 10.00 10.00
8 A2 ½a black, *green* 1.40 1.40
a. "Eeudatory" 16.00 16.00
b. "postage" with small "p" 1.40 1.40
c. First "a" of "anna" inverted 14.00
9 A2 1a black, *yellow* 3.25 3.25
a. "Eeudatory" 35.00 *40.00*
b. "postage" with small "p" 2.00 2.00
c. "annas" 65.00 65.00
10 A2 2a black, *rose lilac* 4.75 4.75
a. "Eeudatory" 60.00 *67.50*
11 A2 4a black, *rose lilac* 35.00 35.00
a. "Eeudatory" 150.00 150.00
12 A2 8a black, *rose lilac* 10.00 10.00
a. "BAMBA" 100.00 100.00
b. "Foudatory" & "Postage" 100.00 100.00
c. "postage" with small "p" 10.00 10.00
13 A2 1r black, *rose lilac* 32.50 32.50
a. "BAMBA" 140.00 140.00
b. "Eeudatory" 150.00 150.00
c. "postage" with small "p" 32.50 32.50
Nos. 7-13 (7) 87.90 87.90

1893

14 A2 ¼a black, *rose* .90 .90
a. "postage" with small "p" .90 .90
15 A2 ¼a black, *magenta* .90 .90
a. "postage" with small "p" .90 .90
b. "AM" of "BAMRA" invtd.
c. "M" OF "BAMRA" invtd.
d. "AMRA" of "BAMRA" inverted 22.50
e. "M" and 2nd "A" of "BAMRA" inverted 52.50 52.50
f. First "a" of "anna" inverted 27.50 27.50
16 A2 2a black, *rose* 1.40 1.40
a. "postage" with small "p" 1.40 1.40
17 A2 4a black, *rose* 3.25 3.25
a. "postage" with small "p" 3.25 3.25
b. "BAMBA" 210.00 210.00
18 A2 8a black, *rose* 5.00 5.00
a. "postage" with small "p" 5.00 5.00
19 A2 1r black, *rose* 18.00 20.00
a. "postage" with small "p" 30.00 30.00
Nos. 14-19 (6) 29.45 31.45

The central ornament varies in size and may be found in various positions.

Bamra stamps became obsolete Dec. 31, 1894.

BARWANI

bər-'wän-ē

LOCATION — A Feudatory State of Central India, in the Malwa Agency.
AREA — 1,178 sq. mi.
POP. — 141,110
CAPITAL — Barwani

The stamps of Barwani were all typographed and normally issued in booklets containing panes of four. Exceptions are noted (Nos. 14-15, 20-25). The majority were completely perforated, but some of the earlier printings were perforated only between the stamps, leaving one or two sides imperf. Nos. 1-25 were issued without gum. Many shades exist.

Rana Ranjit Singh
A1 A2

1921, April (?) **Unwmk.** ***Pin-Perf 7***
Toned Medium Wove Paper
Clear Impression

1 A1 ¼a dull Prus grn 75.00 *225.00*
2 A1 ½a dull blue 175.00 *350.00*

1921 ***Coarse Perf. 7 x Imperf.***
White Thin Wove Paper
Blurred Impression

3 A1 ¼a dull green 17.50 *75.00*
4 A1 ½a pale blue 15.00 *100.00*

1921 **Toned Laid Paper** ***Imperf.***

5 A1 ¼a light green 15.00
6 A1 ½a light green 3.00
a. Perf. 11, top or bottom only 2.50

1921 ***Coarse Perf. 7, 7 x Imperf.***
Thick Wove Paper
Very Blurred Impression

7 A1 ¼a dull blue 15.00
8 A1 ½a dull green 22.50

In 1927 #7-8 were printed on thin hard paper.

1922 ***Perf. 7 x Imperf.***
Thick Glazed Paper

9 A1 ¼a dull ultra 50.00

Rough Perf. 11 x Imperf.

10 A2 1a vermilion 2.00 *18.00*
11 A2 2a violet 2.00 *20.00*
a. Double impression 225.00
Nos. 9-11 (3) 54.00

Shades of No. 11 include purple. No. 11 was also printed on thick dark toned paper.

1923-26 ***Perf.***

Wove, Laid Paper

12 A1 ¼a grayish ultra, perf. 8½ 1.60 *30.00*
13 A1 ¼a black, perf. 7 x imperf. 55.00 *150.00*
14 A1 ¼a dull rose, perf. 11½-12 1.25 *7.50*
15 A1 ¼a dk bl, perf. 11 ('26) 1.25 *7.50*
16 A1 ½a grn, perf. 11ximperf. 1.25 *15.00*
Nos. 12-16 (5) 60.35

No. 12 was also printed on pale gray thin toned paper.

No. 14 was printed on horizontally laid paper in horizontal sheets of 12 containing three panes of 4.

No. 15 was printed on vertically laid paper in horizontal sheets of 8.

Rana Ranjit Singh — A3

1927-28 ***Perf. 7***

Thin Wove Paper

17 A3 4a dull orange 55.00 *250.00*

No. 17 was also printed in light brown on thick paper, pin-perf. 6, and in orange brown on thick paper, rough perf. 7.

1928 ***Coarse Perf. 7***

Thick Glazed Paper

18 A1 ¼a bright blue 9.00
19 A1 ½a bright yel green 18.00

1928, Nov. ***Rough Perf. 10½***

20 A1 ¼a deep ultra 3.25
a. Tête bêche pair 8.50
21 A1 ½a yellow green 4.00
a. Tête bêche pair 7.50

1929-31 ***Perf. 11***

22 A1 ¼a blue 2.00 *7.50*
a. ¼a ultramarine 1.50 *10.00*
23 A1 ½a emerald green 2.50 *10.00*
24 A2 1a car pink ('31) 10.00 *25.00*
25 A3 4a salmon 40.00 *125.00*
Nos. 22-25 (4) 54.50

Nos. 20-25 were printed in sheets of 8 (4x2).

No. 22 had five printings in various shades (bright to deep blue) in horizontal or vertical format.

No. 23 also printed in dark myrtle green.

Rana Devi Singh
A4 A5

1932-48 ***Perf. 11, 12***

Glazed Paper

26 A4 ¼a dark gray 1.40 *9.50*
27 A4 ½a blue green 1.40 *9.50*
28 A4 1a brown 1.50 *9.00*
a. 1a chocolate, perf. 8½ ('48) 10.00 30.00
29 A4 2a deep red violet 2.75 *15.00*
a. Perf. 12x11
b. 2a red lilac 12.50
30 A4 4a olive green 8.50 *17.00*
Nos. 26-30 (5) 15.55 *60.00*

Types of 1921-27

1934-48 ***Perf. 11***

31 A1 ¼a slate gray 2.25 *17.50*
32 A1 ½a green 3.50 *22.50*
33 A2 1a dark brown 9.00 *17.50*
a. 1a brown, perf. 8½ ('48) 9.00 *25.00*
34 A2 2a brt purple ('38) 60.00 *150.00*
35 A2 2a rose car ('46) 20.00 *75.00*
36 A3 4a olive green 20.00 *37.50*
Nos. 31-36 (6) 114.75

In the nine printings of Nos. 26-36, several plate settings spaced the cliches from 2 to 9mm apart. Hence the stamps come in different overall sizes. Not all values were in each printing. Values are for the commonest varieties.

No. 36 was also printed in pale sage green.

1938

37 A5 1a dark brown 22.50 *40.00*
a. Booklet pane of 4 50.00

Stamps of type A5 in red are revenues. Barwani stamps became obsolete 7/1/48.

BHOPAL

bō-'päl

LOCATION — A Feudatory State of Central India, in the Bhopal Agency.
AREA — 6,924 sq. mi.
POP. — 995,745
CAPITAL — Bhopal

Inscription in Urdu in an octagon embossed on Nos. 1-83, in a circle embossed on Nos. 84-90. On designs A1-A3, A7, A11-A12, A14-A15, A19-A21 the embossing makes up the central part of the design.

The embossing may be found inverted or sideways.

Expect irregular perfs on the perforated stamps, Nos. 19-77, due to a combination of imperfect perforating methods and the fragility of the papers.

Nos. 1-90 issued without gum.

A1

A2

Double Lined Frame

1876 **Unwmk.** **Litho.** ***Imperf.***

1 A1 ¼a black 300.00 250.00
a. "EGAM" 1,000. 1,000.
b. "BFGAM" 1,000. 1,000.
c. "BEGAN" 650.00 650.00
2 A1 ½a red 17.50 17.50
a. "EGAM" 50.00 *90.00*
b. "BFGAM" 50.00 *90.00*
c. "BEGAN" 35.00 *60.00*

Single Lined Frame

1877

3 A2 ¼a black *4,000.*
a. "NWAB"
4 A2 ½a red 20.00 *37.00*
a. "NWAB" 100.00 *150.50*

A3

A4

1878

5 A3 ¼a black 5.00 *8.50*
a. "J" diagonal, plate II 5.00 *10.00*

All stamps of type A3 are lettered "EEGAM" for "BEGAM."

1878

6 A4 ½a pale red 4.50 *10.00*
a. ½a brown red 20.00 27.50
b. "NWAB" 15.00
c. "JAHN" 24.00
d. "EECAM" 24.00

A5 A6

1879-80

7 A5 ¼a green 9.00 *15.00*
8 A5 ½a red 10.00 *15.00*

Perf.

9 A5 ¼a green 7.00 *10.00*
10 A5 ½a red 10.00
Nos. 7-10 (4) 36.00 *40.00*

Nos. 7 and 9 have the value in parenthesis; Nos. 8 and 10 are without parenthesis.

1881 ***Imperf.***

11 A6 ¼a green 5.00
a. "NAWA" 20.00
b. "CHAH" 50.00

Perf.

12 A6 ¼a green 7.00
a. "NAWA" 27.50
b. "CHAH" 75.00

A7

1881-89 ***Imperf.***

13 A7 ¼a black 4.00 *10.00*
a. "NWAB" 8.00
14 A7 ½a red 3.00 *7.50*
a. "NWAB" 7.00
15 A7 1a brown 2.75 *8.00*
a. "NWAB" 6.50
16 A7 2a blue 1.50 *8.00*
a. "NWAB" 4.00
17 A7 4a yellow 10.00 *32.50*
a. "NWAB" 25.00
Nos. 13-17 (5) 21.25 66.00

A8

A9

1884 ***Perf.***

19 A8 ¼a green 110.00 *140.00*
a. "JAN" 110.00 *140.00*
b. "BEGM" 325.00
c. "NWAB" 550.00
d. "SHAHAN" 550.00
e. "JN" 375.00
f. "JAHA" 250.00
20 A9 ¼a green 3.00 *8.50*
a. "ANAWAB" 10.00

On type A9 there is a dash at the left of "JA" of "JAHAN" instead of a character like a comma as on types A5 and A6.

Imitations of No. 19 were printed about 1904 in black on wove paper and in red on laid paper, both imperf. and pin-perf.

A10

1884 **Laid Paper** ***Imperf.***

21 A10 ¼a blue green 90.00 *100.00*
a. "NWAB" 250.00
b. "NAWAJANAN" 250.00
c. "SAH" 250.00
22 A10 ½a black 1.60 1.25
a. "NWAB" 7.00
b. "NAWAJANAN" 7.00
c. "SAH" 7.00

Perf.

23 A10 ¼a blue green .50 *2.50*
a. "NWAB" 3.00
b. "NAWAJANAN" 3.00
c. "SAH" 3.00
24 A10 ½a black .40 *1.75*
a. "NWAB" 2.75
b. "NAWAJANAN" 2.75
c. "SAH" 2.75
Nos. 21-24 (4) 92.50 105.50

Type Redrawn

1886 **Wove Paper** ***Imperf.***

25 A10 ¼a grayish green .35 *2.00*
a. ¼a green .35 *2.00*
b. "NWAB" 2.00
c. "NAWA" 1.50
d. "NAWAA" 2.00
e. "NAWABABEGAAM" 2.00
f. "NWABA" 2.00
26 A10 ½a red .30 .30
a. "SAH" 3.00
b. "NAWABA" 2.75

Perf.

27 A10 ¼a green 1.50 *2.50*
a. "NWAB" 8.00
b. "NAWA" 8.00
c. "NAWAA" 8.00
d. "NAWABABEGAAM" 8.00
e. "NWABA" 8.00
28 A10 ½a red 2.50 2.50
a. "SAH" 12.00
b. "NAWABA" 12.00
Nos. 25-28 (4) 4.65 7.30

On Nos. 25-28 the inscriptions are closer to the value than on Nos. 21-24.

A11

A12

1886 ***Imperf.***

29 A11 ½a red 1.40 6.00
a. "BEGAM" 7.50
b. "NWAB" 7.50

Laid Paper

30 A12 4a yellow 6.00
a. "EEGAM" 10.00
b. Wove paper 500.00
c. As "a," wove paper *650.00*

Perf.

31 A12 4a yellow 2.50 *10.00*
a. "EEGAM" 5.00 *15.00*
Nos. 29-31 (3) 9.90

A13

A14

1889 **Wove Paper** ***Imperf.***

32 A13 ¼a green .50 .75
a. "SAH" 3.00 *4.75*
b. "NAWA" 3.00 *4.75*
33 A14 ¼a black 1.10 1.25
a. "EEGAN" 7.25

Perf.

34 A13 ¼a green .50 1.25
a. "SAH" 3.25
b. "NAWA" 3.25
c. Imperf. vertically
35 A14 ¼a black 1.00 3.00
a. "EEGAN" 9.00 *20.00*
b. Horiz. pair, imperf. between 175.00
Nos. 32-35 (4) 3.10 6.25

Type A13 has smaller letters in the upper corners than Type A10.

A15

A16

1890 ***Imperf.***

36 A15 ¼a black 1.00 .80
37 A15 1a brown .90 *3.00*
a. "EEGAM" 10.00 *15.00*
b. "BBGAM" 10.00 *15.00*
38 A7 2a greenish blue .80 1.00
a. "BBEGAM" 6.50 *9.00*
b. "NAWAH" 6.50 *9.00*
39 A7 4a yellow 1.00 *2.10*
40 A16 8a blue 30.00 *57.50*
a. "HAH" 45.00
b. "JABAN" 45.00
Nos. 36-40 (5) 33.70 64.40

An imperf. imitation of Nos. 36 and 41 was printed about 1904 in black on wove paper.

Perf.

41 A15 ¼a black 1.25 2.10
a. Pair, imperf. between 7.50
42 A15 1a brown .90 3.00
a. "EECAM" 17.50 20.00
b. "BBGAM" 17.50 20.00
43 A7 2a greenish blue .85 1.50
a. "BBEGAM" 6.00 12.00
b. "NAWAH" 6.00 12.00
44 A7 4a yellow 1.50 4.00
45 A16 8a blue 32.50 60.00
a. "HAH" 45.00
b. "JABAN" 45.00
Nos. 41-45 (5) 37.00 70.60

Nos. 40 and 45 have a frame line around each stamp.

Imperf

46 A12 ½a red (BECAM) .90 1.10
47 A13 ½a red (NWAB) .75 .60
a. Inverted "N"
b. "SAH" 7.50

Perf.

48 A12 ½a red (BECAM) .60 .60
a. Without embossing
49 A13 ½a red (NWAB) .75 .85
a. Inverted "N"
b. "SAH" 7.50
Nos. 46-49 (4) 3.00 3.15

1891-93 Laid Paper *Imperf.*

50 A16 8a deep green 40.00 75.00
a. "HAH" 55.00
b. "JABAN" 55.00

Perf.

51 A16 8a deep green 40.00 75.00
a. "HAH" 60.00
b. "JABAN" 60.00

For overprint, see No. 83.

1894 Redrawn *Imperf.*

53 A10 ¼a green .60 .60
a. "NAWAH" 5.00 6.00
54 A11 ½a brick red 1.00 .75
55 A16 8a blue black 15.00 15.00
a. Laid paper 27.50

Perf.

56 A10 ¼a green 1.60 1.25
a. "NAWAH" 7.50 7.50
57 A11 ½a brick red .60 1.00
58 A16 8a blue black 20.00 24.00
Nos. 53-58 (6) 38.80 42.60

The ¼a redrawn has letters in corners larger; value in very small characters.

The 8a redrawn has no frame to each stamp but a frame to the sheet.

1898 *Imperf.*

60 A16 8a black 24.00 35.00
b. "E" of "BEGAM" inverted 55.00

A17

A18

A19

A20 A21

1895

Laid Paper

61 A17 ¼a green 1.50 1.50
62 A18 ¼a red 1.75 1.75
63 A19 ¼a black .75 .75
a. "NAWB" 4.25 4.25
64 A20 ½a black .75 .75
65 A21 ½a red .90 1.10

Perf.

66 A17 ¼a green 3.25 3.25
67 A18 ¼a red 1.60 1.60
68 A19 ¼a black 2.50 2.50
a. "NAWB" 18.00
69 A20 ½a black 1.60 1.60
70 A21 ½a red 1.60 1.60
Nos. 61-69 (9) 14.60 14.80

Imperf. imitations of Nos. 65 and 70 were printed about 1904 in deep red on laid paper and in black on wove paper.

Wove Paper

Small Pin-perf.

71 A16 8a blue black

A22

A23

1898 *Imperf.*

72 A22 ¼a black .30 .30
a. "SHAN" 2.50
73 A22 ¼a green .35 .35
a. "SHAN" 2.50
74 A23 ¼a black 1.50 .50
Nos. 72-74 (3) 2.15 1.15

1899

75 A13 ½a black ("NWAB") 2.25 3.00
a. "SHN" 14.00 17.50
b. "NWASBAHJAHNJ" 14.00 17.50
c. "SIIAN"
d. "SBAH" 7.00 8.50
e. "SBAN" 14.00 17.50
f. "NWIB" 14.00 17.50
g. "BEIAM" 14.00 17.50

A24

Coat of Arms — A25

1902

76 A24 ¼a red 1.10 2.25
77 A24 ½a black 1.60 2.75
a. Printed on both sides 365.00
78 A24 1a brown 2.75 6.75
79 A24 2a blue 4.00 5.50
80 A24 4a orange 32.50 47.50
81 A24 8a violet 50.00 80.00
82 A24 1r rose 125.00 150.00
Nos. 76-82 (7) 216.95 294.75

No. 50 Overprinted in Red

1903

83 A16 8a deep green 75.00 75.00
a. Inverted overprint 160.00 160.00

There are two types of the overprint which is the Arabic S, initial of the Begum.

Inscription in Circle Embossed on Each Stamp

1903

84 A24 ¼a red .35 1.75
85 A24 ½a black .45 2.25
86 A24 1a brown .55 2.75
87 A24 2a blue 1.50 10.50
88 A24 4a orange 16.00 24.00
89 A24 8a violet 27.50 57.50
90 A24 1r rose 35.00 77.50
Nos. 84-90 (7) 81.35 176.25

The embossing in a circle, which was first used in 1903, has been applied to many early stamps and impressions from redrawn plates of early issues. So far as is now known, these should be classed as reprints.

1908 Engr. *Perf. 13½*

99 A25 1a yellow green 3.00 3.00
a. Printed on both sides 90.00

OFFICIAL STAMPS

O1

Size: 20½x25mm

Overprinted

1908 Unwmk. Engr. *Perf. 13½*

O1 O1 ½a yellow green 1.50 .20
a. Pair, one without ovpt. 300.00
b. Inverted overprint 100.00
c. Double ovpt., one invtd. 100.00
O2 O1 1a carmine 2.75 .20
a. Inverted overprint 60.00
O3 O1 2a blue 16.00 .20
O4 O1 4a red brown 7.25 .20
Nos. O1-O4 (4) 27.50 .80

Overprinted

O5 O1 ½a yellow green 2.50 .20
O6 O1 1a carmine 6.00 .90
O7 O1 2a blue 3.00 .20
a. Inverted overprint 20.00
O8 O1 4a red brown 45.00 .20
a. Inverted overprint 17.50 50.00
Nos. O5-O8 (4) 56.50 1.50

The difference in the two overprints is in the shape of the letters, most noticeable in the "R."

Type of 1908 Issue
Size: 25½x30½mm

Overprinted **SERVICE**

1930-31 Litho. *Perf. 14*

O9 O1 ½a gray green ('31) 5.25 .70
O10 O1 1a carmine 6.00 .20
O11 O1 2a blue 5.75 .20
O12 O1 4a brown 5.25 .40
Nos. O9-O12 (4) 22.25 1.50

½a, 2a, 4a are inscribed "POSTAGE" on the left side; 1a "POSTAGE AND REVENUE."

Similar to Type O1
Size: 21x25mm
"POSTAGE" at left
"BHOPAL STATE" at right

1932-33 *Perf. 11½, 13, 13½, 14*

O13 O1 ¼a orange yellow 1.75 .20
a. Pair, one without overprint 85.00
b. Perf. 13½ 5.25 2.75
c. Perf. 14 10.00 .20

"BHOPAL GOVT." at right

Perf. 13½

O14 O1 ½a yellow green 3.00 .20
O15 O1 1a brown red 5.50 .20
O16 O1 2a blue 5.50 .20
O17 O1 4a brown 4.25 .50
Nos. O13-O17 (5) 20.00 1.30

No. O14, O16-O17 Surcharged in Red, Violet, Black or Blue:

a

b

HALF ANNA
ONE ANNA
SERVICE
c

1935-36 *Perf. 13½*

O18 O1(a) ¼a on ½a (R) 17.00 9.00
a. Inverted surcharge 125.00 60.00
O19 O1(b) 3p on ½a (R) 2.10 2.50
O20 O1(a) ¼a on 2a (R) 17.00 11.50
a. Inverted surcharge 110.00 50.00
O21 O1(b) 3p on 2a (R) 3.00 2.75
a. Inverted surcharge 45.00 27.50
O22 O1(a) ¼a on 4a (R) 590.00 160.00
O23 O1(a) ¼a on 4a (Bk) ('36) 45.00 16.00
O24 O1(b) 3p on 4a (R) 67.50 32.50
O25 O1(b) 3p on 4a (Bk) ('36) 2.10 2.25
O26 O1(c) 1a on ½a (V) 2.50 1.25
a. Inverted surcharge 50.00 35.00
O27 O1(c) 1a on 2a (R) 1.90 1.50
a. Inverted surcharge 50.00 50.00
O28 O1(c) 1a on 2a (Bk) ('36) .60 .90
O29 O1(c) 1a on 4a (Bl) 3.25 3.50
Nos. O18-O29 (12) 751.95 243.65

Nos. O18-O25 are arranged in composite sheets of 100. The 2 top horizontal rows of each value are surcharged "a" and the next 5 rows as "b." The next 3 rows as "b" but in a narrower setting.

Various errors of spelling or inverted letters are found on Nos. O18-O29.

Arms of Bhopal — O2

1935 Litho.

O30 O2 1a3p claret & blue 2.50 .20
a. Overprint omitted 45.00 45.00

Inscribed: "Bhopal State Postage"
Ovptd. "SERVICE" 11mm long

1937 *Perf. 12*

O31 O2 1a6p dk claret & blue 1.50 .25
a. Overprint omitted 90.00 75.00

See Nos. O42, O45.

Arms of Bhopal — O3

Brown or Black Overprint

1936-38 Typo.

O32 O3 ¼a orange (Br) .60 .20
a. Black overprint 7.50 .50
c. Inverted overprint — 200.00
d. As "a," inverted — 175.00
O32B O3 ¼a yellow (Br) ('38) 2.00 .50
O33 O3 1a carmine 1.10 .20
Nos. O32-O33 (3) 3.70 .90

Moti Mahal O4

Overprinted "SERVICE"

1936 *Perf. 11½*

O34 O4 ½a green & chocolate .50 .40
a. Double impression of stamp .75 12.50

Moti Masjid — O5

4a, Taj Mahal and Be-Nazir Palaces.

Overprinted "SERVICE"

1937 *Perf. 11½*

O35 O5 2a dk blue & brown 1.25 .20
a. Inverted overprint 175.00 175.00
O36 O5 4a bister brn & blue 2.50 .30

Types of 1937
Overprinted "SERVICE" in Black or Brown

1938-44

Designs: 4a, Taj Mahal. 8a, Ahmadabad Palace. 1r, Rait-Ghat.

O37 O4 ½a dp grn & brn .50 .20
O38 O5 2a violet & dp grn 5.00 .20
O39 O5 4a red brn & brt bl 2.00 .35

O40 O5 8a red vio & blue 3.00 .75
a. "SERAICE" 225.00 *300.00*
b. Overprint omitted — 100.00
c. Double overprint — 110.00
O41 O5 1r bl & red vio (Br) 9.50 3.50
a. Black overprint ('44) 12.00 3.50
b. "SREVICE" 100.00 125.00
c. Overprint omitted
d. Double overprint 450.00
Nos. O37-O41 (5) 20.00 5.00

#O39 measures 36½x22½mm, #O40 39x24mm, #O41 45½x27¾mm.

Type of 1935

1939 ***Perf. 12***

O42 O2 1a6p dark claret 4.00 .50

Tiger — O6

Design: 1a, Deer.

1940 **Typo.** ***Perf. 11½***

O43 O6 ¼a ultramarine 2.50 .75
O44 O6 1a red violet 14.00 1.00

Type of 1935
Inscribed: "Bhopal State Postage"

1941

O45 O2 1a3p emerald .75 *.85*

Moti Palace — O7

Coat of Arms — O8

2a, Moti Mosque. 4a, Be-Nazir Palaces.

Perf. 11½, 12

1944-46 **Unwmk.** **Typo.**

O46 O8 3p ultramarine .30 .30
O47 O7 ½a light green .50 .45
O48 O8 9p orange brn ('46) 4.25 1.60
a. Imperf., pair 60.00
O49 O8 1a brt red vio ('45) 2.25 .80
O50 O8 1½a deep plum .70 .35
O51 O7 2a red violet ('45) 3.50 2.00
O52 O8 3a yellow ('46) 4.50 6.00
a. Imperf., pair 60.00
O53 O7 4a brown ('45) 2.25 1.00
O54 O8 6a brt rose ('46) 6.75 *22.50*
a. Imperf., pair 75.00
Nos. O46-O54 (9) 25.00 35.00

For surcharges see Nos. O58-O59.

1946-47 **Unwmk.** ***Perf. 11½***

O55 O8 1a violet 5.75 1.75
O56 O7 2a violet ('47) 8.75 *9.75*
O57 O8 3a deep orange 60.00 47.50
a. Imperf., pair — 125.00
Nos. O55-O57 (3) 74.50 59.00

No. O50 Surcharged "2 As." and Bars

1949 ***Perf. 12***

O58 O8 2a on 1½a dp plum 2.00 *4.50*
a. Inverted surcharge
b. Double surcharge
c. Imperf., pair 140.00 *150.00*

Same Surcharged "2 As." and Rosettes

1949 ***Perf. 12, Imperf.***

O59 O8 2a on 1½a dp plum 450.00 450.00

Three or more types of "2" in surcharge. Bhopal stamps became obsolete in 1950.

BHOR

'bō̤ə̤r

LOCATION — A Feudatory State in the Kolhapur Residency and Deccan States Agency.
AREA — 910 sq. mi.
POP. — 141,546
CAPITAL — Bhor

A1

A2

1879 **Handstamped Unwmk.** ***Imperf.***
Without Gum

1 A1 ½a carmine 1.75 *2.00*
2 A2 1a carmine 1.75 *2.00*

Pant Sachiv Shankarrao — A3

1901 **Typo.**
Without Gum

3 A3 ½a red 5.50 *27.50*

BIJAWAR

bi-'jä-wər

LOCATION — A Feudatory State in the Bundelkhand Agency of Central India.
AREA — 973 sq. mi.
POP. — 115,852
CAPITAL — Bijawar

Maharaja Sir Sawant Singh
A1 A2

1935-36 **Typo.** **Unwmk.** ***Perf. 10½***

1 A1 3p brown 2.50 1.50
a. Imperf., pair 7.00
b. Rouletted 7 ('36) .95 *2.00*
2 A1 6p carmine 2.25 1.50
a. Rouletted 7 ('36) 2.25 2.50
3 A1 9p purple 2.25 1.50
a. Rouletted 7 ('36) 4.00 4.00
4 A1 1a dark blue 2.75 1.75
a. Rouletted 7 ('36) 4.25 4.25
5 A1 2a slate green 2.75 2.00
a. Rouletted 7 ('36) 4.25 7.50

1937 ***Perf. 9***

6 A2 4a red orange 4.75 *7.00*
7 A2 6a yellow 4.75 *14.00*
8 A2 8a emerald 5.25 *16.00*
9 A2 12a turquoise blue 5.75 *14.00*
10 A2 1r purple 25.00 *35.00*
a. "1Rs" instead of "1R" 45.00 *67.50*
Nos. 1-10 (10) 58.00 *94.25*

Bijawar stamps became obsolete in 1939.

BUNDI

'bün-dē

LOCATION — A Feudatory State in the Rajputana Agency of India.
AREA — 2,220 sq. mi.
POP. — 216,722
CAPITAL — Bundi

Katar (Indian Dagger) — A1

A2

A3

Laid Paper

1894 **Unwmk.** **Litho.** ***Imperf.***
Without Gum
Gutters between Stamps

1 A1 ½a slate 2,750. *2,000.*

Redrawn; Blade Does Not Touch Oval
No Gutters between Stamps
Wove Paper

1A A1 ½a slate 15.00 13.00
b. Value above, name below 175.00 175.00
c. Top right ornament omitted 500.00 500.00

On No. 1A, the dagger is thinner and its point does not touch the oval inner frame.

1896
Laid Paper
Without Gum

2 A2 ½a slate 5.00 5.25

1897-98 **Without Gum**

3 A3 1a red 6.50 6.00
4 A3 2a yellow green 8.00 *10.00*
5 A3 4a yellow green 17.00 *18.00*
6 A3 8a red 32.50 *40.00*
7 A3 1r yellow, *blue* 50.00 *52.50*
Nos. 3-7 (5) 114.00 126.50

A4

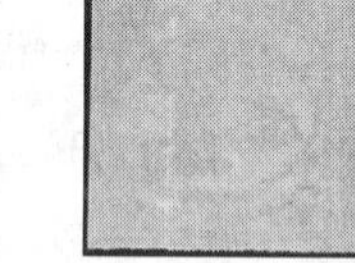

A5

Redrawn; Blade Wider and Diamond-shaped

1898-1900 **Without Gum**

8 A3 ½a slate .40 .40
9 A3 1a red .75 .60
10 A3 2a emerald 4.50 4.50
a. 1st 2 characters of value omitted 300.00 300.00
11 A3 4a emer (value above) 8.00 8.00
12 A4 8a red 8.00 *9.50*
13 A5 1r yellow, *blue* 5.00 *10.00*
a. Wove paper 8.50 8.50
Nos. 8-13 (6) 26.65 *33.00*

On Nos. 9-10, the blade is wider and nearly diamond-shaped.

Point of Dagger to Left

14 A3 4a green 5.00 5.00

Maharao Rajah with Symbols of Spiritual and Temporal Power — A6

Rouletted 11 to 13 in Color

1915 **Typo.**
Without Gum
"Bundi" in 3 Characters (word at top right)

15 A6 ¼a blue .60 .60
a. Laid paper 7.25 6.25
16 A6 ½a black .85 .85
17 A6 1a vermilion 1.10 1.10
a. Laid paper 9.25 9.25
18 A6 2a emerald 1.25 1.25
19 A6 2½a yellow 3.50 *4.25*
20 A6 3a brown 2.00 *4.25*
21 A6 4a yel green 4.25 4.25
23 A6 6a ultramarine 8.50 *21.00*
a. 6a deep blue 8.50
24 A6 8a orange 6.25 6.25
25 A6 10a olive 7.75 7.75
26 A6 12a dark green 11.50 11.50
27 A6 1r violet 27.50 *35.00*
28 A6 2r car brn & blk 35.00 *42.50*
29 A6 3r blue & brown 85.00 *125.00*
30 A6 4r pale grn & red brown 240.00 *250.00*
31 A6 5r ver & pale grn 250.00 *350.00*
Nos. 15-31 (16) 685.05 865.55

Minor differences in lettering in top and bottom panels may be divided into 8 types, but not all values come in each type. In one subtype the top appears as one word. Nos. 30-31 have an ornamental frame around the design.

For overprints see Nos. O1-O39.

1941 ***Perf. 11***
"Bundi" in 4 Characters (word at top right)

32 A6 ¼a light blue 4.50 4.50
33 A6 ½a black 37.50 37.50
34 A6 1a carmine 17.50 *27.50*
35 A6 2a yellow green 32.50
Nos. 32-35 (4) 92.00

The 4-character spelling of "Bundi" is found also on stamps rouletted in color: on ½a and 4a in small characters, and on ¼a, ½a, 1a, 4a, 4r and 5r in large characters like those on Nos. 32-35.

For overprints see Nos. O41-O48.

Arms of Bundi — A7

1941-45 **Typo.** ***Perf. 11***

36 A7 3p bright ultra .20 *.30*
37 A7 6p indigo .30 *.50*
38 A7 1a red orange .50 *1.00*
39 A7 2a fawn 4.75 *8.00*
a. 2a brown ('45) 4.75 *10.50*
40 A7 4a brt yel green 5.25 *12.00*
41 A7 8a dull green 9.00 *19.00*
42 A7 1r royal blue 11.00 *30.00*
Nos. 36-42 (7) 31.00 *70.80*

The 1st printing of Nos. 36-42 was gummed. All later printings were without gum. **Values are for copies without gum.**

For overprints see Nos. O49-O55.

A8

Maj. Maharao Rajah Bahadur Singh — A9

View of Bundi — A10

1947 ***Perf. 11***

43 A8 ¼a deep green .30
44 A8 ½a purple .30
45 A8 1a yellow green .30
46 A9 2a red .50
47 A9 4a deep orange 1.50
48 A10 8a violet blue 2.50
49 A10 1r chocolate 5.50
Nos. 43-49 (7) 10.90

For overprints see Rajasthan Nos. 1-14.

OFFICIAL STAMPS

Regular Issue of 1915 Handstamped in Black, Red or Green

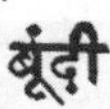

a

सरविस

Rouletted 11 to 13 in Color

1918 **Unwmk.**

Without Gum

No.	Type	Description	Unused	Used
O1	A6	¼a dark blue	.45	
O2	A6	½a black	2.50	
O3	A6	1a vermilion	1.10	
O4	A6	2a emerald	2.50	
O5	A6	2½a yellow	3.00	
O6	A6	3a brown	3.00	
O7	A6	4a yel green	6.00	
O8	A6	6a blue	4.75	
O9	A6	8a orange	9.00	
O10	A6	10a olive green	9.00	
O11	A6	12a dark green	11.00	
O12	A6	1r violet	15.00	
O13	A6	2r car brn & blk	90.00	
O14	A6	3r blue & brown	150.00	
O15	A6	4r pale grn & red brn	275.00	
O16	A6	5r ver & pale grn	275.00	
		Nos. O1-O16 (16)	857.30	

All values come with black handstamp and most exist in red. The overprint is found in various positions, double, inverted, etc.

Several denominations exist in two or more types. See notes following Nos. 31 and 35.

Regular Issue of 1915 Handstamped in Black, Red or Green

b

1919 **Without Gum**

No.	Type	Description	Unused	Used
O17	A6	¼a dark blue	1.50	
O18	A6	½a black	3.00	
O19	A6	1a vermilion	3.50	
O20	A6	2a emerald	6.00	
O21	A6	2½a yellow	15.00	
O22	A6	3a brown	21.00	
O23	A6	4a yel green	15.00	
O24	A6	6a blue	15.00	
O25	A6	8a orange	30.00	
O26	A6	10a olive green	35.00	
O27	A6	12a dark green	35.00	
O28	A6	1r violet	30.00	
O29	A6	2r car brn & blk	110.00	
O30	A6	3r blue & brown	160.00	
O31	A6	4r pale grn & red brn	325.00	
O32	A6	5r ver & pale grn	325.00	
		Nos. O17-O32 (16)	1,130.	

Note following No. O16 applies to this issue.

Regular Issue of 1915 Handstamped in Carmine or Black

BUNDI

c

SERVICE

1919 ***Rouletted in Color***

Without Gum

No.	Type	Description	Unused	Used
O33	A6	¼a blue	5.00	5.00
O34	A6	½a black	3.50	
O35	A6	1a vermilion	7.50	
O36	A6	2a yel green	9.00	
O37	A6	8a orange	45.00	
O38	A6	10a olive	45.00	
O39	A6	12a dark green	75.00	
		Nos. O33-O39 (7)	190.00	

Nos. 33 and 35 Handstamped Type "a" in Black or Carmine

1941 ***Perf. 11***

No.	Type	Description	Unused	Used
O41	A6	½a black	55.00	
O42	A6	2a yellow green	55.00	

Nos. 32 and 35 Handstamped Type "b" in Black or Carmine

No.	Type	Description	Unused	Used
O43	A6	¼a light blue	47.50	
O44	A6	2a yellow green	80.00	

Nos. 32-35 Handstamped Type "c" in Black or Carmine

1941

No.	Type	Description	Unused	Used
O45	A6	¼a light blue	65.00	
O46	A6	½a black	65.00	
O47	A6	1a carmine	75.00	
O48	A6	2a yellow green	27.50	
		Nos. O45-O48 (4)	232.50	

Nos. 36 to 42 Overprinted in Black or Carmine **SERVICE**

1941 ***Perf. 11***

No.	Type	Description	Unused	Used
O49	A7	3p brt ultra (C)	1.25	*1.75*
O50	A7	6p indigo (C)	3.00	*3.50*
O51	A7	1a red orange	3.50	*4.75*
O52	A7	2a fawn	6.00	*9.00*
O53	A7	4a brt yel green	24.00	*30.00*
O54	A7	8a dull green	35.00	*45.00*
O55	A7	1r royal blue (C)	45.00	*60.00*
		Nos. O49-O55 (7)	117.75	*154.00*

BUSSAHIR

'bus-ə-ˌhiˌəˌr

(Bashahr)

LOCATION — A Feudatory State in the Punjab Hill States Agency

AREA — 3,439 sq. mi.

POP. — 100,192

CAPITAL — Bashahr

Tiger

A1 A2

A3

A4

A5

A6

A7

A8

Overprinted "R S" in Violet, Rose, or Blue Green (BG)

Laid Paper

1895 **Unwmk.** **Litho.** ***Imperf.***

No.	Type	Description	Unused	Used
1	A1	¼a pink (V)	875.00	
2	A2	½a slate (R)	250.00	
3	A3	1a red (V)	100.00	
4	A4	2a yellow (V,R)	30.00	*110.00*
5	A5	4a violet (V,R)	60.00	
6	A6	8a brown (V,BG)	60.00	*125.00*
a.		Without overprint	150.00	
7	A7	12a green (R)	150.00	
8	A8	1r ultra (R)	50.00	
		Nos. 1-8 (8)	1,575.	

Perf. 7 to 14

No.	Type	Description	Unused	Used
9	A1	¼a pink (V,BG)	27.50	*60.00*
10	A2	½a slate (R)	13.00	*67.50*
11	A3	1a red (V)	13.00	*55.00*
a.		Pin-perf.	65.00	*100.00*
12	A4	2a yel (V,R,BG)	19.00	*60.00*
a.		Pin-perf. (V,R)	25.00	*50.00*
13	A5	4a violet (V,R,BG)	13.00	*65.00*
a.		Pin-perf. (R)	50.00	
14	A6	8a brown (V,BG)	13.50	*67.50*
15	A7	12a green (V,R)	40.00	*82.50*
a.		Pin-perf. (R)	65.00	
b.		Without overprint	47.50	
16	A8	1r ultra (V,R)	21.00	*67.50*
a.		Pin-perf. (R)	65.00	
		Nos. 9-16 (8)	160.00	*525.00*

"R. S." are the initials of Tika Raghunath Singh, son of the Raja.

A9

A10

A11

A12

A13

A14

Overprinted "R S" Like Nos. 1-16

Wove Paper

1896 **Engr.** ***Pin-perf.***

No.	Type	Description	Unused	Used
17	A9	¼a dk gray vio (R)	—	550.00
18	A10	½a blue gray (R)	400.00	125.00

1900 **Litho.** ***Imperf.***

No.	Type	Description	Unused	Used
19	A9	¼a red (V,BG)	2.50	*5.50*
20	A9	¼a violet (V,R)	3.75	
21	A10	½a blue (V,R)	6.00	*15.00*
22	A11	1a olive (R)	8.75	*20.00*
23	A11	1a red (V,BG)	2.50	*7.50*
24	A12	2a yellow (V)	26.00	
a.		2a ocher (R)	26.00	
25	A13	2a yellow (V)	26.00	
a.		2a ocher (V)	26.00	
26	A14	4a brn vio (V,R,BG)	27.50	*75.00*
		Nos. 19-26 (8)	103.00	

Pin-perf.

No.	Type	Description	Unused	Used
27	A9	¼a red (V,BG)	2.40	*5.50*
28	A9	¼a violet (R)	12.00	11.00
29	A10	½a blue (V,R)	7.75	20.00
30	A11	1a olive (V,R)	14.50	
31	A11	1a red (V)	—	150.00
32	A11	1a vermilion (BG)	3.75	*7.50*
33	A12	2a yellow (BG)	340.00	*350.00*
34	A13	2a yellow (V,R)	27.50	*47.50*
a.		2a ocher (V)	35.00	
35	A14	4a brn vio (V,R,BG)	37.50	
		Nos. 27-35 (8)	445.40	

Obsolete March 31, 1901.

Stamps overprinted with the monogram above (RNS) or with the monogram "PS" were never issued for postal purposes. They are either reprints or remainders to which this overprint has been applied. Many other varieties have appeared since the stamps became obsolete. It is probable that all or nearly all of them are reprints.

CHARKHARI

chər-'kär-ē

LOCATION — A Feudatory State in the Bundelkhand Agency in Central India.

AREA — 880 sq. mi.

POP. — 120,351

CAPITAL — Maharajnagar

A1

Thin White or Blue Wove Paper

1894 **Unwmk.** **Typo.** ***Imperf.***

Value in the Plural

Without Gum

No.	Type	Description	Unused	Used
1	A1	1a green	1,500.	*2,000.*
2	A1	2a green	1,700.	
3	A1	4a green	1,000.	

1897

Value in the Singular

Without Gum

No.	Type	Description	Unused	Used
3A	A1	¼a rose	875.00	650.00
4	A1	¼a purple	2.50	2.25
5	A1	½a purple	2.50	2.25
6	A1	1a green	5.00	4.50
7	A1	2a green	7.00	6.25
8	A1	4a green	7.00	6.25
		Nos. 4-8 (5)	24.00	21.50

In a later printing, the numerals of Nos. 4-8 are smaller or of different shape.

Proofs are known on paper of various colors.

A2

A3

Size: 19½x23mm

1909 **Litho.** ***Perf. 11***

No.	Type	Description	Unused	Used
9	A2	1p red brown	2.10	*32.50*
10	A2	1p pale blue	.90	.60
11	A2	½a scarlet	1.25	.85
12	A2	1a light green	1.40	*1.75*
13	A2	2a ultra	2.10	*2.75*
14	A2	4a deep green	2.10	*2.75*
15	A2	8a brick red	5.00	*13.00*
16	A2	1r red brown	8.75	*24.00*
		Nos. 9-16 (8)	23.60	*78.20*

See #22-27, 39-43. For surcharges see #37-38A.

1919 **Handstamped** ***Imperf.***

Without Gum

No.	Type	Description	Unused	Used
21	A3	1p violet	6.50	4.50
c.		Double frameline	27.50	

The 1p black, type A3, is a proof.

A3a

Wove Paper

1922 ***Imperf.***

Without Gum

No.	Type	Description	Unused	Used
21A	A3a	1a violet	57.50	*65.00*
b.		Perf. 11, laid paper	57.50	*90.00*

Type of 1909 Issue Redrawn

Size: 20x23½mm

1930-40 **Typo.**

Without Gum

No.	Type	Description	Unused	Used
22	A2	1p dark blue	.30	*11.50*
23	A2	½a olive green	.85	*11.50*
23A	A2	½a cop brown ('40)	4.00	*19.00*
24	A2	1a light green	.60	*11.50*
25	A2	1a chocolate	5.50	*19.00*
25A	A2	1a dull red ('40)	65.00	47.50
26	A2	2a light blue	1.00	*14.00*
a.		Tête bêche pair	60.00	
27	A2	4a carmine	2.75	*16.00*
a.		Tête bêche pair	11.00	
		Nos. 22-27 (8)	80.00	*150.00*

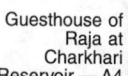

Guesthouse of Raja at Charkhari Reservoir — A4

Imlia Palace — A5

Industrial School — A6

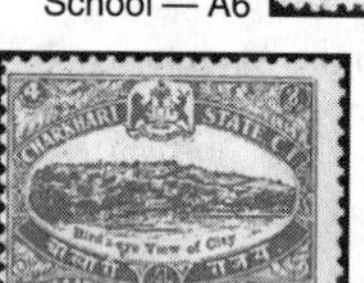
View of City — A7

Maharajnagar Fort, Charkhari City — A8

Guesthouse A9

Palace Gate — A10

Temples at Rampur — A11

Govordhan Temple — A12

1931 ***Perf. 11, 11½, 12***

28	A4	½a dull green	.70	.20
29	A5	1a black brown	.80	.20
30	A6	2a purple	.50	.20
31	A7	4a olive green	.70	.20
32	A8	8a magenta	.80	.20
33	A9	1r rose & green	1.25	.20
34	A10	2r brown & red	2.25	.20
35	A11	3r bl grn & choc	5.50	.20
36	A12	5r violet & blue	5.50	.20
		Nos. 28-36 (9)	18.00	1.80

Size range of A4-A12: 30-31x19½-24mm.
Many errors of perforation and printing exist. Used values are for canceled to order copies.

Nos. 15-16 Surcharged in Black **½ As.**

1940 ***Perf. 11***

37	A2	½a on 8a brick red	22.50	*100.00*
a.		Surcharge inverted	200.00	
b.		"1" of "½" inverted	190.00	
38	A2	1a on 1r red brown	65.00	*275.00*
b.		Surcharge inverted	240.00	
38A	A2	"1 ANNA" on 1r red brown	400.00	*450.00*

Type of 1930

1943 Unwmk. Typo. ***Imperf.***
Size: 20x23½mm

39	A2	1p violet	12.50	*95.00*
a.		Tête bêche pair	50.00	
40	A2	1p apple green	37.50	*125.00*
41	A2	½a orange red	15.00	*30.00*
42	A2	½a black	42.50	*110.00*
43	A2	2a grayish green	32.50	*40.00*
a.		Tête bêche pair	65.00	
		Nos. 39-43 (5)	140.00	*400.00*

COCHIN

kō-'chin

LOCATION — A Feudatory State in the Madras States Agency in Southern India.
AREA — 1,480 sq. mi.
POP. — 1,422,875 (1941)
CAPITAL — Ernakulam

See the United State of Travancore and Cochin.

6 Puttans = 5 Annas
12 Pies = 1 Anna
16 Annas = 1 Rupee

A1

State Seal — A1a

1892 Unwmk. Typo. ***Perf. 12***

1	A1	½p yellow	2.25	2.25
a.		Imperf., pair	—	—
b.		Laid paper	350.00	350.00
2	A1	1p red violet	2.25	1.60
a.		1p purple (error)	150.00	110.00
3	A1	2p purple	1.75	1.75
a.		Imperf.	—	—
		Nos. 1-3 (3)	6.25	5.60

Nos. 1 to 3 sometimes have watermark large umbrella in the sheet.

Wmk. Coat of Arms and Inscription in Sheet

1896

4	A1a	1p violet	65.00	*65.00*

Wmk. 43

4A	A1a	1p violet	17.50	*30.00*

Originally intended for revenue use, Nos. 4-4A were later authorized for postal use.

1894 **Wmk. 41**

Thin Paper

5	A1	½p orange	1.25	1.25
a.		Imperf., pair		
6	A1	1p magenta	5.50	4.25
7	A1	2p purple	3.00	3.00
a.		Imperf., pair	—	—
		Nos. 5-7 (3)	9.75	8.50

A2

A3

A4

A5

Thin (1898) or Thick (1903) Paper

1898-1903

8	A2	3p ultra	.20	.20
9	A3	½p gray green	.55	.20
a.		Pair, one sideways	650.00	650.00
10	A4	1p rose	1.40	.25
a.		Laid paper		1,500.
b.		Tete beche pair	2,500.	2,000.
c.		As "a," tete beche pair		*6,500.*
11	A5	2p purple	2.00	.35
a.		Double impression	*700.00*	250.00
		Nos. 8-11 (4)	4.15	1.00

Type of 1898 Surcharged

1909

13	A2	2p on 3p red violet	.40	.35
a.		Inverted surcharge	72.50	72.50
b.		Pair, stamps tete beche	100.00	*125.00*
c.		Pair, stamps & surch. tete beche	140.00	*150.00*

The surcharge is also known in a thin "2" measuring 5½x7mm, with curving foot. Value $250.

Sri Rama Varma I — A6

1911-13 Engr. ***Perf. 14***

14	A6	2p brown	.20	.20
a.		Imperf., pair		
15	A6	3p blue	.40	.20
a.		Perf. 14x12½	25.00	2.50
16	A6	4p yel green	1.10	.20
17	A6	9p car rose	.80	.20
18	A6	1a orange buff	2.00	.20
19	A6	1½a lilac	4.00	.50
20	A6	2a gray	5.50	.50
21	A6	3a vermilion	26.00	26.00
		Nos. 14-21 (8)	40.00	28.00

For surcharge and overprints see Nos. 34, O2-O9, O23-O24, O27.

Sri Rama Varma II
A7 A8

1918-23 Engr. ***Perf. 14***

23	A7	2p brown	4.50	.20
24	A7	4p green	.80	.20
25	A7	6p red brown ('22)	1.90	.20
26	A7	8p black brown ('23)	1.25	.20
27	A7	9p carmine rose	12.00	.25
28	A7	10p deep blue	1.90	.20
29	A8	1a brown orange	9.75	.90
30	A7	1½a red violet ('21)	1.90	.20
31	A7	2a gray	3.50	.20
32	A7	2¼a yel green ('22)	3.50	2.50
33	A7	3a vermilion	9.00	.35
		Nos. 23-33 (11)	50.00	5.40

The 1a is found in two types, the difference lying in the first of the three characters directly above the maharaja's head.

For surcharges and overprints see Nos. 36-40, 52-53, O10-O22, O25-O26, O28-O36, O71A.

No. 15 Surcharged **2** **Two pies**

Type I - Numeral 8mm high. Curved foot. Top begins with a ball. (As illustrated.)
Type II - Numeral 9mm high. Curved foot. Top begins with a curved line.
Type III - Numeral 6mm high. Straight foot. "Two pies" 15mm wide.
Type IV - "2" as in type III. Capital "P" in "Pies." "Two Pies" 13mm wide.
Type V - Heavy gothic numeral. Capital "P" in "Pies."

1922-29

34	A6	2p on 3p blue (Type I)	.40	.20
a.		Type II	2.00	.90
b.		Type III	3.25	.25
c.		Type IV	.30	.20
d.		Type V	80.00	*100.00*
e.		Double surcharge, I	300.00	300.00
f.		Double surcharge II	500.00	

Types II and III exist with a capital "P" in "Pies." It occurs once in each sheet of the second and third settings. There are four settings.

Type V is the first stamp, fourth row, of the fourth setting.

No. 32 Surcharged **ONE ANNA** **ഒരു അണ** **ANCHAL & REVENUE**

1928

36	A7	1a on 2¼a yel green	4.50	*10.50*
a.		Double surcharge	350.00	350.00

Nos. 24, 26 and 28 Surcharged in Black

1932-33

38	A7	3p on 4p green	.95	.70
39	A7	3p on 8p black brown	.95	*1.90*
40	A7	9p on 10p deep blue	1.10	*2.40*
		Nos. 38-40 (3)	3.00	5.00

Sri Rama Varma III
A9 A10

1933-38 Engr. ***Perf. 13x13½***

41	A9	2p brown ('36)	.55	.20
42	A9	4p green	1.40	.20
43	A9	6p red brown	.95	.20
44	A10	1a brown org ('34)	.50	.20
45	A9	1a8p rose red	5.25	3.00
46	A9	2a gray black ('38)	1.25	.55
47	A9	2¼a yellow green	1.25	.20
48	A9	3a red org ('38)	2.25	1.10
49	A9	3a4p violet	1.10	1.10
50	A9	6a8p black brown	3.50	7.25
51	A9	10a deep blue	3.50	8.50
		Nos. 41-51 (11)	21.50	22.50

See Nos. 55-58. For overprints and surcharges see Nos. 54, 59-62, 73A-74, 76-77, 89, O37-O57, O70-O71, O72-O77A, O89.

6

Nos. 26 and 28 Surcharged in Red

Six Pies

1934 *Perf. 13½*
52 A7 6p on 8p black brown 2.25 .75
53 A7 6p on 10p dark blue 2.25 2.25

No. 44 Overprinted in Black

a

1939 **Engr.**
54 A10 1a brown orange 2.25 .50

Types of 1933-38

1938-41 **Litho.** *Perf. 11, 13*
55 A9 2p dull brown .80 .40
56 A9 4p dull green ('41) .85 .20
57 A9 6p red brown 1.90 .20
c. Perf. 13 2,500.
57A A10 1a brown orange 55.00 67.50
58 A10 2¼a yellow green 5.25 .20
Nos. 55-58 (5) 63.80 68.50

Type of 1934 Overprinted in Black Type "a" or

b

1941-42 *Perf. 11 (#59), 13 (#60)*
59 A10(a) 1a brown orange 200.00 1.00
a. Perf. 13 250.00
60 A10(b) 1a brown org ('42) 10.00 .75
a. Perf. 11 2.50 2.50

No. 45 Surcharged in Black

c

1943-44 **Engr.** *Perf. 13x13½*
61 A9 3p on 1a8p rose red ('44) 2.50 6.50
62 A9 1a3p on 1a8p rose red 1.60 .20

Maharaja Sri Kerala Varma
A11 A12

1943 Litho. Wmk. 294 *Perf. 11, 13*
63 A11 2p dull gray brn, wmk. 41 1.00 1.60
a. Wmk. 294 22.50 2.00
64 A11 4p gray green 3.00 2.75
a. Wmk. 41 500.00 250.00
65 A11 6p red brown 8.00 1.10
66 A11 9p ultramarine 24.00 .80
67 A12 1a brown orange 19.00 32.50
a. Wmk. 41 90.00 90.00
68 A11 2¼a lt ol green 20.00 1.75
Nos. 63-68 (6) 75.00 40.50

For surcharges and overprints see Nos. 69-73, 75, 78, 78B, O58-O69.

No. 64 Surcharged Type "c"
69 A11 3p on 4p gray green 2.75 .20
a. Wmk. 41 55.00 15.00

Nos. 64, 64a and 65 Surcharged in Black

d

1944-48 **Wmk. 294**
70 A11 2p on 6p red brown .70 2.10
71 A11 3p on 4p gray green 3.25 .20
72 A11 3p on 6p red brown .80 .20
73 A11 4p on 6p red brown 2.75 7.50
Nos. 70-73 (4) 7.50 10.00

ANCHAL

Nos. 57A, 67a Surcharged in Black

NINE PIES

1944 **Litho.** **Wmk. 41**
73A A10 6p on 1a brown org 200.00 125.00
74 A10 9p on 1a brown org 190.00 32.50
75 A12 9p on 1a brown org 4.50 2.00
Nos. 73A-75 (3) 394.50 159.50

No. 56 Surcharged Type "c" in Black
76 A9 3p on 4p dull green 5.50 3.75

ANCHAL

Nos. 57A, 67a Surcharged in Black

SURCHARGED NINE PIES

1944
77 A10 9p on 1a brown orange 12.50 4.00
78 A12 9p on 1a brown orange 4.00 2.25

No. 67a Surcharged Type "c"

1944 **Wmk. 41**
78B A12 1a3p on 1a brn org 2,750.

Maharaja Ravi Varma
A13 A15

1944-46 **Wmk. 294** *Perf. 13*
79 A13 9p ultra ('46) 5.50 7.75
a. Perf. 11 10.00 2.00
80 A13 1a3p magenta 4.00 4.75
81 A13 1a9p ultra ('46) 6.50 7.25
Nos. 79-81 (3) 16.00 19.75

For overprints and surcharges see Nos. O78-O80, Travancore 12, 14, O10.

1946-50 **Litho.** *Perf. 13*
82 A15 2p dull brown 1.10 .20
a. Perf. 11 13.00 .75
b. Perf. 11x13 250.00 80.00
83 A15 3p carmine rose .45 .20
83A A15 4p gray green ('50) 1,750. 27.50
84 A15 6p red brown ('47) 16.00 3.00
a. Perf. 11 125.00 .20
85 A15 9p ultramarine .45 .20
86 A15 1a dp orange ('47) 4.50 24.00
a. Perf. 11 375.00
87 A15 2a gray ('47) 62.50 7.00
a. Perf. 11 95.00 .20
88 A15 3a vermilion 40.00 .40
Nos. 82-83,84-88 (7) 125.00 35.00

For surcharges and overprints see Nos. 98-99, O81-O88, Travancore 8, 13, 15-15A, O11.

No. 45 Surcharged Type "d"
Perf. 13x13½

1947-48 **Wmk. 41** **Engr.**
89 A9 6p on 1a8p rose red 2.75 18.00

Maharaja Sri Kerala Varma II — A16

1948-49 **Wmk. 294** *Perf. 11*
90 A16 2p olive brown 1.10 .20
91 A16 3p car ('49) .55 .20
92 A16 4p gray green 7.50 1.50
a. Horiz. pair, imperf. vert. 360.00
93 A16 6p red brown 9.25 .20
94 A16 9p ultra ('49) 1.60 .20
95 A16 2a black 32.50 .50
96 A16 3a ver ('49) 37.50 .50
97 A16 3a4p violet ('49) 60.00 300.00
Nos. 90-97 (8) 150.00 303.30

For overprints see Nos. O90-O97, Travancore 9-11, O8-O9.

No. 86 Surcharged Type "d" in Black

1949
98 A15 6p on 1a dp orange 55.00 110.00
99 A15 9p on 1a dp orange 75.00 110.00

Dutch Palace A17

Design: 2a, Chinese fishing net.

1949 **Unwmk.** *Perf. 11*
100 A17 2a gray 2.50 5.50
a. Imperf. vert., horiz. pair 425.00
101 A17 2¼a gray green 2.50 5.00

See Travancore-Cochin for succeeding issues.

OFFICIAL STAMPS

Stamps and Type of 1911-14 Overprinted

h

1913-14 **Wmk. 41** **Engr.** *Perf. 14*
O2 A6 4p yel green 8.00 .20
a. Inverted overprint — 250.00
b. Double inverted overprint
O3 A6 9p car rose 82.50 .20
O4 A6 1½a red violet 32..50 .20
a. Double overprint 375.00
O5 A6 2a gray 12.00 .20
O6 A6 3a vermilion 47.50 .35
O7 A6 6a violet 37.50 1.60
O8 A6 12a blue 35.00 4.75
O9 A6 1½r deep green 25.00 42.50
Nos. O2-O9 (8) 280.00 50.00

Stamps and Type of 1918-23 Overprinted

h

1918-34
O10 A7 4p green 4.75 .20
a. Double overprint — 350.00
O11 A7 6p red brn ('22) 4.75 .20
a. Double overprint — 325.00
O12 A7 8p blk brn ('26) 7.50 .20
O13 A7 9p carmine rose 19.00 .20
O14 A7 10p dp blue ('23) 8.00 .20
O16 A7 1½a red vio ('21) 5.00 .20
a. Double overprint 200.00
O17 A7 2a gray 30.00 .20
O18 A7 2¼a yel grn ('22) 7.50 .20
b. Double overprint 300.00
O19 A7 3a ver ('22) 18.00 .20
a. Double overprint 325.00
O20 A7 6a violet ('22) 22.50 .40
O21 A7 12a blue ('29) 25.00 2.40
O22 A7 1½r dk green ('34) 27.50 70.00
Nos. O10-O22 (12) 179.50 74.60

On Nos. O2-O22, width of overprint varies from 14¾mm to 16½mm.

No. 15 Overprinted in Red

j

On
C G
S

1921
O23 A6 3p blue 100.00 .75

Nos. O3 and O13 Surcharged with New Values

1923-29
O24 A6 8p on 9p car rose 200.00 1.25
O25 A7 8p on 9p car rose 70.00 .20
a. Double surcharge 250.00
O26 A7 10p on 9p car rose ('25) 60.00 .50
a. Double surcharge 300.00
O27 A6 10p on 9p car rose ('29) 300.00 13.00
Nos. O24-O27 (4) 630.00 14.95

Regular Issue of 1918-23 Overprinted

k

ON
C G
S

1933-34
O28 A7 4p green 17.00 1.10
O29 A7 6p red brown ('34) 10.50 .20
O30 A7 8p black brown 5.50 .20
O31 A7 10p deep blue 4.75 .20
O32 A7 2a gray ('34) 21.00 .20
O33 A7 3a vermilion 6.25 .20
O34 A7 6a dk violet ('34) 60.00 2.40
Nos. O28-O34 (7) 125.00 4.50

Same with Additional Surcharge on Type of Regular Issue of 1918-23 in Red

O35 A7 6p on 8p black brown 1.75 .20
O36 A7 6p on 10p dk blue ('34) 4.00 .20

Regular Issue of 1933 Overprinted Type "k" in Black as in 1933-34

1933-35 *Perf. 13x13½*
O37 A9 4p green .90 .20
O38 A9 6p red brown 1.10 .20
O39 A10 1a brown orange 7.50 .20
O40 A9 1a8p rose red 2.50 .25
O41 A9 2a gray 7.50 .20
O42 A9 2¼a yellow green 3.50 .20
O43 A9 3a vermilion 35.00 .20
O44 A9 3a4p violet 3.25 .20
O45 A9 6a8p black brown 3.25 .20
O46 A9 10a deep blue 3.25 .40
Nos. O37-O46 (10) 67.75 2.25

Regular Stamps of 1934-38 Overprinted in Black

m

ON
C G
S

1939-41 *Perf. 11, 13x13½*

O47 A10 1a brown orange 32.50 .50
O48 A9 2a gray black 18.00 1.25
O49 A9 3a red orange 9.50 1.25
Nos. O47-O49 (3) 60.00 3.00

Similar Overprint on Types of 1933-36
Perf. 11, 13x13½

1939-41 **Litho.** **Wmk. 294**

O50 A9 4p dull green ('41) 32.50 12.00

Wmk. 41

O51 A9 6p red brown ('41) 4.50 2.25
a. Wmk. 294 32.50 1.10
O52 A10 1a brown orange .50 .20
a. Wmk. 294 2.25 .30
O53 A9 3a orange ('40) 1.50 .80
b. Wmk. 294 10.00 1.50
Nos. O50-O53 (4) 39.00 15.25

Similar Overprint in Narrow Serifed Capitals on No. 57

Wmk. 41 *Perf. 11*

O53A A9 6p red brown 700.00 275.00

Type of 1933-36 Overprinted in Black

o

ON
C G
S

Perf. 10½, 11, 13x13½

O54 A9 4p dull green ('41) 12.50 1.75
O55 A9 6p red brown ('41) 11.00 .45
O56 A9 2a gray black 9.00 .80
Nos. O54-O56 (3) 32.50 3.00

Type of 1934 Overprinted in Black

p

ON
C G

S

1941 *Perf. 11*

O57 A10 1a brown orange 160.00 2.50

Stamps and Types of 1944 Overprinted in Black

q

Perf. 11, 13x13½

1944-48 **Wmk. 294**

O58 A11 4p gray green 11.00 3.25
a. Perf. 11 60.00 5.00
O59 A11 6p red brown .75 .20
O60 A11 2a gray black 2.00 .45
O61 A11 2¼a dull yel green 1.25 .60
a. Additional ovpt. on back 75.00
O62 A11 3a red orange 3.00 .50
Nos. O58-O62 (5) 18.00 5.00

Same Overprint with Additional Surcharge **THREE PIES**

O63 A11 3p on 4p gray green 1.25 .20
a. Additional overprint on back
O64 A12 3p on 1a brown org 8.25 3.75
O65 A11 9p on 6p red brown 3.50 1.90
O66 A12 1a3p on 1a brown org 3.00 1.25
Nos. O63-O66 (4) 16.00 7.10

Same Overprint in Black on Types of 1944 Surcharged Type "c"

O67 A11 3p on 4p gray green 2.75 .30
O68 A11 9p on 6p red brown .20 .20
O69 A12 1a3p on 1a brown org 3.50 .20
Nos. O67-O69 (3) 6.45 .70

Nos. O52 and O16 Surcharged Type "d"

1944 **Wmk. 41** *Perf. 11, 13x13½, 14*

O70 A10 3p on 1a brown org 1.25 *2.50*
O71 A10 9p on 1a brown org 110.00 30.00

Engr.

O71A A7 9p on 1½a red vio 200.00 17.50

No. O52 Surcharged Type "c"

O72 A10 1a3p on 1a brn org 250.00 80.00

ON
No. 76 Overprinted in Black

C G
S

Perf. 13

O72A A9 3p on 4p dull green 100.00 50.00

No. 45 Overprinted Type "k" and Surcharged Type "d"

1944-48 **Wmk. 41** *Perf. 13x13½*

O73 A9 9p on 1a8p rose red 100.00 20.00
O74 A9 1a9p on 1a8p rose red 1.75 1.25

No. 45 Overprinted Type "k" and Surcharged Type "c"

O75 A9 3p on 1a8p rose red 2.75 1.10
O76 A9 1a9p on 1a8p rose red 1.00 .20

ON
Type of 1939-41 Overprinted in Black

C G
S

1946 **Wmk. 294** *Perf. 11*

O77 A9 2a gray 50.00 1.00
O77A A9 2¼a yellow green 750.00 15.00

Same Overprint in Black on #79-81

1946 **Litho.** *Perf. 13*

O78 A13 9p ultramarine 2.10 .20
O79 A13 1a3p magenta 1.25 .20
a. Double overprint 24.00 18.00
O80 A13 1a9p ultramarine .30 *.70*
Nos. O78-O80 (3) 3.65 1.10

Types and Stamps of 1946-48 Overprinted Type "h"

1946-48

O81 A15 3p car rose .60 .20
O82 A15 4p gray green 24.00 4.50
O83 A15 6p red brown 5.50 .70
O84 A15 9p ultra .75 .20
O85 A15 1a3p magenta 2.25 .50
O86 A15 1a9p ultra 1.90 .40
O87 A15 2a gray black 13.00 2.75
O88 A15 2¼a olive green 17.00 2.75
Nos. O81-O88 (8) 65.00 12.00

No. 56 Overprinted Type "q" and Surcharged Type "d"

1947 **Wmk. 41** **Engr.** *Perf. 13x13½*

O89 A9 3p on 4p dull green 18.00 5.50

Stamps and Type of 1948-49 Overprinted Type "o"

1948-49 **Wmk. 294** **Litho.** *Perf. 11*

O90 A16 3p carmine ('49) 1.00 .20
O91 A16 4p gray green .90 .30
O92 A16 6p red brown 2.00 .20
O93 A16 9p ultramarine 2.00 .20
O94 A16 2a black ('49) 1.00 .20
O95 A16 2¼a lt ol green ('49) 2.75 *4.50*
O96 A16 3a vermilion ('49) .90 .40
O97 A16 3a4p deep pur ('49) 26.00 22.50
Nos. O90-O97 (8) 36.55 28.50

See Travancore-Cochin for succeeding issues.

DHAR

'där

LOCATION — A Feudatory State in the Malwa Agency in Central India.
AREA — 1,800 sq. mi.
POP. — 243,521
CAPITAL — Dhar

A1

Arms of Dhar — A2

The stamps of type A1 have an oval control mark handstamped in black.

Unwmk.

1897-1900 **Typeset** *Imperf.*
Without Gum

1 A1 ½p black, *red* 2.25 *2.50*
a. Characters for "pice" transposed 15.00
b. Five characters in first word .75
c. Without control mark 82.50
2 A1 ¼a black, *org red* ('00) 2.25 *3.00*
a. Without control mark 100.00
3 A1 ½a black, *lil rose* 3.50 *4.00*
4 A1 1a black, *bl grn* 7.00 *10.50*
5 A1 2a black, *yel* ('00) 25.00 *35.00*
Nos. 1-5 (5) 40.00 *55.00*

1898-1900 **Typo.** *Perf. 11½*

6 A2 ½a red .85 .85
7 A2 ½a rose ('00) 1.50 1.50
a. Imperf., pair 35.00
8 A2 1a maroon 1.00 1.00
9 A2 1a violet ('00) 1.25 1.25
10 A2 1a claret ('00) 1.00 1.00
11 A2 2a dark green ('00) 3.25 *5.00*
Nos. 6-11 (6) 8.85 *10.60*

Obsolete Mar. 31, 1901.

DUTTIA

'dət-ē-ə

(Datia)

LOCATION — A Feudatory State in the Bundelkhand Agency in Central India.
AREA — 912 sq. mi.
POP. — 158,834
CAPITAL — Datia

Ganesh, Elephant-headed God
A1 A2

All Duttia stamps have a circular control mark, about 23mm in diameter, handstamped in blue or black. All were issued without gum.

1893 **Typeset** **Unwmk.** *Imperf.*

1 A1 ¼a black, *org red* 2,500.
2 A1 ½a blk, *grysh grn* 6,000.
3 A2 1a black, *red* 2,000.
4 A1 2a black, *yellow* 1,750.
5 A1 4a black, *rose* 1,250.

Type A2 with Frameline around God, Rosettes in Lower Corners

1896 (?)

5A A2 ½ black, *green* *3,000.*
5C A2 2a dk blue, *lemon* *2,000.*

A 1a in this revised type has been reported.

1897

6 A2 ½a black, *green* 18.00 *150.00*
7 A2 1a black 70.00 *175.00*
a. Laid paper 15.00
8 A2 2a black, *yellow* 22.50 *160.00*
9 A2 4a black, *rose* 18.00 *125.00*
Nos. 6-9 (4) 128.50 *610.00*

A3

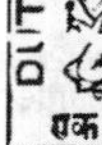
A4

10 A3 ½a black, *green* 60.00
11 A3 1a black 110.00
12 A3 2a black, *yellow* 67.50
13 A3 4a black, *rose* 62.50
Nos. 10-13 (4) 300.00

1899-1900
Rouletted in Colored Lines on 2 or 3 Sides

14 A4 ¼a red (shades) 2.40
b. Tete beche pair *2,500.*
15 A4 ½a black, *green* 2.50
16 A4 1a black 2.75
17 A4 2a black, *yellow* 2.50
18 A4 4a black, *rose red* 3.50
a. Tete beche pair
Nos. 14-18 (5) 13.65

1904 *Imperf.*

22 A4 ¼a carmine 3.00
23 A4 ½a black, *green* 16.00
24 A4 1a black 11.50
Nos. 22-24 (3) 30.50

1911 *Perf. 13½*

25 A4 ¼a carmine 5.50 *25.00*

1916 *Imperf.*

26 A4 ¼a dull blue 5.00 *17.50*
27 A4 ½a green 5.00 *20.00*
28 A4 1a violet 4.50 *20.00*
a. Tete beche pair 20.00
29 A4 2a brown 12.00 *24.00*
29A A4 4a brick red 67.50
Nos. 26-29A (5) 94.00 81.50

1918

31 A4 ½a ultramarine 3.50 12.50
32 A4 1a rose 3.00 14.00
33 A4 2a violet 5.25 *25.00*

Perf. 12

34 A4 ¼a black 4.25 20.00
Nos. 31-34 (4) 16.00 71.50

1920 *Rouletted*

35 A4 ¼a blue 2.00 10.00
36 A4 ½a rose 2.75 14.00

Perf. 7

37 A4 ½a dull red 10.00 25.00
Nos. 35-37 (3) 14.75 49.00

Duttia stamps became obsolete in 1921.

FARIDKOT

fe-'rēd-ˌkōt

LOCATION — A Feudatory State in the Punjab Agency of India.
AREA — 638 sq. mi.
POP. — 164,364
CAPITAL — Faridkot

4 Folus or Paisas = 1 Anna

A1

A2

A3

Handstamped

1879-86 **Unwmk.** *Imperf.*
Without Gum

1 A1 1f ultramarine 1.50 3.00
a. Laid paper 16.00 16.00
b. Tete beche pair 200.00

2 A2 1p ultramarine 2.50 7.50
a. Laid paper 50.00 75.00
3 A3 1p ultramarine 1.25
a. Tete beche pair 175.00
Nos. 1-3 (3) 5.25

Several other varieties exist, but it is believed that only the stamps listed here were issued for postal use. They became obsolete Dec. 31, 1886. See Faridkot under Convention States for issues of 1887-1900.

HYDERABAD (DECCAN)

'hīd-ə-ˌrə-ˌbad

LOCATION — Central India
AREA — 82,313 sq. mi.
POP. — 16,338,534 (1941)
CAPITAL — Hyderabad

This independent princely state was occupied and annexed by India in 1948.

Catalogue values for unused stamps in this State are for Never Hinged items, beginning with Scott 51 in the regular postage section, and Scott O54 in the officials section.

Expect irregular perfs on the Nos. 1-14 and O1-O20 due to the nature of the paper.

A1

A2

1869-71 Engr. Unwmk. *Perf. 11½*
1 A1 ½a brown ('71) 5.50 6.00
2 A2 1a olive green 10.00 5.50
a. Imperf. horiz., pair 110.00 85.00
3 A1 2a green ('71) 27.50 24.00
Nos. 1-3 (3) 43.00 35.50

For overprints see Nos. O1-O3, O11-O13.
The reprints are perforated 12½.

A3

A4

Wove Paper

1871-1909 *Perf. 12½*
4 A3 ½a orange brown .20 .20
a. ½a red brown .20 .20
b. ½a magenta (error) 25.00 11.00
c. Perf. 11½ 15.00 15.00
d. ½a rose .20 .20
e. ½a bright vermilion .20 .20
5 A3 1a dark brown .50 .38
a. Imperf., pair 25.00
b. Pair, imperf. between 50.00
c. Perf. 11½ 37.50 37.50
6 A3 1a black ('09) .95 .20
7 A3 2a green .20 .20
a. 2a olive green ('09) .20 .20
b. Perf. 11½ 110.00
8 A3 3a yellow brown .30 .20
a. Perf. 11½ 22.50 22.50
9 A3 4a slate .40 .30
a. Imperf. horiz., pair 200.00 200.00
b. Perf. 11½ 50.00 50.00
10 A3 4a deep green .80 .45
a. 4a olive green 2.50 2.25
11 A3 8a bister brown .95 .55
a. Perf. 11½
12 A3 12a blue 1.40 1.40
a. Perf. 11½ 95.00 95.00
b. 12a slate green 1.25 1.25
Nos. 4-12 (9) 5.70 3.88

For overprints see Nos. 13, O4-O10, O14-O20, O25-O26.

Surcharged

1900
13 A3 ¼a on ½a brt ver 1.00 1.10
a. Inverted surcharge 27.50 19.00

1902
14 A4 ¼a blue 2.00 1.90

Seal of the Nizam
A5 A6

Engraved by A. G. Wyon

1905 Wmk. 42
17 A5 ¼a blue 2.00 .20
18 A5 ½a red 4.75 .20
19 A5 ½a orange 4.75 .20
Nos. 17-19 (3) 11.50 .60

For overprints see Nos. O21-O23.

Perf. 11, 11½, 12½, 13½ and Compound

1908-11
20 A5 ¼a gray .40 .20
21 A5 ½a green .85 .20
22 A5 1a carmine .50 .20
23 A5 2a lilac .35 .20
24 A5 3a brn orange ('09) .85 .20
25 A5 4a olive green ('09) .85 .25
26 A5 8a violet ('11) .50 .20
27 A5 12a blue green ('11) 6.00 2.75
Nos. 20-27 (8) 10.30 4.20

For overprints see Nos. O24, O27-O38.

Engr. by Bradbury, Wilkinson & Co.

1912
28 A5 ¼a brown violet .20 .20
29 A5 ½a deep green 2.00 .20
a. Imperf., pair 20.00

The frame of type A5 differs slightly in each denomination.
Nos. 20-21 measure 19½x20½mm.
Nos. 28-29 measure 20x21½mm.
For overprints see Nos 37, O39-O40, O44.

1915-16
30 A6 ½a green .60 .20
31 A6 1a carmine rose .60 .20
32 A6 1a red 6.00 .20
Nos. 30-32 (3) 7.20 .60

Unless used, imperf. stamps of types A5 and A6 are from plate proof sheets.
See #58. For overprints see #38, O41-O43, O45.

A7

1927 Wmk. 211 *Perf. 13½*
36 A7 1r yellow 6.00 5.75

Stamps of 1912-16 Surcharged in Red

(4 pies)

(8 pies)

1930
37 A5 4p on ¼a brn vio .20 .20
a. Perf. 11 125.00
b. Double surcharge
38 A6 8p on ½a green .20 .20
a. Perf. 11 125.00 90.00

For overprints see Nos. O44-O45.

Seal of Nizam — A8

Char Minar — A9

High Court of Justice
A10

Reservoir for City of Hyderabad
A11

Bidar College — A13

Entrance to Ajanta Caves
A12

Victory Tower at Daulatabad
A14

Wmk. 211

1931-48 Engr. *Perf. 13½*
39 A8 4p black .20 .20
a. Laid paper ('47) 5.25 3.25
39B A8 6p car lake ('48) 1.00 .60
40 A8 8p green .20 .20
a. 8p yel grn, laid paper ('47) 5.25 3.25
b. Imperf., pair 47.50
41 A9 1a dark brown .20 .20
42 A10 2a dark violet .25 .20
a. Imperf., pair 100.00
43 A11 4a ultramarine .60 .20
a. Imperf., pair 130.00
44 A12 8a deep orange 1.00 .60
45 A13 12a scarlet 2.00 *2.50*
46 A14 1r yellow 2.75 2.75
Nos. 39-46 (9) 8.20 7.45

On No. 39B, "POSTAGE" has been moved to ribbon at bottom of design.
Nos. 39a and 40a are printed from worn plates. The background of the design is unshaded.
See #59. For overprints see #O46-O53, O56.

Unani General Hospital
A15

Osmania General Hospital
A16

Osmania University
A17

Osmania Jubilee Hall — A18

Perf. 13½x14

1937, Feb. 13 Litho. Unwmk.
47 A15 4p violet & black .20 .20
48 A16 8p brown & black .20 .20
49 A17 1a dull orange & gray .20 .20
50 A18 2a dull green & gray .50 .50
Nos. 47-50 (4) 1.10 1.10

The Nizam's Silver Jubilee.

Catalogue values for unused stamps in this section, from this point to the end of the section, are for Never Hinged items.

Returning Soldier — A19

1946 Typo. *Perf. 13½*
51 A19 1a dark blue .20 .20

Wmk. 211
52 A19 1a blue .20 .20

Wmk. Nizam's Seal in Sheet
Laid Paper
53 A19 1a dark blue .50 .35
Nos. 51-53 (3) .90 .75

Victory of the Allied Nations in WW II.

Town Hall, Hyderabad
A20

1947, Feb. 17 Litho. Wove Paper
54 A20 1a black .20 .20

Inauguration of the Reformed Legislature, Feb. 17th, 1947.

Power House, Hyderabad
A21

Designs: 3a, Kaktyai Arch, Warangal Fort. 6a, Golkunda Fort.

Perf. 13½x14

1947-49 Typo. Wmk. 211
55 A21 1a4p dark green .20 .20
56 A21 3a blue .20 .20
57 A21 6a olive brown 4.00 4.00
a. 6a red brown ('49) 35.00 35.00
b. Imperf., pair 90.00
Nos. 55-57 (3) 4.40 4.40

Seal Type of 1915

1947 Engr. *Perf. 13½*
58 A6 ½a rose lake .35 .20

For overprint see No. O54.

Seal Type of 1931

1949 Litho.
59 A8 2p brown 1.25 .20

For overprint see No. O55.

OFFICIAL STAMPS

Regular Issues of 1869-71 Overprinted

1873 Unwmk. *Perf. 11½, 12½*

Red Overprint

O1 A1 ½a brown 21.00
O2 A2 1a olive green 50.00 25.00
O3 A1 2a green 35.00
O4 A3 ½a red brown 3.50 3.50
O5 A3 1a dark brown 6.50 4.25
O6 A3 2a green 6.50 4.00
O7 A3 3a yel brown 8.50 7.00
O8 A3 4a slate 7.00 6.25
O9 A3 8a bister 8.50 8.50
O10 A3 12a blue 11.00 9.00

Black Overprint

O11 A1 ½a brown 15.00
O12 A2 1a olive green 20.00
O13 A1 2a green 27.50
O14 A3 ½a red brown 3.00 1.75
O15 A3 1a dark brown 2.00 1.75
O16 A3 2a green 2.25 .60
O17 A3 3a yel brown 2.00 1.00
O18 A3 4a slate 2.75 2.75
O19 A3 8a bister 5.00 5.00
O20 A3 12a blue 8.00 8.00

The above official stamps became obsolete in August, 1878. Since that date the "Official" overprint has been applied to the reprints and probably to original stamps. Two new varieties of the overprint have also appeared, both on the reprints and on the current stamps. These are overprinted in various colors, positions and combinations.

Same Ovpt. On Regular Issues of 1905-11

1908 Wmk. 42

O21 A5 ½a green 2.00 .20
O22 A5 1a carmine 2.00 .20
O23 A5 2a lilac 3.25 .20
Nos. O21-O23 (3) 7.25 .60

Perf. 11, 11½, 12½, 13½ and Compound

1909-11

O24 A5 ½a red 1.75 .20
O25 A3 1a black 1.00 .20
O26 A3 2a olive green 1.75 .30
O27 A5 3a brown orange 10.00 5.00
O28 A5 4a olive green ('11) 1.50 .30
O29 A5 8a violet ('11) 1.75 .35
O30 A5 12a blue green ('11) 2.50 .35
Nos. O24-O30 (7) 20.25 6.70

Regular Issue of 1908-11 Overprinted

1911-12

O31 A5 ¼a gray .20 .20
O32 A5 ½a green .30 .20
O33 A5 1a carmine .20 .20
O34 A5 2a lilac .20 .20
O35 A5 3a brown orange 1.00 .20
O36 A5 4a olive green .75 .20
O37 A5 8a violet 1.00 .20
O38 A5 12a blue green 2.25 .50
Nos. O31-O38 (8) 5.90 1.90

Same Overprint on Regular Issue of 1912

1912

O39 A5 ¼a brown violet .20 .20
a. ¼a gray violet .20 .20
O40 A5 ½a deep green .20 .20

Same Ovpt. On Regular Issue of 1915-16

1917

O41 A6 ½a green .60 .20
O42 A6 1a carmine rose 1.00 .20
O43 A6 1a red 1.00 .20
Nos. O41-O43 (3) 2.60 .60

Same Overprint on Nos. 37 and 38

1930

O44 A5 4p on ¼a brown violet .80 .20
O45 A6 8p on ½a green .80 .20

Same Overprint on Regular Issue of 1931

1934-47 Wmk. 211 *Perf. 13½*

O46 A8 4p black .20 .20
a. Laid paper ('47) .30
b. Imperf., pair 50.00
O47 A8 8p green .20 .20
a. 8p yel grn, laid paper ('47) 2.00 .30
b. Inverted overprint 145.00 145.00
O48 A9 1a dark brown .25 .20
O49 A10 2a dark violet .25 .20
O50 A11 4a ultramarine .65 .20
O51 A12 8a deep orange 2.00 .20
O52 A13 12a scarlet 2.00 .25
O53 A14 1r yellow 2.75 .30
Nos. O46-O53 (8) 8.30 1.75

Catalogue values for unused stamps in this section, from this point to the end of the section, are for Never Hinged items.

Same Overprint on Nos. 58-59, 39B

1947-50 *Perf. 13½*

O54 A6 ½a rose lake 3.25 1.00
O55 A8 2p brown ('49) 2.50 1.25
O56 A8 6p car lake ('50) 4.00 3.00
Nos. O54-O56 (3) 9.75 5.25

IDAR

ˈē-dər

LOCATION — A Feudatory State in the Western India States Agency.
AREA — 1,669 sq. mi.
POP. — 262,660
CAPITAL — Himmatnagar

Stamps of Idar are in booklet panes of four. All stamps have one or two straight edges.

Maharaja Shri Himatsinhji
A1 A2

1939 Unwmk. Typo. *Perf. 11*

1 A1 ½a light green 2.75 *14.00*

1941 Same Redrawn

2 A1 ½a green 4.50

The panels containing denomination and name of state are shaded.

1944 Unwmk. *Perf. 12*

3 A2 ½a green .75 *14.00*
4 A2 1a purple .40
a. Imperf., pair 135.00
5 A2 2a blue .45
6 A2 4a red 1.40
Nos. 3-6 (4) 3.00

INDORE

in-ˈdō̦ə̦r

(Holkar)

LOCATION — A Feudatory State in the Indore Agency in Central India.
AREA — 9,902 sq. mi.
POP. — 1,513,966
CAPITAL — Indore

Maharaja Tukoji Rao II — A1

A2

1886 Unwmk. Litho. *Perf. 15*

1 A1 ½a lilac 2.00 2.00

1889 Handstamped *Imperf.*

3 A2 ¼a black, *rose* 1.75 *1.90*

No. 3 exists in two types.

The originals of this stamp are printed in water color. The reprints are in oil color and on paper of a deeper shade of rose.

Maharaja Shivaji Rao — A3

1889-92 Engr. *Perf. 15*

4 A3 ¼a orange .20 .20
5 A3 ½a brown violet .20 .20
6 A3 1a green .50 .50
7 A3 2a vermilion 1.25 .65
Nos. 4-7 (4) 2.15 1.55

For overprint see No. 14.

Maharaja Tukoji Rao III
A4 A5

1904-08 *Perf. 13½, 14*

8 A4 ¼a orange .20 .20
9 A5 ½a lake ('08) 5.00 .20
a. Imperf., pair 17.50
10 A5 1a green ('07) 3.75 .20
a. Imperf., pair 100.00
11 A5 2a brown ('05) 2.50 .20
a. Imperf., pair 62.50
12 A5 3a violet 2.25 .45
13 A5 4a ultramarine 2.50 .45
Nos. 8-13 (6) 16.20 1.70

For overprints see Nos. O1-O7.

No. 5 Surcharged

1905 *Perf. 15*

14 A3 ¼a on ½a brown violet 1.75 1.60

Maharaja Yeshwant Rao II
A6 A7

1928-38 Engr. *Perf. 13½*

15 A6 ¼a orange .20 .20
16 A6 ½a claret .20 .20
17 A6 1a green .20 .20
18 A6 1¼a green ('33) .35 .20
19 A6 2a dark brown .90 .65
20 A6 2a Prus blue ('36) .50 .30
21 A6 3a dull violet .90 .90
22 A6 3½a dull violet ('34) 1.00 1.00
23 A6 4a ultramarine 1.00 1.00
24 A6 4a bister ('38) 1.75 .50
25 A6 8a gray 2.00 2.00
26 A6 8a red orange ('38) 7.50 3.25
27 A6 12a rose red ('34) 7.00 7.00

Perf. 14

28 A7 1r lt blue & black 11.00 *15.00*
29 A7 2r car lake & blk 22.50 *25.00*
30 A7 5r org brn & black 30.00 30.00
Nos. 15-30 (16) 87.00 87.40

Imperforates of types A6 and A7 were used with official sanction at Indore City during a stamp shortage in 1938. They were from sheets placed by the printers (Perkins, Bacon) on top of packets of 100 perforated sheets as identification.

Stamps of 1929-33 Surcharged in Black

1940 *Perf. 13, 14*

31 A7 ¼a on 5r org brn & blk .65 .20
a. Dbl. surch., black over green 190.00
32 A7 ½a on 2r car lake & blk 1.00 .20
33 A6 1a on 1¼a green 1.10 .20
a. Inverted surcharge 75.00
Nos. 31-33 (3) 2.75 .60

Stamps with green surcharge only are proofs.

A8

1941-47 Typo. *Perf. 11*

34 A8 ¼a orange .20 .20
35 A8 ½a rose lilac .50 .20
36 A8 1a dk olive green .65 .20
37 A8 1¼a yellow green .75 .20
a. Imperf., pair 125.00
38 A8 2a turquoise blue 6.00 1.75
39 A8 4a bister ('47) 16.00 16.00

Size: 23x28¼mm

40 A8 2r car lake & blk ('47) 12.50 *25.00*
41 A8 5r brn org & blk 14.00 *30.00*
Nos. 34-41 (8) 50.60 *73.55*

OFFICIAL STAMPS

Stamps and Type of 1904-08 Overprinted

1904-06 *Perf. 13½, 14*

O1 A5 ½a lake .20 .20
a. Inverted overprint 14.00
b. Double overprint 14.00
c. Imperf., pair 20.00
O2 A5 1a green .20 .20
O3 A5 2a brown ('05) .20 .20
O4 A5 3a violet ('06) .75 .75
a. Imperf., pair 110.00
O5 A5 4a ultra ('05) 1.25 1.25
Nos. O1-O5 (5) 2.60 2.60

Same Overprint on No. 8

1907

O6 A4 ¼a orange .20 .20

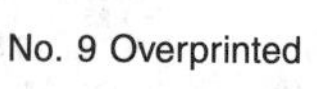

No. 9 Overprinted

O7 A5 ½a lake .20 .20

#O1, O7 differ mainly in the shape of the "R."

JAIPUR

ˈjī-ˌpu̇ər

LOCATION — A Feudatory State in the Jaipur Residency of India.
AREA — 15,610 sq. mi.
POP. — 3,040,876
CAPITAL — Jaipur

Catalogue values for unused stamps in this State are for Never Hinged items, beginning with Scott 49 in the regular postage section, and Scott O30 in the officials section.

Chariot of Surya, Sun God—A1a
A1

Pin-perf. 14x14½

1904 Typo. Unwmk.

1	A1	½a ultramarine	6.25	6.25
a.		½a pale blue	16.00	16.00
b.		½a gray blue		250.00
c.		As "b," imperf.	325.00	375.00
1D	A1a	½a blue	1.75	2.00
e.		½a ultramarine	1.75	2.00
f.		Imperf.		
2	A1	1a dull red	1.75	1.90
a.		1a chestnut	12.50	12.50
3	A1	2a pale green	2.75	2.75
a.		2a emerald	4.25	4.50
		Nos. 1-3 (4)	12.50	12.90

No. 1 has 36 varieties (on 2 plates), differing in minor details. Nos. 1b and 1c are from plate II. No. 1D has 24 varieties (one plate).

Chariot of Surya — A2

Perf. 12½x12 and 13½

1904-06 Engr.

4	A2	¼a olive green ('06)	.20	.20
5	A2	½a deep blue	.20	.20
6	A2	1a carmine	.40	.30
7	A2	2a dark green	.75	.65
8	A2	4a red brown	3.75	2.00
9	A2	8a violet	2.50	1.90
10	A2	1r yellow	3.75	4.00
		Nos. 4-10 (7)	11.55	9.25

For overprints see Nos. 21-22.

A3

A4

1911 Typo. *Imperf.*
Without Gum

11	A3	¼a yellow green	1.50	1.75
a.		¼a olive green	1.50	1.75
b.		"¼" inverted	2.00	2.00
12	A3	¼a olive yellow	.20	.20
b.		¼a blue (error)		
13	A3	½a ultramarine	.20	.20
a.		½a dull blue	.20	.20
b.		"½" for "½"	5.00	
14	A3	1a carmine	.30	.30
15	A3	2a deep green	2.50	2.75
a.		2a gray green	2.50	2.75
		Nos. 11-15 (5)	4.70	5.20

There are six types for each value and several settings of the ¼a and ½a in the 1911 issue.

Wmk. "Dorling & Co., London" in Sheet

1913-18 *Perf. 11*

16	A4	¼a olive bister	.20	.20
a.		Pair, imperf. between	75.00	75.00
17	A4	½a ultramarine	.20	.20
18	A4	1a carmine ('18)	.20	.20
a.		1a scarlet	.20	.20
b.		Vert. pair, imperf. btwn.	87.50	87.50
19	A4	2a green ('18)	2.00	2.00
20	A4	4a red brown	.60	.60
		Nos. 16-20 (5)	3.20	3.20

For overprints see Nos. O1-O6, O9-O10.

Stamps of 1904-06 Surcharged

1926 Unwmk. Engr. *Perf. 13½*

21	A2	3a on 8a violet	.75	.85
a.		Inverted surcharge	125.00	125.00
22	A2	3a on 1r yellow	.75	.85
a.		Inverted surcharge	125.00	125.00

Wmk. "Overland Bank" in Sheet

1928 Typo. *Perf. 12*

17a	A4	½a ultramarine	4.75	4.75
18c	A4	1a rose red	12.50	7.50
18d	A4	1a scarlet	12.50	7.50
19a	A4	2a green	24.00	18.00
20a	A4	4a pale brown		
23	A4	8a violet		
23A	A4	1r red orange	125.00	125.00

Durbar Commemorative Issue

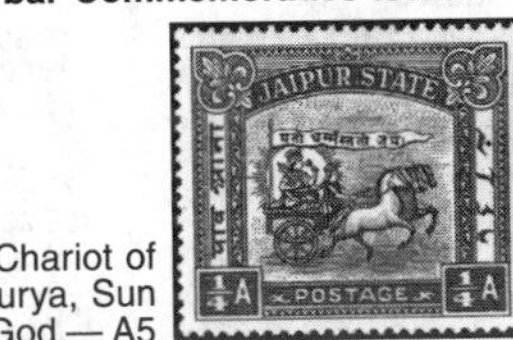

Chariot of Surya, Sun God — A5

Maharaja Man Singh II — A6

Elephant with Standard — A7

Sowar in Armor — A8

Blue Peafowl — A9

Royal Bullock Carriage — A10

Royal Elephant Carriage — A11

Albert Museum — A12

Sireh-Deorhi Gate — A13

Chandra Palace — A14

Amber Palace — A15

Rajas Jai Singh II and Man Singh II — A16

Perf. 13½x14, 14, 14x13½

1931, Mar. 14 Typo. Unwmk.

24	A5	¼a red brn & blk	.25	.20
25	A6	½a dull vio & blk	.40	.20
26	A7	1a blue & black	1.90	.90
27	A8	2a ocher & black	1.90	.90
28	A9	2½a rose & black	8.50	15.00
29	A10	3a dk grn & blk	8.50	14.00
30	A11	4a dull grn & blk	5.50	11.50
31	A12	6a dk blue & blk	5.50	11.50
32	A13	8a brown & black	6.50	14.00
33	A14	1r olive & black	10.00	22.50
34	A15	2r lt green & blk	10.00	27.50
35	A16	5r violet & black	14.00	32.50
		Nos. 24-35 (12)	72.95	150.70

Investiture of the Maharaja Man Singh II with full ruling powers.

Eighteen sets of this issue were overprinted in red "INVESTITURE—MARCH 14, 1931" for presentation to distinguished personages.

For surcharges see Nos. 47, 48, 58. For overprints see Nos. O12-O16, Rajasthan 16.

Man Singh II Type of 1931 and

Raja Man Singh II — A18

1932-46 *Perf. 14*

36	A6	¼a red brn & blk	.20	.20
36A	A6	¾a brn orange & black ('43)	.20	.20
37	A18	1a blue & black	.20	.20
37A	A6	1a blue & black	.50	.20
38	A18	2a ocher & black	.20	.20
38A	A6	2a ocher & blk ('45)	.75	.20
39	A6	2½a dk car & blk	.20	.20
40	A6	3a green & blk	.25	.20
41	A18	4a gray grn & blk	.75	.75
41A	A6	4a gray green & blk ('45)	1.25	.75
42	A6	6a blue & black	.65	.65
43	A18	8a choc & black	.65	.65
43A	A6	8a choc & blk ('45)	2.00	3.00
44	A18	1r bis & gray blk	7.50	10.00
44A	A6	1r bis & gray blk ('46)	7.50	10.00
45	A18	2r yel grn & blk	37.50	50.00
		Nos. 36-45 (16)	60.30	77.40

For overprints see Nos. O17-O30, Rajasthan Nos. 15, 17-25.

Stamps of 1931-32 Surcharged in Red or Black

One Rupee

1936 *Perf. 14x13½, 13½x14*

46	A18	1r on 2r yel grn & blk (R)	2.25	3.75
47	A16	1r on 5r violet & blk	2.00	3.75

No. 25 Surcharged in Red

पाव आना

1938 *Perf. 14x13½*

48	A6	¼a on ½a dull vio & blk	2.25	2.25

Catalogue values for unused stamps in this section, from this point to the end of the section, are for Never Hinged items.

Amber Palace A19

Designs: ¼a, Palace gate. ¾a, Map of Jaipur. 1a, Observatory. 2a, Palace of the Winds. 3a, Arms of the Raja. 4a, Gate of Amber Fort. 8a, Chariot of the Sun. 1r, Raja Man Singh II.

1947-48 Unwmk. Engr. *Perf. 14*

49	A19	¼a dk green & red brn ('48)	.20	.20
50	A19	½a blue vio & dp grn	.20	.20
51	A19	¾a dk car & blk ('48)	.20	.25
52	A19	1a dp ultra & choc	.25	.35
53	A19	2a car & blue vio	.20	.35
54	A19	3a dk gray & grn ('48)	.30	.50
55	A19	4a choc & dp ultra	.40	.70
56	A19	8a dk brown & red	.50	.70
57	A19	1r dk red vio & bl grn ('48)	1.25	2.25
		Nos. 49-57 (9)	3.50	5.50

25th anniv. of the enthronement of Raja Man Singh II.

No. 25 Surcharged in Carmine with New Value and Bars

1947

58	A6	3p on ½a	15.00	15.00
a.		"3 PIE"	50.00	50.00
b.		Inverted surcharge	52.50	52.50
c.		Double surch., one inverted	100.00	100.00
d.		As "a," inverted surcharge	225.00	225.00

For overprint see No. O31.

OFFICIAL STAMPS

Regular Issue of 1913-22 Overprinted in Black or Red

1929 Unwmk. *Perf. 12½x12, 11*

O1	A4	¼a olive green	.35	.20
O2	A4	½a ultramarine	.35	.20
a.		Inverted overprint		90.00
O3	A4	½a ultra (R)	.35	.20
O4	A4	1a red	.50	.20
O5	A4	2a green	.45	.25
O6	A4	4a red brown	2.25	.90
O7	A4	8a purple (R)	18.00	18.00
O8	A4	1r red orange	35.00	35.00
		Nos. O1-O8 (8)	57.25	54.95

The 8a and 1r not issued without overprint.
For overprint see No. O11.

Regular Issue of 1913-22 Overprinted in Black or Red

b **SERVICE**

1931 ***Perf. 11, 12½x12***

O9 A4 ½a ultra 75.00 .20
O10 A4 ½a ultra (R) 90.00 .20
O10A A4 8a purple 200.00 200.00
O10B A4 1r red orange 200.00 200.00
Nos. O9-O10B (4) 565.00 400.40

No. O5 Surcharged

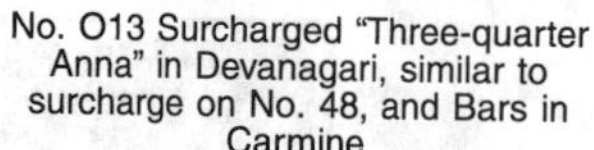

1932

O11 A4 ½a on 2a green 125.00 .25

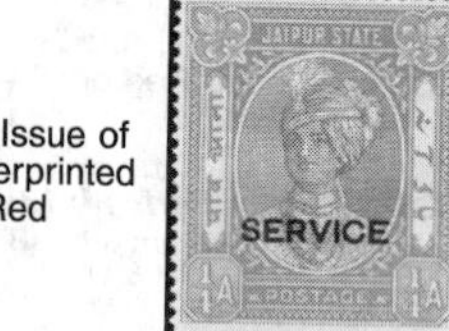

Regular Issue of 1931 Overprinted in Red

1931-37 ***Perf. 13½x14, 14***

O12 A6 ¼a red brn & blk ('36) .20 .20
O13 A6 ½a dull vio & blk .20 .20
O14 A7 1a blue & black 175.00 1.50
O15 A8 2a ocher & blk ('36) .90 .45
O16 A11 4a dl grn & blk ('37) 7.50 3.00

For overprint see No. O32.

Same on Regular Issue of 1932 in Red

1932-37 ***Perf. 14***

O17 A18 1a blue & black .30 .30
O18 A18 2a ocher & black .30 .30
O19 A18 4a gray grn & blk ('37) *175.00 110.00*
O20 A18 8a choc & black 2.50 2.50
O21 A18 1r bis & gray blk 9.00 9.00
Nos. O17-O21 (5) *187.10 122.10*

No. 36 Overprinted Type "b" in Black

1939 ***Perf. 14***

O22 A6 ¼a red brown & blk 45.00 35.00

Nos. 36A, 38A, 39, 41A, 43A, 44A and Type of 1931 Overprinted in Carmine

1941-46 **Unwmk.** ***Perf. 13½, 14***

O23 A6 ¾a brn org & blk ('43) .20 .20
O24 A6 1a blue & blk ('41) .30 .20
O25 A6 2a ocher & black .45 .20
O26 A6 2½a dk car & blk ('46) 1.25 *4.50*
O27 A6 4a gray grn & blk ('46) .60 .30
O28 A6 8a choc & black 1.25 .60
O29 A6 1r bis & gray blk *150.00*
Nos. O23-O28 (6) 4.05 *6.00*

Catalogue values for unused stamps in this section, from this point to the end of the section, are for Never Hinged items.

No. O24 Surcharged with New Value and Bars in Carmine

1947 ***Perf. 13½***

O30 A6 9p on 1a blue & blk .25 .25

No. 58 Overprinted in Red "SERVICE"

Perf. 14

O31 A6 3p on ½a 3.50 *5.00*
a. Inverted surcharge 1,200. 1,100.
b. Double surch., one inverted 65.00 65.00
c. "3 PIE" 300.00 300.00

No. O13 Surcharged "Three-quarter Anna" in Devanagari, similar to surcharge on No. 48, and Bars in Carmine

1949 ***Perf. 14x13½***

O32 A6 ¾a on ½a dl vio & blk 10.00 6.00

For later issues see Rajasthan.

JAMMU AND KASHMIR

'jəm-ˌü and 'kash-ˌmiˌəˌr

LOCATION — A Feudatory State in the Kashmir Residency in the extreme north of India.
AREA — 82,258 sq. mi.
POP. — 4,021,616 (1941)
CAPITAL — Srinagar

All stamps of Jammu and Kashmir were issued without gum.

½ Anna — A1

1 Anna — A2

¼ Rupee — A3

Native Grayish Laid Paper

Handstamped

1866-67 **Unwmk.** ***Imperf.***

Printed in Water Colors

1 A1 ½a gray black 225.00 110.00
Cut to shape 25.00 20.00
2 A2 1a dull blue 400.00 110.00
a. 1a ultramarine 400.00 110.00
b. 1a royal blue 550.00 375.00
Cut to shape 40.00 15.00
3 A2 1a gray black 1,250. 1,000.
Cut to shape 75.00 75.00
4 A3 ¼r dull blue *900.00 400.00*
a. ¼r ultramarine *900.00 400.00*
b. ¼r indigo *2,100. 1,000.*
Cut to shape 900.00 400.00
5 A3 ¼r gray black 1,350. —
Cut to shape 1,350. —
Nos. 1-5 (5) 4,125. 1,620.

It has now been proved by the leading authorities on Indian stamps that all stamps of ½ anna and 1 anna printed from the so-called Die A are forgeries and that no such die was ever in use.

See Nos. 24-59.

JAMMU

A part of the Feudatory State of Jammu & Kashmir, both being ruled by the same sovereign.

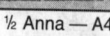

½ Anna — A4

1 Anna — A5

Printed in blocks of four, three types of the ½a and one of the 1a.

Native Grayish Laid Paper

Printed in Water Colors

1867-77 **Unwmk.** ***Imperf.***

6 A4 ½a black 100.00 125.00
7 A4 ½a indigo 250.00 200.00
a. ½a deep ultramarine 200.00 150.00
b. ½a deep violet blue 150.00 75.00
8 A4 ½a red 2.25 1.90
a. ½a orange red 32.50 16.00
b. ½a orange 47.50 47.50
9 A5 1a black 1,200. 800.00
10 A5 1a indigo 500.00 275.00
a. 1a deep ultramarine 500.00 275.00
b. 1a deep violet blue 500.00 275.00
11 A5 1a red 2.75 2.75
a. 1a orange red 16.00 17.50
b. 1a orange 425.00

1876

12 A4 ½a emerald 1,300. 800.00
13 A4 ½a bright blue 1,000. 225.00
14 A5 1a emerald 2,250. 1,400.
15 A5 1a bright blue 300.00 *325.00*

Native Grayish Laid Paper

1877 **Printed in Oil Colors**

16 A4 ½a red 8.00 7.00
a. ½a brown red — 35.00
17 A4 ½a black 750.00
18 A5 1a red 25.00 20.00
a. 1a brown red — 100.00
19 A5 1a black *1,600.*

The formerly listed ½a dark blue, ½a dark green, 1a dark blue and 1a dark green are believed to be reprints.

European White Laid Paper

20 A4 ½a red — *800.00*
a. Thin laid bâtonné paper *1,000.*
21 A5 1a red *310.00*
a. Thin laid bâtonné paper *3,500.*

European White Wove Paper

22 A4 ¼a red *375.00*
23 A5 1a red

RE-ISSUES
For Jammu Only

Native Grayish Laid Paper

Printed in Water Colors

1869-76 ***Imperf.***

24 A1 ½a deep black *16.50 150.00*
25 A1 ½a bright blue 225.00 *300.00*
26 A1 ½a orange red 175.00 55.00
a. ½a orange 90.00 *100.00*
b. ½a red 5.00 2.50
27 A1 ½a emerald 75.00 *175.00*
28 A1 ½a yellow 450.00 750.00
29 A2 1a deep black 200.00
30 A2 1a bright blue 85.00 *275.00*
31 A2 1a orange red 150.00 *200.00*
b. 1a red 11.00 8.00
32 A2 1a emerald 75.00 *175.00*
33 A2 1a yellow 600.00
34 A3 ¼r deep black 200.00 —
35 A3 ¼r bright blue 140.00
a. ¼r indigo 900.00 550.00
36 A3 ¼r orange red 110.00 160.00
a. ¼r orange —
b. ¼r red 50.00 *90.00*
37 A3 ¼r emerald 175.00 *300.00*
38 A3 ¼r yellow 350.00

Native Grayish Laid Paper

1877 **Printed in Oil Colors**

39 A1 ½a red 25.00 *45.00*
40 A1 ½a black 25.00 *45.00*
41 A1 ½a slate blue 100.00 *175.00*
42 A1 ½a sage green 100.00
43 A2 1a red 30.00 *150.00*
45 A2 1a slate blue 20.00 *200.00*
46 A2 1a sage green 110.00
47 A3 ¼r red 175.00 *400.00*
50 A3 ¼r sage green 110.00

European White Laid Paper

51 A1 ½a red 650.00
52 A1 ½a black 20.00 *42.50*
53 A1 ½a slate blue 32.50 *200.00*
54 A1 ½a yellow 100.00
56 A2 1a slate blue 42.50 *350.00*
57 A3 ¼r red 350.00 350.00
58 A3 ¼r sage green *1,000.*

European Brownish Wove Paper

59 A1 ½a red *850.00*

It is probable that the issues of 1876, 1877 and the re-issues of the circular stamps were made to supply the demands of philatelists more than for postal needs. They were, however, available for postage.

There exist also reprints, printed in a variety of colors, on native and European thin wove paper. Collectors are warned against official imitations, which are very numerous. They are printed on several kinds of paper and in a great variety of colors.

A5a

Handstamped in Oil Color

1877, Nov.

60 A5a (½a) red 950.00

This provisional, made with a canceling device, was used only in Nov. 1877, at Jammu city.

KASHMIR

A part of the Feudatory State of Jammu & Kashmir, both being ruled by the same sovereign.

½ Anna — A6

Printed in Water Colors
Native Grayish Laid Paper
Printed from a Single Die

1866 **Unwmk.** ***Imperf.***

62 A6 ½a black 2,000. 300.00

¼ Anna — A7

½ Anna — A8

1 Anna A9

2 Annas A10

4 Annas — A11

8 Annas — A12

The ¼a, 1a and 2a are printed in strips of five varieties, the ½a in sheets of twenty varieties and the 4a and 8a from single dies.

1866-70

63 A7 ¼a black 2.00 2.00
64 A8 ½a black *1,000. 140.00*
65 A8 ½a ultra 2.00 1.25
a. ½a blue 3.75 1.50
66 A9 1a black 1,750. 350.00
67 A9 1a red orange 7.50 7.50
68 A9 1a Venetian red 11.00 8.00
69 A9 1a orange brown 10.00 7.50
70 A9 1a ultra *2,600. 1,200.*
71 A10 2a olive yellow 10.00 *12.50*
72 A11 4a emerald 27.50 26.00
73 A12 8a red 27.50 27.50

All the stamps printed in oil colors are reprints.

As in Jammu, official imitations are numerous and are found in many colors and on various papers.

JAMMU & KASHMIR

¼ Anna — A13

½ Anna — A14

1 Anna — A15

2 Annas — A16

4 Annas — A17

8 Annas — A18

Laid Paper

Printed in Oil Colors

1878 ***Rough Perf. 10-14***

74	A13	¼a red	—	—
75	A14	½a red	12.50	*15.00*
a.		Wove paper		*175.00*
76	A14	½a slate blue	75.00	50.00
77	A15	1a red	1,000.	
78	A15	1a bright violet	—	—

1878-80 ***Imperf.***

79	A13	¼a red	17.50	12.50
80	A14	½a red	7.50	7.50
81	A14	½a slate	13.00	12.50
82	A15	1a red	7.50	7.50
83	A15	1a violet	20.00	20.00
a.		1a dull purple	30.00	30.00
84	A16	2a red	60.00	60.00
85	A16	2a bright violet	27.50	25.00
86	A16	2a dull ultra	*75.00*	75.00
87	A17	4a red	150.00	125.00

Thick Wove Paper

88	A14	½a red	22.50	*45.00*
89	A15	1a red	40.00	17.50
90	A16	2a red	15.00	17.50

Thin Toned Wove Paper

1879-80

91	A13	¼a red	2.50	*2.75*
92	A14	½a red	.50	.50
93	A15	1a red	2.00	*2.50*
94	A16	2a red	2.75	3.50
95	A17	4a red	6.25	6.25
96	A18	8a red	6.50	7.00
		Nos. 91-96 (6)	20.50	22.50

Thin Laid Bâtonné Paper

1880 **Printed in Water Color**

97	A13	¼a ultramarine	675.00	400.00

Thin Toned Wove Paper

1881 **Printed in Oil Colors**

98	A13	¼a orange	7.00	*8.50*
99	A14	½a orange	16.00	11.00
100	A15	1a orange	15.00	8.00
101	A16	2a orange	12.50	8.00
102	A17	4a orange	25.00	*35.00*
103	A18	8a orange	50.00	*55.00*
		Nos. 98-103 (6)	125.50	125.50

⅛ Anna — A19

Thin White or Yellowish Wove Paper

1883-94

104	A19	⅛a yellow brown	.70	*1.00*
a.		⅛a yellow	.70	*1.00*
105	A13	¼a brown	.55	.50
a.		Double impression	1,000.	
106	A14	½a red	1.00	.35
a.		½a rose	1.10	.60
106B	A19	½a bright blue	35.00	
c.		½a dull blue	4.00	
107	A15	1a bronze green	.75	.50
108	A15	1a yel green	.75	.50
109	A15	1a blue green	1.00	
110	A15	1a bister	—	
111	A17	4a green	2.75	2.75
112	A17	4a olive green	2.50	*3.25*
113	A18	8a deep blue	7.50	*8.50*
114	A18	8a dark ultra	6.75	*8.00*
115	A18	8a gray violet	9.00	*14.50*

Printed in Water Color

116	A18	8a gray blue	100.00	90.00

Printed in Oil Colors

Yellow Pelure Paper

117	A16	2a red	2.25	2.25

Yellow Green Pelure Paper

118	A16	2a red	2.00	*2.50*

Deep Green Pelure Paper

119	A16	2a red	10.00	10.00

Coarse Yellow Wove Paper

120	A16	2a red	1.50	.90
		Nos. 104-120 (17)	184.00	145.50

Thin Creamy Laid Paper

1886-94

121	A19	⅛a yellow	35.00	*45.00*
122	A13	¼a brown	8.00	5.50
123	A14	½a vermilion	6.00	4.50
124	A14	½a rose red		55.00
125	A15	1a green	90.00	90.00
126	A17	4a green	—	—

Printed in Water Color

127	A18	8a gray blue	140.00	125.00
		Nos. 121-127 (6)	279.00	325.00

Impressions of types A13 to A19 in colors other than the issued stamps are proofs. Forgeries to defraud the post exist, and some are common.

¼ Anna

Stamps of the above type, printed in red or black, were never placed in use.

OFFICIAL STAMPS

Same Types as Regular Issues
White Laid Paper

1878 **Unwmk.** ***Rough Perf. 10-14***

O1	A14	½a black		1,100.

Imperf

O3	A14	½a black	80.00	80.00
O4	A15	1a black	50.00	50.00
O5	A16	2a black	45.00	42.50
		Nos. O3-O5 (3)	175.00	172.50

Thin White or Yellowish Wove Paper

1880

O6	A13	¼a black	.65	*.75*
O7	A14	½a black	.20	*.30*
O8	A15	1a black	.20	*.50*
O9	A16	2a black	.30	*.45*
O10	A17	4a black	.40	*.75*
O11	A18	8a black	1.25	1.00
		Nos. O6-O11 (6)	3.00	3.75

Thin Creamy Laid Paper

1890-91

O12	A13	¼a black	4.50	4.50
O13	A14	½a black	3.00	3.50
O14	A15	1a black	1.40	3.00
O15	A16	2a black	40.00	
O16	A17	4a black	45.00	45.00
O17	A18	8a black	30.00	45.00
		Nos. O12-O17 (6)	123.90	101.00

Obsolete October 31, 1894.

JASDAN

LOCATION — A Feudatory State in the Kathiawar Agency in Western India.
AREA — 296 sq. mi.
POP. — 34,056 (1931)
CAPITAL — Jasdan

In 1948 Jasdan was incorporated in the United State of Saurashtra (see Soruth).

Catalogue values for all unused stamps in this state are for Never Hinged items.

Sun — A1

Perf. 8½ to 10½

1942 **Unwmk.** **Typo.**

1	A1	1a green	2.75	

Issued in booklet panes of 4 and 8.
The 1a carmine is a revenue stamp.
Jasdan's stamp became obsolete Feb. 15, 1948.

JHALAWAR

'jäl-ə-ˌwär

LOCATION — A Feudatory State in the Rajputana Agency of India.
AREA — 813 sq. mi.
POP. — 107,890
CAPITAL — Jhalrapatan

Apsaras, Hindu Nymph
A1 A2

Laid Paper

1887-90 **Unwmk.** ***Imperf.***

Without Gum

1	A1	1p yellow green	2.00	3.25
2	A2	¼a green	.75	1.25

Obsolete October 31, 1900.

JIND

'jind

(Jhind)

LOCATION — A State of India in the north Punjab.
AREA — 1,299 sq. mi.
POP. — 361,812 (1941)
CAPITAL — Sangrur

A1

A2

A3

A4

A5

1874 **Unwmk.** **Litho.** ***Imperf.***

Thin White Wove Paper

Without Gum

1	A1	½a blue	5.50	3.50
2	A2	1a lilac	7.50	7.50
3	A3	2a yellow	1.25	1.25
4	A4	4a green	27.50	5.50
5	A5	8a dark violet	150.00	40.00
		Nos. 1-5 (5)	191.75	57.75

1875

Thick Blue Laid Paper

Without Gum

6	A1	½a blue	.25	.25
7	A2	1a red violet	.50	.50
8	A3	2a brown orange	.75	.75
9	A4	4a green	.85	.85
10	A5	8a purple	4.25	4.25
		Nos. 6-10 (5)	6.60	6.60

1885 **Without Gum** ***Perf. 12***

11	A1	½a blue	4.25	4.25

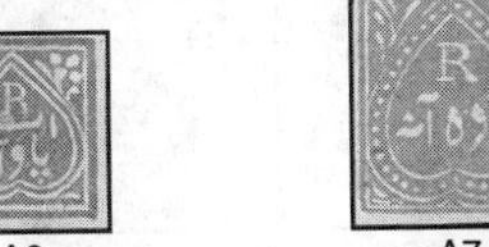

A6 A7

A8

A9

A10 A11

1882-84 **Without Gum** ***Imperf.***

Thin Yellowish Wove Paper

12	A6	¼a buff	.20	.20
a.		Double impression		
13	A7	½a yellow	.55	.55
14	A8	1a brown	1.40	1.40
15	A9	2a blue	.55	.55
16	A10	4a green	.65	.65
17	A11	8a red	2.00	1.40
		Nos. 12-17 (6)	5.35	4.75

Perf. 12

18	A6	¼a buff	.30	.30
19	A7	½a yellow	.40	.40
20	A8	1a brown	.85	.85
21	A9	2a blue	1.50	1.75
22	A10	4a green	2.75	2.75
23	A11	8a red	6.75	6.75
a.		Thick white paper	6.75	6.75
		Nos. 18-23 (6)	12.55	12.80

Laid Paper

Imperf

24	A6	¼a buff	3.50	3.50
25	A7	½a yellow	1.00	1.00
26	A8	1a brown	1.00	1.00
27	A9	2a blue	55.00	55.00
28	A11	8a red	3.75	3.75
		Nos. 24-28 (5)	64.25	64.25

Perf. 12

29	A6	¼a buff	11.00	11.00
30	A7	½a yellow	15.00	11.00
31	A8	1a brown	3.75	3.75
32	A11	8a red	5.00	5.00
		Nos. 29-32 (4)	34.75	30.75

As postage stamps these issues became obsolete in July, 1885, but some possibly remained in use as revenue stamps.

For later issues see Jind under Convention States.

KISHANGARH

'kish-ən-ˌgär

LOCATION — A Feudatory State in the Jaipur Residency of India.
AREA — 858 sq. mi.
POP. — 85,744
CAPITAL — Kishangarh

Kishangarh was incorporated in Rajasthan in 1947-49.

Stamps were issued without gum except Nos. 27-35.

Coat of Arms — A1

1899-1900 **Unwmk.** **Typo.** ***Imperf.***

Soft Porous Paper

1	A1	1a green	21.00	21.00

2 A1 1a blue ('00) *450.00*

Pin-perf

3 A1 1a green 47.50 47.50

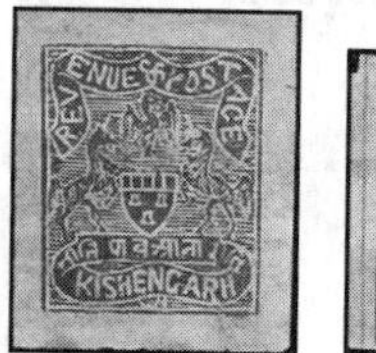

A2

A3

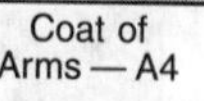

Coat of Arms — A4

Maharaja Sardul Singh — A5

A6

A7

Coat of Arms—A9

A8

Thin Wove Paper

1899-1900 Handstamped *Imperf.*

4 A2 ¼a carmine .45 .45
5 A2 ¼a green 125.00
6 A3 ½a blue .90 .60
7 A3 ½a green 13.00 13.00
8 A3 ½a carmine 13.00 13.00
9 A3 ½a violet 30.00 *35.00*
10 A4 1a gray violet .60 .45
a. 1a gray .60 .45
11 A4 1a rose 60.00 *65.00*
11A A5 2a orange 4.00 4.00
12 A6 4a chocolate 1.90 1.90
a. Laid paper 45.00 45.00
13 A7 1r dull green 18.00
13A A7 1r light brown 50.00 45.00
14 A8 2r brown red 70.00
a. Laid paper 55.00
15 A9 5r violet 45.00
a. Laid paper 75.00

Pin-perf

16 A2 ¼a magenta .25 .25
a. ¼a rose .25
17 A2 ¼a green *150.00* 65.00
a. Imperf. vertically 250.00 250.00
18 A3 ½a blue .30 .30
a. ½a dark blue .60 .60
19 A3 ½a green 12.00 12.00
a. Imperf. vert., pair 60.00 60.00
20 A4 1a gray violet .55 .45
a. 1a gray .75 .75
b. 1a red lilac 6.00
d. As "b," laid paper 30.00 22.50
20E A4 1a rose 40.00 27.50
21 A5 2a orange 7.00 4.50
21B A6 4a pale red brown 1.50 1.25
c. 4a chocolate 1.50 1.25
22 A7 1r dull green 14.00 *19.00*
b. Laid paper 100.00
23 A8 2r brown red 42.50 42.50
b. Laid paper 60.00
24 A9 5r red violet 32.50
d. Laid paper 90.00

Nos. 4-24 exist tête bêche and sell for a slight premium.

For overprints see #O1-O11, Rajasthan #26-28, 30-32.

A9a

A9b

Soft Porous Paper

1901 Typo.

24A A9a ½a rose 10.00 10.00
24B A9b 1a dull violet 18.00 18.00

For overprint see No. O12.

A10

A11

1903 Stout Hard Paper *Imperf.*

25 A10 ½a pink 6.50 5.25
a. Printed on both sides *1,000.*

1904 Thin Wove Paper *Pin-perf.*

25B A11 8a gray 6.50 6.50

Exists tête bêche. Slight premium.

For overprints see #O13, O33, Rajasthan #29.

A11a

Maharaja Sardul Singh — A12

25D A11a 1r green 27.50 27.50

For overprint see No. O13A.

1903 *Imperf.*

Stout Hard Paper

26 A12 2a yellow 4.50 4.50

For overprints see Nos. O14, O34.

Maharaja Madan Singh

A13 A14

1904-05 Engr. *Perf. 12½, 13½*

27 A13 ¼a carmine .35 .20
28 A13 ½a chestnut .35 .20
29 A13 1a deep blue 1.50 .50
30 A13 2a orange 13.50 13.50
31 A13 4a dark brown 4.00 4.00
32 A13 8a purple ('05) 8.00 8.00
33 A13 1r dark green 11.00 11.00
34 A13 2r lemon yellow 17.00 *27.50*
35 A13 5r purple brown 22.50 *42.50*
Nos. 27-35 (9) 78.20 *107.40*

For overprints see Nos. O15-O22, O35-O38, Rajasthan Nos. 33-39.

Thin Wove Paper

1913 Typo. *Rouletted 9½*

37 A14 2 "ANNA" violet 2.50 2.50

Exists tete beche. Slight premium.

See #40-50. For overprint see Rajasthan #43.

Maharaja Madan Singh

A15 A16

Thick, Chalk-surfaced Paper

1913 *Rouletted 6½, 12*

38 A15 ¼a pale blue .20 .20
a. "Kishangahr" 3.25 3.25
b. Imperf., pair 4.50
39 A16 2a purple 13.00 13.00
a. "Kishangahr" 85.00 85.00

For overprint see No. O23.

1913-16 *Rouletted 12, 14½*

40 A14 ¼a pale blue .20 .20
41 A14 ½a green ('15) .20 .20
a. Printed on both sides 200.00
42 A14 1a carmine .90 .90
43 A14 2 "ANNAS" pur 2.75 *3.50*
44 A14 4a ultramarine 5.75 *9.00*
45 A14 8a brown 5.75 *12.00*
46 A14 1r rose lilac 12.00 *24.00*
47 A14 2r dark green 30.00 *35.00*
48 A14 5r brown 45.00 *60.00*
Nos. 40-48 (9) 102.55 *144.80*

On Nos. 40-48 the halftone screen covers the entire design.

Nos. 41-48 have ornaments on both sides of value in top panel.

For overprints see Nos. O24-O30, O39-O43, Rajasthan Nos. 40-42, 44-48.

Type of 1913-16 Redrawn

1918 *Rouletted*

50 A14 1a rose red .90 .90

The redrawn stamp is 24¾mm wide instead of 26mm. There is a white oval around the portrait with only traces of the red line. There is less shading outside the wreath.

For overprint see No. O44.

Maharaja Jagjanarajan Singh

A17 A18

Thick Glazed Paper

1928-29 *Pin-perf. 14½ to 16*

52 A17 ¼a light blue .20 .20
53 A17 ½a lt yellow green .30 .30
a. Imperf., pair 35.00 35.00
54 A18 1a carmine rose .55 .55
55 A18 2a red violet 2.00 2.00
56 A17 4a yellow brown 1.50 1.50
57 A17 8a purple 4.00 4.00
58 A17 1r green 4.00 4.00
59 A17 2r lemon 15.00 *24.00*
60 A17 5r red brown 30.00 *35.00*
a. Imperf., pair 105.00
Nos. 52-60 (9) 57.55 *71.55*

Thick Soft Unglazed Paper

1945-47

52a A17 ¼a gray blue 1.25 1.25
b. ¼a greenish blue ('47) 1.25 1.25
53b A17 ½a deep green 1.25 1.25
54a A18 1a dull carmine 2.50 2.50
b. 1a dark violet blue
55a A18 2a deep red violet 5.00 5.00
b. 2a violet brown, imperf. 20.00
56a A17 4a brown 25.00 25.00
57a A17 8a violet 32.50 *40.00*
58a A17 1r deep green 40.00 *55.00*

The 2r and 5r exist on same paper.

For overprints see Rajasthan Nos. 49-58.

For later issues see Rajasthan.

OFFICIAL STAMPS

Used values are for CTO copies.

Regular Issues of 1899-1916 Handstamped

Black Handstamp

On Issue of 1899-1900

1918 Unwmk. *Imperf.*

O1 A2 ¼a carmine 8.50
O2 A4 1a gray violet 3.50 2.25
O3 A6 4a chocolate 17.00 17.00

Pin-perf

O4 A2 ¼a carmine .50 .50
O4A A2 ¼a green 40.00
O4B A3 ½a blue 27.50
O6 A4 1a gray violet 3.50 1.50
O7 A5 2a orange
O8 A6 4a chocolate 15.00 15.00
O9 A7 1r dull green 60.00 60.00
O10 A8 2r brown red 110.00 110.00
O11 A9 5r red violet 150.00 150.00

See tete beche note after No. 24.

On Issue of 1901

O12 A9b 1a dull violet

On Issue of 1904

O13 A11 8a gray 32.50 32.50
O13A A11a 1r green

Imperf.

O14 A12 2a yellow 17.00 17.00

On Issue of 1904-05

Perf. 12½, 13

O15 A13 ¼a carmine 15.00 12.50
O16 A13 ½a chestnut .60 .50
O17 A13 1a deep blue 9.25 4.00
O18 A13 2a orange
O19 A13 4a dark brown 15.00 15.00
O20 A13 8a purple 60.00 50.00
O21 A13 1r dark green 200.00 200.00
O22 A13 5r purple brn

On Issue of 1913

Rouletted

O23 A15 ¼a pale blue 8.50

On Issue of 1913-16

O24 A14 ¼a pale blue .75 .35
O25 A14 ½a green 1.40 .60
O26 A14 1a carmine 1.40 .65
O27 A14 2a purple 2.00 2.00
O28 A14 4a ultra 22.50 22.50
O29 A14 8a brown 42.50 42.50
O30 A14 1r rose lilac 85.00 85.00
O31 A14 2r dark green 250.00
O32 A14 5r brown 350.00

Red Handstamp

On Issue of 1904

Pin-perf

O33 A11 8a gray 42.50 42.50

Imperf

O34 A12 2a yellow 35.00 35.00

On Issue of 1904-05

Perf. 12½, 13

O35 A13 1a deep blue 12.00 12.00
O36 A13 4a dark brown 15.00 15.00
O37 A13 8a purple 25.00 *35.00*
O38 A13 1r dark green 45.00 *72.50*

On Issue of 1913-16

Rouletted

O39 A14 ¼a pale blue 8.50 8.50
O40 A14 ½a green 8.50 8.50
O41 A14 2a purple 22.50 22.50
O42 A14 4a ultra 42.50 42.50
O43 A14 8a brown 42.50 42.50

On Issue of 1918

Redrawn

O44 A14 1a rose red

The overprint on Nos. O1 to O44 is handstamped and, as usual with that style of overprint, is found inverted, double, etc. In this instance there is evidence that many of the varieties were deliberately made.

LAS BELA

ləs 'bāl-ə

LOCATION — A Feudatory State in the Baluchistan District.
AREA — 7,132 sq. mi.
POP. — 63,008
CAPITAL — Bela

A1

A2

1897-98 Unwmk. Typo. *Perf. 12*

1	A1	½a black, *white*	9.75	9.75
2	A1	½a black, *gray*	2.75	2.50
3	A1	½a blk, *blue* ('98)	5.50	5.50
		Nos. 1-3 (3)	18.00	17.75

1901

4 A2 1a black, *red orange* 9.75 9.75

1904 ***Pin-perf***

5 A1 ½a black, *lt blue* 6.00 6.00

Granite Paper

6 A1 ½a black, *greenish gray* 3.75 3.75

Las Bela stamps became obsolete in Mar. 1907.

MORVI

'mor-vē

LOCATION — A Feudatory State in the Kathiawar Agency, Western India.
AREA — 822 sq. mi.
POP. — 113,023
CAPITAL — Morvi

In 1948 Morvi was incorporated in the United State of Saurashtra (see Soruth).

Sir Lakhdhirji Waghji The Thakur Sahib of Morvi — A1

1931 Unwmk. Typo. *Perf. 12*
Size: 21½x26½mm

1	A1	3p red	.95	*1.10*
a.		3p deep blue (error)	6.00	
2	A1	½a deep blue	1.50	1.25
3	A1	1a red brown	2.00	*2.50*
4	A1	2a yellow brown	4.00	*4.75*
		Nos. 1-4 (4)	8.45	*9.60*

Nos. 1-4 and 1a were printed in two blocks of four, with stamps 5½mm apart, and perforated on four sides. Nos. 1 and 2 were also printed in blocks of four, with stamps 10mm apart, and perforated on two or three sides.

A2

A3

1932 Size: 21x25½mm *Perf. 11*

5	A2	3p rose	.35	*.75*
6	A2	6p gray green	1.25	*1.50*
7	A2	6p emerald	1.25	*2.50*
8	A2	1a ultramarine	1.10	*1.60*
9	A2	2a violet	7.25	*9.00*
		Nos. 5-9 (5)	11.20	*15.35*

1934-48 *Perf. 14, Rough Perf. 11*

10	A3	3p carmine rose	.25	*.30*
a.		3p red	.30	*.30*
11	A3	6p emerald	.30	*.60*
a.		6p green	.30	*.60*
12	A3	1a red brown	1.10	*1.50*
a.		1a brown	1.25	1.75
13	A3	2a violet	1.10	*1.50*
		Nos. 10-13 (4)	2.75	*3.90*

The 1934 London printing of Nos. 10-13 is perf. 14; the later Morvi Press printing is rough perf. 11.
Morvi stamps became obsolete Feb. 15, 1948.

NANDGAON

'nän,d,-,gaun

LOCATION — A Feudatory State in the Chhattisgarh States Agency in Central India.
AREA — 871 sq. mi.
POP. — 182,380
CAPITAL — Rajnandgaon

A1

White Paper

1892, Feb. Unwmk. Typo. *Imperf.*
Without Gum

1	A1	½a blue	2.50
2	A1	2a rose	12.00

Some authorities claim that No. 2 was a revenue stamp.
For overprints see Nos. O1-O2.

A2

1893 Without Gum

4	A2	½a green	9.00
5	A2	2a rose	10.50

For overprint see No. O5.

Same Redrawn

1894 Without Gum

6	A2	½a yellow green	13.00	9.50
7	A2	1a rose	30.00	30.00
a.		Laid paper	125.00	

The redrawn stamps have smaller value characters and wavy lines between the stamps.
For overprints see Nos. O3-O4.

OFFICIAL STAMPS

Regular Issues Handstamped in Violet

1893-94 Unwmk. *Imperf.*
Without Gum

O1	A1	½a blue	*50.00*	
O2	A1	2a red	*65.00*	
O3	A2	½a yellow green	.55	.55
O4	A2	1a rose	2.00	
a.		Laid paper	6.50	
O5	A2	2a rose	3.00	3.00

Some authorities believe that this handstamp was used as a control mark, rather than to indicate a stamp for official mail.
The 1 anna has been reprinted in brown and in blue.
Nandgaon stamps became obsolete in July, 1895.

NOWANUGGUR

,nau-ə-'nəg-ər

(Navanagar)

LOCATION — A Feudatory State in the Kathiawar Agency, Western India.
AREA — 3,791 sq. mi.
POP. — 402,192
CAPITAL — Navanagar

Stamps of Nowanuggur were superseded by those of India.

6 Dokra = 1 Anna
16 Annas = 1 Rupee

Kandjar (Indian Dagger) — A1

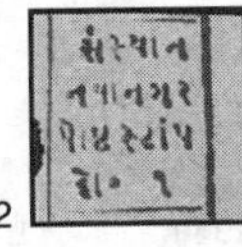

A2

1877 Unwmk. Typo. *Imperf.*
Without Gum
Laid Paper

1	A1	1d dull blue	.50	*10.00*
a.		1d ultramarine	.50	*10.00*
b.		Tete beche pair	900.00	

Perf. 12½

2	A1	1d slate	65.00	65.00
a.		Tete beche pair	1,650.	
b.		Wove paper		

1877-88 *Imperf.*
Without Gum
Wove Paper

3	A2	1d black, *red violet*	.45	*.90*
a.		1d black, *rose*	.45	*.90*
b.		Characters at beginning of 3rd line read "4102" instead of "418"		
4	A2	2d black, *green*	.60	*.90*
a.		2d black, *blue green*	.75	*1.25*
b.		"4102" instead of "418"		
5	A2	3d black, *yellow*	1.10	*1.50*
a.		3d black, *orange yellow*	1.25	*1.75*
b.		"4102" instead of "418"		
c.		Laid paper	32.50	
d.		2d black, *yellow* (error in sheet of 3d)	325.00	
		Nos. 3-5 (3)	2.15	*3.30*

Nos. 3-5 range in width from 14 to 19mm.

Seal of the State — A3

1893 Thick Paper *Imperf.*
Without Gum

6 A3 1d black 60.00

Perf. 12

7	A3	1d black	7.50
8	A3	3d orange	4.50

Imperf
Thin Paper

9	A3	1d black	50.00
10	A3	2d dark green	50.00
11	A3	3d orange	42.50
		Nos. 9-11 (3)	142.50

Perf. 12

12	A3	1d black	.20	*.30*
13	A3	2d green	.45	.45
14	A3	3d orange	.60	.60
a.		Imperf. vert., pair		
		Nos. 12-14 (3)	1.25	1.35

Obsolete at end of 1895.

ORCHHA

'or-chə

(Orcha)

LOCATION — A Feudatory State in the Bundelkhand Agency in Central India.
AREA — 2,080 sq. mi.
POP. — 314,661
CAPITAL — Tikamgarh

Seal of Orchha — A1

1913-17 Unwmk. Litho. *Imperf.*
Without Gum

1	A1	¼a ultra ('15)	.20	*.25*
2	A1	½a emerald ('14)	.20	*.30*
a.		Background of arms unshaded	20.00	*30.00*
3	A1	1a carmine ('14)	1.60	*2.25*
a.		Background of arms unshaded	20.00	
4	A1	2a brown ('17)	4.50	*5.50*
5	A1	4a orange ('14)	7.50	*8.25*
		Nos. 1-5 (5)	14.00	*16.55*

Essays similar to Nos. 2-5 are in different colors.

Maharaja Singh Dev
A2 A3

1939-40 *Perf. 13½, 13½x14*

6	A2	¼a chocolate	.25	*10.00*
7	A2	½a yellow green	.25	*8.50*
8	A2	¾a ultramarine	.25	*13.00*
9	A2	1a rose red	.25	*8.50*
10	A2	1¼a deep blue	.25	*13.00*
11	A2	1½a lilac	.25	*12.50*
12	A2	2a vermilion	1.25	*10.00*
13	A2	2½a turq green	1.60	*8.50*
14	A2	3a dull violet	1.60	*12.00*
15	A2	4a blue gray	2.50	*13.00*
16	A2	8a rose lilac	6.00	*30.00*
17	A3	1r sage green	10.00	*40.00*
18	A3	2r lt violet ('40)	25.00	*65.00*
19	A3	5r yel org ('40)	80.00	*160.00*
20	A3	10r blue	160.00	*250.00*
		Nos. 6-20 (15)	289.45	*654.00*

POONCH

'pünch

LOCATION — A Feudatory State in the Kashmir Residency in India.
AREA — 1,627 sq. mi.
POP. — 287,000 (estimated)
CAPITAL — Poonch

Poonch was feudatory to Jammu and Kashmir. Cancellations of Jammu and Kashmir are found on Poonch stamps, which became obsolete in 1894. The stamps are all printed in watercolor and handstamped from single dies. They may be found on various papers, including wove, laid, wove batonne, laid batonne and ribbed, in various colors and tones. Nearly all Poonch stamps exist tete beche and impressed sideways. Issued without gum.

A1

White Paper
Handstamped

1876 Unwmk. *Imperf.*
Size: 22x21mm

1 A1 6p red 110.

1877
Size: 19x17mm

1A A1 ½a red 4,500. *1,250.*

1879
Size: 21x19mm

1B A1 ½a red 650.

A2

A3

A4

A5

A6

1880-88

White Paper

2	A2	1p red ('84)	12.00	10.50
3	A3	½a red	4.75	3.00
4	A4	1a red	4.25	4.25
5	A5	2a red	10.50	10.50
6	A6	4a red	10.50	

Yellow Paper

7	A2	1p red	1.50	1.50
8	A3	½a red	1.90	1.50
9	A4	1a red	3.75	3.50
10	A5	2a red	1.90	*2.75*
11	A6	4a red	1.10	1.10

Blue Paper

12	A2	1p red	7.75	7.75
13	A4	1a red	2.00	2.00

Orange Paper

14	A2	1p red	.30	.30
15	A3	½a red	4.75	4.75
16	A5	2a red	10.50	10.50
17	A6	4a red	6.50	6.50

Green Paper

18	A3	½a red	5.50	5.50
19	A4	1a red	2.75	2.75
20	A5	2a red	2.50	*3.75*
21	A6	4a red	10.00	*12.00*

Lavender Paper

22	A2	1p red	24.00	24.00
23	A4	1a red	12.00	12.00
24	A5	2a red	.90	.90

OFFICIAL STAMPS

White Paper

Handstamped

1888 **Unwmk.** ***Imperf.***

O1	A2	1p black	.35	.60
O2	A3	½a black	.50	.75
O3	A4	1a black	.75	.75
O4	A5	2a black	1.00	1.00
O5	A6	4a black	1.50	1.50
		Nos. O1-O5 (5)	4.10	4.60

1890

Yellowish Paper

O6	A2	1p black	1.10	
O7	A3	½a black	4.25	4.25
O8	A4	1a black	10.00	7.00
O9	A5	2a black	3.50	3.75
O10	A6	4a black	10.00	
		Nos. O6-O10 (5)	28.85	

Obsolete since 1894.

RAJASTHAN

'rä-jə-ˌstän

(Greater Rajasthan Union)

AREA — 128,424 sq. miles
POP. — 13,085,000

The Rajasthan Union was formed in 1947-49 by 14 Indian States, including the stamp-issuing States of Bundi, Jaipur and Kishangarh.

Catalogue values for all unused stamps in this state are for Never Hinged items.

Bundi Nos. 43 to 49 Overprinted

a

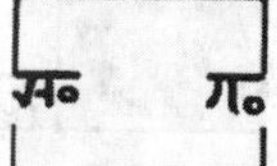

1948 **Unwmk.** ***Perf. 11***

Handstamped in Black, Violet or Blue

1	A8	¼a dp grn (Bk, V)	3.50	
a.		Blue overprint	20.00	
2	A8	½a purple (Bk, V)	2.25	
a.		Blue overprint	20.00	
3	A8	1a yel green (Bk)	3.50	
4	A9	2a red (Bk)	6.00	
5	A9	4a dp orange (V)	16.00	
a.		Black overprint	25.00	
6	A10	8a vio bl (Bk, V)	3.50	
7	A10	1r chocolate (Bl)	55.00	
a.		Black overprint		
b.		Violet overprint	140.00	
		Nos. 1-7 (7)	89.75	

Typo. in Black

12	A9	4a deep orange	2.00	
13	A10	8a violet blue	55.00	
14	A10	1r chocolate	7.50	
		Nos. 12-14 (3)	64.50	

Stamps of Jaipur, 1931-47, Overprinted in Blue or Carmine

1949 **Center in Black** ***Perf. 14***

15	A6	¼a red brown (Bl)	3.00	*2.50*
16	A6	½a dull violet	3.00	*2.50*
17	A6	¾a brown org (Bl)	4.00	*2.50*
18	A6	1a blue	3.50	*3.25*
19	A6	2a ocher	4.00	*3.25*
20	A6	2½a rose (Bl)	5.75	*3.25*
21	A6	3a green	6.25	*4.00*
22	A6	4a gray green	6.25	*4.75*
23	A6	6a blue	7.00	*6.50*
24	A6	8a chocolate	9.50	*20.00*
25	A6	1r bister	10.50	*27.50*
		Nos. 15-25 (11)	62.75	*80.00*

Kishangarh Stamps and Types of 1899-1904 Handstamped Type "a" in Rose

1949 ***Pin-perf., Rouletted***

26	A3	½a blue (#18)	25.00	
27	A4	1a dull lilac (#20)	14.00	
28	A6	4a pale red brown (#21B)	15.00	
29	A11	8a gray (#25B)	27.50	
30	A7	1r dull green (#22)	22.50	
31	A8	2r brown red (#23)	25.00	
32	A9	5r red violet (#24)	30.00	
		Nos. 26-32 (7)	159.00	

Kishangarh Nos. 28, 31-36 Handstamped Type "a" in Rose or Green

1949 **Engr.** ***Perf. 13½, 12½***

33	A13	½a chestnut (R)	10.50	
34	A13	4a dark brown (G)	13.00	
35	A13	4a dark brown (R)	13.00	
36	A13	8a purple (R)	13.00	
37	A13	1r dark green (R)	21.00	
38	A13	2r lemon yellow (R)	21.00	
39	A13	5r purple brown (R)	25.50	
		Nos. 33-39 (7)	117.00	

Kishangarh Nos. 40-42, 37, 43, 46-48 Handstamped Type "a" in Rose

1949 **Typo.** ***Rouletted***

40	A14	¼a pale blue	8.00	8.00
41	A14	½a green	8.00	8.00
42	A14	1a carmine	7.50	7.50
43	A14	2 "anna" violet	7.50	7.50
44	A14	2 "annas" purple	7.50	7.50
45	A14	8a brown	7.50	7.50
46	A14	1r rose lilac	9.00	9.00
47	A14	2r dark green	12.50	12.50
48	A14	5r brown	32.50	32.50
		Nos. 40-48 (9)	100.00	100.00

Kishangarh Stamps and Types of 1928-29 Handstamped Type "a" in Rose

1949 ***Pin-perf***

49	A17	¼a greenish blue	13.00	13.00
50	A17	½a yel green	6.50	6.50
51	A18	1a car rose	9.00	9.00
52	A18	2a red violet	12.00	12.00
53	A17	4a yel brown	2.50	2.50
54	A17	8a purple	9.00	7.25
55	A17	1r deep green	7.50	7.50
56	A17	2r lemon	24.00	24.00
57	A17	5r red brown	25.00	25.00
		Nos. 49-57 (9)	108.50	106.75

Type of Kishangarh 1928-29, Handstamped Type "a" in Rose

1949 ***Pin-perf***

58 A18 1a dark violet blue

No. 58 exists imperf.

Rajasthan stamps became obsolete Apr. 1, 1950.

RAJPEEPLA

räj-'pē-plə

(Rajpipla)

LOCATION — A Feudatory State near Bombay in the Gujarat States Agency in India.
AREA — 1,517 sq. mi.
POP. — 206,086
CAPITAL — Nandod

4 Paisas = 1 Anna

Kandjar (Indian Daggers) — A1

A2

A3

1880 **Unwmk.** **Litho.** ***Perf. 11, 12½***

Without Gum

1	A1	1pa ultramarine	1.00	*4.75*
2	A2	2a green	6.25	*6.75*
a.		Horiz. pair, imperf. btwn.	625.00	625.00
3	A3	4a red	4.50	4.50
		Nos. 1-3 (3)	11.75	*16.00*

The stamps of Rajpeepla have been obsolete since 1886.

SIRMOOR

sir-'muˌə˛r

(Sirmur)

LOCATION — A Feudatory State in the Punjab District of India.
AREA — 1,046 sq. mi.
POP. — 148,568
CAPITAL — Nahan

A1

Raja Sir Shamsher Prakash — A2

1879 **Unwmk.** ***Perf. 11½***

Wove Paper

1	A1	1p green	6.00	6.00
a.		Imperf., pair		

Laid Paper

2	A1	1p blue	3.00	*30.00*
a.		Imperf., pair		

1885-88 **Litho.** ***Perf. 14 and 14½.***

3	A2	3p brown	.20	.20
4	A2	3p orange	.20	.20
5	A2	6p green	.60	.60
6	A2	1a blue	.45	.45
7	A2	2a carmine	2.00	2.00
		Nos. 3-7 (5)	3.45	3.45

There are several printings, dies and minor variations of this issue.

For overprints see Nos. O1-O16.

A3

Elephant — A4

1893 ***Perf. 11½***

9	A3	1p yellow green	.30	.30
a.		1pa dark blue green	.30	.30
10	A3	1p ultramarine	.50	.50
b.		Imperf., pair	60.00	

Nos. 9 and 10 are re-issues, which were available for postage.

The printed perforation, which is a part of the design, is in addition to the regular perforation.

1895-99 **Engr.** ***Perf. 14***

11	A4	3p orange	.60	.20
12	A4	6p green	.90	.25
13	A4	1a dull blue	1.10	.30
14	A4	2a dull red	1.10	.45
15	A4	3a yellow green	2.00	2.00
16	A4	4a dark green	2.00	2.00
17	A4	8a deep blue	5.50	*7.50*
18	A4	1r vermilion	7.50	*9.00*
		Nos. 11-18 (8)	20.70	*21.70*

Sir Surendar Bikram Prakash — A5

1899

19	A5	3a yellow green	2.75	*6.00*
20	A5	4a dark green	3.50	*7.25*
21	A5	8a blue	4.00	*7.75*
22	A5	1r vermilion	6.50	*15.00*
		Nos. 19-22 (4)	16.75	*36.00*

OFFICIAL STAMPS

Regular Stamps Overprinted

Black Overprint

1890-91 **Unwmk.** ***Perf. 14, 14½***

O1	A2	3p orange	1.40	
O2	A2	6p green	1.40	.90
a.		Double overprint		
b.		Double ovpt., one in red	1,050.	
O3	A2	1a blue	12.00	12.00
O4	A2	2a carmine	9.00	9.00
		Nos. O1-O4 (4)	23.80	

1890-92

Red Overprint

O5	A2	6p green	4.50	4.00
O6	A2	1a blue	17.00	9.00

O7	A2	6p green	2.50	1.60
a.		Double overprint		
b.		Inverted overprint		
O8	A2	1a blue	6.00	2.00
a.		Inverted overprint		200.00
b.		Double overprint		200.00

1892

Black Overprint

O9 A2 3p orange	.20	.20
a. Inverted overprint	75.00	
O10 A2 6p green	.75	.75
O11 A2 1a blue	3.25	3.25
a. Double overprint	125.00	
O12 A2 2a carmine	2.50	2.50
a. Inverted overprint	125.00	110.00
Nos. O9-O12 (4)	6.70	6.70

Black Overprint

O13 A2 3p orange	3.25	1.50
a. Inverted overprint		
O14 A2 6p green	2.75	.50
O15 A2 1a blue	1.90	.75
O16 A2 2a carmine	4.75	4.25
Nos. O13-O16 (4)	12.65	7.00

There are several settings of some of these overprints, differing in the sizes and shapes of the letters, the presence or absence of the periods, etc.

The overprints on Nos. O1-O16 are press printed. In addition, nine varieties of handstamped overprints were applied in 1894-96. Most of the handstamps are very similar to the press printed overprints.

Obsolete Mar. 31, 1901.

SORUTH

(Sorath)

(Junagarh)

(Saurashtra)

LOCATION — A Feudatory State near Bombay in the Western India States Agency in India.

AREA — 3,337 sq. mi.

POP. — 670,719

CAPITAL — Junagarh

The United State of Saurashtra (area 31,885 sq. mi.; population 2,900,000) was formed in 1948 by 217 States, including the stamp-issuing States of Jasdan, Morvi, Nowanuggur and Wadhwan.

Nos. 1-27 were issued without gum.

Catalogue values for unused stamps in this State are for Never Hinged items, beginning with Scott 39 in the regular postage section, and Scott O19 in the officials section.

Junagarh

A1

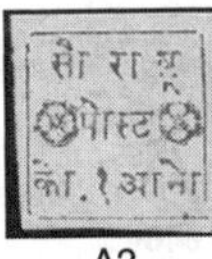

A2

Handstamped in Watercolor

1864 Unwmk. *Imperf.*

Laid Paper

1 A1 (1a) black, *bluish*	360.00	24.00
a. Wove paper		80.00
1B A1 (1a) black, *gray*	360.00	24.00

Wove Paper

2 A1 (1a) black, *cream*		100.00

1868 Typo. *Imperf.*

Wove Paper

3 A2 1a black, *yellowish*		
4 A2 1a red, *green*		1,200.
5 A2 1a red, *blue*		1,200.
6 A2 1a black, *pink*	175.00	42.00
7 A2 2a black, *yellow*		1,750.

Laid Paper

8 A2 1a black, *blue*	25.00	10.00
a. Left character, 3rd line, omitted		
9 A2 1a red	20.00	20.00
a. Left character, 3rd line, omitted		
10 A2 4a black	110.00	*125.00*
a. Left character, 3rd line, omitted		

A 1a black on white laid paper exists in type A2.

In 1890 official imitations of 1a and 4a stamps, type A2, were printed in sheets of 16 and 4. Original sheets have 20 stamps. Four of these imitations are perf. 12, six are imperf.

A3

A4

1877-86 Laid Paper *Imperf.*

11 A3 1a green	.20	.20
a. Printed on both sides	210.00	
12 A4 4a vermilion	.75	.75
a. Printed on both sides	210.00	
13 A4 4a scarlet, *bluish*	.90	.90
Nos. 11-13 (3)	1.85	1.85

Perf. 12

14 A3 1a green	.20	.20
a. 1a blue (error)	350.00	350.00
c. Imperf., pair	6.50	6.50
d. Wove paper	.75	.75
e. As "a," wove paper	350.00	350.00
f. As "d," imperf. btwn., pair	10.50	10.50
15 A3 1a green, *bluish*	.80	.80
a. Pair, imperf. btwn.	42.50	42.50
16 A4 4a red	.90	.90
a. 4a carmine	.90	.90
c. Wove paper	1.75	1.75
d. As "c," imperf., pair	12.00	12.00
17 A4 4a scarlet, *bluish*	1.50	1.50
Nos. 14-17 (4)	3.40	3.40

Nos. 14d and 16c Surcharged

1913-14 *Perf. 12*

18 A3 3p on 1a green	.20	.20
a. Laid paper		30.00
b. Inverted surcharge	20.00	
c. Imperf., pair		
19 A4 1a on 4a red	1.00	1.00
a. Laid paper	5.00	5.00
b. Imperf., pair		
c. Double surcharge	175.00	

A5

A6

1914 *Perf. 12*

20 A5 3p green	.50	.50
a. Imperf., pair	1.00	1.00
21 A6 1a rose carmine	.50	.60
a. Imperf., pair	4.00	4.00
b. Laid paper	20.00	15.00

Nawab Mahabat Khan III
A7 A8

1923-29 Wove Paper *Perf. 12*

22 A7 3p violet	.45	.45
a. Imperf.		
b. Laid paper ('29)	.75	.75
c. As "b," imperf. ('29)	1.40	1.40
d. As "b," horiz. pair, imperf. between	30.00	
23 A8 1a red	1.50	1.50
a. Imperf., pair		
b. Laid paper	2.00	2.00

Surcharged with New Value

27 A8 3p on 1a red	1.50	1.50

Two types of surcharge.

Junagarh City and The Girnar
A9

Gir Lion — A10

Nawab Mahabat Khan III — A11

Kathi Horse
A12

1929 *Perf. 14*

30 A9 3p dk green & blk	1.00	.20
31 A10 ½a dk blue & blk	3.75	.20
32 A11 1a claret & blk	2.25	.60
33 A12 2a org buff & blk	9.00	.35
34 A9 3a car rose & blk	2.50	.25
35 A10 4a dull vio & blk	10.50	.30
36 A12 8a apple grn & blk	12.00	*8.75*
37 A11 1r dull blue & blk	3.50	*7.00*
Nos. 30-37 (8)	44.50	*17.65*

For surcharges see Nos. 40-42, O20-O25. For overprints see Nos. O1-O14.

Type of 1929
Inscribed "Postage and Revenue"

1937

38 A11 1a claret & black	2.00	.50

For overprint see No. O15.

Catalogue values for unused stamps in this section, from this point to the end of the section, are for Never Hinged items.

United State of Saurashtra

A13

Bhavnagar Court Fee Stamp Overprinted in Black
"U.S.S. Revenue & Postage Saurashtra"

1949 Unwmk. Typo. *Perf. 11*

39 A13 1a deep claret	1.75	1.75
a. "POSTAGE" omitted	100.00	100.00
b. Double overprint	100.00	100.00
c. "REVENUE & POSTAGE" omitted	100.00	100.00

Nos. 30, 31 Surcharged in Black or Carmine "POSTAGE & REVENUE ONE ANNA"

1949-50 *Perf. 14*

40 A9 1a on 3p dk grn & blk (bl) ('50)	10.00	10.00
a. "OSTAGE"	110.00	110.00
41 A10 1a on ½a dk bl & blk (C)	7.00	1.40
a. Double surcharge	100.00	100.00

For overprint see No. O19.

No. 33 Surcharged in Green "Postage & Revenue ONE ANNA"

1949

42 A12 1a on 2a org buff & blk	5.75	2.00

For overprint see No. O26.

OFFICIAL STAMPS

Regular Issue of 1929 Overprinted in Red

a

1929 Unwmk. *Perf. 14*

O1 A9 3p dk green & black	.20	.20
O2 A10 ½a dk blue & black	.40	.20
O3 A11 1a claret & black	.20	.20
O4 A12 2a org buff & black	.75	.20
O5 A9 3a car rose & black	.40	.20
O6 A10 4a dull violet & blk	.75	.20
O7 A12 8a apple green & blk	1.25	.20
O8 A11 1r dull blue & blk	1.90	2.00
Nos. O1-O8 (8)	5.85	3.40

For surcharges see Nos. O20-O24.

Regular Issue of 1929 Overprinted in Red

b

1933-49

O9 A9 3p dk grn & black ('49)	150.00	4.25
O10 A10 ½a dk bl & black ('49)	210.00	4.25
O11 A9 3a car rose & blk	9.50	4.50
O12 A10 4a dull vio & blk	22.50	13.00
O13 A12 8a apple grn & blk	22.50	15.00
O14 A11 1r dull blue & blk	25.00	20.00

The 3p is also known with ms. "SARKARI" overprint in carmine.

For surcharge see No. O25.

No. 38 Overprinted Type "a" in Red

1938

O15 A11 1a claret & black	2.50	.50

Catalogue values for unused stamps in this section, from this point to the end of the section, are for Never Hinged items.

United State of Saurashtra

No. 41 with Manuscript "Service" in Carmine

1949

O19 A10 1a on ½a dk bl & blk (C)	27.50	

No. 42 is also known with carmine ms. "Service" overprint in English or Gujarati.

Nos. O4-O8 and O14 Surcharged "ONE ANNA" in Blue or Black

1949

Surcharge 2¼mm high

O20 A12 1a on 2a (Bl)	850.00	24.00
O21 A9 1a on 3a	850.00	24.00
O22 A10 1a on 4a	125.00	22.50
O23 A12 1a on 8a	125.00	22.50

Surcharge 4mm High, Handstamped

O24 A11 1a on 1r (#O8)	200.00	15.00
O25 A11 1a on 1r (#O14)	110.00	27.50
Nos. O20-O25 (6)	2,260.	135.50

No. 42 Overprinted Type "b" in Carmine

1949 Unwmk. *Perf. 14*

O26 A12 1a on 2a	20.00	6.75

TRAVANCORE

ˈtrav-ən-ˌkōˌəˌr

LOCATION — A Feudatory State in the Madras States Agency, on the extreme southwest coast of India.
AREA — 7,662 sq. mi.
POP. — 6,070,018 (1941)
CAPITAL — Trivandrum

16 Cash = 1 Chuckram
2 Chuckrams = 1 Anna

Conch Shell (State Seal)
A1 A2

1888 Unwmk. Typo. *Perf. 12*
Laid Paper

1 A1 1ch ultramarine 6.00 4.50
2 A1 2ch orange red 5.50 4.75
3 A1 4ch green 22.50 22.50
Nos. 1-3 (3) 34.00 31.75

The frame and details of the central medallion differ slightly on each denomination of type A1.
Laid paper printings of Nos. 1-3, 5-7 in completely different colors are essays.

1889-99 Wmk. 43
Wove Paper

4 A1 ½ch violet .20 .20
5 A1 1ch ultramarine .20 .20
a. Vertical pair, imperf. between
6 A1 2ch scarlet .90 .20
a. Horizontal pair, imperf. between 75.00
7 A1 4ch dark green 1.25 .30
Nos. 4-7 (4) 2.55 .90

Shades exist for each denomination.
For surcharges see #10-11. For type surcharged see #20. For overprints see #O1-O2, O4, O6, O18, O24-O25, O27B, O32-O33, O42.

1901-32

8 A2 ¾ch black 1.25 .20
9 A2 ¾ch brt violet ('32) 1.25 .20
a. Horizontal pair, imperf. between

For overprints see Nos. O26-O27, O44, O52.

No. 4 Surcharged

1906

10 A1 ¼ch on ½ch violet .45 .20
a. Inverted surcharge 35.00 35.00
11 A1 ⅜ch on ½ch violet .20 .20
a. Pair, one without surcharge
b. Inverted surcharge
c. Double surcharge

A3 A4

1908-11

12 A3 4ca rose .20 .20
13 A1 6ca red brown ('10) .90 .20
a. Printed on both sides
14 A4 3ch purple ('11) .75 .20
Nos. 12-14 (3) 1.85 .60

For surcharge & overprints see #19, O3, O5, O8, O13, O15, O20, O22, O30-O31, O53.

A5 A6

1916

15 A5 7ch red violet 1.90 .30
16 A6 14ch orange 4.00 2.50

For overprints see Nos. O11-O12, O34-O35.

A7 A8

1920-33

17 A7 1¼ch claret 1.25 .20
18 A7 1½ch light red ('33) 1.25 .20

For surcharges see Nos. 27-28. For overprints see Nos. O7, O17, O28-O29, O38, O56.

No. 12 and Type of 1888 Surcharged

1921

19 A3 1ca on 4ca rose .20 .20
a. Inverted surcharge 10.50 6.50
20 A1 5ca on 1ch dull bl (R) .20 .20
a. Inverted surcharge 13.00 4.00
b. Double surcharge 18.00 13.00

1921-32

21 A8 5ca bister .20 .20
22 A8 5ca brown ('32) 1.25 .20
23 A8 10ca rose .20 .20
Nos. 21-23 (3) 1.65 .60

For surcharges & overprints see #29-30, O9-O10, O14, O16, O19, O21, O23, O36-O37.

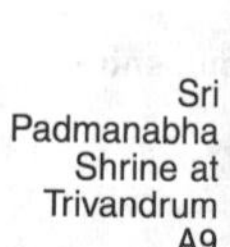

Sri Padmanabha Shrine at Trivandrum
A9

State Chariot — A10

Maharaja Sir Bala Rama Varma — A11

1931, Nov. 6

24 A9 6ca emerald & black .30 .30
25 A10 10ca ultra & black .30 .30
26 A11 3ch violet & black .55 .55
Nos. 24-26 (3) 1.15 1.15

Investiture of Sir Bala Rama Varma with full ruling powers.

No. 17 Surcharged

1932, Jan. 14

27 A7 1ca on 1¼ch claret .20 .20
a. Inverted surcharge 5.00 5.00
b. Double surcharge 16.00 16.00
28 A7 2ca on 1¼ch claret .20 .20
a. Inverted surcharge 5.00 5.00
b. Double surcharge 16.00 16.00
c. Pair, one without surcharge 75.00 75.00

Type of 1932 and No. 23 Surcharged like Nos. 19-20

1932, Mar. 5

29 A8 1ca on 5ca vio brown .20 .20
a. Inverted surcharge 13.00 12.00
b. Double surcharge 13.00 13.00
c. Pair, one without surcharge 55.00
30 A8 2ca on 10ca rose .30 .20
a. Inverted surcharge 9.00 9.00
b. Double surcharge 21.00 21.00

Untouchables Entering Temple and Maharaja — A12

Designs: Different temples and frames.

Perf. 11½, 12½

1937, Mar. 29 Litho.

32 A12 6ca carmine .20 .20
33 A12 12ca ultramarine .20 .20
34 A12 1½ch light green .20 .20
35 A12 3ch purple .30 .20
Nos. 32-35 (4) .90 .80

Temple Entry Bill.

Lake Ashtamudi
A13

A14 A15

Sir Bala Rama Varma — A16

Sri Padmanabha Shrine — A17

View of Cape Comerin
A18

Pachipara Reservoir
A19

Perf. 11, 12, 12½ or Compound

1939, May 9 Litho.

36 A13 1ch yellow green .20 .20
37 A14 1½ch carmine .45 .20
a. Perf. 13½ 18.00 18.00
38 A15 2ch orange .20 .20
39 A16 3ch chocolate .25 .20
40 A17 4ch henna brown .30 .20
41 A18 7ch light blue 1.50 1.10
42 A19 14ch turq green 3.00 2.00
Nos. 36-42 (7) 5.90 4.10

27th birthday of Maharaja Sir Bala Rama Varma.
For surcharges and overprints see Nos. 45, O45-O51, Travancore-Cochin 3-7, O3-O7.

Maharaja Sir Bala Rama Varma and Aruvikara Falls
A20

Maharaja and Marthanda Varma Bridge, Alwaye
A21

1941, Oct. 20 Typo.

43 A20 6ca violet black .20 .20
44 A21 ¾ch dull brown .30 .20

29th birthday of the Maharaja, Oct. 20, 1941.
For overprints & surcharges see #46-47, 49, O54-O55, Travancore-Cochin 1, O1.

Stamps and Types of 1939-41 Surcharged in Black

Perf. 11, 12½

1943, Sept. 17 Wmk. 43

45 A14 2ca on 1½ch carmine .20 .20
46 A21 4ca on ¾ch dull brown .20 .20
47 A20 8ca on 6ca red .45 .20
Nos. 45-47 (3) .85 .60

For overprints see Nos. O57-O59.

Maharaja Sir Bala Rama Varma — A22

1946, Oct. 24 Typo. *Perf. 11, 12*

48 A22 8ca rose red 1.25 .50

For overprint see No. O60. For surcharges see Travancore-Cochin Nos. 2, O2.

No. O54 Overprinted "SPECIAL" Vertically in Orange

1946 *Perf. 12½*

49 A20 6ca violet black 6.50 6.00

OFFICIAL STAMPS

Nos. O1-O60 were issued without gum.

Regular Issues of 1889-1911 Overprinted in Red or Black

Perf. 12, 12½

1911, Aug. 16 Wmk. 43

O1 A1 1ch indigo (R) .40 .20
a. Inverted overprint 8.75 5.50
b. "nO" for "On" 50.00 50.00
c. Double overprint 37.50 37.50

O2 A1 2ch scarlet .50 .20
a. Inverted overprint 11.00 10.00
O3 A4 3ch purple .40 .20
a. Inverted overprint 11.00 10.00
b. Double overprint 40.00 40.00
O4 A1 4ch dark green .50 .20
a. Inverted overprint 12.50 11.00
b. Double overprint 40.00 40.00
Nos. O1-O4 (4) 1.80 .80

Same Ovpt. on Regular Issues of 1889-1920

1918-20

O5 A3 4ca rose .20 .20
a. Imperf., pair 37.50 37.50
b. Inverted overprint 12.50 7.50
c. Double overprint 17.50 5.50
O6 A1 ½ch violet (R) .20 .20
a. Inverted overprint 7.00 3.50
O7 A7 1¼ch claret .30 .20
a. Inverted overprint 12.50 7.50
b. Double overprint 21.00 17.50
Nos. O5-O7 (3) .70 .60

Same Ovpt. on Regular Issues of 1909-21

1921

O8 A1 6ca red brown .25 .20
a. Inverted overprint 8.75 7.50
O9 A8 10ca rose .50 .20
a. Inverted overprint 22.50 12.50
b. Double overprint 27.50 17.50

Same Overprint on Regular Issue of 1921

1922

O10 A8 5ca bister .20 .20
a. Inverted overprint 7.00 3.50

For surcharge see No. O39B.

Same Overprint on Regular Issue of 1916

1925

O11 A5 7ch plum 1.10 .20
O12 A6 14ch orange 1.60 .20

Same Overprint in Blue on Regular Issues of 1889-1921

O13 A3 4ca rose 15.00 1.40
O14 A8 5ca bister
O15 A1 6ca red brown 8.50 1.40
O16 A8 10ca rose 21.00 4.50
O17 A7 1¼ch claret 24.00 6.50
O18 A1 4ch dark green 35.00 9.00

Some authorities question the authenticity of No. O14.

1930

Black Overprint

O19 A8 5ca brown .20 .20

Regular Issues of 1889-1932 Overprinted in Black or Red

1930-34

O20 A3 4ca rose 8.00 6.00
O21 A8 5ca brown 18.00 13.00
a. Inverted overprint 90.00 90.00
O22 A1 6ca org brown .20 .20
O23 A8 10ca rose 1.90 .25
O24 A1 ½ch violet ('34) .35 .20
O25 A1 ½ch purple (R) .20 .20
O26 A2 ¾ch black (R) ('32) .60 .20
O27 A2 ¾ch brt vio ('33) .20 .20
O27B A1 1ch gray blue (R) ('33) .75 .20
O28 A7 1¼ch claret 1.50 .45
O29 A7 1½ch dull red ('32) .30 .20
O30 A4 3ch purple ('33) 1.50 .20
O31 A4 3ch purple (R) .65 .20
O32 A1 4ch dp grn (R) 1.25 .20
O33 A1 4ch deep green 2.75 1.40
O34 A5 7ch maroon 1.75 .20
O35 A6 14ch orange ('31) 2.50 .40
Nos. O20-O35 (17) 42.40 23.70

The overprint on Nos. O22, O26 and O28 is smaller than the illustration. There are two sizes of the overprint on No. O27.

For surcharges see Nos. O39, O40-O41.

Type of 1921-32 and No. 17 Surcharged and Overprinted

1932

O36 A8 6ca on 5ca dk brown .20 .20
O36A A8 6ca on 5ca bister .75 .20
O37 A8 12ca on 10a rose .35 .20
a. New value inverted 8.50 8.50
O38 A7 1ch8ca on 1¼ch cl .45 .20
Nos. O36-O38 (4) 1.75 .80

12 c

Nos. O21, O10, O23 and O28 Surcharged in Black

O39 A8 6ca on 5ca dk brown .25 .20
a. New value inverted
O39B A8 6ca on 5ca bis .60 .20
O40 A8 12ca on 10ca rose .40 .20
a. New value inverted 8.50 8.50
b. "On S S" inverted
c. Ovpt. & surch. inverted 21.00 21.00
O41 A7 1ch8ca on 1¼ch cl .60 .20
a. New value inverted
Nos. O39-O41 (4) 1.85 .80

On

Regular Issue of 1889-94 Overprinted

S S

1933

O42 A1 ½ch violet 1.75 1.25

Regular Issue of 1901 Overprinted in Red

1933

O44 A2 ¾ch black .35 .20

Regular Issue of 1939 Overprinted in Black

a

1939 *Perf. 11, 12, 12½*

O45 A13 1ch yellow green .20 .20
a. Inverted overprint 15.00 15.00
b. Double overprint 15.00 15.00
O46 A14 1½ch carmine .35 .20
a. "SESVICE" 20.00 20.00
O47 A15 2ch orange .45 .20
a. "SESVICE" 21.00 21.00
O48 A16 3ch chocolate .35 .20
a. "SESVICE" 20.00 20.00
O49 A17 4ch henna brown .75 .25
O50 A18 7ch light blue 1.75 .40
O51 A19 14ch turq green 3.00 .50
Nos. O45-O51 (7) 6.85 1.95

27th birthday of Maharaja Sir Bala Rama Varma.

No. 9 Overprinted

b **SERVICE**

1939 **Wmk. 43** *Perf. 12.*

O52 A2 ¾ch violet 1.75 .20

No. 13 Overprinted Type "b"

1941

O53 A1 6ca red brown .50 .20

Nos. 43-44 Overprinted Type "a"

1941 *Perf. 12½*

O54 A20 6ca violet black .30 .20
O55 A21 ¾ch dull brown .30 .20

29th birthday of the Maharaja, Oct. 20, 1941.

For overprint see No. 49.

No. 18 Overprinted Type "b"

1945 *Perf. 12*

O56 A7 1½ch light red .65 .20

Nos. 45-48 Overprinted Type "a"

1945-49 *Perf. 11, 12*

O57 A14 2ca on 1½ch car .20 .20
O58 A21 4ca on ¾ch dull brn .30 .20
O59 A20 8ca on 6ca red .25 .20
O60 A22 8ca rose red ('49) 1.25 .80
a. Double impression of stamp 30.00 30.00
Nos. O57-O60 (4) 2.00 1.40

Travancore stamps became obsolete June 30, 1949.

TRAVANCORE-COCHIN

'trav-ən-,kō,ə,r kō-'chin

LOCATION — Southern India
AREA — 9,155 sq. mi.
POP. — 7,492,000

The United State of Travancore-Cochin was established July 1, 1949.

Catalogue values for all unused stamps in this state are for Never Hinged items.

Travancore Stamps of 1939-47 Surcharged in Red or Black

a **HALF ANNA**

Perf. 11, 12, 12½

1949, July 1 **Wmk. 43**

1 A20 2p on 6ca vio blk (R) 1.10 .70
2 A22 4p on 8ca rose red .50 .20
3 A13 ½a on 1ch yel grn 1.40 .20
a. Inverted surcharge 7.00 7.00
b. "NANA" 100.00 70.00
4 A15 1a on 2ch orange 1.50 .20
5 A17 2a on 4ch hn brn 1.25 .45
a. Inverted surcharge — 200.00
6 A18 3a on 7ch lt blue 4.50 2.75
7 A19 6a on 14ch turq grn 6.00 13.00
Nos. 1-7 (7) 16.25 17.50

For overprints see Nos. O1-O7, O12-O17. For types overprinted see Nos. O18-O23.

Cochin Nos. 80, 91 and Types of 1944-46 Surcharged in Black or Carmine

b

1949-50 **Wmk. 294** *Perf. 11, 13*

8 A15 3p on 9p ultra 6.75 14.00
9 A16 3p on 9p ultra 1.75 1.75
10 A16 3p on 9p ultra (C) 2.75 2.00
11 A16 6p on 9p ultra (C) .75 .30
12 A13 6p on 1a3p mag ('50) 3.25 3.50
13 A15 6p on 1a3p magenta 11.00 12.00
14 A13 1a on 1a9p ultra (C) .80 1.00
15 A15 1a on 1a9p ultra (C) 3.00 1.75
Nos. 8-15 (8) 30.05 36.30

The surcharge exists with line of Hindi characters varying from 16½ to 23mm wide.

For overprints see Nos. O10-O11, O24.

Cochin No. 86 Overprinted

1949

15A A15 1a deep orange 4.00 .40

Conch Shell — A23

View of River — A24

Wmk. 196

1950, Oct. **Litho.** *Perf. 14*

16 A23 2p rose red 1.40 1.40
17 A24 4p ultramarine 2.00 10.00

Cochin No. 86 and Type of 1948-50 Overprinted in Black

1950, Apr. 1 **Wmk. 294** *Perf. 13, 11*

18 A15 1a deep orange 5.50 40.00
19 A16 1a deep orange

The existence of No. 19 has been questioned.

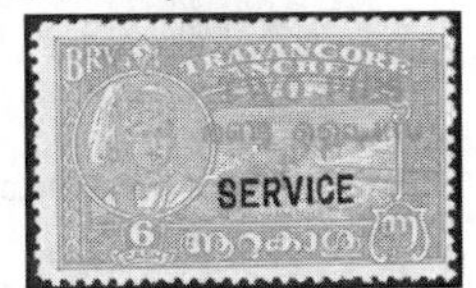

No. 18 Surcharged in Black

20 A15 6p on 1a deep orange 2.50 32.50
21 A15 9p on 1a deep orange 2.00 25.00

OFFICIAL STAMPS

Travancore Stamps of 1939-46 Surcharged Type "a" in Red or Black and Overprinted

c

1949 **Wmk. 43** *Perf. 11, 12, 12½*

O1 A20 2p on 6ca vio blk (R) .75 .20
O2 A22 4p on 8ca rose red 1.75 .50
O3 A13 ½a on 1ch yel grn .35 .20
O4 A15 1a on 2ch orange 13.00 4.00
O5 A17 2a on 4ch hn brn .90 .60
O6 A18 3a on 7ch lt blue 3.25 1.25
O7 A19 6a on 14ch turq grn 9.00 5.25
Nos. O1-O7 (7) 29.00 12.00

Cochin Nos. O90-O91 Surcharged Type "b" in Black

1950 **Wmk. 294** *Perf. 11*

O8 A16 6p on 3p carmine .75 .50
a. Double surcharge — 250.00
O9 A16 9p on 4p gray grn .50 1.50

No. O9 exists with Hindi characters varying from 18 to 22mm wide.

Travancore-Cochin Nos. 14-15 Overprinted "ON C G S"

Perf. 13

O10 A13 1a on 1a9p ultra .60 .40
O11 A15 1a on 1a9p ultra 17.50 13.00

Nos. 2-7 Overprinted in Black

d

1949-51	**Wmk. 43**	***Perf. 11, 12½***	
O12 A22	4p on 8ca rose red	.20	.20
O13 A13	½a on 1ch yel green	.25	.20
O14 A15	1a on 2ch orange	.20	.20
O15 A17	2a on 4ch hn brn	1.25	.70
O16 A18	3a on 7ch lt blue	2.50	.95
O17 A19	6a on 14ch turq grn	.60	*2.75*
	Nos. O12-O17 (6)	5.00	5.00

Types of 1949 Overprinted Type "d"

1951	**Wmk. 294**		
O18 A13	½a on 1ch yel green	.35	.35
O19 A15	1a on 2ch orange	.40	.35

Type of 1949 Overprinted Type "c"

Unwmk.

O20 A22	4p on 8ca rose red	1.40	1.10

No. O20 is not from an unwatermarked part of sheet with wmk. 294 but is printed on paper entirely without watermark.

Nos. 1, 3 and 5 Overprinted Type "c"

Wmk. 294

O21 A13	½a on 1ch yel green	1.10	.50
O22 A20	2p on 6ca violet black	.20	*1.00*
O23 A17	2a on 4ch henna brown	1.10	.75
	Nos. O21-O23 (3)	2.40	2.25

No. 9 Overprinted in Black

1951			
O24 A16	3p on 9p ultra	.60	.55

WADHWAN

wə-ˈdwän

LOCATION — A Feudatory State in Kathiawar Agency, Western India.
AREA — 242 sq. mi.
POP. — 44,259
CAPITAL — Wadhwan

Coat of Arms — A1

1888	**Litho.**	**Unwmk.**	***Pin-perf.***
	Thin Paper		
1 A1	½p black	27.50	
	Perf. 12½		
2 A1	½p black	8.00	*30.00*

1889		***Perf. 12 and 12½***	
	Thick Paper		
3 A1	½p black	5.50	*6.00*
	Nos. 1-3 (3)	41.00	

INDO-CHINA

ˌin-ˌdō-ˈchī-nə

LOCATION — French possessions on the Cambodian Peninsula in southeastern Asia, bordering on the South China Sea and the Gulf of Siam
GOVT. — French Colony and Protectorate
AREA — 280,849 sq. mi.
POP. — 27,030,000 (estimated 1949)
CAPITAL — Hanoi

In 1949, Indo-China was divided into Cambodia, Laos and Viet Nam each issuing its own stamps.

100 Centimes = 1 Franc
100 Cents = 1 Piaster (1918)

Stamps of French Colonies Surcharged in Black or Red:

INDO-CHINE 89 5 R D
a

INDO-CHINE 1889 5 R—D
b

1889 Unwmk. *Perf. 14x13½*

1	A9(a)	5c on 35c dp vio, *org*	6.75	*7.00*
a.		Without date	160.00	140.00
2	A9(b)	5c on 35c dp vio, *org* (R)	62.50	52.50
a.		Date in smaller type	150.00	150.00
b.		Inverted surcharge, #2	900.00	900.00
c.		Inverted surcharge, #2a	1,600.	1,600.

Issue dates: No. 1, Jan. 8; No. 2, Jan. 10.
"R" is the Colonial Governor, P. Richaud, "D" is the Saigon P.M. General P. Demars.

For other overprints on designs A3-A27a see various issues of French Offices in China.

Navigation & Commerce
A3

France
A4

Name of Colony in Blue or Carmine

1892-1900 Typo. *Perf. 14x13½*

3	A3	1c blk, *lil bl*	.60	.55
4	A3	2c brn, *buff*	.70	.70
5	A3	4c claret, *lav*	.70	.70
6	A3	5c grn, *grnsh*	1.10	.70
7	A3	5c yel grn ('00)	.55	.50
8	A3	10c blk, *lavender*	3.75	.80
9	A3	10c red ('00)	1.40	1.00
10	A3	15c blue, quadrille paper	17.50	.75
11	A3	15c gray ('00)	4.25	1.00
12	A3	20c red, *grn*	5.00	.30
13	A3	25c blk, *rose*	8.75	1.50
a.		"INDO-CHINE" omitted	*4,250.*	*3,750.*
14	A3	25c blue ('00)	12.00	1.50
15	A3	30c brn, *bis*	13.00	4.50
16	A3	40c red, *straw*	13.50	5.00
17	A3	50c car, *rose*	27.50	10.00
18	A3	50c brn, *az* ('00)	14.50	5.00
19	A3	75c dp vio, *org*	17.00	9.00
a.		"INDO-CHINE" inverted	*4,750.*	*4,500.*
20	A3	1fr brnz grn, *straw*	30.00	18.00
a.		"INDO-CHINE" double	700.00	700.00
21	A3	5fr red lil, *lav* ('96)	90.00	65.00
		Nos. 3-21 (19)	261.80	126.50

Perf. 13½x14 stamps are counterfeits.
For surcharges and overprints see Nos. 22-23, Q2-Q4.

Nos. 11 and 14 Surcharged in Black

1903

22	A3	5c on 15c gray	.60	.50
23	A3	15c on 25c blue	.90	.60

Issue dates: No. 22, Dec. 4; No. 23, Aug. 8.

1904-06

24	A4	1c olive grn	.40	.30
25	A4	2c vio brn, *buff*	.50	.30
26	A4	4c claret, *bluish*	.40	.30
27	A4	5c deep green	.40	.30
28	A4	10c carmine	.70	.40
29	A4	15c org brn, *bl*	.70	.40
30	A4	20c red, *grn*	1.50	.70
31	A4	25c deep blue	8.50	.80
32	A4	30c pale brn	3.25	2.00
33	A4	35c blk, *yel* ('06)	12.00	1.50
34	A4	40c blk, *bluish*	3.25	1.00
35	A4	50c bister brn	5.00	2.00
36	A4	75c red, *org*	30.00	18.00
37	A4	1fr pale grn	11.50	5.00
38	A4	2fr brn, *org*	32.50	26.00
39	A4	5fr dp vio, *lil*	140.00	110.00
40	A4	10fr org brn, *grn*	140.00	110.00
		Nos. 24-40 (17)	390.60	279.00

For surcharges see Nos. 59-64.

Annamite Girl — A5

Cambodian Girl — A6

Cambodian Woman — A7

Annamite Women — A8

Hmong Woman — A9

Laotian Woman — A10

Cambodian Woman — A11

1907 *Perf. 14x13½*

41	A5	1c ol brn & blk	.20	.20
42	A5	2c yel brn & blk	.20	.20
43	A5	4c blue & blk	.50	.35
44	A5	5c grn & blk	.60	.20
45	A5	10c red & blk	.25	.20
46	A5	15c vio & blk	.65	.50
47	A6	20c vio & blk	2.00	1.50
48	A6	25c bl & blk	4.00	.35
49	A6	30c brn & blk	6.50	3.25
50	A6	35c ol grn & blk	.90	.45
51	A6	40c yel brn & blk	3.00	1.00
52	A6	45c org & blk	5.00	3.25
53	A6	50c car & blk	8.00	3.50

Perf. 13½x14

54	A7	75c ver & blk	7.00	4.25
55	A8	1fr car & blk	35.00	12.50
56	A9	2fr grn & blk	9.00	6.50
57	A10	5fr blue & blk	30.00	22.50
58	A11	10fr pur & blk	65.00	55.00
		Nos. 41-58 (18)	177.80	115.70

For surcharges see Nos. 65-93, B1-B7.

Stamps of 1904-06 Surcharged in Black or Carmine

a

b

1912, Nov. *Perf. 14x13½*

59	A4	5c on 4c cl, *bluish*	3.50	3.50
60	A4	5c on 15c org brn, *bl* (C)	.60	.60
61	A4	5c on 30c pale brn	.70	.70
62	A4	10c on 40c blk, *bluish* (C)	.70	.70
63	A4	10c on 50c bis brn (C)	.70	.70
64	A4	10c on 75c red, *org*	3.25	3.25
		Nos. 59-64 (6)	9.45	9.45

Two spacings between the surcharged numerals are found on Nos. 59-64.

Nos. 41-58 Surcharged with New Values in Cents or Piasters in Black, Red or Blue

1919, Jan.

65	A5	⅖c on 1c	.20	.20
66	A5	⅘c on 2c	.50	.40
67	A5	1⅗c on 4c (R)	.90	.40
68	A5	2c on 5c	.35	.20
a.		Inverted surcharge	75.00	
69	A5	4c on 10c (Bl)	.60	.20
a.		Closed "4"	3.50	.60
b.		Double surcharge	90.00	
70	A5	6c on 15c	3.25	.50
a.		Inverted surcharge	70.00	
71	A6	8c on 20c	2.00	1.00
72	A6	10c on 25c	1.50	.35
73	A6	12c on 30c	3.50	.50
74	A6	14c on 35c	1.00	.25
a.		Closed "4"	5.00	3.00
75	A6	16c on 40c	3.00	.95
76	A6	18c on 45c	4.00	1.50
77	A6	20c on 50c (Bl)	5.00	.60
78	A7	30c on 75c (Bl)	6.00	1.25
79	A8	40c on 1fr (Bl)	11.00	1.60
80	A9	80c on 2fr (R)	12.50	2.75
a.		Double surcharge	200.00	150.00
81	A10	2pi on 5fr (R)	60.00	60.00
82	A11	4pi on 10fr (R)	100.00	85.00
		Nos. 65-82 (18)	215.30	157.65

Types of 1907 Issue Surcharged with New Values in Black or Red

Nos. 88-92

No. 93

1922

88	A5	1c on 5c ocher & blk	.65	
89	A5	2c on 10c gray grn & blk	1.25	
90	A6	6c on 30c lt red & blk	1.40	
91	A6	10c on 50c lt bl & blk	1.50	
92	A6	11c on 55c vio & blk, *bluish*	1.50	
93	A6	12c on 60c lt bl & blk, *pnksh* (R)	1.60	
		Nos. 88-93 (6)	7.90	

Nos. 88-93 were sold officially in Paris but were never placed in use in the colony.

Nos. 88-93 exist without surcharge but were not regularly issued in that condition. Value, Nos. 88-89, each $110; Nos. 90-91, each $90; Nos. 92-93, each $65.

A12

A13

"CENTS" below Numerals

1922-23 *Perf. 14x13½*

94	A12	1/10c blk & sal ('23)	.20	.20
a.		Double impression of frame		
95	A12	⅕c blue & blk	.20	.20
96	A12	⅖c ol brn & blk	.20	.20
a.		Head and value doubled	150.00	150.00
97	A12	⅘c rose & blk, *lav*	.20	.20
98	A12	1c yel brn & blk	.20	.20
99	A12	2c gray grn & blk	.40	.30
100	A12	3c vio & blk	.20	.20
101	A12	4c org & blk	.20	.20
a.		Head and value doubled	110.00	110.00
102	A12	5c car & blk	.20	.20
a.		Head and value doubled	200.00	200.00
103	A13	6c dl red & blk	.30	.30
104	A13	7c grn & blk	.50	.40
105	A13	8c blk, *lav*	1.00	.70
106	A13	9c ocher & blk, *grnsh*	.90	.60
107	A13	10c bl & blk	.40	.30
108	A13	11c vio & blk	.40	.30
109	A13	12c brn & blk	.30	.30
a.		Head and value double (11c+12c)	350.00	350.00
110	A13	15c org & blk	.60	.30
111	A13	20c bl & blk, *straw*	.70	.30
112	A13	40c ver & blk, *bluish*	1.50	.80
113	A13	1pi bl grn & blk, *grnsh*	3.50	3.50
114	A13	2pi vio brn & blk, *pnksh*	6.00	6.00
		Nos. 94-114 (21)	18.10	15.70

For overprints see Nos. O17-O32.

Plowing near Tower of Confucius
A14

Bay of Along
A15

Angkor Wat, Cambodia
A16

Carving Wood A17

That Luang Temple, Laos A18

Founding of Saigon A19

1927, Sept. 26

No.	Type	Denom.	Color	Unused	Used
115	A14	1/10c	lt olive grn	.20	.20
116	A14	1/5c	yellow	.20	.20
117	A14	2/5c	light blue	.20	.20
118	A14	4/5c	dp brn	.20	.20
119	A14	1c	orange	.20	.20
120	A14	2c	blue grn	.45	.20
121	A14	3c	indigo	.20	.20
122	A14	4c	lil rose	.45	.40
123	A14	5c	dp vio	.35	.20
a.			Booklet pane of 10	*140.00*	
124	A15	6c	deep red	1.25	.30
a.			Booklet pane of 10	*140.00*	
125	A15	7c	lt brn	.80	.30
126	A15	8c	gray green	.90	.75
127	A15	9c	red vio	.80	.65
128	A15	10c	light blue	1.10	.60
129	A15	11c	orange	.85	.75
130	A15	12c	myrtle grn	.55	.30
131	A16	15c	dl rose & ol brn	4.75	4.50
132	A16	20c	vio & slate	2.10	1.00
133	A17	25c	org brn & lil rose	4.75	3.50
134	A17	30c	dp bl & ol gray	2.50	2.00
135	A18	40c	ver & lt bl	3.75	1.50
136	A18	50c	lt grn & slate	4.25	1.75
137	A19	1pi	dk bl, blk & yel	12.00	5.50
a.			Yellow omitted	100.00	
138	A19	2pi	red, dp bl & org	14.00	8.00
			Nos. 115-138 (24)	56.80	33.40

Common Design Types pictured following the introduction.

Colonial Exposition Issue

Common Design Types
Surcharged with New Values

1931, Apr. 13 Engr. ***Perf. 12½***

Name of Country in Black

No.	Type	Description	Unused	Used
140	CD71	4c on 50c violet	1.40	1.25
141	CD72	6c on 90c red org	1.60	1.50
142	CD73	10c on 1.50fr dl bl	2.40	2.25
		Nos. 140-142 (3)	5.40	5.00

Junk — A20

Tower at Ruins of Angkor Thom — A21

Planting Rice — A22

Apsaras, Celestial Dancer A23

1931-41 Photo. ***Perf. 13½x13***

No.	Type	Denom.	Color	Unused	Used
143	A20	1/10c	Prus blue	.20	.20
144	A20	1/5c	lake	.20	.20
145	A20	2/5c	org red	.20	.20
146	A20	1/2c	red brn	.20	.20
147	A20	4/5c	dk vio	.20	.20
148	A20	1c	blk brn	.20	.20
149	A20	2c	dk grn	.20	.20
150	A21	3c	dp brn	.20	.20
151	A21	3c	dk grn ('34)	3.00	.85
152	A21	4c	dk bl	.40	.20
153	A21	4c	dk grn ('38)	.30	.20
153A	A21	4c	yel org ('40)	.20	.20
154	A21	5c	dp vio	.20	.20
154A	A21	5c	dp grn ('41)	.20	.20
155	A21	6c	org red	.20	.20
a.			Bklt. pane 5 + 1 label		
156	A21	7c	blk ('38)	.20	.20
157	A21	8c	rose lake ('38)	.20	.20
157A	A21	9c	blk, *yel* ('41)	.30	.20
158	A22	10c	dark blue	.40	.20
158A	A22	10c	ultra, *pink* ('41)	.30	.20
159	A22	15c	dk brn	3.50	.60
160	A22	15c	dk bl ('33)	.20	.20
161	A22	18c	blue ('38)	.20	.20
162	A22	20c	rose	.20	.20
163	A22	21c	olive grn	.20	.20
164	A22	22c	dk grn ('38)	.20	.20
165	A22	25c	dp vio	2.00	.80
165A	A22	25c	dk bl ('41)	.20	.20
166	A22	30c	org brn ('32)	.30	.20

Perf. 13½

No.	Type	Denom.	Color	Unused	Used
167	A23	50c	dk brn	.30	.20
168	A23	60c	dl vio ('32)	.30	.20
168A	A23	70c	lt bl ('41)	.30	.20
169	A23	1pi	yel grn	.60	.35
170	A23	2pi	red	.60	.35
			Nos. 143-170 (34)	16.60	8.75

With "RF," see Nos. 226A-226D.
For surcharge & overprints see #214A, O1-O16.

Emperor Bao-Dai A24

King Sisowath Monivong A25

For Use in Annam

1936, Nov. 20 Engr. ***Perf. 13***

No.	Type	Denom.	Color	Unused	Used
171	A24	1c	brown	.55	.50
172	A24	2c	green	.55	.50
173	A24	4c	violet	.65	.60
174	A24	5c	red brn	.85	.80
175	A24	10c	lil rose	1.10	1.00
176	A24	15c	ultra	1.50	1.40
177	A24	20c	scarlet	1.60	1.50
178	A24	30c	plum	2.10	2.00
179	A24	50c	slate grn	2.10	2.00
180	A24	1pi	rose vio	3.25	3.00
181	A24	2pi	black	3.50	3.25
			Nos. 171-181 (11)	17.75	16.55

For Use in Cambodia

No.	Type	Denom.	Color	Unused	Used
182	A25	1c	brown	.55	.50
183	A25	2c	green	.55	.50
184	A25	4c	violet	.75	.70
185	A25	5c	red brn	.75	.70
186	A25	10c	lil rose	1.75	1.60
187	A25	15c	ultra	2.10	2.00
188	A25	20c	scarlet	1.60	1.50
189	A25	30c	plum	1.60	1.50
190	A25	50c	slate grn	1.60	1.50
191	A25	1pi	rose vio	2.25	2.00
192	A25	2pi	black	3.25	3.00
			Nos. 182-192 (11)	16.75	15.50

Paris International Exposition Issue

Common Design Types

1937, Apr. 15

No.	Type	Description	Unused	Used
193	CD74	2c dp vio	.55	.55
194	CD75	3c dk grn	.55	.55
195	CD76	4c car rose	.45	.45
196	CD77	6c dk brn	.65	.65
197	CD78	9c red	.65	.65
198	CD79	15c ultra	.65	.65
		Nos. 193-198 (6)	3.50	3.50

Colonial Arts Exhibition Issue

Souvenir Sheet
Common Design Type

1937, Apr. 15 ***Imperf.***

No.	Type	Description	Unused	Used
199	CD79	30c dull violet	4.75	4.50

Governor-General Paul Doumer — A26

1938, June 8 Photo. ***Perf. 13½x13***

No.	Type	Description	Unused	Used
200	A26	5c rose car	.40	.25
201	A26	6c brown	.40	.25
202	A26	18c brt bl	.40	.20
		Nos. 200-202,C18 (4)	1.45	.90

Trans-Indo-Chinese Railway, 35th anniv.

New York World's Fair Issue

Common Design Type

1939, May 10 Engr. ***Perf. 12½x12***

No.	Type	Description	Unused	Used
203	CD82	13c car lake	.25	.25
204	CD82	23c ultra	.45	.45

Mot Cot Pagoda, Hanoi — A27

1939, June 12 ***Perf. 13***

No.	Type	Description	Unused	Used
205	A27	6c blk brn	.45	.45
206	A27	9c vermilion	.45	.45
207	A27	23c ultra	.45	.45
208	A27	39c rose vio	.45	.45
		Nos. 205-208 (4)	1.80	1.80

Golden Gate International Exposition.

Angkor Wat and Marshal Pétain A27a

1941 Engr. ***Perf. 12½x12***

No.	Type	Description	Unused	Used
209	A27a	10c dk car	.35	
209A	A27a	25c blue	.35	

Nos. 209-209A were issued by the Vichy government in France, but were not placed on sale in Indo-China.
For overprints, see Nos. 262-263. For surcharges, see B21A-B21B.

Gum
#210-261 issued without gum.

King Norodom Sihanouk of Cambodia A28

Harnessed Elephant on Parade A29

Pin-perf. 12½

1941, Oct. 15 Unwmk. Litho.

No.	Type	Description	Unused	Used
210	A28	1c red org	.60	.60
211	A28	6c violet	1.40	1.40
212	A28	25c dp ultra	12.00	12.00
		Nos. 210-212 (3)	14.00	14.00

Coronation of Norodom Sihanouk, King of Cambodia, October, 1941.

1942, Mar. 29

No.	Type	Description	Unused	Used
213	A29	3c reddish brown	.80	.70
214	A29	6c crimson	.90	.70

Fête of Nam-Giao in Annam.

No. 165 Surcharged in Black

1942 ***Perf. 13***

No.	Type	Description	Unused	Used
214A	A22	10c on 25c dp vio	.30	.20

View of Saigon Fair — A30

1942, Dec. 20 ***Perf. 13½***

No.	Type	Description	Unused	Used
215	A30	6c carmine rose	.25	.25

Saigon Fair of 1942.

Nam-Phuong, Empress of Annam — A31

Marshal Pétain — A32

1942, Sept. 1 ***Pin-perf. 11½***

No.	Type	Description	Unused	Used
216	A31	6c carmine rose	.60	.30

1942-44 ***Perf. 12, 13½***

No.	Type	Description	Unused	Used
217	A32	1c blk brn	.20	.20
218	A32	3c olive brn ('43)	.20	.20
219	A32	6c rose red	.20	.20
220	A32	10c dull grn ('43)	.20	.20
221	A32	40c dk blue ('43)	.30	.30
222	A32	40c slate bl ('44)	.60	.60
		Nos. 217-222 (6)	1.70	1.70

Bao-Dai, Emperor of Annam A33

Norodom Sihanouk, King of Cambodia A34

1942 ***Perf. 13½***

No.	Type	Description	Unused	Used
223	A33	1/2c brown	.35	.20
224	A33	6c carmine rose	.55	.30

Issue dates: ½c, Nov. 1; 6c, Sept. 1.

1943 ***Perf. 11½***

No.	Type	Description	Unused	Used
225	A34	1c brown	.35	.30
226	A34	6c red	.35	.20

Issue dates: 1c, Mar. 10; 6c, May 10.

Types of 1931-32 Without "RF"

1943 Photo. ***Perf. 13½x13***

No.	Type	Description	Unused	Used
226A	A22	30c orange brown	.65	
226B	A23	50c dark brown	.65	
226C	A23	1pi yellow green	.90	
226D	A23	2pi red	1.40	
		Nos. 226A-226D (4)	3.60	

Nos. 226A-226D were issued by the Vichy government in France, but were not placed on sale in Indo-China.

Sisavang-Vong, King of Laos — A35

Family, Country and Labor — A36

1943

227 A35 1c bister brown .20 .20
228 A35 6c carmine rose .45 .30

Issue dates: 1c, Mar. 10; 6c, June 1.

1943, Nov. 5 ***Perf. 12***

229 A36 6c carmine rose .20 .20

National revolution, 3rd anniversary.

Admiral Rigault de Genouilly A37

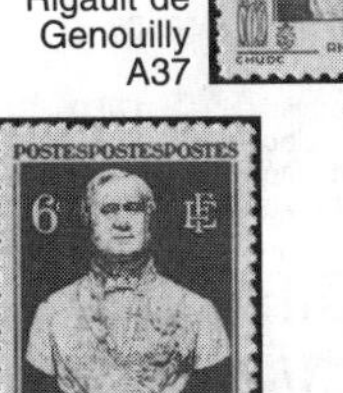

François Chasseloup-Laubat A38

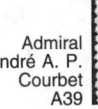

Admiral André A. P. Courbet A39

1943 ***Perf. 11½, 12, 12x11½***

230 A37 6c carmine rose .20 .20
231 A38 6c carmine rose .20 .20
232 A39 6c carmine rose .35 .20
Nos. 230-232 (3) .75 .60

Issued: #230, 232, Sept. 1; #231, Oct. 5.

A 5c dull brown, type A37, was not regularly issued without the Viet Nam overprint. Value, $2.

A 3c light brown, type A39, was prepared but not issued. Value, $5.

Pigneau de Behaine, Bishop of Adran — A40

Alexandre Yersin — A41

1943, June 10 ***Perf. 12***

233 A40 20c dull red .45 .45

1943-45 ***Perf. 12x11½***

234 A41 6c carmine rose .50 .50
235 A41 15c vio brn ('44) .20 .20
236 A41 1pi yel grn ('45) .30 .30
Nos. 234-236 (3) 1.00 1.00

Issued to honor Dr. Alexandre Yersin (1863-1943), the Swiss bacteriologist who introduced rubber culture into Indo-China.

Issued: 6c, 10/5; 15c, 12/10; 1pi, 1/10.

Lt. M. J. François Garnier A42

1943, Sept. ***Perf. 12***

237 A42 1c dull olive bister .40 .25

A 15c brown violet was prepared but not issued. Value, $10.

Alexandre de Rhodes A43

1943-45 ***Pin-perf., Perf. 12***

238 A43 15c dk vio brn ('45) .20 .20
239 A43 30c org brn .20 .20
a. 30c yellow brown, perf. 13½ .20 .20

Nos. 239, 239a carry the monogram "EF."

Issue dates: 15c, Mar. 10; 30c, June 15.

Athlete Giving Olympic Salute A44

1944, July 10 ***Perf. 12***

241 A44 10c dk vio brn & yel 1.50 1.40
242 A44 50c dl red 1.50 1.40

Adm. Pierre de La Grandière A45

1943-45

243 A45 1c dull brn .20 .20
244 A45 5c dark brn ('45) .30 .20

The upper left corner of No. 244 contains the denomination "5c" instead of "EF" monogram.

Issue dates: 1c, Aug.; 5c, Jan. 10.

Auguste Pavie A46

1944 ***Perf. 12***

245 A46 4c org yel .20 .20
246 A46 10c dl grn .30 .20

Issue dates: 4c, Feb. 10; 10c, Jan. 5.

A 20c dark red, type A46, was not regularly issued without the Viet Nam overprint. Value without overprint, $5.

Governor-General Pierre Pasquier — A47

1944

247 A47 5c brn vio .30 .30
248 A47 10c dl grn .30 .20

Issue dates: 5c, Nov. 1; 10c, Sept.

Joost Van Vollenhoven — A48

1944, Oct. 10

249 A48 1c olive brown .30 .20
250 A48 10c green .30 .30

Governor-General J. M. A. de Lanessan — A49

1944

251 A49 1c dl gray brn .30 .20
252 A49 15c dl rose vio .30 .30

Issued: 1c, Dec. 10; 15c, Oct. 16.

Governor-General Paul Doumer — A50

1944

253 A50 2c red vio .20 .20
254 A50 4c lt brn .25 .20
255 A50 10c yel grn .30 .20
Nos. 253-255 (3) .75 .60

Issue dates: 2c, May 15; 4c, June 15; 10c, Jan. 5.

Admiral Charner A51

Doudart de Lagrée A52

1944

256 A51 10c green .20 .20
257 A51 20c brn red .25 .20
258 A51 1pi pale yel grn .40 .25
Nos. 256-258 (3) .85 .65

Issue dates: 10c, 20c, Aug. 10; 1pi, July.

1944-45

259 A52 1c dl gray brn ('45) .20 .20
260 A52 15c dl rose vio .25 .20
261 A52 40c brt bl .30 .20
Nos. 259-261 (3) .75 .60

Issue dates: 1c, Jan. 10; 15c, 40c, Nov.

Nos. 209-209A Overprinted in Black

1946 **Unwmk.** ***Perf. 12½x12***

262 A27a 10c dk car .30 .30
263 A27a 25c blue 1.20 1.20

SEMI-POSTAL STAMPS

No. 45 Surcharged

1914 **Unwmk.** ***Perf. 14x13½***

B1 A5 10c +5c red & blk .50 .50

Nos. 44-46 Surcharged

1915-17

B2 A5 5c + 5c grn & blk ('17) .50 .35
a. Double surcharge 125.00 125.00
B3 A5 10c + 5c red & blk 1.00 .65
B4 A5 15c + 5c vio & blk ('17) 1.00 .65
a. Triple surcharge 110.00 110.00
b. Quadruple surcharge 100.00 100.00
Nos. B2-B4 (3) 2.50 1.65

Nos. B2-B4 Surcharged with New Values in Blue or Black

1918-19

B5 A5 4c on 5c + 5c (Bl) 2.75 3.00
a. Closed "4" 140.00 140.00
B6 A5 6c on 10c + 5c 2.25 2.50
B7 A5 8c on 15c + 5c ('19) 8.00 9.00
a. Double surcharge 140.00 140.00
Nos. B5-B7 (3) 13.00 14.50

France Nos. B5-B10 Surcharged

1918 (?)

B8 SP5 10c on 15c + 10c .75 1.00
B9 SP5 16c on 25c + 15c 2.75 2.75
B10 SP6 24c on 35c + 25c 4.00 4.25
a. Double surcharge 425.00
B11 SP7 40c on 50c + 50c 7.50 7.50
B12 SP8 80c on 1fr + 1fr 20.00 18.00
B13 SP8 4pi on 5fr + 5fr 150.00 150.00
Nos. B8-B13 (6) 185.00 183.50

Curie Issue

Common Design Type

Inscription and Date in Upper Margin

1938, Oct. 24 **Engr.** ***Perf. 13***

B14 CD80 18c + 5c brt ultra 6.00 6.00

French Revolution Issue

Common Design Type

Name and Value Typo. in Black

1939, July 5 **Photo.**

B15 CD83 6c + 2c green 6.00 5.50
B16 CD83 7c + 3c brown 6.00 5.50
B17 CD83 9c + 4c red org 6.00 5.50
B18 CD83 13c + 10c rose pink 6.00 5.50
B19 CD83 23c + 20c blue 6.00 5.50
Nos. B15-B19 (5) 30.00 27.50

Common Design Type and

Tonkinese Sharpshooter SP1

Legionary SP2

1941 **Photo.** ***Perf. 13½***

B19A SP1 10c + 10c red .75
B19B CD86 15c + 30c maroon .75
B19C SP2 25c + 10c blue .75
Nos. B19A-B19C (3) 2.25

Nos. B19A-B19C were issued by the Vichy government in France, but were not placed on sale in Indo-China.

Nos. 209-209A were surcharged "OEUVRES COLONIALES" and surtax (including change of denomination of the 25c to 5c). These were issued in 1944 by the Vichy government and not placed on sale in the colony.

Portal and Flags, City University, Hanoi — SP3

Coat of Arms and Sword — SP4

Perf. 11½

1942, June 1 Unwmk. Litho.

B20 SP3 6c + 2c car rose .40 .40
B21 SP3 15c + 5c brn vio .40 .40

Petain Type of 1941 Surcharged in Black or Red

1944 Engr. *Perf. 12½x12*

B21A 5c + 15c on 25c blue (R) .35
B21B + 25c on 10c dk car .35

Colonial Development Fund.

Nos. B21A-B21B were issued by the Vichy government in France, but were not placed on sale in Indo-China.

No. B20 Surcharged in Black

1944, June 10

B22 SP3 10c + 2c on 6c + 2c .30 .20

1942, Aug. 1 *Perf. 12*

B23 SP4 6c + 2c red & blue .30 .20
B24 SP4 15c + 5c vio blk, red & bl .40 .30

#B23 Surcharged in Black Like #B22

1944, Mar. 15

B25 SP4 10c + 2c on 6c + 2c .30 .20

Aviator Do-Huu-Vi SP5

1943, Aug. 1

B26 SP5 6c + 2c car rose .25 .20

#B26 Surcharged in Black Like #B22

1944, Feb. 10

B27 SP5 10c + 2c on 6c + 2c .25 .20

Surcharge arranged to fit size of stamp.

Aviator Roland Garros — SP6

1943, Nov. 15

B28 SP6 6c + 2c rose car .20 .20

#B28 Surcharged in Black Like #B22

1944, Feb. 10

B29 SP6 10c + 2c on 6c + 2c .20 .20

Cathedral of Orléans SP7

1944, Dec. 20

B30 SP7 15c + 60c brn vio .50 .40
B31 SP7 40c + 1.10pi blue .60 .60

Type of France, 1945, Surcharged in Black

1945 Unwmk. Engr. *Perf. 13*

B32 A152 50c + 50c on 2fr green .25 .25
B33 A152 1pi + 1pi on 2fr hn brn .25 .25
B34 A152 2pi + 2pi on 2fr Prus grn .35 .35
Nos. B32-B34 (3) .85 .85

AIR POST STAMPS

Airplane AP1

1933-41 Unwmk. Photo. *Perf. 13½*

C1 AP1 1c ol brn .20 .20
C2 AP1 2c dk grn .20 .20
C3 AP1 5c yel grn .20 .20
C4 AP1 10c red brn .25 .20
C5 AP1 11c rose car ('38) .20 .20
C6 AP1 15c dp bl .25 .20
C6A AP1 16c brt pink ('41) .20 .20
C7 AP1 20c grnsh gray .35 .25
C8 AP1 30c org brn .20 .20
C9 AP1 36c car rose 1.40 .20
C10 AP1 37c ol grn ('38) .20 .20
C10A AP1 39c dk ol grn ('41) .20 .20
C11 AP1 60c dk vio .20 .20
C12 AP1 66c olive grn .35 .20
C13 AP1 67c brt bl ('38) .75 .60
C13A AP1 69c brt ultra ('41) .35 .25
C14 AP1 1pi black .35 .20
C15 AP1 2pi yel org .75 .20
C16 AP1 5pi purple 1.40 .25
C17 AP1 10pi deep red 2.50 .55
Nos. C1-C17 (20) 10.50 4.90

Issue dates: 11c, 37c, June 8; 67c, Oct. 5; 16c, 39c, 69c, Feb. 5; others, June 1, 1933.

See Nos. C18A-C18O, C27-C28.

Trans-Indo-Chinese Railway Type

1938, June 8 *Perf. 13½x13*

C18 A26 37c red orange .25 .20

Type of 1933-38 Without "RF"

1942-44 *Perf. 13½*

C18A AP1 5c yellow green .20
C18B AP1 10c red brown .20
C18C AP1 11c rose carmine .20
C18D AP1 15c deep blue .20
C18E AP1 20c greenish gray .20
C18F AP1 36c carmine rose .20
C18G AP1 37c olive green .30
C18H AP1 60c dark violet .30
C18I AP1 66c brown olive .30
C18J AP1 67c bright blue .35
C18K AP1 69c br ultramarine .45
C18L AP1 1pi black .60
C18M AP1 2pi yellow orange .75
C18N AP1 5pi purple 1.10
C18O AP1 10pi deep red 1.60
Nos. C18A-C18O (15) 6.95

Nos. C18A-C18O were issued by the Vichy government in France, but were not placed on sale in Indo-China.

Victory Issue

Common Design Type

Perf. 12½

1946, May 8 Unwmk. Engr.

C19 CD92 80c red org .40 .25

Chad to Rhine Issue

Common Design Types

1946, June 6

C20 CD93 50c yel grn .35 .35
C21 CD94 1pi violet .40 .40
C22 CD95 1.50pi carmine .50 .50
C23 CD96 2pi vio brn .50 .50
C24 CD97 2.50pi dp bl .50 .50
C25 CD98 5pi org red .75 .75
Nos. C20-C25 (6) 3.00 3.00

UPU Issue

Common Design Type

1949, July 4 *Perf. 13*

C26 CD99 3pi dp bl, dk vio, grn & red 2.10 1.75

Plane Type of 1933-41

1949, June 13 Photo. *Perf. 13½*

C27 AP1 20pi dk bl grn 7.00 4.00
C28 AP1 30pi brown 7.50 4.00

AIR POST SEMI-POSTAL STAMPS

French Revolution Issue

Common Design Type

Unwmk.

1939, July 5 Photo. *Perf. 13*

Name and Value Typo. in Orange

CB1 CD83 39c + 40c brn blk 14.00 12.50

Poor Family — SPAP1

Orphans SPAP2

Caring for Children — SPAP3

Perf. 13½x12½, 13 (#CB4)

Photo, Engr. (#CB4)

1942, June 22

CB2 SPAP1 15c + 35c green .50
CB3 SPAP2 20c + 60c brown .50
CB4 SPAP3 30c + 90c car red .60
Nos. CB2-CB4 (3) 1.60

Native children's welfare fund.

Nos. CB2-CB4 were issued by the Vichy government in France, but were not placed on sale in Indo-China.

Colonial Education Fund

Common Design Type

Perf. 12½x13½

1942, June 22 Engr.

CB5 CD86a 12c + 18c blue & red .50

No. CB5 was issued by the Vichy government in France, but was not placed on sale in Indo-China.

POSTAGE DUE STAMPS

French Colonies No. J21 Surcharged

1904, June 26 Unwmk. *Imperf.*

J1 D1 5c on 60c brn, *buff* 7.50 6.00

French Colonies Nos. J10-J11 Surcharged in Carmine

1905, July 22

J2 D1 5c on 40c black 17.00 5.50
J3 D1 10c on 60c black 17.00 10.00
J4 D1 30c on 60c black 17.00 10.00
Nos. J2-J4 (3) 51.00 25.50

Dragon from Steps of Angkor Wat

D1 D2

1908 Typo. *Perf. 14x13½*

J5 D1 2c black .80 .60
J6 D1 4c dp bl .80 .60
J7 D1 5c bl grn .90 .60
J8 D1 10c carmine 2.00 .60
J9 D1 15c violet 2.00 1.50
J10 D1 20c chocolate 1.00 .70
J11 D1 30c ol grn 1.00 .70
J12 D1 40c claret 5.00 4.50
J13 D1 50c grnsh bl 4.00 .70
J14 D1 60c orange 7.00 5.50
J15 D1 1fr gray 13.50 10.00
J16 D1 2fr yel brn 13.50 8.00
J17 D1 5fr red 22.50 22.50
Nos. J5-J17 (13) 74.00 56.50

Surcharged with New Values in Cents or Piasters

1919

J18 D1 4/5c on 2c blk 1.00 .50
J19 D1 1 3/5c on 4c dp bl .85 .50
J20 D1 2c on 5c bl grn 2.00 .75
J21 D1 4c on 10c car 2.00 .50
J22 D1 6c on 15c vio 5.00 1.50
J23 D1 8c on 20c choc 3.25 1.50
J24 D1 12c on 30c ol grn 4.50 .90
J25 D1 16c on 40c cl 4.50 .75
J26 D1 20c on 50c grnsh bl 6.00 3.25
J27 D1 24c on 60c org 1.40 1.00
a. Closed "4" 12.00 9.00
J28 D1 40c on 1fr gray 2.50 1.00
a. Closed "4" 12.50 10.00
J29 D1 80c on 20c yel brn 24.00 11.00
J30 D1 2pi on 5fr red 32.50 25.00
a. Double surcharge 125.00 100.00
b. Triple surcharge 125.00 90.00
Nos. J18-J30 (13) 89.50 48.15

"CENTS" below Numerals

1922, Oct.

J31 D2 2/5c black .20 .20
J32 D2 4/5c red .20 .20
J33 D2 1c buff .30 .20
J34 D2 2c gray grn .40 .20
J35 D2 3c violet .40 .20
J36 D2 4c orange .40 .20
a. "4 CENTS" omitted 325.00
b. "4 CENTS" double 100.00 100.00
J37 D2 6c ol grn 1.00 .25
J38 D2 8c blk, *lav* .60 .20
J39 D2 10c dp bl 1.00 .20
J40 D2 12c ocher, *grnsh* .60 .45
J41 D2 20c dp bl, *straw* .90 .35
J42 D2 40c red, *bluish* 1.00 .35
J43 D2 1pi brn vio, *pnksh* 3.00 2.00
Nos. J31-J43 (13) 10.00 5.00

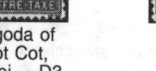

Pagoda of Mot Cot, Hanoi — D3

Dragon of Annam — D4

Perf. 14x13½, 13½x14

1927, Sept. 26

J44 D3 2/5c vio brn & org .20 .20
J45 D3 4/5c vio & blk .20 .20
J46 D3 1c brn red & sl .60 .40
J47 D3 2c grn & brn ol .75 .50

J48	D3	3c red brn & bl	.75	.50
J49	D3	4c ind & brn	.60	.50
J50	D3	6c dp red & ver	.85	.70
J51	D3	8c ol brn & vio	.75	.50
J52	D4	10c dp bl	1.25	.35
J53	D4	12c olive	4.00	3.00
J54	D4	20c rose	1.75	.75
J55	D4	40c bl grn	2.50	1.50
J56	D4	1pi red org	13.00	11.00
		Nos. J44-J56 (13)	27.20	20.10

D5

Value Surcharged in Black or Blue

1931-41 ***Perf. 13***

J57	D5	⅕c red, *org* ('38)	.20	.20
J58	D5	⅖c red, *org*	.20	.20
J59	D5	⅘c red, *org*	.20	.20
J60	D5	1c red, *org*	.20	.20
J61	D5	2c red, *org*	.20	.20
J62	D5	2.5c red, *org* ('40)	.20	.20
J63	D5	3c red, *org* ('38)	.20	.20
J64	D5	4c red, *org*	.20	.20
J65	D5	5c red, *org* ('38)	.20	.20
J66	D5	6c red, *org*	.20	.20
J67	D5	10c red, *org*	.20	.20
J68	D5	12c red, *org*	.20	.20
J69	D5	14c red, *org* ('38)	.20	.20
J70	D5	18c red, *org* ('41)	.20	.20
J71	D5	20c red, *org*	.20	.20
J72	D5	50c red, *org*	.20	.20
J72A	D5	1pi red, *org*	6.00	5.00
J73	D5	1pi red, *org* (Bl)	1.10	.60
		Nos. J57-J73 (18)	10.30	8.80

D6 D7

Perf. 12, 13½ and Compound

1943-44 Litho. Unwmk.

J74	D6	1c red, *org*	.20	.20
J75	D6	2c red, *org*	.20	.20
J76	D6	3c red, *org*	.20	.20
J77	D6	4c red, *org*	.20	.20
J78	D6	6c red, *org*	.20	.20
J79	D6	10c red, *org*	.20	.20
J80	D7	12c blue, *pnksh*	.20	.20
J81	D7	20c blue, *pnksh*	.20	.20
J82	D7	30c blue, *pnksh*	.20	.20
		Nos. J74-J82 (9)	1.80	1.80

Issued: 2c, 3c, 7/15/43; 6c-30c, 8/43; 1c, 4c, 6/10/44.

OFFICIAL STAMPS

Regular Issues of 1931-32 Overprinted in Blue or Red

Overprinted

Perf. 13, 13½

1933, Feb. 27 Unwmk.

O1	A20	1c black brown (Bl)	.40	.20
O2	A20	2c dark green (Bl)	.40	.20

Overprinted

O3	A21	3c deep brown (Bl)	.50	.40
a.		Inverted overprint	75.00	
O4	A21	4c dark blue (R)	.40	.40
a.		Inverted overprint	75.00	
O5	A21	5c deep violet (Bl)	1.25	.20
O6	A21	6c orange red (Bl)	1.10	.20

Overprinted

O7	A22	10c dk blue (R)	.50	.35
O8	A22	15c dk brown (Bl)	2.00	1.00
O9	A22	20c rose (Bl)	1.40	.25
O10	A22	21c olive grn (Bl)	1.90	.75
O11	A22	25c dp violet (Bl)	.90	.30
O12	A22	30c orange brn (Bl)	1.50	.50

Overprinted

O13	A23	50c dark brown (Bl)	7.25	2.50
O14	A23	60c dull violet (Bl)	1.75	1.25
O15	A23	1pi yellow green (Bl)	17.00	6.25
O16	A23	2pi red (Bl)	6.75	6.25
		Nos. O1-O16 (16)	45.00	21.00

Type of Regular Issue, 1922-23 Overprinted diagonally in Black or Red "SERVICE"

1934, Oct. 4 ***Perf. 14x13***

O17	A13	1c olive green	.55	.35
O18	A13	2c brown orange	.55	.35
O19	A13	3c yellow green	.50	.25
O20	A13	4c cerise	1.00	.75
O21	A13	5c yellow	.60	.30
O22	A13	6c orange red	3.50	3.50
O23	A13	10c gray grn (R)	1.50	1.25
O24	A13	15c ultra	1.50	.80
O25	A13	20c gray black (R)	.80	.80
O26	A13	21c light violet	5.50	5.00
O27	A13	25c rose lake	6.00	5.50
O28	A13	30c lilac gray	.85	.50
O29	A13	50c brt violet	4.00	3.75
O30	A13	60c gray	6.50	6.50
O31	A13	1pi blue (R)	17.50	15.00
O32	A13	2pi deep red	27.50	22.50
		Nos. O17-O32 (16)	78.35	67.10

The value tablet has colorless numeral and letters on solid background.

PARCEL POST STAMPS

French Colonies No. 50 Overprinted

1891 Unwmk. ***Perf. 14x13½***

Q1	A9	10c black, *lavender*	9.00	2.50

The overprint on No. Q1 was also handstamped in shiny ink. Value unused, $400.

Indo-China No. 8 Overprinted

1898

Q2	A3	10c black, *lavender*	12.50	12.50

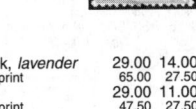

Nos. 8 and 9 Overprinted

1902

Q3	A3	10c black, *lavender*	29.00	14.00
a.		Inverted overprint	65.00	27.50
Q4	A3	10c red	29.00	11.00
a.		Inverted overprint	47.50	27.50
b.		Double overprint	47.50	27.50

INDONESIA

ˌin-də-ˈnē-zhə

LOCATION — In the East Indies
GOVT. — Republic
AREA — 741,101 sq. mi.
POP. — 195,280,000 (1995 est.)
CAPITAL — Jakarta

Formerly Netherlands Indies, Indonesia achieved independence late in 1949 as the United States of Indonesia and became the Republic of Indonesia August 15, 1950. See Netherlands Indies for earlier issues.

100 Sen = 1 Rupiah

Catalogue values for all unused stamps in this country are for Never Hinged items.

Watermark

Wmk. 228

United States of Indonesia

Mountain, Palms and Flag of Republic — A49

Perf. 12½x12

1950, Jan. 17 Photo. Unwmk.

Size: 20½x26mm

333	A49	15s red	.80	.20

1950, June ***Perf. 11½***

Size: 18x23mm

334	A49	15s red	5.50	.30

Netherlands Indies Nos. 307-315 Overprinted in Black

1950 ***Perf. 11½, 12½***

335	A42	1s gray	.40	.20
336	A42	2s claret	.40	.20
337	A42	2½s olive brown	.50	.20
338	A42	3s rose pink	.40	.20
339	A42	4s green	.50	.20
340	A42	5s blue	.25	.20
341	A42	7½s dark green	.50	.20
342	A42	10s violet	.50	.20
343	A42	12½s bright red	.70	.20

Perf. 11½, 1s, 5s. Perf. 12½, 7½s, 12½s. Others, both perfs.

Netherlands Indies Nos. 317-330 Overprinted in Black

Perf. 11½, 12½

345	A43	20s gray black	5.00	2.25
346	A43	25s ultra	.50	.20
347	A44	30s bright red	2.75	1.40
348	A44	40s gray green	.50	.20
349	A44	45s claret	1.25	.20
350	A45	50s orange brown	.85	.20
351	A45	60s brown	3.75	1.75
352	A45	80s scarlet	2.00	.20

Perf. 11½, 20s, 45s, 50s. Others, both perfs.

Overprint 12mm High

Perf. 12½

353	A46	1r purple	1.25	.20
354	A46	2r olive green	175.00	75.00
355	A46	3r red violet	160.00	25.00
356	A46	5r dark brown	50.00	19.00
357	A46	10r gray	90.00	15.00
358	A46	25r orange brown	30.00	6.25
		Nos. 335-358 (23)	527.00	148.65
		Set, hinged	300.00	

For overprints see Riau Archipelago #17-22.

Republic of Indonesia

Arms of the Republic A50

Doves in Flight A51

Perf. 12½x12

1950, Aug. 17 Photo. Unwmk.

359	A50	15s red	2.50	.25
360	A50	25s dull green	3.50	1.10
361	A50	1r sepia	12.00	1.40
		Nos. 359-361 (3)	18.00	2.75

5th anniv. of Indonesia's proclamation of independence.

1951, Oct. 24 Engr. *Perf. 12*

362 A51	7½s	blue green	5.75	.70
363 A51	10s	violet	1.25	.20
364 A51	20s	red	1.25	.20
365 A51	30s	carmine rose	1.25	.50
366 A51	35s	ultra	1.25	.90
367 A51	1r	sepia	21.00	2.00
		Nos. 362-367 (6)	31.75	4.50

6th anniv. of the UN and the 1st anniv. of the Republic of Indonesia as a member.

A52

Post Office — A53

Mythological Hero — A54

Pres. Sukarno — A55

1951-53 Photo. *Perf. 12½*

368 A52	1s	gray	.20	.20
369 A52	2s	plum	.20	.20
370 A52	2½s	brown	4.75	.40
371 A52	5s	car rose	.20	.20
372 A52	7½s	green	.20	.20
373 A52	10s	blue	.20	.20
374 A52	15s	purple	.20	.20
375 A52	20s	rose red	.20	.20
376 A52	25s	deep green	.20	.20
377 A53	30s	red orange	.20	.20
378 A53	35s	purple	.20	.20
379 A53	40s	dull green	.20	.20
380 A53	45s	deep claret	.20	.20
381 A53	50s	brown	8.75	.20
382 A54	60s	dark brown	.20	.20
383 A54	70s	gray	.20	.20
384 A54	75s	ultra	.20	.20
385 A54	80s	claret	.20	.20
386 A54	90s	gray green	.20	.20
		Nos. 368-386 (19)	16.90	4.00

Perf. 12½x12

387 A55	1r	purple	.20	.20
388 A55	1.25r	dp orange	1.40	.20
389 A55	1.50r	brown	.20	.20
390 A55	2r	green	.20	.20
391 A55	2.50r	rose brown	.20	.20
392 A55	3r	blue	.20	.20
392A A55	4r	apple green	.20	.20
393 A55	5r	brown	.20	.20
394 A55	6r	rose lilac	.20	.20
395 A55	10r	slate	.20	.20
396 A55	15r	yellow	.20	.20
397 A55	20r	sepia	.20	.20
398 A55	25r	scarlet	.60	.20
399 A55	40r	yellow green	.60	.20
400 A55	50r	violet	.95	.20
		Nos. 387-400 (15)	5.75	3.00

Nos. 368-376, 387, 390, 392, 393, 395, 398 were issued in 1951; Nos. 377-386, 388-389, 391, 392A, 394, 396-397, 399-400 in 1953.

Values are for the later Djakarta printings which have thicker numerals and a darker over-all impression. Earlier printings by Joh. Enschede and Sons, Haarlem, Netherlands, sell for more.

For surcharge see No. B68. For overprints see Riau Archipelago Nos. 1-16, 32-40.

Melati Flowers — A56

Crowd Releasing Doves — A57

1953, Dec. 22 *Perf. 12½*

401 A56	50s	blue green	10.50	.50

25th anniv. of the formation of the Indonesian Women's Congress.

1955, Apr. 18 *Perf. 13x12½*

402 A57	15s	gray	.90	.20
403 A57	35s	brown	.90	.20
404 A57	50s	deep magenta	1.90	.20
405 A57	75s	blue green	.75	.20
		Nos. 402-405 (4)	4.45	.80

Asian-African Conf., Bandung, April 18-24.

Proclamation of Independence A58

1955, Aug. 17 Photo. *Perf. 12½*

406 A58	15s	green	.75	.25
407 A58	35s	ultra	1.25	.25
408 A58	50s	brown	7.25	.25
409 A58	75s	magenta	1.25	.25
		Nos. 406-409 (4)	10.50	1.00

Ten years of independence.

Voters — A59

1955, Sept. 29 *Perf. 12*

Without gum

410 A59	15s	rose violet	.60	.20
411 A59	35s	green	.60	.20
412 A59	50s	carmine rose	1.90	.20
413 A59	75s	lt ultra	.85	.20
		Nos. 410-413 (4)	3.95	.80

First free elections in Indonesia.

Mas Soeharto Postmaster General A60

Helmet, Wreath and Monument A61

1955, Sept. 27 *Perf. 12½*

414 A60	15s	brown	1.25	.45
415 A60	35s	dark carmine	1.25	.45
416 A60	50s	ultra	6.75	1.00
417 A60	75s	dull green	1.25	.35
		Nos. 414-417 (4)	10.50	2.25

Issued to mark 10 years of Indonesia's Postal, Telegraph and Telephone system.

1955, Nov. 10

418 A61	25s	bluish green	1.25	.60
419 A61	50s	ultra	1.25	.35
420 A61	1r	dk car rose	9.50	.30
		Nos. 418-420 (3)	12.00	1.25

Issued in honor of the soldiers killed in the war of liberation from the Netherlands.

Torch, Book and Map A62

Lesser Malay Chevrotain A63

1956, May 26 Photo.

421 A62	25s	ultra	1.40	.75
422 A62	50s	carmine rose	7.00	.40
423 A62	1r	dark green	1.60	.40
		Nos. 421-423 (3)	10.00	1.55

Asia-Africa Student Conf., Bandung, May, 1956.

1956 Unwmk. *Perf. 12½x13½*

Animals: 5s, 10s, Lesser Malay chevrotain. 20s, 25s, Otter. 35s, Malayan pangolin. 50s, Banteng. 75s, Asiatic two-horned rhinoceros.

424 A63	5s	deep ultra	.25	.20
425 A63	10s	yellow brown	.25	.20
426 A63	15s	rose violet	.40	.20
427 A63	20s	dull green	.40	.20
428 A63	25s	deep claret	.40	.20
429 A63	35s	brt violet blue	.40	.20
430 A63	50s	brown	.75	.20
431 A63	75s	dark brown	.40	.20
		Nos. 424-431 (8)	3.25	1.60

See Nos. 450-456. For overprints see Riau Archipelago Nos. 23-31.

Dancing Girl and Gate — A64

Telegraph Key — A65

1956, Oct. 7 *Perf. 12½x12*

432 A64	15s	slate green	1.25	.25
433 A64	35s	brown violet	1.25	.25
434 A64	50s	blue black	2.50	.30
435 A64	75s	deep claret	2.50	.20
		Nos. 432-435 (4)	7.50	1.00

Founding of the city of Jogjakarta, 200th anniv.

1957, May 10 Unwmk.

436 A65	10s	lt crimson	2.10	.20
437 A65	15s	brt blue	.50	.20
438 A65	25s	gray	.50	.20
439 A65	50s	brown red	.65	.20
440 A65	75s	lt blue green	.80	.20
		Nos. 436-440 (5)	4.55	1.00

Indonesian telegraph system centenary.

Thrift Symbolism A66

Douglas DC-3 A67

Design: 15s, 1r, People and hands holding wreath of rice and cotton.

1957, July 12 Photo. *Perf. 12½*

441 A66	10s	blue	.45	.20
442 A66	15s	rose carmine	.55	.20
443 A66	50s	green	1.00	.30
444 A66	1r	brt violet	1.00	.20
		Nos. 441-444 (4)	3.00	.90

Cooperation Day, July 12.

1958, Apr. 9 *Perf. 12½x12*

Aircraft: 15s, Helicopter. 30s, Miles Magister. 50s, Two-motor plane of Indonesian Airways. 75s, De Havilland Vampire.

445 A67	10s	reddish brown	.45	.20
446 A67	15s	blue	.45	.20
447 A67	35s	orange	.45	.20
448 A67	50s	bright green	.45	.20
449 A67	75s	gray	.45	.20
		Nos. 445-449 (5)	2.25	1.00

Issued for National Aviation Day, April 9.

Animal Type of 1956

Animals: 30s, Otter. 40s, 45s, Malayan pangolin. 60s, 70s, Banteng. 80s, 90s, Asiatic two-horned rhinoceros.

1958 Photo. *Perf. 12½x13½*

450 A63	30s	orange	.20	.20
451 A63	40s	brt yellow grn	.25	.20
452 A63	45s	rose lilac	.25	.20
453 A63	60s	dark blue	.40	.20
454 A63	70s	orange ver	.40	.20
455 A63	80s	red	.55	.20
456 A63	90s	yellow green	.55	.20
		Nos. 450-456 (7)	2.60	1.40

Thomas Cup A68

1958, Aug. 15 *Perf. 13½x13*

457 A68	25s	rose carmine	.20	.20
458 A68	50s	orange	.25	.20
459 A68	1r	brown	.25	.20
		Nos. 457-459 (3)	.70	.60

Indonesia's victory in the 1958 Thomas Cup World Badminton Championship.

Satellite Circling Globe — A69

1958, Oct. 15 Litho. *Perf. 12½x12*

460 A69	10s	dk grn, pink & lt bl	.90	.20
461 A69	15s	vio, gray & pale blu-ish grn	.30	.20
462 A69	35s	brown, blue & pink	.30	.20
463 A69	50s	bl, redsh brn & gray	.30	.20
464 A69	75s	black, vio & buff	.30	.20
		Nos. 460-464 (5)	2.10	1.00

International Geophysical Year, 1957-58.

Bicyclist and Map A70

1958, Nov. 15 Photo. *Perf. 13½x13*

465 A70	25s	bright blue	.30	.20
466 A70	50s	brown carmine	.65	.20
467 A70	1r	gray	.30	.20
		Nos. 465-467 (3)	1.25	.60

Bicycle Tour of Java, Aug. 15-30.

Man Looking into Light A71

Wild Boar (Babirusa) A72

Designs: 15s, Hands and flame. 35s, Woman holding candle. 50s, Family hailing torch. 75s, Torch and "10."

1958, Dec. 10 *Perf. 12½x12*

468 A71	10s	gray brown	.20	.20
469 A71	15s	dull red brn	.20	.20
470 A71	35s	ultra	.20	.20
471 A71	50s	pale brown	.25	.20
472 A71	75s	lt blue grn	.30	.20
		Nos. 468-472 (5)	1.15	1.00

10th anniv. of the signing of the Universal Declaration of Human Rights.

1959, June 1 Photo. *Perf. 12*

Animals: 15s, Anoa (smallest buffalo). 20s, Orangutan. 50s, Javan rhinoceros. 75s, Komodo dragon (lizard). 1r, Malayan tapir.

473 A72	10s	olive bis & sepia	.20	.20
474 A72	15s	org brn & sepia	.20	.20
475 A72	20s	lt ol grn & sepia	.20	.20
476 A72	50s	bister brn & sepia	.50	.20
477 A72	75s	dp rose & sepia	.70	.20
478 A72	1r	blue grn & blk	.90	.20
		Nos. 473-478 (6)	2.70	1.20

Issued to publicize wildlife preservation.

A73

Factories — A74

1959, Aug. 17 Litho. *Perf. 12*

479 A73 20s blue & red .20 .20
480 A73 50s rose red & blk .20 .20
481 A73 75s brown & red .20 .20
482 A73 1.50r lt green & blk .40 .40
Nos. 479-482 (4) 1.00 1.00

Introduction of the constitution of 1945 embodying "guided democracy."

1959, Oct. 26 Photo. *Perf. 12*

Designs: 20s, 75s, Cogwheel and train. 1.15r, Means of transportation.

483 A74 15s brt green & blk .20 .20
484 A74 20s dull org & blk .20 .20
485 A74 50s red & black .20 .20
486 A74 75s brt grnsh bl & blk .20 .20
487 A74 1.15r magenta & blk .20 .20
Nos. 483-487 (5) 1.00 1.00

11th Colombo Plan Conference, Jakarta.

Mother & Child, WRY Emblem — A75

15s, 75s, Destroyed town & fleeing family. 20s, 1.15r, World Refugee Year emblem.

1960, Apr. 7 Unwmk. *Perf. 12½x12*

488 A75 10s claret & blk .20 .20
489 A75 15s bister & blk .20 .20
490 A75 20s org brn & blk .20 .20
491 A75 50s green & blk .20 .20
492 A75 75s dk blue & blk .20 .20
493 A75 1.15r scarlet & blk .20 .20
Nos. 488-493 (6) 1.20 1.20

World Refugee Year, 7/1/59-6/3/60.

Tea Plantation — A76

5s, Oil palms. 10s, Sugar cane and railroad. 15s, Coffee. 20s, Tobacco. 50s, Coconut palms. 75s, Rubber plantation. 1.15r, Rice.

1960 *Perf. 12x12½*

494 A76 5s gray .20 .20
495 A76 10s red brown .20 .20
496 A76 15s plum .20 .20
497 A76 20s ocher .20 .20
498 A76 25s brt blue grn .20 .20
499 A76 50s deep blue .20 .20
500 A76 75s scarlet .20 .20
501 A76 1.15r plum .20 .20
Nos. 494-501 (8) 1.60 1.60

For surcharges see Nos. B132-B134.

Anopheles Mosquito — A77

1960, Nov. 12 Photo. *Perf. 12x12½*

502 A77 25s carmine rose .20 .20
503 A77 50s orange brown .20 .20
504 A77 75s brt green .20 .20
505 A77 3r orange .30 .30
Nos. 502-505 (4) .90 .90

World Health Day, Nov. 12, 1960, and to promote malaria control.

Pres. Sukarno with Hoe — A78

1961, Feb. 15 *Perf. 12½x12*

506 A78 75s gray .30 .20

Planned National Development.

Dayak Dancer of Borneo A79

Designs: 10s, Ambonese boat. 15s, Tangkubanperahu crater. 20s, Bull races. 50s, Toradja houses. 75s, Balinese temple. 1r, Lake Toba. 1.50r, Balinese dancer and musicians. 2r, Buffalo hole, view. 3r, Borobudur Temple, Java.

1961 *Perf. 13½x13*

507 A79 10s rose lilac .65 .20
508 A79 15s gray .65 .20
509 A79 20s orange .65 .20
510 A79 25s orange ver .65 .20
511 A79 50s carmine rose .65 .20
512 A79 75s red brown .65 .20
513 A79 1r brt green 1.25 .20
514 A79 1.50r bister brn 1.25 .20
515 A79 2r grnsh blue 1.60 .30
516 A79 3r gray 1.75 .30
Set of 4 souvenir sheets 17.50 1.90
Nos. 507-516 (10) 9.75 2.20

Issued for tourist publicity.

The four souvenir sheets among them contain one each of Nos. 507-516 imperf., with two or three stamps to a sheet and English marginal inscriptions: "Visit Indonesia" and "Visit the Orient Year." Size: 139x105mm or 105x139mm.

Sports Hall and Thomas Cup A80

Perf. 13½x12½

1961, June 1 Photo.

517 A80 75s pale violet & blue .20 .20
518 A80 1r citron & dk grn .20 .20
519 A80 3r salmon pink & dk bl .20 .20
Nos. 517-519 (3) .60 .60

1961 Thomas Cup World Badminton Championship.

New Buildings and Workers A81

1961, July 6 Unwmk.

520 A81 75s violet & grnsh bl .20 .20
521 A81 1.50r emerald & buff .20 .20
522 A81 3r dk red & salmon .20 .20
Nos. 520-522 (3) .60 .60

16th anniversary of independence.

Sultan Hasanuddin — A82

Portraits: 20s, Abdul Muis. 30s, Surjopranoto. 40s, Tengku Tjhik Di Tiro. 50s, Teuku Umar. 60s, K. H. Samanhudi. 75s, Captain Pattimura. 1r, Raden Adjeng Kartini. 1.25r, K. H. Achmad Dahlan. 1.50r, Tuanku Imam Bondjol. 2r, Si Singamangaradja XII. 2.50r, Mohammad Husni Thamrin. 3r, Ki Hadjar Dewantoro. 4r, Djenderal Sudirman. 4.50r, Dr. G. S. S. J. Ratulangie. 5r, Pangeran Diponegoro. 6r, Dr. Setyabudi. 7.50r, H. O. S. Tjokroaminoto. 10r, K. H. Agus Salim. 15r, Dr. Soetomo.

Perf. 13½x12½

1961-62 Unwmk. Photo.

Black Inscriptions; Portraits in Sepia

523 A82 20s olive .20 .20
524 A82 25s gray olive .20 .20
525 A82 30s brt lilac .20 .20
526 A82 40s brown orange .50 .20
527 A82 50s bluish green .50 .20
528 A82 60s green ('62) .20 .20
529 A82 75s lt red brown .50 .20
530 A82 1r lt blue .55 .20
531 A82 1.25r lt ol grn ('62) .20 .20
532 A82 1.50r emerald .50 .20
533 A82 2r org red ('62) .20 .20
534 A82 2.50r rose claret .50 .20
535 A82 3r gray blue .70 .20
536 A82 4r olive green .90 .20
537 A82 4.50r red lilac ('62) .55 .20
538 A82 5r brick red 1.10 .20
539 A82 6r bister ('62) .55 .20
540 A82 7.50r violet bl ('62) .70 .20
541 A82 10r green ('62) .90 .20
542 A82 15r dp org ('62) 1.10 .20
Nos. 523-542 (20) 10.75 4.00

National heroes. The 25s, 75s, 1.50r, 5r issued on 8/17, Independence Day; 40s, 50s, 4r on 10/5, Army Day; 20s, 30s, 1r, 2.50r, 3r on 11/10, Republic Day; 60s, 2r, 7.50r, 15r on 10/5/62; 1.25r, 4.50r, 6r, 10r on 11/10/62.

Symbols of Census A83

1961, Sept. 15 *Perf. 13½x12½*

543 A83 75s rose violet .20 .20

First census in Indonesia.

Djataju — A84

Scenes from Ramayana Ballet: 40s, Hanuman. 1r, Dasamuka. 1.50r, Kidang Kentiana. 3r, Dewi Sinta. 5r, Rama.

Perf. 12x12½

1962, Jan. 15 Unwmk.

544 A84 30s ocher & red brn .20 .20
545 A84 40s rose lilac & vio .30 .20
546 A84 1r green & claret .60 .20
547 A84 1.50r sal pink & dk grn .75 .20
548 A84 3r pale grn & dp bl 1.10 .20
549 A84 5r brn org & dk brn 1.60 .20
Nos. 544-549 (6) 4.55 1.20

Asian Games Emblem — A85

Main Stadium — A86

Designs: 10s, Basketball. 15s, Main Stadium, Jakarta. 20s, Weight lifter. 25s, Hotel Indonesia. 30s, Cloverleaf intersection. 40s, Discus thrower. 50s, Woman diver. 60s, Soccer. 70s, Press House. 75s, Boxers. 1r, Volleyball. 1.25r, 2r, 3r, 5r, Asian Games emblem. 1.50r, Badminton. 1.75r, Wrestlers. 2.50r, Woman rifle shooter. 4.50r, Hockey. 6r, Water polo. 7.50r, Tennis. 10r, Table tennis. 15r, Bicyclist. 20r, Welcome Monument.

1962 Photo. *Perf. 12½*

550 A85 10s green & yel .20 .20
551 A86 15s grnsh blk & bis .20 .20
552 A85 20s red lil & lt grn .20 .20
553 A86 25s car & lt grn .20 .20
554 A86 30s bl grn & yel .30 .20
555 A85 40s ultra & pale bl .30 .20
556 A85 50s choc & gray .30 .20
557 A85 60s lil rose & vio gray .30 .20
558 A85 70s dk brn & rose .30 .20
559 A85 75s choc & org .30 .20
560 A85 1r purple & lt bl .30 .20
561 A85 1.25r dk bl & rose car .30 .20
562 A85 1.50r red org & lil .30 .20
563 A85 1.75r dk car & rose .35 .20
564 A85 2r brn & yel grn .35 .20
565 A85 2.50r dp bl & lt grn .35 .20
566 A85 3r black & dk red .60 .20
567 A85 4.50r dk grn & red .60 .20
568 A85 5r gray grn & lem .60 .20
569 A85 6r brn red & dp yel .65 .20
570 A85 7.50r red brn & sal .65 .20
571 A85 10r dk blue & blue .65 .20
572 A85 15r dl vio & pale vio .85 .20
573 A85 20r dk grn & ol bis 1.40 .20
Nos. 550-573 (24) 10.55 4.80

4th Asian Games, Jakarta.

Malaria Eradication Emblem — A87

1962, Apr. 7 *Perf. 12½x12*

574 A87 40s dull bl & vio bl .20 .20
575 A87 1.50r yel org & brn .20 .20
576 A87 3r green & indigo .20 .20
577 A87 6r lilac & blk .20 .20
Nos. 574-577 (4) .80 .80

WHO drive to eradicate malaria. The 1.50r and 6r have Indonesian inscription on top.

Atom Diagram — A88

1962, Sept. 24 Photo. *Perf. 12x12½*

578 A88 1.50r dk blue & yel .20 .20
579 A88 4.50r brick red & yel .20 .20
580 A88 6r green & yel .20 .20
Nos. 578-580 (3) .60 .60

Development through science.

Pacific Travel Association Emblem — A89

Mechanized Plow — A90

1.50r, Prambanan Temple and Mount Merapi. 6r, Balinese Meru (Buildings), Pura Taman Ajun.

1963, Mar. 14 **Unwmk.**

581	A89	1r grn & indigo	.20	.20
582	A89	1.50r olive & indigo	.20	.20
583	A89	3r ocher & indigo	.20	.20
584	A89	6r dp org & indigo	.40	.20
		Nos. 581-584 (4)	1.00	.80

12th conf. of the Pacific Area Travel Assoc., Bandung.

1963, Mar. 21 ***Perf. 12½x12, 12x12½***

1r, 3r, Hand holding rice stalks, vert.

585	A90	1r blue & yel	.20	.20
586	A90	1.50r brt grn & indigo	.20	.20
587	A90	3r rose car & org	.20	.20
588	A90	6r orange & blk	.20	.20
		Nos. 585-588 (4)	.80	.80

FAO "Freedom from Hunger" campaign. English inscription on 3r and 6r.

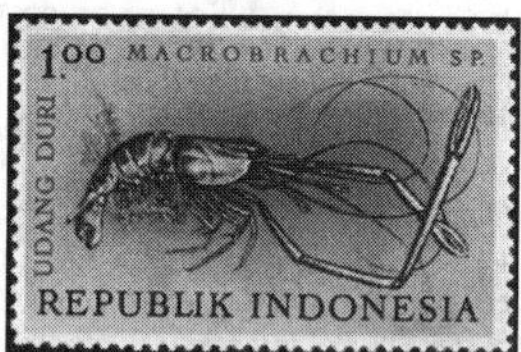

Long-Armed Lobster — A91

Fish: 1.50r, Little tuna. 3r, River roman. 6r, Chinese pompano.

1963, Apr. 6 ***Perf. 12½x12***

589	A91	1r ver, blk & yel	.30	.20
590	A91	1.50r ultra, blk & yel	.30	.20
591	A91	3r Prus bl, bis & car	.40	.20
592	A91	6r ol grn, blk & ocher	.40	.20
		Nos. 589-592 (4)	1.40	.80

Pen and Conference Emblem — A92

Designs: 1.50r, Pen, Emblem and map of Africa and Southeast Asia. 3r, Globe, pen and broken chain, vert. 6r, Globe, hand holding pen and broken chain, vert.

Perf. 12½x12, 12x12½

1963, Apr. 24 **Photo.** **Unwmk.**

593	A92	1r lt bl & dp org	.20	.20
594	A92	1.50r pale vio & mar	.20	.20
595	A92	3r olive, bl & blk	.20	.20
596	A92	6r brick red & blk	.30	.20
		Nos. 593-596 (4)	.90	.80

Asian-African Journalists' Conference.

"Indonesia's Flag from Sabang to Merauke" — A93

4.50r, Parachutist landing in New Guinea. 6r, Bird of paradise & map of New Guinea.

1963, May 1 ***Perf. 12½x12***

597	A93	1.50r org brn, blk & red	.20	.20
598	A93	4.50r multicolored	.20	.20
599	A93	6r multicolored	.20	.20
		Nos. 597-599 (3)	.60	.60

Issued to mark the acquisition of Netherlands New Guinea (West Irian).

Centenary Emblem — A94

Design: 1.50r, 6r, Red Cross.

1963, May 8 ***Perf. 12***

600	A94	1r brt grn & red	.20	.20
601	A94	1.50r lt bl & red	.20	.20
602	A94	3r gray & red	.20	.20
603	A94	6r yel bis & red	.20	.20
		Nos. 600-603 (4)	.80	.80

Centenary of the International Red Cross.

Bank of Indonesia, Djalan A95

Daneswara, God of Prosperity A96

1963, July 5 **Photo.** ***Perf. 12***

604	A95	1.75r lt bl & pur	.20	.20
605	A96	4r citron & sl grn	.20	.20
606	A95	6r lt green & brn	.20	.20
607	A96	12r org & dk red brn	.20	.20
		Nos. 604-607 (4)	.80	.80

Issued for National Banking Day.

Standard Bearers — A97

Designs: 1.75r, "Pendet" dance. 4r, GANEFO building, Senajan, Jakarta. 6r, Archery. 10r, Badminton. 12r, Javelin. 25r, Sailing. 50r, Torch.

1963, Nov. 10 **Unwmk.** ***Perf. 12½***

608	A97	1.25r gray vio & dk brn	.20	.20
609	A97	1.75r org & ol grn	.20	.20
610	A97	4r emer & dk brn	.20	.20
611	A97	6r rose brn & blk	.20	.20
612	A97	10r lt ol grn & dk brn	.20	.20
613	A97	12r rose car & grnsh blk	.25	.20
614	A97	25r blue & dk blue	.35	.20
615	A97	50r red & black	.40	.20
		Nos. 608-615 (8)	2.00	1.60

1st Games of the New Emerging Forces, GANEFO, Jakarta, Nov. 10-22.

Pres. Sukarno — A98

1964 **Photo.** ***Perf. 12½x12***

616	A98	6r brown & dk bl	.20	.20
617	A98	12r bister & plum	.20	.20
618	A98	20r blue & org	.20	.20
619	A98	30r red org & bl	.20	.20
620	A98	40r green & brn	.20	.20
621	A98	50r red & dp grn	.20	.20
622	A98	75r vio & red org	.20	.20
623	A98	100r sil & red brn	.20	.20
624	A98	250r dk blue & sil	.20	.20
625	A98	500r red & gold	.20	.20
		Nos. 616-625 (10)	2.00	2.00

See Nos. B165-B179. For surcharges see Nos. 661, 663-667.

Trailer Truck — A99

Designs: 1r, Oxcart. 1.75r, Freighter. 2r, Lockheed Electra plane. 2.50r, Buginese sailboat, vert. 4r, Mailman with bicycle. 5r, Dakota plane. 7.50r, Teletype operator. 10r, Diesel train. 15r, Passenger ship. 25r, Convair Coronado Plane. 35r, Telephone switchboard operator.

1964 ***Perf. 12x12½, 12½x12***

626	A99	1r dull claret	.20	.20
627	A99	1.25r red brown	.20	.20
628	A99	1.75r Prus blue	.20	.20
629	A99	2r red orange	.20	.20
630	A99	2.50r brt blue	.20	.20
631	A99	4r bluish grn	.20	.20
632	A99	5r olive bister	.20	.20
633	A99	7.50r brt green	.20	.20
634	A99	10r orange	.20	.20
635	A99	15r dark blue	.20	.20
636	A99	25r violet blue	.20	.20
637	A99	35r red brown	.20	.20
		Nos. 626-637 (12)	2.40	2.40

For surcharges see Nos. 659-660, 662.

Ramses II — A100

Design: 6r, 18r, Kiosk of Trajan, Philae.

1964, Mar. 8 ***Perf. 12½x12***

638	A100	4r ol bis & ol grn	.20	.20
639	A100	6r grnsh bl & ol grn	.20	.20
640	A100	12r rose & ol grn	.25	.20
641	A100	18r emer & ol grn	.35	.20
		Nos. 638-641 (4)	1.00	.80

UNESCO world campaign to save historic monuments in Nubia.

Stamps of Netherlands Indies and Indonesia — A101

1964, Apr. 1 ***Perf. 12½***

642	A101	10r gold, dk bl & red org	.70	.20

Centenary of postage stamps in Indonesia.

Indonesian Pavilion — A102

1964, May 16 ***Perf. 12½x12***

643	A102	25r sil, blk, red & dk bl	.40	.20
644	A102	50r gold, Prus bl, red & grn	.70	.20

New York World's Fair, 1964-65.

Thomas Cup — A103

1964, Aug. 15 ***Perf. 12½x13½***

645	A103	25r brt grn, gold & red	.20	.20
646	A103	50r ultra, gold & red	.25	.20
647	A103	75r purple, gold & red	.45	.20
		Nos. 645-647 (3)	.90	.60

Thomas Cup Badminton World Championship, 1964.

Cruisers and Map of West Irian — A104

30r, Submarine. 40r, Torpedo boat.

Perf. 12½x12

1964, Oct. 5 **Photo.** **Unwmk.**

648	A104	20r yellow & brn	.30	.20
649	A104	30r rose & blk	.35	.20
650	A104	40r brt grn & ultra	.35	.20
		Nos. 648-650 (3)	1.00	.60

Issued to honor the Indonesian Navy.

Map of Africa and Asia and Mosque — A105

15r, 50r, Mosque and clasped hands.

1965, Mar. 6 **Photo.** ***Perf. 12½***

651	A105	10r lt blue & pur	.20	.20
652	A105	15r org & red brn	.25	.20
653	A105	25r brt grn & brn	.35	.20
654	A105	50r brn red & blk	.35	.20
		Nos. 651-654 (4)	1.15	.80

Afro-Asian Islamic Conf., Bandung, Mar. 1965.

Hand Holding Scroll — A106

Design: 25r, 75r, Conference emblem (globe, cotton and grain).

1965, Apr. 18 **Unwmk.** ***Perf. 12½***

655	A106	15r silver & dp car	.25	.20
656	A106	25r aqua, gold & red	.25	.20
657	A106	50r gold & dp ultra	.35	.20
658	A106	75r pale vio, gold & red	.35	.20
		Nos. 655-658 (4)	1.20	.80

10th anniv. of the First Afro-Asian Conf.

Nos. 618-623 and Nos. 634-636 Surcharged in Revalued Currency in Orange or Black

1965, Dec. ***Perf. 12x12½, 12½x12***

659	A99	10s on 10r (B)	.20	.20
660	A99	15s on 15r	.20	.20
661	A98	20s on 20r	.20	.20
662	A99	25s on 25r (B)	.20	.20
663	A98	30s on 30r	.20	.20
664	A98	40s on 40r	.20	.20
665	A98	50s on 50r	.20	.20

No.	Type	Value / Description	Unused	Used
666	A98	75s on 75r	.20	.20
667	A98	100s on 100r	.20	.20
		Nos. 659-667 (9)	1.80	1.80

The surcharge on Nos. 659-660 and No. 662 is in two lines and larger.

Pres. Sukarno — A107

1966-67 Photo. *Perf. 12½x12*

No.	Type	Value / Description	Unused	Used
668	A107	1s sep & Prus grn	.20	.20
669	A107	3s sep & lt ol grn	.20	.20
670	A107	5s sep & dp car	.20	.20
671	A107	8s sep & Prus grn	.20	.20
672	A107	10s sep & vio bl	.20	.20
673	A107	15s sep & blk	.20	.20
674	A107	20s sep & dp grn	.20	.20
675	A107	25s sep & dk red brn	.20	.20
676	A107	30s sep & dp bl	.20	.20
677	A107	40s sep & red brn	.20	.20
678	A107	50s sep & brt vio	.20	.20
679	A107	80s sep & org	.20	.20
680	A107	1r sep & emer	.20	.20
681	A107	1.25r sep & dk gray ol	.20	.20
682	A107	1.50r sep & emer	.20	.20
683	A107	2r sep & mag	.20	.20
684	A107	2.50r sep & gray	.20	.20
685	A107	5r sep & ocher	.20	.20
686	A107	10r sep & ol grn	.20	.20
686A	A107	12r grn & org ('67)	.20	.20
686B	A107	25r grn & brt pur ('67)	.20	.20
		Nos. 668-686B (21)	4.20	4.20

The 12r is inscribed "1967" instead of "1966."

Dockyard Workers — A108

Gen. Ahmad Yani — A109

Designs: 40s, Lighthouse. 50s, Fishermen. 1r, Maritime emblem (wheel and eagle). 1.50r, Sailboat. 2r, Loading dock. 2.50r, Diver emerging from water. 3r, Liner at pier.

1966 Photo. *Perf. 12x12½*

No.	Type	Value / Description	Unused	Used
687	A108	20s lt ultra & grn	.20	.20
688	A108	40s pink & dk bl	.20	.20
689	A108	50s green & brn	.20	.20
690	A108	1r salmon, bl & yel	.20	.20
691	A108	1.50r dull lil & dl grn	.20	.20
692	A108	2r gray & dp org	.20	.20
693	A108	2.50r rose lil & dk red	.20	.20
694	A108	3r brt green & blk	.20	.20
a.		Souvenir sheet	7.50	2.90
		Nos. 687-694 (8)	1.60	1.60

Maritime Day. Issued: #687-690, Sept. 23; #691-694, Oct. 23.

No. 694a contains one imperf. stamp similar to No. 694.

1966, Nov. 10

Heroes of the Revolution: #696, Lt. Gen. R. Suprapto. #697, Lt. General Harjono. #698, Lt. Gen. S. Parman. #699, Maj. Gen. D. I. Pandjaitan. #700, Maj. Gen. Sutojo Siswomihardjo. #701, Brig. General Katamso. #702, Colonel Soegijono. #703, Capt. Pierre Andreas Tendean. #704, Adj. Insp. Karel Satsuit Tubun.

Deep Blue Frame

No.	Type	Value / Description	Unused	Used
695	A109	5r org brn	.20	.20
696	A109	5r brt grn	.20	.20
697	A109	5r gray brn	.20	.20
698	A109	5r olive	.20	.20
699	A109	5r gray	.20	.20
700	A109	5r brt purple	.20	.20
701	A109	5r red lilac	.20	.20
702	A109	5r slate green	.20	.20
703	A109	5r dull rose lil	.20	.20
704	A109	5r orange	.20	.20
		Nos. 695-704 (10)	2.00	2.00

Issued to honor military men killed during the Communist uprising, October, 1965.

Tjlempung, Java — A110

Musical Instruments and Maps: 1r, Sasando, Timor. 1.25r, Foi doa, Flores. 1.50r, Kultjapi, Sumatra. 2r, Arababu, Sangihe and Talaud Islands. 2.50r, Drums, West New Guinea. 3r, Katjapi, Celebes. 4r, Hape, Borneo. 5r, Gangsa, Bali. 6r, Serunai, Sumatra. 8r, Rebab, Java. 10r, Trompet, West New Guinea. 12r, Totobuang, Moluccas. 15r, Drums, Nias. 20r, Kulintang, Celebes. 25r, Keledi, Borneo.

1967 Unwmk. Photo. *Perf. 12½x12*

No.	Type	Value / Description	Unused	Used
705	A110	50s red & gray	.20	.20
706	A110	1r brn & dp org	.20	.20
707	A110	1.25r mar & ultra	.20	.20
708	A110	1.50r grn & lt vio	.20	.20
709	A110	2r vio bl & yel bis	.20	.20
710	A110	2.50r ol grn & dl red	.20	.20
711	A110	3r brt grn & dl cl	.20	.20
712	A110	4r vio bl & org	.20	.20
713	A110	5r dull red & bl	.20	.20
714	A110	6r blk & brt pink	.20	.20
715	A110	8r red brn & brt grn	.25	.20
716	A110	10r lilac & red	.35	.20
717	A110	12r ol grn & lil	.40	.20
718	A110	15r vio & lt ol grn	.55	.20
719	A110	20r gray & sepia	.75	.20
720	A110	25r black & green	.90	.20
		Nos. 705-720 (16)	5.20	3.20

Issued: 1.25r, 10r, 12r, 15r, 20r, 25r, Mar. 1; others Feb. 1.

For surcharges see Nos. J118-J137.

Aviator and MiG-21 — A111

1967, Apr. 9 *Perf. 12½*

Aviation Day: 4r, Traffic control tower and 990A Convair jetliner. 5r, Hercules transport plane.

No.	Type	Value / Description	Unused	Used
721	A111	2.50r multicolored	.20	.20
722	A111	4r multicolored	.40	.20
723	A111	5r multicolored	.50	.20
		Nos. 721-723 (3)	1.10	.60

Thomas Cup with Victory Dates — A112

Design: 12r, Thomas Cup and globe.

1967, May 31 *Perf. 12x12½*

No.	Type	Value / Description	Unused	Used
724	A112	5r multicolored	.20	.20
725	A112	12r multicolored	.45	.20

Issued to commemorate the Thomas Cup Badminton World Championship of 1967.

Balinese Girl in Front of Temple Gate — A113

1967, July 1 Photo. *Perf. 12½*

No.	Type	Value / Description	Unused	Used
726	A113	12r multicolored	.75	.20
a.		Souv. sheet of 1, imperf.	3.00	.65

Intl. Tourist Year, 1967. See No. 739.

Heroes of the Revolution Monument, Lubang Buaja — A114

Designs: 5r, Full view of monument, horiz. 7.50r, Shrine at monument.

Perf. 12x12½, 12½x12

1967, Aug. 17 Photo.

No.	Type	Value / Description	Unused	Used
727	A114	2.50r pale grn & dk brn	.20	.20
728	A114	5r brt rose lil & pale brn	.30	.20
729	A114	7.50r pink & Prus grn	.50	.20
		Nos. 727-729 (3)	1.00	.60

Issued to publicize the "Heroes of the Revolution" Monument in Lubang Buaja.

Forest Fire, by Raden Saleh A115

50r, Fight to Death, by Raden Saleh.

1967, Oct. 30 Photo. *Perf. 12½*

No.	Type	Value / Description	Unused	Used
730	A115	25r org & gray grn	.20	.20
a.		Souvenir sheet of 1	3.00	1.10
731	A115	50r vio brn & org	.50	.45

Indonesian painter Raden Saleh (1813-80).

Human Rights Flame — A116

1968, Jan. 1 Photo. *Perf. 12½*

No.	Type	Value / Description	Unused	Used
732	A116	5r grn, lt vio bl & red	.20	.20
733	A116	12r grn, ol bis & red	.35	.20

International Human Rights Year 1968.

Armed Forces College Emblem — A117

1968, Jan. 29 Litho. *Perf. 12½*

No.	Type	Value / Description	Unused	Used
734	A117	10r lt blue, yel & brn	.35	.20

Integration of the Armed Forces College.

WHO Emblem and "20" — A118

20th anniv. of WHO: 20r, WHO emblem.

1968, Apr. 7 Photo. *Perf. 12½*

No.	Type	Value / Description	Unused	Used
735	A118	2r dp yel, pale yel & dk brn	.20	.20
736	A118	20r emerald & blk	.40	.20

Trains of 1867 and 1967 and Railroad's Emblem — A119

1968, May 15 Photo. *Perf. 12½x12*

No.	Type	Value / Description	Unused	Used
737	A119	20r multicolored	.20	.20
738	A119	30r multicolored	.30	.20

Indonesian railroad centenary (in 1967).

Tourist Type of 1967

Tourist Publicity: 30r, Butterfly dancer from West Java.

1968, July 1 *Perf. 12½*

No.	Type	Value / Description	Unused	Used
739	A113	30r gray & multi	1.00	.20
a.		Souv. sheet of 1 + label	4.00	1.10

Bosscha Observatory and Andromeda Nebula — A120

30r, Observatory, globe and sky, vert.

1968, Sept. 20 Photo. *Perf. 12½x12*

No.	Type	Value / Description	Unused	Used
740	A120	15r ultra & yellow	.30	.20
741	A120	30r violet & orange	.55	.20

Bosscha Observatory, 40th anniversary.

Weight Lifting — A121

Designs: 7.50r+7.50r, Sailing, horiz. 12r, Basketball. 30r, Dove, Olympic flame and emblem, horiz.

1968, Oct. 12 *Perf. 12½*

742 A121 5r ocher, blk & grn .20 .20
743 A121 Pair .25 .20
 a. 7.50r Left half .20 .20
 b. 7.50r Right half .20 .20
 c. Souvenir sheet 4.00 .85
744 A121 12r blue & multi .25 .20
745 A121 30r blue grn & multi .40 .20
 Nos. 742-745 (4) 1.10 .80

19th Olympic Games, Mexico City, Oct. 12-27. No. 743 is perforated vertically in the center, dividing it into two separate stamps, each inscribed "Republic Indonesia" and "7.50r." There is no gutter along the center perforation; and the design is continous over the two stamps.

No. 743c contains one No. 743 with track design surrounding the stamps.

Eugenia Aquea Burm. f. — A122

Fruits: 15r, Papaya. 30r, Durian, vert.

Perf. 12½x12, 12x12½

1968, Dec. 20 **Photo.**

746 A122 7.50r multicolored .20 .20
747 A122 15r multicolored .40 .20
 a. Souvenir sheet of 1 *2.00* .50
748 A122 30r multicolored .75 .20
 a. Souvenir sheet of 1 *4.00* 1.00
 Nos. 746-748 (3) 1.35 .60

Issued for the 11th Social Day.

Globe, ILO and UN Emblems A123

Designs: 7.50r, 25r, ILO and UN emblems.

1969, Feb. 1 **Photo.** *Perf. 12½*

749 A123 5r yel grn & scar .20 .20
750 A123 7.50r org & dk grn .20 .20
751 A123 15r lilac & org .20 .20
752 A123 25r bl grn & dull red .30 .20
 Nos. 749-752 (4) .90 .80

50th anniv. of the ILO.

R. Dewi Sartika A124

Red Crosses A125

#754, Tjoet Nja Din. #755, Tjoet Nja Meuthia. #756, General Gatot Subroto. #757, Sutan Sjahrir. #758, Dr. F. L. Tobing. #753-755 show portraits of women.

1969, Mar. 1 **Photo.** *Perf. 12½x12*

753 A124 15r green & pur .30 .20
754 A124 15r red lilac & grn .30 .20
755 A124 15r dk blue & ver .30 .20
756 A124 15r lilac & dk blue .30 .20
757 A124 15r lemon & red .30 .20
758 A124 15r pale brn & blue .30 .20
 Nos. 753-758 (6) 1.80 1.20

Heroes of Indonesian independence.

1969, May 5 **Photo.** *Perf. 12*

20r, Red Cross surrounded by arms.

759 A125 15r green & dp red .30 .20
760 A125 20r org yel & red .50 .20

50th anniversary of the League of Red Cross Societies.

"Family Planning Leads to National Development and Prosperity" — A126

Design: 10r, Family, birds and factories.

1969, June 2 **Photo.** *Perf. 12½*

761 A126 10r blue grn & org .30 .20
762 A126 20r gray & magenta .50 .20

Planned Parenthood Conference of Southeast Asia and Oceania, Bandung, June 1-7.

Map of Bali and Mask A127

Designs: 15r, Map of Bali and woman carrying basket with offerings on head. 30r, Map of Bali and cremation ceremony.

1969, July 1 **Litho.** *Perf. 12½x12*

763 A127 12r gray & multi .45 .20
764 A127 15r lilac & multi .60 .20
765 A127 30r multicolored .95 .20
 a. Souvenir sheet of 1 4.00 1.00
 Nos. 763-765 (3) 2.00 .60

Issued for tourist publicity.

Agriculture A128

Designs: 5r, Religious coexistence (roofs of mosques and churches). 10r, Social welfare (house and family). 12r, Import-export (cargo and ship). 15r, Clothing industry (cloth and spindles). 20r, Education (school children). 25r, Research (laboratory). 30r, Health care (people and syringe). 40r, Fishing (fish and net). 50r, Statistics (charts).

Radar, Djatiluhur Station — A129

1969 **Photo.** *Perf. 12x12½*

766 A128 5r yel grn & bl .20 .20
767 A128 7.50r rose brn & yel .20 .20
768 A128 10r slate & red .30 .20
769 A128 12r blue & dp org .40 .20
770 A128 15r slate grn & org .55 .20
771 A128 20r purple & yel .60 .20
772 A128 25r orange & blk .65 .20
773 A128 30r car rose & gray .70 .20
774 A128 40r green & org .95 .20
775 A128 50r sepia & org 1.00 .20
 Nos. 766-775 (10) 5.55 2.00

Five-year Development Plan.
See No. 968a.

1969, Sept. 29 *Perf. 12½*

30r, Communications satellite and earth.

776 A129 15r multicolored .35 .20
777 A129 30r multicolored .70 .20

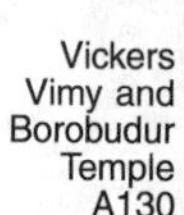

Vickers Vimy and Borobudur Temple A130

100r, Vickers Vimy and map of Indonesia.

1969, Nov. 1 *Perf. 13½x12½*

778 A130 75r dp org & dull pur .35 .20
779 A130 100r yellow & green .45 .20

50th anniv. of the 1st flight from England to Australia (via Java).

EXPO '70, Indonesian Pavilion — A131

Designs: 15r, Garuda, symbol of Indonesian EXPO '70 committee. 30r, like 5r.

1970, Feb. 15 **Photo.** *Perf. 12x12½*

780 A131 5r brown, yel & grn .40 .20
781 A131 15r dk bl, yel grn & red .80 .20
782 A131 30r red, yel & dk bl 1.40 .20
 Nos. 780-782 (3) 2.60 .60

Issued to publicize EXPO '70 International Exposition, Osaka, Japan, Mar. 15-Sept. 13.

Upraised Hands, Bars and Scales of Justice — A132

1970, Mar. 15 **Photo.** *Perf. 12½*

783 A132 10r red orange & pur .65 .20
784 A132 15r brt green & pur .80 .20

Rule of law and justice in Indonesia.

UPU Monument, Bern — A133

Dancers — A134

Design: 30r, UPU Headquarters, Bern.

1970, May 20 **Photo.** *Perf. 12x12½*

785 A133 15r emer & copper red .75 .20
786 A133 30r ocher & blue 1.25 .20

Inauguration of the new UPU Headquarters in Bern, Switzerland.

1970, July 1 **Photo.** *Perf. 12*

787 A134 20r Timor dancers 1.00 .20
788 A134 45r Bali dancers 2.25 .20
 a. Souvenir sheet of 1 7.75 1.10

Tourist publicity. No. 788a sold for 60r.

Asian Productivity Year — A135

Independence Proclamation Monument — A136

1970, Aug. 1 **Photo.** *Perf. 12*

789 A135 5r emerald, org & red .45 .20
790 A135 30r violet, org & red 1.25 .20

1970, Aug. 17

791 A136 40r lt ultra & magenta 13.50 3.50

The 25th anniversary of independence.

Post and Telecommunications Emblems — A137

Postal Worker and Telephone Dial — A138

Perf. 12x12½, 12½x12

1970, Sept. 27 **Photo.**

792 A137 10r green, ocher & yel 5.75 .20
793 A138 25r pink, blk & yel 7.75 .25

25th anniversary of the postal service.

UN Emblem A139

Education Year and UNESCO Emblems A140

1970, Oct. 10 **Photo.** *Perf. 12½*

794 A139 40r pur, red & yel grn 13.50 1.40

25th anniversary of the United Nations.

1970, Nov. 16 **Photo.** *Perf. 12½*

Design: 50r, similar to 25r, but without oval background.

795 A140 25r yel, dk red & brn 10.50 1.25
796 A140 50r lt blue, blk & red 15.00 1.90

International Education Year.

Batik Worker — A141

50r, Woman with bamboo musical instrument (angklung). 75r, Menangkabau house & family in traditional costumes.

1971, May 26 **Litho.** *Perf. 12½*

797 A141 20r multi 3.75 .20
798 A141 50r multi, vert. 5.75 .20
 a. Souvenir sheet of 1 50.00 1.50
799 A141 75r multi 8.00 .20
 Nos. 797-799 (3) 17.50 .60

"Visit Asian lands." No. 798a sold for 70r.

Fatahillah Park, Djakarta — A142

30f, City Hall. 65r, Lenong Theater performance. 80r, Ismail Marzuki Cultural Center.

1971, June 19 Photo. *Perf. 12½*
800 A142 15r yel grn, brn & bl 1.25 .35
801 A142 65r org brn, dk brn & lt grn 5.50 .35
802 A142 80r olive, bl & mag 8.00 1.00
Nos. 800-802 (3) 14.75 1.70

Souvenir Sheet

803 A142 30r bl, yel & lil rose 21.00 3.75

444th anniv. of Djakarta. #803 sold for 60r.

Rama and Sita — A143

Design: 100r, Rama with bow.

1971, Aug. 31
804 A143 30r yellow, grn & blk 1.25 .20
805 A143 100r blue, red & blk 4.50 .25

International Ramayana Festival.

Carrier Pigeon and Conference Emblem — A144

1971, Sept. 20
806 A144 50r ocher & dp brown 1.75 .20

5th Asian Regional Postal Conference.

Globes and UPU Monument, Berne — A145

1971, Oct. 4 Photo. *Perf. 13½x13*
807 A145 40r blue & dull vio 2.00 .20

Universal Postal Union Day.

Boy Writing, UNICEF Emblem — A146

40r, Boy with sheaf of rice, emblem.

1971, Dec. 11 *Perf. 12½*
808 A146 20r orange & multi 2.50 .20
809 A146 40r blue & multi 2.75 .20

25th anniv. UNICEF.

Lined Tang A147

Fish: 30r, Moorish goddess. 40r, Imperial angelfish.

1971, Dec. 27 Litho. *Perf. 12½*
810 A147 15r lilac & multi 4.75 .35
811 A147 30r dull grn & multi 11.00 .60
812 A147 40r blue & multi 12.50 1.50
Nos. 810-812 (3) 28.25 2.45

See #834-836, 859-861, 926-928, 959-961.

UN Emblem A148

Radio Tower A149

Design: 100r, Road and dam.

1972, Mar. 28 Photo. *Perf. 12½*
813 A148 40r lt grnsh bl & bl 2.25 .20
814 A149 75r dk car, yel & grnsh bl 3.00 .20
815 A148 100r green, yel & blk 4.00 .20
Nos. 813-815 (3) 9.25 .60

UN Economic Commission for Asia and the Far East (ECAFE), 25th anniv.

"Your Heart is your Health" — A150

Woman Weaver, Factories — A151

1972, Apr. 7
816 A150 50r multicolored 2.00 .20

World Health Day.

1972, Apr. 22
817 A151 35r orange, yel & pur 2.00 .20

Textile Technology Institute, 50th anniv.

Book Readers A152

1972, May 15 *Perf. 13½x12½*
818 A152 75r blue & multi 3.00 .20

International Book Year 1972.

Weather Satellite — A153

1972, July 20 Photo. *Perf. 12½*
819 A153 35r shown 2.50 .20
820 A153 50r Astronaut on moon 2.50 .20
821 A153 60r Indonesian rocket Kartika 1 5.25 .20
Nos. 819-821 (3) 10.25 .60

Space achievements.

Hotel Indonesia — A154

1972, Aug. 5
822 A154 50r grn, lt bl & car 2.60 .20

Hotel Indonesia, 10th anniversary.

Silat (Self Defense) A155

Family, Houses of Worship A156

Olympic Emblems and: 35r, Running. 50r, Diving. 75r, Badminton. 100r, Olympic Stadium.

1972, Aug. 26 Photo.
823 A155 20r lt blue & multi 1.10 .20
824 A155 35r multicolored 1.75 .20
825 A155 50r yel grn & multi 2.25 .20
826 A155 75r multicolored 3.50 .20
827 A155 100r multicolored 3.75 .20
Nos. 823-827 (5) 12.35 1.00

20th Olympic Games, Munich, 8/26-9/11.

1972, Sept. 27 *Perf. 12½x13½*

Family planning: 75r, Healthy family. 80r, Working family (national prosperity).

828 A156 30r lemon & multi 1.50 .20
829 A156 75r lilac & multi 3.75 .20
830 A156 80r multicolored 5.00 .20
Nos. 828-830 (3) 10.25 .60

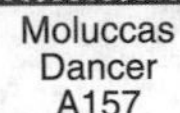

Moluccas Dancer A157

Thomas Cup, Shuttlecock A158

60r, Man, woman and Toradja house, Celebes. 100fr, West Irian house, horiz.

Perf. 12½x13½, 13½x12½

1972, Oct. 28 Photo.
831 A157 30r olive pink & brn 2.10 .20
832 A157 60r multicolored 3.75 .20
833 A157 100r lt bl, brn & dl yel 6.25 .25
Nos. 831-833 (3) 12.10 .65

Fish Type of 1971

Fish: 30r, Butterflyfish. 50r, Regal angelfish. 100r, Spotted triggerfish.

1972, Dec. 4 Litho. *Perf. 12½*
834 A147 30r blue & multi 5.00 .20
835 A147 50r blue & multi 8.00 .20
836 A147 100r blue & multi 19.00 .25
Nos. 834-836 (3) 32.00 .65

1973, Jan. 2 Litho. *Perf. 12½*

Thomas Cup, Shuttlecock and: 75r, National monument & Istora Sports Hall. 80r, Indonesian flag & badminton player.

837 A158 30r emerald & brt bl .50 .20
838 A158 75r dull grn & dk car 2.50 .20
839 A158 80r gold & red 2.50 .20
Nos. 837-839 (3) 5.50 .60

Thomas Cup Badminton World Championship 1973.

WMO Emblem, Anemometer, Wayang Figure — A159

Perf. 13½x12½

1973, Feb. 15 Litho.
840 A159 80r blue, grn & claret 2.00 .20

Cent. of intl. meteorological cooperation.

"Health Begins at Home" — A160

1973, Apr. 7 Photo. *Perf. 12½*
841 A160 80r dk grn, org & ultra 1.90 .20

25th anniv. of WHO.

Ceremonial Mask, Java — A161

1973, June 1 Photo. *Perf. 12½*
842 A161 30r shown 4.50 .20
843 A161 60r Mask, Kalimantan 8.00 .20
844 A161 100r Mask, Bali 12.50 .25
Nos. 842-844 (3) 25.00 .65

Tourist publicity.

Hand Putting Coin into Bank — A162

1973, July 2 Photo. *Perf. 12½*

30r, Symbolic coin bank and hand, horiz.

845 A162 25r yellow, lt brn & blk 1.10 .20
846 A162 30r green, yel & gold 1.60 .20

National savings movement.

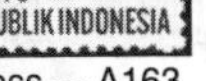

Chess — A163

INTERPOL Emblem and Policemen — A164

8th National Sports Week: 60r, Karate. 75r, Hurdling, horiz.

1973, Aug. 4 Photo. *Perf. 12½*
847 A163 30r red, yellow & blk 2.00 .20
848 A163 60r black, ocher & lt grn 2.50 .20
849 A163 75r black, lt bl & rose 4.00 .35
Nos. 847-849 (3) 8.50 .75

1973, Sept. 3

Design: 50r, INTERPOL emblem and guard statue from Sewu Prambanan Temple, vert.

850 A164 30r yellow, grn & blk 1.40 .20
851 A164 50r yellow, brn & blk 2.00 .20

50th anniv. of Intl. Police Organization.

Batik Worker and Parang Rusak Pattern A165

Batik designs: 80r, Man and Pagi Sore pattern. 100r, Man and Merak Ngigel pattern.

1973, Oct. 9 Photo. *Perf. 12½*

852	A165	60r multicolored	4.00	.20
853	A165	80r multicolored	4.75	.20
854	A165	100r multicolored	6.25	.25
		Nos. 852-854 (3)	15.00	.65

Farmer, Grain, UN and FAO Emblems — A166

1973, Oct. 24 Photo. *Perf. 12½*

855	A166	30r lilac & multi	2.50	.20

World Food Program, 10th anniversary.

Houses of Worship — A167

Family planning: 30r, Classroom. 60r, Family and home.

1973, Nov. 10

856	A167	20r dk bl, lt bl & ver	1.10	.20
857	A167	30r ocher, blk & yel	1.40	.20
858	A167	60r lt grn, yel & blk	3.00	.20
		Nos. 856-858 (3)	5.50	.60

Fish Type of 1971

Fish: 40r, Acanthurus leucosternon. 65r, Chaetodon trifasciatus. 100r, Pomacanthus annularis.

1973, Dec. 10 Litho. *Perf. 12½*

859	A147	40r multicolored	3.25	.20
860	A147	65r multicolored	4.75	.20
861	A147	100r multicolored	8.00	.30
		Nos. 859-861 (3)	16.00	.70

Adm. Sudarso and Battle of Arafuru — A168

1974, Jan. 15

862	A168	40r brt blue & multi	2.50	.20

12th Navy Day.

Bengkulu Costume A169

Designs: Regional Costumes.

1974, Mar. 28 Litho. *Perf. 12½*

863	A169	5r shown	14.00	1.10
864	A169	7.50r Kalimantan, Timor	8.00	1.10
865	A169	10r Kalimantan, Tengah	4.75	.80
866	A169	15r Jambi	1.25	.80
867	A169	20r Sulawesi, Tenggara	1.25	.80
868	A169	25r Nusatenggara, Timor	1.40	.80
869	A169	27.50r Maluku	1.40	*2.50*
870	A169	30r Lampung	1.40	*1.50*
871	A169	35r Sumatra, Barat	1.40	.80
872	A169	40r Aceh	1.40	.80
873	A169	45r Nusatenggara, Barat	3.50	.80
874	A169	50r Riouw	2.75	*2.00*
875	A169	55r Kalimantan, Barat	2.75	.80
876	A169	60r Sulawesi, Utara	2.75	.80
877	A169	65r Sulawesi, Tengah	2.75	.80
878	A169	70r Sumatra, Selatan	2.75	.80
879	A169	75r Java, Barat	2.75	.80
880	A169	80r Sumatra, Utara	2.75	.80
881	A169	90r Yogyakarta	2.75	*5.00*
882	A169	95r Kalimantan, Selatan	2.75	.80
883	A169	100r Java, Timor	2.75	1.60
884	A169	120r Irian, Java	7.00	1.10
885	A169	130r Java, Tengah	7.00	.80
886	A169	135r Sulawesi, Selatan	6.25	.80
887	A169	150r Bali	6.25	.80
888	A169	160r Djakarta	6.25	1.60
		Nos. 863-888 (26)	100.00	31.10

Baladewa A170

Designs (Figures from Shadow Plays): 80r, Kresna. 100r, Bima.

1974, June 1 Photo. *Perf. 12½*

889	A170	40r lt violet & multi	3.25	.20
890	A170	80r salmon & multi	5.75	.20
891	A170	100r rose	7.00	.20
		Nos. 889-891 (3)	16.00	.60

Pres. Suharto A171

Family and WPY Emblem A172

1974-76 Photo. *Perf. 12½*

Portrait in Dark Brown

901	A171	40r lt green & blk	.40	.20
903	A171	50r ultra & blk	.80	.20
906	A171	65r brt pink & blk	1.10	.20
908	A171	75r yellow & blk	1.40	.20
912	A171	100r buff & blk	1.90	.20
913	A171	150r citron & blk	2.75	.30
914	A171	200r green & blue	3.25	.40
915	A171	300r brn org & car	5.50	.55
916	A171	400r green & yellow	7.50	.75
917	A171	500r lilac & car	9.25	1.00
		Nos. 901-917 (10)	33.85	4.00

#914-917 have wavy lines in background.

Issued: #901-913, 8/17/74; #914-917, 8/17/76.

1974, Aug. 19

918	A172	65r ultra, gray & ocher	1.60	.20

World Population Year 1974.

"Welfare" A173

"Development" A174

"Religion" A175

1974, Sept. 9

919	A173	25r green & multi	.80	.20
920	A174	40r yellow grn & multi	1.60	.20
921	A175	65r dk vio brn & multi	2.25	.20
		Nos. 919-921 (3)	4.65	.60

Family planning.

Mailmen with Bicycles, UPU Emblem — A176

UPU cent.: 40r, Horse-drawn mail cart. 65r, Mailman on horseback. 100r, Sailing ship, 18th century.

1974, Oct. 9

922	A176	20r dk green & multi	.90	.20
923	A176	40r dull blue & multi	1.10	.20
924	A176	65r black brn & yel	2.50	.20
925	A176	100r maroon & multi	4.50	.20
		Nos. 922-925 (4)	9.00	.80

Fish Type of 1971

Fish: 40fr, Zebrasoma veliferum. 80r, Euxiphipops navarchus. 100r, Synchiropus splendidus.

1974, Oct. 30 Photo. *Perf. 12½*

926	A147	40r blue & multi	4.00	.20
927	A147	80r blue & multi	6.00	.20
928	A147	100r blue & multi	6.00	.20
		Nos. 926-928 (3)	16.00	.60

Drill Team Searching for Oil — A177

Designs (Pertamina Emblem and): 75r, Oil refinery. 95r, Pertamina telecommunications and computer center. 100r, Gasoline truck and station. 120r, Plane over storage tanks. 130r, Pipes and tanker. 150r, Petro-chemical storage tanks. 200r, Off-shore drilling platform. 95r, 100r, 120r, 130r, vertical.

1974, Dec. 10 *Perf. 13½*

929	A177	40r black & multi	.25	.20
930	A177	75r black & multi	.45	.20
931	A177	95r black & multi	.70	.20
932	A177	100r black & multi	.70	.20
933	A177	120r black & multi	.85	.25
934	A177	130r black & multi	.90	.25
935	A177	150r black & multi	1.10	.30
936	A177	200r black & multi	1.50	.40
		Nos. 929-936 (8)	6.45	2.00

Pertamina State Oil Enterprise, 17th anniv.

Spittoon, Sumatra A178

Artistic Metalware: 75r, Condiment dish, Sumatra. 100r, Condiment dish, Kalimantan.

1975, Feb. 24 Photo. *Perf. 12½*

937	A178	50r red & black	1.90	.20
938	A178	75r green & black	2.25	.20
939	A178	100r brt blue & multi	3.75	.20
		Nos. 937-939 (3)	7.90	.60

Blood Donors' Emblem A179

Globe, Standard Meter and Kilogram A180

1975, Apr. 7

940	A179	40r yellow, red & grn	1.40	.20

"Give blood, save lives."

1975, May 20

941	A180	65r blue, red & yel	2.50	.20

Cent. of Intl. Meter Convention, Paris, 1875.

Farmer, Teacher, Mother, Policewoman and Nurse — A181

IWY Emblem — A182

1975, June 26 Photo. *Perf. 12½*

942	A181	40r multicolored	1.25	.20
943	A182	100r multicolored	2.75	.20

International Women's Year 1975.

Dendrobium Pakarena A183

Stupas and Damaged Temple — A184

Orchids: 70r, Aeridachnis bogor. 85r, Vanda genta.

1975, July 21

944	A183	40r multicolored	3.50	.20
945	A183	70r multicolored	5.50	.20
946	A183	85r multicolored	9.50	.25
		Nos. 944-946 (3)	18.50	.65

See Nos. 1010-1012, 1036-1038.

1975, Aug. 10 *Perf. 12½*

Designs (UNESCO Emblem and): 40r, Buddha statues, stupas and damaged wall. 65r,

Stupas and damaged wall, horiz. 100r, Buddha statue and stupas, horiz.

947 A184 25r yellow, brn & org 2.60 .20
948 A184 40r black, grn & yel 4.25 .20
949 A184 65r lemon, cl & grn 8.50 .20
950 A184 100r bister, brn & sl bl 12.50 .20
Nos. 947-950 (4) 27.85 .80

UNESCO campaign to save Borobudur Temple, Java.

Banjarmasin Battle — A185

Battle Scenes: 40r, Batua, 9/8/46. 75r, Margarana, 11/20/46. 100r, Palembang, 1/1/47.

1975, Aug. 17
951 A185 25r yellow & blk .55 .20
952 A185 40r org ver & red .95 .20
953 A185 75r vermilion & blk 1.75 .20
954 A185 100r orange & blk 2.75 .20
Nos. 951-954 (4) 6.00 .80

Indonesian independence, 30th anniversary.

"Education" A186

Heroes' Monument, Surabaya A187

Family plannings: 25r, "Religion." 40r, "Prosperity."

1975, Oct. 20 Photo. *Perf. 12½*
955 A186 20r blue, salmon & blk 1.00 .20
956 A186 25r emerald, sal & blk 1.25 .20
957 A186 40r dp org, blue & blk 1.50 .20
Nos. 955-957 (3) 3.75 .60

1975, Nov. 10
958 A187 100r maroon & green 3.00 .25

War of independence, 30th anniversary.

Fish Type of 1971

Fish: 40r, Coris angulata. 75r, Chaetodon ephippium. 150r, Platax pinnatus, vert.

1975, Dec. 15 Litho. *Perf. 12½*
959 A147 40r multicolored 2.25 .20
960 A147 75r multicolored 4.25 .20
961 A147 150r multicolored 8.50 .30
Nos. 959-961 (3) 15.00 .70

Thomas Cup — A188

40r, Uber Cup. 100r, Thomas & Uber Cups.

1976, Jan. 31 Photo. *Perf. 12½*
962 A188 20r blue & multi .75 .20
963 A188 40r multicolored 1.10 .20
964 A188 100r green & multi 2.75 .20
Nos. 962-964 (3) 4.60 .60

Indonesia, Badminton World Champions.

Refugees on Truck and New Village — A189

Designs: 50r, Neglected and restored village streets. 100r, Derelict and rebuilt houses.

1976, Feb. 28 Photo. *Perf. 12½*
965 A189 30r yellow & multi .75 .20
966 A189 50r blue & multi 1.25 .20
967 A189 100r ocher & multi 2.25 .20
Nos. 965-967 (3) 4.25 .60

World Human Settlements Day.

Telephones, 1876 and 1976 — A190

1976, Mar. 10 Photo. *Perf. 12½*
968 A190 100r yel, org & brn 1.60 .20
a. Bklt. pane of 8, 4 #968, 4 #775 + 2 labels ('78) 7.75

Centenary of first telephone call by Alexander Graham Bell, Mar. 10, 1876.
Stamps from #968a have straight edges.

Eye and WHO Emblem — A191

Design: 40r, Blind man, eye and World Health Organization emblem.

1976, Apr. 7 Photo. *Perf. 12½*
969 A191 20r yel, lt grn & blk .75 .20
970 A191 40r yel, blue & blk .95 .20

Foresight prevents blindness.

Montreal Stadium — A192

1976, May 17
971 A192 100r ultra 1.60 .20

21st Olympic Games, Montreal, Canada, July 17-Aug. 1.

Lake Tondano, Celebes — A193

Tourist publicity: 40r, Lake Kelimutu, Flores. 75r, Lake Maninjau, Sumatra.

1976, June 1
972 A193 35r lt green & blk .90 .20
973 A193 40r gray, rose & lt grn 1.10 .20
974 A193 75r blue & sl grn 2.00 .20
a. Bklt. pane of 8 (7 #974, #998, 2 labels) ('78) 7.75
Nos. 972-974 (3) 4.00 .60

Stamps from #974a have straight edges.

Radar Station — A194

Designs: 50r, Master control radar station. 100r, Apalata satellite.

1976, July 8 Photo. *Perf. 12½*
975 A194 20r multicolored .65 .20
976 A194 50r green & blk 1.25 .20
977 A194 100r multicolored 2.25 .20
a. Bklt. pane of 9 (4 #977, 5 #987, label) ('78) 13.50
Nos. 975-977 (3) 4.15 .60

Inauguration of domestic satellite system. Stamps from #977a have straight edges.

Arachnis Flos-aeris — A195

Orchids: 40r, Vanda putri serang. 100r, Coelogyne pandurata.

1976, Sept. 7
978 A195 25r multicolored 1.40 .20
a. Souvenir sheet of 1 *72.50*
979 A195 40r multicolored 2.00 .20
980 A195 100r multicolored 6.00 .40
Nos. 978-980 (3) 9.40 .80

Tree and Mountain — A196

1976, Oct. 4
981 A196 20r green, blue & brn 1.10 .20

16th National Reforestation Week.

Dagger and Sheath from Timor — A197

Historic Daggers and Sheaths: 40r, from Borneo. 100r, from Aceh.

1976, Nov. 1 *Perf. 12½*
982 A197 25r multicolored 1.25 .20
983 A197 40r multicolored 2.00 .20
a. Souvenir sheet of 1, imperf 9.00 5.75
984 A197 100r green & multi 4.00 .40
Nos. 982-984 (3) 7.25 .80

No. 983a exists perf. Value *$21.*

Open Book A198

Children Reading A199

1976, Dec. 8 Photo. *Perf. 12½*
985 A198 20r multicolored .80 .20
986 A199 40r multicolored 1.50 .20

Better books for children.

UNICEF Emblem A200

Ballot Box A201

1976, Dec. 11
987 A200 40r multicolored 1.50 .20

UNICEF, 30th anniv.

1977, Jan. 5 Photo. *Perf. 12½*

1977 elections: 75r, Ballot box, grain and factory. 100r, Coat of arms.

988 A201 40r multicolored 1.50 .20
989 A201 75r multicolored 3.00 .20
990 A201 100r multicolored 4.00 .25
Nos. 988-990 (3) 8.50 .65

Camp and Flags Scout Emblems, A202

Designs: 30r, Tent, emblems and trees. 40r, Boy and Girl Scout flags and emblems.

1977, Feb. 28
991 A202 25r multicolored 1.60 .20
992 A202 30r multicolored 1.75 .20
993 A202 40r multicolored 2.00 .20
Nos. 991-993 (3) 5.35 .60

11th National Scout Jamboree.

Letter with "AOPU" — A203

Anniversary Emblem, Djakarta Arms — A204

Design: 100r, Stylized bird and letter.

1977, Apr. 1 Photo. *Perf. 12½*
994 A203 65r multicolored 1.00 .20
995 A203 100r multicolored 1.50 .20

Asian-Oceanic Postal Union, 15th convention.

1977, May 23 Photo. *Perf. 12½*

Designs: Anniversary emblem and arms of Djakarta in different arrangements.

996 A204 20r orange & blue .75 .20
997 A204 40r emerald & blue 1.00 .20
998 A204 100r slate & blue 2.00 .25
a. Souvenir sheet of 1 *7.00* 1.50
Nos. 996-998 (3) 3.75 .65

450th anniversary of Djakarta. No. 998a also issued imperf.

Rose — A205

Various Sports Emblems — A206

1977, May 26 Photo. *Perf. 12½*
999 A205 100r shown 2.00 .30
a. Souvenir sheet 8.00 2.00

1000 A205 100r Envelope 2.00 .30
a. Souvenir sheet of 4 9.50 3.25
b. Pair, Nos. 999-1000 4.00 .60

Amphilex 77 Phil. Exhib., Amsterdam, May 26-June 5. No. 999a contains one stamp similar to No. 999 with blue background. No. 1000a contains 2 each of Nos. 999-1000.
Nos. 999a, 1000a exist imperf.
See No. 1013a.

1977, June 22

9th Natl. Sports Week: 50r, 100r, Different sports emblems.

1001 A206 40r silver & multi 2.25 .20
1002 A206 50r silver & multi 3.25 .20
1003 A206 100r gold & multi 8.00 .45
Nos. 1001-1003 (3) 13.50 .85

Contest Trophy A207

Emblem A208

1977, July 20
1004 A207 40r green & multi 1.90 .20
1005 A208 100r yellow & multi 3.75 .30

10th Natl. Koran Reading Contest, 7/20-27.

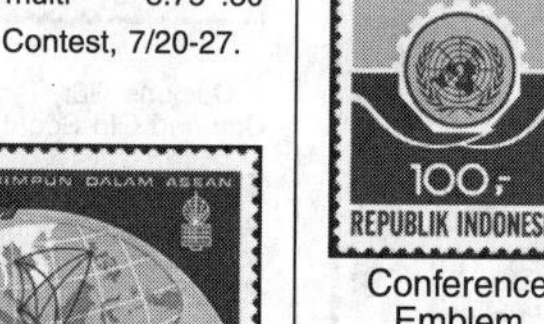

Map of ASEAN Countries, Satellite — A209

35r, Map of ASEAN countries. 50r, Flags of founding members: Indonesia, Malaysia, Philippines, Singapore & Thailand; ship, plane & train.

1977, Aug. 8
1006 A209 25r multicolored 1.50 .20
1007 A209 35r multicolored 1.90 .20
1008 A209 50r multicolored 2.50 .20
Nos. 1006-1008 (3) 5.90 .60

Association of South East Asian Nations (ASEAN), 10th anniversary.

Uniform, Jakarta Regiment A210

1977, Aug. 19
1009 A210 25r green, gold & brn .65 .20

Indonesia-Pakistan Economic and Cultural Organization, 1968-1977.

Orchid Type of 1975

Orchids: 25r, Taeniophyllum. 40r, Phalaenopsis violacea. 100r, Dendrobium spectabile.

1977, Oct. 28 Photo. *Perf. 12½*
1010 A183 25r orange & multi 1.75 .20
1011 A183 40r blue & multi 2.75 .20
1012 A183 100r yel grn & multi 5.75 .25
a. Souvenir sheet of 1, imperf 12.00 1.90
Nos. 1010-1012 (3) 10.25 .65

No. 1012a contains one stamp similar to No. 1012 with blue background. No. 1012a exists perf. Value *$16.*

Child and Mosquito A211

1977, Nov. 7 *Perf. 12½*
1013 A211 40r brt grn, red & blk .60 .20
a. Bklt. pane of 9+label (4 #999, 5 #1013) ('78) 7.75

Natl. Health campaign to eradicate malaria.
Stamps from #1013a have straight edges.
Issue date: No. 1013a, Sept. 27, 1978.

Proboscis Monkey — A212

Designs: 40r, Indian elephant. 100r, Tiger.

1977, Dec. 22
1014 A212 20r multicolored .70 .20
1015 A212 40r multicolored 1.40 .20
1016 A212 100r multicolored 5.50 .90
a. Souvenir sheet of 1 6.75 2.25
Nos. 1014-1016 (3) 7.60 1.30

Wildlife protection. #1016a exists imperf.

Conference Emblem A213

Mother and Child A214

1978, Mar. 27 Photo. *Perf. 12½*
1017 A213 100r lt blue & ultra 1.25 .25

United Nations Conference on Technical Cooperation among Developing Countries.

1978, Apr. 7 Photo. *Perf. 12½*

75r, Mother and child, symbolic design.

1018 A214 40r lt green & blue .65 .20
1019 A214 75r orange red & brn 1.00 .20

Promotion of breast feeding.

Dome of The Rock, Jerusalem — A215

1978, May 15 Photo. *Perf. 12½*
1020 A215 100r multicolored 1.50 .20

Palestinian fighters and their families.

Argentina '78 Emblem A216

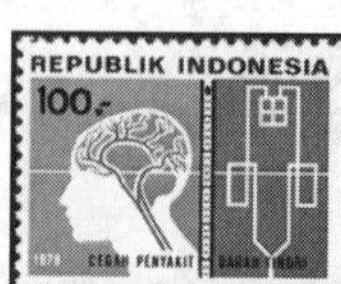

Head and "Blood Circulation" A217

1978, June 1
1021 A216 40r multicolored .55 .20
1022 A216 100r multicolored 1.40 .20

11th World Cup Soccer Championships, Argentina, June 1-25.

1978, June 17 Photo. *Perf. 12½*
1023 A217 100r black, blue & red 1.25 .20

World Health Day and drive against hypertension.

Leather Puppets — A218

Art from Wayang Museum, Djakarta: 75r, Wooden puppets. 100r, Actors with puppet masks.

1978, July 22 Litho. *Perf. 12½*
1024 A218 40r multicolored 1.75 .20
1025 A218 75r multicolored 4.00 .30
1026 A218 100r multicolored 4.25 .40
Nos. 1024-1026 (3) 10.00 .90

Congress Emblem A219

IAAY Emblem A220

1978, Aug. 1
1027 A219 100r slate 1.25 .20

27th Congress of World Confederation of Organizations of Teachers (WCOTP), Djakarta, June 26-Aug. 2.

1978, Aug. 16 Photo. *Perf. 12½*
1028 A220 100r org & dk blue 1.50 .20

International Anti-Apartheid Year.

Congress Emblem A221

Youth Pledge Emblem A222

Design: 100r, People and trees.

1978, Oct. 16 Photo. *Perf. 12½*
1029 A221 40r emerald & blue .30 .20
1030 A221 100r emerald & blk .95 .20

8th World Forestry Congress, Djakarta.

1978, Oct. 28
1031 A222 40r dk brown & red .45 .20
1032 A222 100r salmon, brn & red 1.60 .20

50th anniv. of Youth Pledge. See #1044a.

Wildlife Protection — A223

1978, Nov. 1
1033 A223 40r Porcupine anteater 1.60 .20
1034 A223 75r Deer 2.75 .25
a. Souv. sheet of 5, #1034, 4 #1035 + label 13.00
1035 A223 100r Clouded tiger 4.50 .30
a. Souvenir sheet of 1 4.50
Nos. 1033-1035 (3) 8.85 .75

Stamps in No. 1034a are in changed colors. Souvenir sheets inscribed for Essen 2nd Intl. Stamp Fair.

Orchid Type of 1975

Orchids: 40r, Phalaenopsis sri rejeki. 75r, Dendrobium macrophilium. 100r, Cymbidium fynlaysonianum.

1978, Dec. 22 Photo. *Perf. 12½*
1036 A183 40r multicolored 1.25 .20
1037 A183 75r multicolored 2.25 .20
1038 A183 100r multicolored 3.50 .20
a. Souvenir sheet of 1 4.25 1.50
Nos. 1036-1038 (3) 7.00 .60

Douglas DC-3, 1949, over Volcano — A224

Designs: 75r, Douglas DC-9 over village. 100r, Douglas DC-10 over temple.

1979, Jan. 26 Photo. *Perf. 12½*
1039 A224 40r multicolored .75 .20
1040 A224 75r multicolored 1.25 .20
1041 A224 100r multicolored 2.25 .20
Nos. 1039-1041 (3) 4.25 .60

Garuda Indonesian Airways, 30th anniv.

A225

40r, Thomas Cup and badminton player.

1979, Feb. 24 Photo. *Perf. 12½*
1042 A225 40r Thomas Cup & player .50 .20
1043 A225 100r Player hitting ball 1.10 .20
1044 A225 100r Player facing left 1.40 .20
a. Pair, #1043-1044 2.50
b. Blkt. pane, 3 each #1032, 1043-1044 + label 7.75
Nos. 1042-1044 (3) 3.00 .60

11th Thomas Cup, Djakarta, May 24-June 2.
#1044a forms a continuous design.
Stamps from #1044b have straight edges.

Paphiopedilum Lowii — A227

Orchids: 100r, 300r, Vanda limbata. 125r, Phalaenopsis gigantea. 250r, as 60r.

1979, Mar. 22 Photo. *Perf. 12½*
1045 A227 60r multi 1.40 .20
1046 A227 100r multi 2.00 .30
1047 A227 125r multi 2.75 .35
a. Souvenir sheet of 1 4.25
b. Souv. sheet of 2 (250r, 300r) 10.00
Nos. 1045-1047 (3) 6.15 .85

No. 1047b, issued for Asian Phil. Exhib., Dortmund, West Germany, May 24-27. Sold for 650r.

Family and Houses — A228

Third Five-year Plan: 60r, Pylon and fields. 100r, School and clinic. 125r, Factories and trucks. 150r, Motorized mail delivery.

1979-82

1047C A228 12.50r Plane, food ('80) .20 .20
1047D A228 17.50r Bridge ('82) .20 .20
1048 A228 35r green & olive .20 .20
1049 A228 60r blue & olive .35 .20
1050 A228 100r blue & dk brn .60 .20
1051 A228 125r red brn & ol .85 .25
1052 A228 150r carmine & yel .90 .30
Nos. 1047C-1052 (7) 3.30 1.55

See No. 1058a.

R. A. Kartini and Girls' School A229

1979, Apr. 21 Photo. *Perf. 12½*
1053 A229 100r Kartini 1.00 .30
1054 A229 100r School 1.00 .30
a. Pair, #1053-1054 2.00 .75

Mrs. R. A. Kartini, educator, birth centenary.

Bureau of Education, UNESCO Emblems — A231

1979, May 25 Photo. *Perf. 12½*
1055 A231 150r multicolored 1.90 .20

50th anniversary of the statutes of the International Bureau of Education.

Self Defense A232

Cooperation Emblem A233

Designs: 125r, Games' emblem. 150r, Senayan Main Stadium.

1979, June 21 Photo. *Perf. 12½*
1056 A232 60r multicolored .60 .20
1057 A232 125r multicolored 1.10 .25
1058 A232 150r multicolored 1.50 .30
a. Bklt. pane of 6+4 labels (#1052, 5 #1058) 7.75
Nos. 1056-1058 (3) 3.20 .75

10th So. East Asia Games, Djakarta, Sept. 21-30.
Stamps from #1058a have straight edges.
Issue date: No. 1058a, Sept. 27.

1979, July 12 Photo. *Perf. 12½*
1059 A233 150r multicolored 1.25 .25

32nd Indonesian Cooperative Day.

A234

Designs: 60r, IYC and natl. IYC emblems. 150r, IYC emblem.

1979, Aug. 4 Photo. *Perf. 12½*
1060 A234 60r emerald & blk .55 .20
1061 A234 150r blue & blk 1.00 .25

International Year of the Child.

A235

1979, Sept. 20 Photo. *Perf. 12½*
1062 A235 150r TELECOM 79 1.25 .25

3rd World Telecommunications Exhibition, Geneva, Sept. 20-26.

Fight Drug Abuse — A236

1979, Oct. 17 Photo. *Perf. 12½*
1063 A236 150r deep rose & blk 1.25 .30

Dolphin — A237

Wildlife Protection: 125r, Freshwater dolphin. 150r, Leatherback turtle.

1979, Nov. 24 Photo. *Perf. 12½*
1064 A237 60r multi 1.40 .20
1065 A237 125r multi 2.75 .20
1066 A237 150r multi 4.25 .25
Nos. 1064-1066 (3) 8.40 .65

Souvenir Sheet

1066A A237 200r like #1066 6.00 .40

Ship Made of Cloves — A238

Spice Race, Jakarta-Amsterdam (Sailing Ships): 60r, Penisi, vert. 150r, Madurese boat, vert.

1980, Mar. 12 Photo. *Perf. 12½*
1067 A238 60r bright blue .50 .20
1068 A238 125r red brown 1.00 .20
1069 A238 150r red lilac 1.50 .25
Nos. 1067-1069 (3) 3.00 .65

1980

Souvenir Sheets

1069A A238 300r like #1068 5.50 1.10
1069B A238 500r like #1067 7.50 1.75

Issue dates: 300r, Mar. 12. 500r, May 6. 500r for London 1980 Intl. Stamp Exhib.

Rubber Raft in Rapids A239

Perf. 13½x13, 13x13½

1980, Mar. 21 Photo.
1070 A239 60r shown .40 .20
1071 A239 125r Mountain climbing, vert. 1.10 .20
1072 A239 150r Hang gliding, vert. 1.50 .25
Nos. 1070-1072 (3) 3.00 .65

Souvenir Sheet

1072A A239 300r like #1070 5.00 .75

A240

A241

1980, Apr. 15 *Perf. 12½*
1073 A240 150r multicolored 1.25 .30

Anti-smoking Campaign.

1980, Apr. 21 Photo. *Perf. 12½*
1074 A241 125r Flowers In vase 1.10 .20
1075 A241 150r Bouquet 1.60 .25

2nd Flower Festival, Jakarta, Apr. 19-21.
See No. 1080a-1080b.

A242

A243

1980, Apr. 24 *Perf. 13x13½*

Conference building.

1076 A242 150r gold & lil rose 1.50 .25

Souvenir Sheet

1076A A242 300r multicolored 4.50 .75

1st Asian-African Conf., 25th anniv.

1980, May 2 *Perf. 12½*

Designs: 60r, Male figure. 125r, Elephant stone. 150r, Taman Bali Stone Sarcophagus, 2000 B.C.

1077 A243 60r multicolored .65 .20
1078 A243 125r multicolored 1.25 .20
1079 A243 150r multicolored 1.75 .25
Nos. 1077-1079 (3) 3.65 .65

Flower and Sculpture Types of 1980
Souvenir Sheet

1980 Photo. *Perf. 12½*
1080 Sheet of 8 17.00 3.00
a. A241 100r like #1074 1.10 .20
b. A241 100r like #1075 1.10 .20
c. A243 200r like #1077 2.00 .45
d. A243 200r like #1079 2.00 .45

London 1980 Intl. Stamp Exhib., May 6-14. No. 1080 contains 2 stamps of each design (4x2).

Draftsman in Wheelchair A244

Discus Thrower A245

1980, May 18 Photo. *Perf. 12½*
1081 A244 100r multicolored 1.00 .20

Disabled Veterans Corp, 30th anniversary.

1980, May 18
1082 A245 75r dp orange & sep 1.00 .20

Olympics for the Disabled, Arnhem, Netherlands, June 21-July 5.

Pres. Suharto — A246

A246a

A246b

Perf. 13½x12½, 12½

1980-83 Photo.
1083 A246 12.50r lt grn & grn .20 .20
1084 A246 50r lt grn & bl .40 .20
1084A A246 55r red rose & red lil .20 .20
1085 A246 75r lem & gldn brn .55 .20
1086 A246 100r brt pink & bl .60 .20
a. Bklt pane of 8 + 2 labels (6 #1086, 2 #1088, Inscribed 1981) 6.00
1087 A246a 110r dull org & dp red lil .30 .20
1088 A246 200r dull org & brn 1.10 .40
1088A A246a 250r dull org & brn 2.25 .50
1089 A246a 275r lt ap grn & dk grn .90 .20
1090 A246 300r rose lil & gold 2.75 .60
1091 A246 400r multicolored 3.75 .80

Engr.

Perf. 12½x13

1092 A246b 500r dk red brown 3.75 1.00
Nos. 1083-1092 (12) 16.75 4.70

Issued: 12.50r, 50r, 75r, 100r, 200r, 6/8; 300r, 400r, 8/8/81; 250r, 9/82; 500r, 3/11/83; 55r, 7/83; 110r, 275r, 9/27/83.
See Nos. 1257-1261, 1265, 1268. For surcharge see No. 1527.

Map of Indonesia, People — A247

1980, July 17 *Perf. 12½*
1093 A247 75r blue & pink .45 .20
1094 A247 200r blue & dull yel 1.50 .40

1980 population census.

Ship Laying Cable — A248

1980, Aug. 8 Photo. *Perf. 12½*
1095 A248 75r multicolored .45 .20
1096 A248 200r multicolored 1.50 .40

Singapore-Indonesia submarine cable opening.

50s Stamp of 1946 — A249

100r, 15s Battle of Surabaya stamp, 1946, horiz. 200r, 15s Independence Fund stamp, 1946.

1980, Aug. 17
1097 A249 75r dk brn & dp org .60 .20
1098 A249 100r gold & purple 1.00 .20
1099 A249 200r multicolored 1.90 .40
Nos. 1097-1099 (3) 3.50 .80

Independence, 35th anniversary.

Asian Oceanic Postal Training School — A250

OPEC Anniv. Emblem — A251

1980, Sept. 10 Photo. *Perf. 12½*
1100 A250 200r multicolored 1.50 .40

1980, Sept. 14
1101 A251 200r multicolored 1.60 .40

Organization of Petroleum Exporting Countries, 20th anniversary.

Armed Forces, 35th Anniversary — A252

1980, Oct. 5 Photo. *Perf. 13½x13*
1102 A252 75r shown .45 .20
1103 A252 200r Service men and emblem 1.25 .40

Vulturine Parrot — A253

One Day Beauty Orchid — A254

Designs: Parrots.

1980, Nov. 25 Photo. *Perf. 13x12½*
1104 A253 75r shown 1.90 .20
1105 A253 100r Yellow-backed lory 3.50 .25
1106 A253 200r Red lory 6.50 .55
Nos. 1104-1106 (3) 11.90 1.00

Souvenir Sheet
Perf. 12½
1106A Sheet of 3 21.00 2.50
b. A253 250r like #1105 3.75 .50
c. A253 350r like #1104 6.00 .70
d. A253 400r like #1106 6.75 .80

1980, Dec. 10 *Perf. 13x13½*
Designs: Orchids.
1107 A254 75r *shown* 1.25 .20
1108 A254 100r *Dendrobium discolor* 2.50 .20
1109 A254 200r *Dendrobium lasianthera* 4.50 .40
Nos. 1107-1109 (3) 8.25 .80

Souvenir Sheet
1980 *Perf. 13x13½*
1110 Sheet of 2 19.00 1.75
a. A254 250r like #1109 8.00 .65
b. A254 350r like #1108 10.50 1.00

Heinrich von Stephan (1831-1897), UPU Founder — A255

1981, Jan. 7 *Perf. 13½x12½*
1111 A255 200r brt bl & dk bl 1.25 .35

6th Asian Pacific Scout Jamboree A256

1981 *Perf. 13½x12½, 12½x13½*
1112 A256 75r Emblems .65 .20
1113 A256 100r Scouts, vert. 1.00 .20
1114 A256 200r Emblems, diff. 1.60 .40
Nos. 1112-1114 (3) 3.25 .80

Souvenir Sheet
1115 A256 150r like #1113 5.50 .60

Issued: #1112-1114, 2/22; #1115, 8/14.

4th Asian-Oceanian Postal Union Congress A257

Blood Donor Campaign A258

1981, Mar. 18 *Perf. 12½*
1116 A257 200r multicolored 1.75 .40

1981, Apr. 22
1117 A258 75r Girl holding blood drop .50 .20
1118 A258 100r Hands holding blood drop .90 .20
1119 A258 200r Hands, blood, diff. 1.60 .40
Nos. 1117-1119 (3) 3.00 .80

Intl. Family Planning Conference — A259

1981, Apr. 26
1120 A259 200r multicolored 1.00 .40

Natl. Education Day — A260

Traditional Bali Paintings: Nos. 1121-1122, Song of Sritanjung. No. 1123, Birth of the Eagle.

1981, May 2
1121 100r multicolored 1.10 .20
1122 200r multicolored 2.10 .40
a. A260 Pair #1121-1122 3.20 .60

Souvenir Sheet
1123 Sheet of 2 12.00 3.00
a. A260 400r multicolored 3.50 .75
b. A261 600r multicolored 6.00 1.25

No. 1123 has margin showing WIPA '81 emblem. Sheets exist with marginal inscription "Indonesien grusst WIPA."

A262

A263

1981, May 9
1124 A262 200r multicolored 1.75 .40

ASEAN Building Jakarta, opening.

1981, May 22
1125 A263 200r multicolored 3.00 .40

Uber Cup '81 Badminton Championship, Tokyo.

World Environment Day — A264

Bas-reliefs, Candhi Merut Buddhist Temple, Central Java: 75r, Tree of Life. 200r, Reclining Buddha.

1981, June 5
1126 A264 75r multicolored .50 .20
1127 A264 200r multicolored 1.50 .40

12th Koran Reading Competition, June 7-14 — A265

1981, June 7 *Perf. 13½x12½*
1128 A265 200r multicolored 1.25 .40

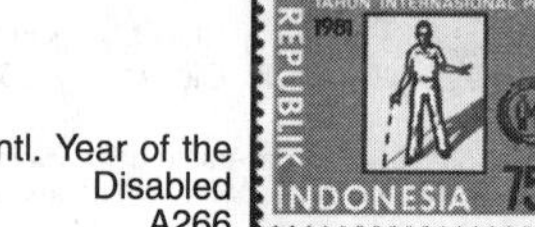

Intl. Year of the Disabled A266

1981, July 31 *Perf. 12½*
1129 A266 75r Blind man .45 .20
1130 A266 200r Speech, hearing disabilities 1.10 .40

Soekarno-Hatta Independence Monument, Jakarta — A267

1981, Aug. 17
1131 A267 200r multicolored 1.75 .40

Natl. Sports Week, Sept. 19-30 — A268

World Food Day — A268a

1981, Sept. 19
1132 A268 75r Skydiving .50 .20
1133 A268 100r Skin diving, horiz. .90 .20
1134 A268 200r Equestrian 1.60 .40
Nos. 1132-1134 (3) 3.00 .80

The horse on No. 1134 is brown black, See Nos. 1374-1375 for souvenir sheets containing No. 1134 in different colors.

1981, Oct. 16
1135 A268a 200r multicolored 3.50 .40

Provincial Arms — A269

Natl. Arms A270

1981-83
1136 A269 100r Aceh 1.75 .30
1137 A269 100r Bali 1.75 .30
1138 A269 100r Bengkulu 1.75 .30
1139 A269 100r Jakarta 1.75 .30
1140 A269 100r West Irian 1.75 .30
1141 A269 100r West Java 1.75 .30
1142 A269 100r Jambi 1.75 .30
1143 A269 100r Central Java 1.75 .30
1144 A269 100r East Java 1.75 .30
1145 A269 100r South Kalimantan 1.75 .30
1146 A269 100r East Kalimantan 1.75 .30
1147 A269 100r West Kalimantan 1.75 .30
1148 A269 100r Lampung 1.75 .30
1149 A269 100r Central Kalimantan 1.75 .30
1150 A269 100r Moluccas 1.75 .30
1151 A269 100r West Nusa Tenggara 1.75 .30
1152 A269 100r East Nusa Tenggara 1.75 .30
1153 A269 100r Southeast Celebes 1.75 .30
1154 A269 100r Central Celebes 1.75 .30
1155 A269 100r West Sumatra 1.75 .30
1156 A269 100r North Celebes 1.75 .30
1157 A269 100r North Sumatra 1.75 .30
1158 A269 100r South Sumatra 1.75 .30
1159 A269 100r Riau 1.75 .30
1160 A269 100r South Sulawesi 1.75 .30
1161 A269 100r Yogyakarta 1.75 .30
1161A A269 100r Timor .50 .20
1162 A270 250r shown 4.00 .75
Nos. 1136-1162 (28) 50.00 8.75

Issued: Nos. 1136-1140, 1981; Nos. 1141-1161, 1162, 1982; No. 1161A, 1983.

Pink-crested Cockatoo — A271

1981, Dec. 10
1163 A271 75r shown 2.50 .20
1164 A271 100r Sulphur-crested cockatoo 3.25 .20
1165 A271 200r King cockatoo 6.75 .40
Nos. 1163-1165 (3) 12.50 .80

Souvenir Sheet
1166 Sheet of 2 21.00 1.25
a. A271 150r like #1164 4.75 .30
b. A271 350r like #1165 15.00 .70

Bumiputra Mutual Life Insurance Co., 70th Anniv. — A272

1982, Feb. 12

1167 A272 75r Family .50 .20
1168 A272 100r Family, diff. .85 .20
1169 A272 200r Hands holding symbols 1.40 .40
Nos. 1167-1169 (3) 2.75 .80

Search and Rescue Institute, 10th Anniv. — A273

General Election — A274

1982, Feb. 28 ***Perf. 12½x13½***

1170 A273 250r multicolored 1.75 .50

1982, Mar. 1 ***Perf. 12½***

1171 A274 75r Ballot, houses .50 .20
1172 A274 100r Farm .85 .20
1173 A274 200r Arms 1.40 .40
Nos. 1171-1173 (3) 2.75 .80

2nd UN Conference on Exploration and Peaceful Uses of Outer Space, Vienna, Aug. 9-21 — A275

1982, Apr. 19 ***Perf. 13x13½***

1174 A275 150r Couple 1.10 .30
1175 A275 250r Emblem 2.50 .30

12th Thomas Badminton Cup, London, May — A276

1982, May 19

1176 A276 250r multicolored 2.50 .50
a. Souvenir sheet of 2 8.50

No. 1176a also exists overprinted "INDONESIE SALUE PHILEXFRANCE" in red or black.

1982 World Cup — A277

1982, June 14

1177 A277 250r multi 3.25 .50
a. Souvenir sheet of 2 10.00
b.-c. Souvenir sheets of 2, each *110.00*

#1177b overprinted in black; #1177c in red.

60th Anniv. of Taman Siswa Educational System — A278

1982, July 3

1178 A278 250r multicolored 1.10 .50

15th Anniv. of Assoc. of South East Asian Nations (ASEAN) — A279

1982, Aug. 8 **Photo.** ***Perf. 12½***

1179 A279 150r Members' flags 2.50 .30

Balinese Starling A280

Red Birds of Paradise A281

1982, Oct. 11 **Photo.** ***Perf. 13x13½***

1180 A280 100r shown 2.40 .20
1181 A280 250r King birds of paradise 4.50 .50

Souvenir Sheet

1181A A280 500r like 100r 12.50 1.00

3rd World Natl. Park Cong., Denpasar Bali.

1982, Dec. 20 ***Perf. 12½x13½***

1182 A281 100r Lawe's six-wired parotia 2.75 .20
1183 A281 150r Twelve-wired birds of paradise 4.50 .30
1184 A281 250r shown 6.25 .50
Nos. 1182-1184 (3) 13.50 1.00

Souvenir Sheet

Perf. 12½x13½

1184A Sheet of 2 20.00 1.00
b. A281 200r like 100r 7.00 .40
c. A281 300r like 250r 11.00 .60

Scouting Year A282

1983, Feb. 22 **Photo.** ***Perf. 13½x13***

1185 A282 250r multi 2.50 .50

Restoration of Borobudur Temple — A283

1983, Feb. 23 ***Perf. 12½***

1186 A283 100r Scaffolding, crane, vert. 1.75 .20
1187 A283 150r Buddha statue, stupas, vert. 2.75 .20
1188 A283 250r Statue, temple 4.50 .35
Nos. 1186-1188 (3) 9.00 .75

Souvenir Sheet

1189 A283 500r Temple 16.00 1.00

Gas Plant — A284

World Communications Year — A285

1983, May 16 **Photo.** ***Perf. 12½***

1190 A284 275r multi 1.75 .40

7th Intl. Liquefied Natural Gas Conference and Exhibition, Jakarta, May 16-19.

1983, May 17 ***Perf. 12½x13½***

1191 A285 75r Dove, ships .55 .20
1192 A285 110r Satellite .70 .20
1193 A285 175r Dish antenna, jet 1.10 .30
1194 A285 275r Airmail envelope, globe 1.40 .40
Nos. 1191-1194 (4) 3.75 1.10

See Nos. 1215-1216.

13th Natl. Koran Reading Competition, Padang, May 23-31 — A286

1983, May 23 ***Perf. 13½x13***

1195 A286 275r multi 1.75 .35

Total Solar Eclipse, June 11 — A287

1983, June 11 ***Perf. 12½***

1196 A287 110r Map, eclipse 1.10 .20
1197 A287 275r Map 2.25 .40

Souvenir Sheet

1198 A287 500r like 275r 10.50 .80

Launch of Palapa B Satellite — A288

Agricultural Census — A289

1983, June 18 ***Perf. 12½x13½***

1199 A288 275r multi 1.75 .25

1983, July 1 **Photo.** ***Perf. 12½***

1200 A289 110r Produce .80 .20
1201 A289 275r Farmer 1.60 .20

15th Anniv. of Indonesia-Pakistan Economic and Cultural Cooperation Org. — A290

Weavings.

1983, Aug. 19

1202 A290 275r Indonesian, Lombok 2.00 .20
1203 A290 275r Pakistani, Baluchistan 2.00 .20

Krakatoa Eruption Centenary A291

1983, Aug. 26

1204 A291 110r Volcano 1.00 .20
1205 A291 275r Map 2.00 .20

CN-235, Light Air Transport — A292

1983, Sept. 10 **Photo.** ***Perf. 12½***

1206 A292 275r multi 1.75 .20

Tropical Fish — A293

1983, Oct. 17 **Photo.** ***Perf. 12½***

1207 A293 110r Puntius tetrazona 2.50 .20
1208 A293 175r Rasbora einthoveni 4.00 .20
1209 A293 275r Toxotes jaculator 7.00 .20
Nos. 1207-1209 (3) 13.50 .60

Canderawasih Birds — A294

1983, Nov. 30 **Photo.** ***Perf. 12½***

1210 A294 110r Diphyllodes respublica 1.60 .20
1211 A294 175r Epimachus fastuosus 2.25 .20
1212 A294 275r Drepanornis albertisi 4.25 .20
1213 A294 500r as #1212 6.75 .40
a. Souvenir sheet of 1 20.00 .80
Nos. 1210-1213 (4) 14.85 1.00

Inalienable Rights of the Palestinian People A295

1983, Dec. 20 ***Perf. 13½x13***

1214 A295 275r multi 1.75 .20

WCY Type of 1983

Souvenir Sheets

1983 **Photo.** ***Perf. 12½x13½***

1215 A285 400r like No. 1192 6.00 .35
1216 A285 500r like No. 1194 7.25 .50

Telecom '83 exhib., Geneva, Oct. 26-Nov. 1 (400r). Philatelic Museum opening, Jakarta (500r). Issued: 400r, Oct. 26; 500r, Sept. 29.

Fight Against Polio — A296

4th Five-Year Development Plan — A297

1984, Feb. 17 Photo. *Perf. 12½*
1217 A296 110r Emblem .65 .20
1218 A296 275r Stylized person 1.50 .20

1984, Apr. 1 Photo. *Perf. 12½*
1219 A297 55r Fertilizer industry .25 .20
1220 A297 75r Aviation .35 .20
1221 A297 110r Shipping .50 .20
1222 A297 275r Communications 1.25 .20
Nos. 1219-1222 (4) 2.35 .80

Forestry Resources A298

1984, May 17 Photo. *Perf. 12½*
1223 A298 75r Forest, paper mill .65 .20
1224 A298 110r Seedling 1.10 .20
1225 A298 175r Tree cutting 1.50 .20
1226 A298 275r Logs 2.75 .20
a. Souv. sheet of 2, #1225-1226 12.50 .35
Nos. 1223-1226 (4) 6.00 .80

17th Annual Meeting of ASEAN Foreign Ministers — A299

1984, July 9 Photo. *Perf. 12½*
1227 A299 275r Flags 2.75 .20

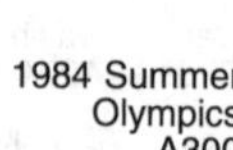

1984 Summer Olympics A300

Horse Dancers, Central Java — A301

1984, July 28 Photo. *Perf. 12½*
1228 A300 75r Pole vault .75 .20
1229 A300 110r Archery .75 .20
1230 A300 175r Boxing 1.25 .20
1231 A300 250r Shooting 2.25 .25
1232 A300 275r Weight lifting 2.50 .25
1233 A300 325r Swimming 2.50 .30
Nos. 1228-1233 (6) 10.00 1.40

1984, Aug. 17 *Perf. 12½x13½*
Processions.
1234 A301 75r shown .75 .20
1235 A301 110r Reyog Ponorogo, East Java 1.25 .20
1236 A301 275r Lion Dance, West Java 3.00 .20
1237 A301 325r Barong of Bali 3.50 .25
Nos. 1234-1237 (4) 8.50 .85

Natl. Sports Day A302

1984, Sept. 9 Photo. *Perf. 13½x13*
1238 A302 110r Thomas Cup victory .75 .20
1239 A302 275r Gymnastics 2.00 .20

Postcode System Inauguration A303

1984, Sept. 27 Photo. *Perf. 12½*
1240 A303 110r multi .55 .20
1241 A303 275r multi 1.25 .20

Birds of Irian Jaya — A304

Oath of the Youth — A305

1984, Oct. 15 *Perf. 12½x13½*
1242 A304 75r Chlamydera lauterbachi 1.60 .20
1243 A304 110r Sericulus aureus 2.50 .20
1244 A304 275r Astrapia nigra 6.00 .25
1245 A304 325r Lophorhina superba 6.50 .30
a. Souv. sheet of 2, #1242, 1245 21.00 4.00
Nos. 1242-1245 (4) 16.60 .95

No. 1245a for PHILAKOREA '84.

1984, Oct. 28 *Perf. 12½*
1246 A305 275r Emblem 1.60 .20

ICAO, 40th Anniversary — A306

1984, Dec. 7 Photo. *Perf. 13½x12½*
1247 A306 275r Airplane, Emblem 1.75 .20

Indonesia Netherlands Marine Exped., 1984-85 — A307

75th Intl. Women's Day — A308

Survey ship Snellius II and: 50r, Marine geological and geophysical exploration. 100r, Mapping ocean currents. 275r, Studying marine flora and fauna.

1985, Feb. 27 Photo. *Perf. 13x13½*
1248 A307 50r multi .50 .20
1249 A307 100r multi 1.00 .20
1250 A307 275r multi 3.00 .25
Nos. 1248-1250 (3) 4.50 .65

1985, Mar. 8
1251 A308 100r Emblem 2.25 .20
1252 A308 275r Silhouettes, emblem 6.75 .20

Five Year Plan A309

1985, Apr. 1 *Perf. 13½x13*
1254 A309 75r Mecca pilgrimage program .35 .20
1255 A309 140r Compulsory education .65 .20
1256 A309 350r Cement industry, Padang works 1.75 .30
Nos. 1254-1256 (3) 2.75 .70

Suharto Type of 1980-83 and

A310

A310a

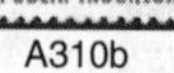

A310b

A310c

Perf. 13½x12½, 12½ (A310, A310a, A310b, A310c)

1983-93 Photo.
1257 A246 10r pale grn & dk grn .20 .20
1258 A246 25r pale org & dk cop red .30 .20
1259 A246 50r beige & dk brn .20 .20
1260 A246 55r sal rose & rose .25 .20
1261 A246 100r lt blue green & ultra .40 .20
1262 A310 140r rose & dp brn .65 .20
1263 A310c 150r yel grn & multi .55 .20
1264 A310b 200r pink, bl & red .55 .20
1265 A246 300r lt dull grn, bl grn & gold 1.40 .20
1266 A310c 300r multicolored 1.10 .20
1267 A310 350r red & brt lil 1.75 .30
1268 A246 400r blue grn, int blue & gold 1.90 .25
1268A A310b 700r pale grn, rose lil & grn 2.00 .30
1268B A310c 700r red & multi 2.75 1.00
1269 A310a 1000r multi 4.75 .70
Nos. 1257-1269 (15) 18.75 4.55

Issued: 10r, 25r, 3/11; 140r, 350r, 4/10/85; 50r, 100r, #1265, 12/24/86; 55r, 400r, 12/87; 200r, 12/89; 700r, 3/90; 1000r, 8/17/88; 150r, #1266, 1268B, 8/17/93.

For surcharge see No. 1527.

Asia-Africa Conference, 30th Anniv. — A311

1985, Apr. 24 *Perf. 12½*
1270 A311 350r Emblem, inscription 2.50 .30

Intl. Youth Year — A312

UN Decade for Women — A313

1985, July 12 *Perf. 12½x13½*
1271 A312 75r Three youths, globe 1.00 .20
1272 A312 140r Youths supporting globe 2.00 .20

1985, July 26
1273 A313 55r Profiles of women, emblem .55 .20
1274 A313 140r Globe, emblem 1.25 .20

Indonesian Trade Fair — A314

1985, Aug. 1
1275 A314 140r Hydro-electric plant 1.00 .20
1276 A314 350r Farmer, industrial plant 2.50 .25

Republic of Indonesia, 40th anniv.

11th Natl. Sports Week, Jakarta, Sept. 9-20 A315

Perf. 13½x12½, 12½x13½
1985, Sept. 9 Photo.
1277 A315 55r Sky diving .40 .20
1278 A315 100r Combat sports .75 .20
1279 A315 140r High jump 1.00 .20
1280 A315 350r Wind surfing, vert. 2.50 .25
Nos. 1277-1280 (4) 4.65 .85

Org. of Petroleum Exporting Countries, OPEC, 25th Anniv. — A316

1985, Sept. 14 *Perf. 12½*
1281 A316 140r multi 1.50 .20

Natl. Oil Industry, Cent. A317

1985, Oct. 8 *Perf. 13½x13*
1282 A317 140r Oil tankers .80 .20
1283 A317 250r Refinery 1.40 .20
1284 A317 350r Offshore oil rig 2.00 .25
Nos. 1282-1284 (3) 4.20 .65

UN, 40th Anniv. — A318

Design: 140r, Doves, 40, emblem. 300r, Bombs transformed into plants.

1985, Oct. 24 ***Perf. 12½***
1285 A318 140r multicolored .85 .20
1286 A318 300r multicolored 1.60 .20

Wildlife A318a

1985, Dec. 27 Photo. ***Perf. 14½x13***
1286A A318a 75r Rhinoceros sondaicus 1.00 .20
1286B A318a 150r Anoa depressicornis 2.00 .20
1286C A318a 300r Varanus komodoensis 4.00 .20
Nos. 1286A-1286C (3) 7.00 .60

1986 Industrial Census — A319

1986, Feb. 8 Photo. ***Perf. 12½***
1287 A319 Pair 1.75 .40
a. 175r Census emblem .85 .20
b. 175r Symbols of industry .85 .20

UN Child Survival Campaign A320

1986, Mar. 15 Photo. ***Perf. 12½***
1288 A320 75r Breastfeeding .80 .20
1289 A320 140r Immunization 1.40 .20

UNICEF, 40th anniv.

4th 5-year Development Plan — A321

14th Thomas Cup, 13th Uber Cup, Jakarta — A322

1986, Apr. 1 Photo. ***Perf. 12½***
1290 A321 140r Construction .25 .20
1291 A321 500r Agriculture 1.00 .25

1986, Apr. 22
1292 A322 55r Cup, racket .90 .20
1293 A322 150r Cups, horiz. 2.00 .20

EXPO '86, Vancouver — A323

1986, May 2 ***Perf. 12½x14½***
1294 A323 75r Pinisi junk .65 .20
1295 A323 150r Kentongan, satellite 1.25 .20
1296 A323 300r Pavilion emblem 2.25 .30
Nos. 1294-1296 (3) 4.15 .70

Natl. Scout Jamboree, JAMNAS '86, Cibubur Jakarta East A324

Perf. 13½x12½, 12½x13½
1986, June 21 Photo.
1297 A324 100r Saluting flag 1.25 .20
1298 A324 140r Cookout 1.75 .20
1299 A324 210r Map-reading, vert. 2.50 .25
Nos. 1297-1299 (3) 5.50 .65

Air Show '86, Jakarta, June 22-July 1 A325

1986, June 23 ***Perf. 13½x12½***
1300 A325 350r multi 2.25 .25

Folk Dances — A326

1986, July 30 Photo. ***Perf. 12½***
1301 A326 140r Legong Kraton 1.25 .20
1302 A326 350r Barong 3.25 .35
1303 A326 500r Kecak 4.50 .45
Nos. 1301-1303 (3) 9.00 1.00

19th Congress of Intl. Society of Sugar Cane Technologists, Jakarta — A327

1986, Aug. 5 ***Perf. 12½x13½***
1304 A327 150r Planting .90 .20
1305 A327 300r Sugar 1.75 .30

Sea-Me-We Submarine Cable Inauguration — A328

1986, Sept. 8 ***Perf. 12½***
1306 A328 140r shown .75 .20
1307 A328 350r Map, diff. 2.25 .35

Southeast Asia, Middle East, Western Europe Submarine Cable.

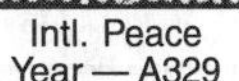

Intl. Peace Year — A329

1987 General Election — A330

1986, Dec. 17 Photo. ***Perf. 12½***
1308 A329 350r shown 1.25 .20
1309 A329 500r Dove circling Earth 2.50 .35

1987, Jan. 19

75r, Tourism, party emblems, industry. 350r, Emblems, natl. eagle, ballot box.

1310 A330 75r multi .35 .20
1311 A330 140r multi .70 .20
1312 A330 350r multi 1.60 .35
Nos. 1310-1312 (3) 2.65 .75

A331

A332

1987, Mar. 21 Photo. ***Perf. 12½***
1313 A331 350r Satellite, horiz. 1.00 .20
1314 A331 500r shown 2.25 .35

Launch of Palapa B-2P, Cape Canaveral.

1987, Apr. 1
1315 A332 140r Boy carving figurines, horiz. .35 .20
1316 A332 350r shown .90 .30

4th 5-Year Development Plan.

Folk Costumes — A333

1987, May 25 ***Perf. 13x13½***
1317 A333 140r Kalimantan Timur *4.75* .20
1318 A333 350r Daerah Aceh *11.00* .35
1319 A333 400r Timor Timur *12.50* .45
Nos. 1317-1319 (3) *28.25* 1.00

See Nos. 1358-1363, 1412-1417, 1448-1453, 1464-1469.

14th Southeast Asia Games, Jakarata, Sept. 9-20 A334

Anniv. Emblems A335

1987, June 10 ***Perf. 12½***
1320 A334 140r Weight lifting .70 .20
1321 A334 250r Swimming 1.40 .25
1322 A334 350r Running 1.90 .35
Nos. 1320-1322 (3) 4.00 .80

1987, June 20
1323 A335 75r multi, horiz. 1.75 .20
1324 A335 100r shown 2.25 .20

City of Jakarta, 460th anniv.; Jakarta Fair, 20th anniv.

Children's Day — A336

ASEAN Headquarters, Jakarta — A337

1987, July 23
1325 A336 100r Education, horiz. .60 .20
1326 A336 250r Universal immunization 1.40 .25

1987, Aug. 8
1327 A337 350r multi 2.00 .25

ASEAN, 20th anniv.

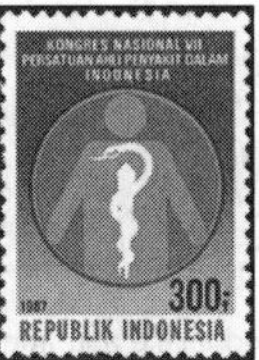

Assoc. of Physicians Specializing in Internal Diseases, 30th Anniv. — A338

1987, Aug. 23 **Photo.**
1328 A338 300r Stylized man, caduceus 1.40 .25

Sand Craters, Mt. Bromo, Timur A339

1987, Oct. 20 ***Perf. 13½x12½***
1329 A339 140r shown .75 .20
1330 A339 350r Bratan (Bedugul) Lake, Bali 2.75 .35
1331 A339 500r Sea gardens, Bunaken Is. 4.00 .45
Nos. 1329-1331 (3) 7.50 1.00

Tourism. See Nos. 1367-1370A, 1408-1410, 1420-1422.

Role of Women in the Fight for Independence A340

1987, Nov. 10 ***Perf. 12½***
1332 A340 75r Veteran .65 .20
1333 A340 100r Soldiers, barbed wire (Laskar Wanita) .85 .20

Fish — A341

1987, Dec. 30
1334 A341 150r Osphronemus goramy 1.25 .20
1335 A341 200r Cyprinus carpio 1.75 .20
1336 A341 500r Clarias batrachus 4.50 .50
Nos. 1334-1336 (3) 7.50 .90

Natl. Veteran's League, 31st Anniv. — A342

1988, Jan. 2

1337 A342 250r blue grn & org 1.40 .25

Occupational Health and Safety for Greater Efficiency and Productivity — A343

1988, Jan. 12 ***Perf. 13½x12½***

1338 A343 350r Worker using safety equipment 1.75 .35

See No. 1419.

Natl. Craft Council, 8th Anniv. — A344

Crafts: 120r, Carved wood snake and frog. 350r, Cane rocking chair. 500r, Ornate carved bamboo containers and fan.

1988, Mar. 3 Photo. ***Perf. 12½***

1339 A344 120r ultra & dark brn .60 .20
1340 A344 350r lt blue & dark brn 1.40 .25
1341 A344 500r yel grn & dark brn 2.00 .35
Nos. 1339-1341 (3) 4.00 .80

Pelita IV (Five-Year Development Plan) — A345

1988, Apr. 1

1342 A345 140r Oil rig, refinery .30 .20
1343 A345 400r Crayfish, trawler .95 .20

World Expo '88, Brisbane, Australia A346

Intl. Red Cross and Red Crescent Organizations, 125th Annivs. A347

Designs: 200r, Two children, Borobudur Temple in silhouette. 300r, Boy wearing armor and headdress. 350r, Girl, boy and a Tongkonan house, Toraja, South Sulawesi.

1988, Apr. 30 Photo. ***Perf. 12½***

1344 A346 200r multi .90 .20
1345 A346 300r multi 1.40 .25
1346 A346 350r multi 1.90 .35
a. Souv. sheet of 3, #1344-1346 *12.50* 2.00
Nos. 1344-1346 (3) 4.20 .80

No. 1346a exists imperf.

1988, May 8

1347 A347 350r black & red 1.50 .25

Orchids — A348

1988, May 17 ***Perf. 13x13½***

1348 A348 400r Dendrobium none 1.75 .30
1349 A348 500r Dendrobium abang 2.25 .35

1988 Summer Olympics, Seoul — A349

Intl. Council of Women, Cent. — A350

1988, June 15 Photo. ***Perf. 12½***

1350 A349 75r Running .50 .20
1351 A349 100r Weight lifting .55 .20
1352 A349 200r Archery 1.10 .20
1353 A349 300r Table tennis 1.60 .20
1354 A349 400r Swimming 2.25 .30
a. Souv. sheet of 3 + label, #1351-1352, 1354, imperf *15.00* 2.25
1355 A349 500r Tennis 2.75 .35
a. Souv. sheet of 3 + label, #1350, 1353, 1355, imperf *15.00* 2.50
Nos. 1350-1355 (6) 8.75 1.45

Sheets exist perf. Value, each *$20.*

1988, June 26

1356 A350 140r brt blue & blk 1.00 .20

7th Natl. Farmers' Week — A351

1988, July 9

1357 A351 350r lake & bister 1.75 .25

Folk Costumes Type of 1987

Traditional wedding attire from: 55r, West Sumatra. 75p, Jambi. 100r, Bengkulu. 120r, Lampung. 200r, Moluccas. 250r, East Nusa.

1988, July 15 ***Perf. 12½x14½***

1358 A333 55r multicolored .55 .20

Perf. 12½x13½

1359 A333 75r multicolored .80 .20
1360 A333 100r multicolored 1.00 .20
1361 A333 120r multicolored 1.25 .20

Perf. 12½x14½

1362 A333 200r multicolored 1.90 .20
1363 A333 250r multicolored 2.50 .20
Nos. 1358-1363 (6) 8.00 1.20

A352

A353

1988, Sept. 29 Photo. ***Perf. 12½***

1364 A352 500r multicolored 2.00 .25

13th Congress of the Non-Aligned News Agencies Pool, Jakarta, Sept. 29-Oct. 1.

1988, Oct. 9

1365 A353 140r multi 1.00 .20

Intl. Letter Writing Week.

Transportion and Communications Decade for Asia and the Pacific (1985-1995) A354

1988, Oct. 24

1366 A354 350r blk & lt blue 1.75 .25

Tourism Type of 1987

Architecture: 250r, Al Mashun Mosque, Medan. 300r, Pagaruyung Palace, Batusangkar. 500r, 1000r, Keong Emas Taman Theater, Jakarta.

1988-89 Photo. ***Perf. 13½x13***

1367 A339 250r multi 1.25 .20
1368 A339 300r multi 1.50 .20
1369 A339 500r multi 2.50 .35
Nos. 1367-1369 (3) 5.25 .75

Souvenir Sheets

Imperf

1370 A339 1000r multi *7.00* .70

Perf. 14½x13

1370A Sheet of 2 *15.00* 3.75
b. A339 1500r like No. 1367 *5.75* 1.25
c. A339 2500r like No. 1368 *9.25* 2.25

No. 1370 exists perf 14½x12½. Value *$18.*

Issue dates: No. 1370A, Nov. 1989; others, Nov. 25, 1988. World Stamp Expo '89, Washington, DC.

Butterflies A356

Flora A357

1988, Dec. 20 ***Perf. 12½x13½***

1371 A356 400r *Papilio gigon* 2.75 .30
1372 A356 500r *Graphium androcles* 3.75 .35

Souvenir Sheet

Imperf

1373 A356 1000r like 500r *10.00* .70

No. 1373 exists perf. 12½x14½. Value *$26.*

Equestrian Type of 1981 Souvenir Sheets

1988 ***Imperf.***

1374 Sheet of 4 *12.50* .65
a. A268 200r blk, dark red & grn .50 .20
1375 Sheet of 1 + label, dk bl, dark red & deep org *12.50* .20

FILACEPT '88, The Hague, Oct. 18-23, 1988. Nos. 1374-1375 exist perf. 12½. Value, each *$17.*

1989, Jan. 7 Photo. ***Perf. 13½x13***

1376 A357 200r *Rafflesia* .90 .20
1377 A357 1000r *Amorphophallus titanum* 4.50 .70

Souvenir Sheet

Perf. 13½x14½

1378 A357 1000r like No. 1377, value in blk *35.00* .70

Garuda Indonesia Airlines, 40th Anniv. — A358

1989, Jan. 26 ***Perf. 12½***

1379 A358 350r bl grn & brt bl 2.00 .25

World Wildlife Fund — A359

Orangutans, *Pongo pygmaeus.*

1989, Mar. 6 Photo. ***Perf. 12½***

1380 A359 75r Adult and young *3.00* .20
1381 A359 100r Adult hanging in tree *3.00* .20
a. Souv. sheet of 2, #1380-1381 *75.00*
1382 A359 140r Adult, young in tree *3.00* .20
1383 A359 500r Adult's head *9.25* .40
a. Souv. sheet of 2, #1382-1383 *75.00*
Nos. 1380-1383 (4) *18.25* 1.00

Use of Postage Stamps in Indonesia, 125th Anniv. — A360

1989, Apr. 1

1384 A360 1000r grn, rose lilac & deep blue 2.75 .70

5th Five-year Development Plan — A361

Industries.

1989, Apr. 1

1385 A361 55r Fertilizer .20 .20
1386 A361 150r Cilegon Iron and Steel Mill .30 .20
1387 A361 350r Petroleum .80 .25
Nos. 1385-1387 (3) 1.30 .65

See Nos. 1427-1428, 1461-1462, 1488-1489, 1530-1532.

Natl. Education Day — A362

Ki Hadjar Dewantara (b. 1889), founder of Taman Siswa school and: 140r, Graduate. 300r, Pencil, globe and books.

1989, May 2

1388 A362 140r ver, lake & brt rose lil .60 .20
1389 A362 300r vio & pale grn 1.40 .20

Terbuka University (140r) and freedom from illiteracy (300r).

Asia-Pacific Telecommunity, 10th Anniv. — A363

Sudirman Cup, Flag — A364

1989, July 1 Photo. ***Perf. 12½***

1390 A363 350r green & vio 1.40 .25

1989, July 3

1391 A364 100r scar, gold & dark red brn 1.75 .20

Sudirman Cup world badminton mixed team championships, Jakarta, May 24-28.

Natl. Children's Day — A365

CIRDAP, 10th Anniv. — A366

1989, July 23

1392 A365 100r Literacy .50 .20
1393 A365 250r Physical fitness 1.25 .20

1989, July 29

1394 A366 140r blue & dark red brn 1.00 .20

Center on Integrated Rural Development for Asia and the Pacific.

A367 A368

Paleoanthropological Discoveries in Indonesia: Fossils of *Homo erectus* and *Homo sapiens* men.

1989, Aug. 31

1395 A367 100r Sangiran 17 .65 .20
1396 A367 150r Perning 1 .95 .20
1397 A367 200r Sangiran 10 1.40 .20
1398 A367 250r Wajak 1 1.60 .20
1399 A367 300r Sambungmacan 1 1.90 .20
1400 A367 350r Ngandong 7 2.25 .25
Nos. 1395-1400 (6) 8.75 1.25

Nos. 1398-1400 vert.

1989, Sept. 4

1401 A368 350r deep blue & yel grn 1.50 .25

Interparliamentary Union, Cent.

12th Natl. Sports Week — A369

1989, Sept. 18

1402 A369 75r Tae kwando .35 .20
1403 A369 100r Tennis .45 .20
1404 A369 140r Judo .65 .20
1405 A369 350r Volleyball 1.60 .25
1406 A369 500r Boxing 2.25 .35
1407 A369 1000r Archery 4.50 .70
Nos. 1402-1407 (6) 9.80 1.90

Tourism Type of 1987

Structures in Miniature Park: 120r, Taman Burung. 350r, Natl. Philatelic Museum. 500r, Istana Anak-Anak, vert.

Perf. 13½x12½, 12½x13½

1989, Oct. 9

1408 A339 120r multicolored .65 .20
1409 A339 350r multicolored 1.75 .30
1410 A339 500r multicolored 2.50 .50
Nos. 1408-1410 (3) 4.90 1.00

Film Festival — A370

1989, Nov. 11 Photo. *Perf. 12½*

1411 A370 150r yel bister & blk 1.50 .20

Folk Costumes Type of 1987

Traditional wedding attire from: 50r, North Sumatra. 75r, South Sumatra. 100r, Jakarta. 140r, North Sulawesi. 350r, Mid Sulawesi. 500r, South Sulawesi. 1500r, North Sulawesi.

1989, Dec. 11 *Perf. 13x13½*

1412 A333 50r multicolored .25 .20
1413 A333 75r multicolored .35 .20
1414 A333 100r multicolored .50 .20
1415 A333 140r multicolored .65 .20
1416 A333 350r multicolored 1.75 .20
1417 A333 500r multicolored 2.50 .25
Nos. 1412-1417 (6) 6.00 1.25

Souvenir Sheet

Imperf

1418 A333 1500r multicolored *8.50* .75

No. 1418 exists perf. 12½x13½. Value *$11.*

Health and Safety Type of 1988

1990, Jan. 12 *Perf. 13x12½*

Size: 29x21mm

1419 A343 200r Lineman, power lines 1.00 .20

Tourism Type of 1987

Architecture: 200r, Fort Marlborough, Bengkulu. 400r, 1000r, National Museum, Jakarta. 500r, 1500r, Mosque of Baiturrahman, Banda Aceh.

1990, Feb. 1 *Perf. 13½x13*

1420 A339 200r multicolored .75 .20
1421 A339 400r multicolored 1.60 .20
1422 A339 500r multicolored 2.00 .30
Nos. 1420-1422 (3) 4.35 .70

Souvenir Sheet

1423 Sheet of 2 *12.00* 1.25
a. A339 1000r multicolored *4.75* .50
b. A339 1500r multicolored *7.25* .75

Flora A371

1990, Mar. 1

1424 A371 75r Mammilaria fragilis .20 .20
1425 A371 1000r Gmelina elliptica 3.00 1.00

Souvenir Sheet

1426 A371 1500r like #1425 *15.00* 3.00

5th Five-year Development Plan Type of 1989

1990, Apr. 1 *Perf. 12½*

1427 A361 200r Road construction .35 .20
1428 A361 1000r Lighthouse, ship 1.90 .50

Visit Indonesia Year, 1991 A372

Perf. 13½x12½, 12½x13½

1990, May 1

1429 A372 100r shown .35 .20
1430 A372 500r Steps, ruin 1.90 .25

Souvenir Sheet

Perf. 14½x12½

1430A A372 5000r like #1429 *17.50* 2.50

No. 1430A, Stamp World London '90.

A373 A374

1990, May 18 *Perf. 12½*

1431 A373 1000r gray grn & brn org 2.25 .50

Disabled Veterans Corps, 40th anniv.

1990, June 8 *Perf. 12½*

1432 A374 75r shown .45 .20
1433 A374 150r multi, diff. .90 .20
1434 A374 400r multi, diff. 2.25 .25
Nos. 1432-1434 (3) 3.60 .65

Souvenir Sheet

1435 A374 1500r multi *12.00* .75

World Cup Soccer Championships, Italy.

Family Planning in Indonesia, 20th Anniv. — A375

1990, June 29

1436 A375 60r brown & red .60 .20

Natl. Census — A376

1990, July 1

1437 A376 90r yel grn & dk grn .60 .20

Natl. Children's Day — A377

1990, July 23

1438 A377 500r multicolored 1.40 .25

Souvenir Sheet

Traditional Lampung Wedding Costumes — A378

Perf. 12½x14½

1990, June 10 Photo.

1439 A378 2000r multicolored *9.00* 1.00

Natl. Philatelic Exhibition, Stamp World London '90 and New Zealand '90.

Independence, 45th Anniv. — A379

1990, Aug. 17 *Perf. 12½x13½*

1440 A379 200r Soldier raising flag .65 .20
1441 A379 500r Skyscraper, highway 1.50 .40

Souvenir Sheet

1442 A379 1000r like #1442 *9.00* .85

Indonesia-Pakistan Economic & Cultural Cooperation Organization — A380

Designs: 400r, Woman dancing in traditional costume, vert.

Perf. 13½x12½, 12½x13½

1990, Aug. 19 Litho.

1443 A380 75r multicolored .35 .20
1444 A380 400r multicolored 1.60 .50

Asian Pacific Postal Training Center, 20th Anniv. — A381

1990, Sept. 10 Photo. *Perf. 12½*

1445 A381 500r vio bl, bl & ultra 1.40 .40

A382 A383

1990, Sept. 14

1446 A382 200r gray, blk & org 1.00 .20

Organization of Petroleum Exporting Countries (OPEC), 30th anniv.

1990, Oct. 24

1447 A383 1000r multicolored 2.75 .85

Environmental Protection Laws, 40th anniv.

Folk Costumes Type of 1987

Traditional wedding attire from: 75r, West Java. 100r, Central Java. 150r, Yogyakarta. 200r, East Java. 400r, Bali. 500r, West Nusa Tenggara.

1990, Nov. 1 *Perf. 13x13½*

1448 A333 75r multicolored .25 .20
1449 A333 100r multicolored .35 .20
1450 A333 150r multicolored .55 .20
1451 A333 200r multicolored .70 .20
1452 A333 400r multicolored 1.40 .35
1453 A333 500r multicolored 1.60 .45
Nos. 1448-1453 (6) 4.85 1.60

A385 A386

Visit Indonesia Year 1991: Women in traditional costumes.

1991, Jan. 1 Photo. *Perf. 12½x13½*

1454 A385 200r multicolored .60 .20
1455 A385 500r multicolored 1.75 .30
1456 A385 1000r multicolored 3.00 .50
Nos. 1454-1456 (3) 5.35 1.00

1991, Feb. 4 *Perf. 12½*

1457 A386 200r yel, grn & bl grn 1.00 .20

16th natl. Koran reading competition, Jogjakarta.

Palace of Sultan Ternate, the Moluccas A387

Design: 1000r, 2500r, Bari House, Palembang, South Sumatra.

1991, Mar. 1 *Perf. 13½x12½*

1458 A387 500r multicolored 1.10 .25
1459 A387 1000r multicolored 2.00 .50

Souvenir Sheet

1460 A387 2500r multicolored *9.00* 1.25

5th Five Year Development Plan Type of 1989

1991, Apr. 1 *Perf. 12½*

1461 A361 75r Steel mill, vert. .20 .20
1462 A361 200r Computers .55 .20

Danger of Smoking — A388

1991, May 31 **Photo.** *Perf. 12½*

1463 A388 90r multicolored .75 .20

Folk Costumes Type of 1987

Traditional wedding attire from: 100r, West Kalimantan. 200r, Mid Kalimantan. 300r, South Kalimantan. 400r, Southeast Sulawesi. 500r, Riau. 1000r, Irian Jaya.

1991, June 15 *Perf. 13x13½*

1464 A333 100r multicolored .20 .20
1465 A333 200r multicolored .40 .20
1466 A333 300r multicolored .60 .20
1467 A333 400r multicolored .80 .20
1468 A333 500r multicolored 1.00 .25
1469 A333 1000r multicolored 2.00 .50
Nos. 1464-1469 (6) 5.00 1.55

Natl. Scouting Jamboree, Cibubur A389

Monument A390

1991, June 15 *Perf. 12½*

1470 A389 200r multicolored 1.40 .20

1991, July 6

1471 A390 200r multicolored .90 .20

Natl. Farmers' Week — A391

Indonesian Chemical Society, 4th Natl. Congress — A392

1991, July 15

1472 A391 500r brt bl, yel & grn 1.75 .25

1991, July 28

1473 A392 400r grn, ver & dull grn 1.25 .20

Chemindo '91.

A393 A394

1991, Aug. 24 **Photo.** *Perf. 12½*

1474 A393 300r blk, red & gray 1.40 .30

5th Junior Men's and 4th Women's Asian Weightlifting Championships.

1991, Aug. 30

1475 A394 500r lilac & sky blue 1.40 .45

World Cup Parachuting Championships.

A395 A396

1991, Sept. 17

1476 A395 200r multicolored 1.25 .20

Indonesian Red Cross, 46th aAnniv.

1991, Oct. 6

1477 A396 300r yellow & blue 1.40 .30

Intl. Amateur Radio Union, 8th regional conf., Bandung.

Istiqlal (Independence) Festival, Jakarta — A397

1991, Oct. 15

1478 A397 200r gray, blk & ver 1.40 .20

Intl. Conference on the Great Apes — A398

Pongo pygmaeus: 200r, Sitting in tree. 500r, Walking. 1000r, 2500r, Sitting on ground.

1991, Dec. 18 *Perf. 12½x13½*

1479 A398 200r multicolored .60 .20
1480 A398 500r multicolored 1.40 .45
1481 A398 1000r multicolored 3.00 .85
Nos. 1479-1481 (3) 5.00 1.50

Souvenir Sheet

1481A A398 2500r multicolored *11.00* 1.25

Intl. Convention on Quality Control Circles, Bali — A399

1991, Oct. 22 *Perf. 12½*

1482 A399 500r multicolored 1.75 .45

Automation of the Post Office — A400

200r, P.O. 500r, Mail sorting equipment.

1992, Jan. 9 **Photo.** *Perf. 13½x13*

1483 A400 200r multicolored .40 .20
1484 A400 500r multicolored .95 .30

National Elections A401

1992, Feb. 10 *Perf. 12½*

1485 A401 75r shown .20 .20
1486 A401 100r Ballot boxes, globe .20 .20
1487 A401 500r Hands dropping ballots in ballot boxes 1.00 .30
Nos. 1485-1487 (3) 1.40 .70

5th Five-year Development Plan Type of 1989

1992, Apr. 1 **Photo.** *Perf. 12½*

1488 A361 150r Construction worker .25 .20
1489 A361 300r Aviation technology .55 .20

Visit Asia Year, 1992 A402

1992, Mar. 1 *Perf. 13½x13*

1490 A402 300r Lembah Baliem, Irian Jaya .65 .20
1491 A402 500r Tanah Lot, Bali 1.10 .30
1492 A402 1000r Lombah Anai, Sumatra Barat 2.25 .50
Nos. 1490-1492 (3) 4.00 1.00

Souvenir Sheet

1493 A402 3000r like #1491 *7.50* 1.75

Birds — A403

1992, July 1 **Photo.** *Perf. 12½x13½*

1494 A403 100r Garrulax leucolophus .25 .20
1495 A403 200r Dinopium javanense .50 .20
1496 A403 400r Buceros rhinoceros 1.00 .25
1497 A403 500r Alisterus amboinensis 1.25 .35
Nos. 1494-1497 (4) 3.00 1.00

Souvenir Sheet

1498 A403 3000r like #1494 *9.25* 1.75

Children's Day — A404

75r, Street scene. 100r, Children with balloons. 200r, Boating scene. 500r, Girl feeding bird.

1992, July 23 *Perf. 12½*

1499 A404 75r multicolored .20 .20
1500 A404 100r multicolored .25 .20
1501 A404 200r multicolored .55 .20
1502 A404 500r multicolored 1.40 .30
Nos. 1499-1502 (4) 2.40 .90

1992 Summer Olympics, Barcelona — A405

Designs: No. 1508a, 2000r, like #1504. b, 3000r, like #1507.

1992, June 1 *Perf. 12½x13½*

1503 A405 75r Weight lifting .20 .20
1504 A405 200r Badminton .35 .20
1505 A405 300r Symbols of events .55 .20
1506 A405 500r Women's tennis .90 .30
1507 A405 1000r Archery 1.90 .60
Nos. 1503-1507 (5) 3.90 1.50

Souvenir Sheet

1508 A405 Sheet of 2, #a.-b. *12.00* 3.75

ASEAN, 25th Anniv. A406

1992, Aug. 8 *Perf. 13½x12½*

1509 A406 200r shown .45 .20
1510 A406 500r Flags, map 1.10 .30
1511 A406 1000r Flags on poles 2.25 .60
Nos. 1509-1511 (3) 3.80 1.10

Flowers A407

Designs: 200r, Phalaenopsis ambilis. 500r, Rafflesia arnoldii. 1000r, 2000r, Jasminum sambae.

Perf. 13½x12½

1992, Jan. 20 **Photo.**

1512 A407 200r multicolored .40 .20
1513 A407 500r multicolored 1.00 .30
1514 A407 1000r multicolored 2.00 .60
Nos. 1512-1514 (3) 3.40 1.10

Souvenir Sheet

Perf. 13½x13

1515 A407 2000r multicolored *8.50* 1.90

A408

A409

Perf. 12½x13½

1992, Sept. 6 Photo.

1516 A408 200r shown .45 .20
1517 A408 500r Flags, emblem 1.10 .30

10th Non-Aligned Summit, Jakarta.

1992, Nov. 29 Photo. *Perf. 12½*

1518 A409 200r green & blue .85 .20

Intl. Planned Parenthood Federation, 40th anniv.

A410

A411

Perf. 12½x13½

1992, Aug. 16 Photo.

1519 A410 200r Globe, satellite .40 .20
1520 A410 500r Palapa satellite 1.00 .30
1521 A410 1000r Old, new telephones 2.00 .60
Nos. 1519-1521 (3) 3.40 1.10

Satellite Communications in Indonesia, 16th anniv.

1992, Oct. 1 *Perf. 12½x13½*

Traditional Dances: 200r, 3000r, Tari Ngremo, Timor. 500r, Tari Gending Sriwijaya, Sumatra.

1522 A411 200r multicolored .55 .20
1523 A411 500r multicolored 1.25 .30

Souvenir Sheet

1524 A411 3000r like #1518 3.50 1.75

No. 1523 was withdrawn from sale on 10/5.
See Nos. 1564-1567, 1596-1600, 1628-1632, 1688-1692, 1747-1751, 1815-1820.

Antara News Agency, 55th Anniv. — A412

1992, Dec. 13 Photo. *Perf. 12½*

1525 A412 500r blue & black 1.00 .20

Natl. Afforestation Campaign — A413

Perf. 13½x12½

1992, Dec. 24 Photo.

1526 A413 500r multicolored 1.00 .30

No. 1260 Surcharged **50r**

1993, Feb. 1 Photo. *Perf. 13½x12½*

1527 A246 50r on 55r #1260 .60 .20

1993 General Session of the People's Consultative Assembly — A414

1993, Mar. 1 Photo. *Perf. 13½x12½*

1528 A414 300r Building exterior .40 .20
1529 A414 700r Building interior .95 .40

5th Five Year Development Plan Type of 1989

300r, Soldier's silhouettes over city. 700r, Immunizing children. 1000r, Runners.

1993, Apr. 1 *Perf. 12½*

1530 A361 300r multicolored .30 .20
1531 A361 700r multicolored .70 .40
1532 A361 1000r multicolored 1.00 .55
Nos. 1530-1532 (3) 2.00 1.15

Ornithoptera Goliath — A415

1993, Apr. 20 Photo. *Perf. 12½*

1533 A415 1000r multicolored 1.25 .60

For overprint see No. 1540.

Surabaja, 700th Anniv. A416

Designs: 300r, Siege of Yamato Hotel. 700r, World Habitat Award, Surabaya skyline. 1000r, Candi Bajang Ratu, natl. monument.

Perf. 13½x12½

1993, May 29 Photo.

1534 A416 300r multicolored .40 .20
1535 A416 700r multicolored .95 .40
1536 A416 1000r multicolored 1.40 .60
Nos. 1534-1536 (3) 2.75 1.20

For overprints see Nos. 1538-1539, 1541.

Nos. 1533-1536 Ovptd. in Red

and

Indopex '93 — A417

1993 *Perfs. as Before*

1538 A416 300r on #1534 .45 .20
1539 A416 700r on #1535 1.10 .40
1540 A415 1000r on #1533 1.50 .60
1541 A416 1000r on #1536 1.50 .60
Nos. 1538-1541 (4) 4.55 1.80

Souvenir Sheet

Perf. 13½x12½

1542 A417 3500r multicolored 5.00 3.00

Location of overprint varies. Issued: No. 1540, Apr. 20; others, May 29.

Environmental Protection — A418

Flowers: Nos. 1543a, 1545a, Jasminum sambac. No. 1543b, Phalaenopsis amabilis. No. 1543c, Rafflesia arnoldi.
Wildlife: Nos. 1544a, 1545b, Varanus komodoensis. No. 1544b, Scleropages formasus. No. 1544c, Spizaetus bartelsi.

Perf. 12½x13½

1993, June 5 Photo.

1543 A418 300r Tripytch, #a.-c. 1.50 .55
1544 A418 700r Tripytch, #a.-c. 3.50 1.25

Souvenir Sheet of 2

1545 A418 1500r #a.-b. *7.50* 1.75

1st World Community Development Camp — A419

Designs: 300r, Boy scouts working on road. 700r, Pres. Suharto shaking hands with scout.

Perf. 13½x12½

1993, July 27 Photo.

1546 A419 300r multicolored .40 .20
1547 A419 700r multicolored .95 .40

Papilio Blumei — A420

Armed Forces Day — A421

Perf. 12½x13½

1993, Aug. 24 Photo.

1548 A420 700r multicolored 1.00 .40

Souvenir Sheets

1549 A420 3000r multicolored *6.75* 1.75
1550 A420 3000r multicolored *6.75* 1.75

Inscription at top of No. 1549 is like that on No. 1548. No. 1550 contains a stamp inscribed "1993," a se-tenant label and Bangkok '93 Philatelic Exhibition inscription in sheet margin.

1993, Oct. 5 *Perf. 12½*

1551 A421 300r Soedirman .45 .20
1552 A421 300r Oerip Soemohardjo .45 .20
a. Pair, #1551-1552 .90 .40

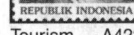

Tourism — A422

13th Natl. Sports Week — A423

300r, 3000r, Waterfall. 700r, Cave formations. 1000r, Dormant volcanic crater, horiz.

Perf. 12½x13½, 13½x12½

1993, Oct. 4

1553 A422 300r multicolored .35 .20
1554 A422 700r multicolored .80 .40
1555 A422 1000r multicolored 1.25 .60
Nos. 1553-1555 (3) 2.40 1.20

Souvenir Sheet

1556 A422 3000r multicolored *4.50* 1.75

1993, Sept. 9 *Perf. 12½x13½*

1557 A423 150r Swimming .20 .20
1558 A423 300r Cycling .35 .20
1559 A423 700r Mascot .80 .40
1560 A423 1000r High jump 1.10 .55
Nos. 1557-1560 (4) 2.45 1.35

Souvenir Sheet

1561 A423 3500r like No. 1560 *5.00* 2.00

Flora and Fauna — A424

Designs: a, Michelia champaca. b, Cananga odorata. c, Copsychus pyrropygus. d, Gracula religiosa robusta.

1993, Nov. 5 Photo. *Perf. 12½x13½*

1562 A424 300r Block of 4, #a.-d. 3.00 .55

Migratory Farm Workers — A425

1993, Dec. 4 *Perf. 12½*

1563 A425 700r Field workers .90 .40

Traditional Dance Type of 1992

Dance and region: 300r, Gending Sriwijaya, South Sumatra. 700r, Tempayan, West Kalimantan. 1000r, 3500r, Tifa, Irian Jaya.

1993, Dec. 22 *Perf. 12½x13½*

1564 A411 300r multicolored .50 .20
1565 A411 700r multicolored 1.00 .40
1566 A411 1000r multicolored 1.50 .55
Nos. 1564-1566 (3) 3.00 1.15

Souvenir Sheet

1567 A411 3500r multicolored 5.50 1.90

Intl. Year of the Family A426

1994, Mar. 1 Photo. *Perf. 13½x12½*

1568 A426 300r multicolored .50 .20

Indonesian Postage Stamps, 130th Anniv. — A427

Design: 700r, Netherlands Indies #B7, #N7, Indonesia #B214.

1994, Apr. 1 *Perf. 12½*

1569 A427 700r multicolored .90 .45

Souvenir Sheet

Imperf

1569A A427 3500r like #1569 4.25 2.00

PHILAKOREA '94 (#1569A).

6th Five Year Development Plan — A428

Buddhist dieties and: 100r, Professional women. 700r, Education. 2000r, Medical care for children.

1994, Apr. 1 *Perf. 12½*

1570 A428 100r multicolored .20 .20
1571 A428 700r multicolored .75 .40
1572 A428 2000r multicolored 1.90 .95
Nos. 1570-1572 (3) 2.85 1.55

Tropical Fish A429

Designs: 300r, Telmatherina ladigesi. 700r, 3500r, Melanotaenia boesemani.

1994, Apr. 20 Photo. *Perf. 13*
1573 A429 300r multicolored .35 .20
1574 A429 700r multicolored .75 .35

Souvenir Sheet

1575 A429 3500r multicolored 3.75 1.90

No. 1575 has continuous design.

Intl. Federation of Red Cross & Red Crescent Societies, 75th Anniv. — A429a

1994, May 5 *Perf. 12½x13*
1575A A429a 300r multicolored .50 .20

Second Asian and Pacific Ministerial Conference on Women, Jakarta — A430

1994, June 13 *Perf. 13½x12½*
1576 A430 700r multicolored .90 .40

A431

1994 World Cup Soccer Championships, US: 150r, Player dribbling ball, vert. 300r, Mascot chasing ball, vert. 700r, 1994 Tournament emblem. 1000r, Ball in net. 3500r, Soccer ball in net.

1994, June 17 *Perf. 12½x13½*
1577 A431 150r multicolored .20 .20
1578 A431 300r multicolored .35 .20

Perf. 13½x12½

1579 A431 700r multicolored .90 .40
1580 A431 1000r multicolored 1.25 .55
Nos. 1577-1580 (4) 2.70 1.35

Souvenir Sheet

1581 A431 3500r multicolored *5.00* 1.75

Thomas & Uber Cups — A432

Designs: a, Uber Cup. b, Thomas Cup.

1994, June 22 *Perf. 12½*
1582 A432 300r Pair, #a.-b. .90 .35

Souvenir Sheet of 2

1583 A432 1750r #a.-b. *4.25* 1.90

A433

A434

Perf. 12½x13½

1994, July 27 Photo.
1584 A433 700r multicolored .90 .40

Human Rights Day.

Perf. 13]x13½

1994, Aug. 19 Photo.
1585 A434 300r Brown pottery vase .35 .20
1586 A434 700r Blue & white vase .75 .35

Indonesia-Pakistan Econiomic & Cultural Cooperation Organization.
See Pakistan Nos. 822-823.

Bogoriense Zooligical Museum, Cent. — A435

700r, Skeleton of Javan rhinoceros. 1000r, 3500r, Skeleton of blue whale.

1994, Aug. 20 *Perf. 13½x13*
1587 A435 700r multicolored .75 .35

Size: 80x22mm

1588 A435 1000r multicolored 1.25 .60

Souvenir Sheet

Perf. 13x13½

1588A A435 3500r multicolored 4.25 2.25

12th Asian Games, Hiroshima 1994 A436

1994, Oct. 2 Litho. *Perf. 13½x13*
1589 A436 300r Mascots .35 .20
1590 A436 700r Hurdlers .75 .40

Bakosurtanal, 25th Anniv. — A437

1994, Oct. 17 Litho. *Perf. 13½x13*
1591 A437 700r multicolored .90 .40

Flora & Fauna — A438

Designs: a, Morus macroura. b, Oncosperma tigillaria. c, Eucalyptus urophylla. d, Phalaenopsis amabilis. e, Pometia pinnata. f, Argusianus argus. g, Loriculus pusillus. h, Philemon buceroides. i, Alisterus amboinensis. j, Seleucidis melanoleuca.
3500r, Philemon buceroides, diff.

1994, Nov. 5 Photo. *Perf. 12½x13½*
1592 A438 150r Block or strip of 10, #a.-j. *8.00* .80

Souvenir Sheet

1593 A438 3500r multicolored *4.25* 1.90
a. With added inscription in blue 10.00

Inscription in sheet margin of No. 1593a contains emblem and "PRIMERA '95." Issued: No. 1593a, 8/21/95.
See Nos. 1622, 1680-1682, 1737-1738, 1812-1814.

Asian-Pacific Economic Cooperation Summit (APEC '94) — A439

Design: 700r, Presidential retreat, Bogor.

1994, Nov. 15 *Perf. 13½X13*
1594 A439 700r multicolored .90 .40

For overprint see No. 1616A.

ICAO, 50th Anniv. A440

1994, Dec. 7
1595 A440 700r multicolored .90 .40

Traditional Dance Type of 1992

Dance, region: 150r, Mengaup, Jambi. 300r, Mask, West Java. 700r, Anging Mamiri, South Sulawesi. 1000r, Pisok, North Sulawesi. 2000r, Bidu, East Nusa Tenggara. 3500r, Mask dance, West Java.

1994, Dec. 27 *Perf. 12½x13½*
1596 A411 150r multicolored .20 .20
1597 A411 300r multicolored .30 .20
1598 A411 700r multicolored .70 .40
1599 A411 1000r multicolored 1.00 .55
1600 A411 2000r multicolored 2.10 1.10
a. Bklt. pane, 2 ea #1596-1600 12.50
Complete booklet, #1600a 12.50
Nos. 1596-1600 (5) 4.30 2.45

Souvenir Sheet

1601 A411 3500r multicolored 4.25 3.75

World Tourism Organization, 20th Anniv. — A441

Designs: 300r, Yogyakarta Palace. 700r, Floating market. 1000r, Pasola Sumba ritual.

1995, Jan. 2 *Perf. 13½x12½*
1602 A441 300r multicolored .25 .20
1603 A441 700r multicolored .60 .35
1604 A441 1000r multicolored .75 .45
Nos. 1602-1604 (3) 1.60 1.00

Indonesian Children, First Lady & Pres. Suharto A442

Perf. 13½x12½

1995, Mar. 11 Photo.
1605 A442 700r multicolored .65 .35

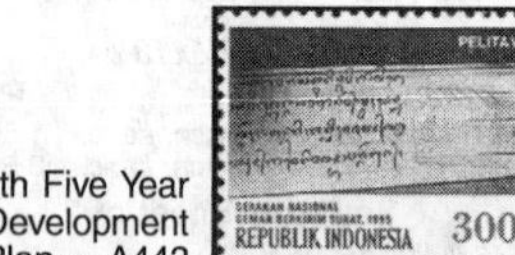

6th Five Year Development Plan — A443

Designs: 300r, Letter from King of Klungung, 18th-19th cent. 700r, Carrier pigeon mascot of natl. letter writing campaign.

1995, Apr. 1 Photo. *Perf. 12½*
1606 A443 300r multicolored .30 .20
1607 A443 700r multicolored .70 .40

4th Intl. Bamboo Conference — A444

Designs: 300r, Schizostachyum brachycladum. 700r, Dendrocalamus asper.

Perf. 12½x13½

1995, June 19 Photo.
1608 A444 300r multicolored .30 .20
1609 A444 700r multicolored .70 .30

First Flight of N250 Turboprop Commuter Airplane A445

1995, Aug. 10 *Perf. 13½x12½*
1610 A445 700r multicolored .65 .30

Independence, 50th Anniv. — A446

1995, Aug. 17
1611 A446 300r Anniv. emblem .25 .20
1612 A446 700r Boy, natl. flag .65 .30

Souvenir Sheet

1612A A446 2500r like No. 1612 3.75 1.25

JAKARTA '95, 8th Asian Intl. Philatelic Exhibition A447

Scenes in Jakarta: 300r, Kota Intan Drawbridge. 700r, Fatahillah Historical Museum.

1995, Aug. 19
1613 A447 300r multicolored .25 .20
1614 A447 700r multicolored .60 .30

No. 1613 exists in 7 souvenir sheets of 1, each with different color margins.

Sail Indonesia '95 A448

1995, Aug. 19
1615 A448 700r multicolored .65 .30

Souvenir Sheet

1616 A448 2500r multicolored 2.75 1.25

No. 1594 Overprinted "PRIMERA '95" in Blue

1995, Aug. 21 Photo. *Perf. 13½x13*
1616A A439 700r on #1594 2.00 2.00

Istiqlal (Independence) Festival II 1995, Jakarta — A449

1995, Sept. 23 *Perf. 12½x13½*
1617 A449 700r multicolored .60 .35

Takeover of Post, Telegraph, & Telephone Headquarters, 50th Anniv. — A450

1995, Sept. 27 *Perf. 13½x12½*
1618 A450 700r multicolored .60 .35

FAO, 50th Anniv. — A451

UN, 50th Anniv. — A452

1995, Oct. 16 *Perf. 12½x13½*
1619 A451 700r multicolored .65 .35

1995, Oct. 24 *Perf. 12½*

UN emblem, "50," and: 300r, Flags of nations. 700r, Rainbow over earth.

1620 A452 300r multicolored .25 .20
1621 A452 700r multicolored .65 .35

Flora and Fauna Type of 1994

Designs: a, Cyrtostachys renda. b, Panthera tigris sumatrae. c, Bouea macrophylla. d, Rhinoceros sondaicus. e, Santalum album. f, Varanus komodoensis. g, Diospyros celebica. h, Macrocephalon maleo. i, Nephleium ramboutan-ake. j, Polyplectron schleiermacheri.
2500r, Panthera tigris sumatrae.

1995, Nov. 5 Photo. *Perf. 12½x13½*
1622 A438 150r Block of 10, #a.-j. 1.50 .75

Souvenir Sheet

1623 A438 2500r multicolored *8.00* 1.25

1995 Aga Khan Award for Architecture — A453

Designs: 300r, Masjid Agung, Kraton Yogyakarta. 700r, Kraton Surakarta.

1995, Nov. 23 *Perf. 13½x13*
1624 A453 300r multicolored .30 .20
1625 A453 700r multicolored .70 .35

Sir Rowland Hill (1795-1879) — A454

300r, Hill, letter carriers on motorcycles. 700r, Hill, Indonesian postal service logo.

1995, Dec. 3 *Perf. 13½x12½*
1626 A454 300r multicolored .30 .20
1627 A454 700r multicolored .70 .35

Traditional Dance Type of 1992

Dance and region: 150r, Nguri, West Nusa Tenggara. 300r, Muli Betanggai, Lampung. 700r, Mutiara, Maluku. 1000r, Gantar, East Kalimantan. 2500r, Tari Nguri, Nusa Tenggara Barrat.

1995, Dec. 27 *Perf. 12½x13½*
1628 A411 150r multicolored .20 .20
1629 A411 300r multicolored .25 .20
1630 A411 700r multicolored .65 .35
1631 A411 1000r multicolored .90 .45
Nos. 1628-1631 (4) 2.00 1.20

Souvenir Sheet

1632 A411 2500r multicolored *3.75* 1.30

1996 Economic Census — A455

Design: 300r, Economic sectors, vert.

1996, Jan. 2 *Perf. 12½*
1633 A455 300r multicolored .30 .20
1634 A455 700r multicolored .70 .35

Greetings Stamps — A456

Various flowers.

1996, Feb. 1 Photo. *Perf. 12½*
1635 A456 150r multicolored .20 .20
1636 A456 300r multicolored .25 .20
1637 A456 700r multicolored .65 .35
Nos. 1635-1637 (3) 1.10 .75

See Nos. 1657-1659.

PWI Journalists' Assoc., 50th Anniv. — A457

Designs: 300r, RM Soemanang Soeriowinoto. 700r, Djamaluddin Adinegoro.

1996, Feb. 9
1638 A457 300r multicolored .30 .20
1639 A457 700r multicolored .70 .35

Australian Spotted Cuscus — A458

Design: Nos. 1640, 1642a, shown. Nos. 1641, 1642b, Indonesian bear cuscus.

1996, Mar.22 Photo. *Perf. 13x13½*
1640 A458 300r multicolored .25 .20
1641 A458 300r multicolored .25 .20
a. Pair, Nos. 1640-1641 .50 .30
b. Sheet of 5 #1641a *21.00* *10.50*

Souvenir Sheet

1642 A458 1250r Sheet of 2, #a.-b. *3.00* 1.25
c. #1642 with added inscription, ovpt. *5.00* 1.25

Indonesia '96 (#1641b).
No. 1642c has black CHINA '96 exhibition emblem in upper right corner. The bottom sheet margin contains gold overprint: "CHINA '96 - 9th Asian International Philatelic Exhibition" in both Chinese and English.
No. 1641b exists folded and affixed to a booklet cover. Value, $11.
See Australia Nos. 1489-1490.

A459

Launching of Palapa C Satellite — A460

1996, Jan. 31 *Perf. 13*
1643 A459 300r multicolored .30 .20

Perf. 12½

1644 A460 700r multicolored .70 .35

Indonesia '96, World Junior Philatelic Exhibition A461

Designs: 300r, No. 1647a, Building. 700r, No. 1647b, Decorated sun umbrellas.

1996, Mar. 21 *Perf. 13½x13*
1645 A461 300r multicolored .25 .20
1646 A461 700r multicolored .65 .35

Souvenir Sheet of 2

1647 A461 1250r #a.-b. *5.00* 1.25

No. 1647 exists imperf with different color margins. A souvenir sheet containg No. 1645-1646 and progressive color proofs of No. 1646 exists.

Education Day A462

Children's drawings: 150r, Teachers, students with outstretched arms. 300r, Children carrying books to school. 700r, Classroom instruction.

1996, May 2 Photo. *Perf. 13½x13*
1648 A462 150r multicolored .20 .20
1649 A462 300r multicolored .25 .20
1650 A462 700r multicolored .65 .35
Nos. 1648-1650 (3) 1.10 .75

Natl. Youth Kirab A463

1996, June 8
1651 A463 300r shown .30 .20
1652 A463 700r Holding flag, emblem .70 .35

1996 Summer Olympics, Atlanta A464

1996, May 15
1653 A464 300r Archery .25 .20
1654 A464 700r Weight lifting .65 .30
1655 A464 1000r Badminton .90 .50
Nos. 1653-1655 (3) 1.80 1.00

Souvenir Sheet

1656 A464 2500r like #1653 3.00 1.25

No. 1656 is a continuous design.

Greetings Type of 1996

1996, Apr. 15 Photo. *Perf. 12½*
1657 A456 150r Roses .20 .20
1658 A456 300r Orchids .25 .20
1659 A456 700r Chrysanthemums .65 .35
Nos. 1657-1659 (3) 1.10 .75

Maritime and Aviation Year — A465

300r, N-2130 aircraft, control tower at Soekarno-Hatta Airport. 700r, Inter-island passenger ship.

1996, June 22
1660 A465 300r multicolored .30 .20
1661 A465 700r multicolored .70 .35

1996 Natl. Scout Jamboree A466

Designs: a, Climbing rope. b, Sliding down rope. c, Girls at bottom of ropes. d, Girls assembling wood and rope ladder. e, Riding unicycle, eagle emblem, boys building scaffolding. f, Girls building scaffolding, campground. g, Two boys with project. h, Woman seated at control center.
No. 1662I, like #1662a-1662d. No. 1662J, like #1662e-1662h.

1996, June 26
1662 A466 150r Block of 8, #a.-h. 1.10 .55

Souvenir Sheets

1662I A466 1250d multicolored 1.50 .75
1662J A466 1250d multicolored 1.50 .75

Istanbul '96 (#1662I-1662J). Nos. 1662I-1662J each contain one 64x48mm stamp.
Nos. 1662a-1662d, 1663e-1662h are continuous designs.

Bank BNI, 50th Anniv. A467

1996, July 5
1663 A467 300r shown .30 .20
1664 A467 700r Sailing ship .70 .35

UNICEF, 50th Anniv. A468

1996, July 23 *Perf. 13½x13*
1665 A468 300r Child reading .25 .20
1666 A468 700r Two children .65 .30
1667 A468 1000r Three children .90 .50
Nos. 1665-1667 (3) 1.80 1.00

Ibu Tien Suharto (1923-96) First Lady — A469

1996, Aug. 5 *Perf. 12½x13½*
1668 A469 700r multicolored .70 .35

Souvenir Sheet

1669 A469 2500r like #1668 3.00 1.25

No. 1669 is a continuous design.

14th Natl. Sports Week, Jakarta
A470

Perf. 13½x12½

1996, Sept. 2 **Photo.**

1670 A470 300r Softball .25 .20
1671 A470 700r Field hockey .65 .30
1672 A470 1000r Basketball .90 .50
Nos. 1670-1672 (3) 1.80 1.00

World Wildlife Fund
A471

Rhinoceros sondaicus: a, #1674a, Adult. b, Adult with young. Dicerorhinus sumatrensis: c, Up close. d, #1674b, Adult.

1996, Oct. 2 **Photo.** ***Perf. 13½x13***

1673 A471 300r Block of 4, #a.-d. 1.10 .55
e. Souvenir sheet, 2 #1673 5.50 2.75
f. As "e," ovptd. in sheet margin 2.25 1.10

Overprint in margin of No. 1673f reads: "Bursa Filateli SEA Games XIX / Jakarta, 11-19 Oktober 1997" in gold.

1674 A471 1500r Sheet of 2, #a.-b. 4.00 1.50

Greetings Stamps — A472

Bouquets of various flowers.

1996, Oct. 15 **Photo.** ***Perf. 12½***

Background Colors

1675 A472 150r yellow & blue .20 .20
1676 A472 300r yellow & green .25 .20
1677 A472 700r pink & blue .65 .35
Nos. 1675-1677 (3) 1.10 .75

Financial Day, 50th Anniv.
A473

1996, Oct. 30 ***Perf. 13½x12½***

1678 A473 700r multicolored .65 .35

Flora & Fauna Type of 1994

Fauna: No. 1680: a, Aceros cassidix. b, Orcaella brevirostris. c, Oriolus chinensis. d, Helarctos malayanus. e, Leucopsar rothschildi.

Flora: f, Borassus flabellifer. g, Coelogyne pandurata. h, Michelia alba. i, Amorphophallus titanum. j, Dysoxyleum densiflorium.

No. 1681, Like #1680e. No. 1682, Like #1680g.

1996, Nov. 5 **Litho.** ***Perf. 12½x13½***

1680 A438 300r Block or strip of 10, #a.-j. 2.60 1.25
a.-j. Any single .25 .20

Souvenir Sheets

1681 A438 1250r multicolored *2.00* .65
1682 A438 1250r multicolored *2.00* .65

Souvenir Sheet

Aceros Cassidix — A474

Perf. 12½x13½

1996, Dec. 14 **Photo.**

1683 A474 2000r multicolored *7.00* .95

ASEANPEX '96.

Scenes from Timor
A475

Designs: 300r, Deep sea diving. 700r, Sailing ships entering harbor, 18th cent.

1996-97 ***Perf. 13½x12½***

1684 A475 300r multicolored .30 .20
1685 A475 700r multicolored .70 .35

Souvenir Sheet

1685A A475 2000d like #1685 2.00 1.00

Hong Kong '97 (#1685A).

Issued: #1686-1687, 12/18/96; #1685A, 2/12/97.

Foster Parents
A476

150r, Children at playground, vert. 300r, Children, adult's hand holding picture of girl.

Perf. 12½x13½, 13½x12½

1996, Dec. 20

1686 A476 150r multicolored .20 .20
1687 A476 300r multicolored .30 .20

Traditional Dance Type of 1992

Dance, region: 150r, Tari Baksa Kembang, Kalimantan Selatan. 300r, 2000r, Tari Ngarojeng, Jakarta. 700r, Tari Rampai, Aceh. 1000r, Tari Boituka, Timor.

1996, Dec. 27 ***Perf. 12½x13½***

1688 A411 150r multicolored .20 .20
1689 A411 300r multicolored .20 .20
1690 A411 700r multicolored .45 .25
1691 A411 1000r multicolored .65 .35
Nos. 1688-1691 (4) 1.50 1.00

Souvenir Sheet

1692 A411 2000r multicolored 1.90 .95

Telecommunications Year — A477

Designs: 300r, Satellite dish, men at computers, map. 700r, Telephone keypad, woman using telephone, satellite in earth orbit.

1997, Jan. 1 ***Perf. 13½x12½***

1693 A477 300r multicolored .20 .20
1694 A477 700r multicolored .55 .25

Greetings Stamps — A478

Designs: No. 1695, Heart, ribbon. No. 1696, Children, "Happy Birthday."

1997, Jan. 15 ***Perf. 12½***

1695 A478 600r multicolored .50 .25
1696 A478 600r multicolored .50 .25

1997 General Election
A479

Ballot box and: 300r, Means of transportion. 700r, Indonesian Archipelago, House of Representatives Building. 1000r, Map, symbols of development.

1997, Feb. 3 ***Perf. 13½x13***

1697 A479 300r multicolored .20 .20
1698 A479 700r multicolored .55 .25
1699 A479 1000r multicolored .75 .35
Nos. 1697-1699 (3) 1.50 .80

Birth of Indonesia's 200-millionth Citizen — A480

Perf. 13½x12½

1997, Mar. 24 **Litho.**

1700 A480 700r Pres. Suharto, baby .55 .25

A481 A482

Indonesian Philatelists Assoc., 75th Anniv.: 300r, Youth examining stamps, #1672. 700r, Magnifying glass, #1660, #1592h, #1580.

1997, Mar. 29 ***Perf. 12½x13½***

1701 A481 300r multicolored .25 .20
1702 A481 700r multicolored .60 .30

1997, Apr. 30 **Litho.** ***Perf. 13x13½***

Indonesian Artists: 300r, Wage Rudolf Soepratman (1903-38), composer, violinist. 700r, Usmar Ismail (1921-71), film pioneer, director. 1000r, Affandi (1907-90), painter.

1703 A482 300r multicolored .25 .20
1704 A482 700r multicolored .60 .30
1705 A482 1000r multicolored .80 .40
b. Sheet, 3 each #1703-1705 + label 5.75 2.75
Nos. 1703-1705 (3) 1.65 .90

Souvenir Sheet

1705A A482 2000r like #1705 2.00 1.00

Indonesia 2000
A483

Gemstones: 300r, Picture jasper. 700r, Chrysocolla. 1000r, Geode. 2000r, Banded agate.

1997, May 20 **Litho.** ***Perf. 13½x13***

1706 A483 300r multicolored .25 .20
1707 A483 700r multicolored .60 .30
1708 A483 1000r multicolored .85 .40
a. Sheet, 3 each, #1706-1708 + label 5.75 2.75
b. As "a," control No. in margin *14.00* *7.00*
Nos. 1706-1708 (3) 1.70 .90

Souvenir Sheet

1709 A483 2000r multicolored 2.50 .85
a. Control No. in margin *4.75* *2.50*

Nos. 1708b, 1709a promote INDONESIA 2000, Jakarta, Aug. 15-21, 2000. Nos. 1708a-1709 and 1708b-1709a were issued in presentation packs with certificate of authenticity.

See Nos. 1764-1767A, 1848-1851.

A484

1997, May 31 **Photo.** ***Perf. 12½***

1710 A484 1000r multicolored .85 .40

World Day to Stop Smoking.

World Environment Day — A485

1997, June 5 **Litho.** ***Perf. 13x13½***

Various marine life of the coral reefs.

1711 A485 150r multicolored .20 .20
1712 A485 300r multicolored .25 .20
1713 A485 700r multicolored .55 .30
Nos. 1711-1713 (3) 1.00 .70

Souvenir Sheet

1714 A485 2000r multicolored 1.90 .95

ASEAN, 30th Anniv.
A486

300r, Hands reaching out to each other. 700r, Rice stalks arranged to form number 30, globe.

1997, Aug. 8 **Litho.** ***Perf. 13½x13***

1715 A486 300r multicolored .25 .20
1716 A486 700r multicolored .60 .30

19th Southeast Asia Games, Jakarta — A487

#1717, Logo, "Hanoman" mascot. #1718, Runner carrying torch, flags of participating nations, logo. #1719, Runner, track, discus thrower. #1720, Hurdler, runners.

1997, Sept. 9 **Litho.** ***Perf. 12½***

1717 A487 300r multicolored .20 .20
1718 A487 300r multicolored .20 .20
a. Pair, #1717-1718 .40 .20
1719 A487 700r multicolored .45 .25
1720 A487 700r multicolored .45 .25
a. Pair, #1719-1720 .90 .45
b. Bklt. pane, 2 ea #1717-1720 3.00
Complete booklet, 1 #1720b 3.00
Nos. 1717-1720 (4) 1.30 .90

Transportation — A488

1997, Sept. 17

1721 A488 300r Buses, ox cart .20 .20
1722 A488 300r Trains .20 .20
a. Pair, #1721-1722 .40 .20
1723 A488 700r Ships .45 .25
1724 A488 700r Airplanes .45 .25
a. Pair, #1723-1724 .90 .50
Nos. 1721-1724 (4) 1.30 .90

Souvenir Sheet

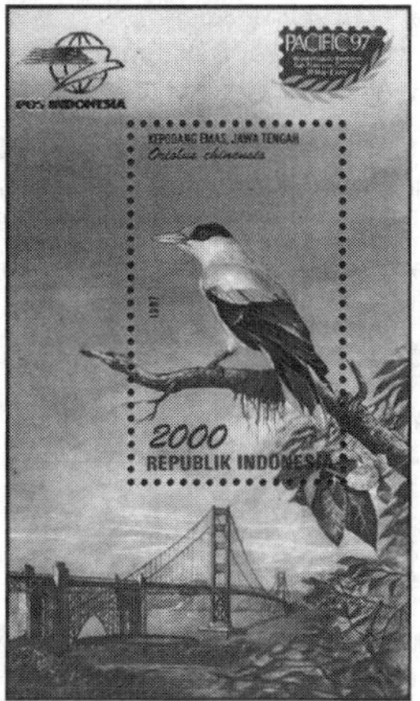
Oriolus Chinensis — A489

1997, May 29 ***Perf. 12½x13½***

1725 A489 2000r multicolored 1.90 .95

PACIFIC 97.

Nusantara Royal Palace Festival A490

Royal carriages: 300r, Singa Baraong wooden carriage, 1549, with carving of mythical animal. 700r, Paksi Naga Liman carriage, phoenix-like bird.

1997, July 1 Litho. ***Perf. 13½x12½***

1726 A490 300r multicolored .30 .20
1727 A490 700r multicolored .70 .35

18th Natl. Koran Reading Contest — A491

Designs: 300r, Decorated roof peaks, windows. 700r, Al-Ikhsaniah Mosque.

1997, July 9 ***Perf. 12½***

1728 A491 300r multicolored .30 .20
1729 A491 700r multicolored .70 .35

Indonesian Membership in UPU, 50th Anniv. — A492

Emblem of UPU and: 300r, Mas Soeharto. 700r, Heinrich von Stephan.

1997, Sept. 27 Litho. ***Perf. 13½x13***

1730 A492 300r multicolored .20 .20
1731 A492 700r multicolored .40 .20

1997-98 General Session of People's Consultative Assembly — A493

1997, Oct. 1 ***Perf. 12½***

1732 A493 700r multicolored .40 .20

Indonesian Armed Forces Day A494

Designs: a, ABRI Village Program. b, Jalesveva Jayamahe Monument. c, Blue Falcon Flight Demonstration Team. d, Police Fast Reaction Unit.

1997, Oct. 5 ***Perf. 13½x12½***

1733 A494 300r Block of 4, #a.-d. .80 .20

Flora and Fauna Type of 1994

Fauna: No. 1737: a, Chitala lopis. b, Haliastur indus. c, Rhinoplax vigil. d, Cervus timorensis. e, Bubalus depressicornis.

Flora: f, Lansium domesticum. g, Salacca zalacca. h, Shorea stenoptera. i, Diospyros macrophylla. j, Diplocaulobium utile.

#1738: a, Shorea stenoptera. b, Haliastur indus.

1997, Nov. 5 ***Perf. 12½x13½***

1737 A438 300r Block of 10 2.50 1.25
a.-j. Any single .25 .20

Souvenir Sheet

1738 A438 1250r Sheet of 2, #a.-b. 1.60 .80

A495

Indonesian Cooperatives Day — A496

Designs: No. 1739, Cooperatives Monument, Tasikmalaya. No. 1740, Cooperatives Monument, Jakarta. No. 1741, Adult taking child's hand. No. 1742, Globe, movement towards globalization. No. 1743, Dr. Mohammad Hatta, Pres. Suharto.

1997, July 12 Litho. ***Perf. 12½x13½***

1739 A495 150r multicolored .20 .20
1740 A495 150r multicolored .20 .20
a. Pair, #1739-1740 .20 .20
1741 A495 300r multicolored .25 .20
1742 A495 300r multicolored .25 .20
a. Pair, #1741-1742 .50 .25

Perf. 12½

1743 A496 700r multicolored .60 .30
Nos. 1739-1743 (5) 1.50 1.10

ASCOPE '97 (Asian Council on Petroleum) A497

a, LNG tanker. b, Petroleum trucks. c, Drilling rig, pumping wells. d, Refinery.

1997, Nov. 24 ***Perf. 13½x12½***

1744 A497 300r Block of 4, #a.-d. .75 .35

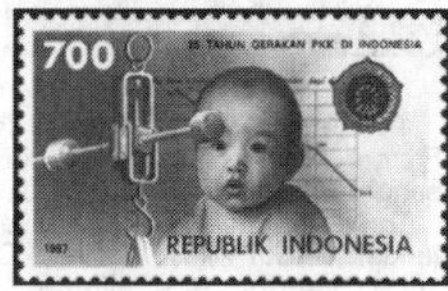
Foster Parents Natl. Movement A498

1997, Dec. 20 **Photo.**

1745 A498 700r multicolored .50 .25

Family Welfare Movement, 25th Anniv. A499

1997, Dec. 27 **Litho.**

1746 A499 700r multicolored .50 .25

Traditional Dance Type of 1992

Dance, region: 150r, Mopuputi Cengke (clove picking), Central Sulawesi. 300r, Mandau Talawang Nyai Balau, Central Kalimantan. 600r, 2000r, Gambyong, Central Java. 700r, Cawan (bowl,) North Sumatra. 1000r, Legong Keraton, Bali.

1997, Dec. 27

1747 A411 150r multicolored .20 .20
1748 A411 300r multicolored .20 .20
1749 A411 600r multicolored .35 .25
1750 A411 700r multicolored .45 .30
1751 A411 1000r multicolored .60 .40
Nos. 1747-1751 (5) 1.80 1.35

Souvenir Sheet

Perf. 12½x13½

1752 A411 2000r multicolored 2.00 1.00

No. 1752 is a continuous design.

Souvenir Sheet

Sulawesi Selatan — A500

Illustration reduced.

1997, Oct. 11 Litho. ***Perf. 13½x12½***

1753 A500 2000r multicolored 1.25 .65

Makasser '97 National Philatelic Exhibition.

Year of Art and Culture 1998 — A501

Designs: 300r, Erau Festival, East Kalimantan. 700r, Tabot Festival, Bengkulu.

1998, Jan. 1 Litho. ***Perf. 12½***

1754 A501 300r multicolored .20 .20
1755 A501 700r multicolored .45 .20

Indonesian Folktales A502

Folktale, region - No. 1759; a-e, Malin Kundang, West Sumatra. f-j: Sangkuriang, West Java. k-o, Roro Jonggrang, Central Java. p-t: Tengger, East Java. Each horizontal strip of 5 has continuous design.

2500r, Kasodo Ceremony, Tenegger, East Java.

1998, Feb. 2 ***Perf. 13½x12½***

1759 Sheet of 20 5.00 2.75
a.-t. A502 300r Any single .25 .20

Souvenir Sheet

1760 A502 2500r like #1759e 2.00 1.00

See Nos. 1828-1829, 1886-1887.

Presidential Palaces — A503

Designs: a, Jakarta. b, Bogor. c, Cipanas. d, Yogyakarta. e, Tampak Siring.

1998, Apr. 1

1761 A503 300r Strip of 5, #a.-e. 1.25 .65

World Health Organization, 50th Anniv. — A504

Designs: 300r, Pregnant woman, man, vert. 700r, Woman holding baby.

1998, Apr. 7 Litho. ***Perf. 12½***

1762 A504 300r multicolored .30 .20
1763 A504 700r multicolored .75 .40

Indonesia 2000 Type of 1997

Gemstones: 300r, Chrysopal. 700r, Tektite. 1000r, Amethyst. #1767, Petrified wood. #1767A, opal.

1998, May 20 ***Perf. 13½x12½***

1764 A483 300r multicolored .20 .20
1765 A483 700r multicolored .20 .20
1766 A483 1000r multicolored .20 .20
a. Sheet, 3 each #1764-1766 + label *1.00* *.50*
Nos. 1764-1766 (3) .60 .60

Souvenir Sheets

1767 A483 2500r multicolored .50 .25

Perf. 13½x14

1767A A483 2500r multicolored 2.50 1.25
b. Sheet, 2 each, #1764-1766, 1 each #1767, 1767A 7.00 6.75

Nos. 1767A, 1764b were issued in presentation packs with control numbers printed in margin and certificate of authenticity.

No. 1767A sold for 10,000r. No. 1767Ab sold for 25,000r.

1998 World Cup Soccer Championships, France — A505

Young boys playing soccer in Indonesia: 300r, Outside school, boy on bicycle. 700r, In neighborhood lot. 1000r, 2500r, In rural area.

1998, June 1

1768 A505 300r multicolored .30 .20
1769 A505 700r multicolored .70 .35
1770 A505 1000r multicolored 1.00 .45
Nos. 1768-1770 (3) 2.00 1.00

Souvenir Sheet

1771 A505 2500r multicolored 2.50 2.50

World Environment Day — A506

Trees along river bank, denomination at: No. 1772, lower right. No. 1773, lower left.

1998, June 5

1772 A506 700r multicolored .70 .35
1773 A506 700r multicolored .70 .35
a. Pair, #1772-1773 1.40 .70

Souvenir Sheet

Juvalux '98, World Philatelic Exhibition, Luxembourg — A507

1998, June 18 ***Perf. 12½x13½***

1774 A507 5000r Felis viverrina 5.00 2.50

World Day to Fight Drug Abuse and Illicit Drug Trafficking — A508

Cartoons depicting how to say no to drugs.

1998, June 26

1775 A508 700r red & multi .70 .35
1776 A508 700r yellow & multi .70 .35
a. Pair, #1775-1776 1.40 .70
b. Tete beche pair, #1775-1776 1.40 .70

Tourism — A509

Temples, shrines in Bali: Nos. 1777, 1779, Pura Besakih. No. 1778, Pura Taman Ayun.

1998, July 1 ***Perf. 12½***

1777 A509 700r multicolored .70 .35
1778 A509 700r shown .70 .35
a. Pair, #1777-1778 1.40 .70

Souvenir Sheet

Perf. 13½x13

1779 A509 2500r multicolored 2.50 1.25

No. 1777 is 64x24mm. No. 1779 contains one 41x25mm stamp.

Souvenir Sheet

Panthera Tigris — A510

Illustration reduced.

1998, July 23 Litho. ***Perf. 13½x12½***

1780 A510 5000r multicolored 1.00 .50

Singpex '98.

Trains A511

Train going right: a, Cattle, freight cars. b, Freight, box cars. c, Passenger cars. d, Passenger car, tender. e, Locomotive 850.
Train going left: f, Locomotive D52. g, Coal tender. h, Car with 2 doors. i, Dining car with large windows. j, Car with two windows.
2500r, Locomotive.

1998, Aug. 10

1781 A511 300r Block of 10, #a.-j. .60 .30

Souvenir Sheet

1782 A511 2500r multicolored .50 .25

No. 1781 issued in sheets of 20 stamps consisting of two tete-beche blocks of 10. No. 1782 contains one 41x25mm stamp.

Pres. H.B.J. Habibie — A512

1998, Aug. 17 ***Perf. 12½x13½***

1783 A512 300r pink & multi .20 .20
1784 A512 700r blue & multi .20 .20
1785 A512 4500r green & multi .95 .45
1786 A512 5000r yellow & multi 1.00 .50
Nos. 1783-1786 (4) 2.35 1.35

13th Asian Games A513

1998, Sept. 9 ***Perf. 13½x12½***

1787 A513 300r Fencing .20 .20
1788 A513 700r Taekwondo .20 .20
1789 A513 4000r Wushu .85 .40
a. Sovenir sheet, #1787-1789 1.10 .55
Nos. 1787-1789 (3) 1.25 .80

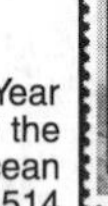

Intl. Year of the Ocean A514

Perf. 13½x12½

1998, Sept. 26 **Litho.**

1790 A514 700r multicolored .20 .20

Souvenir Sheets

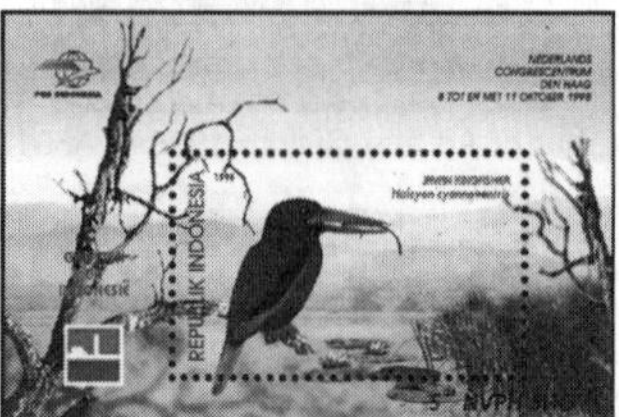

5th NVPH (Netherlands Philatelic Congress) Exhibition, The Hague — A514a

Birds: 5000r, Halcyon cyannoventris. 35,000r, Vannelus macropterus, vert.
Illustration reduced.

1998, Oct. 8 Litho. ***Perf. 13½x12½***

1790A A514a 5000r multi 1.10 .55
1790B A514a 35,000r multi 7.75 3.75

A515

A516

1998, Oct. 9 ***Perf. 12½x13½***

1791 A515 700r #922 .20 .20
1792 A515 700r #414 .20 .20
a. Pair, #1791-1792 .30 .20

World Stamp Day.

Litho. (#1793-1799, 1805)

1998 ***Perf. 12½***

Ducks and Geese: 250r, #1805, Aythya australis. 500r, Anas superciliosa. 700r, Anas gibberifrons. 1000r, Nettapus coromandelianus. 1500r, Nettapus pulchelus. 2500r, Dendrocygna javanica. 3500r, Dendrocygna arcuata. 4000r, Anseranas semipalmata. #1801, Dendrocygna guttata. 10,000r, Anas waigiuensis. 15,000r, Tadorna radjah. 20,000r, Cairina scutulata.

1793 A516 250r multi .20 .20
1794 A516 500r multi .20 .20
1795 A516 700r multi .20 .20
1796 A516 1000r multi .25 .20
1797 A516 1500r multi .35 .20
1798 A516 2500r multi .60 .30
1799 A516 3500r multi .80 .40

Litho. With Hologram

Perf. 13½x12½

Size: 42x25mm

1800 A516 4000r horiz. .90 .45
1801 A516 5000r horiz. 1.10 .55
1802 A516 10,000r horiz. 2.25 1.10
1803 A516 15,000r horiz. 3.50 1.75
1804 A516 20,000r horiz. 4.50 2.25
a. Sheet of 5, #1800-1804, + 4 labels 14.00 7.00
Nos. 1793-1804 (12) 14.85 7.80

Souvenir Sheet

Perf. 12½

1805 A516 5000r lt blue sky 1.10 .55

Soaking in water may affect the hologram on #1800-1804.

Issued: #1793-1799, 1805, 12/1; others 10/19.

Souvenir Sheet

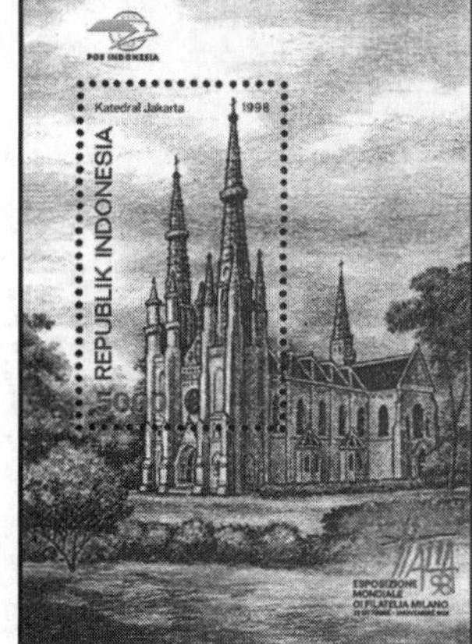

Italia '98 — A516a

Illustration reduced.

1998, Oct. 23 ***Perf. 12½x13½***

1805A A516a 5000r Jakarta Cathedral 1.25 .65

National Flag — A517

Mountains and: #1806, Flagpole at right. #1807, Flagpole at left.

1998, Oct. 28 Litho. ***Perf. 12½x13½***

1806 A517 700r multicolored .20 .20
1807 A517 700r multicolored .20 .20
a. Pair, #1806-1807 .30 .20

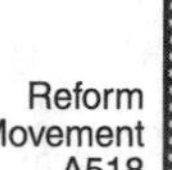

Reform Movement A518

No. 1809, Dove, national flag. No. 1810, Students, Parliament Building.

1998, Oct. 28 ***Perf. 13½x12½***

1808 A518 700r shown .20 .20
1809 A518 700r multicolored .20 .20
a. Pair, #1808-1809 .30 .20

Size: 83x25mm

1810 A518 1000r multicolored .25 .20

Flora and Fauna Type of 1994

Flora - #1812: a, Stelechocarpus burahol. b, Polianthes tuberosa. c, Mirabilis jalapa. d, Mangifera casturi. e, Ficus minahassae.
Fauna - f, Geopelia striata. g, Gallus varius. h, Elephas maximus. i, Nasalis larvatus. j, Tarsius spectrum.
No. 1813, like #1812b. No. 1814, like #1812i.

1998, Nov. 5 ***Perf. 12½x13½***

1812 A438 500r Block of 10 1.25 .60
a.-j. Any single .20 .20

Souvenir Sheets

1813 A438 2500r multicolored .60 .30
1814 A438 2500r multicolored .60 .30

Traditional Dance Type of 1992

Dance, region: 300r, Oreng-oreng Gae, Southeast Sulawesi. 500r, Tribute dance, Bengkulu. 700r, Fan dance, Riau. 1000r, Srimpi, Yogyakarta. 2000r, 5000r, Tribute dance, West Sumatra.

1998, Dec. 27

1815 A411 300r multicolored .20 .20
1816 A411 500r multicolored .20 .20
1817 A411 700r multicolored .20 .20
1818 A411 1000r multicolored .25 .20
1819 A411 2000r multicolored .55 .20
Nos. 1815-1819 (5) 1.40 1.00

Souvenir Sheet

1820 A411 5000r multicolored 1.10 .55

Creation and Engineering Year — A519

Designs: 500r, Hydroelectric turbine, power lines. 700r, Plumbing fixture, water pipes.

1999, Jan. 1 Litho. ***Perf. 12½***

1821 A519 500r multicolored .20 .20
1822 A519 700r multicolored .20 .20

7th Far East & South Pacific Games for Disabled A520

Garuda Indonesia Airways, 50th Anniv. A521

1999, Jan. 10 ***Perf. 12½x13½***

1823 A520 500r Throwing shotput .20 .20
1824 A520 500r Medals, wheelchair .20 .20
a. Pair, #1823-1824 .25 .20

1999, Jan. 26 *Perf. 13x13½*

1825 A521 500r Logo .20 .20
1826 A521 700r Aircraft maintenance .20 .20
1827 A521 2000r Pilot, attendant .45 .25
Nos. 1825-1827 (3) .85 .65

Indonesian Folktales Type of 1998

Folktale, region - #1828: a-e, Danau Toba, North Sumatra. f-j, Banjarmasin, South Kalimantan. k-o, Buleleng, Bali. p-t, Woiram, Irian Jaya.
5000r, like #1828e.

1999, Feb. 15 *Perf. 13½x12½*

1828 Sheet of 20 2.50 1.25
a.-e. A502 500r Strip of 5 .60 .30
f.-j. A502 500r Strip of 5 .60 .30
k.-o. A502 500r Strip of 5 .60 .30
p.-t. A502 500r Strip of 5 .60 .30

Souvenir Sheet

1829 A502 5000r multicolored 1.10 .55

Nos. 1829 is a continuous design.

Souvenir Sheet

Surabaya '99, Natl. Philatelic Exhibition — A522

Illustration reduced.

1999, Mar. 4 Litho. *Perf. 13½x12½*

1830 A522 5000r Apples 1.25 .65
a. Ovptd. in sheet margin 1.25 .65

No. 1830a Overprinted in Gold in Sheet Margin with "APPI SHOW '99 / SURABAYA, 10-18 JULI 1999" and Emblem. Issued, 7/10.

Souvenir Sheet

Australia '99, World Stamp Expo — A523

Illustration reduced.

1999, Mar. 19 *Perf. 12½x13½*

1831 A523 5000r Tarsius spectrum 1.25 .65
a. Ovptd. in sheet margin 1.25 .65

No. 1831a Overprinted in Gold in Sheet Margin with "The 13th / Thaipex / China / Stamp Exhibition / Bangkok '99 / 4 -15. 8. 99" and Emblem. Issued, 8/15.

Mushrooms — A524

No. 1832: a, Mutinus bambusinus. b, Ascosparassis heinricherii. c, Mycena sp.
No. 1833: a, Microporus xanthopus. b, Gloeophyllum imponens. c, Termitomyces eurrhizus.
No. 1834: a, Aseroe rubra. b, Calostoma orirubra. c, Boedijnopeziza insititia.
5000r, Termitomyces eurrhizus.

1999, Apr. 1 *Perf. 12½*

1832 A524 500r Triptych, #a.-c. .40 .20
1833 A524 700r Triptych, #a.-c. .55 .30
1834 A524 1000r Triptych, #a.-c. .75 .40
d. Souvenir sheet, #1832-1834 1.75 .90

Souvenir Sheet

1835 A524 5000r multicolored 1.25 .65

Booklet Stamps

Size:32x24mm

1836 A524 500r Like #1832a .20 .20
1837 A524 500r Like #1832b .20 .20
1838 A524 500r Like #1832c .20 .20
a. Booklet pane, 3 each #1836-1838, + label 1.50
Complete booklet, #1838a 1.50
Nos. 1836-1838 (3) .60 .60

No. 1835 contains one 25x41mm stamp. Numbers have been reserved for additional values in this set.

Public Health Care Insurance — A525

1999, Apr. 7 *Perf. 13½x12½*

1845 A525 700r multicolored .20 .20

Souvenir Sheet

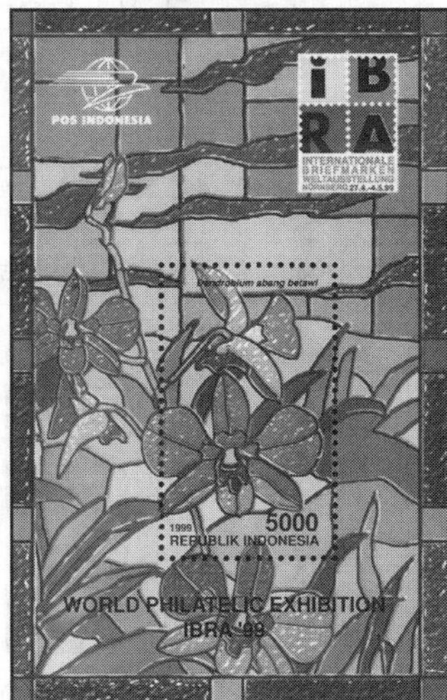

IBRA '99, Intl. Philatelic Exhibition, Nuremberg — A526

Illustration reduced.

1999, Apr. 27 *Perf. 12½x13½*

1846 A526 5000r Dendrobium abang betawi 1.25 .65

Y2K Millennium Bug — A527

Designs: a, "Bug." b, Circuit, android.

1999, May 2 *Perf. 13½x12½*

1847 A527 500r Pair, #a.-b. .30 .20

Indonesia 2000 Type of 1997

1999, May 20 Litho. *Perf. 13½x12¾*

1848 A483 500r Chrysoprase .20 .20
1849 A483 1000r Smoky quartz .30 .20
1850 A483 2000r Opal blue .60 .30
a. Sheet, 3 ea #1848-1850 + label 3.25 3.25
Nos. 1848-1850 (3) 1.10 .70

Souvenir Sheet

1851 A483 4000r Silicified coral 1.25 .65
1851A A483 4000r Javan jade 2.75 2.75
b. Sheet, #1851-1851A, 2 ea # 1849-1850, 4 #1848 8.25 8.25

Nos. 1851A, 1851Ab were issued in presentation packs with certificate of authenticity. Control numbers and silver overpint "1 Tahun/ Lagi / 1 Year / to Go" printed in margin. No. 1851A sold for 10,000r; No. 1851b for 30,000r.

Environmental Care — A528

Winning designs of 1999 Ecophila Stamp Design Contest: 500r, Girl wrapped in blanket, people walking through water. 1000r, 3000r, Boy swimming with duck, plant, cherry. 2000r, Elderly woman drinking water from pitcher, outdoor scene.

1999, June 5

1852 A528 500r multicolored .20 .20
1853 A528 1000r multicolored .30 .20
1854 A528 2000r multicolored .60 .30
Nos. 1852-1854 (3) 1.10 .70

Souvenir Sheet

1855 A528 3000r multicolored .90 .45

1999 General Election — A529

Designs: a, "48," Banner, people standing in line to vote. b, People waiting turn to enter election booth, map.

1999, June 4

1856 A529 1000r Pair, #a.-b. .60 .30

Souvenir Sheet

PhilexFrance '99 — A530

1999, July 2 Litho. *Perf. 12¾x13½*

1858 A530 5000r multi 1.40 .70

Red Cross / Red Crescent Millennium Year Campaign — A531

Photo. & Litho.

1999, Aug. 12 *Perf. 12½*

1859 A531 1000r multicolored .30 .20

National Heroes — A532

No. 1860: a, Dr. W. Z. Johannes (1895-1924). b, Martha Christina Tijahahu (1800-18), freedom fighter. c, Frans Kaisiepo (1921-79), politician. d, Maria Walanda Maramis (1872-1924), educator.

Litho. & Engr.

1999, Aug. 17 *Perf. 12½*

1860 Strip of 4 .55 .25
a.-d. A532 500r any single .20 .20
e. Booklet pane of 4, #1860a .65
f. Booklet pane of 4, #1860b .65
g. Booklet pane of 4, #1860c .65
h. Booklet pane of 4, #1860d .65
Complete bklt., #1860e-1860h 2.75

Complete booklet sold for 10,000r.

Souvenir Sheet

China 1999 World Philatelic Exhibition — A533

Illustration reduced.

Perf. 13½x12¾

1999, Aug. 21 **Litho.**

1861 A533 5000r multi 1.40 .70

Gadjah Mada University, 50th Anniv. — A534

1999, Sept. 19 *Perf. 12½*

1862 A534 500r shown .20 .20
1863 A534 1000r Building, diff. .25 .20

Intl. Year of Older Persons — A535

1999, Oct. 1 *Perf. 13½x12¾*

1864 A535 500r multi .20 .20

UPU, 125th Anniv. — A536

1999, Oct. 9 ***Perf. 12½***

1865	A536 500r Postman on horse	.20	.20
1866	A536 500r Postman on motorcycle	.20	.20
a.	Pair, #1865-1866 + label	.30	.20
1866B	Pair + 2 labels	—	—
c.	A536 1000r Like #1865, 30x32mm	—	—
d.	A536 1000r Like #1866, 30x32mm	—	—

No. 1866B issued in sheets of 5 pairs. As the labels could be personalized, sheets were available only through special orders with Indonesia Post and sold for 20,000r.

Batik Designs — A537

1999, Oct. 1

1867	A537 500r Cirebon	.20	.20
1868	A537 500r Madura	.20	.20
1869	A537 500r Jambi	.20	.20
1870	A537 500r Yogyakarta	.20	.20
	Nos. 1867-1870 (4)	.80	.80

Domesticated Animals — A538

1999, Nov. 5 ***Perf. 13½x12¾***

1871	A538 500r Dogs	.20	.20
1872	A538 500r Chickens	.20	.20
a.	Pair, #1871-1872	.30	.20
1873	A538 500r Cat	.20	.20
1874	A538 500r Rabbits	.20	.20
a.	Pair, #1873-1874	.30	.20
1875	A538 1000r Pigeon	.25	.20
1876	A538 1000r Geese	.25	.20
a.	Pair, #1875-1876	.50	.25
b.	Sheet of 6, #1871-1876	1.10	.55
	Nos. 1871-1876 (6)	1.30	1.20

Souvenir Sheet

1877	A538 4000r Like #1874	1.10	.55

Millennium — A539

Designs: No. 1878, 1000r, No. 1880, 20,000r, 1999 agenda book. No. 1879, 1000r, No. 1881, 20,000r, Clock, child.

Litho. & Photo.

1999-2000 ***Perf. 13½x12¾***

1878-1879	A539 Set of 2	.70	.35
a.	Sheet of 20 + 20 labels	10.50	10.50

Souvenir Sheets

1880-1881	A539 Set of 2	13.00	6.50

Labels on No. 1879a could be personalized. The sheet sold for 38,000r.

Issued: Nos. 1878, 1880, 12/31/99; Nos. 1879, 1879a, 1881, 1/1/00.

Visit Indonesia Decade — A540

Designs: 500r, Satellite, fish. 1000r, Hydroponic agriculture.

2000, Jan. 1 ***Perf. 12¾x13½***

1882-1883	A540 Set of 2	.40	.20

University of Indonesia, 50th Anniv. — A541

Designs: 500r, Salemba campus. 1000r, University building, Depok.

2000, Feb. 2 ***Perf. 12½***

1884-1885	A541 Set of 2	.40	.20

Indonesian Folktales Type of 1998

Folktale, region - #1886: a-e, Tapak Tuan, Aceh. f-j, Batu Ballah, West Kalimantan. k-o, Sawerigading, South Sulawesi. p-t, 7 Putri kahyangan, Moluccas.

5000r, Like #1886e

2000, Feb. 5 ***Perf. 13½x12¾***

1886	Sheet of 20	2.60	1.40
a.-e.	500r Strip of 5	.65	.35
f.-j.	500r Strip of 5	.65	.35
k.-o.	500r Strip of 5	.65	.35
p.-t.	500r Strip of 5	.65	.35

Souvenir Sheet

1887	A502 5000r multi	1.40	.70

Indonesia 2000 Type of 1997

Designs: 500r, Prehnite. 1000r, Chalcedony. 2000r, Volcanic obsidian.

2000, Mar. 1

1888-1890	A483 Set of 3	.95	.50
1890a	Souvenir sheet, 3 each #1888-1890 + label	3.00	1.50

Souvenir Sheet

1891	A483 5000r Jasperized limestone	1.40	.70
a.	Sheet, #1891, 14 #1888, 2 #1889, 3 #1890 + 20 labels	8.50	—

No. 1891a sold for 41,000r with labels personalized.

Comic Strip Characters — A542

Designs: No. 1892, 500r, I Brewok, by Gungun. No. 1893, 500r, Pak Tuntung, by Basuki. No. 1894, Pak Bei, by Masdi Sunardi. No. 1895, 500r, Mang Ohle, by Didin D. Basuni. No. 1896, 500r, Panji Koming, by Dwi Koendoro.

Perf. 12¾x13½

2000, Mar. 13 **Photo.**

1892-1896	A542 Set of 5	.70	.35
1896a	Souvenir sheet, 3 each #1892-1896 + label	2.10	1.10

World Meteorological Organization, 50th Anniv. — A543

Litho. & Photo.

2000, Mar. 23 ***Perf. 12½***

1897	A543 500r multi	.20	.20

Souvenir Sheet

Bangkok 2000 Stamp Exhibition — A544

Illustration reduced.

2000, Mar. 23 ***Perf. 13½x12¾***

1898	A544 5000r multi	1.40	.70

15th Natl. Sports Week — A545

Designs: 500r, Cycling. 1000r, Canoeing. 2000r, High jump.

2000, Apr. 1

1899-1901	A545 Set of 3	.90	.45

Souvenir Sheet

The Stamp Show 2000, London — A546

Illustration reduced.

2000, May 22

1902	A546 5000r multi	1.25	.60

Environmental Care — A547

Designs; 500r, Birds in nest. 1000r, Monkeys. 2000r, Fish.

2000, June 5

1903-1905	A547 Set of 3	.80	.40

Souvenir Sheet

1906	A547 4000r Like #1904	.95	.45

2000 Summer Olympics, Sydney — A548

No. 1907, 500r: a, Boxing. b, Judo.

No. 1908, 1000r: a, Badminton. b, Weight lifting.

No. 1909, 2000r: a, Swimming. b, Running.

Illustration reduced.

2000, July 1

Pairs, #a-b

1907-1909	A548 Set of 3	1.50	.75

Souvenir Sheet

1910	A548 5000r Like #1908b	1.10	.55

Worldwide Fund for Nature (WWF) — A549

Komodo dragon: No. 1911, 500r, No. 1915a, 2500r, With tongue extended. No. 1912, 500r, On log. No. 1913, 500r, Pair walking. No. 1914, 500r, No. 1915b, 2500r, Pair fighting.

2000, Aug. 13

1911-1914	A549 Set of 4	.50	.25
a.	Souvenir sheet, 2 each #1911-1914	1.00	.50

Souvenir Sheet

1915	A549 2500r Sheet of 2, #a-b	1.25	.60

Souvenir Sheet

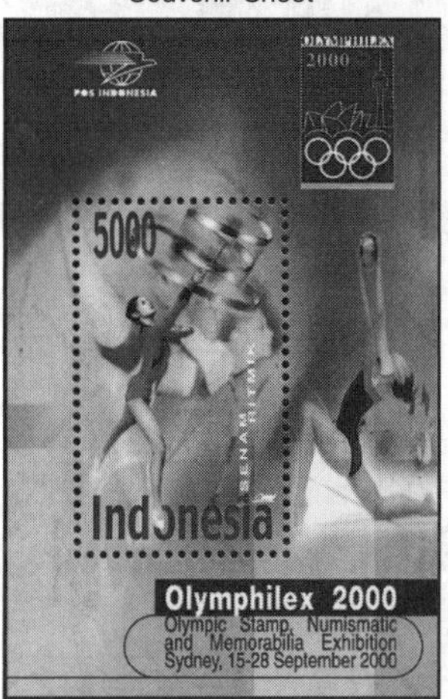

Olymphilex 2000 Stamp Exhibition — A550

2000, Sept. 15 ***Perf. 12¾x13½***

1916	A550 5000r multi	1.25	.60

A551

No. 1917: a, Pres. Abdurrahman Wahid. b, Vice Pres. Megawati Soekarnoputri

Illustration reduced.

Photo. & Engr.

2000, Sept. 27 ***Perf. 12½***

1917	A551 1000r Pair, #a-b	.45	.20

Ducks and Geese Type of 1998

2000, Sept. 27 **Photo.** ***Perf. 12½***

1918	A516 800r Like #1798	.20	.20
1919	A516 900r Like #1793	.20	.20

Traditional Costumes A552

Provinces and regions: a, Aceh. b, Jambi. c, Banten. d, Yogyakarta. e, Central Kalimantan (Kalimantan Tengah). f, Southeast Sulawesi (Sulawesi Tenggara). g, East Nusa Tenggara (Nusa Tenggara Timur). h, North Sumatra (Sumatera Utara). i, Bengkulu. j, Jakarta. k, East Java (Jawa Timur). l, East Kalimantan (Kalimantan Timur). m, South Sulawesi (Sulawesi Selatan). n, Maluku. o, West Sumatra (Sumatera Barat). p, South Sumatra (Sumatera Selatan). q, West Java (Jawa Barat). r, West Kalimantan (Kalimantan Barat). s, North Sulawesi (Sulawesi Utara). t, Bali. u, North Maluku (Maluku Utara). v, Riau. w, Lampung. x, Central Java (Jawa Tengah). y, South Kalimantan (Kalimantan Selatan). z, Central Sulawesi (Sulawesi Tengah). aa, West Nusa Tenggara (Nusa Tenggara Barat). ab, Irian Jaya.

Litho. & Photo.

2000, Oct. 28 ***Perf. 12½***

1920 Sheet of 28 + 7 labels 5.50
a.-ab. A552 900r Any single .20 .20

Artists and Entertainers — A553

No. 1921, horiz.: a, Bing Slamet (1927-74), singer, comedian. b, S. Sudjojono (1913-86), painter. c, I Ketut Maria (1897-1968), dancer. d, Chairil Anwar (1922-49), poet. e, Ibu Sud (1908-93), musician.

2000, Nov. 1 ***Perf. 13½x12¾***

1921 Horiz. strip of 5 1.00 .50
a.-e. A553 900r Any single .20 .20

Souvenir Sheet

1922 A553 4000r Chairil Anwar .90 .45

Indonesia Post in the 21st Century — A554

Designs: 800r, Philately, vert. 900r, Business communications. 1000r, Business financial services, vert. 4000r, Business logistics, vert.

Litho. & Photo.

2000, Dec. 20 ***Perf. 12½***

1923 A554 800r multi .20 .20
1924 A554 900r multi .20 .20
1925 A554 1000r multi .20 .20
1926 A554 4000r multi .85 .40
Nos. 1923-1926 (4) 1.45 1.00

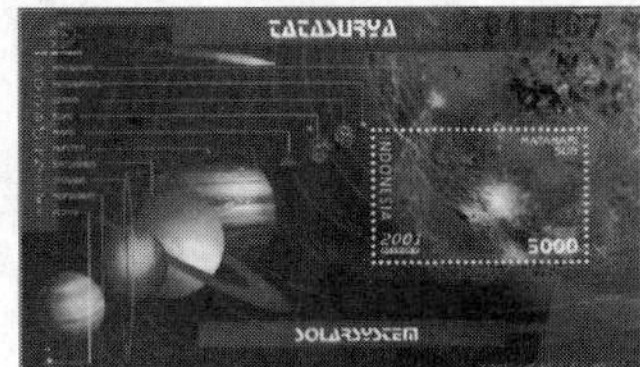

Solar System — A555

No. 1927: a, Sun. b, Mercury. c, Venus. d, Earth. e, Mars. f, Jupiter. g, Saturn. h, Uranus. i, Neptune. j, Pluto.
Illustration reduced.

2001, Jan. 1 Litho. ***Perf. 13½x12¾***

1927 Block of 10 + 5 labels 1.90
a.-j. A555 900r Any single .20 .20
k. Sheet of 10 + 5 labels 1.90
l. Sheet of 20 + 20 labels 7.75 7.75

Souvenir Sheet

1928 A555 5000r Sun 1.10 .55

Labels on No. 1927l could be personalized. The sheet sold for 36,000r.

Indonesian Folktales Type of 1998

Folktale, region - No. 1929: a-e, Batang Tuaka, Riau. f-j, Si Pitung, Jakarta. k-o, Terusan Nusa, Central Kalimantan. p-t, Ile Mauraja, East Nusa Tenggara.
5000r, Like No. 1929h.

Litho. & Photo.

2001, Feb. 2 ***Perf. 13½x12¾***

1929 Sheet of 20 3.75 1.90
a.-e. A502 900r Strip of 5 .90 .45
f.-j. A502 900r Strip of 5 .90 .45
k.-o. A502 900r Strip of 5 .90 .45
p.-t. A502 900r Strip of 5 .90 .45

Souvenir Sheet

1930 A502 5000r multi 1.10 .55

Masks — A556

No. 1931, 500r - Arsa Wijaya, Bali: a, Denomination at L. b, Denomination at R.
No. 1932, 800r - Asmat, Irian Jaya: a, Denomination at L. b, Denomination at R.
No. 1933, 800r - Cirebon, West Java: a, Denomination at L. b, Denomination at R.
No. 1934, 900r - Hudoq, East Kalimantan: a, Denomination at L. b, Denomination at R.
No. 1935, 900r - Wayang Wong, Yogyakarta: a, Denomination at L. b, Denomination at R.
5000r, Like No. 1934b.

2001, Mar. 2 ***Perf. 12¾x13½***

Pairs, #a-b

1931-1935 A556 Set of 5 1.50 .75
c. Sheet, #1931-1935 +2 labels 1.50

Souvenir Sheet

1936 A556 5000r multi 1.00 .50
a. Ovptd. in margin in silver 1.50 .75

Issued: No. 1936a, 10/16/01. No. 1936 overprinted with "HAFNIA '01 / World Philatelic Exhibition / Copenhagen / 16-21 October 2001," show emblem and new price of 7500r.

Traditional Communication Instruments — A557

No. 1937: a, Beduk. b, Bendé. c, Kentongan. d, Nafiri.

2001, Mar. 10 ***Perf. 12½***

1937 Vert. strip of 4 .70 .35
a.-d. A557 900r Any single .20 .20
e. Sheet, 2 each #1937a-1937d 1.40

Greetings—A558 — 1938

Various flowers. Denominations: 800, 900, 1000, 1500, 2000, 4000, 5000, 10000r

Litho. & Typo.

2001, Apr. 21 ***Perf. 12½***

1938-1945 A558 Set of 8 4.50 2.25

A558a

Greetings — A558b

Illustration A558a reduced.

Perf. 13½x12¾

2001, Apr. 21 Litho. & Typo.

1945A A558a 900r multi + label .35 .35

Perf. 12½

1945B A558b 900r multi + label .35 .35

No. 1945A was issued in sheets of 20 + 20 labels that could be personalized. The sheet sold for 36,000r. No. 1945B was issued in sheets of 10 + 10 labels that could be personalized. The sheet sold for 20,000r.

Environmental Care — A559

Children and: 800r, Fish. 900r, 5000r, Deer. 100r, Sea turtle.

Litho. & Photo.

2001, June 5 ***Perf. 13½x12¾***

1946 A559 800r multi .20 .20
a. Tete-beche pair .30 .30
1947 A559 900r multi .20 .20
a. Tete-beche pair .30 .30
1948 A559 1000r multi .20 .20
a. Tete-beche pair .35 .35
Nos. 1946-1948 (3) .60 .60

Souvenir Sheet

1949 A559 3000r multi .55 .25

No. 1949 exists imperf.

Pres. Sukarno (1901-70) — A560

Various portraits: 500, 800, 900, 1000r. 5000r, Sukarno at microphone.

2001, June 6 ***Perf. 12½***

1950-1953 A560 Set of 4 .55 .30
a. Sheet, 2 each #1950-1953 1.10

Souvenir Sheet

Perf. 13½x12¾

1954 A560 5000r multi .90 .45

No. 1954 contains one 41x25mm stamp

National Police — A561

Police and: a, Children. b, Helicopter.
Illustration reduced.

2001, July 1 Photo. ***Perf. 13½x12¾***

1955 A561 1000r Horiz. pair, #a-b .35 .20

National Scouting Jamboree — A562

Scouts: a, Raising flag. b, Pitching tent.
Illustration reduced.

2001, July 3

1956 A562 1000r Horiz. pair, #a-b .35 .20

Children's Games A563

Designs: 800r, Kaki Siapa. 900r, Egrang Bambu. 1000r, Dakon. 2000r, Kuda Pelepah Pisang.

Litho. & Photo.

2001, July 23 ***Perf. 13½x12¾***

1957-1960 A564 Set of 4 1.10 .55
a. Sheet, 2 each #1957-1960 2.25

Souvenir Sheet

Phila Nippon '01, Japan — A564

2001, Aug. 1 **Photo.**

1961 A564 10,000r multi 2.25 1.10

Dr. R. Soeharso Orthopedic Hospital, Surakarta, 50th Anniv. A565

Litho. & Photo.

2001, Aug. 28 ***Perf. 13½x12¾***

1962 A565 1000r multi .20 .20

Traditional Transportation — A566

Designs: No. 1963, 1000r, Rowboat. No. 1964, 1000r, Trishaw. No. 1965, Horse-drawn carriage.

2001, Sept. 17

1963-1965 A566 Set of 3 .65 .30
a. Sheet, 3 each #1963-1965 +label 2.00 1.00

Post Offices A567

Buildings in: 800r, Makassar. 900r, Bandung. 1000r, Balikpapan. 2000r, Padang.

2001, Sept. 27

1966-1969 A567 Set of 4 .95 .45

Gemstones — A568

Designs: 800r, Rose quartz. 900r, Brecciated jasper. 1000r, Malachite. 5000r, Diamond.

2001, Oct. 1

1970-1972 A568 Set of 3 .55 .25
 a. Sheet, 3 each #1970-1972 + label 1.75 .85

Souvenir Sheet

1973 A568 5000r multi 1.00 .50

Year of Dialogue Among Civilizations — A569

2001, Oct. 9 Litho. *Perf. 12¾x13½*

1974 A569 1000r multi .20 .20

Beetles — A570

Designs: 800r, Agestrata dehaan. 900r, Mormolyce phyllodes. No. 1977, 1000r, Batocera rosenbergi. No. 1978, 1000r, Chrysochroa buqueti. 2000r, 5000r, Chalcosoma caucasus.

2001, Nov. 5 Litho. & Photo.

1975-1979 A570 Set of 5 1.10 .55
 a. Booklet pane, #1975-1979 + label 1.10 —
 Booklet, 2 #1979a 2.25

Souvenir Sheet

1980 A570 5000r multi .95 .45

Folktales — A571

No. 1981, 1000r - Pulau Kembara, South Sumatra: a, Four people, lanterns. b, Two men, woman, boat. c, Man and woman standing in boat. d, Man and woman in water. e, Boat, snake, fish.

No. 1982, 1000r - Nyi Koro Kidul, Yogyakarta: a, Woman at tight pointing. b, Woman at foreground with hand at mouth. c, Two men with hats at right. d, Woman in sea. e, Sea and island.

No. 1983, 1000r - Aji Tatin, East Kalimantan: a, Bird in tree, woman, man with hand outstretched. b, Woman, bird boat. c, Sinking boat. d, Woman and tree. e, Bird in tree.

No. 1984, 1000r - Danau Tondano, North Sulawesi: a, Woman with long hair in foreground. b, Man holding spear. c, Man at left with arm to head. d, Man and woman embracing. e, Sea and island.

5000r, Like No. 1981e.

Illustration reduced.

Litho. & Photo.

2002, Feb. 2 *Perf. 13½x12¾*

Blocks of 5, #a-e

1981-1984 A571 Set of 4 4.00 2.00

Souvenir Sheet

1985 A571 5000r multi 1.00 .50

Nos. 1981-1984 are printed in sheets of four blocks of five. Stamp "e" is always adjacent to the LL stamp in the block of the remaining four stamps, and is found tete beche to both stamps "a" and "e" from adjacent blocks of five.

2002 World Cup Soccer Championships, Japan and Korea — A572

Celebrations: 1000r, Player lifting shirt over face. 1500r, Four players with fists raised, horiz. 2000r, 5000r, Player with arms outstretched.

Perf. 12¾x13½, 13½x12¾

2002, Apr. 1 Litho. & Photo.

1986-1988 A572 Set of 3 .95 .45

Souvenir Sheet

1989 A572 5000r multi 1.10 .55

Indonesian Cancer Foundation, 25th Anniv. — A573

2002, Apr. 17 *Perf. 12¾x13½*

1990 A573 1000r multi .25 .20
 a. Tete-beche pair .50 .25

Telecommunications — A574

No. 1991: a, Woman using telephone (2/4). b, Man using cellular phone (1/4). c, Satellite above Earth (4/4). d, Satellite, world map, computer, satellite dish (3/4).

2002, May 17

1991 A574 1000r Block of 4, #a-d .90 .45
 e. Sheet, 2 each #1991a-1991d 1.80 .90
 f. Booklet pane, 4 #1991a .90
 g. Booklet pane, 4 #1991b .90
 h. Booklet pane, 4 #1991c .90
 i. Booklet pane, 4 #1991d .90
 Booklet, #1991f-1991i 3.60

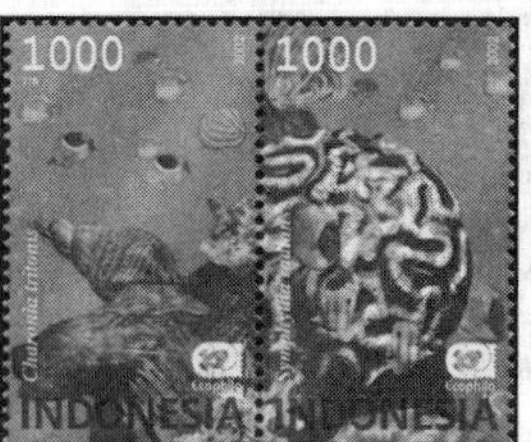

Marine Life — A575

No. 1992, 1000r: a, Charonia tritonis. b, Symphyllia radians.

No. 1993, 1500r: a, Cromileptes altivelis. b, Acanthaster planci.

No. 1994, 2000r, horiz.: a, Paracanthurus hepatus. b, Tridacna gigas.

5000r, Acanthaster planci.

2002, June 5

Horiz. Pairs, #a-b

1992-1994 A575 Set of 3 2.00 1.00
 c. Sheet, #1992, 1993, 1994a, 1994b 2.00 1.00

Souvenir Sheet

1995 A575 5000r multi 1.10 .55

Aceh Province — A576

Designs: 1500r, Student, Aceh dance, map of Aceh. 3500r, Masjid Raya Banda Aceh, map of Indonesia.

2002, June 15 *Perf. 12½*

1996-1997 A576 Set of 2 1.10 .55

Natl. Family Day A577

Perf. 13½x12¾

2002, June 29 Litho. & Typo.

1998 A577 1000r multi .25 .20

33rd Intl. Physics Olympiad, Bali — A578

No. 1999: a, Eclipse (1/2). b, Spectrum colors and Balinese symbols (2/2).

2002, July 14 *Perf. 12¾x13½*

1999 A578 1000r Horiz. pair, #a-b .45 .20

Kites A579

No. 2000: a, Popotengan (bird-shaped) (1/5). b, Barong (dragon head) (2/5). c, Fighting (3/5). d, Bebean (4/5). e, Modern (box and wing) (5/5).

5000r, Popotengan.

Litho. & Photo.

2002, July 15 *Perf. 13½x12¾*

2000 Horiz. strip of 5 1.10 .55
 a.-e. A579 1000r Any single .20 .20

Souvenir Sheet

2001 A579 5000r multi 1.10 .55

Fruit — A580

Designs: 300r, Morinda citrifolia. 500r, Mangifera indica. 1500r, Averrhoa carambola. 3000r, Durio zibethinus.

2002, Aug. 1 Photo. *Perf. 13½x12¾*

2002 A580 300r multi .20 .20
2003 A580 500r multi .20 .20
2004 A580 1500r multi .30 .20
2005 A580 3000r multi .65 .30
 Nos. 2002-2005 (4) 1.35 .90

Souvenir Sheet

Philakorea 2002 World Stamp Exhibition, Seoul — A581

2002, Aug. 2 Litho. *Perf. 12¾x13½*

2006 A581 7000r multi 1.60 .80

Mohammad Hatta (1902-80), Prime Minister — A582

No. 2007, 1000r: a, Denomination at left. b, Denomination at right.

No. 2008, 1500r: a, Denomination at left. b, Denomination at right.

5000r, Hatta standing.

Litho. & Photo.

2002, Aug. 12 *Perf. 12½*

Pairs, #a-b

2007-2008 A582 Set of 2 1.10 .55
 c. Sheet, 2 each #2007-2008 + 2 labels 2.25 1.10

Souvenir Sheet

Perf. 12¾x13½

2009 A582 5000r multi 1.10 .55

No. 2009 contains one 25x41mm stamp.

President and Vice-President — A583

No. 2010: a, Pres. Megawati Soekarnoputri. b, Vice-president Hamzah Haz.
Illustration reduced.

Photo. with Foil Application

2002, Aug. 17 ***Perf. 12½***
2010 A583 1500r Horiz. pair, #a-b, + central label .70 .35

Souvenir Sheet

Amphilex 2002 Intl. Stamp Exhibition, Amsterdam — A584

Perf. 13½x12¾
2002, Aug. 30 **Photo.**
2011 A584 7000r multi 1.60 .80

Souvenir Sheet

Panfila 2002 Philatelic Exhibition, Yogyakarta — A585

2002, Sept. 19 ***Perf. 12¾x13½***
2012 A585 6000r multi 1.40 .70

Paintings — A586

No. 2013, 1000r: a, Seko, Guerrilla Vanguard, by S. Sudjojono. b, Cat, by Popo Iskandar.
No. 2014, 1500r, vert.: a, Catching Lice, by Hendra Gunawan. b, Gatut Kaca with Prigiwa and Prigiwati, by R. Basuki Abdullah.

Litho. & Photo.

2002, Sept. 27 ***Perf. 12½***
Pairs, #a-b
2013-2014 A586 Set of 2 1.10 .55
c. Sheet, 2 each #2013-2014 2.25 1.10

Souvenir Sheet

España 2002 Youth Philatelic Exhibition, Salamanca — A587

2002, Oct. 4 **Photo.** ***Perf. 13½x12¾***
2015 A587 7000r multi 1.60 .80

Flora and Fauna A588

No. 2016, 1000r: a, Trimeresurus hageni. b, Rafflesia micropylora.
No. 2017, 1500r: a, Panthera pardus. b, Terminalia catappa.
No. 2018, 2000r: a, Papilionanthe hookeriana. b, Varanus salvator.
3500r, Panthera pardus.

Litho. & Photo.

2002, Nov. 5 ***Perf. 12¾x13½***
Horiz. Pairs, #a-b
2016-2018 A588 Set of 3 2.00 1.00

Souvenir Sheet
2019 A588 3500r multi .80 .40

Antara, Indonesian News Agency — A589

Litho. & Typo.

2002, Dec. 13 ***Perf. 12½***
2020 A589 1500r multi .35 .20

Happy Birthday — A590

No. 2021: a, Food platter. b, Birthday cake.

2003 **Photo.** ***Perf. 12½***
2021 Strip of 2 stamps and 2 alternating labels 1.00 .50
a.-b. A590 1500r Any single .50 .25
c. Sheet of 5 #2021 6.75 —

No. 2021 was printed in sheets containing 10 strips with labels that could be personalized. The sheet sold for 45,000r. The labels on No. 2021c could also be personalized, and that sheet sold for 30,000r.

Folklore — A591

No. 2022 - Scenes from Danau Ranau, Lampung (#a.-e.), Kongga Owose, Southeast Sulawesi (#f.-j.), Putri Gading Cempaka, Bengkulu (#k.-o.), Putri Mandalika Nyale, West Nusa Tenggara (#p.-t.) and stamp numbers: a, 01/20. b, 02/20. c, 03/20. d, 04/20. e, 05/20. f, 06/20. g, 07/20. h, 08/20. i, 09/20. j, 10/20. k, 11/20. l, 12/20. m, 13/20. n, 14/20. o, 15/20. p, 16/20. q, 17/20. r, 18/20. s, 19/20. t, 20/20.
5000r, Like #2022e.

Litho. & Photo.

2003, Feb. 2 ***Perf. 13½x12¾***
2022 A591 1500r Sheet of 20, #a-t 6.75 3.50

Souvenir Sheet
2023 A591 5000r multi 1.10 .55

SEMI-POSTAL STAMPS

Symbols of Olympic Games SP43

Wings and Flame SP44

Perf. 12½x12
1951, Jan. 2 **Photo.** **Unwmk.**
B58 SP43 5s + 3s gray grn .20 .20
B59 SP43 10s + 5s dk vio bl .20 .20
B60 SP43 20s + 5s org red .20 .20
B61 SP43 30s + 10s dk brn .65 .25
B62 SP43 35s + 10s ultra 2.25 1.00
Nos. B58-B62 (5) 3.50 1.85

Issued to publicize the Asiatic Olympic Games of 1951 at New Delhi, India.

1951, Oct. 15
B63 SP44 5s + 3s olive green .20 .20
B64 SP44 10s + 5s dull blue .20 .20
B65 SP44 20s + 5s red .25 .20
B66 SP44 30s + 10s brown .35 .20
B67 SP44 35s + 10s ultra .70 .20
Nos. B63-B67 (5) 1.70 1.00

2nd Natl. Games, Djakarta, 10/21-28/51.

No. 378 Surcharged in Black

1953, May 8 ***Perf. 12½***
B68 A53 35s + 10s purple .35 .20

The surcharge reads "Natural Disaster." Surtax was for emergency relief following volcanic eruption and floods.

Merapi Erupting SP45

Young Musicians SP46

1954, Apr. 15 **Litho.** ***Perf. 12½x12***
B69 SP45 15s + 10s bl grn .20 .20
B70 SP45 35s + 15s pur .20 .20
B71 SP45 50s + 25s red .20 .20
B72 SP45 75s + 25s vio bl .25 .20
B73 SP45 1r + 25s car .40 .20
B74 SP45 2r + 50s blk brn .85 .40
B75 SP45 3r + 1r gray grn 11.50 2.75
B76 SP45 5r + 2.50r org brn 16.00 3.75
Nos. B69-B76 (8) 29.60 7.90

The surtax was for victims of the Merapi volcano eruption.

1954, Dec. 22 **Photo.** ***Perf. 12½***

15s+10s, Parasol dance. 35s+15s, Girls playing dakon. 50s+15s, Boy on stilts. 75s+25s, Bamboo flute players. 1r+25s, Javanese dancer.

B77 SP46 10s + 10s dk pur .20 .20
B78 SP46 15s + 10s dk grn .20 .20
B79 SP46 35s + 15s car rose .20 .20
B80 SP46 50s + 15s rose brn .25 .20
B81 SP46 75s + 25s ultra .35 .20
B82 SP46 1r + 25s red org .60 .20
Nos. B77-B82 (6) 1.80 1.20

The surtax was for child welfare.

Scout Emblem SP47

Scout Signaling SP48

Designs: 50s+25s, Campfire. 75s+25s, Scout feeding fawn. 1r+50s, Scout saluting.

1955, June 27 **Unwmk.** ***Perf. 12½***
B83 SP47 15s + 10s bl grn .20 .20
B84 SP48 35s + 15s ultra .20 .20
B85 SP48 50s + 25s scar .35 .20
B86 SP48 75s + 25s brn .40 .20
B87 SP48 1r + 50s vio .65 .20
Nos. B83-B87 (5) 1.80 1.00

First National Boy Scout Jamboree.

Blind Weaver SP49

Red Cross and Heart SP50

35s+15s, Basket weaver. 50s+25s, Boy studying map. 75s+50s, Woman reading Braille.

1956, Jan. 4
B88 SP49 15s + 10s dp grn .20 .20
B89 SP49 35s + 15s yel brn .25 .20
B90 SP49 50s + 25s rose car 2.25 .20
B91 SP49 75s + 50s ultra 1.00 .20
Nos. B88-B91 (4) 3.70 .80

The surtax was for the benefit of the blind.

1956, July 26 **Litho.**

Designs: 35s+15s, 50s+15s, Transfusion bottle. 75s+25s, 1r+25s, Outstretched hands.

Cross in Red
B92 SP50 10s + 10s ultra .20 .20
B93 SP50 15s + 10s carmine .20 .20
B94 SP50 35s + 15s lt brn .20 .20
B95 SP50 50s + 15s bl grn .35 .20
B96 SP50 75s + 25s orange .35 .20
B97 SP50 1r + 25s brt pur .35 .20
Nos. B92-B97 (6) 1.65 1.20

Surtax for the Indonesian Red Cross.

Invalids Doing Batik Work — SP51

Designs: 15s+10s, Amputee painting. 35s+15s, Lathe operator. 50s+15s, Crippled child learning to walk. 75s+25s, Treating amputee. 1r+25s, Painting with artificial hand.

1957, Mar. 26 **Photo.** ***Perf. 12½***
B98 SP51 10s + 10s dp blue .20 .20
B99 SP51 15s + 10s brown .25 .20
B100 SP51 35s + 15s red .25 .20
B101 SP51 50s + 15s dp vio .25 .20
B102 SP51 75s + 25s green .40 .20
B103 SP51 1r + 25s dk car rose .40 .20
Nos. B98-B103 (6) 1.75 1.20

The surtax was for rehabilitation of invalids.

Kembodja Flower SP52

Designs: 15s+10s, Michelia. 35s+15s, Sunflower. 50s+15s, Jasmine. 75s+50s, Orchid.

1957, Dec. 23 *Perf. 13½x12½*

Flowers in Natural Colors

B104 SP52 10s + 10s blue 1.60 .20
B105 SP52 15s + 10s dp yel grn 1.25 .20
B106 SP52 35s + 15s dk red brn .40 .20
B107 SP52 50s + 15s ol & dk brn .40 .20
B108 SP52 75s + 60s rose brn .40 .20
Nos. B104-B108 (5) 4.05 1.00

Children SP53

Indonesian Scout Emblem SP54

15s+10s, 50s+25s, 1r+50s, Girl and boy.

1958, July 1 Photo. *Perf. 12½x12*

B109 SP53 10s + 10s blue .20 .20
B110 SP53 15s + 10s rose brn .20 .20
B111 SP53 35s + 15s gray green .20 .20
B112 SP53 50s + 25s gray olive .20 .20
B113 SP53 75s + 50s brn car .20 .20
B114 SP53 1r + 50s brown .25 .20
Nos. B109-B114 (6) 1.25 1.20

The surtax was for orphans.

1959, July 17 Photo. Unwmk.

Design: 15s + 10s, 50s + 25s, 1r + 50s, Scout emblem and compass.

Emblem in Red

B115 SP54 10s + 5s bister .20 .20
B116 SP54 15s + 10s bluish grn .20 .20
B117 SP54 20s + 10s lilac gray .20 .20
B118 SP54 50s + 25s olive .20 .20
B119 SP54 75s + 35s yel brn .30 .20
B120 SP54 1r + 50s dark gray .40 .20
Nos. B115-B120 (6) 1.50 1.20

10th World Scout Jamboree, Makiling National Park near Manila, July 17-26.

Palm-leaf Ribs, Gong and 5 Rings SP55

Young Couple Holding Sharpened Bamboo Weapon SP56

Design: 20s+10s, 75s+35s, Bamboo musical instrument and 5-ring emblem.

1960, Feb. 14 *Perf. 12½x12*

B121 SP55 15s + 5s bis & dk brn .20 .20
B122 SP55 20s + 10s grn & blk .20 .20
B123 SP55 50s + 25s bl & pur .20 .20
B124 SP55 75s + 35s ol & dk grn .20 .20
B125 SP56 1.15r + 50s car & blk .35 .20
Nos. B121-B125 (5) 1.15 1.00

All-Indonesian Youth Cong., Bandung, 2/14-21/60.

Social Emblem SP57

Pineapple SP58

Designs: 15s+15s, Rice, lotus and cotton. 20s+20s, Lotus blossom and tree. 50s+25s, Girl and boy. 75s+25s, Watering of plant in man's hand. 3r+50s, Woman nursing infant.

Perf. 12½x12

1960, Dec. 20 Photo. Unwmk.

Inscribed: "Hari Sosial Ke III"

B126 SP57 10s + 10s ocher & blk .20 .20
B127 SP57 15s + 15s dp cl & blk .20 .20
B128 SP57 20s + 20s bl & blk .20 .20
B129 SP57 50s + 25s bis brn & blk .20 .20
B130 SP57 75s + 25s emer & blk .20 .20
B131 SP57 3r + 50s red & blk .30 .20
Nos. B126-B131 (6) 1.30 1.20

3rd Social Day, Dec. 20.

Type of 1960 Surcharges: "BENTJANA ALAM 1961"

1961, Feb. 17 *Perf. 12x12½*

B132 A76 15s + 10s plum .20 .20
B133 A76 20s + 15s ocher .20 .20
B134 A76 75s + 25s scarlet .20 .20
Nos. B132-B134 (3) .60 .60

The surtax was for flood relief.

1961, Dec. 20 *Perf. 12½x13½*

4th Social Day: 75s+25s, Mangosteen. 3r+1r, Rambutan.

B135 SP58 20s + 10s bl, yel & red .35 .20
B136 SP58 75s + 25s gray, grn & dp claret .40 .20
B137 SP58 3r + 1r grn, yel & red 1.25 .20
Nos. B135-B137 (3) 2.00 .60

Istiqlal Mosque, Djakarta — SP59

40s+20s, 3r+1r, Different view of mosque.

1962, Feb. 22 *Perf. 12½x12*

B138 SP59 30s + 20s Prus grn & yel .20 .20
B139 SP59 40s + 20s dk red & yel .20 .20
B140 SP59 1.50r + 50s brn & yel .50 .20
B141 SP59 3r + 1r grn & yel .55 .20
Nos. B138-B141 (4) 1.45 .80

Issued for the benefit of the new Istiqlal Mosque.

National Monument, Djakarta — SP60

1.50r+50s, 6r+1.50r, Aerial view of monument.

1962, May 20 Photo. *Perf. 12x12½*

B142 SP60 1r + 50s org brn & blk .20 .20
B143 SP60 1.50r + 50s ol grn & ultra .20 .20
B144 SP60 3r + 1r lil rose & dk grn .25 .20
B145 SP60 6r + 1.50r vio bl & red .35 .20
Nos. B142-B145 (4) 1.00 .80

Vanda Tricolor SP61

Orchids: 1.50r+50s, Phalaenopsis amabilis, vert. 3r+1r, Dendrobium phalaenopsis, vert. 6r+1.50r, Paphiopedilum praestans.

Perf. 13½x12½, 12½x13½

1962, Dec. 20 Unwmk.

Orchids in Natural Colors

B146 SP61 1r + 50s ultra & yel .25 .20
B147 SP61 1.50r + 50s grnsh bl & ver .25 .20
B148 SP61 3r + 1r dp bl & ocher .25 .20
B149 SP61 6r + 1.50r org & dl vio .25 .20
Nos. B146-B149 (4) 1.00 .80

Issued for the 5th Social Day.

West Irian Monument, Djakarta — SP62

1963, Feb. 15 *Perf. 12½x13½*

B150 SP62 1r + 50s rose red & blk .20 .20
B151 SP62 1.50r + 50s mag & dk brn .20 .20
B152 SP62 3r + 1r bl & dk brn .20 .20
B153 SP62 6r + 1.50r grn & brn .25 .20
Nos. B150-B153 (4) .85 .80

The surtax was for the construction of the West Irian Monument in Djakarta.

Erupting Volcano SP63

1963, June 29 Photo. *Perf. 13½x13*

B154 SP63 4r + 2r rose red .20 .20
B155 SP63 6r + 3r grnsh bl .20 .20

The surtax was for victims of national natural disasters.

Papilio Blumei, Celebes — SP64

Butterflies: 4r+1r, Charaxes dehaani, Java. 6r+1.50r, Graphium, West Irian. 12r+3r, Troides amphrysus, Sumatra.

1963, Dec. 20 *Perf. 12x12½*

B156 SP64 1.75r + 50s multi .20 .20
B157 SP64 4r + 1r multi .20 .20
B158 SP64 6r + 1.50r multi .20 .20
B159 SP64 12r + 3r multi .40 .20
Nos. B156-B159 (4) 1.00 .80

Issued for the 6th Social Day.

Malaysian Fantails — SP65

Birds: 6r+1.50r, Zebra doves. 12r+3r, Black drongos. 20r+5r, Black-naped orioles. 30r+7.50r, Javanese sparrows.

Perf. 12½x13½

1965, Jan. 25 Photo. Unwmk.

B160 SP65 4r + 1r dl yel, lil & blk .35 .20
B161 SP65 6r + 1.50 grn, blk & pink .35 .20
B162 SP65 12r + 3r ol & blk .35 .20
B163 SP65 20r + 5r gray, yel & red .35 .20
B164 SP65 30r + 7.50r car rose, sl bl & blk .35 .20
Nos. B160-B164 (5) 1.75 1.00

Issued for the 7th Social Day.

Type of Regular Issue, 1964, Inscribed Vertically "Conefo"

1965 *Perf. 12½x12*

B165 A98 1r + 1r org red & brn .20 .20
B166 A98 1.25r + 1.25r org red & brn .20 .20
B167 A98 1.75r + 1.75r org, red & brn blk .20 .20
B168 A98 2r + 2r org red & sl grn .20 .20
B169 A98 2.50r + 2.50r org red & red brn .20 .20
B170 A98 4r + 3.50r org red & dp bl .20 .20
B171 A98 6r + 4r org red & emer .20 .20
B172 A98 10r + 5r org red & yel grn .20 .20
B173 A98 12r + 5.50r org red & org .20 .20
B174 A98 15r + 7.50r org red & bl grn .20 .20
B175 A98 20r + 10r org red & dk gray .20 .20
B176 A98 25r + 10r org red & pur .20 .20
B177 A98 40r + 15r ver & plum .20 .20
B178 A98 50r + 15r org red & dp vio .20 .20
B179 A98 100r + 25r org red & dk ol gray .20 .20
Nos. B165-B179 (15) 3.00 3.00

Conference of New Emerging Forces.

Makara Mask and Magic Rays — SP66

1965, July 17 *Perf. 12*

B180 SP66 20r + 10r red & dk bl .20 .20
B181 SP66 30r + 15r bl & dk red .20 .20

Issued to publicize the fight against cancer.

Family and Produce SP67

State Principles: 20r+10r, Humanitarianism; clasped hands, globe, flags and chain. 25r+10r, Nationalism; map of Indonesia and tree. 40r+15r, Democracy; conference and bull's head. 50r+15r, Belief in God; houses of worship and star.

1965, Aug. 17 Photo. *Perf. 12½*

B182 SP67 10r + 5r fawn, yel & blk .25 .20
B183 SP67 20r + 10r dp yel, red & blk .25 .20
B184 SP67 25r + 10r rose red, red, grn & blk .25 .20
B185 SP67 40r + 15r bl, red & blk .25 .20
B186 SP67 50r + 15r lil, yel & blk .25 .20
Nos. B182-B186 (5) 1.25 1.00

Samudra Beach Hotel and Pres. Sukarno — SP68

Designs: 25r+10r, 80r+20r, Ambarrukmo Palace Hotel and Pres. Sukarno.

1965, Dec. 1 Photo. *Perf. 12½*

B187 SP68 10r + 5r dk bl & lt bl grn .20 .20
B188 SP68 25r + 10r vio blk & yel grn .20 .20
B189 SP68 40r + 15r dk brn & vio bl .30 .20
B190 SP68 80r + 20r dk pur & org .30 .20
Nos. B187-B190 (4) 1.00 .80

Issued for tourist publicity.

Gloriosa — SP69

40r+15r, Magaguabush. 80r+20r, Balsam. 100r+25r, Crape myrtle.

1965, Dec. 20 Photo. *Perf. 12*
Flowers in Natural Colors

B191 SP69 30r + 10r deep blue .20 .20
B192 SP69 40r + 15r deep blue .30 .20
B193 SP69 80r + 20r deep blue .40 .20
B194 SP69 100r + 25r deep blue .60 .20
Nos. B191-B194 (4) 1.50 .80

Dated "1966"

10s+5s, Senna. 20s+5s, Crested barleria. 30s+10s, Scarlet ixora. 40s+10s, Rose of China (hibiscus).

1966, Feb. 10
Flowers in Natural Colors

B195 SP69 10s + 5s Prus bl .30 .20
B196 SP69 20s + 5s grn .30 .20
B197 SP69 30s + 10s grn .30 .20
B198 SP69 40s + 10s Prus bl .45 .20
Nos. B195-B198 (4) 1.35 .80

Nos. B191-B198 issued for the 8th Social Day, Dec. 20, 1965. An imperf. souvenir sheet contains one No. B198. Size: 58x78mm.

Type of 1965 Inscribed: "BENTJANA ALAM / NASIONAL 1966"

15s+5s, Gloriosa. 25s+5s, Magaguabush. 30s+10s, Balsam. 80s+20s, Crape myrtle.

1966, May 2
Flowers in Natural Colors

B199 SP69 15s + 5s blue .20 .20
B200 SP69 25s + 5s dk bl .20 .20
B201 SP69 30s + 10s dk bl .25 .20
B202 SP69 80s + 20s lt bl .60 .20
Nos. B199-B202 (4) 1.25 .80

The surtax was for victims of national natural disasters.

Reticulated Python — SP70

Reptiles: 3r+50s, Bloodsucker. 4r+75s. Saltwater crocodile. 6r+1r, Hawksbill turtle (incorrectly inscribed *chelonia mydas,* "green turtle").

1966, Dec. 20 Photo. *Perf. 12½x12*

B203 SP70 2r + 25s multi .20 .20
B204 SP70 3r + 50s multi .20 .20
B205 SP70 4r + 75s multi .25 .20
B206 SP70 6r + 1r multi .35 .20
Nos. B203-B206 (4) 1.00 .80

Flooded Village SP71

Buddha & Stupa, Borobudur Temple SP72

2.50r+25s, Landslide. 4r+40s, Fire destroying village. 5r+50s, Erupting volcano.

1967, Dec. 20 Photo. *Perf. 12½*

B207 SP71 1.25r + 10s dl vio bl & yel .20 .20
B208 SP71 2.50r + 25s dl vio bl & yel .20 .20
B209 SP71 4r + 40s dp org & blk .25 .20
B210 SP71 5r + 50s dp org & blk .35 .20
a. Souv. sheet of 2, #B209-B210 16.50 10.00
Nos. B207-B210 (4) 1.00 .80

Surtax for victims of natl. natural disasters.

1968, Mar. 1 Photo. *Perf. 12½*

Designs: No. B211, Musicians. No. B212, Sudhana and Princess Manohara. No. B213, Procession with elephant and horses.

B211 SP72 2.50r + 25s brt grn & gray ol .45 .20
B212 SP72 2.50r + 25s brt grn & gray ol .45 .20
B213 SP72 2.50r + 25s brt grn & gray ol .45 .20
a. Souv. sheet of 3, #B211-B213 16.50 7.50
b. Strip of 3, #B211-B213 1.40 .30
B214 SP72 7.50r + 75s org & gray ol .45 .20
Nos. B211-B214 (4) 1.80 .80

The surtax was to help save Borobudur Temple in Central Java, c. 800 A.D.

No. B213b has continuous design showing a frieze from Borobudur.

Scout with Pickax — SP73

Designs: 10r+1r, Bugler. 30r+3r, Scouts singing around campfire, horiz.

1968, June 1 Photo. *Perf. 12½*
Size: 28½x44½mm

B215 SP73 5r + 50 dp org & brn .25 .20
B216 SP73 10r + 1r brn & gray ol .35 .20

Size: 68x28½mm

B217 SP73 30r + 3r ol gray & grn .75 .45
Nos. B215-B217 (3) 1.35 .85

Surtax for Wirakarya Scout Camp.

Woman with Flower SP74

1969, Apr. 21 *Perf. 13½x12½*

B218 SP74 20r + 2r emer, red & yel .65 .20

Emancipation of Indonesian women.

Noble Voluta — SP75

Sea shells: 7.50r+50s, Common hairy triton. 10r+1r, Spider conch. 15r+1.50r, Murex ternispina.

1969, Dec. 20 Photo. *Perf. 12½*

B219 SP75 5r + 50s multi .20 .20
B220 SP75 7.50r + 50s multi .30 .20
B221 SP75 10r + 1r multi .45 .20
B222 SP75 15r + 1.50r multi .65 .20
Nos. B219-B222 (4) 1.60 .80

Issued for the 12th Social Day, Dec. 20.

Chrysocoris Javanus SP76

Insects: 15r+1.50r, Dragonfly. 20r+2r, Carpenter bee.

1970, Dec. 21 Photo. *Perf. 12½*

B223 SP76 7.50r + 50c multi 6.00 .20
B224 SP76 15r + 1.50r multi 15.00 .20
B225 SP76 20r + 2r multi 19.00 .20
Nos. B223-B225 (3) 40.00 .60

The 13th Social Day, Dec. 20.

Fight Against Cancer — SP77

Patient receiving radiation treatment, Jakarta Hospital.

1983, July 1 Photo. *Perf. 12½*

B226 SP77 55r + 20r multi .70 .20
B227 SP77 75r + 25r multi 1.00 .20

Children's Day SP78

Children's Drawings. Surtax was for Children's Palace building fund.

1984, June 17 Photo. *Perf. 13½x13*

B228 SP78 75r + 25r multi .80 .20
B229 SP78 110r + 25r multi 1.10 .20
B230 SP78 175r + 25r multi 1.50 .20
B231 SP78 275r + 25r multi 2.50 .20
a. Souv. sheet of 2, #B230-B231 18.00 .40
b. Souv. sheet of 4 + 2 labels 16.00 .80
Nos. B228-B231 (4) 5.90 .80

AUSIPEX '84. No. B231b for FILACENTO '84, Netherlands, Sept. 6-9.

SP79

SP80

1987, May 12 Photo. *Perf. 12½*

B232 SP79 350r +25r dark ultra & yel 1.50 .25

Yayasan Cancer Medical Assoc., 10th anniv.

1991, June 1 Photo. *Perf. 12½*

B233 SP80 200r +25r multi .85 .20

Natl. Fed. for Welfare of Mentally Handicapped, 24th anniv.

Yayasan Cancer Medical Assoc., 15th Anniv. — SP81

1992, May 12 Photo. *Perf. 12½*

B234 SP81 200r +25r brown & mag .35 .20
B235 SP81 500r +50r blue & mag .90 .35

Natl. Kidney Foundation — SP82

Perf. 13½x12½

1994, Apr. 30 Photo.

B236 SP82 300r +30r multi .60 .20

Rehibilitation Intl., 10th Asia & Pacific Regional Conference — SP83

Design: 700r+100r, Painting, Mother's Love, by disabled artist Patricia Saerang.

Perf. 13½x12½

1995, Sept. 12 Photo.

B238 SP83 700r +100r multi .75 .40

March 1, 1949, Day of Total Attack SP84

Designs: No. B239, Natl. flag, tanks, map. No. B240, Soldiers fighting, soldiers standing at attention, natl. flag.

1996, Mar. 1 Photo. *Perf. 13½x12½*

B239 SP84 700r +100r multi .80 .40
B240 SP84 700r +100r multi .80 .40
a. Pair, #B239-B240 1.60 .80

World AIDS Day SP85

1997, Dec. 1 Photo. *Perf. 13½x12½*

B241 SP85 700r +100r multi .65 .35

PETA (Pembela Tanah Air) Volunteer Army — SP86

Perf. 12½x13½

1998, Nov. 10 **Litho.**

B242 SP86 700r Statue, museum .20 .20

SPECIAL DELIVERY STAMPS

Garuda SD1

Perf. 13½x12½

1967 **Unwmk.** **Photo.**

E1 SD1 10r lt ultra & dl pur .40 .20
E2 SD1 15r org & dl pur 1.10 .20
Nos. E1-E2 (2) 1.50 .40

Inscribed "1968"

1968

E3 SD1 10r lt ultra & dl pur .50 .20
E4 SD1 15r org & dl pur .70 .20
E5 SD1 20r yel & dl pur .80 .20
E6 SD1 30r brt grn & dl pur 1.10 .25
E7 SD1 40r lil & dl pur 1.50 .35
Nos. E3-E7 (5) 4.60 1.20

Same Inscribed "1969"

1969

E8 SD1 20r yel & dl pur .50 .20
E9 SD1 30r brt grn & dl pur .75 .20
E10 SD1 40r lil & dl pur .85 .25
Nos. E8-E10 (3) 2.10 .65

POSTAGE DUE STAMPS

Netherlands Indies Nos. J57 to J59 Surcharged in Black

1950 **Wmk. 228** ***Perf. 14½x14***

J60 D7 2½s on 50c yellow .75 .25
J61 D7 5s on 100c apple grn 2.25 .65
J62 D7 10s on 75c aqua 4.50 .75
Nos. J60-J62 (3) 7.50 1.65

D8

"1966" — D9

Wmk. 228

1951-52 **Litho.** ***Perf. 12½***

J63 D8 2½s vermilion .20 .20
J64 D8 5s vermilion .20 .20
J65 D8 10s vermilion .20 .20
J66 D8 20s blue ('52) .20 .20
J67 D8 25s olive bister ('52) .85 .50
J68 D8 50s vermilion 8.50 3.75
J69 D8 1r citron 1.50 *4.25*
Nos. J63-J69 (7) 11.65 9.30

1953-55 **Unwmk.**

J70 D8 15s lt magenta ('55) .35 .20
J71 D8 30s red brown .20 .20
J72 D8 40s green .35 .20
Nos. J70-J72 (3) .90 .60

1958-61 ***Perf. 13½x12½***

J73 D8 10s orange .20 .20
J74 D8 15s orange ('59) .20 .20
J74A D8 20s orange ('61) .20 .20
J75 D8 25s orange .20 .20
J76 D8 30s orange ('60) .20 .20
J77 D8 50s orange 1.25 .40
J78 D8 100s orange ('60) .60 .20
Nos. J73-J78 (7) 2.85 1.60

1962-65 ***Perf. 13½x12½***

J79 D8 50s light bluish green .20 .20
J80 D8 100s bister .20 .20
J81 D8 250s blue .20 .20
J82 D8 500s dull yellow .20 .20
J83 D8 750s pale lilac .25 .20
J84 D8 1000s salmon .35 .20
J85 D8 50r red ('65) .20 .20
J86 D8 100r maroon ('65) .25 .20
Nos. J79-J86 (8) 1.85 1.60

1966-67 **Unwmk.** **Photo.**

J91 D9 5s dl grn & dl yel .20 .20
J92 D9 10s red & lt bl .20 .20
J93 D9 20s dk bl & pink .20 .20
J94 D9 30s brn & rose .20 .20
J95 D9 40s plum & bis .20 .20
J96 D9 50s ol grn & pale lil .20 .20
J97 D9 100s dk red & yel grn .25 .20
J98 D9 200s brt grn & pink ('67) .30 .20
J99 D9 500s yel & lt bl ('67) .40 .20
J100 D9 1000s rose lil & yel ('67) .65 .20
Nos. J91-J100 (10) 2.80 2.00

Dated "1967"

1967

J101 D9 50s ol grn & pale lil .20 .20
J102 D9 100s dk red & yel grn .25 .20
J103 D9 200s brt grn & pink .35 .20
J104 D9 500s yel & lt bl .60 .20
J105 D9 1000s rose lil & yel 1.00 .20
J106 D9 15r org & gray .80 .20
J107 D9 25r lil & citron 1.40 .25
Nos. J101-J107 (7) 4.60 1.45

Similar stamps inscribed "Bajar" or "Bayar", year date and "Sumbangan Ongkos Tjetak" or ". . . Cetak" are revenues.

Dated "1973"
Inscribed "BAYAR PORTO"

1973

J108 D9 25r lilac & citron .85

Dated "1974"
Inscribed "BAYAR PORTO"

1974

J109 D9 65r olive grn & bister 1.60 .65
J110 D9 125r lil & pale pink 5.00 1.25

Dated "1975"
Inscribed "BAYAR PORTO"

1975 **Photo.** ***Perf. 13½x12½***

J111 D9 25r lilac & citron 1.25 .25

"1976" — D10

1976

J112 D10 125r lil & pale pur 2.50 .40

Dated "1977"

1977

J113 D10 100r dp vio & pale pink .40 .40
J114 D10 200r brt bl & lt lil .85 .85
J115 D10 300r choc & lt sal 1.25 1.25
J116 D10 400r brt grn & tan 1.50 1.50
J117 D10 500r red & tan 2.00 2.00
Nos. J113-J117 (5) 6.00 6.00

See Nos. J138, J139, J142.

Nos. 706, 709, 712-713, 716, 718 Surcharged in Red

1978 **Photo.** ***Perf. 12½x12***

J118 A110 25r on 1r .25
J119 A110 50r on 2r .50
J120 A110 100r on 4r 1.50
J121 A110 200r on 5r 3.00
J122 A110 300r on 10r 4.00
J123 A110 400r on 15r 5.75
Nos. J118-J123 (6) 15.00

Surcharged in Black

J124 A110 25r on 1r .25
J125 A110 50r on 2r .55
J126 A110 100r on 4r 1.60
J127 A110 200r on 5r 3.25
J128 A110 300r on 10r 4.00
J129 A110 400r on 15r 5.50
Nos. J124-J129 (6) 15.15

Nos. 710, 717 Surcharged

1978 **Photo.** ***Perf. 12½x12***

J130 A110 40r on 2.50r .95
J131 A110 40r on 12r .95
J132 A110 65r on 2.50r 1.50
J133 A110 65r on 12r 1.50
J134 A110 125r on 2.50r 3.50
J135 A110 125r on 12r 3.50
J136 A110 150r on 2.50r 4.25
J137 A110 150r on 12r 4.25
Nos. J130-J137 (8) 20.40

Type of 1976 Dated "1979"

1979 ***Perf. 13½x12½***

J138 D10 25r lilac & citron .50 .20

Type of 1976 and

D11

Perf. 13½x12½, 13½x13 (#J144-J148, J150-J153), 14½x13 (#J154-J156A)

1980-90 **Photo.**

Dated "1980"

J139 D10 25r dk lil & beige .20 .20
J140 D11 50r multi .40 .20
J141 D11 75r rose lake & rose .60 .20
J142 D10 125r rose lil & lt pink .60 .25
Nos. J139-J142 (4) 1.80 .85

Dated "1981"

J144 D11 25r brt vio & pale yel grn .20 .20
J145 D11 50r sl grn & lt vio .25 .20
J146 D11 75r rose vio & pink .40 .20
J147 D11 125r pur & yel grn .70 .25
Nos. J144-J147 (4) 1.55 .85

Dated "1982"

J148 D11 125r dp rose lil & pink .65 .25

Dated "1983"

J149 D11 125r dp rose & lil pink .25 .20
J150 D11 200r dp vio & lt bl .40 .20
J151 D11 300r dk grn & cit .60 .20
J152 D11 400r ol grn & brn ol .75 .25
J153 D11 500r sepia & beige 1.00 .30
Nos. J149-J153 (5) 3.00 1.15

Dated "1984"

J154 D11 25r brt vio & pale yel grn .45 .20
J155 D11 50r sl grn & lt vio .45 .20
J156 D11 125r rose lil & lt pink .50 .20
J156A D11 500r sepia & beige 1.60 .40
Nos. J154-J156A (4) 3.00 1.00

Dated "1988"

J157 D11 1000r dp vio & gray .95 .20
J158 D11 2000r red & dp rose lil 2.00 .35
J159 D11 3000r brn & dl org 3.00 .55
J160 D11 5000r grn & bl grn 4.75 .90
Nos. J157-J160 (4) 10.70 2.00

Dated "1990"

J161 D11 2000r emer & brt yel 3.50 1.75
J162 D11 3000r dk bl grn & rose lil 5.00 2.50
J163 D11 4000r brn vio & brt yel grn 6.75 3.50
Nos. J161-J163 (3) 15.25 7.75

RIAU ARCHIPELAGO

(Riouw Archipelago)
100 Sen = 1 Rupiah
(1 rupiah = 1 Malayan dollar)

Indonesia Nos. 371-386 Overprinted in Black

a

b

Overprint "a"

1954 **Unwmk.** ***Perf. 12½***

1 A52 5s car rose 21.00 20.00
2 A52 7½s green .40 .40
3 A52 10s blue 24.00 24.00
4 A52 15s purple 1.00 1.00
5 A52 20s rose red 1.00 1.00
6 A52 25s dp green 50.00 25.00

Overprint "b"

7 A53 30s red orange 2.10 2.10
8 A53 35s purple .40 .40
9 A53 40s dull green .40 .40
10 A53 45s dp claret .40 .40
11 A53 50s brown 175.00 40.00
12 A54 60s dk brown .40 .40
13 A54 70s gray 1.00 1.00
14 A54 75s ultra 3.50 2.50
15 A54 80s claret .70 .70
16 A54 90s gray green .70 .70

Netherlands Indies Nos. 325-330 Overprinted Type "a" in Black
Perf. 12½x12

17 A46 1r purple 4.75 3.00
18 A46 2r olive grn 1.00 1.00
19 A46 3r red violet 1.50 1.50
20 A46 5r dk brown 1.50 1.50
21 A46 10r gray 2.10 2.10
22 A46 25r orange brn 2.10 2.10
Nos. 1-22 (22) 294.95 131.20

Mint values are for stamps with somewhat tropicalized gum (stained brown and cracked). Stamps with clean, clear gum sell for about twice as much.

Indonesia Nos. 424-428, 450 and 430 Overprinted Type "b" or

1957-64 **Photo.** ***Perf. 12½x13½***

23 A63(b) 5s dp ultra .30 .30
24 A63 10s yellow brn 13.00 10.00
25 A63(b) 10s yellow brn .30 .30
26 A63(b) 15s rose vio ('64) .30 *.30*
27 A63(b) 20s dull grn ('60) .30 .30
27A A63 25s dp claret *40.00 40.00*
28 A63(b) 25s dp claret .30 .30
29 A63(b) 30s orange .30 .30
30 A63 50s brown 13.00 10.00
31 A63(b) 50s brown .30 .30

The "b" overprint measures 12mm in this set.

Sukarno Type of Indonesia Overprinted Type "a"

1960 ***Perf. 12½x12***

32 A55 1.25r dp orange 3.00 3.00
33 A55 1.50r brown 3.00 3.00
34 A55 2.50r rose brown 4.50 4.50
35 A55 4r apple green .80 *.30*
36 A55 6r rose lilac .80 *.30*
37 A55 15r yellow .80 *.30*
38 A55 20r sepia .80 .80
39 A55 40r yellow grn .80 *.30*
40 A55 50r violet 2.50 *.30*
Nos. 23-40 (19) 85.10 74.90

Nos. 26, 35-37, 39-40 are valued CTO with Bandung cancels. Postally used sell for much more.

INHAMBANE

ˌin-yəm-ˈban-ə

LOCATION — East Africa
GOVT. — A district of Mozambique, former Portuguese colony
AREA — 21,000 sq. mi. (approx.)
POP. — 248,000 (approx.)

CAPITAL — Inhambane

1000 Reis = 1 Milreis
100 Centavos = 1 Escudo (1913)

Stamps of Mozambique Overprinted

CENTENARIO
DE
S. ANTONIO
—
Inhambane
MDCCCXCV

On 1886 Issue

1895, July 1 Unwmk. *Perf. 12½*
Without Gum

1 A2 5r black 37.50 30.00
2 A2 10r green 35.00 25.00
a. Perf. 13½ 80.00 75.00
3 A2 20r rose 60.00 30.00
4 A2 25r lilac *250.00 250.00*
5 A2 40r chocolate 55.00 40.00
6 A2 50r blue 55.00 32.50
a. Perf. 13½ 50.00 50.00
7 A2 100r yellow brown *400.00 400.00*
8 A2 200r gray violet 50.00 40.00
9 A2 300r orange 50.00 40.00
Nos. 1-9 (9) *992.50 887.50*

On 1894 Issue
Perf. 11½

10 A3 50r lt blue 42.50 35.00
a. Perf. 12½ 55.00 42.50
11 A3 75r rose 55.00 40.00
12 A3 80r yellow green 45.00 37.50
13 A3 100r brown, *buff* 140.00 60.00
14 A3 150r carmine, *rose* 50.00 45.00
Nos. 10-14 (5) 332.50 217.50

700th anniv. of the birth of St. Anthony of Padua.

The status of Nos. 4 and 7 is questionable. No. 3 is always discolored.

Forged overprints exist. Genuine overprints are 21mm high.

King Carlos — A1

1903, Jan. 1 Typo. *Perf. 11½*
Name and Value in Black except 500r

15 A1 2½r gray .30 .30
16 A1 5r orange .30 .30
17 A1 10r lt green .60 .40
18 A1 15r gray green 1.00 .75
19 A1 20r gray violet .85 .55
20 A1 25r carmine .70 .55
21 A1 50r brown 1.75 1.25
22 A1 65r dull blue 17.50 15.00
23 A1 75r lilac 2.00 1.40
24 A1 100r dk blue, *blue* 2.75 1.25
25 A1 115r org brn, *pink* 5.00 5.00
26 A1 130r brown, *straw* 5.00 5.00
27 A1 200r red vio, *pink* 5.00 4.25
28 A1 400r dull bl, *straw* 8.25 7.50
29 A1 500r blk & red, *bl* 16.00 12.00
30 A1 700r gray blk, *straw* 16.00 13.00
Nos. 15-30 (16) 83.00 68.50

For surcharge & overprints see #31-47, 88-101.

No. 22 Surcharged in Black

1905

31 A1 50r on 65r dull blue 2.75 2.00

Nos. 15-21, 23-30 Overprinted in Carmine or Green

1911

32 A1 2½r gray .20 .20
33 A1 5r orange .20 .20
34 A1 10r lt green .20 .20
35 A1 15r gray green .30 .30
36 A1 20r gray violet .30 .30
37 A1 25r carmine (G) .70 .50
38 A1 50r brown .50 .50
39 A1 75r lilac .50 .50
40 A1 100r dk blue, *bl* .50 .50
41 A1 115r org brn, *pink* 1.00 .95
42 A1 130r brown, *straw* 1.00 .95
43 A1 200r red vio, *pink* 1.00 .95
44 A1 400r dull bl, *straw* 1.25 1.00
45 A1 500r blk & red, *bl* 1.50 1.00
46 A1 700r gray blk, *straw* 1.75 1.50
Nos. 32-46 (15) 10.90 9.55

No. 31 Overprinted in Red

REPUBLICA

1914

47 A1 50r on 65r dull blue 1.75 1.25
a. "Republica" inverted 25.00 25.00

Vasco da Gama Issue of Various Portuguese Colonies

Common Design Types CD20-CD27 Surcharged

1913

On Stamps of Macao

48 CD20 ¼c on ½a bl grn 1.25 1.25
49 CD21 ½c on 1a red 1.25 1.25
50 CD22 1c on 2a red vio 1.25 1.25
a. Inverted surcharge 35.00 35.00
51 CD23 2½c on 4a yel grn 1.25 1.25
52 CD24 5c on 8a dk bl 1.25 1.25
53 CD25 7½c on 12a vio brn 2.25 2.25
54 CD26 10c on 16a bis brn 1.75 1.75
55 CD27 15c on 24a bis 1.75 1.75
Nos. 48-55 (8) 12.00 12.00

On Stamps of Portuguese Africa

56 CD20 ¼c on 2½r bl grn 1.00 1.00
57 CD21 ½c on 5r red 1.00 1.00
58 CD22 1c on 10r red vio 1.00 1.00
59 CD23 2½c on 25r yel grn 1.00 1.00
60 CD24 5c on 50r dk bl 1.00 1.00
61 CD25 7½c on 75r vio brn 2.00 2.00
62 CD26 10c on 100r bis brn 1.50 1.50
63 CD27 15c on 150r bis 1.50 1.50
Nos. 56-63 (8) 10.00 10.00

On Stamps of Timor

64 CD20 ¼c on ½a bl grn 1.25 1.25
a. Inverted surcharge 35.00 35.00
65 CD21 ½c on 1a red 1.25 1.25
66 CD22 1c on 2a red vio 1.25 1.25
67 CD23 2½c on 4a yel grn 1.25 1.25
68 CD24 5c on 8a dk bl 1.25 1.25
69 CD25 7½c on 12a vio brn 2.50 2.50
70 CD26 10c on 16a bis brn 1.75 1.75
71 CD27 15c on 24a bis 1.75 1.75
Nos. 64-71 (8) 12.25 12.25
Nos. 48-71 (24) 34.25 34.25

Ceres — A2

1914 Typo. *Perf. 15x14*
Name and Value in Black

72 A2 ¼c olive brown .50 .50
73 A2 ½c black .50 .50
a. Imperf.
74 A2 1c blue green .50 .50
75 A2 1½c lilac brown .50 .50
76 A2 2c carmine .50 .50
77 A2 2½c lt violet .35 .35
78 A2 5c deep blue .80 .80
79 A2 7½c yellow brown 1.25 1.25
80 A2 8c slate 1.25 1.25
81 A2 10c orange brown 1.10 1.10
82 A2 15c plum 1.60 1.60
83 A2 20c yellow green 1.60 1.60
84 A2 30c brown, *grn* 2.50 2.50
85 A2 40c brown, *pink* 2.75 2.75
86 A2 50c orange, *sal* 4.50 4.50
87 A2 1e green, *blue* 5.00 5.00
Nos. 72-87 (16) 25.20 25.20

No. 31 Overprinted in Carmine

1915 *Perf. 11½*

88 A1 50c on 65r dull blue 8.00 6.00

Nos. 15-21, 23-30 Overprinted Locally

1917

89 A1 2½r gray 25.00 25.00
90 A1 5r orange 25.00 25.00
91 A1 15r gray green 2.50 2.50
92 A1 20r gray violet 2.00 2.00
93 A1 50r brown 2.00 2.00
94 A1 75r lilac 2.00 2.00
95 A1 100r blue, *blue* 3.00 2.50
96 A1 115r org brn, *pink* 3.00 2.50
97 A1 130r brn, *straw* 3.00 2.50
98 A1 200r red vio, *pink* 3.00 2.50
99 A1 400r dull bl, *straw* 4.00 3.00
100 A1 500r blk & red, *bl* 5.00 3.00
101 A1 700r gray blk, *straw* 14.00 8.00
Nos. 89-101 (13) 93.50 82.50

The stamps of Inhambane have been superseded by those of Mozambique.

ININI

ˌē-ni-ˈnē

LOCATION — In northeastern South America, adjoining French Guiana
GOVT. — Territory of French Guiana
AREA — 30,301 sq. mi.
POP. — 5,024 (1946)
CAPITAL — St. Elie

Inini was separated from French Guiana in 1930 and reunited with it in when the colony became an integral part of the Republic, acquiring the same status as the departments of Metropolitan France, under a law effective Jan. 1, 1947.

100 Centimes = 1 Franc

Used values are for canceled-to-order copies.

Stamps of French Guiana, 1929-40, Overprinted in Black, Red or Blue:

Nos. 1-9

Nos. 10-26

Nos. 27-40

1932-40 Unwmk. *Perf. 13½x14*

1 A16 1c gray lil & grnsh bl .20 .20
2 A16 2c dk red & bl grn .20 .20
3 A16 3c gray lil & grnsh bl ('40) .20 .20
4 A16 4c ol brn & red vio ('38) .30 .30
5 A16 5c Prus bl & red org .30 .30
6 A16 10c magenta & brn .20 .20
7 A16 15c yel brn & red org .20 .20
8 A16 20c dk bl & ol grn .20 .20
9 A16 25c dk red & dk brn .30 .30

Perf. 14x13½

10 A17 30c dl grn & lt grn .80 .80
11 A17 30c grn & brn ('40) .20 .20
12 A17 35c Prus grn & ol ('38) .40 .40
13 A17 40c org brn & ol gray .30 .30
14 A17 45c ol grn & lt grn ('40) .50 .50
15 A17 50c dk bl & ol gray .20 .20
16 A17 55c vio bl & car ('38) 2.00 2.00
17 A17 60c sal & grn ('40) .20 .20
18 A17 65c sal & grn ('38) .50 .50
19 A17 70c ind & sl bl ('40) .25 .25
20 A17 75c ind & sl bl (Bl) 1.00 1.00
21 A17 80c blk & vio bl (R) ('38) .35 .30
22 A17 90c dk red & ver .45 .45
23 A17 90c red vio & brn ('39) .25 .25
24 A17 1fr lt vio & brn 9.00 9.00
25 A17 1fr car & lt red ('38) .50 .50
26 A17 1fr blk & vio bl ('40) .25 .25
27 A18 1.25fr blk brn & bl grn ('33) .50 .50
28 A18 1.25fr rose & lt red ('39) .30 .30
29 A18 1.40fr ol brn & red vio ('40) .35 .35
30 A18 1.50fr dk bl & lt bl .30 .30
31 A18 1.60fr ol brn & bl grn ('40) .35 .35
32 A18 1.75fr brn, red & blk brn ('33) 13.50 13.50
33 A18 1.75fr vio bl ('38) .65 .60
34 A18 2fr dk grn & rose red .50 .50
35 A18 2.25fr vio bl ('39) .40 .40
36 A18 2.50fr cop red & brn ('40) .40 .40
37 A18 3fr brn red & red vio .50 .50
38 A18 5fr dl vio & yel grn .50 .50
39 A18 10fr ol gray & dp ultra (R) .50 .50
40 A18 20fr indigo & ver .60 .60
Nos. 1-40 (40) 38.60 38.50

Without "RF," see Nos. 46-49.

Common Design Types pictured following the introduction.

Colonial Arts Exhibition Issue
Souvenir Sheet
Common Design Type

1937 *Imperf.*

41 CD75 3fr red brown 9.00 *10.00*

New York World's Fair Issue
Common Design Type

1939, May 10 Engr. *Perf. 12½x12*

42 CD82 1.25fr car lake 2.25 2.25
43 CD82 2.25fr ultra 2.25 2.25

French Guiana Nos. 170A-170B Overprinted "ININI" in Green or Red

1941 Engr. *Perf. 12½x12*

44 A21a 1fr deep lilac .40
45 A21a 2.50fr blue (R) .40

Nos. 44-45 were issued by the Vichy government in France, but were not placed on sale in Inini.

For surcharges, see Nos. B9-B10.

Types of 1932-40 Without "RF"
Methods and Perfs as Before

1942

46 A16 20c dk bl & ol grn .60
47 A17 1fr black & ultra .50
48 A18 10fr ol gr & dp ultra (R) .60
49 A18 20fr indigo & ver .90
Nos. 46-49 (4) 2.60

Nos. 46-49 were issued by the Vichy government in France, but were not placed on sale in Inini.

SEMI-POSTAL STAMPS

Common Design Type
Photo.; Name & Value Typo. in Black

1939, July 5 Unwmk. *Perf. 13*

B1 CD83 45c + 25c green 7.50 7.50
B2 CD83 70c + 30c brown 7.50 7.50
B3 CD83 90c + 35c red org 7.50 7.50

B4 CD83 1.25fr + 1fr rose pink 7.50 7.50
B5 CD83 2.25fr + 2fr blue 7.50 7.50
Nos. B1-B5 (5) 37.50 37.50

Common Design Type and French Guiana Nos. B9 and B11 Overprinted "ININI" in Blue or Red

1941 Photo. *Perf. 13½*
B6 SP1 1fr + 1fr red (B) .85
B7 CD86 1.50fr + 3fr maroon .85
B8 SP2 2.50fr + 1fr blue (R) .85
Nos. B6-B8 (3) 2.55

Nos. B6-B8 were issued by the Vichy government in France, but were not placed on sale in Inini.

Petain Type of 1941 Surcharged in Black or Red

1944 Engr. *Perf. 12½x12*
B9 50c + 1.50fr on 2.50fr deep blue (R) .40
B10 + 2.50fr on 1fr dp lilac .40

Colonial Development Fund.

Nos. B9-B10 were issued by the Vichy government in France, but were not placed on sale in Inini.

AIR POST SEMI-POSTAL STAMPS

Nurse with Mother & Child — SPAP1

Unwmk.
1942, June 22 Engr. *Perf. 13*
CB1 SPAP1 1.50fr + 50c green .60
CB2 SPAP1 2fr + 6fr brn & red .60

Native children's welfare fund.

Nos. CB1-CB2 were issued by the Vichy government in France, but were not placed on sale in Inini.

Colonial Education Fund
Common Design Type
1942, June 22
CB3 CD86a 1.20fr + 1.80fr blue & red .50

No. CB3 was issued by the Vichy government in France, but was not placed on sale in Inini.

POSTAGE DUE STAMPS

Postage Due Stamps of French Guiana, 1929, Overprinted in Black

1932, Apr. 7 Unwmk. *Perf. 13½x14*
J1 D3 5c indigo & Prus bl .20 .20
J2 D3 10c bis brn & Prus grn .25 .25
J3 D3 20c grn & rose red .25 .25
J4 D3 30c ol brn & rose red .25 .25
J5 D3 50c vio & ol brn .40 .40
J6 D3 60c brn red & ol brn .40 .40

Overprinted in Black or Red

J7 D4 1fr dp bl & org brn .50 .50
J8 D4 2fr brn red & bluish grn .75 .75
J9 D4 3fr vio & blk (R) 5.50 5.50
J10 D4 3fr vio & blk 1.00 1.00
Nos. J1-J10 (10) 9.50 9.50

IONIAN ISLANDS

ī-'ō-nē-ən 'ī-ləndṡ

LOCATION — Seven Islands, of which six-Corfu, Paxos, Lefkas (Santa Maura), Cephalonia, Ithaca and Zante-are in the Ionian Sea west of Greece, and a seventh-Cerigo (Kithyra)-is in the Mediterranean south of Greece
GOVT. — Integral part of Kingdom of Greece
AREA — 752 sq. miles
POP. — 231,510 (1938)

These islands were acquired by Great Britain in 1815 but in 1864 were ceded to Greece on request of the inhabitants.

In 1941 the islands were occupied by Italian forces. The Italians withdrew in 1943 and German forces continued the occupation, using current Greek stamps without overprinting, except for Zante.

For stamps of the Italian occupation of Corfu, see Corfu.

10 Oboli = 1 Penny
12 Pence = 1 Shilling
100 Lepta = 1 Drachma
100 Centesimi = 1 Lira

Watermarks

Wmk. 138- "2" Wmk. 139- "1"

Queen Victoria — A1

1859 Unwmk. Engr. *Imperf.*
1 A1 (½p) orange 70.00 *500.00*
Wmk. 138
2 A1 (1p) blue 20.00 *190.00*
Wmk. 139
3 A1 (2p) lake 20.00 *190.00*
Nos. 1-3 (3) 110.00 *880.00*

Forged cancellations are plentiful.

ISSUED UNDER ITALIAN OCCUPATION

Values of stamps overprinted by letterpress in pairs are for unsevered pairs. Single stamps, unused, sell for one third the price of a pair; used, one half the price of a pair.

Handstamped overprints were also applied to pairs, with "isola" instead of "isole."

Issue for Cephalonia and Ithaca

Stamps of Greece, 1937-38, Overprinted in Pairs Vertically, Reading Down, or Horizontally (H) in Black

Perf. 12½x12, 13½x12, 12x13½
1941 Wmk. 252, Unwmk.
N1 A69 5 l brn red & bl 2.75 *3.25*
N2 A70 10 l bl & red brn (#413) (H) 2.75 *3.25*
a. On No. 397 30.00 *35.00*
N3 A71 20 l blk & grn (H) 2.75 *3.25*
a. Overprint inverted 90.00
N4 A72 40 l green & blk 2.75 *3.25*
N5 A73 50 l brown & blk 2.75 *3.25*
N6 A74 80 l ind & yel brn (H) 8.00 5.00
a. Overprint inverted 80.00 80.00
N7 A67 1d green (H) 55.00 29.00
N8 A84 1.50d green (H) 40.00 22.50
a. Overprint inverted 75.00 75.00
N9 A75 2d ultra 3.75 3.25
N10 A76 5d red 17.00 8.50
N11 A77 6d olive brown 17.00 8.50
N12 A78 7d dark brown 17.00 8.50
N13 A67 8d dp blue (H) 42.50 19.00
N14 A79 10d red brn 21.00 9.25
N15 A80 15d green 32.50 18.00
N16 A81 25d dk blue (H) 42.50 37.50
a. Overprint inverted 140.00 110.00
N17 A84 30d org brn (H) 140.00 92.50
a. Overprint inverted 225.00 160.00
Nos. N1-N17 (17) 450.00 277.75

A variety with wrong font "C" in "Cephalonia" is found in several positions in each sheet of all denominations except those overprinted on single stamps. It sells for about three times the price of a normal pair.

Several other minor spelling errors in the overprint occur on several denominations in one of the printings.

Forgeries exist of many of the higher valued stamps and minor varieties of Nos. N1-N17, NC1-NC11 and NRA1-NRA5.

Overprint Reading Up
N1a A69 5 l 13.50 *16.00*
N4a A72 40 l 7.00 *8.50*
N5a A73 50 l 7.00 *8.50*
N9a A75 2d 50.00 42.50
N10a A76 5d 60.00 50.00
N11a A77 6d 42.50 24.00
N12a A78 7d 42.50 24.00
N14a A79 10d 42.50 30.00
N15a A80 15d 50.00 50.00
Nos. N1a-N15a (9) 315.00 *253.50*

General Issue

Stamps of Italy, 1929, Overprinted in Red or Black

1941 Wmk. 140 *Perf. 14*
N18 A90 5c olive brn (R) .30 *.55*
N19 A92 10c dk brown (R) .30 *.55*
N20 A91 20c rose red .30 *.55*
N21 A94 25c deep green .30 *.55*
N22 A95 30c olive brn (R) .30 *.55*
a. "SOLE" for "ISOLE" 35.00
N23 A95 50c purple (R) .30 *.55*
N24 A94 75c rose red .30 *.55*
N25 A94 1.25 l dp blue (R) .30 *.55*
Nos. N18-N25 (8) 2.40 *4.40*

The stamps overprinted "Isole Jonie" were issued for all the Ionian Islands except Cerigo which used regular postage stamps of Greece.

ISSUED UNDER GERMAN OCCUPATION

Zante Issue

Nos. N21 and N23 with Additional Handstamped Overprint in Black

1943 Wmk. 140 *Perf. 14*
N26 A94 25c deep green 22.50 *45.00*
a. Carmine overprint 40.00 *75.00*
N27 A95 50c purple 22.50 *45.00*
a. Carmine overprint 40.00 *75.00*

No. N19 with this overprint is a proof. Value, black $40; carmine $85.

Nos. N26-N27 were in use 8 days, then were succeeded by stamps of Greece.

Forgeries of Nos. N26-N27, NC13 and their cancellations are plentiful.

Greek stamps with Italian overprints for the islands of Cerigo (Kithyra), Paxos and Lefkas (Santa Maura) are fraudulent.

OCCUPATION AIR POST STAMPS

Issued under Italian Occupation

Issue for Cephalonia and Ithaca

Stamps of Greece Overprinted in Pairs Vertically, Reading Down, or Horizontally (H) in Black Like Nos. N1-N17

Perf. 13x12½, 12½x13
1941 Unwmk.
On Greece Nos. C22, C23, C25 and C27 to C30
Grayish Paper
NC1 AP16 1d dp red 17.50 17.50
NC1A AP17 2d dl bl 42.50
NC2 AP19 7d bl vio (H) 90.00 90.00
NC3 AP21 25d rose (H) 80.00 75.00
a. Overprint inverted 190.00 190.00
NC4 AP22 30d dk grn 65.00 65.00
a. Overprint reading up 85.00 70.00
b. Horizontal overprint on single stamp *150.00 125.00*
c. As "b," inverted *250.00*
NC5 AP23 50d vio (H) *275.00* 225.00
NC6 AP24 100d brown 210.00 175.00
a. Overprint reading up 275.00 *300.00*

No. NC1A is known only with overprint reading up.

On Greece Nos. C31-C34
Reengraved; White Paper
NC7 AP16 1d red 9.00 7.50
NC8 AP17 2d gray bl 9.00 7.50
a. Overprint reading up 9.00 7.50
b. Horiz. ovpt. on pair *150.00 90.00*
c. Horizontal overprint on single stamp
NC9 AP18 5d vio (H) 12.50 10.00
a. Overprint inverted 90.00
b. Vert. ovpt. on single stamp, up or down 90.00
NC10 AP19 7d dp ultra (H) 20.00 20.00
a. Overprint inverted 60.00 50.00

Overprinted Horizontally on No. C36
Rouletted 13½
NC11 D3 50 l vio brn 35.00 32.50
a. Pair, one without ovpt. *80.00*
b. On No. C36a *190.00*

See footnote following No. N17.

General Issue

Italy No. C13 Overprinted in Red Like Nos. N18-N25

1941 Wmk. 140 *Perf. 14*
NC12 AP3 50c olive brown .50 1.00
a. "SOLE" for "ISOLE" 35.00

Used in all the Ionian Islands except Cerigo which used air post stamps of Greece.

No. NC12 with additional overprint "BOLLO" is a revenue stamp.

Issued under German Occupation

ZANTE ISSUE

No. NC12 with Additional Handstamped Overprint in Black Like Nos. N26-N27

1943 **Wmk. 140** ***Perf. 14***

NC13 AP3 50c olive brown	25.00	*50.00*
a. "SOLE" for "ISOLE"	*300.00*	
b. Carmine overprint	110.00	*190.00*

See note after No. N27.

OCCUPATION POSTAGE DUE STAMPS

General Issue

Postage Due Stamps of Italy, 1934, Overprinted in Black Like Nos. N18-N25

1941 **Wmk. 140** ***Perf. 14***

NJ1 D6 10c blue	.60	*.75*
NJ2 D6 20c rose red	.60	*.75*
NJ3 D6 30c red orange	.60	*.75*
NJ4 D7 1 l red orange	.60	*.75*
Nos. NJ1-NJ4 (4)	2.40	*3.00*

See footnote after No. N25.

OCCUPATION POSTAL TAX STAMPS

Issued under Italian Occupation

Issue for Cephalonia and Ithaca

Greece No. RA56 with Additional Overprint on Horizontal Pair in Black Like Nos. N1-N17

Serrate Roulette 13½

1941 **Unwmk.**

NRA1 D3 10 l car (Bl+Bk)	3.75	3.75
a. Blue overprint double	35.00	35.00
b. Inverted overprint	55.00	55.00

Same Overprint Reading Down on Vertical Pairs of Nos. RA61-RA63

Perf. 13½x12

NRA2 PT7 10 l brt rose, *pale rose*	7.50	7.50
a. Overprint on horiz. pair	100.00	40.00
b. Horizontal overprint on single stamp	*200.00*	
c. Overprint reading up	12.50	12.50
NRA3 PT7 50 l gray grn, *pale grn*	2.25	2.25
a. Overprint reading up	6.00	6.00
b. Ovpt. on horiz. pair	20.00	20.00
c. Horizontal overprint on single stamp	*250.00*	
NRA4 PT7 1d dl bl, *lt bl*	14.00	12.00
a. Overprint reading up	27.50	21.00

Same Overprint Reading Down on Vertical Pair of No. RA65

NRA5 PT7 50 l gray grn, *pale grn*	150.00	
a. Overprint reading up	180.00	

Nos. NRA5 and NRA5a were not placed in use on any compulsory day.

See footnote following No. N17.

IRAN

i-ˈrän

(Persia)

LOCATION — Western Asia, bordering on the Persian Gulf and the Gulf of Oman

GOVT. — Islamic republic

AREA — 636,000 sq. mi.

POP. — 65,179,752 (1999 est.)

CAPITAL — Tehran

20 Shahis (or Chahis) = 1 Kran
10 Krans = 1 Toman
100 Centimes = 1 Franc = 1 Kran (1881)
100 Dinars = 1 Rial (1933)
100 Rials = 1 Pahlavi
100 Rials = 1 Toman

Catalogue values for unused stamps in this country are for Never Hinged items, beginning with Scott 1054 in the regular postage section, Scott B36 in the semi-postal section, Scott C83 in the airpost section, Scott O72 in the officials section, Scott Q36 in the parcel post section, and Scott RA4 in the postal tax section.

Values of early stamps vary according to condition. Quotations for Nos. 1-20, 33-40 are for fine copies. Very fine to superb specimens sell at much higher prices, and inferior or poor copies sell at reduced prices, depending on the condition of the individual specimen.

Cracked gum on unused stamps does not detract from the value.

Watermarks

Wmk. 161- Lion

Wmk. 306- Arms of Iran

Wmk. 316- Persian Inscription

Wmk. 349- Persian Inscription and Crown in Circle

Illustration of Wmk. 349 shown sideways. Circles in Wmk. 349 are 95mm apart.

Wmk. 353- Persian Inscription and Coat of Arms in Circle

Wmk. 381- "Islamic Republic of Iran" in Persian (Partial Illustration)

Many issues have handstamped surcharges. As usual with such surcharges there are numerous inverted, double and similar varieties.

Coat of Arms
A1 A2

Design A2 has value numeral below lion.

1870 **Unwmk.** **Typo.** ***Imperf.***

1 A1 1s dull violet	65.00	
2 A1 2s green	50.00	
3 A1 4s greenish blue	75.00	
4 A1 8s red	75.00	
Nos. 1-4 (4)	265.00	

Values for used copies of Nos. 1-4 are omitted, since this issue was only pen canceled. After 1875, postmarked remainders were sold to collectors. Values same as unused.

Printed in blocks of 4. Many shades exist. Forgeries exist.

Printed on Both Sides

1a A1 1s	950.
2a A1 2s	700.
3a A1 4s	1,750.
4a A1 8s	1,100.

Vertically Rouletted 10½ on 1 or 2 Sides

1875 **Thick Wove Paper**

11 A2 1s black	90.00	50.00
a. Imperf., pair	*400.00*	*400.00*
12 A2 2s blue	95.00	47.50
a. Tête bêche pair	*10,000.*	
b. Imperf., pair	*575.00*	*575.00*
13 A2 4s vermilion	110.00	42.50
a. Imperf., pair	*625.00*	*625.00*
b. 4s bright red, thin paper, imperf.	525.00	
14 A2 8s yellow green	90.00	40.00
a. Tête bêche pair	*10,000.*	*5,000.*
b. Imperf., pair	*300.00*	*125.00*
Nos. 11-14 (4)	385.00	180.00

Four varieties of each.

Nos. 11-14 were printed in horizontal strips of 4 with 3-10mm spacing between stamps. The strips were then cut very close all around (generally touching or cutting the outer framelines). Then they were hand-rouletted between the stamps. Values are for stamps with rouletting on both sides and margins clear at top and bottom. Stamps showing the rouletting on only one side sell for considerably less.

Nos. 11 to 14 also exist pin-perforated and percé en scie.

No. 13b has spacing of 2-3mm.

See Nos. 15-20, 33-40.

Medium to Thin White or Grayish Paper

1876 ***Imperf.***

15 A2 1s gray black	25.00	25.00
a. Printed on both sides	750.00	
b. Laid paper	500.00	
16 A2 2s gray blue	250.00	*250.00*
a. Printed on both sides	600.00	
17 A2 2s black	600.00	
a. Tête bêche pair	*5,750.*	
18 A2 4s vermilion	125.00	45.00
a. Printed on both sides	800.00	450.00
19 A2 1k rose	160.00	50.00
a. Printed on both sides		475.00
b. Laid paper	450.00	150.00
c. 1k yellow (error)	*9,500.*	
d. Tête bêche pair		*15,000.*
20 A2 4k yellow	550.00	70.00
a. Printed on both sides		*825.00*
b. Laid paper	600.00	110.00
c. Tête bêche pair		*9,000.*

Nos. 15-16, 18-20 were printed in blocks of 4, with spacing of 2mm or less, No. 15 also in vertical strip of 4. No. 17 in a vertical strip of 4.

The 2s black and the vertical-strip printing on the 1s are on medium to thick grayish wove paper. Both printings of the 1s are found in black as well as gray black. Forgeries exist.

Official reprints of the 1s and 4s are on thick coarse white paper without gum.

Unofficial Reprints:
1875 and 1876 issues.

The reprints of the 1s and 1k stamps are readily told; the pearls of the circle are heavier, the borders of the circles containing the Persian numeral of value are wider and the figure "1" below the lion is always Roman.

The reprints of the 2s have the outer line of the frame at the left and at the bottom broken and on some specimens entirely missing.

A distinguishing mark by which to tell the 4s and 4k stamps is the frame, the outer line of which is of the same thickness as the inner line, while on the originals the inner line is very thin and the outer line thick; another feature of most of the reprints is a gash in the lower part of the circle below the figure "4."

In the reprints of the 8s stamps the small scroll nearest to the circles with Persian numerals at the bottom of the stamp touches the frame below it; the inner and outer lines of the frame are of equal thickness, while in the originals the outer line is much heavier than the inner one.

All reprints are found canceled to order.

Nasser-eddin Shah Qajar — A3

Perf. 10½, 11, 12, 13, and Compounds

1876 **Litho.**

27	A3	1s lilac & blk	17.50	6.00
28	A3	2s green & blk	15.00	6.50
29	A3	5s rose & blk	25.00	4.00
30	A3	10s blue & blk	35.00	8.00
		Nos. 27-30 (4)	92.50	24.50

Bisects of the 5s and 1s, the latter used with 2s stamps, were used to make up the 2½ shahis postcard rate. Bisects of the 10s were used in the absence of 5s stamps to make up the letter rate.

The 10s was bisected and surcharged "5 Shahi" or "5 Shahy" for local use in Azerbaijan province and Khoy in 1877.

"Imperfs" of the 5s are envelope cutouts.

Forgeries and official reprints exist.

Very fine examples will have perforations cutting the background net on one side. Genuine stamps withs perfs clear of net on all four sides are very scarce.

1878 **Typo.** ***Imperf.***

33	A2	1k car rose	200.00	87.50
34	A2	1k red, *yellow*	*1,000.*	70.00
a.		Tête bêche pair		*4,750.*
35	A2	4k ultramarine	140.00	60.00
36	A2	5k gold	*2,000.*	200.00
37	A2	5k violet	850.00	200.00
38	A2	5k red bronze	*2,000.*	350.00
39	A2	5k vio bronze	*3,000.*	600.00
40	A2	1t bronze, *bl*	*16,000.*	*5,500.*

Four varieties of each except for 4k which has 3.

Nos. 33 and 34 are printed from redrawn clichés. They have wide colorless circles around the corner numerals.

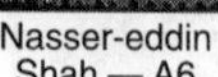

Nasser-eddin Shah — A6

Sun — A7

Perf. 10½, 12, 13, and Compounds

1879 **Litho.**

41	A6	1k brown & blk	100.00	3.00
a.		Imperf., pair	*425.00*	
b.		Inverted center		2,400.
42	A6	5k blue & blk	50.00	3.00
a.		Imperf., pair	*400.00*	140.00
b.		Inverted center		750.00

1880

43	A6	1s red & black	40.00	3.00
44	A6	2s yellow & blk	70.00	5.00
45	A6	5s green & blk	50.00	2.00
46	A6	10s violet & blk	250.00	15.00
		Nos. 43-46 (4)	410.00	25.00

Forgeries and official reprints exist.

The 2, 5 and 10sh of this issue and the 1 and 5kr of the 1879 issue have been reprinted from a new die which resembles the 5 shahi envelope. The aigrette is shorter than on the original stamps and touches the circle above it.

Imperf., Pair

43a	A6	1s	350.00	
44a	A6	2s	550.00	*400.00*
46a	A6	10s	—	*600.00*

1881 **Litho.** ***Perf. 12, 13, 12x13***

47	A7	5c dull violet	20.00	5.00
48	A7	10c rose	25.00	5.00
49	A7	25c green	850.00	65.00
		Nos. 47-49 (3)	895.00	75.00

1882 **Engr., Border Litho.**

50	A7	5c blue vio & vio	15.00	3.00
51	A7	10c dp pink & rose	15.00	3.00
52	A7	25c deep grn & grn	110.00	10.00
		Nos. 50-52 (3)	140.00	16.00

Very fine examples of Nos. 50-52 will have perforations cutting the outer colored border but clear of the inner framelines.

Counterfeits of Nos. 50-52, 53, 53a are plentiful and have been used to create forgeries of Nos. 66, 66a, 70 and 70a. They usually have a strong, complete inner frameline at right. On genuine stamps that line is weak or missing.

A8

Shah Nasr-ed-Din
A9 A10

A11

Type I

Type II (error)

Type I: Three dots at right end of scroll.
Type II: Two dots at right end of scroll.

1882-84 **Engr.**

53	A8	5s green, type I	15.00	1.50
a.		5s green, type II	30.00	7.50
54	A9	10s buff, org & blk	20.00	3.50
55	A10	50c buff, org & blk	50.00	20.00
56	A10	50c gray & blk ('84)	35.00	10.00
57	A10	1fr blue & black	35.00	6.00
58	A10	5fr rose red & blk	40.00	5.00
59	A11	10fr buff, red & blk	65.00	11.00
		Nos. 53-59 (7)	260.00	57.00

Crude forgeries of Nos. 58-59 exist. Halves of the 10s, 50c and 1fr surcharged with Farsi characters in red or black are frauds. The 50c and 1fr surcharged with a large "5" surrounded by rays are also frauds.

No. 59 used is valued for c-t-o.

For overprints and surcharges see #66-72.

Very fine examples of Nos. 53-59 will have perforations cutting the outer colored border but clear of the inner framelines.

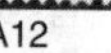

A12

A13

1885, March **Litho.**

59A	A12	5c blue	250.00	35.00
a.		5c violet blue	250.00	50.00
b.		5c ultramarine	250.00	50.00
c.		5c dp reddish lilac	300.00	75.00
d.		As "c," imperf	—	

No. 59A was issued because of an urgent need for 5c stamps, pending the arrival of No. 62 in July.

1885-86 **Typo.**

60	A12	1c green	10.00	1.00
61	A12	2c rose	10.00	1.00
62	A12	5c dull blue	15.00	.50
63	A13	10c brown	7.50	1.00
64	A13	1k slate	7.50	2.00
65	A13	5k dull vio ('86)	80.00	7.00
		Nos. 60-65 (6)	130.00	12.50

Nos. 53, 54, 56 and 58 Surcharged in Black:

a

b

c

d

e

f

1885

66	(a)	6c on 5s grn, type I	30.00	4.00
a.		6c on 5s green, type II	55.00	20.00
67	(b)	12c on 50c gray & blk	70.00	15.00
68	(c)	18c on 10s buff, org & black	70.00	15.00
69	(d)	1t on 5fr rose red & black	60.00	15.00
		Nos. 66-69 (4)	230.00	49.00

1887

70	(e)	3c on 5s grn, type I	25.00	7.00
a.		3c on 5s green, type II	55.00	20.00
71	(a)	6c on 10s buff, org & blk	25.00	7.50
72	(f)	8c on 50c gray & blk	75.00	20.00
		Nos. 70-72 (3)	125.00	34.50

The word "OFFICIEL" indicated that the surcharged stamps were officially authorized.

Surcharges on the same basic stamps of values other than those listed are believed to be bogus.

Counterfeits of Nos. 66-72 abound.

Very fine examples of Nos. 66-72 will have perforations cutting the outer colored border but clear of the inner framelines.

A14

A15

1889 **Typo.** ***Perf. 11, 13½, 11x13½***

73	A14	1c pale rose	.60	.30
74	A14	2c pale blue	.60	.30
75	A14	5c lilac	.60	.30
76	A14	7c brown	7.50	.75
77	A15	10c black	1.25	.30

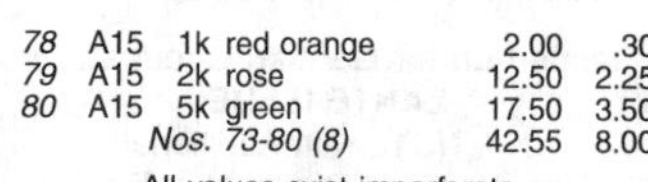

78	A15	1k red orange	2.00	.30
79	A15	2k rose	12.50	2.25
80	A15	5k green	17.50	3.50
		Nos. 73-80 (8)	42.55	8.00

All values exist imperforate.

Canceled to order copies of No. 76 abound.

For surcharges see Nos. 622-625.

Nos. 73-80 with average centering, faded colors and/or toned paper sell for much less.

A16

A17

1891 ***Perf. 10½, 11½***

81	A16	1c black	1.00	.20
82	A16	2c brown	1.00	.20
83	A16	5c deep blue	.50	.20
84	A16	7c gray	60.00	7.00
85	A16	10c rose	1.60	.20
86	A16	14c orange	2.00	.20
87	A17	1k green	17.50	2.00
88	A17	2k orange	140.00	7.00
89	A17	5k ocher yellow	4.50	4.50
		Nos. 81-89 (9)	228.10	21.50

For surcharges see Nos. 626-629.

A18

Nasser-eddin Shah — A19

1894 ***Perf. 12½***

90	A18	1c lilac	1.00	.20
91	A18	2c blue green	1.00	.20
92	A18	5c ultramarine	1.00	.20
93	A18	8c brown	1.00	.20

Perf. 11½x11

94	A19	10c orange	1.00	.75
95	A19	16c rose	6.00	*10.00*
96	A19	1k red & yellow	3.00	.75
97	A19	2k brn org & pale bl	3.00	1.00
98	A19	5k violet & silver	4.00	1.50
99	A19	10k red & gold	12.00	10.00
100	A19	50k green & gold	10.00	7.50
		Nos. 90-100 (11)	43.00	32.30

Canceled to order copies sell for one-third of listed values.

Reprints exist. They are hard to distinguish from the originals. Value, set $15.

See Nos. 104-112, 136-144. For overprints see Nos. 120-128, 152-167, 173-181. For surcharges see Nos. 101-103, 168, 206, 211.

Nos. 93, 98 With Violet or Magenta Surcharge

a

b

1897 ***Perf. 12½, 11½x11***

101	A18(a)	5c on 8c brown (V)	3.50	1.00
102	A19(b)	1k on 5k vio & sil (V)	5.00	3.50
103	A19(b)	2k on 5k vio & sil (M)	7.50	5.00
		Nos. 101-103 (3)	16.00	9.50

Forgeries exist.

Lion Type of 1894 and

Shah Muzaffar-ed-Din
A22

1898 Typo. Perf. 12½

104 A18	1c	gray	1.00	.35
105 A18	2c	pale brown	1.00	.35
106 A18	3c	dull violet	5.00	3.00
107 A18	4c	vermilion	5.00	3.00
108 A18	5c	yellow	1.00	.25
109 A18	8c	orange	10.00	7.00
110 A18	10c	light blue	3.00	.50
111 A18	12c	rose	3.00	1.00
112 A18	16c	green	10.00	7.00
113 A22	1k	ultramarine	6.00	1.00
114 A22	2k	pink	5.00	2.00
115 A22	3k	yellow	5.00	3.00
116 A22	4k	gray	5.00	3.00
117 A22	5k	emerald	5.00	3.00
118 A22	10k	orange	20.00	10.00
119 A22	50k	bright vio	35.00	20.00
		Nos. 104-119 (16)	120.00	64.45

Unauthorized reprints of Nos. 104-119 were made from original clichés. Paper shows a vertical mesh. These abound unused and canceled to order. Value unused, hinged, $16.

See Nos. 145-151. For overprints see Nos. 129-135, 182-188. For surcharges see Nos. 169, 171, 207, 209, 215.

Reprints have been used to make counterfeits of Nos. 120-135, 152-167.

Stamps of 1898 Handstamped in Violet:

a

b

c

d

e

f

g

h

1899

120 (a)	1c	gray	3.00	3.00
121 (b)	2c	pale brown	3.00	3.00
122 (b)	3c	dull violet	10.00	10.00
123 (c)	4c	vermilion	12.00	12.00
124 (c)	5c	yellow	3.00	3.00
125 (d)	8c	orange	10.00	10.00
126 (d)	10c	light blue	4.00	4.00
127 (d)	12c	rose	4.00	4.00
128 (d)	16c	green	15.00	15.00
129 (e)	1k	ultramarine	5.00	5.00
130 (f)	2k	pink	12.00	12.00
131 (f)	3k	yellow	75.00	100.00
132 (g)	4k	gray	75.00	100.00
133 (g)	5k	emerald	20.00	20.00
134 (h)	10k	orange	40.00	40.00
135 (h)	50k	brt violet	75.00	100.00
		Nos. 120-135 (16)	366.00	441.00

The handstamped control marks on Nos. 120-135 exist sideways, inverted and double. Counterfeits are plentiful.

Types of 1894-98

1899 Typo. Perf. 12½

136 A18	1c	gray, *green*	1.00	.35
137 A18	2c	brown, *green*	1.00	.35
138 A18	3c	violet, *green*	7.00	5.00
139 A18	4c	red, *green*	7.00	5.00
140 A18	5c	yellow, *green*	1.00	.20
141 A18	8c	orange, *green*	7.00	5.00
142 A18	10c	pale blue, *grn*	5.00	.20
143 A18	12c	lake, *green*	5.00	1.25
144 A18	16c	green, *green*	10.00	5.00
145 A22	1k	red	10.00	1.00
146 A22	2k	deep green	15.00	8.50
147 A22	3k	lilac brown	25.00	17.00
148 A22	4k	orange red	25.00	17.00
149 A22	5k	gray brown	25.00	17.00
150 A22	10k	deep blue	100.00	30.00
151 A22	50k	brown	60.00	30.00
		Nos. 136-151 (16)	304.00	142.85

Canceled to order copies abound.

Unauthorized reprints of Nos. 136-151 were made from original clichés. Paper is chalky and has white gum. The design can be seen through the back of the reprints. Value unused, hinged, $18.

For surcharges and overprints see Nos. 171, 173-188, 206-207, 209, 211, 215.

Nos. 104-111 Handstamped in Violet

(Struck once on every two stamps.)

1900

152 A18	1c	gray	25.00	15.00
153 A18	2c	pale brown	35.00	20.00
154 A18	3c	dull violet	70.00	40.00
155 A18	4c	vermilion	70.00	40.00
156 A18	5c	yellow	20.00	10.00
158 A18	10c	light blue	—	—
159 A18	12c	rose	70.00	40.00
		Nos. 152-159 (6)	290.00	165.00

Values are for single authenticated copies. Pairs are worth 4-6 times the single value.

This control mark, in genuine state, was not applied to the 8c orange (Nos. 109, 125).

Same Overprint Handstamped on Nos. 120-127 in Violet

(Struck once on each block of 4.)

160 A18	1c	gray	75.00	40.00
163 A18	4c	vermilion	150.00	100.00
164 A18	5c	yellow	35.00	20.00
166 A18	10c	light blue	150.00	100.00
167 A18	12c	rose	65.00	45.00
		Nos. 160-167 (5)	475.00	305.00

Values are for single authenticated copies. Blocks are rare and worth much more.

Counterfeits exist of Nos. 152-167.

No. 93 Surcharged in Violet

1900

168 A18	5c on 8c brown	12.00	1.00

No. 145 Surcharged in Violet

1901

169 A22	12c on 1k red	40.00	40.00
a.	Blue surcharge	40.00	40.00

Counterfeits exist.

Some specialists state that No. 169 with black surcharge was made for collectors.

A23

1902 Violet Surcharge

171 A23	5k on 50k brown	80.00	80.00
a.	Blue surcharge	90.00	90.00

Counterfeits exist. See No. 207.

Nos. 136-151 Overprinted in Black

1902

173 A18	1c	gray, *green*	5.00	2.50
174 A18	2c	brown, *green*	5.00	2.50
175 A18	3c	violet, *green*	7.00	5.00
176 A18	4c	red, *green*	7.00	5.00
177 A18	5c	yellow, *green*	5.00	1.50
178 A18	8c	orange, *green*	7.00	5.00
179 A18	10c	pale blue, *grn*	10.00	3.00
180 A18	12c	lake, *green*	10.00	4.00
181 A18	16c	green, *green*	10.00	10.00
182 A22	1k	red	10.00	6.00
183 A22	2k	deep green	—	—
188 A22	50k	brown	—	—

Overprinted on No. 168

206 A18	5c on 8c brown	30.00	20.00

Overprinted on Nos. 171 and 171a

207 A23	5k on 50k brown	70.00	60.00
a.	On #171a	100.00	80.00

Overprinted on Nos. 169 and 169a

209 A22	12c on 1k red	30.00	30.00
a.	On #169a	30.00	30.00

Counterfeits of the overprint of Nos. 173-183, 188, 206-207, 209 are plentiful. Practically all examples with overprint sideways, inverted, double and double with one inverted are frauds.

Nos. 142 and 145 Surcharged in Violet

1902

211 A18 5c on 10c pale bl, *grn* 40.00 15.00

Surcharges in different colors were made for collectors.

Initials of Victor Castaigne, Postmaster of Meshed — A24

1902 **Typo.** ***Imperf.***

222 A24 1c black 500.00 200.00
a. Inverted frame —
b. Inverted center *3,250.* *1,750.*
223 A24 2c black 400.00 200.00
a. Inverted frame —
b. "2" in right upper corner *3,000.* *1,750.*
c. Frame printed on both sides 1,000.
224 A24 3c black 600.00 500.00
225 A24 5c violet 350.00 150.00
a. "5" in right upper corner —
b. Frame printed on both sides *2,250.* *1,000.*
c. Inverted center —
226 A24 5c black 600.00 200.00
a. Persian "5" in lower left corner —
b. Inverted center —
227 A24 12c dull blue 850.00 500.00
a. Inverted frame —
b. Inverted center —
228 A24 1k rose 10,000. 2,500.

The design of No. 228 differs slightly from the illustration.

Nos. 222-228 were printed in three operations. Inverted centers have frames and numerals upright. Inverted frames have centers and numerals upright.

Pin-perforated

234 A24 12c dull blue 1,000. 500.00

The post office at Meshed having exhausted its stock of stamps, the postmaster issued the above series provisionally. The center of the design is the seal of the postmaster who also wrote his initials upon the upper part, using violet ink for the 1k and red for the others.

Unauthorized reprints, including pinperforated examples of Nos. 222-226, and forgeries exist.

Expert knowledge or certificates of authenticity are required.

A25

TWO TYPES:

Type I - "CHAHI" or "KRANS" are in capital letters.

Type II - Only "C" of "Chahi" or "K" of "Krans" is a capital.

The 3c and 5c sometimes have a tall narrow figure in the upper left corner. The 5c is also found with the cross at the upper left broken or missing. These varieties are known with many of the overprints.

Stamps of Design A25 have a faint fancy background in the color of the stamp. All issued stamps have handstamped controls as listed.

Handstamp Overprinted in Black

1902 **Typeset** ***Imperf.***

Type I

235 A25 1c gray & buff *75.00* 75.00
236 A25 2c brown & buff *75.00* 75.00
237 A25 3c green & buff *85.00* 85.00
238 A25 5c red & buff *75.00* 50.00
239 A25 12c ultra & buff *85.00* 85.00
Nos. 235-239 (5) *395.00* 370.00

Counterfeits abound. Type II stamps with this overprint are forgeries.

The 3c with violet overprint is believed not to have been regularly issued.

Handstamp Overprinted in Rose

1902 **Type I**

247 A25 1c gray & buff 4.00 2.00
a. With Persian numerals "2" 50.00 *75.00*
248 A25 2c brown & buff 8.00 2.00
249 A25 3c dp grn & buff 10.00 2.00
250 A25 5c red & buff 3.00 .75
251 A25 10c ol yel & buff 10.00 2.00
252 A25 12c ultra & buff 15.00 2.00
253 A25 1k violet & bl 35.00 3.00
254 A25 2k ol grn & bl 45.00 10.00
256 A25 10k dk bl & bl 125.00 25.00
257 A25 50k red & blue 300.00 250.00
Nos. 247-257 (10) 555.00 298.75

A 5k exists but its' status is doubtful.

Nos. 247-257 and the 12c on brown paper and on blue paper with blue quadrille lines are known without overprint but are not believed to have been regularly issued in this condition.

The 1c to 10k, A25 type I, with violet overprint are believed not to have been regularly issued. Five denominations also exist with overprint in blue, black or green.

Type II

280 A25 1c gray & yellow 40.00 40.00
281 A25 2c brown & yel 40.00 40.00
282 A25 3c dk grn & yel 40.00 40.00
a. "Persans" 60.00 60.00
283 A25 5c red & yellow 20.00 3.00
284 A25 10c ol yel & yel 20.00 5.00
285 A25 12c blue & yel 20.00 10.00
290 A25 50k org red & bl 300.00 250.00

The same overprint in violet was applied to nine denominations of the Type II stamps, but these are believed not to have been regularly issued. The overprint also exists in blue, black and green.

Reprints, counterfeits, counterfeit overprints, with or without cancellations, re plentiful for Nos. 247-257, 280-290.

Five stamps of type A25, type II, in high denominations (10, 20, 25, 50 and 100 tomans), with "Postes 1319" lion overprint in blue, were used only on money orders, not for postage. They are usually numbered on the back in red, blue or black.

Handstamp Surcharged in Black

1902

Type I

308 A25 5k on 5k ocher & bl *150.00* *50.00*

Counterfeits of No. 308 abound.

This surcharge in rose, violet, blue or green is considered bogus.

This surcharge on 50k orange red and blue, and on 5k ocher and blue, type II, is considered bogus.

Handstamp Overprinted Diagonally in Black

1902

Type I

315 A25 2c brown & buff 100.00 60.00
a. Rose overprint 150.00 100.00

Type II

316 A25 2c brown & yel — —
a. Rose overprint — —

"P. L." stands for "Poste Locale."

Counterfeits of Nos. 315-316 exist.

Some specialists believe that Type II stamps were not used officially for this overprint.

Handstamp Overprinted in Black or Rose

1902 **Type II**

317 A25 2c brn & yellow 100.00 60.00
318 A25 2c brown & yel (R) 150.00 100.00

Counterfeits of Nos. 317-318 exist.

Overprinted in Blue

1903

Type I

321 A25 1k violet & blue 45.00 45.00

Type II

336 A25 1c gray & yellow 30.00 30.00
337 A25 2c brown & yellow 30.00 30.00
338 A25 5c red & yellow 25.00 25.00
339 A25 10c olive yel & yel 35.00 35.00
340 A25 12c blue & yellow 35.00 35.00
Nos. 321-340 (6) 200.00 200.00

The overprint also exists in violet and black, but it is doubtful whether such items were regularly issued.

Forgeries of Nos. 321, 336-340 abound. Genuine unused examples are seldom found.

Arms of Persia A26

Shah Muzaffar-ed-Din A27

1903-04 **Typo.** ***Perf. 12½***

351 A26 1c violet .50 .20
352 A26 2c gray .50 .20
353 A26 3c green .50 .20
354 A26 5c rose .50 .20
355 A26 10c yellow brn .75 1.50
356 A26 12c blue 1.00 .50

Engr.

Perf. 11½x11

357 A27 1k violet 2.50 .50
358 A27 2k ultramarine 3.50 .50
359 A27 5k orange brn 6.00 .75
360 A27 10k rose red 8.50 1.00
361 A27 20k orange ('04) 10.00 4.00
362 A27 30k green ('04) 25.00 7.50
363 A27 50k green 160.00 50.00
Nos. 351-363 (13) 219.25 67.05

No. 355 exists with blue diagonal surcharge "1 CHAHI"; its status is questioned.

See Nos. 428-433. For surcharges and overprints see #364-420, 446-447, 464-469, O8-O28, P1.

No. 353 Surcharged in Violet or Blue

1903

364 A26 1c on 3c green (V) 15.00 10.00
365 A26 2c on 3c green (Bl) 15.00 10.00

A 2c surcharge on No. 354 exists, but its status is dubious.

No. 360 Surcharged in Blue

366 A27 12c on 10k rose red 15.00 10.00
a. Black surcharge 15.00 15.00
b. Violet surcharge 15.00 15.00
Nos. 364-366 (3) 45.00 30.00

Used values for Nos. 366a-366b are for c-t-o copies.

No. 363 Surcharged in Blue or Black

1903

368 A27 2t on 50k grn (Bl) 100.00 35.00
a. Rose surcharge 125.00 75.00
b. Black surcharge 125.00 75.00
370 A27 3t on 50k grn (Bk) 100.00 35.00
a. Violet surcharge 100.00 35.00
b. Rose surcharge 150.00 100.00

No. 363 Surcharged in Blue or Black

1904

372 A27 2t on 50k grn (Bl) 100.00 35.00
375 A27 3t on 50k grn (Bk) 100.00 35.00

The 2t on 50k also exists with surcharge in rose, violet, black and magenta; the 3t on 50k in rose, violet and blue. Values about the same unused; about 50 percent higher used.

No. 352 Overprinted in Violet

1904 ***Perf. 12½***

393 A26 2c gray 30.00 15.00
a. Black overprint 30.00 15.00
b. Rose overprint 30.00 15.00

This overprint also exists in blue, violet blue, maroon and gray, but these were not regularly issued.

The 2c overprinted "Controle" in various types is said to be a revenue stamp.

Stamps of 1903 Surcharged in Black:

a

b

c

1904

400 A26(a) 3c on 5c rose 10.00 .50
401 A26(b) 6c on 10c brown 15.00 .50
402 A27(c) 9c on 1k violet 30.00 1.00
Nos. 400-402 (3) 55.00 2.00

Stamps of 1903 Surcharged in Black, Magenta or Violet:

1905-06

404 A26 1c on 3c green ('06) 35.00 15.00
405 A27 1c on 1k violet 35.00 15.00
406 A27 2c on 5k orange brn 40.00 25.00
407 A26 1c on 3c grn (M) ('06) 15.00 5.00
408 A27 1c on 1k violet (M) 20.00 10.00
409 A27 2c on 5k org brn (V) 30.00 15.00
Nos. 404-409 (6) 175.00 85.00

Nos. 355 and 358 Surcharged in Violet

419 A26 1c on 10c brown *150.00 200.00*
420 A27 2c on 2k ultra *250.00 350.00*

Forgeries of Nos. 419-420 are common. Forgeries of No. 420, especially, are hard to distinguish since the original handstamp was used. Genuine used copies may, in some cases, be identified by the cancellation.

A28

Typeset; "Provisoire" Overprint Handstamped in Black

1906 ***Imperf.***

422 A28 1c violet 2.00 .75
a. Irregular pin perf. or perf. 10½ 10.00 5.00
423 A28 2c gray 2.00 2.00
424 A28 3c green 2.00 .75
425 A28 6c red 2.00 .50
426 A28 10c brown 25.00 20.00
427 A28 13c blue 10.00 7.00
Nos. 422-427 (6) 43.00 31.00

Stamps of type A28 have a faint background pattern of tiny squares within squares, an ornamental frame and open rectangles for the value corners.

The 3c and 6c also exist perforated.

Nos. 422-427 are known without overprint but were probably not issued in that condition. Nearly all values are known with overprint inverted and double.

Forgeries are plentiful.

Lion Type of 1903 and

Shah Mohammed Ali
A29 A30

1907-09 **Typo.** ***Perf. 12½***

428 A26 1c vio, *blue* 1.00 .25
429 A26 2c gray, *blue* 1.00 .25
430 A26 3c green, *blue* 1.00 .25
431 A26 6c rose, *blue* 1.00 .25
432 A26 9c org, *blue* 1.50 .30
433 A26 10c brown, *blue* 2.00 1.00

Engr.
Perf. 11, 11½

434 A29 13c dark blue 3.00 1.00
435 A29 1k red 3.00 1.00
436 A29 26c red brown 3.00 1.00
437 A29 2k deep grn 7.00 1.50
438 A29 3k pale blue 10.00 1.00
439 A29 4k brt yellow 200.00 10.00
440 A29 4k bister 10.00 3.00
441 A29 5k dark brown 10.00 3.00
442 A29 10k pink 10.00 3.00
443 A29 20k gray black 20.00 10.00
444 A29 30k dark violet 20.00 15.00
445 A30 50k gold, ver & black ('09) 40.00 25.00
Nos. 428-445 (18) 343.50 76.80

Frame of No. 445 lithographed. Nos. 434-444 were issued in 1908.

Remainders canceled to order abound. Used values for Nos. 437-445 are for c-t-os.

Nos. 428-429 Overprinted in Black

1909 ***Perf. 12½***

446 A26 1c violet, *blue* 35.00 20.00
447 A26 2c gray, *blue* 35.00 20.00

Counterfeits of Nos. 446-447 exist.

Coat of Arms — A31

1909 **Typo.** ***Perf. 12½x12***

448 A31 1c org & maroon .50 .35
449 A31 2c vio & maroon .50 .35
450 A31 3c yel grn & mar .50 .35
451 A31 6c red & maroon .50 .35
452 A31 9c gray & maroon .50 .35
453 A31 10c red vio & mar .50 .35
454 A31 13c dk blue & mar .50 2.00
455 A31 1k sil, vio & bis brown 1.00 2.00
456 A31 26c dk grn & mar 1.00 3.00
457 A31 2k sil, dk grn & bis brown 1.00 2.00
458 A31 3k sil, gray & bis brown 1.00 3.50
459 A31 4k sil, by & bis brn 1.00 3.50
460 A31 5k gold, brn & bis brown 2.50 3.50
461 A31 10k gold, org & bis brown 5.00 10.00
462 A31 20k gold, ol grn & bister brn 7.00 20.00
463 A31 30k gold, car & bis brown 12.00 20.00
Nos. 448-463 (16) 35.00 71.60

Unauthorized reprints of Nos. 448-463 abound. Originals have clean, bright colors, centers stand out clearly, and paper is much thinner. Nos. 460-463 originals have gleaming gold margins; reprint margins appear as blackish yellow. Centers of reprints of Nos. 448-454, 456 are brown.

Values above are for unused reprints and for authenticated used stamps. Original unused stamps sell for much higher prices.

For surcharges & overprints see #541-549. 582-585, 588-594, 597, 601-606, 707-722, C1-C16, O31-O40.

Nos. 428-444, Imperf., Surcharged in Red or Black:

1910 **Blue Paper** ***Imperf.***

464 A26 1c on 1c violet 75.00 50.00
465 A26 1c on 2c gray 75.00 50.00
466 A26 1c on 3c green 75.00 50.00
467 A26 1c on 6c rose (Bk) 75.00 50.00
468 A26 1c on 9c orange 75.00 50.00
469 A26 1c on 10c brown 75.00 50.00

White Paper

470 A29 2c on 13c dp bl 80.00 50.00
471 A29 2c on 26c red brown (Bk) 80.00 50.00
472 A29 2c on 1k red (Bk) 80.00 50.00
473 A29 2c on 2k dp grn 80.00 50.00
474 A29 2c on 3k pale bl 80.00 50.00
475 A29 2c on 4k brt yel 80.00 50.00
476 A29 2c on 4k bister 80.00 50.00
477 A29 2c on 5k dk brn 80.00 50.00
478 A29 2c on 10k pink (Bk) 80.00 50.00
479 A29 2c on 20k gray blk 80.00 50.00
480 A29 2c on 30k dk vio 80.00 50.00
Nos. 464-480 (17) 1,330. 850.00

Nos. 464-480 were prepared for use on newspapers, but nearly the entire printing was sold to stamp dealers. The issue is generally considered speculative. Counterfeit surcharges exist on trimmed stamps.

Used values are for c-t-o.

Shah Ahmed — A32

Engr. center, Typo. frame ***Perf. 11½, 11½x11, 11½x12***

Engr. center, Typo. frame

1911-13

481 A32 1c green & org .50 .20
482 A32 2c red & sepia .50 .20
483 A32 3c gray brn & grn .50 .20
a. 3c bister brown & green .50 1.00
484 A32 5c brn & car ('13) .50 .75
485 A32 6c gray & car .50 .20
486 A32 6c grn & red brown ('13) .50 .20
487 A32 9c yel brn & vio .75 .20
488 A32 10c red & org brn .75 .20
489 A32 12c grn & ultra ('13) .50 .50
490 A32 13c violet & ultra 1.00 2.00
491 A32 1k ultra & car 1.00 .50
492 A32 24c vio & grn ('13) 1.00 1.00
493 A32 26c ultra & green 1.00 5.00
494 A32 2k grn & red vio 2.00 1.00
495 A32 3k violet & blk 2.00 1.50
496 A32 4k ultramarine & gray ('13) 2.00 20.00
497 A32 5k red & ultra 3.00 2.00
498 A32 10k ol bis & cl 5.00 3.00
499 A32 20k vio brn & bis 6.00 4.00
500 A32 30k red & green 7.00 5.00
Nos. 481-500 (20) 36.00 47.65

Values for Nos. 481-500 unused are for reprints, which cannot be distinguished from the late printings of the stamps. These are perf 11½ (11½x12 for the 4k) with the distance between the inner lines of the inscription tablets at top and bottom of the portrait being 19mm. Unused stamps with other perfs or a shorter vignette sell for much higher prices.

The reprints include inverted centers for some denominations.

For surcharges and overprints see Nos. 501-540, 586-587, 595, 598, 600, 607-609, 630-634, 646-666.

Stamps of 1911 Overprinted in Black

1911

501 A32 1c grn & orange 3.00 .75
502 A32 2c red & sepia 3.00 .75
503 A32 3c gray brn & grn 3.00 .75
504 A32 6c gray & carmine 3.00 .75
505 A32 9c yel brn & vio 3.00 .75
506 A32 10c red & org brn 3.00 .75
507 A32 13c vio & ultra 25.00 5.00
508 A32 1k ultra & car 25.00 2.00
509 A32 26c ultra & green 50.00 10.00
510 A32 2k grn & red vio 30.00 1.00
511 A32 3k vio & black 40.00 1.00
512 A32 5k red & ultra 45.00 1.50
513 A32 10k ol bis & claret 125.00 3.50
514 A32 20k vio brn & bis 140.00 5.00
515 A32 30k red & green 150.00 10.00
Nos. 501-515 (15) 648.00 43.50

The "Officiel" overprint does not signify that the stamps were intended for use on official correspondence but that they were issued by authority. It was applied to the stocks in Tabriz and all post offices in the Tabriz region after a large quantity of stamps had been stolen during the Russian occupation of Tabriz.

The "Officiel" overprint has been counterfeited.

Stamps of 1911 Overprinted in Black

On #449-451, 454

1911, Oct.

516 A32 2c red & sepia 50.00 15.00
517 A32 3c gray brn & grn 50.00 15.00
518 A32 6c gray & carmine 50.00 15.00
519 A32 13c vio & ultra 80.00 35.00

On #482-483, 485, 490

520 A32 2c red & sepia *50.00* 15.00
521 A32 3c gray brn & grn *50.00* 15.00
522 A32 6c gray & car *50.00* 15.00
523 A32 13c violet & ultra *80.00 35.00*

Stamps were sold at a 10% discount to stagecoach station keepers on the Tehran-Recht route. To prevent speculation, these stamps were overprinted "Stagecoach Stations" in French and Farsi.

Forgeries exist, usually overprinted on reprints of the 1909 issue and used copies of the 1911 issue. Values are for authenticated copies.

In 1912 this overprint, reading "Sultan Mohammed Ali Shah Kajar," was handstamped on outgoing mail in the Persian Kurdistan region occupied by the forces of the former Shah Mohammed Ali. It was applied after the stamps were on cover and is found on 8 of the Shah Ahmed stamps of 1911 (1c, 2c, 3c, 6c, 9c, 13c, 1k and 26c). Some specialists add the 10c. Forgeries are abundant.

Nos. 490 and 493 Surcharged:

a

b

1914

535 A32(a) 1c on 13c 15.00 2.00
536 A32(b) 3c on 26c 15.00 4.00

In 1914 a set of 19 stamps was prepared as a coronation issue. The 10 lower values each carry a different portrait; the 9 higher values show buildings and scenes. The same set printed with black centers was overprinted in red "SERVICE." The stamps were never placed in use, but were sold to stamp dealers in 1923.

Nos. 484 and 489 Surcharged in Black or Violet:

c

d

1915

537	A32(c) 1c on 5c	15.00	2.00
538	A32(c) 2c on 5c (V)	15.00	2.00
539	A32(c) 2c on 5c	65.00	20.00
540	A32(d) 6c on 12c	20.00	2.00
	Nos. 537-540 (4)	115.00	26.00

Nos. 455, 454 Surcharged:

e

f

1915 ***Perf. 12½x12***

541	A31(e) 5c on 1k multi	25.00	5.00
542	A31(f) 12c on 13c multi	30.00	7.00

Counterfeit surcharges on reprints abound.

Nos. 448-453, 455 Overprinted

1915

543	A31	1c org & maroon	15.00	2.00
544	A31	2c vio & maroon	15.00	2.00
545	A31	3c grn & maroon	15.00	2.00
546	A31	6c red & maroon	15.00	2.00
547	A31	9c gray & maroon	15.00	3.00
548	A31	10c red vio & mar	20.00	5.00
549	A31	1k sil, vio & bis brn	20.00	5.00
		Nos. 543-549 (7)	115.00	21.00

This overprint ("1333") also exists on the 2k, 10k, 20k and 30k, but they were not issued.

Counterfeit overprints, usually on reprints, abound.

Imperial Crown — A33

King Darius, Farohar overhead — A34

Ruins of Persepolis — A35

Perf. 11½ or Compound 11x11½
Engr., Typo.

1915, Mar. **Wmk. 161**

560	A33	1c car & indigo	.20	*2.00*
561	A33	2c bl & carmine	.20	*2.00*
562	A33	3c dark green	.20	*2.00*
	a.	Inverted center	—	
564	A33	5c red	.20	*2.50*
565	A33	6c olive grn & car	.20	*2.00*
	a.	Inverted center	—	
566	A33	9c yel brn & vio	.20	*2.00*
567	A33	10c bl grn & yel brn	.20	*2.00*
568	A33	12c ultramarine	.20	*2.00*
569	A34	1k sil, yel brn & gray	.65	*5.00*
570	A33	24c yel brn & dk brn	.25	*5.00*
571	A34	2k silver, bl & rose	.65	*5.00*
572	A34	3k sil, vio & brn	.65	*5.00*
573	A34	5k sil, brn & green	.65	*7.00*
574	A35	1t gold, pur & blk	.65	*10.00*
575	A35	2t gold, grn & brn	1.00	*10.00*
576	A35	3t gold, cl & red brn	1.00	*10.00*
577	A35	5t gold, blue & ind	1.00	*10.00*
		Nos. 560-577 (17)	8.10	*83.50*

Coronation of Shah Ahmed.

Nos. 560-568, 570 are engraved. Nos. 569, 571-573 are engraved except for silver margins. Nos. 574-577 have centers engraved, frames typographed.

The 3c and 6c with inverted centers are considered genuine errors. Unauthorized reprints exist of these varieties and of other denominations with inverted centers. **Values unused for Nos. 560-577 are for reprints.**

For surcharges and overprints see Nos. 610-616, 635-646, O41-O57, Q19-Q35.

Nos. 455, 461-463 Overprinted

1915 Unwmk. Typo. ***Perf. 12½x12***

582	A31	1k sil, vio & bis brn	*2.00*	*20.00*
583	A31	10k multicolored	*5.00*	*30.00*
584	A31	20k multicolored	*7.00*	*100.00*
585	A31	30k multicolored	*12.00*	*60.00*
		Nos. 582-585 (4)	*26.00*	210.00

Genuine unused examples are rare. Most unused copies offered in the marketplace are reprints, and the unused values above are for reprints. Used values for for authenticated copies.

Forgeries abound of Nos. 582-585.

No. 491 Surcharged

1917 ***Perf. 11½***

586	A32 12c on 1k multi	*450.00*	*450.00*
587	A32 24c on 1k multi	*300.00*	*300.00*

Issued during the Turkish occupation of Kermanshah. Forgeries exist.

No. 448 Overprinted "1335" in Persian Numerals

1917 ***Perf. 12½x12***

588	A31 1c org & maroon	*250.00*	150.00

Overprint on No. 588 is similar to date in "k" and "l" surcharges. Forgeries exist.

Nos. 449, 452-453, 456 Surcharged:

k l

1917

589	A31(k) 1c on 2c	20.00	3.00
590	A31(k) 1c on 9c	25.00	4.00
591	A31(k) 1c on 10c	20.00	3.00
592	A31(l) 3c on 9c	25.00	4.00
593	A31(l) 3c on 10c	20.00	3.00
594	A31(l) 3c on 26c	30.00	5.00

Same Surcharge on No. 488

595	A32(k) 1c on 10c	20.00	1.50
596	A32(l) 3c on 10c	20.00	1.50

Nos. 454 & 491 Surcharged Type "e"

597	A31 5c on 13c	25.00	5.00
598	A32 5c on 1k	20.00	2.00

Counterfeit surcharges on "canceled" reprints of Nos. 449, 452-454, 456 abound.

No. 489 Surcharged

600	A32 6c on 12c grn & ultra	20.00	1.50

No. 457 Overprinted

1918

601	A31 2k multi	50.00	10.00

Nos. 459-460 Surcharged:

1918

602	A31 24c on 4k multi	60.00	10.00
603	A31 10k on 5k multi	65.00	15.00

The surcharges of Nos. 602-603 have been counterfeited.

Nos. 457-463 Overprinted

1918

603A	A31	2k multicolored	*3.00*	*65.00*
604	A31	3k multicolored	*3.00*	*15.00*
604A	A31	4k multicolored	*5.00*	*150.00*
604B	A31	5k multicolored	*5.00*	*75.00*
605	A31	10k multicolored	*8.00*	*50.00*
605A	A31	20k multicolored	*20.00*	*200.00*
606	A31	30k multicolored	*15.00*	*100.00*
		Nos. 603A-606 (7)	*59.00*	*655.00*

Genuine unused examples are rare. Most unused copies offered in the marketplace are reprints, and the unused values above are for reprints. Used values for for authenticated copies.

Forgeries abound of Nos. 603A-606.

Nos. 489, 488 and 491 Surcharged:

m

n

607	A32(m) 3c on 12c	20.00	1.50
608	A32(n) 6c on 10c	20.00	1.50
609	A32(m) 6c on 1k	20.00	1.50
	Nos. 607-609 (3)	60.00	4.50

Nos. 571-577 Overprinted in Black or Red

1918 **Wmk. 161**

610	A34	2k sil, blue & rose	7.00	*10.00*
611	A34	3k sil, vio & brn (R)	7.00	*10.00*
612	A34	5k sil, brn & grn (R)	7.00	*10.00*
613	A35	1t gold, pur & black (R)	12.00	*15.00*
614	A35	2t gold, grn & brn	12.00	*15.00*
615	A35	3t gold, cl & red brn	12.00	*15.00*
616	A35	5t gold, bl & ind (R)	12.00	*20.00*
		Nos. 610-616 (7)	69.00	95.00

The overprint commemorates the end of World War I. Counterfeits of this overprint are plentiful.

A36

Color Litho., Black Typo.

1919 **Unwmk.** ***Perf. 11½***

617	A36	1c yel & black	5.00	.30
618	A36	3c green & black	5.00	.30
619	A36	5c rose & black	7.00	2.00
620	A36	6c vio & black	5.00	.25
621	A36	12c blue & black	20.00	3.00
		Nos. 617-621 (5)	42.00	5.85

Nos. 617-621 exist imperf., in colors other than the originals, with centers inverted and double impressions. Some specialists call them fraudulent, others call them reprints.

Counterfeits having double line over "POSTES" abound.

Nos. 75, 85-86 Surcharged in Various Colors

1919 ***Perf. 10½, 11, 11½, 13½***

622	A14	2k on 5c lilac (Bk)	5.00	5.00
623	A14	3k on 5c lilac (Br)	5.00	5.00
624	A14	4k on 5c lilac (G)	5.00	5.00
625	A14	5k on 5c lilac (V)	5.00	5.00
626	A16	10k on 10c rose (Bl)	7.00	7.00
627	A16	20k on 10c rose (G)	10.00	10.00
628	A16	30k on 10c rose (Br)	10.00	10.00
629	A16	50k on 14c org (V)	15.00	15.00
		Nos. 622-629 (8)	62.00	62.00

Nos. 622-629 exist with inverted and double surcharge. Some specialists consider these fraudulent.

Nos. 486, 489 Handstamp Surcharged

1921 ***Perf. 11½, 11½x11***

630	A32 10c on 6c	55.00	15.00
631	A32 1k on 12c	55.00	15.00

Counterfeits exist.

No. 489 Surcharged

632	A32 6c on 12c	200.00	7.00

Nos. 486, 489 Surcharged in Violet:

1921

633 A32 10c on 6c 65.00 15.00
634 A32 1k on 12c 65.00 15.00

Counterfeits exist.

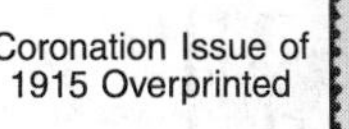

Coronation Issue of 1915 Overprinted

1921, May Wmk. 161 *Perf. 11, 11½*

635 A33 3c dark grn 10.00
 a. Center and overprint inverted —
636 A33 5c red 10.00
637 A33 6c olive grn & car 10.00
638 A33 10c bl grn & yel brn 10.00
639 A33 12c ultramarine 10.00
640 A34 1k sil, yel brn & gray 15.00
641 A34 2k sil, blue & rose 15.00
642 A34 5k sil, brn & green 15.00
643 A35 2t gold, grn & brn 20.00
644 A35 3t gold, cl & red brn 20.00
645 A35 5t gold, blue & ind 20.00
 Nos. 635-645 (11) 155.00

Counterfeits of this Feb. 21, 1921, overprint are plentiful. Inverted overprints exist on all values; some specialists consider them fraudulent.

Stamps of 1911-13 Overprinted

1922 Unwmk. *Perf. 11½, 11½x11*

646 A32 1c grn & orange 3.00 .20
 a. Inverted overprint —
647 A32 2c red & sepia 3.00 .20
648 A32 3c gray brn & green 8.00 .20
 a. 3c bister brown & green 8.00 .20
649 A32 5c brown & car 65.00 25.00
650 A32 6c grn & red brn 5.00 .20
651 A32 9c yel brn & vio 5.00 .20
652 A32 10c red & org brn 6.00 .20
 a. Double ovpt., on inverted
653 A32 12c green & ultra 10.00 .50
654 A32 1k ultra & car 15.00 1.00
655 A32 24c vio & green 15.00 1.00
656 A32 2k grn & red vio 25.00 1.00
657 A32 3k vio & black 35.00 1.50
658 A32 4k ultra & gray 60.00 20.00
659 A32 5k red & ultra 40.00 2.00
660 A32 10k ol bis & cl 175.00 5.00
661 A32 20k vio brn & bis 175.00 7.00
662 A32 30k red & green 175.00 10.00
 Nos. 646-662 (17) 820.00 75.20

The status of inverted overprints on 5c and 12c is dubious. Unlisted inverts on other denominations are generally considered fraudulent. Counterfeits of this overprint exist.

Nos. 653, 655 Surcharged

1922

663 A32 3c on 12c 30.00 1.00
664 A32 6c on 24c 40.00 2.00

Nos. 661-662 Surcharged:

1923

665 A32 10c on 20k 50.00 10.00
666 A32 1k on 30k 65.00 15.00

Shah Ahmed — A37

Perf. 11½, 11x11½, 11½x11

1924-25 Engr.

667 A37 1c orange 2.50 .20
668 A37 2c magenta 2.50 .20
669 A37 3c orange brown 2.50 .20
670 A37 6c black brown 2.50 .20
671 A37 9c dark green 5.00 .75
672 A37 10c dark violet 5.00 .30
673 A37 12c red 5.00 .30
674 A37 1k dark blue 5.00 .35
675 A37 2k indigo & red 5.00 1.00
 a. Center inverted —
676 A37 3k dk vio & red brown 27.50 1.25
677 A37 5k red & brown 40.00 20.00
678 A37 10k choc & lilac 50.00 25.00
679 A37 20k dk grn & brn 60.00 30.00
680 A37 30k org & blk brn 80.00 40.00
 Nos. 667-680 (14) 292.50 119.75

For overprints see Nos. 703-706.

A38

SIX CHAHIS

Type I

Type II

Dated 1924

Color Litho., Black Typo.

1924 *Perf. 11*

681 A38 1c yel brn & blk 3.00 1.00
682 A38 2c gray & blk 3.00 1.00
683 A38 3c dp rose & blk 3.00 1.00
684 A38 6c orange & blk (I) 5.00 1.50
 a. 6c orange & blk (II) 5.00 2.00
 Nos. 681-684 (4) 14.00 4.50

The 1c was surcharged "Chahis" by error. Later the "s" was blocked out in black.

Counterfeits having double line over "POSTES" are plentiful.

Dated 1925

1925

686 A38 2c yel grn & blk 3.00 .50
687 A38 3c red & blk 3.00 .50
689 A38 6c chalky bl & blk 3.00 .50
690 A38 9c lt brn & blk 8.00 1.00
691 A38 10c gray & blk 12.00 2.00
694 A38 1k emer & blk 30.00 5.00
695 A38 2k lilac & blk 75.00 20.00
 Nos. 686-695 (7) 134.00 29.50

Counterfeits having double line over "POSTES" are plentiful.

A39

Gold Overprint on Treasury Department Stamps

1925

697 A39 1c red 5.00 3.00
698 A39 2c yellow 5.00 3.00
699 A39 3c yellow green 5.00 3.00
700 A39 5c dark gray 15.00 15.00
701 A39 10c deep orange 5.00 4.00
702 A39 1k ultramarine 10.00 10.00
 Nos. 697-702 (6) 45.00 38.00

Deposition of Shah Ahmed and establishment of provisional government of Riza Khan Pahlavi.

#697-702 have same center (Persian lion in sunburst) with 6 different frames. Overprint reads: "Post / Provisional Government / of Pahlavi / 9th Abanmah / 1304 / 1925."

Nos. 667-670 Overprinted

1926 *Perf. 11½, 11x11½, 11½x11*

703 A37 1c orange 1.50 .50
704 A37 2c magenta 1.50 .50
705 A37 3c orange brown 1.50 .75
706 A37 6c black brown 52.50 35.00
 Nos. 703-706 (4) 57.00 36.75

Overprinted to commemorate the Pahlavi government of 1925. Counterfeits exist.

Nos. 448-463 Overprinted

1926 *Perf. 11½, 12½x12*

707 A31 1c org & maroon 5.00 .25
 a. Inverted overprint 300.00
708 A31 2c vio & maroon 5.00 .25
709 A31 3c yel grn & mar 5.00 .25
 a. Inverted overprint 300.00
710 A31 6c red & maroon 5.00 .25
711 A31 9c gray & maroon 5.00 .25
712 A31 10c red vio & mar 5.00 .35
713 A31 13c dk bl & mar 10.00 .35
714 A31 1k multi 20.00 .35
715 A31 26c dk grn & mar 10.00 .35
716 A31 2k multi 20.00 .50
717 A31 3k multi 50.00 .50
718 A31 4k sil, bl & bis brn 60.00 10.00
719 A31 5k multi 100.00 8.00
720 A31 10k multi 300.00 8.50
721 A31 20k multi 300.00 10.00
722 A31 30k multi 300.00 12.00
 Nos. 707-722 (16) 1,200. 52.15

Overprinted to commemorate the Pahlavi government in 1926.

Values for Nos. 707-722 are for stamps perf. 11½, on thick paper. Copies perf. 12½x12 on thin paper are worth substantially more.

Forgeries exist perf. 12½x12, with either machine overprints or handstamps. Most of these fakes can be identified by the absence of the top serif of the "1" in "1926."

Riza Shah Pahlavi
A40 A41

1926-29 Typo. *Perf. 11*

723 A40 1c yellow green 2.00 .20
724 A40 2c gray violet 2.00 .20
725 A40 3c emerald 2.00 .20
727 A40 6c magenta 3.00 .25
728 A40 9c rose 10.00 .50
729 A40 10c bister brown 20.00 5.00
730 A40 12c deep orange 25.00 3.00
731 A40 15c pale ultra 30.00 2.00
733 A41 1k dull bl ('27) 50.00 10.00
734 A41 2k brt vio ('29) 110.00 50.00
 Nos. 723-734 (10) 254.00 71.35

1928 Redrawn

740 A40 1c yellow green 10.00 .25
741 A40 2c gray violet 10.00 .25
742 A40 3c emerald 10.00 .25
743 A40 6c rose 15.00 .50
 Nos. 740-743 (4) 45.00 1.25

On the redrawn stamps much of the shading of the face, throat, collar, etc., has been removed.

The letters of "Postes Persanes" and those in the circle at upper right are smaller. The redrawn stamps measure 20¼x25¾mm instead of 19¾x25¼mm.

A42

Riza Shah Pahlavi — A43

Perf. 11½, 12, 12½, Compound

1929 Photo.

744 A42 1c yel grn & cer 1.50 .25
745 A42 2c scar & brt blue 1.50 .25
746 A42 3c mag & myr grn 1.50 .25
747 A42 6c yel brn & ol grn 2.00 .25
748 A42 9c Prus bl & ver 3.00 .25
749 A42 10c bl grn & choc 4.00 .25
750 A42 12c gray blk & pur 6.00 .30
751 A42 15c citron & ultra 7.00 .30
752 A42 1k dull bl & blk 10.00 .50
753 A42 24c ol grn & red brn 7.00 .50

Engr.

Perf. 11½

754 A42 2k brn org & dk vio 15.00 1.50
755 A42 3k dark grn & dp rose 80.00 2.00
756 A42 5k red brn & dp green 30.00 2.00
757 A42 1t ultra & dp rose 40.00 5.00
758 A42 2t carmine & blk 50.00 15.00

Engr. and Typo.

759 A43 3t gold & dp vio 100.00 25.00
 Nos. 744-759 (16) 358.50 53.60

For overprints see Nos. 810-817.

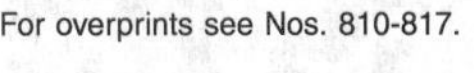

Riza Shah Pahlavi — A44

1931-32 Litho. *Perf. 11*

760 A44 1c ol brn & ultra 3.00 .20
761 A44 2c red brn & blk 3.00 .20
762 A44 3c lilac rose & ol 3.00 .20
763 A44 6c red org & vio 3.00 .20
764 A44 9c ultra & red org 10.00 .40
765 A44 10c ver & gray 10.00 .70
766 A44 11c bl & dull red 17.50 10.00
767 A44 12c turq blue & lil rose 30.00 .70
768 A44 16c black & red 30.00 1.75
769 A44 1k car & turq bl 60.00 1.75
770 A44 27c dk gray & dl bl 45.00 1.75
 Nos. 760-770 (11) 214.50 17.85

For overprints see Nos. 818-826.

Riza Shah Pahlavi
A45 A46

1933-34

771 A45 5d olive brown 1.00 .25
772 A45 10d blue 1.00 .25
773 A45 15d gray 1.00 .25
774 A45 30d emerald 1.00 .25
775 A45 45d turq blue 1.50 .50
776 A45 50d magenta 2.00 .50
777 A45 60d green 3.00 .50
778 A45 75d brown 5.00 1.00
779 A45 90d red 5.00 1.50
780 A46 1r dk rose & blk 15.00 1.00
781 A46 1.20r gray blk & rose 20.00 1.00
782 A46 1.50 citron & bl 25.00 1.00
783 A46 2r lt bl & choc 30.00 1.00
784 A46 3r mag & green 40.00 2.00
785 A46 5r dk brn & red org 150.00 20.00
Nos. 771-785 (15) 300.50 31.00

For overprints see Nos. 795-809.

"Justice"
A47

"Education"
A49

Ruins of Persepolis
A48

Tehran Airport
A50

Sanatorium at Sakhtessar — A51

Cement Factory, Chah-Abdul-Azim — A52

Gunboat "Palang"
A53

Railway Bridge over Karun River
A54

Post Office and Customs Building, Tehran
A55

1935, Feb. 21 Photo. *Perf. 12½*

786 A47 5d red brn & grn 1.00 .75
787 A48 10d red org & gray black 1.00 .75
788 A49 15d mag & Prus bl 1.50 .75
789 A50 30d black & green 1.50 .75
790 A51 45d ol grn & red brn 2.00 .75
791 A52 75d grn & dark brn 6.00 1.00
792 A53 90d blue & car rose 20.00 5.00
793 A54 1r red brn & pur 50.00 20.00
794 A55 1½r violet & ultra 25.00 10.00
Nos. 786-794 (9) 108.00 39.75

Reign of Riza Shah Pahlavi, 10th anniv.

Stamps of 1933-34 Overprinted in Black

1935 *Perf. 11*

795 A45 5d olive brown 1.00 .50
796 A45 10d blue 1.00 .50
797 A45 15d gray 1.00 .50
798 A45 30d emerald 1.00 .50
799 A45 45d turq blue 7.00 1.75
800 A45 50d magenta 3.50 .50
801 A45 60d green 3.50 .50
802 A45 75d brown 7.50 5.00
803 A45 90d red 20.00 10.00
804 A46 1r dk rose & blk 55.00 55.00
805 A46 1.20r gray black & rose 8.50 1.50
806 A46 1.50r citron & bl 8.50 1.50
807 A46 2r lt bl & choc 20.00 1.50
808 A46 3r mag & green 50.00 7.00
809 A46 5r dk brn & red org 150.00 150.00
Nos. 795-809 (15) 337.50 236.25

Same Overprint on Stamps of 1929

1935 *Perf. 12, 12x12½*

810 A42 1c yel green & cer 300.00 300.00
811 A42 2c scar & brt blue 200.00 200.00
812 A42 3c mag & myr grn 125.00 100.00
813 A42 6c yel brn & ol grn 100.00 75.00
814 A42 9c Prus bl & ver 60.00 40.00

Perf. 11½

815 A42 1t ultra & dp rose 30.00 15.00
816 A42 2t carmine & blk 35.00 20.00
817 A43 3t gold & dp vio 50.00 25.00
Nos. 810-817 (8) 900.00 775.00

No. 817 is overprinted vertically.
Forged overprints exist.

Same Ovpt. on Stamps of 1931-32

1935 *Perf. 11*

818 A44 1c ol brn & ultra 275.00 200.00
819 A44 2c red brn & blk 100.00 75.00
820 A44 3c lilac rose & ol 75.00 60.00
821 A44 6c red org & vio 150.00 110.00
822 A44 9c ultra & red org 175.00 140.00
823 A44 11c blue & dull red 10.00 2.00
824 A44 12c turq bl & lil rose 300.00 300.00
825 A44 16c black & red 12.00 3.00
826 A44 27c dk gray & dull bl 15.00 3.00
Nos. 818-826 (9) 1,112. 893.00

Forged overprints exist.

Riza Shah Pahlavi — A56

1935 Photo. *Perf. 11*

Size: 19x27mm

827 A56 5d violet 1.00 .20
828 A56 10d lilac rose 1.00 .20
829 A56 15d turquoise bl 1.00 .20
830 A56 30d emerald 1.50 .20
831 A56 45d orange 1.50 .20
832 A56 50d dull lt brn 2.75 .30
833 A56 60d ultramarine 10.00 .65
834 A56 75d red orange 10.00 .75
835 A56 90d rose 12.50 .75

Size: 21½x31mm

836 A56 1r dull lilac 15.00 .50
837 A56 1.50r blue 20.00 2.00
838 A56 2r dk olive grn 25.00 .75
839 A56 3r dark brown 27.50 2.00
840 A56 5r slate black 160.00 15.00
Nos. 827-840 (14) 288.75 23.70

Riza Shah Pahlavi
A57 A58

1936-37 Litho. *Perf. 11*

Size: 20x27mm

841 A57 5d bright vio 1.00 .20
842 A57 10d magenta 1.00 .20
843 A57 15d bright ultra 1.00 .20
844 A57 30d yellow green 1.00 .20
845 A57 45d vermilion 1.50 .20
846 A57 50d black brn ('37) 2.00 .20
847 A57 60d brown orange 2.00 .20
848 A57 75d rose lake 3.00 .25
849 A57 90d rose red 5.00 .35

Size: 23x31mm

850 A57 1r turq green 15.00 .25
851 A57 1.50r deep blue 15.00 .35
852 A57 2r bright blue 20.00 .35
853 A57 3r violet brown 25.00 .70
854 A57 5r slate green 40.00 1.25
855 A57 10r dark brown & ultra ('37) 125.00 15.00
Nos. 841-855 (15) 257.50 19.90

1938-39 *Perf. 11*

Size: 20x27mm

856 A58 5d light violet 2.00 .20
857 A58 10d magenta 2.00 .20
858 A58 15d violet blue 2.00 .20
859 A58 30d bright green 2.00 .20
860 A58 45d vermilion 2.00 .20
861 A58 50d black brown 2.00 .20
862 A58 60d brown orange 2.00 .20
863 A58 75d rose lake 2.00 .20
864 A58 90d rose red ('39) 5.00 .25

Size: 22½x30mm

865 A58 1r turq green 10.00 .25
866 A58 1.50r deep blue 15.00 .30
867 A58 2r lt blue ('39) 20.00 .30
868 A58 3r violet brown 30.00 .45
869 A58 5r gray grn ('39) 35.00 1.25
870 A58 10r dark brown & ultra ('39) 90.00 7.50
Nos. 856-870 (15) 221.00 11.90

A58a

1939, Mar. 15 *Perf. 13*

870A A58a 5d gray blue 1.50 1.00
870B A58a 10d brown 1.50 1.00
870C A58a 30d green 1.50 1.00
870D A58a 60d dark brown 1.50 1.00
870E A58a 90d red 2.50 2.00
870F A58a 1.50r blue 7.50 3.00
870G A58a 5r lilac 20.00 15.00
870H A58a 10r carmine 40.00 40.00
Nos. 870A-870H (8) 76.00 63.01

60th birthday of Riza Shah Pahlavi. Printed in sheets of 4, perf. 13 and imperf. The imperf. sell for 50% more. The 1r violet and 2r orange were not available to the public. Value unused $10 each.

Crown Prince and Princess Fawziya
A59

1939, Apr. 25 Photo. *Perf. 11½*

871 A59 5d red brown .50 .30
872 A59 10d bright violet .50 .30
873 A59 30d emerald 1.50 .35
874 A59 90d red 5.00 1.25
875 A59 1.50r bright blue 10.00 2.00
Nos. 871-875 (5) 17.50 4.20

Wedding of Crown Prince Mohammed Riza Pahlavi to Princess Fawziya of Egypt.

Bridge over Karun River
A60

Veresk Bridge, North Iran — A61

Granary, Ahwaz
A62

Train and Bridge
A63

Museum, Side View
A64 A67

Ministry of Justice
A65

School Building
A66

Mohammed Riza Pahlavi
A68 A69

1942-46 Unwmk. Litho. *Perf. 11*

876 A60 5d violet 1.00 .20
877 A60 5d red org ('44) .50 .20
878 A61 10d magenta 1.00 .20
879 A61 10d pck grn ('44) .50 .20
880 A62 20d lt red violet 1.50 .25
881 A62 20d mag ('44) .75 .25
882 A63 25d rose carmine 17.50 2.00
883 A63 25d violet ('44) 3.50 .50
884 A64 35d emerald 1.50 .30
885 A65 50d ultramarine 1.50 .30
886 A65 50d emerald ('44) 1.25 .20
887 A66 70d dull vio brn 1.50 .35
888 A67 75d rose lake 10.00 .35
889 A67 75d rose car ('46) 10.00 .35
890 A68 1r carmine 10.00 .25
891 A68 1r maroon ('45) 10.00 .25
892 A68 1.50r red 7.50 .25
893 A68 2r light blue 12.00 .30

894 A68 2r sage grn ('44) 12.00 .30
895 A68 2.50r dark blue 15.00 .30
896 A68 3r peacock grn 85.00 1.00
897 A68 3r brt vio ('44) 35.00 .35
898 A68 5r sage green 150.00 7.50
899 A68 5r lt blue ('44) 25.00 .50
900 A69 10r brn org & blk 40.00 3.00
901 A69 10r dk org brn & black ('44) 20.00 1.00
902 A69 20r choc & vio 400.00 50.00
903 A69 20r orange & black ('44) 30.00 4.00
904 A69 30r gray blk & emerald *900.00* 50.00
905 A69 30r emer & black ('44) 45.00 5.00
906 A69 50r dl bl & brn red 125.00 25.00
907 A69 50r brt vio & black ('45) 50.00 10.00
908 A69 100r rose red & blk ('45) 375.00 50.00
909 A69 200r bl & blk ('45) 275.00 50.00
Nos. 876-909 (34) 2,673. 264.65

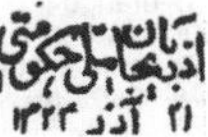

Sixteen denominations of this issue were handstamped at Tabriz in 1945-46 in Persian characters: "Azerbaijan National Government, Dec. 12, 1945." A rebel group did this overprinting while the Russian army held that area.

Flag of Iran A70

Designs: 50d, Docks at Bandar Shapur. 1.50r, Motor convoy. 2.50r, Gorge and railway viaduct. 5r, Map and Mohammed Riza Pahlavi.

Inscribed: "En souvenir des efforts de l'Iran pour la Victoire"

Engr. & Litho.

1949, Apr. 28 ***Perf. 12½***

910 A70 25d multicolored 2.00 1.00

Engr.

911 A70 50d purple 2.00 1.00
912 A70 1.50r carmine rose 9.00 1.25
913 A70 2.50r deep blue 12.00 1.50
914 A70 5r green 22.50 2.50
Nos. 910-914 (5) 47.50 7.25

Iran's contribution toward the victory of the Allied Nations in World War II.

Bridge over Zaindeh River — A71

National Bank — A72

Former Ministry of P.T.T. A73

Mohammed Riza Pahlavi — A74

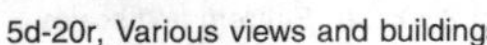

5d-20r, Various views and buildings.

1949-50 Unwmk. Litho. ***Perf. 10½***

915 A71 5d rose & dk grn .35 .20
916 A71 10d ultra & brown .35 .20
917 A71 20d vio & ultra .35 .25
918 A71 25d blk brn & dp blue .40 .20
919 A71 50d grn & ultra .75 .20
920 A71 75d dk brn & red 1.50 .25
921 A72 1r vio & green 2.00 .20
922 A72 1.50r dk grn & ver 2.00 .20
923 A72 2r dp car & blk brn 3.00 .25
924 A72 2.50r chlky bl & bl 3.00 .25
925 A72 3r vio bl & red orange 5.00 .20
926 A72 5r dp car & vio 9.00 .20
927 A73 10r car & blue green ('50) 35.00 .50
a. Inverted center 1,100.
928 A73 20r brown black & red ('50) 250.00 20.00
929 A74 30r choc & deep blue ('50) 75.00 10.00
930 A74 50r red & deep blue ('50) 75.00 10.00
Nos. 915-930 (16) 462.70 43.10

Globes and Pigeons A75

Symbols of UPU — A76

1950, Mar. 16 **Photo.**

931 A75 50d brn carmine 17.50 17.50
932 A76 2.50r deep blue 25.00 25.00

UPU, 75th anniv. (in 1949).

Riza Shah Pahlavi and his Tomb — A77

1950, May 8

933 A77 50d brown 12.00 6.25
934 A77 2r sepia 21.00 9.00

Re-burial of Riza Shah Pahlavi, May 12, 1950.

Mohammed Riza Pahlavi, 31st Birthday — A78

Various portraits.

1950, Oct. 26 Engr. ***Perf. 12½***

Center in Black

935 A78 25d carmine 7.50 .75
936 A78 50d orange 7.50 .75
937 A78 75d brown 20.00 7.50
938 A78 1r green 17.00 1.60
939 A78 2.50r deep blue 19.00 1.60
940 A78 5r brown lake 35.00 4.50
Nos. 935-940 (6) 106.00 16.70

Shah and Queen Soraya A79

A80

1951, Feb. 12 Litho. ***Perf. 10½***

941 A79 5d rose violet 1.50 .60
942 A79 25d orange red 2.50 .75
943 A79 50d emerald 4.00 2.00
944 A80 1r brown 4.50 2.00
945 A80 1.50r carmine 7.00 2.00
946 A80 2.50r blue 10.00 2.50
Nos. 941-946 (6) 29.50 9.85

Wedding of Mohammed Riza Pahlavi to Soraya Esfandiari.

Farabi — A81

1951, Feb. 20

947 A81 50d red 5.00 1.40
948 A81 2.50r blue 10.00 2.50

Death millenary of Farabi, Persian philosopher.

Mohammed Riza Pahlavi
A82 A83

1951-52 Unwmk. Photo. ***Perf. 10½***

950 A82 5d brown orange .50 .20
951 A82 10d violet .50 .20
952 A82 20d choc ('52) 1.10 .35
953 A82 25d blue ('52) .90 .20
954 A82 50d green 1.50 .20
955 A82 75d rose 1.50 .30
956 A83 1r gray green 1.50 .20
957 A83 1.50r cerise 1.50 .45
958 A83 2r chocolate 5.00 .20
959 A83 2.50r deep blue 5.00 .25
960 A83 3r red orange 6.00 .20
961 A83 5r dark green 12.00 .20
962 A83 10r olive ('52) 35.00 .50
963 A83 20r org brn ('52) 20.00 3.00
964 A83 30r vio bl ('52) 15.00 2.00
965 A83 50r blk brn ('52) 30.00 4.00
Nos. 950-965 (16) 137.00 12.45

See Nos. 975-977.

Oil Well and Mosque — A84

Oil Well, Mosque and Monument A85

1953, Feb. 20 **Litho.**

966 A84 50d green & yel 1.75 .20
967 A85 1r lil rose & yel 2.00 .30
968 A84 2.50r blue & yellow 3.00 .80
969 A85 5r blk brn & yel 5.75 2.50
Nos. 966-969 (4) 12.50 3.80

Discovery of oil at Qum.

Abadan Oil Refinery A86

Super Fractionators — A87

Designs: 1r, Storage tanks. 5r, Pipe lines. 10r, Abadan refinery.

1953, Mar. 20 **Photo.**

970 A86 50d blue green .65 .45
971 A86 1r rose 1.50 .45
972 A87 2.50r bright ultra 6.00 1.10
973 A86 5r red orange 6.50 1.25
974 A86 10r dark violet 8.00 1.90
Nos. 970-974 (5) 22.65 5.15

Nationalization of oil industry, 2nd anniv.

Shah Types of 1951-52

1953-54 Photo. ***Perf. 10½***

975 A82 50d dark gray grn 15.00 .35
976 A83 1r dk blue green 1.50 .20
977 A83 1.50r cerise ('54) 1.50 .20
Nos. 975-977 (3) 18.00 .75

The background has been highlighted on the 1r and 1.50r.

Gymnast — A88

Archery A89

Designs: 3r, Climbing Mt. Demavend. 5r, Ancient polo. 10r, Lion hunting.

1953, Oct. 26

978 A88 1r deep green 2.00 1.10
979 A89 2.50fr brt grnsh bl 10.00 3.00
980 A89 3r gray 20.00 3.75
981 A88 5r bister 15.00 8.00
982 A88 10r rose lilac 30.00 10.00
Nos. 978-982 (5) 77.00 25.85

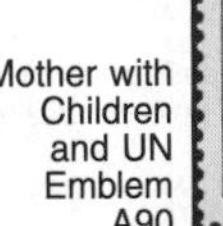

Mother with Children and UN Emblem A90

1953, Oct. 24
983 A90 1r bl grn & dk grn 1.10 .20
984 A90 2.50r lt bl & indigo 1.40 .50

United Nations Day, Oct. 24.

Herring
A91

Refrigeration Compressor — A92

Processing Equipment, National Fisheries — A93

Designs: 2.50r, Sardines. 10r, Sturgeon.

1954, Jan. 31
985 A91 1r multi 3.75 .90
986 A91 2.50r multi 30.00 4.50
987 A92 3r vermilion 11.00 4.50
988 A93 5r deep bl grn 13.00 8.00
989 A91 10r multi 20.00 13.00
Nos. 985-989 (5) 77.75 30.90

Nationalization of fishing industry.

Broken Shackles — A94

Mother Feeding Baby — A95

3r, Torch flag. 5r, Citizen holding flag of Iran.

1954, Aug. 19 **Litho.**
990 A94 2r multicolored 4.50 .65
991 A94 3r multicolored 7.50 1.50
992 A94 5r multicolored 10.00 2.75
Nos. 990-992 (3) 22.00 4.90

Return of the royalist government, 1st anniv.

1954, Oct. 24 **Photo.**
993 A95 2r red lil & org 1.75 .75
994 A95 3r vio bl & org 1.75 1.25

Issued to honor the United Nations.

Woodsman Felling Tree — A96

Designs: 2.50r, Laborer carrying firewood. 5r, Worker operating saw. 10r, Wooden galley.

1954, Dec. 11
995 A96 1r brn & grnsh black 12.50 12.50
996 A96 2.50r grnsh blk & bl 24.00 20.00
997 A96 5r lil & dk brn 45.00 30.00
998 A96 10r bl & claret 60.00 40.00
Nos. 995-998 (4) 141.50 102.50

4th World Forestry Congress, Dehra Dun, India, 1954.

Mohammed Riza Pahlavi
A97 A98

1954-55 **Unwmk.**
999 A97 5d yellow brn .30 .25
1000 A97 10d violet .30 .25
1001 A97 25d scarlet .30 .20
1002 A97 50d black brn .30 .20
1003 A98 1r blue green .45 .20
1004 A98 1.50r cerise .45 .25
1005 A98 2r ocher .45 .25
1006 A98 2.50r blue 1.00 .20
1007 A98 3r olive 1.25 .25
1008 A98 5r dk sl grn 5.00 .25
1009 A98 10r lilac rose 20.00 1.00
1010 A98 20r indigo 30.00 2.00
1011 A98 30r dp yel brn 150.00 7.50
1012 A98 50r dp orange 30.00 5.00
1013 A98 100r light vio 375.00 40.00
1014 A98 200r yellow 125.00 20.00
Nos. 999-1014 (16) 739.80 77.80

See Nos. 1023-1036.

Regional Costume — A99

Regional Costumes: 1r, 2r, Men's costumes. 2.50r, 3r, 5r, Women's costumes.

1955, June 26 **Photo.** ***Perf. 11***
1015 A99 1r bluish gray & multi 1.50 .90
1016 A99 2r dl rose & multi 3.75 1.75
1017 A99 2.50r buff & multi 15.00 2.75
1018 A99 3r rose lil & multi 8.00 3.25
1019 A99 5r gray brn & multi 15.00 6.50
Nos. 1015-1019 (5) 43.25 15.15

Parliament Gate — A100

Designs: 3r, Statue of Liberty, vert. 5r, Old Gate of Parliament.

1955, Aug. 6 **Wmk. 306** ***Perf. 11***
1020 A100 2r red vio & grn 1.60 .55
1021 A100 3r dk bl & aqua 5.25 1.60
1022 A100 5r Prus grn & red org 6.50 4.25
Nos. 1020-1022 (3) 13.35 6.40

50th anniversary of constitution.

Shah Types of 1954-55

1955-56 **Wmk. 306** ***Perf. 11***
1023 A97 5d violet ('56) 2.00 1.00
1024 A97 10d carmine ('56) .50 .20
1025 A97 25d brown .50 .20
1026 A97 50d dk carmine .50 .20
1027 A98 1r dark bl grn .50 .20
1028 A98 1.50r red brn ('56) 35.00 3.00
1029 A98 2r ol grn ('56) 1.00 .25
1030 A98 2.50r blue ('56) 1.50 .30
1031 A98 3r bister 3.25 .20
1032 A98 5r red lilac 3.00 .20
1033 A98 10r brt grnsh bl 8.00 .35
1034 A98 20r slate green 17.50 2.00
1035 A98 30r red org ('56) 125.00 14.00
1036 A98 50r red brn ('56) 100.00 16.50
Nos. 1023-1036 (14) 298.25 38.60

UN Emblem and Globes
A101

1955, Oct. 24 ***Perf. 11x12½***
1039 A101 1r dp car & org 1.25 .50
1040 A101 2.50r dk bl & grnsh blue 1.75 1.25

UN, 10th anniv.Nations, Oct. 24, 1955.

Wrestlers
A102

1955, Oct. 26 **Wmk. 306** ***Perf. 11***
1041 A102 2.50r multi 5.00 2.00

Victory in intl. wrestling competitions.

Garden, Nemazi Hospital — A103

Soldier — A105

Nemazi Hospital, Shiraz
A104

5r, Gate of the Koran. 10r, Hafiz of Shiraz.

1956, Mar. 21 ***Perf. 11x12½***
1042 A103 50d multi 1.60 .60
1043 A104 1r multi 4.00 1.00
1044 A105 2.50r multi 5.00 6.00
1045 A104 5r multi 11.00 4.00
1046 A105 10r multi 20.00 7.00
Nos. 1042-1046 (5) 41.60 18.60

Opening of Nemazi Hospital, Shiraz.

Arms of Iran and Olympic Rings — A106

Tomb at Maragheh
A107

1956, May 15 **Wmk. 306**
1047 A106 5r rose lilac 22.50 15.00

National Olympic Committee, 10th anniv.

1956, May 26 **Photo.** ***Perf. 11x12½***

2.50r, Astrolabe. 5r, Nasr-ud-Din of Tus.

1048 A107 1r orange 2.50 .90
1049 A107 2.50r deep ultra 5.00 .90
1050 A107 5r sepia & pur 7.75 1.75
Nos. 1048-1050 (3) 15.25 3.55

700th death anniv. of Nasr-up-Din of Tus, mathematician and astronomer.

WHO Emblem — A108

Perf. 11x12½
1956, Sept. 19 **Wmk. 306**
1051 A108 6r cerise 2.25 1.00

6th Regional Congress of the WHO.

Scout Bugler and Camp
A109

5r, Scout badge and Shah in scout uniform.

1956, Aug. 5 ***Perf. 12½x11***
1052 A109 2.50r ultra & blue 10.50 5.00
1053 A109 5r lil & red lil 14.00 7.50

National Boy Scout Jamboree.

Catalogue values for unused stamps in this section, from this point to the end of the section, are for Never Hinged items.

Former Telegraph Office, Tehran
A110

6r, Telegraph lines & ancient monument.

1956, Oct. 26
1054 A110 2.50r brt bl & grn, *bluish* 8.50 3.50
1055 A110 6r rose car & lil 11.00 5.00

Centenary of Persian telegraph system.

UN Emblem and People of the World
A111

Design: 2.50r, UN Emblem and scales.

1956, Oct. 24

1056	A111	1r bluish green	1.40	.30
1057	A111	2.50r blue & green	2.75	.55

United Nations Day, Oct. 24.

Shah and Pres. Iskander Mirza of Pakistan A112

1956, Oct. 31

1058	A112	1r multicolored	2.00	.60

Visit of Pres. General Iskander Mirza of Pakistan to Tehran, Oct. 31-Nov. 10.

Mohammed Riza Pahlavi
A113 A114

Perf. 13½x11

1956-57 Wmk. 306 Photo.

1058A	A113	5d brt car & red	.45	*1.00*
1058B	A113	10d vio bl & dl vio	.45	*1.00*
1059	A113	25d dk brn & brn	.65	.35
1059A	A113	50d brn & ol brn	.70	.20
b.		Inverted center	*2,500.*	
1060	A113	1r brn & brt grn	.70	.20
1061	A113	1.50r brt lil & brown	.70	.20
1062	A113	2r red vio & red	.70	.20
1063	A113	2.50r ultra & blue	1.00	.20
1064	A113	3r brn & dk ol bis	1.00	.20
1065	A113	5r ver & mar	1.00	.20
1066	A114	6r dk vio & brn lil	6.00	.25
1067	A114	10r lt blue & grn	12.00	.20
1068	A114	20r green & blue	25.00	3.00
1069	A114	30r rose red & org	30.00	5.00
1070	A114	50r dk grn & ol grn	25.00	5.00
1071	A114	100r lilac & cer	300.00	27.50
1072	A114	200r dp plum & vio bl	175.00	15.00
		Nos. 1058A-1072 (17)	580.35	59.70

Issued: 1.50r, 2r, 3r, 5r, 6r, 1956; others, 1957.

See Nos. 1082-1098.

Lord Baden-Powell A115

Train and Map A117

1957, Feb. 22 ***Perf. 12½***

1073	A115	10r dk grn & brn	7.00	4.00

Birth cent. of Robert Baden-Powell, founder of the Boy Scout movement.

Railroad Tracks — A116

1957, May 2 ***Perf. 11x12½, 12½x11***

Design: 10r, Train and mosque.

1074	A116	2.50r grnsh blk, bl & ocher	7.25	1.00
1075	A117	5r multi	9.50	5.00
1076	A116	10r blk, yel & bl	18.00	9.00
		Nos. 1074-1076 (3)	34.75	15.00

Opening of the Tehran Meshed-Railway.

Pres. Giovanni Gronchi of Italy and Shah — A118

Design: 6r, Ruins of Persepolis and Colosseum in Rome and flags.

Wmk. 316

1957, Sept. 7 Photo. ***Perf. 11***

1077	A118	2r slate bl, grn & red	3.25	1.00
1078	A118	6r slate bl, grn & red	6.75	2.00

Visit of Pres. Giovanni Gronchi of Italy to Iran, Sept. 7.

Queen Soraya and Hospital A119

1957, Sept. 29 Wmk. 316 ***Perf. 11***

1079	A119	2r lt bl & grn	2.50	.45

Sixth Medical Congress, Ramsar.

Globes Showing Location of Iran — A120

1957, Oct. 22 Litho. ***Perf. 12½x11***

1080	A120	10r blk, lt bl, yel & red	7.00	2.00

Intl. Cartographic Conference, Tehran.

Shah and King Faisal II — A121

1957, Oct. 18 Photo.

1081	A121	2r slate bl, grn & red	2.50	.45

Visit of King Faisal of Iraq, Oct. 19.

Shah Types of 1956-57

1957-58 Wmk. 316 ***Perf. 11***

1082	A114	5d violet & pur	.25	*2.00*
1083	A114	10d claret & rose car	.25	*2.00*
1084	A114	25d rose car & brick red	.50	.35
1085	A114	50d grn & olive grn	.40	.20
1086	A114	1r dark green	.40	.20
1087	A114	1.50r claret & red lil	.50	.25
1088	A114	2r bl & grnsh blue	1.65	.20
1089	A114	2.50r dk bl & blue	1.65	.25
1090	A114	3r rose car & ver	1.65	.20
1091	A114	5r violet blue	1.65	.20
1092	A113	6r bright blue	1.65	.20
1093	A113	10r deep green	3.00	.30
1094	A113	20r grn & olive grn	10.00	.45
1095	A113	30r vio bl & dk brn	20.00	4.00
1096	A113	50r dk brn & lt brn	25.00	5.00
1097	A113	100r rose lil & car rose	140.00	25.00
1098	A113	200r vio & yel brn	87.50	20.00
		Nos. 1082-1098 (17)	296.05	60.80

Issued: 1.50r, 2r, 3r, 1957; others, 1958.

Weight Lifter — A122

Modern and Old Houses, Radio Transmitter A123

1957, Nov. 8 ***Perf. 11x14½***

1099	A122	10r bl, grn & red	2.50	.60

Iran's victories in weight lifting.

1958, Feb. 22 Litho.

1100	A123	10r brn, ocher & bl	5.00	1.50

30th anniversary of radio in Iran.

Oil Derrick and Symbolic Flame — A124

Train on Viaduct — A125

Wmk. 316

1958, Mar. 10 Photo. ***Perf. 11***

1101	A124	2r gray & multi	3.25	.80
1102	A124	10r multicolored	8.50	1.25

Drilling of Iran's 1st oil well, 50th anniv.

1958, Apr. 24 Wmk. 306 ***Perf. 11***

Design: 8r, Train and map.

1103	A125	6r dull purple	15.00	4.00
1104	A125	8r green	20.00	8.00

Opening of Tehran-Tabriz railway line.

Exposition Emblem A126

1958, Apr. 17 ***Perf. 12½x11***

1105	A126	2.50r bl & light bl	.60	.20
1106	A126	6r car & salmon	1.25	.20

World's Fair, Brussels, Apr. 17-Oct. 19.

Mohammed Riza Pahlavi — A127 UN Emblem and Map of Iran — A128

1958-59 Wmk. 316 Photo. ***Perf. 11***

1107	A127	5d blue violet	.50	.25
1108	A127	10d lt vermilion	.50	.25
1109	A127	25d crimson	.50	.25
1110	A127	50d brt blue	.50	.25
1111	A127	1r dark green	1.00	.20
1113	A127	2r dark brown	8.00	.25
1115	A127	3r dk red brown	15.00	.20
1117	A127	6r bright blue	6.00	.45
1118	A127	8r magenta	5.00	.35
1120	A127	14r blue violet	12.00	1.75
1121	A127	20r green	20.00	.45
a.		Wmk. 306	25.00	10.00
1122	A127	30r brt car rose	17.00	1.75
1123	A127	50r rose violet	55.00	6.00
1124	A127	100r red orange	20.00	4.50
1125	A127	200r slate green	60.00	9.00
		Nos. 1107-1125 (15)	221.00	25.90

See Nos. 1138-1151, 1173-1179.

1958, Oct. 24

1126	A128	6r bright blue	1.25	.75
1127	A128	10r dk violet & grn	2.25	1.00

Issued for United Nations Day, Oct. 24.

Globe and Hands A129

1958, Dec. 10

1128	A129	6r dk red brn & brn	.75	.30
1129	A129	8r dk grn & gray grn	1.25	.40

Universal Declaration of Human Rights, 10th anniv.

Rudagi — A130

Wrestlers, Flag and Globe — A131

Flag
A130a

Design: 5r, Rudagi, different pose.

1958, Dec. 24 Photo. Wmk. 306

1130 A130 2.50r bluish black 6.50 .90
1131 A130 5r violet 12.50 1.50
1132 A130 10r dark brown 21.00 2.75
Nos. 1130-1132 (3) 40.00 5.15

1100th birth anniv. of Rudagi, blind Persian poet.

Perf. 14½x11

1959, May 8 Wmk. 316

1132A A130a 1r multicolored 1.00 .50
1132B A130a 6r multicolored 2.25 .75

Centenary of the Red Cross.

1959 Litho. *Perf. 11x12½*

1133 A131 6r multicolored 10.00 2.50

World Wrestling Championships, Tehran.

Globe, UN Building and Hand Holding Torch of Freedom
A132

1959, Oct. 24 Photo. *Perf. 11*

1134 A132 6r gray brn, red & bister 1.50 .50

Issued for United Nations Day, Oct. 24.

Shah and Pres. Ayub Khan of Pakistan — A133

1959, Nov. 9 Litho. *Perf. 11x16*

1135 A133 6r multicolored 5.00 .75

Visit of Pres. Khan to Iran.

ILO
Emblem — A134

1959, Nov. 12 *Perf. 16*

1136 A134 1r blue 1.10 .30
1137 A134 5r brown 1.90 .45

ILO, 40th anniversary.

Shah Type of 1958-59

1959-63 Wmk. 316 Photo. *Perf. 11*

1138 A127 5d red brn ('60) .35 .30
1139 A127 10d Prus grn ('60) .35 .30
a. 10d Prussian blue ('63) .50 .50
1140 A127 25d orange 1.00 .20
a. Perf. 12x11½ 20.00 10.00
1141 A127 50d scarlet 1.00 .25
1142 A127 1r deep violet 1.00 .20
1143 A127 3r olive 3.00 .20
1144 A127 8r brown olive 1.50 .20
1145 A127 10r ol blk ('60) 1.50 .20
1146 A127 14r yel green 1.75 .25
1147 A127 20r sl grn ('60) 6.00 .35
1148 A127 30r choc ('60) 6.50 .65
1149 A127 50r dp blue ('60) 6.50 .60
1150 A127 100r green ('60) 110.00 10.00
1151 A127 200r cer ('60) 225.00 15.00
Nos. 1138-1151 (14) 365.45 28.70

Pahlavi Foundation Bridge, Karun River — A135

Design: 5r, Bridge, different view.

1960, Feb. 29 Litho. *Perf. 16x11*

1152 A135 1r dk brn & brt bl 1.00 .20
1153 A135 5r blue & emerald 2.00 .50

Opening of Pahlavi Foundation Bridge at Khorramshahr on the Karun River.

Uprooted Oak Emblem
A136

Design: 6r, Arched frame.

1960, Apr. 7 *Perf. 11*

1154 A136 1r brt ultra .50 .20
1155 A136 6r gray olive .65 .20

World Refugee Year, 7/1/59-6/30/60.

Mosquito — A137

Man with Spray Gun — A138

Design: 3r, Mosquito on water.

1960, Apr. 7 Wmk. 316

1156 A137 1r blk & red, *yel* 1.10 .20
1157 A138 2r lt bl, ultra & blk 1.75 .30
1158 A137 3r blk & red, *yel grn* 3.75 .65
Nos. 1156-1158 (3) 6.60 1.15

Issued to publicize malaria control.

Polo
Player — A139

Design: 6r, Persian archer.

1960, June 9 Litho. Wmk. 316

1159 A139 1r deep claret 1.00 .30
1160 A139 6r dk blue & lt blue 2.00 .75

17th Olympic Games, Rome, 8/25-9/11.

Shah and King Hussein of Jordan — A140

1960, July 6 *Perf. 11*

1161 A140 6r multicolored 5.00 .65

Visit of King Hussein of Jordan to Tehran.

Iranian Scout Emblem in Flower — A141

Tents and Pillars of Persepolis
A142

1960, July 18

1162 A141 1r green .50 .25
1163 A142 6r brn, brt bl & buff 1.00 .50

3rd National Boy Scout Jamboree.

Shah and Queen Farah — A143

1960, Sept. 9 Litho. *Perf. 11*

1164 A143 1r green 3.50 .50
1165 A143 5r blue 7.50 1.00

Marriage of Shah Mohammed Riza Pahlavi and Farah Diba.

UN Emblem and Globe — A144

1960, Oct. 24 Wmk. 316

1166 A144 6r bl, blk & lt brn .50 .20

15th anniversary of the United Nations.

Shah and Queen Elizabeth II
A145

1961, Mar. 2 Litho. *Perf. 11*

1167 A145 1r lt red brown 1.50 .35
1168 A145 6r bright ultra 3.00 .75

Visit of Queen Elizabeth II to Tehran, Feb. 1961.

Girl Playing Arganoon — A146

Safiaddin Amavi — A147

1961, Apr. 10 Wmk. 316 *Perf. 11*

1169 A146 1r dk brown & buff .75 .40
1170 A147 6r greenish gray 1.75 .60

International Congress of Music, Tehran.

Shah Type of 1958-59 Redrawn

1961-62 Litho. *Perf. 11*

1173 A127 25d orange 1.50 .50
1174 A127 50d scarlet 1.50 .40
1175 A127 1r deep violet 3.00 .20
1176 A127 2r chocolate 4.00 .20
1177 A127 3r olive brown 5.00 .50
1178 A127 6r brt blue ('62) 50.00 3.50
1179 A127 8r brown ol ('62) 20.00 2.25
Nos. 1173-1179 (7) 85.00 7.55

On Nos. 1173-1179 (lithographed), a single white line separates the lower panel from the shah's portrait. On Nos. 1107-1125, 1138-1151 (photogravure), two lines, one in color and one in white, separate panel from portrait. Other minor differences exist.

Shah and Queen Farah Holding Crown Prince — A148

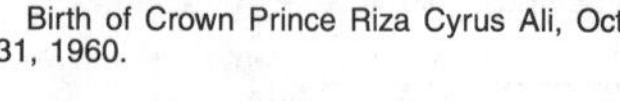

1961, June 2 Litho.

1186 A148 1r bright pink 1.75 .75
1187 A148 6r light blue 6.00 2.25

Birth of Crown Prince Riza Cyrus Ali, Oct. 31, 1960.

Swallows and UN Emblem — A149

Planting Tree — A150

1961, Oct. 24 ***Perf. 11***
1188 A149 2r blue & car rose 1.00 .20
1189 A149 6r blue & violet 1.50 .30

Issued for United Nations Day, Oct. 24.

1962, Jan. 11
1190 A150 2r ol grn, citron & dk bl 1.00 .20
1191 A150 6r ultra, grn & pale bl 1.50 .30

Tree Planting Day.

Worker and Symbols of Labor and Agriculture A151

Map, Family and Cogwheel A152

1962, Mar. 15 **Litho.**
1192 A151 2r bl grn, brn & blk 1.00 .20
1193 A151 6r lt ultra, brn & blk 1.50 .30

Issued for Workers' Day.

1962, Mar. 20 ***Perf. 11***
1194 A152 2r black, yel & lil 1.00 .20
1195 A152 6r black, bl & ultra 1.50 .30

Social Insurance Week.

Sugar Refinery, Khuzistan — A153

1962, Apr. 14 **Wmk. 316**
1196 A153 2r dk & lt blue & grn 1.50 .25
1197 A153 6r ultra, buff & blue 2.00 .40

Opening of sugar refinery in Khuzistan.

Karaj Dam — A154

1962, May 15
1198 A154 2r dk brn & gray grn 1.50 .25
1199 A154 6r vio bl & lt blue 2.00 .40

Inauguration of Karaj Dam, renamed Amir Kabir Dam.

Sefid Rud Dam A155

1962, May 19 **Litho.**
1200 A155 2r dk grn, lt bl & buff 1.50 .25
1201 A155 6r red brn, sl grn & lt blue 2.00 .50

Inauguration of Sefid Rud Dam.

"UNESCO" and UN Emblem — A156

1962, June 2 **Wmk. 316** ***Perf. 11***
1202 A156 2r black, emer & red 1.00 .20
1203 A156 6r blue, emer & red 2.00 .40

15th anniv. of UNESCO.

Malaria Eradication Emblem and Sprayer A157

2r, Emblem & arrow piercing mosquito, horiz. 10r, Emblem & globe, horiz. Sizes: 2r, 10r, 40x25mm; 6r, 29½x34½mm.

1962, June 20
1204 A157 2r black & bluish grn 1.00 .20
1205 A157 6r pink & vio blue 1.50 .30
1206 A157 10r lt blue & ultra 2.50 .50
Nos. 1204-1206 (3) 5.00 1.00

WHO drive to eradicate malaria.

Oil Field and UN Emblem A158

1962, Sept. 1 **Photo.**
1207 A158 6r grnsh blue & brn 2.00 .30
1208 A158 14r gray & sepia 3.50 .70

2nd Petroleum Symposium of ECAFE (UN Economic Commission for Asia and the Far East).

Mohammed Riza Pahlavi — A159

Palace of Darius, Persepolis A160

Perf. 11, 10½x11

1962 **Photo.** **Wmk. 316**
1209 A159 5d green 1.00 .25
1210 A159 10d chestnut 1.00 .50
1211 A159 25d dark blue 1.00 .35
1212 A159 50d Prus green 1.00 .20
1213 A159 1r orange 3.00 .20
1214 A159 2r violet blue 2.00 .20
1215 A159 5r dark brown 3.00 .20
1216 A160 6r blue 12.00 2.50
1217 A160 8r yellow grn 5.00 1.00
1218 A160 10r grnsh blue 8.00 .50
1219 A160 11r slate green 9.00 .65
1220 A160 14r purple 10.00 .65
1221 A160 20r red brown 11.00 1.50
1222 A160 50r vermilion 15.00 1.50
Nos. 1209-1222 (14) 82.00 10.20

See Nos. 1331-1344.

Hippocrates and Avicenna — A161

1962, Oct. 7 **Litho.**
1226 A161 2r brown, buff & ultra 2.50 .35
1227 A161 6r grn, pale grn & ultra 3.00 .60

Near and Middle East Medical Congress.

Hands Laying Bricks A162

Design: 6r, Houses and UN emblem, vert.

1962, Oct. 24
1228 A162 6r dk blue & ultra 2.00 .35
1229 A162 14r dk blue & emer 3.00 .60

Issued for United Nations Day, Oct. 24.

Crown Prince Receiving Flowers — A163

1962, Oct. 31
1230 A163 6r blue gray 5.00 .90
1231 A163 14r dull green 10.00 1.75

Children's Day, Oct. 31; 2nd birthday of Crown Prince Riza.

Map of Iran and Persian Gulf — A164

Hilton Hotel, Tehran — A165

1962, Dec. 12 **Wmk. 316** ***Perf. 11***
1232 A164 6r dk & lt bl, vio bl & rose 2.00 .35
1233 A164 14r dk & lt bl, pink & rose 3.00 .60

The Persian Gulf Seminar.

1963, Jan. 21 **Photo.**
1234 A165 6r deep blue 3.00 .45
1235 A165 14r dark red brown 5.00 .55

Opening of the Royal Tehran Hilton Hotel.

Mohammed Riza Shah Dam A166

1963, Mar. 14 **Litho.**
Center Multicolored
1236 A166 6r violet blue 3.50 .40
1237 A166 14r dark brown 6.00 .65

Mohammed Riza Shah Dam inauguration (later Dez Dam).

Worker with Pickax — A167

Stylized Bird over Globe — A168

1963, Mar. 15
1238 A167 2r cream & black 1.10 .20
1239 A167 6r lt blue & blk 2.00 .30

Issued for Labor Day.

1963, Mar. 21 ***Perf. 11***

Designs: 6r, Stylized globe and "FAO." 14r, Globe in space and wheat emblem.

1240 A168 2r ultra, lt bl & bis 1.50 .20
1241 A168 6r lt ultra, ocher & blk 2.25 .30
1242 A168 14r slate bl & ocher 3.75 .85
Nos. 1240-1242 (3) 7.50 1.35

FAO "Freedom from Hunger" campaign.

Shah and List of Bills — A169

1963, Mar. 21 **Wmk. 316**
1243 A169 6r green & lt blue 5.00 1.50
1244 A169 14r green & dull yel 7.50 2.00

Signing of six socioeconomic bills by Shah, 1st anniv.

Shah and King of Denmark — A170

1963, May 3 Litho. *Perf. 11*

1245 A170 6r indigo & dk ultra 3.50 .55
1246 A170 14r dk brn & red brn 5.00 1.00

Visit of King Frederik IX of Denmark.

Flags, Shah Mosque, Isfahan, and Taj Mahal, Agra A171

1963, May 19

1247 A171 6r blue, yel grn & red 3.50 .65
1248 A171 14r multicolored 5.00 1.25

Visit of Dr. Sarvepalli Radhakrishnan, president of India.

Chahnaz Dam — A172

Cent. Emblem with Red Lion and Sun — A173

1963, June 8 Wmk. 316 *Perf. 11*

1249 A172 6r ultra, bl & grn 3.50 .45
1250 A172 14r dk grn, bl & buff 3.50 .75

Inauguration of Chahnaz Dam (later Hamadan Dam).

1963, June 10

1251 A173 6r blue, gray & red 3.50 .65
1252 A173 14r buff, gray & red 5.50 .90

Centenary of International Red Cross.

Shah and Queen Juliana A174

Perf. 11x10½

1963, Oct. 3 Wmk. 349

1253 A174 6r ultra & blue 4.00 .50
1254 A174 14r sl grn & dull grn 6.00 .75

Visit of Queen Juliana of the Netherlands.

Literacy Corps Emblem and Soldier Teaching Village Class — A175

1963, Oct. 15 Litho. *Perf. 10½*

1255 A175 6r multicolored 4.50 1.00
1256 A175 14r multicolored 6.50 1.00

Issued to publicize the Literacy Corps.

Gen. Charles de Gaulle and View of Persepolis — A176

1963, Oct. 16

1257 A176 6r ultra & blue 4.50 1.00
1258 A176 14r brn & pale brn 5.50 1.00

Visit of General de Gaulle of France.

Fertilizer Plant, Oil Company Emblem and Map — A177

Design: 14r, Factory and Iranian Oil Company emblem, horiz.

Perf. 10½x11, 11x10½

1963, Oct. 18 Wmk. 316

1259 A177 6r black, yel & red 4.50 .50
1260 A177 14r black, bl & yel 5.50 1.50

Opening of Shiraz Chemical Factory.

Pres. Heinrich Lübke of Germany and Mosque in Tehran A178

1963, Oct. 23 Wmk. 349 *Perf. 10½*

1261 A178 6r ultra & dk blue 4.25 .65
1262 A178 14r gray & brown 5.00 1.60

Visit of Pres. Lubke of Germany.

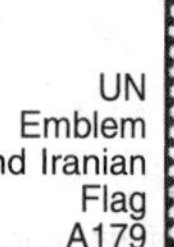

UN Emblem and Iranian Flag A179

1963, Oct. 24

1263 A179 8r multicolored 2.75 .50

Issued for United Nations Day.

UN Emblem and Jets A180

1963, Oct. 24

1264 A180 6r multicolored 2.75 .50

Iranian jet fighters with UN Force in the Congo.

Crown Prince Riza — A181

1963, Oct. 31

1265 A181 2r brown 1.75 .25
1266 A181 6r blue 4.50 .50

Children's Day; Crown Prince Riza's 3rd birthday.

Pres. Brezhnev of USSR — A182

1963, Nov. 16 Wmk. 349 *Perf. 10½*

1267 A182 6r dk brn, yel & bl 3.25 .30
1268 A182 11r dk brn, yel & red 6.00 .75

Visit of Pres. Leonid I. Brezhnev.

Atatürk's Mausoleum, Ankara — A183

1963, Nov. 28 Litho.

1269 A183 4r shown 3.25 .20
1270 A183 5r Kemal Ataturk 3.25 .25

25th death anniv. of Kemal Atatürk, president of Turkey.

Scales and Globe — A184

1963, Dec. 10

1271 A184 6r brt yel grn, blk & ultra 2.75 .30
1272 A184 14r org brn, blk & buff 3.25 .35

Universal Declaration of Human Rights, 15th anniv.

Mother and Child — A185

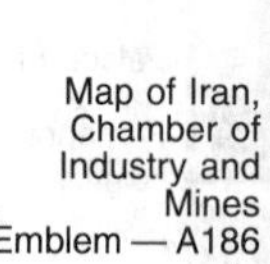

Map of Iran, Chamber of Industry and Mines Emblem — A186

1963, Dec. 16

1273 A185 2r multicolored 2.25 .25
1274 A185 4r multicolored 3.25 .50

Issued for Mother's Day.

1963, Dec. 17 Litho.

1275 A186 8r bl grn, buff & dk bl 4.00 .40

Chamber of Industry and Mines.

Factories and Hand Holding Bill — A187

Designs: 4r, Factories and bills on scale. 6r, Man on globe carrying torch of education. 8r, Tractor, map and yardstick. 10r, Forest. 12r, Gate of Parliament and heads of man and woman.

1964, Jan. 26 Wmk. 349 *Perf. 10½*

1276 A187 2r multicolored 3.00 .75
1277 A187 4r brown & gray 4.00 .75
1278 A187 6r multicolored 5.00 .75
1279 A187 8r multicolored 6.00 1.00
1280 A187 10r multicolored 7.00 1.25
1281 A187 12r red org & brn 8.00 1.50
Nos. 1276-1281 (6) 33.00 6.00

2nd anniv. of six socioeconomic bills: 2r, Shareholding for factory workers. 4r, Sale of shares in government factories. 6r, Creation of Army of Education. 8r, Land reforms. 10r, Nationalization of forests. 12r, Reforms in parliamentary elections.

"ECAFE" and UN Emblem A188

1964, Mar. 2 Wmk. 349

1282 A188 14r brt green & blk 3.00 .45

20th session of ECAFE (Economic Commission for Asia and the Far East), Mar. 2-17.

Flowering Branch — A189

1964, Mar. 5 *Perf. 10½*

1283 A189 50d emerald, blk & org .45 .25
1284 A189 1r brt blue, blk & org .55 .25

Novrooz, Iranian New Year, Mar. 21.

Anemometer A190

Mosque and Arches, Isfahan — A191

1964, Mar. 23 Litho.

1285 A190 6r brt blue & vio bl 1.50 .25

4th World Meteorological Day.

1964, Apr. 7 *Perf. 10½*

11r, Griffon & winged bull, Persepolis.

1286 A191 6r lilac, grn & blk 3.00 .40
1287 A191 11r orange, brn & blk 4.00 .55

Issued for tourist publicity.

Rudaki and Musical Instrument A192

1964, May 16 Photo. Wmk. 349

1288 A192 6r blue	2.50	.45
1289 A192 8r red brown	4.50	.55

Opening of an institute for the blind. The inscription translates: "Wisdom is better than eye and sight."

Sculpture, Persepolis A193

Designs: 4r, Achaemenian horse-drawn mail cart, map of Iran, horiz. 6r, Vessel with sculptured animals. 10r, Head of King Shapur, sculpture.

1964, June 5 Wmk. 349 Litho.

1290 A193 2r gray & blue	4.00	1.00
1291 A193 4r vio bl, lt bl & bl	8.00	1.40
1292 A193 6r brown & yellow	8.00	1.40
1293 A193 10r yel & ol grn	10.00	2.00
Nos. 1290-1293 (4)	30.00	5.80

Opening of the "7000 Years of Persian Art" exhibition in Washington, D.C.

Shah and Emperor Haile Selassie A194

1964, Sept. 14 Wmk. 349 *Perf. 10½*

1294 A194 6r ultra & lt blue	3.00	.40

Visit of Emperor Haile Selassie of Ethiopia.

Tooth and Dentists' Assoc. Emblem A195

"2 I.D.A." A196

1964, Sept. 14 Litho.

1295 A195 2r blue, red & dk blue	2.00	.30
1296 A196 4r ultra, bl & pale brn	2.50	.35

Iranian Dentists' Association, 2nd congress.

Research Institute, Microscope, Wheat and Locust — A197

Beetle under Magnifying Glass — A198

1964, Sept. 23 Wmk. 349 *Perf. 10½*

1297 A197 2r red, orange & brn	3.00	.30
1298 A198 6r blue, brn & indigo	4.00	.50

Fight against plant diseases and damages.

Mithras (Mehr) on Ancient Seal — A199

Eleanor Roosevelt (1884-1962) A200

1964, Oct. 8 Litho.

Size: 26x34mm

1299 A199 8r org & brn org	2.00	.75

Mehragan celebration. See No. 1406.

1964, Oct. 11

1300 A200 10r vio bl & rose vio	4.00	.35

Clasped Hands and UN Emblem — A201

Symbolic Airplane and UN Emblem — A202

1964, Oct. 24 Wmk. 349 *Perf. 10½*

1301 A201 6r ultra, yel, red & blk	1.50	.30
1302 A202 14r org, ultra & red	2.25	.50

Issued for United Nations Day.

Persian Gymnast — A203

Polo Player A204

1964, Oct. 26

1303 A203 4r tan, sep & Prus bl	2.00	.35
1304 A204 6r red & black	2.50	.40

18th Olympic Games, Tokyo, Oct. 10-25.

Crown Prince Riza — A205

1964, Oct. 31 Litho.

1305 A205 1r dull green & brn	1.40	.30
1306 A205 2r deep rose & ultra	2.75	.50
1307 A205 6r ultra & red	4.00	.65
Nos. 1305-1307 (3)	8.15	1.45

Children's Day; Crown Prince Riza's 4th birthday.

UN Emblem, Flame and Smokestack — A206

1964, Nov. 16 Wmk. 349 *Perf. 10½*

1308 A206 6r black, lt bl & car	1.50	.35
1309 A206 8r black, emer & car	2.50	.40

Petro-Chemical Conference and Gas Seminar, Nov.-Dec. 1964.

Shah and King Baudouin — A207

1964, Nov. 17

1310 A207 6r black, org & yel	1.75	.35
1311 A207 8r black, org & emer	3.00	.75

Visit of King Baudouin of Belgium.

Rhazes A208

1964, Dec. 27 Wmk. 349 *Perf. 10½*

1312 A208 2r multicolored	2.50	.35
1313 A208 6r multicolored	3.50	.60

1100th birth anniv. of Rhazes (abu-Bakr Muhammad ibn-Zakariya al-Razi), Persian-born Moslem physician.

Shah and King Olav V A209

1965, Jan. 7 Litho.

1314 A209 2r dk brown & lilac	2.50	.35
1315 A209 4r brown & green	3.50	.75

Visit of King Olav V of Norway.

Map of Iran and Six-pointed Star — A210

1965, Jan. 26 Wmk. 349 *Perf. 10½*

1316 A210 2r black, brt bl & org	1.50	.20

Shah's six socioeconomic bills, 3rd anniv.

Woman and UN Emblem — A211

Green Wheat and Tulip — A212

1965, Mar. 1 Wmk. 349 *Perf. 10½*

1317 A211 6r black & blue	.85	.20
1318 A211 8r ultra & red	1.25	.20

18th session of the UN commission on the status of women.

1965, Mar. 6

1319 A212 50d multicolored	.30	.20
1320 A212 1r multicolored	.30	.20

Novrooz, Iranian New Year, Mar. 21.

Pres. Habib Bourguiba and Minarets of Tunis Mosque — A213

1965, Mar. 14 Litho. *Perf. 10½*

1321 A213 4r multicolored	1.50	.35

Visit of Pres. Habib Bourguiba of Tunisia.

Map of Iran and Trade Mark of Iranian Oil Co. A214

1965, Mar. 20 **Litho.**

1322 A214 6r multicolored 2.50 .25
1323 A214 14r multicolored 3.50 .55

Oil industry nationalization, 14th anniv.

ITU Emblem, Old and New Communication Equipment — A215

1965, May 17 Wmk. 349 *Perf. 10½*

1324 A215 14r dp car rose & gray 1.25 .25

ITU, centenary.

ICY Emblem A216

1965, June 22 Litho. *Perf. 10½*

1325 A216 10r sl grn & gray bl 2.25 .35

International Cooperation Year, 1965.

Iran Airways Emblem A217

1965, July 17 Wmk. 349 *Perf. 10½*

1326 A217 14r multicolored 2.25 .45

Tenth anniversary of Iran Airways.

Hands Holding Book A218

Map and Flags of Turkey, Iran and Pakistan A219

1965, July 21 **Litho.**

1327 A218 2r dk brn, org brn & buff .75 .20
1328 A219 4r multicolored 1.25 .20

Signing of the Regional Cooperation for Development Pact by Turkey, Iran and Pakistan, 1st anniv.

Iranian Scout Emblem and Ornament A220

1965, July 23

1329 A220 2r multicolored 1.00 .20
a. Vert. pair, imperf. horiz. 75.00

Middle East Rover Moot (senior Boy Scout assembly).

Majlis Gate A221

1965, Aug. 5 Wmk. 349 *Perf. 10½*

1330 A221 2r lilac rose & brn .75 .20

60th anniversary of Iranian constitution.

Types of Regular Issue, 1962

Wmk. 349

1964-65 Photo. *Perf. 10½*

1331	A159	5d dk sl grn ('65)	.35	.30
a.		Wmk. 353	.35	.30
1332	A159	10d chestnut	.35	.30
1333	A159	25d dk blue ('65)	.50	.25
1334	A159	50d Prus green	.75	.20
1335	A159	1r orange	.75	.20
1336	A159	2r violet blue	.50	.20
1337	A159	5r dark brown	3.00	.50
1338	A160	6r blue ('65)	11.00	1.00
1339	A160	8r yel grn ('65)	3.50	.25
1340	A160	10r grnsh bl ('65)	3.00	.25
1341	A160	11r sl grn ('65)	10.00	1.50
1342	A160	14r purple ('65)	7.00	1.40
1343	A160	20r red brn ('65)	6.00	2.00
1344	A160	50r org ver ('65)	7.50	2.00
		Nos. 1331-1344 (14)	54.20	10.35

Perf. 11x10½

1331b	A159	5d Wmk. 353	4.00	1.00
1332a	A159	10d	.55	.50
1333a	A159	25d	.80	.25
1334a	A159	50d	3.00	2.00
1335a	A159	1r	3.00	2.00
1337a	A159	5r	6.00	.50
		Nos. 1331b-1337a (6)	17.35	6.25

Dental Congress Emblem — A222

1965, Sept. 7 Litho. *Perf. 10½*

1345 A222 6r gray, ultra, & car .60 .25

Iranian Dentists' Association, 3rd congress.

Classroom and Literacy Corps Emblem A223

Mohammed Riza Pahlavi — A225

Emblem of Persian Medical Society A226

Alphabets on Globe — A224

Designs: 6r, UNESCO emblem and open book (diamond shape). 8r, UNESCO emblem and inscription, horiz. 14r, Shah Riza Pahlavi and inscription in six languages.

1965, Sept. 8

1346 A223 2r multi .35 .20
1347 A224 5r multi .40 .25

Size: 30x30mm

1348 A223 6r multi .80 .30

Size: 35x23mm

1349 A223 8r dk bl, car emer & buff .80 .25

Size: 34x46mm

1350 A223 14r cit, dk bl & brn 2.00 .30
Nos. 1346-1350 (5) 4.35 1.30

World Congress Against Illiteracy, Tehran, Sept. 8-19.

1965, Sept. 16 Litho. *Perf. 10½*

1351 A225 1r crim, rose red & gray 1.50 .25
1352 A225 2r dk red, rose red & yel 1.50 .35

Reign of Shah, 25th anniv.

1965, Sept. 21 **Wmk. 349**

1353 A226 5r ultra, dp ultra & gold .50 .25

14th Medical Congress, Ramsar.

Pres. Jonas of Austria A227

1965, Sept. 30

1354 A227 6r bl, brt bl & gray 1.50 .25

Visit of President Franz Jonas of Austria.

Mithras (Mehr) on Ancient Seal — A228

1965, Oct. 8 Litho. Wmk. 353

1355 A228 4r brt grn, gold, brn & blk 1.00 .20

Mehragan celebration during month of Mehr, Sept. 23-Oct. 22. Persian inscription of watermark vertical on No. 1355.

UN Emblem — A229

1965, Oct. 24 Wmk. 353 *Perf. 10½*

1356 A229 5r bl, grn & rose car .55 .20

20th anniversary of the United Nations.

Symbolic Arches A230

1965, Oct. 26

1357 A230 3r vio bl, blk, yel & red .55 .20

Exhibition of Iranian Commodities.

Crown Prince Riza A231

1965, Oct. 31

1358 A231 2r brown & yellow 1.10 .45

Children's Day; Crown Prince Riza's 5th birthday.

Weight Lifters — A232

1965, Nov. 1

1359 A232 10r brt bl, vio & brt pink .60 .20

World Weight Lifting Championships, Tehran.

Open Book A233

1965, Dec. 1 Wmk. 353 *Perf. 10½*

1360 A233 8r bl, brt pink & blk .60 .20

Issued for Book Week.

Shah and King Faisal A234

1965, Dec. 8 **Litho.**

1361 A234 4r olive bister & brn 1.50 .35

Visit of King Faisal of Saudi Arabia.

Scales and Olive Branch A235

1965, Dec. 12

1362 A235 14r multicolored .60 .20

Human Rights Day (Dec. 10).

Tractor, "Land Reform" A236

Symbols of Reform Bills: 2r, Trees, nationalization of forests. 3r, Factory and gear wheel, sale of shares in government factories. 4r, Wheels, shareholding for factory workers. 5r, Parliament gate, women's suffrage. 6r, Children before blackboard, Army of Education. 7r, Caduceus, Army of Hygiene. 8r, Scales, creation of rural courts. 9r, Two girders, creation of Army of Progress.

1966, Jan. 26 Wmk. 353 *Perf. 10½*

1363	A236	1r orange & brown	.25	.20
1364	A236	2r dl grn & green	.25	.20
1365	A236	3r silver & gray	.25	.20
1366	A236	4r light & dk vio	.35	.20
1367	A236	5r rose & brown	.50	.20
1368	A236	6r olive & brown	.75	.20
1369	A236	7r bl & vio blue	1.00	.20
1370	A236	8r ultra & dp ultra	1.25	.20
1371	A236	9r brn org & dk brn	1.25	.20
		Nos. 1363-1371 (9)	5.85	1.80

Parliamentary approval of the Shah's reform plan.

Shah — A237

Ruins of Persepolis A238

Wmk. 353

1966-71 Photo. *Perf. 10½*

1372	A237	5d green	.25	.25
1373	A237	10d chestnut	.25	.25
1374	A237	25d dark blue	.25	.25
1375	A237	50d Prussian green	.50	.25
a.		50d blue green ('71)	.50	.30
1376	A237	1r orange	.50	.20
1377	A237	2r violet	.50	.20
1377A	A237	4r cl brn ('68)	6.00	1.00
1378	A237	5r dark brn	1.00	.25
1379	A238	6r deep blue	1.00	.20
1380	A238	8r yellow grn	1.00	.25
a.		8r dull green ('71)	1.00	.25
1381	A238	10r Prus bl	1.50	.20
1382	A238	11r slate grn	1.50	.20
1383	A238	14r purple	2.00	.25
1384	A238	20r brown	17.00	.50
1385	A238	50r cop red	7.50	1.50
1386	A238	100r brt blue	17.00	2.50
1387	A238	200r chnt brn	12.50	4.50
		Nos. 1372-1387 (17)	70.25	12.75

Set, except 4r, issued Feb. 22, 1966.

Student Nurse Taking Oath A239

Narcissus A240

1966, Feb. 24 Litho.

1388	A239	5r brt pink & mag	1.00	.50
1389	A239	5r lt bl & brt bl	1.00	.50

Nurses' Day. Nos. 1388-1389 printed in sheets of 50 arranged checkerwise.

1966, Mar. 7

1390	A240	50d ultra, yel & emer	.25	.20
1391	A240	1r lilac, yel & emer	.25	.20

Novrooz, Iranian New Year, Mar. 21.

Oil Derricks in Persian Gulf — A241

1966, Mar. 20 *Perf. 10½*

1392	A241	14r blk, brt bl & brt rose lil	2.00	.40

Formation of six offshore oil companies.

Radio Tower — A242

2r, Radar, horiz. 6r, Emblem & waves. 8r, Compass rose & waves. 10r, Tower & waves.

1966, Apr. 27 Litho. Wmk. 349

1393	A242	2r dark grn	.20	.20
1394	A242	4r ultra & dp org	.20	.20
1395	A242	6r gray ol & plum	.30	.20
1396	A242	8r brt bl & dk bl	.35	.30
1397	A242	10r brn & bister	.55	.30
		Nos. 1393-1397 (5)	1.60	1.20

Inauguration of the radio telecommunication system of the Central Treaty Organization of the Middle East (CENTO).

WHO Headquarters, Geneva — A243

1966, May 3 Wmk. 353

1398	A243	10r brt bl, yel & blk	.75	.30

Opening of the WHO Headquarters, Geneva.

World Map — A244

1966, May 14 Litho.

1399	A244	6r bl & multi	.55	.30
1400	A244	8r multicolored	.65	.30

Intl. Council of Women, 18th Conf., Tehran, May 1966.

Globe, Map of Iran and Ruins of Persepolis — A245

1966, Sept. 5 Wmk. 353 *Perf. 10½*

1401	A245	14r multicolored	1.25	.40

International Iranology Congress, Tehran.

Emblem of Iranian Medical Society A246

1966, Sept. 21

1402	A246	4r ultra, grnsh bl & bis	.50	.30

15th Medical Congress, held at Ramsar.

Gate of Parliament, Mt. Demavend and Congress Emblem — A247

8r, Senate building, Mt. Demavend & emblem.

1966, Oct. 2 Wmk. 353 *Perf. 10½*

1403	A247	6r brick red, ultra & dk grn	.55	.30
1404	A247	8r lt lil, ultra & dk grn	.65	.30

55th Interparliamentary Union Conf., Tehran.

Visit of President Cevdet Sunay of Turkey — A248

1966, Oct. 2 Litho.

1405	A248	6r vio & dk brn	.50	.20

Mithras Type of 1964

1966, Oct. 8

Size: 30x40mm

1406	A199	6r olive bister & brn	.50	.30

Mehragan celebration.

Farmers — A249

1966, Oct. 13

1407	A249	5r olive bister & brn	2.00	.75

Establishment of rural courts of justice.

UN Emblem — A250

1966, Oct. 24 Wmk. 353 *Perf. 10½*

1408	A250	6r brn org & blk	.50	.30

21st anniversary of United Nations.

Crown Prince Riza — A251

1966, Oct. 31 Litho.

1409	A251	1r ultramarine	.75	.50
1410	A251	2r violet	1.25	.50
a.		Pair, #1409-1410	2.50	2.00

Children's Day; Crown Prince Riza's 6th birthday.

Symbolic Woman's Face — A252

1966, Nov. 6

1411	A252	5r gold, blk & ultra	.50	.20

Founding of the Iranian Women's Org.

Film Strip and Song Bird A253

1966, Nov. 6

1412	A253	4r blk, red lil & vio	.65	.25

First Iranian children's film festival.

"Census Count" — A254

1966, Nov. 11
1413 A254 6r dk brn & gray .50 .20

National census.

Book Cover — A255

1966, Nov. 15
1414 A255 8r tan, brn & ultra .50 .20

Issued to publicize Book Week.

Riza Shah Pahlavi A256

Design: 2r, Riza Shah Pahlavi without kepi.

1966, Nov. 16 **Litho.**
1415 A256 1r slate blue 2.50 .50
1416 A256 1r brown 2.50 .50
a. Pair, #1415-1416 6.00 2.00
1417 A256 2r gray green 2.50 .50
1418 A256 2r violet blue 2.50 .50
a. Pair, #1417-1418 6.00 2.00
Nos. 1415-1418 (4) 10.00 2.00

Riza Shah Pahlavi (1877-1944), founder of modern Iran.

EROPA Emblem and Map of Persia A257

1966, Dec. 4 Wmk. 353 *Perf. 10½*
1419 A257 8r dk brn & emerald .65 .20

4th General Assembly of the Org. of Public Administrators, EROPA.

Shah Giving Land Reform Papers to Farmers A258

1967, Jan. 9 Wmk. 353 *Perf. 10½*
1420 A258 6r ol bis, yel & brn 1.50 .20

Approval of land reform laws, 5th anniv.

Shah and 9-Star Crescent — A259

Design: 2r, Torch and 9-star crescent.

1967, Jan. 26 Wmk. 353 Litho.
1421 A259 2r multicolored 1.50 .50
1422 A259 6r multicolored 2.25 .50

5th anniv. of Shah's reforms, the "White Revolution."

Ancient Sculpture of Bull — A260

Designs: 5r, Sculptured mythical animals. 8r, Pillar from Persepolis.

1967, Feb. 25 Wmk. 353 *Perf. 10½*
1423 A260 3r dk brn & ocher .75 .25
1424 A260 5r Prus grn, brn & ocher 1.00 .25
1425 A260 8r vio, blk & sil 1.50 .40
Nos. 1423-1425 (3) 3.25 .90

Issued to publicize Museum Week.

Planting Tree — A261

1967, Mar. 6
1426 A261 8r brn org & grn .50 .20

Tree Planting Day.

Goldfish — A262

1967, Mar. 11
Size: 26x20mm
1427 A262 1r shown .35 .20
Size: 35x27mm
1428 A262 8r Swallows 1.00 .30

Issued for Novrooz, Iranian New Year.

Microscope, Animals and Emblem — A263

1967, Mar. 11 *Perf. 10½*
1429 A263 5r blk, gray & mag .50 .20

Second Iranian Veterinary Congress.

Pres. Arif of Iraq, Mosque — A264

1967, Mar. 14 Litho. Wmk. 353
1430 A264 6r brt bl & grn .50 .30

Visit of Pres. Abdul Salam Mohammed Arif.

Fireworks A265

1967, Mar. 17
1431 A265 5r vio bl & multi .50 .20

Issued for United Nations Stamp Day.

Map of Iran and Oil Company Emblem — A266

1967, Mar. 20
1432 A266 6r multicolored 2.00 .45

Nationalization of Iranian Oil Industry.

Fencers A267

1967, Mar. 23
1433 A267 5r vio & bister .75 .20

Intl. Youth Fencing Championships, Tehran.

Shah and King of Thailand A268

1967, Apr. 23 Wmk. 353 *Perf. 10½*
1434 A268 6r brn org & dk brn 1.50 .25

Visit of King Bhumibol Adulyadej.

Old and Young Couples A269

1967, Apr. 24 Litho.
1435 A269 5r ol bis & vio bl .50 .20

15th anniversary of Social Insurance.

Skier and Iranian Olympic Emblem A270

Designs: 6r, Assyrian soldiers, Olympic rings and tablet inscribed "I.O.C." 8r, Wrestlers and Iranian Olympic emblem.

1967, May 5
1436 A270 3r brown & black .65 .20
1437 A270 6r multicolored .75 .30
1438 A270 8r ultra & brown 1.00 .50
Nos. 1436-1438 (3) 2.40 1.00

65th Intl. Olympic Cong., Tehran, May 2-11.

Lions International — A271

1967, May 11
Size: 41½x30½mm
1439 A271 3r shown .75 .25
Size: 36x42mm
1440 A271 7r Emblem, vert. 1.25 .35

50th anniversary of Lions International.

Visit of Pres. Chivu Stoica of Romania — A272

1967, May 13
1441 A272 6r orange & dk bl .50 .20

International Tourist Year Emblem — A273

1967, June 6 Wmk. 353 *Perf. 10½*
1442 A273 3r brick red & ultra .50 .20

Iranian Pavilion and Ornament A274

1967, June 7 Litho.
1443 A274 4r dk brn, red & gold .50 .20
1444 A274 10r red, dk brn & gold .90 .20

EXPO '67, Montreal, Apr. 28-Oct. 27.

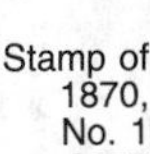

Stamp of 1870, No. 1
A275

1967, July 23 Wmk. 353 *Perf. 10½*

1445 A275 6r multri .50 .20
1446 A275 8r multi .75 .25

Centenary of first Persian postage stamp.

World Map and School Children — A276

1967, Sept. 8 Litho. Wmk. 353

1447 A276 3r ultra & brt & brt bl .40 .20
1448 A276 5r brown & yellow .60 .20

World campaign against illiteracy.

Globe and Oriental Musician — A277

1967, Sept. 10 *Perf. 10½*

1449 A277 14r brn org & dk brn .75 .50

Intl. Conf. on Music Education in Oriental Countries, Sept. 1967.

Child's Hand Holding Adult's — A278

1967, Sept. 14 Litho. Wmk. 353

1450 A278 8r dk brn & yel 4.50 2.50

Introduction of Children's Villages in Iran. (Modelled after Austrian SOS Villages for homeless children).

Winged Wild Goat — A279

1967, Sept. 19

1451 A279 8r dk brn & lemon .60 .25

Festival of Arts, Persepolis.

UN Emblem
A280

1967, Oct. 17

1452 A280 6r olive bister & vio bl .35 .20

Issued for United Nations Day.

Shah and Empress Farah — A281

1967, Oct. 26 Wmk. 353 *Perf. 10½*
Various Frames

1453 A281 2r sil, bl & brn .90 .35
1454 A281 10r sil, bl & vio 1.10 .55
1455 A281 14r lt bl, bl, gold & vio 2.50 1.00
Nos. 1453-1455 (3) 4.50 1.90

Coronation of Shah Mohammed Riza Pahlavi and Empress Farah, Oct. 26, 1967.
Exist part perf., ungummed.

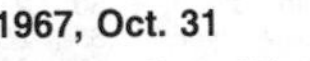

1967, Oct. 31 Litho.

Design: Crown Prince Riza.

1456 A281 2r silver & violet 1.00 .35
1457 A281 8r sil & red brown 1.50 .45

Children's Day; Crown Prince Riza's 7th birthday.

Visit of Pres. Georgi Traikov of Bulgaria — A283

1967, Nov. 20

1458 A283 10r lilac & dk brn .50 .20

Persian Boy Scout Emblem
A284

1967, Dec. 3 Wmk. 353 *Perf. 10½*

1459 A284 8r olive & red brn 1.00 .40

Cooperation Week of the Iranian Boy Scouts, Dec. 5-12.

Hands Holding Chain Link
A285

1967, Dec. 6 Litho.

1460 A285 6r multicolored .50 .20

Issued to publicize Cooperation Year.

Visit of Sheik Sabah of Kuwait — A286

1968, Jan. 10 Wmk. 353 *Perf. 10½*

1461 A286 10r lt bl & slate grn .60 .20

List of Shah's 12 Reform Laws — A287

1968, Jan. 27 Litho. Wmk. 353

1462 A287 2r sl grn, brn & sal .60 .30
1463 A287 8r vio, dk grn & lt grn 1.40 .35
1464 A287 14r brn, pink & lt lil 2.00 .50
Nos. 1462-1464 (3) 4.00 1.15

"White Revolution of King and People."

Almond Blossoms
A288

Haji Firooz (New Year Singer)
A289

Design: 2r, Tulips.

1968, Mar. 12 Wmk. 353 *Perf. 10½*

1465 A288 1r multi .30 .20
1466 A288 2r bluish gray & multi .30 .20
1467 A288 2r brt rose lil & multi .30 .20
1468 A289 6r multi 1.00 .30
Nos. 1465-1468 (4) 1.90 .90

Issued for Novrooz, Iranian New Year.

Oil Worker and Derrick
A290

1968, Mar. 20 Litho.

1469 A290 14r grn, blk & org yel 1.00 .35

Oil industry nationalization, 17th anniv.

WHO Emblem
A291

1968, Apr. 7 Wmk. 353 *Perf. 10½*

1470 A291 14r brn, bl & org .85 .30

WHO, 20th anniversary.

Marlik Chariot, Ancient Sculpture
A292

1968, Apr. 13

1471 A292 8r blue, brn & buff .50 .20

Fifth World Congress of Persian Archaeology and Art, Tehran.

Shah and King Hassan II
A293

1968, Apr. 16

1472 A293 6r bright vio & buff 1.10 .25

Visit of King Hassan II of Morocco.

Human Rights Flame — A294

Soccer Player — A295

Design: 14r, Frameline inscription reads, "International Conference on Human Rights Tehran 1968"; "Iran" at left.

1968, May 5 Wmk. 353 *Perf. 10½*

1473 A294 8r red & dk grn .45 .25
1474 A294 14r vio bl & bl .75 .30

Intl. Human Rights Year. The 8r commemorates the Iranian Human Rights Committee; the 14r, the Intl. Conference on Human Rights, Tehran, 1968.

1968, May 10 Litho.

1475 A295 8r multicolored .45 .25
1476 A295 10r multicolored .75 .30

Asian Soccer Cup Finals, Tehran.

Tehran Oil Refinery
A296

1968, May 21 Wmk. 353 *Perf. 10½*

1477 A296 14r brt bl & multi 1.25 .35

Opening of the Tehran Oil Refinery.

Queen Farah as Girl Guide — A297

1968, June 24 Litho. *Perf. 10½*

1478 A297 4r brt rose lil & bl green 1.75 .50
1479 A297 6r car & brn 2.25 .75

Great Camp of Iranian Girl Guides.

Anopheles Mosquito, Congress Emblem — A298

Winged Figure with Banner, and Globe — A299

1968, Sept. 7 Wmk. 353 *Perf. 10½*

1480 A298 6r brt pur & blk .60 .30
1481 A298 14r dk grn & mag .90 .35

8th Intl. Congress on Tropical Medicine and Malaria, Tehran, Sept. 7-15.

1968, Sept. 8 Litho.

1482 A299 6r lt vio, bis & bl .50 .25
1483 A299 14r dl yel, sl grn & brn .80 .30

World campaign against illiteracy.

Oramental Horse and Flower — A300

1968, Sept. 11

1484 A300 14r sl grn, org & yel grn .75 .20

2nd Festival of Arts, Shiraz-Persepolis.

INTERPOL Emblem and Globe — A301

1968, Oct. 6 Wmk. 353 *Perf. 10½*

1485 A301 10r dk brn & bl .75 .20

37th General Assembly of the Intl. Police Org. (INTERPOL) in Tehran.

Police Emblem on Iran Map in Flag Colors — A302

Peace Dove and UN Emblem — A303

1968, Oct. 7 Litho.

1486 A302 14r multicolored 1.25 .30

Issued for Police Day.

1968, Oct. 24

1487 A303 14r bl & vio bl 1.00 .25

Issued for United Nations Day.

Empress Farah — A304

Designs: 8r, Shah Mohammed Riza Pahlavi. 10fr, Shah, Empress and Crown Prince.

1968, Oct. 26

1488 A304 6r multi 6.00 3.00
1489 A304 8r multi 7.00 3.00
1490 A304 10r multi 8.00 3.00
Nos. 1488-1490 (3) 21.00 9.00

Coronation of Shah Riza Pahlavi and Empress Farah, 1st anniv.

Shah's Crown and Bull's Head Capital — A305

UNICEF Emblem and Child's Drawing — A306

1968, Oct. 30

1491 A305 14r ultra, gold, sil & red .75 .20

Festival of Arts and Culture.

1968, Oct. 31 Litho.

Children's Drawings and UNICEF Emblem: 3r, Boat on lake, house and trees, horiz. 5r, Flowers, horiz.

1492 A306 2r dk brn & multi .25 .20
1493 A306 3r dk grn & multi .35 .20
1494 A306 5r multicolored .50 .25
Nos. 1492-1494 (3) 1.10 .65

Issued for Children's Day.

Labor Union Emblem A307

Factory and Insurance Company Emblem A308

Designs: 8r, Members of Army of Hygiene, and Insurance Company emblem. 10r, Map of Persia, Insurance Company emblem, car, train, ship and plane.

1968, Nov. 6 Wmk. 353 *Perf. 10½*

1495 A307 4r sil & vio bl .35 .20
1496 A308 5r multicolored .50 .25
1497 A308 8r ultra, gray & yel .65 .25
1498 A308 10r multicolored .75 .30
Nos. 1495-1498 (4) 2.25 1.00

Issued to publicize Insurance Day.

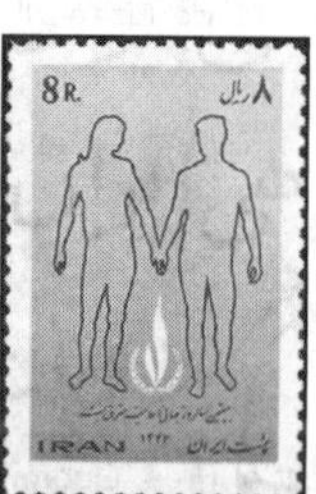

Human Rights Flame, Man and Woman — A309

1968, Dec. 10 Litho. *Perf. 10½*

1499 A309 8r lt bl, vio bl & car .60 .20

International Human Rights Year.

Symbols of Shah's Reform Plan — A310

Design: Each stamp shows symbols of 3 of the Shah's reforms. No. 1503a shows the 12 symbols in a circle with a medallion in the center picturing 3 heads and a torch.

1969, Jan. 26 Wmk. 353 *Perf. 10½*

1500 2r ocher, grn & lil 1.25 .25
1501 4r lil, ocher & grn 1.25 .30
1502 6r lil, ocher & grn 1.50 .40
1503 8r lil, ocher & grn 2.50 .80
a. A310 Block of 4, #1500-1503 7.50 3.50

Declaration of the Shah's Reform Plan.

Shah and Crowd A311

1969, Feb. 1 Litho.

1504 A311 6r red, bl & brn 2.00 .35

10,000th day of the reign of the Shah.

European Goldfinch A312

2r, Ring-necked pheasant. 8r, Roses.

1969, Mar. 6 Wmk. 353 *Perf. 10½*

1505 A312 1r multicolored .30 .20
1506 A312 2r multicolored .35 .20
1507 A312 8r multicolored 1.00 .20
Nos. 1505-1507 (3) 1.65 .60

Issued for Novrooz, Iranian New Year.

"Woman Lawyer" Holding Scales of Justice — A313

Workers, ILO and UN Emblems — A314

1969, Apr. 8 Litho. *Perf. 10½*

1508 A313 6r blk & brt bl .50 .20

15th General Assembly of Women Lawyers, Tehran, Apr. 8-14.

1969, Apr. 30 Wmk. 353 *Perf. 10½*

1509 A314 10r bl & vio bl .65 .20

ILO, 50th anniversary.

Freestyle Wrestlers and Ariamehr Cup — A315

1969, May 6 Litho.

1510 A315 10r lilac & multi 1.50 .50

Intl. Freestyle Wrestling Championships, 3rd round.

Birds and Flower A316

1969, June 10 Wmk. 353 *Perf. 10½*
1511 A316 10r vio bl & multi .75 .20

Issued to publicize Handicrafts Day.

Boy Scout Symbols A317

1969, July 9 Wmk. 353 *Perf. 10½*
1512 A317 6r lt bl & multi 1.25 .30

Philia 1969, an outdoor training course for Boy Scout patrol leaders.

Lady Serving Wine, Safavi Miniature, Iran — A318

#1514, Lady on Balcony, Mogul miniature, Pakistan. #1515, Sultan Suleiman Receiving Sheik Abdul Latif, 16th cent. miniature, Turkey.

1969, July 21 Litho.
1513 A318 25r multi 2.50 .65
1514 A318 25r multi 2.50 .65
1515 A318 25r multi 2.50 .70
Nos. 1513-1515 (3) 7.50 2.00

Signing of the Regional Cooperation for Development Pact by Turkey, Iran and Pakistan, 5th anniv.

Neil A. Armstrong and Col. Edwin E. Aldrin on Moon — A319

1969, July 26
1516 A319 24r bister, bl & brn 7.50 3.00

See note after Algeria No. 427.

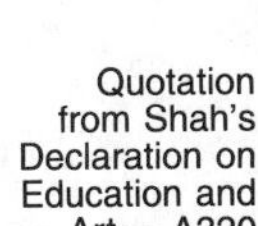

Quotation from Shah's Declaration on Education and Art — A320

1969, Aug. 6 Wmk. 353 *Perf. 10½*
1517 A320 10r car, cream & emer .75 .20

Anniv. of educational and art reforms.

Offshore Oil Rig in Persian Gulf — A321

1969, Sept. 1 Litho.
1518 A321 8r multicolored 1.40 .35

Marine drillings by the Iran-Italia Oil Co., 10th anniv.

Dancers Forming Flower — A322

Crossed-out Fingerprint, Moon and Rocket — A323

1969, Sept. 6 Wmk. 353 *Perf. 10½*
1519 A322 6r multicolored .45 .25
1520 A322 8r multicolored .65 .25

3rd Festival of Arts, Shiraz and Persepolis, Aug. 30-Sept. 9.

1969, Sept. 8 Litho.
1521 A323 4r multicolored .40 .20

World campaign against illiteracy.

Persepolis, Simulated Stamp with UPU Emblem, and Shah — A324

1969, Sept. 28
1522 A324 10r lt bl & multi 2.50 .60
1523 A324 14r multicolored 3.00 .70

16th Congress of the UPU, Tokyo.

Fair Emblem — A325

14r, like 8r, inscribed "ASIA 69." 20r, Fair emblem, world map and "ASIA 69," horiz.

1969, Oct. 5 Wmk. 353 *Perf. 10½*
1524 A325 8r rose & multi .60 .30
1525 A325 14r blue & multi .75 .30
1526 A325 20r tan & multi 1.25 .40
Nos. 1524-1526 (3) 2.60 1.00

2nd Asian Trade Fair, Tehran.

Justice — A326

1969, Oct. 13 Litho.
1527 A326 8r bl grn & dk brn .60 .20

Rural Courts of Justice Day.

UN Emblem A327

1969, Oct. 24
1528 A327 2r lt bl & dp bl .40 .20

25th anniversary of the United Nations.

Emblem and Column Capital, Persepolis — A328

1969, Oct. 28
1529 A328 2r deep blue & multi .60 .25

2nd Festival of Arts and Culture. See Nos. 1577, 1681, 1735.

Child's Drawing and UNICEF Emblem A329

Children's Drawings and UNICEF Emblem: 1r, Boy and birds, vert. 5r, Dinner.

1969, Oct. 31 Wmk. 353 *Perf. 10½*
Size: 28x40mm, 40x28mm
1530 A329 1r lt blue & multi .30 .20
1531 A329 2r lt grn & multi .40 .20
1532 A329 5r lt lil & multi .75 .25
Nos. 1530-1532 (3) 1.45 .65

Children's Week. See Nos. 1578-1580.

Globe Emblem A330

1969, Nov. 6
1533 A330 8r dk brn & bl .60 .20

Meeting of the Natl. Society of Parents and Educators, Tehran.

Satellite Communications Station — A331

1969, Nov. 19 Litho.
1534 A331 6r blk brn & bis 1.00 .30

1st Iranian Satellite Communications Earth Station, Hamadan.

Mahatma Gandhi (1869-1948) A332

1969, Dec. 29 Wmk. 353 *Perf. 10½*
1535 A332 14r gray & dk rose brn 8.00 3.00

Globe, Flags and Emblems A333

Design: 6r, Globe and Red Cross, Red Lion and Sun, and Red Crescent Emblems.

1969, Dec. 31
1536 A333 2r red & multi .75 .30
1537 A333 6r red & multi 1.25 .40

League of Red Cross Societies, 50th anniv.

Symbols of Reform Laws and Shah A334

1970, Jan. 26 Litho. Wmk. 353
1538 A334 1r bister & multi 1.25 .40
1539 A334 2r multicolored 1.50 .60

Declaration of the Shah's Reform Plan.

Pansies A335

New Year's Table A336

1970, Mar. 6 Wmk. 353 *Perf. 10½*

1540 A335 1r multicolored .35 .20
1541 A336 8r multicolored 1.75 .30

Issued for the Iranian New Year.

Chemical Plant, Kharg Island, and Iranian Oil Company Emblem — A337

Designs (Iranian Oil Company Emblem and): 2r, Shah's portrait and quotation. 4r, Laying of gas pipe line and tractor. 8r, Tankers at pier of Kharg Island, vert. 10r, Tehran refinery.

1970, Mar. 20 Wmk. 353 *Perf. 10½*

1542 A337 2r gray & multi 1.25 .25
1543 A337 4r multicolored 1.50 .30
1544 A337 6r lt bl & multi 1.75 .40
1545 A337 8r multicolored 2.00 .50
1546 A337 10r multicolored 2.50 .75
Nos. 1542-1546 (5) 9.00 2.20

Nationalization of the oil industry, 20th anniv.

EXPO '70 Emblem — A338

Radar, Satellite and Congress Emblem — A339

1970, Mar. 27 Litho.

1547 A338 4r brt rose lil & vio bl .40 .20
1548 A338 10r lt bl & pur .75 .20

EXPO '70, Osaka, Japan, Mar. 15-Sept. 13.

1970, Apr. 20 Wmk. 353 *Perf. 10½*

1549 A339 14r multicolored 1.25 .35

Asia-Australia Telecommunications Congress, Tehran.

UPU Headquarters, Bern — A340

1970, May 10

1550 A340 2r gray, brn & lil rose .50 .25
1551 A340 4r lil, brn & lil rose .75 .25

Inauguration of the new UPU Headquarters, Bern.

Asia Productivity Year Emblem — A341

1970, May 19 Wmk. 353 *Perf. 10½*

1552 A341 8r gray & multi .55 .20

Asian Productivity Year, 1970.

Bird Bringing Baby A342

1970, June 15 Litho.

1553 A342 8r brn & dk blue .65 .25

Iranian School for Midwives, 50th anniv.

Tomb of Cyrus the Great, Meshed-Morghab in Fars — A343

Designs: 8r, Pillars of Apadana Palace, Persepolis, vert. 10r, Bas-relief from a Mede tomb, Iraq. 14r, Achaemenian officers, bas-relief, Persepolis.

1970, June 21 Photo. *Perf. 13*

1554 A343 6r gray, red & vio 1.75 .25
1555 A343 8r pale rose, blk & bl grn 2.00 .50
1556 A343 10r yel, red & brn 2.25 .65
1557 A343 14r bl, blk & red brn 2.50 1.00
Nos. 1554-1557 (4) 8.50 2.40

2500th anniversary of the founding of the Persian Empire by Cyrus the Great.
See #1561-1571, 1589-1596, 1605-1612.

Seeyo-Se-Pol Bridge, Isfahan — A344

#1559, Saiful Malook Lake, Pakistan, vert. #1560, View of Fethiye, Turkey, vert.

Wmk. 353

1970, July 21 Litho. *Perf. 10½*

1558 A344 2r multicolored 1.00 .25
1559 A344 2r multicolored 1.00 .25
1560 A344 2r multicolored 1.00 .25
Nos. 1558-1560 (3) 3.00 .75

Signing of the Regional Cooperation for Development Pact by Iran, Turkey and Pakistan, 6th anniv.

Queen Buran, Dirhem Coin A345

Wine Goblet with Lion's Head — A346

Designs: No. 1562, Achaemenian eagle amulet. No. 1563, Mithridates I, dirhem coin. No. 1564, Sassanidae art (arch, coin, jugs). No. 1566, Shapur I, dirhem coin. No. 1567, Achaemenian courier. No. 1568, Winged deer. No. 1569, Ardashir I, dirhem coin. No. 1570, Seal of Darius I (chariot, palms, lion). 14r, Achaemenian tapestry.

1970 Wmk. 353 Photo. *Perf. 13*

1561 A345 1r gold & multi 1.25 .50
1562 A346 2r gold & multi 1.50 .40
1563 A345 2r gold & multi 1.50 .50
1564 A346 2r lilac & multi 1.50 .50
1565 A346 6r lilac & multi 1.75 .40
1566 A345 6r lilac & multi 1.75 .60
1567 A345 6r lilac & multi 2.00 .60
1568 A346 8r lilac & multi 2.00 .50
1569 A345 8r lilac & multi 2.00 .75
1570 A345 8r lilac & multi 2.25 .75
1571 A345 14r lt bl & multi 2.50 1.10
Nos. 1561-1571 (11) 20.00 6.60

2500th anniversary of the founding of the Persian Empire by Cyrus the Great.
Issued: 1r, #1563, 1566, 1569, 8/22; #1562, 1565, 1568, 14r, 8/6; others, 9/22.

Candle and Globe — A347

Persian Decoration A348

1970, Sept. 8 Litho. *Perf. 10½*

1572 A347 1r lt bl & multi .25 .20
1573 A347 2r pale sal & multi .30 .20

Issued to publicize World Literacy Day.

1970, Sept. 14

1574 A348 6r multi .45 .20

Isfahan Intl. Cong. of Architects, Sept. 1970.

Emblem — A349

UN Emblem, Dove and Scales — A350

1970, Sept. 28 *Perf. 10½*

1575 A349 2r lt bl & pur .30 .20

Congress of Election Committees of Persian States and Tehran.

1970, Oct. 24 Litho. Wmk. 353

1576 A350 2r lt bl, mag & dk bl .30 .20

Issued for United Nations Day.

Festival Type of 1969

1970, Oct. 28 *Perf. 10½*

1577 A328 2r org & multi .40 .20

3rd Festival of Arts and Culture.

UNICEF Type of 1969

Children's Drawings and UNICEF Emblem: 50d, Herdsman and goats. 1r, Family picnic. 2r, Mosque.

1970, Oct. 31

Size: 43½x31mm

1578 A329 50d black & multi .25 .20
1579 A329 1r black & multi .30 .20
1580 A329 2r black & multi .45 .20
Nos. 1578-1580 (3) 1.00 .60

Issued for Children's Week.

Shah Mohammed Riza Pahlavi A351

1971, Jan. 26 Wmk. 353 *Perf. 10½*

1581 A351 2r lt bl & multi 3.00 .75

Publicizing the "White Revolution of King and People" and the 12 reform laws.

Sheldrake — A352

2r, Ruddy shelduck. 8r, Flamingo, vert.

1971, Jan. 30 Litho.

1582 A352 1r multicolored 1.25 .30
1583 A352 2r multicolored 1.50 .40
1584 A352 8r multicolored 2.75 .80
Nos. 1582-1584 (3) 5.50 1.50

Intl. Wetland and Waterfowl Conf., Ramsar.

Riza Shah Pahlavi — A353

1971, Feb. 22 Wmk. 353 *Perf. 10½*
1585 A353 6r multicolored 4.50 1.25

50th anniversary of the Pahlavi dynasty's accession to power.

Rooster A354

2r, Barn swallow and nest. 6r, Hoopoe.

1971, Mar. 6 Photo. *Perf. 13½x13*

1586 A354 1r multicolored	1.00	.30
1587 A354 2r multicolored	1.50	.40
1588 A354 6r multicolored	2.75	.80
Nos. 1586-1588 (3)	5.25	1.50

Novrooz, Iranian New Year.

Shapur II Hunting — A355

Bull's Head, Persepolis A356

1r, Harpist, mosaic. #1591, Investiture of Ardashir I, bas-relief. 5r Winged lion ornament. 6r, Persian archer, bas-relief. 8r, Royal audience, bas-relief. 10r, Bronze head of Parthian prince.

1971 Litho. *Perf. 10½*

1589 A356 1r multicolored	1.50	.45
1590 A355 2r blk & brn org	1.75	.45
1591 A355 2r lil, gldn brn & blk	1.75	.45
1592 A356 4r pur & multi	1.75	.45
1593 A356 5r multicolored	2.00	.55
1594 A356 6r multicolored	2.00	.55
1595 A356 8r lt bl & multi	2.75	.80
1596 A356 10r dp bis, blk & slate	2.75	.90
Nos. 1589-1596 (8)	16.25	4.60

2500th anniversary of the founding of the Persian Empire by Cyrus the Great.
Issued: 4r, 5r, 6r, 8r, 5/15; others, 6/15.

Prisoners Leaving Jail — A357

1971, May 20 Litho. Wmk. 353
1597 A357 6r multicolored 1.75 .20
1598 A357 8r multicolored 3.00 .20

Rehabilitation of Prisoners Week.

Religious School, Chaharbagh, Ispahan A358

#1600, Mosque of Selim, Edirne, Turkey. #1601, Badshahi Mosque, Lahore, Pakistan, horiz.

1971, July 21 Litho. *Perf. 10½*

1599 A358 2r multicolored	.40	.20
1600 A358 2r multicolored	.40	.20
1601 A358 2r multicolored	.40	.20
Nos. 1599-1601 (3)	1.20	.60

7th anniversary of Regional Cooperation among Iran, Pakistan and Turkey.

"Fifth Festival of Arts" — A359

1971, Aug. 26 Litho. & Typo.
1602 A359 2r lt & dk grn, red & gold .70 .20

5th Festival of Arts, Shiraz-Persepolis.

"Fight Against Illiteracy" — A360

1971, Sept. 8 Litho.
1603 A360 2r grn & multi .50 .20

International Literacy Day, Sept. 8.

Kings Abdullah and Hussein II of Jordan A361

1971, Sept. 11
1604 A361 2r yel grn, blk & red .50 .25

Hashemite Kingdom of Jordan, 50th anniv.

Shahyad Aryamehr Monument — A362

Designs: 1r, Aryamehr steel mill, near Isfahan. 3r, Senate Building, Tehran. 11r, Shah Abbas Kabir Dam, Zayandeh River.

1971, Sept. 22

1605 A362 1r blue & multi	1.50	.45
1606 A362 2r multicolored	1.75	.45
1607 A362 3r brt pink & multi	1.75	.45
1608 A362 11r org & multi	2.50	.90
Nos. 1605-1608 (4)	7.50	2.25

2500th anniversary of the founding of the Persian empire by Cyrus the Great.

Shah Mohammed Riza Pahlavi — A363

Designs: 2r, Riza Shah Pahlavi. 5r, Stone tablet with proclamation of Cyrus the Great, horiz. 10r, Crown of present empire (erroneously inscribed *Le* Couronne).

1971, Oct. 12

1609 A363 1r gold & multi	4.00	2.00
1610 A363 2r gold & multi	4.00	2.00
1611 A363 5r gold & multi	5.00	2.50
1612 A363 10r gold & multi	6.00	3.00
Nos. 1609-1612 (4)	19.00	9.50

2500th anniversary of the founding of the Persian empire by Cyrus the Great.

Ghatour Railroad Bridge — A364

1971, Oct. 7
1613 A364 2r multicolored 1.50 .50

Iran-Turkey railroad.

Racial Equality Emblem A365

Mohammed Riza Pahlavi — A366

1971, Oct. 24
1614 A365 2r lt blue & multi .25 .20

Intl. Year Against Racial Discrimination.

Perf. 13½x13
1971, Oct. 26 Photo. Wmk. 353
Size: 20½x28mm

1615 A366 5d lilac	.20	.20
1616 A366 10d henna brown	.20	.20
1617 A366 50d brt bl grn	.25	.20
1618 A366 1r dp yel grn	.30	.20
1619 A366 2r brown	.30	.20

Size: 27x36½mm

1620 A366 6r slate green	1.10	.20
1621 A366 8r violet blue	1.60	1.10
1622 A366 10r red lilac	1.40	.30
1623 A366 11r blue green	5.00	1.10
1624 A366 14r brt blue	8.50	.50
1625 A366 20r car rose	8.00	.65
1626 A366 50r yellow bis	6.75	1.25
Nos. 1615-1626 (12)	33.60	6.10

See Nos. 1650-1661B, 1768-1772.

Child's Drawing and Emblem — A367

Designs: No. 1631, Ruins of Persepolis, vert. No. 1632, Warrior, mosaic, vert.

1971, Oct. 31 Litho. *Perf. 10½*

1630 A367 2r multicolored	.40	.20
1631 A367 2r multicolored	.40	.20
1632 A367 2r multicolored	.40	.20
Nos. 1630-1632 (3)	1.20	.60

Children's Week.

UNESCO Emblem and "25" A368

1971, Nov. 4
1633 A368 6r ultra & rose claret .50 .20

25th anniversary of UNESCO.

Domestic Animals and Emblem A369

1971, Nov. 22
1634 A369 2r gray, blk & car .40 .20

4th Iranian Veterinarians' Congress.

ILO Emblem, Cog Wheels and Globe A370

1971, Dec. 4
1635 A370 2r black, org & bl .40 .20

7th ILO Conference for the Asian Region.

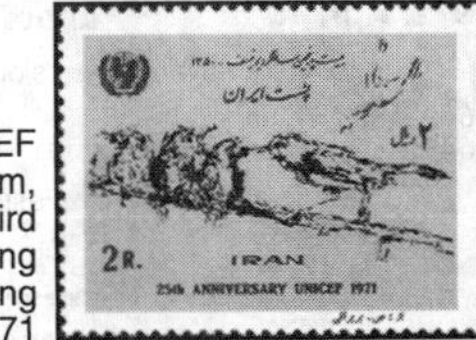
UNICEF Emblem, Bird Feeding Young A371

1971, Dec. 16 *Perf. 13x13½*
1636 A371 2r lt bl, mag & blk .40 .20

25th anniversary of UNICEF.

Mohammed Riza Pahlavi A372

1972, Jan. 26 Wmk. 353 *Perf. 10½*

1637 A372 2r lt green & multi	3.00	1.00
a. 20r Souvenir sheet	12.00	8.00

"White Revolution of King and People" and the 12 reform laws. No. 1637a contains one stamp with simulated perforations.

Pintailed Sandgrouse — A373

#1639, Rock ptarmigan. 2r, Yellow-billed waxbill and red-cheeked cordon-bleu.

1972, Mar. 6 Litho. *Perf. 13x13½*

1638 A373 1r lt green & multi	.75	.30
1639 A373 1r lt blue & multi	.75	.30
1640 A373 2r yellow & multi	1.50	.40
Nos. 1638-1640 (3)	3.00	1.00

Iranian New Year.

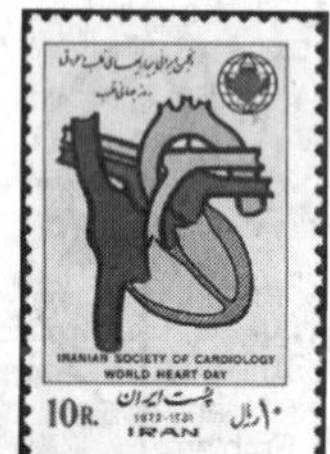

"Your Heart is your Health" — A374

Film Strip and Winged Antelope A375

1972, Apr. 4 *Perf. 10½*

1641 A374 10r lemon & multi	2.00	.30

World Health Day; Iranian Society of Cardiology.

1972, Apr. 16 Litho. & Engr.

8r, Film strips and winged antelope.

1642 A375 6r ultra & gold	1.00	.30
1643 A375 8r yellow & multi	1.75	.35

Tehran International Film Festival.

Rose and Bud — A376

1972, May 5 Litho.

1644 A376 1r shown	.35	.25
1645 A376 2r Yellow roses	.65	.25
1646 A376 5r Red rose	.80	.25
Nos. 1644-1646 (3)	1.80	.75

See Nos. 1711-1713.

Persian Woman, by Behzad A377

Paintings: No. 1648, Fisherman, by Cevat Dereli (Turkey). No. 1649, Young Man, by Abdur Rehman Chughtai (Pakistan).

1972, July 21 Wmk. 353

1647 A377 5r gray & multi	1.40	.30
1648 A377 5r gray & multi	1.40	.30
1649 A377 5r gray & multi	1.40	.30
Nos. 1647-1649 (3)	4.20	.90

Regional Cooperation for Development Pact among Iran, Turkey and Pakistan, 8th anniv.

Shah Type of 1971

1972-73 Photo. *Perf. 13½x13*

Bister Frame & Crown

Size: 20½x28mm

1650	A366 5d lilac	.20	.20
1651	A366 10d henna brown	.20	.20
1652	A366 50d brt blue grn	.25	.20
1653	A366 1r dp yel grn	.30	.20
a.	Brn frame & crown ('73)	.55	.20
1654	A366 2r brown	.50	.20

Size: 27x36½mm

1655	A366 6r slate grn	.75	.20
1656	A366 8r violet blue	.75	.20
1657	A366 10r red lilac	1.00	.20
1658	A366 11r blue green	1.40	.80
1659	A366 14r dull blue	5.50	.60
1660	A366 20r car rose	8.50	.50
1661	A366 50r grnsh blue	3.75	1.00
1661A	A366 100r violet ('73)	5.00	2.00
1661B	A366 200r slate ('73)	11.00	3.50
	Nos. 1650-1661B (14)	39.10	10.00

Festival Emblem A378

1972, Aug. 31 Litho. *Perf. 10½*

1662 A378 6r emerald, red & blk	1.10	.20
1663 A378 8r brt mag, blk & grn	1.60	.25

6th Festival of Arts, Shiraz-Persepolis, Aug. 31-Sept. 8.

Pens and Emblem A379

"10" and Emblems A380

1972, Sept. 8

1664 A379 1r lt blue & multi	.25	.20
1665 A379 2r yellow & multi	.40	.20

World Literacy Day, Sept. 8.

1972, Sept. 18

1666 A380 1r lilac & multi	.25	.20
1667 A380 2r dull yel & multi	.45	.25

10th Congress of Iranian Dentists' Assoc., Sept. 18-22.

Asian Broadcasting Union Emblem — A381

No. 450 on Cover — A382

1972, Oct. 1

1668 A381 6r lt green & multi	.75	.20
1669 A381 8r gray & multi	1.50	.20

9th General Assembly of Asian Broadcasting Union, Tehran, Oct. 1972.

1972, Oct. 9

1670 A382 10r lt blue & multi	2.25	.25

International Stamp Day.

Chess and Olympic Rings — A383

Olympic Rings and: 2r, Hunter. 3r, Archer. 5r, Equestrians. 6r, Polo. 8r, Wrestling.

1972, Oct. 17

1671 A383 1r brown & multi	2.00	1.50
1672 A383 2r blue & multi	2.00	.50
1673 A383 3r lilac & multi	2.50	.50
1674 A383 5r bl grn & multi	2.50	.75
1675 A383 6r red & multi	2.50	.75
1676 A383 8r yel grn & multi	2.50	.75
a. Souv. sheet of 6, #1671-1676, imperf.	15.00	10.00
Nos. 1671-1676 (6)	14.00	4.75

20th Olympic Games, Munich, 8/26-9/11.

Communications Symbol, UN Emblem — A384

Children and Flowers — A385

1972, Oct. 24

1677 A384 10r multicolored	2.00	.20

United Nations Day.

1972, Oct. 31 Litho. Wmk. 353

Children's Drawings and Emblem: No. 1679, Puppet show. 6r, Boys cutting wood, horiz.

1678 A385 2r gray & multi	.35	.20
1679 A385 2r bister & multi	.70	.20
1680 A385 6r pink & multi	1.40	.20
Nos. 1678-1680 (3)	2.45	.60

Children's Week.

Festival Type of 1969

Design: 10r, Crown, emblems and column capital, Persepolis.

1972, Nov. 11

1681 A328 10r dp blue & multi	6.00	1.00

10th anniv. of White Revolution; Festival of Culture and Art.

Family Planning Emblem A386

1972, Dec. 5

1682 A386 1r blue & multi	.30	.20
1683 A386 2r brt pink & multi	.40	.20

To promote family planning.

Iranian Scout Organization, 20th anniv. — A387

1972, Dec. 9

1684 A387 2r multicolored	.50	.20

Ancient Seal A388

Designs: Various ancient seals.

1973, Jan. 5 *Perf. 10½*

1685 A388 1r blue, red & brn	.60	.20
1686 A388 1r yellow & multi	.60	.20
1687 A388 1r pink & multi	.60	.20
1688 A388 2r lt brick red & multi	.60	.20
1689 A388 2r dull org & multi	.60	.20
1690 A388 2r olive & multi	.60	.20
Nos. 1685-1690 (6)	3.60	1.20

Development of writing.

Books and Book Year Emblem A389

Design: 6r, Illuminated page, 10th century, from Shahnameh, by Firdousi.

1973, Jan. 10

1691 A389 2r black & multi .75 .20
1692 A389 6r yellow & multi 1.10 .20

International Book Year.

"12 Improvements by the King" — A390

Designs: 2r, 10r, 12 circles symbolizing 12 improvements. 6r, like 1r.

1973, Jan. 26 **Litho.**

Size: 29x43mm

1693 A390 1r gold, ultra, red & yel .30 .20
1694 A390 2r sil, plum, ol & yel .35 .20

Size: 65x84mm

1695 A390 6r gold, ultra, red & yel 2.00 1.00
Nos. 1693-1695 (3) 2.65 1.40

Souvenir Sheet

Imperf

1696 A390 10r sil, plum, ol & yel 3.25 1.50

Introduction of the King's socioeconomic reforms, 10th anniv.

Blue Surgeonfish A391

Fish: No. 1698, Gilthead. No. 1699, Banded sergeant major. No. 1700, Porkfish. No. 1701, Black-spot snapper.

1973, Mar. 6 **Wmk. 353** ***Perf. 10½***

1697 A391 1r multicolored .65 .20
1698 A391 1r multicolored .65 .20
1699 A391 2r multicolored .95 .20
1700 A391 2r multicolored .95 .20
1701 A391 2r multicolored .95 .20
Nos. 1697-1701 (5) 4.15 1.00

Iranian New Year.

WHO Emblem A392

1973, Apr. 7 **Litho.** **Wmk. 353**

1702 A392 10r brn, grn & red 1.25 .20

25th anniversary of the WHO.

Soccer — A393

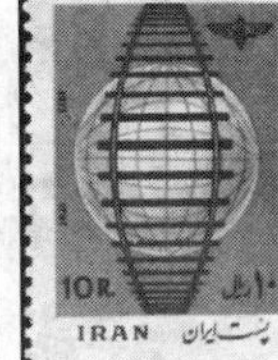

Tracks and Globe — A394

1973, Apr. 13

1703 A393 14r orange & multi 1.40 .25

15th Asian Youth Football (soccer) Tournament.

1973, May 10 **Wmk. 353** ***Perf. 10½***

1704 A394 10r dk grn, lil & vio bl 1.50 .40

13th International Railroad Conference.

Clay Tablet with Aryan Script — A395

Designs: Clay tablets with various scripts.

1973, June 5 ***Perf. 10½***

1705 A395 1r shown .50 .20
1706 A395 1r Kharoshthi .50 .20
1707 A395 1r Achaemenian .50 .20
1708 A395 2r Parthian (Mianeh) .90 .20
1709 A395 2r Parthian (Arsacide) .90 .20
1710 A395 2r Gachtak (Dabireh) .90 .20
Nos. 1705-1710 (6) 4.20 1.20

Development of writing.

Flower Type of 1972

1973, June 20

1711 A376 1r Orchid .20 .20
1712 A376 2r Hyacinth .55 .20
1713 A376 6r Columbine 1.25 .20
Nos. 1711-1713 (3) 2.00 .60

Regional Cooperation for Development Pact Among Iran, Turkey and Pakistan, 9th Anniv. — A396

Designs: No. 1714, Head from mausoleum of King Antiochus I (69-34 B.C.), Turkey. No. 1715, Statue, Shahdad Kerman, Persia, 4000 B.C. No. 1716, Street, Mohenjo-Daro, Pakistan.

1973, July 21

1714 A396 2r brown & multi .35 .20
1715 A396 2r green & multi .35 .20
1716 A396 2r blue & multi .35 .20
a. Strip of 3, #1714-1716 1.25 .75

Shah, Oil Pump, Refinery and Tanker A397

1973, Aug. 4

1717 A397 5r blue & black 1.75 .50

Nationalization of oil industry.

Soldiers and Rising Sun — A398

1973, Aug. 19 **Litho.** **Wmk. 353**

1718 A398 2r ultra & multi .45 .20

20th anniversary of return of monarchy.

Gymnasts and Globe — A399

1973, Aug. 23 ***Perf. 10½***

1719 A399 2r olive & multi .30 .20
1720 A399 2r violet bl & multi .30 .20

7th Intl. Congress of Physical Education and Sports for Girls and Women, Tehran, Aug. 19-25.

Shahyad Monument (later Azadi Monument), Rainbow and WMO Emblem — A400

1973, Sept. 4

1721 A400 5r multicolored .75 .20

Intl. meteorological cooperation, centenary.

Festival Emblem — A401

1973, Aug. 31

1722 A401 1r silver & multi .30 .20
1723 A401 5r gold & multi .50 .20

7th Festival of Arts, Shiraz-Persepolis.

Wrestlers A402

1973, Sept. 6 **Litho.** **Wmk. 353**

1724 A402 6r lt green & multi .85 .30

World Wrestling Championships, Tehran, Sept. 6-14.

"Literacy as Light" — A403

1973, Sept. 8

1725 A403 2r multicolored .30 .20

World Literacy Day, Sept. 8.

Audio-Visual Equipment A404

1973, Sept. 11

1726 A404 10r yellow & multi .80 .25

Tehran Intl. Audio-Visual Exhib., Sept. 11-24.

Warrior Taming Winged Bull A405

1973, Sept. 16

1727 A405 8r blue gray & multi .75 .20

Intl. Council of Military Sports, 25th anniv.

abu-al-Rayhan al-Biruni (973-1048), Philosopher and Mathematician A406

1973, Sept. 16

1728 A406 10r brown & black 1.10 .35

Soccer Cup — A407

1973, Oct. 2 Wmk. 353 *Perf. 10½*

1729 A407 2r lilac, blk & buff .35 .20

Soccer Games for the Crown Prince's Cup.

INTERPOL Emblem — A408

1973, Oct. 7

1730 A408 2r multicolored .35 .20

50th anniversary of INTERPOL.

Symbolic Arches and Globe A409

1973, Oct. 8

1731 A409 10r orange & multi .55 .25

World Federation for Mental Health, 25th anniv.

UPU Emblem, Letter, Post Horn — A410

1973, Oct. 9

1732 A410 6r blue & orange .50 .20

World Post Day, Oct. 9.

Honeycomb A411

1973, Oct. 24

1733 A411 2r lt brown & multi .30 .20
1734 A411 2r gray olive & multi .30 .20

UN Volunteer Program, 5th anniv.

Festival Type of 1969

2r, Crown & column capital, Persepolis.

1973, Oct. 26

1735 A328 2r yellow & multi .40 .20

Festival of Culture and Art.

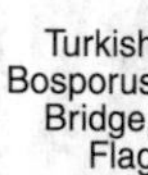

Turkish Bosporus Bridge, Flag A412

8r, Kemal Ataturk & Riza Shah Pahlavi.

1973, Oct. 29 Litho. *Perf. 10½*

1736 A412 2r multicolored .75 .20
1737 A412 8r multicolored 1.25 .25

50th anniversary of the Turkish Republic.

Mother and Child, Emblem — A413

Children's Drawings and Emblem: No. 1739, Wagon, horiz. No. 1740, House and garden with birds.

1973, Oct. 31

1738 A413 2r multicolored .30 .20
1739 A413 2r multicolored .30 .20
1740 A413 2r multicolored .30 .20
Nos. 1738-1740 (3) .90 .60

Children's Week.

Cow, Wheat and FAO Emblem A414

1973, Nov. 4

1741 A414 10r multicolored 1.00 .20

10th anniversary of World Food Program.

Proclamation of Cyrus the Great; Red Cross, Lion and Crescent Emblems A415

1973, Nov. 8

1742 A415 6r lt blue & multi .75 .20

22nd Intl. Red Cross Conf., Tehran, 1972.

"Film Festival" — A416

1973, Nov. 26 Wmk. 353 *Perf. 10½*

1743 A416 2r black & multi .35 .20

2nd International Tehran Film Festival.

Globe and Travelers — A417

1973, Nov. 26 Litho.

1744 A417 10r orange & multi .60 .20

12th annual Congress of Intl. Assoc. of Tour Managers.

Human Rights Flame A418

Score and Emblem — A419

1973, Dec. 10

1745 A418 8r lt blue & multi .75 .20

Universal Declaration of Human Rights, 25th anniv.

1973, Dec. 21

Design: No. 1747, Score and emblem, diff.

1746 A419 10r yel grn, red & blk .75 .25
1747 A419 10r lt bl, ultra & red .75 .25

Dedicated to the art of music.

Forestry, Printing, Education — A420

Designs (Symbols of Reforms): No. 1749, Land reform, sales of shares, women's suffrage. No. 1750, Army of progress, irrigation, women's education. No. 1751, Hygiene, rural courts, housing.

1974, Jan. 26 Litho. *Perf. 10½*

1748 1r lt blue & multi .20 .20
1749 1r lt blue & multi .20 .20
1750 2r lt blue & multi .25 .20
1751 2r lt blue & multi .25 .20
a. A420 Block of 4, #1748-1751 1.25 .90

Imperf

Size: 76½x102mm

1752 A420 20r multicolored 4.00 2.00

"White Revolution of King and People" and 12 reform laws.

Pir Amooz Ketabaty Script — A421

Various Scripts: No. 1754, Mo Eghely Ketabaty. No. 1755, Din Dabireh, Avesta script. No. 1756, Pir Amooz, Naskh style. No. 1757, Pir Amooz, decorative style. No. 1758, Decorative and architectural style.

1974, Feb. 14 Wmk. 353 *Perf. 10½*

1753 A421 1r silver, ocher & multi .75 .30
1754 A421 1r gold, gray & multi .75 .30
1755 A421 1r silver, yel & multi .75 .30
1756 A421 2r gold, gray & multi .75 .30
1757 A421 2r gold, slate & multi .75 .30
1758 A421 2r gold, claret & multi .75 .30
Nos. 1753-1758 (6) 4.50 1.80

Development of writing.

Fowl, Syringe and Emblem A422

1974, Feb. 23

1759 A422 6r red brown & multi .60 .20

5th Iranian Veterinary Congress.

Monarch Butterfly A423

Designs: Various butterflies.

1974, Mar. 6 Litho. *Perf. 10½*

1760 A423 1r rose lilac & multi .80 .20
1761 A423 1r brt rose & multi .80 .20
1762 A423 2r lt blue & multi 1.00 .30
1763 A423 2r green & multi 1.00 .30
1764 A423 2r bister & multi 1.00 .30
Nos. 1760-1764 (5) 4.60 1.30

Novrooz, Iranian New Year.

Jalaludin Mevlana (1207-1273), Poet — A424

1974, Mar. 12 *Perf. 13*

1765 A424 2r pale violet & multi .50 .25

Shah Type of 1971

1974 Photo. *Perf. 13½x13*

Size: 20½x28mm

1768 A366 50d orange & bl .45 .20
1769 A366 1r emerald & bl .50 .20
1770 A366 2r red & blue .80 .20

Size: 27x36½mm

1771 A366 10r lt green & bl 7.00 .20
1772 A366 20r lilac & bl 4.25 .20
Nos. 1768-1772 (5) 13.00 1.00

Palace of the Forty Columns, Hippocrates, Avicenna — A425

1974, Apr. 11 Litho. *Perf. 10½*
1773 A425 10r multicolored .75 .20

9th Medical Congress of the Near and Middle East, Isfahan.

Onager — A426

Athlete and Games Emblem — A427

1974, Apr. 13

1774 A426 1r shown	.50	.20
1775 A426 2r Great bustard	.75	.20
1776 A426 6r Fawn and deer	1.50	.35
1777 A426 8r Caucasian black grouse	2.25	.40
a. Strip of 4, #1774-1777	6.00	3.00

Intl. Council for Game and Wildlife Preservation.

1974, Apr. 30

1778 A427 1r shown	.55	.20
1779 A427 1r Table tennis	.55	.20
1780 A427 2r Boxing	1.00	.20
1781 A427 2r Hurdles	1.00	.20
1782 A427 6r Weight lifting	1.60	.20
1783 A427 8r Basketball	2.50	.20
Nos. 1778-1783 (6)	7.20	1.20

7th Asian Games, Tehran; first issue.

Lion of Venice — A428

Painting: 8r, Audience with the Doge of Venice.

1974, May 5

1784 A428 6r multicolored	.55	.25
1785 A428 8r multicolored	1.00	.35

Safeguarding Venice.

Links and Grain — A429

1974, May 13 Litho. *Perf. 10½*
1786 A429 2r multicolored .30 .20

Cooperation Day.

Military Plane, 1924 A430

1974, June 1

1787 A430 10r shown	2.00	.40
1788 A430 10r Jet, 1974	2.00	.40

50th anniversary of Iranian Air Force.

Swimmer and Games Emblem A431

Bicyclists and Games Emblem A432

1974, July 1 Wmk. 353 *Perf. 10½*

1789 A431 1r shown	.65	.20
1790 A431 1r Tennis, men's doubles	.65	.20
1791 A431 2r Wrestling	.80	.20
1792 A431 2r Hockey	.80	.20
1793 A431 4r Volleyball	1.25	.40
1794 A431 10r Tennis, women's singles	2.50	.50
Nos. 1789-1794 (6)	6.65	1.70

7th Asian Games, Tehran; second issue.

1974, Aug. 1

1795 A432 2r shown	.90	.20
1796 A432 2r Soccer	.90	.20
1797 A432 2r Fencing	.90	.20
1798 A432 2r Small-bore rifle shooting	.90	.20
Nos. 1795-1798 (4)	3.60	.80

7th Asian Games, Tehran; third issue.

Ghaskai Costume — A433

Gold Winged Lion Cup — A434

Regional Costumes: No. 1800, Kurdistan, Kermanshah District. No. 1801, Kurdistan, Sanandaj District. No. 1802, Mazandaran. No. 1803, Bakhtiari. No. 1804, Torkaman.

1974, July 6

1799 A433 2r lt ultra & multi	1.40	.50
1800 A433 2r buff & multi	1.40	.50
1801 A433 2r green & multi	1.40	.50
1802 A433 2r lt blue & multi	1.40	.50
1803 A433 2r gray & multi	1.40	.50
1804 A433 2r dull grn & multi	1.40	.50
a. Block of 6, #1799-1804	8.50	4.50

1974, July 13
1805 A434 2r dull green & multi .30 .20

Iranian Soccer Cup.

Tabriz Rug, Late 16th Century — A435

King Carrying Vases, Bas-relief — A436

Designs: No. 1807, Anatolian rug, 15th century. No. 1808, Kashan rug, Lahore.

1974, July 21

1806 A435 2r brown & multi	.45	.20
1807 A435 2r blue & multi	.45	.20
1808 A435 2r red & multi	.45	.20
a. Strip of 3, #1806-1808	1.40	.30

Regional Cooperation for Development Pact among Iran, Turkey and Pakistan, 10th anniv.

1974, Aug. 15 Litho. *Perf. 10½*
1809 A436 2r black & multi .30 .20

8th Iranian Arts Festival, Shiraz-Persepolis.

Aryamehr Stadium, Tehran — A437

#1811, Games' emblem and inscription. #1812, Aerial view of games' site.

1974
1810 A437 6r multicolored 1.00 .20

Souvenir Sheets

1811 A437 10r multicolored	*3.00*	*1.50*
1812 A437 10r multicolored	*3.00*	*1.50*

7th Asian Games, Tehran; fourth and fifth issues. Nos. 1811-1812 contain one imperf 51x38mm stamp each.
Issued: #1811-1812, 9/1; #1810, 9/16.

"Welfare" — A438

"Education" A439

1974, Sept. 11

1813 A438 2r orange & multi	.30	.20
1814 A439 2r blue & multi	.30	.20

Welfare and free education.

Map of Hasanlu, 1000-800 B.C. — A440

1974, Sept. 24
1815 A440 8r multicolored .70 .20

2nd Intl. Congress of Architecture, Shiraz-Persepolis, Sept. 1974.

Achaemenian Mail Cart and UPU Emblem — A441

Design: 14r, UPU emblem and letters.

1974, Oct. 9 Wmk. 353 *Perf. 10½*

1816 A441 6r orange, grn & blk	1.00	.40
1817 A441 14r multicolored	1.50	.50

Centenary of Universal Postal Union.

Road Through Farahabad Park — A442

1974, Oct. 16

1818 A442 1r shown	.30	.20
1819 A442 2r Recreation Bldg.	.35	.20

Inauguration of Farahabad Park, Tehran.

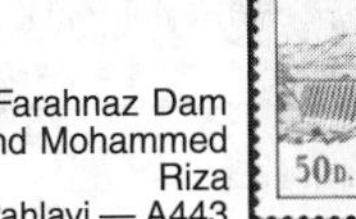
Farahnaz Dam and Mohammed Riza Pahlavi — A443

Designs: 5d, Kharg Island petro-chemical plant. 10d, Ghatour Railroad Bridge. 1r, Tehran oil refinery. 2r, Satellite communication station, Hamadan, and Mt. Alvand. 6r, Aryamehr steel mill, Isfahan. 8r, University of

Tabriz. 10r, Shah Abbas Kabir Dam. 14r, Rudagi (later Vahdat) Music Hall. 20r, Shayad Monument. 50r, Aryamehr Stadium.

1974-75 Photo. *Perf. 13x13½*
Size: 28x21mm
Frame & Shah in Brown

1820 A443 5d slate green .30 .20
1821 A443 10d orange .30 .20
1822 A443 50d blue green .30 .20
1823 A443 1r ultra .30 .20
1824 A443 2r deep lilac .30 .20

Size: 36x26½mm
Frame & Shah in Dark Blue

1825 A443 6r brown .50 .25
1826 A443 8r grnsh blue .50 .25
1827 A443 10r deep lilac .80 .35
 a. Value in Farsi omitted *30.00* 30.00
1828 A443 14r deep green 17.00 .60
1829 A443 20r magenta 3.50 .50
1830 A443 50r violet 4.50 1.40
 Nos. 1820-1830 (11) 28.30 4.35

Issued: 50d, 1r, 2r, 10/16/74; 14r, 11/1974; others 3/6/75.

See Nos. 1831-1841. For overprints see Nos. 2008, 2010.

1975-77
Size: 28x21mm
Frame & Shah in Green

1831 A443 5d orange ('77) .30 .20
1832 A443 10d rose mag ('77) .30 .20
1833 A443 50d lilac .30 .20
1834 A443 1r dark blue .30 .20
1835 A443 2r brown .30 .20

Size: 36x26½mm
Frame & Shah in Brown

1836 A443 6r vio bl ('76) .40 .35
1837 A443 8r deep org ('77) 2.00 .30
1838 A443 10r dp yel grn ('76) 1.60 .20
1839 A443 14r lilac 8.00 .20
1840 A443 20r brt green ('76) 3.50 .40
1841 A443 50r dp blue ('76) 3.00 .90
 Nos. 1831-1841 (11) 20.00 3.35

Festival Emblem, Crown and Column Capital, Persepolis — A444

1974, Oct. 26 Litho. *Perf. 10½*

1842 A444 2r multicolored .40 .20

Festival of Culture and Art.

Destroyer "Palang" and Flag — A445

1974, Nov. 5

1843 A445 10r multicolored 1.50 .35

Navy Day.

Girl at Spinning Wheel A446

Designs: Children's drawings.

1974, Nov. 7 *Perf. 10½*

1844 A446 2r shown .35 .20
1845 A446 2r Scarecrow, vert. .35 .20
1846 A446 2r Picnic .35 .20
 Nos. 1844-1846 (3) 1.05 .60

Children's Week.

Winged Ibex — A447

1974, Nov. 25 Litho. Wmk. 353

1847 A447 2r vio, org & blk .35 .20

Third Tehran International Film Festival.

WPY Emblem A448

1974, Dec. 1

1848 A448 8r orange & multi .60 .20

World Population Year.

Gold Bee A449

Design: 8r, Gold crown, gift of French people to Empress Farah. Bee pin was gift of the Italian people.

1974, Dec. 20

1849 A449 6r multicolored .70 .30
1850 A449 8r multicolored .90 .35

14th wedding anniv. of Shah and Empress Farah.

Angel with Banner — A450

1975, Jan. 7 Litho. *Perf. 10½*

1851 A450 2r org & vio bl .30 .20

International Women's Year.

Symbols of Agriculture, Industry and the Arts — A451

1975, Jan. 26 Wmk. 353

1852 A451 2r multicolored .30 .20

"White Revolution of King and People."

Tourism Year 75 Emblem — A452

1975, Feb. 17

1853 A452 6r multicolored .30 .20

South Asia Tourism Year.

"Farabi" in Shape of Musical Instrument or Alembic — A453

1975, Mar. 1

1854 A453 2r brn red & multi .30 .20

Abu-Nasr al-Farabi (870?-950), physician, musician and philosopher, 1100th birth anniversary.

Ornament, Rug Pattern — A454

1975, Mar. 6

1855 A454 1r shown .25 .20
1856 A454 1r Blossoms and cypress trees .25 .20
1857 A454 1r Shah Abbasi flower .25 .20
 a. Strip of 3, #1855-1857 1.00 .60

Novrooz, Iranian New Year. Nos. 1855-1857 printed in sheets of 45 stamps + 5 labels.

Nasser Khosrov, Poet, Birth Millenary — A455

Formula — A456

1975, Mar. 11

1858 A455 2r blk, gold & red .30 .20

1975, May 5 Litho. *Perf. 10½*

1859 A456 2r buff & multi .40 .20

5th Biennial Symposium of Iranian Biochemical Society.

Charioteer, Bas-relief, Persepolis — A457

Design: 2r, Heads of Persian warriors, bas-relief from Persepolis, vert.

1975, May 5

1860 A457 2r lt brn & multi 1.75 .50
1861 A457 10r blue & multi 3.75 1.00

Rotary International, 70th anniversary.

Signal Fire, Persian Castle A458

Design: 8r, Communications satellite.

1975, May 17

1862 A458 6r multicolored .70 .30
1863 A458 8r lil & multi .80 .40

7th World Telecommunications Day.

Cooperation Day — A459

1975, May 13

1864 A459 2r multicolored .30 .20

Jet, Shayad Monument, Statue of Liberty — A460

1975, May 29 Litho. Wmk. 353

1865 A460 10r org & multi .80 .40

Iran Air's 1st flight to New York, May 1975.

Emblem — A461

1975, June 5

1866 A461 6r blue & multi .45 .20

World Environment Day.

Dam A462

1975, June 10

1867 A462 10r multicolored .70 .20

9th Intl. Congress on Irrigation & Drainage.

Resurgence Party Emblem — A463

Girl Scout Symbols A464

1975, July 1 Wmk. 353 ***Perf. 10½***

1868 A463 2r multicolored .30 .20

Organization of Resurgence Party.

1975, July 16

1869 A464 2r multicolored .50 .25

2nd Natl Girl Scout Camp, Tehran, July 1976.

Festival of Tus — A465

1975, July 17

1870 A465 2r gray, lil & vio .30 .20

Festival of Tus in honor of Firdausi (940-1020), Persian poet born near Tus in Khorasan.

Ceramic Plate, Iran A466

#1872, Camel leather vase, Pakistan, vert. #1873, Porcelain vase, Turkey, vert.

1975, July 21

1871 A466 2r bister & multi .35 .20
1872 A466 2r bister & multi .35 .20
1873 A466 2r bister & multi .35 .20
Nos. 1871-1873 (3) 1.05 .60

Regional Cooperation for Development Pact among Iran, Pakistan and Turkey.

Majlis Gate A467

1975, Aug. 5 Litho. ***Perf. 10½***

1874 A467 10r multi .75 .20

Iranian Constitution, 70th anniversary.

Column with Stylized Branches — A468

1975, Aug. 21 Litho. Wmk. 353

1875 A468 8r red & multi .60 .20

9th Iranian Arts Festival, Shiraz-Persepolis.

Flags over Globe — A469

1975, Sept. 8

1876 A469 2r vio bl & multi .30 .20

Intl. Literacy Symposium, Persepolis.

Stylized Globe — A470

World Map and Envelope — A471

1975, Sept. 13

1877 A470 2r vio & multi .30 .20

3rd Tehran International Trade Fair.

1975, Oct. 9 Litho. ***Perf. 10½***

1878 A471 14r ultra & multi 1.00 .20

World Post Day, Oct. 9.

Crown, Column Capital, Persepolis — A472

1975, Oct. 26 Litho. Wmk. 353

1879 A472 2r ultra & multi .35 .20

Festival of Culture and Art. See No. 1954.

Face and Film — A473

1975, Nov. 2

1880 A473 6r multicolored .65 .20

Tehran Intl. Festival of Children's Films.

"Mother's Face" — A474

Girl — A475

Design: No. 1882, 2r, "Our House," horiz. All designs after children's drawings.

1975, Nov. 5

1881 A474 2r multicolored .35 .20
1882 A475 2r multicolored .35 .20
1883 A475 2r multicolored .35 .20
Nos. 1881-1883 (3) 1.05 .60

Children's Week.

"Film" — A476

1975, Dec. 4 Wmk. 353 ***Perf. 10½***

1884 A476 8r multicolored .60 .20

4th Tehran International Film Festival.

Symbols of Reforms — A477

People — A478

1976, Jan. 26 Litho. ***Perf. 10½***

1885 A477 2r shown .35 .20
1886 A478 2r shown .35 .20
1887 A477 2r Five reform symbols .35 .20
Nos. 1885-1887 (3) 1.05 .60

"White Revolution of King and People."

Motorcycle Policeman A479

Police Helicopter — A480

1976, Feb. 16

1888 A479 2r multicolored .75 .30
1889 A480 6r multicolored 1.25 .50

Highway Police Day.

Soccer Cup — A481

Candlestick A482

1976, Feb. 24 Litho. Wmk. 353
1890 A481 2r org & multi .30 .20

3rd Intl. Youth Soccer Cup, Shiraz and Ahvaz.

1976, Mar. 6

Designs: No. 1892, Incense burner. No. 1893, Rose water container.

1891 A482 1r olive & multi .30 .20
1892 A482 1r claret & multi .30 .20
1893 A482 1r Prus bl & multi .30 .20
a. Strip of 3, #1891-1893 1.00 .60

Novrooz, Iranian New Year.

Telephones, 1876 and 1976 — A483

Eye Within Square — A484

1976, Mar. 10
1894 A483 10r multicolored .75 .20

Centenary of first telephone call by Alexander Graham Bell, Mar. 10, 1876.

1976, Apr. 29 Litho. *Perf. 10½*
1895 A484 6r blk & multi 1.00 .20
a. Perf. 12½ 6.00 4.00

World Health Day: "Foresight prevents blindness."

Nurse with Infant A485

Young Man Holding Old Man's Hand — A486

1976, May 10
1896 A485 2r shown .50 .20
1897 A485 2r Engineering apprentices .50 .20
1898 A486 2r shown .50 .20
Nos. 1896-1898 (3) 1.50 .60

Royal Org. of Social Services, 30th anniv.

Map of Iran, Men Linking Hands — A487

Waves and Ear Phones — A488

1976, May 13 Wmk. 353
1899 A487 2r yel & multi .30 .20

Iranian Cooperatives, 10th anniversary.

1976, May 17
1900 A488 14r gray & multi .75 .20

World Telecommunications Day.

Emblem, Woman with Flag, Man with Gun — A489

1976, June 6
1901 A489 2r bister & multi .35 .20

To publicize the power of stability.

Map of Iran, Columns of Persepolis, Nasser Khosrov — A490

1976, July 6 Litho. *Perf. 10½*
1902 A490 6r yel & multi .50 .20

Tourist publicity.

Riza Shah Pahlavi — A491

1976, July 21 Litho. Wmk. 353

6r, Mohammed Ali Jinnah. 8r, Kemal Ataturk.

1903 A491 2r gray & multi .50 .20
1904 A491 6r gray & multi .60 .20
1905 A491 8r gray & multi .75 .25
Nos. 1903-1905 (3) 1.85 .65

Regional Cooperation for Development Pact among Iran, Turkey and Pakistan, 12th anniversary.

Torch, Montreal and Iranian Olympic Emblems A492

1976, Aug. 1
1906 A492 14r multicolored 1.00 .25

21st Olympic Games, Montreal, Canada, July 17-Aug. 1.

Riza Shah Pahlavi in Coronation Robe — A493

Festival Emblem — A494

Designs: 2r, Shahs Riza and Mohammed Riza Pahlavi, horiz. 14r, 20r, Shah Mohammed Riza Pahlavi in coronation robe and crown.

1976, Aug. 19 Wmk. 353 *Perf. 10½*
1907 A493 2r lilac & multi .80 .35
1908 A493 6r blue & multi 1.75 .45
1909 A493 14r grn & multi 2.25 .65
Nos. 1907-1909 (3) 4.80 1.45

Souvenir Sheet

1976, Oct. 8 *Imperf.*
1910 A493 20r multi 7.50 4.00

50th anniv. of Pahlavi dynasty; 35th anniv. of reign of Shah Mohammed Riza Pahlavi. No. 1910 contains one stamp 43x62mm.

1976, Aug. 29 Litho. *Perf. 10½*
1911 A494 10r multicolored .65 .20

10th Iranian Arts Festival, Shiraz-Persepolis.

Iranian Scout Emblem — A495

1976, Oct. 2 Litho. *Perf. 10½*
1912 A495 2r lt bl & multi .30 .20

10th Asia Pacific Conference, Tehran 1976.

Cancer Radiation Treatment — A496

1976, Oct. 6
1913 A496 2r black & multi .30 .20

Fight against cancer.

Target, Police Woman Receiving Decoration A497

1976, Oct. 7
1914 A497 2r lt bl & multi .30 .20

Police Day.

UPU Emblem, No. 1907 on Cover A498

1976, Oct. 9
1915 A498 10r multicolored 1.00 .20

International Post Day.

Crown Prince Riza with Cup — A499

1976, Oct. 10
1916 A499 6r multicolored .50 .20

Natl. Soc. of Village Culture Houses, anniv.

Shahs Riza and Mohammed Riza, Railroad A500

1976, Oct. 15
1917 A500 8r black & multi 3.00 .50

Railroad Day.

Emblem & Column Capital, Persepolis — A501

Census Emblem — A502

1976, Oct. 26
1918 A501 14r blue & multi 1.00 .30

Festival of Culture and Art.

1976, Oct. 30
1919 A502 2r gray & multi .30 .20

Natl. Population & Housing Census, 1976.

Flowers and Birds — A503 / Mohammed Ali Jinnah — A504

Designs: No. 1921, Flowers and bird. No. 1922, Flowers and butterfly. Designs are from covers of children's books.

1976, Oct. 31 *Perf. 10½*

1920	A503	2r multicolored	.35	.20
1921	A503	2r multicolored	.35	.20
1922	A503	2r multicolored	.35	.20
		Nos. 1920-1922 (3)	1.05	.60

Children's Week.

1976, Dec. 25 Litho. Wmk. 353

1923 A504 10r multicolored .60 .20

Jinnah (1876-1948), 1st Governor General of Pakistan.

Development and Agriculture Corps — A505

17-Point Reform Law: 5d, Land reform. 10d, Nationalization of forests. 50d, Sale of shares of state-owned industries. 1r, Profit sharing for factory workers. 2r, Parliament Gate, Woman suffrage. 3r, Education Corps formation. 5r, Health Corps. 8r, Establishment of village courts. 10r, Nationalization of water resources. 12r, Reconstruction program, urban and rural. 14r, Administrative and educational reorganization. 20r, Sale of factory shares. 30r, Commodity pricing. 50r, Free education. 100r, Child care. 200r, Care of the aged (social security).

1977, Jan. 26 Photo. *Perf. 13x13½*

Frame and Shah's Head in Gold

Size: 28x21mm

1924	A505	5d rose & green	.20	.20
1925	A505	10d lt grn & brn	.20	.20
1926	A505	50d yel & vio bl	.20	.20
1927	A505	1r lil & vio bl	.20	.20
1928	A505	2r org & green	.20	.20
1929	A505	3r lt bl & red	.40	.20
1930	A505	5r bl grn & mag	.40	.20

Size: 37x27mm

1931	A505	6r brn, mar & black	.55	.20
1932	A505	8r ultra, mar & blk	.55	.20
1933	A505	10r lt grn, bl & black	1.50	.20
1934	A505	12r vio, mar & black	1.10	.20
1935	A505	14r org, red & blk	1.60	.75
1936	A505	20r gray, ocher & black	3.25	.50
1937	A505	30r bl, grn & blk	3.25	.65
1938	A505	50r yel, brn & blk	5.50	.60
1939	A505	100r multi	5.00	1.25
1940	A505	200r multi	11.00	2.50
		Nos. 1924-1940 (17)	35.10	8.45

"White Revolution of King and People" reform laws.

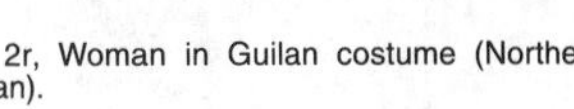

Man in Guilan Costume — A506 / Electronic Tree — A507

2r, Woman in Guilan costume (Northern Iran).

1977, Mar. 6 Wmk. 353 *Perf. 13*

1941	A506	1r multicolored	.30	.20
1942	A506	2r multicolored	.35	.20

Novrooz, Iranian New Year.

1977, May 17 Photo. *Perf. 13*

1943 A507 20r multicolored 1.25 .35

World Telecommunications Day.

Riza Shah Dam A508

1977, May 31 *Perf. 13x13½*

1944 A508 5r multicolored .40 .20

Inauguration of Riza Shah Dam.

Olympic Rings A509

1977, June 23 Litho. *Perf. 10½*

1945 A509 14r multicolored .90 .20

Olympic Day.

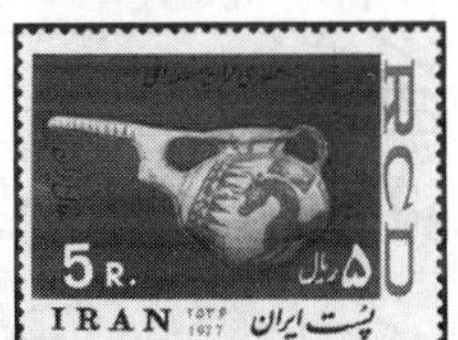

Terra-cotta Jug, Iran A510

#1947, Terra-cotta bullock cart, Pakistan. #1948, Terra-cotta pot with human face, Turkey.

Perf. 13x13½

1977, July 21 Photo. Wmk. 353

1946	A510	5r violet & multi	.40	.20
1947	A510	5r emer & multi	.40	.20
1948	A510	5r green & multi	.40	.20
		Nos. 1946-1948 (3)	1.20	.60

Regional Cooperation for Development Pact among Iran, Turkey and Pakistan, 13th anniv.

Flowers with Scout Emblems, Map of Asia — A511

1977, Aug. 5 Litho. *Perf. 13*

1949 A511 10r multicolored 1.00 .25

2nd Asia-Pacific Jamboree, Nishapur.

Map of Eastern Hemisphere with Iran — A512 / Tree of Learning, Symbolic Letters — A513

1977, Sept. 20 Photo. Wmk. 353

1950 A512 3r multicolored .35 .20

9th Asian Electronics Conference, Tehran.

1977, Oct. 8 Wmk. 353 *Perf. 13*

1951 A513 10r multicolored .60 .20

Honoring the teachers.

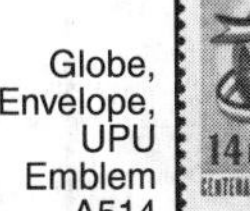

Globe, Envelope, UPU Emblem A514

1977, Oct. 9 Photo.

1952 A514 14r multicolored 1.00 .20

Iran's admission to the UPU, cent.

Folk Art — A515

1977, Oct. 16

1953 A515 5r multicolored .40 .20

Festival of Folk Art.

Festival Type of 1975

Design: 20r, similar to 1975 issue, but with small crown within star.

1977, Oct. 26 *Perf. 10½*

1954 A472 20r bis, grn, car & blk 1.25 .20

Festival of Culture and Art.

Joust — A516 / Emblem — A517

#1956, Rapunzel. #1957, Little princess with attendants.

1977, Oct. 31 Photo.

1955	A516	3r multicolored	.30	.20
1956	A516	3r multicolored	.30	.20
1957	A516	3r multicolored	.30	.20
a.		Strip of 3, #1955-1957	1.25	.60

Children's Week.

1977, Nov. 7 Wmk. 353 *Perf. 13*

1958 A517 5r multicolored .40 .20

First Regional Seminar on the Education and Welfare of the Deaf.

Mohammad Iqbal A518 / African Sculpture A519

1977, Nov. 9 Litho. *Perf. 10½*

1959 A518 5r multicolored .45 .20

Iqbal (1877-1938) of Pakistan, poet and philosopher.

1977, Dec. 14

1960 A519 20r multicolored 3.25 .55

African art.

Shah Mosque, Isfahan — A520

Designs: 1r, Ruins, Persepolis. 2r, Khajou Bridge, Isfahan. 5r, Imam Riza Shrine, Meshed. 9r, Warrior frieze, Persepolis. 10r, Djameh Mosque, Isfahan. 20r, King on throne, bas-relief. 25r, Sheik Lotfollah Mosque. 30r, Ruins, Persepolis, diff. view. 50r, Ali Ghapou Palace, Isfahan. 100r, Bas-relief, Tagh Bastan. 200r, Horseman and prisoners, bas-relief, Naqsh Rostam.

1978-79 Photo. *Perf. 13x13½*

"Iran" and Head in Gold

Size: 28x21mm

1961	A520	1r deep brn	.30	.25
1962	A520	2r emerald	.30	.25
1963	A520	3r magenta	.50	.25
1964	A520	5r Prus blue	.70	.25

Size: 36x27mm

1965	A520	9r sepia ('79)	1.40	.55
1966	A520	10r brt bl ('79)	5.50	.70
1967	A520	20r rose	1.75	.55
1968	A520	25r ultra ('79)	25.00	9.75
1969	A520	30r magenta	2.75	.55
1970	A520	50r deep yel grn ('79)	4.50	3.50
1971	A520	100r dk bl ('79)	15.00	9.75
1972	A520	200r vio bl ('79)	19.00	19.00
		Nos. 1961-1972 (12)	76.70	45.35

For overprints see Nos. 2009, 2011-2018.

Persian Rug — A521

Designs: Persian rugs.

1978, Feb. 11 Litho. *Perf. 10½*

1973	A521	3r sil & multi	.35	.25
1974	A521	5r sil & multi	.45	.25
1975	A521	10r sil & multi	.75	.35
		Nos. 1973-1975 (3)	1.55	.85

Opening of Carpet Museum.

Mazanderan Man — A522

Design: 5r, Mazanderan woman.

1978, Mar. 6 ***Perf. 13***

1976 A522 3r yel & multi	.35	.20
1977 A522 5r lt bl & multi	.55	.20

Novrooz, Iranian New Year.

Mohammed Riza Pahlavi — A523

1978, Jan. 26

1978 A523 20r multicolored	4.00	1.25

Shah's White Revolution, 15th anniv.

Riza Shah Pahlavi and Crown Prince Inspecting Girls' School — A524

Designs (Riza Shah Pahlavi and Crown Prince Mohammed Riza Pahlavi): 5r, Inauguration of Trans-Iranian railroad. 10r, At stairs of Palace, Persepolis. 14r, Shah handing Crown Prince (later Shah) officer's diploma at Tehran Officers' Academy.

1978, Mar. 15

1979 A524 3r multicolored	.50	.25
1980 A524 5r multicolored	.75	.35
1981 A524 10r multicolored	1.25	.40
1982 A524 14r multicolored	1.75	.70
Nos. 1979-1982 (4)	4.25	1.70

Riza Shah Pahlavi (1877-1944), founder of Pahlavi dynasty.

Communications Satellite over Map of Iran — A525

1978, Apr. 19 **Litho.** ***Perf. 10½***

1983 A525 20r multicolored	1.25	.30

ITU, 7th meeting, Tehran; 10th anniv. of Iran's membership.

Antenna, ITU Emblem A526

1978, May 17 **Litho.** ***Perf. 10½***

1984 A526 15r multicolored	.90	.30

10th World Telecommunications Day.

Welfare Legion Emblem — A527

1978, June 13 **Photo.** ***Perf. 13x13½***

1985 A527 10r multicolored	.60	.30

Universal Welfare Legion, 10th anniversary.

Pink Roses, Iran — A528

Designs: 10r, Yellow rose, Turkey. 15r, Red roses, Pakistan.

Perf. 13½x13

1978, July 21 **Wmk. 353**

1986 A528 5r multicolored	.60	.25
1987 A528 10r multicolored	.90	.25
1988 A528 15r multicolored	1.00	.40
Nos. 1986-1988 (3)	2.50	.90

Regional Cooperation for Development Pact among Iran, Turkey and Pakistan, 14th anniversary.

Rhazes, Pharmaceutical Tools — A529

1978, Aug. 26 **Wmk. 353** ***Perf. 13***

1989 A529 5r multicolored	.60	.25

Pharmacists' Day. Rhazes (850-923), chief physician of Great Hospital in Baghdad.

Girl Scouts, Aryamehr Arch A530

1978, Sept. 2 ***Perf. 10½***

1990 A530 5r multicolored	.60	.25

23rd World Girl Scouts Conference, Tehran, Sept. 1978.

Shah Riza Pahlavi A531

Design: 5r, Mohammed Riza Shah Pahlavi.

1978, Sept. 11 **Litho.** ***Perf. 10½***

1991 A531 3r multicolored	1.50	.40
1992 A531 5r multicolored	1.75	.50

Bank Melli Iran, 50th anniversary.

Girl and Bird A532

1978, Oct. 31 **Photo.** ***Perf. 13***

1993 A532 3r multicolored	.75	.30

Children's Week.

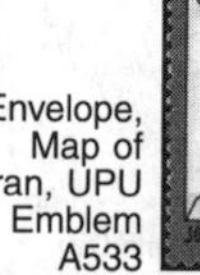
Envelope, Map of Iran, UPU Emblem A533

1978, Nov. 22 ***Perf. 13x13½***

1994 A533 14r gold & multi	1.50	.40

World Post Day, Oct. 22.

Communications Symbols and Classroom — A534

1978, Nov. 22 ***Perf. 10½***

1995 A534 10r multicolored	1.25	.40

Faculty of Communications, 50th anniv.

Human Rights Flame A535

1978, Dec. 17 **Photo.** ***Perf. 13***

1996 A535 20r bl, blk & gold	3.50	.50

Universal Declaration of Human Rights, 30th anniv.

Kurdistani Man — A536

Design: 5r, Kurdistani woman.

1979, Mar. 17

1997 A536 3r multicolored	.90	.25
1998 A536 5r multicolored	1.25	.25

Rose — A537

1979, Mar. 17

1999 A537 2r multicolored	.25	.20

Novrooz, Iranian New Year.

See No. 2310i.

Islamic Republic

Demonstrators — A538

Islamic revolution: 3r, Demonstrators. 5r, Hands holding rose, gun and torch breaking through newspaper. 20r, Hands breaking prison bars, and dove, vert.

1979, Apr. 20 ***Perf. 10½***

2000 A538 3r multicolored	1.50	.30
2001 A538 5r multicolored	1.10	.30
2002 A538 10r multicolored	1.10	.50
2003 A538 20r multicolored	2.50	.65
Nos. 2000-2003 (4)	6.20	1.75

Nos. 1837-1838, 1966, 1970 and Type A520 Overprinted

Designs: 15r, Warriors on horseback, bas-relief, Naqsh-Rostam. 19r, Chehel Sotoon Palace, Isfahan.

1979 **Wmk. 353** ***Perf. 13x13½***

2008 A443	8r org & brown	*3.00*	1.00
2009 A520	9r gold & dp brn	1.50	1.50
2010 A443	10r dp yel grn	*50.00*	10.00
2011 A520	10r gold & brt bl	1.75	1.00
2012 A520	15r gold & red lil	1.75	1.00
2013 A520	19r gold & slate grn	1.75	1.00
2016 A520	50r gold & dp yel grn	5.00	2.00
2017 A520	100r gold & vio bl	10.00	4.00
2018 A520	200r gold & vio bl	12.50	8.50
	Nos. 2008-2018 (9)	*87.25*	30.00

Overprint means Islamic revolution. Forgeries of No. 2010 exist.

Symbolic Tulip — A539

1979, June 5 **Photo.** ***Perf. 13***

2019 A539 5r multicolored	1.50	.40

Potters, by Kamalel Molk A540

#2021, at the Well, by Allah Baksh, Pakistan. #2022, Plowing, by Namik Ismail, Turkey.

1979, July 21 **Litho.** ***Perf. 10½***

2020 A540 5r multicolored	3.25	.30
2021 A540 5r multicolored	2.50	.30
2022 A540 5r multicolored	2.50	.30
Nos. 2020-2022 (3)	8.25	.90

Regional Cooperation for Development Pact among Iran, Turkey and Pakistan, 15th anniv.

"TELECOM 79" — A541

1979, Sept. 20 ***Perf. 10½***

2023 A541 20r multicolored	*7.00*	.25

3rd World Telecommunications Exhibition, Geneva, Sept. 20-26.

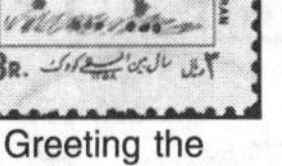

Greeting the Sunrise — A542

Persian Rug Design — A543

Children's Drawings and IYC Emblem: 2r, Tulip over wounded man. 2r, Children with banners.

1979, Sept. 23

2024 A542 2r multicolored .85 .50
2025 A542 3r multicolored .85 .50
2026 A542 5r multicolored 1.60 .50
Nos. 2024-2026 (3) 3.30 1.50

International Year of the Child.

1979-80 Photo. *Perf. 13½x13*

2027 A543 50d brn & pale sal .20 .20
2028 A543 1r dark & lt bl .20 .20
2029 A543 2r red & yellow .20 .20
2030 A543 3r dk bl & lt lil .20 .20
2031 A543 5r slate grn & lt grn .20 .20
2032 A543 10r blk & salmon pink ('80) .30 .20
2033 A543 20r brn & gray ('80) .55 .20

Size: 27x37½mm

2034 A543 50r dp violet & gray ('80) 1.40 .50
2035 A543 100r blk & slate grn ('80) 5.00 1.40
2036 A543 200r dk bl & cr ('80) 5.50 2.75
Nos. 2027-2036 (10) 13.75 6.05

Globe in Envelope — A544

1979, Oct. 9 Litho. *Perf. 10½*

2041 A544 10r multicolored *3.00* .40

World Post Day.

Ghyath-al-din Kashani, Astrolabe A545

1979, Dec. 5 Litho. *Perf. 10½*

2042 A545 5r ocher & blk *1.50* .40

Kashani, mathematician, 550th death anniv.

Ka'aba, Flame and Mosque A546

Hegira (Pilgrimage Year): 5r, Koran open over globe, vert. 10r, Salman Farsi (follower of Mohammed), map of Iran.

1980, Jan. 19

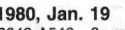

2043 A546 3r multicolored .20 .20
2044 A546 5r multicolored .25 .20
2045 A546 10r multicolored .55 .25
Nos. 2043-2045 (3) 1.00 .65

Reissued in May-June, 1980, with shiny gum and watermark position changed.

People, Map and Flag of Iran — A547

Islamic Revolution, 1st Anniversary: 3r, Blood dripping on broken sword. 5r, Window open on sun of Islam, people.

1980, Feb. 11

2046 A547 1r multicolored .20 .20
2047 A547 3r multicolored .35 .25
2048 A547 5r multicolored .65 .30
Nos. 2046-2048 (3) 1.20 .75

For similar stamps measuring 24x36mm see Nos. 2310a, 2310b, 2310d.

Dehkhoda, Dictionary Editor, Birth Cent. — A548

1980, Feb. 26

2049 A548 10r multicolored .30 .20

East Azerbaijani Woman A549

Mohammed Mossadegh A550

Novrooz (Iranian New Year): 5r, East Azerbaijani man.

1980, Mar. 5

2050 A549 3r multicolored .20 .20
2051 A549 5r multicolored .25 .20

1980, Mar. 19 Photo. *Perf. 13x13½*

2052 A550 20r multi .60 .20

Oil industry nationalization, 29th anniv.; Mohammed Mossadegh, prime minister who initiated nationalization, birth cent.

Professor Morteza Motahhari, 1st Death Anniversary — A551

1980, May 1 Litho. *Perf. 10½*

2053 A551 10r black & red .50 .20

World Telecommunications Day — A552

1980, May 17 Photo. *Perf. 13x13½*

2054 A552 20r multicolored .50 .20

Interior of Mosque A553

1980, June 11 Litho. *Perf. 10½*

2055 A553 50d shown .20 .20
2056 A553 1r Demonstration .20 .20
2057 A553 3r Avicenna, al-Biruni, Farabi .40 .20
2058 A553 5r Hegira emblem .30 .20
Nos. 2055-2058 (4) 1.10 .80

Hegira, 1400th anniv.

Ali Sharyati, Educator A554

1980, June 15 Photo. *Perf. 13x13½*

2059 A554 5r multicolored .30 .20

Holy Ka'aba and Hand Waving Banner — A555

1980, June 28

2060 A555 5r multicolored .30 .20

Hazrat Mehdi, 12th Imam's birth anniv.

A556

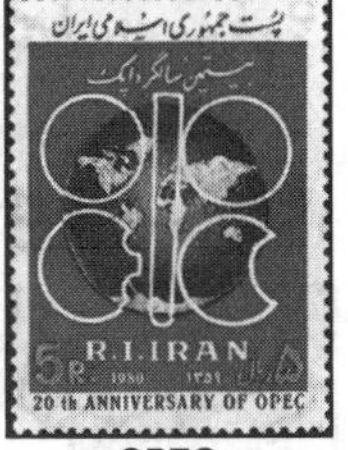

OPEC Emblem — A557

1980, Sept. 10 *Perf. 13½x13*

2061 A556 5r multicolored .30 .20

Ayatollah Seyed Mahmood Talegani, death anniv. Compare with design A829.

1980, Sept. 15

2062 A557 5r shown .30 .20
2063 A557 10r Men holding OPEC emblem .60 .20

20th anniversary of OPEC.

"Let Us Liberate Jerusalem" A558

Tulip and Fayziyye Mosque, Qum A559

1980, Oct. 9 *Perf. 13x13½*

2064 A558 5r multicolored .25 .20
2065 A558 20r multicolored .85 .20

1981, Feb. 11 *Perf. 13*

2066 A559 3r shown .20 .20
2067 A559 5r Blood spilling on tulip .20 .20
2068 A559 20r Tulip, Republic emblem .50 .20
Nos. 2066-2068 (3) .90 .60

Islamic Revolution, 2nd anniversary.

See Nos. 2310c, 2310e, 2310j, watermark 381 (3r, unserifed "R" in denomination. 5r, bright yellow background; 20r, light blue background behind flower.)

Lorestani Man — A560

Telecommunications Day — A561

Novrooz (Iranian New Year): 10r, Lorestani woman.

1981, Mar. 11

2069 A560 5r multicolored .20 .20
2070 A560 10r multicolored .30 .20

Perf. 13½x13

1981, May 17 Photo. Wmk. 353

2071 A561 5r dk grn & org .20 .20

Ayatollah Kashani Birth Centenary — A562

Adult Education A563

Perf. 13x13½

1981, July 21 Wmk. 381

2072 A562 15r dk grn & dl pur .40 .20

Perf. 13x13½, 13½x13 (5r, 10r, 200r)

1981, Aug.

50d, Citizens bearing arms. 2r, Irrigation. 3r, Friday prayer service. 5r, Paasdaar emblem and members. 10r, Koran text. 20r, Hejaab (women's veil). 50r, Industrial development. 100r, Religious ceremony, Mecca. 200r, Mosque interior. 5r, 10r, 200r vert.

2073 A563 50d blk & dp bister .20 .20
2074 A563 1r dl pur & grn .20 .20
2075 A563 2r brn & grnsh bl .20 .20

Size: 38x28mm, 28x38mm

2076 A563 3r brt yel grn & black .20 .20
2077 A563 5r dk bl & brn org .20 .20

2078 A563 10r dk bl & grnsh blue .25 .20
2079 A563 20r red & black .60 .20
2080 A563 50r lilac & black 1.40 .30
2081 A563 100r org brn & blk 3.00 .60
2082 A563 200r blk & bl grn 5.75 1.25
Nos. 2073-2082 (10) 12.00 3.55

Islamic Iranian Army
A564

1981, Sept. 21 Photo. *Perf. 13*
2087 A564 5r multicolored .20 .20

World Post Day and 12th UPU Day — A565

Perf. 13x13½
1981, Oct. 9 Wmk. 381
2088 A565 20r black & blue .50 .25

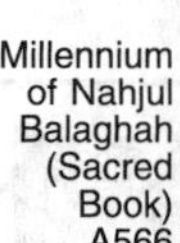

Millennium of Nahjul Balaghah (Sacred Book)
A566

1981, Oct. 17 *Perf. 13*
2089 A566 25r multicolored .60 .20

Martyrs' Memorial — A567

1981, Nov. 9 Photo. *Perf. 13*
2090 A567 3r June 28, 1981 victims .20 .20
2091 A567 5r Pres. Rajai, Prime Minister Bahonar .20 .20
2092 A567 10r Gen. Chamran .25 .20
Nos. 2090-2092 (3) .65 .60

Ayatollah M. H. Tabatabaee, Scholar — A568

1981, Dec. 25 Photo. *Perf. 13*
2093 A568 5r multicolored .20 .20

Literacy Campaign
A569

Islamic Revolution, 3rd Anniv. — A570

1982, Jan. 20 Photo. *Perf. 13x13½*
2094 A569 5r blue & gold .20 .20

1982, Feb. 11 Wmk. 381 *Perf. 13*
2095 A570 5r Map .20 .20
2096 A570 10r Tulip .25 .20
2097 A570 20r Globe .50 .20
a. Strip of 3, #2095-2097 .90 .40

See Nos. 2310f, 2310g, 2310k (5r, orange background, Arabian "5" 6mm above black panel. 10r, dark green background, gray dove with thick black lines around it. 20r, pink background, bright blue globe, faint latitude and longitude lines.)

Unity Week — A571

Khuzestan Man — A573

Koran Verse Relative to Christ
A572

1982, Feb. 20 Photo. *Perf. 13*
2098 A571 25r multicolored 1.00 .20

1982, Mar. 11 Photo. Wmk. 381
2099 A572 20r multicolored .50 .20

1982, Mar. 13
2100 A573 3r shown .20 .20
2101 A573 5r Khuzestan woman .20 .20
a. Pair, #2100-2101 .20 .20

Novrooz (New Year).

3rd Anniv. of Islamic Revolution
A574

1982, Apr. 1
2102 A574 30r multicolored .90 .25

Seyed Mohammad Bagher Sadr — A575

1982, Apr. 8 Photo. *Perf. 13½x13*
2103 A575 50r multicolored 1.00 .40

Martyrs of Altar (Ayatollahs Madani and Dastgeyb) — A576

1982, Apr. 21 *Perf. 13*
2104 A576 50r multicolored 1.00 .40

A577

A578

1982, May 1 Photo. *Perf. 13½x13*
2105 A577 100r multi 2.25 .80

Intl. Workers' Solidarity Day.

1982, May 17 *Perf. 13x13½*
2106 A578 100r multi 2.25 .80

14th World Telecommunications Day.

Mab'as Day (Mohammad's Appointment as Prophet) — A579

1963 Islamic Rising, 19th Anniv. — A580

1982, May 21 *Perf. 13½x13*
2107 A579 32r multicolored .90 .30

1982, June 5 Wmk. 381 *Perf. 13*
2108 A580 28r multicolored .60 .30

Lt. Islambuli, Assassin of Anwar Sadat — A581

1st Death Anniv. of Ayatollah Beheshti — A582

1982, June 17
2109 A581 2r multicolored .40 .20

1982, June 28
2110 A582 10r multicolored .40 .20
a. Missing dot in Arabic numeral 1.00 1.00

Iran-Iraq War
A583

1982, July 7 *Perf. 13x13½*
2111 A583 5r multicolored .20 .20

Universal Jerusalem Day
A584

1982, July 15 *Perf. 13*
2112 A584 1r Dome of the Rock .20 .20

Pilgrimage to Mecca — A585

13th World UPU Day — A586

1982, Sept. 28
2113 A585 10r multicolored .30 .20

1982, Oct. 9 *Perf. 13½x13*
2114 A586 30r multicolored .75 .25

4th Anniv. of Islamic Revolution — A587

1983, Feb. 11 Photo. *Perf. 13*
2115 A587 30r multicolored .75 .25

See No. 2310n for stamp with orange or orange red crowd and thick sharp lettering in black panels.

4th Anniv. of Islamic Republic — A588

1983, Apr. 1 Photo. *Perf. 13*
2116 A588 10r multicolored .30 .20

Teachers' Day — A589

World Communications Year — A590

Perf. 13½x13

1983, May 1 **Wmk. 381**

2117 A589 5r multicolored .25 .20

1983, May 17

2118 A590 20r multicolored .60 .20

First Session of Islamic Consultative Assembly — A591

1983, May 28 ***Perf. 13***

2119 A591 5r multicolored .20 .20

20th Anniv. of Islamic Movement — A592

1983, June 5 **Photo.** ***Perf. 13***

2120 A592 10r multicolored .30 .20

Iraqi MiG Bombing Now Rooz Oil Well A593

1983, June 11 ***Perf. 13x13½***

2121 A593 5r multicolored .50 .20

Ecology week.

Ayatollah Mohammad Sadooghi — A594

1983, July 2 **Photo.** ***Perf. 13½***

2122 A594 20r blk & dl red .60 .20

Universal Day of Jerusalem — A595

Government Week — A596

1983, July 8

2123 A595 5r Dome of the Rock .20 .20

1983, Aug. 30 **Wmk. 381** ***Perf. 13***

2124 A596 3r multicolored .20 .20

Death of Pres. Rajai and Prime Minister Bahonar, 2nd anniv.

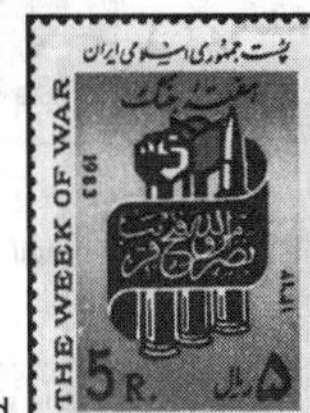

Iran-Iraq War, 3rd Anniv. — A597

1983, Sept. 28 **Photo.** ***Perf. 13***

2125 A597 5r rose red & blk .20 .20

Ayatollah Ashrafi Esphahani, Martyr of Altar — A598

Mirza Kuchik Khan — A599

1983, Oct. 15 **Photo.** ***Perf. 13***

2126 A598 5r multicolored .20 .20

1983-84 **Photo.** ***Perf. 13***

Religious and Political Figures: 1r, Sheikh Mohammad Khiabani. 3r, Seyd Majtaba Navab Safavi. 5r, Seyd Jamal-ed-Din Assadabadi. 10r, Seyd Hassan Modaress. 20r, Sheikh Fazel Assad Nouri. 30r, Mirza Mohammed Hossein Naiyni. 50r, Sheikh Mohammad Hossein Kashef. 100r, Seyd Hassan Shirazi. 200r, Mirza Reza Kermani.

2128 A599 1r black & pink .20 .20
2129 A599 2r org & black .20 .20
2130 A599 3r brt bl & blk .20 .20
2131 A599 5r rose red & blk .20 .20
2132 A599 10r yel grn & blk .30 .20
2133 A599 20r lilac & blk .60 .20
2134 A599 30r gldn brn & blk .90 .30
2135 A599 50r blk & lt bl 1.50 .50
2136 A599 100r blk & org 3.00 1.00
2137 A599 200r blk & bluish grn 6.00 2.00
Nos. 2128-2137 (10) 13.10 5.00

Issue dates: 1r, 50r-200r, Feb. 1984. Others, Oct. 23, 1983.

UPU Day A600

1983, Oct. 9 **Photo.** **Wmk. 381**

2138 A600 10r multi .25 .20

Takeover of the US Embassy, 4th Anniv. — A601

1983, Nov. 4 **Photo.** ***Perf. 13***

2139 A601 28r multicolored .50 .50

UN Day A602

1983, Oct. 24 ***Perf. 13½***

2140 A602 32r multicolored .90 .25

Protest of veto by US, Russia, People's Rep. of China, France and Great Britain.

Intl. Medical Seminar, Tehran — A603

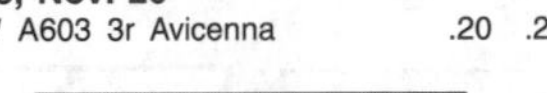

1983, Nov. 20

2141 A603 3r Avicenna .20 .20

People's Forces Preparation Day — A604

1983, Nov. 26 ***Perf. 13***

2142 A604 20r multicolored .60 .20

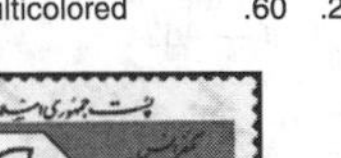

Conference on Crimes of Iraqi Pres. Saddam Hussein — A605

1983, Nov. 28 ***Perf. 13½x13***

2143 A605 5r multicolored .20 .20

Mohammad Mofatteh — A606

1983, Dec. 18 **Photo.** ***Perf. 13***

2144 A606 10r multicolored .30 .20

Birth Anniversary of the Prophet Mohammed A607

1983, Dec. 22 **Photo.** ***Perf. 13***

2145 A607 5r multicolored .45 .20

Approximately 700,000 copies of No. 2145 were issued before a spelling error was discovered, and the remainder of the issue was then withdrawn from sale.

5th Anniv. of Islamic Revolution — A608

1984, Feb. 11 **Photo.** ***Perf. 13x13½***

2146 A608 10r multicolored .75 .20

See No. 2310h for stamp with splotchy colors in blue background and denomination, flag colors and darker, thicker black lines around tulips. Background and denominations on No. 2146 have a screened appearance.

Nurses' Day A609

1984, Feb. 24 ***Perf. 13***

2147 A609 20r Attending wounded soldiers .45 .20

Invalids' Day — A610

Local Flowers — A611

1984, Feb. 29

2148 A610 5r Man in wheelchair .20 .20

1984, Mar. 10 ***Perf. 13½x13***

2149 A611 3r Lotus gebelia .20 .20
2150 A611 5r Tulipa chrysantha .20 .20
2151 A611 10r Glycyrhiza glabra .25 .20
2152 A611 20r Matthiola alyssifolia .45 .20
a. Block of 4, #2149-2152 1.00 .75

Novrooz (New Year).

Islamic Republic, 5th Anniv. — A612

Sheik Ragheb Harb, Lebanese Religious Leader — A614

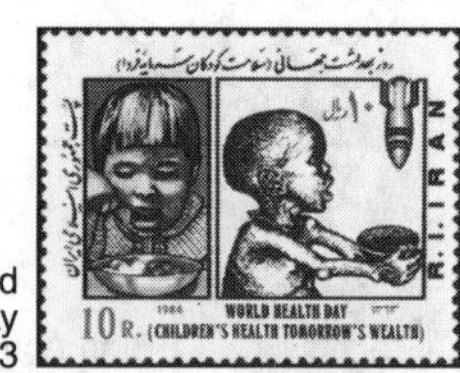

World Health Day
A613

1984, Apr. 1 Photo. *Perf. 13*
2153 A612 5r Flag, globe, map .20 .20

1984, Apr. 7
2154 A613 10r Children .30 .20

1984, Apr. 18
2155 A614 5r multicolored .20 .20

World Red Cross Day — A615

16th World Telecommunications Day — A616

1984, May 8 Photo. *Perf. 13½x13*
2156 A615 5r multicolored .20 .20

1984, May 17
2157 A616 20r multicolored .45 .20

Martyrdom of Seyyed Ghotb — A617

1984, May 28 *Perf. 13*
2158 A617 10r multicolored .30 .20

Struggle Against Discrimination — A618

1984, Mar. 21 Photo. *Perf. 13*
2159 A618 5r Malcolm X .20 .20

Conquest of Mecca Anniv.
A619

1984, June 20
2160 A619 5r Holy Ka'aba, idol destruction .20 .20

Universal Day of Jerusalem
A620

Id Al-fitr Feast
A621

1984, June 29
2161 A620 5r Map, Koran .20 .20
2162 A621 10r Moon, praying crowd, mosque .25 .20
a. Pair, #2161-2162 .40 .20

Tchogha Zanbil Excavation, Susa — A622

Cultural Heritage Preservation: b, Emamzadeh Hossein Shrine, Kazvin. c, Emam Mosque, Isfahan. d, Ark Fortress, Tabriz. e, Mausoleum of Daniel Nabi, Susa.

1984, Aug. 20 *Perf. 13½*
2163 Strip of 5 .75 .25
a.-e. A622 5r, any single .20 .20

"Eid Ul-Adha"
A623

Perf. 13x13½
1984, Sept. 6 Photo. Wmk. 381
2164 A623 10r Holy Ka'aba .30 .20

Feast of Sacrifices (end of pilgrimage to Mecca).

10th Tehran Intl. Trade Fair — A624

Iraq-Iran War, 4th Anniv. — A625

1984, Sept. 11
2165 A624 10r multicolored .30 .20

1984, Sept. 22 Photo. *Perf. 13x13½*
2166 A625 5r Flower, bullets .20 .20

UPU Day
A626

1984, Oct. 9 *Perf. 13½*
2167 A626 20r Dove, UPU emblems .50 .20

Haj Seyyed Mostafa Khomeini Memorial
A627

1984, Oct. 23
2168 A627 5r multicolored .20 .20

Ghazi Tabatabaie Memorial — A628

Mohammed's Birthday, Unity Week — A630

Intl. Saadi Congress
A629

1984, Nov. 1 *Perf. 13x13½*
2169 A628 5r Portrait .20 .20

1984, Nov. 25 *Perf. 13½*
2170 A629 10r Portrait, mausoleum, emblem .50 .20

Saadi (c. 1213-1292), Persian poet.

1984, Dec. 6 Photo. *Perf. 13x13½*
2171 A630 5r Koran, mosque .25 .20

Islamic Revolution, 6th Anniv. — A631

Arbor Day — A632

1985, Feb. 11 *Perf. 13x13½*
2172 A631 40r multicolored .90 .40

See No. 2310o for stamp with bright pink denomination and dove tail.

1985, Mar. 6 *Perf. 13*
2173 A632 3r Sapling, deciduous trees .20 .20
2174 A632 5r Maturing trees .20 .20
a. Pair, #2173-2174 .30 .20

Local Flowers — A633

1985, Mar. 9 *Perf. 13½x13*
2175 A633 5r Fritillaria imperialis .20 .20
2176 A633 5r Ranunculus ficarioides .20 .20
2177 A633 5r Crocus sativus .20 .20
2178 A633 5r Primula heterochroma stapf .20 .20
a. Block of 4, #2175-2178 .50 .30

Novrooz (New Year).

Women's Day — A634

Republic of Iran, 6th Anniv. — A635

1985, Mar. 13 *Perf. 13x13½*
2179 A634 10r Procession of women .30 .20

Birth anniv. of Mohammed's daughter, Fatima.

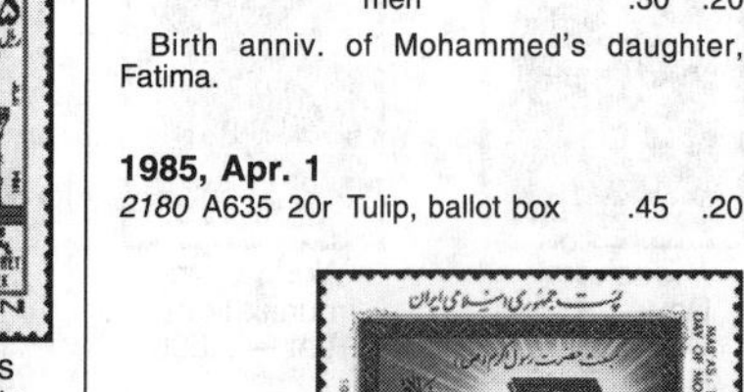

1985, Apr. 1
2180 A635 20r Tulip, ballot box .45 .20

Mab'as Festival
A636

1985, Apr. 18
2181 A636 10r Holy Koran .30 .20

Religious festival celebrating the recognition of Mohammed as the true prophet.

Day of the Oppressed
A637

World Telecommunications Day
A638

1985, May 6
2182 A637 5r Koran, flag, globe .20 .20

Birthday of the 12th Imam.

1985, May 17 *Perf. 13½x13*
2183 A638 20r ITU emblem .45 .20

Liberation of Khorramshahr, 1st Anniv. — A639

1985, May 24
2184 A639 5r Soldier, bridge .20 .20

Fist, Theological Seminary, Qum — A640

Day of Jerusalem
A642

World Handicrafts Day
A641

1985, June 5 ***Perf. 13x13½***
2185 A640 10r multicolored .50 .20

1963 Uprising, 22nd Anniv.

1985, June 10 ***Perf. 13½***
2186 A641 20r Plates, flasks .45 .20

1985, June 14
2187 A642 5r multicolored .20 .20

Id Al-fitr Feast — A643

Founding of the Islamic Propagation Org. — A644

1985, June 20 ***Perf. 13x13½***
2188 A643 5r multicolored .20 .20

1985, June 22
2189 A644 5r tan & emerald .20 .20

Ayatollah Sheikh Abdolhossein Amini — A645

1985, July 3 **Photo.** ***Perf. 13***
2190 A645 5r multicolored .25 .20

Pilgrimage to Mecca — A646

Goharshad Mosque Uprising, 50th Anniv. — A648

Cultural Heritage Preservation — A647

1985, July 20 **Photo.** ***Perf. 13½***
2191 A646 10r multicolored .30 .20

1985, Aug. 20

Ceramic plates from Nishabur: a, Swords. b, Farsi script. c, Peacock. d, Four leaves.

2192 Block of 4 .60 .20
a.-d. A647 5r, any single .20 .20

1985, Aug. 21 ***Perf. 13x13½***
2193 A648 10r multicolored .20 .20

Week of Government A649

Bleeding Tulips A650

Designs: a, Industry and communications. b, Industry and agriculture. c, Health care, red crescent. d, Education.

1985, Aug. 30 **Photo.** ***Perf. 13x13½***
2194 Block of 4 .60 .20
a.-d. A649 5r, any single .20 .20

1985, Sept. 8
2195 A650 10r multicolored .30 .20

17th Shahrivar, Bloody Friday memorial.

OPEC, 25th Anniv. — A651

Design: No. 2196b, OPEC emblem and 25.

1985, Sept. 14 ***Perf. 13½***
2196 Pair .50 .20
a.-b. A651 5r, any single .25 .20

Iran-Iraq War, 5th Anniv. — A652

Designs: a, Dead militiaman. b, Mosque and Ashura in Persian. c, Rockets descending on doves. d, Palm grove, rifle shot exploding rocket.

1985, Sept. 22
2197 Block of 4 .60 .20
a.-d. A652 5r any single .20 .20

Ashura mourning.

Ash-Sharif Ar-Radi — A653

1985, Sept. 26 **Photo.** ***Perf. 13x13½***
2198 A653 20r brt bl, lt bl & gold .60 .20

Ash-Sharif Ar-Radi, writer, death millennium.

UPU Day A654

1985, Oct. 9 ***Perf. 13½***
2199 A654 20r multicolored .60 .20

World Standards Day A655

1985, Oct. 14
2200 A655 20r Natl. Standards Office emblem .60 .20

Agricultural Training and Development Year — A656

Takeover of US Embassy, 6th Anniv. — A657

1985, Oct. 19 ***Perf. 13x13½***
2201 A656 5r Hand, wheat .20 .20

1985, Nov. 4 ***Perf. 13***
2202 A657 40r multicolored .60 .40

Moslem Unity Week A658

High Council of the Cultural Revolution A659

1985, Nov. 25 ***Perf. 13x13½***
2203 A658 10r Holy Ka'aba .30 .20

Birth of prophet Mohammed, 1015th anniv.

1985, Dec. 10
2204 A659 5r Roses .20 .20

Intl. Youth Year — A660

Designs: a, Education. b, Defense. c, Construction. d, Sports.

1985, Dec. 18 **Photo.** ***Perf. 13x13½***
2205 Block of 4 .60 .20
a.-d. A660 5r, any single .20 .20

Ezzeddin al-Qassam, 50th Death Anniv. — A661

1985, Dec. 20 ***Perf. 13½***
2206 A661 20r sil, sep & hn brn .60 .20

Map, Fists, Bayonets A662

1985, Dec. 25 **Wmk. 381**
2207 A662 40r multi 1.25 .40

Occupation of Afghanistan and Moslem resistance, 6th anniv.

Mirza Taqi Khan Amir Kabir (d. 1851) — A663

1986, Jan. 8 **Litho.** ***Perf. 13***
2208 A663 5r multicolored 1.25 .20

Students Destroying Statue of the Shah, Tulips — A664

Women's Day — A666

Sulayman Khater, 40th Death Anniv. — A665

1986, Feb. 11 Photo. *Perf. 13½*
2209 A664 20r multicolored .60 .20

Iranian Revolution, 7th anniv.
See No. 2310l for 24x36mm stamp with yellow Arabic script.

1986, Feb. 15 *Perf. 13*
2210 A665 10r multicolored .30 .20

1986, Mar. 3 *Perf. 13½*
2211 A666 10r multicolored .30 .20

Birth anniv. of Mohammed's daughter, Fatima.

Flowers — A667

a, Papaver orientale. b, Anemone coronaria. c, Papaver bracteatum. d, Anemone biflora.

1986, Mar. 11 Photo. *Perf. 13½*
2212 Block of 4 .60 .20
a. A667 5r any single .20 .20

Novrooz (New Year).

2000th Day of Sacred Defense A668

Intl. Day Against Racial Discrimination A669

1986, Mar. 14 Photo. *Perf. 13x13½*
2213 A668 5r scarlet & grn .20 .20

1986, Mar. 21
2214 A669 5r multicolored .20 .20

Islamic Republic of Iran, 7th Anniv. — A670

1986, Apr. 1 *Perf. 13*
2215 A670 10r Flag, map .30 .20

Mab'as Festival A671

1986, Apr. 7
2216 A671 40r multicolored .60 .20

Army Day — A672

Day of the Oppressed — A673

1986, Apr. 18 *Perf. 13½*
2217 A672 5r multicolored .20 .20

1986, Apr. 25 *Perf. 13x13½*
2218 A673 10r blk, gold & dk red .20 .20

Helicopter Crash — A674

Teacher's Day — A675

1986, Apr. 25 Wmk. 381
2219 A674 40r multicolored 1.25 .40

US air landing at Tabass Air Base, 6th anniv.

1986, May 2 Photo. *Perf. 13x13½*
2220 A675 5r multicolored .20 .20

World Telecommunications Day — A676

1986, May 17 *Perf. 13½x13*
2221 A676 20r blk, sil & ultra .60 .20

Universal Day of the Child — A677

1986, June 1 *Perf. 13*
2222 A677 15r Child's war drawing .45 .20
2223 A677 15r Hosein Fahmide, Iran-Iraq war hero .45 .20
a. Pair, #2222-2223 .90 .30

1963 Uprising, 23rd Anniv. — A678

1986, June 5 *Perf. 13x13½*
2224 A678 10r Qum Theological Seminary .30 .20

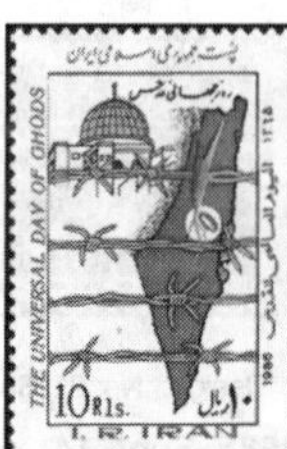

Day of Jerusalem — A679

1986, June 6
2225 A679 10r multicolored .30 .20

Id Al-Fitr Feast A680

1986, June 9 *Perf. 13*
2226 A680 10r Moslems praying .75 .20

World Handicrafts Day A681

a, Baluchi cross-hatched rug. b, Craftsman. c, Qalamkar flower rug. d, Copper repousse vase.

1986, June 10 *Perf. 13½*
2227 Block of 4 1.25 .40
a.-d. A681 10r, any single .30 .20

Intl. Day for Solidarity with Black So. Africans — A682

Ayatollah Beheshti — A683

1986, June 26
2228 A682 10r multicolored .30 .20

1986, June 28 *Perf. 13x13½*
2229 A683 10r multicolored .30 .20

Death of Beheshti and Islamic Party workers, Tehran headquarters bombing, 5th anniv.

Ayatollah Mohammad Taqi Shirazi, Map of Iraq — A684

Shrine of Imam Reza — A685

1986, June 30 Photo. Wmk. 381
2230 A684 20r multicolored .60 .20

Iraqi Moslem uprising against the British.

1986, July 19 *Perf. 13½*
2231 A685 10r multicolored .30 .20

Eid Ul-Adha, Feast of Sacrifice — A686

Eid Ul-Ghadir Feast — A688

Cultural Heritage Preservation — A687

1986, Aug. 17 *Perf. 13x13½*
2232 A686 10r multicolored .30 .20

1986, Aug. 20

Designs: No. 2233, Bam Fortress. No. 2234, Kabud (Blue) Mosque, Tabriz. No. 2235, Mausoleum of Sohel Ben Ali at Astenah, Arak. No. 2236, Soltanieh Mosque, Zendjan Province.

2233 A687 5r Hilltop .25 .20
2234 A687 5r shown .25 .20
2235 A687 5r Intact roof .25 .20
2236 A687 5r Damaged roof .25 .20
Nos. 2233-2236 (4) 1.00 .80

1986, Aug. 25
2237 A688 20r multicolored .60 .20

Population and Housing Census — A689

Iran-Iraq War, 6th Year — A690

1986, Sept. 9 ***Perf. 13½x13***
2238 A689 20r multicolored .40 .20

1986, Sept. 22 ***Perf. 13***
2239 A690 10r Battleship Paykan .30 .20
2240 A690 10r Susangerd .30 .20
2241 A690 10r Khorramshahr .30 .20
2242 A690 10r Howeizeh .30 .20
2243 A690 10r Siege of Abadan .30 .20
Nos. 2239-2243 (5) 1.50 1.00

10th Asian Games, Seoul A691

1986, Oct. 2 **Photo.** **Wmk. 381**
2244 A691 15r Wrestling .40 .20
2245 A691 15r Rifle shooting .40 .20

World Post Day A692

1986, Oct. 9
2246 A692 20r multicolored .60 .20

UNESCO, 40th Anniv. — A693

1986, Nov. 4 **Photo.** ***Perf. 13x13½***
2247 A693 45r blk, sky bl & brt rose 1.25 .45

Ayatollah Tabatabaie (d. 1981) — A694

1986, Nov. 15 **Photo.** ***Perf. 13½x13***
2248 A694 10r multicolored .30 .20

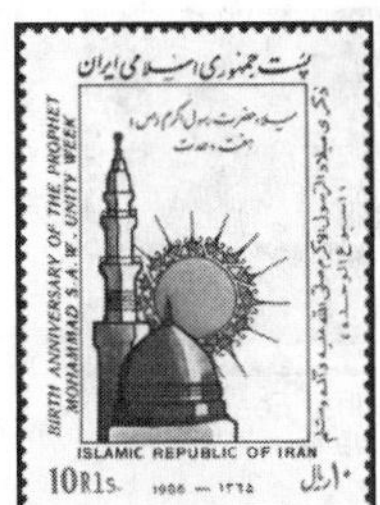

Unity Week — A695

1986, Nov. 20
2249 A695 10r multicolored .30 .20

Birth anniv. of Mohammed.

People's Militia — A696

1986, Nov. 26 ***Perf. 13***
2250 A696 5r multicolored .20 .20

Mobilization of the Oppressed Week.

Afghan Resistance Movement, 7th Anniv. — A697

1986, Dec. 27
2251 A697 40r multicolored 1.25 .40

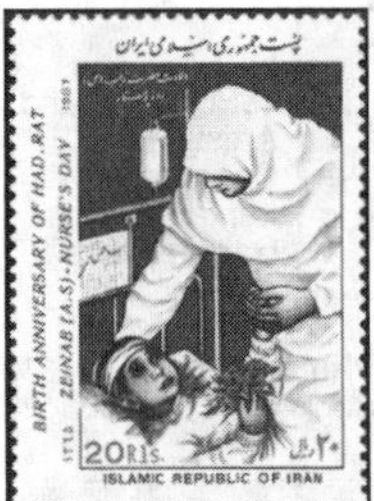

Nurses' Day — A698

1987, Jan. 12 **Photo.** ***Perf. 13***
2252 A698 20r multicolored .60 .20

Hazrat Zainab birth anniv.

Fifth Islamic Theology Conference, Tehran — A699

Wmk. 381

1987, Jan. 29 **Photo.** ***Perf. 13***
2253 A699 20r multicolored .60 .20

Islamic Revolution, 8th Anniv. — A700

1987, Feb. 11
2254 A700 20r multicolored .60 .20

See No. 2310m for 24x36mm stamp.

Islamic Revolutionary Committees, 8th Anniv. — A701

1987, Feb. 12
2255 A701 10r brt bl, scar & yel .30 .20

Women's Day — A702

1987, Feb. 19
2256 A702 10r multicolored .30 .20

Birthday of Fatima, daughter of Mohammed.

Iran Air, 25th Anniv. A703

1987, Feb. 24
2257 A703 30r multicolored .90 .30

Ayatollah Mirza Mohammad Hossein Naeini, 50th Death Anniv. — A704

1987, Mar. 6 **Photo.** ***Perf. 13***
2258 A704 10r multicolored .30 .20

New Year — A705

Mab'as Festival A706

Flowers: a, Iris persica. b, Rosa damascena. c, Iris paradoxa. d, Tulipa clusiana.

1987, Mar. 11 ***Perf. 13½x13***
2259 Block of 4 2.00 .50
a.-d. A705 5r, any single .50 .20

See Nos. 2313, 2361, 2411, 2443.

1987, Mar. 28 ***Perf. 13***
2260 A706 45r gold, dk grn & grn 1.40 .45

Universal Day of the Oppressed A707

1987, Apr. 14
2261 A707 20r multicolored .60 .20

Savior Mahdi's birthday.

Memorial to Lebanese Hizbollah Martyrs — A708

1987, Apr. 5
2262 A708 10r grn, gray & brt car .30 .20

Revolutionary Guards Day — A709

1987, Apr. 2
2263 A709 5r multi .20 .20

Imam Hossein's birthday.

8th Anniv. of Islamic Republic A710

1987, Apr. 1
2264 A710 20r multicolored .60 .20

World Health Day — A711

Child survival through immunization: 3r, Intravenous. 5r, Oral.

1987, Apr. 7 ***Perf. 13x13½***
2265 A711 3r multicolored .20 .20
2266 A711 5r multicolored .30 .20
a. Pair, #2265-2266 .50 .25

Int'l. Labor Day — A712

1987, May 1 Photo. ***Perf. 13***
2267 A712 5r multicolored .20 .20

Teachers' Day — A713

1987, May 2 **Wmk. 381**
2268 A713 5r Ayatollah Mottahari .20 .20

A714

1987, May 17 ***Perf. 13½x13***
2269 A714 20r multicolored .70 .20

World Telecommunications Day.

A715

1987, May 18 ***Perf. 13***
2270 A715 20r Sassanian silver gilt vase .60 .20
2271 A715 20r Bisque pot, Rey, 12th cent. .60 .20

Intl. Museum Day.

Universal Day of Jerusalem A716

1963 Uprising, 24th Anniv. A718

World Crafts Day A717

1987, May 22 ***Perf. 13½x13***
2272 A716 20r multicolored .60 .20

1987, June 10 ***Perf. 13x13½***

a, Blown glass tea service. b, Stained glass window. c, Ceramic plate. d, Potter.

2273 Block of 4 .75 .20
a.-d. A717 5r any single .20 .20

1987, June 5 Photo. ***Perf. 13½***
2274 A718 20r multicolored .60 .20

Tax Reform Week — A719

1987, July 10 ***Perf. 13***
2275 A719 10r black, sil & gold .30 .20

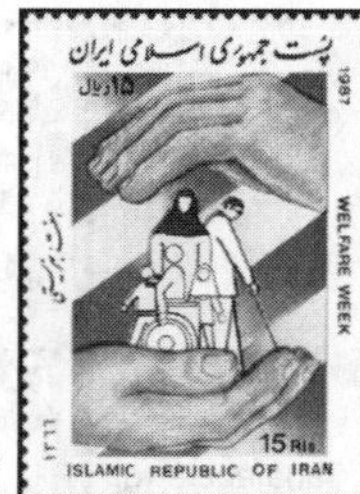
Welfare Week — A720

1987, July 17
2276 A720 15r multicolored .45 .20

Eid Ul-adha, Feast of Sacrifice — A721

1987, Aug. 6
2277 A721 12r sil, blk & Prus grn .45 .20

Eid Ul-Ghadir Festival A722

Banking Week — A723

1987, Aug. 14
2278 A722 18r black, green & gold .55 .20

1987, Aug. 17 ***Perf. 13½x13***
2279 A723 15r red brn, gold & pale grnsh bl .45 .20

1st Cultural and Artistic Congress of Iranian Calligraphers A724

1987, Aug. 21 Photo. ***Perf. 13x13½***
2280 A724 20r multicolored .60 .20

Memorial to Iranian Pilgrims Killed in Mecca — A725

1987, Aug. 26 Wmk. 381 ***Perf. 13***
2281 A725 8r multicolored .30 .20

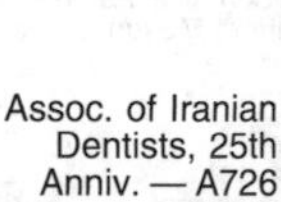
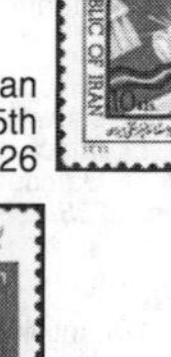
Assoc. of Iranian Dentists, 25th Anniv. — A726

Intl. Peace Day — A727

1987, Aug. 27 Photo. ***Perf. 13½x13***
2282 A726 10r multicolored .30 .20

1987, Sept. 1 ***Perf. 13***
2283 A727 20r gold & lt ultra .60 .20

Iran-Iraq War, 7th Anniv. — A728

Police Day — A729

1987, Sept. 22 ***Perf. 13½x13***
2284 A728 25r shown .75 .25
2285 A728 25r Soldier, battle scene .75 .25
a. Pair, #2284-2285

1987, Sept. 28
2286 A729 10r multicolored .30 .20

Intl. Social Security Week, Oct. 4-10 — A730

World Post Day — A731

1987, Oct. 4 **Wmk. 381**
2287 A730 15r blk, gold & brt blue .45 .20

1987, Oct. 9 ***Perf. 13x13½***

UPU emblem and: No. 2288, M. Ghandi, minister of the Post and Telecommunications Bureau. No. 2289, Globe, dove.

2288 A731 15r multicolored .45 .20
2289 A731 15r multicolored .45 .20

Importation Prohibited
Importation of stamps was prohibited effective Oct. 29, 1987.

A732

A733

Wmk. 381

1987, Nov. 4 Photo. *Perf. 13*
2290 A732 40r multicolored

Takeover of US Embassy, 8th anniv.

1987, Nov. 5
2291 A733 20r multicolored

1st Intl. Tehran Book Fair.

Mohammed's Birthday, Unity Week — A734

1987, Nov. 10
2292 A734 25r multicolored

Ayatollah Modarres Martyrdom, 50th Anniv. — A735

1987, Dec. 1
2293 A735 10r brn & bister

Agricultural Training and Extension Week — A736

1987, Dec. 6
2294 A736 10r multicolored

Afghan Resistance, 8th Anniv. — A737

1987, Dec. 27
2295 A737 40r multicolored

Main Mosques A738

1987-92 *Perf. 13x13½, 13½x13*

Silver Background

2295A A738 1r Shoushtar
2296 A738 2r Ouroumieh
2296A A738 3r Kerman
2297 A738 5r Kazvin
2298 A738 10r Varamin
a. Unwatermarked ('91)
2299 A738 20r Saveh
a. Unwatermarked ('91)
2300 A738 30r Natanz, vert.
2301 A738 40r Shiraz
a. Unwatermarked ('92)
2302 A738 50r Isfahan, vert.
a. Unwatermarked ('91)
2303 A738 100r Hamadan
a. Unwatermarked ('91)
2304 A738 200r Dezfoul, vert.
a. Unwatermarked ('91)
2305 A738 500r Yazd, vert.
a. Unwatermarked ('91)

Issued: 10r, 12/1; 5r, 12/30; 500r, 1/10/88; 20r, 1/14/88; 2r, 1/24/88; 50r, 1/24/89; 100r, 10/21/89; 200r, 10/28/89; 30r, 40r, 3/17/90; 1r, 3r, 3/92.

For surcharges see #2750-2751.

Watermarks on this issue can be difficult to discern. The paper of the unwatermarked stamps show fluoresence under long wave ultraviolet light.

Qum Uprising, 10th Anniversary — A739

1988, Jan. 9 *Perf. 13*
2306 A739 20r multicolored

Bombing of Schools by Iraq — A740

1988, Feb. 1 *Perf. 13x13½*
2307 A740 10r multicolored

Gholamreza Takhti, World Wrestling Champion — A741

1988, Feb. 4 *Perf. 13½*
2308 A741 15r multicolored

Women's Day — A742

1988, Feb. 9 *Perf. 13*
2309 A742 20r multicolored

Birth anniv. of Mohammed's daughter, Fatima.

Souvenir Sheet

Types of 1979-88 and

Islamic Revolution, 9th Anniv. — A743

Perf. 13, Imperf

1988, Feb. 11 Wmk. 381
2310 Sheet of 16
a. A547 1r like #2046
b. A547 3r like #2047
c. A559 3r like #2066
d. A547 5r like #2048
e. A559 5r like #2067
f. A570 5r like #2095
g. A570 10r like #2096
h. A608 10r like #2146
i. A537 18r like #1999
j. A559 20r like #2068
k. A570 20r like #2097
l. A664 20r like #2209
m. A700 20r like #2254
n. A587 30r like #2115
o. A631 40r like #2172
p. A743 40r shown

Nos. 2310a, 2310b, 2310d, 2310l, 2310m are smaller than the original issues. See original issues for distinguishing features on other stamps.

Tabriz Uprising, 10th Anniv. — A744

1988, Feb. 18 *Perf. 13*
2311 A744 25r multicolored

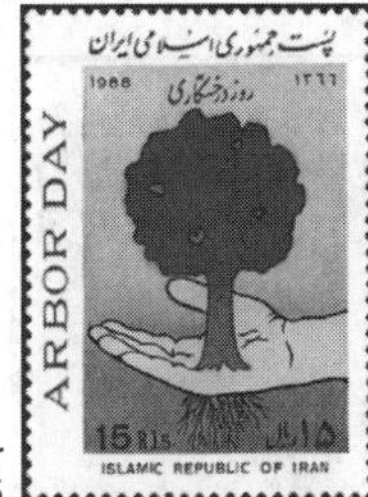

Arbor Day — A745

1988, Mar. 5
2312 A745 15r multicolored

New Year Festival Type of 1987

Flowers: a, Anthemis hyalina. b, Malva silvestria. c, Viola odorata. d, Echium amaenum.

1988, Mar. 10 *Perf. 13½x13*
2313 Block of 4
a.-d. A705 10r any single

Islamic Republic, 9th Anniv. — A746

1988, Apr. 1 *Perf. 13*
2314 A746 20r multicolored

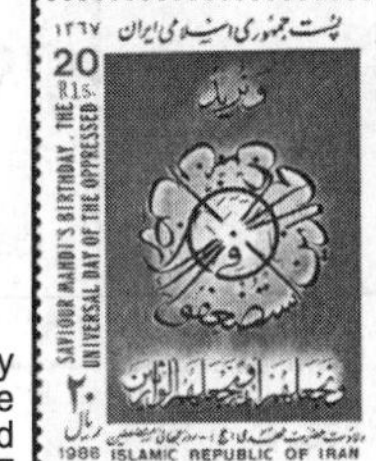
Universal Day of the Oppressed A747

1988, Apr. 3
2314A A747 20r multicolored

Savior Mahdi's Birthday.

Cultural Heritage — A748

1988, Apr. 18
2315 A748 10r Mosque
2316 A748 10r Courtyard
a. Pair, #2315-2316
2317 A748 10r Minarets, vert.
2318 A748 10r Corridor, vert.
a. Pair, #2317-2318

Chemical Bombardment of Halabja, Iraq — A749

1988, Apr. 26
2319 A749 20r multicolored

A750

A750a

Palestinian Uprising
A750b

1988, May 13

2320 Strip of 5
- *a.* A750 10r multi
- *b.* A750a 10r multi
- *c.* A750b 10r multi
- *d.* A750b 10r multi, diff.
- *e.* A750b 10r Rock in hand, rioters

World Telecommunications Day — A751

1988, May 17 ***Perf. 13x13½***

2321 A751 20r green & blue

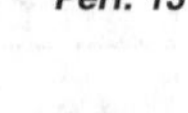

Intl. Museum Day — A752

Designs: a, Ceramic vase, 1982. b, Bastan Museum, entranceway. c, Tabriz silk rug, 14th cent. d, Gold ring, 7th cent. B.C.

1988, May 18 ***Perf. 13***

2322 Block of 4
- *a.-d.* A752 10r any single

Mining Day — A753

1988, May 22 Photo. Wmk. 381

2323 A753 20r multicolored

Intl. Day of the Child — A754

1988, June 1

2324 A754 10r multicolored

June 5th Uprising, 25th Anniv. — A755

1988, June 5

2325 A755 10r multicolored

World Crafts Day
A756

1988, June 10 ***Perf. 13x13½***

2326 A756 10r Straw basket
2327 A756 10r Weaver
- *a.* Pair, #2326-2327

2328 A756 10r Tapestry, vert.
2329 A756 10r Miniature, vert.
- *a.* Pair, #2328-2329

Child Health Campaign
A757

1988, July 6 ***Perf. 13***

2330 A757 20r blk, blue & green

Tax Reform Week — A758

1988, July 10

2331 A758 20r multicolored

A759

1988, July 15 ***Perf. 13½x13***

2332 A759 20r Allameh Balkhi

A760

1988, July 21 ***Perf. 13***

2333 A760 10r Holy Ka'aba, dove, stars
2334 A760 10r shown

Massacre of Muslim Pilgrims at Mecca.

Destruction of Iranian Airliner — A761

1988, Aug. 11

2335 A761 45r multicolored

A762

A763

1988, Aug. 13

2336 A762 20r Seyyed Ali Andarzgou

1988, Sept. 1 ***Perf. 13½x13***

2337 A763 20r multicolored

Islamic Banking Week.

Divine Day of 17 Shahrivar, 10th Anniv. — A764

1988, Sept. 8

2338 A764 25r multicolored

1988 Summer Olympics, Seoul — A765

Designs: a, Weightlifting. b, Pommel horse. c, Judo. d, Soccer. e, Wrestling.

1988, Sept. 10

2339 Strip of 5
- *a.-e.* A765 10r any single

A766

A767

1988, Sept. 17 ***Perf. 13½x13***

2340 A766 30r blk, grn & yel

Agricultural census.

1988, Sept. 22 ***Perf. 13x13½***

2341 A767 20r multicolored

Iran-Iraq War, 8th anniv.

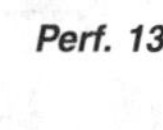

World Post Day
A768

1988, Oct. 9 ***Perf. 13***

2342 A768 20r blk, ultra & grn

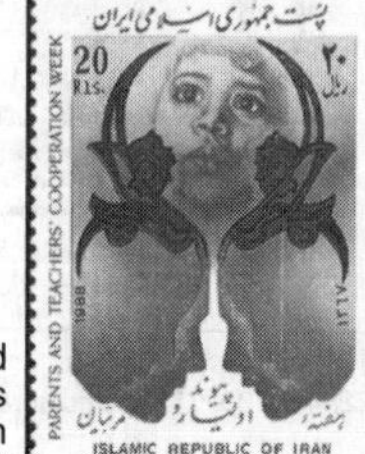

Parents and Teachers Cooperation Week — A769

1988, Oct. 16

2343 A769 20r multicolored

Mohammed's Birthday, Unity Week — A770

1988, Oct. 29
2344 A770 10r multicolored

A771

A772

1988, Nov. 4
2345 A771 45r multicolored

Takeover of US embassy, 9th anniv.

1988, Nov. 6 ***Perf. 13½x13***
2346 A772 10r multicolored

Insurance Day.

Intl. Congress on the Writings of Hafiz — A773

Illustration reduced.

1988, Nov. 19 ***Perf. 13x13½***
2347 A773 20r blue, gold & pink

Agricultural Training and Extension Week — A774

1988, Dec. 6 ***Perf. 13***
2348 A774 15r multicolored

Scientists, Artists and Writers A775

1988, Dec. 18 ***Perf. 13x13½***
2349 A775 10r Parvin E'Tessami
2350 A775 10r Jalal Al-Ahmad
2351 A775 10r Muhammad Mo'in
a. Pair, #2350-2351
2352 A775 10r Qaem Maqam Farahani
2353 A775 10r Kamal Al-Molk
a. Pair, #2352-2353

See Nos. 2398-2402.

Afghan Resistance, 9th Anniv. — A776

1988, Dec. 27 ***Perf. 13***
2354 A776 40r multicolored

Transportion and Communication Decade — A777

Perf. 13x13½
1989, Jan. 16 **Wmk. 381**
2355 A777 20r Satellite, envelopes, microwave dish
2356 A777 20r Cargo planes
a. Pair, #2355-2356
2357 A777 20r Train, trucks
2358 A777 20r Ships
a. Pair, #2357-2358

Prophethood of Mohammed A778

1989, Mar. 6 ***Perf. 13***
2359 A778 20r multicolored

Mab'as festival.

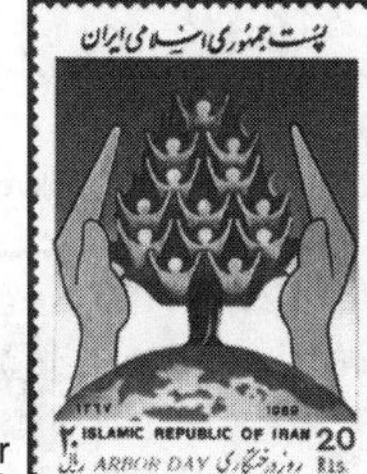

Arbor Day — A779

1989, Mar. 6
2360 A779 20r multicolored

New Year Festival Type of 1987

Flowers: a, Cephalanthera kurdica. b, Dactylorhiza romana. c, Comperia comperiana. d, Orchis mascula.

1989, Mar. 11 ***Perf. 13½x13***
2361 Block of 4
a.-d. A705 10r any single

A780

A781

1989, Mar. 23
2362 A780 20r shown
2363 A780 30r Meteorological devices, ship
a. Pair, #2362-2363

World Meteorology Day.

1989, Apr. 1 ***Perf. 13***
2364 A781 20r multicolored

Islamic Republic, 10th anniv.

Reconstruction of Abadan Refinery A782

1989, Apr. 1
2365 A782 20r multicolored

Ayatollah Morteza Motahhari, 10th Death Anniv. — A783

1989, May 2
2366 A783 20r multi

Teachers' Day.

A784

A785

1989, May 5
2367 A784 30r multicolored

Universal Day of Jerusalem.

1989, May 17 ***Perf. 13½x13***
2368 A785 20r multicolored

World Telecommunications Day.

A786

A787

Intl. Museum Day: Gurgan pottery, 6th cent.

1989, May 18 ***Perf. 13x13½***
2369 A786 20r Jar
2370 A786 20r Bottle
a. Pair, #2369-2370

1989, June 4 ***Perf. 13***
2371 A787 20r multicolored

Nomads' Day.

World Crafts Day A788

1989, July 5 ***Perf. 13x13½***
2372 A788 20r Engraver
2373 A788 20r Copper vase
a. Pair, #2372-2373
2374 A788 20r Copper plate, vert.
2375 A788 20r Copper wall hanging, vert.
a. Pair, #2374-2375

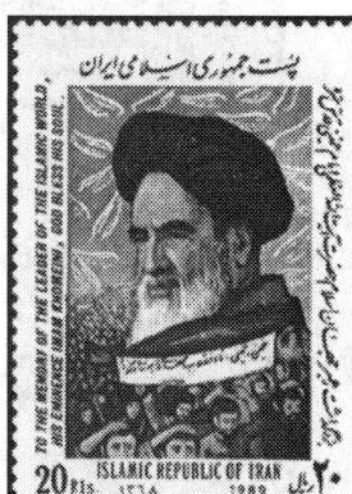

Ayatollah Khomeini (1900-89) A789

1989, July 6 ***Perf. 13***
2376 A789 20r multicolored

Pasteur and Avicenna A790

1989, July 7
2377 A790 30r multicolored
2378 A790 50r multicolored
a. Pair, #2377-2378

PHILEXFRANCE.

Asia-Pacific Telecommunity, 10th Anniv. — A791

1989, July 25
2379 A791 30r blk, org brn & bl

Mehdi Araghi, 10th Death Anniv. — A792

1989, Aug. 30
2380 A792 20r brn org & org brn

M.H. Shahryar, Poet — A793

1989, Sept. 17
2381 A793 20r multicolored

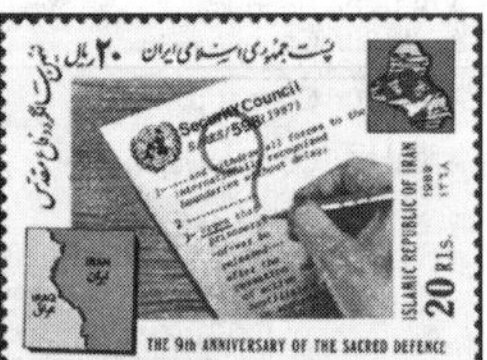

Iran-Iraq War, 9th Anniv. — A794

1989, Sept. 22
2382 A794 20r UN Security Council res. 598

Ayatollah Khomeini — A795

Designs: 1r, Khomeini's birthplace, flower. 2r, Portrait as youth. 3r, Giving speech. 5r, Map, rifles, exile. 10r, Khomeini returns to Iran, Feb. 1, 1979. 20r, Khomeini seated before microphone. 30r, Khomeini with grandson.40r, Other mullahs. 50r, Khomeini gesturing with hands. 70r, On balcony before crowd. 100r, Slogan. 200r, Empty lectern. 500r, Mausoleum. 1000r, Sun rays.

1989-92 Litho. Unwmk. *Perf. 13½*
2382A A795 1r green & multi
2382B A795 2r green & multi
2383 A795 3r green & multi
2384 A795 5r brt vio & multi
2385 A795 10r brt bl & multi
2386 A795 20r blue & multi
2387 A795 30r pink & multi
2388 A795 40r red & multi
2389 A795 50r gray & multi
2390 A795 70r brt grn & multi
2391 A795 100r ultra & multi
2392 A795 200r red brn & multi
2393 A795 500r black & multi
2393A A795 1000r multicolored

Issued: 1r, 1/3/91; 3r, 3/16/90; 5r, 12/13; 10r, 10/22; 20r, 30r, 50r, 9/23/90; 40r, 2/9/90; 100, 200r, 9/26/90; 70r, 500r, 6/4/91; 2r, 1000r, 3/16/92.

World Post Day A796

Wmk. 381
1989, Oct. 9 Photo. *Perf. 13*
2394 A796 20r multicolored

Mohammed's Birthday, Unity Week — A797

1989, Oct. 18
2395 A797 10r multi

Takeover of US Embassy, 10th Anniv. — A798

1989, Nov. 4 *Perf. 13½x13*
2396 A798 40r multicolored

Bassij of the Oppressed (Militia), 10th Anniv. — A799

1989, Nov. 27 *Perf. 13*
2397 A799 10r multicolored

Scientists, Artists and Writers Type of 1988

1989, Dec. 18 *Perf. 13x13½*
2398 A775 10r Mehdi Elahi Ghomshei
2399 A775 10r Dr. Abdulazim Gharib
2400 A775 10r Seyyed Hossein Mirkhani
a. Pair, #2399-2400
2401 A775 10r Ayatollah Seyyed Hossein Boroujerdi
2402 A775 10r Ayatollah Sheikh Abdulkarim Haeri
a. Pair, #2401-2402

Intl. Literacy Year — A800

Wmk. 381
1990, Jan. 1 Photo. *Perf. 13½*
2403 A800 20r multicolored

Cultural Heritage A801

Designs: No. 2404, Drinking vessel, 1980. No. 2405, Footed vase, 1979.

1990, Jan. 21 *Perf. 13*
2404 A801 20r blk & deep org
2405 A801 20r blk & yel grn
a. Pair, #2404-2405

New Identification Card System — A802

1990, Feb. 9
2406 A802 10r multicolored

Islamic Revolution, 11th Anniv. — A803

1990, Feb. 11
2407 A803 50r multicolored

Intl. Koran Recitation Competition A804

1990, Feb. 23
2408 A804 10r blk, bl & grn

A805

A806

1990, Mar. 2 *Perf. 13½x13*
2409 A805 10r multicolored

Invalids of Islamic Revolution.

1990, Mar. 6 *Perf. 13*
2410 A806 20r multicolored

Arbor Day.

New Year Festival Type of 1987

Flowers: a, Coronilla varia. b, Astragalus cornu-caprae. c, Astragalus obtusifolius. d, Astragalus straussii.

1990, Mar. 11 *Perf. 13½x13*
2411 Block of 4
a.-d. A705 10r any single

Islamic Republic, 11th Anniv. — A807

1990, Apr. 1 *Perf. 13*
2412 A807 30r multicolored

World Health Day — A808

1990, Apr. 7
2413 A808 40r multicolored

A809

1990, June 4 Unwmk. ***Perf. 11x10½***
2414 A809 50r multicolored

Ayatollah Khomeini, 1st death anniv.

A810

1990, Dec. 15 Litho. ***Perf. 10½***
2415 A810 100r multicolored

Jerusalem Day.

A811

A812

1990, Oct. 20 ***Perf. 13***
2416 A811 20r Turkoman jewelry
2417 A811 50r Gilded steel bird
a. Pair, #2416-2417

World Crafts Day.

1990, Nov. 17 ***Perf. 10½***
2418 A812 20r multicolored

Intl. Day of the Child.

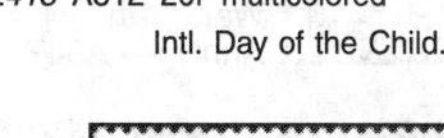

Aid to Earthquake Victims — A813

1990, Nov. 19 ***Perf. 13x13½***
2419 A813 100r multicolored

Return and Tribute to Former Prisoners of Iran-Iraq War — A814

1990, Nov. 21 ***Perf. 13***
2420 A814 250r multicolored

Ferdowsi Intl. Congress — A815

Illustration reduced.

1990, Dec. 22 Litho. ***Imperf.***
Size: 60x75mm

2421 A815 100r Portrait
2422 A815 100r Statue
2423 A815 100r Monument
2424 A815 100r Slogan, diamond cartouche
2425 A815 100r Rectangular slogan
2426 A815 100r Slogan, diff.
2427 A815 200r Two riders embracing
2428 A815 200r Archer, birds
2429 A815 200r Six men
2430 A815 200r White elephant
2431 A815 200r Warrior, genie, horse
2432 A815 200r Hunting scene
2433 A815 200r Riding through fire
2434 A815 200r Four slogan tablets
2435 A815 200r Man with feet shackled
2436 A815 200r Palace scene

Conference on epic poem "Book of Kings" by Ferdowsi.

In 1991 some imperf between blocks of 4 were released.

"Victory Over Iraq" — A816

1991, Feb. 25 ***Perf. 13***
2437 A816 100r multicolored

Intl. Museum Day — A817

Designs: No. 2438, Gold jug with Kufric inscription, 10th cent. A.D. No. 2439, Silver-inlaid brass basin, 14th cent. A.D.

1991, Feb. 25
2438 A817 50r multicolored
2439 A817 50r multicolored
a. Pair, #2438-2439

A818

A819

1991, Mar. 12 ***Perf. 10½***
2440 A818 50r multicolored

World Telecommunications Day.

1991, Feb. 25 ***Perf. 13***
2441 A819 200r org brn & blk

Opening of Postal Museum.

Islamic Revolution, 12th Anniv. — A820

1991, Feb. 11 Photo. ***Perf. 13***
2442 A820 100r multicolored

New Year Festival Type of 1987

Designs: No. 2443a, Iris spuria. b, Iris lycotis. c, Iris demawendica. d, Iris meda.

1991, Mar. 11 ***Perf. 13½x13***
2443 A705 20r Block of 4, #a.-d.

Saleh Hosseini, 10th Death Anniv. — A821

1991, Mar. 19 ***Perf. 13½x13***
2444 A821 30r red & black

Mab'as Festival A822

1991, Mar. 19 ***Perf. 13x13½***
2445 A822 100r multicolored

Universal Day of the Oppressed A823

1991, Mar. 25 ***Perf. 13***
2446 A823 50r multicolored

Savior Mahdi's Birthday.

Revolutionaries, 25th Death Anniv. — A824

1990, June 16
2447 A824 50r maroon & red org

Dated 1990.

Islamic Republic, 12th Anniv. — A825

Unwmk.
1991, Apr. 1 Photo. ***Perf. 13***
2448 A825 20r blk, slate, grn & red

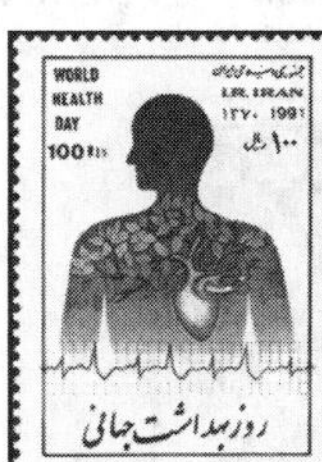

World Health Day — A826

1991, Apr. 7 ***Perf. 13½x13***
2449 A826 100r multicolored

Day of Jerusalem A827

1991, Apr. 12 *Perf. 13*
2450 A827 100r bl, blk & brn

A828 A829

1991, Apr. 12 Litho. *Perf. 10½*
2451 A828 50r multicolored

Women's Day. Birth anniv. of Mohammed's daughter, Fatima.

Perf. 13½x13
1991, Apr. 28 Photo. Unwmk.
2452 A829 200r bl grn & blk

Ayatollah Borujerdi, 30th death anniv.

Teachers' Day — A830

Illustration reduced.

1991, May 2 *Perf. 13x13½*
2453 A830 50r multicolored

Decade for Natural Disaster Reduction A831

1991, May 11 Litho. *Perf. 10½*
2454 A831 100r multicolored

World Telecommunications Day — A832

Perf. 13½x13
1991, May 17 Photo. Unwmk.
2455 A832 100r multicolored

Intl. Museum Day — A833

Flags — A834

Ewers, Kashan, 13th cent.: 20r, With spout. 40r, Baluster.

1991, May 18 *Perf. 13*
2456 A833 20r multicolored
2457 A833 40r multicolored
a. Pair, #2456-2457

1991, May 24 *Perf. 13x13½*
2458 A834 30r multicolored

Liberation of Khorramshahr, 7th anniv.

Abol-Hassan Ali-ebne-Mosa Reza, Birth Anniv. — A835

Views of shrine, Meshed.

1991, May 26 *Perf. 13*
2459 10r Mausoleum
2460 30r Gravestone
a. A835 Pair, #2459-2460

First Intl. Conf. on Seismology and Earthquake Engineering A836

1991, May 27 *Perf. 13½x13*
2461 A836 100r multicolored

World Child Day — A837

1991, June 1 Photo. *Perf. 13½*
2462 A837 50r multicolored

Holy Shrine at Karbola, Iraq Destroyed by Invasion — A838

Unwmk.
1991, June 3 Photo. *Perf. 13*
2463 A838 70r multicolored

Ayatollah Khomeini, 2nd Death Anniv. — A839

1991, June 4
2464 A839 100r multicolored

World Handicrafts Day — A840

Designs: No. 2465, Engraved brass wares. No. 2466, Gilded samovar set.

1991, June 10 *Perf. 13½x13*
2465 A840 40r multicolored
2466 A840 40r multicolored
a. Pair #2465-2466

Intl. Congress on Poet Nezami — A841

1991, June 22 *Perf. 13*
2467 A841 50r multicolored

A842

A843

1991, July 15 Photo. *Perf. 13*
2468 A842 50r multicolored

Ali Ibn Abi Talib, 1330th death anniv.

Unwmk.
1991, July 29 Photo. *Perf. 13*
2469 A843 50r multicolored

Blood Transfusion Week.

Return of Prisoners of War, First Anniv. — A844

Illustration reduced.

1991, Aug. 27 *Perf. 13x13½*
2470 A844 100r multicolored

Ayatollah Marashi, Death Anniv. — A845

Illustration reduced.

1991, Aug. 29 *Perf. 13½x13*
2471 A845 30r multicolored

Ayatollah-ol-Ozma Seyyed Abdol-Hossein Lary, Revolutionary — A846

Design includes 1909 stamp issued by Lary.

1991, Sept. 9 *Perf. 13x13½*
2472 A846 30r multicolored

Start of Iran-Iraq War, 11th Anniv. — A847

1991, Sept. 22 *Perf. 13½x13*
2473 A847 20r multicolored

Mosque, Kaaba, Unity Week — A848

1991, Sept. 22 *Perf. 13*
2474 A848 30r multicolored

World Tourism Day A849

1991, Sept. 27 Photo. ***Perf. 13½***
2475 A849 200r multicolored

Dr. Mohammed Gharib, Pediatrician A849a

1991, Sept. 29 Photo. ***Perf. 13***
2475A A849a 100r bl & blk

Official first day covers are dated 1/19/1991.

World Post Day A850

Unwmk.
1991, Oct. 9 Photo. ***Perf. 13***
2476 A850 70r #2071 on cover

Khaju-ye Kermani Intl. Congress — A851

1991, Oct. 15
2477 A851 30r multicolored

A852

A853

1991, Oct. 16
2478 A852 80r multicolored

World Food Day.

1991, Oct. 19 ***Perf. 13½x13***
2479 A853 40r bl vio & gold

Intl. Conference Supporting Palestinians.

Illustrators of Children's Books, 1st Asian Biennial A854

1991, Oct. 25 ***Perf. 13***
2480 A854 100r Hoopoe

"Children" misspelled.

World Standards Day — A855

1991, Oct. 14 ***Perf. 13½***
2481 A855 100r multicolored

1st Seminar on Adolescent and Children's Literature A856

1991, Nov. 3 ***Perf. 13***
2482 A856 20r multicolored

Roshid Intl. Educational Film Festival A857

1991, Nov. 6
2483 A857 50r multicolored

7th Ministerial Meeting of the Group of 77 — A858

1991, Nov. 16
2484 A858 30r vio & bl grn

Bassij of the Oppressed (Militia), 12th Anniv. — A859

1991, Nov. 25
2485 A859 30r multicolored

Ayatollah Aref Hosseini — A860

1991, Dec. 18 ***Perf. 13½***
2486 A860 50r multicolored

Sadek Ghanji A861

1991, Dec. 20
2487 A861 50r multicolored

Agricultural Training and Extension Week — A862

1991, Dec. 22 ***Perf. 13***
2488 A862 70r multicolored

World Telecommunications Day — A863

#2489: a, 20r, Telegraph key. b, 20r, Phone lines. c, 20r, Early telephones. d, 40r, Satellite dishes. e, 40r, Telecommunications satellite.

1992, May 17 Photo. ***Perf. 13***
2489 A863 Strip of 5, #a.-e.

New Year — A863a

Flora of Iran: Nos. 2490a, 2490d, 20r. Nos. 2490b, 2490c, 40r.

1992, Apr. 18 ***Perf. 13½x13***
2490 A863a Block of 4, #a.-d.

Mosque of Jerusalem A864

1992, Mar. 27 ***Perf. 13x13½***
2491 A864 200r multicolored

Day of Jerusalem and honoring A. Mousavi, the Shiva leader of Lebanon, with Sheikh Ragheb Harb in background.

Reunification of Yemen — A865

1992, May 22 ***Perf. 13½x13***
2492 A865 50r multicolored

World Child Day A866

1992, June 1 ***Perf. 13x13½***
2493 A866 50r multicolored

Intl. Conference of Surveying and Mapping A867

1992, May 25 ***Perf. 13***
2494 A867 40r multicolored

21st FAO Regional Conference A868

1992, May 17 *Perf. 13x13½*
2495 A868 40r blk, bl & grn

South and West Asia Postal Union — A869

Mosques: No. 2496, Imam's Mosque, Isfahan. No. 2497, Lahore Mosque, Pakistan. No. 2498, St. Sophia Mosque, Turkey.

1992, Mar. 27 *Perf. 13½x13*
2496 A869 50r multicolored
2497 A869 50r multicolored
2498 A869 50r multicolored

Economic Cooperation Organization Summit — A870

Design: 20r, Flags, emblem, vert.

1992 *Perf. 13½x13, 13x13½*
2499 A870 20r multicolored
2500 A870 200r multicolored

Issued: 20r, Apr. 25; 200r, Feb. 17.

Natural Resources A871

Islamic Republic, 13th Anniv. — A872

1992, Apr. 15 Litho. *Perf. 13½x13*
2501 A871 100r multicolored

1992, Apr. 1 *Perf. 13½x13*
2502 A872 50r multicolored

Establishment of Postal Airline — A873

1992, Apr. 1 *Perf. 13x13½*
2503 A873 60r multicolored

Islamic Revolution, 13th Anniv. — A874

Unwmk.

1992, Feb. 11 Photo. *Perf. 13*
2504 30r multicolored
2505 50r multicolored
a. A874 Pair, #2504-2505

A875

A876

1992, Mar. 23 Photo. *Perf. 13½x13*
2506 A875 100r multicolored

World Meteorological Day.

1991-92 *Perf. 13x13½*

Famous Men: No. 2507, Mohammed Bagher Madjlessi. No. 2508, Hadi Sabzevari, wearing turban. No. 2509, Omman Samani, wearing fez. No. 2510, Chapter of praise from Koran (Arabic script), by Ostad Mir Emad.

2507 A876 50r shown
2508 A876 50r brown & multi
2509 A876 50r multicolored
2510 A876 50r multicolored

Issued: #2510, 12/18/91; others, 5/17/92. First day covers of #2507-2509 may be dated 12/18/91.

Intl. Museum Day A877

#2511, Gray ceramic ware, 1st millennium B.C. #2512, Painted ceramic bowl.

1992, May 18
2511 A877 40r multicolored
2512 A877 40r multicolored

Ayatollah Khomeini, 3rd Anniv. of Death — A878

1992, June 4 *Perf. 13*
2513 A878 100r multicolored

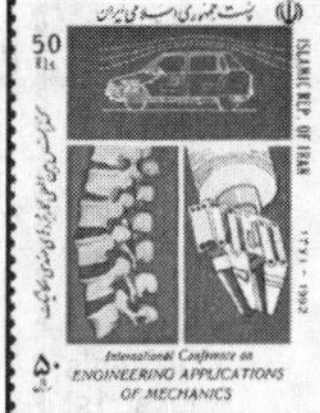
Intl. Conference on Engineering Applications of Mechanics A879

1992, June 9 *Perf. 13½x13*
2514 A879 50r multicolored

A880

1992, June 13 *Perf. 13x13½*
2515 A880 20r multicolored

In memory of clergy-lady Amini.

Sixth Conference of Nonaligned News Agencies — A881

1992, June 15
2516 A881 100r multicolored

A882

A883

1992, June 23 *Perf. 13x13½*
2517 A882 100r grn, blk & gold

Meeting of Ministers of Industry and Technology.

1992, June 26 *Perf. 13½x13*
2518 A883 100r multicolored

World Anti-narcotics Day.

Holy Ka'aba — A884

Prayer Calligraphy A885

Designs: No. 2520, Ayatollah Khomeini in prayer. No. 2521, Khomeini holding prayer beads. No. 2522, Khomeini unwrapping turban. Nos. 2523-2524, Islamic prayers.

1992 Photo. *Perf. 13½x13*
2519 A884 50r multicolored
2520 A884 50r multicolored
2521 A884 50r multicolored
2522 A884 50r multicolored

Perf. 13x13½
2523 A885 50r dk green & lt green
2524 A885 50r dk blue & lt blue

Issue dates: July 27, Aug. 24.

Iran Shipping Line, 25th Anniv. A886

1992, Aug. 24 Photo. *Perf. 13x13½*
2525 A886 200r multicolored

A887

A888

1992, Sept. 15 *Perf. 13½x13*
2526 A887 40r multicolored

Mohammad's Birthday, Unity Week.

Perf. 13½x13, 13x13½

1992, Sept. 22

Iranian Defense Forces: 20r, Soldiers on patrol. 40r, Soldier seated at water's edge, horiz.

2527 A888 20r multicolored
2528 A888 40r multicolored

Intl. Congress on the History of Islamic Medicine — A889

1992, Sept. 23 Litho. *Perf. 13*
2529 A889 20r Avicenna, child
2530 A889 40r Physician's instruments
a. Pair, #2529-2530

Mobarake Steel Plant — A890

1992, Sept. 26 Photo. ***Perf. 13x13½***
2531 20r Inside plant
2532 70r Outside plant
a. A890 Pair, #2531-2532

Intl. Tourism Day A891

1992, Sept. 27 ***Perf. 13x13½***
2533 A891 20r Mazandaran
2534 A891 20r Isfahan
2535 A891 30r Bushehr (Bushire)
2536 A891 30r Hormozgan

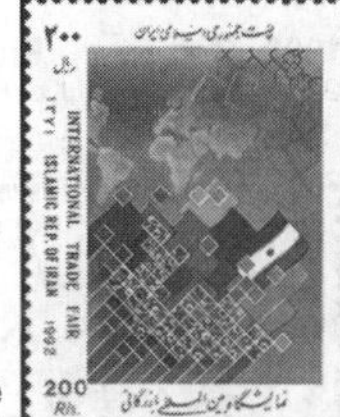
Intl. Trade Fair — A892

1992, Oct. 2 ***Perf. 13½x13***
2537 A892 200r multicolored

World Post Day A893

1992, Oct. 9 ***Perf. 13x13½***
2538 A893 30r Early post office

World Food Day A894

1992, Oct. 16 ***Perf. 13***
2539 A894 100r blk, bl & yel

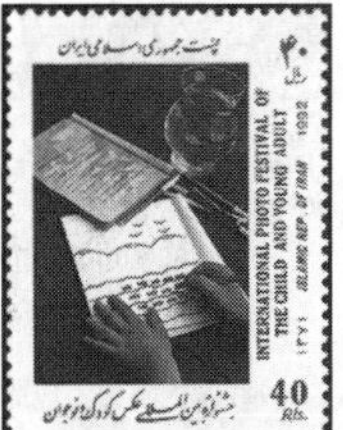
Intl. Youth Photo Festival — A895

1992, Nov. 1 Photo. ***Perf. 13½x13***
2540 A895 40r multicolored

A896

1992, Nov. 4 ***Perf. 13***

a, Seizure of US embassy, 12th anniv. b, Student's day (Eagles flying over dead doves). c, Khomeini's exile (Eagles, dove).

2541 A896 100r Strip of 3, #a.-c.

Fighting in Bosnia and Herzegovina A897

Islamic Development Bank — A898

1992, Nov. 4 ***Perf. 13½x13***
2542 A897 40r multicolored

1992, Nov. 10 Litho. ***Perf. 13½x13***
2543 A898 20r multicolored

Iran-Azerbaijan Telecommunications — A899

1992, Nov. 21 Photo. ***Perf. 13x13½***
2544 A899 40r multicolored

Azad (Open) University, 10th Anniv. — A900

1992, Nov. 23 ***Perf. 13½x13***
2545 A900 200r dark grn & emer

Week of the Basij (Militia) A901

1992, Nov. 26 ***Perf. 13x13½***
2546 A901 40r multicolored

Seyed Mohammed Hosseyn Shahrian, Poet — A902

1992, Dec. 1
2547 A902 80r multicolored

Women's Day — A903

1992, Dec. 15
2548 A903 70r multicolored

Birth anniv. of Fatima.

Famous Iranians — A904

Scientists and writers: No. 2551a, Ayatollah Mirza Abolhassan Shar'rani (in turban). b, Prof. Mahmoud Hessabi, U=o formula. c, Mohiyt Tabatabaiy, books on shelves. d, Mehrdad Avesta, calligraphy.

1992, Dec. 18
2549 A904 20r Block of 4, #a.-d.

Natl. Iranian Oil Drilling Co. A905

1992, Dec. 22
2550 A905 100r shown
2551 A905 100r Ocean drilling platform

A906 A907

1992, Dec. 28 ***Perf. 13½x13***
2552 A906 80r multicolored

Promotion of literacy.

1993-95 Photo. ***Perf. 13½x13***
2553 A907 20r Narcissus
2554 A907 30r Iris
2555 A907 35r Tulips
2556 A907 40r Tuberose
2557 A907 50r White jasmine
2558 A907 60r Guelder rose
2559 A907 70r Pansies
2560 A907 75r Snapdragons
2561 A907 100r Lily
2562 A907 120r Petunia
2563 A907 150r Hyacinth
2564 A907 200r Damascus rose
2565 A907 500r Morning glory
2566 A907 1000r Corn rose

The 60r exists with inverted flowers. Value, unused about $20.

Issued: 20r, 1/12/93; 40r, 2/22/93; 100r, 4/21/93; 200r, 4/29/93; 500r, 6/27/93; 1000r, 7/19/93; 30r, 60r, 10/93; 50r, 8/93; 120r, 5/94; 35r, 75r, 3/95; 70r, 150r, 5/95.

For surcharges see Nos. 2759-2760, 2792-2794.

Prophethood of Mohammed — A908

1993, Jan. 21 Photo. ***Perf. 13x13½***
2567 A908 200r multicolored

Mab'as Festival.

Day of the Disabled — A909

Designs: 40r, Player wearing medal, team members with hands raised.

1993, Jan. 27
2568 20r multicolored
2569 40r multicolored
a. A909 Pair, #2568-2569

Cultural Heritage Preservation A910

Planning Day — A911

1993, Jan. 31 ***Perf. 13½x13***
2570 A910 40r Mosque, exterior
2571 A910 40r Mosque, interior
a. Pair, #2570-2571

1993, Jan. 31 ***Perf. 13***
2572 A911 100r multicolored

Universal Day of the Oppressed A912

1993, Feb. 8 Litho. ***Perf. 13***
2573 A912 60r multicolored

Savior Mahdi's Birthday.

Islamic Revolution, 14th Anniv. A913

a, Iranian flag. b, Flag, soldiers. c, Soldiers, shellbursts. d, Oil derricks, storage tanks, people harvesting. e, Crowd, car, Ayatollah Khomeini.

1993, Feb. 11 Photo. ***Perf. 13x13½***
2574 A913 20r Strip of 5, #a.-e.

A914

1st Islamic Women's Games: a, Volleyball. b, Basketball. c, Medal. d, Swimming. e, Running.

1993, Feb. 13 ***Perf. 13***
2575 A914 40r Strip of 5, #a.-e.

A915

1993, Feb. 16 ***Perf. 13½***
2576 A915 40r Morteza Ansari

Arbor Day A916

1993, Mar. 6
2577 A916 70r multicolored

New Year A917

a, 20r, Butterfly, tulip. b, 20r, Butterfly, lily. c, 40r, Butterfly, flowers. d, 40r, Butterfly, 3 roses.

1993, Mar. 11 ***Perf. 13½x13***
2578 A917 Block of 4, #a.-d.

World Jerusalem Day — A918

End of Ramadan A919

1993, Mar. 14 ***Perf. 13½x13***
2579 A918 20r multicolored

1993, Mar. 26 ***Perf. 13½x13***
2580 A919 100r multicolored

Islamic Republic, 14th Anniv. A920

1993, Apr. 1 ***Perf. 13x13½***
2581 A920 40r Natl. anthem

Intl. Congress on the Millennium of Sheik Mofeed — A921

1993, Apr. 17 ***Perf. 13***
2582 A921 80r multicolored

A922

A924

1993, Apr. 21 ***Perf. 13½x13***
2583 A922 100r multicolored

13th Conference of Asian and Pacific Labor Ministers.

1993, May 17 ***Perf. 13½x13***
2585 A924 50r multicolored

Intl. Congress for Advancement of Science and Technology in Islamic World.

A925

A928

1993, May 1
2586 A925 40r multicolored

Intl. Museum Day.

1993, June 1 **Photo.** ***Perf. 13½x13***
2589 A928 50r multicolored

Intl. Child Day.

Ayatollah Khomeini, 4th Death Anniv. — A929

1993, June 4 ***Perf. 13***
2590 A929 20r multicolored

World Crafts Day A930

World Population Day — A931

1993, June 10 ***Perf. 13½x13***
2591 A930 70r multicolored

1993, July 11 ***Perf. 13***
2592 A931 30r multicolored

1st Cultural-Athletic Olympiad of Iran University Students — A932

Various sports.

1993, July 22 ***Perf. 13x13½***
Background Colors
2593 A932 20r blue
2594 A932 40r henna brown
2595 A932 40r ocher

Intl. Festival of Films for Children and Young Adults, Isfahan — A935

1993, Sept. 11 **Photo.** ***Perf. 13***
2598 A935 60r multicolored

World Post Day — A937

1993, Oct. 9 **Photo.** ***Perf. 13***
2600 A937 60r multicolored

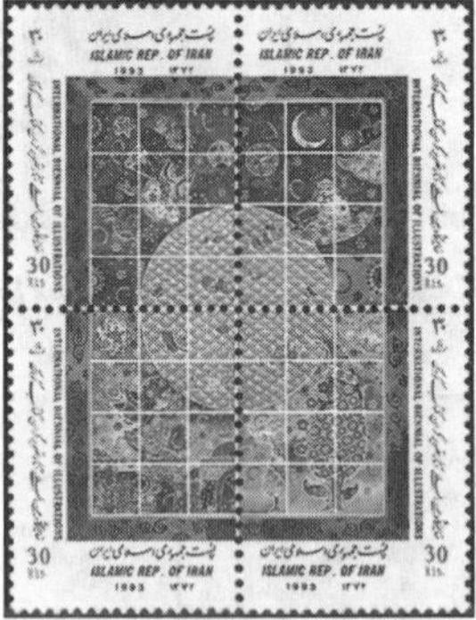
A939

World of water with fish and: a, Birds. b, Girl. c, Angel with trumpet. d, Trees.

1993, Nov. 5 **Photo.** ***Perf. 13½x13***
2602 A939 30r Block of 4, #a.-d.

Illustrators of Children's Books, Intl. Biennial.

A940

1993, Nov. 16 **Photo.** ***Perf. 13***
2603 A940 30r multicolored

Khaje Nassireddin Tussy, scientist and astronomer.

Week of the Bassij (Militia) A941

Designs: No. 2604, Woman tying bandana around militiman's head. No. 2605, Militiaman facing line of tanks.

1993, Dec. 1 ***Perf. 13x13½***
2604 A941 50r multicolored
2605 A941 50r multicolored

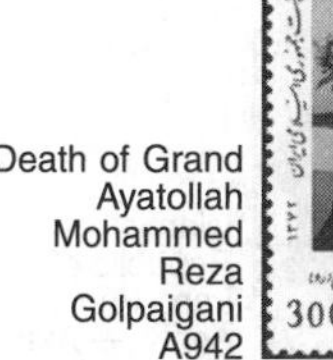

Death of Grand Ayatollah Mohammed Reza Golpaigani A942

1993, Dec. 20 ***Perf. 13***
2606 A942 300r multicolored

Support for Bosnia and Herzegovina A943

#2607, Children playing hopscotch. #2608, Soldier, minaret. #2609, Woman, mosque.

1993, Dec. 27
2607 A943 40r multicolored
2608 A943 40r multicolored
2609 A943 40r multicolored
a. Strip of 3, #2607-2609

Day of Invalids — A944

1994, Jan. 18
2610 A944 80r multicolored

Agriculture Week — A945

1994, Jan. 23
2611 A945 60r multicolored

Conf. on Islamic Law — A946

1994, Feb. 20
2612 A946 60r multicolored

Islamic Revolution, 15th Anniv. — A947

Designs: a, Town, farm, telephone lines. b, Flag, Ayatollah Khomeini, revolutionaries. c, Fisherman, bridge. d, Women working.

1994, Feb. 11
2613 A947 40r Block of 4, #a.-d.

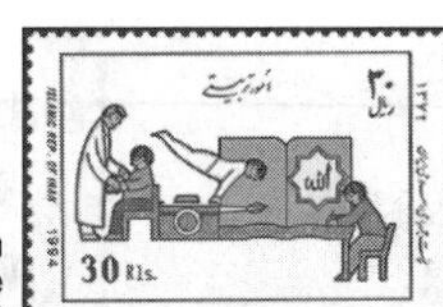

Youth Welfare A948

1994, Mar. 1
2614 A948 30r multicolored

A949

A951

A950

1994, Mar. 28 **Photo.** ***Perf. 13½x13***
2615 A949 30r multicolored

25th Iranian Mathematics Conference, Shareef Industrial University.

1994, Mar. 11 ***Perf. 13***
2616 A950 50r multicolored

World Jerusalem Day.

1994, Mar. 16 ***Perf. 13x13½, 13½x13***
2617 A951 40r Partridges, horiz.
2618 A951 40r Heron
2619 A951 40r Bustard
2620 A951 40r Pheasants, horiz.

New year.

Islamic Republic, 15th Anniv. — A952

1994, Apr. 1 **Photo.** ***Perf. 13***
2621 A952 40r multicolored

A953

1994, Apr. 7
2622 A953 100r multicolored

Intl. congress of Dentist's Assoc. and World Health Day.

Re-els Ali Delvary, 80th Anniv. of Death A954

1994, Apr. 9 ***Perf. 13x13½***
2623 A954 50r multicolored

Intl. Year of the Family — A955

1994, May 10 **Photo.** ***Perf. 13½x13***
2624 A955 50r multicolored

World Telecommunications Day — A956

1994, May 17 ***Perf. 13x13½***
2625 A956 50r multicolored

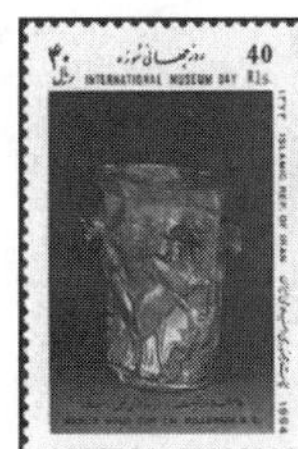

A957

A958

1994, May 18 ***Perf. 13***
2626 A957 40r Marlik gold cup

World Museum Day.

1994, May 21

Cultural Preservation: 40r, Enameled pot with Kufic inscription, 13th cent.

2627 A958 40r multicolored

Ayatollah Khomeini, 5th Death Anniv. — A959

1994, June 4
2628 A959 30r multicolored

Ayatollah Motahari, 15th Anniv. of Death — A961

1994, June 10
2630 A961 30r multicolored

World Crafts Day — A962

1994, June 10 **Photo.** ***Perf. 13***
2631 A962 60r Weaver
2632 A962 60r Glass pitcher

Islamic University Students' Solidarity Games — A963

1994, July 18
2633 A963 60r multicolored

Mohammed's Birthday, Unity Week — A964

1994, Aug. 26
2634 A964 30r multicolored

Seyed Mortaza Avini, Sacred Defense Week A965

1994, Sept. 22 ***Perf. 13x13½***
2635 A965 70r multicolored

World Post Day A966

1994, Oct. 9
2636 A966 50r multicolored

Women's Day — A967

A968

1994, Nov. 24 ***Perf. 13***
2637 A967 70r multicolored

Birth anniv. of Fatima.

1994, Nov. 26
2638 A968 30r multicolored

Week of the Bassij (Militia).

Book Week — A969

1994, Dec. 10
2639 A969 40r multicolored

Support for Moslems of Bosnia & Herzegovina A970

1994, Dec. 27
2640 A970 80r Moslem family
2641 A970 80r Map, arms, homes

Grand Ayatollah Araky — A971

1995, Jan. 5
2642 A971 100r multicolored

Universal Day of the Oppressed A972

1995, Jan. 17
2643 A972 50r multicolored

Savior Mahdi's birthday.

Major General Mehdi Zin-el-Din A973

Major General Mehdi Bakeri — A974

Major General Hasan Bagheri A975

Martyred commanders: #2647, Major General Hosein Kherazi.

1995, Feb. 2
2644 A973 50r multicolored
2645 A974 50r multicolored
2646 A975 50r multicolored
2647 A975 50r multi, diff.

A976

A977

1995, Feb. 11
2648 A976 100r multicolored

Islamic Revolution, 16th anniv.

1995, Feb. 24
2649 A977 100r multicolored

World Jerusalem Day.

Arbor Day — A978

New Year — A979

1995, Mar. 6
2650 A978 50r multicolored

1995, Mar. 16 ***Perf. 13½x13***
2651 A979 50r shown
2652 A979 50r Pansies
2653 A979 50r Hyacinths
2654 A979 50r Tulips, fish bowl

Opening of Bafq-Bandar Abbas Railway Line — A980

1995, Mar. 17
2655 A980 100r multicolored

Islamic Republic of Iran, 16th Anniv. — A981

1995, Apr. 1 **Photo.** ***Perf. 13***
2656 A981 100r multicolored

Second Press Fesitval A982

1995, Apr. 26
2657 A982 100r multicolored

Ayatollah Ahmad Khomeini A983

1995, Apr. 27
2658 A983 50r multicolored

Day of Invalids — A984

1995, June 1
2659 A984 80r Arabic script

Ayatollah Ali Vaziri — A985

1995, May 4
2660 A985 100r multicolored

World Telecommunications Day — A986

1995, May 17
2661 A986 100r multicolored

Ayatollah Khomeini, 6th Death Anniv. — A987

1995, June 4
2662 A987 100r multicolored

UN, 50th Anniv. — A988

a, Infant, hand holding vaccination (WHO). b, Child laughing (UNICEF). c, Shafts of grain, world map (FAO). d, Woman reading (UNESCO).

1995, June 10 ***Perf. 13x13½***
2663 A988 100r Block of 4, #a.-d.

Iqbal Ashtiany, Writer — A989

1995, Aug. 14 ***Perf. 13***
2664 A989 100r multicolored

Government Week — A990

1995, Aug. 28 ***Perf. 13x13½***
2665 A990 100r Workers, dam

Construction of the Karun dam and hydo-electric power station.

Sacred Defense Week — A991

1995, Sept. 22 ***Perf. 13***
2666 A991 100r Gun, Koran

World Post Day — A992

1995, Oct. 9 ***Perf. 13½x13***
2667 A992 100r Globe, envelopes

M.J. Tondgooyan, Oil Minister A993

1995, Dec. 20 ***Perf. 13***
2668 A993 100r multicolored

Prophet Mohammed A994

1995, Dec. 20
2669 A994 100r Arabic calligraphy

Fathi Shaghaghi, Islamic Jihad Secretary General A995

1995, Dec. 31
2670 A995 100r multicolored

Islamic Revolution, 17th Anniv. — A996

1996, Feb. 11
2671 A996 100r multicolored

World Jerusalem Day — A997

1996, Feb. 17
2672 A997 100r Dome of the Rock

Birds A998

1996, Mar. 15
2673 A998 100r shown
2674 A998 100r Crested head
2675 A998 100r blue & multi
2676 A998 100r yel, grn & multi

New year.

Air Force Maj. Gen. Abbas Babai — A999

Major Ali Akbar Shiroody A1000

Maj. Gen. Mahammed Ebrahim Hemmat A1001

Maj. Gen. Mohammed Broujerdi A1002

1996, Mar. 18
2677 A999 100r multicolored
2678 A1000 100r multicolored
2679 A1001 100r multicolored
2680 A1002 100r multicolored

See Nos. 2700-2707 for similar stamps dated 1997.

Islamic Republic of Iran, 17th Anniv. — A1003

1996, Mar. 31 **Photo.** ***Perf. 13***
2681 A1003 200r multicolored

Intl. Book Fair, Tehran A1004

1996, May 8
2682 A1004 85r multicolored

For surcharge see No. 2759A.

Mashhad-Sarakhs-Tajan Intl. Railway — A1005

1996, May 13
2683 A1005 200r multicolored

Turkmenistan intl. railway link,

Prisoners of War — A1006

1996, May 29
2684 A1006 200r multicolored

Captives and Missing Day.

Ayatollah Khomeini, 7th Death Anniv. — A1007

1996, June 3
2685 A1007 200r multicolored

World Crafts Day — A1008

1996, June 24 Photo. *Perf. 13*
2686 A1008 200r multicolored

Third PTT Ministerial Conference, Tehran A1009

1996, July 8
2687 A1009 200f multicolored

Prophet Mohammed's Birthday, Unity Week — A1010

Designs: a, Zouqeblateyne Mosque. b, Tomb of Imam Hossein (red flag on top of dome). c, Mohammed's Mosque (dome without flag). d, Tomb of Imam Riza (green flag on top of dome). e, Qaba Mosque (four minarets).

1996, Aug. 3
2688 A1010 200r Strip of 5, #a.-e.

Government Week — A1011

Flag colors and: a, Tehran Subway. b, Iron works, Isfahan. c, Merchant fleet. d, Oil refinery, Bandar-e-Imam (clouds in sky). e, Satellite dish, Boumehen.

1996, Aug. 23
2689 A1011 200r Strip of 5, #a.-e.

Ayatollah Moqddas Ardebily A1012

1996, Sept. 12 Photo. *Perf. 13*
2690 A1012 200r multicolored

Sacred Defense Week — A1013

1996, Sept. 21
2691 A1013 200r multicolored

World Standards Day — A1014

1996, Oct. 13
2692 A1014 200r multicolored

World Food Day — A1015

1996, Oct. 16
2693 A1015 200r multicolored

Natl. Census A1016

1996, Oct. 22
2694 A1016 200r multicolored

2nd World University Wrestling Championships, Tehran — A1017

1996, Dec. 10
2695 A1017 500r multicolored

Islamic Revolution, 18th Anniv. — A1018

a, Ayatollah Khomeini holding man to his chest. b, Martyrs. c, Khomeini waving. d, Khomeini, leaders, airplane. e, Soldiers wearing helmets.

1997, Feb. 10
2696 A1018 200r Strip of 5, #a.-e.

Arbor Day — A1019

1997, Mar. 5
2697 A1019 200r multicolored

Islamic Republic, 18th Anniv. — A1020

1997, Apr. 1
2698 A1020 200r multicolored

8th Intl. Conference on Rainwater Catchment Systems A1021

1997, Apr. 21
2699 A1021 200r multicolored

Sheikh Fazlollah Mahallati A1022

Brig. Gen. Abbas Karimi A1023

Brig. Gen. Alireza Movahed Danesh A1024

Sheikh Abdollah Mishmi A1025

Brig. Gen. Naser Kazemi A1026

Gen. Mohammed Reza Vasture A1027

Maj. Gen. Yousef Kolahdooz A1028

Brig. Gen. Yadollah Kalhor A1029

1997, May 4
2700 A1022 100r multicolored
2701 A1023 100r multicolored
2702 A1024 100r multicolored
2703 A1025 100r multicolored
2704 A1026 100r multicolored
2705 A1027 100r multicolored
2706 A1028 100r multicolored
2707 A1029 100r multicolored

Martyred commanders. See Nos. 2677-2680 for similar stamps.

Post, Telecommunications — A1030

1997, May 22
2708 A1030 200r multicolored

Ayatollah Khomeini, 8th Death Anniv. — A1031

1997, June 4
2709 A1031 200r multicolored

Montreal Protocol on Substances that Deplete Ozone Layer, 10th Anniv. — A1032

1997, Sept. 16 Photo. *Perf. 13*
2710 A1032 200r multicolored

Tehran Subway — A1033

Designs: 50r, Grain elevator. 65r, Medals, Students' Science Olympiad. 70r, Mobarake Steel Plant. 100r, Telecommunications. 130r, Port facilities. 150r, Bandar Abbas Oil Refinery. 200r, Rajai Dam. 350r, Rajai power station. 400r, Front of Foreign Affairs office. 500r, Child receiving oral polio vaccine. 650r, Printing house for Koran. 1000r, Imam Khomeini Intl. Airport. 2000r, Prayer place and tomb of Ayatollah Khomeini, Teheran.

1997 Photo. *Perf. 13½x13*
2711 A1033 40r multicolored
2712 A1033 50r multicolored
2713 A1033 65r multicolored
2714 A1033 70r multicolored
2715 A1033 100r multicolored
2716 A1033 130r multicolored
2717 A1033 150r multicolored
2718 A1033 200r multicolored
2719 A1033 350r multicolored
2720 A1033 400r multicolored
2721 A1033 500r multicolored
2722 A1033 650r multicolored
2723 A1033 1000r multicolored
2724 A1033 2000r multicolored

Issued: 2000r, 10/22; others, Sept.

Sacred Defense Week — A1034

1997, Sept. 28 Photo. *Perf. 13*
2725 A1034 200r multicolored

Poets — A1035

#2726, Maitre Eqbal Lahouri. #2727, Molana Djalaleddin Mohammad Molavi.

1997, Oct. 15
2726 A1035 200r green & multi
2727 A1035 200r salmon & multi

World Post Day — A1036

1997, Oct. 15
2728 A1036 200r multicolored

Naim Frasheri (1846-1900), Albanian Moslem Poet — A1037

1997, Nov. 5
2729 A1037 200r multicolored

Eighth Islamic Summit A1038

Various ornate designs, Islamic texts: a, Seven ornaments. b, Ornament at bottom. c, Ornament at right. d, Ornament at upper left. e, Ornament above crescent.

1997, Dec. 9
2730 A1038 300r Strip of 5, #a.-e.

2nd Islamic Countries Women's Sports Games, Tehran A1039

1997, Dec. 12
2731 A1039 200r multicolored

Islamic Revolution, 19th Anniv. A1040

a, Natl. flags. b, Harvesting grain, factory. c, Soldiers carrying flags. d, Crowd cheering, picture of Ayatollah Khomeini. e, Ayatollah Khomeini.

1998, Feb. 11
2732 A1040 200r Strip of 5, #a.-e.

World Jerusalem Day — A1041

1998, Feb. 17
2733 A1041 250r multicolored

New Year — A1042

1998, Mar. 5
2734 A1042 200r Still life

Arbor Day A1043

1998, Mar. 11
2735 A1043 200r multicolored

Islamic Republic, 19th Anniv. — A1044

1998, Apr. 1 Photo. *Perf. 13*
2736 A1044 250r multicolored

A1045

A1046

1998, May 17 *Perf. 13½x13*
2737 A1045 200r multicolored

World Telecommunications Day.

1998, May 23 Photo. *Perf. 13*
2738 A1046 200r multicolored

Election day.

War Martyrs

A1047

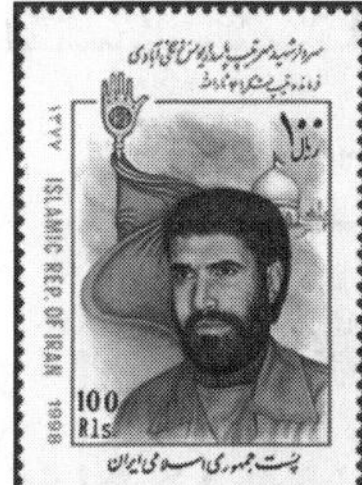

A1048

A1049

A1050

1998, May 24 **Photo.** ***Perf. 13***
2739 A1047 100r multicolored
2740 A1048 100r multicolored
2741 A1049 100r multicolored
2742 A1050 100r multicolored

Shahriyar, Poet — A1051

1998, May 27
2743 A1051 200r multicolored

Ayatollah Khomeini, 9th Death Anniv. — A1052

1998, June 4 ***Perf. 13***
2744 A1052 200r multicolored

2nd Congress of the South West Asia Postal Union, Tehran A1053

1998, June 8
2745 A1053 250r multicolored

1998 World Cup Soccer Championships, France — A1054

1998, June 10
2746 A1054 500r multicolored

A1055

A1056

1998, June 10
2747 A1055 200r multicolored

World Handicrafts Day.

1998, Sept. 4
2748 A1056 250r Union Day

1000th Friday of Public Prayer A1057

1998, Oct. 30 **Litho.** ***Perf. 13***
2749 A1057 250r multicolored

Nos. 2295A & 2296A Surcharged in Black or Green

1998, Nov. 11 ***Perf. 13x13½***
2750 A738 200r on 1r Shoustar
2751 A738 200r on 3r Kerman (G)

Intl. Year of the Ocean A1058

1998, Nov. 14 ***Perf. 13***
2752 A1058 250r multicolored

Sacred Defense Week — A1059

1998, Nov. 23
2753 A1059 250r multicolored

World Post Day A1060

1998, Dec. 2
2754 A1060 200r multicolored

1998 World Wrestling Championships, Tehran — A1061

1998, Dec. 8
2755 A1061 250r multicolored

Children and Cancer A1062

1998, Dec. 13
2756 A1062 250r multicolored

Cultural Development A1063

1998, Dec. 16 **Photo.** ***Perf. 13***
2757 A1063 250r multicolored

Islamic Revolution, 20th Anniv. — A1064

1999, Feb. 11 **Photo.** ***Perf. 13***
2758 A1064 250r multicolored

#2554, 2682, 2555 Surcharged in Black or Red

#2759, 2760

#2759A

1999, Feb. **Photo.** ***Perf. 13, 13½x13***
2759 A907 200r on 35r (#2555)
2759A A1004 250r on 85r (R, #2682)
2760 A907 900r on 30r (#2554)

Establishment of Islamic Republic, 20th Anniv. — A1065

1999, Apr. 1 **Photo.** ***Perf. 13***
2761 A1065 250r multicolored

Ghadir Khom Religious Feast — A1066

1999, Apr. 5 **Photo.** ***Perf. 13***
2762 A1066 250r multicolored

Ayatollah Khomeini's Charity Account — A1067

1999, Apr. 10 **Photo.** ***Perf. 13***
2763 A1067 250r Houses
2764 A1067 250r Village, palm trees

Army Day A1068

1999, Apr. 18
2765 A1068 250r multicolored

Mullah Sadra — A1069

1999, May 22
2766 A1069 250r multicolored

Ayatollah Khomeini, 10th Anniv. of Death — A1070

1999, May 25
2767 A1070 250r multicolored

Islamic Parliament, 20th Anniv. — A1071

1999, May 28 Photo. *Perf. 13*
2768 A1071 250r multicolored

Islamic Inter-parliamentary Conference — A1072

1999, June 15 Photo. *Perf. 13*
2769 A1072 250r multicolored

Unity Week A1073

1999, July 1 Photo. *Perf. 13*
2770 A1073 250r multicolored

Handicrafts Day — A1074

1999, July 25 Photo. *Perf. 13*
2771 A1074 250r multicolored

Total Solar Eclipse, Aug. 11 — A1075

Designs: a, Moon over right portion of sun. b, Baily's beads at top. c, Totality. d, Baily's beads at right. e, Moon over left portion of sun.

1999, Feb. 11 Photo. *Perf. 13*
2772 A1075 250r Strip of 5, #a.-e.

Birds — A1076

1999-2002 Photo. *Perf. 13x13½*

2776	A1076	100r	Hoopoe
2778	A1076	150r	Kingfisher
2779	A1076	200r	Robin
2780	A1076	250r	Lark
2782	A1076	300r	Red-backed shrike
2782A	A1076	400r	Blue tit
2783	A1076	500r	Eurasian bee-eater
2784	A1076	1000r	Redwing
2785	A1076	2000r	Twite
2786	A1076	3000r	White throat
2786A	A1076	4500r	Turtle dove

Numbers have been reserved for additional values in this set.
Issued: 150r, 8/6; 250r, 8/4; 100r, 6/17/00; 300r, 5/31/00; 500r, 8/30/00; 1000r, 10/30/00; 2000r, 1/13/01; 3000r, 1/23/01. 200r, 4/24/02; 400r, 5/18/02; 4500r, 7/16/02.

UPU, 125th Anniv. A1077

1999, Oct. 2 Photo. *Perf. 13*
2787 A1077 250r multicolored

Children's Day — A1078

a, Iranian girl. b, Latin American boy. c, Eskimo boy. d, African girl. e, Russian boy. f, French girl. g, Chinese girl. h, Asian Indian girl. i, American Indian girl. j, Arabian boy.

1999, Oct. 8
2788 A1078 150r Strip of 10, #a.-j.

Order of stamps in strip varies.

Intl. Exhibition of Children's Book Illustrators A1079

Background colors: a, Blue. b, Yellow. c, Red. d, Green.

1999, Nov. 15
2789 A1079 250r Block of 4, #a.-d.

Ayatollah Mohammed Taghi Jafari — A1080

1999, Nov. 16
2790 A1080 250r multicolored

Islamic Revolution, 21st Anniv. — A1081

2000, Feb. 11 Photo. *Perf. 13*
2791 A1081 300r multi

Nos. 2558, 2560, 2562 Surcharged Like No. 2759

Methods and Perfs. as Before

2000, Feb.
2792 A907 250r on 60r
2793 A907 250r on 75r
2794 A907 250r on 120r

The 60r stamp with the inverted flowers footnoted after No. 2566 is known with the 250r surcharge.

New Year — A1082

2000, Mar. 13 Photo. *Perf. 13*
2795 A1082 300r multi

Science & Technology University, 70th Anniv. — A1083

2000, July 9 Photo. *Perf. 13*
2796 A1083 300r multi

Dated 1999.

Dr. Mohammed Mofatteh (1928-79), Martyr — A1084

2000, July 22
2797 A1084 300r multi

A1085

A1086

A1087

A1088

A1089

A1090

A1091

Martyrs A1092

2000

2798 A1085 150r multi
2799 A1086 150r multi
2800 A1087 150r multi
2801 A1088 150r multi
2802 A1089 150r multi
2803 A1090 150r multi
2804 A1091 150r multi
2805 A1092 150r multi

Issued: Nos. 2798-2801, 8/6/00; Nos. 2802-2805, 7/30/01.

National Archives Day — A1093

2000, May 5 **Photo.** ***Perf. 13***
2806 A1093 300r multi

University Jihad Movement A1094

2000, Aug. 6
2807 A1094 300r multi

8th Asia-Pacific Postal Union Congress, Tehran — A1095

2000, Sept. 12
2808 A1095 300r multi

World Space Week A1096

Satellite and: No. 2809, 500r, Dish at R. No. 2810, 500r, Dish at L.

2000, Oct. 4
2809-2810 A1096 Set of 2

World Breastfeeding Week A1097

2000, Oct.
2811 A1097 300r multi

Ghadir Khom Festival A1098

2001, Mar. 14
2812 A1098 500r multi

Year of H. H. Ali — A1099

2001, Mar. 14
2813 A1099 500r multi

New Year — A1100

Birds: No. 2814, 300r, shown. No. 2815, 300r, Bird, diff., vert.

2001, Mar. 18 ***Perf. 13x13½, 13½x13***
2814-2815 A1100 Set of 2

Belgica 2001 Intl Stamp Exhibition, Brussels — A1101

Designs: No. 2816, 350r, Chaffinch (shown). No. 2817, 350r, Waxwing. No. 2818, 350r, National Garden, vert.

2001, June 9 ***Perf. 13***
2816-2818 A1101 Set of 3

Phila Nippon '01, Japan A1102

Emblem and: No. 2819, 250r, Mount Fuji, Japan. No. 2820, 250r, Mount Damavand, Iran.

2001, Aug. 1 **Photo.** ***Perf. 13***
2819-2820 A1102 Set of 2

World Tourism Day — A1103

2001, Sept. 22
2821 A1103 500r multi

Police Week — A1104

No. 2822: a, Helicopters, parachutists, police cars, motorcycle police. b, Parachutists, officer saluting flag, motorcycle police, naval patrol.

Illustration reduced.

2001, Sept. 29 ***Perf. 13x13½***
2822 A1104 250r Horiz. pair, #a-b

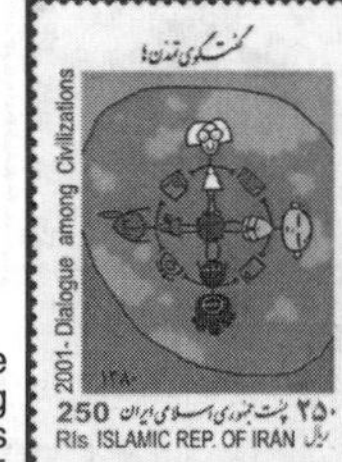

Year of Dialogue Among Civilizations A1105

Designs: No. 2823, 250r, Shown. No. 2824, 250r, Cubist and Oriental art, horiz.

2001, Oct. 9 ***Perf. 13***
2823-2824 A1105 Set of 2

Third Moslem Women's Games, Tehran — A1106

2001, Oct. 24
2825 A1106 250r multi

Spring of the Holy Koran — A1107

2001, Nov. 26
2826 A1107 500r multi

Honeybee — A1108

2001, Dec. 3
2827 A1108 500r multi

UN High Commissioner for Refugees, 50th Anniv. — A1109

2001, Dec. 10
2828 A1109 500r multi

Transportation Day — A1110

No. 2829: a, Truck on road. b, Truck on bridge, truck on road, gate.
Illustration reduced.

2001, Dec. 17 ***Perf. 13x13½***
2829 A1110 350r Horiz. pair, #a-b

Navy Day A1111

No. 2830, 500r: a, Ship heading right. b, Ship heading left.
No. 2831, 500r: a, Helicopter, hovercraft. b, Submarine.

2001, Nov. 28 **Photo.** ***Perf. 13***
Vert. Pairs, #a-b
2830-2831 A1111 Set of 2

Tehran Subway A1112

No. 2832: a, Train headed right. b, Train headed left.

2001, Dec. 13
2832 A1112 500r Vert. pair, #a-b

Iranian-made Automobiles — A1113

Designs: No. 2833, 500r, shown. No. 2834, 500r, Automobile, vert.

2002, Jan. 15
2833-2834 A1113 Set of 2

Arbor Day — A1114

2002, Mar. 6
2835 A1114 500r multi

A1115

New Year's Day — A1116

No. 2836: a, Bird with yellow breast. b, Parrot.
No. 2837: a, Stork facing left. b, Hoopoe facing right.
Illustration reduced.

2002, Mar. 16
2836 A1115 500r Horiz. pair, #a-b
2837 A1116 500r Horiz. pair, #a-b

Imam Hossein — A1117

Illustration reduced.

2002, July 8 **Photo.** ***Imperf.***
2838 A1117 400r multi

Butterflies — A1118

No. 2839: a, Danaus sita. b, Polygonia c-album. c, Precis orithya. d, Vanessa cardui. e, Papilio maacki.

2002, July 29 ***Perf. 13***
2839 Horiz. strip of 5
a.-e. A1118 400r Any single

A1119

PhilaKorea 2002 World Stamp Exhibition, Seoul — A1120

No. 2840 - Flowers: a, Hyoscyamus muticus. b, Frittillaria. c, Calotropis procera. d, Ranuculus.
No. 2841 - Horse breeds: a, Caspian. b, Kurd. c, Turkoman. d, Arab.
Illustrations reduced.

2002, Aug. 2
2840 A1119 400r Block of 4, #a-d, + 2 labels
2841 A1120 400r Block of 4, #a-d, + 2 labels

Ayatollah Khomeini (1900-89) A1121

2002, Aug. 20
2842 A1121 400r multi

Jerusalem Day — A1122

2002, Nov. 29
2843 A1122 400r multi

Iran - Brazil Diplomatic Relations, Cent. — A1123

No. 2844: a, Iranian ceramics. b, Brazilian ceramics.

2002, Dec. 15
2844 Horiz. pair + label
a.-b. A1123 400r Either single

See Brazil No.

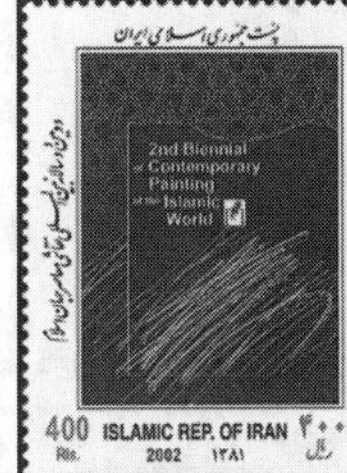

2nd Biennial of Contemporary Painting of the Islamic World — A1124

2002, Dec. 25
2845 A1124 400r multi

Esco Production Line, 30th Anniv. — A1125

Illustration reduced.

2003, Jan. 13 ***Perf. 13x13½***
2846 A1125 400r multi

SEMI-POSTAL STAMPS

Lion and Bull, Persepolis SP1

Persian Soldier, Persepolis — SP2

Palace of Darius the Great — SP3

Tomb of Cyrus the Great, Pasargadae SP4

King Darius on his Throne — SP5

Perf. 13x13½, 13½x13

1948, Jan. 30 **Engr.** **Unwmk.**

B1	SP1	50d + 25d emer	1.75	1.75
B2	SP2	1r + 50d red	1.75	1.75
B3	SP3	2½r + 1¼r blue	1.75	1.75
B4	SP4	5r + 2½r pur	2.75	2.75
B5	SP5	10r + 5r vio brn	2.75	2.75
		Nos. B1-B5 (5)	10.75	10.75

The surtax was for reconstruction of the tomb of Avicenna (980-1037), Persian physician and philosopher, at Hamadan.

Ardashir II — SP6

Shapur I and Valerian SP7

Designs: 1r+50d, King Narses, Naqsh-i-Rustam. 5r+2½r, Taq-i-Kisra, Ctesiphon. 10r+5r, Ardashir I and Ahura Mazda.

1949, June 11

B6	SP6	50d + 25d green	1.50	1.50
B7	SP6	1r + 50d ver	1.50	1.50
B8	SP7	2½r + 1½r blue	1.50	1.50
B9	SP7	5r + 2½r magenta	3.00	3.00
B10	SP7	10r + 5r grnsh gray	3.00	3.00
		Nos. B6-B10 (5)	10.50	10.50

The surtax was for reconstruction of Avicenna's tomb at Hamadan.

Gunbad-i-Ali — SP8

Alaviyan, Hamadan SP9

Seldjukide Coin — SP10

Designs: 1r+½r, Masjid-i-Jami, Isfahan. 5r+2½r, Masjid-i-Jami, Ardistan.

1949, Dec. 22

B11	SP8	50d + 25d bl grn	1.25	1.25
B12	SP8	1r + ½r dk brn	1.25	1.25
B13	SP9	2½r + 1¼r blue	1.25	1.25
B14	SP9	5r + 2½r red	2.25	2.25
B15	SP10	10r + 5r olive gray	2.40	2.40
		Nos. B11-B15 (5)	8.40	8.40

The surtax was for reconstruction of Avicenna's tomb at Hamadan.

Koran, Crescent and Flag — SP11

1950, Oct. 2 Litho. *Perf. 11*

B16	SP11	1.50r + 1r multi	22.50	15.00

Economic Conference of the Islamic States.

Tomb of Baba Afzal at Kashan SP12

Gorgan Vase — SP13

Designs: 2½r+1¼r, Tower of Ghazan. 5r+2½r, Masjid-i Gawhar. 10r+5r, Mihrab of the Mosque at Rezaieh.

Perf. 13x13½, 13½x13

1950, Aug. 23 Engr.

B17	SP12	50d + 25d dk grn	1.25	*1.25*
B18	SP13	1r + ½r blue	1.25	*1.25*
B19	SP13	2½r + 1¼r choc	1.25	*1.25*
B20	SP12	5r + 2½r red	2.25	*2.25*
B21	SP12	10r + 5r gray	2.40	*2.40*
		Nos. B17-B21 (5)	8.40	8.40

The surtax was for reconstruction of Avicenna's tomb at Hamadan.

Mohammed Riza Pahlavi and Map — SP14

Monument to Fallen Liberators of Azerbaijan SP15

Designs: 1r+50d, Marching troops. 1.50r+75d, Running advance with flag. 2.50r+1.25r, Mohammed Riza Pahlavi. 3r+1.50r, Parade of victors.

1950, Dec. 12 Litho.

B22	SP14	10d + 5d blk brn	7.00	3.50
B23	SP15	50d + 25d blk brn	7.50	3.50
B24	SP15	1r + 50d brown lake	15.00	4.50
B25	SP14	1.50r + 75d org ver	15.00	9.00
B26	SP14	2.50r + 1.25r blue	16.00	11.00
B27	SP15	3r + 1.50r ultra	21.00	8.50
		Nos. B22-B27 (6)	81.50	40.00

Liberation of Azerbaijan Province from communists, 4th anniv.

The surtax was for families of Persian soldiers who died in the struggle.

Koran Gate at Shiraz SP16

Saadi — SP17

Design: 50d+50d, Tomb of Saadi, Shiraz.

Perf. 11x10½, 10½x11

1952, Apr. 30 Photo. Unwmk.

B28	SP16	25d + 25d dl bl grn	2.75	1.50
B29	SP16	50d + 50d brn ol	3.00	1.75
B30	SP17	1.50r + 50d vio bl	10.50	6.00
		Nos. B28-B30 (3)	16.25	9.25

770th birthday of Saadi, Persian poet. The surtax was to help complete Saadi's tomb at Shiraz.

Three stamps of same denominations and colors, with values enclosed in tablets, were prepared but not officially issued.

View of Hamadan SP18

Avicenna — SP19

Designs: 2½r+1¼r, Gonbad Qabus (tower of tomb). 5r+2½r, Old tomb of Avicenna. 10r+5r, New tomb.

Perf. 13x13½, 13½x13

1954, Apr. 21 Engr. Unwmk.

B31	SP18	50d + 25d dp grn	1.25	1.25
B32	SP19	1r + ½r vio brn	1.25	1.25
B33	SP19	2½r + 1¼r blue	1.25	1.25
B34	SP18	5r + 2½r ver	2.00	2.00
B35	SP18	10r + 5r ol gray	3.00	3.00
		Nos. B31-B35 (5)	8.75	8.75

The surtax was for reconstruction of Avicenna's tomb at Hamadan.

Catalogue values for unused stamps in this section, from this point to the end of the section, are for Never Hinged items.

Mother with Children and Ruins — SP20

Wmk. 316

1963, Feb. 4 Litho. *Perf. 10½*

B36	SP20	14r + 6r dk bl grn & lt brn	1.75	.50

The surtax was for the benefit of survivors of the Kazvin earthquake.

For overprints see Nos. C86-C88.

AIR POST STAMPS

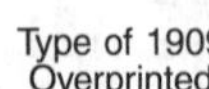

Type of 1909 Overprinted

1927 Unwmk. Typo. *Perf. 11½*

C1	A31	1c org & maroon	2.00	1.00
C2	A31	2c vio & maroon	2.00	1.00
C3	A31	3c grn & maroon	2.00	1.00
C4	A31	6c red & maroon	2.00	1.00
C5	A31	9c gray & maroon	4.00	1.00
C6	A31	10c red vio & mar	6.00	1.00
C7	A31	13c dk bl & mar	8.00	2.50
C8	A31	1k sil, vio & bis brown	8.00	2.50
C9	A31	26c dk grn & mar	8.00	2.50
C10	A31	2k sil, dk grn & bis brown	15.00	2.50
C11	A31	3k sil, gray & bis brown	20.00	4.00
C12	A31	4k sil, bl & bis brown	30.00	9.00
C13	A31	5k gold, brn & bis brown	30.00	9.00
C14	A31	10k gold, org & bis brown	250.00	200.00
C15	A31	20k gold, ol grn & bis brn	250.00	200.00
C16	A31	30k gold, car & bis brown	250.00	200.00
		Nos. C1-C16 (16)	887.00	638.00

Counterfeit overprints are plentiful. They are found on Nos. 448-463, perf. 12½x12 instead of 11½.

Exist without overprint. Value, set $600.

AP1

AP2

AP3

AP4

AP5

Airplane, Value and "Poste aérièn" Surcharged on Revenue Stamps

1928 *Perf. 11*

C17	AP1	3k yellow brn	90.00	40.00
C18	AP2	5k dark brown	30.00	10.00
C19	AP3	1t gray vio	22.50	10.00
C20	AP4	2t olive bister	22.50	10.00
C21	AP5	3t deep green	35.00	15.00
		Nos. C17-C21 (5)	200.00	85.00

AP6

AP7

"Poste aerienne"

1928-29

C22	AP6	1c emerald	1.00	.25
a.		1c yellow green	1.00	.20
b.		Double overprint	35.00	
C23	AP6	2c light blue	1.00	.20
C24	AP6	3c bright rose	1.00	.20
C25	AP6	5c olive brn	1.00	.20
a.		"5" omitted	550.00	*650.00*
b.		Horiz. pair, imperf. btwn.	*200.00*	
C26	AP6	10c dark green	1.00	.20
a.		"10" omitted	15.00	
b.		"1" inverted	20.00	
C27	AP7	1k dull vio	2.00	1.00
a.		"1" inverted	25.00	
C28	AP7	2k orange	4.00	2.00
a.		"S" for "s" in "Krs"	35.00	
		Nos. C22-C28 (7)	11.00	4.05

Counterfeits exist.

Revenue Stamps Similar to Nos. C17 to C21, Overprinted like Nos. C22 to C28: "Poste aerienne"

1929

C29	AP1	3k yellow brn	80.00	25.00
C30	AP2	5k dark brn	15.00	5.00
C31	AP3	10k violet	25.00	10.00

C32 AP4 20k olive grn 30.00 10.00
C33 AP5 30k deep grn 40.00 15.00
Nos. C29-C33 (5) 190.00 65.00

Riza Shah Pahlavi and Eagle — AP8

1930, July 6 Photo. *Perf. 12½x11½*

C34 AP8 1c ol bis & brt bl .50 .50
C35 AP8 2c blue & gray blk .50 .50
C36 AP8 3c ol grn & dk vio .50 .50
C37 AP8 4c dk vio & pck bl .50 .50
C38 AP8 5c lt grn & mag .50 .50
C39 AP8 6c mag & bl grn .50 .50
C40 AP8 8c dk gray & dp violet .50 .50
C41 AP8 10c dp ultra & ver .50 .50
C42 AP8 12c slate & org .50 .50
C43 AP8 15c org brn & ol green .50 .50
C44 AP8 1k Prus bl & scar 5.00 2.50

Engr.

C45 AP8 2k black & ultra 5.00 2.50
C46 AP8 3k dk brn & gray green 6.50 3.00
C47 AP8 5k dp red & gray black 6.50 4.00
C48 AP8 1t orange & vio 20.00 6.00
C49 AP8 2t dk grn & red brown 20.00 6.00
C50 AP8 3t brn vio & sl bl 150.00 50.00
Nos. C34-C50 (17) 218.00 79.00

Same Overprinted in Black

1935 Photo.

C51 AP8 1c ol bis & brt bl .50 .50
C52 AP8 2c blue & gray blk .50 .50
C53 AP8 3c ol grn & dk vio .50 .50
C54 AP8 4c dk vio & pck bl .50 .50
C55 AP8 5c lt grn & mag .50 .50
C56 AP8 6c mag & bl grn .50 .50
C57 AP8 8c dk gray & dp violet .50 .50
C58 AP8 10c dp ultra & ver .50 .50
C59 AP8 12c slate & org .50 .50
C60 AP8 15c org brn & ol green .50 .50
C61 AP8 1k Prus bl & scar 17.50 *22.50*

Engr.

C62 AP8 2k blk & ultra 17.50 *22.50*
C63 AP8 3k dk brn & gray green 25.00 15.00
C64 AP8 5k dp red & gray black 10.00 10.00
C65 AP8 1t orange & vio 150.00 125.00
C66 AP8 2t dk grn & red brown 20.00 15.00
C67 AP8 3t brn vio & sl bl 30.00 15.00
Nos. C51-C67 (17) 275.00 230.00

Plane Over Mt. Demavend AP9

Plane above Mosque AP10

Unwmk.

1953, Jan. 21 Photo. *Perf. 11*

C68 AP9 50d bl green 1.00 .20
C69 AP10 1r car rose 1.00 .20
C70 AP10 2r dark blue 1.00 .20
C71 AP10 3r dark brn 1.00 .20
C72 AP10 5r purple 3.00 .20
C73 AP10 10r org ver 3.00 .30
C74 AP10 20r vio blue 3.00 .50
C75 AP10 30r olive 7.00 1.00
C76 AP10 50r brown 15.00 2.50
C77 AP10 100r black brn 60.00 12.00
C78 AP10 200r dk bl grn 35.00 14.00
Nos. C68-C78 (11) 130.00 31.30

AP11

Golden Dome Mosque and Oil Well AP12

1953, May 4 Litho. *Perf. 10½*

Mosque in Deep Yellow

C79 AP11 3r violet 10.00 5.00
C80 AP12 5r chocolate 17.00 5.00
C81 AP11 10r bl green 45.00 12.00
C82 AP12 20r red vio 90.00 30.00
Nos. C79-C82 (4) 162.00 52.00

Discovery of oil at Qum.

Catalogue values for unused stamps in this section, from this point to the end of the section, are for Never Hinged items.

Globe and UN Emblem AP13

Perf. 10½x12½

1957, Oct. 24 Photo. Wmk. 316

C83 AP13 10r brt red lil & rose 3.00 .75
C84 AP13 20r dl vio & rose vio 6.00 1.25

United Nations Day, Oct. 24, 1957.

UNESCO Emblem AP14

Wmk. 353

1966, June 20 Litho. *Perf. 10½*

C85 AP14 14r multi .95 .20

20th anniversary of UNESCO.

No. B36 Surcharged in Maroon, Brown or Red

1969, Dec. 4 Wmk. 316 *Perf. 10½*

C86 SP20 4r on 14r + 6r (M) 2.00 .65
C87 SP20 10r on 14r + 6r (B) 2.00 .65
C88 SP20 14r on 14r + 6r (R) 2.00 .65
Nos. C86-C88 (3) 6.00 1.95

1st England-Australia flight, via Iran, made by Capt. Ross Smith and Lt. Keith Smith, 50th anniv.

IATA Emblem and Persepolis AP15

Perf. 13x13½

1970, Oct. 27 Photo. Wmk. 353

C89 AP15 14r multi 5.00 .50

26th meeting of the Intl. Air Transport Assoc. (IATA), Tehran.

"UIT" AP16

1972, May 17 Litho. *Perf. 10½*

C90 AP16 14r multicolored 2.50 .50

4th World Telecommunications Day.

Shah and Jet AP17

1974, June 1 Photo. *Perf. 13*

C91 AP17 4r org & black .50 .20
C92 AP17 10r blue & black 1.75 .20
C93 AP17 12r dull yel & blk 1.75 .35
C94 AP17 14r lt green & blk 1.90 .35
C95 AP17 20r red lilac & blk 2.50 .50
C96 AP17 50r dull bl & blk 6.75 1.40
Nos. C91-C96 (6) 15.15 3.00

Crown Prince at Controls of Light Aircraft — AP18

1974, Oct. 31 Litho. *Perf. 10½*

C97 AP18 14r gold & multi 1.40 .45

Crown Prince Riza's 14th birthday.

Importation Prohibited
Importation of stamps was prohibited effective Oct. 29, 1987.

Islamic Revolution, 10th Anniv. — AP19

1989, Feb. 11 *Perf. 13x13½*

C98 AP19 40r red vio, blk & gold .75 .50
C99 AP19 50r bl vio, blk & gold .75 .50
a. Pair, #C98-C99 1.75 1.50

Ayatollah Khomeini — AP20

1989, July 11 *Perf. 13*

C100 AP20 70r multicolored 1.00 .50

OFFICIAL STAMPS

Four bicolored stamps of this design (1s, 2s, 5s, 10s), with centers embossed, exist, but were never issued or used in Iran. They are known imperforate and in many trial colors.

Shah Muzaffar-ed-Din O1

No. 145 Surcharged in Black

1902 *Perf. 12½*

O5 O1 5c on 1k red 8.50 5.00
O6 O1 10c on 1k red 8.50 5.00
O7 O1 12c on 1k red 8.50 5.00
Nos. O5-O7 (3) 25.50 15.00

Nos. 351-363 Overprinted in Black

1903-06

O8 A26 1c violet .60 .20
O9 A26 2c gray .60 .20
O10 A26 3c green .60 .20
O11 A26 5c rose .60 .20
O12 A26 10c yel brown .60 .20
O13 A26 12c blue .60 .20

Perf. 11½x11

O14 A27 1k violet 1.50 .50
O15 A27 2k ultra 3.00 .50
a. Violet overprint 6.00 5.00
O16 A27 5k org brown 6.00 .80
O17 A27 10k rose red 7.50 1.00
a. Violet overprint 12.50
O18 A27 20k orange ('06) 25.00 7.00
O19 A27 30k green ('06) 30.00 7.00
O20 A27 50k green 110.00 45.00
Nos. O8-O20 (13) 186.60 63.00

Overprinted on Nos. 368, 370a

O21 A27 2t on 50k grn (Bl) 80.00 35.00
O22 A27 3t on 50k grn (V) 80.00 35.00

Overprinted on Nos. 372, 375, New Value Surcharged in Blue or Black

1905

O23 A27 2t on 50k grn (Bl) 80.00 35.00
O28 A27 3t on 50k grn (Bk) 80.00 35.00

The 2t on 50k also exists with surcharge in black and magenta; the 3t on 50k in violet and magenta. Values about the same.

Regular Issue of 1909 Overprinted

There is a space between the word "Service" and the Persian characters.

1911 ***Perf. 12½x12***

No.	Type	Description	Unused	Used
O31	A31	1c org & maroon	6.00	3.00
O32	A31	2c vio & maroon	6.00	3.00
O33	A31	3c yel grn & mar	6.00	3.00
O34	A31	6c red & maroon	6.00	3.00
O35	A31	9c gray & maroon	12.00	5.00
O36	A31	10c multicolored	16.00	5.00
O38	A31	1k multicolored	20.00	10.00
O40	A31	2k multicolored	40.00	20.00
		Nos. O31-O40 (8)	112.00	52.00

The 13c, 26c and 3k to 30k denominations were not regularly issued with this overprint.

Dangerous counterfeits exist, usually on reprints.

Regular Issue of 1915 Overprinted

1915 **Wmk. 161** ***Perf. 11, 11½***

No.	Type	Description	Unused	Used
O41	A33	1c car & indigo	*2.00*	*2.00*
O42	A33	2c bl & carmine	*2.00*	*2.00*
O43	A33	3c dark green	*2.00*	*2.00*
O44	A33	5c red	*2.00*	*2.00*
O45	A33	6c ol grn & car	*2.00*	*2.00*
O46	A33	9c yel brn & vio	*2.00*	*2.00*
O47	A33	10c multicolored	*2.00*	*2.00*
O48	A33	12c ultramarine	*2.00*	*2.00*
O49	A34	1k multicolored	*5.00*	*5.00*
O50	A33	24c multicolored	*3.00*	*3.00*
O51	A34	2k sil, bl & rose	*5.00*	*5.00*
O52	A34	3k sil, vio & brn	*5.00*	*5.00*
O53	A34	5k multicolored	*5.00*	*5.00*
O54	A35	1t gold, pur & blk	*7.00*	*7.00*
O55	A35	2t gold, grn & brn	*7.00*	*7.00*
O56	A35	3t multicolored	*9.00*	*9.00*
O57	A35	5t gold, bl & ind	*10.00*	*10.00*
		Nos. O41-O57 (17)		*72.00*

Coronation of Shah Ahmed.

Reprints have dull rather than shiny overprint. **Value, set, $17.50.**

Coat of Arms
O2 O3

1941 **Unwmk.** **Litho.** ***Perf. 11***

For Internal Postage

No.	Type	Description	Unused	Used
O58	O2	5d violet	2.50	.20
O59	O2	10d magenta	2.50	.20
O60	O2	25d carmine	2.50	.20
O61	O2	50d brown black	2.50	.20
O62	O2	75d claret	4.00	.45

Size: 22½x30mm

No.	Type	Description	Unused	Used
O63	O2	1r peacock grn	5.00	.45
O64	O2	1½r deep blue	7.00	1.50
O65	O2	2r light blue	10.00	1.50
O66	O2	3r vio brown	15.00	1.50
O67	O2	5r gray green	20.00	2.00
O68	O2	10r dk brn & bl	150.00	5.00
O69	O2	20r chlky bl & brt pink	225.00	20.00
O70	O2	30r vio & brt grn	400.00	45.00
O71	O2	50r turq grn & dk brown	750.00	175.00
		Nos. O58-O71 (14)	1,596.	253.20

Catalogue values for unused stamps in this section, from this point to the end of the section, are for Never Hinged items.

Perf. 13½x13

1974, Feb. 25 **Photo.** **Wmk. 353**

Size: 20x28mm

No.	Type	Description	Unused	Used
O72	O3	5d vio & lilac	.30	.25
O73	O3	10d mag & grnsh bl	.30	.25
O74	O3	50d org & lt green	.30	.20
O75	O3	1r green & gold	.40	.20
O76	O3	2r emerald & org	.70	.20

Perf. 13

Size: 23x37mm

No.	Type	Description	Unused	Used
O77	O3	6r slate grn & org	.75	.20
O78	O3	8r ultra & yellow	1.00	.20
O79	O3	10r dk bl & lilac	4.25	.25
O80	O3	11r pur & light bl	1.75	.25
O81	O3	14r red & lt ultra	1.75	.60
O82	O3	20r vio blue & org	3.50	.50
O83	O3	50r dk brn & brt grn	9.00	1.75
		Nos. O72-O83 (12)	24.00	4.85

1977-79 **Wmk. 353** ***Perf. 13½x13***

Size: 20x28mm

No.	Type	Description	Unused	Used
O87	O3	1r black & lt grn	.35	.20
O88	O3	2r brown & gray	.40	.20
O89	O3	3r ultra & orange	.50	.20
O90	O3	5r green & rose	.65	.20

Perf. 13

Size: 23x37mm

No.	Type	Description	Unused	Used
O91	O3	6r dk bl & lt bl ('78)	.75	.45
O92	O3	8r red & bl grn ('78)	.80	.50
O93	O3	10r dk grn & yel grn	.80	.25
O94	O3	11r dk blue & brt yellow ('79)	1.75	.50
O95	O3	14r dl grn & gray	1.75	.50
O96	O3	15r bl & rose lil ('78)	3.25	1.00
O97	O3	20r purple & yel	3.25	.40
O98	O3	30r brn & ocher ('78)	3.75	1.25
O99	O3	50r blk & gold ('78)	10.00	1.25
		Nos. O87-O99 (13)	28.00	6.90

NEWSPAPER STAMP

No. 429 Overprinted

1909 **Typo.** **Unwmk.** ***Perf. 12½***

No.	Type	Description	Unused	Used
P1	A26	2c gray, *blue*	*15.00*	*10.00*

PARCEL POST STAMPS

Regular issues of 1907-08 (types A26, A29) with the handstamp above in blue, black or green are of questionable status as issued stamps. The handstamp probably is a cancellation.

No. 436 Overprinted in Black

1909 **Engr.** ***Perf. 11½***

No.	Type	Description	Unused	Used
Q18	A29	26c red brown	5.00	3.00

The overprint is printed.

Regular Issue of 1915 Overprinted in Black

1915 **Wmk. 161** ***Perf. 11, 11½***

No.	Type	Description	Unused	Used
Q19	A33	1c car & indigo	*2.00*	*2.00*
Q20	A33	2c bl & carmine	*2.00*	*2.00*
Q21	A33	3c dark green	*2.00*	*2.00*
Q22	A33	5c red	*2.00*	*2.00*
Q23	A33	6c ol green & car	*2.00*	*2.00*
Q24	A33	9c yel brn & vio	*2.00*	*2.00*
Q25	A33	10c bl grn & yel brn	*2.00*	*2.00*
Q26	A33	12c ultramarine	*2.00*	*2.00*
Q27	A34	1k multicolored	*5.00*	*5.00*
Q28	A33	24c multicolored	*3.00*	*3.00*
Q29	A34	2k multicolored	*5.00*	*5.00*
Q30	A34	3k multicolored	*5.00*	*5.00*
Q31	A34	5k multicolored	*5.00*	*5.00*
Q32	A35	1t multicolored	*7.00*	*7.00*
Q33	A35	2t gold, grn & brn	*7.00*	*7.00*
Q34	A35	3t multicolored	*9.00*	*9.00*
Q35	A35	5t multicolored	*10.00*	*10.00*
		Nos. Q19-Q35 (17)		*72.00*

Coronation of Shah Ahmed.

Reprints have dull rather than shiny overprint. **Value, set, $16.**

Catalogue values for unused stamps in this section, from this point to the end of the section, are for Never Hinged items.

Post Horn — PP1

Black frame and "IRAN" (reversed) are printed on back of Nos. Q36-Q65, to show through when stamp is attached to parcel.

1958 **Wmk. 306** **Typo.** ***Perf. 12½***

No.	Type	Description	Unused	Used
Q36	PP1	50d olive bis	.20	.20
Q37	PP1	1r carmine	.20	.20
Q38	PP1	2r blue	.30	.20
a.		Imperf., pair	32.50	
Q39	PP1	3r green	.30	.20
Q40	PP1	5r purple	.70	.20
Q41	PP1	10r orange brn	2.75	.20
Q42	PP1	20r dp orange	2.75	.20
Q43	PP1	30r lilac	3.75	1.40
Q44	PP1	50r dk carmine	4.50	1.75
Q45	PP1	100r yellow	11.00	2.25
Q46	PP1	200r light grn	19.00	4.50
		Nos. Q36-Q46 (11)	45.45	11.30

1961-66 **Wmk. 316**

No.	Type	Description	Unused	Used
Q51	PP1	5r purple ('66)	1.25	.40
Q52	PP1	10r org brn ('62)	4.25	1.50
Q53	PP1	20r orange	5.25	1.90
Q54	PP1	30r red lil ('63)	6.50	2.10
Q55	PP1	50r dk car ('63)	8.50	3.25
Q56	PP1	100r yellow ('64)	17.50	7.50
Q57	PP1	200r emer ('64)	21.00	8.25
		Nos. Q51-Q57 (7)	64.25	24.90

1967-74 **Wmk. 353**

No.	Type	Description	Unused	Used
Q58	PP1	2r blue ('74)	.20	.20
Q59	PP1	5r dk pur ('69)	.20	.20
Q60	PP1	10r orange brn	.40	.25
Q61	PP1	20r orange ('69)	2.00	.50
Q62	PP1	30r red lilac	1.50	.25
Q63	PP1	50r red brn ('68)	2.00	1.25
Q64	PP1	100r yellow	3.50	1.50
Q65	PP1	200r emerald ('69)	6.00	5.00
		Nos. Q58-Q65 (8)	15.80	9.15

Perf. 13½x13

1981 **Typo.** **Wmk. 353**

Without Black Frame and IRAN on Back

No.	Type	Description	Unused	Used
Q67	PP1	50r orange brown	*10.00*	
Q69	PP1	200r green	*6.00*	

Nos. Q67, Q69 printed from new dies. Numerals are larger and higher in the value tablet on No. Q67. Numerals read down from upper left to lower right in value tablet on No. Q69.

The editors would like to see a 100r in this design.

POSTAL TAX STAMPS

Iranian Red Cross Lion and Sun Emblem PT1

1950 **Unwmk.** **Litho.** ***Perf. 11***

No.	Type	Description	Unused	Used
RA1	PT1	50d grn & car rose	10.00	.90
RA2	PT1	2r vio & lil rose	4.00	1.50

1955 **Wmk. 306**

No.	Type	Description	Unused	Used
RA3	PT1	50d emer & car rose	*75.00*	5.00

Catalogue values for unused stamps in this section, from this point to the end of the section, are for Never Hinged items.

1957-58 **Wmk. 316**

No.	Type	Description	Unused	Used
RA4	PT1	50d emer & rose lil	4.00	.90
RA5	PT1	2r vio & car rose ('58)	2.50	1.00

1965 **Wmk. 349** ***Perf. 10½***

No.	Type	Description	Unused	Used
RA6	PT1	50d emer & car rose	2.00	.50
RA7	PT1	2r vio & lil rose	2.50	.65

1965-66 **Wmk. 353**

No.	Type	Description	Unused	Used
RA8	PT1	50d emer & car rose (I)	1.00	.20
a.		Type II	3.00	.20
RA9	PT1	2r vio & car rose ('66)	3.00	.35

No. RA8 was printed in two types: I. Without diagonal line before Persian "50." II. With line.

1976, Sept.-78 **Photo.** ***Perf. 13x13½***

No.	Type	Description	Unused	Used
RA10	PT1	50d emerald & red	2.50	.30
RA11	PT1	2r slate & red ('78)	2.50	*2.50*

Nos. RA10-RA11 are redrawn and have vertical watermark.

Nos. RA1-RA11 were obligatory on all mail. 50d stamps were for registered mail, 2r stamps for parcel post. The tax was for hospitals.

The 2.25r and 2.50r of type PT1 were used only on telegrams.

IRAQ

i-räk

LOCATION — In western Asia, bounded on the north by Syria and Turkey, on the east by Iran, on the south by Saudi Arabia, and on the west by Jordan
GOVT. — Republic
AREA — 167,925 sq. mi.
POP. — 22,427,150 (1999 est.)
CAPITAL — Baghdad

Iraq, formerly Mesopotamia, a province of Turkey, was mandated to Great Britain in 1920. The mandate was terminated in 1932. For earlier issues, see Mesopotamia.

16 Annas = 1 Rupee
1000 Fils = 1 Dinar (1932)

Catalogue values for unused stamps in this country are for Never Hinged items, beginning with Scott 79 in the regular postage section, Scott C1 in the air post section, Scott CO1 in the air post official section, Scott O90 in the officials section, Scott RA1 in the postal tax section, and Scott RAC1 in the air post postal tax section.

Issues under British Mandate

Sunni Mosque — A1

Gufas on the Tigris — A2

Assyrian Winged Bull — A4

Ctesiphon Arch — A5

Motif of Assyrian Origin — A3

Colors of the Dulaim Camel Corps — A6

Golden Shiah Mosque of Kadhimain — A7

Conventionalized Date Palm or "Tree of Life" — A8

1923-25 Engr. Wmk. 4 *Perf. 12*

No.	Type	Value	Unused	Used
1	A1	½a olive grn	.40	.20
2	A2	1a brown	.65	.20
3	A3	1½a car lake	.30	.20
4	A4	2a brown org	.30	.20
5	A5	3a dp blue	.65	.20
6	A6	4a dull vio	1.25	.25
7	A7	6a blue grn	.80	.25
8	A6	8a olive bis	1.40	.60
9	A8	1r grn & brn	3.00	.70
10	A1	2r black	12.00	6.50
11	A1	2r bister ('25)	35.00	3.00
12	A6	5r orange	30.00	13.00
13	A7	10r carmine	40.00	20.00
		Nos. 1-13 (13)	125.75	45.30

For overprints see Nos. O1-O24, O42, O47, O51-O53.

King Faisal I — A9

1927

No.	Type	Value	Unused	Used
14	A9	1r red brown	5.00	1.00

See No. 27. For overprint and surcharges see Nos. 43, O25, O54.

King Faisal I
A10 A11

1931

No.	Type	Value	Unused	Used
15	A10	½a green	.30	.20
16	A10	1a chestnut	.30	.20
17	A10	1½a carmine	.60	.25
18	A10	2a orange	.60	.20
19	A10	3a light blue	.70	.20
20	A10	4a pur brown	1.00	.60
21	A10	6a Prus blue	1.00	.60
22	A10	8a dark green	1.50	1.00
23	A11	1r dark brown	3.00	1.25
24	A11	2r yel brown	5.00	3.00
25	A11	5r dp orange	16.00	*25.00*
26	A11	10r red	50.00	*60.00*
27	A9	25r violet	450.00	*650.00*
		Nos. 15-27 (13)	530.00	*742.50*

See Nos. 44-60. For overprints see Nos. O26-O41, O43-O46, O48-O50, O54-O71.

Issues of the Kingdom

Nos. 6, 15-27 Surcharged in "Fils" or "Dinars" in Red, Black or Green:

a

b

c

1 Dinar

d

1932, Apr. 1

No.	Type	Value	Unused	Used
28	A10(a)	2f on ½a (R)	.20	.20
29	A10(a)	3f on ½a	.20	.20
a.		Double surcharge	160.00	
b.		Inverted surcharge	*160.00*	
30	A10(a)	4f on 1a (G)	.75	.25
31	A10(a)	5f on 1a	.25	.20
a.		Double surcharge	250.00	
b.		Inverted Arabic "5"	*30.00*	*35.00*
32	A10(a)	8f on 1½a	.30	.25
a.		Inverted surcharge	*150.00*	
33	A10(a)	10f on 2a	.40	.20
34	A10(a)	15f on 3a	.75	1.00
35	A10(a)	20f on 4a	1.25	1.00
36	A6(b)	25f on 4a	2.00	2.50
a.		"Flis" for "Fils"	*350.00*	*350.00*
b.		Inverted Arabic "5"	*400.00*	*500.00*
37	A10(a)	30f on 6a	1.50	.65
38	A10(a)	40f on 8a	2.25	2.00
39	A11(c)	75f on 1r	2.00	2.00
40	A11(c)	100f on 2r	6.00	4.00
41	A11(c)	200f on 5r	15.00	*20.00*
42	A11(d)	½d on 10r	65.00	*75.00*
a.		Bar in "½" omitted	*675.00*	*700.00*
43	A9(d)	1d on 25r	125.00	*150.00*
		Nos. 28-43 (16)	222.85	*259.45*

King Faisal I
A12 A13

A14

Values in "Fils" and "Dinars"

1932, May 9 Engr.

No.	Type	Value	Unused	Used
44	A12	2f ultra	.20	.20
45	A12	3f green	.20	.20
46	A12	4f vio brown	.20	.20
47	A12	5f gray green	.20	.20
48	A12	8f deep red	.20	.20
49	A12	10f yellow	.20	.20
50	A12	15f deep blue	.50	.20
51	A12	20f orange	.50	.25
52	A12	25f rose lilac	.50	.20
53	A12	30f olive grn	.50	.20
54	A12	40f dark violet	1.00	1.00
55	A13	50f deep brown	.55	.25
56	A13	75f lt ultra	1.60	1.50
57	A13	100f deep green	2.75	.45
58	A13	200f dark red	9.00	3.00
59	A14	½d gray blue	27.50	25.00
60	A14	1d claret	65.00	65.00
		Nos. 44-60 (17)	110.60	98.25

For overprints see Nos. O55-O71.

A15

A16

King Ghazi — A17

1934-38 Unwmk.

No.	Type	Value	Unused	Used
61	A15	1f purple ('38)	.20	.20
62	A15	2f ultra	.20	.20
63	A15	3f green	.20	.20
64	A15	4f pur brown	.20	.20
65	A15	5f gray green	.20	.20
66	A15	8f deep red	.20	.20
67	A15	10f yellow	.20	.20
68	A15	15f deep blue	.20	.20
69	A15	20f orange	.25	.20
70	A15	25f brown vio	.50	.25
71	A15	30f olive grn	.50	.20
72	A15	40f dark vio	.50	.20
73	A16	50f deep brown	.80	.20
74	A16	75f ultra	1.10	.30
75	A16	100f deep green	1.75	.35
76	A16	200f dark red	4.00	.70
77	A17	½d gray blue	14.00	7.50
78	A17	1d claret	25.00	10.00
		Nos. 61-78 (18)	50.00	21.50

For overprints see Nos. 226, O72-O89.

Catalogue values for unused stamps in this section, from this point to the end of the section, are for Never Hinged items.

Sitt Zubaidah Mosque — A18

Mausoleum of King Faisal I — A19

Lion of Babylon — A20

Malwiye of Samarra (Spiral Tower) — A21

Oil Wells — A22

Mosque of the Golden Dome, Samarra — A23

Perf. 14, 13½, 12½, 12x13½, 13½x12, 14x13½

1941-42 Engr.

No.	Type	Value	Unused	Used
79	A18	1f dark violet ('42)	.20	.20
80	A18	2f chocolate ('42)	.20	.20
81	A19	3f brt green ('42)	.20	.20
82	A19	4f purple ('42)	.20	.20
83	A19	5f dk car rose ('42)	.20	.20
84	A20	8f carmine	.40	.25
85	A20	8f ocher ('42)	.20	.20
86	A20	10f ocher	8.00	.40
87	A20	10f carmine ('42)	.20	.20
88	A20	15f dull blue	.50	.20
89	A20	15f black ('42)	.20	.20
90	A20	20f black	3.00	.45
91	A20	20f dull blue ('42)	.20	.20
92	A21	25f dark violet	.20	.20
93	A21	30f deep orange	.20	.20
94	A21	40f brn orange	2.00	.30
95	A21	40f chestnut ('42)	.75	.20
96	A21	50f ultra	.40	.20
97	A21	75f rose violet	.60	.25
98	A22	100f olive green ('42)	1.10	.30
99	A22	200f dp orange ('42)	4.25	.75
100	A23	½d lt bl, perf. 12x13½ ('42)	7.25	1.00
a.		Perf. 14	6.00	2.50
101	A23	1d grnsh bl ('42)	15.00	6.50
		Nos. 79-101 (23)	45.45	13.00

Nos. 92-95 measure 17¾x21½mm, Nos. 96-97 measure 21x24mm.

For overprints see #O90-O114, O165, RA5.

King Faisal II
A24 A25

Photo.; Frame Litho.

1942 *Perf. 13 x 13½*

No.	Type	Value	Unused	Used
102	A24	1f violet & brown	.20	.20
103	A24	2f dk blue & brown	.20	.20
104	A24	3f lt green & brown	.20	.20
105	A24	4f dull brown & brn	.20	.20
106	A24	5f sage green & brn	.20	.20
107	A24	6f red orange & brn	.20	.20
108	A24	10f dl rose red & lt brn	.20	.20
109	A24	12f yel green & brown	.20	.20
		Nos. 102-109 (8)	1.60	1.60

For overprints see Nos. O115-O122.

Perf. 11½x12
1948, Jan. 15 Engr. Unwmk.
Size: 17¾x20½mm

110 A25 1f slate .20 .20
111 A25 2f sepia .20 .20
112 A25 3f emerald .20 .20
113 A25 4f purple .20 .20
114 A25 5f rose lake .20 .20
115 A25 6f plum .20 .20
116 A25 8f ocher 1.50 .20
117 A25 10f rose red .20 .20
118 A25 12f dark olive .20 .20
119 A25 15f black 1.50 .20
120 A25 20f blue .20 .20
121 A25 25f rose violet .20 .20
122 A25 30f red orange .20 .20
123 A25 40f orange brn .30 .20

Perf. 12x11½
Size: 22x27½mm

124 A25 60f deep blue .75 .20
125 A25 75f lilac rose 1.25 .25
126 A25 100f olive green 3.00 .30
127 A25 200f deep orange 2.75 .45
128 A25 ½d blue 7.00 2.00
129 A25 1d green 22.50 10.00
Nos. 110-129 (20) 42.75 16.00

Sheets of 6 exist, perforated and imperforate, containing Nos. 112, 117, 120 and 125-127, with arms and Arabic inscription in blue green in upper and lower margins. Value each, $25.

See Nos. 133-138. For overprints see Nos. 188-194, O123-O142, O166-O177, O257, O272, O274, O277, O282, RA1-RA4, RA6.

Post Rider and King Ghazi — A26

Designs: 40f, Equestrian statue & Faisal I. 50f, UPU symbols & Faisal II.

1949, Nov. 1 *Perf. 13x13½*

130 A26 20f blue 1.40 1.00
131 A26 40f red orange 1.90 1.00
132 A26 50f purple 4.25 3.50
Nos. 130-132 (3) 7.55 5.50

75th anniv. of the UPU.

Type of 1948

1950-51 Unwmk. *Perf. 11½x12*
Size: 17¾x20½mm

133 A25 3f rose lake 3.00 .20
134 A25 5f emerald 5.00 .30
135 A25 14f dk olive ('50) .50 .20
136 A25 16f rose red 2.00 .30
137 A25 28f blue 1.00 .30

Perf. 12x11½
Size: 22x27½mm

138 A25 50f deep blue ('50) 1.50 .35
Nos. 133-138 (6) 13.00 1.65

For overprints see Nos. 160, O143-O148, O258, O273, O275-O276.

King Faisal II
A27 A28

1953, May 2 Engr. *Perf. 12*

139 A27 3f deep rose car .50 .40
140 A27 14f olive 1.00 .45
141 A27 28f blue 3.00 .65
b. Souv. sheet of 3, #139-141 60.00 40.00
Nos. 139-141 (3) 4.50 1.50

Coronation of King Faisal II, May 2, 1953.

1954-57 *Perf. 11½x12*
Size: 18x20½mm

141A A28 1f blue ('56) .20 .20
142 A28 2f chocolate .20 .20
143 A28 3f rose lake .20 .20
144 A28 4f violet .20 .20
145 A28 5f emerald .20 .20
146 A28 6f plum .20 .20
147 A28 8f ocher .20 .20
148 A28 10f blue .20 .20
149 A28 15f black .75 .30
149A A28 16f brt rose ('57) 1.50 1.00
150 A28 20f olive .40 .20
151 A28 25f rose vio ('55) .40 .20
152 A28 30f ver ('55) .50 .20
153 A28 40f orange brn .50 .20

Size: 22x27½mm

154 A28 50f blue 1.00 .20
155 A28 75f pink 2.00 .35
156 A28 100f olive green 4.00 .75
157 A28 200f orange 6.00 1.00
Nos. 141A-157 (18) 18.65 6.00

For overprints see Nos. 158-159, 195-209, 674, 676, 678, O148A-O161A, O178-O191, O259-O260, O283-O291.

No. 143, 148 and 137 Overprinted in Black

1955, Apr. 6 *Perf. 11½x12*

158 A28 3f rose lake .50 .25
159 A28 10f blue .50 .25
160 A25 28f blue .85 .40
Nos. 158-160 (3) 1.85 .90

Abrogation of Anglo-Iraq treaty of 1930.

King Faisal II — A29

1955, Nov. 26 *Perf. 13½x13*

161 A29 3f rose lake .60 .25
162 A29 10f light ultra .60 .35
163 A29 28f blue 1.25 .75
Nos. 161-163 (3) 2.45 1.35

6th Arab Engineers' Conf., Baghdad, 1955.
For surcharge see No. 227.

Faisal II and Globe — A30

1956, Mar. 3 *Perf. 13x13½*

164 A30 3f rose lake .60 .35
165 A30 10f light ultra .75 .35
166 A30 28f blue 1.10 .60
Nos. 164-166 (3) 2.45 1.30

Arab Postal Conf., Baghdad, Mar. 3.
For overprint see #173. For surcharge see #251.

Mechanical Loom A31

Designs: 3f, Dam. 5f, Modern city development. 10f, Pipeline. 40f, Tigris Bridge.

1957, Apr. 8 Photo. *Perf. 11½*
Granite Paper

167 A31 1f Prus bl & org yel .20 .20
168 A31 3f multicolored .25 .20
169 A31 5f multicolored .25 .20
170 A31 10f lt bl, ocher & red .40 .20
171 A31 40f lt bl, blk & ocher .90 .35
Nos. 167-171 (5) 2.00 1.15

Development Week, 1957. See #185-187.

Fair Emblem — A32

1957, June 1 Unwmk.
Granite Paper

172 A32 10f brown & buff .60 .50

Agricultural and Industrial Exhibition, Baghdad, June 1.

No. 166 Overprinted in Red

1957, Nov. 14 *Perf. 13x13½*

173 A30 28f blue 2.25 1.00
a. Double overprint 200.00 *225.00*

Iraqi Red Crescent Soc., 25th anniv.

King Faisal II — A33

Perf. 11½x12
1957-58 Unwmk. Engr.

174 A33 1f blue .20 .25
175 A33 2f chocolate .20 .25
176 A33 3f dark car ('57) .20 .25
177 A33 4f dull violet .20 .25
177A A33 5f emerald .35 *.35*
178 A33 6f plum .35 .35
179 A33 8f ocher .70 .60
180 A33 10f blue .55 .50
Nos. 174-180 (8) 2.75 *2.80*

Higher denominations exist without Republic overprint. They were probably not regularly issued.

See note below No. 225.

For overprints see Nos. 210-225, 675, O162-O164, O192-O199, O292-O294. For types overprinted see #677, 679, O261, O295.

Tanks — A34

King Faisal II — A35

Army Day, Jan. 6: 10f, Marching soldiers. 20f, Artillery and planes.

1958, Jan. 6 *Perf. 13x13½*

181 A34 8f green & black .40 .40
182 A34 10f brown & black .65 .60
183 A34 20f blue & red brown .70 .60
184 A35 30f car & purple 1.25 .75
Nos. 181-184 (4) 3.00 2.35

Type of 1957

3f, Sugar beet, bag & refining machinery, vert. 5f, Farm. 10f, Dervendi Khan dam.

1958, Apr. 26 Photo. *Perf. 11½*
Granite Paper

185 A31 3f gray vio, grn & lt gray .25 .20
186 A31 5f multicolored .30 .25
187 A31 10f multicolored .75 .40
Nos. 185-187 (3) 1.30 .85

Development Week, 1958.

Republic

Stamps of 1948-51 Overprinted

Perf. 11½x12, 12x11½
1958 Engr. Unwmk.
Size: 17¾x20½mm

188 A25 12f dark olive .50 .20
189 A25 14f olive .60 .20
190 A25 16f rose red 8.00 2.25
191 A25 28f blue .80 .45

Size: 22x27½mm

192 A25 60f deep blue 2.10 .45
193 A25 ½d blue 13.00 3.25
194 A25 1d green 25.00 11.00
Nos. 188-194 (7) 50.00 17.80

Other denominations of type A25 exist with this overprint, but these were probably not regularly issued.

Same Overprint on Stamps of 1954-57
Size: 18x20½mm

195 A28 1f blue .40 .20
196 A28 2f chocolate .40 .20
196A A28 4f violet .40 .20
196B A28 5f emerald .40 .20
197 A28 6f plum .40 .20
198 A28 8f ocher .40 .20
199 A28 10f blue .50 .20
200 A28 15f black .65 .20
201 A28 16f bright rose 1.50 .35
202 A28 20f olive .75 .40
203 A28 25f rose violet .50 .20
204 A28 30f vermilion .75 .25
205 A28 40f orange brn .75 .20

Size: 22½x27½mm

206 A28 50f blue 3.25 2.00
207 A28 75f pink 2.50 1.50
208 A28 100f olive green 3.00 2.00
209 A28 200f orange 8.00 4.00
Nos. 195-209 (17) 24.55 12.50

The lines of this overprint are found transposed on Nos. 195, 196 and 199.

Same Overprint on Stamps and Type of 1957-58
Size: 18x20mm

210 A33 1f blue 2.00 .50
211 A33 2f chocolate .40 .20
212 A33 3f dark carmine .40 .20
213 A33 4f dull violet .40 .20
214 A33 5f emerald .40 .20
215 A33 6f plum .40 .20
216 A33 8f ocher .40 .20
217 A33 10f blue .40 .20
218 A33 20f olive .40 .20
219 A33 25f rose violet .75 .55
220 A33 30f vermilion 1.00 .20
221 A33 40f orange brn 2.75 .90

Size: 22x27½mm

222 A33 50f rose violet 2.25 .50
223 A33 75f olive 2.25 .90
224 A33 100f orange 2.75 .90
225 A33 200f blue 7.50 1.40
Nos. 210-225 (16) 24.45 7.45

#218-225 were not issued without overprint.

The lines of this overprint are found transposed on Nos. 210 and 214.

Many errors of overprint exist of #188-226.

For overprint see No. O198.

Same Overprint on No. 78
Perf. 12

226 A17 1d claret 17.50 15.00

No. 163 Surcharged in Red

1958, Nov. 26 *Perf. 13x13½*

227 A29 10f on 28f blue .90 .50

Arab Lawyers' Conf., Baghdad, Nov. 26.

Soldier and Flag A36

1959, Jan. 6 Photo. *Perf. 11½*

228 A36 3f bright blue .20 .20
229 A36 10f olive green .30 .25
230 A36 40f purple 1.00 .35
Nos. 228-230 (3) 1.50 .80

Issued for Army Day, Jan. 6.

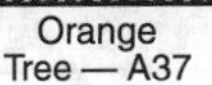

Orange Tree — A37

Emblem of Republic — A38

1959, Mar. 21 Unwmk. *Perf. 11½*

231	A37	10f green, dk grn & org	.50	.20

Issued for Arbor Day.

1959-60 Litho. & Photo. *Perf. 11½*

Granite Paper

Emblem in Gold, Red and Blue; Blue Inscriptions

232	A38	1f gray	.20	.20
233	A38	2f salmon	.20	.20
234	A38	3f pale violet	.20	.20
235	A38	4f bright yel	.20	.20
236	A38	5f light blue	.20	.20
237	A38	10f bright pink	.20	.20
238	A38	15f light green	.20	.20
239	A38	20f bister brn	.20	.20
240	A38	30f light gray	.20	.20
241	A38	40f orange yel	.25	.20
242	A38	50f yel green	2.75	.60
243	A38	75f pale grn ('60)	.75	.20
244	A38	100f orange ('60)	1.40	.30
245	A38	200f lilac ('60)	2.25	.65
246	A38	500f bister ('60)	6.00	1.75
247	A38	1d brt grn ('60)	10.00	5.00
		Nos. 232-247 (16)	25.20	10.50

See Nos. 305A-305B. For overprints see Nos. 252, 293-295, O200-O221.

Worker and Buildings — A39

Victorious Fighters A40

Perf. 12½x13, 13x12½

1959, July 14 Photo.

248	A39	10f ocher & blue	.30	.30
249	A40	30f ocher & emerald	.75	.50

1st anniv. of the Revolution of July 14 (1958), which overthrew the kingdom.

Harvest — A41

1959, July 14 *Perf. 11½*

250	A41	10f lt grn & dk grn	.35	.20

No. 166 Surcharged in Dark Red

1959, June 1 Engr. *Perf. 13x13½*

251	A30	10f on 28f blue	.75	.40

Issued for Children's Day, 1959.

No. 237 Overprinted

Litho. and Photo.

1959, Oct. 23 *Perf. 11½*

252	A38	10f multicolored	.50	.30

Health and Sanitation Week.

Abdul Karim Kassem and Army Band — A42

Abdul Karim Kassem and: 16f, Field maneuvers, horiz. 30f, Antiaircraft. 40f, Troops at attention, flag and bugler. 60f, Fighters and flag, horiz.

1960, Jan. 6 Photo. *Perf. 11½*

253	A42	10f blue, grn & mar	.20	.25
254	A42	16f brt blue & red	.45	.30
255	A42	30f ol grn, yel & brn	.45	.30
256	A42	40f deep vio & buff	.75	.40
257	A42	60f dk brown & buff	1.40	.50
		Nos. 253-257 (5)	3.25	1.75

Issued for Army Day, Jan. 6.

Prime Minister Abdul Karim Kassem — A43

Maroof el Rasafi — A44

1960, Feb. 1 Engr. *Perf. 12½*

258	A43	10f lilac	.35	.20
259	A43	30f emerald	.70	.30

Issued to honor Prime Minister Kassem on his recovery from an assassination attempt.

1960, May 10 Photo. *Perf. 13½x13*

260	A44	10f maroon & blk	1.50	1.00
a.		Inverted overprint	100.00	100.00

Exists without overprint. Value $4.

Symbol of the Republic — A45

Unknown Soldier's Tomb and Kassem with Freedom Torch — A46

1960, July 14 *Perf. 11½*

261	A45	6f ol grn, red & gold	.35	.25
262	A46	10f green, blue & red	.35	.25
263	A46	16f vio, blue & red	.45	.35
264	A45	18f ultra, red & gold	.45	.35
265	A45	30f brown, red & gold	.60	.45
266	A46	60f dk brn, bl & red	1.25	.70
		Nos. 261-266 (6)	3.45	2.35

2nd anniv. of the July 14, 1958 revolution.

Gen. Kassem and Marching Troops — A47

Gen. Kassem and Arch — A48

1961, Jan. 6 *Perf. 11½*

Granite Paper

267	A47	3f gray ol, emer, yel & gold	.20	.20
268	A47	6f pur, emer, yel & gold	.20	.20
269	A47	10f sl, emer, yel & gold	.30	.20
270	A48	20f bl grn, blk & buff	.40	.25
271	A48	30f bis brn, blk & buff	.40	.25
272	A48	40f ultra, black & buff	.75	.30
		Nos. 267-272 (6)	2.25	1.40

Issued for Army Day, Jan. 6.

Gen. Kassem and Children A49

1961, June 1 Photo. Unwmk.

Granite Paper

273	A49	3f yellow & brown	.40	.25
274	A49	6f blue & brown	.60	.25
275	A49	10f pink & brown	.80	.25
276	A49	30f yellow & brown	.80	.25
277	A49	50f lt grn & brown	1.40	.35
		Nos. 273-277 (5)	4.00	1.35

Issued for World Children's Day.

Gen. Kassem and Flag — A50

5f, 30f, 40f, Gen. Kassem saluting and flags.

1961, July 14 *Perf. 11½*

Granite Paper

278	A50	1f multicolored	.20	.20
279	A50	3f multicolored	.20	.20
280	A50	5f multicolored	.20	.20
281	A50	6f multicolored	.20	.20
282	A50	10f multicolored	.20	.20
283	A50	30f multicolored	.40	.20
284	A50	40f multicolored	.55	.25
285	A50	50f multicolored	1.10	.25
286	A50	100f multicolored	3.25	1.60
		Nos. 278-286 (9)	6.30	3.30

3rd anniv. of the July 14, 1958 revolution.

Gen. Kassem and Flag — A51

Gen. Kassem and Symbol of Republic A52

Perf. 11½

1962, Jan. 6 Unwmk. Photo.

Granite Paper

287	A51	1f multicolored	.20	.20
288	A51	3f multicolored	.20	.20
289	A51	6f multicolored	.20	.20
290	A52	10f blk, lilac & gold	.30	.20
291	A52	30f black, org & gold	.60	.30
292	A52	50f blk, pale grn & gold	1.00	.50
		Nos. 287-292 (6)	2.50	1.60

Issued for Army Day, Jan. 6.

Nos. 234, 237 and 240 Overprinted

Litho. & Photo.

1962, May 29 *Perf. 11½*

293	A38	3f multicolored	.20	.20
294	A38	10f multicolored	.20	.20
295	A38	30f multicolored	.60	.35
		Nos. 293-295 (3)	1.00	.75

Fifth Islamic Congress.

Hands Across Map of Arabia and North Africa — A53

1962, July 14 Photo.

296	A53	1f brn, org, grn & gold	.20	.20
297	A53	3f brn, yel grn, grn & gold	.20	.20
298	A53	6f blk, lt brn, grn & gold	.20	.20
299	A53	10f brn, lil, grn & gold	.25	.20
300	A53	30f brn, rose, grn & gold	.40	.30
301	A53	50f brn, gray, grn & gold	.75	.45
		Nos. 296-301 (6)	2.00	1.55

Revolution of July 14, 1958, 4th anniv.

al-Kindi A54

Emblem of Republic A54a

Designs: 3f, Horsemen with standards and trumpets. 10f, Old map of Baghdad and Tigris. 40f, Gen. Kassem, modern building and flag.

Perf. 14x13½

1962, Dec. 1 Litho. Unwmk.

302	A54	3f multicolored	.20	.20
303	A54	6f multicolored	.20	.20
304	A54	10f multicolored	.30	.20
305	A54	40f multicolored	.90	.40
		Nos. 302-305 (4)	1.60	1.00

9th century Arab philosopher al-Kindi; millenary of the Round City of Baghdad.

1962, Dec. 20 ***Perf. 13½x14***

305A	A54a	14f brt green & blk	1.25	.40
305B	A54a	35f ver & black	1.75	.60

Nos. 305A-305B were originally sold affixed to air letter sheets, obliterating the portrait of King Faisal II. They were issued in sheets for general use in 1966.

For overprints see Nos. RA15-RA16.

Tanks on Parade and Gen. Kassem — A55

Malaria Eradication Emblem — A56

1963, Jan. 6 Photo. ***Perf. 11½***

306	A55	3f black & yellow	.20	.20
307	A55	5f brown & plum	.20	.20
308	A55	6f blk & lt green	.20	.20
309	A55	10f blk & lt blue	.20	.20
310	A55	10f black & pink	.20	.20
311	A55	20f black & ultra	.40	.20
312	A55	40f blk & rose lilac	.55	.25
313	A55	50f brn & brt ultra	.75	.40
		Nos. 306-313 (8)	2.70	1.85

Issued for Army Day, Jan. 6.

1962, Dec. 31 ***Perf. 14***

Republic Emblem in Red, Blue & Gold

314	A56	3f yel grn, blk & dk grn	.20	.20
315	A56	10f org, blk & dark blue	.45	.20
316	A56	40f lilac, black & blue	.75	.30
		Nos. 314-316 (3)	1.40	.70

WHO drive to eradicate malaria.

Gufas on the Tigris — A57

Shepherd and Sheep A58

Designs: 2f, 500f, Spiral tower, Samarra. 4f, 15f, Ram's head harp, Ur. 5f, 75f, Map and Republic emblem. 10f, 50f, Lion of Babylon. 20f, 40f, Baghdad University. 30f, 200f, Kadhimain mosque. 100f, 1d, Winged bull, Khorsabad.

Engr.; Engr. and Photo. (bicolored)

1963, Feb. 16 Unwmk. ***Perf. 12x11***

317	A57	1f green	.45	.20
318	A57	2f purple	.45	.20
319	A57	3f black	.45	.20
320	A57	4f black & yel	.45	.20
321	A57	5f lilac & lt grn	.50	.20
322	A57	10f rose red	.65	.20
323	A57	15f brn & buff	1.00	.20
324	A57	20f violet blue	1.10	.20
325	A57	30f orange	.70	.25
326	A57	40f brt green	1.25	.20
327	A57	50f dark brown	5.00	.40
328	A57	75f blk & lt grn	2.50	.30
329	A57	100f brt lilac	2.75	.20
330	A57	200f brown	5.00	.35
331	A57	500f blue	7.00	1.60
332	A57	1d deep claret	9.75	3.00
		Nos. 317-332 (16)	39.00	7.90

For overprints see Nos. RA7-RA12.

1963, Mar. 21 Litho. ***Perf. 13½x14***

10f, Man holding sheaf. 20f, Date palm grove.

333	A58	3f emerald & gray	.20	.20
334	A58	10f dp brn & lil rose	.30	.20
335	A58	20f dk bl & red brn	.75	.35
a.		Souv. sheet of 3, #333-335	3.50	
		Nos. 333-335 (3)	1.25	.75

FAO "Freedom from Hunger" campaign. No. 335a sold for 50f.

No. 335a was overprinted in 1970 in black to commemorate the UN 25th anniv. Denominations on the 3 stamps were obliterated, leaving "Price 50 Fils" in the margin.

Cent. Emblem — A59

Rifle, Helmet and Flag — A60

Design: 30f, Iraqi Red Crescent Society Headquarters, horiz.

Perf. 11x11½, 11½x11

1963, Dec. 30 Photo.

336	A59	3f violet & red	.20	.20
337	A59	10f gray & red	.20	.20
338	A59	30f blue & red	.50	.20
		Nos. 336-338 (3)	.90	.60

Centenary of International Red Cross.

1964, Jan. 6 Unwmk. ***Perf. 11½***

Granite Paper

339	A60	3f brn, blue & emer	.20	.20
340	A60	10f brn, pink & emer	.25	.20
341	A60	30f brown, yel & emer	.45	.20
		Nos. 339-341 (3)	.90	.60

Issued for Army Day, Jan. 6.

Flag and Soldiers Storming Government Palace — A61

1964, Feb. 8 ***Perf. 11½***

Granite Paper

342	A61	10f pur, red, grn & blk	.30	.20
343	A61	30f red brn, red, grn & blk	.50	.25
a.		Souv. sheet of 2, imperf	4.25	2.75
b.		Souv. sheet of 2 (4th anniv.) ('67)	4.25	2.75

Revolution of Ramadan 14, 1st anniv. #343a contains stamps similar to #342-343 in changed colors (10f olive, red, green & black; 30f ultra, red, green & black). Sold for 50f.

No. 343b consists of various block-outs and overprints on No. 343a. It commemorates the 4th anniv. of the Revolution of Ramadan 14. Sold for 70f. Issued Feb. 8, 1967.

Hammurabi and a God from Stele in Louvre — A62

Design: 10f, UN emblem and scales.

1964, June 10 Litho. ***Perf. 13½***

344	A62	6f lilac & pale grn	.30	.25
345	A62	10f org & vio blue	.45	.25
346	A62	30f blue & pale grn	.75	.35
		Nos. 344-346 (3)	1.50	.85

15th anniv. (in 1963) of the Universal Declaration of Human Rights.

"Industrialization of Iraq" — A63

Soldier Planting New Flag — A64

1964, July 14 ***Perf. 11***

347	A63	3f gray, org & black	.20	.20
348	A64	10f rose red, blk & emer	.20	.20
349	A64	20f rose red, blk & emer	.30	.20
350	A63	30f gray, org & black	.50	.20
		Nos. 347-350 (4)	1.20	.80

6th anniv. of the July 14, 1958 revolution.

Star and Fighters A65

1964, Nov. 18 Photo. ***Perf. 11½***

351	A65	5f sepia & orange	.20	.20
352	A65	10f lt bl & orange	.20	.20
353	A65	50f vio & red orange	.60	.30
		Nos. 351-353 (3)	1.00	.70

Revolution of Nov. 18, 1963, 1st anniv.

Musician with Lute — A66

Perf. 13x13½

1964, Nov. 28 Litho. Unwmk.

354	A66	3f bister & multi	.65	.20
355	A66	10f dl grn & multi	.65	.20
356	A66	30f dl rose & multi	.90	.60
		Nos. 354-356 (3)	2.20	1.00

International Arab Music Conference.

Map of Arab Countries and Emblem A67

1964, Dec. 13 ***Perf. 12½x14***

357	A67	10f lt grn & rose lilac	.35	.20

9th Arab Engineers' Conference, Baghdad.

Arab Postal Union Emblem — A67a

Soldier, Flag and Rising Sun — A68

1964, Dec. 21 Photo. ***Perf. 11***

358	A67a	3f sal pink & blue	.20	.20
359	A67a	10f brt red lil & brn	.30	.20
360	A67a	30f orange & blue	.60	.25
		Nos. 358-360 (3)	1.10	.65

10th anniv. of Permanent Office of APU

For overprint see No. 707.

Perf. 14x12½

1965, Jan. 6 Litho. Unwmk.

361	A68	5f dull green & multi	.20	.20
362	A68	15f henna brn & multi	.20	.20
363	A68	30f black brn & multi	.60	.20
		Nos. 361-363 (3)	1.00	.60

Issued for Army Day, Jan. 6.

An imperf. souvenir sheet carries a revised No. 363 with "30 FILS" omitted, and a portrait of Pres. Abdul Salam Arif. Violet inscriptions including "PRICE 60 FILS."

Symbols of Agriculture and Industry A69

1965, Jan. 8 ***Perf. 12½x14***

364	A69	10f ultra, brn & blk	.25	.20

Arab Labor Ministers' Conference.

Tanker A70

1965, Jan. 30 ***Perf. 14***

365	A70	10f multicolored	.60	.25

Inauguration (in 1962) of the deep sea terminal for oil tankers.

Soldier with Flag and Rifle — A71

Tree Week — A72

1965, Feb. 8 Litho. ***Perf. 13½***

366	A71	10f multicolored	.35	.20

Revolution of Ramadan 14, 2nd anniv.

1965, Mar. 6 Unwmk. ***Perf. 13***

367	A72	6f multicolored	.20	.20
368	A72	20f multicolored	.75	.20

Federation Emblem — A73

Dagger in Map of Palestine — A74

1965, Mar. 24 Unwmk. *Perf. 14*

369 A73 3f lt bl, vio bl & gold .20 .20
370 A73 10f gray, black & gold .20 .20
371 A73 30f rose, car & gold .50 .30
Nos. 369-371 (3) .90 .70

Arab Federation of Insurance.

1965, Apr. 9 Litho. *Perf. 14x12½*

372 A74 10f gray & black .40 .20
373 A74 20f lt brn & dk blue .75 .25

Deir Yassin massacre, Apr. 9, 1948.

Smallpox Attacking People — A75

1965, Apr. 30 Litho. *Perf. 14*

374 A75 3f multicolored .25 .20
375 A75 10f multicolored .30 .20
376 A75 20f multicolored .70 .25
Nos. 374-376 (3) 1.25 .65

WHO's fight against smallpox. Exist imperf. Value $2.

ITU Emblem, Old and New Telecommunication Equipment — A76

1965, May 17 *Perf. 14, Imperf.*

377 A76 10f multicolored .35 .20
378 A76 20f multicolored .90 .20
a. Souv. sheet of 2, #377-378 6.00 5.50

ITU, centenary. No. 378a sold for 40f and exists imperf.

Map of Arab Countries and Banner — A77

1965, May 26 Litho. *Perf. 14x12½*

379 A77 10f multicolored .25 .20

Anniversary of the treaty with the UAR.

Library Aflame and Lamp A78

1965, June Photo. *Perf. 11*

380 A78 5f black, grn & red .25 .20
381 A78 10f blk, green & red .40 .20

Burning of the Library of Algiers, 6/2/62.

Revolutionist with Torch, Cannon and Flames — A79

1965, June 30 Litho. *Perf. 13*

382 A79 5f multicolored .20 .20
383 A79 10f multicolored .25 .20

45th anniversary, Revolution of 1920.

Mosque — A80

1965, July 12 Photo. *Perf. 12*

384 A80 10f multicolored .40 .30

Prophet Mohammed's birthday. A souvenir sheet contains one imperf. stamp similar to No. 384. Sold for 50f. Value $5

Factories and Grain — A81

Arab Fair Emblem — A82

1965, July 14 Litho. *Perf. 13*

385 A81 10f multicolored .25 .20

7th anniv. of the July 14, 1958 Revolution.

1965, Oct. 22 Unwmk. *Perf. 13*

386 A82 10f multicolored .25 .20

Second Arab Fair, Baghdad.

Pres. Abdul Salam Mohammed Arif — A83

1965, Nov. 18 Photo. *Perf. 11½*
Granite Paper

387 A83 5f org, buff & dk blue .25 .20
388 A83 10f lt ultra, gray & dk brn .35 .20
389 A83 50f lil, pale pink & sl blk 1.40 .60
Nos. 387-389 (3) 2.00 1.00

Revolution of Nov. 18, 1963, 2nd anniv.

Census Chart and Adding Machine — A84

1965, Nov. 29 Litho. *Perf. 13*

390 A84 3f gray & plum .30 .20
391 A84 5f brown red & brn .35 .20
392 A84 15f olive bis & dl bl .70 .20
Nos. 390-392 (3) 1.35 .60

Issued to publicize the 1965 census.

Date Palms — A85

Soldiers' Monument A86

1965, Dec. 27 Litho. *Perf. 13½x14*

393 A85 3f olive bis & multi .20 .20
394 A85 10f car rose & multi .30 .20
395 A85 15f blue & multi .80 .30
Nos. 393-395 (3) 1.30 .70

2nd FAO Intl. Dates Conference, Baghdad, Dec. 1965.

For surcharges see Nos. 694-695.

1966, Jan. 6 Photo. *Perf. 12*

396 A86 2f car rose & multi .20 .20
397 A86 5f multicolored .20 .20
398 A86 40f yel grn & multi 1.10 .75
Nos. 396-398 (3) 1.50 1.15

Issued for Army Day.

Eagle and Flag of Iraq — A87

Perf. 12½

1966, Feb. 8 Photo. Unwmk.

399 A87 5f dl bl & multi .20 .20
400 A87 10f orange & multi .40 .20

3rd anniv. of the Revolution of Ramadan 14, which overthrew the Kassem government.

Arab League Emblem — A88

Soccer Players — A89

1966, Mar. 22 *Perf. 11x11½*

401 A88 5f org, brn & brt grn .20 .20
402 A88 15f ol, rose lil & ultra .40 .20

Arab Publicity Week.

1966, Apr. 1 *Perf. 12*

5f, Player and goal post. 15f, As 2f. 50f, Legs of player, ball and emblem, horiz.

403 A89 2f multicolored .30 .20
404 A89 5f multicolored .20 .20
405 A89 15f multicolored .90 .45
Nos. 403-405 (3) 1.40 .85

Miniature Sheet

Imperf

406 A89 50f vio & multi 4.25 *10.50*

3rd Arab Soccer Cup, Baghdad, Apr. 1-10.

Steam Shovel Within Cogwheel A90

1966, May 1 Litho. *Perf. 13½*

407 A90 15f multicolored .20 .20
408 A90 25f red, blk, & sil .25 .20

Issued for Labor Day, May 1, 1966.

Queen Nefertari — A91

Facade of Abu Simbel A92

Perf. 12½x13, 13½

1966, May 20 Litho.

409 A91 5f olive, yel & blk .20 .20
410 A91 15f blue, yel & brn .20 .20
411 A92 40f bis brn, red & blk 1.25 1.00
Nos. 409-411 (3) 1.65 1.40

UNESCO world campaign to save historic monuments in Nubia.

President Arif and Flag — A93

1966, July 14 Photo. *Perf. 11½*

412 A93 5f multicolored .20 .20
413 A93 15f multicolored .25 .20
414 A93 50f multicolored .75 .25
Nos. 412-414 (3) 1.20 .65

8th anniv. of the July 14, 1958 revolution.

A94

1966, July 22 Litho. *Perf. 12*
Multicolored Vignette

415 A94 5f lt olive green .20 .20
416 A94 15f lt greenish blue .20 .20
417 A94 30f lt yellow green .25 .20
Nos. 415-417 (3) .65 .60

Mohammed's 1,396th birthday.

Iraqi Museum, Baghdad A95

Designs: 50f, Golden headdress, Ur. 80f, Carved Sumerian head, vert.

1966, Nov. 9 Litho. *Perf. 14*

418 A95 15f multicolored .25 .20
419 A95 50f lt bl, blk, gold & pink .90 .50
420 A95 80f crim, blk, bl & gold 2.25 .75
Nos. 418-420 (3) 3.40 1.45

Opening of New Iraqi Museum, Baghdad.

UNESCO Emblem — A96

Iraqi Citizens — A97

1966, Dec. *Perf. 13½*

421 A96 5f blue, black & tan .20 .20
422 A96 15f brt org brn, blk & gray .20 .20

20th anniv. of UNESCO.

1966, Nov. 18 *Perf. 13½x13*

423 A97 15f multicolored .40 .35
424 A97 25f multicolored .65 .85

3rd anniv. of the Revolution of 11/18/63.

Rocket Launchers and Soldier A98

1967, Jan. 6 Photo. *Perf. 11½*

425 A98 15f citron, dk brn & dp bis .20 .20
426 A98 20f brt lil, dk brn & dp bis .40 .20

Issued for Army Day, Jan. 6.

Oil Derrick, Pipeline, Emblem — A99

15f, 50f, Refinery and emblem, horiz.

1967, Mar. 6 Litho. *Perf. 14*

427 A99 5f ol grn, pale yel & blk .20 .20
428 A99 15f multicolored .20 .20
429 A99 40f vio, yel & blk .20 .20
430 A99 50f multicolored .40 .30
Nos. 427-430 (4) 1.00 .90

6th Arab Petroleum Cong., Baghdad, Mar. 1967.

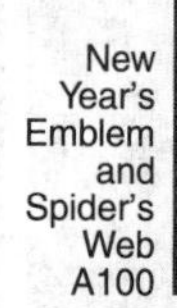

New Year's Emblem and Spider's Web A100

1967, Apr. 11 Litho. *Perf. 13½*

431 A100 5f multicolored .20 .20
432 A100 15f multicolored .20 .20

Issued for the Hajeer Year (New Year).

Worker Holding Cogwheel and Map of Arab Countries — A101

1967, May 1 *Perf. 12½x13*

433 A101 10f gray & multi .20 .20
434 A101 15f lt ultra & multi .20 .20

Issued for Labor Day.

A102

1967, June 20 Litho. *Perf. 14*

435 A102 5f multicolored .20 .20
436 A102 15f blue & multi .25 .20

Mohammed's 1,397th birthday.

Flag, Hands with Clubs — A103

1967, July 7 *Perf. 13x13½*

437 A103 5f multicolored .20 .20
438 A103 15f multicolored .20 .20

47th anniversary of Revolution of 1920.

Um Qasr Harbor A104

10f, 15f, Freighter loading in Um Qasr harbor.

1967, July 14 Litho. *Perf. 14x13½*

439 A104 5f multicolored .20 .20
440 A104 10f multicolored .20 .20
441 A104 15f multicolored .45 .20
442 A104 40f multicolored 1.60 .20
Nos. 439-442 (4) 2.45 .80

9th anniv. of the July 14, 1958 revolution and the inauguration of the port of Um Qasr.

Iraqi Man — A105

President Arif — A106

Iraqi Costumes: 5f, 15f, 25f, Women's costumes. 10f, 20f, 30f, Men's costumes.

1967, Nov. 10 Litho. *Perf. 13*

443 A105 2f pale brn & multi .20 .20
444 A105 5f ver & multi .20 .20
445 A105 10f multicolored .20 .20
446 A105 15f ultra & multi .25 .20
447 A105 20f lilac & multi .50 .20
448 A105 25f lemon & multi .50 .20
449 A105 30f fawn & multi .50 .25
Nos. 443-449,C19-C21 (10) 6.10 2.45

For overprints see Nos. 597-599, RA17.

Perf. 11x11½, 11½x11

1967, Nov. 18

15f, Pres. Arif and map of Iraq, horiz.

450 A106 5f bl, vio blk & yel .20 .20
451 A106 15f rose & multi .50 .25

4th anniversary of Nov. 18th revolution.

Ziggurat of Ur — A107

Designs: 5f, Gate with Nimrod statues. 10f, Gate, Babylon. 15f, Minaret of Mosul, vert. 25f, Arch and ruins of Ctesiphon.

1967, Dec. 1 Litho. *Perf. 13*

452 A107 2f orange & multi .20 .20
453 A107 5f lilac & multi .20 .20
454 A107 10f orange & multi .20 .20
455 A107 15f rose red & multi .30 .20
456 A107 25f vio bl & multi .40 .20
Nos. 452-456,C22-C26 (10) 32.75 16.15

International Tourist Year.
For overprints see Nos. 593, 680, RA18.

Iraqi Girl Scout Emblem and Sign — A108

5f, Girl Scouts at campfire & Girl Scout emblem. 10f, Boy Scout emblem & Boy Scout sign. 15f, Boy Scouts pitching tent & Boy Scout sign.

1967, Dec. 15

457 A108 2f orange & multi .80 .20
458 A108 5f blue & multi 1.00 .25
459 A108 10f green & multi 1.10 .40

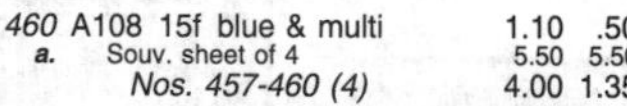

460 A108 15f blue & multi 1.10 .50
a. Souv. sheet of 4 5.50 5.50
Nos. 457-460 (4) 4.00 1.35

Issued to honor the Scout movement.
No. 460a contains 4 stamps similar to Nos. 457-460 with simulated perforations. Sold for 50f.
For overprint see No. RA19.

Soldiers on Maneuvers A109

1968, Jan. 6 Photo. *Perf. 11½*

461 A109 5f lt bl, brn & brt grn .20 .20
462 A109 15f lt bl, ind & olive .40 .20

Issued for Army Day 1968.

White-cheeked Bulbul — A110

Birds: 10f, Hoopoe. 15f, Eurasian jay. 25f, Peregrine falcon. 30f, White stork. 40f, Black partridge. 50f, Marbled teal.

1968, Jan. Litho. *Perf. 14*

463 A110 5f org & black .20 .20
464 A110 10f blue, blk & brn .25 .20
465 A110 15f pink & multi .50 .20
466 A110 25f dl org & multi .60 .40
467 A110 30f emer, blk & brn .65 .20
468 A110 40f rose lil & multi 1.90 .20
469 A110 50f multicolored 2.00 .45
Nos. 463-469 (7) 6.10 1.85

Fighting Soldiers A111

1968, Feb. 8 *Perf. 11½*

470 A111 15f blk, org & brt bl 1.90 .20

Revolution of Ramadan 14, 5th anniv.

Factories, Tractor and Grain — A112

1968, May 1 Litho. *Perf. 13*

471 A112 15f lt bl & multi .20 .20
472 A112 25f multicolored .25 .20

Issued for Labor Day.

Soccer A113

5f, 25f, Goalkeeper holding ball, vert.

1968, June 14 *Perf. 13½*
473 A113 2f multicolored .20 .20
474 A113 5f multicolored .20 .20
475 A113 15f multicolored .25 .20
476 A113 25f multicolored 1.50 .50
a. Souv. sheet, 70f, imperf. 5.00 *8.50*
Nos. 473-476 (4) 2.15 1.10

23rd C.I.S.M. (Conseil Internationale du Sports Militaire) Soccer Championships.
No. 476a shows badge of Military Soccer League.

Soldier, Flag, Chain and Rising Sun — A114

1968, July 14 **Photo.** *Perf. 13½x14*
478 A114 15f multicolored .25 .20

10th anniv. of the July 14, 1958 revolution.

World Health Organization Emblem — A115

5f, 10f, Staff of Aesculapius over emblem, vert.

1968, Nov. 29 **Litho.** *Perf. 13½*
479 A115 5f multicolored .20 .20
480 A115 10f multicolored .20 .20
481 A115 15f blue, red & black .25 .20
482 A115 25f yel grn, red & blk .50 .20
Nos. 479-482 (4) 1.15 .80

WHO, 20th anniv. Exist imperf.

Human Rights Flame — A116

Mother and Children — A117

1968, Dec. 22 **Litho.** *Perf. 13½*
483 A116 10f lt bl, yel & car .20 .20
484 A116 25f lt yel grn, yel & car .25 .20
a. Souv. sheet, 100f, imperf. 3.00 3.00

International Human Rights Year.

1968, Dec. 31 **Litho.** *Perf. 13½*
485 A117 15f multi .25 .20
486 A117 25f bl & multi .75 .20
a. Souv. sheet, 100f, imperf 5.00 3.25

UNICEF. For overprints see Nos. 624-625.

Tanks A118

1969, Jan. 6 **Photo.**
487 A118 25f vio, car & brn 2.00 1.00

Issued for Army Day, Jan. 6.

Harvester A119

1969, Feb. **Photo.** *Perf. 13½*
488 A119 15f yel brn & multi .25 .20

6th anniv. of the Revolution of Ramadan 14.

Mosque - A119a

1969, Mar. 19 **Photo.** *Perf. 13x13½*
488A A119a 15f multicolored .20 .20

Issued for Hajeer (pilgrimage) Year.

Emblem A120

1969, Apr. 12 **Litho.** *Perf. 12½x12*
489 A120 10f yel grn & multi .40 .20
490 A120 15f orange & multi .60 .20

1st conference of the Arab Veterinary Union, Baghdad, Apr. 1969.

Barbus Grypus A121

Fish: 3f, Barbus puntius sharpeyi. 10f, Pampus argenteus. 100f, Barbus esocinus.

1969, May 9 *Perf. 14*
491 A121 2f multicolored .85 .20
492 A121 3f multicolored .90 .20
493 A121 10f multicolored 1.00 .20
494 A121 100f multicolored 3.25 2.00
Nos. 491-494 (4) 6.00 2.60

Holy Kaaba, Mecca A122

1969, May 28 **Photo.** *Perf. 12*
495 A122 15f blue & multi .20 .20

Mohammed's 1,399th birthday.

ILO Emblem A123

1969, June 6 **Litho.** *Perf. 13x12½*
496 A123 5f lt vio, yel & blk .20 .20
497 A123 15f grnsh gray, yel & black .20 .20
498 A123 50f rose, yel & blk .70 .50
a. Souv. sheet, 100f, imperf. 3.00 *5.00*
Nos. 496-498 (3) 1.10 .90

ILO, 50th anniv.

Weight Lifting — A124

Coat of Arms, Symbols of Industry — A125

Design: 5f, 35f, High jump.

1969, June 20 *Perf. 13½x13*
500 A124 3f org yel & multi .20 .20
501 A124 5f blue & multi .20 .20
502 A124 10f rose pink & multi .20 .20
503 A124 35f yellow & multi .70 .25
a. Souv. sheet of 4, #500-503, imperf. 6.25 6.25
Nos. 500-503 (4) 1.30 .85

19th Olympic Games, Mexico City, Oct. 12-27, 1968. No. 503a sold for 100f.

1969, July 14 **Photo.** *Perf. 13*
504 A125 10f brn org & multi .20 .20
505 A125 15f multicolored .30 .20

11th anniv. of the July 14, 1958 revolution.

Street Fighting A126

Pres. Ahmed Hassan al-Bakr — A127

Wheat and Fair Emblem — A128

Design: 20f, Baghdad International Airport.

1969, July 17 *Perf. 13½*
506 A126 10f yel & multi .30 .20
507 A126 15f blue & multi .30 .20
508 A126 20f blue & multi .90 .25
509 A127 200f gold & multi 9.00 5.00
Nos. 506-509 (4) 10.50 5.65

Coup of July 17, 1968, 1st anniv. #508 also for the inauguration of Baghdad Intl. Airport.

1969, Oct. 1 **Photo.** *Perf. 13½*
510 A128 10f brt grn, gold & dl red .20 .20
511 A128 15f ultra, gold & red .20 .20

6th International Fair, Baghdad.
For overprints see Nos. 567A-567B.

Motor Ship Al-Waleed A129

Designs: 15f, Floating crane Antara. 30f, Pilot ship Al-Rasheed. 35f, Suction dredge Hillah. 50f, Survey ship Al-Fao.

1969, Oct. 8 **Litho.** *Perf. 12½*
512 A129 15f black & multi .25 .20
513 A129 20f black & multi .30 .25
514 A129 30f black & multi .48 .30
515 A129 35f black & multi .95 .55
516 A129 50f black & multi 2.75 1.40
Nos. 512-516 (5) 4.73 2.70

50th anniversary of Basrah Harbor.

Radio Tower and Map of Palestine A130

"Search for Knowledge" A131

1969, Nov. 9 **Litho.** *Perf. 12½x13*
517 A130 15f multicolored .60 .20
518 A130 50f multicolored 1.60 .40

10th anniversary of Iraqi News Agency.
For overprints see Nos. 698-699.

1969, Nov. 21 **Photo.** *Perf. 13*
519 A131 15f blue & multi .20 .20
520 A131 20f green & multi .20 .20

Campaign against illiteracy.

Front Page of First Baghdad Newspaper A132

1969, Dec. 26 **Litho.** *Perf. 13½*
521 A132 15f yel, org & black .50 .30

Centenary of the Iraqi press.
For overprint see No. 552.

Soldier, Map of Iraq and Plane — A133

1970, Jan. 6 **Photo.** *Perf. 13*
522 A133 15f lt vio & multi .40 .20
523 A133 20f yellow & multi .80 .30

Issued for Army Day 1970.

Soldier, Farmer and Worker Shoring up Wall in Iraqi Colors — A134

Poppies — A135

1970, Feb. 8 **Photo.** *Perf. 13*
524 A134 10f multicolored .25 .20
525 A134 15f brick red & multi .50 .25

7th anniv. of the Revolution of Ramadan 14.

1970, June 12 Litho. *Perf. 13*

Flowers: 3f, Poet's narcissus. 5f, Tulip. 10f, 50f, Carnations. 15f, Rose.

526 A135 2f emer & multi .20 .20
527 A135 3f blue & multi .20 .20
528 A135 5f multicolored .20 .20
529 A135 10f lt grn & multi .20 .20
530 A135 15f pale sal & multi .70 .20
531 A135 50f lt grn & multi 1.50 .75
Nos. 526-531 (6) 3.00 1.75

The overprinted sets Nos. 532-543 were released before Nos. 526-531.

For overprints see Nos. 621-623, RA20. For surcharge see No. 726.

Nos. 526-531 Overprinted in Ultramarine

1970, Mar. 21

532 A135 2f emer & multi .20 .20
533 A135 3f lt bl & multi .20 .20
534 A135 5f multicolored .20 .20
535 A135 10f lt grn & multi .40 .20
536 A135 15f pale sal & multi .75 .20
537 A135 50f lt grn & multi 3.25 1.50
Nos. 532-537 (6) 5.00 2.50

Issued for Novrooz (New Year).

Nos. 526-531 Overprinted in Black

1970, Apr. 18

538 A135 2f emer & multi .20 .20
539 A135 3f lt bl & multi .20 .20
540 A135 5f multicolored .20 .20
541 A135 10f lt grn & multi .25 .20
542 A135 15f pale sal & multi .45 .20
543 A135 50f lt grn & multi 2.25 .75
Nos. 538-543 (6) 3.55 1.75

Issued for the Spring Festival, Mosul.

Map of Arab Countries, Slogans — A136

50f, 150f, People, flag, sun and map of Iraq.

1970, Apr. 7 *Perf. 13x12½*

544 A136 15f gold & multi .20 .20
545 A136 35f sil & multi .25 .20
546 A136 50f red & multi .55 .30
a. Souv. sheet, 150f, imperf. 3.00 3.00
Nos. 544-546 (3) 1.00 .70

23rd anniversary of Al-Baath Party.

Workers and Cogwheel — A137

1970, May 1

547 A137 10f silver & multi .20 .20
548 A137 15f silver & multi .25 .20
549 A137 35f silver & multi .80 .40
Nos. 547-549 (3) 1.25 .80

Issued for Labor Day.

Kaaba, Mecca, and Koran A138

1970, May 17 Photo. *Perf. 13*

550 A138 15f brt bl & multi .20 .20
551 A138 20f orange & multi .20 .20

Mohammed's 1,400th birthday.

No. 521 Overprinted "1970" and Arabic Inscription in Prussian Blue

1970, June 15 Litho. *Perf. 13½*

552 A132 15f yel, org & black .20 .20

Day of Iraqi press.

Revolutionists and Guns — A139

Designs: 35f, Revolutionist and rising sun.

1970, June 30 Litho. *Perf. 13*

553 A139 10f blk & apple grn .20 .20
554 A139 15f black & gold .20 .20
555 A139 35f blk & red org .50 .20
a. Souv. sheet, 100f, imperf. 2.25 2.25
Nos. 553-555 (3) .90 .60

50th anniversary, Revolution of 1920.

Broken Chain and New Dawn — A140

1970, July 14 *Perf. 13x13½*

557 A140 15f multicolored .20 .20
558 A140 20f multicolored .20 .20

12th anniv. of the July 14, 1958 revolution.

Map of Arab Countries and Hands — A141

1970, July 17 *Perf. 13*

559 A141 15f gold & multi .20 .20
560 A141 25f gold & multi .20 .20

2nd anniversary of coup of July 17, 1968.

Pomegranates A142

1970, Aug. 21 *Perf. 14*

561 A142 3f shown .20 .20
562 A142 5f Grapefruit .20 .20
563 A142 10f Grapes .20 .20
564 A142 15f Oranges .50 .20
565 A142 35f Dates .90 .30
Nos. 561-565 (5) 2.00 1.10

The Latin inscriptions on the 5f and 10f have been erroneously transposed.

For overprints & surcharge see #613-615, 725.

Kaaba, Mecca, Moon over Mountain and Spider Web — A143

1970, Sept. 4 Photo. *Perf. 13*

566 A143 15f multicolored .20 .20
567 A143 25f multicolored .20 .20

Issued for Hajeer (Pilgrimage) Year.

Nos. 510-511 Overprinted in Red

1970, Sept. Photo. *Perf. 13½*

567A A128 10f multi 1.10 1.10
567B A128 15f multi 1.60 *2.00*

7th International Fair, Baghdad.

Intl. Education Year Emblem A144

1970, Nov. 13 Photo. *Perf. 13*

568 A144 5f yel green & multi .20 .20
569 A144 15f brick red & multi .20 .20

Flag and Map of Arab League Countries A145

1970 *Perf. 11*

570 A145 15f olive & multi .20 .20
571 A145 35f gray & multi .25 .20

25th anniversary of the Arab League.

Baghdad Hospital and Emblem A146

1970, Dec. 7 Litho. *Perf. 12*

572 A146 15f yellow & multi .20 .20
573 A146 40f lt green & multi .50 .25

Iraqi Medical Society, 50th anniv.

Sugar Beet — A147

15f, Sugar factory, horiz. 30f, like 5f.

Perf. 13x13½, 13½x13

1970, Dec. 25 Photo.

574 A147 5f ocher, grn & blk .20 .20
575 A147 15f black & multi .20 .20
576 A147 30f org ver, grn & blk .20 .20
Nos. 574-576 (3) .60 .60

Publicity for Mosul sugar factory.

OPEC Emblem A148

1970, Dec. 30 Litho. *Perf. 13x13½*

577 A148 10f rose claret, bis & bl .40 .20
578 A148 40f emer, bis & blue 1.60 .70

OPEC, 10th anniversary.

Soldiers — A149

Soldiers, Maps of Arab Countries and Israel — A150

Perf. 13½x14, 11½x12½

1971, Jan. 6

579 A149 15f multicolored .30 .20
580 A150 40f red org & multi 1.75 .50
a. Souv. sheet of 2, #579-580, imperf. 4.00 *6.25*

Army Day, 50th anniversary.
No. 580a sold for 100f.

Marchers and Map of Arab Countries — A151

1971, Feb. 8 Litho. *Perf. 11½x12½*

581 A151 15f yellow & multi .25 .20
582 A151 40f pink & multi .75 .30

Revolution of Ramadan 14, 8th anniversary.

Spider Web, Pilgrims
A152

1971, Feb. 26 Photo. *Perf. 13*

583 A152 10f pink & multi	.20	.20
584 A152 15f buff & multi	.20	.20

Hajeer (New) Year.

President al-Bakr
A153

1971, Mar. 11 Litho. *Perf. 14*

585 A153 15f orange & multi	.50	.20
586 A153 100f emer & multi	2.75	.85

First anniversary of Mar. 11th Manifesto.

Marshland
A154

Tourist Publicity: 10f, Stork flying over Baghdad. 15f, "Summer Resorts." 100f, Return of Sindbad the Sailor.

1971, Mar. 15 *Perf. 13*

587 A154 5f multicolored	.25	.20
588 A154 10f lt grn & multi	.30	.20
589 A154 15f pink & multi	.70	.50
590 A154 100f multicolored	4.75	3.00
Nos. 587-590 (4)	6.00	3.90

Blacksmith Taming Serpent — A155

1971, Mar. 21 *Perf. 11½x12*

591 A155 15f multicolored	.50	.20
592 A155 25f yel & multi	1.00	.40

Novrooz Festival.

No. 455 Overprinted

1971, Mar. 23 Litho. *Perf. 13*

593 A107 15f rose red & multi	3.75	2.50

World Meteorological Day. See No. C39.

Workers, Soldier, Map of Arab Countries — A156

1971, Apr. 7

594 A156 15f yel & multi	.75	.25
595 A156 35f multicolored	1.25	.50
596 A156 250f multicolored	10.00	6.25
Nos. 594-596 (3)	12.00	7.00

24th anniv. of the Al Baath Party. No. 596 has circular perforation around vignette set within a white square of paper, perforated on 4 sides. The design of No. 596 is similar to Nos. 594-595, but with denomination within the circle and no inscriptions in margin.

Nos. 443-444, 448 Overprinted

1971, Apr. 14

597 A105 2f pale brn & multi	.45	.20
598 A105 5f ver & multi	.45	.20
599 A105 25f lemon & multi	1.75	1.00
Nos. 597-599 (3)	2.65	1.40

Mosul Festival.

Worker, Farm Woman with Torch
A157

1971, May 1 Litho. *Perf. 13*

600 A157 15f ocher & multi	.20	.20
601 A157 40f olive & multi	.75	.20

Labor Day.

Muslim Praying in Mecca
A158

1971, May 7

602 A158 15f yellow & multi	.25	.20
603 A158 100f pink & multi	2.75	1.00

Mohammed's 1,401st birthday.

People, Fists, Map of Iraq
A159

1971, July 14 Photo. *Perf. 14*

604 A159 25f green & multi	.20	.20
605 A159 50f lt bl & multi	.40	.25

13th anniv. of the July 14, 1958 revolution.

Surveyor, Preacher, Rising Sun
A160

1971, July 17 *Perf. 13*

606 A160 25f multicolored	.25	.20
607 A160 70f orange & multi	.75	.45

3rd anniversary of July 17, 1968, coup.

Rafidain Bank Emblem
A161

1971, Sept. 24 Photo. *Perf. 13½*

Diameter: 27mm

608 A161 10f multicolored	.45	*.85*
609 A161 15f multicolored	.85	.85
610 A161 25f multicolored	1.60	*2.75*

Diameter: 32mm

611 A161 65f multicolored	8.50	4.25
612 A161 250f multicolored	21.00	12.50
Nos. 608-612 (5)	32.40	21.20

30th anniversary of Rafidain Bank. Nos. 608-612 have circular perforation around design within a white square of paper, perforated on 4 sides.

Nos. 561, 564-565 Overprinted

1971, Oct. 15 Litho. *Perf. 14*

613 A142 3f bl grn & multi	.30	.20
614 A142 15f red & multi	1.00	.50
615 A142 35f orange & multi	2.00	.75
Nos. 613-615 (3)	3.30	1.45

Agricultural census, Oct. 15, 1971.

Nos. 527-528, 530 Overprinted and Surcharged

Soccer
A162

Designs: 25f, Track and field. 35f, Table tennis. 75f, Gymnastics. 95f, Volleyball and basketball.

1971, Nov. 17 Litho. *Perf. 13½*

616 A162 15f green & multi	.25	.20
617 A162 25f pink & multi	.50	.30
618 A162 35f lt bl & multi	.75	.70
619 A162 70f lt grn & multi	3.25	1.00
620 A162 95f yel grn & multi	5.25	2.00
a. Souvenir sheet of 5	11.00	5.50
Nos. 616-620 (5)	10.00	4.20

4th Pan-Arab Schoolboys Sports Games, Baghdad. No. 620a contains 5 stamps similar to Nos. 616-620 with simulated perforations. Sold for 200f.

1971, Nov. 23 Litho. *Perf. 13*

621 A135 15f multicolored	.80	.25
622 A135 25f on 5f multi	1.50	.75
623 A135 70f on 3f multi	5.50	2.00
Nos. 621-623 (3)	7.80	3.00

Students' Day. The 15f has only first 3 lines of Arabic overprint.

Nos. 485-486 Overprinted

1971, Dec. 11 Litho. *Perf. 13½*

624 A117 15f multicolored	2.00	.75
625 A117 25f blue & multi	4.75	2.00

25th anniv. of UNICEF.

Children Crossing Street
A162a

1971, Dec. 17 Litho. *Perf. 13x12½*

625A A162a 15f yel & multi	1.00	.50
625B A162a 25f brt rose & multi	2.00	1.00

2nd Traffic Week. For overprints see #668-669.

Arab Postal Union Emblem
A163

1971, Dec. 24 Photo. *Perf. 11½*

626 A163 25f emer, yel & brn	.30	.20
627 A163 70f vio bl, yel & red	1.10	.45

25th anniv. of the Conf. of Sofar, Lebanon, establishing Arab Postal Union.

Racial Equality Emblem — A164

1971, Dec. 31 *Perf. 13½x14*

628 A164 25f brt grn & multi	.25	.20
629 A164 70f orange & multi	.65	.35

Intl. Year Against Racial Discrimination.

Soldiers with Flag and Torch — A165

Workers A166

1972, Jan. 6 Photo. *Perf. 14x13½*
630 A165 25f blue & multi .70 .40
631 A165 70f brt grn & multi 2.75 1.50

Army Day, Jan. 6.

1972, Feb. 8
632 A166 25f brt grn & multi .80 .40
633 A166 95f lilac & multi 5.75 1.50

Revolution of Ramadan 14, 9th anniv.

Mosque, Minaret, Crescent and Caravan A167

1972, Feb. 26 Litho. *Perf. 12½x13*
634 A167 25f bl grn & multi .25 .20
635 A167 35f purple & multi .35 .20

Hegira (Pilgrimage) Year.

Peace Symbols and "11" — A168

1972, Mar. 11 Photo. *Perf. 11x12½*
636 A168 25f lt blue & blk .85 .25
637 A168 70f brt lilac & blk 2.50 .75

2nd anniversary of Mar. 11 Manifesto.

Mountain Range and Flowers — A169

1972, Mar. 21 *Perf. 11½x11*
638 A169 25f vio blue & multi .90 .20
639 A169 70f vio blue & multi 2.75 1.00

Novrooz, New Year Festival.

Party Emblem A170

Symbolic Design — A171

Perf. 14 (A170), 13 (A171)

1972 Litho.
640 A170 10f brn org & multi .20 .20
641 A171 25f bister & multi .25 .25
642 A170 35f brn org & multi .40 .50
643 A171 70f red & multi 2.50 .75
Nos. 640-643 (4) 3.35 1.70

Iraqi Arab Baath Socialist Party, 25th anniv. Issued: 25f, 70f, Mar. 23; 10f, 35f, Apr. 7.

Emblem, Map, Weather Balloons and Chart — A172

Cogwheel and Ship — A173

1972, Mar. 23 Photo. *Perf. 14x13½*
644 A172 25f multicolored .65 .20
645 A172 35f yel & multi .95 .25

12th World Meteorological Day.

1972, Mar. 25 *Perf. 11x11½*
646 A173 25f ocher & multi .25 .20
647 A173 35f pink & multi .40 .20

Arab Chamber of Commerce.

Derrick and Flame A174

Quill Pens, Map of Arab Countries A175

1972, Apr. 7 *Perf. 13x13½*
648 A174 25f multicolored .50 .25
649 A174 35f multicolored .75 .30

Opening of North Rumaila (INOC, North Iraq Oil Fields).

1972, Apr. 17 Photo. *Perf. 11x11½*
650 A175 25f orange & multi .30 .20
651 A175 35f blue & multi .55 .20

3rd Congress of Arab Journalists.

Women's Federation Emblem A176

1972, Apr. 22 Litho. *Perf. 13½*
652 A176 25f green & multi .30 .20
653 A176 35f lilac & multi .55 .20

Iraqi Women's Federation, 4th anniversary.

Hand Holding Globe-shaped Wrench — A177

1972, May 1 Photo. *Perf. 11½*
654 A177 25f yel grn & multi .30 .20
655 A177 35f orange & multi .55 .20

Labor Day.

Kaaba, Mecca, and Crescent — A178

1972, May 26
656 A178 25f green & multi .30 .20
657 A178 35f purple & multi .55 .20

Mohammed's 1,402nd birthday.

Soldier, Civilian and Guns — A179

1972, July 14 Photo. *Perf. 13½x14*
658 A179 35f multicolored .60 .25
659 A179 70f lilac & multi 1.90 .75

14th anniv. of July 14, 1958, revolution.

Dome of the Rock, Arab Countries' Map, Fists A180

1972, July 17 *Perf. 13*
660 A180 25f citron & multi .60 .20
661 A180 95f blue & multi 1.90 .75

4th anniv. of July 17, 1968 coup.

Congress Emblem, Scout Saluting Iraqi Flag — A182

1972, Aug. 12 Photo. *Perf. 13½x14*
664 A182 20f multicolored 1.00 .55
665 A182 25f lilac & multi 2.00 .80

10th Arab Boy Scouts Jamboree and Conference, Mosul, Aug. 10-19.

1972, Aug. 24

Congress emblem and Girl Guide in camp.

666 A182 10f yellow & multi 1.00 .45
667 A182 45f multicolored 3.00 .90

4th Arab Guides Camp & Conf., Mosul, Aug. 24-30.

No. 625A Overprinted and Surcharged, No. 625B Overprinted with New Date:

1972, Oct. 4 Photo. *Perf. 13x12½*
668 A162a 25f brt rose & multi 3.75 1.75
669 A162a 70f on 15f multi 5.00 4.50

Third Traffic Week.

Central Bank of Iraq A183

1972, Nov. 16 Photo. *Perf. 13*
670 A183 25f lt blue & multi .35 .30
671 A183 70f lt green & multi 1.00 .70

25th anniversary, Central Bank of Iraq.

UIC Emblem A184

1972, Dec. 29
672 A184 25f dp rose & multi .65 .20
673 A184 45f brt vio & multi 1.40 .50

50th anniv., Intl. Railroad Union (UIC).

Nos. 148-149, 151, 180 and Type of 1957-58 Overprinted with 3 Bars

1973, Jan. 29 Engr. *Perf. 11½x12*
674 A28 10f blue .40 .20
675 A33 10f blue .40 .20
676 A28 15f black .80 .35
677 A33 15f black .80 .35
678 A28 25f rose violet 1.50 .50
679 A33 25f rose violet 1.50 .50
Nos. 674-679 (6) 5.40 2.10

The size and position of the bottom bar of overprint differs; the bar can be same size as 2 top bars, short and centered or moved to the right.

No. 455 Overprinted

1973, Mar. 25 Litho. *Perf. 13*
680 A107 15f rose red & multi 6.00 2.50

Intl. History Cong. See Nos. C52-C53.

Workers and Oil Wells A185

Ram's-head Harp — A186

1973, June 1 Litho. *Perf. 13*
681 A185 25f yel & multi 1.25 .50
682 A185 70f rose & multi 5.50 2.00

1st anniv. of nationalization of oil industry.

1973, June Litho. *Perf. 13x12½*

Designs: 25f, 35f, 45f, Minaret, Mosul, 50f, 70f, 95f, Statue of goddess. 10f, 20f, like 5f.

683 A186 5f orange & blk .20 .20
684 A186 10f bister & blk .20 .20
685 A186 20f brt rose & blk .20 .20
686 A186 25f ultra & blk .20 .20
687 A186 35f emer & blk .25 .20
688 A186 45f blue & black .30 .25
689 A186 50f olive & yel .35 .25
690 A186 70f violet & yel .50 .35
691 A186 95f brown & yel .65 .50
Nos. 683-691 (9) 2.85 2.35

For overprint see No. RA21.

People with Flags, Grain A187

1973, July 14
692 A187 25f multicolored .20 .25
693 A187 35f multicolored .40 .30

July Festivals.

Nos. 393 and 395 Surcharged

1973 Litho. *Perf. 13½x14*
694 A85 25f on 3f multi 2.50 1.50
695 A85 70f on 15f multi 6.75 4.00

Festival of Date Trees.

INTERPOL Headquarters — A188

1973, Sept. 20 Litho. *Perf. 12*
696 A188 25f multicolored .30 .20
697 A188 70f brt bl & multi .65 .35

50th anniv. of Intl. Criminal Police Org.

Nos. 517-518 Overprinted in Silver

1973, Sept. 29 Litho. *Perf. 12½x13*
698 A130 15f multicolored 3.50 1.00
699 A130 50f multicolored 6.00 3.00

Meeting of Intl. Org. of Journalists' Executive Committee, Sept. 26-29.

Flags and Fair Emblem — A189

WMO Emblem — A190

1973, Oct. 10 Photo. *Perf. 11*
700 A189 10f brt grn & dk brn .20 .20
701 A189 20f ocher & multi .35 .20
702 A189 65f blue & multi .80 .60
Nos. 700-702 (3) 1.35 1.00

10th International Baghdad Fair, Oct. 1-21.

1973, Nov. 15 Litho. *Perf. 12*
703 A190 25f org, blk & green .50 .20
704 A190 35f brt rose, blk & grn .70 .25

Intl. meteorological cooperation, cent.

Flags of Arab League and Iraq, Maghreb Emblem A191

1973, Dec. 1 Photo. *Perf. 14*
705 A191 20f dl org & multi .25 .20
706 A191 35f blue & multi .35 .20

11th session of Civil Aviation Council of Arab States, Baghdad, Dec. 1973.

No. 360 Overprinted

1973, Dec. 12 Photo. *Perf. 11*
707 A67a 30f orange & blue 3.00 2.25

6th Executive Council Meeting of APU.

Human Rights Flame — A192

1973, Dec. 25 *Perf. 11½*
708 A192 25f multicolored .20 .20
709 A192 70f ultra & multi .60 .35

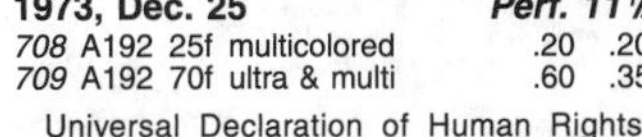
Universal Declaration of Human Rights, 25th anniv.

Military College Crest and Cadets A193

1974, Jan. 6 *Perf. 12x11½*
710 A193 25f ocher & multi .20 .20
711 A193 35f ultra & multi .30 .20

50th anniversary of the Military College.

UPU and Arab Postal Union Emblems A194

1974, May 28 Photo. *Perf. 11½x12*
712 A194 25f gold & multi .45 .20
713 A194 35f gold & multi .45 .30
714 A194 70f gold & multi .90 .75
Nos. 712-714 (3) 1.80 1.25

Centenary of the Universal Postal Union.

Symbols of Ancient Mesopotamia and Oil Industry — A195

1974, June 1 Litho. *Perf. 12½*
715 A195 10f blue & multi .20 .20
716 A195 25f ocher & multi .30 .25
717 A195 70f rose & multi 1.00 .75
Nos. 715-717 (3) 1.50 1.20

Nationalization of the oil industry, 2nd anniv.

Festival A196

1974, July 17 *Perf. 11½x12*
718 A196 20f lilac & multi .20 .20
719 A196 35f dull org & multi .45 .20

July Festivals.

National Front Emblem and People A197

1974, July 17 *Perf. 12x11½*
720 A197 25f blue & multi .25 .20
721 A197 70f brt grn & multi .65 .35

1st anniv. of Progressive National Front.

Cement Plant and Brick Wall — A198

1974, Oct. 19 *Perf. 11½x12*
722 A198 20f gray bl & multi .25 .20
723 A198 25f red & multi .30 .20
724 A198 70f emerald & multi .75 .60
Nos. 722-724 (3) 1.30 1.00

25th anniversary of Iraqi Cement Plant.

Nos. 561 and 527 Surcharged

a

b

1975, Jan. 9 Litho. *Perf. 13, 14*
725 A142 (a) 10f on 3f multi 2.25 1.50
726 A135 (b) 25f on 3f multi 7.00 5.00

Globe and WPY Emblem A199

1975, Jan. 30 *Perf. 11½x12*
727 A199 25f dull bl & blk .35 .20
728 A199 35f brt pink & ind .75 .25
729 A199 70f yel grn & vio 1.75 .75
Nos. 727-729 (3) 2.85 1.20

World Population Year 1974.

Festival Symbols — A200

1975, July 17 Litho. *Perf. 12x11½*
730 A200 5f lt brn & multi .20 .20
731 A200 10f lt brn & multi .20 .20
732 A200 35f lt brn & multi .85 .75
Nos. 730-732 (3) 1.25 1.15

Festivals, July 1975.

Map of Arab Countries A201

1975, Aug. 5 Photo. *Perf. 13*

733 A201 25f rose & multi	.25	.20
734 A201 35f multicolored	.30	.25
735 A201 45f multicolored	.45	.35
Nos. 733-735 (3)	1.00	.80

Arab Working Org., 10th anniv.

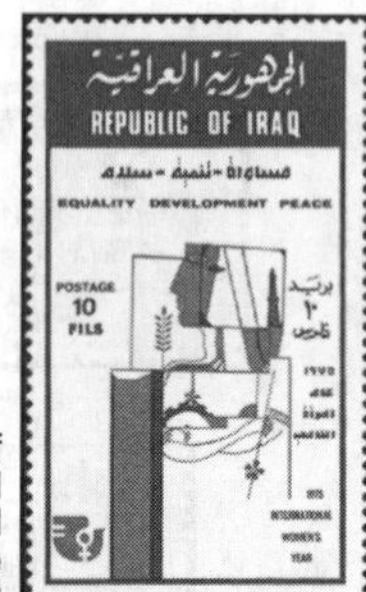
Symbols of Women, Oil Industry and Agriculture A202

1975, Aug. 15 *Perf. 14*

736 A202 10f lilac & multi	.30	.20
737 A202 35f multicolored	.65	.50
738 A202 70f bl & multi	2.50	1.00
a. Souv. sheet, 100f, imperf.	9.00	*11.00*
Nos. 736-738 (3)	3.45	1.70

International Women's Year.

Euphrates Dam and Causeway — A203

1975, Sept. 5 Litho. *Perf. 12x11½*

739 A203 3f orange & multi	.20	.20
740 A203 25f purple & multi	.40	.20
741 A203 70f rose red & multi	1.60	.50
Nos. 739-741 (3)	2.20	.90

Intl. Commission on Irrigation and Drainage, 25th anniv.

National Insurance Co. Seal A204

1975, Oct. 11 Photo. *Perf. 13*

742 A204 20f brt bl & multi	.55	.20
743 A204 25f crim & multi	.70	.30
a. Souv. sheet, 100f, imperf.	7.00	*8.50*

Natl. Insurance Co., Baghdad, 25th anniv.

Musician Entertaining King — A205

1975, Nov. 21 *Perf. 14*

744 A205 25f silver & multi	.30	.20
745 A205 45f gold & multi	.45	.25

Baghdad Intl. Music Conf., Nov. 1975.

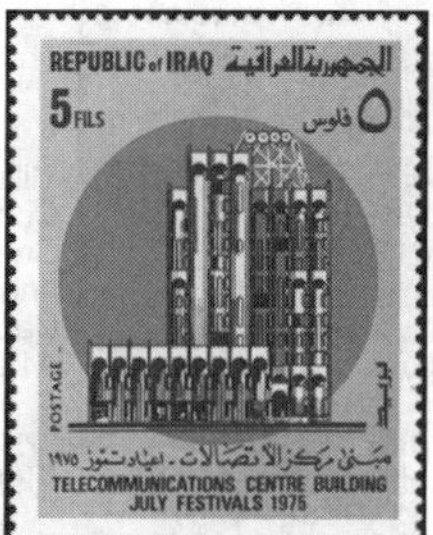
Telecommunications Center — A206

1975, Dec. 22 Litho. *Perf. 12½*

746 A206 5f lil rose & multi	.20	.20
747 A206 10f blue & multi	.20	.20
748 A206 60f green & multi	1.00	.50
Nos. 746-748 (3)	1.40	.90

Inauguration of Telecommunications Center Building during July 1975 Festival.

Diesel Locomotive — A207

Conference Emblem and: 30f, Diesel passenger locomotive #511. 35f, 0-3-0 steam tank locomotive with passenger train. 50f, 2-3-0 German steam locomotive, c. 1914.

1975, Dec. 22 Photo. *Perf. 14*

749 A207 25f tan & multi	2.25	.40
750 A207 30f tan & multi	3.50	.75
751 A207 35f yel grn & multi	4.50	1.50
752 A207 50f yel grn & multi	6.75	4.00
Nos. 749-752 (4)	17.00	6.65

15th Taurus Railway Conference, Baghdad.

A208

A209

Design: Soldier on guard.

1976, Jan. 6 *Perf. 13*

753 A208 5f silver & multi	.20	.20
754 A208 25f silver & multi	.25	.20
755 A208 50f gold & multi	.75	.40
Nos. 753-755 (3)	1.20	.80

55th Army Day.

1976, Jan. 8 Photo. *Perf. 13½x13*

Fingerprint crossed out, Arab world.

756 A209 5f violet & multi	.20	.20
757 A209 15f blue & multi	.30	.20
758 A209 35f green & multi	1.00	.75
Nos. 756-758 (3)	1.50	1.15

Statue of Goddess — A210

20f-30f, Two female figures forming column. 35f-75f, Head of bearded man.

1976, Jan. 1 Litho. *Perf. 13x12½*

759 A210 5f lilac & multi	.20	.20
760 A210 10f rose & multi	.20	.20
761 A210 15f yellow & multi	.20	.20
762 A210 20f bister & multi	.20	.20
763 A210 25f lt grn & multi	.20	.20
764 A210 30f blue & multi	.20	.20
765 A210 35f lil rose & multi	.20	.20
766 A210 50f citron & multi	.30	.25
767 A210 75f violet & multi	.50	.40
Nos. 759-767 (9)	2.20	2.05

Iraq Earth Station A211

1976, Feb. 8 *Perf. 13x13½*

768 A211 10f silver & multi	.25	.20
769 A211 25f silver & multi	.75	.30
770 A211 75f gold & multi	3.00	1.25
Nos. 768-770 (3)	4.00	1.75

Revolution of Ramadan 14, 13th anniv.

Telephones 1876 and 1976 — A212

Map of Maghreb, ICATU Emblem — A213

1976, Mar. 17 Litho. *Perf. 12x12½*

771 A212 35f multicolored	.80	.30
772 A212 50f multicolored	1.60	.50
773 A212 75f multicolored	2.50	.75
Nos. 771-773 (3)	4.90	1.55

Centenary of first telephone call by Alexander Graham Bell, Mar. 10, 1876.

1976, Mar. 24 Photo. *Perf. 13½*

774 A213 5f green & multi	.20	.20
775 A213 10f multicolored	.25	.20
Nos. 774-775,C54 (3)	4.45	2.40

20th Intl. Conf. of Arab Trade Unions.

Map of Iraq, Family, Torch and Wreath — A214

1976, Apr. 1 *Perf. 12½*

776 A214 5f multicolored	.20	.20
777 A214 15f lilac & multi	.30	.20
778 A214 35f multicolored	.50	.25
Nos. 776-778 (3)	1.00	.65

Police Day.

Pipeline, Map of Iraq — A215

Pres. A. H. al-Bakr Embracing Vice Pres. Saddam Hussein — A216

1976, June 1 Photo. *Perf. 13*

779 A215 25f multicolored	1.50	.75
780 A215 75f multicolored	4.50	2.00

Souvenir Sheet

Imperf

781 A216 150f multicolored	17.50	20.00

4th anniversary of oil nationalization.

"Festival" — A217

1976, July 17 *Perf. 14*

782 A217 15f orange & multi	.25	.20
783 A217 35f orange & multi	.75	.50

Festivals, July 1976.

Archbishop Capucci, Map of Palestine A218

1976, Aug. 18 Litho. *Perf. 12*

784 A218 25f multicolored	.50	.20
785 A218 35f multicolored	1.00	.20
786 A218 75f multicolored	2.50	1.00
Nos. 784-786 (3)	4.00	1.40

Detention of Archbishop Hilarion Capucci in Israel, Aug. 18, 1974.

Common Kingfisher — A219

"15" — A220

10f, Turtle dove. 15f, Pin-tailed sandgrouse. 25f, Blue rock thrush. 50f, Purple and gray herons.

1976, Sept. 15 Litho. *Perf. 13½x14*

787 A219 5f multicolored .20 .20
788 A219 10f multicolored .25 .20
789 A219 15f multicolored .35 .20
790 A219 25f multicolored .50 .25
791 A219 50f multicolored 2.00 .35
Nos. 787-791 (5) 3.30 1.20

1976, Nov. 23 Photo. *Perf. 13½*

792 A220 30f multicolored 1.00 .50
793 A220 70f multicolored 2.50 .75

15th anniv. of National Students Union.

Oil Tanker and Emblems A221

25f, 50f, Pier, refinery, pipeline.

1976, Dec. 25 *Perf. 12½x12*

794 A221 10f multicolored .50 .20
795 A221 15f multicolored .75 .25
796 A221 25f multicolored 1.75 .50
797 A221 50f multicolored 2.50 .70
Nos. 794-797 (4) 5.50 1.65

1st Iraqi oil tanker (10f, 15f) and Nationalization of Basrah Petroleum Co. Ltd., 1st anniv. (25f, 50f).

Happy Children — A222

Ornament A223

UNESCO Emblem and: 25f, Children with flowers and butterflies. 75f, Children planting flowers around flagpole.

1976, Dec. 25 *Perf. 12x12½*

798 A222 10f multicolored .25 .20
799 A222 25f multicolored 1.75 .30
800 A222 75f multicolored 3.00 .90
Nos. 798-800 (3) 5.00 1.40

30th anniv. of UNESCO, and Books for Children Campaign.

1977, Mar. 2 Photo. *Perf. 13½*

801 A223 25f gold & multi .50 .20
802 A223 35f gold & multi .70 .25

Birthday of Mohammed (570-632).

Peace Dove — A224

Dahlia — A225

1977, Mar. 11 *Perf. 14x13½*

803 A224 25f lt bl & multi .30 .20
804 A224 30f buff & multi .35 .20

Peace Day.

1977, Mar. 21 Litho. *Perf. 12½*

Flowers: 10f, Sweet peas. 35f, Chrysanthemums. 50f, Verbena.

805 A225 5f multicolored .20 .20
806 A225 10f multicolored .25 .20
807 A225 35f multicolored .80 .25
808 A225 50f multicolored 1.50 .50
Nos. 805-808 (4) 2.75 1.15

Spring Festivals, Baghdad.

Emblem with Doves A226

Designs: 75f, Emblem with flame. 100f, Dove with olive branch.

1977, Apr. 7 Photo. *Perf. 13*

809 A226 25f yel & multi .60 .20
810 A226 75f yel & multi 2.25 .40

Souvenir Sheet

Imperf

811 A226 100f multicolored 4.75 *6.50*

Al Baath Party, 30th anniversary. No. 811 contains one 49x35mm stamp.

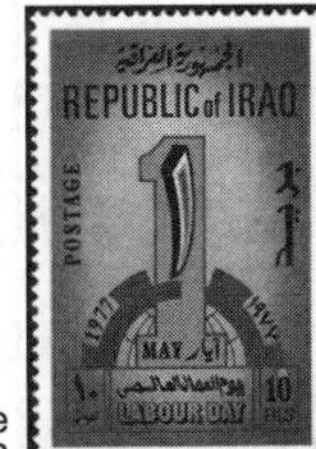

APU Emblem, Members' Flags A227

1977, Apr. 12 Litho. *Perf. 14*

812 A227 25f orange & multi .30 .20
813 A227 35f gray & multi .40 .20

25th anniversary of Arab Postal Union.

Cogwheel, Globe and "1" — A228

1977, May 1 Litho. *Perf. 14½x14*

814 A228 10f multicolored .20 .20
815 A228 30f multicolored .30 .20
816 A228 35f multicolored .40 .20
Nos. 814-816 (3) .90 .60

Labor Day.

Weight Lifting A229

75f, Weight lifter, standing up. 100f, Symbolic weight lifter with Iraqi coat of arms, laurel wreath.

1977, May 8 Photo. *Perf. 14*

817 A229 25f multicolored .60 .60
818 A229 75f multicolored 1.00 .85

Souvenir Sheet

Imperf

819 A229 100f multicolored 6.00 *7.50*

8th Asian Weight Lifting Championship, Baghdad, May 1977. No. 819 contains one 42x52mm stamp.

Arabian Garden A230

Grain and Dove — A231

Arab Tourist Year: 10f, View of town with minarets, horiz. 30f, Landscape with bridge and waterfall. 50f, Hosts welcoming tourists, and drum, horiz.

Perf. 11½x12, 12x11½

1977, June 15 Litho.

820 A230 5f multicolored .20 .20
821 A230 10f multicolored .20 .20
822 A230 30f multicolored .60 .20
823 A230 50f multicolored 1.75 1.25
Nos. 820-823 (4) 2.75 1.85

1977, July 17 Photo. *Perf. 14*

824 A231 25f multicolored .30 .20
825 A231 30f multicolored .35 .20

Festivals, July 1977.

Map of Arab Countries A232

1977, Sept. 9 Photo. *Perf. 13½x14*

826 A232 30f multicolored .40 .25
827 A232 70f multicolored 1.60 .50

UN Conference on Desertification, Nairobi, Kenya, Aug. 29-Sept. 9.

Census Emblem — A233 Festival Emblem — A234

1977, Oct. 17 Litho. *Perf. 14x14½*

828 A233 20f ultra & multi .25 .20
829 A233 30f brown & multi .35 .20
830 A233 70f gray & multi .70 .35
Nos. 828-830 (3) 1.30 .75

Population Census Day, Oct. 17.

1977, Nov. 1 Photo. *Perf. 14*

831 A234 25f silver & multi .30 .20
832 A234 50f gold & multi .60 .25

Al Mutanabby Festival, Nov. 1977.

A235 A236

Junblatt, caricatures of Britain, US, Israel.

1977, Nov. 16 Photo. *Perf. 14*

833 A235 20f multicolored .25 .20
834 A235 30f multicolored .35 .20
835 A235 70f multicolored .80 .35
Nos. 833-835 (3) 1.40 .75

Kemal Junblatt, Druse leader, killed in Lebanese war.

1977, Dec. 12 Photo. *Perf. 14*

836 A236 30f gold & multi .40 .20
837 A236 35f silver & multi .50 .20

Hegira (Pilgrimage) Year.

Young People and Flags — A237

Coins and Coin Bank — A238

1978, Apr. 7 Photo. *Perf. 11½x11*

838 A237 10f multicolored .20 .20
839 A237 15f multicolored .25 .20
840 A237 35f multicolored .55 .20
Nos. 838-840 (3) 1.00 .60

Youth Day.

1978, Apr. 15

841 A238 15f multicolored .20 .20
842 A238 25f multicolored .30 .20
843 A238 35f multicolored .40 .20
Nos. 841-843 (3) .90 .60

6th anniversary of postal savings law.

Microwave Transmission and Receiving A239

Emblems and Flags of Participants — A240

1978, May 17 Photo. *Perf. 14*

844 A239 25f org & multi .20 .20
845 A239 35f lilac & multi .30 .20
846 A239 75f emer & multi .60 .35
Nos. 844-846 (3) 1.10 .75

10th World Telecommunications Day and 1st anniversary of commissioning of national microwave network.

Perf. 12½x11½

1978, June 19 Litho.

847 A240 25f multicolored .55 .20
848 A240 35f multicolored .85 .20

Conference of Postal Ministers of Arabian Gulf Countries, Baghdad (Saudi Arabia, United Arab Emirates, Qatar, Bahrain, Kuwait, Oman, People's Republic of Yemen).

Ancient Coin — A241

Designs: Ancient Iraqi coins. 75f vertical.

Perf. 11½x12½

1978, June 25 Photo.

849 A241 1f citron & multi .20 .20
850 A241 2f blue & multi .20 .20
851 A241 3f salmon & multi .20 .20
852 A241 4f salmon & multi .20 .20
853 A241 75f bl grn & multi 2.25 .40
Nos. 849-853 (5) 3.05 1.20

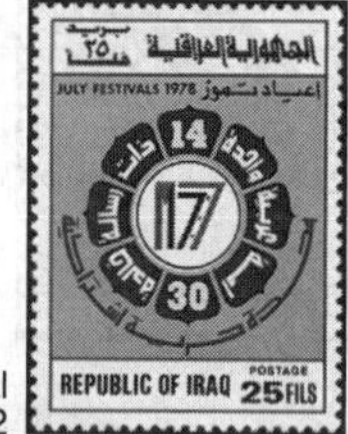

Festival Emblem — A242

Festival Poster — A243

1978, July 17 *Perf. 13½x13*

854 A242 25f multicolored .20 .20
855 A242 35f multicolored .30 .20

Souvenir Sheet

Perf. 13x13½

856 A243 100f multicolored 4.25 *5.00*

Festivals, July 1978.

WHO Emblem, Nurse, Hospital, Sick Child A244

1978, Aug. 18 Photo. *Perf. 14*

857 A244 25f multicolored .25 .20
858 A244 35f multicolored .30 .20
859 A244 75f multicolored .70 .35
Nos. 857-859 (3) 1.25 .75

Eradication of smallpox.

Maritime Union Emblem A245

1978, Aug. 30 Photo. *Perf. 11½x12*

860 A245 25f multicolored .30 .20
861 A245 75f multicolored .90 .35

1st World Maritime Day.

Workers A246

1978, Sept. 12 *Perf. 14*

862 A246 10f multicolored .20 .20
863 A246 25f multicolored .40 .20
864 A246 35f multicolored .70 .20
Nos. 862-864 (3) 1.30 .60

10th anniv. of People's Work Groups.

Fair Emblem with Atom Symbol — A247

Map of Iraq, Ruler and Globe — A248

1978, Oct. 1

865 A247 25f multicolored .25 .20
866 A247 35f multicolored .30 .20
867 A247 75f multicolored .70 .35
Nos. 865-867 (3) 1.25 .75

15th International Fair, Baghdad, Oct. 1-15.

1978, Oct. 14

868 A248 25f multicolored .25 .20
869 A248 35f multicolored .30 .20
870 A248 75f multicolored .70 .35
Nos. 868-870 (3) 1.25 .75

World Standards Day.

Altharthar-Euphrates Dam — A249

1978 Photo. *Perf. 11½*

871 A249 5f multicolored .20 .20
872 A249 10f multicolored .20 .20
873 A249 15f multicolored .20 .20
874 A249 25f multicolored .30 .20
875 A249 35f multicolored .40 .20
876 A249 50f multicolored .60 .25
Nos. 871-876 (6) 1.90 1.25

Arab Summit Conference A250

Surgeons' Conference Emblem — A251

1978, Nov. 2 Photo. *Perf. 14*

890 A250 25f multicolored .25 .20
891 A250 35f multicolored .45 .25
892 A250 75f multicolored .90 .55
Nos. 890-892 (3) 1.60 1.00

9th Arab Summit Conference, Baghdad, Nov. 2-5.

1978, Nov. 8 Litho. *Perf. 12x11½*

893 A251 25f multicolored .25 .20
894 A251 75f multicolored .80 .35

4th Cong. of the Assoc. of Thoracic & Cardiovascular Surgeons of Asia, Baghdad, Nov. 6-10.

Pilgrims at Mt. Arafat and Holy Ka'aba A252

1978, Nov. 9 Photo. *Perf. 14*

895 A252 25f multicolored .25 .20
896 A252 35f multicolored .35 .20

Pilgrimage to Mecea.

Atom Symbol, Map of South America, Africa, Arabia A253

1978, Nov. 11 *Perf. 13½*

897 A253 25f multicolored .65 .20
898 A253 50f multicolored .55 .25
899 A253 75f multicolored .80 .35
Nos. 897-899 (3) 2.00 .80

Technical Cooperation Among Developing Countries Conf., Buenos Aires, Argentina, Sept. 1978.

Hands Holding Emblem — A254

Globe and Flame Emblem — A255

1978, Nov. 30 Litho. *Perf. 13½x13*

900 A254 25f multicolored .30 .20
901 A254 50f multicolored .60 .25
902 A254 75f multicolored .95 .35
Nos. 900-902 (3) 1.85 .80

Anti-Apartheid Year.

1978, Dec. 20 *Perf. 14*

903 A255 25f multicolored .20 .20
904 A255 75f multicolored .60 .35

Declaration of Human Rights, 30th anniv.

Candle and Emblem — A256

Book, Pencil and Flame — A257

1979, Jan. 9 Photo. *Perf. 14*

905 A256 10f multicolored .20 .20
906 A256 25f multicolored .20 .20
907 A256 35f multicolored .30 .20
Nos. 905-907 (3) .70 .60

Police Day.

1979, Feb. 15 Photo. *Perf. 14*

908 A257 15f multicolored .25 .20
909 A257 25f multicolored .35 .20
910 A257 35f multicolored .65 .20
Nos. 908-910 (3) 1.25 .60

Application of Compulsory Education Law, anniversary.

Pupils, School and Teacher A258

1979, Mar. 1 *Perf. 13*

911 A258 10f multicolored .20 .20
912 A258 15f multicolored .20 .20
913 A258 50f multicolored .80 .25
Nos. 911-913 (3) 1.20 .65

Teacher's Day.

Pupils, Flag, Pencil — A259

1979, Mar. 10 *Perf. 13½x13*

914 A259 15f multicolored .20 .20
915 A259 25f multicolored .30 .20
916 A259 35f multicolored .50 .20
Nos. 914-916 (3) 1.00 .60

National Comprehensive Compulsory Literacy Campaign.

Book, World Map, Arab Achievements A260

1979, Mar. 22 *Perf. 13*

917 A260 35f multicolored .30 .20
918 A260 75f multicolored .60 .40

Achievements of the Arabs.

Girl Playing Flute — A261

1979, Apr. 15 Litho. *Perf. 13½*

919	A261	15f multicolored	.25	.20
920	A261	25f multicolored	.35	.20
921	A261	35f multicolored	.75	.30
		Nos. 919-921 (3)	1.35	.70

Mosul Spring Festival.

Iraqi Flag, Globe, UPU Emblem A262

1979, Apr. 22 Photo. *Perf. 13x13½*

922	A262	25f multicolored	.40	.20
923	A262	35f multicolored	.45	.20
924	A262	75f multicolored	1.00	.50
		Nos. 922-924 (3)	1.85	.90

50th anniv. of Iraq's admission to the UPU.

Soccer Tournament Emblem A263

1979, May 4 Photo. *Perf. 13*

925	A263	10f multicolored	.20	.20
926	A263	15f multicolored	.30	.20
927	A263	50f multicolored	1.00	.50
		Nos. 925-927 (3)	1.50	.90

5th Arabian Gulf Soccer Championship.

Child With Globe and Candle A264

Design: 100f, IYC emblem, boy and girl reaching for UN emblem, vert.

1979, June 1 Photo. *Perf. 13x13½*

928	A264	25f multicolored	.40	.20
929	A264	75f multicolored	1.25	.65

Souvenir Sheet

930	A264	100f multicolored	21.00	17.50

International Year of the Child.
No. 930 contains one 30x42mm stamp.

Leaf and Flower — A265

1979, July 17 Litho. *Perf. 12½*

931	A265	15f multicolored	.20	.20
932	A265	25f multicolored	.20	.20
933	A265	35f multicolored	.30	.20
		Nos. 931-933 (3)	.70	.60

July festivals.

Students Holding Globe, UNESCO Emblem A266

1979, July 25

934	A266	25f multicolored	.40	.20
935	A266	40f multicolored	.70	.30
936	A266	100f multicolored	2.00	.50
		Nos. 934-936 (3)	3.10	1.00

Intl. Bureau of Education, Geneva, 50th anniv.

S. al Hosari, Philosopher A267

Designs: No. 938, Mustapha Jawad, historian. No. 939, Jawad Selim, sculptor.

1979, Oct. 15 Litho. *Perf. 12½*

937	A267	25f multicolored	.30	.20
938	A267	25f multicolored	.30	.20
939	A267	25f multicolored	.30	.20
		Nos. 937-939 (3)	.90	.60

Pilgrimage to Mecca A268

1979, Oct. 25 Litho. *Perf. 12½*

940	A268	25f multicolored	.30	.20
941	A268	50f multicolored	.60	.25

Iraqi News Agency, 20th Anniversary A269

1979, Nov. 9 Photo. *Perf. 11½*

942	A269	25f multicolored	.20	.20
943	A269	50f multicolored	.40	.25
944	A269	75f multicolored	.60	.35
		Nos. 942-944 (3)	1.20	.80

Telecom 79 — A270

1979, Nov. 20 Litho. *Perf. 11½*

945	A270	25f multicolored	.25	.20
946	A270	50f multicolored	.50	.30
947	A270	75f multicolored	.75	.50
		Nos. 945-947 (3)	1.50	1.00

3rd World Telecommunications Exhibition, Geneva, Sept. 20-26.

International Palestinian Solidarity Day — A271

1979, Nov. 29 Photo. *Perf. 11½x12*

948	A271	25f multicolored	.60	.20
949	A271	50f multicolored	1.10	.30
950	A271	75f multicolored	1.50	.50
		Nos. 948-950 (3)	3.20	1.00

A272

A273

Designs: 25f, 75f, Ahmad Hassan Al-Bakr. 35f, 100f, Pres. Saddam Hussein.

1979, Dec. 1 Photo. *Perf. 13x13½*

951	A272	25f multicolored	.25	.20
952	A272	35f multicolored	.35	.20
953	A272	75f multicolored	.65	.30
954	A272	100f multicolored	2.75	1.60
		Nos. 951-954 (4)	4.00	2.30

1979, Dec. 10 *Perf. 14*

Vanguard Emblem and: 10f, Boy and violin. 15f, Children, map of Iraq. 25f, Youths. 35f, Vanguard emblem alone.

955	A273	10f multicolored	.20	.20
956	A273	15f multicolored	.20	.20
957	A273	25f multicolored	.25	.20
958	A273	35f multicolored	.35	.20
		Nos. 955-958 (4)	1.00	.80

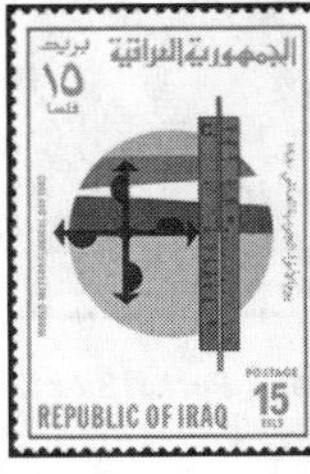

World Meteorological Day — A274

World Health Day — A275

1980, Mar. 23 Photo. *Perf. 14*

959	A274	15f multicolored	.20	.20
960	A274	25f multicolored	.25	.20
961	A274	35f multicolored	.35	.20
		Nos. 959-961 (3)	.80	.60

1980, Apr. 7 Photo. *Perf. 14*

962	A275	25f multicolored	.25	.20
963	A275	35f multicolored	.35	.20
964	A275	75f multicolored	1.25	.40
		Nos. 962-964 (3)	1.85	.80

Festivals Emblem — A276

Pres. Hussein — A277

1980, July 17 Photo. *Perf. 13½x13*

965	A276	25f multicolored	.25	.20
966	A276	35f multicolored	.30	.20

Souvenir Sheet

Perf. 13½

967	A277	100f multicolored	3.75	3.75

July Festivals.

Hurdles, Moscow '80 Emblem A278

1980, July 30 Photo. *Perf. 14*

968	A278	15f shown	.20	.20
969	A278	20f Weight lifting, vert.	.30	.25
970	A278	30f Boxing	.55	.35
971	A278	35f Soccer, vert.	1.10	.55
		Nos. 968-971 (4)	2.15	1.35

Souvenir Sheet

972	A278	100f Wrestling	4.75	4.75

22nd Summer Olympic Games, Moscow, July 19-Aug. 3.

Fruits — A279

1980, Aug. 15

973	A279	5f Blackberries	.20	.20
974	A279	15f Apricots	.20	.20
975	A279	20f Pears	.35	.20
976	A279	25f Apples	.50	.20
977	A279	35f Plums	1.00	.20
		Nos. 973-977 (5)	2.25	1.00

World Tourism Conference, Manila, Sept. 27 — A279a

1980, Aug. 30 Litho. *Perf. 12½*

978 A279a 25f multicolored .30 .20
979 A279a 50f multicolored .60 .25
980 A279a 100f multicolored 1.10 .55
Nos. 978-980 (3) 2.00 1.00

Postal Union Emblem, Posthorn, Map of Arab States — A280

1980, Sept. 8 *Perf. 12*

981 A280 10f multicolored .20 .20
982 A280 30f multicolored .35 .20
983 A280 35f multicolored .45 .20
Nos. 981-983 (3) 1.00 .60

Arab Postal Union, 11th Congress, Baghdad.

20th Anniversary of OPEC — A281

1980, Sept. 30

984 A281 30f multicolored 1.00 .25
985 A281 75f multicolored 1.50 .50

Papilio Machaon A282

1980, Oct. 20 Photo. *Perf. 13½x14*

987 A282 10f shown .35 .20
988 A282 15f Danaus chrysippus .45 .20
989 A282 20f Vanessa atalanta .60 .25
990 A282 30f Colias croceus 1.00 .25
Nos. 987-990 (4) 2.40 .90

Hegira, 1,500th Anniv. A283

1980, Nov. 9 Litho. *Perf. 11½x12*

991 A283 15f multicolored .20 .20
992 A283 25f multicolored .30 .20
993 A283 35f multicolored .40 .20
Nos. 991-993 (3) .90 .60

International Palestinian Solidarity Day — A284

1980, Nov. 29

994 A284 25f multicolored .30 .20
995 A284 35f multicolored .40 .20
996 A284 75f multicolored .80 .40
Nos. 994-996 (3) 1.50 .80

Army Day — A285

February Revolution, 18th Anniversary A286

1981, Jan. 6 Photo. *Perf. 14x13½*

997 A285 5f multicolored .20 .20
998 A285 30f multicolored .35 .20
999 A285 75f multicolored .90 .40
Nos. 997-999 (3) 1.45 .80

1981, Feb. 8 *Perf. 12*

1000 A286 15f multicolored .20 .20
1001 A286 30f multicolored .30 .20
1002 A286 35f multicolored .40 .20
Nos. 1000-1002 (3) .90 .60

Map of Arab Countries A287

1981, Mar. 22 Litho. *Perf. 12½*

1003 A287 5f multicolored .20 .20
1004 A287 25f multicolored .30 .20
1005 A287 35f multicolored .40 .20
Nos. 1003-1005 (3) .90 .60

Battle of Qadisiya — A288

1981, Apr. 7 Photo. *Perf. 13½x13*

1006 A288 30f multicolored .35 .20
1007 A288 35f multicolored .40 .20
1008 A288 75f multicolored .80 .40
Nos. 1006-1008 (3) 1.55 .80

Souvenir Sheet

1009 A288 100f multicolored 4.50 *5.50*

No. 1009 contains one horiz. stamp.

Helicopters and Tank A289

1981, June 1 Photo.

1010 A289 5f shown .20 .20
1011 A289 10f Plane .30 .20
1012 A289 15f Rocket .50 .20
Nos. 1010-1012,C66 (4) 2.00 1.35

Air Force, 50th anniv.

Natl. Assembly Election, First Anniv. — A290

1981, June 20 *Perf. 12½*

1013 A290 30f multicolored .35 .20
1014 A290 35f multicolored .40 .20
1015 A290 45f multicolored .55 .25
Nos. 1013-1015 (3) 1.30 .65

July Festivals A291

1981, July 17 Photo.

1016 A291 15f multicolored .20 .20
1017 A291 25f multicolored .30 .20
1018 A291 35f multicolored .40 .20
Nos. 1016-1018 (3) .90 .60

Pottery Maker — A292

Designs: Popular industries.

1981, Aug. 15 *Perf. 14*

1019 A292 5f Straw weaver .20 .20
1020 A292 30f Metal worker .35 .20
1021 A292 35f shown .45 .20
1022 A292 50f Rug maker, horiz. 1.00 .30
Nos. 1019-1022 (4) 2.00 .90

Islamic Pilgrimage — A293

1981, Oct. 7 Photo. *Perf. 12x11½*

1023 A293 25f multicolored .30 .20
1024 A293 45f multicolored .55 .25
1025 A293 50f multicolored .60 .30
Nos. 1023-1025 (3) 1.45 .75

World Food Day A294

1981, Oct. 16 Photo. *Perf. 14*

1026 A294 30f multicolored .35 .20
1027 A294 45f multicolored .50 .25
1028 A294 75f multicolored .80 .45
Nos. 1026-1028 (3) 1.65 .90

Intl. Year of the Disabled — A295

1981, Nov. 15

1029 A295 30f multicolored .30 .20
1030 A295 45f multicolored .50 .25
1031 A295 75f multicolored .70 .45
Nos. 1029-1031 (3) 1.50 .90

5th Anniv. of United Arab Shipping Co. A296

1981, Dec. 2 *Perf. 13x13½*

1032 A296 50f multicolored .75 .30
1033 A296 120f multicolored 2.25 .75

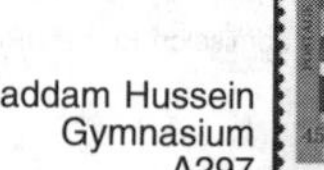

Saddam Hussein Gymnasium A297

1981, Sept. 26 Litho. *Perf. 12x12½*

1034 A297 45f shown .50 .25
1035 A297 50f Palace of Conferences .50 .30
1036 A297 120f like #1035 1.25 .75
1037 A297 150f like #1034 1.40 .90
Nos. 1034-1037 (4) 3.65 2.20

For surcharges see Nos. 1097-1099.

35th Anniv. of Al Baath Party — A298

Mosul Spring Festival — A299

1982, Apr. 7 Photo. *Perf. 13½x13*

1038 A298 25f Pres. Hussein, flowers .25 .20
1039 A298 30f "7 7 7" .25 .20
1040 A298 45f like 25f .40 .25
1041 A298 50f like 30f .45 .35
Nos. 1038-1041 (4) 1.35 1.00

Souvenir Sheet

Imperf

1042 A298 150f multicolored 1.75 1.25

1982, Apr. 15 Litho. *Perf. 11½x12*

1043 A299 25f Birds .30 .20
1044 A299 30f Girl .35 .20
1045 A299 45f like 25f .55 .25
1046 A299 50f like 30f .60 .35
Nos. 1043-1046 (4) 1.80 1.00

Intl. Workers' Day A300

1982, May 1 ***Perf. 12½***

1047 A300 25f multicolored .20 .20
1048 A300 45f multicolored .35 .25
1049 A300 50f multicolored .45 .30
Nos. 1047-1049 (3) 1.00 .75

14th World Telecommunications Day — A301

1982, May 17 Photo. ***Perf. 13x13½***

1050 A301 5f multicolored .20 .20
1051 A301 45f multicolored .35 .25
1052 A301 100f multicolored .80 .55
Nos. 1050-1052 (3) 1.35 1.00

10th Anniv. of Oil Nationalization A302

1982, June 1 Litho. ***Perf. 12½***

1053 A302 5f Oil gusher .20 .20
1054 A302 25f like 5f .60 .20
1055 A302 45f Statue 1.25 .25
1056 A302 50f like 45f 1.40 .35
Nos. 1053-1056 (4) 3.45 1.00

Martyrs' Day — A303

Women's Day — A304

1981, Dec. 1 Photo. ***Perf. 14***

1057 A303 45f multicolored .35 .25
1058 A303 50f multicolored .40 .30
1059 A303 120f multicolored 1.00 .75
Nos. 1057-1059,O339A-O339C (6) 3.50 2.50

1982, Mar. 4 Litho. ***Perf. 12½x13***

1060 A304 25f multicolored .30 .20
1061 A304 45f multicolored .55 .25
1062 A304 50f multicolored .60 .30
Nos. 1060-1062 (3) 1.45 .75

A305

A305a

1982, Apr. 12 ***Perf. 12½***

1063 A305 25f multicolored .30 .20
1064 A305 45f multicolored .55 .25
1065 A305 50f multicolored .60 .30
Nos. 1063-1065 (3) 1.45 .75

Arab Postal Union, 30th anniv.

1982, June 7 Photo. ***Perf. 14***

1065A A305a 30f Nuclear power emblem, lion .50 .20
1065B A305a 45f shown .75 .30
1065C A305a 50f like 30f .90 .40
1065D A305a 120f like 45f 2.00 1.00
Nos. 1065A-1065D (4) 4.15 1.90

First anniv. of attack on nuclear power reactor.

July Festivals — A306

1982, July 17 Photo. ***Perf. 14½x14***

1066 A306 25f multicolored .40 .20
1067 A306 45f multicolored .55 .25
1068 A306 50f multicolored .60 .30
Nos. 1066-1068 (3) 1.55 .75

Lacerta Viridis A307

1982, Aug. 20 Litho. ***Perf. 12½***

1069 A307 25f shown .30 .20
1070 A307 30f Vipera aspis .35 .20
1071 A307 45f Lacerta virdis, diff. .55 .25
1072 A307 50f Natrix tessellata .60 .35
Nos. 1069-1072 (4) 1.80 1.00

7th Non-aligned Countries Conference, Baghdad, Sept. — A308

#1073, Tito. #1074, Nehru. #1075, Nasser. #1076, Kwame Nkrumah. #1077, Hussein.

1982, Sept. 6 Photo. ***Perf. 13x13½***

1073 A308 50f multicolored .55 .40
1074 A308 50f multicolored .55 .40
1075 A308 50f multicolored .55 .40
1076 A308 50f multicolored .55 .40
1077 A308 100f multicolored 1.10 .55
Nos. 1073-1077 (5) 3.30 2.15

TB Bacillus Centenary A309

1982, Oct. 1 ***Perf. 14x14½***

1078 A309 20f multicolored .20 .20
1079 A309 50f multicolored .55 .30
1080 A309 100f multicolored 1.10 .40
Nos. 1078-1080 (3) 1.85 .90

1982 World Cup — A310

Designs: Various soccer players. 150f horiz.

1982, July 1 Litho. ***Perf. 11½x12***

1081 A310 5f multicolored .20 .20
1082 A310 45f multicolored .50 .25
1083 A310 50f multicolored .55 .30
1084 A310 100f multicolored 1.10 .60
Nos. 1081-1084 (4) 2.35 1.35

Souvenir Sheet

Perf. 12½

1085 A310 150f multicolored 1.75 1.25

13th UPU Day A311

1982, Oct. 9 ***Perf. 12x11½***

1086 A311 5f multicolored .20 .20
1087 A311 45f multicolored .40 .25
1088 A311 100f multicolored .90 .55
Nos. 1086-1088 (3) 1.50 1.00

Musical Instruments A312

1982, Nov. 15 ***Perf. 12½x13***

1089 A312 5f Drums .20 .20
1090 A312 10f Zither .20 .20
1091 A312 35f Stringed instrument .65 .35
1092 A312 100f Lute 1.75 .85
Nos. 1089-1092 (4) 2.80 1.60

Birth Anniv. of Mohammed — A313

Mecca Mosque views.

1982, Dec. 27 Litho. ***Perf. 12x11½***

1093 A313 25f multicolored .20 .20
1094 A313 30f multicolored .30 .25
1095 A313 45f multicolored .35 .25
1096 A313 50f multicolored .40 .30
Nos. 1093-1096 (4) 1.25 1.00

Nos. 1034-1036 Surcharged

1983, May 15 Litho. ***Perf. 12x12½***

1097 A297 60f on 50f multi .75 .30
1098 A297 70f on 45f multi .90 .45
1099 A297 160f on 120f multi 2.00 .90
Nos. 1097-1099 (3) 3.65 1.65

July Festivals A314

1983, July 17 Litho. ***Perf. 14½x14***

1100 A314 30f multicolored .35 .20
1101 A314 60f multicolored .75 .35
1102 A314 70f multicolored .90 .45
Nos. 1100-1102 (3) 2.00 1.00

Local Flowers — A315

1983, June 15 Photo. ***Perf. 15x14***

Border Color

1103 A315 10f shown, light blue .20 .20
1104 A315 20f Flowers, diff., pale yellow .20 .20
1105 A315 30f like 10f, yellow .25 .20
1106 A315 40f like 20f, gray .35 .25
1107 A315 50f like 10f, pale green .40 .30
1108 A315 100f like 20f, pink .80 .60
 a. Bklt. pane of 6, #1103-1108 3.00
Nos. 1103-1108 (6) 2.20 1.75

Nos. 1103-1108 issued in booklets only.
For surcharges see Nos. 1501-1506.

A316

Battle of Thi Qar — A317

1983, Oct. 30 Photo. ***Perf. 12½x13***

1109 A316 20f silver & multi .25 .20
1110 A317 50f silver & multi .60 .30
1111 A316 60f gold & multi .70 .35
1112 A317 70f gold & multi 1.10 .40
Nos. 1109-1112 (4) 2.65 1.25

World Communications Year — A318

25f, 70f show emblem and hexagons.

1983, Oct. 20 Photo. *Perf. 11½x12*

1113 A318 5f brt yel grn & multi .20 .20
1114 A318 25f rose lil & multi .30 .20
1115 A318 60f brt org yel & multi .70 .35
1116 A318 70f brt bl vio & multi 1.10 .40
Nos. 1113-1116 (4) 2.30 1.15

Souvenir Sheet

1117 A318 200f apple grn & multi 3.75 3.75

Baghdad Intl. Fair — A319

Symbolic "9" — A320

1983, Nov. 1 Photo. *Perf. 12½*

1118 A319 60f multicolored .50 .30
1119 A319 70f multicolored .55 .40
1120 A319 160f multicolored 1.25 .90
Nos. 1118-1120 (3) 2.30 1.60

1983, Nov. 10 Photo. *Perf. 14*

9th Natl. Congress of Arab Baath Socialist Party: 30f, 70f, Symbols of development. 60f, 100f, Torch, eagle, globe, open book.

1121 A320 30f multicolored .25 .20
1122 A320 60f multicolored .50 .30
1123 A320 70f multicolored .55 .40
1124 A320 100f multicolored .80 .55
Nos. 1121-1124 (4) 2.10 1.45

Festival Crowd — A321

Various Paintings.

1983, Nov. 20 Litho. *Perf. 12½*

1125 A321 60f shown .50 .30
1126 A321 60f Men hauling boat, vert. .50 .30
1127 A321 60f Decorations .50 .30
1128 A321 70f Village .55 .40
1129 A321 70f Crowd .55 .40
Nos. 1125-1129 (5) 2.60 1.70

Sabra and Shattela Palestinian Refugee Camp Massacre A322

Various Victims.

1983, Nov. 29 *Perf. 11½x12*

1130 A322 10f multicolored .20 .20
1131 A322 60f multicolored 1.00 .30
1132 A322 70f multicolored 1.10 .40
1133 A322 160f multicolored 2.00 .90
Nos. 1130-1133 (4) 4.30 1.80

Pres. Hussein, Map — A323

1983 Photo. *Perf. 13½x13*

1134 A323 60f multicolored .60 .30
1135 A323 70f multicolored .70 .40
1136 A323 250f multicolored 2.50 1.60
Nos. 1134-1136 (3) 3.80 2.30

Hussein as head of Al Baath Party, 4th anniv.

Modern Building — A324

Various buildings.

1983, Dec. 31 Litho. *Perf. 14*

1137 A324 60f multicolored .50 .30
1138 A324 70f multicolored .55 .40
1139 A324 160f multicolored 1.25 .90
1140 A324 200f multicolored 1.60 1.10
Nos. 1137-1140,O340-O341 (6) 4.95 3.40

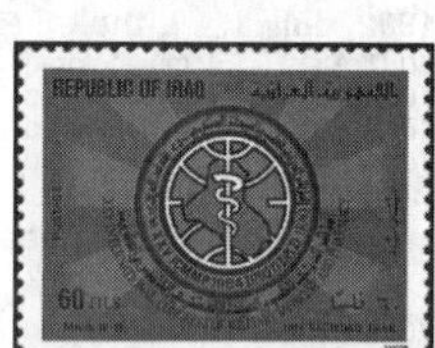
Medical Congress Emblem A325

1984, Mar. 10 *Perf. 13x12½*

1141 A325 60f multicolored .60 .30
1142 A325 70f multicolored .70 .40
1143 A325 200f multicolored 2.00 1.10
Nos. 1141-1143 (3) 3.30 1.80

25th Intl. Congress of Military Medicine and Pharmacy, Baghdad, Mar. 10-15.

Pres. Hussein's Birthday — A326

Various portraits of Hussein.

1984, Apr. 28 Litho. *Perf. 12½x13*

1144 A326 60f multicolored .50 .30
1145 A326 70f multicolored .55 .40
1146 A326 160f multicolored 1.25 .90
1147 A326 200f multicolored 1.60 1.10
Nos. 1144-1147 (4) 3.90 2.70

Souvenir Sheet

Imperf

1148 A326 250f multicolored 2.00 1.75

Gold ink on Nos. 1144-1147 and dark green ink in "margin" of No. 1148 was applied by a thermographic process, producing a raised effect. No. 1148 has perf. 12½x13 label picturing Pres. Hussein.

1984 Summer Olympics, Los Angeles — A327

1984, Aug. 12 Litho. *Perf. 12x11½*

1149 A327 50f Boxing .30 .25
1150 A327 60f Weight lifting .40 .25
1151 A327 70f like 50f .45 .30
1152 A327 100f like 60f .65 .45

Size: 80x60mm

Imperf

1153 A327 200f Soccer 1.40 .95
Nos. 1149-1153 (5) 3.20 2.20

Nos. 1153 contains one 32x41mm perf. 12½ label within the stamp.

A328

A329

50f, 70f, Pres. Hussein, flaming horses heads, map. 60f, 100f, Abstract of woman, sapling, rifle. 200f, Shield, heraldic eagle.

1984, Sept. 22 *Perf. 11½x12*

1154 A328 50f multicolored .30 .25
1155 A328 60f multicolored .40 .25
1156 A328 70f multicolored .45 .30
1157 A328 100f multicolored .65 .45

Size: 80x60mm

Imperf

1158 A328 200f multicolored 1.40 .95
Nos. 1154-1158 (5) 3.20 2.20

Battle of Qadisiya. No. 1158 contains one 32x41mm perf. 12½ label within the stamp.

1984, Dec. 1 *Perf. 13½*

Martyrs' Day: 50f, 70f, Natl. flag as flame. 60f, 100f, Woman holding rifle, medal.

1159 A329 50f multicolored .30 .25
1160 A329 60f multicolored .40 .25
1161 A329 70f multicolored .45 .30
1162 A329 100f multicolored .65 .45
Nos. 1159-1162 (4) 1.80 1.25

Pres. Hussein's Visit to Al-Mustansiriyah University, 5th Anniv. — A330

1985, Apr. 2 Photo. *Perf. 12x11½*

1163 A330 60f dk bl gray & dk pink .40 .25
1164 A330 70f myr grn & dk pink .45 .30
1165 A330 250f blk & dk pink 1.75 1.15
Nos. 1163-1165 (3) 2.60 1.70

Iraqi Air Force, 54th Anniv. — A331

Pres. Hussein, 48th Birthday — A332

10f, 160f, Pres. Hussein, fighter planes, pilot's wings. 60f, 70f, 200f, Planes, flag, "54," horiz.

Perf. 13x12½, 13½ (60f, 70f)

1985, Apr. 22 Litho.

1166 A331 10f multicolored .20 .20
1167 A331 60f multicolored .40 .25
1168 A331 70f multicolored .45 .30
1169 A331 160f multicolored 1.10 .70
Nos. 1166-1169 (4) 2.15 1.45

Souvenir Sheet

Perf. 12½

1170 A331 200f multicolored 1.40 .95

1985, Apr. 28 *Perf. 13½*

30f, 70f, Pres. Hussein, sunflower. 60f, 100f, Pres., candle & flowers. 200f, Flowers & text.

1171 A332 30f multicolored .20 .20
1172 A332 60f multicolored .40 .25
1173 A332 70f multicolored .45 .30
1174 A332 100f multicolored .65 .45
Nos. 1171-1174 (4) 1.70 1.20

Souvenir Sheet

Perf. 13x12½

1175 A332 200f multicolored 1.40 .95

Posts and Telecommunications Development Program — A333

Designs: 20f, 60f, Graph, woman in modern office. 50f, 70f, Satellite dish and graphs.

1985, June 30 *Perf. 12½*

1176 A333 20f multicolored .20 .20
1177 A333 50f multicolored .30 .25
1178 A333 60f multicolored .40 .25
1179 A333 70f multicolored .45 .30
Nos. 1176-1179 (4) 1.35 1.00

Battle of Qadisiya A334

Designs: 10f, 60f, Shown. 20f, 70f, Pres. Hussein, Al-Baath Party emblem. 200f, Dove, natl. flag as shield, soldier.

1985, Sept. 4 *Perf. 11½x12*

1180 A334 10f multicolored .20 .20
1181 A334 20f multicolored .20 .20
1182 A334 60f multicolored .40 .25
1183 A334 70f multicolored .45 .35
Nos. 1180-1183 (4) 1.25 1.00

Souvenir Sheet

Perf. 12x12½

1184 A334 200f multicolored 1.40 .95

No. 1184 contains one stamp 30x45mm.

Solar Energy Research Center A335

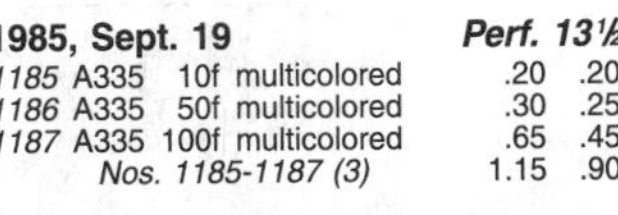

1985, Sept. 19 *Perf. 13½*

1185	A335	10f multicolored	.20	.20
1186	A335	50f multicolored	.30	.25
1187	A335	100f multicolored	.65	.45
		Nos. 1185-1187 (3)	1.15	.90

UN Child Survival Campaign A336

Al Sharif, Poet, Death Millennium A337

Designs: 10f, 50f, Stop Polio Campaign. 15f, 100f, Girl, infant.

1985, Oct. 10

1188	A336	10f multicolored	.20	.20
1189	A336	15f multicolored	.20	.20
1190	A336	50f multicolored	.30	.25
1191	A336	100f multicolored	.65	.45
		Nos. 1188-1191 (4)	1.35	1.10

1985, Oct. 20

1192	A337	10f multicolored	.20	.20
1193	A337	50f multicolored	.30	.25
1194	A337	100f multicolored	.65	.45
		Nos. 1192-1194 (3)	1.15	.90

UN, 40th Anniv. A338

1985, Oct. 24

1195	A338	10f multicolored	.20	.20
1196	A338	40f multicolored	.30	.20
1197	A338	100f multicolored	.65	.45
		Nos. 1195-1197 (3)	1.15	.85

Death of Iraqi Prisoners of War in Iran — A339

30f, 100f, Knife, Geneva Convention declaration, red crescent, red cross. 70f, 200f, POWs, gun shell, natl. flag, cherub & dove.

1985, Nov. 10 *Perf. 14*

1198	A339	30f multicolored	.20	.20
1199	A339	70f multicolored	.45	.30
1200	A339	100f multicolored	.65	.45
1201	A339	200f multicolored	1.40	.95

Size: 110x80mm

Imperf

1202	A339	250f multicolored	2.75	1.10
		Nos. 1198-1202 (5)	5.45	3.00

No. 1202 contains 2 perf. 14 labels similar to 100f and 200f designs within the stamp.

Intl. Palestinian Solidarity Day A341

1985, Nov. 29 **Litho.** *Perf. 13½*

1207	A341	10f multicolored	.20	.20
1208	A341	50f multicolored	.50	.30
1209	A341	100f multicolored	1.00	.50
		Nos. 1207-1209 (3)	1.70	1.00

Martyrs' Day — A342

1985, Dec. 1 *Perf. 11½x12*

1210	A342	10f multicolored	.20	.20
1211	A342	40f multicolored	.30	.20
1212	A342	100f multicolored	.70	.50
		Nos. 1210-1212 (3)	1.20	.90

Intl. Youth Year — A343

1985, Dec. 12 **Litho.** *Perf. 11½x12*

IYY emblem and: 40f, 100f, Soldier holding flag. 50f, 200f, Youths, flag. 250f, Flag, cogwheel, rifle muzzle, symbols of industry.

1213	A343	40f multicolored	.40	.20
1214	A343	50f multicolored	.45	.25
1215	A343	100f multicolored	.90	.45
1216	A343	200f multicolored	2.00	.95
		Nos. 1213-1216 (4)	3.75	1.85

Souvenir Sheet

Perf. 12x12½

1217	A343	250f multicolored	2.50	1.10

No. 1217 contains one stamp 30x45mm. Exists imperf.

Army Day A344

Pres. Hussein, "6" and: 10f, 50f, Soldier, flowers, vert. 40f, 100f, Flag, cogwheel, rockets. 200f, Al-Baath Party emblem, rifle, waves.

1986, Jan. 6 *Perf. 11½x12, 12x11½*

1218	A344	10f multicolored	.20	.20
1219	A344	40f multicolored	.40	.20
1220	A344	50f multicolored	.50	.25
1221	A344	100f multicolored	.90	.45
		Nos. 1218-1221 (4)	2.00	1.10

Miniature Sheet

Perf. 12½x11½

1222	A344	200f multicolored	2.00	.95

No. 1222 contains one stamp 52x37mm.

Women's Day A345

Designs: 30f, 100f, Women in traditional and modern occupations, vert. 50f, 150f, Emblem, green flag, battle scene, grapes.

Perf. 11½x12, 12x11½

1986, Mar. 8 **Litho.**

1223	A345	30f multicolored	.25	.20
1224	A345	50f multicolored	.35	.25
1225	A345	100f multicolored	.70	.50
1226	A345	150f multicolored	1.10	.70
		Nos. 1223-1226 (4)	2.40	1.65

Pres. Hussein, 49th Birthday A346

Designs: 30f, 100f, Children greeting Pres. 50f, 150f, Portrait. 250f, Portrait, flag, flowers.

1986, Apr. 28 **Litho.** *Perf. 11½x12*

1227	A346	30f multicolored	.30	.20
1228	A346	50f multicolored	.45	.25
1229	A346	100f multicolored	.90	.45
1230	A346	150f multicolored	1.25	.65

Size: 80x60mm

Imperf

1231	A346	250f multicolored	2.50	1.10
		Nos. 1227-1231 (5)	5.40	2.65

Oil Nationalization Day, June 1 — A347

Labor Day — A348

Designs: 10f, 100f, Symbols of industry, horiz. 40f, 150f, Oil well, pipeline to refinery.

Perf. 12x11½, 11½x12

1986, July 25 **Litho.**

1232	A347	10f multicolored	.20	.20
1233	A347	40f multicolored	.45	.20
1234	A347	100f multicolored	.85	.45
1235	A347	150f multicolored	1.25	.65
		Nos. 1232-1235 (4)	2.75	1.50

1986, July 28 *Perf. 11½x12*

Designs: 10f, 100f, Laborer, cog wheel. 40f, 150f, May Day emblem.

1236	A348	10f multicolored	.20	.20
1237	A348	40f multicolored	.30	.20
1238	A348	100f multicolored	.65	.45
1239	A348	150f multicolored	.95	.65
		Nos. 1236-1239 (4)	2.10	1.50

Iraqi Air Force, 55th Anniv. A349

Designs: 30f, 100f, Fighter plane, pilot's wings, natl. flag. 50f, 150f, Fighter planes. 250f, Medal, aircraft in flight.

1986, July 28 *Perf. 12x11½*

1240	A349	30f multicolored	.30	.20
1241	A349	50f multicolored	.40	.25
1242	A349	100f multicolored	.85	.45
1243	A349	150f multicolored	1.25	.65

Size: 81x61mm

Imperf

1244	A349	250f multicolored	2.50	1.10
		Nos. 1240-1244 (5)	5.30	2.65

No. 1244 also exists perf.

July Festivals A350

Pres. Hussein and: 20f, 100f, Flag. 30f, 150f, "17." 250f, Inscription, portrait inside medal of honor.

1986, July 29 *Perf. 11½x12*

1245	A350	20f multicolored	.20	.20
1246	A350	30f multicolored	.25	.20
1247	A350	100f multicolored	.65	.45
1248	A350	150f multicolored	.95	.65

Size: 81x61mm

Imperf

1249	A350	250f multicolored	1.60	1.10
		Nos. 1245-1249 (5)	3.65	2.60

1st Qadisiya Battle — A351

Designs: 20f, 70f, Warrior, shield, vert. 60f, 100f, Pres. Hussein, star, battle scene.

Perf. 13x13½, 13½x13

1986, Sept. 4 **Litho.**

1250	A351	20f multicolored	.20	.20
1251	A351	60f multicolored	.40	.30
1252	A351	70f multicolored	.50	.35
1253	A351	100f multicolored	.70	.50
		Nos. 1250-1253 (4)	1.80	1.35

Battle between the Arabs and Persian Empire.

Hussein's Battle of Qadisiya — A352

30f, 100f, Pres. Hussein, soldiers saluting peace, vert. 40f, 150f, Pres., armed forces. 250f, Pres., soldiers, flags, military scenes.

Perf. 11½x12½, 12½x11½

1986, Sept. 4

1254	A352	30f multicolored	.25	.20
1255	A352	40f multicolored	.30	.20
1256	A352	100f multicolored	.70	.50
1257	A352	150f multicolored	1.10	.70

Size: 80x60mm

Imperf

1258	A352	250f multicolored	1.75	1.10
		Nos. 1254-1258 (5)	4.10	2.70

Intl. Peace Year — A353

1986, Nov. 15 Litho. *Perf. 11½x12*

1259 A353 50f Dove, flag, G clef .30 .25
1260 A353 100f Globe, dove, rifle .65 .50
1261 A353 150f like 50f 1.00 .70
1262 A353 250f like 100f 1.60 1.10

Size: 80x69mm

Imperf

1263 A353 200f Emblem, flag, map, fist 1.25 1.00
Nos. 1259-1263 (5) 4.80 3.55

Pres. Hussein
A354 A355

1986 *Perf. 12½x12*

1264 A354 30f multicolored .20 .20
1265 A355 30f multicolored .20 .20
1266 A354 50f multicolored .30 .25
1267 A355 50f multicolored .30 .25
1268 A354 100f multicolored .65 .45
1269 A355 100f multicolored .65 .45
1270 A354 150f multicolored 1.00 .70
1271 A355 150f multicolored 1.00 .70
1272 A354 250f multicolored 1.60 1.10
1273 A354 350f multicolored 2.25 1.50
Nos. 1264-1273 (10) 8.15 5.80

For overprints & surcharges see #1347-1348, 1455, 1480-1481, 1484, 1499-1500, 1518-1519.

Army Day — A356

1987, Jan. 6 Litho. *Perf. 12x12½*

1274 A356 20f shown .20 .20
1275 A356 40f Hussein, armed forces .25 .25
1276 A356 90f like 20f .60 .60
1277 A356 100f like 40f .65 .65
Nos. 1274-1277 (4) 1.70 1.70

United Arab Shipping Co., 10th Anniv. (in 1986) A357

1987, Apr. 3 Litho. *Perf. 12½*

1278 A357 50f Cargo ship .35 .25
1279 A357 100f Container ship Chaleb Ibn Al Waleeb .70 .45
1280 A357 150f like 50f 1.10 .70
1281 A357 250f like 100f 1.75 1.10

Size: 102x91mm

Imperf

1282 A357 200f Loading cargo aboard the Waleeb 1.25 1.00
Nos. 1278-1282 (5) 5.15 3.50

Arab Baath Socialist Party, 40th Anniv. — A358

1987, Apr. 7 Litho. *Perf. 12x12½*

1283 A358 20f shown .20 .20
1284 A358 40f Hussein, "7," map .25 .25
1285 A358 90f like 20f .60 .60
1286 A358 100f like 40f .65 .65
Nos. 1283-1286 (4) 1.70 1.70

Pres. Hussein's 50th Birthday A359

1987, Apr. 28 *Perf. 12½x12*

1287 A359 20f shown .20 .20
1288 A359 40f Portrait .25 .25
1289 A359 90f like 20f .60 .60
1290 A359 100f like 40f .65 .65
Nos. 1287-1290 (4) 1.70 1.70

July Festivals — A360

UNICEF, 40th Anniv. — A361

1987, July 17 *Perf. 12½x12, 12x12½*

1291 A360 20f Hussein, star, flag, horiz. .20 .20
1292 A360 40f shown .25 .25
1293 A360 90f like 20f, horiz. .60 .60
1294 A360 100f like 40f .65 .65
Nos. 1291-1294 (4) 1.70 1.70

1987, Oct. 4 *Perf. 12x12½, 12½x12*

1295 A361 20f shown .20 .20
1296 A361 40f "40," horiz. .25 .25
1297 A361 90f like 20f .60 .60
1298 A361 100f like 40f, horiz. .65 .65
Nos. 1295-1298 (4) 1.70 1.70

Census Day A362

1987, Nov. 1 *Perf. 12x11½*

1299 A362 20f shown .20 .20
1300 A362 30f Graph, Arabs, diff. .20 .20
1301 A362 50f like 30f .35 .35
1302 A362 500f like 20f 3.25 3.25
Nos. 1299-1302 (4) 4.00 4.00

Army Day A363

Perf. 11½x12, 12x11½

1988, Jan. 6 Litho.

1303 A363 20f "6," Hussein, troops, vert. .20 .20
1304 A363 30f shown .20 .20
1305 A363 50f like 20f, vert. .35 .20
1306 A363 150f like 30f 1.00 .40
Nos. 1303-1306 (4) 1.75 1.00

Art Day — A364

A365

1988, Jan. 8 Litho. *Perf. 11½x12*

1307 A364 20f shown .20 .20
1308 A364 30f Hussein, rainbow, gun barrel, music .25 .20
1309 A364 50f like 20f .40 .20
1310 A364 100f like 30f .75 .25

Size: 60x80mm

Imperf

1311 A364 150f Notes, instruments, floral ornament 1.25 .80
Nos. 1307-1311 (5) 2.85 1.65

1988, Feb. 8 *Perf. 11½x12, 12x11½*

1312 A365 20f "8," troops, Hussein, horiz. .20 .20
1313 A365 30f "8," Hussein, eagle .25 .20
1314 A365 50f like 20f, horiz. .40 .20
1315 A365 150f like 30f 1.25 .40
Nos. 1312-1315 (4) 2.10 1.00

Popular Army, 18th anniv. (20f, 50f); Feb. 8th Revolution, 25th anniv. (30f, 150f).

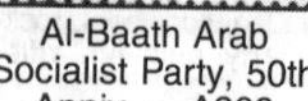

Al-Baath Arab Socialist Party, 50th Anniv. — A366

President Hussein's 41st Birthday — A367

1988, Apr. 7 *Perf. 12x12½, 12½x12*

1316 A366 20f Flag, grain, convention, horiz. .20 .20
1317 A366 30f shown .25 .20
1318 A366 50f like 20f, horiz. .40 .20
1319 A366 150f like 30f 1.25 .40
Nos. 1316-1319 (4) 2.10 1.00

1988, Apr. 28 *Perf. 12x12½*

1320 A367 20f shown .20 .20
1321 A367 30f Hussein, 3 hands, flowers .25 .20
1322 A367 50f like 20f .40 .20
1323 A367 100f like 50f .75 .25

Size: 90x99mm

Imperf

1324 A367 150f Sun, Hussein, heart, flowers 1.25 .80
Nos. 1320-1324 (5) 2.85 1.65

World Health Organization, 40th Anniv. — A368

Regional Marine Environment Day, Apr. 4 — A369

1988, June 1 *Perf. 12½x12, 12x12½*

1325 A368 20f WHO anniv. emblem, horiz. .20 .20
1326 A368 40f shown .30 .20
1327 A368 90f like 20f, horiz. .70 .25
1328 A368 100f like 40f .80 .25
Nos. 1325-1328 (4) 2.00 .90

1988, Apr. 24 *Perf. 12x12½, 12½x12*

1329 A369 20f shown .20 .20
1330 A369 40f Flag in map, fish, horiz. .30 .20
1331 A369 90f like 20f .70 .25
1332 A369 100f like 40f, horiz. .80 .25
Nos. 1329-1332 (4) 2.00 .90

Shuhada School Victims Memorial A370

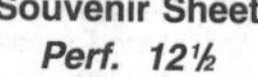

A371

1988, June 1 *Perf. 11½x12, 12x11½*

1333 A370 20f shown .20 .20
1334 A370 40f Girl caught in explosion, horiz. .30 .20
1335 A370 90f like 20f .75 .25
1336 A370 100f like 40f, horiz. .80 .25
Nos. 1333-1336 (4) 2.05 .90

Souvenir Sheet

Perf. 12½

1337 A371 150f red, blk & brt grn 1.10 .75

Pilgrimage to Mecca — A372

1988, July 24 Litho. *Perf. 13½*

1338 A372 90f multicolored .70 .25
1339 A372 100f multicolored .80 .35
1340 A372 150f multicolored 1.25 .40
Nos. 1338-1340 (3) 2.75 1.00

Basra, 1350th Anniv. A373

1988, Oct. 22 *Perf. 12x11½*

1341 A373 100f multicolored .75 .25

Natl. Flag, Grip on Lightning — A374

Pres. Hussein, Natl. Flag — A375

1988, July 17 *Perf. 12x12½*

1342 A374 50f shown .40 .20
1343 A374 90f Map, Hussein, desert .70 .25
1344 A374 100f like 50f .80 .25
1345 A374 150f like 90f 1.10 .35

Size: 90x70mm

Imperf

1346 A375 250f shown 2.00 .65
Nos. 1342-1346 (5) 5.00 1.70

July Festivals and 9th anniv. of Pres. Hussein's assumption of office.

Nos. 1272-1273 Overprinted

1988, Aug. 7 Litho. *Perf. 12½x12*

1347 A354 250f multicolored 2.90 .95
1348 A354 350f multicolored 4.00 1.40

Victory.

Navy Day — A376

1988, Aug. 12 *Perf. 12x12½*

1349 A376 50f shown .60 .20
1350 A376 90f Map, boats 1.10 .35
1351 A376 100f like 50f 1.25 .40
1352 A376 150f like 90f 1.75 .60

Size: 91x70mm

Imperf

1353 A376 250f Emblem, Pres. Hussein decorating officers 3.50 1.10
Nos. 1349-1353 (5) 8.20 2.65

1988 Summer Olympics, Seoul — A377

1988, Sept. 19 *Perf. 12x12½*

1354 A377 100f Boxing, character trademark 1.25 .40
1355 A377 150f Flag, emblems 1.75 .60

Size: 101x91mm

Imperf

1356 A377 500f Emblem, trademark, Hussein, trophy 7.00 2.40
Nos. 1354-1356 (3) 10.00 3.40

Liberation of Fao — A378

1988, Sept. 1 *Perf. 12x11½*

1357 A378 100f multicolored 1.25 .40
1358 A378 150f multicolored 1.75 .60

Size: 60x80mm

Imperf

1359 A378 500f Hussein, text 7.00 2.40
Nos. 1357-1359 (3) 10.00 3.40

Mosul A379

Baghdad A380

Ancient cities.

1988, Oct. 22 *Perf. 12x11½, 11½x12*

1360 A379 50f Fortress .60 .20
1361 A380 150f Astrolabe, modern architecture 1.75 .60

Al-Hussein Missile — A381

1988, Sept. 10 *Perf. 11½x12*

1362 A381 100f multicolored .80 .30
1363 A381 150f multicolored 1.25 .45

Size: 80x60mm

Imperf

1364 A381 500f Hussein, map, missile 3.75 1.25
Nos. 1362-1364 (3) 5.80 2.00

2nd Intl. Festival, Babylon — A382

1988, Sept. 30 *Perf. 11½x12*

1365 A382 100f multicolored .80 .25
1366 A382 150f multicolored 1.10 .40

Size: 60x80mm

Imperf

1367 A382 500f Medallions 3.75 1.25
Nos. 1365-1367 (3) 5.65 1.90

Victorious Iraq A383

1988, Aug. 8 Litho. *Perf. 12x11½*

1368 A383 50f multicolored .40 .20
1369 A383 100f multicolored .80 .30
1370 A383 150f multicolored 1.25 .40
Nos. 1368-1370 (3) 2.45 .90

Birthday of Mohammed A384

1988, Oct. 23 Litho. *Perf. 11½x12*

1371 A384 100f multicolored .75 .25
1372 A384 150f multicolored 1.10 .40
1373 A384 1d multicolored 7.50 2.50
Nos. 1371-1373 (3) 9.35 3.15

Martyrs' Day A385

1988, Dec. 1 Litho. *Perf. 13½*

1374 A385 100f multicolored .75 .25
1375 A385 150f multicolored 1.10 .40
1376 A385 500f multicolored 3.75 1.25
Nos. 1374-1376 (3) 5.60 1.90

Police Day A386

1989, Jan. 9 Litho. *Perf. 12x11½*

1377 A386 50f multicolored .40 .20
1378 A386 100f multicolored .75 .25
1379 A386 150f multicolored 1.10 .40
Nos. 1377-1379 (3) 2.25 .85

Postal Savings Bank — A387

a

1988 Litho. *Perf. 11½x12*

1380 A387 50f shown 1.00 .50

Size: 23½x25mm

Perf. 13½x13

1381 A387(a) 100f multi 2.00 1.00
1382 A387(a) 150f multi 3.00 1.50
Nos. 1380-1382 (3) 6.00 3.00

#1381-1382 have a line of Arabic at the top.

#1381-1382 without overprint are postal savings stamps.

For surcharges see #1507-1510, 1512-1514.

Arab Cooperation Council A388

1989, Feb. 12 Litho. *Perf. 12x11½*

1383 A388 100f shown .80 .25
1384 A388 150f Statesmen, diff. 1.10 .40

52nd Birthday of Pres. Hussein A392

1989, Apr. 28 Litho. *Perf. 12x11½*

1392 A392 100f multicolored .70 .25
1393 A392 150f multicolored 1.00 .30

Size: 60x81mm

Imperf

1394 A392 250f Hussein, diff. 1.75 .60
Nos. 1392-1394 (3) 3.45 1.15

Fao Liberation, 1st Anniv. — A393

1989, Apr. 18 *Perf. 12x11½*

1395 A393 100f multi .70 .25
1396 A393 150f multi 1.00 .30

Size: 60x81mm

Imperf

1397 A393 250f Calendar 1.75 .60
Nos. 1395-1397 (3) 3.45 1.15

Gen. Adnan Khairalla — A394

Reconstruction of Basra — A395

1989, May 6 Litho. *Perf. 13½*

1398 A394 50f gold & multi .50 .20
1399 A394 100f copper & multi .95 .30
1400 A394 150f silver & multi 1.40 .50
Nos. 1398-1400 (3) 2.85 1.00

Gen. Adnan Khairalla (1940-1989), deputy commander-in-chief of the armed forces and minister of defense.

1989, June 14

1401 A395 100f multi .95 .30
1402 A395 150f multi 1.40 .50

Reconstruction of Fao — A396

Women — A397

1989, June 25

1403 A396 100f multi .95 .30
1404 A396 150f multi 1.40 .50

1989, June 25 Litho. *Perf. 11½x12*

1405 A397 100f yel & multi .60 .20
1406 A397 150f brt pink & multi .90 .30
1407 A397 1d brt blue & multi 5.75 2.00
1408 A397 5d white & multi 28.75 9.50
Nos. 1405-1408 (4) 36.00 12.00

For surcharges see Nos. 1485-1486, 1511, 1522.

July Festivals — A398

1989, July 17 Litho. *Perf. 12x12½*

1409 A398 50f multicolored .40 .20
1410 A398 100f multicolored .80 .25
1411 A398 150f multicolored 1.25 .40
Nos. 1409-1411 (3) 2.45 .85

Election of Pres. Hussein, 10th anniv.

Family A399

1989, July 19 *Perf. 13½*

1412 A399 50f multicolored .40 .20
1413 A399 100f multicolored .80 .25
1414 A399 150f multicolored 1.25 .40
Nos. 1412-1414 (3) 2.45 .85

A400

Victory Day — A401

1989, Aug. 8 *Perf. 12x12½*

1415 A400 100f multicolored .75 .25
1416 A400 150f multicolored 1.25 .40

Size: 71x91mm

Imperf

1417 A401 250f multicolored 2.00 .70
Nos. 1415-1417 (3) 4.00 1.35

Interparliamentary Union, Cent. — A402

1989, Sept. 15 *Perf. 12½x12*

1418 A402 25f multicolored .20 .20
1419 A402 100f multicolored .80 .25
1420 A402 150f multicolored 1.25 .40
Nos. 1418-1420 (3) 2.25 .85

Ancient Cities A403

1989, Oct. 15 *Perf. 11½x12½*

1421 A403 100f Dhi Qar-ur .80 .25
1422 A403 100f Erbil .80 .25
1423 A403 100f An Najaf .80 .25
Nos. 1421-1423 (3) 2.40 .75

5th Session of the Arab Ministers of Transport Council, Baghdad, Oct. 21 A404

Designs: 100f, Land, air and sea transport, diff. 150f, Modes of transport, flags, vert.

1989, Oct. 21 *Perf. 12x11½, 11½x12*

1424 A404 50f shown .40 .20
1425 A404 100f multicolored .80 .25
1426 A404 150f multicolored 1.25 .40
Nos. 1424-1426 (3) 2.45 .85

Iraqi News Agency, 30th Anniv. A405

1989, Nov. 9 *Perf. 13½*

1427 A405 50f multicolored .40 .20
1428 A405 100f multicolored .80 .25
1429 A405 150f multicolored 1.25 .40
Nos. 1427-1429 (3) 2.45 .85

Declaration of Palestinian State, 1st Anniv. — A406

Flowers — A407

1989, Nov. 15 *Perf. 12x12½*

1430 A406 25f shown .20 .20
1431 A406 50f Palestinian uprising .40 .20
1432 A406 100f like 25f .80 .25
1433 A406 150f like 50f 1.25 .35
Nos. 1430-1433 (4) 2.65 1.00

1989, Nov. 20 *Perf. 13½x13*

1434 A407 25f *Viola sp.* .20 .20
1435 A407 50f *Antirrhinum majus* .40 .20
1436 A407 100f *Hibiscus trionum* .80 .25
1437 A407 150f *Mesembryanthemum sparkles* 1.25 .40
Nos. 1434-1437 (4) 2.65 1.05

Miniature Sheet

Perf. 12½x11½

1438 Sheet of 4 4.00 4.00
a. A407 25f like No. 1434 1.00 1.00
b. A407 50f like No. 1435 1.00 1.00
c. A407 100f like No. 1436 1.00 1.00
d. A407 150f like No. 1437 1.00 1.00

No. 1438 has a continuous design. No. 1438 sold for 500f.

For overprints and surcharges see Nos. 1450-1451, 1456, 1516, 1524.

A408 A409

1989, Oct. 25 Litho. *Perf. 13½*

1439 A408 100f multicolored .80 .25
1440 A408 150f multicolored 1.10 .40

Reconstruction of Fao.

1989, Dec. 4 Litho. *Perf. 13½*

1441 A409 50f multicolored .40 .20
1442 A409 100f multicolored .80 .25
1443 A409 150f multicolored 1.10 .40
Nos. 1441-1443 (3) 2.30 .85

Martyrs' Day.

Iraqi Red Crescent Soc. — A410

1989, Dec. 10 Litho. *Perf. 13½*

1444 A410 100f multicolored .40 .20
1445 A410 150f multicolored 1.10 .40
1446 A410 500f multicolored 3.75 1.25
Nos. 1444-1446 (3) 5.25 1.85

Arab Cooperation Council, 1st Anniv. — A411

1990, Feb. 16 Litho. *Perf. 13x13½*

1447 A411 50f yellow & multi .75 .30
1448 A411 100f orange & multi 1.75 .55

Size: 80x62mm

Imperf

1449 A411 250f blue & multi 5.00 1.60
Nos. 1447-1449 (3) 7.50 2.45

For surcharge see No. 1523.

Nos. 1435, 1437 Ovptd.

1990, May 28 Litho. *Perf. 13½x13*

1450 A407 50f multicolored
1451 A407 150f multicolored

Arab League Summit Conf., Baghdad.

Importation Prohibited

The importation of stamps from Iraq was prohibited on Aug. 2, 1990. Iraqi stamps issued after that date have not been valued.

End of Iran-Iraq War, 2nd Anniv. — A412

1990, Aug. 30 Litho. *Perf. 13½x13*

1452 A412 50f purple & multi
1453 A412 100f blue & multi

Imperf

Size: 59x81mm

1454 A412 250f Saddam Hussein, dove

For surcharge see No. 1525.

No. 1269 Surcharged

1992(?) Litho. *Perf. 12½x12*

1455 A355 1d on 100f #1269

No. 1434 Surcharged

عشرة دنانير

❖❖*❖

Type I

عشرة دنانير

Type II

1993, Aug. 1 Litho. *Perf. 13½x13*
1456 A407 10d on 25f Type I
a. Type II

No. RA23 Surcharged

1992 Photo. *Perf. 14*
1457 PT3 100f on 5f multi

Reconstruction of Iraq — A413

Designs: 250f, Satellite dish. 500f, Bridges. 750f, Power plant, horiz. 1d, Factory.

1993, Sept. Photo. *Perf. 14*
1459 A413 250f red & multi
1460 A413 500f blue & multi
1461 A413 750f yellow & multi
1462 A413 1d multicolored

Stamps of this issue may be poorly centered or have perforations running through the design.

For surcharge see No. 1526.

Peace Ship A414

1993 Photo. *Perf. 14*
1463 A414 2d red & multi
1464 A414 5d green & multi

No. RA23 Surcharged

b

c

دينار واحد

d

دينار واحد

e

دينار واحد

f

دينار واحـد

g

دينـــارين

h

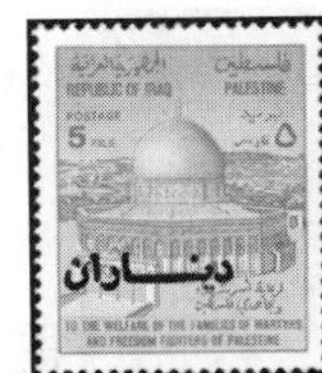

i

j

k

٥ دينـــار

l

٥ دينـــار

m

n

o

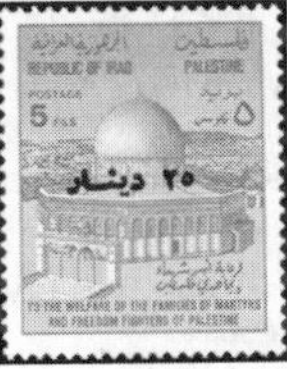

p

q

٢٥ دينـــار

r

* ٢٥ دينار *

s

t

1994, Feb. 5 Photo. *Perf. 14*
1465 PT3(b) 500f on 5f multi
1466 PT3(c) 1d on 5f multi
1467 PT3(d) 1d on 5f multi
a. PT3(e) 1d on 5f multi
b. PT3(f) 1d on 5f multi
c. PT3(g) 1d on 5f multi
1468 PT3(h) 2d on 5f multi
1469 PT3(i) 2d on 5f multi
1470 PT3(j) 3d on 5f multi
1471 PT3(k) 3d on 5f multi
1472 PT3(l) 5d on 5f multi
a. PT3(m) 5d on 5f multi
b. PT3(n) 5d on 5f multi
1473 PT3(o) 5d on 5f multi
1474 PT3(p) 10d on 5f multi
1475 PT3(q) 25d on 5f multi
a. PT3(r) 25d on 5f multi
1476 PT3(s) 25d on 10d on 5f
1477 PT3(t) 50d on 5f multi

No. 1273 Surcharged

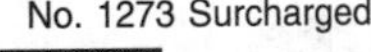

u

ميلاد القائد
٩٤/٤/٢٨
* ٥ دينار *

v

1994, Apr. 28 Litho. *Perf. 12½x12*
1480 A354(u) 5d on 350f #1273
1481 A354(v) 5d on 350f #1273
a. Pair, #1480-1481

Alqa'id Two-Deck Bridge A415

1994, July 17 *Perf. 14*
1482 A415 1d pink & multi
1483 A415 3d blue & multi
a. Pair, #1482-1483

No. 1273 Surcharged

عيد النصر
٩٩٤/٨/٨
* ٥ دينار *

1994, Aug. 8 *Perf. 12½x12*
1484 A354 5d on 350f #1273

No. 1406 Surcharged

w

x

1995, Jan. 2 *Perf. 11½x12*
1485 A397(w) 5d on 150f #1406
1486 A397(x) 5d on 150f #1406

Baghdad Clock — A416

Saddam Tower — A417

1995, Feb. 28 *Perf. 11*
1487 A416 7d blue & black

Size: 76x98mm

Imperf

1488 A416 25d multicolored

1995, Mar. 12 *Perf. 14*
1489 A417 2d multicolored
1490 A417 5d multicolored
a. Vert. pair, #1489-1490

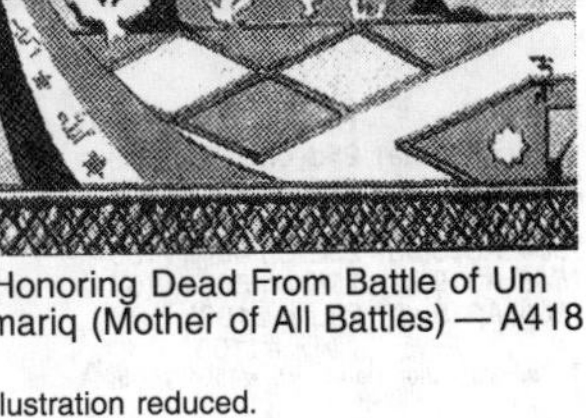

Honoring Dead From Battle of Um Almariq (Mother of All Battles) — A418

Illustration reduced.

1995 *Imperf.*
1491 A418 100d multicolored

Saddam Hussein, 58th Birthday — A419

Design: No. 1492, Saddam seated, flowers & flag behind him, vert.
Illustration reduced.

1995, Apr. 28 *Imperf.*
1492 A419 25d multicolored
1493 A419 25d multicolored

Saddam River Canal Project — A420

1995, July 17 *Perf. 11*
1494 A420 4d olive yellow & blue
1495 A420 4d red & blue

Size: 97x57mm

Imperf

1496 A420 25d multicolored

Embargo of Iraq — A421

1995, Aug. 6 *Perf. 11*
1497 A421 10d blue green & rose lilac

Size: 77x100mm

Imperf

1498 A421 25d multicolored

No. 1273 Surcharged

Referendum
15/10/1995
❋25 Dinars❋

y

يوم الاستفتاء
١٩٩٥/١٠/١٥
* ٢٥ دينار *

z

1995, Oct. 15 Litho. *Perf. 12½x12*
1499 A354(y) 25d on 350f #1273
1500 A354(z) 25d on 350f #1273

Nos. 1103-1108 Surcharged

aa ab

1995(?) **Photo.** ***Perf. 15x14***

1501 A315(aa) 25d on 10f #1103
1502 A315(ab) 25d on 20f #1104
1503 A315(aa) 25d on 30f #1105
1504 A315(ab) 25d on 40f #1106
1505 A315(aa) 25d on 50f #1107
1506 A315(ab) 25d on 100f #1108
a. Bklt. pane of 6, #1501-1506

No. 1380, Postal Savings Stamps Similar to Type A387 Surcharged in Red or Black

ac ad

ae

1995(?) **Litho.** ***Perf. 11½x12***

Size: 23½x25mm

1507 A387(ac) 25d on 100f multi
1508 A387(ac) 25d on 150f blue & multi
1509 A387(ad) 50d on 250f yel & multi (R)
1510 A387(ae) 50d on 50f #1380

No. 1406 Surcharged

1995(?)

1511 A397 100d on 150f multi

Postal Savings Stamps Similar to Type A387 Surcharged in Red

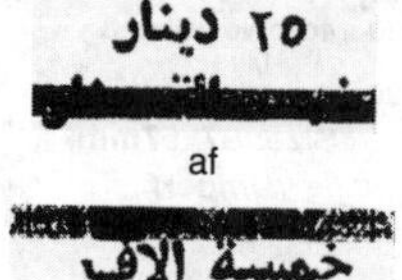

af

ag

ah

1996 **Litho.** ***Perf. 11½x12***

Size: 23½x25mm

On 250f Yellow & Multi

1512 A387(af) 25d on 1000d
1513 A387(ag) 25d on 5000d
1514 A387(ah) 50d on 1500d

A421a

A421b

Children, Bank—A421c

1996 **Litho.** ***Perf. 13½***

1514A A421a 25d on 10f grn & multi
1514B A421b 25d on 25f bl & multi
1514C A421c 50d on 10f grn & multi

Children, Bank — A422

1996 **Litho.** ***Perf. 13½***

1515 A422 50d on 50f multi

No. 1515 without surcharge is a postal savings stamp.

No. 1435 Surcharged

1996 ***Perf. 13½x13***

1516 A407 100d on 50f multi

No. O341 Surcharged

1996 ***Perf. 14***

1517 A324 100d on 70f #O341

No. 1273 Surcharged

ak al

1996 **Litho.** ***Perf. 12½x12***

1517A A354(ak) 25d on 350f
1519A A354(al) 1000d on 350f

No. 1273 Surcharged in Blue or Black

ai

aj

1996 ***Perf. 12½x12***

1518 A354(ai) 250d on 350f (Bl)
1519 A354(aj) 350d on 350f

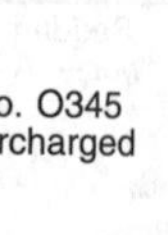

No. O345 Surcharged

1996 **Litho.** ***Perf. 13½***

1519B A329 100d on 60f

Battle of Um Al Maarik — A423

1997, Feb. 13 **Photo.** ***Perf. 11***

1520 A423 25d blk, red & green
1521 A423 100d blue, red & grn
a. Arabic word at right center reversed

No. 1406 Surcharged

1997, Apr. 22 **Litho.** ***Perf. 11½x12***

1522 A397 25d on 150f #1406

Post Day.

No. 1448 Surcharged

1997 ***Perf. 13x13½***

1523 A411 25d on 100f #1448

Baath Party, 50th anniv.

No. 1450 Surcharged like No. 1516

1997 **Litho.** ***Perf. 13½***

1524 A407 100d on 50f multi

No. 1452 Surcharged

1997 ***Perf. 13½x13***

1525 A412 100d on 50f multi

No. 1459 Surcharged

1997 ***Perf. 14***

1526 A413 25d on 250f multi

A424

A425

Referendum Day: 250d, Saddam Hussein, map of Arab nations.

1997 ***Perf. 14***

1527 A424 25d shown
1527A A424 100d multicolored

Imperf

Size: 91x77mm

1528 A424 250d multicolored

1997, Dec. 19 ***Perf. 14***

Saddam Hussein and: 25d, 100d, #1531, Water irrigating trees, grain. #1532, Water pipeline, flowers, grain.

Self-Adhesive (#1530)

1529 A425 25d multicolored
1530 A425 100d multicolored

Imperf

Size: 68x81mm

1531 A425 250d multicolored

Size: 64x82mm

1532 A425 250d multicolored

Wafa'a Alqa'id project.

Saladin (1169-1250), Founder of Ayyubid Dynasty, Saddam Hussein — A426

1998, Feb. **Litho.** ***Perf. 14***

Self-Adhesive

1533 A426 25d multicolored
1534 A426 100d multicolored

Size: 79x67mm

Imperf

1535 A426 250d multicolored

Nos. 1533-1534 exist imperf. No. 1535 has water-activated gum.

New Year — A427

Illustration reduced.

1998, Mar. 21 ***Imperf.***

1536 A427 250d Zinnias
1537 A427 250d Irises

1998 World Cup Soccer Championship, France — A428

Illustration reduced.

1998, June ***Imperf.***

1538 A428 250d shown

Size: 63x76mm

1539 A428 250d Two players, vert.

Souvenir Sheet

Arab Police & Security Leaders Conf., 25th Anniv. — A429

Illustration reduced.

1998, July 12 **Litho.** ***Imperf.***

1540 A429 250d multicolored

A430

"Zad" Day (Arabic Alphabet) — A431

1998, Oct. 25 ***Perf. 14***

1541 A430 25d multicolored
1542 A431 100d multicolored

Flowers — A432

Designs: 25d, Chamomilla recutita. 50d, Helianthus annuus. 1000d, Carduus nutans.

1998, Oct. 27

1543 A432 25d multicolored
1544 A432 50d brown leaves
1545 A432 50d green leaves
1546 A432 1000d multicolored

Self-Adhesive

1547 A432 25d like #1543

No. 1547 is printed on glossy paper.

A433

Martyr's Day — A434

1998, Dec. 1

1548 A433 25d multicolored
1549 A434 100d multicolored

Nos. 1548-1549 exist imperf.

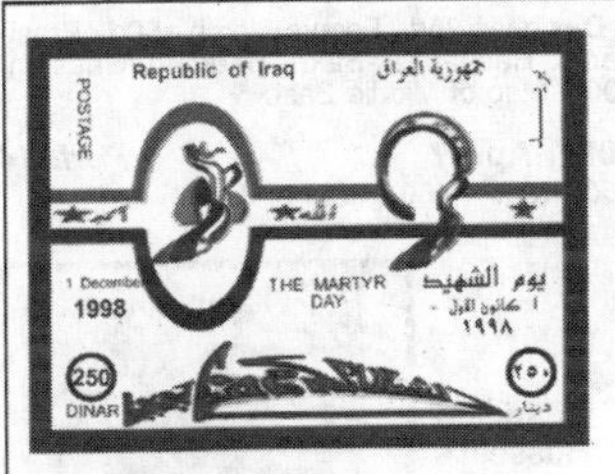

Martyr's Day — A434a

Illustration reduced.

1998, Dec. 1 **Litho.**

Imperf

1550 A434a 250d multicolored

Anthocharis Euphome — A435

1998, Dec. 20

1551 A435 100d Precis orithya
1552 A435 150d shown

Exist imperf.

Intl. Conference on Tower of Babel and Ziggurat of Borsippa — A436

1999, Jan. 23 **Litho.** ***Perf. 14***

1553 A436 25d multicolored
1554 A436 50d multicolored

Imperf

Size: 71x89mm

1555 A436 250d multicolored

Great Dam — A437

Saddam Hussein, 62nd Birthday — A439

Saddam Theater — A438

1999, Apr. 28 ***Perf. 14***

1556 A437 25d Dam
1557 A437 100d Dam, Saddam Hussein

Imperf

Size: 70x92mm

1558 A437 250d Like #1557

1999, May 7 ***Perf. 14***

1559 A438 25d Saddam Hussein, emblem
1560 A438 100d Al-Saddamiyah City

Imperf

Size: 92x70mm

1561 A438 250d Clock tower

1999, May 17 ***Perf. 14***

1562 A439 25d multicolored
1563 A439 50d multicolored
1564 A439 150d multicolored
1565 A439 500d multicolored
1566 A439 1000d multicolored
1567 A439 5000d multi, horiz.

1998 World Cup, France — A440

Honey Bees — A441

1999, July 17

1568 A440 25d Two players
1569 A440 100d Goalie save, horiz.

1999, Sept. 18

1570 A441 25d brown & multi
1571 A441 50d black & multi

Al Fat'h Day A442

Saddam Hussein and: 25d, Eagle, flowers. 50d, People. 250d, Eagle, flag.

1999, Dec. 12 **Litho.** ***Perf. 14***

1572-1573 A442 Set of 2

Imperf

Size: 93x71mm

1574 A442 250d multi

A443

A444

A445

Jerusalem Day A446

2000, Feb. ***Perf. 14***

1575 A443 25d multi
1576 A444 50d multi
1577 A445 100d multi
1578 A446 150d multi

Imperf

Size: 93x71mm

1579 A446 250d multi

A447

Saddam Hussein's Birthday A448

2000, May 17 ***Perf. 14***

1580 A447 25d multi

1581 A448 50d multi

Imperf

Size: 92x71mm

1582 A448 500d Saddam Hussein, stars

Sculpture A449

Text "July Festivals 2000": a, At right. b, At left. c, At bottom center on two lines. d, At lower left. e, At bottom center on 3 lines.

2000, July 12 ***Perf. 14***

1583 Horiz. strip of 5
a.-e. A449 25d Any single

Exists imperf.

Victory Day — A450

Designs: 25d, 250d, Saddam Hussein. 50d, Saddam Hussein, flag.

2000, Aug. 8 ***Perf. 14***

1584-1585 A450 Set of 2

Imperf

Size: 71x91mm

1586 A450 250d multi

Birds A451

Designs: 25d, Anas platyrhynchos. 50d, Passer domesticus. 150d, Porphyrio poliocephalus.

2000, Aug. 28 ***Perf. 14***

1587-1589 A451 Set of 3

Imperf

Size: 93x71mm

1590 A451 500d Carduelis carduelis

Prophet Mohammad's Birthday — A452

Designs: 25d, Green background. 50d, Tan background.

2000, Oct. 11 ***Perf. 14***

1591-1592 A452 Set of 2

A453

Referendum Day — A454

2000, Oct. 15 ***Perf. 14***

1593 A453 25d multi
1594 A454 50d multi

Imperf

Size: 93x72mm

1595 A453 250d Saddam Hussein, crowd

Baytol Hikma, 1200th Anniv. — A455

2001, Jan. ***Perf. 14***

1596-1597 A455 Set of 2

A456

A457

Writing, 5th Millennium A458

2001, Mar. **Litho.** ***Perf. 14***

1598 A456 25d multi
1599 A457 50d multi
1600 A456 75d multi
1601 A457 100d multi
1602 A458 150d multi
1603 A458 250d multi

Bombing of Al Amiriya Shelter, 10th Anniv. A459

Designs: 25d, 150d, Mother, injured child, rescue workers. 50d, Doves, wreath, picture frames, vert.

2001, Mar. ***Perf. 14***

1604-1605 A459 Set of 2

Imperf

Size: 91x71mm

Without Gum

1606 A459 150d multi

Al Baath Party, 54th Anniv. A460

Designs: 25d, People, torch. 50d, Presidents Hassan al-Bakr, Saddam Hussein. 100d, Map of Middle East.

2001, Apr. 7 ***Perf. 14***

1607-1609 A460 Set of 3

Saddam Hussein's 64th Birthday A461

Saddam Hussein: 25d, Seated, with flowers, vert. 50d, Seated. 100d, Seated, with people. 250d, Standing, with crowd.

2001, Apr. 28 ***Perf. 14***

1610-1612 A461 Set of 3

Imperf

Size: 89x69mm

Without Gum

1613 A461 250d multi

Fish A462

Designs: 25d, Barbus sharpeyi. 50d, Barbus esocinus. 100d, Barbus xanthopterus. 150d, Pampus argenteus.

2001, Aug. 4 ***Perf. 14***

1614-1617 A462 Set of 4

Battle of Um Al Maarik, 10th Anniv. — A463

Frame color: 25d, Red. 100d, Black.

2001, Aug.

1618-1619 A463 Set of 2

Mammals A464

Designs: 100d, Gazella subgutturosa. 250d, Lepus europaeus. 500d, Camelus dromedarius.
1000d, Various mammals.

2001, Aug. ***Perf. 14***

1620-1622 A464 Set of 3

Imperf

Size: 92x70mm

Without Gum

1623 A464 1000d multi

Nationalization of Oil Industries, 29th Anniv. — A465

Designs: 25d, Oil rig, workers, soldier, Iraqi flag. 50d, Oil rig, refinery, pipeline.

2001, Sept. 15 **Litho.** ***Perf. 14***

1624-1625 A465 Set of 2

Support for Palestinians A466

Designs: No. 1626, 25d, Saddam Hussein, map of Israel and Iraq. No. 1627, 25d, Dome of the Rock, Palestinian flag, gunman, vert. 50d, Dome of the Rock, Palestinian flag, gunman with arms raised, vert.
No. 1629, 250d, Dome of the Rock, Israeli tank and Palestinian rock-thrower. No. 1630, 250d, Dome of the Rock, doves, Palestinian flag and Mohammad J. Durra and father.

2001, Sept. 20

1626-1628 A466 Set of 3

Imperf

Size: 88x67mm

Without Gum

1629-1630 A466 Set of 2

2001 Youth Soccer World Cup A467

Designs: 25d, Players, map of world. 50d, Map of Asia, player, trophy, vert.

2001, Oct. 7 ***Perf. 14***

1631-1632 A467 Set of 2

Iraqi Claim of Depleted Uranium US Bombs Dropped on Iraqi Citizens — A468

Falling bombs and: No. 1633, 25d, Woman and children. No. 1634, 25d, No. 1636, 250d, Disfigured people. 50d, People, Iraqi flag, horiz.

2001, Nov.

1633-1635 A468 Set of 3

Imperf
Size: 70x91mm
Without Gum

1636 A468 250d multi

Army Day — A469

Designs: 25d, Iraqi flag, soldiers, airplanes, ship and tank. No. 1638, 50d, No. 1640, 250d, Monument, vert. 100d, Soldier, Iraqi flag, tank, vert.

2002, Jan. 6 ***Perf. 14***
1637-1639 A469 Set of 3

Imperf
Size: 73x91mm
Without Gum

1640 A469 250d multi

Liberation of Fao — A470

Saddam Hussein and : 25d, Mosque. 100d, Soldier, map of Iraq, horiz.

2002, Apr. 17 ***Perf. 14***
1641-1642 A470 Set of 2

Jerusalem Day — A471

Frame color: 25d, Blue. 50d, Yellow. 100d, Pink.

2002, Apr.
1643-1645 A471 Set of 3

Hegira, Year 1423 A472

Designs: 25d, Mosques, Holy Kaaba. 50d, Minaret and mosque, vert. 75d, Bird, spider web.

2002, Apr.
1646-1648 A472 Set of 3

Bombardment of Al Amirya Shelter, 11th Anniv. — A473

Frame color: 25d, Black. 50d, Red.

2002, Apr.
1649-1650 A473 Set of 2

War Against Iraq, 11th Anniv. — A474

2002, Apr.
1651 A474 100d multi

Flowers — A475

Designs: 25d, Roses. 50d, Roses, diff. 150d, Poppies, carnations.
250d, Roses, diff.

2002, Apr. ***Perf. 14***
1652-1654 A475 Set of 3

Imperf
Size: 73x91mm
Without Gum

1655 A475 250d multi

Saddam Hussein's 65th Birthday — A476

Color of vignette frame and country name: 25d, Red. 50d, Purple. 75d, Green. 100d, Dark blue.
No. 1660, 250d, Saddam Huseein, hearts and flowers. No. 1661, 250d, Saddam Hussein with headdress.

2002, Apr. 28 ***Perf. 14***
1656-1659 A476 Set of 4

Imperf
Size: 74x91mm
Without Gum

1660-1661 A476 Set of 2

Palestinian Unity — A477

2002 **Litho.** ***Perf. 14***
1662 A477 5000d multi

Mosques — A478

Designs: 25d, Sheikh Maroof Mosque. 50d, Al-Mouiz Mosque. 75d, Um Al Marik Mosque.

2002
1663-1665 A478 Set of 3

Post Day — A479

Air mail envelope and: 50d, Stamp with dove. 100d, Airplane, ship, train, map of world.
250d, Globe and dove.

2002
1666-1667 A479 Set of 2

Imperf
Size: 70x91mm
Without Gum

1668 A479 250d multi

2002 World Cup Soccer Championships, Japan and Korea — A480

World Cup, various players and background color of: 50d, Blue. 100d, Yellow. 150d, Red violet.
250d, Purple.

2002 ***Perf. 14***
1669-1671 A480 Set of 3

Imperf
Size: 70x92mm
Without Gum

1672 A480 250d multi

Ancient Ships A481

Various ships: 150d, 250d, 500d.

2002 ***Perf. 14***
1673-1675 A481 Set of 3

Victory Day — A482

Frame color: 25d, Blue. 50d, Pink.
150d, Eagle, vert.

2002 ***Perf. 14***
1676-1677 A482 Set of 2

Imperf
Size: 71x90mm
Without Gum

1678 A482 150d multi

A483

A484

A485

A486

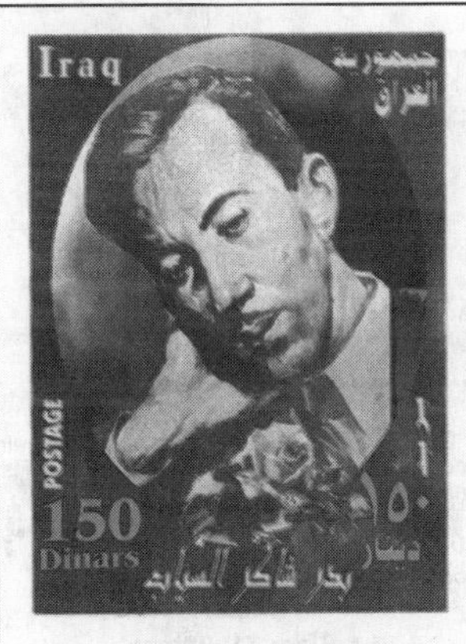

Poets — A487

Illustration A487 reduced.

2002 **Litho.** ***Perf. 14***
1679 A483 25d multi
1680 A484 50d multi
1681 A485 75d multi
1682 A486 100d multi

Imperf
Size: 70x92mm
Without Gum

1683 A487 150d multi

A488

A489

A490

Baghdad Day — A491

Illustration A491 reduced.

2002 ***Perf. 14***

1684	A488	25d multi	
1685	A489	50d multi	
1686	A490	75d multi	

Imperf

Size: 91x70mm

Without Gum

1687 A491 250d multi

Referendum Day — A492

Designs: 100d, 250d, Saddam Hussein, people, hands, heart and flowers. 150d, Fist, ballot box.

2002 ***Perf. 14***

1688-1689 A492 Set of 2

Imperf

Size: 71x92mm

Without Gum

1690 A492 250d multi

Mammals A493

Designs: 25d, Oryx leucoryx. 50d, Acionyx jubatus, vert. 75d, 250d, Panthera leo persica, vert. 100d, Castor fiber. 150d, Equus hemionus hemippus.

2002 ***Perf. 14***

1691-1695 A493 Set of 5

Imperf

Size: 70x93mm

Without Gum

1696 A493 250d multi

Saddam University A494

Background colors: 50d, Brown. 100d, Blue.

2002 ***Perf. 14***

1697-1698 A494 Set of 2

AIR POST STAMPS

Catalogue values for unused stamps in this section are for Never Hinged items.

Basra Airport — AP1

Diyala Railway Bridge — AP2

Vickers Viking over: 4f, 20f, Kut Dam. 5f, 35f, Faisal II Bridge.

Perf. 11½, 11½x12

1949, Feb. 1 **Engr.** **Unwmk.**

C1	AP1	3f blue green	.20	.20
C2	AP1	4f red violet	.20	.20
C3	AP1	5f red brown	.20	.20
C4	AP1	10f carmine	2.25	.75
C5	AP1	20f blue	1.00	.40
C6	AP1	35f red orange	1.00	.40
C7	AP2	50f olive	1.50	.60
C8	AP2	100f violet	4.00	1.25
		Nos. C1-C8 (8)	10.35	4.00

Sheets exist, perf. and imperf., containing one each of Nos. C1-C8, with arms and Arabic inscription in blue green in upper and lower margin. Value (2 sheets) $70.

Republic

ICY Emblem — AP3

1965, Aug. 13 **Litho.** ***Perf. 13½***

C9	AP3	5f brn org & black	.40	.20
C10	AP3	10f citron & dk brn	.60	.20
C11	AP3	30f ultra & black	1.60	.50
		Nos. C9-C11 (3)	2.60	.90

International Cooperation Year.

Trident 1E Jet Plane AP4

1965, Dec. 1 **Photo.** ***Perf. 11½***

Granite Paper

C12	AP4	5f multicolored	.20	.20
C13	AP4	10f multicolored	.20	.20
C14	AP4	40f multicolored	2.50	.50
		Nos. C12-C14 (3)	2.90	.90

Introduction by Iraqi Airways of Trident 1E jet planes.

Arab International Tourist Union Emblem — AP5

Travelers on Magic Carpet AP6

1966, Dec. 3 **Litho.** ***Perf. 13½, 14***

C15	AP5	2f multicolored	.20	.20
C16	AP6	5f yellow & multi	.20	.20
C17	AP5	15f blue & multi	.25	.20
C18	AP6	50f multicolored	.90	.40
		Nos. C15-C18 (4)	1.55	1.00

Meeting of the Arab Intl. Tourist Union, Baghdad.

For overprint see No. RAC1.

Costume Type of Regular Issue

Iraqi Costumes: 40f, Woman's head. 50f, Woman's costume. 80f, Man's costume.

1967, Nov. 10 **Litho.** ***Perf. 13***

C19	A105	40f multicolored	.30	.20
C20	A105	50f blue & multi	.45	.25
C21	A105	80f green & multi	3.00	.55
		Nos. C19-C21 (3)	3.75	1.00

International Tourist Year Type of Regular Issue

Designs: 50f, Female statue, Temples of Hatra. 80f, Spiral Tower (Malwiye of Samarra). 100f, Adam's Tree. 200f, Aladdin's Cave. 500f, Golden Shiah Mosque of Kadhimain. 50f, 80f, 100f and 200f are vert.

1967, Dec. 1 **Litho.**

C22	A107	50f multicolored	.60	.25
C23	A107	80f multicolored	1.10	.40
C24	A107	100f multicolored	2.25	.50
C25	A107	200f ver & multi	3.50	2.00
C26	A107	500f brn & multi	24.00	12.00
		Nos. C22-C26 (5)	31.45	15.15

For overprints see Nos. C39, C52, C53.

Arabian AP7

Animals: 2f, Striped hyena. 3f, Leopard. 5f, Mountain gazelle. 200f, Arabian stallion.

1969, Sept. 1 **Litho.** ***Perf. 14***

C27	AP7	2f multicolored	.20	.20
C28	AP7	3f multicolored	.20	.20
C29	AP7	5f multicolored	.20	.20
C30	AP7	10f multicolored	.25	.20
C31	AP7	200f multicolored	6.50	3.50
		Nos. C27-C31 (5)	7.35	4.30

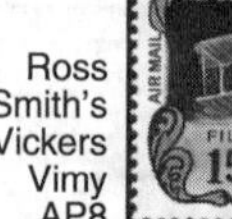
Ross Smith's Vickers Vimy AP8

1969, Dec. 4 **Litho.** ***Perf. 14***

C32	AP8	15f dk bl & multi	.80	.35
C33	AP8	35f multicolored	1.60	.50
a.		Souv. sheet of 2, #C32-C33, imperf.	7.50	6.00

50th anniv. of the first England to Australia flight of Capt. Ross Smith and Lt. Keith Smith. No. C33a sold for 100f.

View Across Euphrates — AP9

Iraqi Banknotes and Pres. Hassan al-Bakr AP10

1970, Oct. 30 **Litho.** ***Perf. 13***

C34	AP9	10f brt bl & multi	.75	.20
C35	AP9	15f multicolored	.75	.20
C36	AP10	1d multicolored	18.00	7.50
		Nos. C34-C36 (3)	19.50	7.90

National Development Plan.

For overprints see Nos. C42-C43.

Telecommunications Emblem — AP11

1970, Dec. 15 **Litho.** ***Perf. 14x13½***

C37	AP11	15f gray & multi	.25	.20
C38	AP11	25f lt bl & multi	.50	.35

10th Conf. of Arab Telecommunications Union.

No. C23 Overprinted

1971, Apr. 23 ***Perf. 13***

C39 A107 80f multicolored 5.50 4.00

World Meteorological Day.

Iraqi Philatelic Society Emblem — AP12

1972, Feb. 25 **Litho.** ***Perf. 13***

C40	AP12	25f multicolored	.80	.50
C41	AP12	70f pink & multi	2.50	1.50

Iraqi Philatelic Society, 20th anniversary.

Nos. C34-C35 Overprinted

1972, Feb. 25

C42	AP9	10f brt bl & multi	1.00	.25
C43	AP9	15f multicolored	2.00	1.00

9th Cong. of Natl. Union of Iraqi Students.

Soccer and C.I.S.M. Emblem AP13

20f, 35f, Players, soccer ball, C.I.S.M. emblem. 100f, Winged lion, Olympic & C.I.S.M. emblems.

1972, June 9 Litho. *Perf. 13½*

C46 AP13 10f lt bl & multi .35 .20
C47 AP13 20f dp bl & multi .70 .20
C48 AP13 25f green & multi .70 .20
C49 AP13 35f brt bl & multi 2.75 .50
a. Souv. sheet, 100f, imperf. 8.00 8.00
Nos. C46-C49 (4) 4.50 1.10

25th Military Soccer Championships (C.I.S.M.), Baghdad, June 9-19.

Statue of Athlete — AP14

Design: 70f, Mesopotamian archer on horseback, ancient and modern athletes.

1972, Nov. 15 Photo. *Perf. 14x13½*

C50 AP14 25f multicolored .75 .50
C51 AP14 70f multicolored 2.25 1.50

Cong. of Asian and World Body Building Championships, Baghdad, Nov. 15-23, 1972.

Nos. C23, C26 Overprinted

1973, Mar. 25 Litho. *Perf. 13*

C52 A107 80f multi 11.00 4.50
C53 A107 500f multi 37.50 *52.50*

International History Congress.

ICATU Type of 1976

1976, Mar. 24 Photo. *Perf. 13½*

C54 A213 75f blue & multi 4.00 2.00

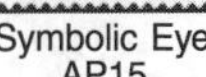

Symbolic Eye AP15

Basketball AP16

1976, June 20 Photo. *Perf. 14*

C55 AP15 25f ultra & dk brn .20 .20
C56 AP15 35f brt grn & dk brn .25 .20
C57 AP15 50f orange & multi .40 .25
Nos. C55-C57 (3) .85 .65

World Health Day: Foresight prevents blindness.

1976, July 30 Litho. *Perf. 12x12½*

Montreal Olympic Games Emblem and: 35f, Volleyball. 50f, Wrestling. 75f, Boxing. 100f, Target shooting, horiz.

C58 AP16 25f yel & multi .50 .20
C59 AP16 35f blue & multi .75 .25
C60 AP16 50f ver & multi 1.00 .50
C61 AP16 75f yel grn & multi 1.50 .70
Nos. C58-C61 (4) 3.75 1.65

Souvenir Sheet

Imperf

C62 AP16 100f grn & multi 6.00 6.00

21st Olympic Games, Montreal, Canada, July 17-Aug. 1.

13th World Telecommunications Day — AP17

1981, May 17 Photo. *Perf. 12½*

C63 AP17 25f multicolored .20 .20
C64 AP17 50f multicolored .40 .25
C65 AP17 75f multicolored .60 .40
Nos. C63-C65 (3) 1.20 .85

Air Force Type of 1981

1981, June 1 Photo. *Perf. 14x13½*

C66 A289 120f Planes, vert. 1.00 .75

AIR POST OFFICIAL STAMP

Catalogue values for all unused stamps in this section are for Never Hinged items.

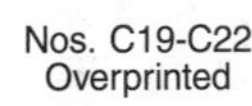

Nos. C19-C22 Overprinted

1971 Litho. *Perf. 13*

CO1 A105 40f multicolored 3.25 1.00
CO2 A105 50f multicolored 4.25 1.00
CO3 A105 80f multicolored 4.00 1.00

"Official" Reading Down

CO4 A107 50f multicolored 3.50 2.25
Nos. CO1-CO4 (4) 15.00 5.25

Nos. C27-C28, C30 Overprinted or Surcharged

1971 *Perf. 14*

CO5 AP7 10f multicolored .60 .25
CO6 AP7 15f on 3f multi .80 .50
CO7 AP7 25f on 2f multi 1.60 1.00
Nos. CO5-CO7 (3) 3.00 1.75

No bar and surcharge on No. CO5.

OFFICIAL STAMPS

British Mandate

Regular Issue of 1923 Overprinted:

k

l

1923 Wmk. 4 *Perf. 12*

O1 A1(k) ½a olive grn .50 .20
O2 A2(k) 1a brown .60 .20
O3 A3(l) 1½a car lake 1.50 .35
O4 A4(k) 2a brown org 1.10 .20
O5 A5(k) 3a deep blue 2.25 .60
O6 A6(l) 4a dull violet 2.25 .40
O7 A7(k) 6a blue green 3.00 1.10
O8 A6(l) 8a olive bister 3.50 1.10
O9 A8(l) 1r green & brn 4.00 1.10
O10 A1(k) 2r black (R) 14.00 6.25
O11 A6(l) 5r orange 42.50 20.00
O12 A7(k) 10r carmine 60.00 42.50
Nos. O1-O12 (12) 135.20 74.00

Regular Issue of 1923-25 Overprinted:

m

n

1924-25

O13 A1(m) ½a olive green .85 .20
O14 A2(m) 1a brown .65 .20
O15 A3(n) 1½a car lake .65 .20
O16 A4(m) 2a brown org 1.10 .20
O17 A5(m) 3a deep blue 1.50 .20
O18 A6(n) 4a dull violet 3.00 .25
O19 A7(m) 6a blue green 1.50 .20
O20 A6(n) 8a olive bister 3.00 .30
O21 A8(n) 1r green & brn 7.75 .85
O22 A1(m) 2r bister ('25) 25.00 3.00
O23 A6(n) 5r orange 40.00 35.00
O24 A7(m) 10r brown red 55.00 35.00
Nos. O13-O24 (12) 140.00 75.60

For overprint see Nos. O42, O47, O51-O53.

No. 14 Overprinted Type "n"

1927

O25 A9 1r red brown 5.50 1.50

Regular Issue of 1931 Overprinted Vertically

o

1931

O26 A10 ½a green .20 .20
O27 A10 1a chestnut .20 .20
O28 A10 1½a carmine 7.50 5.00
O29 A10 2a orange .25 .20
O30 A10 3a light blue .30 .20
O31 A10 4a purple brown .50 .20
O32 A10 6a Pruss blue 16.00 1.25
O33 A10 8a dark green 12.00 1.50

Overprinted Horizontally

p

O34 A11 1r dark brown 7.50 1.10
O35 A11 2r yellow brown 12.50 12.50
O36 A11 5r deep orange 32.50 40.00
O37 A11 10r red 60.00 70.00
Nos. O26-O37 (12) 149.45 132.35

Overprinted Vertically Reading Up

O38 A9(p) 25r violet 525.00 *750.00*

For overprints see Nos. O39-O41, O43-O46, O48-O50, O54.

Kingdom

Nos. O15, O19, O22-O24, O26-O31, O33-O35, O38 Surcharged with New Values in Fils and Dinars, like Nos. 28-43

1932, Apr. 1

O39 A10 3f on ½a .35 .35
O40 A10 4f on 1a (G) .20 .20
O41 A10 5f on 1a .20 .20
a. Inverted Arabic "5" *40.00* *35.00*
O42 A3 8f on 1½a .70 .20
O43 A10 10f on 2a .25 .20
O44 A10 15f on 3a .40 .20
O45 A10 20f on 4a .45 .20
O46 A10 25f on 4a .50 .25
O47 A7 30f on 6a .60 .35
O48 A10 40f on 8a 1.10 .35
a. "Flis" for "Fils" *300.00* *450.00*
O49 A11 50f on 1r 1.75 .80
O50 A11 75f on 1r 3.00 2.75
O51 A1 100f on 2r 6.00 1.00
O52 A6 200f on 5r 12.00 8.00
O53 A7 ½d on 10r 35.00 32.50
a. Bar in "½" omitted *700.00*
O54 A9 1d on 25r 87.50 80.00
Nos. O39-O54 (16) 150.00 127.55

Regular Issue of 1932 Overprinted Vertically like Nos. O26-O33

1932, May 9

O55 A12 2f ultramarine .20 .20
O56 A12 3f green .20 .20
O57 A12 4f violet brn .20 .20
O58 A12 5f gray .20 .20
O59 A12 8f deep red .20 .20
O60 A12 10f yellow .20 .20
O61 A12 15f deep blue 1.25 .20
O62 A12 20f orange .25 .20
O63 A12 25f rose lilac 3.50 .40
O64 A12 30f olive grn .75 .40
O65 A12 40f dark violet 1.40 .40

Overprinted Horizontally Like Nos. O34 to O37

O66 A13 50f deep brown 1.40 .50
O67 A13 75f lt ultra 2.00 .25
O68 A13 100f deep green 5.25 .50
O69 A13 200f dark red 14.00 2.75

Overprinted Vertically like No. O38

O70 A14 ½d gray blue 14.00 3.50
O71 A14 1d claret 35.00 *50.00*
Nos. O55-O71 (17) 80.00 *60.30*

Regular Issue of 1934-38 Overprinted Type "o" Vertically Reading up in Black

1934-38 Unwmk.

O72 A15 1f purple ('38) .90 .35
O73 A15 2f ultramarine .75 .20
O74 A15 3f green .45 .20
O75 A15 4f purple brn .85 .20
O76 A15 5f gray green .75 .20
O77 A15 8f deep red 3.00 .20
O78 A15 10f yellow .30 .20
O79 A15 15f deep blue 6.75 1.00
O80 A15 20f orange .65 .20
O81 A15 25f brown violet 13.50 4.00
O82 A15 30f olive green 3.00 .20
O83 A15 40f dark violet 4.00 .20

Overprinted Type "p"

O84 A16 50f deep brown .60 .50
O85 A16 75f ultramarine 4.25 .55
O86 A16 100f deep green 1.25 .70
O87 A16 200f dark red 3.00 1.60

Overprinted Type "p" Vertically Reading Up

O88 A17 ½d gray blue 8.50 *12.00*
O89 A17 1d claret 32.50 *37.50*
Nos. O72-O89 (18) 85.00 60.00

Catalogue values for unused stamps in this section, from this point to the end of the section, are for Never Hinged items.

Stamps of 1941-42 Overprinted in Black or Red:

r

s

Perf. 11½x13½, 13 to 14 and Compound

1941-42

O90 A18(r) 1f dk vio ('42) .20 .20
O91 A18(r) 2f choc ('42) .20 .20
O92 A19(r) 3f brt grn ('42) .20 .20
O93 A19(r) 4f pur (R) ('42) .20 .20
O94 A19(r) 5f dk car rose ('42) .20 .20
O95 A20(s) 8f carmine .50 .20
O96 A20(s) 8f ocher ('42) .20 .20
O97 A20(s) 10f ocher 2.00 .20
O98 A20(s) 10f car ('42) .20 .20
O99 A20(s) 15f dull blue 5.50 .35
O100 A20(s) 15f blk (R) ('42) .20 .20
O101 A20(s) 20f black (R) 1.00 .20
O102 A20(s) 20f dl bl ('42) .40 .20
O103 A21(s) 25f dark vio 1.50 .20
O104 A21(r) 25f dk vio ('42) .30 .20
O105 A21(s) 30f dp orange 1.10 .20
O106 A21(r) 30f dk org ('42) .25 .20
O107 A21(s) 40f brown org 1.10 .25
O108 A21(r) 40f chnt ('42) .50 .25
O109 A21(r) 50f ultra 1.00 .20
O110 A21(r) 75f rose vio .40 .30
O111 A22(s) 100f ol grn ('42) .60 .40
O112 A22(s) 200f dp org ('42) 1.60 1.60
O113 A23(r) ½d blue ('42) 8.00 5.00
O114 A23(r) 1d grnsh bl ('42) 13.00 10.00
Nos. O90-O114 (25) 40.35 21.55

The space between the English and Arabic on overprints "r" and "s" varies with the size of the stamps.

For overprints see Nos. O165, RA5.

Stamps of 1942 Overprinted in Black

1942 Unwmk. *Perf. 13x13½*

O115 A24 1f violet & brown .20 .20
O116 A24 2f dark blue & brn .20 .20
O117 A24 3f lt green & brn .20 .20
O118 A24 4f dl brown & brn .20 .20
O119 A24 5f sage green & brn .20 .20
O120 A24 6f red orange & brn .20 .20
O121 A24 10f dl rose red & brn .20 .20
O122 A24 12f yel green & brn .20 .20
Nos. O115-O122 (8) 1.60 1.60

Stamps of 1948 Overprinted in Black

1948, Jan. 15 *Perf. 11½x12*

Size: 17¾x20½mm

O123 A25 1f slate .20 .20
O124 A25 2f sepia .20 .20
O125 A25 3f emerald .20 .20
O126 A25 4f purple .20 .20
O127 A25 5f rose lake .20 .20
O128 A25 6f plum .20 .20
O129 A25 8f ocher .20 .20
O130 A25 10f rose red .20 .20
O131 A25 12f dark olive .20 .20
O132 A25 15f black .25 .75
O133 A25 20f blue .20 .20
O134 A25 25f rose violet .20 .20
O135 A25 30f red orange .20 .20
O136 A25 40f orange brn .25 .20

Perf. 12x11½

Size: 22x27½mm

O137 A25 60f deep blue .35 .25
O138 A25 75f lilac rose .40 .40
O139 A25 100f olive grn .55 .35
O140 A25 200f dp orange 1.10 1.00
O141 A25 ½d blue 5.00 2.75
O142 A25 1d green 10.00 5.50
Nos. O123-O142 (20) 20.30 13.60

For overprints see Nos. O166-O177, O257, O272, O274, O277, O282, RA1, RA3, RA4.

Same Overprint on Nos. 133-138

1949-51 *Perf. 11½x12*

Size: 17¾x20½mm

O143 A25 3f rose lake ('51) .80 .35
O144 A25 5f emerald ('51) .80 .35
O145 A25 14f dk olive ('50) .80 .20
O146 A25 16f rose red ('51) .80 .35
O147 A25 28f blue ('51) .80 .25

Perf. 12x11½

Size: 22x27½mm

O148 A25 50f deep blue 1.25 .50
Nos. O143-O148 (6) 5.25 2.00

For overprints see #O258, O273, O275, O276.

Same Overprint in Black on Stamps and Type of 1954-57

1955-59 *Perf. 11½x12*

O148A A28 1f blue ('56) .20 .20
O149 A28 2f chocolate .20 .20
O150 A28 3f rose lake .20 .20
O151 A28 4f violet .20 .20
O152 A28 5f emerald .20 .20
O153 A28 6f plum ('56) .20 .20
O154 A28 8f ocher ('56) .20 .20
O155 A28 10f blue .20 .20
O155A A28 16f brt rose ('57) 12.50 11.00
O156 A28 20f olive .20 .20
O157 A28 25f rose violet .80 .50
O158 A28 30f vermilion .20 .20
O159 A28 40f orange brn .30 .20

Size: 22½x27½mm

O160 A28 50f blue 2.00 .30
O161 A28 60f pale purple 7.00 3.00
O161A A28 100f ol grn ('59) 15.00 3.00
Nos. O148A-O161A (16) 39.60 20.00

Dates of issue for Nos. O155A and O161A are suppositional.

For overprints see Nos. O178-O191, O259-O260, O283-O291.

Same Ovpt. on Stamps of 1957-58

O162 A33 1f blue 2.50 .60
O162A A33 2f chocolate 3.00 1.00
O162B A33 3f dk carmine 3.75 1.50
O162C A33 4f dull violet 4.50 .80
O162D A33 5f emerald 2.50 .80
O163 A33 6f plum 2.50 .80
O164 A33 10f blue 2.50 .80
Nos. O162-O164 (7) 21.25 6.30

For overprints see #O192-O199, O292-O293.

Republic

Official Stamps of 1942-51 with Additional Overprint

Perf. 13½x14

1958-59 Engr. Unwmk.

O165 A22 200f dp orange 3.25 2.50

Perf. 11½x12, 12x11½

O166 A25 12f dk olive .60 .45
O167 A25 14f olive .60 .50
O168 A25 15f black .35 .25
O169 A25 16f rose red 1.40 1.40
O170 A25 25f rose vio 2.00 1.25
O171 A25 28f blue 1.00 1.00
O172 A25 40f orange brn .60 .50
O173 A25 60f deep blue 1.50 1.40
O174 A25 75f lilac rose 1.25 1.00
O175 A25 200f dp orange 1.50 1.50
O176 A25 ½d blue 10.00 3.50
O177 A25 1d green 16.00 7.25
Nos. O166-O177 (12) 36.80 20.00

Other denominations of types A22 and A25 exist with this overprint, but these were probably not regularly issued.

Same Ovpt. on Nos. O148A-O161A

O178 A28 1f blue .20 .20
O179 A28 2f chocolate .20 .20
O180 A28 3f rose lake .20 .20
O181 A28 4f violet .20 .20
O181A A28 5f emerald .40 .20
O182 A28 6f plum .20 .20
O183 A28 8f ocher .30 .20
O183A A28 10f blue .80 .25
O184 A28 16f bright rose 3.25 2.00
O185 A28 20f olive .30 .20
O186 A28 25f rose violet .30 .20
O187 A28 30f vermilion .40 .20
O188 A28 40f orange brn .50 .25
O189 A28 50f blue .60 .45
O190 A28 60f pale purple .75 .55
O191 A28 100f olive grn .80 .50
Nos. O178-O191 (16) 9.40 6.00

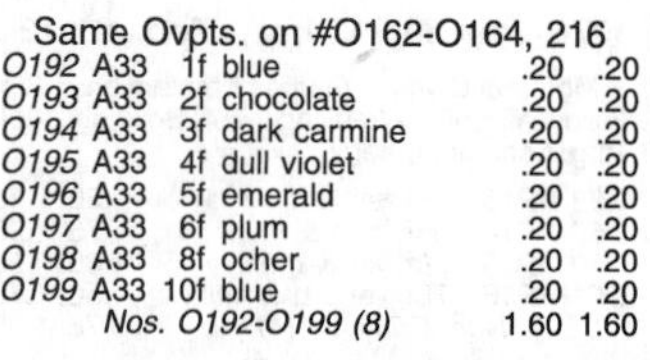

Same Ovpts. on #O162-O164, 216

O192 A33 1f blue .20 .20
O193 A33 2f chocolate .20 .20
O194 A33 3f dark carmine .20 .20
O195 A33 4f dull violet .20 .20
O196 A33 5f emerald .20 .20
O197 A33 6f plum .20 .20
O198 A33 8f ocher .20 .20
O199 A33 10f blue .20 .20
Nos. O192-O199 (8) 1.60 1.60

Nos. 232-233, 235-237, 242 Overprinted

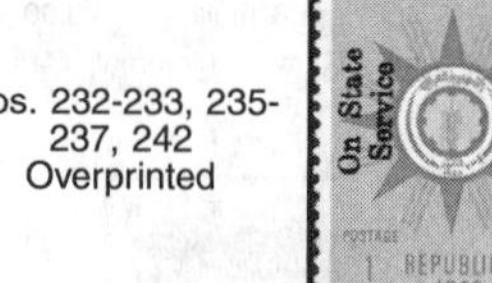

Litho. & Photo.

1961, Apr. 1 Unwmk. *Perf. 11½*

O200 A38 1f multi .20 .20
O201 A38 2f multi .20 .20
O202 A38 4f multi .20 .20
O203 A38 5f multi .25 .20
O204 A38 10f multi .45 .35
O205 A38 50f multi 5.00 2.00
Nos. O200-O205 (6) 6.30 3.15

Nos. 232-247 Overprinted

1961

Emblem in Gold, Red and Blue; Blue Inscriptions

O206 A38 1f gray .20 .20
O207 A38 2f salmon .20 .20
O208 A38 3f pale violet .20 .20
O209 A38 4f bright yel .20 .20
O210 A38 5f light blue .20 .20
O211 A38 10f bright pink .20 .20
O212 A38 15f lt green .20 .20
O213 A38 20f bister brn .20 .20
O214 A38 30f light gray .25 .20
O215 A38 40f orange yel .25 .20
O216 A38 50f yel green .30 .20
O217 A38 75f pale green .45 .25
O218 A38 100f orange .55 .40
O219 A38 200f lilac 1.10 .55
O220 A38 500f bister 7.50 3.75
O221 A38 1d brt green 15.00 7.50
Nos. O206-O221 (16) 27.00 14.65

Nos. 480-482 Overprinted

1971 Litho. *Perf. 13½*

O222 A115 10f multicolored .50 1.00
O223 A115 15f blue & multi 5.00 1.00
O224 A115 25f multicolored 5.00 2.00
Nos. O222-O224 (3) 10.50 4.00

Overprint lines are spaced 16mm on No. O222, 32½mm on Nos. O223-O224.

Same Overprint on Nos. 453, 455-456

1971 *Perf. 13*

O225 A107 5f lilac & multi 4.75 .20
O226 A107 15f rose red & multi 4.75 .35
O227 A107 25f vio bl & multi 7.50 1.00
Nos. O225-O227 (3) 17.00 1.55

Overprint horizontal on Nos. O225 and O227; vertical, reading down on No. O226. Distance between English and Arabic words: 8mm.

Nos. 446, 448-449 Overprinted

1971 Litho. *Perf. 13*

O228 A105 15f multicolored 1.00 .50
O229 A105 15f multicolored 45.00 5.00
O230 A105 25f multicolored 8.00 2.00
O231 A105 30f multicolored 8.00 2.00
Nos. O228-O231 (4) 62.00 9.50

No. O229 overprinted "Official" horizontally.

Same Overprint on Nos. 483-486

1972 *Perf. 13½*

O232 A116 10f multicolored 1.90 .50
O233 A116 25f multicolored 4.00 1.00

1972

O234 A117 15f multicolored 2.50 .50
O235 A117 25f multicolored 4.00 1.00

Same Overprint, "Official" Reading Down on Nos. 562-565

1972

O240 A142 5f multicolored .50 .25
O241 A142 10f multicolored 1.75 .50
O242 A142 15f multicolored 4.50 .50
O243 A142 35f multicolored 5.25 1.00
Nos. O240-O243 (4) 12.00 2.25

Latin inscription on Nos. O240-O241 obliterated with heavy bar.

No. 487 Overprinted "Official" like No. CO5

1972 Photo. *Perf. 13½*

O244 A118 25f multicolored .20 .20

#O134, O148 Ovptd. with 3 Bars

Perf. 11½x12, 12x11½

1973, Jan. 29 Engr.

O257 A25 25f rose violet 4.00 1.00
O258 A25 50f deep blue 4.00 3.50

Same on Nos. O157 and O160

O259 A28 25f rose violet 4.00 1.00
O260 A28 50f blue 4.00 3.50

Type of 1957 Overprinted

Size: 22x27½mm

O261 A33 50f rose violet 4.00 3.50
Nos. O257-O261 (5) 20.00 12.50

See note after No. 679. No. O261 not issued without overprints.

King Faisal Issues Overprinted

Two sizes of overprint: Arabic 6½mm or 9mm.

1973

O263 A28 15f black (#149) 4.00 1.00
O264 A33 15f black 4.00 1.00
O265 A25 25f rose vio (#121) 10.00 10.00
O266 A28 25f rose vio (#151) 4.00 1.00
O267 A33 25f rose violet 4.00 1.00

Same Overprint on Nos. 674-677

O268 A28 10f blue 2.50 2.00
O269 A33 10f blue 20.00 15.00
O270 A28 15f black 20.00 15.00
O271 A33 15f black 2.50 2.00
Nos. O263-O271 (9) 71.00 48.00

Official Stamps of 1948-51 Overprinted

Overprint design faces left or right.

1973

O272	A25	12f (#O131)	1.00	.20
O273	A25	14f (#O145)	1.00	.30
O274	A25	15f (#O132)	1.00	.30
O275	A25	16f (#O146)	2.00	.50
O276	A25	28f (#O147)	4.00	.75
O277	A25	30f (#O135)	4.00	.55
O278	A25	40f (#O136)	4.00	.90
O279	A25	60f (#O137)	4.00	3.00
O280	A25	100f (#O139)	13.00	5.00
O281	A25	½d (#O141)	32.50	13.00
O282	A25	1d (#O142)	67.50	67.50
		Nos. O272-O282 (11)	134.00	92.00

Same Overprint on Official Stamps of 1955-59

O283	A28	3f (#O150)	1.00	.35
O284	A28	6f (#O153)	1.00	.35
O285	A28	8f (#O154)	1.00	.35
O286	A28	16f (#O155A)	*10.00*	*10.00*
O287	A28	20f (#O156)	1.00	.35
O288	A28	30f (#O158)	1.00	.60
O289	A28	40f (#O159)	1.00	1.00
O290	A28	60f (#O161)	8.75	2.00
O291	A28	100f (#O161A)	*17.50*	*5.00*
		Nos. O283-O291 (9)	*42.25*	*20.00*

Same Overprint on 1957-58 Issues

O292	A33	3f dk car (#O162B)	3.00	.75
O293	A33	6f plum (#O163)	3.00	.75
O294	A33	8f ocher (#179)	3.00	.75
O295	A33	30f red orange	3.00	.75
		Nos. O292-O295 (4)	12.00	3.00

The overprint on Nos. O294-O295 includes the "On State Service" overprint; No. O295 was not issued without overprints. The overprint leaf design faces left or right and varies in size.

Nos. 403, 497, 681 Overprinted

Perf. 12½, 13x12½, 13½

1974 (?) **Photo., Litho.**

O296	A89	2f multicolored	1.00	
O297	A123	15f multicolored	1.00	.50
O298	A185	25f multicolored	3.00	1.00
		Nos. O296-O298 (3)	5.00	

Size of "Official" on Nos. O297-O298 9mm.

Nos. 683-691 Overprinted

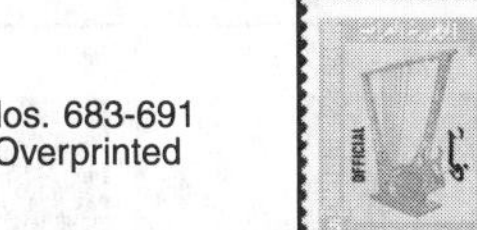

1974 **Litho.** ***Perf. 13x12½***

O299	A186	5f orange & blk	.20	.20
O300	A186	10f bister & blk	.20	.20
O301	A186	20f brt rose & blk	.35	.20
O302	A186	25f ultra & blk	.75	.75
O303	A186	35f emerald & blk	.75	.30
O304	A186	45f blue & black	.75	.35
O305	A186	50f olive & yel	1.00	.40
O306	A186	70f violet & yel	1.00	.55
O307	A186	95f brown & yel	1.50	.75
		Nos. O299-O307 (9)	6.50	3.70

Nos. 455 and 467 Overprinted

1975 **Litho.** ***Perf. 13, 14***

O308	A107	15f multicolored	1.00	.35
O311	A110	30f multicolored	4.00	.60

Space between Arabic and English lines of overprint is 4mm on No. O308, 13mm on No. O311.

Nos. 491-493 Overprinted or Surcharged like Nos. CO5-CO7

1975 ***Perf. 14***

O312	A121	10f multicolored	1.50	.70
O312A	A121	15f on 3f multi	6.00	1.00
O313	A121	25f on 2f multi	5.00	1.00
		Nos. O312-O313 (3)	12.50	2.70

Nos. 322-325 Overprinted

Engr.; Engr. & Photo.

1975 ***Perf. 12x11***

O314	A57	10f rose red	8.00	.60
O315	A57	15f brown & buff	8.00	.75
O316	A57	20f violet blue	8.00	.75
O317	A57	30f orange	15.00	.80
		Nos. O314-O317 (4)	39.00	2.90

Arms of Iraq — O1

Altharthar - Euphrates Canal — O2

1975 **Photo.** ***Perf. 14***

O318	O1	5f multicolored	.20	.20
O319	O1	10f blue & multi	.20	.20
O320	O1	15f yel & multi	.25	.25
O321	O1	20f ultra & multi	.35	.35
O322	O1	25f org & multi	.50	.50
O323	O1	30f rose & multi	.60	.60
O324	O1	50f multicolored	1.00	1.00
O325	O1	100f multicolored	2.00	2.00
		Nos. O318-O325 (8)	5.10	5.10

Nos. 787-791 Overprinted "OFFICIAL" in English and Arabic

1976, Sept. 15 **Litho.** ***Perf. 13½x14***

O327	A219	5f multicolored	.35	.25
O328	A219	10f multicolored	.35	.30
O329	A219	15f multicolored	1.00	.35
O330	A219	25f multicolored	1.50	.75
O331	A219	50f multicolored	3.00	1.50
		Nos. O327-O331 (5)	6.20	3.15

1978 **Photo.** ***Perf. 11½***

O332	O2	5f multicolored	.20	.20
O333	O2	10f multicolored	.20	.20
O334	O2	15f multicolored	.25	.20
O335	O2	25f multicolored	.50	.20
		Nos. O332-O335 (4)	1.15	.80

Baghdad University Entrance — O3

1981, Oct. 21 **Litho.** ***Perf. 12x12½***

O336	O3	45f multicolored	.35	.25
O337	O3	50f multicolored	.40	.30

Nos. O336-O337 Surcharged

1983, May 15 **Litho.** ***Perf. 12x12½***

O338	O3	60f on 45f multi	.50	.30
O339	O3	70f on 50f multi	.60	.45

Martyrs Type of 1981

1981 **Photo.** ***Perf. 14***

O339A	A303	45f silver border	.35	.25
O339B	A303	50f gold border	.40	.30
O339C	A303	120f metallic bl border	1.00	.65
		Nos. O339A-O339C (3)	1.75	1.20

Building Type of 1983

1982, Dec. 31 **Litho.** ***Perf. 14***

O340	A324	60f multicolored	.50	.30
O341	A324	70f multicolored	.55	.40

For surcharge see No. 1517.

Martyr Type of 1984

1984, Dec. 1 ***Perf. 13½***

O342	A329	20f multicolored	.20	.20
O343	A329	30f multicolored	.20	.20
O344	A329	50f multicolored	.30	.25
O345	A329	60f multicolored	.40	.25
		Nos. O342-O345 (4)	1.10	.90

No. RA22 Overprinted

1985 (?) **Litho.** ***Perf. 13x12½***

O346	PT2	5f bister, blk & yel	.30	.30

POSTAL TAX STAMPS

Catalogue values for unused stamps in this section are for Never Hinged items.

Nos. O125 and 115 Surcharged in Carmine or Black

مالية
فلسان
انقاذ فلسطين

1949 **Unwmk.** ***Perf. 11½x12***

RA1	A25	2f on 3f emer (C)	*15.00*	*7.50*
RA2	A25	2f on 6f plum	*27.50*	*7.00*

Similar Overprint in Carmine or Black on Nos. O124, O127 and O94 Middle Arabic Line Omitted

Perf. 11½x12

RA3	A25	2f sepia (C)	*15.00*	*3.00*
RA4	A25	5f rose lake	*30.00*	*10.00*

Perf. 12x13½, 14

RA5	A19	5f dark car rose	*20.00*	*4.00*

Larger overprint on #RA5, 20½mm wide.

No. 115 Surcharged in Black

Perf. 11½x12

RA6	A25	5f on 6f plum	*27.50*	*10.50*

The tax on Nos. RA1-RA6 was to aid the war in Palestine.

Nos. 317, 322-326 Surcharged

Engr.; Engr. & Photo.

1963 ***Perf. 12x11***

RA7	A57	5f on 1f green	.60	.60
RA8	A57	5f on 10f rose red	.60	.60
RA9	A57	5f on 15f brn & buff	.60	.60
RA10	A57	5f on 20f vio blue	.60	.60
RA11	A57	5f on 30f orange	.60	.60
RA12	A57	5f on 40f brt green	.60	.60
		Nos. RA7-RA12 (6)	3.60	3.60

Surtax was for the Defense Fund.

PT1

b

1967, Aug. **Photo.** ***Perf. 13½***

RA13	PT1	5f brown	.35	.20

Surtax was for flood victims.

Same Overprinted "b"

1967, Nov.

RA14	PT1	5f brown	.35	.35

Surtax was for Defense Fund.

Nos. 305A-305B with Surcharge Similar to Nos. RA7-RA12

1972 **Litho.** ***Perf. 13½x14***

RA15	A54a	5f on 14f	4.00	3.75
RA16	A54a	5f on 35f	4.00	3.75

Surtax was for the Defense Fund. The 2 disks obliterating old denominations are on one line at the bottom. Size of Arabic inscription: 17x12mm.

No. 452 with Surcharge Similar to Nos. RA7-RA12, and Nos. 443, 457 and 526 Surcharged:

1973 **Litho.** ***Perf. 13***

RA17	A105	5f on 2f multi	5.75	.40
RA18	A107	5f on 2f multi	5.75	.40
RA19	A108	5f on 2f multi	5.75	.40
RA20	A135	5f on 2f multi	5.75	.40
		Nos. RA17-RA20 (4)	23.00	1.60

Surtax was for the Defense Fund. Surcharges on Nos. RA17-RA20 are adjusted to fit shape of stamps and to obliterate old denominations.

No 683 Overprinted

1974 **Litho.** ***Perf. 13x12½***

RA21	A186	5f orange & blk	2.50	2.50

Soldier PT2

Dome of the Rock, Jerusalem PT3

1974

RA22	PT2	5f bister, blk & yel	.50	.30

Surtax of Nos. RA21-RA22 was for the Defense Fund.

For overprint see No. O346.

1977 **Photo.** ***Perf. 14***

RA23	PT3	5f multicolored	2.00	.20

Surtax was for families of Palestinians.

For surcharges see Nos. 1457, 1465-1477.

AIR POST POSTAL TAX STAMPS

Catalogue values for unused stamps in this section are for Never Hinged items.

#C15 Surcharged Like #RA17-RA20

1973 **Litho.** ***Perf. 13½***

RAC1	AP5	5f on 2f multi	5.00	5.00

Surtax was for the Defense Fund.

IRELAND

'īr-lənd

(Eire)

LOCATION — Comprises the entire island of Ireland, except 5,237 square miles at the extreme north
GOVT. — Republic
AREA — 27,136 sq. mi.
POP. — 3,626,087 (1996)
CAPITAL — Dublin

12 Pence = 1 Shilling
100 Pence = 1 Pound (Punt) (1971)
100 Cents = 1 Euro (2002)

Catalogue values for unused stamps in this country are for Never Hinged items, beginning with Scott 99 in the regular postage section, Scott C1 in the air post section, and Scott J5 in the postage due section.

Watermarks

Wmk. 44- SE in Monogram

The letters "SE" are the initials of "Saorstat Eireann" (Irish Free State).

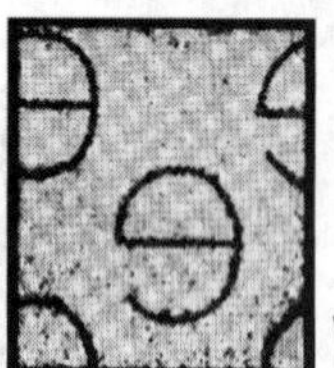

Wmk. 262- Multiple "e"

Overprinted by Dollard, Ltd.

Great Britain Nos. 159-167, 170-172, 179-181 Overprinted

Overprint measures 15x17½mm

This overprint means "Provisional Government of Ireland."

Black or Gray Black Overprint

1922, Feb. 17 Wmk. 33 ***Perf. 15x14***

1	A82 ½p green	.90	.30
	Never hinged	1.10	
a.	Inverted overprint	350.00	550.00
2	A83 1p scarlet	1.25	.30
	Never hinged	1.50	
a.	Inverted overprint	225.00	300.00
b.	Double overprint		—
3	A86 2½p ultra	1.75	4.00
	Never hinged	3.00	
4	A87 3p violet	3.75	3.00
	Never hinged	10.00	
5	A88 4p slate green	3.50	8.00
	Never hinged	7.75	
6	A89 5p yel brown	3.75	6.75
	Never hinged	9.50	
7	A90 9p black brown	9.50	17.00
	Never hinged	30.00	
8	A90 10p light blue	7.50	35.00
	Never hinged	20.00	
	Nos. 1-8 (8)	31.90	74.35

The ½p with red overprint is a proof.

Red or Carmine Overprint

1922, Apr.-July

9	A86 2½p ultra	1.50	3.00
	Never hinged	2.75	
10	A88 4p slate green (R)	9.50	15.00
	Never hinged	18.00	
10A	A88 4p slate green (C)	45.00	65.00
	Never hinged	70.00	
11	A90 9p black brown	16.00	17.00
	Never hinged	35.00	
	Nos. 9-11 (4)	72.00	100.00

Overprinted in Black

Overprint measures 21½x14mm

There is a variation that is 21x14mm. The "h" and "é" are 1mm apart. See Nos. 36-38.

1922, Feb. 17 Wmk. 34 ***Perf. 11x12***

12	A91 2sh6p brown	35.00	60.00
	Never hinged	65.00	
13	A91 5sh car rose	60.00	110.00
	Never hinged	125.00	
14	A91 10sh gray blue	125.00	225.00
	Never hinged	250.00	
	Nos. 12-14 (3)	220.00	395.00

Overprinted by Alex. Thom & Co.

Overprinted in Black

Overprint measures 14½x16mm

TWO PENCE

Die I - Four horizontal lines above the head. Heavy colored lines above and below the bottom tablet. The inner frame line is closer to the central design than it is to the outer frame line.

Die II - Three lines above the head. Thinner lines above and below the bottom tablet. The inner frame line is midway between the central design and the outer frame line.

1922, Feb. 17 Wmk. 33 ***Perf. 15x14***

15	A84 1½p red brown	1.00	1.00
	Never hinged	2.75	
a.	"PENCF"	350.00	250.00
16	A85 2p orange (II)	2.25	.50
	Never hinged	3.75	
a.	Inverted overprint (II)	275.00	400.00
b.	2p orange (I)	2.25	.90
	As "b," never hinged	3.75	
c.	Inverted overprint (I)	175.00	225.00
17	A89 6p red violet	8.75	14.00
	Never hinged	19.00	
18	A90 1sh bister	14.00	8.50
	Never hinged	27.50	
	Nos. 15-18 (4)	26.00	24.00

Important: see Nos. 25-26, 31, 35.

Overprinted by Harrison & Sons

Coil Stamps

Overprinted in Black in Glossy Black Ink

Overprint measures 15¼x17mm

1922, June

19	A82 ½p green	2.50	11.00
	Never hinged	4.50	
20	A83 1p scarlet	2.50	6.50
	Never hinged	3.50	
21	A84 1½p red brown	5.50	35.00
	Never hinged	8.00	
22	A85 2p orange (I)	15.00	30.00
	Never hinged	26.00	
a.	2p orange (II)	18.00	30.00
	Never hinged	30.00	
	Nos. 19-22 (4)	25.50	82.50

In Harrison overprint, "i" of "Rialtas" extends below the base of the other letters.

The Harrison stamps were issued in coils, either horizontal or vertical. The paper is double where the ends of the strips were overlapped. Mint pairs with the overlap sell for about three times the price of a single. The perforations are often clipped.

Overprinted by Alex. Thom & Co.

Stamps of Great Britain, 1912-22 Overprinted as Nos. 15 to 18, in Shiny to Dull Blue Black, or Red

Overprint measures 14½x16mm

Note: The blue black overprints can best be distinguished from the black by use of 50-power magnification with a light source behind the stamp.

1922, July-Nov. ***Perf. 15x14***

23	A82 ½p green	2.40	.70
	Never hinged	3.00	
24	A83 1p scarlet	1.60	.45
	Never hinged	2.25	
25	A84 1½p red brown	4.50	3.00
	Never hinged	8.75	
26	A85 2p orange (II)	2.75	.45
	Never hinged	4.50	
a.	Inverted overprint (II)	275.00	500.00
b.	2p orange (I)	18.00	1.75
	Never hinged	32.50	
27	A86 2½p ultra (R)	6.25	17.50
	Never hinged	11.50	
28	A87 3p violet	3.00	1.90
	Never hinged	4.25	
29	A88 4p slate green (R)	3.50	4.75
	Never hinged	5.50	
30	A89 5p yellow brown	4.50	8.25
	Never hinged	11.00	
31	A89 6p red violet	8.25	3.00
	Never hinged	12.00	
32	A90 9p blk brn (R)	12.50	15.00
	Never hinged	25.00	
33	A90 9p ol grn (R)	5.50	32.50
	Never hinged	11.00	
34	A90 10p light blue	27.50	50.00
	Never hinged	42.50	
35	A90 1sh bister	9.50	11.00
	Never hinged	24.00	
	Nos. 23-35 (13)	91.75	148.50

Nos. 23, 24, 28, 34 overprinted in black were not generally issued and may be proofs.

Overprinted as Nos. 12 to 14 in Blue Black (Shiny to Dull)

Overprint measures 21x13½mm

The "h" and "é" are ½mm apart.

1922 Wmk. 34 ***Perf. 11x12***

36	A91 2sh6p gray brown	200.	310.
	Never hinged	325.	
37	A91 5sh car rose	225.	350.
	Never hinged	350.	
38	A91 10sh gray blue	925.	1,250.
	Never hinged	1,650.	
	Nos. 36-38 (3)	1,350.	1,910.

Overprinted in Blue Black

Overprint measures 15¾x16mm

1922, Dec. Wmk. 33 ***Perf. 15x14***

39	A82 ½p green	.50	1.50
	Never hinged	1.75	
40	A83 1p scarlet	2.75	2.00
	Never hinged	5.00	
41	A84 1½p red brown	2.25	8.00
	Never hinged	5.00	
42	A85 2p orange (II)	9.50	6.00
	Never hinged	14.00	
43	A90 1sh bister	27.50	42.50
	Never hinged	42.50	
	Nos. 39-43 (5)	42.50	60.00

Stamps of Great Britain, 1912-22, Overprinted in Shiny to Dull Blue Black or Red

This overprint means "Irish Free State"

Overprint measures 15x8½mm

"1922" is 6¼mm long

The inner loop of the "9" is an upright oval.

The measurement of "1922" is made across the bottom of the numerals and does not include the serif at the top of the "1."

There were 5 plates for printing the overprint on Nos. 44-55. In the impressions from plate I the 12th stamp in the 15th row has no accent on the 2nd "A" of "SAORSTAT." To correct this an accent was inserted by hand, sometimes this was in a reversed position.

On Nos. 56-58 the accent was omitted on the 2nd stamp in the 3rd and 8th rows. Damage to the plate makes the accent look reversed on the 4th stamp in the 7th row. The top of the "t" slants down in a line with the so-called accent.

1922-23 Wmk. 33 ***Perf. 15x14***

44	A82 ½p green	.75	.30
	Never hinged	1.00	
a.	Accent omitted	950.00	800.00
b.	Accent added	85.00	95.00
45	A83 1p scarlet	.75	.40
	Never hinged	1.00	
a.	Accent omitted	7,000.	5,000.
b.	Accent added	125.00	150.00
c.	Accent and final "t" omitted	6,000.	4,250.
d.	Accent and final "t" added	200.00	225.00
46	A84 1½p red brown	2.50	8.00
	Never hinged	5.25	
47	A85 2p orange (II)	1.50	.90
	Never hinged	4.00	
48	A86 2½p ultra (R)	2.50	7.50
	Never hinged	4.75	
a.	Accent omitted	125.00	150.00
49	A87 3p violet	6.00	10.00
	Never hinged	13.50	
a.	Accent omitted	225.00	250.00
50	A88 4p sl green (R)	2.75	6.00
	Never hinged	5.50	
a.	Accent omitted	140.00	160.00
51	A89 5p yel brown	3.00	4.50
	Never hinged	5.25	
52	A89 6p dull violet	2.50	1.90
	Never hinged	4.75	
a.	Accent added	700.00	700.00
53	A90 9p ol green (R)	3.25	5.00
	Never hinged	7.50	
a.	Accent omitted	225.00	290.00
54	A90 10p lt blue	15.00	50.00
	Never hinged	32.50	
55	A90 1sh bister	9.00	10.00
	Never hinged	24.00	
a.	Accent omitted	5,500.	6,500.
b.	Accent added	600.00	650.00

Perf. 11x12

Wmk. 34

56	A91 2sh6p lt brown	32.50	52.50
	Never hinged	70.00	
a.	Accent omitted	325.00	375.00
57	A91 5sh car rose	60.00	110.00
	Never hinged	125.00	
a.	Accent omitted	425.00	475.00
58	A91 10sh gray blue	140.00	250.00
	Never hinged	350.00	
a.	Accent omitted	2,000.	2,500.
	Nos. 44-58 (15)	282.00	517.00

Overprinted by Harrison & Sons

Coil Stamps

Same Ovpt. in Black or Blue Black

1923 Wmk. 33 ***Perf. 15x14***

59	A82 ½p green	1.50	8.50
	Never hinged	3.00	
a.	Tall "1"	7.50	45.00
	Never hinged	15.00	
60	A83 1p scarlet	3.50	8.50
	Never hinged	7.50	
a.	Tall "1"	35.00	140.00
	Never hinged	80.00	
61	A84 1½p red brown	5.25	35.00
	Never hinged	8.25	
a.	Tall "1"	80.00	200.00
	Never hinged	125.00	
62	A85 2p orange (II)	5.75	8.00
	Never hinged	9.00	
a.	Tall "1"	10.00	45.00
	Never hinged	20.00	
	Nos. 59-62 (4)	16.00	60.00

These stamps were issued in coils, made by joining horizontal or vertical strips of the stamps. See 2nd paragraph after #22. In some strips there were two stamps with the "1" of "1922" 2½mm high and with serif at foot.

In this setting the middle "e" of "eireann" is a trifle above the line of the other letters, making the word appear slightly curved. The lower end of the "1" of "1922" is rounded on #59-62 instead of flat as on #44-47.

The inner loop of the "9" is round.

See Nos. 77b, 78b and 79b.

Booklet Panes

For very fine the perforation holes at top or bottom of the pane should be visible, though not necessarily perfect half circles.

"Sword of Light" — A1

Map of Ireland — A2

Coat of Arms — A3

Celtic Cross — A4

Perf. 15x14

1922-23 Typo. Wmk. 44

65	A1 ½p emerald	.70	.90
	Never hinged	.85	
a.	Booklet pane of 6	300.00	
66	A2 1p car rose	.70	.20
	Never hinged	1.25	
a.	Booklet pane of 6	350.00	
b.	Booklet pane of 3 + 3 labels	250.00	
67	A2 1½p claret	1.50	2.25
	Never hinged	5.00	
68	A2 2p deep green	1.50	.20
	Never hinged	1.00	
a.	Booklet pane of 6	275.00	
b.	Perf. 15 horiz. ('35)	12,500.	1,500.

No. 68b is valued in the grade of fine.

69 A3 2½p chocolate 4.00 4.00
Never hinged 6.00
70 A4 3p ultra 1.90 .75
Never hinged 5.25
71 A3 4p slate 1.90 3.25
Never hinged 7.00
72 A1 5p deep violet 7.75 9.75
Never hinged 37.50
73 A1 6p red violet 4.25 3.50
Never hinged 8.50
74 A3 9p violet 15.00 8.25
Never hinged 75.00
75 A4 10p brown 8.75 19.00
Never hinged 35.00
76 A1 1sh light blue 17.00 5.50
Never hinged 70.00
Nos. 65-76 (12) 64.95 57.55

The 2p was issued in 1922; other denominations in 1923.

No. 68b is a vertical coil stamp.

See Nos. 87, 91-92, 105-117, 137-138, 225-226, 326. For types overprinted see Nos. 118-119.

Overprinted by the Government Printing Office, Dublin Castle and British Board of Inland Revenue at Somerset House, London

Great Britain Nos. 179-181 Ovptd. in Black or Gray Black

"1922" is 5½mm long

The measurement of "1922" is made across the bottom of the numerals and does not include the serif at the top of the "1."

1925 Wmk. 34 *Perf. 11x12*

77 A91 2sh6p gray brown 35.00 75.00
Never hinged 55.00
78 A91 5sh rose red 47.50 100.00
Never hinged 70.00
79 A91 10sh gray blue 110.00 225.00
Never hinged 225.00
Nos. 77-79 (3) 192.50 400.00

In 1927 the 2sh6p, 5sh and 10sh stamps were overprinted from a plate in which the Thom and Castle clichés were combined, thus including wide and narrow "1922" in the same setting.

Overprinted by British Board of Inland Revenue at Somerset House, London

Pair with "1922" Wide and Narrow

1927

77a A91 2sh6p 250.00
Never hinged 425.00
78a A91 5sh 425.00
Never hinged 725.00
79a A91 10sh 1,200.
Never hinged 1,900.
Nos. 77a-79a (3) 1,875.

Wide "1922"

"1922" is 6¼mm long

1927-28

77b A91 2sh6p 30.00 50.00
Never hinged 65.00
78b A91 5sh ('28) 65.00 87.50
Never hinged 125.00
79b A91 10sh ('28) 175.00 190.00
Never hinged 325.00
Nos. 77b-79b (3) 270.00 327.50

Daniel O'Connell — A5

Perf. 15x14

1929, June 22 Wmk. 44

80 A5 2p dark green .35 .30
Never hinged .50
81 A5 3p dark blue 3.75 8.50
Never hinged 10.00
82 A5 9p dark violet 4.00 8.00
Never hinged 12.50
Nos. 80-82 (3) 8.10 16.80

Catholic Emancipation in Ireland, centenary.

Shannon River Hydroelectric Station — A6

1930, Oct. 15

83 A6 2p black brown .75 .50
Never hinged 2.00

Opening of the hydroelectric development of the River Shannon.

Farmer with Scythe A7

Cross of Cong and Chalice A8

1931, June 12

84 A7 2p pale blue .80 .40
Never hinged 1.40

Bicentenary of Royal Dublin Society.

1932, May 12

85 A8 2p dark green .80 .50
Never hinged 2.25
86 A8 3p bright blue 2.00 4.75
Never hinged 5.75

International Eucharistic Congress.

Coil Stamp

Type of 1922-23 Issue

1933-34 *Perf. 15 Horizontally*

87 A2 1p rose ('34) 22.50 30.00
Never hinged 35.00
a. 1p carmine rose 95.00 175.00
Never hinged 160.00

No. 87a has a single perforation at each side near the top, while No. 87 is perforated top and bottom only.

See No. 68b.

Adoration of the Cross A9

Hurling A10

1933, Sept. 18 *Perf. 15x14*

88 A9 2p slate green .45 .25
Never hinged .75
89 A9 3p deep blue 2.50 2.50
Never hinged 6.25

Holy Year.

1934, July 27

90 A10 2p green .90 .55
Never hinged 1.60

50th anniv. of the Gaelic Athletic Assoc.

Coil Stamps

Types of 1922-23

Wmk. 44 Sideways

1934 *Perf. 14 Vertically*

91 A1 ½p green 30.00 37.50
Never hinged 42.50
92 A2 2p gray green 45.00 70.00
Never hinged 80.00

Overprinted by Harrison & Sons and British Board of Inland Revenue at Somerset House, London

Great Britain Nos. 222-224 Overprinted in Black

1935 Wmk. 44 *Perf. 11x12*

93 A91 2sh6p brown 35.00 35.00
Never hinged 60.00
94 A91 5sh carmine 90.00 100.00
Never hinged 225.00
95 A91 10sh dark blue 350.00 350.00
Never hinged 800.00
Nos. 93-95 (3) 475.00 485.00

Waterlow printing can be distinguished by the crossed lines in the background of portrait. Previous issues have horizontal lines only.

St. Patrick and Paschal Fire — A11

1937, Sept. 8 Wmk. 44 *Perf. 14x15*

96 A11 2sh6p bright green 55.00 55.00
Never hinged 160.00
97 A11 5sh brown violet 80.00 80.00
Never hinged 190.00
98 A11 10sh dark blue 50.00 50.00
Never hinged 160.00
Nos. 96-98 (3) 185.00 185.00

See Nos. 121-123.

Catalogue values for unused stamps in this section, from this point to the end of the section, are for Never Hinged items.

Allegory of Ireland and Constitution A12

1937, Dec. 29 *Perf. 15x14*

99 A12 2p plum 1.25 .25
100 A12 3p deep blue 5.75 3.75

Constitution Day.

See Nos. 169-170.

Father Theobald Mathew A13

1938, July 1

101 A13 2p black brown 1.50 .25
102 A13 3p ultramarine 10.50 6.00

Temperance Crusade by Father Mathew, centenary.

Washington, US Eagle and Harp — A14

1939, Mar. 1

103 A14 2p bright carmine .90 .30
104 A14 3p deep blue 8.50 6.50

US Constitution, 150th anniv.

Coil Stamp

Type of 1922-23

1940-46 Wmk. 262 *Perf. 15 Horiz.*

105 A2 1p car rose ('46) 27.50 15.00
a. Perf. 14 horiz. 50.00 40.00

Types of 1922-23

1940-42 *Perf. 15x14*

Size: 18x22mm

106 A1 ½p emerald ('41) 1.75 .20
a. Booklet pane of 6 350.00
107 A2 1p car rose ('41) .20 .20
a. Booklet pane of 6 5.00
b. Bklt. pane of 3 + 3 labels 1,250.
108 A2 1½p claret ('41) 9.50 .20
a. Booklet pane of 6 140.00
109 A2 2p deep green .25 .20
a. Booklet pane of 6 12.50
110 A3 2½p choc ('41) 6.50 .20
a. Booklet pane of 6 95.00
111 A4 3p dull blue ('41) .30 .20
a. Booklet pane of 6 40.00
112 A3 4p slate .35 .20
a. Booklet pane of 6 65.00
113 A1 5p deep violet .50 .20
114 A1 6p red violet ('42) .60 .20
115 A3 9p violet .70 .20
116 A4 10p olive brown 1.75 .30
117 A1 1sh blue 70.00 21.00
Nos. 106-117 (12) 92.40 23.30

Types of 1922-23 Overprinted in Green or Violet

Overprint reads: "In memory of the Rebellion of 1916."

1941, Apr. 12 *Perf. 15x14*

118 A2 2p yellow orange 2.00 .50
119 A4 3p blue (V) 37.50 17.50

Volunteer Soldier and Dublin Post Office A15

1941, Oct. 27

120 A15 2½p bluish black 1.00 .60

Nos. 118-120 commemorate the 25th anniv. of the Easter Rebellion.

St. Patrick Type of 1937

1943-45 Wmk. 262 *Perf. 14x15*

121 A11 2sh6p bright green 5.00 .65
122 A11 5sh brown violet 8.00 2.25
123 A11 10sh dark blue ('45) 17.00 4.00
Nos. 121-123 (3) 30.00 6.90

Dr. Douglas Hyde A16

Sir Rowan Hamilton A17

1943, July 31 *Perf. 15x14*

124 A16 ½p green .50 .60
125 A16 2½p red lilac 1.25 .50

50th anniv. of the Gaelic League.

1943, Nov. 13 Typo. Wmk. 262

126 A17 ½p deep green .50 .60
127 A17 2½p dk red brown 2.25 .40

Centenary of discovery of the mathematical formula of Quaternions by William Rowan Hamilton.

Brother Michael O'Clery — A18

1944, June 30 *Perf. 14x15*

128 A18 ½p emerald .20 .25
a. Booklet pane of 6 25.00
129 A18 1sh reddish brown .90 .25

300th anniv. of the death of Michael O'Clery, Irish historian.

Edmund Rice — A19

Sower — A20

1944, Aug. 29 *Perf. 15x14*

130 A19 2½p slate .80 .40

Death centenary of Edmund Ignatius Rice, founder of the Christian Brothers of Ireland.

1945, Sept. 15

131 A20 2½p ultramarine 1.50 .20
132 A20 6p red violet 7.25 4.25

Commemorates the work of the Young Irelanders and the death centenary of Thomas Davis, Sept. 16, 1845.

Plowman A21

1946, Sept. 16 **Typo.**

133 A21 2½p red 1.50 .20
134 A21 3p dark blue 4.25 3.50

Birth centenary of Charles Stewart Parnell and Michael Davitt, leaders in the struggle for Irish political independence.

Theobald Wolfe Tone A22

Perf. 15x14

1948, Nov. 19 **Wmk. 262**

135 A22 2½p deep plum 1.50 .20
136 A22 3p deep violet 6.50 4.25

Insurrection of 1798, 150th anniversary.

Types of 1922-23

1949

137 A1 8p bright red .80 .25
138 A4 11p carmine rose 1.60 1.00

Leinster House, Dublin A23

1949, Nov. 21

139 A23 2½p red brown 1.60 .40
140 A23 3p violet blue 7.00 3.50

International recognition of the Republic, Easter Monday, 1949.

James Clarence Mangan A24

Statue of St. Peter A25

1949, Dec. 5

141 A24 1p dark green 3.00 .50

Mangan (1803-1849), poet.

Wmk. 262

1950, Sept. 11 **Engr.** ***Perf. 12½***

142 A25 2½p violet 1.00 .30
143 A25 3p blue 10.00 7.50
144 A25 9p brown 10.00 8.00
Nos. 142-144 (3) 21.00 15.80

Holy Year, 1950.

Thomas Moore — A26

Irish Harp — A27

1952, Nov. 10 ***Perf. 13***

145 A26 2½p deep plum .20 .20
146 A26 3½p dk olive green 3.50 2.75

Death centenary of Thomas Moore (1779-1852), poet.

1953, Feb. 9 **Typo.** ***Perf. 14x15***

147 A27 2½p bright green .75 .20
148 A27 1sh4p bright blue 25.00 24.00

Ireland's National festival "An Tostal."

Robert Emmet — A28

Madonna by della Robbia — A29

1953, Sept. 21 **Engr.** ***Perf. 12½x13***

149 A28 3p deep green 3.25 .25
150 A28 1sh3p carmine rose 47.50 11.50

150th anniv. of the execution of Robert Emmet (1778-1803), Irish nationalist.

1954, May 24 ***Perf. 15***

151 A29 3p blue 1.00 .20
152 A29 5p deep green 8.25 5.00

Marian Year, 1953-54.

John Henry Cardinal Newman A30

Statue of John Barry A31

1954, July 19 **Typo.** ***Perf. 15x14***

153 A30 2p rose lilac 2.50 .20
154 A30 1sh3p blue 17.50 6.00

Opening of the Catholic University of Ireland, centenary.

1956, Sept. 16 **Engr.** ***Perf. 15***

155 A31 3p dull purple .75 .20
156 A31 1sh3p blue 11.00 8.00

John Barry (1745-1803), "Father of the American Navy," on the occasion of the unveiling of a statue in Wexford, Ireland, his birthplace.

Redmond A32

O'Crohan A33

Perf. 14x15

1957, June 11 **Wmk. 262**

157 A32 3p dark blue 1.00 .20
158 A32 1sh3p rose lake 13.00 9.00

Birth cent. of John Edward Redmond (1856-1918), Irish political leader.

1957, July 1

159 A33 2p dull purple 1.50 .20
160 A33 5p violet 5.50 5.00

Birth cent. of Thomas O'Crohan (Tomas O'Criomhthain) (1856-1937), fisherman and author.

Brown A34

Father Luke Wadding A35

1957, Sept. 23 **Typo.** ***Perf. 15x14***

161 A34 3p blue 2.25 .50
162 A34 1sh3p carmine rose 37.50 16.00

Adm. William (Guillermo) Brown (1777-1857), founder of the Argentine Navy.

1957, Nov. 25 **Engr.** ***Perf. 15***

163 A35 3p dark blue 1.50 .50
164 A35 1sh3p deep claret 19.00 7.00

Luke Wadding (1588-1657), Irish Franciscan friar and historian.

Clarke A36

Aikenhead A37

1958, July 28 **Wmk. 262**

165 A36 3p deep green .95 .20
166 A36 1sh3p red brown 13.50 7.50

Thomas J. Clarke (1858-1916), patriot.

1958, Oct. 20 ***Perf. 15x14***

167 A37 3p blue 1.25 .20
168 A37 1sh3p carmine 17.00 8.50

Mother Mary Aikenhead (1787-1858), founder of the Irish Sisters of Charity.

Constitution Type of 1937

1958, Dec. 29 **Typo.** **Wmk. 262**

169 A12 3p brown .55 .20
170 A12 5p bright green 5.00 4.50

21st anniv. of the constitution.

Arthur Guinness — A38

1959, July 20 **Engr.** ***Perf. 15***

171 A38 3p rose lake 2.00 .20
172 A38 1sh3p dark blue 18.00 8.50

Bicentenary of Guinness Brewery.

Flight of the Holy Family A39

1960, June 20 ***Perf. 15***

173 A39 3p rose violet .25 .20
174 A39 1sh3p sepia 1.00 *2.00*

World Refugee Year, 7/1/59-6/30/60.

Europa Issue

Symbolic Wheel CD3

1960, Sept. 19 **Engr.** ***Perf. 15***

175 CD3 6p orange brown 22.50 4.00
176 CD3 1sh3p violet 52.50 25.00

No. 176 has fugitive ink.

De Havilland Dragon, Boeing 707 Jet and Dublin Airport A41

1961, June 26 ***Perf. 15***

177 A41 6p dull blue 1.90 1.90
178 A41 1sh3p green 4.25 4.25

25th anniv. of the founding of Aer Lingus, Irish International Airlines.

St. Patrick — A42

1961, Sept. 25 ***Perf. 14½***

179 A42 3p blue .60 .20
180 A42 8p pale purple 1.90 *4.50*
181 A42 1sh3p green 2.00 1.40
Nos. 179-181 (3) 4.50 6.10

1,500th anniv. of St. Patrick's death.

John O'Donovan and Eugene O'Curry A43

1962, Mar. 26 ***Perf. 15***

182 A43 3p crimson .40 .20
183 A43 1sh3p purple 4.75 3.75

Death centenaries of John O'Donovan (1806-1861) and Eugene O'Curry (1794-1862), Gaelic scholars and translators.

Europa Issue

19 Leaves on Young Tree CD5

1962, Sept. 17 **Engr.** **Wmk. 262**

184 CD5 6p pink & dark red .75 *1.00*
185 CD5 1sh3p bluish grn & dk blue grn 1.50 *1.75*

Wheat Emblem and Globe A45

1963, Mar. 21 **Wmk. 262**

186 A45 4p violet .20 .20
187 A45 1sh3p red 2.00 *2.50*

FAO "Freedom from Hunger" campaign.

Europa Issue

Stylized Links, Symbolizing Unity CD6

1963, Sept. 16 ***Perf. 15***

188 CD6 6p rose carmine 2.25 2.25
189 CD6 1sh3p dark blue 4.50 4.50

Centenary Emblem A47

1963, Dec. 2 **Photo.** ***Perf. 14½x14***

190 A47 4p gray & red .25 .20
191 A47 1sh3p brt green, gray & red 1.25 *1.75*

Centenary of the International Red Cross.

Wolfe Tone
A48

1964, Apr. 13 Engr. *Perf. 15*
192 A48 4p black .70 .20
193 A48 1sh3p dark blue 4.00 3.50

Birth bicentenary of Theobald Wolfe Tone (1763-1798), Irish revolutionist.

Irish
Pavilion
A49

1964, July 20 Photo. *Perf. 14½x14*
194 A49 5p multicolored .75 .20
a. Brown omitted 1,000.
195 A49 1sh5p multicolored 4.25 4.00

New York World's Fair, 1964-65.

Europa Issue

CEPT Daisy (22 Petals) — CD7

Perf. 14x14½
1964, Sept. 14 Litho. Wmk. 262
196 CD7 8p dull grn & ultra 2.50 1.50
197 CD7 1sh5p red brown & org 7.50 5.00

ITU Emblem, Globe and Communication Waves — A51

1965, May 17 Photo. *Perf. 14½x14*
198 A51 3p dp blue & emerald .50 .20
199 A51 8p black & emerald 2.25 2.25

ITU, cent.

William Butler
Yeats — A52

1965, June 14 *Perf. 15*
200 A52 5p orange brn & blk .50 .25
201 A52 1sh5p gray green, brn & black 4.50 3.75

Birth centenary of William Butler Yeats (1865-1939), poet and dramatist.

ICY
Emblem
A53

1965, Aug. 16 Photo. *Perf. 15*
202 A53 3p brt blue & vio bl 2.50 .50
203 A53 10p redsh brn & dk brn 15.00 *5.00*

International Cooperation Year.

Europa Issue

Leaves and
Fruit — CD8

1965, Sept. 27 *Perf. 15*
204 CD8 8p brick red & blk 1.10 1.00
205 CD8 1sh5p lt blue & claret 5.25 4.50

James
Connolly
A55

Designs: No. 207, Thomas J. Clarke. No. 208, Patrick Henry Pearse. No. 209, Symbolic of lives lost in fight for independence, and of Ireland marching into freedom. No. 210, Eamonn Ceannt. No. 211, Sean MacDiarmada. No. 212, Thomas MacDonagh. No. 213, Joseph Plunkett.

1966, Apr. 12 Wmk. 262 *Perf. 15*
206 A55 3p blue & black 1.00 .35
207 A55 3p olive green 1.00 .35
a. Pair, #206-207 3.00 *1.50*
208 A55 5p olive & black 1.10 .35
209 A55 5p brt grn, blk & orange 1.10 .35
a. Pair, #208-209 3.25 *1.75*
210 A55 7p dull org & blk 1.25 *2.50*
211 A55 7p blue grn & blk 1.25 *2.50*
a. Pair, #210-211 3.75 *7.50*
212 A55 1sh5p grnsh bl & blk 1.25 *2.00*
213 A55 1sh5p emerald & blk 1.25 *2.00*
a. Pair, #212-213 4.50 *9.50*
Nos. 206-213 (8) 9.20 10.40

50th anniv. of the Easter Week Rebellion, and to honor the signers of the Proclamation of the Irish Republic.

Roger
Casement
A56

Symbolic
Sailboat
CD9

1966, Aug. 3 *Perf. 15*
214 A56 5p black .20 .20
215 A56 1sh dark red brown .90 .80

50th death anniv. of Roger Casement (1864-1916), British consular agent and Irish rebel who was executed for treason.

Europa Issue

1966, Sept. 26 Photo. *Perf. 15*
216 CD9 7p orange & green 1.25 .40
217 CD9 1sh5p gray & green 3.75 1.60

Ballintubber
Abbey
A58

1966, Nov. 8 *Perf. 15*
218 A58 5p red brown .20 .20
219 A58 1sh black .40 .40

750th anniversary of Ballintubber Abbey.

Cross and Sword Types of 1922

1966-67 Photo. *Perf. 15*
Size: 17x20½mm
225 A4 3p blue ('67) .50 .25
226 A1 5p brt vio, type II ('68) .50 .30
a. Booklet pane of 6, No. 226b 25.00
b. Type I ('66) 4.75 4.75

Type I has irregularly spaced lines in shading behind sword.

Europa Issue

Cogwheels — CD10

1967, May 2
232 CD10 7p green & gold 2.00 .75
233 CD10 1sh5p dk red & gold 5.50 1.50

Maple
Leaves
A60

1967, Aug. 28 Photo.
234 A60 5p multicolored .20 .20
235 A60 1sh5p multicolored .55 *.80*

Centenary of the Canadian Confederation.

Rock of
Cashel
A61

1967, Sept. 25 Wmk. 262 *Perf. 15*
236 A61 7p sepia .20 *.30*
237 A61 10p Prussian blue .50 *.60*

International Tourist Year.

One Cent
Fenian
Fantasy — A62

Swift's Bust
and St.
Patrick's
Cathedral,
Dublin — A63

Design: 1sh, 24c Fenian fantasy.

1967, Oct. 23 Photo. *Perf. 15*
238 A62 5p lt green & slate grn .20 .20
239 A62 1sh pale pink & gray .35 *.50*

Fenian Rising, centenary. The Fenian fantasy was created by S. Allan Taylor.

1967, Nov. 30 *Perf. 15*

Design: 1sh5p, Gulliver, Lilliputian army.

240 A63 3p gray & sepia .20 .20
241 A63 1sh5p lt blue & sepia .30 *.50*

Birth tercentenary of Jonathan Swift (1667-1745), author of Gulliver's Travels.

Europa Issue

Golden Key
with CEPT
Emblem
CD11

1968, Apr. 29 Photo. Wmk. 262
242 CD11 7p multicolored .85 .85
243 CD11 1sh5p multicolored 2.00 1.40

St. Mary's
Cathedral,
Limerick
A65

1968, Aug. 26 Engr. *Perf. 15*
244 A65 5p dull blue .20 .20
245 A65 10p olive .40 *.80*

800th anniv. of the founding of St. Mary's Cathedral by Donal Mor O'Brien, last King of Munster.

Countess
Markievicz
A66

1968, Sept. 23 Photo. Wmk. 262
246 A66 3p black .20 .20
247 A66 1sh5p dark blue .35 *.50*

Birth centenary of Countess Constance Markievicz (1868-1927), champion of Irish Independence and first Minister of Labor.

James
Connolly — A67

1968, Sept. 23 *Perf. 15*
248 A67 6p brown, dk brn & blk .20 *.40*
249 A67 1sh dull grn, grn & blk .30 *.40*

Birth centenary of James Connolly (1868-1916), founder of the Irish Socialist Party, editor of "Workers' Republic" and Commander of the Irish Citizen Army.

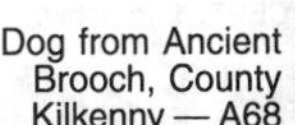
Dog from Ancient
Brooch, County
Kilkenny — A68

Winged Ox
from
Lichfield
Gospel
Book
A69

Designs: ½p, 1p, 2p, 3p, 4p, 5p, 6p, Dog. 7p, 8p, 9p, 10p, 1sh, 1sh9p, Stag from ancient bowl, Kent. 2sh6p, 5sh, Winged ox. 10sh, Eagle, from ancient manuscript.

1968-70 Photo. Wmk. 262 *Perf. 15*
250 A68 ½p orange .20 .30
251 A68 1p yellow green .20 .20
252 A68 2p ocher .75 .20
253 A68 3p bright blue .50 .20
254 A68 4p dark red .45 .20
255 A68 5p deep green .75 .45
256 A68 6p brown .45 .20
a. Booklet pane of 6 ('70) 25.00
257 A68 7p yel & brown .65 *3.25*
258 A68 8p red org & blk .65 *1.40*
259 A68 9p ol grn & dk bl .75 .20
260 A68 10p violet & dk brn 2.25 1.60
261 A68 1sh dk red brn & brown .65 .20
262 A68 1sh9p grnsh bl & dk brown 5.75 1.60
263 A69 2sh6p red org, bl, ol & dull yel 2.50 .30
264 A69 5sh ol, gray, bis & yel 4.50 1.60
265 A69 10sh dk red brn, yel & dp org 6.50 3.50
Nos. 250-265 (16) 27.50 15.40

Issued: 2p, 8p, 2sh6p, 10sh, 10/14/68; 6p, 9p, 1sh9p, 5sh, 2/24/69; 4p, 5p, 10p, 1sh, 3/31/69; ½p, 1p, 3p, 7p, 6/9/69.
See #290-304, 343-359, 395-402, 466-475.

Coil Stamps

1970 *Perf. 14x15*
251a A68 1p yellow green 1.25 3.00
252a A68 2p ocher 1.25 3.00
253a A68 3p bright blue 1.25 3.00
Nos. 251a-253a (3) 3.75 9.00

Human Rights Flame — A70

1968, Nov. 4 Wmk. 262 *Perf. 15*
266 A70 5p black, ocher & gold .20 .20
267 A70 7p crim, ocher & gold .35 .45

International Human Rights Year.

First Meeting of Irish Parliament A71

1969, Jan. 21 *Perf. 15x14½*
268 A71 6p dark slate green .20 .20
269 A71 9p dark blue gray .35 .45

50th anniv. of the first meeting of the Dail Eireann at the Mansion House, Dublin, Jan. 21, 1919.

"EUROPA" and "CEPT" CD12

1969, Apr. 28 Photo. *Perf. 15*
270 CD12 9p ultra, gray & ocher 1.25 1.25
271 CD12 1sh9p car, gray & gold 2.00 2.00

Europa and CEPT, 10th anniv.

ILO Emblem — A73

1969, July 14 *Perf. 15*
272 A73 6p gray & black .20 .20
273 A73 9p yellow & black .30 .40

ILO, 50th anniv.

Last Supper and Crucifixion, by Evie Hone A74

Perf. 15x14½

1969, Sept. 1 Photo. Wmk. 262
274 A74 1sh multicolored .70 1.75

The design is after a stained-glass window by Evie Hone (1894-1955) in the Eton College Chapel.

Mahatma Gandhi A75

1969, Oct. 2 *Perf. 15*
275 A75 6p dk yel grn & blk .20 .20
276 A75 1sh9p yel, grn & black .40 .70

Mohandas K. Gandhi (1869-1948), leader in India's fight for independence.

Stylized Bird, Tree and Shamrock A76

1970, Feb. 23 *Perf. 15*
277 A76 6p olive bister & black .20 .20
278 A76 9p violet & black .75 .90

Nature Conservation Year.

Europa Issue

Interwoven Threads CD13

1970, May 4 Photo. *Perf. 15*
279 CD13 6p purple & silver 1.25 .20
280 CD13 9p yel brn & silver 1.75 1.40
281 CD13 1sh9p dk gray & sil 2.50 2.00
Nos. 279-281 (3) 5.50 3.60

Sailing Boats, by Peter Monamy (1670-1749) A78

1970, July 13 *Perf. 15*
282 A78 4p gold & multi .20 .20

250th anniv. of the Royal Cork Yacht Club.

Madonna of Eire, by Mainie Jellett (1896-1943) A79

Tomás MacCurtain A80

1970, Sept. 1 Photo. *Perf. 15*
283 A79 1sh violet blue & multi .50 .50

1970, Oct. 26 *Perf. 15*

Nos. 285, 287, Terence MacSwiney.

284 A80 9p violet & black 1.10 .90
285 A80 9p violet & black 1.10 .90
a. Pair, #284-285 3.00 3.50
286 A80 2sh9p brt blue & blk 3.00 2.75
287 A80 2sh9p brt blue & blk 3.00 2.75
a. Pair, #286-287 7.50 10.00

50th anniv. of the deaths of Tomás MacCurtain (1884-1920) and Terence MacSwiney (1879-1920), lord mayors of Cork, who died during the Irish war of independence.

Kevin Barry A81

1970, Nov. 2
288 A81 6p olive green .20 .20
289 A81 1sh2p violet blue .65 .80

50th anniv. of the death of Kevin Barry (1902-1920), who was hanged during the Irish war of independence.

Decimal Currency Issue

Types of 1968-69 (Numerals only)

Designs: ½p, 1p, 1½p, 2p, 2½p, 3p, 3½p, 4p, No. 298A, Dog. No. 298, 6p, 7p, 7½p, 9p, Stag. 10p, 12p, 20p, Winged ox. 50p, Eagle.

Two types of 10p:
I - Ox outlined in brown
II - Outlined in dull lilac

1971-75 Wmk. 262 Photo. *Perf. 15*
290 A68 ½p yellow green .20 .20
a. Booklet pane of 6 25.00
291 A68 1p bright blue .55 .20
a. Booklet pane of 6 1.50
c. Bklt. pane of 5 + label ('74) 1.50
292 A68 1½p brown red .20 .20
293 A68 2p dark green .20 .20
b. Booklet pane of 5 + label ('75) 1.25
294 A68 2½p sepia .20 .20
a. Booklet pane of 6 5.00
295 A68 3p yel orange .20 .20
296 A68 3½p deep orange .20 .20
297 A68 4p violet .20 .20
298 A68 5p ap grn & brn .95 .20
298A A68 5p apple grn ('74) 3.75 .45
c. Booklet pane of 6 ('74) 6.00
d. Bklt. pane of 5 + label ('74) 2.00
299 A68 6p blue gray & dk brown 4.75 .30
299A A68 7p ol green & ind ('74) 5.25 1.00
300 A68 7½p rose vio & dk brown .65 .85
301 A68 9p bl grn & blk 1.00 .35
302 A69 10p lil & multi (I) 20.00 9.50
b. Type II 17.00 1.25
302A A69 12p multi ('74) .80 .80
303 A69 20p slate & multi 1.00 .20
304 A69 50p rose brn & multi 2.40 .75
Nos. 290-304 (18) 42.50 16.00

Booklet panes have watermark sideways.
Issued: #298A, 7p, 12p, 1/29/74; others, 2/15/71.
See Nos. 343-359, 395-402, 466-475.

Coil Stamps

1971-74 *Perf. 14x15*
291b A68 1p bright blue .90 .50
292a A68 1½p brown red .25 .50
293a A68 2p dark green ('72) .30 .40
294b A68 2½p sepia .30 .75
c. Strip of 3 (1p, 1½p, 2½p) 1.25 1.50
297a A68 4p violet ('72) 1.00 .70
b. Strip of 4 (1½p, 2p, 2½p, 4p) ('72) 2.00 2.00
298b A68 5p apple green ('74) 1.00 .90
e. Strip of 4 (2x1½p, 2p, 5p) ('74) 2.00 2.00

Europa Issue, 1971

Common Design Type

Size: 36½x21mm

1971, May 3 Wmk. 262 *Perf. 15*
305 CD14 4p apple green & blk .75 .20
306 CD14 6p blue & black 3.00 2.25

John M. Synge — A82

An Island Man, by Jack B. Yeats — A83

1971, July 19 Photo. *Perf. 15*
307 A82 4p gray, black & gold .20 .20
308 A82 10p org, black & gold .80 1.00

Birth cent. of John Millington Synge (1871-1909), poet and dramatist.

1971, Aug. 30 *Perf. 15*
309 A83 6p multicolored .70 .70

Jack Butler Yeats (1871-1957), painter.

Racial Equality Emblem A84

Madonna, by John Hughes, Loughrea Cathedral A85

Perf. 14x14½

1971, Oct. 18 Litho. Unwmk.
310 A84 4p red .20 .20
311 A84 10p black .70 .80

Intl. Year Against Racial Discrimination.

1971, Nov. 15 Photo. *Perf. 15*
312 A85 2½p dp bl grn, gold & slate .20 .20
313 A85 6p ultra, gold & slate .60 .70

Christmas.

"Your Heart is your Health" A86

1972, Apr. 7 Photo. Wmk. 262
314 A86 2½p gold & brown .25 .25
315 A86 12p silver & black 2.25 2.25

World Health Day.

Europa Issue

Sparkles, Symbolic of Communications — CD15

1972, May 1 *Perf. 15*
316 CD15 4p red, black & sil 3.25 .75
317 CD15 6p blue, black & sil 9.25 5.00

Dove Soaring Past Rising Moon — A88

1972, June 1 Photo.
318 A88 4p gray blue, org & dk bl .25 .25
319 A88 6p olive, yel & dk green .75 .55

The patriot dead of 1922-23.

Black Lake, by Gerard Dillon A89

1972, July 10 *Perf. 15*
320 A89 3p indigo & multi .45 .40

Rider from Clonmacnoise Slab and Olympic Rings — A90

1972, Aug. 28 Photo. Wmk. 262

321 A90 3p yellow, black & gold .20 .20
322 A90 6p salmon, black & gold .70 .70

20th Olympic Games, Munich, Aug. 26-Sept. 11, and 50th anniversary of the Olympic Council of Ireland.

Madonna and Child — A91

Ireland No. 68 — A92

1972, Oct. 16 Unwmk. *Perf. 15*

323 A91 2½p dk green & multi .20 .20
324 A91 4p tan & multi .45 .30
325 A91 12p multicolored 1.10 1.00
Nos. 323-325 (3) 1.75 1.50

Christmas. The design is after a miniature in the Book of Kells, 9th century.

1972, Dec. 6 Photo.

326 A92 6p blue gray & dp grn .50 *.85*
a. Souvenir sheet of 4 8.50 *10.00*

50th anniv. of 1st Irish postage stamp.

Recurrent Celtic Head Motif — A93

1973, Jan. 1 Unwmk.

327 A93 6p orange & multi .40 *.50*
328 A93 12p green & multi 1.60 1.50

Ireland's entry into the European Community.

Europa Issue

Post Horn of Arrows CD16

1973, Apr. 30

329 CD16 4p bright ultra 1.25 .20
330 CD16 6p black 3.25 2.00

"Berlin Blues I," by William Scott A95

Perf. 15x14½

1973, Aug. 9 Photo. Unwmk.

331 A95 5p lt blue, blue & dk brn .55 .45

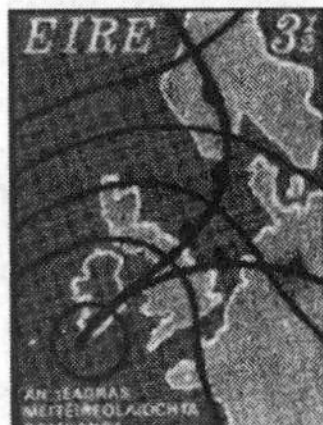

Weather Map of Northwest Europe — A96

1973, Sept. 4 *Perf. 14½x15*

332 A96 3½p ultra & multi .25 .20
333 A96 12p lilac & multi 1.50 1.50

Intl. meteorological cooperation, cent.

Tractor Plowing and Birds A97

1973, Oct. 5 *Perf. 15x14½*

334 A97 5p emerald & multi .25 .20
335 A97 7p emerald & multi 1.50 .70

World Plowing Championships, Wellington Bridge, County Wexford, Oct. 1-7.

Flight into Egypt, by Jan de Cock — A98

1973, Nov. 1 *Perf. 15*

336 A98 3½p black & multi .20 .20
337 A98 12p gold & multi 1.25 *1.40*

Christmas.

Rescue, by Bernard Gribble A99

Design: Ballycotton lifeboat rescuing crew of Daunt Rock Lightship, 1936.

1974, Mar. 28 Photo. Wmk. 262

338 A99 5p multicolored .50 .45

Sesquicentennial of the founding of the Royal National Lifeboat Institution.

Edmund Burke, by John Henry Foley — A100

Oliver Goldsmith, by John Henry Foley — A101

Europa Issue

Perf. 14½x15

1974, Apr. 29 Unwmk.

339 A100 5p lt ultra & black 1.75 .20
340 A100 7p lt green & black 8.25 2.50

1974, June 24 Photo.

341 A101 3½p brt citron & blk .25 .20
342 A101 12p emerald & black 1.50 1.40

Oliver Goldsmith (1728-1774), writer.

Types of 1968-69

½p, 1p, 2p, 3p, 3½p, 5p, #350, 352, Dog. #349, 351, 8p, 9p, Stag. 10p, 15p, 20p, Winged ox. 50p, £1, Eagle.

1974-78 Unwmk. *Perf. 15*

343 A68 ½p yel green ('78) .70 .20
344 A68 1p brt blue ('75) .20 .20
345 A68 2p dark green ('76) .20 .20
346 A68 3p ocher ('75) .20 .20
347 A68 3½p deep orange 5.25 *6.25*
348 A68 5p apple green 1.40 .20
349 A68 6p bl gray & dk brn 2.00 *2.25*
350 A68 6p blue gray ('75) .45 .20
351 A68 7p ol grn & indigo 1.60 .60
352 A68 7p olive green ('75) .80 .20
a. Bklt. pane of 5 + label ('77) 14.00
353 A68 8p brown & dk brn ('75) 1.40 .75
354 A68 9p bl grn & black ('75) 1.60 .45
355 A69 10p lil & multi ('75) 2.25 .45
356 A69 15p multi ('75) 1.25 .60
357 A69 20p slate & multi 1.10 .25
358 A69 50p rose brown & multi ('75) 1.60 .50
359 A69 £1 multi ('75) 4.00 .50
Nos. 343-359 (17) 26.00 14.00

Two types of No. 358 differ in clarity of screening, date on tail, etc.

Coil Stamps

1977, Mar. 21 *Perf. 14x15*

344b A68 1p bright blue .60 .60
345b A68 2p dark green .40 *.50*
348b A68 5p apple green .90 *1.00*
c. Strip of 4 (1p, 2x2p, 5p) 1.75 *2.00*

Kitchen Table, by Norah McGuinness A102

1974, Aug. 19 Photo. *Perf. 14x15*

360 A102 5p multicolored .60 .40

Rugby A103

1974, Sept. 2 Engr. *Perf. 15x14*

361 A103 3½p slate green .60 .25
a. 3½ deep slate green 7.00 4.50
362 A103 12p multicolored 2.50 2.50

Centenary of Irish Rugby Union.

No. 361a was printed from a reengraved plate with more deeply engraved lines. The original printing (No. 361) was considered to be of unsatisfactory quality.

UPU "Postmark" A104

Virgin and Child, by Bellini — A105

1974, Oct. 9 Photo. *Perf. 14½x15*

363 A104 5p emerald & black .30 .20
364 A104 7p ultra & multi .80 1.00

Centenary of Universal Postal Union.

block newblock=y>

1974, Nov. 14

365 A105 5p multicolored .25 .20
366 A105 15p multicolored 1.25 *1.50*

Christmas.

"Peace" — A106

1975, Mar. 25 Photo. *Perf. 14½x15*

367 A106 8p dp rose lil & ultra .30 .20
368 A106 15p ultra & emerald 1.10 .90

International Women's Year.

Europa Issue

Castletown Hunt (detail), by Robert Healy A107

1975, Apr. 28 Photo. *Perf. 15x14½*

369 A107 7p black 2.50 .25
370 A107 9p green 4.50 2.50

Chipping from the Fringe A108

1975, June 26 Photo. *Perf. 15x14½*

371 A108 6p shown .40 .20
372 A108 9p Putting 1.40 1.25

9th European Amateur Golf Team Championships, Killarney.

Bird of Prey, by Oisín Kelly A109

1975, July 28

373 A109 15p ocher .80 *1.10*

Nano Nagle and Pupils, Engraving by Charles Turner — A110

Clock Tower, St. Ann's Church, Shandon — A111

1975, Sept. 1 Photo. *Perf. 14½x15*
374 A110 5p light blue & black .20 .20
375 A110 7p buff & black .60 .35

Presentation Order of Nuns, bicentenary.

1975, Oct. 6 Photo. *Perf. 12½*

Designs: 7p, 9p, Holycross Abbey.

376 A111 5p sepia .30 .20
377 A111 6p ultra & multi .60 .90
378 A111 7p sapphire .75 .30
379 A111 9p multicolored 1.10 .70
Nos. 376-379 (4) 2.75 2.10

European Architectural Heritage Year.

St. Oliver Plunkett, by Imogen Stuart — A112

Madonna and Child, by Fra Filippo Lippi — A113

1975, Oct. 13 Engr. *Perf. 14x14½*
380 A112 7p black .30 .20
381 A112 15p dull red 1.10 .85

Canonization of Oliver Plunkett (1625-1681), Primate of Ireland.

1975, Nov. 13 Photo. *Perf. 15*
382 A113 5p multicolored .20 .20
383 A113 7p multicolored .30 .20
384 A113 10p gold & multi .65 .50
Nos. 382-384 (3) 1.15 .90

Christmas.

James Larkin — A114

Bell Making First Call — A115

1976 Jan. 21 Photo. *Perf. 14½x15*
385 A114 7p gray & slate grn .20 .20
386 A114 11p ocher & brown 1.25 .80

James Larkin (1876-1947), trade union leader.

1976, Mar. 10 Photo. *Perf. 14½x15*
387 A115 9p multicolored .30 .25
388 A115 15p multicolored 1.25 .60

Centenary of first telephone call by Alexander Graham Bell, March 10, 1876.

13 Stars and Stripes A116

Designs: 8p, 50 stars, and stripes. 9p, 15p, Benjamin Franklin on Albany essay of 1847.

1976, May 17 Litho. *Perf. 15x14*
389 A116 7p ultra, sil & red .25 .20
a. Silver (inscription) omitted 275.00
390 A116 8p ultra, sil & red .40 .80
391 A116 9p bl, sil & ocher .70 .40
392 A116 15p red, sil & bl .80 .80
a. Souvenir sheet of 4, #389-392 7.25 7.50
b. Silver (inscription) omitted, #392 950.00 900.00
Nos. 389-392 (4) 2.15 2.20

American Bicentennial. No. 392a exists with silver omitted.

Irish Delft Spirit Barrel A117

Europa: 11p, Bowl, Irish Delft. Designs show mark of Henry Delamain's Factory, Dublin, both pieces c. 1756.

1976, July 1 Photo. *Perf. 15x14½*
393 A117 9p gray & magenta 1.00 .25
394 A117 11p gray & blue 1.75 1.75

Types of 1968

Designs: 8p, 9p, 9½p, No. 399, Dog. No. 398, 11p, 12p, Stag. 17p, Winged ox.

1976-79 Photo. Unwmk. *Perf. 15*
395 A68 8p brown .35 .20
396 A68 9p blue green .55 .20
397 A68 9½p red ('79) .55 .20
398 A68 10p lilac & black 1.50 .30
399 A68 10p purple ('77) .65 .20
400 A68 11p carmine & black .90 .20
401 A68 12p emer & black ('77) .90 .20
402 A69 17p ol, bl & ocher ('77) .80 .20
Nos. 395-402 (8) 6.20 1.70

The Lobster Pots, by Paul Henry A118

1976, Aug. 30 Photo. *Perf. 15*
405 A118 15p gold & multi .80 .50

Paul Henry (1876-1958), birth centenary.

Radio Waves A119

Radio Tower and Waves, Globe — A120

Perf. 14½x14, 14x14½
1976, Oct. 5 Litho.
406 A119 9p brt blue & black .20 .20
407 A120 11p black & multi 1.10 1.40

Irish broadcasting, 50th anniversary.

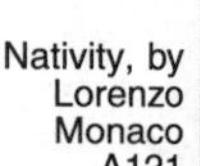

Nativity, by Lorenzo Monaco A121

1976, Nov. 11 *Perf. 15x14½*
408 A121 7p multicolored .25 .20
409 A121 9p multicolored .50 .25
410 A121 15p multicolored 1.00 .55
Nos. 408-410 (3) 1.75 1.00

Christmas.

Irish Manuscript, 16th Century A122

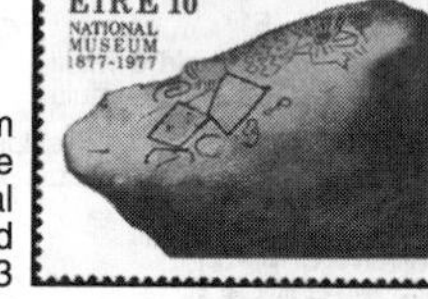

Stone from Newgrange Burial Mound A123

1977, May 9 Photo. *Perf. 15x14½*
411 A122 8p multicolored .30 .20
412 A123 10p multicolored .65 .60

Centenaries of National Library (8p) and National Museum (10p).

Europa Issue

View of Ballynahinch A124

Lugalla Lake — A125

1977, June 27 Litho. *Perf. 14x14½*
413 A124 10p multicolored 2.50 .30
414 A125 12p multicolored 7.50 2.50

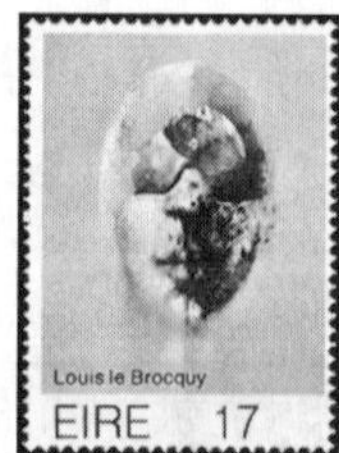

Head, by Louis le Brocquy, 1973 — A126

1977, Aug. 8 *Perf. 14x14½*
415 A126 17p multicolored 1.00 .90

Girl Guide and Tents A127

Design: 17p, Boy Scout and tents.

1977, Aug. 22 Photo. *Perf. 15x14½*
416 A127 8p multicolored .45 .25
417 A127 17p multicolored 1.00 1.25

European Scout and Guide Conference, Ireland, and 50th anniversary of Catholic Boy Scouts of Ireland.

The Shanachie, by Jack B. Yeats — A128

Eriugena A129

Perf. 14x14½, 14½x14
1977, Sept. 12 Litho.
418 A128 10p black .40 .30
419 A129 12p black 1.10 1.25

Folklore of Ireland Society, 50th anniv. and 1100th death anniv. of Johannes Scottus Eriugena, philospher, poet and mystic.

"Electricity," Mural by Robert Ballagh — A130

Bulls, from Contemporary Coin — A131

Greyhound A132

Litho. (10p, 17p); Photo. (12p)
Perf. 14½x14; 15x14½ (12p)
1977, Oct. 10
420 A130 10p multicolored .30 .20
421 A131 12p multicolored .70 1.10
422 A132 17p multicolored .55 .80
Nos. 420-422 (3) 1.55 2.10

50th anniversaries of: Electricity Supply Board (10p); Agricultural Credit Act (12p); introduction of greyhound racing (17p).

Holy Family, by Giorgione — A133

Bremen, Junkers Monoplane A134

1977, Nov. 3 Photo. ***Perf. 14½x15***
423 A133 8p multicolored .35 .20
424 A133 10p multicolored .55 .30
425 A133 17p multicolored .95 .50
Nos. 423-425 (3) 1.85 1.00

Christmas.

1978, Apr. 13 Litho. ***Perf. 14***
426 A134 10p ultra & black .30 .30
427 A134 17p lt brown & black .80 .60

50th anniversary of first East-West transatlantic flight from Baldonnel, County Dublin, to Greenly Island, Gulf of St. Lawrence.

Spring Gentian — A135

Wild flowers: 10p, Strawberry tree. 11p, Large-flowered butterwort. 17p, St. Daboec's heath.

1978, June 12 Litho. ***Perf. 14x14½***
428 A135 8p multicolored .20 .20
429 A135 10p multicolored .50 .35
430 A135 11p multicolored .65 *.85*
431 A135 17p multicolored .80 *.95*
Nos. 428-431 (4) 2.15 *2.35*

Catherine McAuley — A136

William Orpen, Self-portrait — A138

Vaccination, lithograph by Manigaud — A137

1978, Sept. 18 Litho. ***Perf. 14***
432 A136 10p multicolored .30 .20
433 A137 11p multicolored .50 .50
434 A138 17p multicolored 1.00 .80
Nos. 432-434 (3) 1.80 1.50

Catherine McAuley (1778-1841), founder of Sisters of Mercy (10p); eradication of smallpox (11p); William Orpen (1878-1931), painter (17p).

Offshore Oil Well — A139

Virgin and Child, by Guercino — A141

Woodcock on Farthing A140

1978, Oct. 18 Litho. ***Perf. 14***
435 A139 10p multicolored .40 .20

First natural gas coming in off the Irish Coast at Kinsale.

1978, Oct. 26 Photo. ***Perf. 15x14½***

Coins: 10p, Salmon on florin. 11p, Hen and chicks on penny. 17p, Horse on half crown.

436 A140 8p multicolored .30 .20
437 A140 10p multicolored .40 .20
438 A140 11p multicolored .40 .40
439 A140 17p multicolored .55 .55
Nos. 436-439 (4) 1.65 1.35

Irish currency, 50th anniversary.

1978, Nov. 16 Photo. ***Perf. 14½x15***
440 A141 8p multicolored .30 .20
441 A141 10p multicolored .35 .20
442 A141 17p multicolored .65 .60
Nos. 440-442 (3) 1.30 1.00

Christmas.

Conolly Folly, Castletown A142

Europa: 11p, Belvedere on Tower Hill at Dromoland.

1978, Dec. 6 ***Perf. 15x14½***
443 A142 10p brown 4.00 .25
444 A142 11p dull green 4.50 1.00

Cross-country Runners — A143

1979, Aug. 20 Litho. ***Perf. 14½x14***
445 A143 8p multicolored .30 .25

7th World Cross-country Championships, Greenpark Racecourse, Limerick, March 25.

Rowland Hill, Bronze Statue — A144

"European Communities" (7 Languages) A145

1979, Aug. 20 ***Perf. 14x14½***
446 A144 17p multicolored .50 .55

Sir Rowland Hill (1795-1879), originator of penny postage.

1979, Aug. 20 Photo. ***Perf. 14½x15***
447 A145 10p lt greenish gray .40 .40
448 A145 11p rose lilac .45 .45

European Parliament, first direct elections, June 7-10.

Wren A146

Birds: 10p, Great crested grebe. 11p, Greenland white-fronted geese. 17p, Peregrine falcon.

1979, Aug. 30 Litho. ***Perf. 14½x14***
449 A146 8p multicolored .35 .20
450 A146 10p multicolored .45 .45
451 A146 11p multicolored .50 .50
452 A146 17p multicolored .95 1.10
Nos. 449-452 (4) 2.25 2.25

A Happy Flower A147

Children's Drawings: 11p, "Me and my skipping rope," vert. 17p, "Swans on a lake."

Perf. 14½x14, 14x14½
1979, Sept. 13 Litho.
453 A147 10p multicolored .30 .30
454 A147 11p multicolored .35 *.45*
455 A147 17p multicolored .50 *.60*
Nos. 453-455 (3) 1.15 *1.35*

International Year of the Child.

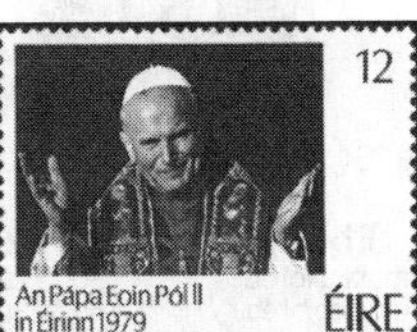

Pope John Paul II A148

1979, Sept. 29 Litho. ***Perf. 14½x14***
456 A148 12p multicolored .40 .20

Visit of Pope John Paul II to Ireland.

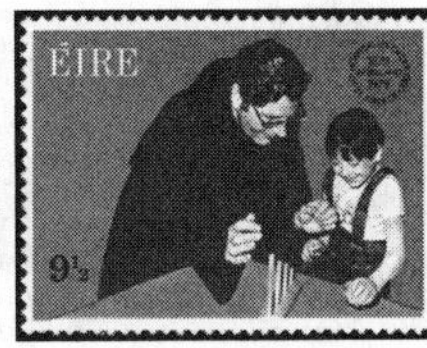
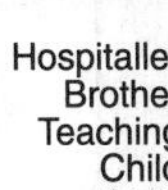

Hospitaller Brother Teaching Child A149

1979, Oct. 4
457 A149 9½p rose & black .30 .30

Hospitaller Order of St. John of God, centenary in Ireland.

Windmill and Sun — A150

1979, Oct. 4 Photo. ***Perf. 14½x15***
458 A150 11p multicolored .40 .40

Energy conservation.

"Seated Figure," by F.E. McWilliam A151

1979, Oct. 4 Litho. ***Perf. 14½x14***
459 A151 20p multicolored .60 *.70*

Patrick Pearse A152

1979, Nov. 10 Photo. ***Perf. 15x14½***
460 A152 12p multicolored .40 .20

Patrick Henry Pearse (1879-1916), Irish writer and leader of Easter Rebellion.

Mother and Child, Panel, Domnach Argid Shrine — A153

1979, Nov. 15 Photo. ***Perf. 14½x15***
461 A153 9½p multicolored .30 .20
462 A153 20p multicolored .60 .35

Christmas.

Europa Issue

Bianconi Long Car, 1836 A154

Laying Transatlantic Cable, Steamer William Cory, 1866 — A155

1979, Dec. 6 Litho. *Perf. 15x14*

463 A154 12p multicolored .75 .50
464 A155 13p multicolored 3.75 1.00

Type of 1968

Designs: 13p, 16p, Stag; others, Dog.

1980-82 Photo. *Perf. 15*

466 A68 12p green .45 .20
467 A68 13p red brown & dk brn .50 .30
468 A68 15p ultra .45 .20
469 A68 16p olive green & blk .65 .30

Litho.

470 A68 18p dull red brn ('81) .45 .20
471 A68 19p dull blue ('81) .70 .55
472 A68 22p gray blue ('81) .60 .20
473 A68 24p brown olive ('81) .70 .40
474 A68 26p bluish green ('82) .70 .20
475 A68 29p dp rose lilac ('82) 1.25 .80
Nos. 466-475 (10) 6.45 3.35

St. Jean Baptiste de la Salle — A156

1980, Mar. 19 Litho. *Perf. 14x15*

477 A156 12p multicolored .40 .20

The Brothers of the Christian School (founded by St. Jean Baptiste), centenary in Ireland.

Europa Issue

George Bernard Shaw, by Alick Ritchie A157

Oscar Wilde, by Toulouse-Lautrec A158

1980, May 7 Litho. *Perf. 14x15*

478 A157 12p multicolored 1.10 .35
479 A158 13p multicolored 1.10 .75

Irish Ermine — A159

Bodhran Drum and Whistle Players — A160

1980, July 30 Litho. *Perf. 14x15*

480 A159 12p shown .30 .20
481 A159 15p Irish hare .40 .20
482 A159 16p Fox .40 .30
483 A159 25p Red deer .90 .60
a. Miniature sheet of 4, #480-483 3.00 *4.25*
Nos. 480-483 (4) 2.00 1.30

1980, Sept. 25 Photo. *Perf. 14x15*

484 A160 12p shown .35 .25
485 A160 15p Piper, Uilleann pipes .40 .30
486 A160 25p Irish jig .65 .45
Nos. 484-486 (3) 1.40 1.00

Sean O'Casey (1880-1964), Playwright A161

Gold Painting No. 57, by Patrick Scott — A162

1980, Oct. 23 Litho. *Perf. 14x14½*

487 A161 12p multicolored .35 .25

1980, Oct. 23 *Perf. 14x15*

488 A162 25p multicolored .70 .55

A163

A164

1980, Dec. 4 Photo. *Perf. 15x14½*

489 A163 12p multicolored .30 .20
490 A163 15p multicolored .40 .30
491 A163 25p multicolored .70 .50
Nos. 489-491 (3) 1.40 1.00

Christmas.

1981, Mar. 12 Litho. *Perf. 14x14½*

Scientists and Inventions: 12p, Robert Boyle (1627-1691), and Air Pump, 1659. 15p, Harry Ferguson (1884-1960), hydraulic tractor, 1936. 16p, Charles Parsons (1854-1931), Parsons' turbine, 1884. 25p, John Holland (1841-1914), Holland submarine, 1878.

492 A164 12p multicolored .25 .20
493 A164 15p multicolored .30 .25
494 A164 16p multicolored .35 .35
495 A164 25p multicolored .55 *.70*
Nos. 492-495 (4) 1.45 1.50

The Cock and the Pot, Rubbing, 1841 — A165

Europa: 19p, The Scales of Judgment, rubbing, 1827.

1981, May 4 Litho. *Perf. 14½x15*

496 A165 18p multicolored 1.50 .30
497 A165 19p multicolored 2.00 *.60*

Hiking A166

Perf. 14x15, 15x14

1981, June 24 Litho.

498 A166 15p Bicycling, vert. .35 .20
499 A166 18p shown .45 .30
500 A166 19p Mountain climbing .45 .45
501 A166 30p Rock climbing, vert. .75 .60
Nos. 498-501 (4) 2.00 1.55

Youth Hostel Assn., 50th anniv.

Jeremiah O'Donovan Rossa (1831-1915), Journalist — A167

Railway Embankment, by William John Leech (1881-1968) — A168

Perf. 14½x15, 15x14½

1981, Aug. 31

502 A167 15p multicolored .35 .30
503 A168 30p multicolored .75 .70

James Hoban (1762-1831), White House Architect — A169

1981, Sept. 29 *Perf. 15x14*

504 A169 18p multicolored .55 .30

Same design used for US Nos. 1935-1936.

Draft Horse King of Diamonds A170

Famous Horses: No. 505, Show-jumper Boomerang. No. 506, Steeplechaser Arkle. 24p, Flat racer Ballymoss. 36p, Connemara pony Coosheen Finn.

1981, Oct. 23 Litho. *Perf. 15x14*

505 A170 18p multicolored .65 .40
506 A170 18p multicolored .65 .40
a. Pair, #505-506 1.40 1.40
507 A170 22p multicolored .65 .40
508 A170 24p multicolored .65 *.80*
509 A170 36p multicolored 1.00 1.00
Nos. 505-509 (5) 3.60 3.00

A171

A172

Nativity, by Federico Barocci (Christmas 1981).

1981, Nov. 19 Litho. *Perf. 14x15*

510 A171 18p multicolored .45 .20
511 A171 22p multicolored .55 .25
512 A171 36p multicolored .90 .55
Nos. 510-512 (3) 1.90 1.00

1981, Dec. 10 Litho. *Perf. 14x14½*

513 A172 18p multicolored .50 .20

Land Law Act centenary.

250th Anniv. of Royal Dublin Society A173

1981, Dec. 10 *Perf. 14½x14*

514 A173 22p multicolored .60 .55

50th Anniv. of Killarney Natl. Park A174

1982, Feb. 26 Litho. *Perf. 14½x14*

515 A174 18p Upper Lake .50 .30
516 A174 36p Eagle's Nest .85 .70

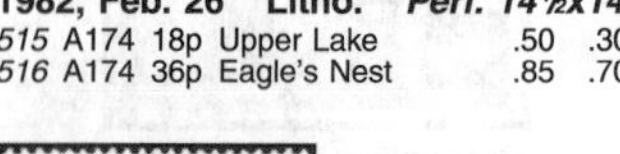

The Stigmatization of St. Francis, by Sassetta — A175

Francis Makemie, Old Presbyterian Church, Ramelton — A176

1982, Apr. 2 — *Perf. 14x15, 15x14*

517 A175 22p multicolored .50 .35
518 A176 24p brown .70 .50

800th birth anniv. of St. Francis of Assisi; 300th anniv. of Francis Makemie's ordination (father of American Presbyterianism).

Europa Issue

Great Famine of 1845-50 — A177

Conversion of Ireland to Christianity (St. Patrick and his Followers, by Vincenzo Valdre) A178

1982, May 4

519 A177 26p tan & brown 5.50 1.00
520 A178 29p multicolored 6.50 5.00

Padraic O'Connaire (1882-1928), Writer — A179

Designs: 26p, James Joyce (1882-1941), writer and poet, by Brancusi. 29p, John Field (1782-1837), Composer and pianist, Nocturne score. 44p, Charles Joseph Kickham (1828-1882), journalist and writer. 29p, 44p by Colin Harrison.

1982, June 16 — Litho. — *Perf. 14x15*

521 A179 22p blue & black .50 .30
522 A179 26p black & brown .65 .50
523 A179 29p black & blue .85 .85
524 A179 44p gray green & black 1.25 1.25
Nos. 521-524 (4) 3.25 2.90

Porbeagle Shark A180

1982, July 29 — *Perf. 15x14*

525 A180 22p shown .70 .40
526 A180 22p Oyster .70 .40
527 A180 26p Salmon 1.00 .40
528 A180 29p Dublin Bay prawn 1.10 1.10
Nos. 525-528 (4) 3.50 2.30

Currach A181

1982, Sept. 21 — *Perf. 15x14, 14x15*

529 A181 22p shown .70 .35
530 A181 22p Galway hooker, vert. .70 .35
531 A181 26p Asgard II training ship 1.00 .40
532 A181 29p Howth 17-footer, vert. 1.25 1.40
Nos. 529-532 (4) 3.65 2.50

The Irish House of Commons, by Francis Wheatley A182

1982, Oct. 14 — Litho. — *Perf. 14½x14*

533 A182 22p multicolored .55 .30

Bicentenary of Grattan's Parliament.

A183

A183a

Eamon de Valera (1882-1975), President, by Robert Ballagh.

1982, Oct. 14 — *Perf. 14x14½*

534 A183 26p multicolored .70 .30

1982, Nov. 11 — Litho. — *Perf. 14½x15*

Madonna and Child, by Andrea della Robbia (1435-1525)

535 A183a 22p lt violet & multi .50 .30
536 A183a 26p gray & multi .70 .40

Christmas.

A184

A185

Killarney Cathedral, 1855 — A186

Designs: 1p-5p, Central Pavilion, Dublin Botanical Gardens. 6p, 7p, 10p, 12p, Dr. Steeven's Hospital, Dublin. 15p, 20p, 22p, Aughnanure Castle, Oughterard, 16th cent. 23p, 26p, Cormac's Chapel, 1134. 29p, 30p, St. Mac Dara's Church. 50p, Casino, Marino. £1, Cahir Castle, 15th century. £5 Central Bus Station, Dublin, 1953.

50p, £1, £5 horiz.

1982-90 — Litho. — *Perf. 14x15, 15x14*

537 A184 1p dull blue .20 .20
538 A184 2p gray green .20 .20
539 A184 3p black .20 .20
540 A184 4p rose lake .20 .20
 a. Perf. 13½ on 3 or 4 sides .20 .20
541 A184 5p brown .20 .20
542 A184 6p dull blue .20 .20
543 A184 7p gray green .20 .20
544 A184 10p black .25 .20
545 A184 12p rose lake .30 .20
546 A185 15p gray green .40 .20
547 A185 20p rose lake .50 .30
548 A185 22p dull blue .55 .30
 a. Bklt. pane of 7+label (3 4p, 4 22p) ('88) 3.60
549 A185 23p gray green .55 .35
550 A185 26p black .60 .40
 a. Bklt. pane, 2 ea 2p, 22p, 26p 2.25
 b. Bklt. pane, 4 ea 2p, 22p, 26p 4.50
 c. Bklt. pane, 3 4p, 5 22p, 4 26p ('88) 6.00
 d. Perf. 13½ on 3 sides .60 .60
551 A184 29p gray green .70 .40
552 A184 30p black .70 .45
 a. Perf. 13½ on 3 or 4 sides .70 .70

Perf. 14x15, 15x14

553 A186 44p gray & black 1.10 .70
554 A186 50p gray & dull blue 1.25 .75
555 A186 £1 gray & brown 6.25 2.75
556 A186 £5 gray & rose lake 12.00 7.25
Nos. 537-556 (20) 26.55 15.65

Stamps from #550c imprinted "Booklet Stamp" in green on reverse side. #550c sold for £2.

Issued: 4p, 6p-7p, 20p, 23p, 30p, 50p, 3/16/83; 1p-3p, 5p, 10p-15p, 7/6/83; #540a, 550d, 552a, 5/3/90; others, 12/15/82.

See Nos. 638-645, 803a, 804b.

Dublin Chamber of Commerce Bicentenary A187

Bank of Ireland Bicentenary — A188

1983, Feb. 23 — Litho.

557 A187 22p Ouzel Galley goblet .60 .30
558 A188 26p Bank .75 .45

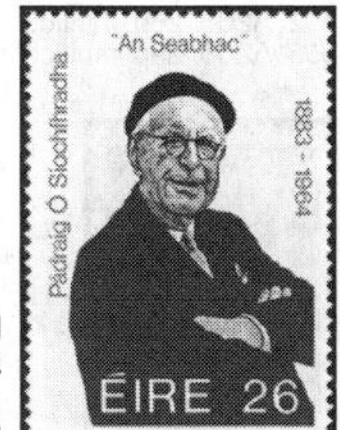

Padraig Siochfhradha (1883-1964), Writer — A189

Boys' Brigade Centenary A190

1983, Apr. 7 — Litho. — *Perf. 14x14½*

559 A189 26p multicolored .65 .30
560 A190 29p multicolored .95 .95

Europa A191

Design: 26p, Newgrange Winter Solstice, Neolithic Pattern Drawing by Louis le Brocquy. 29p, Quaternion formula, by William Rowan Hamilton (1805-1865).

1983, May 4 — Litho. — *Perf. 14½x14*

561 A191 26p black & gold 3.75 .75
562 A191 29p multicolored 8.25 5.50

Kerry Blue Terrier A192

Drawings of dogs by Wendy Walsh.

1983, June 23

563 A192 22p shown .70 .70
564 A192 26p Irish wolfhound .80 .80
565 A192 26p Irish water spaniel .80 .80
566 A192 29p Irish terrier .95 .95
567 A192 44p Irish setters 1.40 1.40
 a. Miniature sheet of 5, #563-567 7.00 6.00
Nos. 563-567 (5) 4.65 4.65

Sean Mac Diarmada (1883-1916), Nationalist A193

Society for the Prevention of Cruelty to Animals A194

Society of St. Vincent de Paul Sesquicentennial A195

Industrial Credit Co., 50th Anniv. A196

US Pres. Andrew Jackson (1767-1845) A197

Perf. 14x14½, 14½x14

1983, Aug. 11

568 A193 22p multicolored .85 .85
569 A194 22p multicolored .85 .85
570 A195 26p multicolored 1.10 1.00
571 A196 26p multicolored 1.10 1.00
572 A197 44p gray 2.00 2.00
Nos. 568-572 (5) 5.90 5.70

WCY — A198

Handicrafts A199

1983, Sept. 15 Litho. *Perf. 14x15*

573 A198 22p	Mailman	.50	.35
574 A198 29p	Dish antenna	.70	.70

1983, Oct. 13 Litho. *Perf. 14x15*

575 A199 22p	Weaving	.75	.45
576 A199 26p	Basketweaving	.85	.50
577 A199 29p	Irish crochet	1.00	.90
578 A199 44p	Harpmaking	1.40	1.30
	Nos. 575-578 (4)	4.00	3.15

La Natividad by Rogier van der Weyden — A200

1983, Nov. 30 Litho. *Perf. 14x14½*

579 A200 22p	multicolored	.50	.35
580 A200 26p	multicolored	.60	.50

Christmas.

Irish Railways Sesquicentenary — A201

Locomotives: 23p, Princess, Dublin and Kingstown Railway. 26p, Macha, Great Southern Railways. 29p, Kestrel, Great Northern Railway. 44p, Link-Hoffman railcar, Coras Iompair Eireann.

1984, Jan. 30 *Perf. 14½x14*

581 A201 23p	multicolored	1.10	1.10
582 A201 26p	multicolored	.65	.65
583 A201 29p	multicolored	1.25	1.25
584 A201 44p	multicolored	2.00	2.00
a.	Souvenir sheet of 4, #581-584	6.50	5.50
	Nos. 581-584 (4)	5.00	5.00

Private Overprints

Nos. 584a, 684a, 708a, 708b, 803a, 804a, 811a, 826a, 847a, 855a, 876b, and others, exist with privately applied show overprints.

Local Trees A202

1984, Mar. 1 Litho. *Perf. 15x14*

585 A202 22p	Irish whitebeam	.85	.55
586 A202 26p	Irish yew	1.00	.75
587 A202 29p	Irish willow	1.25	.85
588 A202 44p	Birch	1.75	1.25
	Nos. 585-588 (4)	4.85	3.40

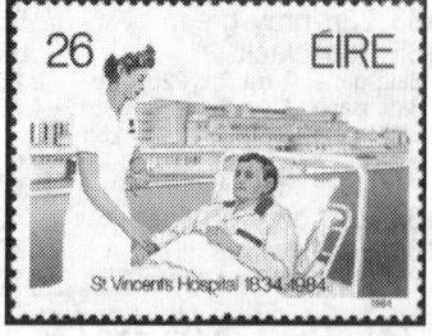

St. Vincent's Hospital, Dublin, Sesquicentenary — A203

Royal College of Surgeons in Ireland Bicentenary — A204

1984, Apr. 12 Litho.

589 A203 26p	multicolored	.75	.65
590 A204 44p	multicolored	1.25	1.10

2nd European Parliament Election A205

1984, May 10 Litho. *Perf. 15x14*

591 A205 26p	multicolored	.85	.45

Europa (1959-84) A206

1984, May 10

592 A206 26p	multicolored	*4.00*	3.00
593 A206 29p	multicolored	*5.00*	3.75

John McCormack (1884-1945), Singer — A207

1984, June 6 Litho. *Perf. 14x14½*

594 A207 22p	multicolored	.60	.35

See US No. 2090.

1984 Summer Olympics A208

1984, June 21 Litho. *Perf. 14½x14*

595 A208 22p	Hammer throw	.60	.45
596 A208 26p	Hurdles	.75	.55
597 A208 29p	Running	.85	.80
	Nos. 595-597 (3)	2.20	1.80

Gaelic Athletic Assoc. Centenary A209

1984, Aug. 23 Litho. *Perf. 14x15*

598 A209 22p	Hurlers	.50	.35
599 A209 26p	Soccer, vert.	.65	.45

Mayoral City of Galway, 500th Anniv. — A210

St. Brendan (484-577) A211

1984, Sept. 18 *Perf. 14x15, 15x14*

600 A210 26p	Medal	.75	.65
601 A211 44p	Portrait, manuscript	1.25	1.25

Post Office Bicentenary — A212

1984, Oct. 19 *Perf. 15x14*

602 A212 26p	Handing sealed letter	.70	.35

A213

Virgin And Child by Sassoferrato A214

Perf. 14½x14, 14x14½

1984, Nov. 26 Litho.

603 A213 17p	multicolored	.45	.20
604 A214 22p	multicolored	.55	.30
605 A214 26p	multicolored	.75	.35
	Nos. 603-605 (3)	1.75	.85

Christmas.

Love A215

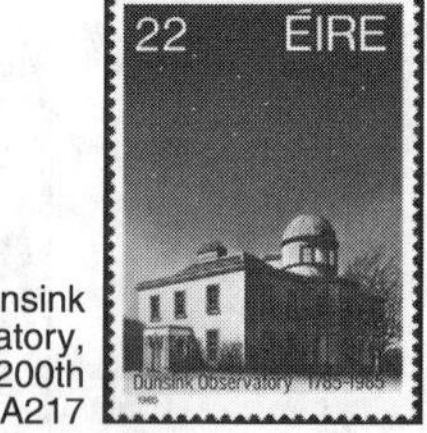

A216

1985, Jan. 31 Litho. *Perf. 15x14*

606 A215 22p	Heart-shaped balloon	.60	.30
607 A216 26p	Bouquet of hearts	.85	.35

Dunsink Observatory, 200th Anniv. — A217

Cork City Charter, 800th Anniv. A218

Royal Irish Academy, 200th Anniv. — A219

1st Manned Flight in Ireland, 200th Anniv. — A220

1985, Mar. 14 Litho.

608 A217 22p	black	.50	.45
609 A218 26p	multicolored	.65	.50
610 A219 37p	multicolored	.85	.85
611 A220 44p	multicolored	1.00	1.00
	Nos. 608-611 (4)	3.00	2.80

Butterflies A221

1985, Apr. 11 Litho. *Perf. 14x15*

612 A221 22p	Common blue	1.25	1.10
613 A221 26p	Red admiral	1.40	1.25
614 A221 28p	Brimstone	1.60	1.25
615 A221 44p	Marsh fritillary	2.25	2.00
	Nos. 612-615 (4)	6.50	5.60

Europa A222

26p, Charles Villiers Stanford (1852-1924), composer. 37p, Turlough O'Carolan (1670-1738), Composer.

1985, May 16 Litho. *Perf. 15x14*

616 A222 26p multicolored 3.50 1.00
617 A222 37p multicolored 7.00 6.00

European Music Year — A223

Composers: No. 618, Giuseppe Domenico Scarlatti (1685-1757). No. 619, George Frideric Handel (1685-1759). No. 620, Johann Sebastian Bach (1685-1750).

1985, May 16 Litho. *Perf. 14x15*

618 A223 22p multicolored 1.50 1.50
619 A223 22p multicolored 1.50 1.50
a. Pair, #618-619 3.00 3.00
620 A223 26p multicolored 1.50 1.50
Nos. 618-620 (3) 4.50 4.50

Irish UN Defense Forces in the Congo, 1960 A224

Thomas Ashe (1885-1917), Patriot and Educator — A225

Bishop George Berkeley (1685-1753), Philosopher and Educator — A226

Perf. 15x14, 14x15

1985, June 20 Litho.

621 A224 22p multicolored .90 .60
622 A225 26p multicolored 1.00 .70
623 A226 44p multicolored 1.60 1.50
Nos. 621-623 (3) 3.50 2.80

Irish forces as part of the UN Defense Forces, 25th anniv. (22p).

Intl. Youth Year — A227

1985, Aug. 1 Litho.

624 A227 22p multi, horiz. .85 .65
625 A227 26p multicolored 1.00 .75

Architecture Type of 1982

Designs: 24p, 39p, Aughnanure Castle. 28p, 32p, 37p, St. Mac Dara's Church. 46p, Cahir Castle. £1, Killarney Cathedral. £2, Casino, Marino. 46p, £2, horiz.

Perf. 15x14, 14x15 (A184, No. 644)

1985-88 Litho.

638 A185 24p brown .45 .30
639 A184 28p rose lake .50 .30
a. Bklt. pane, 4 2p, 2 24p, 1 4p, 5 28p ('88) 5.75
c. Bklt. pane, 2 2p, 3 4p, 3 24p, 4 28p ('88) 6.00
640 A184 32p brown .65 .40
641 A184 37p dull blue .75 .45
642 A185 39p rose lake .80 .50
643 A186 46p gray & gray grn .95 .60
644 A186 £1 gray & dull bl 1.90 1.10
645 A186 £2 gray & gray grn 6.00 3.00
Nos. 638-645 (8) 12.00 6.65

Issued: 24p, 28p, 37p, £1, June 27, 1985; 32p, 39p, 46p, May 1, 1986; £2, July 26, 1988.

Industrial Innovations A228

Institution of Engineers, 150th Anniv. A229

1985, Oct. 3 Litho. *Perf. 15x14*

646 A228 22p Computer technology .55 .50
647 A228 26p Peat production .70 .65
648 A229 44p The Key Man, by Sean Keating 1.10 1.10
Nos. 646-648 (3) 2.35 2.25

Candle, Holly — A230

Virgin and Child in a Landscape, by Adrian van Ijsenbrandt A231

Christmas: No. 651, The Holy Family, by Murillo. 26p, Adoration of the Shepherds, by Louis Le Nain, horiz.

Perf. 14x15, 15x14

1985, Nov. 26 Litho.

649 A230 22p shown .55 .30
650 A231 22p shown .55 .30
651 A231 22p multicolored .55 .30
a. Pair, #650-651 1.10 .75
652 A231 26p multicolored .65 .30
Nos. 649-652 (4) 2.30 1.20

#649 was issued in discount sheets of 16 that sold for £3.

Love — A232

1986, Jan. 30 *Perf. 14x15*

653 A232 22p shown .90 .50
654 A232 26p Heart-shaped mailbox 1.10 .55

Ferns — A233

Europa — A234

1986, Mar. 20 Litho. *Perf. 14½x15*

655 A233 24p Hart's tongue .80 .30
656 A233 28p Rusty-back .95 .45
657 A233 46p Killarney 1.60 1.25
Nos. 655-657 (3) 3.35 2.00

1986, May 1 *Perf. 14x15, 15x14*

658 A234 28p Industry and nature 12.50 1.50
659 A234 39p Hedgerows, horiz. 25.00 7.00

Aer Lingus, 50th Anniv. A235

1986, May 27 *Perf. 15x14*

660 A235 28p Jet, 1986 1.40 .45
661 A235 46p The Eagle, 1936 2.25 1.50

Inland Waterways A236

1986, May 27 *Perf. 15x14, 14x15*

662 A236 24p Robertstown Grand Canal .85 .45
663 A236 28p Fishing, County Mayo, vert. .95 .55
664 A236 30p Yachting, River Shannon 1.00 1.00
Nos. 662-664 (3) 2.80 2.00

British & Irish Steam Packet Co., 150th Anniv. A237

1986, July 10 *Perf. 15x14*

665 A237 24p Steamer Severn, 1836 .85 .65
666 A237 28p M.V. Leinster, 1986 1.00 .70

Lighthouses A238

1986, July 10 *Perf. 14½x15*

667 A238 24p Kish, helicopter 1.25 1.00
668 A238 30p Fastnet 1.75 1.50

Dublin Council of Trade Unions, Cent. — A239

Arthur Griffith (1871-1922), Statesman A240

Women in Society, Construction Surveyor — A241

A242

Intl. Peace Year A242a

Perf. 14½x15, 14x15 (#670, 672), 15x14½, 15x14

1986, Aug. 21

669 A239 24p multicolored .85 .65
670 A240 28p multicolored .95 .70
671 A241 28p multicolored .95 .70
672 A242 30p multi, vert. 1.00 .90
673 A242a 46p shown 1.60 1.40
Nos. 669-673 (5) 5.35 4.35

See Nos. 699, 711, 749, 807, 836.

William Mulready (1786-1863), Letter Sheet Designer — A243

Carriages by Charles Bianconi (1786-1875) — A244

Perf. 15x14, 14x15

1986, Oct. 2 Litho.

674 A243 24p multicolored .70 .50
675 A244 28p multi, vert. .80 .60
676 A244 39p shown 1.10 1.10
Nos. 674-676 (3) 2.60 2.20

Adoration of the Shepherds, by Francesco Pascucci A245

Adoration of the Magi, by Frans Francken III (1542-1616) A246

1986, Nov. 20 ***Perf. 15x14, 14½x15***

677 A245 21p multicolored .95 .45
678 A246 28p multicolored 1.25 .60

Christmas. #677 was issued in discount sheets of 16 that sold for £2.50.

Love A247

Perf. 15x14, 14x15

1987, Jan. 27 **Litho.**

679 A247 24p Flowers, butterfly .90 .45
680 A247 28p Postman, vert. 1.10 .55

Trolleys A248

1987, Mar. 4 **Litho.** ***Perf. 15x14***

681 A248 24p Cork Electric .80 .40
682 A248 28p Dublin Standard 1.00 .50
683 A248 30p Howth (G.N.R.) 1.10 .70
684 A248 46p Galway Horse 1.60 1.40
a. Miniature sheet of 4, #681-684 6.00 6.00
Nos. 681-684 (4) 4.50 3.00

See note following No. 584.

Waterford Chamber of Commerce, 200th Anniv. A249

Muintir Na Tire, 50th Anniv. A250

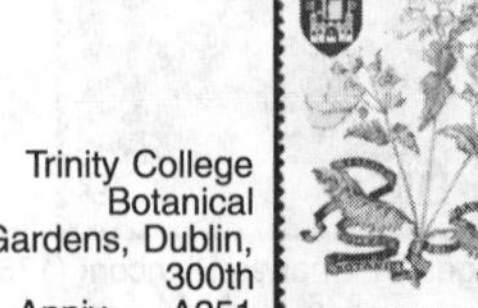

Trinity College Botanical Gardens, Dublin, 300th Anniv. — A251

Medical Missionaries of Mary, 50th Anniv. — A252

Anniversaries and events: 24p, Three ships, Chamber crest. 28p, Canon Hayes (1887-1957), founder, and symbols of Muintir Na Tire activities. 30p, College crest, Calceolaria burbidgei. 39p, Intl. Missionary Training Hospital, Drogheda, and Mother Mary Martin.

Perf. 15x14, 14x15

1987, Apr. 9 **Litho.**

685 A249 24p vio bl, blk & dk grn .75 .40
686 A250 28p multicolored .85 .45
687 A251 30p multicolored .90 .50
688 A252 39p multicolored 1.25 1.00
Nos. 685-688 (4) 3.75 2.35

Europa A253

Modern architecture, art: 28p, Borda na Mona headquarters, Dublin, and The Turf Cutter, by sculptor John Behan. 39p, St. Mary's Church and ruins of Romanesque monastery at Cong.

1987, May 14 ***Perf. 15x14***

689 A253 28p multicolored 3.50 2.50
690 A253 39p multicolored 8.00 6.75

Cattle A254

1987, July 2

691 A254 24p Kerry 1.00 .45
692 A254 28p Friesian 1.25 .60
693 A254 30p Hereford 1.25 .70
694 A254 39p Shorthorn 1.50 1.25
Nos. 691-694 (4) 5.00 3.00

Festivals A255

1987, Aug. 27 ***Perf. 14x15***

695 A255 24p Fleadh Nua, Ennis .70 .35
696 A255 28p Festival Queen, Tralee .85 .45
697 A255 30p Wexford opera festival .90 .60
698 A255 46p Ballinasloe horse fair 1.40 1.40
Nos. 695-698 (4) 3.85 2.80

Nos. 695-696 vert.

Statesmen Type of 1986 and

Ewer and Chalice, Company Crest A256

Harp in Shield, Preamble Excerpt A257

Woman Leading Board Meeting — A258

Design: No. 699, Cathal Brugha, vert.

Perf. 14x15, 15x14

1987, Oct. 1 **Litho.**

699 A240 24p black .80 .80
700 A256 24p multicolored .80 .80
701 A257 28p multicolored .90 .90
702 A258 46p multicolored 1.50 1.50
Nos. 699-702 (4) 4.00 4.00

Company of Goldsmiths of Dublin, 350th anniv. (No. 700); Irish Constitution, 50th anniv. (28p); Women in Society, (46p).

A259

Christmas A260

21p, 12 Days of Christmas (1st 3 days). 24p, Embroidery (detail), Waterford Vestments, 15th cent. 28p, Neapolitan creche (detail), 1850.

Perf. 15x14, 14x15

1987, Nov. 17 **Litho.**

703 A259 21p multicolored .75 .35
704 A260 24p multicolored .85 .40
705 A260 28p multicolored .95 .45
Nos. 703-705 (3) 2.55 1.20

No. 703 issued in discount sheets of 14 + center label; sheet sold for £2.90.

Love A261

Perf. 15x14½, 14½x15

1988, Jan. 27 **Litho.**

706 A261 24p shown 1.10 1.10
707 A261 28p Pillar box, vert. 1.25 1.25

Dublin Millennium A262

1988, Mar. 1 ***Perf. 15x14***

708 A262 28p multicolored .85 .45
a. Booklet pane of 4, Gaelic 3.50
b. Booklet pane of 4, English 3.50

Nos. 708a, 708b consist of two vert. pairs separated by a history in Gaelic or English.

See note following No. 584.

A263

Impact of the Irish Abroad A264

Designs: No. 709, Robert O'Hara Burke (1820-1861), by Sir Sidney Nolan; 19th cent. map of Australia with Burke & Wills expedition route. 46p, Mural (detail) of the Eureka Stockade by Nolan.

1988, Mar. 1

709 A263 24p multicolored .90 .40
710 A264 46p multicolored 1.60 1.50

Statesmen Type of 1986 and

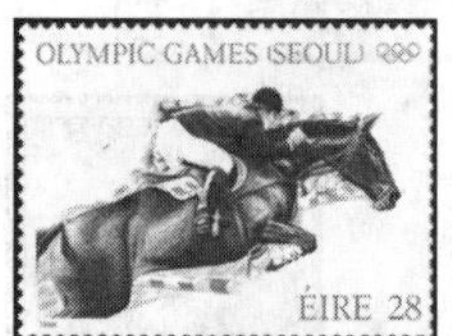

1988 Summer Olympics, Seoul A265

Order of Malta Ambulance Corps, 50th Anniv. A266

Barry Fitzgerald (1888-1961), Actor — A267

Designs: 24p, William T. Cosgrave (1880-1965), president of the United Ireland and Fine Gael party. No. 713, Cycling.

Perf. 14x15, 15x14

1988, Apr. 7 **Litho.**

711 A240 24p black .70 .45
712 A265 28p multicolored .85 .50
713 A265 28p multicolored .85 .50
a. Pair, #712-713 1.75 1.25
714 A266 30p multicolored 1.10 1.10
715 A267 50p multicolored 1.50 .85
Nos. 711-715 (5) 5.00 3.40

Nos. 712-713 printed in sheets of 5 each plus two labels.

Sirius Sailing from Passage West, County Cork A268

1988, May 12 **Litho.** ***Perf. 15x14***

716 A268 24p multicolored 1.00 .50

1st scheduled transatlantic crossing by steamship, sesquicentennial.

Europa A269

28p, Air traffic controllers and A320 Airbus. 39p, Europe on globe, letters.

1988, May 12 Litho. *Perf. 15x14*

717 A269 28p multicolored 4.00 1.25
718 A269 39p multicolored 5.50 3.75

Maia and Mercury Flying Boats in Foynes Harbor A269a

1988, May 12 Litho. *Perf. 15x14*

719 A269a 46p multicolored 1.75 1.75

1st east-west transatlantic crossing by seaplane, 50th anniv.

Conservation of Flora — A270

1988, June 21 Litho. *Perf. 14x15*

720 A270 24p Otanthus maritimus .80 .35
721 A270 28p Saxifraga hartii .90 .45
722 A270 46p Astragalus danicus 1.40 1.40
Nos. 720-722 (3) 3.10 2.20

Irish Security Forces A271

1988, Aug. 23 Litho. *Perf. 15x14*

723 A271 28p Garda Siochana (police) .75 .40
724 A271 28p Army .75 .40
725 A271 28p Navy, air corps .75 .40
726 A271 28p FCA, Slua Muiri .75 .40
a. Block or strip of 4, #723-726 3.00 3.00

Institute of Chartered Accountants, Cent. — A272

Defeat of the Spanish Armada, 400th Anniv. A273

Perf. 14x15, 15x14

1988, Oct. 6 Litho.

727 A272 24p multicolored .90 .40
728 A273 46p Duquesa Santa Ana off Donegal Coast 1.60 1.60

John F. Kennedy, Portrait by James Wyeth A274

1988, Nov. 24 Litho. *Perf. 15x14*

729 A274 28p multicolored 1.00 .50

A275

Christmas A276

1988, Nov. 24 *Perf. 14x15*

730 A275 21p St. Kevin's Church, Glendalough .60 .30
731 A276 24p Adoration of the Magi .70 .35
732 A276 28p Flight into Egypt .85 .40
733 A276 46p Holy Family 1.40 1.40
Nos. 730-733 (4) 3.55 2.45

No. 730 issued only in discount sheets of 14. Sheet sold for £2.90.

Love A277

The Sonnet, by William Mulready (1786-1863) A278

Perf. 15x14, 14x15

1989, Jan. 24 Litho.

734 A277 24p multicolored .80 .35
735 A278 28p multicolored .90 .45

Mulready, designer of Rowland Hill's first stamped envelope.

Classic Automobiles — A279

1989, Apr. 11 Litho. *Perf. 15x14*

736 A279 24p Silver Stream .65 .30
737 A279 28p Benz Comfortable .75 .45
a. Booklet pane, 2 each 24p, 28p 3.25
738 A279 39p Thomond Car 1.10 1.00
739 A279 46p Chambers Car 1.25 1.25
a. Booklet pane of 4, #736-739 4.25
Nos. 736-739 (4) 3.75 3.00

Parks and Gardens A280

1989, Apr. 11

740 A280 24p Garinish Is. .75 .35
741 A280 28p Glenveagh .85 .45
742 A280 32p Connemara Natl. Park 1.00 .50
743 A280 50p St. Stephen's Green 1.60 1.60
Nos. 740-743 (4) 4.20 2.90

Europa A281

1989, May 11

744 A281 28p Ring-a-ring-a-rosie 1.40 .50
745 A281 39p Hopscotch 2.00 1.50

Irish Red Cross Soc., 50th Anniv. — A282

1989, May 11 *Perf. 14x15*

746 A282 24p multicolored .70 .35

European Parliament 3rd Elections — A283

1989, May 11

747 A283 28p Stars from flag .75 .40

Sts. Kilian, Colman and Totnan (d. 689), Martyred Missionaries, and Shamrock — A284

1989, June 15 Litho. *Perf. 13½*

748 A284 28p multicolored .75 .40
a. Booklet pane of 4, English 3.00
b. Booklet pane of 4, Gaelic 3.00
c. Booklet pane of 4, German 3.00
d. Booklet pane of 4, Latin 3.00

See Federal Republic of Germany No. 1580.

Statesmen Type of 1986 and

RIAI Emblem — A285

Dublin-Cork Coach, 1789 — A286

Singer, Scene from La Boheme A287

Nehru — A288

Design: 24p, Sean Thomas O'Kelly (1883-1966), 2nd president.

Perf. 14x15, 15x14

1989, July 25 Litho.

749 A240 24p black .75 .40
750 A285 28p multicolored .85 .45
751 A286 28p multicolored .85 .45
752 A287 30p multicolored .95 .95
753 A288 46p red brown 1.50 1.50
Nos. 749-753 (5) 4.90 3.75

Royal Institute of Architects, 150th anniv.; Mail coach in Ireland, bicent.; Margaret Burke Sheridan (1889-1958), soprano; Jawaharlal Nehru, 1st prime minister of independent India.

Flags and *Sail Ireland Yacht Rounding Cape Horn,* by Des Fallon A289

1989, Aug. 31 Litho. *Perf. 15x14*

754 A289 28p multicolored 1.00 .45

Whitbread round of the World Yacht Race 1989-90.

Wildlife: Game Birds — A290

1989, Oct. 5 Litho. *Perf. 13½*

755 A290 24p *Lagopus lagopus* .95 .40
756 A290 28p *Vanellus vanellus* 1.10 .50
757 A290 39p *Scolopax rusticola* 1.50 1.25
758 A290 46p *Phasianus colchicus* 1.90 1.60
a. Miniature sheet of 4, #755-758 6.00 6.00
Nos. 755-758 (4) 5.45 3.75

Children and Creche — A291

Miniatures from a Flemish Psalter, 13th Cent. — A292

1989, Nov. 14 Litho. *Perf. 14x15*

759 A291 21p multicolored .65 .35
760 A292 24p Annunciation .75 .40
761 A292 28p Nativity .90 .45
762 A292 46p Adoration of the Magi 1.50 1.50
Nos. 759-762 (4) 3.80 2.70

No. 759 issued only in discount sheets of 14. Sheet sold for £2.90.

Ireland's Presidency of the European Communities — A293

European Tourism Year A294

1990, Jan. 9 Litho. *Perf. 15x14*

763 A293 30p multicolored 1.00 1.00
764 A294 50p multicolored 2.00 1.75

Love Issue — A295

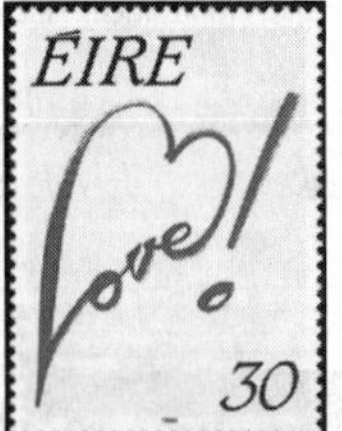

Love Issue — A296

1990, Jan. 30 Litho. *Perf. 14x15*

765 A295 26p shown 1.25 1.25
766 A296 30p "Love!" 1.25 1.25

Enamel Latchet Brooch — A297

Ardagh Chalice A298

Art treasures of Ireland: 1p, 2p, Silver Kite Brooch, vert. 4p, 5p, Dunamase Food Vessel, vert. 10p, Derrinboy Armlets. 20p, Gold Dress Fastener. 26p, 28p, Lismore Crosier, vert. 32p, Broighter Collar. 34p, 37p, 38p, 40p, Gleninsheen Collar, vert. 41p, 44p, 45p, Silver thistle brooch, vert. 50p, 52p, Broighter boat, vert. £2, Tara Brooch. £5, St. Patrick's Bell Shrine, vert.

1990-95 Litho. *Perf. 15x14, 14x15*

767 A297 1p blue & blk .20 .20
768 A297 2p orange & blk .20 .20
770 A297 4p violet & blk .20 .20
a. Perf. 13x13½ .20 .20
b. Photo. .20 .20
771 A297 5p green & blk .30 .20
774 A297 10p orange & blk .45 .30
777 A297 20p yel & blk (I) .80 .45
778 A297 26p violet & blk .90 .60
a. Perf. 13½ on 3 or 4 sides 2.50 2.50
779 A297 28p org & blk (I) 1.00 .65
a. Bklt. pane, 3 #770, 4 #779 + label 4.50
b. Photo. .85 .85
780 A297 30p brt blue & blk 1.10 .70
a. Perf. 13½ 2.50 2.50
b. Bklt. pane, 3 #540a, 1 #550d, 2 #778a, 2 #780a 5.50
c. Bklt. pane, #768, 3 #770, #778, 2 #780 + label 4.00
781 A297 32p green & blk 1.10 .75
a. Bklt. pane, 2 #770b, #779b, 2 #781d 3.25
b. Perf. 13½x13 1.25 1.25
c. Bklt. pane, #770a, 3 #781b 3.75
d. Photo. 1.00 1.00
e. Booklet pane, 1 #770, 3 #781 3.75
782 A297 34p yellow & blk 1.75 1.40
783 A297 37p green & blk 2.25 1.75
784 A297 38p purple & blk 2.25 1.75
785 A297 40p blue & black 2.25 1.75
786 A297 41p orange & blk 1.75 1.10
787 A297 44p yellow & blk 1.75 1.10
788 A297 45p violet & black 2.25 2.00
789 A297 50p yellow & blk 2.25 1.40
790 A297 52p blue & blk (I) 2.50 2.00
791 A298 £1 yellow & blk 3.00 2.10
792 A298 £2 green & blk 5.75 4.25
793 A298 £5 blue & blk 14.00 10.50

Self-Adhesive

Die cut perf 11

Size: 27x21mm

794 A297 32p like #781 1.50 .90
a. Die cut perf. 11½ 1.50 .90
Nos. 767-794 (23) 49.50 36.25

Issued: 26p, 30p, 32p, 41p, 50p, £1, 3/8; #780b, 5/3; 1p, 2p, 4p, 10p, 34p, £2, 7/26; #780c, 11/15; 5p, 20p, £5, 1/26/91; #781a, 5/14/91; 28p, 37p, 38p, 44p, 52p, 4/3/91; #779a, 10/17/91; #794, 10/31/91; 40p, 45p, 5/14/92; #770a, 781b, 9/24/93; #781e, 11/16/95.

£1
#791-793

£1
Type IV

Nos. 777a-790a (type II):
Type I - Coarse background dot structure.
Type II - Fine background dot structure.

Perf. 14x15, 15x14

1995, Nov. 15 Litho.

777a A297 20p Type II 2.50 2.00
779c A297 28p Type II 2.50 2.00
790a A297 52p Type II 3.25 2.50
791a A298 £1 Type IV 5.25 4.25
792a A298 £2 Type IV 10.50 8.25
793a A298 £5 Type IV 24.00 19.00
Nos. 777a-793a (6) 48.00 38.00

A299

A300

1990, Mar. 22 Litho. *Perf. 14x15*

Booklet Stamps

795 A299 26p Gift boxes 3.00 2.75
796 A299 26p Nosegay 3.00 2.75
797 A299 30p Horseshoe 3.00 2.75
798 A299 30p Balloons 3.00 2.75
a. Bklt. pane of 4, #795-798 English labels 12.50
b. As "a," 4 English, 4 Gaelic labels 12.50

Greetings. Available only in discount booklets containing #798a, 798b. Bklts. sold for £1.98.

1990, Apr. 5 Litho. *Perf. 14x15*

799 A300 30p Tackle 1.75 *2.00*
800 A300 30p Heading the ball 1.75 *2.00*
a. Pair, #799-800 3.50 *4.00*

1990 World Cup Soccer Championships, Italy.
Printed in sheets of 8 plus label.

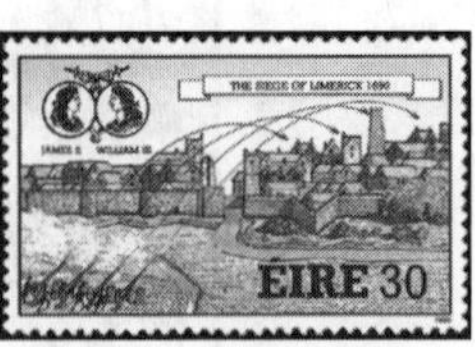

Williamite Wars, 300th Anniv. — A301

1990, Apr. 5 Litho. *Perf. 13½*

801 A301 30p Siege of Limerick 1.25 1.25
802 A301 30p Battle of the Boyne 1.25 1.25
a. Pair, #801-802 2.50 2.50

Penny Black, 150th Anniv. A302

1990, May 3 Litho. *Perf. 15x14*

803 A302 30p #780 1.10 .90
a. Bklt. pane, #803, 2 each #552a, 780a 6.50
804 A302 50p #68, 255, 550, 780 1.75 1.40
a. Bklt. pane, 2 ea #803-804 7.50
b. Bklt. pane of 4, #552a, 780a, 803-804 6.50

See note following No. 584.

Europa 1990 — A303

Post offices.

1990, May 3 *Perf. 14x15*

805 A303 30p GPO, Dublin 1.50 1.00
806 A303 41p Westport P.O., County Mayo 1.75 1.75

Printed in sheets of 10+2 labels.

Statesman Type of 1986

1990, June 21 Litho. *Perf. 14x15*

807 A240 30p Michael Collins 2.25 1.25

Irish Missionaries — A304

Design: 50p, Working at water pump.

1990, June 21 *Perf. 15x14*

808 A304 26p multicolored .80 .80
809 A304 50p multicolored 1.60 1.60

Garden Flowers — A305

1990, Aug. 30 Litho. *Perf. 14x15*

810 A305 26p Narcissus .80 .70
811 A305 30p Rosa x hibernica .95 .95
a. Bklt. pane, 2 each #810-811 6.00
812 A305 41p Primula 1.40 1.40
813 A305 50p Erica erigena 1.60 1.60
a. Booklet pane of 4, #810-813 6.50
Nos. 810-813 (4) 4.75 4.65

See note following No. 584.

Theater A306

Designs: No. 814, Playboy of the Western World. No. 815, Juno and the Paycock. No. 816, The Field. No. 817, Waiting for Godot.

1990, Oct. 18 Litho. *Perf. 13½*

814 A306 30p multicolored 1.50 *1.75*
815 A306 30p multicolored 1.50 *1.75*
816 A306 30p multicolored 1.50 *1.75*
817 A306 30p multicolored 1.50 *1.75*
a. Block or strip of 4, #814-817 6.00 *7.00*

A307

Christmas A308

1990, Nov. 15 Litho. *Perf. 14x15*

818 A307 26p Child praying .90 .90
819 A308 26p Nativity scene .90 .90
820 A308 30p Madonna and Child 1.10 1.10
821 A308 50p Adoration of the Magi 1.75 1.75
Nos. 818-821 (4) 4.65 4.65

No. 818 sold only in discount sheets of 12 for £2.86.

Love — A309

Irish Cycles — A310

1991, Jan. 29 Litho. *Perf. 14x15*

822 A309 26p shown .90 .90
823 A309 30p Boy, girl kissing 1.10 1.10

1991, Mar. 5

824 A310 26p Starley rover .90 .75
825 A310 30p Child's horse tricycle 1.10 1.10
826 A310 50p Penny farthing 1.75 1.75
a. Souvenir sheet of 3, #824-826 3.75 3.75
Nos. 824-826 (3) 3.75 3.60

See note following No. 584.

1916 Rising, 75th Anniv. A311

Design: Statue of Cuchulainn by Oliver Sheppard, 1916 Proclamation.

1991, Apr. 3 Litho. *Perf. 15x14*

827 A311 32p multicolored 1.25 1.00

Dublin, European City of Culture A312

Designs: 28p, La Traviata, performed by Dublin Grand Opera Society. 32p, Dublin City Hall. 44p, St. Patrick's Cathedral, 800th anniv. 52p, Custom House, 200th anniv.

1991, Apr. 11 *Perf. 15x14*

828 A312 28p multicolored .85 .85
829 A312 32p multicolored 1.00 1.00
830 A312 44p multicolored 1.25 1.25
a. Booklet pane of 3, #828-830 3.75

Size: 41x25mm

Perf. 13½

831 A312 52p multicolored 1.50 1.50
a. Booklet pane of 4, #828-831 4.00
Nos. 828-831 (4) 4.60 4.60

50th anniv. of Dublin Grand Opera Soc. (No. 828).

Europa A313

1991, May 14 Litho. *Perf. 15x14*

832 A313 32p Giotto probe 1.25 1.25
833 A313 44p Hubble telescope 2.00 2.00

Williamite Wars, 300th Anniv. A314

1991, May 14

834 A314 28p Siege of Athlone 1.10 1.10
835 A314 28p Treaty of Limerick 1.10 1.10
a. Pair, #834-835 2.25 2.25

Statesman Type of 1986 and

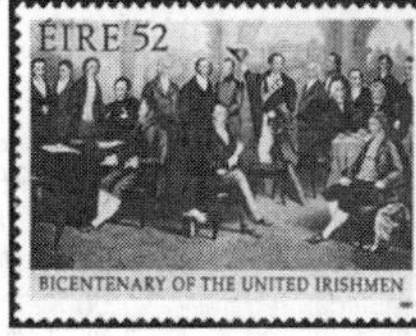

Charles Stewart Parnell (1846-1891), Politician — A315

Society of United Irishmen, Bicent. A316

28p, John A. Costello (1891-1976), politician.

Perf. 14x15, 15x14

1991, July 2 Litho.

836 A240 28p black 1.00 1.00
837 A315 32p multicolored 1.10 1.10
838 A316 52p multicolored 1.90 1.90
Nos. 836-838 (3) 4.00 4.00

A317

Perf. 15x14, 14x15

1991, Sept. 3 Litho.

839 A317 28p Golfer putting, horiz. 1.10 .75
840 A317 32p shown 1.40 1.00

Walker Cup Competition, Portmarnock Golf Club (No. 839).

Irish Sheep — A318

1991, Sept. 3 *Perf. 14x15, 15x14*

841 A318 32p Wicklow Cheviot 1.00 .75
842 A318 38p Donegal Blackface 1.50 1.50
843 A318 52p Galway, horiz. 2.00 2.00
Nos. 841-843 (3) 4.50 4.25

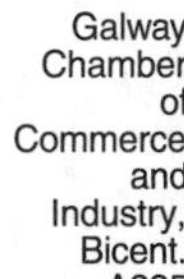

Fishing Fleet A319

1991, Oct. 17 Litho. *Perf. 15x14*

844 A319 28p Boatyard .60 .60
845 A319 32p Inshore trawler .80 .80
a. Bklt. pane of 5, #845, 2 each #768, 783 4.00
b. Bklt. pane, 2 each #844, 845 4.00
846 A319 44p Inshore potter 1.60 1.60
847 A319 52p Factory ship 2.00 2.00
a. Booklet pane of 4, #844-847 5.00
Nos. 844-847 (4) 5.00 5.00

See note following No. 584.

A320

Christmas A321

1991, Nov. 14 Litho. *Perf. 14x15*

848 A320 28p Wise men, star .85 .85
849 A321 28p Annunciation .95 .80
850 A321 32p Nativity 1.00 .90
851 A321 52p Adoration of the Magi 1.75 1.75
Nos. 848-851 (4) 4.55 4.30

No. 848 issued only in discount sheets of 13+2 labels which sold for £3.36.

Love A322

Design: 32p, Rainbow over meadow, love etched in stone, vert.

Perf. 15x14, 14x15

1992, Jan. 28 Litho.

852 A322 28p shown .90 .90
853 A322 32p multicolored 1.10 1.10

1992 Summer Olympics, Barcelona A323

1992, Feb. 25 Litho. *Perf. 15x14*

854 A323 32p Boxing 1.00 1.00
855 A323 44p Sailing 1.40 1.40
a. Sheet of 4, 2 each #854-855 6.00 *6.50*

See note following No. 584.

Healthy Lifestyle — A324

1992, Feb. 25 *Perf. 14x15*

856 A324 28p multicolored 1.10 1.10

Galway Chamber of Commerce and Industry, Bicent. A325

1992, Apr. 2 Litho. *Perf. 15x14*

857 A325 28p multicolored .90 .90

Intl. Maritime Heritage Year A326

Perf. 15x14, 14x15

1992, Apr. 2 Litho.

858 A326 32p Mari Cog 1.25 1.00
859 A326 52p Ovoca, vert. 1.75 1.75

Greetings — A327

1992, Apr. 2 *Perf. 14x15*

860 A327 28p Coastline 1.50 1.50
861 A327 28p Mountain 1.50 1.50
862 A327 32p Flowers 1.50 1.50
863 A327 32p Pond 1.50 1.50
a. Bklt. pane of 4, #860-863, 8 English labels 7.50
b. Bklt. pane of 4, #860-863, 4 English labels + 4 Gaelic labels 7.50
Nos. 860-863 (4) 6.00 6.00

#863a contains #860-863 in order. #863b contains #862, 863, 860 and 861 in order.

Discovery of America, 500th Anniv. A328

Europa: 44p, Landing in New World.

1992, May 14 Litho. *Perf. 15x14*

864 A328 32p multicolored 1.25 1.25
865 A328 44p multicolored 1.50 1.50

Irish in the Americas — A329

Design: No. 867, The White House, bridge, railroad workers, musicians, workers.

1992, May 14 *Perf. 13½*

866 A329 52p multicolored 1.75 1.75
867 A329 52p multicolored 1.75 1.75
a. Pair, #866-867 3.50 3.50

Pine Marten A330

1992, July 9 Litho. *Perf. 15x14*

868 A330 28p shown 1.40 .75
869 A330 32p In tree 1.40 .90
870 A330 44p With young 2.25 2.00
871 A330 52p Holding bird 2.50 2.25
Nos. 868-871 (4) 7.55 5.90

World Wildlife Fund.

Trinity College, Dublin, 400th Anniv. — A331

1992, Sept. 2 Litho. *Perf. 13½*

872 A331	32p	Library	1.10	1.10
873 A331	52p	Main entrance	1.75	1.75

Views of Dublin by James Malton, Bicent. A332

1992, Sept. 2 *Perf. 15x14*

874 A332	28p	Rotunda, Assembly rooms	.90	.75
875 A332	44p	Charlemont House	1.50	1.50

Single European Market A333

1992, Oct. 15 Litho. *Perf. 15x14*

876 A333	32p	multicolored	1.00	1.00
a.		Bklt. pane of 3	3.00	
b.		Bklt. pane of 4	3.50	

No. 876b comes with stamps in three formats: four singles, two pairs, and block of four. See note following No. 584.

Food and Farming — A334

1992, Oct. 15 *Perf. 14x15*

877 A334	32p	Fresh food	1.10	1.00
878 A334	32p	Cattle	1.10	1.00
879 A334	32p	Combine harvesting grain	1.10	1.00
880 A334	32p	Growing vegetables	1.10	1.00
a.		Strip of 4, #877-880	4.40	4.40

A335

Christmas A336

Designs: No. 881, Rural churchyard. No. 882, The Annunciation, manuscript illustration, Chester Beatty Library, Dublin. 32p, Adoration of the Shepherds, by Jocopo da Empoli. 52p, Adoration of the Magi, by Johann Rottenhammer.

1992, Nov. 19

881 A335	28p	multicolored	.90	.60
882 A336	28p	multicolored	.95	.65
883 A336	32p	multicolored	1.10	1.00
884 A336	52p	multicolored	1.75	1.75
		Nos. 881-884 (4)	4.70	4.00

No. 881 issued only in discount sheets of 13+2 labels which sold for £3.36.

Love A337

Design: 28p, Queen of Hearts, vert.

Perf. 14x15, 15x14

1993, Jan. 26 Litho.

885 A337	28p	multicolored	.80	.80
886 A337	32p	multicolored	.95	.95

Irish Impressionist Paintings — A338

Designs: 28p, Evening at Tangier, by Sir John Lavery. 32p, The Goose Girl, by William J. Leech. 44p, La Jeune Bretonne, by Roderic O'Conor, vert. 52p, Lustre Jug, by Walter Osborne, vert.

1993, Mar. 4 *Perf. 13*

887 A338	28p	multicolored	.80	.70
888 A338	32p	multicolored	.95	.80
a.		Booklet pane of 2, #887-888	3.00	
889 A338	44p	multicolored	1.25	1.25
890 A338	52p	multicolored	1.50	1.50
a.		Booklet pane of 2, #889-890	3.50	
b.		Booklet pane of 4, #887-890	5.00	
		Nos. 887-890 (4)	4.50	4.25

No. 890b exists in two formats with different margin inscriptions.

Orchids — A339

1993, Apr. 20 Litho. *Perf. 14x15*

891 A339	28p	Bee orchid	.80	.45
892 A339	32p	O'Kelly's orchid	.95	.75
893 A339	38p	Dark red helleborine	1.60	1.60
894 A339	52p	Irish lady's tresses	1.90	1.90
a.		Souvenir sheet of 4, #891-894	6.00	6.00
b.		As "a," with blue inscription	10.00	10.00
		Nos. 891-894 (4)	5.25	4.70

No. 894b has a larger top margin than No. 894a. Added Inscription includes text and flags of Ireland and Thailand.

Contemporary Paintings — A340

Europa: 32p, Pears in a Copper Pan, by Hilda van Stockum. 44p, Arrieta Orzola, by Tony O'Malley.

1993, May 18 Litho. *Perf. 13x13½*

895 A340	32p	multicolored	1.00	.80
896 A340	44p	multicolored	1.25	1.25

Issued in sheets of 10 + 2 labels.

Gaelic League, Cent. A341

Design: 52p, Illuminated manuscript presented to founder Douglas Hyde, vert.

Perf. 15x14, 14x15

1993, July 8 Litho.

897 A341	32p	multicolored	1.25	1.00
898 A341	52p	multicolored	1.75	1.75

Irish Amateur Swimming Assoc., Cent. A342

Designs: No. 899, Swimmer diving into water. No. 900, Woman swimming.

1993, July 8 *Perf. 15x14*

899 A342	32p	multicolored	1.25	1.25
900 A342	32p	multicolored	1.25	1.25
a.		Pair, #899-900	2.50	2.50

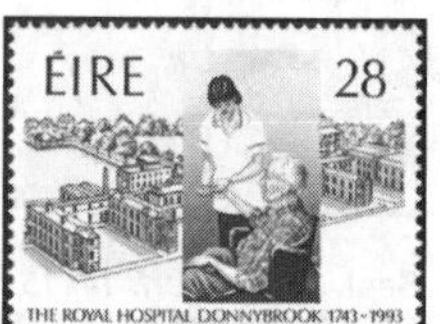

Royal Hospital Donnybrook, 250th Anniv. — A343

Ceide Fields, County Mayo A345

Carlow College, Bicent. — A344

Edward Bunting (1773-1843), Composer — A346

Perf. 15x14, 14x15, 13½ (52p)

1993, Sept. 2 Litho.

901 A343	28p	multicolored	.80	.55
902 A344	32p	multicolored	.95	.60
903 A345	44p	multicolored	1.25	1.25
904 A346	52p	multicolored	1.50	1.50
		Nos. 901-904 (4)	4.50	3.90

Irish Buses A347

Designs: 28p, Great Northern Railways Gardner. 32p, CIE Leyland Titan. No. 907, Horse-drawn omnibus. No. 908, Char-a-banc.

1993, Oct. 12 Litho. *Perf. 15x14*

905 A347	28p	multicolored	.80	.80
906 A347	32p	multicolored	.85	.80
a.		Booklet pane, 2 each #905-906	4.00	
907 A347	52p	multicolored	1.75	1.75
908 A347	52p	multicolored	1.75	1.75
a.		Pair, #907-908	3.50	3.50
b.		Booklet pane of 4, #905-908	5.00	
		Nos. 905-908 (4)	5.15	5.10

A348

Christmas A349

Designs: 32p, Mary placing infant Jesus in manger. 52p, Adoration of the shepherds.

Perf. 14x15, 15x14

1993, Nov. 16 Litho.

909 A348	28p	multicolored	.80	.70
910 A349	28p	multicolored	.80	.70
911 A349	32p	multicolored	.90	.75
912 A349	52p	multicolored	1.50	1.50
		Nos. 909-912 (4)	4.00	3.65

No. 909 issued only in discount sheets of 13+2 labels which sold for £3.36.

Love A350

32p, Man, woman in shape of heart, vert.

Perf. 15x14, 14x15

1994, Jan. 27 Litho.

913 A350	28p	multicolored	.80	.80
914 A350	32p	multicolored	.95	.95

Greetings Stamps — A351

1994, Jan. 27 ***Perf. 14x15***

915 A351 32p Face in sun 1.60 1.60
916 A351 32p Face in flower 1.60 1.60
917 A351 32p Face in heart 1.60 1.60
a. Souv. sheet of 3, #915-917 7.50 7.50
918 A351 32p Face in rose 1.60 1.60
a. Booklet pane of 4, #915-918, 4 English + 4 Gaelic labels 6.00
b. As "a," 8 English labels 6.00
Nos. 915-918 (4) 6.40 6.40

New Year 1994 (Year of the Dog), Hong Kong '94 (#917a).
#918a contains 915-918 in order. #918b contains 917, 918, 915, 916 in order.

Macra na Feirme, 50th Anniv. A352

The Taking of Christ, by Caravaggio A353

Irish Co-operative Organization Society, Cent. — A354

Irish Congress of Trade Unions, Cent. A355

1994, Mar. 2 **Litho.** ***Perf. 15x14***

919 A352 28p blue & gold .80 .70
920 A353 32p multicolored .95 .75
921 A354 38p multicolored 1.10 1.10
922 A355 52p blue, blk & lt blue 1.50 1.50
Nos. 919-922 (4) 4.35 4.05

Voyages of St. Brendan (487-577) A356

Europa: 32p, St. Brendan, Irish monks sailing past volcano. 44p, St. Brendan on island with sheep, monks in boat.

1994, Apr. 18 **Litho.** ***Perf. 15x14***

923 A356 32p multicolored 1.00 .80
924 A356 44p multicolored 1.50 1.50
a. Miniature sheet of 2, #923-924 3.00 3.00

See Faroe Islands Nos. 264-265; Iceland Nos. 780-781.

Parliamentary Anniversaries — A357

#925, 1st meeting of the Dail, 1919. #926, 4th direct elections to European Parliament.

1994, Apr. 27

925 A357 32p multicolored 1.10 1.00
926 A357 32p multicolored 1.10 1.00
a. Booklet pane, 1 each #925-926 2.00
b. Booklet pane, 2 each #925-926 4.25

1994 World Cup Soccer Championships, US — A358

Players from: No. 927, Argentina in striped shirt, Ireland in green. No. 928, Ireland, Germany.

1994, May 31 ***Perf. 14x15***

927 A358 32p multicolored 1.50 1.50
928 A358 32p multicolored 1.50 1.50
a. Pair, #927-928 3.00 3.00

Women's Hockey A359

32p, 1994 Women's Hockey World Cup, Dublin. 52p, Irish Ladies' Hockey Union, cent.

1994, May 31 ***Perf. 13x13½***

929 A359 32p multicolored 1.25 1.00
930 A359 52p multicolored 1.50 1.50

Moths A360

1994, July 12 **Litho.** ***Perf. 14½x14***

931 A360 28p Garden tiger .90 .75
932 A360 32p Burren green 1.00 .80
933 A360 38p Emperor 1.25 1.25
934 A360 52p Elephant hawkmoth 1.60 1.60
a. Souvenir sheet of 4, #931-934 5.50 5.50
b. As "a," overprinted 6.75 6.75
Nos. 931-934 (4) 4.75 4.40

Size: 34x23mm

Self-Adhesive

Die Cut Perf. 11½

935 A360 32p like #932 1.25 1.25
936 A360 32p like #931 1.25 1.25
937 A360 32p like #934 1.25 1.25
938 A360 32p like #933 1.25 1.25
a. Strip of 4, #935-938 4.00 4.00

Overprint on #934b shows PHILAKOREA '94 exhibition emblem and Chinese inscription.

A361

A362

A363

Anniversaries and Events — A364

28p, Medieval view of Drogheda. #940, Edmund Ignatius Rice (1762-1844), philantropist. #941, Edmund Burke (1729-97), political commentator. #942, Eamonn Andrews (1922-87), broadcaster. #943, Vickers Vimy aircraft.

1994, Sept. 6 **Litho.** ***Perf. 13½***

939 A361 28p multicolored .90 .90

Perf. 14x14½

940 A362 32p multicolored 1.00 1.00

Perf. 14x13½

941 A363 32p multicolored 1.00 1.00
942 A363 52p multicolored 1.60 1.60

Perf. 15x14

943 A364 52p multicolored 1.60 1.60
Nos. 939-943 (5) 6.10 6.10

Drogheda, 800th anniv. (#939). First Newfoundland-Ireland transatlantic flight, 75th anniv. (#943).

Nobel Prize Winners A365

#944, George Bernard Shaw (1856-1950), dramatist, essayist. #945, Samuel Beckett (1906-89), playwright. 32p, Sean McBride (1904-88), statesman. 52p, William Butler Yeats (1865-1939), poet.

1994, Oct. 18 **Litho.** ***Perf. 15x14***

944 A365 28p multicolored .90 .90
945 A365 28p multicolored .90 .90
a. Pair, #944-945 1.80 1.80
946 A365 32p multicolored 1.00 1.00
a. Booklet pane of 3, #944-946 2.80
b. Bklt. pane, #944-945, 2 #946 3.80
947 A365 52p multicolored 1.60 1.60
a. Booklet pane, 1 #946, 2 #947 4.25
b. Booklet pane of 4, #944-947 4.50
Prestige bklt., #946a-946b, 947a-947b 17.50
Nos. 944-947 (4) 4.40 4.40

A366

Christmas A367

#948, Stained glass nativity scene. #949, Annunciation, detail, 11th cent. ivory plaque. 32p, Flight Into Egypt, 15th cent. wood carving. 52p, Nativity, detail, 11th cent. ivory plaque.

1994, Nov. 17 **Litho.** ***Perf. 14x15***

948 A366 28p multicolored .80 .80
949 A367 28p multicolored .90 .90
950 A367 32p multicolored 1.00 1.00
951 A367 52p multicolored 1.60 1.60
Nos. 948-951 (4) 4.30 4.30

No. 948 issued only in discount sheets of 13+2 labels which sold for £3.36.

Greetings Stamps — A368

1995, Jan. 24 **Litho.** ***Perf. 14x15***

952 A368 32p Tree of hearts 1.25 1.25

Booklet Stamps

953 A368 32p Teddy bear, balloon 1.25 1.25
954 A368 32p Clown juggling hearts 1.25 1.25
955 A368 32p Bouquet of flowers 1.25 1.25
a. Booklet pane, #952-955 + 4 English, 4 Gaelic labels 5.50
b. As "a," 8 English labels 5.50
Complete booklet, #955a-955b 8.00
c. Souvenir sheet, #952, 954-955 + 3 English, 3 Gaelic labels 6.00 6.00

New Year 1995 (Year of the Boar) (#955c).
No. 955a contains #953-954, 952, 955 in order. No. 955b contains #952, 955, 953-954 in order.

Narrow Gauge Railways A369

1995, Feb. 28 **Litho.** ***Perf. 15x14***

956 A369 28p West Clare .90 .90
957 A369 32p Co. Donegal 1.10 1.10
958 A369 38p Cork & Muskerry 1.25 1.25
959 A369 52p Cavan & Leitrim 1.75 1.75
a. Souvenir sheet of 4, #956-959 5.50 5.50
Nos. 956-959 (4) 5.00 5.00

No. 959a exists with Singapore '95 overprint in sheet margin.

Peace & Freedom A370

Europa: Nos. 960, 962, Stylized dove, reconstructed city. 44p, No. 963, Stylized dove, map of Europe.

1995, Apr. 6 **Litho.** ***Perf. 15x14***

960 A370 32p multicolored 1.10 1.00
961 A370 44p multicolored 1.90 1.90

Size: 34½x23mm
Self-Adhesive
Die Cut Perf. 11½

962 A370 32p multicolored 1.25 1.25
963 A370 32p multicolored 1.25 1.25
Nos. 960-963 (4) 5.50 5.40

Nos. 962-963 are coil stamps, printed in horizontal rolls of 100, with 50 of each value alternating.

1995 Rugby World Cup A371

1995, Apr. 6 ***Perf. 14***

964 A371 32p shown 1.10 1.00
965 A371 52p Player being tackled 1.60 1.60

Souvenir Sheet

966 A371 £1 like #964 3.75 3.75

No. 966 has a continuous design.

A372 A373

32p, Irish soldiers, Cross of Fontenoy.

1995, May 15 Photo. ***Perf. 11½***

967 A372 32p multicolored 1.10 1.10

Battle of Fontenoy, 250th Anniv. See Belgium No. 1583.

1995, May 15 Litho. ***Perf. 14x15***

Military uniforms: 28p, Irish Brigade, French Army, 1745. No. 969, Tercio Irlanda, Army of Flanders, 1605. No. 970, Royal Dublin Fusiliers, 1914. 38p, St. Patrick's Battalion, Papal Army, 1860. 52p, The Fighting 69th, Army of Potomac, 1861.

968 A373 28p multicolored .90 .45
969 A373 32p multicolored 1.00 .50
a. Bklt. pane, 2 ea #968-969 3.50
970 A373 32p multicolored 1.00 .50
971 A373 38p multicolored 1.25 .60
a. Bklt. pane of 3, #968-969, #971 3.25
972 A373 52p multicolored 1.75 .85
a. Bklt. pane of 3, #968-969, 972 3.00
b. Bklt. pane of 4, #968-969, 971-972 3.75
Prestige booklet, #969a, 971a, 972a, 972b 16.00
Nos. 968-972 (5) 5.90 2.90

Radio, Cent. A374

Designs: No. 973, Guglielmo Marconi, transmitting equipment. No. 974, Radio channel dial.

1995, June 8 Litho. ***Perf. 13½***

973 A374 32p multicolored 1.10 1.10
974 A374 32p multicolored 1.10 1.10
a. Pair, #973-974 2.25 2.25

See Germany #1900, Italy #2038-2039, San Marino #1336-1337, Vatican City #978-979.

A375

A376

A377

Anniversaries & Events A378

Designs: 28p, Dr. Bartholomew Mosse, Rotunda Hospital. No. 976, Piper, laurel wreath over map of Europe. No. 977, St. Patrick's College. 52p, Geological map of Ireland.

1995, July 27 Litho. ***Perf. 14½x14***

975 A375 28p multicolored .90 .90
976 A376 32p multicolored 1.00 1.00

Perf. 14½

977 A377 32p multicolored 1.00 1.00

Perf. 13½

978 A378 52p multicolored 1.60 1.60
Nos. 975-978 (4) 4.50 4.50

Rotunda Hospital, 250th anniv. (#975). End of World War II, 50th anniv. (#976). St. Patrick's College, Maynooth, bicent. (#977). Geological survey of Ireland, 150th anniv. (#978).

Reptiles & Amphibians — A379

1995, Sept. 1 Litho. ***Perf. 15x14***

979 A379 32p Natterjack toad 1.00 1.00
980 A379 32p Common lizard 1.00 1.00
981 A379 32p Smooth newt 1.00 1.00
982 A379 32p Common frog 1.00 1.00
a. Strip of 4, #979-982 4.00 4.00

Die Cut Perf. 9¼
Size: 34½x22½mm
Self-Adhesive

982B A379 32p like No. 979 1.00 1.00
982C A379 32p like No. 980 1.00 1.00
982D A379 32p like No. 981 1.00 1.00
982E A379 32p like No. 982 1.00 1.00
f. Strip of 4, Nos. 982B-982E 4.00

Natl. Botanic Gardens, Bicent. — A380

Designs: 32p, Crinum moorei. 38p, Sarracenia x moorei. 44p, Solanum crispum "glasnevin."

1995, Oct. 9 Litho. ***Perf. 14x15***

983 A380 32p multicolored 1.00 .75
984 A380 38p multicolored 1.10 1.10
985 A380 44p multicolored 1.40 1.40
a. Booklet pane of 3, #983-985 3.75
b. Bklt. pane of 3, #984-985, 2 #983 4.75
Complete booklet, #985a-985b 8.50
Nos. 983-985 (3) 3.50 3.25

UN, 50th Anniv. A381

1995, Oct. 19 ***Perf. 13x13½***

986 A381 32p shown 1.00 .75
987 A381 52p UN, "50" emblem 1.50 1.50

A382

Christmas A383

Designs: No. 988, Adoration of the Magi. No. 989, Adoration of the Shepherds. 32p, Adoration of the Magi. 52p, Nativity.

1995, Nov. 16 Litho. ***Perf. 14½x14***

988 A382 28p multicolored .90 .90
989 A383 28p multicolored .90 .90
990 A383 32p multicolored 1.10 1.10
991 A383 52p multicolored 1.60 1.60
Nos. 988-991 (4) 4.50 4.50

No. 988 issued only in discount sheets of 13+2 labels, which sold for £3.36.

Greetings/Love Stamps — A384

Television cartoon characters from "Zog, Zig and Zag:" No. 992, With hearts. No. 993, Waving hands. No. 994, In car, wearing space helmets. No. 995, Holding out hands, wearing hats.

1996, Jan. 23 Litho. ***Perf. 14x15***

992 A384 32p multicolored 1.50 1.00

Booklet Stamps

993 A384 32p multicolored 1.50 1.50
994 A384 32p multicolored 1.50 1.50
995 A384 32p multicolored 1.50 1.50
a. Booklet pane, Nos. 992-995, 5 English, 3 Gaelic labels 5.75
b. As "a," 7 English, 1 Gaelic label 5.75
Complete booklet, #995a-995b 8.00
c. Souvenir sheet, Nos. 992, 994-995 + 4 English, 2 Gaelic labels, 1 large label with Chinese inscription 6.50 6.50

No. 995a contains Nos. 993-995, 992 in order. No. 995b contains Nos. 995, 992-994 in order.

New Year 1996 (Year of the Rat) (#995c).

A385

1996 Summer/Paralympic Games, Atlanta — A386

1996, Feb. 1

996 A385 28p show .80 .75
997 A386 32p Discus .90 .90
998 A386 32p Canoeing .90 .90
999 A386 32p Running .90 .90
a. Strip of 3, Nos. 997-999 2.75 2.75

No. 999a printed in sheets of 9 stamps.

L'Imaginaire Irlandais — A387

1996, Mar. 12 Litho. ***Perf. 15x14***

1000 A387 32p multicolored 1.00 .90

Irish Horse Racing A388

1996, Mar. 12 Litho. ***Perf. 15x14***

1001 A388 28p Fairyhouse .90 .90
1002 A388 32p Punchestown 1.00 1.00
1003 A388 32p The Curragh 1.00 1.00
a. Pair, #1002-1003 2.00 2.00
b. Booklet pane, 2 #1001, 1 each #1002-1003 4.00
c. Souv. sheet, #1002-1003 15.00 15.00
1004 A388 38p Galway 1.25 1.25
a. Booklet pane, 2 #1002, 1 #1004 3.75
1005 A388 52p Leopardstown 1.60 1.60
a. Bklt. pane, #1005, 2 #1003 3.75
b. Bklt. pane, 1 ea #1002-1005 4.75
Prestige booklet, Nos. 1003b, 1004a, 1005a, 1005b 15.60
Nos. 1001-1005 (5) 5.75 5.75

No. 1003c for China '96.

UNESCO World Heritage Site A389

UNICEF, 50th Anniv. A390

Designs: 28p, Passage tombs, Bru na Bóinne National Monument, Boyne Valley. 32p, Children.

1996, Apr. 2 Litho. *Perf. 14*

1006	A389	28p	sepia & black	1.00	.50
1007	A390	32p	multicolored	1.25	.75

Europa A391

32p, Louie Bennett (1870-1956), Suffragette, trade unionist. 44p, Lady Augusta Gregory (1852-1932), playwright, co-founder of Abbey Theatre.

1996, Apr. 2 *Perf. 15x14*

1008	A391	32p	violet	1.10	1.00
1009	A391	44p	green	1.50	1.50

Die Cut 9¼

Self-Adhesive Coil Stamps

1009A	A391	32p	like #1008	1.50	1.50
1009B	A391	32p	like #1009	1.50	1.50

Nos. 962-963 are coil stamps, printed in horizontal rolls with each value alternating.

Irish Winners of Tourist Trophy Motorcycle Races — A392

32p, Stanley Woods. 44p, Artie Bell. No. 1012, Alec Bennett. 52p, No. 1014, Robert & Joey Dunlop.

1996, May 30 *Perf. 14*

1010	A392	32p	multicolored	.85	.75
1011	A392	44p	multicolored	1.25	1.25
1012	A392	50p	multicolored	1.60	1.60
1013	A392	52p	multicolored	1.60	1.60
			Nos. 1010-1013 (4)	5.30	5.20

Souvenir Sheet

1014	A392	50p	multicolored	1.75	1.75

See Isle of Man Nos. 701-705.

Michael Davitt (1846-1906), Nationalist Leader — A393

1996, July 4 Litho. *Perf. 13½x13*

1015	A393	28p	multicolored	.90	.90

Ireland's Presidency of the European Union A394

1996, July 4 *Perf. 13x13½*

1016	A394	32p	multicolored	1.00	1.00

Thomas A. McLaughlin (1896-1971), Designer of Ardnacrusha Hydro-electric Power Station — A395

1996, July 4

1017	A395	38p	multicolored	1.25	1.25

Bord na Móna (Irish Peat Corp.), 50th Anniv. A396

1996, July 4

1018	A396	52p	multicolored	1.60	1.60

Irish Naval Service, 50th Anniv. A397

Designs: 32p, Coastal patrol vessel. 44p, Corvette. 52p, Motor torpedo boat, vert.

1996, July 18 *Perf. 15x14*

1019	A397	32p	multicolored	1.00	.75
	a.		Booklet pane, 3 #1019	3.00	
1020	A397	44p	multicolored	1.50	1.50
1021	A397	52p	multicolored	1.75	1.75
	a.		Booklet pane of 3, #1019-1021	4.50	
			Complete booklet, #1019a, 1021a	7.00	
			Nos. 1019-1021 (3)	4.25	4.00

People with Disabilities A398

1996, Sept. 3 Litho. *Perf. 14x15*

1022	A398	28p	Man in wheel-chair	.90	.90
1023	A398	28p	Blind woman, child	.90	.90
	a.		Pair, #1022-1023	1.80	1.80

Freshwater Ducks A399

Designs: 32p, Anas crecca. 38p, Anas clypeata. 44p, Anas penelope. 52p, Anas platyrhynchos.

1996, Sept. 24 *Perf. 15x14*

1024	A399	32p	multicolored	1.00	.75
1025	A399	38p	multicolored	1.25	1.00
1026	A399	44p	multicolored	1.40	1.40
1027	A399	52p	multicolored	1.75	1.75
	a.		Souvenir sheet, #1024-1027	5.50	5.50
			Nos. 1024-1027 (4)	5.40	4.90

No. 1027a is a continuous design.

Motion Pictures, Cent. A400

1996, Oct. 17 Litho. *Perf. 13½*

1028	A400	32p	Man of Aran	1.00	1.00
1029	A400	32p	My Left Foot	1.00	1.00
1030	A400	32p	The Commit-ments	1.00	1.00
1031	A400	32p	The Field	1.00	1.00
	a.		Strip of 4, #1028-1031	4.00	4.00

A401

Christmas A402

#1032, Stained glass scene of Holy Family. #1033, Adoration of the Magi. 32p, The Annunciation. 52p, Shepherds receive news of Christ's birth.

1996, Nov. 19 *Perf. 14*

1032	A401	28p	multicolored	.90	.75
1033	A402	28p	multicolored	.90	.90
1034	A402	32p	multicolored	1.00	.90
1035	A402	52p	multicolored	1.75	1.75
			Nos. 1032-1035 (4)	4.55	4.30

No. 1032 sold only in discount sheets of 15 for £3.92.

Spideog Robin — A403

Greenland White-fronted Goose — A404

Perf. 15x14, 14x15

1997, Jan. 16 Litho.

1036	A403	28p	Blue tit, horiz.	.90	.75
1037	A403	32p	shown	1.00	.80
	b.		Perf. 14	1.00	1.00
1038	A403	44p	Puffin	1.40	1.10
1039	A403	52p	Barn owl	1.75	1.40
1040	A404	£1	shown	3.25	2.50

Booklet Stamp

Size: 18x21mm, 21x18mm

1040A	A403	32p	Like #1037	1.00	.80
	b.		Booklet pane, 3 #1040A, 1 #770	3.15	
			Complete booklet, #1040b	3.15	

Size: 20x23mm

Perf. 14x15

1040C	A403	32p	Like #1037, "Eire" 8½mm wide ('99)	1.00	.80
	d.		Bklt. pane of 5 + 5 labels	5.00	
			Complete booklet	5.00	
			Nos. 1036-1040C (7)	10.30	8.15

On Nos. 1037,1037b "Eire" is 9mm wide, and size of design is 21x24mm.

See Nos. 1053-1054, 1067, 1076-1081A, 1094, 1105-1115C.

Compare with Nos. 1353-1373.

Issued: No. 1040C, 6/30/99

Greetings Stamps — A405

Designs: No. 1041, Doves on tree limb. No. 1042, Cow jumping over moon. No. 1043, Pig going to market. No. 1044, Rooster on fence.

1997, Jan. 28 Litho. *Perf. 14x15*

1041	A405	32p	multicolored	1.25	1.25

Booklet Stamps

1042	A405	32p	multicolored	1.25	1.25
1043	A405	32p	multicolored	1.25	1.25
1044	A405	32p	multicolored	1.25	1.25
	a.		Booklet pane, #1041-1044, 5 English, 3 Gaelic labels	4.50	
	b.		As "a," #1041-1044, 7 English, 1 Gaelic label	4.50	
			Complete booklet, #1044a, 1044b	8.00	3.00
	c.		Souvenir sheet, 1042-1044, 3 English, 3 Gaelic labels + 1 large label with "Year of the Ox," Hong Kong '97	6.50	6.50

#1044a contains #1042, 1041, 1043-1044 in order. #1044b contains #1043-1044, 1041-1042 in order.

Irish State, 75th Anniv. A406

Designs: No. 1045, Dáil, national flag, constitution. No. 1046, Defense forces, badges, UN flag. No. 1047, Four Courts, scales of justice. No. 1048, Garda badge, Garda Siochána.

1997, Feb. 18 *Perf. 15x14*

1045	A406	32p	multicolored	1.00	1.00
1046	A406	32p	multicolored	1.00	1.00
	a.		Pair, #1045-1046	2.00	2.00
1047	A406	52p	multicolored	1.50	1.50
1048	A406	52p	multicolored	1.50	1.50
	a.		Pair, #1047-1048	3.00	3.00

See #1055-1058, 1082-1084, 1095-1096.

Marine Mammals A407

Designs: 28p, Halichoerus grypus, vert. 32p, Tursiops truncatus, vert. 44p, Phocaena phocaena. 52p, Orcinus orca.

Perf. 14x15, 15x14

1997, Mar. 6 Litho.

1049	A407	28p	multicolored	.85	.85
1050	A407	32p	multicolored	1.00	1.00
1051	A407	44p	multicolored	1.40	1.40
1052	A407	52p	multicolored	1.75	1.75
	a.		Souvenir sheet, #1049-1052	5.50	5.50
			Nos. 1049-1052 (4)	5.00	5.00

Bird Type of 1997

Die Cut Perf. 9x9½

1997, Mar. 6 Litho.

Self-Adhesive Coil Stamps

1053	A403	32p	Peregrine fal-con	1.75	1.75
1054	A403	32p	like #1037	1.75	1.75
	a.		Pair, #1053-1054	3.50	

Die Cut Perf. 11x11¼

1054B	A403	32p	Like #1053	1.75	1.75
1054C	A403	32p	Like #1054	1.75	1.75
	d.		Pair, #1054B-1054C	2.00	
			Nos. 1053-1054C (4)	7.00	7.00

Issued: #1053-1054, 3/6/97; #1054B-1054C, 4/97.

Irish State, 75th Anniv. Type of 1997

#1055, Singer, violinist, bodhran player. #1056, Athlete, soccer and hurling players. #1057, Irish currency, blueprint, food processing plant. #1058, Abbey Theatre emblem, books, palette, paintbrushes, Séamus Heaney manuscript.

1997, Apr. 3 *Perf. 15x14*

1055	A406	32p	multicolored	1.00	1.00
1056	A406	32p	multicolored	1.00	1.00
	a.		Pair, #1055-1056	2.00	2.00
1057	A406	52p	multicolored	1.75	1.75
1058	A406	52p	multicolored	1.75	1.75
	a.		Pair, #1057-1058	3.40	3.40

Irish Coinage, Millennium A408

1997, Apr. 3 ***Perf. 15x14***

1059 A408 32p First Irish coin 1.00 1.00

Stories and Legends A409

Europa: 32p, "The Children of Lir" flying as swans. 44p, "Oisin & Niamh" on horse.

1997, May 14 Litho. ***Perf. 14***

1060 A409 32p multicolored 1.00 .75
1061 A409 44p multicolored 1.75 1.75

Die Cut Perf. 9x9½

Self-Adhesive Coil Stamps

1062 A409 32p like #1060 1.00 1.00
1063 A409 32p like #1061 1.00 1.00
  a. Pair, #1062-1063 2.00

The Great Famine, 150th Anniv. A410

Designs: 28p, Passengers waiting to board emigrant ship. 32p, Family group attending dying child. 52p, Irish Society of Friends soup kitchen.

1997, May 14 Litho. ***Perf. 15x14***

1064 A410 28p multicolored .90 .70
1065 A410 32p multicolored 1.00 .80
1066 A410 52p multicolored 1.75 1.75
  Nos. 1064-1066 (3) 3.65 3.25

Bird Type of 1997

Souvenir Sheet

1997, May 29 ***Perf. 14***

1067 A404 £2 Pintail, horiz. 9.00 9.00

PACIFIC 97.

No. 1067 shows the duck's head in brown. See #1111 for stamp with duck's head in black.

Kate O'Brien (1897-1974), Novelist — A411

1997, July 1 Litho. ***Perf. 14***

1068 A411 28p multicolored .90 .90

St. Columba (521-97), Irish Patron Saint — A412

1997, July 1 ***Perf. 14x15***

1069 A412 28p multicolored .90 .90

A413

A414

Designs: 32p, Daniel O'Connell (1775-1847), politician. 52p, John Wesley (1703-91), founder of Methodism, first visit to Ireland, 250th anniv.

1997, July 1 ***Perf. 14x14½***

1070 A413 32p multicolored 1.00 1.00
1071 A414 52p multicolored 1.75 1.75

Lighthouses — A415

Designs: No. 1072, Baily. No. 1073, Tarbert. 38p, Hook Head, vert. 50p, Fastnet.

1997, July 1 ***Perf. 15x14, 14x15***

1072 A415 32p multicolored 1.00 1.00
1073 A415 32p multicolored 1.00 1.00
  a. Pair, #1072-1073 2.00 2.00
  b. Bklt. pane, #1073, 2 #1072 2.75
  c. Bklt. pane, 2 ea #1072-1073 3.00
1074 A415 38p multicolored 1.25 1.25
1075 A415 50p multicolored 1.60 1.60
  a. Booklet pane, #1074-1075 2.75
  b. Bklt. pane of 4, #1073a, 1074-1075 4.50
  Complete booklet, #1073b, 1073c, 1075a, 1075b 17.50

Bird Types of 1997

Perf. 14x15, 15x14

1997, Aug. 27 **Litho.**

1076 A403 1p Magpie .20 .20
1077 A403 2p Gannet .20 .20
1078 A403 4p Corncrake .20 .20
1079 A403 10p Kingfisher .20 .20
1080 A403 20p Lapwing .30 .20
1081 A404 £5 Shelduck 15.00 12.50

Booklet Stamp

Size: 18x21mm

1081A A403 4p Like #1078 .20 .20
  Nos. 1076-1081A (7) 16.30 13.70

Irish State, 75th Anniv. Type of 1997

28p, Quill, page from Annals of Four Masters, #128. 32p, Stained glass window, #82. 52p, Aer Lingus airplane, letter, #C7.

1997, Aug. 27 ***Perf. 15x14***

1082 A406 28p multicolored .80 .80
1083 A406 32p multicolored .95 .95
1084 A406 52p multicolored 1.50 1.50
  Nos. 1082-1084 (3) 3.25 3.25

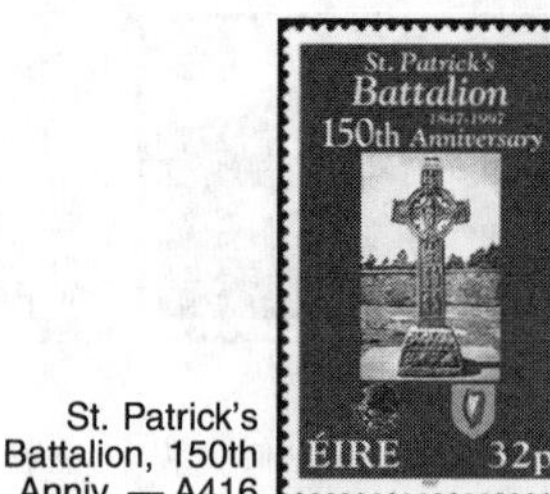

St. Patrick's Battalion, 150th Anniv. — A416

1997, Sept. 12 Litho. ***Perf. 14x13½***

1085 A416 32p multicolored 1.00 1.00

See Mexico No. 2049.

Bram Stoker's "Dracula" A417

Scenes of Dracula: 28p, Being transformed into a bat, vert. 32p, With potential victim, vert. 38p, Emerging from coffin. 52p, With wolf.

1997, Oct. 1 ***Perf. 14x15, 15x14***

1086 A417 28p multicolored .80 .80
1087 A417 32p multicolored .95 .95
  a. Souvenir sheet of 1 1.75 1.75
1088 A417 38p multicolored 1.10 1.10
1089 A417 52p multicolored 1.50 1.50
  a. Souv. sheet of 4, #1086-1089 5.00 5.00
  Nos. 1086-1089 (4) 4.35 4.35

Stamps from Nos. 1087a, 1089a have souvenir sheet background framing vignette.

A418

Christmas — A419

#1090-1092: Different images of Holy Family in stained glass. #1093, Christmas tree.

1997, Nov. 18 Litho. ***Perf. 14x15***

1090 A418 28p multicolored .75 .75
1091 A418 32p multicolored .85 .85
1092 A418 52p multicolored 1.40 1.40
  Nos. 1090-1092 (3) 3.00 3.00

Self-Adhesive

Serpentine Die Cut 9x9½

1093 A419 28p multicolored .80 .80
  a. Booklet pane, 20 #1093 16.00

By its nature, No. 1093a is a complete booklet. The peelable paper backing serves as a booklet cover.

No. 1093 sold only in discount booklets for £5.32.

Bird Type of 1997

Perf. 15x14 (on 3 Sides)

1997, Dec. 6 **Litho.**

Booklet Stamp

1094 A403 32p like #1053 .95 .95
  a. Bklt. pane, #1081A, 3 #1094 3.00
  Complete booklet, #1094a 4.00

Irish State, 75th Anniv. Type of 1997

No. 1095, General Post Office, #68.

No. 1096: a, like #1048. b, like #1047. c, like #1057. d, like #1058. e, like #1082. f, like #1084.

1997, Dec. 6 Litho. ***Perf. 15x14***

1095 A406 32p multicolored 1.25 1.25

Sheet of 12

1096 A406 32p #a.-f. + #1045-1046, 1055-1056, 1083, 1095 13.00 *13.50*

Greetings Stamps — A420

Love is: No. 1097, "...from my heart." No. 1098, "...a birthday wish." No. 1099, "...thinking of you." No. 1100, "...keeping in touch."

1998, Jan. 26 Litho. ***Perf. 14x15***

1097 A420 32p multicolored 1.10 1.10
1098 A420 32p multicolored 1.10 1.10
1099 A420 32p multicolored 1.10 1.10
1100 A420 32p multicolored 1.10 1.10
  a. Bklt. pane, #1097-1100 + 8 labels 4.50
  Complete booklet, 2 #1100a 11.00
  b. Souv. sheet, #1098-1100 + 7 labels 2.90 1.40

No. 1100a exists with stamps in two different orders. No. 1100b has 1 English, 4 Chinese, 1 Gaelic labels + 1 large label with "Year of the Tiger," in English and Chinese.

See Nos. 1120-1123.

Aviation Pioneers A421

28p, Lady Mary Heath (Sophie Catherine Pierce), 1st solo flight, Capetown-Croydon via Cairo, 1928. 32p, Col. James Fitzmaurice, navigator on "Bremen," 1st east-west Atlantic flight, 1928. 44p, Capt. J.P. (Paddy) Saul, navigator aboard Southern Cross, Dublin-Newfoundland, 1930. 52p, Capt. Charles Blair, 1st non-stop commercial flight Foynes-NYC, 1942.

1998, Feb. 24 ***Perf. 15x14***

1101 A421 28p multicolored .80 .80
1102 A421 32p multicolored .95 .95
  a. Bklt. pane, 2 ea #1101-1102 3.00
1103 A421 44p multicolored 1.25 1.25
  a. Bklt. pane, #1103, 2 #1102 3.00
1104 A421 52p multicolored 1.50 1.50
  a. Bklt. pane, #1102, 2 #1104 3.50
  b. Bklt. pane of 4, #1101-1104 3.75
  Complete booklet, #1102a, 1103a, 1104a, 1104b 17.00
  Nos. 1101-1104 (4) 4.50 4.50

Bird Types of 1997

No. 1111A: b, Like #1107. c, Like #1080. d, Like #1077. e, Like #1078. f, Like #1076. g, Like #1106B, "Eire" 8½mm wide. h, Like #1079. i, Like #1053. j, Like #1039. k, Like #1037. l, Like #1109. m, Like #1106, "Eire" 8½mm wide. n, Wren. o, Pied wagtail. p, Like #1038.

1998-99 Litho. ***Perf. 15x14, 14x15***

1105 A403 5p Woodpigeon, horiz. .40 .40
1106 A403 30p Blackbird .75 .75
  d. Perf. 14 .75 .75
1106B A403 30p Goldcrest, bklt. stamp .90 .90
  c. Booklet pane, 5 each #1106, 1106B 9.00
  Complete booklet, #1106Bc 9.00
1107 A403 35p Stonechat 1.00 1.00
  a. Perf. 14 1.00 1.00
1108 A403 40p Ringed plover, horiz. 1.25 1.25
  a. Perf. 14 1.25 1.25
1109 A403 45p Song thrush 1.50 1.50
  a. Perf. 14 1.50 1.50
1110 A403 50p Sparrowhawk, horiz. 1.75 1.75
  a. Perf. 14 1.75 1.75
1111 A404 £2 Pintail 5.25 5.25

Sheet of 15

1111A A403 30p #b.-p. 12.50 12.50

See note under #1067.

Booklet Stamps

Size: 18x21mm, 21x18mm

1112 A403 5p Like #1105 .40 .40
1113 A403 30p Like #1106 .90 .90
a. Booklet pane, 2 #1112, 3 #1113 3.00
Complete booklet, #1113a 3.00
1113B A403 30p like #1106B .75 .75
c. Bklt. pane, 2 #1112, 3 #1113B + label 3.00
Complete booklet, #1113c 3.00

Size: 20x23mm

1113D A403 45p Like #1109, "Eire" 8½mm wide 1.40 1.40
e. Booklet pane of 4 + 4 labels 5.75
Complete booklet 5.75

Size: 21x24mm

1113F A403 30p Like #1106, "Eire" 8½mm wide .65 .35
1113G A403 30p Like #1106B, "Eire" 8½mm wide .65 .35
h. Booklet pane, 5 each #1113F-1113G 6.50 —
Booklet, #1113Gh 6.50

Die Cut Perf. 9x9½

Self-Adhesive

1114 A403 30p like #1106 1.25 1.25
1115 A403 30p like #1106B 1.25 1.25
a. Pair, #1114-1115 2.50

Litho.

Die Cut Perf. 11x11¼

Self-Adhesive Coil Stamps

1115B A403 30p Like #1114 1.25 1.25
1115C A403 30p Like #1115 1.25 1.25
d. Pair, #1115B-1115C 1.80

Issued: #1115B-1115C, 5/98; #1106B, 1113B, 9/4/98; #1111A, 2/16/99; #1113D, 6/30/99; #1113F, 1113G, 5/3/01.

Equestrian Sports A422

30p, Show jumping. 32p, Three-day event. 40p, Gymkhana. 45p, Dressage, vert.

1998, Apr. 2

1116 A422 30p multicolored .90 .75
1117 A422 32p multicolored .95 .75
1118 A422 40p multicolored 1.25 1.25
1119 A422 45p multicolored 1.40 1.40
a. Souvenir sheet, #1116-1119 4.50 4.50
Nos. 1116-1119 (4) 4.50 4.15

Greetings Type of 1998

1998, May 6 Litho. *Perf. 14x15*

Booklet Stamps

1120 A420 30p like #1098 1.00 1.00
1121 A420 30p like #1099 1.00 1.00
1122 A420 30p like #1100 1.00 1.00
1123 A420 30p like #1097 1.00 1.00
a. Bklt. pane, #1120-1123 + 8 labels 3.50
Complete booklet, 2 #1123a 10.50

No. 1123a exists with stamps in different order. Complete booklet contains two different panes.

Festivals A423

Europa: 30p, Crinniú na mBáid, Kinvara (sailboats). 40p, Puck Fair, Killorglin.

1998, May 6 *Perf. 15x14*

1124 A423 30p multicolored 1.50 1.25
1125 A423 40p multicolored 1.50 1.50

Serpentine Die Cut Perf 9x9½

Self-Adhesive

1126 A423 30p like #1124 1.10 1.10
1127 A423 30p like #1125 1.10 1.10
a. Pair, #1126-1127 2.25
Nos. 1124-1127 (4) 5.20 4.95

1798 Rebellion, Bicent. A424

Battle scene and: No. 1128, "Liberty." No. 1129, Pikeman. No. 1130, French soldier. No. 1131, Wolfe Tone. No. 1132, Henry Joy McCracken.

1998, May 6

1128 A424 30p multicolored .90 .90
1129 A424 30p multicolored .90 .90
1130 A424 30p multicolored .90 .90
a. Strip of 3, #1128-1130 2.75 2.75
1131 A424 45p multicolored 1.40 1.40
1132 A424 45p multicolored 1.40 1.40
a. Pair, #1131-1132 3.00 3.00

Tour de France Bicycle Race A425

#1133, 4 cyclists. #1134, 2 cyclists, 1 wearing dark glasses. #1135, 2 cyclists, 1 wearing hat. #1136, Leading rider in yellow jersey.

1998, June 2 Litho. *Perf. 15x14*

1133 A425 30p multicolored .85 .85
1134 A425 30p multicolored .85 .85
1135 A425 30p multicolored .85 .85
1136 A425 30p multicolored .85 .85
a. Strip of 4, #1133-1136 3.40 1.60

Democracy Stamps A426

Designs: 30p, Local government (Ireland Act), cent. 32p, Entrance into European Union, 25th anniv. 35p, Women's vote in local elections, cent. 45c, Republic of Ireland Act, 50th anniv.

1998, June 2

1137 A426 30p multicolored .85 .85
1138 A426 32p multicolored .90 .90
1139 A426 35p multicolored 1.00 1.00
1140 A426 45p multicolored 1.25 1.25
Nos. 1137-1140 (4) 4.00 4.00

1998 Tall Ships Race — A427

Perf. 14x15, 15x14

1998, July 20 Litho.

1141 A427 30p Asgard II .75 .75
a. Perf. 15 1.00 1.00
1142 A427 30p Eagle 1.00 1.00
a. Pair, #1141-1142 1.75 1.75
b. Perf. 15 1.25 1.25
c. Bklt. pane, #1142b, 2 #1141a 2.25
1143 A427 45p Boa Esperanza, horiz. 1.25 1.25
a. Perf. 15 1.50 1.50
1144 A427 £1 T.S. Royalist, horiz. 2.75 2.75
a. Perf. 15 3.00 3.00
b. Bklt. pane of 3, #1142b-1144a 2.75
Complete booklet, #1142b, 1144a 10.50
Nos. 1141-1144 (4) 5.75 5.75

Souvenir Sheet

1145 A427 £2 like #1143 6.50 6.50

Die Cut Perf. 9x9½, 9½x9

Self-Adhesive

1145A A427 30p like #1143 .90 .90
1145B A427 30p like #1141 .90 .90
1145C A427 30p like #1142 .90 .90
1145D A427 30p like #1144 .90 .90
e. Strip of 4, #1145A-1145D 3.50

Portugal '98 (#1145).
Issued: £2, 9/4; others, 7/20.

Postboxes — A428

1998, Sept. 3

No. 1146, Ashworth, 1856. No. 1147, Wallbox, 1922. No. 1148, Double Pillarbox, 1899. No. 1149, Penfold, 1866.

1146 A428 30p multicolored .80 .90
1147 A428 30p multicolored .80 .90
1148 A428 30p multicolored .80 .90
1149 A428 30p multicolored .80 .90
a. Strip of 4, #1146-1149 3.25 3.25

Mary Immaculate College, Limerick, Cent. — A429

Newton School, Waterford, Bicent. — A430

1998, Sept. 3 *Perf. 15x14, 14x15*

1150 A429 30p multicolored .80 .65
1151 A430 40p multicolored 1.10 1.10

Universal Declaration of Human Rights, 50th Anniv. A431

1998, Sept. 3 *Perf. 15x14*

1152 A431 45p multicolored 1.25 1.25

Endangered Animals — A432

#1153, Cheetah. #1154, Scimitar-horned oryx. 40p, Golden lion tamarin. 45p, Tiger.

1998, Oct. 8 Litho. *Perf. 14*

1153 A432 30p multi 1.10 1.10
1154 A432 30p multi 1.10 1.10
a. Pair, #1153-1154 2.25 2.25
1155 A432 40p multi, vert. 1.10 1.10
1156 A432 45p multi, vert. 1.25 1.25
a. Souvenir sheet, #1153-1156, perf. 15 5.50 5.50
b. As "a," inscription on extended margin 9.00 9.00
Nos. 1153-1156 (4) 4.55 4.55

Stamps on Nos. 1156a, 1156b have a white border. No. 1156b contains exhibition logo and "National Stamp Exhibition RDS-Dublin-6-8 November 1998" in sheet margin.

A433

Christmas — A434

#1157, Holy family. 32p, Adoration of the Shepherds. 45p, Adoration of the Magi.
No. 1160, Choir singers.

1998, Nov. 17 Litho. *Perf. 14x15*

1157 A433 30p multicolored .80 .80
1158 A433 32p multicolored .85 .85
1159 A433 45p multicolored 1.25 1.25
Nos. 1157-1159 (3) 2.90 2.90

Booklet Stamp

Self-Adhesive

Serpentine Die Cut Perf. 11x11½

1160 A434 30p multicolored .80 .80
a. Booklet pane of 20 14.00

No. 1160a is a complete booklet. The Peelable paper backing serves as a booklet cover. No. 1160 sold only in discount booklets at £5.40.

A435

Pets greetings stamps.

1999, Jan. 26 Litho. *Perf. 14x15*

1161 A435 30p Dog .80 .80

Booklet Stamps

1162 A435 30p Cat .80 .80
1163 A435 30p Fish .80 .80
1164 A435 30p Rabbit .80 .80
a. Booklet pane, #1161-1164 + 5 English, 3 Gaelic labels 3.25
b. Booklet pane, #1161-1164 + 7 English, 1 Gaelic label 3.25
Complete booklet, #1164a-1164b 6.50
c. Souvenir sheet, #1162-1164 (see footnote) 2.50 2.50

No. 1164a contains Nos. 1161-1164 in order. No. 1164b contains stamps in reverse order. No. 1164c has 1 English, 2 Chinese, 3 Gaelic labels + 1 large label with "Year of the Rabbit" in English and Chinese.

New Year 1999 (Year of the Rabbit) (#1164c).

A436

Irish Actors: 30p, Micheál Mac Liammóir (1899-1978). 45p, Siobhán McKenna (1923-86). 50p, Noel Purcell (1900-85).

1999, Feb. 16 Litho. *Perf. 14x15*

1165 A436 30p brown .80 .40
1166 A436 45p green 1.25 .60
1167 A436 50p blue 1.40 .70
Nos. 1165-1167 (3) 3.45 1.70

Irish Emigration A437

1999, Feb. 26 Litho. *Perf. 15x14*

1168 A437 45p multicolored 1.25 .60

See US No. 3286.

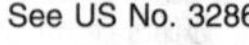

Maritime Heritage A438

30p, Polly Woodside. 35p, Ilen. 45p, Royal Natl. Lifeboat Institution. £1, Titanic.

1999, Mar. 19 Litho. *Perf. 14*

1169 A438 30p multi, vert. .80 .40
1170 A438 35p multi, vert. .95 .45
1171 A438 45p multi 1.25 .60
1172 A438 £1 multi 2.75 1.40
a. Souvenir sheet of 2 5.50 5.50
b. As "a" ovptd. in sheet margin 5.50 5.50
Nos. 1169-1172 (4) 5.75 2.85

Souvenir Sheet

Perf. 14x14½

1173 Sheet of 2, #1173a, Australia #1729 2.50 1.25
a. A438 30p like #1169 .80 .40

Australia '99, World Stamp Expo. (#1172b, #1173). See Australia No. 1729a. No. 1172b is overprinted in gold in sheet margin with Australia '99, World Stamp Expo exhibition emblem.

Sky is gray blue, country and denomination are 3mm high on #1169. Sky is blue, country and denomination are 4mm high on #1173a.

Natl. Parks A438a

Europa: #1174, 1176, Whooping swans, Kilcolman Nature Reserve. 40p, #1177, Fallow deer, Wellington Memorial Obelisk, Phoenix Park.

1999, Apr. 29 Litho. *Perf. 15x14*

1174 A438a 30p multicolored 1.25 1.25
1175 A438a 40p multicolored 1.50 1.50

Die Cut Perf. 9x9½

Self-adhesive

1176 A438a 30p Like #1174 1.00 1.00
1177 A438a 30p Like #1175 1.00 1.00
a. Pair, #1176-1177 1.60

A439

A441

A440

1999, Apr. 29 Litho. *Perf. 14x15*

1178 A439 30p green & black .80 .40

Prime Minister Sean Lemass (1899-1971).

1999, Apr. 29 *Perf. 15x14*

1179 A440 30p multicolored .80 .40

Introduction of the Euro. No. 1179 is denominated in both pence and euros.

1999, Apr. 29 *Perf. 14x15*

1180 A441 45p multicolored 1.00 .50

Council of Europe, 50th anniv.

Intl. Year of Older Persons A442

1999, June 15 *Perf. 15x14*

1181 A442 30p multicolored .80 .40

UPU, 125th Anniv. A443

1999, June 15

1182 A443 30p Modern mail truck .80 .40
1183 A443 30p Early mail truck .80 .40
a. Pair, #1182-1183 1.60 1.60

Pioneer Total Abstinence Assoc., Cent. — A444

1999, June 15 *Perf. 14x15*

1184 A444 32p Fr. James Cullen .85 .40

Gaelic Football Team of the Millennium A445

No. 1185: a, Danno Keeffe. b, Enda Colleran. c, Joe Keohane. d, Seán Flanagan. e, Seán Murphy. f, John Joe Reilly. g, Martin O'Connell. h, Mick O'Connell. i, Tommy Murphy. j, Seán O'Neill. k, Seán Purcell. l, Pat Spillane. m. Mikey Sheehy. n, Tom Langan. o, Kevin Heffernan.

Perf. 14¾x14¼

1999, Aug. 17 Litho.

1185 Sheet of 15 + label 12.50 12.50
a.-o. A445 30p any single .80 .40

Booklet Stamps

Size: 33x22mm

Self-Adhesive

Serpentine Die Cut Perf. 11¼x11½

1186 A445 30p like #1185a .80 .40
1187 A445 30p like #1185c .80 .40
1188 A445 30p like #1185e .80 .40
1189 A445 30p like #1185h .80 .40
1190 A445 30p like #1185l .80 .40
1191 A445 30p like #1185m .80 .40
a. Bklt. pane, #1186-1189, 2 each #1190-1191 6.50
1192 A445 30p like #1185d .80 .40
1193 A445 30p like #1185b .80 .40
1194 A445 30p like #1185n .80 .40
1195 A445 30p like #1185k .80 .40
a. Bklt. pane, 2 ea #1192-1195 6.50
1196 A445 30p like #1185o .80 .40
1197 A445 30p like #1185g .80 .40
1198 A445 30p like #1185i .80 .40
a. Bklt. pane, 3 ea #1196-1197, 2 #1198 6.50
1199 A445 30p like #1185f .80 .40
1200 A445 30p like #1185j .80 .40
a. Bklt. pane, 4 ea #1199-1200 6.50

Nos. 1191a, 1195a, 1198a, 1200a are each complete booklets. The peelable paper backing serves as a booklet cover. #1185 exists imperf.

Airplanes A446

Designs: 30p, Douglas DC-3. 32p, Britten Norman Islander. 40p, Boeing 707. 45p, Lockheed Constellation.

1999, Sept. 9 Litho. *Perf. 14¾x14¼*

1201 A446 30p multicolored .80 .40
a. Booklet pane of 4 3.25
1202 A446 32p multicolored .90 .45
a. Bklt. pane, 2 ea #1201, 1202 3.50
1203 A446 40p multicolored 1.10 .55
a. Bklt. pane, #1203, 2 #1201 2.75
1204 A446 45p multicolored 1.25 .60
a. Booklet pane, #1201-1204 4.25
Complete bkt., #1201a-1204a 14.00
Nos. 1201-1204 (4) 4.05 2.00

Extinct Irish Animals A447

Perf. 14¼x14¾, 14¾x14¼

1999, Oct. 11 Litho.

1205 A447 30p Mammoth, vert. .80 .40
1206 A447 30p Giant deer, vert. .80 .40
a. Pair, #1205-1206 1.60 1.60
1207 A447 45p Wolf 1.25 .60
1208 A447 45p Brown bear 1.25 .60
a. Pair, #1207-1208 2.50 2.50
b. Souvenir sheet, #1205-1208, perf. 14¾ 4.25 4.25

Stamps from No. 1208b do not have white border.

Die Cut Perf. 9¼x9½, 9½x9¼

1999, Oct. 11 Litho.

Self-Adhesive

1209 A447 30p Like #1208 .80 .40
1210 A447 30p Like #1205 .80 .40
1211 A447 30p Like #1207 .80 .40
1212 A447 30p Like #1206 .80 .40
a. Strip, #1209-1212 3.20

Christmas A448

1999, Nov. 4 Litho. *Perf. 14¾x14¼*

1213 A448 30p Holy Family .80 .40
1214 A448 32p Shepherds .85 .40
1215 A448 45p Magi 1.25 .60
Nos. 1213-1215 (3) 2.90 1.40

Self-Adhesive Booklet Stamp

Size: 19x27mm

Die Cut 11x11¼

1216 A448 30p Angel, vert. .80 .40
a. Booklet pane of 20 16.00

No. 1216a sold for £5.40 and is a complete booklet.

Millennium — A449

People of the 20th Century - No. 1217: a, Grace Kelly. b, Jesse Owens. c, John F. Kennedy. d, Mother Teresa. e, John McCormack. f, Nelson Mandela.

Irish Historic Events - No. 1218, horiz.: a, Norman invasion, 1169. b, Flight of the Earls, 1607. c, Irish Parliament, 1782. d, Land league. e, Irish independence. f, UN peacekeeping.

Discoveries - No. 1219: a, Rev. Nicholas Callan, electrical scientist. b, Birr Telescope. c, Thomas Edison. d, Albert Einstein. e, Marie Curie. f, Galileo.

The Arts - No. 1220: a, Ludwig van Beethoven. b, Dame Ninette de Valois, ballet director. c, James Joyce. d, Mona Lisa, by Leonardo da Vinci. e, Painting by Sir John Lavery. f, William Shakespeare.

World Events - No. 1221, horiz.: a, French Revolution, 1789. b, Industrial Revolution. c, Peace, 1945. d, Women's liberation. e, Fall of the Berlin Wall, 1989. f, Modern communications.

Epic Journeys - No. 1222, horiz.: a, Marco Polo. b, Capt. James Cook. c, Australian explorers Robert O'Hara Burke and William Wills. d, Antarctic explorer Ernest Shackleton. e, Charles Lindbergh. f, Astronaut on moon.

Perf. 14¼x14¾, 14¾x14¼

1999-2000 Litho.

1217 Sheet of 12, 2 ea #a.-f. 9.00 4.50
a.-f. A449 30p Any single .75 .35
1218 Sheet of 12, 2 ea #a.-f. 9.00 4.50
a.-f. A449 30p Any single .75 .35
1219 Sheet of 12, 2 each #a.-f. 8.50 8.50
a.-f. A449 30p Any single .70 .35
1220 Sheet of 12, 2 each #a.-f. 8.50 8.50
a.-f. A449 30p Any single .70 .35
1221 A449 Sheet of 12, 2 each #a-f 8.75 8.75
a.-f. 30p Any single .70 .35
1222 A449 Sheet of 12, 2 each #a-f 8.75 8.75
a.-f. 30p Any single .70 .35

Issued: #1217, 12/31; #1218, 1/1/00; #1219, 2/29/00; #1221, 12/31/00; #1222, 1/1/01.

Mythical Creatures — A450

2000, Jan. 26 Litho. *Perf. 14¼x14¾*

1223 A450 30p Frog Prince .75 .35
1224 A450 30p Pegasus .75 .35
1225 A450 30p Unicorn .75 .35
1226 A450 30p Dragon .75 .35
a. Booklet pane, #1223-1226, + 3 Gaelic, 5 English labels 3.00
b. Booklet pane, #1223-1226, + 2 Gaelic, 6 English labels 3.00
c. Booklet pane, #1223, 1226, + 14 labels 1.50
Complete booklet, #1226a-1226c 7.50

d. Souvenir sheet, #1224-1226, + 7 labels 2.25 2.25
Nos. 1223-1226 (4) 3.00 1.40

New Year 2000 (Year of the Dragon), No. 1226d.

Emigrant Ship Jeanie Johnston A451

2000, Mar. 9 Litho. *Perf. 14¾x14¼*
1227 A451 30p multi .70 .70

Europa, 2000
Common Design Type

2000, May 9 Litho. *Perf. 14¼x14¾*
1230 CD17 32p multi .75 .35

Die Cut Perf 9½x9¼
Self-Adhesive
Size: 22x34mm

1231 CD17 30p multi .70 .35

Oscar Wilde (1854-1900), Playwright — A453

#1232, Portrait. #1233, The Happy Prince. #1234, The Importance of Being Earnest. #1235, The Picture of Dorian Gray. #1236, £2, Like #1232, signature at left.

Perf. 14¼x14¾, 14¼x14 (#1236)
2000, May 22 Litho.
1232 A453 30p multi .70 .35
1233 A453 30p multi .70 .35
1234 A453 30p multi .70 .35
1235 A453 30p multi .70 .35
a. Block, #1232-1235 2.80 1.40

Size: 27x27mm

1236 A453 30p multi + label 1.25 1.25
Sheet of 20 25.00
Nos. 1232-1236 (5) 4.05 2.65

Souvenir Sheet

1237 A453 £2 multi 4.50 4.50

No. 1236 was printed in sheets of 20 stamps and 20 labels for £10. These sheets were not available at Irish post offices, but were sold through special mail orders through the Irish Post, and at the Irish Post booth at The Stamp Show 2000 in London. Labels were blank, but purchasers could provide Irish Post with photographic images or other artwork that would be reproduced on the labels.

2000 Summer Olympics, Sydney A454

2000, July 7 Litho. *Perf. 13¼*
1238 A454 30p Running .70 .35
1239 A454 30p Javelin .70 .35
a. Pair, #1238-1239 1.40 .70
1240 A454 50p Long jump 1.25 .60
1241 A454 50p High jump 1.25 .60
a. Pair, #1240-1241 2.50 1.25

Stampin' the Future A455

Children's Stamp Design Contest Winners: 30p, Marguerite Nyhan (rocket and flowers), vert. 32p, Kyle Staunton (2000). No. 1244, Jennifer Branagan (Earth, sun and moon). No. 1245, Diarmuid O'Ceochain (rocket, building on moon).

Perf. 14¼x14¾, 14¾x14¼
2000, July 7
1242 A455 30p multi .70 .35
1243 A455 32p multi .75 .35
1244 A455 45p multi 1.00 .50
1245 A455 45p multi 1.00 .50
a. Pair, #1244-1245 2.00 1.00
Nos. 1242-1245 (4) 3.45 1.70

Team of the Millennium Type of 1999

Hurling - No. 1246: a, Tony Reddin. b, Bobby Rackard. c, Nick O'Donnell. d, John Doyle. e, Brian Whelahan. f, John Keane. g, Paddy Phelan. h, Lory Meagher. i, Jack Lynch. j, Jim Langton. k, Mick Mackey. l, Christy Ring. m, Jimmy Doyle. n, Ray Cummins. o, Eddie Keher.

2000, Aug. 2 Litho. *Perf. 14¾x14¼*
1246 Sheet of 15 + label 10.50 10.50
a.-o. A445 30p Any single .70 .35

Booklet Stamps
Self-Adhesive
Size: 33x22mm
Serpentine Die Cut 11¼x11½

1247 A445 30p Like #1246a .70 .35
1248 A445 30p Like #1246m .70 .35
1249 A445 30p Like #1246d .70 .35
a. Booklet, 3 each #1247-1248, 4 #1249 7.00
1250 A445 30p Like #1246b .70 .35
1251 A445 30p Like #1246c .70 .35
a. Booklet, 5 each #1250-1251 7.00
1252 A445 30p Like #1246k .70 .35
1253 A445 30p Like #1246e .70 .35
1254 A445 30p Like #1246f .70 .35
a. Booklet, 4 #1252, 3 each #1253-1254 7.00
1255 A445 30p Like #1246g .70 .35
1256 A445 30p Like #1246j .70 .35
1257 A445 30p Like #1246h .70 .35
1258 A445 30p Like #1246o .70 .35
a. Booklet, 2 each #1255-1256, 3 each #1257-1258 7.00
1259 A445 30p Like #1246i .70 .35
1260 A445 30p Like #1246n .70 .35
1261 A445 30p Like #1246l .70 .35
a. Booklet, 3 each #1259-1260, 4 #1261 7.00
Nos. 1247-1261 (15) 10.50 5.25

No. 1246 exists imperf.

Butterflies A456

Designs: 30p, Peacock. 32p, Small tortoiseshell. 45p, Silver-washed fritillary. 50p, Orange-tip.

2000, Sept. 6 *Perf. 13¼x12¾*
1262 A456 30p multi .65 .30
1263 A456 32p multi .75 .40
1264 A456 45p multi 1.00 .50
1265 A456 50p multi 1.10 .55
a. Souvenir sheet, #1262-1265 3.50 3.50

Stamps from No. 1265a lack year date.

Military Aircraft A457

Designs: No. 1266, Bristol F.2b Mk II fighter. No. 1267, Hawker Hurricane Mk IIc. No. 1268, Alouette III helicopter. No. 1269, De Havilland DH.115 Vampire T.55.

2000, Oct. 9 Litho. *Perf. 14¾x14¼*
1266 A457 30p multi .65 .30
1267 A457 30p multi .65 .30
a. Pair, #1266-1267 1.50 1.50
b. Booklet pane, 2 each #1266-1267 2.60
1268 A457 45p multi 1.00 .50
a. Booklet pane, #1266-1268 2.40
1269 A457 45p multi 1.00 .50
a. Pair, #1268-1269 2.00 2.00
b. Booklet pane, 2 each #1268-1269 4.00
c. Booklet pane, #1266-1269 3.50
Booklet, #1267b, 1268a, 1269b, 1269c 12.50
Nos. 1266-1269 (4) 3.30 1.60

Coil Stamps
Self-Adhesive
Die Cut Perf. 9¼x9½

1270 A457 30p Like #1266 .65 .30
1271 A457 30p Like #1267 .65 .30
1272 A457 30p Like #1269 .65 .30
1273 A457 30p Like #1268 .65 .30
a. Strip, #1270-1273 2.60

Dept. of Agriculture, Cent. A458

2000, Nov. 14 Litho. *Perf. 13½*
1274 A458 50p multi 1.25 .60

Christmas A459

Designs: No. 1275, Nativity. 32p, Adoration of the Magi. 45p, Adoration of the Shepherds. No. 1278, Flight to Egypt.

2000, Nov. 14 *Perf. 14¼x14¾*
1275 A459 30p multi .70 .35
1276 A459 32p multi .75 .40
1277 A459 45p multi 1.10 .55

Booklet Stamp
Self-Adhesive
Size: 21x26mm
Serpentine Die Cut 11¼

1278 A459 30p multi .65 .35
a. Booklet of 24 16.00
Nos. 1275-1278 (4) 3.20 1.65

No. 1278 sold for £6.60.

Pets — A460

Designs: Nos. 1279, 1283, Goldfish, hearts. Nos. 1280a, 1284, Snake. Nos. 1280b, 1282, Frog, four-leaf clover. Nos. 1280c, 1285, Turtle, stars. No. 1281, Lizard, daisy.

2001, Jan. 24 Litho. *Perf. 14¼x14¾*
1279 A460 30p multi .70 .35

Souvenir Sheet

1280 Sheet of 3 2.10 1.25
a.-c. A460 30p Any single .70 .35

Booklet Stamps
Size: 25x30mm
Self-Adhesive
Serpentine Die Cut 12

1281 A460 30p multi .70 .35
1282 A460 30p multi .70 .35
1283 A460 30p multi .70 .35
1284 A460 30p multi .70 .35
1285 A460 30p multi .70 .35
a. Booklet, 2 each #1281-1285 + 10 labels 7.00
Nos. 1281-1285 (5) 3.50 1.75

Broadcasting in Ireland — A461

Designs: 30p, Camera, audience, man. 32p, Microphone, announcers. 45p, People listening to radio. 50p, Television.

2001, Feb. 27 *Perf. 14¾x14¼*
1286 A461 30p multi .70 .35
1287 A461 32p multi .75 .40
1288 A461 45p multi 1.10 .55
1289 A461 50p multi 1.25 .60
Nos. 1286-1289 (4) 3.80 1.90

Literary Anniversaries A462

Designs: 30p, Marsh's Library, first public library in Ireland, 300th anniv. 32p, Book of Common Prayer, first book printed in Ireland, 450th anniv.

2001, Mar. 14 *Perf. 14¼x14¾*
1290 A462 30p multi .70 .35
1291 A462 32p multi .75 .40

Comhaltas Ceoltóirí Eirann, 50th Anniv. — A463

Musician with: No. 1292, Bagpipes. No. 1293, Tambourine. No. 1294, Flute, horiz. No. 1295, Violin, horiz.

Perf. 14¼x14¾, 14¾x14¼
2001, Mar. 14
1292 A463 30p multi .70 .35
1293 A463 30p multi .70 .35
a. Pair, #1292-1293 1.40 .70
1294 A463 45p multi 1.00 .50
1295 A463 45p multi 1.00 .50
a. Pair, #1294-1295 2.00 1.00
Nos. 1292-1295 (4) 3.40 1.70

Race Cars A464

Designs: Nos. 1296, 1300, 1301, Jordan Grand Prix Formula 1. Nos. 1297, 1304, Hillman Imp, Tulip Rally. Nos. 1298, 1303, Mini Cooper S, Monte Carlo Rally. Nos. 1299, 1302, Mercedes SSK, Irish Grand Prix.

2001, Apr. 26 *Perf. 13¾x14¼*
1296 A464 30p multi .65 .35
1297 A464 32p multi .70 .35
1298 A464 45p multi 1.00 .50
1299 A464 £1 multi 2.25 1.10
Nos. 1296-1299 (4) 4.60 2.30

Souvenir Sheet

1300 A464 £2 multi 4.50 2.25
a. With Belgica show emblem in margin 4.50 2.25

Booklet Stamps
Size: 36x24mm
Self-Adhesive
Serpentine Die Cut 11¾

1301 A464 30p multi .65 .35
1302 A464 30p multi .65 .35
1303 A464 30p multi .65 .35
1304 A464 30p multi .65 .35
a. Booklet, 4 #1301, 2 each #1302-1304 6.50
Nos. 1301-1304 (4) 2.60 1.40

Issued: No. 1300a, 6/9/01.

Irish Heriatge in Australia
A465

2001, May 3 ***Perf. 14¾x14¼***

1305 A465 30p Ned Kelly .65 .35
1306 A465 30p Peter Lalor .65 .35
a. Pair, #1305-1306 1.30 .70
1307 A465 45p Settlers 1.00 .50
1308 A465 45p Emigrants 1.00 .50
a. Pair, #1307-1308 2.00 1.00
Nos. 1305-1308 (4) 3.30 1.70

Souvenir Sheet

1309 A465 £1 Like #1305 2.25 1.10

Europa
A466

2001, May 16 Litho. ***Perf. 14¾x14¼***

1310 A466 30p Wading .65 .35
1311 A466 32p Fishing .70 .35

Europa Type of 2001
Die Cut Perf. 9¼x9½

2001, May 16 **Litho.**

Coil Stamps
Self-Adhesive

1312 A466 30p Wading .65 .35
1313 A466 30p Fishing .65 .35
a. Strip, #1312-1313 1.30

Bird Types of 1997 With Added Euro Denominations

Designs: Nos. 1314, 1319A, Blackbird. 1319B, Goldcrest. 32p, Robin. 35p, Puffin. 40p, Wren. 45p, Song thrush. £1, Greenland white-fronted goose.

Perf. 14¼x14¾

2001, June 11 **Litho.**

1314 A403 30p multi .65 .30
1315 A403 32p multi .70 .35
1316 A403 35p multi .80 .40
1317 A403 40p multi .90 .45
1318 A403 45p multi 1.00 .50

Perf. 14¾x14¼

1319 A404 £1 multi 2.25 1.10

Self-Adhesive
Coil Stamps
Size: 21x26mm

1319A A403 30p multi .65 .30
1319B A403 30p multi .65 .30
c. Pair, #1319A-1319B 1.30
Nos. 1314-1319 (6) 6.30 3.10

Battle of Kinsale, 400th Anniv.
A467

Designs: No. 1320, Soldiers on horseback. No. 1321, Soldiers in stream. 32p, Soldiers and ramparts. 45p, View of Kinsale.

2001, July 10 ***Perf. 13½***

1320 A467 30p multi .65 .35
1321 A467 30p multi .65 .35
a. Pair, #1320-1321 1.30 .70
1322 A467 32p multi .70 .35
1323 A467 45p multi 1.00 .50
Nos. 1320-1323 (4) 3.00 1.55

Hall of Fame Athletes
A468

Designs: Nos. 1324, 1328, Padraic Carney, soccer player. Nos. 1325, 1329, Frank Cummins, hurler. Nos. 1326, 1330, Jack O'Shea, soccer player. Nos. 1327, 1331, Nicky Rackard, hurler.

2001, Sept. 5 Litho. ***Perf. 14¾x14***

1324 A468 30p multi .70 .35
1325 A468 30p multi .70 .35
1326 A468 30p multi .70 .35
1327 A468 30p multi .70 .35
a. Horiz. strip, #1324-1327 2.80 1.40

Booklet Stamps
Size: 33x22mm
Self-Adhesive
Serpentine Die Cut 11x11½

1328 A468 30p multi .70 .35
1329 A468 30p multi .70 .35
1330 A468 30p multi .70 .35
1331 A468 30p multi .70 .35
a. Booklet, 2 each #1328, 1331, 3 each #1329-1330 7.00
Nos. 1324-1331 (8) 5.60 2.80

Sailboats — A469

Designs: No. 1332, Ruffian 23. No. 1333, Howth 17. No. 1334, 1720 Sportsboat. No. 1335, The Glen. No. 1336, Ruffian 23. No. 1337, Howth 17. No. 1338, The Glen. No. 1339, 1720 Sportsboat.

2001, Sept. 5 ***Perf. 14x14¾***

1332 A469 30p multi .70 .35
1333 A469 32p multi .75 .40
1334 A469 45p multi 1.10 .55
1335 A469 45p multi 1.10 .55
a. Horiz. pair, #1334-1335 2.20 1.10
Nos. 1332-1335 (4) 3.65 1.85

Coil Stamps
Self-Adhesive

1336 A469 30p multi .70 .35
1337 A469 30p multi .70 .35
1338 A469 30p multi .70 .35
1339 A469 30p multi .70 .35
a. Strip of 4, #1336-1339 2.80

Numbers have been reserved for additional stamps in this set.

Bird Type of 1997
Serpentine Die Cut 11¼

2001, Oct. 9 **Litho.**

Booklet Stamps
Self-Adhesive

1340 A403 N Blackbird .70 .35
1341 A403 N Goldcrest .70 .35
a. Booklet, 5 each #1340-1341 7.00
1342 A403 E Robin .75 .40
a. Booklet of 10 + 10 etiquettes 7.50
1343 A403 W Song thrush 1.00 .55
a. Booklet of 10 + 10 etiquettes 10.00
Nos. 1340-1343 (4) 3.15 1.65

Fish
A470

Designs: 30p, Perch. No. 1345, Arctic char. No. 1346, Pike. 45p, Common bream.

2001, Oct. 9 ***Perf. 14¾x14***

1344 A470 30p multi .70 .35
1345 A470 32p multi .75 .40
1346 A470 32p multi .75 .40
a. Horiz. pair, #1345-1346 1.50 .80
1347 A470 45p multi 1.00 .50
a. Booklet pane, #1344-1347 3.25 —
b. Booklet pane, #1345, 1346, 2 #1347 3.50 —
c. Booklet pane, 2 each #1344, 1347 3.50 —
Booklet, #1347b, 1347c, 2 #1347a 13.50

No. 1347a exists with stamps in different order. The booklet contains the two different panes.

Governmental Support of Arts, 50th Anniv. — A471

2001, Nov. 5 ***Perf. 14x14¾***

1348 A471 50p multi 1.10 .55

Christmas — A472

Designs: No. 1349, Nativity. 32p, Annunciation. 45p, Presentation in the Temple. No. 1352, Madonna and Child.

2001, Nov. 5 ***Perf. 14x14¾***

1349 A472 30p multi .70 .35
1350 A472 32p multi .75 .40
1351 A472 45p multi 1.00 .50

Booklet Stamp
Size: 21x27mm
Self-Adhesive
Serpentine Die Cut 11x11¼

1352 A472 30p multi .65 .30
a. Booklet of 24 16.00
Nos. 1349-1352 (4) 3.10 1.55

No. 1352a sold for £6.60.

100 Cents = 1 Euro (€)

A473

Birds (With Euro Denominations Only) — A474

Designs: 1c, Magpie. 2c, Gannet. 3c, Blue tit, horiz. 4c, Corncrake. 5c, Wood pigeon, horiz. 10c, Kingfisher. 20c, Lapwing. Nos. 1360, 1371, 1372, 38c, Blackbird. No. 1373, 38c, Goldcrest. 41c, Chaffinch. 44c, Robin. 50c, Gray heron, horiz. 51c, Roseate tern, horiz. 57c, Curlew. €1, Barnacle goose. €2, Greenland white-fronted goose, vert. €5, Pintail. €10, Shelduck, vert.

Perf. 14x14¾, 14¾x14

2002, Jan. 1 **Litho.**

1353 A473 1c multi .20 .20
1354 A473 2c multi .20 .20
1355 A473 3c multi .20 .20
1356 A473 4c multi .20 .20
1357 A473 5c multi .20 .20
1358 A473 10c multi .20 .20
1359 A473 20c multi .35 .20
1360 A473 38c multi .65 .30
1361 A473 41c multi .70 .35
1362 A473 44c multi .75 .40
1363 A473 50c multi .85 .45
1364 A473 51c multi .90 .45
1365 A473 57c multi 1.00 .50
1366 A474 €1 multi 1.75 .85
1367 A474 €2 multi 3.50 1.75
1368 A474 €5 multi 8.75 4.50
1369 A474 €10 multi 17.50 8.75

Booklet Stamps
Size: 18x20mm
Perf. 14¾x14¼ on 3 Sides

1370 A473 10c multi .20 .20
1371 A473 38c multi .65 .30
a. Booklet pane, #1370, 5 #1371 3.50 —
Booklet, #1371a 3.50

Coil Stamps
Size: 21x26mm
Self-Adhesive
Serpentine Die Cut 11x11¼

1372 A473 38c multi .65 .30
1373 A473 38c multi .65 .30
a. Pair, #1372-1373 1.30
Nos. 1353-1373 (21) 40.05 20.80

Introduction of the Euro
A475

Designs: 38c, 1 euro coin introduced in 2002. 41c, 50p coin used from 1971-2001. 57c, 1p coin used from 1928-71.

2002, Jan. 1 Litho. ***Perf. 14¾x14¼***

1374 A475 38c multi .65 .30
1375 A475 41c multi .70 .35
1376 A475 57c multi 1.00 .50
Nos. 1374-1376 (3) 2.35 1.15

Toys — A476

Designs: Nos. 1377, 1379, Teddy bear. Nos. 1378a, 1381, Rocking horse. Nos. 1378b, 1382, Wooden locomotive. Nos. 1378c, 1380, Doll. No. 1383, Blocks.

2002, Jan. 22 ***Perf. 14¼x14¾***

1377 A476 38c multi .65 .30

Souvenir Sheet
Perf. 14¼x14¾ on 3 or 4 Sides

1378 Sheet of 3 2.00 1.00
a.-c. A476 38c Any single .65 .30

Booklet Stamps
Self-Adhesive
Size: 21x27mm
Serpentine Die Cut 11¼

1379 A476 38c multi .65 .30
1380 A476 38c multi .65 .30
1381 A476 38c multi .65 .30
1382 A476 38c multi .65 .30
1383 A476 38c multi .65 .30
a. Booklet of 10, 2 each #1379-1383, + 10 labels 6.50
Nos. 1379-1383 (5) 3.25 1.50

Steeplechasing in Ireland, 250th Anniv. — A477

2002, Mar. 12 ***Perf. 14¾x14¼***

1384 A477 38c Arkle .65 .30
1385 A477 38c L'Escargot .65 .30
1386 A477 38c Dawn Run .65 .30
1387 A477 38c Istabraq .65 .30
a. Horiz. strip of 4, #1384-1387 2.60 1.25

Scouting A478

Designs: No. 1388, Scout with peg and mallet. No. 1389, Scouts and leader around camp fire. No. 1390, Scouts on hike. No. 1391, Scouts kayaking.

2002, Mar. 12

1388 A478 41c multi .75 .40
1389 A478 41c multi .75 .40
a. Horiz. pair, #1388-1389 1.50 .80
1390 A478 57c multi 1.00 .50
1391 A478 57c multi 1.00 .50
a. Horiz. pair, #1390-1391 2.00 1.00
Nos. 1388-1391 (4) 3.50 1.80

Bird Type of 2002

Designs: 47c, Kestrel, horiz. 55c, Oystercatcher, horiz. 60c, Jay, horiz.

2002, June 17 Litho. *Perf. 14¾x14*

1392 A473 47c multi .90 .45
1393 A473 55c multi 1.10 .55
1394 A473 60c multi 1.25 .60
Nos. 1392-1394 (3) 3.25 1.60

Issued: 47c, 55c, 60c, 6/17.

Bird Type of 2002

Designs: No. 1395, Chaffinch. No. 1396, Goldcrest. 44c, Robin. 57c, Song thrush.

Serpentine Die Cut 11x11¼

2002 Litho.

Self-Adhesive

Size: 21x26mm

1395 A473 41c multi .75 .35
1396 A473 41c multi .75 .35
a. Coil pair, #1395-1396 1.50
b. Booklet of 10, 5 each #1395-1396 7.50

Booklet Stamps

1397 A473 44c multi .80 .40
a. Booklet of 10 8.00
1398 A473 57c multi 1.00 .50
a. Booklet of 10 10.00
Nos. 1395-1398 (4) 3.30 1.60

Issued: Nos. 1395-1398, 4/2. This is an expanding set.

Compare Nos. 1395-1396 with Nos. 1433-1434.

Mammals A479

Designs: 41c, Meles meles. 50c, ꞋꞋ5, Lutra lutra. 57c, Sciurus vulgaris, vert. ꞋꞋ1, Erinaceus europaeus, vert.

Perf. 14¾x14¼, 14¼x14¾

2002, Apr. 23 Litho.

1399 A479 41c multi .75 .35
1400 A479 50c multi .90 .45
1401 A479 57c multi 1.00 .50
1402 A479 ꞋꞋ1 multi 1.90 .95
Nos. 1399-1402 (4) 4.55 2.25

Souvenir Sheet

1403 A479 ꞋꞋ5 multi 9.25 4.50

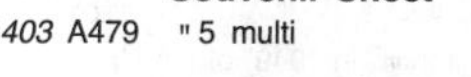

Europa A480

Designs: Nos. 1404, 1406, Clown. Nos. 1405, 1407, Equestrian act.

2002, May 14 Litho. *Perf. 14¾x14*

1404 A480 41c multi .75 .35
1405 A480 44c multi .80 .40

Coil Stamps

Size: 34x23mm

Self-Adhesive

Die Cut Perf. 9¼x9½

1406 A480 41c multi .75 .35
1407 A480 41c multi .75 .75
a. Horiz. pair, #1406-1407 1.50
Nos. 1404-1407 (4) 3.05 1.85

Soccer Stars A481

Designs: Nos. 1408, 1415, Packie Bonner. Nos. 1409, 1412, Roy Keane, vert. Nos. 1410, 1413, Paul McGrath, vert. Nos. 1411, 1414, David O'Leary, vert.

2002, May 14 *Perf. 14¾x14, 14x14¾*

1408 A481 41c multi .75 .35
1409 A481 41c multi .75 .35
1410 A481 41c multi .75 .35
1411 A481 41c multi .75 .35
a. Vert. strip of 3, #1409-1411 2.25 1.10

Booklet Stamps

Sizes: 23x34, 34x23mm

Self-Adhesive

Serpentine Die Cut 11½x11¾, 11¾x11½

1412 A481 41c multi .75 .35
1413 A481 41c multi .75 .35
1414 A481 41c multi .75 .35
1415 A481 41c multi .75 .35
a. Booklet, 3 #1412-1413, 2 #1414-1415 7.50

Canonization of St. Pio of Pietrelcina (1887-1968) A482

2002, June 17 Litho. *Perf. 14x14¾*

1416 A482 41c multi .80 .40

BrianBorú, 1000th Anniv of High Kingship A483

Designs: 41c, Leading troops into battle. 44c, Commanding ships. 57c, On throne. ꞋꞋ1, Decreeing Armagh as the primacy of the Irish church.

2002, July 9 *Perf. 14¾x14*

1417 A483 41c multi .80 .40
1418 A483 44c multi .90 .45
1419 A483 57c multi 1.10 .55
1420 A483 ꞋꞋ1 multi 2.00 1.00
Nos. 1417-1420 (4) 4.80 2.40

Bird Type of 2002

Designs: No. 1421, Goldcrest. No. 1422, 36c, Wren. No. 1423, Chaffinch.

Perf. 14x14¾ on 3 Sides

2002, Aug. 6 Litho.

Booklet Stamps

1421 A473 41c multi .80 .40
a. Booklet pane of 10, 5 each #1361, 1421 8.00 —
Booklet, #1421a 8.00

Size: 18x21mm

Perf. 14¾x14¼ on 3 Sides

1422 A473 36c multi .70 .35
1423 A473 41c multi .80 .40
a. Booklet pane of 5, #1422, 4 #1423 + label 3.90 —
Booklet, #1423a 3.90

Paintings in National Gallery A484

Designs: No. 1424, Before the Start, by Jack B. Yeats. No. 1425, The Conjuror, by Nathaniel Hone. No. 1426, The Colosseum and Arch of Constantine, Rome, by Giovanni Paolo Panini. No. 1427, The Gleaners, by Jules Breton.

2002, Aug. 29 *Perf. 14¾x14*

1424 A484 41c multi .80 .40
a. Booklet pane of 4 3.20 —
1425 A484 41c multi .80 .40
a. Booklet pane of 4 3.20 —
1426 A484 41c multi .80 .40
a. Booklet pane of 4 3.20 —
1427 A484 41c multi .80 .40
a. Horiz. strip, #1424-1427 3.20 1.60
b. Booklet pane of 4 3.20 —
Booklet, #1424a, 1425a, 1426a, 1427b 13.00

Archbishop Thomas Croke (1823-1902) A485

2002, Sept. 17 *Perf. 14x14¾*

1428 A485 44c multi .90 .45

Hall of Fame Athletes Type of 2001

Designs: No. 1429, Peter McDermott, soccer player. No. 1430, Jimmy Smyth, hurler. No. 1431, Matt Connor, soccer player. No. 1432, Seanie Duggan, hurler.

2002, Sept. 17 *Perf. 14¾x14*

1429 A468 41c multi .80 .40
1430 A468 41c multi .80 .40
1431 A468 41c multi .80 .40
1432 A468 41c multi .80 .40
a. Horiz. strip, #1429-1432 3.20 1.60

Bird Type of 2002 Redrawn

Designs: No. 1433, Chaffinch. No. 1434, Goldcrest

Serpentine Die Cut 11x11¼

2002, Oct. 17 Photo.

Coil Stamps

Self-Adhesive

1433 A473 41c multi .80 .40
1434 A473 41c multi .80 .40
a. Coil pair, #1433-1434 1.60

Text appears grayer on Nos. 1433-1434 than on Nos. 1395-1396. On No. 1433, the second "h" of "Chaffinch" touches the branch, while it does not touch on No. 1395. On No. 1434, the points of the pine needles at the bottom of the stamp are shown, while they are cut off on No. 1396.

Irish Rock Musicians A486

Designs: Nos. 1435, 1439, U2. Nos. 1436, 1440, Phil Lynott. Nos. 1437, 1441, Van Morrison. Nos. 1438, 1442, Rory Gallagher.

2002, Oct. 17 Litho. *Perf. 13¼x12¾*

1435 A486 41c multi .80 .40
1436 A486 41c multi .80 .40
a. Horiz. pair, #1435-1436 1.60 .80
1437 A486 57c multi 1.10 .55
1438 A486 57c multi 1.10 .55
a. Horiz. pair, #1437-1438 2.20 1.10
Nos. 1435-1438 (4) 3.80 1.90

Souvenir Sheets

Perf. 12¾x13¼

1439 A486 ꞋꞋ2 multi 4.00 2.00
1440 A486 ꞋꞋ2 multi 4.00 2.00
1441 A486 ꞋꞋ2 multi 4.00 2.00
1442 A486 ꞋꞋ2 multi 4.00 2.00

Christmas — A487

Scenes from *Les Très Riches Heures du Duc de Berry*: No. 1443, Adoration of the Magi. 44c, The Annunciation. 57c, Angels Announcing Birth to Shepherds.

No. 1446, Adoration of the Shepherds.

2002, Nov. 7 Litho. *Perf. 14¼x14¾*

1443 A487 41c multi .85 .40
1444 A487 44c multi .90 .45
1445 A487 57c multi 1.10 .55

Booklet Stamp

Self-Adhesive

Size: 21x27mm

Serpentine Die Cut 11x11¼

1446 A487 41c multi .85 .40
a. Booklet pane of 24 21.00
Nos. 1443-1446 (4) 3.70 1.80

No. 1446a sold for ꞋꞋ9.43.

AIR POST STAMPS

Catalogue values for unused stamps in this section are for Never Hinged items.

Angel over Rock of Cashel AP1

Designs: 1p, 1sh3p, 1sh5p, Rock of Cashel. 3p, Lough Derg. 6p, Croagh Patrick. 1sh, Glendalough.

Perf. 15x14

1948-65 Wmk. 262 Engr.

C1 AP1 1p dk brown ('49) 2.00 3.50
C2 AP1 3p blue 3.50 2.25
C3 AP1 6p rose lilac 1.00 1.50
C4 AP1 8p red brown ('54) 7.50 6.50
C5 AP1 1sh green ('49) 1.00 1.50
C6 AP1 1sh3p ver ('54) 8.50 1.25

Perf. 15

C7 AP1 1sh5p dark blue ('65) 3.25 1.00
Nos. C1-C7 (7) 26.75 17.50

POSTAGE DUE STAMPS

D1

1925 Typo. Wmk. 44 *Perf. 14x15*

J1 D1 ½p emerald 21.00 22.50
Never hinged 75.00
J2 D1 1p carmine 12.00 7.25
Never hinged 35.00
J3 D1 2p dark green 21.00 6.75
Never hinged 75.00
J4 D1 6p plum 6.00 8.50
Never hinged 25.00
Nos. J1-J4 (4) 60.00 45.00

Catalogue values for unused stamps in this section, from this point to the end of the section, are for Never Hinged items.

1940-70 Wmk. 262

J5 D1 ½p emerald ('43) 35.00 22.50
J6 D1 1p brt carmine ('41) 1.10 .50
J7 D1 1½p vermilion ('52) 2.25 *5.00*
J8 D1 2p dark green 2.25 .55
J9 D1 3p blue ('52) 1.75 1.25
J10 D1 5p royal purple ('43) 3.00 *3.50*
J11 D1 6p plum ('60) 2.25 1.50
J12 D1 8p orange ('62) 7.50 5.00

J13	D1	10p red lilac ('65)	7.75	5.00
J14	D1	1sh lt yel grn ('69)	15.00	6.00
		Nos. J5-J14 (10)	77.85	50.80

1971, Feb. 15 Typo. Wmk. 262

J15	D1	1p sepia	.20	.20
J16	D1	1½p bright green	.20	.20
J17	D1	3p gray green	.90	.70
J18	D1	4p orange	1.25	.80
J19	D1	5p bright blue	2.25	1.40
J20	D1	7p yellow	.30	.20
J21	D1	8p scarlet	.30	.20
		Nos. J15-J21 (7)	5.40	3.70

1978 Unwmk.

J25	D1	3p gray green	2.50	*6.00*
J26	D1	4p orange	4.00	*10.50*
J27	D1	5p bright blue	2.50	*6.00*
		Nos. J25-J27 (3)	9.00	*22.50*

Celtic Knot — D2

D3

1980-85 Photo. *Perf. 15*

J28	D2	1p brt yel green	.20	.20
J29	D2	2p ultramarine	.20	.20
J30	D2	4p dark green	.40	.35
J31	D2	6p yel orange	.55	.50
J32	D2	8p violet blue	.75	.65
J33	D2	18p green	1.60	1.40
J33A	D2	20p org brown ('85)	1.40	1.10
J34	D2	24p emerald	2.25	1.90
J35	D2	30p plum ('85)	1.75	1.50
J36	D2	50p rose pink ('85)	3.25	3.00
		Nos. J28-J36 (10)	12.35	10.80

Issue dates: 1p, 2p, 4p, 6p, 8p, 18p, 24p, June 11; 20p, 30p, 50p, Aug. 22.

1988, Oct. 6 Litho. *Perf. 14x15*

J37	D3	1p blk, dp yel & brt red	.20	.20
J38	D3	2p blk, vio brn & brt red	.20	.20
J39	D3	3p blk, dull vio & brt red	.20	.20
J40	D3	4p blk, vio & brt red	.20	.20
J41	D3	5p blk, vio bl & brt red	.20	.20
J42	D3	17p blk, brt ol grn & brt red	.50	.25
J43	D3	20p blk, bluish gray & brt red	.60	.30
J44	D3	24p blk, bl grn & brt red	.70	.35
J45	D3	30p blk & brt red	.90	.45
J46	D3	50p blk, gray & brt red	1.50	.75
J47	D3	£1 blk, dk ol brn & brt red	3.00	1.50
		Nos. J37-J47 (11)	8.20	4.60

ISRAEL

'iz-rē-əl

LOCATION — Western Asia, bordering on the Mediterranean Sea
GOVT. — Republic
AREA — 8,017 sq. mi.
POP. — 5,749,760 (1999 est.)
CAPITAL — Jerusalem

When the British mandate of Palestine ended in May 1948, the Jewish state of Israel was proclaimed by the Jewish National Council in Palestine.

1000 Mils = 1 Pound
1000 Prutot = 1 Pound (1949)
100 Agorot = 1 Pound (1960)
100 Agorot = 1 Shekel (1980)

Catalogue values for all unused stamps in this country are for Never Hinged items.

Tabs

Stamps of Israel are printed in sheets with tabs (labels) usually attached below the bottom row, sometimes at the sides.

Tabs of the following numbers are in two parts, perforated between: 9, 15, 23-37, 44, 46-47, 50, 55, 62-65, 70-72, 74-77, 86-91, 94-99, 104-118, 123-126, 133-136B, 138-141, 143-151, 160-161, 165-167, 178-179, 182, 187-189, 203, 211-213, 222-223, 228-237, 243-244, 246-250, 256-258, 269-270, 272-273, 275, 294-295, 312, 337-339, 341-344, 346-347, 353-354, C1-C13, C22-C30. Both parts must be present to quaify for with tab value. Stamps with only one part sell for about one-quarter to one-third of full tab prices.

Watermarks

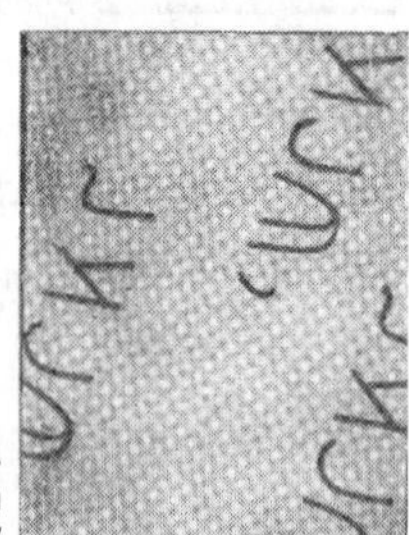

Wmk. 301- ISRAEL in Hebrew

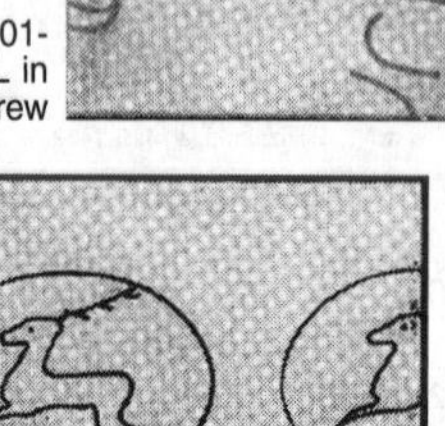

Wmk. 302- Multiple Stag

Ancient Judean Coins
A1 A2

Designs: Nos. 1-6, Various coins.

Perf. 10, 11 and Compound

1948, May 16 Typo. Unwmk.

1	A1	3m orange	.25	.20
2	A1	5m yellow grn	.25	.20
3	A1	10m red violet	.40	.20
4	A1	15m red	.65	.20
5	A1	20m bright ultra	2.10	.20
6	A1	50m orange brown	8.50	.20
		Nos. 1-6 (6)	12.15	1.20
		Set, hinged tabs	100.00	
		Nos. 1-6 (6) with tabs	210.00	

Size: 34½x22mm

7	A2	250m dark sl grn	32.50	9.50
8	A2	500m red brn, *cr*	140.00	47.50

Size: 36½x24mm

9	A2	1000m blk bl, *pale bl*	210.00	95.00
		Nos. 7-9 (3)	382.50	152.00
		Nos. 7-9 with tabs	*4,750.*	
		Set, hinged	190.00	

Nos. 1-9 exist imperf.
See design A6. For overprints see #J1-J5.

Rouletted

1a	A1	3m	.40	.20
2b	A1	5m	.60	.20
3b	A1	10m	10.00	.70
		Nos. 1a-3b (3)	11.00	1.10
		Set, with tabs	225.00	
		Set with tabs, hinged	100.00	

Flying Scroll — A3

1948, Sept. 26 Litho. *Perf. 11½*

10	A3	3m brn red & ultra	.30	.20
11	A3	5m dl grn & ultra	.30	.20
12	A3	10m dp car & ultra	.30	.20
13	A3	20m dp ultra & ultra	1.25	.55
14	A3	65m brown & red	10.50	3.75
		Nos. 10-14 (5)	12.65	4.90
		With tabs	225.00	
		With tabs, hinged	100.00	

Jewish New Year, 5709.

Flag of Israel — A4

1949, Mar. 31

15	A4	20m bright blue	.40	.25
		With tab	40.00	

Appointment of the government by the Knesset.

Souvenir Sheet

A5

1949, May 1 *Imperf.*

16	A5	Sheet of 4	72.50	25.00
a.		10m dark carmine rose	17.50	4.00

1st anniv. of Israeli postage stamps.
The sheet was sold at "TABUL," First National Stamp Exhibition, in Tel Aviv, May 1-6, 1949. Tickets, costing 100 mils, covered the entrance fee and one sheet.

Bronze Half-Shekel of 67 A.D. — A6

Approach to Jerusalem — A8

Hebrew University, Jerusalem A7

"The Negev" by Reuven Rubin — A9

1949-50 Unwmk. *Perf. 11½, 14*

17	A6	3p gray black	.25	.20
18	A6	5p purple	.20	.20
19	A6	10p green	.20	.20
20	A6	15p deep rose	.25	.20
21	A6	30p dark blue	.30	.20
22	A6	50p brown	1.25	.20
23	A7	100p Prus grn	.30	.20
		With tab	18.00	
24	A8	250p org brn & gray	1.00	.65
		With tab	32.50	
25	A9	500p dp org & brown	6.25	5.50
		With tab	210.00	
		Nos. 17-25 (9)	10.00	7.55
		Nos. 17-22 with tabs (6)	70.00	
		Tete beche pairs, Nos. 18-21	80.00	80.00

Each of Nos. 17-22 portrays a different coin.
25th anniv. of the Hebrew University in Jerusalem (No. 23).
Issued: 250p, 2/16; 3p-50p, 12/18; 100p, 5/9/50; 500p, 12/26/50.
See Nos. 38-43, 56-61, 80-83, and design A1. For overprints see Nos. O1-O4.

Well at Petah Tikva — A10

1949, Aug. 10 *Perf. 11*

27	A10	40p dk grn & brn	6.50	.30
		With tab	75.00	

70th anniv. of Petah Tikva.

Arms and Service Insignia A11

1949, Sept. 20 *Perf. 11½*

28	A11	5p Air Force	.35	.25
29	A11	10p Navy	.95	.40
30	A11	35p Army	4.25	2.75
		Nos. 28-30 (3)	5.55	3.40
		With tabs	525.00	

Jewish New Year, 5710.

Running Stag — A12

1950, Mar. 26

31	A12	40p purple	.50	.20
a.		Booklet pane of 4	3.50	
32	A12	80p rose red	.50	.20
a.		Booklet pane of 4	7.00	
b.		Nos. 31 and 32 tête bêche	45.00	25.00
		With tabs	65.00	

75th anniv. (in 1949) of the UPU.

Struggle for Free Immigration A13

Arrival of Immigrants A14

1950, Apr. 23

33 A13 20p dull brown 2.50 1.25
34 A14 40p dull green 5.00 3.25
With tabs 450.00

Independence Day, Apr. 22, 1950.

Fruit and Star of David — A15

1950, Aug. 31 Litho. *Perf. 14*

35 A15 5p vio blue & org .20 .20
36 A15 15p red brn & grn .35 .20
With tabs 42.50

Jewish New Year, 5711.

Runner and Track A16

1950, Oct. 1

37 A16 80p olive & sl blk 1.60 .50
With tab 55.00

3rd Maccabiah, Ramat Gan, Sept. 27, 1950.

Coin Type of 1949 Redrawn

Designs: Various coins.

1950

38 A6 3p gray black .20 .20
39 A6 5p purple .20 .20
a. Tête bêche pair 3.00 3.00
40 A6 10p green .20 .20
a. Tête bêche pair 1.25 1.00
41 A6 15p deep rose .20 .20
a. Tête bêche pair 2.00 1.75
42 A6 30p dark blue .20 .20
a. Tête bêche pair 4.00 4.00
43 A6 50p brown .20 .20
Nos. 38-43 (6) 1.20 1.20
With tabs 2.90

Inscription at left measures 11mm on Nos. 38-43; 9mm on Nos. 17-22.

Detail from Tablet, "Founding of Tel Aviv" A17

1951, Mar. 22

44 A17 40p dark brown .30 .20
With tab 20.00

40th anniversary of Tel Aviv.

Young Man Holding Outline Map of Israel — A18

1951, Apr. 30 Litho.

45 A18 80p red brown .20 .20
With tab 3.75

Issued to promote the sale of Independence Bonds.

Metsudat Yesha A19

Hakastel A20

1951, May 9 Unwmk.

46 A19 15p red brown .20 .20
47 A20 40p deep blue .50 .20
With tabs 40.00

Proclamation of State of Israel, 3rd anniv.

Tractor and Wheat — A21

Tree — A22

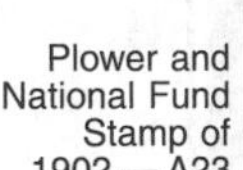

Plower and National Fund Stamp of 1902 — A23

1951, June 24 *Perf. 14*

48 A21 15p red brown .20 .20
49 A22 25p Prussian green .20 .20
50 A23 80p dull blue .35 .20
Nos. 48-50 (3) .75 .60
With tabs 82.50

Jewish National Fund, 50th anniversary.

Theodor Zeev Herzl — A24

Carrier Pigeons — A25

1951, Aug. 14

51 A24 80p gray green .20 .20
With tab 4.00

23rd Zionist Congress, Jerusalem.

1951, Sept. 16

Designs: 15p, Girl holding dove and fruit. 40p, Scrolls of the law.

52 A25 5p blue .20 .20
53 A25 15p cerise .20 .20
54 A25 40p rose violet .20 .20
Nos. 52-54 (3) .60 .60
With tabs 2.25

Jewish New Year, 5712.

Menorah and Emblems of Twelve Tribes — A26

1952, Feb. 27

55 A26 1000p dk bl & gray 16.00 7.00
With tab 225.00

Redrawn Coin Type of 1950

Designs: Various coins.

1952, Mar. 30

56 A6 20p orange .20 .20
a. Tête bêche pair 2.50 2.50
57 A6 35p olive green .20 .20
58 A6 40p orange brown .20 .20
59 A6 45p red violet .20 .20
a. Tête bêche pair 4.50 4.50
60 A6 60p carmine .20 .20
61 A6 85p aquamarine .20 .20
Nos. 56-61 (6) 1.20 1.20
With tabs 12.00

Thistle and Yad Mordecai Battlefield A27

Battlefields: 60p, Cornflower and Deganya. 110p, Anemone and Safed.

1952, Apr. 29

62 A27 30p lil rose & vio brn .20 .20
63 A27 60p ultra & gray blk .20 .20
64 A27 110p crimson & gray .35 .25
Nos. 62-64 (3) .75 .65
With tabs 19.00

Proclamation of State of Israel, 4th anniv.

Manhattan Skyline and American Zionists' House A28

1952, May 13

65 A28 220p dark blue & gray .35 .20
With tab 11.00

Opening of American Zionists' House, Tel Aviv.

Figs — A29

Unwmk.

1952, Sept. 3 Litho. *Perf. 14*

66 A29 15p shown .20 .20
67 A29 40p Lily .20 .20
68 A29 110p Dove .20 .20
69 A29 220p Nut cluster .25 .20
Nos. 66-69 (4) .85 .80
With tabs 21.00

Jewish New Year, 5713.

Pres. Chaim Weizmann (1874-1952) and Presidential Standard — A30

1952, Dec. 9

70 A30 30p slate .20 .20
71 A30 110p black .25 .20
With tabs 8.50

Weizmann, president of Israel 1948-52.

Numeral Incorporating Agricultural Scenes — A31

1952, Dec. 31

72 A31 110p brown, buff & emer .20 .20
With tab 8.00

70th anniversary of B.I.L.U. (Bet Yaakov Lechu Venelcha) immigration.

Five Anemones and State Emblem — A32

1953, Apr. 19

73 A32 110p grnsh bl, bl blk & red .20 .20
With tab 4.25

5th anniversary of State of Israel.

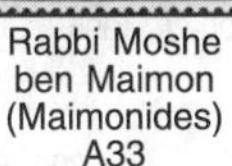

Rabbi Moshe ben Maimon (Maimonides) A33

Holy Ark, Jerusalem A34

1953, Aug. 3 Wmk. 301 *Perf. 14x13*

74 A33 110p brown .35 .35
With tab 8.25

7th International Congress of History of Science, Jerusalem, Aug. 4-11.

1953, Aug. 11

Holy Arks: 45p, Petah Tikva. 200p, Safed.

75 A34 20p sapphire .20 .20
76 A34 45p brown red .20 .20
77 A34 200p purple .20 .20
Nos. 75-77 (3) .60 .60
With tabs 8.00

Jewish New Year, 5714.

Combined Ball-Globe A35

Desert Rose A36

Unwmk.

1953, Sept. 20 Litho. *Perf. 14*
78 A35 110p blue & dark brn .20 .20
With tab 4.25

4th Maccabiah, Sept. 20-29, 1953.

1953, Sept. 22
79 A36 200p multicolored .20 .20
With tab 4.50

Conquest of the Desert Exhib., 9/22-10/14.

Redrawn Type of 1950

Designs: Various coins.

1954, Jan. 5
80 A6 80p olive bister .20 .20
81 A6 95p blue green .20 .20
82 A6 100p fawn .20 .20
83 A6 125p violet blue .20 .20
Nos. 80-83 (4) .80 .80
With tabs 2.50

Marigold and Ruins at Yehiam — A37

350p, Narcissus and bridge at Gesher.

1954, May 5 Litho.
84 A37 60p dk bl, mag & ol gray .20 .20
85 A37 350p dk brn, grn & yel .20 .20
With tabs 1.75

Memorial Day and 6th anniversary of proclamation of State of Israel.

Theodor Zeev Herzl (1860-1904), Founder of Zionist Movement — A38

1954, July 21 Wmk. 302
86 A38 160p dk bl, dk brn & cr .20 .20
With tab .85

Bearers with Grape Cluster A39

1954, Sept. 8 *Perf. 13x14*
87 A39 25p dark brown .20 .20
With tab .20

Jewish New Year, 5715.

19th Century Mail Coach and Jerusalem Post Office A40

200p, Mail truck & present G.P.O., Jerusalem.

1954, Oct. 13 *Perf. 14*
88 A40 60p blue, blk & yel .20 .20
89 A40 200p dk grn, blk & red .20 .20
With tabs 3.00

TABIM, National Stamp Exhibition, Jerusalem, Oct. 13-18.

Baron Edmond de Rothschild (1845-1934) and Grape Cluster — A41

1954, Nov. 23 *Perf. 13x14*
90 A41 300p dark blue green .20 .20
With tab .85

Lighted Oil Lamp A42

1955, Jan. 13 *Perf. 13x14*
91 A42 250p dark blue .20 .20
With tab .75

Teachers' Association, 50th anniversary.

Parachutist and Barbed Wire — A43

1955, Mar. 31 Litho. *Perf. 14*
92 A43 120p dk Prus green .20 .20
With tab .45

Jewish volunteers from Palestine who served in British army in World War II.

Lighted Menorah A44

1955, Apr. 26
93 A44 150p dk grn, blk & org .20 .20
With tab .35

Proclamation of State of Israel, 7th anniv.

Immigration by Ship — A45

Designs: 10p, Immigration by plane. 25p, Agricultural training. 30p, Gardening. 60p, Vocational training. 750p, Scientific education.

1955, May 10 Unwmk. *Perf. 14*
94 A45 5p brt blue & black .20 .20
95 A45 10p red & black .20 .20
96 A45 25p deep grn & black .20 .20
97 A45 30p orange & black .20 .20
98 A45 60p lilac rose & blk .20 .20
99 A45 750p olive bis & blk .25 .20
Nos. 94-99 (6) 1.25 1.20
With tabs 1.75

Israel's Youth Immigration Institution, 20th anniv.

Musicians with Tambourine and Cymbals A46

Mandrake, Reuben A48

Ambulance A47

Musician with: 60p, Ram's Horn. 120p, Loud Trumpet. 250p, Harp.

1955, Aug. 25 Photo. Wmk. 302
100 A46 25p dark green & org .20 .20

Unwmk.

101 A46 60p dk gray & orange .20 .20
102 A46 120p dark blue & yel .20 .20
103 A46 250p red brn & org .20 .20
#100-103, with tabs .50

Jewish New Year, 5716.
See Nos. 121-123.

1955, Nov. 1 Wmk. 301 *Perf. 14*
104 A47 160p grn, red & blk .20 .20
With tab .30

Magen David Adom (Israeli Red Cross), 25th anniv.

1955-57 Wmk. 302 *Perf. 13x14*

Twelve Tribes: 20p, Gates of Sechem, Simeon. 30p, Ephod, Levi. 40p, Lion, Judah. 50p, Scales, Dan. 60p, Stag, Naphtali. 80p, Tents, Gad. 100p, Tree, Asher. 120p, Sun and stars, Issachar. 180p, Ship, Zebulon. 200p, Sheaf of wheat, Joseph. 250p, Wolf, Benjamin.

105 A48 10p bright green .20 .20
106 A48 20p red lilac ('56) .20 .20
107 A48 30p bright ultra .20 .20
108 A48 40p brown ('56) .20 .20
109 A48 50p grnsh bl ('56) .20 .20
110 A48 60p lemon .20 .20
111 A48 80p deep vio ('56) .20 .20
112 A48 100p vermilion .20 .20
113 A48 120p olive ('56) .20 .20
114 A48 180p lil rose ('56) .20 .20
115 A48 200p green ('56) .20 .20
116 A48 250p gray ('56) .20 .20
#105-116, with tabs 2.00

See Nos. 133-136B.

Albert Einstein (1879-1955) and Equation of his Relativity Theory — A49

1956, Jan. 3 *Perf. 13x14*
117 A49 350p brown .20 .20
With tab .60

Technion, Haifa A50

1956, Jan. 3 Wmk. 302
118 A50 350p lt ol grn & blk .20 .20
With tab .20

Israel Institute of Technology, 30th anniv.

"Eight Years of Israel" — A51

Jaffa Oranges — A52

1956, Apr. 12 Litho. *Perf. 14*
119 A51 150p multicolored .20 .20
With tab .20

Proclamation of State of Israel, 8th anniv.

1956, May 20 Wmk. 302 *Perf. 14*
120 A52 300p bl grn & orange .20 .20
With tab .20

4th Intl. Congress of Mediterranean Citrus Growers.

New Year Type of 1955

Musician with: 30p, Lyre. 50p, Cymbals. 150p, Double oboe, horiz.

1956, Aug. 14 Photo. *Perf. 14x13*
121 A46 30p brown & brt blue .20 .20

Perf. 14

122 A46 50p purple & orange .20 .20
123 A46 150p dk bl grn & org .20 .20
#121-123, with tabs .25

Jewish New Year, 5717.

Haganah Insignia A54

Bezalel Museum and Antique Lamp A55

1957, Jan. 1 *Perf. 13x14*
124 A54 20p + 80p brt grn .20 .20
125 A54 50p + 150p car rose .20 .20
126 A54 50p + 350p ultra .20 .20
#124-126, with tabs .25

Defense issue. Divided denomination used to show increased postal rate.

1957, Apr. 29 Litho. *Perf. 14*
127 A55 400p multicolored .20 .20
With tab .20

Bezalel Natl. Museum, Jerusalem, 50th anniv.

Jet Plane and "9" — A56

Horse and Seal — A57

1957, Apr. 29
128 A56 250p deep bl & blk .20 .20
With tab .20

Proclamation of State of Israel, 9th anniv.

1957, Sept. 4 Wmk. 302 *Perf. 14*

Ancient Seals: 160p, Lion. 300p, Gazelle.

129 A57 50p ocher & blk, *lt bl* .20 .20

Perf. 14x13
Photo. Unwmk.

130 A57 160p grn & blk, *bis brn* .20 .20
131 A57 300p dp car & blk, *pink* .20 .20
#130-131, with tabs .25

Jewish New Year, 5718.

TABIL
Souvenir Sheet

Bet Alpha Synagogue Mosaic — A58

1957, Sept. 17 Litho. *Roulette 13*
132 A58 Sheet of 4 .30 .30
a. 100p multicolored .20 .20
b. 200p multicolored .20 .20
c. 300p multicolored .20 .20
d. 400p multicolored .20 .20

1st Intl. stamp exhib. in Israel, Tel Aviv, 9/17-23.

Tribes Type of 1955-57
Perf. 13x14

1957-59 Unwmk. Photo.
133 A48 10p brt grn ('58) .20 .20
133A A48 20p red lilac .20 .20
133C A48 40p brown ('59) .55 .45
134 A48 50p greenish blue .20 .20
135 A48 60p lemon .20 .20
136 A48 100p vermilion .20 .20
136B A48 120p olive ('58) .20 .20
Nos. 133-136B (7) 1.75 1.65
With tabs 42.50

Hammer Thrower — A59

1958, Jan. 20 *Perf. 14x13*
137 A59 500p bister & car .20 .20
With tab .25

Maccabiah Games, 25th anniversary.

Ancient Ship — A60

Ships: 20p, Three-master used for "illegal immigration." 30p, Cargo ship "Shomron." 1000p, Passenger ship "Zion."

Wmk. 302
1958, Jan. 27 Litho. *Perf. 14*
Size: 36½x22½mm
138 A60 10p ocher, red & blk .20 .20

Perf. 13x14
Photo.
139 A60 20p brt grn, blk & brn .20 .20
140 A60 30p red, blk & grnsh bl .20 .20

Size: 56½x22½mm
141 A60 1000p brt bl, blk & grn .20 .20
#138-141, with tabs .35

Issued to honor Israel's merchant fleet.

Menorah and Olive Branch — A61

Unwmk.
1958, Apr. 21 Litho. *Perf. 14*
142 A61 400p gold, blk & grn .20 .20
With tab .20

Memorial Day and 10th anniversary of proclamation of State of Israel.

Dancing Youths Forming "10" — A62

1958, July 2
143 A62 200p dk org & dk grn .20 .20
With tab .20

First World Conference of Jewish Youth, Jerusalem, July 28-Aug. 1.

Convention Center, Jerusalem A63

1958, July 2
144 A63 400p vio & org, *yellow* .20 .20
With tab .20

10th Anniversary of Independence Exhibition, Jerusalem, June 5-Aug. 21.

Wheat — A64

1958, Aug. 27 Photo. *Perf. 14x13*
145 A64 50p shown .20 .20
146 A64 60p Barley .20 .20
147 A64 160p Grapes .20 .20
148 A64 300p Figs .20 .20
#145-148, with tabs .30

Jewish New Year, 5719.

"Love Thy Neighbor . . ." — A65

1958, Dec. 10 Litho. *Perf. 14*
149 A65 750p yel, gray & grn .20 .20
With tab .90

Universal Declaration of Human Rights, 10th anniversary.

Designing and Printing Stamps A66

Radio and Telephone — A67

120p, Mobile post office. 500p, Teletype.

1959, Feb. 25 Wmk. 302 *Perf. 14*
150 A66 60p olive, blk & red .20 .20
151 A66 120p olive, blk & red .20 .20
152 A67 250p olive, blk & red .20 .20
153 A67 500p olive, blk & red .20 .20
#150-153, with tabs .45

Decade of postal activities in Israel.

Shalom Aleichem A68

Cyclamen A69

Portraits: No. 155, Chaim Nachman Bialik. No. 156, Eliezer Ben-Yehuda.

1959 Unwmk. Photo. *Perf. 14x13*
154 A68 250p yel grn & red brn .20 .20
155 A68 250p ocher & ol gray .20 .20
#154-155, with tabs .35

Perf. 14
Litho.
156 A68 250p bl & vio bl .20 .20
With tab .40

Birth cent. of Aleichem (Solomon Rabinowitz), Yiddish writer (No. 154); 25th death anniv. of Bialik, Hebrew poet (No. 155); birth cent. of Ben-Yehuda, father of modern Hebrew (No. 156).
Issued: #154, 3/30; #155, 7/22; #156, 11/25.

1959, May 11 Wmk. 302 *Perf. 14*

Flowers: 60p, Anemone. 300p, Narcissus.

Flowers in Natural Colors
157 A69 60p deep green .20 .20
158 A69 120p deep plum .20 .20
159 A69 300p blue .20 .20
#157-159, with tabs .35

Memorial Day and 11th anniversary of proclamation of State of Israel.

Buildings, Tel Aviv — A70

1959, May 4
160 A70 120p multicolored .20 .20
With tab .20

50th anniversary of Tel Aviv.

Bristol Britannia and Windsock A71

1959, July 22
161 A71 500p multicolored .20 .20
With tab .30

Civil Aviation in Israel, 10th anniversary.

Pomegranates A72

Perf. 14x13
1959, Sept. 9 Photo. Unwmk.
162 A72 60p shown .20 .20
163 A72 200p Olives .20 .20
164 A72 350p Dates .20 .20
Nos. 162-164 (3) .60 .60
With tabs 1.50

Jewish New Year, 5720.

Merhavya A73

Settlements: 120p, Yesud Ha-Maala. 180p, Deganya.

1959, Nov. 25 Photo. *Perf. 13x14*
165 A73 60p citron & dk grn .20 .20
166 A73 120p red brn & ocher .20 .20
167 A73 180p blue & dk grn .20 .20
Nos. 165-167 (3) .60 .60
With tabs 1.90

Settlements of Merhavya and Deganya, 50th anniv.; Yesud Ha-Maala, 75th anniv.

Judean Coin (66-70 A.D.) — A74

1960 Unwmk. *Perf. 13x14*
Denominations in Black
168 A74 1a brn, *pinkish* .20 .20
a. On surface colored paper .20 .20
As "a," with tab .75
b. Black overprint omitted
169 A74 3a brt red, *pinkish* .20 .20
170 A74 5a gray, *pinkish* .20 .20
171 A74 6a brt grn, *lt bl* .20 .20
171A A74 7a gray, *bluish* .20 .20
172 A74 8a mag, *lt blue* .20 .20
173 A74 12a grnsh bl, *lt bl* .20 .20
a. Black overprint omitted
174 A74 18a orange .20 .20
175 A74 25a blue .20 .20
176 A74 30a carmine .20 .20
177 A74 50a bright lilac .20 .20
#168-177, with tabs 1.75

Issue dates: 7a, July 6; others, Jan. 6.

Operation "Magic Carpet" A75

Design: 50a, Resettled family in front of house, grapes and figs.

1960, Apr. 7 Unwmk. *Perf. 13x14*
178 A75 25a red brown .20 .20
179 A75 50a green .20 .20
#178-179, with tabs .35

World Refugee Year, July 1, 1959-June 30, 1960.

Sand Lily — A76

Design: 32a, Evening primrose.

1960, Apr. 27 Litho. *Perf. 14*

180 A76 12a multicolored	.20	.20
181 A76 32a brn, yel & grn	.20	.20
#180-181, with tabs	.55	

Memorial Day; proclamation of State of Israel, 12th anniv. See #204-206, 238-240.

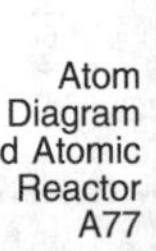

Atom Diagram and Atomic Reactor A77

1960, July 6 Wmk. 302 *Perf. 14*

182 A77 50a blue, red & blk	.20	.20
With tab	.60	

Installation of Israel's first atomic reactor.

Theodor Herzl and Rhine at Basel — A78

King Saul — A79

1960, Aug. 31 Litho. *Perf. 14*

183 A78 25a gray brown	.20	.20
With tab	.40	

1960, Aug. 31 Wmk. 302

Designs: 25a, King David. 40a, King Solomon.

Kings in Multicolor

184 A79 7a emerald	.20	.20

Unwmk.

185 A79 25a brown	.20	.20
186 A79 40a blue	.25	.20
Nos. 185-186 (2)	.45	.40
With tabs	1.25	

Jewish New Year, 5721. See Nos. 208-210.

Jewish Postal Courier, Prague, 18th Century A80

Perf. 13x14

1960, Oct. 9 Photo. Unwmk.

187 A80 25a olive blk, *gray*	.25	.20
With tab	2.50	
a. Souvenir sheet	11.00	6.00

TAVIV Natl. Stamp Exhib., Tel Aviv, Oct. 9-19.

No. 187a sold only at Exhibition for 50a.

Henrietta Szold and Hadassah Medical Center A81

1960, Dec. 14 *Perf. 13x14*

188 A81 25a turq bl & vio gray	.20	.20
With tab	.30	

Birth cent. of Henrietta Szold, founder of Hadassah, American Jewish women's organization.

Shields of Jerusalem and First Zionist Congress A82

1960, Dec. 14 Unwmk. *Perf. 14*

189 A82 50a vio bl & turq blue	.20	.20
With tab	1.10	

25th Zionist Congress, Jerusalem, 1960.

Ram — A83

Signs of Zodiac — A84

1961, Feb. 27 Photo. *Perf. 13x14*

190 A83 1a Ram	.20	.20
191 A83 2a Bull	.20	.20
192 A83 6a Twins	.20	.20
193 A83 7a Crab	.20	.20
194 A83 8a Lion	.20	.20
a. Booklet pane of 6 ('65)	.45	
195 A83 10a Virgin	.20	.20
196 A83 12a Scales	.20	.20
a. Booklet pane of 6 ('65)	.45	
197 A83 18a Scorion	.20	.20
198 A83 20a Archer	.20	.20
199 A83 25a Goat	.20	.20
200 A83 32a Water bearer	.20	.20
201 A83 50a Fishes	.20	.20

Perf. 14

Litho.

202 A84 £1 dk bl, gold & lt bl	.25	.20
Nos. 190-202 (13)	2.65	2.60
With tabs	5.25	

Booklet pane sheets (Nos. 194a, 196a) of 36 (9x4) contain 6 panes of 6, with gutters dividing the sheet in four sections. Each sheet yields 4 tete beche pairs and 4 tete beche gutter pairs, or strips. See Nos. 215-217.

Vertical strips of 6 of the 1a, 10a and No. 216 (5a) are from larger sheets from which coils were produced. Regular sheets of 50 are arranged 10x5.

Javelin Thrower and "7" — A85

1961, Apr. 18 Litho. *Perf. 14*

203 A85 25a multicolored	.20	.20
With tab	.45	

7th Intl. Congress of the Hapoel Sports Org., Ramat Gan, May 1961.

Flower Type of 1960

7a, Myrtle. 12a, Sea onion. 32a, Oleander.

1961, Apr. 18 Unwmk.

Flowers in Natural Colors

204 A76 7a green	.20	.20
205 A76 12a rose carmine	.20	.20
206 A76 32a brt greenish bl	.20	.20
Nos. 204-206 (3)	.60	.60
With tabs	1.00	

Memorial Day; proclamation of State of Israel, 13th anniv.

Scaffold Around "10" and Sapling — A86

1961, June 14 Photo. *Perf. 14*

207 A86 50a Prussian blue	.20	.20
With tab	.55	

Israel bond issue 10th anniv.

Type of 1960

Designs: 7a, Samson. 25a, Judas Maccabaeus. 40a, Bar Cocheba.

1961, Aug. 21 Litho. *Perf. 14*

Multicolored Designs

208 A79 7a red orange	.20	.20
209 A79 25a gray	.20	.20
210 A79 40a lilac	.20	.20
Nos. 208-210 (3)	.60	.60
With tabs	1.25	

Jewish New Year, 5722.

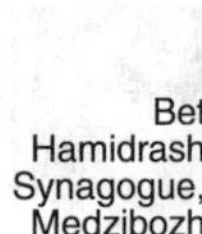

Bet Hamidrash Synagogue, Medzibozh A87

1961, Aug. 21 Photo. *Perf. 13x14*

211 A87 25a dk brn & yel	.20	.20
With tab	.40	

Bicentenary of death of Rabbi Israel Baal-Shem-Tov, founder of Hasidism.

Pine Cone A88

Design: 30a, Symbolic trees.

1961, Dec. 26 Unwmk. *Perf. 13x14*

212 A88 25a green, yel & blk	.20	.20
213 A88 30a org, green & ind	.20	.20
#212-213, with tabs	2.00	

Achievements of afforestation program.

Cello, Harp, French Horn and Kettle Drum — A89

1961, Dec. 26 Litho. *Perf. 14*

214 A89 50a multicolored	.25	.25
With tab	2.00	

Israel Philharmonic Orchestra, 25th anniv.

Zodiac Type of 1961 Surcharged with New Value

1962, Mar. 18 Photo. *Perf. 13x14*

215 A83 3a on 1a lt lilac	.20	.20
a. Without overprint	80.00	
216 A83 5a on 7a gray	.20	.20
217 A83 30a on 32a emerald	.20	.20
a. Without overprint	32.50	
#215-217, with tabs	.25	

See note after No. 202.

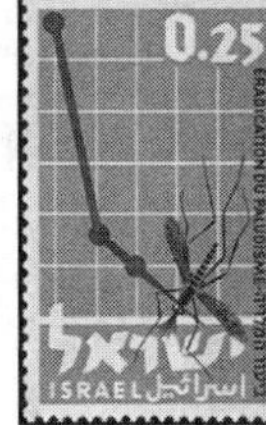

Anopheles Maculipennis and Chart Showing Decline of Malaria in Israel — A90

View of Rosh Pinna — A91

1962, Apr. 30 *Perf. 14x13*

218 A90 25a ocher, red & blk	.20	.20
With tab	.50	

WHO drive to eradicate malaria.

1962, Apr. 30 Unwmk.

219 A91 20a yel, green & brn	.20	.20
With tab	.50	

Rosh Pinna agricultural settlement, 80th anniv.

Flame ("Hear, O Israel . . .") A92

Yellow Star of David and Six Candles A93

1962, Apr. 30 Photo.

220 A92 12a black, org & red	.20	.20

Perf. 14

221 A93 55a multicolored	.20	.20
#220-221, with tabs	1.40	

Heroes and Martyrs Day, in memory of the 6,000,000 Jewish victims of Nazi persecution.

Vautour Fighter-Bomber — A94

Design: 30a, Fighter-Bombers in formation.

1962, Apr. 30 *Perf. 13x14*

222 A94 12a blue	.20	.20
223 A94 30a olive green	.20	.20
#222-223, with tabs	1.75	

Memorial Day; proclamation of the state of Israel, 14th anniv.

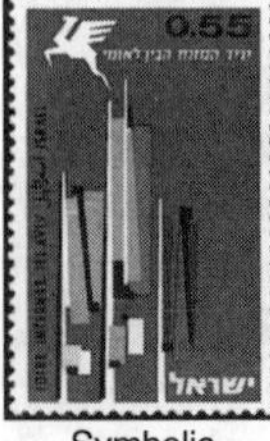

Symbolic Flags — A95

Wolf and Lamb, Isaiah 11:6 — A96

1962, June 5 *Perf. 14*

224 A95 55a multicolored	.20	.20
With tab	1.00	

Near East Intl. Fair, Tel Aviv, June 5-July 5.

1962, Sept. 5

Designs: 28a, Leopard and kid, Isaiah 11:6. 43a, Child and asp, Isaiah 11:8.

225 A96 8a buff, red & black .20 .20
226 A96 28a buff, lilac & black .20 .20
227 A96 43a buff, org & black .20 .20
Nos. 225-227 (3) .60 .60
With tabs 3.00

Jewish New Year, 5723.

Boeing 707 — A97

1962, Nov. 7 ***Perf. 13x14***
228 A97 55a bl, dk bl & rose lil .30 .20
With tab 1.10
a. Souvenir sheet 1.90 1.25

El Al Airlines; El Al Philatelic Exhibition, Tel Aviv, Nov. 7-14. Issued in sheets of 15.

No. 228a contains one stamp in greenish blue, dark blue & rose lilac with greenish blue color continuing into margin design (No. 228 has white perforations). Sold for £1 for one day at philatelic counters in Jerusalem, Haifa and Tel Aviv and for one week at the El Al Exhibition.

Cogwheel Symbols of UJA Activities A98

1962, Dec. 26 Unwmk. ***Perf. 13x14***
229 A98 20a org red, sil & bl .20 .20
With tab .50

25th anniv. of the United Jewish Appeal (United States) and its support of immigration, settlement, agriculture and care of the aged and sick.

Janusz Korczak A99

1962, Dec. 26 **Photo.**
230 A99 30a olive grn & blk .20 .20
With tab .45

Dr. Janusz Korczak (Henryk Goldszmit, 1879-1942), physician, teacher and writer, killed in Treblinka concentration camp.

Orange butterflyfish A100

Red Sea fish: 3a, Pennant Coral Fish. 8a, Lionfish. 12a, Zebra-striped angelfish.

1962, Dec. 26 Litho. ***Perf. 14***
Fish in Natural Colors
231 A100 3a green .20 .20
232 A100 6a purple .20 .20
233 A100 8a brown .20 .20
234 A100 12a dark blue .20 .20
#231-234, with tabs .60

See Nos. 246-249.

Stockade at Dawn A101

Design: 30a, Completed stockade at night.

1963, Mar. 21 Unwmk. ***Perf. 14***
235 A101 12a yel brn, blk & yel .20 .20
236 A101 30a dp plum, blk & lt bl .20 .20
#235-236, with tabs .85

25th anniv. of the "Stockade and Tower" villages.

Hand Offering Food to Bird A102

1963, Mar. 21 Photo. ***Perf. 13x14***
237 A102 55a gray & black .25 .20
With tab .80
a. Booklet pane of 4 32.50

FAO "Freedom from Hunger" campaign.

Issued in sheets of 15 (5x3) with 5 tabs. The booklet pane sheet of 16 (4x4) is divided into 2 panes of 8 (4x2) by horizontal gutter. The 4 stamps at left in each pane are inverted in relation to the 4 at right, making 4 horizontal tete beche pairs down the center of the sheet.

Flower Type of 1960

8a, White lily. 30a, Hollyhock. 37a, Tulips.

1963, Apr. 25 Litho. ***Perf. 14***
Flowers in Natural Colors
238 A76 8a slate .20 .20
239 A76 30a yellow green .20 .20
240 A76 37a sepia .20 .20
Nos. 238-240 (3) .60 .60
With tabs 2.75

Memorial Day; proclamation of the State of Israel, 15th anniv.

Typesetter, 19th Century — A103

1963, June 19 Photo. ***Perf. 14x13***
241 A103 12a tan & vio brn .50 .40
With tab 1.60
a. Sheet of 16 42.50 *65.00*

Hebrew press in Palestine, cent. The background of the sheet shows page of 1st issue of "Halbanon" newspaper, giving each stamp a different background.

"The Sun Beat upon the Head of Jonah" — A104

Hoe Clearing Thistles — A105

Designs: 30a, "There was a mighty tempest in the sea." 55a, "Jonah was in the belly of the fish." 30a, 55a horiz.

1963, Aug. 21 ***Perf. 14x13, 13x14***
242 A104 8a org, lil & blk .20 .20
243 A104 30a multicolored .20 .20
244 A104 55a multicolored .20 .20
Nos. 242-244 (3) .60 .60
With tabs 2.75

Jewish New Year, 5724.

1963, Aug. 21 ***Perf. 14***
245 A105 37a multicolored .20 .20
With tab .90

80 years of agricultural settlements in Israel; "Year of the Pioneers."

Fish Type of 1962

Red Sea Fish: 2a, Undulate triggerfish. 6a, Radiate turkeyfish. 8a, Bigeye. 12a, Imperial angelfish.

1963, Dec. 16 Litho. ***Perf. 14***
Fish in Natural Colors
246 A100 2a violet blue .20 .20
247 A100 6a green .20 .20
248 A100 8a orange .20 .20
249 A100 12a olive green .20 .20
Nos. 246-249 (4) .80 .80
With tabs .90

S.S. Shalom, Sailing Vessel and Ancient Map of Coast Line — A106

1963, Dec. 16 Photo. ***Perf. 13x14***
250 A106 £1 ultra, brt grn & lil .85 .45
With tab 8.00

Maiden voyage of S.S. Shalom.

"Old Age and Survivors Insurance" A107

Pres. Izhak Ben-Zvi (1884-1963) A108

Designs (Insurance): 25a, Maternity. 37a, Large family. 50a, Workers' compensation.

1964, Feb. 24 Litho. ***Perf. 14***
251 A107 12a multicolored .20 .20
252 A107 25a multicolored .20 .20
253 A107 37a multicolored .20 .20
254 A107 50a multicolored .30 .30
Nos. 251-254 (4) .90 .90
With tabs 7.75

Natl. Insurance Institute 10th anniv.

1964, Apr. 13 Photo. ***Perf. 14x13***
255 A108 12a dark brown .20 .20
With tab .20

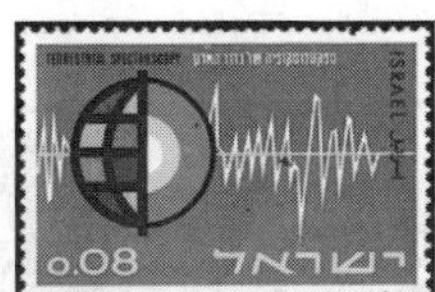

Terrestrial Spectroscopy — A109

Designs: 35a, Macromolecules of the living cell. 70a, Electronic computer.

1964, Apr. 13 ***Perf. 14***
256 A109 8a multicolored .20 .20
257 A109 35a multicolored .20 .20
258 A109 70a multicolored .20 .20
Nos. 256-258 (3) .60 .60
With tabs 3.50

Proclamation of the State of Israel, 16th anniv.; Israel's contribution to science.

Basketball Players A110

Serpent of Aesculapius and Menorah A111

8a, Runner. 12a, Discus thrower. 50a, Soccer.

1964, June 24 ***Perf. 14x13***
259 A110 8a brt brick red & dk brown .20 .20
260 A110 12a rose lil & dk brn .20 .20
261 A110 30a bl, car & dk brn .20 .20
262 A110 50a yel grn, org red & dk brown .20 .20
Nos. 259-262 (4) .80 .80
With tabs .90

Israel's participation in the 18th Olympic Games, Tokyo, Oct. 10-25.

1964, Aug. 5 **Unwmk.**
263 A111 £1 ol bis & slate grn .40 .30
With tab .75

6th World Congress of the Israel Medical Association, Haifa, Aug. 3-13.

Ancient Glass Vase — A112

Different glass vessels, 1st-3rd centuries.

1964, Aug. 5 **Litho.**
264 A112 8a vio, brn & org .20 .20
265 A112 35a ol, grn & bl grn .20 .20
266 A112 70a brt car rose, blue & violet blue .20 .20
Nos. 264-266 (3) .60 .60
With tabs .85

Jewish New Year, 5725.

Steamer Bringing Immigrants A113

Eleanor Roosevelt (1884-1962) A114

1964, Nov. 2 Litho. ***Perf. 14***
267 A113 25a slate bl, bl grn & blk .20 .20
With tab .35

30th anniv. of the blockade runners bringing immigrants to Israel.

1964, Nov. 2 Photo. ***Perf. 14x13***
268 A114 70a dull purple .20 .20
With tab .45

Chess Board, Knight and Emblem of Chess Olympics — A115

1964, Nov. 2 ***Perf. 13x14***
269 A115 12a shown .20 .20
270 A115 70a Rook .35 .30
With tabs 1.90

16th Chess Olympics, Tel Aviv, Nov. 1964.

"Africa-Israel Friendship" — A116

1964, Nov. 30 Photo. *Perf. 14x13*

271 A116 57a ol, blk, gold & red brown .35 .20
With tab 2.00
a. Souvenir sheet 1.40 1.40

TABAI, Natl. Stamp Exhibition, dedicated to African-Israel friendship, Haifa, Nov. 30-Dec. 6. No. 271a contains one imperf. stamp. Sold for £1.

View of Masada from West A117

Designs: 36a, Northern Palace, lower terrace. £1, View of Northern Palace, vert.

1965, Feb. 3 Photo. *Perf. 13x14*

272 A117 25a dull green .20 .20
273 A117 36a bright blue .20 .20
274 A117 £1 dark red brn .20 .20
Nos. 272-274 (3) .60 .60
With tabs 1.75

Ruins of Masada, the last stronghold in the war against the Romans, 66-73 A.D.

Book Fair Emblem A118

1965, Mar. 24 Photo. *Perf. 13x14*

275 A118 70a gray ol, brt bl & blk .20 .20
With tab .30

2nd Intl. Book Fair, Jerusalem, April.

Arms of Ashdod — A119

1965-66 *Perf. 13x14*

Town Emblems: 1a, Lydda (Lod). 2a, Qiryat Shemona. 5a, Petah Tikva. 6a, Nazareth. 8a, Beersheba. 10a Bet Shean. 12a, Tiberias. 20a, Elat. 25a, Acre (Akko). 35a, Dimona. 37a, Zefat. 50a, Rishon Leziyyon. 70a, Jerusalem. £1, Tel Aviv-Jaffa. £3, Haifa.

Size: 17x22½mm

276 A119 1a brown .20 .20
277 A119 2a lilac rose .20 .20
278 A119 5a gray .20 .20
279 A119 6a violet .20 .20
280 A119 8a orange .20 .20
a. Booklet pane of 6 .45
281 A119 10a emerald .20 .20
282 A119 12a dark purple .20 .20
a. Booklet pane of 6 .50
283 A119 15a green .20 .20
284 A119 20a rose red .20 .20
285 A119 25a ultramarine .20 .20
286 A119 35a magenta .20 .20
287 A119 37a olive .20 .20
288 A119 50a greenish bl .20 .20

Perf. 14x13

Size: 22x27mm

289 A119 70a dark brown .20 .20
290 A119 £1 dark green .25 .20
291 A119 £3 dk carmine rose .55 .20
Nos. 276-291 (16) 3.60 3.20
With tabs 9.25

Issued: #283-286, 3/24/65; #290, 11/24/65; #291, 3/14/66; others, 2/2/66.
The uncut booklet pane sheets of 36 are divided into 4 panes (2 of 6 stamps, 2 of 12) by horizontal and vertical gutters. alf of the stamps in the 2 panes of 12 are inverted, causing 4 horizontal tête bêche pairs and 4 horizontal tête bêche gutter pairs.
Vertical strips of 6 of the 1a, 5a and 10a are from larger sheets, released Jan. 10, 1967, from which coils were produced. Regular sheets of 50 are arranged 10x5.
No. 290 also comes tagged (1975).
See Nos. 334-336, 386-393.

Hands Reaching for Hope, and Star of David — A120

"Irrigation of the Desert" — A121

1965, Apr. 27 Unwmk. *Perf. 14x13*

292 A120 25a gray, black & yel .20 .20
With tab .40

Liberation of Nazi concentration camps, 20th anniv.

1965, Apr. 27 Photo.

293 A121 37a olive bister & blue .20 .20
With tab .20

Memorial Day; proclamation of the state of Israel, 17th anniv.

Telegraph Pole and Syncom Satellite A122

1965, July 21 Unwmk. *Perf. 13x14*

294 A122 70a vio, blk & grnsh bl .20 .20
With tab .45

ITU, centenary.

Symbol of Cooperation and UN Emblem A123

1965, July 21 Litho. *Perf. 14*

295 A123 36a gray, dp claret, bl, red & bis .20 .20
With tab .30

International Cooperation Year.

Dead Sea Extraction Plant A124

"Let There be Light . . ." A125

1965, July 21

296 A124 12a Crane .20 .20
297 A124 50a shown .20 .20
#296-297, with tabs .70

Dead Sea chemical industry.

1965, Sept. 7 Photo. *Perf. 13x14*

Genesis 1, The Creation: 8a, Firmament and Waters. 12a, Dry land and vegetation. 25a, Heavenly lights. 35a, Fish and fowl. 70a, Man.

298 A125 6a dk pur, lil & gold .20 .20
299 A125 8a brt grn, dk bl & gold .20 .20
300 A125 12a red brn, blk & gold .20 .20
301 A125 25a dk pur, pink & gold .20 .20
302 A125 35a lt & dk bl & gold .20 .20
303 A125 70a dp cl, car & gold .35 .25
Nos. 298-303 (6) 1.35 1.25
With tabs 1.50

Jewish New Year, 5726. Sheets of 20 (10x2).

Charaxes Jasius A126

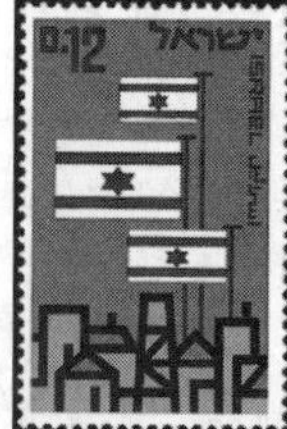

Flags over Rooftops A127

Butterflies & Moths: 6a, Papilio alexanor maccabaeus. 8a, Daphnis nerii. 12a, Zegris eupheme uarda.

1965, Dec. 15 Litho. *Perf. 14*

Butterflies in Natural Colors

304 A126 2a lt olive green .20 .20
305 A126 6a lilac .20 .20
306 A126 8a ocher .20 .20
307 A126 12a blue .20 .20
#304-307, with tabs .60

1966, Apr. 20 Litho. *Perf. 14*

Designs: 30a, Fireworks over Tel Aviv. 80a, Warships and Super Mirage jets, Haifa.

308 A127 12a multi .20 .20
309 A127 30a multi .20 .20
310 A127 80a multi .20 .20
#308-310, with tabs .45

Proclamation of state of Israel, 18th anniv.

Memorial, Upper Galilee — A128

1966, Apr. 20 Photo. *Perf. 14x13*

311 A128 40a olive gray .20 .20
With tab .20

Issued for Memorial Day.

Knesset Building, Jerusalem — A129

1966, June 22 Photo. *Perf. 13x14*

312 A129 £1 deep blue .25 .20
With tab .50

Inauguration of the Knesset Building (Parliament). Sheets of 12.

Road Sign and Motorcyclist A130

Spice Box A131

Road Signs and: 5a, Bicyclist. 10a, Pedestrian. 12a, Child playing ball. 15a, Automobile.

1966, June 22 *Perf. 14*

313 A130 2a sl, red brn & lil rose .20 .20
314 A130 5a ol bis, sl & lil rose .20 .20
315 A130 10a vio, lt bl & lil rose .20 .20
316 A130 12a bl, grn & lil rose .20 .20
317 A130 15a grn, red & lil rose .20 .20
#313-317, with tabs .25

Issued to publicize traffic safety.

1966, Aug. 24 Photo. *Perf. 13x14*

Ritual Art Objects: 15a, Candlesticks. 35a, Kiddush cup. 40a, Torah pointer. 80a, Hanging lamp.

318 A131 12a sil, gold, blk & bl .20 .20
319 A131 15a sil, gold, blk & lil .20 .20
320 A131 35a sil, gold, blk & emer .20 .20
321 A131 40a sil, gold, blk & vio bl .20 .20
322 A131 80a sil, gold, blk & red .20 .20
#318-322, with tabs .75

Jewish New Year, 5727.

Bronze Panther, Avdat, 1st Century, B.C. — A132

30a, Stone menorah, Tiberias, 2nd Cent. 40a, Phoenician ivory sphinx, 9th cent., B.C. 55a, Gold earring (calf's head), Ashdod, 6th-4th cents. B.C. 80a, Miniature gold capital, Persia, 5th cent., B.C. £1.15, Gold drinking horn (ram's head), Persia, 5th cent., B.C., vert.

1966, Oct. 26 Litho. *Perf. 14*

323 A132 15a dp bl & yel brn .20 .20
324 A132 30a vio brn & bister .20 .20
325 A132 40a sepia & yel bis .20 .20
326 A132 55a Prus grn, dp yel & brown .25 .20
327 A132 80a lake, dp yel & brown .40 .25

Perf. 13x14

328 A132 £1.15 vio, gold & brn .75 .50
Nos. 323-328 (6) 2.00 1.55
With tabs 5.00

Israel Museum, Jerusalem. Sheets of 12.

Coach and Mailman of Austrian Levant — A133

Microscope and Cells — A134

Designs: 15a, Turkish mailman and caravan. 40a, Palestinian mailman and locomotive. £1, Israeli mailman and jet liner.

1966, Dec. 14 Photo. *Perf. 14*

329 A133 12a ocher & green .20 .20
330 A133 15a lt grn, brn & dp car .20 .20
331 A133 40a brt rose & dk blue .20 .20
332 A133 £1 grnsh bl & brown .20 .20
Nos. 329-332 (4) .80 .80
With tabs .80

Issued for Stamp Day.

1966, Dec. 14 *Perf. 14x13*

333 A134 15a red & dark slate grn .20 .20
With tab .20

Campaign against cancer.

Arms Type of 1965-66

Town Emblems: 40a, Mizpe Ramon. 55a, Ashkelon. 80a, Rosh Pinna.

1967, Feb. 8 Unwmk. *Perf. 13x14*

334 A119 40a dark olive .20 .20
335 A119 55a dk carmine rose .20 .20
336 A119 80a red brown .20 .20
Nos. 334-336 (3) .60 .60
With tabs 1.75

Port of Acre A135

Ancient Ports: 40a, Caesarea. 80a, Jaffa.

1967, Mar. 22 Photo. *Perf. 13x14*

337 A135 15a dark brown .20 .20
338 A135 40a dark blue grn .20 .20
339 A135 80a deep blue .20 .20
Nos. 337-339 (3) .60 .60
With tabs 1.00

Page of Shulhan Aruk and Crowns — A136

1967, Mar. 22 *Perf. 13½x13*

340 A136 40a dk & lt bl, gray & gold .20 .20
With tab .25

400th anniv. of the publication (in 1565) of the Shulhan Aruk, a compendium of Jewish religious and civil law, by Joseph Karo (1488-1575).

War of Independence Memorial — A137

1967, May 10 Unwmk. *Perf. 13x14*

341 A137 55a lt bl, indigo & sil .20 .20
With tab .40

Issued for Memorial Day, 1967.

Auster Plane over Convoy on Jerusalem Road A138

Military Aircraft: 30a, Mystère IV jet fighter over Dead Sea area. 80a, Mirage jet fighters over Masada.

1967, May 10 Photo.

342 A138 15a lt ol grn & dk bl grn .20 .20
343 A138 30a ocher & dark brn .20 .20
344 A138 80a grnsh bl & vio bl .20 .20
Nos. 342-344 (3) .60 .60
With tabs .80

Issued for Independence Day, 1967.

Israeli Ships in Straits of Tiran A139

15a, Star of David, sword & olive branch, vert. 80a, Wailing (Western) Wall, Jerusalem.

1967, Aug. 16 *Perf. 14x13, 13x14*

345 A139 15a dk red, blk & yel .20 .20
346 A139 40a Prussian green .20 .20
347 A139 80a deep violet .20 .20
#345-347, with tabs .25

Victory of the Israeli forces, June, 1967.

Torah, Scroll of the Law — A140

Various ancient, decorated Scrolls of the Law.

1967, Sept. 13 *Perf. 13x14*

348 A140 12a gold & multi .20 .20
349 A140 15a silver & multi .20 .20
350 A140 35a gold & multi .20 .20
351 A140 40a silver & multi .20 .20
352 A140 80a gold & multi .20 .20
#348-352, with tabs .70

Jewish New Year, 5728. Sheets of 20 (10x2).

Chaim Weizmann A141

Design: 40a, Lord Balfour.

1967, Nov. 2 Photo. *Perf. 13x14*

353 A141 15a dark green .20 .20
354 A141 40a brown .20 .20
#353-354, with tabs .25

50th anniv. of the Balfour Declaration, which established the right to a Jewish natl. home in Palestine. Issued in sheets of 15.

Emblem and Doll — A142

Nubian Ibex — A143

Inscriptions: 30a, Hebrew. 40a, French.

1967, Nov. 2 Litho. *Perf. 14*

355 A142 30a yellow & multi .20 .20
356 A142 40a brt bl & multi .20 .20
357 A142 80a brt grn & multi .20 .20
#355-357, with tabs .45

Intl. Tourist Year. Issued in sheets of 15.

1967, Dec. 27 Litho. *Perf. 13*

18a, Caracal lynx. 60a, Dorcas gazelles.

Animal in Ocher & Brown

358 A143 12a dull purple .20 .20
359 A143 18a bright green .20 .20
360 A143 60a bright blue .20 .20
#358-360, with tabs .40

Flags Forming Soccer Ball — A144

1968, Mar. 11 Photo. *Perf. 13*

361 A144 80a ocher & multi .20 .20
With tab .25

Pre-Olympic soccer tournament.

Welcoming Immigrants A145

Resistance Fighter A146

Design: 80a, Happy farm family.

1968, Apr. 24 Litho. *Perf. 14*

362 A145 15a lt green & multi .20 .20
363 A145 80a cream & multi .20 .20
#362-363, with tabs .25

Issued for Independence Day, 1968.

1968, Apr. 24 Photo. *Perf. 14x13*

364 A146 60a brown olive .20 .20
With tab .20

Warsaw Ghetto Uprising, 25th anniv. Design from Warsaw Ghetto Memorial.

Sword and Laurel A147

Rifles and Helmet A148

1968, Apr. 24 Litho. *Perf. 14*

365 A147 40a gold & multi .20 .20
366 A148 55a black & multi .20 .20
#365-366, with tabs .30

Zahal defense army, Independence Day (No. 365); Memorial Day (No. 366).

Candle and Prison Window A149

Prime Minister Moshe Sharett (1894-1965) A150

1968, June 5 Photo. *Perf. 14x13*

367 A149 80a blk, gray & sepia .20 .20
With tab .20

Issued to honor those who died for freedom.

1968, June 5 Unwmk.

368 A150 £1 deep brown .20 .20
With tab .20

27th Zionist Congress.

Knot Forming Star of David — A151

Dome of the Rock and Absalom's Tomb — A152

1968, Aug. 21 Litho. *Perf. 13*

369 A151 30a multi .20 .20
With tab .20

50 years of Jewish Scouting. Sheets of 15.

1968, Aug. 21 Photo. *Perf. 14x13*

Views of Jerusalem: 15a, Church of the Resurrection. 35a, Tower of David and City Wall. 40a, Yemin Moshe District and Mount of Olives. 60a, Israel Museum and "Shrine of the Book."

370 A152 12a gold & multi .20 .20
371 A152 15a gold & multi .20 .20
372 A152 35a gold & multi .20 .20
373 A152 40a gold & multi .20 .20
374 A152 60a gold & multi .20 .20
#370-374, with tabs .50

Jewish New Year, 5729. Sheets of 15.

Detail from Lions' Gate, Jerusalem (St. Stephen's Gate) A153

1968, Oct. 8 Unwmk. *Perf. 13x14*

375 A153 £1 brown org .20 .20
With tab .20
a. Souvenir sheet .35 .30

TABIRA Natl. Philatelic Exhibition. No. 375a contains one imperf. stamp. Sold only at exhibition for £1.50. No. 375 Issued in sheets of 15.

Abraham Mapu A154

Wheelchair Basketball A155

1968, Oct. 8 Photo. *Perf. 14x13*

376 A154 30a dark olive grn .20 .20
With tab .20

Mapu (1808-1867), novelist and historian.

1968, Nov. 6 Photo. *Perf. 14x13*

377 A155 40a green & yel grn .20 .20
With tab .20

17th Stoke-Mandeville Games for the Paralyzed, Nov. 4-13. Sheets of 15.

Port of Elat — A156

Ports of Israel: 60a, Ashdod. £1, Haifa.

1969, Feb. 19 Unwmk. *Perf. 13x14*

378 A156 30a deep magenta .20 .20
379 A156 60a brown .20 .20
380 A156 £1 dull green .20 .20
Nos. 378-380 (3) .60 .60
With tabs 2.00

Tank A157

1969, Apr. 16 Photo. *Perf. 13x14*

381 A157 15a shown .20 .20
382 A157 80a Destroyer .20 .20
#381-382, with tabs .40

Issued for Independence Day 1969.

Israel's Flag at Half-mast — A158

1969, Apr. 16

383 A158 55a vio, gold & bl .20 .20
With tab .25

Issued for Memorial Day.

Worker and ILO Emblem A159

1969, Apr. 16

384 A159 80a dark blue grn .20 .20
With tab .25

ILO, 50th anniversary.

Hand Holding Torch A160

Arms of Hadera A161

1969, July 9 Photo. *Perf. 14x13*

385 A160 60a gold & multi .20 .20
With tab .60

Issued to publicize the 8th Maccabiah.

1969-73 *Perf. 13x14*

Town Emblems: 3a, Hertseliya. 5a, Holon. 15a, Bat Yam. 18a, Ramla. 20a, Kefar Sava. 25a, Giv'atayim. 30a, Rehovot. 40a, Netanya. 50a, Bene Beraq. 60a, Nahariyya. 80a, Ramat Gan.

386 A161 2a green .20 .20
387 A161 3a deep magenta .20 .20
388 A161 5a orange .20 .20
389 A161 15a bright rose .20 .20
c. Bklt. pane of 6 (2 #389 + 4 #389A) ('71) .65
389A A161 18a ultra ('70) .20 .20
d. Bklt. pane of 6 ('71) .70
e. Bklt. pane of 6 (1 #281 + 5 #389A) ('73) .65
389B A161 20a brown ('70) .20 .20
f. Bklt. pane of 5 + label ('73) .90
390 A161 25a dark blue .20 .20
390A A161 30a brt pink ('70) .20 .20
391 A161 40a purple .20 .20
392 A161 50a greenish bl .20 .20
392A A161 60a olive ('70) .20 .20
393 A161 80a dark green .20 .20
Nos. 386-393 (12) 2.40 2.40
With tabs 3.75

Nos. 389c and 389d were also sold in uncut sheets of 36, No. 389e in uncut sheet of 18. See note after No. 291 about similar sheets.

Noah Building the Ark — A162

The Story of the Flood: 15a, Animals boarding the Ark. 35a, The Ark during the flood. 40a, Noah sending out the dove. 60a, Noah and the rainbow.

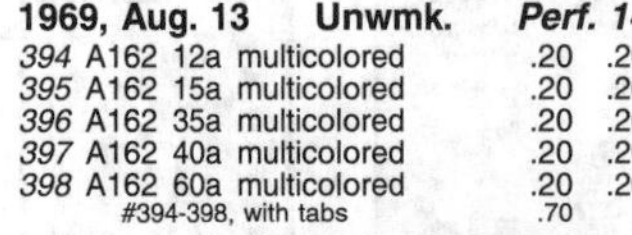

1969, Aug. 13 Unwmk. *Perf. 14*

394 A162 12a multicolored .20 .20
395 A162 15a multicolored .20 .20
396 A162 35a multicolored .20 .20
397 A162 40a multicolored .20 .20
398 A162 60a multicolored .20 .20
#394-398, with tabs .70

Jewish New Year, 5730. Sheets of 15.

King David by Marc Chagall A163

1969, Sept. 24 Photo. *Perf. 14*

399 A163 £3 multicolored .65 .55
With tab 1.25

Atom Diagram and Test Tube — A164

1969, Nov. 3 *Perf. 14x13*

400 A164 £1.15 vio bl & multi .70 .45
With tab 2.25

Weizmann Institute of Science, 25th anniv.

Joseph Trumpeldor A165

Dum Palms, Emeq Ha-Arava A166

1970, Jan. 21 Photo. *Perf. 14x13*

401 A165 £1 dark purple .25 .20
With tab .60

50th anniv. of the defense of Tel Hay under the leadership of Joseph Trumpeldor.

1970, Jan. 21

Views: 3a, Tahana Waterfall. 5a, Nahal Baraq Canyon, Negev. 6a, Cedars in Judean Hills. 30a, Soreq Cave, Judean Hills.

402 A166 2a olive .20 .20
403 A166 3a deep blue .20 .20
404 A166 5a orange red .20 .20
405 A166 6a slate green .20 .20
406 A166 30a brt purple .20 .20
#402-406, with tabs .35

Issued to publicize nature reserves.

Magic Carpet Shaped as Airplane A167

Prime Minister Levi Eshkol (1895-1969) A168

1970, Jan. 21 Litho. *Perf. 13*

407 A167 30a multicolored .20 .20
With tab .20

20th anniv. of "Operation Magic Carpet" which airlifted the Yemeni Jews to Israel.

1970, Mar. 11 Litho. *Perf. 14*

408 A168 15a bl & multi .20 .20
With tab .20

Mania Shochat — A169

Camel and Train — A170

Portrait: 80a, Ze'ev Jabotinsky (1880-1940), writer and Zionist leader.

1970, Mar. 11 Photo. *Perf. 14x13*

409 A169 40a dp plum & buff .20 .20
410 A169 80a green & cream .20 .20
#409-410, with tabs 1.10

Ha-Shomer (Watchmen defense organization), 60th anniv. (No. 409); defense of Jerusalem, 50th anniv. (No. 410)

1970, Mar. 11 Litho. *Perf. 13*

411 A170 80a orange & multi .40 .25
With tab .75

Opening of Dimona-Oron Railroad.

Scene from "The Dibbuk" — A171

1970, Mar. 11 Photo. *Perf. 14x13*

412 A171 £1 multicolored .20 .20
With tab .60

Habimah Natl. Theater, 50th anniv.

Memorial Flame A172

Orchis Laxiflorus A173

1970, May 6 Photo. *Perf. 13x14*

413 A172 55a vio, pink & blk .20 .20
With tab .25

Issued for Memorial Day, 1970.

1970, May 6 Litho. *Perf. 14*

Flowers: 15a, Iris mariae. 80a, Lupinus pilosus.

414 A173 12a pale gray, plum & grn .20 .20
415 A173 15a multicolored .20 .20
416 A173 80a pale bl & multi .30 .30
Nos. 414-416 (3) .70 .70
With tabs .95

Issued for Independence Day, 1970.

Charles Netter — A174

420 Class Yachts — A175

80a, Agricultural College (Mikwe Israel) & garden.

1970, May 6 Photo. *Perf. 14x13*

417 A174 40a lt grn, dk brn & gold .20 .20
418 A174 80a gold & multi .20 .20
With tabs 1.25

Centenary of first agricultural college in Israel; its founder, Charles Netter.

1970, July 8 Photo. *Perf. 14x13*

Designs: Various 420 Class yachts.

419 A175 15a grnsh bl, blk & sil .20 .20
420 A175 30a ol, red, blk & sil .20 .20
421 A175 80a ultra, blk & silver .25 .20
Nos. 419-421 (3) .65 .60
With tabs 1.10

World "420" Class Sailing Championships.

Hebrew Letters Shaped Like Ship and Buildings A176

1970, July 8 *Perf. 13x14*

422 A176 40a gold & multi .20 .20
With tab .20

Keren Hayesod, a Zionist Fund to maintain schools and hospitals in Palestine, 50th anniv.

Arava Plane A177

1970, July 8

423 A177 £1 brt blue, blk & sil .20 .20
With tab .35

First Israeli designed and built aircraft.

Bird (Exiles) and Sun (Israel) A178

1970, Sept. 7 Litho. *Perf. 14*

424 A178 80a yel & multi .20 .20
With tab .25

"Operation Ezra and Nehemiah," the exodus of Iraqi Jews.

Old Synagogue, Cracow — A179

Historic Synagogues: 15a, Great Synagogue, Tunis. 35a, Portuguese Synagogue, Amsterdam. 40a, Great Synagogue, Moscow. 60a, Shearith Israel Synagogue, New York.

Perf. 14, 13 (15a)

1970, Sept. 7 Photo.

425 A179 12a gold & multi .20 .20
426 A179 15a gold & multi .20 .20
427 A179 35a gold & multi .20 .20

No.	Description	Unused	Used
428	A179 40a gold & multi	.20	.20
429	A179 60a gold & multi	.20	.20
	#425-429, with tabs	.40	

Jewish New Year, 5731.

Tel Aviv Post Office, 1920 — A180

1970, Oct. 18 Photo. *Perf. 14*

No.	Description	Unused	Used
430	A180 £1 multicolored	.20	.20
	With tab	.25	
a.	Souvenir sheet	1.25	1.50

TABIT Natl. Stamp Exhibition, Tel Aviv, Oct. 18-29. No. 430a contains an imperf. stamp similar to No. 430. Sold for £1.50.

Mother and Child A181

1970, Oct. 18 *Perf. 13x14*

No.	Description	Unused	Used
431	A181 80a dp grn, yel & gray	.20	.20
	With tab	.45	

WIZO, Women's Intl. Zionist Org., 50th anniv.

Paris Quai, by Camille Pissarro — A182

Paintings from Tel Aviv Museum: 85a, The Jewish Wedding, by Josef Israels. £2, Flowers in a Vase, by Fernand Leger.

1970, Dec. 22 Litho. *Perf. 14*

No.	Description	Unused	Used
432	A182 85a black & multi	.20	.20
433	A182 £1 black & multi	.20	.20
434	A182 £2 black & multi	.50	.30
	Nos. 432-434 (3)	.90	.70
	With tabs	1.75	

Hammer and Menorah Emblem — A183

Persian Fallow Deer — A184

1970, Dec. 22

No.	Description	Unused	Used
435	A183 35a gold & multi	.20	.20
	With tab	.20	

General Federation of Labor in Israel (Histadrut), 50th anniversary.

1971, Feb. 16 Litho. *Perf. 13*

Animals of the Bible: 3a, Asiatic wild ass. 5a, White oryx. 78a, Cheetah.

No.	Description	Unused	Used
436	A184 2a multicolored	.20	.20
437	A184 3a multicolored	.20	.20
438	A184 5a multicolored	.20	.20
439	A184 78a multicolored	.20	.20
	#436-439, with tabs	.45	

"Samson and Dalila," Israel National Opera — A185

Theater Art in Israel: No. 441, Inn of the Ghosts, Cameri Theater. No. 442, A Psalm of David, Inbal Dance Theater.

1971, Feb. 16 *Perf. 14x13*

No.	Description	Unused	Used
440	A185 50a bister & multi	.20	.20
441	A185 50a lt grn & multi	.20	.20
442	A185 50a blue & multi	.20	.20
	Nos. 440-442 (3)	.60	.60
	With tabs	.60	

Basketball A186

Defense Forces Emblem A187

No. 444, Runner. No. 445, Athlete on rings.

1971, Apr. 13 Litho. *Perf. 14*

No.	Description	Unused	Used
443	A186 50a green & multi	.20	.20
444	A186 50a ocher & multi	.20	.20
445	A186 50a lt vio & multi	.20	.20
	#443-445, with tabs	.50	

9th Hapoel Games.

1971, Apr. 13 Photo. *Perf. 14x13*

No.	Description	Unused	Used
446	A187 78a multicolored	.20	.20
	With tab	.25	

Memorial Day, 1971, and the war dead.

Jaffa Gate, Jerusalem — A188

Gates of Jerusalem: 18c, New Gate. 35c, Damascus Gate. 85c, Herod's Gate.

1971, Apr. 13 *Perf. 14*
Size: 41x41mm

No.	Description	Unused	Used
447	A188 15a gold & multi	.20	.20
448	A188 18a gold & multi	.20	.20
449	A188 35a gold & multi	.25	.20
450	A188 85a gold & multi	.60	.40
a.	Souvenir sheet of 4	3.50	3.50
	Nos. 447-450 (4)	1.25	1.00
	With tabs	2.00	

Independence Day, 1971. No. 450a contains 4 stamps similar to Nos. 447-450, but smaller (27x27mm). Sold at the Jerusalem Exhibition for £2.

See Nos. 488-491.

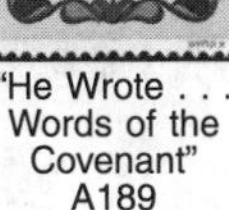

"He Wrote . . . Words of the Covenant" A189

"You shall rejoice in your feast" A190

85a, "First Fruits . . ." Exodus 23:19. £1.50, ". . . Feast of Weeks" Exodus 34:22. The quotation on 50a is from Exodus 34:28. The quotations are in English on the tabs.

1971, May 25 Photo. *Perf. 14x13*

No.	Description	Unused	Used
451	A189 50a yellow & multi	.20	.20
452	A189 85a yellow & multi	.25	.20
453	A189 £1.50 yellow & multi	.45	.30
	Nos. 451-453 (3)	.90	.70
	With tabs	1.75	

For the Feast of Weeks (Shabuoth).

1971, Aug. 24 Photo. *Perf. 14x13*

Designs: 18a, "You shall dwell in booths for seven days . . ." Leviticus 23:42. 20a, "That I made the people of Israel dwell in booths . . ." Lev. 23:43. 40a, ". . . when you have gathered in the produce of the land" Lev. 23:39. 65a, ". . . then I will give you your rains in their season" Lev. 26:4. The quotation on 15a is from Deuteronomy 16:14. The quotations are in English on tabs.

No.	Description	Unused	Used
454	A190 15a yellow & multi	.20	.20
455	A190 18a yellow & multi	.20	.20
456	A190 20a yellow & multi	.20	.20
457	A190 40a yellow & multi	.20	.20
458	A190 65a yellow & multi	.20	.20
	#454-458, with tabs	.75	

For the Feast of Tabernacles (Sukkoth).

Sun Shining on Fields A191

1971, Aug. 24 *Perf. 14*

No.	Description	Unused	Used
459	A191 40a gold & multi	.20	.20
	With tab	.20	

1st cooperative settlement in Israel, at Emeq (Valley of Israel), 50th anniv.

Retort and Grain — A192

1971, Oct. 25 Litho. *Perf. 14*

No.	Description	Unused	Used
460	A192 £1 green & multi	.20	.20
	With tab	.25	

50th anniversary of Volcani Institute of Agricultural Research.

Tagging

Starting in 1975, vertical luminescent bands were overprinted on various regular and commemorative stamps.

In the 1971-75 regular series, values issued both untagged and tagged are: 20a, 25a, 30a, 35a, 45a, 50a, 65a, £1.10, £1.30, £2 and £3. Also No. 290 was re-issued with tagging in 1975.

Regular issues from 1975 onward, including the £1.70, are tagged unless otherwise noted.

Tagged commemoratives include Nos. 562-563 and all from Nos. 567-569 onward unless otherwise noted.

Negev — A193

1971-75 Photo. *Perf. 13x14*

Landscapes: 3a, Judean desert. 5a, Gan Ha-Shelosha. 18a, Kinneret. 20a, Tel Dan. 22a, Fishermen, Yafo. 25a, Arava. 30a, En Avedat. 35a, Brekhat Ram, Golan Heights. 45a, Grazing sheep, Mt. Hermon. 50a, Rosh Pinna. 55a, Beach and park, Netanya. 65a, Plain of Zebulun. 70a, Shore, Engedi. 80a, Beach at Elat. 88a, Boats in Akko harbor. 95a, Hamifratz Hane'elam (lake). £1.10, Aqueduct near Akko. £1.30, Zefat. £1.70, Upper Nazareth. £2, Coral Island. £3, Haifa.

No.	Description	Unused	Used
461	A193 3a deep blue	.20	.20
462	A193 5a green	.20	.20
463	A193 15a deep org	.20	.20
464	A193 18a bright mag	.65	.20
464A	A193 20a dark green	.20	.20
465	A193 22a brt blue	1.00	.25
465A	A193 25a orange red	.20	.20
466	A193 30a brt rose	.20	.20
466A	A193 35a plum	.20	.20
467	A193 45a dull vio blue	.20	.20
468	A193 50a green	.20	.20
469	A193 55a olive	.20	.20
469A	A193 65a black	.20	.20
470	A193 70a deep car	.20	.20
470A	A193 80a deep ultra	.20	.20
471	A193 88a greenish blue	1.00	.20
472	A193 95a org ver	.80	.20
472A	A193 £1.10 olive	.20	.20
472B	A193 £1.30 deep blue	.20	.20
472C	A193 £1.70 dark brown	.40	.20
473	A193 £2 brown	.40	.20
474	A193 £3 deep violet	.55	.20
	Nos. 461-474 (22)	7.80	4.45
	With tabs	12.00	

Issued: 15a, 18a, 50a, 88a, 10/25; 22a, 55a, 70a, 1/4/72; 3a, 5a, 30a, £3, 11/7/72; 45a, 95a, £2, 1/16/73; 20a, 65a, 10/23/73; 35a, £1.10, 12/20/73; 25a, 80a, £1.30, 11/5/74; £1.70, 6/17/75.

See No. 592.

"Get Wisdom" Proverbs 4:7 — A194

Abstract Designs: 18a, Mathematical and scientific formula. 20a, Tools and engineering symbols. 40a, Abbreviations of various college degrees.

1972, Jan. 4 Litho. *Perf. 14*

No.	Description	Unused	Used
475	A194 15a brt grn & multi	.20	.20
476	A194 18a multicolored	.20	.20
477	A194 20a multicolored	.20	.20
478	A194 40a red, blk & gold	.20	.20
	#475-478, with tabs	.30	

The Scribe, Sculpture by Boris Schatz A195

Works by Israeli Artists: 55a, Young Girl (Sarah), by Abel Pann. 70a, Zefat (landscape), by Menahem Shemi, horiz. 85a, Old Jerusalem, by Jacob Steinhardt. £1, Resurrection (abstract), by Aharon Kahana.

Perf. 13x14 (40a, 85a), 14

1972, Mar. 7

No.	Description	Unused	Used
479	A195 40a black & tan	.20	.20
480	A195 55a red brn & multi	.20	.20
481	A195 70a lt grn & multi	.20	.20
482	A195 85a blk & yellow	.25	.20
483	A195 £1 blk & multi	.30	.25
	Nos. 479-483 (5)	1.15	1.05
	With tabs	1.40	

Exodus — A196

Passover: 45a, Baking unleavened bread. 95a, Seder.

1972, Mar. 7 Litho. *Perf. 13*

484 A196 18a buff & multi	.20	.20
485 A196 45a buff & multi	.20	.20
486 A196 95a buff & multi	.30	.20
Nos. 484-486 (3)	.70	.60
With tabs	1.25	

"Let My People Go" — A197

1972, Mar. 7 *Perf. 14*

487 A197 55a blk, bl & yel grn	.45	.30
With tab	3.00	

No. 487 inscribed in Hebrew, Arabic, Russian and English.

Gate Type of 1971

Gates of Jerusalem: 15a, Lions' Gate. 18a, Golden Gate. 45a, Dung Gate. 55a, Zion Gate.

1972, Apr. 17 Photo. *Perf. 14*
Size: 40x40mm

488 A188 15a gold & multi	.20	.20
489 A188 18a gold & multi	.20	.20
490 A188 45a gold & multi	.25	.25
491 A188 55a gold & multi	.35	.35
a. Souvenir sheet of 4	2.60	2.60
Nos. 488-491 (4)	1.00	1.00
With tabs	2.25	

Independence Day. #491a contains 4 27x27mm stamps similar to #488-491. Sold for £2.

Jethro's Tomb — A198

1972, Apr. 17 Litho. *Perf. 13*

492 A198 55a multicolored	.20	.20
With tab	.25	

Memorial Day — A199

1972, Apr. 17 *Perf. 14*

493 A199 55a Flowers	.20	.20
With tab	.25	

Hebrew Words Emerging from Opened Ghetto — A200

1972, June 6 *Perf. 13*

494 A200 70a blue & multi	.45	.35
With tab	2.00	

Rabbi Isaac ben Solomon Ashkenazi Luria ("Ari") (1534-72), Palestinian cabalist.

International Book Year — A201

1972, June 6 *Perf. 14x13*

495 A201 95a Printed page	.25	.20
With tab	.35	

Satellite Earth Station, Satellite and Rainbow — A202

1972, June 6 *Perf. 13*

496 A202 £1 tan & multi	.20	.20
With tab	.30	

Opening of satellite earth station in Israel.

17th Cent. Ark, Ancona — A203

Menorah and "25" — A204

Holy Arks from: 45a, Padua, 1729. 70a, Parma, 17th century. 95a, Reggio Emilia, 1756. Arks moved to Israel from Italian synagogues.

1972, Aug. 8 Photo. *Perf. 14x13*

497 A203 15a deep brn & yel	.20	.20
498 A203 45a dp grn, yel grn & gold	.20	.20
499 A203 70a brn red, yel & bl	.20	.20
500 A203 95a magenta & gold	.20	.20
Nos. 497-500 (4)	.80	.80
With tabs	1.50	

Jewish New Year, 5733.

1972, Aug. 8

501 A204 £1 silver, bl & mag	.20	.20
With tab	.25	

25th anniversary of the State of Israel.

Brass Menorah, Morocco, 18th-19th Century A205

Menorahs: 25a, Brass, Poland, 18th century. 70a, Silver, Germany, 17th century.

1972, Nov. 7 Litho. *Perf. 14x13*

502 A205 12a emer, blk & bl grn	.20	.20
503 A205 25a lil rose, blk & org	.20	.20
504 A205 70a blue, blk & vio	.20	.20
#502-504, with tabs	.55	

Hanukkah (Festival of Lights), 1972.

Child's Drawing — A206

Pendant — A207

Designs: Children's drawings.

1973, Jan. 16 Litho. *Perf. 14*
Sizes: 22½x37mm (2a, 55a); 17x48mm (3a)

505 A206 2a blk & multi	.20	.20
506 A206 3a multicolored	.20	.20
507 A206 55a multicolored	.20	.20
#505-507, with tabs	.30	

Youth Wing of Israel Museum, Jerusalem (2a, 3a) and Youth Workshops, Tel Aviv Museum (55a).

1973, Jan. 16 Photo. *Perf. 14x13*

508 A207 18a silver & multi	.20	.20
With tab	.20	

Immigration of North African Jews.

Levi, by Marc Chagall A208

Tribes of Israel: #510, Simeon. #511, Reuben. #512, Issachar. #513, Zebulun. #514, Judah. #515, Dan. #516, Gad. #517, Asher. #518, Naphtali. #519, Joseph. No.520, Benjamin.

1973 Litho. *Perf. 14*

509 A208 £1 multicolored	.40	.40
510 A208 £1 gray grn & multi	.40	.40
511 A208 £1 olive & multi	.40	.40
512 A208 £1 gray bl & multi	.40	.40
513 A208 £1 lemon & multi	.40	.40
514 A208 £1 gray & multi	.40	.40
515 A208 £1 bl grn & multi	.40	.40
516 A208 £1 gray & multi	.40	.40
517 A208 £1 yel grn & multi	.40	.40
518 A208 £1 sepia & multi	.40	.40
519 A208 £1 olive & multi	.40	.40
520 A208 £1 tan & multi	.40	.40
Nos. 509-520 (12)	4.80	4.80
With tabs	8.50	

Designs from stained glass windows by Marc Chagall, Hadassah-Hebrew University Medical Center Synagogue, Jerusalem.
Issued: #509-514, 3/26; #515-520, 8/21.

Israel's Declaration of Independence — A209

1973, May 3 Photo. *Perf. 14*

521 A209 £1 ocher & multi	.20	.20
With tab	.25	
a. Souvenir sheet	.65	.75

25 years of Independence. No. 521a sold for £1.50.

Star of David and Runners A210

1973, May 3 Litho.

522 A210 £1.10 multicolored	.20	.20
With tab	.25	

9th Maccabiah.

Prison-cloth Hand — A211

1973, May 3 Photo.

523 A211 55a blue black	.20	.20
With tab	.20	

Heroes and martyrs of the Holocaust, 1933-1945.

Flame A212

Prophets A213

1973, May 3 Litho.

524 A212 65a multicolored	.20	.20
With tab	.25	

Memorial Day.

1973, Aug. 21 Photo. *Perf. 13x14*

525 A213 18a Isaiah	.20	.20
526 A213 65a Jeremiah	.20	.20
527 A213 £1.10 Ezekiel	.20	.20
#525-527, with tabs	.25	

Jewish New Year, 5734.

Torch of Learning, Cogwheel — A214

1973, Oct. 23 *Perf. 14x13*

528 A214 £1.25 slate & multi	.20	.20
With tab	.25	

50th anniversary of the Technion, Israel Institute of Technology.

Rescue Boat and Danish Flag — A215

1973, Oct. 23 ***Perf. 13x14***

529 A215 £5 bister, red & blk .40 .30
With tab .50

30th anniversary of the rescue by the Danes of the Jews in Denmark.

Spectators at Stamp Show — A216

Design: £1, Spectators, different design.

1973, Dec. 20 **Litho.** ***Perf. 13***

530 A216 20a brown & multi .20 .20
531 A216 £1 brown & multi .20 .20
#530-531, with tabs .20

JERUSALEM '73 Philatelic Exhibition, Mar. 25-Apr. 2, 1974.

Souvenir Sheets

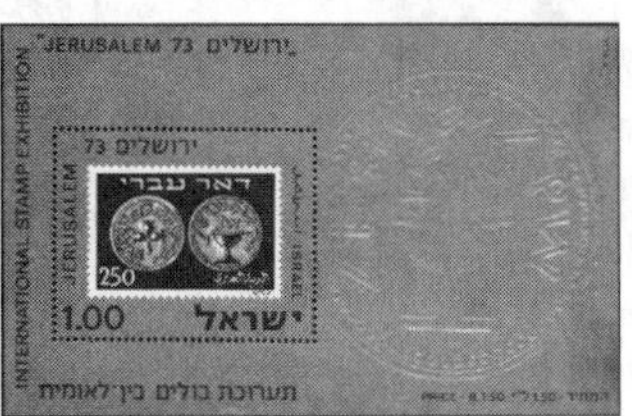

Israel No. 7 — A217

Designs: £2, No. 8. £3, No. 9.

1974, Mar. 25 **Photo.** ***Perf. 14x13***

532 A217 £1 silver & dk slate grn .20 .20
533 A217 £2 silver & red brn .20 .20
534 A217 £3 silver & blk blue .20 .20
Nos. 532-534 (3) .60 .60

Jerusalem '73 Philatelic Exhibition, Mar. 25-Apr. 2, 1974 (postponed from Dec. 1973), 25th anniv. of State of Israel. Each sheet was sold with a 50 per cent surcharge.

Soldier with Prayer Shawl A218

Quill and Inkwell with Hebrew Letters A219

1974, Apr. 23 ***Perf. 13x14***

535 A218 £1 blk & light bl .20 .20
With tab .20

Memorial Day.

1974, Apr. 23 ***Perf. 14x13***

536 A219 £2 gold & black .20 .20
With tab .25

50th anniversary of Hebrew Writers Assn.

Lady in Blue, by Moshe Kisling A220

Designs: £2, Mother and Child, Sculpture by Chana Orloff. £3, Girl in Blue, by Chaim Soutine.

1974, June 11 **Litho.** ***Perf. 14***

537 A220 £1.25 multicolored .20 .20
538 A220 £2 multicolored .20 .20
539 A220 £3 multicolored .30 .30
#537-539, with tabs .65

Art works from Tel Aviv, En Harod and Jerusalem Museums.

Wrench A221

1974, June 11

540 A221 25a multicolored .20 .20
With tab .20

50th anniv. of Working Youth Movement.

Istanbuli Synagogue, Jerusalem — A222

Designs: Interiors of restored synagogues in Jerusalem's Old City.

1974, Aug. 6 **Photo.** ***Perf. 13x14***

541 A222 25a shown .20 .20
542 A222 70a Emtzai Synagogue .20 .20
543 A222 £1 Rabbi Yohanan Synagogue .20 .20
#541-543, with tabs .25

Jewish New Year, 5735.

Lady Davis Technical Center "AMAL," Tel Aviv — A223

60a, Elias Sourasky Library, Tel Aviv University. £1.45, Mivtahim Rest Home, Zikhron Yaaqov.

1974, Aug. 6 ***Perf. 13½x14***

544 A223 25a violet black .20 .20
545 A223 60a dark blue .20 .20
546 A223 £1.45 maroon .20 .20
#544-546, with tabs .25

Modern Israeli architecture.

David Ben-Gurion — A224

1974, Nov. 5 ***Perf. 14***

547 A224 25a brown .20 .20
548 A224 £1.30 slate green .20 .20
#547-549, with tabs .25

David Ben-Gurion (1886-1973), first Prime Minister and Minister of Defense of Israel.

Arrows on Globe — A225

Dove Delivering Letter — A226

1974, Nov. 5 **Litho.** ***Perf. 14***

549 A225 25a black & multi .20 .20

Photo.

550 A226 £1.30 gold & multi .20 .20
#549-550, with tabs .25

Centenary of Universal Postal Union.

Hebrew University, Mount Scopus, Jerusalem — A227

1975, Jan. 14 **Litho.** ***Perf. 13***

551 A227 £2.50 multicolored .20 .20
With tab .25

Hebrew University, 50th anniv.

Girl Carrying Plant — A228

Welder — A229

Arbor Day: 35a, Bird singing in tree. £2, Boy carrying potted plant.

1975, Jan. 14 ***Perf. 14***

552 A228 1a multicolored .20 .20
553 A228 35a multicolored .20 .20
554 A228 £2 multicolored .20 .20
#552-554, with tabs .25

1975, Jan. 14 **Photo.** ***Perf. 14x13***

80a, Tractor driver. £1.20, Electrical lineman.

555 A229 30a multicolored .20 .20
556 A229 80a multicolored .20 .20
557 A229 £1.20 ultra & multi .20 .20
#555-557, with tabs .25

Occupational safety and publicity for the Institute for Safety and Hygiene.

Hebrew University Synagogue, Jerusalem — A230

Modern Israeli architecture: £1.30, Yad Mordecai Museum. £1.70, Bat Yam City Hall.

Perf. 14, 13½x14 (#559)

1975, Mar. 4 **Photo.**

558 A230 80a brown .20 .20
559 A230 £1.30 slate green .20 .20
560 A230 £1.70 brown olive .20 .20
#558-560, with tabs .40

US President Harry S Truman (1884-1972) — A231

1975, Mar. 4 **Engr.** ***Perf. 14***

561 A231 £5 dark brown .35 .20
With tab .40

Eternal Flame over Soldier's Grave — A232

Memorial Tablet — A233

1975, Apr. 10 **Photo.** ***Perf. 14x13***

562 A232 £1.45 black & multi .20 .20
With tab .25

Memorial Day.

1975, Apr. 10

563 A233 £1.45 blk, red & gray .20 .20
With tab .25

In memory of soldiers missing in action.

Hurdling A234

1975, Apr. 10 ***Perf. 13x14***

564 A234 25a shown .20 .20
565 A234 £1.70 Bicycling .20 .20
566 A234 £3 Volleyball .20 .20
#564-566, with tabs .40

10th Hapoel Games; 50th anniv. of Hapoel Org.

Yom Kippur, by Maurycy Gottlieb A235

Paintings of religious holidays: £1.00 Hanukkah, by Mortiz D. Oppenheim. 1.40, The Purim Players, by Jankel Adler, horiz.

1975, June 17 **Litho.** ***Perf. 14***

567 A235 £1 multicolored .20 .20
568 A235 £1.40 multicolored .20 .20
569 A235 £4 multicolored .20 .20
#567-569, with tabs .50

Old Couple A236

1975, June 17 **Photo.** ***Perf. 13x14***

570 A236 £1.85 multicolored .20 .20
With tab .25

International Gerontological Association, 10th triennial conference, Jerusalem.

Pres. Zalman Shazar (1889-1974) — A237

1975, Aug. 5 Photo. *Perf. 14x13*

571 A237 35a silver & blk .20 .20
With tab .20

Pioneer Women, 50th Anniv. — A238

1975, Aug. 5 *Perf. 14½*

572 A238 £5 Emblem .30 .20
With tab .35

Judges of Israel — A239

1975, Aug. 5 *Perf. 13x14*

573 A239 35a Gideon .20 .20
574 A239 £1 Deborah .20 .20
575 A239 £1.40 Jephthah .20 .20
#573-575, with tabs .35

Jewish New Year, 5736.

Hebrew University, Mt. Scopus — A240

1975, Oct. 14 Photo. *Perf. 14x13*

576 A240 £4 multicolored .20 .20
With tab .25

Return of Hadassah to Mt. Scopus, Jerusalem.

Collared Pratincoles A241

Protected Birds: £1.70, Spur-winged plover. £2, Black-winged stilts.

1975, Oct. 14 Litho. *Perf. 13*

577 A241 £1.10 pink & multi .20 .20
578 A241 £1.70 lemon & multi .20 .20
579 A241 £2 multicolored .20 .20
#577-579, with tabs .40

Butterfly and Factory (Air Pollution) — A242

Designs: 80a, Fish and tanker (water pollution). £1.70, Ear and jet (noise pollution).

1975, Dec. 9 Photo. *Perf. 14*

580 A242 50a car & multi .20 .20
581 A242 80a green & multi .20 .20
582 A242 £1.70 orange & multi .20 .20
Nos. 580-582 (3) .60 .60
With tabs .45

Environmental protection.

Star of David — A243

1975-80 *Perf. 13x14*

583 A243 75a vio bl & car .20 .20
584 A243 £1.80 violet bl & gray .20 .20
585 A243 £1.85 vio bl & lt brn .20 .20
586 A243 £2.45 vio bl & brt green .20 .20
587 A243 £2.70 vio bl & purple .20 .20
588 A243 £4.30 ultra & red .20 .20
589 A243 £5.40 vio bl & ol .30 .20
590 A243 £8 vio bl & bl .40 .20
Nos. 583-590 (8) 1.90 1.60
With tabs 2.25

Issued: £1.85, 12/9; £2.45, 6/22/76; 75a, 12/77; £5.40, 5/23/78; £1.80, £8, 5/22/79; £2.70, 12/25/79; £4.30, 5/26/80.

Landscape Type of 1971-75

Design: £10, View of Elat and harbor.

1976, Aug. 17 Photo. *Perf. 14x14½*

592 A193 £10 Prussian blue .80 .20
With tab .90

No. 592 issued both tagged and untagged.

"In the days of Ahasuerus." — A247

Designs (from Book of Esther): 80a, "He set the royal crown on her head." £1.60, "Thus shall it be done to the man whom the king delights to honor."

1976, Feb. 17 Photo. *Perf. 14*

593 A247 40a multicolored .20 .20
594 A247 80a multicolored .20 .20
595 A247 £1.60 multicolored .20 .20
a. Souv. sheet of 3, #593-595, perf 13x14 .35 .35
#593-595, with tabs .30

Purim Festival. No. 595a sold for £4.

Border Settlement, Barbed Wire — A248

1976, Feb. 17

596 A248 £1.50 olive & multi .20 .20
With tab .25

Border settlements, part of Jewish colonization of Holy Land.

Symbolic Key — A249

1976, Feb. 17

597 A249 £1.85 multicolored .20 .20
With tab .25

Bezalel Academy of Arts and Design, Jerusalem, 70th anniv.

"200" US Flag A250

1976, Apr. 25 Photo. *Perf. 13x14*

598 A250 £4 gold & multi .25 .20
With tab .30

American Bicentennial.

Dancers of Meron, by Reuven Rubin A251

1976, Apr. 25 Litho. *Perf. 14*

599 A251 £1.30 multicolored .20 .20
With tab .25

Lag Ba-Omer festival.

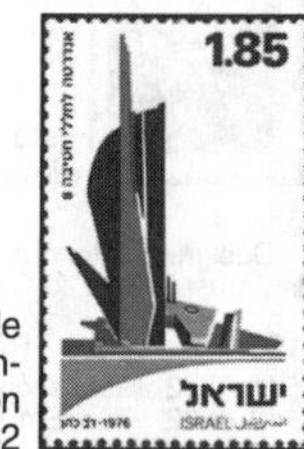

8th Brigade Monument, Ben-Gurion Airport — A252

1976, Apr. 25 Photo. *Perf. 14x13*

600 A252 £1.85 multicolored .20 .20
With tab .25

Memorial Day.

Souvenir Sheet

Tourism, Sport and Industry — A253

1976, Apr. 25

601 A253 Sheet of 3 .60 .50
a. £1 multicolored .20 .20
b. £2 multicolored .20 .20
c. £4 multicolored .35 .25

No. 601 sold for £10.

High Jump A254

1976, June 22 *Perf. 13x14*

602 A254 £1.60 shown .20 .20
603 A254 £2.40 Diving .20 .20
604 A254 £4.40 Gymnastics .30 .25
#602-604, with tabs .65

21st Olympic Games, Montreal, Canada, July 17-Aug. 1.

Tents and Suns — A255

1976, June 22 *Perf. 14*

605 A255 £1.50 green & multi .20 .20
With tab .25

Israel Camping Union.

"Truth" A256

Pawn A257

Design: £1.50, "Judgment" (scales). £1.90, "Peace" (dove and olive branch).

1976, Aug. 17 Photo. *Perf. 14x13*

Tagged

606 A256 45a gold & multi .20 .20
607 A256 £1.50 gold & multi .20 .20
608 A256 £1.90 gold & multi .20 .20
#606-608, with tabs .30

Festivals 5737.

1976, Oct. 19 Litho. *Perf. 14*

609 A257 £1.30 shown .20 .20
610 A257 £1.60 Rook .20 .20
#609-610, with tabs .35

22nd Men's and 7th Women's Chess Olympiad, Haifa, Oct. 24-Nov. 11.

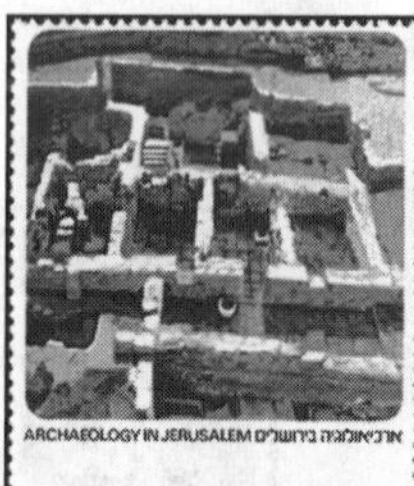

Byzantine Building, 6th Century A258

70a, City wall, 7th cent. B.C. £2.40, Robinson's Arch. £2.80, Steps to Gate of Hulda. Both from area leading to 2nd Temple, 1st cent. B.C. £5, Wall, Omayyad Palace, 8th cent. A.D.

1976 Litho. *Perf. 14*

611 A258 70a multicolored .20 .20
612 A258 £1.30 multicolored .20 .20
613 A258 £2.40 multicolored .20 .20
614 A258 £2.80 multicolored .35 .20
615 A258 £5 multicolored .45 .40
Nos. 611-615 (5) 1.40 1.20
With tabs 1.75

Excavations in Old Jerusalem.
Issued: #612-614, 10/19; #611, 615, 12/23.

Clearing the Land, 1890 A259

Designs: 10a, Building harbor wall. 60a, Road building, vert. £1.40, Plower and horse-drawn plow. £1.80, Planting trees.

1976, Dec. 23 Photo. *Perf. 13*

616 A259 5a brown & gold .20 .20
617 A259 10a purple & gold .20 .20
618 A259 60a gold & car .20 .20

619	A259	£1.40 gold & blue	.20	.20
620	A259	£1.80 green & gold	.20	.20
		#616-620, with tabs	.40	

Work of the pioneers.

"Let's Pull up Grandfather's Carrot" — A260

1977, Feb. 15 Litho. *Perf. 14*

621	A260	£2.60 multicolored	.25	.20
		With tab	.30	

Voluntary service.

Doves, Jew and Arab Shaking Hands A261

£1.40, Arab & Jew holding hands, and flowers. £2.70, Peace dove, Arab and Jew dancing. Illustrations for the book "My Shalom-My Peace."

1977, Feb. 15

622	A261	50a multicolored	.20	.20
623	A261	£1.40 multicolored	.20	.20
624	A261	£2.70 multicolored	.25	.25
		622-#624, with tabs	.55	

Children's drawings for peace.

"By the Rivers of Babylon . . ." — A262

Drawings by Efraim Moshe Lilien: £1.80, Abraham, vert. £2.10, "May our eyes behold thee when thou returnest to Zion in compassion."

Perf. 14x13, 13x14

1977, Feb. 15 Photo.

625	A262	£1.70 gray, brn & blk	.20	.20
626	A262	£1.80 yel, blk & brn	.20	.20
627	A262	£2.10 lt grn & dk grn	.25	.20
		Nos. 625-627 (3)	.65	.60
		With tabs	.75	

Souvenirs for 5th Zionist Congress, 1902.

Trumpet A263

Embroidered Sabbath Cloth A264

1977, Apr. 19 Litho. *Perf. 14*

628	A263	£1.50 shown	.20	.20
629	A263	£2 Lyre	.20	.20
630	A263	£5 Cymbals	.25	.20
		#628-630, with tabs	.55	

Ancient musical instruments, Haifa Music Museum and Amli Library.

1977, Apr. 19 *Perf. 13x14*

631	A264	£3 buff & multi	.25	.20
		With tab	.30	

Importance of Sabbath observation in Jewish life.

Parachutists' Memorial, Bilu-Gedera, Tel Aviv — A265

1977, Apr. 19 *Perf. 13x14*

632	A265	£3.30 gray, blk & grn	.30	.25
		With tab	.40	

Memorial Day.

10th Maccabiah — A266

1977, June 23 Photo. *Perf. 14x13*

633	A266	£1 Fencing	.20	.20
634	A266	£2.50 Shot put	.20	.20
635	A266	£3.50 Judo	.25	.20
		Nos. 633-635 (3)	.65	.60
		With tabs	.70	

ZOA Convention Emblem — A267

1977, June 23 *Perf. 14*

636	A267	£4 silver & multi	.30	.20
		With tab	.40	

Convention of Zionist Organization of America (ZOA), Jerusalem, June 1977.

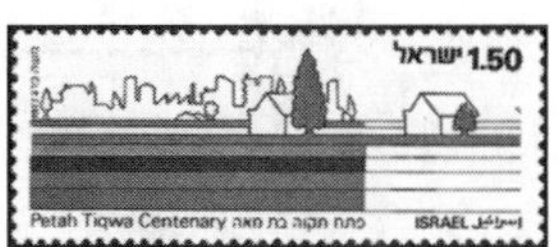

Petah Tikva Centenary — A268

1977, June 23 *Perf. 14x13*

637	A268	£1.50 multicolored	.20	.20
		With tab	.20	

Matriarchs of the Bible — A269

1977, Aug. 16 Photo. *Perf. 14*

638	A269	70a Sarah	.20	.20
639	A269	£1.50 Rebekah	.20	.20
640	A269	£2 Rachel	.20	.20
641	A269	£3 Leah	.20	.20
		#638-641, with tabs	.75	

Jewish New Year, 5738.

Police — A270

Illuminated Page — A271

1977, Aug. 16 Litho. *Perf. 14*

642	A270	£1 shown	.20	.20
643	A270	£1 Frontier Guards	.20	.20
644	A270	£1 Civil Guard	.20	.20
		#642-644, with tabs	.35	

Israel Police Force, established Mar. 26, 1948.

1977, July 21 Photo. *Perf. 14x13*

645	A271	£4 multicolored	.20	.20
		With tab	.25	

4th cent. of Hebrew printing at Safad.

Farm Growing from Steel Helmet A272

Koffler Accelerator A273

1977, Oct. 18 Litho. *Perf. 14*

646	A272	£3.50 multicolored	.20	.20
		With tab	.25	

Fighting Pioneer Youth (NAHAL), established 1949.

1977, Oct. 18 Photo. *Perf. 14x13*

647	A273	£8 black & blue	.60	.40

Inauguration of Koffler accelerator at Weizmann Institute of Science, Rehovot. Untagged.

Caesarea — A274

Scenes: £1, Arava on the Dead Sea. £20, Rosh Pinna.

1977-78 *Perf. 13½x14*

Size: 27x22mm

649	A274	10a violet blue	.20	.20
664	A274	£1 olive bister	.20	.20

Perf. 14½x14

Size: 27½x26½mm

672	A274	£20 org & dk grn ('78)	.80	.20
		#649-672, with tabs	1.10	

The 10a is untagged. The £1, £20 issued tagged and untagged.

Issued: 10a, £1, 10/18/77; £20, 7/4/78.

First Holy Land Locomotive A276

Locomotives: £1.50, Jezreel Valley train. £2, British Mandate period. £2.50, Israel Railways.

1977, Dec. 13 Photo. *Perf. 13x14*

674	A276	65a multicolored	.20	.20
675	A276	£1.50 multicolored	.20	.20
676	A276	£2 multicolored	.20	.20
677	A276	£2.50 multicolored	.25	.25
a.		Souvenir sheet of 4, #674-677	1.25	1.25
		#674-677, with tabs	.80	

Railways in the Holy Land. #677a sold for £10.

Cypraea Isabella — A277

Designs: Red Sea shells.

1977, Dec. 13 Litho. *Perf. 14*

678	A277	£2 shown	.20	.20
679	A277	£2 Lioconcha castrensis	.20	.20
680	A277	£2 Gloripallium pallium	.20	.20
681	A277	£2 Malea pomum	.20	.20
		#678-681, with tabs	.50	

Street in Jerusalem, by Haim Glicksberg (1904-1970) A278

Paintings: £3.80, Thistles, by Leopold Krakauer (1890-1954). £4.40, An Alley in Zefat, by Mordekhai Levanon (1901-1968).

1978, Feb. 14

682	A278	£3 multicolored	.20	.20
683	A278	£3.80 multicolored	.20	.20
684	A278	£4.40 multicolored	.25	.25
		Nos. 682-684 (3)	.65	.65
		With tabs	.65	

Marriage Contract, Netherlands, 1648 — A279

Marriage Contracts (Ketubah): £3.90, Morocco, 1897. £6, Jerusalem, 1846.

1978, Feb. 14

685	A279	75a multicolored	.20	.20
686	A279	£3.90 multicolored	.20	.20
687	A279	£6 multicolored	.30	.20
		#685-687, with tabs	.65	

Eliyahu Golomb — A280

Designs: Portraits.

1978, Apr. 23 Photo. *Perf. 14x13*

688	A280	£2 shown	.20	.20
689	A280	£2 Dr. Moshe Sneh	.20	.20
690	A280	£2 David Raziel	.20	.20
691	A280	£2 Yitzhak Sadeh	.20	.20
692	A280	£2 Abraham Stern	.20	.20
		#688-692, with tabs	.60	

Heroes of underground movement. Nos. 688-692 issued in sheets of 15.

See Nos. 695-696, 699-700, 705-706, 712-714, 740-742.

Souvenir Sheet

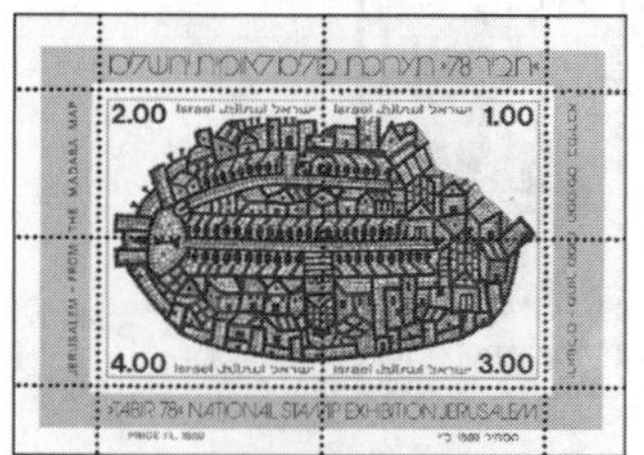

Jerusalem, Mosaic, from Madaba Map — A281

1978, Apr. 23 Litho. *Perf. 14*

693 A281 Sheet of 4 1.40 1.40
- *a.* £1 multicolored .20 .20
- *b.* £2 multicolored .25 .20
- *c.* £3 multicolored .40 .35
- *d.* £4 multicolored .50 .45

Tabir '78 National Stamp Exhibition, Jerusalem, Apr. 23. No. 693 sold for £15.

Flowers A282

Design: Flowers, after children's paintings on Memorial Wall in Yad-Lebanim Museum, Petah Tikva. Each stamp shows different flowers.

1978, Apr. 23 *Perf. 14*

694 Sheet of 15 1.40 1.25
- *a.-o.* A282 £1.50 single stamp .20 .20

Memorial Day.

Heroes Type

Designs: No. 695, Theodor Herzl. No. 696, Chaim Weizmann.

1978, July 5 Photo. *Perf. 14x13*

695 A280 £2 gray & gray ol .20 .20
696 A280 £2 buff & vio bl .20 .20
#695-696, with tabs .25

Herzl, founder of Zionism; Weizmann, 1st President of Israel.

Hatiqwa, 1st Verse A285

YMCA Building, Jerusalem A286

1978, July 4 *Perf. 13x14*

697 A285 £8.40 multicolored .45 .35
With tab .50

Centenary of Israeli National Anthem, Hatiqwa, by poet Naftali Herz Imber.

1978, July 4 Litho. *Perf. 13*

698 A286 £5.40 multicolored .25 .20
With tab .35

Centenary of YMCA in Jerusalem.

Heroes Type

Designs: No. 699, Rabbi Kook (1865-1935). No. 700, Rabbi Ouziel (1880-1963).

1978, Aug. 22 Photo. *Perf. 14x13*

699 A280 £2 pale gray & slate grn .20 .20
700 A280 £2 pale gray & dk pur .20 .20
#699-700, with tabs .25

Patriarchs A288

1978, Aug. 22 *Perf. 14*

701 A288 £1.10 Abraham & Isaac .20 .20
702 A288 £5.20 Isaac .25 .25
703 A288 £6.60 Jacob .30 .30
#701-703, with tabs .70

Festivals 5739.

Families and Houses A289

1978, Aug. 22 *Perf. 13x14*

704 A289 £5.10 multicolored .30 .20
With tab .35

Social welfare.

Heroes Type

Designs: No. 705, David Ben-Gurion. No. 706, Ze'ev Jabotinsky.

1978, Oct. 31 Photo. *Perf. 14x13*

705 A280 £2 buff & vio brn .20 .20
706 A280 £2 gray & indigo .20 .20
#705-706, with tabs .25

30 years of independence. Ben-Gurion, first Prime Minister, and Ze'ev Vladimir Jabotinsky (1880-1940), leader of World Union of Zionist Revisionists.

Star of David and Growing Tree — A291

1978, Oct. 31 Litho. *Perf. 14*

707 A291 £8.40 multicolored .45 .35
With tab .50

United Jewish Appeal, established 1939 in US to help Israel.

Old and New Hospital Buildings A292

1978, Oct. 31

708 A292 £5.40 multicolored .25 .20
With tab .30

Opening of new Shaare Zedek Medical Center, Jerusalem.

Silver and Enamel Vase, India — A293

Iris Lortetii — A295

£3, Elephant with howdah, Persia, 13th cent. £4, Mosque lamp, glass and enamel, Syria, 14th cent.

1978, Oct. 31

709 A293 £2.40 multicolored .20 .20
710 A293 £3 multicolored .20 .20
711 A293 £4 multicolored .20 .20
Nos. 709-711 (3) .60 .60
With tabs .65

Leo Arie Mayer Memorial Museum for Islamic Art, Jerusalem.

Heroes Type

#712, Menachem Ussishkin (1863-1941). #713, Berl Katzenelson (1878-1944). #714, Max Nordau (1849-1923).

1978, Dec. 26 Photo. *Perf. 14x13*

712 A280 £2 citron & sl grn .20 .20
713 A280 £2 gray & vio blue .20 .20
714 A280 £2 buff & black .20 .20
#712-714, with tabs .45

30th anniversary of independence.

1978, Dec. 26 Litho. *Perf. 14*

Protected Wild Flowers: £5.40, Iris haynei. £8.40, Iris nazarena.

715 A295 £1.10 multicolored .20 .20
716 A295 £5.40 multicolored .30 .25
717 A295 £8.40 multicolored .45 .35
Nos. 715-717 (3) .95 .80
With tabs .95

Agricultural Mechanization A296

Symbolic Designs: £2.40, Seawater desalination. £4.30, Electronics. £5, Chemical fertilizers.

1979, Feb. 13 Litho. *Perf. 13*

718 A296 £1.10 multicolored .20 .20
719 A296 £2.40 multicolored .20 .20
720 A296 £4.30 multicolored .20 .20
721 A296 £5 multicolored .20 .20
#718-721, with tabs .70

Technological Achievements.

"Hope from Darkness" A297

1979, Feb. 13

722 A297 £5.40 multicolored .30 .25
With tab .35

Salute to "the Righteous among Nations," an award to those who helped during Nazi period.

Jewish Brigade Flag — A298

1979, Feb. 13 Photo. *Perf. 14*

723 A298 £5.10 blue, yel & blk .25 .25
With tab .30

Jewish Brigade served with British Armed Forces during WWII.

Paper (Prayer for Peace) in Crevice of Western Wall — A299

1979, Mar. 26 Photo. *Perf. 14x13*

724 A299 £10 multicolored .35 .25
With tab .40
- *a.* Souv. sheet of 1, imperf. .40 .45

Signing of peace treaty between Israel and Egypt, Mar. 26.

11th Hapoel Games — A300

1979, Apr. 23 Litho. *Perf. 13*

725 A300 £1.50 Weightlifting .20 .20
726 A300 £6 Tennis .30 .20
727 A300 £11 Gymnastics .50 .40
Nos. 725-727 (3) 1.00 .80
With tabs 1.00

"50" and Rotary Emblem — A301

1979, Apr. 23 Photo. *Perf. 14x13*

728 A301 £7 multicolored .35 .25
With tab .40

Rotary Intl. in Israel, 50th anniv.

Navy Memorial, Ashdod A302

1979, Apr. 23

729 A302 £5.10 multicolored .25 .20
With tab .30

Memorial Day.

Rabbi Yehoshua ben Hananya A303

Flag Colors as Search Light A304

Craftsmen-Sages: £8.50, Rabbi Meir Baal Ha-Ness, scribe. £13, Rabbi Johanan, sandal maker.

1979, Sept. 4 Photo. *Perf. 14x13*

730 A303 £1.80 multicolored .20 .20
731 A303 £8.50 multicolored .20 .20
732 A303 £13 multicolored .35 .30
Nos. 730-732 (3) .75 .70
With tabs .75

Jewish New Year 5740.

1979, Sept. 4

733 A304 £10 multicolored .25 .20
With tab .30

Jewish Agency, 50th anniversary.

Hot Springs, Tiberias
A305

Boy Riding Rainbow
A306

Design: £12, Dead Sea health resorts.

1979, Sept. 4 Litho. *Perf. 14*

734 A305 £8 multicolored .20 .20
735 A305 £12 multicolored .30 .25
#734-735, with tabs .55

1979, Nov. 13 Photo. *Perf. 13x14*

736 A306 £8.50 multicolored .20 .20
With tab .25

International Year of the Child.

Jerusalem — A307

Children's Drawings of Jerusalem: £4, People of different nationalities, horiz. £5, Praying at the Western Wall, horiz.

1979, Nov. 13 *Perf. 14*

737 A307 £1.80 multicolored .20 .20
738 A307 £4 multicolored .20 .20
739 A307 £5 multicolored .20 .20
#737-739, with tabs .30

Heroes Type

Designs: £7, Arthur Ruppin (1876-1943). £9, Joseph Trumpeldor (1880-1920). £13, Aaron Aaronsohn (1876-1919).

1979, Nov. 13 Photo. *Perf. 14x13*

740 A280 £7 gray & magenta .20 .20
741 A280 £9 pale grn & Prus bl .25 .25
742 A280 £13 pale yel & dk ol .35 .35
Nos. 740-742 (3) .80 .80
With tabs .85

Sorek Cave — A308

1980, Jan. 15 Litho. *Perf. 13x14*

743 A308 £50 multicolored 1.00 .50
With tab 1.25

Star of David in Cogwheel
A309

Scolymus Maculatus
A310

1980, Jan. 15 *Perf. 14*

744 A309 £13 multicolored .40 .40
With tab .45

Organization for Rehabilitation through Training (ORT), centenary.

1980, Jan. 15

Thistles: £5.50, Echinops viscosus. £8.50, Cynara syriaca.

745 A310 50a multicolored .20 .20
746 A310 £5.50 multicolored .20 .20
747 A310 £8.50 multicolored .25 .20
#745-747, with tabs .50

Men and Drop of Blood — A311

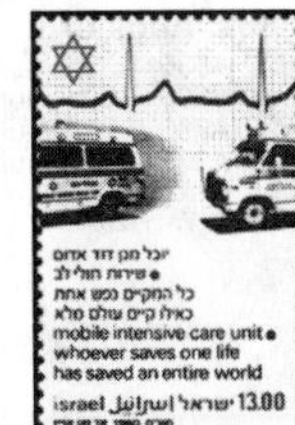

Mobile Intensive Care Unit — A312

1980, Apr. 15 Photo. *Perf. 14x13*

748 A311 £2.70 multicolored .20 .20
749 A312 £13 multicolored .30 .30
a. Souv. sheet, 2 each #748-749 1.00 1.00
#748-749, with tabs .45

Magen David Adom (Red Star of David), 50th anniv.

Road of Courage Monument
A313

Sabbath Lamp, Netherlands, 18th Century
A314

1980, Apr. 15 Litho. *Perf. 14*

750 A313 £12 multicolored .30 .25
With tab .35

Memorial Day.

1980, Aug. 5 Photo. *Perf. 13x14*

Sabbath Lamps: £20, Germany, 18th century. £30, Morocco, 19th century.

751 A314 £4.30 multicolored .20 .20
752 A314 £20 multicolored .30 .30
753 A314 £30 multicolored .50 .50
Nos. 751-753 (3) 1.00 1.00
With tabs 1.10

Yizhak Gruenbaum
A315

Renewal of Jewish Settlement in Gush Etzion
A316

1980, Aug. 5 *Perf. 14x13*

754 A315 £32 sepia .80 .70
With tab .85

Yizhak Gruenbaum (1879-1970), first minister of the interior.

1980, Aug. 5

755 A316 £19 multicolored .35 .30
With tab .40

View of Haifa and Mt. Carmel, 17th Century — A317

1980, Sept. 28 Litho. *Perf. 14x13*

756 A317 Sheet of 2 1.60 *2.00*
a. 2s multicolored .60 *.70*
b. 3s multicolored .85 *1.00*

Haifa 80 National Stamp Exhibition, Haifa, Sept. 28-Oct. 7.

A318

1980-81 Photo. *Perf. 13x14*

757 A318 5a brt yel grn & green .20 .20
758 A318 10a red & brt mag .20 .20
759 A318 20a grnsh bl & dk blue .20 .20
760 A318 30a lil & dp vio .20 .20
761 A318 50a red org & red brown .20 .20
762 A318 60a brt yel grn & dk brown .20 .20
762A A318 70a Prus bl & black .20 .20
763 A318 1s brt mag & dk green .20 .20
764 A318 2s dk bl grn & brn red .25 .20
765 A318 2.80s brown & grn .30 .20
766 A318 3.20s gray & red .35 .20
767 A318 4.20s ultra & dk pur .40 .20
768 A318 5s green & blk .55 .20
769 A318 10s brn org & brn 1.25 .20
#757-769, with tabs 4.50

Issued: 70a, 5/5/81; others, 12/16/80.
See Nos. 784-786, 807-808

Prime Minister Golda Meir (1898-1978) — A319

1981, Feb. 10 Photo. *Perf. 14x13*

770 A319 2.60s rose violet .40 .40
With tab .45

View of Jerusalem, by Mordechai Ardon — A320

1981, Feb. 10 Litho. *Perf. 14*

Paintings of Jerusalem by: 50a, Anna Ticho. 1.50s, Joseph Zaritsky, vert.

771 A320 50a multicolored .20 .20
772 A320 1.50s multicolored .25 .20
773 A320 2.50s multicolored .40 .35
Nos. 771-773 (3) .85 .75
With tabs .95

Hand Putting Coin in Light Bulb — A321

1981, Mar. 17 Photo. *Perf. 14*

774 A321 2.60s shown .25 .25
775 A321 4.20s Hand squeezing solar energy .40 .35
#774-775, with tabs .80

Shmuel Yosef Agnon (1880-1970), Writer — A322

Wind Surfing — A323

Designs: 2.80s, Moses Montefiore (1784-1885), first knighted English Jew. 3.20s, Abba Hillel Silver (1893-1963), statesman.

Perf. 14x13, 14 (3.20s)

1981, Mar. 17

776 A322 2s dk blue & blk .25 .25
777 A322 2.80s dk bl grn & blk .30 .30
778 A322 3.20s deep bis & blk .35 .30
Nos. 776-778 (3) .90 .85
With tabs 1.00

1981, May 5 *Perf. 14x13*

779 A323 80a shown .20 .20
780 A323 4s Basketball .55 .55
781 A323 6s High jump .75 .75
Nos. 779-781 (3) 1.50 1.50
With tabs 1.50

11th Maccabiah Games, July 8-16.

Biq'at Hayarden Memorial
A324

Jewish Family Heritage
A325

1981, May 5 *Perf. 13x14*

782 A324 1s red & black .20 .20
With tab .25

1981, May 5 Litho. *Perf. 14*

783 A325 3s multicolored .40 .35
With tab .45

Type of 1980

1981, Aug. 25 Photo. *Perf. 13x14*

784 A318 90a dp vio & brn org .20 .20
785 A318 3s red & dk blue .45 .30
786 A318 4s dk brn vio & dp lil rose .50 .35
Nos. 784-786 (3) 1.15 .85
With tabs 1.25

The Burning Bush
A326

Roses
A327

Festivals 5742 (Book of Exodus): 1s "Let my people go . . ." 3s, Crossing of the Red Sea. 4s, Moses with Tablets.

1981, Aug. 25
787 A326 70a multicolored .20 .20
788 A326 1s multicolored .20 .20
789 A326 3s multicolored .35 .35
790 A326 4s multicolored .45 .40
Nos. 787-790 (4) 1.20 1.15
With tabs 1.25

1981, Oct. 22 Litho. *Perf. 14*
791 A327 90a Rosa damascena .20 .20
792 A327 3.50s Rosa phoenicia .40 .35
793 A327 4.50s Rosa hybrida .50 .45
Nos. 791-793 (3) 1.10 1.00
With tabs 1.50

Ha-Shiv'a Interchange, Morasha-Ashod Highway — A328

1981, Oct. 22 Photo. *Perf. 14x13*
794 A328 8s multicolored .70 .65
With tab .75

Elat Stone
A329

Arbutus Andrachne
A330

1981, Dec. 29 Litho. *Perf. 14*
795 A329 2.50s shown .25 .25
796 A329 5.50s Star sapphire .55 .55
797 A329 7s Emerald .70 .70
Nos. 795-797 (3) 1.50 1.50
With tabs 2.25

1981, Dec. 29
798 A330 3s shown .30 .30
799 A330 3s Cercis siliquastrume .30 .30
800 A330 3s Quercus ithaburensis .30 .30
a. Vert. or horiz. strip of 3, #798-800 1.00 1.00
#800a, horiz. strip of 3 with tabs 1.25

Sheets of 9.

Road Safety — A331

1982, Mar. 2 Photo. *Perf. 14x13*
801 A331 7s multicolored .70 .70
With tab 1.00
a. Souvenir sheet 1.25 1.25

No. 801a sold for 10s.

Joseph Gedalyah Klausner (1874-1958), Historian and Philosopher
A331a

7s, Perez Bernstein (1890-1971), writer and editor. 8s, Rabbi Arys Levin (1885-1969).

1982, Mar. 2
802 A331a 7s multi .50 .50
803 A331a 8s multi .55 .55
804 A331a 9s cream & dk bl .65 .65
Nos. 802-804 (3) 1.70 1.70
With tabs 1.90

Type of 1980 and

Produce — A332

1982-83 Photo. *Perf. 13 x 14*
805 A332 40a Prus bl & grn .20 .20
806 A332 80a lt bl & pur .20 .20
807 A318 1.10s ol & red .20 .20
808 A318 1.20s bl & red .20 .20
809 A332 1.40s ol grn & red .20 .20
810 A332 6s red vio & brn org .25 .20
811 A332 7s brn org & ol .20 .20
812 A332 8s brt grn & red brn .20 .20
813 A332 9s ol & brn .25 .20
814 A332 15s ver & brt grn .40 .20
Nos. 805-814 (10) 2.30 2.00
With tabs 4.50

Issued: 1.10s, 2/11; 1.20s, 3/16; 1.40s, 6/22/82; 40a, 80a, 6s, 1/11/83; 7s-15s, 10/11/83.
See Nos. 876-879.

Tel Aviv Landscape, by Aryeh Lubin (d. 1980) — A333

Landscapes by: 8s, Sionah Tagger, vert. 15s, Israel Paldi (1892-1979).

1982, Apr. 22 Litho. *Perf. 14*
815 A333 7s multicolored .50 .50
816 A333 8s multicolored .50 .50
817 A333 15s multicolored 1.00 1.00
Nos. 815-817 (3) 2.00 2.00
With tabs 2.75

Gedudei Nouar Youth Corps
A334

Armour Memorial, En Zetim
A335

1982, Apr. 22 Photo. *Perf. 14x13*
818 A334 5s multicolored .40 .35
With tab .55

1982, Apr. 22 Litho. *Perf. 14*
819 A335 1.50s multicolored .20 .20
With tab .20

Memorial Day.

Joshua Addressing Crowd — A336

Festivals 5743 (Book of Joshua): 5.50s, Crossing River Jordan. 7.50s, Blowing down walls of Jericho. 9.50s, Battle with five kings of Amorites.

1982, Aug. 10 *Perf. 14*
820 A336 1.50s multicolored .20 .20
821 A336 5.50s multicolored .30 .30
822 A336 7.50s multicolored .45 .45
823 A336 9.50s multicolored .55 .55
Nos. 820-823 (4) 1.50 1.50
With tabs 1.50

Hadassah, 70th Anniv. — A337

1982, Aug. 10 Litho.
824 A337 12s multicolored .85 .70
With tab 1.25

Rosh Pinna Settlement Centenary
A338

1982 Photo. *Perf. 13x14*
825 A338 2.50s shown .20 .20
826 A338 3.50s Rishon Leziyyon .20 .20
827 A338 6s Zikhron Yaaqov .35 .30
828 A338 9s Mazkeret Batya .65 .60
Nos. 825-828 (4) 1.40 1.30
With tabs 1.50

Issued: 2.50s, 3.50s, Aug. 10; others, Oct. 5.
See Nos. 849-850.

Olive Branch
A339

Emblem of Council for a Beautiful Israel
A340

1982, Sept. 12
829 A339 multicolored .20 .20
With tab .40
a. Booklet pane of 8 + 8 ('84) 3.00

Sold at various values.

1982, Oct. 5 Litho. *Perf. 14*
830 A340 17s multicolored .90 .75
With tab 1.00
a. Souv. sheet of 1, imperf. 1.60 1.50

No. 830a was for Beer Sheva '82 National Stamp Exhibition. Sold for 25s.

Eliahu Bet Tzuri — A341

Independence Martyrs: b, Hannah Szenes. c, Shlomo Ben Yosef. d, Yosef Lishanski. e, Naaman Belkind. f, Eliezer Kashani. g, Yechiel Dresner. h, Dov Gruner. i, Mordechai Alkachi. j, Eliahu Hakim. k, Meir Nakar. l, Avshalom Haviv. m, Yaakov Weiss. n, Meir Feinstein. o, Moshe Barazani. p, Eli Cohen. q, Samuel Azaar. r, Moshe Marzouk. s, Shalom Salih. t, Yosef Basri.

1982, Dec. *Perf. 14x13½*
831 Sheet of 20 5.50 5.50
a.-t. A341 3s multicolored .20 .20

Anti-Smoking Campaign
A342

1983, Feb. 15 Litho. *Perf. 13*
832 A342 7s Candy in ash tray .35 .25
With tab .50

Beekeeping
A343

1983, Feb. 15 Photo. *Perf. 13x14*
833 A343 30s multi 1.60 1.50
With tab 1.75

A343a

1983, Feb. 15 Litho. *Perf. 14*
834 A343a 8s Golan .30 .30
835 A343a 15s Galil .65 .55
836 A343a 20s Yehuda and Shomeron .95 .70
Nos. 834-836 (3) 1.90 1.55
With tabs 3.00

Memorial Day (Apr. 17) — A344

1983, Apr. 12 *Perf. 13*
837 A344 3s Division of Steel Memorial, Besor Region .20 .20
With tab .20

Independence Day — A345

1983, Apr. 12 *Perf. 14*
838 A345 25s multicolored 1.25 1.00
With tab 1.40
a. Souvenir sheet, imperf. 2.25 2.00

No. 838a sold for 35s.

12th Hapoel Games — A346

1983, Apr. 12 *Perf. 14x13*
839 A346 6s multicolored .25 .25
With tab .35

50th Anniv. of Israel Military Industries — A347

1983, Apr. 12
840 A347 12s multicolored .55 .55
With tab .60

Souvenir Sheet

WWII Uprising Leaders — A348

Designs: a, Yosef Glazman (1908-1943), Founder of United Partisans Org. b, Text.1 c, Mordechai Anilewicz (1919-1943), leader of Warsaw Ghetto revolt. No. 841 sold for 45s.

1983, June 7 ***Perf. 14***
841 A348 Sheet of 3 2.25 2.25
a. 10s multicolored .60 .50
b. 10s multicolored .60 .50
c. 10s multicolored .60 .50

Raoul Wallenberg (1912-1945), Swedish Diplomat — A349

1983, June 7 ***Perf. 14x13***
842 A349 14s multicolored .65 .45
With tab .80

The Last Way, by Yosef Kuzkovski — A350

1983, June 7 ***Perf. 14***
843 A350 35s multicolored 1.10 1.10
With tab 1.25

Ohel Moed Synagogue, Tel Aviv A351

1983, Aug. 23
844 A351 3s shown .20 .20
845 A351 12s Yeshurun Society, Jerusalem .35 .35
846 A351 16s Ohel Aharon, Haifa .50 .50
847 A351 20s Eliyahu Khakascni, Beer Sheva .60 .60
Nos. 844-847 (4) 1.65 1.65
With tabs 1.90

View of Afula, Jezreel Valley — A352

1983, Aug. 23
848 A352 15s multicolored .65 .55
With tab .80

Settlement Type of 1982

1983, Aug. 23
849 A338 11s Yesud Ha-Maala .45 .40
850 A338 13s Nes Ziyyona .50 .45
#849-850, with tabs 1.25

Souvenir Sheet

Tel Aviv Seashore Promenade — A353

1983, Sept. 25 ***Perf. 14x13***
851 A353 Sheet of 2 7.25 7.25
a. 30s multicolored 2.00 2.00
b. 50s multicolored 3.50 3.50

Tel Aviv '83, 13th Natl. Stamp Show, Sept. Sold for 120s.

KFIR-C2 Tactical Fighter — A354

1983, Dec. 13 Photo. ***Perf. 14***
852 A354 8s shown .20 .20
853 A354 18s Reshef class missile boat .25 .25
854 A354 30s Merkava-MK1 battle tank .45 .45
Nos. 852-854 (3) .90 .90
With tabs .90

Rabbi Meir Bar-Ilan (1880-1949), Founder of Mizrachi Movement — A355

1983, Dec. 13 Photo. ***Perf. 14x13***
855 A355 9s multicolored .20 .20
With tab .20

Jewish Immigration from Germany, 50th Anniv. A356

1983, Dec. 13 Photo. ***Perf. 13x14***
856 A356 14s multicolored .40 .35
With tab .45

Michael Halperin (1860-1919), Zionist — A357

Uri Zvi Grinberg (1896-1981), Poet — A358

15s, Yigal Allon (1918-1980), military commander, founder of Israel Labor Party.

1984, Mar. 15 Photo. ***Perf. 14x13***
857 A357 7s multicolored .20 .20

Litho.
Perf. 14
858 A357 15s multicolored .25 .25

Perf. 13
859 A358 16s multicolored .30 .30
Nos. 857-859 (3) .75 .75
With tabs 1.00

Hevel Ha-Besor Settlement — A359

1984, Mar. 15 ***Perf. 14***
860 A359 12s shown .20 .20
861 A359 17s Arava .30 .25
862 A359 40s Gaza Strip .75 .50
Nos. 860-862 (3) 1.25 .95
With tabs 1.50

Monument of Alexander Zaid, by David Polus A360

Monuments: No. 864, Tel Hay Defenders (seated lion), by Abraham Melnikov (1892-1960). No. 865, Dov Gruner, by Chana Orloff (1888-1968).

1984, Mar. 15 ***Perf. 13x14***
863 A360 15s multicolored .35 .25
864 A360 15s multicolored .35 .25
865 A360 15s multicolored .35 .25
Nos. 863-865 (3) 1.05 .75
With tabs 1.35

Memorial Day — A361

Natl. Labor Fed., 50th Anniv. — A362

Design: Oliphant House (Druse military memorial), Dalyat Al Karmil.

1984, Apr. 26 Photo. ***Perf. 14x13***
866 A361 10s multicolored .20 .20
With tab .20

1984, Apr. 26
867 A362 35s multicolored .35 .25
With tab .40

Produce Type of 1982-83

1984 Photo. ***Perf. 13x14***
876 A332 30s vio brn & red .35 .25
877 A332 50s dp bis & rose mag .65 .40
878 A332 100s gray & green 1.25 .80
879 A332 500s dp org & bl blk 1.10 .90
Nos. 876-879 (4) 3.35 2.35
With tabs 7.00

Issued: 500s, 11/27; others 4/26.

Leon Pinsker (1821-91), A363

Gen. Charles O. Wingate (1903-44) A364

1984, July 3 ***Perf. 14x13***
880 A363 20s Hovevei Zion founder .20 .20
881 A364 20s British soldier .20 .20
#880-881, with tabs .50

Hearts, Stars — A365

1984, July 3
882 A365 30s multicolored .25 .25
With tab .30

70th anniv. of American Jewish Joint Distribution Committee (philanthropic org. created during World War I).

1984 Summer Olympics A366

1984, July 3 Litho. ***Perf. 14***
883 A366 80s Dove .70 .70
With tab .90

Souvenir Sheet
Perf. 14x13
884 A366 240s like 80s 5.00 4.25

No. 884 contains one 23x32mm stamp. Sold for 350s.

Biblical Women A367

David Wolffsohn (1856-1914), Jewish Colonial Trust Founder A368

1984, Sept. 4 Photo. ***Perf. 13x14***
885 A367 15s Hannah .20 .20
886 A367 70s Ruth .35 .35
887 A367 100s Huldah .60 .60
Nos. 885-887 (3) 1.15 1.15
With tabs 1.25

1984, Sept. 4 ***Perf. 14x14½***
888 A368 150s multicolored .90 .60
With tab 1.25

Nahalal Settlement (Founded 1921) A369

1984, Sept. 4 ***Perf. 14***

889 A369 80s multicolored .50 .45
With tab .60

World Food Day, Oct. 16 — A370

1984, Nov. 27 **Litho.**

891 A370 200s Bread, wheat 1.00 .65
With tab 1.10

Rabbi Isaac Herzog (1888-1959), Statesman, Scholar — A371

1984, Nov. 27 **Photo.** ***Perf. 14½***

892 A371 400s multicolored 1.60 1.40
With tab 1.75

A372

Perf. 14, 13 (30s)

1984, Nov. 27 **Litho.**

Children's Book Illustrations (Authors and their books): 20s, Apartment to Let, by Leah Goldberg (1911-70). 30s, Why is the Zebra Wearing Pajamas, by Omer Hillel (b. 1926) (30x30mm). 50s, Across the Sea, by Haim Nahman Bialik (1873-1934).

893 A372 20s multicolored .20 .20
894 A372 30s multicolored .20 .20
895 A372 50s multicolored .30 .20
Nos. 893-895 (3) .70 .60
With tabs .80

Birds of Prey — A373

1985, Feb. 5 **Litho.** ***Perf. 14***

896 A373 100s Lappet faced vulture .30 .30
897 A373 200s Bonelli's eagle .55 .55
898 A373 300s Sooty falcon .75 .75
899 A373 500s Griffon vulture 1.40 1.40
Nos. 896-899 (4) 3.00 3.00
With tabs 5.75

Souvenir Sheet

899A Sheet of 4 7.25 3.75
b. A373 100s like #896 .35 .35
c. A373 200s like #897 .75 .65
d. A373 300s like #898 1.10 1.00
e. A373 500s like #899 1.60 1.50

No. 899A sold for 1650s. Nos. 899Ab-899Ad do not have inscriptions below the design.

Aviation in the Holy Land A374

1985, Apr. 2 **Litho.** ***Perf. 14***

900 A374 50s Bleriot XI, 1913 .20 .20
901 A374 150s Scipio-Short S-17 Kent, 1931 .50 .40
902 A374 250s Tiger Moth DH-82, 1934 .80 .70
903 A374 300s Scion-Short S-16, 1937 .85 1.00
Nos. 900-903 (4) 2.35 2.30
With tabs 2.75

Natl. Assoc. of Nurses — A375

1985, Apr. 2 **Litho.** ***Perf. 14***

904 A375 400s multicolored 1.00 .95
With tab 1.50

Golani Brigade Memorial and Museum — A376

1985, Apr. 2 **Photo.** ***Perf. 14x13***

905 A376 50s multicolored .25 .20
With tab .45

Zivia (1914-1978) and Yitzhak (1915-1981) Zuckerman, Resistance Heroes, Warsaw Ghetto — A377

1985, Apr. 2 **Photo.** ***Perf. 13x14***

906 A377 200s multicolored .65 .50
With tab .80

Souvenir Sheets

Dome of the Rock A378

16th Cent. Bas-relief, Ottoman Period A379

Adam, Eve and the Serpent (detail) — A380

#907b, The Western Wall. #907c, Church of the Holy Sepulchre. #908b, Hand, 18th cent. bas-relief, Jewish Quarter. #908c, Rosette carving, 12th-13th cent. Crusader capital. #909, Frontispiece and detail, Schocken Bible, South Germany, ca. 1290.

1985, May 14 **Litho.** ***Perf. 13x14***

907 Sheet of 3 2.40 2.40
a.-c. A378 200s any single .70 .65

Sold for 900s.

Perf. 14x13

908 Sheet of 3 3.50 3.50
a.-c. A379 350s any single 1.10 1.10

Sold for 1500s.

Perf. 14

909 A380 800s multi 3.25 3.25
Nos. 907-909 (3) 9.15 9.15

Sold for 1200s.

The Israeli postal administration authorized the Intl. Philatelic Federation (FIP) to overprint a limited number of these souvenir sheets for sale exclusively at ISRAPHIL '85 to raise funds. The FIP overprints have control numbers and are inscribed "Under the Patronage of the Philatelic Federation" in the sheet margin. The sheets remained valid for postage but were not sold by the post office.

12th Maccabiah Games A381

1985 Festivals A382

1985, July 16 **Litho.** ***Perf. 14***

910 A381 400s Basketball .75 .75
911 A381 500s Tennis .90 .90
912 A381 600s Windsurfing 1.10 1.10
Nos. 910-912 (3) 2.75 2.75
With tabs 4.00

1985, July 16 **Litho.** ***Perf. 14***

Tabernacle utensils: 100sh, Ark of the Covenant. 150sh, Acacia showbread table. 200sh, Menora. 300sh, Incense altar.

913 A382 100s multi .20 .20
914 A382 150s multi .30 .30
915 A382 200s multi .35 .35
916 A382 300s multi .55 .55
Nos. 913-916 (4) 1.40 1.40
With tabs 2.25

A383

A384

1985, July 16 **Litho.** ***Perf. 14***

917 A383 150s Emblem, badges .40 .25
With tab .55

Intl. Youth Year.

1985, Nov. 5 **Litho.** ***Perf. 14***

918 A384 200s multi .80 .25
With tab .95

Leon Yehuda Recanati (1890-1945), financier and philanthropist.

Meir Dizengoff (1861-1936), Founder and Mayor of Tel Aviv — A385

1985, Nov. 5

919 A385 500s multi 1.00 .65
With tab 1.25

Gedera Settlement, Cent. A386

1985, Nov. 5 **Photo.** ***Perf. 13x14***

920 A386 600s multi 1.10 .80
With tab 1.40

Theodor Herzl A388

Capital, Second Temple, Jerusalem A389

The Kibbutz — A387

1985, Nov. 5 **Litho.** ***Perf. 14***

921 A387 900s multi 1.25 1.10
With tab 1.50

Designs: 1s, Corinthian, A.D. 1st cent. 3s, Ionic, 1st cent. B.C.

1986, Jan. 1 **Photo.** ***Perf. 13x14***

922 A388 1a red & ultra .20 .20
923 A388 2a green & ultra .20 .20
924 A388 3a brown & ultra .20 .20
925 A388 5a blue & ultra .20 .20
926 A388 10a org & ultra .20 .20
927 A388 20a pink & ultra .20 .20
928 A388 30a lemon & ultra .25 .25
929 A388 50a pur & ultra .45 .40
930 A389 1s multi 1.00 .95
931 A389 3s multi 2.75 2.75
Nos. 922-931 (10) 5.65 5.55
With tabs 6.25

1s and 3s designs with 1000a and 1500a values were not issued.

See Nos. 1014-1020.

Red Sea Coral A390

1986, Mar. 4 Litho. *Perf. 14*

932 A390 30a Balanophyllia .35 .35
933 A390 40a Goniopora .50 .50
934 A390 50a Dendronephthya .65 .65
Nos. 932-934 (3) 1.50 1.50
With tabs 3.00

Arthur Rubinstein (1887-1982), Pianist — A391

1986, Mar. 4 Photo. *Perf. 13x14*

935 A391 60a Picasso portraits .90 .80
With tab 1.25

Broadcasting from Jerusalem, 50th Anniv. — A392

1986, Mar. 4 Litho. *Perf. 14*

936 A392 70a Map and microphone, 1936 .90 .90
With tab 1.10

Negev Brigade Memorial, Beer Sheva — A393

1986, May 4 Litho. *Perf. 13*

937 A393 20a multicolored .30 .30
With tab .40

Memorial Day.

Al Jazzar Mosque, Akko — A394

1986, May 4 Photo. *Perf. 14x13*

938 A394 30a multicolored .40 .40
With tab .50

Id Al-Fitr Feast.

Institutes of Higher Learning in the US — A395

Designs: No. 939, 942a, Hebrew Union College, Jewish Institute of Religion, 1875, Cincinnati. No. 940, 942b, Yeshiva University, 1886, NYC. No. 941, 942c, Jewish Theological Seminary of America, 1886, NYC.

1986, May 4 Litho. *Perf. 14*

939 A395 50a multicolored .60 .60
940 A395 50a multicolored .60 .60
941 A395 50a multicolored .60 .60
Nos. 939-941 (3) 1.80 1.80
With tabs 2.25

Souvenir Sheet

942 Sheet of 3 + label 4.00 4.00
a.-c. A395 75a any single 1.25 1.25

AMERIPEX '86. Size of Nos. 942a-942c: 36x23mm. No. 942 sold for 3s.

Ben Gurion Airport, 50th Anniv. A396

1986, July 22 *Perf. 14x13*

943 A396 90a Terminal from aircraft 1.25 1.25
With tab 1.50

"No to Racism" in Graffiti — A397

1986, July 22 *Perf. 14*

944 A397 60a multicolored .90 .80
With tab 1.10

Druze Feast of Prophet Nabi Sabalan A398

1986, July 22 Photo. *Perf. 14*

945 A398 40a Tomb, Hurfeish .50 .50
With tab .60

Joseph Sprinzak (1885-1959), 1st Speaker of Knesset — A399

1986, July 22 Litho. *Perf. 13*

946 A399 80a multicolored 1.00 1.00
With tab 1.10

Worms Illuminated Mahzor, 13th Cent. — A400

1986, Sept. 23 Litho. *Perf. 13x14*

947 A400 20a Gates of Heaven .25 .25
948 A400 40a Sheqalim, prayer .50 .50
949 A400 90a Rose flower prayer introduction 1.10 1.10
Nos. 947-949 (3) 1.85 1.85
With tabs 2.25

David Ben-Gurion (1886-1973) — A401

1986, Oct. 19 Litho. *Perf. 14x13*

950 A401 1s multicolored 1.25 1.25
With tab 1.40

Souvenir Sheet

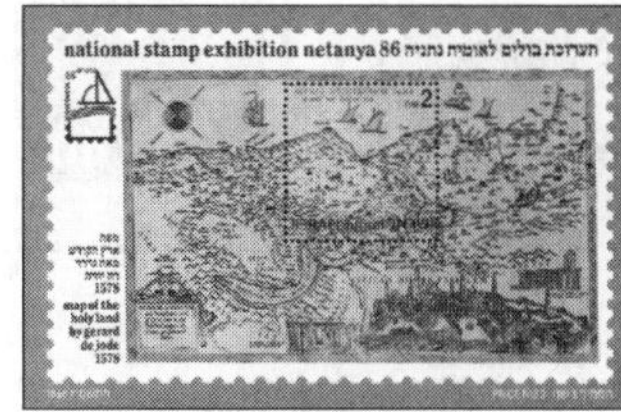

Map of the Holyland, by Gerard de Jode, 1578 — A402

1986, Oct. 19 *Perf. 14½*

951 A402 2s multicolored 4.00 3.50

NATANYA '86 Stamp Exhibition; Organized philately in Natanya, 50th anniv. Sold for 3s.

Israel Meteorological Service, 50th Anniv. — A403

1986, Dec. 18 Litho. *Perf. 13*

952 A403 50a multicolored .70 .70
With tab 1.25

Basilica of the Annunciation, Nazareth — A404

1986, Dec. 18 Litho. *Perf. 14*

953 A404 70a multicolored .90 .90
With tab 1.60

Israel Philharmonic Orchestra, 50th Anniv. — A405

1986, Dec. 18

954 A405 1.50s Bronislaw Huberman, violinist 2.25 2.00
955 A405 1.50s Arturo Toscanini, conductor 2.25 2.00
a. Pair, #954-955 4.50 4.00
With tabs 6.75

Owls A406

1987, Feb. 24 Litho. *Perf. 14x13*

956 A406 30a Bubo bubo .55 .55
957 A406 40a Otus brucei .70 .70
958 A406 50a Tyto alba .90 .90
959 A406 80a Strix butleri 1.50 1.50
Nos. 956-959 (4) 3.65 3.65
With tabs 8.00

Souvenir Sheet

960 Sheet of 4 8.50 8.50
a. A406 30a like #956 1.25 1.25
b. A406 40a like #957 1.60 1.60
c. A406 50a like #958 2.10 2.10
d. A406 80a like #959 3.25 3.25

Sold for 3s. Nos. 960a-960d do not have inscriptions below the design.

Ammunition Hill Memorial, Jerusalem A407

1987, Apr. 16 Litho. *Perf. 14*

961 A407 30a multicolored .40 .40
With tab .65

Memorial Day.

13th Hapoel Games A408

1987, Apr. 16

962 A408 90a multicolored 1.10 1.10
With tab 1.60

Souvenir Sheet

HAIFA '87 Stamp Exhibition — A409

1987, Apr. 16 *Perf. 14x13*

963 A409 2.70s No. C8 5.75 5.75

Sold for 4s.

Amateur Radio Operators — A410

1987, June 14 Litho. *Perf. 14*

964 A410 2.50s multi 3.75 3.75
With tab 4.50

World Dog Show, June 23-27 — A411

1987, June 14

965 A411 40a Saluki .90 .70
966 A411 50a Sloughi 1.10 .90
967 A411 2s Canaan 5.00 4.00
Nos. 965-967 (3) 7.00 5.60
With tabs 9.00

Clean Environment A412

1987, June 14 *Perf. 13*

968 A412 40a multicolored .75 .45
With tab .85

Rabbi Moshe Avigdor Amiel (1883-1945), Founder of Yeshivas — A413

1987, Sept. 10 Litho. *Perf. 14*

969 A413 1.40s multi 1.40 1.40
With tab 1.50

Synagogue Models, Nahum Goldmann Museum, Tel Aviv A414

Kupat Holim Health Insurance Institute, 75th Anniv. A415

1987, Sept. 10 *Perf. 13x14*

970 A414 30a Altneuschul, Prague, 13th cent. .40 .40
971 A414 50a Aleppo, Syria, 9th cent. .60 .60
972 A414 60a Florence, Italy, 19th cent. .75 .75
Nos. 970-972 (3) 1.75 1.75
With tabs 1.90

See Nos. 996-998.

1987, Sept. 10 *Perf. 14*

973 A415 1.50s multi 1.50 1.50
With tab 1.75

Pinhas Rosen (1887-1978), First Minister of Justice — A416

1987, Nov. 24 Litho. *Perf. 13*

974 A416 80a multicolored .90 .90
With tab 1.25

A417

1987, Nov. 24 *Perf. 14*

Exploration of the Holy Land, 19th cent.: 30a, Thomas Howard Molyneux (1847) and Christopher Costigan (1835). 50a, William Francis Lynch (1848). 60a, John MacGregor (1868-1869).

975 A417 30a multi .40 .40
976 A417 50a multi .65 .65
977 A417 60a multi .75 .50
Nos. 975-977 (3) 1.80 1.55
With tabs 2.00

Souvenir Sheet

978 Sheet of 3 3.50 3.50
a. A417 40a like #975 .75 .75
b. A417 50a like #976 1.00 1.00
c. A417 80a like #977 1.60 1.60

No. 978 sold for 2.50s.

A418 A419

1988, Jan. 26

979 A418 10a Computer technology .20 .20
980 A418 80a Genetic engineering .95 .95
981 A418 1.40s Medical engineering 1.60 1.60
Nos. 979-981 (3) 2.75 2.75
With tabs 3.00

Industrialization of Israel, cent.

1988, Jan. 26

982 A419 40a multicolored .50 .50
With tab .60

Water conservation.

Australia Bicentennial — A420

1988, Jan. 26 *Perf. 14*

983 A420 1s multi 1.25 1.25
With tab 1.50

Sunflower — A421

1988, Mar. 9 Photo. *Perf. 13x14*

984 A421 (30a) dk yel grn & yel .25 .25
With tab .35

A422

Design: Anne Frank (1929-45), Amsterdam house where she hid.

1988, Apr. 19 Litho.

985 A422 60a multicolored .50 .50
With tab .60

Independence 40 Stamp Exhibition, Jerusalem A423

1988, Apr. 19

Design: Modern Jerusalem.

986 A423 1s shown .90 .90
With tab 1.00

Souvenir Sheet

987 A423 2s detail from 1s 3.25 3.25

No. 987 sold for 3s.

Memorial Day A424

1988, Apr. 19 *Perf. 14x13*

988 A424 40a multicolored .35 .35
With tab .45
a. Souvenir sheet of 1 .75 .75

Natl. independence, 40th anniv. No. 988a contains one stamp like No. 988 but without copyright inscription LR. Sold for 60a.

Souvenir Sheet

Israel's 40th Anniv. Exhibition, Tel Aviv — A425

Stamps on stamps: a, No. 245. b, No. 297. c, No. 120. d, No. 96. e, Like No. 794. f, No. 252. g, No. 333. h, No. 478.

1988, June 9 Litho. *Perf. 14*

989 Sheet of 8 + label 2.50 2.50
a.-h. A425 20a any single .25 .25

Sold for 2.40s. Center label pictures Israel 40 emblem.

B'nai B'rith in Jerusalem, Cent. — A426

1988, June 27 *Perf. 14*

990 A426 70a multicolored .70 .70
With tab .75

Nature Reserves in the Negev A427

1988, June 27

991 A427 40a Ein Zin .50 .40
992 A427 60a She'Zaf .70 .60
993 A427 70a Ramon .90 .75
Nos. 991-993 (3) 2.10 1.75
With tabs 2.40

See Nos. 1052-1054, 1154-1156.

Agents Executed During World War II — A428

Portraits: 40a, Havivah Reik (1914-1944). 1.65s, Enzo Hayyim Sereni (1905-1944).

1988, Sept. 1 Litho.

994 A428 40a multicolored .35 .35
995 A428 1.65s multicolored 1.40 1.40
#994-995, with tabs 1.90

Synagogue Models Type of 1987

Models in the Nahum Goldmann Museum, Tel Aviv: 35a, Kai-Feng Fu Synagogue, 12th cent., China. 60a, Zabludow Synagogue, 17th cent., Poland. 70a, Touro Synagogue, 1763, Newport, Rhode Island, designed by Peter Harrison.

1988, Sept. 1 *Perf. 13x14*

996 A414 35a multicolored .30 .30
997 A414 60a multicolored .55 .55
998 A414 70a multicolored .65 .65
Nos. 996-998 (3) 1.50 1.50
With tabs 1.60

A429

1988, Nov. 9 *Perf. 14*

999 A429 80a multicolored .85 .85
With tab 1.00

Kristallnacht, Nazi pogrom in Germany, 50th anniv.

Moshe Dayan (1915-1981), Foreign Minister, Minister of Defense — A430

1988, Nov. 9 *Perf. 13*

1000 A430 40a multicolored .40 .40
With tab .50

Jewish Legion, 70th Anniv. A431

1988, Nov. 9 *Perf. 14*

1001 A431 2s yel brn, sepia & lem 1.60 1.60
With tab 1.75

Agricultural Achievements — A433

50a, Avocado (fruit-growing). 60a, Lilium longiflorum (horticulture). 90a, Irrigation.

1988, Dec. 22 *Perf. 14*

1004 A433 50a multicolored .45 .45
1005 A433 60a multicolored .55 .55
1006 A433 90a multicolored .85 .85
Nos. 1004-1006 (3) 1.85 1.85
With tabs 2.00

Natl. Tourism — A434

1989, Mar. 12 Litho. *Perf. 13*

1007 A434 40a Red Sea .40 .30
1008 A434 60a Dead Sea .55 .45
1009 A434 70a Mediterranean Sea .65 .50
1010 A434 1.70s Sea of Galilee 1.60 1.25
Nos. 1007-1010 (4) 3.20 2.50
With tabs 3.50

Rabbi Judah Leib Maimon (1875-1962) — A435

1989, Mar. 12 *Perf. 14*

1011 A435 1.70s multi 1.75 1.25
With tab 2.00

Rashi, Rabbi Solomon Ben Isaac (b. 1039), Talmudic Commentator — A436

1989, Mar. 12

1012 A436 4s buff & black 4.25 3.00
With tab 4.50

Memorial Day — A437

UNICEF — A438

Fallen Airmen's Memorial at Har Tayassim.

1989, Apr. 30 Litho. *Perf. 14*

1013 A437 50a multi .50 .45
With tab .60

Archaeology Type of 1986

Gates of Huldah, Temple Compound, Mt. Moriah: 40a, Rosettes and rhomboids, frieze and columns, facade of the eastern gate, 1st cent. B.C. 60a, Corinthian capital, 6th cent.

70a, Bas-relief from the Palace of Umayade Caliphs, 8th cent. 80a, Corinthian capital from the Church of Ascension on the Mount of Olives, 12-13th cent. 90a, Star of David, limestone relief, northern wall, near the new gate, Suleiman's Wall. 2s, Mamluk relief, 14th century. 10s, Carved frieze from a sepulcher entrance, end of the Second Temple Period.

1988-90 Litho. *Perf. 14*

1014 A389 40a multi .35 .30
1015 A389 60a multi .50 .40
1016 A389 70a multi .55 .40
1017 A389 80a multi .65 .45
1018 A389 90a multi .65 .45
1019 A389 2s multi 1.40 .95
1020 A389 10s multi 8.75 5.75
Nos. 1014-1020 (7) 12.85 8.70
With tabs 14.00

Issued: 40a, 60a, 12/22/88; 70a, 80a, 6/11/89; 10s, 4/30/89; 90a, 10/17/89; 2s, 6/12/90.

1989, Apr. 30 *Perf. 14*

1022 A438 90a multicolored .80 .65
With tab .90

Moshe Smoira (1888-1961), 1st Pres. of Israeli Supreme Court — A439

1989, June 11 Litho. *Perf. 13*

1023 A439 90a deep blue .80 .65
With tab .90

13th Maccabiah Games, July 3-13 A440

1989, June 11 *Perf. 13x14*

1024 A440 80a multi .80 .65
With tab .90

Ducks — A441

Designs: a, Garganey. b, Mallard. c, Teal. d, Shelduck.

1989, July 18 Litho. *Perf. 14*

1025 Strip of 4 5.75 5.75
With tabs 9.00
a.-d. A441 80a any single 1.25 .85

Souvenir Sheet

1025E Sheet of 4 7.00 7.00
f. A441 80a like No. 1025d 1.60 1.60
g. A441 80a like No. 1025b 1.60 1.60
h. A441 80a like No. 1025a 1.60 1.60
i. A441 80a like No. 1025c 1.60 1.60

World Stamp Expo '89. No. 1025E contains four 29x33mm stamps. Sold for 5s.

Graphic Design Industry — A442

1989, July 18

1026 A442 1s multi 1.00 .75
With tab 1.10

Souvenir Sheet

French Revolution, Bicent. — A443

1989, July 7

1027 A443 3.50s multi 6.50 6.50

Sold for 5s.

Hebrew Language Council, Cent. — A444

1989, Sept. 3 Litho. *Perf. 13x14*

1028 A444 1s multi .95 .70
With tab 1.10

Rabbi Yehuda Hai Alkalai (1798-1878), Zionist — A445

1989, Sept. 3 *Perf. 14*

1029 A445 2.50s multi 5.00 1.75
With tab 6.50

Mizrah Festival A446

Paper cutouts: 50a, Menorah and lions, by Gadoliahu Neminsky, Holbenisk, Ukraine, 1921. 70a, Menorah and hands, Morocco, 19th-20th cent. 80a, "Misrah," hunting scene and deer, Germany, 1818.

1989, Sept. 3 *Perf. 14x13*

1030 A446 50a multi .45 .35
1031 A446 70a multi .65 .50
1032 A446 80a multi .75 .55
Nos. 1030-1032 (3) 1.85 1.40
With tabs 2.00

Tevel '89 Youth Stamp Exhibition, Oct. 15-21 A447

1989, Oct. 12 Photo. *Perf. 13x14*

1033 A447 50a multi .45 .30
With tab .60

1st Israeli Stamp Day — A448

1989, Oct. 17 Litho. *Perf. 14*

1034 A448 1s multi .85 .75
With tab .95

Special Occasions A449

1989, Nov. 17 Photo. *Perf. 13½x14*

1035 A449 (50a) Good luck .45 .35
1036 A449 (50a) With love .45 .35
a. Booklet pane of 10 5.00
1037 A449 (50a) See you again .45 .35
a. Booklet pane of 10 + 2 labels 5.75
b. Sheet of 20 + 5 labels 11.50
Nos. 1035-1037 (3) 1.35 1.05
With tabs 1.75

Nos. 1036a, 1037a contain 5 tete-beche pairs, No. 1037b contains 10 tete-beche pairs.

#1037a-1037b had value of 80a when released.

Issued: No. 1036a, Aug. 7, 1990. Nos. 1037a-1037b, June 22, 1993.

See Nos. 1059-1061, 1073-1075.

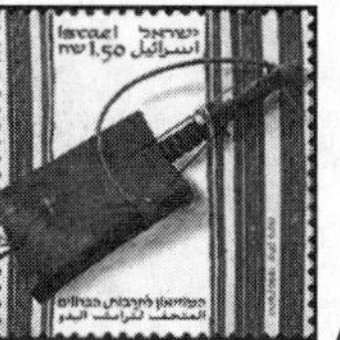

A450

Design: Tapestry and Rebab, a Stringed Instrument, from the Museum of Bedouin Culture.

1990, Feb. 13 Litho. *Perf. 13*

1038 A450 1.50s multicolored 1.25 .95
With tab 1.50

The Circassians in Israel — A451

1990, Feb. 13 Photo. *Perf. 14x13*

Designs: Circassian folk dancers.

1039 A451 1.50s multicolored 1.25 .95
With tab 1.50

Rehovot City, Cent. A452

1990, Feb. 13 *Perf. 14*

1040 A452 2s multicolored 1.90 1.40
With tab 2.25

Souvenir Sheet

Isaiah's Vision of Eternal Peace, by Mordecai Ardon — A453

Series of 3 stained-glass windows, The Hall of Eternal Jewishness and Humanism, Hebrew University Library, Jerusalem: a, "Roads to Jerusalem" (inscription at L). b, Isaiah's prophecy of broken guns beaten into ploughshares (inscription at R).

1990, Apr. 17 Litho. *Perf. 14*

1041 Sheet of 2 5.00 5.00
a.-b. A453 1.50s any single 2.50 2.50

Stamp World London '90. Sold for 4.50s. Also exists imperf.

Architecture — A454

Design: 75a, School, Deganya Kibbutz, 1930. 1.10s, Dining hall, Kibbutz Tel Yosef by Leopold Krakauer, 1933. 1.20s, Engel House by Ze'ev Rechter, 1933. 1.40s, Home of Dr. Chaim Weizmann, Rehovot by Erich Mendelsohn, 1936. 1.60s, Jewish Agency for Palestine, Jerusalem, by Yohanan Ratner, 1932.

1990-92 Photo. *Perf. 14x13½*

1044 A454 75a black, pale grn & buff .60 .55
1046 A454 1.10s blk, yel & grn .95 .95
1047 A454 1.20s blk, bl & yel 1.10 1.10
1049 A454 1.40s blk, lt lil & buff 1.25 1.25
1051 A454 1.60s multicolored 1.10 1.10
a. Dotted rose lilac background 1.10 1.10
Nos. 1044-1051 (5) 5.00 4.95
With tabs 5.25

No. 1051 has a solid bluish lilac background.

Issued: 75a, 4/17; 1.10s, 1.20s, 12/12; 1.40s, 4/9/91; 1.60s, 4/26/92; #1051a, 7/14/96.

This is an expanding set. Numbers will change if necessary.

Nature Reserves Type of 1988

1990, Apr. 17 Litho. *Perf. 14*

1052 A427 60a Gamla, Yehudiyya .55 .45
1053 A427 80a Huleh .75 .55
1054 A427 90a Mt. Meron .90 .65
Nos. 1052-1054 (3) 2.20 1.65
With tabs 2.50

Memorial Day A456

1990, Apr. 17 Photo. *Perf. 13x14*

1055 A456 60a Artillery Corps Memorial .60 .45
With tab .80

Intl. Folklore Festival, Haifa — A457

1990, June 12 Litho. *Perf. 14*

1056	1.90s Denom at UL	2.50 2.50
1057	1.90s Denom at UR	2.50 2.50
a.	A457 Pair, #1056-1057	5.00 5.00
	With tabs	6.00

Hagana, 70th Anniv. — A459

1990, June 12

1058	A459 1.50s multicolored	1.40 1.40
	With tab	1.50

Special Occasions Type of 1989

1990, June 12 *Perf. 13½x14*

1059	A449 55a Good luck	.50 .35
1060	A449 80a See you again	.75 .50
1061	A449 1s With love	.95 .60
	Nos. 1059-1061 (3)	2.20 1.45
	With tabs	2.50

Spice Boxes — A460

55a, Austro-Hungarian spice box, 19th cent. 80a, Italian, 19th cent. 1s, German, 18th cent.

1990, Sept. 4 Litho. *Perf. 13x14*

1062	A460 55a sil, gray & blk	.40 .40
1063	A460 80a sil, gray & blk	.60 .60
1064	A460 1s multicolored	.75 .75
a.	Bklt. pane of 6 (3 #1062, 2 #1063, #1064)	4.00 4.00
	Nos. 1062-1064 (3)	1.75 1.75
	With tabs	1.90

A461

1990, Sept. 4 *Perf. 13*

1065	A461 1.10s Aliya absorption	.85 .85
	With tab	.90

Electronic Mail — A462

1990, Sept. 4 *Perf. 14x13*

1066	A462 1.20s black & grn	.90 .90
	With tab	1.00

Souvenir Sheet

Beersheba '90 Stamp Exhibition — A463

1990, Sept. 4 *Perf. 13x14*

1067	A463 3s multicolored	4.75 4.75

Sold for 4s.

Computer Games — A464

1990, Dec. 12 Litho. *Perf. 13x14*

1068	A464 60a Basketball	.45 .45
1069	A464 60a Chess	.45 .45
1070	A464 60a Auto racing	.45 .45
	Nos. 1068-1070 (3)	1.35 1.35
	With tabs	1.50

Ze'ev Jabotinsky (1880-1940), Zionist Leader — A465

1990, Dec. 12 Litho. *Perf. 13x14*

1071	A465 1.90s multicolored	1.40 1.40
	With tab	1.50

Philately Day — A466

1990, Dec. 12 *Perf. 14*

1072	A466 1.20s P.O., Yafo, #5	.90 .90
	With tab	1.00

Special Occasions Type of 1989

1991, Feb. 19 Photo. *Perf. 13½x14*

1073	A449 (60a) Happy birthday	.45 .35
1074	A449 (60a) Keep in touch	.45 .35
a.	Booklet pane of 10 + 2 labels	5.75
b.	Sheet of 20 + 5 labels	11.50
1075	A449 (60a) Greetings	.45 .35
	Nos. 1073-1075 (3)	1.35 1.05
	With tabs	1.50

No. 1074a contains 5 tete-beche pairs. No. 1074b contains 10 tete-beche pairs.

Nos. 1074a-1074b had value of 85a when released.

Issued: Nos. 1074a-1074b, 4/18/94.

Famous Women A467

Designs: No. 1076, Sarah Aaronsohn (1890-1917), World War I heroine. No. 1077, Rahel Bluwstein (1890-1931), poet. No. 1078, Lea Goldberg (1911-1970), poet.

1991, Feb. 19 *Perf. 14*

1076	A467 1.30s multicolored	1.10 1.10
1077	A467 1.30s multicolored	1.10 1.10
1078	A467 1.30s multicolored	1.10 1.10
	Nos. 1076-1078 (3)	3.30 3.30
	With tabs	3.50

See Nos. 1096-1097, 1102-1103.

Hadera, Cent. — A468

1991, Feb. 19 *Perf. 13*

1079	A468 2.50s multicolored	2.00 2.00
	With tab	2.25

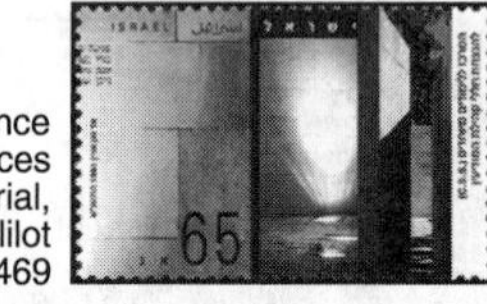
Intelligence Services Memorial, G'lilot A469

1991, Apr. 9 Litho. *Perf. 14*

1080	A469 65a multicolored	.60 .60
	With tab	.70

14th Hapoel Games A470

1991, Apr. 9

1081	A470 60a multicolored	.55 .50
1082	A470 90a multicolored	.75 .70
1083	A470 1.10s multicolored	.95 .90
	Nos. 1081-1083 (3)	2.25 2.10
	With tabs	2.50

Electrification A471

Designs: 70a, First power station, Tel Aviv, 1923. 90a, Yarden Power Station, Naharayim, 1932. 1.20s, Rutenberg Power Station, Ashqelon, 1991.

1991, June 11 Litho. *Perf. 13*

1084	A471 70a multicolored	.65 .60
1085	A471 90a multicolored	.80 .75
1086	A471 1.20s multicolored	1.10 1.00
	Nos. 1084-1086 (3)	2.55 2.35
	With tabs	2.75

Rabbi Shimon Hakham (1843-1910) A472

1991, June 11

1087	A472 2.10s multicolored	1.90 1.50
	With tab	2.00

Souvenir Sheet

Postal and Philatelic Museum, Tel Aviv — A473

Israel #5, Palestine #70, Turkey #133.

1991, June 11 *Perf. 14x13*

1088	A473 3.40s multicolored	4.50 4.50

No. 1088 sold for 5s. Exists imperf.

A474

Jewish Festivals: 65a, Man blowing ram's horn, Rosh Hashanah. 1s, Father blessing children, Yom Kippur. 1.20s, Family seated at harvest table, Sukkoth.

1991, Aug. 27 Litho. *Perf. 14*

1089	A474 65a multicolored	.50 .50
1090	A474 1s multicolored	.75 .75
1091	A474 1.20s multicolored	.90 .90
	Nos. 1089-1091 (3)	2.15 2.15
	With tabs	2.50

Jewish Chronicle, 150th Anniv. — A475

1991, Aug. 27

1092	A475 1.50s multicolored	1.10 1.10
	With tab	1.25

Baron Maurice De Hirsch (1831-1896), Founder of Jewish Colonization Assoc. — A476

1991, Aug. 27 *Perf. 14*

1093	A476 1.60s multicolored	1.25 1.25
	With tab	1.40

Souvenir Sheet

Haifa, by Gustav Bauernfeind — A477

1991, Aug. 27 *Perf. 14x13*

1094	A477 3s multicolored	6.25 5.00

Haifa '91, Israeli-Polish Philatelic Exhibition. Sold for 4s.

Philately Day — A478

1991, Dec. 2 Litho. *Perf. 13*

1095 A478 70a #2 on piece	.50	.50
With tab	.60	

Famous Women Type of 1991

Designs: 1s, Rahel Yanait Ben-Zvi (1886-1979), politician. 1.10s, Dona Gracia (Nasi, 1510?-1569), philanthropist.

1991, Dec. 2 Litho. *Perf. 14*

1096 A467 1s multicolored	.70	.70
1097 A467 1.10s multicolored	.75	.75
#1096-1097, with tabs	1.60	

1992 Summer Olympics, Barcelona — A479

1991, Dec. 2

1098 A479 1.10s multicolored	.85	.85
With tab	1.40	

Lehi — A480

Etzel — A481

1991, Dec. 2 *Perf. 14*

1099 A480 1.50s multicolored	1.00	1.00
With tab	1.25	

1991, Dec. 2

1100 A481 1.50s blk & red	1.00	1.00
With tab	1.25	

Wolfgang Amadeus Mozart, Death Bicent. — A482

1991, Dec. 2 *Perf. 13*

1101 A482 2s multicolored	2.75	1.75
With tab	3.25	
a. Booklet pane of 4	11.00	

One pair in No. 1101a is tete beche.

Famous Women Type of 1991

80a, Hanna Rovina (1889-1980), actress. 1.30s, Rivka Guber (1902-81), educator.

1992, Feb. 18 Litho. *Perf. 14*

1102 A467 80a multicolored	.50	.50
1103 A467 1.30s multicolored	.90	.90
#1102-1103, with tabs	1.50	

Sea of Galilee A483

Anemone A483a

1992, Feb. 18

1104 A483 85a Trees	1.50	.70
1105 A483 85a Sailboat	1.50	.70
1106 A483 85a Fish	1.50	.70
a. Strip of 3, #1104-1106	4.50	2.10
With tabs	5.00	

1992, Feb. 18 Photo. *Perf. 13x14*

1107 A483a (75a) multi	.50	.45
With tab	.60	

PALMAH, 50th Anniv. A484

The Samaritans A485

1992, Feb. 18 Litho. *Perf. 14*

1108 A484 1.50s multicolored	1.00	1.00
With tab	1.25	

1992, Feb. 18

1109 A485 2.60s multicolored	1.75	1.75
With tab	2.25	

Rabbi Hayyim Joseph David Azulai (1724-1806) A486

Rabbi Joseph Hayyim Ben Elijah (1834-1909) A487

1992, Apr. 26 *Perf. 13*

1110 A486 85a multicolored	.60	.60
Perf. 14		
1111 A487 1.20s multicolored	.80	.80
#1110-1111, with tabs	1.75	

Discovery of America, 500th Anniv. A488

1992, Apr. 26 *Perf. 14*

1112 A488 1.60s multicolored	1.25	1.25
With tab	1.40	

Memorial Day — A488a

1992, Apr. 26 Litho. *Perf. 13*

1113 A488a 85a multicolored	.55	.55
With tab	.60	

Souvenir Sheet

Expulsion of Jews from Spain, 500th Anniv. A489

Designs: No. 1114a, 80a, Map of Palestine. b, 1.10s, Map of Italy, Sicily, Greece and central Mediterranean. c, 1.40s, Map of Spain and Portugal.

1992, Apr. 26 *Perf. 14*

1114 A489 Sheet of 3, #a.-c.	3.50	3.50

Jaffa-Jerusalem Railway, Cent. — A490

Different train and four scenes on each stamp showing railroad equipment and memorabilia.

1992

1115 A490 85a multicolored	.55	.55
1116 A490 1s multicolored	.70	.70
1117 A490 1.30s multicolored	.90	.90
1118 A490 1.60s multicolored	1.10	1.10
#1115-1118, with tabs	3.50	
a. Bklt. pane of 4, #1115-1118	3.25	

Souvenir Sheet

1118B Sheet of 4 + 4 labels	3.75	3.75
c. A490 50a like #1118	.90	.90
d. A490 50a like #1117	.90	.90
e. A490 50a like #1115	.90	.90
f. A490 50a like #1116	.90	.90

Nos. 1115 and 1118, 1116 and 1117 are tete beche in No. 1118a. Nos. 1118c and 1118f, 1118d and 1118e are tete beche in No. 1118B.

Issued: #1118B, Sept. 17; others June 16.

Rabbi Hayyim Benatar (1696-1743) A491

Rabbi Shalom Sharabi (1720-1777) A492

1992, June 16 *Perf. 13*

1119 A491 1.30s multicolored	.90	.90
1120 A492 3s multicolored	2.00	2.00
#1119-1120, with tabs	3.25	

Jewish Natl. & University Library, Jerusalem, Cent. — A493

85a, Parables, 1491. 1s, Italian manuscript, 15th cent. 1.20s, Bible translation by Martin Buber.

1992, Sept. 17 Litho. *Perf. 13x14*

1121 A493 85a multicolored	.55	.55
1122 A493 1s multicolored	.65	.65
1123 A493 1.20s multicolored	.80	.80
Nos. 1121-1123 (3)	2.00	2.00
With tabs	2.25	

Supreme Court A494

1992, Sept. 17 *Perf. 14*

1124 A494 3.60s multicolored	2.10	2.10
With tab	2.25	

Wild Animals A495

#1125, Panthera pardus saxicolor. #1126, Elephas maximus. #1127, Pan troglodytes. #1128, Panthera leo persica.

1992, Sept. 17

1125 A495 50a multicolored	.40	.40
1126 A495 50a multicolored	.40	.40
1127 A495 50a multicolored	.40	.40
1128 A495 50a multicolored	.40	.40
a. Strip of 4, #1125-1128	1.60	1.60
With tabs	1.75	

European Unification A496

1992, Dec. 8 Litho. *Perf. 13*

1129 A496 1.50s multicolored	.90	.90
With tab	1.00	

Stamp Day.

First Hebrew Film, 75th Anniv. — A497

Films: 80a, Liberation of the Jews, 1918. 2.70s, Oded, the Vagabond, 1932, first Hebrew feature film. 3.50s, The Promised Land, 1935, first Hebrew talkie.

1992, Dec. 8

1130 A497 80a multicolored	.60	.60
1131 A497 2.70s multicolored	1.90	1.90
1132 A497 3.50s multicolored	2.50	2.50
Nos. 1130-1132 (3)	5.00	5.00
With tabs	5.25	

Birds — A498

1992-98 Photo. *Perf. 13x14*

1133 A498 10a Wallcreeper	.20	.20
1134 A498 20a Tristram's grackle	.20	.20
1135 A498 30a White wagtail	.20	.20
1137 A498 50a Palestine sunbird	.30	.20
1141 A498 85a Sinai rosefinch	.45	.30
1142 A498 90a Swallow	.60	.60
1142A A498 1s Trumpeter finch	.65	.65
b. Violet background	.65	.65
1143 A498 1.30s Graceful warbler	.70	.45
1144 A498 1.50s Black-eared wheatear	.85	.55
1146 A498 1.70s Common bulbul	.85	.55
Nos. 1133-1146 (10)	5.00	3.90
With tabs	5.25	

No. 1142A has a gray background.

Souvenir Sheet

Designs: a, like #1133. b, like #1137. c, like #1135. d, like #1134. e, like #1141. f, like #1144. g, like #1146. h, like #1142A. i, like #1143. j, like #1142.

Litho. *Perf. 14*

1152 Sheet of 10	2.00	2.00
a.-j. A498 30a Any single	.20	.20

Nos. 1152a-1152j, issued for China '96, 9th Asian Intl. Philatelic Exhibition, have color variations and a gray border.

Issued: 10a, 20a, 30a, 90a, 12/8; 1.30s, 1.70s, 12/9/93; 50a, 1.50s, 2/16/93; 85a, 2/8/94; 1s, 6/7/95; #1152, 4/17/96; #1142Ab, 11/22/98.

This is an expanding set. Numbers may change.

Menachem Begin (1913-92), Prime Minister 1977-83 — A499

1993, Feb. 16 Litho. *Perf. 13*

1153 A499 80a multicolored .45 .45
With tab .50

Nature Reserves Type of 1988

1993, Feb. 16 *Perf. 14*

1154 A427 1.20s Hof Dor .70 .70
1155 A427 1.50s Nahal Ammud .90 .90
1156 A427 1.70s Nahal Ayun .95 .95
Nos. 1154-1156 (3) 2.55 2.55
With tabs 2.75

Baha'i World Center, Haifa — A500

1993, Feb. 16 *Perf. 13*

1157 A500 3.50s multicolored 3.25 2.25
With tab 5.25

Medical Corps Memorial — A501

1993, Apr. 18 Litho. *Perf. 13*

1158 A501 80a multicolored .45 .45
With tab .55

Scientific Concepts A502

Warsaw Ghetto Uprising, 50th Anniv. A503

1993, Apr. 18 *Perf. 14*

1159 A502 80a Principle of lift .50 .50
1160 A502 80a Waves .50 .50
1161 A502 80a Color mixing .50 .50
1162 A502 80a Eye's memory .50 .50
a. Strip of 4, #1159-1162 2.00 2.00
With tabs 2.25

1993, Apr. 18 *Perf. 14*

1163 A503 1.20s gray, black & yel .80 .80
With tab .85

See Poland No. 3151.

Independence, 45th Anniv. — A504

1993, Apr. 18 *Perf. 14*

1164 A504 3.60s multicolored 2.25 2.25
With tab 2.50

Giulio Racah (1909-1965), Physicist — A505

1.20s, Aharon Katchalsky-Katzi (1913-72), chemist.

1993, June 29 Photo. *Perf. 13x14*

1165 A505 80a magenta, bister & blue .45 .45
1166 A505 1.20s magenta, bister & blue .65 .65
#1165-1166, with tabs 1.25

Traffic Safety — A506

Fight Against Drugs — A507

Children's drawings: 80a, Family crossing street. 1.20s, Traffic signs. 1.50s, Traffic director with hand as face.

1993, June 29 Litho. *Perf. 14*

1167 A506 80a multicolored .50 .50
1168 A506 1.20s multicolored .80 .80
1169 A506 1.50s multicolored .95 .95
Nos. 1167-1169 (3) 2.25 2.25
With tabs 2.50

1993, June 29 *Perf. 14*

1170 A507 2.80s multicolored 1.75 1.75
With tab 1.90

14th Maccabiah Games A508

1993, June 29 *Perf. 14*

1171 A508 3.60s multicolored 2.25 2.25
With tab 2.50

Respect for the Elderly A509

Festivals A510

1993, Aug. 22 Litho. *Perf. 14*

1172 A509 80a multicolored .50 .50
With tab .55

1993, Aug. 22 *Perf. 14*

1173 A510 80a Wheat .55 .55
1174 A510 1.20s Grapes .75 .75
1175 A510 1.50s Olives .95 .95
Nos. 1173-1175 (3) 2.25 2.25
With tabs 2.50

Environmental Protection — A511

1993, Aug. 22

1176 A511 1.20s multicolored .80 .80
With tab .85

B'nai B'rith, 150th Anniv. — A512

1993, Aug. 22 *Perf. 13*

1177 A512 1.50s multicolored .90 .90
With tab 1.00

Souvenir Sheet

Telafila '93, Israel-Romania Philatelic Exhibition — A513

3.60s, Immigrant Ship, by Marcel Janco.

1993, Aug. 21 Litho. *Perf. 14x13*

1178 A513 3.60s multicolored 2.50 2.50

Hebrew Magazines for Children, Cent. A514

1993, Dec. 9 Litho. *Perf. 14*

1179 A514 1.50s multicolored .90 .90
With tab 1.00

Philately Day.

Hanukkah A515

Hanukkah lamp with candles lit and: 90a, Oil lamp, Talmudic Period. 1.30s, Hanukkah Lamp, Eretz Israel carved stone, 20th cent. 2s, Lighting the Hanukkah Lamp, Rothschild Miscellany illuminated manuscript, c. 1470. #1183, Moroccan lamp, Mazagan. #1184: Folding Hanukkah Lamp, Lodz Ghetto, 1944. 2.10s, Coin of the Bar-Kokhba War. 1.80s, Cubic copper savivon (dreidel). 2.15s, Hanukkah lamp "Mattathias the Hasmonean," by Boris Schatz.

1993-99

1180 A515 90a multicolored .55 .55
1181 A515 1.30s multicolored .80 .80
1182 A515 2s multicolored 1.25 1.25
1183 A515 1.50s multicolored .90 .90
1184 A515 1.50s multicolored 1.00 1.00
1185 A515 2.10s multicolored 1.25 1.25
1186 A515 1.80s multicolored 1.00 1.00
1187 A515 2.15s multicolored 1.10 1.10
Nos. 1180-1187 (8) 7.85 7.85
With tabs 8.75

The numbering of this set reflects the lighting of the candles on the Menorah.

Issued: 90a, 1.30s, 2s, 12/9/93; #1183, 11/27/94; #1184, 12/14/95; #1185-1186, 12/23/97; 2.15s, 1/5/99.

This is an expanding set. Numbers have been reserved for additional values.

Beetles A516

#1189, Graphopterus serrator. #1190, Potosia cuprea. #1191, Coccinella septempunctata. #1192, Chlorophorus varius.

1994, Feb. 8 Litho. *Perf. 14*

1189 A516 85a multicolored .45 .40
1190 A516 85a multicolored .45 .40
1191 A516 85a multicolored .45 .40
1192 A516 85a multicolored .45 .40
a. Bklt. pane, 2 each #1189-1192 4.25
Nos. 1189-1192 (4) 1.80 1.60
With tabs 1.90

Health — A517

1994, Feb. 8 *Perf. 13*

1193 A517 85a Exercise .55 .40
1194 A517 1.30s Don't smoke .75 .60
1195 A517 1.60s Eat sensibly .95 .75
Nos. 1193-1195 (3) 2.25 1.75
With tabs 2.50

Mordecai Haffkine (1860-1930), Developer of Cholera Vaccine — A518

1994, Feb. 8 *Perf. 14*

1196 A518 3.85s multicolored 2.25 1.75
With tab 2.50

Intl. Style Architecture in Tel Aviv, 1930-39 A519

#1197, Citrus House, by Karl Rubin, 1936-38. #1198, Assuta Hospital, by Yosef Neufeld, 1934-35. #1199, Cooperative Workers' Housing, by Arieh Sharon, 1934-36.

1994, Apr. 5 Litho. *Perf. 14*

1197 A519 85a multicolored .50 .50
1198 A519 85a multicolored .50 .50
1199 A519 85a multicolored .50 .50
Nos. 1197-1199 (3) 1.50 1.50
With tabs 1.60

Memorial Day — A520

85a, Monument to fallen soldiers of Communications, Electronics & Computer Corps, Yehud.

1994, Apr. 5 Litho. *Perf. 14*

1200 A520 85a multicolored .50 .50
With tab .55

Prevent Violence — A521

1994, Apr. 5 *Perf. 13*

1201 A521 3.85s black & red 2.10 2.10
With tab 2.25

Saul Adler (1895-1966), Scientist — A522

1994, Apr. 5 *Perf. 14*

1202 A522 4.50s multicolored 2.60 2.60
With tab 2.75

Hot Air Ballooning A523

#1203, Filling balloon. #1204, Balloons in flight. #1205, Marking target.

1994, June 21 Litho. *Perf. 14*

1203 A523 85a multicolored .50 .50
1204 A523 85a multicolored .50 .50
1205 A523 85a multicolored .50 .50
Nos. 1203-1205 (3) 1.50 1.50
With tabs 1.60

Tarbut Elementary Schools, 75th Anniv. A524

1994, June 21

1206 A524 1.30s multicolored .80 .80
With tab .90

Antoine de St. Exupery (1900-44) A525

1994, June 21

1207 A525 5s multicolored 3.00 3.00
With tab 3.25

Intl. Olympic Committee, Cent. — A526

Peace — A527

1994, June 21

1208 A526 2.25s multicolored 1.40 1.40
With tab 1.50

1994, Aug. 23 Litho. *Perf. 14*

1209 A527 90a multicolored .55 .55
With tab .60

Peace Between Arabs and Israelis.

Children's Drawings of Bible Stories A528

Designs: 85a, Adam and Eve. 1.30s, Jacob's Dream. 1.60s, Moses in the Bulrushes. 4s, Parting of the Red Sea.

1994, Aug. 23

1210 A528 85a multicolored .50 .50
1211 A528 1.30s multicolored .80 .80
1212 A528 1.60s multicolored .95 .95
Nos. 1210-1212 (3) 2.25 2.25
With tabs 2.50

Souvenir Sheet

Perf. 13x14

1213 A528 4s multicolored 2.75 2.75

No. 1213 contains one 40x51mm stamp.

Immigration to Israel — A529

1994, Aug. 23 *Perf. 13*

1214 A529 1.40s Third Aliya .80 .80
1215 A529 1.70s Fourth Aliya .95 .95
#1214-1215, with tabs 1.90

Israel-Jordan Peace Treaty — A530

1994, Oct. 26 Litho. *Perf. 14*

1216 A530 3.50s multicolored 2.00 2.00
With tab 2.25

Public Transportation — A531

Designs: 90a, Ford Model T's, 1920's. 1.40s, White Super buses, 1940's. 1.70s, Leyland Royal Tiger buses, 1960's.

1994, Nov. 27

1217 A531 90a multicolored .55 .55
1218 A531 1.40s multicolored .90 .90
1219 A531 1.70s multicolored 1.00 1.00
Nos. 1217-1219 (3) 2.45 2.45
With tabs 2.75

Computerization of Post Offices — A532

1994, Nov. 27

1220 A532 3s multicolored 1.90 1.90
With tab 2.00

Dreyfus Affair, Cent. A533

1994, Nov. 27

1221 A533 4.10s multicolored 2.50 2.50
With tab 2.75

Outdoor Sculpture A534

Designs: 90a, Serpentine, by Itzhak Danziger (1916-77), Yarkon Park, Tel Aviv. 1.40s, Stabile, by Alexander Calder (1898-1976), Mount Herzl, Jerusalem. 1.70s, Gate to the Hall of Remembrance, by David Palombo (1920-66), Yad Vashem, Jerusalem.

1995, Feb. 7 Litho. *Perf. 14x13*

1222 A534 90a multicolored .55 .55
1223 A534 1.40s multicolored .90 .90
1224 A534 1.70s multicolored 1.00 1.00
Nos. 1222-1224 (3) 2.45 2.45
With tabs 2.75

Jewish Composers A535

Title of work, composer: No. 1225, Schelomo, by Ernest Bloch (1880-1959). No. 1226, Symphony No. 1 - Jeremiah, by Leonard Bernstein (1918-90).

1995, Feb. 7

1225 A535 4.10s multicolored 2.50 2.50
1226 A535 4.10s multicolored 2.50 2.50
#1225-1226, with tabs 5.50

See Nos. 1231-1232, 1274-1275.

Ordnance Corps Monument, Netanya — A536

1995, Apr. 25 Litho. *Perf. 13*

1227 A536 1s multicolored .65 .65
With tab .70

End of World War II, Liberation of Concentration Camps, 50th Anniv. — A537

1995, Apr. 25 *Perf. 14x13*

1228 A537 1s multicolored .65 .65
With tab .70

Souvenir Sheet

1229 A537 2.50s like #1228 1.60 1.60

No. 1229 contains one 51x40mm stamp.

UN, 50th Anniv. A538

1995, Apr. 25 *Perf. 14*

1230 A538 1.50s multicolored .90 .90
With tab 1.00

Composer Type of 1995

#1231, Arnold Schoenberg (1874-1951). #1232, Darius Milhaud (1892-1974).

1995, Apr. 25

1231 A535 2.40s multicolored 1.50 1.50
1232 A535 2.40s multicolored 1.50 1.50
#1231-1232, with tabs 3.25

Souvenir Sheet

Jewish Volunteers to British Army in World War II — A539

Illustration reduced.

1995, Apr. 25

1233 A539 2.50s multicolored 1.75 1.75
With tab 2.00

15th Hapoel Games, Ramat Gan A540

1995, June 7 Litho. *Perf. 14*

1234 A540 1s Kayak .65 .65
With tab .70

Kites — A541

Designs: No. 1235, Hexagonal "Tiara" kite, bird-shaped kite, rhombic Eddy kite. No. 1236, Drawing of kite glider, "Cody War Kite," box kite. No. 1237, Rhombic aerobatic kites, aerobatic "Delta" kite, drawing by Otto Lilienthal.

1995, June 7

1235 1s multicolored .65 .65
1236 1s multicolored .65 .65
1237 1s multicolored .65 .65
a. A541 Strip of 3, #1235-1237 2.00 2.00
With tabs 2.25

Children's Books A542

Designs: 1s, Stars in a Bucket, by Anda Amir-Pinkerfeld. 1.50s, Hurry, Run, Dwarfs, by Miriam Yallan-Stekelis. 1.80s, Daddy's Big Umbrella, by Levin Kipnis.

1995, June 7

1238 A542 1s multicolored .65 .65
1239 A542 1.50s multicolored 1.00 1.00
1240 A542 1.80s multicolored 1.25 1.25
Nos. 1238-1240 (3) 2.90 2.90
With tabs 3.25

Zim Israel Navigation Co. Ltd., 50th Anniv. A543

1995, June 7

1241 A543 4.40s multicolored 3.00 3.00
With tab 3.25

Festivals A544

Designs: 1s, Elijah's Chair for circumcision, linen cloth. 1.50s, Tallit bag, usually a Bar-

Mitzvah gift. 1.80s, Marriage Stone for breaking glass at wedding, cloth.

1995, Sept. 4 Litho. *Perf. 14*

1242 A544 1s multicolored .65 .65
1243 A544 1.50s multicolored 1.00 1.00
1244 A544 1.80s multicolored 1.25 1.25
Nos. 1242-1244 (3) 2.90 2.90
With tabs 3.25

Jerusalem, 3000th Anniv. A545

Designs: 1s, 6th Cent. mosaic pavement, Gaza Synagogue. 1.50s, 19th Cent. illustration of city from map of Eretz Israel, by Rabbi Pinie of Safed. 1.80s, Aerial photograph of Knesset, Supreme Court.

1995, Sept. 4

1245 A545 1s multicolored .65 .65
1246 A545 1.50s multicolored 1.00 1.00
1247 A545 1.80s multicolored 1.25 1.25
Nos. 1245-1247 (3) 2.90 2.90
With tabs 3.25

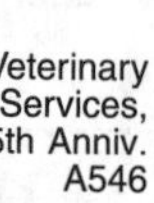

Veterinary Services, 75th Anniv. A546

1995, Sept. 4

1248 A546 4.40s multicolored 3.00 3.00
With tab 3.25

Yitzhak Rabin (1922-95), Prime Minister A547

1995, Dec. 5

1249 A547 5s multicolored 3.25 3.25
With tab 3.50

Fire Fighting and Rescue Service, 70th Anniv. A548

Designs: No. 1250, Fighting fire. No. 1251, Rescue vehicle, fireman beside car.

1995, Dec. 14

1250 A548 1s multicolored .65 .65
1251 A548 1s multicolored .65 .65
#1250-1251, with tabs 1.50

Model Planes A549

1995, Dec. 14

1252 A549 1.80s multicolored 1.25 1.25
With tab 1.40

Philately Day.

Motion Pictures, Cent. A550

Silhouettes of people in theater viewing: 4.40s, Marx Brothers, Simone Signoret, Peter Sellers, Danny Kaye, Al Jolson.

1995, Dec. 14

1253 A550 4.40s multicolored 3.00 3.00
With tab 3.25

Souvenir Sheet

Jerusalem, City of David, 3000th Anniv. A551

Designs: a, Mosaic pavement of King David playing harp, Gaza Synagogue, 6th cent. CE. b, Map of Eretz Israel drawn by Rabbi Pinie, 19th cent. c, Present day aerial view of Knesset and Supreme Court.

1995, Dec. 16

1254 Sheet of 3 2.75 2.75
a. A551 1s multicolored .60 .60
b. A551 1.50s multicolored .90 .90
c. A551 1.80s multicolored 1.25 1.25

Sports — A552

1996-98 Photo. *Perf. 13x14*

1256 A552 1.05s Mountain cycling .65 .65
1257 A552 1.10s Horseback riding .65 .65
a. Booklet pane of 20 13.00
Complete booklet, #1257a 13.00
1257B A552 1.80s Water skiing 1.00 1.00
1258 A552 1.90s Paragliding 1.25 1.25
1259 A552 2s Women's volleyball 1.25 1.25
1259A A552 2.20s Whitewater rafting 1.25 1.25
1260 A552 3s Beach bat & ball 1.75 1.75
1262 A552 5s Archery 3.00 3.00
1264 A552 10s Rappelling 5.75 5.75
Nos. 1256-1264 (9) 16.55 16.55
With tabs 18.50

Issued: 1.05s, 1.90s, 2s, 2/20/96; 1.10s, 5s, 2/13/97; 10s, 7/8/97; 3s, 9/23/97; 1257A, 1259A, 2/17/98.

This is an expanding set. Numbers may change.

Souvenir Sheet

Synagogue, Dura-Europos, Syria, 3rd Century A.D. — A553

Murals from synagogue walls: a, Temple, walls of Jerusalem. b, Torah Ark niche. c, Anointing of David as king by Prophet Samuel.

1996, Feb. 20 Litho. *Perf. 14x13*

1266 A553 Sheet of 3 2.75 2.75
a. 1.05s multicolored .60 .60
b. 1.60s multicolored .90 .90
c. 1.90s multicolored 1.25 1.25

Jerusalem, 3000th anniv.

Israel Cattle Breeders' Assoc., 70th Anniv. A554

1996, Feb. 20 *Perf. 14*

1267 A554 4.65s multicolored 3.00 3.00
With tab 3.25

Hebrew Writers' Assoc., 75th Anniv. — A555

No. 1269: a, M.J. Berdyczewski. b, Yehuda Burla. c, Devorah Baron. d, Haim Hazaz. e, J.L. Gordon. f, Joseph Hayyim Brenner. g, Abraham Shlonsky. h, Yaakov Shabtai. i, I.L. Peretz. j, Nathan Alterman. k, Saul Tchernichowsky. l, Amir Gilboa. m, Yokheved Bat-Miriam. n, Mendele Mokher Sefarim.

1996, Apr. 17 Litho. *Perf. 14*

1269 Pane of 14 3.50 3.50
a.-n. A555 40a Any single .25 .25

Manufacturers Assoc. of Israel, 75th Anniv. — A556

1996, Apr. 17

1271 A556 1.05s multicolored .65 .65
With tab .75

Monument to the Fallen Israel Police A557

1996, Apr. 17

1272 A557 1.05s multicolored .65 .65
With tab .75

Settlement of Metulla, Cent. — A558

1996, Apr. 17

1273 A558 1.90s multicolored 1.25 1.25
With tab 1.40

Composer Type of 1995

Designs: No. 1274, Felix Mendelssohn (1809-47). No. 1275, Gustav Mahler (1860-1911).

1996 Litho. *Perf. 14*

1274 A535 4.65s multicolored 3.00 3.00
1275 A535 4.65s multicolored 3.00 3.00
#1274-1275, with tabs 6.50

Issued: #1275, 4/17/96; #1274, 6/25/96.

A559

A560

1996, June 25

1276 A559 1.05s multicolored .65 .65
With tab .75

Eleven Jewish settlements in Negev Desert, 50th Anniv.

1996, June 25

1277 A560 1.05s Fencing .65 .65
1278 A560 1.60s Pole vault 1.00 1.00
1279 A560 1.90s Wrestling 1.25 1.25
a. Booklet pane of 6, 1 #1277, 2 #1278, 3 #1279 6.50
Complete booklet, #1279a 6.50
Nos. 1277-1279 (3) 2.90 2.90
With tabs 3.25

1996 Summer Olympics, Atlanta.

Fruit A561

1.05s, Orange, "sweety", kumquat, lemon. 1.60s, Avocado, persimmon, date, mango, grapes. 1.90s, Carambola, lychee, papaya.

1996, June 25

1280 A561 1.05s multicolored .65 .65
1281 A561 1.60s multicolored 1.00 1.00
1282 A561 1.90s multicolored 1.25 1.25
Nos. 1280-1282 (3) 2.90 2.90
With tabs 3.25

Public Works Department, 75th Anniv. — A562

1996, Sept. 3 Litho. *Perf. 14*

1283 A562 1.05s multicolored .65 .65
With tab .75

Festivals A563

Stylized designs: 1.05s, Bowl of honey, two lighted candles, Rosh Hashanah. 1.60s, Sukka booth, Sukkot. 1.90s, Inside of synagogue during Torah reading, Simchat Torah.

1996, Sept. 3

1284 A563 1.05s multicolored .65 .65
1285 A563 1.60s multicolored 1.00 1.00
1286 A563 1.90s multicolored 1.25 1.25
Nos. 1284-1286 (3) 2.90 2.90
With tabs 3.25

1st Zionist Congress, Cent. — A564

Designs: 4.65s, Tapestry of Theodore Herzl, David's Tower, shining sun. 5s, Casino building, Basel, site of first congress.

1996, Sept. 3

1287 A564 4.65s multicolored 3.00 3.00
With tab 3.25

Souvenir Sheet

1288 A564 5s multicolored 3.00 3.00

No. 1288 contains one 40x51mm stamp.

Hanukkah A565

Serpentine Die Cut 11

1996, Oct. 22 Photo.

1289 A565 2.50s multicolored 1.50 1.50
With tab 1.60

See US No. 3118.

Ha-Shilo'ah, Cent., edited by Ahad Ha'am (1856-1927) — A566

1996, Dec. 5 Litho. *Perf. 14*
1290 A566 1.15s multicolored .70 .70
With tab .80

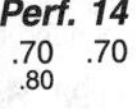

Coexistence: Man and Animals — A567

1996, Dec. 5
1291 A567 1.10s Birds, aircraft .65 .65
1292 A567 1.75s Pets 1.10 1.10
1293 A567 2s Dolphins 1.25 1.25
Nos. 1291-1293 (3) 3.00 3.00
With tabs 3.25

Space Research in Israel A568

1996, Dec. 5
1294 A568 2.05s multicolored 1.25 1.25
With tab 1.40

Philately Day.

UOAD (Umbrella Organization of Associations for the Disabled) — A569

1996, Dec. 5
1295 A569 5s multicolored 3.00 3.00
With tab 3.25

Souvenir Sheet

Inventors — A570

Designs: a, 1.50s, Alexander Graham Bell (1847-1922). b, 2s, Thomas Alva Edison (1847-1931).

1997, Feb. 13 Litho. *Perf. 13*
1296 A570 Sheet of 2, #a.-b. 2.25 2.25

Hong Kong '97.

Ethnic Costumes A571

1.10s, Ethiopia. 1.70s, Kurdistan. 2s, Salonica.

1997, Feb. 13 *Perf. 14*
1297 A571 1.10s multicolored .65 .65
1298 A571 1.70s multicolored 1.00 1.00
1299 A571 2s multicolored 1.25 1.25
Nos. 1297-1299 (3) 2.90 2.90
With tabs 3.25

Miguel de Cervantes (1547-1616), Writer — A572

1997, Feb. 13
1300 A572 3s multicolored 1.75 1.75
With tab 2.00

Mounument to the Fallen Soldiers of the Logistics Corps A573

1997, Apr. 30 Litho. *Perf. 14*
1301 A573 1.10s multicolored .65 .65
With tab .70

A574 A575

Jewish monuments in Prague: No. 1302, Tombstone of Rabbi Judah Loew MaHaRal. No. 1303, Altneuschul Synagogue.

1997, Apr. 30
1302 A574 1.70s blue & multi 1.00 1.00
1303 A574 1.70s red & multi 1.00 1.00
a. Sheet, 4 each, #1302-1303 8.00 8.00
#1302-1303, with tabs 2.25

Stamps in No. 1303a do not have tabs.
See Czech Republic Nos. 3009-3010.

1997, Apr. 30

Design: "The Vilna Gaon," Rabbi Elijah Ben Solomon Zalman (1720-97).

1304 A575 2s multicolored 1.25 1.25
With tab 1.40

Organized Clandestine Immigration (1934-48) — A576

1997, Apr. 30
1305 A576 5s multicolored 3.00 3.00
With tab 3.25

Souvenir Sheet

Discovery of the Cairo Geniza, Cent., Discovery of Dead Sea Scrolls, 50th Anniv. — A577

Designs: a, 2s, Ben Ezra Synagogue, Cairo. b, 3s, Cliffs, Dead Sea, Prof. Sukenik examining scrolls.

1997, May 29 Litho. *Perf. 13*
1306 A577 Sheet of 2, #a.-b. 3.00 3.00

Pacific '97.

Hello First Grade A578

1997, July 8 Litho. *Perf. 14*
1307 A578 1.10s multicolored .65 .65
With tab .70

Road Safety — A579

#1308, "Keep in Lane," car sinking into lake, fish. #1309, "Keep Your Distance," car with bird on front grille. #1310, "Don't Drink and Drive," man holding drink, car balanced on edge of cliff.

1997, July 8 *Perf. 13*
1308 A579 1.10s multicolored .65 .65
1309 A579 1.10s multicolored .65 .65
1310 A579 1.10s multicolored .65 .65
Nos. 1308-1310 (3) 1.95 1.95
With tabs 2.25

15th Maccabiah Games A580

1997, July 8 *Perf. 14*
1311 A580 5s Ice skating 3.00 3.00
With tab 3.25

Festival Stamps — A581

The Visiting Patriarchs, Sukkot: 1.10s, Abraham. 1.70s, Isaac. 2s, Jacob.

1997, Sept. 23 Litho. *Perf. 14*
1312 A581 1.10s multicolored .60 .60
1313 A581 1.70s multicolored .95 .95
1314 A581 2s multicolored 1.10 1.10
a. Booklet pane, 1 #1312, 2 #1313, 3 #1314 5.75
Complete booklet, #1314a 5.75
Nos. 1312-1314 (3) 2.65 2.65
With tabs 3.00

Compare with Nos. 1375-1378.

Music and Dance in Israel — A582

Designs: 1.10s, Zimriya, World assembly of choirs. 2s, Karmiel Dance Festival. 3s, Festival of Klezmers (musical instruments).

1997, Sept. 23 *Perf. 13*
1315 A582 1.10s multicolored .60 .60
1316 A582 2s multicolored 1.10 1.10
1317 A582 3s multicolored 1.75 1.75
Nos. 1315-1317 (3) 3.45 3.45
With tabs 3.75

UN Resolution on Creation of Jewish State, 50th Anniv. — A583

1997, Sept. 23 *Perf. 13x14*
1318 A583 5s multicolored 2.75 2.75
With tab 3.00

Souvenir Sheet

Pushkin's "Eugene Onegin," Translated by Abraham Shlonsky — A584

Illustration reduced.

1997, Nov. 19 *Perf. 14x13*
1319 A584 5s multicolored 2.75 2.75

See Russia No. 6418.

State of Israel, 50th Anniv. in 1998 — A585

1997, Dec. 23 *Perf. 14*
1320 A585 (1.10s) multicolored .60 .60
With tab .65
a. Size: 17x22mm .60 .60
With tab .65
b. Booklet pane, 20 #1320a 12.00
Complete booklet, #1320b 12.00
c. As "a," perf. 13x14, photo. .60 .60
With tab .65

No. 1320b consists of two blocks of 10 stamps, tete-beche in relationship to each other. No. 1320 is 18x23mm. No. 1320a has brighter blue stripes in flag.

Issued: #1320a, 2/17/98; #1320c, 5/3/98.

"MACHAL," Overseas Volunteers A586

Designs: 1.80s, "GACHAL," recruitment in the Diaspora.

1997, Dec. 23
1321 A586 1.15s multicolored .65 .65
1322 A586 1.80s multicolored 1.00 1.00
#1321-1322, with tabs 1.75

Chabad's Children of Chernobyl A587

1997, Dec. 23

1323 A587 2.10s multicolored 1.10 1.10
With tab 1.25

A588

A589

1997, Dec. 23

1324 A588 2.50s Julia Set Fractal 1.40 1.40
With tab 1.50

Philately Day.

1998, Feb. 17 Litho. *Perf. 14x13*

Three battle fronts during war: Nos. 1325, 1328a (1.50s), Northern Front, photograph of people, Zefat, 1948. Nos. 1326, 1328b (2.50s), Central Front, drawing over photograph of vehicles coming down mountain, outskirts of Jerusalem, 1948. Nos. 1327, 1328c (3s), Southern Front, raising Israeli flag, Elat, 1949.

1325 A589 1.15s multicolored .65 .65
1326 A589 1.15s multicolored .65 .65
1327 A589 1.15s multicolored .65 .65
Nos. 1325-1327 (3) 1.95 1.95
With tabs 2.25

Souvenir Sheet

1328 A589 Sheet of 3, #a.-c. 3.90 3.90

War of Independence, 1947-49. No. 1328b is 51x40mm.

Chaim Herzog (1918-97), President of Israel A590

1998, Feb. 17 *Perf. 14*

1329 A590 5.35s multicolored 3.00 3.00
With tab 3.25

A591

A592

Jewish Contributions to Modern World Culture: a, Franz Kafka (1883-1924), writer. b, George Gershwin. c, Lev Davidovich Landau (1908-68), physicist. d, Albert Einstein. e, Leon Blum (1872-1950), statesman. f, Elizabeth Rachel Felix (1821-58), actress.

1998, Apr. 27 Litho. *Perf. 14*

1330 Sheet of 6 + 6 labels 3.00 3.00
a.-f. A591 90a Any single .50 .50

1998, Apr. 27

1331 A592 1.15s multicolored .60 .60
With tab .65

Memorial Day.

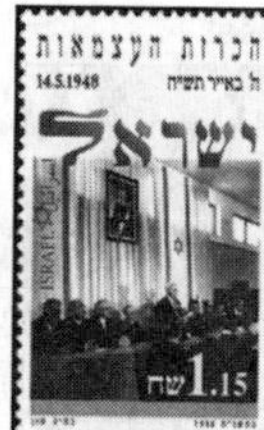

A593

A594

1998, Apr. 27

1332 A593 1.15s multicolored .60 .60
With tab .65

Declaration of the Establishment of the State of Israel, 50th anniv.

1998, Apr. 27

1333 A594 5.35s multicolored 3.00 3.00
With tab 3.25

Israel Defense Forces, 50th anniv.

Holocaust Memorial Day — A595

Non-Jews who risked their lives to save Jews during Holocaust: Giorgio Perlasca, Aristides de Sousa Mendes, Carl Lutz, Sempo Sugihara, Selahattin Ulkumen. Illustration reduced.

1998, Apr. 27 *Perf. 13*

1334 A595 6s multicolored 3.25 3.25
With tab 3.50

Children's Pets — A596

Israel '98: a, Cat. b, Dog. c, Bird. d, Goldfish. e, Hamster. f, Rabbit.

1998, May 13

1335 Sheet of 6 2.00 2.00
a.-f. A596 60a Any single .35 .35

No. 1335 contains diagonal perforations so that lower left corner of each stamp can be removed leaving denominated portion in shape of a pentagon.

Postal and Philatelic Museum A597

Illustrations by Kariel Gardosh featuring cartoon character, "Srulik:" a, At post office counter. b, Looking at stamp with magnifying glass. c, Putting mail into post box.

1998, May 13 *Perf. 14*

1336 Sheet of 3 3.75 3.75
a. A597 1.50s multicolored .80 .80
b. A597 2.50s multicolored 1.25 1.25
c. A597 3s multicolored 1.60 1.60

Aircraft Used in War of Independence, 1948 — A598

1998, May 3 Litho. *Perf. 14*

1337 A598 2.20s Dragon Rapide 1.25 1.25
1338 A598 2.20s Spitfire 1.25 1.25
1339 A598 2.20s B-17 Flying Fortress 1.25 1.25
a. Strip of 3, #1337-1339 3.75 3.75
With tabs 4.00 4.00

Israel '98.

No. 1339a was issued in sheets containing 2 strips printed tete beche separated by strip of three labels.

A limited edition booklet exist. It contained the following panes: 1 #1305, 1 #1318, 1 #1320, 1 #1320b, 1 each #1321-1322, 1 each #1325-1327, 1 #1332, 1 #1333, 1 #1339a.

Souvenir Sheet

Mosaic of a Young Woman, Zippori — A599

Illustration reduced.

1998, May 13

1340 A599 5s multicolored 3.25 3.25

Israel '98. Sold for 6s

Souvenir Sheet

King Solomon's Temple — A600

a, Drawing of the temple. b, Inscribed ivory pomegranate. Illustration reduced.

1998, May 13

1341 A600 Sheet of 2 4.00 4.00
a. 2s multicolored 1.60 1.60
b. 3s multicolored 2.40 2.40

Israel '98. Sold for 7s

Israel Jubilee Exhibition A601

1998, Aug. 3 Litho. *Perf. 14x13*

1342 A601 5.35s multicolored 2.50 2.50
With tab 2.75

Child's Drawing "Living in a World of Mutual Respect" A602

1998, Sept. 8 *Perf. 14*

1343 A602 1.15s multicolored .55 .55
With tab .60

Holy Cities A603

1998, Sept. 8

1344 A603 1.80s Hebron .85 .85
1345 A603 2.20s Jerusalem 1.00 1.00
#1344-1345, with tabs 2.10

1999

1346 A603 1.15s Zefat .60 .60
1347 A603 5.35s Tiberias 2.75 2.75
#1346, with tabs 3.75

Festival Stamps A604

Holy ark curtains: 1.15s, Peacocks on both sides of menorah, text, Star of David. 1.80s, Menorah, text, two lions. 2.20s, Text surrounded by ornate floral pattern.

1998, Sept. 8

1348 A604 1.15s multicolored .55 .55
1349 A604 1.80s multicolored .85 .85
1350 A604 2.20s multicolored 1.00 1.00
Nos. 1348-1350 (3) 2.40 2.40
With tabs 2.75

Natl. Flag A605

Hyacinth A606

1998, Dec. 17 Litho. *Die Cut*

Self-Adhesive

1351 A605 1.15s dk bl & bl .55 .55
1352 A605 2.15s dk bl & grn 1.00 1.00
1353 A605 3.25s dk bl & rose red 1.60 1.60
1354 A605 5.35s dk bl & yel org 2.75 2.75
Nos. 1351-1354 (4) 5.90 5.90

1999, Feb. 1 Photo. *Perf. 15*

1355 A606 ( ) multicolored .60 .60
With tab .65

Knesset, 50th Anniv. A607

1999, Feb. 1 Litho. *Perf. 14*

1356 A607 1.80s multicolored .90 .90
With tab 1.00

Manuscript of Rabbi Shalem Shabazi (1619-80), Poet — A608

1999, Feb. 1

1357 A608 2.20s multicolored 1.10 1.10
With tab 1.25

Jewish Colonial Trust, Cent. A609

Drawings from one pound sterling share.

1999, Feb. 16

1358 A609 1.80s multicolored .90 .90
With tab 1.00

Ethnic Costumes A610

Designs: 2.15s, Yemenite Jewry, Yemen. 3.25s, Bene Israel Community, India.

1999, Feb. 16

1359 A610 2.15s multicolored 1.10 1.10
1360 A610 3.25s multicolored 1.60 1.60
#1359-1360, with tabs 3.00

Souvenir Sheet

Ancient Boat from Sea of Galilee — A611

a, 3s, Reconstructed boat. b, 5s, Ancient boat.

1999, Mar. 19 Litho. *Perf. 13*

1361 A611 Sheet of 2, #a.-b. 4.00 4.00

Australia '99, World Stamp Expo.

Jewish Contributions to Modern World Culture Type of 1998

Designs: a, Emile Durkheim (1858-1917), social scientist. b, Paul Erlich (1854-1915), medical researcher. c, Rosa Luxemburg (1870-1919), politician. d, Norbert Wiener (1894-1964), mathematician, developer of computer science. e, Sigmund Freud (1856-1939), psychologist, founder of psychoanalysis. f, Martin Buber (1878-1965), religious philosopher.

1999, Apr. 18 Litho. *Perf. 14*

1362 Sheet of 6 + 6 labels 2.75 2.75
a.-f. A591 90a Any single .45 .45

Monument for Fallen Bedouin Soldiers A612

1999, Apr. 18

1363 A612 1.20s multicolored .60 .60
With tab .65

Israel's Admission to UN, 50th Anniv. A613

1999, Apr. 18

1364 A613 2.30s multicolored 1.10 1.10
With tab 1.25

Simcha Holtzberg (1924-94), Holocaust Survivor, "Father of Wounded Soldiers" A614

1999, Apr. 18

1365 A614 2.50s multicolored 1.25 1.25
With tab 1.40

Painting, "My Favorite Room," by James Ensor (1860-1949) — A614a

1999, May 16 Photo. *Perf. 11½*

1365A A614a 2.30s multi 1.10 1.10
With tab 1.25

See Belgium No. 1738.

"Lovely Butterfly," Children's Television Show A615

Puppets: No. 1366, Ouza, the goose. No. 1367, Nooly, the chick & Shabi, the snail. No. 1368, Batz, the tortoise, and Pingi, the penguin.

1999, June 22 Litho. *Perf. 14*

1366 A615 1.20s multicolored .60 .60
1367 A615 1.20s multicolored .60 .60
1368 A615 1.20s multicolored .60 .60
a. Strip of 3, #1366-1368 1.80 1.80
With tabs 2.00

Pilgrimage to the Holy Land A616

1999, June 22

1369 A616 3s Nazareth 1.50 1.50
1370 A616 3s River Jordan 1.50 1.50
1371 A616 3s Jerusalem 1.50 1.50
Nos. 1369-1371 (3) 4.50 4.50
With tabs 5.00

Rabbi Or Sharga (?-1794) — A617

Illustration from Musa-Nameh manuscript, by Shahin, depicting battle of Isreal over Amalek.

1999, June 22

1372 A617 5.60s multicolored 2.75 2.75
With tab 3.00

Ethnic Costumes Type of 1999

Designs: 2.30s, Jewish woman in traditional Moroccan costume. 3.40s, Jewish man in traditional costume of Bukhara.

1999, Sept. 1 Litho. *Perf. 14*

1373 A610 2.30s multicolored 1.10 1.10
1374 A610 3.40s multicolored 1.60 1.60
#1373-1374, with tab 3.00

"Ushpizin," Guests in the Sukkah, Festival of Sukkoth — A619

1999, Sept. 1

1375 A619 1.20s Joseph .60 .60
1376 A619 1.90s Moses .90 .90
1377 A619 2.30s Aaron 1.10 1.10
1378 A619 5.60s David 2.75 2.75
a. Bklt. pane, #1376-1378, 3 #1375 6.75 6.75
Complete booklet, #1378a 6.75
Nos. 1375-1378 (4) 5.35 5.35
With tabs 6.00

Stamp Day A620

1999, Sept. 1

1379 A620 5.35s multicolored 2.50 2.50
With tab 2.75

Ceramic Urns, Museum of Jewish Culture, Bratislava, Slovakia — A621

Designs: No. 1380, Urn from 1776 showing man on sick bed, denomination at UL. No. 1381, Urn from 1734 showing funeral procession, denomination at UR.

1999, Nov. 23 Litho. *Perf. 14*

1380 A621 1.90s multi .95 .95
1381 A621 1.90s multi .95 .95
#1380-1381, with tabs 2.10

See Slovakia Nos. 344-345.

Kiryat Shemona, 50th Anniv. A622

1999, Dec. 7

1382 A622 1.20s multicolored .60 .60
With tab .65

Proclamation of Jerusalem as Israel's Capital, 50th Anniv. — A623

1999, Dec. 7 *Perf. 13x14*

1383 A623 3.40s multicolored 1.60 1.60
With tab 1.75

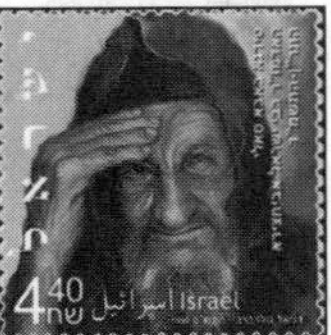

Sidna "Baba Sali" The Admor, Israel Abihssira (1890-1984) A624

1999, Dec. 7 *Perf. 13*

1384 A624 4.40s multi 2.25 2.25
With tab 2.50

Millennium A625

Designs: 1.40s, Joggers in park. 1.90s, Researcher with flask. 2.30s, Man at computer. 2.80s, Astronaut in space.

2000, Jan. 1

1385 A625 1.40s multi .70 .70
1386 A625 1.90s multi .95 .95
1387 A625 2.30s multi 1.10 1.10
1388 A625 2.80s multi 1.40 1.40
Nos. 1385-1388 (4) 4.15 4.15
With tabs 4.75

Stampin' the Future Children's Stamp Design Contest Winners A626

Various children's drawings.

2000, Jan. 1 *Perf. 13x13½*

Background Colors

1389 A626 1.20s blue .60 .60
1390 A626 1.90s yel org .95 .95
1391 A626 2.30s red 1.10 1.10
1392 A626 3.40s green 1.60 1.60
Nos. 1389-1392 (4) 4.25 4.25
With tabs 4.75

Fairy Tales of Hans Christian Andersen (1805-75) A627

1.20s, The Little Mermaid. 1.90s, The Emperor's New Clothes. 2.30s, The Ugly Duckling.

2000, Feb. 15 Litho. *Perf. 13x14*

1393 A627 1.20s multi .60 .60
1394 A627 1.90s multi .95 .95
1395 A627 2.30s multi 1.10 1.10
Nos. 1393-1395 (3) 2.65 2.65
With tabs 3.00

Pilgrimage to the Holy Land A628

Churches: 1.40s, All Apostles, Capernaum. 1.90s, St. Andrew's, Jerusalem. 2.30s, Church of the Visitation, Ein Kerem.

2000, Feb. 15 *Perf. 14x13*

1396 A628 1.40s multi .70 .70
1397 A628 1.90s multi .95 .95
1398 A628 2.30s multi 1.10 1.10
Nos. 1396-1398 (3) 2.75 2.75
With tabs 3.00

King Hussein of Jordan (1935-99) A629

Shuni Historic Site A630

2000, Feb. 15 Litho. *Perf. 14*

1399 A629 4.40s multi 2.25 2.25
With tab 2.50

Perf. 14 Syncopated Type A

2000, Feb. 15 Photo.

1400 A630 2.30s multi 1.10 1.10
With tab 1.25

See #1409, 1427.

A631

A632

Worldwide Fund for Nature: Various depictions of Blanford's fox.

2000, May 3 Litho. *Perf. 14*

Denomination Color

1401 A631 1.20s red violet .60 .60
1402 A631 1.20s green .60 .60
1403 A631 1.20s blue .60 .60

1404 A631 1.20s yellow .60 .60
a. Strip, #1401-1404 + central label 2.40 2.40
With tabs 2.75

2000, May 3
1405 A632 1.20s multi .60 .60
With tab .65

Memorial Day.

Intl. Communications Day — A633

2000, May 3 ***Perf. 13***
1406 A633 2.30s multi 1.10 1.10
With tab 1.25

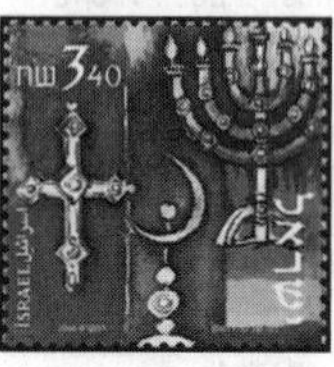

Land of Three Religions A634

2000, May 3
1407 A634 3.40s multi 1.60 1.60
With tab 1.75

Johann Sebastian Bach (1685-1750) A635

2000, May 3
1408 A635 5.60s multi 2.75 2.75
With tab 3.00

Historic Site Type of 2000

Perf. 14 Syncopated Type A

2000, July 25 **Photo.**
1409 A630 1.20s Juara .60 .60
With tab .70
a. Perf. 14¾x15 Sync. Type A .60 .60
With tab .70

The line containing the country name in English and Arabic is 10mm long on No. 1409, 11 mm long on No. 1409a.
Issued: #1409a, 2001.

2000 Summer Olympics, Sydney — A636

2000, July 25 **Litho.** ***Perf. 13***
1410 A636 2.80s multi 1.40 1.40
With tab 1.50

A637

A638

2000, July 25 ***Perf. 14***
1411 A637 4.40s multi 2.25 2.25
With tab 2.50

King Hassan II of Morocco (1929-99).

2000, June 25 ***Perf. 13½x13***

Israeli food.

1412 A638 1.40s Couscous .70 .70
1413 A638 1.90s Gefilte fish .95 .95
1414 A638 2.30s Falafel 1.10 1.10
a. Booklet pane, #1412, 2 #1413, 3 #1414 6.00
Booklet, #1414a 6.00
Nos. 1412-1414 (3) 2.75 2.75
With tabs 3.00

Dental Health A639

2000, Sept. 19 **Litho.** ***Perf. 14***
1415 A639 2.20s multi 1.10 1.10
With tab 1.25

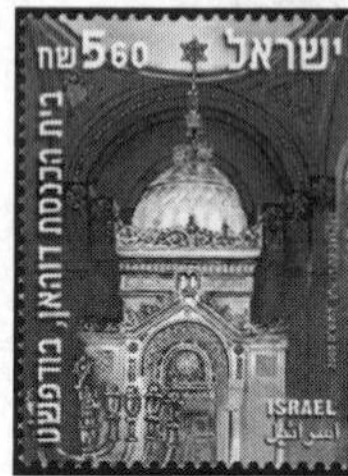

Dohany Synagogue, Budapest A640

2000, Sept. 19 ***Perf. 13x14***
1416 A640 5.60s multi 2.75 2.75
With tab 3.00

See Hungary No. 3710.

Jewish New Year Cards — A641

Designs: 1.20s, Boy giving girl a gift. 1.90s, Girl holding Zionist flag. 2.30s, Man giving flowers and greetings to woman.

2000, Sept. 19 ***Perf. 14***
1417 A641 1.20s multi .60 .60
1418 A641 1.90s multi .95 .95
1419 A641 2.30s multi 1.10 1.10
Nos. 1417-1419 (3) 2.65 2.65
With tabs 3.00

Aleppo Codex — A642

2000, Dec. 5 ***Perf. 13***
1420 A642 4.40s multi 2.10 2.10
With tab 2.40

Dinosaurs A643

Designs: No. 1421, Struthiomimuses on beach. No. 1422, Struthiomimuses in forest. No. 1423. Struthiomimus on hill.

2000, Dec. 5 **Litho.** ***Perf. 13***
1421 A643 2.20s multi 1.10 1.10
1422 A643 2.20s multi 1.10 1.10
1423 A643 2.20s multi 1.10 1.10
a. Strip of 3, #1421-1423 3.30 3.30
With tabs 3.50

Science Fiction A644

Designs: 2.80s, Robot. 3.40s, Time travel. 5.60s, Space flight.

2000, Dec. 5 ***Perf. 14***
1424 A644 2.80s multi 1.40 1.40
1425 A644 3.40s multi 1.75 1.75
1426 A644 5.60s multi 2.75 2.75
Nos. 1424-1426 (3) 5.90 5.90
With tabs 6.50

Historic Sites Type of 2000

Perf. 14 Syncopated Type A

2000-2001 **Photo.**
1427 A630 2.20s Mitzpe Revivim 1.10 1.10
With tab 1.25
1428 A630 3.40s Ilaniyya 1.75 1.75
With tab 1.90

Issued: 2.20s, 12/5; 3.40s, 2/13/01.

Settlements, Cent. — A645

2001, Feb. 13 **Litho.** ***Perf. 14***
1429 A645 2.50s Yavne'el 1.25 1.25
1430 A645 4.70s Menahamia 2.25 2.25
1431 A645 5.90s Kefar Tavor 3.00 3.00
Nos. 1429-1431 (3) 6.50 6.50
With tabs 7.25

Hebrew Letters Aleph and Beth — A646

No. 1432: a, Aleph. b, Beth. c, Gimel. d, Daleth. e, He. f, Waw. g, Zayin. h, Heth. i, Teth. j, Yod. k, Kaph. l, Lamed. m, Mem. n, Nun. o, Samekh. p, Ayin. q, Pe. r, Sadhe. s, Qoph. t, Resh. u, Sin. v, Taw.
No. 1433 - End-of-word letters: a, Kaph. b, Mem. c, Nun. d, Pe. e, Sadhe.

2001, Feb. 13 **Photo.** ***Perf. 15***
1432 Sheet of 22 1.10 1.10
a.-v. A646 10a Any single .20 .20

Litho.

Perf. 14

1433 Horiz. strip of 5 .25 .25
a.-e. A646 10a Any single .20 .20
1434 A646 1s shown .50 .50
With tab .55

No. 1433 issued in sheets of two tete-beche strips. The horizontal strips of stamps in No. 1432 are printed tete-beche.

Worldwide Fund for Nature Type of 2000 Without WWF Emblem

Designs: 1.20s, Lesser kestrel. 1.70s, Kuhl's pipistrelle. 2.10s, Roe deer. 2.50s, Greek tortoise.

2001, Mar. 18 **Litho.** ***Perf. 14***
1435 A631 1.20s multi .60 .60
1436 A631 1.70s multi .80 .80
1437 A631 2.10s multi 1.00 1.00
1438 A631 2.50s multi 1.25 1.25
a. Booklet pane, 2 each #1435-1438 7.50
Nos. 1435-1438 (4) 3.65 3.65
With tabs 4.00

Flowers — A647

No. 1439: a, Prairie gentian (purple). b, Barberton daisy (yellow) c, Star of Bethlehem (orange). d, Calla lily (white).

2001, Mar. 18
1439 Horiz. strip of 4 + 6 labels 2.40 2.40
a.-d. A647 1.20s Any single .60 .60

No. 1439 was printed in sheets of four strips. The second and fourth strips in the sheet have the stamps in reverse order. Sheets sold at the Jerusalem 2001 Stamp Exhibition could have their labels personalized by the purchaser.

Souvenir Sheet

Jerusalem 2001 Stamp Exhibition — A648

2001, Mar. 18
1440 A648 10s multi 5.00 5.00

Monument to Fallen Nahal Soldiers — A649

2001, Apr. 18 **Litho.** ***Perf. 13***
1441 A649 1.20s multi .55 .55
With tab .60

Memorial Day.

Historic Sites Type of 2000

Perf. 14 Syncopated Type A

2001, May 23 **Photo.**
1442 A630 2s Sha'ar HaGay Inn .95 .95
With tab 1.10

Shrine of the Báb Terraces, Haifa — A650

2001, May 23 ***Perf. 13x13¼***
1443 A650 3s multi 1.40 1.40
With tab 1.60

Karaite Jews — A651

2001, May 23 **Litho.** ***Perf. 14***
1444 A651 5.60s multi 2.75 2.75
With tab 3.00

Souvenir Sheet

Belgica 2001 Intl. Stamp Exhibition, Brussels — A652

Cut diamonds: a, 1.40s, Marquise. b, 1.70s, Round. c, 4.70s, Square.

2001, May 23 ***Perf. 14¾x14½***

1445 A652 Sheet of 3 4.75 4.75
a. 1.40s multi .85 .85
b. 1.70s multi 1.00 1.00
c. 4.70s multi 2.75 2.75

No. 1445 sold for 10s.

Youth Movements — A653

2001, July 17 ***Perf. 14***

1446 A653 5.60s multi 2.75 2.75
With tab 3.00

Bezalel School of Art Ceramic Facade Tiles — A654

Landscapes of: 1.20s, Hebron. 1.40s, Jaffa. 1.90s, Haifa. 2.30s, Tiberias.

2001, July 17 ***Perf. 13x14***

1447 A654 1.20s multi .55 .55
1448 A654 1.40s multi .65 .65
1449 A654 1.90s multi .90 .90
1450 A654 2.30s multi 1.10 1.10
Nos. 1447-1450 (4) 3.20 3.20
With tabs 3.50

Souvenir Sheet

Phila Nippon '01, Japan — A655

Children's stamp design contest winners: a, 1.20s, Balloons. b, 1.40s, Cat. c, 2.50s, Veterinarian with dog. d, 4.70s, Dolphins.

2001, July 17 ***Perf. 14¾***

1451 A655 Sheet of 4 4.75 4.75
a. 1.20s multi .55 .55
b. 1.40s multi .70 .70
c. 2.50s multi 1.25 1.25
d. 4.70s multi 2.25 2.25

No. 1451 sold for 10s.

Shota Rustaveli (c. 1172-c. 1216), Georgian Poet — A656

2001, Sept. 3 Litho. ***Perf. 13x14***

1452 A656 3.40s multi 1.60 1.60
With tab 1.75

Yehuda Amichai (1924-2000), Poet — A657

2001, Sept. 3

1453 A657 5.60s multi 2.60 2.60
With tab 2.75

Jewish National Fund, Cent A658

2001, Sept. 3 ***Perf. 14***

1454 A658 5.60s multi 2.60 2.60
With tab 2.75

Jewish New Year Cards Type of 2000

Designs: 1.20s, Soldier, dove with olive branch. 1.90s, Two women. 2.30s, Boy with flowers.

2001, Sept. 3

1455 A641 1.20s multi .55 .55
1456 A641 1.90s multi .90 .90
1457 A641 2.30s multi 1.10 1.10
Nos. 1455-1457 (3) 2.55 2.55
With tabs 2.75

Selection of Col. Ilan Ramon as Israel's First Astronaut — A659

2001, Dec. 11 Litho. ***Perf. 13***

1458 A659 1.20s multi .55 .55
With tab .65

Akim Association for the Rehabilitation of the Mentally Handicapped, 50th Anniv. — A660

2001, Dec. 11 ***Perf. 13x14***

1459 A660 2.20s multi 1.00 1.00
With tab 1.10

Heinrich Heine (1797-1856), Poet — A661

2001, Dec. 11

1460 A661 4.40s multi 2.10 2.10
With tab 2.40

Institute for the Blind, Jerusalem, Cent. A662

Litho. & Embossed

2001, Dec. 11 ***Perf. 14¾***

1461 A662 5.60s multi 2.60 2.60
With tab 3.00

Coastal Conservation A663

2001, Dec. 11 Litho. ***Perf. 13***

1462 A663 10s multi 4.75 4.75
With tab 5.25

Flower Type of 2001

2002, Feb. 24 Litho. ***Perf. 14***

1463 A647 1.20s Yellow lily .55 .55
With tab .60

No. 1463 has small picture of flower at left, while No. 1439b has small picture of flower at right.

Languages A664

2002, Feb. 24 ***Perf. 13x14***

1464 A664 2.10s Yiddish .90 .90
1465 A664 2.10s Ladino .90 .90
With tabs 2.00

Mushrooms A665

Designs: 1.90s, Agaricus campester. 2.20s, Amanita muscaria. 2.80s, Suillus granulatus.

2002, Feb. 24

1466 A665 1.90s multi .80 .80
1467 A665 2.20s multi .95 .95
1468 A665 2.80s multi 1.25 1.25
Nos. 1466-1468 (3) 3.00 3.00
With tabs 3.50

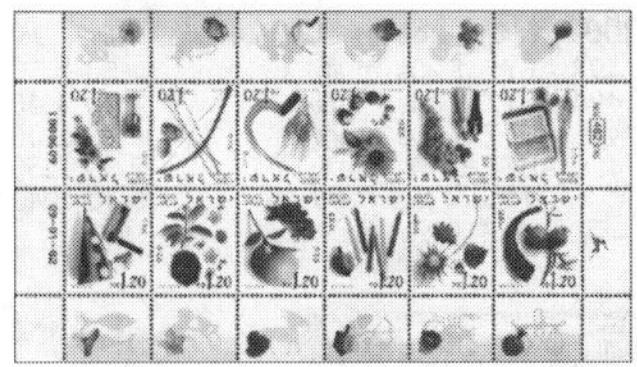

Months of the Year — A666

Designs: a, Tishrei (shofar, pomegranates). b, Heshvan (dried leaves). c, Kislev (dreidel, Hanukkah candles). d, Tevet (orange, flowers). e, Shevat (seedling, flowers, seeds). f, Adar (party hat, noisemaker, hamentashen). g, Nisan (cup, matzoh, flowers). h, Iyyar (bow and arrows, seeds). i, Sivan (wheat, sickle). j, Tammuz (flower, shells). k, Av (bride, groom, grapes). l, Elul, (cotton, dates, prayer book).

2002, Feb. 24 Photo. ***Perf. 14x14¼***

1469 A666 Sheet of 12 6.25 6.25
a.-l. 1.20s Any single .50 .50

Self-Adhesive

Serpentine Die Cut 16

1470 A666 Booklet of 12 6.25
a.-l. 1.20s Any single .50 .50

Monument to Fallen Military Police A667

2002, Apr. 10 Litho. ***Perf. 14***

1471 A667 1.20s multi .50 .50
With tab .60

Hakhel Le Yisrael — A668

2002, Apr. 10 ***Perf. 13x14***

1472 A668 4.70s multi 2.00 2.00
With tab 2.25

Israel Foundation for Handicapped Children, 50th Anniv. — A669

2002, Apr. 10

1473 A669 5.90s multi 2.50 2.50
With tab 2.75

Historians — A670

Designs: No. 1474, Heinrich Graetz (1817-91). No. 1475, Simon Dubnow (1860-1941). No. 1476, Benzion Dinur (1884-1973). No. 1477, Yitzhak Baer (1888-1980).

2002, Apr. 10 ***Perf. 14***

1474 A670 2.20s multi .90 .90
1475 A670 2.20s multi .90 .90
1476 A670 2.20s multi .90 .90
1477 A670 2.20s multi .90 .90
Nos. 1474-1477 (4) 3.60 3.60
With tabs 4.00

Historic Sites Type of 2000

Perf. 14 Syncopated

2002, June 18 Photo.

1478 A630 3.30s Hatsar Kinneret 1.40 1.40
With tab 1.60

Cable Cars — A671

2002, June 18 Litho. ***Perf. 14***

1479 A671 2.20s Haifa .95 .95
1480 A671 2.20s Massada .95 .95
1481 A671 2.20s Menara .95 .95
1482 A671 2.20s Rosh Haniqra .95 .95
Nos. 1479-1482 (4) 3.80 3.80
With tabs 4.25

Souvenir Sheet

Geology — A672

2002, June 18

1483 A672 Sheet of 3 5.00 5.00
a. 2.20s Fish fossil 1.10 1.10
b. 3.40s Copper minerals 1.75 1.75
c. 4.40s Ammonite 2.10 2.10

No. 1483 sold for 12s.

Rechavam Ze'evy (1926-2001), Assassinated Tourism Minister A673

Baruch Spinoza (1632-77), Philosopher A674

2002, Aug. 27 Litho. *Perf. 14*

1484 A673 1.20s multi .50 .50
With tab .60

2002, Aug. 27 *Perf. 13x14*

1485 A674 5.90s multi 2.50 2.50
With tab 2.75 2.75

Wine — A675

Designs: 1.20s, Clippers, bunch of grapes. 1.90s, Corkscrew, cork. 2.30s, Wine glass, bottle.

2002, Aug. 27 *Perf. 14*

1486 A675 1.20s multi .50 .50
1487 A675 1.90s multi .80 .80
1488 A675 2.30s multi 1.00 1.00
Nos. 1486-1488 (3) 2.30 2.30
With tabs 2.60

Birds of the Jordan Valley A676

2002, Aug. 27 *Perf. 14½x14*

1489 A676 2.20s Golden eagle .95 .95
1490 A676 2.20s Black stork .95 .95
1491 A676 2.20s Common crane .95 .95
Nos. 1489-1491 (3) 2.85 2.85
With tabs 3.25

Historic Sites Type of 2000

Perf. 14 Syncopated

2002, Aug. 27 Photo.

1492 A630 4.60s Kadoorie School 2.00 2.00
With tab 2.25

Political Journalists A677

Designs: 1.20s, Abba Ahimeir (1897-1962). 3.30s, Israel Eldad (1910-96). 4.70s, Moshe Beilinson (1890-1936). 5.90s, Rabbi Binyamin (1880-1957).

2002, Nov. 26 Litho. *Perf. 14*

1493 A677 1.20s multi .50 .50
1494 A677 3.30s multi 1.40 1.40
1495 A677 4.70s multi 2.00 2.00
1496 A677 5.90s multi 2.50 2.50
Nos. 1493-1496 (4) 6.40 6.40
With tabs 7.25

Toys A678

Menorah A679

2002, Nov. 26

1497 A678 2.20s Five Stones .95 .95
1498 A678 2.20s Marbles .95 .95
1499 A678 2.20s Spinning top .95 .95
1500 A678 2.20s Yo-yo .95 .95
Nos. 1497-1500 (4) 3.80 3.80
With tabs 4.25

2002, Nov. 26 Photo. *Perf. 15x14¾*

1502 A679 30a gray olive .20 .20
1505 A679 1s purple .40 .40
With tabs .65

AIR POST STAMPS

Doves Pecking at Grapes — AP1

Marisa Eagle — AP2

Designs: 30p, Beth Shearim eagle. 40p, Mosaic bird. 50p, Stylized dove. 250p, Mosaic dove and olive branch.

Perf. 11½

1950, June 25 Unwmk. Litho.

C1 AP1 5p brt grnsh bl .60 .20
C2 AP1 30p gray .30 .20
C3 AP1 40p dark green .30 .20
C4 AP1 50p henna brown .30 .20
C5 AP2 100p rose car 10.50 10.00
C6 AP2 250p dk gray bl 1.50 .35
Nos. C1-C6 (6) 13.50 11.15
With tabs 250.00

Haifa Bay and City Seal AP3

120p, Haifa, Mt. Carmel and city seal.

1952, Apr. 13 *Perf. 14*

Seal in Gray

C7 AP3 100p ultramarine .30 .20
C8 AP3 120p purple .20 .20
#C7-C8, with tabs 15.00

Stamps were available only on purchase of a ticket to the National Stamp Exhibition, Haifa. Price, including ticket, 340p.

Olive Tree — AP4

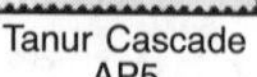

Tanur Cascade AP5

Coast at Tel Aviv-Jaffa AP6

70p, En Gev, Sea of Galilee. 100p, Road to Jerusalem. 150p, Lion Rock. 350p, Bay of Elat, Red Sea. 750p, Lake Hule. 3000p, Tomb of Rabbi Meir Baal Haness, Tiberias.

1953-56 Litho.

C9 AP4 10p olive grn .20 .20
C10 AP4 70p violet .20 .20
C11 AP4 100p green .20 .20
C12 AP4 150p orange brn .20 .20
C13 AP4 350p car rose .20 .20
C14 AP5 500p dull & dk bl .20 .20
C15 AP6 750p brown .20 .20
C16 AP6 1000p deep bl grn 1.90 .75
With tab 90.00
C17 AP6 3000p claret .20 .20
Nos. C9-C17 (9) 3.50 2.35
Nos. C9-C15, C17 with tabs 5.00

Issued: 1000p, 3/16/53; 10p, 100p, 500p, 3/2/54; 70p, 150p, 350p, 4/6/54; 750p, 8/21/56; 3000p, 11/13/56.

Old Town, Zefat — AP7

Houbara Bustard — AP9

Port of Elat ('Aqaba) — AP8

Designs: 20a, Ashkelon, Afridar Center. 25a, Acre, tower and boats. 30a, Haifa, view from Mt. Carmel. 35a, Capernaum, ancient synagogue, horiz. 40a, Jethro's tomb, horiz. 50a, Jerusalem, horiz. 65a, Tiberias, tower and lake, horiz. £1, Jaffa, horiz.

1960-61 Photo. *Perf. 13x14, 14x13*

C18 AP7 15a light lil & blk .20 .20
C19 AP7 20a brt yel grn & blk .20 .20
C20 AP7 25a orange & blk ('61) .20 .20
C21 AP7 30a grnsh bl & blk ('61) .20 .20
C22 AP7 35a yel grn & blk ('61) .20 .20
C23 AP7 40a lt vio & blk ('61) .20 .20
C24 AP7 50a olive & blk ('61) .20 .20
C25 AP7 65a lt ultra & black .20 .20
C26 AP7 £1 pink & blk ('61) .40 .30
Nos. C18-C26 (9) 2.00 1.90
With tabs 11.00

Issued: #C18, C19, C25, 2/24/60; #C20-C22, 6/14/61; #C23, C24, C26, 10/26/61.

Wmk. 302

1962, Feb. 21 Litho. *Perf. 14*

C27 AP8 £3 multicolored 1.60 1.00
With tab 8.50

Perf. 13x14, 14x13

1963 Unwmk. Photo.

Birds: 5a, Sinai rose finch, horiz. 20a, White-breasted kingfisher, horiz. 28a, Mourning wheatear, horiz. 30a, Blue-cheeked bee eater. 40a, Graceful prinia. 45a, Palestine sunbird. 70a, Scops owl. £1, Purple heron. £3, White-tailed Sea eagle.

C28 AP9 5a dp vio & multi .20 .20
C29 AP9 20a red & multi .20 .20
C30 AP9 28a emerald & multi .20 .20
C31 AP9 30a orange & multi .20 .20
C32 AP9 40a multicolored .20 .20
C33 AP9 45a yellow & multi .20 .20
C34 AP9 55a multicolored .20 .20
C35 AP9 70a black & multi .20 .20
C36 AP9 £1 multicolored .35 .35
C37 AP9 £3 ultra & multi .85 .70
Nos. C28-C37 (10) 2.80 2.65
With tabs 5.75

Issue dates: #C28-C30, Apr. 15; #C31-C33, June 19; #C34-C36, Feb. 13; #C37, Oct. 23.

Diamond and Boeing 707 AP10

Boeing 707 and: 10a, Textiles. 30a, Symbolic stamps. 40a, Vase, jewelry. 50a, Chick, egg. 55a, Melon, avocado, strawberries. 60a, Gladioli. 80a, Electronic equipment, chart. £1, Heavy oxygen isotopes (chemical apparatus). £1.50, Women's fashions.

1968 Photo. *Perf. 13x14*

C38 AP10 10a ultra & multi .20 .20
C39 AP10 30a gray & multi .20 .20
C40 AP10 40a multicolored .20 .20
C41 AP10 50a multicolored .20 .20
C42 AP10 55a multicolored .20 .20
C43 AP10 60a sl grn, lt grn & red .20 .20
C44 AP10 80a yel, brn & lt bl .20 .20
C45 AP10 £1 dark bl & org .20 .20

C46	AP10	£1.50 multicolored	.25	.20
C47	AP10	£3 pur & lt bl	.30	.25
		Nos. C38-C47 (10)	2.15	2.05
		With tabs	3.00	

Israeli exports. Sheets of 15 (5x3).
Issued: #C38-C41, 3/11; #C47, 2/7; #C42-C43, C45, 11/6; #C44, C46, 12/23.

POSTAGE DUE STAMPS

Types of Regular Issue Overprinted in Black

Various coins, as on postage denominations.

Unwmk.
1948, May 28 Typo. *Perf. 11*
Yellow Paper

J1	A1	3m orange	2.75	1.25
J2	A1	5m yellow green	3.75	1.75
J3	A1	10m red violet	6.50	4.00
J4	A1	20m ultramarine	12.00	8.00
J5	A1	50m orange brown	50.00	47.50
		Nos. J1-J5 (5)	75.00	62.50
		With tabs (blank)	*1,700.*	

The 3m, 20m and 50m are known with overprint omitted.
Nos. J1-J5 exist imperf.

D1

Running Stag — D2

1949, Dec. 18 Litho. *Perf. 11½*

J6	D1	2p orange	.20	.20
J7	D1	5p purple	.20	.20
J8	D1	10p yellow green	.20	.20
J9	D1	20p vermilion	.20	.20
J10	D1	30p violet blue	.25	.20
J11	D1	50p orange brown	.45	.25
		Nos. J6-J11 (6)	1.50	1.25
		With tabs (blank)	110.00	

1952, Nov. 30 Unwmk. *Perf. 14*

J12	D2	5p orange brown	.20	.20
J13	D2	10p Prussian blue	.20	.20
J14	D2	20p magenta	.20	.20
J15	D2	30p gray black	.20	.20
J16	D2	40p green	.20	.20
J17	D2	50p brown	.20	.20
J18	D2	60p purple	.20	.20
J19	D2	100p red	.20	.20
J20	D2	250p blue	.20	.20
		Nos. J12-J20 (9)	1.80	1.80
		With tabs (blank)	4.50	

OFFICIAL STAMPS

Redrawn Type of 1950 Overprinted in Black

1951, Feb. 1 Unwmk. *Perf. 14*

O1	A6	5p bright red violet	.20	.20
O2	A6	15p vermilion	.20	.20
O3	A6	30p ultramarine	.20	.20
O4	A6	40p orange brown	.20	.20
		Nos. O1-O4 (4)	.80	.80
		With tabs	17.50	

ITALIAN COLONIES

ə-ˈtal-yən ˈkä-lə-nēz

General Issues for all Colonies

100 Centesimi = 1 Lira

Used values in italics are for postaly used stamps. CTO's or stamps with fake cancels sell for about the same as unused, hinged stamps.

Watermark

Wmk. 140

Type of Italy, Dante Alighieri Society Issue, in New Colors and Overprinted in Red or Black

1932, July 11 Wmk. 140 *Perf. 14*

1	A126	10c gray blk	.50	*.55*
2	A126	15c olive brn	.50	*.55*
3	A126	20c slate grn	.50	.25
4	A126	25c dk grn	.50	.25
5	A126	30c red brn (Bk)	.50	.35
6	A126	50c bl blk	.50	.20
7	A126	75c car rose (Bk)	.80	.80
8	A126	1.25 l dk bl	.80	*1.00*
9	A126	1.75 l violet	1.00	*2.10*
10	A126	2.75 l org (Bk)	1.00	*5.25*
11	A126	5 l + 2 l ol grn	1.00	*6.50*
12	A126	10 l + 2.50 l dp bl	1.00	*8.25*
		Nos. 1-12,C1-C6 (18)	15.00	*46.75*

Types of Italy, Garibaldi Issue, in New Colors and Inscribed: "POSTE COLONIALI ITALIANE"

1932, July 1 Photo.

13	A138	10c green	1.90	*2.50*
14	A138	20c car rose	1.90	1.75
15	A138	25c green	1.90	1.75
16	A138	30c green	1.90	1.75
17	A138	50c car rose	1.90	1.75
18	A141	75c car rose	1.90	*3.00*
19	A141	1.25 l deep blue	1.90	*3.00*
20	A141	1.75 l + 25c dp bl	3.25	*5.25*
21	A144	2.55 l + 50c ol brn	3.25	*7.75*
22	A145	5 l + 1 l dp bl	3.25	*9.50*
		Nos. 13-22,C8-C12 (15)	38.10	*62.75*

See Nos. CE1-CE2.

Plowing with Oxen — A1

Pack Camel — A2

Lioness — A3

1933, Mar. 27 Wmk. 140

23	A1	10c ol brn	2.75	*2.50*
24	A2	20c dl vio	2.75	*2.50*
25	A3	25c green	2.75	2.50
26	A1	50c purple	2.75	2.50
27	A2	75c carmine	2.75	*3.00*
28	A3	1.25 l blue	2.75	*3.00*
29	A1	2.75 l red orange	4.25	5.25
30	A2	5 l + 2 l gray grn	7.00	*11.00*
31	A3	10 l + 2.50 l org brn	7.00	*14.50*
		Nos. 23-31,C13-C19 (16)	70.05	*93.25*

Annexation of Eritrea by Italy, 50th anniv.

Agricultural Implements A4

Arab and Camel — A5

"Eager with New Life" — A7

Steam Roller — A6

1933 Photo. *Perf. 14*

32	A4	5c orange	2.75	*2.10*
33	A5	25c green	2.75	*2.10*
34	A6	50c purple	2.75	*1.75*
35	A4	75c carmine	2.75	*3.00*
36	A5	1.25 l deep blue	2.75	*3.00*
37	A6	1.75 l rose red	2.75	*3.00*
38	A4	2.75 l dark blue	2.75	*5.50*
39	A5	5 l brnsh blk	4.25	*7.00*
40	A6	10 l bluish blk	4.25	*7.75*
41	A7	25 l gray black	7.25	*12.00*
		Nos. 32-41,C20-C27 (18)	70.75	*94.45*

10th anniversary of Fascism. Each denomination bears a different inscription.
Issue dates: 25 l, Dec. 26; others, Oct. 5.

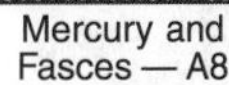

Mercury and Fasces — A8

Soccer Kickoff — A10

Scoring a Goal — A9

1934, Apr. 18

42	A8	20c red orange	.50	*1.75*
43	A8	30c slate green	.50	*1.75*
44	A8	50c indigo	.50	*1.75*
45	A8	1.25 l blue	.50	*3.50*
		Nos. 42-45 (4)	2.00	*8.75*

15th annual Trade Fair, Milan.

1934, June 5

46	A9	10c olive green	15.00	*18.00*
47	A9	50c purple	30.00	11.50
48	A9	1.25 l blue	30.00	*45.00*
49	A10	5 l brown	37.50	*112.50*
50	A10	10 l gray blue	37.50	*112.50*
		Nos. 46-50,C29-C35 (12)	302.50	*600.00*

2nd World Soccer Championship.

SEMI-POSTAL STAMPS

Many issues of Italy and Italian Colonies include one or more semi-postal denominations. To avoid splitting sets, these issues are generally listed as regular postage, airmail, etc., unless all values carry a surtax.

AIR POST STAMPS

Italian Air Post Stamps for Dante Alighieri Society Issue in New Colors and Overprinted in Red or Black Like #1-12

1932, July 11 Wmk. 140 *Perf. 14*

C1	AP10	50c gray blk (R)	.70	*1.40*
C2	AP11	1 l indigo (R)	.70	*1.40*
C3	AP11	3 l gray (R)	1.25	*1.90*
C4	AP11	5 l ol brn (R)	1.25	*3.00*
C5	AP10	7.70 l + 2 l car rose	1.25	*5.25*
C6	AP11	10 l + 2.50 l org	1.25	*7.75*
		Nos. C1-C6 (6)	6.40	*20.70*

Leonardo da Vinci — AP1

1932, Sept. 7 Photo. *Perf. 14½*

C7	AP1	100 l dp grn & brn	7.75	*22.50*

Types of Italian Air Post Stamps, Garibaldi Issue, in New Colors and Inscribed: "POSTE AEREA COLONIALE ITALIANA"

1932, July 1

C8	AP13	50c car rose	1.90	*2.50*
C9	AP14	80c green	1.90	*2.50*
C10	AP13	1 l + 25c ol brn	3.75	*6.00*
C11	AP13	2 l + 50c ol brn	3.75	*6.00*
C12	AP14	5 l + 1 l ol brn	3.75	*7.75*
		Nos. C8-C12 (5)	15.05	*24.75*

Eagle AP2

Savoia Marchetti 55 — AP3

Savoia Marchetti 55 Over Map of Eritrea AP4

1933 *Perf. 14*

C13	AP2	50c org brn	1.90	*2.50*
C14	AP2	1 l blk vio	1.90	*2.50*
C15	AP3	3 l carmine	5.25	*4.25*
C16	AP3	5 l olive brn	5.25	*4.25*
C17	AP2	7.70 l + 2 l slate	7.00	*11.00*
C18	AP3	10 l + 2.50 l dp bl	7.00	*11.00*
C19	AP4	50 l dk vio	7.00	*11.00*
		Nos. C13-C19 (7)	35.30	*46.50*

50th anniv. of Italian Government of Eritrea.
Issue dates: 50 l, June 1; others, Mar. 27.

Macchi-Costoldi Seaplane — AP5

Savoia S73 — AP6

Winding Propeller AP7

"More Efficient Machinery" AP8

1933-34

C20 AP5	50c org brn	3.25	2.50
C21 AP6	75c red vio	3.25	2.50
C22 AP5	1 l bis brn	3.25	2.50
C23 AP6	3 l olive gray	3.25	*6.00*
C24 AP5	10 l dp vio	3.25	*6.00*
C25 AP6	12 l bl grn	3.25	*7.75*
C26 AP7	20 l gray blk	5.75	*9.50*
C27 AP8	50 l blue ('34)	10.50	*10.50*
Nos. C20-C27 (8)		35.75	*47.25*

Tenth anniversary of Fascism.
Issue dates: 50 1, Dec. 26; others, Oct. 5.

Natives Hailing Dornier Wal — AP9

1934, Apr. 24

C28 AP9	25 l brown olive	16.00	*35.00*

Issued in honor of Luigi Amadeo, Duke of the Abruzzi (1873-1933).

Airplane over Stadium AP10

Goalkeeper Leaping — AP11

Seaplane and Soccer Ball AP12

1934, June

C29 AP10	50c yel brn	7.50	*19.00*
C30 AP10	75c dp vio	7.50	*19.00*
C31 AP11	5 l brn blk	27.50	*37.50*
C32 AP11	10 l red org	27.50	*37.50*
C33 AP10	15 l car rose	27.50	*37.50*
C34 AP11	25 l green	27.50	75.00
C35 AP12	50 l bl grn	27.50	75.00
Nos. C29-C35 (7)		152.50	*300.50*

World Soccer Championship Games, Rome. Issued: 50 l, June 21; others, June 5.

AIR POST SPECIAL DELIVERY STAMPS

Garibaldi Type of Italy

Wmk. 140

1932, Oct. 6 Photo. *Perf. 14*

CE1 APSD1	2.25 l + 1 l dk vio & sl	2.75	*6.00*
CE2 APSD1	4.50 l + 1.50 l dk brn & grn	3.00	*7.75*

ITALIAN E. AFRICA

ə-'tal-yən 'ēst 'a-fri-kə

LOCATION — In eastern Africa, bordering on the Red Sea and Indian Ocean
GOVT. — Italian Colony
AREA — 665,977 sq. mi. (estimated)
POP. — 12,100,000 (estimated)
CAPITAL — Asmara

This colony was formed in 1936 and included Ethiopia and the former colonies of Eritrea and Italian Somaliland. For previous issues see listings under these headings.

100 Centesimi = 1 Lira

Used values in italics are for postaly used stamps. CTO's or stamps with fake cancels sell for about the same as unused, hinged stamps.

Grant's Gazelle — A1

Eagle and Lion — A2

Victor Emmanuel III — A3

Fascist Legionary — A5

Statue of the Nile — A4

Desert Road — A6

Wmk. 140

1938, Feb. 7 Photo. *Perf. 14*

1	A1	2c red orange	.20	*.45*
2	A2	5c brown	.25	.20
3	A3	7½c dk violet	.40	*1.10*
4	A4	10c olive brown	1.10	.20
5	A5	15c slate green	.25	.20
6	A3	20c crimson	.25	.20
7	A6	25c green	1.00	.20
8	A1	30c olive brown	.40	.35
9	A2	35c sapphire	.90	*1.75*
10	A3	50c purple	.25	.20

Engr.

11	A5	75c carmine lake	1.00	.20
12	A6	1 l olive green	.55	.20
13	A3	1.25 l deep blue	.90	.20
14	A4	1.75 l orange	13.00	.20
15	A2	2 l cerise	.80	.20
16	A6	2.55 l dark brown	5.75	*7.00*
17	A1	3.70 l purple	17.00	11.00
18	A5	5 l purple	4.50	1.10
19	A2	10 l henna brown	5.75	3.50
20	A4	20 l dull green	10.50	7.00
Nos. 1-20,C1-C11,CE1-CE2 (33)			116.80	59.15

Augustus Caesar (Octavianus) A7

Goddess Abundantia A8

1938, Apr. 25 Photo. *Perf. 14*

21	A7	5c bister brn	.20	*.50*
22	A8	10c copper red	.20	*.45*
23	A7	25c deep green	.60	*.45*
24	A8	50c purple	.60	*.35*
25	A7	75c crimson	.60	*.85*
26	A8	1.25 l deep blue	.60	*1.75*
Nos. 21-26,C12-C13 (8)			3.45	*6.45*

Bimillenary of the birth of Augustus Caesar (Octavianus), first Roman emperor.

Rome-Berlin Axis.
Four stamps of type AP8, without "Posta Aerea," were prepared in 1941, but not issued. Value, each $1,500.

Native Boat — A9

Native Soldier — A10

Statue Suggesting Italy's Conquest of Ethiopia — A11

1940, May 11 Wmk. 140

27	A9	5c olive brown	.20	*.35*
28	A10	10c red orange	.20	*.35*
29	A11	25c green	.85	.60
30	A9	50c purple	.85	.35
31	A10	75c rose red	.85	*1.00*
32	A11	1.25 l dark blue	.85	.80
33	A10	2 l + 75c carmine	.85	*4.25*
Nos. 27-33,C14-C17 (11)			8.15	*13.50*

Issued in connection with the first Triennial Overseas Exposition held at Naples.

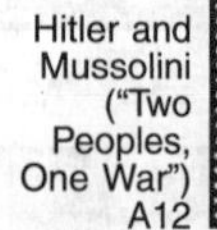

Hitler and Mussolini ("Two Peoples, One War") A12

1941, June 19

34	A12	5c ocher	.20
35	A12	10c chestnut	.20
36	A12	20c black	.80
37	A12	25c turquoise grn	.80
38	A12	50c rose lilac	.80
39	A12	75c rose car	.80
40	A12	1.25 l brt ultra	.80
Nos. 34-40,C18-C19 (9)			32.40

SEMI-POSTAL STAMPS

Many issues of Italy and Italian Colonies include one or more semi-postal denominations. To avoid splitting sets, these issues are generally listed as regular postage, airmail, etc., unless all values carry a surtax.

AIR POST STAMPS

Plane Flying over Mountains AP1

Mussolini Carved in Stone Cliff — AP2

Airplane over Lake Tsana AP3

Bataleur Eagle — AP4

Eagle Attacking Serpent — AP5

Wmk. Crowns (140)

1938, Feb. 7 Photo. *Perf. 14*

C1 AP1	25c slate green	1.25	*1.10*
C2 AP2	50c olive brown	29.00	.20
C3 AP3	60c red orange	.80	*3.00*
C4 AP1	75c orange brn	1.25	.80
C5 AP4	1 l slate blue	.20	.20

Engr.

C6 AP2	1.50 l violet	.50	.20
C7 AP3	2 l slate blue	.50	.45
C8 AP1	3 l carmine lake	.80	1.75
C9 AP4	5 l red brown	1.75	1.25
C10 AP2	10 l violet brn	4.50	2.50
C11 AP1	25 l slate blue	9.00	6.00
Nos. C1-C11 (11)		49.55	17.45

1938, Apr. 25 Photo.

C12 AP5	50c bister brown	.25	.85
C13 AP5	1 l purple	.40	*1.25*

Bimillenary of the birth of Augustus Caesar (Octavianus), first Roman emperor.

Triennial Overseas Exposition Type

#C14, C16, Tractor. #C15, C17, Plane over city.

1940, May 11

C14 A10	50c olive gray	.75	*1.40*
C15 A9	1 l purple	.75	*1.40*
C16 A10	2 l + 75c gray blue	1.00	*1.50*
C17 A9	5 l + 2.50 l red brn	1.00	*1.50*
Nos. C14-C17 (4)		3.50	*5.80*

Hitler and Mussolini ("Two Peoples, One War") AP8

AP9

1941, Apr. 24

C18 AP8 1 l slate blue 25.00
C19 AP9 1 l slate blue 3.00

Rome-Berlin Axis.

AIR POST SPECIAL DELIVERY STAMPS

Plow and Airplane — APSD1

Wmk. 140

1938, Feb. 7 Engr. *Perf. 14*

CE1 APSD1 2 l slate blue 1.25 *2.50*
CE2 APSD1 2.50 l dark brown 1.25 *3.75*

SPECIAL DELIVERY STAMPS

Victor Emmanuel III — SD1

Wmk. 140

1938, Apr. 16 Engr. *Perf. 14*

E1 SD1 1.25 l dark green .65 1.25
E2 SD1 2.50 l dark carmine .65 *4.00*

POSTAGE DUE STAMPS

Italy, Nos. J28 to J40, Overprinted in Black

1941 Wmk. 140 *Perf. 14*

J1 D6 5c brown .40
J2 D6 10c blue .40
J3 D6 20c rose red 1.10
J4 D6 25c green 1.10
J5 D6 30c red orange 2.75
J6 D6 40c black brown 2.75
J7 D6 50c violet 2.75
J8 D6 60c slate black 5.25
J9 D7 1 l red orange 11.00
J10 D7 2 l green 11.00
J11 D7 5 l violet 11.00
J12 D7 10 l blue 11.00
J13 D7 20 l carmine rose 11.00
Nos. J1-J13 (13) 71.50

In 1943 a set of 11 "Segnatasse" stamps, picturing a horse and rider and inscribed "A. O. I.," was prepared but not issued. Value, $10.

ITALIAN STATES

ə-'tal-yən 'stāts

Watermarks

Wmk. 157- Large Letter "A"

Wmk. 184- Interlaced Wavy Lines

Wmk. 184 has double lined letters diagonally across the sheet readihng: "II R R POSTE TOSCANE."

Wmk. 185- Crowns in the sheet

The watermark consists of twelve crowns, arranged in four rows of three, with horizontal and vertical lines between them. Only parts of the watermark appear on each stamp. (Reduced illustration.)

Wmk. 186- Fleurs-de-Lis in Sheet

MODENA

LOCATION — In northern Italy
GOVT. — Duchy
AREA — 1,003 sq. mi.
POP. — 448,000 (approx.)
CAPITAL — Modena

In 1852, when the first postage stamps were issued, Modena was under the rule of Duke Francis V of the House of Este-Lorraine. In June, 1859, he was overthrown and the Duchy was annexed to the Kingdom of Sardinia which on March 17, 1861, became the Kingdom of Italy.

100 Centesimi = 1 Lira

Values of Modena stamps vary tremendously according to condition. Values are for very fine examples, and values for unused stamps are for examples with original gum as defined in the catalogue introduction. Extremely fine or superb copies sell at much higher prices, and fine or poor copies sell at greatly reduced prices. In addition, very fine unused copies without gum sell for about 20% of the values shown.

Coat of Arms
A1 A2

1852 Unwmk. Typo. *Imperf.*

Without Period After Figures of Value

1 A1 5c blk, *green* 1450. 100.00
a. Pair, #1, 6 1,750. *1,250.*
2 A1 10c blk, *rose* 350.00 70.00
a. "EENT. 10" *4,500. 1,650.*
b. "1" of "10" inverted *4,500. 1,650.*
c. "CNET" *875.00 1,200.*
d. No period after "CENT" *1,250.* 575.00
e. Pair, #2, 7 800.00 *1,650.*
3 A1 15c blk, *yellow* 32.50 20.00
a. "CETN 15." *4,250. 725.00*
b. No period after "CENT" 175.00 *400.00*
4 A1 25c blk, *buff* 35.00 22.50
a. No period after "CENT" 400.00 *700.00*
b. "ENT.25" omitted *575.00* —
c. 25c black, *green* (error) 1,750. 1,000.
d. "N" of "CENT" omitted 475.00 *1,000.*
5 A1 40c blk, *blue* 275.00 95.00
a. 40c black, *pale blue* *9,750.* 925.00
b. No period after "CENT" *1,200. 1,200.*
c. As "a," no period after "CENT" — —
d. Pair, #5, 8 *450.00 1,750.*

Unused examples of No. 5a lack gum.
See Nos. PR3-PR4.

With Period After Figures of Value

6 A1 5c blk, *green* 20.00 *35.00*
a. 5c black, *olive green* 275.00 92.50
As "a," without gum 17.50
b. "ENT" — *1,550.*
c. "CNET" *2,900. 2,500.*
d. As "a," "CNET" *1,450. 1,450.*
e. "E" of "CENT" sideways — 3,750.
f. As "a," "CEN1" *1,600. 1,600.*
g. As "a," no period after "5" 375.00 *375.00*
h. Double impression *825.00* —
i. As "a," double impression *800.00* —
j. Pair, #6a, 6g 800.00 *1,550.*
7 A1 10c blk, *rose* 275.00 200.00
a. "CENE" 875.00 *1,200.*
b. "CNET" 450.00 *550.00*
c. "CE6T" 875.00 *1,200.*
d. "N" of "CENT" sideways *5,500. 2,750.*
e. Double impression 800.00 *2,750.*
8 A1 40c blk, *blue* 32.50 *92.50*
a. "CNET" 190.00 *575.00*
b. "CENE" 375.00 *1,200.*
c. "CE6T" 375.00 *1,200.*
d. "49" 190.00 *575.00*
e. "4C" 375.00 *1,200.*
f. "CEN.T" *19,500.* —

Unused examples of No. 6h lack gum.

Wmk. 157

9 A1 1 l black 45.00 *1,750.*
a. Period after "LIRA" 110.00 *3,250.*
b. No period after "1" 110.00 *2,600.*

Provisional Government

1859 Unwmk.

10 A2 5c green 1,100. *525.00*
a. 5c emerald 1,200. *550.00*
b. 5c dark green 1,200. *550.00*
11 A2 15c brown 1,900. *2,750.*
a. 15c gray brown 225.00
b. 15c black brown *2,100. 3,350.*
c. No period after "15" *2,200. 3,000.*
d. Period before "CENT" *2,900. 4,350.*
e. Double impression (#11a) *1,000.*
12 A2 20c lilac 47.50 *775.00*
a. 20c violet 2,650. 110.00
b. 20c blue violet 1,450. 110.00
c. No period after "20" 70.00 *875.00*
d. "ECNT" 175.00 *1,950.*
e. "N" inverted 150.00 *1,400.*
f. Double impression (#12b) *3,400.*
13 A2 40c carmine 150.00 *950.00*
a. 40c brown rose 150.00 *950.00*
b. No period after "40" 275.00 *1,750.*
c. Period before "CENT" 275.00 *1,750.*
d. Inverted "5" before the "C" 19,500. —
14 A2 80c buff 140.00 *14,500.*
a. 80c brown orange 140.00 *14,500.*
b. "CENT 8" 275.00 —
c. "CENT 0" 825.00 —
d. No period after "80" 275.00 —
e. "N" inverted 275.00 —

The reprints of the 1859 issue have the word "CENT" and the figures of value in different type from the originals. There is no frame line at the bottom of the small square in the lower right corner.

NEWSPAPER TAX STAMPS

NT1

NT2

B. G. CEN. 9 — Type I
B. G. CEN. 9. — Type II

1853 Unwmk. Typo. *Imperf.*

PR1 NT1 9c blk, *violet* (I) — *2,200.*
PR2 NT1 9c blk, *violet* (II) 475.00 57.50
a. No period after "9" *650.00* 200.00

All known unused examples of #PR1 lack gum.

1855-57

PR3 A1 9c blk, *violet* 2.00
a. No period after "9" 3.00
b. No period after "CENT" 4.75
PR4 A1 10c blk, *gray vio* ('57) 45.00 *200.00*
a. "CEN1" 225.00 *1,000.*

No. PR3 was never placed in use.

1859

PR5 NT2 10c black 675.00 *1,450.*
a. Double impression *12,500. 15,000.*
b. Vert. guidelines between stamps 775.00

No. PR5 has horizontal guide lines between stamps. No. PR5b is a second printing, which was not issued.

These stamps did not pay postage, but were a fiscal tax collected by the postal authorities on newspapers arriving from foreign countries. The stamps of Modena were superseded by those of Sardinia in February, 1860.

PARMA

LOCATION — Comprising the present provinces of Parma and Piacenza in northern Italy.
GOVT. — Independent Duchy
AREA — 2,750 sq. mi. (1860)
POP. — 500,000 (1860)
CAPITAL — Parma

Parma was annexed to Sardinia in 1860.

100 Centesimi = 1 Lira

Values of Parma stamps vary tremendously according to condition. Values are for very fine examples, and values for unused stamps are for examples with original gum as defined in the catalogue introduction except for No. 8 which is known only without gum. Extremely fine or superb copies sell at much higher prices, and fine or poor copies sell at greatly reduced prices. In addition, very fine unused copies without gum sell for about 20% of the values shown.

Crown and Fleur-de-lis
A1 A2

1852 Unwmk. Typo. *Imperf.*

1 A1 5c blk, *yellow* 72.50 *95.00*
2 A1 10c blk, *white* 72.50 *95.00*
3 A1 15c blk, *pink* 2,200. 45.00
a. Tête bêche pair *67,500.*
b. Double impression *2,900.*
4 A1 25c blk, *violet* *9,250.* 150.00
5 A1 40c blk, *blue* 1,750. 240.00
a. 40c black, *pale blue* — 300.00

1854-55

6 A1 5c org yel *4,250.* 500.00
a. 5c lemon yellow *5,500.* 575.00
b. Double impression *12,500.*
7 A1 15c red *5,000.* 110.00
8 A1 25c red brn ('55) — 250.00
a. Double impression *25,000.*

No. 8 unused is without gum.

1857-59

9 A2 15c red ('59) 200.00 *300.00*
10 A2 25c red brown 375.00 160.00
11 A2 40c bl, wide "0" ('58) 45.00 *375.00*
a. Narrow "0" in "40" 47.50 *400.00*

Provisional Government

A3

1859

12 A3 5c yel grn 525.00 *14,250.*
a. 5c blue green 2,000. *2,750.*
13 A3 10c brown 925.00 *375.00*
a. 10c deep brown 925.00 *375.00*
b. "1" of "10" inverted 1,850. —
c. Thick "0" in "10" 1,100. *450.00*
14 A3 20c pale blue 925.00 140.00
a. 20c deep blue 925.00 160.00
b. Thick "0" in "20" 1,100. 175.00
15 A3 40c red 525.00 *5,500.*
a. 40c brown red *15,000.* *8,000.*
b. Thick "0" in "40," (#15) 625.00 *6,750.*
c. Thick "0" in "40," (#15a) *16,500.* *9,000.*
16 A3 80c olive yellow *5,750.* 135,000.
a. 80c org yel *8,000.*
d. Thick "0" in "80," (#16) *8,500.*
e. Thick "0" in "80," (#16a) *6,750.*

Nos. 12-16 exist in two other varieties: with spelling "CFNTESIMI" and with small "A" in "STATI." These are valued about 50 per cent more than normal stamps.

See Nos. PR1-PR2.

NEWSPAPER TAX STAMPS

Type of 1859

1853-57 Unwmk. Typo. *Imperf.*
Normal Paper ('53)

PR1 A3 6c black, *deep rose* 1,750. 240.00
PR2 A3 9c black, *blue* 950.00 *12,500.*

Full margins = 1¼mm.

Thin, Semitransparent Paper ('57)

PR1a A3 6c black, *rose* ('57) 77.50
PR2a A3 9c black, *blue* 35.00

These stamps belong to the same class as the Newspaper Tax Stamps of Modena, Austria, etc. No. PR1 and PR2 were not regularly issued. The paper for PR1 and PR2 is very thin and semitransparent. The paper for PR1a and PR2a is normal and non-transparent.

Note following #16 also applies to #PR1-PR2.

The stamps of Parma were superseded by those of Sardinia in 1860.

ROMAGNA

LOCATION — Comprised the present Italian provinces of Forli, Ravenna, Ferrara and Bologna.
GOVT. — Formerly one of the Roman States
AREA — 5,626 sq. mi.
POP. — 1,341,091 (1853)
CAPITAL — Ravenna

Postage stamps were issued when a provisional government was formed pending the unification of Italy. In 1860 Romagna was annexed to Sardinia and since 1862 the postage stamps of Italy have been used.

100 Bajocchi = 1 Scudo

Values of Romagna stamps vary tremendously according to condition. Values are for very fine examples, and values for unused stamps are for examples with original gum as defined in the catalogue introduction. Extremely fine or superb copies sell at much higher prices, and fine or poor copies sell at greatly reduced prices. In addition, very fine unused copies without gum sell for about 20% of the values shown.

A1

1859 Unwmk. Typo. *Imperf.*

1 A1 ½b blk, *straw* 20.00 *250.00*
a. Half used as ¼b on cover *10,750.*
2 A1 1b blk, *drab* 20.00 *110.00*
3 A1 2b blk, *buff* 35.00 *125.00*
a. Half used as 1b on cover *4,000.*
4 A1 3b blk, *dk grn* 40.00 *260.00*
5 A1 4b blk, *fawn* 525.00 125.00
a. Half used as 2b on cover *21,000.*
6 A1 5b blk, *gray vio* 50.00 *300.00*
7 A1 6b blk, *yel grn* 275.00 *6,000.*
a. Half used as 3b on cover *87,500.*
8 A1 8b blk, *rose* 175.00 *1,450.*
a. Half used as 4b on cover *87,500.*
9 A1 20b blk, *gray grn* 175.00 *2,000.*

These stamps have been reprinted several times. The reprints usually resemble the originals in the color of the paper but there are impressions on incorrect colors and also in colors on white paper. They often show broken letters and other injuries. The Y shaped ornaments between the small circles in the corners are broken and blurred and the dots outside the circles are often missing or joined to the circles.

Forged cancellations are plentiful.

Bisects used Oct. 12, 1859 to Mar. 1, 1860.

The stamps of Romagna were superseded by those of Sardinia in February, 1860.

ROMAN STATES

LOCATION — Comprised most of the central Italian Peninsula, bounded by the former Kingdom of Lombardy-Venetia and Modena on the north, Tuscany on the west, and the Kingdom of Naples on the southeast.
GOVT. — Under the direct government of the See of Rome.
AREA — 16,000 sq. mi.
POP. — 3,124,758 (1853)
CAPITAL — Rome

Upon the formation of the Kingdom of Italy, the area of the Roman States was greatly reduced and in 1870 they disappeared from the political map of Europe. Postage stamps of Italy have been used since that time.

100 Bajocchi = 1 Scudo
100 Centesimi = 1 Lira (1867)

Values of Roman States stamps vary tremendously according to condition. Values are for very fine examples, and values for unused stamps are for examples with original gum as defined in the catalogue introduction. Extremely fine or superb copies sell at much higher prices, and fine or poor copies sell at greatly reduced prices. In addition, very fine unused copies without gum sell for about 20% of the values shown.

Papal Arms
A1 A2

A3

A4

A5

A6

A7

A8

A9

A10

A11

1852 Unwmk. Typo. *Imperf.*

1 A1 ½b blk, *dl vio* 35.00 *95.00*
a. ½b black, *gray blue* 475.00 65.00
b. ½b black, *gray lilac* 475.00 200.00
c. ½b black, *gray* 475.00 65.00
d. ½b black, *reddish violet* 1,900. 1,000.
e. ½b black, *dark violet* 200.00 210.00
f. Tête bêche pair *23,250.*
h. As "a," half used as ¼b on wrapper *46,500.*
1. Pen cancel *8,500.*
i. Double impression — *4,500.*
j. Impression on both sides — *8,750.*
2 A2 1b blk, *gray grn* 190.00 8.75
a. 1b black, *bl green* 260.00 14.50
b. Half used as ½b on cover 400.00
c. Grayish greasy ink 650.00 29.00
d. Double impression *4,350.*
e. Impression on both sides — *8,750.*
3 A3 2b blk, *grnsh white* 8.75 *40.00*
a. 2b black, *yellow green* 125.00 9.50
b. As #3, half used as 1b on cover *4,650.*
c. As "a," half used as 1b on cover 350.00
d. Grayish greasy ink 750.00 29.00
e. No period after "BAJ" 140.00 32.50
f. As "a" and "e" 260.00 19.00
g. Double impression *4,000.*
4 A4 3b blk, *brown* 110.00 47.50
a. 3b black, *light brown* 3,750. 87.50
b. 3b black, *yellow brown* 1,900. 29.00
c. 3b black, *yellow buff* 1,900. *29.00*
d. 3b black, *chrome yellow* 24.00 *125.00*
e. One-third used as 1b on circular *2,600.*
f. Two-thirds used as 2b on circular *8,000.*
g. Grayish greasy ink 4,500. 125.00
h. Impression on both sides — *8,750.*
i. Double impression — *4,500.*
j. Half used as 1½b on cover *10,500.*
5 A5 4b blk, *lemon* 160.00 52.50
a. 4b black, *yellow* 160.00 52.50
b. 4b black, *rose brown* 5,000. 82.50
c. 4b black, *gray brown* 4,750. 52.50
d. Half used as 2b on cover *1,950.*
e. One-quarter used as 1b on cover *20,000.*
f. Impression on both sides — *17,500.*
g. Ribbed paper 150.00 45.00
h. Grayish greasy ink *9,500.* 200.00
i. As "a," half used as 2b on cover *3,250.*
j. As "a," one-quarter used as 1b on cover *17,500.*
6 A6 5b blk, *rose* 160.00 9.50
a. 5b black, *pale rose* 175.00 10.50
c. Impression on both sides *9,000.*
d. Double impression *4,350.*
e. Grayish greasy ink 1,100. 29.00
f. Half used as 2½b on cover *50,000.*
7 A7 6b blk, *grnsh grn* 550.00 45.00
a. 6b black, *gray* 1,200. 47.50
b. 6b black, *grayish lilac* 875.00 160.00
c. Grayish greasy ink 2,900. 150.00
d. Double impression — *4,350.*
e. Half used as 3b on cover *4,350.*
f. One-third used as 2b on cover *16,000.*
8 A8 7b blk, *blue* 875.00 52.50
a. Half used as 3½b on cover *25,000.*
b. Double impression — *4,000.*
c. Grayish greasy ink 2,350. 90.00
9 A9 8b black 425.00 27.50
a. Half used as 4b on cover *7,250.*
b. Quarter used as 2b on cover *60,000.*
c. Double impression — —
d. Grayish greasy ink *1,900.* 175.00
10 A10 50b dull blue *10,500.* 1,300.
a. 50b deep blue (worn impression) *16,000.* 2,200.
11 A11 1sc rose *2,750.* *2,500.*

Counterfeits exist of Nos. 10-11. Fraudulent cancellations are found on No. 11.

A12

A13

A14 A15

A16

A17

A18

1867 *Imperf.*
Glazed Paper

12 A12 2c blk, *green* 87.50 *175.00*
a. No period after "Cent" 100.00 *190.00*
13 A13 3c blk, *gray* 775.00 *5,500.*
a. 3c black, *lilac gray* 1,900. *1,750.*
14 A14 5c blk, *lt bl* 125.00 *150.00*
a. No period after "5" 260.00 *290.00*
15 A15 10c blk, *vermilion* 875.00 47.50
a. Double impression *5,000.*
16 A16 20c blk, *cop red* (unglazed) 110.00 65.00
a. No period after "20" 400.00 150.00
b. No period after "CENT" 400.00 150.00
17 A17 40c blk, *yellow* 150.00 *150.00*
a. No period after "40" 175.00 *190.00*
18 A18 80c blk, *lil rose* 150.00 *375.00*
a. No period after "80" 225.00 *575.00*
Nos. 12-18 (7) 2,272. 6,462.

Imperforate stamps on unglazed paper, or in colors other than listed, are unfinished remainders of the 1868 issue.

Fraudulent cancellations are found on Nos. 13, 14, 17, 18.

1868 Glazed Paper *Perf. 13*

19 A12 2c blk, *green* 8.75 *50.00*
a. No period after "CENT" 10.00 *57.50*
20 A13 3c blk, *gray* 37.50 *2,350.*
a. 3c black, *lilac gray* *5,500.* *14,500.*
21 A14 5c blk, *lt bl* 10.00 *35.00*
a. No period after "5" 11.50 *40.00*
b. No period after "Cent" 65.00 *190.00*
c. 5c black, *lt bl* (unglazed, imperf., without gum) 45.00 —
22 A15 10c blk, *org ver* 3.00 *9.25*
a. 10c black, *vermilion* 57.50 11.50
b. 10c black, *ver* (unglazed) .80 —
c. 10c black, *ver* (unglazed, imperf., without gum) .75 —
23 A16 20c blk, *dp crim* 3.00 *19.00*
a. 20c black, *magenta* 4.50 *32.50*
b. 20c blk, *mag* (unglazed) 200.00 *24.00*
c. 20c blk, *mag* (imperf., without gum) 1.50 —
d. 20c blk, *cop red* (unglazed) 1,000. 35.00
e. 20c blk, *dp crim* (imperf., without gum) 1.50 —
f. No period after "20" *(copper red)* *1,500.* 210.00
g. No period after "20" *(mag)* 19.00 *150.00*
h. No period after "20" *(deep crimson)* 19.00 *160.00*
i. No period after "CENT" *(copper red)* *1,500.* 210.00
j. No period after "CENT" *(magenta)* 19.00 *150.00*
k. No period after "CENT" *(deep crimson)* 19.00 *150.00*
24 A17 40c blk, *grnsh yel* 5.75 *87.50*
a. 40c black, *yellow* 200.00 *70.00*
b. 40c black, *orange yellow* 72.50 *575.00*
c. No period after "40" 7.00 *87.50*
25 A18 80c blk, *rose lilac* 175.00 *260.00*
a. 80c black, *bright rose* *3,350.* *27,500.*
b. 80c black, *rose lilac* (unglazed) 47.50 —
c. No period after "80" *rose lilac*(unglazed) 77.50 *400.00*
d. 80c black, *pale rose lilac* (unglazed) 65.00 —
e. 80c black, *pale rose* (unglazed) 26.00 *260.00*
f. As "e," no period after "80" 37.50 *425.00*
g. As "a," no period after "80" *4,250.* —
h. As "e," double impression — —
Nos. 19-25 (7) 243.00 2,810.

All values except the 3c are known imperforate vertically or horizontally.

Double impressions are known of the 5c, 10c, 20c (all three colors), 40c and 80c.

Fraudulent cancellations are found on Nos. 20, 24 and 25.

The stamps of the 1867 and 1868 issues have been privately reprinted; many of these reprints are well executed and it is difficult to distinguish them from the originals. Most reprints show more or less pronounced defects of the design. On the originals the horizontal lines between stamps are unbroken, while on most of the reprints these lines are broken. Most of the perforated reprints gauge 11½.

Roman States stamps were replaced by those of Italy in 1870.

SARDINIA

LOCATION — An island in the Mediterranean Sea off the west coast of Italy and a large area in northwestern

Italy, including the cities of Genoa, Turin and Nice.

GOVT. — Kingdom

As a result of war and revolution, most of the former independent Italian States were joined to the Kingdom of Sardinia in 1859 and 1860. On March 17, 1861, the name was changed to the Kingdom of Italy.

100 Centesimi = 1 Lira

Values of Sardinia stamps vary tremendously according to condition. Values are for very fine examples, and values for unused stamps are for examples with original gum as defined in the catalogue introduction. Extremely fine or superb copies sell at much higher prices, and fine or poor copies sell at greatly reduced prices. In addition, very fine unused copies without gum sell for about 20-30% of the values shown.

A1

A2

A3

King Victor Emmanuel II — A4

1851 Unwmk. Litho. *Imperf.*

1 A1 5c gray blk 6,500. 1,600.
 a. 5c black 6,500. 1,600.
2 A1 20c blue 5,750. 125.00
 a. 20c deep blue 5,750. 125.00
 b. 20c pale blue 5,750. 190.00
3 A1 40c rose 10,000. *3,000.*
 a. 40c violet rose 10,000. *4,500.*

1853 Embossed

4 A2 5c *bl grn* 10,000. 1,000.
 a. Double embossing *2,000.*
5 A2 20c *dl bl* 11,500. 110.00
 a. Double embossing 950.00
6 A2 40c *pale rose* 7,750. 775.00
 a. Double embossing 8,750. *950.00*

Lithographed and Embossed

1854

7 A3 5c yellow grn *26,000.* 500.00
 a. Double embossing *1,000.*
 b. 5c grayish green 1,900. —
8 A3 20c blue *12,750.* 110.00
 a. Double embossing *400.00*
 b. 20c indigo 725.00 —
9 A3 40c rose *75,000.* 2,300.
 a. Double embossing *4,350.*
 b. 40c brown rose 160.00 —

Nos. 7b, 8b and 9b, differing in shade from the original stamps, were prepared but not issued.

Typographed Frame in Color, Colorless Embossed Center

1855-63 Unwmk. *Imperf.*

Stamps of this issue vary greatly in color, paper and sharpness of embossing as between the early (1855-59) printings and the later (1860-63) ones. Year dates after each color name indicate whether the stamp falls into the Early or Late printing group.

As a rule, early printings are on smooth thick paper with sharp embossing, while later printings are usually on paper varying from thick to thin and of inferior quality with embossing less distinct and printing blurred. The outer frame shows a distinct design on the early printings, while this design is more or less blurred or even a solid line on the later printings.

10 A4 5c green ('62-63) 4.75 *11.50*
 a. 5c yellow green ('62-63) 11.50 *16.00*
 b. 5c olive green ('60-61) 290.00 100.00
 c. 5c yellow green ('55-59) *575.00* 110.00
 d. 5c myrtle green ('57) *3,000.* 325.00
 e. 5c emerald ('55-57) *2,000.* 260.00
 f. Head inverted — *2,200.*
 g. Double head, one inverted — *2,200.*
11 A4 10c bis ('63) 4.50 *11.50*
 a. 10c ocher ('62) 65.00 14.50
 b. 10c olive bister ('62) 57.50 20.00
 c. 10c olive green ('61) 175.00 30.00
 d. 10c reddish brown ('61) 575.00 67.50
 e. 10c gray brown ('61) 125.00 40.00
 f. 10c olive gray ('60-61) 200.00 47.50
 g. 10c gray ('60) 800.00 125.00
 h. 10c grayish brown ('59) 45.00 110.00
 i. 10c violet brown ('59) 375.00 190.00
 j. 10c dark brown ('58) *500.00* 260.00
 k. Head inverted — *2,600.*
 l. Double head, one inverted — *2,600.*
 m. Pair, one without embossing *1,900.* —
 n. Half used as 5c on cover *60,000.*
12 A4 20c indigo ('62) 87.50 32.50
 a. 20c blue ('61) 100.00 17.50
 b. 20c light blue ('60-61) 100.00 17.50
 c. 20c Prussian bl ('59-60) 375.00 25.00
 d. 20c indigo ('57-58) 350.00 37.50
 e. 20c sky blue ('55-56) *2,900.* 150.00
 f. 20c cobalt ('55) *1,750.* 92.50
 g. Head inverted 1,900. *1,000.*
 h. Double head, one inverted — —
 i. Pair, one without embossing *1,000.* —
 j. Half used as 10c on cover *82,500.*
13 A4 40c red ('63) 17.50 *29.00*
 a. 40c rose ('61-62) 92.50 45.00
 b. 40c carmine ('60) 375.00 225.00
 c. 40c light red ('57) *1,750.* 100.00
 d. 40c vermilion ('55-57) *1,750.* 250.00
 e. Head inverted — *3,600.*
 f. Double head, one inverted — *3,500.*
 g. Pair, one without embossing *1,600.* —
 h. Half used as 20c on cover *47,500.*
14 A4 80c org yel ('62) 24.00 *325.00*
 a. 80c yellow ('60-61) 26.00 *300.00*
 b. 80c yellow ocher ('59) *575.00* 450.00
 c. 80c ocher ('58) 150.00 *350.00*
 d. 80c brown orange ('58) 150.00 *350.00*
 e. Head inverted — *13,000.*
 f. Half used as 40c on cover
15 A4 3 l bronze ('61) 325.00 *2,350.*
 Nos. 10-15 (6) 463.25 2,759.

Forgeries of the inverted and double head varieties have been made by applying a faked head embossing to printer's waste without head. These forgeries are plentiful.

Fraudulent cancellations are found on #13-15.

The 5c, 20c and 40c have been reprinted; the embossing of the reprints is not as sharp as that of the originals, the colors are dull and blurred.

NEWSPAPER STAMPS

N1

Typographed and Embossed

1861 Unwmk. *Imperf.*

P1 N1 1c black 5.75 *8.00*
 a. Numeral "2" 525.00 *1,650.*
 b. Figure of value inverted 1,350. *24,000.*
 c. Double impression —
P2 N1 2c black 110.00 67.50
 a. Numeral "1" *6,500.* *20,000.*
 b. Figure of value inverted *1,400.* *24,000.*

Forgeries of the varieties of the embossed numerals have been made from printer's waste without numerals.

See Italy No. P1 for 2c buff.

The stamps of Sardinia were superseded in 1862 by those of Italy, which were identical with the 1855 issue of Sardinia, but perforated. Until 1863, imperforate and perforated stamps were issued simultaneously.

TUSCANY

LOCATION — In the north central part of the Apennine Peninsula.

GOVT. — Grand Duchy

AREA — 8,890 sq. mi.

POP. — 2,892,000 (approx.)

CAPITAL — Florence

Tuscany was annexed to Sardinia in 1860.

60 Quattrini = 20 Soldi = 12 Crazie = 1 Lira

100 Centesimi = 1 Lira (1860)

Values of Tuscany stamps vary tremendously according to condition. Values are for very fine examples, and values for unused stamps are for examples with original gum as defined in the catalogue introduction. Extremely fine or superb copies sell at much higher prices, and fine or poor copies sell at greatly reduced prices. In addition, very fine unused copies without gum sell for about 20% of the values shown.

Lion of Tuscany — A1

1851-52 Typo. Wmk. 185 *Imperf.*

Blue, Grayish Blue or Gray Paper

1 A1 1q black ('52) 7,250. 1,150.
2 A1 1s ocher, *grayish* 8,750. 1,650.
 a. 1s orange, *grayish* 10,000. 1,350.
 b. 1s yellow, *bluish* 10,750. 1,450.
3 A1 2s scarlet *29,000.* 4,250.
4 A1 1cr carmine 4,500. 77.50
 a. 1cr brown carmine 5,750. 77.50
5 A1 2cr blue 2,600. 87.50
 a. 2cr greenish blue 2,900. 110.00
6 A1 4cr green 4,750. 110.00
 a. 4cr bluish green 4,750. 110.00
7 A1 6cr slate blue 5,250. 160.00
 a. 6cr blue 4,750. 160.00
 b. 6cr indigo 5,250. 160.00
8 A1 9cr gray lilac 11,500. 125.00
 a. 9cr deep violet 11,500. 125.00
9 A1 60cr red ('52) *52,500.* *15,000.*

The first paper was blue, later paper more and more grayish. Stamps on distinctly blue paper sell about 20 percent higher, except Nos. 3 and 9 which were issued on blue paper only. Examples without watermark are proofs.

Reprints of Nos. 3 and 9 have re-engraved value labels, color is too brown and impressions blurred and heavy. Paper same as originals.

1857-59 Wmk. 184

White Paper

10 A1 1q black 950.00 675.00
11 A1 1s yellow *26,000.* 3,250.
12 A1 1cr carmine 5,750. 350.00
13 A1 2cr blue 1,600. 87.50
14 A1 4cr blue green 5,250. 110.00
15 A1 6cr deep blue *6,500.* 150.00
16 A1 9cr gray lilac ('59) *23,250.* *3,250.*

Provisional Government

Coat of Arms — A2

1860

17 A2 1c brn lilac 1,750. 575.00
 a. 1c red lilac 2,250. 650.00
 b. 1c gray lilac 1,750. 575.00
18 A2 5c green 7,000. 175.00
 a. 5c olive green 7,750. 190.00
 b. 5c yellow green 8,750. 250.00
19 A2 10c deep brn 2,000. 32.50
 a. 10c gray brown 1,600. 29.00
 b. 10c purple brown 1,600. 29.00
20 A2 20c blue 5,750. 110.00
 a. 20c deep blue 5,750. 125.00
 b. 20c gray blue 6,000. 125.00
21 A2 40c rose 8,750. 190.00
 a. 40c carmine 8,750. 190.00
 b. Half used as 20c on cover *115,000.*
22 A2 80c pale red brn *17,500.* 925.00
 a. 80c brown orange *17,500.* 925.00
23 A2 3 l ocher *120,000.* *56,500.*

Dangerous counterfeits exist of #1-PR1c.

NEWSPAPER TAX STAMP

NT1

1854 Unwmk. Typo. *Imperf.*

Yellowish Pelure Paper

PR1 NT1 2s black 47.50
 a. Tête bêche pair 500.00
 b. as "a," one stamp on back 500.00
 c. Double impression 375.00

This stamp represented a fiscal tax on newspapers coming from foreign countries. It was not canceled when used.

The stamps of Tuscany were superseded by those of Sardinia in 1861.

TWO SICILIES

LOCATION — Formerly comprised the island of Sicily and the lower half of the Apennine Peninsula.

GOVT. — Independent Kingdom

CAPITAL — Naples

The Kingdom was annexed to Sardinia in 1860.

200 Tornesi = 100 Grana = 1 Ducat

Values of Two Sicilies stamps vary tremendously according to condition. Values are for very fine examples, and values for unused stamps are for examples with original gum as defined in the catalogue introduction. Extremely fine or superb copies sell at much higher prices, and fine or poor copies sell at greatly reduced prices. In addition, very fine unused copies without gum sell for about 20-30% of the values shown.

Naples

Coat of Arms
A1 A2

A3

A4

A5

A6

A7

1858 Engr. Wmk. 186 *Imperf.*

1 A1 ½g pale lake 1,450. 250.00
 a. ½g rose lake 1,500. 250.00
 b. ½g lake 1,750. 375.00
 c. ½g carmine lake 1,950. 500.00
 d. Half used as ¼g on newspaper *132,500.*
2 A2 1g pale lake 725.00 35.00
 a. 1g rose lake 350.00 32.50
 b. 1g brown lake 775.00 65.00
 c. 1g carmine lake 525.00 50.00
 d. Printed on both sides *1,300.*
 e. Double impression —
3 A3 2g pale lake 210.00 9.25
 a. 2g rose lake 210.00 9.25
 b. 2g lake 375.00 16.00
 c. 2g carmine lake 450.00 16.00
 d. Impression of 1g on reverse *1,150.*
 e. Double impression *7,250.*
 f. Printed on both sides *1,250.*
4 A4 5g brown lake 2,000. 40.00
 a. 5g rose lake 1,750. 40.00
 b. 5g carmine lake 2,450. 45.00
 c. Double impression — —
 d. Printed on both sides *3,250.*
 e. 5g rose carmine 3,600. 110.00
 f. 5g bright carmine 4,000. 140.00
 g. 5g dark carmine 4,250. 200.00
5 A5 10g rose lake 3,750. 125.00
 a. 10g lake 4,000. 190.00
 b. 10g carmine lake 4,000. 190.00
 c. Printed on both sides *11,000.*
 d. Double impression 12,250.
6 A6 20g rose lake 3,250. 450.00
 a. 20g lake 3,250. 500.00
 b. Double impression *36,250.* —
 c. 20g pale rose *5,250.* 1,000.
 d. 20g pale car rose *6,000.* 1,200.
7 A7 50g rose lake *7,750.* 2,250.
 a. 50g lake *7,750.* 2,250.
 b. Double impression — —

As a secret mark, the engraver, G. Masini, placed a minute letter of his name just above the lower outer line of each stamp. There were three plates of the 2g, one plate of the 50g, and two plates of each of the other values.

Nos. 1-2, 4-7 have been reprinted in bright rose and Nos. 1 and 7 in dull brown. The *reprints are on thick unwatermarked paper. Value $8 each.*

Provisional Government

A8

A9

1860

8	A8 ½t deep blue		*130,000.*	*8,000.*
9	A9 ½t blue		*30,000.*	2,900.
a.	½t deep blue		*30,000.*	2,900.

100 varieties of each.

No. 8 was made from the plate of No. 1, which was altered by changing the "G" to "T."

No. 9 was made from the same plate after a second alteration erasing the coat of arms and inserting the Cross of Savoy. Dangerous counterfeits exist of Nos. 8-9.

Sicily

Ferdinand II — A10

1859 Unwmk. Engr. *Imperf.*

10	A10 ½g orange	500.00	*575.00*
a.	½g yellow	*5,000.*	*1,800.*
b.	½g olive yellow	—	*24,750.*
c.	Printed on both sides	—	*23,250.*
11	A10 1g dk brn	*13,000.*	550.00
a.	1g olive brown (I)	*24,500.*	7,000.
12	A10 1g ol grn (III)	875.00	190.00
a.	1g grysh olive grn (II)	2,000.	150.00
b.	1g olive brown (II)	700.00	110.00
c.	Double impression	*2,600.*	*2,600.*
13	A10 2g blue	2,000.	80.00
a.	2g deep blue	*2,900.*	260.00
b.	Printed on both sides	—	*14,500.*
14	A10 5g deep rose	550.00	425.00
a.	5g carmine	500.00	400.00
b.	5g brick red	*7,250.*	*4,250.*
15	A10 5g vermilion	375.00	*1,100.*
a.	5g orange vermilion	200.00	*1,150.*
16	A10 10g dark blue	575.00	250.00
a.	10g indigo	625.00	275.00
17	A10 20g dk gray vio	575.00	450.00
18	A10 50g dk brn red	550.00	*3,600.*

There were three plates each for the 1g and 2g, two each for the ½g and 5g and one plate each for the other values.

Nos. 10a, 10b, 11, 11a, 14, 14a, 14b and 15 are printed from Plate I on which the stamps are 2 to 2½mm apart. On almost all stamps from Plate I, the S and T of POSTA touch.

Nos. 12a, and 15a are from Plate II and No. 12 is from Plate III. On both Plates II and III stamps are spaced 1½mm apart. Most stamps from Plate II have a white line about 1mm long below the beard.

The ½g blue is stated to be a proof of which two copies are known used on cover.

Fraudulent cancellations are known on Nos. 10, 15, 15a and 18.

Neapolitan Provinces

King Victor Emmanuel II — A11

Lithographed, Center Embossed

1861 Unwmk. *Imperf.*

19	A11 ½t green	8.75	*125.00*
a.	½t yellow green	300.00	*150.00*
b.	½t emerald	2,600.	400.00
c.	½t black (error)	*30,000.*	*37,500.*
d.	Head inverted (green)	150.00	
e.	Head inverted (yel grn)		*7,500.*
f.	Printed on both sides		*17,500.*
20	A11 ½g bister	110.00	*150.00*
a.	½g brown	110.00	*150.00*
b.	½g gray brown	140.00	*150.00*
c.	Head inverted	1,150.	—
21	A11 1g black	275.00	19.00
a.	Head inverted		*1,150.*
22	A11 2g blue	72.50	9.25
a.	2g deep blue	72.50	9.25
b.	Head inverted	*210.00*	*550.00*
c.	2g black (error)		*40,000.*
23	A11 5g car rose	125.00	87.50
a.	5g vermilion	125.00	100.00
b.	5g lilac rose	160.00	140.00
c.	Head inverted	*650.00*	*5,250.*
e.	Printed on both sides		*9,250.*
25	A11 10g orange	87.50	*160.00*
a.	10g ocher	*750.00*	400.00
b.	10g bister	100.00	*175.00*
26	A11 20g yellow	375.00	*1,600.*
a.	Head inverted		*18,750.*
27	A11 50g gray	20.00	*6,375.*
a.	50g slate	23.00	*6,375.*
b.	50g slate blue	29.00	*7,750.*
	Nos. 19-27 (8)	1,073.	8,525.

Counterfeits of the inverted head varieties of this issue are plentiful. See note on forgeries after Sardinia No. 15.

Fraudulent cancellations are found on Nos. 19-20, 23-27.

Stamps similar to those of Sardinia 1855-61, type A4 but with inscriptions in larger, clearer lettering, were prepared in 1861 for the Neapolitan Provinces. They were not officially issued although a few are known postally used. Denominations: 5c, 10c, 20c, 40c and 80c.

Stamps of Two Sicilies were replaced by those of Italy in 1862.

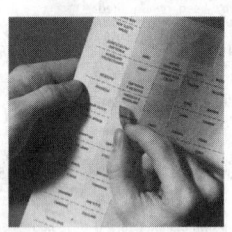

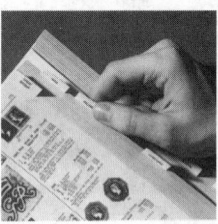

ITALY

ˈi-tᵊl-ē

LOCATION — Southern Europe
GOVT. — Republic
AREA — 119,764 sq. mi.
POP. — 56,735,130 (1999 est.)
CAPITAL — Rome

Formerly a kingdom, Italy became a republic in June 1946

100 Centesimi = 1 Lira
100 Cents = 1 Euro (2002)

Catalogue values for unused stamps in this country are for Never Hinged items, beginning with Scott 691 in the regular postage section, Scott B47 in the semi-postal section, Scott C129 in the airpost section, Scott D21 in the pneumatic post section, Scott E32 in the special delivery section, Scott EY11 in the authorized delivery section, Scott J83 in the postage due section, Scott Q77 in the parcel post section, Scott QY5 in the parcel post authorized delivery section, Scott 1N1 in the A.M.G. section, Scott 1LN1 in the Venezia Giulia section, 1LNC1 in the occupation air post section, 1LNE1 in the occupation special delivery section, and all of the items in the Italian Social Republic area.

Watermarks

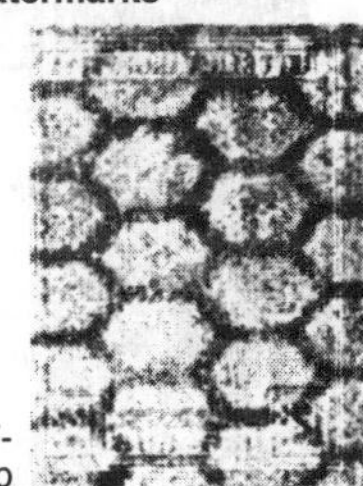

Wmk. 87-Honeycomb

Wmk. 140-Crown

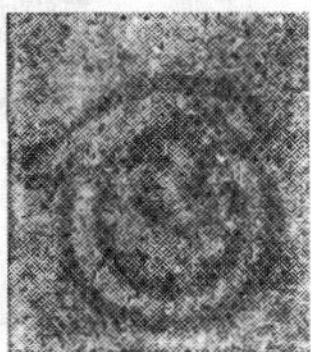

Wmk. 277-Winged Wheel

Wmk. 303-Multiple Stars

Values of Italy stamps vary tremendously according to condition. Quotations are for very fine examples, and values for unused stamps are for examples with original gum as defined in the catalogue introduction. Extremely fine or superb copies sell at much higher prices, and fine or poor copies sell at greatly reduced prices. In addition, unused copies without gum are discounted severely.

Very fine examples of Nos. 17-21, 24-75, J2-J27, O1-O8 and Q1-Q6 will have perforations barely clear of the frameline or design due to the narrow spacing of the stamps on the plates.

King Victor Emmanuel II
A4 A5

Typographed; Head Embossed

1862 Unwmk. *Perf. 11½x12*

17	A4	10c bister	*5,500.*	150.00
19	A4	20c dark blue	8.75	*19.00*
20	A4	40c red	160.00	82.50
21	A4	80c orange	30.00	*1,000.*

The outer frame shows a distinct design on the early printings, while this design is more or less blurred, or even a solid line, on the later printings.

Numerous shades of Nos. 17-21 exist. Some are very expensive. For listings, see the *Scott Classic Catalogue.*

The 20c and 40c exist perf. 11½. These are remainders of Sardinia with forged perforations.

Counterfeit cancellations are often found on No. 21.

Lithographed; Head Embossed

1863 *Imperf.*

22	A4	15c blue	40.00	27.50
a.		Head inverted		*35,000.*
b.		Double head	62.50	45.00
c.		Head omitted	225.00	21,000.

See note after Sardinia No. 15.

No. 22c is valued with original gum only.

Two types of No. 23:

Type I - First "C" in bottom line nearly closed.

Type II - "C" open. Line broken below "Q."

1863 Litho.

23	A5	15c blue, Type II	2.50	*4.50*
a.		Type I	350.00	13.50
		Without gum, type I	27.50	

A6

A7

A8

A13

1863-77 Typo. Wmk. 140 *Perf. 14*

24	A6	1c gray green	1.75	1.50
a.		Imperf., pair		*8,500.*
25	A7	2c org brn ('65)	6.25	1.00
a.		Imperf., pair	100.00	*160.00*
26	A8	5c slate grn	1,000.	1.50
27	A8	10c buff	1,600.	1.75
a.		10c orange brown	1,600.	1.75
28	A8	10c blue ('77)	4,250.	2.00
29	A8	15c blue	1,600.	2.00
a.		Imperf.		*3,250.*
30	A8	30c brown	5.50	2.75
a.		Imperf.		*4,500.*
31	A8	40c carmine	3,250.	2.25
a.		40c rose	3,250.	2.25
32	A8	60c lilac	6.25	*9.00*
33	A13	2 l vermilion	12.50	*45.00*

Nos. 26 to 32 have the head of type A8 but with different corner designs for each value.

Early printings of Nos. 24-27, 29-33 were made in London, later printings in Turin. Values are for Turin printings. London printings of 1c, 2c, 30c, 60c and 2 l sell for more.

For overprints see Italian Offices Abroad Nos. 1-5, 8-11.

No. 29 Surcharged in Brown

1865

Type I - Dots flanking stars in oval, and dot in eight check-mark ornaments in corners.

Type II - Dots in oval, none in corners.

Type III - No dots.

34	A8	20c on 15c bl (I)	425.00	1.75
a.		Type II	3,750.	10.00
b.		Type III	1,200.	3.75
c.		Inverted surcharge (I)		*35,000.*

A15

1867-77 Typo.

35	A15	20c blue	550.	.75
36	A15	20c orange ('77)	3,150.	2.00

For overprints see Italian Offices Abroad #9-10.

Official Stamps Surcharged in Blue

1877

37	O1	2c on 2c lake	90.00	7.50
38	O1	2c on 5c lake	100.00	10.00
39	O1	2c on 20c lake	500.00	2.25
40	O1	2c on 30c lake	350.00	3.25
41	O1	2c on 1 l lake	325.00	2.25
42	O1	2c on 2 l lake	350.00	4.00
43	O1	2c on 5 l lake	475.00	5.00
44	O1	2c on 10 l lake	325.00	6.75
		Nos. 37-44 (8)	2,515.	41.00

Inverted Surcharge

37a	O1	2c on 2c		900.00
38a	O1	2c on 5c		650.00
39a	O1	2c on 20c	*18,750.*	550.00
40a	O1	2c on 30c		550.00
41a	O1	2c on 1 l	*22,500.*	600.00
42a	O1	2c on 2 l	*22,500.*	675.00
43a	O1	2c on 5 l		675.00
44a	O1	2c on 10 l		625.00

King Humbert I — A17

1879 Typo. *Perf. 14*

45	A17	5c blue green	5.50	.75
46	A17	10c claret	290.00	.90
47	A17	20c orange	250.00	.75
48	A17	25c blue	425.00	1.75
49	A17	30c brown	90.00	*1,100.*
50	A17	50c violet	8.00	6.25
51	A17	2 l vermilion	32.50	*175.00*

Nos. 45-51 have the head of type A17 with different corner designs for each value.

Beware of forged cancels on No. 49, both off and on cover.

For surcharges and overprints see Nos. 64-66, Italian Offices Abroad 12-17.

Arms of Savoy — A24

Humbert I — A25

A26

A27

A28

A29

1889

52	A24	5c dark green	475.00	1.40
53	A25	40c brown	6.00	5.00
54	A26	45c gray green	1,100.	3.25
55	A27	60c violet	7.50	*11.50*
56	A28	1 l brown & yel	7.50	4.50
a.		1 l brown & orange	10.00	5.00
57	A29	5 l grn & claret	11.50	*325.00*

Forged cancellations exist on #51, 57.

Parcel Post Stamps of 1884-86 Surcharged in Black

1890

58	PP1	2c on 10c ol gray	3.25	3.50
a.		Inverted surcharge	200.00	*1,400.*
59	PP1	2c on 20c blue	2.90	3.50
60	PP1	2c on 50c claret	35.00	20.00
a.		Inverted surcharge		*17,500.*
61	PP1	2c on 75c blue grn	2.50	*3.25*
62	PP1	2c on 1.25 l org	22.50	17.50
a.		Inverted surcharge	*32,500.*	*16,250.*
63	PP1	2c on 1.75 l brn	10.00	*30.00*
		Nos. 58-63 (6)	76.15	*77.75*

Stamps of 1879 Surcharged

1890-91

64 A17 2c on 5c bl grn ('91) 10.00 *30.00*
a. "2" with thin tail 72.50 *175.00*
65 A17 20c on 30c brown 225.00 4.00
66 A17 20c on 50c violet 275.00 19.00
Nos. 64-66 (3) 510.00 *53.00*

On Nos. 65-66 the period is omitted in the surcharge.

Arms of Savoy — A33

Humbert I — A34

A35

A36

A37

A38

1891-96 Typo.

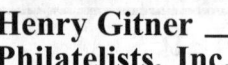

67 A33 5c green 350.00 .90
68 A34 10c claret ('96) 4.00 .75
69 A35 20c orange ('95) 4.00 .75
70 A36 25c blue 4.00 2.00
71 A37 45c ol grn ('95) 4.00 2.00
72 A38 5 l blue & rose 37.50 *72.50*

Arms of Savoy — A39

A40

A41

1896-97

73 A39 1c brown 3.50 2.50
74 A40 2c orange brown 3.50 .80
75 A41 5c green ('97) 16.00 .65
Nos. 73-75 (3) 23.00 3.95

A42

Coat of Arms
A43 A44

Victor Emmanuel III
A45 A46

1901-26

76 A42 1c brown .20 .20
a. Imperf., pair 375.00 *575.00*
77 A43 2c org brn .20 .20
a. Double impression 62.50 *125.00*
b. Imperf., pair 110.00
78 A44 5c blue grn 30.00 .25
a. Imperf., pair —
79 A45 10c claret 37.50 .65
a. Imperf., pair — *5,250.*
80 A45 20c orange 7.00 .65
81 A45 25c ultra 60.00 .90
a. 25c dp blue 65.00 1.00
82 A46 25c grn & pale grn ('26) .25 .20
83 A45 40c brown 275.00 3.00
84 A45 45c olive grn 3.00 .20
a. Imperf., pair 190.00 *325.00*
85 A45 50c violet 200.00 6.00
86 A46 75c dk red & rose ('26) 2.50 .20
87 A46 1 l brown & grn 1.50 .20
a. Imperf., pair 90.00 *72.50*
88 A46 1.25 l bl & ultra ('26) 3.50 .20
89 A46 2 l dk grn & org ('23) 16.50 1.75
90 A46 2.50 l dk grn & org ('26) 35.00 2.50
91 A46 5 l blue & rose 11.00 2.00
Nos. 76-91 (16) 683.15 19.10

Nos. 83, 85, unused, are valued in fine condition.

The borders of Nos. 79-81, 83-85, 87, 89 and 91 differ slightly for each denomination.

On Nos. 82, 86, 88 and 90, the value is expressed as "Cent. 25," etc.

See No. 87b in set following No. 174G.

For surcharges and overprints see Nos. 148-149, 152, 158, 174F-174G, B16; Austria N20-N21, N27, N30, N52-N53, N58, N60, N64-N65, N71, N74; Dalmatia 1, 6-7.

Overprints & Surcharges See Offices in China, Crete, Africa, Turkish Empire (Albania to Valona) and Aegean Islands for types A36-A58 overprinted or surcharged.

No. 80 Surcharged in Black

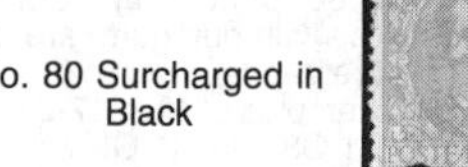

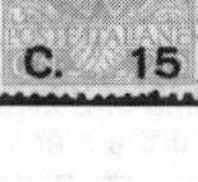

1905

92 A45 15c on 20c org 50.00 .75
a. Double surcharge *2,250.*

No. 93 No. 111 No. 123

A47

1906 Unwmk. Engr. *Perf. 12*

93 A47 15c slate 50.00 .50
a. Imperf. horiz. or vert., pair 80.00 *95.00*
b. Booklet pane of 6 *500.00*

A48

A49

1906-19 Wmk. 140 Typo. *Perf. 14*

94 A48 5c green .30 .20
a. Imperf., pair 55.00 *24.00*
b. Printed on both sides 95.00
95 A48 10c claret .75 .20
a. Imperf., pair 55.00 *24.00*
96 A48 15c slate ('19) 1.00 .25
a. Imperf., pair 150.00 *67.50*
Nos. 94-96 (3) 2.05 .65

The frame of #95 differs in several details.

See Nos. 96b-96d following No. 174G.

For overprints and surcharge see Nos. 142A-142B, 150, 174A, B5, B9-B10; Austria N22-N23, N31, N54-N55, N61-N62, N66-N67; Dalmatia 2-5.

1908-27

97 A49 20c brn org ('25) 1.00 .50
98 A49 20c green ('25) .30 .20
99 A49 20c lil brn ('26) 1.50 .20
100 A49 25c blue 1.25 .20
a. Imperf., pair 100.00 *85.00*
b. Printed on both sides 110.00 *175.00*
101 A49 25c lt grn ('27) 5.50 *4.50*
102 A49 30c org brn ('22) 1.50 .40
b. Imperf., pair 100.00 *175.00*
103 A49 30c gray ('25) 2.25 .20
104 A49 40c brown 2.40 .20
a. Imperf., pair 125.00 *125.00*
105 A49 50c violet .90 .20
a. Imperf., pair 125.00 *175.00*
106 A49 55c dl vio ('20) 6.00 5.00
107 A49 60c car ('17) 1.50 .25
108 A49 60c blue ('23) 5.75 *17.50*
109 A49 60c brn org ('26) 4.50 .35
110 A49 85c red brn ('20) 4.00 1.75
Nos. 97-110 (14) 38.35 *31.45*

The upper panels of Nos. 104 and 105 are in solid color with white letters. A body of water has been added to the background.

See Nos. 100c-105j following No. 174G.

For overprints & surcharges see #142C-142D, 147, 151, 153-157, 174B-174E, B7-B8, B12-B15A; Austria N24-N26, N28-N29, N32, N56-N57, N59, N63, N68-N70, N72-N73.

A50

A51

Redrawn

Perf. 13x13½, 13½x14

1909-17 Typo. Unwmk.

111 A50 15c slate black 200.00 1.00
112 A50 20c brown org ('16) 30.00 .75

No. 111 is similar to No. 93, but the design has been redrawn and the stamp is 23mm high instead of 25mm. There is a star at each side of the coat collar, but one is not distinct. See illustrations next to A47.

For overprints see Nos. B6, B11.

Wmk. 140 *Perf. 14*

113 A50 20c brn org ('17) 3.00 .25
a. Imperf., pair 22.50 *35.00*

Stamps overprinted "Prestito Nazionale, 1917," or later dates, are Thrift or Postal Savings Stamps.

1910, Nov. 1

114 A51 10 l gray grn & red 50.00 10.00

For surcharge see Dalmatia No. 8.

Giuseppe Garibaldi
A52 A53

Perf. 14x13½

1910, Apr. 15 Unwmk.

115 A52 5c green 10.00 *12.50*
116 A52 15c claret 21.00 *25.00*

50th anniversary of freedom of Sicily.

1910, Dec. 1

117 A53 5c claret 100.00 57.50
118 A53 15c green 210.00 82.50

50th anniversary of the plebiscite of the southern Italian provinces in 1860.

Used values in italics are for postaly used stamps. CTO's sell for about the same as unused, hinged stamps.

Symbols of Rome and Turin — A54

Symbol of Valor — A55

Genius of Italy — A56

Glory of Rome — A57

1911, May 1 Engr. *Perf. 14x13½*
119 A54 2c brown 1.25 *1.50*
120 A55 5c deep green 8.25 *10.00*
121 A56 10c carmine 9.50 *17.50*
122 A57 15c slate 12.50 *21.00*
Nos. 119-122 (4) 31.50 *50.00*

50th anniv. of the union of Italian States to form the Kingdom of Italy.
Nos. 115 to 122 were sold at a premium over their face value.
For surcharges see Nos. 126-128.

Victor Emmanuel III — A58

Campanile, Venice — A59

1911, Oct. Re-engraved *Perf. 13½*
123 A58 15c slate 22.50 .50
a. Imperf., pair 100.00 *150.00*
b. Printed on both sides 150.00 *225.00*
c. Bklt. pane of 6 *200.00*

The re-engraved stamp is 24mm high. The stars at each side of the coat collar show plainly and the "C" of "Cent" is nearer the frame than in No. 93. See illustrations next to A47.
For surcharge see No. 129.

1912, Apr. 25 *Perf. 14x13½*
124 A59 5c indigo 3.75 3.75
125 A59 15c dk brn 13.50 *16.50*

Re-erection of the Campanile at Venice.

Nos. 120-121 Surcharged in Black

1913, Mar. 1
126 A55 2c on 5c dp grn 1.00 *2.00*
127 A56 2c on 10c car 1.00 *2.00*

No. 122 Surcharged in Violet

128 A57 2c on 15c slate 1.00 *2.00*
Nos. 126-128 (3) 3.00 6.00
Set, never hinged 6.75

No. 123 Surcharged CENT 20

1916
129 A58 20c on 15c slate 11.50 .50
Never hinged 22.50
a. Bklt. pane of 6 125.00
b. Inverted surcharge 200.00 200.00
c. Double surcharge 125.00 125.00

Old Seal of Republic of Trieste A60

Allegory of Dante's Divine Comedy A61

Italy Holding Laurels for Dante — A62

Dante Alighieri — A63

Wmk. 140
1921, June 5 Litho. *Perf. 14*
130 A60 15c blk & rose 1.75 *14.00*
131 A60 25c bl & rose 1.75 *14.00*
132 A60 40c brn & rose 1.75 *14.00*
Nos. 130-132 (3) 5.25 *42.00*
Set, never hinged 10.50

Reunion of Venezia Giulia with Italy.

1921, Sept. 28 Typo.
133 A61 15c vio brn 2.00 *8.75*
a. Imperf., pair 55.00
134 A62 25c gray grn 2.00 *8.75*
a. Imperf., pair 55.00
135 A63 40c brown 2.00 *8.75*
a. Imperf., pair 55.00
Nos. 133-135 (3) 6.00 *26.25*
Set, never hinged 15.00

600th anniversary of the death of Dante.
A 15c gray was not issued. Value, $20.
Nos. 133-135 exist in part perforate pairs.

"Victory" — A64

Perf. 14, 14x13½
1921, Nov. 1 Engr.
136 A64 5c olive green .25 *.75*
137 A64 10c red .50 *.85*
138 A64 15c slate green 1.25 *3.75*
139 A64 25c ultra .50 *2.00*
Nos. 136-139 (4) 2.50 *7.35*
Set, never hinged 6.40

3rd anniv. of the victory on the Piave.
Nos. 136-137, 139 exist imperf.
For surcharges see Nos. 171-174.

Flame of Patriotism Tempering Sword of Justice — A65

Giuseppe Mazzini — A66

Mazzini's Tomb A67

1922, Sept. 20 Typo. *Perf. 14*
140 A65 25c maroon 3.75 *12.50*
141 A66 40c vio brn 7.50 *14.00*
142 A67 80c dk bl 3.75 *20.00*
Nos. 140-142 (3) 15.00 *46.50*
Set, never hinged 38.00

Mazzini (1805-1872), patriot and writer.

Nos. 95, 96, 100 and 104 Overprinted in Black

1922, June 4 Wmk. 140 *Perf. 14*
142A A48 10c claret 150.00 100.00
142B A48 15c slate 110.00 90.00
142C A49 25c blue 95.00 90.00
142D A49 40c brown 160.00 100.00
Nos. 142A-142D (4) 515.00 380.00
Set, never hinged 1,525.

9th Italian Philatelic Congress, Trieste. Counterfeits exist.

Christ Preaching The Gospel — A68

Portrait at upper right and badge at lower right differ on each value. Portrait at upper left is of Pope Gregory XV. Others: 20c, St. Theresa. 30c, St. Dominic. 50c, St. Francis of Assisi. 1 l, St. Francis Xavier.

1923, June 11
143 A68 20c ol grn & brn org 1.10 *30.00*
144 A68 30c claret & brn org 1.10 *30.00*
145 A68 50c vio & brn org 1.10 *30.00*
146 A68 1 l bl & brn org 1.10 *30.00*
Nos. 143-146 (4) 4.40 *120.00*
Set, never hinged 14.00

300th anniv. of the Propagation of the Faith. Practically the entire issue was delivered to speculators.
Nos. 143-146 exist imperf. and part perf.

Stamps of Previous Issues, Surcharged:

a

b

c

d

Lire 1,75
e

1923-25
147 A49(a) 7½c on 85c .25 .75
a. Double surcharge — *750.00*
148 A42(b) 10c on 1c .25 .20
a. Inverted surcharge 15.00 *22.50*
149 A43(b) 10c on 2c .25 .20
a. Inverted surcharge 37.50 *55.00*
150 A48(c) 10c on 15c .25 .20
151 A49(a) 20c on 25c .25 .20
152 A45(d) 25c on 45c .25 *7.50*
153 A49(a) 25c on 60c 1.50 .60
154 A49(a) 30c on 50c .20 .20
155 A49(a) 30c on 55c .35 .20
156 A49(a) 50c on 40c 4.00 .25
a. Inverted surcharge 110.00 *160.00*
b. Double surcharge 70.00 *80.00*
157 A49(a) 50c on 55c 20.00 5.00
a. Inverted surcharge *500.00* *875.00*
158 A51(e) 1.75 l on 10 l 10.00 13.50
Nos. 147-158 (12) 37.55 28.80
Set, never hinged 77.50

Years of issue: Nos. 148-149, 156-157, 1923; Nos. 147, 152-153, 1924; others, 1925.

Emblem of the New Government A69

Wreath of Victory, Eagle and Fasces A70

Symbolical of Fascism and Italy — A71

Unwmk.
1923, Oct. 24 Engr. *Perf. 14*
159 A69 10c dark green 2.25 *2.10*
a. Imperf., pair 475.00
160 A69 30c dark violet 2.25 *2.10*
161 A69 50c brown carmine 3.25 *4.50*

Wmk. 140 Typo.
162 A70 1 l blue 5.50 2.50
163 A70 2 l brown 5.50 *4.50*
164 A71 5 l blk & bl 10.00 *25.00*
a. Imperf., pair 225.00
Nos. 159-164 (6) 28.75 *40.70*
Set, never hinged 57.50

Anniv. of the March of the Fascisti on Rome.

Fishing Scene A72

Designs: 15c, Mt. Resegone. 30c, Fugitives bidding farewell to native mountains. 50c, Part of Lake Como. 1 l, Manzoni's home, Milan. 5 l, Alessandro Manzoni. The first four designs show scenes from Manzoni's work "I Promessi Sposi."

1923, Dec. 29 *Perf. 14*
165 A72 10c brn red & blk 3.75 *37.50*
166 A72 15c bl grn & blk 3.75 *37.50*
167 A72 30c blk & slate 3.75 *37.50*
a. Imperf., pair —
Never hinged 1,400.
168 A72 50c org brn & blk 3.75 *37.50*
169 A72 1 l blue & blk 60.00 *150.00*
a. Imperf., pair, no gum 1750. —
170 A72 5 l vio & blk 325.00 *1,200.*
a. Imperf., pair —
Never hinged 950.00
Nos. 165-170 (6) 400.00 *1,500.*
Set, never hinged 1,000.

50th anniv. of the death of Alessandro Manzoni.

Nos. 136-139 Surcharged

1924, Feb.
171 A64 1 l on 5c ol grn 9.50 *50.00*
172 A64 1 l on 10c red 5.50 *50.00*
173 A64 1 l on 15c slate grn 9.50 *50.00*
174 A64 1 l on 25c ultra 5.50 *50.00*
Nos. 171-174 (4) 30.00 *200.00*
Set, never hinged 76.00

Surcharge forgeries exist.

Perf. 14x13½

171a	A64	1 l on 5c	19.00	*62.50*
172a	A64	1 l on 10c	11.50	*62.50*
173a	A64	1 l on 15c	19.00	*62.50*
174h	A64	1 l on 25c	11.50	*62.50*
		Nos. 171a-174h (4)	61.00	*250.00*
		Set, never hinged	120.00	

Nos. 95, 102, 105, 108, 110, 87 and 89 Overprinted in Black or Red

1924, Feb. 16

174A	A48	10c claret	1.10	*7.50*
174B	A49	30c org brn	1.10	*7.50*
174C	A49	50c violet	1.10	*7.50*
174D	A49	60c bl (R)	7.50	*30.00*
174E	A49	85c choc (R)	4.00	*30.00*
174F	A46	1 l brn & grn	32.50	*140.00*
174G	A46	2 l dk grn & org	26.00	*140.00*
		Nos. 174A-174G (7)	73.30	*362.50*
		Set, never hinged	160.00	

These stamps were sold on an Italian warship which made a cruise to South American ports in 1924.

Overprint forgeries exist of #174D-174G.

Stamps of 1901-22 with Advertising Labels Attached

Perf. 14 all around, Imperf. between

1924-25

96b	A48	15c + Bitter Campari	1.40	5.25
96c	A48	15c + Cordial Campari	1.40	5.25
96d	A48	15c + Columbia	17.00	17.50
100c	A49	25c + Abrador	45.00	45.00
100d	A49	25c + Coen	95.00	17.50
100e	A49	25c + Piperno	750.00	225.00
100f	A49	25c + Reinach	45.00	32.50
100g	A49	25c + Tagliacozzo	325.00	240.00
102a	A49	30c + Columbia	14.50	*16.00*
105b	A49	50c + Coen	750.00	32.50
105c	A49	50c + Columbia	8.50	4.75
105d	A49	50c + De Montel	1.25	5.25
105e	A49	50c + Piperno	825.00	70.00
105f	A49	50c + Reinach	95.00	24.00
105g	A49	50c + Siero Casali	7.75	*16.00*
105h	A49	50c + Singer	1.40	*2.25*
105i	A49	50c + Tagliacozzo	*1,150.*	175.00
105j	A49	50c + Tantal	125.00	47.50
87b	A46	1 l + Columbia	325.00	275.00
		Nos. 96b-87b (19)	4,583.	1,256.
		Set, never hinged	7,500.	

No. 113 with Columbia label and No. E3 with Cioccolato Perugina label were prepared but not issued. Values $20, $5.

King Victor Emmanuel III — A78

Perf. 11, 13½ (No. 177)

1925-26 Engr. Unwmk.

175	A78	60c brn car	.20	.20
a.		Perf. 13½	2.75	.75
b.		Imperf., pair	125.00	
176	A78	1 l dk bl	.20	.20
a.		Perf. 13½	3.50	1.00
b.		Imperf., pair	125.00	—
177	A78	1.25 l dk bl ('26)	1.75	.75
a.		Perf. 11	62.50	20.00
b.		Imperf., pair	290.00	—
		Nos. 175-177 (3)	2.15	1.15
		Set, never hinged	7.50	

25th year of the reign of Victor Emmanuel III.

Nos. 175 to 177 exist with sideways watermark of fragments of letters or a crown, which are normally on the sheet margin.

St. Francis and His Vision A79

Monastery of St. Damien A80

Assisi Monastery A81

St. Francis' Death A82

St. Francis — A83

1926, Jan. 30 Wmk. 140 ***Perf. 14***

178	A79	20c gray grn	.20	.35
179	A80	40c dk vio	.20	.35
180	A81	60c red brn	.20	.35
a.		Imperf., pair	—	

Unwmk. ***Perf. 11***

181	A83	30c slate blk	.20	.35
a.		Perf. 13½	7.50	3.00
		Never hinged	19.00	
182	A82	1.25 l dark blue	.50	.35
a.		Perf. 13½	275.00	8.75
		Never hinged	675.00	

Perf. 13½

183	A83	5 l + 2.50 l dk brn	5.00	*40.00*
		Nos. 178-183 (6)	6.30	*41.75*
		Set, never hinged	14.90	

St. Francis of Assisi, 700th death anniv.

Alessandro Volta — A84

1927 Wmk. 140 Typo. ***Perf. 14***

188	A84	20c dk car	.35	.30
189	A84	50c grnsh blk	.75	.25
190	A84	60c chocolate	1.00	1.25
191	A84	1.25 l ultra	2.10	1.75
		Nos. 188-191 (4)	4.20	3.55
		Set, never hinged	10.55	

Cent. of the death of Alessandro Volta.

The 20c in purple is Cyrenaica No. 25 with overprint omitted. Value, $2,500.

A85 A86

1927-29 Size: 17½x22mm ***Perf. 14***

192	A85	50c brn & slate	1.60	.25
a.		Imperf., pair	—	—

Unwmk.

Engr. ***Perf. 11***

Size: 19x23mm

193	A85	1.75 l dp brn	2.25	.20
a.		Perf. 13½ ('29)	*12,000.*	875.00
		Never hinged	*18,000.*	
b.		Perf. 11x13½ ('29)	—	800.00
c.		Perf. 13½x11 ('29)	—	800.00
194	A85	1.85 l black	.55	.40
195	A85	2.55 l brn car	3.00	*3.75*
196	A85	2.65 l dp vio	3.00	*20.00*
		Nos. 192-196 (5)	10.40	*24.60*
		Set, never hinged	27.50	

1928-29 Wmk. 140 Typo. ***Perf. 14***

197	A86	7½c lt brown	1.75	*3.25*
198	A86	15c brown org ('29)	2.25	.20
199	A86	35c gray blk ('29)	4.50	4.25
200	A86	50c dull violet	8.75	.20
		Nos. 197-200 (4)	17.25	*7.90*
		Set, never hinged	42.50	

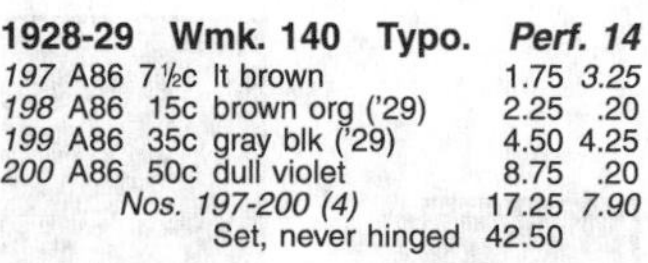

Emmanuel Philibert, Duke of Savoy — A87

Statue of Philibert, Turin — A88

Philibert and Italian Soldier of 1918 — A89

1928 ***Perf. 11, 14***

201	A87	20c red brn & ultra	1.00	1.25
a.		Perf. 13½	65.00	27.50
202	A87	25c dp red & bl grn	1.00	1.25
a.		Perf. 13½	24.00	11.00
203	A87	30c bl grn & red brn	1.00	1.75
a.		Center inverted	*21,000.*	*3,250.*
b.		Perf. 13½	10.00	6.50
204	A89	50c org brn & bl	.75	.40
205	A89	75c dp red	1.00	.75
206	A88	1.25 l bl & blk	1.00	.75
207	A89	1.75 l bl grn	3.25	4.00
208	A87	5 l vio & bl grn	8.00	*32.50*
209	A89	10 l blk & pink	19.00	*75.00*
210	A88	20 l vio & blk	37.50	*275.00*
		Nos. 201-210 (10)	73.50	*392.65*
		Set, never hinged	175.00	

400th anniv. of the birth of Emmanuel Philibert, Duke of Savoy; 10th anniv. of the victory of 1918; Turin Exhibition.

She-wolf Suckling Romulus and Remus

A90 A95a

Julius Caesar A91

Augustus Caesar A92

"Italia" — A93

A94

A95

1929-42 Wmk. 140 Photo. ***Perf. 14***

213	A90	5c olive brn	.20	.20
214	A91	7½c deep vio	.20	.20
215	A92	10c dark brn	.20	.20
216	A93	15c slate grn	.20	.20
217	A91	20c rose red	.20	.20
218	A94	25c dp green	.20	.20
219	A95	30c olive brn	.20	.20
a.		Imperf., pair	225.00	
220	A93	35c dp blue	.20	.20
221	A95	50c purple	.20	.20
a.		Imperf., pair	75.00	*110.00*
222	A94	75c rose red	.20	.20
222A	A91	1 l dk pur ('42)	.20	.20
223	A94	1.25 l dp blue	.20	.20
224	A92	1.75 l red org	.20	.20
225	A93	2 l car lake	.20	.20
226	A95a	2.55 l slate grn	.20	.20
226A	A95a	3.70 l pur ('30)	.20	.20
227	A95a	5 l rose red	.40	.20
228	A93	10 l purple	.75	.20
229	A91	20 l lt green	2.25	*2.75*
230	A92	25 l bluish sl	5.00	*12.00*
231	A94	50 l dp violet	6.00	*16.00*
		Nos. 213-231 (21)	17.60	*34.35*
		Set, never hinged	37.50	

Stamps of the 1929-42 issue overprinted "G.N.R." are 1943 local issues of the Guardia Nazionale Republicana.

See Nos. 427-438, 441-459.

For surcharge and overprints see Nos. 460, M1-M13, 1N10-1N13, 1LN1-1LN1A, 1LN10; Italian Social Republic 1-5A; Yugoslavia-Ljubljana N36-N54.

Courtyard of Monte Cassino A96

Monks Laying Cornerstone — A98

St. Benedict of Nursia — A100

Designs: 25c, Fresco, "Death of St. Benedict." 75c+15c, 5 l+1 l, Monte Cassino Abbey.

1929, Aug. 1 Photo. Wmk. 140

232	A96	20c red orange	.90	.25
233	A96	25c dk green	.90	.25
234	A98	50c + 10c ol brn	2.25	*4.25*
235	A98	75c + 15c crim	2.75	*7.00*
236	A96	1.25 l + 25c saph	3.50	*7.75*
237	A98	5 l + 1 l dk vio	5.75	*25.00*

Unwmk.

Engr.

238	A100	10 l + 2 l slate grn	7.75	*50.00*
		Nos. 232-238 (7)	23.80	*94.50*
		Set, never hinged	57.50	

14th cent. of the founding of the Abbey of Monte Cassino by St. Benedict in 529 A.D. The premium on some of the stamps was given to the committee for the celebration of the centenary.

Prince Humbert and Princess Marie José A101

1930, Jan. 8 Photo. Wmk. 140

239	A101	20c orange red	.25	.25
240	A101	50c + 10c ol brn	.95	*1.10*
241	A101	1.25 l + 25c dp bl	1.50	*3.50*
		Nos. 239-241 (3)	2.70	*4.85*
		Set, never hinged	7.50	

Marriage of Prince Humbert of Savoy with Princess Marie José of Belgium.

The surtax on Nos. 240 and 241 was for the benefit of the Italian Red Cross Society.

The 20c in green is Cyrenaica No. 35 with overprint omitted. Value, $10,000.

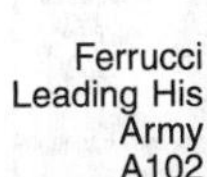

Ferrucci Leading His Army A102

Fabrizio Maramaldo Killing Ferrucci A103

Francesco Ferrucci — A104

1930, July 10

242 A102	20c rose red	.30	.35
243 A103	25c deep green	.60	.35
244 A103	50c purple	.30	.25
245 A103	1.25 l deep blue	2.50	1.50
246 A104	5 l + 2 l org red	5.00	*55.00*
	Nos. 242-246 (5)	8.70	*57.45*
	Set, never hinged	27.50	
	Nos. 242-246,C20-C22 (8)	15.95	*174.45*
	Set, never hinged	40.00	

4th cent. of the death of Francesco Ferrucci, Tuscan warrior.

Overprints

See Aegean Islands for types A103-A145 Overprinted.

Helenus and Aeneas A106

Designs: 20c, Anchises and Aeneas watch passing of Roman Legions. 25c, Aeneas feasting in shade of Albunea. 30c, Ceres and her children with fruits of Earth. 50c, Harvesters at work. 75c, Woman at loom, children and calf. 1.25 l, Anchises and his sailors in sight of Italy. 5 l+1.50 l, Shepherd piping by fireside. 10 l+2.50 l, Aeneas leading his army.

1930, Oct. 21 Photo. *Perf. 14*

248 A106	15c olive brn	.30	.20
249 A106	20c orange	.30	.20
250 A106	25c green	.35	.20
251 A106	30c dull vio	.45	.20
252 A106	50c violet	.30	.20
253 A106	75c rose red	.70	.55
254 A106	1.25 l blue	.90	.45

Unwmk. Engr.

255 A106	5 l +1.50 l red brn	27.50	*50.00*
256 A106	10 l +2.50 l gray grn	27.50	*50.00*
	Nos. 248-256 (9)	58.30	*102.00*
	Set, never hinged	175.00	
	Nos. 248-256,C23-C26 (13)	143.80	*490.50*
	Set, never hinged	300.00	

Bimillenary of the birth of Virgil. Surtax on Nos. 255-256 was for the National Institute Figli del Littorio.

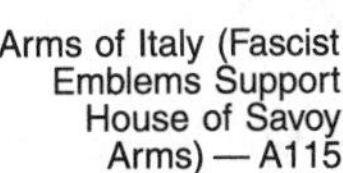
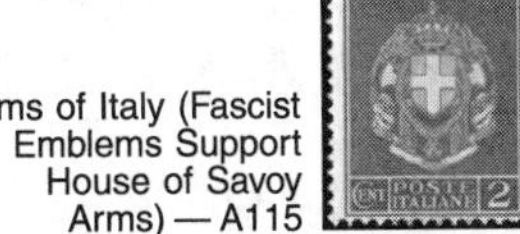
Arms of Italy (Fascist Emblems Support House of Savoy Arms) — A115

1930, Dec. 16 Photo. Wmk. 140

257 A115	2c deep orange	.20	.20
	Never hinged	.30	

St. Anthony being Installed as a Franciscan A116

Olivares Hermitage, Portugal A118

St. Anthony Freeing Prisoners A120

St. Anthony's Death A121

St. Anthony Succoring the Poor — A122

Designs: 25c, St. Anthony preaching to the fishes. 50c, Basilica of St. Anthony, Padua.

Wmk. 140

1931, Mar. 9 Photo. *Perf. 14*

258 A116	20c dull violet	.40	.20
259 A116	25c gray green	.60	.20
260 A118	30c brown	.75	.25
261 A118	50c violet	.40	.20
262 A120	1.25 l blue	2.50	.70

Unwmk. Engr.

263 A121	75c brown red	3.50	1.25
a.	Perf. 12	50.00	*57.50*
	Never hinged, #263a	190.00	
264 A122	5 l + 2.50 l ol grn	14.00	*47.50*
	Nos. 258-264 (7)	22.15	*50.30*
	Set, never hinged	92.50	

7th centenary of the death of Saint Anthony of Padua.

Tower of Meloria — A123

Training Ship "Amerigo Vespucci" A124

Cruiser "Trento" A125

1931, Nov. 29 Photo. Wmk. 140

265 A123	20c rose red	1.10	.30
266 A124	50c purple	1.25	.25
267 A125	1.25 l dk bl	5.00	.75
	Nos. 265-267 (3)	7.35	1.30
	Set, never hinged	22.50	

Royal Naval Academy at Leghorn (Livorno),50th anniv.

Giovanni Boccaccio A126

Designs: 15c, Niccolo Machiavelli. 20c, Paolo Sarpi. 25c, Count Vittorio Alfieri. 30c, Ugo Foscolo. 50c, Count Giacomo Leopardi. 75c, Giosue Carducci. 1.25 l, Carlo Giuseppe Botta. 1.75 l, Torquato Tasso. 2.75 l, Francesco Petrarca. 5 l+2 l, Ludovico Ariosto. 10 l+2.50 l, Dante Alighieri.

1932, Mar. 14 *Perf. 14*

268 A126	10c olive brn	.85	.30
269 A126	15c slate green	1.25	.20
270 A126	20c rose red	1.25	.20
271 A126	25c dp green	1.25	.20
272 A126	30c olive brn	3.00	.20
273 A126	50c violet	1.25	.20
274 A126	75c car rose	5.00	1.00
275 A126	1.25 l dp blue	2.00	.70
276 A126	1.75 l orange	3.00	1.00
277 A126	2.75 l gray	7.75	*9.00*
278 A126	5 l + 2 l car rose	14.00	*45.00*
279 A126	10 l + 2.50 l ol grn	16.00	*55.00*
	Nos. 268-279 (12)	56.60	*113.00*
	Set, never hinged	125.00	
	Nos. 268-279,C28-C34 (20)	157.50	*288.50*
	Set, never hinged	207.50	

Dante Alighieri Society, a natl. literary association founded to promote development of the Italian language and culture. The surtax was added to the Society funds to help in its work.

View of Caprera A138

Garibaldi Carrying His Dying Wife A141

Garibaldi Memorial A144

Giuseppe Garibaldi A145

Designs: 20c, 30c, Garibaldi meeting Victor Emmanuel II. 25c, 50c, Garibaldi at Battle of Calatafimi. 1.25 l, Garibaldi's tomb. 1.75 l+25c, Rock of Quarto.

1932, Apr. 6

280 A138	10c gray blk	.40	.20
281 A138	20c olive brn	.40	.20
282 A138	25c dull grn	.80	.30
283 A138	30c orange	.95	.30
284 A138	50c violet	.45	.20
285 A141	75c rose red	2.50	1.00
286 A141	1.25 l dp blue	2.25	.80
287 A141	1.75 l + 25c bl gray	14.00	*24.00*
288 A144	2.55 l + 50c red brn	14.00	*30.00*
289 A145	5 l + 1 l cop red	15.00	*35.00*
	Nos. 280-289 (10)	50.75	*92.00*
	Set, never hinged	150.00	
	Nos. 280-289,C35-C39,CE1-CE2 (17)	80.10	*222.00*
	Set, never hinged	207.50	

50th anniv. of the death of Giuseppe Garibaldi, patriot.

Plowing with Oxen and Tractor A146

10c, Soldier guarding mountain pass. 15c, Marine, battleship & seaplane. 20c, Head of Fascist youth. 25c, Hands of workers & tools. 30c, Flags, Bible & altar. 35c, "New roads for the new Legions." 50c, Mussolini statue, Bologna. 60c, Hands with spades. 75c, Excavating ruins. 1 l, Steamers & galleons. 1.25 l, Italian flag, map & points of compass. 1.75 l, Flag, athlete & stadium. 2.55 l, Mother & child. 2.75 l, Emblems of drama, music, art & sport. 5 l+2.50 l, Roman emperor.

1932, Oct. 27 Photo.

290 A146	5c dk brown	1.00	.20
291 A146	10c dk brown	1.00	.20
292 A146	15c dk gray grn	1.00	.20
293 A146	20c car rose	1.00	.20
294 A146	25c dp green	1.00	.20
295 A146	30c dk brown	1.00	.45
296 A146	35c dk blue	2.00	1.90
297 A146	50c purple	1.00	.20
298 A146	60c orange brn	2.00	1.25
299 A146	75c car rose	1.60	.40
300 A146	1 l black vio	3.25	.65
301 A146	1.25 l dp blue	1.60	.35
302 A146	1.75 l orange	3.50	.35
303 A146	2.55 l dk gray	12.50	12.00
304 A146	2.75 l slate grn	13.00	13.00
305 A146	5 l + 2.50 l car rose	45.00	*57.50*
	Nos. 290-305 (16)	91.45	*89.05*
	Set, never hinged	180.00	
	Nos. 290-305,C40-C41,E16-E17 (20)	101.60	*193.10*
	Set, never hinged	200.00	

10th anniv. of the Fascist government and the March on Rome.

Statue of Athlete — A162

Cross in Halo, St. Peter's Dome — A163

1933, Aug. 16 *Perf. 14*

306 A162	10c dk brown	.20	.20
307 A162	20c rose red	.20	.25
308 A162	50c purple	.20	.20
309 A162	1.25 l blue	1.40	1.25
	Nos. 306-309 (4)	2.00	1.90
	Set, never hinged	5.50	

Intl. University Games at Turin, Sept., 1933.

1933, Oct. 23

Designs: 25c, 50c, Angel with cross. 1.25 l, as 20c. 2.55 l, + 2.50 l, Cross with doves.

310 A163	20c rose red	.20	.20
311 A163	25c green	1.40	.40
312 A163	50c purple	.40	.20
313 A163	1.25 l dp blue	1.25	.65
314 A163	2.55 l + 2.50 l blk	3.75	*50.00*
	Nos. 310-314 (5)	7.00	*51.45*
	Set, never hinged	17.50	
	Nos. 310-314,CB1-CB2 (7)	8.55	*58.95*
	Set, never hinged	22.50	

Issued at the solicitation of the Order of the Holy Sepulchre of Jerusalem to mark the Holy Year.

Anchor of the "Emanuele Filiberto" A166

Antonio Pacinotti A172

Designs: 20c, Anchor. 50c, Gabriele d'Annunzio. 1.25 l, St. Vito's Tower. 1.75 l, Symbolizing Fiume's annexation. 2.55 l+2 l, Victor Emmanuel III arriving aboard "Brindisi." 2.75 l+2.50 l, Galley, gondola and battleship.

1934, Mar. 12

315	A166	10c dk brown	3.00	.30
316	A166	20c rose red	.25	.20
317	A166	50c purple	.25	.20
318	A166	1.25 l blue	.40	*.90*
319	A166	1.75 l + 1 l indigo	.45	*12.00*
320	A166	2.55 l + 2 l dull vio	.45	*16.00*
321	A166	2.75 l + 2.50 l ol grn	.50	*18.00*
		Nos. 315-321 (7)	5.30	*47.60*
		Set, never hinged	7.00	
		Nos. 315-321,C56-C61,CE5-CE7 (16)	8.60	*130.10*
		Set, never hinged	17.50	

10th anniversary of annexation of Fiume.

1934, May 23

322	A172	50c purple	.70	.20
323	A172	1.25 l sapphire	.70	.90
		Set, never hinged	3.25	

75th anniv. of invention of the dynamo by Antonio Pacinotti (1841-1912), scientist.

Guarding the Goal — A173

Players — A175

Soccer Players A174

1934, May 23

324	A173	20c red orange	3.00	1.25
325	A174	25c green	3.00	.60
326	A174	50c purple	3.00	.20
327	A174	1.25 l blue	9.00	3.25
328	A175	5 l + 2.50 l brn	35.00	*67.50*
		Nos. 324-328 (5)	53.00	*72.80*
		Set, never hinged	190.00	
		Nos. 324-328,C62-C65 (9)	126.00	*503.30*
		Set, never hinged	340.00	

2nd World Soccer Championship.
For overprints see Aegean Islands #31-35.

Luigi Galvani — A176

1934, Aug. 16

329	A176	30c brown, *buff*	1.00	.25
330	A176	75c carmine, *rose*	1.00	1.25
		Set, never hinged	3.50	

Intl. Congress of Electro-Radio-Biology.

Carabinieri Emblem — A177

Cutting Barbed Wire A178

Designs: 20c, Sardinian Grenadier and soldier throwing grenade. 25c, Alpine Infantry. 30c, Military courage. 75c, Artillery. 1.25 l, Acclaiming the Service. 1.75 l+1 l, Cavalry. 2.55 l+2 l, Sapping Detail. 2.75 l+2 l, First aid.

1934, Sept. 6 Photo. Wmk. 140

331	A177	10c dk brown	.50	.30
332	A178	15c olive grn	.65	.60
333	A178	20c rose red	.60	.25
334	A177	25c green	.75	.25
335	A178	30c dk brown	1.25	.75
336	A178	50c purple	1.25	.20
337	A178	75c car rose	2.50	1.40
338	A178	1.25 l dk blue	2.25	1.00
339	A177	1.75 l + 1 l red org	8.75	*20.00*
340	A178	2.55 l + 2 l dp cl	9.50	*22.50*
341	A178	2.75 l + 2 l vio	12.00	*24.00*
		Nos. 331-341 (11)	40.00	*71.25*
		Set, never hinged	105.00	
		Nos. 331-341,C66-C72 (18)	61.25	*170.00*
		Set, never hinged	145.00	

Centenary of Military Medal of Valor.
For overprints see Aegean Islands #36-46.

Man Holding Fasces A187

Standard Bearer, Bayonet Attack A188

Design: 30c, Eagle and soldier.

1935, Apr. 23 *Perf. 14*

342	A187	20c rose red	.30	.20
343	A187	30c dk brown	1.00	1.10
344	A188	50c purple	.25	.20
		Nos. 342-344 (3)	1.55	1.50
		Set, never hinged	4.50	

Issued in honor of the University Contests.

Fascist Flight Symbolism A190

Leonardo da Vinci — A191

1935, Oct. 1

345	A190	20c rose red	2.50	.50
346	A190	30c brown	7.50	1.25
347	A191	50c purple	17.50	.35
348	A191	1.25 l dk blue	20.00	1.50
		Nos. 345-348 (4)	47.50	3.60
		Set, never hinged	250.00	

International Aeronautical Salon, Milan.

Vincenzo Bellini — A192

Bellini's Villa — A194

Bellini's Piano A193

1935, Oct. 15

349	A192	20c rose red	.80	.30
350	A192	30c brown	1.25	.45
351	A192	50c violet	.80	.25
352	A192	1.25 l dk blue	2.75	1.40
353	A193	1.75 l + 1 l red org	14.00	*30.00*
354	A194	2.75 l + 2 l ol blk	19.00	*35.00*
		Nos. 349-354 (6)	38.60	*67.40*
		Set, never hinged	160.00	
		Nos. 349-354,C79-C83 (11)	75.60	*271.90*
		Set, never hinged	200.00	

Bellini (1801-35), operatic composer.

Map of Italian Industries A195

Designs: 20c, 1.25 l, Map of Italian Industries. 30c, 50c, Cogwheel and plow.

1936, Mar. 23

355	A195	20c red	.20	.25
356	A195	30c brown	.20	.30
357	A195	50c purple	.20	.20
358	A195	1.25 l blue	1.00	.75
		Nos. 355-358 (4)	1.60	1.50
		Set, never hinged	3.75	

The 17th Milan Trade Fair.

Flock of Sheep A197

Ajax Defying the Lightning A199

Bust of Horace A200

Designs: 20c, 1.25 l+1 l, Countryside in Spring. 75c, Capitol. 1.75 l+1 l, Pan piping. 2.55 l+1 l, Dying warrior.

Wmk. Crowns (140)

1936, July 1 Photo. *Perf. 14*

359	A197	10c dp green	1.75	.30
360	A197	20c rose red	1.10	.25
361	A199	30c olive brn	1.50	.50
362	A200	50c purple	1.10	.20
363	A197	75c rose red	2.25	1.10
364	A197	1.25 l + 1 l dk bl	10.50	*25.00*
365	A199	1.75 l + 1 l car rose	12.00	*40.00*
366	A197	2.55 l + 1 l sl blk	17.00	*50.00*
		Nos. 359-366 (8)	47.20	*117.35*
		Set, never hinged	150.00	
		Nos. 359-366,C84-C88 (13)	77.95	*339.85*
		Set, never hinged	200.00	

2000th anniv. of the birth of Quintus Horatius Flaccus (Horace), Roman poet.

Child Holding Wheat — A204

Child Giving Salute — A205

Child and Fasces — A206

"Il Bambino" by della Robbia — A207

1937, June 28

367	A204	10c yellow brn	1.25	.25
368	A205	20c car rose	1.25	.25
369	A204	25c green	1.25	.30
370	A206	30c dk brown	2.50	.40
371	A205	50c purple	1.50	.20
372	A207	75c rose red	3.00	.75
373	A205	1.25 l dk blue	6.50	1.00
374	A206	1.75 l + 75c org	30.00	30.00
375	A207	2.75 l + 1.25 l dk bl grn	14.00	*32.50*
376	A205	5 l + 3 l bl gray	14.00	*35.00*
		Nos. 367-376 (10)	75.25	*100.65*
		Set, never hinged	175.00	
		Nos. 367-376,C89-C94 (16)	117.25	*391.90*
		Set, never hinged	250.00	

Summer Exhibition for Child Welfare. The surtax on Nos. 374-376 was used to support summer camps for children.

Rostral Column — A208

15c, Army Trophies. 20c, Augustus Caesar (Octavianus) offering sacrifice. 25c, Cross Roman Standards. 30c, Julius Caesar and Julian Star. 50c, Augustus receiving acclaim. 75c, Augustus Caesar. 1.25 l, Symbolizing maritime glory of Rome. 1.75 l+1 l, Sacrificial Altar. 2.55 l+2 l, Capitol.

1937, Sept. 23

377	A208	10c myrtle grn	.80	.25
378	A208	15c olive grn	.80	.35
379	A208	20c red	.80	.25
380	A208	25c green	.80	.20
381	A208	30c olive bis	1.00	.30
382	A208	50c purple	.80	.20
383	A208	75c scarlet	1.25	1.10
384	A208	1.25 l dk blue	2.00	1.25
385	A208	1.75 l + 1 l plum	17.50	*30.00*
386	A208	2.55 l + 2 l sl blk	22.50	*32.50*
		Nos. 377-386 (10)	48.25	*66.40*
		Set, never hinged	125.00	
		Nos. 377-386,C95-C99 (15)	101.75	*239.90*
		Set, never hinged	175.00	

Bimillenary of the birth of Emperor Augustus Caesar (Octavianus) on the occasion of the exhibition opened in Rome by Mussolini, Sept. 22, 1937.
For overprints see Aegean Islands #47-56.

Gasparo Luigi Pacifico Spontini A218

Antonius Stradivarius A219

Count Giacomo Leopardi A220

Giovanni Battista Pergolesi A221

Giotto di Bondone — A222

1937, Oct. 25

No.	Type	Description	Unused	Used
387	A218	10c dk brown	.40	.20
388	A219	20c rose red	.40	.20
389	A220	25c dk green	.40	.20
390	A221	30c dk brown	.40	.30
391	A220	50c purple	.40	.20
392	A221	75c crimson	1.10	.75
393	A222	1.25 l dp blue	1.60	.90
394	A218	1.75 l dp orange	1.60	.90
395	A219	2.55 l + 2 l gray grn	8.25	*22.50*
396	A222	2.75 l + 2 l red brn	8.25	*24.00*
		Nos. 387-396 (10)	22.80	*50.15*
		Set, never hinged	55.00	

Centennials of Spontini, Stradivarius, Leopardi, Pergolesi and Giotto.

For overprints see Aegean Islands #57-58.

Guglielmo Marconi A223

Augustus Caesar (Octavianus) A224

1938, Jan. 24

No.	Type	Description	Unused	Used
397	A223	20c rose pink	.45	.20
398	A223	50c purple	.20	.20
399	A223	1.25 l blue	.80	.60
		Nos. 397-399 (3)	1.45	1.00
		Set, never hinged	5.00	

Guglielmo Marconi (1874-1937), electrical engineer, inventor of wireless telegraphy.

1938, Oct. 28

10c, Romulus Plowing. 25c, Dante. 30c, Columbus. 50c, Leonardo da Vinci. 75c, Victor Emmanuel II and Garibaldi. 1.25 l, Tomb of Unknown Soldier, Rome. 1.75 l, Blackshirts' March on Rome, 1922. 2.75 l, Map of Italian East Africa and Iron Crown of Monza. 5 l, Victor Emmanuel III.

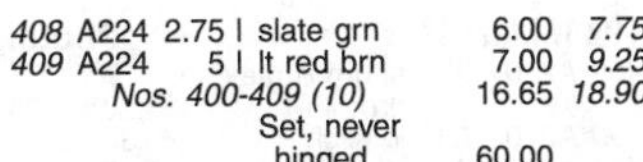

No.	Type	Description	Unused	Used
400	A224	10c brown	.30	.20
401	A224	20c car rose	.30	.20
402	A224	25c dk green	.30	.20
403	A224	30c olive brn	.30	.20
404	A224	50c lt violet	.30	.20
405	A224	75c rose red	.55	.30
406	A224	1.25 l dp blue	.70	.30
407	A224	1.75 l vio blk	.90	.30
408	A224	2.75 l slate grn	6.00	*7.75*
409	A224	5 l lt red brn	7.00	*9.25*
		Nos. 400-409 (10)	16.65	*18.90*
		Set, never hinged	60.00	
		Nos. 400-409,C100-C105 (16)	38.10	*122.65*
		Set, never hinged	90.00	

Proclamation of the Empire.

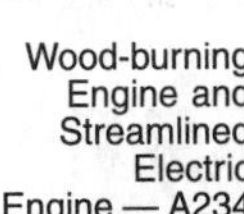

Wood-burning Engine and Streamlined Electric Engine — A234

1939, Dec. 15 Photo. *Perf. 14*

No.	Type	Description	Unused	Used
410	A234	20c rose red	.20	.20
411	A234	50c brt violet	.20	.20
412	A234	1.25 l dp blue	.40	.60
		Nos. 410-412 (3)	.80	1.00
		Set, never hinged	3.50	

Centenary of Italian railroads.

Adolf Hitler and Benito Mussolini A235

Hitler and Mussolini A236

1941 Wmk. 140

No.	Type	Description	Unused	Used
413	A235	10c dp brown	.45	.45
414	A235	20c red orange	.45	.45
415	A235	25c dp green	.45	.45
416	A236	50c violet	1.00	.40
417	A236	75c rose red	1.75	.75
418	A236	1.25 l deep blue	1.75	1.25
		Nos. 413-418 (6)	5.85	3.75
		Set, never hinged	20.00	

Rome-Berlin Axis.

Stamps of type A236 in the denominations and colors of Nos. 413-415 were prepared but not issued. They were sold for charitable purposes in 1948. Value $10 each.

Galileo Teaching Mathematics at Padua — A237

Designs: 25c, Galileo presenting telescope to Doge of Venice. 50c, Galileo Galilei (1564-1642). 1.25 l, Galileo studying at Arcetri.

1942, Sept. 28

No.	Type	Description	Unused	Used
419	A237	10c dk org & lake	.25	.20
420	A237	25c gray grn & grn	.25	.20
421	A237	50c brn vio & vio	.25	.20
a.		Frame missing	*400.00*	
422	A237	1.25 l Prus bl & ultra	.25	.75
		Nos. 419-422 (4)	1.00	1.35
		Set, never hinged	2.25	

Statue of Rossini — A241

Gioacchino Rossini — A242

1942, Nov. 23 Photo.

No.	Type	Description	Unused	Used
423	A241	25c deep green	.20	.20
424	A241	30c brown	.20	.20
425	A242	50c violet	.20	.20
426	A242	1 l blue	.20	.50
		Nos. 423-426 (4)	.80	1.10
		Set, never hinged	1.50	

Gioacchino Antonio Rossini (1792-1868), operatic composer.

"Victory for the Axis" A243

"Discipline is the Weapon of Victory" A244

"Everything and Everyone for Victory" A245

"Arms and Hearts Must Be Stretched Out Towards the Goal" A246

Perf. 14 all around, Imperf. between

1942 Photo. Wmk. 140

No.	Type	Description	Unused	Used
427	A243	25c deep green	.35	.30
428	A244	25c deep green	.35	.30
429	A245	25c deep green	.35	.30
430	A246	25c deep green	.35	.30
431	A243	30c olive brown	.35	.75
432	A244	30c olive brown	.35	.75
433	A245	30c olive brown	.35	.75
434	A246	30c olive brown	.35	.75
435	A243	50c purple	.35	.30
436	A244	50c purple	.35	.30
437	A245	50c purple	.35	.30
438	A246	50c purple	.35	.30
		Nos. 427-438 (12)	4.20	*5.40*
		Set, never hinged	7.00	

Issued in honor of the Italian Army.

The left halves of #431-438 are type A95.

For overprints see Italian Socal Republic #6-17.

She-Wolf Suckling Romulus and Remus — A247

Perf. 10½x11½, 11x11½, 11½, 14

1944, Jan. Litho. Wmk. 87

Without Gum

No.	Type	Description	Unused	Used
439	A247	50c rose vio & bis rose	.30	.40

Unwmk.

No.	Type	Description	Unused	Used
440	A247	50c rose vio & pale rose	.20	.20

Nos. 439-440 exist imperf., part perf.

Types of 1929

1945, May Unwmk. *Perf. 14*

No.	Type	Description	Unused	Used
441	A93	15c slate green	.20	.20
442	A93	35c deep blue	.20	.20
443	A91	1 l deep violet	.20	.20
		Nos. 441-443 (3)	.60	.60
		Set, never hinged	1.50	

Types of 1929 Redrawn Fasces Removed

Victor Emmanuel III A248

Julius Caesar A249

Augustus Caesar A250

"Italia" A251

A252

1944-45 Wmk. 140 Photo. *Perf. 14*

No.	Type	Description	Unused	Used
444	A248	30c dk brown	.20	.20
445	A248	50c purple	.40	.60
446	A248	60c slate grn ('45)	.20	.20
447	A249	1 l dp violet ('45)	.80	.20
		Nos. 444-447 (4)	1.60	1.20
		Set, never hinged	4.50	

1945 Unwmk. *Perf. 14*

No.	Type	Description	Unused	Used
448	A250	10c dk brown	.20	.20
448A	A249	20c rose red	.20	.20
449	A251	50c dk violet	.20	.20
450	A248	60c slate grn	.20	.20
451	A251	60c red org	.20	.20
452	A249	1 l dp violet	.20	.20
452A	A249	1 l dp vio, redrawn	.20	.20
452B	A251	2 l dp car	2.25	.20
452C	A251	10 l purple	1.75	1.25
		Nos. 448-452C (9)	5.40	2.85
		Set, never hinged	15.00	

1945 Wmk. 277

No.	Type	Description	Unused	Used
453	A249	20c rose red	.20	.20
454	A248	60c slate grn	.20	.20
455	A249	1 l dp violet	.20	.20
456	A251	1.20 l dk brown	.20	.20
457	A251	2 l dk red	.20	.20
458	A252	5 l dk red	.20	.20
459	A251	10 l purple	2.00	1.25
		Nos. 453-459 (7)	3.20	2.45
		Set, never hinged	10.00	

Nos. 452A and 457 are redrawings of types A249 and A251. In the redrawn 1 l, the "L" of "LIRE" extends under the "IRE" and the letters of "POSTE ITALIANE" are larger. In the original the "L" extends only under the "I."

In the redrawn 2 l, the "2" is smaller and thinner, and the design is less distinct.

For overprints see Nos. 1LN2-1LN8.

No. 224 Surcharged in Black

1945, Mar. Wmk. 140

No.	Type	Description	Unused	Used
460	A92	2.50 l on 1.75 l red org	.20	.20
		Never hinged	.20	
a.		Six bars at left	.70	.90

Loggia dei Mercanti, Bologna A253

Basilica of San Lorenzo, Rome A254

Stamps of Italian Social Republic Surcharged in Black

1945, May 2 Photo. *Perf. 14*

461 A253 1.20 l on 20c crim .20 .20
462 A254 2 l on 25c green .20 .20
a. 2½ mm between "2" and "LIRE" .45 .70
Set, never hinged .30

Breaking Chain A255

United Family and Scales A256

Planting Tree — A257

Tying Tree — A258

Torch A259

"Italia" and Sprouting Oak Stump A260

1945-47 Wmk. 277 Photo. *Perf. 14*

463 A255 10c rose brown .20 .20
464 A256 20c dk brown .20 .20
464A A259 25c brt bl grn ('46) .20 .20
465 A257 40c slate .20 .20
465A A255 50c dp vio ('46) .20 .20
466 A258 60c dk green .20 .20
467 A255 80c car rose .20 .20
468 A257 1 l dk green .20 .20
469 A259 1.20 l chestnut .20 .20
470 A258 2 l dk claret brn .20 .20
471 A259 3 l red .20 .20
471A A259 4 l red org ('46) .25 .20
472 A256 5 l deep blue .20 .20
472A A257 6 l dp vio ('47) .45 .20
473 A255 10 l slate .20 .20
473A A257 15 l dp bl ('46) .90 .20
474 A259 20 l dk red vio .20 .20
475 A260 25 l dk grn 1.90 .20
476 A260 50 l dk vio brn .75 .20
Nos. 463-476 (19) 7.05 3.80
Set, never hinged 40.00

See Nos. 486-488.

For overprints see Nos. 1LN11-1LN12, 1LN14-1N19, Trieste 1-13, 15-17, 30-32, 58-68, 82-83.

United Family and Scales A261

1946 Engr. *Perf. 14*

477 A261 100 l car lake 65.00 .85
Never hinged 210.00
a. Perf. 14x13½ 77.50 1.10
Never hinged 240.00

For overprints see #1LN13, Trieste 14, 69.

Cathedral of St. Andrea, Amalfi — A262

Church of St. Michael, Lucca — A263

"Peace" from Fresco at Siena A264

Signoria Palace, Florence A265

View of Cathedral Domes, Pisa A266

Republic of Genoa A267

"Venice Crowned by Glory," by Paolo Veronese A268

Oath of Pontida A269

1946, Oct. 30

478 A262 1 l brown .20 .20
479 A263 2 l dk blue .20 .20
480 A264 3 l dk bl grn .20 .20
481 A265 4 l dp org .20 .20
482 A266 5 l dp violet .20 .20
483 A267 10 l car rose .20 .20
484 A268 15 l dp ultra .25 .30
485 A269 20 l red brown .20 .20
Nos. 478-485 (8) 1.70
Set, never hinged 1.40

Proclamation of the Republic.

Types of 1945

1947-48 Wmk. 277 Photo. *Perf. 14*

486 A255 8 l dk green ('48) .80 .20
487 A256 10 l red orange 7.00 .20
488 A259 30 l dk blue ('48) 67.50 .25
Nos. 486-488 (3) 75.30 .65
Set, never hinged 240.00

St. Catherine Giving Mantle to Beggar — A270

5 l, St. Catherine carrying cross. 10 l, St. Catherine, arms outstretched. 30 l, St. Catherine & scribe.

1948, Mar. 1 Photo.

489 A270 3 l yel grn & gray grn .20 .20
490 A270 5 l vio & bl .30 .35
491 A270 10 l red brn & vio 2.00 .40
492 A270 30 l bis & gray brn 8.00 2.25
Nos. 489-492 (4) 10.50 3.20
Set, never hinged 17.50
Nos. 489-492,C127-C128 (6) 48.50 31.95
Set, never hinged 100.00

600th anniv. of the birth of St. Catherine of Siena, Patroness of Italy.

"Constitutional Government" — A271

1948, Apr. 12

493 A271 10 l rose vio .40 .35
494 A271 30 l blue 1.00 .70
Set, never hinged 3.50

Proclamation of the constitution of 1/1/48.

Uprising at Palermo, Jan. 12, 1848 A272

Designs (Revolutionary scenes): 4 l, Rebellion at Padua. 5 l, Proclamation of statute, Turin. 6 l, "Five Days of Milan." 8 l, Daniele Manin proclaiming the Republic of Venice. 10 l, Defense of Vicenza. 12 l, Battle of Curtatone. 15 l, Battle of Gioto. 20 l, Insurrection at Bologna. 30 l, "Ten Days of Brescia." 50 l, Garibaldi in Rome fighting. 100 l, Death of Goffredo Mameli.

1948, May 3

495 A272 3 l dk brown .20 .20
496 A272 4 l red violet .20 .20
497 A272 5 l dp blue .20 .20
498 A272 6 l dp yel grn .20 .35
499 A272 8 l brown .20 .30
500 A272 10 l orange red .35 .20
501 A272 12 l dk gray grn .50 *1.00*
502 A272 15 l gray blk 1.50 .45
503 A272 20 l car rose 4.25 3.25
504 A272 30 l brt ultra 1.90 .30
505 A272 50 l violet 30.00 1.25
506 A272 100 l blue blk 37.50 9.50
Nos. 495-506 (12) 77.00 17.20
Set, never hinged 375.00
Nos. 495-506,E26 (13) 92.00 27.20
Set, never hinged 400.00

Centenary of the Risorgimento, uprisings of 1848-49 which led to Italian unification.

For overprints see Trieste Nos. 18-29, E5.

Alpine Soldier and Bassano Bridge A273

1948, Oct. 1 Wmk. 277 *Perf. 14*

507 A273 15 l dark green 1.00 1.00
Never hinged 2.00

Bridge of Bassano, re-opening, Oct. 3, 1948.

For overprint see Trieste No. 33.

Gaetano Donizetti — A274

1948, Oct. 23 Photo.

508 A274 15 l dark brown .70 *.95*
Never hinged 1.40

Death cent. of Gaetano Donizetti, composer.

For overprint see Trieste No. 34.

Fair Buildings A275

1949, Apr. 12

509 A275 20 l dark brown 2.40 1.75
Never hinged 8.50

27th Milan Trade Fair, April 1949.

For overprint see Trieste No. 35.

Standard of Doges of Venice — A276

15 l, Clock strikers, Lion Tower and Campanile of St. Mark's. 20 l, Lion standard and Venetian galley. 50 l, Lion tower and gulls.

1949, Apr. 12

Buff Background

510 A276 5 l red brown .20 .20
511 A276 15 l dk green .75 .95
512 A276 20 l dp red brn 1.90 .20
513 A276 50 l dk blue 14.00 .95
Nos. 510-513 (4) 16.85 2.30
Set, never hinged 65.00

Biennial Art Exhibition of Venice, 50th anniv.

For overprints see Trieste Nos. 36-39.

"Transportation" and Globes — A277

1949, May 2 Wmk. 277 *Perf. 14*

514 A277 50 l brt ultra 19.00 3.75
Never hinged 52.50

75th anniv. of the UPU.

For overprint see Trieste No. 40.

Workman and Ship — A278

1949, May 30 Photo.

515 A278 5 l dk green 1.60 1.75
516 A278 15 l violet 9.25 *10.00*
517 A278 20 l brown 21.00 10.50
Nos. 515-517 (3) 31.85 *22.25*
Set, never hinged 77.50

European Recovery Program.

For overprints see Trieste Nos. 42-44.

The Vascello, Rome A279

1949, May 18

518 A279 100 l brown 77.50 52.50
Never hinged 200.00

Centenary of Roman Republic.

For overprint see Trieste No. 41.

Giuseppe Mazzini — A280

Vittorio Alfieri — A281

1949, June 1

519 A280 20 l gray 1.75 1.60
Never hinged 9.75

Erection of a monument to Giuseppe Mazzini (1805-72), Italian patriot and revolutionary.
For overprint see Trieste No. 45.

1949, June 4 **Photo.**

520 A281 20 l brown 1.90 1.25
Never hinged 7.75

200th anniv. of the birth of Vittorio Alfieri, tragic dramatist.
For overprint see Trieste No. 46.

Basilica of St. Just, Trieste A282

1949, June 8

521 A282 20 l brown red 7.25 7.75
Never hinged 11.00

Trieste election, June 12, 1949.
For overprint see Trieste No. 47.

Staff of Aesculapius, Globe — A283

1949, June 13 **Wmk. 277** ***Perf. 14***

522 A283 20 l violet 9.00 6.00
Never hinged 37.50

2nd World Health Cong., Rome, 1949.
For overprint see Trieste No. 49.

Lorenzo de Medici A284

Andrea Palladio A285

1949, Aug. 4

523 A284 20 l violet blue 1.75 1.25
Never hinged 9.75

Birth of Lorenzo de Medici, 500th anniv.
For overprint see Trieste No. 50.

1949, Aug. 4

524 A285 20 l violet 6.50 3.75
Never hinged 13.00

Andrea Palladio (1518-1580), architect.
For overprint see Trieste No. 51.

Tartan and Fair Buildings A286

1949, Aug. 16

525 A286 20 l red 1.60 1.25
Never hinged 5.25

133th Levant Fair, Bari, September, 1949.
For overprint see Trieste No. 52.

Voltaic Pile — A287

Alessandro Volta — A288

1949, Sept. 14 **Engr.** ***Perf. 14***

526 A287 20 l rose car 1.25 .85
a. Perf. 13x14 7.75 4.25
527 A288 50 l deep blue 25.00 14.00
a. Perf. 13x14 97.50 36.00
Set, never hinged 85.00

Invention of the Voltaic Pile, 150th anniv.
For overprints see Trieste Nos. 53-54.

Holy Trinity Bridge — A289

1949, Sept. 19 **Photo.**

528 A289 20 l deep green 1.75 1.25
Never hinged 6.50

Issued to publicize plans to reconstruct Holy Trinity Bridge, Florence.
For overprint see Trieste No. 55.

Gaius Valerius Catullus A290

Domenico Cimarosa A291

1949, Sept. 19 **Wmk. 277** ***Perf. 14***

529 A290 20 l brt blue 3.00 1.25
Never hinged 10.50

2000th anniversary of the death of Gaius Valerius Catullus, Lyric poet.
For overprint see Trieste No. 56.

1949, Dec. 28

530 A291 20 l violet blk 2.50 1.00
Never hinged 9.00

Bicentenary of the birth of Domenico Cimarosa, composer.
For overprint see Trieste No. 57.

Milan Fair Scene A292

1950, Apr. 12 **Photo.**

531 A292 20 l brown 1.75 1.25
Never hinged 3.75

The 28th Milan Trade Fair.
For overprint see Trieste No. 70.

Flags and Italian Automobile A293

1950, Apr. 29

532 A293 20 l vio gray 2.50 .85
Never hinged 9.00

32nd Intl. Auto Show, Turin, May 4-14, 1950.
For overprint see Trieste No. 71.

Pitti Palace, Florence A294

"Perseus" by Cellini — A295

Composite of Italian Cathedrals and Churches — A296

1950, May 22

533 A294 20 l olive grn 1.60 1.10
534 A295 55 l blue 18.00 5.75
Set, never hinged 60.00

5th General Conf. of UNESCO.
For overprints see Trieste Nos. 72-73.

1950, May 29

535 A296 20 l violet 2.10 .35
536 A296 55 l blue 24.00 1.00
Set, never hinged 77.50

Holy Year, 1950.
For overprints see Trieste Nos. 74-75.

Gaudenzio Ferrari A297

Radio Mast and Tower of Florence A298

1950, July 1 **Wmk. 277** ***Perf. 14***

537 A297 20 l gray grn 4.00 1.25
Never hinged 13.00

Issued to honor Gaudenzio Ferrari.
For overprint see Trieste No. 76.

1950, July 15 **Photo.**

538 A298 20 l purple 4.50 4.25
539 A298 55 l blue 55.00 70.00
Set, never hinged 175.00

Intl. Shortwave Radio Conf., Florence, 1950.
For overprints Trieste see Nos. 77-78.

Ludovico A. Muratori A299

Guido d'Arezzo A300

1950, July 22

540 A299 20 l brown 1.75 .95
Never hinged 5.75

200th anniv. of the death of Ludovico A. Muratori, writer.
For overprint see Trieste No. 79.

1950, July 29

541 A300 20 l dark green 4.50 1.00
Never hinged 16.00

900th anniv. of the death of Guido d'Arezzo, music teacher and composer.
For overprint see Trieste No. 80.

Tartan and Fair Buildings A301

1950, Aug. 21

542 A301 20 l chestnut brown 3.00 .85
Never hinged 9.00

Levant Fair, Bari, September, 1950.
For overprint see Trieste No. 81.

G. Marzotto and A. Rossi — A302

Tobacco Plant — A303

1950, Sept. 11

543 A302 20 l indigo .90 .60
Never hinged 1.75

Pioneers of the Italian wool industry.
For overprint see Trieste No. 84.

1950, Sept. 11

Designs: 20 l, Mature plant, different background. 55 l, Girl holding tobacco plant.

544 A303 5 l dp claret & grn .50 *.85*
545 A303 20 l brown & grn .50 .45
546 A303 55 l dp ultra & brn 20.00 11.00
Nos. 544-546 (3) 21.00 12.30
Set, never hinged 52.50

Issued to publicize the European Tobacco Conference, Rome, 1950.
For overprints see Trieste Nos. 85-87.

Arms of the Academy of Fine Arts — A304

Augusto Righi — A305

1950, Sept. 16

547 A304 20 l ol brn & red brn 1.60 1.00
Never hinged 3.75

200th anniv. of the founding of the Academy of Fine Arts, Venice.
For overprint see Trieste No. 88.

1950, Sept. 16

548 A305 20 l cream & gray blk 1.60 1.00
Never hinged 3.75

Centenary of the birth of Augusto Righi, physicist.
For overprint see Trieste No. 89.

Blacksmith, Aosta Valley — A306

1851 Stamp of Tuscany — A307

Designs: 1 l, Auto mechanic. 2 l, Mason. 5 l, Potter. 6 l, Lace-making. 10 l, Weaving, 12 l, Sailor steering boat. 15 l, Shipbuilding. 20 l, Fisherman. 25 l, Sorting oranges. 30 l, Woman carrying grapes. 35 l, Olive picking. 40 l, Wine cart. 50 l, Shepherd and flock. 55 l, Plowing. 60 l, Grain cart. 65 l, Girl worker in hemp field. 100 l, Husking corn. 200 l, Woodcutter.

1950, Oct. 20 Wmk. 277 *Perf. 14*

549	A306	50c vio blue	.20	.20
550	A306	1 l dk bl vio	.20	.20
551	A306	2 l sepia	.20	.20
552	A306	5 l dk gray	.20	.20
553	A306	6 l chocolate	.20	.20
554	A306	10 l dp green	1.10	.20
555	A306	12 l dp blue grn	.50	.20
556	A306	15 l dk gray bl	.40	.20
557	A306	20 l blue vio	2.25	.20
558	A306	25 l brn org	.75	.20
559	A306	30 l magenta	.40	.20
560	A306	35 l crimson	1.90	.35
561	A306	40 l brown	.20	.20
562	A306	50 l violet	3.25	.20
563	A306	55 l dp blue	.20	.20
564	A306	60 l red	.80	.20
565	A306	65 l dk grn	.20	.20

Perf. 13x14, 14x13

Engr.

566	A306	100 l brn org	14.50	.20
a.		Perf. 13	14.00	.20
b.		Perf. 14	16.00	.20
567	A306	200 l ol brn	4.75	1.00
a.		Perf. 14	5.00	1.00
		Nos. 549-567 (19)	32.20	4.75
		Set, never hinged	100.00	

See Nos. 668-673A. For overprints see Trieste Nos. 90-108, 122-124, 178-180.

1951, Mar. 27 Photo. *Perf. 14*

Design: 55 l, Tuscany 6cr.

568	A307	20 l red vio & red	1.25	1.10
569	A307	55 l ultra & blue	16.00	14.00
		Set, never hinged	40.00	

Centenary of Tuscany's first stamps.
For overprints see Trieste Nos. 109-110.

Italian Automobile A308

1951, Apr. 2

570	A308	20 l dk green	4.00	1.40
		Never hinged	16.00	

33rd Intl. Automobile Exhib., Turin, Apr. 4-15, 1951.
For overprint see Trieste No. 111.

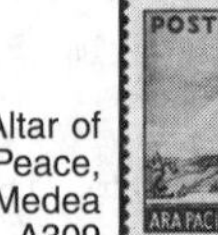

Altar of Peace, Medea A309

1951, Apr. 11

571	A309	20 l blue vio	2.25	1.40
		Never hinged	11.00	

Consecration of the Altar of Peace at Redipuglia Cemetery, Medea.
For overprint see Trieste No. 112.

Helicopter over Leonardo da Vinci Heliport — A310

P. T. T. Building, Milan Fair — A311

1951, Apr. 12 Photo.

572	A310	20 l brown	3.75	.70
573	A311	55 l dp blue	22.50	20.00
		Set, never hinged	82.50	

29th Milan Trade Fair.
For overprints see Trieste Nos. 113-114.

Symbols of the International Gymnastic Festival A312

Statue of Diana, Spindle and Turin Tower A313

Wmk. 277

1951, May 18 Photo. *Perf. 14*

Fleur-de-lis in Red

574	A312	5 l dk brown	15.00	*110.00*
575	A312	10 l Prus green	15.00	*110.00*
576	A312	15 l vio blue	15.00	*110.00*
		Nos. 574-576 (3)	45.00	*330.00*
		Set, never hinged	72.50	

International Gymnastic Festival and Meet, Florence, 1951.
Fake cancellations exist on Nos. 574-576.
For overprints see Trieste Nos. 115-117.

1951, Apr. 26

577	A313	20 l purple	5.00	1.75
		Never hinged	24.00	

Tenth International Exhibition of Textile Art and Fashion, Turin, May 2-16.
For overprint see Trieste No. 118.

Landing of Columbus A314

1951, May 5

578	A314	20 l Prus green	5.00	1.75
		Never hinged	22.50	

500th anniversary of birth of Columbus.
For overprint see Trieste No. 119.

Reconstructed Abbey of Montecassino — A315

Design: 55 l, Montecassino Ruins.

1951, June 18

579	A315	20 l violet	2.40	.85
580	A315	55 l brt blue	35.00	24.00
		Set, never hinged	77.50	

Issued to commemorate the reconstruction of the Abbey of Montecassino.
For overprints see Trieste Nos. 120-121.

Pietro Vannucci (Il Perugino) A316

Stylized Vase A317

Cartouche of Amenhotep III and Pitcher A318

1951, July 23

581	A316	20 l brn & red brn	1.40	1.50
		Never hinged	4.25	

500th anniversary (in 1950) of the birth of Pietro Vannucci, painter.
For overprint see Trieste No. 125.

1951, July 23

582	A317	20 l grnsh gray & blk	3.50	1.25
583	A318	55 l vio bl & pale sal	19.00	11.00
		Set, never hinged	47.50	

Triennial Art Exhibition, Milan, 1951.
For overprints see Trieste Nos. 126-127.

Cyclist — A319

1951, Aug. 23

584	A319	25 l gray black	1.75	1.40
		Never hinged	10.00	

World Bicycle Championship Races, Milan, Aug.-Sept. 1951.
For overprint see Trieste No. 128.

Tartan and Globes A320

1951, Sept. 8 Photo.

585	A320	25 l deep blue	1.90	1.10
		Never hinged	6.75	

15th Levant Fair, Bari, September 1951.
For overprint see Trieste No. 129.

"La Figlia di Jorio" by Michetti A321

1951, Sept. 15 Wmk. 277 *Perf. 14*

586	A321	25 l dk brown	1.50	1.10
		Never hinged	6.75	

Centenary of the birth of Francesco Paolo Michetti, painter.
For overprint see Trieste No. 130.

Sardinia Stamps of 1851 A322

1951, Oct. 5

587	A322	10 l shown	1.25	1.75
588	A322	25 l 20c stamp	1.60	1.50
589	A322	60 l 40c stamp	5.75	5.75
		Nos. 587-589 (3)	8.60	9.00
		Set, never hinged	21.00	

Centenary of Sardinia's 1st postage stamp.
For overprints see Trieste Nos. 131-133.

Mercury — A323

Roman Census A324

1951, Oct. 31

590	A323	10 l green	.60	.85
591	A324	25 l vio gray	1.25	.70
		Set, never hinged	5.75	

3rd Industrial and the 9th General Italian Census.
For overprints see Trieste Nos. 134-135.

Winter Scene — A325

Trees A326

1951, Nov. 21

592	A325	10 l ol & dl grn	.60	*.95*
593	A326	25 l dull grn	1.50	.75
		Set, never hinged	7.75	

Issued to publicize the Festival of Trees.
For overprints see Trieste Nos. 136-137.

Giuseppe Verdi A327

Portraits of Verdi, various backgrounds.

1951, Nov. 19 Engr.

594	A327	10 l vio brn & dk grn	.70	*1.25*
595	A327	25 l red brn & dk brn	3.50	.85
596	A327	60 l dp grn & indigo	7.50	4.25
		Nos. 594-596 (3)	11.70	6.35
		Set, never hinged	42.50	

50th anniversary of the death of Giuseppe Verdi, composer.
For overprints see Trieste Nos. 138-140.

Vincenzo Bellini — A328

Wmk. 277

1952, Jan. 28 Photo. *Perf. 14*

597 A328 25 l gray & gray blk 1.00 .55
Never hinged 4.50

150th anniversary of the birth of Vincenzo Bellini, composer.
For overprint see Trieste No. 141.

Palace of Caserta and Statuary A329

1952, Feb. 1

598 A329 25 l dl grn & ol bis 1.00 .50
Never hinged 3.50

Issued to honor Luigi Vanvitelli, architect.
For overprint see Trieste No. 142.

Statues of Athlete and River God Tiber — A330

1952, Mar. 22

599 A330 25 l brn & sl blk .35 .45
Never hinged 1.10

Issued on the occasion of the first International Exhibition of Sports Stamps.
For overprint see Trieste No. 143.

Milan Fair Buildings A331

1952, Apr. 12 Engr.

600 A331 60 l ultra 6.00 4.00
Never hinged 30.00

30th Milan Trade Fair.
For overprint see Trieste No. 144.

Leonardo da Vinci — A332

Virgin of the Rocks — A332a

1952 Wmk. 277 Photo. *Perf. 14*

601 A332 25 l deep orange .20 .20

Unwmk.

Engr. *Perf. 13*

601A A332a 60 l ultra 1.25 *3.00*

Wmk. 277

601B A332 80 l brn car 5.25 .20
c. Perf. 14x13 4.25 .40
Set, never hinged 32.50

Leonardo da Vinci, 500th birth anniv.
For overprints see Trieste #145, 163-164.

First Stamps and Cathedral Bell Towers of Modena and Parma A333

1952, May 29 *Perf. 14*

602 A333 25 l blk & red brn .70 .35
603 A333 60 l blk & ultra 3.50 3.75
Set, never hinged 10.00

Cent. of the 1st postage stamps of Modena and Parma.
For overprints see Trieste Nos. 146-147.

Globe and Torch — A334

Lion of St. Mark — A335

1952, June 7

604 A334 25 l bright blue .75 .40
Never hinged 2.50

Issued to honor the Overseas Fair at Naples and Italian labor throughout the world.
For overprint see Trieste No. 148.

1952, June 14

605 A335 25 l black & yellow .50 .40
Never hinged 2.25

26th Biennial Art Exhibition, Venice.
For overprint see Trieste No. 149.

"P" and Basilica of St. Anthony A336

Flag and Basilica of St. Just A337

1952, June 19

606 A336 25 l bl gray, red & dk bl 1.00 .40
Never hinged 3.25

30th International Sample Fair of Padua.
For overprint see Trieste No. 150.

1952, June 28

607 A337 25 l dp grn, dk brn & red .65 .40
Never hinged 2.25

4th International Sample Fair of Trieste.
For overprint see Trieste No. 151.

Fair Entrance and Tartan A338

1952, Sept. 6 Wmk. 277 *Perf. 14*

608 A338 25 l dark green .40 .40
Never hinged 1.90

16th Levant Fair, Bari, Sept. 1952.
For overprint see Trieste No. 152.

Girolamo Savonarola A339

Mountain Peak and Climbing Equipment A340

1952, Sept. 20

609 A339 25 l purple .65 .40
Never hinged 5.50

500th anniversary of the birth of Girolamo Savonarola.
For overprint see Trieste No. 153.

1952, Oct. 4

610 A340 25 l gray .40 .30
Never hinged .80

Issued to publicize the National Exhibition of the Alpine troops, Oct. 4, 1952.
For overprint see Trieste No. 154.

Colosseum and Plane A341

1952, Sept. 29

611 A341 60 l vio bl & dk bl 9.25 5.50
Never hinged 16.00

Issued to publicize the first International Civil Aviation Conference, Rome, Sept. 1952.
For overprint see Trieste No. 155.

Guglielmo Cardinal Massaia and Map A342

1952, Nov. 21 Engr. *Perf. 13*

612 A342 25 l brn & dk brn .70 .40
Never hinged 1.75

Centenary of the establishment of the first Catholic mission in Ethiopia.
For overprint see Trieste No. 156.

Symbols of Army, Navy and Air Force A343

Sailor, Soldier and Aviator A344

Design: 60 l, Boat, plane and tank.

1952, Nov. 3 Photo. *Perf. 14*

613 A343 10 l dk green .20 .20
614 A344 25 l blk & dk brn .40 .20
615 A344 60 l black & blue 1.75 1.50
Nos. 613-615 (3) 2.35 1.90
Set, never hinged 8.00

Armed Forces Day, Nov. 4, 1952.
For overprints see Trieste Nos. 157-159.

Antonio Mancini — A345

Vincenzo Gemito — A346

1952, Dec. 6

616 A345 25 l dark green .40 .35
617 A346 25 l brown .40 .30
Set, never hinged 2.00

Birth centenaries of Antonio Mancini, painter, and Vincenzo Gemito, sculptor.
For overprints see Trieste Nos. 160-161.

Martyrs, Jailer and Artist Boldini A347

1952, Dec. 31

618 A347 25 l gray blk & dk blue 1.00 .45
Never hinged 2.50

Centenary of the deaths of the five Martyrs of Belfiore.
For overprint see Trieste No. 162.

Antonello da Messina — A349

1953, Feb. 21 Photo. *Perf. 14*

621 A349 25 l car lake .85 .40
Never hinged 2.25

Messina Exhibition of the paintings of Antonello and his 15th cent. contemporaries.
For overprint see Trieste No. 165.

Racing Cars A350

1953, Apr. 24

622 A350 25 l violet .85 .30
Never hinged 1.10

20th 1,000-mile auto race.
For overprint see Trieste No. 166.

Decoration "Knights of Labor" Bee and Honeycomb A351

Arcangelo Corelli A352

1953, Apr. 30

623 A351 25 l violet .50 .30
Never hinged 1.10

For overprint see Trieste No. 167.

1953, May 30

624 A352 25 l dark brown .40 .30
Never hinged 1.10

300th anniv. of the birth of Arcangelo Corelli, composer.
For overprint see Trieste No. 168.

St. Clare of Assisi and Convent of St. Damien A353

"Italia" after Syracusean Coin A354

1953, June 27

625 A353 25 l brown & dull red .25 .20
Never hinged .80

St. Clare of Assisi, 700th death anniv.
For overprint see Trieste No. 169.

1953-54 Wmk. 277 *Perf. 14*
Size: 17x21mm

626 A354 5 l gray .20 .20
627 A354 10 l org ver .20 .20
628 A354 12 l dull green .20 .20
628A A354 13 l brt lil rose ('54) .20 .20
629 A354 20 l brown .85 .20
630 A354 25 l purple .70 .20
631 A354 35 l rose car .25 .20
632 A354 60 l blue 2.25 .20
633 A354 80 l orange brn 14.00 .20
Nos. 626-633 (9) 18.85 1.80
Set, never hinged 110.00

See Nos. 661-662, 673B-689, 785-788, 998A-998W, 1288-1290. For overprints see Trieste Nos. 170-177.

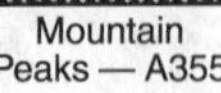

Mountain Peaks — A355

Tyche, Goddess of Fortune — A356

1953, July 11

634 A355 25 l blue green .75 .20
Never hinged 1.60

Festival of the Mountain.
For overprint see Trieste No. 181.

1953, July 16

635 A356 25 l dark brown .35 .20
636 A356 60 l deep blue 1.25 .75
Set, never hinged 4.75

Intl. Exposition of Agriculture, Rome, 1953.
For overprints see Trieste Nos. 182-183.

Continents Joined by Rainbow A357

1953, Aug. 6

637 A357 25 l org & Prus bl 2.75 .20
638 A357 60 l lil rose & dk vio bl 6.00 1.40
Set, never hinged 16.00

Signing of the North Atlantic Treaty, 4th anniv.
For overprints see Trieste Nos. 184-185.

Luca Signorelli A358

Agostino Bassi A359

1953, Aug. 13

639 A358 25 l dk brn & dull grn .30 .20
Never hinged .90

Issued to publicize the opening of an exhibition of the works of Luca Signorelli, painter.
For overprint see Trieste No. 186.

1953, Sept. 5

640 A359 25 l dk gray & brown .25 .20
Never hinged .80

6th International Microbiology Congress, Rome, Sept. 6-12, 1953.
For overprint see Trieste No. 187.

Siena — A360

Rapallo A361

Views: 20 l, Seaside at Gardone. 25 l, Mountain, Cortina d'Ampezzo. 35 l, Roman ruins, Taormina. 60 l, Rocks and sea, Capri.

1953, Dec. 31 *Perf. 14*

641 A360 10 l dk brn & red brn .20 .20
642 A361 12 l lt blue & gray .20 .20
643 A361 20 l brn org & dk brn .25 .20
644 A360 25 l dk grn & pale bl .25 .20
645 A361 35 l cream & brn .50 .20
646 A361 60 l bl grn & ind .75 .35
Nos. 641-646 (6) 2.15 1.35
Set, never hinged 8.75

For overprints see Trieste Nos. 188-193, 204-205.

Lateran Palace, Rome — A362

Television Screen and Aerial — A363

1954, Feb. 11

647 A362 25 l dk brown & choc .25 .20
648 A362 60 l blue & ultra 1.00 1.00
Set, never hinged 4.00

Signing of the Lateran Pacts, 25th anniv.
For overprints see Trieste Nos. 194-195.

1954, Feb. 25

649 A363 25 l purple .50 .20
650 A363 60 l dp blue grn 2.00 1.75
Set, never hinged 7.75

Introduction of regular natl. television service.
For overprints see Trieste Nos. 196-197.

"Italia" and Quotation from Constitution A364

1954, Mar. 20

651 A364 25 l purple .70 .20
Never hinged 2.00

Propaganda for the payment of taxes.
For overprint see Trieste No. 198.

Vertical Flight Trophy — A365

Eagle Perched on Ruins — A366

1954, Apr. 24

652 A365 25 l gray black .40 .40
Never hinged .90

Issued to publicize the experimental transportation of mail by helicopter, April 1954.
For overprint see Trieste No. 199.

1954, June 1

653 A366 25 l gray, org brn & blk .20 .20
Never hinged .40

10th anniv. of Italy's resistance movement.
For overprint see Trieste No. 200.

Alfredo Catalani, Composer, Birth Centenary — A367

1954, June 19 *Perf. 14*

654 A367 25 l dk grnsh gray .20 .20
Never hinged .40

For overprint see Trieste No. 201.

Marco Polo, Lion of St. Mark and Dragon A368

1954, July 8 Engr. *Perf. 14*

655 A368 25 l red brown .25 .20

Perf. 13

656 A368 60 l gray green 1.50 1.75
a. Perf. 13x12 7.50 4.00
Set, never hinged 4.75

700th anniv. of the birth of Marco Polo.
For overprints see Trieste Nos. 202-203.

Automobile and Cyclist A369

1954, Sept. 6 Photo. *Perf. 14*

657 A369 25 l dp green & red .20 .20
Never hinged .50

Italian Touring Club, 60th anniv.
For overprint see Trieste No. 206.

St. Michael Overpowering the Devil — A370

1954, Oct. 9

658 A370 25 l rose red .25 .20
659 A370 60 l blue .85 1.10
Set, never hinged 1.50

23rd general assembly of the International Criminal Police, Rome 1954.
For overprints see Trieste Nos. 207-208.

Pinocchio and Group of Children — A371

1954, Oct. 26

660 A371 25 l rose red .20 .20
Never hinged .60

Carlo Lorenzini, creator of Pinocchio.

Italia Type of 1953-54

1954, Dec. 28 Engr. *Perf. 13*
Size: 22½x27½mm

661 A354 100 l brown 26.00 .20
662 A354 200 l dp blue 4.75 .20
Set, never hinged 150.00

Madonna, Perugino A372

Amerigo Vespucci and Map A373

60 l, Madonna of the Pieta, Michelangelo.

1954, Dec. 31 Photo. *Perf. 14*

663 A372 25 l brown & bister .25 .20
664 A372 60 l black & cream .70 *1.10*
Set, never hinged 2.25

Issued to mark the end of the Marian Year.

1954, Dec. 31 Engr. *Perf. 13*

665 A373 25 l dp plum .25 .20
a. Perf. 13x14 2.25 .50
666 A373 60 l blue blk .85 *1.10*
a. Perf. 13x14 .45 *1.10*
Set, never hinged 2.75

500th anniv. of the birth of Amerigo Vespucci, explorer, 1454-1512.

Silvio Pellico (1789-1854), Dramatist — A374

Wmk. 277

1955, Jan. 24 Photo. *Perf. 14*

667 A374 25 l brt blue & vio .30 .20
Never hinged .40

Italy at Work Type of 1950

1955-57 Wmk. 303

668 A306 50c vio bl .20 .20
669 A306 1 l dk bl vio .20 .20
670 A306 2 l sepia .20 .20
671 A306 15 l dk gray bl .65 .25
672 A306 30 l magenta 17.00 .50
673 A306 50 l violet 12.00 .25
673A A306 65 l dk grn ('57) 5.75 *18.00*
Nos. 668-673A (7) 36.00 19.60
Set, never hinged 110.00

Italia Type of 1953-54 and

St. George, by Donatello — A374a

1955-58 Wmk. 303 Photo. *Perf. 14*
Size: 17x21mm

673B A354 1 l gray ('58) .20 .20
674 A354 5 l slate .20 .20
675 A354 6 l ocher ('57) .20 .20
676 A354 10 l org ver .20 .20
677 A354 12 l dull green .20 .20
678 A354 13 l brt lil rose .20 .20
679 A354 15 l gray vio ('56) .20 .20
680 A354 20 l brown .20 .20
681 A354 25 l purple .20 .20
682 A354 35 l rose car .20 .20
683 A354 50 l olive ('58) .25 .20
685 A354 60 l blue .20 .20
686 A354 80 l brown org .20 .20
687 A354 90 l lt red brn ('58) .20 .20

Engr. ***Perf. 13½***
Size: 22½x28mm

688	A354	100 l brn ('56)	3.00	.20
a.		Perf. 13½x12	3.00	.20
b.		Perf. 13½x14	300.00	15.00
689	A354	200 l gray bl ('57)	3.00	.20
690	A374a	500 l grn ('57)	.75	.20
b.		Perf. 14x13½	.60	.20
690A	A374a	1000 l rose car ('57)	.95	.20
c.		Perf. 14x13½	1.25	.20
		Nos. 673B-690A (18)	10.55	3.60
		Set, never hinged	37.50	

Nos. 690-690A were printed on ordinary and fluorescent paper.

See Nos. 785-788. See Nos. 998A-998W for small-size set.

Catalogue values for unused stamps in this section, from this point to the end of the section, are for Never Hinged items.

"Italia"
A375

Oil Derrick and Old Roman Aqueduct
A376

1955, Mar. 15 **Photo.** ***Perf. 14***
691 A375 25 l rose vio 2.00 .20

Issued as propaganda for the payment of taxes.

1955, June 6

60 l, Marble columns and oil field on globe.

692 A376 25 l olive green .40 .20
693 A376 60 l henna brown .95 *1.25*

4th World Petroleum Cong., Rome, June 6-15, 1955.

Antonio Rosmini, Philosopher, Death Centenary — A377

1955, July 1 **Wmk. 303** ***Perf. 14***
694 A377 25 l sepia 1.00 .20

Girolamo Fracastoro and Stadium at Verona
A378

1955, Sept. 1
695 A378 25 l gray blk & brn .70 .20

Intl. Medical Congress, Verona, Sept. 1-4.

Basilica of St. Francis, Assisi
A379

1955, Oct. 4
696 A379 25 l black & cream .40 .20

Issued in honor of St. Francis and for the 7th centenary (in 1953) of the Basilica in Assisi.

Young Man at Drawing Board — A380

1955, Oct. 15
697 A380 25 l Prus green .40 .20

Centenary of technical education in Italy.

Harvester — A381

FAO Headquarters, Rome — A382

1955, Nov. 3
698 A381 25 l rose red & brn .20 .20
699 A382 60 l blk & brt pur .80 .75

Intl. Institute of Agriculture, 50th anniv. and FAO, successor to the Institute, 10th anniv.

A383

A384

1955, Nov. 10
700 A383 25 l rose brown 1.10 .20

70th anniversary of the birth of Giacomo Matteotti, Italian socialist leader.

1955, Nov. 19
701 A384 25 l dark green .35 .20

Death of Battista Grassi, zoologist, 30th anniv.

"St. Stephen Giving Alms" — A385

"St. Lorenzo Giving Alms"
A386

1955, Nov. 26
702 A385 10 l black & cream .20 .20
703 A386 25 l ultra & cream .40 .20

Death of Fra Angelico, painter, 500th anniv.

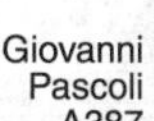

Giovanni Pascoli
A387

1955, Dec. 31
704 A387 25 l gray black .30 .20

Centenary of the birth of Giovanni Pascoli, poet.

Ski Jump "Italia"
A388

Stadiums at Cortina: 12 l, Skiing. 25 l, Ice skating. 60 l, Ice racing, Lake Misurina.

1956, Jan. 26 **Photo.**
705 A388 10 l blue grn & org .20 .20
706 A388 12 l yellow & blk .20 .20
707 A388 25 l vio blk & org brn .35 .20
708 A388 60 l sapphire & org 2.25 1.00
Nos. 705-708 (4) 3.00 1.60

VII Winter Olympic Games at Cortina d'Ampezzo, Jan. 26-Feb. 5, 1956.

Mail Coach and Tunnel Exit
A389

1956, May 19 **Wmk. 303** ***Perf. 14***
709 A389 25 l dk blue grn 6.00 .20

50th anniv. of the Simplon Tunnel.

Arms of Republic and Symbols of Industry
A390

1956, June 2
710 A390 10 l gray & slate bl .30 .20
711 A390 25 l pink & rose red .45 .20
712 A390 60 l lt bl & brt bl 2.75 1.40
713 A390 80 l orange & brn 7.00 .20
Nos. 710-713 (4) 10.50 2.00

Tenth anniversary of the Republic.

Amedeo Avogadro
A391

1956, Sept. 8
714 A391 25 l black vio .25 .20

Centenary of the death of Amedeo Avogadro, physicist.

Europa Issue

"Rebuilding Europe" — A392

1956, Sept. 15
715 A392 25 l dark green .75 .20
716 A392 60 l blue 6.75 .35

Issued to symbolize the cooperation among the six countries comprising the Coal and Steel Community.

Globe and Satellites
A393

1956, Sept. 22
717 A393 25 l intense blue .20 .20

7th Intl. Astronautical Cong., Rome, Sept. 17-22.

Globe — A394

1956, Dec. 29 **Litho.** **Unwmk.**
718 A394 25 l red & bl grn, *pink* .20 .20
719 A394 60 l bl grn & red, *pale bl grn* .40 .20

Italy's admission to the United Nations.

The design, viewed through red and green glasses, becomes three-dimensional.

Postal Savings Bank and Notes
A395

1956, Dec. 31 **Photo.** **Wmk. 303**
720 A395 25 l sl bl & dp ultra .20 .20

80th anniversary of Postal Savings.

Ovid
A396

Antonio Canova
A397

Paulina Borghese as Venus
A398

1957, June 10 ***Perf. 14***
721 A396 25 l ol grn & blk .30 .20

2000th anniversary of the birth of the poet Ovid (Publius Ovidius Naso).

1957, July 15 **Engr.**

60 l, Sculpture: Hercules and Lichas.

722 A397 25 l brown .20 .20
723 A397 60 l gray .25 .60
724 A398 80 l vio blue .25 .20
Nos. 722-724 (3) .70 1.00

Birth of Antonio Canova, sculptor, 200th anniv.

Traffic Light
A399

"United Europe"
A400

Wmk. 303

1957, Aug. 7 Photo. ***Perf. 14***

725 A399 25 l green, blk & red .35 .20

Campaign for careful driving.

1957, Sept. 16 Litho. ***Perf. 14***

Flags in Original Colors

726 A400 25 l light blue .20 .20

Perf. 13

727 A400 60 l violet blue 1.10 .20

United Europe for peace and prosperity.

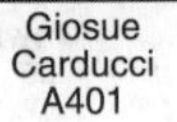

Giosue Carducci A401

Filippino Lippi A402

1957, Oct. 14 Engr. ***Perf. 14***

728 A401 25 l brown .30 .20

Death of the poet Giosue Carducci, 50th anniv.

1957, Nov. 25 Wmk. 303 ***Perf. 14***

729 A402 25 l reddish brown .30 .20

Birth of Filippino Lippi, painter, 500th anniv.

2000th Anniv. of the Death of Marcus Tullius Cicero, Roman Statesman and Writer — A403

1957, Nov. 30 **Photo.**

730 A403 25 l brown red .20 .20

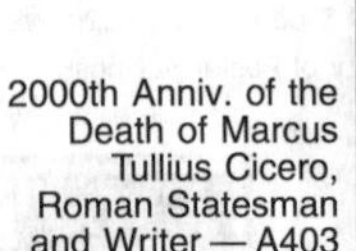

St. Domenico Savio and Students of Various Races A404

1957, Dec. 14

731 A404 15 l brt lil & blk .20 .20

Cent. of the death of St. Domenico Savio.

St. Francis of Paola A405

Giuseppe Garibaldi A406

1957, Dec. 21 **Engr.**

732 A405 25 l black .25 .20

450th anniv. of the death of St. Francis of Paola, patron saint of seafaring men.

1957, Dec. 14 ***Perf. 14x13, 13x14***

Design: 110 l, Garibaldi monument, horiz.

733 A406 15 l slate green .20 .20

734 A406 110 l dull purple .35 .20

150th anniv. of the birth of Giuseppe Garibaldi.

Peasant, Dams and Map of Sardinia A407

1958, Feb. 1 Engr. ***Perf. 14***

738 A407 25 l bluish grn .20 .20

Completion of the Flumendosa-Mulargia irrigation system.

Immaculate Conception Statue, Rome, and Lourdes Basilica — A408

1958, Apr. 16 Wmk. 303 ***Perf. 14***

739 A408 15 l rose claret .20 .20

740 A408 60 l blue .20 .20

Apparition of the Virgin Mary at Lourdes, cent.

Book and Symbols of Labor Industry and Agriculture A409

Designs: 60 l, "Tree of Freedom," vert. 110 l, Montecitorio Palace.

1958, May 9 Photo. ***Perf. 14***

741 A409 25 l bl grn & ocher .20 .20

742 A409 60 l blk brn & bl .20 .20

743 A409 110 l ol bis & blk brn .25 .20

Nos. 741-743 (3) .65 .60

10th anniversary of the constitution.

Brussels Fair Emblem A410

Prologue from Pagliacci A411

1958, June 12

744 A410 60 l blue & yellow .20 .20

Intl. and Universal Exposition at Brussels.

1958, July 10

745 A411 25 l dk bl & dk red .20 .20

Birth of Ruggiero Leoncavallo, composer, cent.

Scene from La Bohème A412

1958, July 10 Engr. Unwmk.

746 A412 25 l dark blue .20 .20

Birth of Giacomo Puccini, composer, cent.

Giovanni Fattori, Self-portrait A413

"Ave Maria on the Lake" by Giovanni Segantini A414

1958, Aug. 7 Wmk. 303 ***Perf. 13x14***

747 A413 110 l redsh brown .35 .20

Death of Giovanni Fattori, painter, 50th anniv.

1958, Aug. 7 ***Perf. 14***

748 A414 110 l slate, *buff* .40 .20

Birth of Giovanni Segantini, painter, cent.

Map of Brazil, Plane and Arch of Titus A415

1958, Aug. 23 Photo. ***Perf. 14***

749 A415 175 l Prus green .40 .20

Italo-Brazilian friendship on the occasion of Pres. Giovanni Gronchi's visit to Brazil.

Common Design Types pictured following the introduction.

Europa Issue, 1958

Common Design Type

1958, Sept. 13

Size: 20½x35½mm

750 CD1 25 l red & blue .20 .20

751 CD1 60 l blue & red .20 .20

Issued to show the European Postal Union at the service of European integration.

½g Stamp of Naples A416

Evangelista Torricelli A417

Design: 60 l, 1g Stamp of Naples.

Perf. 14x13½, 13½

1958, Oct. 4 Engr. Unwmk.

752 A416 25 l brown red .20 .20

753 A416 60 l blk & red brn .20 .20

Centenary of the stamps of Naples.

1958, Oct. 20 Wmk. 303 ***Perf. 14***

754 A417 25 l rose claret .65 .20

350th anniv. of the birth of Evangelista Torricelli, mathematician and physicist.

"The Triumph of Caesar," Montegna A418

Persian Style Bas-relief, Sorrento A419

25 l, Coats of Arms of Trieste, Rome & Trento, horiz. 60 l, War memorial bell of Rovereto.

1958, Nov. 3 Engr. ***Perf. 14x13½***

755 A418 15 l green .20 .20

756 A418 25 l gray .20 .20

757 A418 60 l rose claret .20 .20

Nos. 755-757 (3) .60 .60

40th anniv. of Italy's victory in World War I.

1958, Nov. 27 **Photo.**

758 A419 25 l sepia, *bluish* .20 .20

759 A419 60 l vio bl, *bluish* .45 .60

Visit of the Shah of Iran to Italy.

Eleonora Duse — A420

Dancers and Antenna — A421

Unwmk.

1958, Dec. 11 Engr. ***Perf. 14***

760 A420 25 l brt ultra .20 .20

Cent. of the birth of Eleonora Duse, actress.

1958, Dec. 29 Photo. Wmk. 303

Design: 60 l, Piano, dove and antenna.

761 A421 25 l red, bl & blk .20 .20

762 A421 60 l ultra & blk .20 .20

10th anniv. of the Prix Italia (International Radio and Television Competitions).

Stamp of Sicily — A422

Design: 60 l, Stamp of Sicily, 5g.

Perf. 14x13½

1959, Jan. 2 Engr. Unwmk.

763 A422 25 l Prus green .20 .20

764 A422 60 l dp orange .20 .20

Centenary of the stamps of Sicily.

Dome of St. Peter's and Tower of Lateran Palace A423

Wmk. 303

1959, Feb. 11 Photo. ***Perf. 14***

765 A423 25 l ultra .20 .20

30th anniversary of the Lateran Pacts.

Map of North Atlantic and NATO Emblem A424

1959, Apr. 4

766 A424 25 l dk bl & ocher .20 .20
767 A424 60 l dk bl & green .20 .20

10th anniv. of NATO.

Arms of Paris and Rome A425

1959, Apr. 9

768 A425 15 l blue & red .20 .20
769 A425 25 l blue & red .20 .20

Cultural ties between Rome and Paris.

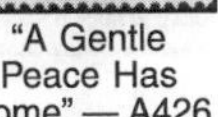

"A Gentle Peace Has Come" — A426

Statue of Lord Byron — A427

1959, Apr. 13 Engr. Unwmk.

770 A426 25 l olive green .20 .20

International War Veterans Association convention, Rome.

1959, Apr. 21

771 A427 15 l black .20 .20

Unveiling in Rome of a statue of Lord Byron by Bertel Thorvaldson, Danish sculptor.

Camillo Prampolini — A428

1959, Apr. 27 Unwmk. *Perf. 14*

772 A428 15 l car rose 1.90 .20

Camillo Prampolini, socialist leader and reformer, birth centenary.

Fountain of Dioscuri and Olympic Rings — A429

Baths of Carcalla A430

Designs: 25 l, Capitoline tower. 60 l, Arch of Constantine. 110 l, Ruins of Basilica of Massentius.

1959, June 23 Photo. Wmk. 303
Designs in Dark Sepia

773 A429 15 l red orange .20 .20
774 A429 25 l blue .20 .20
775 A430 35 l bister .20 .20
776 A430 60 l rose lilac .25 .20
777 A430 110 l yellow .25 .20
Nos. 773-777 (5) 1.10 1.00

1960 Olympic Games in Rome.

Victor Emanuel II, Garibaldi, Cavour, Mazzini A431

Battle of San Fermo A432

25 l, "After the Battle of Magenta" by Fattori and Red Cross, vert. 60 l, Battle of Palestro. 110 l, "Battle of Magenta" by Induno, vert.

Engr., Cross Photo. on 25 l
1959, June 27 Unwmk.

778 A431 15 l gray .20 .20
779 A431 25 l brn & red .20 .20
780 A432 35 l dk violet .20 .20
781 A432 60 l ultra .20 .20
782 A432 110 l magenta .20 .20
Nos. 778-782 (5) 1.00 1.00

Cent. of the war of independence. No. 779 for the centenary of the Red Cross idea.

Labor Monument, Geneva A433

Stamp of Romagna A434

1959, July 20 *Perf. 14x13, 14*

783 A433 25 l violet .20 .20
784 A433 60 l brown .20 .20

40th anniv. of the ILO.

Italia Type of 1953-54
Photo.; Engr. (100 l, 200 l)
1959-66 Wmk. 303 *Perf. 14*
Size: 17x21mm

785 A354 30 l bis brn ('60) .25 .20
786 A354 40 l lil rose ('60) 1.25 .20
786A A354 70 l Prus grn ('60) .35 .20
787 A354 100 l brown .45 .20
787A A354 130 l gray & dl red ('66) .25 .20
788 A354 200 l dp blue .45 .20
Nos. 785-788 (6) 3.00 1.20

1959, Sept. 1 Photo.

Design: 60 l, Stamp of Romagna, 20b.

789 A434 25 l pale brn & blk .20 .20
790 A434 60 l gray grn & blk .20 .20

Centenary of the stamps of Romagna.

Europa Issue, 1959
Common Design Type
1959, Sept. 19
Size: 22x27½mm

791 CD2 25 l olive green .20 .20
792 CD2 60 l blue .20 .20

Stamp of 1953 with Facsimile Cancellation A435

Aeneas Fleeing with Father and Son, by Raphael A436

1959, Dec. 20 Wmk. 303 *Perf. 14*

793 A435 15 l gray, rose car & blk .20 .20

Italy's first Stamp Day, Dec. 20, 1959.

1960, Apr. 7 Engr. Unwmk.

794 A436 25 l lake .20 .20
795 A436 60 l gray violet .20 .20

World Refugee Year, 7/1/59-6/30/60. Design is detail from "The Fire in the Borgo."

Garibaldi's Proclamation to the Sicilians — A437

King Victor Emmanuel and Garibaldi Meeting at Teano — A438

60 l, Volunteers embarking, Quarto, Genoa.

Wmk. 303
1960, May 5 Photo. *Perf. 14*

796 A437 15 l brown .20 .20

Perf. 13x14, 14x13
Engr. Unwmk.

797 A438 25 l rose claret .20 .20
798 A437 60 l ultramarine .20 .20

Cent. of the liberation of Southern Italy (Kingdom of the Two Sicilies) by Garibaldi.

Emblem of 17th Olympic Games — A439

Olympic Stadium A440

Statues: 15 l, Roman Consul on way to the games. 35 l, Myron's Discobolus. 110 l, Seated boxer. 200 l, Apoxyomenos by Lysippus.

Stadia: 25 l, Velodrome. 60 l, Sports palace. 150 l, Small sports palace.

Photogravure, Engraved
Perf. 14x13½, 13½x14
1960 Wmk. 303, Unwmk.

799 A439 5 l yellow brn .20 .20
800 A440 10 l dp org & dk bl .20 .20
801 A439 15 l ultra .20 .20
802 A440 25 l lt vio & brn .20 .20
803 A439 35 l rose cl .20 .20
804 A440 60 l bluish grn & brn .20 .20
805 A439 110 l plum .20 .20
806 A440 150 l blue & brn 1.00 .55
807 A439 200 l green .50 .20
Nos. 799-807 (9) 2.90 2.15

17th Olympic Games, Rome, 8/25-9/11.

The photo. denominations (5-10, 25, 60, 150 l) are wmkd.; the engraved (15, 35, 110, 200 l) are unwmkd.

Bottego Statue, Parma A441

Michelangelo da Caravaggio A442

1960 Unwmk. Engr. *Perf. 14*

808 A441 30 l brown .20 .20

Birth cent. of Vittorio Bottego, explorer.

Europa Issue, 1960
Common Design Type
1960 Photo. Wmk. 303
Size: 37x27mm

809 CD3 30 l dk grn & bis brn .20 .20
810 CD3 70 l dk bl & salmon .20 .20

1960 Unwmk. Engr. *Perf. 13x13½*

811 A442 25 l orange brn .20 .20

350th anniv. of the death of Michelangelo da Caravaggio (Merisi), painter.

Mail Coach and Post Horn A443

1960 Wmk. 303 Photo. *Perf. 14*

812 A443 15 l blk brn & org brn .20 .20

Issued for Stamp Day, Dec. 20.

Slave, by Michelangelo — A444

Designs from Sistine Chapel by Michelangelo: 5 l, 10 l, 115 l, 150 l, Heads of various "slaves." 15 l, Joel. 20 l, Libyan Sybil. 25 l, Isaiah. 30 l, Eritrean Sybil. 40 l, Daniel. 50 l, Delphic Sybil. 55 l, Cumaean Sybil. 70 l, Zachariah. 85 l, Jonah. 90 l, Jeremiah. 100 l, Ezekiel. 200 l, Self-portrait. 500 l, Adam. 1000 l, Eve.

Wmk. 303
1961, Mar. 6 Photo. *Perf. 14*
Size: 17x21mm

813 A444 1 l gray .20 .20
814 A444 5 l brown org .20 .20
815 A444 10 l red org .20 .20
816 A444 15 l brt lil .20 .20
817 A444 20 l Prus grn .20 .20
818 A444 25 l brown .30 .20
819 A444 30 l purple .20 .20
820 A444 40 l rose red .20 .20
821 A444 50 l olive .45 .20
822 A444 55 l red brn .20 .20
823 A444 70 l blue .20 .20
824 A444 85 l slate grn .20 .20
825 A444 90 l lil rose .40 .20
826 A444 100 l vio gray .75 .20
827 A444 115 l ultra .25 .20

Engr.

828 A444 150 l chocolate 1.10 .20
829 A444 200 l dark blue 1.75 .20
a. Perf. 13½ 1.75 .20

Perf. 13½
Size: 22x27mm

830 A444 500 l blue grn 3.50 .20
831 A444 1000 l brown red 3.25 .50
Nos. 813-831 (19) 13.75 4.10

Map Showing Flight from Italy to Argentina
A445

185 l, Italy to Uruguay. 205 l, Italy to Peru.

1961, Apr. Photo. *Perf. 14*

832	A445	170 l ultra	4.50	4.50
833	A445	185 l dull green	4.50	4.50
834	A445	205 l violet blk	9.00	9.00
a.		205 l rose lilac	1,500.	
		Nos. 832-834 (3)	18.00	18.00

Visit of Pres. Gronchi to South America, 4/61.

Nos. 832-833 and 834a were issued Apr. 4, to become valid on Apr. 6. The map of Peru on No. 834a was drawn incorrectly and the stamp was therefore withdrawn on Apr. 4. A corrected design in new color (No. 834) was issued Apr. 6. Forgeries of No. 834a exist.

Statue of Pliny, Como Cathedral
A446

Ippolito Nievo (1831-61), Writer
A447

1961, May 27

835	A446	30 l brown	.20	.20

1900th anniversary of the birth of Pliny the Younger, Roman consul and writer.

1961, June 8 Wmk. 303 *Perf. 14*

836	A447	30 l multi	.20	.20

St. Paul Aboard Ship
A448

1961, June 28

837	A448	30 l multi	.20	.20
838	A448	70 l multi	.30	.30

1,900th anniversary of St. Paul's arrival in Rome. The design is after a miniature from the Bible of Borso D'Este.

Cavalli Gun and Gaeta Fortress
A449

Cent. of Italian unity: 30 l, Carignano palace, Turin. 40 l, Montecitorio palace, Rome. 70 l, Palazzo Vecchio, Florence. 115 l, Villa Madama, Rome. 300 l, Steel construction, Italia '61 Exhibition, Turin.

1961, Aug. 12 Photo.

839	A449	15 l dk bl & redsh brn	.20	.20
840	A449	30 l dk bl & red brn	.20	.20
841	A449	40 l bl & brn	.35	.20
842	A449	70 l brn & pink	.50	.20
843	A449	115 l org brn & dk bl	1.75	.20
844	A449	300 l brt grn & red	5.00	4.00
		Nos. 839-844 (6)	8.00	5.00

Europa Issue, 1961

Common Design Type

1961, Sept. 18 Wmk. 303 *Perf. 14*

Size: 36½x21mm

845	CD4	30 l carmine	.20	.20
846	CD4	70 l yel grn	.20	.20

Giandomenico Romagnosi — A450

Perf. 13½

1961, Nov. 28 Unwmk. Engr.

847	A450	30 l green	.20	.20

Bicentenary of the birth of Giandomenico Romagnosi, jurist and philosopher.

Design from 1820 Sardinia Letter Sheet
A451

Wmk. 303

1961, Dec. 3 Photo. *Perf. 14*

848	A451	15 l lil rose & blk	.20	.20

Issued for Stamp Day 1961.

Family Scene "I am the Lamp that Glows so Gently . . ."
A452

1962, Apr. 6 Wmk. 303 *Perf. 14*

849	A452	30 l red	.20	.20
850	A452	70 l blue	.25	.30

Death of Giovanni Pascoli, poet, 50th anniv.

Pacinotti's Dynamo
A453

1962, June 12

851	A453	30 l rose & blk	.20	.20
852	A453	70 l ultra & blk	.25	.30

Antonio Pacinotti (1841-1912), physicist and inventor of the ring winding dynamo.

St. Catherine of Siena, by Andrea Vanni — A454

Lion of St. Mark — A455

70 l, St. Catherine, 15th century woodcut.

1962, June 26 Photo.

853	A454	30 l black	.20	.20

Engraved and Photogravure

854	A454	70 l red & blk	.25	.40

500th anniversary of the canonization of St. Catherine of Siena, Patroness of Italy.

1962, Aug. 25 Photo.

Design: 30 l, Stylized camera eye.

855	A455	30 l bl & blk	.20	.20
856	A455	70 l red org & blk	.20	.20

Intl. Film Festival in Venice, 30th anniv.

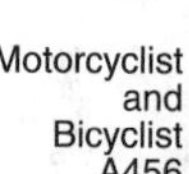

Motorcyclist and Bicyclist
A456

70 l, Group of cyclists. 300 l, Bicyclist.

1962, Aug. 30

857	A456	30 l grn & blk	.20	.20
858	A456	70 l bl & blk	.20	.20
859	A456	300 l dp org & blk	4.00	2.50
		Nos. 857-859 (3)	4.40	2.90

World Bicycle Championship Races.

Europa Issue, 1962

Common Design Type

1962, Sept. 17

Size: 37x21mm

860	CD5	30 l carmine	.30	.20
861	CD5	70 l blue	.30	.25

Swiss and Italian Flags, Eugenio and Angela Lina Balzan Medal
A457

1962, Oct. 25 Wmk. 303 *Perf. 14*

862	A457	70 l rose red, grn & brn	.30	.20

1st distribution of the Balzan Prize by the Intl. Balzan Foundation for Italian-Swiss Cooperation.

Malaria Eradication Emblem — A458

Stamps of 1862 and 1961 — A459

1962, Oct. 31 Photo.

863	A458	30 l light violet	.20	.20
864	A458	70 l light blue	.25	.25

WHO drive to eradicate malaria.

1962, Dec. 2

865	A459	15 l pur, buff & bister	.20	.20

Stamp Day and cent. of Italian postage stamps.

A460

A461

Holy Spirit Descending on Apostles.

1962, Dec. 8

866	A460	30 l org & dk bl grn, *buff*	.20	.20
867	A460	70 l dk bl grn & org, *buff*	.20	.20

21st Ecumenical Council of the Roman Catholic Church, Vatican II. The design is an illumination from the Codex Syriacus.

1962, Dec. 10 Engr. Unwmk.

Statue of Count Camillo Bensi di Cavour.

868	A461	30 l dk grn	.20	.20

Centenary of Court of Accounts.

Count Giovanni Pico della Mirandola
A462

Gabriele D'Annunzio
A463

Wmk. 303

1963, Feb. 25 Photo. *Perf. 14*

869	A462	30 l gray blk	.20	.20

Mirandola (1463-94), Renaissance scholar.

1963, Mar. 12 Engr. Unwmk.

870	A463	30 l dk grn	.20	.20

Issued to commemorate the centenary of the birth of Gabriele d'Annunzio, author and soldier.

Sower — A464

Design: 70 l, Harvester typing sheaf, sculpture from Maggiore Fountain, Perugia.

1963, Mar. 21 Photo. Wmk. 303

871	A464	30 l rose car & brn	.20	.20
872	A464	70 l bl & brn	.30	.30

FAO "Freedom from Hunger" campaign.

Mt. Viso, Alpine Club Emblem, Ax and Rope — A465

Map of Italy and "INA" Initials — A466

1963, Mar. 30 Wmk. 303 *Perf. 14*

873	A465	115 l dk brn & brt bl	.20	.20

Italian Alpine Club founding, cent.

1963, Apr. 4

874	A466	30 l grn & blk	.20	.20

50th anniv. of the Natl. Insurance Institute.

Globe and Stamp
A467

1963, May 7 Photo. *Perf. 14*

875	A467	70 l bl & grn	.20	.20

1st Intl. Postal Conf., Paris, 1863.

Crosses and Centenary Emblem on Globe — A468

1963, June 8 Wmk. 303 *Perf. 14*

876 A468 30 l dk gray & red .20 .20
877 A468 70 l dl bl & red .25 .25

International Red Cross founding, cent.

Roman Column, Globe and Highways A469

1963, Aug. 21 Wmk. 303 *Perf. 14*

878 A469 15 l gray ol & dk bl .20 .20
879 A469 70 l dl bl & brn .20 .20

UN Tourist Conf., Rome, Aug. 21-Sept. 5.

Europa Issue, 1963

Common Design Type

1963, Sept. 16

Size: 27½x23mm

880 CD6 30 l rose & brn .20 .20
881 CD6 70 l brn & grn .20 .20

Bay of Naples, Vesuvius and Sailboats A470

Athlete on Greek Vase A471

1963, Sept. 21 Wmk. 303 *Perf. 14*

882 A470 15 l bl & org .20 .20
883 A471 70 l dk grn & org brn .20 .20

4th Mediterranean Games, Naples, Sept. 21-29.

Giuseppe Gioachino Belli (1791-1863), Poet — A472

Stamps Forming Flower — A473

1963, Nov. 14 Wmk. 303 *Perf. 14*

884 A472 30 l red brn .20 .20

1963, Dec. 1

885 A473 15 l bl & car .20 .20

Issued for Stamp Day.

Pietro Mascagni and Old Costanzi Theater, Rome — A474

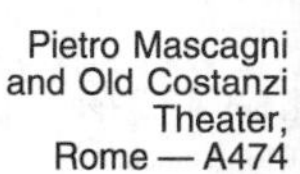

#886, Giuseppe Verdi & La Scala, Milan.

1963 Photo.

886 A474 30 l gray grn & yel brn .20 .20
887 A474 30 l yel brn & gray grn .20 .20

Verdi (1813-1901), and Mascagni (1863-1945), composers. Issued: #886, Oct. 10; #887, Dec. 7.

Galileo Galilei A475

Nicodemus by Michelangelo A476

1964, Feb. 15 Wmk. 303 *Perf. 14*

888 A475 30 l org brn .20 .20
889 A475 70 l black .20 .20

Galilei (1564-1642), astronomer & physicist.

1964, Feb. 18 Photo.

890 A476 30 l brown .20 .20

Michelangelo Buonarroti (1475-1564), artist. Head of Nicodemus (self-portrait?) from the Pieta, Florence Cathedral. See No. C137.

Carabinieri A477

70 l, Charge of Pastrengo, 1848, by De Albertis.

1964, June 5 Wmk. 303 *Perf. 14*

891 A477 30 l vio bl & red .20 .20
892 A477 70 l brown .20 .20

150th anniv. of the Carabinieri (police corps).

Giambattista Bodoni — A478

Perf. 14x13

1964, July 30 Engr. Unwmk.

893 A478 30 l carmine .20 .20
a. Perf. 13 .20 .20

Death of Giambattista Bodoni (1740-1813), printer & type designer (Bodoni type), 150th anniv.

Europa Issue, 1964

Common Design Type

Wmk. 303

1964, Sept. 14 Photo. *Perf. 14*

Size: 21x37mm

894 CD7 30 l brt rose lilac .20 .20
895 CD7 70 l blue green .20 .20

Walled City — A479

Left Arch of Victor Emmanuel Monument, Rome — A480

1964, Oct. 15 Photo. *Perf. 14*

896 A479 30 l emer & dk brn .20 .20
897 A479 70 l bl & dk brn .20 .20

Unwmk. Engr.

898 A479 500 l red 1.00 .50
Nos. 896-898 (3) 1.40 .90

7th Congress of European Towns. The buildings in design are: Big Ben, London; Campodoglio, Rome; Town Hall, Bruges; Römer, Frankfurt; Town Hall, Paris; Belfry, Zurich; Gate, Kampen (Holland).

1964, Nov. 4 Photo. Wmk. 303

899 A480 30 l dk red brn .20 .20
900 A480 70 l blue .20 .20

Pilgrimage to Rome of veterans living abroad.

Giovanni da Verrazano and Verrazano-Narrows Bridge, New York Bay — A481

1964, Nov. 21 Wmk. 303 *Perf. 14*

901 A481 30 l blk & brn .20 .20

Opening of the Verrazano-Narrows Bridge connecting Staten Island and Brooklyn, NY, and to honor Giovanni da Verrazano (1485-1528), discoverer of New York Bay. See No. C138.

Italian Sports Stamps, 1934-63 — A482

1964, Dec. 6 Photo. *Perf. 14*

902 A482 15 l gldn brn & dk brn .20 .20

Issued for Stamp Day.

Italian Soldiers in Concentration Camp — A483

Victims Trapped by Swastika A484

15 l, Italian soldier, sailor and airman fighting for the Allies. 70 l, Guerrilla fighters in the mountains. 115 l, Marchers with Italian flag. 130 l, Ruins of city and torn Italian flag.

1965, Apr. 24 Photo. Wmk. 303

903 A483 10 l black .20 .20
904 A483 15 l grn & rose car .20 .20
905 A484 30 l plum .20 .20
906 A483 70 l deep blue .20 .20
907 A484 115 l rose car .20 .20
908 A484 130 l grn, sepia & red .20 .20
Nos. 903-908 (6) 1.20 1.20

Italian resistance movement during World War II, 20th anniv.

Antonio Meucci, Guglielmo Marconi and ITU Emblem A485

1965, May 17 *Perf. 14*

909 A485 70 l red & dk grn .20 .20

Cent. of the ITU.

Sailboats of Flying Dutchman Class A486

Designs: 70 l, Sailboats of 5.5-meter class, vert. 500 l, Sailboats, Lightning class.

1965, May 31 Photo. Wmk. 303

910 A486 30 l blk & dl rose .20 .20
911 A486 70 l blk & ultra .20 .20
912 A486 500 l blk & gray bl .40 .30
Nos. 910-912 (3) .80 .70

Issued to publicize the World Yachting Championships, Naples and Alassio.

Mont Blanc and Tunnel A487

1965, June 16 Wmk. 303 *Perf. 14*

913 A487 30 l black .20 .20

Opening of the Mont Blanc Tunnel connecting Entrayes, Italy, and Le Polerins, France.

Alessandro Tassoni and Scene from "Seccia Rapita" — A488

Unwmk.

1965, Sept. 20 Photo. *Perf. 14*

914 A488 40 l blk & multi .20 .20

Tassoni (1565-1635), poet. Design is from 1744 engraving by Bartolomeo Soliani.

Europa Issue, 1965

Common Design Type

1965, Sept. 27 Wmk. 303

Size: 36½x27mm

915 CD8 40 l ocher & ol grn .20 .20
916 CD8 90 l ultra & ol grn .20 .20

Dante, 15th Century Bust — A489

Designs (from old Manuscripts): 40 l, Dante in Hell. 90 l, Dante in Purgatory led by Angel of Chastity. 130 l, Dante in Paradise interrogated by St. Peter on faith, horiz.

Perf. 13½x14, 14x13½

1965, Oct. 21 Photo. Unwmk.

917 A489 40 l multi .20 .20
918 A489 90 l multi .20 .20
919 A489 130 l multi .20 .20

Wmk. 303 *Perf. 14*

920 A489 500 l slate grn .40 .30
Nos. 917-920 (4) 1.00 .90

Dante Alighieri (1265-1321), poet.

House under Construction — A490

1965, Oct. 31 Wmk. 303 *Perf. 14*
921 A490 40 l buff, blk & org brn .20 .20

Issued for Savings Day.

Jet Plane, Moon and Airletter Border A491

Design: 40 l, Control tower and plane.

1965, Nov. 3
922 A491 40 l dk Prus bl & red .20 .20

Unwmk.
923 A491 90 l red, grn, dp bl & buff .20 .20

Night air postal network.

Map of Italy with Milan-Rome Highway — A492

Two-Man Bobsled — A493

1965, Dec. 5 Photo. *Perf. 13x14*
924 A492 20 l bl, blk, ocher & gray .20 .20

Issued for Stamp Day.

1966, Jan. 24 Wmk. 303 *Perf. 14*

Design: 90 l, Four-man bobsled.

925 A493 40 l dl bl, gray & red .20 .20
926 A493 90 l vio & bl .20 .20

Intl. Bobsled Championships, Cortina d'Ampezzo.

Woman Skater — A494

Benedetto Croce — A495

Winter University Games: 40 l, Skier holding torch, horiz. 500 l, Ice hockey.

1966, Feb. 5 Photo.
927 A494 40 l blk & red .20 .20
928 A494 90 l vio & red .20 .20
929 A494 500 l brn & red .40 .30
Nos. 927-929 (3) .80 .70

1966, Feb. 25 Wmk. 303 *Perf. 14*
930 A495 40 l brown .20 .20

Benedetto Croce (1866-1952), philosopher, statesman and historian.

Arms of Venice and Other Cities in Venezia — A496

1966, Mar. 22 Photo. Unwmk.
932 A496 40 l gray & multi .20 .20

Centenary of Venezia's union with Italy.

Battle of Bezzecca — A497

1966, July 21 Wmk. 303 *Perf. 14*
933 A497 90 l ol grn .20 .20

Centenary of the unification of Italy and of the Battle of Bezzecca.

Umbrella Pine — A498

Carnations62 A499

25 l, Apples. 50 l, Florentine iris. 55 l, Cypresses. 90 l, Daisies. 170 l, Olive tree. 180 l, Juniper.

1966-68 Unwmk. *Perf. 13½x14*
934 A498 20 l multi .20 .20
934A A498 25 l multi ('67) .20 .20
935 A499 40 l multi .20 .20
935A A498 50 l multi ('67) .20 .20
935B A498 55 l multi ('68) .20 .20
936 A499 90 l multi .20 .20
937 A498 170 l multi .25 .20
937A A498 180 l multi ('68) .25 .20
Nos. 934-937A (8) 1.70 1.60

Tourist Attractions A500

"I" in Flag Colors — A501

1966, May 28 Wmk. 303 *Perf. 14*
938 A500 20 l yel, org & blk .20 .20

Issued for tourist publicity and in connection with the National Conference on Tourism, Rome.

Perf. 13½x14
1966, June 2 Photo. Unwmk.
939 A501 40 l multi .20 .20
940 A501 90 l multi .20 .20

20th anniversary of the Republic of Italy.

Singing Angels, by Donatello — A502

Madonna, by Giotto — A503

Perf. 13½x14
1966, Sept. 24 Photo. Unwmk.
941 A502 40 l multi .20 .20

Donatello (1386-1466), sculptor.

Europa Issue, 1966
Common Design Type

1966, Sept. 26 Wmk. 303 *Perf. 14*
Size: 22x38mm
942 CD9 40 l brt pur .20 .20
943 CD9 90 l brt bl .20 .20

Perf. 13½x14
1966, Oct. 20 Photo. Unwmk.
944 A503 40 l multi .20 .20

700th anniversary of the birth of Giotto di Bondone (1266?-1337), Florentine painter.

Italian Patriots A504

1966, Nov. 3 Wmk. 303 *Perf. 14*
945 A504 40 l gray & dl grn .20 .20

50th anniv. of the execution by Austrians of 4 Italian patriots: Fabio Filzi, Cesare Battisti, Damiano Chiesa and Nazario Sauro.

Postrider — A505

Perf. 14x13½
1966, Dec. 4 Photo. Unwmk.
946 A505 20 l multi .20 .20

Issued for Stamp Day.

Globe and Compass Rose A506

1967, Mar. 20 Photo. Wmk. 303
947 A506 40 l dull blue .20 .20

Centenary of Italian Geographical Society.

Arturo Toscanini (1867-1957), Conductor — A507

1967, Mar. 25 *Perf. 14*
948 A507 40 l dp vio & cream .20 .20

Seat of Parliament on Capitoline Hill, Rome A508

1967, Mar. 25 *Perf. 14*
949 A508 40 l sepia .20 .20
950 A508 90 l rose lil & blk .20 .20

10th anniv. of the Treaty of Rome, establishing the European Common Market.

Europa Issue, 1967
Common Design Type

1967, Apr. 10 Wmk. 303 *Perf. 14*
Size: 22x28mm
951 CD10 40 l plum & pink .20 .20
952 CD10 90 l ultra & pale gray .20 .20

Alpine Ibex, Grand Paradiso Park — A509

National Parks: 40 l, Brown bear, Abruzzi Apennines, horiz. 90 l, Red deer, Stelvio Pass, Ortler Mountains, horiz. 170 l, Oak and deer, Circeo.

Perf. 13½x14, 14x13½
1967, Apr. 22 Photo.
953 A509 20 l multi .20 .20
954 A509 40 l multi .20 .20
955 A509 90 l multi .20 .20
956 A509 170 l multi .20 .20
Nos. 953-956 (4) .80 .80

Claudio Monteverdi and Characters from "Orfeo" A510

1967, May 15 *Perf. 14*
957 A510 40 l bis brn & brn .20 .20

Monteverdi (1567-1643), composer.

Bicyclists and Mountains A511

50th Bicycle Tour of Italy: 90 l. Three bicyclists on the road. 500 l, Group of bicyclists.

Perf. 14x13½

1967, May 15 Photo. Unwmk.

958 A511 40 l multi .20 .20
959 A511 90 l brt bl & multi .20 .20
960 A511 500 l yel grn & multi .95 .45
Nos. 958-960 (3) 1.35 .85

Luigi Pirandello and Stage A512

1967, June 28 ***Perf. 14x13***

961 A512 40 l blk & multi .20 .20

Pirandello (1867-1936), novelist & dramatist.

Stylized Mask A513

1967, June 30 Wmk. 303 ***Perf. 14***

962 A513 20 l grn & blk .20 .20
963 A513 40 l car rose & blk .20 .20

10th "Festival of Two Worlds," Spoleto.

Postal Card with Postal Zone Number A514

Design: 40 l, 50 l, Letter addressed with postal zone number.

Wmk. 303, Unwmkd, (20 l, 40 l)

1967-68

964 A514 20 l multi .20 .20
965 A514 25 l multi ('68) .20 .20
966 A514 40 l multi .20 .20
967 A514 50 l multi ('68) .20 .20
Nos. 964-967 (4) .80 .80

Introduction of postal zone numbers, 7/1/67.

Pomilio PC-1 Biplane and 1917 Airmail Postmark A515

1967, July 18 Photo. Wmk. 303

968 A515 40 l blk & lt bl .20 .20

1st airmail stamp, Italy #C1, 50th anniv.

St. Ivo Church, Rome — A516

Umberto Giordano and "Improvisation" from Opera Andrea Chenier — A517

1967, Aug. 2 Unwmk. ***Perf. 14***

969 A516 90 l multi .20 .20

Francesco Borromini (1599-1667), architect.

1967, Aug. 28 Wmk. 303

970 A517 20 l blk & org brn .20 .20

Umberto Giordano (1867-1948), composer.

Oath of Pontida, by Adolfo Cao — A518

ITY Emblem — A519

1967, Sept. 2

971 A518 20 l dk brn .20 .20

800th anniv. of the Oath of Pontida, which united the Lombard League against Emperor Frederick I.

Perf. 13½x14

1967, Oct. 23 Photo. Unwmk.

972 A519 20 l blk, cit & brt bl .20 .20
973 A519 50 l blk, org & brt bl .20 .20

Issued for International Tourist Year, 1967.

Lions Emblem — A520

Soldier at the Piave — A521

1967, Oct. 30 ***Perf. 14x13½***

974 A520 50 l multi .20 .20

50th anniversary of Lions International.

1967, Nov. 9 ***Perf. 13x14***

975 A521 50 l multi .20 .20

50th anniversary of Battle of the Piave.

Enrico Fermi at Los Alamos and Model of 1st Atomic Reactor — A522

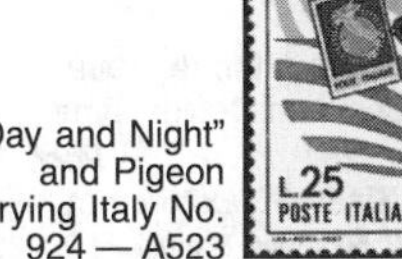

"Day and Night" and Pigeon Carrying Italy No. 924 — A523

Wmk. 303

1967, Dec. 2 Photo. ***Perf. 14***

976 A522 50 l org brn & blk .20 .20

25th anniv. of the 1st atomic chain reaction under Enrico Fermi (1901-54), Chicago, IL.

1967, Dec. 3 Unwmk. ***Perf. 13½x14***

977 A523 25 l multi .20 .20

Issued for Stamp Day, 1967.

Scouts at Campfire — A524

St. Aloysius Gonzaga, by Pierre Legros — A525

1968, Apr. 23 ***Perf. 13x14***

978 A524 50 l multi .20 .20

Issued to honor the Boy Scouts.

Europa Issue, 1968

Common Design Type

Perf. 14x13

1968, Apr. 29 Wmk. 303

Size: 36½x26mm

979 CD11 50 l blk, rose & sl grn .20 .20
980 CD11 90 l blk, bl & brn .20 .20

Perf. 13½x14

1968, May 28 Photo. Wmk. 303

981 A525 25 l red brn & dl vio .20 .20

Aloysius Gonzaga (1568-1591), Jesuit priest who ministered to victims of the plague.

Arrigo Boito and Mephistopheles — A526

1968, June 10 Unwmk. ***Perf. 14***

982 A526 50 l multi .20 .20

Boito (1842-1918), composer and librettist.

Francesco Baracca and "Planes," by Giacomo Balla A527

1968, June 19

983 A527 25 l multi .20 .20

Major Francesco Baracca (1888-1918), World War I aviator.

Giambattista Vico — A528

Bicycle Wheel and Velodrome, Rome — A529

Designs: No. 985, Tommaso Campanella. No. 986, Gioacchino Rossini.

Perf. 14x13½

1968 Engr. Wmk. 303

984 A528 50 l ultra .20 .20
985 A528 50 l black .20 .20
a. Perf. 13½ .90 .20
986 A528 50 l car rose .20 .20
Nos. 984-986 (3) .60 .60

Vico (1668-1744), philosopher; Campanella (1568-1639), Dominican monk, philosopher poet and teacher; Rossini (1792-1868), composer.

Issued: #984, 6/24; #985, 9/5; #986, 10/25.

Perf. 13x14

1968, Aug. 26 Photo. Unwmk.

90 l, Bicycle and Sforza Castle, Imola.

987 A529 25 l slate, rose & brown .20 .20
988 A529 90 l slate, blue & ver .20 .20

Bicycling World Championships: 25 l for the track championships at the Velodrome in Rome; 90 l, the road championships at Imola.

"The Small St. Mark's Place," by Canaletto — A531

1968, Sept. 30 Unwmk. ***Perf. 14***

989 A531 50 l pink & multi .20 .20

Canaletto (Antonio Canale, 1697-1768), Venetian painter.

"Mobilization" — A533

Symbolic Designs: 25 l, Trench war. 40 l, The Navy. 50 l, The Air Force. 90 l, The Battle of Vittorio Veneto. 180 l, The Unknown Soldier.

1968, Nov. 2 Photo. Unwmk.

990 A533 20 l brn & multi .20 .20
991 A533 25 l bl & multi .20 .20
992 A533 40 l multi .20 .20
993 A533 50 l multi .20 .20
994 A533 90 l grn & multi .20 .20
995 A533 180 l bl & multi .20 .20
Nos. 990-995 (6) 1.20 1.20

50th anniv. of the Allies' Victory in WW I.

Emblem — A534

1968, Nov. 20 ***Perf. 14x13½***

996 A534 50 l blk, bl grn & red .20 .20

50th anniv. of the Postal Checking Service.

Parabolic Antenna, Fucino A535

1968, Nov. 25 Photo. ***Perf. 14***

997 A535 50 l multi .20 .20

Issued to publicize the expansion of the space communications center at Fucino.

Development of Postal Service — A536

1968, Dec. 1 Wmk. 303

998 A536 25 l car & yel .20 .20

Issued for the 10th Stamp Day.

Fluorescent Paper was introduced in 1968 for regular and special delivery issues. These stamps are about 1mm. smaller each way than the non-fluorescent ones they replaced, except Nos. 690-690A which remained the same size.

Commemorative or nonregular stamps issued only on fluorescent paper are Nos. 935B, 937A, 965, 967 and from 981 onward unless otherwise noted.

Italia Type of 1953-54

Small Size: 16x19½-20mm

Photo.; Engr. (100, 150, 200-400 l)

1968-76 Wmk. 303 ***Perf. 14***

No.	Type	Value	Color	Unused	Used
998A	A354	1 l	dk gray	.20	.20
998B	A354	5 l	slate	.20	.20
998C	A354	6 l	ocher	.20	.20
998D	A354	10 l	org ver	.20	.20
998E	A354	15 l	gray vio	.20	.20
998F	A354	20 l	brown	.20	.20
998G	A354	25 l	purple	.20	.20
998H	A354	30 l	bis brn	.20	.20
998I	A354	40 l	lil rose	.20	.20
998J	A354	50 l	olive	.20	.20
998K	A354	55 l	vio ('69)	.20	.20
998L	A354	60 l	blue	.20	.20
998M	A354	70 l	Prus grn	.20	.20
998N	A354	80 l	brn org	.20	.20
998O	A354	90 l	lt red brn	.20	.20
998P	A354	100 l	redsh brn	.20	.20
998Q	A354	125 l	ocher & lil ('74)	.20	.20
998R	A354	130 l	gray & dl red	.20	.20
998S	A354	150 l	vio ('76)	.20	.20
998T	A354	180 l	gray & vio brn ('71)	.25	.20
998U	A354	200 l	slate blue	.20	.20
998V	A354	300 l	Prus grn ('72)	.30	.20
998W	A354	400 l	dull red ('76)	.30	.20
			Nos. 998A-998W (23)	4.85	4.60

Memorial Medal — A537

Unwmk.

1969, Apr. 22 Photo. ***Perf. 14***

999 A537 50 l pink & blk .20 .20

Centenary of the State Audit Bureau.

Europa Issue, 1969

Common Design Type

1969, Apr. 28 ***Perf. 14x13***

Size: 35½x25½mm

1000 CD12 50 l mag & multi .20 .20

1001 CD12 90 l bl & multi .20 .20

Niccolo Machiavelli A538

ILO Emblem A539

1969, May 3 ***Perf. 14x13½***

1002 A538 50 l blue & multi .20 .20

Niccolo Machiavelli (1469-1527), statesman and political philosopher.

Wmk. 303

1969, June 7 Photo. ***Perf. 14***

1003 A539 50 l grn & blk .20 .20

1004 A539 90 l car & blk .20 .20

50th anniv. of the ILO.

Federation Emblem, Tower of Superga Basilica and Matterhorn A540

1969, June 26 Unwmk. ***Perf. 14***

1005 A540 50 l gold, bl & car .20 .20

Federation of Italian Philatelic Societies, 50th anniv.

Sondrio-Tirano Stagecoach, 1903 — A541

1969, Dec. 7 Engr. Wmk. 303

1006 A541 25 l violet blue .20 .20

Issued for the 11th Stamp Day.

Downhill Skier — A542

90 l, Sassolungo & Sella Group, Dolomite Alps.

Perf. 13x14

1970, Feb. 6 Unwmk. Photo.

1007 A542 50 l blue & multi .20 .20

1008 A542 90 l blue & multi .20 .20

World Alpine Ski Championships, Val Gardena, Bolzano Province, Feb. 6-15.

Galatea, by Raphael A543

Painting: 50 l, Madonna with the Goldfinch (detail), by Raphael, 1483-1520.

1970, Apr. 6 Photo. ***Perf. 14x13***

1009 A543 20 l multi .20 .20

1010 A543 50 l multi .20 .20

Symbol of Flight, Colors of Italy and Japan A544

1970, May 2 Unwmk. ***Perf. 14***

1011 A544 50 l multi .20 .20

1012 A544 90 l multi .20 .20

50th anniv. of Arturo Ferrarin's flight from Rome to Tokyo, Feb. 14-May 31, 1920.

Europa Issue, 1970

Common Design Type

1970, May 4 Wmk. 303

Size: 36x20mm

1013 CD13 50 l red & org .20 .20

1014 CD13 90 l bl grn & org .20 .20

Gattamelata, Bust by Donatello — A545

1970, May 30 Engr. ***Perf. 14x13***

1015 A545 50 l slate green .20 .20

Erasmo de' Narni, called Il Gattamelata (1370-1443), condottiere.

Runner A546

Unwmk.

1970, Aug. 26 Photo. ***Perf. 14***

1016 A546 20 l shown .20 .20

1017 A546 180 l Swimmer .20 .20

1970 World University Games, Turin, 8/26-9/6.

Dr. Maria Montessori and Children A547

1970, Aug. 31 ***Perf. 14x13***

1018 A547 50 l multi .20 .20

Montessori (1870-1952), educator & physician.

Map of Italy and Quotation of Count Camillo Cavour — A548

1970, Sept. 19 Unwmk. ***Perf. 14***

1019 A548 50 l multi .20 .20

Union of the Roman States with Italy, cent.

Loggia of St. Mark's Campanile, Venice A549

Perf. 14x13½

1970, Sept. 26 Engr. Wmk. 303

1020 A549 50 l red brown .20 .20

Iacopo Tatti "Il Sansovino" (1486-1570), architect.

Garibaldi at Battle of Dijon A550

1970, Oct. 15 Photo. ***Perf. 14***

1021 A550 20 l gray & dk bl .20 .20

1022 A550 50 l brt rose lil & dk bl .20 .20

Cent. of Garibaldi's participation in the Franco-Prussian War during Battle of Dijon.

Tree and UN Emblem — A551

1970, Oct. 24 Unwmk. ***Perf. 13x14***

1023 A551 25 l blk, sep & grn .20 .20

1024 A551 90 l blk, brt bl & yel grn .20 .20

25th anniversary of the United Nations.

Rotary Emblem A552

1970, Nov. 12 Wmk. 303 ***Perf. 14***

1025 A552 25 l bluish vio & org .20 .20

1026 A552 90 l bluish vio & org .20 .20

Rotary International, 65th anniversary.

Telephone Dial and Trunk Lines A553

1970, Nov. 24

1027 A553 25 l yel grn & dk red .20 .20
1028 A553 90 l ultra & dk red .20 .20

Issued to publicize the completion of the automatic trunk telephone dialing system.

"Man Damaging Nature" — A554

Virgin and Child, by Fra Filippo Lippi — A556

Mail Train A555

1970, Nov. 28 Wmk. 303 *Perf. 14*

1029 A554 20 l car lake & grn .20 .20
1030 A554 25 l dk bl & emer .20 .20

For European Nature Conservation Year.

1970, Dec. 6 Engr.

1031 A555 25 l black .20 .20

For the 12th Stamp Day.

1970, Dec. 12 Photo. Unwmk.

1032 A556 25 l multi .20 .20

Christmas 1970. See No. C139.

Saverio Mercadante (1795-1870), Composer — A557

1970, Dec. 17 Wmk. 303

1033 A557 25 l vio & gray .20 .20

Mercury, by Benvenuto Cellini — A558

Bramante's Temple, St. Peter in Montorio — A559

1971, Mar. 20 Photo. *Perf. 14*

1034 A558 50 l Prussian blue .20 .20

Benvenuto Cellini (1500-1571), sculptor.

Photogravure and Engraved

1971, Apr. 8 *Perf. 13x14*

1035 A559 50 l ocher & blk .20 .20

Honoring Bramante (Donato di Angelo di Antonio, 1444-1514), architect.

Adenauer, Schuman, De Gasperi A560

Perf. 14x13½

1971, Apr. 28 Photo. Wmk. 303

1036 A560 50 l blk & lt grnsh bl .20 .20
1037 A560 90 l blk & lil rose .20 .20

European Coal & Steel Community, 20th anniv.

Europa Issue, 1971

Common Design Type

1971, May 3 *Perf. 14*

1038 CD14 50 l ver & dk red .20 .20
1039 CD14 90 l brt rose lil & dk lil .20 .20

Giuseppe Mazzini, Italian Flag — A561

Perf. 14x13½

1971, June 12 Unwmk.

1040 A561 50 l multi .20 .20
1041 A561 90 l multi .20 .20

25th anniversary of the Italian Republic.

Kayak Passing Between Poles A562

Design: 90 l, Kayak in free descent.

1971, June 16 Photo. *Perf. 14*

1042 A562 25 l multi .20 .20
1043 A562 90 l multi .20 .20

Canoe Slalom World Championships, Merano.

Skiing, Basketball, Volleyball — A563

50 l, Gymnastics, cycling, track and swimming.

Perf. 13½x14

1971, June 26 Photo. Unwmk.

1044 A563 20 l emer, ocher & blk .20 .20
1045 A563 50 l dl bl, org & blk .20 .20

Youth Games.

Plane Circling Globe and "A" — A564

Designs: 50 l, Ornamental "A." 150 l, Tail of B747 in shape of "A."

1971, Sept. 16 *Perf. 14x13½*

1046 A564 50 l multi .20 .20
1047 A564 90 l multi .20 .20
1048 A564 150 l multi .20 .20
Nos. 1046-1048 (3) .60 .60

ALITALIA, Italian airlines founding, 25th anniv.

Grazia Deledda (1871-1936), Novelist — A565

Photogravure and Engraved

Perf. 13½x14

1971, Sept. 28 Wmk. 303

1049 A565 50 l blk & salmon .20 .20

Child in Barrel Made of Banknote — A566

Perf. 13x14

1971, Oct. 27 Photo. Unwmk.

1050 A566 25 l blk & multi .20 .20
1051 A566 50 l multi .20 .20

Publicity for postal savings bank.

UNICEF Emblem and Children A567

90 l, Children hailing UNICEF emblem.

1971, Nov. 26 *Perf. 14x13*

1052 A567 25 l pink & multi .20 .20
1053 A567 90 l multi .20 .20

25th anniv. of UNICEF.

Packet Tirrenia and Postal Ensign A568

1971, Dec. 5 Wmk. 303 *Perf. 14*

1054 A568 25 l slate green .20 .20

Stamp Day.

Nativity A569

Christmas: 90 l, Adoration of the Kings. Both designs are from miniatures in Evangelistary of Matilda in Nonantola Abbey, 12th-13th centuries.

Perf. 14x13

1971, Dec. 10 Photo. Unwmk.

1055 A569 25 l gray & multi .20 .20
1056 A569 90 l gray & multi .20 .20

Giovanni Verga and Sicilian Cart A570

1972, Jan. 27

1057 A570 25 l org & multi .20 .20
1058 A570 50 l multi .20 .20

Verga (1840-1922), writer & playwright.

Giuseppe Mazzini (1805-1872), Patriot and Writer — A571

Wmk. 303

1972, Mar. 10 Engr. *Perf. 13*

1059 A571 25 l blk & Prus grn .20 .20
1060 A571 90 l black .20 .20
1061 A571 150 l blk & rose red .20 .20
Nos. 1059-1061 (3) .60 .60

Flags, Milan Fair A572

Designs: 50 l, 90 l, Different abstract views.

Perf. 14x13½

1972, Apr. 14 Photo. Unwmk.

1062 A572 25 l emer & blk .20 .20
1063 A572 50 l dp org & blk .20 .20
1064 A572 90 l bl & blk .20 .20
Nos. 1062-1064 (3) .60 .60

50th anniversary of the Milan Sample Fair.

Europa Issue 1972

Common Design Type

1972, May 2 *Perf. 13x14*

Size: 26x36mm

1065 CD15 50 l multi .20 .20
1066 CD15 90 l multi .20 .20

Alpine Soldier and Pack Mule A573

50 l, Mountains, Alpinist's hat, pick & laurel. 90 l, Alpine soldier & mountains.

1972, May 10 *Perf. 14x13*

1067 A573 25 l ol & multi .20 .20
1068 A573 50 l bl & multi .20 .20
1069 A573 90 l grn & multi .20 .20
Nos. 1067-1069 (3) .60 .60

Centenary of the Alpine Corps.

Brenta Mountains, Society Emblem A574

Emblem and: 50 l, Mountain climber & Brenta Mountains. 180 l, Sunset over Mt. Crozzon.

Perf. 14x13

1972, Sept. 2 Photo. Unwmk.

1070 A574 25 l multi .20 .20
1071 A574 50 l multi .20 .20
1072 A574 180 l multi .20 .20
Nos. 1070-1072 (3) .60 .60

Tridentine Alpinist Society centenary.

Conference Emblem, Seating Diagram
A575

1972, Sept. 21

1073 A575 50 l multi .20 .20
1074 A575 90 l multi .20 .20

60th Conference of the Inter-Parliamentary Union, Montecitorio Hall, Rome.

St. Peter Damian, by Giovanni di Paoli, c. 1445
A576

1972, Sept. 21 Photo.

1075 A576 50 l multi .20 .20

St. Peter Damian (1007-72), church reformer, cardinal, papal legate.

The Three Graces, by Antonio Canova (1757-1822), Sculptor — A577

1972, Oct. 13 Engr. Wmk. 303

1076 A577 50 l black .20 .20

Page from Divine Comedy, Foligno Edition
A578

Designs (Illuminated First Pages): 90 l, Mantua edition, vert. 180 l, Jesina edition.

Perf. 14x13½, 13½x14

1972, Nov. 23 Photo. Unwmk.

1077 A578 50 l ocher & multi .20 .20
1078 A578 90 l multi .20 .20
1079 A578 180 l multi .20 .20
Nos. 1077-1079 (3) .60 .60

500th anniversary of three illuminated editions of Dante's Divine Comedy.

Angel — A579

Christmas: 25 l, Christ Child in cradle, horiz. 150 l, Angel. All designs from 18th century Neapolitan crèche.

Perf. 13x14, 14x13

1972, Dec. 6 Photo.

1080 A579 20 l multi .20 .20
1081 A579 25 l multi .20 .20
1082 A579 150 l multi .20 .20
Nos. 1080-1082 (3) .60 .60

Passenger and Mail Autobus
A580

1972, Dec. 16 Engr. Wmk. 303

1083 A580 25 l magenta .20 .20

Stamp Day.

Leòn Battista Alberti — A581

Lorenzo Perosi — A582

1972, Dec. 16 *Perf. 14*

1084 A581 50 l ultra & ocher .20 .20

Leòn Battista Alberti (1404-1472), architect, painter, organist and writer.

1972, Dec. 20 Photo. Unwmk.

1085 A582 50 l dk vio brn & org .20 .20
1086 A582 90 l blk & yel grn .20 .20

Lorenzo Perosi (1872-1956), priest & composer.

Luigi Orione and Boys — A583

Ship Exploring Ocean Floor — A584

1972, Dec. 30

1087 A583 50 l lt bl & dk bl .20 .20
1088 A583 90 l ocher & slate grn .20 .20

Orione (1872-1940), founder of CARITAS; Catholic Welfare Organization.

1973, Feb. 15 Photo. *Perf. 13x14*

1089 A584 50 l multi .20 .20

Cent. of the Naval Hydrographic Institute.

Palace Staircase, Caserta
A585

1973, Mar. 1 Engr. *Perf. 14x13½*

1090 A585 25 l gray olive .20 .20

Luigi Vanvitelli (1700-1773), architect.

Schiavoni Shore — A586

The Tetrarchs, 4th Century Sculpture — A587

50 l, "Triumph of Venice," by Vittore Carpaccio. 90 l, Bronze horses from St. Mark's. 300 l, St. Mark's Square covered by flood.

1973 Photo. *Perf. 14*

1091 A586 20 l ultra & multi .20 .20
1092 A587 25 l ultra & multi .20 .20
1093 A586 50 l ultra & multi .20 .20
1094 A587 90 l ultra & multi .20 .20
1095 A586 300 l ultra & multi .50 .30
Nos. 1091-1095 (5) 1.30 1.10

Save Venice campaign. Issued: #1091, 3/5; others 4/10.

Verona Fair Emblem — A588

Title Page for Book about Rosa — A589

1973, Mar. 10 *Perf. 13x14*

1096 A588 50 l multi .20 .20

75th International Fair, Verona.

1973, Mar. 15 *Perf. 14*

1097 A589 25 l org & blk .20 .20

Salvator Rosa (1615-1673), painter & poet.

G-91 Jet Fighters
A590

Designs: 25 l, Formation of S-55 seaplanes. 50 l, G-91Y fighters. 90 l, Fiat CR-32's flying figure 8. 180 l, Camprini-Caproni jet, 1940.

1973, Mar. 28 *Perf. 14x13½*

1098 A590 20 l multi .20 .20
1099 A590 25 l multi .20 .20
1100 A590 50 l multi .20 .20
1101 A590 90 l multi .20 .20
1102 A590 180 l multi .20 .20
Nos. 1098-1102,C140 (6) 1.30 1.20

50th anniversary of military aviation.

Soccer Field and Ball
A591

Design: 90 l, Soccer players and goal.

1973, May 19 Photo. *Perf. 14x13½*

1103 A591 25 l ol, blk & lt grn .20 .20
1104 A591 90 l grn & multi .60 .20

75th anniv. of Italian Soccer Federation.

Alessandro Manzoni, by Francisco Hayez — A592

Villa Rotunda, by Andrea Palladio (1508-80), Architect. — A593

1973, May 22 Engr.

1105 A592 25 l blk & brn .20 .20

Manzoni (1785-1873), novelist and poet.

1973, May 30 Photo. Unwmk.

Perf. 13x14

1106 A593 90 l blk, yel & lem .20 .20

Spiral and Cogwheels
A594

1973, June 20 *Perf. 14x13*

1107 A594 50 l gold & multi .20 .20

50th anniversary of the State Supply Office.

Europa Issue 1973

Common Design Type

1973, June 30 Litho. *Perf. 14*

Size: 36x20mm

1108 CD16 50 l lil, gold & yel .20 .20
1109 CD16 90 l lt bl grn, gold & yel .20 .20

Catcher and Diamond
A595

Design: 90 l, Diamond and batter.

1973, July 21 Photo. *Perf. 14x13½*

1110 A595 25 l multi .20 .20
1111 A595 90 l multi .20 .20

International Baseball Cup.

Viareggio by Night — A596

1973, Aug. 10 Photo. *Perf. 13x14*

1112 A596 25 l blk & multi .20 .20

Viareggio Carnival.

Assassination of Giovanni Minzoni — A597

1973, Aug. 23 *Perf. 14x13*

1113 A597 50 l multi .20 .20

Minzoni (1885-1923), priest & social worker.

Gaetano Salvemini (1873-1957), Historian, Anti-Fascist — A598

1973, Sept. 8 ***Perf. 14x13½***

1114 A598 50 l pink & multi .20 .20

Palazzo Farnese, Caprarola, by Vignola A599

1973, Sept. 21 Engr. ***Perf. 14x13½***

1115 A599 90 l choc & yel .20 .20

Giacomo da Vignola (real name, Giacomo Barocchio), 1507-1573, architect.

St. John the Baptist, by Caravaggio A600

Lithographed & Engraved

1973, Sept. 28 ***Perf. 14***

1116 A600 25 l blk & dl yel .20 .20

400th anniversary of the birth of Michelangelo da Caravaggio (1573-1610?), painter.

Tower of Pisa — A601

1973, Oct. 8 **Photo.**

1117 A601 50 l multi .20 .20

8th century of Leaning Tower of Pisa.

Sandro Botticelli — A602

1973-74 Photo. ***Perf. 14x13½***

1118 A602 50 l shown .20 .20
1119 A602 50 l Giambattista Piranesi .20 .20
1120 A602 50 l Paolo Veronese .20 .20
1121 A602 50 l Andrea del Verrocchio .20 .20
1122 A602 50 l Giovanni Battista Tiepolo .20 .20
1123 A602 50 l Francesco Borromini .20 .20
1124 A602 50 l Rosalba Carriera .20 .20
1125 A602 50 l Giovanni Bellini .20 .20
1126 A602 50 l Andrea Mantegna .20 .20
1127 A602 50 l Raphael .20 .20
Nos. 1118-1127 (10) 2.00 2.00

Famous artists.

Issued: #1118-1122, 11/5; #1123-1127, 5/25/74.

See #1204-1209, 1243-1247, 1266-1270.

Trevi Fountain, Rome — A603

Designs: No. 1129, Immacolatella Fountain, Naples. No. 1130, Pretoria Fountain, Palermo.

Photogravure and Engraved

1973, Nov. 10 ***Perf. 13½x14***

1128 A603 25 l blk & multi .20 .20
1129 A603 25 l blk & multi .20 .20
1130 A603 25 l blk & multi .20 .20
Nos. 1128-1130 (3) .60 .60

See Nos. 1166-1168, 1201-1203, 1251-1253, 1277-1279, 1341-1343, 1379-1381.

Angels, by Agostino di Duccio — A604

Sculptures by Agostino di Duccio: 25 l, Virgin and Child. 150 l, Angels with flute and trumpet.

1973, Nov. 26

1131 A604 20 l yel grn & blk .20 .20
1132 A604 25 l lt bl & blk .20 .20
1133 A604 150 l yel & blk .20 .20
Nos. 1131-1133 (3) .60 .60

Christmas 1973.

Map of Italy, Rotary Emblems — A605

1973, Nov. 28 **Photo.**

1134 A605 50 l red, grn & dk bl .20 .20

50th anniv. of Rotary International of Italy.

Caravelle A606

Wmk. 303

1973, Dec. 2 Engr. ***Perf. 14***

1135 A606 25 l Prussian blue .20 .20

15th Stamp Day.

Gold Medal of Valor, 50th Anniv. — A607

Perf. 13½x14

1973, Dec. 10 Photo. Unwmk.

1136 A607 50 l gold & multi .20 .20

Enrico Caruso (1873-1921), Operatic Tenor — A608

1973, Dec. 15 **Engr.**

Design: 50 l, Caruso as Duke in Rigoletto.

1137 A608 50 l magenta .20 .20

Christ Crowning King Roger — A609

Norman art in Sicily: 50 l, King William II offering model of church to the Virgin, mosaic from Monreale Cathedral. The design of 20 l, is from a mosaic in Martorana Church, Palermo.

Lithographed and Engraved

1974, Mar. 4 ***Perf. 13½x14***

1138 A609 20 l ind & buff .20 .20
1139 A609 50 l red & lt grn .20 .20

Luigi Einaudi (1874-1961), Pres. of Italy — A610

1974, Mar. 23 Engr. ***Perf. 14x13½***

1140 A610 50 l green .20 .20

Guglielmo Marconi (1874-1937), Italian Inventor and Physicist — A611

Design: 90 l, Marconi and world map.

1974, Apr. 24 Photo. ***Perf. 14x13½***

1141 A611 50 l bl grn & gray .20 .20
1142 A611 90 l vio & multi .20 .20

David, by Giovanni L. Bernini — A612

Europa: 90 l, David, by Michelangelo.

1974, Apr. 29 Photo. ***Perf. 13½x14***

1143 A612 50 l sal, ultra & gray .20 .20
1144 A612 90 l grn, ultra & buff .20 .20

Customs Frontier Guards, 1774, 1795, 1817 A613

Uniforms of Customs Service: 50 l, Lombardy Venetia, 1848, Sardinia, 1815, Tebro Battalion, 1849. 90 l, Customs Guards, 1866, 1880 and Naval Marshal, 1892. 180 l, Helicopter pilot, Naval and Alpine Guards, 1974. All bordered with Italian flag colors.

1974, June 21 Photo. ***Perf. 14***

1145 A613 40 l multi .20 .20
1146 A613 50 l multi .20 .20
1147 A613 90 l multi .20 .20
1148 A613 180 l multi .20 .20
Nos. 1145-1148 (4) .80 .80

Customs Frontier Guards bicentenary.

Sprinter A614

1974, June 28 Photo. ***Perf. 14x13***

1149 A614 40 l shown .20 .20
1150 A614 50 l Pole vault .20 .20

European Athletic Championships, Rome.

Sharpshooter — A615

Design: 50 l, Bersaglieri emblem.

1974, June 27

1151 A615 40 l multi .20 .20
1152 A615 50 l grn & multi .20 .20

Bersaglieri Veterans Association, 50th anniv.

View of Portofino — A616

1974, July 10 ***Perf. 14***

1153 A616 40 l shown .20 .20
1154 A616 40 l View of Gradara .20 .20

Tourist publicity.

See Nos. 1190-1192, 1221-1223, 1261-1265, 1314-1316, 1357-1360, 1402-1405, 1466-1469, 1520-1523, 1563A-1563D, 1599-1602, 1630-1633, 1708-1711, 1737-1740, 1776-1779, 1803-1806, 1830-1833, 1901-1904.

Petrarch (1304-74), Poet — A617

50 l, Petrarch at his desk (from medieval manuscript).

Lithographed and Engraved

1974, July 19 *Perf. 13½x14*

1155 A617 40 l ocher & multi .20 .20
1156 A617 50 l ocher, yel & bl .20 .20

Niccolo Tommaseo (1802-1874), Writer, Venetian Education Minister — A618

Tommaseo Statue, by Ettore Ximenes, Shibenik.

1974, July 19

1157 A618 50 l grn & pink .20 .20

Giacomo Puccini (1858-1924), Composer A619

1974, Aug. 16 **Photo.**

1158 A619 40 l multi .20 .20

Lodovico Ariosto (1474-1533), Poet — A620

1974, Sept. 9 **Engr.** *Perf. 14x13½*

1159 A620 50 l King Roland, woodcut .20 .20

The design is from a contemporary illustration of Ariosto's poem "Orlando Furioso."

Quotation from Menippean Satire by Varro A621

1974, Sept. 21

1160 A621 50 l ocher & dk red .20 .20

Marcus Terentius Varro (116-27 BC), Roman scholar and writer.

"October," 15th Century Mural A622

1974, Sept. 28 **Photo.** *Perf. 14*

1161 A622 50 l multi .20 .20

14th International Wine Congress, Trento.

"UPU" and Emblem A623

Design: 90 l, Letters, "UPU" and emblem.

1974, Oct. 19 **Photo.** *Perf. 14*

1162 A623 50 l multi .20 .20
1163 A623 90 l multi .20 .20

Centenary of Universal Postal Union.

St. Thomas Aquinas, by Francesco Traini — A624

1974, Oct. 25 *Perf. 13x14*

1164 A624 50 l multi .20 .20

St. Thomas Aquinas (1225-1274), scholastic philosopher, 700th death anniversary.

Bas-relief from Ara Pacis — A625

1974, Oct. 26

1165 A625 50 l multi .20 .20

Centenary of the Ordini Forensi (Bar Association).

Fountain Type of 1973

Designs: No. 1166, Oceanus Fountain, Florence. No. 1167, Neptune Fountain, Bologna. No. 1168, Fontana Maggiore, Perugia.

Photogravure and Engraved

1974, Nov. 9 *Perf. 13x14*

1166 A603 40 l blk & multi .20 .20
1167 A603 40 l blk & multi .20 .20
1168 A603 40 l blk & multi .20 .20
Nos. 1166-1168 (3) .60 .60

St. Francis Adoring Christ Child, Anonymous — A626

Photogravure and Engraved

1974, Nov. 26 *Perf. 14x13½*

1169 A626 40 l multi .20 .20

Christmas 1974.

Masked Dancers — A627

1974, Dec. 1 **Photo.** *Perf. 13½x14*

1170 A627 40 l Pulcinella .20 .20
1171 A627 50 l shown .20 .20
1172 A627 90 l Pantaloon .20 .20
Nos. 1170-1172 (3) .60 .60

16th Stamp Day 1974.

God Admonishing Adam, by Jacopo della Quercia — A628

Courtyard, Uffizi Gallery, Florence, by Giorgio Vasari A629

1974, Dec. 20 **Engr.** *Perf. 14*

1173 A628 90 l dk vio bl .20 .20

Lithographed and Engraved

1174 A629 90 l multi .20 .20

Italian artists: Jacopo della Quercia (1374-c. 1438), sculptor, and Giorgio Vasari (1511-1574), architect, painter and writer.

Angel with Tablet — A630

Angel with Cross — A632

Angels' Bridge, Rome — A631

Holy Year 1975: 50 l, Angel holding column. 150 l, Angel holding Crown of Thorns. The angels are statues by Giovanni Bernini on the Angels' Bridge (San Angelo).

1975, Mar. 25 **Photo.** *Perf. 14*

1175 A630 40 l multi .20 .20
1176 A630 50 l bl & multi .20 .20
1177 A631 90 l bl & multi .20 .20
1178 A630 150 l vio & multi .20 .20
1179 A632 180 l multi .20 .20
Nos. 1175-1179 (5) 1.00 1.00

Pitti Madonna, by Michelangelo A633

Works of Michelangelo: 50 l, Niche in Vatican Palace. 90 l, The Flood, detail from Sistine Chapel.

1975, Apr. 18 **Engr.** *Perf. 13½x14*

1180 A633 40 l dl grn .20 .20
1181 A633 50 l sepia .20 .20
1182 A633 90 l red brn .20 .20
Nos. 1180-1182 (3) .60 .60

Michelangelo Buonarroti (1475-1564), sculptor, painter and architect.

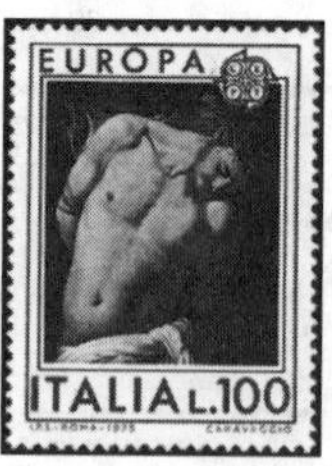

Flagellation of Jesus, by Caravaggio A634

Europa: 150 l, Apparition of Angel to Hagar and Ishmael, by Tiepolo (detail).

1975, Apr. 29 **Photo.** *Perf. 13x14*

1183 A634 100 l multi .20 .20
1184 A634 150 l multi .20 .20

Four Days of Naples, by Marino Mazzacurati A635

Resistance Fighters of Cuneo, by Umberto Mastroianni A636

Design: 100 l, Martyrs of Ardeatine Caves, by Francesco Coccia.

1975, Apr. 23

1185 A635 70 l multi .20 .20
1186 A636 100 l ol & multi .20 .20
1187 A636 150 l multi .20 .20
Nos. 1185-1187 (3) .60 .60

Resistance movement victory, 30th anniv.

Globe and IWY Emblem A637

1975, May *Perf. 14x13½*

1188 A637 70 l multi .20 .20

International Women's Year 1975.

Satellite, San Rita Launching Platform — A638

1975, May 28 *Perf. 13½x14*

1189 A638 70 l multi .20 .20

San Marco satellite project.

Tourist Type of 1974

Paintings: No. 1190, View of Isola Bella. No. 1191, Baths of Montecatini. No. 1192, View of Cefalù.

1975, June 16 Photo. *Perf. 14*

1190 A616 150 l grn & multi .20 .20
1191 A616 150 l bl grn & multi .20 .20
1192 A616 150 l red brn & multi .20 .20
Nos. 1190-1192 (3) .60 .60

Artist and Model, Armando Spadini — A640

Painting: No. 1194, Flora, by Guido Reni.

1975, June 20 Engr. *Perf. 14*

1193 A640 90 l blk & multi .20 .20
1194 A640 90 l multi .20 .20

50th death anniv. of Armando Spadini and 400th birth anniv. of Guido Reni.

Giovanni Pierluigi da Palestrina (1525-94), Composer of Sacred Music — A641

1975, June 27 Engr. *Perf. 13½x14*

1195 A641 100 l magenta & tan .20 .20

Emmigrants and Ship A642

1975, June 30 Photo. *Perf. 14x13½*

1196 A642 70 l multi .20 .20

Italian emigration centenary.

Emblem of United Legal Groups A643

and *Perf. 14x13½*

1975, July 25 Photo. Engr.

1197 A643 100 l yel, grn & red .20 .20

Unification of Italian legal organizations, cent.

Locomotive Wheels A644

1975, Sept. 15 Photo. *Perf. 14x13½*

1198 A644 70 l multi .20 .20

Intl. Railroad Union, 21st cong., Bologna.

Salvo D'Acquisto, by Vittorio Pisano A645

1975, Sept. 23

1199 A645 100 l multi .20 .20

D'Acquisto died in 1943 saving 22 people.

Stylized Syracusean Italia — A646

1975, Sept. 26 Photo. *Perf. 13½x14*

1200 A646 100 l org & multi .20 .20

Cent. of unification of the State Archives.

Fountain Type of 1973

Designs: No. 1201, Rosello Fountain, Sassari. No. 1202, Fountain of the 99 Faucets, Aquila. No. 1203, Piazza Fontana, Milan.

Photogravure and Engraved

1975, Oct. 30 *Perf. 13x14*

1201 A603 70 l blk & multi .20 .20
1202 A603 70 l blk & multi .20 .20
1203 A603 70 l blk & multi .20 .20
Nos. 1201-1203 (3) .60 .60

Botticelli Type of 1973-74

1975, Nov. 14 Photo. *Perf. 14x13½*

1204 A602 100 l Alessandro Scarlatti .20 .20
1205 A602 100 l Antonio Vivaldi .20 .20
1206 A602 100 l Gaspare Spontini .20 .15
1207 A602 100 l F. B. Busoni .20 .20
1208 A602 100 l Francesco Cilea .20 .20
1209 A602 100 l Franco Alfano .20 .20
Nos. 1204-1209 (6) 1.20 1.15

Famous musicians.

Annunciation to the Shepherds A648

Christmas: 100 l, Nativity. 150 l, Annunciation to the Kings. Designs from painted wood panels, portal of Alatri Cathedral, 14th century.

Lithographed and Engraved

1975, Nov. 25 *Perf. 13½x14*

1210 A648 70 l grn & multi .20 .20
1211 A648 100 l ultra & multi .20 .20
1212 A648 150 l brn & multi .20 .20
Nos. 1210-1212 (3) .60 .60

"The Magic Orchard" — A649

Children's Drawings: 70 l, Children on Horseback, horiz. 150 l, Village and procession, horiz.

Perf. 14x13½, 13½x14

1975, Dec. 7 Photo.

1213 A649 70 l multi .20 .20
1214 A649 100 l multi .20 .20
1215 A649 150 l multi .20 .20
Nos. 1213-1215 (3) .60 .60

17th Stamp Day.

Boccaccio, by Andrea del Castagno — A650

Design: 150 l, Frontispiece for "Fiammetta," 15th century woodcut.

Engraved and Lithographed

1975, Dec. 22 *Perf. 13½x14*

1216 A650 100 l yel grn & blk .20 .20
1217 A650 150 l buff & multi .20 .20

Giovanni Boccaccio (1313-1375), writer.

State Advocate's Office, Rome — A651

1976, Jan. 30 Photo. *Perf. 13½x14*

1218 A651 150 l multi .20 .20

State Advocate's Office, centenary.

ITALIA 76 Emblem — A652

Design: 180 l, Milan Fair pavilion.

1976, Mar. 27 Photo. *Perf. 13½x14*

1219 A652 150 l blk, red & grn .20 .20
1220 A652 180 l blk, red, grn & bl .20 .20

ITALIA 76 International Philatelic Exhibition, Milan, Oct. 14-24.

Tourist Type of 1974

Tourist publicity: #1221, Fenis Castle. #1222, View of Ischia. #1223, Itria Valley.

1976, May 21 Photo. *Perf. 14*

1221 A616 150 l grn & multi .20 .20
1222 A616 150 l plum & multi .20 .20
1223 A616 150 l yel & multi .20 .20
Nos. 1221-1223 (3) .60 .60

Majolica Plate, Deruta — A653

Europa: 180 l, Ceramic vase in shape of woman's head, Caltagirone.

1976, May 22 *Perf. 13½x14*

1224 A653 150 l multi .20 .20
1225 A653 180 l brn & multi .30 .20

Italian Flags — A654

Italian Presidents A655

1976, June 1

1226 A654 100 l multi .20 .20
1227 A655 150 l multi .20 .20

30th anniversary of Italian Republic.

Fortitude, by Giacomo Serpotta, 1656-1732 A656

Paintings: No. 1229, Woman at Table, by Umberto Boccioni, 1882-1916. No. 1230, The Gunner's Letter, by F. T. Marinetti, 1876-1944.

1976, July 26 Engr. *Perf. 14*

1228 A656 150 l blue .20 .20

Lithographed and Engraved

1229 A656 150 l multi .20 .20
1230 A656 150 l blk & red .20 .20
Nos. 1228-1230 (3) .60 .60

Italian art.

Paintings by Vittore Carpaccio (1460-1526), Venetian Painter — A657

#1230, St. George. #1231, Dragon, after painting in Church of St. George Schiavoni, Venice.

1976, July 30 Engr. *Perf. 14x13½*

1231 A657 150 l rose lake .20 .20
1232 A657 150 l rose lake .20 .20
a. Pair, #1231-1232 + label .40 .20

Flora, by Titian A658

1976, Sept. 15 Engr. *Perf. 14*

1233 A658 150 l carmine .25 .20

Titian (1477-1576), Venetian painter.

St. Francis, 13th Century Fresco — A659

1976, Oct. 2 Engr. *Perf. 14*
1234 A659 150 l brown .20 .20

St. Francis of Assisi, 750th death anniv.

Cart, from Trajan's Column A660

100 l, Emblem of Kingdom of Sardinia. 150 l, Marble mask, 19th cent. mail box. 200 l, Hand canceler, 19th cent. 400 l, Automatic letter sorting machine.

1976, Oct. 14 Photo. *Perf. 14x13½*
1235 A660 70 l multi .20 .20
1236 A660 100 l multi .20 .20
1237 A660 150 l multi .20 .20
1238 A660 200 l multi .25 .20
1239 A660 400 l multi .45 .20
Nos. 1235-1239 (5) 1.30 1.00

ITALIA 76 International Philatelic Exhibition, Milan, Oct. 14-24.

Girl and Animals — A661

Designs (Children' Drawings): 100 l, Trees, rabbit and flowers. 150 l, Boy healing tree.

1976, Oct. 17 *Perf. 13½x14*
1240 A661 40 l multi .20 .20
1241 A661 100 l multi .20 .20
1242 A661 150 l multi .20 .20
Nos. 1240-1242 (3) .60 .60

18th Stamp Day and nature protection.

Botticelli Type of 1973-74

1976, Nov. 22 Photo. *Perf. 14x13½*
1243 A602 170 l Lorenzo Ghiberti .20 .20
1244 A602 170 l Domenico Ghirlandaio .20 .20
1245 A602 170 l Sassoferrato .20 .20
1246 A602 170 l Carlo Dolci .20 .20
1247 A602 170 l Giovanni Piazzetta .20 .20
Nos. 1243-1247 (5) 1.00 1.00

Famous painters.

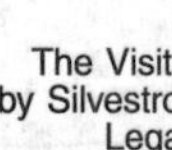

The Visit, by Silvestro Lega A662

1976, Dec. 7 Photo. *Perf. 14x13½*
1248 A662 170 l multi .25 .20

Silvestro Lega (1826-1895), painter.

Adoration of the Kings, by Bartolo di Fredi — A663

Christmas: 120 l, Nativity, by Taddeo Gaddi.

1976, Dec. 11 *Perf. 13½x14*
1249 A663 70 l multi .20 .20
1250 A663 120 l multi .20 .20

Fountain Type of 1973

Designs: No. 1251, Antique Fountain, Gallipoli. No. 1252, Madonna Fountain, Verona. No. 1253, Silvio Cosini Fountain, Palazzo Doria, Genoa.

Lithographed and Engraved

1976, Dec. 21 *Perf. 13½x14*
1251 A603 170 l blk & multi .25 .20
1252 A603 170 l blk & multi .25 .20
1253 A603 170 l blk & multi .25 .20
Nos. 1251-1253 (3) .75 .60

Snakes Forming Net A664

Design: 170 l, Drug addict and poppy.

1977, Feb. 28 Photo. *Perf. 14x13½*
1254 A664 120 l multi .20 .20
1255 A664 170 l multi .25 .20

Fight against drug abuse.

Micca Setting Fire A665

1977, Mar. 5
1256 A665 170 l multi .20 .20

Pietro Micca (1677-1706), patriot who set fire to the powder magazine of Turin Citadel.

Globe with Cross in Center — A666

Design: 120 l, People of the World united as brothers by St. John Bosco.

1977, Mar. 29 Photo. *Perf. 13x13½*
1257 A666 70 l multi .20 .20
1258 A666 120 l multi .20 .20

Honoring the Salesian missionaries.

Italian Constitution, Article 53 — A667

1977, Apr. 14 Photo. *Perf. 14*
1259 A667 120 l bis, brn & blk .20 .20
1260 A667 170 l lt grn, grn & blk .20 .20

"Pay your taxes."

Tourist Type of 1974

Europa (Europa Emblem and): 170 l, Taormina. 200 l, Castle del Monte.

1977, May 2
1261 A616 170 l multi .25 .20
1262 A616 200 l multi .45 .20

Tourist Type of 1974

Paintings: No. 1263, Canossa Castle. No. 1264, Fermo. No. 1265, Castellana Caves.

1977, May 30 Photo. *Perf. 14*
1263 A616 170 l brn & multi .25 .20
1264 A616 170 l vio & multi .25 .20
1265 A616 170 l gray & multi .25 .20
Nos. 1263-1265 (3) .75 .60

Botticelli Type of 1973-74

1977, June 27 *Perf. 14x13½*
1266 A602 70 l Filippo Brunelleschi .20 .20
1267 A602 70 l Pietro Aretino .20 .20
1268 A602 70 l Carlo Goldoni .20 .20
1269 A602 70 l Luigi Cherubini .20 .20
1270 A602 70 l Eduardo Bassini .20 .20
Nos. 1266-1270 (5) 1.00 1.00

Famous artists, writers and scientists.

Justice, by Andrea Delitio A669

Painting: No. 1272, Winter, by Giuseppe Arcimboldi, 1527-c.1593.

Engraved and Lithographed

1977, Sept. 5 *Perf. 14*
1271 A669 170 l multi .25 .20
1272 A669 170 l multi .25 .20

Corvette Caracciolo — A670

Italian Ships: No. 1274, Hydrofoil gunboat Sparviero. No. 1275, Paddle steamer Ferdinando Primo. No. 1276, Passenger liner Saturnia.

Photogravure and Engraved

1977, Sept. 23 *Perf. 14x13½*
1273 170 l multi .25 .20
1274 170 l multi .25 .20
1275 170 l multi .25 .20
1276 170 l multi .25 .20
a. A670 Block or strip of 4, #1273-1276 + 2 labels 1.00 .50

See #1323-1326, 1382-1385, 1435-1438.

Fountain Type of 1973

Designs: No. 1277, Pacassi Fountain, Gorizia. No. 1278, Fraterna Fountain, Isernia. No. 1279, Palm Fountain, Palmi.

Lithographed and Engraved

1977, Oct. 18 *Perf. 13x14*
1277 A603 120 l blk & multi .20 .20
1278 A603 120 l blk & multi .20 .20
1279 A603 120 l blk & multi .20 .20
Nos. 1277-1279 (3) .60 .60

Volleyball — A671

Designs (Children's Drawings): No. 1281, Butterflies and net. No. 1282, Flying kites.

1977, Oct. 23 Photo. *Perf. 13x14*
1280 A671 120 l multi .20 .20
1281 A671 120 l multi .20 .20
1282 A671 120 l multi .20 .20
a. Block of 3, #1280-1282 + label .50 .30

19th Stamp Day.

Symbolic Blood Donation A672

Design: 70 l, Blood donation symbolized.

1977, Oct. 26 *Perf. 14x13½*
1283 A672 70 l multi .20 .20
1284 A672 120 l multi .30 .20

Blood donors.

Quintino Sella and Italy No. 24 — A673

1977, Oct. 23 *Perf. 13½x14*
1285 A673 170 l olive & blk brn .30 .20

Quintino Sella (1827-1884), statesman, engineer, mineralogist, birth sesquicentenary.

Italia Type of 1953-54 and

Italia — A674

1977-87 Wmk. 303 *Perf. 14*
Size: 16x20mm
Photo.
1288 A354 120 l dk bl & emer .20 .20
Photo. & Engr.
1289 A354 170 l grn & ocher .25 .20
Litho. & Engr.
1290 A354 350 l red, ocher & pur .40 .20

Perf. 14x13½
Engr. Unwmk.
1291 A674 1500 l multi 1.50 .20
1292 A674 2000 l multi 1.90 .20
1293 A674 3000 l multi 3.00 .20
1294 A674 4000 l multi 3.75 .20
1295 A674 5000 l multi 5.00 .40
1296 A674 10,000 l multi 9.50 1.40
1297 A674 20,000 l multi 22.50 12.00
Nos. 1288-1297 (10) 48.00 15.20

Issued: 120 l, 170 l, 350l, 11/22/77; 5,000 l, 12/4/78; 4,000 l, 2/12/79; 3,000 l, 3/12/79; 2,000 l, 4/12/79; 1,500 l, 5/14/79; 10,000 l, 6/27/83; 20,000 l, 1/5/87.

Dina Galli (1877-1951), Actress — A675

Perf. 13½x14
1977, Dec. 2 Photo. Unwmk.
1309 A675 170 l multi .25 .20

Adoration of the Shepherds, by Pietro Testa — A676

Christmas: 120 l, Adoration of the Shepherds, by Gian Jacopo Caraglio.

Lithographed and Engraved

1977, Dec. 13 ***Perf. 14***
1310 A676 70 l blk & ol .20 .20
1311 A676 120 l blk & bl grn .20 .20

La Scala Opera House, Milan, Bicent. — A677

Designs: 170 l, Facade. 200 l, Auditorium.

1978, Mar. 15 Litho. ***Perf. 13½x14***
1312 A677 170 l multi .25 .20
1313 A677 200 l multi .30 .20

Tourist Type of 1974

Paintings: 70 l, Gubbio. 200 l, Udine. 600 l, Paestum.

1978, Mar. 30 Photo. ***Perf. 14***
1314 A616 70 l multi .20 .20
1315 A616 200 l multi .25 .20
1316 A616 600 l multi .75 .40
Nos. 1314-1316 (3) 1.20 .80

Giant Grouper A678

Designs (outline of "Amerigo Vespucci" in background): No. 1318, Leatherback turtle. No. 1319, Mediterranean monk seal. No. 1320, Audouin's gull.

1978, Apr. 3 ***Perf. 14x13***
1317 A678 170 l multi .45 .20
1318 A678 170 l multi .45 .20
1319 A678 170 l multi .45 .20
1320 A678 170 l multi .45 .20
a. Strip of 4, #1317-1320 + label 1.90 1.00

Endangered species in Mediterranean.

Castel Nuovo, Angevin Fortifications, Naples — A679

Europa: 200 l, Pantheon, Rome.

1978, Apr. 29 Litho. ***Perf. 14x13½***
1321 A679 170 l multi .35 .20
1322 A679 200 l multi .35 .20

Ship Type of 1977

Designs: No. 1323, Cruiser Benedetto Brin. No. 1324, Frigate Lupo. No. 1325, Ligurian brigantine Fortuna. No. 1326, Container ship Africa.

1978, May 8 Litho. & Engr.
1323 170 l multi .55 .20
1324 170 l multi .55 .20
1325 170 l multi .55 .20
1326 170 l multi .55 .20
a. A670 Block of 4, #1323-1326 + 2 labels 2.25 .75

Matilde Serao — A680

Designs: Portraits of famous Italians.

1978, May 10 Engr. ***Perf. 14x13½***
1327 A680 170 l shown .25 .20
1328 A680 170 l Vittorino da Feltre .25 .20
1329 A680 170 l Victor Emmanuel II .25 .20
1330 A680 170 l Pope Pius IX .25 .20
1331 A680 170 l Marcello Malpighi .25 .20
1332 A680 170 l Antonio Meucci .25 .20
a. Block of 6, #1327-1332 1.50 .75

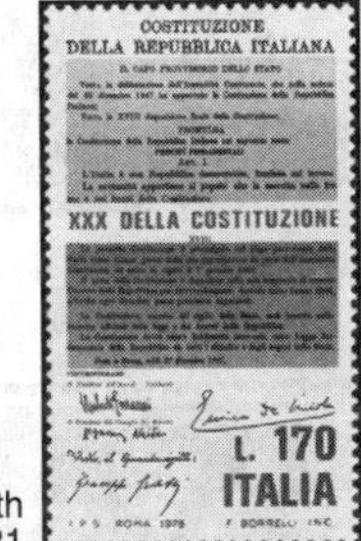

Constitution, 30th Anniv. — A681

1978, June 2 Litho. ***Perf. 13½x14***
1333 A681 170 l multi .25 .20

Telegraph Wires and Lens — A682

1978, June 30 Photo.
1334 A682 120 l lt bl & gray .20 .20

Photographic information.

The Lovers, by Tranquillo Cremona (1837-1878) — A683

Design: 520 l, The Cook (woman with goose), by Bernardo Strozzi (1581-1644).

Engraved and Lithographed

1978, July 12 ***Perf. 14***
1335 A683 170 l multi .55 .20
1336 A683 520 l multi 2.25 .75

Holy Shroud of Turin, by Giovanni Testa, 1578 — A684

1978, Sept. 8 Photo. ***Perf. 14***
1337 A684 220 l yel, red & blk .30 .20

400th anniversary of the transfer of the Holy Shroud from Savoy to Turin.

Volleyball — A685

Design: 120 l, Volleyball, diff.

1978, Sept. 20
1338 A685 80 l multi .45 .20
1339 A685 120 l multi .45 .20

Men's Volleyball World Championship.

Mother and Child, by Masaccio — A686

1978, Oct. 18 Engr. ***Perf. 13½x14***
1340 A686 170 l indigo .25 .20

Masaccio (real name Tommaso Guidi; 1401-28), painter.

Fountain Type of 1973

Designs: No 1341, Neptune Fountain, Trent. No. 1342, Fortuna Fountain, Fano. No. 1343, Cavallina Fountain, Genzano di Lucania.

1978, Oct. 25 Litho. & Engr.
1341 A603 120 l blk & multi .20 .20
1342 A603 120 l blk & multi .20 .20
1343 A603 120 l blk & multi .20 .20
Nos. 1341-1343 (3) .60 .60

Virgin and Child, by Giorgione — A687

Adoration of the Kings, by Giorgione — A688

1978, Nov. 8 Engr. ***Perf. 13x14***
1344 A687 80 l dark red .20 .20

Photo. ***Perf. 14x13½***
1345 A688 120 l multi .20 .20

Christmas 1978.

Flags as Flowers — A689

Designs: No. 1347, European flags. No. 1348, "People hailing Europe."

1978, Nov. 26 Photo. ***Perf. 13x14***
1346 A689 120 l multi .20 .20
1347 A689 120 l multi .20 .20
1348 A689 120 l multi .20 .20
Nos. 1346-1348 (3) .60 .60

20th Stamp Day on theme "United Europe."

State Printing Office, Stamps A690

Design: 220 l, Printing press and stamps.

1979, Jan. 6 Photo. ***Perf. 14x13½***
1349 A690 170 l multi .20 .20
1350 A690 220 l multi .30 .20

1st stamps printed by State Printing Office, 50 anniv.

St. Francis Washing Lepers, 13th Century Painting A691

1979, Jan. 22
1351 A691 80 l multi .20 .20

Leprosy relief.

Bicyclist Carrying Bike — A692

1979, Jan. 27 ***Perf. 13½x14***
1352 A692 170 l multi .20 .20
1353 A692 220 l multi .30 .20

World Crosscountry Bicycle Championships.

Virgin Mary, by Antonello da Messina A693

Painting: 520 l, Haystack, by Ardengo Soffici (1879-1964).

1979, Feb. 15 Engr. ***Perf. 14***
1354 A693 170 l multi .30 .20
1355 A693 520 l multi .70 .45

Albert Einstein (1879-1955), Theoretical Physicist and His Equation. — A694

Lithographed and Engraved

1979, Mar. 14 ***Perf. 13x14***
1356 A694 120 l multi .20 .20

Tourist Type of 1974

Paintings: 70 l, Asiago. 90 l, Castelsardo. 170 l, Orvieto. 220 l, Scilla.

1979, Mar. 30 Photo. ***Perf. 14***
1357 A616 70 l grn & multi .20 .20
1358 A616 90 l car & multi .20 .20
1359 A616 170 l ultra & multi .25 .20
1360 A616 220 l gray & multi .35 .20
Nos. 1357-1360 (4) 1.00 .80

Famous Italians — A695

No. 1361, Carlo Maderno (1556-1629), architect. No. 1362, Lazzaro Spallanzani (1729-1799), physiologist. No. 1363, Ugo Foscolo (1778-1827), writer. No. 1364 Massimo Bontempelli (1878-1960), journalist. No. 1365, Francesco Severi (1879-1961), mathematician.

1979, Apr. 23 Engr. ***Perf. 14x13½***
1361 A695 170 l multi .20 .20
1362 A695 170 l multi .20 .20
1363 A695 170 l multi .20 .20
1364 A695 170 l multi .20 .20
1365 A695 170 l multi .20 .20
Nos. 1361-1365 (5) 1.00 1.00

Telegraph A696

Europa: 220 l, Carrier pigeons.

1979, Apr. 30 Photo. ***Perf. 14***
1366 A696 170 l multi .30 .20
1367 A696 220 l multi .45 .20

Flags and "E" — A697

1979, May 5 ***Perf. 14x13½***
1368 A697 170 l multi .20 .20
1369 A697 220 l multi .30 .20

European Parliament, first direct elections, June 7-10.

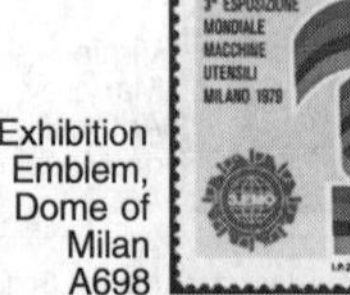

Exhibition Emblem, Dome of Milan A698

1979, June 22 Photo. ***Perf. 14***
1370 A698 170 l multi .20 .20
1371 A698 220 l multi .30 .20

3rd World Machine Tool Exhib., Milan, Oct. 10-18.

Aeneas and Rotary Emblem — A699

1979, June 9 ***Perf. 13½x14***
1372 A699 220 l multi .35 .20

70th World Rotary Cong., Rome, June 1979.

Basket — A700

1979, June 13 ***Perf. 14***
1373 A700 80 l shown .20 .20
1374 A700 120 l Basketball players .30 .20

21st European Basketball Championship, June 9-20.

A701

Patient & Physician, 16th cent. woodcut.

1979, June 16 Photo. & Engr.
1375 A701 120 l multi .20 .20

Digestive Ailments Study Week.

A702

Lithographed and Engraved

1979, July 9 ***Perf. 13x14***

Design: Ottorino Respighi (1879-1936), composer, Roman landscape.

1376 A702 120 l multi .20 .20

Woman Making Phone Call A703

200 l, Woman with old-fashioned phone.

1979, Sept. 20 Photo. ***Perf. 14***
1377 A703 170 l red & gray .20 .20
1378 A703 220 l grn & slate .30 .20

3rd World Telecommunications Exhibition, Geneva, Sept. 20-26.

Fountain Type of 1973

Designs: No. 1379, Great Fountain, Viterbo. No. 1380, Hot Springs, Acqui Terme. No. 1381, Pomegranate Fountain, Issogne Castle.

Lithographed and Engraved

1979, Sept. 22 ***Perf. 13x14***
1379 A603 120 l multi .30 .20
1380 A603 120 l multi .30 .20
1381 A603 120 l multi .30 .20
Nos. 1379-1381 (3) .90 .60

Ship Type of 1977

Designs: No. 1382, Cruiser Enrico Dandolo. No. 1383, Submarine Carlo Fecia. No. 1384, Freighter Cosmos. No. 1385, Ferry Deledda.

1979, Oct. 12 ***Perf. 14x13½***
1382 170 l multi .30 .20
1383 170 l multi .30 .20
1384 170 l multi .30 .20
1385 170 l multi .30 .20
a. A670 Block of 4, #1382-1385 + 2 labels 1.60 .75

Penny Black, Rowland Hill A704

1979, Oct. 25 Photo.
1386 A704 220 l multi .30 .20

Minstrels and Church A705

1979, Nov. 7 Photo. ***Perf. 14x13½***
1387 A705 120 l multi .20 .20

Christmas 1979.

Black and White Boys Holding Hands A706

Children's Drawings: 120 l, Children of various races under umbrella map, vert. 150 l, Children and red balloons.

Perf. 14x13½, 13½x14

1979, Nov. 25 Photo.
1388 A706 70 l multi .20 .20
1389 A706 120 l multi .20 .20
1390 A706 150 l multi .20 .20
Nos. 1388-1390 (3) .60 .60

21st Stamp Day.

Solar Energy Panels A707

Energy Conservation: 170 l, Sun & pylon.

1980, Feb. 25 Photo. ***Perf. 14x13½***
1391 A707 120 l multi .20 .20
1392 A707 170 l multi .25 .20

St. Benedict of Nursia, 1500th Birth Anniv. — A708

1980, Mar. 21 Engr. ***Perf. 13½x14***
1393 A708 220 l dark blue .30 .20

Royal Palace, Naples — A709

Lithographed and Engraved

1980, Apr. 16 ***Perf. 13½x14***
1394 A709 220 l multi .30 .20

20th International Philatelic Exhibition, Europa '80, Naples, Apr. 26-May 4.

Antonio Pigafetta, Caravel A710

Europa: 220 l, Antonio Lo Surdo (1880-1949) geophysicist.

1980, Apr. 28 Litho. ***Perf. 14x13½***
1395 A710 170 l multi .25 .20
1396 A710 220 l multi .35 .20

St. Catherine, Reliquary Bust — A711

1980, Apr. 29 Photo.
1397 A711 170 l multi .25 .20

St. Catherine of Siena (1347-1380).

Italian Red Cross A712

1980, May 15 Photo. ***Perf. 14x13½***
1398 A712 70 l multi .20 .20
1399 A712 80 l multi .20 .20

Temples of Philae, Egypt — A713

1980, May 20
1400 Pair + label .60 .20
a. A713 220 l shown .25 .20
b. A713 220 l Temple of Philae, diff. .25 .20

Italian civil engineering achievements (Temples of Philae saved from ruin by Italian engineers).

Soccer Player A714

1980, June 11
1401 A714 80 l multi 1.75 .75

European Soccer Championships, Milan, Turin, Rome, Naples, June 9-22.

Tourist Type of 1974

Paintings: 80 l, Erice. 150 l, Villa Rufolo, Ravello. 200 l, Roseto degli Abruzzi. 670 l, Public Baths, Salsomaggiore Terme.

1980, June 28 *Perf. 14*
1402 A616 80 l multi .20 .20
1403 A616 150 l multi .30 .20
1404 A616 200 l multi .35 .20
1405 A616 670 l multi .70 .40
Nos. 1402-1405 (4) 1.55 1.00

Cosimo I with his Artists, by Giorgio Vasari, and Armillary sphere — A715

1980, July 2 *Perf. 13½x14*
1406 A715 Pair + label .50 .50
a. 170 l Cosimo I .20 .20
b. 170 l Armillary sphere .20 .20

The Medici in Europe of the 16th Century Exhibition, Florence.

Fonte Avellana Monastery Millennium A716

1980, Sept. 3 **Engr.** *Perf. 14x13½*
1407 A716 200 l grn & brn .30 .20

St. Angelo Castle, Rome — A717

Designs: Castles.

Perf. 14x13½
1980, Sept. 22 **Engr.** **Wmk. 303**
1408 5 l shown .20 .20
1409 10 l Sforzesco, Milan .20 .20
1410 20 l Del Monte, Andria .20 .20
1411 40 l Ursino, Catania .20 .20
1412 50 l Rocca di Calascio .20 .20
1413 60 l Norman Tower, St. Mauro Fort .20 .20
1414 90 l Isola Capo Rizzuto .20 .20
1415 100 l Aragonese, Ischia .20 .20
1416 120 l Estense, Ferrara .20 .20
1417 150 l Miramare, Trieste .20 .20
1418 170 l Ostia, Rome .25 .20
1419 180 l Gavone, Savona .25 *1.00*
1420 200 l Cerro al Volturno, Isernia .25 .20
1421 250 l Rocca di Mondavio .35 .20
1422 300 l Svevo, Bari .40 .20
1423 350 l Mussomeli, Caltanissetta .45 .20
1424 400 l Imperatore-Prato, Florence .55 .20
1425 450 l Bosa, Nuoro .60 .20
1426 500 l Rovereto, Trento .70 .20
1427 600 l Scaligero, Sirmione .75 .20
1428 700 l Ivrea, Turin 1.00 .20
1429 800 l Rocca Maggiore, Assisi 1.10 .20
1430 900 l St. Pierre, Aosta 1.25 .20
1431 1000 l Montagnana, Padua 1.25 .20
Nos. 1408-1431 (24) 11.15 5.60

Coil Stamps
Perf. 14 Vert.
Size: 16x21mm

1432 30 l St. Severna, Rome .20 .20
1433 120 l Lombardia, Enna .25 .20
a. Pair, Nos. 1432-1433 .40 .20
1434 170 l Serralunga d'Alba, Cuneo .30 .20
a. Pair, Nos. 1432, 1434 .75 .75
Nos. 1432-1434 (3) .75 .60

No. 1412 exists dated "1980."
See #1475-1484, 1657-1666, 1863-1868.

Ship Type of 1977

#1435, Corvette Gabbiano. #1436, Torpedo boat Audace. #1437, Sailing ship Italia. #1438, Floating dock Castoro Sei.

Lithographed and Engraved
1980, Oct. 11 *Perf. 14x13½*
1435 200 l multi *1.25* .20
1436 200 l multi *1.25* .20
1437 200 l multi *1.25* .20
1438 200 l multi *1.25* .20
a. A670 Block of 4, #1435-1438 + 2 labels *7.00* 1.00

Philip Mazzei (1730-1816), Political Writer in US — A718

1980, Oct. 18 **Photo.** *Perf. 13½x14*
1439 A718 320 l multi .45 .20

Villa Foscari Malcontenta, Venezia — A719

Villas: 150 l, Barbaro Maser, Treviso. 170 l, Godi Valmarana, Vicenza.

Lithographed and Engraved
1980, Oct. 31 *Perf. 14x13½*
1440 A719 80 l multi .40 .20
1441 A719 150 l multi .40 .20
1442 A719 170 l multi .40 .20
Nos. 1440-1442 (3) 1.20 .60

See Nos. 1493-1495, 1528-1530, 1565-1568, 1606-1609, 1646-1649, 1691-1695.

St. Barbara, by Palma the Elder (1480-1528) — A720

Design: No. 1444, Apollo and Daphne, by Gian Lorenzo Bernini (1598-1680).

1980, Nov. 20 *Perf. 14*
1443 A720 520 l multi .70 .45
1444 A720 520 l multi .70 .45

Nativity Sculpture by Federico Brandini, 16th Cent. — A721

1980, Nov. 22 **Engr.**
1445 A721 120 l brn org & blk .20 .20

Christmas 1980.

View of Verona A722

22nd Stamp Day: Views of Verona drawings by school children.

1980, Nov. 30 **Photo.** *Perf. 14x13½*
1446 A722 70 l multi .20 .20
1447 A722 120 l multi .20 .20
1448 A722 170 l multi .25 .20
Nos. 1446-1448 (3) .65 .60

Daniele Comboni (1831-1881), Savior of the Africans — A723

1981, Mar. 14 **Engr.**
1449 A723 80 l multi .20 .20

Alcide de Gasperi (1881-1954), Statesman A724

1981, Apr. 3 *Perf. 13½x14*
1450 A724 200 l olive green .25 .20

International Year of the Disabled — A725

1981, Apr. 11 **Photo.**
1451 A725 300 l multi .50 .20

A726

1981, Apr. 27 **Photo.** *Perf. 13½x14*
1452 A726 200 l Roses .30 .20
1453 A726 200 l Anemones .30 .20
1454 A726 200 l Oleanders .30 .20
Nos. 1452-1454 (3) .90 .60

See Nos. 1510-1512, 1555-1557.

Europa — A727

Designs: No. 1455, Chess game with human pieces, Marostica. No. 1456, Horse race, Siena.

1981, May 4
1455 A727 300 l shown .40 .20
1456 A727 300 l multicolored .40 .20

St. Rita Offering Thorn — A728

1981, May 22
1457 A728 600 l multi .60 .35

St. Rita of Cascia, 600th birth anniversary.

Ciro Menotti (1798-1831), Patriot — A729

1981, May 26 **Engr.** *Perf. 14x13½*
1458 A729 80 l brn & blk .20 .20

G-222 Aeritalia Transport Plane — A730

1981, June 1 **Photo.**
1459 200 l shown .30 .20
1460 200 l MB-339 Aermacchi jet .30 .20
1461 200 l A-109 Agusta helicopter .30 .20
1462 200 l P-68 Partenavia transport plane .30 .20
a. A730 Block of 4, #1459-1462 + 2 labels 1.35 .65

See Nos. 1505-1508, 1550-1553.

Hydro-geological Research — A731

1981, June 8 *Perf. 13½x14*
1463 A731 80 l multi .20 .20

Sao Simao Dam and Power Station, Brazil — A732

Civil Engineering Works Abroad: No. 1465, High Island Power Station, Hong Kong.

1981, June 26 Engr. *Perf. 14x13½*

1464 A732 300 l dark blue .45 .20
1465 A732 300 l red .45 .20
a. Pair, #1464-1465 + label .90 .30

See Nos. 1516-1517, 1538-1539.

Tourist Type of 1974

1981, July 4 Photo. *Perf. 14*

1466 A616 80 l View of Matera .20 .20
1467 A616 150 l Lake Garda .20 .20
1468 A616 300 l St. Teresa di Gallura beach .60 .20
1469 A616 900 l Tarquinia 1.75 .40
Nos. 1466-1469 (4) 2.75 1.00

Naval Academy, Livorno and Navy Emblem A735

Naval Academy of Livorno Centenary: 150 l, View. 200 l, Cadet with sextant, training ship Amerigo Vespucci.

1981, July 24 *Perf. 14x13½*

1472 A735 80 l multi .20 .20
1473 A735 150 l multi .20 .20
1474 A735 200 l multi .25 .20
Nos. 1472-1474 (3) .65 .60

Castle Type of 1980

Perf. 14x13½

1981-84 Photo. Wmk. 303

1475 A717 30 l Aquila .20 .20
1476 A717 70 l Aragonese, Reggio Calabria .20 .20
1477 A717 80 l Sabbionara, Avio .20 .20

Perf. 13½

1478 A717 550 l Rocca Sinibalda .65 .20
1479 A717 1400 l Caldoresco, Vasto 2.00 .60
Nos. 1475-1479 (5) 3.25 1.40

Issue dates: Nos. 1475-1477, Aug. 20, 1981; Nos. 1478-1479, Feb. 14, 1984.

Coil Stamps

1981-88 Engr. *Perf. 14 Vert.*

Size: 16x21mm

1480 A717 50 l Scilla .20 .20
1481 A717 200 l Angionia, Lucera *2.75 2.00*
1482 A717 300 l Norman Castle, Melfi .60 .20
1483 A717 400 l Venafro .45 .20
1484 A717 450 l Piobbico Pesaro .40 .20
a. Pair, #1480, 1484 .60 .25
Nos. 1480-1484 (5) *4.40 2.80*

Issued: #1481-1482, 9/30; #1483, 6/25/83; #1480, 1484, 7/25/85; #1484a, 3/1/88.

Palazzo Spada, Rome (Council Seat) A736

1981, Aug. 31 Engr. Unwmk.

1485 A736 200 l multi .25 .20

State Council sesquicentennial.

World Cup Races — A737

1981, Sept. 4 Photo. *Perf. 13½x14*

1486 A737 300 l multi .40 .20

Harbor View, by Carlo Carra (1881-1966) — A738

#1488, Castle, by Guiseppe Ugonia (1881-1944).

Lithographed and Engraved

1981, Sept. 7 *Perf. 14*

1487 A738 200 l multi .30 .20
1488 A738 200 l multi .30 .20

See #1532-1533, 1638-1639, 1697-1698, 1732.

Riace Bronze, 4th Cent. B.C. — A739

1981, Sept. 9 Photo. *Perf. 13½x14*

1489 200 l Statue .30 .20
1490 200 l Statue, diff. .30 .20
a. A739 Pair, #1489-1490 .65 .30

Greek statues found in 1972 in sea near Reggio di Calabria.

Virgil, Mosaic, Treviri A740

1981, Sept. 19 *Perf. 14*

1491 A740 600 l multi .65 .40

Virgil's death bimillennium.

Food and Wine, by Gregorio Sciltian A741

1981, Oct. 16 Litho. *Perf. 14*

1492 A741 150 l multi .30 .20

World Food Day.

Villa Type of 1980

Lithographed and Engraved

1981, Oct. 17 *Perf. 14x13½*

1493 A719 100 l Villa Campolieto, Ercolano .20 .20
1494 A719 200 l Cimbrone, Ravello .30 .20
1495 A719 300 l Pignatelli, Naples .50 .20
Nos. 1493-1495 (3) 1.00 .60

Adoration of the Magi, by Giovanni de Campione d'Italia (Christmas 1981) — A743

1981, Nov. 21 Engr. *Perf. 14*

1496 A743 200 l multi .35 .20

Pope John XXIII (1881-1963) A744

1981, Nov. 25 Photo. *Perf. 13½x14*

1497 A744 200 l multi .25 .20

Stamp Day — A745

Photogravure, Photogravure and Engraved (200 l)

Perf. 14x13½, 13½x14

1981, Nov. 29

1498 A745 120 l Letters, horiz. .20 .20
1499 A745 200 l Angel, letter chest .35 .20
1500 A745 300 l Letter seal .55 .20
Nos. 1498-1500 (3) 1.10 .60

St. Francis of Assisi, 800th Birth Anniv. — A746

Design: St. Francis Receiving the Stigmata, by Pietro Cavaro.

1982, Jan. 6 *Perf. 13½x14*

1501 A746 300 l dk bl & brn .45 .20

Niccolo Paganini (1782-1840), Composer, Violinist — A748

1982, Feb. 19 Photo. *Perf. 13½x14*

1503 A748 900 l multi 1.25 .70

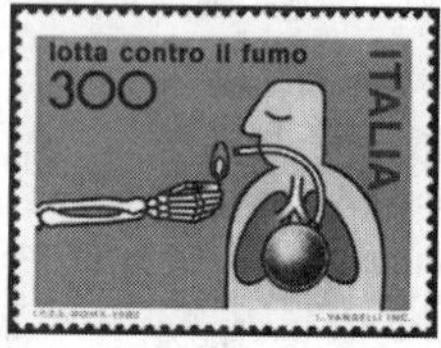

Anti-smoking Campaign — A749

1982, Mar. 2 Photo. *Perf. 14x13½*

1504 A749 300 l multi .45 .20

Aircraft Type of 1981

1982, Mar. 27 Litho. *Perf. 14x13½*

1505 300 l Aeritalia MRCA .45 .20
1506 300 l SIAI 260 Turbo .45 .20
1507 300 l Piaggio 166-dl3 Turbo .45 .20
1508 300 l Nardi NH-500 .45 .20
a. A730 Block of 4, #1505-1508 + 2 labels 3.75

Sicilian Vespers, 700th Anniv. — A750

1982, Mar. 31 Engr. *Perf. 13½x14*

1509 A750 120 l multi .20 .20

Flower Type of 1981

1982, Apr. 10 Photo.

1510 A726 300 l Cyclamens .55 .20
1511 A726 300 l Camellias .55 .20
1512 A726 300 l Carnations .55 .20
Nos. 1510-1512 (3) 1.65 .60

Europa — A751

Photogravure and Engraved

1982, May 3 *Perf. 13½x14*

1513 A751 200 l Coronation of Charlemagne, 799 .40 .20
1514 A751 450 l Treaty of Rome signatures, 1957 .90 .20

Engineering Type of 1981

1982, May 29 Photo. *Perf. 14x13½*

1516 A732 450 l Microwaves across Red Sea .70 .20
1517 A732 450 l Automatic letter sorting .70 .20
a. Pair, #1516-1517 + label 1.40 .60

Giuseppe Garibaldi (1807-82) A753

1982, June 2 *Perf. 13½x14*
1518 A753 200 l multi .65 .20

Game of the Bridge, Pisa — A754

1982, June 5
1519 A754 200 l multi .35 .20

See Nos. 1562, 1603, 1628-1629, 1655, 1717, 1749, 1775, 1807.

Tourist Type of 1974

1982, June 28 *Perf. 14*
1520 A616 200 l Frasassi Caves .40 .20
1521 A616 200 l Paganella Valley .40 .20
1522 A616 450 l Temple of Agrigento .70 .20
1523 A616 450 l Rodi Garganico Beach .70 .20
Nos. 1520-1523 (4) 2.20 .80

World Junior Canoeing Championship — A755

1982, Aug. 4 Photo. *Perf. 14*
1524 A755 200 l multi .40 .20

Duke Federico da Montefeltro (1422-1482) — A756

Photogravure and Engraved

1982, Sept. 10 *Perf. 14x13½*
1525 A756 200 l Urbino Palace, Gubbio Council House .30 .20

Italy's Victory in 1982 World Cup A757

1982, Sept. 12 Photo. *Perf. 14*
1526 A757 1000 l World Cup 1.75 .75

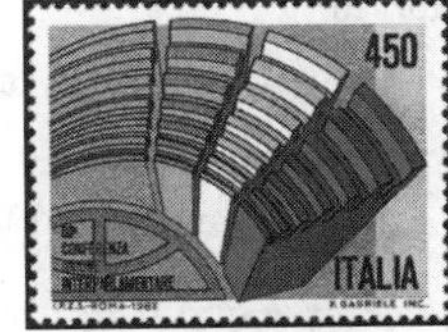

69th Inter-Parliamentary Conference, Rome — A758

1982, Sept. 14 *Perf. 14x13½*
1527 A758 450 l multi .60 .20

Villa Type of 1980

Designs: 150 l, Temple of Aesculapius, Villa Borghese, Rome. 250 l, Villa D'Este, Tivoli, Rome. 350 l, Villa Lante, Bagnaia, Viterbo.

Photogravure and Engraved

1982, Oct. 1 *Perf. 14x13½*
1528 A719 150 l multi .25 .20
1529 A719 250 l multi .40 .20
1530 A719 350 l multi 1.75 .20
Nos. 1528-1530 (3) 2.40 .60

Thurn and Taxis Family Postal Service — A759

1982, Oct. 23 Engr. *Perf. 13½x14*
1531 A759 300 l Franz von Taxis (1450-1517) .45 .20

Art Type of 1981

Paintings: No. 1532, The Fortune Teller by G.B. Piazzetta (1682-1754). No. 1533, Antonietta Negroni Prati Morosini as a Little Girl by Francesco Hayez (1791-1882).

Lithographed and Engraved

1982, Nov. 3 *Perf. 14*
1532 A738 300 l multi .60 .20
1533 A738 300 l multi .60 .20

24th Stamp Day A761

Children's Drawings.

1982, Nov. 28 Photo. *Perf. 14x13½*
1534 A761 150 l multi .20 .20
1535 A761 250 l multi .30 .20
1536 A761 350 l multi .50 .20
Nos. 1534-1536 (3) 1.00 .60

Cancer Research — A762

1983, Jan. 14 Photo. *Perf. 13½x14*
1537 A762 400 l multi .50 .20

Engineering Type of 1981

1983, Jan. 20 *Perf. 13½*
1538 A732 400 l Globe, factories .45 .20
1539 A732 400 l Automated assembly line .45 .20
a. Pair, #1538-1539 1.25 .60

Crusca Academy, 400th Anniv. — A763

1983, Jan. 25 Engr. *Perf. 14x13½*
1540 A763 400 l Emblem .50 .20

World Biathlon Championship — A764

1983, Feb. 5 Photo. *Perf. 14*
1541 A764 200 l multi .30 .20

Gabriele Rossetti (1783-1854), Writer — A765

1983, Feb. 28 Engr. *Perf. 14x13½*
1542 A765 300 l dk brn & dk bl .40 .20

Francesco Guicciardini (1483-1540), Historian — A766

1983, Mar. 5 Engr. *Perf. 13½x14*
1543 A766 450 l sepia .60 .20

Umberto Saba (1883-1957), Poet — A767

1983, Mar. 9 Photo. *Perf. 14x13½*
1544 A767 600 l multi .80 .20

Pope Pius XII (1876-1958) A768

1983, Mar. 21 Engr. *Perf. 13½x14*
1545 A768 1400 l dark blue 1.60 .30

Holy Year — A769

1983, Mar. 25 Photo. *Perf. 14*
1546 A769 250 l St. Paul's Basilica .20 .20
1547 A769 300 l St. Maria Maggiore Church .30 .20
1548 A769 400 l San Giovanni Church .40 .20
1549 A769 500 l St. Peter's Church 1.10 .20
Nos. 1546-1549 (4) 2.00 .80

Aircraft Type of 1981

1983, Mar. 28 Litho. *Perf. 14x13½*
1550 400 l Caproni C22J glider .45 .20
1551 400 l Aeritalia Macchi jet fighter .45 .20
1552 400 l SIAI-211 jet trainer .45 .20
1553 400 l A-129 Agusta helicopter .45 .20
a. A730 Block or strip of 4, #1550-1553 + 2 labels 2.75

Intl. Workers' Day (May 1) — A770

1983, Apr. 29 Engr. *Perf. 14x13½*
1554 A770 1200 l blue 1.50 .40

Flower Type of 1981

1983, Apr. 30 Photo. *Perf. 13½x14*
1555 A726 200 l Mimosa .60 .20
1556 A726 200 l Rhododendron 1.00 .20
1557 A726 200 l Gladiolus 1.00 .20
Nos. 1555-1557 (3) 2.60 .60

Europa 1983 A771

Litho. & Engr.

1983, May 2 *Perf. 14x13½*
1558 A771 400 l Galileo, telescope, 160l *3.75* .40
1559 A771 500 l Archimedes and his screw *3.75* .60

Ernesto T. Moneta (1833-1918), Nobel Peace Prize Winner, 1907 — A772

1983, May 5 Engr. *Perf. 14x13½*
1560 A772 500 l multi .60 .20

Monument, Globe, Computer Screen A773

20th Natl. Eucharistic Congress A775

1983, May 9 Photo. *Perf. 13½x14*
1561 A773 500 l multi .60 .20

3rd Intl. Congress of Jurisdicial Information.

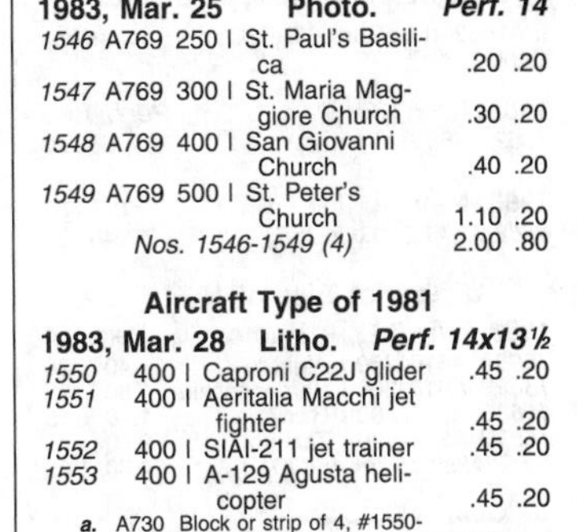

Folk Celebration Type of 1982

#1562, La Corsa Dei Ceri Procession, Gubbio.

1983, May 13 ***Perf. 13½***
1562 A754 300 l multi .55 .20

1983, May 14 ***Perf. 14***
1563 A775 300 l multi .40 .20

Tourist Type of 1974

1983, July 30 Photo. ***Perf. 14***
1563A A616 250 l Alghero .40 .20
1563B A616 300 l Bardonecchia .80 .25
1563C A616 400 l Riccione 1.40 .35
1563D A616 500 l Taranto 2.00 .40
Nos. 1563A-1563D (4) 4.60 1.20

Girolamo Frescobaldi (1583-1643), Composer A776

1983, Sept. 14 Engr. ***Perf. 13½x14***
1564 A776 400 l brn & grn .55 .25

Villa Type of 1980

Designs: 250 l, Fidelia, Spello. 300 l, Imperiale, Pesaro. 400 l, Michetti Convent, Francavilla al Mare. 500 l, Riccia.

Photogravure and Engraved

1983, Oct. 10 ***Perf. 14x13½***
1565 A719 250 l multi .75 .20
1566 A719 300 l multi .60 .20
1567 A719 400 l multi 1.25 .25
1568 A719 500 l multi 1.40 .35
Nos. 1565-1568 (4) 4.00 1.00

Francesco de Sanctis (1817-1883), Writer — A777

1983, Oct. 28 **Photo.**
1569 A777 300 l multi .40 .20

Christmas 1983 — A778

Raphael Paintings: 250 l, Madonna of the Chair. 400 l, Sistine Madonna. 500 l, Madonna of the Candelabra.

1983, Nov. 10 ***Perf. 13½x14***
1570 A778 250 l multi .20 .20
1571 A778 400 l multi .40 .25
1572 A778 500 l multi 1.40 .30
Nos. 1570-1572 (3) 2.00 .75

25th Stamp Day, World Communications Year — A779

Children's Drawings. 200 l, 400 l horiz.

Perf. 14x13½, 13½x14

1983, Nov. 27
1573 A779 200 l Letters holding hands .20 .20
1574 A779 300 l Spaceman .60 .20
1575 A779 400 l Flag train, globe 1.00 .25
Nos. 1573-1575 (3) 1.80 .65

Road Safety A780

Perf. 13½x14, 14x13½

1984, Jan. 20 **Photo.**
1576 A780 300 l Bent road sign, vert. .40 .20
1577 A780 400 l Accident .55 .30

Promenade in Bois de Boulogne, by Giuseppe de Nittis (1846-1884) — A781

Design: 400 l, Portrait of Paul Guillaume, 1916, by Amedeo Modigliani (1884-1920).

Lithographed and Engraved

1984, Jan. 25 ***Perf. 14***
1578 A781 300 l multi .60 .20
1579 A781 400 l multi .60 .25

Galaxy-Same Tractor — A782

Italian-made vehicles.

1984, Mar. 10 Photo. ***Perf. 14x13½***
1580 A782 450 l shown .55 .30
1581 A782 450 l Alfa-33 car .55 .30
1582 A782 450 l Maserati Biturbo car .55 .30
1583 A782 450 l Iveco 190-38 truck .55 .30
a. Block of 4, #1580-1583 + 2 labels 4.75 1.50

See Nos. 1620-1623, 1681-1684.

A783

1984, Apr. 10
1584 A783 300 l Mosaic, furnace .40 .20
1585 A783 300 l Glass Blower .40 .20
a. Pair, #1584-1585 + label 1.00 .45

2nd European Parliament Elections — A784

1984, Apr. 16
1586 A784 400 l Parliament Strasbourg .55 .25

Forest Preservation — A785

1984, Apr. 24 Photo. ***Perf. 14x13½***
1587 A785 450 l Helicopter fire patrol .55 .30
1588 A785 450 l Hedgehog, squirrel, badger .55 .30
1589 A785 450 l Riverside waste dump .55 .30
1590 A785 450 l Plant life, animals .55 .30
a. Block of 4, #1587-1590 7.50 1.50

Italia '85 A786

1984, Apr. 26 ***Perf. 14***
1591 A786 450 l Ministry of Posts, Rome .80 .30
1592 A786 550 l Via Appia Antiqua, Rome 1.00 .35

Rome Pacts, 40th Anniv. A787

Trade Unionists: Giuseppe di Vittorio, Bruno Buozzi, Achille Grandi.

1984, Apr. 30 ***Perf. 14x13½***
1593 A787 450 l multi .70 .30

Europa (1959-84) A788

1984, May 5
1594 A788 450 l multi *1.60* .55
1595 A788 550 l multi *4.75* .70

Intl. Telecommunications Symposium, Florence, May — A789

1984, May 7 ***Perf. 14***
1596 A789 550 l multi .85 .35

Italian Derby Centenary A790

Lithographed and Engraved

1984, May 12 ***Perf. 14x13½***
1597 A790 250 l Racing 1.40 .20
1598 A790 400 l Racing, diff. 1.75 .25

Tourist Type of 1974

1984, May 19 Photo. ***Perf. 14***
1599 A616 350 l Campione d'Italia .80 .25
1600 A616 400 l Chianciano Terme baths .80 .25
1601 A616 450 l Padula 1.60 .30
1602 A616 550 l Greek ampitheater, Syracuse 1.60 .35
Nos. 1599-1602 (4) 4.80 1.15

Folk Celebration Type of 1982

Design: La Macchina Di Santa Rosa.

1984, Sept. 3 Photo. ***Perf. 13½x14***
1603 A754 400 l multi .70 .25

Peasant Farming A792

1984, Oct. 1 Photo. ***Perf. 14x13½***
1604 A792 250 l Grain harvester, thresher .35 .20
1605 A792 350 l Cart, hand press .55 .20

Villa Type of 1980

Designs: 250 l, Villa Caristo, Stignano. 350 l, Villa Doria Pamphili, Genoa. 400 l, Villa Reale, Stupinigi. 450 l, Villa Mellone, Lecce.

Lithographed and Engraved

1984, Oct. 6 ***Perf. 14x13½***
1606 A719 250 l multi .75 .20
1607 A719 350 l multi .75 .20
1608 A719 400 l multi 1.50 .25
1609 A719 450 l multi 1.50 .25
Nos. 1606-1609 (4) 4.50 .90

Italia '85 — A793

1984, Nov. 9 ***Perf. 13½x14***
1610 A793 550 l Etruscan bronze statue .60 .30
1611 A793 550 l Italia '85 emblem .60 .30
1612 A793 550 l Etruscan silver mirror .60 .30
a. Strip of 3, #1610-1612 3.50 1.50

Journalistic Information A794

1985, Jan. 15 Photo. ***Perf. 13½x14***
1613 A794 350 l Globe, paper tape, microwave dish .40 .20

Modern Problems — A795

1985, Jan. 23 Photo. ***Perf. 13½x14***
1614 A795 250 l Aging .40 .20

A796

Italia '85. No. 1615, The Hunt, by Raphael (1483-1520). No. 1616, Emblem. No. 1617, Detail from fresco by Baldassare Peruzzi (1481-1536) in Bishop's Palace, Ostia Antica.

Photo. and Engr., Photo. (#1616)

1985, Feb. 13 ***Perf. 13½x14***

1615 A796 600 l multi .60 .30
1616 A796 600 l multi .60 .30
1617 A796 600 l multi .60 .30
a. Strip of 3, #1615-1617 3.00 1.50

Faience Tiles, Plate, Flask and Covered Bowl — A797

Italian ceramics: No. 1619, Tile mural, gladiators in combat.

1985, Mar. 2 Photo. ***Perf. 14x13½***

1618 A797 600 l multi .60 .30
1619 A797 600 l multi .60 .30
a. Pair, #1618-1619 + label 2.00 .75

Italian Vehicle Type of 1984

1985, Mar. 21

1620 A782 450 l Lancia Thema .45 .25
1621 A782 450 l Fiat Abarth .45 .25
1622 A782 450 l Fiat Uno .45 .25
1623 A782 450 l Lamborghini .45 .25
a. Block of 4, #1620-1623 + 2 labels *9.00* 1.50

A799

Italia '85: No. 1624, Church of St. Mary of Peace, Rome, by Pietro de Cortona (1596-1669). No. 1625, Exhibition emblem. No. 1626, Church of St. Agnes, Rome, fountain and obelisk.

Photo. and Engr., Photo. (#1625)

1985, Mar. 30 ***Perf. 13½x14***

1624 A799 250 l multi .40 .20
1625 A799 250 l multi .40 .20
1626 A799 250 l multi .40 .20
a. Strip of 3, #1624-1626 1.50 .50

Pope Sixtus V, (1520-1590), 400th Anniv. of Papacy — A800

Sixtus V, dome of St. Peter's Basilica, Rome.

1985, Apr. 24 Litho. and Engr.

1627 A800 1500 l multi 1.75 .90

Folk Celebration Type of 1982

Folktales: No. 1628, The March of the Turks, Potenza. No. 1629, San Marino Republican Regatta, Amalti.

1985, May 29 Photo.

1628 A754 250 l multi .70 .20
1629 A754 350 l multi 1.10 .20

Tourist Type of 1974

Scenic views: 350 l, Bormio town center. 400 l, Mt. Vesuvius from Castellamare di Stabia. 450 l, Stromboli Volcano from the sea. 600 l, Beach, old town at Termoli.

1985, June 1 ***Perf. 14***

1630 A616 350 l multi .40 .20
1631 A616 400 l multi .80 .25
1632 A616 450 l multi 1.00 .30
1633 A616 600 l multi 2.25 .35
Nos. 1630-1633 (4) 4.45 1.10

Nature Conservation A803

1985, June 5 ***Perf. 13½x14***

1634 A803 500 l European beaver .55 .30
1635 A803 500 l Primula .55 .30
1636 A803 500 l Nebrodi pine .55 .30
1637 A803 500 l Italian sandpiper .55 .30
a. Block of 4, #1634-1637 *9.00* 1.50

Art Type of 1981

Designs: No. 1638, Madonna bu Il Sassoferrato, G.B. Salvi, 1609-1685. No. 1639, Pride of the Work by Mario Sironi, 1885-1961.

Lithographed and Engraved

1985, June 15 ***Perf. 14***

1638 A738 350 l multi .80 .20
1639 A738 400 l multi 1.10 .25

Europa — A805

Tenors and Composers: 500 l, Aureliano Pertile (1885-1969) and Giovanni Martinelli (1885-1962). 600 l, Johann Sebastian Bach (1685-1750) and Vincenzo Bellini (1801-1835).

1985, June 20 Photo. ***Perf. 13½x14***

1640 A805 500 l multi *3.00* .50
1641 A805 600 l multi *6.00* .75

San Salvatore Abbey, Monte Amiata, 950th Anniv. A806

Lithographed and Engraved

1985, Aug. 1 ***Perf. 14x13½***

1642 A806 450 l multi .65 .25

World Cycling Championships — A807

1985, Aug. 21 Photo.

1643 A807 400 l multi 1.10 .25

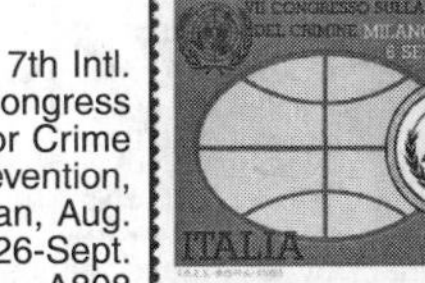

7th Intl. Congress for Crime Prevention, Milan, Aug. 26-Sept. 6 — A808

1985, Aug. 26

1644 A808 600 l multi 1.00 .35

Intl. Youth Year A809

1985, Sept. 3

1645 A809 600 l multi 1.00 .35

Villa Type of 1980

Designs: 300 l, Nitti, Maratea. 400 l, Aldrovandi Mazzacorati, Bologna. 500 l, Santa Maria, Pula. 600 l, De Mersi, Villazzano.

Lithographed and Engraved

1985, Oct. 1 ***Perf. 14x13½***

1646 A719 300 l multi .90 .20
1647 A719 400 l multi 1.10 .25
1648 A719 500 l multi 1.75 .30
1649 A719 600 l multi 2.25 .35
Nos. 1646-1649 (4) 6.00 1.10

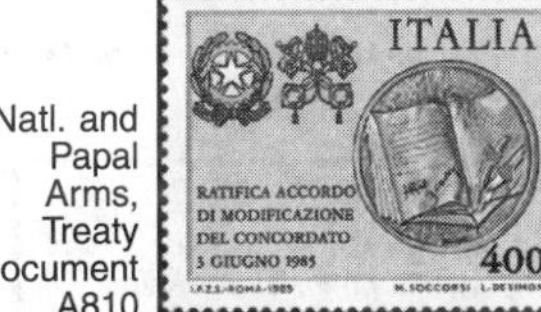

Natl. and Papal Arms, Treaty Document A810

1985, Oct. 15 Photo.

1650 A810 400 l multi .75 .25

Ratification of new Concordat with the Vatican.

Souvenir Sheets

Parma #10, View of Parma A812

Switzerland #3L1 A813

Sardinia #1, Great Britain #1 — A814

No. 1651: b, Two Sicilies #3, Naples. c, Two Sicilies #10, Palermo. d, Modena #3, Modena. e, Roman States #8, Rome. f, Tuscany #5, Florence. g, Sardinia #15, Turin. h, Romagna #7, Bologna. i, Lombardy-Venetia #4, Milan.

No. 1652b, Japan #1. c, US #2. d, Western Australia #1. e, Mauritius #4.

Illustration A814 reduced.

Lithographed and Engraved

1985, Oct. 25 ***Perf. 14***

1651 Sheet of 9 4.25 2.00
a.-i. A812 300 l, any single .35 .20

Perf. 14x13½

1652 Sheet of 5 + label 4.25 1.50
a.-e. A813 500 l, any single .60 .30

Imperf

1653 A814 4000 l multi 4.75 2.50

Italia '85, Rome, Oct. 25-Nov. 3.

Long-distance Skiing — A815

1986, Jan. 25 Photo. ***Perf. 14x13½***

1654 A815 450 l multi .60 .30

Folk Celebration Type of 1982

Design: Procession of St. Agnes, Le Candelore Folk Festival, Catania.

1986, Feb. 3 ***Perf. 13½x14***

1655 A754 450 l multi .75 .30

Amilcare Ponchielli (1834-1886), Composer — A816

Photogravure and Engraved

1986, Mar. 8 ***Perf. 14x13½***

1656 A816 2000 l Scene from La Giaconda 2.25 1.25

Castle Type of 1980

Designs: 380 l, Vignola, Modena. 650 l, Montecchio Castle, Castiglion Fiorentino. 750 l, Rocca di Urbisaglia.

Perf. 14x13½

1986-90 Photo. Wmk. 303

1657 A717 380 l multi ('87) .40 .30
1658 A717 650 l multi .70 .30

Engr.

1659 A717 750 l multi ('90) 1.25 .75
Nos. 1657-1659 (3) 2.35 1.35

Issue date: 750 l, Sept. 20.

Coil Stamps

Perf. 14 Vert.

1988-91 Engr. Wmk. 303

Size: 16x21mm

1661 A717 100 l St. Severa .20 .20
1662 A717 500 l Norman Castle, Melfi .80 .40
1663 A717 600 l Scaligero, Sirmione 1.10 .55
1664 A717 650 l Serralunga D'Alba 1.00 .50
1665 A717 750 l Venafro 1.25 .60
1666 A717 800 l Rocca Maggiore, Assisi 1.50 .75
Nos. 1661-1666 (6) 5.85 3.00

Issued: 600 l, 800 l, 2/20/91; others, 3/1/88.

Giovanni Battista Pergolesi (1710-1736), Musician — A817

Perf. 13½x14

1986, Mar. 15 Photo. Unwmk.

1667 A817 2000 l multi 3.00 1.25

The Bay, Acitrezza — A818

1986, Mar. 24 *Perf. 14*

1668 A818 350 l shown .65 .25
1669 A818 450 l Piazetta, Capri .90 .30
1670 A818 550 l Kursaal, Merano 1.00 .35
1671 A818 650 l Lighthouse, San Benedetto del Tronto 1.25 .45
Nos. 1668-1671 (4) 3.80 1.35

Europa 1986 — A819

Trees in special shapes: a, Heart (life). b, Star (poetry). c, Butterfly (color). d, Sun (energy).

1986, Apr. 28 Photo. *Perf. 13x14*

1672 Block of 4 6.75 2.00
a.-d. A819 650 l, any single .90 .45

25th Intl. Opthalmological Congress, Rome, May 4-10 — A820

1986, May 3 Photo. *Perf. 14*

1673 A820 550 l multi .75 .40

Police in Uniform — A821

1986, May 10

1674 A821 550 l multi 1.60 .40
1675 A821 650 l multi 1.90 .45

European Police Conference, Chianciano Terme, May 10-12. Nos. 1674-1675 printed se-tenant with labels picturing male or female police.

Battle of Bezzecca, 120th Anniv. A822

1986, May 31 *Perf. 14x13½*

1676 A822 550 l multi .75 .35

Memorial Day for Independence Martyrs — A823

1986, May 31 *Perf. 14*

1677 A823 2000 l multi 3.00 1.40

Bersaglieri Corps of Mountain Troops, 150th Anniv. — A824

1986, June 1 *Perf. 13½x14*

1678 A824 450 l multi .70 .30

Telecommunications — A825

1986, June 16 *Perf. 14x13½*

1679 A825 350 l multi .40 .25

Sacro Monte di Varallo Monastery — A826

1986, June 28 Engr. *Perf. 14*

1680 A826 2000 l Prus bl & sage grn 3.00 1.40

Italian Vehicle Type of 1984

1986, July 4 Photo. *Perf. 14x13½*

1681 A782 450 l Alfa Romeo AR8 Turbo .60 .30
1682 A782 450 l Innocenti 650 SE .60 .30
1683 A782 450 l Ferrari Testarossa .60 .30
1684 A782 450 l Fiatallis FR 10B .60 .30
a. Block of 4, #1681-1684 + 2 labels *9.50*

Ladies' Fashions — A827

Breda Heavy Industry — A828

Olivetti Computer Technology — A829

1986, July 14

1685 A827 450 l shown .65 .30
1686 A827 450 l Men's fashions .65 .30
a. Pair, #1685-1686 + label *3.00* .75
1687 A828 650 l shown *3.00* .45
1688 A829 650 l shown *3.00* .45
Nos. 1685-1688 (4) *7.30* 1.50

Alitalia, Italian Airlines, 40th Anniv. A830

1986, Sept. 16 Photo. *Perf. 14x13½*

1689 A830 550 l Anniv. emblem 1.00 .40
1690 A830 650 l Jet, runway lights 1.25 .50

Villa Type of 1980

1986, Oct. 1 Photo. & Engr.

1691 A719 350 l Necker, Trieste .65 .25
1692 A719 350 l Borromeo, Cassano D'Adda .65 .25
1693 A719 450 l Palagonia, Bagheria .85 .35
1694 A719 550 l Medicea, Poggio a Caiano 1.00 .40
1695 A719 650 l Castello d'Issogne, Issogne 1.25 .50
Nos. 1691-1695 (5) 4.40 1.75

Christmas — A831

Madonna and Child, bronze sculpture by Donatello, Basilica del Santo, Padua.

1986, Oct. 10 Engr. *Perf. 14*

1696 A831 450 l brown olive .70 .35

Art Type of 1981

Designs: 450 l, Seated Woman Holding a Book, drawing by Andrea del Sarto, Uffizi, Florence, vert. 550 l, Daphne at Pavarola, painting by Felice Casorati, Museum of Modern Art, Turin, vert.

1986, Oct. 11 Litho. & Engr.

1697 A738 450 l blk & pale org 1.75 .35
1698 A738 550 l multi 2.25 .40

Memorial, Globe, Plane — A832

Plane, Cross, Men — A833

1986, Nov. 11 Photo. *Perf. 13½x14*

1699 A832 550 l multi .80 .40
1700 A833 650 l multi .95 .50

Intl. Peace Year, memorial to Italian airmen who died at Kindu, Zaire, while on a peace mission.

Stamp Day A834

1986, Nov. 29 *Perf. 14x13½*

1701 A834 550 l Die of Sardinia No. 2 1.50 .45

Francesco Matraire, printer of first Sardinian stamps.

A835

Industries — A836

Perf. 14½x13½

1987, Feb. 27 Photo.

1702 A835 700 l Marzotto Textile, 1836 1.10 .55
1703 A836 700 l Italgas Energy Corp., 1837 1.10 .55

Environmental Protection — A837

Designs: a, Volturno River. b, Garda Lake. c, Trasimeno Lake. d, Tirso River.

1987, Mar. 6 Litho. *Perf. 14x13½*

1704 Block of 4 8.00 2.00
a.-d. A837 500 l, any single .80 .40

Antonio Gramsci (1891-1937), Author and Artist — A838

1987, Apr. 27 Litho. *Perf. 14x13½*

1705 A838 600 l scar & gray black .95 .50

Europa 1987 A839

Modern architecture: 600 l, Church of Sun Motorway, Florence, designed by Michelucci. 700 l, Railway station, Rome, designed by Nervi.

1987, May 4 Photo.

1706 A839 600 l multi 1.50 .50
1707 A839 700 l multi 1.75 .55

Tourist Type of 1974

1987, May 9 *Perf. 14*

1708 A616 380 l Verbania Pallanza .75 .30
1709 A616 400 l Palmi .80 .35
1710 A616 500 l Vasto 1.00 .40
1711 A616 600 l Villacidro 1.25 .50
Nos. 1708-1711 (4) 3.80 1.55

Naples Soccer Club, Nat'l. Champions A840

1987, May 18 Litho. *Perf. 13½x14*

1712 A840 500 l multi 1.90 .40

The Absinthe Drinkers, by Degas — A841

1987, May 29

1713 A841 380 l multi .80 .30

Fight against alcoholism.

St. Alfonso M. de Liguori (1696-1787) and Gulf of Naples — A842

1987, Aug. 1 *Perf. 14x13½*

1714 A842 400 l multi .65 .30

Events A843

Emblems and natl. landmarks: No. 1715, OLYMPHILEX '87, Intl. Olympic Committee Building, Foro Italico, Rome. No. 1716, World Athletics Championships, Olympic Stadium, Rome.

1987, Aug. 29 Photo. *Perf. 14x14½*

1715 A843 700 l multi .90 .55
1716 A843 700 l multi .90 .55

Folk Celebration Type of 1982

Design: Quintana Joust, Foligno.

Perf. 13½x14½

1987, Sept. 12 **Photo.**

1717 A754 380 l multi .70 .30

Piazzas A844

380 l, Piazza del Popolo, Ascoli Piceno. 500 l, Piazza Giuseppe Verdi, Palermo. 600 l, Piazza San Carlo, Turin. 700 l, Piazza dei Signori, Verona.

Litho. & Engr.

1987, Oct. 10 *Perf. 14x13½*

1718 A844 380 l multi .75 .30
1719 A844 500 l multi 1.00 .40
1720 A844 600 l multi 1.25 .50
1721 A844 700 l multi 1.40 .55
Nos. 1718-1721 (4) 4.40 1.75

See Nos. 1747-1748, 1765-1766.

Christmas A845

Paintings by Giotto: 500 l, Adoration in the Manger, Basilica of St. Francis, Assisi. 600 l, The Epiphany, Scrovegni Chapel, Padua.

1987, Oct. 15 Photo. *Perf. 13½x14*

1722 A845 500 l multi .90 .40
1723 A845 600 l multi 1.10 .50

Battle of Mentana, 120th Anniv. A846

Litho. & Engr.

1987, Nov. 3 *Perf. 14x13½*

1724 A846 380 l multi .70 .35

Il Pantocrator (Christ), Mosaic, Monreale Cathedral — A847

Coat of Arms and San Carlo Theater, Naples, from an 18th Cent. Engraving — A848

1987, Nov. 4 *Perf. 14*

1725 A847 500 l multi 1.50 .45
1726 A848 500 l multi 1.50 .45

Artistic heritage. See Nos. 1768-1769.

Nunziatella Military School, 200th Anniv. A849

1987, Nov. 14 *Perf. 14x13½*

1727 A849 600 l multi 1.00 .50

Stamp Day — A850

Philatelist Marco DeMarchi (d. 1936) holding magnifying glass and stamp album, Milan Cathedral.

1987, Nov. 20 Photo. *Perf. 13½x14*

1728 A850 500 l multi 1.60 .45

Homo Aeserniensis (Flint Knapper) — A851

Photo. & Engr.

1988, Feb. 6 *Perf. 13½x14*

1729 A851 500 l multi .75 .40

Remains of Isernia Man, c. 736,000 years-old, discovered near Isernia.

E. Quirino Visconti School, Rome A852

Litho. & Engr.

1988, Mar. 1 Unwmk. *Perf. 14x13½*

1730 A852 500 l multi .75 .40

See Nos. 1764, 1824, 1842.

St. John Bosco (1815-1888), Educator — A853

1988, Apr. 2 Photo. *Perf. 13½x14*

1731 A853 500 l multi .75 .40

Art Type of 1981

Painting: *The Archaeologists,* by Giorgio de Chirico (1888-1978).

1988, Apr. 7 Engr. *Perf. 14*

1732 A738 650 l multi, vert. 1.90 .55

1st Printed Hebrew Bible, 500th Anniv. A854

Soncino Bible excerpt, 15th cent.

1988, Apr. 22 Photo. *Perf. 14x13½*

1733 A854 550 l multi .90 .45

Epilepsy Foundation A855

Design: St. Valentine, electroencephalograph readout, epileptic in seizure and medieval crest.

1988, Apr. 23

1734 A855 500 l multi .80 .40

Europa 1988 A856

Transport and communication: 650 l, ETR 450 locomotive. 750 l, Electronic mail, map of Italy.

1988, May 2

1735 A856 650 l multi 1.40 .55
1736 A856 750 l multi 1.60 .65

Tourist Type of 1974

Scenic views: 400 l, Castiglione della Pescaia. 500 l, Lignano Sabbiadoro. 650 l, Noto. 750 l, Vieste.

1988, May 7 Photo. *Perf. 14*

1737 A616 400 l multi .60 .30
1738 A616 500 l multi .80 .40
1739 A616 650 l multi 1.00 .50
1740 A616 750 l multi 1.10 .55
Nos. 1737-1740 (4) 3.50 1.75

A858

1988, May 16

1741 A858 500 l Golf .80 .40

1990 World Cup Soccer Championships — A859

1988, May 16 Litho. *Perf. 14x13½*

1742 A859 3150 l blk, grn & dark red 4.00 2.50

1988 Natl. Soccer Championships, Milan — A860

1988, May 23 *Perf. 13½x14*

1743 A860 650 l multi 1.00 .50

Bronze Sculpture, Pergola — A861

1988, June 4 Engr. *Perf. 14*

1744 A861 500 l Horse .75 .40
1745 A861 650 l Woman .95 .50

Bologna University, 900th Anniv. — A862

1988, June 10 Engr. *Perf. 13½x14*

1746 A862 500 l violet .75 .40

Piazza Type of 1987

Designs: 400 l, Piazza del Duomo, Pistoia. 550 l, Piazza del Unita d'Italia, Trieste.

Litho. & Engr.

1988, July 2 *Perf. 14x13½*

1747 A844 400 l multi .70 .30
1748 A844 550 l multi .95 .40

Folk Celebration Type of 1982

Discesa Dei Candelieri, Sassari: Man wearing period costume, column and bearers.

1988, Aug. 13 Photo. *Perf. 13½x14*

1749 A754 550 l multi 1.40 .40

Intl. Gastroenterology and Digestive Endoscopy Congress, Rome — A863

1988, Sept. 5

1750 A863 750 l multi 1.00 .55

Surrealistic Films A864

Italian films amd directors: 500 l, *Ossessione,* 1942, by Luchino Visconti. 650 l, *Ladri di Biciclette,* 1948, by Vittorio DeSica. 2400 l, *Roma Citta Aperta,* 1945, by Roberto Rossellini. 3050 l, *Riso Amaro,* 1949, by Giuseppe DeSantis.

1988, Oct. 13 Litho. *Perf. 14x13½*

1751 A864 500 l multi .80 .40
1752 A864 650 l multi 1.10 .55
1753 A864 2400 l multi 3.75 1.90
1754 A864 3050 l multi 4.75 2.50
Nos. 1751-1754 (4) 10.40 5.35

Elsag — A865

Aluminia — A866

State Mint and Polygraphic Insitute — A867

Italian Industries.

1988, Oct. 19 Photo.

1755 A865 750 l multi .85 .65
1756 A866 750 l multi .85 .65

Photo. & Engr.

1757 A867 750 l multi .85 .65
Nos. 1755-1757 (3) 2.55 1.95

Christmas: *Nativity,* by Pasquale Celommi, Church of the Virgin's Assumption A868

1988, Oct. 29 Photo. *Perf. 13½x14*

1758 A868 650 l multi 1.40 .55

Christmas A869

Photo. & Engr.

1988, Nov. 12 *Perf. 14x13½*

1759 A869 500 l dark blue grn & chest brn 1.40 .40

St. Charles Borromeo (1538-1584), Ecclesiastical Reformer — A870

1988, Nov. 4 Litho. & Engr.

1760 A870 2400 l multi 3.00 1.75

Stamp Day — A871

Japan #69 & stamp designer Edoardo Chiossone.

1988, Dec. 9 Photo. *Perf. 13½x14*

1761 A871 500 l multi .80 .40

Campaign Against AIDS — A872

1989, Jan. 13

1762 A872 650 l multi 1.00 .50

Paris-Peking Rally — A873

1989, Jan. 21 *Perf. 14½x13½*

1763 A873 3150 l Map, Itala race car 5.00 2.50

School Type of 1988

1989 Photo. & Engr. *Perf. 14x13½*

1764 A852 650 l multi .90 .50

Piazza Type of 1987

No. 1765, Piazza Del Duomo, Catanzaro. No. 1766, Piazza Di Spagna, Rome.

Litho. & Engr.

1989, Apr. 10 *Perf. 14x13½*

1765 A844 400 l multi .85 .30
1766 A844 400 l multi .85 .30

Velo World Yachting Championships A875

1989, Apr. 8 Photo. *Perf. 14*

1767 A875 3050 l multi 4.50 2.25

Artistic Heritage Type of 1987

Art and architecture: 500 l, King with scepter and orb, Palazzo Della Ragione, Padova, vert. 650 l, Crypt of St. Nicolas, St. Nicolas Basilica, Bari, vert.

1989, Apr. 8 Litho. & Engr., Engr.

1768 A847 500 l multi .75 .40
1769 A847 650 l indigo 1.00 .50

Europa 1989 — A876

Children's games.

Perf. 14x13½, 13½x14

1989, May 8 Photo.

1770 A876 500 l Leapfrog, horiz. 1.00 .35
1771 A876 650 l shown 1.40 .45
1772 A876 750 l Sack race, horiz. 1.60 .55
Nos. 1770-1772 (3) 4.00 1.35

European Parliament 3rd Elections — A877

1989, June 3 *Perf. 13½x14*

1773 A877 500 l multi 1.00 .35

No. 1773 also inscribed in European Currency Units "ECU 0,31."

Pisa University — A878

1989, May 29 Engr. *Perf. 14x13½*

1774 A878 500 l violet .75 .35

Folk Celebration Type of 1982

Priest and Flower Feast street scene.

1989, May 27 Photo. *Perf. 13½x14*

1775 A754 400 l multi .60 .30

Landscape Type of 1974

1989, June 10 Photo. *Perf. 14*

1776 A616 500 l Naxos Gardens 1.00 .35
1777 A616 500 l Spotorno 1.00 .35
1778 A616 500 l Pompei 1.00 .35
1779 A616 500 l Grottammare 1.00 .35
Nos. 1776-1779 (4) 4.00 1.40

Ministry of Posts, Cent. A879

1989, June 24 *Perf. 14x13½*

1780 A879 500 l Posthorn, No. 52 .70 .35
1781 A879 2400 l Posthorn, Earth 3.25 1.60

INTER Soccer Championships — A880

1989, June 26

1782 A880 650 l multi .90 .45

Interparliamentary Union, Cent. — A881

1989, June 28

1783 A881 750 l multi 1.00 .50

French Revolution, Bicent. — A882

1989, July 7 Photo. *Perf. 14*
1784 A882 3150 l multi 4.75 2.25

Fortified Walls of Corinaldo, by Francesco di Giorgio Martini (1439-1502) — A883

Litho. & Engr.

1989, Sept. 2 *Perf. 14*
1785 A883 500 l multi .90 .40

Charlie Chaplin (1889-1977) — A884

1989, Sept. 23 Engr. *Perf. 14x13½*
1786 A884 750 l black & sepia 1.40 .55

Naples-Portici Railway, 150th Anniv. — A885

Illustration reduced.

1989, Oct. 3 Litho. & Engr.
1787 550 l Denom at UL .80 .40
1788 550 l Denom at UR .80 .40
a. A885 Pair, #1787-1788 1.75 1.00

Adoration of the Kings, by Correggio — A887

1989, Oct. 21 Photo. *Perf. 13½x14*
1789 500 l multicolored .75 .40
1790 500 l multicolored .75 .40
a. A887 Pair, #1789-1790 2.00 .90

Christmas.

Fidardo Castle, the Stradella, Accordion — A889

Industries.

1989, Oct. 14 Photo. *Perf. 14x13½*
1791 A889 450 l Music .70 .35
1792 A889 450 l Arnoldo World Publishing .70 .35

Stamp Day — A890

1989, Nov. 24 *Perf. 13½x14*
1793 A890 500 l Emilio Diena 1.00 .40

1990 World Soccer Championships, Italy — A891

1989, Dec. 9 Engr. *Perf. 13½x14*
1794 A891 450 l multicolored .75 .35

Columbus's First Voyage, 1474-1484 — A892

1990, Feb. 24 Photo.
1795 700 l Denom at UL 1.10 .55
1796 700 l Denom at UR 1.10 .55
a. A892 Pair, #1795-1796 2.25 1.50

Souvenir Sheets

1990 World Cup Soccer Championships, Italy — A894

Soccer club emblems and stadiums in Italy.

No. 1797: a, Italy. b, US. c, Olympic Stadium, Rome. d, Municipal Stadium, Florence. e, Austria. f, Czechoslovakia.

No. 1798: a, Argentina. b, Russia. c, St. Paul Stadium, Naples. d, New Stadium, Bari. e, Cameroun. f, Romania.

No. 1799: a, Brazil. b, Costa Rica. c, Alps Stadium, Turin. d, Ferraris Stadium, Genoa. e, Sweden. f, Scotland.

No. 1800: a, UAE. b, West Germany. c, Dall'ara Stadium, Bologna. d, Meazza Stadium, Milan. e, Colombia. f, Yugoslavia.

No. 1801: a, Belgium. b, Uruguay. c, Bentegodi Stadium, Verona. d, Friuli Stadium, Udine. e, South Korea. f, Spain.

No. 1802: a, England. b, Netherlands. c, Sant'elia Stadium, Cagliari. d, La Favorita Stadium, Palermo. e, Ireland. f, Egypt.

1990, Mar. 24 *Perf. 14x13½*
1797 Sheet of 6 3.50 1.75
a.-f. A894 450 l any single .55 .25
1798 Sheet of 6 4.50 2.25
a.-f. A894 600 l any single .75 .35
1799 Sheet of 6 5.00 2.50
a.-f. A894 650 l any single .80 .40
1800 Sheet of 6 5.25 2.75
a.-f. A894 700 l any single .85 .45
1801 Sheet of 6 6.00 3.00
a.-f. A894 800 l any single 1.00 .50
1802 Sheet of 6 9.00 4.50
a.-f. A894 1200 l any single 1.50 .75
Nos. 1797-1802 (6) 33.25 16.75

See No. 1819.

Tourist Type of 1974

1990, Mar. 30 Photo. *Perf. 14*
1803 A616 600 l Sabbioneta .90 .45
1804 A616 600 l Montepulciano .90 .45
1805 A616 600 l Castellammare del Golfo .90 .45
1806 A616 600 l San Felice Circeo .90 .45
Nos. 1803-1806 (4) 3.60 1.80

Folk Celebration Type of 1982

Design: Horse race, Merano.

1990, Apr. 9 *Perf. 13½x14*
1807 A754 600 l multicolored .95 .45

Aurelio Saffi, Death Cent. A895

1990, Apr. 10 *Perf. 14*
1808 A895 700 l multicolored 1.00 .55

Giovanni Giorgi (1871-1950) — A896

1990, Apr. 23 *Perf. 14x13½*
1809 A896 600 l multicolored .85 .55

Metric System in Italy, 55th. anniv.

Labor Day, Cent. — A897

1990, Apr. 28 Photo. *Perf. 13½x14*
1810 A897 600 l multicolored .85 .55

Naples Soccer Club, Italian Champions A898

1990, Apr. 30 *Perf. 13½x14*
1811 A898 700 l multicolored 1.25 .65

Europa A899

Post Offices: 700 l, San Silvestro Piazza, Rome. 800 l, Fondaco Tedeschi, Venice.

1990, May 7 *Perf. 14x13½*
1812 A899 700 l multicolored 1.40 .65
1813 A899 800 l multicolored 1.50 .75

Giovanni Paisiello (1740-1816), Composer A900

1990, May 9 *Perf. 14x13½*
1814 A900 450 l multicolored .65 .40

Dante Alighieri (1265-1321), Poet — A901

1990, May 12 *Perf. 14x13½*
1815 A901 700 l multicolored 1.00 .60

Dante Alighieri Soc., cent.

Mosaic (Detail) — A902

Sculpture — A903

Photo. (#1816), Litho. & Engr. (#1817)

1990, May 19 *Perf. 13½x14*
1816 A902 450 l multicolored .70 .40
1817 A903 700 l multicolored 1.00 .60

Malatestiana Music Festival, Rimini, 40th Anniv. — A904

1990, June 15 Photo. *Perf. 14*
1818 A904 600 l multicolored .85 .60

World Cup Soccer Type of 1990 Inscribed "Campione Del Mondo"

1990, July 9 Litho. *Perf. 14x13½*
1819 A894 600 l like No. 1800b 1.50 .60

Still Life, by Giorgio Morandi (1890-1964) — A905

1990, July 20 Engr. *Perf. 14*
1820 A905 750 l black 1.10 .55

Greco-Roman Wrestling, World Championships — A906

1990, Oct. 11 Litho. *Perf. 14x13½*
1821 A906 3200 l multicolored 4.75 2.25

Christmas — A907

Paintings of the Nativity by: 600 l, Emidio Vangelli. 750 l, Pellegrino.

1990, Oct. 26 *Perf. 14*
1822 A907 600 l multicolored .85 .40
1823 A907 750 l multicolored 1.00 .50

School Type of 1988 and

Italian Schools — A908

Designs: 600 l, Bernardino Telesio gymnasium, Cosenza. 750 l, University of Catania.

Litho. & Engr.

1990, Nov. 5 *Perf. 14x13½*
1824 A852 600 l multicolored .85 .40

Engr.

1825 A908 750 l multicolored 1.00 .50

Stamp Day — A909

Self-portrait, Corrado Mezzana (1890-1952).

1990, Nov. 16 Litho. *Perf. 13½x14*
1826 A909 600 l multicolored 1.10 .55

A910

1991, Jan. 5 Litho. *Perf. 13½x14*
1827 A910 600 l The Nativity .95 .45

Genoa Flower Show — A911

1991, Jan. 10 *Perf. 14*
1828 A911 750 l multicolored 1.10 .55

Seal of the Univ. of Siena — A912

1991, Jan. 15 Photo. *Perf. 13½x14*
1829 A912 750 l multicolored 1.00 .50

Tourist Type of 1974

1991 Photo.
1830 A616 600 l San Remo .90 .45
1831 A616 600 l Roccaraso .90 .45
1832 A616 600 l La Maddalena .90 .45
1833 A616 600 l Calgi .90 .45
Nos. 1830-1833 (4) 3.60 1.80

United Europe — A913

Perf. 14x13½

1991, Mar. 12 Photo. Unwmk.
1834 A913 750 l multi 1.25 .60

#1834 also carries .48 ECU denomination.

Discovery of America, 500th Anniv. (in 1992) — A914

1991, Mar. 22 Litho.
1835 750 l Ships leaving port 1.10 .55
1836 750 l Columbus, Queen's court 1.10 .55
a. A914 Pair, #1835-1836 2.25 1.10

Giuseppe Gioachino Belli (1791-1863), Poet — A916

1991, Apr. 15 Litho. *Perf. 14x13½*
1837 A916 600 l bl & gray blk .85 .40

Church of St. Gregory, Rome — A917

1991, Apr. 20 Photo. *Perf. 14x13½*
1838 A917 3200 l multicolored 3.75 1.90

Europa A918

1991, Apr. 29 Photo. *Perf. 14x13½*
1839 A918 750 l DRS satellite 1.40 .70
1840 A918 800 l Hermes space shuttle 1.50 .75

Santa Maria Maggiore Church, Lanciano — A919

1991, May 2 Engr. *Perf. 13½x14*
1841 A919 600 l brown .90 .45

Schools Type of 1988

Design: D. A. Azuni school, Sassari.

Litho. & Engr.

1991, May 3 *Perf. 14x13½*
1842 A852 600 l multicolored .95 .45

Team Genoa, Italian Soccer Champions, 1990-91 — A920

1991, May 27 Photo. *Perf. 13½x14*
1843 A920 3000 l multicolored 3.75 2.50

Basketball, Cent. — A921

1991, June 5
1844 A921 500 l multicolored .75 .40

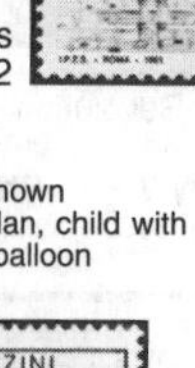

Children's Rights — A922

1991, June 14
1845 A922 600 l shown .95 .45
1846 A922 750 l Man, child with balloon 1.10 .55

Art and Culture A923

Designs: 600 l, Sculpture by Pericle Fazzini (b. 1913). 3200 l, Exhibition Hall, Turin, designed by Pier Luigi Nervi (1891-1979).

Litho. & Engr.

1991, June 21 *Perf. 14*
1847 A923 600 l multicolored .75 .40
1848 A923 3200 l multicolored 4.25 2.00

Egyptian Museum, Turin — A924

1991, Aug. 31 Litho. *Perf. 13½x14*
1849 A924 750 l grn, yel & gold 1.10 .55

Luigi Galvani (1737-1798), Electrophysicist — A925

1991, Sept. 24 *Perf. 14x13½*
1850 A925 750 l multicolored 1.10 .55

Radio, cent. (in 1995). See Nos. 1873, 1928, 1964.

Nature Protection A926

1991, Oct. 10 Photo. *Perf. 14x13½*
1851 A926 500 l Marevivo posidonia .90 .45
1852 A926 500 l Falco pellegrino .90 .45
1853 A926 500 l Cervo sardo .90 .45
1854 A926 500 l Orso marsicano .90 .45
Nos. 1851-1854 (4) 3.60 1.80

World Wildlife Fund.

Wolfgang Amadeus Mozart, Death Bicent. — A927

1991, Oct. 7 ***Perf. 13½x14***

1855 A927 800 l multicolored		1.25	.60

Christmas A928

1991, Oct. 18

1856 A928 600 l multicolored		.90	.45

Giulio and Alberto Bolaffi, Philatelists — A929

1991, Oct. 25 ***Perf. 14***

1857 A929 750 l multicolored		1.10	.55

Stamp Day.

Pietro Nenni (1891-1980), Politician — A930

1991, Oct. 30

1858 A930 750 l multicolored		1.10	.55

Fountain of Neptune, Florence, by Bartolomeo Ammannati (1511-1592) A931

1992, Feb. 6 Photo. ***Perf. 13½x14***

1859 A931 750 l multicolored		1.00	.50

22nd European Indoor Track Championships — A932

1992, Jan. 30 ***Perf. 14x13½***

1860 A932 600 l multicolored		1.00	.50

University of Ferrara, 600th Anniv. — A933

1992, Mar. 4 Photo. ***Perf. 13½x14***

1861 A933 750 l multicolored		1.00	.50

Castle Type of 1980

Perf. 14x13½

1992-94 Photo. Wmk. 303

1862 A717	200 l Cerro al Volturno	.25	.20
1863 A717	250 l Mondavio	.30	.20
1864 A717	300 l Bari	.40	.20
1865 A717	450 l Bosa	.55	.30
1866 A717	850 l Arechi, Salerno	1.50	.75
	Nos. 1862-1866 (5)	3.00	1.65

Issued: 200 l, 250 l, 300 l, 450 l, 2/24/94; 850 l, 3/7/92.

This is an expanding set. Numbers will change if necessary.

University of Naples — A934

1992, Mar. 9 Unwmk. ***Perf. 14x13½***

1872 A934 750 l multicolored		1.00	.50

Radio Cent. Type of 1991

Alessandro Volta (1745-1827), Italian physicist.

1992, Mar. 26

1873 A925 750 l multicolored		1.25	.60

Radio, cent. (in 1995).

Genoa '92 Intl. Philatelic Exhibition — A935

1992, Mar. 27 ***Perf. 13½x14***

1874 A935 750 l multicolored		1.10	.55

Lorenzo de Medici (1449-1492) A936

1992, Apr. 8 ***Perf. 14***

1875 A936 750 l bl & org brn		1.10	.55

Filippini Institute, 300th Anniv. — A937

1992, May 2 Photo. ***Perf. 13½x14***

1876 A937 750 l multicolored		1.10	.55

Discovery of America, 500th Anniv. A938

#1877, Columbus seeking Queen Isabella's support. #1878, Columbus' fleet. #1879, Sighting land. #1880, Landing in New World.

1992, Apr. 24 Photo. ***Perf. 14x13½***

1877 A938	500 l multicolored	.90	.45
1878 A938	500 l multicolored	.90	.45
1879 A938	500 l multicolored	.90	.45
1880 A938	500 l multicolored	.90	.45
a.	Block of 4, #1877-1880	3.75	1.90

See US Nos. 2620-2623.

Discovery of America, 500th Anniv. — A939

Designs: 750 l, Monument to Columbus, Genoa. 850 l, Globe, Genoa '92 Exhibition emblem.

1992, May 2 ***Perf. 13½x14***

1881 A939	750 l multicolored	1.40	.70
1882 A939	850 l multicolored	1.60	.80

Europa.

Miniature Sheets

Voyages of Columbus — A940

Columbus: #1883: a, Presenting natives. b, Announcing his discovery. c, In chains.

#1884: a, Welcomed at Barcelona. b, Restored to favor. c, Describing his 3rd voyage.

#1885: a, In sight of land. b, Fleet. c, Queen Isabella pledging her jewels.

#1886: a, Soliciting aid from Isabella. b, At La Rabida. c, Recall.

#1887: a, Landing. b, Santa Maria. c, Queen Isabella and Columbus. #1888, Columbus.

#1883-1888 are similar in design to US #230-245.

1992, May 22 Engr. ***Perf. 10½***

1883 A940	Sheet of 3	5.75	3.00
a.	50 l olive black	.20	.20
b.	300 l dark blue green	.35	.20
c.	4000 l red violet	5.25	2.50
1884 A940	Sheet of 3	5.25	2.50
a.	100 l brown violet	.20	.20
b.	800 l magenta	1.00	.50
c.	3000 l green	4.00	1.90
1885 A940	Sheet of 3	3.50	1.75
a.	200 l dark blue	.25	.20
b.	900 l ultra	1.25	.60
c.	1500 l orange	1.90	.95
1886 A940	Sheet of 3	2.75	1.40
a.	400 l chocolate	.50	.25
b.	700 l vermillion	.95	.45
c.	1000 l slate blue	1.25	.65
1887 A940	Sheet of 3	4.25	2.00
a.	500 l brown violet	.65	.30
b.	600 l dark green	.75	.35
c.	2000 l crimson lake	2.75	1.25
1888 A940	5000 l Sheet of 1	6.75	3.25
	Nos. 1883-1888 (6)	28.25	13.90

See US Nos. 2624-2629, Portugal Nos. 1918-1923 and Spain Nos. 2677-2682.

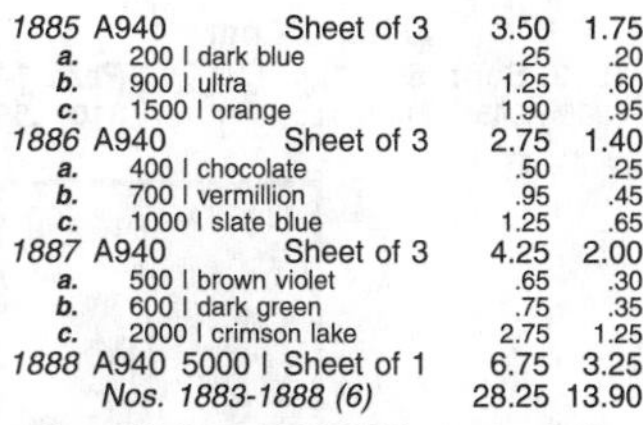

Tour of Italy Bicycle Race A941

1992, May 23 Photo. ***Perf. 14x13½***

1889 A941	750 l Ocean	1.50	.75
1890 A941	750 l Mountains	1.50	.75
a.	Pair, #1889-1890	3.00	1.50

No. 1890a printed in continuous design.

Milan, Italian Soccer Champions A942

1992, May 25 ***Perf. 13½x14***

1891 A942 750 l black, red & grn		1.50	.75

Beach Resorts A943

1992 ***Perf. 14x13½***

1892 A943	750 l Viareggio	1.00	.50
1893 A943	750 l Rimini	1.00	.50

Issued: #1892, May 30; #1893, June 13.

Tazio Nuvolari (1892-1953), Race Car Driver — A944

1992, June 5 ***Perf. 14x13½***

1900 A944 3200 l multicolored		4.75	2.50

Tourism Type of 1974

1992, June 30 ***Perf. 14***

1901 A616	600 l Arcevia	.85	.40
1902 A616	600 l Maratea	.85	.40
1903 A616	600 l Braies	.85	.40
1904 A616	600 l Pantelleria	.85	.40
	Nos. 1901-1904 (4)	3.40	1.60

The Shepherds, by Jacopo da Ponte — A945

Litho. & Engr.

1992, Sept. 5 *Perf. 14*

1905 A945 750 l multicolored 1.10 .55

Discovery of America, 500th Anniv. — A946

500 l, Columbus' house, Genoa. 600 l, Columbus' fleet. 750 l, Map. 850 l, Columbus pointing to land. 1200 l, Coming ashore. 3200 l, Columbus, art by Michelangelo.

1992, Sept. 18 Photo. *Perf. 13½x14*

1906 A946 500 l multicolored .65 .30
1907 A946 600 l multicolored .80 .40
1908 A946 750 l multicolored 1.00 .50
1909 A946 850 l multicolored 1.10 .55
1910 A946 1200 l multicolored 1.60 .80
1911 A946 3200 l multicolored 4.25 2.00
Nos. 1906-1911 (6) 9.40 4.55

Genoa '92.

Stamp Day — A947

1992, Sept. 22 *Perf. 14*

1912 A947 750 l multicolored 1.25 .70

Self-Adhesive

Perf. 13½

1913 A947 750 l multicolored 2.25 .70

Lions Intl., 75th Anniv. A948

1992, Sept. 24 *Perf. 14x13½*

1914 A948 3000 l multicolored 3.75 1.90

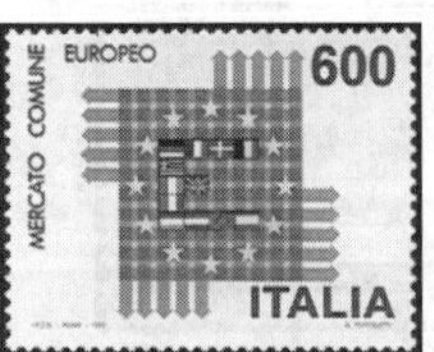

Single European Market A949

1992, Oct. 5 Photo. *Perf. 14x13½*

1915 A949 600 l multicolored .85 .40

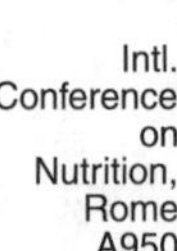

Intl. Conference on Nutrition, Rome A950

1992, Oct. 16 Photo. *Perf. 14x13½*

1916 A950 500 l multicolored .75 .35

Christmas A951

1992, Oct. 31

1917 A951 600 l multicolored .90 .45

Miniature Sheet

United Europe — A952

Buildings on natl. flags, inscriptions in native language: a, Italy (Benvenuta). b, Belgium (Vienvenue, Welkom). c, Denmark (Velkommen). d, France (Bienvenue L'Europe). e, Germany (Willkommen). f, Greece. g, Ireland (Failte). h, Luxembourg (Bienvenue Europe). i, Netherlands (Welkom). j, Portugal (Bem-Vinda). k, United Kingdom (Welcome). l, Spain (Bienvenida).

1993, Jan. 20 Photo. *Perf. 13½x14*

Sheet of 12

1918 A952 750 l #a.-l. 12.50 12.50

Meeting of Veterans of 1943 Battle of Nikolayev, Ukraine A953

1993, Jan. 23 Litho. *Perf. 14x13½*

1919 A953 600 l multicolored .85 .40

Carlo Goldoni (1707-93), Playwright A954

Paintings depicting scenes from plays: No. 1920, Nude man leaning on picture. No. 1921, Woman seated in front of harlequins.

1993, Feb. 6 Photo. *Perf. 13½x14*

1920 A954 500 l multicolored .70 .35
1921 A954 500 l multicolored .70 .35

Mosaic from the Piazza Armerina A955

Photo. & Engr.

1993, Feb. 20 *Perf. 14*

1922 A955 750 l multicolored 1.10 .55

Natl. Health Day Promoting a Healthy Heart A956

1993, Mar. 5 Photo. *Perf. 14x13½*

1923 A956 750 l multicolored 1.10 .55

Cats A957

1993, Mar. 6 *Perf. 14x13½,13½x14*

1924 A957 600 l European .80 .40
1925 A957 600 l Maine coon, vert. .80 .40
1926 A957 600 l Devon Rex, vert. .80 .40
1927 A957 600 l White Persian .80 .40
Nos. 1924-1927 (4) 3.20 1.60

Radio Cent. Type of 1991

Design: 750 l, Temistocle Calzecchi Onesti.

1993, Mar. 26 Litho. *Perf. 14x13½*

1928 A925 750 l multicolored 1.10 .55

Radio cent. (in 1995).

City Scene, by Francesco Guardi (1712-1793) — A958

Photo. & Engr.

1993, Apr. 6 *Perf. 14*

1929 A958 3200 l multicolored 4.25 2.00

Horace (Quintus Horatius Flaccus), Poet and Satirist, 2000th Anniv. of Death — A959

1993, Apr. 19 Photo. *Perf. 13½x14*

1930 A959 600 l multicolored .85 .40

Contemporary Paintings — A960

Europa: 750 l, Carousel Animals, by Lino Bianchi Barriviera. 850 l, Abstract, by Gino Severini.

1993, May 3

1931 A960 750 l multicolored 1.25 .60
1932 A960 850 l multicolored 1.40 .70

Natl. Soccer Champions, Milan — A961

1993, May 24

1933 A961 750 l multicolored 1.10 .55

Natl. Academy of St. Luke, 400th Anniv. — A962

1993, May 31 **Photo.**

1934 A962 750 l multicolored 1.10 .55

St. Giuseppe Benedetto Cottolengo (1786-1842) A963

1993, May **Photo. & Engr.**

1935 A963 750 l multicolored 1.10 .55

Family Fest '93 — A964

1993, June 5 Photo. *Perf. 14x13½*

1936 A964 750 l multicolored 1.10 .55

Tourism A965

1993, June 28 Photo. *Perf. 14x13½*

1937 A965 600 l Palmanova .80 .40
1938 A965 600 l Senigallia .80 .40
1939 A965 600 l Carloforte .80 .40
1940 A965 600 l Sorrento .80 .40
Nos. 1937-1940 (4) 3.20 1.60

See Nos. 1972-1975, 2032-2035.

1993 World Kayaking Championships, Trentino — A966

1993, July 1 *Perf. 13½x14*

1941 A966 750 l multicolored 1.10 .55

Regina Margherita Observatory, Cent. — A967

1993, Sept. 4 Photo. ***Perf. 14x13½***

No.	Type	Denom.	Description	Unused	Used
1942	A967	500 l	multicolored	.80	.40

Museum Treasures A968

Designs: No. 1943, Concert, by Bartolomeo Manfredi. No. 1944, Ancient map of Foggia. 750 l, Illuminated page with "S," vert. 850 l, The Death of Adonis, by Sebastiano Del Piombo.

Perf. 14x13½, 13½x14

1993, Nov. 27 Litho.

No.	Type	Denom.	Description	Unused	Used
1943	A968	600 l	multicolored	.80	.40
1944	A968	600 l	multicolored	.80	.40
1945	A968	750 l	multicolored	.95	.45
1946	A968	850 l	multicolored	1.10	.55
			Nos. 1943-1946 (4)	3.65	1.80

Holy Stairway, Veroli — A969

1993, Sept. 25 Photo. ***Perf. 13½x14***

No.	Type	Denom.	Description	Unused	Used
1947	A969	750 l	multicolored	1.10	.55

World War II — A970

Events of 1943: No. 1948, Deportation of Jews from Italy, Oct. 16, 1943. No. 1949, Soldiers, helmet (Battle of Naples). No. 1950, Execution of the Cervi Brothers.

1993, Sept. 25

No.	Type	Denom.	Description	Unused	Used
1948	A970	750 l	multicolored	1.00	.50
1949	A970	750 l	multicolored	1.00	.50
1950	A970	750 l	multicolored	1.00	.50
			Nos. 1948-1950 (3)	3.00	1.50

See Nos. 1984-1986.

Thurn and Taxis Postal History A971

#1951, Coach. #1952, Coat of arms. # 1953, Cart. #1954, Post rider on galloping horse. #1955, Post rider on walking horse.

1993, Oct. 2 ***Perf. 14x13½***

No.	Type	Denom.	Description	Unused	Used
1951	A971	750 l	multicolored	1.00	.50
1952	A971	750 l	multicolored	1.00	.50
1953	A971	750 l	multicolored	1.00	.50
1954	A971	750 l	multicolored	1.00	.50
1955	A971	750 l	multicolored	1.00	.50
			Nos. 1951-1955 (5)	5.00	2.50

Perf. 14 Horiz.

No.	Type	Denom.	Description	Unused	Used
1951a	A971	750 l		1.00	.50
1952a	A971	750 l		1.00	.50
1953a	A971	750 l		1.00	.50
1954a	A971	750 l		1.00	.50
1955a	A971	750 l		1.00	.50
b.			Booklet pane of 5, #1951a-1955a	5.00	

Bank of Italy, Cent. A972

1993, Oct. 15 ***Perf. 14x13½***

No.	Type	Denom.	Description	Unused	Used
1956	A972	750 l	Bank exterior	1.25	.60
1957	A972	1000 l	1000 Lire note	1.50	.75

Christmas A973

Designs: 600 l, Living Creche in the town of Corchiano. 750 l, Detail of The Annunciation, by Piero Della Francesca.

1993, Oct. 26 Litho. ***Perf. 13½x14***

No.	Type	Denom.	Description	Unused	Used
1958	A973	600 l	multicolored	.85	.40
1959	A973	750 l	multicolored	1.00	.50

Stamp Day A974

1993, Nov. 12 Photo. ***Perf. 14***

No.	Type	Denom.	Description	Unused	Used
1960	A974	600 l	blue & red	.85	.40

First Italian colonial postage stamps, cent.

Circus — A975

1994, Jan. 8 Litho. ***Perf. 13½x14***

No.	Type	Denom.	Description	Unused	Used
1961	A975	600 l	Acrobat, horses	.75	.40
1962	A975	750 l	Clown performing	.90	.45

Presence of Women in the Home A976

1994, Feb. 14 Photo. ***Perf. 14***

No.	Type	Denom.	Description	Unused	Used
1963	A976	750 l	multicolored	.95	.45

Radio Cent. Type of 1991

750 l, Augusto Righi (1850-1920), physicist.

Perf. 14x13½

1994, Mar. 11 Photo. Unwmk.

No.	Type	Denom.	Description	Unused	Used
1964	A925	750 l	multicolored	1.10	.55

Radio cent. (in 1995).

Dogs A977

1994, Mar. 12 ***Perf. 14x13***

No.	Type	Denom.	Description	Unused	Used
1965	A977	600 l	German shepherd	.75	.35
1966	A977	600 l	Abruzzi sheepdog	.75	.35
1967	A977	600 l	Boxer	.75	.35
1968	A977	600 l	Dalmatian	.75	.35
			Nos. 1965-1968 (4)	3.00	1.40

Italian Cuisine — A978

1994, Mar. 24 ***Perf. 13x14***

No.	Type	Denom.	Description	Unused	Used
1969	A978	500 l	Breads	.65	.30
1970	A978	600 l	Pasta	.75	.40

Procession Honoring Apparition of Christ, Tarquinia — A979

1994, Apr. 2 ***Perf. 13½***

No.	Type	Denom.	Description	Unused	Used
1971	A979	750 l	multicolored	1.00	.50

Tourism Type of 1993

1994, Apr. 23 Photo. ***Perf. 14x13½***

No.	Type	Denom.	Description	Unused	Used
1972	A965	600 l	Orta San Giulio	.75	.35
1973	A965	600 l	Santa Marinella	.75	.35
1974	A965	600 l	Messina	.75	.35
1975	A965	600 l	Monticchio, Potenza	.75	.35
			Nos. 1972-1975 (4)	3.00	1.40

A981

Nobel Prize Winners: 750 l, Camillo Golgi (1844-1926), Physician, Medicine, 1906. 850 l, Guilio Natta (1903-), Chemistry, 1963.

1994, May 2 Photo. ***Perf. 13½x14***

No.	Type	Denom.	Description	Unused	Used
1976	A981	750 l	multicolored	.90	.45
1977	A981	850 l	multicolored	1.00	.50

Publication of "Summa de Arithemtica, Geometria, Proportioni et Proportionalita," 500th Anniv. — A982

Fra Luca Pacioli (c. 1445-1514), mathematician.

1994, May 2 Photo. ***Perf. 14x13***

No.	Type	Denom.	Description	Unused	Used
1978	A982	750 l	multicolored	.95	.45

Lajos Kossuth (1802-94) — A983

1994, Apr. 30 Photo. ***Perf. 13½x14***

No.	Type	Denom.	Description	Unused	Used
1979	A983	3750 l	multicolored	4.25	2.00

Milan, Winners of 1993-94 Italian Soccer Championships — A984

1994, May 2 ***Perf. 14x13½***

No.	Type	Denom.	Description	Unused	Used
1980	A984	750 l	multicolored	1.10	.55

World Swimming Championships A985

1994, May 2 Photo. ***Perf. 13½x14***

No.	Type	Denom.	Description	Unused	Used
1981	A985	600 l	Diving	.80	.40
1982	A985	750 l	Water polo	1.00	.50

Archaeology Exhibition, Rimini — A986

1994, May 6

No.	Type	Denom.	Description	Unused	Used
1983	A986	750 l	multicolored	1.00	.50

World War II Type of 1993

Events of 1944: No. 1984, Destruction of Monte Cassino. No. 1985, Massacre of the Ardeatine Caves. No. 1986, Massacre at Marzabotto.

1994, May 18

No.	Type	Denom.	Description	Unused	Used
1984	A970	750 l	multicolored	.90	.45
1985	A970	750 l	multicolored	.90	.45
1986	A970	750 l	multicolored	.90	.45
			Nos. 1984-1986 (3)	2.70	1.35

22nd Natl. Eucharistic Congress, Siena — A987

1994, May 28 Photo. ***Perf. 13½x14***

No.	Type	Denom.	Description	Unused	Used
1987	A987	600 l	multicolored	.85	.40

Ariadne, Venus and Bacchus, by Tintoretto (1518-94) — A988

1994, May 31 ***Perf. 14***
1988 A988 750 l multicolored 1.00 .50

Brotherhood of Mercy, Florence, 700th Anniv. — A989

1994, June 4 ***Perf. 14x13½***
1989 A989 750 l multicolored 1.00 .50

European Parliamentary Elections — A990

1994, June 11 Photo. ***Perf. 13½x14***
1990 A990 600 l multicolored .85 .40

Natl. Museums — A991

#1991, Attic Krater, Natl. Archaeological Museum. #1992, Ancient drawing, Natl. Archives. 750 l, Statue, Natl. Roman Museum. 850 l, Medallion, Natl. Archives.

1994, June 16
1991 A991 600 l multicolored .70 .35
1992 A991 600 l multicolored .70 .35
1993 A991 750 l multicolored .90 .45
1994 A991 850 l multicolored 1.00 .50
Nos. 1991-1994 (4) 3.30 1.65

Intl. Olympic Committee, Cent. — A992

1994, June 23
1995 A992 850 l multicolored 1.10 .55

G-7 Summit, Naples — A993

1994, July 8
1996 A993 600 l multicolored .85 .40

A 750 l in this this design was printed but not issued.

A995

A996

1994, Sept. 8 Photo. ***Perf. 14***
1998 A995 500 l multicolored .80 .40

Basilica of Loreto, 500th anniv.

1994, Sept. 19
1999 A996 750 l multicolored 1.00 .50

Frederick II (1194-1250), Holy Roman Emperor.

Stamp Day — A998

Designs: 600 l, Pietro Miliani (1744-1817), paper manufacturer. 750 l, Convent of San Domenico.

1994, Sept. 16 Photo. ***Perf. 13½x14***
2001 A998 600 l multicolored .80 .40
2002 A998 750 l multicolored .95 .45

Basilica of St. Mark, 900th Anniv. A999

1994, Oct. 8 Photo. ***Perf. 13½x13***
2003 A999 750 l multicolored 1.10 .55
a. Souvenir sheet of 2, tete beche 2.25 2.25

No. 2003 printed with se-tenant label. No. 2003a contains one each No. 2003 and San Marino No. 1314. Only No. 2003 was valid for postage in Italy. See San Marino No. 1314.

Christmas A1000

600 l, The Annunciation, by Melozzo da Forli. 750 l, Madonna and Child, by Lattanzio da Rimini.

1994, Nov. 5 Photo. ***Perf. 13½x14***
2004 A1000 600 l multicolored .80 .40
2005 A1000 750 l multicolored 1.00 .50

Italian Touring Club, Cent. — A1001

1994, Nov. 8
2006 A1001 600 l multicolored .85 .40

CREDIOP, 75th Anniv. — A1002

1994, Nov. 11
2007 A1002 750 l multicolored 1.10 .55

Giovanni Gentile (1875-1944), Philosopher A1003

1994, Nov. 21
2008 A1003 750 l multicolored 1.00 .50

Querini Dubois Palace, Venice — A1004

1994 ***Perf. 13½x14***
2009 A1004 600 l red & silver .90 .45

New Italian Postal Emblem A1005

1994 ***Perf. 14x13½***
2010 A1005 750 l red, black & green 1.10 .55
2011 A1005 750 l red brown 1.10 .55
a. Pair, #2010-2011 2.25 1.10

See Nos. 2059-2060.

World Speed Skating Championships — A1006

1995, Feb. 6 Photo. ***Perf. 14x13½***
2012 A1006 750 l multicolored 1.00 .50

Achille Beltrame (1871-1945) A1007

Design: 500 l, Cover of first issue of LA DOMENICA DEL CORRIERE.

1995, Feb. 18 Photo. ***Perf. 13½x14***
2013 A1007 500 l multicolored .75 .35

Italian Food — A1008

1995, Mar. 4
2014 A1008 500 l Rice .65 .30
2015 A1008 750 l Olives, olive oil .95 .45

See Nos. 2068-2069.

Birds A1009

1995, Mar. 11 Photo. ***Perf. 14x13½***
2016 A1009 600 l Heron .75 .35
2017 A1009 600 l Vulture .75 .35
2018 A1009 600 l Royal eagle .75 .35
2019 A1009 600 l Alpine chaffinch .75 .35
Nos. 2016-2019 (4) 3.00 1.40

UN, 50th Anniv. A1010

1995, Mar. 24 Photo. ***Perf. 14x13½***
2020 A1010 850 l multicolored 1.10 .55

Fifth Day of Milan War Memorial, by Giuseppe Grandi, Cent. A1011

1995, Mar. 25 Photo. ***Perf. 14x13½***
2021 A1011 750 l gold, black & blue .95 .45

Miniature Sheet

End of World War II, 50th Anniv. — A1012

Designs: a, Mafalda de Savoy, concentration camp, barbed wire. b, Allied DUKW, Battles of Anzio and Nettuno. c, Women in World War II, Teresa Gullace. d, Gold Medal of Valor, Palazzo Vecchio, Florence. e, Gold Medal of Valor, building, Vittorio Veneto. f, Gold Medal of Valor, Cathedral, Cagliari. g. Mountain Battalion. h, Air dropping supplies, Balkans. i, Atlantic fleet.

1995, Mar. 31 Photo. *Perf. 14x13½*
2022 A1012 750 l Sheet of 9, #a.-i. 8.00 4.00

Natl. Treasures A1013

Designs: No. 2023, Illuminated manuscript with "P," State Archives, Rome. No. 2024, Painting of Port of Naples, by Tavola Strozzi, Natl. Museum of San Martino, horiz. No. 2025, Illuminated manuscript with "I," Christ, State Archives, Mantua. No. 2026, Painting, Sacred and Profane Love, by Titian, Borghese Gallery and Museum, Rome, horiz.

Perf. 13½x14, 14x13½
1995, Apr. 28 Photo.
2023 A1013 500 l multicolored .55 .25
2024 A1013 500 l multicolored .55 .25
2025 A1013 750 l multicolored .90 .45
2026 A1013 850 l multicolored 1.00 .50
Nos. 2023-2026 (4) 3.00 1.45

Venice Biennial, Cent. — A1014

1995, Apr. 29 *Perf. 13½x14*
2027 A1014 750 l multicolored .95 .45

Basilica of Santa Croce, Florence A1015

1995, May 3 Engr.
2028 A1015 750 l deep brn blk .95 .45

Peace & Freedom A1016

Europa: 750 l, Family, liberating soldiers, Italian flag. 850 l, Stars of European flag, church, mosque.

1995, May 5 Photo. *Perf. 13½x14*
2029 A1016 750 l multicolored 1.00 .50
2030 A1016 850 l multicolored 1.10 .55

Volleyball, Cent. — A1017

1995, May 8
2031 A1017 750 l multicolored 1.00 .50

Tourism Type of 1993

1995, May 12 Photo. *Perf. 14x13½*
2032 A965 750 l Nuoro .90 .45
2033 A965 750 l Susa .90 .45
2034 A965 750 l Alatri .90 .45
2035 A965 750 l Venosa .90 .45
Nos. 2032-2035 (4) 3.60 1.80

Discovery of the X-Ray, Cent. A1018

1995, June 2
2036 A1018 750 l multicolored .95 .45

1994-95 Natl. Soccer Championship Team, Juventus A1019

1995, June 5 *Perf. 13½x14*
2037 A1019 750 l multicolored 1.00 .50

Radio, Cent. A1020

Designs: 750 l, Griffone House. 850 l, Guglielmo Marconi, transmitting equipment.

1995, June 8 *Perf. 14x13½*
2038 A1020 750 multicolored .90 .45

Perf. 14
2039 A1020 850 l multicolored 1.00 .50

No. 2039 is 36x21mm. See Germany No. 1900, Ireland No. 974a, San Marino Nos. 1336-1337, Vatican City Nos. 978-979.

A1021

St. Anthony of Padua (1195-1231) — A1022

Perf. 13½x14, 14x13½
1995, June 13
2040 A1021 750 l multicolored .90 .45
2041 A1022 850 l multicolored 1.00 .50

See Portugal Nos. 2054-2057.

Historical Public Gardens A1023

Designs: No. 2042, Durazzo Pallavicini, Pegli. No. 2043, Boboli, Firenze. No. 2044, Ninfa, Cisterna di Latina. No. 2045, Royal Park, Caserta.

Litho. & Engr.
1995, June 24 *Perf. 14x13½*
2042 A1023 750 l multicolored .90 .45
2043 A1023 750 l multicolored .90 .45
2044 A1023 750 l multicolored .90 .45
2045 A1023 750 l multicolored .90 .45
Nos. 2042-2045 (4) 3.60 1.80

Congress of European Society of Ophthalmology A1024

1995, June 24 Litho. *Perf. 13½x14*
2046 A1024 750 l multicolored .95 .45

The Sailors' Wives, by Massimo Campigli (1895-1971) — A1025

1995, July 4 Photo. *Perf. 14*
2047 A1025 750 l multicolored 1.10 .55

14th World Conference on Relativity, Florence A1026

1995, Aug. 7 Litho. *Perf. 14x13*
2048 A1026 750 l Galileo, Einstein 1.00 .50

Motion Pictures, Cent. — A1027

#2049, Son of the Shiek, Rudolph Valentino. #2050, L'oro Di Napoli, Toto. #2051, Le Notti Di Cabiria, F. Fellini. #2052, Cinecitta '95.

Litho. & Engr.
1995, Aug. 29 *Perf. 13½x14*
2049 A1027 750 l multicolored .90 .45
2050 A1027 750 l multicolored .90 .45
2051 A1027 750 l multicolored .90 .45
2052 A1027 750 l multicolored .90 .45
Nos. 2049-2052 (4) 3.60 1.80

See #2099-2101, 2170-2172, 2269-2271.

FAO, 50th Anniv. A1028

1995, Sept. 1 Photo. *Perf. 14x13½*
2053 A1028 850 l multicolored 1.10 .55

Basilica of Pontida & Death of St. Albert of Prezzate, 900th Anniv. A1029

1995, Sept. 2 Engr.
2054 A1029 1000 l blue & brown 1.25 .60

ROMA '95, First World Military Games — A1030

1995, Sept. 6 Photo. *Perf. 13½x14*
2055 A1030 850 l multicolored 1.10 .55

Italian News Agency (ANSA), 50th Anniv. A1031

1995, Oct. 27 Photo. *Perf. 14x13½*
2056 A1031 750 l multicolored 1.00 .50

Christmas A1032

Designs: 750 l, Nativity figurines, Cathedral of Polignano a Mare, by Stefano da Putignano. 850 l, Adoration of the Magi, by Fra Angelico.

1995, Nov. 18
2057 A1032 750 l multicolored 1.10 .55
2058 A1032 850 l multicolored 1.25 .65

New Italian Postal Emblem Type of 1994

1995, Dec. 9 Photo. *Perf. 13½x14*
Size: 26x18mm
2059 A1005 750 l like No. 2011 1.00 .50
a. Booklet pane of 8 8.00
Complete booklet, #2059a 8.00
2060 A1005 850 l like No. 2010 1.00 .50
a. Booklet pane of 8 8.00
Complete booklet, #2060a 8.00

Renato Mondolfo A1033

1995, Dec. 9 Photo. ***Perf. 14x13½***
2061 A1033 750 l multicolored .95 .45

Philately Day.

F.T. Marinetti (1876-1944), Science Fiction Writer — A1034

1996, Jan. 19 Photo. ***Perf. 14***
2062 A1034 750 l multicolored 1.10 .55

Collections from Natl. Museum and Archives A1035

#2063, Arms of the Academy of Georgofili, Florence. #2064, Illuminated manuscript from Lucca (1372), vert. #2065, Manuscript of Gabriele D'Annunzio (1863-1938), author, soldier, political leader. #2066, French miniature, c. 1486.

1996, Feb. 26 ***Perf. 14x13½, 13½x14***
2063 A1035 750 l multicolored 1.10 .55
2064 A1035 750 l multicolored 1.10 .55
2065 A1035 850 l multicolored 1.25 .65
2066 A1035 850 l multicolored 1.25 .65
Nos. 2063-2066 (4) 4.70 2.40

Sarah and the Angel, by Tiepolo (1696-1770) — A1036

1996, Mar. 5 ***Perf. 14***
2067 A1036 1000 l multicolored 1.40 .70

Italian Food Type of 1995

1996, Mar. 20 ***Perf. 13½x14***
2068 A1008 500 l White wine, grapes .75 .40
2069 A1008 750 l Red wine, grapes 1.10 .55

CHINA '96, 9th Asian Intl. Philatelic Exhibition A1037

1996, Mar. 22 ***Perf. 14x13½***
2070 A1037 1250 l multicolored 1.75 .90

Marco Polo's return from China, 700th anniv. (in 1995).

See San Marino No. 1350.

Cathedral of Milan — A1038

No. 2071, Front entrance. No. 2072, Corner, side view.

1996, Mar. 23 ***Perf. 13½x14***
2071 A1038 750 l multicolored 1.10 .55
2072 A1038 750 l multicolored 1.10 .55
a. Pair, #2071-2072 2.20 1.10
b. Booklet pane, 4 #2072a 10.00
Complete booklet, #2072b 10.00

No. 2072a is a continuous design.
ITALIA '98, Intl. Philatelic Exhibition, Milan.

A1039

1996, Apr. 3 ***Perf. 13½x14, 14x13½***
2073 A1039 750 l shown 1.10 .55
2074 A1039 750 l Globe, "100" 1.10 .55

Natl. Press Federation, 50th anniv. (#2073). "La Gazzetta dello Sport," cent. (#2074), horiz.

Intl. Museum of Postal Images, Belvedere Ostrense A1040

1996, Apr. 13 Photo. ***Perf. 13½x14***
2075 A1040 500 l multicolored .75 .40

Academy of Finance Police, Cent. — A1040a

1996, Apr. 13
2076 A1040a 750 l multicolored 1.10 .55

RAMOGE Agreement Between France, Italy, Monaco, 20th Anniv. A1041

Photo. & Engr.

1996, May 14 ***Perf. 14x13½***
2077 A1041 750 l multicolored 1.00 .50

See France No. 2524, Monaco No. 1998.

Rome-New York Trans-Continental Drive — A1042

1996, Apr. 13 Photo. ***Perf. 13½x14***
2078 A1042 4650 l multicolored 7.00 3.50

Europa (Famous Women) A1043

750 l, Carina Negrone, pilot. 850 l, Adelaide Ristori, actress.

1996, Apr. 29 Photo. ***Perf. 13½x14***
2079 A1043 750 l multicolored 1.10 .55
2080 A1043 850 l multicolored 1.25 .65

St. Celestine V (1215-96) A1044

Litho. & Engr.

1996, May 18 ***Perf. 14x13½***
2081 A1044 750 l multicolored 1.10 .55

Tourism A1045

#2082, Pienza Cathedral. #2083, St. Anthony's Church, Diano Marina. #2084, Belltower of Church of St. Michael the Archangel, Monte Sant'Angelo. #2085, Prehistoric stone dwelling, Lampedusa.

1996, May 18 Photo. ***Perf. 14x13½***
2082 A1045 750 l multicolored 1.10 .55
2083 A1045 750 l multicolored 1.10 .55
2084 A1045 750 l multicolored 1.10 .55
2085 A1045 750 l multicolored 1.10 .55
Nos. 2082-2085 (4) 4.40 2.20

Consecration of Reconstructed Farfa Abbey, 500th Anniv. — A1046

1996, May 18 Photo. ***Perf. 13½x14***
2086 A1046 1000 l multicolored 1.40 .70

Mediterranean Fair, Palermo — A1047

1996, May 25 ***Perf. 14x13½***
2087 A1047 750 l multicolored 1.10 .55

Italian Republic, 50th Anniv. — A1048

1996, June 1 ***Perf. 13½x14***
2088 A1048 750 l multicolored 1.10 .55

Production of Vespa Motor Scooters, 50th Anniv. — A1049

1996, June 20
2089 A1049 750 l multicolored 1.10 .55

First Meeting of European Economic Community, Messina and Venice, 40th Anniv. — A1050

1996, June 21 ***Perf. 14***
2090 A1050 750 l multicolored 1.10 .55

Modern Olympic Games, Cent. A1051

Designs: 500 l, Runners, 1896. 750 l, Discus, Atlanta skyline, vert. 850 l, Gymnast on rings, basketball, Atlanta stadium. 1250 l, 1896 stadium, Athens, 1996 stadium, Atlanta, vert.

Perf. 14x13½, 13½x14

1996, July 1 Photo.
2091 A1051 500 l multicolored .75 .40
2092 A1051 750 l multicolored 1.10 .55
2093 A1051 850 l multicolored 1.25 .65
2094 A1051 1250 l multicolored 1.90 .95
Nos. 2091-2094 (4) 5.00 2.55

Butterflies A1052

#2095, Melanargia arge. #2096, Papilio hospiton. #2097, Zygaena rubicundus. #2098, Acanthobrahmaea europaea.

1996, Aug. 26 ***Perf. 14x13½***
2095 A1052 750 l multicolored 1.10 .55
2096 A1052 750 l multicolored 1.10 .55
2097 A1052 750 l multicolored 1.10 .55
2098 A1052 750 l multicolored 1.10 .55
Nos. 2095-2098 (4) 4.40 2.20

Motion Picture Type of 1995

#2099, Massimo Troisi in "Scusate Il Ritardo." #2100, Aldo Fabrizi in "Prima Comunione." #2101, Bartolomeo Pagano as Maciste in "Cabiria."

Photo. & Engr.

1996, Aug. 30 ***Perf. 13½x14***
2099 A1027 750 l multicolored 1.10 .55
2100 A1027 750 l multicolored 1.10 .55
2101 A1027 750 l multicolored 1.10 .55
Nos. 2099-2101 (3) 3.30 1.65

A1054

1996, Sept. 7 Photo. ***Perf. 13½x14***
2102 A1054 750 l multicolored 1.10 .55

Milan, 1995-96 national soccer champions.

The Duomo, Cathedral of Santa Maria del Fiore, Florence, 700th Anniv. A1055

1996, Sept. 7 Engr. ***Perf. 14x13½***
2103 A1055 750 l dark blue 1.10 .55

13th Intl. Congress of Prehistoric Science — A1056

1996, Sept. 9 Photo. ***Perf. 13½x14***
2104 A1056 850 l multicolored 1.25 .65

Levant Fair, Bari A1057

1996, Sept. 13 Photo. ***Perf. 14x13½***
2105 A1057 750 l multicolored 1.10 .55

1997 Mediterranean Games, Bari — A1058

1996, Sept. 13 ***Perf. 13½x14***
2106 A1058 750 l multicolored 1.10 .55

Juventus, 1995-96 European Soccer Champions A1059

1996, Sept. 14
2107 A1059 750 l multicolored 1.10 .55

Alessandro Pertini (1896-1990), Former President A1060

1996, Sept. 25 Photo. ***Perf. 13½x14***
2108 A1060 750 l multicolored 1.10 .55

Eugenio Montale (1896-1981), Poet — A1061

1996, Oct. 12 Litho. & Engr.
2109 A1061 750 l blue & brown 1.10 .55

Annunciation, by Pietro da Cortona (1596-1669) A1062

1996, Oct. 31 Photo.
2110 A1062 500 l multicolored .75 .35

Invitation to Philately A1063

Designs: 750 l, Tex Willer, western scene. 850 l, Seagulls, gondola, city, Corto Maltese.

Litho. & Engr.

1996, Oct. 31 ***Perf. 14x13½***
2111 A1063 750 l multicolored 1.10 .55
2112 A1063 850 l multicolored 1.25 .65

Stamp Day — A1064

1996, Nov. 8 Photo. ***Perf. 13½x14***
2113 A1064 750 l multicolored .90 .45

Universities of Italy — A1065

Perf. 13½x14, 14x13½

1996, Nov. 9 Engr.

Designs: No. 2114, Agrarian School, cent., University of Perugia. No. 2115, University of Sassari (1562-1996), horiz. No. 2116, University of Salerno

2114 A1065 750 l brown .90 .45
2115 A1065 750 l green .90 .45
2116 A1065 750 l blue .90 .45
Nos. 2114-2116 (3) 2.70 1.35

World Food Day — A1066

1996, Nov. 13 Photo. ***Perf. 14x13½***
2117 A1066 850 l green & black 1.00 .50

Christmas A1067

Designs: 750 l, Madonna and Child, by Pisanello. 850 l, Santa, toys, horiz.

Perf. 13½x14, 14x13½

1996, Nov. 15
2118 A1067 750 l multicolored .90 .45
2119 A1067 850 l multicolored 1.00 .50

UNESCO, 50th Anniv. — A1068

850 l, Baby, globe, emblem.

1996, Nov. 20 ***Perf. 13½x14***
2120 A1068 750 l multicolored .90 .45
2121 A1068 850 l multicolored 1.00 .50

Natl. Institute of Statistics, 70th Anniv. — A1069

1996, Nov. 26
2122 A1069 750 l multicolored .90 .45

First Edition of "Strega," 50th Anniv. — A1070

1996, Nov. 29
2123 A1070 3400 l multicolored 4.00 2.00

First Natl. Flag, Bicent. — A1071

1997, Jan. 7 Photo. ***Perf. 13½x14***
2124 A1071 750 l multicolored 1.00 .50

Sestrieres '97, World Alpine Skiing Championships A1072

1997, Feb. 1 Photo. ***Perf. 13½x14***
2125 A1072 750 l shown 1.00 .50
2126 A1072 850 l Ski of colors 1.10 .60

Galileo Ferraris (1847-97), Physicist, Electrical Engineer A1073

1997, Feb. 7 ***Perf. 14x13½***
2127 A1073 750 l multicolored 1.00 .50

Emanuela Loi (1967-92),Police Woman Killed by Mafia — A1074

1997, Mar. 8
2128 A1074 750 l multicolored 1.00 .50

Italia '98, World Philatelic Exhibition, Milan — A1075

Designs: a, Airmail philately. b, Topical philately. c, Postal history. d, Philatelic literature.

1997, Mar. 21 Litho. ***Perf. 13½x14***
2129 Sheet of 4 4.00 2.00
a.-d. A1075 750 l any single 1.00 .50

Statue of Marcus Aurelius (121-180), Roman Emperor A1076

1997, Mar. 25 **Photo.**
2130 A1076 750 l multicolored 1.00 .50

Treaty of Rome, 40th anniv.

St. Ambrose (339-397), Bishop of Milan — A1077

Litho. & Engr.

1997, Apr. 4 ***Perf. 14***
2131 A1077 1000 l multicolored 1.25 .65

St. Geminian, 1600th Death Anniv. — A1078

1997, Apr. 4 Photo. ***Perf. 13½x14***
2132 A1078 750 l multicolored 1.00 .50

University of Rome A1079

Design: No. 2134, University of Padua.

1997, Apr. 14 Engr. ***Perf. 14x13½***
2133 A1079 750 l claret 1.00 .50
2134 A1079 750 l blue 1.00 .50

Founding of Rome, 2750th Anniv. A1080

1997, Apr. 21 Photo. ***Perf. 14x13½***
2135 A1080 850 l multicolored 1.10 .55

Timoleontee Wall, Gela — A1081

1997, Apr. 24
2136 A1081 750 l multicolored 1.00 .50

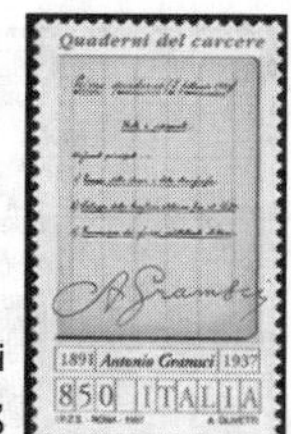

Antonio Gramsci (1891-1937), Politician — A1082

1997, Apr. 26 Photo. ***Perf. 14***
2137 A1082 850 l multicolored 1.25 .65

Monastery Church, Pavia, 500th Anniv. — A1083

1997, May 3 ***Perf. 13½x14***
2138 A1083 1000 l multicolored 1.40 .70

Stories and Legends A1084

Europa: 800 l, Cobbler's workshop. 900 l, Street singer, vert.

Perf. 14x13, 13x14

1997, May 5 **Photo.**
2139 A1084 800 l multicolored 1.00 .50
2140 A1084 900 l multicolored 1.25 .60

Massimo Theatre, Palermo, Cent. — A1085

1997, May 16 Photo. ***Perf. 13½x14***
2141 A1085 800 l multicolored 1.10 .55

Tourism A1086

Designs: No. 2142, St. Vitalian Basilica, Ravenna. No. 2143, Tomb of Marcus Tullius Cicero (106-43BC), Formia. No. 2144, College of Assumption of the Holy Mary, Positano. No. 2145, St. Sebastian Church, Acireale.

1997, May 17 Photo. ***Perf. 14x13***
2142 A1086 800 l multicolored 1.10 .55
2143 A1086 800 l multicolored 1.10 .55
2144 A1086 800 l multicolored 1.10 .55
2145 A1086 800 l multicolored 1.10 .55
Nos. 2142-2145 (4) 4.40 2.20

Book Fair, Turin — A1087

1997, May 22 ***Perf. 13½x14***
2146 A1087 800 l multicolored 1.10 .55

Queen Paola of Belgium, 60th Birthday A1088

1997, May 23 Photo. ***Perf. 14x13½***
2147 A1088 750 l San Angelo Castle 1.10 .55

See Belgium No. 1652.

Rome Fair A1089

1997, May 24 Photo. ***Perf. 14x13½***
2148 A1089 800 l multicolored 1.10 .55

Cathedral of Orvieto — A1090

1997, May 31 Engr. ***Perf. 13x14***
2149 A1090 450 l deep violet .60 .30

Fr. Giuseppe Morosini (1913-44) A1091

1997, June 4 **Photo.**
2150 A1091 800 l multicolored 1.00 .50

Bologna Fair A1092

1997, June 7 ***Perf. 14x13***
2151 A1092 800 l multicolored 1.00 .50

Juventus, 1996-97 Italian Soccer Champions A1093

1997, June 7 ***Perf. 13½x14***
2152 A1093 800 l multicolored 1.10 .55

Abruzzo Natl. Park, 75th Anniv. — A1094

1997, June 7 Photo. ***Perf. 13½x14***
2153 A1094 800 l multicolored 1.00 .50

Italian Naval League, Cent. — A1095

1997, June 10 Photo. ***Perf. 13½x14***
2154 A1095 800 l multicolored 1.10 .55

13th Mediterranean Games, Bari — A1096

1997, June 13 ***Perf. 14x13½***
2155 A1096 900 l multicolored 1.25 .60

Public Gardens A1097

Designs: No. 2156, Miramare-Trieste Park. No. 2157, Cavour-Santena. No. 2158, Villa Sciarra, Rome. No. 2159, Orto Botanical Gardens, Palermo.

Photo. & Engr.

1997, June 14 ***Perf. 14x13½***
2156 A1097 800 l multicolored 1.00 .50
2157 A1097 800 l multicolored 1.00 .50
2158 A1097 800 l multicolored 1.00 .50
2159 A1097 800 l multicolored 1.00 .50
Nos. 2156-2159 (4) 4.00 2.00

Italian Labor Force — A1098

Perf. 13½x14, 14x13½

1997, June 20

2160 A1098 800 l Industry 1.00 .50
2161 A1098 900 l Agriculture, horiz. 1.10 .60

John Cabot's Voyage to Canada, 500th Anniv. A1099

1997, June 24 Litho. *Perf. 14*

2162 A1099 1300 l multicolored 1.75 .85

See Canada No. 1649.

Pietro Verri (1728-97), Economist, Journalist A1100

1997, June 28 *Perf. 13½x14*

2163 A1100 3600 l multicolored 4.75 2.25

Madonna of the Rosary by Pomarancio il Vecchio (Niccolo Cercignani)(d. 1597) — A1101

650 l, The Miracle of Ostia, by Paolo de Dono Uccello (1397-1475).

1997, July 19 Photo. *Perf. 13½x14*

2164 A1101 450 l multicolored .65 .35

Size: 26x37mm

2165 A1101 650 l multicolored .95 .45

Varia di Palmi Festival — A1102

1997, Aug. 2 *Perf. 13½x14*

2166 A1102 800 l multicolored 1.25 .60

Universiade 97, Sicily A1103

1997, Aug. 19 Photo. *Perf. 14x13½*

2167 A1103 450 l Basketball .60 .30
2168 A1103 800 l High jump 1.10 .55

Antonio Rosmini (1797-1855), Priest, Philosopher — A1104

1997, Aug. 26

2169 A1104 800 l multicolored 1.10 .55

Motion Picture Type of 1995

#2170, Pietro Germi in "The Railway Man." #2171, Anna Magnani in "Mamma Roma." #2172, Ugo Tognazzi in "My Dear Friends."

Photo. & Engr.

1997, Aug. 27 *Perf. 13½x14*

2170 A1027 800 l multicolored 1.10 .55
2171 A1027 800 l multicolored 1.10 .55
2172 A1027 800 l multicolored 1.10 .55
Nos. 2170-2172 (3) 3.30 1.65

Viareggio Literary Prize A1106

1997, Aug. 30 Photo. *Perf. 14x13½*

2173 A1106 4000 l multicolored 5.50 2.75

Intl. Fair, Bolzano A1107

1997, Sept. 1

2174 A1107 800 l multicolored 1.10 .55

A1108

Artifacts and Paintings from Natl. Museums and Galleries: 450 l, Bronze head, 500BC, National Museum, Reggio Calabria. 650 l, Madonna and Child with Two Vases of Roses, by Ercole di Roberti, Natl. Picture Gallery, Ferrara. 800 l, Miniature of troubadour, Sordello da Goito, Arco Palace Museum, Manta. 900 l, St. George and the Dragon, Vitale da Bologna, Natl. Picture Gallery, Bologna.

1997, Sept. 13 Photo. *Perf. 13½x14*

2175 A1108 450 l multicolored .60 .30
2176 A1108 650 l multicolored .85 .40
2177 A1108 800 l multicolored 1.00 .50
2178 A1108 900 l multicolored 1.25 .60
Nos. 2175-2178 (4) 3.70 1.80

Pope Paul VI (1897-1978) A1109

1997, Sept. 26 Engr. *Perf. 13x14*

2179 A1109 4000 l dark blue 5.25 2.50

Milan Fair A1110

1997, Sept. 30 Photo. *Perf. 14x13*

2180 A1110 800 l multicolored 1.00 .50

Marshall Plan, 50th Anniv. — A1111

1997, Oct. 17

2181 A1111 800 l multicolored 1.00 .50

Christmas A1112

Nativity scenes: 800 l, Molded polychrome, from Church of St. Francis, Leonessa. 900 l, Fresco, from Baglioni Chapel, St. Mother Mary Church, Spello.

1997, Oct. 18

2183 A1112 800 l multicolored 1.00 .50
2184 A1112 900 l multicolored 1.25 .60

Aristide Merloni (1897-1970) A1113

1997, Oct. 24 *Perf. 13x14*

2185 A1113 800 l multicolored 1.00 .50

Giovanni Battista Cavalcaselle (1819-97), Art Historian A1114

Litho. & Engr.

1997, Oct. 31 *Perf. 13½x14*

2186 A1114 800 l multicolored 1.10 .55

Philately Day — A1115

1997, Dec. 5 Photo.

2187 A1115 800 l multicolored 1.10 .55

Emigration of Italian Population of Dalmatia, Istria & Fiume, 50th Anniv. A1116

1997, Dec. 6 *Perf. 14x13½*

2188 A1116 800 l multicolored 1.10 .55

State Highway Police, 50th Anniv. A1117

1997, Dec. 12

2189 A1117 800 l multicolored 1.10 .55

Constitution, 50th Anniv. — A1118

1998, Jan. 2 Photo. *Perf. 13½x14*

2190 A1118 800 l multicolored 1.10 .55

Hercules and the Hydra, by Antonio Del Pollaiolo (1429-98) A1119

1998, Jan. 3 *Perf. 14*

2191 A1119 800 l multicolored 1.10 .55

See Nos. 2278, 2319.

Famous Writers A1120

450 l, Bertolt Brecht (1898-1956), playwright. 650 l, Federico Garcia Lorca (1898-1936), poet, dramatist. 800 l, Curzio Malaparte (Kurt Suckert) (1898-1957), journalist, writer. 900 l, Leonida Repaci (1898-1985), writer.

1998, Feb. 2 *Perf. 14x13½*

2192 A1120 450 l multi .60 .30
2193 A1120 650 l multi .90 .45
2194 A1120 800 l multi 1.10 .55
2195 A1120 900 l multi, vert. 1.20 .60
Nos. 2192-2195 (4) 3.80 1.90

Verona Fair, Cent. A1121

1998, Feb. 11 Photo. *Perf. 14x13½*

2196 A1121 800 l multicolored 1.10 .55

Jewish Emancipation, 150th Anniv. — A1122

1998, Mar. 28 ***Perf. 14***

2197 A1122 800 l multicolored 1.10 .55

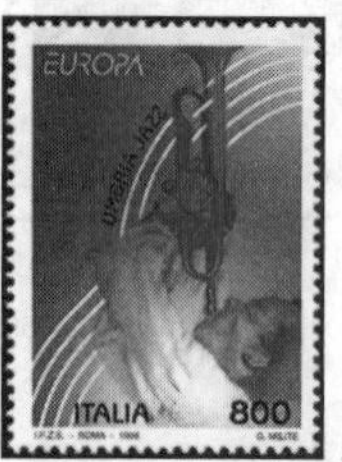

National Festivals A1123

1998, Apr. 3 Litho. ***Perf. 13½x14***

2198 A1123 800 l Umbria Jazz 1.10 .55
2199 A1123 900 l Giffoni Film 1.25 .65

Europa.

Completion of "The Last Supper," by Leonardo da Vinci (1452-1519), 500th Anniv. — A1124

1998, Apr. 4 Engr. ***Perf. 14x13½***

2200 A1124 800 l red brown 1.10 .55

Gaetano Donizetti (1797-1848), Composer — A1125

1998, Apr. 8 **Photo.**

2201 A1125 800 l multicolored 1.10 .55

Italian Opera, 400th Anniv. — A1126

1998, Apr. 8 ***Perf. 13½x14***

2202 A1126 800 l multicolored 1.10 .55

Cathedral of Turin, 500th anniv., and Shroud of Turin — A1127

1998, Apr. 18 Photo. ***Perf. 13½x14***

2203 A1127 800 l multicolored 1.10 .55

Tourism A1128

#2204, Castle, Otranto. #2205, Mori Fountain and Castle, Marino. #2206, Village and chapel, Livigno. #2207, Marciana Marina, Elba Island.

1998, Apr. 18 Litho. ***Perf. 14x13½***

2204 A1128 800 l multicolored 1.10 .55
2205 A1128 800 l multicolored 1.10 .55
2206 A1128 800 l multicolored 1.10 .55
2207 A1128 800 l multicolored 1.10 .55
Nos. 2204-2207 (4) 4.40 2.20

See Nos. 2283-2286.

Sardinia Intl. Fair A1129

1998, Apr. 23 Photo. ***Perf. 14x13½***

2208 A1129 800 l multicolored 1.10 .55

The Charge of Carabinieri at Pastrengo, by Sebastiano de Albertis (1828-97) A1130

1998, Apr. 30 ***Perf. 13½x14***

2209 A1130 800 l multicolored 1.10 .55

A1131

1998, May 11 Photo. ***Perf. 13½x14***

2210 A1131 800 l Padua Fair 1.00 .50

Juventus, 1997-98 Italian Soccer Champions A1132

1998, May 18

2211 A1132 800 l multicolored 1.00 .50

Polytechnical School, Turin — A1133

1998, May 18 Engr. ***Perf. 14x13½***

2212 A1133 800 l dark blue 1.00 .50

World Food Program — A1134

1998, May 22 **Photo.**

2213 A1134 900 l multicolored 1.25 .60

4th Intl. Convention on Fossils, Evolution, and Environment, Pergola — A1135

1998, May 30 Photo. ***Perf. 14x13½***

2214 A1135 800 l multicolored 1.00 .50

Carthusian Monastery of Santa Maria di Pesio, 825th Anniv. A1136

1998, May 30

2215 A1136 800 l multicolored 1.00 .50

A1137

1998, June 2 ***Perf. 13½x14***

2216 A1137 800 l multicolored 1.00 .50

Honoring the fallen of the Italian police corps.

6th World Congress of Endoscopic Surgery — A1138

1998, June 3

2217 A1138 900 l multicolored 1.25 .60

Italian Museums A1139

#2218, Regional Archeological Museum, Agrigento. #2219, Natl. Museum of the Risorgimento, Turin. #2220, Peggy Guggenheim Collection, Venier Dei Leoni Palace, Venice.

1998, June 6 ***Perf. 13½x14, 14x13½***

2218 A1139 800 l multi 1.00 .50
2219 A1139 800 l multi, horiz. 1.00 .50
2220 A1139 800 l multi, horiz. 1.00 .50
Nos. 2218-2220 (3) 3.00 1.50

A1140

1998, June 13 ***Perf. 13½x14***

2221 A1140 800 l Vicenza Fair 1.00 .50

Giacomo Leopardi (1798-1837), Poet — A1141

1998, June 29 Photo. ***Perf. 14x13½***

2222 A1141 800 l dark brn & sep 1.10 .55

Women in Art — A1142

Paintings: 100 l, "Young Velca," Etruscan tomb. 450 l, Detail from, "Herod's Feast," by Filippo Lippi. 650 l, Woman in profile, by Fra Benci. 800 l, "Lady with the Unicorn," by Raphael. 1000 l, sculpture of Constanza Buonarelli, by Gian Lorenzo Bernini.

1998, July 8 Photo. ***Perf. 14x13½***

2223 A1142 100 l blk & multi .20 .20
2224 A1142 450 l vio & multi .65 .30
2225 A1142 650 l gray grn & multi .90 .45

Engr.

Wmk. 303

2226 A1142 800 l red brn & multi 1.10 .55
2227 A1142 1000 l grn bl & multi 1.40 .70
Nos. 2223-2227 (5) 4.25 2.20

Denominated in Lira and Euros

1999, Jan. 28 Photo. ***Perf. 14x13½***

2228 A1142 100 l blk & multi .20 .20
2229 A1142 450 l vio & multi .55 .30
2230 A1142 650 l gray grn & multi .80 .40

Engr.

Wmk. 303

2231 A1142 800 l red brn & multi 1.00 .50
2232 A1142 1000 l grn bl & multi 1.25 .65
Nos. 2228-2232 (5) 3.80 2.05

33rd World Baseball Cup A1143

Perf. 14x13½

1998, July 21 Photo. Unwmk.
2251 A1143 900 l multicolored 1.25 .65

Columbus' Landing in Venezuela and Exploration of Amerigo Vespucci, 500th Anniv. A1144

1998, Aug. 12
2252 A1144 1300 l multicolored 1.75 .90

See Venezuela No. 1595.

Riccione Intl. Stamp Fair, 50th Anniv. — A1145

1998, Aug. 28 ***Perf. 13½x14***
2253 A1145 800 l multicolored 1.10 .55

Mother Teresa (1910-97) A1146

1998, Sept. 5 ***Perf. 14x13½, 13½x14***
2254 A1146 800 l shown 1.10 .55
2255 A1146 900 l Portrait, vert. 1.25 .65

See Albania Nos. 2578-2579.

Father Pio da Pietrelcina (1887-1968) — A1147

1998, Sept. 23 Engr. ***Perf. 14x13½***
2256 A1147 800 l deep blue 1.10 .55

1998 World Equestrian Championships, Rome — A1148

1998, Oct. 2 Photo. ***Perf. 14x13½***
2257 A1148 4000 l multicolored 5.50 2.75

School of Higher Education in Telecommunications, Rome — A1149

1998, Oct. 9 Engr. ***Perf. 14x13½***
2258 A1149 800 l deep blue 1.10 .55

Italia '98, Intl. Philatelic Exhibition — A1150

1998, Oct. 23 Photo. ***Perf. 14***
2259 A1150 800 l Pope John Paul II 1.00 .50

Armed Forces Day A1151

Emblem from branch of the military and: No. 2260, Aircraft carrier "Giuseppe Garibaldi," Navy. No. 2261, Eurofighter 2000, Air Force. No. 2262, Officer, Carabinieri (police force), vert. No. 2263, Italian monument, El Alamein battlefield, vert.

Perf. 14x13½, 13½x14

1998, Oct. 24 Photo.
2260 A1151 800 l multicolored 1.10 .55
2261 A1151 800 l multicolored 1.10 .55
2262 A1151 800 l multicolored 1.10 .55
2263 A1151 800 l multicolored 1.10 .55
Nos. 2260-2263 (4) 4.40 2.20

Nos. 2260-2263 were printed se-tenant with Italia '98 label. Air Force, 75th anniv. (#2261).

Art Day — A1152

1998, Oct. 25 ***Perf. 13½x14***
2264 A1152 800 l Dionysus 1.10 .55

Italia '98.

Enzo Ferrari (1898-1988) Automobile Manufacturer — A1153

a, 1931 Bobbio-Passo del Penice. b, 1952 Ferrari F1. c, 1963 Ferrari GTO. d, 1998 Ferrari F1.

1998, Oct. 26 Litho. ***Perf. 13½***
2265 A1153 800 l Sheet of 4, #a.-d. 4.25 2.10

Italia '98.

Universal Declaration of Human Rights, 50th Anniv. — A1154

1998, Oct. 27 Photo. ***Perf. 14x13½***
2266 A1154 1400 l multicolored 1.90 .95

Printed se-tenant with a label. Italia '98.

Europe Day — A1155

1998, Oct. 28 ***Perf. 13½x14***
2267 A1155 800 l multicolored 1.10 .55

Die Cut Perf. 11

Self-Adhesive

Booklet Stamp

2268 A1155 800 l multicolored 1.10 .55
a. Booklet pane of 6 6.75
Complete booklet, #2268a 6.75

Motion Picture Type of 1995

Motion pictures, stars: 450 l, "Ti Conosco Mascherina," Eduardo de Filippo. 800 l, "Fantasmi a Roma," Antonio Pietrangeli. 900 l, "Il Signor Max," Mario Camerini.

1998, Oct. 29 Litho. & Engr.
2269 A1027 450 l multicolored .65 .30
2270 A1027 800 l multicolored 1.10 .55
2271 A1027 900 l multicolored 1.25 .60
Nos. 2269-2271 (3) 3.00 1.45

Nos. 2269-2271 each printed se-tenant with label. Italia '98.

Communications Day — A1156

1998, Oct. 31 Photo.
2272 A1156 800 l multicolored 1.10 .55

Souvenir Sheet

Stamp Day — A1157

Illustration reduced.

1998, Nov. 1 Litho.
2273 A1157 4000 l multicolored 5.50 2.75

Italia '98.

Christmas A1158

800 l, Sculpture, "The Epiphany," Church of St. Mark, Seminara, vert. 900 l, Adoration of the shepherds, drawing by Giulio Romano.

Perf. 13½x14, 14x13½

1998, Nov. 28 Engr.
2274 A1158 800 l deep blue 1.00 .50
2275 A1158 900 l brown 1.25 .60

The Ecstasy of St. Teresa, Sculpture by Gian Lorenzo Bernini — A1159

1998, Dec. 1 Photo. ***Perf. 13½x14***
2276 A1159 900 l multicolored 1.25 .60

Emancipation of Valdesi, 150th Anniv. — A1160

1998, Dec. 4 ***Perf. 14***
2277 A1160 800 l multicolored 1.00 .50

Art Type of 1998

Conception of Space, by Lucio Fontana (1899-1968).

1999, Feb. 19 Photo. ***Perf. 14***
2278 A1119 450 l multicolored .55 .30

National Parks A1162

Europa: 800 l, Wolf, Calabria, vert. 900 l, Birds, Tuscan Archipelago.

Perf. 13¼x14, 14x13¼

1999, Mar. 12 Photo.
2279 A1162 800 l multicolored 1.00 .50
2280 A1162 900 l multicolored 1.10 .55

Holy Year 2000 — A1163

1999, Mar. 13 ***Perf. 13¼x13¾***
2281 A1163 1400 l Holy Door 1.75 .90

St. Egidio Church, Cellere A1164

1999, Apr. 10 Engr. ***Perf. 13¾x13½***
2282 A1164 800 l brown lake 1.00 .50

Tourism Type of 1998

#2283, Earthen pyramids, Segonzano. #2284, Waterfalls, river, Terni. #2285, Buildings, Lecce. #2286, Walls around Lipari.

1999, Apr. 17 Photo. *Perf. 14x13¼*

2283 A1128 800 l multicolored 1.00 .50
2284 A1128 800 l multicolored 1.00 .50
2285 A1128 800 l multicolored 1.00 .50
2286 A1128 800 l multicolored 1.00 .50
Nos. 2283-2286 (4) 4.00 2.00

Museums A1165

#2287, Swan on Lake, Casina della Civette, Rome. #2288, "Iulia Bela," International Ceramics Museaum, Faenza, vert. #2289, Bells, Marinelli Historic Bell Museum, Agnone.

Perf. 14x13¼, 13¼x14

1999, Apr. 17 Photo.

2287 A1165 800 l multicolored 1.00 .50
2288 A1165 800 l multicolored 1.00 .50
2289 A1165 800 l multicolored 1.00 .50
Nos. 2287-2289 (3) 3.00 1.50

Constitutional Court — A1166

Perf. 13¾x13¼

1999, Apr. 23 Photo.

2290 A1166 800 l multicolored 1.00 .50

Natl. Firefighting Service A1167

1999, Apr. 29

2291 A1167 800 l multicolored 1.00 .50

Military Academy of Modena — A1168

1999, May 3 Photo. *Perf. 13¼x14*

2292 A1168 800 l multicolored 1.00 .50

50th Anniv. of Death of Grande Torino Soccer Team in Airplane Crash A1169

1999, May 4 Photo. *Perf. 14x13¼*

2293 A1169 800 l Plane, team members 1.00 .50
2294 A1169 900 l Superga Basilica, names 1.00 .50

Council of Europe, 50th Anniv. A1170

1999, May 5 Photo. *Perf. 14x13¼*

2295 A1170 800 l multicolored 1.00 .50

Milan, 1998-99 Italian Soccer Champions A1171

1999, June 7 Photo. *Perf. 13¼x14*

2296 A1171 800 l multicolored 1.00 .50

Elections for European Parliament, 20th Anniv. A1172

1999, June 10 Photo. *Perf. 14x13¼*

2297 A1172 800 l multicolored 1.00 .50

Priority Mail A1173

Typo. & Silk-screened

1999, June 14 *Die Cut 11¼*

Self-Adhesive

2298 A1173 1200 l multicolored 1.50 .75
a. Bklt. pane of 4 + 4 etiquettes 6.00
Complete booklet, #2298a 6.00
b. Bklt. pane of 8, no etiquettes 12.00
Complete booklet, #2298b 12.00

No. 2298 was intended for Priority Mail service. Self-adhesive blue etiquettes to be used with each stamp on mail were provided on the sheets and in booklets of 4 stamps.

The backing paper from the sheet stamps is rouletted, while the backing paper in the booklets is not.

See No. 2324.

Fausto Coppi (1919-60), Cyclist A1174

1999, June 12 Photo. *Perf. 14x13¼*

2299 A1174 800 l multi .90 .45

Fiat Automobile Co., Cent. — A1175

1999, July 10 Photo. *Perf. 13¼x14*

2300 A1175 4800 l multi 6.00 3.00

Statue of Our Lady of the Snows, Mt. Rocciamelone, Cent. — A1176

1999, July 19

2301 A1176 800 l multi 1.00 .50

Eleonora de Fonseca Pimentel (1752-1799), Writer — A1177

1999, Aug. 20 *Perf. 14x13¼*

2302 A1177 800 l multi 1.00 .50

30th World Canoe Championships — A1178

1999, Aug. 26

2303 A1178 900 l multi 1.10 .55

Johann Wolfgang von Goethe (1749-1832), German Poet — A1179

1999, Aug. 28

2304 A1179 4000 l multi 4.75 2.40

World Cycling Championships A1180

1999, Sept. 15 Photo. *Perf. 13¼x14*

2305 A1180 1400 l multi 1.60 .80

Stamp Day — A1181

1999, Sept. 25 Photo. *Perf. 13¼x14*

2306 A1181 800 l multi .90 .45

Basilica of St. Francis, Assisi — A1182

Litho. & Engr.

1999, Sept. 25 *Perf. 14x13¼*

2307 A1182 800 l multi .90 .45

Giuseppe Parini (1729-99), Poet — A1183

1999, Oct. 2 Engr. *Perf. 13¼x14*

2308 A1183 800 l blue gray .90 .45

Alessandro Volta's Pile, Bicent. — A1184

1999, Oct. 11 Photo.

2309 A1184 3000 l multi 3.50 1.75

UPU, 125th Anniv. A1185

1999, Oct. 18 *Perf. 14x13¼*

2310 A1185 900 l multi 1.00 .50

Goffredo Mameli (1827-49), Lyricist of Natl. Anthem, Nos. 506, 518 — A1186

1999, Oct. 22 *Perf. 14*

2311 A1186 1500 l multi 1.75 .85

"Stamps, Our Friends" — A1187

Various abstract designs: a, 450 l. b, 650 l. c, 800 l. d, 1000 l.

1999, Oct. 23 *Perf. 13¼x14*

2312 A1187 Sheet of 4, #a.-d. 3.25 1.60

A1188

1999, Nov. 4

2313 A1188 900 l 1899 Military Conscript 1.00 .50

Christmas
A1189

Designs: 800 l, Santa Claus, reindeer and sleigh. 1000 l, Nativity, By Dosso Dossi.

1999, Nov. 5 **Photo.**

2314 A1189 800 l multi .90 .45
2315 A1189 1000 l multi 1.10 .55

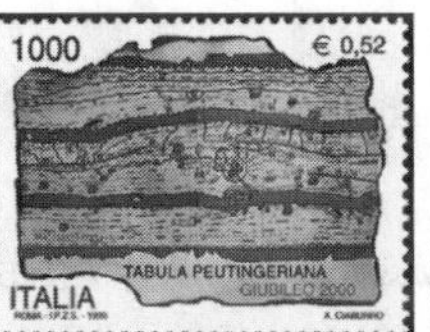

Holy Year
2000
A1190

#2316, Map by Conrad Peutinger, 1507. #2317, 18th cent. print of pilgrims in Rome. #2318, Bas-relief, facade of Fidenza Duomo.

1999, Nov. 24 Photo. *Perf. 14x13¼*

2316 A1190 1000 l multi 1.10 .55
2317 A1190 1000 l multi 1.10 .55
2318 A1190 1000 l multi 1.10 .55
Nos. 2316-2318 (3) 3.30 1.65

Art Type of 1998

Design: Restless Leopard, by Antonio Ligabue (1899-1965), horiz.

1999, Nov. 27 Photo. *Perf. 14*

2319 A1119 1000 l multi 1.10 .55

Schools
A1191

Designs: 450 l, State Institute of Art, Urbino. 650 l, Normal Superior School, Pisa.

1999, Nov. 27 Engr. *Perf. 14x13¼*

2320 A1191 450 l black .50 .25
2321 A1191 650 l brown .75 .35

Year 2000
A1192

1999, Nov. 27 **Photo.**

2322 A1192 4800 l multi 5.50 2.75

Souvenir Sheet

Millennium — A1193

Designs: a, The past. b, The future.

2000, Jan. 1 Litho. *Perf. 14x13¼*

2323 A1193 Sheet of 2 4.50 2.25
a.-b. A1193 2000 l Any single 2.25 1.10

See #2330-2332, 2365.

Priority Mail Type of 1999 Redrawn With Yellow Rectangle at Center

Typo. & Silk-Screened

2000, Jan. 10 ***Die Cut 11¼***

Self-Adhesive

2324 A1173 1200 l multi 1.25 .65

No. 2324 was intended for Priority Mail service. A self-adhesive blue etiquette is adjacent to the stamp. See No. 2393 for similar stamp with Posta Prioritaria in lower case letters.

First Performance of Opera "Tosca," Cent. — A1194

Litho. & Engr.

2000, Jan. 14 ***Perf. 14x13¼***

2325 A1194 800 l multi .80 .40

Basilica of St. Paul — A1195

2000, Jan. 18 Photo. *Perf. 13¼x14*

2326 A1195 1000 l multi 1.00 .50

Holy Year 2000.

Six Nation Rugby Tournament — A1196

2000, Feb. 5 ***Perf. 14x13¼***

2327 A1196 800 l multi .80 .40

5th Symposium on Breast Diseases
A1197

2000, Feb. 12 ***Perf. 13¼x14***

2328 A1197 800 l shown .80 .40
2329 A1197 1000 l Woman holding rose 1.00 .50

Millennium Type of 2000

Souvenir Sheet

No. 2330: a, Art. b, Science.
No. 2331: a, Nature. b, The city.
No. 2332: a, Generations. b, Space.

2000 Litho. *Perf. 14x13¼*

2330 Sheet of 2 1.60 .80
a.-b. A1193 800 l Any single .80 .40
2331 Sheet of 2 1.75 .90
a.-b. A1193 800 l Any single .85 .45
2332 Sheet of 2 1.60 .80
a.-b. A1193 800 l Any single .80 .40

Issued: #2330, 3/4; #2331, 5/4; #2332, 7/4.

Skiing World Cup — A1198

2000, Mar. 7 Photo. *Perf. 13¼x14*

2333 A1198 4800 l multi 5.00 2.50

Souvenir Sheet

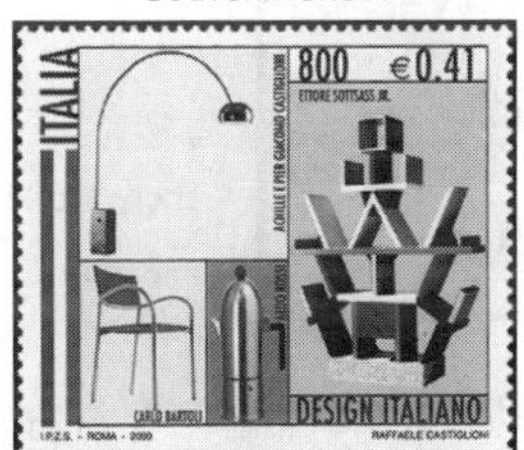

Italian Design — A1199

Household furnishings designed by:
a, Achille & Pier Giacomo Castiglioni, Ettore Sottsass, Jr. Carlo Bartoli, Aldo Rossi. b, Mario Bellini, Alessandro Mendini, Vico Magistretti, Alberto Meda & Paolo Rizzatto. c, Gio Ponti, Gatti Paolini Teodoro, Massimo Morozzi, Tobia Scarpa. d, Pietro Chiesa, Joe Colombo, Cini Boeri & Tomu Katayanagi, Lodovico Acerbis & Giotto Stoppino. e, Gaetano Pesce, Antonio Citterio & Oliver Loew, Enzo Mari, De Pas D'Urbino Lomazzi. f, Marco Zanuso, Anna Castelli Ferrieri, Michele de Lucchi & Giancarlo Fassina, Bruno Munari.

2000, Mar. 9 Litho. *Perf. 13¼*

2334 Sheet of 6 5.00 2.50
a.-f. A1199 800 l Any single .80 .40

Holy Year
2000
A1200

Paintings depicting the life of Jesus:
450 l, The Adoration of the Shepherds, by Ghirlandaio. 650 l, The Baptism and Temptation of Christ, by Veronese, vert. 800 l, The Last Supper, by Ghirlandaio, vert. 1000 l, Fresco from Episodes of the Life of the Virgin Mary and Christ, by Giotto. 1200 l, The Resurrection of Christ, by Piero della Francesca, vert.

Perf. 14x13¼, 13¼x14

2000, Mar. 10 **Litho.**

2335 A1200 450 l multi .45 .25
2336 A1200 650 l multi .65 .30
2337 A1200 800 l multi .80 .40
2338 A1200 1000 l multi 1.00 .50
2339 A1200 1200 l multi 1.25 .65
Nos. 2335-2339 (5) 4.15 2.10

La Civiltá Cattolica, 150th Anniv.
A1201

2000, Apr. 6 Photo. *Perf. 14x13¼*

2340 A1201 800 l multi .90 .45

San Giuseppe de Merode College, Rome, 150th Anniv.
A1202

2000, Apr. 8

2341 A1202 800 l multi .90 .45

Intl. Cycling Union, Cent. — A1203

2000, Apr. 14 Photo. *Perf. 13¼x14*

2342 A1203 1500 l multi 1.60 .80

Tourism — A1204

Designs: No. 2343, Terre di Franciacorta, Brescia. No. 2344, Dunarobba Petrified Forest, Avigliano Umbro. No. 2345, Ercolano. No. 2346, Bella di Taormina Island.

2000, Apr. 14 ***Perf. 14x13¼***

2343 A1204 800 l multi .80 .40
2344 A1204 800 l multi .80 .40
2345 A1204 800 l multi .80 .40
2346 A1204 800 l multi .80 .40
Nos. 2343-2346 (4) 3.20 1.60

Little Holy Society, Caltanissetta — A1205

2000, Apr. 19

2347 A1205 800 l multi .80 .40

Niccolò Piccinni (1728-1800), Opera Composer
A1206

2000, May 6 ***Perf. 13¼x14***

2348 A1206 4000 l multi 4.25 2.10

Europa, 2000
Common Design Type

2000, May 9
2349 CD17 800 l multi .85 .40

Post and Telecommunications Historical Museum — A1207

No. 2350, Ship, telecommunications equipment. No. 2351, #19, 20.

2000, May 9 Litho. ***Perf. 14x13¼***
2350 A1207 800 l multi .80 .40
2351 A1207 800 l multi .80 .40

Lazio, 1999-2000 Soccer Champions A1208

2000, May 20 Photo. ***Perf. 13¼x14***
2352 A1208 800 l multi .80 .40

Monza Cathedral A1209

2000, May 31
2353 A1209 800 l multi .85 .40

Rome, Headquarters of UN Food and Agriculture Agencies A1210

2000, June 17 Photo. ***Perf. 13¼x14***
2354 A1210 1000 l multi 1.00 .50

Jesus the Redeemer Monument, Nuoro, Cent. — A1211

2000, June 24
2355 A1211 800 l multi .80 .40

Società Italiana per Condotte d'Acqua, Construction Company, 120th Anniv. — A1212

2000, June 28 ***Perf. 14x13¼***
2356 A1212 800 l multi .80 .40

Stampin' the Future Children's Stamp Design Contest Winner — A1213

2000, July 7 ***Perf. 13¼x14***
2357 A1213 1000 l multi 1.00 .50

Archery World Championships, Campagna A1214

2000, July 8
2358 A1214 1500 l multi 1.50 .75

World Cycling Championships A1215

2000, July 31 Photo. ***Perf. 13¼x14***
2359 A1215 800 l multi .80 .40

Madonna and Child, by Carlo Crivelli A1216

Litho. & Engr.

2000, Aug. 8 ***Perf. 14***
2360 A1216 800 l multi .80 .40

Sant'Orso Fair, 1000th Anniv. A1217

2000, Aug. 8 Photo. ***Perf. 14x13¼***
2361 A1217 1000 l multi 1.00 .50

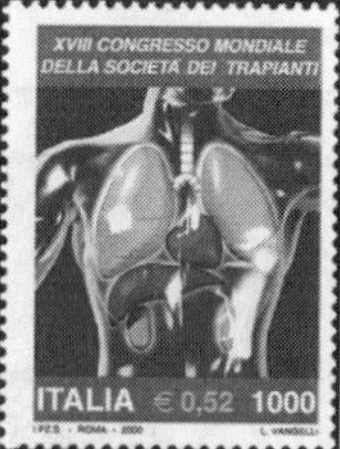

18th World Congress of Transplantation Society A1218

2000, Aug. 26 Photo. ***Perf. 13¼x14***
2362 A1218 1000 l multi 1.00 .50

2000 Summer Olympics, Sydney — A1219

Designs: 800 l, Celebrating athlete, Olympic stadium, Sydney. 1000 l, Myron's Discobolus, Sydney skyline.

2000, Sept. 1
2363 A1219 800 l multi .80 .40
2364 A1219 1000 l multi 1.00 .50

Millennium Type of 2000
Souvenir Sheet

No. 2365, vert.: a, War. b, Peace.

2000 Litho. ***Perf. 13¼x14***
2365 Sheet of 2 1.60 .80
a.-b. A1193 800 l Any single .80 .40

Issued: No. 2365, 9/4.

Millennium Type of 2000

No. 2366: a, Meditation. b, Expression.

2000, Nov. 4 Litho. ***Perf. 14x13¼***
2366 Sheet of 2 1.60 .80
a.-b. A1193 800 l Any single .80 .40

Issued: No. 2366, 11/4.

Battle of Marengo, Bicent. — A1220

2000, Sept. 8 Photo. ***Perf. 13¼x14***
2367 A1220 800 l multi .80 .40

Fellini Film Year — A1221

2000, Sept. 20 Photo. ***Perf. 13¼x14***
2368 A1221 800 l multi .80 .40

Philately Day A1222

2000, Sept. 23 Photo. ***Perf. 14x13¼***
2369 A1222 800 l multi .80 .40

Father Luigi Maria Monti (1825-1900) — A1223

2000, Sept. 30 Photo. ***Perf. 14x13¼***
2370 A1223 800 l multi .80 .40

Antonio Salieri (1750-1825), Composer A1224

2000, Sept. 30 ***Perf. 13¼x14***
2371 A1224 4800 l multi 4.75 2.40

2000 Paralympics, Sydney — A1225

2000, Oct. 2 Photo. ***Perf. 13¼x14***
2372 A1225 1500 l multi 1.50 .75

World Mathematics Year — A1226

2000, Oct. 14 Photo. ***Perf. 14x13¼***
2373 A1226 800 l multi .80 .40

Voluntarism A1227

2000, Oct. 18 ***Perf. 13¼x14***
2374 A1227 800 l multi .80 .40

Giordano Bruno (1548-1600), Philosopher — A1228

2000, Oct. 20 ***Perf. 14x13¼***
2375 A1228 800 l multi .80 .40

Madonna and Child, by Luca Della Robbia
A1229

Litho. & Engr.

2000, Oct. 25 *Perf. 14*
2376 A1229 800 l multi .80 .40

Accademia Roveretana Degli Agaiti, 250th Anniv. — A1230

2000, Oct. 26 Photo. *Perf. 13¼x14*
2377 A1230 800 l multi .80 .40

Gaetano Martino (1900-67), Statesman — A1231

2000, Nov. 3 Photo. *Perf. 14*
2378 A1231 800 l multi .80 .40

Perseus, by Benvenuto Cellini (1500-71), Sculptor — A1232

Litho. & Engr.

2000, Nov. 3 *Perf. 14*
2379 A1232 1200 l multi 1.25 .60

Schools
A1233

Designs: 800 l, Camerino University. 1000 l, Calabria University, Cosenza.

2000, Nov. 6 Engr. *Perf. 14x13¼*
2380 A1233 800 l blue .80 .40
2381 A1233 1000 l blue 1.00 .50

Christmas
A1234

Designs: 800 l, Snowflakes. 1000 l, Creche, Matera Cathedral, horiz.

Perf. 13¼x14, 14x13¼

2000, Nov. 6 Photo.
2382 A1234 800 l multi .90 .45
2383 A1234 1000 l multi 1.00 .50

World Snowboarding Championships
A1235

2001, Jan. 15 Photo. *Perf. 13¼x14*
2384 A1235 1000 l multi 1.00 .50

The Annunciation, by Botticelli — A1236

2001, Jan. 18 *Perf. 14*
2385 A1236 1000 l multi 1.00 .50

Exhibit of Italian art at Natl. Museum of Western Art, Tokyo.

Souvenir Sheet

Opera Composers — A1237

No. 2386: a, Vincenzo Bellini (1801-35). b, Domenico Cimarosa (1749-1801). c, Gaspare Luigi Pacifico Spontini (1774-1851). d, Giuseppe Verdi (1813-1901).

2001, Jan. 27 Litho. *Perf. 13¼x14*
2386 A1237 Sheet of 4 3.25 1.60
a.-d. 800 l Any single .80 .40

St. Rose of Viterbo (1235-1252)
A1238

2001, Mar. 6 Photo. *Perf. 13¼x14*
2387 A1238 800 l multi .80 .40

Souvenir Sheet

Ferrari, 2000 Formula 1 World Champions — A1239

2001, Mar. 9 Litho. *Perf. 14x13¼*
2388 A1239 5000 l multi 5.00 2.50

Santa Maria Abbey, Sylvis — A1240

2001, Mar. 10 Engr. *Perf. 14*
2389 A1240 800 l blue .80 .40

Postage Stamp Sesquicentennials — A1241

Designs: No. 2390, Tuscany #1. No. 2391, Sardinia #1. No. 2392, Lombardy-Venetia #1.

2001, Mar. 31 Photo. *Perf. 13¼x14*
2390 A1241 800 l multi .80 .40
2391 A1241 800 l multi .80 .40
2392 A1241 800 l multi .80 .40
Nos. 2390-2392 (3) 2.40 1.20

Priority Mail
A1242

Serpentine Die Cut 11
Typo & Silk Screened
2001, Apr. 10
Self-Adhesive

2393 A1242 1200 l multi 1.25 .60
a. Booklet pane of 4 + 4 etiquettes 5.00
Booklet, #2393a 5.00

Compare with No. 2324. No. 2393 was intended for Priority Mail service. A self-adhesive blue etiquette is adjacent to the stamp.

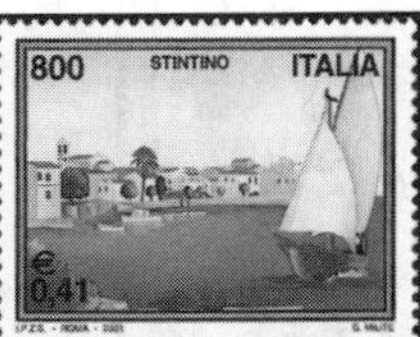

Tourism
A1243

2001, Apr. 14 Photo. *Perf. 14x13¼*
2394 A1243 800 l Stintino .80 .40
2395 A1243 800 l Comacchio .80 .40
2396 A1243 800 l Diamante .80 .40
2397 A1243 800 l Pioraco .80 .40
Nos. 2394-2397 (4) 3.20 1.60

Nature and the Environment
A1244

Designs: 450 l, Campanula. 650 l, Marmots. 800 l, Storks. 1000 l, World Day Against Desertification.

2001, Apr. 21 *Perf. 13¼x14*
2398 A1244 450 l multi .45 .25
2399 A1244 650 l multi .65 .30
2400 A1244 800 l multi .80 .40
2401 A1244 1000 l multi 1.00 .50
Nos. 2398-2401 (4) 2.90 1.45

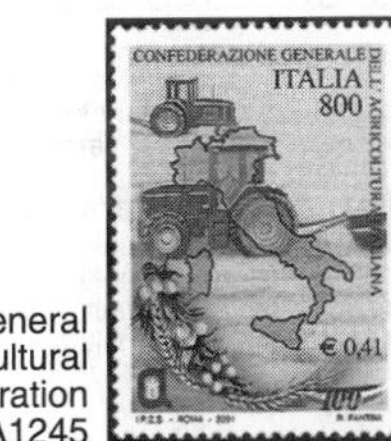

General Agricultural Confederation
A1245

2001, Apr. 24 Photo. *Perf. 13¼x14*
2402 A1245 800 l multi .80 .40

Gorizia, 1000th Anniv.
A1246

2001, Apr. 28 *Perf. 14x13¼*
2403 A1246 800 l multi .80 .40

Europa
A1247

2001, May 4 Photo. *Perf. 14x13¼*
2404 A1247 800 l multi .80 .40

European Union's Charter of Fundamental Rights — A1248

2001, May 9 Photo. *Perf. 14x13¼*
2405 A1248 800 l multi .80 .40

Order of the Knights of Labor, Cent. — A1249

2001, May 9 Photo. ***Perf. 13¼x14***
2406 A1249 800 l multi .80 .40

Workplace Injury Memorial Day — A1250

2001, May 19
2407 A1250 800 l multi .80 .40

Art and Student Creativity Day A1251

Children's art by: No. 2408, Lucia Catena. No. 2409, Luigi Di Cristo. No. 2410, Barbara Grilli. No. 2411, Rita Vergari, vert.

2001, May 26 ***Perf. 13¼x14, 14x13¼***
2408 A1251 800 l multi .80 .40
2409 A1251 800 l multi .80 .40
2410 A1251 800 l multi .80 .40
2411 A1251 800 l multi .80 .40
Nos. 2408-2411 (4) 3.20 1.60

Masaccio (1401-28), Painter — A1252

2001, June 1 ***Perf. 13¼x14***
2412 A1252 800 l multi .80 .40

Madonna of Senigallia, by Piero della Francesca A1253

Litho. & Engr.

2001, June 9 ***Perf. 14***
2413 A1253 800 l multi .80 .40

Panathlon International, 50th Anniv. — A1254

2001, June 12 Photo. ***Perf. 13¼x14***
2414 A1254 800 l multi .80 .40

Republic of San Marino, 1700th Anniv. — A1255

2001, June 23
2415 A1255 800 l multi .80 .40

Rome, 2000-2001 Soccer Champions A1256

2001, June 23 Photo. ***Perf. 13¼x14***
2416 A1256 800 l multi .80 .40

Harbormaster's Corps and Coast Guard — A1257

2001, July 20 Photo. ***Perf. 14x13¼***
2417 A1257 800 l multi .80 .40

Salvatore Quasimodo (1901-68), Writer — A1258

2001, Aug. 20 ***Perf. 13¼x14***
2418 A1258 1500 l multi 1.50 .75

Octagonal Room, Domus Aurea (Golden House of Nero), Rome — A1259

2001, Aug. 31 Engr. ***Perf. 14***
2419 A1259 1000 l multi 1.00 .50

Italian Design A1260

Household furnishings designed by: a, Piero Lissoni, Patricia Urquiola and Anna Bartoli. b, Monica Graffeo and Rodolfo Dordoni. c, Ferruccio Laviani and Massimo Iosa Ghini. d, Anna Gili and Miki Astori. e, Marco Ferreri, M. Cananzi and R. Semprini. f, Stefano Giovannoni and Massimiliano Datti.

2001, Sept. 1 Litho. ***Perf. 13¼***
2420 Sheet of 6 5.00 2.40
a.-f. A1260 800 l Any single .80 .40

Cent. of Il Quarto Stato, Painting by Giuseppe Pellizza da Volpedo — A1261

2001, Sept. 15 Engr. ***Perf. 14x13¼***
2421 A1261 1000 l brown 1.00 .50

Discovery of Mummified Man "Otzi" in Melting Glacier, 10th Anniv. — A1262

2001, Sept. 19 Photo. ***Perf. 13¼x14***
2422 A1262 800 l multi .80 .40

Stamp Day A1263

2001, Sept. 22 ***Perf. 14x13¼***
2423 A1263 800 l multi .80 .40

Enrico Fermi (1901-54), Physicist — A1264

2001, Sept. 29 ***Perf. 13¼x14***
2424 A1264 800 l multi .80 .40

Schools A1265

Designs: No. 2425, Pavia University. No. 2426, Bari University, vert. No. 2427, Camilo Cavour State Science High School, Rome.

Perf. 14x13¼, 13¼x14

2001, Sept. 29 Engr.
2425 A1265 800 l blue .80 .40
2426 A1265 800 l red brown .80 .40
2427 A1265 800 l Prus blue .80 .40
Nos. 2425-2427 (3) 2.40 1.20

Latin Union A1266

2001, Oct. 12 Photo. ***Perf. 14x13¼***
2428 A1266 800 l multi .80 .40

Natl. Archaeological Museum, Taranto — A1267

2001, Oct. 12 Photo. ***Perf. 14x13¼***
2429 A1267 1000 l multi 1.00 .50

Intl. Food and Agriculture Organizations A1268

Wheat and emblem of: a, Intl. Fund for Agricultural Development. b, Food and Agriculture Organization and farmer (49x27mm). c, World Food Program.

2001, Oct. 16 Photo. ***Perf. 14x13¼***
2430 Horiz. strip of 3 2.40 1.25
a.-c. A1268 800 l Any single .80 .40

Enthroned Christ and Angels, Sancta Sanctorum, St. John Lateran Basilica A1269

Litho. & Engr.

2001, Oct. 19 ***Perf. 14***
2431 A1269 800 l multi .80 .40

Madonna and Child, by Macrino d'Alba A1270

2001, Oct. 20
2432 A1270 800 l multi .80 .40

A1271

Christmas A1272

2001, Oct. 30 Photo. ***Perf. 14x13¼***
2433 A1271 800 l multi .80 .40
2434 A1272 1000 l multi 1.00 .50

Souvenir Sheet

Italian Silk Industry — A1273

Silk-screened on Silk

2001, Nov. 29 *Imperf.*
2435 A1273 5000 l multi 5.25 5.25

100 Cents = 1 Euro (")

Women in Art Type of 1998 With Denominations in Euros Only

Designs: 1c, Hebe, sculpture by Antonio Canova. 2c, Profile of woman from Syracuse tetradrachm. 3c, Queen of Sheba from "The Meeting of King Solomon and the Queen of Sheba," painting by Piero della Francesa. 5c, "Young Velca," Etruscan tomb. 10c, Head of terra cotta statue, 3rd cent. BC. 20c, Danae, painting by Correggio. 23c, Detail from "Herod's Feast," by Fra Filippo Lippi. 41c, "Lady with the Unicorn," by Raphael. 50c, "Antea," by Parmigianino. 77c, "Primavera," by Botticelli.

2002 Photo. *Perf. 14x13¼*
2436 A1142 1c multi .20 .20
2437 A1142 2c multi .20 .20
2438 A1142 3c multi .20 .20
2440 A1142 5c multi .20 .20
2441 A1142 10c multi .20 .20
2443 A1142 20c multi .35 .20
2444 A1142 23c multi .40 .20

Engr.

Wmk. 303

2446 A1142 41c multi .70 .35
2448 A1142 50c multi .85 .45
2451 A1142 77c multi 1.25 .65
Nos. 2436-2451 (10) 4.55 2.85

Issued: 2c, 5c, 10c, 23c, 41c, 50c, 77c, 1/1. 1c, 3c, 20c, 3/1.This is an expanding set.

Italia — A1274

2002 Engr. Unwmk. *Perf. 14x13¼*
2454 A1274 " 1 multi 1.75 .80
2455 A1274 " 1.24 multi 2.25 1.10
2457 A1274 " 1.55 multi 2.75 1.40
2459 A1274 " 2.17 multi 3.75 1.90
2461 A1274 " 2.58 multi 4.50 2.25
2463 A1274 " 3.62 multi 6.25 3.00
2465 A1274 " 6.20 multi 11.00 5.50
Nos. 2454-2465 (7) 32.25 15.95

Issued: " 1, " 1.24, " 1.55, " 2.17, " 2.58, " 3.62, 1/2. " 6.20, 3/1.

Priority Mail Type of 2001 with Euro Denominations Only

Typo. & Silk Screened

2002, Jan. 2 *Serpentine Die Cut 11*

Self-Adhesive

Background Color

2466 A1242 62c yellow 1.10 .55
Booklet, 4 #2466 4.50
2467 A1242 77c blue green 1.40 .70
2468 A1242 " 1 blue 1.75 .85
2469 A1242 " 1.24 yel green 2.10 1.10
2470 A1242 " 1.86 rose 3.25 1.60
2471 A1242 " 4.13 lilac 7.25 3.50
Nos. 2466-2471 (6) 16.85 8.30

A self-adhesive etiquette is adjacent to each stamp.

Introduction of the Euro — A1275

No. 2472: a, 1285 Venetian ducat. b, 1252 Genoan genovino and Florentine florin.

No. 2473: a, Euro symbol and flags. b, 1946 Italian 1-lira coin and new 1-euro coin.

Illustration reduced.

2002, Jan. 2 Photo. *Perf. 14x13¼*
2472 A1275 Horiz. pair 1.40 .70
a.-b. 41c Either single .70 .35
2473 A1275 Horiz. pair 1.40 .70
a.-b. 41c Either single .70 .35

Blessed Josemaría Escrivá (1902-75), Founder of Opus Dei A1276

2002, Jan. 9
2474 A1276 41c multi .75 .35

Luigi Bocconi and Luigi Bocconi Commercial University, Milan A1277

2002, Jan. 24
2475 A1277 41c multi .75 .35

Parma Stamps, 150th Anniv. — A1278

2002, Jan. 26 *Perf. 13¼x14*
2476 A1278 41c No. 1 .75 .35

Intl. Year of Mountains A1279

2001, Feb. 1
2477 A1279 41c multi .75 .35

2006 Winter Olympics, Turin — A1280

2002, Feb. 23
2478 A1280 41c multi .75 .35

Malato Alla Fonte, Sculpture by Arnolfo de Cambio — A1281

2002, Mar. 8 Engr. *Perf. 14*
2479 A1281 41c red lilac .75 .35

Tourism A1282

Designs: No. 2480, Venaria Reale. No. 2481, San Gimignano. No. 2482, Sannicandro di Bari. No. 2483, Capo d'Orlando.

2002, Mar. 23 Photo. *Perf. 14x13¼*
2480 A1282 41c multi .75 .35
2481 A1282 41c multi .75 .35
2482 A1282 41c multi .75 .35
2483 A1282 41c multi .75 .35
Nos. 2480-2483 (4) 3.00 1.40

Santa Maria Della Grazie Sanctuary, Spezzano Albanese — A1283

2002, Apr. 3 Engr. *Perf. 14*
2484 A1283 41c red brown .75 .35

State Police, 150th Anniv. A1284

2002, Apr. 12 Photo. *Perf. 14x13¼*
2485 A1284 41c multi .75 .35

Fr. Matteo Ricci (1552-1610), Missionary in China, Geographer — A1285

2002, Apr. 20
2486 A1285 41c multi .75 .35

Europa A1286

2002, May 4 Photo. *Perf. 14x13¼*
2487 A1286 41c multi .75 .35

Francesco Morosini Naval School, Venice A1287

2002, May 4
2488 A1287 41c multi .75 .35

Italian Cinema — A1288

Designs: No. 2489, Umberto D., directed by Vittorio De Sica. No. 2490, Miracle in Milan, written by Cesare Zavattini.

Litho. & Engr.

2002, May 10 *Perf. 13¼x14*
2489 A1288 41c multi .75 .35
2490 A1288 41c multi .75 .35

Juventus, 2001-02 Italian Soccer Champions A1289

2002, May 18 **Photo.**
2491 A1289 41c multi .80 .40

Giovanni Falcone (1939-92) and Paolo Borsellino (1940-92), Judges Assassinated by Mafia — A1290

2002, May 23 *Perf. 14x13¼*
2492 A1290 62c multi 1.25 .60

NATO-Russia Summit Meeting, Rome — A1291

2002, May 28 Photo. *Perf. 14x13¼*
2493 A1291 41c multi .80 .40

World Kayak Championships, Valsesia — A1292

2002, May 30 *Perf. 13¼x14*
2494 A1292 52c multi 1.00 .50

Italian Military Forces in Peace Missions — A1293

2002, June 1
2495 A1293 41c multi .80 .40

Modena Stamps, 150th Anniv. — A1294

2002, June 1 Photo. ***Perf. 13¼x14***
2496 A1294 41c multi .80 .40

Alfredo Binda (1902-86), Cyclist — A1295

2002, June 14 Photo. ***Perf. 13¼x14***
2497 A1295 41c multi .80 .40

St. Pio of Pietrelcina (1887-1968) — A1296

2002, June 16 ***Perf. 14***
2498 A1296 41c multi .80 .40

Monument to the Massacre of the Acqui Division — A1297

2002, June 21 ***Perf. 13¼x14***
2499 A1297 41c multi .80 .40

The Crucifixion, by Cimabue A1298

Litho. & Engr.

2002, June 22 ***Perf. 14***
2500 A1298 " 2.58 multi 5.00 2.50

Prefectural Institute, Bicent. A1299

2002, June 24 Photo. ***Perf. 14x13¼***
2501 A1299 41c multi .80 .40

St. Maria Goretti (1890-1902) A1300

2002, July 6 ***Perf. 13¼x14***
2502 A1300 41c multi .80 .40

Jules Cardinal Mazarin (1602-61), and Birthplace A1301

2002, July 13 Photo. ***Perf. 14x13¼***
2503 A1301 41c multi .80 .40

Italians Around the World — A1302

2002, Aug. 8 ***Perf. 13¼x14***
2504 A1302 52c multi 1.00 .50

Monument to Sant'Anna di Stazzema Massacre A1303

2002, Aug. 17
2505 A1303 41c multi .80 .40

UNESCO World Heritage Sites — A1304

Designs: 41c, Pisa. 52c, Aeolian Islands. Illustration reduced.

2002, Oct. 30 ***Perf. 14***
2506 A1304 41c multi + label .80 .40
2507 A1304 52c multi + label 1.00 .50

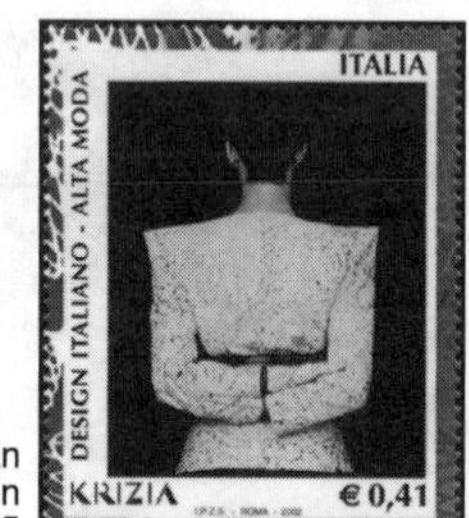

Italian Design A1305

Apparel by: a, Krizia. b, Dolce e Gabbana. c, Gianfranco Ferre. d, Giorgio Armani. e, Laura Biagiotti. f, Prada.

2002, Aug. 30 **Litho.**
2508 Sheet of 6 5.00 2.50
a.-f. A1305 41c Any single .80 .40

Carlo Alberto Dalla Chiesa (1920-82), Prefect of Palermo Assassinated by Mafia — A1306

2002. Sept. 3 Photo. ***Perf. 13¼x14***
2509 A1306 41c multi .80 .40

Concordia Theater, Monte Castello de Vibio — A1307

Litho. & Engr.

2002, Sept. 7 ***Perf. 14***
2510 A1307 41c multi .80 .40

Sailboat Gathering, Imperia A1308

2002, Sept. 11 Photo. ***Perf. 14x13¼***
2511 A1308 41c multi .80 .40

Santa Giulia Museum, Brescia — A1309

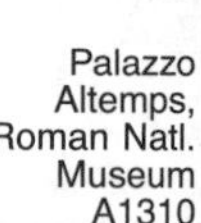

Palazzo Altemps, Roman Natl. Museum A1310

Perf. 13¼x14, 14x13¼

2002, Oct. 4 **Photo.**
2512 A1309 41c multi .80 .40
2513 A1310 41c multi .80 .40

Roman States Postage Stamps, 150th Anniv. — A1311

2002, Oct. 4 Photo. ***Perf. 13¼x14***
2514 A1311 41c Roman States #6 .80 .40

Flora and Fauna — A1312

2002, Oct. 11
2515 A1312 23c Orchid .45 .25
2516 A1312 52c Lynx 1.00 .50
2517 A1312 77c Stag beetle 1.50 .75
Nos. 2515-2517 (3) 2.95 1.50

World Food Day — A1313

2002, Oct. 16 Photo. ***Perf. 13¼x14***
2518 A1313 41c multi .80 .40

Forestry Corps — A1314

2002, Oct. 22
2519 A1314 41c multi .85 .40

Father Carlo Gnocchi (1902-56), Founder of Fondazione Pro Juventute A1315

2002, Oct. 25
2520 A1315 41c multi .85 .40

2002 Muscular Dystrophy Telethon A1316

2002, Oct. 31 ***Perf. 14x13¼***
2521 A1316 41c multi .85 .40

Christmas A1317

Designs: 41c, Nativity. 62c, Child with candle, Christmas tree, vert.

Perf. 14x13¼, 13¼x14

2002, Oct. 31 **Photo.**
2522 A1317 41c multi .85 .40
2523 A1317 62c multi 1.25 .60

SEMI-POSTAL STAMPS

Many issues of Italy and Italian Colonies include one or more semi-postal denominations. To avoid splitting sets, these issues are generally listed as regular postage, airmail, etc., unless all values carry a surtax.

Italian Flag — SP1

Italian Eagle Bearing Arms of Savoy — SP2

1915-16 Typo. Wmk. 140 *Perf. 14*

B1 SP1 10c + 5c rose 1.50 *3.75*
B2 SP2 15c + 5c slate 2.00 *3.00*
B3 SP2 20c + 5c orange 7.00 *18.50*
Nos. B1-B3 (3) 10.50 *25.25*
Set, never hinged 26.25

No. B2 Surcharged

1916

B4 SP2 20c on 15c + 5c 4.50 *11.50*
Never hinged 11.25
a. Double overprint 300.00 —
Never hinged —
b. Inverted overprint 300.00 450.00
Never hinged —

Regular Issues of 1906-16 Overprinted in Blue or Red **B.L.P.**

1921

B5 A48 10c claret (Bl) *450.00* 300.00
B6 A50 20c brn org (Bl) *625.00* 125.00
B7 A49 25c blue (R) 75.00 37.50
B8 A49 40c brn (Bl) 30.00 3.75
a. Inverted overprint 45.00 25.00
Nos. B5-B8 (4) *1,180.* 466.25
Set, never hinged 1,800.

Regular Issues of 1901-22 Overprinted in Red, Black, Blue, Brown or Orange

1922-23

B9 A48 10c cl ('23) (Bk) 32.50 16.00
a. Blue overprint 32.50 17.50
Never hinged 62.50
b. Brown overprint 32.50 17.50
Never hinged 62.50
B10 A48 15c slate (Org) 150.00 125.00
a. Blue overprint 300.00 210.00
Never hinged 600.00
B11 A50 20c brn org (Bk) 110.00 110.00
a. Blue overprint 275.00 110.00
Never hinged 550.00
B12 A49 25c blue (Bk; '23) 50.00 30.00
b. Red overprint 125.00 110.00
Never hinged 250.00
B12A A49 30c org brn (Bk) 80.00 45.00
B13 A49 40c brn (Bl) 67.50 30.00
a. Black overprint 67.50 30.00
Never hinged 140.00
b. As "a," invtd. ovpt. 100.00 —
B14 A49 50c vio ('23) (Bk) 300.00 210.00
a. Blue overprint —
B15 A49 60c car (Bk) *1,150.* 675.00
B15A A49 85c choc (Bk) 110.00 110.00
B16 A46 1 l brn & grn ('23) (Bk) *1,850.* 800.00
a. Inverted overprint *1,850.*
Nos. B9-B16 (10) *3,900.* 2,151.
Set, never hinged 6,237.

The stamps overprinted "B. L. P." were sold by the Government below face value to the National Federation for Assisting War Invalids. Most of them were affixed to special envelopes (Buste Lettere Postali) which bore advertisements. The Federation was permitted to sell these envelopes at a reduction of 5c from the face value of each stamp. The profits for the war invalids were derived from the advertisements.

Values of Nos. B5-B16 unused are for stamps with original gum. Most copies without gum or with part gum sell for about a quarter of values quoted. Uncanceled stamps affixed to the special envelopes usually sell for about half value.

The overprint on Nos. B9-B16 is wider (13½mm) than that on Nos. B5-B8 (11mm). The 1922-23 overprint exists both typo. and litho. on 10c, 15c, 20c and 25c; only litho. on 40c, 50c, 60c and 1 l; and only typo. on 30c and 85c.

Counterfeits of the B.L.P. overprints exist.

Administering Fascist Oath — SP3

1923, Oct. 29 *Perf. 14x14½*

B17 SP3 30c + 30c brown 20.00 *37.50*
B18 SP3 50c + 50c violet 20.00 *37.50*
B19 SP3 1 l + 1 l gray 20.00 *37.50*
Nos. B17-B19 (3) 60.00 *112.50*
Set, never hinged 150.00

The surtax was given to the Benevolent Fund of the Black Shirts (the Italian National Militia).

Anniv. of the March of the Fascisti on Rome.

St. Maria Maggiore SP4

Pope Opening Holy Door SP8

Designs: 30c+15c, St. John Lateran. 50c+25c, St. Paul's Church. 60c+30c, St. Peter's Basilica. 5 l+2.50 l, Pope closing Holy Door.

1924, Dec. 24 *Perf. 12*

B20 SP4 20c + 10c dk grn & brn 1.40 *4.50*
B21 SP4 30c + 15c dk brn & brn 1.40 *4.50*
B22 SP4 50c + 25c vio & brn 1.40 *4.50*
B23 SP4 60c + 30c dp rose & brn 1.40 *13.50*
B24 SP8 1 l + 50c dp bl & vio 1.40 *11.50*
B25 SP8 5 l + 2.50 l org brn & vio 2.25 *30.00*
Nos. B20-B25 (6) 9.25 *68.50*
Set, never hinged 22.75

The surtax was contributed toward the Holy Year expenses.

Castle of St. Angelo SP10

Victor Emmanuel II — SP14

50c+20c, 60c+30c, Aqueduct of Claudius. 1.25 l+50c, 1.25 l+60c, Capitol, Roman Forum. 5 l+2 l, 5 l+2.50 l, People's Gate.

Unwmk.

1926, Oct. 26 Engr. *Perf. 11*

B26 SP10 40c + 20c dk brn & blk 1.10 *3.75*
B27 SP10 60c + 30c brn red & ol brn 1.10 *3.75*
B28 SP10 1.25 l + 60c bl grn & blk 1.10 *11.00*
B29 SP10 5 l + 2.50 l dk bl & blk 1.75 *50.00*
Nos. B26-B29 (4) 5.05 *68.50*
Set, never hinged 12.25

Stamps inscribed "Poste Italiane" and "Fiere Campionaria di Tripoli" are listed in Libya.

1928, Mar. 1

B30 SP10 30c + 10c dl vio & blk 3.75 *9.00*
B31 SP10 50c + 20c ol grn & sl 3.75 *7.50*
B32 SP10 1.25 l + 50c dp bl & blk 10.00 *21.00*
B33 SP10 5 l + 2 l brn red & blk 17.50 *62.50*
Nos. B30-B33 (4) 35.00 *100.00*
Set, never hinged 86.00

The tax on Nos. B26 to B33 was devoted to the charitable work of the Voluntary Militia for National Defense.

See Nos. B35-B38.

1929, Jan. 4 Photo. *Perf. 14*

B34 SP14 50c + 10c olive green 1.75 *3.25*
Never hinged 4.25

50th anniv. of the death of King Victor Emmanuel II. The surtax was for veterans.

Type of 1926 Issue

Designs in same order.

1930, July 1 Engr.

B35 SP10 30c + 10c dk grn & vio .50 *6.75*
B36 SP10 50c + 10c dk grn & bl grn .75 *4.25*
B37 SP10 1.25 l + 30c ind & grn 2.50 *13.50*
B38 SP10 5 l + 1.50 l blk brn & ol brn 3.75 *50.00*
Nos. B35-B38 (4) 7.50 *74.50*
Set, never hinged 18.65

The surtax was for the charitable work of the Voluntary Militia for National Defense.

Militiamen at Ceremonial Fire with Quotation from Leonardo da Vinci — SP15

Symbolical of Pride for Militia — SP16

Symbolical of Militia Guarding Immortality of Italy SP17

Militia Passing Through Arch of Constantine SP18

1935, July 1 Photo. Wmk. 140

B39 SP15 20c + 10c rose red 3.75 *4.25*
B40 SP16 25c + 15c green 3.75 *6.75*
B41 SP17 50c + 30c purple 3.75 *8.75*
B42 SP18 1.25 l + 75c blue 3.75 *12.50*
Nos. B39-B42 (4) 15.00 *32.25*
Set, never hinged 37.00
Nos. B39-B42,CB3 (5) 18.75 *44.75*
Set, never hinged 46.25

The surtax was for the Militia.

Roman Battle SP19

Roman Warriors SP20

1941, Dec. 13

B43 SP19 20c + 10c rose red .20 *.55*
B44 SP19 30c + 15c brown .20 *.70*
B45 SP20 50c + 25c violet .25 *.85*
B46 SP20 1.25 l + 1 l blue .30 *.90*
Nos. B43-B46 (4) .95 *3.00*
Set, never hinged 4.50

2,000th anniv. of the birth of Livy (59 B.C.-17 A.D.), Roman historian.

Catalogue values for unused stamps in this section, from this point to the end of the section, are for Never Hinged items.

Aid for Flood Victims — SP21

1995, Jan. 2 Photo. *Perf. 13½x14*

B47 SP21 750 l +2250 l multi 4.00 3.50

Queen Helen (1873-1952) SP22

2002, Mar. 2 Photo. *Perf. 13¼x14*

B48 SP22 41c + 21c multi 1.10 1.10

Surtax for breast cancer research and prevention.

AIR POST STAMPS

Used values for Nos. C1-C105 are for postally used stamps with legible cancellations. Forged cancels on these issues abound, and expertization is srongly recommended.

Special Delivery Stamp No. E1 Overprinted

1917, May Wmk. 140 *Perf. 14*

C1 SD1 25c rose red 7.25 *19.00*
Never hinged 17.50

Type of SD3 Surcharged in Black

1917, June 27

No.	Type	Description	Unused	Used
C2	SD3	25c on 40c violet	9.50	*25.00*
		Never hinged	24.00	

Type SD3 was not issued without surcharge.

AP2

1926-28 **Typo.**

No.	Type	Description	Unused	Used
C3	AP2	50c rose red ('28)	3.50	5.50
C4	AP2	60c gray	1.75	*5.50*
C5	AP2	80c brn vio & brn ('28)	15.00	*47.50*
C6	AP2	1 l blue	6.00	*5.50*
C7	AP2	1.20 l brn ('27)	15.00	*70.00*
C8	AP2	1.50 l buff	9.50	17.00
C9	AP2	5 l gray grn	22.50	*62.50*
		Nos. C3-C9 (7)	73.25	*213.50*
		Set, never hinged	175.00	

Nos. C4 and C6 Surcharged

1927, Sept. 16

No.	Type	Description	Unused	Used
C10	AP2	50c on 60c gray	5.50	*30.00*
a.		Pair, one without surcharge	375.00	
C11	AP2	80c on 1 l blue	19.00	*125.00*
		Set, never hinged	60.00	

Pegasus AP3

Wings AP4

Spirit of Flight — AP5

Arrows AP6

1930-32 **Photo.** **Wmk. 140**

No.	Type	Description	Unused	Used
C12	AP4	25c dk grn ('32)	.20	.20
C13	AP3	50c olive brn	.20	.20
C14	AP5	75c org brn ('32)	.20	.20
C15	AP4	80c org red	.20	.40
C16	AP5	1 l purple	.20	.20
C17	AP6	2 l deep blue	.20	.20
C18	AP3	5 l dk green	.20	.75
C19	AP3	10 l dp car	.20	2.75
		Nos. C12-C19 (8)	1.60	4.90
		Set, never hinged	3.00	

The 50c, 1 l and 2 l were reprinted in 1942 with labels similar to those of Nos. 427-438, but were not issued. Value, set of 3, $100.

For overprints see Nos. MC1-MC5. For overprints and surcharges on design AP6 see Nos. C52-C55; Yugoslavia-Ljubljana NB9-NB20, NC11-NC17.

Ferrucci Type of Postage

Staue of Ferrucci.

1930, July 10

No.	Type	Description	Unused	Used
C20	A104	50c purple	1.50	*11.00*
C21	A104	1 l orange brn	1.50	*13.50*
C22	A104	5 l + 2 l brn vio	4.25	*92.50*
		Nos. C20-C22 (3)	7.25	*117.00*
		Set, never hinged	17.50	

For overprinted types see Aegean Islands Nos. C1-C3.

Virgil Type of Postage

Jupiter sending forth his eagle.

1930, Oct. 21 **Photo.** **Wmk. 140**

No.	Type	Description	Unused	Used
C23	A106	50c lt brown	6.50	*9.50*
C24	A106	1 l orange	6.50	*14.00*

Engr.

Unwmk.

No.	Type	Description	Unused	Used
C25	A106	7.70 l + 1.30 l vio brn	32.50	*175.00*
C26	A106	9 l + 2 l indigo	40.00	*190.00*
		Nos. C23-C26 (4)	85.50	*388.50*
		Set, never hinged	210.00	

The surtax on Nos. C25-C26 was for the National Institute Figli del Littorio.

For overprinted types see Aegean Islands Nos. C4-C7.

Trans-Atlantic Squadron — AP9

1930, Dec. 15 **Photo.** **Wmk. 140**

No.	Type	Description	Unused	Used
C27	AP9	7.70 l Prus bl & gray	210.00	*775.00*
		Never hinged	425.00	
a.		Seven stars instead of six	650.00	—
		Never hinged	1,300.	

Flight by Italian aviators from Rome to Rio de Janeiro, Dec. 1930-Jan. 12, 1931.

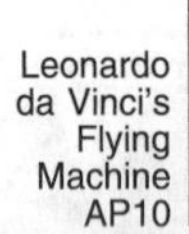

Leonardo da Vinci's Flying Machine AP10

Leonardo da Vinci AP11

Leonardo da Vinci — AP12

1932

No.	Type	Description	Unused	Used
C28	AP10	50c olive brn	1.50	*1.50*
C29	AP11	1 l violet	2.40	*2.00*
C30	AP11	3 l brown red	3.50	*6.50*
C31	AP11	5 l dp green	3.50	*8.00*
C32	AP10	7.70 l + 2 l dk bl	6.00	*27.50*
C33	AP11	10 l + 2.50 l blk brn	6.50	*30.00*
		Nos. C28-C33 (6)	23.40	*75.50*
		Set, never hinged	55.00	

Engr.

Unwmk.

No.	Type	Description	Unused	Used
C34	AP12	100 l brt bl & grnsh blk	22.50	*100.00*
		Never hinged	50.00	
a.		Thin paper	37.50	*150.00*

Dante Alighieri Soc. and especially Leonardo da Vinci, to whom the invention of a flying machine has been attributed. Surtax was for the benefit of the Society.

Inscription on No. C34: "Man with his large wings by beating against the air will be able to dominate it and lift himself above it".

Issued: #C28-C33, Mar. 14; #C34, Aug. 6.

For overprinted types see Aegean Islands Nos. C8-C13.

Garibaldi's Home at Caprera AP13

Farmhouse where Anita Garibaldi Died AP14

50c, 1 l+25c, Garibaldi's home, Caprera. 2 l+50c, Anita Garibaldi. 5 l+1 l, Giuseppe Garibaldi.

1932, Apr. 6 **Photo.** **Wmk. 140**

No.	Type	Description	Unused	Used
C35	AP13	50c copper red	1.75	*4.75*
C36	AP14	80c deep green	2.10	*8.75*
C37	AP13	1 l + 25c red brn	3.75	*22.50*
C38	AP13	2 l + 50c dp bl	6.75	*32.50*
C39	AP14	5 l + 1 l dp grn	7.25	*37.50*
		Nos. C35-C39 (5)	21.60	*106.00*
		Set, never hinged	52.50	

50th anniv. of the death of Giuseppe Garibaldi, patriot. The surtax was for the benefit of the Garibaldi Volunteers.

For overprinted types see Aegean Islands Nos. C15-C19.

March on Rome Type of Postage

50c, Eagle sculpture and airplane. 75c, Italian buildings from the air.

1932, Oct. 27 ***Perf. 14***

No.	Type	Description	Unused	Used
C40	A146	50c dark brown	1.50	*5.75*
C41	A146	75c orange brn	5.50	*22.50*
		Set, never hinged	16.00	

Graf Zeppelin Issue

Zeppelin over Pyramid of Caius Cestius AP19

Designs: 5 l, Tomb of Cecilia Metlella. 10 l, Stadium of Mussolini. 12 l, St. Angelo Castle and Bridge. 15 l, Roman Forum. 20 l, Imperial Avenue.

1933, Apr. 24

No.	Type	Description	Unused	Used
C42	AP19	3 l black & grn	10.50	52.50
C43	AP19	5 l green & brn	10.50	*65.00*
C44	AP19	10 l car & dl bl	10.50	*140.00*
C45	AP19	12 l dk bl & red org	10.50	*225.00*
C46	AP19	15 l dk brn & gray	10.50	*275.00*
C47	AP19	20 l org brn & bl	10.50	*300.00*
a.		Vertical pair, imperf. between	2,750.	
		Never hinged	4,500.	
		Nos. C42-C47 (6)	63.00	*1,057.*
		Set, never hinged	150.00	

Balbo's Trans-Atlantic Flight Issue

Italian Flag

King Victor Emmanuel III

Allegory "Flight" — AP25

#C49, Colosseum at Rome, Chicago skyline. #C48-C49 consist of 3 parts; Italian flag, Victor Emmanuel III, & scene arranged horizontally.

1933, May 20

No.	Type	Description	Unused	Used
C48	AP25	5.25 l + 19.75 l red, grn & ultra	110.00	*600.00*
		Never hinged	175.00	
a.		Left stamp without ovpt.	*10,000.*	
		Never hinged	15,000.	
C49	AP25	5.25 l + 44.75 l grn, red & ultra	110.00	*600.00*
		Never hinged	175.00	

Transatlantic Flight, Rome-Chicago, of 24-seaplane squadron led by Gen. Italo Balbo. Center and right sections paid postage. At left is registered air express label overprinted "APPARECCHIO" and abbreviated pilot's name. Twenty triptychs of each value differ in name overprint.

No. C49 overprinted "VOLO DI RITORNO/ NEW YORK-ROMA" was not issued; flight canceled. Value never hinged, $35,000.

For overprints see Nos. CO1, Aegean Islands C26-C27.

Type of Air Post Stamp of 1930 Surcharged in Black

1934, Jan. 18

No.	Type	Description	Unused	Used
C52	AP6	2 l on 2 l yel	3.00	*37.50*
C53	AP6	3 l on 2 l yel grn	3.00	*57.50*
C54	AP6	5 l on 2 l rose	3.00	*110.00*
C55	AP6	10 l on 2 l vio	3.00	*175.00*
		Nos. C52-C55 (4)	12.00	*380.00*
		Set, never hinged	30.00	

For use on mail carried on a special flight from Rome to Buenos Aires.

Annexation of Fiume Type of Postage

25c, 75c, View of Fiume Harbor. 50c, 1 l+50c, Monument to the Dead. 2 l+1.50 l, Venetian Lions. 3 l+2 l, Julian wall.

1934, Mar. 12

No.	Type	Description	Unused	Used
C56	A166	25c green	.30	*2.75*
C57	A166	50c brown	.30	*1.50*
C58	A166	75c org brn	.30	*6.75*
C59	A166	1 l + 50c dl vio	.30	*12.50*
C60	A166	2 l + 1.50 l dl bl	.30	*16.00*
C61	A166	3 l + 2 l blk brn	.30	*17.50*
		Nos. C56-C61 (6)	1.80	*57.00*
		Set, never hinged	7.50	

Airplane and View of Stadium AP32

Soccer Player and Plane AP33

Airplane and Stadium Entrance AP35

Airplane over Stadium AP34

1934, May 24

No.	Type	Description	Unused	Used
C62	AP32	50c car rose	5.25	12.50
C63	AP33	75c gray blue	7.75	*18.00*
C64	AP34	5 l + 2.50 l ol grn	30.00	*175.00*
C65	AP35	10 l + 5 l brn blk	30.00	*225.00*
		Nos. C62-C65 (4)	73.00	*430.50*
		Set, never hinged	175.00	

2nd World Soccer Championships.

For overprinted types see Aegean Islands Nos. C28-C31.

Zeppelin under Fire AP36

Air Force Memorial — AP40

Designs: 25c, 80c, Zeppelin under fire. 50c, 75c, Motorboat patrol. 1 l+50c, Desert infantry. 2 l+1 l, Plane attacking troops.

1934, Apr. 24

C66	AP36	25c dk green	1.25	3.00
C67	AP36	50c gray	1.25	4.50
C68	AP36	75c dk brown	1.25	5.75
C69	AP36	80c slate blue	1.50	7.00
C70	AP36	1 l + 50c red brn	3.50	22.50
C71	AP36	2 l + 1 l brt bl	4.75	26.00
C72	AP40	3 l + 2 l brn blk	7.75	30.00
		Nos. C66-C72 (7)	21.25	98.75
		Set, never hinged	52.50	

Cent. of the institution of the Military Medal of Valor.

For overprinted types see Aegean Islands Nos. C32-C38.

King Victor Emmanuel III — AP41

1934, Nov. 5

C73	AP41	1 l purple	1.10	25.00
C74	AP41	2 l brt blue	1.10	32.50
C75	AP41	4 l red brown	3.00	110.00
C76	AP41	5 l dull green	3.00	150.00
C77	AP41	8 l rose red	9.00	210.00
C78	AP41	10 l brown	13.00	250.00
		Nos. C73-C78 (6)	30.20	777.50
		Set, never hinged	75.00	

65th birthday of King Victor Emmanuel III and the nonstop flight from Rome to Mogadiscio.

For overprint see No. CO2.

Muse Playing Harp AP42

Angelic Dirge for Bellini AP43

Scene from Bellini Opera, La Sonnambula — AP44

1935, Sept. 24

C79	AP42	25c dull yellow	1.50	4.75
C80	AP42	50c brown	1.50	3.75
C81	AP42	60c rose carmine	4.00	8.50
C82	AP43	1 l + 1 l purple	12.00	77.50
C83	AP44	5 l + 2 l green	18.00	110.00
		Nos. C79-C83 (5)	37.00	204.50
		Set, never hinged	90.00	

Vincenzo Bellini, (1801-35), operatic composer.

Quintus Horatius Flaccus Type of Postage

25c, Seaplane in Flight. 50c, 1 l+1 l, Monoplane over valley. 60c, Oak and eagle. 5 l+2 l, Ruins of ancient Rome.

1936, July 1

C84	A197	25c dp green	1.50	3.75
C85	A197	50c dk brown	2.25	3.75
C86	A197	60c scarlet	3.00	7.50
C87	A197	1 l + 1 l vio	10.50	82.50
C88	A197	5 l + 2 l slate bl	13.50	125.00
		Nos. C84-C88 (5)	30.75	222.50
		Set, never hinged	75.00	

Child of the Balilla AP49

Heads of Children AP50

1937, June 28

C89	AP49	25c dk bl grn	3.00	7.50
C90	AP50	50c brown	6.00	3.75
C91	AP49	1 l purple	4.50	7.50
C92	AP50	2 l + 1 l dk bl	6.00	67.50
C93	AP49	3 l + 2 l org	10.50	95.00
C94	AP50	5 l + 3 l rose lake	12.00	110.00
		Nos. C89-C94 (6)	42.00	291.25
		Set, never hinged	100.00	

Summer Exhibition for Child Welfare. The surtax on Nos. C92-C94 was used to support summer camps for poor children.

Prosperous Italy AP51

50c, Prolific Italy. 80c, Apollo's steeds. 1 l+1 l, Map & Roman Standard. 5 l+1 l, Augustus Caesar.

1937, Sept. 23

C95	AP51	25c red vio	3.00	6.75
C96	AP51	50c olive brn	3.00	5.75
C97	AP51	80c orange brn	6.50	8.50
C98	AP51	1 l + 1 l dk bl	15.00	57.50
C99	AP51	5 l + 1 l dl vio	26.00	95.00
		Nos. C95-C99 (5)	53.50	173.50
		Set, never hinged	125.00	

Bimillenary of the birth of Augustus Caesar (Octavianus) on the occasion of the exhibition opened in Rome by Mussolini on Sept. 22nd, 1937.

For overprinted types see Aegean Islands Nos. C39-C43.

King Victor Emmanuel III — AP56

25c, 3 l, King Victor Emmanuel III. 50c, 1 l, Dante Alighieri. 2 l, 5 l, Leonardo da Vinci.

1938, Oct. 28

C100	AP56	25c dull green	2.10	3.75
C101	AP56	50c dk yel brn	2.10	3.75
C102	AP56	1 l violet	2.75	5.25
C103	AP56	2 l royal blue	3.25	21.00
C104	AP56	3 l brown car	4.75	30.00
C105	AP56	5 l dp green	6.50	40.00
		Nos. C100-C105 (6)	21.45	103.75
		Set, never hinged	52.50	

Proclamation of the Empire.

Plane and Clasped Hands AP59

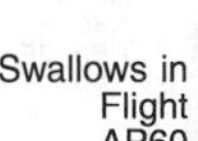

Swallows in Flight AP60

1945-47 Wmk. 277 Photo. *Perf. 14*

C106	AP59	1 l slate bl	.20	.20
C107	AP60	2 l dk blue	.20	.20
C108	AP59	3.20 l red org	.20	.20
C109	AP60	5 l dk green	.20	.20
C110	AP59	10 l car rose	.20	.20
C111	AP60	25 l dk bl ('46)	4.50	2.75
C112	AP60	25 l brown ('47)	.20	.20
C113	AP59	50 l dk grn ('46)	6.75	6.00
C114	AP59	50 l violet ('47)	.20	.20
		Nos. C106-C114 (9)	12.65	10.15
		Set, never hinged	32.50	

Issued: #C111, C113, 7/13/46; #C112, C114, 4/21/47.

See Nos. C130-C131. For surcharges and overprints see Nos. C115, C136, 1LNC1-1LNC7, Trieste C1-C6, C17-C22.

No. C108 Surcharged in Black

1947, July 1

C115	AP59	6 l on 3.20 l	.20	.20
		Never hinged	.20	
	a.	Pair, one without surcharge	975.00	
	b.	Inverted surcharge		5,500.

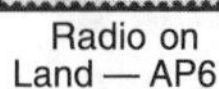

Radio on Land — AP61

Plane over Capitol Bell Tower — AP65

Designs: 6 l, 25 l, Radio on land. 10 l, 35 l, Radio at sea. 20 l, 50 l, Radio in the skies.

1947, Aug. 1 Photo. *Perf. 14*

C116	AP61	6 l dp violet	.20	.20
C117	AP61	10 l dk car rose	.20	.20
C118	AP61	20 l dp orange	.75	.20
C119	AP61	25 l aqua	.45	.20
C120	AP61	35 l brt blue	.45	.40
C121	AP61	50 l lilac rose	.95	1.00
		Nos. C116-C121 (6)	3.00	2.20
		Set, never hinged	7.00	

50th anniv. of radio.

For overprints see Trieste Nos. C7-C12.

1948

C123	AP65	100 l green	3.00	.20
C124	AP65	300 l lilac rose	.30	.20
C125	AP65	500 l ultra	.40	.30

Engr.

C126	AP65	1000 l dk brown	1.40	.85
	a.	Vert. pair, imperf. btwn.	250.00	250.00
	b.	Perf. 14x13	1.90	1.40
		Nos. C123-C126 (4)	5.10	1.55
		Set, never hinged	7.50	

See No. C132-C135. For overprints see Trieste Nos. C13-C16, C23-C26.

St. Catherine Carrying Cross AP66

200 l, St. Catherine with outstretched arms.

1948, Mar. 1 Photo.

C127	AP66	100 l bl vio & brn org	30.00	21.00
C128	AP66	200 l dp blue & bis	8.00	7.75
		Set, never hinged	80.00	

600th anniversary of the birth of St. Catherine of Siena, patroness of Italy.

Catalogue values for unused stamps in this section, from this point to the end of the section, are for Never Hinged items.

Giuseppe Mazzini (1805-1872), Patriot — AP67

1955, Dec. 31 Wmk. 303 *Perf. 14*

C129	AP67	100 l Prus green	1.60	.75

Types of 1945-46, 1948

1955-62 Wmk. 303 *Perf. 14*

C130	AP60	5 l green ('62)	.20	.20
C131	AP59	50 l vio ('57)	.20	.20
C132	AP65	100 l green	.75	.20
C133	AP65	300 l lil rose	.85	.55
C134	AP65	500 l ultra ('56)	1.00	.90

Engr.

Perf. 13½

C135	AP65	1000 l maroon ('59)	1.50	1.40
		Nos. C130-C135 (6)	4.50	3.45

Fluorescent Paper

See note below No. 998.

No. C132 was issued on both ordinary and fluorescent paper. The design of the fluorescent stamp is smaller.

Airmail stamps issued only on fluorescent paper are Nos. C139-C140.

Type of 1945-46 Surcharged in Ultramarine

1956, Feb. 24

C136	AP59	120 l on 50 l mag	1.10	1.25

Visit of Pres. Giovanni Gronchi to the US and Canada.

Madonna of Bruges, by Michelangelo AP68

Wmk. 303

1964, Feb. 18 Photo. *Perf. 14*

C137	AP68	185 l black	.30	.30

Michelangelo Buonarroti (1475-1564), artist.

Verrazano Type of Regular Issue

1964, Nov. 21 Wmk. 303 *Perf. 14*

C138	A481	130 l blk & dull grn	.20	.20

See note after No. 901.

Adoration of the Kings, by Gentile da Fabriano — AP69

1970, Dec. 12 Photo. Unwmk.

C139 AP69 150 l multicolored .30 .20

Christmas 1970.

Aviation Type of Regular Issue

Design: F-140S Starfighter over Aeronautical Academy, Pozzuoli.

1973, Mar. 28 Photo. *Perf. 14x13½*

C140 A590 150 l multicolored .30 .20

AIR POST SEMI-POSTAL STAMPS

Holy Year Type of Postage

Dome of St. Peter's, dove with olive branch, Church of the Holy Sepulcher.

Wmk. 140

1933, Oct. 23 Photo. *Perf. 14*

CB1 A163 50c + 25c org brn .70 3.00
CB2 A163 75c + 50c brn vio .85 4.50
Set, never hinged 5.00

Symbolical of Military Air Force — SPAP2

1935, July 1

CB3 SPAP2 50c + 50c brown 3.75 12.50
Never hinged 9.25

The surtax was for the Militia.

AIR POST SPECIAL DELIVERY STAMPS

Garibaldi, Anita Garibaldi, Plane APSD1

Wmk. 140

1932, June 2 Photo. *Perf. 14*

CE1 APSD1 2.25 l + 1 l 3.75 11.50
CE2 APSD1 4.50 l + 1.50 l 4.00 12.50
Set, never hinged 10.00

Death of Giuseppe Garibaldi, 50th anniv.

For overprinted types see Aegean Islands Nos. CE1-CE2.

Airplane and Sunburst APSD2

1933-34

CE3 APSD2 2 l gray blk ('34) .20 .45
CE4 APSD2 2.25 l gray blk 1.50 45.00
Set, never hinged 7.50

For overprint and surcharge see Nos. MCE1; Yugoslavia-Ljubljana NCE1.

Annexation of Fiume Type

Flag raising before Fascist headquarters.

1934, Mar. 12

CE5 A166 2 l + 1.25 l 1.10 11.50
CE6 A166 2.25 l + 1.25 l .20 6.50
CE7 A166 4.50 l + 2 l .20 7.50
Nos. CE5-CE7 (3) 1.50 25.50
Set, never hinged 3.50

Triumphal Arch in Rome APSD4

1934, Aug. 31

CE8 APSD4 2 l + 1.25 l brown 6.25 17.50
CE9 APSD4 4.50 l + 2 l cop red 6.75 17.50
Set, never hinged 32.50

Centenary of the institution of the Military Medal of Valor.

For overprinted types see Aegean Islands Nos. CE3-CE4.

AIR POST OFFICIAL STAMPS

Balbo Flight Type of Air Post Stamp of 1933 Overprinted

SERVIZIO DI STATO

1933 Wmk. 140 *Perf. 14*

CO1 AP25 5.25 l + 44.75 l red, grn & red vio 1,250. 6,750.
Never hinged 1,800.

Type of Air Post Stamp of 1934 Overprinted in Gold Crown and "SERVIZIO DI STATO"

1934

CO2 AP41 10 l blue blk 350.00 5,250.
Never hinged 700.00

65th birthday of King Victor Emmanuel III and the non-stop flight from Rome to Mogadiscio.

PNEUMATIC POST STAMPS

PN1

1913-28 Wmk. 140 Typo. *Perf. 14*

D1 PN1 10c brown 1.00 5.25
D2 PN1 15c brn vio ('28) 1.00 3.25
a. 15c dull violet ('21) 2.75 8.00
D3 PN1 15c rose red ('28) 1.00 5.25
D4 PN1 15c claret ('28) 1.75 3.25
D5 PN1 20c brn vio ('25) 4.50 10.50
D6 PN1 30c blue ('23) 3.50 17.50
D7 PN1 35c rose red ('27) 7.25 40.00
D8 PN1 40c dp red ('26) 10.00 47.50
Nos. D1-D8 (8) 30.00 132.50

Nos. D1, D2a, D5-D6, D8 Surcharged Like Nos. C10-C11

1924-27

D9 PN1 15c on 10c 1.75 7.00
D10 PN1 15c on 20c ('27) 4.25 7.75
D11 PN1 20c on 10c ('25) 3.75 11.00
D12 PN1 20c on 15c ('25) 4.75 5.50
D13 PN1 35c on 40c ('27) 11.00 37.50
D14 PN1 40c on 30c ('25) 4.75 27.50
Nos. D9-D14 (6) 30.25 96.25

Dante Alighieri PN2

Galileo Galilei PN3

1933, Mar. 29 Photo.

D15 PN2 15c dark violet .20 .50
D16 PN3 35c rose red .20 .50

Similar to Types of 1933, Without "REGNO"

1945, Oct. 22 Wmk. 277

D17 PN2 60c dull brown .20 .20
D18 PN3 1.40 l dull blue .20 .20

Minerva — PN6

1947, Nov. 15

D19 PN6 3 l rose lilac 5.00 9.00
D20 PN6 5 l aqua .20 .20
Set, never hinged 13.00

Catalogue values for unused stamps in this section, from this point to the end of the section, are for Never Hinged items.

1958-66 Wmk. 303

D21 PN6 10 l rose red .20 .20
D22 PN6 20 l sapphire ('66) .20 .20

SPECIAL DELIVERY STAMPS

Victor Emmanuel III — SD1

1903-26 Typo. Wmk. 140 *Perf. 14*

E1 SD1 25c rose red 17.50 .50
a. Imperf., pair 100.00 150.00
E2 SD1 50c dl red ('20) 1.50 .60
E3 SD1 60c dl red ('22) 2.25 .50
E4 SD1 70c dl red ('25) .20 .20
E5 SD1 1.25 l dp bl ('26) .20 .20
Nos. E1-E5 (5) 21.65 2.00

No. E1 is almost always found poorly centered, and it is valued thus.

For overprints and surcharges see Nos. C1, E11, E13, Austria NE1-NE2, Dalmatia E1, Offices in Crete, Offices in Africa, Offices in Turkish Empire.

Victor Emmanuel III — SD2

1908-26

E6 SD2 30c blue & rose .75 1.25
E7 SD2 2 l bl & red ('25) 3.00 22.50
E8 SD2 2.50 l bl & red ('26) 1.00 2.25
Nos. E6-E8 (3) 4.75 26.00

The 1.20 lire blue and red (see No. E12) was prepared in 1922, but not issued. Value $70.

For surcharges and overprints see Nos. E10, E12, Austria MNE3, Dalmatia E2, Offices in China, Offices in Africa, Offices in Turkish Empire.

SD3

1917, Nov.

E9 SD3 25c on 40c violet 12.50 22.50

Type SD3 not issued without surcharge.
For surcharge see No. C2.

No. E6 Surcharged

1921, Oct.

E10 SD2 1.20 l on 30c .75 4.25
a. Comma in value omitted 1.60 18.00
b. Double surcharge 32.50

No. E2 Surcharged **Cent. 60**

1922, Jan. 9

E11 SD1 60c on 50c dull red 15.00 .50
a. Inverted surcharge 30.00 55.00
b. Double surcharge 350.00
c. Imperf., pair 110.00 250.00

Type of 1908 Surcharged

1924, May

E12 SD2 1.60 l on 1.20 l bl & red 1.00 15.00
a. Double surch., one inverted 27.50 60.00

No. E3 Surcharged like No. E11

1925, Apr. 11

E13 SD1 70c on 60c dull red .50 .40
a. Inverted surcharge 32.50 65.00

Victor Emmanuel III — SD4

1932-33 Photo.

E14 SD4 1.25 l green .20 .20
E15 SD4 2.50 l deep org ('33) .20 1.00

For overprints and surcharges see Nos. ME1, Italian Social Republic E1-E2, Yugoslavia-Ljubljana NB5-NB8, NE1.

March on Rome Tyoe of Postage

1.25 l Ancient Pillars and Entrenchments. 2.50 l, Head of Mussolini, trophies of flags, etc.

1932, Oct. 27

E16 A146 1.25 l deep green .40 .80
E17 A146 2.50 l deep orange 2.75 75.00
Set, never hinged 7.00

"Italia" SD7

1945, Aug. Wmk. 277 *Perf. 14*

E18 SD7 5 l rose carmine .20 .20

Winged Foot SD8

Rearing Horse and Torch-Bearer — SD9

1945-51

E19 SD8 5 l henna brn .20 .20
E20 SD9 10 l deep blue .20 .20
E21 SD9 15 l dk car rose ('47) 2.00 .20
E22 SD8 25 l brt red org ('47) 18.00 .20
E23 SD8 30 l dp vio ('46) 4.00 .20
E24 SD8 50 l lil rose ('51) 12.00 .20
E25 SD9 60 l car rose ('48) 12.00 .20
Nos. E19-E25 (7) 48.40 1.40
Set, never hinged 110.00

See No. E32. For overprints see Nos. 1LNE1-1LNE2, Trieste E1-E4, E6-E7.

Type of Regular Issue of 1948 Inscribed: "Espresso"

1948, Sept. 18 Photo. *Perf. 14*

E26 A272 35 l violet *(Naples)* 15.00 10.00
Never hinged 25.00

Catalogue values for unused stamps in this section, from this point to the end of the section, are for Never Hinged items.

Type of 1945-51

1955, July 7 Wmk. 303 *Perf. 14*

E32 SD8 50 l lilac rose 4.00 .20

Etruscan Winged Horses SD10

1958-76 Photo.

Size: 36½x20¼mm

E33 SD10 75 l magenta .20 .20

Size: 36x20mm

E34 SD10 150 l dl bl grn ('68) .25 .20
a. Size: 36½x20¼mm ('66) 1.25 .20
E35 SD10 250 l blue ('74) .50 .20
E36 SD10 300 l brown ('76) .50 .20
Nos. E33-E36 (4) 1.45 .80

Nos. E34-E36 are fluorescent.

AUTHORIZED DELIVERY STAMPS

For the payment of a special tax for the authorized delivery of correspondence privately instead of through the post office.

AD1

1928 Wmk. 140 Typo. *Perf. 14*

EY1 AD1 10c dull blue 1.25 .20
a. Perf. 11 10.00 .60

Coat of Arms — AD2

1930 Photo. *Perf. 14*

EY2 AD2 10c dark brown .20 .20

For surcharge and overprint see Nos. EY3, Italian Social Republic EY1.

No. EY2 Surcharged in Black

1945

EY3 AD2 40c on 10c dark brown .20 .20

Coat of Arms — AD3

"Italia" — AD4

1945-46 Photo. Wmk. 277

EY4 AD3 40c dark brown .20 .25
EY5 AD3 1 l dk brown ('46) 1.75 .75

For overprint see Trieste No. EY1.

1947-52

Size: 27½x22½mm

EY6 AD4 1 l brt grnsh bl .20 .20
EY7 AD4 8 l brt red ('48) 9.00 .20

Size: 20½x16½mm

EY8 AD4 15 l violet ('49) 24.00 .20
EY9 AD4 20 l rose vio ('52) 2.00 .20
Set, never hinged 125.00

For overprints see Trieste Nos. EY2-EY5.

Catalogue values for unused stamps in this section, from this point to the end of the section, are for Never Hinged items.

Italia Type of 1947

1955-90 Wmk. 303 Photo. *Perf. 14*

Size: 20½x16½mm

EY11 AD4 20 l rose vio .20 .20
EY12 AD4 30 l Prus grn ('65) .20 .20
EY13 AD4 35 l ocher ('74) .20 .20
EY14 AD4 110 l lt ultra ('77) .20 .20
EY15 AD4 270 l brt pink ('84) .30 .20

Size: 19½x16½mm

EY16 AD4 300 l rose & grn ('87) .60 .20
EY17 AD4 370 l tan & brn vio .65 .40
Nos. EY11-EY17 (7) 2.35 1.60

Issue date: 370 l, Sept. 24, 1990.

POSTAGE DUE STAMPS

Unused values for Postage Due stamps are for examples with full original gum. Stamps without gum, with part gum or privately gummed sell for much less.

D1

D2

1863 Unwmk. Litho. *Imperf.*

J1 D1 10c yellow 1,250. 90.00
a. 10c yellow orange 1,250. 110.00
Without gum 65.00

1869 Wmk. 140 Typo. *Perf. 14*

J2 D2 10c buff 2,500. 20.00

D3

D4

1870-1925

J3 D3 1c buff & mag 2.50 5.00
J4 D3 2c buff & mag 9.00 11.50
J5 D3 5c buff & mag .30 .30
J6 D3 10c buff & mag ('71) .35 .30
b. Imperf. *1,000.*
J7 D3 20c buff & mag ('94) 2.00 .30
a. Imperf., pair 85.00 *100.00*
J8 D3 30c buff & mag 1.40 .45
b. Imperf. *7,500.* 725.00
J9 D3 40c buff & mag 1.75 .90
J10 D3 50c buff & mag 1.40 .40
b. Imperf. *800.00*
J11 D3 60c buff & mag 87.50 1.75
J12 D3 60c buff & brn ('25) 12.50 3.75
J13 D3 1 l lt bl & brn 3,250. 6.50
J14 D3 1 l bl & mag ('94) 3.75 .40
a. Imperf., pair 85.00 85.00
J15 D3 2 l lt bl & brn 3,250. 12.50
J16 D3 2 l bl & mag ('03) 20.00 1.25
J17 D3 5 l bl & brn ('74) 190.00 15.00
J18 D3 5 l bl & mag ('03) 80.00 6.50
J19 D3 10 l bl & brn ('74) *4,250.* 15.00
J20 D3 10 l bl & mag ('94) 62.50 2.75

Early printings of 5c, 10c, 30c, 40c, 50c and 60c were in buff and magenta, later ones (1890-94) in stronger shades. The earlier, paler shades and their inverted-numeral varieties sell for considerably more than those of the later shades. Values are for the later shades.

For surcharges and overprints see Nos. J25-J27, Austria NJ1-NJ16, Dalmatia J1-J4, Offices in China, Offices in Turkish Empire.

Numeral Inverted

J3a D3 1c 2,500. 1,500.
J4a D3 2c *5,900.* 2,500.
J5a D3 5c 2.00 2.00
J6a D3 10c 3.25 3.25
J7b D3 20c 13.50 12.50
J8a D3 30c 4.50 *7.00*
J9a D3 40c 275.00 *300.00*
J10a D3 50c 32.50 32.50
J11a D3 60c 175.00 160.00
J13a D3 1 l *15,000.*
J14b D3 1 l 1,750. 1,250.
J15a D3 2 l *1,450.*
J16a D3 2 l *1,500.* *1,350.*
J17a D3 5 l 800.00
J19a D3 10 l 225.00

1884-1903

J21 D4 50 l green 27.50 27.50
J22 D4 50 l yellow ('03) 40.00 19.00
J23 D4 100 l claret 27.50 10.00
J24 D4 100 l blue ('03) 32.50 9.00
Nos. J21-J24 (4) 127.50 65.50

Nos. J3 & J4 Surcharged in Black

1890-91

J25 D3 10c on 2c 62.50 15.00
J26 D3 20c on 1c 250.00 11.50
a. Inverted surcharge *4,500.*
J27 D3 30c on 2c 825.00 4.50
a. Inverted surcharge *1,300.*
Nos. J25-J27 (3) 1,137. 31.00

Coat of Arms
D6 D7

1934 Photo.

J28 D6 5c brown .35 .20
J29 D6 10c blue .35 .20
J30 D6 20c rose red .35 .20
J31 D6 25c green .35 .20
J32 D6 30c red org .35 .20
J33 D6 40c blk brn .35 *1.10*
J34 D6 50c violet .35 .20
J35 D6 60c slate blk .35 *3.50*
J36 D7 1 l red org .35 .20
J37 D7 2 l green .35 .20
J38 D7 5 l violet .75 .45
J39 D7 10 l blue 2.25 1.10
J40 D7 20 l car rose 3.50 *6.25*
Nos. J28-J40 (13) 10.00 14.00

For overprints and surcharges see Italian Social Republic #J1-J13, Yugoslavia-Ljubljana NJ14-NJ22.

D8

D9

1945-46 Unwmk. *Perf. 14*

J41 D8 5c brn, *grayish* ('46) 2.00 *2.50*
J42 D8 10c blue .45 *.70*
J43 D8 20c rose red, *grayish* ('46) 2.00 *.70*
J44 D8 25c dk grn .45 *.70*
J45 D8 30c red org .45 *.70*
J46 D8 40c blk brn .45 *.70*
J47 D8 50c violet .45 *.70*
J48 D8 60c black .45 *2.50*
J49 D9 1 l red org .45 *.70*
J50 D9 2 l green .45 *.70*
J51 D9 5 l violet .45 *.70*
J52 D9 10 l blue .45 *.70*
J53 D9 20 l car rose .45 *1.25*
Nos. J41-J53 (13) 8.95 13.25

Nos. J41 and J43 have yellow gum.

Wmk. 277

J54 D8 10c dark blue .20 .20
J55 D8 25c dk grn .45 .45
J56 D8 30c red org .45 .60
J57 D8 40c blk brn .20 .20
J58 D8 50c vio ('46) 2.00 .45
J59 D8 60c bl blk ('46) 2.25 1.25
J60 D9 1 l red org .20 .20
J61 D9 2 l dk grn .20 .20
J62 D9 5 l violet 5.25 .30
J63 D9 10 l dark blue 8.00 4.00
J64 D9 20 l car rose 11.00 .75
Nos. J54-J64 (11) 30.20 8.60
Set, never hinged 82.50

For overprints see Trieste Nos. J1, J3-J5.

D10

1947-54 Photo. *Perf. 14*

J65 D10 1 l red orange .20 .20
J66 D10 2 l dk green .20 .20
J67 D10 3 l carmine .20 .45
J68 D10 4 l brown .30 .25
J69 D10 5 l violet .45 .20
J70 D10 6 l vio blue 1.00 .25
J71 D10 8 l rose vio 2.25 .60
J72 D10 10 l deep blue .75 .20
J73 D10 12 l golden brn 1.40 .60
J74 D10 20 l lil rose 24.00 .20
J75 D10 25 l dk red ('54) 30.00 .45
J76 D10 50 l aqua 19.00 .20
J77 D10 100 l org yel ('52) 1.90 .20

Engr.

Perf. 13½x14

J78 D10 500 l dp bl & dk car ('52) 3.50 .20
a. Perf. 11x13 4.50 .25
b. Perf. 13 4.50 .20
Nos. J65-J78 (14) 85.15 4.20
Set, never hinged 300.00

For overprints see Trieste Nos. J2, J6-J29.

Catalogue values for unused stamps in this section, from this point to the end of the section, are for Never Hinged items.

1955-91 Wmk. 303 Photo. *Perf. 14*

J83 D10 5 l violet .20 .20
J85 D10 8 l rose vio 250.00 200.00
J86 D10 10 l deep blue .20 .20
J87 D10 20 l lil rose .20 .20
J88 D10 25 l dk red .20 .20
J89 D10 30 l gray brn ('61) .20 .20
J90 D10 40 l dl brn ('66) .20 .20
J91 D10 50 l aqua .20 .20
a. Type II .25 .20
J92 D10 100 l org yel ('58) .20 .20

Engr.

J93 D10 500 l dp bl & dk car ('61) .90 .20
J94 D10 900 l dp car & gray grn ('84) .80 .25
J95 D10 1500 l brown & orange 3.00 1.60
Nos. J83,J86-J95 (11) 6.30 3.65

Type I imprint on No. J91 reads: "1ST POL. STATO OFF. CARET VALORI". Type II imprint reads: "I.P.Z.S. OFF. CARTE VALORI" (1992). No. J91 has lighter background with more distinguishable lettering and design.

No. J92 exists with both Type I & Type II imprints.

Nos. J92 and J93 exist with "I. P. Z. S. ROMA" imprint.

Issue date: 1500 l, Feb. 20, 1991.

MILITARY STAMPS

Regular Stamps, 1929-42, Overprinted

1943 Wmk. 140 *Perf. 14*

M1 A90 5c ol brn .25 .30
M2 A92 10c dk brn .25 .30
M3 A93 15c slate grn .25 .30
M4 A91 20c rose red .25 .30
M5 A94 25c dp grn .25 .30
M6 A95 30c ol brn .25 .30
M7 A95 50c purple .25 .20
M8 A91 1 l dk pur 1.10 *4.50*
M9 A94 1.25 l deep blue .25 *.35*
M10 A92 1.75 l red org .25 *.30*
M11 A93 2 l car lake .25 *.35*
M12 A95a 5 l rose red .25 *1.00*
M13 A93 10 l purple 1.10 *6.50*
Nos. M1-M13 (13) 4.95 *15.00*

Due to a shortage of regular postage stamps during 1944-45, this issue was used for ordinary mail. "P. M." stands for "Posta Militare."

MILITARY AIR POST STAMPS

Air Post Stamps, 1930 Overprinted Like Nos. M1-M13 in Black

1943 Wmk. 140 *Perf. 14*

MC1 AP3 50c olive brown .25 *.45*
MC2 AP5 1 l purple .25 *.45*
MC3 AP6 2 l deep blue .25 *1.25*
MC4 AP3 5 l dark green 1.10 *3.00*
MC5 AP3 10 l deep carmine 1.10 *5.50*
Nos. MC1-MC5 (5) 2.95 *10.65*

MILITARY AIR POST SPECIAL DELIVERY STAMP

#CE3 Overprinted Like #M1-M13

1943 Wmk. 140 *Perf. 14*

MCE1 APSD2 2 l gray black .60 *5.50*

MILITARY SPECIAL DELIVERY STAMP

#E14 Overprinted Like #M1-M13

1943 Wmk. 140 *Perf. 14*

ME1 SD4 1.25 l green .20 *.70*

OFFICIAL STAMPS

O1

1875 Wmk. 140 Typo. *Perf. 14*

O1 O1 2c lake .65 *1.25*
O2 O1 5c lake .65 *1.25*
O3 O1 20c lake .25 *.40*
O4 O1 30c lake .25 *.50*
O5 O1 1 l lake 1.40 *4.25*
O6 O1 2 l lake 8.50 *15.00*
O7 O1 5 l lake 50.00 *70.00*
O8 O1 10 l lake 90.00 47.50
Nos. O1-O8 (8) 151.70 *140.15*

For surcharges see Nos. 37-44.

Stamps inscribed "Servizio Commissioni" were used in connection with the postal service but not for the payment of postage.

NEWSPAPER STAMP

N1

Typographed, Numeral Embossed

1862 Unwmk. *Imperf.*

P1 N1 2c buff 27.50 *62.50*
a. Numeral double 275.00 *825.00*

Black 1c and 2c stamps of similar type are listed under Sardinia.

PARCEL POST STAMPS

King Humbert I — PP1

1884-86 Wmk. 140 Typo. *Perf. 14*

Various Frames

Q1 PP1 10c olive gray 80.00 25.00
Q2 PP1 20c blue 137.50 40.00
Q3 PP1 50c claret 6.00 5.00
Q4 PP1 75c blue grn 5.50 5.00
Q5 PP1 1.25 l orange 13.00 12.50
Q6 PP1 1.75 l brown 16.00 *57.50*
Nos. Q1-Q6 (6) 258.00 145.00

For surcharges see Nos. 58-63.

Parcel Post stamps from No. Q7 onward were used by affixing them to the waybill so that one half remained on it following the parcel, the other half staying on the receipt given the sender. Most used halves are right halves. Complete stamps were and are obtainable canceled, probably to order.

Both unused and used values are for complete stamps.

PP2

1914-22 Wmk. 140 *Perf. 13*

Q7 PP2 5c brown 1.00 *2.25*
Q8 PP2 10c deep blue 1.00 *2.25*
Q9 PP2 20c black ('17) 2.00 *2.25*
Q10 PP2 25c red 3.00 *2.25*
Q11 PP2 50c orange 3.00 3.00
Q12 PP2 1 l violet 4.00 1.25
Q13 PP2 2 l green 5.00 2.25
Q14 PP2 3 l bister 6.25 4.00
Q15 PP2 4 l slate 10.50 4.00
Q16 PP2 10 l rose lil ('22) 30.00 6.50
Q17 PP2 12 l red brn ('22) 87.50 *110.00*
Q18 PP2 15 l ol grn ('22) 87.50 *110.00*
Q19 PP2 20 l brn vio ('22) 62.50 *125.00*
Nos. Q7-Q19 (13) 303.25 *375.00*

Halves Used

Q7-Q15 .20
Q16 .20
Q17-Q19 .75

Imperfs exist. Value per pair: 20c, 25c, 50c, 2 l, 4 l, 10 l, $50 each; 3 l, $60; 12 l, 15 l, 20 l, $200 each.

No. Q7 Surcharged

Q20 PP2 30c on 5c brown .60 *2.75*
Half stamp .20
Q21 PP2 60c on 5c brown .95 *2.75*
Half stamp .20
Q22 PP2 1.50 l on 5c brown 3.00 *18.00*
Half stamp .25
a. Double surcharge 25.00

No. Q16 Surcharged

LIRE 3 LIRE 3

Q23 PP2 3 l on 10 l rose lilac 3.00 *10.00*
Half stamp .20
Nos. Q20-Q23 (4) 7.55 *33.50*

PP3

1927-39 Wmk. 140

Q24 PP3 5c brn ('38) .45 *.50*
Q25 PP3 10c dp bl ('39) .45 *.50*
Q26 PP3 25c red ('32) .45 *.50*
Q27 PP3 30c ultra .45 *.75*
Q28 PP3 50c org ('32) .45 *.50*
Q29 PP3 60c red .45 *.75*
Q30 PP3 1 l lilac ('31) .45 *.50*
Q31 PP3 1 l brn vio ('36) 12.50 11.50
Q32 PP3 2 l grn ('32) .45 *.75*
Q33 PP3 3 l bister .45 *1.50*
a. Printed on both sides 15.00
Q34 PP3 4 l gray .45 *1.50*
Q35 PP3 10 l rose lil ('34) 1.25 *4.25*
Q36 PP3 20 l lil brn ('33) 1.75 *6.50*
Nos. Q24-Q36 (13) 20.00 *30.00*

Value of used halves, Nos. Q24-Q36, each 15 cents.

For overprints see Italian Social Republic Nos. Q1-Q12.

Nos. Q24-Q30, Q32-Q36 Overprinted Between Halves in Black

1945 Wmk. 140 *Perf. 13*

Q37 PP3 5c brown .40 .45
Q38 PP3 10c dp blue .40 .45
Q39 PP3 25c red .40 .45
Q40 PP3 30c ultra 6.00 1.90
Q41 PP3 50c orange .40 .20
Q42 PP3 60c red .40 .20
Q43 PP3 1 l lilac .40 .20
Q44 PP3 2 l green .40 .20
Q45 PP3 3 l bister .40 .30
Q46 PP3 4 l gray .40 .25
Q47 PP3 10 l rose lilac 1.90 *3.75*
Q48 PP3 20 l lilac brn 8.00 *8.00*
Nos. Q37-Q48 (12) 19.50 *16.35*
Set, never hinged 40.00

Halves Used

Q37-Q39, Q41-Q47 .20
Q40 .20
Q48 .20

Type of 1927

With Fasces Removed

1946 Typo.

Q55 PP3 1 l lilac .55 .20
Q56 PP3 2 l green .40 .20
Q57 PP3 3 l yellow org .70 .30
Q58 PP3 4 l gray 1.00 .20
Q59 PP3 10 l rose lilac 20.00 3.00
Q60 PP3 20 l lilac brn 26.00 9.75
Nos. Q55-Q60 (6) 48.65 13.65
Set, never hinged 150.00

Halves Used

Q55-Q58 .20
Q59 .25
Q60 .30

PP4

PP5

Perf. 13, 13x14, 12½x13

1946-54 Photo. Wmk. 277

Q61 PP4 25c dl vio bl ('48) .20 .20
Q62 PP4 50c brown ('47) .20 .20
Q63 PP4 1 l golden brn ('47) .20 .20
Q64 PP4 2 l lt bl grn ('47) .20 .20
Q65 PP4 3 l red org ('47) .20 .20
Q66 PP4 4 l gray blk ('47) .90 *1.40*
Q67 PP4 5 l lil rose ('47) .20 .20
a. Perf. 13 .20 .20
Q68 PP4 10 l violet 1.25 .20
a. Perf. 13 1.60 .90
Q69 PP4 20 l lilac brn .70 .25
a. Perf. 13 4.50 .45
Q70 PP4 30 l plum ('52) 1.10 1.25
a. Perf. 13 .70 *.90*
Q71 PP4 50 l rose red 3.50 .55
a. Perf. 13 3.50 .70
Q72 PP4 100 l sapphire 11.50 7.00
a. Perf. 13 70.00 11.00
Q73 PP4 200 l green ('48) 14.00 14.00
a. Perf. 13 18.00 18.00
Q74 PP4 300 l brn car ('48) 675.00 175.00
a. Perf. 13 675.00 175.00
Q75 PP4 500 l brown ('48) 40.00 35.00

Engr.

Perf. 13

Q76 PP5 1000 l ultra ('54) 1,300. 975.00
Nos. Q61-Q76 (16) 2,049. 1,210.
Set, never hinged 5,000.

Halves Used

Q61-Q69, Q70, Q71, Q72 .20
Q69a, Q70a, Q71a .20
Q72a .20
Q73,Q75 .20
Q73a .25
Q74 .30
Q74a .40
Q76 1.25

For overprints see Trieste Nos. Q1-Q26.

Catalogue values for unused stamps in this section, from this point to the end of the section, are for Never Hinged items.

Perf. 12½x13

1955-59 Wmk. 303 Photo.

Without Imprint

Q77 PP4 25c vio bl .30 *.40*
Q77A PP4 50c brn ('56) 8.00 *11.50*
Q78 PP4 5 l lil rose ('59) .20 .20
Q79 PP4 10 l violet .20 .20
Q80 PP4 20 l lil brn .20 .20
Q81 PP4 30 l plum ('56) .20 .20
Q82 PP4 40 l dl vio ('57) .20 .20
Q83 PP4 50 l rose red .20 .20
Q84 PP4 100 l sapphire .20 .20
Q85 PP4 150 l org brn ('57) .20 .20
Q86 PP4 200 l grn ('56) .30 .20
Q87 PP4 300 l brn car ('58) .45 .40
Q88 PP4 400 l gray blk ('57) .55 .45
Q89 PP4 500 l brn ('57) 1.00 .60

Engr.

Perf. 13

Q90 PP5 1000 l ultra ('57) 1.25 .95
Q91 PP5 2000 l red brn & car ('57) 3.25 1.90
Nos. Q77-Q91 (16) 16.70 *18.00*

Halves Used

Q77-Q89 .20
Q90-Q91 .40

1960-66 Photo. *Perf. 12½x13*

Q92 PP4 60 l bright lilac .20 .20
Q93 PP4 140 l dull red .25 .30
Q94 PP4 280 l yellow .60 .45
Q95 PP4 600 l olive bister .70 .75
Q96 PP4 700 l blue ('66) 1.10 .75
Q97 PP4 800 l dp org ('66) 1.25 .95
Nos. Q92-Q97 (6) 4.10 3.40

Halves Used

Q92-Q93 .20
Q94 .20
Q95 .40
Q96-Q97 .25

Imprint: "I.P.S.-Off. Carte Valori-Roma"

1973, Mar. Photo. Wmk. 303

Q98 PP4 20 l lilac brown .20 .20
Q99 PP4 30 l plum .20 .20

PARCEL POST AUTHORIZED DELIVERY STAMPS

For the payment of a special tax for the authorized delivery of parcels privately instead of through the post office.

PAD1

1953 Wmk. 277 Photo. *Perf. 13*

QY1 PAD1 40 l orange red 1.75 *2.25*
QY2 PAD1 50 l ultra 65.00 *72.50*
QY3 PAD1 75 l brown 40.00 *45.00*
QY4 PAD1 110 l lil rose 40.00 *50.00*
Nos. QY1-QY4 (4) 146.75 *169.75*
Set, never hinged 450.00

Halves Used

QY1 .30
QY2 .60
QY3 1.50
QY4 1.90

For overprints see Trieste Nos. QY1-QY4.

Catalogue values for unused stamps in this section, from this point to the end of the section, are for Never Hinged items.

1956-58 Wmk. 303 *Perf. 12½x13*

QY5 PAD1 40 l orange red 1.60 .90
QY6 PAD1 50 l ultra 3.25 2.25
QY7 PAD1 60 l brt vio bl ('58) 9.00 5.25
QY8 PAD1 75 l brown 350.00 150.00
QY9 PAD1 90 l lil ('58) .35 .20
QY10 PAD1 110 l lil rose 350.00 125.00

QY11 PAD1 120 l grnsh bl ('58) .35 .20
Nos. QY5-QY11 (7) 714.55 283.80

Halves Used

QY5-QY6 .20
QY7 .90
QY8,QY10 4.00
QY9 .30
QY11 .25

1960-81

QY12 PAD1 70 l green ('66) 35.00 35.00
QY13 PAD1 80 l brown .40 .40
QY14 PAD1 110 l org yel .40 .40
QY15 PAD1 140 l black .45 .50
QY16 PAD1 150 l car rose ('68) .30 .50
QY17 PAD1 180 l red ('66) .40 .60
QY18 PAD1 240 l dk bl ('66) .45 .70

Engr.

Perf. 13½

QY19 PAD1 500 l ocher ('76) 1.40 1.40
QY20 PAD1 600 l bl grn ('79) 1.40 1.40
QY21 PAD1 900 l ultra ('81) 1.10 1.40
Nos. QY12-QY21 (10) 41.30 42.30

Halves Used

QY12 4.00
QY13-QY15, QY18, QY21 .20
QY16, QY17, QY19 .25
QY20 .35

PAD2

Perf. 14x13½

1984 Photo. Wmk. 303

QY22 PAD2 3000 l multi 3.50 3.50

OCCUPATION STAMPS

Issued under Austrian Occupation

Emperor Karl of Austria
OS1 OS2

Austria #M49-M67 Surcharged in Black

1918 Unwmk. *Perf. 12½*

N1 OS1 2c on 1h grnsh bl .35 *.70*
N2 OS1 3c on 2h red org .35 *.70*
N3 OS1 4c on 3h ol gray .35 *.70*
N4 OS1 6c on 5h ol grn .35 *.70*
N5 OS1 7c on 6h vio .35 *.70*
a. Perf. 12½x11½ 28.00 *55.00*
N6 OS1 11c on 10h org brn .35 *.70*
N7 OS1 13c on 12h blue .35 *.70*
N8 OS1 16c on 15h brt rose .35 *.70*
N9 OS1 22c on 20h red brn .35 *.70*
a. Perf. 11½ 14.00 *28.00*
N10 OS1 27c on 25h ultra .50 *1.00*
N11 OS1 32c on 30h slate .35 *.70*
N12 OS1 43c on 40h ol bis .35 *.70*
a. Perf. 11½ 14.00 *28.00*
N13 OS1 53c on 50h dp grn .35 *.70*
N14 OS1 64c on 60h rose .35 *.70*
N15 OS1 85c on 80h dl bl .35 *.70*
N16 OS1 95c on 90h dk vio .35 *.70*
N17 OS2 2 l 11c on 2k rose, *straw* .35 .70
N18 OS2 3 l 16c on 3k grn, *bl* 1.00 2.00
N19 OS2 4 l 22c on 4k rose, *grn* 1.00 2.00
Nos. N1-N19 (19) 8.10 *16.20*

Emperor Karl — OS3

Austria #M69-M81 Surcharged in Black

1918

N20 OS3 2c on 1h grnsh bl 6.00
N21 OS3 3c on 2h orange 6.00
N22 OS3 4c on 3h ol gray 6.00
N23 OS3 6c on 5h yel grn 6.00
N24 OS3 11c on 10h dk brn 6.00
N25 OS3 22c on 20h red 6.00
N26 OS3 27c on 25h blue 6.00
N27 OS3 32c on 30h bister 6.00
N28 OS3 48c on 45h dk sl 6.00
N29 OS3 53c on 50h dp grn 6.00
N30 OS3 64c on 60h violet 6.00
N31 OS3 85c on 80h rose 6.00
N32 OS3 95c on 90h brn vio 6.00
N33 OS3 1 l 6c on 90h brn vio 6.00
Nos. N20-N33 (14) 84.00

Nos. N20 to N33 inclusive were never placed in use in the occupied territory. They were, however, on sale at the Post Office in Vienna for a few days before the Armistice.

OCCUPATION SPECIAL DELIVERY STAMPS

Bosnia #QE1-QE2 Surcharged

1918 Unwmk. *Perf. 12½*

NE1 SH1 3c on 2h ver 5.50 *11.00*
NE2 SH1 6c on 5h dp grn 5.50 *11.00*

Nos. NE1-NE2 are on yellowish paper. Reprints on white paper sell for about 70 cents a set.

OCCUPATION POSTAGE DUE STAMPS

Bosnia #J16, J18-J19, J21-J24 Surcharged Like Nos. NE1-NE2

1918 Unwmk. *Perf. 12½*

NJ1 D2 6c on 5h red 1.90 *3.75*
a. Perf. 11½ 5.50 *11.00*
NJ2 D2 11c on 10h red 1.90 *3.75*
a. Perf. 11½ 5.50 *11.00*
NJ3 D2 16c on 15h red .90 *1.90*
NJ4 D2 27c on 25h red .90 *1.90*
NJ5 D2 32c on 30h red .90 *1.90*
NJ6 D2 43c on 40h red .90 *1.90*
NJ7 D2 53c on 50h red .90 *1.90*
Nos. NJ1-NJ7 (7) 8.30 *17.00*

OCCUPATION NEWSPAPER STAMPS

Austrian #MP1-MP4 Surcharged

1918 Unwmk. *Perf. 12½*

NP1 MN1 3c on 2h blue .20 *.25*
a. Perf. 11½ 2.75 *5.50*
NP2 MN1 7c on 6h org .45 *.90*
NP3 MN1 11c on 10h car .45 *.90*
NP4 MN1 22c on 20h brn .35 *.70*
a. Perf. 11½ 15.00 *30.00*
Nos. NP1-NP4 (4) 1.45 *2.75*

A.M.G.

Issued jointly by the Allied Military Government of the United States and Great Britain, for civilian use in areas under Allied occupation.

Catalogue values for unused stamps in this section are for Never Hinged items.

OS4

Offset Printing
"Italy Centesimi" (or "Lira") in Black

1943 Unwmk. *Perf. 11*

1N1 OS4 15c pale orange 1.00 .80
1N2 OS4 25c pale citron 1.00 .80
1N3 OS4 30c light gray 1.00 .80
1N4 OS4 50c light violet 1.00 .80
1N5 OS4 60c orange yellow 1.00 1.90
1N6 OS4 1 l lt yel green 1.00 .80
1N7 OS4 2 l deep rose 2.25 1.60
1N8 OS4 5 l light blue 3.25 *2.75*
1N9 OS4 10 l buff 3.25 *4.00*
Nos. 1N1-1N9 (9) 14.75*14.25*

Italy Nos. 217, 220 and 221 Overprinted in Blue, Vermilion, Carmine or Orange

1943, Dec. 10 Wmk. 140 *Perf. 14*

1N10 A91 20c rose red (Bl) 1.50 *3.00*
1N11 A93 35c dp blue (C) 17.50 *17.50*
a. 35c deep blue (V) 35.00 *50.00*
1N13 A95 50c purple (C) .75 *1.10*
a. 50c purple (O) .90 *2.00*
Nos. 1N10-1N13 (3) 19.75 *21.60*

Nos. 1N1-1N9 were for use in Sicily, Nos. 1N10-1N13 for use in Naples.

VENEZIA GIULIA

Catalogue values for unused stamps in this section are for Never Hinged items.

Stamps of Italy, 1929 to 1945 Overprinted in Black:

a

b

On Stamps of 1929

1945-47 Wmk. 140 *Perf. 14*

1LN1 A92 (a) 10c dk brown .30 *.35*
1LN1A A91 (a) 20c rose red ('47) .40 *.50*

On Stamps of 1945

1945 Wmk. 277 *Perf. 14*

1LN2 A249 (a) 20c rose red .35 *.50*
1LN3 A248 (a) 60c sl grn .45 .35
1LN4 A249 (a) 1 l dp vio .30 .35
1LN5 A251 (a) 2 l dk red .35 .35
1LN6 A252 (b) 5 l dk red .65 .50
1LN7 A251 (a) 10 l purple .90 *1.25*
Nos. 1LN2-1LN7 (6) 3.00 *3.30*

On Stamps of 1945

1945-46 Unwmk.

1LN7A A250(a) 10c dk brn ('46) .30 .25
1LN7B A249(a) 20c rose red ('46) .25 *.50*
1LN8 A251(a) 60c red org .25 .25
Nos. 1LN7A-1LN8 (3) .80 *1.00*

On Air Post Stamp of 1930

1945 Wmk. 140 *Perf. 14*

1LN9 AP3 (a) 50c olive brn .25 *.50*

On Stamp of 1929

1946

1LN10 A91 (a) 20 l lt green 2.25 *3.50*

On Stamps of 1945

Wmk. 277

1LN11 A260 (a) 25 l dk green 4.25 *6.50*
1LN12 A260 (a) 50 l dk vio brn 4.75 *7.50*

Italy No. 477 Overprinted in Black

1LN13 A261 100 l car lake 17.50 *25.00*
Nos. 1LN10-1LN13 (4) 28.75 *42.50*

Stamps of Italy, 1945-47 Overprinted Type "a" in Black

1947

1LN14 A259 25c brt bl grn .25 .30
1LN15 A258 2 l dk claret brn .60 *.75*
1LN16 A259 3 l red .45 .30
1LN17 A259 4 l red org .70 .40
1LN18 A257 6 l deep violet 1.75 *1.40*
1LN19 A259 20 l dk red vio *45.00* 2.25
Nos. 1LN14-1LN19 (6) *48.75* 5.40

Some denominations of the Venezia Giulia A.M.G. issues exist with inverted overprint; several values exist in horizontal and vertical pairs, one stamp without overprint.

OCCUPATION AIR POST STAMPS

Catalogue values for unused stamps in this section are for Never Hinged items.

Italy Nos. C106-C107 and C109-C113 Overprinted Like 1LN13 in Black

1946-47 Wmk. 277 *Perf. 14*

1LNC1 AP59 1 l sl blue ('47) .25 *3.25*
1LNC2 AP60 2 l dk blue ('47) .25 *1.75*
1LNC3 AP60 5 l dk green ('47) 1.75 *1.00*
1LNC4 AP59 10 l car rose ('47) 1.75 *1.00*
1LNC5 AP60 25 l dk blue 1.75 *1.00*
1LNC6 AP60 25 l brown ('47) 22.50 *22.50*
1LNC7 AP59 50 l dk green 3.25 *3.00*
Nos. 1LNC1-1LNC7 (7) 31.50 *33.50*

Nos. 1LNC5 and 1LNC7 exist with inverted overprint; No. 1LNC5 with double overprint, one inverted.

OCCUPATION SPECIAL DELIVERY STAMPS

Catalogue values for unused stamps in this section are for Never Hinged items.

Italy Nos. E20 and E23 Overprinted Like 1LN13 in Black

1946 Wmk. 277 *Perf. 14*

1LNE1 SD9 10 l deep blue 3.50 *4.50*
1LNE2 SD8 30 l deep violet 8.75 *12.50*

ITALIAN SOCIAL REPUBLIC

On Sept. 15, 1943, Mussolini proclaimed the establishment of a Republican fascist party and a new fascist government. This government's authority covered only the Northern Italy area occupied by the Germans.

Catalogue values for unused stamps in this section are for Never Hinged items.

Italy Nos. 218, 219, 221 to 223 and 231 Overprinted in Black or Red:

a

b

c

1944 Wmk. 140 *Perf. 14*

1	A94(a)	25c deep grn	.25	.20
2	A95(b)	30c ol brn (R)	.25	.20
3	A95(c)	50c pur (R)	.25	.20
4	A94(a)	75c rose red	.25	.20
5	A94(b)	1.25 l dp bl (R)	.25	.20
5A	A94(b)	50 l dp vio (R)	700.00	*1,900.*
		Nos. 1-5 (5)	1.25	1.00

Nos. 1 to 5 exist with overprint inverted. No. 1 exists with overprint "b." Counterfeits of No. 5A exist.

Italy Nos. 427 to 438 Overprinted Same in Black or Red

6	A243(a)	25c deep green	.35	*.55*
7	A244(a)	25c deep green	.35	*.55*
8	A245(a)	25c deep green	.35	*.55*
9	A246(a)	25c deep green	.35	*.55*
10	A243(b)	30c olive brown (R)	.40	*.75*
11	A244(b)	30c olive brown (R)	.40	*.75*
12	A245(b)	30c olive brown (R)	.40	*.75*
13	A246(b)	30c olive brown (R)	.40	*.75*
14	A243(c)	50c purple (R)	.35	*.55*
15	A244(c)	50c purple (R)	.35	*.55*
16	A245(c)	50c purple (R)	.35	*.55*
17	A246(c)	50c purple (R)	.35	*.55*
		Nos. 6-17 (12)	4.40	*7.40*

Loggia dei Mercanti, Bologna — A1

Basilica of San Lorenzo, Rome — A2

Drummer Boy — A3

1944 Photo. *Perf. 14*

18	A1	20c crimson	.20	.20
19	A2	25c green	.20	.20
20	A3	30c brown	.20	.20
21	A3	75c dark red	.20	.20
		Nos. 18-21 (4)	.80	.80

For surcharges see Italy Nos. 461-462.

Church of St. Ciriaco, Ancona A4

Monte Cassino Abbey A5

Loggia dei Mercanti, Bologna A6

Basilica of San Lorenzo, Rome A7

Statue of "Rome" A8

Basilica of St. Maria delle Grazie, Milan A9

1944 Unwmk.

22	A4	5c brown	.20	.20
23	A5	10c brown	.20	.20
24	A6	20c rose red	.20	.20
25	A7	25c deep green	.20	.20
26	A3	30c brown	.20	.20
27	A8	50c purple	.20	.20
28	A3	75c dark red	.20	.20
29	A5	1 l purple	.20	.20
30	A9	1.25 l blue	.20	*.30*
31	A9	3 l deep green	.20	*15.00*
		Nos. 22-31 (10)	2.00	*16.90*

Bandiera Brothers — A10

1944, Dec. 6

32	A10	25c deep green	.20	*.25*
33	A10	1 l purple	.20	*.25*
34	A10	2.50 l rose red	.20	*2.75*
		Nos. 32-34 (3)	.60	*3.25*

Cent. of the execution of Attilio (1811-44) and Emilio Bandiera (1819-44), revolutionary patriots who were shot at Cosenza, July 23, 1844, by Neapolitan authorities after an unsuccessful raid.

This set was overprinted in 1945 by the committee of the National Philatelic Convention to publicize that gathering at Venice.

SPECIAL DELIVERY STAMPS

Catalogue values for unused stamps in this section are for Never Hinged items.

Italy Nos. E14 and E15 Overprinted in Red or Black

1944 Wmk. 140 *Perf. 14*

E1	SD4	1.25 l green (R)	.20	*.25*
E2	SD4	2.50 l deep orange	.20	*1.25*

Cathedral, Palermo SD1

1944 Photo.

E3	SD1	1.25 l green	.25	*.55*

AUTHORIZED DELIVERY STAMP

Catalogue values for unused stamps in this section are for Never Hinged items.

Italy No. EY2 Overprinted

1944 Wmk. 140 *Perf. 14*

EY1	AD2	10c dark brown	.30	.20

POSTAGE DUE STAMPS

Catalogue values for unused stamps in this section are for Never Hinged items.

Italy #J28-J40 Overprinted Like #EY1

1944 Wmk. 140 *Perf. 14*

J1	D6	5c brown	.20	*.40*
J2	D6	10c blue	.20	*.40*
J3	D6	20c rose red	.20	*.40*
J4	D6	25c green	.20	*.40*
J5	D6	30c red org	.20	*1.10*
J6	D6	40c blk brn	.20	*1.50*
J7	D6	50c violet	.20	*.25*
J8	D6	60c slate blk	1.00	*4.50*
J9	D7	1 l red org	.20	*.25*
J10	D7	2 l green	1.50	*3.00*
J11	D7	5 l violet	20.00	*25.00*
J12	D7	10 l blue	40.00	*55.00*
J13	D7	20 l car rose	40.00	*55.00*
		Nos. J1-J13 (13)	104.10	*147.20*

PARCEL POST STAMPS

Both unused and used values are for complete stamps.

Catalogue values for unused stamps in this section are for Never Hinged items.

Italian Parcel Post Stamps and Types of 1927-39 Overprinted Like No. EY1

1944 Wmk. 140 *Perf. 13*

Q1	PP3	5c brown	2.25	1.75
Q2	PP3	10c deep blue	2.25	1.75
Q3	PP3	25c carmine	2.25	1.75
Q4	PP3	30c ultra	2.25	1.75
Q5	PP3	50c orange	2.25	1.75
Q6	PP3	60c red	2.25	1.75
Q7	PP3	1 l lilac	2.50	2.00
Q8	PP3	2 l green	160.00	160.00
Q9	PP3	3 l yel grn	4.50	4.75
Q10	PP3	4 l gray	4.50	4.75
Q11	PP3	10 l rose lilac	125.00	125.00
Q12	PP3	20 l lilac brn	290.00	290.00
		Nos. Q1-Q12 (12)	600.00	597.00

No parcel post service existed in 1944. Nos. Q1-Q12 were used undivided, for regular postage.

ITALIAN OFFICES ABROAD

Stamps listed under this heading were issued for use in the Italian Post Offices which, for various reasons, were maintained from time to time in foreign countries.

100 Centesimi = 1 Lira

GENERAL ISSUE

Values of Italian Offices Abroad stamps vary tremendously according to condition. Quotations are for very fine examples, and values for unused stamps are for examples with original gum as defined in the catalogue introduction. Extremely fine or superb copies sell at much higher prices, and fine or poor copies sell at greatly reduced prices. In addition, unused copies without gum are discounted severely.

Very fine examples of Nos. 1-17 will have perforations barely clear of the frameline or design due to the narrow spacing of the stamps on the plates.

Italian Stamps with Corner Designs Slightly Altered and Overprinted

1874-78 Wmk. 140 *Perf. 14*

1	A6	1c olive green	2.50	*7.50*
a.		Inverted overprint	*12,500.*	
c.		2 dots in lower right corner	15.00	*82.50*
d.		Three dots in upper right corner	125.00	*600.00*
e.		Without overprint	23,750.	
2	A7	2c orange brn	3.00	*10.00*
a.		Without overprint	23,750.	33,750.
3	A8	5c slate grn	250.00	9.00
a.		Lower right corner not altered	*7,250.*	950.00
4	A8	10c buff	625.00	17.50
a.		Upper left corner not altered	*8,750.*	475.00
b.		None of the corners altered	—	*27,500.*
c.		Lower corners not altered		*2,200.*
5	A8	10c blue ('78)	110.00	5.00
6	A15	20c blue	575.00	9.50
7	A15	20c org ('78)	2,250.	4.50
8	A8	30c brown	1.00	*5.75*
a.		None of the corners altered		*16,500.*
b.		Right lower corner not altered	—	—
c.		Double overprint	—	—
9	A8	40c rose	1.00	*4.50*
10	A8	60c lilac	2.00	*30.00*
11	A13	2 l vermilion	45.00	*225.00*

1881

12	A17	5c green	1.50	*3.50*
13	A17	10c claret	1.50	*2.75*
14	A17	20c orange	1.50	*2.00*
a.		Double overprint, on piece		—
15	A17	25c blue	1.50	*3.50*
16	A17	50c violet	3.50	*22.50*
17	A17	2 l vermilion	7.50	—
		Nos. 12-17 (6)	17.00	
		Nos. 12-16 (5)		34.25

The "Estero" stamps were used in various parts of the world, South America, Africa, Turkey, etc.

Forged cancellations exist on Nos. 1-2, 9-11, 16.

OFFICES IN CHINA

100 Cents = 1 Dollar

PEKING

PECHINO
2 CENTS

Italian Stamps of 1901-16 Handstamped

Wmk. 140, Unwmk.

1917 *Perf. 12, 13½, 14*

1	A48	2c on 5c green	87.50	47.50
c.		4c on 5c green	*2,750.*	
3	A48	4c on 10c claret (No. 95)	175.00	87.50
c.		4c on 10c claret (No. 79)	—	
5	A58	6c on 15c slate	350.00	190.00
b.		8c on 15c slate	1,600.	1,200.
7	A58	8c on 20c on 15c slate	2,000.	875.00
8	A50	8c on 20c brn org (No. 112)	*3,000.*	1,000.
9	A49	20c on 50c vio	*16,750.*	*10,000.*
b.		40c on 50c violet	*6,000.*	*5,500.*
11	A46	40c on 1 l brn & grn	*110,000.*	*14,250*

Inverted surcharges are found on Nos. 1, 3, 3c, 5, 7-9; values same. Double surcharge one inverted exist on Nos. 1, 3; value about double.

Excellent forgeries exist of the higher valued stamps of Offices in China.

Italian Stamps of 1901-16 Overprinted

1917-18

12	A42	1c brown	8.75	*12.00*
13	A43	2c orange brown	8.75	*12.00*
a.		Double overprint	150.00	
14	A48	5c green	2.60	*3.50*
a.		Double overprint	87.50	
15	A48	10c claret	2.60	*3.50*
16	A50	20c brn org (No. 112)	77.50	*60.00*
17	A49	25c blue	2.60	*6.00*
18	A49	50c violet	2.60	*6.50*

19	A46	1 l brown & grn	5.25	*11.00*
20	A46	5 l blue & rose	8.75	*17.50*
21	A51	10 l gray grn & red	77.50	*160.00*
		Nos. 12-21 (10)	196.90	*292.00*

Italy No. 113, the watermarked 20c brown orange, was also overprinted "Pechino," but not issued. Value $2.50.

Italian Stamps of 1901-16 Surcharged:

a

2
dollari

Pechino
b

TWO DOLLARS:
Type I - Surcharged "2 dollari" as illustration "b."
Type II - Surcharged "2 DOLLARI."
Type III - Surcharged "2 dollari." "Pechino" measures 11½mm wide, instead of 13mm.

1918-19 ***Perf. 14***

22	A42	½c on 1c brown	72.50	*62.50*
a.		Surcharged "1 cents"	260.00	*275.00*
23	A43	1c on 2c org brn	2.50	*4.50*
a.		Surcharged "1 cents"	150.00	*150.00*
24	A48	2c on 5c green	2.50	*4.50*
25	A48	4c on 10c claret	2.50	*4.50*
26	A50	8c on 20c brn org (No. 112)	12.50	*8.75*
27	A49	10c on 25c blue	6.00	*8.75*
28	A49	20c on 50c violet	7.00	*8.75*
29	A46	40c on 1 l brown & green	87.50	*100.00*
30	A46	$2 on 5 l bl & rose (type I)	160.00	*260.00*
a.		Type II	*30,000.*	*24,500.*
b.		Type III	*4,400.*	*3,250.*
		Nos. 22-30 (9)	353.00	*462.25*

Italy No. 100 Surcharged

1919

32	A49	10c on 25c blue	3.00	*8.25*

PEKING SPECIAL DELIVERY STAMPS

Italian Special Delivery Stamp 1908 Overprinted Like Nos. 12-21

1917 **Wmk. 140** ***Perf. 14***

E1	SD2	30c blue & rose	5.25	*15.00*

No. E1 Surcharged

1918

E2	SD2	12c on 30c bl & rose	37.50	*110.00*

PEKING POSTAGE DUE STAMPS

Italian Postage Due Stamps Overprinted Like Nos. 12-21

1917 **Wmk. 140** ***Perf. 14***

J1	D3	10c buff & magenta	2.10	*5.25*
J2	D3	20c buff & magenta	2.10	*5.25*
J3	D3	30c buff & magenta	2.10	*5.25*
J4	D3	40c buff & magenta	4.00	*5.25*
		Nos. J1-J4 (4)	10.30	*21.00*

Nos. J1-J4 Surcharged Like No. E2

1918

J5	D3	4c on 10c	*30,000.*	*24,500.*
J6	D3	8c on 20c	11.00	*15.00*
J7	D3	12c on 30c	37.50	*45.00*
J8	D3	16c on 40c	190.00	*250.00*

In 1919, the same new values were surcharged on Italy Nos. J6-J9 in a different style: four lines to cancel the denomination, and "-PECHINO- 4 CENTS." These were not issued. Value $1.10 each.

TIENTSIN

TIENTSIN
2 CENTS

Italian Stamps of 1906 Handstamped

Wmk. 140, Unwmk.

1917 ***Perf. 12, 13½, 14***

1	A48	2c on 5c green	175.00	140.00
c.		4c on 5c green	*3,750.*	
2	A48	4c on 10c claret	300.00	175.00
4	A58	6c on 15c slate	700.00	450.00
b.		4c on 15c slate	2,000.	1,600.
		Nos. 1-4 (3)	1,175.	765.00

Italian Stamps of 1901-16 Overprinted

1917-18

5	A42	1c brown	8.75	*12.00*
a.		Inverted overprint	150.00	150.00
6	A43	2c orange brn	8.75	*12.00*
7	A48	5c green	2.75	*3.50*
8	A48	10c claret	2.75	*3.50*
9	A50	20c brn org (#112)	77.50	*60.00*
10	A49	25c blue	2.75	*6.00*
11	A49	50c violet	2.75	*6.50*
12	A46	1 l brown & grn	5.50	*10.00*
13	A46	5 l blue & rose	8.75	*17.50*
14	A51	10 l gray grn & red	77.50	*160.00*
		Nos. 5-14 (10)	197.75	*291.00*

Italy No. 113, the watermarked 20c brown orange was also overprinted "Tientsin," but not issued. Value $2.50.

Italian Stamps of 1901-16 Surcharged:

a

b

TWO DOLLARS:
Type I - Surcharged "2 Dollari" as illustration "b".
Type II - Surcharged "2 dollari".
Type III - Surcharged "2 Dollari". "Tientsin" measures 10mm wide instead of 13mm.

1918-21 ***Perf. 14***

15	A42	½c on 1c brown	72.50	*62.50*
a.		Inverted surcharge	175.00	*175.00*
b.		Surcharged "1 cents"	275.00	*260.00*
16	A43	1c on 2c org brn	2.25	*4.50*
a.		Surcharged "1 cents"	175.00	*175.00*
b.		Inverted surcharge	160.00	160.00
17	A48	2c on 5c green	2.25	*4.50*
18	A48	4c on 10c claret	2.25	*4.50*
19	A50	8c on 20c brn org (#112)	12.50	*8.75*
20	A49	10c on 25c blue	6.00	*8.75*
21	A49	20c on 50c violet	7.25	*8.75*
22	A46	40c on 1 l brn & grn	87.50	*100.00*
23	A46	$2 on 5 l bl & rose (type I)	160.00	*275.00*
a.		Type II	*4,850.*	*3,600.*
b.		Type III ('21)	*4,350.*	*3,250.*
		Nos. 15-23 (9)	352.50	*477.25*

SPECIAL DELIVERY STAMPS

Italian Special Delivery Stamp of 1908 Overprinted

1917 **Wmk. 140** ***Perf. 14***

E1	SD2	30c blue & rose	5.25	*15.00*

No. E1 Surcharged

1918

E2	SD2	12c on 30c bl & rose	37.50	*110.00*

POSTAGE DUE STAMPS

Italian Postage Due Stamps Overprinted

1917 **Wmk. 140** ***Perf. 14***

J1	D3	10c buff & magenta	2.10	*5.25*
a.		Double overprint	150.00	
J2	D3	20c buff & magenta	2.10	*5.25*
J3	D3	30c buff & magenta	2.10	*5.25*
a.		Double overprint	150.00	
J4	D3	40c buff & magenta	4.25	*5.25*
		Nos. J1-J4 (4)	10.55	*21.00*

Nos. J1-J4 Surcharged

1918

J5	D3	4c on 10c	*1,350.*	*1,600.*
J6	D3	8c on 20c	11.00	*15.00*
J7	D3	12c on 30c	37.50	*45.00*
J8	D3	16c on 40c	190.00	*250.00*

In 1919, the same new values were surcharged on Italy Nos. J6-J9 in a different style: four lines to cancel the denomination, and "-TIENTSIN- 4 CENTS." These were not issued. Value $4.00 each.

OFFICES IN CRETE

40 Paras = 1 Piaster
100 Centesimi = 1 Lira (1906)

Italy Nos. 70 and 81 Surcharged in Red or Black

a

b

1900-01 **Wmk. 140** ***Perf. 14***

1	A36(a)	1pi on 25c blue	4.50	*27.50*
2	A45(b)	1pi on 25c dp bl (Bk) ('01)	2.25	*50.00*

Italian Stamps Overprinted

1906

On Nos. 76-79, 92, 81, 83-85, 87, 91

3	A42	1c brown	.45	*1.10*
a.		Pair, one without ovpt.	375.00	
4	A43	2c org brn	.45	*1.10*
a.		Imperf., pair	750.00	
b.		Double overprint	160.00	
5	A44	5c bl grn	.90	*1.40*
6	A45	10c claret	75.00	55.00
7	A45	15c on 20c org	1.10	*1.50*
8	A45	25c blue	4.50	4.50
9	A45	40c brown	4.00	*4.50*
10	A45	45c ol grn	3.50	*4.50*
11	A45	50c violet	4.50	*6.00*
12	A46	1 l brn & grn	26.00	*26.00*
13	A46	5 l bl & rose	125.00	*125.00*
		Nos. 3-13 (11)	245.40	*230.60*

On Nos. 94-95, 100, 104-105

1907-10

14	A48	5c green	.75	*1.10*
a.		Inverted overprint	175.00	
15	A48	10c claret	.75	*1.10*
16	A49	25c blue	1.50	*3.50*
17	A49	40c brown	15.00	*17.50*
18	A49	50c violet	1.50	*3.50*
		Nos. 14-18 (5)	19.50	*26.70*

On No. 111 in Violet

1912 **Unwmk.** ***Perf. 13x13½***

19	A50	15c slate black	1.50	*2.75*

SPECIAL DELIVERY STAMP

Special Delivery Stamp of Italy Overprinted

1906 **Wmk. 140** ***Perf. 14***

E1	SD1	25c rose red	4.00	*7.75*

OFFICES IN AFRICA

40 Paras = 1 Piaster
100 Centesimi = 1 Lira (1910)

BENGASI

Italy No. 81 Surcharged in Black

1901 **Wmk. 140** ***Perf. 14***

1	A45	1pi on 25c dp bl	22.50	*65.00*

Same Surcharge on Italy No. 100

1911

2	A49	1pi on 25c blue	25.00	*65.00*

TRIPOLI

Italian Stamps of 1901-09 Overprinted in Black or Violet

1909 **Wmk. 140**

2	A42	1c brown	2.50	*2.25*
a.		Inverted overprint	150.00	
3	A43	2c orange brn	.90	*1.25*
4	A48	5c green	55.00	4.50
a.		Double overprint	160.00	
5	A48	10c claret	1.75	*1.25*
a.		Double overprint	125.00	*125.00*
6	A49	25c blue	1.50	*1.25*
7	A49	40c brown	3.75	*3.00*
8	A49	50c violet	5.25	*4.00*

Perf. 13½x14

Unwmk.

9	A50	15c slate blk (V)	2.25	*2.25*
		Nos. 2-9 (9)	97.90	*84.75*

Italian Stamps of 1901 Overprinted

1909 **Wmk. 140** ***Perf. 14***

10	A46	1 l brown & grn	60.00	40.00
11	A46	5 l blue & rose	17.50	100.00

Same Overprint on Italy Nos. 76-77

1915

12	A42	1c brown	1.50	
13	A43	2c orange brown	1.50	

Nos. 12-13 were prepared but not issued.

SPECIAL DELIVERY STAMPS

Italy Nos. E1, E6 Overprinted Like Nos. 10-11

1909 Wmk. 140 *Perf. 14*

E1	SD1	25c rose red	3.00	*6.00*
E2	SD2	30c blue & rose	8.75	*8.75*

Tripoli was ceded by Turkey to Italy in Oct., 1912, and became known as the Colony of Libia. Later issues will be found under Libya.

OFFICES IN TURKISH EMPIRE

40 Paras = 1 Piaster

Various powers maintained post offices in the Turkish Empire before World War I by authority of treaties which ended with the signing of the Treaty of Lausanne in 1923. The foreign post offices were closed Oct. 27, 1923.

GENERAL ISSUE

Italian Stamps of 1906-08 Surcharged

Printed at Turin

1908 Wmk. 140

1	A48	10pa on 5c green	.90	*.90*
2	A48	20pa on 10c claret	.90	*.90*
3	A49	40pa on 25c blue	1.75	*1.50*
4	A49	80pa on 50c violet	2.75	*2.10*

See Janina Nos. 1-4.

Surcharged in Violet

Unwmk.

5	A47	30pa on 15c slate	1.25	*1.50*
		Nos. 1-5 (5)	7.55	*6.90*

Nos. 1, 2, 3 and 5 were first issued in Janina, Albania, and subsequently for general use. They can only be distinguished by the cancellations.

Italian Stamps of 1901-08 Surcharged:

Nos. 6-8

1 PIASTRA

No. 9

2 PIASTRE

Nos. 10-12

Printed at Constantinople

1908 First Printing

6	A48	10pa on 5c green	100.00	87.50
a.		Vert. pair, one without surcharge	925.00	
7	A48	20pa on 10c claret	100.00	87.50
8	A47	30pa on 15c slate	300.00	260.00
9	A49	1pi on 25c blue	300.00	260.00
a.		"PIASTRE"	400.00	
10	A49	2pi on 50c violet	950.00	875.00
11	A46	4pi on 1 l brn & grn	*4,250.*	*3,250.*
12	A46	20pi on 5 l bl & rose	*12,500*	*7,750.*

On Nos. 8, 9 and 10 the surcharge is at the top of the stamp. No. 11 has the "4" closed at the top. No. 12 has the "20" wide.

Second Printing

Surcharged:

Nos. 13-15

No. 16

Nos. 17-19

13	A48	10pa on 5c green	3.00	*4.25*
14	A48	20pa on 10c claret	3.00	*4.25*
15	A47	30pa on 15c slate	12.00	*11.00*
a.		Double surcharge	72.50	72.50
b.		Triple surcharge	150.00	150.00
16	A49	1pi on 25c blue	3.00	*3.25*
a.		"PIPSTRA"	60.00	60.00
b.		"1" omitted	60.00	60.00
17	A49	2pi on 50c violet	27.50	*27.50*
a.		Surcharged "20 PIASTRE"	650.00	650.00
b.		"20" with "0" scratched out	190.00	190.00
c.		"2" 5mm from "PIASTRE"	125.00	125.00
18	A46	4pi on 1 l brn & grn	475.00	375.00
19	A46	20pi on 5 l bl & rose	1,800.	1,150.
		Nos. 13-19 (7)	2,323.	1,575.

On No. 18 the "4" is open at the top.

Third Printing

Surcharged in Red

20	A47	30pa on 15c slate	1.50	*1.60*
a.		Double surcharge	125.00	125.00

Fourth Printing

Surcharged:

4 4 PIASTRE 20 20 PIASTRE

20B	A46	4pi on 1 l brn & grn	29.00	27.50
c.		Inverted "S"	75.00	75.00
20D	A46	20pi on 5 l bl & rose	87.50	*95.00*
i.		Inverted "S"	210.00	210.00

Fifth Printing

Surcharged

20 20 PIASTRE

20E	A46	4pi on 1 l brn & grn	27.50	32.50
f.		Surch. "20 PIASTRE"	775.00	
20G	A46	20pi on 5 l bl & rose	27.50	32.50
h.		Double surcharge	600.00	*600.00*

Italian Stamps of 1906-19 Surcharged

1921

21	A48	1pi on 5c green	75.00	*150.00*
22	A48	2pi on 15c slate	3.00	*5.00*
23	A50	4pi on 20c brn org (No. 113)	35.00	*30.00*
24	A49	5pi on 25c blue	35.00	*30.00*
a.		Double surcharge	160.00	
25	A49	10pi on 60c carmine	1.50	*2.75*
		Nos. 21-25 (5)	149.50	*217.75*

No. 21 is almost always found poorly centered, and it is valued thus.

On No. 25 the "10" is placed above "PIASTRE."

Italian Stamps of 1901-19 Surcharged

n

o

1922

26	A42(n)	10pa on 1c brown	1.25	*1.75*
27	A43(n)	20pa on 2c org brn	1.25	*1.75*
28	A48(n)	30pa on 5c green	2.40	*3.00*
29	A48(o)	1pi20pa on 15c slate	3.50	*1.75*
30	A50(n)	3pi on 20c brn org (#113)	4.25	*8.25*
31	A49(o)	3pi30pa on 25c blue	1.75	*1.75*
32	A49(o)	7pi20pa on 60c carmine	3.50	*3.00*
33	A46(n)	15pi on 1 l brn & grn	15.00	*25.00*
		Nos. 26-33 (8)	32.90	*46.25*

No No. 32, the distance between the two lines is 2mm. See note after No. 58A.

Italy No. 100 Surcharged

34	A49	3.75pi on 25c blue	1.50	1.75

Italian Stamps of 1901-20 Surcharged:

q

r

1922

35	A48	30pi on 5c green	3.00	*6.00*
36	A49	1.50pi on 25c blue	1.40	*3.00*
37	A49	3.75pi on 40c brown	1.90	*3.50*
38	A49	4.50pi on 50c violet	5.25	*10.00*
39	A49	7.50pi on 60c carmine	4.50	*7.50*
40	A49	15pi on 85c red brn	7.50	*15.00*
41	A46	18.75pi on 1 l brn & grn	3.75	*12.00*

On No. 40 the numerals of the surcharge are above "PIASTRE."

On No. 42 the figure "4" is open at top. See note after No. 61.

On No. 43 the figure "9" has a curved or arched bottom. See note after No. 62.

Surcharged

45 PIASTRE

42	A46	45pa on 5 l bl & rose	210.00	*250.00*
43	A51	90pa on 10 l gray grn & red	225.00	*290.00*

Italian Stamps of 1901-17 Surcharged Type "q" or:

44	A43	30pa on 2c org brn	1.40	*1.60*
45	A50	1.50pi on 20c brn org (#113)	1.40	*1.60*
		Nos. 35-45 (11)	465.10	*600.20*

Italian Stamps of 1901-20 Surcharged in Black or Red

46	A48	30pa on 5c green	.90	*1.75*
47	A48	1½pi on 10c claret	1.25	*1.75*
48	A49	3pi on 25c blue	8.75	4.50
49	A49	3¾pi on 40c brown	1.60	*1.75*
50	A49	4½pi on 50c violet	26.00	22.50
51	A49	7½pi on 85c red brn	4.50	*5.25*
a.		"PIASIRE"	30.00	*30.00*
52	A46	7½pi on 1 l brn & grn (R)	5.25	*6.50*
a.		Double surcharge	100.00	100.00
b.		"PIASIRE"	35.00	*35.00*
53	A46	15pi on 1 l brn & grn	40.00	*82.50*
54	A46	45pi on 5 l blue & rose	65.00	*52.50*
55	A51	90pi on 10 l gray grn & red	52.50	*87.50*
		Nos. 46-55 (10)	205.75	*266.50*

Italian Stamps of 1901-20 Surcharged Type "o" or:

No. 58

No. 59

Nos. 61-62

1923

56	A49	1pi20pa on 25c blue	6.50	
57	A49	3pi30pa on 40c brown	6.50	
58	A49	4pi20pa on 50c violet	19.00	
58A	A49	7pi20pa on 60c car	6.50	
59	A49	15pi on 85c red brn	6.50	
60	A46	18pi30pa on 1 l brn & grn	6.50	
a.		Double surcharge	*160.00*	
61	A46	45pi on 5 l bl & rose	19.00	
62	A51	90pi on 10 l gray grn & red	17.50	
		Nos. 56-62 (8)	88.00	

On No. 58A the distance between the lines is 1.5mm. On No. 61 the figure "4" is closed at top. On No. 62 the figure "9" is nearly rectilinear at bottom.

Nos. 56-62 were not issued.

SPECIAL DELIVERY STAMPS

Italian Special Delivery Stamps Surcharged

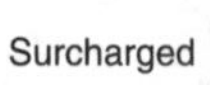
Surcharged

1908 Wmk. 140 *Perf. 14*

E1	SD1	1pi on 25c rose red	1.75	*2.10*

Surcharged

1910

E2	SD2	60pa on 30c blue & rose	2.75	*3.25*

Surcharged

1922

E3 SD2 15pi on 1.20 l on 30c bl & rose 13.00 *27.50*

On No. E3, lines obliterate the first two denominations.

Surcharged

15
PIASTRE

1922

E4 SD2 15pi on 30c bl & rose 160.00 *275.00*

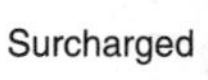

Surcharged

1923

E5 SD2 15pi on 1.20 l blue & red 7.50

No. E5 was not regularly issued.

ALBANIA

Stamps of Italy Surcharged in Black

1902 **Wmk. 140** ***Perf. 14***

1 A44 10pa on 5c green 1.90 *.90*
2 A45 35pa on 20c orange 3.25 *2.50*
3 A45 40pa on 25c blue 6.50 2.50
Nos. 1-3 (3) 11.65 *5.90*

Nos. 1-3 with red surcharges are proofs.

1907

4 A48 10pa on 5c green 25.00 *30.00*
5 A48 20pa on 10c claret 14.50 *12.50*
6 A45 80pa on 50c violet 14.50 *12.50*
Nos. 4-6 (3) 54.00 *55.00*

No. 5 is almost always found poorly centered, and it is valued thus.

CONSTANTINOPLE

Stamps of Italy Surcharged in Black or Violet

Wmk. 140, Unwmk. (#3)

1909-11 ***Perf. 14, 12***

1 A48 10pa on 5c green .90 *1.40*
2 A48 20pa on 10c claret .90 *1.40*
3 A47 30pa on 15c slate (V) .90 *1.40*
4 A49 1pi on 25c blue .90 *1.40*
a. Double surcharge 125.00 *125.00*
5 A49 2pi on 50c violet 1.25 *1.60*

Surcharged

6 A46 4pi on 1 l brn & grn 1.50 *1.90*
7 A46 20pi on 5 l bl & rose 32.50 30.00
8 A51 40pi on 10 l gray grn & red 2.75 *15.00*
Nos. 1-8 (8) 41.60 *54.10*

Italian Stamps of 1901-19 Surcharged:

Nos. 10, 12-13

Nos. 9, 11

1922

9 A48 20pa on 5c green 10.00 *13.00*
10 A48 1pi20pa on 15c slate 1.00 *1.50*
11 A49 3pi on 30c org brn 1.00 *1.50*
12 A49 3pi30pa on 40c brown 1.00 *1.50*
13 A46 7pi20pa on 1 l brn & grn 1.00 *1.50*
Nos. 9-13 (5) 14.00 *19.00*

Italian Stamps of 1901-20 Surcharged

1923

14 A48 30pa on 5c green 1.50 *1.60*
15 A49 1pi20pa on 25c blue 1.50 *1.60*
16 A49 3pi30pa on 40c brown 1.50 *1.40*
17 A49 4pi20pa on 50c violet 1.50 *1.40*
18 A49 7pi20pa on 60c car 1.50 *1.40*
19 A49 15pi on 85c red brn 1.50 *2.50*
20 A46 18pi30pa on 1 l brn & grn 2.25 *5.00*
21 A46 45pi on 5 l bl & rose 2.25 *5.00*
22 A51 90pi on 10 l gray grn & red 2.25 *5.50*
Nos. 14-22 (9) 15.75 *25.40*

CONSTANTINOPLE SPECIAL DELIVERY STAMP

Unissued Italian Special Delivery Stamp of 1922 Surcharged in Black

1923 **Wmk. 140** ***Perf. 14***

E1 SD2 15pi on 1.20 l bl & red 3.75 *15.00*

CONSTANTINOPLE POSTAGE DUE STAMPS

Italian Postage Due Stamps of 1870-1903 Overprinted

Costantinopoli

1922 **Wmk. 140** ***Perf. 14***

J1 D3 10c buff & mag 22.50 *32.50*
J2 D3 30c buff & mag 22.50 *32.50*
J3 D3 60c buff & mag 22.50 *32.50*
J4 D3 1 l blue & mag 22.50 *32.50*
J5 D3 2 l blue & mag 550.00 *825.00*
J6 D3 5 l blue & mag 190.00 *300.00*
Nos. J1-J6 (6) 830.00 *1,255.*

A circular control mark with the inscription "Poste Italiane Constantinopoli" and with the arms of the Kingdom of Italy (Savoy Cross) in the center was applied to each block of four of these stamps in black.

DURAZZO

Stamps of Italy Surcharged in Black or Violet

Wmk. 140, Unwmk. (#3)

1909-11 ***Perf. 14, 12***

1 A48 10pa on 5c green .45 *.90*
2 A48 20pa on 10c claret .45 *.90*
3 A47 30pa on 15c slate (V) 21.00 1.75
4 A49 1pi on 25c blue .75 *1.25*
5 A49 2pi on 50c violet .75 *1.25*

Surcharged

6 A46 4pi on 1 l brn & grn 1.75 *1.50*
7 A46 20pi on 5 l bl & rose 100.00 95.00
8 A51 40pi on 10 l gray grn & red 5.00 *47.50*
Nos. 1-8 (8) 130.15 150.05

No. 3 Surcharged

1916 **Unwmk.** ***Perf. 12***

9 A47 20c on 30pa on 15c slate 2.50 *11.00*

JANINA

Stamps of Italy Surcharged

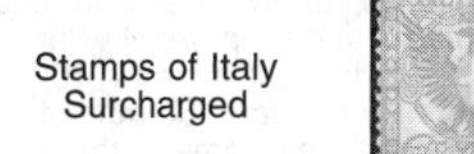

1902-07 **Wmk. 140** ***Perf. 14***

1 A44 10pa on 5c green 4.25 1.40
2 A45 35pa on 20c orange 2.50 *1.60*
3 A45 40pa on 25c blue 14.50 4.00
4 A45 80pa on 50c vio ('07) 32.50 *25.00*
Nos. 1-4 (4) 53.75 *32.00*

Surcharged in Black or Violet

Wmk. 140, Unwmk. (#7)

1909-11 ***Perf. 14, 12***

5 A48 10pa on 5c green .40 *.45*
6 A48 20pa on 10c claret .40 *.45*
7 A47 30pa on 15c slate (V) .45 *.60*
8 A49 1pi on 25c blue .45 *.60*
9 A49 2pi on 50c violet .90 *.80*

Surcharged

10 A46 4pi on 1 l brn & grn .90 *.90*
11 A46 20pi on 5 l bl & rose 125.00 140.00
12 A51 40pi on 10 l gray grn & red 6.00 *42.50*
Nos. 5-12 (8) 134.50 186.30

JERUSALEM

Stamps of Italy Surcharged in Black or Violet

Wmk. 140, Unwmk. (#3)

1909-11 ***Perf. 14, 12***

1 A48 10pa on 5c green 1.90 *4.00*
2 A48 20pa on 10c claret 1.90 *4.00*
3 A47 30pa on 15c slate (V) 1.90 *5.25*
4 A49 1pi on 25c blue 1.90 *4.00*
5 A49 2pi on 50c violet 8.75 *10.50*

Surcharged

6 A46 4pi on 1 l brn & grn 12.00 *17.50*
7 A46 20pi on 5 l bl & rose 450.00 *275.00*
8 A51 40pi on 10 l gray grn & red 16.00 *150.00*
Nos. 1-8 (8) 494.35 *470.25*

Forged cancellations exist on Nos. 1-8.

SALONIKA

Stamps of Italy Surcharged in Black or Violet

Wmk. 140, Unwmk. (#3)

1909-11 ***Perf. 14, 12***

1 A48 10pa on 5c green .45 *.55*
2 A48 20pa on 10c claret .45 *.55*
3 A47 30pa on 15c slate (V) .75 *.90*
4 A49 1pi on 25c blue .75 *.90*
5 A49 2pi on 50c violet .90 *1.10*

Surcharged

6 A46 4pi on 1 l brn & grn 1.25 *1.40*
7 A46 20pi on 5 l bl & rose 190.00 190.00
8 A51 40pi on 10 l gray grn & red 6.00 *35.00*
Nos. 1-8 (8) 200.55 230.40

SCUTARI

Stamps of Italy Surcharged in Black or Violet

Wmk. 140, Unwmk. (#3)

1909-11 ***Perf. 14, 12***

1 A48 10pa on 5c green .35 *.75*
2 A48 20pa on 10c claret .35 *.75*
3 A47 30pa on 15c slate (V) 13.00 3.00
4 A49 1pi on 25c blue .35 *1.25*
5 A49 2pi on 50c violet .60 *1.50*

Surcharged

6 A46 4pi on 1 l brn & grn .75 *1.75*
7 A46 20pi on 5 l bl & rose 15.00 *21.00*
8 A51 40pi on 10 l gray grn & red 35.00 *75.00*
Nos. 1-8 (8) 65.40 *105.00*

Surcharged like Nos. 1-5

1915
9 A43 4pa on 2c orange brn 1.50 *3.00*

No. 3 Surcharged

1916 Unwmk. *Perf. 12*
10 A47 20c on 30pa on 15c slate 3.50 *13.00*

SMYRNA

Stamps of Italy Surcharged in Black or Violet

Wmk. 140, Unwmk. (#3)

1909-11 *Perf. 14, 12*
1 A48 10pa on 5c green .35 *.55*
2 A48 20pa on 10c claret .35 *.55*
3 A47 30pa on 15c slate (V) 1.10 *1.25*
4 A49 1pi on 25c blue 1.10 *1.25*
5 A49 2pi on 50c violet 1.50 *1.75*

Surcharged

6 A46 4pi on 1 l brn & grn 1.75 *2.25*
7 A46 20pi on 5 l bl & rose 82.50 87.50
8 A51 40pi on 10 l gray grn & red 8.75 *52.50*
Nos. 1-8 (8) 97.40 *147.60*

Italian Stamps of 1901-22 Surcharged:

Nos. 10, 12-13

Nos. 9, 11

1922
9 A48 20pa on 5c green 15.00
10 A48 1pi20pa on 15c slate .40
11 A49 3pi on 30c org brn .40
12 A49 3pi30pa on 40c brown .75
13 A46 7pi20pa on 1 l brn & grn .75
Nos. 9-13 (5) 17.30

Nos. 9-13 were not issued.

VALONA

Stamps of Italy Surcharged in Black or Violet

Wmk. 140, Unwmk. (#3)

1909-11 *Perf. 14, 12*
1 A48 10pa on 5c green .20 *.90*
2 A48 20pa on 10c claret .20 *.90*
3 A47 30pa on 15c slate (V) 10.50 3.00
4 A49 1pi on 25c blue .75 *1.10*
5 A49 2pi on 50c violet .75 *1.40*

Surcharged

6 A46 4pi on 1 l brn & grn 1.10 *1.75*
7 A46 20pi on 5 l bl & rose 29.00 32.50
8 A51 40pi on 10 l gray grn & red 32.50 *77.50*
Nos. 1-8 (8) 75.00 *119.05*

Italy No. 123 Surcharged in Violet or Red Violet

1916
9 A58 30pa on 15c slate (V) 3.00 *7.50*
a. Red violet surcharge 6.00 *15.00*

No. 9 Surcharged

10 A58 20c on 30pa on 15c slate 1.25 *8.75*

AEGEAN ISLANDS

(Dodecanese)

A group of islands in the Aegean Sea off the coast of Turkey. They were occupied by Italy during the Tripoli War and were ceded to Italy by Turkey in 1924 by the Treaty of Lausanne. Stamps of Italy overprinted with the name of the island were in use at the post offices maintained in the various islands.

Rhodes, on the island of the same name, was capital of the entire group.

100 Centesimi = 1 Lira

GENERAL ISSUE

Italian Stamps of 1907-08 Overprinted

1912 Wmk. 140 *Perf. 14*
1 A49 25c blue 26.00 *15.00*
a. Inverted overprint 150.00 *150.00*
2 A49 50c violet 26.00 *15.00*
a. Inverted overprint 150.00 *150.00*

Virgil Issue

Types of Italian Stamps of 1930 Overprinted in Red or Blue

1930 Photo. Wmk. 140 *Perf. 14*
3 A106 15c vio blk .90 *5.25*
4 A106 20c org brn .90 *5.25*
5 A106 25c dk green .90 *2.25*
6 A106 30c lt brown .90 *2.25*
7 A106 50c dull vio .90 *2.25*
8 A106 75c rose red .90 *5.25*
9 A106 1.25 l gray bl .90 *7.50*

Engr.

Unwmk.
10 A106 5 l + 1.50 l dk vio 2.10 *15.00*
11 A106 10 l + 2.50 l ol brn 2.10 *15.00*
Nos. 3-11,C4-C7 (13) *18.00* 120.00

St. Anthony of Padua Issue

Types of Italian Stamps of 1931 Overprinted in Blue or Red

1932 Photo. Wmk. 140 *Perf. 14*
12 A116 20c black brn 13.00 *8.25*
13 A116 25c dull grn 13.00 8.25
14 A118 30c brown org 13.00 *9.50*
15 A118 50c dull vio 13.00 6.50
16 A120 1.25 l gray bl 13.00 11.00

Engr.

Unwmk.
17 A121 75c lt red 13.00 *12.50*
18 A122 5 l + 2.50 l dp org 13.00 *47.50*
Nos. 12-18 (7) 91.00 *103.50*

Dante Alighieri Society Issue

Types of Italian Stamps of 1932 Overprinted

1932 Photo. Wmk. 140
19 A126 10c grnsh gray .85 *2.10*
20 A126 15c black vio .85 *2.10*
21 A126 20c brown org .85 *2.10*
22 A126 25c dp green .85 2.10
23 A126 30c dp org .85 *2.10*
24 A126 50c dull vio .85 .90
25 A126 75c rose red .85 *2.60*
26 A126 1.25 l blue .85 *2.10*
27 A126 1.75 l ol brn .95 *2.60*
28 A126 2.75 l car rose 1.00 *2.60*
29 A126 5 l + 2 l dp vio 1.10 *8.25*
30 A126 10 l + 2.50 l dk brn 1.10 *12.00*
Nos. 19-30 (12) 10.95 *41.55*

See Nos. C8-C14.

Soccer Issue

Types of Italy, "Soccer" Issue, Overprinted in Black or Red

1934
31 A173 20c brn rose (Bk) 35.00 35.00
32 A174 25c green (R) 35.00 35.00
33 A174 50c violet (R) 125.00 17.50
34 A174 1.25 l gray bl (R) 35.00 *60.00*
35 A175 5 l +2.50 l bl (R) 35.00 *150.00*
Nos. 31-35 (5) 265.00 *297.50*

See Nos. C28-C31.

Same Overprint on Types of Medal of Valor Issue of Italy, in Red or Black

1935
36 A177 10c sl gray (R) 26.00 *25.00*
37 A178 15c brn (Bk) 26.00 *25.00*
38 A178 20c red org (Bk) 26.00 *25.00*
39 A177 25c dp grn (R) 26.00 *25.00*
40 A178 30c lake (Bk) 26.00 *25.00*
41 A178 50c ol grn (Bk) 26.00 *25.00*
42 A178 75c rose red (Bk) 26.00 *25.00*
43 A178 1.25 l dp bl (R) 26.00 *25.00*
44 A177 1.75 l + 1 l pur (R) 17.00 *25.00*
45 A178 2.55 l + 2 l dk car (Bk) 17.00 *25.00*
46 A178 2.75 l + 2 l org brn (Bk) 17.00 *25.00*
Nos. 36-46 (11) 259.00 *275.00*

See Nos. C32-C38, CE3-CE4.

Types of Italy, 1937, Overprinted in Blue or Red

1938 Wmk. 140 *Perf. 14*
47 A208 10c dk brn (Bl) 1.75 2.50
48 A208 15c pur (R) 1.75 2.50
49 A208 20c yel bis (Bl) 1.75 2.50
50 A208 25c myr grn (R) 1.75 2.50
51 A208 30c dp cl (Bl) 1.75 2.50
52 A208 50c sl grn (R) 1.75 4.50
53 A208 75c rose red (Bl) 1.75 4.50
54 A208 1.25 l dk bl (R) 1.75 4.50
55 A208 1.75 l + 1 l dp org (Bl) 2.50 *8.25*
56 A208 2.55 l + 2 l ol brn (R) 2.50 *8.25*
Nos. 47-56 (10) 19.00 42.50

Bimillenary of birth of Augustus Caesar (Octavianus), first Roman emperor.

See Nos. C39-C43.

Same Overprint of Type of Italy, 1937, in Red

1938
57 A222 1.25 l deep blue .85 *1.50*
58 A222 2.75 l + 2 l brown 1.00 *6.00*

600th anniversary of the death of Giotto di Bondone, Italian painter.

Statue of Roman Wolf — A1

Arms of Rhodes — A2

Dante's House, Rhodes A3

1940 Photo.
59 A1 5c lt brown .20 .55
60 A2 10c pale org .20 .55
61 A3 25c blue grn .55 1.00
62 A1 50c rose vio .55 1.00
63 A2 75c dull ver .55 1.40
64 A3 1.25 l dull blue .55 1.60
65 A2 2 l + 75c rose .55 8.75
Nos. 59-65,C44-C47 (11) 6.15 26.80

Triennial Overseas Exposition, Naples.

AIR POST STAMPS

Ferrucci Issue

Types of Italian Air Post Stamps of 1930 Overprinted in Blue or Red Like Nos. 12-18

1930 Wmk. 140 *Perf. 14*
C1 A104 50c brn vio (Bl) 4.50 *8.75*
C2 A104 1 l dk bl (R) 4.50 *8.75*
C3 A104 5 l + 2 l dp car (Bl) 9.75 *26.00*
Nos. C1-C3 (3) 18.75 *43.50*

Nos. C1-C3 were sold at Rhodes only.

Virgil Issue

Types of Italian Air Post Stamps of 1930 Overprinted in Red or Blue Like Nos. 3-11

1930 **Photo.**

C4 A106 50c dp grn (R) 1.25 *10.50*
C5 A106 1 l rose red (Bl) 1.25 *12.00*

Engr.

Unwmk.

C6 A106 7.70 l + 1.30 l dk brn (R) 2.50 *15.00*
C7 A106 9 l + 2 l gray (R) 2.50 *22.50*
Nos. C4-C7 (4) 7.50 *60.00*

Dante Alighieri Society Issue

Types of Italian Air Post Stamps of 1932 Overprinted Like Nos. 19-30

1932 **Wmk. 140**

C8 AP10 50c car rose .90 *2.10*
C9 AP11 1 l dp grn .90 *2.10*
C10 AP11 3 l dl vio .90 *2.25*
C11 AP11 5 l dp org .90 *2.25*
C12 AP10 7.70 l + 2 l ol brn 1.25 *6.00*
C13 AP11 10 l + 2.50 l dk bl 1.25 *10.50*
Nos. C8-C13 (6) 6.10 *25.20*

Leonardo da Vinci — AP12

1932 **Photo.** ***Perf. 14½***

C14 AP12 100 l dp bl & grnsh gray 13.00 *60.00*

Garibaldi Types of Italian Air Post Stamps of 1932 Overprinted in Red or Blue Like Nos. 12-18

1932

C15 AP13 50c deep green 22.50 *45.00*
C16 AP14 80c copper red 22.50 *45.00*
C17 AP13 1 l + 25c dl bl 22.50 *45.00*
C18 AP13 2 l + 50c red brn 22.50 *45.00*
C19 AP14 5 l + 1 l bluish sl 22.50 *45.00*
Nos. C15-C19 (5) 112.50 *225.00*

See Nos. CE1-CE2.

Graf Zeppelin over Rhodes AP17

1933 ***Perf. 14***

C20 AP17 3 l olive brn 27.50 *65.00*
C21 AP17 5 l dp vio 27.50 *75.00*
C22 AP17 10 l dk green 27.50 *140.00*
C23 AP17 12 l dk blue 27.50 *150.00*
C24 AP17 15 l car rose 27.50 *150.00*
C25 AP17 20 l gray blk 27.50 *150.00*
Nos. C20-C25 (6) 165.00 *730.00*

Balbo Flight Issue

Types of Italian Air Post Stamps of 1933 Overprinted

1933 **Wmk. 140** ***Perf. 14***

C26 AP25 5.25 l + 19.75 l grn, red & bl gray 21.00 *52.50*
C27 AP25 5.25 l + 44.75 l red, grn & bl gray 21.00 *52.50*

Soccer Issue

Types of Italian Air Post Stamps of 1934 Overprinted in Black or Red Like #31-35

1934

C28 AP32 50c brown (R) 4.00 *22.50*
C29 AP33 75c rose red) 4.00 *22.50*
C30 AP34 5 l + 2.50 l red org 11.00 *45.00*
C31 AP35 10 l + 5 l grn (R) 11.00 *60.00*
Nos. C28-C31 (4) 30.00 *150.00*

Types of Medal of Valor Issue of Italy Overprinted in Red or Black Like #31-35

1935

C32 AP36 25c dp grn 32.50 *42.50*
C33 AP36 50c blk brn (R) 32.50 *42.50*
C34 AP36 75c rose 32.50 *42.50*
C35 AP36 80c dk brn 32.50 *42.50*
C36 AP36 1 l + 50c ol grn 26.00 *42.50*
C37 AP36 2 l + 1 l dp bl (R) 26.00 *42.50*
C38 AP40 3 l + 2 l vio (R) 26.00 *42.50*
Nos. C32-C38 (7) 208.00 *297.50*

Types of Italy Air Post Stamps, 1937,

Overprinted in Blue or Red Like #47-56

1938 **Wmk. 140** ***Perf. 14***

C39 AP51 25c dl gray vio (R) 1.90 2.25
C40 AP51 50c grn (R) 1.90 2.25
C41 AP51 80c brt bl (R) 1.90 6.50
C42 AP51 1 l + 1 l rose lake 2.75 9.50
C43 AP51 5 l + 1 l rose red 5.00 *21.00*
Nos. C39-C43 (5) 13.45 41.50

Bimillenary of the birth of Augustus Caesar (Octavianus).

Statues of Stag and Roman Wolf AP18

Plane over Government Palace, Rhodes — AP19

1940 **Photo.**

C44 AP18 50c olive blk .75 1.60
C45 AP19 1 l dk vio .75 1.60
C46 AP18 2 l + 75c dk bl .75 3.25
C47 AP19 5 l + 2.50 l cop brn .75 5.50
Nos. C44-C47 (4) 3.00 11.95

Triennial Overseas Exposition, Naples.

AIR POST SPECIAL DELIVERY STAMPS

Type of Italian Garibaldi Air Post Special Delivery Stamps Overprinted in Blue or Ocher Like Nos. 12-18

1932 **Wmk. 140** ***Perf. 14***

CE1 APSD1 2.25 l + 1 l bl & rose & (Bl) 30.00 *52.50*
CE2 APSD1 4.50 l + 1.50 l ocher & gray (O) 30.00 *52.50*

Type of Medal of Valor Issue of Italy, Overprinted in Black Like Nos. 31-35

1935

CE3 APSD4 2 l + 1.25 l dp bl 26.00 *42.50*
CE4 APSD4 4.50 l + 2 l grn 26.00 *42.50*

ISSUES FOR THE INDIVIDUAL ISLANDS

Italian Stamps of 1901-20 Overprinted with Names of Various Islands as

a

b

c

The 1912-22 issues of each island have type "a" overprint in black on all values except 15c (type A58) and 20c on 15c, which have type "b" overprint in violet.

The 1930-32 Ferruci and Garibaldi issues are types of the Italian issues overprinted type "c."

CALCHI

Overprinted "Karki" in Black or Violet

1912-22 **Wmk. 140** ***Perf. 13½, 14***

1 A43 2c orange brn 4.25 4.00
a. Double overprint 175.00
2 A48 5c green 1.40 *4.00*
a. Double overprint 160.00
3 A48 10c claret .35 *4.00*
4 A48 15c slate ('22) 2.50 *22.50*
a. Double overprint 175.00
5 A50 20c brn org ('21) 2.50 *21.00*
6 A49 25c blue .35 *4.00*
7 A49 40c brown .35 *4.00*
8 A49 50c violet .35 *6.50*

Unwmk.

9 A58 15c slate (V) 19.00 7.50
10 A50 20c brn org ('17) 65.00 *75.00*
Nos. 1-10 (10) 96.05 *152.50*

No. 9 Surcharged

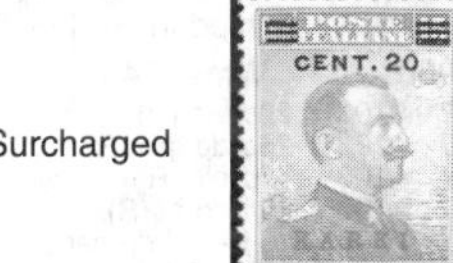

1916 ***Perf. 13½***

11 A58 20c on 15c slate 1.10 *13.00*

Ferrucci Issue

Overprinted in Red or Blue

1930 **Wmk. 140** ***Perf. 14***

12 A102 20c vio (R) 1.25 *2.50*
13 A103 25c dk grn (R) 1.25 *2.50*
14 A103 50c blk (R) 1.25 *4.25*
15 A103 1.25 l dp bl (R) 1.25 *4.25*
16 A104 5 l + 2 l dp car (Bl) 1.90 *6.50*
Nos. 12-16 (5) 6.90 *20.00*

Garibaldi Issue

Overprinted "CARCHI" in Red or Blue

1932

17 A138 10c brown 5.25 *8.75*
18 A138 20c red brn (Bl) 5.25 *8.75*
19 A138 25c dp grn 5.25 *8.75*
20 A138 30c bluish sl 5.25 *8.75*
21 A138 50c red vio (Bl) 5.25 *8.75*
22 A141 75c cop red (Bl) 5.25 *8.75*
23 A141 1.25 l dl bl 5.25 *8.75*
24 A141 1.75 l + 25c brn 5.25 *8.75*
25 A144 2.55 l + 50c org (Bl) 5.25 *8.75*
26 A145 5 l + 1 l dl vio 5.25 *8.75*
Nos. 17-26 (10) 52.50 *87.50*

CALINO

Overprinted "Calimno" in Black or Violet

1912-21 **Wmk. 140** ***Perf. 13½, 14***

1 A43 2c orange brn 4.25 4.00
2 A48 5c green 1.25 *4.00*
3 A48 10c claret .35 *4.00*
4 A48 15c slate ('21) 2.25 *22.50*
5 A50 20c brn org ('21) 2.25 *22.50*
6 A49 25c blue 3.75 *4.00*
7 A49 40c brown .35 *4.00*
8 A49 50c violet .35 *6.50*

Unwmk.

9 A58 15c slate (V) 16.00 7.50
10 A50 20c brn org ('17) 50.00 *75.00*
Nos. 1-10 (10) 80.80 *154.00*

No. 9 Surcharged Like Calchi No. 11

1916 ***Perf. 13½***

11 A58 20c on 15c slate 8.75 *15.00*

Ferrucci Issue

Overprinted in Red or Blue

1930 **Wmk. 140** ***Perf. 14***

12 A102 20c violet (R) 1.25 *2.50*
13 A103 25c dk green (R) 1.25 *2.50*
14 A102 50c black (R) 1.25 *4.25*
15 A102 1.25 l dp bl (R) 1.25 *4.25*
16 A104 5 l + 2 1 dp car (Bl) 1.90 *6.50*
Nos. 12-16 (5) 6.90 *20.00*

Garibaldi Issue

Overprinted in Red or Blue

1932

17 A138 10c brown 5.25 *8.75*
18 A138 20c red brn (Bl) 5.25 *8.75*
19 A138 25c dp grn 5.25 *8.75*
20 A138 30c bluish sl 5.25 *8.75*
21 A138 50c red vio (Bl) 5.25 *8.75*
22 A141 75c cop red (Bl) 5.25 *8.75*
23 A141 1.25 l dull blue 5.25 *8.75*
24 A141 1.75 l + 25c brn 5.25 *8.75*
25 A144 2.55 l + 50c org (Bl) 5.25 *8.75*
26 A145 5 l + 1 l dl vio 5.25 *8.75*
Nos. 17-26 (10) 52.50 *87.50*

CASO

Overprinted "Caso" in Black or Violet

1912-21 **Wmk. 140** ***Perf. 13½, 14***

1 A43 2c orange brn 4.25 4.00
2 A48 5c green 1.40 *4.00*
3 A48 10c claret .35 *4.00*
4 A48 15c slate ('21) 2.25 *22.50*
5 A50 20c brn org ('20) 1.75 *17.50*
6 A49 25c blue .35 *4.00*
7 A49 40c brown .35 *4.00*
8 A49 50c violet .35 *6.50*

Unwmk.

9 A58 15c slate (V) 19.00 *7.50*
10 A50 20c brn org ('17) 65.00 *75.00*
Nos. 1-10 (10) 95.05 *149.00*

No. 9 Surcharged Like Calchi No. 11

1916 ***Perf. 13½***

11 A58 20c on 15c slate .55 *10.50*

Ferrucci Issue

Overprinted in Red or Blue

1930 **Wmk. 140** ***Perf. 14***

12 A102 20c vio (R) 1.25 *2.50*
13 A103 25c dk grn (R) 1.25 *2.50*
14 A103 50c blk (R) 1.25 *4.25*
15 A103 1.25 l dp bl (R) 1.25 *4.25*
16 A104 5 l + 2 l dp car (Bl) 1.90 *6.50*
Nos. 12-16 (5) 6.90 *20.00*

Garibaldi Issue

Overprinted in Red or Blue

1932

17 A138 10c brown 5.25 *8.75*
18 A138 20c red brn (Bl) 5.25 *8.75*
19 A138 25c dp grn 5.25 *8.75*
20 A138 30c bluish sl 5.25 *8.75*
21 A138 50c red vio (Bl) 5.25 *8.75*
22 A141 75c cop red (Bl) 5.25 *8.75*
23 A141 1.25 l dl bl 5.25 *8.75*
24 A141 1.75 l + 25c brn 5.25 *8.75*
25 A144 2.55 l + 50c org (Bl) 5.25 *8.75*
26 A145 5 l + 1 l dl vio 5.25 *8.75*
Nos. 17-26 (10) 52.50 *87.50*

COO

(Cos, Kos)

Overprinted "Cos" in Black or Violet

1912-22 **Wmk. 140** ***Perf. 13½, 14***

1 A43 2c orange brn 4.25 4.00
2 A48 5c green 42.50 4.00
3 A48 10c claret 1.90 *4.00*
4 A48 15c slate ('22) 2.50 *30.00*
5 A50 20c brn org ('21) 1.75 *17.50*
6 A49 25c blue 16.00 4.00
7 A49 40c brown .35 *4.00*
8 A49 50c violet .35 *6.50*

Unwmk.

9 A58 15c slate (V) 19.00 7.50
10 A50 20c brn org ('17) 25.00 *75.00*
Nos. 1-10 (10) 113.60 *156.50*

No. 9 Surcharged Like Calchi No. 11

1916 ***Perf. 13½***

11 A58 20c on 15c slate 8.75 *17.50*

Ferrucci Issue
Overprinted in Red or Blue

1930 Wmk. 140 *Perf. 14*
12 A102 20c vio (R) 1.25 *2.50*
13 A103 25c dk grn (R) 1.25 *2.50*
14 A103 50c blk (R) 1.25 *4.25*
15 A103 1.25 l dp bl (R) 1.25 *4.25*
16 A104 5 l + 2 l dp car (Bl) 1.90 *6.50*
Nos. 12-16 (5) 6.90 *20.00*

Garibaldi Issue
Overprinted in Red or Blue

1932
17 A138 10c brown 5.25 *8.75*
18 A138 20c red brn (Bl) 5.25 *8.75*
19 A138 25c dp grn 5.25 *8.75*
20 A138 30c bluish sl 5.25 *8.75*
21 A138 50c red vio (Bl) 5.25 *8.75*
22 A141 75c cop red (Bl) 5.25 *8.75*
23 A141 1.25 l dl bl 5.25 *8.75*
24 A141 1.75 l + 25c brn 5.25 *8.75*
25 A144 2.55 l + 50c org (Bl) 5.25 *8.75*
26 A145 5 l + 1 l dl vio 5.25 *8.75*
Nos. 17-26 (10) 52.50 *87.50*

LERO

Overprinted "Leros" in Black or Violet

1912-22 Wmk. 140 *Perf. 13½, 14*
1 A43 2c orange brn 4.25 4.00
2 A48 5c green 3.00 *4.00*
3 A48 10c claret .60 *4.00*
4 A48 15c slate ('22) 2.50 *19.00*
5 A50 20c brn org ('21) 82.50 50.00
6 A49 25c blue 17.50 4.00
7 A49 40c brown 2.50 *4.00*
8 A49 50c violet .35 *6.50*

Unwmk.
9 A58 15c slate (V) 32.50 7.50
10 A50 20c brn org ('17) 25.00 *75.00*
Nos. 1-10 (10) 170.70 *178.00*

No. 9 Surcharged Like Calchi No. 11

1916 *Perf. 13½*
11 A58 20c on 15c slate 8.75 *15.00*

Ferrucci Issue
Overprinted in Red or Blue

1930 *Perf. 14*
12 A102 20c violet (R) 1.25 *2.50*
13 A103 25c dk green (R) 1.25 *2.50*
14 A103 50c black (R) 1.25 *4.25*
15 A103 1.25 l dp bl (R) 1.25 *4.25*
16 A104 5 l + 2 l dp car (Bl) 1.90 *6.50*
Nos. 12-16 (5) 6.90 *20.00*

Garibaldi Issue
Overprinted in Red or Blue

1932
17 A138 10c brown 5.25 *8.75*
18 A138 20c red brn (Bl) 5.25 *8.75*
19 A138 25c dp grn 5.25 *8.75*
20 A138 30c bluish sl 5.25 *8.75*
21 A138 50c red vio (Bl) 5.25 *8.75*
22 A141 75c cop red (Bl) 5.25 *8.75*
23 A141 1.25 l dl bl 5.25 *8.75*
24 A141 1.75 l + 25c brn 5.25 *8.75*
25 A144 2.55 l + 50c org (Bl) 5.25 *8.75*
26 A145 5 l + 1 l dl vio 5.25 *8.75*
Nos. 17-26 (10) 52.50 *87.50*

LISSO

Overprinted "Lipso" in Black or Violet

1912-22 Wmk. 140 *Perf. 13½, 14*
1 A43 2c orange brn 4.25 4.00
2 A48 5c green 1.60 *4.00*
3 A48 10c claret .75 *4.00*
4 A48 15c slate ('22) 2.50 *19.00*
5 A50 20c brn org ('21) 2.50 *22.50*
6 A49 25c blue .35 *4.00*
7 A49 40c brown 1.10 *4.00*
8 A49 50c violet .35 *6.50*

Unwmk.
9 A58 15c slate (V) 17.50 7.50
10 A50 20c brn org ('17) 40.00 *75.00*
Nos. 1-10 (10) 70.90 *150.50*

No. 9 Surcharged Like Calchi No. 11

1916 *Perf. 13½*
11 A58 20c on 15c slate .65 *14.00*

Ferrucci Issue
Overprinted in Red or Blue

1930 Wmk. 140 *Perf. 14*
12 A102 20c vio (R) 1.25 *2.50*
13 A103 25c dk grn (R) 1.25 *2.50*
14 A103 50c blk (R) 1.25 *4.25*
15 A103 1.25 l dp bl (R) 1.25 *4.25*
16 A104 5 l + 2 l dp car (Bl) 1.90 *6.50*
Nos. 12-16 (5) 6.90 *20.00*

Garibaldi Issue
Overprinted "LIPSO" in Red or Blue

1932
17 A138 10c brown 5.25 *8.75*
18 A138 20c red brn (bl) 5.25 *8.75*
19 A138 25c dp grn 5.25 *8.75*
20 A138 30c bluish sl 5.25 *8.75*
21 A138 50c red vio (Bl) 5.25 *8.75*
22 A141 75c cop red (Bl) 5.25 *8.75*
23 A141 1.25 l dl bl 5.25 *8.75*
24 A141 1.75 l + 25c brn 5.25 *8.75*
25 A144 2.55 l + 50c org (Bl) 5.25 *8.75*
26 A145 5 l + 1 l dl vio 5.25 *8.75*
Nos. 17-26 (10) 52.50 *87.50*

NISIRO

Overprinted "Nisiros" in Black or Violet

1912-22 Wmk. 140 *Perf. 13½, 14*
1 A43 2c orange brn 4.25 4.00
2 A48 5c green 1.40 *4.00*
3 A48 10c claret .35 *4.00*
4 A48 15c slate ('22) 12.00 *21.00*
5 A50 20c brn org ('21) 50.00 *55.00*
6 A49 25c blue 1.25 *4.00*
7 A49 40c brown .35 *4.00*
8 A49 50c violet 2.50 *6.50*

Unwmk.
9 A58 15c slate (V) 16.00 7.50
10 A50 20c brn org ('17) 65.00 *75.00*
Nos. 1-10 (10) 153.10 *185.00*

No. 9 Surcharged Like Calchi No. 11

1916 *Perf. 13½*
11 A58 20c on 15c slate .65 *14.00*

Ferrucci Issue
Overprinted in Red or Blue

1930 Wmk. 140 *Perf. 14*
12 A102 20c vio (R) 1.25 *2.50*
13 A103 25c dp grn (R) 1.25 *2.50*
14 A103 50c blk (R) 1.25 *4.25*
15 A103 1.25 l dp bl (R) 1.25 *4.25*
16 A104 5 l + 2 l dp car (Bl) 1.90 *6.50*
Nos. 12-16 (5) 6.90 *20.00*

Garibaldi Issue
Overprinted in Red or Blue

1932
17 A138 10c brown 5.25 *8.75*
18 A138 20c red brn (Bl) 5.25 *8.75*
19 A138 25c dp grn 5.25 *8.75*
20 A138 30c bluish slate 5.25 *8.75*
21 A138 50c red vio (Bl) 5.25 *8.75*
22 A141 75c cop red (Bl) 5.25 *8.75*
23 A141 1.25 l dull blue 5.25 *8.75*
24 A141 1.75 l + 25c brn 5.25 *8.75*
25 A144 2.55 l + 50c org (Bl) 5.25 *8.75*
26 A145 5 l + 1 l dl vio 5.25 *8.75*
Nos. 17-26 (10) 52.50 *87.50*

PATMO

Overprinted "Patmos" in Black or Violet

1912-22 Wmk. 140 *Perf. 13½, 14*
1 A43 2c orange brn 4.25 4.00
2 A48 5c green 1.40 *4.00*
3 A48 10c claret 1.25 *4.00*
4 A48 15c slate ('22) 2.50 *22.50*
5 A50 20c brn org ('21) 82.50 75.00
6 A49 25c blue .45 *4.00*
7 A49 40c brown 2.25 *4.00*
8 A49 50c violet .35 *4.00*

Unwmk.
9 A58 15c slate (V) 16.00 7.50
10 A50 20c brn org ('17) 40.00 *75.00*
Nos. 1-10 (10) 150.95 *204.00*

No. 9 Surcharged Like Calchi No. 11

1916 *Perf. 13½*
11 A58 20c on 15c slate 8.75 *17.50*

Ferrucci Issue
Overprinted in Red or Blue

1930 Wmk. 140 *Perf. 14*
12 A102 20c vio (R) 1.25 *2.50*
13 A103 25c dk grn (R) 1.25 *2.50*
14 A103 50c blk (R) 1.25 *4.25*
15 A103 1.25 l dp bl (R) 1.25 *4.25*
16 A104 5 l + 2 l dp car (Bl) 1.90 *6.50*
Nos. 12-16 (5) 6.90 *20.00*

Garibaldi Issue
Overprinted in Red or Blue

1932
17 A138 10c brown 5.25 *8.75*
18 A138 20c red brn (Bl) 5.25 *8.75*
19 A138 25c dp grn 5.25 *8.75*
20 A138 30c bluish slate 5.25 *8.75*
21 A138 50c red vio (Bl) 5.25 *8.75*
22 A141 75c cop red (Bl) 5.25 *8.75*
23 A141 1.25 l dl bl 5.25 *8.75*
24 A141 1.75 l + 25c brn 5.25 *8.75*
25 A144 2.55 l + 50c org (Bl) 5.25 *8.75*
26 A145 5 l + 1 l dl vio 5.25 *8.75*
Nos. 17-26 (10) 52.50 *87.50*

PISCOPI

Overprinted "Piscopi" in Black or Violet

1912-21 Wmk. 140 *Perf. 13½, 14*
1 A43 2c orange brn 4.25 4.00
2 A48 5c green 1.40 *4.00*
3 A48 10c claret .35 *4.00*
4 A48 15c slate ('21) 8.75 *22.50*
5 A50 20c brn org ('21) 25.00 *32.50*
6 A49 25c blue .35 *4.00*
7 A49 40c brown .35 *4.00*
8 A49 50c violet .35 *6.50*

Unwmk.
9 A58 15c slate (V) 19.00 7.50
10 A50 20c brn org ('17) 40.00 *75.00*
Nos. 1-10 (10) 99.80 *164.00*

No. 9 Surcharged Like Calchi No. 11

1916 *Perf. 13½*
11 A58 20c on 15c slate .65 *13.00*

Ferrucci Issue
Overprinted in Red or Blue

1930 Wmk. 140 *Perf. 14*
12 A102 20c vio (R) 1.25 *2.50*
13 A103 25c dk grn (R) 1.25 *2.50*
14 A103 50c blk (R) 1.25 *4.25*
15 A103 1.25 l dp bl (R) 1.10 *4.25*
16 A104 5 l + 2 l dp car (Bl) 1.90 *6.50*
Nos. 12-16 (5) 6.75 *20.00*

Garibaldi Issue
Overprinted in Red or Blue

1932
17 A138 10c brown 5.25 *8.75*
18 A138 20c red brn (Bl) 5.25 *8.75*
19 A138 25c dp grn 5.25 *8.75*
20 A138 30c bluish sl 5.25 *8.75*
21 A138 50c red vio (Bl) 5.25 *8.75*
22 A141 75c cop red (Bl) 5.25 *8.75*
23 A141 1.25 l dl bl 5.25 *8.75*
24 A141 1.75 l + 25c brn 5.25 *8.75*
25 A144 2.55 l + 50c org (Bl) 5.25 *8.75*
26 A145 5 l + 1 l dl vio 5.25 *8.75*
Nos. 17-26 (10) 52.50 *87.50*

RHODES

(Rodi)
Overprinted "Rodi" in Black or Violet

1912-24 Wmk. 140 *Perf. 13½, 14*
1 A43 2c org brn .35 *4.00*
2 A48 5c green 1.25 *4.00*
a. Double overprint 175.00
3 A48 10c claret .35 *4.00*
4 A48 15c slate ('21) 75.00 32.50
5 A45 20c org ('16) 1.75 *3.75*
6 A50 20c brn org ('19) 4.00 *8.75*
a. Double overprint 60.00
7 A49 25c blue 1.25 *4.00*
8 A49 40c brown 1.90 *4.00*
9 A49 50c violet .35 *6.50*
10 A49 85c red brn ('22) 35.00 *52.50*
11 A46 1 l brn & grn ('24) 1.75

No. 11 was not regularly issued.

Unwmk.
12 A58 15c slate (V) 21.00 7.50
13 A50 20c brn org ('17) 87.50 75.00
Nos. 1-13 (13) 231.45 206.50

No. 12 Surcharged Like Calchi No. 11

1916 *Perf. 13½*
14 A58 20c on 15c slate 65.00 *70.00*

Windmill, Rhodes — A1

Medieval Galley — A2

Christian Knight — A3

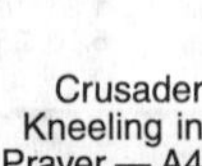

Crusader Kneeling in Prayer — A4

Crusader's Tomb — A5

No Imprint

1929 Unwmk. Litho. *Perf. 11*
15 A1 5c magenta 3.00 .90
16 A2 10c olive brn 3.00 .75
17 A3 20c rose red 3.00 .20
18 A3 25c green 3.00 .20
19 A4 30c dk blue 3.00 .35
20 A5 50c dk brown 3.00 .20
21 A5 1.25 l dk blue 3.00 .90
22 A4 5 l magenta 32.50 *40.00*
23 A4 10 l olive brn 82.50 *100.00*
Nos. 15-23 (9) 136.00 *143.50*

Visit of the King and Queen of Italy to the Aegean Islands. The stamps are inscribed "Rodi" but were available for use in all the Aegean Islands.

Nos. 15-23 and C1-C4 were used in eastern Crete in 1941-42 with Greek postmarks.

See Nos. 55-63.

Ferrucci Issue
Overprinted in Red or Blue

1930 Wmk. 140 *Perf. 14*
24 A102 20c violet (R) 1.25 *2.50*
25 A103 25c dk green (R) 1.25 *2.50*
26 A103 50c black (R) 1.25 *4.25*
27 A103 1.25 l dp blue (R) 1.25 *4.25*
28 A104 5 l + 2 l dp car (Bl) 1.90 *6.50*
Nos. 24-28 (5) 6.90 *20.00*

Hydrological Congress Issue
Rhodes Issue of 1929 Overprinted

1930 Unwmk. *Perf. 11*
29 A1 5c magenta 8.75 *7.50*
30 A2 10c olive brn 10.50 *7.50*
31 A3 20c rose red 17.50 *6.50*
32 A3 25c green 22.50 6.50
33 A4 30c dk blue 10.50 *7.50*
34 A5 50c dk brown 325.00 25.00
35 A5 1.25 l dk blue 250.00 37.50
36 A4 5 l magenta 125.00 *160.00*
37 A4 10 l olive grn 125.00 *190.00*
Nos. 29-37 (9) 894.75 *448.00*

Rhodes Issue of 1929 Overprinted in Blue or Red

1931

No.	Type	Description	Unused	Used
38	A1	5c magenta (Bl)	3.00	*5.25*
39	A2	10c olive brn (R)	3.00	*5.25*
40	A3	20c rose red (Bl)	3.00	*8.25*
41	A3	25c green (R)	3.00	*8.25*
42	A4	30c dk blue (R)	3.00	*8.25*
43	A5	50c dk brown (R)	25.00	19.00
44	A5	1.25 l dk bl (R)	19.00	*35.00*
		Nos. 38-44 (7)	59.00	89.25

Italian Eucharistic Congress, 1931.

Garibaldi Issue

Overprinted in Red or Blue

1932 Wmk. 140 *Perf. 14*

No.	Type	Description	Unused	Used
45	A138	10c brown	8.25	*8.75*
46	A138	20c red brn (Bl)	8.25	*8.75*
47	A138	25c dp grn	8.25	*8.75*
48	A138	30c bluish sl	8.25	*8.75*
49	A138	50c red vio (Bl)	8.25	*8.75*
50	A141	75c cop red (Bl)	8.25	*8.75*
51	A141	1.25 l dl bl	8.25	*8.75*
52	A141	1.75 l + 25c brn	8.25	*8.75*
53	A144	2.55 l + 50c org (Bl)	8.25	*8.75*
54	A145	5 l + 1 l dl vio	8.25	*8.75*
		Nos. 45-54 (10)	82.50	*87.50*

Types of Rhodes Issue of 1929

Imprint: "Officina Carte-Valori Roma"

1932

No.	Type	Description	Unused	Used
55	A1	5c rose lake	.75	.20
56	A2	10c dk brn	.75	.20
57	A3	20c red	.75	.20
58	A3	25c dl grn	.75	.20
59	A4	30c dl bl	.75	.20
60	A5	50c blk brn	.75	.20
61	A5	1.25 l dp bl	.75	.20
62	A4	5 l rose lake	.75	1.10
63	A4	10 l ol brn	1.50	*2.50*
		Nos. 55-63 (9)	7.50	5.00

Aerial View of Rhodes A6

Map of Rhodes — A7

1932 Wmk. 140 Litho. *Perf. 11*

Shield in Red

No.	Type	Description	Unused	Used
64	A6	5c blk & grn	4.50	*7.50*
65	A6	10c blk & vio bl	4.50	4.50
66	A6	20c blk & dl yel	4.50	4.50
67	A6	25c lil & blk	4.50	4.50
68	A6	30c blk & pink	4.50	4.50

Shield and Map Dots in Red

No.	Type	Description	Unused	Used
69	A7	50c blk & gray	4.50	4.50
70	A7	1.25 l red brn & gray	4.50	*10.00*
71	A7	5 l dk bl & gray	13.00	*30.00*
72	A7	10 l dk grn & gray	37.50	*50.00*
73	A7	25 l choc & gray	250.00	*550.00*
		Nos. 64-73 (10)	332.00	*670.00*

20th anniv. of the Italian occupation and 10th anniv. of Fascist rule.

Deer and Palm — A8

1935, Apr. Photo. Wmk. 140

No.	Type	Description	Unused	Used
74	A8	5c orange	7.50	*11.00*
75	A8	10c brown	7.50	*11.00*
76	A8	20c car rose	7.50	*12.00*
77	A8	25c green	7.50	*12.00*
78	A8	30c purple	7.50	*13.00*
79	A8	50c red brn	7.50	*13.00*
80	A8	1.25l blue	7.50	*32.50*
81	A8	5 l yellow	82.50	*140.00*
		Nos. 74-81 (8)	135.00	*244.50*

Holy Year.

WEIHNACHTEN WEIHNACHTEN
1944 1944

The above overprints on No. 55 are stated to have been prepared locally for use on German military correspondence, but banned by postal authorities in Berlin.

RHODES SEMI-POSTAL STAMPS

Rhodes Nos. 55-62 Surcharged in Black or Red

1943 Wmk. 140 *Perf. 14*

No.	Type	Description	Unused	Used
B1	A1	5c + 5c rose lake	.45	.45
B2	A2	10c + 10c dk brn	.45	.45
B3	A3	20c + 20c red	.45	.45
B4	A3	25c + 25c dl grn	.45	.45
B5	A4	30c + 30c dl bl (R)	.75	.60
B6	A5	50c + 50c blk brn	.75	.90
B7	A5	1.25 l + 1.25 l dp bl (R)	1.25	1.25
B8	A4	5 l + 5 l rose lake	55.00	55.00
		Nos. B1-B8 (8)	59.55	59.55

The surtax was for general relief.

Rhodes Nos. 55 to 58, 60 and 61 Surcharged in Black or Red

1944

No.	Type	Description	Unused	Used
B9	A1	5c + 3 l rose lake	1.10	*1.75*
B10	A2	10c + 3 l dk brn (R)	1.10	*1.75*
B11	A3	20c + 3 l red	1.10	*1.75*
B12	A3	25c + 3 l dl grn (R)	1.10	*1.75*
B13	A5	50c + 3 l blk brn (R)	1.10	*1.75*
B14	A5	1.25 l + 5 l dp bl (R)	17.50	*21.00*
		Nos. B9-B14 (6)	23.00	*29.75*

The surtax was for war victims.

Rhodes Nos. 62 and 63 Surcharged in Red

1945

No.	Type	Description	Unused	Used
B17	A4	5 l + 10 l rose lake	5.50	*8.50*
B18	A4	10 l + 10 l ol brn	5.50	*8.50*

The surtax was for the Red Cross.

RHODES AIR POST STAMPS

Symbolical of Flight — AP18

1934 Typo. Wmk. 140 *Perf. 14*

No.	Type	Description	Unused	Used
C1	AP18	50c black & yellow	.20	.20
C2	AP18	80c black & mag	.65	*1.50*
C3	AP18	1 l black & green	.45	.20
C4	AP18	5 l black & red vio	1.10	*2.75*
		Nos. C1-C4 (4)	2.40	*4.65*

RHODES AIR POST SEMI-POSTAL STAMPS

Rhodes Nos. C1-C4 Surcharged in Silver

1944 Wmk. 140 *Perf. 14*

No.	Type	Description	Unused	Used
CB1	AP18	50c + 2 l	6.00	2.25
CB2	AP18	80c + 2 l	7.50	4.50
CB3	AP18	1 l + 2 l	8.75	5.25
CB4	AP18	5 l + 2 l	45.00	*50.00*
		Nos. CB1-CB4 (4)	67.25	*62.00*

The surtax was for war victims.

RHODES SPECIAL DELIVERY STAMPS

Stag — SD1

1936 Photo. Wmk. 140 *Perf. 14*

No.	Type	Description	Unused	Used
E1	SD1	1.25 l green	1.50	1.25
E2	SD1	2.50 l vermilion	2.25	*2.50*

Nos. 58 and 57 Surcharged in Black

1943

No.	Type	Description	Unused	Used
E3	A3	1.25 l on 25c dl grn	.35	*1.10*
E4	A3	2.50 l on 20c red	.35	*1.10*

RHODES SEMI-POSTAL SPECIAL DELIVERY STAMPS

Rhodes Nos. E1 and E2 Surcharged in Red or Black

LRE 1,25 PRO
ASSISTENZA EGEO

1943 Wmk. 140 *Perf. 14*

No.	Type	Description	Unused	Used
EB1	SD1	1.25 l + 1.25 l (R)	26.00	16.00
EB2	SD1	2.50 l + 2.50 l	32.50	21.00

The surtax was for general relief.

RHODES POSTAGE DUE STAMPS

Maltese Cross PD1

Immortelle PD2

1934 Photo. Wmk. 140 *Perf. 13*

No.	Type	Description	Unused	Used
J1	PD1	5c vermilion	.75	*.90*
J2	PD1	10c carmine	.75	*.90*
J3	PD1	20c dk green	.75	*.55*
J4	PD1	30c purple	.75	*.75*
J5	PD1	40c dk blue	.75	*1.90*
J6	PD2	50c vermilion	.75	*.55*
J7	PD2	60c carmine	.75	*3.00*
J8	PD2	1 l dk green	.75	*3.00*
J9	PD2	2 l purple	.75	*1.90*
		Nos. J1-J9 (9)	6.75	13.45

RHODES PARCEL POST STAMPS

Both unused and used values are for complete stamps.

PP1

PP2

1934 Photo. Wmk. 140 *Perf. 13*

No.	Type	Description	Unused	Used
Q1	PP1	5c vermilion	1.40	1.40
Q2	PP1	10c carmine	1.40	1.40
Q3	PP1	20c dk green	1.40	1.40
Q4	PP1	25c purple	1.40	1.40
Q5	PP1	50c dk blue	1.40	1.40
Q6	PP1	60c black	1.40	1.40
Q7	PP2	1 l vermilion	1.40	1.40
Q8	PP2	2 l carmine	1.40	1.40
Q9	PP2	3 l dk green	1.40	1.40
Q10	PP2	4 l purple	1.40	1.40
Q11	PP2	10 l dk blue	1.40	1.40
		Nos. Q1-Q11 (11)	15.40	15.40

Value of used halves, Nos. Q1-Q11, each 20 cents.

See note preceding No. Q7 of Italy.

SCARPANTO

Overprinted "Scarpanto" in Black or Violet

1912-22 Wmk. 140 *Perf. 13½, 14*

No.	Type	Description	Unused	Used
1	A43	2c orange brn	4.25	4.00
2	A48	5c green	1.40	*4.00*
3	A48	10c claret	.35	*4.00*
4	A48	15c slate ('22)	8.75	*16.00*
5	A50	20c brown org ('21)	25.00	25.00
6	A49	25c blue	4.25	4.00
7	A49	40c brown	.35	*4.00*
8	A49	50c violet	1.25	*6.50*

Unwmk.

No.	Type	Description	Unused	Used
9	A58	15c slate (V)	15.00	7.50
10	A50	20c brown org ('17)	65.00	*75.00*
		Nos. 1-10 (10)	125.60	*150.00*

No 9 Surcharged Like Calchi No. 11

1916 *Perf. 13½*

No.	Type	Description	Unused	Used
11	A58	20c on 15c slate	.65	*15.00*

Ferrucci Issue

Overprinted in Red or Blue

1930 Wmk. 140 *Perf. 14*

No.	Type	Description	Unused	Used
12	A102	20c violet (R)	1.25	*2.50*
13	A103	25c dk green (R)	1.25	*2.50*
14	A103	50c black (R)	1.25	*4.25*
15	A103	1.25 l dp blue (R)	1.25	*4.25*
16	A104	5 l + 2 l dp car (Bl)	1.90	*6.50*
		Nos. 12-16 (5)	6.90	*20.00*

Garibaldi Issue

Overprinted in Red or Blue

1932

No.	Type	Description	Unused	Used
17	A138	10c brown	5.25	*8.75*
18	A138	20c red brown (Bl)	5.25	*8.75*
19	A138	25c dp green	5.25	*8.75*
20	A138	30c bluish slate	5.25	*8.75*
21	A138	50c red vio (Bl)	5.25	*8.75*

22 A141 75c cop red (Bl) 5.25 8.75
23 A141 1.25 l dull blue 5.25 8.75
24 A141 1.75 l + 25c brown 5.25 8.75
25 A144 2.55 l + 50c org (Bl) 5.25 8.75
26 A145 5 l + 1 l dl vio 5.25 8.75
Nos. 17-26 (10) 52.50 87.50

SIMI

Overprinted "Simi" in Black or Violet

1912-21 Wmk. 140 Perf. 13½, 14
1 A43 2c orange brn 4.25 4.00
2 A48 5c green 12.50 4.00
3 A48 10c claret .35 4.00
4 A48 15c slate ('21) 65.00 32.50
5 A50 20c brown org ('21) 32.50 19.00
6 A49 25c blue 1.60 4.00
7 A49 40c brown .35 4.00
8 A49 50c violet .35 6.50

Unwmk.
9 A58 15c slate (V) 25.00 7.50
10 A50 20c brn org ('17) 32.50 52.50
Nos. 1-10 (10) 174.40 138.00

No. 9 Surcharged Like Calchi No. 11

1916 Perf. 13½
11 A58 20c on 15c slate 5.25 12.00

Ferrucci Issue

Overprinted in Red or Blue

1930 Wmk. 140 Perf. 14
12 A102 20c violet (R) 1.25 2.50
13 A103 25c dk green (R) 1.25 2.50
14 A103 50c blk (R) 1.25 4.25
15 A103 1.25 l dp blue (R) 1.25 4.25
16 A104 5 l + 2 l dp car (Bl) 1.90 6.50
Nos. 12-16 (5) 6.90 20.00

Garibaldi Issue

Overprinted in Red or Blue

1932
17 A138 10c brown 5.25 8.75
18 A138 20c red brn (Bl) 5.25 8.75
19 A138 25c deep green 5.25 8.75
20 A138 30c bluish slate 5.25 8.75
21 A138 50c red vio (Bl) 5.25 8.75
22 A141 75c cop red (Bl) 5.25 8.75
23 A141 1.25 l dl bl 5.25 8.75
24 A141 1.75 l + 25c brn 5.25 8.75
25 A144 2.55 l + 50c org (Bl) 5.25 8.75
26 A145 5 l + 1 l dl vio 5.25 8.75
Nos. 17-26 (10) 52.50 87.50

STAMPALIA

Overprinted "Stampalia" in Black or Violet

1912-21 Wmk. 140 Perf. 13½, 14
1 A43 2c org brn 4.25 4.00
2 A48 5c green .35 4.00
3 A48 10c claret .35 4.00
4 A48 15c slate ('21) 6.00 16.00
5 A50 20c brn org ('21) 25.00 25.00
6 A49 25c blue .45 4.00
7 A49 40c brown 1.90 4.00
8 A49 50c violet .35 6.50

Unwmk.
9 A58 15c slate (V) 19.00 7.50
10 A50 20c brn org ('17) 42.50 52.50
Nos. 1-10 (10) 100.15 127.50

No. 9 Surcharged Like Calchi No. 11

1916 Perf. 13½
11 A58 20c on 15c slate .55 10.50

Ferrucci Issue

Overprinted in Red or Blue

1930 Wmk. 140 Perf. 14
12 A102 20c violet (R) 1.25 2.50
13 A103 25c dk green (R) 1.25 2.50
14 A103 50c black (R) 1.25 4.25
15 A103 1.25 l dp blue (R) 1.25 4.25
16 A104 5 l + 2 l dp car (Bl) 1.90 6.50
Nos. 12-16 (5) 6.90 20.00

Garibaldi Issue

Overprinted in Red or Blue

1932
17 A138 10c brown 5.25 8.75
18 A138 20c red brn (Bl) 5.25 8.75
19 A138 25c dp green 5.25 8.75
20 A138 30c bluish slate 5.25 8.75
21 A138 50c red vio (Bl) 5.25 8.75
22 A141 75c cop red (Bl) 5.25 8.75
23 A141 1.25 l dull blue 5.25 8.75
24 A141 1.75 l + 25c brn 5.25 8.75
25 A144 2.55 l + 50c org (Bl) 5.25 8.75
26 A145 5 l + 1 l dl vio 5.25 8.75
Nos. 17-26 (10) 52.50 87.50

TRIESTE

A free territory (1947-1954) on the Adriatic Sea between Italy and Yugoslavia. In 1954 the territory was divided, Italy acquiring the northern section and seaport, Yugoslavia the southern section (Zone B).

Catalogue values for all unused stamps in this country are for Never Hinged items.

ZONE A

Issued jointly by the Allied Military Government of the United States and Great Britain

Stamps of Italy 1945-47 Overprinted:

a

b

c

1947, Oct. 1 Wmk. 277 Perf. 14
1 A259(a) 25c brt bl grn .20 1.25
2 A255(a) 50c dp vio .20 1.25
3 A257(a) 1 l dk grn .20 .20
4 A258(a) 2 l dk cl brn .20 .20
5 A259(a) 3 l red .20 .20
6 A259(a) 4 l red org .20 .20
7 A256(a) 5 l deep blue .20 .20
8 A257(a) 6 l dp vio .20 .20
9 A255(a) 10 l slate .20 .20
10 A257(a) 15 l deep blue .70 .20
11 A259(a) 20 l dk red vio 2.25 .20
12 A260(b) 25 l dk grn 3.75 2.50
13 A260(b) 50 l dk vio brn 4.50 2.10

Perf. 14x13½
14 A261(c) 100 l car lake 24.00 10.50
Nos. 1-14 (14) 37.00 19.40

The letters "F. T. T." are the initials of "Free Territory of Trieste."

Italy Nos. 486-488 Ovptd. Type "a"

1948, Mar. 1 Perf. 14
15 A255 8 l dk green 2.50 2.50
16 A256 10 l red org 7.50 .25
17 A259 30 l dk blue 150.00 4.00
Nos. 15-17 (3) 160.00 6.75

Italy Nos. 495 to 506 Overprinted

d

1948, July 1
18 A272 3 l dk brn .25 .20
19 A272 4 l red vio .25 .20
20 A272 5 l deep blue .25 .20
21 A272 6 l dp yel grn .35 .25
22 A272 8 l brown .25 .20
23 A272 10 l org red .35 .20
24 A272 12 l dk gray grn .45 1.10
25 A272 15 l gray blk 10.00 7.00
26 A272 20 l car rose 15.00 7.00
27 A272 30 l brt ultra 2.00 1.10
28 A272 50 l violet 9.00 9.00
29 A272 100 l bl blk 27.50 27.50
Nos. 18-29 (12) 65.65 53.95

Italy, Nos. 486 to 488, Overprinted in Carmine

1948, Sept. 8
30 A255 8 l dk green .30 .25
31 A256 10 l red org .30 .25
32 A259 30 l dk blue 1.75 1.75
Nos. 30-32,C17-C19 (6) 4.10 4.40

The overprint is embossed.

Italy, No. 507, Overprinted Type "d" in Carmine

1948, Oct. 15
33 A273 15 l dk green 1.75 1.60

Italy, No. 508, Overprinted in Green

e

1948, Nov. 15
34 A274 15 l dk brown 9.00 1.50

Italy, No. 509, Overprinted Type "d" in Red

1949, May 2 Wmk. 277 Perf. 14
35 A275 20 l dk brown 9.00 2.25

Italy, Nos. 510 to 513, Overprinted

f

1949, May 2 Buff Background
36 A276 5 l red brown .75 1.25
37 A276 15 l dk green 7.50 9.25
38 A276 20 l dp red brn 4.50 1.25
39 A276 50 l dk blue 10.00 5.00
Nos. 36-39 (4) 22.75 16.75

Italy, No. 514, Overprinted Type "d" in Red

1949, May 2
40 A277 50 l brt ultra 4.00 3.25

Italy, No. 518, Overprinted Type "d" in Red

1949, May 30
41 A279 100 l brown 62.50 75.00

Italy, Nos. 515-517, Ovptd. Type "f"

1949, June 15
42 A278 5 l dk green 10.00 5.25
43 A278 15 l violet 10.00 11.00
44 A278 20 l brown 10.00 7.75
Nos. 42-44 (3) 30.00 24.00

Italy, Nos. 519 and 520, Overprinted Type "e" in Carmine

1949, July 16
45 A280 20 l gray 9.00 4.00
46 A281 20 l brown 9.00 4.00

Italy, No. 521 Overprinted in Green

g

1949, June 8
47 A282 20 l brown red 5.00 2.25

Italy, No. 522, Overprinted Type "f" in Carmine

1949, July 8
49 A283 20 l violet 15.00 5.00

Italy, No. 523 Overprinted Type "e", without Periods, in Black

1949, Aug. 27
50 A284 20 l violet blue 7.75 3.25

Italy, No. 524 Ovptd. Type "f"

1949, Aug. 27
51 A285 20 l violet 17.50 13.00

Italy, No. 525, Overprinted Type "d" in Green

1949, Sept. 10
52 A286 20 l red 10.00 3.75

Italy Nos. 526 and 527 Overprinted

h

Wmk. 277
1949, Nov. 7 Photo. Perf. 14
53 A287 20 l rose car 3.00 3.00
54 A288 50 l deep blue 12.00 12.00

Same Overprint on No. 528

1949, Nov. 7
55 A289 20 l dp grn 4.50 2.75

Same Overprint on No. 529

1949, Nov. 7
56 A290 20 l brt blue 3.25 2.75

Same Overprint in Red on No. 530

1949, Dec. 28
57 A291 20 l violet blk 4.50 2.00

Same Overprint in Black on Italian Stamps of 1945-48

1949-50 Photo.
58 A257 1 l dk green .20 .80
59 A258 2 l dk cl brn .20 .20
60 A259 3 l red .20 .20
61 A256 5 l deep blue .20 .20
62 A257 6 l dp violet .20 .20
63 A255 8 l dk green 21.00 9.50
64 A256 10 l red org .20 .20
65 A257 15 l deep blue 2.50 .60
66 A259 20 l dk red vio 1.25 .20
67 A260 25 l dk grn ('50) 24.00 1.90
68 A260 50 l dk vio brn ('50) 30.00 1.50

Engr.
69 A261 100 l car lake 95.00 9.50
Nos. 58-69 (12) 174.95 25.00

Issued: 3 l, 20 l, 10/21; 5 l, 11/5; 10 l, 11/7; 100 l, 11/23; 15 l, 11/28; 1 l, 2 l, 6 l, 8 l, 12/28; 50 l, 1/19; 25 l, 2/25.

Italy, No. 531, Overprinted Type "g" in Carmine

1950, Apr. 12
70 A292 20 l brown 3.75 1.50

Same Overprint in Carmine on Italy, No. 532

1950, Apr. 29
71 A293 20 l vio gray 1.50 2.00

Same Overprint in Carmine on Italy, Nos. 533 and 534

1950, May 22
72 A294 20 l olive green 2.50 1.60
73 A295 55 l blue 10.00 12.00

Italy, Nos. 535 and 536, Overprinted Type "h" in Black

1950, May 29
74 A296 20 l violet 3.75 1.60
75 A296 55 l blue 12.00 12.00

Italy, No. 537, Overprinted Type "g" in Carmine

1950, July 10
76 A297 20 l gray grn 2.75 2.00

Same Overprint in Carmine on Italy, Nos. 538-539

1950, July 15

77 A298 20 l purple 5.75 4.50
78 A298 55 l blue 18.00 18.00

Italy, No. 540, Overprinted Type "h"

1950, July 22

79 A299 20 l brown 4.50 2.25

Italy, No. 541 Overprinted in Carmine

i

1950, July 29

80 A300 20 l dk grn 4.50 2.25

Italy, No. 542, Overprinted Type "g"

1950, Aug. 21

81 A301 20 l chnt brn 2.50 2.00

Italy, Nos. 473A and 474, Overprinted

1950, Aug. 27

82 A257 15 l deep blue 3.00 2.25
83 A259 20 l dk red vio 3.00 .75

Trieste Fair.

Italy, No. 543, Overprinted Type "i" in Carmine

1950, Sept. 11

84 A302 20 l indigo 1.25 1.10

Italy Nos. 544-546, Ovptd. Type "h"

1950, Sept. 16 Wmk. 277 *Perf. 14*

85 A303 5 l dp cl & grn .50 1.75
86 A303 20 l brn & grn 1.50 1.75
87 A303 55 l dp ultra & brn 22.50 21.00
Nos. 85-87 (3) 24.50 24.50

Same, in Black, on Italy No. 547

1950, Sept. 16

88 A304 20 l ol brn & red brn 2.75 1.75

Same, in Black, on Italy No. 548

1950, Sept. 16

89 A305 20 l cr & gray blk 5.00 1.75

Italy, Nos. 549 to 565, Overprinted Type "g" in Black

1950, Oct. 20

90 A306 50c violet blue .20 .20
91 A306 1 l dk blue vio .20 .20
92 A306 2 l sepia .20 .20
93 A306 5 l dk gray .20 .20
94 A306 6 l chocolate .25 .20
95 A306 10 l deep green .25 .20
96 A306 12 l dp blue grn .35 1.00
97 A306 15 l dk gray bl 1.00 .20
98 A306 20 l blue vio 1.00 .20
99 A306 25 l brown org 2.00 .20
100 A306 30 l magenta .75 .60
101 A306 35 l crimson 2.00 1.50
102 A306 40 l brown 1.25 .80
103 A306 50 l violet .25 .30
104 A306 55 l deep blue .25 .60
105 A306 60 l red 6.75 3.75
106 A306 65 l dk green .25 .55

Italy Nos. 566 and 567 Overprinted

k

Perf. 14, 14x13½

Engr.

107 A306 100 l brown org 2.50 .45
108 A306 200 l olive brn 2.50 5.50
Nos. 90-108 (19) 22.15 16.85

Italy Nos. 568 and 569 Overprinted Type "k" in Black

1951, Mar. 27 Photo. *Perf. 14*

109 A307 20 l red vio & red 2.00 1.75
110 A307 55 l ultra & bl 30.00 27.50

Italy No. 570 Overprinted Type "g"

1951, Apr. 2

111 A308 20 l dk grn 1.50 1.75

Same, on Italy No. 571

1951, Apr. 11

112 A309 20 l bl vio 2.00 1.75

Italy Nos. 572 and 573 Overprinted

1951, Apr. 12

113 A310(h) 20 l brown 1.60 1.25
114 A311(g) 55 l deep blue 3.25 3.50

Italy Nos. 574 to 576 Overprinted Type "h" in Black

1951, May 18 Fleur-de-Lis in Red

115 A312 5 l dk brown 5.75 11.00
116 A312 10 l Prus grn 5.75 11.00
117 A312 15 l vio bl 5.75 11.00
Nos. 115-117 (3) 17.25 33.00

Italy No. 577 Overprinted

m

1951, Apr. 26

118 A313 20 l purple 1.60 2.00

Italy No. 578 Overprinted Type "h"

1951, May 5

119 A314 20 l Prus green 2.75 3.25

Italy Nos. 579-580 Ovptd. Type "g"

1951, June 18

120 A315 20 l violet .60 1.25
121 A315 55 l brt blue 1.90 3.50

Nos. 94, 98 and 104 Overprinted

1951, June 24

122 A306 6 l chocolate .40 .75
123 A306 20 l blue violet .55 .60
124 A306 55 l deep blue .70 1.25
Nos. 122-124 (3) 1.65 2.60

Issued to publicize the Trieste Fair, 1951.

Italy No. 581 Overprinted

n

1951, July 23

125 A316 20 l brn & red brn 1.00 1.10

Italy Nos. 582 and 583 Overprinted Types "n" and "h" in Red

1951, July 23

126 A317(n) 20 l grnsh gray & blk 1.10 1.25
127 A318(h) 55 l vio bl & pale sal 2.50 3.75

Italy No. 584 Overprinted Type "g" in Carmine

1951, Aug. 23

128 A319 25 l gray blk 1.00 1.10

Overprint "g" on Italy No. 585

1951, Sept. 8

129 A320 25 l deep blue 1.00 1.10

Italy No. 586 Overprinted Type "h" in Red

1951, Sept. 15

130 A321 25 l dk brn 1.00 1.10

Italy Nos. 587-589 Overprinted in Blue

o

1951, Oct. 11

131 A322 10 l dk brn & gray .40 .75
132 A322 25 l rose red & bl grn .75 .75
133 A322 60 l vio bl & red org 1.10 1.50
Nos. 131-133 (3) 2.25 3.00

Italy Nos. 590-591 Overprinted

p

1951, Oct. 31 Photo.

Overprint Spaced to Fit Design

134 A323 10 l green .75 .90
135 A324 25 l vio gray .75 .90

Italy Nos. 592-593 Ovptd. Type "k"

1951, Nov. 21

136 A325 10 l ol & dull grn .80 1.25
137 A326 25 l dull green 1.00 .80

Italy Nos. 594-596 Overprinted Types "k" or "p" in Black

1951, Nov. 23

Overprint "p" Spaced to Fit Design

138 A327(p) 10 l vio brn & dk grn .50 .90
139 A327(k) 25 l red brn & dk brn .90 .90
140 A327(p) 60 l dp grn & ind 1.40 1.90
Nos. 138-140 (3) 2.80 3.70

Italy No. 597 Overprinted Type "p"

1952, Jan. 28 Wmk. 277 *Perf. 14*

Overprint Spaced to Fit Design

141 A328 25 l gray & gray blk 1.00 .70

Italy No. 598 Overprinted Type "k"

1952, Feb. 2

142 A329 25 l dl grn & ol bis 1.00 .70

Same on Italy No. 599

1952, Mar. 26

143 A330 25 l brn & sl blk .85 .70

Same on Italy No. 600

1952, Apr. 12

144 A331 60 l ultra 2.50 3.25

Same on Italy No. 601

1952, Apr. 16

145 A332 25 l dp orange .75 .20

Stamps of Italy Overprinted "AMG FTT" in Various Sizes and Arrangements

On Nos. 602-603

1952, June 14 Wmk. 277 *Perf. 14*

146 A333 25 l blk & red brn .65 .60
147 A333 60 l blk & ultra 1.10 1.75

On No. 604

1952, June 7

148 A334 25 l bright blue .90 .70

On No. 605

1952, June 14

149 A335 25 l black & yellow .90 .70

On No. 606

1952, June 19

150 A336 25 l bl gray, red & dk bl (R) .90 .70

On No. 607

1952, June 28

151 A337 25 l dp grn, dk brn & red .90 .70

On No. 608

1952, Sept. 6

152 A338 25 l dark green .90 .70

On No. 609 in Bronze

1952, Sept. 20

153 A339 25 l purple .90 .70

On No. 610

1952, Oct. 4

154 A340 25 l gray .90 .70

On No. 611

1952, Oct. 1

155 A341 60 l vio bl & dk bl 2.25 3.25

On No. 612

1952, Nov. 21 *Perf. 13*

156 A342 25 l brn & dk brn .90 .70

On Nos. 613-615

1952, Nov. 3 *Perf. 14*

157 A343 10 l dk green .20 .35
158 A344 25 l blk & dk brn .80 .30
159 A344 60 l blk & blue .80 1.50
Nos. 157-159 (3) 1.80 2.15

On Nos. 616-617

1952, Dec. 6

160 A345 25 l dk green .90 .70
161 A346 25 l brown .90 .70

On No. 618

1953, Jan. 5

162 A347 25 l gray blk & dk bl (Bl) .90 .70

On Nos. 601A-601B

1952, Dec. 31

163 A332a 60 l ultra (G) .75 1.25
164 A332 80 l brown car 1.60 .50

On No. 621

1953, Feb. 21

165 A349 25 l car lake .90 .70

On No. 622

1953, Apr. 24

166 A350 25 l violet .90 .70

On No. 623

1953, Apr. 30

167 A351 25 l violet .90 .70

On No. 624

1953, May 30

168 A352 25 l dark brown .90 .70

On No. 625

1953, June 27

169 A353 25 l brn & dull red .90 .70

On Nos. 626-633

1953-54

170 A354 5 l gray .20 .20
171 A354 10 l org ver .25 .20
172 A354 12 l dull grn .25 .20
172A A354 13 l brt lil rose ('54) .25 .20
173 A354 20 l brown .25 .20
174 A354 25 l purple .25 .20
175 A354 35 l rose car .50 .90

176 A354 60 l blue .60 1.25
177 A354 80 l org brn .65 1.40
Nos. 170-177 (9) 3.20 4.75

Issue dates: 13 l, Feb. 1. Others, June 16.

Italy, Nos. 554, 558 and 564 Overprinted in Red or Green

1953, June 27

178 A306 10 l dp green (R) .40 .60
179 A306 25 l brown org .50 .40
180 A306 60 l red .60 1.00
Nos. 178-180 (3) 1.50 2.00

5th International Sample Fair of Trieste.

On No. 634

1953, July 11

181 A355 25 l blue green .95 .70

On Nos. 635-636

1953, July 16

182 A356 25 l dark brown .45 .50
183 A356 60 l deep blue .70 1.00

On Nos. 637-638

1953, Aug. 6

184 A357 25 l org & Prus bl 1.00 .70
185 A357 60 l lil rose & dk vio bl 3.00 3.25

On No. 639

1953, Aug. 13

186 A358 25 l dk brn & dl grn .90 .70

On No. 640

1953, Sept. 5

187 A359 25 l dk gray & brn .90 .70

On Nos. 641-646

1954, Jan. 26

188 A360 10 l dk brn & red brn .25 .30
189 A361 12 l lt bl & gray .30 .50
190 A361 20 l brn org & dk brn .40 .35
191 A360 25 l dk grn & pale bl .40 .20
192 A361 35 l cream & brn .40 .80
193 A361 60 l bl grn & ind .55 1.00
Nos. 188-193 (6) 2.30 3.15

On Nos. 647-648

1954, Feb. 11

194 A362 25 l dk brn & choc .45 .50
195 A362 60 l bl & ultra .65 1.00

On Nos. 649-650

1954, Feb. 25

196 A363 25 l purple .45 .35
197 A363 60 l dp bl grn .95 1.50

On No. 651

1954, Mar. 20

198 A364 25 l purple .90 .50

On No. 652

1954, Apr. 24

199 A365 25 l gray blk .90 .70

On No. 653

1954, June 1

200 A366 25 l gray, org brn & blk .90 .70

On No. 654

1954, June 19

201 A367 25 l dk grnsh gray .90 .70

On Nos. 655-656

1954, July 8

202 A368 25 l red brown .40 .55
203 A368 60 l gray green .95 1.25

FIERA DI TRIESTE 1954

Nos. 644, 646 With Additional Overprint

1954, June 17

204 A360 25 l dk grn & pale bl .45 .50
205 A361 60 l bl grn & indigo .65 1.00

International Sample Fair of Trieste.

On No. 657

1954, Sept. 6

206 A369 25 l dp grn & red .90 .70

On Nos. 658-659

1954, Oct. 30

207 A370 25 l rose red .30 .40
208 A370 60 l blue .55 .65

OCCUPATION AIR POST STAMPS

Air Post Stamps of Italy, 1945-47, Overprinted Type "c" in Black

1947, Oct. 1 Wmk. 277 Perf. 14

C1 AP59 1 l slate bl .20 .20
C2 AP60 2 l dk blue .20 .20
C3 AP60 5 l dk green 3.25 2.25
C4 AP59 10 l car rose 3.25 2.25
C5 AP60 25 l brown 7.25 3.50
C6 AP59 50 l violet 45.00 5.50
Nos. C1-C6 (6) 59.15 13.90

Italy, Nos. C116 to C121, Overprinted Type "b" in Black

1947, Nov. 19

C7 AP61 6 l dp violet 1.25 1.75
C8 AP61 10 l dk car rose 1.25 1.75
C9 AP61 20 l dp org 9.50 4.25
C10 AP61 25 l aqua 1.75 2.00
C11 AP61 35 l brt blue 1.75 2.50
C12 AP61 50 l lilac rose 9.50 2.50
Nos. C7-C12 (6) 25.00 14.75

Italy, Nos. C123 to C126, Overprinted Type "f" in Black

1948

C13 AP65 100 l green 82.50 2.25
C14 AP65 300 l lil rose 11.50 13.00
C15 AP65 500 l ultra 13.50 19.00
C16 AP65 1000 l dk brown 140.00 160.00
Nos. C13-C16 (4) 247.50 194.25

Issue date: Nos. C13-C15, Mar. 1.

Italy, No. C110, C113 and C114, Overprinted in Black

(Reduced Illustration)

1948, Sept. 8

C17 AP59 10 l carmine rose .35 .35
C18 AP60 25 l brown .70 .90
C19 AP59 50 l violet .70 .90
Nos. C17-C19 (3) 1.75 2.15

The overprint is embossed.

Italy Air Post Stamps of 1945-48 Overprinted Type "h" in Black

1949-52

C20 AP59 10 l car rose .20 .20
C21 AP60 25 l brown ('50) .20 .20
C22 AP59 50 l violet .20 .20
C23 AP65 100 l green .55 .20
C24 AP65 300 l lil rose ('50) 8.75 9.25
C25 AP65 500 l ultra ('50) 15.00 11.00
C26 AP65 1000 l dk brn ('52) 32.50 29.00
Nos. C20-C26 (7) 57.40 50.05

No. C26 is found in two perforations: 14 and 14x13.

Issued: 100 l, 11/7; 50 l, 12/5; 10 l, 12/28; 25 l, 1/23; 300 l, 500 l, 11/25; 1000 l, 2/18.

OCCUPATION SPECIAL DELIVERY STAMPS

Special Delivery Stamps of Italy 1946-48 Overprinted Type "c"

1947-48 Wmk. 277 Perf. 14

E1 SD9 15 l dk car rose .20 .20
E2 SD8 25 l brt red org ('48) 37.50 5.75
E3 SD8 30 l dp vio .40 .30
E4 SD9 60 l car rose ('48) 30.00 8.75
Nos. E1-E4 (4) 68.10 15.00

Issue dates: Oct. 1, 1947. Mar. 1, 1948.

Italy No. E26, Overprinted Type "d"

1948, Sept. 24

E5 A272 35 l violet 2.50 3.00

Italy No. E25, Overprinted Type "h"

1950, Sept. 27

E6 SD9 60 l car rose 6.25 1.50

Italy No. E32 Overprinted Type "k"

1952, Feb. 4

E7 SD8 50 l lilac rose 6.25 1.50

OCCUPATION AUTHORIZED DELIVERY STAMPS

Authorized Delivery Stamp of Italy, 1946 Overprinted Type "a" in Black

1947, Oct. 1 Wmk. 277 Perf. 14

EY1 AD3 1 l dark brown .25 .25

Italy, No. EY7 Overprinted in Black

1947, Oct. 29

EY2 AD4 8 l bright red 9.75 1.75

Italy, No. EY8, Overprinted Type "a" in Black

1949, July 30

EY3 AD4 15 l violet 35.00 7.50

Same, Overprinted Type "h" in Black

1949, Nov. 7

EY4 AD4 15 l violet 1.25 .50

Italy No. EY9 Overprinted Type "h" in Black

1952, Feb. 4

EY5 AD4 20 l rose violet 8.75 .50

OCCUPATION POSTAGE DUE STAMPS

Postage Due Stamps of Italy, 1945-47, Overprinted Type "a"

1947, Oct. 1 Wmk. 277 Perf. 14

J1 D9 1 l red orange .20 .25
J2 D10 2 l dk green .20 .35
J3 D9 5 l violet 6.00 .25
J4 D9 10 l dk blue 8.75 1.75
J5 D9 20 l car rose 24.00 1.75
J6 D10 50 l aqua 1.40 .50
Nos. J1-J6 (6) 40.55 4.85

Same Overprint on Postage Due Stamps of Italy, 1947

1949

J7 D10 1 l red orange .20 .50
J8 D10 3 l carmine .55 1.25
J9 D10 4 l brown 7.50 11.00
J10 D10 5 l violet 82.50 15.00
J11 D10 6 l vio blue 22.50 21.00
J12 D10 8 l rose vio 47.50 50.00
J13 D10 10 l deep blue 110.00 15.00
J14 D10 12 l golden brn 17.00 18.00
J15 D10 20 l lilac rose 17.00 4.50
Nos. J7-J15 (9) 304.75 136.25

Issued: 3 l, 4 l, 6 l, 8 l, 12 l, 1/24; others, 4/15.

Postage Due Stamps of Italy, 1947-54, Overprinted Type "h"

1949-54

J16 D10 1 l red orange .25 .20
J17 D10 2 l dk green .25 .20
J18 D10 3 l car ('54) .35 .70
J20 D10 5 l violet .45 .20
J21 D10 6 l vio bl ('50) .35 .20
J22 D10 8 l rose vio ('50) .35 .20
J23 D10 10 l deep blue .50 .20
J24 D10 12 l gldn brn ('50) 1.10 .70
J25 D10 20 l lilac rose 1.90 .50
J26 D10 25 l dk red ('54) 4.75 6.50
J27 D10 50 l aqua ('50) 3.25 .20
J28 D10 100 l org yel ('52) 5.25 .50
J29 D10 500 l dp bl & dk car ('52) 30.00 12.00
Nos. J16-J29 (13) 48.75 22.30

Issued: 5 l, 10 l, 11/7; 1 l, 11/22; 2 l, 20 l, 12/28; 6 l, 8 l, 12 l, 5/16; 50 l, 11/25; 100 l, 11/11; 500 l, 6/19; 3 l, 1/24; 25 l, 2/1.

OCCUPATION PARCEL POST STAMPS

See note preceding Italy No. Q7.

Parcel Post Stamps of Italy, 1946-48, Overprinted:

1947-48 Wmk. 277 Perf. 13½

Q1 PP4 1 l golden brn .25 .40
Q2 PP4 2 l lt bl grn .35 .50
Q3 PP4 3 l red org .40 .60
Q4 PP4 4 l gray blk .50 .75
Q5 PP4 5 l lil rose ('48) 1.40 2.00
Q6 PP4 10 l violet 2.75 4.00
Q7 PP4 20 l lilac brn 4.00 6.00
Q8 PP4 50 l rose red 6.50 9.00
Q9 PP4 100 l sapphire 8.00 12.00
Q10 PP4 200 l grn ('48) 325.00 450.00
Q11 PP4 300 l brn car ('48) 160.00 225.00
Q12 PP4 500 l brn ('48) 95.00 140.00
Nos. Q1-Q12 (12) 604.15 850.25

Halves Used

Q1-Q4 .20
Q5 .20
Q6-Q7 .20
Q8 .20
Q9 .25
Q10 5.75
Q11 4.50
Q12 1.90

Issued: #Q1-Q4, Q6-Q9, Oct. 1; others, Mar. 1.

Parcel Post Stamps of Italy, 1946-54, Overprinted:

1949-54

Q13 PP4 1 l gldn brn ('50) 1.10 1.25
Q14 PP4 2 l lt bl grn ('51) .25 .30
Q15 PP4 3 l red org ('51) .25 .30
Q16 PP4 4 l gray blk ('51) .35 .30
Q17 PP4 5 l lilac rose .35 .40
Q18 PP4 10 l violet .45 .30
Q19 PP4 20 l lil brn .50 .30
Q20 PP4 30 l plum ('52) .65 .70
Q21 PP4 50 l rose red ('50) .80 .30
Q22 PP4 100 l saph ('50) 2.50 3.00
Q23 PP4 200 l green 22.50 32.50
Q24 PP4 300 l brn car ('50) 67.50 85.00
Q25 PP4 500 l brn ('51) 42.50 50.00

Perf. 13x13½

Q26 PP5 1000 l ultra ('54) 160.00 160.00
Nos. Q13-Q26 (14) 299.70 334.65

Halves Used

Q13-Q18, Q20 .20
Q19, Q22 .20
Q21 .20
Q23 .20
Q24 .60
Q25 .70
Q26 1.40

Pairs of Q18 exist with 5mm between overprints instead of 11mm. Value $800.

Issued: 20 l, 200 l, 11/22; 5 l, 10 l, 11/28; 300 l, 1/19; 50 l, 3/10; 1 l, 10/7; 100 l, 11/9; 500 l, 11/25; 2 l, 3 l, 4 l, 8/1; 30 l, 3/6; 1000 l, 8/12.

PARCEL POST AUTHORIZED DELIVERY STAMPS

For the payment of a special tax for the authorized delivery of parcels privately instead of through the post office. Both unused and used values are for complete stamps.

Parcel Post Authorized Delivery Stamps of Italy 1953 Overprinted in Black like Nos. Q13-Q26

1953, July 8 Wmk. 277

QY1 PAD1 40 l org red 2.50 1.00
QY2 PAD1 50 l ultra 2.50 1.00
QY3 PAD1 75 l brown 2.50 1.00
QY4 PAD1 110 l lilac rose 2.50 1.00
Nos. QY1-QY4 (4) 10.00 4.00

Halves Used

QY1 .20
QY2 .20
QY3-QY4 .35

IVORY COAST

'iv-rē 'kōst

LOCATION — West coast of Africa, bordering on Gulf of Guinea
GOVT. — Republic
AREA — 127,520 sq. mi.
POP. — 15,818,068 (1999 est.)
CAPITAL — Yamoussoukro

The former French colony of Ivory Coast became part of French West Africa and used its stamps, starting in 1945. On December 4, 1958, Ivory Coast became a republic, with full independence on August 7, 1960.

100 Centimes = 1 Franc

Catalogue values for unused stamps in this country are for Never Hinged items, beginning with Scott 167 in the regular postage section, Scott B15 in the semi-postal section, Scott C14 in the airpost section, Scott J19 in the postage due section, Scott M1 in the military section, and Scott O1 in the official section.

Navigation and Commerce — A1

Perf. 14x13½

1892-1900 Typo. Unwmk.

Colony Name in Blue or Carmine

No.	Type	Description	Unused	Used
1	A1	1c black, *lil bl*	.75	.75
2	A1	2c brown, *buff*	1.25	1.25
3	A1	4c claret, *lav*	2.00	1.75
4	A1	5c green, *grnsh*	6.00	4.25
5	A1	10c black, *lavender*	8.50	5.50
6	A1	10c red ('00)	75.00	65.00
7	A1	15c blue, quadrille paper	9.00	6.75
8	A1	15c gray ('00)	5.50	2.00
9	A1	20c red, *green*	9.75	8.00
10	A1	25c black, *rose*	12.00	2.00
11	A1	25c blue ('00)	17.50	11.00
12	A1	30c brown, *bister*	17.00	12.50
13	A1	40c red, *straw*	12.50	6.00
14	A1	50c car, *rose*	50.00	35.00
15	A1	50c brn, *azure* ('00)	17.50	9.00
16	A1	75c deep vio, *org*	17.50	14.00
17	A1	1fr brnz grn, *straw*	25.00	19.00
		Nos. 1-17 (17)	286.75	203.75

Perf. 13½x14 stamps are counterfeits.
For surcharges see Nos. 18-20, 37-41.

Nos. 12, 16-17 Surcharged in Black

1904

No.	Type	Description	Unused	Used
18	A1	0,05c on 30c brn, *bis*	47.50	47.50
19	A1	0,10c on 75c vio, *org*	8.50	8.50
20	A1	0,15c on 1fr brnz grn, *straw*	9.50	9.50
		Nos. 18-20 (3)	65.50	65.50

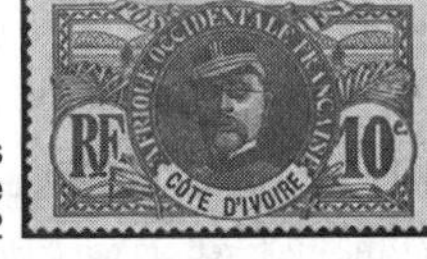

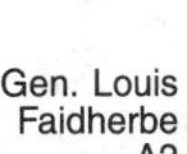

Gen. Louis Faidherbe A2

Oil Palm — A3

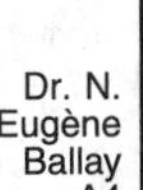

Dr. N. Eugène Ballay A4

1906-07

Name of Colony in Red or Blue

No.	Type	Description	Unused	Used
21	A2	1c slate	.65	.65
22	A2	2c chocolate	.75	.70
23	A2	4c choc, *gray bl*	1.25	1.25
a.		Name double	125.00	125.00
24	A2	5c green	1.60	1.25
25	A2	10c carmine (B)	3.25	2.50
26	A3	20c black, *azure*	4.25	3.50
27	A3	25c bl, *pinkish*	3.50	2.25
28	A3	30c choc, *pnksh*	5.75	3.50
30	A3	35c black, *yel*	7.25	2.75
31	A3	45c choc, *grnsh*	7.50	5.25
32	A3	50c deep violet	7.00	5.50
33	A3	75c blue, *org*	8.50	5.50
34	A4	1fr black, *azure*	22.50	16.00
35	A4	2fr blue, *pink*	30.00	30.00
36	A4	5fr car, *straw* (B)	57.50	57.50
		Nos. 21-36 (15)	161.25	138.10

Stamps of 1892-1900 Surcharged in Carmine or Black

1912

No.	Type	Description	Unused	Used
37	A1	5c on 15c gray (C)	.40	.40
38	A1	5c on 30c brn, *bis* (C)	.80	.80
39	A1	10c on 40c red, *straw*	.80	.80
a.		Pair, one without surcharge	62.50	
40	A1	10c on 50c brn, *az* (C)	1.00	1.00
41	A1	10c on 75c dp vio, *org*	4.50	4.50
		Nos. 37-41 (5)	7.50	7.50

Two spacings between the surcharged numerals are found on Nos. 37 to 41.

River Scene A5

1913-35

No.	Type	Description	Unused	Used
42	A5	1c vio brn & vio	.20	.20
43	A5	2c brown & blk	.20	.20
44	A5	4c vio & vio brn	.20	.20
45	A5	5c yel grn & bl grn	.30	.25
46	A5	5c choc & ol brn ('22)	.20	.20
47	A5	10c red org & rose	.50	.30
48	A5	10c yel grn & bl grn ('22)	.20	.20
49	A5	10c car rose, *bluish* ('26)	.20	.20
50	A5	15c org & rose ('17)	.40	.20
51	A5	20c black & gray	.30	.20
52	A5	25c ultra & bl	4.75	2.75
53	A5	25c blk & vio ('22)	.20	.20
54	A5	30c choc & brn	.65	.50
55	A5	30c red org & rose ('22)	.90	.90
56	A5	30c lt bl & rose red ('26)	.20	.20
57	A5	30c dl grn & grn ('27)	.20	.20
58	A5	35c vio & org	.35	.20
59	A5	40c gray & bl grn	.75	.40
60	A5	45c red org & choc	.35	.25
61	A5	45c dp rose & mar ('34)	3.00	2.75
62	A5	50c black & vio	2.25	1.50
63	A5	50c ultra & bl ('22)	.45	.45
64	A5	50c ol grn & bl ('25)	.25	.25
65	A5	60c vio, *pnksh* ('25)	.20	.20
66	A5	65c car rose & ol grn ('26)	.85	.85
67	A5	75c brn & rose	.35	.30
68	A5	75c ind & ultra ('34)	2.00	2.00
69	A5	85c red vio & blk ('26)	.85	.85
70	A5	90c brn red & rose ('30)	7.50	7.50
71	A5	1fr org & black	.65	.60
72	A5	1.10fr dl grn & dk brn ('28)	3.75	3.75
73	A5	1.50fr lt bl & dp bl ('30)	4.00	3.25
74	A5	1.75fr lt ultra & mag ('35)	8.50	3.75
75	A5	2fr brn & blue	2.25	.90
76	A5	3fr red vio ('30)	4.00	3.25
77	A5	5fr dk bl & choc	4.00	2.25
		Nos. 42-77 (36)	55.90	42.15

Nos. 45, 47, 50 and 58 exist on both ordinary and chalky paper.
For surcharges see Nos. 78-91, B1.

Stamps and Type of 1913-34 Surcharged

1922-34

No.	Type	Description	Unused	Used
78	A5	50c on 45c dp rose & maroon ('34)	1.90	1.25
79	A5	50c on 75c indigo & ultra ('34)	1.10	.90
80	A5	50c on 90c brn red & rose ('34)	1.10	1.10
81	A5	60c on 75c vio, *pnksh*	.25	.25
82	A5	65c on 15c orange & rose ('25)	.50	.50
83	A5	85c on 75c brown & rose ('25)	.65	.50
		Nos. 78-83 (6)	5.50	4.50

Stamps and Type of 1913 Surcharged with New Value and Bars

1924-27

No.	Type	Description	Unused	Used
84	A5	25c on 2fr (R)	.40	.40
85	A5	25c on 5fr	.40	.40
86	A5	90c on 75c brn red & cer ('27)	.60	.45
87	A5	1.25fr on 1fr dk bl & ultra (R) ('26)	.35	.25
88	A5	1.50fr on 1fr lt bl & dk blue ('27)	.50	.50
89	A5	3fr on 5fr brn red & bl grn ('27)	1.75	1.75
90	A5	10fr on 5fr dl red & rose lil ('27)	9.00	8.25
91	A5	20fr on 5fr bl grn & ver ('27)	10.00	10.00
		Nos. 84-91 (8)	23.00	22.00

Common Design Types pictured following the introduction.

Colonial Exposition Issue

Common Design Types

Name of Country in Black

1931 Engr. *Perf. 12½*

No.	Type	Description	Unused	Used
92	CD70	40c deep green	1.40	1.40
93	CD71	50c violet	3.25	3.25
94	CD72	90c red orange	1.40	1.40
95	CD73	1.50fr dull blue	3.50	3.50
		Nos. 92-95 (4)	9.55	9.55

Stamps of Upper Volta 1928, Overprinted

1933 *Perf. 13½x14*

No.	Type	Description	Unused	Used
96	A5	2c brown & lilac	.20	.20
97	A5	4c blk & yellow	.20	.20
98	A5	5c ind & gray bl	.35	.30
99	A5	10c indigo & pink	.30	.30
100	A5	15c brown & blue	.75	.55
101	A5	20c brown & green	.75	.55
102	A6	25c brn & yellow	1.25	1.10
103	A6	30c dp grn & brn	1.25	1.10
104	A6	45c brown & blue	4.25	4.00
105	A6	65c indigo & bl	1.60	1.50
106	A6	75c black & lilac	2.00	1.50
107	A6	90c brn red & lil	1.60	1.60

Overprinted

No.	Type	Description	Unused	Used
108	A7	1fr brown & green	2.25	1.75
109	A7	1.50fr ultra & grysh	2.25	1.75

Surcharged

No.	Type	Description	Unused	Used
110	A6	1.25fr on 40c blk & pink	1.25	1.25
111	A6	1.75fr on 50c blk & green	2.25	1.75
		Nos. 96-111 (16)	22.50	19.40

Baoulé Woman — A6

Rapids on Comoe River — A9

Mosque at Bobo-Dioulasso — A7

Coastal Scene A8

1936-44 *Perf. 13*

No.	Type	Description	Unused	Used
112	A6	1c carmine rose	.20	.20
113	A6	2c ultramarine	.20	.20
114	A6	3c dp grn ('40)	.20	.20
115	A6	4c chocolate	.20	.20
116	A6	5c violet	.20	.20
117	A6	10c Prussian bl	.20	.20
118	A6	15c copper red	.20	.20
119	A7	20c ultramarine	.20	.20
120	A7	25c copper red	.20	.20
121	A7	30c blue green	.20	.20
122	A7	30c brown ('40)	.20	.20
123	A6	35c dp grn ('38)	.50	.35
124	A7	40c carmine rose	.20	.20
125	A7	45c brown	.35	.30
126	A7	45c blue grn ('40)	.20	.20
127	A7	50c plum	.30	.30
128	A7	55c dark vio ('38)	.30	.30
129	A8	60c car rose ('40)	.20	.20
130	A8	65c red brown	.35	.25
131	A8	70c red brn ('40)	.25	.25
132	A8	75c dark violet	.65	.40
133	A8	80c blk brn ('38)	.75	.40
134	A8	90c carmine rose	4.50	3.00
135	A8	90c dk grn ('39)	.25	.25
136	A8	1fr dark green	1.90	.80
137	A8	1fr car rose ('38)	.25	.20
138	A8	1fr dk vio ('40)	.20	.20
139	A8	1.25fr copper red	.30	.20
140	A8	1.40fr ultra ('40)	.20	.20
141	A8	1.50fr ultramarine	.30	.20
141A	A8	1.50fr grnsh blk ('44)	.50	.50
142	A8	1.60fr blk brn ('40)	.40	.40
143	A9	1.75fr carmine rose	.30	.20
144	A9	1.75fr dull bl ('38)	.35	.25
145	A9	2fr ultramarine	.35	.20
146	A9	2.25fr dark bl ('39)	.50	.50
147	A9	2.50fr rose red ('40)	.60	.60
148	A9	3fr green	.40	.25
149	A9	5fr chocolate	.50	.40

150 A9 10fr violet .75 .55
151 A9 20fr copper red 1.40 1.00
Nos. 112-151 (41) 20.20 15.25

Stamps of types A7-A9 without "RF," see Nos. 166A-166D.
For surcharges see Nos. B8-B11.

Paris International Exposition Issue
Common Design Types

1937 ***Perf. 13***
152 CD74 20c deep violet .60 .60
153 CD75 30c dark green .60 .60
154 CD76 40c carmine rose .80 .80
155 CD77 50c dk brn & bl .60 .60
156 CD78 90c red .60 .60
157 CD79 1.50fr ultra .80 .80
Nos. 152-157 (6) 4.00 4.00

Colonial Arts Exhibition Issue
Souvenir Sheet
Common Design Type

1937 ***Imperf.***
158 CD76 3fr sepia 4.00 4.00

Louis Gustave Binger A10

1937 ***Perf. 13***
159 A10 65c red brown .20 .20

Death of Governor General Binger; 50th anniv. of his exploration of the Niger.

Caillie Issue
Common Design Type

1939 **Engr.** ***Perf. 12½x12***
160 CD81 90c org brn & org .40 .40
161 CD81 2fr bright violet .60 .60
162 CD81 2.25fr ultra & dk bl .60 .60
Nos. 160-162 (3) 1.60 1.60

New York World's Fair Issue
Common Design Type

1939
163 CD82 1.25fr carmine lake .65 .55
164 CD82 2.25fr ultramarine .65 .55

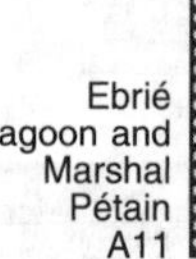

Ebrié Lagoon and Marshal Pétain A11

1941
165 A11 1fr green .40 *.60*
166 A11 2.50fr deep blue .40 *.60*

For surcharges, see Nos. B14A-B14B.

Types of 1936-40 Without "RF"

1944 ***Perf. 13***
166A A7 30c brown .90
166B A8 60c car rose 1.00
166C A8 1fr dark violet 1.00
166D A9 20fr copper red 2.00
Nos. 166A-166D (4) 4.90

Nos. 166A-166D were issued by the Vichy government in France, but were not placed on sale in Ivory Coast.

For other stamps inscribed Cote d'Ivoire and Afrique Occidental Francaise see French West Africa Nos. 58, 72, 77.

Catalogue values for unused stamps in this section, from this point to the end of the section, are for Never Hinged items.

Republic

Elephant A12

President Felix Houphouet-Boigny A13

1959, Oct. 1 **Engr.** ***Perf. 13***
167 A12 10fr black & emerald .20 .20
168 A12 25fr vio brn & olive .30 .20
169 A12 30fr ol blk & grnsh bl .35 .25
Nos. 167-169 (3) .85 .65

Imperforates
Most Ivory Coast stamps from 1959 onward exist imperforate in issued and trial colors, and also in small presentation sheets in issued colors.

1959, Dec. 4 **Unwmk.**
170 A13 25fr violet brown .30 .20

Proclamation of the Republic, 1st anniv.

Bété Mask — A14

Designs: Masks of 5 tribes: Bété, Gueré, Baoulé, Senufo and Guro. #174-176 horiz.

1960 ***Perf. 13***
171 A14 50c pale brn & vio brn .20 .20
172 A14 1fr violet & mag .20 .20
173 A14 2fr ultra & bl grn .20 .20
174 A14 4fr dk grn & org .20 .20
175 A14 5fr ver & brown .20 .20
176 A14 6fr dark brn & vio .20 .20
177 A14 45fr dk grn & brn vio .60 .25
178 A14 50fr dk brn & grnsh bl .65 .25
179 A14 85fr car & slate grn 1.10 .60
Nos. 171-179 (9) 3.55 2.30

C.C.T.A. Issue
Common Design Type

1960, May 16 **Engr.** ***Perf. 13***
180 CD106 25fr grnsh bl & vio .40 .40

Emblem of the Entente A14a

Blood Lilies A16

Young Couple with Olive Branch and Globe — A15

1960, May 29 **Photo.** ***Perf. 13x13½***
181 A14a 25fr multicolored .40 .40

1st anniv. of the Entente (Dahomey, Ivory Coast, Niger and Upper Volta).

1961, Aug. 7 **Engr.** ***Perf. 13***
182 A15 25fr emer, bister & blk .30 .20

First anniversary of Independence.

1961-62

Designs: Various Local Plants & Orchids.

183 A16 5fr dk grn, red & orange ('62) .20 .20
184 A16 10fr ultra, claret & yel .20 .20
185 A16 15fr org, rose lil & green ('62) .20 .20
186 A16 20fr brn, dk red & yel .25 .20
187 A16 25fr grn, red brn & yel .40 .20
188 A16 30fr blk, car & green .40 .25
189 A16 70fr green, ver & yel .90 .40
190 A16 85fr brn, lil, yel & grn 1.25 .75
Nos. 183-190 (8) 3.80 2.40

Early Letter Carrier and Modern Mailman — A17

1961, Oct. 14 **Unwmk.** ***Perf. 13***
191 A17 25fr choc, emer & bl .35 .25

Issued for Stamp Day.

Ayamé Dam — A18

1961, Nov. 18 **Engr.**
192 A18 25fr grnsh bl, blk & grn .30 .20

Swimming Race A19

1961, Dec. 23 **Unwmk.** ***Perf. 13***
193 A19 5fr shown .20 .20
194 A19 20fr Basketball .20 .20
195 A19 25fr Soccer .25 .20
Nos. 193-195 (3) .65 .60

Abidjan Games, Dec. 24-31. See No. C17.

Palms — A20

1962, Feb. 5 **Photo.** ***Perf. 12x12½***
196 A20 25fr brn, blue & org .30 .20

Commission for Technical Co-operation in Africa South of the Sahara, 17th session, Abidjan, 2/5-16.

Fort Assinie and Assinie River — A21

1962, May 26 **Engr.** ***Perf. 13***
197 A21 85fr Prus grn, grn & dl red brn 1.00 .55

Centenary of the Ivory Coast post.

African and Malagasy Union Issue
Common Design Type

1962, Sept. 8 **Photo.** ***Perf. 12½x12***
198 CD110 30fr multicolored .75 .55

African and Malagasy Union, 1st anniv.

Fair Emblem, Cotton and Spindles — A22

1963, Jan. 26 **Engr.** ***Perf. 13***
199 A22 50fr grn, brn org & sepia .45 .25

Bouake Fair, Jan. 26-Feb. 4.

Stylized Map of Africa A23

1963, May 25 **Photo.** ***Perf. 12½x12***
200 A23 30fr ultra & emerald .40 .40

Conference of African heads of state for African unity, Addis Ababa.

Hartebeest A24

UNESCO Emblem, Scales and Globe A25

Designs: 1fr, Yellow-backed duiker, horiz. 2fr, Potto. 4fr, Beecroft's hyrax, horiz. 5fr, Water chevrotain. 15fr, Forest hog, horiz. 20fr, Wart hog, horiz. 25fr, Bongo (antelope). 45fr, Cape hunting dogs, or hyenas, horiz. 50fr, Black-and-white colobus (monkey).

1963-64 **Engr.** ***Perf. 13***
201 A24 1fr choc, grn & yellow ('64) .20 .20
202 A24 2fr blk, dk bl, gray ol & brown ('64) .20 .20
203 A24 4fr red brn, dk bl, brn & black ('64) .20 .20
204 A24 5fr sl grn, brn & citron ('64) .20 .20
205 A24 10fr ol grn & ocher .20 .20
206 A24 15fr red brn, grn & black ('64) .25 .20
207 A24 20fr red org grn & blk .40 .20
208 A24 25fr red brn & green .40 .20
209 A24 45fr choc, bl grn & yel green .75 .40

210 A24 50fr red brn, grn & blk .80 .40
a. Min. sheet of 4, #205, 207, 209-210 1.75 1.75
Nos. 201-210 (10) 3.60 2.40

See Nos. 218-220.

1963, Dec. 10 **Unwmk.**
211 A25 85fr dk bl, blk & org .80 .50

Universal Declaration of Human Rights, 15th anniv.

Sun Radiating from Ivory Coast over Africa A26

Weather Station and Balloon A27

1964, Mar. 17 **Photo.** ***Perf. 12x12½***
212 A26 30fr grn, dl vio & red .35 .20

Inter-African Conference of Natl. Education Ministers.

1964, Mar. 23 ***Perf. 13x12½***
213 A27 25fr multicolored .30 .25

World Meteorological Day, Mar. 23.

Physician Vaccinating Child — A28

1964, May 8 **Engr.** ***Perf. 13***
214 A28 50fr dk brn, bl & red .55 .35

Issued to honor the National Red Cross.

Wrestlers, Globe and Torch — A29

1964, June 27 **Unwmk.** ***Perf. 13***
215 A29 35fr Globe, torch, athletes, vert. .45 .35
216 A29 65fr shown .80 .65

18th Olympic Games, Tokyo, Oct. 10-25.

Europafrica Issue, 1964

Common Design Type

Design: 30fr, White man and black man beneath tree of industrial symbols.

1964, July 20 **Photo.** ***Perf. 12x13***
217 CD116 30fr multicolored .30 .20

Animal Type of 1963-64

Designs: 5fr, Manatee, horiz. 10fr, Pygmy hippopotamus, horiz. 15fr, Royal antelope.

1964, Oct. 17 **Engr.** ***Perf. 13***
218 A24 5fr yel grn, sl grn & brn .20 .20
219 A24 10fr sep, Prus grn & dp cl .20 .20
220 A24 15fr lil rose, grn & org brn .35 .20
Nos. 218-220 (3) .75 .60

Co-operation Issue

Common Design Type

1964, Nov. 7 **Unwmk.** ***Perf. 13***
221 CD119 25fr grn, dk brn & red .30 .25

Korhogo Mail Carriers with Guard, 1914 — A30

1964, Nov. 28 **Engr.**
222 A30 85fr blk, brn, bl & brn red .80 .60

Issued for Stamp Day.

Potter A31

Artisans: 10fr, Wood carvers. 20fr, Ivory carver. 25fr, Weaver.

1965, Mar. 27 **Engr.** ***Perf. 13***
223 A31 5fr mag, green & blk .20 .20
224 A31 10fr red lil, grn & blk .20 .20
225 A31 20fr bis, dp bl & dk brn .20 .20
226 A31 25fr brn, olive & car .25 .20
Nos. 223-226 (4) .85 .80

Unloading Mail, 1900 A32

1965, Apr. 24 **Unwmk.** ***Perf. 13***
227 A32 30fr multicolored .35 .25

Issued for Stamp Day.

A32a

ITU emblem, old and new telecommunication equipment.

1965, May 17
228 A32a 85fr mar, brt grn & dk bl .90 .60

ITU, centenary.

Abidjan Railroad Station A33

1965, June 12 **Engr.** ***Perf. 13***
229 A33 30fr magenta, bl & brn ol .35 .25

Pres. Felix Houphouet-Boigny and Map of Ivory Coast — A34

1965, Aug. 7 **Photo.** ***Perf. 12½x13***
230 A34 30fr multicolored .35 .25

Fifth anniversary of Independence.

Hammerhead Stork — A35

Baoulé Mother and Child, Carved in Wood — A37

Mail Train, 1906 — A36

Birds: 1fr, Bruce's green pigeon, horiz. 2fr, Spur-winged goose, horiz. 5fr, Stone partridge. 15fr, White-breasted guinea fowl. 30fr, Namaqua dove, horiz. 50fr, Lizard buzzard, horiz. 75fr, Yellow-billed stork. 90fr, Forest (or Latham's) francolin.

1965-66 **Engr.** ***Perf. 13***
231 A35 1fr yel grn, pur & yellow ('66) .20 .20
232 A35 2fr slate grn, blk & red ('66) .20 .20
233 A35 5fr dk ol, dk brn & brn red ('66) .20 .20
234 A35 10fr red lil, blk & red brown .20 .20
235 A35 15fr sl grn, gray & ver .20 .20
236 A35 30fr sl grn, mar & red brown .35 .20
237 A35 50fr brn, blk & chlky bl .60 .35
238 A35 75fr org, mar & sl grn .80 .40
239 A35 90fr emerald, blk & brown ('66) 1.25 .65
Nos. 231-239 (9) 4.00 2.60

1966, Mar. 26 **Engr.** ***Perf. 13***
240 A36 30fr grn, blk & mar .40 .25

Issued for Stamp Day.

1966, Apr. 9 **Unwmk.**

Designs: 10fr, Unguent vessel, Wamougo mask lid, 20fr, Atié carved drums. 30fr, Bété female ancestral figure.

241 A37 5fr blk & emerald .20 .20
242 A37 10fr purple & blk .20 .20
243 A37 20fr orange & blk .35 .25
244 A37 30fr red & black .45 .25
Nos. 241-244 (4) 1.20 .90

Intl. Negro Arts Festival, Dakar, Senegal, 4/1-24.

Hotel Ivoire A38

1966, Apr. 30 **Engr.** ***Perf. 13***
245 A38 15fr bl, grn, red & olive .20 .20

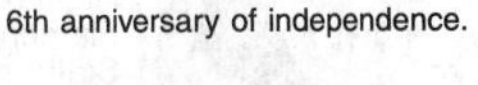
Farm Tractor A39

1966, Aug. 7 **Photo.** ***Perf. 12½x12***
246 A39 30fr multicolored .30 .25

6th anniversary of independence.

Uniformed Teacher and Villagers A40

1966, Sept. 1 **Engr.** ***Perf. 13***
247 A40 30fr dk red, indigo & dk brn .30 .25

National School of Administration.

Veterinarian Treating Cattle A41

1966, Oct. 22 **Engr.** ***Perf. 13***
248 A41 30fr ol, bl & dp brn .35 .25

Campaign against cattle plague.

Man, Waves, UNESCO Emblem — A42

Delivery of Gift Parcels — A43

1966, Nov. 14 **Engr.** ***Perf. 13***
249 A42 30fr dp bl & vio brn .35 .25

UNESCO, 20th anniv.

1966, Dec. 11 **Engr.** ***Perf. 13***
250 A43 30fr dk bl, brn & blk .35 .25

UNICEF, 20th anniv.

Bouaké Hospital and Red Cross A44

1966, Dec. 20
251 A44 30fr red brn, red & lilac .35 .25

Sikorsky S-43 Seaplane and Boats — A45

1967, Mar. 25 **Engr.** ***Perf. 13***
252 A45 30fr indigo, bl grn & brn .40 .25

Stamp Day. 30th anniv. of the Sikorsky S-43 flying boat route.

Pineapple Harvest A46

1967 **Engr.** ***Perf. 13***
253 A46 20fr shown .20 .20
254 A46 30fr Cabbage tree .30 .20
255 A46 100fr Bananas 1.10 .60
Nos. 253-255 (3) 1.60 1.00

Issue dates: 30fr, June 24; others, Mar. 25.

Genie, Protector of Assamlangangan A47

1967, July 31 Engr. *Perf. 13*
256 A47 30fr grn, blk & maroon .30 .20

Intl. PEN Club (writers' organization), 25th Congress, Abidjan, July 31-Aug. 5.

Old and New Houses A48

1967, Aug. 7 Photo. *Perf. 12½x12*
257 A48 30fr multicolored .30 .20

7th anniversary of independence.

Lions Emblem and Elephant's Head A49

1967, Sept. 2 Photo. *Perf. 12½x13*
258 A49 30fr lt bl & multi .40 .30

50th anniversary of Lions International.

Monetary Union Issue
Common Design Type

1967, Nov. 4 Engr. *Perf. 13*
259 CD125 30fr car, slate grn & blk .25 .20

Allegory of French Recognition of Ivory Coast — A50

Tabou Radio Station — A51

1967, Nov. 17 Photo. *Perf. 13x12½*
260 A50 90fr multicolored .80 .50

Days of Recognition, 20th anniv. See No. 298.

1968, Mar. 9 Engr. *Perf. 13*
261 A51 30fr dk grn, brn & brt grn .35 .20

Issued for Stamp Day.

Cotton Mill — A52

Designs: 5fr, Palm oil extraction plant. 15fr, Abidjan oil refinery. 20fr, Unloading raw cotton and spinning machine, vert. 30fr, Flour mill. 50fr, Cacao butter extractor. 70fr, Instant coffee factory, vert. 90fr, Saw mill and timber.

1968 Engr. *Perf. 13*
262 A52 5fr ver, slate grn & blk .20 .20
263 A52 10fr dk grn, gray & ol bis .20 .20
264 A52 15fr ver, lt ultra & blk .20 .20
265 A52 20fr Prus blue & choc .20 .20
266 A52 30fr dk grn, brt bl & brown .35 .20
267 A52 50fr red, brt grn & blk .45 .25
268 A52 70fr dk brn, bl & brn .65 .35
269 A52 90fr dp bl, blk & brn .90 .40
Nos. 262-269 (8) 3.15 2.00

Issued: 5fr, 15fr, June 8; 10fr, 20fr, 90fr, Mar. 23; others, Oct. 5.

Canoe Race A53

1968, Apr. 6 Engr. *Perf. 13*
270 A53 30fr shown .35 .20
271 A53 100fr Runners 1.00 .60

19th Olympic Games, Mexico City, 10/12-27.

Queen Pokou Sacrificing her Son — A54

1968, Aug. 7 Photo. *Perf. 12½x12*
272 A54 30fr multicolored .30 .20

8th anniversary of independence.

Vaccination, WHO Emblem and Elephant's Head A55

1968, Sept. 28 Engr. *Perf. 13*
273 A55 30fr choc, brt bl & maroon .35 .20

WHO, 20th anniversary.

Antelope in Forest — A56

1968, Oct. 26 Engr. *Perf. 13*
274 A56 30fr ultra, brn & olive .40 .20

Protection of fauna and flora.

Abidjan Anthropological Museum and Carved Screen — A57

1968, Nov. 2
275 A57 30fr vio bl, ol & rose mag .30 .20

Human Rights Flame and Statues of "Justitia" A58

1968, Nov. 9 Engr. *Perf. 13*
276 A58 30fr slate, org & dk brn .35 .20

International Human Rights Year.

"Ville de Maranhao" at Grand Bassam A59

1969, Mar. 8 Engr. *Perf. 13*
277 A59 30fr brn, brt bl & grn .38 .20

Issued for Stamp Day.

Opening of Hotel Ivoire, Abidjan — A60

1969, Mar. 29
278 A60 30fr ver, bl & grn .30 .20

Carved Figure — A61

Mountains and Radio Tower, Man — A62

1969, July 5 Engr. *Perf. 13*
279 A61 30fr red lil, blk & red org .30 .20

Ivory Coast art exhibition, Fine Arts Museum, Vevey, Switzerland, 7/12-9/22.

1969, Aug. 7 Engr. *Perf. 13*
280 A62 30fr dl brn, sl & grn .35 .20

9th anniversary of independence.

Development Bank Issue
Common Design Type

Design: Development Bank emblem and Ivory Coast coat of arms.

1969, Sept. 6
281 CD130 30fr ocher, grn & mar .30 .20

Arms of Bouake — A63

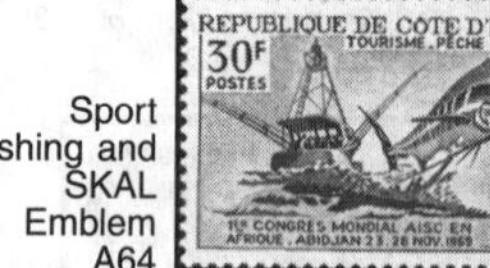

Sport Fishing and SKAL Emblem A64

Coats of Arms: 15fr, Abidjan. 30fr, Ivory Coast.

1969 Photo. *Perf. 13*
282 A63 10fr multicolored .20 .20
283 A63 15fr multicolored .20 .20
284 A63 30fr multicolored .25 .20
Nos. 282-284 (3) .65 .60

Issued: 10fr, 10/25; 15fr, 12/27; 30fr, 12/20.
See Nos. 335-336, designs A113, A297.

1969, Nov. 22 Engr. *Perf. 13*
285 A64 30fr shown .35 .20
286 A64 100fr Vacation village, SKAL emblem 1.00 .50

1st Intl. Congress in Africa of the SKAL Tourist Assoc., Abidjan, Nov. 23-28.

ASECNA Issue
Common Design Type

1969, Dec. 13 Engr. *Perf. 13*
287 CD132 30fr vermilion .30 .20

University Center, Abidjan — A65

1970, Feb. 26 Engr. *Perf. 13*
288 A65 30fr indigo & yel grn .25 .20

Higher education in Ivory Coast, 10th anniv.

Gabriel Dadié and Telegraph Operator A66

1970, Mar. 7 Engr. *Perf. 13*
289 A66 30fr dk red, sl grn & blk .25 .20

Stamp Day; Gabriel Dadié (1891-1953) 1st native-born postal administrator.

University of Abidjan — A67

1970, Mar. 21 Photo.
290 A67 30fr Prus bl, dk pur & dk yel grn .25 .20

3rd General Assembly of the Assoc. of French-language Universities (A.U.P.E.L.F.).

Safety Match Production — A68

1970, May 9 Engr. *Perf. 13*
291 A68 5fr shown .20 .20
292 A68 20fr Textile industry .20 .20
293 A68 50fr Shipbuilding .40 .20
Nos. 291-293 (3) .80 .60

Radar, Classroom with Television — A69

1970, May 17
294 A69 40fr red, grn & gray olive .40 .35

Issued for World Telecommunications Day.

UPU Headquarters Issue
Common Design Type

1970, May 20
295 CD133 30fr lil, brt grn & olive .35 .20

UN Emblem, Lion, Antelopes and Plane A70

1970, June 27 Engr. *Perf. 13*
296 A70 30fr dk red brn, ultra & dk green .40 .25

25th anniversary of the United Nations.

Coffee Branch and Bags Showing Increased Production A71

1970, Aug. 7 Engr. *Perf. 13*
297 A71 30fr org, bluish grn & gray .25 .20

Tenth anniversary of independence.

Type of 1967

1970, Oct. 29 Photo. *Perf. 12x12½*
298 A50 40fr multicolored .40 .20

Ivory Coast Democratic Party, 5th Congress.

Power Plant at Uridi — A73

1970, Nov. 21 Engr. *Perf. 13*
299 A73 40fr multicolored .40 .20

Independence, 10th Anniv. — A73a

Designs: Nos. 299A, 299D, Pres. Houphouet-Boigny, Gen. Charles DeGaulle. Nos. 299B, 299F, Pres. Houphouet-Boigny, elephants. Nos. 299C, 299E, Coat of arms.

1970, Nov. 27 Embossed *Perf. 10½*
Die Cut

299A A73a 300fr Silver 10.00
299B A73a 300fr Silver 10.00
299C A73a 300fr Silver 10.00
g. Pair, #299B-299C 22.50
299D A73a 1000fr Gold 20.00
299E A73a 1000fr Gold 20.00

Litho. & Embossed

299F A73a 1200fr Gold & multi 25.00
h. Pair, #299E-299F 45.00

Nos. 299B, 299F are airmail.

Postal Service Autobus, 1925 A74

1971, Mar. 6 Engr. *Perf. 13*
300 A74 40fr dp grn, dk brn & gldn brn .35 .20

Stamp Day.

Marginella Desjardini A75

Marine Life: 1fr, Aporrhaispes gallinae. 5fr, Neptunus validus. 10fr, Hermodice carunculata, vert. No. 305, Natica fanel, vert. No. 306, Goniaster cuspidatus, vert. No. 307, Xenorhora digitata. 25fr, Conus prometheus. 35fr, Polycheles typhlops, vert. No. 310, Conus genuanus. No. 311, Chlamys flabellum. 45fr, Strombus bubonius. 50fr, Enoplometopus callistus, vert. 65fr, Cypraea stercoraria.

1971-72 Engr. *Perf. 13*

301 A75 1fr olive & multi .20 .20
302 A75 5fr red & multi .20 .20
303 A75 10fr emer & multi .20 .20
304 A75 15fr brt bl & multi .20 .20
305 A75 15fr dp car & multi .20 .20
306 A75 20fr ocher & car .20 .20
307 A75 20fr ver & multi .25 .20
308 A75 25fr dk car, rose brn & black .25 .20
309 A75 35fr yel & multi .30 .20
310 A75 40fr emer & multi .45 .25
311 A75 40fr brown & multi .40 .20
312 A75 45fr multi .40 .25
313 A75 50fr green & multi .60 .40
314 A75 65fr bl, rose brn & sl grn .60 .40
Nos. 301-314 (14) 4.45 3.30

Issued: #304, 306, 310, 4/24/71; 5fr, 35fr, 50fr, 6/5/71; 1fr, 10fr, #311, 10/23/71; 25fr, 65fr, 1/29/72; #305, 307, 45fr, 4/3/72.

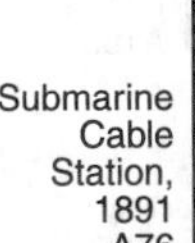
Submarine Cable Station, 1891 A76

1971, May 17
315 A76 100fr bl, ocher & olive .75 .45

3rd World Telecommunications Day.

Apprentice and Lathe — A77

1971, June 19 Engr. *Perf. 13*
316 A77 35fr grn, slate & org brn .30 .20

Technical instruction and professional training.

Map of Africa and Telecommunications System — A78

1971, June 26 *Perf. 13x12½*
317 A78 45fr magenta & multi .40 .20

Pan-African Telecommunications system.

Bondoukou Market — A79

1971, Aug. 7 Engr. *Perf. 13*
Size: 48x27mm
318 A79 35fr ultra, brn & slate .30 .20

11th anniv. of independence. See No. C46.

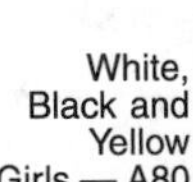

White, Black and Yellow Girls — A80

1971, Oct. 10 Photo. *Perf. 13*
319 A80 40fr shown .35 .20
320 A80 45fr Boys around globe .40 .20

Intl. Year Against Racial Discrimination.

Gaming Table and Lottery Tickets A81

1971, Nov. 13 *Perf. 12½*
321 A81 35fr green & multi .25 .20

National lottery.

Electric Power Installations — A82

1971, Dec. 18 *Perf. 13*
322 A82 35fr red brn & multi .35 .20

Cogwheel and Workers A83

1972, Mar. 18 Engr. *Perf. 13*
323 A83 35fr org, bl & dk brn .25 .20

Technical Cooperation Week.

"Your Heart is Your Health" — A84

Girls Reading, Book Year Emblem — A85

1972, Apr. 7 Photo. *Perf. 12½x13*
324 A84 40fr blue, olive & red .35 .20

World Health Day.

Perf. 12½x13, 13x12½
1972, Apr. 22 Engr.
325 A85 35fr Boys reading, horiz. .25 .20
326 A85 40fr shown .35 .20

International Book Year.

Postal Sorting Center, Abidjan A86

1972, May 13 *Perf. 13*
327 A86 40fr dk grn, rose lil & bis .35 .20

Stamp Day.

Radio Tower, Abobo, and ITU Emblem — A87

1972, May 17 Engr. *Perf. 13*
328 A87 40fr blue, red & grn .35 .20

4th World Telecommunications Day.

Computer Operator, Punch Card A88

1972, June 24
329 A88 40fr brt grn, bl & red .35 .20

Development of computerized information.

View of Odienné — A89

1972, Aug. 7 Engr. *Perf. 13*
330 A89 35fr bl, grn & brn .25 .20

12th anniversary of independence.

West African Monetary Union Issue
Common Design Type

1972, Nov. 2 Engr. *Perf. 13*
331 CD136 40fr brn, gray & red lilac .30 .20

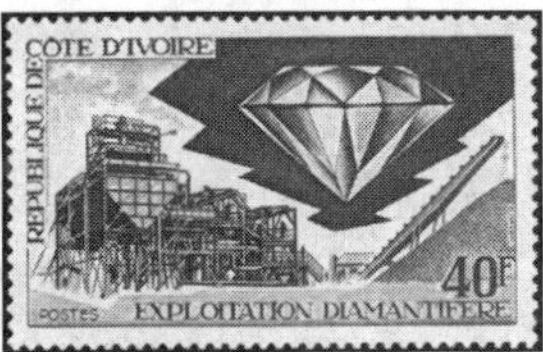

Diamond and Diamond Mine — A90

1972, Nov. 4
332 A90 40fr Prus bl, slate & org brn .35 .20

Pasteur Institute, Louis Pasteur A91

1972, Nov. 21
333 A91 35fr vio bl, grn & brn .30 .20

Pasteur (1822-1895), chemist and bacteriologist.

Children at Village Pump
A92

1972, Dec. 9 **Engr.** ***Perf. 13***

334 A92 35fr dk red, grn & blk .25 .20

Water campaign. See No. 360.

Arms Type of 1969

1973 **Photo.** ***Perf. 12***

335 A63 5fr Daloa .20 .20
336 A63 10fr Gagnoa .20 .20

Nos. 335-336 are 16½-17x22mm and have "DELRIEU" below design at right. Nos. 282-284 are 17x23mm and have no name at lower right.

Dr. Armauer G. Hansen — A93

1973, Feb. 3 **Engr.** ***Perf. 13***

342 A93 35fr lil, dp bl & brn .30 .20

Centenary of the discovery of the Hansen bacillus, the cause of leprosy.

Lake Village Bletankoro — A94

1973, Mar. 10 **Engr.** ***Perf. 13***

343 A94 200fr choc, bl & grn 1.50 .80

Balistes Capriscus
A95

Fish: 20fr, Pseudupeneus prayensis. 25fr, Cephalopholis taeniops. 35fr, Priacanthus arenatus. 50fr, Xyrichthys novacula.

1973-74 **Engr.** ***Perf. 13***

344 A95 15fr ind & slate grn .20 .20
345 A95 20fr lilac & multi .20 .20
346 A95 25fr slate grn & rose ('74) .20 .20
347 A95 35fr rose red & slate grn .30 .20
348 A95 50fr blk, ultra & rose red .40 .30
Nos. 344-348 (5) 1.30 1.10

Issued: 50fr, 3/24; 15fr, 20fr, 7/7; 35fr, 12/1; 25fr, 3/2.

Children
A96

1973, Apr. 7 **Engr.** ***Perf. 13***

354 A96 40fr grn, blk & dl red .35 .20

Establishment of first children's village in Africa (SOS villages for homeless children).

Parliament, Abidjan — A97

1973, Apr. 24 **Photo.** ***Perf. 13x12½***

355 A97 100fr multicolored .70 .40

112th session of the Inter-parliamentary Council.

Teacher and PAC Store
A98

1973, May 12 **Photo.** ***Perf. 13x12½***

356 A98 40fr multicolored .25 .20

Commercial Action Program (PAC).

Mother, Typist, Dress Form and Pot — A99

1973, May 26

357 A99 35fr multicolored .25 .20

Technical instruction for women.

Farmers, African Scout Emblem
A100

1973, July 16 **Photo.** ***Perf. 13x12½***

358 A100 40fr multicolored .25 .20

24th Boy Scout World Conference, Nairobi, Kenya, July 16-21.

Party Headquarters, Yamoussokro — A101

1973, Aug. 7 **Photo.** ***Perf. 13***

359 A101 35fr multicolored .25 .20

Children at Dry Pump
A102

1973, Aug. 16 **Engr.**

360 A102 40fr multicolored .25 .20

African solidarity in drought emergency.

African Postal Union Issue

Common Design Type

1973, Sept. 12 **Engr.** ***Perf. 13***

361 CD137 100fr pur, blk & red .65 .40

Decorated Arrow Heads, Abidjan Museum — A103

1973, Sept. 15 **Photo.** ***Perf. 12½x13***

362 A103 5fr blk, brn red & brn .20 .20

Ivory Coast No. 1 — A104

1973, Oct. 9 **Engr.** ***Perf. 13***

363 A104 40fr emer, blk & org .30 .20

Stamp Day.

Highway Intersection
A105

1973, Oct. 13

364 A105 35fr blue, blk & grn .25 .20

Indenie-Abidjan intersection.

Map of Africa, Federation Emblem — A106

Elephant Emblem — A107

1973, Oct. 26 **Photo.** ***Perf. 13***

365 A106 40fr ultra, red brn & vio bl .25 .20

Intl. Social Security Federation, 18th General Assembly, Abidjan, Oct. 26-Nov. 3.

1973, Nov. 19

366 A107 40fr blk & bister .25 .20

7th World Congress of the Universal Federation of World Travel Agents' Associations, Abidjan.

Kong Mosque — A108

1974, Mar. 9

367 A108 35fr bl, grn & brn .20 .20

People and Sun
A109

1974, Apr. 20 **Photo.** ***Perf. 13***

368 A109 35fr multicolored .20 .20

Permanent Mission to UN.

Grand Lahou Post Office — A110

1974, May 17 **Engr.** ***Perf. 13***

369 A110 35fr multicolored .20 .20

Stamp Day.

Map and Flags of Members
A110a

1974, May 29 **Photo.** ***Perf. 13x12½***

370 A110a 40fr blue & multi .25 .20

15th anniversary of the Council of Accord.

Pres. Houphouet-Boigny
A111 A112

1974-76 **Engr.** ***Perf. 13***

371 A111 25fr grn, org & brn .20 .20
 a. Booklet pane of 10 1.60
 b. Booklet pane of 20 3.50
373 A112 35fr org, grn & brn .20 .20
 a. Booklet pane of 10 2.25
 b. Booklet pane of 20 4.50
374 A112 40fr grn, org & brn .25 .20
 a. Booklet pane of 10 2.50
375 A112 60fr bl, car & brn ('76) .35 .20
376 A112 65fr car, bl & brn ('76) .35 .20
Nos. 371-376 (5) 1.35 1.00

See Nos. 783-792.

Arms of Ivory Coast
A113

WPY Emblem
A114

1974, June 29 **Photo.** ***Perf. 12***

377 A113 30fr emer, brn & gold
378 A113 35fr brn, emer & gold .20 .20
 a. Booklet pane of 10 2.25
 b. Booklet pane of 20 4.50
379 A113 40fr vio, bl, emer & gold .20 .20
 a. Booklet pane of 10 2.50
 b. Booklet pane of 20 5.50

1976, Jan.
Inscribed: "COTE D'IVOIRE"

380 A113 60fr car, gold & emer .30 .20
381 A113 65fr grn, gold & emer .35 .20
382 A113 70fr bl, gold & emer .40 .20
Nos. 378-382 (5) 1.45 1.00

See design A297.

1974, Aug. 19 Engr. *Perf. 13*
383 A114 40fr emerald & blue .25 .20

World Population Year.

Cotton Harvest — A115

1974, Sept. 21 Litho. *Perf. 12½x13*
384 A115 50fr multicolored .25 .20

UPU Centenary A116

1974, Oct. 9 Engr. *Perf. 13*
385 A116 40fr multicolored .25 .20

See Nos. C59-C60.

Plowing Farmer, Service Emblem A117

1974, Dec. 7 Photo. *Perf. 13*
386 A117 35fr multicolored .20 .20

14th anniversary of independence.

National Library, First Anniv. — A118

1975, Jan. 9 Photo. *Perf. 13*
387 A118 40fr multicolored .25 .20

Raoul Follereau and Blind Students — A119

1975, Jan. 26 Engr. *Perf. 13*
388 A119 35fr multicolored .20 .20

Follereau, educator of the blind and lepers.

Congress Emblem — A120

Coffee Cultivation A121

1975, Mar. 4 Photo. *Perf. 12½x13*
389 A120 40fr blk & emerald .25 .20

52nd Congress of the Intl. Assoc. of Seed Crushers, Abidjan, Mar. 2-7.

1975, Mar. 15 *Perf. 13½x13*
390 A121 5fr Flowering branch .20 .20
391 A121 10fr Branch with beans .20 .20

Sassandra Wharf — A122

1975, Apr. 19 Engr. *Perf. 13*
392 A122 100fr multicolored .50 .35

Letter Sorting A123

1975, Apr. 26 Photo. *Perf. 13*
393 A123 40fr multicolored .25 .20

Stamp Day.

Cotton Flower — A124

Cotton Bolls — A125

1975, May 3 Photo. *Perf. 13*
394 A124 5fr multicolored .20 .20
395 A125 10fr multicolored .20 .20

Cotton cultivation.

Marie Kore, Women's Year Emblem — A126

1975, May 19 Engr. *Perf. 13*
396 A126 45fr lt bl, yel grn & brn .25 .20

International Women's Year.

Fort Dabou — A127

1975, June 7 Engr. *Perf. 13*
397 A127 50fr multicolored .25 .20

Abidjan Harbor — A128

40fr, Grand Bassam wharf, 1906. 100fr, Planned harbor expansion on Locodjro.

1975, July 1 Photo. *Perf. 13*
398 A128 35fr multicolored .20 .20

Miniature Sheet

399 Sheet of 3 1.10 1.10
a. A128 40fr multi, vert. .20 .20
b. A128 100fr multi .50 .50

25th anniversary of Abidjan Harbor. No. 399 contains Nos. 398, 399a, 399b.

Cacao Pods on Tree — A129

1975, Aug. 2
400 A129 35fr multicolored .20 .20

Farm Workers A130

1975, Oct. 4 Photo. *Perf. 13x12½*
401 A130 50fr multicolored .25 .20

Natl. Org. for Rural Development.

Railroad Bridge, N'zi River — A131

1975, Dec. 7 Photo. *Perf. 13*
402 A131 60fr multicolored .35 .20

15th anniversary of independence.

Baoulé Mother and Child, Carved in Wood — A132

1976, Jan. 24 Litho. *Perf. 13*
403 A132 65fr black & multi .40 .25

Baoulé Mask A133

Chief Abron's Chair A133a

1976, Feb. 7 Photo. *Perf. 12½*
404 A133 20fr multicolored .20 .20
405 A133a 150fr multicolored .80 .50

Senufo Statuette — A134

1976, Feb. 21 *Perf. 13x13½*
406 A134 25fr ocher & multi .20 .20

Telephones 1876 and 1976 — A135

1976, Mar. 10 Litho. *Perf. 12*
407 A135 70fr multicolored .40 .25

Centenary of first telephone call by Alexander Graham Bell, Mar. 10, 1876.

Ivory Coast Map, Pigeon, Carving
A136

1976, Apr. 10 Photo. *Perf. 12½*

408	A136	65fr multicolored	.35	.25

20th Stamp Day.

Smiling Trees and Cat — A137

Children with Books — A138

1976, June 5 Litho. *Perf. 12½*

409	A137	65fr multicolored	.35	.20

Nature protection.

1976, July 3 Photo. *Perf. 12½x13*

410	A138	65fr multicolored	.35	.25

Runner, Maple Leaf, Olympic Rings — A139

1976, July 17 Litho. *Perf. 12*

411	A139	60fr Javelin, vert.	.35	.25
412	A139	65fr shown	.35	.25

21st Olympic Games, Montreal, Canada, July 17-Aug. 1.

Mohammad Ali Jinnah — A139a

1976, Aug. 14 Litho. *Perf. 13*

412A	A139a	50fr multicolored		

1st Governor-General of Pakistan.

Cashew
A140

1976, Sept. 18 *Perf. 12½*

413	A140	65fr blue & multi	.35	.20

Highway and Conference Emblem — A141

1976, Oct. 25 Litho. *Perf. 12½x12*

414	A141	60fr multicolored	.35	.25

3rd African Highway Conference, Abidjan, July 25-30.

Pres. Houphouet-Boigny
A142

1976-77 Photo. *Perf. 13½x12½*

415	A142	35fr brn, red lil & blk ('77)		
416	A142	40fr brt grn, ocher & brn blk	.20	.20
a.		Bklt. pane of 12 (8#416, 4#417)	7.50	
417	A142	45fr ocher, brt grn & brn blk	.25	.20
418	A142	60fr brn, mag & brn blk	.35	.20
419	A142	65fr grn, org & brn blk	.35	.20
		Nos. 416-419 (4)	1.15	.80

The 40fr and 45fr issued in booklet and coil; 35fr, 60fr and 65fr in coil only.

Stamps from booklets are imperf. on one side or two adjoining sides. Coils have control number on back of every 10th stamp.

John Paul Jones, American Marine and Ship — A143

American Bicentennial: 125fr, Count de Rochambeau and grenadier of Touraine Regiment. 150fr, Admiral Count Jean Baptiste d'Estaing and French marine. 175fr, Lafayette and grenadier of Soissons Regiment. 200fr, Jefferson, American soldier, Declaration of Independence. 500fr, Washington, US flag, Continental officer.

1976, Nov. 27 Litho. *Perf. 11*

421	A143	100fr multicolored	.60	.30
422	A143	125fr multicolored	.80	.35
423	A143	150fr multicolored	1.00	.40
424	A143	175fr multicolored	1.10	.45
425	A143	200fr multicolored	1.25	.50
		Nos. 421-425 (5)	4.75	2.00

Souvenir Sheet

426	A143	500fr multicolored	3.00	1.40

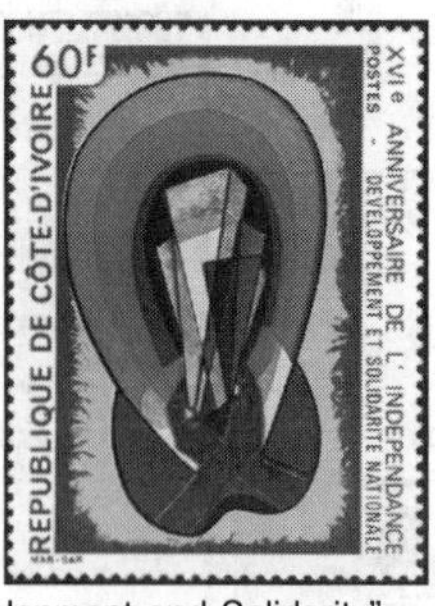

"Development and Solidarity" — A144

1976, Dec. 7 Photo. *Perf. 13*

427	A144	60fr multicolored	.35	.20

16th anniversary of independence.

Benin Head, Ivory Coast Arms — A145

1977, Jan. 15 Photo. *Perf. 13*

428	A145	65fr gold, dk brn & grn	.35	.20

2nd World Black and African Festival, Lagos, Nigeria, Jan. 15-Feb. 12.

Musical Instruments — A146

1977, Mar. 5 Engr. *Perf. 13*

429	A146	5fr Baoule bells	.20	.20
430	A146	10fr Senufo balafon	.20	.20
431	A146	20fr Dida drum	.20	.20
		Nos. 429-431 (3)	.60	.60

Air Afrique Plane Unloading Mail
A147

1977, Apr. 9 Litho. *Perf. 13*

432	A147	60fr multicolored	.35	.25

Stamp Day.

Sassenage Castle, Grenoble — A148

1977, May 21 Litho. *Perf. 12½*

433	A148	100fr multicolored	.50	.35

Intl. French Language Council, 10th anniv.

Orville and Wilbur Wright, "Wright Flyer," 1903 — A149

History of Aviation: 75fr, Louis Bleriot crossing English Channel, 1909. 100fr, Ross Smith and Vickers-Vimy (flew England-Australia, 1919). 200fr, Charles A. Lindbergh and "Spirit of St. Louis" (flew New York-Paris, 1927). 300fr, Supersonic jet Concorde, 1976. 500fr, Lindbergh in flying suit and "Spirit of St. Louis."

1977, June 27 Litho. *Perf. 14*

434	A149	60fr multi	.40	.20
435	A149	75fr multi	.50	.20
436	A149	100fr multi	.65	.20
437	A149	200fr multi	1.25	.40
438	A149	300fr multi	2.00	.60
		Nos. 434-438 (5)	4.80	1.60

Souvenir Sheet

439	A149	500fr multi	3.25	1.40

Santos Dumont's "Ville de Paris," 1907 — A150

65fr, LZ1 at takeoff. 150fr, "Schwaben" LZ10 over Germany. 200fr, "Bodensee" LZ120, 1919. 300fr, LZ127 over Sphinx & pyramids.

1977, Sept. 3 Litho. *Perf. 11*

440	A150	60fr multi	.40	.20
441	A150	65fr multi	.40	.20
442	A150	150fr multi	.90	.35
443	A150	200fr multi	1.25	.50
444	A150	300fr multi	1.75	.75
		Nos. 440-444 (5)	4.70	2.00

History of the Zeppelin. Exist imperf.

See No. C63.

Congress Emblem — A151

1977, Sept. 12 Photo. *Perf. 12½*

445	A151	60fr lt & dk grn	.35	.25

17th Intl. Congress of Administrative Sciences in Africa, Abidjan, Sept. 12-16.

A152

1977, Nov. 12 Photo. *Perf. 13½x14*

446	A152	65fr multicolored	.35	.25

Yamoussoukro, 1st Ivory Coast container ship.

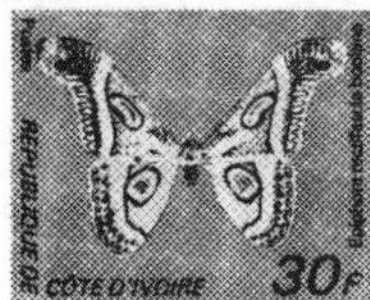

Butterflies A152a

Designs: 30fr, Epiphora rectifascia boolana. 60fr, Charaxes jasius epijasius. 65fr, Imbrasia arata. 100fr, Palla decius.

1977, Nov. Photo. *Perf. 14x13*

No.	Type	Description	Unused	Used
446A	A152a	30fr multicolored	*1.50*	*.50*
446B	A152a	60fr multicolored	*9.00*	*4.50*
446C	A152a	65fr multicolored	*2.50*	*1.00*
446D	A152a	100fr multicolored	*3.00*	*1.50*
		Nos. 446A-446D (4)	*16.00*	*7.50*

A153

Hand Holding Produce, Generators, Factories.

1977, Dec. 7 Photo. *Perf. 13½*

No.	Type	Description	Unused	Used
447	A153	60fr multicolored	.35	.25

17th anniversary of independence.

Flowers — A153a

1977 Photo. *Perf. 13x14*

No.	Type	Description	Unused	Used
447A	A153a	5fr Strophanthus hispidus	*2.00*	*1.00*
447B	A153a	20fr Anthurium cultorum	*3.00*	*1.50*
447C	A153a	60fr Arachnis flos-aeris	*5.00*	*2.50*
447D	A153a	65fr Renanthera storiei	*6.00*	*3.00*
		Nos. 440-444 (5)	*4.70*	*2.00*

Presidents Giscard d'Estaing and Houphouet-Boigny — A154

1978, Jan. 11 *Perf. 13*

No.	Type	Description	Unused	Used
448	A154	60fr multicolored	.35	.25
449	A154	65fr multicolored	.35	.25
450	A154	100fr multicolored	.50	.40
a.		Souvenir sheet, 500fr	3.25	1.40
		Nos. 448-450 (3)	1.20	.90

Visit of Pres. Valery Giscard d'Estaing. No. 450a contains one stamp.

St. George and the Dragon, by Rubens A155

Paintings by Peter Paul Rubens (1577-1640): 150fr, Child's head. 250fr, Annunciation. 300fr, The Birth of Louis XIII. 500fr, Virgin & Child.

1978, Mar. 4 Litho. *Perf. 13½*

No.	Type	Description	Unused	Used
451	A155	65fr gold & multi	.40	.20
452	A155	150fr gold & multi	.90	.40
453	A155	250fr gold & multi	1.60	.55
454	A155	300fr gold & multi	1.90	.70
		Nos. 451-454 (4)	4.80	1.85

Souvenir Sheet

No.	Type	Description	Unused	Used
455	A155	500fr gold & multi	3.25	1.40

Royal Guards — A156

1978, Apr. 1 Litho. *Perf. 12½*

No.	Type	Description	Unused	Used
456	A156	60fr shown	.30	.20
457	A156	65fr Cosmological figures	.35	.20

Rural Postal Center — A157

1978, Apr. 8

No.	Type	Description	Unused	Used
458	A157	60fr multicolored	.30	.20

Stamp Day.

Antenna, ITU Emblem A158

1978, May 17 *Perf. 13*

No.	Type	Description	Unused	Used
459	A158	60fr multicolored	.30	.20

10th World Telecommunications Day.

Svante August Arrhenius, Electrolytic Apparatus — A159

Nobel Prize Winners: 75fr, Jules Bordet, child, mountains, eagle and Petri dish. 100fr, André Gide, and St. Peter's, Rome. 200fr, John Steinbeck and horse farm. 300fr, Children with flowers and UNICEF emblem. 500fr, Max Planck, rockets and earth.

1978, May 27 Litho. *Perf. 13½*

No.	Type	Description	Unused	Used
460	A159	60fr multi	.40	.20
461	A159	75fr multi	.45	.25
462	A159	100fr multi	.60	.30
463	A159	200fr multi	1.40	.60
464	A159	300fr multi	1.90	.90
		Nos. 460-464 (5)	4.75	2.25

Souvenir Sheet

No.	Type	Description	Unused	Used
465	A159	500fr multi	3.25	1.40

Soccer Ball, Player and Argentina '78 Emblem — A160

Soccer Ball, Argentina '78 Emblem and: 65fr, Player, vert. 100fr, Player, diff. 150fr, Goalkeeper. 300fr, Ball as sun, and player, vert. 500fr, Ball as globe with Argentina on map of South America.

1978, June 17

No.	Type	Description	Unused	Used
466	A160	60fr multi	.40	.20
467	A160	65fr multi	.45	.20
468	A160	100fr multi	.60	.30
469	A160	150fr multi	.90	.40
470	A160	300fr multi	1.90	.90
		Nos. 466-470 (5)	4.25	2.00

Souvenir Sheet

No.	Type	Description	Unused	Used
471	A160	500fr multi	2.50	1.40

11th World Cup Soccer Championship, Argentina, June 1-25.

Miniodes Discolor A161

Butterflies: 65fr, Charaxes lactetinctus. 100fr, Papilio zalmoxis. 200fr, Papilio antimachus.

1978, July 8 Photo. *Perf. 14x13*

No.	Type	Description	Unused	Used
472	A161	60fr multicolored	.30	.20
473	A161	65fr multicolored	.35	.20
474	A161	100fr multicolored	.50	.30
475	A161	200fr multicolored	1.00	.60
		Nos. 472-475 (4)	2.15	1.30

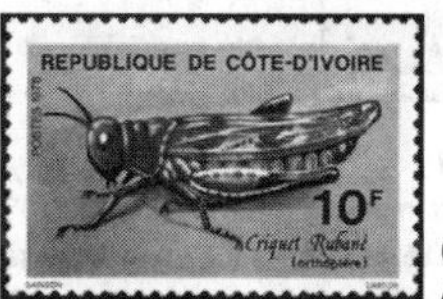

Cricket A162

Insects: 20fr, 60fr, Various hemiptera. 65fr, Goliath beetle.

1978, Aug. 26 Litho. *Perf. 12½*

No.	Type	Description	Unused	Used
476	A162	10fr multicolored	.20	.20
477	A162	20fr multicolored	.20	.20
478	A162	60fr multicolored	.25	.20
479	A162	65fr multicolored	.35	.40
		Nos. 476-479 (4)	1.00	1.00

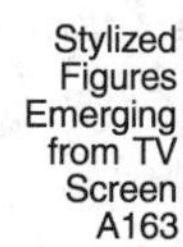

Stylized Figures Emerging from TV Screen A163

65fr, Passengers on train made up of TV sets.

1978, Sept. 18 *Perf. 13*

No.	Type	Description	Unused	Used
480	A163	60fr multicolored	.30	.20
481	A163	65fr multicolored	.35	.25

Educational television programs.

Map of Ivory Coast, Mobile Drill Platform Ship A164

Map of Ivory Coast, Ram at Discovery Site and: 65fr, Gold goblets. 500fr, Pres. Houphouet-Boigny holding gold goblets.

1978, Oct. 18 Litho. *Perf. 12½x12*

No.	Type	Description	Unused	Used
482	A164	60fr multicolored	.30	.20
483	A164	65fr multicolored	.35	.25

Souvenir Sheet

No.	Type	Description	Unused	Used
484	A164	500fr multicolored	2.50	1.40

Announcement of oil discovery off the coast of Ivory Coast, 1st anniv.

National Assembly, Paris, UPU Emblem A165

1978, Dec. 2 Litho. *Perf. 13½*

No.	Type	Description	Unused	Used
485	A165	200fr multicolored	1.25	.60

Congress of Paris, centenary.

Drummer A166

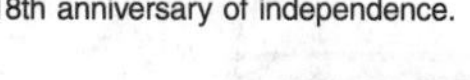

1978, Dec. 7 Photo. *Perf. 12½x13*

No.	Type	Description	Unused	Used
486	A166	60fr multicolored	.30	.20

18th anniversary of independence.

Poster — A167

Design: 65fr, Arrows made of flags, and television screen.

1978, Dec. 12

No.	Type	Description	Unused	Used
487	A167	60fr multicolored	.30	.20
488	A167	65fr multicolored	.35	.25

Technical cooperation among developing countries with the help of educational television.

Plowing — A168

1979, Jan. 27 Photo. *Perf. 13*
489 A168 100fr multicolored .50 .30

King Hassan II, Pres. Houphouet-Boigny, Flags and Map of Morocco and Ivory Coast — A169

1979, Jan. 27 Photo. *Perf. 13*
490 A169 60fr multicolored 10.00
491 A169 65fr multicolored 10.00
492 A169 500fr multicolored 10.00
Nos. 490-492 (3) 30.00

Visit of King Hassan of Morocco to Ivory Coast. The visit never took place and the stamps were not issued. To recover the printing costs the stamps were sold in Paris for one day.

Horus — A170

1979, Feb. 17 Litho. *Perf. 12½*
493 A170 200fr multi 1.00 .60
494 A170 500fr Vulture with ankh, cartouches 2.50 1.50

UNESCO drive to save Temples of Philae.

Flowers — A171

1979, Feb. 24
495 A171 30fr Locranthus .20 .20
496 A171 60fr Vanda Josephine .30 .20
497 A171 65fr Renanthera storiei .35 .25
Nos. 495-497 (3) .85 .65

Wildlife Protection A172

1979, Mar. 24 Photo. *Perf. 13x13½*
498 A172 50fr Hippopotamus .35 .25

Globe and Emblem — A173

Child Riding Dove — A174

1979, Apr. 1 Litho. *Perf. 12x12½*
499 A173 60fr multicolored .40 .30
500 A174 65fr multicolored .45 .35
501 A173 100fr multicolored .65 .55
502 A174 500fr multicolored 3.50 2.50
Nos. 499-502 (4) 5.00 3.70

International Year of the Child.

Rural Mail Delivery — A175

1979, Apr. 7 *Perf. 12½*
503 A175 60fr multicolored .40 .30

Stamp Day.

Korhogo Cathedral — A176

1979, Apr. 9 *Perf. 13*
504 A176 60fr multicolored .40 .30

Arrival of Catholic missionaries, 75th anniv.

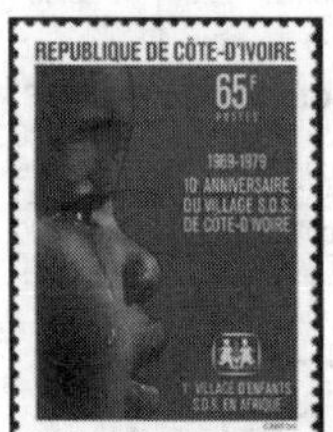

Crying Child — A177

1979, May 17 Litho. *Perf. 12½*
505 A177 65fr multicolored .40 .35

10th anniv. of SOS Village (for homeless children).

Euphaedra Xypete A178

Butterflies: 65fr, Pseudacraea bois duvali. 70fr, Auchenisa schausi.

1979, May 26 *Perf. 13x13½*
506 A178 60fr multicolored .40 .25
507 A178 65fr multicolored .40 .25
508 A178 70fr multicolored .45 .30
Nos. 506-508 (3) 1.25 .80

Endangered Animals — A179

1979, June 2
509 A179 5fr Antelopes .20 .20
510 A179 20fr Duikerbok .20 .20
511 A179 60fr Aardvark .40 .25
Nos. 509-511 (3) .80 .65

UPU Emblem, Radar, Truck and Ship — A180

#513, Ancestral figure & antelope, vert.

1979, June 8 Engr. *Perf. 13*
512 A180 70fr multi .45 .30

Photo.

513 A180 70fr multi .45 .30

Philexafrique II, Libreville, Gabon, June 8-17. Nos. 512, 513 each printed in sheets of 10 with 5 labels showing exhibition emblem.

Rowland Hill, Steam Locomotive, Great Britain No. 75 — A181

Rowland Hill, Locomotives and: 75fr, Ivory Coast #125. 100fr, Hawaii #4. 150fr, Japan #30, syll. 3. 300fr, France #2. 500fr, Ivory Coast #123.

1979, July 7 Litho. *Perf. 13½*
514 A181 60fr multi .40 .25
515 A181 75fr multi .50 .30
516 A181 100fr multi .65 .40
517 A181 150fr multi 1.00 .60
518 A181 300fr multi 2.00 1.25
Nos. 514-518 (5) 4.55 2.80

Souvenir Sheet

519 A181 500fr multi 3.50

Sir Rowland Hill (1795-1879), originator of penny postage.

Insects — A181a

A181b

1979 Photo. *Perf. 14x13, 13x14*
519A A181a 30fr Wasp, horiz. 2.00 1.00
519B A181a 60fr Praying mantis 3.50 1.50
519C A181a 65fr Cricket, horiz. 4.00 1.50
Nos. 519A-519C (3) 9.50 4.00

1979 Photo. *Perf. 13x14*

Musical instruments.

519D A181b 100fr Harp 10.00 4.00
519E A181b 150fr Whistles 15.00 6.00

"TELECOM 79" — A182

Culture Day — A183

1979, Sept. 20 Litho. *Perf. 13x12½*
520 A182 60fr multicolored .40 .25

3rd World Telecommunications Exhibition, Geneva, Sept. 20-26.

1979, Oct. 13 *Perf. 12½*
521 A183 65fr multicolored .40 .25

Fish — A183a

1979 Photo. *Perf. 14x13*
521A A183a 60fr Pterois volitans
521B A183a 65fr Coelacanth

Boxing — A184

1979, Oct. 27 Litho. *Perf. 14x13½*
522 A184 60fr shown .40 .25
523 A184 65fr Running .40 .25
524 A184 100fr Soccer .65 .40
525 A184 150fr Bicycling 1.00 .70
526 A184 300fr Wrestling 2.00 1.40
Nos. 522-526 (5) 4.45 3.00

Souvenir Sheet

527 A184 500fr Gymnastics 3.50 2.00

Pre-Olympic Year.

Wildlife Fund Emblem and Jentink's Duiker — A185

Wildlife Protection: 60fr, Colobus Monkey. 75fr, Manatees. 100fr, Epixerus ebii. 150fr, Hippopotamus. 300fr, Chimpanzee.

1979, Nov. 3 Litho. *Perf. 14½*
528 A185 40fr multi 2.10 .25
529 A185 60fr multi 2.50 .40
530 A185 75fr multi 3.25 .50
531 A185 100fr multi 4.75 .60
532 A185 150fr multi 6.75 .85
533 A185 300fr multi 13.00 1.75
Nos. 528-533 (6) 32.35 4.35

Raoul Follerau Institute, Adzope — A186

1979, Dec. 6 Litho. *Perf. 12½*
534 A186 60fr multi .40 .25

Independence, 19th Anniversary A187

1979, Dec. 7 Litho. *Perf. 14x13½*
535 A187 60fr multicolored .40 .25

Fireball A188

Local Flora: 5fr, Clerodendron thomsonae, vert. 50fr, Costus incanusiamus, vert. 60fr, Ficus elastica abidjan, vert.

1980 Litho. *Perf. 12½*
536 A188 5fr multicolored .20 .20
537 A188 10fr multicolored .20 .20
538 A188 50fr multicolored .35 .20
539 A188 60fr multicolored .40 .25
Nos. 536-539 (4) 1.15 .85

Issued: 5fr, 10fr, Jan. 26; 50fr, 60fr, Feb. 16.

Rotary Intl., 75th Anniv. — A189

1980, Feb. 23 Photo. *Perf. 13½*
540 A189 65fr multicolored .40 .30

International Archives Day — A190

1980, Feb. 26 Litho.
541 A190 65fr multicolored .40 .30

Astronaut Shaking Hands with Boy — A191

Path of Apollo 11 — A192

1980, July 6 Photo.
542 A191 60fr multicolored .40 .25
543 A192 65fr multicolored .40 .30
544 A191 70fr multicolored .45 .35
545 A192 150fr multicolored 1.00 .65
Nos. 542-545 (4) 2.25 1.55

Apollo 11 moon landing, 10th anniv. (1979).

Jet and Map of Africa A193

1980, Mar. 22 *Perf. 12½*
546 A193 60fr multicolored .40 .25

ASECNA (Air Safety Board), 20th anniv.

Boys and Stamp Album, Globe — A194

1980, Apr. 12 Litho. *Perf. 12½*
547 A194 65fr bl grn & red brn .40 .25

Stamp Day; Youth philately.

Missionary and Church, Aboisso A195

1980, Apr. 26 Photo. *Perf. 13x13½*
548 A195 60fr multicolored .40 .25

Settlement of the Holy Fathers at Aboisso, 75th anniversary.

Fight Against Cigarette Smoking A196

1980, May 3 *Perf. 12½*
549 A196 60fr multicolored .40 .25

Pope John Paul II, Pres. Houphouet-Boigny — A197

1980, May 10 Photo. *Perf. 13*
550 A197 65fr multicolored .40 .30

Visit of Pope John Paul II to Ivory Coast.

Le Belier Locomotive A198

1980, May 17 Litho. *Perf. 13*
551 A198 60fr shown .40 .25
552 A198 65fr Abidjan Railroad Station, 1904 .40 .30
553 A198 100fr Passenger car, 1908 .65 .40
554 A198 150fr Steam locomotive, 1940 1.00 .60
Nos. 551-554 (4) 2.45 1.55

Central Bank of West African States, 1st Anniversary A199

1980, May 26 Litho. *Perf. 12x12½*
555 A199 60fr multicolored .40 .25

Lujtanus Sebae A200

1980, Apr. 19 Photo. *Perf. 14*
556 A200 60fr shown .40 .25
557 A200 65fr Monodactylus sebae, vert. .40 .30
558 A200 100fr Colisa fasciata .65 .45
Nos. 556-558 (3) 1.45 1.00

Snake — A201

1980, July 12 Litho. *Perf. 12½*
559 A201 60fr shown .40 .25
560 A201 150fr Toad 1.00 .55

Tourists in Village, by K. Ehouman Pierre A202

Conference Emblem — A203

1980, Aug. 9
561 A202 60fr multicolored .40 .25
562 A203 65fr multicolored .40 .25

National Tourist Office, Abidjan; World Tourism Conference, Manila.

Forticula Auricularia A204

Perf. 14x13, 13x14
1980, Sept. 6 Photo.
563 A204 60fr shown .40 .25
564 A204 65fr Praying mantis, vert. .40 .25

Perf. 13½x13, 13x13½
1980, Oct. 11 Photo.

Designs: 60fr, 200fr, Various grasshoppers.

565 A204 60fr multi, vert. .40 .25
566 A204 200fr multi 1.40 .70

Hands Free from Chain, Map of Ivory Coast, Pres. Houphouet-Boigny — A205

Pres. Houphouet-Boigny, Symbols of Development — A206

Perf. 12½x13, 14x14½ (A206)
1980, Oct. 18
567 A205 60fr shown .40 .25
568 A206 65fr shown .40 .25
569 A205 70fr Map, colors, document .45 .25
570 A205 150fr like #567 1.00 .55
571 A206 300fr like #568 2.00 1.10
Nos. 567-571 (5) 4.25 2.40

Pres. Houphouet-Boigny, 75th birthday.

7th PDCI and RDA Congress A207

1980, Oct. 25 *Perf. 12½*
572 A207 60fr multicolored .40 .25
573 A207 65fr multicolored .40 .25

River Cruise Boat Sotra A208

1980, Dec. 6 Litho. *Perf. 13x13½*
574 A208 60fr multicolored .40 .25

View of Abidjan — A209

1980, Dec. 7 ***Perf. 13x12½***

575 A209 60fr multicolored .40 .25

20th anniversary of independence.

Universities Association Emblem — A210

African Postal Union, 5th Anniversary A211

1980, Dec. 16 ***Perf. 12½***

576 A210 60fr multicolored .40 .25

African Universities Assoc., 5th General Conf.

1980, Dec. 24 Photo. ***Perf. 13½***

577 A211 150fr multi 1.00 .55

Herichtys Cyanoguttatum — A212

1981, Mar. 14 Litho. ***Perf. 12½***

578 A212 60fr shown .40 .25
579 A212 65fr Labeo bicolor .40 .25
580 A212 200fr Tetraodon fluviatilis 1.40 1.75
Nos. 578-580 (3) 2.20 2.25

Birds — A212a

1980, Dec. 30 Photo. ***Perf. 14½x14***

580A A212a 60fr Spreo superbus
580B A212a 65fr Tockus camurus
580C A212a 65fr Balearica pavonina
580D A212a 100fr Ephippiorhynchus

Post Office, Grand Lahou A213

25th Anniv. of Ivory Coast Philatelic Club A214

1981, May 2 Litho. ***Perf. 12½***

581 A213 60fr multicolored .40 .25
582 A214 65fr multicolored .40 .25

Stamp Day.

13th World Telecommunications Day — A215

1981, May 17

583 A215 30fr multicolored .20 .20
584 A215 60fr multicolored .40 .25

Viking Satellite Landing, 1976 — A216

Space Conquest: Columbia space shuttle.

1981, June 13 Litho. ***Perf. 13½***

585 A216 60fr multi .40 .25
586 A216 75fr multi .50 .30
587 A216 125fr multi .80 .50
588 A216 300fr multi 2.00 1.10
Nos. 585-588 (4) 3.70 2.15

Souvenir Sheet

589 A216 500fr multi 3.50 1.50

Local Flowers — A217

Prince Charles and Lady Diana, Coach — A218

1981, July 4 Photo. ***Perf. 14½x14***

590 A217 50fr Amorphophallus .35 .20
591 A217 60fr Sugar Cane .40 .25
592 A217 100fr Heliconia ivoirea .65 .40
Nos. 590-592 (3) 1.40 .85

1981, Aug. 8 Litho. ***Perf. 12½***

Royal Wedding: Couple and coaches.

593 A218 80fr multi .55 .30
594 A218 100fr multi .65 .40
595 A218 125fr multi .80 .40
Nos. 593-595 (3) 2.00 1.10

Souvenir Sheet

596 A218 500fr multi 3.50 1.50

For overprints see Nos. 642-645.

Elephant on Flag and Map — A219

1981, Sept. Litho. ***Perf. 12½***

597 A219 80fr multicolored .55 .30
598 A219 100fr multicolored .65 .40
599 A219 125fr multicolored .80 .40
Nos. 597-599 (3) 2.00 1.10

See Nos. 662-666, 833.

Soccer Players A220

Soccer players.

1981, Sept. 19 ***Perf. 14***

600 A220 70fr multi, horiz. .45 .25
601 A220 80fr multi, horiz. .55 .30
602 A220 100fr multi .65 .35
603 A220 150fr multi 1.00 .60
604 A220 350fr multi 2.25 1.40
Nos. 600-604 (5) 4.90 2.90

Souvenir Sheet

605 A220 500fr multi, horz. 3.50 1.50

ESPANA '82 World Cup Soccer Championship.

For overprints see Nos. 651-656.

West African Rice Development Assoc., 10th Anniv. — A221

1981, Oct. 3 ***Perf. 12½***

606 A221 80fr multicolored .55 .30

World Food Day A222

1981, Oct. 18

607 A222 100fr multicolored .65 .40

Post Day — A223

1981, Oct. 9 Litho. ***Perf. 12½***

608 A223 70fr multicolored .45 .25
609 A223 80fr multicolored .55 .30
610 A223 100fr multicolored .65 .35
Nos. 608-610 (3) 1.65 .90

75th Anniv. of Grand Prix — A224

Designs: Winners and their cars.

1981, Nov. 21 ***Perf. 14***

611 A224 15fr Felice Nazarro, 1907 .20 .20
612 A224 40fr Jim Clark, 1962 .25 .20
613 A224 80fr Fiat, 1907 .55 .30
614 A224 100fr Auto Union, 1936 .65 .40
615 A224 125fr Ferrari, 1961 .80 .40
Nos. 611-615 (5) 2.45 1.50

Souvenir Sheet

616 A224 500fr 1933 car 3.50 1.90

21st Anniv. of Independence — A225

1981, Dec. 7 ***Perf. 13x12½***

617 A225 50fr multicolored .35 .20
618 A225 80fr multicolored .55 .30

Traditional Hairstyle — A226

Rotary Emblem on Map of — A228

Stamp Day Africa — A227

Designs: Various hairstyles.

1981, Dec. 19 Photo. *Perf. 14½x14*

619 A226 80fr multicolored .55 .30
620 A226 100fr multicolored .65 .40
621 A226 125fr multicolored .80 .50
Nos. 619-621 (3) 2.00 1.20

1982, Apr. 3 Litho. *Perf. 12½x12*

622 A227 100fr Bingerville P.O., 1902 .65 .40

1982, Apr. 13 *Perf. 12½*

623 A228 100fr ultra & gold .65 .40

Pres. Houphouet-Boigny's Rotary Goodwill Conference, Abidjan, Apr. 13-15.

250th Birth Anniv. of George Washington — A229

Anniversaries: 100fr, Auguste Piccard (1884-1962), Swiss physicist. 350fr, Goethe (1749-1832). 450fr, 500fr, Princess Diana, 21st birthday (portraits).

1982, May 15 Litho. *Perf. 13*

624 A229 80fr multi .55 .30
625 A229 100fr multi .65 .40
626 A229 350fr multi 2.25 1.25
627 A229 450fr multi 3.00 1.90
Nos. 624-627 (4) 6.45 3.85

Souvenir Sheet

628 A229 500fr multi 3.50 2.00

Visit of French Pres. Mitterand, May 21-24 — A230

1982, May 21 Photo. *Perf. 13½*

629 A230 100fr multicolored .65 .40

14th World Telecommunications Day — A231

1982, May 29 Litho. *Perf. 13*

630 A231 80fr multicolored .55 .30

Scouting Year — A232

Scouts sailing, diff. 80fr, 150fr, 350fr, 500fr vert.

1982, May 29 *Perf. 12½*

631 A232 80fr multi .55 .30
632 A232 100fr multi .65 .40
633 A232 150fr multi 1.00 .60
634 A232 350fr multi 2.25 1.25
Nos. 631-634 (4) 4.45 2.55

Souvenir Sheet

635 A232 500fr multi 3.50 2.00

TB Bacillus Centenary A233

1982, June 5 Photo. *Perf. 13x13½*

636 A233 30fr brown & multi .20 .20
637 A233 80fr lt grn & multi .55 .30

UN Conference on Human Environment, 10th Anniv. — A234

1982, July Photo. *Perf. 13½x13*

638 A234 40fr multicolored .25 .20
639 A234 80fr multicolored .55 .30

League of Ivory Coast Secretaries, First Congress — A235

1982, Aug. 9 Litho. *Perf. 12½x13*

640 A235 80fr tan & multi .55 .30
641 A235 100fr silver & multi .65 .40

593-596 Overprinted in Blue: "NAISSANCE / ROYALE 1982"

1982, Aug. 21 *Perf. 12½*

642 A218 80fr multi .55 .30
643 A218 100fr multi .65 .40
644 A218 125fr multi .80 .50
Nos. 642-644 (3) 2.00 1.20

Souvenir Sheet

645 A218 500fr multi 3.50 2.00

Birth of Prince William of Wales, June 21.

La Colombe de l'Avenir, 1962, by Pablo Picasso (1881-1973) — A236

Picasso Paintings: 80fr, Child with Dove, 1901. 100fr, Self-portrait, 1901. 185fr, Les Demoiselles d'Avignon, 1907. 350fr, The Dream, 1932. Nos. 646-649 vert.

1982, Sept. 4 Litho. *Perf. 13*

646 A236 80fr multi .55 .30
647 A236 100fr multi .65 .40
648 A236 185fr multi 1.25 .70
649 A236 350fr multi 2.25 1.40
650 A236 500fr multi 3.50 2.00
Nos. 646-650 (5) 8.20 4.80

Nos. 600-605 Overprinted with World Cup Winners 1966-1982 in Black on Silver

1982, Oct. 9 Litho. *Perf. 14*

651 A220 70fr multi .45 .25
652 A220 80fr multi .55 .30
653 A220 100fr multi .65 .40
654 A220 150fr multi .75 .45
655 A220 350fr multi 2.25 1.40
Nos. 651-655 (5) 4.65 2.80

Souvenir Sheet

656 A220 500fr multi 2.75 1.50

Italy's victory in 1982 World Cup.

13th World UPU Day — A237

Designs: 80fr, P.O. counter. 100fr, Postel-2001 building, Abidjan, vert. 350fr, Postal workers. 500fr, Postel-2001 interior.

1982, Oct. 23 *Perf. 12½*

657 A237 80fr multi .55 .30
658 A237 100fr multi .70 .40
659 A237 350fr multi 2.25 1.40

Size: 48x37mm

Perf. 13

660 A237 500fr multi 3.50 1.50
Nos. 657-660 (4) 7.00 3.60

22nd Anniv. of Independence — A238

1982, Dec. 7 *Perf. 13*

661 A238 100fr multicolored .65 .40

Elephant Type of 1981

1982-84

662 A219 5fr multicolored .20 .20
662A A219 10fr multi ('84) .20 .20
662B A219 20fr multicolored .20 .20
663 A219 25fr multicolored .20 .20
664 A219 30fr multicolored .20 .20
665 A219 40fr multicolored .25 .20
666 A219 50fr multicolored .35 .20
Nos. 662-666 (7) 1.60 1.40

Man Waterfall A238a

1982 Photo. *Perf. 15x14*

666A A238a 80fr shown .55 .30
666B A238a 80fr Boisee Savanna .55 .30
666C A238a 500fr like #666A 3.50 1.90
Nos. 666A-666C (3) 4.60 2.50

Issued: #666B, Dec. 18; others, Nov. 27.

20th Anniv. of West African Monetary Union A239

1982, Dec. 21 Litho. *Perf. 12½*

667 A239 100fr Emblem .65 .40

Abouissa Children's Village A240

1983, Mar. 5 Photo. *Perf. 13½x13*

668 A240 125fr multicolored .80 .40

Anteater A241

1983, Mar. 12 Litho. *Perf. 12½x13*

669 A241 35fr Pangolin, vert. .25 .20
670 A241 90fr shown .60 .35
671 A241 100fr Colobus monkey, vert. .65 .40
672 A241 125fr Buffalo .80 .40
Nos. 669-672 (4) 2.30 1.35

Stamp Day — A242

1983, Mar. 19 Litho. *Perf. 12½*

673 A242 100fr Grand Bassam P.O., 1903 .65 .40

Easter 1983 A243

Paintings by Rubens (1577-1640). 100fr, 400fr, 500fr vert.

1983, Apr. 9 *Perf. 13*

674 A243 100fr Descent from the Cross .65 .40
675 A243 125fr Resurrection .80 .40
676 A243 350fr Crucifixion 2.25 1.40
677 A243 400fr Piercing of the Sword 2.50 1.50
678 A243 500fr Descent, diff. 3.50 1.90
Nos. 674-678 (5) 9.70 5.60

25th Anniv. of UN Economic Commission for Africa — A244

1983, Apr. 29 Litho. *Perf. 13x12½*

679 A244 100fr multicolored .65 .40

Gray Parakeet A245

1983, June 11

680 A245 100fr Fish eagle, vert. .65 .40
681 A245 125fr shown .80 .40
682 A245 150fr Touracoes 1.00 .50
Nos. 680-682 (3) 2.45 1.30

World Communications Year — A245a

1983, July 16 ***Perf. 12½x13***

682A A245a 100fr shown
682B A245a 125fr diff.

A246

1983, Sept. 3 Litho. ***Perf. 12½***

683 A246	50fr Flali, Gouro	.35	.20
684 A246	100fr Masked dancer, Guere	.65	.35
685 A246	125fr Stilt dancer, Yacouba	.80	.45
	Nos. 683-685 (3)	1.80	1.00

20th Anniv. of the Ivory Hotel, Abidjan — A249

1983, Sept. 7 ***Perf. 13***

693 A249 100fr multicolored .65 .40

Ecology in Action A250

1983, Oct. 24 Litho.

694 A250	25fr Forest after fire	.20	.20
695 A250	100fr Animals fleeing	.30	.20
696 A250	125fr Animals grazing	.40	.25
	Nos. 694-696 (3)	.90	.65

Raphael (1483-1520), 500th Birth Anniv. — A252

Paintings: 100fr, Christ and St. Peter. 125fr, Study for St. Joseph, vert. 350fr, Virgin of the House of Orleans, vert. 500fr, Virgin with the Blue Diadem, vert.

1983, Nov. 5 Litho. ***Perf. 13***

698 A252	100fr multi	.30	.20
699 A252	125fr multi	.40	.20
700 A252	350fr multi	1.10	.60
701 A252	500fr multi	1.60	1.00
	Nos. 698-701 (4)	3.40	2.00

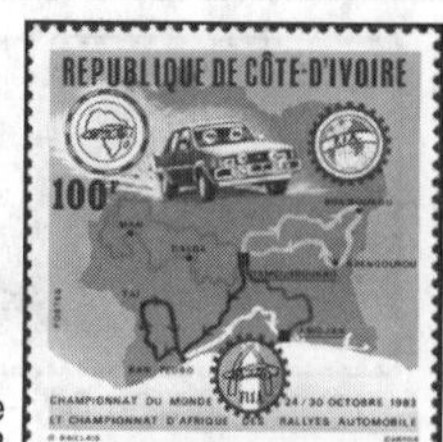

Auto Race A253

1983, Oct. 24 Litho. ***Perf. 12½***

702 A253 100fr Car, map .30 .20

Flowers — A254

1983, Nov. 26 Photo. ***Perf. 14x15***

703 A254	100fr Fleurs d'Ananas	*20.00*
704 A254	125fr Heliconia Rostrata	*20.00*
705 A254	150fr Rose de Porcelaine	*20.00*

23rd Anniv. of Independence — A255

1983, Dec. 7

706 A255 100fr multicolored .30 .20

First Audio-visual Forum, Abidjan — A256

1984, Jan. 25 Litho. ***Perf. 13x12½***

707 A256 100fr Screen, arrow .30 .20

14th African Soccer Cup — A257

1984, Mar. 4 Photo. ***Perf. 12½***

708 A257	100fr Emblem	.30	.20
709 A257	200fr Maps shaking hands	.60	.35

Local Insects A258

1984, Mar. 24 Litho. ***Perf. 13***

710 A258	100fr Argiope, vert.	.30	.20
711 A258	125fr Polistes gallicus	.40	.20

Stamp Day — A259

1984, Apr. 7 Litho. ***Perf. 12½***

712 A259 100fr Abidjan P.O., 1934 .30 .20

Lions Emblem A260

1984, Apr. 27 ***Perf. 13½x13***

713 A260	100fr multicolored	.30	.20
714 A260	125fr multicolored	.40	.25

3rd Convention of Multi-district 403, Abidjan, Apr. 27-29.

16th World Telecommunications Day — A261

1984, May 17 ***Perf. 12½***

715 A261 100fr multi .30 .20

Council of Unity, 25th Anniv. — A262

1984, May 29

716 A262	100fr multicolored	.30	.20
717 A262	125fr multicolored	.40	.25

First Governmental Palace, Grand-Bassam — A263

1984, July 14 Litho. ***Perf. 12½***

718 A263	100fr shown	.30	.20
719 A263	125fr Palace of Justice, Grand-Bassam	.40	.20

Men Playing Eklan — A264

1984, Aug. 11 ***Perf. 13***

720 A264	100fr Board	.30	.20
721 A264	125fr shown	.40	.20

Locomotive "Gazelle" — A265

1984 ***Perf. 12½***

722 A265	100fr shown	.30	.20
723 A265	100fr Cargo ship	.30	.20
724 A265	125fr Superpacific	.40	.20
725 A265	125fr Cargo ship, diff.	.40	.20
726 A265	350fr Pacific type 10	1.10	.60
727 A265	350fr Ocean liner	1.10	.60
728 A265	500fr Mallet class GT2	1.50	.90
729 A265	500fr Ocean liner, diff.	1.50	.90
	Nos. 722-729 (8)	6.60	3.80

Issue dates: trains, Aug. 25; ships, Sept. 1.

Stamp Day A266

1984, Oct. 20 Litho. ***Perf. 12½***

730 A266 100fr Map, post offices .25 .20

10th Anniv., West African Union A267

1984, Oct. 27 Litho. ***Perf. 13½***

731 A267 100fr Map, member nations .25 .20

Wildlife — A267a

1984, Nov. 3 Photo. ***Perf. 14½x15***

731A A267a	100fr Tragelaphus scriptus	*20.00*	*7.50*
731B A267a	150fr Felis serval	*20.00*	*7.50*

Tourism A267b

1984, Nov. 10 Photo. ***Perf. 15x14½***

731C A267b	50fr Le Club Valtur	*17.50*	*3.00*
731D A267b	100fr Grand Lahou	*17.50*	*4.50*

Flowers — A267c

1984, Nov. 17 Photo. ***Perf. 14½x15***
731E A267c 100fr Allamanda carthartica *20.00 7.50*
731F A267c 125fr Baobob *20.00 7.50*

90th Anniv., Ivory Coast Postage Stamps A268

1984, Nov. 23 Litho. ***Perf. 12½***
732 A268 125fr Book cover .35 .20

24th Anniv. of Independence — A269

1984, Dec. 7 Litho. ***Perf. 12½***
733 A269 100fr Citizens, outline map .25 .20

Rotary Intl. Conf. — A270

1985, Jan. 16 Litho. ***Perf. 12½x13***
734 A270 100fr multicolored .25 .20
735 A270 125fr multicolored .35 .20

Traditional Costumes A271

1985, Feb. 16 Litho. ***Perf. 13½***
736 A271 90fr Dan le Babou .25 .20
737 A271 100fr Post-natal gown .25 .20

Birds — A271a

1985, Mar. Photo. ***Perf. 14½x15***
737A A271a 25fr Marabout 35.00
737B A271a 100fr Jacana 35.00
737C A271a 350fr Ibis 35.00

Stamp Day — A272

1985, Apr. 13 Litho. ***Perf. 12½***
738 A272 100fr Riverboat Adjame .25 .20

18th District of Zonta Intl., 7th Conference, Abidjan, Apr. 25-27 — A273

1985, Apr. 25 Litho. ***Perf. 13½***
739 A273 125fr Zonta Intl. emblem .35 .20

Bondoukou — A273a

100fr, Marche de Bondoukou. 125fr, Mosque, Samatiguila.

1985 Litho. ***Perf. 14½x13½***
739A A273a 100fr multicolored *35.00 5.00*
739B A273a 125fr multicolored *35.00 5.00*
739C A273a 200fr multicolored *35.00 5.00*
Nos. 739A-739C (3) 105.00 15.00

PHILEXAFRICA '85, Lome — A274

1985, May 15 ***Perf. 13***
740 A274 200fr Factory, jet, van .55 .25
741 A274 200fr Youth sports, farming .55 .25
a. Pair, Nos. 740-741 + label 1.10 .50

African Development Bank, 20th Anniv. — A275

1985, June 18
742 A275 100fr Senegal chemical industry .25 .20
743 A275 125fr Gambian tree nursery .35 .20

Intl. Youth Year — A276

1985, July 20 ***Perf. 12½***
744 A276 125fr Map, profiles, dove .40 .20

Natl. Armed Forces, 25th Anniv. — A277

Emblems: No. 745, Presidential Guard. No. 746, F.A.N.C.I. 125fr, Air Transport & Liaison Group, G.A.T.L. 200fr, National Marines. 350fr, National Gendarmerie.

1985, July 27 ***Perf. 12½x13***
745 A277 100fr dp rose lil & gold .30 .20
746 A277 100fr dark bl & gold .30 .20
747 A277 125fr blk brn & gold .40 .20
748 A277 200fr blk brn & gold .60 .30
749 A277 350fr brt ultra & sil 1.00 .50
Nos. 745-749 (5) 2.60 1.40

1986 World Cup Soccer Preliminaries, Mexico — A279

1985, Aug. ***Perf. 13***
751 A279 100fr Heading the ball .30 .20
752 A279 150fr Tackle .40 .20
753 A279 200fr Dribbling .60 .30
754 A279 350fr Passing 1.00 .50
Nos. 751-754 (4) 2.30 1.20

Souvenir Sheet

755 A279 500fr Power shot 1.40 .65

Ivory Coast - Sovereign Military Order of Malta Postal Convention, Dec. 19, 1984 — A280

1985, Aug. 31 ***Perf. 13x12½***
756 A280 125fr Natl. arms .40 .20
757 A280 350fr S.M.O.M. arms 1.00 .50

Visit of Pope John Paul II — A281

1985, Sept. 24 ***Perf. 13***

Overprint in Black

758 A281 100fr Portrait, St. Paul's Cathedral, Abidjan .30 .20

The overprint, "Consecration de la Cathedrale Saint Paul d'Abidjon," was added to explain the reason for the visit of the Pope. Copies without overprint exist but were not issued.

UN Child Survival Campaign A282

1985, Oct. 5 Litho. ***Perf. 13½x14***
759 A282 100fr Breast-feeding .35 .20
760 A282 100fr Oral rehydration therapy .35 .20
761 A282 100fr Mother and child .35 .20
762 A282 100fr Vaccination .35 .20
Nos. 759-762 (4) 1.40 .80

UN 40th Anniv. — A283

1985, Oct. 31 ***Perf. 13***
763 A283 100fr multicolored .35 .20

Admission to UN, 25th anniv.

World Wildlife Fund — A284

Striped antelopes.

1985, Nov. 30
764 A284 50fr multicolored *5.50* .50
765 A284 60fr multicolored *6.50* .75
766 A284 75fr multicolored *13.00* 1.00
767 A284 100fr multicolored *20.00* 1.50
Nos. 764-767 (4) 45.00 3.75

City Skyline — A285

1985, Nov. 21 Litho. ***Perf. 13***
768 A285 125fr multicolored .40 .20

Expo '85 national industrial exhibition.

Return to the Land Campaign A286

Handicrafts A287

1985, Dec. 7 ***Perf. 12½***
769 A286 125fr multicolored .40 .20

Natl. independence, 25th anniv.

Flowers — A286a

100fr, L'Amorphophallus staudtii. 125fr, Crinum scillifolium. 200fr, Triphyophyllum peltatum.

1985, Dec. 28 **Litho.** ***Perf. 14x15***
769A A286a 100fr multi *35.00 5.00*
769B A286a 125fr multi *35.00 5.00*
769C A286a 200fr multi *35.00 5.00*
Nos. 769A-769C (3) *105.00 15.00*

1986, Jan. ***Perf. 13½***
770 A287 125fr Spinning thread .65 .30
771 A287 155fr Painting .80 .40

Flora — A288

Cooking Utensils, Natl. Museum, Abidjan — A289

1986, Feb. 22 **Litho.** ***Perf. 13½***
772 A288 40fr Omphalocarpum elatum .25 .20
773 A288 50fr Momordica charantia .30 .20
774 A288 125fr Millettia takou .70 .35
775 A288 200fr Costus afer 1.10 .55
Nos. 772-775 (4) 2.35 1.30

1986, Mar. 6 ***Perf. 13x12½, 12½x13***
776 A289 20fr We bowl .20 .20
777 A289 30fr Baoule bowl .20 .20
778 A289 90fr Baoule platter .50 .25
779 A289 125fr Dan scoop .70 .35
780 A289 440fr Baoule lidded pot 2.50 1.25
Nos. 776-780 (5) 4.10 2.25

Nos. 776-778 horiz.

Natl. Pedagogic and Vocational School, 10th Anniv. — A290

1986, Mar. 20 ***Perf. 13½***
781 A290 125fr multicolored .70 .35

Cable Ship Stephan, 1910 — A291

1986, Apr. 12 **Litho.** ***Perf. 12½***
782 A291 125fr multicolored .70 .35

Stamp Day.

Houphouet-Boigny Type of 1974-76

1986, Apr. **Engr.** ***Perf. 13***
783 A112 5fr dk red, dp rose lil & brn .20 .20
784 A112 10fr gray grn, brt bl & brn .20 .20
785 A112 20fr brt ver, blk brn & brn .20 .20
786 A112 25fr bl, dp rose lil & brn .20 .20
787 A112 30fr brt ver, blk brn & brn .20 .20
789 A112 50fr lake, dk vio & brn .30 .20
790 A112 90fr dk brn vio, rose lake & brn .50 .25
791 A112 125fr brt lil rose, brt ver & brn .70 .35
792 A112 155fr dk brn vio, Prus bl & brn .85 .40
Nos. 783-792 (9) 3.35 2.20

The 1986 printing of the 40fr is in slightly darker colors than No. 374.

Natl. Youth and Sports Institute, 25th Anniv. — A293

1986, May 9 **Litho.** ***Perf. 12½***
793 A293 125fr brt org & dk yel grn .70 .35

Fish A294

5fr, Polypterus endlicheri. 125fr, Synodontis punctifer. 150fr, Protopterus annectens. 155fr, Synodontis koensis. 440fr, Malapterurus electricus.

1986, July 5 **Litho.** ***Perf. 14½x13½***
794 A294 5fr multi .20 .20
795 A294 125fr multi .75 .40
796 A294 150fr multi .90 .45
797 A294 155fr multi .95 .50
798 A294 440fr multi 2.75 2.00
Nos. 794-798 (5) 5.55 3.55

Enthronement of a Chief, Agni District — A295

1986, July 19 ***Perf. 13½x14½***
799 A295 50fr Drummer, vert. .25 .20
800 A295 350fr Chief in litter 2.00 1.00
801 A295 440fr Royal entourage 2.75 2.00
Nos. 799-801 (3) 5.00 3.20

Rural Houses — A296

1986, Aug. 2 **Litho.** ***Perf. 14x15***
802 A296 125fr Baoule aoulo .75 .40
803 A296 155fr Upper Antiam eva .95 .50
804 A296 350fr Lobi soukala 2.00 1.00
Nos. 802-804 (3) 3.70 1.90

Coat of Arms A297

Coastal Landscapes A298

1986-87 **Engr.** ***Perf. 13***
807 A297 50fr bright org .30 .20
810 A297 125fr dark green .75 .40
813 A297 155fr crimson .95 .50
815 A297 195fr blue ('87) 1.10 .55
Nos. 807-815 (4) 3.10 1.65

Issue dates: 50fr, 125fr, 155fr, Aug. 23.
This is an expanding set. Numbers will change if necessary.

Perf. 14x15, 15x14

1986, Aug. 30 **Litho.**
820 A298 125fr Grand Bereby .75 .40
821 A298 155fr Sableux Boubele, horiz. .95 .50

Oceanographic Research Center — A299

Perf. 14½x13½

1986, Sept. 13 **Litho.**
822 A299 125fr Fishing grounds .70 .35
823 A299 155fr Net fishing .85 .40

Intl. Peace Year — A300

1986, Oct. 16 **Litho.** ***Perf. 14x13½***
824 A300 155fr multicolored .85 .40

Research and Development — A301

1986, Nov. 15 ***Perf. 13½x14***
825 A301 125fr Bull .70 .35
826 A301 155fr Wheat .85 .40

Natl. Independence, 26th Anniv. — A302

1986, Dec. 6 **Litho.** ***Perf. 13½x14***
827 A302 155fr multicolored .85 .40

Rural Housing A303

1987, Mar. 14 **Litho.** ***Perf. 13½x14***
828 A303 190fr Guesseple Dan 1.10 .55
829 A303 550fr M'Bagui Senoufo 3.00 1.50

Stamp Day — A304

Jean Mermoz College, 25th Anniv. — A305

1987, Apr. 4 ***Perf. 13x13½***
830 A304 155fr Mailman, 1918 .85 .40

1987, Apr. 9 ***Perf. 13***
831 A305 40fr Cock, elephant .25 .20
832 A305 155fr Dove, children .85 .40

Elephant Type of 1981

1987, Apr. 9
833 A219 35fr multicolored .20 .20

This is an expanding set. Numbers will change if necessary.

Fouilles, by Krah N'Guessan A306

Paintings by local artists: 500fr, Cortege Ceremonial, by Santoni Gerard.

1987, Aug. 14 **Litho.** ***Perf. 14½x15***
841 A306 195fr multi 1.40 .70
842 A306 500fr multi 3.50 1.75

World Post Day, Express Mail Service A307

1987, Oct. 9 ***Perf. 13½***
843 A307 155fr multi 1.10 .55
844 A307 195fr multi 1.25 .65

Intl. Trade Cent. A308

1987, Oct. 24

845 A308 155fr multi 1.10 .55

A309

1987, Dec. 5 Litho. ***Perf. 14x13½***

846 A309 155fr multicolored 1.10 .55

Natl. Independence, 27th anniv.

A310

1988, Feb. 20 Litho. ***Perf. 14x13½***

847 A310 155fr multicolored 1.10 .55

Lions Club for child survival.

The Modest Canary, by Monne Bou A311

Paintings by local artists: 20fr, The Couple, by K.J. Houra, vert. 150fr, The Eternal Dance, by Bou, vert. 155fr, La Termitiere, by Mathilde Moro, vert. 195fr, The Sun of Independence, by Michel Kodjo, vert.

1988, Jan. 30 ***Perf. 12½x13, 13x12½***

848 A311	20fr multi		.20	.20
849 A311	30fr shown		.20	.20
850 A311	150fr multi		1.10	.55
851 A311	155fr multi		1.10	.55
852 A311	195fr multi		1.40	.70
	Nos. 848-852 (5)		4.00	2.20

Stamp Day A312

1988, Apr. 4 Litho. ***Perf. 13***

853 A312 155fr Bereby P.O., c. 1900 1.10 .55

A313

1988, Apr. 18 Litho. ***Perf. 15x14***

854 A313 195fr blk & dark red 1.25 .65

15th French-Language Nations Cardiology Congress, Abidjan, Apr. 18-20.

A314

1988, May 21 Litho. ***Perf. 12x13***

855 A314 195fr multicolored 1.40 .70

Intl. Fund for Agricultural Development (IFAD), 10th anniv.

1st Intl. Day for the Campaign Against Drug Abuse and Drug Trafficking A315

1988, Aug. 27 Litho. ***Perf. 13½***

856 A315 155fr multi 1.10 .55

Stone Heads — A316

Natl. Independence 28th Anniv. — A318

World Post Day — A317

Various stone heads from the Niangoran-Bouah Archaeological Collection.

Litho. & Engr.

1988, July 9 ***Perf. 13x14½***

857 A316	5fr beige & sep		.20	.20
858 A316	10fr buff & sep		.20	.20
859 A316	30fr pale grn & sep		.20	.20
860 A316	155fr pale yel & sep		1.10	.55
861 A316	195fr pale yel grn & sep		1.25	.60
	Nos. 857-861 (5)		2.95	1.75

1988, Oct. 15 Litho. ***Perf. 14***

862 A317 155fr multi 1.00 .50

1988, Dec. 6 ***Perf. 11½x12***

Year of the Forest: 40fr, Healthy trees. No. 864, Stop forest fires. No. 865, Planting trees.

863 A318	40fr multi		.25	.20
864 A318	155fr multi		1.00	.50
865 A318	155fr multi		1.00	.50
	Nos. 863-865 (3)		2.25	1.20

History of Money A319

1989, Feb. 25 Litho. ***Perf. 12x11½***

Granite Paper

866 A319	50fr shown		.30	.20
867 A319	195fr Senegal bank notes, 1854, 1901		1.25	.60

See Nos. 885-886, 896-898, 915. For surcharges see Nos. 904-905.

"Valeur d'echange 0fr.25" on 25c Type A5, 1920 A320

1989, Apr. ***Perf. 12½***

868 A320 155fr multi 1.00 .50

Stamp Day.

Jewelry from the National Museum Collection A321

1989, Mar. 25 Litho. ***Perf. 14***

869 A321	90fr Voltaic bracelets	.55	.30
870 A321	155fr Anklets	.95	.50

Sculptures by Christian Lattier A322

Perf. 11½x12, 12x11½

1989, May 13 Granite Paper

871 A322	40fr *The Old Man and the Infant*, vert.	.25	.20
872 A322	155fr *The Saxophone Player*, vert.	.95	.50
873 A322	550fr *The Panther*	3.25	1.60
	Nos. 871-873 (3)	4.45	2.30

For surcharge see No. 903.

Council for Rural Development, 30th Anniv. — A323

1989, May 29 ***Perf. 15x14***

874 A323 75fr Flags, well, tractor, field .45 .25

See Togo No. 1526.

Intl. Peace Congress — A324

1989, June Litho. ***Perf. 13***

875 A324 195fr multi 1.10 .55

Rural Habitat A325

1989, June 10 Litho. ***Perf. 14***

876 A325 155fr Hut, Sirikukube Dida 1.00 .50

For surcharge see No. 902.

Sekou Watara, King of Kong (1710-1745) — A326

Designs: No. 878, Bastille, Declaration of Human Rights and Citizenship.

1989, July 7 Litho. ***Perf. 13***

877 A326	200fr shown	1.25	.60
878 A326	200fr multi	1.25	.60
a.	Pair, Nos. 877-878 + label	2.50	1.25

PHILEXFRANCE '89, French revolution bicent.

Endangered Species — A327

1989, Sept. 16 ***Perf. 12x11½***

Granite Paper

879 A327	25fr *Varanus niloticus*	.20	.20
880 A327	100fr *Crocodylus niloticus*	.65	.30

World Post Day A328

1989, Oct. 9 Litho. ***Perf. 12½x13***

881 A328 195fr multi 1.25 .65

CAPTEAO, 30th Anniv. A329

1989, Oct. 28 Litho. *Perf. 12½*
882 A329 155fr multicolored 1.10 .55

Conference of Postal and Telecommunication Administrations of West African Nations.

A330

A331

1989, Dec. 7 *Perf. 13*
883 A330 155fr multicolored 1.10 .55

Natl. independence, 29th anniv.

1990, Jan. 18 Litho. *Perf. 13*
884 A331 155fr multicolored 1.10 .55

Pan-African Union, 10th anniv.

History of Money Type of 1989

1990, Mar. 17 Litho. *Perf. 12x11½*

Granite Paper

885 A319 155fr 1923 25fr note 1.25 .60
886 A319 195fr 1, 2, 5fr notes 1.50 .75

Stamp Day A332

1990, Apr. 21 Litho. *Perf. 13x12½*
887 A332 155fr Packet Africa 1.25 .60

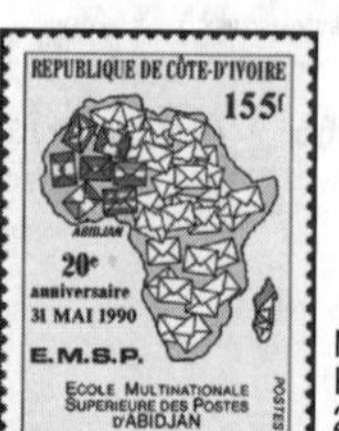
Multinational Postal School, 20th Anniv. — A333

1990, May 31 *Perf. 12½*
888 A333 155fr multicolored 1.25 .60

Rural Village A334

1990, June 30 *Perf. 14*
889 A334 155fr multicolored 1.25 .60

Intl. Literacy Year A335

1990, July 28 *Perf. 15x14*
890 A335 195fr multicolored 1.50 .75

Dedication of Basilica of Notre Dame of Peace, Yamoussoukro — A336

1990, Sept. 8 *Perf. 14½x13½*
891 A336 155fr shown 1.25 .60
892 A336 195fr Basilica, diff. 1.50 .75

Visit of Pope John Paul II — A337

1990, Sept. 9 *Perf. 13*
893 A337 500fr multicolored 4.00 2.00

World Post Day — A338

1990, Oct. 9 Litho. *Perf. 14x15*
894 A338 195fr multicolored 1.75 .90

Independence, 30th Anniv. — A339

1990, Dec. 6 Litho. *Perf. 13½x14½*
895 A339 155fr multicolored 1.40 .70

History of Money Type of 1989

1991, Mar. 1 Litho. *Perf. 11½*

Granite Paper

896 A319 40fr French West Africa 1942 5fr, 100fr notes .30 .20
897 A319 155fr like #896 1.10 .55
898 A319 195fr French West Africa & Togo 50fr, 500fr notes 1.40 .70
Nos. 896-898 (3) 2.80 1.45

For surcharges see Nos. 904-905.

Stamp Day A340

1991, May 18 Litho. *Perf. 13½*
899 A340 150fr multicolored 1.10 .55

Miniature Sheets of 9

French Open Tennis Championships, Cent. — A341

Tennis Players: No. 900a, Henri Cochet. b, Rene Lacoste. c, Jean Borotra. d, Don Budge. e, Marcel Bernard. f, Ken Rosewall. g, Rod Laver. h, Bjorn Borg. i, Yannick Noah.

No. 901a, Suzanne Lenglen. b, Helen Wills Moody. c, Simone Mathieu. d, Maureen Connolly. e, Francoise Durr. f, Margaret Court. g, Chris Evert. h, Martina Navratilova. i, Steffi Graf.

1991, May 24 Litho. *Perf. 13½*
900 A341 200fr #a.-i. 13.50 6.75
901 A341 200fr #a.-i. 13.50 6.75

Nos. 872, 876, 897-898 Surcharged

Perfs. as Before

1991, July 15 Litho.
902 A325 150fr on 155fr #876 1.10 .55

Granite Paper

903 A322 150fr on 155fr #872 1.10 .55
904 A319 150fr on 155fr #897 1.10 .55
905 A319 200fr on 195fr #898 1.50 .75
Nos. 902-905 (4) 4.80 2.40

Location of obliterator and surcharge varies.

Packet Boats A342

1991, June 28 Litho. *Perf. 12x11½*

Granite Paper

906 A342 50fr Europe .40 .20
907 A342 550fr Asia 4.25 2.10

World Post Day A343

1991, Oct. 9 *Perf. 13*
908 A343 50fr shown .40 .20
909 A343 100fr SIPE, globe .80 .40

Tribal Drums — A344

1991 Litho. *Perf. 14x15*
910 A344 5fr We .20 .20
911 A344 25fr Krou, Soubre region .20 .20
912 A344 150fr Sinematiali 1.25 .60
913 A344 200fr Akye, Alepe region 1.60 .80
Nos. 910-913 (4) 3.25 1.80

Independence, 31st Anniv. — A345

1991, Dec. 7 Litho. *Perf. 13½x14½*
914 A345 150fr multicolored 1.25 .65

History of Money Type of 1989

1991, Dec. 8 *Perf. 12x11½*

Granite Paper

915 A319 100fr like #898 .90 .45

Flowers A346

Various flowers.

1991, Dec. 20 Engr. *Perf. 13*
916 A346 150fr grn, blk & mag, vert. 1.25 .65
917 A346 200fr grn, olive & rose car 1.60 .85

African Soccer Championships — A347

Designs: 150fr, Elephants holding trophy, map, soccer ball, vert.

1992, Apr. 22 Litho. *Perf. 13*
918 A347 20fr multicolored .20 .20
919 A347 150fr multicolored 1.25 .65

Animals A348

1992, May 5 Engr. *Perf. 13x12½*
920 A348 5fr Viverra civetta .20 .20
921 A348 40fr Nandinia binotata .35 .20
922 A348 150fr Tragelaphus euryceros 1.25 .65
923 A348 500fr Panthera pardus 4.50 2.25
Nos. 920-923 (4) 6.30 3.30

World Post Day — A349

1992, Oct. 7 Litho. *Perf. 13*

924 A349 150fr black & blue 1.25 .65

First Ivory Coast Postage Stamp, Cent. — A350

Designs: a, #3, #197. b, #182, #909 with mail trucks, post office boxes.

1992, Oct. 7

925 A350 150fr Pair, #a.-b. + label 2.60 1.25

Funeral Monuments A351

Various grave site monuments.

1992, Dec. 30 Engr. *Perf. 13*

926 A351 5fr multicolored .20 .20
927 A351 50fr multicolored .40 .20
928 A351 150fr multicolored 1.25 .60
929 A351 400fr multicolored 3.25 1.60
Nos. 926-929 (4) 5.10 2.60

Intl. Abidjan Marathon A351a

1992, Nov. 20 Litho. *Perf. 11½*
Granite Paper

929A A351a 150fr Flags, runners .65 .30
929B A351a 200fr Runners 1.00 .40

Nos. 929A-929B were not available in the philatelic market until Apr. 1994.

Gold Mine of Ity, 1st Anniv. — A351b

32nd Anniv. of Independence A351c

1992, Nov. 8 Litho. *Perf. 14x15*

929C A351b 200fr multicolored 1.00 .40

No. 929C was not available in the philatelic market until Apr. 1994.

1992, Dec. 4

150fr, People, flag, Statue of Liberty, map.

929D A351c 30fr shown .20 .20
929E A351c 150fr multicolored .65 .30

Nos. 929D-929E were not available in the philatelic market until Apr. 1994.

Tourist Attractions A351d

Environmental Summit A351e

Perf. 14x15, 15x14
1992, Sept. 4 Litho.

929F A351d 10fr Modern hotel, horiz.
929G A351d 25fr Dent de Man
929H A351d 100fr Resort, horiz.
929I A351d 200fr Map of tourist sites

Perf. 11½x12, 12x11½
1992, June 5 Litho.

200fr, Prevent water pollution, horiz.

Granite Paper

929J A351e 150fr multicolored
929K A351e 200fr multicolored

Stamp Day A352

Designs showing children interested in philately: No. 930, Girl, stamp collection, #169. No. 931, Girl, #431, #446B, #186, and #920. 150fr, Boy sitting under tree, stamp exhibition.

1993, Apr. 17 Litho. *Perf. 13½*

930 A352 50fr multicolored .40 .20
931 A352 50fr multicolored .40 .20
932 A352 150fr multicolored 1.25 .60
Nos. 930-932 (3) 2.05 1.00

A353

A354

Medicinal plants.

1993, May 14 Litho. *Perf. 11½x12*
Granite Paper

933 A353 5fr Argemone mexicana .20 .20
934 A353 20fr Hibiscus esculentus .20 .20
935 A353 200fr Cassia alata 1.60 .80
Nos. 933-935 (3) 2.00 1.20

1993, Aug. 27 Photo. *Perf. 12x11½*

Orchids: 10fr, Calyptrochilum emarginatum. 50fr, Plectrelminthus caudathus. 150fr, Eulophia guineensis.

Granite Paper

936 A354 10fr multicolored .20 .20
937 A354 50fr multicolored .40 .20
938 A354 150fr multicolored 1.25 .60
Nos. 936-938 (3) 1.85 1.00

Ivory Coast Colony, Cent. A355

25fr, Organization charter. 100fr, Colonial Governor Louis Gustave Binger, Pres. F. Houphouet-Boigny. 500fr, Natives selecting goods for trade.

1993, Sept. 17 *Perf. 13x12½*

939 A355 25fr green & black .20 .20
940 A355 100fr blue & black .80 .40
941 A355 500fr brown & black 4.00 2.00
Nos. 939-941 (3) 5.00 2.60

Elimination Round of 1994 World Cup Soccer Championships, US — A356

Designs: 150fr, Cartoon soccer players. 200fr, Three players. 300fr, Two players. 400fr, Cartoon players, diff.

1993, Sept. 24 Litho. *Perf. 14x15*

942 A356 150fr multicolored 1.10 .55
943 A356 200fr multicolored 1.50 .75
944 A356 300fr multicolored 2.25 1.10
945 A356 400fr multicolored 3.00 1.50
Nos. 942-945 (4) 7.85 3.90

World Post Day A357

Designs: 30fr, Map of Ivory Coast. 200fr, Post office, Bouake.

1993, Oct. 9 *Perf. 13x13½*

946 A357 30fr multicolored .25 .20
947 A357 200fr multicolored 1.50 .75

African Biennial of Plastic Arts, Abidjan A358

Perf. 14½x13½
1993, Nov. 24 Litho.

948 A358 200fr multicolored .75 .40

Independence, 33rd Anniv. — A359

1993, Dec. 7 Litho. *Perf. 13½x13*

950 A359 200fr multicolored 1.50 .75

Pres. Felix Houphouet-Boigny (1905-93) — A360

Pres. Houphouet-Boigny and: Nos. 951a, 952a, 953a, Modern buildings, technology. Nos. 951b, 952b, 953b, Agriculture, shipping. Nos. 951c, 952c, 953c, Dove, rainbow, Presidential palace.

1994, Feb. 5 Litho. *Perf. 13*

951 A360 150fr Strip of 3, #a.-c. 1.75 .90
952 A360 200fr Strip of 3, #a.-c. 2.25 1.10

Souvenir Sheet
Perf. 12

953 A360 500fr Sheet of 3, #a.-c. 5.75 2.75

Raoul Follereau, Campaign Against Leprosy A361

1994, Feb. 20 Litho. *Perf. 13*

954 A361 150fr multicolored .65 .30

RASCOM (Regional African Satellite Communications Organization), 1st Meeting, Abidjan — A362

1994, Jan. 19 Litho. *Perf. 14x13*

955 A362 150fr multicolored .60 .30

Woman Carrying Basket — A363

Litho. & Engr.
1994-95 *Perf. 13½x13*
Color of Border

956 A363 5fr orange .20 .20
956A A363 10fr green .20 .20
956B A363 20fr red .20 .20
957 A363 25fr blue .20 .20
957A A363 30fr olive bister .20 .20
958 A363 40fr yellow green .20 .20
959 A363 50fr brown .25 .20
960 A363 75fr lilac rose .30 .20
961 A363 150fr bright green .70 .35
961A A363 180fr pale lake .95 .50

961B A363 280fr gray 1.40 .70
962 A363 300fr violet 1.40 .70
Nos. 956-962 (12) 6.20 3.85

Issued: 30fr, 180fr, 280fr, 5/16/95, dated 1994; others, 11/4/94.

Stained Glass Windows, Basilica of Notre Dame of Peace, Yamoussoukro
A364

Designs: 25fr, Christ, world map. 150fr, Christ, fishermen. 200fr, Madonna and Child. 600fr, Aerial view of Cathedral, Yamoussoukro.

1994, Nov. 18 Litho. *Perf. 14*
963 A364 25fr lilac rose & multi .20 .20
964 A364 150fr pale orange & multi .70 .35
965 A364 200fr yellow & mulit .90 .45
Nos. 963-965 (3) 1.80 1.00

Souvenir Sheet

966 A364 600fr multicolored 3.25 1.50

Natl. Independence, 34th Anniv. — A365

1994, Dec. 6 Litho. *Perf. 12*
967 A365 150fr multicolored .70 .35

Snakes
A366

Designs: 10fr, Python regius. 20fr, Philothamnus semivariegatus. 100fr, Dendroaspis veridis. 180fr, Bitis arietans. 500fr, Bitis nasicornis.

1995, June 23 Litho. *Perf. 13*
968 A366 10fr multicolored .20 .20
969 A366 20fr multicolored .20 .20
970 A366 100fr multicolored .50 .25
971 A366 180fr multicolored .90 .45
972 A366 500fr multicolored 2.50 1.25
Nos. 968-972 (5) 4.30 2.35

FAO, 50th Anniv. — A367

UN, 50th Anniv. — A368

1995, Aug. 4 Litho. *Perf. 11½*
973 A367 100fr multicolored .70 .35
974 A368 280fr multicolored 1.50 .75

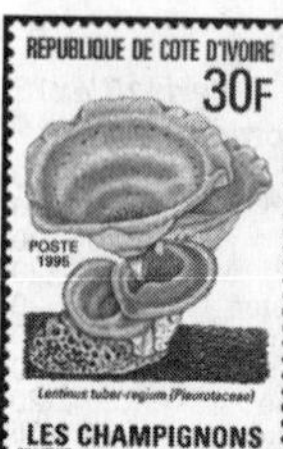

Mushrooms
A369

Designs: 30fr, Lentinus tuber-regium. 50fr, Volvariella volvacea. 180fr, Dictyophora indusiata. 250fr, Termitomyces schimperi.

1995, Sept. 8 *Perf. 14x13½*
975 A369 30fr multicolored .20 .20
976 A369 50fr multicolored .25 .20
977 A369 180fr multicolored .95 .50
978 A369 250fr multicolored 1.25 .65
a. Block of 4, #975-978 2.75 1.50

#978a was issued in sheets of 16 stamps.

Louis Pasteur (1822-95)
A370

1995, Sept. 28 *Perf. 11½*
979 A370 280fr multicolored 1.50 .75

School Philatelic Clubs
A371

1995, Oct. 6 *Perf. 13½*
980 A371 50fr GSR .25 .20
981 A371 180fr LBP .95 .50

Butterflies
A371a

180fr, Pala decius. 280fr, Papilio dardanus. 550fr, Papilio menestheus.

1995 Litho. *Perf. 15x14*
981A A371a 180fr multicolored
981B A371a 280fr multicolored
981C A371a 550fr multicolored

Transportation in Abidjan — A372

Designs: 180fr, People pushing, pulling cart of grain, automobiles, bus on street. 280fr, People getting into bus in middle of traffic.

1996, May 24 *Perf. 13½*
982 A372 180fr multicolored .95 .50
983 A372 280fr multicolored 1.50 .75

Fish
A373

Designs: 50fr, Heterotis niloticus. 180fr, Auchenoglanis occidentalis. 700fr, Schilbe mandibularis.

1996, June
984 A373 50fr multicolored .25 .20
985 A373 180fr multicolored 1.00 .50
986 A373 700fr multicolored 3.75 1.85
Nos. 984-986 (3) 5.00 2.55

A374

A375

Orchids: 40fr, Cyrtorchis arcuata. 100fr, Eulophia horsfalii. 180fr, Eulophidium maculatum. 200fr, Ansellia africana.

1996, July 12 Litho. *Perf. 13½x13*
987 A374 40fr multicolored .20 .20
988 A374 100fr multicolored .55 .35
989 A374 180fr multicolored 1.00 .50
990 A374 200fr multicolored 1.00 .50
Nos. 987-990 (4) 2.75 1.55

1996, Nov. 19
991 A375 200fr Boxing 1.00 .50
992 A375 280fr Running 1.50 .75
993 A375 400fr Long jump 2.00 1.00
994 A375 500fr Natl. Olympic Committee emblem 2.50 1.25
Nos. 991-994 (4) 7.00 3.50

1996 Summer Olympic Games, Atlanta.

Carved Canes
A376

180fr, Cane of Birifor hunter. 200fr, Cane of Chief Lobi. 280fr, Cane of Chief Lobi (Gbobéri).

1996, Sept. 20 Litho. *Perf. 11½*
995 A376 180fr black & green .95 .45
996 A376 200fr black & org yel 1.00 .50
997 A376 280fr black & lilac 1.50 .75
Nos. 995-997 (3) 3.45 1.70

Water Flowers
A377

Designs: 50fr, Nelumbo nucifera. 180fr, Nymphea lotus. 280fr, Nymphea capensis. 700fr, Nymphea alba.

1997, June 20 Litho. *Perf. 13½x14*
998 A377 50fr multicolored .25 .20
999 A377 180fr multicolored .85 .45
1000 A377 280fr multicolored 1.40 .70
1001 A377 700fr multicolored 3.50 1.75
Nos. 998-1001 (4) 6.00 3.10

Basilica of Our Lady of Peace, Yamoussoukro — A378

a, 180fr, Pres. Felix Houphouet-Boigny, exterior view of basilica. b, 200fr, Interior view. c, 280fr, Aerial view, Pope John Paul II.

1997, July 8 Litho. *Perf. 13*
1002 A378 Strip of 3, #a.-c. 3.00 1.50

Traditional Jewelry — A379

Various beaded necklaces.

1997, Aug. 22 *Perf. 11½*
1003 A379 50fr plum & black .25 .20
1004 A379 100fr plum & black .45 .25
1005 A379 180fr plum & black .80 .40
Nos. 1003-1005 (3) 1.50 .85

A379a

A380

Various stone heads of Gohitafla.

1997, Oct. 10 Litho. *Perf. 11½*
Granite Paper
1006 A379a 100fr red & multi .35 .20
1007 A379a 180fr blue & multi .60 .30
1008 A379a 500fr green & multi 1.60 .80
Nos. 1006-1008 (3) 2.55 1.30

1997, Nov. 28 *Perf. 13½*

Work tools: 180fr, Pulley. 280fr, Comb. 300fr, Navette, horiz.

1009 A380 180fr orange & multi .60 .30
1010 A380 280fr green & multi .90 .45
1011 A380 300fr blue & multi 1.00 .50
Nos. 1009-1011 (3) 2.50 1.25

Endangered Species
A381

Designs: 180fr, African manatee. 280fr, Jentink's duiker. 400fr, Kob antelope.

1997, Dec. 19 Photo. *Perf. 11½*
1012 A381 180fr multicolored .60 .30
1013 A381 280fr multicolored .90 .45
1014 A381 400fr multicolored 1.40 .65
Nos. 1012-1014 (3) 2.90 1.40

1998 World Cup Soccer Championships, France — A382

Paris landmarks in background and: 180fr, Player, ball depicted with angry face. 280fr, Flags of nations inside outline of player. 400fr,

Player taking shot on goal. 500fr, Two players, mascot, vert.

Perf. 13x13½, 13½x13

1998, June 5 **Litho.**

1015 A382 180fr multicolored .60 .30
1016 A382 280fr multicolored .95 .45
1017 A382 400fr multicolored 1.25 .65
1018 A382 500fr multicolored 1.60 .85
Nos. 1015-1018 (4) 4.40 2.25

Mushrooms A383

Endemic Plants — A384

50fr, Agaricus bingensis. 180fr, Lactarius gymnocarpus. 280fr, Termitomyces le testui.

1998, June 26 **Litho.** ***Perf. 13½x13***

1019 A383 50fr multicolored .20 .20
1020 A383 180fr multicolored .60 .30
1021 A383 280fr multicolored .95 .50
Nos. 1019-1021 (3) 1.75 1.00

1998, July 10 ***Perf. 12***

Designs: 40fr, Hutchinsonia barbata. 100fr, Synsepalum aubrevillei. 180fr, Cola lorougnonis.

Granite Paper

1022 A384 40fr multicolored .20 .20
1023 A384 100fr multicolored .35 .20
1024 A384 180fr multicolored .60 .30
Nos. 1022-1024 (3) 1.15 .70

Traditional Costumes from Grand-Bassam Museum — A385

1998, Nov. 13 **Litho.** ***Perf. 13½x13***

1025 A385 180fr Tapa .65 .30
1026 A385 280fr Raffia 1.00 .50

Trains of Africa A386

180fr, South African Railway, 1918. 280fr, Garret 2-8-2+2-8-2 Beyer Peacock, 1925. 500fr, Cecil Rhodes.

1999, Feb. 26 **Litho.** ***Perf. 13½***

1027 A386 180fr multicolored .65 .30
1028 A386 280fr multicolored 1.00 .50

Souvenir Sheet

1029 A386 500fr multicolored 1.75 .90

PhilexFrance '99, World Philatelic Exhibition — A387

Animals: 180fr+20fr, Loxodonta africana. 250fr, Syncerus caffer. 280fr, Pan troglodytes. 400fr, Cercopithecus aethiops.

1999, July 2 **Litho.** ***Perf. 13x13¼***

1030 A387 180fr +20fr multi .65 .30
1031 A387 250fr multicolored .80 .40
1032 A387 280fr multicolored .90 .45
1033 A387 400fr multicolored 1.25 .65
Nos. 1030-1033 (4) 3.60 1.80

UPU, 125th Anniv. A388

UPU emblem and: 180fr+20fr, Carved heads. 280fr, Methods of delivering mail.

1999, June 25 ***Perf. 11¾x11½***

1034 A388 180fr +20fr multi .65 .30
1035 A388 280fr multicolored .90 .45

Flowers A389

Ahouakro Rock Formations A390

Designs: 100fr, Ancistrochilus rothschilianus. 180fr+20fr, Brachycorythis pubescens. 200fr, Bulbophyllum barbigerum. 280fr, Habenaria macrandra.

1999, July 27 **Litho.** ***Perf. 13¼x13***

1036 A389 100fr multicolored .30 .30
1037 A389 180fr +20fr multi .65 .65
1038 A389 200fr multicolored .65 .65
1039 A389 280fr multicolored .90 .90
Nos. 1036-1039 (4) 2.50 2.50

Perf. 13¼x14, 14x13¼

1999, Aug. 6 **Litho.**

Various rock formations.

1040 A390 180fr +20fr multi, horiz. .65 .65
1041 A390 280fr multi, horiz. .90 .90
1042 A390 400fr multi 1.25 1.25
Nos. 1040-1042 (3) 2.80 2.80

PhilexFrance 99 — A391

1999, July 2 **Litho.** ***Perf. 13***

1043 A391 280fr multicolored *.90 .90*

No. 1043 has a holographic image. Soaking in water may affect hologram.

Birds — A392

Designs: 50fr, Oriolus auratus. 180fr + 20fr, Nectarinia cinnyris venusta. 280fr, Trenon vinago australis. 300fr, Psittacus eithacus.

1999, Oct. 29 **Litho.** ***Perf. 13¼x13***

1044 A392 50fr multi .20 .20
1045 A392 180fr + 20fr multi .65 .65
1046 A392 280fr multi .90 .90
1047 A392 300fr multi .95 .95
Nos. 1044-1047 (4) 2.70 2.70

Fish A393

Designs: 100fr, Synodontis schall. 180fr + 20fr, Chromidotilapia guntheri. 280fr, Distichodus rostratus.

1999, Nov. 19 ***Perf. 13½x13¼***

1048 A393 100fr multi .30 .30
1049 A393 180fr +20fr multi .65 .65
1050 A393 280fr multi .90 .90
Nos. 1048-1050 (3) 1.85 1.85

Challenges for Ivory Coast in Third Millennium — A394

Designs: 100fr, Education. 180fr +20fr, Agriculture. 200fr, Industry. 250fr, Information. 280fr, Peace. 400fr, Culture.

1999, Dec. 10 ***Perf. 13½x13¾***

1051 A394 100fr multi .30 .30
1052 A394 180fr +20fr multi .65 .65
1053 A394 200fr multi .65 .65
1054 A394 250fr multi .80 .80
1055 A394 280fr multi .90 .90
1056 A394 400fr multi 1.25 1.25
Nos. 1051-1056 (6) 4.55 4.55

Native Masks A395

Perf. 13½x13¼, 13¼x13½

2000, June 30 **Litho.**

1057 A395 30fr Wambélé .20 .20
1058 A395 180fr +20fr Djè .55 .55
1059 A395 400fr Korobla, vert. 1.10 1.10
Nos. 1057-1059 (3) 1.85 1.85

Edible Plants — A396

Designs: 30fr, Blighia sapida. 180fr+20fr, Ricinodendron heudelotii. 300fr, Telfaira occidentalis. 400fr, Napoleonaea vogelii.

2000, July 14 ***Perf. 13¼x13½***

1060 A396 30fr multi .20 .20
1061 A396 180fr +20fr multi .55 .55
1062 A396 300fr multi .85 .85
1063 A396 400fr multi 1.10 1.10
Nos. 1060-1063 (4) 2.70 2.70

Pres. Robert Guei, Elephant, Map and Dove — A397

2000, Aug. 4 ***Perf. 13¾x13¼***

1064 A397 180fr +20fr red & multi .55 .55
1065 A397 400fr yel & multi 1.10 1.10

Independence, 40th anniv., coup d'etat of Robert Guei.

Cacao — A398

Frame colors: 5fr, Dark blue green. 10fr, Light brown. 20fr, Claret. 25fr, Blue. 30fr, Greenish black. 40fr, Cerise. 50fr, Golden brown. 100fr, Brown. 180fr+20fr, Orange. 300fr, Blue violet. 350fr, Prussian blue. 400fr, Emerald. 600fr, Olive green.

Perf. 11½x11¾

2000, Aug. 25 **Photo.**

Granite Paper

1066-1078 A398 Set of 13 6.00 6.00

National Lottery, 30th Anniv. — A399

Denominations: 180fr+20fr, 400fr.

2000, Aug. 30 **Litho.** ***Perf. 13¼x13***

1079-1080 A399 Set of 2 1.75 1.75

2000 Summer Olympics, Sydney A400

Designs: 180fr+20fr, Soccer. 400fr, Kangaroo. 600fr, Runners. 750fr, Bird over stadium.

2000, Sept. 8 ***Perf. 13½x13¼***

1081-1084 A400 Set of 4 5.75 5.75

Hairstyles — A401

Various hairstyles: 180fr+20fr, 300fr, 400fr, 500fr.

2000, Sept. 22 ***Perf. 13¾x13¼***
1085-1088 A401 Set of 4 4.00 4.00

Release of Nelson Mandela, 10th Anniv. — A402

2000, Oct. 6 Photo. ***Perf. 12x11¾***
1089 A402 300fr multi .85 .85

Historic Monuments A403

Designs: 180fr+20fr, Queen Pokou. 400fr, Akwaba. 600fr, Invocation of the Spirits.

2000, Nov. 10 Litho. ***Perf. 13½x13***
1090-1092 A403 Set of 3 3.50 3.50

UN High Commisioner for Refugees, 50th Anniv. — A404

2000 Photo. ***Perf. 11¾x12***
1093 A404 400fr multi 1.10 1.10

Abokouamekro Animal Park — A405

Designs: 50fr, Cattle. 100fr, Rhinoceroses. 180fr+20fr, Rhinoceros. 400fr+20fr, Cattle.

2001, May Litho. ***Perf. 13½x13¼***
1094-1097 A405 Set of 4 2.25 2.25

Sculpted Columns in National Museum — A406

Designs: 100fr, Alingué, Wouo Anouman. 180fr+20fr, Blolo Bian, Blolo B1a. 300fr+20fr, Botoumo. 400fr+20fr, Odi Oka.

2001, June ***Perf. 13¼x13***
1098-1101 A406 Set of 4 3.00 3.00

Elimination Rounds for World Cup Soccer Championships — A407

Various soccer plays: 180fr + 20fr, 400fr + 20fr, 600fr + 20fr, 700fr.

2001 Litho. ***Perf. 13x13¼***
1102-1105 A407 Set of 4 5.25 5.25

SEMI-POSTAL STAMPS

No. 47 Surcharged in Red

1915 Unwmk. ***Perf. 14x13½***
B1 A5 10c + 5c .60 .75
a. Double surcharge 45.00 45.00

Issued on ordinary and chalky paper.

Curie Issue
Common Design Type

1938 ***Perf. 13***
B2 CD80 1.75fr + 50c brt ultra 5.00 6.00

French Revolution Issue
Common Design Type

1939 Photo.
Name and Value Typo. in Black

B3	CD83	45c + 25c grn	4.50	4.00
B4	CD83	70c + 30c brn	4.50	4.00
B5	CD83	90c + 35c red org	4.50	4.00
B6	CD83	1.25fr + 1fr rose pink	4.50	4.00
B7	CD83	2.25fr + 2fr blue	4.50	4.00
		Nos. B3-B7 (5)	22.50	20.00

Stamps of 1936-38 Surcharged in Red or Black

1941

B8	A7	50c + 1fr plum (Bk)	1.00	1.00
B9	A8	80c + 2fr blk brn (R)	6.25	7.00
B10	A8	1.50fr + 2fr ultra (R)	6.75	7.00
B11	A9	2fr + 3fr ultra (Bk)	6.75	7.00
		Nos. B8-B11 (4)	20.75	22.00

Common Design Type and

Native Engineer SP1

Senegalese Light Artillery SP2

1941 Photo. ***Perf. 13½***

B12	SP1	1fr + 1fr red	.60
B13	CD86	1.50fr + 3fr claret	.60
B14	SP2	2.50fr + 1fr blue	.60
		Nos. B12-B14 (3)	1.80

Nos. B12-B14 were issued by the Vichy government in France, but were not placed on sale in Ivory Coast.

Petain Type of 1941 Surcharged in Black or Red

1944 Engr. ***Perf. 12½x12***
B14A 50c + 1.50fr on 2.50fr deep blue (R) .40
B14B + 2.50fr on 1fr green .40

Colonial Development Fund.
Nos. B14A-B14B were issued by the Vichy government in France, but were not placed on sale in Ivory Coast.

Catalogue values for unused stamps in this section, from this point to the end of the section, are for Never Hinged items.

Republic
Anti-Malaria Issue
Common Design Type

1962, Apr. 7 Engr. ***Perf. 12½x12***
B15 CD108 25fr + 5fr ol grn .65 .65

Freedom from Hunger Issue
Common Design Type

1963, Mar. 21 ***Perf. 13***
B16 CD112 25fr + 5fr red lil, dk vio & brn .80 .80

Red Cross - Red Crescent Soc., Child Survival Campaign — SP3

1987, May 8 Litho. ***Perf. 13½***
B17 SP3 195fr +5fr multi 1.10 1.10

No. B17 surcharged "+5fr" in red. Not issued without surcharge. Surtax for the Red Cross - Red Crescent Soc.

Organization of African Unity, 25th Anniv. — SP4

1988, Nov. 19 Litho. ***Perf. 12½x13***
B18 SP4 195fr +5fr multi 1.40 1.40

Marie Therese Houphouet-Boigny and N'Daya Intl. Emblem — SP5

1988, Dec. 9 Litho. ***Perf. 13***
B19 SP5 195fr +5fr multi 1.40 1.40

N'Daya Intl., 1st anniv.

See postage issues, beginning with #1030, for semi-postal stamps that are part of sets with regular postage stamps.

Council of Understanding, Solidarity & Rural Development, 40th Anniv. — SP6

1999, May 29 Litho. ***Perf. 13x13½***
B20 SP6 180fr +20fr multi .65 .30

Independence, 41st Anniv. — SP7

2001 Litho. ***Perf. 13¼x13½***
B21 SP7 180fr +20fr multi .55 .55

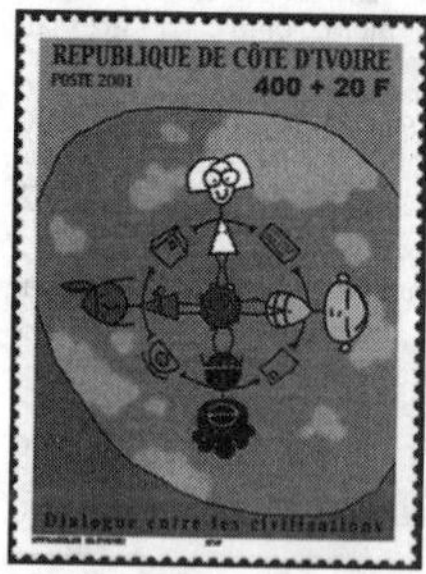

Year of Dialogue Among Civilizations SP8

2001, Oct. 9 ***Perf. 13x13¼***
B22 SP8 400fr +20fr multi 1.25 1.25

Second Republic, 1st Anniv. SP9

2001
B23 SP9 180fr +20fr multi .55 .55

AIR POST STAMPS

Common Design Type

1940 Unwmk. Engr. ***Perf. 12½x12***

C1	CD85	1.90fr ultramarine	.20	.20
C2	CD85	2.90fr dark red	.20	.20
C3	CD85	4.50fr dk gray grn	.25	.25
C4	CD85	4.90fr yel bister	.30	.30
C5	CD85	6.90fr deep orange	.90	.90
		Nos. C1-C5 (5)	1.85	1.85

Common Design Types

1942

C6	CD88	50c car & blue	.20
C7	CD88	1fr brn & black	.20
C8	CD88	2fr dk grn & red brn	.35
C9	CD88	3fr dk blue & scar	.35
C10	CD88	5fr vio & dk red	.35

Frame Engraved, Center Typographed

C11 CD89 10fr multicolored .40
C12 CD89 20fr multicolored .55
C13 CD89 50fr multicolored .80 1.25
Nos. C6-C13 (8) 3.20 .00

There is doubt whether Nos. C6-C12 were officially placed in use.

Catalogue values for unused stamps in this section, from this point to the end of the section, are for Never Hinged items.

Republic

Lapalud Place and Post Office, Abidjan — AP1

Designs: 200fr, Houphouet-Boigny Bridge. 500fr, Ayamé dam.

1959, Oct. 1 Engr. *Perf. 13*
C14 AP1 100fr multicolored 1.10 .40
C15 AP1 200fr multicolored 1.50 1.10
C16 AP1 500fr multicolored 5.25 2.25
Nos. C14-C16 (3) 7.85 3.75

Sports Type of 1961

1961, Dec. 23
C17 A19 100fr High jump .90 .65

Air Afrique Issue
Common Design Type

1962, Feb. 17 Unwmk. *Perf. 13*
C18 CD107 50fr Prus bl, choc & org brn .65 .50

Village in Man Region — AP2

1962, June 23 Engr. *Perf. 13*
C19 AP2 200fr Street in Odienne, vert. 2.25 .90
C20 AP2 500fr shown 4.50 2.00

UN Headquarters, New York — AP3

1962, Sept. 20 *Perf. 13*
C21 AP3 100fr multi 1.10 .70

Admission to the UN, 2nd anniv.

Sassandra Bay — AP4

1963 Unwmk. *Perf. 13*
C22 AP4 50fr Moossou bridge .50 .25
C23 AP4 100fr shown 1.10 .65
C24 AP4 200fr Comoe River 2.00 1.00
Nos. C22-C24 (3) 3.60 1.90

African Postal Union Issue
Common Design Type

1963, Sept. 8 Photo. *Perf. 12½*
C25 CD114 85fr org brn, ocher & red .90 .75

1963 Air Afrique Issue
Common Design Type

1963, Nov. 19 Unwmk. *Perf. 13x12*
C26 CD115 25fr crim, gray, blk & grn .35 .25

Ramses II and Queen Nefertari — AP5

President John F. Kennedy (1917-63) — AP7

Arms of Republic — AP6

1964, Mar. 7 Engr. *Perf. 13*
C27 AP5 60fr car, blk & red brn .80 .65

UNESCO campaign to save historic monuments in Nubia.

1964, June 13 Photo.
C28 AP6 200fr ultra, yel grn & gold 1.75 .75

1964, Nov. 14 Unwmk. *Perf. 12½*
C29 AP7 100fr gray, cl brn & blk 1.25 .80
a. Souvenir sheet of 4 4.00 4.00

Liana Bridge, Lieupleu — AP8

1965, Dec. 4 Engr. *Perf. 13*
C30 AP8 100fr ol grn, dk grn & dk red brn 1.00 .65

Street in Kong — AP9

1966, Mar. 5 Engr. *Perf. 13*
C31 AP9 300fr brt bl, bis brn & vio brn 3.25 1.60

Air Afrique Issue, 1966
Common Design Type

1966, Aug. 20 Photo. *Perf. 13*
C32 CD123 30fr dk grn, blk & gray .35 .20

Air Afrique Headquarters AP10

1967, Feb. 4 Engr. *Perf. 13*
C33 AP10 500fr emer, ind & ocher 5.00 2.00

Opening of Air Afrique headquarters in Abidjan.

African Postal Union Issue, 1967
Common Design Type

1967, Sept. 9 Engr. *Perf. 13*
C34 CD124 100fr blk, vio & car lake 1.10 .65

Senufo Village — AP11

1968 Engr. *Perf. 13*
C35 AP11 100fr shown 1.10 .70
C36 AP11 500fr Tiegba village 4.50 2.00

Issue dates: 100fr, Feb. 17; 500fr, Apr. 27.

PHILEXAFRIQUE Issue

Street in Grand Bassam, by Achalme — AP12

1969, Jan. 11 Photo. *Perf. 12x12½*
C37 AP12 100fr grn & multi 1.10 1.10

PHILEXAFRIQUE Phil. Exhib., Abidjan, Feb. 14-23. Printed with alternating green label.

2nd PHILEXAFRIQUE Issue
Common Design Type

50fr, Ivory Coast #130 & view of San Pedro. 100fr, Ivory Coast #149 & man wearing chief's garments, vert. 200fr, Ivory Coast #77 # Exhibition Hall, Abidjan.

1969, Feb. 14 Engr. *Perf. 13*
C38 CD128 50fr grn, brn red & deep bl .50 .50
C39 CD128 100fr brn, org & dp blue 1.00 1.00
C40 CD128 200fr brn, gray & dp blue 1.75 1.75
a. Min. sheet of 3, #C38-C40 3.50 3.50
Nos. C38-C40 (3) 3.25 3.25

Opening of PHILEXAFRIQUE.

Man Waterfall — AP13

Mount Niangbo — AP14

1970 Engr. *Perf. 13*
C41 AP13 100fr multicolored .75 .45
C42 AP14 200fr multicolored 1.75 .75

Issue dates: 100fr, Jan. 6; 200fr, July 18.

San Pedro Harbor — AP15

1971, Mar. 21 Engr. *Perf. 13*
C43 AP15 100fr multicolored .80 .45

Treichville Swimming Pool — AP16

1971, May 29 Photo. *Perf. 12½*
C44 AP16 100fr multicolored .80 .50

Aerial View of Coast Line — AP17

1971, July 3 Engr. *Perf. 13*
C45 AP17 500fr multi 4.25 2.00

Tourist publicity for the African Riviera.

Bondoukou Market Type of Regular Issue

Design: 200fr, Similar to No. 318, but without people at left and in center.

Embossed on Gold Paper

1971, Aug. 7 *Perf. 12½*
Size: 36x26mm
C46 A79 200fr gold, ultra & blk 1.90 1.50

African Postal Union Issue, 1971
Common Design Type

Design: 100fr, Ivory Coast coat of arms and UAMPT building, Brazzaville, Congo.

1971, Nov. 13 Photo. *Perf. 13x13½*
C47 CD135 100fr bl & multi .80 .45

Lion of St. Mark AP18

1972, Feb. 5 Photo. *Perf. 12½*

C48 AP18 100fr shown 1.00 .65
C49 AP18 200fr Waves, St. Mark's Basilica, Venice 2.25 1.50

UNESCO campaign to save Venice.

Kawara Mosque — AP19

1972, Apr. 29 Engr. *Perf. 13*

C50 AP19 500fr bl, brn & ocher 4.00 1.90

View of Gouessesso — AP20

1972 Engr. *Perf. 13*

C51 AP20 100fr shown .80 .45
C52 AP20 200fr Jacqueville Lake 2.00 .80
C53 AP20 500fr Kossou Dam 4.00 2.00
Nos. C51-C53 (3) 6.80 3.25

Issued: 100fr, 6/10; 200fr, 1/8; 500fr, 11/17.

Akakro Radar Earth Station — AP21

1972, Nov. 27 Engr. *Perf. 13*

C54 AP21 200fr brt bl, sl grn & choc 1.75 .90

The Judgment of Solomon, by Nandjui Legue — AP22

1973, Aug. 26 Photo. *Perf. 13*

C55 AP22 500fr multi 3.75 2.00

6th World Peace Conference for Justice.

Sassandra River Bridge — AP23

1974, May 4 Engr. *Perf. 13*

C56 AP23 100fr blk & yel grn .55 .30
C57 AP23 500fr slate grn & brn 2.50 1.50

Vridi Soap Factory, Abidjan — AP24

1974, July 6 Photo. *Perf. 13*

C58 AP24 200fr multi 1.10 .65

UPU Emblem, Ivory Coast Flag, Post Runner and Jet — AP25

1974, Oct. 9 Photo. *Perf. 13*

C59 AP25 200fr multi 1.10 .90
C60 AP25 300fr multi 1.75 1.25

Centenary of Universal Postal Union.

Fly Whisk and Panga Knife, Symbols of Akans Royal Family — AP26

1976, Apr. 3 Photo. *Perf. 12½x13*

C61 AP26 200fr brt bl & multi 1.10 .65

Tingrela Mosque — AP27

1977, May 7 Engr. *Perf. 13*

C62 AP27 500fr multi 2.50 1.50

Zeppelin Type of 1977
Souvenir Sheet

"Graf Zeppelin" LZ 127 over New York.

1977, Sept. 3 Litho. *Perf. 11*

C63 A150 500fr multi 3.25 1.40

Exists imperf.

Philexafrique II - Essen Issue
Common Design Types

#C64, Elephant and Ivory Coast No. 239. #C65, Pheasant and Bavaria No. 1.

1978, Nov. 1 Litho. *Perf. 13x12½*

C64 CD138 100fr multi .50 .30
C65 CD139 100fr multi .50 .30
a. Pair, #C64-C65 + label 1.00 .75

Gymnast, Olympic Rings — AP28

Various gymnasts. 75fr, 150fr, 350fr, vert.

1980, July 24 Litho. *Perf. 14½*

C66 AP28 75fr multi .50 .30
C67 AP28 150fr multi 1.00 .60
C68 AP28 250fr multi 1.60 1.00
C69 AP28 350fr multi 2.25 1.25
Nos. C66-C69 (4) 5.35 3.15

Souvenir Sheet

C70 AP28 500fr multi 3.50 2.00

22nd Summer Olympic Games, Moscow, July 19-Aug. 3.

President Houphouet-Boigny, 75th Birthday — AP28a

Embossed Die Cut

1980, Oct. 18 *Perf. 10½*

C70A AP28a 2000fr Silver
C70B AP28a 3000fr Gold

Manned Flight Bicentenary — AP29

Various balloons. 100fr, 125fr, 350fr vert.

1983, Apr. 2 Litho. *Perf. 13*

C71 AP29 100fr Montgolfier, 1783 .65 .40
C72 AP29 125fr Hydrogen, 1783 .80 .45
C73 AP29 150fr Mail transport, 1870 1.00 .55
C74 AP29 350fr Double Eagle II, 1978 2.25 1.40
C75 AP29 500fr Dirigible 3.50 1.75
Nos. C71-C75 (5) 8.20 4.55

Pre-Olympic Year — AP30

Various swimming events.

1983, July 9 Litho. *Perf. 14*

C76 AP30 100fr Crawl .25 .20
C77 AP30 125fr Diving .35 .20
C78 AP30 350fr Backstroke .90 .55
C79 AP30 400fr Butterfly 1.10 .60
Nos. C76-C79 (4) 2.60 1.55

Souvenir Sheet

C80 AP30 500fr Water polo 1.40 .80

1984 Summer Olympics — AP31

Pentathlon.

1984, Mar. *Perf. 12½*

C81 AP31 100fr Swimming .30 .20
C82 AP31 125fr Running .40 .25
C83 AP31 185fr Shooting .55 .35
C84 AP31 350fr Fencing 1.10 .70
Nos. C81-C84 (4) 2.35 1.50

Souvenir Sheet

C85 AP31 500fr Equestrian 1.50 .70

Los Angeles Olympics Winners AP32

1984, Dec. 15 Litho. *Perf. 13*

C86 AP32 100fr Tiacoh, silver .25 .20
C87 AP32 150fr Lewis, gold .40 .25
C88 AP32 200fr Babers, gold .65 .35
C89 AP32 500fr Cruz, gold 1.40 .80
Nos. C86-C89 (4) 2.70 1.60

Christmas AP33

Paintings: 100fr, Virgin and Child, by Correggio. 200fr, Holy Family with Angels, by Andrea del Sarto. 400fr, Virgin and Child, by Bellini.

1985, Jan. 12 *Perf. 13*

C90 AP33 100fr multi .25 .20
C91 AP33 200fr multi .65 .35
C92 AP33 400fr multi 1.10 .65
Nos. C90-C92 (3) 2.00 1.20

Nos. C91-C92 have incorrect frame inscriptions.

Audubon Birth Bicentenary — AP34

Birds: 100fr, Mergus serrator. 150fr, Pelecanus erythrorhynchos. 200fr, Mycteria americana. 350fr, Melanitta deglandi.

1985, June 8 Litho. *Perf. 13*

C93 AP34 100fr multi .25 .20
C94 AP34 150fr multi, vert. .40 .20
C95 AP34 200fr multi, vert. .55 .25
C96 AP34 350fr multi .90 .45
Nos. C93-C96 (4) 2.10 1.10

PHILEXAFRICA '85, Lome, Togo — AP35

1985, Nov. 16 Litho. *Perf. 13*

C97 AP35 250fr shown .65 .35
C98 AP35 250fr Soccer, boys and deer .65 .35
a. Pair, #C97-C98 + label 1.30 1.00

Edmond Halley, Computer Drawing of Comet — AP36

Return of Halley's Comet: 155fr, Sir William Herschel, Uranus. 190fr, Space probe, comet. 350fr, MS T-5 probe, comet. 440fr, Skylab, Kohoutek comet.

1986, Jan. Litho. *Perf. 13*

C99 AP36 125fr shown .50 .25
C100 AP36 155fr multi .60 .30
C101 AP36 190fr multi .75 .40
C102 AP36 350fr multi 1.40 .70
C103 AP36 440fr multi 1.75 .85
Nos. C99-C103 (5) 5.00 2.50

1986 World Cup Soccer Championships, Mexico — AP37

Various soccer plays.

1986, Apr. 26 Litho. *Perf. 13*

C104 AP37 90fr multi .50 .25
C105 AP37 125fr multi .70 .35
C106 AP37 155fr multi .85 .40
C107 AP37 440fr multi 2.40 1.25
C108 AP37 500fr multi 2.75 1.40
Nos. C104-C108 (5) 7.20 3.65

Souvenir Sheet

Perf. 13½x13

C109 AP37 600fr multi 3.25 1.75

AP38

1988 Summer Olympics, Seoul — AP39

Sailing sports.

1987, May 23 Litho. *Perf. 12½*

C110 AP38 155fr Soling Class .85 .40
C111 AP38 195fr Windsurfing 1.10 .55
C112 AP38 250fr 470 Class 1.40 .70
C113 AP38 550fr Windsurfing, diff. 3.00 1.50
Nos. C110-C113 (4) 6.35 3.15

Souvenir Sheet

C114 AP39 650fr 470 Class, diff. 3.75 2.00

1988 Summer Olympics, Seoul — AP40

1988, June 18 Litho. *Perf. 13*

C115 AP40 100fr Gymnastic rings .65 .30
C116 AP40 155fr Women's handball 1.00 .50
C117 AP40 195fr Boxing 1.25 .60
C118 AP40 500fr Parallel bars 3.25 1.60
Nos. C115-C118 (4) 6.15 3.00

Souvenir Sheet

C119 AP40 500fr Horizontal bar 3.25 1.60

1990 World Cup Soccer Championships, Italy — AP41

Italian monuments and various athletes.

1989, Nov. 25 Litho. *Perf. 13*

C120 AP41 195fr Milan Cathedral 1.40 .70
C121 AP41 300fr Columbus Monument, Genoa 2.10 1.10
C122 AP41 450fr Turin 3.25 1.60
C123 AP41 550fr Bologna 3.75 3.75
Nos. C120-C123 (4) 10.50 7.15

World Cup Soccer Championships, Italy — AP42

Various plays.

1990, May 31 Litho. *Perf. 13*

C124 AP42 155fr multicolored 1.25 .60
C125 AP42 195fr multicolored 1.50 .75
C126 AP42 500fr multicolored 3.75 1.90
C127 AP42 600fr multicolored 4.75 2.40
Nos. C124-C127 (4) 11.25 5.65

AIR POST SEMI-POSTAL STAMPS

Types of Dahomey Air Post Semi-Postal Issue

Perf. 13½x12½, 13 (#CB3)

Photo, Engr. (#CB3)

1942, June 22

CB1 SPAP1 1.50fr + 3.50fr green .50 *2.75*
CB2 SPAP2 2fr + 6fr brown .50 *2.75*
CB3 SPAP2 3fr + 9fr car red .50 *2.75*
Nos. CB1-CB3 (3) 1.50 *8.25*

Native children's welfare fund.

Colonial Education Fund

Common Design Type

Perf. 12½x13½

1942, June 22 Engr.

CB4 CD86a 1.20fr + 1.80fr blue & red .50 *2.75*

POSTAGE DUE STAMPS

Natives — D1

D2

Perf. 14x13½

1906-07 Unwmk. Typo.

J1 D1 5c grn, *greenish* 1.50 1.50
J2 D1 10c red brown 1.75 1.75
J3 D1 15c dark blue 2.75 2.75
J4 D1 20c blk, *yellow* 4.00 4.00
J5 D1 30c red, *straw* 4.00 4.00
J6 D1 50c violet 3.00 3.00
J7 D1 60c black, *buff* 18.00 18.00
J8 D1 1fr blk, *pinkish* 20.00 20.00
Nos. J1-J8 (8) 55.00 55.00

1914

J9 D2 5c green .20 .20
J10 D2 10c rose .20 .20
J11 D2 15c gray .20 .20
J12 D2 20c brown .20 .20
J13 D2 30c blue .25 .25
J14 D2 50c black .40 .40
J15 D2 60c orange .50 .50
J16 D2 1fr violet .80 .80
Nos. J9-J16 (8) 2.75 2.75

Type of 1914 Issue Surcharged

1927

J17 D2 2fr on 1fr lilac rose .85 .85
J18 D2 3fr on 1fr org brown .85 .85

Catalogue values for unused stamps in this section, from this point to the end of the section, are for Never Hinged items.

Republic

Guéré Mask — D3

Mask — D4

1960 Engr. *Perf. 14x13*

Denomination Typographed in Black

J19 D3 1fr purple .20 .20
J20 D3 2fr bright green .20 .20
J21 D3 5fr orange yellow .25 .25
J22 D3 10fr ultramarine .50 .50
J23 D3 20fr lilac rose .85 .85
Nos. J19-J23 (5) 2.00 2.00

1962, Nov. 3 Typo. *Perf. 13½x14*

Designs: Various masks and heads, Bingerville school of art.

J24 D4 1fr org & brt blue .20 .20
J25 D4 2fr black & red .20 .20
J26 D4 5fr red & dark grn .20 .20
J27 D4 10fr green & lilac .45 .45
J28 D4 20fr dark pur & blk .80 .80
Nos. J24-J28 (5) 1.85 1.85

Baoulé Weight — D5

Gold Weight — D6

Designs: Various Baoulé weights.

1968, May 18 Photo. *Perf. 13*

J29 D5 5fr cit, brn & bl grn .20 .20
J30 D5 10fr lt bl, brn & bl grn .20 .20
J31 D5 15fr sal, brn & bl grn .40 .40
J32 D5 20fr gray, car & bl grn .60 .60
J33 D5 30fr bis, brn & bl grn .70 .70
Nos. J29-J33 (5) 2.10 2.10

1972, May 27 Engr.

Designs: Various gold weights.

J34 D6 20fr vio bl & org red .45 .45
J35 D6 40fr ver & ocher .65 .65
J36 D6 50fr orange & chocolate .90 .90
J37 D6 100fr slate grn & ocher 2.00 2.00
Nos. J34-J37 (4) 4.00 4.00

MILITARY STAMP

The catalogue value for the unused stamp in this section is for Never Hinged.

Coat of Arms — M1

Perf. 13x14

1967, Jan. 1 Unwmk. Typo.

M1 M1 multi 1.60 1.60

OFFICIAL STAMPS

Catalogue values for unused stamps in this section are for Never Hinged items.

Ivory Coast Coat of Arms — O1

1974, Jan. 1 Photo. *Perf. 12*

O1 O1 (35fr) green & multi .40 .20
O2 O1 (75fr) orange & multi .65 .35
O3 O1 (100fr) lil rose & multi .90 .60
O4 O1 (250fr) violet & multi 2.50 1.25
Nos. O1-O4 (4) 4.45 2.40

PARCEL POST STAMPS

Postage Due Stamps of French Colonies Overprinted

Overprinted in Black

1903 Unwmk. *Imperf.*

Q1 D1 50c lilac 25.00 25.00
Q2 D1 1fr rose, *buff* 25.00 25.00

Colis

Overprinted in Black

Postaux

Q3 D1 50c lilac *2,500. 2,500.*
Q4 D1 1fr rose, *buff* *2,500. 2,500.*

Accents on "O" of "COTE"
Nos. Q7-Q8, Q11-Q12, Q15, Q17-Q18, Q21-Q22, Q24-Q25 exist with or without accent.

Overprinted

Red Overprint

Q5 D1 50c lilac 75.00 75.00
a. Inverted overprint 250.00 250.00

Blue Black Overprint

Q6 D1 1fr rose, *buff* 55.00 55.00
a. Inverted overprint 200.00 200.00

Surcharged in Black

Cote d'Ivoire ✕✕ 1FR Colis Postaux
a

Cote d'Ivoire 1FR Colis Postaux
b

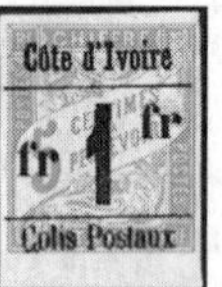
c

Côte d'Ivoire fr 1 fr Colis Postaux
d

e

Cote d'Ivoire fr 1 fr Colis Postaux
f

g

Côte d'Ivoire UN FR Colis Postaux
h

1903

Q7 D1 50c on 15c pale grn 7.50 7.50
a. Inverted surcharge 100.00 100.00
Q8 D1 50c on 60c brn, *buff* 24.00 21.00
a. Inverted surcharge 125.00 125.00
Q9 (a) 1fr on 5c blue *2,750.* *2,750.*
Q10 (b) 1fr on 5c blue *2,750.* *1,600.*
Q11 (c) 1fr on 5c blue 9.00 8.00
a. Inverted surcharge 150.00 150.00
Q12 (d) 1fr on 5c blue 12.00 11.00
Q13 (e) 1fr on 5c blue *3,000.* *2,750.*
Q14 (f) 1fr on 5c blue *6,750.* *6,250.*
Q15 (g) 1fr on 5c blue 60.00 60.00
Q16 (h) 1fr on 5c blue *2,250.* *2,250.*
Q17 (c) 1fr on 10c gray brn 12.00 12.00
a. Inverted surcharge 125.00 125.00
Q18 (d) 1fr on 10c gray brn 25.00 25.00
a. Inverted surcharge 125.00 125.00
Q19 (g) 1fr on 10c gray brn *2,750.* *2,750.*
Q20 (h) 1fr on 10c gray brn *30,000.*

Some authorities regard Nos. Q9 and Q10 as essays. A sub-type of type "a" has smaller, bold "XX" without serifs.

Surcharged in Black:

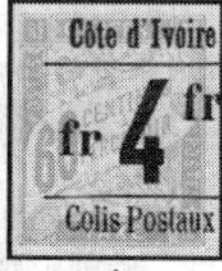
j

Cote d Ivoire fr 4 fr Colis Postaux
k

Côte d'Ivoire fr 4 fr Colis Postaux
l

Q21 (j) 4fr on 60c brn, *buff* 90.00 85.00
a. Double surcharge —
Q22 (k) 4fr on 60c brn, *buff* 250.00 200.00
Q23 (l) 4fr on 60c brn, *buff* 600.00 550.00

Surcharged in Black

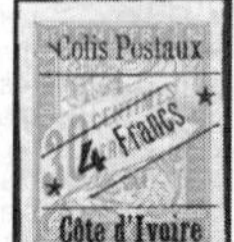

Q24 D1 4fr on 15c green 90.00 90.00
a. One large star 275.00 225.00
b. Two large stars 150.00 150.00
Q25 D1 4fr on 30c rose 90.00 90.00
a. One large star 275.00 225.00
b. Two large stars 150.00 150.00

Overprinted in Black

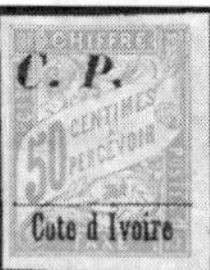

1904

Q26 D1 50c lilac 25.00 25.00
a. Inverted overprint
Q27 D1 1fr rose, *buff* 25.00 25.00
a. Inverted overprint

Overprinted in Black

Q28 D1 50c lilac 25.00 25.00
a. Inverted overprint 125.00 125.00
Q29 D1 1fr rose, *buff* 30.00 30.00
a. Inverted overprint 150.00 150.00

Surcharged in Black

Q30 D1 4fr on 5c blue 190.00 190.00
Q31 D1 8fr on 15c green 190.00 190.00

Overprinted in Black

1905

Q32 D1 50c lilac 60.00 60.00
Q33 D1 1fr rose, *buff* 60.00 60.00

Surcharged in Black

Q34 D1 2fr on 1fr rose, *buff* 175. 175.
Q35 D1 4fr on 1fr rose, *buff* 175. 175.
a. Italic "4" 1,200. 1,200.
Q36 D1 8fr on 1fr rose, *buff* 425. 425.

Vol. 3 Number Additions, Deletions & Changes

Number in 2003 Catalogue	Number in 2004 Catalogue
German States	
Hamburg	
new	5b
Germany	
1725A	1726
1726	1727
1727	1728
1730	1729
1731	1730
1732	1731
1733	1732
1734	1733
1734A	1734
1845	1840
1846	1841
1846A	1842
1847	1843
1848	1844
1848a	1844a
1849	1846
1849a	1846a
1850	1847
1850a	1847a
1850B	1848
1850Bc	1848a
1851	1849
1851A	1850
1852	1851
1853	1852
1854	1853
1855	1854
1856	1855
1856A	1856
1859	1858
1860	1859
1861	1860
Great Britain	
5	5a
5a	5
new	21b
new	28e
new	58a
new	70a
new	85a
new	87a
new	125a
new	J13b
MH264	MH262
MH264A	MH264
MH300	MH308
MH305	MH309
Alderney	
new	81a
new	81b
new	142a
new	143a
Jersey	
new	1012f
Isle of Man	
New	547b
Greenland	
new	120a
Guadeloupe	
new	163A
new	B11A-B11B
new	CB1-CB2
new	CB3
new	J37A-J37C
Haiti	
C515	931
Honduras	
new	8
Hungary	
new	3200a
Indo-China	
new	226A-226D
new	B21A-B21B
new	C18A-C18O
new	CB2-CB4
new	CB5
Iran	
62a	65A
new	65Aa
new	65Ab
new	65Ac
new	65Ad
215	deleted
new	516-523
new	648a
new	652a
new	C28a
Italian States	
Modena	
new	PR5b
Parma	
PR1	PR1a
PR1a	PR1
PR2	PR2a
PR2a	PR2
Italy	
1863	1862
1864	1863
1865	1864
1866	1865
1868	1866
2229	2228
2235	2229
2238	2230
2243	2231
2247	2232

Illustrated Identifier

This section pictures stamps or parts of stamp designs that will help identify postage stamps that do not have English words on them.

Many of the symbols that identify stamps of countries are shown here as well as typical examples of their stamps.

See the Index and Identifier on the previous pages for stamps with inscriptions such as "sen," "posta," "Baja Porto," "Helvetia," "K.S.A.", etc.

Linn's Stamp Identifier is now available. The 144 pages include more 2,000 inscriptions and over 500 large stamp illustrations. Available from Linn's Stamp News, P.O. Box 29, Sidney, OH 45365-0029.

1. HEADS, PICTURES AND NUMERALS

GREAT BRITAIN

Great Britain stamps never show the country name, but, except for postage dues, show a picture of the reigning monarch.

Victoria

Edward VII George V Edward VIII

George VI

Elizabeth II

Some George VI and Elizabeth II stamps are surcharged in annas, new paisa or rupees. These are listed under Oman.

Silhouette (sometimes facing right, generally at the top of stamp)

The silhouette indicates this is a British stamp. It is not a U.S. stamp.

VICTORIA

Queen Victoria

INDIA

Other stamps of India show this portrait of Queen Victoria and the words "Service" and "Annas."

AUSTRIA

YUGOSLAVIA

(Also BOSNIA & HERZEGOVINA if imperf.)

BOSNIA & HERZEGOVINA

Denominations also appear in top corners instead of bottom corners.

HUNGARY

Another stamp has posthorn facing left

BRAZIL

AUSTRALIA

Kangaroo and Emu

GERMANY

Mecklenburg-Vorpommern

SWITZERLAND

2. ORIENTAL INSCRIPTIONS

CHINA

Any stamp with this one character is from China (Imperial, Republic or People's Republic). This character appears in a four-character overprint on stamps of Manchukuo. These stamps are local provisionals, which are unlisted. Other overprinted Manchukuo stamps show this character, but have more than four characters in the overprints. These are listed in People's Republic of China.

Some Chinese stamps show the Sun.

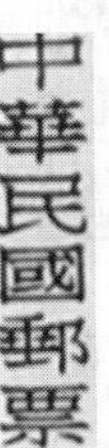

Most stamps of Republic of China show this series of characters.

Stamps with the China character and this character are from People's Republic of China. 人

Calligraphic form of People's Republic of China

Chinese stamps without China character

REPUBLIC OF CHINA

PEOPLE'S REPUBLIC OF CHINA

Mao Tse-tung

MANCHUKUO

Temple

Emperor Pu-Yi

The first 3 characters are common to many Manchukuo stamps.

The last 3 characters are common to other Manchukuo stamps.

Orchid Crest

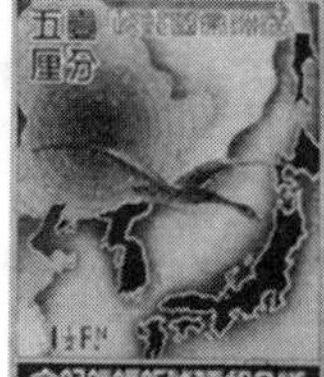
Manchukuo stamp without these elements

JAPAN

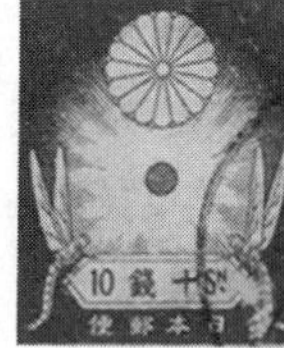

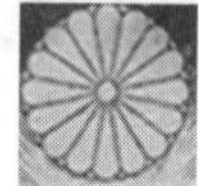
Chrysanthemum Crest

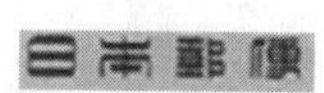
Country Name

Japanese stamps without these elements

The number of characters in the center and the design of dragons on the sides will vary.

RYUKYU ISLANDS

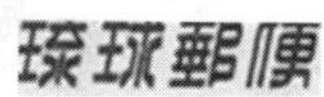
Country Name

PHILIPPINES (Japanese Occupation)

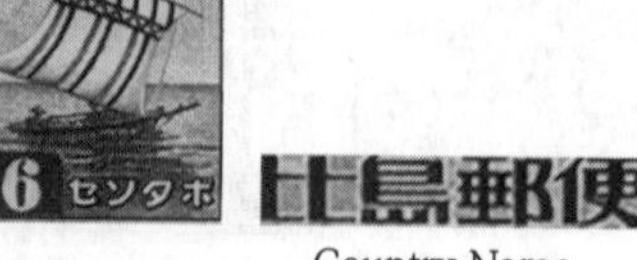
Country Name

NORTH BORNEO (Japanese Occupation)

Indicates Japanese Occupation Country Name

MALAYA (Japanese Occupation)

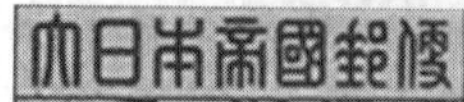
Indicates Japanese Occupation

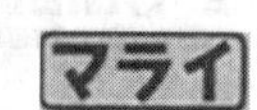
Country Name

BURMA (Japanese Occupation)

Indicates Japanese Occupation

Country Name

Other Burma Japanese Occupation stamps without these elements

Burmese Script

KOREA

These two characters, in any order, are common to stamps from the Republic of Korea (South Korea) or the unlisted stamps of the People's Democratic Republic of Korea (North Korea).

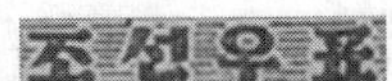

This series of four characters can be found on the stamps of both Koreas.

Yin Yang appears on some stamps.

대한민국우표

Indicates Republic of Korea (South Korea)

South Korean postage stamps issed after 1952 do not show currency expressed in Latin letters. Stamps wiith "HW," "HWAN," "WON," "WN," "W" or "W" with two lines through it, if not illustrated in listings of stamps before this date, are revenues. North Korean postage stamps do not have currency expressed in Latin letters.

THAILAND

Country Name

King Chulalongkorn

King Prajadhipok and Chao P'ya Chakri

3. CENTRAL AND EASTERN ASIAN INSCRIPTIONS

INDIA - FEUDATORY STATES

Alwar **Bhor**

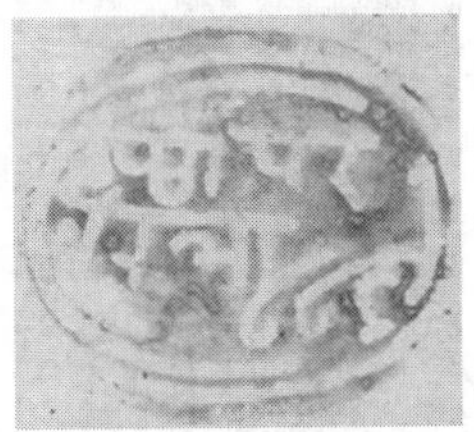

Bundi

Similar stamps come with different designs in corners and differently drawn daggers (at center of circle).

Dhar **Faridkot**

Hyderabad

Similar stamps exist with straight line frame around stamp, and also with different central design which is inscribed "Postage" or "Post & Receipt."

Indore **Jhalawar**

A similar stamp has the central figure in an oval.

Nandgaon

Nowanuggur

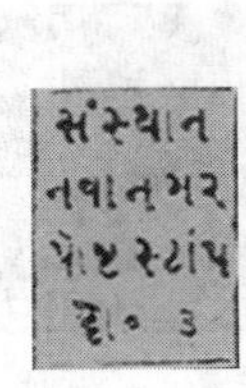

Poonch

Similar stamps exist in various sizes

Rajpeepla **Soruth**

BANGLADESH

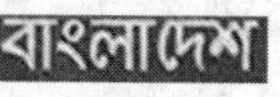

Country Name

NEPAL

Similar stamps are smaller, have squares in upper corners and have five or nine characters in central bottom panel.

TANNU TUVA **ISRAEL**

GEORGIA

This inscription is found on other pictorial stamps.

Country Name

ARMENIA

The four characters are found somewhere on pictorial stamps. On some stamps only the middle two are found.

4. AFRICAN INSCRIPTIONS

ETHIOPIA

5. ARABIC INSCRIPTIONS

AFGHANISTAN

Many early Afghanistan stamps show Tiger's head, many of these have ornaments protruding from outer ring, others show inscriptions in black.

Arabic Script

Mosque Gate & Crossed Cannons
The four characters are found somewhere on pictorial stamps. On some stamps only the middle two are found.

BAHRAIN

EGYPT

Postage

INDIA - FEUDATORY STATES

Jammu & Kashmir

Text and thickness of ovals vary. Some stamps have flower devices in corners.

India-Hyderabad

IRAN

Country Name

Royal Crown

Lion with Sword

Symbol

IRAQ

JORDAN

LEBANON

Similar types have denominations at top and slightly different design.

LIBYA

Country Name in various styles

Other Libya stamps show Eagle and Shield (head facing either direction) or Red, White and Black Shield (with or without eagle in center).

SAUDI ARABIA

Tughra (Central design)

Palm Tree and Swords

SYRIA

THRACE

YEMEN

PAKISTAN

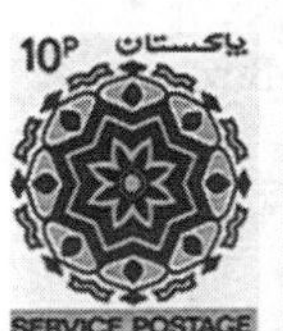

PAKISTAN - BAHAWALPUR

Country Name in top panel, star and crescent

TURKEY

Star & Crescent is a device found on many Turkish stamps, but is also found on stamps from other Arabic areas (see Pakistan-Bahawalpur)

Tughra (similar tughras can be found on stamps of Turkey in Asia, Afghanistan and Saudi Arabia)

Mohammed V

Mustafa Kemal

Plane, Star and Crescent

TURKEY IN ASIA

Other Turkey in Asia pictorials show star & crescent.
Other stamps show tughra shown under Turkey.

6. GREEK INSCRIPTIONS

GREECE

Country Name in various styles
(Some Crete stamps overprinted with the Greece country name are listed in Crete.)

Lepta

Drachma Drachmas Lepton

Abbreviated Country Name ΕΛΛ

Other forms of Country Name

No country name

CRETE

Country Name

These words are on other stamps

Grosion

Crete stamps with a surcharge that have the year "1922" are listed under Greece.

EPIRUS

Country Name

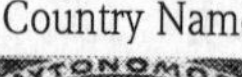

IONIAN IS.

7. CYRILLIC INSCRIPTIONS

RUSSIA

Postage Stamp

Imperial Eagle

ПОЧТА

почта Почта

Postage in various styles

КОП  РОССIЯ

Abbreviation for Kopeck Abbreviation for Ruble Russia

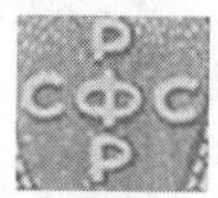

Abbreviation for Russian Soviet Federated Socialist Republic
RSFSR stamps were overprinted (see below)

Abbreviation for Union of Soviet Socialist Republics

This item is footnoted in Latvia

RUSSIA - Army of the North

ОКСА

"OKCA"

RUSSIA - Wenden

RUSSIAN OFFICES IN THE TURKISH EMPIRE

These letters appear on other stamps of the Russian offices.

The unoverprinted version of this stamp and a similar stamp were overprinted by various countries (see below).

ARMENIA

BELARUS

FAR EASTERN REPUBLIC

Country Name

SOUTH RUSSIA

Country Name

FINLAND

Circles and Dots on stamps similar to Imperial Russia issues

BATUM

Forms of Country Name

TRANSCAUCASIAN FEDERATED REPUBLICS

Abbreviation for Country Name

KAZAKHSTAN

ҚАЗАҚСТАН

Country Name

KYRGYZSTAN

КЫРГЫЗСТАН

КЫРГЫЗСТАН Country Name

ROMANIA

TADJIKISTAN

Country Name & Abbreviation

UKRAINE

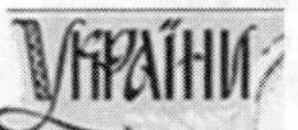

України

Україні

Country Name in various forms

РР

The trident appears on many stamps, usually as an overprint.

Abbreviation for Ukrainian Soviet Socialist Republic

WESTERN UKRAINE

Abbreviation for Country Name

AZERBAIJAN

AZƏRBAYCAN 10q.
POCTU 1992

AZƏRBAYCAN

Country Name

А.С.С.Р.

Abbreviation for Azerbaijan Soviet Socialist Republic

MONTENEGRO

ЦРНЕГОРЕ

ЦРНА ГОРА

Country Name in various forms

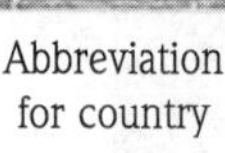

Abbreviation for country name

No country name (A similar Montenegro stamp without country name has same vignette.)

SERBIA

СРПСКА СРБИЈА

Country Name in various forms

К.С.

Abbreviation for country name

No country name

YUGOSLAVIA

Showing country name

No Country Name

MACEDONIA

МАКЕДОНИЈА

МАКЕДОНИЈА

Country Name

МАКЕДОНСКИ

Different form of Country Name

BULGARIA

Country Name Postage

Stotinka

СТОТИНКИ СТОТ.

Stotinki (plural) Abbreviation for Stotinki

Country Name in various forms and styles

БЪЛГАРИЯ

Н Р България

НРБЪЛГАРИЯ

No country name

Abbreviation for Lev, leva

MONGOLIA

ШУУДАН ТӨГРӨГ

Country name in one word Tugrik in Cyrillic

МОНГОЛ ШУУДАН МӨНГӨ

Country name in two words Mung in Cyrillic

Mung in Mongolian

Tugrik in Mongolian

Arms

No Country Name

INDEX AND IDENTIFIER

All page numbers shown are those in this Volume 3.

Postage stamps that do not have English words on them are shown in the Identifier which begins on page 1134.

Pronunciation Symbols

ə .... banana, collide, abut

ˈə, ˌə .... humdrum, abut

ə .... immediately preceding \l\, \n\, \m\, \ŋ\, as in battle, mitten, eaten, and sometimes open \ˈō-pəm\, lock and key \-əŋ-\; immediately following \l\, \m\, \r\, as often in French table, prisme, titre

ər .... further, merger, bird

ˈər-, ˈə-r .... as in two different pronunciations of hurry \ˈhər-ē, ˈhə-rē\

a .... mat, map, mad, gag, snap, patch

ā .... day, fade, date, aorta, drape, cape

ä .... bother, cot, and, with most American speakers, father, cart

ȧ .... father as pronounced by speakers who do not rhyme it with *bother;* French patte

au̇ .... now, loud, out

b .... baby, rib

ch .... chin, nature \ˈnā-chər\

d .... did, adder

e .... bet, bed, peck

ˈē, ˌē .... beat, nosebleed, evenly, easy

ē .... easy, mealy

f .... fifty, cuff

g .... go, big, gift

h .... hat, ahead

hw .... whale as pronounced by those who do not have the same pronunciation for both *whale* and *wail*

i .... tip, banish, active

ī .... site, side, buy, tripe

j .... job, gem, edge, join, judge

k .... kin, cook, ache

k̲ .... German ich, Buch; one pronunciation of loch

l .... lily, pool

m .... murmur, dim, nymph

n .... no, own

ⁿ .... indicates that a preceding vowel or diphthong is pronounced with the nasal passages open, as in French *un bon vin blanc* \œⁿ -bōⁿ -vaⁿ -bläⁿ\

ŋ .... sing \ˈsiŋ\, singer \ˈsiŋ-ər\, finger \ˈfiŋ-gər\, ink \ˈiŋk \

ō .... bone, know, beau

ȯ .... saw, all, gnaw, caught

œ .... French boeuf, German Hölle

œ̄ .... French feu, German Höhle

ȯi .... coin, destroy

p .... pepper, lip

r .... red, car, rarity

s .... source, less

sh .... as in shy, mission, machine, special (actually, this is a single sound, not two); with a hyphen between, two sounds as in *grasshopper* \ˈgras-ˌhä-pər\

t .... tie, attack, late, later, latter

th .... as in thin, ether (actually, this is a single sound, not two); with a hyphen between, two sounds as in *knighthood* \ˈnīt-ˌhu̇d\

t̲h̲ .... then, either, this (actually, this is a single sound, not two)

ü .... rule, youth, union \ˈyün-yən\, few \ˈfyü\

u̇ .... pull, wood, book, curable \ˈkyu̇r-ə-bəl\, fury \ˈfyu̇r-ē\

ue .... German füllen, hübsch

u̅e̅ .... French rue, German fühlen

v .... vivid, give

w .... we, away

y .... yard, young, cue \ˈkyü\, mute \ˈmyüt\, union \ˈyün-yən\

ʸ .... indicates that during the articulation of the sound represented by the preceding character the front of the tongue has substantially the position it has for the articulation of the first sound of *yard,* as in French *digne* \dēnʸ\

z .... zone, raise

zh .... as in vision, azure \ˈa-zhər\ (actually, this is a single sound, not two); with a hyphen between, two sounds as in *hogshead* \ˈhȯgz-ˌhed, ˈhägz-\

\ .... slant line used in pairs to mark the beginning and end of a transcription: \ˈpen\

ˈ .... mark preceding a syllable with primary (strongest) stress: \ˈpen-mən-ˌship\

ˌ .... mark preceding a syllable with secondary (medium) stress: \ˈpen-mən-ˌship\

- .... mark of syllable division

( ) .... indicate that what is symbolized between is present in some utterances but not in others: *factory* \ˈfak-t(ə-)rē\

÷ .... indicates that many regard as unacceptable the pronunciation variant immediately following: *cupola* \ˈkyü-pə-lə, ÷-ˌlō\

INDEX TO ADVERTISERS – 2004 VOLUME 3

2004 VOLUME 3 DEALER DIRECTORY YELLOW PAGE LISTINGS

This section of your Scott Catalogue contains advertisements to help you conveniently find what you need, when you need it...!

Accessories

BROOKLYN GALLERY COIN & STAMP
8725 4th Avenue
Brooklyn, NY 11209
718-745-5701
718-745-2775 Fax
Email: info@brooklyngallery.com
Web: www.brooklyngallery.com

Appraisals

CONNEXUS
P.O. Box 819
Snow Camp, NC 27349
336-376-8207
Email: Connexus1@world.att.net

Approvals-Personalized WW & U.S.

THE KEEPING ROOM
P.O. Box 257
Trumbull, CT 06611
203-372-8436

Asia

MICHAEL ROGERS, INC.
199 E. Welbourne Ave.
Suite 3
Winter Park, FL 32789
407-644-2290 or 800-843-3751
407-645-4434 Fax
Email: mrogersinc@aol.com
Web: www.michaelrogersinc.com

THE STAMP ACT
P.O. Box 1136
Belmont, CA 94002
650-592-3315
650-508-8104 Fax
Email: bchang@ix.netcom.com or bob @thestampact.com
Web: thestampact.com

Auctions

DANIEL F. KELLEHER CO., INC.
24 Farnsworth Street
Suite 605
Boston, MA 02210
617-443-0033
617-443-0789 Fax

JACQUES C. SCHIFF, JR., INC.
195 Main Street
Ridgefield Park, NJ 07660
201-641-5566
From NYC: 662-2777
201-641-5705 Fax

STAMP CENTER/DUTCH COUNTRY AUCTIONS
4115 Concord Pike
Wilmington, DE 19803
302-478-8740
302-478-8779 Fax
Email: scdca@dol.net
Web: www.thestampcenter.com

Auctions - Mail Bid

E. JOSEPH McCONNELL
P.O. Box 683
Monroe, NY 10950
845-496-5916
845-782-0347 Fax
Email: mcconn1@warwick.net
Web: www.EJMcConnell.com

Auctions-Public

ALAN BLAIR STAMPS/AUCTIONS
5407 Lakeside Avenue
Suite 4
Richmond, VA 23228
800-689-5602 Phone/Fax
Email: alanblair@prodigy.net

Austria

JOSEPH EDER
P.O. Box 185529
Hamden, CT 06518
203-281-0742
203-230-2410 Fax
Email: j.eder@worldnet.att.net
Web: www.ederstamps.com

Auctions

British Commonwealth

Booklets- Worldwide

HENRY GITNER PHILATELISTS, INC.
P.O. Box 3077-S
Middletown, NY 10940
845-343-5151 or 800-947-8267
845-343-0068 Fax
Email: hgitner@hgitner.com
Web: www.hgitner.com

British Commonwealth

CENTURY STAMP CO. LTD.
Century House
1723 Lakeshore Rd. West
Mississauga, ON L5J 1J4
CANADA
905-822-5464
905-822-2113 Fax
Email: centurystamps@rogers.com
Web: www.centurystamps.com

EMPIRE STAMP CO.
P.O. Box 8337
Calabasa, CA 91372-8337
800-616-7278 or 818-225-1181
818-225-1182 Fax
Email: info@empirestamps.com
Web: www.empirestamps.com

British Commonwealth

British Commonwealth

JAY'S STAMP CO.
Box 28484
Dept. S
Philadelphia, PA 19149-0184
215-743-0207 Phone/Fax
Email: jasc@comcast.net
Web: www.jaysco.com

METROPOLITAN STAMP CO., INC.
P.O. Box 1133
Chicago, IL 60690-1133
815-439-0142
815-439-0143 Fax
Email: metrostamp@aol.com

VICTORIA STAMP CO.
P.O. Box 745
Ridgewood, NJ 07451
201-652-7283
201-612-0024
Email: VictoriaStampCo@aol.com
Web: www.VictoriaStampCo.com

Central America

GUY SHAW
P.O. Box 10025
Bakersfield, CA 93389
661-834-7135 Phone/Fax
Email: guyshaw@guyshaw.com
Web: www.guyshaw.com

China

MICHAEL ROGERS, INC.
199 E. Welbourne Ave.
Suite 3
Winter Park, FL 32789
407-644-2290 or 800-843-3751
407-645-4434 Fax
Email: mrogersinc@aol.com
Web: www.michaelrogersinc.com

Collections

BOB & MARTHA FRIEDMAN
624 Homestead Place
Joliet, IL 60435
815-725-6666
815-725-4134 Fax

DR. ROBERT FRIEDMAN & SONS
2029 West 75th Street
Woodridge, IL 60517
630-985-1515
630-985-1588 Fax

HENRY GITNER PHILATELISTS, INC.
P.O. Box 3077-S
Middletown, NY 10940
845-343-5151 or 800-947-8267
845-343-0068 Fax
Email: hgitner@hgitner.com
Web: www.hgitner.com

Ducks

METROPOLITAN STAMP CO., INC.
P.O. Box 1133
Chicago, IL 60690-1133
815-439-0142
815-439-0143 Fax
Email: metrostamp@aol.com

MICHAEL JAFFE
P.O. Box 61484
Vancouver, WA 98666
360-695-6161 or 800-782-6770
360-695-1616 Fax
Email:
mjaffe@brookmanstamps.com
Web: www.brookmanstamps.com

Ducks - Foreign

METROPOLITAN STAMP CO., INC.
P.O. Box 1133
Chicago, IL 60690-1133
815-439-0142
815-439-0143 Fax
Email: metrostamp@aol.com

Europa

HENRY GITNER PHILATELISTS, INC.
P.O. Box 3077-S
Middletown, NY 10940
845-343-5151 or 800-947-8267
845-343-0068 Fax
Email: hgitner@hgitner.com
Web: www.hgitner.com

France

JOSEPH EDER
P.O. Box 185529
Hamden, CT 06518
203-281-0742
203-230-2410 Fax
Email: j.eder@worldnet.att.net
Web: www.ederstamps.com

French S. Antarctic

E. JOSEPH McCONNELL
P.O. Box 683
Monroe, NY 10950
845-496-5916
845-782-0347 Fax
Email: mcconn1@warwick.net
Web: www.EJMcConnell.com

German Colonies

COLONIAL STAMP COMPANY
$1 million photo price list, $5.00 (refundable against purchase)
5757 Wilshire Blvd. PH #8
Los Angeles, CA 90036
323-933-9435
323-939-9930 Fax
Email: gwh225@aol.com
Web: www.colonialstamps.com

JOSEPH EDER
P.O. Box 185529
Hamden, CT 06518
203-281-0742
203-230-2410 Fax
Email: j.eder@worldnet.att.net
Web: www.ederstamps.com

German E. Africa (B & G)

COLONIAL STAMP COMPANY
5757 Wilshire Blvd. PH #8
Los Angeles, CA 90036
323-933-9435
323-939-9930 Fax
Email: gwh225@aol.com
Web: www.colonialstamps.com

German New Guinea (B & G)

COLONIAL STAMP COMPANY
5757 Wilshire Blvd. PH #8
Los Angeles, CA 90036
323-933-9435
323-939-9930 Fax
Email: gwh225@aol.com
Web: www.colonialstamps.com

German Occupation

HENRY GITNER PHILATELISTS, INC.
P.O. Box 3077-S
Middletown, NY 10940
845-343-5151 or 800-947-8267
845-343-0068 Fax
Email: hgitner@hgitner.com
Web: www.hgitner.com

JOSEPH EDER
P.O. Box 185529
Hamden, CT 06518
203-281-0742
203-230-2410 Fax
Email: j.eder@worldnet.att.net
Web: www.ederstamps.com

German So West Africa

COLONIAL STAMP COMPANY
5757 Wilshire Blvd. PH #8
Los Angeles, CA 90036
323-933-9435
323-939-9930 Fax
Email: gwh225@aol.com
Web: www.colonialstamps.com

German States

COLONIAL STAMP COMPANY
5757 Wilshire Blvd. PH #8
Los Angeles, CA 90036
323-933-9435
323-939-9930 Fax
Email: gwh225@aol.com
Web: www.colonialstamps.com

Germany

AMEEN STAMPS
8831 Long Point Road
Suite 204
Houston, TX 77055
713-468-0644
713-468-2420 Fax
Email: rameen@ev1.net

CENTURY STAMP CO. LTD.
Century House
1723 Lakeshore Rd. West
Mississauga, ON L5J 1J4
CANADA
905-822-5464
905-822-2113 Fax
Email: centurystamps@rogers.com
Web: www.centurystamps.com

Germany

HENRY GITNER PHILATELISTS, INC.
P.O. Box 3077-S
Middletown, NY 10940
845-343-5151 or 800-947-8267
845-343-0068 Fax
Email: hgitner@hgitner.com
Web: www.hgitner.com

JOSEPH EDER
P.O. Box 185529
Hamden, CT 06518
203-281-0742
203-230-2410 Fax
Email: j.eder@worldnet.att.net
Web: www.ederstamps.com

Germany- Third Reich

JOSEPH EDER
P.O. Box 185529
Hamden, CT 06518
203-281-0742
203-230-2410 Fax
Email: j.eder@worldnet.att.net
Web: www.ederstamps.com

Gold Coast

COLONIAL STAMP COMPANY
5757 Wilshire Blvd. PH #8
Los Angeles, CA 90036
323-933-9435
323-939-9930 Fax
Email: gwh225@aol.com
Web: www.colonialstamps.com

Great Britain

COLONIAL STAMP COMPANY
5757 Wilshire Blvd. PH #8
Los Angeles, CA 90036
323-933-9435
323-939-9930 Fax
Email: gwh225@aol.com
Web: www.colonialstamps.com

Hong Kong

COLONIAL STAMP COMPANY
5757 Wilshire Blvd. PH #8
Los Angeles, CA 90036
323-933-9435
323-939-9930 Fax
Email: gwh225@aol.com
Web: www.colonialstamps.com

Hong Kong

HENRY GITNER PHILATELISTS, INC.
P.O. Box 3077-S
Middletown, NY 10940
845-343-5151 or 800-947-8267
845-343-0068 Fax
Email: hgitner@hgitner.com
Web: www.hgitner.com

THE STAMP ACT
P.O. Box 1136
Belmont, CA 94002
650-592-3315
650-508-8104 Fax
Email: bchang@ix.netcom.com or bob @thestampact.com
Web: thestampact.com

India & States

COLONIAL STAMP COMPANY
5757 Wilshire Blvd. PH #8
Los Angeles, CA 90036
323-933-9435
323-939-9930 Fax
Email: gwh225@aol.com
Web: www.colonialstamps.com

Insurance

COLLECTIBLES INSURANCE AGENCY
P.O. Box 1200 SSC
Westminster, MD 21158
888-837-9537
410-876-9233 Fax
Email: info@insurecollectibles.com
Web: www.collectinsure.com

Iraq

COLONIAL STAMP COMPANY
5757 Wilshire Blvd. PH #8
Los Angeles, CA 90036
323-933-9435
323-939-9930 Fax
Email: gwh225@aol.com
Web: www.colonialstamps.com

Israel

HENRY GITNER PHILATELISTS, INC.
P.O. Box 3077-S
Middletown, NY 10940
845-343-5151 or 800-947-8267
845-343-0068 Fax
Email: hgitner@hgitner.com
Web: www.hgitner.com

Italy

HENRY GITNER PHILATELISTS, INC.
P.O. Box 3077-S
Middletown, NY 10940
845-343-5151 or 800-947-8267
845-343-0068 Fax
Email: hgitner@hgitner.com
Web: www.hgitner.com

Japan

MICHAEL ROGERS, INC.
199 E. Welbourne Ave.
Suite 3
Winter Park, FL 32789
407-644-2290 or 800-843-3751
407-645-4434 Fax
Email: mrogersinc@aol.com
Web: www.michaelrogersinc.com

Korea

MICHAEL ROGERS, INC.
199 E. Welbourne Ave.
Suite 3
Winter Park, FL 32789
407-644-2290 or 800-843-3751
407-645-4434 Fax
Email: mrogersinc@aol.com
Web: www.michaelrogersinc.com

Latin America

GUY SHAW
P.O. Box 10025
Bakersfield, CA 93389
661-834-7135 Phone/Fax
Email: guyshaw@guyshaw.com
Web: www.guyshaw.com

Manchukuo

MICHAEL ROGERS, INC.
199 E. Welbourne Ave.
Suite 3
Winter Park, FL 32789
407-644-2290 or 800-843-3751
407-645-4434 Fax
Email: mrogersinc@aol.com
Web: www.michaelrogersinc.com

New Issues

DAVIDSON'S STAMP SERVICE
P.O. Box 36355
Indianapolis, IN 46236-0355
317-826-2620
Email: davidson@in.net
Web: www.newstampissues.com

Germany

New Issues

New Issues- Retail

BOMBAY PHILATELIC INC.
P.O. Box 540819
Lake Worth, FL 33454
561-791-9557
561-791-9024 Fax
Email: sales@bombaystamps.com
Web: www.bombaystamps.com

STANLEY M. PILLER & ASSOCIATES
3351 Grand Avenue
Oakland, CA 94610
510-465-8290
510-465-7121 Fax
Email: stmpdlr@aol.com
Web: www.smpiller.com

New Issues- Wholesale

BOMBAY PHILATELIC INC.
P.O. Box 540819
Lake Worth, FL 33454
561-791-9557
561-791-9024 Fax
Email: sales@bombaystamps.com
Web: www.bombaystamps.com

Proofs & Essays

HENRY GITNER PHILATELISTS, INC.
P.O. Box 3077-S
Middletown, NY 10940
845-343-5151 or 800-947-8267
845-343-0068 Fax
Email: hgitner@hgitner.com
Web: www.hgitner.com

Publications - Collector

AMERICAN PHILATELIC SOCIETY
Dept. TZ
P.O. Box 8000
State College, PA 16803
814-237-3803
814-237-6128 Fax
Email: flsente@stamps.org
Web: www.stamps.org

South America

GUY SHAW
P.O. Box 10025
Bakersfield, CA 93389
661-834-7135 Phone/Fax
Email: guyshaw@guyshaw.com
Web: www.guyshaw.com

Stamp Shows

ATLANTIC COAST EXHIBITIONS
Division of Beach Philatelics
42 Baltimore Lane
Palm Coast, FL 32137-8850
386-445-4550
386-447-0811 Fax
Email: mrstamp2@aol.com
Web: www.beachphilatelics.com

STAMP STORES

Arizona

B.J.'S STAMPS
Barbara J. Johnson
6342 W. Bell Road
Glendale, AZ 85308
623-878-2080
623-412-3456 Fax
Email: info@bjstamps.com
Web: www.bjstamps.com

STAMP STORES

California

ASHTREE STAMP & COIN
2410 N. Blackstone
Fresno, CA 93703-1747
559-227-7167

BROSIUS STAMP & COIN
2105 Main Street
Santa Monica, CA 90405
310-396-7480
310-396-7455 Fax

COLONIAL STAMP CO./BRITISH EMPIRE SPECIALIST
5757 Wilshire Blvd. PH #8 (by appt.)
Los Angeles, CA 90036
323-933-9435
323-939-9930 Fax
Email: gwh225@aol.com
Web: www.colonialstamps.com

FISCHER-WOLK PHILATELICS
24771 "G" Alicia Parkway
Laguna Hills, CA 92653
949-837-2932
Email: fischerwolk@earthlink.net

STANLEY M. PILLER & ASSOCIATES
3351 Grand Avenue
Oakland, CA 94610
510-465-8290
510-465-7121 Fax
Email: stmpdlr@aol.com
Web: www.smpiller.com

Colorado

ACKLEY'S STAMPS
3230 N. Stone Avenue
Colorado Springs, CO 80907
719-633-1153
Email: ackl9@aol.com

SHOWCASE STAMPS
3865 Wadsworth
Wheat Ridge, CO 80033
303-425-9252
Email: kbeiner@colbi.net
Web: www.showcasestamps.com

Connecticut

MILLER'S STAMP SHOP
41 New London Turnpike
Uncasville, CT 06382
860-848-0468 or 800-67-STAMP
860-848-1926 Fax
Email: millstamps@aol.com
Web: www.millerstamps.com

SILVER CITY COIN & STAMP
41 Colony Street
Meriden, CT 06451
203-235-7634
203-237-4915 Fax

Florida

BEACH PHILATELICS
Daytona Flea Market (Fri.-Sun.)
I 95 Exit 87 (Tamoka Farms Rd.)
Corner Shoppes Bldg.
Booths 70-72
Daytona Beach, FL 32119
386-503-6598

Florida

CORBIN STAMP & COIN, INC.
108 West Robertson Street
Brandon, FL 33511
813-651-3266

R.D.C. STAMPS
7381 SW 24th Street
Miami, FL 33155-1402
305-264-4213
305-262-2919 Fax
Email: rdcstamps@aol.com

SUN COAST STAMP CO.
3231 Gulf Gate Drive
Suite 102
Sarasota, FL 34231
941-921-9761 or 800-927-3351
941-921-1762 Fax
Email: email@suncoaststamp.com
Web: www.stampfinder.com

WINTER PARK STAMP SHOP
Ranch Mall (17-92)
325 S. Orlando Ave.
Suite 1-2
Winter Park, FL 32789-3608
407-628-1120 or 800-845-1819
407-628-0091 Fax
Email: jim@winterparkstampshop.com
Web: www.winterparkstampshop.com

Georgia

STAMPS UNLIMITED OF GEORGIA
133 Carnegie Way
Room 250
Atlanta, GA 30303
404-688-9161

Illinois

DON CLARK'S STAMPS & COINS
937 1/2 W. Galena Blvd.
Aurora, IL 60506
630-896-4606

DR. ROBERT FRIEDMAN & SONS
2029 West 75th Street
Woodridge, IL 60517
630-985-1515
630-985-1588 Fax

Indiana

KNIGHT STAMP & COIN CO.
237 Main Street
Hobart, IN 46342
219-942-4341 or 800-634-2646
Email: knight@knightcoin.com
Web: www.knightcoin.com

Kentucky

COLLECTORS STAMPS LTD.
4012 Dupont Circle #313
Louisville, KY 40207
502-897-9045
Email: csl@aye.net

Maryland

BALTIMORE COIN & STAMP EXCHANGE
10194 Baltimore National Pike
Unit 104
Ellicott City, MD 21042
410-418-8282
410-418-4813 Fax

Maryland

BULLDOG STAMP COMPANY
4641 Montgomery Avenue
Bethesda, MD 20814
301-654-1138

Massachusetts

KAPPY'S COINS & STAMPS
534 Washington Street
Norwood, MA 02062
781-762-5552
781-762-3292 Fax
Email: kappyscoins@aol.com

Michigan

THE MOUSE AND SUCH
696 N. Mill Street
Plymouth, MI 48170
734-454-1515
734-454-9812 Fax
Email: weluvstamps@hotmail.com

New Jersey

AALLSTAMPS
38 N. Main Street
P.O. Box 249
Milltown, NJ 08850
732-247-1093
732-247-1094 Fax
Email: mail@aallstamps.com
Web: www.aallstamps.com

BERGEN STAMPS & COLLECTIBLES
717 American Legion Drive
Teaneck, NJ 07666
201-836-8987

RON RITZER STAMPS INC.
Millburn Mall
2933 Vauxhall Road
Vauxhall, NJ 07088
908-687-0007
908-687-0795 Fax
Email: ritzerstamps@earthlink.net

TRENTON STAMP & COIN CO.
Thomas DeLuca
Store: Forest Glen Plaza
1804 Route 33
Hamilton Square, NJ 08690
Mail: P.O. Box 8574
Trenton, NJ 08650
800-446-8664
609-587-8664 Fax
Email: TOMD4TSC@aol.com

New York

CHAMPION STAMP CO., INC.
432 West 54th Street
New York, NY 10019
212-489-8130
212-581-8130 Fax
Email: championstamp@aol.com
Web: www.championstamp.com

Ohio

FEDERAL COIN & STAMP EXCHANGE
P.O. Box 14579
401 Euclid Ave.
Suite 45
Cleveland, OH 44114
216-861-1160
216-861-5960 Fax

STAMP STORES

Ohio

HILLTOP STAMP SERVICE
Richard A. Peterson
P.O. Box 626
Wooster, OH 44691
330-262-8907 or 330-262-5378
Email: hilltop@bright.net

THE LINK STAMP CO.
3461 E. Livingston Ave.
Columbus, OH 43227
614-237-4125 Phone/Fax
800-546-5726 Phone/Fax

Pennsylvania

PHILLY STAMP & COIN CO., INC.
1804 Chestnut Street
Philadelphia, PA 19103
215-563-7341
215-563-7382 Fax
Email: phillysc@netreach.net
Web: www.phillystampandcoin.com

Tennessee

HERRON HILL, INC.
5007 Black Road
Suite 140
Memphis, TN 38117
901-683-9644

Virginia

KENNEDY'S STAMPS & COINS
7059 Brookfield Plaza
Springfield, VA 22150
703-569-7300
703-569-7644 Fax
Email: kennedy@patriot.net

LATHEROW & CO., INC.
5054 Lee Hwy.
Arlington, VA 22207
703-538-2727 or 800-647-4624
703-538-5210 Fax

Washington

TACOMA MALL BLVD. COIN & STAMP
5225 Tacoma Mall Blvd. E101
Tacoma, WA 98409
253-472-9632
253-472-8948 Fax
Email: kfeldman01@sprynet.com

Wisconsin

JIM LUKES' STAMP & COIN
815 Jay Street
P.O. Box 1780
Manitowoc, WI 54221
920-682-2324 Phone/Fax

Topicals - Columbus

MR. COLUMBUS
Box 1492
Fennville, MI 49408
616-543-4755
Email: columbus@accn.org

Topicals - Miscellaneous

BOMBAY PHILATELIC INC.
P.O. Box 540819
Lake Worth, FL 33454
561-791-9557
561-791-9024 Fax
Email: sales@bombaystamps.com
Web: www.bombaystamps.com

United States

BOB & MARTHA FRIEDMAN
624 Homestead Place
Joliet, IL 60435
815-725-6666
815-725-4134 Fax

BROOKMAN STAMP CO.
P.O. Box 90
Vancouver, WA 98666
360-695-1391 or 800-545-4871
360-695-1616 Fax
Email: dave@brookmanstamps.com
Web: www.brookmanstamps.com

DR. ROBERT FRIEDMAN & SONS
2029 West 75th Street
Woodridge, IL 60517
630-985-1515
630-985-1588 Fax

Want Lists

BROOKMAN INTERNATIONAL
P.O. Box 450
Vancouver, WA 98666
360-695-1391 or 800-545-4871
360-695-1616 Fax
Email: dave@brookmanstamps.com

CHARLES P. SCHWARTZ
P.O. Box 165
Mora, MN 55051
320-679-4705
Email: charlesp@ecenet.com

Want Lists- British Empire 1840-1935 German Cols/Offices

COLONIAL STAMP COMPANY
5757 Wilshire Blvd. PH #8
Los Angeles, CA 90036
323-933-9435
323-939-9930 Fax
Email: gwh225@aol.com
Web: www.colonialstamps.com

Wholesale

HENRY GITNER PHILATELISTS, INC.
P.O. Box 3077-S
Middletown, NY 10940
845-343-5151 or 800-947-8267
845-343-0068 Fax
Email: hgitner@hgitner.com
Web: www.hgitner.com

WWI-WWII

HENRY GITNER PHILATELISTS, INC.
P.O. Box 3077-S
Middletown, NY 10940
845-343-5151 or 800-947-8267
845-343-0068 Fax
Email: hgitner@hgitner.com
Web: www.hgitner.com

Worldwide

S. SEREBRAKIAN, INC.
P.O. Box 448
Monroe, NY 10950
845-783-9791
845-782-0347 Fax
Email: mcconn1@warwick.net

Worldwide-Collections

BOB & MARTHA FRIEDMAN
624 Homestead Place
Joliet, IL 60435
815-725-6666
815-725-4134 Fax

DR. ROBERT FRIEDMAN & SONS
2029 West 75th Street
Woodridge, IL 60517
630-985-1515
630-985-1588 Fax

Worldwide - Price Lists

ROBERT E. BARKER
P.O. Box 1100
Warren, ME 04864
207-273-6200 or 800-833-0217
207-273-4254 or 888-325-5158 Fax
Email: rebarker@rebarker.com
Web: www.rebarker.com

Worldwide-Year Sets

BOMBAY PHILATELIC INC.
P.O. Box 540819
Lake Worth, FL 33454
561-791-9557
561-791-9024 Fax
Email: sales@bombaystamps.com
Web: www.bombaystamps.com

HENRY GITNER PHILATELISTS, INC.
P.O. Box 3077-S
Middletown, NY 10940
845-343-5151 or 800-947-8267
845-343-0068 Fax
Email: hgitner@hgitner.com
Web: www.hgitner.com

WALLACE STAMPS
Box 82
Port Washington, NY 11050
516-883-5578

Topicals